SCOTT®

# 2014 STANDARD POSTAGE STAMP CATALOGUE

ONE HUNDRED AND SEVENTIETH EDITION IN SIX VOLUMES

## VOLUME 3

## COUNTRIES OF THE WORLD G-I

EDITOR Charles Snee
EDITOR EMERITUS James E. Kloetzel
ASSISTANT EDITOR /NEW ISSUES & VALUING Martin J. Frankevicz
ASSOCIATE EDITORS David Akin, Donna Houseman
VALUING ANALYST Steven R. Myers
ADMINISTRATIVE ASSISTANT/CATALOGUE LAYOUT Eric Wiessinger
PRINTING AND IMAGE COORDINATOR Stacey Mahan
CREATIVE DIRECTOR Mark Potter
ADVERTISING Angela Nolte
CIRCULATION/PRODUCT PROMOTION MANAGER Tim Wagner
VICE PRESIDENT/EDITORIAL AND PRODUCTION Steve Collins
PRESIDENT William Fay

Released June 2013
Includes New Stamp Listings through the April 2013 *Linn's Stamp News Special Edition* Catalogue Update



**Scott Publishing Co.**

911 Vandemark Road, Sidney, OH 45365-0828
A division of AMOS PRESS, INC., publishers of *Linn's Stamp News, Linn's Stamp News Special Edition, Coin World* and *Coin World Special Edition.*

# Table of Contents




See Volume 1 for United States, United Nations and Countries of the World A-B
See Volume 2, 4 through 6 for Countries of the World, C-F, J-Z

Volume 2: C-F
Volume 4: J-M
Volume 5: N-Sam
Volume 6: San-Z


**Scott Publishing Mission Statement**

The Scott Publishing Team exists to serve the recreational, educational and commercial hobby needs of stamp collectors and dealers.

We strive to set the industry standard for philatelic information and products by developing and providing goods that help collectors identify, value, organize and present their collections.

Quality customer service is, and will continue to be, our highest priority. We aspire toward achieving total customer satisfaction.




ISBN 0-89487-481-0

Library of Congress Card No. 2-3301

# Scott Publishing Co.

SCOTT 911 VANDEMARK ROAD, SIDNEY, OHIO 45365 937-498-0802

Greetings, Scott Catalogue User:

***Spotlights on Great Britain, Hungary and Italy.***

A hearty welcome to Vol. 3 of the 2014 edition of the Scott *Standard Postage Stamp Catalogue*, which details listings for the countries of the world, G-I. This catalogue is chock-a-block full of countries that garner significant attention among collectors. During the past couple of months, the Scott editors elected to give close looks to Great Britain, Hungary and Italy.

Overall, more than 13,000 value changes are recorded in Vol. 3 of the 2014 Standard catalogue. Hungary and Italy lead the way, with almost 3,000 and more than 2,600 value changes, respectively.

More than 2,200 value changes are recorded for Great Britain, beginning with the British Empire Exhibition issue of 1924. In general, values are down modestly, but there are some increases among issues of the 1990s. The 1995 booklet pane of 10 depicting various paintings (Scott 1605a) moves to $13.50 mint, never hinged, from $11 in 2013.

Great Britain errors also notch some significant gains. Among the more spectacular advances are the two 1969 5-penny Cathedral stamps with bluish violet omitted, Scott 589a and 590a; each is valued at $20,000 mint in the 2014 catalogue, a jump of $13,500 over their 2013 catalogue value of $6,500 each.

Before moving on, a word about values of recent issues. Catalogue users will see that values for some countries are down somewhat for stamps issued during the 1960s through the early 1990s. More recent issues, particularly stamps issued during the past 10 years, are showing healthy gains in value. This follows a pattern the editors began seeing three years ago.

Hungary last fell under the editors' pens for a significant review for the 2011 catalogue. This year, careful scrutiny yielded almost 3,000 changes. Given the softening of the forint against the dollar during the past couple of years, values for 20th-century material and later are down. There are increases among selected classic issues. The 1871-72 Franz Josef I stamps show substantial increases in unused condition. The 15-kreuzer yellow brown, Scott 5, soars to $1,250, from $750 in 2013.

A scarce type variety of the 1953 2-forint Joseph Stalin is newly listed as Scott 1035a, valued at $600 mint, never hinged and $300 used. Distinguishing this stamp from its common counterpart, Scott 1035, involves looking at the background behind the "MAGYAR POSTA" inscription at the bottom of the design. The Type I stamp, Scott 1035a, has a solid background, while Scott 1035, the Type II variety, shows a background of horizontal lines.

We have often reminded catalogue users to look closely at footnotes, which are often added, expanded or clarified from one year to the next. In Hungary, dozens of imperforate sets are described and valued in footnotes beneath the main listings. Here, many value changes also have been made, mostly in a downward direction.

A complete review of modern Italy results in more than 2,200 value changes in the Postage section. For the most part, mild downward adjustments of five to 10 percent are the order of the day. Modest increases in value are noted for issues beginning in mid-2001. Some substantial jumps are seen in used values for various back-of-the-book issues, including semipostals, air post, air post semipostals and pneumatic mail. The set of six surcharged Pneumatic Mail stamps of 1924-27, Scott D9-D14, jumps from $637 used in 2013, to $879 used this year.

Values for used postage due and parcel post stamps of the Italian Social Republic jump dramatically. The 20-lira lilac brown parcel post stamp, Scott Q12, moves to $5,000 used, from $3,750 used last year.

About 700 value changes are seen in Italian Offices Abroad, with both unused and used values rising by 10 percent or more. Some of the increases here are significant: the 20-para on 5-lira blue and rose of Salonika (Scott 7) rises 20 percent in used condition, from $575 in 2013 to $700 this year. The Aegean Islands also see movement in a positive direction, with more than 1,100 value changes recorded. As you look over the various Italy sections, pay particular attention to items described and valued in footnotes — a number of significant value increases are to be seen.

***What is happening in the rest of the 2014 Vol. 3?***

In the Great Britain Machin-head listings, an expanded editorial note has been added after Scott MH382 that explains the code variations of the iridescent "ROYAL MAIL" imprint that appears on selected Machin-head definitive stamps. The codes identify the format from which a given stamp originated. A small number of color-omitted errors from the 1960s are added for the first time, including a lemon-omitted variety of the 1965 3-penny Post Office Tower, Scott 438a, valued at $6,000 mint, never hinged and at $2,250 used.

Iceland weighs in with almost 1,200 value changes. The big news here is the "I GILDI" overprints, which see some hefty jumps in value. The relevant Scott numbers to focus on are 45-68 and their Official counterparts, O20-O30. A fresh analysis from an expert on these stamps provided the Scott editors with useful data to make the needed adjustments. In some cases, values more than double from those in the 2013 catalogue.

Values for the classic issues of Gambia, from Queen Victoria through King George VI (Scott 1-151), were given a careful review. Increases of 10 percent to 15 percent are typical. An expanded footnote for Scott 1-4 clarifies the strength of the embossing to the stated values. And for those collectors on a more limited budget, no-gum values for Scott 1-4 are now provided.

In the German State of Bavaria, a quartet of inverted-overprint errors have been added to the 1920 set of stamps overprinted "Deutsches Reich". These minor varieties are listed as Nos. 257b, 258a, 262a and 264a.

Booklet collectors will be pleased to see the addition of unlettered listings for complete booklets for Guernsey, Jersey and the Isle of Man. Various design and editorial notes for these areas have been corrected and expanded.

In Iran, the catalog listings of two minor varieties of Scott 14, the tete-beche pair (14a) and the imperforate single (14b), have been changed to 14b and 14c, respectively, to avoid confusion with the 1876 1-shahi black, Scott 14A.

For a summary of these and other listing-related changes, you are encouraged to peruse the Number Additions, Deletions & Changes listing, located on page 1479 in this volume.

***What do you think of this year's cover theme?***

Perhaps you were too eager to dive into the catalogue to notice that the theme for this year's covers is women. The Scott editors had a splendid time selecting from among dozens of worthy stamps to determine those that would make the final cut. In some cases, multiple votes had to be taken to determine the winners. The vignettes near the top of each cover picture the faces of women on other stamps that were considered for full-color presentation. The final result is quite spectacular, wouldn't you agree? If you have an idea for a future cover theme, please let us know.

Now sit back, relax and bask in the pleasures of the world's greatest hobby. Cheers!

Chris Snee

Charles Snee/Catalogue Editor

# Acknowledgments

Our appreciation and gratitude go to the following individuals who have assisted us in preparing information included in this year's Scott Catalogues. Some helpers prefer anonymity. These individuals have generously shared their stamp knowledge with others through the medium of the Scott Catalogue.

Those who follow provided information that is in addition to the hundreds of dealer price lists and advertisements and scores of auction catalogues and realizations that were used in producing the catalogue values. It is from those noted here that we have been able to obtain information on items not normally seen in published lists and advertisements. Support from these people goes beyond data leading to catalogue values, for they also are key to editorial changes.

A special acknowledgment to Liane and Sergio Sismondo of The Classic Collector for their extraordinary assistance and knowledge sharing that has aided in the preparation of this year's Standard and Classic Specialized Catalogues.

Vagn Andersen (AFSE)
Roland Austin
Robert Ausubel (Great Britain Collectors Club)
Jack Hagop Barsoumian (International Stamp Co.)
Jules K. Beck
Vladimir Berrio-Lemm
George G. Birdsall
John Birkinbine II
Roger S. Brody
Tom Brougham (Canal Zone Study Group)
Bernard Bujnak
Ronald A. Burns
Alan C. Bush
Mike Bush (Joseph V. Bush, Inc.)
Tina & John Carlson (JET Stamps)
Henry Chlanda
Bob Coale
Frank D. Correl
David Crawford
Tony L. Crumbley (Carolina Coin & Stamp, Inc.)
Christopher Dahle
Stephen R. Datz
Charles Deaton
Chris de Haer
Ubaldo Del Toro
Kenneth E. Diehl
Bob Dumaine
Sister Theresa Durand
Mark Eastzer (Markest Stamp Co.)
Paul G. Eckman
Mehdi Esmaili
Henry Fisher
Robert A. Fisher
Jeffrey M. Forster
Robert S. Freeman
Ernest E. Fricks (France & Colonies Philatelic Society)
Stan Goldfarb
Allan Grant (Rushstamps, Ltd.)
Daniel E. Grau
Fred F. Gregory
Jan E. Gronwall
John Heaton
Bruce Hecht (Bruce L. Hecht Co.)
Clifford O. Herrick (Fidelity Trading Co.)
Armen Hovsepian (Armenstamp)
Philip J. Hughes
Sandeep Jaiswal
John Jamieson (Saskatoon Stamp and Coin)
Peter Jeannopoulos
Stephen Joe (International Stamp Service)
William A. Jones
Allan Katz (Ventura Stamp Co.)
Stanford M. Katz
Patricia A. Kaufmann (Confederate Stamp Alliance)
George Krieger
John R. Lewis (The William Henry Stamp Co.)
Ulf Lindahl
Ignacio Llach (Filatelia Llach S.L.)
Robert L. Markovits (Quality Investors, Ltd.)
Marilyn R. Mattke
William K. McDaniel
Gary N. McLean
Mark S. Miller
Allen Mintz (United Postal Stationery Society)
Gary Morris (Pacific Midwest Co.)
Bruce M. Moyer (Moyer Stamps & Collectibles)
Richard H. Muller
Behruz Nassre
Greg Nelson
Nik & Lisa Oquist
Dr. Everett Parker
John E. Pearson (Pittwater Philatelic Service)
Donald J. Peterson (International Philippine Philatelic Society)
Stanley M. Piller (Stanley M. Piller & Associates)
Todor Drumev Popov
Philippe & Guido Poppe (Poppe Stamps, Inc.)
Siddique Mahmudur Rahman
Ghassan D. Riachi
Eric Roberts
Omar Rodriquez
Robert G. Rufe
Michael Ruggiero
Mehrdad Sadri (Persiphila)
Alex Schauss (Schauss Philatelics)
Jacques C. Schiff, Jr. (Jacques C. Schiff, Jr., Inc.)
Bernard Seckler (Fine Arts Philatelists)
Guy Shaw
Jeff Siddiqui
Sergio & Liane Sismondo (The Classic Collector)
Jay Smith
Frank J. Stanley, III
Kenneth Thompson
Peter Thy
Scott R. Trepel (Siegel Auction Galleries)
Kristian Wang
Daniel C. Warren
Giana Wayman
William R. Weiss, Jr. (Weiss Expertizing)
Ed Wener (Indigo)
Don White (Dunedin Stamp Centre)
Kirk Wolford (Kirk's Stamp Company)
Ralph Yorio
Val Zabijaka
Michal Zika

# Addresses, Telephone Numbers, Web Sites, E-Mail Addresses of General & Specialized Philatelic Societies

Collectors can contact the following groups for information about the philately of the areas within the scope of these societies, or inquire about membership in these groups. Aside from the general societies, we limit this list to groups that specialize in particular fields of philately, particular areas covered by the Scott Standard Postage Stamp Catalogue, and topical groups. Many more specialized philatelic society exist than those listed below. These addresses are updated yearly, and they are, to the best of our knowledge, correct and current. Groups should inform the editors of address changes whenever they occur. The editors also want to hear from other such specialized groups not listed. Unless otherwise noted all website addresses begin with http://

**American Philatelic Society**
100 Match Factory Place
Bellefonte PA 16823-1367
Ph: (814) 933-3803
www.stamps.org
E-mail: apsinfo@stamps.org

**American Stamp Dealers Association, Inc.**
P.O. Box 692
Leesport PA 19553
Ph: (800) 369-8207
www.americanstampdealer.com
E-mail: asda@americanstampdealer.com

**National Stamp Dealers Association**
Dick Keiser, President
2916 NW Bucklin Hill Road #136
Silverdale WA 98383-8514
Ph: (800) 875-6633
www.nsdainc.org
E-mail: gail@nsdainc.org

**International Society of Worldwide Stamp Collectors**
Joanne Berkowitz, MD
P.O. Box 19006
Sacramento CA 95819
www.iswsc.org
E-mail: executivedirector@iswsc.org

**Royal Philatelic Society**
41 Devonshire Place
London, W1G 6JY
UNITED KINGDOM
www.rpsl.org.uk
E-mail: secretary@rpsl.org.uk

**Royal Philatelic Society of Canada**
P.O. Box 929, Station Q
Toronto, ON, M4T 2P1
CANADA
Ph: (888) 285-4143
www.rpsc.org
E-mail: info@rpsc.org

**Young Stamp Collectors of America**
Janet Houser
100 Match Factory Place
Bellefonte PA 16823-1367
Ph: (814) 933-3820
www.stamps.org/ysca/intro.htm
E-mail: ysca@stamps.org

## Philatelic Research Resources

(The Scott editors encourage any additional research organizations to submit data for inclusion in this listing category)

**American Philatelic Research Library**
Tara Murray
100 Match Factory Place
Bellefonte PA 16823
Ph: (814) 933-3803
www.stamplibrary.org
E-mail: aprl@stamps.org

**Institute for Analytical Philately, Inc.**
P.O. Box 8035
Holland MI 49422-8035
Ph: (616) 399-9299
www.analyticalphilately.org
E-mail: info@analyticalphilately.org

**The Western Philatelic Library**
P.O. Box 2219
1500 Partridge Ave.
Sunnyvale CA 94087
Ph: (408) 733-0336
www.fwpf.org

## Groups focusing on fields or aspects found in worldwide philately (some might cover U.S. area only)

**American Air Mail Society**
Stephen Reinhard
P.O. Box 110
Mineola NY 11501
www.americanairmailsociety.org
E-mail: sreinhard1@optonline.net

**American First Day Cover Society**
Douglas Kelsey
P.O. Box 16277
Tucson AZ 85732-6277
Ph: (520) 321-0880
www.afdcs.org
E-mail: afdcs@afdcs.org

**American Revenue Association**
Eric Jackson
P.O. Box 728
Leesport PA 19533-0728
Ph: (610) 926-6200
www.revenuer.org
E-mail: eric@revenuer.com

**American Topical Association**
Vera Felts
P.O. Box 8
Carterville IL 62918-0008
Ph: (618) 985-5100
www.americantopicalassn.org
E-mail: americantopical@msn.com

**Christmas Seal & Charity Stamp Society**
John Denune
234 E. Broadway
Granville OH 43023
Ph: (740) 587-0276
www.seal-society.org
E-mail: jdenune@roadrunner.com

**Errors, Freaks and Oddities Collectors Club**
Don David Price
5320 Eastchester Drive
Sarasota FL 34134-2711
Ph: (717) 445-9420
www.efocc.org
E-mail: ddprice98@hotmail.com

**First Issues Collectors Club**
Kurt Streepy, Secretary
3128 E. Mattatha Drive
Bloomington IN 47401
www.firstissues.org
E-mail: secretary@firstissues.org

**International Society of Reply Coupon Collectors**
Peter Robin
P.O. Box 353
Bala Cynwyd PA 19004
E-mail: peterrobin@verizon.net

**The Joint Stamp Issues Society**
Richard Zimmermann
124, Avenue Guy de Coubertin
Saint Remy Les Chevreuse, F-78470
FRANCE
www.jointstampissues.net
E-mail: contact@jointstampissues.net

**National Duck Stamp Collectors Society**
Anthony J. Monico
P.O. Box 43
Harleysville PA 19438-0043
www.ndscs.org
E-mail: ndscs@ndscs.org

**No Value Identified Club**
Albert Sauvanet
Le Clos Royal B, Boulevard des Pas Enchantes
St. Sebastien-sur Loire, 44230
FRANCE
E-mail: alain.vailly@irin.univ nantes.fr

**The Perfins Club**
Jerry Hejduk
P.O. Box 490450
Leesburg FL 34749-0450
Ph: (352) 326-2117
E-mail: flprepers@comcast.net

**Postage Due Mail Study Group**
John Rawlins
13, Longacre
Chelmsford, CM1 3BJ
UNITED KINGDOM
E-mail: john.rawlins2@ukonline.co.uk.

**Post Mark Collectors Club**
Beverly Proulx
7629 Homestead Drive
Baldwinsville NY 13027
Ph: (315) 638-0532
www.postmarks.org
E-mail: stampdance@yahoo.com

**Postal History Society**
Joseph F. Frasch, Jr.
P.O. Box 20387
Columbus OH 43220-0387
www.stampclubs.com
E-mail: jfrasch@ix.netcom.com

**Precancel Stamp Society**
Jerry Hejduk
P.O. Box 490450
Leesburg FL 34749-0450
Ph: (352) 326-2117
www.precancels.com
E-mail: psspromosec@comcast.net

**United Postal Stationery Society**
Stuart Leven
P.O. Box 24764
San Jose CA 95154-4764
www.upss.org
E-mail: poststat@gmail.com

**United States Possessions Philatelic Society**
David S. Durbin
3604 Darice Lane
Jefferson City MO 65109
Ph: (573) 230-6921
www.uspps.net
E-mail: patlabb@aol.com

## Groups focusing on U.S. area philately as covered in the Standard Catalogue

**Canal Zone Study Group**
Tom Brougham
737 Neilson St.
Berkeley CA 94707
www.CanalZoneStudyGroup.com
E-mail: czsgsecretary@gmail.com

**Carriers and Locals Society**
Martin Richardson
P.O. Box 74
Grosse Ile MI 48138
www.pennypost.org
E-mail: martinr362@aol.com

**Confederate Stamp Alliance**
Patricia A. Kaufmann
10194 N. Old State Road
Lincoln DE 19960
Ph. (302) 422-2656
www.csalliance.org
E-mail: trishkauf@comcast.net

**Hawaiian Philatelic Society**
Kay H. Hoke
P.O. Box 10115
Honolulu HI 96816-0115
Ph: (808) 521-5721

**Plate Number Coil Collectors Club**
Gene Trinks
16415 W. Desert Wren Court
Surprise AZ 85374
Ph: (623) 322-4619
www.pnc3.org
E-mail: gctrinks@cox.net

**Ryukyu Philatelic Specialist Society**
Laura Edmonds, Secy.
P.O. Box 240177
Charlotte NC 28224-0177
Ph: (336) 509-3739
www.ryukyustamps.org
E-mail: secretary@ryukyustamps.org

**United Nations Philatelists**
Blanton Clement, Jr.
P.O. Box 146
Morrisville PA 19067-0146
www.unpi.com
E-mail: bclemjr@yahoo.com

**United States Stamp Society**
Executive Secretary
P.O. Box 6634
Katy TX 77491-6631
www.usstamps.org
E-mail: webmaster@usstamps.org

**U.S. Cancellation Club**
Roger Rhoads
6160 Brownstone Court
Mentor OH 44060
bob.trachimowicz.org/uscchome.htm
E-mail: rrrhoads@aol.com

**U.S. Philatelic Classics Society**
Rob Lund
2913 Fulton St.
Everett WA 98201-3733
www.uspcs.org
E-mail: membershipchairman@uspcs.org

## Groups focusing on philately of foreign countries or regions

**Aden & Somaliland Study Group**
Gary Brown
P.O. Box 106
Briar Hill, Victoria, 3088
AUSTRALIA
E-mail: garyjohn951@optushome.com.au

**American Society of Polar Philatelists (Antarctic areas)**
Alan Warren
P.O. Box 39
Exton PA 19341-0039
www.polarphilatelists.org

**Andorran Philatelic Study Circle**
D. Hope
17 Hawthorn Drive
Stalybridge, Cheshire, SK15 1UE
UNITED KINGDOM
apsc.free.fr
E-mail: apsc@free.fr

**Australian States Study Circle of The Royal Sydney Philatelic Club**
Ben Palmer
GPO 1751
Sydney, N.S.W., 2001
AUSTRALIA

**Austria Philatelic Society**
Ralph Schneider
P.O. Box 23049
Belleville IL 62223
Ph: (618) 277-6152
www.austriaphilatelicsociety.com
E-mail: rschneiderstamps@att.net

**Baltic States Philatelic Society**
Anatoly Chlenov
5719 Drysdale Court
San Jose CA 95124
Ph: (650) 863-1552
www.baltic-philately.com
E-mail: achlenov@localstamps.com

**American Belgian Philatelic Society**
Edward de Bary
11 Wakefield Drive Apt. 2105
Asheville NC 28803

**Bechuanalands and Botswana Society**
Neville Midwood
69 Porlock Lane
Furzton, Milton Keynes, MK4 1JY
UNITED KINGDOM
www.nevsoft.com
E-mail: bbsoc@nevsoft.com

**Bermuda Collectors Society**
John Pare
405 Perimeter Road
Mount Horeb WI 53572
www.bermudacollectorssociety.org
E-mail: science29@comcast.net

**Brazil Philatelic Association**
William V. Kriebel
1923 Manning St.
Philadelphia PA 19103-5728
Ph: (215) 735-3697
www.brazilphilatelic.org
E-mail: info@brazilphilatelic.org

**British Caribbean Philatelic Study Group**
Dr. Reuben A. Ramkissoon
11075 Benton St. #236
Loma Linda CA 92354-3182
www.bcpsg.com
E-mail: rramkissoon@juno.com

**The King George VI Collectors Society (British Commonwealth)**
Brian Livingstone
21 York Mansions, Prince of Wales Drive
London, SW11 4DL
UNITED KINGDOM
www.kg6.info
E-mail: livingstone484@btinternet.com

**British North America Philatelic Society (Canada & Provinces)**
David G. Jones
184 Larkin Drive
Nepean, ON, K2J 1H9
CANADA
www.bnaps.org
E-mail: shibumi.management@gmail.com

**British West Indies Study Circle**
John Seidl
4324 Granby Way
Marietta GA 30062
Ph: (770) 642-6424
www.bwisc.org
E-mail: john.seidl@gmail.com

**Burma Philatelic Study Circle**
Michael Whittaker
1, Ecton Leys, Hillside
Rugby, Warwickshire, CV22 5SL
UNITED KINGDOM
www.burmastamps.homecall.co.uk
E-mail: manningham8@mypostoffice.co.uk

**Cape and Natal Study Circle**
Dr. Guy Dillaway
P.O. Box 181
Weston MA 02493
www.nzsc.demon.co.uk

**Ceylon Study Circle**
R. W. P. Frost
42 Lonsdale Road, Cannington
Bridgewater, Somerset, TA5 2JS
UNITED KINGDOM
www.ceylonsc.org
E-mail: rodney.frost@tiscali.co.uk

**Channel Islands Specialists Society**
Moira Edwards
86, Hall Lane, Sandon
Chelmsford, Essex, CM2 7RQ
UNITED KINGDOM
www.ciss1950.org.uk
E-mail: membership@ciss1950.org.uk

**China Stamp Society**
Paul H. Gault
P.O. Box 20711
Columbus OH 43220
www.chinastampsociety.org
E-mail: secretary@chinastampsociety.org

**Colombia/Panama Philatelic Study Group (COPAPHIL)**
Thomas P. Myers
P.O. Box 522
Gordonsville VA 22942
www.copaphil.org
E-mail: tpmphil@hotmail.com

**Association Filatelic de Costa Rica**
Giana Wayman
c/o Interlink 102, P.O. Box 52-6770
Miami FL 33152
E-mail: scotland@racsa.co.cr

**Society for Costa Rica Collectors**
Dr. Hector R. Mena
P.O. Box 14831
Baton Rouge LA 70808
www.socorico.org
E-mail: hrmena@aol.com

**International Cuban Philatelic Society**
Ernesto Cuesta
P.O. Box 34434
Bethesda MD 20827
www.cubafil.org
E-mail: ecuesta@philat.com

**Cuban Philatelic Society of America Æ**
P.O. Box 141656
Coral Gables FL 33114-1656
www.cubapsa.com
E-mail: cpsa.usa@gmail.com

**Cyprus Study Circle**
Colin Dear
10 Marne Close, Wem
Shropshire, SY4 5YE
UNITED KINGDOM
www.cyprusstudycircle.org/index.htm
E-mail: colindear@talktalk.net

**Society for Czechoslovak Philately**
Tom Cassaboom
P.O. Box 4124
Prescott AZ 86302
www.csphilately.org
E-mail: klfck1@aol.com

**Danish West Indies Study Unit of the Scandinavian Collectors Club**
Arnold Sorensen
7666 Edgedale Drive
Newburgh IN 47630
Ph: (812) 480-6532
www.scc-online.org
E-mail: valbydwi@hotmail.com

**East Africa Study Circle**
Michael Vesey-Fitzgerald
Vernalls Orchard, Gosport Lane
Lyndhurst, S043 7BP
UNITED KINGDOM
www.easc.org.uk
E-mail: secretary@easc.org.uk

**Egypt Study Circle**
Mike Murphy
109 Chadwick Road
London, SE15 4PY
UNITED KINGDOM
Trent Ruebush: North American Agent
E-mail: truebrush@usaid.gov
egyptstudycircle.org.uk
E-mail: egyptstudycircle@hotmail.com

**Estonian Philatelic Society**
Juri Kirsimagi
29 Clifford Ave.
Pelham NY 10803
Ph: (914) 738-3713

**Ethiopian Philatelic Society**
Ulf Lindahl
21 Westview Place
Riverside CT 06878
Ph: (203) 866-3540
home.comcast.net/~fbheiser/ethiopia5.htm
E-mail: ulindahl@optonline.net

**Falkland Islands Philatelic Study Group**
Carl J. Faulkner
Williams Inn, On-the-Green
Williamstown MA 01267-2620
Ph: (413) 458-9371
www.fipsg.org.uk

**Faroe Islands Study Circle**
Norman Hudson
40 Queenís Road, Vicarís Cross
Chester, CH3 5HB
UNITED KINGDOM
www.faroeislandssc.org
E-mail: jntropics@hotmail.com

**Former French Colonies Specialist Society**
COLFRA
BP 628
75367 Paris, Cedex 08
FRANCE
www.colfra.com
E-mail: clubcolfra@aol.com

**France & Colonies Philatelic Society**
Edward Grabowski
111 Prospect St., 4C
Westfield NJ 07090
www.drunkenboat.net/frandcol/
E-mail: edjjg@alum.mit.edu

**Germany Philatelic Society**
P.O. Box 6547
Chesterfield MO 63006
www.germanyphilatelicusa.org

**Gibraltar Study Circle**
David R. Stirrups
10 Crescent Lodge
The Crescent
Middlesbrough, TS5 6SF
UNITED KINGDOM
www.gibraltarstudycircle.wordpress.com
E-mail: stirrups@btinternet.com

**Great Britain Collectors Club**
Steve McGill
10309 Brookhollow Circle
Highlands Ranch CO 80129
www.gbstamps.com/gbcc
E-mail: steve.mcgill@comcast.net

**International Society of Guatemala Collectors**
Jaime Marckwordt
449 St. Francis Blvd.
Daly City CA 94015-2136
www.guatemalastamps.com

**Haiti Philatelic Society**
Ubaldo Del Toro
5709 Marble Archway
Alexandria VA 22315
www.haitiphilately.org
E-mail: u007ubi@aol.com

**Hong Kong Stamp Society**
Ming W. Tsang
P.O. Box 206
Glenside PA 19038
www.hkss.org
E-mail: hkstamps@yahoo.com

**Society for Hungarian Philately**
Robert Morgan
2201 Roscomare Road
Los Angeles CA 90077-2222
Ph; (253) 759-4078
www.hungarianphilately.org
E-mail: ruthandlyman@nventure.com

**India Study Circle**
John Warren
P.O. Box 7326
Washington DC 20044
Ph: (202) 564-6876
www.indiastudycircle.org
E-mail: warren.john@epa.gov

**Indian Ocean Study Circle**
E. S. Hutton
29 Patermoster Close
Waltham Abby, Essex, EN9 3JU
UNITED KINGDOM
www.indianoceanstudycircle.com
E-mail:
secretary@indianoceanstudycircle.com

**Society of Indo-China Philatelists**
Ron Bentley
2600 N. 24th St.
Arlington VA 22207
www.sicp-online.org
E-mail: ron.bentley@verizon.net

**Iran Philatelic Study Circle**
Mehdi Esmaili
P.O. Box 750096
Forest Hills NY 11375
www.iranphilatelic.org
E-mail: m.esmaili@earthlink.net

**Eire Philatelic Association (Ireland)**
David J. Brennan
P.O. Box 704
Bernardsville NJ 07924
www.eirephilatelicassoc.org
E-mail: brennan704@aol.com

**Society of Israel Philatelists**
Howard Rotterdam
P.O. Box 507
Northfield OH 44067
www.israelstamps.com
E-mail: israelstamps@gmail.com

**Italy and Colonies Study Circle**
Richard Harlow
7 Duncombe House, 8 Manor Road
Teddington, TW11 8BE
UNITED KINGDOM
www.icsc.pwp.blueyonder.co.uk
E-mail: harlowr@gmail.com

**International Society for Japanese Philately**
William Eisenhauer
P.O. Box 230462
Tigard OR 97281
www.isjp.org
E-mail: secretary@isjp.org

**Korea Stamp Society**
John E. Talmage
P.O. Box 6889
Oak Ridge TN 37831
www.pennfamily.org/KSS-USA
E-mail: jtalmage@usit.net

**Latin American Philatelic Society**
Jules K. Beck
30½ St. #209
St. Louis Park MN 55426-3551

**Liberian Philatelic Society**
William Thomas Lockard
P.O. Box 106
Wellston OH 45692
Ph: (740) 384-2020
E-mail: tlockard@zoomnet.net

**Liechtenstudy USA (Liechtenstein)**
Paul Tremaine
410 SW Ninth St.
Dundee OR 97115
Ph: (503) 538-4500
www.liechtenstudy.org
E-mail: editor@liechtenstudy.org

**Lithuania Philatelic Society**
John Variakojis
3715 W. 68th St.
Chicago IL 60629
Ph: (773) 585-8649
lithuanianphilately.com/lps
E-mail: variakojis@sbcglobal.net

**Luxembourg Collectors Club**
Gary B. Little
7319 Beau Road
Sechelt, BC, VON 3A8
CANADA
lcc.luxcentral.com
E-mail: gary@luxcentral.com

**Malaya Study Group**
David Tett
P.O. Box 34
Wheathampstead, Herts, AL4 8JY
UNITED KINGDOM
www.m-s-g.org.uk
E-mail: davidtett@aol.com

**Malta Study Circle**
Alec Webster
50 Worcester Road
Sutton, Surrey, SM2 6QB
UNITED KINGDOM
E-mail: alecwebster50@hotmail.com

**Mexico-Elmhurst Philatelic Society International**
Thurston Bland
1022 Ramona Ave.
Corona CA 92879-2123
www.mepsi.org

**Asociacion Mexicana de Filatelia**
AMEXFIL
Jose Maria Rico, 129, Col. Del Valle
Mexico City DF, 03100
MEXICO
www.amexfil.mx
E-mail: alejandro.grossmann@gmail.com

**Society for Moroccan and Tunisian Philately**
206, bld. Pereire
75017 Paris
FRANCE
members.aol.com/Jhaik5814
E-mail: splm206@aol.com

**Nepal & Tibet Philatelic Study Group**
Roger D. Skinner
1020 Covington Road
Los Altos CA 94024-5003
Ph: (650) 968-4163
www.fuchs-online.com/ntpsc/
E-mail: colinhepper@hotmail.co.uk

**American Society for Netherlands Philately**
Hans Kremer
50 Rockport Court
Danville CA 94526
Ph: (925) 820-5841
www.asnp1975.com
E-mail: hkremer@usa.net

**New Zealand Society of Great Britain**
Keith C. Collins
13 Briton Crescent
Sanderstead, Surrey, CR2 0JN
UNITED KINGDOM
www.cs.stir.ac.uk/~rgc/nzsgb
E-mail: rgc@cs.stir.ac.uk

**Nicaragua Study Group**
Erick Rodriguez
11817 SW 11th St.
Miami FL 33184-2501
clubs.yahoo.com/clubs/nicaraguastudygroup
E-mail: nsgsec@yahoo.com

**Society of Australasian Specialists/Oceania**
David McNamee
P.O. Box 37
Alamo CA 94507
www.sasoceania.org
E-mail: dmcnamee@aol.com

**Orange Free State Study Circle**
J. R. Stroud
28 Oxford St.
Burnham-on-sea, Somerset, TA8 1LQ
UNITED KINGDOM
orangefreestatephilately.org.uk
E-mail: richardstroudph@gofast.co.uk

**Pacific Islands Study Circle**
John Ray
24 Woodvale Ave.
London, SE25 4AE
UNITED KINGDOM
www.pisc.org.uk
E-mail: info@pisc.org.uk

**Pakistan Philatelic Study Circle**
Jeff Siddiqui
P.O. Box 7002
Lynnwood WA 98046
E-mail: jeffsiddiqui@msn.com

**Centro de Filatelistas Independientes de Panama**
Vladimir Berrio-Lemm
Apartado 0823-02748
Plaza Concordia Panama
PANAMA
E-mail: panahistoria@gmail.com

**Papuan Philatelic Society**
Steven Zirinsky
P.O. Box 49, Ansonia Station
New York NY 10023
Ph: (718) 706-0616
www.communigate.co.uk/york/pps
E-mail: szirinsky@cs.com

**International Philippine Philatelic Society**
Donald J. Peterson
7408 Alaska Ave., NW
Washington DC 20012
Ph: (202) 291-6229
www.theipps.info
E-mail: dpeterson@comcast.net

**Pitcairn Islands Study Group**
Dr. Everett L. Parker
249 NW Live Oak Place
Lake City FL 32055-8906
Ph: (386) 754-8524
www.pisg.net
E-mail: eparker@hughes.net

**Polonus Philatelic Society (Poland)**
Robert Ogrodnik
P.O. Box 240428
Ballwin MO 63024-0428
Ph: (314) 821-6130
www.polonus.org
E-mail: rvo1937@gmail.com

**International Society for Portuguese Philately**
Clyde Homen
1491 Bonnie View Road
Hollister CA 95023-5117
www.portugalstamps.com
E-mail: cjh1491@sbcglobal.net

**Rhodesian Study Circle**
William R. Wallace
P.O. Box 16381
San Francisco CA 94116
www.rhodesianstudycircle.org.uk
E-mail: bwall8rscr@earthlink.net

**Rossica Society of Russian Philately**
Alexander Kolchinsky
1506 Country Lake Drive
Champaign IL 6821-6428
www.rossica.org
E-mail: alexander.kolchinsky@rossica.org

**St. Helena, Ascension & Tristan Da Cunha Philatelic Society**
Dr. Everett L. Parker
249 NW Live Oak Place
Lake City FL 32055-8906
Ph: (386) 754-8524
www.atlanticislands.org
E-mail: eparker@hughes.net

**St. Pierre & Miquelon Philatelic Society**
James R. (Jim) Taylor
2335 Paliswood Road SW
Calgary, AB, T2V 3P6
CANADA

**Associated Collectors of El Salvador**
Joseph D. Hahn
1015 Old Boalsburg Road Apt G-5
State College PA 16801-6149
www.elsalvadorphilately.org
E-mail: jdhahn2@gmail.com

**Fellowship of Samoa Specialists**
Donald Mee
23 Leo St.
Christchurch, 8051
NEW ZEALAND
www.samoaexpress.org
E-mail: donanm@xtra.co.nz

**Sarawak Specialists' Society**
Stu Leven
P.O. Box 24764
San Jose CA 95154-4764
Ph: (408) 978-0193
www.britborneostamps.org.uk
E-mail: stulev@ix.netcom.com

**Scandinavian Collectors Club**
Steve Lund
P.O. Box 16213
St. Paul MN 55116
www.scc-online.org
E-mail: steve88h@aol.com

**Slovakia Stamp Society**
Jack Benchik
P.O. Box 555
Notre Dame IN 46556

**Philatelic Society for Greater Southern Africa**
Alan Hanks
34 Seaton Drive
Aurora, ON, L4G 2KI
CANADA
Ph: (905) 727-6993
www.psgsa.thestampweb.com
Email: alan.hanks@sympatico.ca

**South Sudan Philatelic Society**
William Barclay
134A Spring Hill Road
South Londonerry VT 05155
E-mail: bill.barclay@wfp.org

**Spanish Philatelic Society**
Robert H. Penn
1108 Walnut Drive
Danielsville PA 18038
Ph: (610) 760-8711
E-mail: roberthpenn@aol.com

**Sudan Study Group**
David Sher
5 Ellis Park Road
Toronto, ON, M6S 2V2
CANADA
www.sudanstamps.org

**American Helvetia Philatelic Society (Switzerland, Liechtenstein)**
Richard T. Hall
P.O. Box 15053
Asheville NC 28813-0053
www.swiss-stamps.org
E-mail: secretary2@swiss-stamps.org

**Tannu Tuva Collectors Society**
Ken R. Simon
P.O. Box 385
Lake Worth FL 33460-0385
Ph: (561) 588-5954
www.tuva.tk
E-mail: yurttuva@yahoo.com

**Society for Thai Philately**
H. R. Blakeney
P.O. Box 25644
Oklahoma City OK 73125
E-mail: HRBlakeney@aol.com

**Transvaal Study Circle**
Jeff Woolgar
c/o 9 Meadow Road
Gravesend, DA11 7LR
UNITED KINGDOM
www.transvaal.org.uk

**Ottoman and Near East Philatelic Society (Turkey and related areas)**
Bob Stuchell
193 Valley Stream Lane
Wayne PA 19087
www.oneps.org
E-mail: rstuchell@msn.com

**Ukrainian Philatelic & Numismatic Society**
Michael G. Matus
157 Lucinda Lane
Wyomissing PA 19610-1026
Ph: (610) 927 3838
www.upns.org
E-mail: michael.matus@verizon.net

**Vatican Philatelic Society**
Sal Quinonez
1 Aldersgate, Apt. 1002
Riverhead NY 11901-1830
Ph: (516) 727-6426
www.vaticanphilately.org

**British Virgin Islands Philatelic Society**
Giorgio Migliavacca
P.O. Box 7007
St. Thomas VI 00801-0007
www.islandsun.com/FEATURES/bviphil9198.html
E-mail: issun@candwbvi.net

**West Africa Study Circle**
Dr. Peter Newroth
Suite 603
5332 Sayward Hill Crescent
Victoria, BC, V8Y 3H8
CANADA
www.wasc.org.uk/

**Western Australia Study Group**
Brian Pope
P.O. Box 423
Claremont, Western Australia, 6910
AUSTRALIA
www.wastudygroup.com
E-mail: black5swan@yahoo.com.au

**Yugoslavia Study Group of the Croatian Philatelic Society**
Michael Lenard
1514 N. Third Ave.
Wausau WI 54401
Ph: (715) 675-2833
E-mail: mjlenard@aol.com

### Topical Groups

**Americana Unit**
Dennis Dengel
17 Peckham Road
Poughkeepsie NY 12603-2018
www.americanaunit.org
E-mail: info@americanaunit.org

**Astronomy Study Unit**
John W. G. Budd
29203 Coharie Loop
San Antonio FL 33576-4643
Ph: (352) 588-4706
www.astronomystudyunit.com
E-mail: jwgbudd@earthlink.net

**Bicycle Stamp Club**
Tony Teideman
P.O. Box 90
Baulkham Hills, NSW, 1755
AUSTRALIA
members.tripod.com/~bicyclestamps
E-mail: tonimaur@bigpond.com

**Biology Unit**
Alan Hanks
34 Seaton Drive
Aurora, ON, L4G 2K1
CANADA
Ph: (905) 727-6993

**Bird Stamp Society**
Graham Horsman
23A E. Main St.
Blackburn West Lothian
Scotland, EH47 7QR
UNITED KINGDOM
www.bird-stamps.org/bss
E-mail: graham_horsman7@msn.com

**Canadiana Study Unit**
Robert Haslewood
5140 Cumberland Avenue
Montreal, Quebec, H4V 2N8
CANADA
E-mail: robert.haslewood058@sympatico.ca

**Captain Cook Study Unit**
Brian P. Sandford
173 Minuteman Drive
Concord MA 01742-1923
www.captaincooksociety.com
E-mail: US@captaincooksociety.com

**Casey Jones Railroad Unit**
Roy W. Menninger MD
85 SW Pepper Tree Lane
Topeka KS 66611-2072
www.uqp.de/cjr/index.htm
E-mail: roymenn@sbcglobal.net

**Cats on Stamps Study Unit**
Mary Ann Brown
3006 Wade Road
Durham NC 27705
www.catsonstamps.org
E-mail: mabrown@nc.rr.com

**Chemistry & Physics on Stamps Study Unit**
Dr. Roland Hirsch
20458 Water Point Lane
Germantown MD 20874
www.cpossu.org
E-mail: rfhirsch@cpossu.org

**Chess on Stamps Study Unit**
Ray C. Alexis
608 Emery St.
Longmont CO 80501
E-mail: chessstuff911459@aol.com

**Christmas Philatelic Club**
Jim Balog
P.O. Box 774
Geneva OH 44041
www.web.295.ca/cpc/
E-mail: jpbstamps@windstream.net

**Columbus Philatelic Society**
Donald R. Ager **Christopher**
P.O. Box 71
Hillsboro NH 03244-0071
Ph: (603) 464-5379
ccps.maphist.nl/
E-mail: meganddon@tds.net

**Collectors of Religion on Stamps**
James Bailey
P.O. Box 937
Brownwood TX 76804
www.coros-society.org
E-mail: corosec@directtv.net

**Dogs on Stamps Study Unit**
Morris Raskin
202A Newport Road
Monroe Township NJ 08831
Ph: (609) 655-7411
www.dossu.org
E-mail: mraskin@cellurian.com

**Earth's Physical Features Study Group**
Fred Klein
515 Magdalena Ave.
Los Altos CA 94024
epfsu.jeffhayward.com

**Ebony Society of Philatelic Events and Reflections, Inc. (African-American topicals)**
Manuel Gilyard
800 Riverside Drive, Suite 4H
New York NY 10032-7412
www.esperstamps.org
E-mail: gilyardmani@aol.com

**Europa Study Unit**
Tonny E. Van Loij
3002 S. Xanthia St.
Denver CO 80231-4237
www.europastudyunit.org/
E-mail: tvanloij@gmail.com

**Fine & Performing Arts**
Deborah L. Washington
6922 S. Jeffery Blvd., #7 - North
Chicago IL 60649
E-mail: brasslady@comcast.net

**Fire Service in Philately**
John Zaranek
81 Hillpine Road
Cheektowaga NY 14227-2259
Ph: (716) 668-3352
E-mail: jczaranek@roadrunner.com

**Gay & Lesbian History on Stamps Club**
Joe Petronie
P.O. Box 190842
Dallas TX 75219-0842
www.glhsc.org
E-mail: glhsc@aol.com

**Gems, Minerals & Jewelry Study Unit**
George Young
P.O. Box 632
Tewksbury MA 01876-0632
Ph: (978) 851-8283
www.rockhounds.com/rockshop/gmjsuapp.txt
E-mail: george-young@msn.com

**Graphics Philately Association**
Mark H. Winnegrad
P.O. Box 380
Bronx NY 10462-0380
www.graphics-stamps.org
E-mail: indybruce1@yahoo.com

**Journalists, Authors & Poets on Stamps**
Ms. Lee Straayer
P.O. Box 6808
Champaign IL 61826
E-mail: lstraayer@dcbnet.com

**Lighthouse Stamp Society**
Dalene Thomas
8612 W. Warren Lane
Lakewood CO 80227-2352
Ph: (303) 986-6620
www.lighthousestampsociety.org
E-mail: dalene@lighthousestampsociety.org

**Lions International Stamp Club**
John Bargus
108-2777 Barry Road RR 2
Mill Bay, BC, V0R 2P2
CANADA
Ph: (250) 743-5782

**Mahatma Gandhi On Stamps Study Circle**
Pramod Shivagunde
Pratik Clinic, Akluj
Solapur, Maharashtra, 413101
INDIA
E-mail: drnanda@bom6.vsnl.net.in

**Masonic Study Unit**
Stanley R. Longenecker
930 Wood St.
Mount Joy PA 17552-1926
Ph: (717) 669-9094
E-mail: natsco@usa.net

**Mathematical Study Unit**
Monty J. Strauss
4209 88th St.
Lubbock TX 79423-2041
www.math.ttu.edu/msu/
E-mail: m.strauss@ttu.edu

**Medical Subjects Unit**
Dr. Frederick C. Skvara
P.O. Box 6228
Bridgewater NJ 08807
E-mail: fcskvara@optonline.net

**Military Postal History Society**
Ed Dubin
1 S. Wacker Drive, Suite 3500
Chicago IL 60606
www.militaryPHS.org
E-mail: dubine@comcast.net

**Mourning Stamps and Covers Club**
James Bailey, Jr.
P.O. Box 937
Brownwood TX 76804
E-mail: jfbailey238@directv.net

**Napoleonic Age Philatelists**
Ken Berry
7513 Clayton Drive
Oklahoma City OK 73132-5636
Ph: (405) 721-0044
www.nap-stamps.org
E-mail: krb2@earthlink.net

**Old World Archeological Study Unit**
Caroline Scannell
11 Dawn Drive
Smithtown NY 11787-1761
www.owasu.org
E-mail: editor@owasu.org

**Petroleum Philatelic Society International**
Dr. Chris Coggins
174 Old Bedford Road
Luton, England, LU2 7HW
UNITED KINGDOM
E-mail: WAMTECH@Luton174.fsnet.co.uk

**Philatelic Computing Study Group**
Robert de Violini
P.O. Box 5025
Oxnard CA 93031-5025
www.pcsg.org
E-mail: dviolini@adelphia.net

**Rotary on Stamps Unit**
Gerald L. Fitzsimmons
105 Calla Ricardo
Victoria TX 77904
rotaryonstamps.org
E-mail: glfitz@suddenlink.net

**Scouts on Stamps Society International**
Lawrence Clay
P.O. Box 6228
Kennewick WA 99336
Ph: (509) 735-3731
www.sossi.org
E-mail: lclay3731@charter.net

**Ships on Stamps Unit**
Les Smith
302 Conklin Ave.
Penticton, BC, V2A 2T4
CANADA
Ph: (250) 493-7486
www.shipsonstamps.org
E-mail: lessmith440@shaw.ca

**Space Unit**
Carmine Torrisi
P.O. Box 780241
Maspeth NY 11378
Ph: (917) 620-5687
stargate.1usa.com/stamps/
E-mail: ctorrisi1@nyc.rr.com

**Sports Philatelists International**
Mark Maestrone
2824 Curie Place
San Diego CA 92122-4110
www.sportstamps.org
Email: president@sportstamps.org

**Stamps on Stamps Collectors Club**
Alf Jordan
156 W. Elm St.
Yarmouth ME 04096
www.stampsonstamps.org
E-mail: ajordan1@maine.rr.com

**Windmill Study Unit**
Walter J. Hollien
P.O. Box 346
Long Valley NJ 07853-0346
Ph: (862) 812-0030
E-mail: whollien@earthlink.net

**Wine On Stamps Study Unit**
Bruce L. Johnson
115 Raintree Drive
Zionsville IN 46077
www.wine-on-stamps.org
E-mail: indybruce@yahoo.com

**Women on Stamps Study Unit**
Hugh Gottfried
2232 26th St.
Santa Monica CA 90405-1902
E-mail: hgottfried@adelphia.net

# Expertizing Services

The following organizations will, for a fee, provide expert opinions about stamps submitted to them. Collectors should contact these organizations to find out about their fees and requirements before submiting philatelic material to them. The listing of these groups here is not intended as an endorsement by Scott Publishing Co.

## General Expertizing Services

**American Philatelic Expertizing Service (a service of the American Philatelic Society)**
100 Match Factory Place
Bellefonte PA 16823-1367
Ph: (814) 237-3803
Fax: (814) 237-6128
www.stamps.org
E-mail: ambristo@stamps.org
Areas of Expertise: Worldwide

**B. P. A. Expertising, Ltd.**
P.O. Box 1141
Guildford, Surrey, GU5 0WR
UNITED KINGDOM
E-mail: sec@bpaexpertising.org
Areas of Expertise: British Commonwealth, Great Britain, Classics of Europe, South America and the Far East

**Philatelic Foundation**
70 W. 40th St., 15th Floor
New York NY 10018
Ph: (212) 221-6555
Fax: (212) 221-6208
www.philatelicfoundation.org
E-mail: philatelicfoundation@verizon.net
Areas of Expertise: U.S. & Worldwide

**Philatelic Stamp Authentication and Grading, Inc.**
P.O. Box 37-2460
Satellite Beach FL 32937
Customer Service: (305) 345-9864
www.psaginc.com
E-mail: info@psaginc.com
Areas of Expertise: U.S., Canal Zone, Hawaii, Philippines, Canada & Provinces

**Professional Stamp Experts**
P.O. Box 6170
Newport Beach CA 92658
Ph: (877) STAMP-88
Fax: (949) 833-7955
www.collectors.com/pse
E-mail: pseinfo@collectors.com
Areas of Expertise: Stamps and covers of U.S., U.S. Possessions, British Commonwealth

**Royal Philatelic Society Expert Committee**
41 Devonshire Place
London, W1N 1PE
UNITED KINGDOM
www.rpsl.org.uk/experts.html
E-mail: experts@rpsl.org.uk
Areas of Expertise: Worldwide

## Expertizing Services Covering Specific Fields Or Countries

**China Stamp Society Expertizing Service**
1050 W. Blue Ridge Blvd.
Kansas City MO 64145
Ph: (816) 942-6300
E-mail: hjmesq@aol.com
Areas of Expertise: China

**Confederate Stamp Alliance Authentication Service**
Gen. Frank Crown, Jr.
P.O. Box 278
Capshaw AL 35742-0396
Ph: (302) 422-2656
Fax: (302) 424-1990
www.csalliance.org
E-mail: csaas@knology.net
Areas of Expertise: Confederate stamps and postal history

**Errors, Freaks and Oddities Collectors Club Expertizing Service**
138 East Lakemont Drive
Kingsland GA 31548
Ph: (912) 729-1573
Areas of Expertise: U.S. errors, freaks and oddities

**Estonian Philatelic Society Expertizing Service**
39 Clafford Lane
Melville NY 11747
Ph: (516) 421-2078
E-mail: esto4@aol.com
Areas of Expertise: Estonia

**Hwaiian Philatelic Society Expertizing Service**
P.O. Box 10115
Honolulu HI 96816-0115
Areas of Expertise: Hawaii

**Hong Kong Stamp Society Expertizing Service**
P.O. Box 206
Glenside PA 19038
Fax: (215) 576-6850
Areas of Expertise: Hong Kong

**International Association of Philatelic Experts United States Associate members:**

Paul Buchsbayew
119 W. 57th St.
New York NY 10019
Ph: (212) 977-7734
Fax: (212) 977-8653
Areas of Expertise: Russia, Soviet Union

William T. Crowe
P.O. Box 2090
Danbury CT 06813-2090
E-mail: wtcrowe@aol.com
Areas of Expertise: United States

John Lievsay
(see American Philatelic Expertizing Service and Philatelic Foundation)
Areas of Expertise: France

Robert W. Lyman
P.O. Box 348
Irvington on Hudson NY 10533
Ph and Fax: (914) 591-6937
Areas of Expertise: British North America, New Zealand

Robert Odenweller
P.O. Box 401
Bernardsville NJ 07924-0401
Ph and Fax: (908) 766-5460
Areas of Expertise: New Zealand, Samoa to 1900

Sergio Sismondo
10035 Carousel Center Drive
Syracuse NY 13290-0001
Ph: (315) 422-2331
Fax: (315) 422-2956
Areas of Expertise: British East Africa, Camerouns, Cape of Good Hope, Canada, British North America

**International Society for Japanese Philately Expertizing Committee**
132 North Pine Terrace
Staten Island NY 10312-4052
Ph: (718) 227-5229
Areas of Expertise: Japan and related areas, except WWII Japanese Occupation issues

**International Society for Portuguese Philately Expertizing Service**
P.O. Box 43146
Philadelphia PA 19129-3146
Ph and Fax: (215) 843-2106
E-mail: s.s.washburne@worldnet.att.net
Areas of Expertise: Portugal and Colonies

**Mexico-Elmhurst Philatelic Society International Expert Committee**
P.O. Box 1133
West Covina CA 91793
Areas of Expertise: Mexico

**Ukrainian Philatelic & Numismatic Society Expertizing Service**
30552 Dell Lane
Warren MI 48092-1862
Areas of Expertise: Ukraine, Western Ukraine

**V. G. Greene Philatelic Research Foundation**
P.O. Box 204, Station Q
Toronto, ON, M4T 2M1
CANADA
Ph: (416) 921-2073
Fax: (416) 921-1282
www.greenefoundation.ca
E-mail: vggfoundation@on.aibn.com
Areas of Expertise: British North America

# Information on Catalogue Values, Grade and Condition

## Catalogue Value

The Scott Catalogue value is a retail value; that is, an amount you could expect to pay for a stamp in the grade of Very Fine with no faults. Any exceptions to the grade valued will be noted in the text. The general introduction on the following pages and the individual section introductions further explain the type of material that is valued. The value listed for any given stamp is a reference that reflects recent actual dealer selling prices for that item.

Dealer retail price lists, public auction results, published prices in advertising and individual solicitation of retail prices from dealers, collectors and specialty organizations have been used in establishing the values found in this catalogue. Scott Publishing Co. values stamps, but Scott is not a company engaged in the business of buying and selling stamps as a dealer.

Use this catalogue as a guide for buying and selling. The actual price you pay for a stamp may be higher or lower than the catalogue value because of many different factors, including the amount of personal service a dealer offers, or increased or decreased interest in the country or topic represented by a stamp or set. An item may occasionally be offered at a lower price as a "loss leader," or as part of a special sale. You also may obtain an item inexpensively at public auction because of little interest at that time or as part of a large lot.

Stamps that are of a lesser grade than Very Fine, or those with condition problems, generally trade at lower prices than those given in this catalogue. Stamps of exceptional quality in both grade and condition often command higher prices than those listed.

Values for pre-1900 unused issues are for stamps with approximately half or more of their original gum. Stamps with most or all of their original gum may be expected to sell for more, and stamps with less than half of their original gum may be expected to sell for somewhat less than the values listed. On rarer stamps, it may be expected that the original gum will be somewhat more disturbed than it will be on more common issues. Post-1900 unused issues are assumed to have full original gum. From breakpoints in most countries' listings, stamps are valued as never hinged, due to the wide availability of stamps in that condition. These notations are prominently placed in the listings and in the country information preceding the listings. Some countries also feature listings with dual values for hinged and never-hinged stamps.

## Grade

A stamp's grade and condition are crucial to its value. The accompanying illustrations show examples of Very Fine stamps from different time periods, along with examples of stamps in Fine to Very Fine and Extremely Fine grades as points of reference. When a stamp seller offers a stamp in any grade from fine to superb without further qualifying statements, that stamp should not only have the centering grade as defined, but it also should be free of faults or other condition problems.

**FINE** stamps (illustrations not shown) have designs that are quite off center, with the perforations on one or two sides very close to the design but not quite touching it. There is white space between the perforations and the design that is minimal but evident to the unaided eye. Imperforate stamps may have small margins, and earlier issues may show the design just touching one edge of the stamp design. Very early perforated issues normally will have the perforations slightly cutting into the design. Used stamps may have heavier than usual cancellations.

**FINE-VERY FINE** stamps will be somewhat off center on one side, or slightly off center on two sides. Imperforate stamps will have two margins of at least normal size, and the design will not touch any edge. For perforated stamps, the perfs are well clear of the design, but are still noticeably off center. *However, early issues of a country may be printed in such a way that the design naturally is very close to the edges. In these cases, the perforations may cut into the design very slightly.* Used stamps will not have a cancellation that detracts from the design.

**VERY FINE** stamps will be just slightly off center on one or two sides, but the design will be well clear of the edge. The stamp will present a nice, balanced appearance. Imperforate stamps will be well centered within normal-sized margins. *However, early issues of many countries may be printed in such a way that the perforations may touch the design on one or more sides. Where this is the case, a boxed note will be found defining the centering and margins of the stamps being valued.* Used stamps will have light or otherwise neat cancellations. This is the grade used to establish Scott Catalogue values.

**EXTREMELY FINE** stamps are close to being perfectly centered. Imperforate stamps will have even margins that are slightly larger than normal. Even the earliest perforated issues will have perforations clear of the design on all sides.

**Scott Publishing Co. recognizes that there is no formally enforced grading scheme for postage stamps, and that the final price you pay or obtain for a stamp will be determined by individual agreement at the time of transaction.**

## Condition

*Grade* addresses only centering and (for used stamps) cancellation. *Condition* refers to factors other than grade that affect a stamp's desirability.

Factors that can increase the value of a stamp include exceptionally wide margins, particularly fresh color, the presence of selvage, and plate or die varieties. Unusual cancels on used stamps (particularly those of the 19th century) can greatly enhance their value as well.

Factors other than faults that decrease the value of a stamp include loss of original gum, regumming, a hinge remnant or foreign object adhering to the gum, natural inclusions, straight edges, and markings or notations applied by collectors or dealers.

Faults include missing pieces, tears, pin or other holes, surface scuffs, thin spots, creases, toning, short or pulled perforations, clipped perforations, oxidation or other forms of color changelings, soiling, stains, and such man-made changes as reperforations or the chemical removal or lightening of a cancellation.

## Grading Illustrations

On the following two pages are illustrations of various stamps from countries appearing in this volume. These stamps are arranged by country, and they represent early or important issues that are often found in widely different grades in the marketplace. The editors believe the illustrations will prove useful in showing the margin size and centering that will be seen on the various issues.

In addition to the matters of margin size and centering, collectors are reminded that the very fine stamps valued in the Scott catalogues also will possess fresh color and intact perforations, and they will be free from defects.

Examples shown are computer-manipulated images made from single digitized master illustrations.

## Stamp Illustrations Used in the Catalogue

It is important to note that the stamp images used for identification purposes in this catlaogue may not be indicative of the grade of stamp being valued. Refer to the written discussion of grades on this page and to the grading illustrations on the following two pages for grading information.

Fine-Very Fine

SCOTT CATALOGUES VALUE STAMPS IN THIS GRADE

Very Fine

Extremely Fine

Fine-Very Fine

SCOTT CATALOGUES VALUE STAMPS IN THIS GRADE

Very Fine

Extremely Fine

Fine-Very Fine

SCOTT CATALOGUES VALUE STAMPS IN THIS GRADE

Very Fine

Extremely Fine

Fine-Very Fine

SCOTT CATALOGUES VALUE STAMPS IN THIS GRADE

Very Fine

Extremely Fine

For purposes of helping to determine the gum condition and value of an unused stamp, Scott Publishing Co. presents the following chart which details different gum conditions and indicates how the conditions correlate with the Scott values for unused stamps. Used together, the Illustrated Grading Chart on the previous pages and this Illustrated Gum Chart should allow catalogue users to better understand the grade and gum condition of stamps valued in the Scott catalogues.

| Gum Categories: | MINT N.H. | ORIGINAL GUM (O.G.) | | | | NO GUM |
|---|---|---|---|---|---|---|
| | <br>**Mint Never Hinged**<br>*Free from any disturbance* | <br>**Lightly Hinged**<br>*Faint impression of a removed hinge over a small area* | 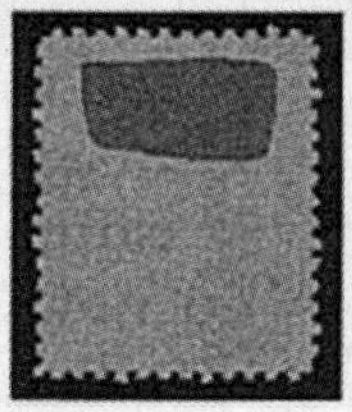<br>**Hinge Mark or Remnant**<br>*Prominent hinged spot with part or all of the hinge remaining* | 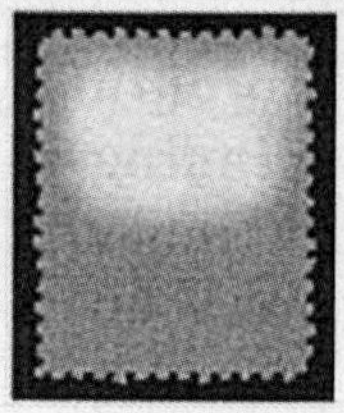<br>**Large part o.g.**<br>*Approximately half or more of the gum intact* | <br>**Small part o.g.**<br>*Approximately less than half of the gum intact* | <br>**No gum**<br>*Only if issued with gum* |
| Commonly Used Symbol: | ★★ | ★ | ★ | ★ | ★ | (★) |
| Pre-1900 Issues (Pre-1881 for U.S.) | *Very fine pre-1900 stamps in these categories trade at a premium over Scott value* | | | Scott Value for "Unused" | | Scott "No Gum" listings for selected unused classic stamps |
| From 1900 to breakpoints for listings of never-hinged stamps | Scott "Never Hinged" listings for selected unused stamps | Scott Value for "Unused" (Actual value will be affected by the degree of hinging of the full o.g.) | | | | |
| From breakpoints noted for many countries | Scott Value for "Unused" | | | | | |

**Never Hinged (NH; ★★):** A never-hinged stamp will have full original gum that will have no hinge mark or disturbance. The presence of an expertizer's mark does not disqualify a stamp from this designation.

**Original Gum (OG; ★):** Pre-1900 stamps should have approximately half or more of their original gum. On rarer stamps, it may be expected that the original gum will be somewhat more disturbed than it will be on more common issues. Post-1900 stamps should have full original gum. Original gum will show some disturbance caused by a previous hinge(s) which may be present or entirely removed. The actual value of a post-1900 stamp will be affected by the degree of hinging of the full original gum.

**Disturbed Original Gum:** Gum showing noticeable effects of humidity, climate or hinging over more than half of the gum. The significance of gum disturbance in valuing a stamp in any of the Original Gum categories depends on the degree of disturbance, the rarity and normal gum condition of the issue and other variables affecting quality.

**Regummed (RG; (★)):** A regummed stamp is a stamp without gum that has had some type of gum privately applied at a time after it was issued. This normally is done to deceive collectors and/or dealers into thinking that the stamp has original gum and therefore has a higher value. A regummed stamp is considered the same as a stamp with none of its original gum for purposes of grading.

# Understanding the Listings

On the opposite page is an enlarged "typical" listing from this catalogue. Below are detailed explanations of each of the highlighted parts of the listing.

**1 Scott number** — Scott catalogue numbers are used to identify specific items when buying, selling or trading stamps. Each listed postage stamp from every country has a unique Scott catalogue number. Therefore, Germany Scott 99, for example, can only refer to a single stamp. Although the Scott catalogue usually lists stamps in chronological order by date of issue, there are exceptions. When a country has issued a set of stamps over a period of time, those stamps within the set are kept together without regard to date of issue. This follows the normal collecting approach of keeping stamps in their natural sets.

When a country issues a set of stamps over a period of time, a group of consecutive catalogue numbers is reserved for the stamps in that set, as issued. If that group of numbers proves to be too few, capital-letter suffixes, such as "A" or "B," may be added to existing numbers to create enough catalogue numbers to cover all items in the set. A capital-letter suffix indicates a major Scott catalogue number listing. Scott generally uses a suffix letter only once. Therefore, a catalogue number listing with a capital-letter suffix will seldom be found with the same letter (lower case) used as a minor-letter listing. If there is a Scott 16A in a set, for example, there will seldom be a Scott 16a. However, a minor-letter "a" listing may be added to a major number containing an "A" suffix (Scott 16Aa, for example).

Suffix letters are cumulative. A minor "b" variety of Scott 16A would be Scott 16Ab, not Scott 16b.

There are times when a reserved block of Scott catalogue numbers is too large for a set, leaving some numbers unused. Such gaps in the numbering sequence also occur when the catalogue editors move an item's listing elsewhere or have removed it entirely from the catalogue. Scott does not attempt to account for every possible number, but rather attempts to assure that each stamp is assigned its own number.

Scott numbers designating regular postage normally are only numerals. Scott numbers for other types of stamps, such as air post, semi-postal, postal tax, postage due, occupation and others have a prefix consisting of one or more capital letters or a combination of numerals and capital letters.

**2 Illustration number** — Illustration or design-type numbers are used to identify each catalogue illustration. For most sets, the lowest face-value stamp is shown. It then serves as an example of the basic design approach for other stamps not illustrated. Where more than one stamp use the same illustration number, but have differences in design, the design paragraph or the description line clearly indicates the design on each stamp not illustrated. Where there are both vertical and horizontal designs in a set, a single illustration may be used, with the exceptions noted in the design paragraph or description line.

When an illustration is followed by a lower-case letter in parentheses, such as "A2(b)," the trailing letter indicates which overprint or surcharge illustration applies.

Illustrations normally are 70 percent of the original size of the stamp. Oversized stamps, blocks and souvenir sheets are reduced even more. Overprints and surcharges are shown at 100 percent of their original size if shown alone, but are 70 percent of original size if shown on stamps. In some cases, the illustration will be placed above the set, between listings or omitted completely. Overprint and surcharge illustrations are not placed in this catalogue for purposes of expertizing stamps.

**3 Paper color** — The color of a stamp's paper is noted in italic type when the paper used is not white.

**4 Listing styles** — There are two principal types of catalogue listings: major and minor.

Major listings are in a larger type style than minor listings. The catalogue number is a numeral that can be found with or without a capital-letter suffix, and with or without a prefix.

Minor listings are in a smaller type style and have a small-letter suffix or (if the listing immediately follows that of the major number) may show only the letter. These listings identify a variety of the major item. Examples include perforation and shade differences, multiples (some souvenir sheets, booklet panes and se-tenant combinations), and singles of multiples.

Examples of major number listings include 16, 28A, B97, C13A, 10N5, and 10N6A. Examples of minor numbers are 16a and C13Ab.

**5 Basic information about a stamp or set** — Introducing each stamp issue is a small section (usually a line listing) of basic information about a stamp or set. This section normally includes the date of issue, method of printing, perforation, watermark and, sometimes, some additional information of note. *Printing method, perforation and watermark apply to the following sets until a change is noted.* Stamps created by overprinting or surcharging previous issues are assumed to have the same perforation, watermark, printing method and other production characteristics as the original. Dates of issue are as precise as Scott is able to confirm and often reflect the dates on first-day covers, rather than the actual date of release.

**6 Denomination** — This normally refers to the face value of the stamp; that is, the cost of the unused stamp at the post office at the time of issue. When a denomination is shown in parentheses, it does not appear on the stamp. This includes the non-denominated stamps of the United States, Brazil and Great Britain, for example.

**7 Color or other description** — This area provides information to solidify identification of a stamp. In many recent cases, a description of the stamp design appears in this space, rather than a listing of colors.

**8 Year of issue** — In stamp sets that have been released in a period that spans more than a year, the number shown in parentheses is the year that stamp first appeared. Stamps without a date appeared during the first year of the issue. Dates are not always given for minor varieties.

**9 Value unused and Value used** — The Scott catalogue values are based on stamps that are in a grade of Very Fine unless stated otherwise. Unused values refer to items that have not seen postal, revenue or any other duty for which they were intended. Pre-1900 unused stamps that were issued with gum must have at least most of their original gum. Later issues are assumed to have full original gum. From breakpoints specified in most countries' listings, stamps are valued as never hinged. Stamps issued without gum are noted. Modern issues with PVA or other synthetic adhesives may appear ungummed. Unused self-adhesive stamps are valued as appearing undisturbed on their original backing paper. Values for used self-adhesive stamps are for examples either on piece or off piece. For a more detailed explanation of these values, please see the "Catalogue Value," "Condition" and "Understanding Valuing Notations" sections elsewhere in this introduction.

In some cases, where used stamps are more valuable than unused stamps, the value is for an example with a contemporaneous cancel, rather than a modern cancel or a smudge or other unclear marking. For those stamps that were released for postal and fiscal purposes, the used value represents a postally used stamp. Stamps with revenue cancels generally sell for less.

Stamps separated from a complete se-tenant multiple usually will be worth less than a pro-rated portion of the se-tenant multiple, and stamps lacking the attached labels that are noted in the listings will be worth less than the values shown.

**10 Changes in basic set information** — Bold type is used to show any changes in the basic data given for a set of stamps. These basic data categories include perforation gauge measurement, paper type, printing method and watermark.

**11 Total value of a set** — The total value of sets of three or more stamps issued after 1900 are shown. The set line also notes the range of Scott numbers and total number of stamps included in the grouping. The actual value of a set consisting predominantly of stamps having the minimum value of 25 cents may be less than the total value shown. Similarly, the actual value or catalogue value of se-tenant pairs or of blocks consisting of stamps having the minimum value of 25 cents may be less than the catalogue values of the component parts.

A6

King George VI
A7

| | | | | | |
|---|---|---|---|---|---|
| **1938-44** | | | **Engr.** | | **Perf. 12½** |
| **54** | A6 | ½p | green | .25 | *2.00* |
| **54A** | A6 | ½p | dk brown ('42) | .25 | *2.25* |
| **55** | A6 | 1p | dark brown | 2.50 | .35 |
| **55A** | A6 | 1p | green ('42) | .25 | 1.*75* |
| **56** | A6 | 1½p | dark carmine | 4.00 | *6.00* |
| **56A** | A6 | 1½p | gray ('42) | .25 | *5.75* |
| **57** | A6 | 2p | gray | 5.00 | 1.25 |
| **57A** | A6 | 2p | dark car ('42) | .25 | *2.00* |
| **58** | A6 | 3p | blue | .60 | 1.00 |
| **59** | A6 | 4p | rose lilac | 1.60 | 2.00 |
| **60** | A6 | 6p | dark violet | 2.00 | 2.00 |
| **61** | A6 | 9p | olive bister | 2.00 | *4.75* |
| **62** | A6 | 1sh | orange & blk | 2.10 | *3.25* |

**Typo.**
**Perf. 14**
**Chalky Paper**

| | | | | | |
|---|---|---|---|---|---|
| **63** | A7 | 2sh | ultra & dl vio, *bl* | 7.00 | *17.50* |
| **64** | A7 | 2sh6p | red & blk, *bl* | 8.00 | *19.50* |
| **65** | A7 | 5sh | red & grn, *yel* | 35.00 | 30.00 |
| **a.** | | | 5sh dk red & dp grn, *yel* ('44) | 55.00 | *140.00* |
| **66** | A7 | 10sh | red & grn, *grn* | 35.00 | *70.00* |

**Wmk. 3**

| | | | | | |
|---|---|---|---|---|---|
| **67** | A7 | £1 | blk & vio, *red* | 30.00 | *45.00* |
| | | | *Nos. 54-67 (18)* | 136.05 | *216.35* |
| | | | Set, never hinged | 220.00 | |

**1** SCOTT NUMBER

**2** ILLUS. NUMBER

**3** PAPER COLOR

**4** LISTING STYLES — MAJORS, MINORS

**5** BASIC INFORMATION ON STAMP OR SET

**6** DENOMINATION

**7** COLOR OR OTHER DESCRIPTION

**8** YEAR OF ISSUE

**9** CATALOGUE VALUES — UNUSED, USED

**10** CHANGES IN BASIC SET INFORMATION

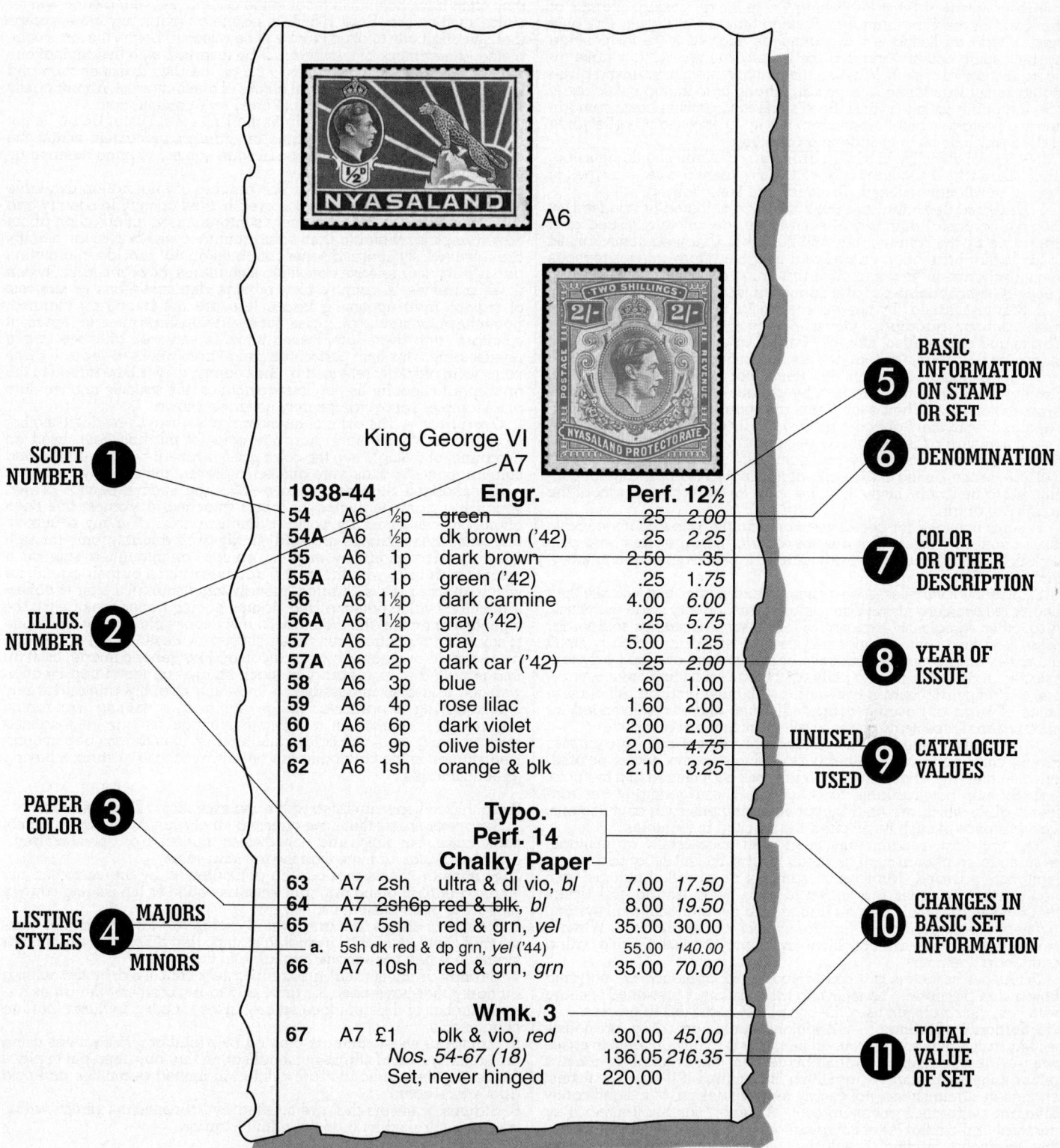

**11** TOTAL VALUE OF SET

# Catalogue Listing Policy

It is the intent of Scott Publishing Co. to list all postage stamps of the world in the *Scott Standard Postage Stamp Catalogue*. The only strict criteria for listing is that stamps be decreed legal for postage by the issuing country and that the issuing country actually have an operating postal system. Whether the primary intent of issuing a given stamp or set was for sale to postal patrons or to stamp collectors is not part of our listing criteria. Scott's role is to provide basic comprehensive postage stamp information. It is up to each stamp collector to choose which items to include in a collection.

It is Scott's objective to seek reasons why a stamp should be listed, rather than why it should not. Nevertheless, there are certain types of items that will not be listed. These include the following:

1. Unissued items that are not officially distributed or released by the issuing postal authority. If such items are officially issued at a later date by the country, they will be listed. Unissued items consist of those that have been printed and then held from sale for reasons such as change in government, errors found on stamps or something deemed objectionable about a stamp subject or design.

2. Stamps "issued" by non-existent postal entities or fantasy countries, such as Nagaland, Occusi-Ambeno, Staffa, Sedang, Torres Straits and others. Also, stamps "issued" in the names of legitimate, stamp-issuing countries that are not authorized by those countries.

3. Semi-official or unofficial items not required for postage. Examples include items issued by private agencies for their own express services. When such items are required for delivery, or are valid as prepayment of postage, they are listed.

4. Local stamps issued for local use only. Postage stamps issued by governments specifically for "domestic" use, such as Haiti Scott 219-228, or the United States non-denominated stamps, are not considered to be locals, since they are valid for postage throughout the country of origin.

5. Items not valid for postal use. For example, a few countries have issued souvenir sheets that are not valid for postage. This area also includes a number of worldwide charity labels (some denominated) that do not pay postage.

6. Intentional varieties, such as imperforate stamps that look like their perforated counterparts and are usually issued in very small quantities. Also, other egregiously exploitative issues such as stamps sold for far more than face value, stamps purposefully issued in artificially small quantities or only against advance orders, stamps awarded only to a selected audience such as a philatelic bureau's standing order customers, or stamps sold only in conjunction with other products. All of these kinds of items are usually controlled issues and/or are intended for speculation. These items normally will be included in a footnote.

7. Items distributed by the issuing government only to a limited group, club, philatelic exhibition or a single stamp dealer or other private company. These items normally will be included in a footnote.

8. Stamps not available to collectors. These generally are rare items, all of which are held by public institutions such as museums. The existence of such items often will be cited in footnotes.

The fact that a stamp has been used successfully as postage, even on international mail, is not in itself sufficient proof that it was legitimately issued. Numerous examples of so-called stamps from non-existent countries are known to have been used to post letters that have successfully passed through the international mail system.

There are certain items that are subject to interpretation. When a stamp falls outside our specifications, it may be listed along with a cautionary footnote.

A number of factors are considered in our approach to analyzing how a stamp is listed. The following list of factors is presented to share with you, the catalogue user, the complexity of the listing process.

**Additional printings** — "Additional printings" of a previously issued stamp may range from an item that is totally different to cases where it is impossible to differentiate from the original. At least a minor number (a small-letter suffix) is assigned if there is a distinct change in stamp shade, noticeably redrawn design, or a significantly different perforation measurement. A major number (numeral or numeral and capital-letter combination) is assigned if the editors feel the "additional printing" is sufficiently different from the original that it constitutes a different issue.

**Commemoratives** — Where practical, commemoratives with the same theme are placed in a set. For example, the U.S. Civil War Centennial set of 1961-65 and the Constitution Bicentennial series of 1989-90 appear as sets. Countries such as Japan and Korea issue such material on a regular basis, with an announced, or at least predictable, number of stamps known in advance. Occasionally, however, stamp sets that were released over a period of years have been separated. Appropriately placed footnotes will guide you to each set's continuation.

**Definitive sets** — Blocks of numbers generally have been reserved for definitive sets, based on previous experience with any given country. If a few more stamps were issued in a set than originally expected, they often have been inserted into the original set with a capital-letter suffix, such as U.S. Scott 1059A. If it appears that many more stamps than the originally allotted block will be released before the set is completed, a new block of numbers will be reserved, with the original one being closed off. In some cases, such as the U.S. Transportation and Great Americans series, several blocks of numbers exist. Appropriately placed footnotes will guide you to each set's continuation.

**New country** — Membership in the Universal Postal Union is not a consideration for listing status or order of placement within the catalogue. The index will tell you in what volume or page number the listings begin.

**"No release date" items** — The amount of information available for any given stamp issue varies greatly from country to country and even from time to time. Extremely comprehensive information about new stamps is available from some countries well before the stamps are released. By contrast some countries do not provide information about stamps or release dates. Most countries, however, fall between these extremes. A country may provide denominations or subjects of stamps from upcoming issues that are not issued as planned. Sometimes, philatelic agencies, those private firms hired to represent countries, add these later-issued items to sets well after the formal release date. This time period can range from weeks to years. If these items were officially released by the country, they will be added to the appropriate spot in the set. In many cases, the specific release date of a stamp or set of stamps may never be known.

**Overprints** — The color of an overprint is always noted if it is other than black. Where more than one color of ink has been used on overprints of a single set, the color used is noted. Early overprint and surcharge illustrations were altered to prevent their use by forgers.

**Personalized Stamps** — Since 1999, the special service of personalizing stamp vignettes, or labels attached to stamps, has been offered to customers by postal administrations of many countries. Sheets of these stamps are sold, singly or in quantity, only through special orders made by mail, in person, or through a sale on a computer website with the postal administrations or their agents for which an extra fee is charged, though some countries offer to collectors at face value personalized stamps having generic images in the vignettes or on the attached labels. It is impossible for any catalogue to know what images have been chosen by customers. Images can be 1) owned or created by the customer, 2) a generic image, or 3) an image pulled from a library of stock images on the stamp creation website. It is also impossible to know the quantity printed for any stamp having a particular image. So from a valuing standpoint, any image is equivalent to any other image for any personalized stamp having the same catalogue number. Illustrations of personalized stamps in the catalogue are not always those of stamps having generic images.

Personalized items are listed with some exceptions. These include:

1. Stamps or sheets that have attached labels that the customer cannot personalize, but which are nonetheless marketed as "personalized," and are sold for far more than the franking value.
2. Stamps or sheets that can be personalized by the customer, but where a portion of the print run must be ceded to the issuing country for sale to other customers.
3. Stamps or sheets that are created exclusively for a particular commercial client, or clients, including stamps that differ from any similar stamp that has been made available to the public.
4. Stamps or sheets that are deliberately conceived by the issuing authority that have been, or are likely to be, created with an excessive number of different face values, sizes, or other features that are changeable.
5. Stamps or sheets that are created by postal administrations using the same system of stamp personalization that has been put in place for use by the public that are printed in limited quantities and sold above face value.
6. Stamps or sheets that are created by licensees not directly affiliated or controlled by a postal administration.

Excluded items may or may not be footnoted.

**Se-tenants** — Connected stamps of differing features (se-tenants) will be listed in the format most commonly collected. This includes pairs, blocks or larger multiples. Se-tenant units are not always symmetrical. An example is Australia Scott 508, which is a block of seven stamps. If the stamps are primarily collected as a unit, the major number may be assigned to the multiple, with minors going to each component stamp. In cases where continuous-design or other unit se-tenants will receive significant postal use, each stamp is given a major Scott number listing. This includes issues from the United States, Canada, Germany and Great Britain, for example.

# Special Notices

## Classification of stamps

The *Scott Standard Postage Stamp Catalogue* lists stamps by country of issue. The next level of organization is a listing by section on the basis of the function of the stamps. The principal sections cover regular postage, semi-postal, air post, special delivery, registration, postage due and other categories. Except for regular postage, catalogue numbers for all sections include a prefix letter (or number-letter combination) denoting the class to which a given stamp belongs. When some countries issue sets containing stamps from more than one category, the catalogue will at times list all of the stamps in one category (such as air post stamps listed as part of a postage set).

The following is a listing of the most commonly used catalogue prefixes.

**Prefix .... Category**
C......... Air Post
M......... Military
P......... Newspaper
N......... Occupation - Regular Issues
O......... Official
Q......... Parcel Post
J.......... Postage Due
RA...... Postal Tax
B......... Semi-Postal
E......... Special Delivery
MR...... War Tax

Other prefixes used by more than one country include the following:
H......... Acknowledgment of Receipt
I.......... Late Fee
CO...... Air Post Official
CQ...... Air Post Parcel Post
RAC.... Air Post Postal Tax
CF...... Air Post Registration
CB...... Air Post Semi-Postal
CBO... Air Post Semi-Postal Official
CE...... Air Post Special Delivery
EY....... Authorized Delivery
S......... Franchise
G......... Insured Letter
GY...... Marine Insurance
MC..... Military Air Post
MQ..... Military Parcel Post
NC...... Occupation - Air Post
NO...... Occupation - Official
NJ........ Occupation - Postage Due
NRA.... Occupation - Postal Tax
NB...... Occupation - Semi-Postal
NE...... Occupation - Special Delivery
QY...... Parcel Post Authorized Delivery
AR...... Postal-fiscal
RAJ..... Postal Tax Due
RAB.... Postal Tax Semi-Postal
F......... Registration
EB....... Semi-Postal Special Delivery
EO...... Special Delivery Official
QE...... Special Handling

## New issue listings

Updates to this catalogue appear each month in the *Linn's Stamp News Special Edition* magazine. Included in this update are additions to the listings of countries found in the *Scott Standard Postage Stamp Catalogue* and the *Specialized Catalogue of United States Stamps and Covers*, as well as corrections and updates to current editions of this catalogue.

From time to time there will be changes in the final listings of stamps from the *Linn's Stamp News Special Edition* to the next edition of the catalogue. This occurs as more information about certain stamps or sets becomes available.

The catalogue update section of the *Linn's Stamp News Special Edition* is the most timely presentation of this material available. Annual subscriptions to *Linn's Stamp News* are available from Linn's Stamp News, Box 926, Sidney, OH 45365-0926.

## Number additions, deletions & changes

A listing of catalogue number additions, deletions and changes from the previous edition of the catalogue appears in each volume. See Catalogue Number Additions, Deletions & Changes in the table of contents for the location of this list.

## Understanding valuing notations

The *minimum catalogue value* of an individual stamp or set is 25 cents. This represents a portion of the cost incurred by a dealer when he prepares an individual stamp for resale. As a point of philatelic-economic fact, the lower the value shown for an item in this catalogue, the greater the percentage of that value is attributed to dealer mark up and profit margin. In many cases, such as the 25-cent minimum value, that price does not cover the labor or other costs involved with stocking it as an individual stamp. The sum of minimum values in a set does not properly represent the value of a complete set primarily composed of a number of minimum-value stamps, nor does the sum represent the actual value of a packet made up of minimum-value stamps. Thus a packet of 1,000 different common stamps — each of which has a catalogue value of 25 cents — normally sells for considerably less than 250 dollars!

The *absence of a retail value* for a stamp does not necessarily suggest that a stamp is scarce or rare. A dash in the value column means that the stamp is known in a stated form or variety, but information is either lacking or insufficient for purposes of establishing a usable catalogue value.

Stamp values in *italics* generally refer to items that are difficult to value accurately. For expensive items, such as those priced at $1,000 or higher, a value in italics indicates that the affected item trades very seldom. For inexpensive items, a value in italics represents a warning. One example is a "blocked" issue where the issuing postal administration may have controlled one stamp in a set in an attempt to make the whole set more valuable. Another example is an item that sold at an extreme multiple of face value in the marketplace at the time of its issue.

One type of warning to collectors that appears in the catalogue is illustrated by a stamp that is valued considerably higher in used condition than it is as unused. In this case, collectors are cautioned to be certain the used version has a genuine and contemporaneous cancellation. The type of cancellation on a stamp can be an important factor in determining its sale price. Catalogue values do not apply to fiscal, telegraph or non-contemporaneous postal cancels, unless otherwise noted.

Some countries have released back issues of stamps in canceled-to-order form, sometimes covering as much as a 10-year period. The Scott Catalogue values for used stamps reflect canceled-to-order material when such stamps are found to predominate in the marketplace for the issue involved. Notes frequently appear in the stamp listings to specify which items are valued as canceled-to-order, or if there is a premium for postally used examples.

Many countries sell canceled-to-order stamps at a marked reduction of face value. Countries that sell or have sold canceled-to-order stamps at *full* face value include United Nations, Australia, Netherlands, France and Switzerland. It may be almost impossible to identify such stamps if the gum has been removed, because official government canceling devices are used. Postally used examples of these items on cover, however, are usually worth more than the canceled-to-order stamps with original gum.

## Abbreviations

Scott Publishing Co. uses a consistent set of abbreviations throughout this catalogue to conserve space, while still providing necessary information.

## COLOR ABBREVIATIONS

| | | | | | |
|---|---|---|---|---|---|
| amb. | amber | crim. | crimson | ol | olive |
| anil.. | aniline | cr | cream | olvn | olivine |
| ap | apple | dk | dark | org | orange |
| aqua | aquamarine | dl | dull | pck | peacock |
| az | azure | dp | deep | pnksh | pinkish |
| bis | bister | db | drab | Prus. | Prussian |
| bl | blue | emer | emerald | pur | purple |
| bld | blood | gldn. | golden | redsh | reddish |
| blk | black | grysh | grayish | res | reseda |
| bril | brilliant | grn | green | ros | rosine |
| brn | brown | grnsh | greenish | ryl | royal |
| brnsh | brownish | hel | heliotrope | sal | salmon |
| brnz. | bronze | hn | henna | saph | sapphire |
| brt | bright | ind | indigo | scar. | scarlet |
| brnt. | burnt | int | intense | sep | sepia |
| car | carmine | lav | lavender | sien. | sienna |
| cer | cerise | lem | lemon | sil | silver |
| chlky | chalky | lil | lilac | sl | slate |
| cham | chamois | lt | light | stl | steel |
| chnt. | chestnut | mag. | magenta | turq | turquoise |
| choc | chocolate | man. | manila | ultra | ultramarine |
| chr | chrome | mar | maroon | Ven | Venetian |
| cit | citron | mv | mauve | ver | vermilion |
| cl | claret | multi | multicolored | vio | violet |
| cob | cobalt | mlky | milky | yel | yellow |
| cop | copper | myr | myrtle | yelsh | yellowish |

When no color is given for an overprint or surcharge, black is the color used. Abbreviations for colors used for overprints and surcharges include: "(B)" or "(Blk)," black; "(Bl)," blue; "(R)," red; and "(G)," green.

Additional abbreviations in this catalogue are shown below:

| | |
|---|---|
| Adm. | Administration |
| AFL | American Federation of Labor |
| Anniv. | Anniversary |
| APS | American Philatelic Society |
| Assoc. | Association |
| ASSR. | Autonomous Soviet Socialist Republic |
| b. | Born |
| BEP | Bureau of Engraving and Printing |
| Bicent. | Bicentennial |
| Bklt. | Booklet |
| Brit. | British |
| btwn. | Between |
| Bur. | Bureau |
| c. or ca. | Circa |
| Cat. | Catalogue |
| Cent. | Centennial, century, centenary |
| CIO | Congress of Industrial Organizations |
| Conf. | Conference |
| Cong. | Congress |
| Cpl. | Corporal |
| CTO | Canceled to order |
| d. | Died |
| Dbl. | Double |
| EDU | Earliest documented use |
| Engr. | Engraved |
| Exhib. | Exhibition |
| Expo. | Exposition |
| Fed. | Federation |
| GB | Great Britain |
| Gen. | General |
| GPO | General post office |
| Horiz. | Horizontal |
| Imperf. | Imperforate |
| Impt. | Imprint |
| Intl. | International |
| Invtd. | Inverted |
| L | Left |
| Lieut., lt. | Lieutenant |
| Litho. | Lithographed |
| LL | Lower left |
| LR | Lower right |
| mm | Millimeter |
| Ms. | Manuscript |
| Natl. | National |
| No. | Number |
| NY | New York |
| NYC | New York City |
| Ovpt. | Overprint |
| Ovptd. | Overprinted |
| P | Plate number |
| Perf. | Perforated, perforation |
| Phil. | Philatelic |
| Photo. | Photogravure |
| PO | Post office |
| Pr. | Pair |
| P.R. | Puerto Rico |
| Prec. | Precancel, precanceled |
| Pres. | President |
| PTT | Post, Telephone and Telegraph |
| R | Right |
| Rio | Rio de Janeiro |
| Sgt. | Sergeant |
| Soc. | Society |
| Souv. | Souvenir |
| SSR | Soviet Socialist Republic, see ASSR |
| St. | Saint, street |
| Surch. | Surcharge |
| Typo. | Typographed |
| UL | Upper left |
| Unwmkd. | Unwatermarked |
| UPU | Universal Postal Union |
| UR | Upper Right |
| US | United States |
| USPOD | United States Post Office Department |
| USSR | Union of Soviet Socialist Republics |
| Vert. | Vertical |
| VP | Vice president |
| Wmk. | Watermark |
| Wmkd. | Watermarked |
| WWI | World War I |
| WWII | World War II |

# Examination

Scott Publishing Co. will not comment upon the genuineness, grade or condition of stamps, because of the time and responsibility involved. Rather, there are several expertizing groups that undertake this work for both collectors and dealers. Neither will Scott Publishing Co. appraise or identify philatelic material. The company cannot take responsibility for unsolicited stamps or covers sent by individuals.

All letters, E-mails, etc. are read attentively, but they are not always answered due to time considerations.

# How to order from your dealer

When ordering stamps from a dealer, it is not necessary to write the full description of a stamp as listed in this catalogue. All you need is the name of the country, the Scott catalogue number and whether the desired item is unused or used. For example, "Japan Scott 422 unused" is sufficient to identify the unused stamp of Japan listed as "422 A206 5y brown."

# Basic Stamp Information

A stamp collector's knowledge of the combined elements that make a given stamp issue unique determines his or her ability to identify stamps. These elements include paper, watermark, method of separation, printing, design and gum. On the following pages each of these important areas is briefly described.

## Paper

Paper is an organic material composed of a compacted weave of cellulose fibers and generally formed into sheets. Paper used to print stamps may be manufactured in sheets, or it may have been part of a large roll (called a web) before being cut to size. The fibers most often used to create paper on which stamps are printed include bark, wood, straw and certain grasses. In many cases, linen or cotton rags have been added for greater strength and durability. Grinding, bleaching, cooking and rinsing these raw fibers reduces them to a slushy pulp, referred to by paper makers as "stuff." Sizing and, sometimes, coloring matter is added to the pulp to make different types of finished paper.

After the stuff is prepared, it is poured onto sieve-like frames that allow the water to run off, while retaining the matted pulp. As fibers fall onto the screen and are held by gravity, they form a natural weave that will later hold the paper together. If the screen has metal bits that are formed into letters or images attached, it leaves slightly thinned areas on the paper. These are called watermarks.

When the stuff is almost dry, it is passed under pressure through smooth or engraved rollers - dandy rolls - or placed between cloth in a press to be flattened and dried.

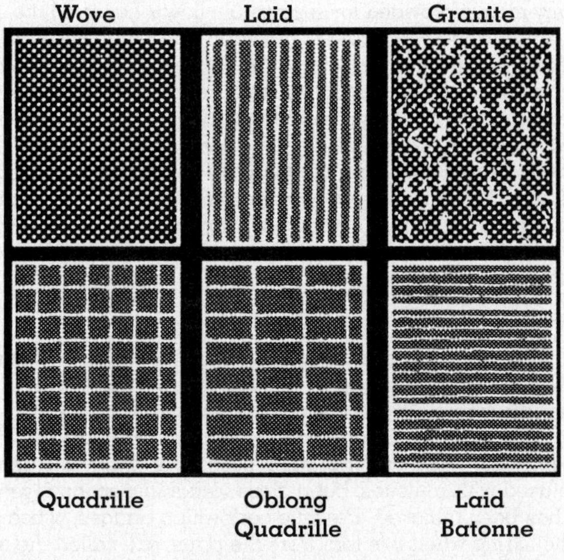


Stamp paper falls broadly into two types: wove and laid. The nature of the surface of the frame onto which the pulp is first deposited causes the differences in appearance between the two. If the surface is smooth and even, the paper will be of fairly uniform texture throughout. This is known as *wove paper*. Early papermaking machines poured the pulp onto a continuously circulating web of felt, but modern machines feed the pulp onto a cloth-like screen made of closely interwoven fine wires. This paper, when held to a light, will show little dots or points very close together. The proper name for this is "wire wove," but the type is still considered wove. Any U.S. or British stamp printed after 1880 will serve as an example of wire wove paper.

Closely spaced parallel wires, with cross wires at wider intervals, make up the frames used for what is known as *laid paper*. A greater thickness of the pulp will settle between the wires. The paper, when held to a light, will show alternate light and dark lines. The spacing and the thickness of the lines may vary, but on any one sheet of paper they are all alike. See Russia Scott 31-38 for examples of laid paper.

*Batonne*, from the French word meaning "a staff," is a term used if the lines in the paper are spaced quite far apart, like the printed ruling on a writing tablet. Batonne paper may be either wove or laid. If laid, fine laid lines can be seen between the batons.

*Quadrille* is the term used when the lines in the paper form little squares. *Oblong quadrille* is the term used when rectangles, rather than squares, are formed. Grid patterns vary from distinct to extremely faint. See Mexico-Guadalajara Scott 35-37 for examples of oblong quadrille paper.

Paper also is classified as thick or thin, hard or soft, and by color. Such colors may include yellowish, greenish, bluish and reddish.

Brief explanations of other types of paper used for printing stamps, as well as examples, follow.

**Colored** — Colored paper is created by the addition of dye in the paper-making process. Such colors may include shades of yellow, green, blue and red. *Surface-colored papers*, most commonly used for British colonial issues in 1913-14, are created when coloring is added only to the surface during the finishing process. Stamps printed on surface-colored paper have white or uncolored backs, while true colored papers are colored through. See Jamaica Scott 71-73.

**Pelure** — Pelure paper is a very thin, hard and often brittle paper that is sometimes bluish or grayish in appearance. See Serbia Scott 169-170.

**Native** — This is a term applied to handmade papers used to produce some of the early stamps of the Indian states. Stamps printed on native paper may be expected to display various natural inclusions that are normal and do not negatively affect value. Japanese paper, originally made of mulberry fibers and rice flour, is part of this group. See Japan Scott 1-18.

**Manila** — This type of paper is often used to make stamped envelopes and wrappers. It is a coarse-textured stock, usually smooth on one side and rough on the other. A variety of colors of manila paper exist, but the most common range is yellowish-brown.

**Silk** — Introduced by the British in 1847 as a safeguard against counterfeiting, silk paper contains bits of colored silk thread scattered throughout. The density of these fibers varies greatly and can include as few as one fiber per stamp or hundreds. U.S. revenue Scott R152 is a good example of an easy-to-identify silk paper stamp.

Silk-thread paper has uninterrupted threads of colored silk arranged so that one or more threads run through the stamp or postal stationery. See Great Britain Scott 5-6 and Switzerland Scott 14-19.

**Granite** — Filled with minute cloth or colored paper fibers of various colors and lengths, granite paper should not be confused with either type of silk paper. Austria Scott 172-175 and a number of Swiss stamps are examples of granite paper.

**Chalky** — A chalk-like substance coats the surface of chalky paper to discourage the cleaning and reuse of canceled stamps, as well as to provide a smoother, more acceptable printing surface. Because the designs of stamps printed on chalky paper are imprinted on what is often a water-soluble coating, any attempt to remove a cancellation will destroy the stamp. *Do not soak these stamps in any fluid.* To remove a stamp printed on chalky paper from an envelope, wet the paper from underneath the stamp until the gum dissolves enough to release the stamp from the paper. See St. Kitts-Nevis Scott 89-90 for examples of stamps printed on this type of chalky paper.

**India** — Another name for this paper, originally introduced from China about 1750, is "China Paper." It is a thin, opaque paper often used for plate and die proofs by many countries.

**Double** — In philately, the term double paper has two distinct meanings. The first is a two-ply paper, usually a combination of a thick and a thin sheet, joined during manufacture. This type was used experimentally as a means to discourage the reuse of stamps.

The design is printed on the thin paper. Any attempt to remove a cancellation would destroy the design. U.S. Scott 158 and other Banknote-era stamps exist on this form of double paper.

The second type of double paper occurs on a rotary press, when the end of one paper roll, or web, is affixed to the next roll to save time feeding the paper through the press. Stamp designs are printed over the joined paper and, if overlooked by inspectors, may get into post office stocks.

**Goldbeater's Skin** — This type of paper was used for the 1866 issue of Prussia, and was a tough, translucent paper. The design was printed in reverse on the back of the stamp, and the gum applied over the printing. It is impossible to remove stamps printed on this type of paper from the paper to which they are affixed without destroying the design.

**Ribbed** — Ribbed paper has an uneven, corrugated surface made by passing the paper through ridged rollers. This type exists on some copies of U.S. Scott 156-165.

Various other substances, or substrates, have been used for stamp manufacture, including wood, aluminum, copper, silver and gold foil, plastic, and silk and cotton fabrics.

## Watermarks

Watermarks are an integral part of some papers. They are formed in the process of paper manufacture. Watermarks consist of small designs, formed of wire or cut from metal and soldered to the surface of the mold or, sometimes, on the dandy roll. The designs may be in the form of crowns, stars, anchors, letters or other characters or symbols. These pieces of metal - known in the paper-making industry as "bits" - impress a design into the paper. The design sometimes may be seen by holding the stamp to the light. Some are more easily seen with a watermark detector. This important tool is a small black tray into which a stamp is placed face down and dampened with a fast-evaporating watermark detection fluid that brings up the watermark image in the form of dark lines against a lighter background. These dark lines are the thinner areas of the paper known as the watermark. Some watermarks are extremely difficult to locate, due to either a faint impression, watermark location or the color of the stamp. There also are electric watermark detectors that come with plastic filter disks of various colors. The disks neutralize the color of the stamp, permitting the watermark to be seen more easily.

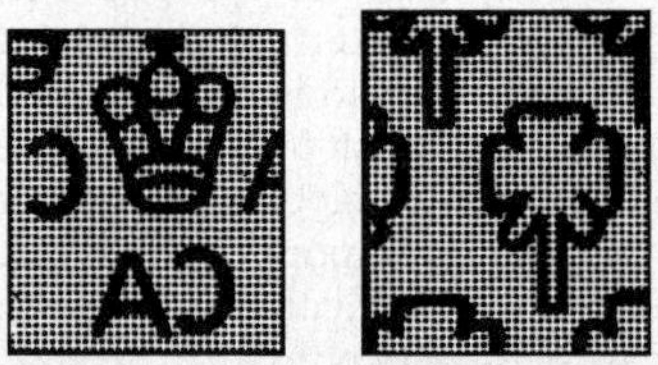

**Multiple watermarks of Crown Agents and Burma**

**Watermarks of Uruguay, Vatican City and Jamaica**

**WARNING: Some inks used in the photogravure process dissolve in watermark fluids (Please see the section on Soluble Printing Inks).** Also, see "chalky paper."

Watermarks may be found normal, reversed, inverted, reversed and inverted, sideways or diagonal, as seen from the back of the stamp. The relationship of watermark to stamp design depends on the position of the printing plates or how paper is fed through the press. On machine-made paper, watermarks normally are read from right to left. The design is repeated closely throughout the sheet in a "multiple-watermark design." In a "sheet watermark," the design appears only once on the sheet, but extends over many stamps. Individual stamps may carry only a small fraction or none of the watermark.

"Marginal watermarks" occur in the margins of sheets or panes of stamps. They occur on the outside border of paper (ostensibly outside the area where stamps are to be printed). A large row of letters may spell the name of the country or the manufacturer of the paper, or a border of lines may appear. Careless press feeding may cause parts of these letters and/or lines to show on stamps of the outer row of a pane.

## Soluble Printing Inks

**WARNING:** Most stamp colors are permanent; that is, they are not seriously affected by short-term exposure to light or water. Many colors, especially of modern inks, fade from excessive exposure to light. There are stamps printed with inks that dissolve easily in water or in fluids used to detect watermarks. Use of these inks was intentional to prevent the removal of cancellations. Water affects all aniline inks, those on so-called safety paper and some photogravure printings - all such inks are known as fugitive colors. *Removal from paper of such stamps requires care and alternatives to traditional soaking.*

## Separation

"Separation" is the general term used to describe methods used to separate stamps. The three standard forms currently in use are perforating, rouletting and die-cutting. These methods are done during the stamp production process, after printing. Sometimes these methods are done on-press or sometimes as a separate step. The earliest issues, such as the 1840 Penny Black of Great Britain (Scott 1), did not have any means provided for separation. It was expected the stamps would be cut apart with scissors or folded and torn. These are examples of imperforate stamps. Many stamps were first issued in imperforate formats and were later issued with perforations. Therefore, care must be observed in buying single imperforate stamps to be certain they were issued imperforate and are not perforated copies that have been altered by having the perforations trimmed away. Stamps issued imperforate usually are valued as singles. However, imperforate varieties of normally perforated stamps should be collected in pairs or larger pieces as indisputable evidence of their imperforate character.

### PERFORATION

The chief style of separation of stamps, and the one that is in almost universal use today, is perforating. By this process, paper between the stamps is cut away in a line of holes, usually round, leaving little bridges of paper between the stamps to hold them together. Some types of perforation, such as hyphen-hole perfs, can be confused with roulettes, but a close visual inspection reveals that paper has been removed. The little perforation bridges, which project from the stamp when it is torn from the pane, are called the teeth of the perforation.

As the size of the perforation is sometimes the only way to differentiate between two otherwise identical stamps, it is necessary to be able to accurately measure and describe them. This is done with a perforation gauge, usually a ruler-like device that has dots or graduated lines to show how many perforations may be counted in the space of two centimeters. Two centimeters is the space universally adopted in which to measure perforations.

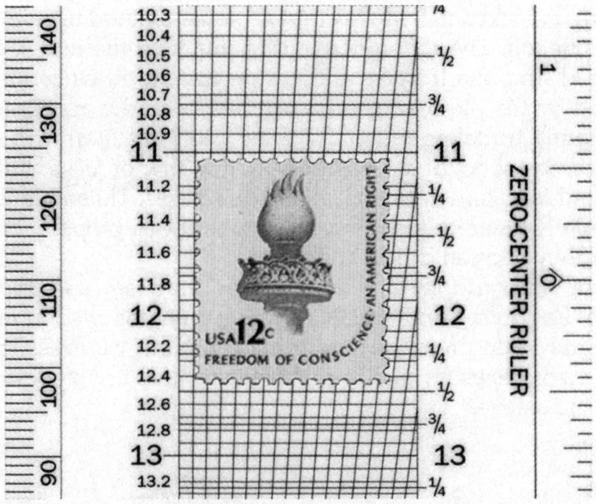


**Perforation gauge**

To measure a stamp, run it along the gauge until the dots on it fit exactly into the perforations of the stamp. If you are using a graduated-line perforation gauge, simply slide the stamp along the surface until the lines on the gauge perfectly project from the center of the bridges or holes. The number to the side of the line of dots or lines that fit the stamp's perforation is the measurement. For example, an "11" means that 11 perforations fit between two centimeters. The description of the stamp therefore is "perf. 11." If the gauge of the perforations on the top and bottom of a stamp differs from that on the sides, the result is what is known as *compound perforations*. In measuring compound perforations, the gauge at top and bottom is always given first, then the sides. Thus, a stamp that measures 11 at top and bottom and 10½ at the sides is "perf. 11 x 10½." See U.S. Scott 632-642 for examples of compound perforations.

Stamps also are known with perforations different on three or all four sides. Descriptions of such items are clockwise, beginning with the top of the stamp.

A perforation with small holes and teeth close together is a "fine perforation." One with large holes and teeth far apart is a "coarse perforation." Holes that are jagged, rather than clean-cut, are "rough perforations." *Blind perforations* are the slight impressions left by the perforating pins if they fail to puncture the paper. Multiples of stamps showing blind perforations may command a slight premium over normally perforated stamps.

The term *syncopated perfs* describes intentional irregularities in the perforations. The earliest form was used by the Netherlands from 1925-33, where holes were omitted to create distinctive patterns. Beginning in 1992, Great Britain has used an oval perforation to help prevent counterfeiting. Several other countries have started using the oval perfs or other syncopated perf patterns.

A new type of perforation, still primarily used for postal stationery, is known as microperfs. Microperfs are tiny perforations (in some cases hundreds of holes per two centimeters) that allows items to be intentionally separated very easily, while not accidentally breaking apart as easily as standard perforations. These are not currently measured or differentiated by size, as are standard perforations.

perce en arc

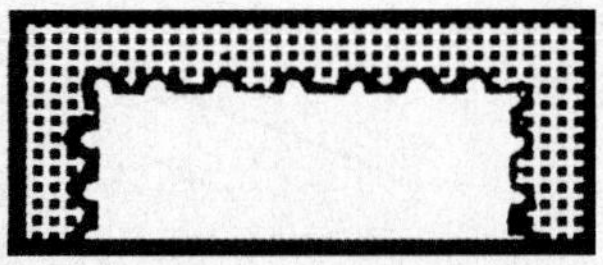

perce en lignes

perce en points

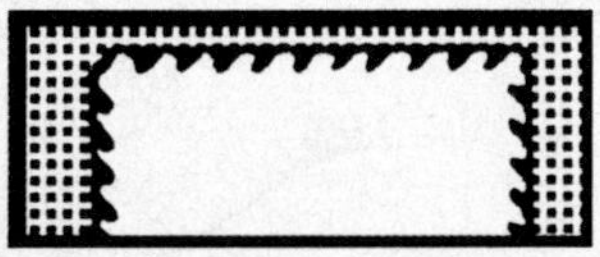

oblique roulette

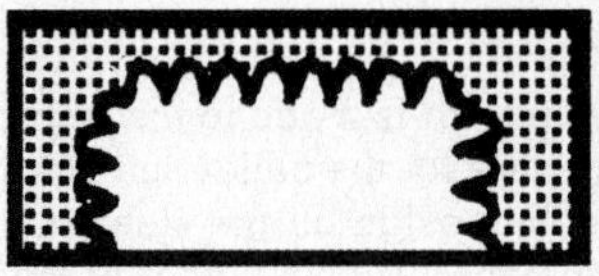

perce en scie

perce serpentin

### ROULETTING

In rouletting, the stamp paper is cut partly or wholly through, with no paper removed. In perforating, some paper is removed. Rouletting derives its name from the French roulette, a spur-like wheel. As the wheel is rolled over the paper, each point makes a small cut. The number of cuts made in a two-centimeter space determines the gauge of the roulette, just as the number of perforations in two centimeters determines the gauge of the perforation.

The shape and arrangement of the teeth on the wheels varies. Various roulette types generally carry French names:

*Perce en lignes* - rouletted in lines. The paper receives short, straight cuts in lines. This is the most common type of rouletting. See Mexico Scott 500.

*Perce en points* - pin-rouletted or pin-perfed. This differs from a small perforation because no paper is removed, although round, equidistant holes are pricked through the paper. See Mexico Scott 242-256.

*Perce en arc* and *perce en scie* - pierced in an arc or saw-toothed designs, forming half circles or small triangles. See Hanover (German States) Scott 25-29.

*Perce en serpentin* - serpentine roulettes. The cuts form a serpentine or wavy line. See Brunswick (German States) Scott 13-18.

Once again, no paper is removed by these processes, leaving the stamps easily separated, but closely attached.

### DIE-CUTTING

The third major form of stamp separation is die-cutting. This is a method where a die in the pattern of separation is created that later cuts the stamp paper in a stroke motion. Although some standard stamps bear die-cut perforations, this process is primarily used for self-adhesive postage stamps. Die-cutting can appear in straight lines, such as U.S. Scott 2522, shapes, such as U.S. Scott 1551, or imitating the appearance of perforations, such as New Zealand Scott 935A and 935B.

## Printing Processes

**ENGRAVING (Intaglio, Line-engraving, Etching)**

**Master die** — The initial operation in the process of line engraving is making the master die. The die is a small, flat block of softened steel upon which the stamp design is recess engraved in reverse.

**Master die**

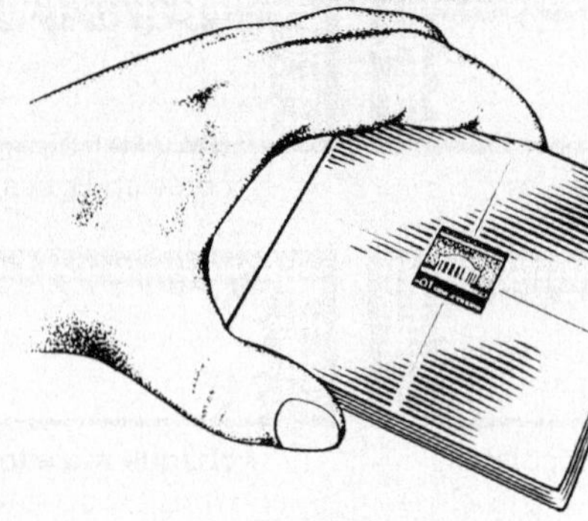

Photographic reduction of the original art is made to the appropriate size. It then serves as a tracing guide for the initial outline of the design. The engraver lightly traces the design on the steel with his graver, then slowly works the design until it is completed. At various points during the engraving process, the engraver hand-inks the die and makes an impression to check his progress. These are known as progressive die proofs. After completion of the engraving, the die is hardened to withstand the stress and pressures of later transfer operations.

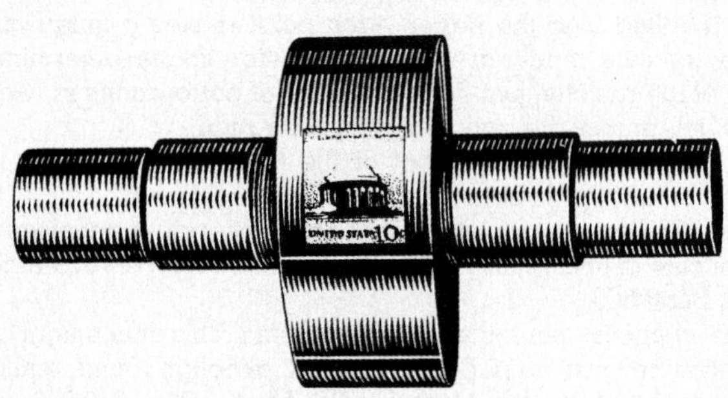

**Transfer roll**

**Transfer roll** — Next is production of the transfer roll that, as the name implies, is the medium used to transfer the subject from the master die to the printing plate. A blank roll of soft steel, mounted on a mandrel, is placed under the bearers of the transfer press to allow it to roll freely on its axis. The hardened die is placed on the bed of the press and the face of the transfer roll is applied to the die, under pressure. The bed or the roll is then rocked back and forth under increasing pressure, until the soft steel of the roll is forced into every engraved line of the die. The resulting impression on the roll is known as a "relief" or a "relief transfer." The engraved image is now positive in appearance and stands out from the steel. After the required number of reliefs are "rocked in," the soft steel transfer roll is hardened.

Different flaws may occur during the relief process. A defective relief may occur during the rocking in process because of a minute piece of foreign material lodging on the die, or some other cause. Imperfections in the steel of the transfer roll may result in a breaking away of parts of the design. This is known as a relief break, which will show up on finished stamps as small, unprinted areas. If a damaged relief remains in use, it will transfer a repeating defect to the plate. Deliberate alterations of reliefs sometimes occur. "Altered reliefs" designate these changed conditions.

**Plate** — The final step in pre-printing production is the making of the printing plate. A flat piece of soft steel replaces the die on the bed of the transfer press. One of the reliefs on the transfer roll is positioned over this soft steel. Position, or layout, dots determine the correct position on the plate. The dots have been lightly marked on the plate in advance. After the correct position of the relief is determined, the design is rocked in by following the same method used in making the transfer roll. The difference is that this time the image is being transferred from the transfer roll, rather than to it. Once the design is entered on the plate, it appears in reverse and is recessed. There are as many transfers entered on the plate as there are subjects printed on the sheet of stamps. It is during this process that double and shifted transfers occur, as well as re-entries. These are the result of improperly entered images that have not been properly burnished out prior to rocking in a new image.

Modern siderography processes, such as those used by the U.S. Bureau of Engraving and Printing, involve an automated form of rocking designs in on preformed cylindrical printing sleeves. The same process also allows for easier removal and re-entry of worn images right on the sleeve.

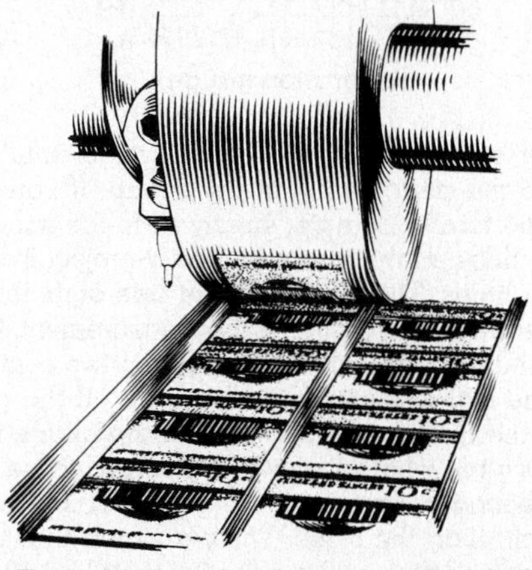

**Transferring the design to the plate**

Following the entering of the required transfers on the plate, the position dots, layout dots and lines, scratches and other markings generally are burnished out. Added at this time by the siderographer are any required *guide lines, plate numbers* or other *marginal markings.* The plate is then hand-inked and a proof impression is taken. This is known as a plate proof. If the impression is approved, the plate is machined for fitting onto the press, is hardened and sent to the plate vault ready for use.

On press, the plate is inked and the surface is automatically wiped clean, leaving ink only in the recessed lines. Paper is then forced under pressure into the engraved recessed lines, thereby receiving the ink. Thus, the ink lines on engraved stamps are slightly raised, and slight depressions (debossing) occur on the back of the stamp. Prior to the advent of modern high-speed presses and more advanced ink formulations, paper had to be dampened before receiving the ink. This sometimes led to uneven shrinkage by the time the stamps were perforated, resulting in improperly perforated stamps, or misperfs. Newer presses use drier paper, thus both *wet* and *dry printings* exist on some stamps.

**Rotary Press** — Until 1914, only flat plates were used to print engraved stamps. Rotary press printing was introduced in 1914, and slowly spread. Some countries still use flat-plate printing.

After approval of the plate proof, older *rotary press plates* require additional machining. They are curved to fit the press cylinder. "Gripper slots" are cut into the back of each plate to receive the "grippers," which hold the plate securely on the press. The plate is then hardened. Stamps printed from these bent rotary press plates are longer or wider than the same stamps printed from flat-plate presses. The stretching of the plate during the curving process is what causes this distortion.

**Re-entry** — To execute a re-entry on a flat plate, the transfer roll is re-applied to the plate, often at some time after its first use on the press. Worn-out designs can be resharpened by carefully burnishing out the original image and re-entering it from the transfer roll. If the original impression has not been sufficiently removed and the transfer roll is not precisely in line with the remaining impression, the resulting double transfer will make the re-entry obvious. If the registration is true, a re-entry may be difficult or impossible to distinguish. Sometimes a stamp printed from a successful re-entry is identified by having a much sharper and clearer impression than its neighbors. With the advent of rotary presses, post-press re-entries were not possible. After a plate was curved for the rotary press, it was impossible to make a re-entry. This is because the plate had already been bent once (with the design distorted).

However, with the introduction of the previously mentioned modern-style siderography machines, entries are made to the preformed cylindrical printing sleeve. Such sleeves are dechromed and softened. This allows individual images to be burnished out and re-entered on the curved sleeve. The sleeve is then rechromed, resulting in longer press life.

**Double Transfer** — This is a description of the condition of a transfer on a plate that shows evidence of a duplication of all, or a portion of the design. It usually is the result of the changing of the registration between the transfer roll and the plate during the rocking in of the original entry. Double transfers also occur when only a portion of the design has been rocked in and improper positioning is noted. If the worker elected not to burnish out the partial or completed design, a strong double transfer will occur for part or all of the design.

It sometimes is necessary to remove the original transfer from a plate and repeat the process a second time. If the finished re-worked image shows traces of the original impression, attributable to incomplete burnishing, the result is a partial double transfer.

With the modern automatic machines mentioned previously, double transfers are all but impossible to create. Those partially doubled images on stamps printed from such sleeves are more than likely re-entries, rather than true double transfers.

**Re-engraved** — Alterations to a stamp design are sometimes necessary after some stamps have been printed. In some cases, either the original die or the actual printing plate may have its "temper" drawn (softened), and the design will be re-cut. The resulting impressions from such a re-engraved die or plate may differ slightly from the original issue, and are known as "re-engraved." If the alteration was made to the master die, all future printings will be consistently different from the original. If alterations were made to the printing plate, each altered stamp on the plate will be slightly different from each other, allowing specialists to reconstruct a complete printing plate.

**Dropped Transfers** — If an impression from the transfer roll has not been properly placed, a dropped transfer may occur. The final stamp image will appear obviously out of line with its neighbors.

**Short Transfer** — Sometimes a transfer roll is not rocked its entire length when entering a transfer onto a plate. As a result, the finished transfer on the plate fails to show the complete design, and the finished stamp will have an incomplete design printed. This is known as a "short transfer." U.S. Scott No. 8 is a good example of a short transfer.

## TYPOGRAPHY (Letterpress, Surface Printing, Flexography, Dry Offset, High Etch)

Although the word "Typography" is obsolete as a term describing a printing method, it was the accepted term throughout the first century of postage stamps. Therefore, appropriate Scott listings in this catalogue refer to typographed stamps. The current term for this form of printing, however, is "letterpress."

As it relates to the production of postage stamps, letterpress printing is the reverse of engraving. Rather than having recessed areas trap the ink and deposit it on paper, only the raised areas of the design are inked. This is comparable to the type of printing seen by inking and using an ordinary rubber stamp. Letterpress includes all printing where the design is above the surface area, whether it is wood, metal or, in some instances, hardened rubber or polymer plastic.

For most letterpress-printed stamps, the engraved master is made in much the same manner as for engraved stamps. In this instance, however, an additional step is needed. The design is transferred to another surface before being transferred to the transfer roll. In this way, the transfer roll has a recessed stamp design, rather than one done in relief. This makes the printing areas on the final plate raised, or relief areas.

For less-detailed stamps of the 19th century, the area on the die not used as a printing surface was cut away, leaving the surface area raised. The original die was then reproduced by stereotyping or electrotyping. The resulting electrotypes were assembled in the required number and format of the desired sheet of stamps. The plate used in printing the stamps was an electroplate of these assembled electrotypes.

Once the final letterpress plates are created, ink is applied to the raised surface and the pressure of the press transfers the ink impression to the paper. In contrast to engraving, the fine lines of letterpress are impressed on the surface of the stamp, leaving a debossed surface. When viewed from the back (as on a typewritten page), the corresponding line work on the stamp will be raised slightly (embossed) above the surface.

## PHOTOGRAVURE (Gravure, Rotogravure, Heliogravure)

In this process, the basic principles of photography are applied to a chemically sensitized metal plate, rather than photographic paper. The design is transferred photographically to the plate through a halftone, or dot-matrix screen, breaking the reproduction into tiny dots. The plate is treated chemically and the dots form depressions, called cells, of varying depths and diameters, depending on the degrees of shade in the design. Then, like engraving, ink is applied to the plate and the surface is wiped clean. This leaves ink in the tiny cells that is lifted out and deposited on the paper when it is pressed against the plate.

Gravure is most often used for multicolored stamps, generally using the three primary colors (red, yellow and blue) and black. By varying the dot matrix pattern and density of these colors, virtually any color can be reproduced. A typical full-color gravure stamp will be created from four printing cylinders (one for each color). The original multicolored image will have been photographically separated into its component colors.

Modern gravure printing may use computer-generated dot-matrix screens, and modern plates may be of various types including metal-coated plastic. The catalogue designation of Photogravure (or "Photo") covers any of these older and more modern gravure methods of printing.

For examples of the first photogravure stamps printed (1914), see Bavaria Scott 94-114.

## LITHOGRAPHY (Offset Lithography, Stone Lithography, Dilitho, Planography, Collotype)

The principle that oil and water do not mix is the basis for lithography. The stamp design is drawn by hand or transferred from engraving to the surface of a lithographic stone or metal plate in a greasy (oily) substance. This oily substance holds the ink, which will later be transferred to the paper. The stone (or plate) is wet with an acid fluid, causing it to repel the printing ink in all areas not covered by the greasy substance.

Transfer paper is used to transfer the design from the original stone or plate. A series of duplicate transfers are grouped and, in turn, transferred to the final printing plate.

**Photolithography** — The application of photographic processes to lithography. This process allows greater flexibility of design, related to use of halftone screens combined with line work. Unlike photogravure or engraving, this process can allow large, solid areas to be printed.

**Offset** — A refinement of the lithographic process. A rubber-covered blanket cylinder takes the impression from the inked lithographic plate. From the "blanket" the impression is *offset* or transferred to the paper. Greater flexibility and speed are the principal reasons offset printing has largely displaced lithography. The term "lithography" covers both processes, and results are almost identical.

### EMBOSSED (Relief) Printing

Embossing, not considered one of the four main printing types, is a method in which the design first is sunk into the metal of the die. Printing is done against a yielding platen, such as leather or linoleum. The platen is forced into the depression of the die, thus forming the design on the paper in relief. This process is often used for metallic inks.

Embossing may be done without color (see Sardinia Scott 4-6); with color printed around the embossed area (see Great Britain Scott 5 and most U.S. envelopes); and with color in exact registration with the embossed subject (see Canada Scott 656-657).

### HOLOGRAMS

For objects to appear as holograms on stamps, a model exactly the same size as it is to appear on the hologram must be created. Rather than using photographic film to capture the image, holography records an image on a photoresist material. In processing, chemicals eat away at certain exposed areas, leaving a pattern of constructive and destructive interference. When the phororesist is developed, the result is a pattern of uneven ridges that acts as a mold. This mold is then coated with metal, and the resulting form is used to press copies in much the same way phonograph records are produced.

A typical reflective hologram used for stamps consists of a reproduction of the uneven patterns on a plastic film that is applied to a reflective background, usually a silver or gold foil. Light is reflected off the background through the film, making the pattern present on the film visible. Because of the uneven pattern of the film, the viewer will perceive the objects in their proper three-dimensional relationships with appropriate brightness.

The first hologram on a stamp was produced by Austria in 1988 (Scott 1441).

### FOIL APPLICATION

A modern technique of applying color to stamps involves the application of metallic foil to the stamp paper. A pattern of foil is applied to the stamp paper by use of a stamping die. The foil usually is flat, but it may be textured. Canada Scott 1735 has three different foil applications in pearl, bronze and gold. The gold foil was textured using a chemical-etch copper embossing die. The printing of this stamp also involved two-color offset lithography plus embossing.

### THERMOGRAPHY

In the 1990s stamps began to be enhanced with thermographic printing. In this process, a powdered polymer is applied over a sheet that has just been printed. The powder adheres to ink that lacks drying or hardening agents and does not adhere to areas where the ink has these agents. The excess powder is removed and the sheet is briefly heated to melt the powder. The melted powder solidifies after cooling, producing a raised, shiny effect on the stamps. See Scott New Caledonia C239-C240.

### COMBINATION PRINTINGS

Sometimes two or even three printing methods are combined in producing stamps. In these cases, such as Austria Scott 933 or Canada 1735 (described in the preceding paragraph), the multiple-printing technique can be determined by studying the individual characteristics of each printing type. A few stamps, such as Singapore Scott 684-684A, combine as many as three of the four major printing types (lithography, engraving and typography). When this is done it often indicates the incorporation of security devices against counterfeiting.

### INK COLORS

Inks or colored papers used in stamp printing often are of mineral origin, although there are numerous examples of organic-based pigments. As a general rule, organic-based pigments are far more subject to varieties and change than those of mineral-based origin.

The appearance of any given color on a stamp may be affected by many aspects, including printing variations, light, color of paper, aging and chemical alterations.

Numerous printing variations may be observed. Heavier pressure or inking will cause a more intense color, while slight interruptions in the ink feed or lighter impressions will cause a lighter appearance. Stamps printed in the same color by water-based and solvent-based inks can differ significantly in appearance. This affects several stamps in the U.S. Prominent Americans series. Hand-mixed ink formulas (primarily from the 19th century) produced under different conditions (humidity and temperature) account for notable color variations in early printings of the same stamp (see U.S. Scott 248-250, 279B, for example). Different sources of pigment can also result in significant differences in color.

Light exposure and aging are closely related in the way they affect stamp color. Both eventually break down the ink and fade colors, so that a carefully kept stamp may differ significantly in color from an identical copy that has been exposed to light. If stamps are exposed to light either intentionally or accidentally, their colors can be faded or completely changed in some cases.

Papers of different quality and consistency used for the same stamp printing may affect color appearance. Most pelure papers, for example, show a richer color when compared with wove or laid papers. See Russia Scott 181a, for an example of this effect.

The very nature of the printing processes can cause a variety of differences in shades or hues of the same stamp. Some of these shades are scarcer than others, and are of particular interest to the advanced collector.

## Luminescence

All forms of tagged stamps fall under the general category of luminescence. Within this broad category is fluorescence, dealing with forms of tagging visible under longwave ultraviolet light, and phosphorescence, which deals with tagging visible only under shortwave light. Phosphorescence leaves an afterglow and fluorescence does not. These treated stamps show up in a range of different colors when exposed to UV light. The differing wavelengths of the light activates the tagging material, making it glow in various colors that usually serve different mail processing purposes.

Intentional tagging is a post-World War II phenomenon, brought about by the increased literacy rate and rapidly growing mail volume. It was one of several answers to the problem of the need for more automated mail processes. Early tagged stamps served the purpose of triggering machines to separate different types of mail. A natural outgrowth was to also use the signal to trigger machines that faced all envelopes the same way and canceled them.

Tagged stamps come in many different forms. Some tagged stamps have luminescent shapes or images imprinted on them as a form of security device. Others have blocks (United States), stripes, frames (South Africa and Canada), overall coatings (United States), bars (Great Britain and Canada) and many other types. Some types of tagging are even mixed in with the pigmented printing ink (Australia Scott 366, Netherlands Scott 478 and U.S. Scott 1359 and 2443).

The means of applying taggant to stamps differs as much as the intended purposes for the stamps. The most common form of tagging is a coating applied to the surface of the printed stamp. Since the taggant ink is frequently invisible except under UV light, it does not interfere with the appearance of the stamp. Another common application is the use of phosphored papers. In this case the paper itself either has a coating of taggant applied before the stamp is printed, has taggant applied during the papermaking process (incorporating it into the fibers), or has the taggant mixed into the coating of the paper. The latter method, among others, is currently in use in the United States.

Many countries now use tagging in various forms to either expedite mail handling or to serve as a printing security device against counterfeiting. Following the introduction of tagged stamps for public use in 1959 by Great Britain, other countries have steadily joined the parade. Among those are Germany (1961); Canada and Denmark (1962); United States, Australia, France and Switzerland (1963); Belgium and Japan (1966); Sweden and Norway (1967); Italy (1968); and Russia (1969). Since then, many other countries have begun using forms of tagging, including Brazil, China, Czechoslovakia, Hong Kong, Guatemala, Indonesia, Israel, Lithuania, Luxembourg, Netherlands, Penrhyn Islands, Portugal, St. Vincent, Singapore, South Africa, Spain and Sweden to name a few.

In some cases, including United States, Canada, Great Britain and Switzerland, stamps were released both with and without tagging. Many of these were released during each country's experimental period. Tagged and untagged versions are listed for the aforementioned countries and are noted in some other countries' listings. For at least a few stamps, the experimentally tagged version is worth far more than its untagged counterpart, such as the 1963 experimental tagged version of France Scott 1024.

In some cases, luminescent varieties of stamps were inadvertently created. Several Russian stamps, for example, sport highly fluorescent ink that was not intended as a form of tagging. Older stamps, such as early U.S. postage dues, can be positively identified by the use of UV light, since the organic ink used has become slightly fluorescent over time. Other stamps, such as Austria Scott 70a-82a (varnish bars) and Obock Scott 46-64 (printed quadrille lines), have become fluorescent over time.

Various fluorescent substances have been added to paper to make it appear brighter. These optical brightners, as they are known, greatly affect the appearance of the stamp under UV light. The brightest of these is known as Hi-Brite paper. These paper varieties are beyond the scope of the Scott Catalogue.

Shortwave UV light also is used extensively in expertizing, since each form of paper has its own fluorescent characteristics that are impossible to perfectly match. It is therefore a simple matter to detect filled thins, added perforation teeth and other alterations that involve the addition of paper. UV light also is used to examine stamps that have had cancels chemically removed and for other purposes as well.

## Gum

The Illustrated Gum Chart in the first part of this introduction shows and defines various types of gum condition. Because gum condition has an important impact on the value of unused stamps, we recommend studying this chart and the accompanying text carefully.

The gum on the back of a stamp may be shiny, dull, smooth, rough, dark, white, colored or tinted. Most stamp gumming adhesives use gum arabic or dextrine as a base. Certain polymers such as polyvinyl alcohol (PVA) have been used extensively since World War II.

The *Scott Standard Postage Stamp Catalogue* does not list items by types of gum. The *Scott Specialized Catalogue of United States Stamps and Covers* does differentiate among some types of gum for certain issues.

Reprints of stamps may have gum differing from the original issues. In addition, some countries have used different gum formulas for different seasons. These adhesives have different properties that may become more apparent over time.

Many stamps have been issued without gum, and the catalogue will note this fact. See, for example, United States Scott 40-47. Sometimes, gum may have been removed to preserve the stamp. Germany Scott B68, for example, has a highly acidic gum that eventually destroys the stamps. This item is valued in the catalogue with gum removed.

## Reprints and Reissues

These are impressions of stamps (usually obsolete) made from the original plates or stones. If they are valid for postage and reproduce obsolete issues (such as U.S. Scott 102-111), the stamps are *reissues*. If they are from current issues, they are designated as *second, third,* etc., *printing*. If designated for a particular purpose, they are called *special printings*.

When special printings are not valid for postage, but are made from original dies and plates by authorized persons, they are *official reprints*. *Private reprints* are made from the original plates and dies by private hands. An example of a private reprint is that of the 1871-1932 reprints made from the original die of the 1845 New Haven, Conn., postmaster's provisional. *Official reproductions* or imitations are made from new dies and plates by government authorization. Scott will list those reissues that are valid for postage if they differ significantly from the original printing.

The U.S. government made special printings of its first postage stamps in 1875. Produced were official imitations of the first two stamps (listed as Scott 3-4), reprints of the demonetized pre-1861 issues (Scott 40-47) and reissues of the 1861 stamps, the 1869 stamps and the then-current 1875 denominations. Even though the official imitations and the reprints were not valid for postage, Scott lists all of these U.S. special printings.

Most reprints or reissues differ slightly from the original stamp in some characteristic, such as gum, paper, perforation, color or watermark. Sometimes the details are followed so meticulously that only a student of that specific stamp is able to distinguish the reprint or reissue from the original.

## Remainders and Canceled to Order

Some countries sell their stock of old stamps when a new issue replaces them. To avoid postal use, the *remainders* usually are canceled with a punch hole, a heavy line or bar, or a more-or-less regular-looking cancellation. The most famous merchant of remainders was Nicholas F. Seebeck. In the 1880s and 1890s, he arranged printing contracts between the Hamilton Bank Note Co., of which he was a director, and several Central and South American countries. The contracts provided that the plates and all remainders of the yearly issues became the property of Hamilton. Seebeck saw to it that ample stock remained. The "Seebecks," both remainders and reprints, were standard packet fillers for decades.

Some countries also issue stamps *canceled-to-order (CTO)*, either in sheets with original gum or stuck onto pieces of paper or envelopes and canceled. Such CTO items generally are worth less than postally used stamps. In cases where the CTO material is far more prevalent in the marketplace than postally used examples, the catalogue value relates to the CTO examples, with postally used examples noted as premium items. Most CTOs can be detected by the presence of gum. However, as the CTO practice goes back at least to 1885, the gum inevitably has been soaked off some stamps so they could pass as postally used. The normally applied postmarks usually differ slightly from standard postmarks, and specialists are able to tell the difference. When applied individually to envelopes by philatelically minded persons, CTO material is known as *favor canceled* and generally sells at large discounts.

## Cinderellas and Facsimiles

*Cinderella* is a catch-all term used by stamp collectors to describe phantoms, fantasies, bogus items, municipal issues, exhibition seals, local revenues, transportation stamps, labels, poster stamps and many other types of items. Some cinderella collectors include in their collections local postage issues, telegraph stamps, essays and proofs, forgeries and counterfeits.

A *fantasy* is an adhesive created for a nonexistent stamp-issuing authority. Fantasy items range from imaginary countries (Occusi-Ambeno, Kingdom of Sedang, Principality of Trinidad or Torres Straits), to non-existent locals (Winans City Post), or nonexistent transportation lines (McRobish & Co.'s Acapulco-San Francisco Line).

On the other hand, if the entity exists and could have issued stamps (but did not) or was known to have issued other stamps, the items are considered *bogus* stamps. These would include the Mormon postage stamps of Utah, S. Allan Taylor's Guatemala and Paraguay inventions, the propaganda issues for the South Moluccas and the adhesives of the Page & Keyes local post of Boston.

*Phantoms* is another term for both fantasy and bogus issues.

*Facsimiles* are copies or imitations made to represent original stamps, but which do not pretend to be originals. A catalogue illustration is such a facsimile. Illustrations from the Moens catalogue of the last century were occasionally colored and passed off as stamps. Since the beginning of stamp collecting, facsimiles have been made for collectors as space fillers or for reference. They often carry the word "facsimile," "falsch" (German), "sanko" or "mozo" (Japanese), or "faux" (French) overprinted on the face or stamped on the back. Unfortunately, over the years a number of these items have had fake cancels applied over the facsimile notation and have been passed off as genuine.

## Forgeries and Counterfeits

Forgeries and counterfeits have been with philately virtually from the beginning of stamp production. Over time, the terminology for the two has been used interchangeably. Although both forgeries and counterfeits are reproductions of stamps, the purposes behind their creation differ considerably.

Among specialists there is an increasing movement to more specifically define such items. Although there is no universally accepted terminology, we feel the following definitions most closely mirror the items and their purposes as they are currently defined.

*Forgeries* (also often referred to as *Counterfeits*) are reproductions of genuine stamps that have been created to defraud collectors. Such spurious items first appeared on the market around 1860, and most old-time collections contain one or more. Many are crude and easily spotted, but some can deceive experts.

An important supplier of these early philatelic forgeries was the Hamburg printer Gebruder Spiro. Many others with reputations in this craft included S. Allan Taylor, George Hussey, James Chute, George Forune, Benjamin & Sarpy, Julius Goldner, E. Oneglia and L.H. Mercier. Among the noted 20th-century forgers were Francois Fournier, Jean Sperati and the prolific Raoul DeThuin.

Forgeries may be complete replications, or they may be genuine stamps altered to resemble a scarcer (and more valuable) type. Most forgeries, particularly those of rare stamps, are worth only a small fraction of the value of a genuine example, but a few types, created by some of the most notable forgers, such as Sperati, can be worth as much or more than the genuine. Fraudulently produced copies are known of most classic rarities and many medium-priced stamps.

In addition to rare stamps, large numbers of common 19th- and early 20th-century stamps were forged to supply stamps to the early packet trade. Many can still be easily found. Few new philatelic forgeries have appeared in recent decades. Successful imitation of well-engraved work is virtually impossible. It has proven far easier to produce a fake by altering a genuine stamp than to duplicate a stamp completely.

*Counterfeit* (also often referred to as *Postal Counterfeit* or *Postal Forgery*) is the term generally applied to reproductions of stamps that have been created to defraud the government of revenue. Such items usually are created at the time a stamp is current and, in some cases, are hard to detect. Because most counterfeits are seized when the perpetrator is captured, postal counterfeits, particularly used on cover, are usually worth much more than a genuine example to specialists. The first postal counterfeit was of Spain's 4-cuarto carmine of 1854 (the real one is Scott 25). Apparently, the counterfeiters were not satisfied with their first version, which is now very scarce, and they soon created an engraved counterfeit, which is common. Postal counterfeits quickly followed in Austria, Naples, Sardinia and the Roman States. They have since been created in many other countries as well, including the United States.

An infamous counterfeit to defraud the government is the 1-shilling Great Britain "Stock Exchange" forgery of 1872, used on telegraph forms at the exchange that year. The stamp escaped detection until a stamp dealer noticed it in 1898.

## Fakes

*Fakes* are genuine stamps altered in some way to make them more desirable. One student of this part of stamp collecting has estimated that by the 1950s more than 30,000 varieties of fakes were known. That number has grown greatly since then. The widespread existence of fakes makes it important for stamp collectors to study their philatelic holdings and use relevant literature. Likewise, collectors should buy from reputable dealers who guarantee their stamps and make full and prompt refunds should a purchased item be declared faked or altered by some mutually agreed-upon authority. Because fakes always have some genuine characteristics, it is not always possible to obtain unanimous agreement among experts regarding specific items. These students may change their opinions as philatelic knowledge increases. More than 80 percent of all fakes on the philatelic market today are regummed, reperforated (or perforated for the first time), or bear forged overprints, surcharges or cancellations.

Stamps can be chemically treated to alter or eliminate colors. For example, a pale rose stamp can be re-colored to resemble a blue shade of high market value. In other cases, treated stamps can be made to resemble missing color varieties. Designs may be changed by painting, or a stroke or a dot added or bleached out to turn an ordinary variety into a seemingly scarcer stamp. Part of a stamp can be bleached and reprinted in a different version, achieving an inverted center or frame. Margins can be added or repairs done so deceptively that the stamps move from the "repaired" into the "fake" category.

Fakers have not left the backs of the stamps untouched either. They may create false watermarks, add fake grills or press out genuine grills. A thin India paper proof may be glued onto a thicker backing to create the appearance an issued stamp, or a proof printed on cardboard may be shaved down and perforated to resemble a stamp. Silk threads are impressed into paper and stamps have been split so that a rare paper variety is added to an otherwise inexpensive stamp. The most common treatment to the back of a stamp, however, is regumming.

Some in the business of faking stamps have openly advertised fool-proof application of "original gum" to stamps that lack it, although most publications now ban such ads from their pages. It is believed that very few early stamps have survived without being hinged. The large number of never-hinged examples of such earlier material offered for sale thus suggests the widespread extent of regumming activity. Regumming also may be used to hide repairs or thin spots. Dipping the stamp into watermark fluid, or examining it under longwave ultraviolet light often will reveal these flaws.

Fakers also tamper with separations. Ingenious ways to add margins are known. Perforated wide-margin stamps may be falsely represented as imperforate when trimmed. Reperforating is commonly done to create scarce coil or perforation varieties, and to eliminate the naturally occurring straight-edge stamps found in sheet margin positions of many earlier issues. Custom has made straight-edged stamps less desirable. Fakers have obliged by perforating straight-edged stamps so that many are now uncommon, if not rare.

Another fertile field for the faker is that of overprints, surcharges and cancellations. The forging of rare surcharges or overprints began in the 1880s or 1890s. These forgeries are sometimes difficult to detect, but experts have identified almost all. Occasionally, overprints or cancellations are removed to create non-overprinted stamps or seemingly unused items. This is most commonly done by removing a manuscript cancel to make a stamp resemble an unused example. "SPECIMEN" overprints may be removed by scraping and repainting to create non-overprinted varieties. Fakers use inexpensive revenues or pen-canceled stamps to generate unused stamps for further faking by adding other markings. The quartz lamp or UV lamp and a high-powered magnifying glass help to easily detect removed cancellations.

The bigger problem, however, is the addition of overprints, surcharges or cancellations - many with such precision that they are very difficult to ascertain. Plating of the stamps or the overprint can be an important method of detection.

Fake postmarks may range from many spurious fancy cancellations to a host of markings applied to transatlantic covers, to adding normally appearing postmarks to definitives of some countries with stamps that are valued far higher used than unused. With the increased popularity of cover collecting, and the widespread interest in postal history, a fertile new field for fakers has come about. Some have tried to create entire covers. Others specialize in adding stamps, tied by fake cancellations, to genuine stampless covers, or replacing less expensive or damaged stamps with more valuable ones. Detailed study of postal rates in effect at the time a cover in question was mailed, including the analysis of each handstamp used during the period, ink analysis and similar techniques, usually will unmask the fraud.

## Restoration and Repairs

Scott Publishing Co. bases its catalogue values on stamps that are free of defects and otherwise meet the standards set forth earlier in this introduction. Most stamp collectors desire to have the finest copy of an item possible. Even within given grading categories there are variances. This leads to a controversial practice that is not defined in any universal manner: stamp *restoration*.

There are broad differences of opinion about what is permissible when it comes to restoration. Carefully applying a soft eraser to a stamp or cover to remove light soiling is one form of restoration, as is washing a stamp in mild soap and water to clean it. These are fairly accepted forms of restoration. More severe forms of restoration include pressing out creases or removing stains caused by tape. To what degree each of these is acceptable is dependent upon the individual situation. Further along the spectrum is the freshening of a stamp's color by removing oxide build-up or the effects of wax paper left next to stamps shipped to the tropics.

At some point in this spectrum the concept of *repair* replaces that of restoration. Repairs include filling thin spots, mending tears by reweaving or adding a missing perforation tooth. Regumming stamps may have been acceptable as a restoration or repair technique many decades ago, but today it is considered a form of fakery.

Restored stamps may or may not sell at a discount, and it is possible that the value of individual restored items may be enhanced over that of their pre-restoration state. Specific situations dictate the resultant value of such an item. Repaired stamps sell at substantial discounts from the value of sound stamps.

# Terminology

**Booklets** — Many countries have issued stamps in small booklets for the convenience of users. This idea continues to become increasingly popular in many countries. Booklets have been issued in many sizes and forms, often with advertising on the covers, the panes of stamps or on the interleaving.

The panes used in booklets may be printed from special plates or made from regular sheets. All panes from booklets issued by the United States and many from those of other countries contain stamps that are straight edged on the sides, but perforated between. Others are distinguished by orientation of watermark or other identifying features. Any stamp-like unit in the pane, either printed or blank, that is not a postage stamp, is considered to be a *label* in the catalogue listings.

Scott lists and values booklet panes. Modern complete booklets also are listed and valued. Individual booklet panes are listed only when they are not fashioned from existing sheet stamps and, therefore, are identifiable from their sheet stamp counterparts.

Panes usually do not have a used value assigned to them because there is little market activity for used booklet panes, even though many exist used and there is some demand for them.

**Cancellations** — The marks or obliterations put on stamps by postal authorities to show that they have performed service and to prevent their reuse are known as cancellations. If the marking is made with a pen, it is considered a "pen cancel." When the location of the post office appears in the marking, it is a "town cancellation." A "postmark" is technically any postal marking, but in practice the term generally is applied to a town cancellation with a date. When calling attention to a cause or celebration, the marking is known as a "slogan cancellation." Many other types and styles of cancellations exist, such as duplex, numerals, targets, fancy and others. See also "precancels," below.

**Coil Stamps** — These are stamps that are issued in rolls for use in dispensers, affixing and vending machines. Those coils of the United States, Canada, Sweden and some other countries are perforated horizontally or vertically only, with the outer edges imperforate. Coil stamps of some countries, such as Great Britain and Germany, are perforated on all four sides and may in some cases be distinguished from their sheet stamp counterparts by watermarks, counting numbers on the reverse or other means.

**Covers** — Entire envelopes, with or without adhesive postage stamps, that have passed through the mail and bear postal or other markings of philatelic interest are known as covers. Before the introduction of envelopes in about 1840, people folded letters and wrote the address on the outside. Some people covered their letters with an extra sheet of paper on the outside for the address, producing the term "cover." Used airletter sheets, stamped envelopes and other items of postal stationery also are considered covers.

**Errors** — Stamps that have some major, consistent, unintentional deviation from the normal are considered errors. Errors include, but are not limited to, missing or wrong colors, wrong paper, wrong watermarks, inverted centers or frames on multicolor printing, inverted or missing surcharges or overprints, double impressions, missing perforations, unintentionally omitted tagging and others. Factually wrong or misspelled information, if it appears on all examples of a stamp, are not considered errors in the true sense of the word. They are errors of design. Inconsistent or randomly appearing items, such as misperfs or color shifts, are classified as freaks.

**Color-Omitted Errors** — This term refers to stamps where a missing color is caused by the complete failure of the printing plate to deliver ink to the stamp paper or any other paper. Generally, this is caused by the printing plate not being engaged on the press or the ink station running dry of ink during printing.

**Color-Missing Errors** — This term refers to stamps where a color or colors were printed somewhere but do not appear on the finished stamp. There are four different classes of color-missing errors, and the catalog indicates with a two-letter code appended to each such listing what caused the color to be missing. These codes are used only for the United States' color-missing error listings.

**FO** = A *foldover* of the stamp sheet during printing may block ink from appearing on a stamp. Instead, the color will appear on the back of the foldover (where it might fall on the back of the selvage or perhaps on the back of the stamp or another stamp). FO also will be used in the case of foldunders, where the paper may fold underneath the other stamp paper and the color will print on the platen.

**EP** = A piece of *extraneous paper* falling across the plate or stamp paper will receive the printed ink. When the extraneous paper is removed, an unprinted portion of stamp paper remains and shows partially or totally missing colors.

**CM** = A misregistration of the printing plates during printing will result in a *color misregistration*, and such a misregistraion may result in a color not appearing on the finished stamp.

**PS** = *A perforation shift* after printing may remove a color from the finished stamp. Normally, this will occur on a row of stamps at the edge of the stamp pane.

**Measurements** – When measurements are given in the Scott catalogues for stamp size, grill size or any other reason, the first measurement given is always for the top and bottom dimension, while the second measurement will be for the sides (just as perforation gauges are measured). Thus, a stamp size of 15mm x 21mm will indicate a vertically oriented stamp 15mm wide at top and bottom, and 21mm tall at the sides. The same principle holds for measuring or counting items such as U.S. grills. A grill count of 22x18 points (B grill) indicates that there are 22 grill points across by 18 grill points down.

**Overprints and Surcharges** — Overprinting involves applying wording or design elements over an already existing stamp. Overprints can be used to alter the place of use (such as "Canal Zone" on U.S. stamps), to adapt them for a special purpose ("Porto" on Denmark's 1913-20 regular issues for use as postage due stamps, Scott J1-J7) or to commemorate a special occasion (United States Scott 647-648).

A *surcharge* is a form of overprint that changes or restates the face value of a stamp or piece of postal stationery.

Surcharges and overprints may be handstamped, typeset or, occasionally, lithographed or engraved. A few hand-written overprints and surcharges are known.

**Personalized Stamps** — In 1999, Australia issued stamps with se-tenant labels that could be personalized with pictures of the customer's choice. Other countries quickly followed suit, with some offering to print the selected picture on the stamp itself within a frame that was used exclusively for personalized issues. As the picture used on these stamps or labels vary, listings for such stamps are for any picture within the common frame (or any picture on a se-tenant label), be it a "generic" image or one produced especially for a customer, almost invariably at a premium price.

**Precancels** — Stamps that are canceled before they are placed in the mail are known as precancels. Precanceling usually is done to expedite the handling of large mailings and generally allow the affected mail pieces to skip certain phases of mail handling.

In the United States, precancellations generally identified the point of origin; that is, the city and state. This information appeared across the face of the stamp, usually centered between parallel lines. More recently, bureau precancels retained the parallel lines, but the city and state designations were dropped. Recent coils have a service inscription that is present on the original printing plate. These show the mail service paid for by the stamp. Since these stamps are not intended to receive further cancellations when used as intended, they are considered precancels. Such items often do not have parallel lines as part of the precancellation.

In France, the abbreviation *Affranchts* in a semicircle together with the word *Postes* is the general form of precancel in use. Belgian precancellations usually appear in a box in which the name of the city appears. Netherlands precancels have the name of the city enclosed between concentric circles, sometimes called a "lifesaver." Precancellations of other countries usually follow these patterns, but may be any arrangement of bars, boxes and city names.

Precancels are listed in the Scott catalogues only if the precancel changes the denomination (Belgium Scott 477-478); if the precanceled stamp is different from the non-precanceled version (such as untagged U.S. precancels); or if the stamp exists only precanceled (France Scott 1096-1099, U.S. Scott 2265).

**Proofs and Essays** — Proofs are impressions taken from an approved die, plate or stone in which the design and color are the same as the stamp issued to the public. Trial color proofs are impressions taken from approved dies, plates or stones in colors that vary from the final version. An essay is the impression of a design that differs in some way from the issued stamp. "Progressive die proofs" generally are considered to be essays.

**Provisionals** — These are stamps that are issued on short notice and intended for temporary use pending the arrival of regular issues. They usually are issued to meet such contingencies as changes in government or currency, shortage of necessary postage values or military occupation.

During the 1840s, postmasters in certain American cities issued stamps that were valid only at specific post offices. In 1861, postmasters of the Confederate States also issued stamps with limited validity. Both of these examples are known as "postmaster's provisionals."

**Se-tenant** — This term refers to an unsevered pair, strip or block of stamps that differ in design, denomination or overprint.

Unless the se-tenant item has a continuous design (see U.S. Scott 1451a, 1694a) the stamps do not have to be in the same order as shown in the catalogue (see U.S. Scott 2158a).

**Specimens** — The Universal Postal Union required member nations to send samples of all stamps they released into service to the International Bureau in Switzerland. Member nations of the UPU received these specimens as samples of what stamps were valid for postage. Many are overprinted, handstamped or initial-perforated "Specimen," "Canceled" or "Muestra." Some are marked with bars across the denominations (China-Taiwan), punched holes (Czechoslovakia) or back inscriptions (Mongolia).

Stamps distributed to government officials or for publicity purposes, and stamps submitted by private security printers for official approval, also may receive such defacements.

The previously described defacement markings prevent postal use, and all such items generally are known as "specimens."

**Tete Beche** — This term describes a pair of stamps in which one is upside down in relation to the other. Some of these are the result of intentional sheet arrangements, such as Morocco Scott B10-B11. Others occurred when one or more electrotypes accidentally were placed upside down on the plate, such as Colombia Scott 57a. Separation of the tete-beche stamps, of course, destroys the tete beche variety.

# Pronunciation Symbols

ə .... banana, collide, abut

ˈə, ˌə .... humdrum, abut

ə .... immediately preceding \l\, \n\, \m\, \ŋ\, as in battle, mitten, eaten, and sometimes open \ˈō-p$^{ə}$m\, lock and key \-$^{ə}$ŋ-\; immediately following \l\, \m\, \r\, as often in French table, prisme, titre

ər .... further, merger, bird

ˈər-, ˈə-r .... as in two different pronunciations of hurry \ˈhər-ē, ˈhə-rē\

a .... mat, map, mad, gag, snap, patch

ā .... day, fade, date, aorta, drape, cape

ä .... bother, cot, and, with most American speakers, father, cart

ȧ .... father as pronounced by speakers who do not rhyme it with *bother*; French patte

au̇ .... now, loud, out

b .... baby, rib

ch .... chin, nature \ˈnā-chər\

d .... did, adder

e .... bet, bed, peck

ˈē, ˌē .... beat, nosebleed, evenly, easy

ē .... easy, mealy

f .... fifty, cuff

g .... go, big, gift

h .... hat, ahead

hw .... whale as pronounced by those who do not have the same pronunciation for both *whale* and *wail*

i .... tip, banish, active

ī .... site, side, buy, tripe

j .... job, gem, edge, join, judge

k .... kin, cook, ache

k̲ .... German ich, Buch; one pronunciation of loch

l .... lily, pool

m .... murmur, dim, nymph

n .... no, own

$^{n}$ .... indicates that a preceding vowel or diphthong is pronounced with the nasal passages open, as in French *un bon vin blanc* \œ$^{n}$ -bō$^{n}$ -va$^{n}$ -blä$^{n}$\

ŋ .... sing \ˈsiŋ\, singer \ˈsiŋ-ər\, finger \ˈfiŋ-gər\, ink \ˈiŋk \

ō .... bone, know, beau

ȯ .... saw, all, gnaw, caught

œ .... French boeuf, German Hölle

œ̄ .... French feu, German Höhle

ȯi .... coin, destroy

p .... pepper, lip

r .... red, car, rarity

s .... source, less

sh .... as in shy, mission, machine, special (actually, this is a single sound, not two); with a hyphen between, two sounds as in *grasshopper* \ˈgras-ˌhä-pər\

t .... tie, attack, late, later, latter

th .... as in thin, ether (actually, this is a single sound, not two); with a hyphen between, two sounds as in *knighthood* \ˈnīt-ˌhu̇d\

t̲h̲ .... then, either, this (actually, this is a single sound, not two)

ü .... rule, youth, union \ˈyün-yən\, few \ˈfyü\

u̇ .... pull, wood, book, curable \ˈkyu̇r-ə-bəl\, fury \ˈfyu̇r-ē\

ue .... German füllen, hübsch

u̅e̅ .... French rue, German fühlen

v .... vivid, give

w .... we, away

y .... yard, young, cue \ˈkyü\, mute \ˈmyüt\, union \ˈyün-yən\

$^{y}$ .... indicates that during the articulation of the sound represented by the preceding character the front of the tongue has substantially the position it has for the articulation of the first sound of *yard*, as in French *digne* \dēn$^{y}$\

z .... zone, raise

zh .... as in vision, azure \ˈa-zhər\ (actually, this is a single sound, not two); with a hyphen between, two sounds as in *hogshead* \ˈhȯgz-ˌhed, ˈhägz-\

\ .... slant line used in pairs to mark the beginning and end of a transcription: \ˈpen\

ˈ .... mark preceding a syllable with primary (strongest) stress: \ˈpen-mən-ˌship\

ˌ .... mark preceding a syllable with secondary (medium) stress: \ˈpen-mən-ˌship\

\- .... mark of syllable division

( ) .... indicate that what is symbolized between is present in some utterances but not in others: *factory* \ˈfak-t(ə-)rē\

÷ .... indicates that many regard as unacceptable the pronunciation variant immediately following: *cupola* \ˈkyü-pə-lə, ÷-ˌlō\

# Currency Conversion

| Country | Dollar | Pound | S Franc | Yen | HK $ | Euro | Cdn $ | Aus $ |
|---|---|---|---|---|---|---|---|---|
| Australia | 0.9588 | 1.5094 | 1.0543 | 0.0103 | 0.1237 | 1.3009 | 0.9607 | — |
| Canada | 0.9980 | 1.5712 | 1.0974 | 0.0108 | 0.1287 | 1.3541 | — | 1.0409 |
| European Union | 0.7370 | 1.1603 | 0.8104 | 0.0080 | 0.0950 | — | 0.7385 | 0.7687 |
| Hong Kong | 7.7541 | 12.207 | 8.5266 | 0.0837 | — | 10.521 | 7.7696 | 8.0873 |
| Japan | 92.697 | 145.93 | 101.93 | — | 11.955 | 125.78 | 92.882 | 96.680 |
| Switzerland | 0.9094 | 1.4317 | — | 0.0098 | 0.1173 | 1.2339 | 0.9112 | 0.9485 |
| United Kingdom | 0.6352 | — | 0.6985 | 0.0069 | 0.0819 | 0.8619 | 0.6365 | 0.6625 |
| United States | — | 1.5743 | 1.0996 | 0.0108 | 0.1290 | 1.3569 | 1.0020 | 1.0430 |

| Country | Currency | U.S. $ Equiv. |
|---|---|---|
| Gabon | Community of French Africa (CFA) franc | .0021 |
| Gambia | dalasy | .0294 |
| Georgia | lari | .6042 |
| Germany | euro | 1.3569 |
| Ghana | cedi | .5240 |
| Gibraltar | pound | 1.5743 |
| Great Britain | pound | 1.5743 |
| Alderney | pound | 1.5743 |
| Guernsey | pound | 1.5743 |
| Jersey | pound | 1.5743 |
| Isle of Man | pound | 1.5743 |
| Greece | euro | 1.3569 |
| Mount Athos | euro | 1.3569 |
| Greenland | Danish krone | .1819 |
| Grenada | East Caribbean dollar | .3704 |
| Grenada Grenadines | East Caribbean dollar | .3704 |
| Guatemala | quetzal | .1279 |
| Guinea | franc | .0001 |
| Guinea-Bissau | CFA franc | .0021 |
| Guyana | dollar | .0049 |
| Haiti | gourde | .0235 |
| Honduras | lempira | .0502 |
| Hong Kong | dollar | .1290 |
| Hungary | forint | .0046 |
| Iceland | krona | .0079 |
| India | rupee | .0188 |
| Indonesia | rupiah | .0001 |
| Iran | rial | .0001 |
| Iraq | dinar | .0009 |
| Ireland | euro | 1.3569 |
| Israel | shekel | .2710 |
| Italy | euro | 1.3569 |
| Ivory Coast | CFA franc | .0021 |

*Source:* ***xe.com****, Feb. 4, 2013. Figures reflect values as of Feb. 4, 2013.*

# COMMON DESIGN TYPE

Pictured in this section are issues where one illustration has been used for a number of countries in the Catalogue. Not included in this section are overprinted stamps or those issues which are illustrated in each country.

## EUROPA

### Europa, 1956

The design symbolizing the cooperation among the six countries comprising the Coal and Steel Community is illustrated in each country.

| | |
|---|---|
| **Belgium** | **496-497** |
| **France** | **805-806** |
| **Germany** | **748-749** |
| **Italy** | **715-716** |
| **Luxembourg** | **318-320** |
| **Netherlands** | **368-369** |

### Europa, 1958

"E" and Dove — CD1

European Postal Union at the service of European integration.

**1958, Sept. 13**

| | |
|---|---|
| Belgium | 527-528 |
| France | 889-890 |
| Germany | 790-791 |
| Italy | 750-751 |
| Luxembourg | 341-343 |
| Netherlands | 375-376 |
| Saar | 317-318 |

### Europa, 1959

6-Link Enless Chain — CD2

**1959, Sept. 19**

| | |
|---|---|
| Belgium | 536-537 |
| France | 929-930 |
| Germany | 805-806 |
| Italy | 791-792 |
| Luxembourg | 354-355 |
| Netherlands | 379-380 |

### Europa, 1960

19-Spoke Wheel CD3

First anniverary of the establishment of C.E.P.T. (Conference Europeenne des Administrations des Postes et des Telecommunications.) The spokes symbolize the 19 founding members of the Conference.

**1960, Sept.**

| | |
|---|---|
| Belgium | 553-554 |
| Denmark | 379 |
| Finland | 376-377 |
| France | 970-971 |
| Germany | 818-820 |
| Great Britain | 377-378 |
| Greece | 688 |
| Iceland | 327-328 |
| Ireland | 175-176 |
| Italy | 809-810 |
| Luxembourg | 374-375 |
| Netherlands | 385-386 |
| Norway | 387 |
| Portugal | 866-867 |
| Spain | 941-942 |
| Sweden | 562-563 |
| Switzerland | 400-401 |
| Turkey | 1493-1494 |

### Europa, 1961

19 Doves Flying as One — CD4

The 19 doves represent the 19 members of the Conference of European Postal and Telecommunications Administrations C.E.P.T.

**1961-62**

| | |
|---|---|
| Belgium | 572-573 |
| Cyprus | 201-203 |
| France | 1005-1006 |
| Germany | 844-845 |
| Great Britain | 383-384 |
| Greece | 718-719 |
| Iceland | 340-341 |
| Italy | 845-846 |
| Luxembourg | 382-383 |
| Netherlands | 387-388 |
| Spain | 1010-1011 |
| Switzerland | 410-411 |
| Turkey | 1518-1520 |

### Europa, 1962

Young Tree with 19 Leaves CD5

The 19 leaves represent the 19 original members of C.E.P.T.

**1962-63**

| | |
|---|---|
| Belgium | 582-583 |
| Cyprus | 219-221 |
| France | 1045-1046 |
| Germany | 852-853 |
| Greece | 739-740 |
| Iceland | 348-349 |
| Ireland | 184-185 |
| Italy | 860-861 |
| Luxembourg | 386-387 |
| Netherlands | 394-395 |
| Norway | 414-415 |
| Switzerland | 416-417 |
| Turkey | 1553-1555 |

### Europa, 1963

Stylized Links, Symbolizing Unity — CD6

**1963, Sept.**

| | |
|---|---|
| Belgium | 598-599 |
| Cyprus | 229-231 |
| Finland | 419 |
| France | 1074-1075 |
| Germany | 867-868 |
| Greece | 768-769 |
| Iceland | 357-358 |
| Ireland | 188-189 |
| Italy | 880-881 |
| Luxembourg | 403-404 |
| Netherlands | 416-417 |
| Norway | 441-442 |
| Switzerland | 429 |
| Turkey | 1602-1603 |

### Europa, 1964

Symbolic Daisy — CD7

5th anniversary of the establishment of C.E.P.T. The 22 petals of the flower symbolize the 22 members of the Conference.

**1964, Sept.**

| | |
|---|---|
| Austria | 738 |
| Belgium | 614-615 |
| Cyprus | 244-246 |
| France | 1109-1110 |
| Germany | 897-898 |
| Greece | 801-802 |
| Iceland | 367-368 |
| Ireland | 196-197 |
| Italy | 894-895 |
| Luxembourg | 411-412 |
| Monaco | 590-591 |
| Netherlands | 428-429 |
| Norway | 458 |
| Portugal | 931-933 |
| Spain | 1262-1263 |
| Switzerland | 438-439 |
| Turkey | 1628-1629 |

### Europa, 1965

Leaves and "Fruit" CD8

**1965**

| | |
|---|---|
| Belgium | 636-637 |
| Cyprus | 262-264 |
| Finland | 437 |
| France | 1131-1132 |
| Germany | 934-935 |
| Greece | 833-834 |
| Iceland | 375-376 |
| Ireland | 204-205 |
| Italy | 915-916 |
| Luxembourg | 432-433 |
| Monaco | 616-617 |
| Netherlands | 438-439 |
| Norway | 475-476 |
| Portugal | 958-960 |
| Switzerland | 469 |
| Turkey | 1665-1666 |

### Europa, 1966

Symbolic Sailboat — CD9

**1966, Sept.**

| | |
|---|---|
| Andorra, French | 172 |
| Belgium | 675-676 |
| Cyprus | 275-277 |
| France | 1163-1164 |
| Germany | 963-964 |
| Greece | 862-863 |
| Iceland | 384-385 |
| Ireland | 216-217 |
| Italy | 942-943 |
| Liechtenstein | 415 |
| Luxembourg | 440-441 |
| Monaco | 639-640 |
| Netherlands | 441-442 |
| Norway | 496-497 |
| Portugal | 980-982 |
| Switzerland | 477-478 |
| Turkey | 1718-1719 |

### Europa, 1967

Cogwheels CD10

**1967**

| | |
|---|---|
| Andorra, French | 174-175 |
| Belgium | 688-689 |
| Cyprus | 297-299 |
| France | 1178-1179 |
| Germany | 969-970 |
| Greece | 891-892 |
| Iceland | 389-390 |
| Ireland | 232-233 |
| Italy | 951-952 |
| Liechtenstein | 420 |
| Luxembourg | 449-450 |
| Monaco | 669-670 |
| Netherlands | 444-447 |
| Norway | 504-505 |
| Portugal | 994-996 |
| Spain | 1465-1466 |
| Switzerland | 482 |
| Turkey | B120-B121 |

### Europa, 1968

Golden Key with C.E.P.T. Emblem CD11

**1968**

| | |
|---|---|
| Andorra, French | 182-183 |
| Belgium | 705-706 |
| Cyprus | 314-316 |
| France | 1209-1210 |
| Germany | 983-984 |
| Greece | 916-917 |
| Iceland | 395-396 |
| Ireland | 242-243 |
| Italy | 979-980 |
| Liechtenstein | 442 |
| Luxembourg | 466-467 |
| Monaco | 689-691 |
| Netherlands | 452-453 |
| Portugal | 1019-1021 |
| San Marino | 687 |
| Spain | 1526 |
| Switzerland | 488 |
| Turkey | 1775-1776 |

### Europa, 1969

"EUROPA" and "CEPT" CD12

Tenth anniversary of C.E.P.T.

**1969**

| | |
|---|---|
| Andorra, French | 188-189 |
| Austria | 837 |
| Belgium | 718-719 |
| Cyprus | 326-328 |
| Denmark | 458 |
| Finland | 483 |
| France | 1245-1246 |
| Germany | 996-997 |
| Great Britain | 585 |
| Greece | 947-948 |
| Iceland | 406-407 |
| Ireland | 270-271 |
| Italy | 1000-1001 |
| Liechtenstein | 453 |
| Luxembourg | 475-476 |
| Monaco | 722-724 |
| Netherlands | 475-476 |
| Norway | 533-534 |
| Portugal | 1038-1040 |
| San Marino | 701-702 |
| Spain | 1567 |

Sweden...814-816
Switzerland...500-501
Turkey...1799-1800
Vatican...470-472
Yugoslavia...1003-1004

**Europa, 1970**

Interwoven Threads
CD13

**1970**

Andorra, French...196-197
Belgium...741-742
Cyprus...340-342
France...1271-1272
Germany...1018-1019
Greece...985, 987
Iceland...420-421
Ireland...279-281
Italy...1013-1014
Liechtenstein...470
Luxembourg...489-490
Monaco...768-770
Netherlands...483-484
Portugal...1060-1062
San Marino...729-730
Spain...1607
Switzerland...515-516
Turkey...1848-1849
Yugoslavia...1024-1025

**Europa, 1971**

"Fraternity, Cooperation, Common Effort"
CD14

**1971**

Andorra, French...205-206
Belgium...803-804
Cyprus...365-367
Finland...504
France...1304
Germany...1064-1065
Greece...1029-1030
Iceland...429-430
Ireland...305-306
Italy...1038-1039
Liechtenstein...485
Luxembourg...500-501
Malta...425-427
Monaco...797-799
Netherlands...488-489
Portugal...1094-1096
San Marino...749-750
Spain...1675-1676
Switzerland...531-532
Turkey...1876-1877
Yugoslavia...1052-1053

**Europa, 1972**

Sparkles, Symbolic of Communications
CD15

**1972**

Andorra, French...210-211
Andorra, Spanish...62
Belgium...825-826
Cyprus...380-382
Finland...512-513
France...1341
Germany...1089-1090
Greece...1049-1050
Iceland...439-440
Ireland...316-317
Italy...1065-1066
Liechtenstein...504
Luxembourg...512-513
Malta...450-453
Monaco...831-832
Netherlands...494-495
Portugal...1141-1143
San Marino...771-772
Spain...1718
Switzerland...544-545
Turkey...1907-1908
Yugoslavia...1100-1101

**Europa, 1973**

Post Horn and Arrows
CD16

**1973**

Andorra, French...219-220
Andorra, Spanish...76
Belgium...839-840
Cyprus...396-398
Finland...526
France...1367
Germany...1114-1115
Greece...1090-1092
Iceland...447-448
Ireland...329-330
Italy...1108-1109
Liechtenstein...528-529
Luxembourg...523-524
Malta...469-471
Monaco...866-867
Netherlands...504-505
Norway...604-605
Portugal...1170-1172
San Marino...802-803
Spain...1753
Switzerland...580-581
Turkey...1935-1936
Yugoslavia...1138-1139

**Europa, 2000**

CD17

**2000**

Albania...2621-2622
Andorra, French...522
Andorra, Spanish...262
Armenia...610-611
Austria...1814
Azerbaijan...698-699
Belarus...350
Belgium...1818
Bosnia & Herzegovina (Moslem)...358
Bosnia & Herzegovina (Serb)...111-112
Croatia...428-429
Cyprus...959
Czech Republic...3120
Denmark...1189
Estonia...394
Faroe Islands...376
Finland...1129
Aland Islands...166
France...2771
Georgia...228-229
Germany...2086-2087
Gibraltar...837-840
Great Britain (Guernsey)...805-809
Great Britain (Jersey)...935-936
Great Britain (Isle of Man)...883
Greece...1959
Greenland...363
Hungary...3699-3700
Iceland...910
Ireland...1230-1231
Italy...2349
Latvia...504
Liechtenstein...1178
Lithuania...668
Luxembourg...1035
Macedonia...187
Malta...1011-1012
Moldova...355
Monaco...2161-2162
Poland...3519
Portugal...2358
Portugal (Azores)...455
Portugal (Madeira)...208
Romania...4370
Russia...6589
San Marino...1480
Slovakia...355
Slovenia...424
Spain...3036
Sweden...2394
Switzerland...1074
Turkey...2762
Turkish Rep. of Northern Cyprus...500
Ukraine...379
Vatican City...1152

The Gibraltar stamps are similar to the stamp illustrated, but none have the design shown above. All other sets listed above include at least one stamp with the design shown, but some include stamps with entirely different designs. Bulgaria Nos. 4131-4132 and Yugoslavia Nos. 2485-2486 are Europa stamps with completely different designs.

**PORTUGAL & COLONIES**
**Vasco da Gama**

Fleet Departing
CD20

Fleet Arriving at Calicut — CD21

Embarking at Rastello
CD22

Muse of History
CD23

San Gabriel, da Gama and Camoens
CD24

Archangel Gabriel, the Patron Saint
CD25

Flagship San Gabriel — CD26

Vasco da Gama — CD27

Fourth centenary of Vasco da Gama's discovery of the route to India.

**1898**

Azores...93-100
Macao...67-74
Madeira...37-44
Portugal...147-154
Port. Africa...1-8
Port. Congo...75-98
Port. India...189-196
St. Thomas & Prince Islands...170-193
Timor...45-52

**Pombal**
**POSTAL TAX**
**POSTAL TAX DUES**

Marquis de Pombal — CD28

Planning Reconstruction of Lisbon, 1755 — CD29

Pombal Monument, Lisbon — CD30

Sebastiao Jose de Carvalho e Mello, Marquis de Pombal (1699-1782), statesman, rebuilt Lisbon after earthquake of 1755. Tax was for the erection of Pombal monument. Obligatory on all mail on certain days throughout the year. Postal Tax Dues are inscribed "Multa."

**1925**

Angola... RA1-RA3, RAJ1-RAJ3
Azores... RA9-RA11, RAJ2-RAJ4
Cape Verde... RA1-RA3, RAJ1-RAJ3
Macao... RA1-RA3, RAJ1-RAJ3
Madeira... RA1-RA3, RAJ1-RAJ3
Mozambique... RA1-RA3, RAJ1-RAJ3
Nyassa... RA1-RA3, RAJ1-RAJ3
Portugal... RA11-RA13, RAJ2-RAJ4
Port. Guinea... RA1-RA3, RAJ1-RAJ3
Port. India... RA1-RA3, RAJ1-RAJ3
St. Thomas & Prince Islands... RA1-RA3, RAJ1-RAJ3
Timor... RA1-RA3, RAJ1-RAJ3

Vasco da Gama
CD34

Mousinho de Albuquerque
CD35

Dam
CD36

Prince Henry the Navigator
CD37

Affonso de Albuquerque
CD38

Plane over Globe
CD39

**1938-39**

Angola...274-291, C1-C9
Cape Verde...234-251, C1-C9
Macao...289-305, C7-C15
Mozambique...270-287, C1-C9
Port. Guinea...233-250. C1-C9
Port. India...439-453, C1-C8
St. Thomas & Prince Islands... 302-319, 323-340, C1-C18
Timor...223-239, C1-C9

## Lady of Fatima

Our Lady of the Rosary, Fatima, Portugal — CD40

**1948-49**

| | |
|---|---|
| Angola | 315-318 |
| Cape Verde | 266 |
| Macao | 336 |
| Mozambique | 325-328 |
| Port. Guinea | 271 |
| Port. India | 480 |
| St. Thomas & Prince Islands | 351 |
| Timor | 254 |

A souvenir sheet of 9 stamps was issued in 1951 to mark the extension of the 1950 Holy Year. The sheet contains: Angola No. 316, Cape Verde No. 266, Macao No. 336, Mozambique No. 325, Portuguese Guinea No. 271, Portuguese India Nos. 480, 485, St. Thomas & Prince Islands No. 351, Timor No. 254. The sheet also contains a portrait of Pope Pius XII and is inscribed "Encerramento do Ano Santo, Fatima 1951." It was sold for 11 escudos.

## Holy Year

Church Bells and Dove CD41

Angel Holding Candelabra CD42

Holy Year, 1950.

**1950-51**

| | |
|---|---|
| Angola | 331-332 |
| Cape Verde | 268-269 |
| Macao | 339-340 |
| Mozambique | 330-331 |
| Port. Guinea | 273-274 |
| Port. India | 490-491, 496-503 |
| St. Thomas & Prince Islands | 353-354 |
| Timor | 258-259 |

A souvenir sheet of 8 stamps was issued in 1951 to mark the extension of the Holy Year. The sheet contains: Angola No. 331, Cape Verde No. 269, Macao No. 340, Mozambique No. 331, Portuguese Guinea No. 275, Portuguese India No. 490, St. Thomas & Prince Islands No. 354, Timor No. 258, some with colors changed. The sheet contains doves and is inscribed 'Encerramento do Ano Santo, Fatima 1951.' It was sold for 17 escudos.

## Holy Year Conclusion

Our Lady of Fatima — CD43

Conclusion of Holy Year. Sheets contain alternate vertical rows of stamps and labels bearing quotation from Pope Pius XII, different for each colony.

**1951**

| | |
|---|---|
| Angola | 357 |
| Cape Verde | 270 |
| Macao | 352 |
| Mozambique | 356 |
| Port. Guinea | 275 |
| Port. India | 506 |
| St. Thomas & Prince Islands | 355 |
| Timor | 270 |

## Medical Congress

CD44

First National Congress of Tropical Medicine, Lisbon, 1952. Each stamp has a different design.

**1952**

| | |
|---|---|
| Angola | 358 |
| Cape Verde | 287 |
| Macao | 364 |
| Mozambique | 359 |
| Port. Guinea | 276 |
| Port. India | 516 |
| St. Thomas & Prince Islands | 356 |
| Timor | 271 |

## Postage Due Stamps

CD45

**1952**

| | |
|---|---|
| Angola | J37-J42 |
| Cape Verde | J31-J36 |
| Macao | J53-J58 |
| Mozambique | J51-J56 |
| Port. Guinea | J40-J45 |
| Port. India | J47-J52 |
| St. Thomas & Prince Islands | J52-J57 |
| Timor | J31-J36 |

## Sao Paulo

Father Manuel da Nobrega and View of Sao Paulo — CD46

Founding of Sao Paulo, Brazil, 400th anniv.

**1954**

| | |
|---|---|
| Angola | 385 |
| Cape Verde | 297 |
| Macao | 382 |
| Mozambique | 395 |
| Port. Guinea | 291 |
| Port. India | 530 |
| St. Thomas & Prince Islands | 369 |
| Timor | 279 |

## Tropical Medicine Congress

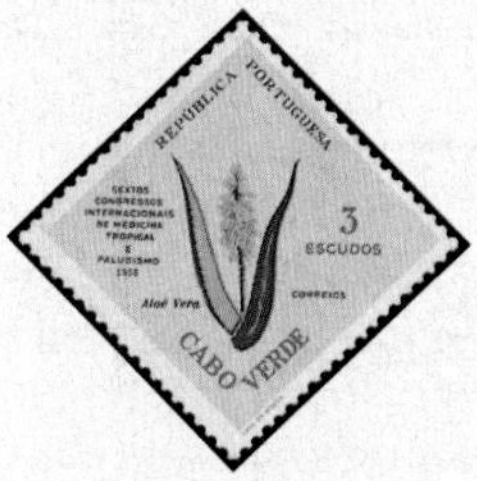


CD47

Sixth International Congress for Tropical Medicine and Malaria, Lisbon, Sept. 1958. Each stamp shows a different plant.

**1958**

| | |
|---|---|
| Angola | 409 |
| Cape Verde | 303 |
| Macao | 392 |
| Mozambique | 404 |
| Port. Guinea | 295 |
| Port. India | 569 |
| St. Thomas & Prince Islands | 371 |
| Timor | 289 |

## Sports

CD48

Each stamp shows a different sport.

**1962**

| | |
|---|---|
| Angola | 433-438 |
| Cape Verde | 320-325 |
| Macao | 394-399 |
| Mozambique | 424-429 |
| Port. Guinea | 299-304 |
| St. Thomas & Prince Islands | 374-379 |
| Timor | 313-318 |

## Anti-Malaria

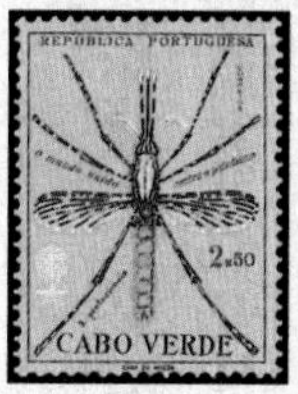


Anopheles Funestus and Malaria Eradication Symbol — CD49

World Health Organization drive to eradicate malaria.

**1962**

| | |
|---|---|
| Angola | 439 |
| Cape Verde | 326 |
| Macao | 400 |
| Mozambique | 430 |
| Port. Guinea | 305 |
| St. Thomas & Prince Islands | 380 |
| Timor | 319 |

## Airline Anniversary

Map of Africa, Super Constellation and Jet Liner — CD50

Tenth anniversary of Transportes Aereos Portugueses (TAP).

**1963**

| | |
|---|---|
| Angola | 490 |
| Cape Verde | 327 |
| Mozambique | 434 |
| Port. Guinea | 318 |
| St. Thomas & Prince Islands | 381 |

## National Overseas Bank

Antonio Teixeira de Sousa — CD51

Centenary of the National Overseas Bank of Portugal.

**1964, May 16**

| | |
|---|---|
| Angola | 509 |
| Cape Verde | 328 |
| Port. Guinea | 319 |
| St. Thomas & Prince Islands | 382 |
| Timor | 320 |

## ITU

ITU Emblem and the Archangel Gabriel — CD52

International Communications Union, Cent.

**1965, May 17**

| | |
|---|---|
| Angola | 511 |
| Cape Verde | 329 |
| Macao | 402 |
| Mozambique | 464 |
| Port. Guinea | 320 |
| St. Thomas & Prince Islands | 383 |
| Timor | 321 |

## National Revolution

CD53

40th anniv. of the National Revolution. Different buildings on each stamp.

**1966, May 28**

| | |
|---|---|
| Angola | 525 |
| Cape Verde | 338 |
| Macao | 403 |
| Mozambique | 465 |
| Port. Guinea | 329 |
| St. Thomas & Prince Islands | 392 |
| Timor | 322 |

## Navy Club

CD54

Centenary of Portugal's Navy Club. Each stamp has a different design.

**1967, Jan. 31**

| | |
|---|---|
| Angola | 527-528 |
| Cape Verde | 339-340 |
| Macao | 412-413 |
| Mozambique | 478-479 |
| Port. Guinea | 330-331 |
| St. Thomas & Prince Islands | 393-394 |
| Timor | 323-324 |

## Admiral Coutinho

CD55

Centenary of the birth of Admiral Carlos Viegas Gago Coutinho (1869-1959), explorer and aviation pioneer. Each stamp has a different design.

**1969, Feb. 17**

| | |
|---|---|
| Angola | 547 |
| Cape Verde | 355 |
| Macao | 417 |
| Mozambique | 484 |
| Port. Guinea | 335 |
| St. Thomas & Prince Islands | 397 |
| Timor | 335 |

### Administration Reform

Luiz Augusto Rebello da Silva — CD56

Centenary of the administration reforms of the overseas territories.

**1969, Sept. 25**

| | |
|---|---|
| Angola | 549 |
| Cape Verde | 357 |
| Macao | 419 |
| Mozambique | 491 |
| Port. Guinea | 337 |
| St. Thomas & Prince Islands | 399 |
| Timor | 338 |

### Marshal Carmona

CD57

Birth centenary of Marshal Antonio Oscar Carmona de Fragoso (1869-1951), President of Portugal. Each stamp has a different design.

**1970, Nov. 15**

| | |
|---|---|
| Angola | 563 |
| Cape Verde | 359 |
| Macao | 422 |
| Mozambique | 493 |
| Port. Guinea | 340 |
| St. Thomas & Prince Islands | 403 |
| Timor | 341 |

### Olympic Games

CD59

20th Olympic Games, Munich, Aug. 26-Sept. 11. Each stamp shows a different sport.

**1972, June 20**

| | |
|---|---|
| Angola | 569 |
| Cape Verde | 361 |
| Macao | 426 |
| Mozambique | 504 |
| Port. Guinea | 342 |
| St. Thomas & Prince Islands | 408 |
| Timor | 343 |

### Lisbon-Rio de Janeiro Flight

CD60

50th anniversary of the Lisbon to Rio de Janeiro flight by Arturo de Sacadura and Coutinho, March 30-June 5, 1922. Each stamp shows a different stage of the flight.

**1972, Sept. 20**

| | |
|---|---|
| Angola | 570 |
| Cape Verde | 362 |
| Macao | 427 |
| Mozambique | 505 |
| Port. Guinea | 343 |
| St. Thomas & Prince Islands | 409 |
| Timor | 344 |

### WMO Centenary

WMO Emblem — CD61

Centenary of international meterological cooperation.

**1973, Dec. 15**

| | |
|---|---|
| Angola | 571 |
| Cape Verde | 363 |
| Macao | 429 |
| Mozambique | 509 |
| Port. Guinea | 344 |
| St. Thomas & Prince Islands | 410 |
| Timor | 345 |

### FRENCH COMMUNITY

**Upper Volta can be found under Burkina Faso in Vol. 1**

**Madagascar can be found under Malagasy in Vol. 3**

### Colonial Exposition

People of French Empire CD70

Women's Heads CD71

France Showing Way to Civilization CD72

"Colonial Commerce" CD73

International Colonial Exposition, Paris.

**1931**

| | |
|---|---|
| Cameroun | 213-216 |
| Chad | 60-63 |
| Dahomey | 97-100 |
| Fr. Guiana | 152-155 |
| Fr. Guinea | 116-119 |
| Fr. India | 100-103 |
| Fr. Polynesia | 76-79 |
| Fr. Sudan | 102-105 |
| Gabon | 120-123 |
| Guadeloupe | 138-141 |
| Indo-China | 140-142 |
| Ivory Coast | 92-95 |
| Madagascar | 169-172 |
| Martinique | 129-132 |
| Mauritania | 65-68 |
| Middle Congo | 61-64 |
| New Caledonia | 176-179 |
| Niger | 73-76 |
| Reunion | 122-125 |
| St. Pierre & Miquelon | 132-135 |
| Senegal | 138-141 |
| Somali Coast | 135-138 |
| Togo | 254-257 |
| Ubangi-Shari | 82-85 |
| Upper Volta | 66-69 |
| Wallis & Futuna Isls. | 85-88 |

### Paris International Exposition Colonial Arts Exposition

"Colonial Resources" CD74 CD77

Overseas Commerce CD75

Exposition Building and Women CD76

"France and the Empire" CD78

Cultural Treasures of the Colonies CD79

Souvenir sheets contain one imperf. stamp.

**1937**

| | |
|---|---|
| Cameroun | 217-222A |
| Dahomey | 101-107 |
| Fr. Equatorial Africa | 27-32, 73 |
| Fr. Guiana | 162-168 |
| Fr. Guinea | 120-126 |
| Fr. India | 104-110 |
| Fr. Polynesia | 117-123 |
| Fr. Sudan | 106-112 |
| Guadeloupe | 148-154 |
| Indo-China | 193-199 |
| Inini | 41 |
| Ivory Coast | 152-158 |
| Kwangchowan | 132 |
| Madagascar | 191-197 |
| Martinique | 179-185 |
| Mauritania | 69-75 |
| New Caledonia | 208-214 |
| Niger | 72-83 |
| Reunion | 167-173 |
| St. Pierre & Miquelon | 165-171 |
| Senegal | 172-178 |
| Somali Coast | 139-145 |
| Togo | 258-264 |
| Wallis & Futuna Isls. | 89 |

### Curie

Pierre and Marie Curie CD80

40th anniversary of the discovery of radium. The surtax was for the benefit of the Intl. Union for the Control of Cancer.

**1938**

| | |
|---|---|
| Cameroun | B1 |
| Cuba | B1-B2 |
| Dahomey | B2 |
| France | B76 |
| Fr. Equatorial Africa | B1 |
| Fr. Guiana | B3 |
| Fr. Guinea | B2 |
| Fr. India | B6 |
| Fr. Polynesia | B5 |
| Fr. Sudan | B1 |
| Guadeloupe | B3 |
| Indo-China | B14 |
| Ivory Coast | B2 |
| Madagascar | B2 |
| Martinique | B2 |
| Mauritania | B3 |
| New Caledonia | B4 |
| Niger | B1 |
| Reunion | B4 |
| St. Pierre & Miquelon | B3 |
| Senegal | B3 |
| Somali Coast | B2 |
| Togo | B1 |

### Caillie

Rene Caillie and Map of Northwestern Africa — CD81

Death centenary of Rene Caillie (1799-1838), French explorer. All three denominations exist with colony name omitted.

**1939**

| | |
|---|---|
| Dahomey | 108-110 |
| Fr. Guinea | 161-163 |
| Fr. Sudan | 113-115 |
| Ivory Coast | 160-162 |
| Mauritania | 109-111 |
| Niger | 84-86 |
| Senegal | 188-190 |
| Togo | 265-267 |

### New York World's Fair

Natives and New York Skyline CD82

**1939**

| | |
|---|---|
| Cameroun | 223-224 |
| Dahomey | 111-112 |
| Fr. Equatorial Africa | 78-79 |
| Fr. Guiana | 169-170 |
| Fr. Guinea | 164-165 |
| Fr. India | 111-112 |
| Fr. Polynesia | 124-125 |
| Fr. Sudan | 116-117 |
| Guadeloupe | 155-156 |
| Indo-China | 203-204 |
| Inini | 42-43 |
| Ivory Coast | 163-164 |
| Kwangchowan | 121-122 |
| Madagascar | 209-210 |
| Martinique | 186-187 |
| Mauritania | 112-113 |
| New Caledonia | 215-216 |
| Niger | 87-88 |
| Reunion | 174-175 |
| St. Pierre & Miquelon | 205-206 |
| Senegal | 191-192 |
| Somali Coast | 179-180 |
| Togo | 268-269 |
| Wallis & Futuna Isls. | 90-91 |

### French Revolution

Storming of the Bastille CD83

French Revolution, 150th anniv. The surtax was for the defense of the colonies.

**1939**

| | |
|---|---|
| Cameroun | B2-B6 |
| Dahomey | B3-B7 |
| Fr. Equatorial Africa | B4-B8, CB1 |
| Fr. Guiana | B4-B8, CB1 |
| Fr. Guinea | B3-B7 |
| Fr. India | B7-B11 |
| Fr. Polynesia | B6-B10, CB1 |
| Fr. Sudan | B2-B6 |
| Guadeloupe | B4-B8 |
| Indo-China | B15-B19, CB1 |
| Inini | B1-B5 |
| Ivory Coast | B3-B7 |

Kwangchowan ... B1-B5
Madagascar ... B3-B7, CB1
Martinique ... B3-B7
Mauritania ... B4-B8
New Caledonia ... B5-B9, CB1
Niger ... B2-B6
Reunion ... B5-B9, CB1
St. Pierre & Miquelon ... B4-B8
Senegal ... B4-B8, CB1
Somali Coast ... B3-B7
Togo ... B2-B6
Wallis & Futuna Isls. ... B1-B5

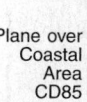

Plane over Coastal Area CD85

All five denominations exist with colony name omitted.

**1940**

Dahomey ... C1-C5
Fr. Guinea ... C1-C5
Fr. Sudan ... C1-C5
Ivory Coast ... C1-C5
Mauritania ... C1-C5
Niger ... C1-C5
Senegal ... C12-C16
Togo ... C1-C5

### Defense of the Empire

Colonial Infantryman — CD86

**1941**

Cameroun ... B13B
Dahomey ... B13
Fr. Equatorial Africa ... B8B
Fr. Guiana ... B10
Fr. Guinea ... B13
Fr. India ... B13
Fr. Polynesia ... B12
Fr. Sudan ... B12
Guadeloupe ... B10
Indo-China ... B19B
Inini ... B7
Ivory Coast ... B13
Kwangchowan ... B7
Madagascar ... B9
Martinique ... B9
Mauritania ... B14
New Caledonia ... B11
Niger ... B12
Reunion ... B11
St. Pierre & Miquelon ... B8B
Senegal ... B14
Somali Coast ... B9
Togo ... B10B
Wallis & Futuna Isls. ... B7

### Colonial Education Fund

CD86a

**1942**

Cameroun ... CB3
Dahomey ... CB4
Fr. Equatorial Africa ... CB5
Fr. Guiana ... CB4
Fr. Guinea ... CB4
Fr. India ... CB3
Fr. Polynesia ... CB4
Fr. Sudan ... CB4
Guadeloupe ... CB3
Indo-China ... CB5
Inini ... CB3
Ivory Coast ... CB4
Kwangchowan ... CB4
Malagasy ... CB5
Martinique ... CB3
Mauritania ... CB4
New Caledonia ... CB4
Niger ... CB4
Reunion ... CB4
St. Pierre & Miquelon ... CB3
Senegal ... CB5
Somali Coast ... CB3
Togo ... CB3
Wallis & Futuna ... CB3

Cross of Lorraine & Four-motor Plane CD87

**1941-5**

Cameroun ... C1-C7
Fr. Equatorial Africa ... C17-C23
Fr. Guiana ... C9-C10
Fr. India ... C1-C6
Fr. Polynesia ... C3-C9
Fr. West Africa ... C1-C3
Guadeloupe ... C1-C2
Madagascar ... C37-C43
Martinique ... C1-C2
New Caledonia ... C7-C13
Reunion ... C18-C24
St. Pierre & Miquelon ... C1-C7
Somali Coast ... C1-C7

Transport Plane CD88

Caravan and Plane CD89

**1942**

Dahomey ... C6-C13
Fr. Guinea ... C6-C13
Fr. Sudan ... C6-C13
Ivory Coast ... C6-C13
Mauritania ... C6-C13
Niger ... C6-C13
Senegal ... C17-C25
Togo ... C6-C13

### Red Cross

Marianne CD90

The surtax was for the French Red Cross and national relief.

**1944**

Cameroun ... B28
Fr. Equatorial Africa ... B38
Fr. Guiana ... B12
Fr. India ... B14
Fr. Polynesia ... B13
Fr. West Africa ... B1
Guadeloupe ... B12
Madagascar ... B15
Martinique ... B11
New Caledonia ... B13
Reunion ... B15
St. Pierre & Miquelon ... B13
Somali Coast ... B13
Wallis & Futuna Isls. ... B9

### Eboue

CD91

Felix Eboue, first French colonial administrator to proclaim resistance to Germany after French surrender in World War II.

**1945**

Cameroun ... 296-297
Fr. Equatorial Africa ... 156-157
Fr. Guiana ... 171-172
Fr. India ... 210-211
Fr. Polynesia ... 150-151
Fr. West Africa ... 15-16
Guadeloupe ... 187-188
Madagascar ... 259-260
Martinique ... 196-197
New Caledonia ... 274-275
Reunion ... 238-239
St. Pierre & Miquelon ... 322-323
Somali Coast ... 238-239

### Victory

Victory — CD92

European victory of the Allied Nations in World War II.

**1946, May 8**

Cameroun ... C8
Fr. Equatorial Africa ... C24
Fr. Guiana ... C11
Fr. India ... C7
Fr. Polynesia ... C10
Fr. West Africa ... C4
Guadeloupe ... C3
Indo-China ... C19
Madagascar ... C44
Martinique ... C3
New Caledonia ... C14
Reunion ... C25
St. Pierre & Miquelon ... C8
Somali Coast ... C8
Wallis & Futuna Isls. ... C1

### Chad to Rhine

Leclerc's Departure from Chad — CD93

Battle at Cufra Oasis — CD94

Tanks in Action, Mareth — CD95

Normandy Invasion — CD96

Entering Paris — CD97

Liberation of Strasbourg — CD98

"Chad to the Rhine" march, 1942-44, by Gen. Jacques Leclerc's column, later French 2nd Armored Division.

**1946, June 6**

Cameroun ... C9-C14
Fr. Equatorial Africa ... C25-C30
Fr. Guiana ... C12-C17
Fr. India ... C8-C13
Fr. Polynesia ... C11-C16
Fr. West Africa ... C5-C10
Guadeloupe ... C4-C9
Indo-China ... C20-C25
Madagascar ... C45-C50
Martinique ... C4-C9
New Caledonia ... C15-C20
Reunion ... C26-C31
St. Pierre & Miquelon ... C9-C14
Somali Coast ... C9-C14
Wallis & Futuna Isls. ... C2-C7

### UPU

French Colonials, Globe and Plane — CD99

Universal Postal Union, 75th anniv.

**1949, July 4**

Cameroun ... C29
Fr. Equatorial Africa ... C34
Fr. India ... C17
Fr. Polynesia ... C20
Fr. West Africa ... C15
Indo-China ... C26
Madagascar ... C55
New Caledonia ... C24
St. Pierre & Miquelon ... C18
Somali Coast ... C18
Togo ... C18
Wallis & Futuna Isls. ... C10

### Tropical Medicine

Doctor Treating Infant CD100

The surtax was for charitable work.

**1950**

| | |
|---|---|
| Cameroun | B29 |
| Fr. Equatorial Africa | B39 |
| Fr. India | B15 |
| Fr. Polynesia | B14 |
| Fr. West Africa | B3 |
| Madagascar | B17 |
| New Caledonia | B14 |
| St. Pierre & Miquelon | B14 |
| Somali Coast | B14 |
| Togo | B11 |

### Military Medal

Medal, Early Marine and Colonial Soldier — CD101

Centenary of the creation of the French Military Medal.

**1952**

| | |
|---|---|
| Cameroun | 322 |
| Comoro Isls. | 39 |
| Fr. Equatorial Africa | 186 |
| Fr. India | 233 |
| Fr. Polynesia | 179 |
| Fr. West Africa | 57 |
| Madagascar | 286 |
| New Caledonia | 295 |
| St. Pierre & Miquelon | 345 |
| Somali Coast | 267 |
| Togo | 327 |
| Wallis & Futuna Isls. | 149 |

### Liberation

Allied Landing, Victory Sign and Cross of Lorraine — CD102

Liberation of France, 10th anniv.

**1954, June 6**

| | |
|---|---|
| Cameroun | C32 |
| Comoro Isls. | C4 |
| Fr. Equatorial Africa | C38 |
| Fr. India | C18 |
| Fr. Polynesia | C22 |
| Fr. West Africa | C17 |
| Madagascar | C57 |
| New Caledonia | C25 |
| St. Pierre & Miquelon | C19 |
| Somali Coast | C19 |
| Togo | C19 |
| Wallis & Futuna Isls. | C11 |

### FIDES

Plowmen CD103

Efforts of FIDES, the Economic and Social Development Fund for Overseas Possessions (Fonds d' Investissement pour le Developpement Economique et Social). Each stamp has a different design.

**1956**

| | |
|---|---|
| Cameroun | 326-329 |
| Comoro Isls. | 43 |
| Fr. Equatorial Africa | 189-192 |
| Fr. Polynesia | 181 |
| Fr. West Africa | 65-72 |
| Madagascar | 292-295 |
| New Caledonia | 303 |
| St. Pierre & Miquelon 350 | |
| Somali Coast | 268 |
| Togo | 331 |

### Flower

CD104

Each stamp shows a different flower.

**1958-9**

| | |
|---|---|
| Cameroun | 333 |
| Comoro Isls. | 45 |
| Fr. Equatorial Africa | 200-201 |
| Fr. Polynesia | 192 |
| Fr. So. & Antarctic Terr. | 11 |
| Fr. West Africa | 79-83 |
| Madagascar | 301-302 |
| New Caledonia | 304-305 |
| St. Pierre & Miquelon | 357 |
| Somali Coast | 270 |
| Togo | 348-349 |
| Wallis & Futuna Isls. | 152 |

### Human Rights

Sun, Dove and U.N. Emblem CD105

10th anniversary of the signing of the Universal Declaration of Human Rights.

**1958**

| | |
|---|---|
| Comoro Isls. | 44 |
| Fr. Equatorial Africa | 202 |
| Fr. Polynesia | 191 |
| Fr. West Africa | 85 |
| Madagascar | 300 |
| New Caledonia | 306 |
| St. Pierre & Miquelon | 356 |
| Somali Coast | 274 |
| Wallis & Futuna Isls. | 153 |

### C.C.T.A.

CD106

Commission for Technical Cooperation in Africa south of the Sahara, 10th anniv.

**1960**

| | |
|---|---|
| Cameroun | 339 |
| Cent. Africa | 3 |
| Chad | 66 |
| Congo, P.R. | 90 |
| Dahomey | 138 |
| Gabon | 150 |
| Ivory Coast | 180 |
| Madagascar | 317 |
| Mali | 9 |
| Mauritania | 117 |
| Niger | 104 |
| Upper Volta | 89 |

### Air Afrique, 1961

Modern and Ancient Africa, Map and Planes — CD107

Founding of Air Afrique (African Airlines).

**1961-62**

| | |
|---|---|
| Cameroun | C37 |
| Cent. Africa | C5 |
| Chad | C7 |
| Congo, P.R. | C5 |
| Dahomey | C17 |
| Gabon | C5 |
| Ivory Coast | C18 |
| Mauritania | C17 |
| Niger | C22 |
| Senegal | C31 |
| Upper Volta | C4 |

### Anti-Malaria

CD108

World Health Organization drive to eradicate malaria.

**1962, Apr. 7**

| | |
|---|---|
| Cameroun | B36 |
| Cent. Africa | B1 |
| Chad | B1 |
| Comoro Isls. | B1 |
| Congo, P.R. | B3 |
| Dahomey | B15 |
| Gabon | B4 |
| Ivory Coast | B15 |
| Madagascar | B19 |
| Mali | B1 |
| Mauritania | B16 |
| Niger | B14 |
| Senegal | B16 |
| Somali Coast | B15 |
| Upper Volta | B1 |

### Abidjan Games

CD109

Abidjan Games, Ivory Coast, Dec. 24-31, 1961. Each stamp shows a different sport.

**1962**

| | |
|---|---|
| Chad | 83-84 |
| Cent. Africa | 19-20 |
| Congo, P.R. | 103-104 |
| Gabon | 163-164, C6 |
| Niger | 109-111 |
| Upper Volta | 103-105 |

### African and Malagasy Union

Flag of Union CD110

First anniversary of the Union.

**1962, Sept. 8**

| | |
|---|---|
| Cameroun | 373 |
| Cent. Africa | 21 |
| Chad | 85 |
| Congo, P.R. | 105 |
| Dahomey | 155 |
| Gabon | 165 |
| Ivory Coast | 198 |
| Madagascar | 332 |
| Mauritania | 170 |
| Niger | 112 |
| Senegal | 211 |
| Upper Volta | 106 |

### Telstar

Telstar and Globe Showing Andover and Pleumeur-Bodou — CD111

First television connection of the United States and Europe through the Telstar satellite, July 11-12, 1962.

**1962-63**

| | |
|---|---|
| Andorra, French | 154 |
| Comoro Isls. | C7 |
| Fr. Polynesia | C29 |
| Fr. So. & Antarctic Terr. | C5 |
| New Caledonia | C33 |
| Somali Coast | C31 |
| St. Pierre & Miquelon | C26 |
| Wallis & Futuna Isls. | C17 |

### Freedom From Hunger

World Map and Wheat Emblem CD112

U.N. Food and Agriculture Organization's "Freedom from Hunger" campaign.

**1963, Mar. 21**

| | |
|---|---|
| Cameroun | B37-B38 |
| Cent. Africa | B2 |
| Chad | B2 |
| Congo, P.R. | B4 |
| Dahomey | B16 |
| Gabon | B5 |
| Ivory Coast | B16 |
| Madagascar | B21 |
| Mauritania | B17 |
| Niger | B15 |
| Senegal | B17 |
| Upper Volta | B2 |

### Red Cross Centenary

CD113

Centenary of the International Red Cross.

**1963, Sept. 2**

| | |
|---|---|
| Comoro Isls. | 55 |
| Fr. Polynesia | 205 |
| New Caledonia | 328 |
| St. Pierre & Miquelon | 367 |
| Somali Coast | 297 |
| Wallis & Futuna Isls. | 165 |

## African Postal Union, 1963

UAMPT Emblem, Radio Masts, Plane and Mail CD114

Establishment of the African and Malagasy Posts and Telecommunications Union.

**1963, Sept. 8**

| | |
|---|---|
| Cameroun | C47 |
| Cent. Africa | C10 |
| Chad | C9 |
| Congo, P.R. | C13 |
| Dahomey | C19 |
| Gabon | C13 |
| Ivory Coast | C25 |
| Madagascar | C75 |
| Mauritania | C22 |
| Niger | C27 |
| Rwanda | 36 |
| Senegal | C32 |
| Upper Volta | C9 |

## Air Afrique, 1963

Symbols of Flight — CD115

First anniversary of Air Afrique and inauguration of DC-8 service.

**1963, Nov. 19**

| | |
|---|---|
| Cameroun | C48 |
| Chad | C10 |
| Congo, P.R. | C14 |
| Gabon | C18 |
| Ivory Coast | C26 |
| Mauritania | C26 |
| Niger | C35 |
| Senegal | C33 |

## Europafrica

Europe and Africa Linked — CD116

Signing of an economic agreement between the European Economic Community and the African and Malagasy Union, Yaounde, Cameroun, July 20, 1963.

**1963-64**

| | |
|---|---|
| Cameroun | 402 |
| Chad | C11 |
| Cent. Africa | C12 |
| Congo, P.R. | C16 |
| Gabon | C19 |
| Ivory Coast | 217 |
| Niger | C43 |
| Upper Volta | C11 |

## Human Rights

Scales of Justice and Globe CD117

15th anniversary of the Universal Declaration of Human Rights.

**1963, Dec. 10**

| | |
|---|---|
| Comoro Isls. | 58 |
| Fr. Polynesia | 206 |
| New Caledonia | 329 |
| St. Pierre & Miquelon | 368 |
| Somali Coast | 300 |
| Wallis & Futuna Isls. | 166 |

## PHILATEC

Stamp Album, Champs Elysees Palace and Horses of Marly CD118

Intl. Philatelic and Postal Techniques Exhibition, Paris, June 5-21, 1964.

**1963-64**

| | |
|---|---|
| Comoro Isls. | 60 |
| France | 1078 |
| Fr. Polynesia | 207 |
| New Caledonia | 341 |
| St. Pierre & Miquelon | 369 |
| Somali Coast | 301 |
| Wallis & Futuna Isls. | 167 |

## Cooperation

CD119

Cooperation between France and the French-speaking countries of Africa and Madagascar.

**1964**

| | |
|---|---|
| Cameroun | 409-410 |
| Cent. Africa | 39 |
| Chad | 103 |
| Congo, P.R. | 121 |
| Dahomey | 193 |
| France | 1111 |
| Gabon | 175 |
| Ivory Coast | 221 |
| Madagascar | 360 |
| Mauritania | 181 |
| Niger | 143 |
| Senegal | 236 |
| Togo | 495 |

## ITU

Telegraph, Syncom Satellite and ITU Emblem CD120

Intl. Telecommunication Union, Cent.

**1965, May 17**

| | |
|---|---|
| Comoro Isls. | C14 |
| Fr. Polynesia | C33 |
| Fr. So. & Antarctic Terr. | C8 |
| New Caledonia | C40 |
| New Hebrides | 124-125 |
| St. Pierre & Miquelon | C29 |
| Somali Coast | C36 |
| Wallis & Futuna Isls. | C20 |

## French Satellite A-1

Diamant Rocket and Launching Installation — CD121

Launching of France's first satellite, Nov. 26, 1965.

**1965-66**

| | |
|---|---|
| Comoro Isls. | C15-C16 |
| France | 1137-1138 |
| Reunion | 358-359 |
| Fr. Polynesia | C40-C41 |
| Fr. So. & Antarctic Terr. | C9-C10 |
| New Caledonia | C44-C45 |
| St. Pierre & Miquelon | C30-C31 |
| Somali Coast | C39-C40 |
| Wallis & Futuna Isls. | C22-C23 |

## French Satellite D-1

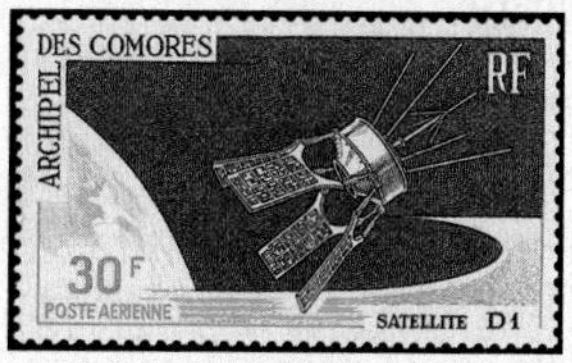


D-1 Satellite in Orbit — CD122

Launching of the D-1 satellite at Hamaguir, Algeria, Feb. 17, 1966.

**1966**

| | |
|---|---|
| Comoro Isls. | C17 |
| France | 1148 |
| Fr. Polynesia | C42 |
| Fr. So. & Antarctic Terr. | C11 |
| New Caledonia | C46 |
| St. Pierre & Miquelon | C32 |
| Somali Coast | C49 |
| Wallis & Futuna Isls. | C24 |

## Air Afrique, 1966

Planes and Air Afrique Emblem — CD123

Introduction of DC-8F planes by Air Afrique.

**1966**

| | |
|---|---|
| Cameroun | C79 |
| Cent. Africa | C35 |
| Chad | C26 |
| Congo, P.R. | C42 |
| Dahomey | C42 |
| Gabon | C47 |
| Ivory Coast | C32 |
| Mauritania | C57 |
| Niger | C63 |
| Senegal | C47 |
| Togo | C54 |
| Upper Volta | C31 |

## African Postal Union, 1967

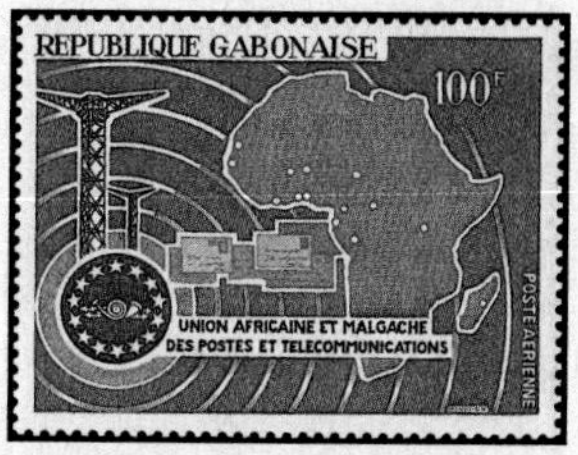


Telecommunications Symbols and Map of Africa — CD124

Fifth anniversary of the establishment of the African and Malagasy Union of Posts and Telecommunications, UAMPT.

**1967**

| | |
|---|---|
| Cameroun | C90 |
| Cent. Africa | C46 |
| Chad | C37 |
| Congo, P.R. | C57 |
| Dahomey | C61 |
| Gabon | C58 |
| Ivory Coast | C34 |
| Madagascar | C85 |
| Mauritania | C65 |
| Niger | C75 |
| Rwanda | C1-C3 |
| Senegal | C60 |
| Togo | C81 |
| Upper Volta | C50 |

## Monetary Union

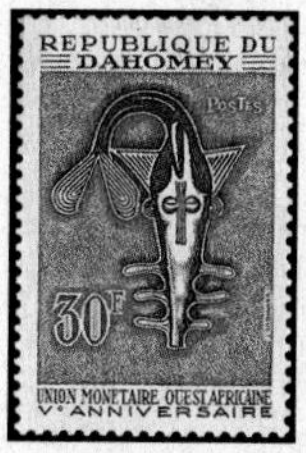


Gold Token of the Ashantis, 17-18th Centuries — CD125

West African Monetary Union, 5th anniv.

**1967, Nov. 4**

| | |
|---|---|
| Dahomey | 244 |
| Ivory Coast | 259 |
| Mauritania | 238 |
| Niger | 204 |
| Senegal | 294 |
| Togo | 623 |
| Upper Volta | 181 |

## WHO Anniversary

Sun, Flowers and WHO Emblem CD126

World Health Organization, 20th anniv.

**1968, May 4**

| | |
|---|---|
| Afars & Issas | 317 |
| Comoro Isls. | 73 |
| Fr. Polynesia | 241-242 |
| Fr. So. & Antarctic Terr. | 31 |
| New Caledonia | 367 |
| St. Pierre & Miquelon | 377 |
| Wallis & Futuna Isls. | 169 |

## Human Rights Year

Human Rights Flame — CD127

**1968, Aug. 10**

| | |
|---|---|
| Afars & Issas | 322-323 |
| Comoro Isls. | 76 |

Fr. Polynesia 243-244
Fr. So. & Antarctic Terr. 32
New Caledonia 369
St. Pierre & Miquelon 382
Wallis & Futuna Isls. 170

### 2nd PHILEXAFRIQUE

CD128

Opening of PHILEXAFRIQUE, Abidjan, Feb. 14. Each stamp shows a local scene and stamp.

**1969, Feb. 14**

Cameroun C118
Cent. Africa C65
Chad C48
Congo, P.R. C77
Dahomey C94
Gabon C82
Ivory Coast C38-C40
Madagascar C92
Mali C65
Mauritania C80
Niger C104
Senegal C68
Togo C104
Upper Volta C62

### Concorde

Concorde in Flight CD129

First flight of the prototype Concorde supersonic plane at Toulouse, Mar. 1, 1969.

**1969**

Afars & Issas C56
Comoro Isls. C29
France C42
Fr. Polynesia C50
Fr. So. & Antarctic Terr. C18
New Caledonia C63
St. Pierre & Miquelon C40
Wallis & Futuna Isls. C30

### Development Bank

Bank Emblem — CD130

African Development Bank, fifth anniv.

**1969**

Cameroun 499
Chad 217
Congo, P.R. 181-182
Ivory Coast 281
Mali 127-128
Mauritania 267
Niger 220
Senegal 317-318
Upper Volta 201

### ILO

ILO Headquarters, Geneva, and Emblem — CD131

Intl. Labor Organization, 50th anniv.

**1969-70**

Afars & Issas 337
Comoro Isls. 83
Fr. Polynesia 251-252
Fr. So. & Antarctic Terr. 35
New Caledonia 379
St. Pierre & Miquelon 396
Wallis & Futuna Isls. 172

### ASECNA

Map of Africa, Plane and Airport CD132

10th anniversary of the Agency for the Security of Aerial Navigation in Africa and Madagascar (ASECNA, Agence pour la Securite de la Navigation Aerienne en Afrique et a Madagascar).

**1969-70**

Cameroun 500
Cent. Africa 119
Chad 222
Congo, P.R. 197
Dahomey 269
Gabon 260
Ivory Coast 287
Mali 130
Niger 221
Senegal 321
Upper Volta 204

### U.P.U. Headquarters

CD133

New Universal Postal Union headquarters, Bern, Switzerland.

**1970**

Afars & Issas 342
Algeria 443
Cameroun 503-504
Cent. Africa 125
Chad 225
Comoro Isls. 84
Congo, P.R. 216
Fr. Polynesia 261-262
Fr. So. & Antarctic Terr. 36
Gabon 258
Ivory Coast 295
Madagascar 444
Mali 134-135
Mauritania 283
New Caledonia 382
Niger 231-232
St. Pierre & Miquelon 397-398
Senegal 328-329
Tunisia 535
Wallis & Futuna Isls. 173

### De Gaulle

CD134

First anniversary of the death of Charles de Gaulle, (1890-1970), President of France.

**1971-72**

Afars & Issas 356-357
Comoro Isls. 104-105
France 1322-1325
Fr. Polynesia 270-271
Fr. So. & Antarctic Terr. 52-53
New Caledonia 393-394
Reunion 377, 380
St. Pierre & Miquelon 417-418
Wallis & Futuna Isls. 177-178

### African Postal Union, 1971

UAMPT Building, Brazzaville, Congo — CD135

10th anniversary of the establishment of the African and Malagasy Posts and Telecommunications Union, UAMPT. Each stamp has a different native design.

**1971, Nov. 13**

Cameroun C177
Cent. Africa C89
Chad C94
Congo, P.R. C136
Dahomey C146
Gabon C120
Ivory Coast C47
Mauritania C113
Niger C164
Rwanda C8
Senegal C105
Togo C166
Upper Volta C97

### West African Monetary Union

African Couple, City, Village and Commemorative Coin — CD136

West African Monetary Union, 10th anniv.

**1972, Nov. 2**

Dahomey 300
Ivory Coast 331
Mauritania 299
Niger 258
Senegal 374
Togo 825
Upper Volta 280

### African Postal Union, 1973

Telecommunications Symbols and Map of Africa — CD137

11th anniversary of the African and Malagasy Posts and Telecommunications Union (UAMPT).

**1973, Sept. 12**

Cameroun 574
Cent. Africa 194
Chad 294
Congo, P.R. 289
Dahomey 311
Gabon 320
Ivory Coast 361
Madagascar 500
Mauritania 304
Niger 287
Rwanda 540
Senegal 393
Togo 849
Upper Volta 297

### Philexafrique II — Essen

CD138

CD139

Designs: Indigenous fauna, local and German stamps. Types CD138-CD139 printed horizontally and vertically se-tenant in sheets of 10 (2x5). Label between horizontal pairs alternately commemoratives Philexafrique II, Libreville, Gabon, June 1978, and 2nd International Stamp Fair, Essen, Germany, Nov. 1-5.

**1978-1979**

Benin C285-C286
Central Africa C200-C201
Chad C238-C239
Congo Republic C245-C246
Djibouti C121-C122
Gabon C215-C216
Ivory Coast C64-C65
Mali C356-C357
Mauritania C185-C186
Niger C291-C292
Rwanda C12-C13
Senegal C146-C147
Togo C363-C364

---

## BRITISH COMMONWEALTH OF NATIONS

The listings follow established trade practices when these issues are offered as units by dealers. The Peace issue, for example, includes only one stamp from the Indian state of Hyderabad. The U.P.U. issue includes the Egypt set. Pairs are included for those varieties issued with bilingual designs se-tenant.

### Silver Jubilee

Windsor Castle and King George V CD301

Reign of King George V, 25th anniv.

**1935**

Antigua 77-80
Ascension 33-36
Bahamas 92-95
Barbados 186-189
Basutoland 11-14
Bechuanaland Protectorate 117-120
Bermuda 100-103
British Guiana 223-226
British Honduras 108-111
Cayman Islands 81-84
Ceylon 260-263
Cyprus 136-139
Dominica 90-93
Falkland Islands 77-80
Fiji 110-113
Gambia 125-128

Gibraltar .......... 100-103
Gilbert & Ellice Islands .......... 33-36
Gold Coast .......... 108-111
Grenada .......... 124-127
Hong Kong .......... 147-150
Jamaica .......... 109-112
Kenya, Uganda, Tanganyika .......... 42-45
Leeward Islands .......... 96-99
Malta .......... 184-187
Mauritius .......... 204-207
Montserrat .......... 85-88
Newfoundland .......... 226-229
Nigeria .......... 34-37
Northern Rhodesia .......... 18-21
Nyasaland Protectorate .......... 47-50
St. Helena .......... 111-114
St. Kitts-Nevis .......... 72-75
St. Lucia .......... 91-94
St. Vincent .......... 134-137
Seychelles .......... 118-121
Sierra Leone .......... 166-169
Solomon Islands .......... 60-63
Somaliland Protectorate .......... 77-80
Straits Settlements .......... 213-216
Swaziland .......... 20-23
Trinidad & Tobago .......... 43-46
Turks & Caicos Islands .......... 71-74
Virgin Islands .......... 69-72

The following have different designs but are included in the omnibus set:

Great Britain .......... 226-229
Offices in Morocco ...... 67-70, 226-229, 422-425, 508-510
Australia .......... 152-154
Canada .......... 211-216
Cook Islands .......... 98-100
India .......... 142-148
Nauru .......... 31-34
New Guinea .......... 46-47
New Zealand .......... 199-201
Niue .......... 67-69
Papua .......... 114-117
Samoa .......... 163-165
South Africa .......... 68-71
Southern Rhodesia .......... 33-36
South-West Africa .......... 121-124

249 stamps

### Coronation

Queen Elizabeth and King George VI
CD302

**1937**

Aden .......... 13-15
Antigua .......... 81-83
Ascension .......... 37-39
Bahamas .......... 97-99
Barbados .......... 190-192
Basutoland .......... 15-17
Bechuanaland Protectorate .......... 121-123
Bermuda .......... 115-117
British Guiana .......... 227-229
British Honduras .......... 112-114
Cayman Islands .......... 97-99
Ceylon .......... 275-277
Cyprus .......... 140-142
Dominica .......... 94-96
Falkland Islands .......... 81-83
Fiji .......... 114-116
Gambia .......... 129-131
Gibraltar .......... 104-106
Gilbert & Ellice Islands .......... 37-39
Gold Coast .......... 112-114
Grenada .......... 128-130
Hong Kong .......... 151-153
Jamaica .......... 113-115
Kenya, Uganda, Tanganyika .......... 60-62
Leeward Islands .......... 100-102
Malta .......... 188-190
Mauritius .......... 208-210
Montserrat .......... 89-91
Newfoundland .......... 230-232
Nigeria .......... 50-52
Northern Rhodesia .......... 22-24
Nyasaland Protectorate .......... 51-53
St. Helena .......... 115-117
St. Kitts-Nevis .......... 76-78
St. Lucia .......... 107-109
St. Vincent .......... 138-140
Seychelles .......... 122-124
Sierra Leone .......... 170-172
Solomon Islands .......... 64-66
Somaliland Protectorate .......... 81-83
Straits Settlements .......... 235-237
Swaziland .......... 24-26
Trinidad & Tobago .......... 47-49
Turks & Caicos Islands .......... 75-77
Virgin Islands .......... 73-75

The following have different designs but are included in the omnibus set:

Great Britain .......... 234
Offices in Morocco .......... 82, 439, 514
Canada .......... 237
Cook Islands .......... 109-111
Nauru .......... 35-38
Newfoundland .......... 233-243
New Guinea .......... 48-51
New Zealand .......... 223-225
Niue .......... 70-72
Papua .......... 118-121
South Africa .......... 74-78
Southern Rhodesia .......... 38-41
South-West Africa .......... 125-132

202 stamps

### Peace

King George VI and Parliament Buildings, London
CD303

Return to peace at the close of World War II.

**1945-46**

Aden .......... 28-29
Antigua .......... 96-97
Ascension .......... 50-51
Bahamas .......... 130-131
Barbados .......... 207-208
Bermuda .......... 131-132
British Guiana .......... 242-243
British Honduras .......... 127-128
Cayman Islands .......... 112-113
Ceylon .......... 293-294
Cyprus .......... 156-157
Dominica .......... 112-113
Falkland Islands .......... 97-98
Falkland Islands Dep. .......... 1L9-1L10
Fiji .......... 137-138
Gambia .......... 144-145
Gibraltar .......... 119-120
Gilbert & Ellice Islands .......... 52-53
Gold Coast .......... 128-129
Grenada .......... 143-144
Jamaica .......... 136-137
Kenya, Uganda, Tanganyika .......... 90-91
Leeward Islands .......... 116-117
Malta .......... 206-207
Mauritius .......... 223-224
Montserrat .......... 104-105
Nigeria .......... 71-72
Northern Rhodesia .......... 46-47
Nyasaland Protectorate .......... 82-83
Pitcairn Island .......... 9-10
St. Helena .......... 128-129
St. Kitts-Nevis .......... 91-92
St. Lucia .......... 127-128
St. Vincent .......... 152-153
Seychelles .......... 149-150
Sierra Leone .......... 186-187
Solomon Islands .......... 80-81
Somaliland Protectorate .......... 108-109
Trinidad & Tobago .......... 62-63
Turks & Caicos Islands .......... 90-91
Virgin Islands .......... 88-89

The following have different designs but are included in the omnibus set:

Great Britain .......... 264-265
  Offices in Morocco .......... 523-524
Aden
  Kathiri State of Seiyun .......... 12-13
  Qu'aiti State of Shihr and Mukalla .......... 12-13
Australia .......... 200-202
Basutoland .......... 29-31
Bechuanaland Protectorate .......... 137-139
Burma .......... 66-69
Cook Islands .......... 127-130
Hong Kong .......... 174-175
India .......... 195-198
  Hyderabad .......... 51
New Zealand .......... 247-257
Niue .......... 90-93
Pakistan-Bahawalpur .......... O16
Samoa .......... 191-194
South Africa .......... 100-102
Southern Rhodesia .......... 67-70
South-West Africa .......... 153-155
Swaziland .......... 38-40
Zanzibar .......... 222-223

164 stamps

### Silver Wedding

King George VI and Queen Elizabeth
CD304 CD305

**1948-49**

Aden .......... 30-31
  Kathiri State of Seiyun .......... 14-15
  Qu'aiti State of Shihr and Mukalla .......... 14-15
Antigua .......... 98-99
Ascension .......... 52-53
Bahamas .......... 148-149
Barbados .......... 210-211
Basutoland .......... 39-40
Bechuanaland Protectorate .......... 147-148
Bermuda .......... 133-134
British Guiana .......... 244-245
British Honduras .......... 129-130
Cayman Islands .......... 116-117
Cyprus .......... 158-159
Dominica .......... 114-115
Falkland Islands .......... 99-100
Falkland Islands Dep. .......... 1L11-1L12
Fiji .......... 139-140
Gambia .......... 146-147
Gibraltar .......... 121-122
Gilbert & Ellice Islands .......... 54-55
Gold Coast .......... 142-143
Grenada .......... 145-146
Hong Kong .......... 178-179
Jamaica .......... 138-139
Kenya, Uganda, Tanganyika .......... 92-93
Leeward Islands .......... 118-119
Malaya
  Johore .......... 128-129
  Kedah .......... 55-56
  Kelantan .......... 44-45
  Malacca .......... 1-2
  Negri Sembilan .......... 36-37
  Pahang .......... 44-45
  Penang .......... 1-2
  Perak .......... 99-100
  Perlis .......... 1-2
  Selangor .......... 74-75
  Trengganu .......... 47-48
Malta .......... 223-224
Mauritius .......... 229-230
Montserrat .......... 106-107
Nigeria .......... 73-74
North Borneo .......... 238-239
Northern Rhodesia .......... 48-49
Nyasaland Protectorate .......... 85-86
Pitcairn Island .......... 11-12
St. Helena .......... 130-131
St. Kitts-Nevis .......... 93-94
St. Lucia .......... 129-130
St. Vincent .......... 154-155
Sarawak .......... 174-175
Seychelles .......... 151-152
Sierra Leone .......... 188-189
Singapore .......... 21-22
Solomon Islands .......... 82-83
Somaliland Protectorate .......... 110-111
Swaziland .......... 48-49
Trinidad & Tobago .......... 64-65
Turks & Caicos Islands .......... 92-93
Virgin Islands .......... 90-91
Zanzibar .......... 224-225

The following have different designs but are included in the omnibus set:

Great Britain .......... 267-268
  Offices in Morocco ..... 93-94, 525-526
Bahrain .......... 62-63
Kuwait .......... 82-83
Oman .......... 25-26
South Africa .......... 106
South-West Africa .......... 159

138 stamps

### U.P.U.

Mercury and Symbols of Communications — CD306

Plane, Ship and Hemispheres — CD307

Mercury Scattering Letters over Globe
CD308

U.P.U. Monument, Bern
CD309

Universal Postal Union, 75th anniversary.

**1949**

Aden .......... 32-35
  Kathiri State of Seiyun .......... 16-19
  Qu'aiti State of Shihr and Mukalla .......... 16-19
Antigua .......... 100-103
Ascension .......... 57-60
Bahamas .......... 150-153
Barbados .......... 212-215
Basutoland .......... 41-44
Bechuanaland Protectorate .......... 149-152
Bermuda .......... 138-141
British Guiana .......... 246-249
British Honduras .......... 137-140
Brunei .......... 79-82
Cayman Islands .......... 118-121
Cyprus .......... 160-163
Dominica .......... 116-119
Falkland Islands .......... 103-106
Falkland Islands Dep. .......... 1L14-1L17
Fiji .......... 141-144
Gambia .......... 148-151
Gibraltar .......... 123-126
Gilbert & Ellice Islands .......... 56-59
Gold Coast .......... 144-147
Grenada .......... 147-150
Hong Kong .......... 180-183
Jamaica .......... 142-145
Kenya, Uganda, Tanganyika .......... 94-97
Leeward Islands .......... 126-129
Malaya
  Johore .......... 151-154
  Kedah .......... 57-60
  Kelantan .......... 46-49
  Malacca .......... 18-21
  Negri Sembilan .......... 59-62
  Pahang .......... 46-49
  Penang .......... 23-26
  Perak .......... 101-104
  Perlis .......... 3-6
  Selangor .......... 76-79
  Trengganu .......... 49-52
Malta .......... 225-228
Mauritius .......... 231-234
Montserrat .......... 108-111
New Hebrides, British .......... 62-65
New Hebrides, French .......... 79-82
Nigeria .......... 75-78
North Borneo .......... 240-243
Northern Rhodesia .......... 50-53
Nyasaland Protectorate .......... 87-90
Pitcairn Islands .......... 13-16
St. Helena .......... 132-135
St. Kitts-Nevis .......... 95-98
St. Lucia .......... 131-134
St. Vincent .......... 170-173

| | |
|---|---|
| Sarawak | 176-179 |
| Seychelles | 153-156 |
| Sierra Leone | 190-193 |
| Singapore | 23-26 |
| Solomon Islands | 84-87 |
| Somaliland Protectorate | 112-115 |
| Southern Rhodesia | 71-72 |
| Swaziland | 50-53 |
| Tonga | 87-90 |
| Trinidad & Tobago | 66-69 |
| Turks & Caicos Islands | 101-104 |
| Virgin Islands | 92-95 |
| Zanzibar | 226-229 |

The following have different designs but are included in the omnibus set:

| | |
|---|---|
| Great Britain | 276-279 |
| Offices in Morocco | 546-549 |
| Australia | 223 |
| Bahrain | 68-71 |
| Burma | 116-121 |
| Ceylon | 304-306 |
| Egypt | 281-283 |
| India | 223-226 |
| Kuwait | 89-92 |
| Oman | 31-34 |
| Pakistan-Bahawalpur | 26-29, O25-O28 |
| South Africa | 109-111 |
| South-West Africa | 160-162 |

319 stamps

### University

Arms of University College CD310

Alice, Princess of Athlone CD311

1948 opening of University College of the West Indies at Jamaica.

**1951**

| | |
|---|---|
| Antigua | 104-105 |
| Barbados | 228-229 |
| British Guiana | 250-251 |
| British Honduras | 141-142 |
| Dominica | 120-121 |
| Grenada | 164-165 |
| Jamaica | 146-147 |
| Leeward Islands | 130-131 |
| Montserrat | 112-113 |
| St. Kitts-Nevis | 105-106 |
| St. Lucia | 149-150 |
| St. Vincent | 174-175 |
| Trinidad & Tobago | 70-71 |
| Virgin Islands | 96-97 |

28 stamps

### Coronation

Queen Elizabeth II — CD312

**1953**

| | |
|---|---|
| Aden | 47 |
| Kathiri State of Seiyun | 28 |
| Qu'aiti State of Shihr and Mukalla | 28 |
| Antigua | 106 |
| Ascension | 61 |
| Bahamas | 157 |
| Barbados | 234 |
| Basutoland | 45 |
| Bechuanaland Protectorate | 153 |
| Bermuda | 142 |
| British Guiana | 252 |
| British Honduras | 143 |
| Cayman Islands | 150 |
| Cyprus | 167 |
| Dominica | 141 |
| Falkland Islands | 121 |
| Falkland Islands Dependencies | 1L18 |
| Fiji | 145 |
| Gambia | 152 |
| Gibraltar | 131 |
| Gilbert & Ellice Islands | 60 |
| Gold Coast | 160 |
| Grenada | 170 |
| Hong Kong | 184 |
| Jamaica | 153 |
| Kenya, Uganda, Tanganyika | 101 |
| Leeward Islands | 132 |
| Malaya | |
| Johore | 155 |
| Kedah | 82 |
| Kelantan | 71 |
| Malacca | 27 |
| Negri Sembilan | 63 |
| Pahang | 71 |
| Penang | 27 |
| Perak | 126 |
| Perlis | 28 |
| Selangor | 101 |
| Trengganu | 74 |
| Malta | 241 |
| Mauritius | 250 |
| Montserrat | 127 |
| New Hebrides, British | 77 |
| Nigeria | 79 |
| North Borneo | 260 |
| Northern Rhodesia | 60 |
| Nyasaland Protectorate | 96 |
| Pitcairn | 19 |
| St. Helena | 139 |
| St. Kitts-Nevis | 119 |
| St. Lucia | 156 |
| St. Vincent | 185 |
| Sarawak | 196 |
| Seychelles | 172 |
| Sierra Leone | 194 |
| Singapore | 27 |
| Solomon Islands | 88 |
| Somaliland Protectorate | 127 |
| Swaziland | 54 |
| Trinidad & Tobago | 84 |
| Tristan da Cunha | 13 |
| Turks & Caicos Islands | 118 |
| Virgin Islands | 114 |

The following have different designs but are included in the omnibus set:

| | |
|---|---|
| Great Britain | 313-316 |
| Offices in Morocco | 579-582 |
| Australia | 259-261 |
| Bahrain | 92-95 |
| Canada | 330 |
| Ceylon | 317 |
| Cook Islands | 145-146 |
| Kuwait | 113-116 |
| New Zealand | 280-284 |
| Niue | 104-105 |
| Oman | 52-55 |
| Samoa | 214-215 |
| South Africa | 192 |
| Southern Rhodesia | 80 |
| South-West Africa | 244-248 |
| Tokelau Islands | 4 |

106 stamps

### Royal Visit 1953

Separate designs for each country for the visit of Queen Elizabeth II and the Duke of Edinburgh.

**1953**

| | |
|---|---|
| Aden | 62 |
| Australia | 267-269 |
| Bermuda | 163 |
| Ceylon | 318 |
| Fiji | 146 |
| Gibraltar | 146 |
| Jamaica | 154 |
| Kenya, Uganda, Tanganyika | 102 |
| Malta | 242 |
| New Zealand | 286-287 |

13 stamps

### West Indies Federation

Map of the Caribbean CD313

Federation of the West Indies, April 22, 1958.

**1958**

| | |
|---|---|
| Antigua | 122-124 |
| Barbados | 248-250 |
| Dominica | 161-163 |
| Grenada | 184-186 |
| Jamaica | 175-177 |
| Montserrat | 143-145 |
| St. Kitts-Nevis | 136-138 |
| St. Lucia | 170-172 |
| St. Vincent | 198-200 |
| Trinidad & Tobago | 86-88 |

30 stamps

### Freedom from Hunger

Protein Food CD314

U.N. Food and Agricultural Organization's "Freedom from Hunger" campaign.

**1963**

| | |
|---|---|
| Aden | 65 |
| Antigua | 133 |
| Ascension | 89 |
| Bahamas | 180 |
| Basutoland | 83 |
| Bechuanaland Protectorate | 194 |
| Bermuda | 192 |
| British Guiana | 271 |
| British Honduras | 179 |
| Brunei | 100 |
| Cayman Islands | 168 |
| Dominica | 181 |
| Falkland Islands | 146 |
| Fiji | 198 |
| Gambia | 172 |
| Gibraltar | 161 |
| Gilbert & Ellice Islands | 76 |
| Grenada | 190 |
| Hong Kong | 218 |
| Malta | 291 |
| Mauritius | 270 |
| Montserrat | 150 |
| New Hebrides, British | 93 |
| North Borneo | 296 |
| Pitcairn | 35 |
| St. Helena | 173 |
| St. Lucia | 179 |
| St. Vincent | 201 |
| Sarawak | 212 |
| Seychelles | 213 |
| Solomon Islands | 109 |
| Swaziland | 108 |
| Tonga | 127 |
| Tristan da Cunha | 68 |
| Turks & Caicos Islands | 138 |
| Virgin Islands | 140 |
| Zanzibar | 280 |

37 stamps

### Red Cross Centenary

Red Cross and Elizabeth II CD315

**1963**

| | |
|---|---|
| Antigua | 134-135 |
| Ascension | 90-91 |
| Bahamas | 183-184 |
| Basutoland | 84-85 |
| Bechuanaland Protectorate | 195-196 |
| Bermuda | 193-194 |
| British Guiana | 272-273 |
| British Honduras | 180-181 |
| Cayman Islands | 169-170 |
| Dominica | 182-183 |
| Falkland Islands | 147-148 |
| Fiji | 203-204 |
| Gambia | 173-174 |
| Gibraltar | 162-163 |
| Gilbert & Ellice Islands | 77-78 |
| Grenada | 191-192 |
| Hong Kong | 219-220 |
| Jamaica | 203-204 |
| Malta | 292-293 |
| Mauritius | 271-272 |
| Montserrat | 151-152 |
| New Hebrides, British | 94-95 |
| Pitcairn Islands | 36-37 |
| St. Helena | 174-175 |
| St. Kitts-Nevis | 143-144 |
| St. Lucia | 180-181 |
| St. Vincent | 202-203 |
| Seychelles | 214-215 |
| Solomon Islands | 110-111 |
| South Arabia | 1-2 |
| Swaziland | 109-110 |
| Tonga | 134-135 |
| Tristan da Cunha | 69-70 |
| Turks & Caicos Islands | 139-140 |
| Virgin Islands | 141-142 |

70 stamps

### Shakespeare

Shakespeare Memorial Theatre, Stratford-on-Avon — CD316

400th anniversary of the birth of William Shakespeare.

**1964**

| | |
|---|---|
| Antigua | 151 |
| Bahamas | 201 |
| Bechuanaland Protectorate | 197 |
| Cayman Islands | 171 |
| Dominica | 184 |
| Falkland Islands | 149 |
| Gambia | 192 |
| Gibraltar | 164 |
| Montserrat | 153 |
| St. Lucia | 196 |
| Turks & Caicos Islands | 141 |
| Virgin Islands | 143 |

12 stamps

### ITU

ITU Emblem CD317

Intl. Telecommunication Union, cent.

**1965**

| | |
|---|---|
| Antigua | 153-154 |
| Ascension | 92-93 |
| Bahamas | 219-220 |
| Barbados | 265-266 |
| Basutoland | 101-102 |
| Bechuanaland Protectorate | 202-203 |
| Bermuda | 196-197 |
| British Guiana | 293-294 |
| British Honduras | 187-188 |
| Brunei | 116-117 |
| Cayman Islands | 172-173 |
| Dominica | 185-186 |
| Falkland Islands | 154-155 |
| Fiji | 211-212 |
| Gibraltar | 167-168 |
| Gilbert & Ellice Islands | 87-88 |
| Grenada | 205-206 |
| Hong Kong | 221-222 |
| Mauritius | 291-292 |
| Montserrat | 157-158 |
| New Hebrides, British | 108-109 |
| Pitcairn Islands | 52-53 |
| St. Helena | 180-181 |
| St. Kitts-Nevis | 163-164 |
| St. Lucia | 197-198 |
| St. Vincent | 224-225 |
| Seychelles | 218-219 |
| Solomon Islands | 126-127 |
| Swaziland | 115-116 |
| Tristan da Cunha | 85-86 |
| Turks & Caicos Islands | 142-143 |
| Virgin Islands | 159-160 |

64 stamps

### Intl. Cooperation Year

ICY Emblem
CD318

**1965**

Antigua ....................155-156
Ascension ....................94-95
Bahamas ....................222-223
Basutoland....................103-104
Bechuanaland Protectorate......204-205
Bermuda....................199-200
British Guiana....................295-296
British Honduras....................189-190
Brunei ....................118-119
Cayman Islands....................174-175
Dominica....................187-188
Falkland Islands ....................156-157
Fiji....................213-214
Gibraltar....................169-170
Gilbert & Ellice Islands............104-105
Grenada....................207-208
Hong Kong ....................223-224
Mauritius....................293-294
Montserrat ....................176-177
New Hebrides, British ............110-111
New Hebrides, French ............126-127
Pitcairn Islands....................54-55
St. Helena ....................182-183
St. Kitts-Nevis....................165-166
St. Lucia ....................199-200
Seychelles ....................220-221
Solomon Islands....................143-144
South Arabia ....................17-18
Swaziland ....................117-118
Tristan da Cunha....................87-88
Turks & Caicos Islands ............144-145
Virgin Islands....................161-162

64 stamps

### Churchill Memorial

Winston Churchill and St. Paul's, London, During Air Attack
CD319

**1966**

Antigua ....................157-160
Ascension ....................96-99
Bahamas ....................224-227
Barbados ....................281-284
Basutoland....................105-108
Bechuanaland Protectorate......206-209
Bermuda....................201-204
British Antarctic Territory............16-19
British Honduras....................191-194
Brunei....................120-123
Cayman Islands....................176-179
Dominica....................189-192
Falkland Islands ....................158-161
Fiji....................215-218
Gibraltar....................171-174
Gilbert & Ellice Islands............106-109
Grenada....................209-212
Hong Kong ....................225-228
Mauritius....................295-298
Montserrat ....................178-181
New Hebrides, British ............112-115
New Hebrides, French ............128-131
Pitcairn Islands....................56-59
St. Helena ....................184-187
St. Kitts-Nevis....................167-170
St. Lucia ....................201-204
St. Vincent....................241-244
Seychelles ....................222-225
Solomon Islands....................145-148
South Arabia ....................19-22
Swaziland ....................119-122
Tristan da Cunha....................89-92
Turks & Caicos Islands ............146-149
Virgin Islands....................163-166

136 stamps

### Royal Visit, 1966

Queen Elizabeth II and Prince Philip
CD320

Caribbean visit, Feb. 4 - Mar. 6, 1966.

**1966**

Antigua ....................161-162
Bahamas ....................228-229
Barbados....................285-286
British Guiana....................299-300
Cayman Islands....................180-181
Dominica....................193-194
Grenada....................213-214
Montserrat ....................182-183
St. Kitts-Nevis....................171-172
St. Lucia ....................205-206
St. Vincent....................245-246
Turks & Caicos Islands ............150-151
Virgin Islands....................167-168

26 stamps

### World Cup Soccer

Soccer Player and Jules Rimet Cup
CD321

World Cup Soccer Championship, Wembley, England, July 11-30.

**1966**

Antigua ....................163-164
Ascension....................100-101
Bahamas ....................245-246
Bermuda....................205-206
Brunei....................124-125
Cayman Islands....................182-183
Dominica....................195-196
Fiji....................219-220
Gibraltar....................175-176
Gilbert & Ellice Islands............125-126
Grenada....................230-231
New Hebrides, British ............116-117
New Hebrides, French ............132-133
Pitcairn Islands....................60-61
St. Helena ....................188-189
St. Kitts-Nevis....................173-174
St. Lucia ....................207-208
Seychelles....................226-227
Solomon Islands....................167-168
South Arabia ....................23-24
Tristan da Cunha....................93-94

42 stamps

### WHO Headquarters

World Health Organization Headquarters, Geneva — CD322

**1966**

Antigua ....................165-166
Ascension....................102-103
Bahamas ....................247-248
Brunei....................126-127
Cayman Islands....................184-185
Dominica....................197-198
Fiji....................224-225
Gibraltar....................180-181
Gilbert & Ellice Islands............127-128
Grenada....................232-233
Hong Kong ....................229-230
Montserrat ....................184-185
New Hebrides, British ............118-119
New Hebrides, French ............134-135
Pitcairn Islands....................62-63
St. Helena ....................190-191
St. Kitts-Nevis....................177-178
St. Lucia ....................209-210
St. Vincent....................247-248
Seychelles ....................228-229
Solomon Islands....................169-170
South Arabia....................25-26
Tristan da Cunha....................99-100

46 stamps

### UNESCO Anniversary

"Education" — CD323

"Science" (Wheat ears & flask enclosing globe). "Culture" (lyre & columns). 20th anniversary of the UNESCO.

**1966-67**

Antigua ....................183-185
Ascension....................108-110
Bahamas ....................249-251
Barbados ....................287-289
Bermuda....................207-209
Brunei ....................128-130
Cayman Islands....................186-188
Dominica....................199-201
Gibraltar....................183-185
Gilbert & Ellice Islands............129-131
Grenada....................234-236
Hong Kong ....................231-233
Mauritius....................299-301
Montserrat ....................186-188
New Hebrides, British ............120-122
New Hebrides, French ............136-138
Pitcairn Islands....................64-66
St. Helena ....................192-194
St. Kitts-Nevis....................179-181
St. Lucia ....................211-213
St. Vincent....................249-251
Seychelles ....................230-232
Solomon Islands....................171-173
South Arabia ....................27-29
Swaziland ....................123-125
Tristan da Cunha....................101-103
Turks & Caicos Islands ............155-157
Virgin Islands....................176-178

84 stamps

### Silver Wedding, 1972

Queen Elizabeth II and Prince Philip — CD324

Designs: borders differ for each country.

**1972**

Anguilla....................161-162
Antigua ....................295-296
Ascension....................164-165
Bahamas ....................344-345
Bermuda....................296-297
British Antarctic Territory............43-44
British Honduras....................306-307
British Indian Ocean Territory......48-49
Brunei ....................186-187
Cayman Islands....................304-305
Dominica....................352-353
Falkland Islands ....................223-224
Fiji....................328-329
Gibraltar....................292-293
Gilbert & Ellice Islands............206-207
Grenada....................466-467
Hong Kong ....................271-272
Montserrat ....................286-287
New Hebrides, British ............169-170
Pitcairn Islands....................127-128
St. Helena ....................271-272
St. Kitts-Nevis....................257-258
St. Lucia ....................328-329
St.Vincent....................344-345
Seychelles ....................309-310
Solomon Islands....................248-249
South Georgia....................35-36
Tristan da Cunha....................178-179
Turks & Caicos Islands ............257-258
Virgin Islands....................241-242

60 stamps

### Princess Anne's Wedding

Princess Anne and Mark Phillips — CD325

Wedding of Princess Anne and Mark Phillips, Nov. 14, 1973.

**1973**

Anguilla....................179-180
Ascension....................177-178
Belize....................325-326
Bermuda....................302-303
British Antarctic Territory............60-61
Cayman Islands....................320-321
Falkland Islands ....................225-226
Gibraltar....................305-306
Gilbert & Ellice Islands............216-217
Hong Kong ....................289-290
Montserrat ....................300-301
Pitcairn Island....................135-136
St. Helena ....................277-278
St. Kitts-Nevis....................274-275
St. Lucia ....................349-350
St. Vincent....................358-359
St. Vincent Grenadines....................1-2
Seychelles....................311-312
Solomon Islands....................259-260
South Georgia ....................37-38
Tristan da Cunha....................189-190
Turks & Caicos Islands ............286-287
Virgin Islands....................260-261

44 stamps

### Elizabeth II Coronation Anniv.

CD326

CD327

CD328

Designs: Royal and local beasts in heraldic form and simulated stonework. Portrait of Elizabeth II by Peter Grugeon. 25th anniversary of coronation of Queen Elizabeth II.

**1978**

Ascension....................229
Barbados....................474
Belize....................397
British Antarctic Territory....................71
Cayman Islands....................404
Christmas Island ....................87
Falkland Islands ....................275
Fiji....................384
Gambia....................380
Gilbert Islands ....................312
Mauritius....................464
New Hebrides, British ....................258
St. Helena ....................317
St. Kitts-Nevis....................354
Samoa....................472

Solomon Islands .......... 368
South Georgia .......... 51
Swaziland .......... 302
Tristan da Cunha .......... 238
Virgin Islands .......... 337

20 sheets

### Queen Mother Elizabeth's 80th Birthday

CD330

Designs: Photographs of Queen Mother Elizabeth. Falkland Islands issued in sheets of 50; others in sheets of 9.

**1980**

Ascension .......... 261
Bermuda .......... 401
Cayman Islands .......... 443
Falkland Islands .......... 305
Gambia .......... 412
Gibraltar .......... 393
Hong Kong .......... 364
Pitcairn Islands .......... 193
St. Helena .......... 341
Samoa .......... 532
Solomon Islands .......... 426
Tristan da Cunha .......... 277

12 stamps

### Royal Wedding, 1981

Prince Charles and Lady Diana — CD331

CD331a

Wedding of Charles, Prince of Wales, and Lady Diana Spencer, St. Paul's Cathedral, London, July 29, 1981.

**1981**

Antigua .......... 623-625
Ascension .......... 294-296
Barbados .......... 547-549
Barbuda .......... 497-499
Bermuda .......... 412-414
Brunei .......... 268-270
Cayman Islands .......... 471-473
Dominica .......... 701-703
Falkland Islands .......... 324-326
Falkland Islands Dep. .......... 1L59-1L61
Fiji .......... 442-444
Gambia .......... 426-428
Ghana .......... 759-761
Grenada .......... 1051-1053
Grenada Grenadines .......... 440-443
Hong Kong .......... 373-375
Jamaica .......... 500-503
Lesotho .......... 335-337
Maldive Islands .......... 906-908
Mauritius .......... 520-522
Norfolk Island .......... 280-282
Pitcairn Islands .......... 206-208
St. Helena .......... 353-355
St. Lucia .......... 543-545
Samoa .......... 558-560
Sierra Leone .......... 509-517
Solomon Islands .......... 450-452
Swaziland .......... 382-384
Tristan da Cunha .......... 294-296
Turks & Caicos Islands .......... 486-488
Caicos Island .......... 8-10
Uganda .......... 314-316
Vanuatu .......... 308-310
Virgin Islands .......... 406-408

### Princess Diana

CD332

CD333

Designs: Photographs and portrait of Princess Diana, wedding or honeymoon photographs, royal residences, arms of issuing country. Portrait photograph by Clive Friend. Souvenir sheet margins show family tree, various people related to the princess. 21st birthday of Princess Diana of Wales, July 1.

**1982**

Antigua .......... 663-666
Ascension .......... 313-316
Bahamas .......... 510-513
Barbados .......... 585-588
Barbuda .......... 544-546
British Antarctic Territory .......... 92-95
Cayman Islands .......... 486-489
Dominica .......... 773-776
Falkland Islands .......... 348-351
Falkland Islands Dep. .......... 1L72-1L75
Fiji .......... 470-473
Gambia .......... 447-450
Grenada .......... 1101A-1105
Grenada Grenadines .......... 485-491
Lesotho .......... 372-375
Maldive Islands .......... 952-955
Mauritius .......... 548-551
Pitcairn Islands .......... 213-216
St. Helena .......... 372-375
St. Lucia .......... 591-594
Sierra Leone .......... 531-534
Solomon Islands .......... 471-474
Swaziland .......... 406-409
Tristan da Cunha .......... 310-313
Turks and Caicos Islands .......... 530A-534
Virgin Islands .......... 430-433

### 250th anniv. of first edition of Lloyd's List (shipping news publication) & of Lloyd's marine insurance.

CD335

Designs: First page of early edition of the list; historical ships, modern transportation or harbor scenes.

**1984**

Ascension .......... 351-354
Bahamas .......... 555-558
Barbados .......... 627-630
Cayes of Belize .......... 10-13
Cayman Islands .......... 522-525
Falkland Islands .......... 404-407
Fiji .......... 509-512
Gambia .......... 519-522
Mauritius .......... 587-590
Nauru .......... 280-283
St. Helena .......... 412-415
Samoa .......... 624-627
Seychelles .......... 538-541
Solomon Islands .......... 521-524
Vanuatu .......... 368-371
Virgin Islands .......... 466-469

### Queen Mother 85th Birthday

CD336

Designs: Photographs tracing the life of the Queen Mother, Elizabeth. The high value in each set pictures the same photograph taken of the Queen Mother holding the infant Prince Henry.

**1985**

Ascension .......... 372-376
Bahamas .......... 580-584
Barbados .......... 660-664
Bermuda .......... 469-473
Falkland Islands .......... 420-424
Falkland Islands Dep. .......... 1L92-1L96
Fiji .......... 531-535
Hong Kong .......... 447-450
Jamaica .......... 599-603
Mauritius .......... 604-608
Norfolk Island .......... 364-368
Pitcairn Islands .......... 253-257
St. Helena .......... 428-432
Samoa .......... 649-653
Seychelles .......... 567-571
Solomon Islands .......... 543-547
Swaziland .......... 476-480
Tristan da Cunha .......... 372-376
Vanuatu .......... 392-396
Zil Elwannyen Sesel .......... 101-105

### Queen Elizabeth II, 60th Birthday

CD337

**1986, April 21**

Ascension .......... 389-393
Bahamas .......... 592-596
Barbados .......... 675-679
Bermuda .......... 499-503
Cayman Islands .......... 555-559
Falkland Islands .......... 441-445
Fiji .......... 544-548
Hong Kong .......... 465-469
Jamaica .......... 620-624
Kiribati .......... 470-474
Mauritius .......... 629-633
Papua New Guinea .......... 640-644
Pitcairn Islands .......... 270-274
St. Helena .......... 451-455
Samoa .......... 670-674
Seychelles .......... 592-596
Solomon Islands .......... 562-566
South Georgia .......... 101-105
Swaziland .......... 490-494
Tristan da Cunha .......... 388-392
Vanuatu .......... 414-418
Zambia .......... 343-347
Zil Elwannyen Sesel .......... 114-118

### Royal Wedding

Marriage of Prince Andrew and Sarah Ferguson CD338

**1986, July 23**

Ascension .......... 399-400
Bahamas .......... 602-603
Barbados .......... 687-688
Cayman Islands .......... 560-561
Jamaica .......... 629-630
Pitcairn Islands .......... 275-276
St. Helena .......... 460-461
St. Kitts .......... 181-182
Seychelles .......... 602-603
Solomon Islands .......... 567-568
Tristan da Cunha .......... 397-398
Zambia .......... 348-349
Zil Elwannyen Sesel .......... 119-120

### Queen Elizabeth II, 60th Birthday

Queen Elizabeth II & Prince Philip, 1947 Wedding Portrait — CD339

Designs: Photographs tracing the life of Queen Elizabeth II.

**1986**

Anguilla .......... 674-677
Antigua .......... 925-928
Barbuda .......... 783-786
Dominica .......... 950-953
Gambia .......... 611-614
Grenada .......... 1371-1374
Grenada Grenadines .......... 749-752
Lesotho .......... 531-534
Maldive Islands .......... 1172-1175
Sierra Leone .......... 760-763
Uganda .......... 495-498

### Royal Wedding, 1986

CD340

Designs: Photographs of Prince Andrew and Sarah Ferguson during courtship, engagement and marriage.

**1986**

Antigua .......... 939-942
Barbuda .......... 809-812
Dominica .......... 970-973
Gambia .......... 635-638
Grenada .......... 1385-1388
Grenada Grenadines .......... 758-761
Lesotho .......... 545-548
Maldive Islands .......... 1181-1184
Sierra Leone .......... 769-772
Uganda .......... 510-513

### Lloyds of London, 300th Anniv.

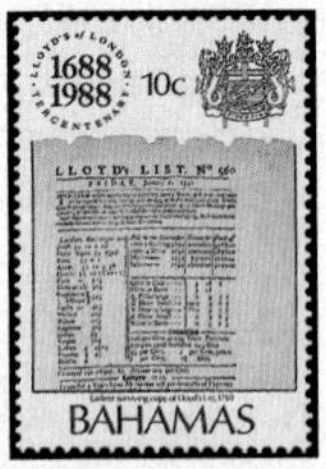


CD341

Designs: 17th century aspects of Lloyds, representations of each country's individual connections with Lloyds and publicized disasters insured by the organization.

**1986**

Ascension .......... 454-457
Bahamas .......... 655-658
Barbados .......... 731-734
Bermuda .......... 541-544
Falkland Islands .......... 481-484
Liberia .......... 1101-1104
Malawi .......... 534-537
Nevis .......... 571-574
St. Helena .......... 501-504
St. Lucia .......... 923-926
Seychelles .......... 649-652
Solomon Islands .......... 627-630

South Georgia..........................131-134
Trinidad & Tobago...................484-487
Tristan da Cunha.....................439-442
Vanuatu ....................................485-488
Zil Elwannyen Sesel.................146-149

### Moon Landing, 20th Anniv.

CD342

Designs: Equipment, crew photographs, spacecraft, official emblems and report profiles created for the Apollo Missions. Two stamps in each set are square in format rather than like the stamp shown; see individual country listings for more information.

**1989**

Ascension Is............................468-472
Bahamas .................................674-678
Belize......................................916-920
Kiribati ...................................517-521
Liberia..................................1125-1129
Nevis.......................................586-590
St. Kitts ..................................248-252
Samoa ....................................760-764
Seychelles ..............................676-680
Solomon Islands......................643-647
Vanuatu ..................................507-511
Zil Elwannyen Sesel.................154-158

### Queen Mother, 90th Birthday

CD343 CD344

Designs: Portraits of Queen Elizabeth, the Queen Mother. See individual country listings for more information.

**1990**

Ascension Is............................491-492
Bahamas .................................698-699
Barbados .................................782-783
British Antarctic Territory..........170-171
British Indian Ocean Territory........106-107
Cayman Islands.......................622-623
Falkland Islands .......................524-525
Kenya.......................................527-528
Kiribati ....................................555-556
Liberia....................................1145-1146
Pitcairn Islands........................336-337
St. Helena ...............................532-533
St. Lucia .................................969-970
Seychelles ...............................710-711
Solomon Islands......................671-672
South Georgia...........................143-144
Swaziland ................................565-566
Tristan da Cunha.....................480-481
Zil Elwannyen Sesel.................171-172

### Queen Elizabeth II, 65th Birthday, and Prince Philip, 70th Birthday

CD345

CD346

Designs: Portraits of Queen Elizabeth II and Prince Philip differ for each country. Printed in sheets of 10 + 5 labels (3 different) between. Stamps alternate, producing 5 different triptychs.

**1991**

Ascension Is............................505-506
Bahamas ..................................730-731
Belize.......................................969-970
Bermuda..................................617-618
Kiribati ....................................571-572
Mauritius.................................733-734
Pitcairn Islands........................348-349
St. Helena ...............................554-555
St. Kitts...................................318-319
Samoa.....................................790-791
Seychelles ...............................723-724
Solomon Islands......................688-689
South Georgia..........................149-150
Swaziland ................................586-587
Vanuatu ..................................540-541
Zil Elwannyen Sesel.................177-178

### Royal Family Birthday, Anniversary

CD347

Queen Elizabeth II, 65th birthday, Charles and Diana, 10th wedding anniversary: Various photographs of Queen Elizabeth II, Prince Philip, Prince Charles, Princess Diana and their sons William and Henry.

**1991**

Antigua .................................1446-1455
Barbuda.................................1229-1238
Dominica................................1328-1337
Gambia..................................1080-1089
Grenada.................................2006-2015
Grenada Grenadines...........1331-1340
Guyana..................................2440-2451
Lesotho....................................871-875
Maldive Islands....................1533-1542
Nevis........................................666-675
St. Vincent............................1485-1494
St. Vincent Grenadines...........769-778
Sierra Leone.........................1387-1396
Turks & Caicos Islands ...........913-922
Uganda ....................................918-927

### Queen Elizabeth II's Accession to the Throne, 40th Anniv.

CD348

CD349

Various photographs of Queen Elizabeth II with local Scenes.

**1992 - CD348**

Antigua ..................................1513-1518
Barbuda.................................1306-1309
Dominica................................1414-1419
Gambia..................................1172-1177
Grenada.................................2047-2052
Grenada Grenadines...........1368-1373
Lesotho......................................881-885
Maldive Islands....................1637-1642
Nevis.........................................702-707
St. Vincent............................1582-1587
St. Vincent Grenadines...........829-834
Sierra Leone.........................1482-1487
Turks and Caicos Islands.........978-987
Uganda.....................................990-995
Virgin Islands............................742-746

**1992 - CD349**

Ascension Islands ....................531-535
Bahamas ..................................744-748
Bermuda..................................623-627
British Indian Ocean Territory........119-123
Cayman Islands.......................648-652
Falkland Islands .......................549-553
Gibraltar..................................605-609
Hong Kong .............................619-623
Kenya......................................563-567
Kiribati ...................................582-586
Pitcairn Islands........................362-366
St. Helena ...............................570-574
St. Kitts ..................................332-336
Samoa ....................................805-809
Seychelles ..............................734-738
Solomon Islands......................708-712
South Georgia .........................157-161
Tristan da Cunha.....................508-512
Vanuatu ..................................555-559
Zambia....................................561-565
Zil Elwannyen Sesel.................183-187

### Royal Air Force, 75th Anniversary

CD350

**1993**

Ascension.................................557-561
Bahamas .................................771-775
Barbados .................................842-846
Belize....................................1003-1008
Bermuda..................................648-651
British Indian Ocean Territory........136-140
Falkland Is. .............................573-577
Fiji ..........................................687-691
Montserrat ..............................830-834
St. Kitts...................................351-355

### Royal Air Force, 80th Anniv.

Design CD350 Re-inscribed

**1998**

Ascension.................................697-701
Bahamas .................................907-911
British Indian Ocean Terr.........198-202
Cayman Islands.......................754-758
Fiji..........................................814-818
Gibraltar..................................755-759
Samoa ....................................957-961
Turks & Caicos Islands ........1258-1265
Tuvalu ....................................763-767
Virgin Islands......................... 879-883

### End of World War II, 50th Anniv.

CD351

CD352

**1995**

Ascension.................................613-617
Bahamas ..................................824-828
Barbados .................................891-895
Belize....................................1047-1050
British Indian Ocean Territory........163-167
Cayman Islands.......................704-708
Falkland Islands .......................634-638
Fiji..........................................720-724
Kiribati ...................................662-668
Liberia..................................1175-1179
Mauritius.................................803-805
St. Helena ...............................646-654
St. Kitts..................................389-393
St. Lucia ..............................1018-1022
Samoa ....................................890-894
Solomon Islands......................799-803
South Georgia & S. Sandwich Is.............198-200
Tristan da Cunha.....................562-566

### UN, 50th Anniv.

CD353

**1995**

Bahamas .................................839-842
Barbados .................................901-904
Belize....................................1055-1058
Jamaica ...................................847-851
Liberia..................................1187-1190
Mauritius.................................813-816
Pitcairn Islands........................436-439
St. Kitts..................................398-401
St. Lucia ..............................1023-1026
Samoa ....................................900-903
Tristan da Cunha.....................568-571
Virgin Islands..........................807-810

### Queen Elizabeth, 70th Birthday

CD354

**1996**

Ascension.................................632-635
British Antarctic Territory..........240-243
British Indian Ocean Territory........176-180
Falkland Islands .......................653-657
Pitcairn Islands........................446-449
St. Helena ...............................672-676
Samoa ....................................912-916
Tokelau ...................................223-227
Tristan da Cunha.....................576-579
Virgin Islands..........................824-828

### Diana, Princess of Wales (1961-97)

CD355

**1998**

Ascension .......................................696
Bahamas ................................901A-902
Barbados .........................................950
Belize............................................1091
Bermuda..........................................753
Botswana ................................659-663
British Antarctic Territory.................258
British Indian Ocean Terr. ...............197
Cayman Islands....................752A-753
Falkland Islands ..............................694
Fiji..........................................819-820
Gibraltar...........................................754
Kiribati ...................................719A-720
Namibia ...........................................909
Niue ................................................706
Norfolk Island ...........................644-645
Papua New Guinea ........................937
Pitcairn Islands...............................487
St. Helena .......................................711
St. Kitts ...............................437A-438
Samoa ..................................955A-956
Seycelles .........................................802
Solomon Islands.......................866-867
South Georgia & S. Sandwich Islands
......................................................220
Tokelau ...............................252B-253
Tonga...............................................980
Niuafo'ou.......................................201
Tristan da Cunha.............................618
Tuvalu .............................................762
Vanuatu ...........................................719
Virgin Islands...................................878

### Wedding of Prince Edward and Sophie Rhys-Jones

CD356

**1999**

Ascension ................................729-730
Cayman Islands.......................775-776
Falkland Islands ......................729-730
Pitcairn Islands.......................505-506
St. Helena ..............................733-734
Samoa ....................................971-972
Tristan da Cunha.....................636-637
Virgin Islands..........................908-909

### 1st Manned Moon Landing, 30th Anniv.

CD357

**1999**

Ascension ................................731-735
Bahamas .................................942-946
Barbados ................................967-971
Bermuda..........................................778
Cayman Islands.......................777-781
Fiji..........................................853-857
Jamaica ..................................889-893
Kiribati ....................................746-750
Nauru......................................465-469
St. Kitts ..................................460-464
Samoa ....................................973-977
Solomon Islands......................875-879
Tuvalu ....................................800-804
Virgin Islands...........................910-914

### Queen Mother's Century

CD358

**1999**

Ascension ................................736-740
Bahamas .................................951-955
Cayman Islands.......................782-786
Falkland Islands ......................734-738
Fiji..........................................858-862
Norfolk Island ..........................688-692
St. Helena ..............................740-744
Samoa ....................................978-982
Solomon Islands......................880-884
South Georgia & South
Sandwich Islands ...............231-235
Tristan da Cunha.....................638-642
Tuvalu ....................................805-809

### Prince William, 18th Birthday

CD359

**2000**

Ascension ................................755-759
Cayman Islands.......................797-801
Falkland Islands ......................762-766
Fiji..........................................889-893
South Georgia .........................257-261
and South Sandwich Islands
Tristan da Cunha.....................664-668
Virgin Islands..........................925-929

### Reign of Queen Elizabeth II, 50th Anniv.

CD360

**2002**

Ascension ................................790-794
Bahamas ..............................1033-1037
Barbados ..............................1019-1023
Belize....................................1152-1156
Bermuda..................................822-826
British Antarctic Territory..........307-311
British Indian Ocean Territory ........239-
243
Cayman Islands.......................844-848
Falkland Islands ......................804-808
Gibraltar..................................896-900
Jamaica ..................................952-956
Nauru......................................491-495
Norfolk Island ..........................758-762
Papua New Guinea .............1019-1023
Pitcairn Islands...............................552
St. Helena ..............................788-792
St. Lucia ...............................1146-1150
Solomon Islands......................931-935
South Georgia & So. Sandwich Is. .......
..............................................274-278
Swaziland ...............................706-710
Tokelau ...................................302-306
Tonga............................................1059
Niuafo'ou.......................................239
Tristan da Cunha.....................706-710
Virgin Islands..........................967-971

### Queen Mother Elizabeth (1900-2002)

CD361

**2002**

Ascension ................................799-801
Bahamas ..............................1044-1046
Bermuda..................................834-836
British Antarctic Territory..........312-314
British Indian Ocean Territory ........245-
247
Cayman Islands.......................857-861
Falkland Islands ......................812-816
Nauru......................................499-501
Pitcairn Islands........................561-565
St. Helena ..............................808-812
St. Lucia ...............................1155-1159
Seychelles .......................................830
Solomon Islands......................945-947
South Georgia & So. Sandwich Isls. ....
..............................................281-285
Tokelau ...................................312-314
Tristan da Cunha.....................715-717
Virgin Islands..........................979-983

### Head of Queen Elizabeth II

CD362

**2003**

Ascension .......................................822
Bermuda..........................................865
British Antarctic Territory.................322
British Indian Ocean Territory .........261
Cayman Islands...............................878
Falkland Islands ..............................828
St. Helena .......................................820
South Georgia & South Sandwich
Islands ..........................................294
Tristan da Cunha.............................731
Virgin Islands.................................1003

### Coronation of Queen Elizabeth II, 50th Anniv.

CD363

**2003**

Ascension ................................823-825
Bahamas ..............................1073-1075
Bermuda..................................866-868
British Antarctic Territory..........323-325
British Indian Ocean Territory ........262-
264
Cayman Islands.......................879-881
Jamaica ..................................970-972
Kiribati ....................................825-827
Pitcairn Islands........................577-581
St. Helena ..............................821-823
St. Lucia ...............................1171-1173
Tokelau ...................................320-322
Tristan da Cunha.....................732-734
Virgin Islands........................1004-1006

### Prince William, 21st Birthday

CD364

**2003**

Ascension .......................................826
British Indian Ocean Territory .........265
Cayman Islands.......................882-884
Falkland Islands ..............................829
South Georgia & South Sandwich
Islands ..........................................295
Tokelau ...........................................323
Tristan da Cunha.............................735
Virgin Islands........................1007-1009

# British Commonwealth of Nations

## Dominions, Colonies, Territories, Offices and Independent Members

Comprising stamps of the British Commonwealth and associated nations.

A strict observance of technicalities would bar some or all of the stamps listed under Burma, Ireland, Kuwait, Nepal, New Republic, Orange Free State, Samoa, South Africa, South-West Africa, Stellaland, Sudan, Swaziland, the two Transvaal Republics and others but these are included for the convenience of collectors.

## 1. Great Britain

Great Britain: Including England, Scotland, Wales and Northern Ireland.

## 2. The Dominions, Present and Past

### AUSTRALIA

The Commonwealth of Australia was proclaimed on January 1, 1901. It consists of six former colonies as follows:

New South Wales
Queensland
South Australia
Victoria
Tasmania
Western Australia

The following islands and territories are, or have been, administered by Australia: Australian Antarctic Territory, Christmas Island, Cocos (Keeling) Islands, Nauru, New Guinea, Norfolk Island, Papua.

### CANADA

The Dominion of Canada was created by the British North America Act in 1867. The following provinces were former sepa- rate colonies and issued postage stamps:

British Columbia and Vancouver Island
New Brunswick
Newfoundland
Nova Scotia
Prince Edward Island

### FIJI

The colony of Fiji became an independent nation with dominion status on Oct. 10, 1970.

### GHANA

This state came into existence Mar. 6, 1957, with dominion status. It consists of the former colony of the Gold Coast and the Trusteeship Territory of Togoland. Ghana became a republic July 1, 1960.

### INDIA

The Republic of India was inaugurated on January 26, 1950. It succeeded the Dominion of India which was proclaimed August 15, 1947, when the former Empire of India was divided into Pakistan and the Union of India. The Republic is composed of about 40 predominantly Hindu states of three classes: governor's provinces, chief commissioner's provinces and princely states. India also has various territories, such as the Andaman and Nicobar Islands.

The old Empire of India was a federation of British India and the native states. The more important princely states were autonomous. Of the more than 700 Indian states, these 43 are familiar names to philatelists because of their postage stamps.

### CONVENTION STATES

Chamba
Faridkot
Gwalior
Jhind
Nabha
Patiala

### FEUDATORY STATES

Alwar
Bahawalpur
Bamra
Barwani
Bhopal
Bhor
Bijawar
Bundi
Bussahir
Charkhari
Cochin
Dhar
Dungarpur
Duttia
Faridkot (1879-85)
Hyderabad
Idar
Indore
Jaipur
Jammu
Jammu and Kashmir
Jasdan
Jhalawar
Jhind (1875-76)
Kashmir
Kishangarh
Kotah
Las Bela
Morvi
Nandgaon
Nowanuggur
Orchha
Poonch
Rajasthan
Rajpeepla
Sirmur
Soruth
Tonk
Travancore
Wadhwan

### NEW ZEALAND

Became a dominion on September 26, 1907. The following islands and territories are, or have been, administered by New Zealand:

Aitutaki
Cook Islands (Rarotonga)
Niue
Penrhyn
Ross Dependency
Samoa (Western Samoa)
Tokelau Islands

### PAKISTAN

The Republic of Pakistan was proclaimed March 23, 1956. It succeeded the Dominion which was proclaimed August 15, 1947. It is made up of all or part of several Moslem provinces and various districts of the former Empire of India, including Bahawalpur and Las Bela. Pakistan withdrew from the Commonwealth in 1972.

### SOUTH AFRICA

Under the terms of the South African Act (1909) the self-governing colonies of Cape of Good Hope, Natal, Orange River Colony and Transvaal united on May 31, 1910, to form the Union of South Africa. It became an independent republic May 3, 1961.

Under the terms of the Treaty of Versailles, South-West Africa, formerly German South-West Africa, was mandated to the Union of South Africa.

### SRI LANKA (CEYLON)

The Dominion of Ceylon was proclaimed February 4, 1948. The island had been a Crown Colony from 1802 until then. On May 22, 1972, Ceylon became the Republic of Sri Lanka.

## 3. Colonies, Past and Present; Controlled Territory and Independent Members of the Commonwealth

Aden
Aitutaki
Antigua
Ascension
Bahamas
Bahrain
Bangladesh
Barbados
Barbuda
Basutoland
Batum
Bechuanaland
Bechuanaland Prot.
Belize
Bermuda
Botswana
British Antarctic Territory
British Central Africa
British Columbia and Vancouver Island
British East Africa
British Guiana

British Honduras
British Indian Ocean Territory
British New Guinea
British Solomon Islands
British Somaliland
Brunei
Burma
Bushire
Cameroons
Cape of Good Hope
Cayman Islands
Christmas Island
Cocos (Keeling) Islands
Cook Islands
Crete,
British Administration
Cyprus
Dominica
East Africa & Uganda
Protectorates
Egypt
Falkland Islands
Fiji
Gambia
German East Africa
Gibraltar
Gilbert Islands
Gilbert & Ellice Islands
Gold Coast
Grenada
Griqualand West
Guernsey
Guyana
Heligoland
Hong Kong
Indian Native States
(see India)
Ionian Islands
Jamaica
Jersey
Kenya
Kenya, Uganda & Tanzania
Kuwait
Labuan
Lagos
Leeward Islands
Lesotho
Madagascar
Malawi
Malaya
Federated Malay States
Johore
Kedah
Kelantan
Malacca
Negri Sembilan
Pahang
Penang
Perak
Perlis
Selangor
Singapore
Sungei Ujong
Trengganu
Malaysia
Maldive Islands
Malta
Man, Isle of
Mauritius
Mesopotamia
Montserrat
Muscat
Namibia
Natal
Nauru
Nevis
New Britain
New Brunswick
Newfoundland
New Guinea
New Hebrides
New Republic
New South Wales
Niger Coast Protectorate
Nigeria
Niue
Norfolk Island
North Borneo
Northern Nigeria
Northern Rhodesia
North West Pacific Islands
Nova Scotia
Nyasaland Protectorate
Oman
Orange River Colony
Palestine
Papua New Guinea
Penrhyn Island
Pitcairn Islands
Prince Edward Island
Queensland
Rhodesia
Rhodesia & Nyasaland
Ross Dependency
Sabah
St. Christopher
St. Helena
St. Kitts
St. Kitts-Nevis-Anguilla
St. Lucia
St. Vincent
Samoa
Sarawak
Seychelles
Sierra Leone
Solomon Islands
Somaliland Protectorate
South Arabia
South Australia
South Georgia
Southern Nigeria
Southern Rhodesia
South-West Africa
Stellaland
Straits Settlements
Sudan
Swaziland
Tanganyika
Tanzania
Tasmania
Tobago
Togo
Tokelau Islands
Tonga
Transvaal
Trinidad
Trinidad and Tobago
Tristan da Cunha
Trucial States
Turks and Caicos
Turks Islands
Tuvalu
Uganda
United Arab Emirates
Victoria
Virgin Islands
Western Australia
Zambia
Zanzibar
Zululand

**POST OFFICES IN FOREIGN COUNTRIES**

Africa
East Africa Forces
Middle East Forces
Bangkok
China
Morocco
Turkish Empire

# Colonies, Former Colonies, Offices, Territories Controlled by Parent States

## Belgium

Belgian Congo
Ruanda-Urundi

## Denmark

Danish West Indies
Faroe Islands
Greenland
Iceland

## Finland

Aland Islands

## France

### COLONIES PAST AND PRESENT, CONTROLLED TERRITORIES

Afars & Issas, Territory of
Alaouites
Alexandretta
Algeria
Alsace & Lorraine
Anjouan
Annam & Tonkin
Benin
Cambodia (Khmer)
Cameroun
Castellorizo
Chad
Cilicia
Cochin China
Comoro Islands
Dahomey
Diego Suarez
Djibouti (Somali Coast)
Fezzan
French Congo
French Equatorial Africa
French Guiana
French Guinea
French India
French Morocco
French Polynesia (Oceania)
French Southern & Antarctic Territories
French Sudan
French West Africa
Gabon
Germany
Ghadames
Grand Comoro
Guadeloupe
Indo-China
Inini
Ivory Coast
Laos
Latakia
Lebanon
Madagascar
Martinique
Mauritania
Mayotte
Memel
Middle Congo
Moheli
New Caledonia
New Hebrides
Niger Territory
Nossi-Be
Obock
Reunion
Rouad, Ile
Ste.-Marie de Madagascar
St. Pierre & Miquelon
Senegal
Senegambia & Niger
Somali Coast
Syria
Tahiti
Togo
Tunisia
Ubangi-Shari
Upper Senegal & Niger
Upper Volta
Viet Nam
Wallis & Futuna Islands

### POST OFFICES IN FOREIGN COUNTRIES

China
Crete
Egypt
Turkish Empire
Zanzibar

## Germany

### EARLY STATES

Baden
Bavaria
Bergedorf
Bremen
Brunswick
Hamburg
Hanover
Lubeck
Mecklenburg-Schwerin
Mecklenburg-Strelitz
Oldenburg
Prussia
Saxony
Schleswig-Holstein
Wurttemberg

### FORMER COLONIES

Cameroun (Kamerun)
Caroline Islands
German East Africa
German New Guinea
German South-West Africa
Kiauchau
Mariana Islands
Marshall Islands
Samoa
Togo

## Italy

### EARLY STATES

Modena
Parma
Romagna
Roman States
Sardinia
Tuscany
Two Sicilies
  Naples
  Neapolitan Provinces
  Sicily

### FORMER COLONIES, CONTROLLED TERRITORIES, OCCUPATION AREAS

Aegean Islands
  Calimno (Calino)
  Caso
  Cos (Coo)
  Karki (Carchi)
  Leros (Lero)
  Lipso
  Nisiros (Nisiro)
  Patmos (Patmo)
  Piscopi
  Rodi (Rhodes)
  Scarpanto
  Simi
  Stampalia
Castellorizo
Corfu
Cyrenaica
Eritrea
Ethiopia (Abyssinia)
Fiume
Ionian Islands
  Cephalonia
  Ithaca
  Paxos
Italian East Africa
Libya
Oltre Giuba
Saseno
Somalia (Italian Somaliland)
Tripolitania

### POST OFFICES IN FOREIGN COUNTRIES

"ESTERO"*
Austria
China
  Peking
  Tientsin
Crete
Tripoli
Turkish Empire
  Constantinople
  Durazzo
  Janina
Jerusalem
Salonika
Scutari
Smyrna
Valona

*Stamps overprinted "ESTERO" were used in various parts of the world.

## Netherlands

Aruba
Netherlands Antilles (Curacao)
Netherlands Indies
Netherlands New Guinea
Surinam (Dutch Guiana)

## Portugal

### COLONIES PAST AND PRESENT, CONTROLLED TERRITORIES

Angola
Angra
Azores
Cape Verde
Funchal
Horta
Inhambane
Kionga
Lourenco Marques
Macao
Madeira
Mozambique
Mozambique Co.
Nyassa
Ponta Delgada
Portuguese Africa
Portuguese Congo
Portuguese Guinea
Portuguese India
Quelimane
St. Thomas & Prince Islands
Tete
Timor
Zambezia

## Russia

### ALLIED TERRITORIES AND REPUBLICS, OCCUPATION AREAS

Armenia
Aunus (Olonets)
Azerbaijan
Batum
Estonia
Far Eastern Republic
Georgia
Karelia
Latvia
Lithuania
North Ingermanland
Ostland
Russian Turkestan
Siberia
South Russia
Tannu Tuva
Transcaucasian Fed. Republics
Ukraine
Wenden (Livonia)
Western Ukraine

## Spain

### COLONIES PAST AND PRESENT, CONTROLLED TERRITORIES

Aguera, La
Cape Juby
Cuba
Elobey, Annobon & Corisco
Fernando Po
Ifni
Mariana Islands
Philippines
Puerto Rico
Rio de Oro
Rio Muni
Spanish Guinea
Spanish Morocco
Spanish Sahara
Spanish West Africa

### POST OFFICES IN FOREIGN COUNTRIES

Morocco
Tangier
Tetuan

# Dies of British Colonial Stamps

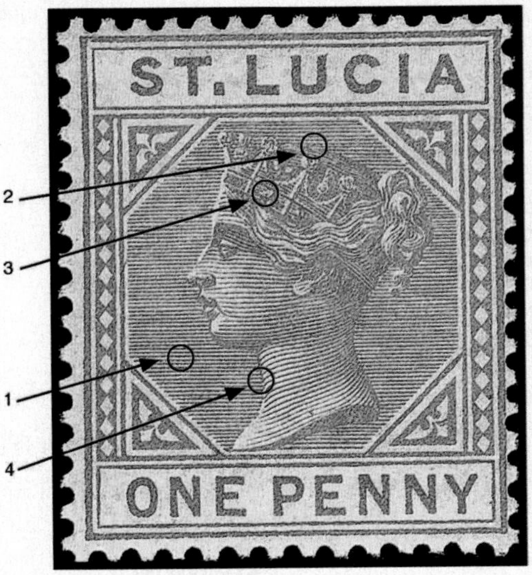


**DIE A:**

**1.** The lines in the groundwork vary in thickness and are not uniformly straight.

**2.** The seventh and eighth lines from the top, in the groundwork, converge where they meet the head.

**3.** There is a small dash in the upper part of the second jewel in the band of the crown.

**4.** The vertical color line in front of the throat stops at the sixth line of shading on the neck.

**DIE B:**

**1.** The lines in the groundwork are all thin and straight.

**2.** All the lines of the background are parallel.

**3.** There is no dash in the upper part of the second jewel in the band of the crown.

**4.** The vertical color line in front of the throat stops at the eighth line of shading on the neck.

**DIE I:**

**1.** The base of the crown is well below the level of the inner white line around the vignette.

**2.** The labels inscribed "POSTAGE" and "REVENUE" are cut square at the top.

**3.** There is a white "bud" on the outer side of the main stem of the curved ornaments in each lower corner.

**4.** The second (thick) line below the country name has the ends next to the crown cut diagonally.

DIE Ia.
1 as die II.
2 and 3 as die I.

DIE Ib.
1 and 3 as die II.
2 as die I.

**DIE II:**

**1.** The base of the crown is aligned with the underside of the white line around the vignette.

**2.** The labels curve inward at the top inner corners.

**3.** The "bud" has been removed from the outer curve of the ornaments in each corner.

**4.** The second line below the country name has the ends next to the crown cut vertically.

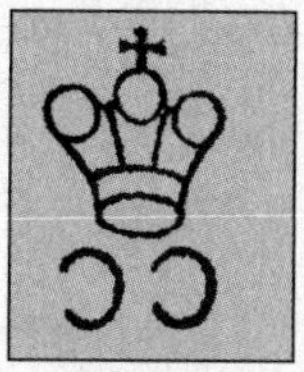

Wmk. 1
Crown and C C

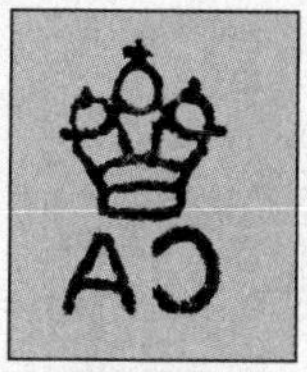

Wmk. 2
Crown and C A

Wmk. 3
Multiple Crown and C A

Wmk. 4
Multiple Crown and Script C A

Wmk. 4a

Wmk. 314
St. Edward's Crown and C A Multiple

Wmk. 373

Wmk. 384

Wmk. 406

# British Colonial and Crown Agents Watermarks

Watermarks 1 to 4, 314, 373, 384 and 406, common to many British territories, are illustrated here to avoid duplication.

The letters "CC" of Wmk. 1 identify the paper as having been made for the use of the Crown Colonies, while the letters "CA" of the others stand for "Crown Agents." Both Wmks. 1 and 2 were used on stamps printed by De La Rue & Co.

Wmk. 3 was adopted in 1904; Wmk. 4 in 1921; Wmk. 314 in 1957; Wmk. 373 in 1974; Wmk. 384 in 1985; Wmk 406 in 2008.

In Wmk. 4a, a non-matching crown of the general St. Edwards type (bulging on both sides at top) was substituted for one of the Wmk. 4 crowns which fell off the dandy roll. The non-matching crown occurs in 1950-52 printings in a horizontal row of crowns on certain regular stamps of Johore and Seychelles, and on various postage due stamps of Barbados, Basutoland, British Guiana, Gold Coast, Grenada, Northern Rhodesia, St. Lucia, Swaziland and Trinidad and Tobago. A variation of Wmk. 4a, with the non-matching crown in a horizontal row of crown-CA-crown, occurs on regular stamps of Bahamas, St. Kitts-Nevis and Singapore.

Wmk. 314 was intentionally used sideways, starting in 1966. When a stamp was issued with Wmk. 314 both upright and sideways, the sideways varieties usually are listed also – with minor numbers. In many of the later issues, Wmk. 314 is slightly visible.

Wmk. 373 is usually only faintly visible.

# GABON

ga-ˈbōⁿ

LOCATION — West coast of Africa, at the equator
GOVT. — Republic
AREA — 102,089 sq. mi.
POP. — 1,225,853 (1999 est.)
CAPITAL — Libreville

Gabon originally was under the control of French West Africa. In 1886, it was united with French Congo. In 1904, Gabon was granted a certain degree of colonial autonomy which prevailed until 1934, when it merged with French Equatorial Africa. Gabon Republic was proclaimed November 28, 1958.

100 Centimes = 1 Franc

**Catalogue values for unused stamps in this country are for Never Hinged items, beginning with Scott 148 in the regular postage section, Scott B4 in the semi-postal section, Scott C1 in the airpost section, Scott CB1 in the airpost semi-postal section, Scott J34 in the postage due section, and Scott O1 in the officials section.**

**Watermark**

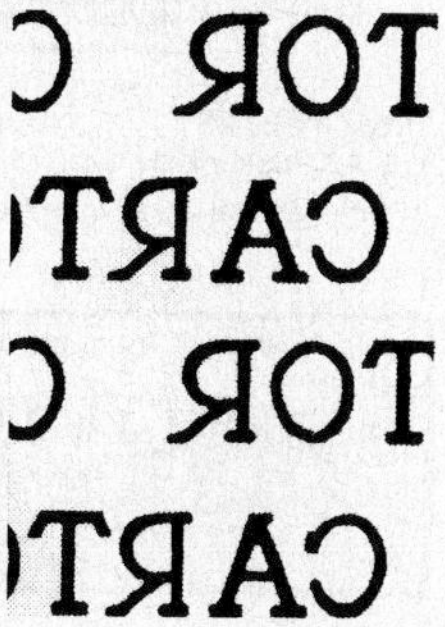

Wmk. 385

For detailed listings of overprint and surcharge varieties of Gabon Nos. 1-15, see the *Scott Classic Specialized Catalogue of Stamps and Covers.*

### Stamps of French Colonies of 1881-86 Handstamp Surcharged in Black

a

b

**1886 Unwmk. Perf. 14x13½**

| | | | | |
|---|---|---|---|---|
| 1 | A9 (a) | 5c on 20c red, *grn* | 550.00 | *600.00* |
| 2 | A9 (b) | 10c on 20c red, *grn* | 525.00 | *550.00* |
| 3 | A9 (b) | 25c on 20c red, *grn* | 100.00 | 72.50 |
| *e.* | | 56-dot diamond grid around "GAB" | *6,400.* | 1,900. |
| 4 | A9 (b) | 50c on 15c bl | 1,500. | *2,100.* |
| 5 | A9 (b) | 75c on 15c bl | 1,900. | *2,300.* |

Nos. 1-3 exist with double surcharge of numeral; No. 3 with "GAB" double or inverted, or with "25" double.

On Nos. 3 and 5 the surcharge slants down; on No. 4 it slants up. The number of dots varies.

Counterfeits of Nos. 1-15 exist.

Handstamp Surcharged in Black — c

**1888-89**

| | | | | |
|---|---|---|---|---|
| 6 | A9 | 15c on 10c blk, *lav* | *5,800.* | 1,500. |
| 7 | A9 | 15c on 1fr brnz grn, *straw* | *2,400.* | 1,200. |
| 8 | A9 | 25c on 5c grn, *grnsh* | 1,500. | 300.00 |
| *a.* | | Double surcharge | *4,000.* | *4,000.* |
| 9 | A9 | 25c on 10c blk, *lav* | *5,900.* | 1,900. |
| 10 | A9 | 25c on 75c car, *rose* | *3,600.* | 1,900. |

*Official reprints exist.*

Postage Due Stamps of French Colonies Handstamp Surcharged in Black — d

**1889 *Imperf.***

| | | | | |
|---|---|---|---|---|
| 11 | D1 | 15c on 5c black | 300.00 | 275.00 |
| 12 | D1 | 15c on 30c black | *5,000.* | *3,800.* |
| 13 | D1 | 25c on 20c black | 140.00 | 120.00 |

Nos. 11 and 13 exist with "GABON," "TIMBRE" or "25" double; "TIMBRE" or "15" omitted, etc.

A8

**1889 Typeset**

| | | | | |
|---|---|---|---|---|
| 14 | A8 | 15c blk, *rose* | 1,900. | 1,200. |
| 15 | A8 | 25c blk, *green* | 1,200. | 950. |

Ten varieties of each. Nos. 14-15 exist with "GAB" inverted, double or omitted, and with small "f" in "Francaise."

Navigation and Commerce — A9

### Name of Colony in Blue or Carmine

**1904-07 Typo. *Perf. 14x13½***

| | | | | |
|---|---|---|---|---|
| 16 | A9 | 1c blk, *lil bl* | 1.20 | 1.20 |
| *a.* | | "GABON" double | 360.00 | 360.00 |
| 17 | A9 | 2c brn, *buff* | 1.60 | 1.60 |
| 18 | A9 | 4c claret, *lav* | 2.75 | 2.00 |
| 19 | A9 | 5c yellow green | 3.25 | 2.40 |
| 20 | A9 | 10c rose | 10.50 | 7.50 |
| 21 | A9 | 15c gray | 11.00 | 7.50 |
| 22 | A9 | 20c red, *grn* | 15.00 | 14.00 |
| 23 | A9 | 25c blue | 14.00 | 7.50 |
| 24 | A9 | 30c yel brn | 16.00 | 15.00 |
| 25 | A9 | 35c blk, *yel* ('06) | 24.00 | 24.00 |
| 26 | A9 | 40c red, *straw* | 25.00 | 20.00 |
| 27 | A9 | 45c blk, *gray grn* ('07) | 37.50 | 32.50 |
| 28 | A9 | 50c brn, *az* | 16.00 | 14.00 |
| 29 | A9 | 75c dp vio, *org* | 25.00 | 25.00 |
| 30 | A9 | 1fr brnz grn, *straw* | 40.00 | 40.00 |
| 31 | A9 | 2fr vio, *rose* | 80.00 | 80.00 |
| 32 | A9 | 5fr lil, *lav* | 125.00 | 125.00 |
| | | *Nos. 16-32 (17)* | 447.80 | 419.20 |

Perf. 13½x14 stamps are counterfeits.

For surcharges see Nos. 72-84.

Fang Warrior — A10

Fang Woman — A12

Libreville A11

### Inscribed: "Congo Français"

**1910 *Perf. 13½x14***

| | | | | |
|---|---|---|---|---|
| 33 | A10 | 1c choc & org | 2.00 | 2.00 |
| 34 | A10 | 2c black & choc | 2.75 | 2.75 |
| 35 | A10 | 4c vio & dp bl | 2.50 | 2.50 |
| 36 | A10 | 5c ol gray & grn | 4.00 | 4.00 |
| 37 | A10 | 10c red & car | 5.75 | 5.75 |
| 38 | A10 | 20c choc & dk vio | 8.00 | 8.00 |
| 39 | A11 | 25c dp bl & choc | 8.00 | 8.00 |
| 40 | A11 | 30c gray blk & red | 40.00 | 40.00 |
| 41 | A11 | 35c dk vio & grn | 24.00 | 24.00 |
| 42 | A11 | 40c choc & ultra | 32.50 | 32.50 |
| 43 | A11 | 45c carmine & vio | 52.50 | 52.50 |
| 44 | A11 | 50c bl grn & gray | 75.00 | 75.00 |
| 45 | A11 | 75c org & choc | 130.00 | 130.00 |
| 46 | A12 | 1fr dk brn & bis | 130.00 | 130.00 |
| 47 | A12 | 2fr carmine & brn | 325.00 | 325.00 |
| 48 | A12 | 5fr blue & choc | 325.00 | 325.00 |
| | | *Nos. 33-48 (16)* | 1,167. | 1,167. |

### *Inscribed: "Afrique Equatoriale"* On Dull Cream Paper

**1910-22**

| | | | | |
|---|---|---|---|---|
| 49 | A10 | 1c choc & org | .30 | *.40* |
| 50 | A10 | 2c black & choc | .30 | *.40* |
| *b.* | | 2c gray black & deep olive | .65 | *.80* |
| 51 | A10 | 4c vio & dp bl | .50 | *.55* |
| 52 | A10 | 5c ol gray & grn | .95 | .55 |
| 53 | A10 | 5c gray blk & ocher ('22) | 1.25 | 1.25 |
| 54 | A10 | 10c red & car | 1.40 | 1.00 |
| 55 | A10 | 10c yel grn & bl grn ('22) | 1.25 | 1.25 |
| 56 | A10 | 15c brn vio & rose ('18) | 1.25 | .80 |
| 57 | A10 | 20c ol brn & dk vio | 6.50 | 5.50 |
| 58 | A11 | 25c dp bl & choc | 1.40 | 1.00 |
| 59 | A11 | 25c Prus bl & blk ('22) | 1.60 | 1.60 |
| 60 | A11 | 30c gray blk & red | 1.60 | 1.60 |
| 61 | A11 | 30c rose & red ('22) | 2.00 | *2.40* |
| 62 | A11 | 35c dk vio & grn | 1.25 | 1.25 |
| 63 | A11 | 40c choc & ultra | 1.60 | 1.60 |
| 64 | A11 | 45c carmine & vio | 1.60 | 1.60 |
| 65 | A11 | 45c blk & red ('22) | 2.75 | *3.25* |
| 66 | A11 | 50c bl grn & gray | 2.00 | 2.00 |
| 67 | A11 | 50c dk bl & bl ('22) | 1.60 | 1.60 |
| 68 | A11 | 75c org & choc | 6.50 | 6.50 |
| 69 | A12 | 1fr dk brn & bis | 3.25 | 3.25 |
| 70 | A12 | 2fr car & brn | 6.50 | *7.25* |
| 71 | A12 | 5fr blue & choc | 8.75 | *9.50* |
| | | *Nos. 49-71 (23)* | 56.10 | 56.10 |

Nos. 49-51, 54, 62, 64 and 66 also exist on white paper. See the *Scott Classic Specialized Catalogue of Stamps and Covers* for listings.

For overprints and surcharges, see Nos 85-119, B1-B3.

### Stamps of 1904-07 Surcharged in Black or Carmine

### Spacing between figures of surcharge 1.5mm (5c), 2mm (10c)

**1912**

| | | | | |
|---|---|---|---|---|
| 72 | A9 | 5c on 2c brn, *buff* | 1.60 | *2.00* |
| 73 | A9 | 5c on 4c cl, *lav* (C) | 1.60 | *2.00* |
| 74 | A9 | 5c on 15c gray (C) | 1.25 | 1.25 |
| 75 | A9 | 5c on 20c red, *grn* | 1.25 | *1.60* |
| 76 | A9 | 5c on 25c bl (C) | 1.25 | *1.60* |
| 77 | A9 | 5c on 30c pale brn (C) | 1.60 | *2.00* |
| 78 | A9 | 10c on 40c red, *straw* | 1.25 | *1.60* |
| *a.* | | Double surcharge | 2,000. | |
| 79 | A9 | 10c on 45c blk, *gray grn* (C) | 1.25 | *1.60* |
| 80 | A9 | 10c on 50c brn, *az* (C) | 1.60 | *2.00* |
| 81 | A9 | 10c on 75c dp vio, *org* | 1.60 | *2.00* |
| 82 | A9 | 10c on 1fr brnz grn, *straw* | 1.60 | *2.00* |
| 83 | A9 | 10c on 2fr vio, *rose* | 1.60 | *2.00* |
| *a.* | | Inverted surcharge | 340.00 | 340.00 |
| 84 | A9 | 10c on 5fr lil, *lav* | 4.50 | *4.75* |
| | | *Nos. 72-84 (13)* | 21.95 | 26.40 |

Two spacings between the surcharged numerals are found on Nos. 72 to 84. For detailed listings, see the *Scott Classic Specialized Catalogue of Stamps and Covers.*

### Stamps of 1910-22 Overprinted in Black, Blue or Carmine

On A10, A12

On A11

**1924-31**

| | | | | |
|---|---|---|---|---|
| 85 | A10 | 1c brown & org | .30 | *.40* |
| 86 | A10 | 2c blk & choc (Bl) | .50 | *.60* |
| 87 | A10 | 4c violet & ind | .30 | *.40* |
| 88 | A10 | 5c gray blk & ocher | .45 | *.55* |
| 89 | A10 | 10c yel grn & bl grn | 1.00 | 1.00 |
| *a.* | | Double overprint (Bk & Bl) | 175.00 | |
| 90 | A10 | 10c dk bl & brn ('26) (C) | .40 | .40 |
| *a.* | | Overprint omitted | 350.00 | 350.00 |
| *b.* | | Double overprint | | 475.00 |
| 91 | A10 | 15c brn vio & rose (Bl) | 1.00 | 1.00 |
| 92 | A10 | 15c rose & brn vio ('31) (Bl) | 1.25 | 1.25 |
| *a.* | | Overprint omitted | 250.00 | |
| 93 | A10 | 20c ol brn & dk vio (C) | 1.00 | 1.00 |
| *a.* | | Inverted overprint | 180.00 | 180.00 |
| *b.* | | Double overprint | | 400.00 |
| *c.* | | Double overprint, both inverted | 525.00 | |
| 94 | A11 | 25c Prus bl & blk (C) | .95 | .95 |
| 95 | A11 | 30c rose & red (Bl) | .90 | *1.00* |
| 96 | A11 | 30c blk & org ('26) | 1.00 | 1.00 |
| *a.* | | Overprint omitted | *10,000.* | |
| 97 | A11 | 30c dk grn & bl grn ('28) | 1.25 | 1.25 |
| *a.* | | Overprint omitted | 1,800. | |
| 98 | A11 | 35c dk vio & grn (Bl) | .80 | *.95* |
| 99 | A11 | 40c choc & ultra (C) | .75 | *.90* |
| 100 | A11 | 45c blk & red (Bl) | 1.50 | 1.50 |
| 101 | A11 | 50c dk bl & bl (C) | 1.00 | 1.00 |
| 102 | A11 | 50c car & grn ('26) | 1.10 | 1.10 |
| 103 | A11 | 65c dp bl & red org ('27) | 4.50 | 4.00 |
| 104 | A11 | 75c org & brn (Bl) | 2.25 | 2.25 |
| 105 | A11 | 90c brn red & rose ('30) | 2.75 | 2.75 |
| 106 | A12 | 1fr dk brn & bis | 1.90 | 1.90 |
| 107 | A12 | 1.10fr dl grn & rose red ('28) | 6.00 | *7.50* |
| 108 | A12 | 1.50fr pale bl & dk bl ('30) | 1.25 | 1.25 |
| *a.* | | Overprint omitted | 290.00 | |
| 109 | A12 | 2fr rose & brn | 2.25 | *2.50* |
| 110 | A12 | 3fr red vio ('30) | 10.50 | 8.25 |
| *a.* | | Overprint omitted | 275.00 | |
| 111 | A12 | 5fr dp bl & choc | 5.50 | 6.50 |
| | | *Nos. 85-111 (27)* | 52.35 | 53.15 |

### Types of 1924-31 Issues Surcharged with New Values in Black or Carmine

**1925-28**

| | | | | |
|---|---|---|---|---|
| 112 | A12 | 65c on 1fr ol grn & brn | 1.25 | 1.25 |
| 113 | A12 | 85c on 1fr ol grn & brn | 1.25 | 1.25 |
| 114 | A11 | 90c on 75c brn red & cer ('27) | 1.60 | 1.60 |
| *a.* | | "90" omitted | 240.00 | |
| 115 | A12 | 1.25fr on 1fr dk bl & ultra (C) | 1.25 | 1.25 |
| 116 | A12 | 1.50fr on 1fr lt bl & dk bl ('27) | 2.00 | 2.00 |
| 117 | A12 | 3fr on 5fr mag & ol brn | 9.25 | 8.75 |
| 118 | A12 | 10fr on 5fr org brn & grn ('27) | 13.00 | *14.00* |

**119** A12 20fr on 5fr red vio & org red ('27) 16.00 *17.50*
*Nos. 112-119 (8)* 45.60 47.60

Bars cover the old denominations on Nos. 114-119.

Common Design Types pictured following the introduction.

**Colonial Exposition Issue**
Common Design Types

**1931** *Perf. 12½*

**Name of Country in Black**

| | | | | |
|---|---|---|---|---|
| **120** | CD70 | 40c dp green | 4.00 | 4.00 |
| **121** | CD71 | 50c violet | 4.00 | 4.00 |
| **122** | CD72 | 90c red orange | 4.00 | 4.00 |
| **123** | CD73 | 1.50fr dull blue | 5.50 | 5.50 |
| | | *Nos. 120-123 (4)* | 17.50 | 17.50 |

Timber Raft on Ogowe River A16

Count Savorgnan de Brazza — A17

Village of Setta Kemma A18

**1932-33** **Photo.** *Perf. 13x13½*

| | | | | |
|---|---|---|---|---|
| **124** | A16 | 1c brown violet | .25 | .25 |
| **125** | A16 | 2c blk, *rose* | .25 | .25 |
| **126** | A16 | 4c green | .30 | .30 |
| **127** | A16 | 5c grnsh blue | .55 | .55 |
| **128** | A16 | 10c red, *yel* | .55 | .55 |
| **129** | A16 | 15c red, *grn* | .70 | .65 |
| **130** | A16 | 20c deep red | .70 | .65 |
| **131** | A16 | 25c brown red | .70 | .50 |
| **132** | A17 | 30c yellow grn | 2.00 | 1.60 |
| **133** | A17 | 40c brown vio | 2.25 | 1.10 |
| **134** | A17 | 45c blk, *dl grn* | 3.25 | 2.40 |
| **135** | A17 | 50c red brown | 1.60 | 1.25 |
| **136** | A17 | 65c Prus blue | 6.50 | 6.50 |
| **137** | A17 | 75c blk, *red org* | 4.00 | 3.25 |
| **138** | A17 | 90c rose red | 4.00 | 3.25 |
| **139** | A17 | 1fr yel grn, *bl* | 27.50 | 24.00 |
| **140** | A18 | 1.25fr dp vio ('33) | 2.25 | 2.00 |
| **141** | A18 | 1.50fr dull blue | 11.00 | 7.25 |
| **142** | A18 | 1.75fr dp green ('33) | 2.50 | 2.00 |
| **143** | A18 | 2fr brn red | 52.50 | 45.00 |
| **144** | A18 | 3fr yel grn, *bl* | 6.00 | 4.50 |
| **145** | A18 | 5fr red brown | 15.00 | 13.50 |
| **146** | A18 | 10fr blk, *red org* | 32.50 | 27.50 |
| **147** | A18 | 20fr dk violet | 47.50 | 40.00 |
| | | *Nos. 124-147 (24)* | 224.35 | 188.80 |

See French Equatorial Africa No. 192 for stamp inscribed "Gabon" and "Afrique Equatoriale Francaise."

**Catalogue values for all unused stamps in this section, from this point to the end of the section, are for Never Hinged items.**

**Republic**

Prime Minister Leon Mba — A19

Flag & Map of Gabon & UN Emblem — A20

**Unwmk.**

**1959, Nov. 28** **Engr.** *Perf. 13*

| | | | | |
|---|---|---|---|---|
| **148** | A19 | 15fr shown | .40 | .25 |
| **149** | A19 | 25fr Mba, profile | .40 | .25 |

Proclamation of the Republic, 1st anniv.

Imperforates
Most Gabon stamps from 1959 onward exist imperforate in issued and trial colors, and also in small presentation sheets in issued colors.

**C.C.T.A. Issue**
Common Design Type

**1960, May 21** **Engr.** *Perf. 13*

**150** CD106 50fr vio brn & Prus bl 1.10 1.10

**1961, Feb. 9**

| | | | | |
|---|---|---|---|---|
| **151** | A20 | 15fr multi | .35 | .25 |
| **152** | A20 | 25fr multi | .55 | .25 |
| **153** | A20 | 85fr multi | 1.90 | 1.10 |
| | | *Nos. 151-153 (3)* | 2.80 | 1.60 |

Gabon's admission to United Nations.

Combretum A21

1fr, 5fr, Tulip tree, vert. 2fr, 3fr, Yellow cassia.

**1961, July 4** **Unwmk.** *Perf. 13*

| | | | | |
|---|---|---|---|---|
| **154** | A21 | 50c rose red & grn | .25 | .25 |
| **155** | A21 | 1fr sl grn, red & bis | .25 | .25 |
| **156** | A21 | 2fr dk grn & yel | .25 | .25 |
| **157** | A21 | 3fr ol grn & yel | .55 | .55 |
| **158** | A21 | 5fr multi | .60 | .60 |
| **159** | A21 | 10fr grn & rose red | .60 | .60 |
| | | *Nos. 154-159 (6)* | 2.50 | 2.50 |

President Leon Mba — A22

**1962** **Engr.**

| | | | | |
|---|---|---|---|---|
| **160** | A22 | 15fr indigo, car & grn | .30 | .25 |
| **161** | A22 | 20fr brn blk, car & grn | .50 | .25 |
| **162** | A22 | 25fr brn, car & grn | .55 | .25 |
| | | *Nos. 160-162 (3)* | 1.35 | .75 |

Issued: 15fr, 2/9; 20fr, 11/15; 25fr, 8/17.

**Abidjan Games Issue**
Common Design Type

**1962, July 21** **Photo.** *Perf. 12½x12*

| | | | | |
|---|---|---|---|---|
| **163** | CD109 | 20fr Foot race, start | .75 | .50 |
| **164** | CD109 | 50fr Soccer | 1.25 | 1.00 |
| | | *Nos. 163-164,C6 (3)* | 5.75 | 3.75 |

**African-Malgache Union Issue**
Common Design Type

**1962, Sept. 8** *Perf. 12½x12*

**165** CD110 30fr emer, bluish grn, red & gold 1.60 1.25

Captain Ntchorere and Flags of France and Gabon A23

**1962, Nov. 23** *Perf. 12*

**166** A23 80fr multi 1.60 1.10

Capt. Ntchorere, who died for France, 6/7/40.

Waves Around Globe A23a

Design: 100fr, Orbit patterns around globe.

**1963, Sept. 19** **Photo.** *Perf. 12½*

| | | | | |
|---|---|---|---|---|
| **167** | A23a | 25fr ultra, grn & org | .55 | .55 |
| **168** | A23a | 100fr grn, ultra & red brn | 2.10 | 1.75 |

Issued to publicize space communications.

UNESCO Emblem, Scales and Tree A23b

**1963, Dec. 10** **Engr.** *Perf. 13*

**169** A23b 25fr grn, dk gray & red brn .60 .25

15th anniv. of the Universal Declaration of Human Rights.

Barograph and WMO Emblem A23c

**1964, Mar. 23** **Unwmk.** *Perf. 13*

**170** A23c 25fr ol bis, sl grn & ultra .90 .60

UN's 4th World Meteorological Day, Mar. 23.

Arms of Gabon — A24

**1964, June 15** **Photo.** *Perf. 13x12½*

**171** A24 25fr ocher & multi .90 .45

Tarpon A25

Designs: 60fr, Gorilla, vert. 80fr, Buffalo.

**1964, July 15** **Engr.** *Perf. 13*

| | | | | |
|---|---|---|---|---|
| **172** | A25 | 30fr brn red, bl & blk | 1.25 | .70 |
| **173** | A25 | 60fr brn, grn & brn red | 2.25 | .90 |
| **174** | A25 | 80fr dk bl, grn & red brn | 2.40 | 1.25 |
| | | *Nos. 172-174 (3)* | 5.90 | 2.85 |

**Cooperation Issue**
Common Design Type

**1964, Nov. 7**

**175** CD119 25fr gray, dk brn & lt bl .90 .60

Dissotis Rotundifolia — A26

5fr, Gloriosa superba. 15fr, Eulophia horsfallii.

**1964, Nov. 16** **Photo.** *Perf. 12x12½*

**Flowers in Natural Colors**

| | | | | |
|---|---|---|---|---|
| **176** | A26 | 3fr deep grn | .40 | .25 |
| **177** | A26 | 5fr green | .75 | .40 |
| **178** | A26 | 15fr dark brn | 1.20 | .80 |
| | | *Nos. 176-178 (3)* | 2.35 | 1.45 |

Sun and IQSY Emblem A27

**1965, Feb. 25** *Perf. 12½x12*

**179** A27 85fr multi 1.75 .80

International Quiet Sun Year, 1964-65.

Morse Telegraph A28

**1965, May 17** **Engr.** *Perf. 13*

**180** A28 30fr multi .85 .60

Cent. of the ITU.

Manganese Crusher, Moanda A29

Design: 60fr, Uranium mining, Mounana.

**1965, June 15** **Unwmk.** *Perf. 13*

| | | | | |
|---|---|---|---|---|
| **181** | A29 | 15fr brt bl, pur & red | .55 | .30 |
| **182** | A29 | 60fr brn, brt bl & red | 1.90 | .90 |

Issued to publicize Gabon's mineral wealth.

Field Ball — A30

Okoukoue Dance — A31

**1965, July 15** **Engr.** *Perf. 13*

**183** A30 25fr brt grn, blk & red .90 .60

1st African Games, Brazzaville, 7/18-25. See No. C35.

**1965, Sept. 15** *Perf. 13*

Design: 60fr, Mukudji dance.

| | | | | |
|---|---|---|---|---|
| **184** | A31 | 25fr brn, grn & yel | .55 | .25 |
| **185** | A31 | 60fr blk, dk red & brn | 1.75 | .90 |

Abraham Lincoln A32

**1965, Sept. 28 Photo.** ***Perf. 12½x13***

| | | | |
|---|---|---|---|
| **186** | A32 50fr vio bl, blk, gold & buff | 1.00 | .50 |

Centenary of death of Abraham Lincoln.

Old & New Post Offices and Mail Transport A33

**1965, Dec. 18 Engr.** ***Perf. 13***

| | | | |
|---|---|---|---|
| **187** | A33 30fr bl, brt grn & choc | .90 | .70 |

Issued for Stamp Day, 1965.

Balumbu Mask — A34

Intl. Negro Arts Festival, Dakar, Senegal, Apr. 1-24:

10fr, Fang ancestral figure, Byeri. 25fr, Fang mask. 30fr, Okuyi mask, Myene. 85fr, Bakota leather mask.

**1966, Apr. 18 Photo.** ***Perf. 12x12½***

| | | | |
|---|---|---|---|
| **188** | A34 5fr red, brn, blk & buff | .30 | .25 |
| **189** | A34 10fr brt grnsh bl, dk brn & yel | .35 | .30 |
| **190** | A34 25fr multicolored | 1.00 | .35 |
| **191** | A34 30fr mar, yel & blk | 1.25 | .70 |
| **192** | A34 85fr multicolored | 3.00 | 1.60 |
| | *Nos. 188-192 (5)* | 5.90 | 3.20 |

WHO Headquarters, Geneva — A35

**1966, May 3 Photo.** ***Perf. 12½x13***

| | | | |
|---|---|---|---|
| **193** | A35 50fr org yel, ultra & blk | 1.40 | .60 |

Inauguration of the WHO Headquarters, Geneva.

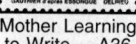

Mother Learning to Write — A36

Soccer Player — A37

**1966, June 22 Photo.** ***Perf. 12x12½***

| | | | |
|---|---|---|---|
| **194** | A36 30fr multi | .90 | .45 |

UNESCO literacy campaign.

**1966, July 15 Engr.** ***Perf. 13***

Design: 90fr, Player facing left.

| | | | |
|---|---|---|---|
| **195** | A37 25fr brn, grn & ultra | .80 | .25 |
| **196** | A37 90fr ultra & dk pur | 2.50 | 1.25 |
| | *Nos. 195-196,C45 (3)* | 6.30 | 2.75 |

8th World Cup Soccer Championship, Wembley, England, July 11-30.

Timber Industry — A38

Economic development: 85fr, Offshore oil rigs.

**1966, Aug. 17** ***Perf. 13***

| | | | |
|---|---|---|---|
| **197** | A38 20fr red brn, lil & dk grn | .80 | .50 |
| **198** | A38 85fr dk brn, brt bl & brt grn | 3.50 | 1.60 |

Woman with Children at Bank Window A39

**1966, Sept. 23 Engr.** ***Perf. 13***

| | | | |
|---|---|---|---|
| **199** | A39 25fr brt bl, vio brn & sl grn | 1.00 | .50 |

Issued to publicize Savings Banks.

Scouts Around Campfire A40

50fr, Boy Scout pledging ceremony, vert.

**1966, Oct. 17 Engr.** ***Perf. 13***

| | | | |
|---|---|---|---|
| **200** | A40 30fr sl bl, car & dk brn | 1.00 | .60 |
| **201** | A40 50fr Prus bl, brn red & dk brn | 1.60 | .70 |

Issued to honor Gabon's Boy Scouts.

Sikorsky S-43 Hydroplane and Map of West Africa A41

**1966, Dec. 17 Photo.** ***Perf. 12½x12***

| | | | |
|---|---|---|---|
| **202** | A41 30fr multi | 2.10 | 1.25 |

Stamp Day and for the 30th anniv. of the 1st air-mail service from Libreville to Port Gentil.

Hippopotami — A42

Animals: 2fr, African crocodiles. 3fr, Water chevrotain. 5fr, Chimpanzees. 10fr, Elephants. 20fr, Leopards.

**1967, Jan. 5 Photo.** ***Perf. 13x14***

| | | | |
|---|---|---|---|
| **203** | A42 1fr multi | .25 | .25 |
| **204** | A42 2fr multi | .45 | .25 |
| **205** | A42 3fr multi | .45 | .25 |
| **206** | A42 5fr multi | .50 | .25 |
| **207** | A42 10fr multi | 1.50 | .80 |
| **208** | A42 20fr multi | 3.50 | .80 |
| | *Nos. 203-208 (6)* | 6.65 | 2.60 |

Lions International Emblem — A43

50fr, Lions emblem, map of Gabon and globe.

**1967, Jan. 14** ***Perf. 12½x13***

| | | | |
|---|---|---|---|
| **209** | A43 30fr multicolored | .80 | .25 |
| **210** | A43 50fr blue & multi | 1.40 | .80 |
| *a.* | Strip of 2, #209-210 + label | 3.25 | 1.75 |

50th anniv. of Lions Intl.

Carnival Masks — A44

**1967, Feb. 4 Photo.** ***Perf. 12x12½***

| | | | |
|---|---|---|---|
| **211** | A44 30fr brn, yel bis & bl | 1.10 | .45 |

Libreville Carnival, Feb. 4-7.

"Transportation" and Tourist Year Emblem — A45

**1967, Feb. 15** ***Perf. 12½x13***

| | | | |
|---|---|---|---|
| **212** | A45 30fr multi | 1.10 | .45 |

International Tourist Year, 1967.

Olympic Diving Tower, Mexico City — A46

Symbolic of Atomic Energy Agency — A47

1968 Olympic Games: 30fr, Sun, snow crystals and Olympic rings. 50fr, Ice skating rink and view of Grenoble.

**1967, Mar. 18 Engr.** ***Perf. 13***

| | | | |
|---|---|---|---|
| **213** | A46 25fr dk vio, grnsh bl & ultra | .75 | .40 |
| **214** | A46 30fr grn, red lil & mar | 1.10 | .50 |
| **215** | A46 50fr ultra, grn & brn | 1.75 | 1.10 |
| | *Nos. 213-215 (3)* | 3.60 | 2.00 |

**1967, Apr. 15 Engr.** ***Perf. 13***

| | | | |
|---|---|---|---|
| **216** | A47 30fr red brn, dk grn & ultra | 1.00 | .25 |

International Atomic Energy Agency.

Pope Paul VI, Papal Arms and Libreville Cathedral A48

**1967, June 1 Engr.** ***Perf. 13***

| | | | |
|---|---|---|---|
| **217** | A48 30fr ultra, grn & blk | 1.10 | .50 |

"Populorum progressio" encyclical by Pope Paul VI concerning underdeveloped countries.

Flags, Tree, Logger, Map of Gabon and Mask — A49

**1967, June 24 Engr.** ***Perf. 13***

| | | | |
|---|---|---|---|
| **218** | A49 30fr multi | 1.00 | .50 |

EXPO '67, International Exhibition, Montreal, Apr. 28-Oct. 27, 1967.

**Europafrica Issue, 1967**

Map of Europe and Africa and Products A50

**1967, July 18 Photo.** ***Perf. 12½x12***

| | | | |
|---|---|---|---|
| **219** | A50 50fr multi | 1.50 | .60 |

UN Emblem, Women and Child A51

**1967, Aug. 10 Engr.** ***Perf. 13***

| | | | |
|---|---|---|---|
| **220** | A51 75fr brt blue, dk brn & emer | 1.60 | .80 |

United Nations Commission for Women.

19th Century Mail Ships — A52

Design: No. 222, Modern mail ships.

**1967, Nov. 17 Photo.** ***Perf. 12½***

| | | | |
|---|---|---|---|
| **221** | A52 30fr multi | 1.90 | .95 |
| **222** | A52 30fr multi | 1.90 | .95 |
| *a.* | Pair, #221-222 | 5.00 | 5.00 |

Stamp Day. No. 222a has continuous design.

Draconea Fragrans — A53

Trees: 10fr, Pycnanthus angolensis. 20fr, Disthemonanthus benthamianus.

**1967, Dec. 5 Engr.** ***Perf. 13***

**Size: 22x36mm**

| | | | |
|---|---|---|---|
| **223** | A53 5fr bl, emer & brn | .75 | .35 |
| **224** | A53 10fr grn, dk grn & bl | .80 | .55 |
| **225** | A53 20fr rose red, grn & ol | 1.20 | .90 |
| | *Nos. 223-225,C61-C62 (5)* | 7.10 | 4.80 |

For booklet pane see No. C62a.

WHO Regional Office A54

**1968, Apr. 8 Engr. *Perf. 13***
**226** A54 20fr multi .85 .50

20th anniv. of the WHO.

Dam, Power Station and UNESCO Emblem A55

**1968, June 18 Engr. *Perf. 13***
**227** A55 15fr lake, org & Prus bl .70 .40

Hydrological Decade (UNESCO), 1965-74.

Pres. Albert Bernard Bongo — A56

30fr, Pres. Bongo & arms of Gabon in background.

**1968, June 24 Photo. *Perf. 12x12½***
**228** A56 25fr grn, buff & blk .65 .25
**229** A56 30fr rose lil, lt bl & blk .75 .25

Tanker, Refinery, and Map of Area Served — A56a

**1968, July 30 Photo. *Perf. 12½***
**230** A56a 30fr multi .85 .50

Port Gentil (Gabon) Refinery opening, 6/12/68.

Open Book, Child and UNESCO Emblem A57

**1968, Sept. 10 Engr. *Perf. 13***
**231** A57 25fr vio bl, dl red & brn 1.60 .25

Issued for International Literacy Day.

A58

A60

A59

**1968, Oct. 15 Engr. *Perf. 13***
**232** A58 20fr Coffee 1.60 .75
**233** A58 40fr Cacao 2.50 1.10

**1968, Nov. 23 Engr. *Perf. 13***
**234** A59 30fr "La Junon" 2.00 .70

Issued for Stamp Day.

**1968, Dec. 10**

Lawyer, globe and human rights flame.

**235** A60 20fr blk, bl grn & car .70 .45

International Human Rights Year.

Okanda Gap — A61

Designs: 15fr, Barracuda. 25fr, Kinguele Waterfall, vert. 30fr, Sitatunga trophies, vert.

**1969, Mar. 28 Engr. *Perf. 13***
**236** A61 10fr brn, bl & sl grn .35 .25
**237** A61 15fr brn red, emer & ind 2.50 .50
**238** A61 25fr bl, pur & ol .75 .35
**239** A61 30fr multi 1.60 .70
*Nos. 236-239 (4)* 5.20 1.80

Year of African Tourism, 1969.

Mvet (Musical Instrument) A62

Musical Instruments: 30fr, Ngombi harp. 50fr, Ebele and Mbe drums. 100fr, Medzang xylophone.

**1969, June 6 Engr. *Perf. 13***
**240** A62 25fr plum, ol & dp car .50 .25
**241** A62 30fr red brn, ol & dk brn .50 .25
**242** A62 50fr plum, ol & dp car 1.10 .65
**243** A62 100fr red brn, ol & dk brn 2.40 1.00
*a.* Min. sheet of 4, #240-243 6.50 6.50
*Nos. 240-243 (4)* 4.50 2.15

Aframomum Polyanthum (Zingiberaceae) A63

Tree of Life A64

African Plants: 2fr, Chlamydocola chlamydantha (Sterculiaceae). 5fr, Costus dinklagei (Zingiberaceae). 10fr, Cola rostrata (Sterculiaceae). 20fr, Dischistocalyx grandifolius (Acanthaceae).

**1969, July 15 Photo. *Perf. 12x12½***
**244** A63 1fr multi .25 .25
**245** A63 2fr lt ol & multi .25 .25
**246** A63 5fr multi .25 .25
**247** A63 10fr slate & multi 1.10 .25
**248** A63 20fr yel & multi 1.75 .70
*Nos. 244-248 (5)* 3.60 1.70

**1969, Aug. 17 Photo.**
**249** A64 25fr multi .60 .50

National renovation.

Drilling for Oil on Land — A65

Workers and ILO Emblem — A66

Design: 50fr, Offshore drilling station.

**1969, Sept. 13 *Perf. 12x12½***
**250** A65 25fr multi .25 .25
**251** A65 50fr multi 2.10 .25
*a.* Strip of 2, #250-251 + label 3.00 3.00

20th anniv. of the ELF-SPAFE oil operations in Gabon.

**1969, Oct. 29 Engr. *Perf. 13***
**252** A66 30fr bl, sl grn & dp car .90 .45

50th anniv. of the ILO.

Arms of Port Gentil — A67

Coats of Arms: 20fr, Lambarene. 30fr, Libreville.

**1969, Nov. 19 Photo. *Perf. 12***
**253** A67 20fr red, gold, sil & blk 1.00 .25
**254** A67 25fr bl, blk & gold 1.40 .25
**255** A67 30fr bl & multi 1.60 .80
*Nos. 253-255 (3)* 4.00 1.30

See Nos. 267-269, 291-293, 321-326, 340-348, 409-417, 492-501.

Canoe Mail Transport A68

**1969, Dec. 18 Engr. *Perf. 13***
**256** A68 30fr brt grn, grnsh bl & red brn 1.25 .80

Issued for Stamp Day 1969.

Satellite, Globe, TV Screen and ITU Emblem A69

**1970, May 17 Engr. *Perf. 13***
**257** A69 25fr dk bl, dk red brn & blk .90 .60

International Telecommunications Day.

**UPU Headquarters Issue**
Common Design Type

**1970, May 20 Engr. *Perf. 13***
**258** CD133 30fr brt grn, brt rose lil & brn .90 .55

Geisha and African Drummer A70

**1970, May 27 Photo. *Perf. 12½x12***
**259** A70 30fr ultra & multi 1.10 .60

EXPO '70 Intl. Exhibition, Osaka, Japan, 3/15-9/13.

**ASECNA Issue**
Common Design Type

**1970, Aug. 26 Engr. *Perf. 13***
**260** CD132 100fr brt grn & bl grn 2.00 .95

UN Emblem, Globe, Dove and Charts A71

**1970, Oct. 24 Photo. *Perf. 12½x12***
**261** A71 30fr Prus bl & multi .90 .60

25th anniversary of the United Nations.

Bushbucks A72

Designs: 15fr, Pels scaly-tailed flying squirrel. 25fr, Gray-cheeked monkey, vert. 40fr, African golden cat. 60fr, Sevaline genet.

**1970, Dec. 14 Photo. *Perf. 12½x13***
**262** A72 5fr yel grn & multi .60 .40
**263** A72 15fr red org & blk .95 .55
**264** A72 25fr vio & multi 1.75 .80
**265** A72 40fr red & multi 2.75 1.10
**266** A72 60fr bl & multi 4.75 2.10
*Nos. 262-266 (5)* 10.80 4.95

**Arms Type of 1969**

20fr, Mouila. 25fr, Bitam. 30fr, Oyem.

**1971, Feb. 16 Photo. *Perf. 12***
**267** A67 20fr ver, blk, sil & gold .90 .25
**268** A67 25fr emer, gold & blk 1.00 .25
**269** A67 30fr emer, gold, blk & red 1.25 .25
*Nos. 267-269 (3)* 3.15 .75

Men of Four Races and Emblem — A73

**1971, Mar. 21 Engr. *Perf. 13***
**270** A73 40fr multi .90 .45

Intl. year against racial discrimination.

Map of Africa and Telecommunications System — A74

**1971, Apr. 30 Photo. *Perf. 13***
**271** A74 30fr org & multi .90 .45

Pan-African telecommunications system.

Charaxes Smaragdalis — A75

Butterflies: 10fr, Euxanthe crossleyi. 15fr, Epiphora rectifascia. 25fr, Imbrasia bouvieri.

**1971, May 26 Photo. *Perf. 13***

**272** A75 5fr yel & multi 2.40 .80
**273** A75 10fr bl & multi 5.00 1.00
**274** A75 15fr grn & multi 9.00 1.10
**275** A75 25fr ol & multi 11.50 2.00
*Nos. 272-275 (4)* 27.90 4.90

Hertzian Center, Nkol Ogoum A76

**1971, June 17 Engr. *Perf. 13***

**276** A76 40fr grn, blk & dk car 1.10 .70

3rd World Telecommunications Day.

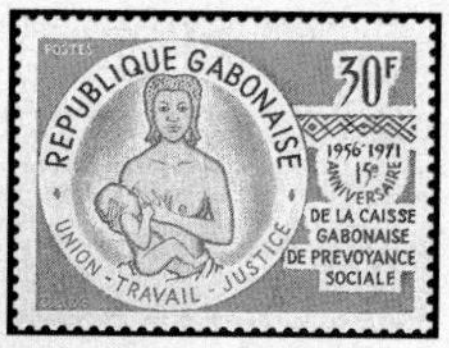


Mother Nursing Child A77

**1971, Aug. 17 Engr. *Perf. 13***

**277** A77 30fr lil rose, sep & ocher .90 .45

Gabonese social security system, 15th anniv.

UN Headquarters and Emblem — A78

**1971, Sept. 30 Photo. *Perf. 13***

**278** A78 30fr red & multi .90 .45

10th anniv. of Gabon's admission to the UN.

Large Egret — A79

Birds: 40fr, African gray parrot. 50fr, Woodland Kingfisher. 75fr, Cameroon bareheaded rock-fowl. 100fr, Gold Coast touraco.

**1971, Oct. 12 Litho. *Perf. 13***

**279** A79 30fr multi 1.75 1.10
**280** A79 40fr multi 2.40 1.50
**281** A79 50fr multi 2.50 1.60
**282** A79 75fr multi 3.50 2.10
**283** A79 100fr multi 4.75 2.50
*Nos. 279-283 (5)* 14.90 8.80

Asystasia Volgeliana A80

Designs: Flowers of Acanthus Family after paintings by Noel Hallé.

**1972, Apr. 4 Photo. *Perf. 13***

**284** A80 5fr pale cit & multi .25 .25
**285** A80 10fr multi .50 .25
**286** A80 20fr multi .75 .50
**287** A80 30fr lil rose & multi 1.10 .70
**288** A80 40fr dk grn & multi 1.90 1.00
**289** A80 65fr red & multi 3.25 1.40
*Nos. 284-289 (6)* 7.75 4.10

Louis Pasteur — A81

**1972, May 15 Engr. *Perf. 13***

**290** A81 80fr dp org, pur & grn 1.25 .60

Sesquicentennial of the birth of Louis Pasteur (1822-1895), scientist and bacteriologist.

**Arms Type of 1969**

30fr, Franceville. 40fr, Makokou. 60fr, Tchibanga.

**1972, June 2 Photo. *Perf. 12***

**291** A67 30fr sil & multi .75 .25
**292** A67 40fr grn & multi .75 .50
**293** A67 60fr blk, grn & sil 1.60 .75
*Nos. 291-293 (3)* 3.10 1.50

Globe and Telecommunications Symbols — A81a

**1972, July 25 *Perf. 13x12½***

**294** A81a 40fr blk, yel & org .90 .45

4th World Telecommunications Day.

Nat King Cole — A82

Black American Jazz Musicians: 60fr, Sidney Bechet. 100fr, Louis Armstrong.

**1972, Sept. 1 Photo. *Perf. 13x13½***

**295** A82 40fr bl & multi 1.60 .35
**296** A82 60fr org & multi 2.40 .70
**297** A82 100fr multi 4.00 1.10
*Nos. 295-297 (3)* 8.00 2.15

Blanding's Rear-fanged Snake — A83

Designs: 2fr, Beauty snake. 3fr, Eggeating snake. 15fr, Striped ground snake. 25fr, Jameson's mamba. 50fr, Gabon viper.

**1972, Oct. 2 Litho. *Perf. 13***

**298** A83 1fr lem & multi .25 .25
**299** A83 2fr red brn & multi .25 .25
**300** A83 3fr brn org & multi .40 .25
**301** A83 15fr multi 1.45 .50
**302** A83 25fr grn & multi 2.75 .55
**303** A83 50fr multi 4.50 1.00
*Nos. 298-303 (6)* 9.60 2.80

See Nos. 330-332, 354-357.

Dr. Armauer G. Hansen, Lambarene Leprosarium — A84

**1973, Jan. 28 Engr. *Perf. 13***

**304** A84 30fr Prus grn, sl grn & brn 1.25 .55

Centenary of the discovery of the Hansen bacillus, the cause of leprosy.

Charaxes Candiope — A85

Designs: Various butterflies.

**1973, Feb. 23 Litho. *Perf. 13***

**305** A85 10fr shown 1.90 .40
**306** A85 15fr Eunica pechueli 2.25 .40
**307** A85 20fr Cyrestis camillus 3.75 .85
**308** A85 30fr Charaxes castor 5.00 1.25
**309** A85 40fr Charaxes ameliae 6.00 1.75
**310** A85 50fr Pseudacrea boisduvali 6.50 2.10
*Nos. 305-310 (6)* 25.40 6.75

Balloon of Santos-Dumont, 1901 — A86

History of Aviation: 1fr, Montgolfier's balloon, 1783, vert. 3fr, Octave Chanute's biplane, 1896. 4fr, Clement Ader's Plane III, 1897. 5fr, Louis Bleriot crossing the Channel, 1909. 10fr, Fabre's hydroplane, 1910.

**1973, May 3 Engr. *Perf. 13***

**311** A86 1fr grn, sl grn & dk red .25 .25
**312** A86 2fr sl grn & brt bl .25 .25
**313** A86 3fr bl, sl & org .25 .25
**314** A86 4fr lil & dk pur .75 .25
**315** A86 5fr slate grn & org 1.10 .35
**316** A86 10fr rose lil & Prus bl 2.10 .50
*Nos. 311-316 (6)* 4.70 1.85

**1977 Coil Stamp**

**316A** A86 10fr aqua 3.50 .25

No. 316A has red control numbers on back of every 10th stamp.

INTERPOL Emblem — A87

**1973, June 26 Engr. *Perf. 13***

**317** A87 40fr magenta & ultra .90 .40

50th anniversary of the International Criminal Police Organization (INTERPOL).

Earth Station "2 Decembre" A88

**1973, July 2 Engr. *Perf. 13***

**318** A88 40fr slate grn, bl & brn .90 .40

Party Headquarters, Libreville — A89

**1973, Aug. 17 Photo.**

**319** A89 30fr multi .90 .25

**African Postal Union Issue**

Common Design Type

**1973, Sept. 12 Engr. *Perf. 13***

**320** CD137 100fr red lil, pur & bl 1.25 .75

**Arms Type of 1969**

5fr, Gamba. 10fr, Ogowe-Lolo. 15fr, Fougamou. 30fr, Kango. 40fr, Booue. 60fr, Koula-Moutou.

**1973-74 Photo. *Perf. 12***

**321** A67 5fr bl & multi ('74) .65 .25
**322** A67 10fr blk, red & gold ('74) .65 .25
**323** A67 15fr grn & multi ('74) .90 .25
**324** A67 30fr red & multi 1.60 .35
**325** A67 40fr red & multi 1.90 .55
**326** A67 60fr emer & multi 3.00 .70
*Nos. 321-326 (6)* 8.70 2.35

Issued Nos. 321-323, 2/13; Nos. 324-326, 10/4.

St. Teresa of Lisieux — A90

40fr, St. Teresa and Jesus carrying cross.

**1973, Dec. 4 Photo. *Perf. 13***

**327** A90 30fr blk & multi .90 .25
**328** A90 40fr blk & multi 1.10 .35

St. Teresa of the Infant Jesus (Thérèse Martin, 1873-97), Carmelite nun.

Human Rights Flame — A91

**1973, Dec. 10 Engr.**

**329** A91 20fr grn, red & ultra .60 .25

25th anniversary of the Universal Declaration of Human Rights.

**Wildlife Type of 1972**

Monkeys: 40fr, Mangabey. 60fr, Cercopithecus cephus. 80fr, Mona monkey.

**1974, Mar. 20 Litho. *Perf. 14***

**330** A83 40fr gray grn & multi 1.50 .65
**331** A83 60fr lt bl & multi 2.50 .80
**332** A83 80fr lil rose & multi 4.00 1.25
*Nos. 330-332 (3)* 8.00 2.70

Ogowe River at Lambarene A93

50fr, Cape Estérias. 75fr, Poubara rope bridge.

**1974, July 30 Photo. *Perf. 13x13½***

**333** A93 30fr multi .60 .25
**334** A93 50fr multi .80 .25
**335** A93 75fr multi 1.75 .90
*Nos. 333-335 (3)* 3.15 1.40

Manioc
A94

Design: 50fr, Palms and dates.

**1974, Nov. 13 Photo. *Perf. 13x12½***

**336** A94 40fr org red & multi .90 .30
**337** A94 50fr bister & multi 1.10 .30

### UDEAC Issue

Presidents and Flags of Cameroun, CAR, Congo, Gabon and Meeting Center — A95

**1974, Dec. 8 Photo. *Perf. 13***

**338** A95 40fr multi .80 .30

See No. C156.

Hôtel du Dialogue — A96

**1975, Jan. 20 Photo. *Perf. 13***

**339** A96 50fr multi .90 .45

Opening of Hôtel du Dialogue.

### Arms Type of 1969

5fr, Ogowe-Ivindo. 10fr, Moabi. No. 342, Moanda. No. 343, Nyanga. 25fr, Mandji. No. 345, Mekambo. No. 346, Omboué. 60fr, Minvoul. 90fr, Mayumba.

**1975-77 Photo. *Perf. 12***

**340** A67 5fr red & multi .25 .25
**341** A67 10fr gold & multi .25 .25
**342** A67 15fr red, sil & blk .45 .25
**343** A67 15fr bl & multi .35 .25
**344** A67 25fr grn & multi .45 .25
**345** A67 50fr blk, gold & red 1.40 .35
**346** A67 50fr multi 1.50 .60
**347** A67 60fr multi 1.40 .60
**348** A67 90fr multi 1.90 .75
*Nos. 340-348 (9)* 7.95 3.55

Issued: Nos. 340-342, Jan. 21, 1975; Nos. 343-345, Aug. 17, 1976; Nos. 346-348, July 12, 1977.

Map of Africa with Lion's Head, and Lions Emblem — A97

**1975, May 2 Typo. *Perf. 13***

**349** A97 50fr grn & multi .90 .30

Lions Club 17th congress, District 403, Libreville.

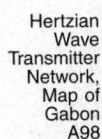

Hertzian Wave Transmitter Network, Map of Gabon
A98

**1975, July 8 Engr. *Perf. 13***

**350** A98 40fr multi .90 .60

City and Rural Women, Car, Train and Building — A99

**1975, July 22 Engr. *Perf. 13***

**351** A99 50fr car, bl & brn 2.10 .80

International Women's Year 1975.

Scoutmaster Ange Mba, Emblems and Rope — A100

Design: 50fr, Hand holding rope, Scout, camp, Boy Scout and Nordjamb 75 emblems.

**1975, July 29**

**352** A100 40fr multi .60 .30
**353** A100 50fr grn, red & dk brn .90 .40

Nordjamb 75, 14th Boy Scout Jamboree, Lillehammer, Norway, July 29-Aug. 7.

### Wildlife Type of 1972

Fish: 30fr, Lutjanus goreensis. 40fr, Galeoides decadactylus. 50fr, Sardinella aurita. 120fr, Scarus hoefleri.

**1975, Sept. 22 Litho. *Perf. 14***

**354** A83 30fr multi .75 .30
**355** A83 40fr multi 1.25 .50
**356** A83 50fr multi 1.75 .50
**357** A83 120fr multi 3.25 1.25
*Nos. 354-357 (4)* 7.00 2.55

Agro-Industrial Complex — A102

**1975, Dec. 15 Litho. *Perf. 12½***

**358** A102 60fr multi 1.00 .50

Inauguration of Agro-Industrial Complex, Franceville.

Tchibanga Bridge — A103

Bridges of Gabon: 10fr, Mouila. 40fr, Kango. 50fr, Lambaréné, vert.

**1976, Jan. 30 Engr. *Perf. 13***

**359** A103 5fr multi .25 .25
**360** A103 10fr multi .35 .25
**361** A103 40fr multi .80 .30
**362** A103 50fr multi 1.10 .45
*Nos. 359-362 (4)* 2.50 1.25

Telephones 1876 and 1976, Satellite, A. G. Bell — A104

**1976, Mar. 10 Engr. *Perf. 13***

**363** A104 60fr dk bl, grn & sl grn 1.10 .40

Centenary of first telephone call by Alexander Graham Bell, Mar. 10, 1876.

Msgr. Jean Remy Bessieux — A105

**1976, Apr. 30 Engr. *Perf. 13***

**364** A105 50fr grn, bl & sepia .90 .45

Death centenary of Msgr. Bessieux.

Athletes, Torch, Map of Africa, Games Emblem — A106

**1976, June 25 Photo. *Perf. 13x12½***

**365** A106 50fr multi .70 .25
**366** A106 60fr org & multi .90 .30

First Central African Games (Zone 5), Libreville, June-July.

Motobécane, France — A107

Motorcycles: 5fr, Bultaco, Spain. 10fr, Suzuki, Japan. 20fr, Kawasaki, Japan. 100fr, Harley-Davidson, US.

**1976, July 20 Litho. *Perf. 12½***

**367** A107 3fr multi .40 .25
**368** A107 5fr org & multi .40 .25
**369** A107 10fr bl & multi .70 .30
**370** A107 20fr multi 1.25 .30
**371** A107 100fr car & multi 4.50 1.00
*Nos. 367-371 (5)* 7.25 2.10

Rice
A108

**1976, Oct. 15 Litho. *Perf. 13x13½***

**372** A108 50fr shown .90 .35
**373** A108 60fr Pepper plants 1.10 .55

**1977, Apr. 22 Litho. *Perf. 13x13½***

50fr, Banana plantation. 60fr, Peanut market.

**374** A108 50fr multi .90 .35
**375** A108 60fr multi 1.10 .55

Telecommunications Emblem and Telephone — A109

**1977, May 17 *Perf. 13***

**376** A109 60fr multi .90 .50

World Telecommunications Day.

View of Oyem
A110

50fr, Cape Lopez. 70fr, Lebamba Cave.

**1977, June 9 Litho. *Perf. 12½***

**377** A110 50fr multi .70 .30
**378** A110 60fr multi .75 .40
**379** A110 70fr multi .85 .45
*Nos. 377-379 (3)* 2.30 1.15

Conference Hall — A111

**1977, June 23 Photo. *Perf. 13x12½***

**380** A111 100fr multi 1.40 .75

Meeting of the OAU, Libreville.

Arms of Gabon — A112

**Size: 23x36mm**

**1977 Engr. *Perf. 13***

**381** A112 50fr blue 1.25 .50

**Size: 17x23mm**

**382** A112 60fr orange 1.10 .50
*a.* Booklet pane of 5 6.00
**383** A112 80fr red 1.60 .65
*Nos. 381-383 (3)* 3.95 1.65

No. 381 issued in coils, No. 382 in booklets only.

Issued: Nos. 381-382, June 23; No. 383, Sept.

Modern Buildings, Libreville — A113

**1977, Aug. 17 Litho. *Perf. 12***

**387** A113 50fr multi .90 .25

National Festival 1977.

Paris to Vienna, 1902 — A114

Renault Automobiles: 10fr, Coupé 1 2 CV, 1921. 30fr, Torpédo Scaphandrier, 1925. 40fr, Reinastella 40 CV, 1929. 100fr, Nerva Grand Sport, 1937. 150fr, Voiturette 1 CV, 1899. 200fr, Alpine Renault V6, 1977.

**1977, Aug 30 Engr. *Perf. 13***

| | | |
|---|---|---|
| **388** A114 5fr multi | .50 | .35 |
| **389** A114 10fr multi | .50 | .35 |
| **390** A114 30fr multi | 1.25 | .50 |
| **391** A114 40fr multi | 2.10 | .60 |
| **392** A114 100fr multi | 5.25 | 2.25 |
| *Nos. 388-392 (5)* | 9.60 | 4.05 |

**Miniature Sheet**

| | | |
|---|---|---|
| **393** Sheet of 2 + label | 18.00 | 18.00 |
| *a.* A114 150fr multi | 5.25 | 5.25 |
| *b.* A114 200fr multi | 7.00 | 7.00 |

Louis Renault, French automobile pioneer, birth centenary. Nos. 383a-393b are perf. on 3 sides, without perforation between stamps and center label showing dark brown portrait of Renault.

See Nos. 395-400.

Globe A115

**1978, Feb. 21 Engr. *Perf. 13x12½***

| | | |
|---|---|---|
| **394** A115 80fr multi | .90 | .60 |

World Leprosy Day.

**Automobile Type of 1977**

Citroen Cars: 10fr, Cabriolet, 1922. 50fr, Taxi, 1927. 60fr, Berline, 1932. 80fr, Berline, 1934. 150fr, Torpedo, 1919. 200fr, Berline, 1948. 250fr, Pallas, 1975.

**1978, May 9 Engr. *Perf. 13***

| | | |
|---|---|---|
| **395** A114 10fr multi | .80 | .35 |
| **396** A114 50fr multi | 1.50 | .45 |
| **397** A114 60fr multi | 2.50 | .95 |
| **398** A114 80fr multi | 2.50 | .95 |
| **399** A114 200fr multi | 6.75 | 2.25 |
| *Nos. 395-399 (5)* | 14.05 | 4.95 |

**Miniature Sheet**

| | | |
|---|---|---|
| **400** Sheet of 2 | 18.00 | 18.00 |
| *a.* A114 150fr multi | 5.25 | 5.25 |
| *b.* A114 250fr multi | 7.00 | 7.00 |

Andre Citroen (1878-1935), automobile designer and manufacturer.

Ndjole on Ogowe River — A116

Views: 40fr, Lambarene lake district. 50fr, Owendo Harbor.

**1978, May 17 Litho. *Perf. 12½***

| | | |
|---|---|---|
| **401** A116 30fr multi | .40 | .25 |
| **402** A116 40fr multi | .70 | .25 |
| **403** A116 50fr multi | .90 | .35 |
| *Nos. 401-403 (3)* | 2.00 | .85 |

Sternotomis Mirabilis — A117

Various Coleopteras.

**1978, June 21 Photo. *Perf. 12½x13***

| | | |
|---|---|---|
| **404** A117 20fr multi | .50 | .30 |
| **405** A117 60fr multi | 2.10 | .65 |
| **406** A117 75fr multi | 2.50 | .75 |
| **407** A117 80fr multi | 3.25 | 1.25 |
| *Nos. 404-407 (4)* | 8.35 | 2.95 |

Anti-Apartheid Emblem — A118

**1978, July 25 Engr. *Perf. 13***

| | | |
|---|---|---|
| **408** A118 80fr multi | .90 | .60 |

**Arms Type of 1969**

**1978-80 Photo. *Perf. 12***

| | | |
|---|---|---|
| **409** A67 5fr Oyem | .25 | .25 |
| **410** A67 5fr Ogowe-Maritime ('79) | .25 | .25 |
| **411** A67 10fr Lastoursville ('79) | .25 | .25 |
| **412** A67 10fr Haut-Ogooue ('80) | .25 | .25 |
| **413** A67 15fr M'Bigou ('79) | .25 | .25 |
| **414** A67 20fr Estuaire ('80) | .25 | .25 |
| **415** A67 30fr Bitam ('80) | .25 | .25 |
| **416** A67 40fr Okondja | .80 | .25 |
| **417** A67 60fr Mimongo | 1.60 | .40 |
| *Nos. 409-417 (9)* | 4.15 | 2.40 |

Issued: Nos. 409, 416-417, 8/17; Nos. 410-411, 413, 3/21/79; Nos. 412, 414, 415, 8/13/80.

A119

**1978, Oct. 24 Engr. *Perf. 13***

| | | |
|---|---|---|
| **419** A119 80fr multi | 1.10 | .65 |

UNESCO campaign to save the Acropolis.

Penicillin Formula, — A120

**1978, Nov. 21 Engr. *Perf. 13***

| | | |
|---|---|---|
| **420** A120 90fr multi | 3.00 | 1.10 |

Alexander Fleming's discovery of antibiotics, 50th anniversary.

The Visitation — A121

80fr, Massacre of the Innocents. Woodcarvings from St. Michael's Church, Libreville.

**1978, Dec. 15 Photo.**

| | | |
|---|---|---|
| **421** A121 60fr gold & multi | .90 | .40 |
| **422** A121 80fr gold & multi | 1.10 | .50 |

Christmas 1978. See Nos. 437-438.

Train and Map A122

**1978, Dec. 27 Litho. *Perf. 12½***

| | | |
|---|---|---|
| **423** A122 60fr multi | 1.50 | .60 |

Inauguration of Trans-Gabon Railroad, Libreville to Njolé.

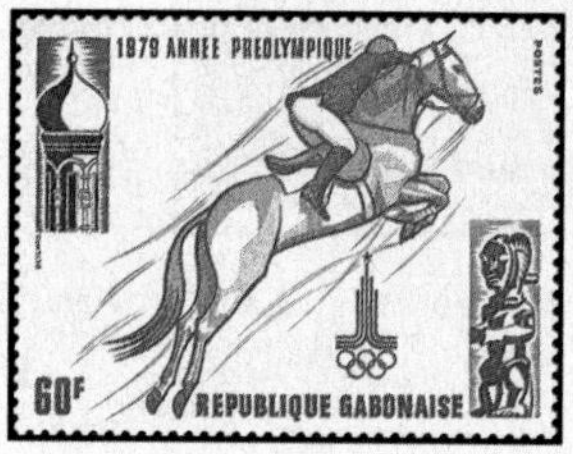


A123

Pre-Olympic Year (Kremlin Towers, Olympic Emblem, Ancestral Figure and): 80fr, Long jump, vert. 100fr, Yachts.

**1979, May 15 Engr. *Perf. 13***

| | | |
|---|---|---|
| **424** A123 60fr multi | .60 | .30 |
| **425** A123 80fr multi | .75 | .40 |
| **426** A123 100fr multi | .95 | .55 |
| *a.* Miniature sheet of 3, #424-426 | 3.75 | 3.75 |
| *Nos. 424-426 (3)* | 2.30 | 1.25 |

Rowland Hill, Messenger and Gabon No. O9 — A124

Allamanda Schottii A125

Designs: 80fr, Bakota mask and tulip tree flowers, vert. 150fr, Pigeon, UPU emblem, truck and canoe. No. 430b, Gloriosa superba. No. 430c, Phaeomeria magnifica, vert. No. 430d, Berlinia bracteosa, vert.

**1979, June 8 Photo. *Perf. 13***

| | | |
|---|---|---|
| **427** A124 50fr multi | 1.10 | 1.10 |
| **428** A124 80fr multi | 2.00 | 1.25 |
| **Engr.** | | |
| **429** A124 150fr multi | 3.25 | 2.00 |
| *Nos. 427-429 (3)* | 6.35 | 4.35 |

**Souvenir Sheet**

**Photo. *Perf. 14***

| | | |
|---|---|---|
| **430** Sheet of 4 | 11.00 | 11.00 |
| *a.* A125 100fr multicolored | 2.00 | |
| *b.* A125 100fr multicolored | 2.00 | |
| *c.* A125 100fr multicolored | 2.00 | |
| *d.* A125 100fr multicolored | 2.00 | |

Philexafrique II, Libreville, June 8-17. Nos. 427-429 each printed in sheets of 10 with 5 labels showing exhibition emblem. No. 427 also commemorates Sir Rowland Hill (1795-1879), originator of penny postage. No. 430 has label with exhibition emblem.

IYC Emblem, Globe, Child with Bird — A126

**1979, June 15 Engr. *Perf. 13***

| | | |
|---|---|---|
| **431** A126 100fr multi | 1.40 | .70 |

International Year of the Child.

"TELECOM 79" — A127

**1979, Sept. 18 Litho. *Perf. 13x12½***

| | | |
|---|---|---|
| **432** A127 80fr multi | 1.00 | .40 |

3rd World Telecommunications Exhibition, Geneva, Sept. 20-26.

Sugar Cane Harvest — A128

**1979, Oct. 9 Photo. *Perf. 12½x13***

| | | |
|---|---|---|
| **433** A128 25fr shown | .45 | .25 |
| **434** A128 30fr Yams | .65 | .25 |

Judo Throw — A129

**1979, Oct. 23 Engr. *Perf. 13***

| | | |
|---|---|---|
| **435** A129 40fr multi | 1.60 | .55 |

World Judo Championships, Paris, Dec.

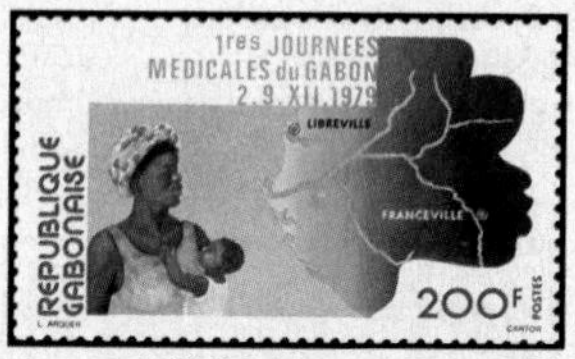


Mother and Child, Map of Congo River Basin — A130

**1979, Dec. 2 Litho. *Perf. 12***

| | | |
|---|---|---|
| **436** A130 200fr multi | 2.50 | .80 |

Medical Week, Dec. 2-9.

**Christmas Type of 1978**

Wood Carvings, St. Michael's Church, Libreville: 60fr, Flight into Egypt. 80fr, The Circumcision.

**1979, Dec. 12** **Photo.** ***Perf. 13***

**437** A121 60fr multi .90 .40
**438** A121 80fr multi 1.10 .40

Pres. Omar Bongo — A131

**1979-80** **Litho.** ***Perf. 12½***

**439** A131 60fr multi .90 .40
**440** A131 80fr multi 2.50 1.25

Bongo's 44th birthday (No. 439); re-election and inauguration (No. 440).
Issued: 60fr, 12/30/79; 80fr, 2/27/80.

OPEC, 20th Anniv. — A132

**1980, Mar. 27** **Litho.** ***Perf. 13½x13***

**441** A132 50fr multi 1.10 .35

Donguila Church — A133

**1980 Apr. 3** **Litho.** ***Perf. 12½***

**442** A133 60fr shown .65 .30
**443** A133 80fr Bizengobibere Church .85 .35

Easter 1980.

De Brazza (1852-1905), Map of Gabon with Franceville — A134

**1980, June 30** **Litho.** ***Perf. 12½***

**444** A134 165fr multi 2.50 1.10

Franceville Foundation centenary, founded by Savorgnan De Brazza.

20th Anniversary of Independence — A135

**1980, Aug. 17** **Photo.** ***Perf. 13***

**445** A135 60fr Leon Mba and Omar Bongo .90 .25

World Tourism Conference, Manila, Sept. 27 — A136

**1980, Sept. 10** **Engr.**

**446** A136 80fr multi .90 .35

20th Anniversary of OPEC — A137

**1980, Sept. 15** **Litho.** ***Perf. 12½***

**447** A137 90fr shown 1.00 .40
**448** A137 120fr Men Holding OPEC emblem, vert. 1.50 .60

Pseudochelidon Eurystomina — A138

**1980, Oct. 15** **Photo.** ***Perf. 14x14½***

**449** A138 50fr shown 3.00 .80
**450** A138 60fr Merops nubicus 3.50 1.10
**451** A138 80fr Pitta angolensis 4.75 1.60
**452** A138 150fr Scotopelia peli 7.50 2.75
*Nos. 449-452 (4)* 18.75 6.25

Statue of Bull, Bizangobibere Church — A139

**1980, Dec. 10** **Photo.** ***Perf. 14x14½***

**453** A139 60fr shown .75 .35
**454** A139 80fr Male statue 1.25 .55

Christmas 1980.

Heinrich von Stephan — A140

**1981, Jan. 7** **Engr.** ***Perf. 13***

**455** A140 90fr brn & dk brn .90 .35

Von Stephan (1831-97), UPU founder.

13th Anniversary of National Renovation Movement — A141

**1981, Mar. 12** **Litho.** ***Perf. 13x12½***

**456** A141 60fr multi .70 .25

Lion Statue, Bizangobibere — A142

**1981, Apr. 12** **Photo.** ***Perf. 14x14½***

**457** A142 75fr multi .90 .40
**458** A142 100fr multi 1.10 .55

Easter 1981.

Port Gentil Lions Club Banner — A143

**1981, May 1** **Litho.** ***Perf. 12½***

**459** A143 60fr shown .75 .25
**460** A143 75fr District 403 .85 .30
**461** A143 80fr Libreville Cocotiers 1.10 .35
**462** A143 100fr Libreville Hibiscus 1.40 .40
**463** A143 165fr Ekwata 2.10 .70
**464** A143 200fr Haut-Ogooue 2.40 .90
*Nos. 459-464 (6)* 8.60 2.90

Lions International, 23rd Congress of District 403, Libreville, May 1-3.

13th World Telecommunications Day — A144

**1981, May 17** **Photo.** ***Perf. 13***

**465** A144 125fr multi 1.60 .55

Unity, Work and Justice — A145

R.P. Klaine (Missionary), 70th Death Anniv. — A146

**1981-96?** **Photo.** ***Perf. 13***

**466** A145 5fr beige & blk .25 .25
**467** A145 10fr pale lil & blk .25 .25
**468** A145 15fr brt yel grn & blk .25 .25
**469** A145 20fr pink & blk .25 .25
**470** A145 25fr vio & blk .25 .25
**471** A145 40fr red org & blk .45 .25
**472** A145 50fr bluish grn & blk .55 .25
**473** A145 75fr bis brn & blk .70 .25
**473A** A145 90fr lt bl & blk ('83) .70 .25
**474** A145 100fr yel & blk 1.00 .40
**474A** A145 125fr grn & blk ('83) 1.10 .35
**474B** A145 150fr brt pink & blk ('86) 1.25 .40
**474C** A145 175fr grnish bl & blk ('96) .55 .55
*Nos. 466-474B (12)* 7.00 3.40

Issued: 5fr, 10fr, 15fr, 20fr, 25fr, 40fr, 50fr, 75fr, 100fr, 7/1. See Nos. 862-871, 959-960.

**1981, July 2** **Litho.**

90fr, Archbishop Walker, 110th birth anniv.

**475** A146 70fr multi .80 .30
**476** A146 90fr multi 1.25 .35

Map of Gabon and Scout Sign — A147

**1981, July 16** ***Perf. 12½***

**477** A147 75fr multi 1.00 .35

4th Pan-African Scouting Congress, Abidjan, Aug.

No. 477 Overprinted: DAKAR / 28e CONFERENCE / MONDIALE DU / SCOUTISME

**1981, July 23**

**478** A147 75fr multi 1.10 .45

28th World Scouting Conf., Dakar, Aug.

Intl. Year of the Disabled — A148

**1981, Aug. 6** **Engr.** ***Perf. 13***

**479** A148 100fr multi 1.10 .45

Hypolimnas Salmacis — A149

**1981, Sept. 10 Litho.** ***Perf. 14½x14***
**480** A149 75fr shown 2.00 .70
**481** A149 100fr Euphaedra themis 2.50 1.00
**482** A149 150fr Amauris niavius 3.50 1.50
**483** A149 250fr Cymothoe lucasi 6.00 2.25
*Nos. 480-483 (4)* 14.00 5.45

Paul as Harlequin, by Pablo Picasso (1881-1973) A150

**1981, Sept. 25** ***Perf. 14½x13½***
**484** A150 500fr multi 7.00 2.50

World Food Day — A151

**1981, Oct. 16 Engr.** ***Perf. 13***
**485** A151 350fr multi 4.00 1.60

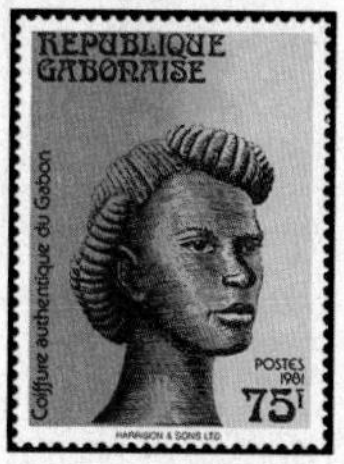


Traditional Hairstyle — A152

Designs: Various hairstyles.

**1981, Nov. 12 Litho.** ***Perf. 14½x15***
**486** A152 75fr multi .90 .55
**487** A152 100fr multi 1.00 .50
**488** A152 125fr multi 1.60 .80
**489** A152 200fr multi 2.50 1.10
*a.* Souvenir sheet of 4, #486-489 6.50 6.50
*Nos. 486-489 (4)* 6.00 2.95

See Nos. 609A-609B, 676.

Christmas 1981 A153

Designs: Children's drawings.

**1981, Dec. 10** ***Perf. 14½x14***
**490** A153 75fr Girls dancing .90 .35
**491** A153 100fr Dinner 1.25 .50

### Arms Type of 1969
***Perf. 12, 13 (#495-497)***

**1982-92** **Photo.**
**492** A67 75fr Moyen-Ogooue .70 .25
**493** A67 90fr Cocobeach .90 .25
**494** A67 100fr Woleu-N'tem 1.00 .25
**495** A67 100fr Lambarene .90 .30
**496** A67 100fr Port Gentil District .90 .35
**497** A67 100fr Medouneu .90 .35
**498** A67 125fr Mouila 1.25 .35
**499** A67 135fr N'Djole 1.40 .40
**500** A67 150fr N'Gounie 1.50 .40
**501** A67 160fr Leconi 1.40 .60
*Nos. 492-501 (10)* 10.85 3.50

Issued: Nos. 492, 494, 500, 1/13/82; Nos. 493, 498, 499, 8/7/84; Nos. 495, 501, 8/11/86; No. 496, 4/17/91; No. 497, 8/12/82.

A154

**1982, Feb. 16 Litho.** ***Perf. 13***
**502** A154 100fr multi 2.40 1.10

Visit of Pope John Paul II, Feb. 17-19.

A155

**1982, Mar. 31 Engr.** ***Perf. 13***
**503** A155 75fr black .80 .30

Alfred de Musset (1810-1857), writer.

Merchant Navy Ships A156

**1982, Apr. 7 Litho.** ***Perf. 14½x14***
**504** A156 75fr Timber carrier .75 .30
**505** A156 100fr Freighter 1.00 .40
**506** A156 200fr Oil tanker 2.00 .85
*Nos. 504-506 (3)* 3.75 1.55

See Nos. 588, 599.

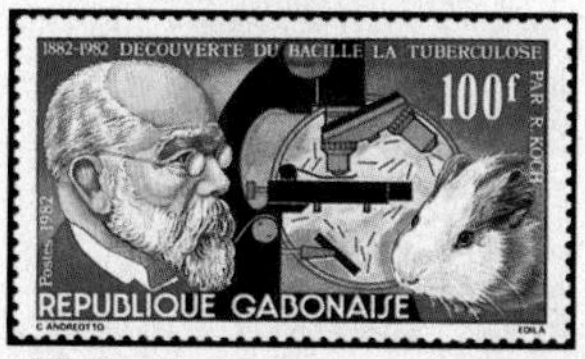


TB Bacillus Centenary — A157

**1982, Apr. 24 Litho.** ***Perf. 13***
**507** A157 100fr multi 1.60 .50

PHILEXFRANCE '82 Stamp Exhibition, Paris, June 11-21 — A158

**1982, Apr. 28** ***Perf. 12½***
**508** A158 100fr Rope bridge .85 .40
**509** A158 200fr Sculptured head 1.90 .55
*a.* Pair, #508-509 + label 4.00 2.75

14th World Telecommunications Day — A159

**1982, May 17** ***Perf. 13***
**510** A159 75fr multi .90 .40

1982 World Cup — A160

Designs: Various soccer players.

**1982, May 19** ***Perf. 14x14½***
**511** A160 100fr multi 1.00 .40
**512** A160 125fr multi 1.10 .45
**513** A160 200fr multi 2.10 .75
*a.* Souvenir sheet of 3, #511-513, perf. 14½ 5.00 5.00
*Nos. 511-513 (3)* 4.20 1.60

For overprints see Nos. 516-518.

2nd UN Conf. on Peaceful Uses of Outer Space, Vienna, Aug. 9-21 — A161

**1982, July 7 Engr.** ***Perf. 13***
**514** A161 250fr Satellites 2.75 1.25

White Carnations A162

Designs: Various carnations.

**1982, June 9 Photo.** ***Perf. 14½x14***
**515** Strip of 3 5.00 4.25
*a.* A162 75fr multi .90 .45
*b.* A162 100fr multi 1.10 .50
*c.* A162 175fr multi 2.25 1.00

### Nos. 511-513a Overprinted in Red with Semi-Finalists or Finalists

**1982, Aug. 19 Litho.** ***Perf. 14x14½***
**516** A160 100fr multi 1.00 .35
**517** A160 125fr multi 1.10 .45
**518** A160 200fr multi 2.10 .75
*a.* Souvenir sheet of 3 5.00 5.00
*Nos. 516-518 (3)* 4.20 1.55

Italy's victory in 1982 World Cup.

Phyllonotus Duplex A163

**1982, Sept. 22** ***Perf. 14½x14***
**519** A163 75fr shown 1.25 .50
**520** A163 100fr Chama crenulata 1.50 .65
**521** A163 125fr Cardium hians 2.25 1.25
*Nos. 519-521 (3)* 5.00 2.40

Okouyi Mask — A164

**1982, Oct. 13 Litho.** ***Perf. 14x14½***
**522** A164 75fr shown .65 .30
**523** A164 100fr Ondoumbo reliquary 1.10 .40
**524** A164 150fr Tsogho statuette 1.90 .55
**525** A164 250fr Fang bellows 2.75 .95
*Nos. 522-525 (4)* 6.40 2.20

Christmas 1982 — A165

**1983, Dec. 15 Litho.** ***Perf. 14x14½***
**526** A165 100fr St. Francis Xavier Church .90 .35

Trans-Gabon Railroad Inauguration — A166

**1983, Jan. 18** ***Perf. 12½***
**527** A166 75fr multi 2.00 .50

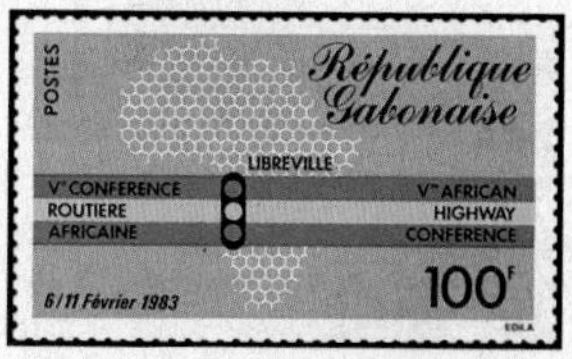


5th African Highway Conference, Libreville, Feb. 6-11 — A167

**1983, Feb. 2** ***Perf. 13***
**528** A167 100fr multi .90 .35

15th Anniv. of Natl. Renewal — A168

Provincial Symbols: a. Bakota mask, Ogowe Ivindo. b. Butterfly, Ogowe Lolo. c. Buffalo, Nyanga. d. Isogho hairdo, Ngounie. e. Tarpon, Ogowe Maritime. f. Manganese, Haut Ogowe. g. Crocodiles, Moyen Ogowe. h. Coffee plant. i. Epitorium trochiformis.

**1983, Mar. 12 Litho.** ***Perf. 13x13½***
**529** Strip of 9 + label 17.50 15.00
*a.* A168 75fr multi 1.00 .45
*b.* A168 90fr multi 1.25 .50
*c.* A168 90fr multi 1.25 .50
*d.* A168 100fr multi 1.40 .60
*e.* A168 125fr multi 1.60 .75
*f.* A168 125fr multi 1.60 .75
*g.* A168 125fr multi 1.60 .75
*h.* A168 135fr multi 1.90 .85
*i.* A168 135fr multi 1.90 .85

25th Anniv. of Intl. Maritime Org. — A169

**1983, Mar. 17** *Perf. 13*
**530** A169 125fr multi 1.40 .50

Pelican A170

**1983, Apr. 20 Litho.** *Perf. 15x14½*
**531** A170 90fr Water musk deer .90 .35
**532** A170 125fr shown 1.25 .45
**533** A170 225fr Elephant 3.25 .85
**534** A170 400fr Iguana 4.50 1.50
*a.* Souv. sheet of 4, #531-534 16.00 16.00
*Nos. 531-534 (4)* 9.90 3.15

25th Anniv. of UN Economic Commission for Africa A171

**1983, Apr. 29 Litho.** *Perf. 12½*
**535** A171 125fr multi 1.25 .50

15th World Telecommunications Day — A172

**1983, May 17 Litho.** *Perf. 13*
**536** A172 90fr multi 1.40 .55
**537** A172 90fr multi 1.40 .55
*a.* Pair, #536-537 4.00 4.00

Denomination of No. 536 in lower right, No. 537, upper left.

Nkoltang Earth Satellite Station — A173

**1983, July 2**
**538** A173 125fr multi 1.25 .50

10th anniv. of station; WCY.

Ivindo River Rapids — A174

**1983, Sept. 7 Engr.** *Perf. 13*
**539** A174 90fr shown .85 .35
**540** A174 125fr Ogooue River 1.40 .60
**541** A174 185fr Wonga Wongue Preserve 2.00 .80
**542** A174 350fr Coastal view 3.75 1.50
*Nos. 539-542 (4)* 8.00 3.25

Hand Drum, Mahongwe A175

**1983, Oct. 12 Litho.** *Perf. 14x14½*
**543** A175 90fr shown .90 .35
**544** A175 125fr Okoukoue dancer 1.40 .45
**545** A175 135fr Four-stringed fiddle 1.50 .60
**546** A175 260fr Ndoumou dancer 3.00 1.10
*Nos. 543-546 (4)* 6.80 2.50

Harmful Insects — A176

**1983, Nov. 9**
**547** A176 90fr Glossinidae 1.60 .80
**548** A176 125fr Belonogaster junceus 2.00 1.10
**549** A176 300fr Aedes aegypti 4.25 1.60
**550** A176 350fr Mylabris 5.25 2.10
*Nos. 547-550 (4)* 13.10 5.60

Christmas 1983 — A177

Wood Carvings, St. Michael's Church, Libreville.

***Perf. 14½x13½***
**1983, Dec. 14 Litho.**
**551** A177 90fr Adultress .80 .35
**552** A177 125fr Good Samaritan 1.40 .65

Boeing 737, No. 202 — A178

**1984, Jan. 12** *Perf. 13x12½*
**553** A178 125fr shown 1.50 .40
**554** A178 225fr Lufthansa jet, Germany No. C2 3.00 .70
*a.* Pair, #553-554 + label 5.50 4.75

19th World UPU Congress, Hamburg, June 19-26.

3rd Anniv. of Africa 1 Radio Transmitter — A179

**1984, Feb. 7 Litho.** *Perf. 12½*
**555** A179 125fr multi 1.25 .35

Local Flowers — A180

Various flowers.

**1984, Apr. 18 Litho.** *Perf. 14x15*
**556** A180 90fr multi 1.25 .45
**557** A180 125fr multi 1.40 .55
**558** A180 135fr multi 1.90 .65
**559** A180 350fr multi 4.00 1.60
*Nos. 556-559 (4)* 8.55 3.25

Fruit Trees A181

**1984, Mar. 1 Litho.** *Perf. 14½x14*
**560** A181 90fr Coconut 1.15 .45
**561** A181 100fr Papaya 1.15 .55
**562** A181 125fr Mango 1.60 .65
**563** A181 250fr Banana 3.00 .85
*Nos. 560-563 (4)* 6.90 2.50

World Telecommunications Day — A182

**1984, May 17** *Perf. 13x13½*
**564** A182 125fr multi 1.25 .45

Black Jazz Musicians A183

**1984, July 5** *Perf. 12½*
**565** A183 90fr Lionel Hampton 1.75 .70
**566** A183 125fr Charlie Parker 2.40 .70
**567** A183 260fr Erroll Garner 3.75 1.75
*Nos. 565-567 (3)* 7.90 3.15

View of Medouneu — A184

**1984, Sept. 1 Litho.** *Perf. 13*
**568** A184 90fr shown .95 .40
**569** A184 125fr Canoes, Ogooue River 1.50 .55
**570** A184 165fr Railroad 2.50 1.25
*Nos. 568-570 (3)* 4.95 2.20

15th World UPU Day — A185

**1984, Oct. 9 Litho.** *Perf. 13½*
**571** A185 125fr UPU emblem, globe, mail 1.40 .50

40th Anniv., International Civil Aviation Organization — A186

**1984, Dec. 1 Litho.** *Perf. 13½*
**572** A186 125fr Icarus 1.40 .50

Masks — A186a

**1984, Oct. 30 Litho.** *Perf. 14x15*
**572A** A186a 90fr Kouele — —
**572B** A186a 125fr Eventail Pounou — —
**572C** A186a 150fr Reliquaire Mahongoue — —
**572D** A186a 250fr Kota du Sud — —

Christmas — A187

**1984, Dec. 14 Litho.** *Perf. 12½*
**573** A187 90fr St. Michael's Church Libreville .90 .45
**574** A187 125fr St. Michael's, diff. 1.40 .65
*a.* Pair, #573-574 3.00 2.50

World Leprosy Day — A188

**1985, Jan. 27 Litho.** *Perf. 12½*
**575** A188 125fr Hospital, Libreville 1.50 .55

International Youth Year — A189

**1985, Feb. 6 Litho.** ***Perf. 13x12½***

**576** A189 125fr Silhouttes, wreath 1.40 .50

Birds A190

**1984, Nov. 16 Litho.** ***Perf. 15x14***

| | | | |
|---|---|---|---|
| **577** A190 | 90fr Crowned crane | 1.25 | .75 |
| **578** A190 | 125fr Hummingbird | 2.00 | 1.00 |
| **579** A190 | 150fr Toucan | 2.50 | 1.25 |
| | *Nos. 577-579 (3)* | 5.75 | 3.00 |

Silhouettes, Emblem — A191

**1985, Mar. 20 Wmk. 385** ***Perf. 12½***

**580** A191 125fr brt ultra, red & bl 1.40 .50

Cultural and Technical Cooperation Agency, 15th anniv.

Wildlife A192

**1985, Apr. 17 Unwmk.** ***Perf. 15x14***

| | | | |
|---|---|---|---|
| **581** A192 | 90fr Aulacode | 1.75 | .60 |
| **582** A192 | 100fr Porcupine | 1.75 | .60 |
| **583** A192 | 125fr Giant pangolin | 2.25 | 1.25 |
| **584** A192 | 350fr Antelope | 5.75 | 2.25 |
| *a.* | Souvenir sheet of 4, #581-584 | 13.00 | 13.00 |
| | *Nos. 581-584 (4)* | 11.50 | 4.70 |

Georges Damas Aleka, Composer A193

**1985, Apr. 30** ***Perf. 13***

**585** A193 90fr Portrait, La Concorde score 1.10 .35

A194

**1985, May 17** ***Perf. 13½***

**586** A194 125fr multi 1.40 .50

World Telecommunications Day. ITU, 120th anniv.

A195

**1985, June 9**

**587** A195 90fr Emblem 1.10 .60

J.O.C., 30th anniv.

**Merchant Navy Ships Type of 1982**

**1985, July 1** ***Perf. 15x14***

**588** A156 185fr Freighter Mpassa 2.10 .80

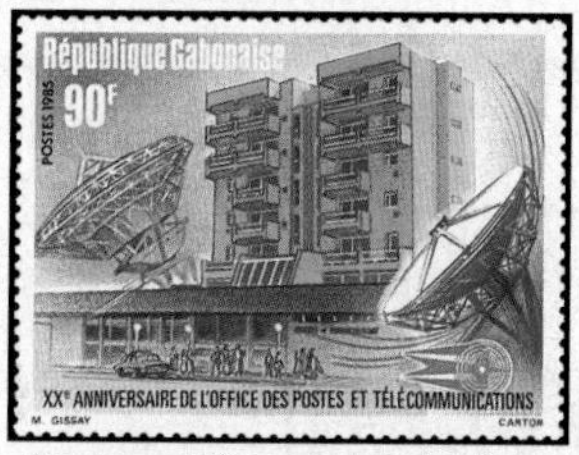


Posts and Telecommunications Administration, 20th Anniv. — A196

**1985, July 25** ***Perf. 13***

**589** A196 90fr Headquarters 1.10 .50

President Bongo — A197

**1985, Aug. 17** ***Perf. 14***

| | | | |
|---|---|---|---|
| **590** A197 | 250fr multi | 3.50 | 1.60 |
| **591** A197 | 500fr multi | 7.75 | 4.00 |
| *a.* | Pair, #590-591 + 3 labels | 14.00 | 14.00 |

***Imperf***

**Size: 120x90mm**

| | | | |
|---|---|---|---|
| **592** A197 | 1000fr View of Libreville | 14.00 | 14.00 |
| | *Nos. 590-592 (3)* | 25.25 | 19.60 |

Natl. Independence, 25th anniv.

No. 592 has non-denominated vignettes of Nos. 590-591.

Org. of Petroleum Exporting Countries, 25th Anniv. — A198

**1985, Sept. 25 Wmk. 385** ***Perf. 13½***

**593** A198 350fr multi 4.00 1.90

Intl. Center of the Bantu Civilizations — A199

***Perf. 15x14***

**1985, Nov. 16 Litho. Unwmk.**

**594** A199 185fr multi 2.00 .95

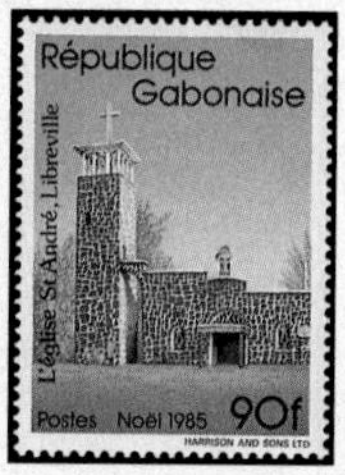


St. Andrew's Church, Libreville — A199a

Design: 125fr, Church interior, horiz.

***Perf. 14x15, 15x14***

**1985, Dec. 16 Litho.**

| | | | |
|---|---|---|---|
| **594A** A199a | 90fr multicolored | — | — |
| **594B** A199a | 125fr multicolored | | — |

Christmas.

UNESCO, 25th Anniv. — A200

**1986, Jan. 5 Litho.** ***Perf. 12½***

**595** A200 100fr multi 1.10 .45

A201

**1986, May 1 Litho.** ***Perf. 13½***

**596** A201 150fr multi 1.75 .60

Rotary Intl. District 915, 4th conf.

A202

**1986, June 16 Litho.** ***Perf. 12½***

**597** A202 150fr multi 1.75 .60

Natl. Week of Cartography, Libreville, June 16-20.

Coffee Flowers, Berries, Beans — A203

**1986, Aug. 27 Litho.** ***Perf. 12½***

**598** A203 125fr multi 1.50 .90

Organization of African and Madagascar Coffee Producers, 25th anniv.

**Merchant Navy Ships Type of 1982**

**1986, June 24 Litho.** ***Perf. 15x14***

**599** A156 250fr Merchantman L'Abanga 3.00 1.25

Natl. Postage Stamp, Cent. — A205

**1986, July 10** ***Perf. 13½x14½***

**600** A205 500fr Boats, No. 4 7.00 3.50

Flowering Plants — A206

**1986, July 23** ***Perf. 14½x15***

| | | | |
|---|---|---|---|
| **601** A206 | 100fr Allamanda neri-ifolia | 1.25 | .50 |
| **602** A206 | 150fr Musa cultivar | 1.90 | .80 |
| **603** A206 | 160fr Dissotis decumbens | 2.10 | .85 |
| **604** A206 | 350fr Campylospermum laeve | 4.75 | 2.10 |
| | *Nos. 601-604 (4)* | 10.00 | 4.25 |

Butterflies A207

**1986, Sept. 18 Litho.** ***Perf. 15x14***

| | | | |
|---|---|---|---|
| **605** A207 | 150fr Machaon | 2.25 | 1.00 |
| **606** A207 | 290fr Urania | 4.50 | 1.75 |

St. Pierre Church, Libreville A208

**1986, Dec. 23 Litho.** ***Perf. 15x14½***

**607** A208 500fr multi 5.00 2.10

Christmas.

Trans-Gabon Railway from Owendo to Franceville, Inauguration — A209

**1986, Dec. 30** ***Perf. 13***
**608** A209 90fr multi 1.40 .50

### Souvenir Sheet

**609** A209 250fr multi 4.50 4.50

### Traditional Hairstyles Type of 1981

**1986, Nov. 10** **Litho.** ***Perf. 14x15***
**609A** A152 100fr black, gray & yellow *150.00 7.50*
**609B** A152 150fr tan, black & red brown 5.00 1.50

Fish A210

**1987, Jan. 15** ***Perf. 15x14½***
**610** A210 90fr Adioryx bastatus 1.25 .60
**611** A210 125fr Scarus boefleri 1.75 .85
**612** A210 225fr Cephalacanthus volitans 2.25 1.25
**613** A210 350fr Dasyatis marmorata 3.25 1.90
*a.* Souv. sheet of 4, Nos. 610-613 11.50 11.50
*Nos. 610-613 (4)* 8.50 4.60

No. 613a issued Oct. 1987.

Raoul Follereau (1903-1977) A211

**1987, Jan. 23** ***Perf. 12½***
**614** A211 125fr multi 1.75 .85

World Leprosy Day.

Pres. Bongo Accepting the 1986 Dag Hammarskjold Peace Prize — A212

**1987, Mar. 31** **Litho.** ***Perf. 13***
**615** A212 125fr multi 1.25 .60

World Telecommunications Day — A213

**1987, May 17** **Litho.** ***Perf. 13½***
**616** A213 90fr multi 1.10 .40

Lions Club of Gabon, 30th Anniv. — A214

**1987, July 18** **Litho.** ***Perf. 12x12½***
**617** A214 90fr multi 1.10 .40

Pierre de Coubertin, Father of the Modern Olympics A215

**1987, Aug. 29**
**618** A215 200fr multi 2.00 .85

Lions Club Intl., 70th Anniv. — A216

**1987, Oct. 1**
**619** A216 165fr multi 1.75 .65

World Post Day — A217

**1987, Oct. 9** **Litho.** ***Perf. 13½***
**620** A217 125fr multi 1.25 .50

Seashells A218

**1987, Feb. 20** ***Perf. 15x14***
**621** A218 90fr Natica fanel 1.00 .30
**622** A218 125fr Natica fulminea cruentata 1.45 .45
*a.* Souv. sheet of 2, Nos. 621-622 7.00 7.00

Intl. Year of Shelter for the Homeless — A219

**1987, Oct. 5** ***Perf. 12½***
**623** A219 90fr multi 1.10 .40

Solidarity with the South West African Peoples' Organization (SWAPO) — A220

**1987, Sept. 15** **Litho.** ***Perf. 14½x15***
**624** A220 225fr Pres. Bongo, SWAPO leader 2.10 .95

St. Anna of Odimba Mission — A221

**1987, Nov. 2** ***Perf. 13½***
**625** A221 90fr multi 1.00 .30

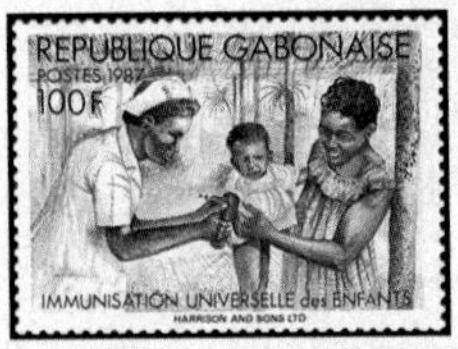


Universal Child Immunization — A222

**1987, Nov. 16** ***Perf. 15x14½***
**626** A222 100fr multi 1.25 .40

20th Anniv. of the Presidency of Omar Bongo A223

**1987, Dec. 2** ***Perf. 14½x13½***
**627** A223 1000fr multi 10.00 5.50

Christmas A224

**1987, Dec. 15** ***Perf. 15x14½***
**628** A224 90fr St. Therese Church, Oyem 1.00 .30

1988 Winter Olympics, Calgary — A225

**1987, Dec. 30** ***Perf. 13½x14½***
**629** A225 125fr multi 1.25 .50

Medicinal Plants — A226

**1988, Jan. 26** **Litho.** ***Perf. 14x15***
**630** A226 90fr Cassia occidentalis 1.10 .55
**631** A226 125fr Tabernanthe iboga 1.60 .55
**632** A226 225fr Cassia alata 2.75 1.10
**633** A226 350fr Anthocleista schweinfurthii 5.50 2.75
*a.* Miniature sheet of 4, #630-633 12.00 12.00
*Nos. 630-633 (4)* 10.95 4.95

World Wildlife Fund — A227

African forest elephant, *Loxodonta africana cyclotis.*

**1988, Feb. 29** **Litho.** ***Perf. 13½***
**634** A227 25fr multi 2.25 .75
**635** A227 40fr multi, diff. 3.00 1.50
**636** A227 50fr multi, diff. 5.00 1.75
**637** A227 100fr multi, diff. 8.25 3.25
*Nos. 634-637 (4)* 18.50 7.25

Traditional Musical Instruments — A228

**1988, Feb. 17** ***Perf. 14***
**638** A228 90fr Obamba hochet 1.10 .70
**639** A228 100fr Fang sanza, vert. 1.20 .70
**640** A228 125fr Mitsogho harp, vert. 1.45 .90
**641** A228 165fr Fang xylophone 2.25 1.00
*a.* Souv. sheet of 4, Nos. 638-641 7.00 7.00
*Nos. 638-641 (4)* 6.00 3.30

World Cup Rugby — A229

***Perf. 13½x14½***

**1987, June 10** **Litho.**

**642** A229 350fr multi 4.25 1.90

Delta Post Office Inauguration — A230

**1988, Mar. 9**

**643** A230 90fr multi 1.00 .30

World Telecommunications Day — A231

**1988, May 17** ***Perf. 13½***

**644** A231 125fr multi 1.25 .45

Storming of the Bastille, July 14, 1789 — A232

**1988, May 30** **Litho.** ***Perf. 13***

**645** A232 125fr multi 1.60 .50

PHILEXFRANCE '89.

Intl. Fund for Agricultural Development (IFAD), 10th Anniv. — A233

**1988, June 20** ***Perf. 13½***

**646** A233 350fr multi 4.25 1.60

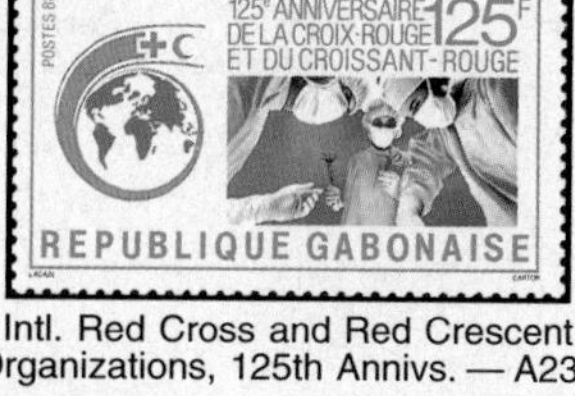


Intl. Red Cross and Red Crescent Organizations, 125th Annivs. — A234

**1988, July 15** **Litho.** ***Perf. 12½***

**647** A234 125fr multi 1.25 .45

1988 Summer Olympics, Seoul A235

**1988, Sept. 17** **Litho.** ***Perf. 15x14***

**648** A235 90fr Tennis 1.00 .35
**649** A235 100fr Swimming 1.00 .45
**650** A235 350fr Running 3.75 1.60
**651** A235 500fr Hurdles 5.75 2.00
*a.* Souv. sheet of 4, #648-651 13.00 13.00
*Nos. 648-651 (4)* 11.50 4.40

World Post Day A236

**1988, Oct. 9** ***Perf. 13½***

**652** A236 125fr blk, brt yel & brt blue 1.25 .45

Christmas A237

**1988, Dec. 20** **Litho.** ***Perf. 15x14***

**653** A237 200fr Medouneu Church 2.00 .70

Natica Fanel — A237a

**1988, July 1** **Litho.** ***Perf. 15x14***

**653A** A237a 90fr shown *18.00 5.00*
**653B** A237a 125fr Natica sp. *22.50 7.50*
*c.* Souv. sheet of 2, #653A-653B — —

A238

**1989, Feb. 21** ***Perf. 13½***

**654** A238 175fr multi 1.50 .60

Chaine des Rotisseurs in Gabon, 10th anniv.

A239

**1989, Mar. 6** **Litho.** ***Perf. 13½***

**655** A239 125fr multi 1.40 .55

Rabi Kounga oil field. See No. 707.

Traditional Games — A240

***Perf. 13½x14½***

**1989, Mar. 20** **Litho.**

**656** A240 90fr multicolored 1.10 .55

Birds — A241

**1989, Apr. 17** **Litho.** ***Perf. 14x15***

**657** A241 100fr White-tufted bittern 1.00 .35
**658** A241 175fr Gabon gray parakeet 1.50 .65
**659** A241 200fr Pygmy hornbill 1.90 .70
**660** A241 500fr Pope's martin 4.75 2.10
*a.* Souv. sheet of 4, Nos. 657-660 11.00 11.00
*Nos. 657-660 (4)* 9.15 3.80

See Nos. 750-753.

A242

**1989, Apr. 27** ***Perf. 13***

**661** A242 125fr multi 1.25 .45

8th Convention of Lions Intl. District 403, Libreville, Apr. 27-29.

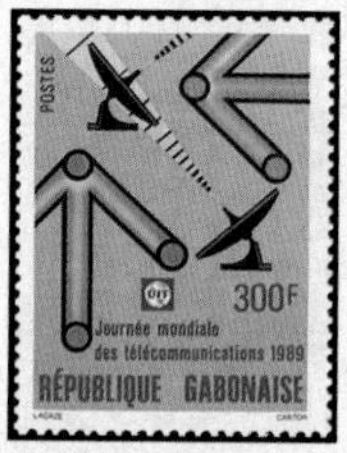


World Telecommunications Day — A243

**1989, May 17** **Wmk. 385** ***Perf. 13½***

**662** A243 300fr multi 3.25 1.10

PHILEXFRANCE '89 — A244

Symbols of the French revolution, 1789.

**Wmk. 385**

**1989, July 7** **Litho.** ***Perf. 13***

**663** A244 175fr multi 2.10 .80

French Revolution, Bicent. — A245

**1989, July 14** **Wmk. 385**

**664** A245 500fr multi 6.50 3.25

Fruit — A246

***Perf. 14½x15***

**1989, May 30** **Litho.** **Unwmk.**

**665** A246 90fr Coconuts 1.00 .45
**666** A246 125fr Cabosse 1.50 .50
**667** A246 175fr Pineapple 2.25 .80
**668** A246 250fr Breadfruit 2.75 1.25
*a.* Souv. sheet of 4, #665-668 8.50 8.50
*Nos. 665-668 (4)* 7.50 3.00

AIMF, 10th Anniv. — A247

**1989, July 27** **Litho.** ***Perf. 13***

**669** A247 100fr multi 1.25 .50

African Development Bank, 25th Anniv. — A248

**1989, Aug. 2** **Litho.** ***Perf. 13***

**670** A248 100fr multi 1.00 .40

*Apples and Oranges,* by Cezanne (1839-1906) — A249

***Perf. 13½x14½***

**1989, June 22** **Litho.**

**671** A249 500fr multicolored 6.00 3.25

1990 World Cup Soccer Championships, Italy — A250

Various athletes.

*Perf. 15x14½*

**1989, Aug. 23 Litho. Unwmk.**

**672** A250 100fr shown .95 .35
**673** A250 175fr multi, diff. 1.75 .65
**674** A250 300fr multi, diff. 3.00 1.25
**675** A250 500fr multi, diff. 4.75 1.90
*a.* Souv. sheet of 4, #672-675 11.00 11.00
*Nos. 672-675 (4)* 10.45 4.15

**Traditional Hairstyles Type of 1981**

**1989, Sept. 16** *Perf. 14½x15*

**676** A152 175fr gray, black & vio 2.00 .85

Post Day — A252

**Granite Paper**

**1989, Sept. 10 Litho.** *Perf. 12*

**677** A252 175fr multicolored 1.75 .80

Postal Service, 125th Anniv. (in 1987) — A255

*Perf. 13½x14½*

**1989 Litho. Unwmk.**

**681** A255 90fr multicolored 11.00 2.75

Dated 1988.

St. Louis Church, Port Gentil A256

**1989, Dec. 15 Litho.** *Perf. 15x14*

**682** A256 100fr multicolored 1.00 .40

Christmas. See Nos. 725-726, 757.

L'Ogooue', N'Gomo

**1989, Nov. 18 Litho.** *Perf. 15x14*

**682A** A256a 100fr multicolored — —

Libreville Coat of Arms — A257

**Wmk. 385**

**1990, Mar. 12 Litho.** *Perf. 13½*

**683** A257 100fr multicolored 1.10 .55

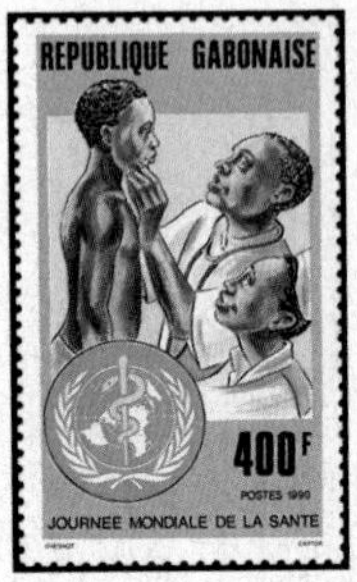


World Health Day — A258

**Unwmk.**

**1990, Apr. 7 Litho.** *Perf. 13*

**684** A258 400fr multicolored 4.50 2.10

Souvenir Sheet

Prehistoric Tools A259

**1990, Feb. 14 Litho.** *Perf. 15x14*

**685** Sheet of 4 30.00 30.00
*a.* A259 100fr Hand axe 1.25 .60
*b.* A259 175fr Knife blade 2.10 1.40
*c.* A259 300fr Arrowhead 3.75 1.50
*d.* A259 400fr Double bladed hand axe 6.25 4.50

See Nos. 727-730.

Fauna — A260

Designs: No. 686, 100fr, Cercopitheque. No. 686A, 175fr, Potamochoerus porcus, horiz. No. 686B, 200fr, Antilope du Gabon, horiz. No. 686C, 500fr, Papio mandrillus sphinx.

**1990, Apr. 13** *Perf. 14*

**686-686C** A260 Set of 4 — —
*686Cd* Souvenir sheet of 4, #686-686C, + label 15.00 15.00

First Postage Stamps, 150th Anniv. — A261

**1991, Jan. 9** *Perf. 13½x14½*

**687** A261 500fr multicolored 7.00 3.50

Independence, 30th Anniv. — A263

**1990, Aug. 17 Litho.** *Perf. 13*

**693** A263 100fr multicolored 1.10 .50

Mushrooms — A263a

Various mushrooms.

**1990, Sept. 12 Litho.** *Perf. 15x14*

**693A** A263a 100fr multicolored *6.00 1.10*
**693B** A263a 175fr multicolored *12.00 2.25*
**693C** A263a 300fr multicolored *17.50 4.25*
**693D** A263a 500fr multicolored *24.50 6.50*
*Nos. 693A-693D (4) 60.00 14.10*

Organization of Petroleum Exporting Countries (OPEC), 30th anniv. — A264

**1990, Sept. 19 Litho.** *Perf. 13*

**694** A264 200fr multicolored 2.00 1.00

1990 World Cup Soccer Championships, Italy — A264a

**1990, June 8 Litho.** *Perf. 15x14*

**694A** A264a 100fr Goalie making save *1.00 .50*
**694B** A264a 175fr Four players, ball *1.75 .80*
**694C** A264a 300fr Goalie reaching for ball — —
**694D** A264a 500fr Player celebrating *4.75 2.25*
*e.* Souvenir sheet, #694A-694D — —

A265

**1990, Oct. 9** *Perf. 13½*

**695** A265 175fr blue, yel & blk 2.00 1.00

World Post Day.

Traditional Bwiti Dancer — A265a

**1990, Apr. 25 Litho.** *Perf. 15x14*

**695A** A265a 100fr Ndjembe dancers —
**695B** A265a 175fr shown —

Flowers A266

**1991, Jan. 9 Litho.** *Perf. 15x14*

**696** A266 100fr Frangipanier 1.25 .60
**697** A266 175fr Boule de feu 2.10 1.00
**698** A266 200fr Flamboyant 2.40 1.10
**699** A266 300fr Rose de porcelaine 3.75 1.75
*a.* Souvenir sheet of 4, #696-699 10.00 10.00
*Nos. 696-699 (4)* 9.50 4.45

Petroglyphs — A267

**1991, Feb. 26 Litho.** *Perf. 15x14*

**700** A267 100fr Lizard figure 1.25 .60
**701** A267 175fr Triangular figure 2.00 1.25
**702** A267 300fr Incused lines 3.50 1.50
**703** A267 500fr Concentric circles, circles in lines 5.75 3.00
*a.* Souvenir sheet of 4, #700-703 75.00 75.00
*Nos. 700-703 (4)* 12.50 6.35

Rubber Trees — A268

**1991, Mar. 20 Litho.** *Perf. 14x15*

**705** A268 100fr multicolored 1.00 .45

World Telecommunications Day — A269

**1991, May 17 Litho.** *Perf. 13½*

**706** A269 175fr multicolored 1.90 .95

**Rabi Kounga Oil Field Type of 1989**

**1991 Litho.** *Perf. 13½*

**707** A239 175fr multicolored *150.00*

Ngounie Women Washing Clothes
A271

**1991, July 17 Litho. *Perf. 13½***
**708** A271 100fr multicolored 1.00 .45

Craftsmen
A272

**1991, June 19 *Perf. 14x15***
**709** A272 100fr Basket maker 1.10 .55
**710** A272 175fr Wood carver 1.90 .95
**711** A272 200fr Weaver 2.25 1.10
**712** A272 500fr Thatch maker 5.75 2.75
*a.* Souvenir sheet of 4, #709-712 — —
*Nos. 709-712 (4)* 11.00 5.35

A273

Gabonese Medals: 100fr, Equatorial Knight's Star. 175fr, Equatorial Officer's Star. 200fr, Equatorial Commander's Star.

**1991, Aug. 18 Litho. *Perf. 14x15***
**Gray Background**
**713** A273 100fr multicolored 1.00 .50
**714** A273 175fr multicolored 1.75 .90
**715** A273 200fr multicolored 2.00 1.00
*Nos. 713-715 (3)* 4.75 2.40

See Nos. 735-737.

Fishing in Gabon
A274

**1991, Sept. 18 *Perf. 15x14***
**716** A274 100fr Bow-net fishing 1.25 .55
**717** A274 175fr Trammel fishing 1.60 .95
**718** A274 200fr Net fishing 2.25 1.10
**719** A274 300fr Seine fishing 3.25 1.75
*a.* Souvenir sheet of 4, #716-719 9.50 9.50
*Nos. 716-719 (4)* 8.35 4.35

World Post Day — A275

**1991, Oct. 9 *Perf. 13½***
**720** A275 175fr blue & multi 2.00 .95

See Nos. 749, 786.

Termite Mounds — A276

**1991, Nov. 6 *Perf. 14x15***
**721** A276 100fr Phallic 1.50 .60
**722** A276 175fr Cathedral 2.50 1.00
**723** A276 200fr Mushroom 3.00 1.10
**724** A276 300fr Arboreal 4.00 1.75
*Nos. 721-724 (4)* 11.00 4.45

**Church Type of 1989**

**1991, Dec. 18 Litho. *Perf. 15x14***
**725** A256 100fr Church of Makokou 1.00 .40
**726** A256 100fr Church of Dibwangui 1.00 .40

Christmas. No. 725 inscribed 1990.

**Prehistoric Tools Type of 1990**

Pottery: 100fr, Neolithic pot. 175fr, Bottle, 8th cent. 200fr, Vase, 8th cent. 300fr, Vase, 8th cent, diff.

**1992, Jan. 9 Litho. *Perf. 14x15***
**727** A259 100fr multi, vert. 1.10 .40
**728** A259 175fr multi, vert. 1.90 .75
**729** A259 200fr multi, vert. 2.50 .85
**730** A259 300fr multi, vert. 3.00 1.25
*a.* Sheet of 4, #727-730 9.50 9.50
*Nos. 727-730 (4)* 8.50 3.25

Occupations
A277

**1992, Feb. 5**
**731** A277 100fr Basket maker 1.10 .55
**732** A277 175fr Blacksmith 1.90 .95
**733** A277 200fr Boat builder 2.10 1.10
**734** A277 300fr Hairdresser 3.25 1.75
*a.* Souvenir sheet of 4, #731-734 9.50 9.50
*Nos. 731-734 (4)* 8.35 4.35

No. 734a issued Feb. 9.

**Gabonese Medals Type of 1991**

Designs: 100fr, Equatorial Grand Officer's Star. 175fr, Grand Cross of Dignity and Equatorial Star. 200fr, Order of Merit.

**1992, Mar. 18 Litho. *Perf. 14x15***
**Aquamarine Background**
**735** A273 100fr multicolored .95 .50
**736** A273 175fr multicolored 1.90 .90
**737** A273 200fr multicolored 2.25 1.00
*Nos. 735-737 (3)* 5.10 2.40

A278

**1992, Apr. 19 *Perf. 13***
**738** A278 500fr multicolored 6.00 3.00

Konrad Adenauer (1876-1967), German Statesman.

A279

**1992, May 17 *Perf. 13½***
**739** A279 175fr multicolored 2.00 .95

World Telecommunications Day.

Butterflies
A280

**1992, June 10 Litho. *Perf. 15x14***
**740** A280 100fr Graphium policenes 1.90 1.25
**741** A280 175fr Acraea egina 2.75 1.75

A281

**1992, July 25 *Perf. 14x15***
**742** A281 100fr Cycling 1.10 .55
**743** A281 175fr Boxing 2.00 1.00
**744** A281 200fr Pole vault 2.25 1.10
*Nos. 742-744 (3)* 5.35 2.65

1992 Summer Olympics, Barcelona.

A282

Tribal masks.

**1992, Sept. 16 Litho. *Perf. 14x15***
**745** A282 100fr Fang 1.00 .50
**746** A282 175fr Mpongwe 1.90 .95
**747** A282 200fr Kwele 2.10 1.00
**748** A282 300fr Pounou 3.25 1.60
*a.* Souvenir sheet of 4, #745-748 9.50 9.50
*Nos. 745-748 (4)* 8.25 4.05

**World Post Day Type of 1991 Inscribed 1992**

**1992, Oct. 9 Litho. *Perf. 13½***
**749** A275 175fr bl grn & multi 2.00 .95

**Bird Type of 1989**

**1992, Nov. 4 Litho. *Perf. 14x15***
**750** A241 100fr African owl 1.90 .90
**751** A241 175fr Coliou strie 3.00 1.50
**752** A241 200fr Vulture 3.75 2.10
**753** A241 300fr Giant kingfisher 6.75 2.75
*a.* Souvenir sheet of 4, #750-753 20.00 20.00
*Nos. 750-753 (4)* 15.40 7.25

Cattle
A283

Various scenes of cattle in pasture.

**1992, Dec. 10 *Perf. 15x14***
**754** A283 100fr multicolored 1.00 .50
**755** A283 175fr multicolored 1.75 .90
**756** A283 200fr multicolored 2.00 1.00
*Nos. 754-756 (3)* 4.75 2.40

**Church Type of 1989**

**1992, Dec. 16**
**757** A256 100fr Tchibanga Church 1.00 .40

Christmas.

Intl. Conference on Nutrition, Rome — A284

**1992, Dec. 20 *Perf. 13½***
**758** A284 100fr multicolored 1.00 .40

Shells
A285

**1993, Jan. 6 Litho. *Perf. 15x14***
**759** A285 100fr Pugilina .90 .40
**760** A285 175fr Conus pulcher 1.90 .70
**761** A285 200fr Fusinus 2.25 .80
**762** A285 300fr Cymatium 3.50 1.25
*a.* Souvenir sheet, #759-762 14.00 14.00
*Nos. 759-762 (4)* 8.55 3.15

World Leprosy Day
A286

**1993, Jan. 28 *Perf. 13½***
**763** A286 175fr multicolored 2.00 .95

Fernan-Vaz Mission
A287

**1993, Feb. 3 *Perf. 15x14***
**764** A287 175fr multicolored 2.50 1.25

Chappe's Semaphore Telegraph, Bicent. — A288

Designs: 100fr, Claude Chappe (1763-1805), engineer and inventor. 175fr, Chappe's signaling device and code. 200fr, Emile Baudot (1845-1903), devising telegraph code, early telegraph equipment. 300fr, Modern satellite, electronic chip and fiber optics.

**1993, Mar. 10 Litho. *Perf. 13½***
**765** A288 100fr multicolored 1.00 .50
**766** A288 175fr multicolored 1.75 .90
**767** A288 200fr multicolored 2.00 1.10
**768** A288 300fr multicolored 3.25 1.60
*a.* Souvenir sheet of 4, #765-768 9.50 9.50
*Nos. 765-768 (4)* 8.00 4.10

Albert Schweitzer's Arrival in Lambarene, 80th Anniv. — A289

**1993, Apr. 6 Litho. *Perf. 13***

**769** A289 500fr multicolored 6.00 2.75
*a.* Booklet pane of 1 6.50

**Booklet Stamps**

**Size: 26x37mm**

***Perf. 13½***

**770** A289 250fr Feeding chick-ens 3.50 1.40
*a.* Booklet pane of 4 20.00
**771** A289 250fr Holding babies 3.50 1.40
*a.* Booklet pane of 4 20.00
*Nos. 769-771 (3)* 13.00 5.55

Booklet containing one of each pane sold for 3000fr. Value $40.

Nicolaus Copernicus, Heliocentric Solar System A290

**1993, May 5 Litho. *Perf. 15x14***

**772** A290 175fr multicolored 1.60 .75

Polska '93.

A291

**1993, May 17 *Perf. 13½***

**773** A291 175fr multicolored 1.60 .75

World Telecommunications Day.

A292

Traditional Wine Making: 100fr, Still. 175fr, Extracting juice from palm roots. 200fr, Man in palm tree.

**1993, June 9 Litho. *Perf. 14***

**774** A292 100fr multicolored 1.00 .45
**775** A292 175fr multicolored 1.60 .80
**776** A292 200fr multicolored 1.90 .95
*a.* Souvenir sheet of 3, #774-776 6.00 6.00
*Nos. 774-776 (3)* 4.50 2.20

Crustaceans — A293

**1993, July 21 Litho. *Perf. 15x14***

**777** A293 100fr Spiny lobster .90 .60
**778** A293 175fr Violin crab 1.45 .95
**779** A293 200fr Crayfish 1.90 1.10
**780** A293 300fr Spider crab 2.75 1.60
*a.* Souvenir sheet of 4, #777-780 — —
*Nos. 777-780 (4)* 7.00 4.25

Paris '94 — A294

**1993, Aug. 10 Litho. *Perf. 13***

**781** A294 100fr multicolored 1.10 .50

Animal Traps A295

**1993, Sept. 15 Litho. *Perf. 15x14***

**782** A295 100fr Squirrel 1.10 .25
**783** A295 175fr Small game 1.75 .55
**784** A295 200fr Large game 1.90 .90
**785** A295 300fr Palm rat 3.25 1.40
*a.* Souvenir sheet of 4, #782-785 6.00 6.00
*Nos. 782-785 (4)* 8.00 3.10

**World Post Day Type of 1991 Inscribed 1993**

**1993, Oct. 9 *Perf. 13½***

**786** A275 175fr yellow & multi 1.60 .75

Making Bamboo Toys — A296

**1993, Oct. 20 *Perf. 11½***

**787** A296 100fr multicolored 1.10 .55

Tourism A297

**1993, Nov. 16**

**788** A297 100fr Leconi Canyon 1.00 .25
**789** A297 175fr La Lope Valley 1.60 .50

Christmas A298

**1993, Dec. 20 *Perf. 15x14***

**790** A298 100fr Catholic Mission, Mandji 1.10 .55

Provincial Map — A299

**1993-94 Litho. *Perf. 14½***

**791** A299 5fr yellow & multi ('94) .25 .25
**792** A299 10fr gray & multi ('93) .25 .25
*a.* Dated 1994 — —
**793** A299 25fr pink & multi ('93) .25 .25
*a.* Dated 1994 — —
**794** A299 50fr grn & multi ('93) — —
**795** A299 75fr lilac & multi ('94) .40 .25
**796** A299 100fr brownish pink & multi ('94) .70 .30
**797** A299 175fr multi ('94) 1.00 .45

Issued: 10fr, 25fr, 50fr, 3/25; 5fr, 75fr, 100fr, 175fr, 1/28/94.
Nos. 792 and 793 are dated 1993.

Vision of Gabon's Future — A300

**1994, Oct. 5 Litho. *Perf. 14½***

**798** A300 500fr multicolored *3.00 1.50*

1994 World Cup Soccer Championships, US — A301

Designs: a, 100fr, Hands on soccer ball. b, 175fr, Two players, ball in air. c, 200fr, Legs of players. d, 300fr, Player, ball.

**1994, Apr. 5 *Perf. 15x14***

**799** A301 Sheet of 4, #a.-d. *30.00 15.00*

UN, 50th Anniv. — A301a

**1995, July 5 Litho. *Perf. 11¾x11½***

**799E** A301a 500fr multi 2.00 2.00

Prehistoric Wildlife — A302

No. 800: a, Sordes. b, Diplodocus (d-e, g-h). c, Eudimorphodon (b). d, Dimetrodon (a). e, Anuroenathus. f, Deinonychus, pachycephalosaurus (e). g, Triceratops (j). h, Hadrosaur (i, k-l). i, Genus Meganeura. j, Longisquama. k, Oviraptor. l, Monoclonius.

No. 801: a, Pistosaurus (d-e, h). b, Pteranodon (c). c, Coelophysis. d, Xenacanthus (g). e, Ischyodus (f, h-i). f, Placochelys. g, Dunkleosteus (j). h, Cymbospondylus (i). i, Enchodus. j, Paracybeloides (k). k, Nautiliod (h). l, Palaeospondylus.

No. 802: a, Tyrannosaurus rex (d). b, Apatosaurus (a, d-e). c, Dimorphodon. d, Stegasaurus (a, e). e, Archaeopteryx. f, Protoceratops. g, Ichthyosaur. h, Phobosuchus, deltoptychius. i, Parasaurolophus (f). j, Scapanorhynchus (g). k, Spathobathis, plesiosaurus (j, l). l, Cladoselacho.

**1995, Sept. 4 Litho. *Perf. 14***

**800** A302 125fr Sheet of 12, #a.-l. 8.00 4.50
**801** A302 225fr Sheet of 12, #a.-l. 13.50 7.50
**802** A302 260fr Sheet of 12, #a.-l. 16.00 8.75
*Nos. 800-802 (3)* 37.50 20.75

Singapore '95 (No. 800).

Nobel Prize Fund Established, Cent. — A303

No. 803 — Nobel Prize recipients: a, Walter H. Brattain, physics, 1956. b, Carl F. Cori, medicine, 1947. c, Gerty T. Cori, medicine, 1947. d, Owen Chamberlain, physics, 1959. e, Christian Anfinsen, chemistry, 1972. f, George de Hevesy, chemistry, 1943. g, Kenichi Fukui, chemistry, 1981. h, Élie Wiesel, peace, 1986. i, Carl F. Braun, physics, 1909.

No. 804: a, Georg Wittig, chemistry, 1979. b, Charles Dawes, peace, 1925. c, Frederic Mistral, literature, 1904. d, Juan Jimenez, literature, 1956. e, Michael S. Brown, medicine, 1985. f, Guglielmo Marconi, physics, 1909. g, Werner Forssmann, medicine, 1956. h, Francis W. Aston, chemistry, 1922. i, Martin Ryle, physics, 1974.

No. 805: a, Leon Jouhaux, peace, 1951. b, Rudolf L. Mossbauer, physics, 1961. c, George Seferis, literature, 1963. d, James Chadwick, physics, 1935. e, Aung San Suu Kyi, peace, 1991. f, John H. Nothrop, chemistry, 1946. g, Eduard Buchner, chemistry, 1907. h, Hans A. Bethe, physics, 1967. i, Nils Dalen, physics, 1912.

No. 806, 1500fr, Hermann Hesse, literature, 1946. No. 807, 1500fr, Albert Schweitzer, peace, 1952. No. 808, 1500fr, Nelson Mandela, peace, 1993.

**1995, Oct. 18 Litho. *Perf. 14***

**803** A303 125fr Sheet of 9, #a.-i. 6.75 3.25
**804** A303 225fr Sheet of 9, #a.-i. 9.00 6.00
**805** A303 260fr Sheet of 9, #a.-i. 14.00 7.00
*Nos. 803-805 (3)* 29.75 16.25

**Souvenir Sheets**

**806-808** A303 Set of 3 27.00 27.00

Monseigneur Bessieux (1803-76), Evangelist A306

**1995, Dec. 25 Litho. *Perf. 13***

**811** A306 500fr multicolored 2.75 1.40

Louis Pasteur (1822-95), Microbiologist — A306a

***Perf. 14¼x14¾***

**1995, Dec. 12 Litho.**

**811A** A306a 500fr multi *17.50 17.50*

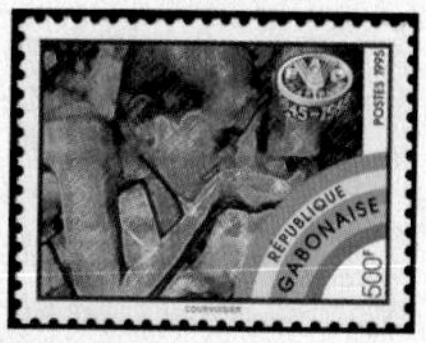


Food and Agriculture Organization, 50th Anniv. — A306b

**1995, Sept. 20** **Litho.** ***Perf. 11¾***
**811B** A306b 500fr multi *17.50 17.50*

Mbigou Rock Sculptor — A306c

***Perf. 14¼x14¾***
**1995, Nov. 15** **Litho.**
**811C** A306c 500fr multi *17.50 17.50*

Miniature Sheet of 8

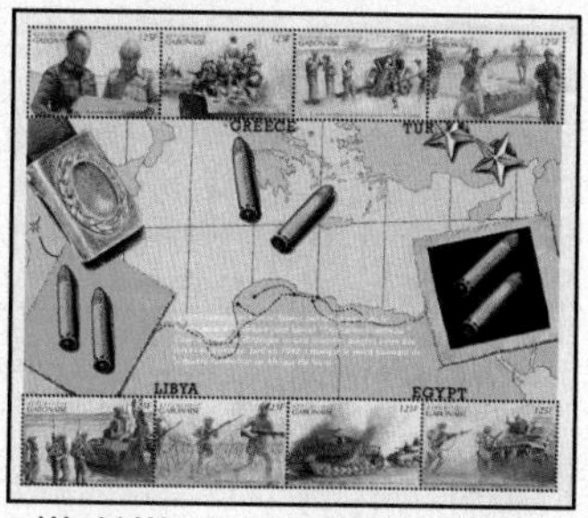


World War II, 50th Anniv. — A307

No. 812: a, German generals planning attack. b, Afrika Korps troops ride tanks into El Agheila. c, German artillary fires on British positions in Tobruk. d, British soldiers surrender. e, British soldiers break siege of Tobruk. f, Allies advancing though barbed wire, El Alamein. g, German tanks retreat to Tunis. h, German tank surrenders.

**1996, Jan. 29** ***Perf. 14***
**812** A307 125fr Sheet of 8, #a.-h. + label 6.50 2.75

World War II, 50th Anniv. A308

No. 813: a, Pres. Franklin D. Roosevelt. b, Pres. Harry S Truman. c, Gen. George Marshall.
1000fr, Flags of US, Great Britain, USSR.

**1996, Jan. 26** **Litho.** ***Perf. 14***
**813** A308 225fr Strip of 3, #a.-c. 4.50 4.50

**Souvenir Sheet**

**814** A308 1000fr multicolored 6.50 6.50

No. 813 was issued in sheets of 9 stamps.

Dogs — A309

No. 815: a, Dalmatian. b, Basset hound. c, Harrier. d, German Shepherd. e, Bernese bouvier. f, Pug. g, West highland white terrier. h, Akita.

**1996, May 13** **Litho.** ***Perf. 14***
**815** A309 125fr Sheet of 8, #a.-h. 6.00 6.00

China '96 Philatelic Exhibition.

St. Pius X Catholic Mission, 10th Anniv. A310

Mgr. Marcel Lefebvre, interior of mission.

**1996, Mar. 4** ***Perf. 13½***
**816** A310 100fr yellow & multi .75 .25
**817** A310 125fr blue & multi .95 .45

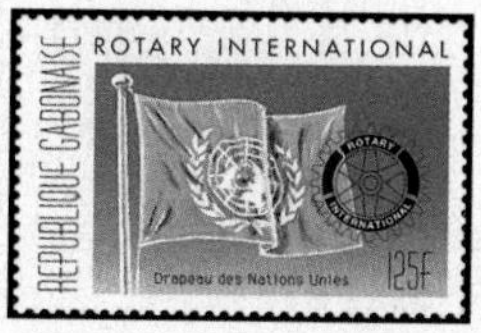


Rotary, Intl. A311

Rotary emblem and: 125fr, UN flag. 225fr, Natl. flag of Gabon. 260fr, Rotary, Intl. flag.
1500fr, Olympic flag.

**1996, July 3** **Litho.** ***Perf. 14***
**818-820** A311 Set of 3 4.00 3.00

**Souvenir Sheet**

**821** A311 1500fr multicolored 9.00 9.00

Boy Scouts — A312

Designs: 125fr, Scout sign. 225fr, Constructing a lean-to. 260fr, Camping.
1500fr, Lord Baden-Powell.

**1996, July 15**
**822-824** A312 Set of 3 4.00 3.25

**Souvenir Sheet**

**825** A312 1500fr multicolored 9.00 9.00

Cercopithecus Solatus — A313

**1996, Mar. 6** ***Perf. 13½x13***
**826** A313 500fr multicolored 3.25 1.75

Fight Against AIDS — A314

**1996, Apr. 3** ***Perf. 13½x13***
**827** A314 500fr multicolored 3.25 1.75

Shells — A315

Designs: 100fr, Fusinus caparti. 260fr, Hexaplex rosarium. 500fr, Conus pulcher, horiz.

**1996** ***Perf. 13½x13, 13x13½***
**828-830** A315 Set of 3 5.00 3.50

1996 Summer Olympic Games, Atlanta A316

**1996, May 8** ***Perf. 11½***
**831** A316 225fr Boxing 1.25 .75
**832** A316 500fr Relay race 2.50 1.60

Campaign Against Use of Illegal Drugs A317

**1996, Aug. 6** **Litho.** ***Perf. 11½***
**833** A317 500fr multicolored 2.75 1.25

Contemporary Paintings, by H. Moundounga A318

**1996, Sept. 10**
**834** A318 100fr Girl .65 .25
**835** A318 125fr Three faces .85 .40
**836** A318 225fr Eyes 1.50 .75
*a.* Souvenir sheet, #834-836 3.25 3.25
*Nos. 834-836 (3)* 3.00 1.40

Souvenir Sheet

Temple in Winter — A319

**1996, May 13** **Litho.** ***Perf. 14***
**837** A319 500fr multicolored 4.50 2.25

China '96 Philatelic Exhibition, No. 837 was not available until March 1997.

Environmental Protection — A320

Endangered species: 100fr, Galago alleni, vert. 125fr, Perodicticus potto. 225fr, Orycteropus afer. 260fr, Manis gigantea.

**1996, June 5** ***Perf. 13½***
**838-841** A320 Set of 4 5.00 3.25

Children's Paintings A321

Designs: 100fr, Woman's arms encircling world, vert. 125fr, People forming circle around animals. 225fr, Slaughtering of elephants, vert.

**1996, Dec. 25** **Litho.** ***Perf. 11½***
**842-844** A321 Set of 3 1.75 1.25

Dated 1996.

Traditional Houses A322

Designs: 100fr, Mud & stick cabin. 125fr, Pygmy hut. 225fr, Bark-sided cabins. 260fr, Wood-sided cabins.

**1996, Nov. 6**
**845-848** A322 Set of 4 4.50 2.75
*a.* Souvenir sheet, #845-848 5.00 5.00

A323

A324

**1996, Oct. 10**
**849** A323 500fr multicolored 2.00 1.25

Investiture of Pres. Nelson Mandela, 3rd anniv.

**1997, Apr. 9** **Litho.** ***Perf. 14***

UNICEF, 50th Anniv.: No. 850: a, Boy holding cup. b, Girl holding cup. c, Boy eating.
1500fr, Boy holding plate.

**850** A324 260fr Sheet of 3, #a.-c. 4.00 4.00

**Souvenir Sheet**

**851** A324 1500fr multicolored 8.50 8.50

UNESCO, 50th Anniv. A325

No. 852, 225fr: a, Kyoto, Japan. b, Puma, Los Katios Natl. Park, Colombia. c, Abu Simbel Monument, Egypt. d, Old Rauma, Finland. e, Rotunda, City of Vicenza, Italy. f, Homes, China. g, Port of Salvador, Brazil. h, Delos Ruins, Greece.

No. 853, 225fr: a, Fasil Ghebbi Monument, Gondar Region, Ethiopia. b, Victoria Falls, Zambia. c, Zambezi Plains, Chewore Safari Areas, Zimbabwe. d, Nature Reserve, Niger. e, Banc D'Arguin Natl. Park, Mauritania. f, Gorée Island, Senegal. g, Djémila Ruins, Algeria. h, Mosque, Medina of Fez, Morocco.

1000fr, Terracotta warriors, Mausoleum of first Qin Emperor, China.

**1997, Apr. 16**

**Sheets of 8, #a-h, + Label**

**852-853** A325 Set of 2 15.00 15.00

**Souvenir Sheet**

**854** A325 1000fr multicolored 7.50 7.50

City Arms — A326

**1997, Mar. 12** **Litho.** ***Perf. 11½x12***

**855** A326 100fr N'Dendé .65 .25
**856** A326 125fr Libreville .85 .35
**857** A326 225fr Mitzic 1.50 .80
*Nos. 855-857 (3)* 3.00 1.40

Return of Hong Kong to China — A327

Designs: 125fr, Skyline. 225fr, Skyline, diff. 260fr, Skyline at night, horiz. 500fr, Skyline at night, Deng Xiaoping (1904-97), horiz.

**1997, July 1** ***Perf. 14***

**858-861** A327 Set of 4 6.00 4.00

Nos. 858-859 were each issued in sheets of 4. Nos. 860-861 are 59x28mm and were issued in sheets of 3.

**Unity, Work and Justice Type of 1981**

**1994-95** **Litho.** ***Perf. 11¾***

**Granite Paper**

**862** A145 5fr green blue & black .25 .25
**863** A145 10fr orange & black .25 .25
**864** A145 25fr grey lilac & black .25 .25
**865** A145 50fr salmon & black .25 .25
**866** A145 75fr tan & blk .25 .25
**867** A145 100fr pink & black .25 .25
**868** A145 125fr yellow green & black .45 .35
**869** A145 175fr yellow & black .55 .40
**870** A145 225fr green & black .70 .55
**871** A145 260fr lt blue & black .80 .60
*Nos. 862-871 (10)* 4.00 3.40

Issued: 50fr, 125fr, 9/30/95; others, 9/20/94.

Paintings — A328

**1995, Oct. 10** **Litho.** ***Perf. 14***

**872** A328 100fr Woman *1.00* .45
**873** A328 125fr Stylized women *1.50* .65
**873A** A328 225fr Masked Face *2.00* *1.10*
*b.* Souvenir sheet of 3, #872-873A — —

Raponda Walker, 25th Death Anniv. — A329

**1995, June 7** ***Perf. 13½***

**874** A329 500fr multicolored *3.00* —

Masks — A330

**1995, Feb. 15**

**875** A330 100fr Bateke *2.50* —
**876** A330 125fr Bavili *2.50*
**877** A330 225fr Fang *2.50*
**878** A330 260fr Bandjabi *2.50*
*a.* Souvenir sheet of 4, #875-878 — —

Shells A331

**1995, Apr. 4**

**879** A331 100fr Cymbium glans —
**880** A331 125fr Muricidae murey —
**880A** A331 225fr Siliquaria — —
**881** A331 260fr Strombus latus —
*a.* Souvenir sheet of 4, #879-880A, 881 — —

Saint-Exupery French Cultural Center — A332

**1996, May 12** ***Perf. 13x13½***

**883** A332 100fr black & multi —
**884** A332 125fr blue & multi —
**885** A332 225fr red & multi —

Inter-Continental Hotel, 50th Anniv. — A333

**1996, Apr. 4** ***Perf. 13½***

**886** A333 125fr creme & blue
**886A** A333 225fr lt yel & blue *1.00* —

Early Post Offices — A333a

**1996, July 20** **Litho.** ***Perf. 12x11½***

**886B** A333a 100fr Port Gentil, 1917 *1.00* *.50*
**886C** A333a 125fr Cap-Lopez, 1888 *1.00* *.65*
**886D** A333a 225fr Libreville, 1862 *1.45* *1.10*

Flowers, Butterflies, Moths, Insects A334

Designs, vert: 125fr, Rubra tigridia pauonia, pieridae. 225fr, Acraeidae, strelitzia reginae. 260fr, Zautedeschia aethiopica, zonabris oculata. 500fr, Bee orchid, iron prominent moth caterpillar.

No. 891, 260fr: a, Liliaceae. b, Macrophylla, phoebis philea. c, Theaceae amugashita. d, Lilium american cultivars, vanessa atalanta. e, Hybrids, hippodamia convergens. f, Sibine stimulea, iridaceae.

No. 892, 260fr: a, Kalmialati. b, G. gandavensis, calopteryx maculata. c, Narcissus pseudonarcissus. d, Ipheton uniflorum, Tlemaris thysbe. e, Rudbackia hirta. f, Tritida grandiflora, danaus plexippus.

No. 893, 1500fr, Papilion zellicaon, geranium pelargonium, vert. No. 894, 1500fr, Anax jumus, gladstoniana, vert.

**1997, Aug. 11** **Litho.** ***Perf. 14***

**887-890** A334 Set of 4 7.25 5.00

**Sheets of 6, #a-f**

**891-892** A334 Set of 2 16.00 16.00

**Souvenir Sheets**

**893-894** A334 Set of 2 15.00 15.00

Protection of Indigenous Animals — A335

Designs: 100fr, Dendrohyrax arboreus. 125fr, Galago elegantulus. 225fr, Stephanoaetus coronatus.

**1997, June 5** ***Perf. 13½x13***

**895-897** A335 Set of 3 3.00 2.00
*897a* Souvenir sheet of 3, #895-897 1.75 1.75

Gabonese Art — A336

Designs: 100fr, Droits de Creatures, vert. 125fr, Ambassadeur, vert. 225fr, Hallucinations.

**1997, May 8** ***Perf. 13½x13, 13x13½***

**898-900** A336 Set of 3 3.00 3.00
*900a* Souvenir sheet of 1, #900 1.50 1.50

Air Gabon, 20th Anniv. A337

**1997, June 1** ***Perf. 13x13½***

**901** A337 125fr multicolored .90 .50
**902** A337 225fr multicolored 1.60 .80

First ACP Summit, Libreville — A338

**1997, Nov. 6** **Litho.** ***Perf. 13½x13***

**903** A338 225fr multicolored 1.40 .70

Lions Club in Gabon, 40th Anniv. — A339

**1997, Oct. 8** ***Perf. 13½x13***

**904** A339 225fr multicolored 1.40 .70

AIPLF, 30th Anniv. A340

**1997, Oct. 30** ***Perf. 12x11½***

**905** A340 260fr multicolored 1.40 .65

Paul Gondjout, 1st Pres. of the Natl. Assembly — A341

**1997, Nov. 11** ***Perf. 14x14½***

**906** A341 500fr multicolored 2.75 1.25

Heinrich von Stephan (1831-97) — A342

**1997, Nov. 17** ***Perf. 11½x12***

**907** A342 500fr multicolored 2.75 1.25

Princess Diana (1961-97) — A343

No. 908: a, 500fr. b, 300fr. c, 260fr. d, 225fr. e, f, 125fr.

3000fr, Diana in white dress.

**1998, Feb. 10** **Litho.** ***Perf. 13½***

**908** A343 Sheet of 6, #a.-f. 10.00 10.00

**Souvenir Sheet**

**909** A343 3000fr multicolored 15.00 15.00

District Arms — A344

Designs: 100fr, Akieni. 125fr, Pana. 225fr, Lebamba.

**1998, June 4** **Litho.** ***Perf. 13½x13***

**910-912** A344 Set of 3 3.00 1.50

Traditional Tools A345

Designs: 100fr, Yanghe. 125fr, Ikanga. 225fr, Ivedili.

**1997, Nov. 5** **Litho.** ***Perf. 14***

**913-915** A345 Set of 3 3.00 1.90

New Horizons Foundation A346

**1998, May 15** **Litho.** ***Perf. 13x13½***

**916** A346 225fr multicolored 1.40 .70

Protected Animals — A347

Designs: 100fr, Hippopotamus amphibius. 125fr, Sylvicapra grimmia. 225fr, Pelecanus rufescens.

**1998, Apr. 17** ***Perf. 13½x13***

**917** A347 100fr multicolored .65 .35
**918** A347 125fr multicolored .95 .65
**919** A347 225fr multicolored 1.25 .75
*a.* Souvenir sheet, #917-919 3.25 3.25

1998 World Cup Soccer Championships, France — A348

Various soccer plays, country flags in background: 100fr, 125fr, 225fr, 260fr.

**1998, July 10** **Litho.** ***Perf. 13½x13***

**920-923** A348 Set of 4 4.75 2.75
*923a* Sheet of 4, #920-923 5.00 5.00

ACCT, 26th Anniv. — A349

**1998, Oct. 10**

**924** A349 260fr multicolored 1.40 .65

Elimination of Land Mines — A350

**1998, May 15** **Litho.** ***Perf. 11½x12***

**925** A350 260fr multicolored 1.60 .80

Gandhi — A351

**1998, Oct. 9**

**926** A351 260fr multicolored 1.60 .80

Mother Teresa (1910-97) — A352

**1998, June 30**

**927** A352 500fr multicolored 2.75 1.40

Deng Xiaoping (1904-97) — A353

**1998, Sept. 14**

**928** A353 500fr multicolored 2.75 1.40

Intl. Year of the Ocean A354

**1999, Oct. 19** **Litho.** ***Perf. 11½***

**929** A354 125fr multicolored 2.50 .85

Dated 1998.

Wooden Tools — A355

**1999**

**930** A355 100fr Mortier .70 .55
**931** A355 125fr Pilon 1.00 .80

Dated 1998.

Universal Declaration of Human Rights A356

**1999, Aug. 10**

**932** A356 225fr multicolored 1.40 .80

Dated 1998.

Space Exploration — A357

Designs: No. 933, 225fr, Gemini 7. No. 934, 225fr, Skylab. No. 935, 225fr, Atlas Moon Explorer. No. 936, 225fr, Space Shuttle.

No. 937: a, Venera 4. b, TDRS. c, Sputnik II. d, Zond II. e, Untethered walk. f, Intelsat 6. g, Luna 16. h, Sputnik III. i, Vostok V. j, Lunar explorer. k, 2nd lunar landing. l, Conrad and Surveyor.

No. 938: a, Sputnik. b, Mariner 2. c, Apollo 11 Lunar Module. d, Gemini 7. e, Mir. f, Atlas Moon Explorer. g, Space Shuttle Orbit. h, Hubbell. i, Soyuz. j, Apollo 11 re-entry. k, Skylab. l, Venture Star.

No. 939: a, Lunar landing II. b, Gemini 7. c, Venture Star. d, Hubbell.

No. 940, 1500fr, Shuttle launch. No. 941, 1500fr, Untethered walk. No. 942, 1500fr, Apollo II. No. 943, 1500fr, Lunar landing module.

**1999, Apr. 30** **Litho.** ***Perf. 14***

**933-936** A357 Set of 4 3.75 2.00
**937** A357 100fr Sheet of 12, #a.-l. 6.00 6.00
**938** A357 125fr Sheet of 12, #a.-l. 8.50 8.50

**Sheet of 4**

**939** A357 225fr Sheet of 4, #a.-d. 4.00 4.00

**Souvenir Sheets**

**940-943** A357 Set of 4 35.00 35.00

Moon landing, 30th anniv.

Traditional Weapons — A358

Designs: 100fr, Sagaie. 125fr, Arbalète. 225fr, Couteau et jet.

**1999, Nov. 10** ***Perf. 13***

**944-946** A358 Set of 3 3.00 1.60

Folklore — A358a

Designs: 125fr, Mitsogho reliquary. 225fr, Bwèri Fang sculpture.

**1999, July 2** **Litho.** ***Perf. 13¼***

**946A** A358a 125fr multi —
**946B** A358a 225fr multi —

The editors suspect that additional stamps may have been issued in this set and would like to examine any examples.

Democracy A359

**1999, Dec. 12** **Litho.** ***Perf. 11¾***

**947** A359 100fr multicolored .75 .50

UPU, 125th Anniv. A360

Designs: 100fr, People, map. 225fr, Emblem, letters, vert. 260fr, Great Wall of China, vert.

**1999, Aug. 21**

**948** A360 100fr multicolored .60 .40
**949** A360 225fr multicolored 1.00 .75
**950** A360 260fr multicolored 1.50 1.00
*Nos. 948-950 (3)* 3.10 2.15

Manufacture of Aspirin, Cent. — A361

**1999, July 6**

**951** A361 225fr multicolored 1.40 .70

Mushrooms — A361a

Designs: 100fr, Amanite panthère. 125fr, Basidomycetes, horiz. 225fr, Basidomycetes, diff., horiz. 260fr, Amanite tue-mouches.

***Perf. 13¼x13, 13x13¼***

**1999, Apr. 30** **Litho.**

**951A-951D** A361a Set of 4 6.50 6.50
*951De* Souvenir sheet of 4, #951A-951D — —

PhilexFrance '99 — A362

**1999, July 2** **Litho.** ***Perf. 13***

**952** A362 225fr multi *3.00 1.40*

No. 952 has a holographic image. Soaking in water may affect hologram.

Elephants A363

**1999** ***Perf. 13x13¼***

**953** A363 100fr multi 1.50 .75

PhilexFrance '99 World Philatelic Exhibition, Paris.

Central African Economic and Monetary Community Days — A364

Map of Africa and: 125fr, Circle of member's flags. 225fr, Rows of member's flags.

**1999, Nov. 23 Litho.** ***Perf. 14½***
**954-955** A364 Set of 2 2.40 2.40

Pope John XXIII, St. Peter's Basilica A365

**1999, Dec. 12 Litho.** ***Perf. 11¾***
**956** A365 100fr multi .75 .75

Announcement of 2nd Vatican Council, 40th anniv., Christmas.

**Unity, Work and Justice Type of 1981**

**1999, Dec. 12 Litho.** ***Perf. 11¾***
**Granite Paper**
**959** A145 40fr lil & blk .25 .25
**960** A145 90fr olive grn & blk — —

Shells A365a

Designs: 100fr, Harpa doris. 125fr, Thais haemastoma. 225fr, Cassis tessellata.

**1999, June 25 Litho.** ***Perf. 13x13½***
**964-966** A365a Set of 3 4.00 4.00

Fish A365b

Designs: 100fr, Epinephelus marginatus, mugil cephalus. 125fr, Brycinus macrolepidotus. 225fr, Oreochromis schwebischi. 260fr, Pomadasys peroteti, caranx hippos, ethmalosa fimbriata.

**1999, Apr. 26**
**967-970** A365b Set of 4 5.50 5.50
*970a* Souvenir sheet of 4, #967-970 — —

Expo 2000, Hanover A366

***Perf. 11¾x11½***
**2000, Feb. 16 Litho.**
**971** A366 225fr multi 1.60 1.60

Protected Animals A367

Designs: 125fr, Haliaetus vocifer. 225fr, Panthera pardus. 260fr, Panthera leo.

**2000, June 5**
**972-974** A367 Set of 3 4.00 4.00
*974a* Souvenir sheet of 3, #972-974 — —

Events of the 20th Century A368

Designs: 100fr, Universal Declaration of Human Rights, vert. 125fr, World War II. 225fr, First man on the moon.

***Perf. 11½x11¾, 11¾x11½***
**2000, July 20**
**975-977** A368 Set of 3 3.00 3.00

Scientific Achievements of the 20th Century — A369

Designs: 100fr, Microprocessor, 1971. 125fr, Nuclear reactor, 1942. 225fr, Structure of DNA, 1953.

**2000, Nov. 28** ***Perf. 11¾x11½***
**978-980** A369 Set of 3 3.00 3.00

See Nos. 1040-1042.

Tourism A370

100fr, Pygmy village. 125fr, Lake region. 225fr, Poubara Waterfall. 260fr, Mt. Brazza.

**2000, Sept. 29** ***Perf. 13x13½***
**981-984** A370 Set of 4 4.75 4.75
*984a* Miniature sheet of 4, #981-984 — —

Y2K Bug — A371

**2000, Dec. 11** ***Perf. 11½x11¾***
**985** A371 225fr multi 1.40 1.40

Dr. Albert Schweitzer (1875-1965) A372

**2000, Jan. 14** ***Perf. 13¼x13***
**986** A372 260fr multi 1.60 1.60

A373

Trains — A374

Designs: No. 987, 100fr, Japanese Hikari trains. 125fr, Hungarian Bo-Bo electric locomotive. No. 989, 500fr, Pakistani electric locomotive. No. 990, 500fr, Belgian locomotive.

No. 991: a, 100fr, Korean Bo-Bo locomotive. b, 100fr, Moroccan electric locomotive. c, 100fr, Spanish electric locomotive. d, 500fr, Yugoslavian Type J2-441. e, 500fr, Chinese electric locomotive. f, 500fr, Norwegian Type E115.

No. 992: a, 100fr, Portuguese Diesel-electric locomotive. b, 100fr, Japanese mag-lev train. c, 100fr, Long Island Railroad diesel car. d, 500fr, German Type 103. e, 500fr, Romanian Co-Co locomotive. f, 500fr, English HST.

No. 993, 1500fr, English train "The Advanced." No. 994, 1500fr, French TGV 001. No. 995, 1500fr, Austrian Transalpine train. No. 996, 1500fr, Stourbridge Lion. No. 997, 1500fr, Puffing Billy, vert. No. 998, 1500fr, Union Pacific 4-8-8-4 Big Boy, vert. No. 999, French TGV, vert.

***Perf. 13¼x13¾, 13¾x13¼***
**2000, Dec. 10 Litho.**
**987-990** A373 Set of 4 6.00 6.00

**Sheets of 6, #a-f**
**991-992** A373 Set of 2 20.00 20.00

**Souvenir Sheets**
**993-995** A373 Set of 3 24.00 24.00
**996-999** A374 Set of 4 30.00 30.00

See Nos. 1024-1027, 1032-1033, 1036-1037.

A375

Prehistoric Animals — A376

Designs: No. 1000, 100fr, Archaeopteryx. No. 1001, 100fr, Velociraptor, vert. No. 1002, 125fr, Torosaurus. No. 1003, 125fr, Corythosaurus, vert. No. 1004, 225fr, Pachycephalosaurus, vert. No. 1005, 500fr, Parasaurolophus.

No. 1006, 100fr, Pterodactylus. No. 1007, 125fr, Allosaurus. No. 1008, 125fr, Struthiomimus, vert. No. 1009, 225fr, Psittacosaurus, vert. No. 1010, 260fr, Parasauraolophus, vert. No. 1011, 500fr, Acanthostega.

No. 1012: a, 125fr, Camarasaurus. b, 125fr, Rhamphorhynchus. c, 125fr, Saltasaurus. d, 225fr, Camptosaurus. e, 225fr, Megalosaurus. f, 225fr, Allosaurus. g, 260fr, Anchisaurus. h, 260fr, Dilophosaurus. i, 260fr, Massospondylus.

No. 1013: a, 100fr, Stegosaurus. b, 100fr, Pteranodon. c, 100fr, Carnotaurus. d, 125fr, Iguanodon. e, 125fr, Pentaceratops. f, 125fr, Styracosaurus. g, 500fr, Deinonychus. h, 500fr, Stegoceras. i, 500fr, Struthiomimus.

No. 1014: a, 125fr, Volcano. b, 125fr, Pterodactylus. c, 125fr, Dimorphodon. d, 125fr, Alamosaurus. e, 225fr, Psittacosaurus. f, 225fr, Deinonychus. g, 225fr, Dromiceiomimus. h, 225fr, Yangchuanosaurus. i, 260fr, Protorosaurus. j, 260fr, Triceratops. k, 260fr, Daspletosaurus. l, 260fr, Pentaceratops.

No. 1015: a, 125fr, Brachiosaurus. b, 125fr, Scaphognathus. c, Mountain and sun. d, 125fr, Pteranodon. e, 225fr, Tyrannosaurus. f, 225fr, Ichthyosaurus. g, 225fr, Macroplata. h, 225fr, Dilophosaurus. i, 500fr, Stegosaurus. j, 500fr, Thecodontosaurus. k, 500fr, Saltosaurus. l, 500fr, Pachyrhinosaurus.

No. 1016, 225fr: a, Tyrannosaurus. b, Criorhynchus. c, Pterodactylus. d, Albertosaurus. e, Dromiceiomimus. f, Opisthocoelicaudia. g, Brachiosaurus. h, Pachycephalosaurus. i, Parasaurolophus. j, Edmontosaurus. k, Pentaceratops. l, Corythosaurus.

No. 1017, 260fr: a, Peteinosaurus. b, Volcanoes. c, Acanthostega. d, Ceresiosaurus. e, Pliosaur. f, Stethacanthus. g, Ichthyosaur. h, Pholidogaster. i, Gerrothorax. j, Diplocaulus. k, Mixosaurus. l, Echinoceras raricostatum.

No. 1018, 1500fr, Tyrannosaurus Rex. No. 1019, 1500fr, Arrhinoceratops. No. 1020, 1500fr, Argentinosaurus, vert. No. 1021, 1500fr, Cetiosaurus, vert. No. 1022, 1500fr, Archaeopteryx. No. 1023, Saltasaurus, vert.

**2000, Dec. 20**
**1000-1005** A375 Set of 6 8.00 8.00
**1006-1011** A376 Set of 6 8.00 8.00

**Sheets of 9, #a-i**
**1012-1013** A375 Set of 2 20.00 20.00

**Sheets of 12, #a-l**
**1014-1015** A375 Set of 2 30.00 30.00
**1016-1017** A376 Set of 2 30.00 30.00

**Souvenir Sheets**
**1018-1021** A375 Set of 4 30.00 30.00
**1022-1023** A376 Set of 2 16.00 16.00

No. 1021 contains one 42x56mm stamp.

**Train Type of 2000 and**

A377

Designs: 100fr, German Type 201. No. 1025, 225fr, German Type 112. No. 1026, 225fr, ICT. No. 1027, 260fr, ICE.

No. 1028, 260fr, French Electric BB9004. No. 1029, 260fr, French Type 232U 4-8-2. No. 1030, 500fr, French Type 241C 4-8-2 "Mountain." No. 1031, 500fr, German TEE.

No. 1032: a, 125fr, German Type 41. b, 125fr, Type 39. c, 125fr, German Type 10. d, 500fr, German Type 99. e, 500fr, German Type 58. f, 500fr, German Type 44.

No. 1033: a, 225fr, German Type 229. b, 225fr, Type 152. c, 225fr, German Type 101. d, 500fr, German Type 250. e, 500fr, German Type 232. f, 500fr, Type 216.

No. 1034: a, 125fr, Prussian Type P8 4-6-0. b, 125fr, Bavarian Type S3/6 4-6-2. c, 125fr, German Type 01 4-6-2. d, 500fr, German Electric "Crocodile." e, 500fr, Swiss Electric Type Be 4/6. f, 500fr, Swiss Electric Type Ae 6/6.

No. 1035: a, 125fr, Stirling 8ft Single 4-2-2 "No. 1," UK. b, 125fr, Greeley Pacific Type A3 4-6-2 "Flying Scotsman," UK. c, 125fr, Stanier Coronation Type 4-6-2 "Coronation Scot," UK. d, 500fr, Baldwin 4-4-0 "The General," US. e, Class J1 Hudson 4-8-4, US. f, "Super Chief" Diesel-electric, US.

No. 1036, 1500fr, Type 91. No. 1037, 1500fr, Type 57. No. 1038, Greeley Pacific Type A4 4-6-2 "Silver Link," UK. No. 1039, J Type 4-8-4, US.

***Perf. 13¼x13½, 13½x13¼***
**2000? Litho.**
**1024-1027** A374 Set of 4 4.00 4.00
**1028-1031** A377 Set of 4 8.00 8.00

**Sheets of 6, #a-f**
**1032-1033** A374 Set of 2 20.00 20.00
**1034-1035** A377 Set of 2 19.00 19.00

**Souvenir Sheets**
**1036-1037** A374 Set of 2 16.00 16.00
**1038-1039** A377 Set of 2 16.00 16.00

Nos. 1038-1039 each contain one 56x42mm stamp.

Raponda Walker Foundation A378

**2000, Dec. 25 Litho.** ***Perf. 11½***
**1039A** A378 225fr multi 1.10 1.10

End of the Millennium A379

**2000, Dec. 11**
**1039B** A379 225fr multi 1.20 1.20

### Scientific Achievements of the 20th Century Type of 2000

Designs: 100fr, Isolation of insulin, 1921. 125fr, Invention of television, 1921. 225fr, Invention of the calculator, 1951.

*Perf. 11¾x11½*
**2000, Nov. 28** **Litho.**
**1040-1042** A369 Set of 3 3.00 3.00

Dancers A380

Designs: 100fr, Mengane dancers. 130fr, Maghouba dancers. 225fr, Ndjobi dancers.

**2001, Apr. 24** **Litho.** *Perf. 11¾*
**1043** A380 100fr multi .50 .30
**1044** A380 130fr multi .50 .30
**1045** A380 225fr multi 1.00 .50
*a.* Souvenir sheet of 3, #1043-1045 — —

Flowers — A381

Design: 100fr, Pseudogardenia kallreyeri. 125fr, Ouratea turnerae. 225fr, Strophantus gratus. 260fr, Spathodea campanulata.

**2001** **Litho.** *Perf. 11¾*
**1046-1049** A381 Set of 4 .50 .25
*1049a* Miniature sheet of 4, #1046-1049 .50 .25

Gabon Poste Emblem A382

Color of denomination: 125fr, Green. 225fr, Blue.

**2003, Apr. 5** **Litho.** *Perf. 13x13¼*
**1050-1051** A382 Set of 2 1.75 1.75

Orchids — A383

Designs: 100fr, Plectrelmintus caudatus. 125fr, Eulophia. 225fr, Jacinthe d'eau.

**2004, Feb. 20** *Perf. 13¼x13*
**1052-1054** A383 Set of 3 2.25 2.25
*1054a* Souvenir sheet, #1052-1054 2.75 2.75

Cooperation Between Gabon and People's Republic of China, 30th Anniv. — A384

No. 1055: a, 125fr, Chinese Prime Minister Wen Jiabao, Gabon Pres. Omar Bongo and flags. b, 225fr, Coats of arms of People's Republic of China and Gabon. No. 1056, 2500fr, Like No. 1055a. No. 1057, 2500fr, Like No. 1055b.

**2004, Apr. 20** *Perf. 12*
**1055** A384 Horiz. pair, #a-b 2.00 2.00

### Souvenir Sheets
### Printed on Wood Veneer
### Self-Adhesive

**1056-1057** A384 Set of 2 8.50 8.50

Nos. 1056 and 1057 are airmail and each contains one 90x50mm stamp.

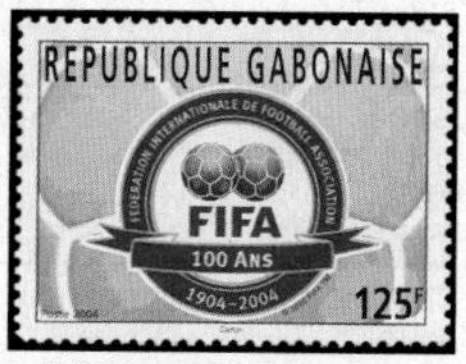


FIFA (Fédération Internationale de Football Association), Cent. — A385

Background color: 125fr, Blue. 225fr, Green.

**2004, Apr. 24** **Litho.** *Perf. 13x13¼*
**1058-1059** A385 Set of 2 1.75 1.75

Biodiversity — A386

Designs: 100fr, Hyperolius kuligae. 125fr, Chameleon, vert. 225fr, Merops malimbicus. 260fr, Owl.

**2004, June 5** *Perf. 13x13¼, 13¼x13*
**1060-1063** A386 Set of 4 5.50 5.50

Rotary International, Cent. — A387

**2005, Feb. 23** **Litho.** *Perf. 13x13¼*
**1064** A387 125fr multi .60 .60

### Souvenir Sheet

**1065** A387 2500fr multi 8.50 8.50

Souvenir Sheet

Lake Evaro — A388

**2005** **Litho.** *Perf. 13¾x13½*
**1066** A388 225fr multi 3.00 2.00

### Souvenir Sheet

**1067** A388 500fr multi 1.90 1.90

Christmas A389

No. 1068 — Carved wooden toys: a, 260fr, Antique car. b, 350fr, Logging truck.

**2005** *Perf. 13x13¼*
**1068** A389 Pair, #a-b 2.00 1.25
*c.* Souvenir sheet of 4, 2 each #1068a-1068b 3.00 2.00

Soccer Players and Flag A390

**2005** *Perf. 13x13¼*
**1069** A390 225fr multi 2.00 1.25

No. 1069 issued in sheets of 4.

Central African Network of Protected Areas — A391

**2007, May 28** *Perf. 13¼*
**1070** A391 500fr multi 2.10 2.10

Petroleum Exploration in Gabon, 80th Anniv. A392

Designs: No. 1071, 250fr, Ship and offshore drilling platform. No. 1072, 250fr, Oil drilling complex in jungle. No. 1073, 250fr, Oil workers. No. 1074, 500fr, Oil tanker at dock. No. 1075, 500fr, Elephants and oil drilling complex in jungle, vert. No. 1076, 500fr, Oil workers, vert.

*Perf. 13x13¼, 13¼x13*
**2008, May 5** **Litho.**
**1071-1076** A392 Set of 6 11.00 11.00
*1076a* Sheet of 6, #1071-1076 11.00 11.00

Souvenir Sheet

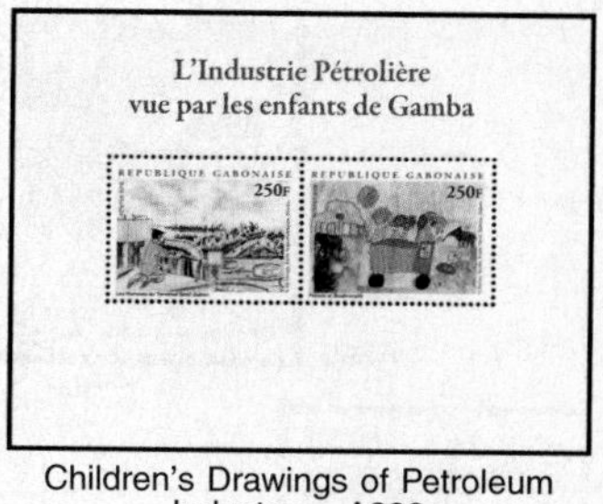


Children's Drawings of Petroleum Industry — A393

No. 1077: a, Workers at Shell Gabon Terminal. b, Petroleum and Biodiversity.

**2008, Sept. 25** **Litho.** *Perf. 13x13¼*
**1077** A393 250fr Sheet of 2, #a-b 2.25 2.25

Rule of Pres. Omar Bongo, 41st Anniv. A394

### Litho. & Embossed

**2008, Dec. 5** *Perf. 13½x13*
**1078** A394 500fr multi 2.25 2.25

### Litho. & Embossed With Foil Application

**1079** A394 5000fr gold & multi 22.50 22.50

Nos. 1078-1079 each were printed in sheets of 4.

Rotary International, 50th Anniv. in Gabon (in 2009) — A396

**2010** **Litho.** *Perf. 13x13¼*
**1082** A396 250fr multi 1.00 .50

Gabon Numerique 2010 A397

**2010, July**
**1083** A397 500fr multi 2.00 1.25

A398

A399

Prize-winning Art in 50th Anniversary of Gabon Art Contest — A400

**2010, Aug.** *Perf. 13¼x13, 13x13¼*

| | | | | |
|---|---|---|---|---|
| **1084** | A398 | 250fr multi | 1.00 | .50 |
| **1085** | A399 | 250fr multi | 1.00 | .50 |
| **1086** | A400 | 250fr multi | 1.00 | .50 |

Pres. Ali Bongo Ondimba — A401

**2010, Aug.** *Perf. 13¼x13*

**1087** A401 500fr multi 2.00 1.25

Gabon Presidents Léon Mba (1902-67), Omar Bongo (1935-2009) and Ali Bongo — A402

**2010, Aug.**

**1088** A402 500fr multi 2.00 1.25

**Souvenir Sheet**

**1089** A402 1500fr multi 20.00 15.00

A403

A404

Intl. Widows Day — A405

**2011, June 23** **Litho.** *Perf. 13x13¼*

**1090** A403 250fr multi — —
**1091** A404 250fr multi — —

*Perf. 13¼x13*

**1092** A405 250fr multi — —

2012 African Cup of Nations Soccer Championships, Gabon and Equatorial Guinea — A406

Flags of Gabon and Equatorial Guinea and mascot: 250fr, Holding ball on ground. 500fr, Dribbling ball.

**2012** *Perf. 13x13¼*

**1093-1094** A406 Set of 2 — —

## SEMI-POSTAL STAMPS

No. 37 Surcharged in Red

**1916** **Unwmk.** *Perf. 13½x14*

| | | | |
|---|---|---|---|
| **B1** A10 10c + 5c red & car | 30.00 | 30.00 |
| *a.* Double surcharge | 200.00 | 225.00 |
| *d.* In pair with unsurcharged stamp | 550.00 | |

**Same Surcharge on No. 54 in Red**

| | | |
|---|---|---|
| **B2** A10 10c + 5c red & car | 37.50 | 37.50 |
| *a.* Double surcharge | 200.00 | 225.00 |
| *b.* Inverted surcharge | 175.00 | |
| *c.* Double surcharge, one inverted | 175.00 | 200.00 |
| *d.* In pair with unsurcharged stamp | 550.00 | |

No. 54 Surcharged in Red

**1917**

**B3** A10 10c + 5c red & car 2.40 2.40

**Catalogue values for unused stamps in this section, from this point to the end of the section, are for Never Hinged items.**

**Republic**

**Anti-Malaria Issue**

Common Design Type

**1962, Apr. 7** **Engr.** *Perf. 12½x12*

**B4** CD108 25fr + 5fr yel grn 1.00 1.00

WHO drive to eradicate malaria.

**Freedom from Hunger Issue**

Common Design Type

**1963, Mar. 21** **Unwmk.** *Perf. 13*

**B5** CD112 25fr + 5fr dk red, grn & brn 1.00 1.00

Red Cross — SP1

**1997, May 8** **Litho.** *Perf. 13½x13*

**B6** SP1 150fr +75fr multi 1.40 1.10

## AIR POST STAMPS

**Catalogue values for unused stamps in this section are for Never Hinged items.**

Dr. Albert Schweitzer — AP1

**Unwmk.**

**1960, July 23** **Engr.** *Perf. 13*

**C1** AP1 200fr grn, dl red brn & ultra 7.50 3.75

For surcharge see No. C11.

Workmen Felling Tree — AP2

**1960, Oct. 8**

**C2** AP2 100fr red brn, grn & blk 4.50 1.90

5th World Forestry Cong., Seattle, WA, Aug. 29-Sept. 10.

**Olympic Games Issue**

French Equatorial Africa No. C37 Surcharged in Red Like Chad No. C1

AP2a

**1960, Dec. 15**

**C3** AP2a 250fr on 500fr grnsh blk, blk & slate 10.00 10.00

17th Olympic Games, Rome, 8/25-9/11.

Lyre-tailed Honey Guide — AP3

**1961, May 30** *Perf. 13*

**C4** AP3 50fr sl grn, red brn & ultra 3.00 1.60

See Nos. C14-C17.

**Air Afrique Issue**

Common Design Type

**1962, Feb. 17** **Engr.** *Perf. 13*

**C5** CD107 500fr sl grn, blk & bis 13.00 7.00

Long Jump — AP3a

**1962, July 21** **Photo.** *Perf. 12x12½*

**C6** AP3a 100fr dk & lt bl, brn & blk 3.75 2.25

Issued to publicize the Abidjan Games.

Breguet 14, 1928 — AP4

Development of air transport: 20fr, Dragon biplane transport. 60fr, Caravelle jet. 85fr, Rocket-propelled aircraft.

**1962, Sept. 4** **Engr.** *Perf. 13*

| | | | |
|---|---|---|---|
| **C7** AP4 10fr dl red brn & sl | .75 | .25 |
| **C8** AP4 20fr dk bl, sl & ocher | 1.10 | .45 |
| **C9** AP4 60fr dk sl grn, blk & brn | 2.75 | 1.00 |
| **C10** AP4 85fr dk bl, blk & org | 2.75 | 1.60 |
| *a.* Souv. sheet of 4, #C7-C10 | 11.00 | 11.00 |
| *Nos. C7-C10 (4)* | 7.35 | 3.30 |

Gabon's 1st phil. exhib., Libreville, Sept. 2-9.

**No. C1 Surcharged in Red: "100F/JUBILE GABONAIS/1913-1963"**

**1963, Apr. 18**

**C11** AP1 100fr on 200fr 4.00 2.10

50th anniv. of Dr. Albert Schweitzer's arrival in Gabon.

Post Office, Libreville — AP5

**1963, Apr. 28** **Photo.** *Perf. 13x12*

**C12** AP5 100fr multi 1.90 1.00

**African Postal Union Issue**

Common Design Type

**1963, Sept. 8** **Unwmk.** *Perf. 12½*

**C13** CD114 85fr brt car, ocher & red 1.90 .80

**Bird Type of 1961**

Birds: 100fr, Johanna's sunbird. 200fr, Blue-headed bee-eater, vert. 250fr, Crowned hawk-eagle, vert. 500fr, Narina trogon, vert.

**1963-64** **Engr.** *Perf. 13*

| | | |
|---|---|---|
| **C14** AP3 100fr dk grn, vio bl & car | 3.75 | 1.25 |
| **C15** AP3 200fr ol, vio bl & red | 8.00 | 3.00 |
| **C16** AP3 250fr grn, blk & dk brn ('64) | 15.00 | 4.00 |
| **C17** AP3 500fr multi | 15.00 | 7.00 |
| *Nos. C14-C17 (4)* | 41.75 | 15.25 |

Issued: Nos. C14-C15, C17, 10/7; No. C16, 9/23/64.

### 1963 Air Afrique Issue

Common Design Type

**1963, Nov. 19 Photo. *Perf. 13x12***

**C18** CD115 50fr lt vio, gray, blk & grn 1.25 .65

### Europafrica Issue

Common Design Type

**1963, Nov. 30 *Perf. 12x13***

**C19** CD116 50fr vio, yel & dk brn 1.60 .75

### Chiefs of State Issue

Map and Presidents of Chad, Congo, Gabon and CAR AP5a

**1964, June 23 *Perf. 12½***

**C20** AP5a 100fr multi 2.10 .90

See note after Central African Republic No. C19.

### Europafrica Issue, 1964

Globe and Emblems of Industry and Agriculture — AP6

**1964, July 20 *Perf. 12x13***

**C21** AP6 50fr red, olive & blue 1.60 .75

See note after Cameroun No. 402.

Start of Race — AP7

Athletes (Greek): 50fr, Massage at gymnasium, vert. 100fr, Anointing with oil before game, vert. 200fr, Four athletes.

**1964, July 30 Engr. *Perf. 13***

**C22** AP7 25fr sl grn, dk brn & org 1.00 .45
**C23** AP7 50fr dk brn, sl grn & org brn 1.60 .60
**C24** AP7 100fr vio bl, ol grn & dk brn 3.00 1.10
**C25** AP7 200fr dk brn, mag & org red 5.25 3.00
*a.* Min. sheet of 4, #C22-C25 14.00 14.00
*Nos. C22-C25 (4)* 10.85 5.15

18th Olympic Games, Tokyo, Oct. 10-25.

Communications Symbols — AP7a

**1964, Nov. 2 Litho. *Perf. 12½x13***

**C26** AP7a 25fr lt grn, dk brn & lt red brn .90 .25

See note after Chad No. C19.

John F. Kennedy (1917-63) — AP8

**1964, Nov. 23 Photo. *Perf. 12½***

**C27** AP8 100fr grn, org & blk 2.25 1.50
*a.* Souv. sheet of 4 11.00 11.00

Telephone Operator, Nurse and Police Woman — AP9

**1964, Dec. 5 Engr. *Perf. 13***

**C28** AP9 50fr car, bl & chocolate 1.40 .40

Social evolution of Gabonese women.

World Map and ICY Emblem — AP10

**1965, Mar. 25 Unwmk. *Perf. 13***

**C29** AP10 50fr org, Prus bl & grnsh bl 1.40 .70

International Cooperation Year.

Merchant Ship, 17th Century — AP11

25fr, Galleon, 16th cent., vert. 85fr, Frigate, 18th cent., vert. 100fr, Brig, 19th cent.

**1965, Apr. 22 Photo. *Perf. 13***

**C30** AP11 25fr lilac & multi 1.25 .55
**C31** AP11 50fr yellow & multi 2.75 .80
**C32** AP11 85fr multi 4.75 1.75
**C33** AP11 100fr multi 6.25 2.10
*Nos. C30-C33 (4)* 15.00 5.20

Red Cross Nurse Carrying Sick Child — AP12

**1965, June 25 Engr. *Perf. 13***

**C34** AP12 100fr brn, slate grn & red 2.25 .75

Issued for the Gabonese Red Cross.

Women's Basketball AP13

**1965, July 15 Unwmk.**

**C35** AP13 100fr sep, red org & brt lil 2.75 .90

African Games, Brazzaville, July 18-25.

Maps of Europe and Africa — AP14

**1965, July 26 Photo. *Perf. 13x12***

**C36** AP14 50fr multi 1.90 .65

See note after Cameroun No. 421.

Pres. Leon Mba AP15

**1965, Aug. 17 *Perf. 12½***

**C37** AP15 25fr multi .90 .50

Fifth anniversary of independence.

Sir Winston Churchill and Microphones — AP16

**1965, Sept. 28 Photo. *Perf. 12½***

**C38** AP16 100fr gold, blk & bl 2.50 1.10

Sir Winston Spencer Churchill (1874-1965), statesman and World War II leader.

Dr. Albert Schweitzer — AP17

### Embossed on Gold Foil

***Die-cut Perf. 14½, Approx.***

**1965, Dec. 4**

**C39** AP17 1000fr gold 75.00 75.00

Dr. Albert Schweitzer (1875-1965), medical missionary, theologian and musician.

Pope John XXIII and St. Peter's — AP18

**1965, Dec. 10 Photo. *Perf. 13x12½***

**C40** AP18 85fr multi 1.75 1.10

Issued in memory of Pope John XXIII.

Anti-Malaria Treatment AP19

**1966, Apr. 8 Photo. *Perf. 12½***

**C41** AP19 50fr shown 1.25 .75
*a.* Min. sheet of 4 8.75 8.75
**C42** AP19 100fr First aid 2.75 1.10
*a.* Min. sheet of 4 14.00 14.00

Issued for the Red Cross.

Diamant Rocket, A-1 Satellite and Map of Africa — AP20

90fr, FR-1 satellite, Diamant rocket and earth.

**1966, May 18 Engr. *Perf. 13***

**C43** AP20 30fr dk pur, brt bl & red brn .85 .45
**C44** AP20 90fr brt lil, red & pur 2.00 .80

French achievements in space.

Soccer and World Map — AP21

**1966, July 15 Engr. *Perf. 13***

**C45** AP21 100fr slate & brn red 3.00 1.25

8th World Soccer Cup Championship, Wembley, England, July 11-30.

Symbols of Industry and Transportation
AP22

**1966, July 26 Photo. *Perf. 12x13***
**C46** AP22 50fr multi 1.50 .65

3rd anniv. of the economic agreement between the European Economic Community and the African and Malgache Union.

### Air Afrique Issue, 1966
Common Design Type

**1966, Aug. 31 Photo. *Perf. 13***
**C47** CD123 30fr org, blk & gray 1.00 .60

Student and UNESCO Emblem — AP23

**1966, Nov. 4 Engr. *Perf. 13***
**C48** AP23 100fr dl bl, ocher & blk 1.75 .85

20th anniv. of UNESCO.

Libreville Airport — AP24

**1966, Nov. 21 Engr. *Perf. 13***
**C49** AP24 200fr dp bl & red brn 4.50 1.50

Inauguration of Libreville Airport.

Farman 190 — AP25

Planes: 300fr, De Havilland Heron. 500fr, Potez 56.

**1967, Apr. 1 Engr. *Perf. 13***
**C50** AP25 200fr ultra, lil & bl grn 4.00 1.75
**C51** AP25 300fr brn, lil & brt bl 6.50 2.10
**C52** AP25 500fr brn car, dk grn & indigo 11.00 4.75
*Nos. C50-C52 (3)* 21.50 8.60

For surcharge see No. C128.

Planes, Runways and ICAO Emblem — AP26

**1967, May 19 Engr. *Perf. 13***
**C53** AP26 100fr plum, brt bl & yel grn 2.00 1.10

International Civil Aviation Organization.

Blood Donor and Bottles — AP27

100fr, Human heart and transfusion apparatus.

**1967, June 26 Photo. *Perf. 12½***
**C54** AP27 50fr ocher, red & sl 1.75 .65
*a.* Souvenir sheet of 4 9.75 9.75
**C55** AP27 100fr yel grn, red & gray 3.50 1.25
*a.* Souvenir sheet of 4 15.00 15.00

Issued for the Red Cross. Nos. C54a, C55a each contain 2 vertical tête bêche pairs.

Jamboree Emblem and Symbols of Orientation
AP28

Design: 100fr, Jamboree emblem, maps and Scouts of Africa and America.

**1967, Aug. 1 Engr. *Perf. 13***
**C56** AP28 50fr multi 1.60 .80
**C57** AP28 100fr brt grn, dp car & bl 2.40 1.60

12th Boy Scout World Jamboree, Farragut State Park, Idaho, Aug. 1-9.

### African Postal Union Issue, 1967
Common Design Type

**1967, Sept. 9 Engr. *Perf. 13***
**C58** CD124 100fr dl bl, ol & red brn 2.25 .95

Mission Church — AP29

**1967, Oct. 18 Engr. *Perf. 13***
**C59** AP29 100fr brt bl, dk grn & blk 2.75 1.25

125th anniv. of the arrival of American Protestant missionaries in Baraka-Libreville.

UN Emblem, Sword, Book and People — AP30

**1967, Nov. 7 Photo. *Perf. 13***
**C60** AP30 60fr dk red, vio bl & bis 1.10 .65

UN Commission on Human Rights.

### Tree Type of Regular Issue

Designs: 50fr, Baillonella toxisperma. 100fr, Aucoumea klaineana.

**1967, Dec. 5 Engr. *Perf. 13***
**Size: 26½x47½mm**
**C61** A53 50fr grn, brt bl & brn 1.60 1.10
**C62** A53 100fr multi 2.75 1.90
*a.* Bklt. pane of 5, #223-225, C61-C62 with gutter btwn. 8.00 8.00

Konrad Adenauer
AP31

**1968, Feb. 20 Photo. *Perf. 12½***
**C63** AP31 100fr blk, dl org & red 2.50 1.10
*a.* Souvenir sheet of 4 12.50 12.50

Issued in memory of Konrad Adenauer (1876-1967), chancellor of West Germany (1949-63). No. C63a includes 1967 CEPT (Europa) emblem.

Madonna of the Rosary by Murillo
AP32

90fr, Christ in Bonds, by Luis de Morales. 100fr, St. John on Patmos, by Juan Mates.

**1968, July 9 Photo. *Perf. 12½x12***
**C64** AP32 60fr multi 1.40 .55
**C65** AP32 90fr multi 2.00 .95
**C66** AP32 100fr multi, horiz. 2.25 1.10
*Nos. C64-C66 (3)* 5.65 2.60

See Nos. C77, C102-C102B, C132-C133, C146-C148.

### Europafrica Issue

Stylized Knot — AP32a

**1968, July 23 Photo. *Perf. 13***
**C67** AP32a 50fr yel brn, emer & lt ultra 1.10 .45

See note after Congo Republic No. C69.

Support for Red Cross — AP33

50fr, Distribution of Red Cross gifts.

**1968, Aug. 13**
**C68** AP33 50fr multi 1.40 .65
**C69** AP33 100fr multi 2.75 1.40
*a.* Bklt. pane of 2, #C68, C69 with gutter btwn. 7.50 7.50

Issued for the Red Cross.

High Jump — AP34

**1968, Sept. 3 Engr.**
**C70** AP34 25fr shown .70 .50
**C71** AP34 30fr Bicycling, vert. .85 .55
**C72** AP34 100fr Judo, vert. 2.25 1.25
**C73** AP34 200fr Boxing 4.25 2.10
*a.* Bklt. pane of 4, #C70-C71, C72-C73 with gutter btwn. 11.00 11.00
*Nos. C70-C73 (4)* 8.05 4.40

Issued to publicize the 19th Summer Olympic Games, Mexico City, Oct. 12-27.

Pres. Mba, Flag and Arms of Gabon
AP35

### Embossed on Gold Foil

**1968, Nov. 28 *Perf. 14½***
**C74** AP35 1000fr gold, grn, yel & dk bl 30.00 30.00

Death of Pres. Léon Mba (1902-67), 1st anniv.

Pres. Bongo, Maps of Gabon and Owendo Harbor — AP36

**1968, Dec. 16 Photo. *Perf. 12½***
**C75** AP36 25fr shown 1.25 .25
**C76** AP36 30fr Owendo Harbor 1.25 .25
*a.* Strip of 2, #C75-C76 + label 3.00 3.00

Laying of the foundation stone for Owendo Harbor, June 24, 1968.

### PHILEXAFRIQUE Issue
### Painting Type of 1968

Design: 100fr, The Convent of St. Mary of the Angels, by Francois Marius Granet.

**1969, Jan. 8 Photo. *Perf. 12½x12***
**C77** AP32 100fr multi 4.25 4.25

Issued to publicize PHILEXAFRIQUE Philatelic Exhibition in Abidjan, Feb. 14-23. Printed with alternating brown label.

Mahatma Gandhi — AP37

Portraits: 30fr, John F. Kennedy. 50fr, Robert F. Kennedy. 100fr, Martin Luther King, Jr.

**1969, Jan. 15** ***Perf. 12½***

**C78** AP37 25fr pink & blk .75 .45
**C79** AP37 30fr lt yel grn & blk .75 .45
**C80** AP37 50fr lt bl & blk 1.10 .45
**C81** AP37 100fr brt rose lil & blk 2.25 .90
*a.* Souv. sheet of 4, #C78-C81 6.00 6.00
*Nos. C78-C81 (4)* 4.85 2.25

Issued to honor exponents of non-violence.

**2nd PHILEXAFRIQUE Issue**

Common Design Type

**1969, Feb. 14** **Engr.** ***Perf. 13***

**C82** CD128 50fr grn, ind & red brn 2.25 2.25

Battle of Rivoli, by Henri Philippoteaux — AP39

100fr, The Oath of the Army, by Jacques Louis David. 250fr, Napoleon with the Children on the Terrace in St. Cloud, by Louis Ducis.

**1969, Apr. 23** **Photo.** ***Perf. 12½x12***

**C83** AP39 50fr brn & multi 2.25 1.10
**C84** AP39 100fr grn & multi 2.75 2.40
**C85** AP39 250fr lil & multi 12.00 7.00
*Nos. C83-C85 (3)* 17.00 10.50

Birth bicentenary of Napoleon I.

Red Cross Plane, Nurse and Biafran Children — AP40

20fr, Dispensary, ambulance & supplies. 25fr, Physician & nurse in children's ward. 30fr, Dispensary & playing children.

**1969, June 20** **Photo.** ***Perf. 14x13½***

**C86** AP40 15fr lt ultra, dk brn & red .80 .25
**C87** AP40 20fr emer, blk, brn & red .75 .45
**C88** AP40 25fr grnsh bl, dk brn & red .75 .45
**C89** AP40 30fr org yel, dk brn & red 1.10 .45
*Nos. C86-C89 (4)* 3.40 1.60

Red Cross help for Biafra.

A souvenir sheet contains four stamps similar to Nos. C86-C89, but lithographed and rouletted 13x13½. Gray margin with red inscription and Red Cross. Size: 118x75mm. Sold in cardboard folder. Value $4.

Astronauts and Lunar Landing Module, Apollo 11 — AP41

**Embossed on Gold Foil**

**1969, July 25** ***Die-cut Perf. 10½x10***

**C90** AP41 1000fr gold 26.00 26.00

See note after Algeria No. 427.

**Europafrica Issue, 1970**

African and European Heads and Symbols — AP42

**1970, June 5** **Photo.** ***Perf. 12x13***

**C91** AP42 50fr multi 1.25 .50

Icarus and Sun — AP43

Designs: 100fr, Leonardo da Vinci's flying man, 1519. 200fr, Jules Verne's space shell approaching moon, 1865.

**1970, June 10** **Engr.** ***Perf. 13***

**C92** AP43 25fr ultra, red & org .85 .50
**C93** AP43 100fr ocher, plum & sl grn 2.00 1.00
**C94** AP43 200fr gray, ultra & dk car 4.75 2.00
*a.* Min. sheet of 3, #C92-C94 8.50 8.50
*Nos. C92-C94 (3)* 7.60 3.50

UAMPT Emblem AP44

**Embossed on Gold Foil**

**1970, June 18** ***Die-cut Perf. 12½***

**C95** AP44 200fr gold, yel grn & bl 3.50 2.40

Meeting of the Afro-Malagasy Union of Posts & Telecommuncations (UAMPT), Libreville, 6/17-23.

Throwing Knives AP45

Gabonese Weapons: 30fr, Assegai and crossbow, vert. 50fr, War knives, vert. 90fr, Dagger and sheath.

**1970, July 10** **Engr.** ***Perf. 13***

**C96** AP45 25fr multi .60 .35
**C97** AP45 30fr multi .80 .40
**C98** AP45 50fr multi 1.00 .50
**C99** AP45 90fr multi 2.40 .90
*a.* Min. sheet of 4, #C96-C99 6.50 6.50
*Nos. C96-C99 (4)* 4.80 2.15

Japanese Masks, Mt. Fuji and Torii at Miyajima — AP46

**Embossed on Gold Foil**

**1970, July 31** ***Die-cut Perf. 10***

**C100** AP46 1000fr multi 25.00 25.00

Issued to publicize EXPO '70 International Exhibition, Osaka, Japan, Mar. 15-Sept. 13.

Pres. Albert Bernard Bongo — AP47

**Lithographed; Gold Embossed**

**1970, Aug. 17** ***Perf. 12½***

**C101** AP47 200fr multi 5.00 2.25

10th anniversary of independence.

**Painting Type of 1968**

Paintings: 50fr, Portrait of a Young Man, School of Raphael. 100fr, Portrait of Jeanne d'Aragon, by Raphael. 200fr, Madonna with Blue Diadem, by Raphael.

**1970, Oct. 16** **Photo.** ***Perf. 12½x12***

**C102** AP32 50fr multi 1.10 .50
**C102A** AP32 100fr blue & multi 2.40 .95
**C102B** AP32 200fr brown & multi 4.75 2.50
*Nos. C102-C102B (3)* 8.25 3.95

Raphael (1483-1520).

Miniature Sheets

AP47a

Hugo Junkers — AP47b

**1970, Dec. 5** **Litho.** ***Perf. 12***

**C103** Sheet of 8 11.00 11.00
*a.* AP47a 15fr Sikorsky S-32
*b.* AP47a 25fr Fokker "Southern Cross"
*c.* AP47a 40fr Dornier DO-18
*d.* AP47a 60fr Dornier DO-X
*e.* AP47a 80fr Breguet "Bizerte"
*f.* AP47a 125fr Douglas "Cloudster"
*g.* AP47a 150fr De Havilland DH-2
*h.* AP47a 200fr Vickers "Vimi"
**C104** Sheet of 4 18.50 18.50
*a.* AP47b 200fr shown
*b.* AP47b 300fr Claude Dornier
*c.* AP47b 400fr Anthony Fokker
*d.* AP47b 500fr Igor Sikorsky

***Imperf***

**C105** Sheet of 8 11.00 11.00
*a.* AP47a 10fr Dornier "Spatz"
*b.* AP47a 20fr Douglas DC-3
*c.* AP47a 30fr Dornier DO-7 "Wal"
*d.* AP47a 50fr Sikorsky S-38
*e.* AP47a 75fr De Havilland "Moth"
*f.* AP47a 100fr Supermarine "Spitfire"
*g.* AP47a 125fr Breguet XIX
*h.* AP47a 150fr Fokker "Universal"

**Size: 80x90mm**

**C106** AP47b 1000fr Claude Dornier 18.50 18.50

Claude Dornier (1884-1969), aviation pioneer. No. C104 exists imperf. Value $17.

Presidents Bongo and Pompidou — AP48

**1971, Feb. 11** **Photo.** ***Perf. 13***

**C107** AP48 50fr multi 2.25 1.10

Visit of Georges Pompidou, Pres. of France.

Apollo 14 — AP48a

**1971, Feb. 19** ***Perf. 14***

**Yellow Inscriptions**

**C108** 15fr Lift off .25 .25
**C108A** 25fr Achieving orbit .45 .30
**C108B** 40fr Lunar module descent .80 .60
**C108C** 55fr Lunar landing 1.00 .65
**C108D** 75fr Lunar liftoff 1.50 1.00
**C108E** 120fr Earth re-entry 2.50 1.50
*Nos. C108-C108E (6)* 6.50 4.30

**Souvenir Sheet**

**C108F** Sheet of 2 7.50 4.25
*g.* AP48a 100fr Modules attached 3.00 1.75
*h.* AP48a 100fr like #C108E 3.00 1.75

Nos. C108-C108F exist imperf. with white inscriptions. Same values.

Flowers and Plane — AP49

25fr, Carnations. 40fr, Roses. 55fr, Daffodils. 75fr, Orchids. 120fr, Tulips.

**1971, May 7 Litho. *Perf. 13½x14***

| | | | | |
|---|---|---|---|---|
| **C109** | AP49 | 15fr yellow & multi | .45 | .25 |
| **C109A** | AP49 | 25fr multi | .70 | .25 |
| **C109B** | AP49 | 40fr pink & multi | 1.10 | .40 |
| **C109C** | AP49 | 55fr blue & multi | 1.40 | .45 |
| **C110** | AP49 | 75fr multi | 2.40 | .60 |
| **C111** | AP49 | 120fr green & multi | 3.00 | .85 |
| *a.* | | Souv. sheet of 2, #C110-C111 | 6.00 | 6.00 |
| | | *Nos. C109-C111 (6)* | 9.05 | 2.80 |

"Flowers by air."

Napoleon's Death Mask AP50

Designs: 200fr, Longwood, St. Helena, by Jacques Marchand, horiz. 500fr, Sarcophagus in Les Invalides, Paris.

**1971, May 12 Photo. *Perf. 13***

| | | | | |
|---|---|---|---|---|
| **C112** | AP50 | 100fr gold & multi | 3.00 | .70 |
| **C113** | AP50 | 200fr gold & multi | 5.00 | .80 |
| **C114** | AP50 | 500fr gold & multi | 12.00 | 3.25 |
| | | *Nos. C112-C114 (3)* | 20.00 | 4.75 |

Napoleon Bonaparte (1769-1821).

Souvenir Sheet

Charles de Gaulle — AP51

Designs: 40fr, President de Gaulle. 80fr, General de Gaulle. 100fr, Quotation.

**1971, June 18 Photo. *Perf. 12½***

| | | | | |
|---|---|---|---|---|
| **C115** | AP51 | Sheet of 5 | 11.00 | 11.00 |
| *a.* | | 40fr dark red & multi | .95 | .95 |
| *b.* | | 80fr dark green & multi | .95 | .95 |
| *c.* | | 100fr green, brown & yel | 2.50 | 2.50 |

In memory of Gen. Charles de Gaulle (1890-1970), Pres. of France.

For surcharge see No. C126.

Red Crosses AP52

**1971, June 29**

| | | | | |
|---|---|---|---|---|
| **C116** | AP52 | 50fr multicolored | 1.40 | .40 |

For the Red Cross of Gabon.

For surcharge see No. C143.

Uranium — AP53

**1971, July 20 Photo. *Perf. 13x12½***

| | | | | |
|---|---|---|---|---|
| **C117** | AP53 | 85fr shown | 7.00 | 3.50 |
| **C118** | AP53 | 90fr Manganese | 8.00 | 4.00 |

Landing Module over Moon — AP54

**Embossed on Gold Foil**

**1971, July 30 *Die-cut Perf. 10***

| | | | | |
|---|---|---|---|---|
| **C119** | AP54 | 1500fr multi | 30.00 | 30.00 |

Apollo 11 and 15 US moon missions.

**African Postal Union Issue, 1971**

Common Design Type

Design: 100fr, Bakota copper mask and UAMPT building, Brazzaville, Congo.

**1971, Nov. 13 Photo. *Perf. 13x13½***

| | | | | |
|---|---|---|---|---|
| **C120** | CD135 | 100fr bl & multi | 2.00 | .70 |

Ski Jump and Miyajima Torii AP55

130fr, Speed skating and Japanese temple.

**1972, Jan. 31 Engr. *Perf. 13***

| | | | | |
|---|---|---|---|---|
| **C121** | AP55 | 40fr hn brn, sl grn & vio bl | 1.25 | .35 |
| **C122** | AP55 | 130fr hn brn, sl grn & vio bl | 3.25 | .75 |
| *a.* | | Souvenir sheet of 2, #C121-C122 + label | 5.00 | 5.00 |

11th Winter Olympic Games, Sapporo, Japan, Feb. 3-13.

The Basin and Grand Canal, by Vanvitelli — AP56

Paintings: 70fr, Rialto Bridge, by Canaletto (erroneously inscribed Caffi), vert. 140fr, Santa Maria della Salute, by Vanvitelli, vert.

**1972, Feb. 7 Photo. *Perf. 13***

| | | | | |
|---|---|---|---|---|
| **C123** | AP56 | 60fr gold & multi | 3.00 | .70 |
| **C124** | AP56 | 70fr gold & multi | 4.50 | 1.00 |
| **C125** | AP56 | 140fr gold & multi | 8.75 | 1.50 |
| | | *Nos. C123-C125 (3)* | 16.25 | 3.20 |

UNESCO campaign to save Venice.

**No. C115 Surcharged in Brown and Gold**

Souvenir Sheet

**1972, Feb. 11 *Perf. 12½***

| | | | | |
|---|---|---|---|---|
| **C126** | AP51 | Sheet of 5 | 20.00 | 20.00 |
| *a.* | | 60fr on 40fr multi | 2.75 | 2.75 |
| *b.* | | 120fr on 80fr multi | 4.00 | 4.00 |
| *c.* | | 180fr on 100fr multi | 8.25 | 8.25 |

Publicity for the erection of a memorial for Charles de Gaulle. Nos. C126a-C126b have surcharge and Cross of Lorraine in gold, 2 bars obliterating old denomination in brown; No. C126c has surcharge, cross and bars in brown. Two Lorraine Crosses and inscription (MEMORIAL DU GENERAL DE GAULLE) in brown added in margin.

Hotel Inter-Continental, Libreville — AP57

**1972, Feb. 26 Engr. *Perf. 13***

| | | | | |
|---|---|---|---|---|
| **C127** | AP57 | 40fr bl, sl grn & org brn | 1.10 | .35 |

**No. C51 Surcharged**

**1972, Mar. 3**

| | | | | |
|---|---|---|---|---|
| **C128** | AP25 | 50fr on 300fr multi | 1.00 | .30 |

Official visit of the Grand Master of the Knights of Malta, March 3.

Discobolus, by Alcamenes AP58

Designs: 100fr, Doryphoros, by Polycletus. 140fr, Borghese gladiator, by Agasias.

**1972, May 10 Engr. *Perf. 13***

| | | | | |
|---|---|---|---|---|
| **C129** | AP58 | 30fr rose cl & gray | .90 | .40 |
| **C130** | AP58 | 100fr rose cl & gray | 1.90 | .50 |
| **C131** | AP58 | 140fr rose cl & gray | 2.50 | .70 |
| *a.* | | Min. of sheet of 3, #C129-C131 | 6.50 | 6.50 |
| | | *Nos. C129-C131 (3)* | 5.30 | 1.60 |

20th Olympic Games, Munich, 8/26-9/10.

For surcharges see Nos. C134-C136.

**Painting Type of 1968**

Paintings: 30fr, Adoration of the Magi, by Peter Brueghel, the Elder, horiz. 40fr, Madonna and Child, by Marco Basaiti.

**1972, Oct. 30 Photo. *Perf. 13***

| | | | | |
|---|---|---|---|---|
| **C132** | AP32 | 30fr gold & multi | 1.10 | .25 |
| **C133** | AP32 | 40fr gold & multi | 1.60 | .25 |

Christmas 1972.

**Nos. C129-C131 Surcharged with New Value, Two Bars and Names of Athletes.**

**1972, Dec. 5 Engr. *Perf. 13***

| | | | | |
|---|---|---|---|---|
| **C134** | AP58 | 40fr on 30fr | 1.10 | .35 |
| **C135** | AP58 | 120fr on 100fr | 2.00 | .65 |
| **C136** | AP58 | 170fr on 140fr | 3.25 | 1.00 |
| | | *Nos. C134-C136 (3)* | 6.35 | 2.00 |

Gold medal winners in 20th Olympic Games: Daniel Morelon, France, Bicycling (C134); Kipchoge Keino, Kenya, steeplechase (C135); Mark Spitz, US, swimming (C136).

Globe with Space Orbits, Simulated Stamps — AP59

**1973, Feb. 20 Photo. *Perf. 13***

| | | | | |
|---|---|---|---|---|
| **C137** | AP59 | 100fr multi | 2.25 | .50 |
| *a.* | | Souv. sheet of 4, perf. 12x12½ | 25.00 | 25.00 |

PHILEXGABON 1973, Phil. Exhib., Libreville, Feb. 19-26. No. C137a exists imperf.

DC10-30 "Libreville" over Libreville Airport — AP60

**1973, Mar. 19 Typo. *Perf. 13***

| | | | | |
|---|---|---|---|---|
| **C138** | AP60 | 40fr blue & multi | 2.25 | .50 |

Kinguélé Hydroelectric Station — AP61

Design: 40fr, Kinguélé Dam.

**1973, June 19 Engr. *Perf. 13***

| | | | | |
|---|---|---|---|---|
| **C139** | AP61 | 30fr slate grn & dk ol | .80 | .25 |
| **C140** | AP61 | 40fr slate grn, dk ol & bl | 1.10 | .25 |
| *a.* | | Strip of 2, #C139-C140 + label | 2.75 | 1.25 |

Hydroelectric installations at Kinguélé.

M'Bigou Stone Sculpture, Woman's Head — AP62

Design: 200fr, Sculpture, man's head.

**1973, July 5**

| | | | | |
|---|---|---|---|---|
| **C141** | AP62 | 100fr blk, bl & grn | 3.25 | .70 |
| **C142** | AP62 | 200fr grn, sep & sl grn | 3.75 | 1.25 |

**No. C116 Surcharged with New Value, 2 Bars, and Overprinted in Ultramarine: "SECHERESSE SOLIDARITE AFRICAINE"**

**1973, Aug. 16 Photo. *Perf. 12½***
**C143** AP52 100fr on 50fr multi 2.25 .65

African solidarity in drought emergency.

Astronauts and Lunar Rover on Moon — AP63

**1973, Sept. 6 Engr. *Perf. 13***
**C144** AP63 500fr multi 10.00 4.00

Apollo 17 US moon mission, 12/7-19/73.

Presidents Houphouet Boigny (Ivory Coast) and De Gaulle — AP64

**1974, Apr. 30 Engr. *Perf. 13***
**C145** AP64 40fr rose lilac & indigo 2.25 .55

30th anniv. of the Conf. of Brazzaville.

**Painting Type of 1968**

Impressionist Paintings: 40fr, Pleasure Boats, by Claude Monet, horiz. 50fr, Ballet Dancer, by Edgar Degas. 130fr, Young Girl with Flowers, by Auguste Renoir.

**1974, June 11 Photo. *Perf. 13***

| | | | |
|---|---|---|---|
| **C146** AP32 | 40fr gold & multi | 3.50 | .50 |
| **C147** AP32 | 50fr gold & multi | 5.50 | .70 |
| **C148** AP32 | 130fr gold & multi | 8.75 | 1.10 |
| | *Nos. C146-C148 (3)* | 17.75 | 2.30 |

Astronaut on Moon, Eagle and Emblems AP65

**1974, July 20 Engr. *Perf. 13***
**C149** AP65 200fr multi 2.75 .90

First men on the moon, 5th anniversary.

UPU Emblem, Letters, Pigeon AP66

UPU cent.: 300fr, UPU emblem, letters, pigeons, diff.

**1974, Oct. 9 Engr. *Perf. 13***

| | | | |
|---|---|---|---|
| **C150** AP66 | 150fr lt bl & Prus bl | 2.50 | .90 |
| **C151** AP66 | 300fr org & claret | 5.00 | 1.75 |

Space Docking, US and USSR Crafts AP67

**1974, Oct. 23 Engr. *Perf. 13***
**C152** AP67 1000fr grn, red & sl 11.00 5.25

Russo-American space cooperation.
For overprint see No. C169.

Soccer and Games Emblem — AP68

Designs: Soccer actions.

**1974, Oct. 25**

| | | | |
|---|---|---|---|
| **C153** AP68 | 40fr grn, red & brn | .70 | .25 |
| **C154** AP68 | 65fr red, brn & grn | 1.00 | .35 |
| **C155** AP68 | 100fr grn, red & brn | 1.50 | .60 |
| *a.* | Souv. sheet of 3, #C153-C155 + 3 labels | 4.50 | 4.50 |
| | *Nos. C153-C155 (3)* | 3.20 | 1.20 |

World Cup Soccer Championship, Munich, June 13-July 7.

**UDEAC Issue**

Presidents and Flags of Cameroun, CAR, Gabon and Congo — AP68a

**1974, Dec. 8 Photo. *Perf. 13***
**C156** AP68a 100fr gold & multi 1.25 .45

Annunciation, Tapestry, 15th Century — AP69

Christmas: 40fr, Visitation from 15th century tapestry, Notre Dame de Beaune, vert.

**1974, Dec. 11**

| | | | |
|---|---|---|---|
| **C157** AP69 | 40fr gold & multi | 1.10 | .30 |
| **C158** AP69 | 50fr gold & multi | 1.25 | .35 |

Dr. Schweitzer and Lambarene Hospital — AP70

**1975, Jan. 14 Engr. *Perf. 13***
**C159** AP70 500fr multi 9.00 3.00

Dr. Albert Schweitzer (1875-1965), medical missionary, birth centenary.

Crucifixion, by Bellini — AP71

Paintings: 150fr, Resurrection, Burgundian School, c. 1500.

**1975, Apr. 8 Photo. *Perf. 13½***
**Size: 26x45mm**
**C160** AP71 140fr gold & multi 2.10 .60
**Size: 36x48mm**
***Perf. 13***
**C161** AP71 150fr gold & multi 2.50 .70

Easter 1975.

Marc Seguin Locomotive, 1829 — AP72

Locomotives: 25fr, The Iron Duke, 1847. 40fr, Thomas Rogers, 1895. 50fr, The Soviet 272, 1934.

**1975, Apr. 8 Engr. *Perf. 13***

| | | | |
|---|---|---|---|
| **C162** AP72 | 20fr multi | 1.60 | .40 |
| **C163** AP72 | 25fr multi | 2.25 | .40 |
| **C164** AP72 | 40fr multi | 2.75 | .65 |
| **C165** AP72 | 50fr lil & multi | 3.50 | .75 |
| | *Nos. C162-C165 (4)* | 10.10 | 2.20 |

Swimming Pool, Montreal Olympic Games' Emblem — AP73

Designs: 150fr, Boxing ring and emblem. 300fr, Stadium, aerial view, and emblem.

**1975, Sept. 30 Litho. *Perf. 13x12½***

| | | | |
|---|---|---|---|
| **C166** AP73 | 100fr multi | 1.50 | .30 |
| **C167** AP73 | 150fr multi | 1.90 | .60 |
| **C168** AP73 | 300fr multi | 3.75 | 1.10 |
| *a.* | Min. sheet of 3, #C166-C168 | 8.00 | 8.00 |
| | *Nos. C166-C168 (3)* | 7.15 | 2.00 |

Pre-Olympic Year 1975.

**No. C152 Surcharged in Violet Blue: "JONCTION / 17 Juillet 1975"**

**1975, Oct. 20 Engr. *Perf. 13***
**C169** AP67 1000fr multi 11.00 4.50

Apollo-Soyuz link-up in space, July 17, 1975.

Annunciation, by Maurice Denis — AP74

Painting: 50fr, Virgin and Child with Two Saints, by Fra Filippo Lippi.

**1975, Dec. 9 Photo. *Perf. 13***

| | | | |
|---|---|---|---|
| **C170** AP74 | 40fr gold & multi | 1.25 | .40 |
| **C171** AP74 | 50fr gold & multi | 1.60 | .55 |

Christmas 1975.

Concorde and Globe — AP75

**1975, Dec. 29 Engr. *Perf. 13***
**C172** AP75 500fr bl, vio bl & red 11.00 3.75

For overprint see No. C198.

No. C172 Surcharged

**1976, Jan. 21**
**C173** AP75 1000fr on 500fr 20.00 8.00

Nos. C172-C173 for the 1st commercial flight of supersonic jet Concorde from Paris to Rio, Jan. 21.

Slalom and Olympic Games Emblem — AP76

Design: 250fr, Speed skating and Winter Olympic Games emblem.

**1976, Apr. 22 Engr. *Perf. 13***

| | | | |
|---|---|---|---|
| **C174** AP76 | 100fr blk, bl & red | 1.50 | .40 |
| **C175** AP76 | 250fr blk, bl & red | 3.25 | 1.40 |
| *a.* | Souvenir sheet | 6.50 | 6.50 |

12th Winter Olympic Games, Innsbruck, Austria, Feb. 4-15. No. C175a contains 100fr and 250fr stamps in continuous design with additional inscription and skier between, but without perforations between the design elements.

Size of perforated area: 125x27mm; size of sheet: 169x90mm.

Jesus Between the Thieves AP77

Design: 130fr, St. Thomas putting finger into wounds of Jesus. Both designs after wood carvings in Church of St. Michael, Libreville.

**1976, Apr. 28 Litho. *Perf. 12½x13***

| | | | |
|---|---|---|---|
| **C176** AP77 | 120fr multi | 1.60 | .65 |
| **C177** AP77 | 130fr multi | 2.25 | .95 |

Easter 1976. See Nos. C188-C189, C220-C221.

Boston Tea Party — AP78

Designs: 150fr, Battle of New York. 200fr, Demolition of statue of George III.

**1976, May 3 Engr. *Perf. 13***

**C178** AP78 100fr multi 1.00 .50
**C179** AP78 150fr multi 1.90 .70
**C180** AP78 200fr multi 2.25 .80
*a.* Triptych, #C178-C180 + 2 labels 8.00 6.50

American Bicentennial.

### Nos. C178-C180 Overprinted: "4 JUILLET 1976"

**1976, July 4 Engr. *Perf. 13***

**C181** AP78 100fr multi 1.00 .50
**C182** AP78 150fr multi 1.90 .70
**C183** AP78 200fr multi 2.25 .80
*a.* Triptych, #C181-C183 + 2 labels 8.00 6.50

Independence Day.

Running — AP79

200fr, Soccer. 260fr, High jump.

**1976, July 27 Litho. *Perf. 12½***

**C184** AP79 100fr multi 1.10 .35
**C185** AP79 200fr multi 2.50 .65
**C186** AP79 260fr multi 3.25 .90
*a.* Souv. sheet of 3, #C184-C186, perf. 13 8.00 3.75
*Nos. C184-C186 (3)* 6.85 1.90

21st Olympic Games, Montreal, Canada, July 17-Aug. 1.

Presidents Giscard d'Estaing and Bongo — AP80

**1976, Aug. 5 Photo. *Perf. 13***

**C187** AP80 60fr blue & multi 1.25 .30

Visit of Pres. Valèrie Giscard d'Estaing of France.

### Sculpture Type of 1976

Christmas: 50fr, Presentation at the Temple. 60fr, Nativity. Designs after wood Carvings in Church of St. Michael, Libreville.

**1976, Dec. 6 Litho. *Perf. 12½x13***

**C188** AP77 50fr multi 1.00 .25
**C189** AP77 60fr multi 1.10 .35

Oklo Fossil Reactor — AP81

**1976, Dec. 15 Litho. *Perf. 13***

**C190** AP81 60fr red & multi 1.10 .30

The Last Supper, by Juste de Gand — AP82

100fr, The Deposition, by Nicolas Poussin.

**1977, Mar. 25 Litho. *Perf. 12½***

**C191** AP82 50fr gold & multi 1.10 .25
**C192** AP82 100fr gold & multi 2.25 .65

Easter 1977.

Air Gabon Plane and Insigne — AP83

**1977, June 3 Litho. *Perf. 12½***

**C193** AP83 60fr multi 1.10 .30

Air Gabon's first intercontinental route.

Beethoven, Piano and Score — AP84

**1977, June 15 Engr. *Perf. 13***

**C194** AP84 260fr slate 3.00 .95

Ludwig van Beethoven (1770-1827).

Lindbergh and Spirit of St. Louis — AP85

**1977, Sept. 13 Engr. *Perf. 13***

**C195** AP85 500fr multi 8.00 2.75

Charles A. Lindbergh's solo transatlantic flight from NY to Paris, 50th anniv.

Soccer — AP86

**1977, Oct. 18 Photo. *Perf. 13x12½***

**C196** AP86 250fr multi 3.25 1.10

Elimination games, World Soccer Cup, Buenos Aires, 1978.

Viking on Mars AP87

**1977, Nov. 17 Engr. *Perf. 13***

**C197** AP87 1000fr multi 13.00 3.50

Viking, US space probe.

### No. C172 Overprinted: "PARIS NEW-YORK / PREMIER VOL / 22.11.77"

**1977, Nov. 22 Engr. *Perf. 13***

**C198** AP75 500fr multi 11.00 2.50

Concorde, 1st commercial flight, Paris to NYC.

Lion Hunt, by Rubens — AP88

Rubens Paintings: 80fr, Hippopotamus Hunt. 200fr, Head of Black Man, vert.

**1977, Nov. 24 Litho. *Perf. 13***

**C199** AP88 60fr gold & multi 1.10 .35
**C200** AP88 80fr gold & multi 1.25 .45
**C201** AP88 200fr gold & multi 3.50 1.10
*a.* Souv. sheet of 3, #C199-C201 8.00 4.00
*Nos. C199-C201 (3)* 5.85 1.90

Peter Paul Rubens (1577-1640).

Adoration of the Kings, by Rubens — AP89

Design: 80fr, Flight into Egypt, by Rubens.

**1977, Dec. 15 Litho. *Perf. 12½***

**C202** AP89 60fr gold & multi 1.10 .30
**C203** AP89 80fr gold & multi 1.25 .45

Christmas 1977; Peter Paul Rubens.

Paul Gauguin, Self-Portrait AP90

150fr, Flowers in vase and Maori statuette.

**1978, Feb. 8 Litho. *Perf. 12½x12***

**C204** AP90 150fr multi 3.00 .60
**C205** AP90 300fr multi 5.50 1.10

Paul Gauguin (1848-1903), French painter.

Pres. Bongo, Map of Gabon, Plane and Train AP91

### Lithographed; Gold Embossed

**1978, Mar. 12 *Perf. 12½***

**C206** AP91 500fr multi 7.00 1.75

10th anniversary of national renewal.

Soccer and Argentina '78 Emblem — AP92

Argentina '78 Emblem and: 120fr, Three soccer players. 200fr, Jules Rimet Cup, vert.

**1978, July 18 Engr. *Perf. 13***

**C207** AP92 100fr red, grn & brn 1.10 .25
**C208** AP92 120fr grn, red & brn 1.25 .40
**C209** AP92 200fr brn & red 2.40 .55
*a.* Min. sheet of 3, #C207-C209 6.50 3.00
*Nos. C207-C209 (3)* 4.75 1.20

11th World Cup Soccer Championship, Argentina, June 1-25.

### Nos. C207-C209a Overprinted in Ultramarine or Black

a

b

c

**1978, July 21 Engr. *Perf. 13***

**C210** AP92(a) 100fr multi 1.00 .30
**C211** AP92(b) 120fr multi 1.25 .40
**C212** AP92(c) 200fr multi 2.10 .65
*a.* Min. sheet of 3 (Bk) 6.00 6.00
*Nos. C210-C212 (3)* 4.35 1.35

Argentina's World Cup victory.

Albrecht Dürer (age 13), Self-portrait AP93

Design: 250fr, Lucas de Leyde, by Dürer.

**1978, Sept. 15 Engr. *Perf. 13***

| | | | | |
|---|---|---|---|---|
| **C213** | AP93 | 100fr red brn & slate | 1.25 | .30 |
| **C214** | AP93 | 250fr blk & red brn | 3.50 | .80 |

Dürer (1474-1528), German painter.

**Philexafrique II-Essen Issue**
Common Design Types

Designs: No. C215, Gorilla and Gabon No. 280. No. C216, Stork and Saxony No. 1.

**1978, Nov. 1 Litho. *Perf. 13x12½***

| | | | | |
|---|---|---|---|---|
| **C215** | CD138 | 100fr multi | 2.75 | 1.40 |
| **C216** | CD139 | 100fr multi | 2.75 | 1.40 |
| *a.* | | Pair, #C215-C216 + label | 9.00 | 5.00 |

No. C216a exists with two different labels: one for PHILEXAFRIQUE II and one for ESSEN '78.

Wright Brothers and Flyer AP94

**1978, Dec. 19 Engr. *Perf. 13***

| | | | | |
|---|---|---|---|---|
| **C217** | AP94 | 380fr multi | 5.00 | 1.10 |

75th anniversary of 1st powered flight.

Pope John Paul II AP95

Design: 200fr, Popes Paul VI and John Paul I, St. Peter's Basilica and Square, horiz.

**1979, Jan. 24 Litho. *Perf. 12½***

| | | | | |
|---|---|---|---|---|
| **C218** | AP95 | 100fr multi | 2.50 | .35 |
| **C219** | AP95 | 200fr multi | 5.50 | .80 |

**Sculpture Type of 1976**

Easter: 100fr, Disciples recognizing Jesus in the breaking of the bread. 150fr, Jesus appearing to Mary Magdalene. Designs after wood carvings in Church of St. Michael, Libreville.

**1979, Apr. 10 Litho. *Perf. 12½x13***

| | | | | |
|---|---|---|---|---|
| **C220** | AP77 | 100fr multi | 1.25 | .45 |
| **C221** | AP77 | 150fr multi | 2.25 | .65 |

Capt. Cook and Ships AP96

**1979, July 10 Engr. *Perf. 13***

| | | | | |
|---|---|---|---|---|
| **C222** | AP96 | 500fr multi | 5.50 | 2.00 |

Capt. James Cook (1728-1779), explorer, death bicentenary.

Flags and Map of England and France, Bleriot, Bleriot XI — AP97

Aviation Retrospect: 1000fr, Astronauts walking on moon (gold embossed inset).

***Perf. 12½x12, 12***

**1979, Aug. 8 Litho.**

| | | | | |
|---|---|---|---|---|
| **C223** | AP97 | 250fr multi | 3.25 | 1.00 |
| **C224** | AP97 | 1000fr multi | 11.00 | 3.75 |

1st flight over English Channel, 70th anniv.; Apollo 11 moon landing, 10th anniv.

Rotary Emblem, Map of Africa, Head — AP98

**1979, Sept. 25 Photo. *Perf. 13***

| | | | | |
|---|---|---|---|---|
| **C225** | AP98 | 80fr multi | 1.10 | .35 |

Rotary International, 75th anniversary.

Eugene Jamot, Tsetse Fly — AP99

**1979, Nov. 23 Engr. *Perf. 13***

| | | | | |
|---|---|---|---|---|
| **C226** | AP99 | 300fr multi | 5.00 | 1.50 |

Eugene Jamot (1879-1937), discoverer of sleeping sickness cure.

Bobsledding, Lake Placid '80 Emblem AP100

**1980, Feb. 25 Litho. *Perf. 12½***

| | | | | |
|---|---|---|---|---|
| **C227** | AP100 | 100fr shown | 1.00 | .40 |
| **C228** | AP100 | 200fr Ski jump | 2.10 | .75 |
| *a.* | | Souv. sheet of 2, #C227-C228 | 4.00 | 1.90 |

13th Winter Olympic Games, Lake Placid, NY, Feb. 12-24.

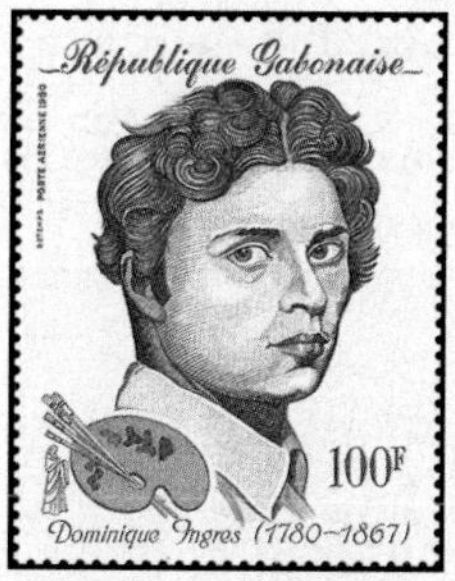


Jean Ingres AP101

**1980, May 14 Engr. *Perf. 13***

| | | | | |
|---|---|---|---|---|
| **C229** | AP101 | 100fr shown | 1.50 | .50 |
| **C230** | AP101 | 200fr Jacques Offenbach | 3.00 | .95 |
| **C231** | AP101 | 360fr Gustave Flaubert | 4.50 | 1.75 |
| | | *Nos. C229-C231 (3)* | 9.00 | 3.20 |

12th World Telecommunications Day — AP102

**1980, May 17 Litho. *Perf. 12½***

| | | | | |
|---|---|---|---|---|
| **C232** | AP102 | 80fr multi | 1.10 | .35 |

Costes, Bellonte and Plane — AP103

Design: 1000fr, Mermoz, sea plane.

**1980, July 16 Engr. *Perf. 13***

| | | | | |
|---|---|---|---|---|
| **C233** | AP103 | 165fr multi | 1.60 | .70 |
| **C234** | AP103 | 1000fr multi | 11.00 | 4.50 |

1st North Atlantic crossing, 50th anniv.; 1st South Atlantic air mail service, 50th anniv.

Running, Moscow '80 Emblem AP104

**1980, July 25 Litho.**

| | | | | |
|---|---|---|---|---|
| **C235** | AP104 | 50fr shown | .55 | .25 |
| **C236** | AP104 | 100fr Pole vault | 1.10 | .45 |
| **C237** | AP104 | 250fr Boxing | 2.90 | 1.00 |
| *a.* | | Souv. sheet of 3, #C235-C237 | 8.50 | 4.00 |
| | | *Nos. C235-C237 (3)* | 4.55 | 1.70 |

22nd Summer Olympic Games, Moscow, July 19-Aug. 3.

**Nos. C235-C237a Overprinted in Red, Brown, Ultramarine or Black**

No. C238

No. C239

No. C240

**1980, Sept. 25 Litho. *Perf. 13***

| | | | | |
|---|---|---|---|---|
| **C238** | AP104 | 50fr (R, vert. & horiz.) | .50 | .25 |
| **C239** | AP104 | 100fr (Br) | .95 | .40 |
| **C240** | AP104 | 250fr (U) | 2.50 | .85 |
| *a.* | | Souv. sheet of 3 (Blk) | 8.50 | 4.00 |
| | | *Nos. C238-C240 (3)* | 3.95 | 1.50 |

Pres. Charles de Gaulle AP105

**1980, Nov. 9 Photo. *Perf. 13***

| | | | | |
|---|---|---|---|---|
| **C241** | AP105 | 100fr shown | 1.25 | .35 |
| **C242** | AP105 | 200fr Pres. & Mrs. de Gaulle | 2.40 | .70 |
| *a.* | | Souv. sheet of 2, #C241-C242 | 6.50 | 3.25 |

Pres. Charles de Gaulle (1890-1970).

AP106

**1981, Feb. 19 Litho. *Perf. 13***

| | | | | | |
|---|---|---|---|---|---|
| **C243** | AP106 | 60fr | Soccer Players | .65 | .25 |
| **C244** | AP106 | 190fr | Soccer player | 2.10 | .75 |

ESPANA '82 World Cup Soccer Championship.

AP107

Spacecraft and Astronauts: 250fr, Yuri Gagarin. 500fr, Alan B. Shepard.

**1981, Mar. 26 Litho. *Perf. 13***

| | | | | | |
|---|---|---|---|---|---|
| **C245** | AP107 | 150fr | multi | 1.40 | .55 |
| **C246** | AP107 | 250fr | multi | 2.40 | .85 |
| **C247** | AP107 | 500fr | multi | 4.75 | 1.75 |
| *a.* | | | Souv. sheet of 3, #C245-C247, perf. 12½ | 9.00 | 4.50 |
| | | | *Nos. C245-C247 (3)* | 8.55 | 3.15 |

200th anniv. of discovery of Uranus by William Herschel (1738-1822).

Map of Africa and Emblems AP108

**1981, June 1 Litho. *Perf. 12½***

| | | | | | |
|---|---|---|---|---|---|
| **C248** | AP108 | 100fr | multi | 1.00 | .40 |

Electric Power Distribution Union, 7th Congress, Libreville, June 1-5.

D-51 Steam Locomotive, Japan, and SNCF Turbotrain TGV-001, France — AP109

200th Birth Anniv. of George Stephenson: 100fr, B&O Mallet 7100, US, Prussian T3 steam locomotive. 350fr, Stephenson and his Rocket, BB Alsthom electric locomotive, Central Africa.

**1981, June 4 Engr. *Perf. 13***

| | | | | | |
|---|---|---|---|---|---|
| **C249** | AP109 | 75fr | multi | 1.10 | .35 |
| **C250** | AP109 | 100fr | multi | 1.60 | .45 |
| **C251** | AP109 | 350fr | multi | 5.25 | 1.50 |
| *a.* | | | Souvenir sheet of 3 | 7.50 | 3.25 |
| | | | *Nos. C249-C251 (3)* | 7.95 | 2.30 |

No. C251a contains No. C249-C251 in changed colors.

**No. C251a Overprinted in 1 line across 3 stamps: "26 fevrier 1981-Record du monde de vitesse 380 km a l'heure"**
Souvenir Sheet

**1981, June 13 Engr. *Perf. 13***

| | | | | | |
|---|---|---|---|---|---|
| **C252** | AP109 | | Sheet of 3 | 6.50 | 3.25 |

New world railroad speed record, set Feb. 26.

Intl. Letter Writing Week, Oct. 9-16 — AP110

**1981, Oct. 9 Photo. *Perf. 13***

| | | | | | |
|---|---|---|---|---|---|
| **C253** | AP110 | 200fr | multi | 2.25 | .90 |

Souvenir Sheet

22nd Anniv. of Independence — AP110a

**1982 Typo. *Perf. 13x12½***
**Self-Adhesive**

| | | | | | |
|---|---|---|---|---|---|
| **C253A** | AP110a | 2000fr | multi | 40.00 | 40.00 |

Printed on wood.

Still Life with a Mandolin, by George Braque (1882-1963) — AP111

Design: 350fr, Boy Blowing Bubbles, by Edouard Manet (1832-1883), vert.

***Perf. 13x12½, 12½x13***
**1982, Oct. 5 Litho.**

| | | | | | |
|---|---|---|---|---|---|
| **C254** | AP111 | 300fr | multi | 3.75 | 1.10 |
| **C255** | AP111 | 350fr | multi | 6.00 | 1.25 |

Pre-olympic Year — AP112

**1983, Feb. 16 Litho. *Perf. 13***

| | | | | | |
|---|---|---|---|---|---|
| **C256** | AP112 | 90fr | Gymnast | .70 | .30 |
| **C257** | AP112 | 350fr | Wind surfing | 4.00 | 1.10 |

Manned Flight Bicentenary AP113

Balloons.

**1983, June 1 Engr. *Perf. 13***

| | | | | | |
|---|---|---|---|---|---|
| **C258** | AP113 | 100fr | Transatlantic flight, 5th anniv. | 1.10 | .40 |
| **C259** | AP113 | 125fr | Montgolfiere, 1783 | 1.25 | .45 |
| **C260** | AP113 | 350fr | Rozier's balloon, 1783 | 4.00 | 1.50 |
| | | | *Nos. C258-C260 (3)* | 6.35 | 2.35 |

Lady with Unicorn, by Raphael (1483-1520) AP114

**1983, June 19 *Perf. 12½x13***

| | | | | | |
|---|---|---|---|---|---|
| **C261** | AP114 | 1000fr | multi | 12.00 | 5.25 |

1984 Winter Olympics — AP115

**1984, Feb. 8 Litho. *Perf. 12½***

| | | | | | |
|---|---|---|---|---|---|
| **C262** | AP115 | 125fr | Hockey | 1.40 | .25 |
| **C263** | AP115 | 350fr | Figure skaters | 3.75 | .70 |

See No. C268.

Paris-Libreville-Paris Air Race, Mar. 15-28 — AP116

**1984, Mar. 15 Litho. *Perf. 13x12½***

| | | | | | |
|---|---|---|---|---|---|
| **C264** | AP116 | 500fr | Planes, emblem | 5.00 | .85 |

The Racetrack, by Edgar Degas — AP117

**1984, Mar. 21 *Perf. 13***

| | | | | | |
|---|---|---|---|---|---|
| **C265** | AP117 | 500fr | multi | 8.00 | 1.25 |

1984 Summer Olympics AP118

**1984, May 31 Litho. *Perf. 12½***

| | | | | | |
|---|---|---|---|---|---|
| **C266** | AP118 | 90fr | Basketball | .80 | .25 |
| **C267** | AP118 | 125fr | Running | 1.25 | .25 |

**Nos. C262-C263, C266-C267 with Added Inscriptions**
Souvenir Sheet

**1984, Oct. 3 Litho. *Perf. 13***

| | | | | |
|---|---|---|---|---|
| **C268** | | Sheet of 4 | 7.50 | 3.50 |
| *a.* | AP118 | 90fr MEDAILLE D'OR: U.S.A. | .65 | .25 |
| *b.* | AP118 | 125fr MEDAILLE D'OR: KORIR | .95 | .25 |
| *c.* | AP115 | 125fr Hockey sur glace: U.R.S.S. | .95 | .25 |
| *d.* | AP115 | 350fr Danse couple: J. Torvill-C. Dean | 2.75 | .55 |

**Souvenir Sheet**

Hamburg '84 Philatelic Exhibition — AP119

**1984 Typo. *Perf. 13x12½***
**Self-Adhesive**

| | | | | | |
|---|---|---|---|---|---|
| **C268A** | AP119 | 1000fr | multi | 21.00 | 21.00 |

Printed on wood.

Dr. Albert Schweitzer (1875-1965) — AP119a

**1985, Sept. 5 Litho. *Perf. 12½***

| | | | | | |
|---|---|---|---|---|---|
| **C269** | AP119a | 350fr | multi | 4.25 | .70 |

Flags of Gabon, UN
AP120

**1985, Sept. 20**
**C270** AP120 225fr multi 2.50 .40

Admission of Gabon to UN, 25th anniv.

Central Post Office, Libreville, UPU and Gabon Postal Emblems — AP121

**1985, Oct. 9**
**C271** AP121 300fr multi 3.25 .60

World Post Day.

UN, 40th Anniv. — AP122

**1985, Oct. 24 Litho. *Perf. 12½***
**C272** AP122 350fr multi 3.75 .70

PHILEXAFRICA '85, Lome, Togo — AP123

100fr, Scout campsite.150fr, Telecommunications, transportation.

**1985, Oct. 30 *Perf. 13***
**C273** AP123 100fr multicolored 2.00 .25
**C274** AP123 150fr multicolored 3.50 .50
*a.* Pair, #C273-C274 + label 6.50 2.00

Gabon's Gift to the UN — AP124

Design: Mother and Child, carved wood statue, and UN emblem.

**1986, Mar. 15 Litho. *Perf. 13½***
**C275** AP124 350fr multi 3.75 1.10

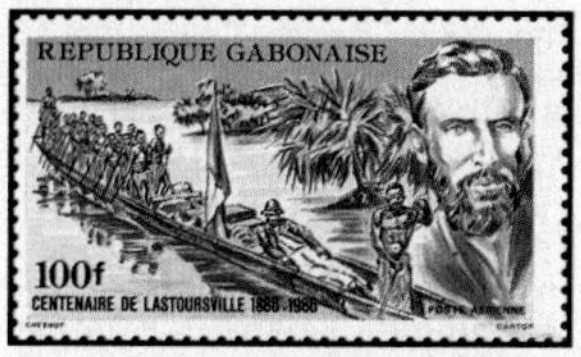


Lastour Arriving in Gabon — AP125

**1986, Mar. 25 Litho. *Perf. 12½***
**C276** AP125 100fr multi 1.50 .45

Lastoursville, cent.

World Telecommunications Day — AP126

**1986, May 17 *Perf. 13½***
**C277** AP126 300fr multi 3.00 .95

1986 World Cup Soccer Championships, Mexico — AP127

100fr, Goal. 150fr, Dribbling, religious carving. 250fr, Players, map, soccer cup. 350fr, Stadium, flags.

**1986, May 31 *Perf. 12½***
**C278** AP127 100fr multi 1.00 .35
**C279** AP127 150fr multi 1.50 .45
**C280** AP127 250fr multi 2.50 .80
**C281** AP127 350fr multi 3.25 1.10
*a.* Souv. sheet of 4, #C278-C281 10.00 4.75
*Nos. C278-C281 (4)* 8.25 2.70

For overprints see Nos. C283-C286.

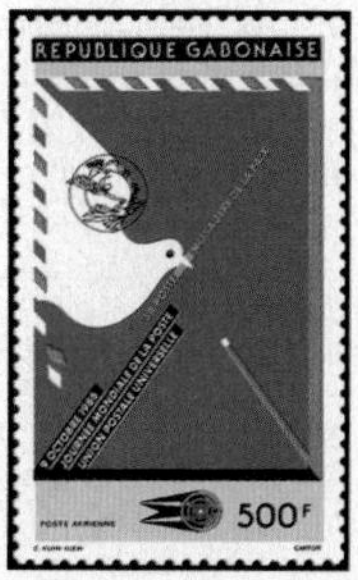


World Post Day — AP128

**1986, Oct. 9 Litho. *Perf. 12½***
**C282** AP128 500fr multi 5.00 1.50

**Nos. C278-C281 Ovptd. "ARGENTINA 3 -R.F.A 2" in One or Two Lines in Red**

**1986, Oct. 23 Litho. *Perf. 12½***
**C283** AP127 100fr multi 1.00 .35
**C284** AP127 150fr multi 1.50 .45
**C285** AP127 250fr multi 2.50 .80
**C286** AP127 350fr multi 3.25 1.10
*Nos. C283-C286 (4)* 8.25 2.70

The Renewal, 19th Anniv.
AP129

**1987, Mar. 12 Litho. *Perf. 13***
**C287** AP129 500fr multi 6.00 2.00

Konrad Adenauer (1876-1967), West German Chancellor
AP130

**1987, Apr. 15 *Perf. 12x12½***
**C288** AP130 300fr mar, chlky bl & blk 4.50 1.25

Schweitzer and Medical Settlement — AP131

**1988, Apr. 17 Litho. *Perf. 12½x12***
**C289** AP131 500fr multi 6.50 2.25

Dr. Albert Schweitzer (1875-1965), missionary physician and founder of the hospital and medical settlement, Lambarene, Gabon.

Port Gentil Refinery, 20th Anniv. — AP132

**1988, Sept. 1 Litho. *Perf. 13½***
**C290** AP132 350fr multi 4.00 1.75

De Gaulle's Call for French Resistance, 50th Anniv. — AP133

**1990, June 18 Litho. *Perf. 13***
**C291** AP133 500fr multicolored 7.50 2.50

Port of Marseilles by J. B. Jongkind (1819-1891) — AP134

**1991, Feb. 9 Litho. *Perf. 13***
**C292** AP134 500fr multicolored 6.00 2.75

Discovery of America, 500th Anniv. — AP135

**1992, Oct. 12 Litho. *Perf. 13***
**C293** AP135 500fr multicolored 5.50 2.50

Antoine de Saint-Exupery (1900-44) — AP136

**1994 Litho. *Perf. 13***
**C294** AP136 500fr multicolored *3.25 1.60*

Opening of the Channel Tunnel — AP137

**1994, Sept. 5**
**C295** AP137 500fr multicolored *3.00 1.50*

---

## AIR POST SEMI-POSTAL STAMPS

**Catalogue values for unused stamps in this section are for Never Hinged items.**

Ramses II Paying Homage to Four Gods, Wadi-es-Sabua — SPAP1

**Unwmk.**

**1964, Mar. 9 Engr. *Perf. 13***
**CB1** SPAP1 10fr + 5fr dk bl & bis brn 1.00 1.00
**CB2** SPAP1 25fr + 5fr dk car rose & vio bl 1.25 1.25
**CB3** SPAP1 50fr + 5fr sl grn & claret 2.10 2.10
*Nos. CB1-CB3 (3)* 4.35 4.35

UNESCO world campaign to save historic monuments in Nubia.

---

## POSTAGE DUE STAMPS

Postage Due Stamps of France Overprinted

**1928 Unwmk. *Perf. 14x13½***

| No. | Type | Description | Unused | Used |
|---|---|---|---|---|
| J1 | D2 | 5c light blue | .40 | *.55* |
| J2 | D2 | 10c gray brown | .40 | *.65* |
| J3 | D2 | 20c olive green | 1.25 | *1.60* |
| J4 | D2 | 25c bright rose | 1.25 | *1.60* |
| J5 | D2 | 30c light red | 1.60 | *2.00* |
| J6 | D2 | 45c blue green | 2.00 | *2.40* |
| J7 | D2 | 50c brown violet | 3.00 | *3.25* |
| J8 | D2 | 60c yellow brown | 3.00 | *3.25* |
| J9 | D2 | 1fr red brown | 3.00 | *3.25* |
| J10 | D2 | 2fr orange red | 4.75 | 4.75 |
| J11 | D2 | 3fr bright violet | 5.50 | 5.50 |
| | | *Nos. J1-J11 (11)* | 26.15 | 28.80 |

Chief Makoko, de Brazza's Aide — D3

Count Savorgnan de Brazza — D4

**1930 Typo. *Perf. 13½x14***

| No. | Type | Description | Unused | Used |
|---|---|---|---|---|
| J12 | D3 | 5c dk bl & olive | 1.25 | 1.25 |
| J13 | D3 | 10c dk red & brn | 1.40 | 1.40 |
| J14 | D3 | 20c green & brn | 1.90 | 1.90 |
| J15 | D3 | 25c lt bl & brn | 1.90 | 1.90 |
| J16 | D3 | 30c bis brn & Prus bl | 2.75 | 2.75 |
| J17 | D3 | 45c Prus bl & ol | 4.50 | 4.50 |
| J18 | D3 | 50c red vio & brn | 4.75 | 4.75 |
| J19 | D3 | 60c gray lil & bl blk | 9.00 | 9.00 |
| J20 | D4 | 1fr bis brn & bl blk | 12.50 | 12.50 |
| J21 | D4 | 2fr violet & brn | 16.00 | 16.00 |
| J22 | D4 | 3fr dp red & brn | 18.00 | 18.00 |
| | | *Nos. J12-J22 (11)* | 73.95 | 73.95 |

Fang Woman — D5

**1932 Photo. *Perf. 13x13½***

| No. | Type | Description | Unused | Used |
|---|---|---|---|---|
| J23 | D5 | 5c dk bl, *bl* | .95 | .95 |
| J24 | D5 | 10c red brown | 1.10 | 1.10 |
| J25 | D5 | 20c chocolate | 1.75 | 1.75 |
| J26 | D5 | 25c yel grn, *bl* | 1.75 | 1.75 |
| J27 | D5 | 30c car rose | 2.10 | 2.10 |
| J28 | D5 | 45c red org, *yel* | 7.75 | 7.75 |
| J29 | D5 | 50c dk violet | 2.50 | 2.50 |
| J30 | D5 | 60c dull blue | 3.75 | 3.75 |
| J31 | D5 | 1fr blk, *red org* | 9.00 | 9.00 |
| J32 | D5 | 2fr dark green | 10.00 | 10.00 |
| J33 | D5 | 3fr rose lake | 9.25 | 9.25 |
| | | *Nos. J23-J33 (11)* | 49.90 | 49.90 |

**Catalogue values for unused stamps in this section, from this point to the end of the section, are for Never Hinged items.**

### Republic

Pineapple — D6

**Unwmk.**

**1962, Dec. 10 Engr. *Perf. 11***

| No. | Type | Description | Unused | Used |
|---|---|---|---|---|
| J34 | D6 | 50c shown | .25 | .25 |
| J35 | D6 | 50c Mangoes | .25 | .25 |
| *a.* | | Pair, #J34-J35 | .35 | |
| J36 | D6 | 1fr Avocados | .25 | .25 |
| J37 | D6 | 1fr Tangerines | .25 | .25 |
| *a.* | | Pair, #J36-J37 | .50 | |
| J38 | D6 | 2fr Coconuts | .25 | .25 |
| J39 | D6 | 2fr Grapefruit | .25 | .25 |
| *a.* | | Pair, #J38-J39 | .50 | |
| J40 | D6 | 5fr Oranges | .35 | .35 |
| J41 | D6 | 5fr Papaya | .35 | .35 |
| *a.* | | Pair, #J40-J41 | 1.00 | |
| J42 | D6 | 10fr Breadfruit | .75 | .75 |
| J43 | D6 | 10fr Guavas | .75 | .75 |
| *a.* | | Pair, #J42-J43 | 2.25 | |
| J44 | D6 | 25fr Lemons | 1.00 | 1.00 |
| J45 | D6 | 25fr Bananas | 1.00 | 1.00 |
| *a.* | | Pair, #J44-J45 | 3.50 | |
| | | *Nos. J34-J45 (12)* | 5.70 | 5.70 |

Pairs se-tenant at the base.

Charaxes Candiope — D7

Butterflies: 10fr, Charaxes ameliae. 25fr, Cyrestis camillus. 50fr, Charaxes castor. 100fr, Pseudacrea boisduvali.

**1978, July 4 Litho. *Perf. 13***

| No. | Type | Description | Unused | Used |
|---|---|---|---|---|
| J46 | D7 | 5fr multi | .30 | .25 |
| J47 | D7 | 10fr multi | .30 | .25 |
| J48 | D7 | 25fr multi | .65 | .30 |
| J49 | D7 | 50fr multi | 1.25 | .50 |
| J50 | D7 | 100fr multi | 2.00 | .95 |
| | | *Nos. J46-J50 (5)* | 4.50 | 2.25 |

## OFFICIAL STAMPS

**Catalogue values for unused stamps in this section are for Never Hinged items.**

Map of Gabon — O1

Flag of Gabon — O2

Designs: 25fr, 30fr, Flag of Gabon. 50fr, 85fr, 100fr, 200fr, Coat of Arms.

**1968 Unwmk. Photo. *Perf. 14***

| No. | Type | Description | Unused | Used |
|---|---|---|---|---|
| O1 | O1 | 1fr olive & multi | .25 | .25 |
| O2 | O1 | 2fr multi | .25 | .25 |
| O3 | O1 | 5fr lilac & multi | .25 | .25 |
| O4 | O1 | 10fr emer & multi | .25 | .25 |
| O5 | O1 | 25fr brn & multi | .50 | .25 |
| O6 | O1 | 30fr org & multi | .50 | .25 |
| O7 | O1 | 50fr multi | .95 | .25 |
| O8 | O1 | 85fr multi | 1.75 | .35 |
| O9 | O1 | 100fr yel & multi | 2.10 | .45 |
| O10 | O1 | 200fr gray & multi | 4.00 | 1.10 |
| | | *Nos. O1-O10 (10)* | 10.80 | 3.65 |

**1971-84 Typo. *Perf. 13x14***

| No. | Type | Description | Unused | Used |
|---|---|---|---|---|
| O11 | O2 | 5fr multi ('81) | .25 | .25 |
| O12 | O2 | 10fr multi | .25 | .25 |
| O13 | O2 | 20fr multi ('81) | .25 | .25 |
| O14 | O2 | 25fr multi ('84) | .25 | .25 |
| O15 | O2 | 30fr multi ('78) | .40 | .25 |
| O16 | O2 | 40fr multi ('72) | .75 | .25 |
| O17 | O2 | 50fr multi ('76) | .85 | .25 |
| O18 | O2 | 60fr multi ('77) | 1.10 | .25 |
| O19 | O2 | 75fr multi ('81) | .75 | .25 |
| O20 | O2 | 80fr multi ('77) | 1.50 | .40 |
| O21 | O2 | 100fr multi ('78) | 1.25 | .25 |
| O22 | O2 | 500fr multi ('78) | 6.25 | 1.25 |
| | | *Nos. O11-O22 (12)* | 13.85 | 4.15 |

# GAMBIA

'gam-bē-ə

LOCATION — Extending inland from the mouth of the Gambia River on the west coast of Africa

GOVT. — Republic in British Commonwealth

AREA — 4,068 sq. mi.

POP. — 1,087,000 (1995 est.)

CAPITAL — Banjul

The British Crown Colony and Protectorate of Gambia became independent in 1965 and a republic in 1970.

12 Pence = 1 Shilling

100 Bututs = 1 Dalasy (1971)

**Catalogue values for unused stamps in this country are for Never Hinged items, beginning with Scott 144.**

Queen Victoria

A1 A2

### Typographed and Embossed

**1869, Jan. Unwmk. *Imperf.***

| No. | Type | Description | Unused | Used |
|---|---|---|---|---|
| 1 | A1 | 4p pale brown | 550.00 | 240.00 |
| | | No gum | 400.00 | |
| *a.* | | 4p brown | 650.00 | 240.00 |
| | | No gum | 475.00 | |
| 2 | A1 | 6p blue | 625.00 | 240.00 |
| | | No gum | 450.00 | |
| *a.* | | 6p deep blue | *650.00* | *240.00* |
| | | No gum | 475.00 | |
| *b.* | | 6p pale blue | *3,250.* | *1,250.* |
| | | No gum | 2,500. | |

**1874, Aug. Wmk. 1**

| No. | Type | Description | Unused | Used |
|---|---|---|---|---|
| 3 | A1 | 4p brown | 450.00 | 240.00 |
| | | No gum | 300.00 | |
| *a.* | | 4p pale brown | 450.00 | 250.00 |
| | | No gum | 300.00 | |
| 4 | A1 | 6p blue | 400.00 | 240.00 |
| | | No gum | 290.00 | |
| *a.* | | 6p deep blue | 400.00 | 250.00 |
| | | No gum | 290.00 | |
| *b.* | | Panel sloping down from left to right | 950.00 | 525.00 |
| | | No gum | 650.00 | |

Nos. 1-4 are often seen with flat embossing. Unused values for are for fine-very fine examples with sharp, detailed embossing. Values for unused stamps without gum and used stamps are for examples with average embossing.

The name panel sloping down variety, No. 4b, is from a top right corner position. A top left corner position exists with a less noticeable sloping of the panel down from right to left; it is worth less.

**1880, June *Perf. 14***

| No. | Type | Description | Unused | Used |
|---|---|---|---|---|
| 5 | A1 | ½p orange | 15.50 | *22.50* |
| 6 | A1 | 1p maroon | 8.50 | *7.00* |
| 7 | A1 | 2p rose | 50.00 | 12.50 |
| 8 | A1 | 3p ultra | 72.50 | 37.50 |
| 9 | A1 | 4p pale brown | 350.00 | 22.50 |
| *a.* | | 4p brown | 350.00 | 22.50 |
| 10 | A1 | 6p blue | 140.00 | 52.50 |
| *a.* | | Panel sloping down from left to right | 375.00 | 175.00 |
| 11 | A1 | 1sh green | 300.00 | 165.00 |
| *a.* | | 1sh deep green | 375.00 | 180.00 |
| | | *Nos. 5-11 (7)* | 936.50 | 319.50 |

The watermark on Nos. 5-11 exists both upright and sideways.

See footnote following No. 4.

**1886-93 Wmk. 2 Sideways**

| No. | Type | Description | Unused | Used |
|---|---|---|---|---|
| 12 | A1 | ½p gray grn | 5.25 | 3.50 |
| 13 | A1 | 1p rose car ('87) | 10.50 | *12.50* |
| *a.* | | 1p maroon | | *17,250.* |
| 14 | | 2p deep orange | 4.00 | *10.50* |
| *b.* | | 2p orange | 15.00 | 5.75 |
| 15 | A1 | 2½p dp br blue | 11.00 | 1.40 |
| 16 | A1 | 3p gray | 10.00 | *17.00* |
| 17 | A1 | 4p dp brown | 14.00 | 2.25 |
| 18 | A1 | 6p slate green ('93) | 19.00 | *67.50* |
| *a.* | | 6p pale olive green ('86) | 100.00 | 60.00 |
| *b.* | | 6p bronze green ('89) | 45.00 | *72.50* |
| *c.* | | As "a," panel sloping down from left to right | 325.00 | 125.00 |
| *d.* | | As "b," panel sloping down from left to right | 95.00 | *180.00* |
| 19 | A1 | 1sh violet | 9.00 | *24.00* |
| *a.* | | 1sh purple | 8.00 | *22.50* |
| | | *Nos. 12-19 (8)* | 82.75 | *138.65* |

See footnote following No. 4.

**1898, Jan. Typo. Wmk. 2**

| No. | Type | Description | Unused | Used |
|---|---|---|---|---|
| 20 | A2 | ½p gray green | 3.25 | 2.00 |
| 21 | A2 | 1p carmine rose | 2.75 | .85 |
| 22 | A2 | 2p brn org & pur | 7.00 | 4.00 |
| 23 | A2 | 2½p ultramarine | 3.50 | *2.75* |
| 24 | A2 | 3p red vio & ultra | 42.50 | 14.00 |
| 25 | A2 | 4p brown & ultra | 16.00 | *37.50* |
| 26 | A2 | 6p ol grn & car rose | 15.00 | *45.00* |
| 27 | A2 | 1sh vio & green | 40.00 | *85.00* |
| | | *Nos. 20-27 (8)* | 130.00 | *191.10* |

King Edward VII — A3

**1902-05 *Perf. 14***

| No. | Type | Description | Unused | Used |
|---|---|---|---|---|
| 28 | A3 | ½p green | 5.00 | *2.75* |
| 29 | A3 | 1p car rose | 11.50 | 1.10 |
| 30 | A3 | 2p org & pur | 3.75 | 2.25 |
| 31 | A3 | 2½p ultramarine | 42.50 | 20.00 |
| 32 | A3 | 3p red vio & ultra | 16.00 | 4.00 |
| 33 | A3 | 4p brn & ultra | 6.25 | *37.50* |
| 34 | A3 | 6p ol grn & rose | 12.50 | *14.00* |
| 35 | A3 | 1sh bluish vio & green | 47.50 | *92.50* |
| 36 | A3 | 1sh6p grn & red, *yel* | 10.00 | *25.00* |
| 37 | A3 | 2sh black & org | 55.00 | *72.50* |
| 38 | A3 | 2sh6p pur & brn, *yel* | 17.50 | *75.00* |
| 39 | A3 | 3sh red & grn, *yel* | 22.50 | *72.50* |
| | | *Nos. 28-39 (12)* | 250.00 | *419.10* |

Numerals of 5p, 7½p, 10p, 1sh6p, 2sh, 2sh6p and 3sh of type A3 are in color on plain tablet.

Issue dates: 1p, Mar. 13. ½p, 3p, Apr. 19. 2p, 2½p, 4p, 6p, 1sh, 2sh, June 14. 1sh6p, 2sh6p, 3sh, Apr. 6, 1905.

For surcharges, see Nos. 65-66.

**1904-09 Wmk. 3**

| No. | Type | Description | Unused | Used |
|---|---|---|---|---|
| 41 | A3 | ½p green | 5.25 | .35 |
| 42 | A3 | 1p car rose | 5.25 | .25 |
| *a.* | | 1p carmine ('09) | 16.00 | .25 |
| 43 | A3 | 2p org & pur ('06) | 14.00 | 2.50 |
| 44 | A3 | 2p gray ('09) | 2.25 | 12.50 |
| 45 | A3 | 2½p br blue ('05) | 10.50 | 5.50 |
| 46 | A3 | 3p red vio & ultra | 14.50 | 2.25 |
| 47 | A3 | 3p vio, *yel* ('09) | 6.25 | 1.10 |
| 48 | A3 | 4p brn & ultra ('06) | 21.00 | *45.00* |
| 49 | A3 | 4p blk & red, *yel* ('09) | 2.75 | .75 |
| 50 | A3 | 5p gray & black | 16.00 | *30.00* |
| 51 | A3 | 5p org & vio ('09) | 2.75 | 1.40 |
| 52 | A3 | 6p ol grn & rose ('06) | 22.00 | *75.00* |
| 53 | A3 | 6p dull vio ('09) | 2.75 | 2.50 |
| 54 | A3 | 7½p blue grn & red | 17.00 | *65.00* |
| 55 | A3 | 7½p brn & ultra ('09) | 4.00 | 2.75 |
| 56 | A3 | 10p ol bis & red | 27.50 | *52.50* |
| 57 | A3 | 10p ol grn & car rose ('09) | 5.25 | *8.00* |
| 58 | A3 | 1sh violet & grn | 37.50 | *62.50* |
| 59 | A3 | 1sh blk, *grn* ('09) | 5.25 | *20.00* |
| 60 | A3 | 1sh 6p vio & grn ('09) | 27.50 | *80.00* |
| 61 | A3 | 2sh black & org | 100.00 | *125.00* |
| 62 | A3 | 2sh vio & bl, *bl* ('09) | 16.00 | *22.50* |
| 63 | A3 | 2sh 6p blk & red, *bl* ('09) | 24.00 | 22.50 |
| 64 | A3 | 3sh yel & grn ('09) | 40.00 | *55.00* |
| | | *Nos. 41-64 (24)* | 429.25 | *694.85* |

**Nos. 38-39 Surcharged in Black**

a

b

Type a (I) — The word "PENNY" is 5mm from the horizontal bars.

Type a (II) — "PENNY" is 4mm from the bars.

**1906, Apr. Wmk. 2**

| No. | Type | Description | Unused | Used |
|---|---|---|---|---|
| 65 | A3 | ½p on 2sh6p, type I | 57.50 | *70.00* |
| *a.* | | Type II | 62.50 | *75.00* |
| 66 | A3 | 1p on 3sh | 62.50 | 35.00 |
| *a.* | | Double surcharge | *2,150.* | *5,750.* |

King George V — A4

**1912-22 Wmk. 3**

| No. | Type | Description | Unused | Used |
|---|---|---|---|---|
| 70 | A4 | ½p dp green | 3.00 | *1.75* |
| 71 | A4 | 1p carmine | 2.75 | 1.75 |
| *a.* | | 1p scarlet ('16) | 7.25 | 1.00 |
| 72 | A4 | 1½p ol brn & grn | .60 | .35 |
| 73 | A4 | 2p gray | .60 | *3.25* |
| 74 | A4 | 2½p dp br blue | 5.00 | 3.50 |
| 75 | A4 | 3p violet, *yel* | 1.10 | .35 |
| 76 | A4 | 4p blk & red, *yel* | 1.10 | *11.50* |
| 77 | A4 | 5p orange & vio | 1.10 | *2.25* |

| | | | | |
|---|---|---|---|---|
| 78 | A4 | 6p dl vio & red violet | 2.00 | 2.75 |
| 79 | A4 | 7½p brn & ultra | 4.25 | 12.00 |
| 80 | A4 | 10p ol grn & car rose | 5.00 | 20.00 |
| 81 | A4 | 1sh blk, *green* | 3.25 | 1.10 |
| a. | | 1sh black, *emerald* | 2.50 | 24.00 |
| 82 | A4 | 1sh6p vio & green | 18.00 | 11.50 |
| 83 | A4 | 2sh vio & bl, *bl* | 6.75 | 7.00 |
| 84 | A4 | 2sh6p blk & red, *bl* | 7.00 | 16.00 |
| 85 | A4 | 3sh yel & green | 13.50 | 45.00 |
| 86 | A4 | 5sh grn & red, *yel* ('22) | 125.00 | 200.00 |
| | | *Nos. 70-86 (17)* | 200.00 | 340.05 |

Numerals of 1½p, 5p, 7½p, 10p, 1sh6p, 2sh, 2sh6p, 3sh, 4sh and 5sh of type A3 are in color on colorless tablet. No. 86 is on chalky paper.

**1921-22** **Wmk. 4**

| | | | | |
|---|---|---|---|---|
| 87 | A4 | ½p green | .35 | 22.50 |
| 88 | A4 | 1p carmine | 1.60 | 9.50 |
| 89 | A4 | 1½p ol grn & bl grn | 2.00 | 19.00 |
| 90 | A4 | 2p gray | 1.10 | 2.75 |
| 91 | A4 | 2½p ultramarine | .60 | 10.50 |
| 92 | A4 | 5p org & violet | 2.00 | 22.50 |
| 93 | A4 | 6p dl vio & red vio | 2.25 | 20.00 |
| 94 | A4 | 7½p brn & ultra | 2.25 | 47.50 |
| 95 | A4 | 10p yel grn & car rose | 8.00 | 25.00 |
| 96 | A4 | 4sh gray & red ('22) | 105.00 | 210.00 |
| | | *Nos. 87-96 (10)* | 125.15 | 389.25 |

No. 96 is on chalky paper.

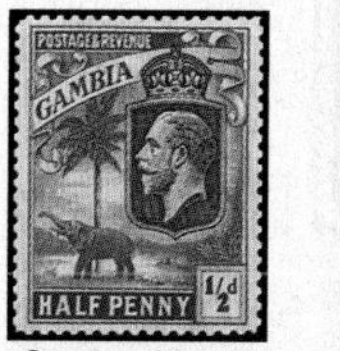
George V and Elephant — A5

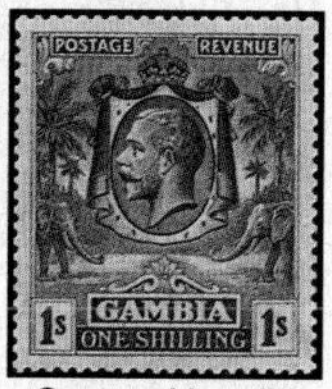
George V — A6

**1922-27** **Engr.** **Wmk. 4**

**Head and Shield in Black**

| | | | | |
|---|---|---|---|---|
| 102 | A5 | ½p green | .65 | .65 |
| 103 | A5 | 1p brown | 1.10 | .30 |
| 104 | A5 | 1½p carmine | 1.10 | .30 |
| 105 | A5 | 2p gray | 1.10 | 4.75 |
| 106 | A5 | 2½p orange | 2.40 | 15.00 |
| 107 | A5 | 3p ultramarine | 1.10 | .25 |
| 108 | A5 | 4p car, *org* ('27) | 21.00 | 30.00 |
| 109 | A5 | 5p yellow green | 4.25 | 16.00 |
| 110 | A5 | 6p claret | 1.50 | .35 |
| 111 | A5 | 7½p vio, *yel* ('27) | 21.00 | 95.00 |
| 112 | A5 | 10p blue | 5.75 | 20.00 |
| 113 | A6 | 1sh vio, *org* ('24) | 3.75 | 2.50 |
| 114 | A6 | 1sh6p blue | 21.00 | 19.00 |
| 115 | A6 | 2sh vio, *blue* | 12.50 | 8.00 |
| 116 | A6 | 2sh6p dark green | 12.50 | 11.00 |
| 117 | A6 | 3sh aniline vio | 26.00 | 90.00 |
| a. | | 3sh black purple | 275.00 | 475.00 |
| 118 | A6 | 4sh brown | 24.00 | 24.00 |
| 119 | A6 | 5sh dk grn, *yel* ('26) | 37.50 | 67.50 |
| 120 | A6 | 10sh yellow green | 85.00 | 145.00 |
| | | *Nos. 102-120 (19)* | 283.20 | 549.60 |

**1922, Sept. 1** **Wmk. 3**

**Head & Shield in Black**

| | | | | |
|---|---|---|---|---|
| 121 | A5 | 4p carmine, *yel* | 5.00 | 6.00 |
| 122 | A5 | 7½p violet, *yel* | 7.50 | 9.50 |
| 123 | A6 | 1sh violet, *orange* | 32.50 | 42.50 |
| 124 | A6 | 5sh dk green, *yel* | 62.50 | 215.00 |
| | | *Nos. 121-124 (4)* | 107.50 | 273.00 |

Common Design Types pictured following the introduction.

## Silver Jubilee Issue

Common Design Type

**1935, May 6** **Wmk. 4** ***Perf. 11x12***

| | | | | |
|---|---|---|---|---|
| 125 | CD301 | 1½p carmine & bl | .75 | 2.40 |
| 126 | CD301 | 3p ultra & brn | 1.30 | 2.25 |
| 127 | CD301 | 6p ol grn & lt bl | 3.00 | 7.25 |
| 128 | CD301 | 1sh brn vio & ind | 13.50 | 15.00 |
| | | *Nos. 125-128 (4)* | 18.55 | 26.90 |
| | | Set, never hinged | 20.00 | |

## Coronation Issue

Common Design Type

**1937, May 12** ***Perf. 11x11½***

| | | | | |
|---|---|---|---|---|
| 129 | CD302 | 1p brown | .25 | 1.30 |
| 130 | CD302 | 1½p dark carmine | .25 | 1.30 |
| 131 | CD302 | 3p deep ultra | .50 | 2.10 |
| | | *Nos. 129-131 (3)* | 1.00 | 4.70 |
| | | Set, never hinged | 1.30 | |

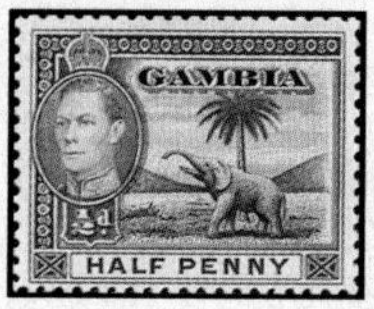
King George VI and Elephant Badge of Gambia — A7

**1938-46** ***Perf. 12***

| | | | | |
|---|---|---|---|---|
| 132 | A7 | ½p bl grn & blk | .25 | .80 |
| 133 | A7 | 1p brn & red vio | .25 | .55 |
| 134 | A7 | 1½p rose red & brn lake | .25 | 2.25 |
| 134A | A7 | 1½p gray black & ultra ('44) | .25 | 1.75 |
| 135 | A7 | 2p gray black & ultra | 3.00 | 3.75 |
| 135A | A7 | 2p rose red & brn lake ('43) | .65 | 2.50 |
| 136 | A7 | 3p blue & brt bl | .40 | .25 |
| 136A | A7 | 5p dk vio brn & olive ('41) | .45 | .60 |
| 137 | A7 | 6p plum & ol grn | 1.25 | .40 |
| 138 | A7 | 1sh vio & sl blk | 1.60 | .25 |
| 138A | A7 | 1sh3p bl & choc ('46) | 2.00 | 2.75 |
| 139 | A7 | 2sh bl & dp rose | 5.00 | 3.75 |
| 140 | A7 | 2sh6p sl grn & sep | 10.00 | 2.75 |
| 141 | A7 | 4sh dk vio & red orange | 17.50 | 2.75 |
| 142 | A7 | 5sh org red & dk blue | 17.50 | 4.50 |
| 143 | A7 | 10sh blk & yel org | 20.00 | 8.00 |
| | | *Nos. 132-143 (16)* | 80.35 | 37.60 |
| | | Set, never hinged | 110.00 | |

Issued: 5p, 3/13; No. 135A, 10/1; No. 134A, 1/22; 1sh3p, 11/28; others, 4/1.

**Catalogue values for unused stamps in this section, from this point to the end of the section, are for Never Hinged items.**

## Peace Issue

Common Design Type

**1946, Aug. 6** **Engr.** ***Perf. 13½***

| | | | | |
|---|---|---|---|---|
| 144 | CD303 | 1½p black | .25 | .50 |
| 145 | CD303 | 3p deep blue | .25 | .45 |

## Silver Wedding Issue

Common Design Types

**1948, Dec. 24** **Photo.** ***Perf. 14x14½***

| | | | | |
|---|---|---|---|---|
| 146 | CD304 | 1½p black | .25 | .25 |

***Perf. 11½x11***

**Engr.; Name Typo.**

| | | | | |
|---|---|---|---|---|
| 147 | CD305 | £1 purple | 22.00 | 21.00 |

## UPU Issue

Common Design Types

**Engr.; Name Typo. on 3p, 6p**

***Perf. 13½, 11x11½***

**1949, Oct. 10** **Wmk. 4**

| | | | | |
|---|---|---|---|---|
| 148 | CD306 | 1½p slate | .40 | 1.60 |
| 149 | CD307 | 3p indigo | 1.75 | 2.10 |
| 150 | CD308 | 6p red lilac | .80 | 3.50 |
| 151 | CD309 | 1sh violet | .55 | .65 |
| | | *Nos. 148-151 (4)* | 3.50 | 7.85 |

## Coronation Issue

Common Design Type

**1953, June 2** **Engr.** ***Perf. 13½x13***

| | | | | |
|---|---|---|---|---|
| 152 | CD312 | 1½p dk blue & black | .45 | .40 |

Palm Wine Tapping — A8

Designs: 1p, 1sh3p, Cutter. 1½p, 5sh, Wollof woman. 2½p, 2sh, Barra canoe. 3p, 10sh, "Lady Wright." 4p, 4sh, James Island. 1sh, 2sh6p, Woman farming. £1, Elephant badge of Gambia.

**1953, Nov. 2** ***Perf. 13½***

| | | | | |
|---|---|---|---|---|
| 153 | A8 | ½p dk green & car | .35 | .25 |
| 154 | A8 | 1p dk brn & ultra | .30 | .35 |
| 155 | A8 | 1½p gray & dk brn | .25 | .45 |
| 156 | A8 | 2½p car & black | .35 | .75 |
| 157 | A8 | 3p pur & indigo | .30 | .25 |
| 158 | A8 | 4p dp blue & blk | .50 | 2.25 |
| 159 | A8 | 6p dp plum & brn | .25 | .25 |
| 160 | A8 | 1sh green & yel brn | .50 | .50 |
| 161 | A8 | 1sh3p blue & vio bl | 8.75 | .55 |
| 162 | A8 | 2sh car & indigo | 6.00 | 3.25 |
| 163 | A8 | 2sh6p brn & bl grn | 4.00 | 2.00 |
| 164 | A8 | 4sh brn org & dp bl | 10.00 | 3.50 |
| 165 | A8 | 5sh ultra & red brn | 2.75 | 2.50 |
| 166 | A8 | 10sh dk yel green & ultra | 18.00 | 11.00 |
| 167 | A8 | £1 black & bl grn | 20.00 | 11.00 |
| | | *Nos. 153-167 (15)* | 72.30 | 38.85 |

Palm Leaf and Elizabeth II, by Annigoni — A9

Design: 3p, 6p, Map of West Africa.

**Wmk. 314**

**1961, Dec. 2** **Engr.** ***Perf. 11½***

| | | | | |
|---|---|---|---|---|
| 168 | A9 | 2p lilac & green | .25 | .40 |
| 169 | A9 | 3p brown & Prus grn | .90 | .25 |
| 170 | A9 | 6p car rose & dk blue | .90 | .65 |
| 171 | A9 | 1sh3p green & violet | .90 | 2.25 |
| | | *Nos. 168-171 (4)* | 2.95 | 3.55 |

Visit of Elizabeth II to Gambia, Dec., 1961.

## Freedom from Hunger Issue

Common Design Type

**1963, June 4** **Photo.** ***Perf. 14x14½***

| | | | | |
|---|---|---|---|---|
| 172 | CD314 | 1sh3p car rose | .50 | .25 |

## Red Cross Centenary Issue

Common Design Type

**1963, Sept. 2** **Litho.** ***Perf. 13***

| | | | | |
|---|---|---|---|---|
| 173 | CD315 | 2p black & red | .25 | .25 |
| 174 | CD315 | 1sh3p ultra & red | .60 | .60 |

Beautiful Long-tailed Sunbird — A10

Birds: 1p, Yellow-mantled whydah. 1½p, Cattle egret. 2p, Yellow-bellied parrot. 3p, Ring-necked parakeet. 4p, Amethyst starling. 6p, Village weaver. 1sh, Rufous-crowned roller. 1sh3p, Red-eyed turtle dove. 2sh6p, Double-spurred francolin. 5sh, Palm-nut vulture. 10sh, Orange-cheeked waxbill. £1, Emerald cuckoo.

***Perf. 12½x13***

**1963, Nov. 4** **Photo.** **Wmk. 314**

**Multicolored Design & Inscription**

| | | | | |
|---|---|---|---|---|
| 175 | A10 | ½p rose buff | .45 | .90 |
| 176 | A10 | 1p gray green | .60 | .25 |
| 177 | A10 | 1½p pale violet | 1.75 | .90 |
| 178 | A10 | 2p buff | 1.75 | .90 |
| 179 | A10 | 3p light gray | 1.75 | .95 |
| 180 | A10 | 4p lt yel green | 1.75 | .95 |
| 181 | A10 | 6p light blue | 1.75 | .25 |
| 182 | A10 | 1sh pale grysh grn | 1.75 | .25 |
| 183 | A10 | 1sh3p light blue | 11.00 | 1.60 |
| 184 | A10 | 2sh6p pale green | 7.25 | 3.00 |
| 185 | A10 | 5sh blue | 7.25 | 3.50 |
| 186 | A10 | 10sh tan | 11.00 | 9.25 |
| 187 | A10 | £1 pale rose | 23.00 | 16.50 |
| | | *Nos. 175-187 (13)* | 71.05 | 39.20 |

For overprints see Nos. 188-191, 193-205.

**Nos. 176, 179, 182 and 183 Overprinted: "SELF GOVERNMENT/1963"**

**1963, Nov. 7**

| | | | | |
|---|---|---|---|---|
| 188 | A10 | 1p multicolored | .25 | .35 |
| 189 | A10 | 3p multicolored | .35 | .25 |
| 190 | A10 | 1sh multicolored | .35 | .35 |
| 191 | A10 | 1sh3p multicolored | .45 | .45 |
| | | *Nos. 188-191 (4)* | 1.40 | 1.40 |

## Shakespeare Issue

Common Design Type

**1964, Apr. 23** **Photo.** ***Perf. 14x14½***

| | | | | |
|---|---|---|---|---|
| 192 | CD316 | 6p ultramarine | .35 | .25 |

**Nos. 175-187 Overprinted: "INDEPENDENCE / 1965"**

***Perf. 12½x13***

**1965, Feb. 18** **Photo.** **Wmk. 314**

**Multicolored Design & Inscription**

| | | | | |
|---|---|---|---|---|
| 193 | A10 | ½p rose buff | .40 | .85 |
| 194 | A10 | 1p gray green | .40 | .25 |
| 195 | A10 | 1½ pale violet | .65 | .85 |
| 196 | A10 | 2p buff | .90 | .30 |
| 197 | A10 | 3p light gray | .90 | .25 |
| 198 | A10 | 4p lt yel green | .90 | 1.50 |
| 199 | A10 | 6p light blue | .90 | .25 |
| 200 | A10 | 1sh pale grysh grn | .90 | .25 |
| 201 | A10 | 1sh3p light blue | .90 | .25 |
| 202 | A10 | 2sh6p pale green | .90 | .65 |
| 203 | A10 | 5sh blue | .90 | .85 |
| 204 | A10 | 10sh tan | 1.75 | 3.50 |
| 205 | A10 | £1 pale rose | 9.00 | 9.00 |
| | | *Nos. 193-205 (13)* | 19.40 | 18.75 |

In the overprint, "1965" is flush at left side under "Independence" on the ½p, 1½p, 6p, 1sh3p and 2sh6p; it is centered on the others.

Flag of Gambia over Gambia River — A11

Design: 2p, 1sh6p, Coat of arms.

**1965, Feb. 18** **Unwmk.** ***Perf. 14***

| | | | | |
|---|---|---|---|---|
| 206 | A11 | ½p slate & multi | .25 | .25 |
| 207 | A11 | 2p lt brown & multi | .25 | .25 |
| 208 | A11 | 7½p dk brown & multi | .40 | .40 |
| 209 | A11 | 1sh6p lt green & multi | .55 | .30 |
| | | *Nos. 206-209 (4)* | 1.45 | 1.20 |

Gambia's Independence.

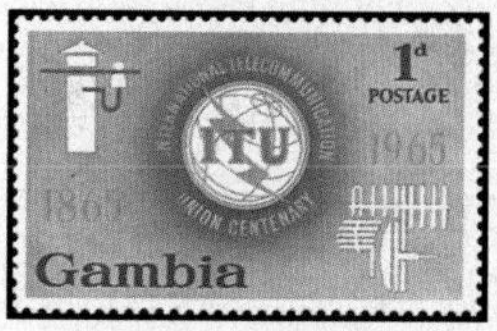
ITU Emblem, Old and New Communication Equipment — A12

**1965, May 17** **Photo.** ***Perf. 14½x14***

| | | | | |
|---|---|---|---|---|
| 210 | A12 | 1p dull blue & silver | .40 | .25 |
| 211 | A12 | 1sh6p violet & gold | 1.25 | .30 |

Cent. of the ITU.

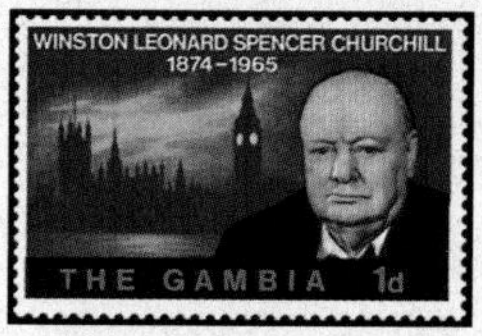
Winston Churchill and Parliament — A13

**1966, Jan. 24** ***Perf. 14x14½***

| | | | | |
|---|---|---|---|---|
| 212 | A13 | 1p multicolored | .25 | .25 |
| 213 | A13 | 6p multicolored | .40 | .25 |
| 214 | A13 | 1sh6p multicolored | .60 | .60 |
| | | *Nos. 212-214 (3)* | 1.25 | 1.10 |

Sir Winston Leonard Spencer Churchill, statesman and WWII leader.

Red-cheeked Cordon Bleu and Emblem — A14

Birds: 1p, White-faced tree duck. 1½p, Red-throated bee eater. 2p, Pied kingfisher. 3p, Yellow-crowned bishop. 4p, Fish eagle. 6p, Bruce's green pigeon. 1sh, Blue-bellied roller. 1sh6p, African pigmy kingfisher. 2sh6p, Spur-winged goose. 5sh, Little woodpecker. 10sh, Violet plantain eater. £1, Pintailed whydah, vert.

***Perf. 12½x13***

**1966, Feb. 18** **Photo.** **Unwmk.**

**Size: 29x25mm**

**Multicolored Design & Inscription**

| | | | | |
|---|---|---|---|---|
| 215 | A14 | ½p gray | .75 | .30 |
| 216 | A14 | 1p bluish green | .25 | .45 |
| 217 | A14 | 1½p yel green | .25 | .35 |
| 218 | A14 | 2p rose lilac | 3.75 | .70 |
| 219 | A14 | 3p lilac | .25 | .25 |
| 220 | A14 | 4p blue | .40 | .30 |
| 221 | A14 | 6p gray | .30 | .25 |
| 222 | A14 | 1sh light green | .30 | .25 |

| | | | | |
|---|---|---|---|---|
| **223** | A14 | 1sh6p bright blue | .75 | .25 |
| **224** | A14 | 2sh6p tan | .75 | .60 |
| **225** | A14 | 5sh gray green | .75 | .75 |
| **226** | A14 | 10sh ocher | .75 | *2.50* |

***Perf. 14x14½***

**Size: 25x39mm**

| | | | | |
|---|---|---|---|---|
| **227** | A14 | £1 pink | 1.00 | *6.00* |
| | | *Nos. 215-227 (13)* | 10.25 | *12.95* |

Coat of Arms, Old and New Views of Bathurst — A15

**Photo.; Silver Impressed (Arms)**

**1966, June 24** ***Perf. 14½x14***

| | | | | |
|---|---|---|---|---|
| **228** | A15 | 1p orange & dk brn | .25 | .25 |
| **229** | A15 | 2p lt ultra & dk brn | .25 | .25 |
| **230** | A15 | 6p emer & dk brown | .25 | .25 |
| **231** | A15 | 1sh6p brt pink & dk brn | .25 | .25 |
| | | *Nos. 228-231 (4)* | 1.00 | 1.00 |

150th anniv. of the founding of Bathurst.

Adonis and Atlantic Hotels and ITY Emblem — A16

**Photo.; Silver Impressed (Emblem)**

**1967, Dec. 20** ***Perf. 14½x14***

| | | | | |
|---|---|---|---|---|
| **232** | A16 | 2p lt yel green & brn | .25 | .25 |
| **233** | A16 | 1sh orange & brown | .25 | .25 |
| **234** | A16 | 1sh6p lilac rose & brn | .25 | .25 |
| | | *Nos. 232-234 (3)* | .75 | .75 |

International Tourist Year.

Handcuffs and Human Rights Flame A17

Intl. Human Rights Year: 1sh, Fort Bullen. 5sh, Methodist Church.

**1968, July 15** **Photo.** ***Perf. 14x13***

| | | | | |
|---|---|---|---|---|
| **235** | A17 | 1p gold & multi | .25 | .25 |
| **236** | A17 | 1sh gold & multi | .25 | .25 |
| **237** | A17 | 5sh gold & multi | .30 | *1.00* |
| | | *Nos. 235-237 (3)* | .80 | 1.50 |

Gambia #1, Victoria and Elizabeth II — A18

Designs: 6p, Gambia #2, Victoria & Elizabeth II. 2sh6p, Gambia #1-2, Elizabeth II.

**Photo. and Embossed**

***Perf. 14x13½***

**1969, Jan. 20** **Wmk. 314**

| | | | | |
|---|---|---|---|---|
| **238** | A18 | 4p dull yel & dk brn | .30 | .25 |
| **239** | A18 | 6p dp yel grn & bl | .30 | .25 |
| **240** | A18 | 2sh6p dk bl gray, brn & bl | .90 | *1.40* |
| | | *Nos. 238-240 (3)* | 1.50 | 1.90 |

Centenary of Gambian postage stamps.

Dornier Wal, Route Gambia to Brazil and Lufthansa Emblem — A19

2p, Plane & ship Westfalen, route Gambia to Brazil & Lufthansa emblem. 1sh6p, Zeppelin, route Gambia to Brazil & Lufthansa emblem.

***Perf. 13½x14***

**1969, Dec. 15** **Litho.** **Unwmk.**

| | | | | |
|---|---|---|---|---|
| **241** | A19 | 2p pink, org red & blk | .75 | .25 |
| **242** | A19 | 1sh buff, dl yel & blk | .75 | .25 |
| **243** | A19 | 1sh6p lt bl, ultra & blk | .80 | *1.40* |
| | | *Nos. 241-243 (3)* | 2.30 | 1.90 |

35th anniversary of pioneer air services.

Runner, Flag and Arms of Gambia A20

**1970, July 16** ***Perf. 14½x14***

**Flag in Red, Blue & Green**

| | | | | |
|---|---|---|---|---|
| **244** | A20 | 1p pink & brown | .25 | .25 |
| **245** | A20 | 1sh ultra & brown | .25 | .25 |
| **246** | A20 | 5sh green & brown | .30 | *.80* |
| | | *Nos. 244-246 (3)* | .80 | 1.30 |

9th Commonwealth Games, Edinburgh, Scotland, July 16-25.

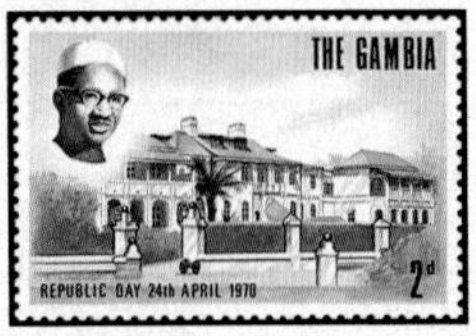


Pres. Jawara and State House A21

Republic Day, Apr. 24, 1970: 1sh, Pres. Sir Dauda Kairaba Jawara, vert. 1sh6p, Pres. Jawara and Gambia flag, vert.

**1970, Nov. 2** **Litho.** ***Perf. 14***

| | | | | |
|---|---|---|---|---|
| **247** | A21 | 2p gray & multi | .25 | .25 |
| **248** | A21 | 1sh multicolored | .25 | .25 |
| **249** | A21 | 1sh6p pink & multi | .50 | .70 |
| | | *Nos. 247-249 (3)* | 1.00 | 1.20 |

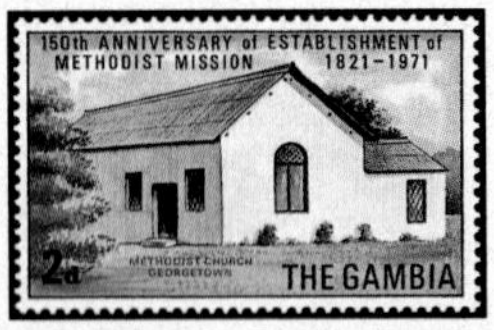


Methodist Church, Georgetown — A22

Designs: 1sh, Map of Africa and cross, vert. 1sh6p, John Wesley.

**1971, Apr. 16** **Unwmk.** ***Perf. 14***

| | | | | |
|---|---|---|---|---|
| **250** | A22 | 2p multicolored | .25 | .25 |
| **251** | A22 | 1sh vio blue & multi | .25 | .25 |
| **252** | A22 | 1sh6p green & multi | .60 | .80 |
| | | *Nos. 250-252 (3)* | 1.10 | 1.30 |

Establishment of Methodist Mission, 150th anniv.

Yellowfin Tuna A23

Fish from Gambian Waters: 4b, Peters' mormyrid. 6b, Tropical two-wing flying fish. 8b, African sleeper goby. 10b, Yellowtail snapper. 13b, Rock hind. 25b, West African eel cat. 38b, Tiger shark. 50b, Electric catfish. 63b, Swamp eel. 1.25d, Smalltooth sawfish. 2.50d, Barracuda. 5d, Brown bullhead.

**1971, July 1** **Litho.** ***Perf. 14***

**Fish in Natural Colors**

| | | | | |
|---|---|---|---|---|
| **253** | A23 | 2b blue | .25 | .25 |
| **254** | A23 | 4b lemon | .25 | .25 |
| **255** | A23 | 6b lt blue green | .25 | .25 |
| **256** | A23 | 8b orange brown | .25 | .25 |
| **257** | A23 | 10b lt Prus blue | .25 | .25 |
| **258** | A23 | 13b orange yel | .25 | .25 |
| **259** | A23 | 25b green | .35 | .50 |
| **260** | A23 | 38b brick red | .40 | .55 |
| **261** | A23 | 50b Prus blue | .70 | .80 |
| **262** | A23 | 63b bister | .85 | *1.60* |
| **263** | A23 | 1.25d yel green | 1.50 | *3.25* |
| **264** | A23 | 2.50d deep rose | 2.50 | *4.50* |
| **265** | A23 | 5d ultramarine | 4.50 | *7.50* |
| | | *Nos. 253-265 (13)* | 12.30 | *20.20* |

Mungo Park, Scottish Landscape, Map of Gambia Basin — A24

Map of Gambia River Basin and: 25b, Park traveling in dugout canoe. 37b, Park's death under attack at Busa Rapids.

***Perf. 13½x14***

**1971, Sept. 10** **Litho.** **Unwmk.**

| | | | | |
|---|---|---|---|---|
| **270** | A24 | 4b ultra & multi | .35 | .25 |
| **271** | A24 | 25b yel green & multi | 1.05 | .45 |
| **272** | A24 | 37b brick red & multi | 1.70 | *2.00* |
| | | *Nos. 270-272 (3)* | 3.10 | 2.70 |

Mungo Park (1771-1806), Scottish explorer of the Gambia and Niger Rivers.

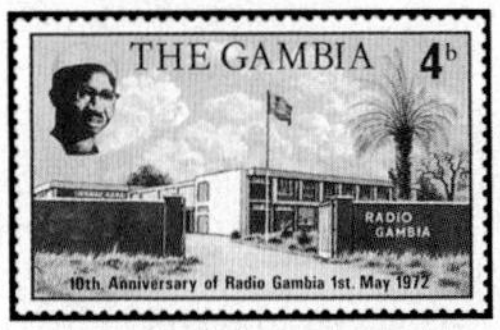


Radio Gambia and Pres. Jawara A25

Designs: 25b, Map showing area reached by Radio Gambia. 37b, Like 4b.

**1972, July 1** ***Perf. 14***

| | | | | |
|---|---|---|---|---|
| **273** | A25 | 4b black & dull yel | .25 | .25 |
| **274** | A25 | 25b black, blue & red | .25 | *.25* |
| **275** | A25 | 37b black & yel green | .30 | *.75* |
| | | *Nos. 273-275 (3)* | .80 | 1.25 |

Radio Gambia, 10th anniv., May 1.

High Jump A26

**1972, Aug. 31** ***Perf. 13½***

| | | | | |
|---|---|---|---|---|
| **276** | A26 | 4b emerald & multi | .25 | .25 |
| **277** | A26 | 25b lt ultra & multi | .25 | .25 |
| **278** | A26 | 37b red & multi | .40 | .40 |
| | | *Nos. 276-278 (3)* | .90 | .90 |

20th Olympic Games, Munich, 8/26-9/11.

Mandingo Woman — A27

Designs: 25b, Musician playing Mandingo 21-stringed lute (kora). 37b, Map of Mali empire and area of Mandingo language.

**1972, Oct. 18** **Litho.** ***Perf. 14x14½***

| | | | | |
|---|---|---|---|---|
| **279** | A27 | 2b rose red & multi | .25 | .25 |
| **280** | A27 | 25b lt ultra & multi | .30 | .30 |
| **281** | A27 | 37b emerald & multi | .40 | .40 |
| | | *Nos. 279-281 (3)* | .95 | .95 |

International Conference on Mandingo Studies, London, June 30-July 3.

Ship Model with Lanterns A28

Christmas: 2b, Lighted ship (lantern) carried by boys.

**1972, Dec. 1** **Litho.** ***Perf. 13x13½***

| | | | | |
|---|---|---|---|---|
| **282** | A28 | 2b violet & multi | .25 | .25 |
| **283** | A28 | 1.25d blue & multi | .65 | .65 |

Peanuts, FAO Emblem — A29

**1973, Mar. 31** **Litho.** ***Perf. 14½x14***

| | | | | |
|---|---|---|---|---|
| **284** | A29 | 2b red & multi | .25 | .25 |
| **285** | A29 | 25b lt blue & multi | .25 | .25 |
| **286** | A29 | 37b emerald & multi | .30 | .30 |
| | | *Nos. 284-286 (3)* | .80 | .80 |

Freedom from Hunger, 2nd UN development campaign.

Planting and Drying Rice — A30

Oil Palms — A31

**1973, Apr. 30** ***Perf. 14½x14***

| | | | | |
|---|---|---|---|---|
| **287** | A30 | 2b shown | .25 | .25 |
| **288** | A30 | 25b Sorghum (Guinea corn) | .25 | .25 |
| **289** | A30 | 37b Rice crop | .40 | .30 |

**1973, July 16**

| | | | | |
|---|---|---|---|---|
| **290** | A31 | 2b shown | .25 | .25 |
| **291** | A31 | 25b Limes | .25 | .25 |
| **292** | A31 | 37b Oil palm fruits | .55 | .45 |

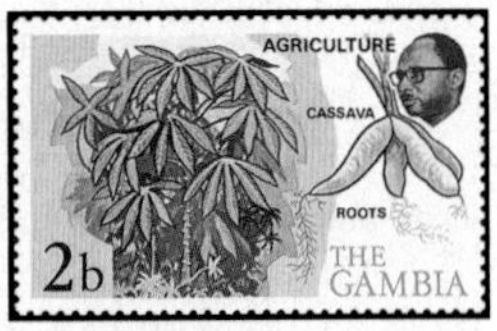


Cassava A32

**1973, Oct. 15**

| | | | | |
|---|---|---|---|---|
| **293** | A32 | 2b shown | .25 | .25 |
| **294** | A32 | 50b Cotton | .55 | .45 |
| | | *Nos. 287-294 (8)* | 2.75 | 2.45 |

Gambian agriculture.

OAU Emblem — A33

**1973, Nov. 1 Unwmk. *Perf. 13½x13***

| | | | | |
|---|---|---|---|---|
| **295** | A33 | 4b green, yel & black | .25 | .25 |
| **296** | A33 | 25b dp mag, yel & black | .25 | .25 |
| **297** | A33 | 37b blue, yel & black | .25 | .25 |
| | | *Nos. 295-297 (3)* | .75 | .75 |

10th anniv. of the OAU.

Red Cross — A34

***Perf. 14½x14***

**1973, Nov. 30 Wmk. 314**

| | | | | |
|---|---|---|---|---|
| **298** | A34 | 4b red & black | .25 | .25 |
| **299** | A34 | 25b ultra, red & black | .25 | .25 |
| **300** | A34 | 37b emer, red & black | .25 | .25 |
| | | *Nos. 298-300 (3)* | .75 | .75 |

25th anniv. of Gambia Red Cross Soc.

Flag of Gambia and Arms of Banjul — A35

***Perf. 13½x13***

**1973, Dec. 17 Litho. Unwmk.**

| | | | | |
|---|---|---|---|---|
| **301** | A35 | 4b yel green & multi | .25 | .25 |
| **302** | A35 | 25b ver & multi | .25 | .25 |
| **303** | A35 | 37b lt ultra & multi | .25 | .25 |
| | | *Nos. 301-303 (3)* | .75 | .75 |

Change of name of Bathurst to Banjul and of St. Mary's Island to Banjul Island.

UPU Emblem — A36

**1974, Aug. 24 Litho. *Perf. 13½x13***

| | | | | |
|---|---|---|---|---|
| **304** | A36 | 4b lilac & multi | .25 | .25 |
| **305** | A36 | 37b blue & multi | .45 | .45 |

Centenary of Universal Postal Union.

Churchill at Harrow — A37

Churchill in Uniform of 4th Hussars — A38

Designs: 50b, Churchill as Prime Minister.

**1974, Nov. 30 Litho. *Perf. 13½***

| | | | | |
|---|---|---|---|---|
| **306** | A37 | 4b multicolored | .25 | .25 |
| **307** | A38 | 37b multicolored | .30 | .25 |
| **308** | A38 | 50b multicolored | .35 | *.65* |
| | | *Nos. 306-308 (3)* | .90 | *1.15* |

Sir Winston Churchill (1874-1965).

WPY Emblem, Races of Man A39

Symbolic Designs and WPY Emblem: 37b, Races multiplying and dividing like atom. 50b, World population.

**1974, Dec. 16 Litho. *Perf. 14***

| | | | | |
|---|---|---|---|---|
| **309** | A39 | 4b multicolored | .25 | .25 |
| **310** | A39 | 37b multicolored | .25 | .25 |
| **311** | A39 | 50b multicolored | .25 | .25 |
| | | *Nos. 309-311 (3)* | .75 | .75 |

World Population Year.

Dr. Schweitzer and Hospital, Lambarene — A40

50b, Dr. Schweitzer examining patient. 1.25d, Dr. Schweitzer in boat on Ogowe River.

**1975, Jan. 14 Litho. *Perf. 14***

| | | | | |
|---|---|---|---|---|
| **312** | A40 | 10b multicolored | .25 | .25 |
| **313** | A40 | 50b multicolored | .60 | .25 |
| **314** | A40 | 1.25d multicolored | 1.10 | .75 |
| | | *Nos. 312-314 (3)* | 1.95 | 1.25 |

Dr. Albert Schweitzer (1875-1965), medical missionary, birth centenary.

Peace Dove A41

10b, Gambia flag. 50b, Gambia coat of arms. 1.25d, Map of Gambia & Gambia River.

**1975, Feb. 18 *Perf. 13***

| | | | | |
|---|---|---|---|---|
| **315** | A41 | 4b multicolored | .25 | .25 |
| **316** | A41 | 10b multicolored | .25 | .25 |
| **317** | A41 | 50b multicolored | .25 | .25 |
| **318** | A41 | 1.25d multicolored | .25 | .40 |
| | | *Nos. 315-318 (4)* | 1.00 | 1.15 |

10th anniversary of independence.

Public Services Graph, A.D.B. Emblem A42

David, by Michelangelo A43

African Development Bank Emblem and: 50b, Plant symbolizing growth of Africa, fed by Development Bank. 1.25d, A.D.B. emblem surrounded by symbols of water, education, roads and hospitals.

**1975, Mar. 31 Litho. *Perf. 14***

| | | | | |
|---|---|---|---|---|
| **319** | A42 | 10b multicolored | .25 | .25 |
| **320** | A42 | 50b multicolored | .25 | .25 |
| **321** | A42 | 1.25d multicolored | .40 | .40 |
| | | *Nos. 319-321 (3)* | .90 | .90 |

African Development Bank, 10th anniv.

**1975, Nov. 14 *Perf. 14½***

Bas-reliefs by Michelangelo: 50b, Madonna of the Steps. 1.25d, Battle of the Centaurs, horiz.

| | | | | |
|---|---|---|---|---|
| **322** | A43 | 10b dull blue & multi | .25 | .25 |
| **323** | A43 | 50b sepia & multi | .35 | .35 |
| **324** | A43 | 1.25d green & multi | .80 | .80 |
| | | *Nos. 322-324 (3)* | 1.40 | 1.40 |

Michelangelo Buonarroti (1475-1564), Italian painter, sculptor and architect.

Gambia High School A44

Designs: 50b, Pupil in laboratory and school emblem. 1.50d, School emblem.

**1975, Nov. 17**

| | | | | |
|---|---|---|---|---|
| **325** | A44 | 10b multicolored | .25 | .25 |
| **326** | A44 | 50b multicolored | .25 | .25 |
| **327** | A44 | 1.50d multicolored | .40 | .40 |
| | | *Nos. 325-327 (3)* | .90 | .90 |

Gambia High School, centenary.

Teacher and IWY Emblem A45

IWY: 10b, Women planting rice. 50b, Nurse holding baby. 1.50d, Woman traffic officer.

**1975, Dec. 15 Litho. *Perf. 14½***

| | | | | |
|---|---|---|---|---|
| **328** | A45 | 4b yellow & multi | .25 | .25 |
| **329** | A45 | 10b multicolored | .25 | .25 |
| **330** | A45 | 50b multicolored | .35 | .25 |
| **331** | A45 | 1.50d blue & multi | .60 | .30 |
| | | *Nos. 328-331 (4)* | 1.45 | 1.05 |

Woman Golfer A46

Designs: 50b, Golfer addressing ball. 1.50d, Golfer finishing iron shot.

**1976, Feb. 18 Litho. *Perf. 14½***

| | | | | |
|---|---|---|---|---|
| **332** | A46 | 10b multicolored | .90 | .25 |
| **333** | A46 | 50b multicolored | 1.60 | .35 |
| **334** | A46 | 1.50d multicolored | 2.50 | 1.10 |
| | | *Nos. 332-334 (3)* | 5.00 | 1.70 |

11th anniversary of independence.

American Militiaman — A47

American Bicent.: 50b, Continental Army soldier. 1.25d, Declaration of Independence.

**1976, May 15 Litho. *Perf. 14x13½***

| | | | | |
|---|---|---|---|---|
| **335** | A47 | 25b multicolored | .25 | .25 |
| **336** | A47 | 50b multicolored | .40 | .40 |
| **337** | A47 | 1.25d multicolored | .75 | .75 |
| *a.* | | Souvenir sheet of 3, #335-337 | 2.00 | *4.00* |
| | | *Nos. 335-337 (3)* | 1.40 | 1.40 |

Mother and Child, Christmas Decoration — A48

**1976, Oct. 28 Litho. *Perf. 14***

| | | | | |
|---|---|---|---|---|
| **338** | A48 | 10b lt ultra & multi | .25 | .25 |
| **339** | A48 | 50b rose & multi | .25 | .25 |
| **340** | A48 | 1.25d yel grn & multi | .30 | .40 |
| | | *Nos. 338-340 (3)* | .80 | .90 |

Christmas.

Serval Cat and Wildlife Fund Emblem — A49

Designs: 25b, Harnessed antelope. 50b, Sitatunga. 1.25d, Leopard.

**1976, Nov. 29 *Perf. 13½x14***

| | | | | |
|---|---|---|---|---|
| **341** | A49 | 10b multicolored | *7.75* | *.50* |
| **342** | A49 | 25b multicolored | *10.00* | *.50* |
| **343** | A49 | 50b multicolored | *19.00* | *1.00* |
| **344** | A49 | 1.25d multicolored | *34.00* | *10.00* |
| *a.* | | Souvenir sheet of 4, #341-344 | *100.00* | *20.00* |
| | | *Nos. 341-344 (4)* | *70.75* | *12.00* |

Abuko Nature Reserve.

Queen's Visit, 1961 — A50

Designs: 50b, The spurs and jeweled sword. 1.25d, The oblation of the sword.

**1977, Feb. 7 Litho. *Perf. 13½x14***

| | | | | |
|---|---|---|---|---|
| **345** | A50 | 25b multicolored | .25 | .25 |
| **346** | A50 | 50b multicolored | .25 | .25 |
| **347** | A50 | 1.25d multicolored | .30 | .40 |
| | | *Nos. 345-347 (3)* | .80 | .90 |

25th anniv. of the reign of Elizabeth II.

Festival Emblem and Weaver A51

**1977, Jan. 12 Litho. *Perf. 14***

| | | | | |
|---|---|---|---|---|
| **348** | A51 | 25b multicolored | .25 | .25 |
| **349** | A51 | 50b multicolored | .30 | .30 |
| **350** | A51 | 1.25d multicolored | .70 | .70 |
| *a.* | | Souvenir sheet of 3, #348-350 | 2.25 | *3.75* |
| | | *Nos. 348-350 (3)* | 1.25 | 1.25 |

2nd World Black and African Festival, Lagos, Nigeria, Jan. 15-Feb. 12.

Stone Circles, near Kuntaur A52

Tourism: 50b, Ruins of Fort on James Island. 1.25d, Mungo Park Monument.

**1977, Feb. 18 Litho. *Perf. 14½***

**351** A52 25b multicolored .25 .25
**352** A52 50b multicolored .30 .30
**353** A52 1.25d multicolored .70 .70
*Nos. 351-353 (3)* 1.25 1.25

Clerodendrum Splendens — A53

Flowers and Shrubs: 4b, White water lily. 6b, Fireball lily. 8b, Mussaenda elegans. 10b, Broad-leaved ground orchid. 13b, Fiber plant. 25b, False kapok. 38b, Baobab. 50b, Coral tree. 63b, Gloriosa lily. 1.25d, Bell-flowered mimosa. 2.50d, Kindin dolo. 5d, African tulip tree. 6b, 8b, 10b, 13b, 25b, 38b, 1.25d, 2.50d, vertical.

**1977, July 1 Litho. *Perf. 14½***

**354** A53 2b multicolored .25 .25
**355** A53 4b multicolored .25 *.25*
**356** A53 6b multicolored .25 *.25*
**357** A53 8b multicolored .25 .25
**358** A53 10b multicolored 1.90 .25
**359** A53 13b yellow & multi 1.50 *1.75*
*a.* Pale olive background *3.00 4.50*
**360** A53 25b multicolored .25 .25
**361** A53 38b multicolored .25 *.70*
**362** A53 50b multicolored .35 .55
**363** A53 63b multicolored .40 *.75*
**364** A53 1.25d multicolored .60 *1.90*
**365** A53 2.50d multicolored .65 *1.90*
**366** A53 5d multicolored .90 *3.00*
*Nos. 354-366 (13)* 7.80 *12.05*

For surcharges see Nos. 390A-390C.

Crowned Crane, Nile Crocodile, Bush Buck — A54

Madonna, Flight into Egypt, by Rubens — A55

Designs: 25b, Banjul Declaration, excerpt, flag colors. 50b, Banjul Declaration. 1.25d, Climbing lily, butterfly and moth.

**1977, Oct. 15 Litho. *Perf. 14***

**367** A54 10b lt blue & black .25 .25
**368** A54 25b multicolored .35 .25
**369** A54 50b multicolored .70 .25
**370** A54 1.25d red & black 2.25 .75
*Nos. 367-370 (4)* 3.55 1.50

Banjul Declaration, for the conservation of flora and fauna, Feb. 18, 1977.

**1977, Dec. 15 Litho. *Perf. 14x13½***

Rubens Paintings: 25b, Education of Mary by St. Ann. 50b, Child's head. 1d, Madonna surrounded by saints.

**371** A55 10b multicolored .25 .25
**372** A55 25b multicolored .25 .25
**373** A55 50b multicolored .45 .35
**374** A55 1d multicolored .75 1.00
*Nos. 371-374 (4)* 1.70 1.85

Peter Paul Rubens (1577-1640). Nos. 371-374 printed in sheets of 5 stamps and decorative label.

Dome of the Rock, Jerusalem — A56

**1978, Jan. 3 Litho. *Perf. 14½***

**375** A56 8b olive green & multi *1.00 .60*
**376** A56 25b red & multi *4.00 2.50*

Palestinian fighters and their families.

Walking on Greased Pole — A57

Designs: 50b, Pillow fight on greased pole. 1.25d, Rowers in long boat.

**1978, Feb. 18 *Perf. 14***

**377** A57 10b multicolored .25 .25
**378** A57 50b multicolored .25 .25
**379** A57 1.25d multicolored .30 .30
*Nos. 377-379 (3)* .80 .80

Independence Regatta celebrating 13th anniversary of independence.

**Elizabeth II Coronation Anniversary Issue**

Souvenir Sheet

Common Design Types

**1978, Apr. 15 Litho. *Perf. 15***

**380** Sheet of 6 1.50 1.50
*a.* CD326 1d White grayhound of Richmond .30 .30
*b.* CD327 1d Elizabeth II .30 .30
*c.* CD328 1d Lion .30 .30

No. 380 contains 2 se-tenant strips of Nos. 380a-380c, separated by horizontal gutter with commemorative and descriptive inscriptions.

Verreaux's Eagle Owl — A58

Birds of Prey and Wildlife Fund Emblem: 25b, Lizard buzzard. 50b, West African harrier hawk. 1.25d, Long-crested hawk eagle.

**1978, Oct. 28 Litho. *Perf. 14x13½***

**381** A58 20b multicolored *22.50 .75*
**382** A58 25b multicolored *22.50 .75*
**383** A58 50b multicolored *35.00 3.00*
**384** A58 1.25d multicolored *50.00 11.00*
*Nos. 381-384 (4) 130.00 15.50*

Abuko Nature Reserve.

MV Lady Wright A59

New river vessels: 25b, River vessel Lady Chilel Jawara. 1d, Cross section of Lady Chilel Jawara.

**1978, Dec. 1 Litho. *Perf. 14½***

**385** A59 8b multicolored .25 .25
**386** A59 25b multicolored .35 .30
**387** A59 1d multicolored 1.25 1.25
*Nos. 385-387 (3)* 1.85 1.80

Motorized Police A60

**1979, Feb. 18 Litho. *Perf. 14***

**388** A60 10b shown .80 .25
**389** A60 50b Fire engine 1.40 .30
**390** A60 1.25d Ambulance 2.25 1.00
*Nos. 388-390 (3)* 4.45 1.55

14th anniversary of independence.

**Nos. 359, 363-364 Surcharged**

**1979 Litho. *Perf. 14½***

**390A** A53 25b on 13b multi .25 *.35*
**390B** A53 25b on 63b multi .25 .25
**390C** A53 25b on 1.25d multi .25 .25
*Nos. 390A-390C (3)* .75 .85

Issued: No. 390A, 3/5; others, 3/26.

Ramsgate Sands, by William P. Frith — A61

Designs: 10b, 25b, IYC emblem and details from painting shown on 1d. 25b, vert.

**1979, May 25 Litho. *Perf. 14***

**Size: 38x21mm, 21x38mm**

**391** A61 10b multicolored .25 .25
**392** A61 25b multicolored .25 .25

**Size: 56x21mm**

**393** A61 1d multicolored .75 .75
*Nos. 391-393 (3)* 1.25 1.25

International Year of the Child.

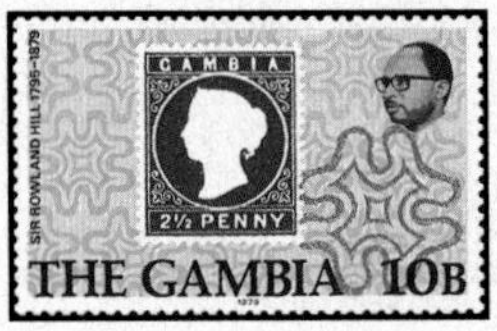


Gambia No. 15, Maltese Cross Postmark A62

Gambian Stamps and Maltese Cross Postmark: 25b, #1. 50b, #208. 1.25d, #125.

**1979, Aug. 16 Litho. *Perf. 14½***

**394** A62 10b multicolored .25 .25
**395** A62 25b multicolored .25 .25
**396** A62 50b multicolored .25 .30
**397** A62 1.25d multicolored .30 .70
*a.* Souvenir sheet of 1 .80 *1.40*
*Nos. 394-397 (4)* 1.05 1.50

Sir Rowland Hill (1795-1879), originator of penny postage.

Abuko Earth Station, Construction — A63

Telecommunications: 50b, Newly opened station. 1d, Intelsat satellites orbiting earth.

**1979, Sept. 20 Litho. *Perf. 14***

**398** A63 25b multicolored .25 .25
**399** A63 50b multicolored .30 .30
**400** A63 1d multicolored .50 .50
*Nos. 398-400 (3)* 1.05 1.05

Apollo 11 Lift-off — A64

**1979, Oct. 17 Litho. *Perf. 14***

**401** A64 25b shown .25 .25
**402** A64 38b Orbiting moon .25 .25
**403** A64 50b Splashdown .55 .55
*a.* Souvenir booklet 5.00
*b.* Pane, 2 each 25b, 38b, 50b 1.90
*c.* Pane of 1 (2d Lunar module) 1.75
*Nos. 401-403 (3)* 1.05 1.05

Apollo 11 moon landing, 10th anniversary. No. 403a contains Nos. 403b-403c printed on peelable, self-adhesive paper backing with Apollo 11 emblems on back. Stamps and panes are die-cut and have 1 to 3 sides rouletted 9½.

Large Spotted Acraea, Wildlife Fund Emblem — A65

Wildlife Fund Emblem and Butterflies: 50b, Yellow pansy. 1d, Veined swallowtail. 1.25d, Foxy charaxes.

**1980, Jan. 3 Litho. *Perf. 13½x14***

**404** A65 25b multicolored *12.00 .50*
**405** A65 50b multicolored *15.50 1.00*
**406** A65 1d multicolored *25.00 2.50*
**407** A65 1.25d multicolored *27.00 3.00*
*a.* Souvenir sheet of 4, #404-407 *110.00 20.00*
*Nos. 404-407 (4) 79.50 7.00*

Abuko Nature Reserve.

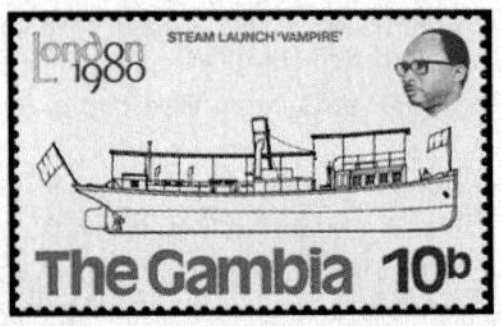


Steam Launch "Vampire" — A66

**1980, May 6 Litho. *Perf. 14½***

**408** A66 10b shown .25 .25
**409** A66 25b "Lady Denham" .35 .25

***Perf. 13½x14½***

**Size: 49x21mm**

**410** A66 50b "Mansa Kila Ba" .50 .50
**411** A66 1.25d "Prince of Wales" .65 *.85*
*Nos. 408-411 (4)* 1.75 1.85

London 80 Intl. Stamp Exhib., May 6-14.
For surcharge see No. 497A.

**Queen Mother Elizabeth Birthday Issue**

Common Design Type

**1980, Aug. 4 Litho. *Perf. 14***

**412** CD330 67b multicolored .40 *.50*

Phoenician Trading Vessel — A67

**1980, Oct. 2 Litho. *Perf. 14½***

**413** A67 8b shown .25 .25
**414** A67 67b Egyptian seagoing ship .70 .60
**415** A67 75b Portuguese caravel .80 .70
**416** A67 1d Spanish galleon 1.00 .90
*Nos. 413-416 (4)* 2.75 2.45

Virgin and Child, by Francesco de Mura — A68

Christmas: 67b, Praying Virgin with Crown of Stars, by Correggio. 75b, Rest on the Flight, after Correggio.

**1980, Dec. 18 Litho. *Perf. 14***

**417** A68 8b multicolored .25 .25
**418** A68 67b multicolored .25 .25
**419** A68 75b multicolored .25 .25
*Nos. 417-419 (3)* .75 .75

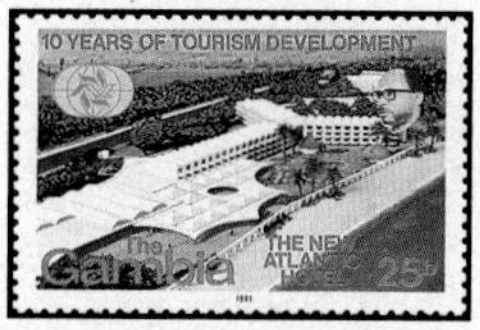

New Atlantic Hotel, Conference Emblem — A69

**1981, Feb. 18 Litho. *Perf. 14***
**420** A69 25b shown .25 .25
**421** A69 75b Ancient stone circle .45 .45
**422** A69 85b Conference emblem .60 .60
*Nos. 420-422 (3)* 1.30 1.30

World Tourism Conference, Manila, Sept. 27 and 16th anniversary of independence.

13th World Telecomunications Day — A70

**1981, May 17 Litho. *Perf. 14***
**423** A70 50b No. 399 .50 .35
**424** A70 50b No. 313 .50 .35
**425** A70 85b ITU, WHO emblems .75 .60
*Nos. 423-425 (3)* 1.75 1.30

**Royal Wedding Issue**
Common Design Type

**1981, July 22 Litho. *Perf. 13½x13***
**426** CD331 75b Bouquet .25 .25
**427** CD331 1d Charles .30 .30
**428** CD331 1.25d Couple .35 .35
*Nos. 426-428 (3)* .90 .90

For surcharges see Nos. 439, 497C.

Planting Rice Seedlings A71

**1981, Sept. 4 Litho. *Perf. 14***
**429** A71 10b shown .25 .25
**430** A71 50b Spraying .25 *.35*
**431** A71 85b Winnowing and drying .35 *.55*
*Nos. 429-431 (3)* .85 *1.15*

West African Rice Development Assoc., 10th anniv.

Abuko Nature Reserve A72

Designs: Wildlife Fund emblem and reptiles.

**1981, Nov. 17 Litho. *Perf. 14***
**432** A72 40b Bosc's monitor *27.50* *.75*
**433** A72 60b Dwarf crocodile *20.00* *1.50*
**434** A72 80b Royal python *37.50* *2.50*
**435** A72 85b Chameleon *42.50* *3.00*
*Nos. 432-435 (4)* *127.50* *7.75*

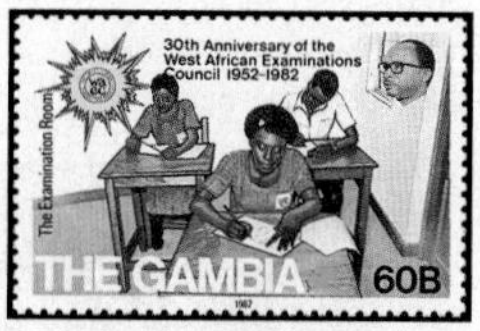

30th Anniv. of West African Examinations Council — A73

**1982, Mar. 16 Litho. *Perf. 14***
**436** A73 60b Test room .55 .40
**437** A73 85b 1st high school .65 .55
**438** A73 1.10d Council office .85 .75
*Nos. 436-438 (3)* 2.05 1.70

**No. 426 Surcharged**

**1982, Apr. 19 Litho. *Perf. 13½x13***
**439** CD331 60b on 75b multi *5.00* *3.00*

Scouting Year A74

**1982, May *Perf. 14***
**440** A74 85b Tree planting 2.50 1.25
**441** A74 1.25d Woodworking 2.75 2.50
**442** A74 1.27d Baden-Powell 3.00 *3.25*
*Nos. 440-442 (3)* 8.25 7.00

1982 World Cup A75

**1982, June 13 Litho. *Perf. 14***
**443** A75 10b Team .25 .25
**444** A75 1.10d Players 1.50 .75
**445** A75 1.25d Stadium 1.50 .80
**446** A75 1.55d Cup 1.75 1.00
*a.* Souvenir sheet of 4, #443-446 6.25 6.25
*Nos. 443-446 (4)* 5.00 2.80

For surcharge see No. 497B.

**Princess Diana Issue**
Common Design Type

**1982, July 1 *Perf. 14½x14***
**447** CD333 10b Arms .25 .25
**448** CD333 85b Diana .65 .65
**449** CD333 1.10d Wedding .85 .85
**450** CD333 2.50d Portrait 1.50 1.50
*Nos. 447-450 (4)* 3.25 3.25

For surcharge see No. 479D.

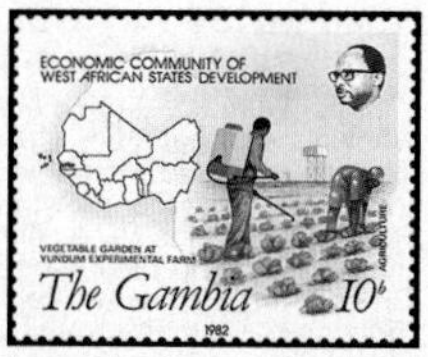

Economic Community of West African States Development A76

Designs: 10b, Yundum Experimental Farm. 60b, Banjul/Kaolack Microwave Tower. 90b, Soap Factory, Denton Bridge Banjul. 1.25d, Control Tower, Yundum.

**1982, Nov. 5 Litho. *Perf. 14x14½***
**451** A76 10b multicolored .30 .25
**452** A76 60b multicolored 2.10 *2.40*
**453** A76 90b multicolored 2.10 *3.25*
**454** A76 1.25d multicolored 3.00 *3.75*
*Nos. 451-454 (4)* 7.50 9.65

Kassina Cassinoides — A77

**1982, Dec. Litho. *Perf. 14***
**455** A77 10b shown 2.25 .25
**456** A77 20b Hylarana galamensis 4.25 .45
**457** A77 85b Euphlyctis occipitalis 7.25 4.50
**458** A77 2d Kassina senegalensis 9.50 *12.00*
*Nos. 455-458 (4)* 23.25 17.20

A78

**1983, Mar. 14 Wmk. 373 *Perf. 12***
**459** A78 10b Globe showing Gambia .25 .25
**460** A78 60b Batik cloth .25 *.35*
**461** A78 1.10d Bagging peanuts .45 *.60*
**462** A78 2.10d Flag .70 *1.25*
*Nos. 459-462 (4)* 1.65 2.45

Commonwealth Day.

Sisters of St. Joseph of Cluny Centenary — A79

**1983, Apr. 8 Litho. *Perf. 14***
**463** A79 10b Founder Anne Marie Javouhey, vert. .25 .25
**464** A79 85b Javouhey with children, house .45 .45

River Boats A80

**1983, July 11 Litho. *Perf. 14***
**465** A80 1b Canoes .25 .25
**466** A80 2b Upstream ferry .25 .25
**467** A80 3b Dredging vessel .25 .25
**468** A80 4b Harbor launch .30 .30
**469** A80 5b Freighter .30 .30
**470** A80 10b 60-foot launch .30 .30
**471** A80 20b Multi-purpose vessel .40 .40
**472** A80 30b Large sailing canoe .40 .40
**473** A80 40b Passenger-cargo ferry .40 .40
**474** A80 50b Cargo liner, diff. .45 .45
**475** A80 75b Fishing boats .55 .50
**476** A80 1d Peanut river train .80 .60
**477** A80 1.25d Groundnutter .85 *1.25*
**478** A80 2.50d Banjul-Barra ferry 1.50 *2.25*
**479** A80 5d Binlang Bolong 2.75 *4.75*
**480** A80 10d Passenger-cargo ferry, diff. 5.75 *8.50*
*Nos. 465-480 (16)* 15.50 *21.15*

For overprints see Nos. 523-524.

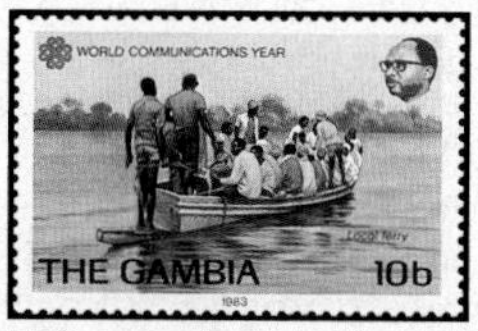

World Communications Year — A81

**1983, Oct. 10**
**481** A81 10b Local ferry .25 .25
**482** A81 85b GPO telex, Banjul .90 .80
**483** A81 90b Radio Gambia 1.00 .90
**484** A81 1.10d Loading mail, Yundum Airport 1.10 1.10
*Nos. 481-484 (4)* 3.25 3.05

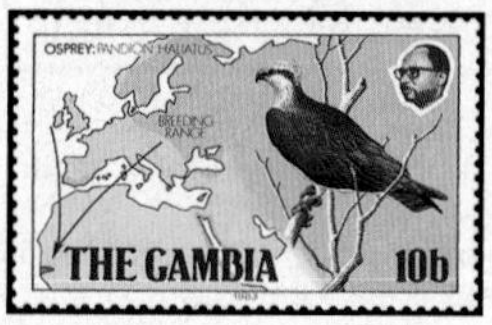

Osprey, Breeding Range A82

Designs: Birds, Maps of Europe and Africa.

**1983, Sept. 12 Litho. *Perf. 14***
**485** A82 10b multicolored 2.75 .65
**486** A82 60b multicolored 4.50 4.25
**487** A82 85b multicolored 5.25 4.75
**488** A82 1.10d multicolored 6.00 *7.25*
*Nos. 485-488 (4)* 18.50 16.90

Raphael, 500th Birth Anniv. A83

Details from St. Paul Preaching at Athens.

**1983, Nov. 1 Litho. *Perf. 14***
**489** A83 60b multicolored .55 .55
**490** A83 85b multicolored .70 .70
**491** A83 1d multicolored .75 .75
*Nos. 489-491 (3)* 2.00 2.00

**Souvenir Sheet**

**492** A83 2d multi, vert. 1.90 1.50

Manned Flight, 200th Anniv. A84

Flown covers and: 60b, Montgolfier Balloon. 85b, British Caledonian Aircraft. 96b, Junkers Airplane. 1.25d, Lunar module. 4d, Zeppelin.

**1983, Dec. 12 Litho. *Perf. 14***
**493** A84 60b multicolored .35 .35
**494** A84 85b multicolored .45 .45
*a.* Bklt. pane, 2 each #493, 494 3.00
**495** A84 90b multicolored .45 .45
**496** A84 1.25d multicolored .50 .50
*a.* Bklt. pane, 2 each #495, 496 5.00
*Nos. 493-496 (4)* 1.75 1.75

**Souvenir Sheet**

**497** A84 4d multicolored 10.00 10.00

No. 497 issued in booklet containing Nos. 497, 494a, 496a.

**Nos. 411, 445, 428 and 449 Surcharged with Black Bars and New Value**
***Perfs. as before***

**1983, Dec. 14 Litho.**
**497A** A66 1.50d on 1.25d, #411 *40.00*
**497B** A75 1.50d on 1.25d, #445 *40.00*
**497C** CD331 2d on 1.25d, #428 *40.00*
**497D** CD333 2d on 1.10d, #449 *40.00*

The status of Nos. 497A-497D is questioned.

Easter A85

Various Disney characters painting Easter eggs.

**1984, Apr. 15 Litho. *Perf. 11***
**498** A85 1b multicolored .25 .25
**499** A85 2b multicolored .25 .25
**500** A85 3b multicolored .25 .25
**501** A85 4b multicolored .25 .25
**502** A85 5b multicolored .25 .25
**503** A85 10b multicolored .25 .25
**504** A85 60b multicolored .55 .45
**505** A85 90b multicolored .85 .70
**506** A85 5d multicolored 3.00 3.00
*Nos. 498-506 (9)* 5.90 5.65

**Souvenir Sheet**
***Perf. 14***

**507** A85 5d multicolored 6.00 6.00

1984 Summer Olympics A86

**1984, Mar. 30 Litho. *Perf. 14***

**508** A86 60b Shot put, vert. .30 .30
**509** A86 85b High jump .45 .45
**510** A86 90b Wrestling, vert. .45 .45
**511** A86 1d Gymnastics, vert. .50 .50
**512** A86 1.25d Swimming .60 .60
**513** A86 2d Diving 1.00 1.00
*Nos. 508-513 (6)* 3.30 3.30

**Souvenir Sheet**

**514** A86 5d Yachting, vert. 3.25 3.25

For overprints see Nos. 570-576.

Nile Crododile A87

**1984, May 23**

**515** A87 4b Young hatching *3.50* *.75*
**516** A87 6b Adult carrying young *3.50* *.75*
**517** A87 90b Adult *24.00* *5.00*
**518** A87 1.50d Adult, diff. *29.00* *6.00*
*Nos. 515-518 (4)* *60.00* *12.50*

**Souvenir Sheet**

As Nos. 515-518, without WWF emblem.

**518A** A87 Sheet of 4 *8.50* *6.00*
***b.-e.*** each single *2.00* *1.50*

**Lloyd's List Issue**
Common Design Type

**1984, June 1 Litho. *Perf. 14***

**519** CD335 60b Banjul Port .85 .60
**520** CD335 85b Bulk cargo carrier 1.05 .90
**521** CD335 90b Sinking of the Dagomba 1.05 *1.10*
**522** CD335 1.25d 19th-cent. frigate 1.90 *1.90*
*Nos. 519-522 (4)* 4.85 4.50

**Nos. 478-479 Overprinted: "19th UPU / CONGRESS HAMBURG"**

**1984, June 19 Litho. *Perf. 14***

**523** A80 2.50d multicolored 1.50 *1.75*
**524** A80 5d multicolored 2.75 *3.50*

1984 Summer Olympics A88

**1984, July 28 Litho. *Perf. 14***

**525** A88 60b Running .50 .40
**526** A88 85b Long jump .60 .55
**527** A88 90b Running, diff. .60 .55
**528** A88 1.25d Long jump, diff. .80 .70
*Nos. 525-528 (4)* 2.50 2.20

Gambia-South America Transatlantic Flight, 50th Anniv. — A89

**1984, Nov. 1 Litho. *Perf. 14***

**529** A89 60b Graf Zeppelin D-LZ127 1.40 1.10
**530** A89 85b Dornier Wal on S.S. Westfalen 2.10 *1.90*
**531** A89 90b Dornier DO-18 D-ABYM 2.50 *2.75*
**532** A89 1.25d Dornier Wal D-2069 2.50 *3.00*
*Nos. 529-532 (4)* 8.50 *8.75*

Butterflies A90

**1984, Nov. 27**

**533** A90 10b Antanartia hippomene .35 .25
**534** A90 85b Pseudacraea eurytus 1.00 1.00
**535** A90 90b Charaxes lactitinctus 1.00 1.00
**536** A90 3d Graphium pylades 2.75 *4.25*
*Nos. 533-536 (4)* 5.10 *6.50*

**Souvenir Sheets**

**537** A90 5d Eurema hapale 12.50 12.50

Marine Life — A90a

**1984, Nov. 27**

**538** A90a 55b Penaeus duorarum .45 .35
**539** A90a 75b Caretta caretta .70 .50
**540** A90a 1.50d Physalia 1.00 1.00
**541** A90a 2.35d Uca pugilator 2.00 1.90
*Nos. 538-541 (4)* 4.15 *3.75*

**Souvenir Sheets**

**542** A90a 5d Cowrie snail 5.50 5.50

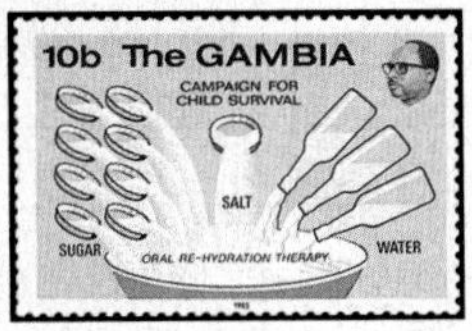


UN Child Survival Campaign A91

**1985, Feb. 27**

**543** A91 10b Oral rehydration therapy .25 .25
**544** A91 85b Growth monitoring .45 .45
**545** A91 1.10d Breast-feeding .60 .60
**546** A91 1.50d Universal immunization .70 .70
*Nos. 543-546 (4)* 2.00 2.00

UN Decade for Women A92

Design: 1d, 1.25d, Woman working in office.

**1985, Mar. 11**

**547** A92 60b multicolored .30 .30
**548** A92 85b multicolored .45 .45
**549** A92 1d multicolored .60 .60
**550** A92 1.25d multicolored .65 .65
*Nos. 547-550 (4)* 2.00 2.00

Audubon Birth Bicent. — A93

Queen Mother, 85th Birthday — A94

Illustrations of North American bird species by John J. Audubon (1785-1851).

**1985, July 15**

**551** A93 60b Cathartes aura 1.60 1.00
**552** A93 85b Anhinga anhinga 2.00 1.75
**553** A93 1.50d Butoroides striatus 2.25 3.75
**554** A93 5d Aix sponsa 4.25 6.25
*Nos. 551-554 (4)* 10.10 12.75

**Souvenir Sheet**

**555** A93 10d Gavia immer 8.50 8.50

**1985, July 24**

**556** A94 85b Inspecting troops .45 .45
**557** A94 3d Portrait 1.40 1.40
**558** A94 5d Portrait, diff. 2.40 2.40
*Nos. 556-558 (3)* 4.25 4.25

**Souvenir Sheet**

**559** A94 10d On parade with Prince Charles 5.00 5.00

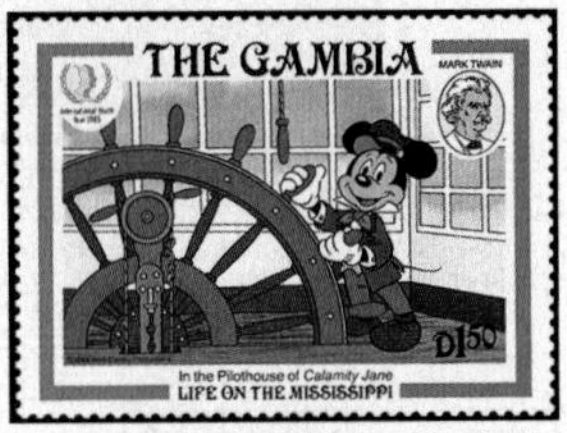


Life on the Mississippi, by Mark Twain (1835-1910) — A95

Walt Disney characters. The 60b, 85b, 2.35d, 5d and No. 569 show scenes from "Faithful John" by the brothers Grimm.

**1985, Oct. 30**

**560** A95 60b Portrait .80 .80
**561** A95 85b Treasure 1.00 1.00
**562** A95 1.50d Helm of Calamity Jane 2.10 2.10
**563** A95 2d Antebellum Mansion, Missouri Shore 2.25 2.25
**564** A95 2.35d Music 2.25 2.25
**565** A95 2.50d Measuring Channel Depth, Natchez 2.75 2.75
**566** A95 3d Card Game aboard the Gold Dust 3.00 3.00
**567** A95 5d Statue 4.00 4.00
*Nos. 560-567 (8)* 18.15 18.15

**Souvenir Sheet**

**568** A95 10d Landing, St. Louis 10.00 10.00
**569** A95 10d Goofy 10.00 10.00

**Nos. 508-514 Ovptd. "GOLD MEDALIST" or "GOLD MEDAL," Name of Winner and Country**

60b, Claudia Losch, West Germany, women's shot put. 85b, Ulrike Meyfarth, West Germany, women's high jump. 90b, Pasquale Passarelli, West Germany, 126-pound Greco-Roman wrestling. 1d, Li Ning, China, men's gymnastic floor exercises. 1.25d, Michael Gross, West Germany, men's 100-meter butterfly and 200-meter freestyle swimming. 2d, Sylvie Bernier, Canada, women's springboard diving. 5d, US, Star Class yachting.

**1985, Nov. 11 *Perf. 14***

**570** A86 60b multicolored .60 .30
**571** A86 85b multicolored .80 .40
**572** A86 90b multicolored .80 .45
**573** A86 1d multicolored .80 .50
**574** A86 1.25d multicolored 1.10 .65
**575** A86 2d multicolored 1.40 1.00
*Nos. 570-575 (6)* 5.50 3.30

**Souvenir Sheet**

**576** A86 5d multicolored 2.60 2.60

UN 40th Anniv. A97

Views of Banjul.

**1985, Nov. 15**

**577** A97 85b Independence Stadium .90 .90
**578** A97 2d Central Bank 2.10 2.10
**579** A97 4d Port 4.50 4.50
**580** A97 6d Oyster Creek Bridge 7.00 7.00
*Nos. 577-580 (4)* 14.50 14.50

Natl. independence, 20th anniv.

UN FAO, 40th Anniv. A98

**1985, Nov. 15**

**581** A98 60b Corn .90 .90
**582** A98 1.10d Paddy 1.75 1.75
**583** A98 3d Cow, calf 5.00 5.00
**584** A98 5d Fruit 7.75 7.75
*Nos. 581-584 (4)* 15.40 15.40

Diocese of Gambia and Guinea, 50th Anniv. A99

Designs: 60b, Fishermen, Fotoba, Guinea. 85b, St. Mary's Primary School, Banjul. 1.10d, St. Mary's Cathedral, Banjul. 1.50d, Mobile Dispensary at Christy, Kunda, 1935-45.

**1985, Dec. 24**

**585** A99 60b multicolored .35 .30
**586** A99 85b multicolored .60 .45
**587** A99 1.10d multicolored .65 .60
**588** A99 1.50d multicolored 1.00 .90
*Nos. 585-588 (4)* 2.60 2.25

Girl Guides, 75th Anniv. — A100

Christmas — A101

**1985, Dec. 27**

**589** A100 60b Application, horiz. .35 .35
**590** A100 85b 2nd Bathurst, horiz. .55 .55
**591** A100 1.50d Lady Baden-Powell 1.10 1.10
**592** A100 5d Rosamond Fowlis, leader 3.50 3.50
*Nos. 589-592 (4)* 5.50 5.50

**Souvenir Sheet**

**593** A100 10d Guides 7.00 7.00

**1985, Dec. 27 *Perf. 15***

Painting details: 60b, Virgin and Child, by Dirck Bouts (c. 1400-1475). 85b, The Annunciation, by Robert Campin (c. 1378-1444). 1.50d, Adoration of the Shepherds, by Gerard David (c. 1460-1523). 5d, The Nativity, by Gerard David. 10d, Adoration of the Magi, by Hieronymus Bosch (1450-1516).

**594** A101 60b multicolored .25 .25
**595** A101 85b multicolored .40 .40
**596** A101 1.50d multicolored .80 .80
**597** A101 5d multicolored 1.50 1.50
*Nos. 594-597 (4)* 2.95 2.95

**Souvenir Sheet**

**598** A101 10d multicolored 5.25 5.25

Intl. Youth Year A102

**1985, Dec. 31 *Perf. 14***

**599** A102 60b Mother's helper .30 .30
**600** A102 85b Wrestling .45 .45
**601** A102 1.10d Griot storyteller .55 *1.00*
**602** A102 1.50d Crocodile pool .90 *1.25*
*Nos. 599-602 (4)* 2.20 3.00

**Souvenir Sheet**

**603** A102 5d Cow herder 3.00 3.00

A103

Halley's Comet — A104

Designs: 10b, Maria Mitchell (1818-1889), American astronomer, Kitt Peak Natl. Observatory, Papago Indian Reservation, Arizona. 20b, Apollo 11, Neil Armstrong steps on moon, 1969. 75b, Skylab 4, Kohoutek Comet, 1973. 1d, NASA Infrared Astronomical Satellite, 1983. 2d, Comet sighting, 1577, Turkish art. No. 609, NASA Intl. Cometary Explorer satellite. No. 610, Comet.

**1986, Mar.**

**604** A103 10b multicolored .35 .25
**605** A103 20b multicolored .65 .25
**606** A103 75b multicolored .90 .55
**607** A103 1d multicolored 1.25 .80
**608** A103 2d multicolored 1.75 1.40
**609** A103 10d multicolored 4.75 5.00
*Nos. 604-609 (6)* 9.65 8.25

**Souvenir Sheet**

**610** A104 10d multicolored 7.50 7.50

For overprints see Nos. 650-656.

**Queen Elizabeth II, 60th Birthday**
Common Design Type

Designs: 1d, Royal family at Royal Tournament, 1936. 2.50d, Christening, 1983. No. 613, State visit to West Germany, 1978. No. 614, At Balmoral, 1935.

**1986, Apr. 21**

**611** CD339 1d lt yel bis & blk .50 .40
**612** CD339 2.50d pale green & multi 1.00 .75
**613** CD339 10d dl lil & multi 3.00 3.00
*Nos. 611-613 (3)* 4.50 4.15

**Souvenir Sheet**

**614** CD339 10d tan & black 3.75 3.75

1986 World Cup Soccer Championships, Mexico — A105

**1986, May 2**

**615** A105 75b Block .60 .60
**616** A105 1d Kneeing the ball .85 .85
**617** A105 2.50d Kick 2.50 2.50
**618** A105 10d Heading the ball 6.00 6.00
*Nos. 615-618 (4)* 9.95 9.95

**Souvenir Sheet**

**619** A105 10d Goalie catching ball 10.00 10.00

For overprints see Nos. 639-643.

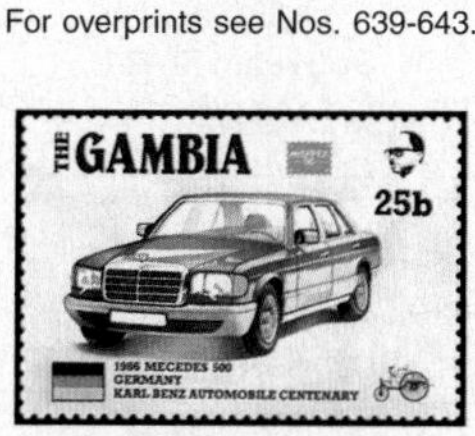


AMERIPEX '86 — A106

Exhibition emblem, automobiles and flags: 25b, 1986 Mercedes 500, Germany. 75b, 1935 Cord 810, US. 1d, 1957 Borgward Isabella Coupe, Germany. 1.25d, 1985-6 Lamborghini Countach, Italy. 2d, 1955 Ford Thunderbird, US. 2.25d, 1956 Citroen DS19, France. 5d, 1936 Bugatti Atlante, France. 10d, 1936 Horch 853, Germany. No. 628, 1913 Benz 8/20, Germany. No. 629, 1924 Steiger 10/50, Germany.

**1986, May 22** *Perf. 15*

**620** A106 25b multi .25 .25
**621** A106 75b multi .40 .35
**622** A106 1d multi .60 .55
**623** A106 1.25d multi .65 .65
**624** A106 2d multi .75 *1.00*
**625** A106 2.25d multi .75 *1.10*
**626** A106 5d multi 1.40 *2.50*
**627** A106 10d multi 3.25 *4.25*
*Nos. 620-627 (8)* 8.05 *10.65*

**Souvenir Sheets**

**628** A106 12d multi 6.50 6.50
**629** A106 12d multi 6.50 6.50

Karl Benz automobile cent.

Statue of Liberty, Cent. A107

Statue and famous emigrants: 20b, John Jacob Astor (1763-1848), financier. 1d, Jacob Riis (1849-1914), journalist. 1.25d, Igor Sikorsky (1889-1972), aeronautics engineer. 5d, Charles Boyer (1899-1978), actor. 10d, Statue, vert.

**1986, June 10** *Perf. 14*

**630** A107 20b multicolored .25 .25
**631** A107 1d multicolored .60 .60
**632** A107 1.25d multicolored .65 .65
**633** A107 5d multicolored 2.75 2.75
*Nos. 630-633 (4)* 4.25 4.25

**Souvenir Sheet**

**634** A107 10d multicolored 5.50 5.50

**Royal Wedding Issue, 1986**
Common Design Type

1d, Engagement of Prince Andrew and Sarah Ferguson. 2.50d, Andrew. 4d, Andrew in flight uniform, other helicopter pilot. 7d, Couple, diff.

**1986, July 23**

**635** CD340 1d multi .60 .60
**636** CD340 2.50d multi 1.40 1.40
**637** CD340 4d multi 2.25 2.25
*Nos. 635-637 (3)* 4.25 4.25

**Souvenir Sheet**

**638** CD340 7d multi 5.00 5.00

**Nos. 615-619 Overprinted "WINNERS / Argentina 3 / W. Germany 2" in Gold**

**1986, Sept. 16** **Litho.** *Perf. 14*

**639** A105 75b multicolored .40 .40
**640** A105 1d multicolored .60 .60
**641** A105 2.50d multicolored 1.25 1.25
**642** A105 10d multicolored 5.00 5.00
*Nos. 639-642 (4)* 7.25 7.25

**Souvenir Sheet**

**643** A105 10d multicolored 6.50 6.50

Christmas, STOCKHOLMIA '86 — A108

Disney characters mailing letters in various countries.

**1986, Nov. 4** *Perf. 11*

**644** A108 1d Great Britain 1.10 .50
**645** A108 1.25d United States 1.25 .70
**646** A108 2d France 1.90 1.25
**647** A108 2.35d Australia 2.10 1.40
**648** A108 5d Germany 2.60 2.00
*Nos. 644-648 (5)* 8.95 5.85

**Souvenir Sheet**

**649** A108 10d Sweden 9.00 9.00

**Nos. 604-610 Ovptd. in Silver**

**1986, Oct. 21** **Litho.** *Perf. 14*

**650** A103 10b multicolored .25 .25
**651** A103 20b multicolored .65 .25
**652** A103 75b multicolored 1.00 .50
**653** A103 1d multicolored 1.10 .60
**654** A103 2d multicolored 1.40 1.50
**655** A103 10d multicolored 4.25 4.50
*Nos. 650-655 (6)* 8.65 7.60

**Souvenir Sheet**

**656** A104 10d multicolored 5.00 5.00

Marc Chagall (1887-1985), Artist A109

Paintings, ceramicware, sculpture: 75b, Snowing. 85b, The Boat, 1957. 1d, Maternity, 1913. 1.25d, The Flute Player. 2.35d, Lovers and the Beast, 1957. 4d,Fishes at Saint Jean. 5d, Entering the Ring, 1968. 10d, Three Acrobats, 1956. No. 665, The Sabbath. No. 666, The Cattle Driver.

**1987, Feb. 6** **Litho.**

**657** A109 75b multi .45 .25
**658** A109 85b multi .55 .30
**659** A109 1d multi .65 .40
**660** A109 1.25d multi .85 .50
**661** A109 2.35d multi 1.40 .80
**662** A109 4d multi 2.00 1.25
**663** A109 5d multi 2.50 1.50
**664** A109 10d multi 4.00 2.50

**Sizes: 110x95mm, 110x68mm**

***Imperf***

**665** A109 12d multi 6.50 6.50
**666** A109 12d multi 6.50 6.50
*Nos. 657-666 (10)* 25.40 20.50

Musical Instruments — A110

Various instruments from the Mandingo Empire.

**1987, Jan. 21** **Litho.** *Perf. 15*

**667** A110 75b Bugarab, tabala .25 .25
**668** A110 1d Balaphong, fiddle .35 .30
**669** A110 1.25d Bolongbato, konting .40 .35
**670** A110 10d Koras 2.25 2.25
*Nos. 667-670 (4)* 3.25 3.15

**Souvenir Sheet**

**671** A110 12d Sabarrs 3.25 3.25

Nos. 669-670 vert.
For overprints see Nos. 750, 856-860.

America's Cup A111

**1987, Apr. 3** *Perf. 14*

**672** A111 20b America, 1851 .25 .25
**673** A111 1d Courageous, 1974 .35 .35
**674** A111 2.50d Volunteer, 1887 .90 .90
**675** A111 10d Intrepid, 1967 4.00 4.00
*Nos. 672-675 (4)* 5.50 5.50

**Souvenir Sheet**

**676** A111 12d Australia II, 1983 5.75 5.75

For overprint see No. 751.

Statue of Liberty, Cent. A112

Photographs of restoration and unveiling in 1986.

**1987, Apr. 9** **Litho.**

**677** A112 1b Shoulder, torch .25 .25
**678** A112 2b Operation Sail flotilla .25 .25
**679** A112 3b Tall ship, ships .25 .25
**680** A112 5b Luxury liner, aircraft carrier .25 .25
**681** A112 50b Statue's coiffure .50 .50
**682** A112 75b Coiffure, diff. .70 .70
**683** A112 1d Workmen scaling statue .85 .85
**684** A112 1.25d Back of statue 1.00 1.00
**685** A112 10d Front of Statue 5.00 5.00
**686** A112 12d Side of statue 5.25 5.25
*Nos. 677-686 (10)* 14.30 14.30

Nos. 677, 681-686 vert.

Flowers from Abuko Nature Reserve — A113

75b, Lantana camara. 1d, Clerodendrum thomsoniae. 1.50d, Haemanthus multiflorus. 1.70d, Gloriosa simplex. 1.75d, Combretum microphyllum. 2.25d, Eulophia guineensis. 5d, Erythrina senegalensis. 15d, Dichrostachys glomerata.

No. 691, Costus spectabilis. No. 691A, Strophanthus preussii.

**1987, May 25**

**687** A113 75b multi .25 .25
**687A** A113 1d multi .25 .25
**688** A113 1.50d multi .45 .40
**688A** A113 1.70d multi .50 .45
**689** A113 1.75d multi .50 .45
**689A** A113 2.25d multi .65 .60
**689B** A113 5d multi 1.40 1.40
**690** A113 15d multi 3.25 3.25
*Nos. 687-690 (8)* 7.25 7.05

**Souvenir Sheets**

**691** A113 15d shown 3.25 3.25
**691A** A113 15d multi 3.25 3.25

Nos. 691-691A are continuous designs.
For overprint see No. 752.

CAPEX '87 A115

Various buses.

**1987, June 15**

**692** A115 20b multi, vert. .55 .25
**693** A115 75b multi .75 .25
**694** A115 1d multi 1.90 .75
**695** A115 10d multi, vert. 3.75 2.00
*Nos. 692-695 (4)* 6.95 3.25

**Souvenir Sheet**

**696** A115 12d multi 7.00 7.00

For overprint see No. 749.

1988 Summer Olympics, Seoul
A116

**1987, July 3**

| | | | | | |
|---|---|---|---|---|---|
| 697 | A116 | 50b | Women's basket-ball | .25 | .25 |
| 698 | A116 | 1d | Volleyball | .60 | .30 |
| 699 | A116 | 3d | Field hockey | 1.10 | .90 |
| 700 | A116 | 10d | Handball | 3.50 | 3.00 |
| | | | *Nos. 697-700 (4)* | 5.45 | 4.45 |

**Souvenir Sheet**

| | | | | | |
|---|---|---|---|---|---|
| 701 | A116 | 15d | Soccer | 5.00 | 5.00 |

Nos. 697-698 vert.

A117

The Twelve Days of Christmas, Medieval Counting Song — A118

Designs: 20b, Partridge in a pear tree. 40b, 2 turtle doves. 60b, 3 French hens. 75b, 4 calling birds. 1d, 5 golden rings. 1.25d, 6 geese a-laying. 1.50d, 7 swans a-swimming. 2d, 8 maids a-milking. 3d, 9 ladies dancing. 5d, 10 lords a-leaping. 10d, 11 pipers piping. 12d, 12 drummers drumming.

**Miniature Sheet**

**1987, Nov. 2 Litho. *Perf. 14***

| | | | | |
|---|---|---|---|---|
| 702 | | Sheet of 12 | 14.50 | 14.50 |
| *a.* | A117 | 20b multicolored | .25 | .25 |
| *b.* | A117 | 40b multicolored | .25 | .25 |
| *c.* | A117 | 60b multicolored | .25 | .25 |
| *d.* | A117 | 75b multicolored | .25 | .25 |
| *e.* | A117 | 1d multicolored | .40 | .40 |
| *f.* | A117 | 1.25d multicolored | .45 | .45 |
| *g.* | A117 | 1.50d multicolored | .60 | .60 |
| *h.* | A117 | 2d multicolored | .75 | .75 |
| *i.* | A117 | 3d multicolored | 1.25 | 1.25 |
| *j.* | A117 | 5d multicolored | 1.90 | 1.90 |
| *k.* | A117 | 10d multicolored | 3.50 | 3.50 |
| *l.* | A117 | 12d multicolored | 4.25 | 4.25 |

**Souvenir Sheet**

| | | | | | |
|---|---|---|---|---|---|
| 703 | A118 | 15d | multi | 5.00 | 5.00 |

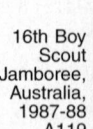

16th Boy Scout Jamboree, Australia, 1987-88
A119

**1987, Nov. 9**

| | | | | | |
|---|---|---|---|---|---|
| 704 | A119 | 75b | Singing around campfire | .25 | .25 |
| 705 | A119 | 1d | Nature study, African katydid | .65 | .30 |
| 706 | A119 | 1.25d | Bird watching, red-tailed tropicbird | .85 | .40 |
| 707 | A119 | 12d | Boarding bus | 6.00 | 3.50 |
| | | | *Nos. 704-707 (4)* | 7.75 | 4.45 |

**Souvenir Sheet**

| | | | | | |
|---|---|---|---|---|---|
| 708 | A119 | 15d | Nature study | 8.75 | 8.75 |

Mickey Mouse, 60th Anniv. — A120

Disney animated characters and historic locomotives: 60b, Richard Trevithick's locomotive, 1804. 75b, Empire State Express 999, 1893. 1d, George Stephenson's Rocket, 1829. 1.25d, Santa Fe Mountain 2-10-2, 1920. 2d, Class GG-1 Pennsylvania, 1933. 5d, Stourbridge Lion, 1829. 10d, Best Friend of Charleston, 1830. 12d, M10001 Union Pacific, 1934. No. 717, Tres Grande Vitesse-SNCF, 1981, France. No. 718, The General, Western & Atlantic, 1855.

**1987, Dec. 9 Litho. *Perf. 14x13½***

| | | | | | |
|---|---|---|---|---|---|
| 709 | A120 | 60b | multicolored | .25 | .25 |
| 710 | A120 | 75b | multicolored | .25 | .25 |
| 711 | A120 | 1d | multicolored | .50 | .30 |
| 712 | A120 | 1.25d | multicolored | .60 | .40 |
| 713 | A120 | 2d | multicolored | .90 | .60 |
| 714 | A120 | 5d | multicolored | 2.25 | 1.50 |
| 715 | A120 | 10d | multicolored | 4.50 | 3.00 |
| 716 | A120 | 12d | multicolored | 5.00 | 3.50 |
| | | | *Nos. 709-716 (8)* | 14.25 | 9.80 |

**Souvenir Sheets**

| | | | | | |
|---|---|---|---|---|---|
| 717 | A120 | 15d | multicolored | 6.50 | 6.50 |
| 718 | A120 | 15d | multicolored | 6.50 | 6.50 |

Fauna and Flora
A121

**1988, Feb. 9 Litho. *Perf. 15***

| | | | | | |
|---|---|---|---|---|---|
| 719 | A121 | 50b | Duiker, acacia | .25 | .25 |
| 720 | A121 | 75b | Red-billed hornbill, casuarina | .25 | .25 |
| 721 | A121 | 90b | West African dwarf crocodile, rice | .25 | .25 |
| 722 | A121 | 1d | Leopard, papyrus | .25 | .25 |
| 723 | A121 | 1.25d | Crested cranes, millet | .30 | .30 |
| 724 | A121 | 2d | Waterbuck, baobab tree | .45 | .45 |
| 725 | A121 | 3d | Oribi, Senegal palm | .70 | .70 |
| 726 | A121 | 5d | Hippopotamus, papaya | 1.00 | 1.00 |
| | | | *Nos. 719-726 (8)* | 3.45 | 3.45 |

**Souvenir Sheets**

| | | | | | |
|---|---|---|---|---|---|
| 727 | A121 | 12d | Great white pelican | 2.50 | 2.50 |
| 728 | A121 | 12d | Red-throated bee-eater | 2.50 | 2.50 |

Nos. 720, 722, 724, 726 and 728 vert.

40th Wedding Anniv. of Queen Elizabeth II and Prince Philip — A122

**1988, Mar. 15 *Perf. 14***

| | | | | | |
|---|---|---|---|---|---|
| 729 | A122 | 75b | Wedding portrait, 1947 | .25 | .25 |
| 730 | A122 | 1d | Couple at leisure | .25 | .25 |
| 731 | A122 | 3d | Wedding portrait, diff. | .75 | .75 |
| 732 | A122 | 10d | Couple, c. 1987 | 3.00 | 3.00 |
| | | | *Nos. 729-732 (4)* | 4.25 | 4.25 |

**Souvenir Sheet**

| | | | | | |
|---|---|---|---|---|---|
| 733 | A122 | 15d | Wedding party | 3.25 | 3.25 |

1988 Summer Olympics, Seoul
A123

**1988, May 3 Litho. *Perf. 14***

| | | | | | |
|---|---|---|---|---|---|
| 734 | A123 | 1d | Archery, vert. | .25 | .25 |
| 735 | A123 | 1.25d | Boxing, vert. | .25 | .25 |
| 736 | A123 | 5d | Gymnastics, vert. | 1.50 | 1.25 |
| 737 | A123 | 10d | 100-Meter sprint | 3.00 | 2.50 |
| | | | *Nos. 734-737 (4)* | 5.00 | 4.25 |

**Souvenir Sheet**

| | | | | | |
|---|---|---|---|---|---|
| 738 | A123 | 15d | Award ceremony, Olympic stadium | 3.75 | 3.75 |

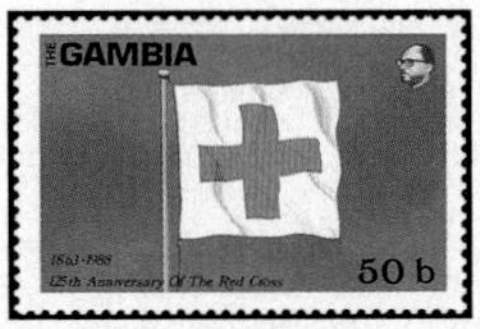

Anniversaries & Events — A124

Designs: 50b, Red Cross flag. 75b, Friendship 7, piloted by John Glenn, 1963. 1d, British Airways Concorde jet. 1.25d, Spirit of St. Louis, piloted by Charles Lindbergh, 1927. 2d, X-15, piloted by Major William Knight, 1967. 3d, Bell X-1, piloted by Capt. Charles Yeager, 1947. 10d, Spanish galleon, British warship, 1588. 12d, The Titanic. No. 747, Kangaroo and joey. No. 748, Cathedral, modern church, vert.

**1988, May 15**

| | | | | | |
|---|---|---|---|---|---|
| 739 | A124 | 50b | multicolored | .75 | .75 |
| 740 | A124 | 75b | multicolored | .75 | .75 |
| 741 | A124 | 1d | multicolored | 1.25 | 1.25 |
| 742 | A124 | 1.25d | multicolored | 1.25 | 1.25 |
| 743 | A124 | 2d | multicolored | 1.75 | 1.75 |
| 744 | A124 | 3d | multicolored | 2.25 | 2.25 |
| 745 | A124 | 10d | multicolored | 5.00 | 5.00 |
| 746 | A124 | 12d | multicolored | 6.00 | 6.00 |
| | | | *Nos. 739-746 (8)* | 19.00 | 19.00 |

**Souvenir Sheets**

| | | | | | |
|---|---|---|---|---|---|
| 747 | A124 | 15d | multicolored | 3.75 | 3.75 |
| 748 | A124 | 15d | multicolored | 3.75 | 3.75 |

Intl. Red Cross, 125th anniv. (50b); first American in space, 25th anniv. in 1987 (75b); 1st London-New York scheduled Concorde flight, 10th anniv. in 1987 (1d); first solo transatlantic flight, 60th anniv. in 1987 (1.25d); fastest speed flown, 6.72 Mach, 20th anniv. in 1987 (2d); 1st supersonic flight, 40th anniv. in 1987 (3d); defeat of the Spanish Armada, 400th anniv. (10d); maiden voyage of the Titanic, 75th anniv. in 1987 (12d); founding of Australia, bicentennial (No. 747); and founding of Berlin, 750th anniv. in 1987 (No. 748).

**Nos. 694, 670, 675 and 690 Ovptd. for Philatelic Exhibitions**

a

b

c

d

**1988, Apr. 19 Litho. *Perf. 14, 15***

| | | | | | |
|---|---|---|---|---|---|
| 749 | A115(a) | 1d | multi | .50 | .50 |
| 750 | A110(b) | 10d | multi | 3.00 | 3.00 |
| 751 | A111(c) | 10d | multi | 3.00 | 3.00 |
| 752 | A113(d) | 15d | multi | 3.50 | 3.50 |
| | | | *Nos. 749-752 (4)* | 10.00 | 10.00 |

Paintings by Titian
A125

Designs: 25b, Emperor Charles V, 1549. 50b, St. Margaret and the Dragon, 1565. 60b, Ranuccio Farnese, 1542. 75b, Tarquin and Lucretia, 1570. 1d, The Knight of Malta, c. 1550. 5d, Spain Succouring Faith, 1571. 10d, Doge Francesco Venier, 1555. 12d, Doge Grimani Before the Faith, c. 1555-1576. No. 761, Jealous Husband, 1511. No. 762, Venus Blindfolding Cupid, 1560.

**1988, July 7 Litho. *Perf. 13½x14***

| | | | | | |
|---|---|---|---|---|---|
| 753 | A125 | 25b | multicolored | .25 | .25 |
| 754 | A125 | 50b | multicolored | .50 | .50 |
| 755 | A125 | 60b | multicolored | .50 | .50 |
| 756 | A125 | 75b | multicolored | .70 | .70 |
| 757 | A125 | 1d | multicolored | .80 | .80 |
| 758 | A125 | 5d | multicolored | 2.75 | 2.75 |
| 759 | A125 | 10d | multicolored | 4.50 | 4.50 |
| 760 | A125 | 12d | multicolored | 5.00 | 5.00 |
| | | | *Nos. 753-760 (8)* | 15.00 | 15.00 |

**Souvenir Sheets**

| | | | | | |
|---|---|---|---|---|---|
| 761 | A125 | 15d | multicolored | 4.00 | 4.00 |
| 762 | A125 | 15d | multicolored | 4.00 | 4.00 |

Tribute to John F. Kennedy
A126

**1988, Sept. 1 Litho. *Perf. 14***

| | | | | | |
|---|---|---|---|---|---|
| 763 | A126 | 75b | Sailing | .25 | .25 |
| 764 | A126 | 1d | Peace Corps enactment | .30 | .30 |
| 765 | A126 | 1.25d | Public address, vert. | .40 | .40 |
| 766 | A126 | 12d | Grave, Arlington Natl. Cemetery | 2.50 | 2.50 |
| | | | *Nos. 763-766 (4)* | 3.45 | 3.45 |

**Souvenir Sheet**

| | | | | | |
|---|---|---|---|---|---|
| 767 | A126 | 15d | Kennedy, vert. | 4.25 | 4.25 |

Entertainers — A127

20b, Emmett Lee Kelly (1898-1979), clown. 1d, Gambia Natl. Ensemble. 1.25d, Jackie Gleason (1916-87), comedian, & The Honeymooners cast. 1.50d, Stan Laurel (1890-1965) & Oliver Hardy (1892-1957), film comedy team. 2.50d, Yul Brynner (c. 1920-85), actor. 3d, Cary Grant (1904-86), actor. 10d, Danny Kaye (1918-87), comedian, actor. 20d, Charlie Chaplin (1889-1977), comedian, actor. No.

776, Harpo (1893-1964), Chico (1891-1961), Zeppo (1901-79) & Groucho (1890-1977) Marx, comedy team. No. 777, Fred Astaire (1899-1987) & Rita Hayworth (1918-87), dancers & film stars. Nos. 768-775 vert.

**1988, Nov. 9** **Litho.**

| | | | | | |
|---|---|---|---|---|---|
| **768** | A127 | 20b | multi | .25 | .25 |
| **769** | A127 | 1d | multi | .50 | .50 |
| **770** | A127 | 1.25d | multi | .60 | .60 |
| **771** | A127 | 1.50d | multi | .65 | .65 |
| **772** | A127 | 2.50d | multi | 1.00 | 1.00 |
| **773** | A127 | 3d | multi | 1.25 | 1.25 |
| **774** | A127 | 10d | multi | 4.00 | 4.00 |
| **775** | A127 | 20d | multi | 6.75 | 6.75 |
| | | | *Nos. 768-775 (8)* | 15.00 | 15.00 |

**Souvenir Sheets**

| | | | | | |
|---|---|---|---|---|---|
| **776** | A127 | 15d | multi | 7.00 | 7.00 |
| **777** | A127 | 15d | multi | 7.00 | 7.00 |

Kelly's name is spelled incorrectly; Brynner's and Grant's dates are incorrect.

Zeppelin LZ7 Deutschland, 1910 — A128

Transportation innovations: 50b, Stephenson's Locomotion, 1825. 75b, General Motors Sun Racer, 1987. 1d, Sprague's Premiere, 1888. 1.25d, Gold Rush bicycle, 1986. 2.50d, 1st Liquid-fuel rocket, invented by Robert Goddard, 1925. 10d, Orukter Amphibolos, 1805. 12d, Sovereign of the Seas, 1988. No. 786, USS Nautilus, 1954, vert. No. 787, Fulton's Nautilus, early 19th cent.

**1988, Nov. 21** **Litho.** ***Perf. 14***

| | | | | | |
|---|---|---|---|---|---|
| **778** | A128 | 25b | multi | .60 | .25 |
| **779** | A128 | 50b | multi | 1.00 | .40 |
| **780** | A128 | 75b | multi | 1.10 | .55 |
| **781** | A128 | 1d | multi | 1.50 | .70 |
| **782** | A128 | 1.25d | multi | 1.50 | .75 |
| **783** | A128 | 2.50d | multi | 2.25 | 1.25 |
| **784** | A128 | 10d | multi | 5.75 | 3.50 |
| **785** | A128 | 12d | multi | 6.75 | 4.00 |
| | | | *Nos. 778-785 (8)* | 20.45 | 11.40 |

**Souvenir Sheets**

| | | | | | |
|---|---|---|---|---|---|
| **786** | A128 | 15d | multi | 4.75 | 4.75 |
| **787** | A128 | 15d | multi | 4.75 | 4.75 |

Discovery of America, 500th Anniv. (in 1992) A129

Designs: 50b, Caravel, Henry the Navigator (1394-1460), Prince of Portugal, and coat of arms, vert. 75b, Jesse Ramsden's sextant, map of Africa, arms, vert. 1d, Hour glass, 15th cent., and map, vert. 1.25d, Henry and Vasco da Gama, vert. 2.50d, Da Gama and 15th cent. caravel, vert. 5d, Mungo Park (1771-1806), Scottish explorer, arms and map of Gambia River. 10d, Map of west African coast, 1563. 12d, Portuguese caravel, arms. No. 796, Caravel off the Gambian coast, 15th cent., vert. No. 797, European ship off Gambian coast, 15th cent., vert.

**1988, Dec. 1** **Litho.** ***Perf. 14***

| | | | | | |
|---|---|---|---|---|---|
| **788** | A129 | 50b | multi | .90 | .90 |
| **789** | A129 | 75b | multi | 1.00 | 1.00 |
| **790** | A129 | 1d | multi | 1.25 | 1.25 |
| **791** | A129 | 1.25d | multi | 1.50 | 1.50 |
| **792** | A129 | 2.50d | multi | 1.75 | 1.75 |
| **793** | A129 | 5d | shown | 3.00 | 3.00 |
| **794** | A129 | 10d | multi | 5.25 | 5.25 |
| **795** | A129 | 12d | multi | 5.50 | 5.50 |
| | | | *Nos. 788-795 (8)* | 20.15 | 20.15 |

**Souvenir Sheets**

| | | | | | |
|---|---|---|---|---|---|
| **796** | A129 | 15d | multi | 5.00 | 5.00 |
| **797** | A129 | 15d | multi | 5.00 | 5.00 |

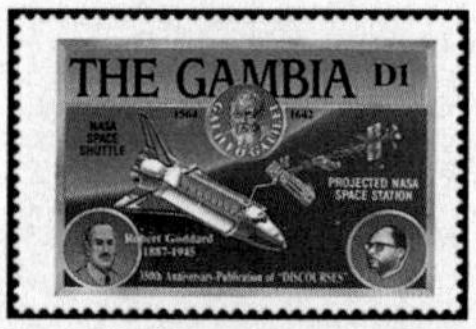


Space Achievements — A130

Galileo and: 50b, Futuristic aerospace plane and Ernst Mach (1838-1916), Austrian physicist, vert. 75b, OAO III astronomical satellite and Niels Bohr (1885-1962), Danish physicist and Nobel laureate in 1922, vert. 1d, NASA space shuttle, future space station and Robert Goddard (1882-1945), American rocket scientist. 1.25d, Flyby of probe past Jupiter, 1979, and Edward Barnard (1857-1923), American astronomer who discovered Jupiter's 5th satellite in 1892. 2d, Hubble Space Telescope and George Hale (1868-1938), American astronomer, vert. 3d, Precision measurement of the distance between the Earth and the Moon by laser and Albert A. Michelson (1852-1931), Nobel laureate in 1907 for research on the speed of light. 10d, HEAO-2 Einstein orbital satellite and Albert Einstein, vert. 20d, Voyager, 1st circumnavigation of the world without refueling, 1987, and the Wright Brothers. No. 806, Moon Ganymede passing the Great Red Spot on Jupiter. No. 807, Apollo and Neil Armstrong, 1st man on the Moon, July 20, 1969, vert.

**1988, Dec. 12** ***Perf. 14***

| | | | | | |
|---|---|---|---|---|---|
| **798** | A130 | 50b | multi | .50 | .30 |
| **799** | A130 | 75b | multi | .60 | .40 |
| **800** | A130 | 1d | multi | .75 | .55 |
| **801** | A130 | 1.25d | multi | .90 | .75 |
| **802** | A130 | 2d | multi | 1.25 | 1.10 |
| **803** | A130 | 3d | multi | 1.50 | 1.50 |
| **804** | A130 | 10d | multi | 3.50 | 3.50 |
| **805** | A130 | 20d | multi | 6.00 | 6.00 |
| | | | *Nos. 798-805 (8)* | 15.00 | 14.10 |

**Souvenir Sheets**

| | | | | | |
|---|---|---|---|---|---|
| **806** | A130 | 15d | multi | 4.75 | 4.75 |
| **807** | A130 | 15d | multi | 4.75 | 4.75 |

350th anniv. of the publication of Discourses, by Galileo.

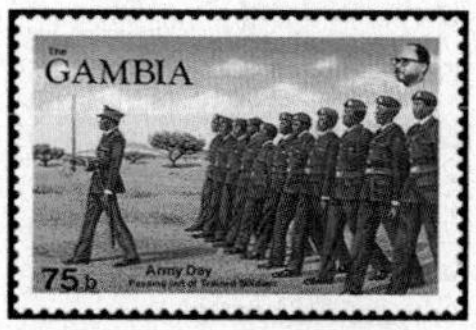


Army Day A131

**1989, Feb. 10** **Litho.** ***Perf. 14***

| | | | | | |
|---|---|---|---|---|---|
| **808** | A131 | 75b | Troops on parade | .25 | .25 |
| **809** | A131 | 1d | Regimental flags | .30 | .30 |
| **810** | A131 | 1.25d | Drummer, vert. | .45 | .45 |
| **811** | A131 | 10d | Atlantic Shooting Cup winner, vert. | 2.50 | 2.50 |
| **812** | A131 | 15d | Assault course, vert. | 4.00 | 4.00 |
| **813** | A131 | 20d | 105-mm gun | 4.50 | 4.50 |
| | | | *Nos. 808-813 (6)* | 12.00 | 12.00 |

Miniature Sheet

Mickey Mouse, 60th Anniv. (in 1988) — A132

Mickey Mouse through the years: a, 1928. b, 1931. c, 1936. d, 1955. e, 1947. f, 1940. g, 1960. h, 1976. i, 1988. 15d, Birthday party.

**1989, Apr. 6** **Litho.** ***Perf. 13x13½***

| | | | | | |
|---|---|---|---|---|---|
| **814** | A132 | | Sheet of 9 | 17.50 | 17.50 |
| *a.-i.* | | | 2d any single | 1.50 | 1.40 |

**Size: 139x110mm**

***Imperf***

| | | | | | |
|---|---|---|---|---|---|
| **815** | A132 | 15d | multi | 8.00 | 8.00 |

Easter A133

Paintings by Rubens: 50b, Le Coup de Lance, 1620. 75b, The Flagellation of Christ, 1617. 1d, The Lamentation for Christ, c. 1617. 1.25d, Descent from the Cross, c. 1611. 2d, The Holy Trinity, c. 1617. 5d, The Doubting Thomas. 10d, Lamentation over Christ, 1614. 12d, Lamentation over Christ with the Virgin and St. John, c. 1613. No. 824, The Last Supper, c. 1631. No. 825, The Raising of the Cross, c. 1610.

**1989, Apr. 14** ***Perf. 13½x14***

| | | | | | |
|---|---|---|---|---|---|
| **816** | A133 | 50b | multi | .45 | .25 |
| **817** | A133 | 75b | multi | .55 | .35 |
| **818** | A133 | 1d | multi | .55 | .35 |
| **819** | A133 | 1.25d | multi | .60 | .50 |
| **820** | A133 | 2d | multi | 1.00 | .80 |
| **821** | A133 | 5d | multi | 1.75 | 1.75 |
| **822** | A133 | 10d | multi | 2.75 | 2.75 |
| **823** | A133 | 12d | multi | 3.00 | 3.00 |
| | | | *Nos. 816-823 (8)* | 10.65 | 9.75 |

**Souvenir Sheets**

| | | | | | |
|---|---|---|---|---|---|
| **824** | A133 | 15d | multi | 4.00 | 4.00 |
| **825** | A133 | 15d | multi | 4.00 | 4.00 |

Indigenous Birds — A134

**1989, Apr. 24** ***Perf. 14***

| | | | | | |
|---|---|---|---|---|---|
| **826** | A134 | 20b | African emerald cuckoo | .80 | .25 |
| **827** | A134 | 60b | Gray-headed bush shrike | 1.10 | .50 |
| **828** | A134 | 75b | Crowned crane | 1.10 | .55 |
| **829** | A134 | 1d | Secretary bird | 1.25 | .60 |
| **830** | A134 | 2d | Red-billed hornbill | 1.50 | .90 |
| **831** | A134 | 5d | Superb sunbird | 2.75 | 2.50 |
| **832** | A134 | 10d | Little owl | 5.00 | 3.75 |
| **833** | A134 | 12d | Bateleur eagle | 5.75 | 4.50 |
| | | | *Nos. 826-833 (8)* | 19.25 | 13.55 |

**Souvenir Sheets**

| | | | | | |
|---|---|---|---|---|---|
| **834** | A134 | 15d | Red-billed fire finch | 5.50 | 5.50 |
| **835** | A134 | 15d | Ostriches | 5.50 | 5.50 |

Indigenous Butterflies — A135

**1989, May 15**

| | | | | | |
|---|---|---|---|---|---|
| **836** | A135 | 50b | Papilio antimachus | .60 | .25 |
| **837** | A135 | 75b | Euphaedra neophron | .75 | .45 |
| **838** | A135 | 1d | Aterica rabena | .75 | .45 |
| **839** | A135 | 1.25d | Salamis parhassus | .90 | .90 |
| **840** | A135 | 5d | Precis rhadama | 2.75 | 2.75 |
| **841** | A135 | 10d | Papilio demodocus | 5.00 | 5.00 |
| **842** | A135 | 12d | Charaxes etesippe | 5.75 | 5.75 |
| **843** | A135 | 15d | Danaus formosa | 7.25 | 7.25 |
| | | | *Nos. 836-843 (8)* | 23.75 | 22.80 |

**Souvenir Sheets**

| | | | | | |
|---|---|---|---|---|---|
| **844** | A135 | 15d | Euphaedra ceres | 8.75 | 8.75 |
| **845** | A135 | 15d | Cymothoe pluto | 8.75 | 8.75 |

Trains of Africa A136

Designs: 50b, Nigerian coal train, 1959. 75b, 14A Class 2-6-6-2 Garratt. 1d, British (Pacific) in Sudan. 1.25d, American 0-8-0, 1925. 5d, Scottish 4-8-2, 1955. 7d, Scottish 4-8-2, 1926. 10d, British 4-6-0. 12d, American-made 2-6-0 in Ghana. No. 854, British 2-8-2 Class 25 facing forward, vert. No. 855, Class 25 facing left, vert.

**1989, June 15** **Litho.** ***Perf. 14***

| | | | | | |
|---|---|---|---|---|---|
| **846** | A136 | 50b | multi | .55 | .30 |
| **847** | A136 | 75b | multi | .65 | .40 |
| **848** | A136 | 1d | multi | .70 | .50 |
| **849** | A136 | 1.25d | multi | .85 | .80 |
| **850** | A136 | 5d | multi | 2.25 | 2.25 |
| **851** | A136 | 7d | multi | 2.50 | 2.50 |
| **852** | A136 | 10d | multi | 4.00 | 4.00 |
| **853** | A136 | 12d | multi | 4.50 | 4.50 |
| | | | *Nos. 846-853 (8)* | 16.00 | 15.25 |

**Souvenir Sheets**

| | | | | | |
|---|---|---|---|---|---|
| **854** | A136 | 15d | multi | 6.00 | 6.00 |
| **855** | A136 | 15d | multi | 6.00 | 6.00 |

**Nos. 667-671 Ovptd. "PHILEXFRANCE / '89"**

**1989, June 23** **Litho.** ***Perf. 15***

| | | | | | |
|---|---|---|---|---|---|
| **856** | A110 | 75b | multi | .25 | .25 |
| **857** | A110 | 1d | multi | .30 | .30 |
| **858** | A110 | 1.25d | multi | .45 | .45 |
| **859** | A110 | 10d | multi | 2.00 | 2.00 |
| | | | *Nos. 856-859 (4)* | 3.00 | 3.00 |

**Souvenir Sheet**

| | | | | | |
|---|---|---|---|---|---|
| **860** | A110 | 12d | multi | 3.25 | 3.25 |

Paintings by Japanese Artists A137

Paintings by Hiroshige unless noted otherwise: 50b, Sparrow and Bamboo. 75b, Peonies and a Canary, by Hokusai. 1d, Crane and Marsh Grasses. 1.25d, Crossbill and Thistle, by Hokusai. 2d, Cuckoo and Azalea, by Hokusai. 5d, Parrot on a Pine Branch. 10d, Mandarin Ducks in a Stream. 12d, Bullfinch and Drooping Cherry, by Hokusai. No. 869, Tit and Peony, horiz. No. 870, Peony and Butterfly, by Shigenobu, horiz.

**1989, July 7** ***Perf. 13½x14, 14x13½***

| | | | | | |
|---|---|---|---|---|---|
| **861** | A137 | 50b | multi | .55 | .30 |
| **862** | A137 | 75b | multi | .75 | .40 |
| **863** | A137 | 1d | multi | .90 | .55 |
| **864** | A137 | 1.25d | multi | 1.00 | .65 |
| **865** | A137 | 2d | multi | 1.25 | 1.00 |
| **866** | A137 | 5d | multi | 2.25 | 2.25 |
| **867** | A137 | 10d | multi | 4.50 | 4.50 |
| **868** | A137 | 12d | multi | 5.00 | 5.00 |
| | | | *Nos. 861-868 (8)* | 16.20 | 14.65 |

**Souvenir Sheets**

| | | | | | |
|---|---|---|---|---|---|
| **869** | A137 | 15d | multi | 5.50 | 5.50 |
| **870** | A137 | 15d | multi | 5.50 | 5.50 |

1990 World Cup Soccer Championships, Italy — A138

Various athletes and Italian landmarks: 75b, Rialto Bridge, Venice. 1.25d, The Baptistery, Pisa. 7d, Casino San Remo. 12d, The Colosseum, Rome. No. 875, St. Mark's Cathedral, Venice. No. 876, Piazza Colonna, Rome.

**1989, Aug 25** *Perf. 14*

**871** A138 75b multi .55 .55
**872** A138 1.25b multi .70 .70
**873** A138 7d multi 3.00 3.00
**874** A138 12d multi 4.75 4.75
*Nos. 871-874 (4)* 9.00 9.00

**Souvenir Sheets**

**875** A138 15d multi 5.75 5.75
**876** A138 15d multi 5.75 5.75

Medicinal Plants — A139

**1989, Sept. 18** **Litho.** *Perf. 14*

**877** A139 20b Vitex doniana .25 .25
**878** A139 50b Ricinus communis .25 .25
**879** A139 75b Palisota hirsuta .35 .35
**880** A139 1d Smilax kraussiana .45 .45
**881** A139 1.25d Aspilia africana .55 .55
**882** A139 5d Newbouldia laevis 1.90 1.90
**883** A139 8d Monodora tenuifolia 3.00 3.00
**884** A139 10d Gossypium arboreum 3.50 3.50
*Nos. 877-884 (8)* 10.25 10.25

**Souvenir Sheets**

**885** A139 15d Kigelia africana 6.00 6.00
**886** A139 15d Spathodea campanulata 6.00 6.00

Fish A140

**1989, Oct. 19** **Litho.** *Perf.*

**887** A140 20b Lookdown .25 .25
**888** A140 75b Boarfish .70 .70
**889** A140 1d Gray triggerfish .75 .75
**890** A140 1.25d Skipjack tuna .85 .85
**891** A140 2d Bermuda chub 1.10 1.10
**892** A140 4d Atlantic manta 2.10 2.10
**893** A140 5d Striped mullet 2.50 2.50
**894** A140 10d Ladyfish 3.75 3.75
*Nos. 887-894 (8)* 12.00 12.00

**Souvenir Sheet**

**895** A140 15d Porcupinefish 7.25 7.25
**896** A140 15d Shortfin makos 7.25 7.25

Souvenir Sheet

The White House, Washington, D.C. — A141

**1989, Nov. 17** **Litho.** *Perf. 14*

**897** A141 10d multicolored 2.75 2.75

World Stamp Expo '89.

World Stamp Expo '89, Washington, D.C. — A142

Disney characters riding carousel horses: 20b, Daniel Muller Indian pony. 50b, Herschell-Spillman steed. 75b, Gustav Dentzel stander. 1d, Muller armored stander. 1.25d, Jumper from the Smithsonian Collection. 2d, Illion "American Beauty." 8d, Zalar jumper. 10d, Parker buckling. No. 906, Philadelphia Tobaggan Co. Carousel, Elitch Gardens, Denver, CO. No. 907, PTC Roman chariot.

**1989, Nov. 29** **Litho.** *Perf. 14x13½*

**898** A142 20b multicolored .70 .25
**899** A142 50b multicolored 1.00 .30
**900** A142 75b multicolored 1.10 .40
**901** A142 1d multicolored 1.10 .50
**902** A142 1.25d multicolored 1.25 .75
**903** A142 2d multicolored 1.75 1.00
**904** A142 8d multicolored 5.00 3.00
**905** A142 10d multicolored 5.00 3.25
*Nos. 898-905 (8)* 16.90 9.45

**Souvenir Sheets**

**906** A142 12d multicolored 7.25 7.25
**907** A142 12d multicolored 7.25 7.25

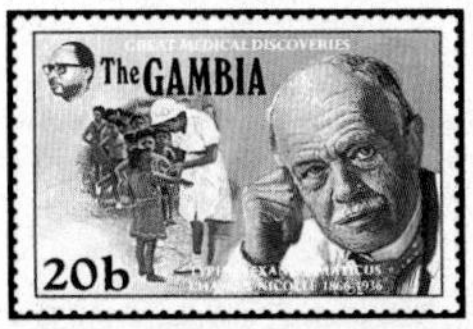

Nobel Prize Winners for Physiology and Great Medical Pioneers — A143

20b, Charles Nicolle (1866-1936), France, 1928 Prize, discovered transmission of typhus by body lice. 50b, Paul Ehrlich (1854-1915), Germany, 1908 Prize, immunology research. 75b, Selman Waksman (1888-1973), Russian-American, 1952 Prize, discovered antibiotic streptomycin, used to treat tuberculosis. 1d, Edward Jenner (1749-1823), Great Britain, discovered smallpox vaccine. 1.25d, Robert Koch (1843-1910), 1905 Prize, isolated the tubercle bacillus. 5d, Sir Alexander Fleming (1881-1955), Scotland, 1945 Prize, developed penicillin. 8d, Max Theiler (1899-1972), US, 1951 Prize, developed yellow fever vaccine. 10d, Louis Pasteur (1822-95), France, proved the germ theory of infection.

#916, C-9 Nightingale Aeromedical Airlift. #917, Hughes Vicking helicopter used in airlift.

**1989, Dec. 12** *Perf. 14*

**908** A143 20b multicolored .85 .30
**909** A143 50b multicolored .95 .40
**910** A143 75b multicolored 1.10 .50
**911** A143 1d multicolored 1.25 .60
**912** A143 1.25d multicolored 1.25 .70
**913** A143 5d multicolored 2.25 1.60
**914** A143 8d multicolored 3.50 2.50
**915** A143 10d multicolored 4.50 3.25
*Nos. 908-915 (8)* 15.65 9.85

**Souvenir Sheets**

**916** A143 15d multicolored 5.50 5.50
**917** A143 15d multicolored 5.50 5.50

Orchids — A144

**1989, Dec. 18** *Perf. 14*

**918** A144 20b Bulbophyllum lepidum .35 .30
**919** A144 75b Tridactyle tridactylites .60 .60
**920** A144 1d Vanilla imperialis .90 .90
**921** A144 1.25d Oeceoclades maculata 1.00 1.00
**922** A144 2d Polystachya affinis 1.40 1.40
**923** A144 4d Ancistrochilus rothschildianus 2.40 2.40
**924** A144 5d Angraecum distichum 2.75 2.75
**925** A144 10d Liparis guineensis 4.50 4.50
*Nos. 918-925 (8)* 13.90 13.85

**Souvenir Sheets**

**926** A144 15d Eulophia guineensis 7.00 7.00
**927** A144 15d Plectrelminthus caudatus 7.00 7.00

Christmas — A145

Disney characters and classic automobiles: 20b, 1922 Pierce Arrow. 50b, 1919 Spyker. 75b, 1929 Packard. 1d, 1920 Daimler. 1.25d, 1924 Hispano Suiza. 2d, Opel Laubfrosch, 1924-27. 10d, 1927 Vauxhall 30/98. 12d, 1923 Peerless. No. 936, 1930 Bentley Supercharged, Santa Claus. No. 937, 1928 Stutz Blackhawk Speedster, picnic.

**1989, Dec. 19** **Litho.** *Perf. 14*

**928** A145 20b multicolored .75 .25
**929** A145 50b multicolored 1.00 .40
**930** A145 75b multicolored 1.10 .55
**931** A145 1d multicolored 1.25 .65
**932** A145 1.25d multicolored 1.40 .90
**933** A145 2d multicolored 1.50 1.25
**934** A145 10d multicolored 4.50 3.00
**935** A145 12d multicolored 5.00 3.25
*Nos. 928-935 (8)* 16.50 10.25

**Souvenir Sheets**

**936** A145 15d multicolored 8.75 8.75
**937** A145 15d multicolored 8.75 8.75

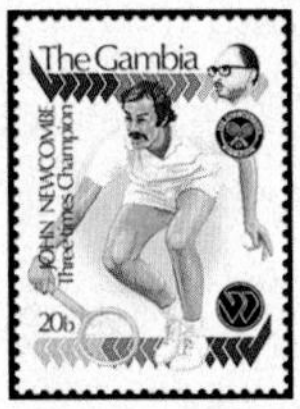

Wimbledon Tennis Champions — A146

**1990, Jan. 2** **Litho.** *Perf. 15x14½*

**938** A146 20b John Newcombe .25 .25
**939** A146 20b G.W. Hillyard .25 .25
*a.* Pair, #938-939 .40 .40
**940** A146 50b Roy Emerson .30 .30
**941** A146 50b Dorothy Chambers .30 .30
*a.* Pair, #940-941 .65 .65
**942** A146 75b Donald Budge .40 .40
**943** A146 75b Suzanne Lenglen .40 .40
*a.* Pair, #942-943 .85 .85
**944** A146 1d Laurence Doherty .45 .45
**945** A146 1d Helen Wills Moody .45 .45
*a.* Pair, #944-945 .95 .95
**946** A146 1.25d Bjorn Borg .50 .50
**947** A146 1.25d Maureen Connolly .50 .50
*a.* Pair, #946-947 1.10 1.10
**948** A146 4d Jean Borotra 1.10 1.10
**949** A146 4d Maria Bueno 1.10 1.10
*a.* Pair, #948-949 2.50 2.50
**950** A146 5d Anthony Wilding 1.40 1.40
**951** A146 5d Louise Brough 1.40 1.40
*a.* Pair, #950-951 3.00 3.00
**952** A146 7d Fred Perry 1.75 1.75
**953** A146 7d Margaret Court 1.75 1.75
*a.* Pair, #952-953 4.00 4.00
**954** A146 10d Bill Tilden 2.50 2.50
**955** A146 10d Billie Jean King 2.50 2.50
*a.* Pair, #954-955 5.75 5.75
**956** A146 12d Rod Laver 2.75 2.75
**957** A146 12d Martina Navratilova 2.75 2.75
*a.* Pair, #956-957 6.25 6.25
*Nos. 938-957 (20)* 22.80 22.80

**Souvenir Sheets**

**958** A146 15d Rod Laver, diff. 6.50 6.50
**959** A146 15d Martina Navratilova, diff. 6.50 6.50

1st Moon Landing, 20th Anniv. (in 1989) — A147

Designs: 20b, Eagle lunar module descending, horiz. 50b, Apollo 11 liftoff. 75b, Astronaut descending ladder, horiz. 1d, Astronaut, US flag over Sea of Tranquillity, horiz. 1.25d, Mission emblem. 1.75d, Crew, horiz. 8d, Lunar module, Sea of Tranquillity, horiz. 12d, Recovery of command module Columbia after splashdown. No. 968, Neil Armstrong returning to Eagle. No. 969, View of Earth.

**1990, Feb. 16** *Perf. 14*

**960** A147 20b multicolored .70 .25
**961** A147 50b multicolored .90 .30
**962** A147 75b multicolored 1.10 .45
**963** A147 1d multicolored 1.25 .55
**964** A147 1.25d multicolored 1.25 .60
**965** A147 1.75d multicolored 1.40 1.00
**966** A147 8d multicolored 4.00 2.25
**967** A147 12d multicolored 5.25 2.75
*Nos. 960-967 (8)* 15.85 8.15

**Souvenir Sheets**

**968** A147 15d multicolored 5.00 5.00
**969** A147 15d multicolored 5.00 5.00

Miniature Sheet

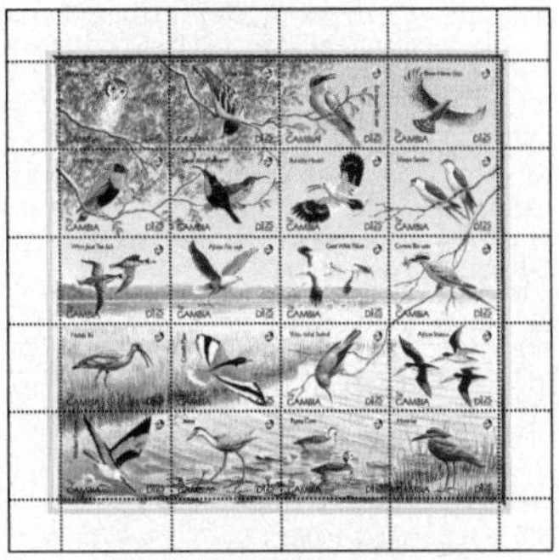
Birds of Africa — A148

No. 970: a, White-faced owl. b, Village weaver. c, Red-throated bee eater. d, Brown harrier eagle. e, Red bishop. f, Scarlet-chested sunbird. g, Red-billed hornbill. h, Mosque swallow. i, White-faced tree duck. j, African fish eagle. k, Great white pelican. l, Carmine bee eater. m, Hadada ibis. n, Crocodile plover. o, Yellow-bellied sunbird. p, African skimmer. q, Woodland kingfisher. r, Jacana. s, Pygmy goose. t, Hamerkop.

**1990, Apr. 12** **Litho.** *Perf. 14*

**970** Sheet of 20 19.00 19.00
*a.-t.* A148 1.25d any single .90 .90

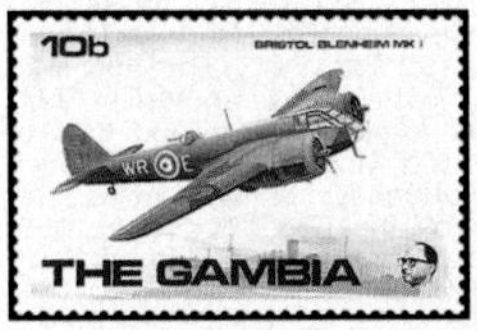

RAF World War II Fighter Planes A149

Designs: 10b, Bristol Blenheim Mk-1. 20b, Battle. 50b, Blenheim 4. 60b, Wellington 1C. 75b, Whitley 5. 1d, Hampden Mk-1. 1.25d, Spitfire 1A and Hurricane 1. 2d, Avro Manchester. 3d, Stirling. 5d, Handley Page Halifax B-2. 10d, Lancaster B-3. 12d, Mosquito B-4. No. 983, Lancaster B-3 over Hamburg. No. 984, Spitfire 1, Battle of Britain.

**1990, Apr. 18** *Perf. 14*

**971** A149 10b multicolored .65 .50
**972** A149 20b multicolored .85 .50
**973** A149 50b multicolored .95 .50
**974** A149 60b multicolored 1.10 .50
**975** A149 75b multicolored 1.10 .50
**976** A149 1d multicolored 1.25 .50
**977** A149 1.25d multicolored 1.25 .50
**978** A149 2d multicolored 1.50 .55
**979** A149 3d multicolored 1.75 .90
**980** A149 5d multicolored 2.40 1.40
**981** A149 10d multicolored 4.25 2.50
**982** A149 12d multicolored 5.25 3.00
*Nos. 971-982 (12)* 22.30 11.85

### Souvenir Sheets

**983** A149 15d multicolored 6.00 6.00
**984** A149 15d multicolored 6.00 6.00

Independence, 25th Anniv. — A150

Designs: 3d, Sir Dawda Jawara, President. 12d, Jet and map showing airport. 18d, National arms.

**1990, June 5 Litho. *Perf. 14***

**985** A150 1d multicolored .25 .25
**986** A150 3d multicolored 1.10 1.10
**987** A150 12d multicolored 5.00 5.00
*Nos. 985-987 (3)* 6.35 6.35

### Souvenir Sheet

**988** A150 18d multicolored 5.50 5.50

Baobab Tree A151

**1990, June 14 Litho. *Perf. 14***

**989** A151 5b shown .60 .60
**990** A151 10b Woodcarving .25 .25
**991** A151 20b Pres. Jawara .25 .25
**992** A151 50b Map .40 .25
**993** A151 75b Batik fabric .25 .25
**994** A151 1d Bakau Beach Resort .25 .25
**995** A151 1.25d Tendaba Camp .30 .30
**996** A151 2d Shrimp industry .45 .45
**997** A151 5d Peanut oil mill .75 *1.25*
**998** A151 10d Pottery, kora 1.25 1.25
**999** A151 15d Ansellia Africana orchid 5.50 5.50
**1000** A151 30d Ancient stone rings, Euryphene gambiae 7.00 7.00
*Nos. 989-1000 (12)* 17.25 17.60

Nos. 990, 999 vert.

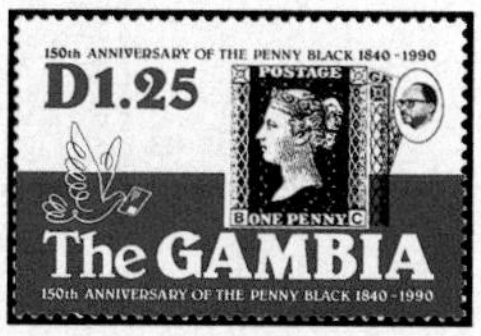


Penny Black, 150th Anniv. A152

**1990, June 18**

**1001** A152 1.25d brt bl & blk .75 .35
**1002** A152 12d dark red & blk 5.50 3.50

### Souvenir Sheet

**1003** A152 15d sil, bis & blk 7.00 7.00

Mickey Visits England — A153

Walt Disney characters at: 20b, 10 Downing Street. 50b, Trafalgar Square. 75b, Cliffs of Dover. 1d, Tower of London. 5d, Hampton Court Palace. 8d, Magdalen Tower, Oxford University. 10d, Old London Bridge. 12d, Rosetta Stone, British Museum. No. 1012, Picadilly Circus. No. 1013, Houses of Parliament and Big Ben on the River Thames.

**1990, June 19 *Perf. 14x13½***

**1004** A153 20b multicolored .45 .30
**1005** A153 50b multicolored .65 .35
**1006** A153 75b multicolored .85 .40
**1007** A153 1d multicolored 1.10 .45
**1008** A153 5d multicolored 2.50 2.50
**1009** A153 8d multicolored 3.00 3.00
**1010** A153 10d multicolored 3.75 3.75
**1011** A153 12d multicolored 4.75 4.75
*Nos. 1004-1011 (8)* 17.05 15.50

### Souvenir Sheets

**1012** A153 18d multicolored 9.00 9.00
**1013** A153 18d multicolored 9.00 9.00

Stamp World London '90. Nos. 1004-1005, 1007, 1009 vert.

A154

**1990, July 19 *Perf. 14***

**1014** 6d Girl facing left 1.50 1.50
**1015** 6d Young girl, diff. 1.50 1.50
**1016** 6d Seated in chair 1.50 1.50
*a.* A154 Strip of 3, #1014-1016 5.50 5.50

### Souvenir Sheet

**1017** A154 18d like No. 1014 5.75 5.75

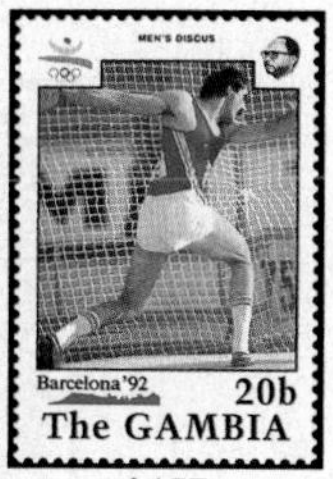


A156 A157

Players from participating countries.

**1990, Sept. 24 Litho. *Perf. 14***

**1018** A156 1d Italy .45 .45
**1019** A156 1.25d Argentina .55 .55
**1020** A156 3d Costa Rica 1.10 1.10
**1021** A156 5d UAE 1.60 1.60
*Nos. 1018-1021 (4)* 3.70 3.70

### Souvenir Sheets

**1022** A156 18d Holland 7.75 7.75
**1023** A156 18d Romania 7.75 7.75

World Cup Soccer Championships, Italy.

**1990, Nov. 1 Litho. *Perf. 14***

**1024** A157 20b Men's discus .40 .25
**1025** A157 50b Men's 100-meter race .45 .25
**1026** A157 75b Women's 400-meter race .50 .30
**1027** A157 1d Men's 200-meter race .55 .55
**1028** A157 1.25d Rhythmic gymnastics .45 .45
**1029** A157 3d Soccer 1.60 1.60
**1030** A157 10d Men's marathon 4.25 4.25
**1031** A157 12d Tornado class sailing 5.25 5.25
*Nos. 1024-1031 (8)* 13.45 12.90

### Souvenir Sheets

**1032** A157 15d Parade of flags 6.75 6.75
**1033** A157 15d Stadium, card section 6.75 6.75

1992 Summer Olympics, Barcelona.

Christmas A158

Entire paintings or different details from: 20b, 7d, The Annunciation with St. Emidius by Crivelli. 50b, The Annunciation by Campin. 75b, The Solly Madonna by Raphael. 1.25d, The Tempi Madonna by Raphael. 2d, Madonna of the Linen Window by Raphael. 10d, The Orleans Madonna by Raphael. 15d, Madonna and Child by Crivelli. No. 1042, The Niccolini-Cowper Madonna by Raphael.

**1990, Dec. 24 Litho. *Perf. 13½x14***

**1034** A158 20b multicolored .45 .25
**1035** A158 50b multicolored .55 .25
**1036** A158 75b multicolored .70 .25
**1037** A158 1.25d multicolored .80 .65
**1038** A158 2d multicolored .90 .90
**1039** A158 7d multicolored 2.50 2.50
**1040** A158 10d multicolored 3.00 3.00
**1041** A158 15d multicolored 4.75 4.75
*Nos. 1034-1041 (8)* 13.65 12.55

### Souvenir Sheet

**1042** A158 15d multicolored 8.00 8.00

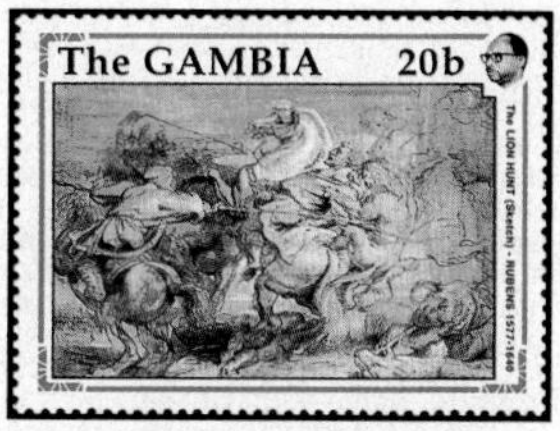


Peter Paul Rubens (1577-1640), Painter — A159

Entire paintings or different details from: 20b, 75b, 10d, No. 1054, The Lion Hunt. 1d, 1.25d, 3d, 15d, The Tiger Hunt. 5d, No. 1055, The Boar Hunt. No. 1056, The Crocodile and Hippopotamus Hunt. No. 1057, Saint George Slays the Dragon, vert.

**1990, Dec. 24 Litho. *Perf. 14x13½***

**1046** A159 20b multicolored .25 .25
**1047** A159 75b multicolored .35 .25
**1048** A159 1d multicolored .40 .40
**1049** A159 1.25d multicolored .55 .55
**1050** A159 3d multicolored 1.25 1.25
**1051** A159 5d multicolored 1.60 1.60
**1052** A159 10d multicolored 2.75 2.75
**1053** A159 15d multicolored 3.75 3.75
*Nos. 1046-1053 (8)* 10.90 10.80

### Souvenir Sheets

**1054** A159 15d multicolored 4.75 4.75
**1055** A159 15d multicolored 4.75 4.75
**1056** A159 15d multicolored 4.75 4.75
**1057** A159 15d multicolored 4.75 4.75

World Summit for Children A160

**1991, Jan. 7 Litho. *Perf. 14***

**1058** A160 1d multicolored .80 .80

Intl. Literacy Year — A161

Walt Disney characters in "The Sword in the Stone": No. 1059a, Wart and Sir Kay. b, Merlin reading book. c, Wart learning geography. d, Wart writing on blackboard. e, Wart as bird, Madam Mim. f, Merlin and Madam Mim. g, Mim as dragon. h, Wart pulling sword from stone. i, Wart as King of England. No. 1060, Merlin, Wart in forest, vert. No. 1061, Knight trying to remove sword from stone, vert.

**1991, Feb. 14 Litho. *Perf. 14x13½***

**1059** A161 3d Sheet of 9, #a-i 15.00 15.00

### Souvenir Sheets

**1060** A161 20d multicolored 9.50 9.50
**1061** A161 20d multicolored 9.50 9.50

### Miniature Sheets

Wildlife — A162

No. 1062: a, Bebearia senegalensis. b, Graphium ridleyanus. c, Precis antilope. d, Charaxes ameliae. e, Addax. f, Sassaby. g, Civet. h, Green monkey. i, Spurwing goose. j, Red-billed hornbill. k, Osprey. l, Glossy ibis. m, Egyptian plover. n, Golden-tailed woodpecker. o, Green woodhoopoe. p, Gaboon viper.

No. 1063: a, Red-billed firefinch. b, Leaflove. c, Piacpiac. d, Emerald cuckoo. e, Red colobus monkey. f, African elephant. g, Duiker. h, Giant eland. i, Oribi. j, West African dwarf crocodile. k, Crowned crane. l, Jackal. m, Yellow-throated longclaw. n, Abyssinian ground hornbill. o, Papilio hesperus. p, Papilio antimachus.

No. 1064: a, Martial eagle. b, Red-cheeked cordon-bleu. c, Red bishop. d, Great white pelican. e, Patas monkey. f, Vervet monkey. g, Roan antelope. h, Western hartebeest. i, Waterbuck. j, Warthog. k, Spotted hyena. l, Olive baboon. m, Palla decius. n, Acraea pharsalus. o, Neptidopsis ophione. p, Acraea caecilia.

No. 1065, African spoonbill, vert. No. 1066, Lion, vert. No. 1067, Buffalo weaver, vert.

**1991, May 31 Litho. *Perf. 14***

**1062** A162 1d Sheet of 16, #a.-p. 5.00 5.00
**1063** A162 1.50d Sheet of 16, #a.-p. 7.25 7.25
**1064** A162 5d Sheet of 16, #a.-p. 23.00 23.00
*Nos. 1062-1064 (3)* 35.25 35.25

### Souvenir Sheets

**1065** A162 18d multicolored 5.50 5.50
**1066** A162 18d multicolored 5.50 5.50
**1067** A162 18d multicolored 5.50 5.50

Butterflies — A163

Designs: 20b, Papilio dardanus. 50b, Bematistes poggei. 1d, Vanessa cardiu. 1.50d, Amphicallia tigris. 3d, Hypolimnes dexithea. 8d, Acraea egina. 10d, Salmis temora. 15d, Precis octavia. No. 1076, Danaus chrysippus. No. 1077, Charaxes jasius. No. 1078, Papilio demodocus. No. 1079, Papilio nireus.

**1991, June 1 Litho. *Perf. 14***

**1068** A163 20b multicolored .35 .35
**1069** A163 50b multicolored .40 .40
**1070** A163 1d multicolored .50 .50
**1071** A163 1.50d multicolored .55 .55
**1072** A163 3d multicolored 1.10 1.10
**1073** A163 8d multicolored 2.75 2.75
**1074** A163 10d multicolored 3.50 3.50
**1075** A163 15d multicolored 5.25 5.25
*Nos. 1068-1075 (8)* 14.40 14.40

### Souvenir Sheets

**1076** A163 18d multicolored 4.75 4.75
**1077** A163 18d multicolored 4.75 4.75
**1078** A163 18d multicolored 4.75 4.75
**1079** A163 18d multicolored 4.75 4.75

While Nos. 1078-1079 have same release date as Nos. 1068-1077, the dollar value of Nos. 1078-1079 were lower when they were released.

### Royal Family Birthday, Anniversary

Common Design Type

**1991, Aug. 12 Litho. *Perf. 14***

**1080** CD347 20b multi .35 .25
**1081** CD347 50b multi .40 .30
**1082** CD347 75b multi .45 .40
**1083** CD347 1d multi .50 .50
**1084** CD347 1.25d multi .65 .65
**1085** CD347 1.50d multi .80 .80
**1086** CD347 12d multi 4.50 4.50
**1087** CD347 15d multi 6.00 6.00
*Nos. 1080-1087 (8)* 13.65 13.40

### Souvenir Sheets

| | | | | | |
|---|---|---|---|---|---|
| 1088 | CD347 | 18d | Elizabeth, Philip | 4.50 | 4.50 |
| 1089 | CD347 | 18d | Diana, sons, Charles | 6.50 | 6.50 |

20b, 75b, 1.50d, 15d, No. 1089, Charles and Diana, 10th wedding anniversary. Others, Queen Elizabeth II, 65th birthday.

Phila Nippon '91 — A164

Walt Disney characters playing Japanese games and sports: 50b, Donald Duck and Mickey Mouse playing Go. 75b, Morty, Ferdie and Pete sumo wrestling. 1d, Minnie Mouse, Clarabelle, Daisy Duck playing battledore and shuttlecock. 1.25d, Goofy, Mickey at Okinawa bullfight, vert. 5d, Mickey as a Hawk Hunter Tagari, vert. 7d, Mickey, Minnie, and Donald play Jan-Ken-Pon, vert. 10d, Goofy as archer. 15d, Morty, Ferdie fly Japanese kites, vert. No. 1098, Goofy batting in Japanese baseball game, vert. No. 1099, Mickey, Scrooge McDuck playing Japanese football, vert. No. 1100, Mickey fly fishing, vert. No. 1101, Mickey climbing Mt. Fuji, vert.

*Perf. 14x13½, 13½x14*

**1991, Aug. 22** Litho.

| | | | | | |
|---|---|---|---|---|---|
| 1090 | A164 | 50b | multicolored | .50 | .30 |
| 1091 | A164 | 75b | multicolored | .60 | .40 |
| 1092 | A164 | 1d | multicolored | .70 | .45 |
| 1093 | A164 | 1.25d | multicolored | .80 | .55 |
| 1094 | A164 | 5d | multicolored | 2.25 | 2.25 |
| 1095 | A164 | 7d | multicolored | 3.00 | 3.00 |
| 1096 | A164 | 10d | multicolored | 4.00 | 4.00 |
| 1097 | A164 | 15d | multicolored | 5.75 | 5.75 |
| | | | *Nos. 1090-1097 (8)* | 17.60 | 16.70 |

### Souvenir Sheets

| | | | | | |
|---|---|---|---|---|---|
| 1098 | A164 | 20d | multicolored | 5.50 | 5.50 |
| 1099 | A164 | 20d | multicolored | 5.50 | 5.50 |
| 1100 | A164 | 20d | multicolored | 5.50 | 5.50 |
| 1101 | A164 | 20d | multicolored | 5.50 | 5.50 |

Intl. Literacy Year — A165

Walt Disney characters in scenes from Rudyard Kipling's "Just So Stories": 50b, How the Whale Got His Throat. 75b, How the Camel Got His Hump. 1d, How the Leopard Got His Spots. 1.25d, The Elephant's Child. 1.50d, Singsong of Old Man Kangaroo. 7d, The Crab that Played with the Sea. 10d, The Cat that Walked by Himself. 15d, The Butterfly that Stamped. No. 1110, How the Alphabet was Made, vert. No. 1111, The Beginning of the Armadillos. No. 1112, How the First Letter was Written, vert. No. 1113, How the Rhinoceros Got His Skin.

**1991, Aug. 28** Litho. *Perf. 14x13½*

| | | | | | |
|---|---|---|---|---|---|
| 1102 | A165 | 50b | multicolored | .75 | .30 |
| 1103 | A165 | 75b | multicolored | .80 | .40 |
| 1104 | A165 | 1d | multicolored | .85 | .45 |
| 1105 | A165 | 1.25d | multicolored | .90 | .55 |
| 1106 | A165 | 1.50d | multicolored | 1.00 | .90 |
| 1107 | A165 | 7d | multicolored | 3.50 | 3.50 |
| 1108 | A165 | 10d | multicolored | 5.00 | 5.00 |
| 1109 | A165 | 15d | multicolored | 7.50 | 7.50 |
| | | | *Nos. 1102-1109 (8)* | 20.30 | 18.60 |

### Souvenir Sheets

*Perf. 13½x14, 14x13½*

| | | | | | |
|---|---|---|---|---|---|
| 1110 | A165 | 20d | multicolored | 6.75 | 6.75 |
| 1111 | A165 | 20d | multicolored | 6.75 | 6.75 |
| 1112 | A165 | 20d | multicolored | 6.75 | 6.75 |
| 1113 | A165 | 20d | multicolored | 6.75 | 6.75 |

Train Cabooses — A166

No. 1114: a, Steel cupola, Canadian Pacific. b, Four-wheel, Cumberland and Pennsylvania. c, Mexican slim gauge. d, All steel cupola, Northern Pacific. e, Four-wheel, Morristown & Erie. f, Streamlined cupola, Burlington Northern. g, Caboose coach, McCloud River. h, Wide vision, Santa Fe. i, Wide vision, Frisco.

No. 1115: a, Narrow gauge, Oahu Railway. b, Standard brake-van, British Railways. c, Wide view steel, Union Pacific. d, Four-wheel, Belt Railway of Chicago. e, Four-wheel, McCloud River. f, Logging, Angelina County Lumber Co. g, Narrow gauge, Coahuila & Zacatecas. h, Three-foot gauge, United Railways of Yucatan. i, Steel cupola, Rio Grande.

No. 1116: a, Four-wheel, Colorado & Southern. b, Transfer, Santa Fe. c, Wooden cupola, Canadian National. d, Transfer steel, Union Pacific. e, Caboose coach, Virginia & Truckee. f, Standard brake-van, British. g, Narrow gauge, Intl. Railways of Central America. h, Steel cupola, Northern Pacific. i, Wood, Burlington Northern.

No. 1117, Pennsylvania electric, vert. No. 1118, Unidentified caboose, trainman with flag, vert. No. 1119, Unidentified green wooden caboose behind yellow freight car.

**1991, Sept. 12** Litho. *Perf. 14x13½*

### Sheets of 9

| | | | | | |
|---|---|---|---|---|---|
| 1114 | A166 | 1d | Sheet of 9, #a.-i. | 5.75 | 5.75 |
| 1115 | A166 | 2d | Sheet of 9, #a.-i. | 7.25 | 7.25 |
| 1116 | A166 | 1.50d | Sheet of 9, #a.-i. | 5.75 | 5.75 |
| | | | *Nos. 1114-1116 (3)* | 18.75 | 18.75 |

### Souvenir Sheets

*Perf. 12x13, 13x12*

| | | | | | |
|---|---|---|---|---|---|
| 1117 | A166 | 20d | multicolored | 6.00 | 6.00 |
| 1118 | A166 | 20d | multicolored | 6.00 | 6.00 |
| 1119 | A166 | 20d | multicolored | 6.00 | 6.00 |

While Nos. 1115-1116 and 1118-1119 have the same issue date as Nos. 1114 and 1117, the dollar value of Nos. 1115-1116 and 1118-1119 was lower when they were released.

Fish — A167

**1991, Oct. 28** Litho. *Perf. 14x14½*

| | | | | | |
|---|---|---|---|---|---|
| 1120 | A167 | 20b | Tiger shark | .25 | .25 |
| 1121 | A167 | 25b | Common jewel fish | .25 | .25 |
| 1122 | A167 | 50b | Five spot fish | .45 | .45 |
| 1123 | A167 | 75b | Smalltooth sawfish | .45 | .45 |
| 1124 | A167 | 1d | Five spot tilapia | .45 | .45 |
| 1125 | A167 | 1.25d | Dwarf jewel fish | .55 | .55 |
| 1126 | A167 | 1.50d | Five spot jewel fish | .65 | .65 |
| 1127 | A167 | 3d | Bumphead | 1.00 | 1.00 |
| 1128 | A167 | 10d | Egyptian mouth-brooder | 3.00 | 3.00 |
| 1129 | A167 | 15d | Burton's mouth-brooder | 4.25 | 4.25 |
| | | | *Nos. 1120-1129 (10)* | 11.30 | 11.30 |

### Souvenir Sheets

| | | | | | |
|---|---|---|---|---|---|
| 1130 | A167 | 18d | Great barracuda | 9.00 | 9.00 |
| 1131 | A167 | 18d | Yellowtail snapper | 9.00 | 9.00 |

While Nos. 1120-1122, 1125, 1129-1131 have the same issue date as Nos. 1123-1124, 1126-1128 the dollar value of Nos. 1120-1122, 1125, 1129-1130 was lower when they were released.

Hummel Figurines — A168

20b, No. 1141a, Girl and boy waving handkerchiefs. 75b, No. 1140a, Boy and girl under umbrella. 1d, No. 1140b, Two girls wearing scarfs. 1.50d, No. 1140c, Girl and boy in window with flower box. 2.50d, No. 1141b, Two girls with basket. 5d, No. 1141c, Boy wearing long pants, boy wearing shorts. 10d, No. 1141d, Two girls on fence. 15d, No. 1140d, Boy with stick, girl with bag.

**1991, Nov. 4** Litho. *Perf. 14*

| | | | | | |
|---|---|---|---|---|---|
| 1132 | A168 | 20b | multicolored | .25 | .25 |
| 1133 | A168 | 75b | multicolored | .25 | .25 |
| 1134 | A168 | 1d | multicolored | .25 | .25 |
| 1135 | A168 | 1.50d | multicolored | .50 | .50 |
| 1136 | A168 | 2.50d | multicolored | .70 | .70 |
| 1137 | A168 | 5d | multicolored | 1.25 | 1.25 |
| 1138 | A168 | 10d | multicolored | 2.50 | 2.50 |
| 1139 | A168 | 15d | multicolored | 3.50 | 3.50 |
| | | | *Nos. 1132-1139 (8)* | 9.20 | 9.20 |

### Souvenir Sheets

| | | | | | |
|---|---|---|---|---|---|
| 1140 | A168 | 4d | Sheet of 4, #a.-d. | 4.50 | 4.50 |
| 1141 | A168 | 5d | Sheet of 4, #a.-d. | 5.50 | 5.50 |

Paintings by Vincent Van Gogh A169

Designs: 20b, The Old Cemetery Tower at Nuenen in the Snow, horiz. 25b, Head of a Peasant Woman with White Cap. 50b, The Green Parrot. 75b, Vase with Carnations. 1d, Vase with Red Gladioli. 1.25b, Beach at Scheveningen in Calm Weather, horiz. 1.50d, Boy Cutting Grass with a Sickle, horiz. 2d, Coleus Plant in a Flowerpot. 3d, Self-portrait, spring-summer 1887. 4d, Self-portrait. 5d, Self-portrait, diff. 6d, Self-portrait, spring 1887. 8d, Still Life with a Bottle, Two Glasses, Cheese and Bread. 10d, Still Life with Cabbage, Clogs and Potatoes, horiz. 12d, Montmartre: The Street Lamps. 15d, Head of a Peasant Woman with Brownish Cap. No. 1158, Arles: View From the Wheat Fields. No. 1159, Autumn Landscape. No. 1160, Montmartre: Quarry, The Mills, horiz. No. 1161, The Potato Eaters, horiz.

*Perf. 13½x14, 14x13½*

**1991, Dec. 5** Litho.

| | | | | | |
|---|---|---|---|---|---|
| 1142 | A169 | 20b | multicolored | .40 | .25 |
| 1143 | A169 | 25b | multicolored | .45 | .25 |
| 1144 | A169 | 50b | multicolored | .50 | .25 |
| 1145 | A169 | 75b | multicolored | .55 | .30 |
| 1146 | A169 | 1d | multicolored | .60 | .35 |
| 1147 | A169 | 1.25d | multicolored | .65 | .45 |
| 1148 | A169 | 1.50d | multicolored | .70 | .55 |
| 1149 | A169 | 2d | multicolored | .75 | .65 |
| 1150 | A169 | 3d | multicolored | .90 | .90 |
| 1151 | A169 | 4d | multicolored | 1.25 | 1.25 |
| 1152 | A169 | 5d | multicolored | 1.50 | 1.50 |
| 1153 | A169 | 6d | multicolored | 2.00 | 2.00 |
| 1154 | A169 | 8d | multicolored | 2.75 | 2.75 |
| 1155 | A169 | 10d | multicolored | 3.25 | 3.25 |
| 1156 | A169 | 12d | multicolored | 4.25 | 4.25 |
| 1157 | A169 | 15d | multicolored | 4.50 | 4.50 |

### Size: 127x102mm

*Imperf*

| | | | | | |
|---|---|---|---|---|---|
| 1158 | A169 | 20d | multicolored | 6.25 | 6.25 |
| 1159 | A169 | 20d | multicolored | 6.25 | 6.25 |
| 1160 | A169 | 20d | multicolored | 6.25 | 6.25 |
| 1161 | A169 | 20d | multicolored | 6.25 | 6.25 |
| | | | *Nos. 1142-1161 (20)* | 50.00 | 48.45 |

While Nos. 1142-1143, 1146, 1148, 1150, 1153, 1155-1156, 1160-1161 have the same issue date as Nos. 1144-1145, 1147, 1149, 1151-1152, 1154, 1157-1159, the dollar value of Nos. 1142-1143, 1146, 1148, 1150, 1153, 1155-1156, 1160-1161 was lower when they were released.

Christmas A170

Paintings by Fra Angelico: 20b, The Madonna of Humility. 50b, Madonna and Child with Angels. 75b, The Virgin and Child with Angels. 1d, Annunciation. 1.25d, Presentation in the Temple. 5d, Annunciation, diff. 10d, Madonna della Stella. 15d, Naming of St. John the Baptist. No. 1170, Annunciation and Adoration of the Magi. No. 1171, Coronation of the Virgin.

**1991, Dec. 23** *Perf. 12*

| | | | | | |
|---|---|---|---|---|---|
| 1162 | A170 | 20b | multicolored | .25 | .25 |
| 1163 | A170 | 50b | multicolored | .25 | .25 |
| 1164 | A170 | 75b | multicolored | .30 | .25 |
| 1165 | A170 | 1d | multicolored | .35 | .30 |
| 1166 | A170 | 1.25d | multicolored | .45 | .45 |
| 1167 | A170 | 5d | multicolored | 1.40 | 1.40 |
| 1168 | A170 | 10d | multicolored | 2.50 | 2.50 |
| 1169 | A170 | 15d | multicolored | 4.00 | 4.00 |
| | | | *Nos. 1162-1169 (8)* | 9.50 | 9.40 |

### Souvenir Sheets

*Perf. 14½*

| | | | | | |
|---|---|---|---|---|---|
| 1170 | A170 | 20d | multicolored | 5.25 | 5.25 |
| 1171 | A170 | 20d | multicolored | 5.25 | 5.25 |

### Queen Elizabeth II's Accession to the Throne, 40th Anniv.

Common Design Type

**1992, Feb. 6** Litho. *Perf. 14*

| | | | | | |
|---|---|---|---|---|---|
| 1172 | CD348 | 20b | multicolored | .25 | .25 |
| 1173 | CD348 | 50b | multicolored | .35 | .25 |
| 1174 | CD348 | 1d | multicolored | .50 | .35 |
| 1175 | CD348 | 15d | multicolored | 5.00 | 5.00 |
| | | | *Nos. 1172-1175 (4)* | 6.10 | 5.85 |

### Souvenir Sheets

| | | | | | |
|---|---|---|---|---|---|
| 1176 | CD348 | 20d | Queen at left, yacht | 5.50 | 5.50 |
| 1177 | CD348 | 20d | Queen at right, boat | 5.50 | 5.50 |

Famous Blues Musicians — A171

**1992, Feb. 12** *Perf. 14*

| | | | | | |
|---|---|---|---|---|---|
| 1178 | A171 | 20b | Son House | .25 | .25 |
| 1179 | A171 | 25b | W. C. Handy | .25 | .25 |
| 1180 | A171 | 50b | Muddy Waters | .40 | .40 |
| 1181 | A171 | 75b | Lightnin Hopkins | .55 | .55 |
| 1182 | A171 | 1d | Ma Rainey | .60 | .60 |
| 1183 | A171 | 1.25d | Mance Lipscomb | .70 | .70 |
| 1184 | A171 | 1.50d | Mahalia Jackson | .80 | .80 |
| 1185 | A171 | 2d | Ella Fitzgerald | .85 | .85 |
| 1186 | A171 | 3d | Howlin Wolf | 1.05 | 1.05 |
| 1187 | A171 | 5d | Bessie Smith | 1.75 | 1.75 |
| 1188 | A171 | 7d | Leadbelly | 2.25 | 2.25 |
| 1189 | A171 | 10d | Joe Willie Wilkins | 3.50 | 3.50 |
| | | | *Nos. 1178-1189 (12)* | 12.95 | 12.95 |

### Souvenir Sheets

| | | | | | |
|---|---|---|---|---|---|
| 1190 | A171 | 20d | Gambian string drummer | 6.00 | 6.00 |
| 1191 | A171 | 20d | Elvis Presley | 6.00 | 6.00 |
| 1192 | A171 | 20d | Billie Holiday | 6.00 | 6.00 |

While all stamps have the same issue date the dollar value of some was lower when they actually were released.

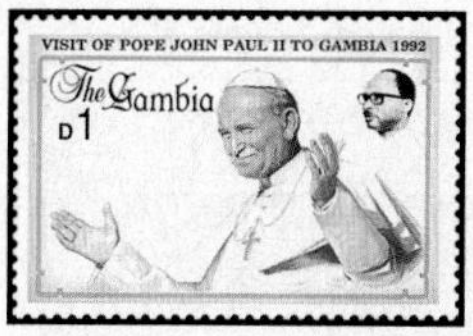


A172

Papal Visit, 1992 — A172a

Designs: 1d, Pope John Paul II. 1.25d, Pope, Pres. Dwada Jawara. 20d, Flags, Papal arms. 25d, Pope at Mass.

**1992, Feb. 23 Litho. *Perf. 14***

**1193** A172 1d multicolored .65 .65
**1194** A172 1.25d multicolored .80 .80
**1195** A172 20d multicolored 6.50 6.50
*Nos. 1193-1195 (3)* 7.95 7.95

**Souvenir Sheet**

**1196** A172 25d multicolored 9.00 9.00

**Embossed**
***Perf. 12***
**Without Gum**
**Size: 65x43mm**

**1196A** A172a 50d gold *37.50*

No. 1196A was not available until late 1993, exists imperf on large card.

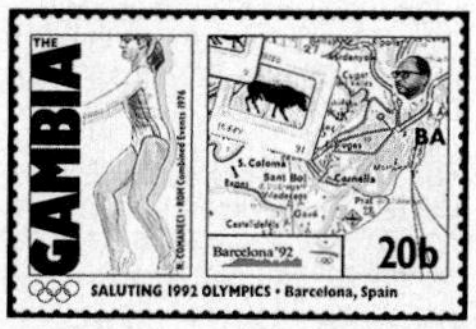


1992 Summer Olympics, Barcelona A173

20b, Map & Nadia Comaneci, gymnastics, Romania, 1976. 50b, D. Moorcraft, 5000 meters, Great Britain, 1984. 75b, M. Nemeth, javelin, Hungary, 1976. 1d, J. Pedraza, 20k walking, Mexico, 1968. 1.25d, Map, Spanish Arms & flag, Yachting soling class, Brazil, 1984. 1.50d, Spanish building, Field hockey, East Germany, 1984. 12d, Map & Michael Jordan, basketball, US, 1984. 15d, V. Borzov, 100 meters, USSR, 1972. No. 1205, Flamenco dancer, vert. No. 1206, Map & Bull.

**1992, Mar. 6 Litho. *Perf. 14***

**1197** A173 20b multicolored .30 .25
**1198** A173 50b multicolored .40 .30
**1199** A173 75b multicolored .45 .40
**1200** A173 1d multicolored .50 .50
**1201** A173 1.25d multicolored .70 .70
**1202** A173 1.50d multicolored .75 .75
**1203** A173 12d multicolored 3.00 3.00
**1204** A173 15d multicolored 5.00 5.00
*Nos. 1197-1204 (8)* 11.10 10.90

**Souvenir Sheet**

**1205** A173 20d multicolored 6.25 6.25
**1206** A173 20d multicolored 6.25 6.25

While Nos. 1197, 1201-1203, 1206 have the same issue date as Nos. 1198-1200, 1204-1205, the value of Nos. 1197, 1201-1203, 1206 was lower when they were released.

Easter A174

Paintings: 20b, Christ Presented to the People, by Rembrandt. 50b, Christ Carrying the Cross, by Mathias Grunewald. 75b, The Crucifixion, by Mathias Grunewald. 1d, The Crucifixion, by Rubens. 1.25d, The Road to Calvary (detail), by Tintoretto. 1.50d, The Road to Calvary (entire), by Tintoretto. 15d, The Crucifixion, by Masaccio. 20d, Descent from the Cross (detail), by Rembrandt. No. 1215, Crowning with Thorns (detail), by Titian. No. 1216, Crowning with Thorns, by Anthony Van Dyck.

**1992, Apr. 16 Litho. *Perf. 13½***

**1207** A174 20b multicolored .25 .25
**1208** A174 50b multicolored .25 .25
**1209** A174 75b multicolored .25 .25
**1210** A174 1d multicolored .30 .25
**1211** A174 1.25d multicolored .45 .35
**1212** A174 1.50d multicolored .55 .40
**1213** A174 15d multicolored 3.75 3.75
**1214** A174 20d multicolored 4.75 4.75
*Nos. 1207-1214 (8)* 10.55 10.25

**Souvenir Sheets**

**1215** A174 25d multicolored 6.25 6.25
**1216** A174 25d multicolored 6.25 6.25

World Columbian Stamp Expo, Chicago A175

Walt Disney characters in Chicago: 50b, Mickey at Navy pier. 1d, Mickey floats by Wrigley Building. 1.25d, Donald graduates from University of Chicago. 12d, Goofy at Chicago's Adler Planetarium. No. 1221, Goofy above Chicago at the Hancock Center, horiz.

**1992, Apr. 8 Litho. *Perf. 13½x14***

**1217** A175 50b multicolored .50 .25
**1218** A175 1d multicolored .65 .50
**1219** A175 1.25d multicolored .80 .75
**1220** A175 12d multicolored 5.50 5.50
*Nos. 1217-1220 (4)* 7.45 7.00

**Souvenir Sheet**
***Perf. 14x13½***

**1221** A175 18d multicolored 8.50 8.50

No. 1220 has name spelled "Alder."

Granada '92 — A176

Mickey Mouse as Columbus: 20b, With map. 75b, Ideas rejected. 1.50d, Explores America. 15d, Returns to Spain. No. 1231, Embarks for America.

**1992, Apr. 8 *Perf. 13½x14***

**1227** A176 20b multicolored .60 .60
**1228** A176 75b multicolored .90 .90
**1229** A176 1.50d multicolored 1.25 1.25
**1230** A176 15d multicolored 5.75 5.75
*Nos. 1227-1230 (4)* 8.50 8.50

**Souvenir Sheet**

**1231** A176 18d multicolored 8.00 8.00

Flowers — A177

**1992, July 21 Litho. *Perf. 14***

**1237** A177 20b Hibiscus .25 .25
**1238** A177 50b Calabash nutmeg .25 .25
**1239** A177 75b Silk cotton tree .30 .30
**1240** A177 1d Oncoba .40 .40
**1241** A177 1.25d Paintbrush plant .50 .50
**1242** A177 1.50d Tree gardenia .55 .55
**1243** A177 2d Glory bower .70 .70
**1244** A177 5d Ashanti blood 1.30 1.30
**1245** A177 10d African peach 2.25 2.25
**1246** A177 12d Butterfly bush 2.50 2.50
**1247** A177 15d Crepe ginger 3.00 3.00
**1248** A177 18d Spider tresses 3.25 3.25
*Nos. 1237-1248 (12)* 15.25 15.25

**Souvenir Sheets**

**1249** A177 20d Water lily 4.50 4.50
**1250** A177 20d Bougainvillea 4.50 4.50
**1251** A177 20d Baobab tree 4.50 4.50
**1252** A177 20d Climbing pea 4.50 4.50

While Nos. 1240, 1242, 1244, 1247, 1250 have the same release date as Nos. 1237, 1241, 1243, 1248-1249, their values in relation to the dollar were higher when they were released.

Riverboats — A178

Riverboat and waterway: 20b, Joven Antonia, Gambia River. 50b, Dresden, Elbe River. 75b, Medway Queen, Medway River. 1d, Lady Wright, Gambia River. 1.25d, Devin, Vltava River. 1.50d, Lady Chilel, Gambia River. 5d, Robert Fulton, Hudson River. 10d, Coonawarra, Murray River. 12d, Nakusp, Columbia River. 15d, Lucy Ashton, Firth of Clyde. No. 1263, Rudesheim, Rhine River. No. 1264, City of Cairo, Mississippi River.

**1992, Aug. 3 Litho. *Perf. 14***

**1253** A178 20b multicolored .25 .25
**1254** A178 50b multicolored .25 .25
**1255** A178 75b multicolored .30 .30
**1256** A178 1d multicolored .40 .40
**1257** A178 1.25d multicolored .50 .50
**1258** A178 1.50d multicolored .60 .60
**1259** A178 5d multicolored 1.50 1.50
**1260** A178 10d multicolored 2.40 2.40
**1261** A178 12d multicolored 2.60 2.60
**1262** A178 15d multicolored 3.50 3.50
*Nos. 1253-1262 (10)* 12.30 12.30

**Souvenir Sheets**

**1263** A178 20d multicolored 6.50 6.50
**1264** A178 20d multicolored 6.50 6.50

Miniature Sheet

World War II in the Pacific — A179

Designs: a, USS Pennsylvania. b, Japanese attack begins. c, USS Ward sinking Japanese submarine. d, Ford Naval Air Station under attack. e, News bulletin announcing attack. f, Front page of Honolulu Star-Bulletin. g, Japanese invade Guam. h, US recovers Wake Island. i, Doolittle raids Japan from USS Hornet. j, Battle of Midway.

**1992 Litho. *Perf. 14½x15***

**1265** A179 2d Sheet of 10, #a.-j. 17.00 17.00

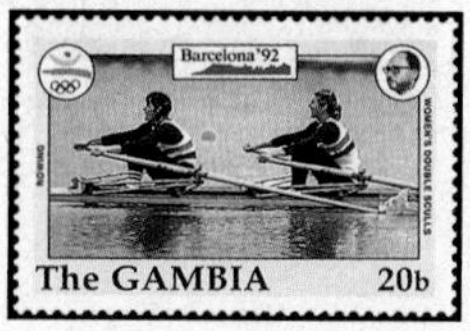


1992 Summer Olympics, Barcelona A180

Designs: 20b, Women's double sculls. 50b, Kayak, vert. 75b, Women's precision rapid-fire shooting. 1d, Judo, vert. 1.25d, Javelin, vert. 1.50d, Gymnastics, vault, vert. 3d, Windsurfing, vert. 5d, High jump. No. 1274, Women's 200-meter backstroke. No. 1275, Table tennis.

**1992, Aug. 10 Litho. *Perf. 14***

**1266** A180 20b multicolored .25 .25
**1267** A180 50b multicolored .45 .45
**1268** A180 75b multicolored .65 .65
**1269** A180 1d multicolored .70 .70
**1270** A180 1.25d multicolored .80 .80
**1271** A180 1.50d multicolored 1.00 1.00
**1272** A180 3d multicolored 1.50 1.50
**1273** A180 5d multicolored 2.25 2.25
*Nos. 1266-1273 (8)* 7.60 7.60

**Souvenir Sheets**

**1274** A180 18d multicolored 5.00 5.00
**1275** A180 18d multicolored 5.00 5.00

1992 Winter Olympics, Albertville — A181

Designs: 2d, Downhill skiing, vert. 10d, Four-man bobsled, vert. 12d, Ski jumping, vert. 15d, Slalom skiing.

No. 1280, 18d, Men's 500-meter speedskating. No. 1281, 18d, Pairs figure skating, vert.

**1992, Aug. 10 Litho. *Perf. 14***

**1276-1279** A181 Set of 4 18.00 18.00

**Souvenir Sheets**

**1280-1281** A181 Set of 2 10.00 10.00

Dinosaurs — A182

20b, Dryosaurus. 25b, Saurolophus. 50b, #1291, Allosaurus. 75b, Fabrosaurus. 1d, Deinonychus. 1.25d, No. 1292A, Cetiosaurus. 1.50d, Camptosaurus. 2d, No. 1292, Ornithosuchus. 3d, Spinosaurus. 5d, Ornithomimus. 10d, Kentrosaurus. 12d, Schlermochus.

**1992, Sept. 21 Litho. *Perf. 14***

**1283** A182 20b multi .45 .45
**1284** A182 25b multi .45 .45
**1284A** A182 50b multi .55 .55
**1284B** A182 75b multi .65 .65
**1284C** A182 1d multi .65 .65
**1285** A182 1.25d multi .75 .75
**1286** A182 1.50d multi .75 .75
**1286A** A182 2d multi .75 .75
**1287** A182 3d multi .80 .80
**1288** A182 5d multi 1.25 1.25
**1289** A182 10d multi 2.25 2.25
**1290** A182 12d multi 2.75 2.75
*Nos. 1283-1290 (12)* 12.05 12.05

**Souvenir Sheets**

**1291** A182 25d multi 7.00 7.00
**1292** A182 25d multi 7.00 7.00
**1292A** A182 25d multi 7.00 7.00

Genoa '92.

Walt Disney's Goofy, 60th Anniv. — A183

Scenes from Disney cartoon films: 50b, Orphan's Benefit, 1934, 1941. 75b, Moose Hunters, 1937. 1d, Mickey's Amateurs, 1937. 1.25d, Lonesome Ghosts, 1937. 5d, Boat Builders, 1938. 7d, The Whalers, 1938. 10d,

Goofy and Wilbur, 1939. 15d, Saludos Amigos, 1941. No. 1301, The Band Concert, 1935, vert. No. 1302, Goofy today, vert.

**1992 Litho. *Perf. 14x13½***

| | | | | | |
|---|---|---|---|---|---|
| **1293** | A183 | 50b | multicolored | .45 | .45 |
| **1294** | A183 | 75b | multicolored | .65 | .65 |
| **1295** | A183 | 1d | multicolored | .80 | .80 |
| **1296** | A183 | 1.25d | multicolored | .80 | .80 |
| **1297** | A183 | 5d | multicolored | 2.00 | 2.00 |
| **1298** | A183 | 7d | multicolored | 2.50 | 2.50 |
| **1299** | A183 | 10d | multicolored | 2.75 | 2.75 |
| **1300** | A183 | 15d | multicolored | 3.50 | 3.50 |
| | *Nos. 1293-1300 (8)* | | | 13.45 | 13.45 |

**Souvenir Sheets**

***Perf. 13½x14***

| | | | | | |
|---|---|---|---|---|---|
| **1301** | A183 | 20d | multicolored | 8.50 | 8.50 |
| **1302** | A183 | 20d | multicolored | 8.50 | 8.50 |

Discovery of America, 500th Anniv. A184

5d, Santa Maria. 12d, Pinta, Santa Maria, and Nina. 18d, Tree branch, green-winged macaw.

**1992, Oct. Litho. *Perf. 14***

| | | | | | |
|---|---|---|---|---|---|
| **1303** | A184 | 5d | multi | 1.25 | 1.25 |
| **1304** | A184 | 12d | multi | 2.25 | 2.25 |

**Souvenir Sheet**

| | | | | | |
|---|---|---|---|---|---|
| **1305** | A184 | 18d | multi, vert. | 5.00 | 5.00 |

Golf — A186

Pres. Jarwara playing golf and: 20b, Map, flag of Australia. 1d, Trophy, Gambian flag. 1.50d, Gambian flag. 2d, Map, flag of Japan. 3d, Map, flag of US. 5d, Trophy, 1985, Gambian flag (small portrait only). No. 1312, Map, flag of Scotland. 12d, Map, flag of Italy. No. 1312B, Pres. Jawara about to tee off. No. 1312C, Gambian flag (small portrait).

**1992 Litho. *Perf. 14***

| | | | | | |
|---|---|---|---|---|---|
| **1306** | A186 | 20b | multi | .55 | .45 |
| **1307** | A186 | 1d | multi | .85 | .85 |
| **1308** | A186 | 1.50d | multi | 1.10 | 1.10 |
| **1309** | A186 | 2d | multi | 1.30 | 1.30 |
| **1310** | A186 | 3d | multi | 1.75 | 1.75 |
| **1311** | A186 | 5d | multi | 2.40 | 2.40 |
| **1312** | A186 | 10d | multi | 3.50 | 3.50 |
| **1312A** | A186 | 12d | multi | 4.25 | 4.25 |
| | *Nos. 1306-1312A (8)* | | | 15.70 | 15.60 |

**Souvenir Sheets**

| | | | | | |
|---|---|---|---|---|---|
| **1312B** | A186 | 10d | multi | 8.00 | 8.00 |
| **1312C** | A186 | 18d | multi, horiz. | 8.00 | 8.00 |

No. 1306, Royal Melbourne Golf Course, Australia. No. 1309, Shinonoseki Golf Course, Japan. No. 1310, US Open, Pebble Beach. No. 1312, St. Andrew's Golf Course, Scotland. No. 1312A, Italian Open, Monticello, Milan.

Issued: 20b, 2d, 5d, Nos. 1312, 1312B, Dec. 8; others, Oct.

Souvenir Sheet

Ellis Island, New York City — A187

**1992, Oct. 28 Litho. *Perf. 14***

| | | | | | |
|---|---|---|---|---|---|
| **1313** | A187 | 18d | multicolored | 5.75 | 5.75 |

Postage Stamp Mega Event '92, New York City.

Christmas A188

Details or entire paintings: 50b, The Holy Family, by Raphael. 75b, Madonna and Child with St. Elizabeth and the Infant St. John (Small Holy Family), by Raphael. 1d, The Holy Family as the Little Holy Family, by Raphael. 1.25d, Escape to Egypt, by Broederlam. 1.50d, Flight Into Egypt, by Isenbrant. No. 1319, The Flight into Egypt, by Cosimo Tura. No. 1320, Flight into Egypt, by Master of Hoogstraelen. No. 1321, The Holy Family, by El Greco. 4d, The Holy Family, by Bernard Van Orley. 5d, Holy Family with Infant Jesus Sleeping, by Charles Le Brun. 10d, Rest on the Flight to Egypt, by Gentileschi. 12d, Rest on the Flight to Egypt, by Orazio Gentileschi. No. 1326, The Holy Family, by Giorgione. No. 1327, Rest on the Flight to Egypt, by Simone Cantarino. No. 1328, The Flight to Egypt, by Vittore Carpaccio.

**1992, Nov. 3 Litho. *Perf. 13½x14***

| | | | | | |
|---|---|---|---|---|---|
| **1314** | A188 | 50b | multicolored | .25 | .25 |
| **1315** | A188 | 75b | multicolored | .35 | .35 |
| **1316** | A188 | 1d | multicolored | .45 | .45 |
| **1317** | A188 | 1.25d | multicolored | .60 | .60 |
| **1318** | A188 | 1.50d | multicolored | .60 | .60 |
| **1319** | A188 | 2d | multicolored | .85 | .85 |
| **1320** | A188 | 2d | multicolored | .85 | .85 |
| **1321** | A188 | 2d | multicolored | .85 | .85 |
| **1322** | A188 | 4d | multicolored | 1.30 | 1.30 |
| **1323** | A188 | 5d | multicolored | 1.60 | 1.60 |
| **1324** | A188 | 10d | multicolored | 3.00 | 3.00 |
| **1325** | A188 | 12d | multicolored | 3.25 | 3.25 |
| | *Nos. 1314-1325 (12)* | | | 13.95 | 13.95 |

**Souvenir Sheets**

| | | | | | |
|---|---|---|---|---|---|
| **1326** | A188 | 25d | multicolored | 4.50 | 4.50 |
| **1327** | A188 | 25d | multicolored | 4.50 | 4.50 |
| **1328** | A188 | 25d | multicolored | 4.50 | 4.50 |

A189 A190

A191

A192

A193

A194 Anniversaries and Events — A195

Designs: No. 1329, Ariane 4 rocket. No. 1330, Berlin airlift, Konrad Adenauer. No. 1331, LZ127 Graf Zeppelin. 6d, Jentink's duiker. 7d, World map. 9d, Wolfgang Amadeus Mozart. No. 1335, America's Cup yacht Enterprise, 1930. No. 1336, Imperial parrot. No. 1337, Lions Intl. emblem. No. 1338, American Space shuttle. 15d, Prisoners of war returning home, Adenauer. 18d, First rigid airship, LZ1. No. 1341, European Space Agency's Hermes space shuttle. No. 1342, Scene from "The Marriage of Figaro." No. 1343, Face of Adenauer. No. 1344, Count Ferdinand von Zeppelin. No. 1345, Earth as seen from space.

**1992-93 Litho. *Perf. 14***

| | | | | | |
|---|---|---|---|---|---|
| **1329** | A189 | 2d | multicolored | .70 | .70 |
| **1330** | A191 | 2d | multicolored | .80 | .80 |
| **1331** | A191 | 2d | multicolored | .70 | .70 |
| **1332** | A192 | 6d | multicolored | 2.25 | 2.25 |
| **1333** | A193 | 7d | multicolored | 2.50 | 2.50 |
| **1334** | A190 | 9d | multicolored | 4.25 | 4.25 |
| **1335** | A194 | 10d | multicolored | 3.50 | 3.50 |
| **1336** | A192 | 10d | multicolored | 2.75 | 2.75 |
| **1337** | A195 | 10d | multicolored | 2.50 | 2.50 |
| **1338** | A189 | 12d | multicolored | 2.50 | 2.50 |
| **1339** | A191 | 15d | multicolored | 4.00 | 4.00 |
| **1340** | A191 | 18d | multicolored | 4.00 | 4.00 |
| | *Nos. 1329-1340 (12)* | | | 30.45 | 30.45 |

**Souvenir Sheets**

| | | | | | |
|---|---|---|---|---|---|
| **1341** | A189 | 18d | multicolored | 7.00 | 7.00 |
| **1342** | A190 | 18d | multicolored | 7.00 | 7.00 |
| **1343** | A191 | 18d | multicolored | 7.00 | 7.00 |
| **1344** | A191 | 18d | multicolored | 7.00 | 7.00 |
| **1345** | A192 | 18d | multicolored | 7.00 | 7.00 |

Intl. Space Year (Nos. 1329, 1338, 1341). Wolfgang Amadeus Mozart, bicent. of death (Nos. 1334, 1342). Konrad Adenauer, 25th anniv. of death (Nos. 1330, 1339, 1343). Count Zeppelin, 75th anniv. of death (Nos. 1331, 1340, 1344). Earth Summit, Rio de Janeiro (Nos. 1332, 1336, 1345). Intl. Conf. on Nutrition, Rome (No. 1333). America's Cup yacht race (No. 1335). Lions Intl., 75th anniv. (No. 1337).

Issued: Nos. 1333, 1335, 1339, 1343, 1/93; others, 12/92.

Peace Corps, 25th Anniv. A196

**1993, Feb.**

| | | | | | |
|---|---|---|---|---|---|
| **1346** | A196 | 2d | multicolored | 1.40 | 1.40 |

Elvis Presley, 15th Anniv. of Death (in 1992) — A197

No. 1347: a, Portrait. b, With guitar. c, Holding microphone.

**1993**

| | | | | | |
|---|---|---|---|---|---|
| **1347** | A197 | 3d | Strip of 3, #a.-c. | 2.75 | 2.75 |

Miniature Sheets

Baseball Films — A198

No. 1348 — Movie and stars: a, Casey at the Bat, Wallace Beery, 1927, Elliott Gould, 1986. b, Babe Comes Home, Anna Q. Nilsson, Babe Ruth, 1927. c, Elmer the Great, Joe E. Brown, 1933. d, The Naughty Nineties, Bud Abbott and Lou Costello, 1945. e, Take Me Out to the Ball Game, Frank Sinatra, Gene Kelly, Esther Williams, 1949. f, Damn Yankees, Tab Hunter, Gwen Verdon, 1958. g, The Pride of St. Louis, Dan Dailey, 1952. h, Brewster's Millions, John Candy, Richard Pryor, 1985.

No. 1349: a, The Jackie Robinson Story, Jackie Robinson, Ruby Dee, 1950. b, Bang the Drum Slowly, Robert DeNiro, 1973. c, The Bingo Long Traveling All-Stars & Motor Kings, James Earl Jones, Billy Dee Williams, 1976. d, Bull Durham, Kevin Costner, Susan Sarandon, 1988. e, Eight Men Out, eight actors, 1988. f, Field of Dreams, Ray Liotta, 1989. g, Major League, Charlie Sheet, 1989. h, Mr. Baseball, Tom Selleck, 1992.

No. 1350, The Babe, John Goodman, 1992. No. 1351, The Natural, Robert Redford. No. 1351A, The Winning Team, Ronald Reagan. No. 351B, A League of Their Own, Tom Hanks, Madonna.

**1993, Mar. 25 Litho. *Perf. 13***

| | | | | | |
|---|---|---|---|---|---|
| **1348** | A198 | 3d | Sheet of 8, #a.-h. | 7.50 | 7.50 |
| **1349** | A198 | 3d | Sheet of 8, #a.-h. | 7.50 | 7.50 |

**Souvenir Sheet**

| | | | | | |
|---|---|---|---|---|---|
| **1350** | A198 | 20d | multi | 5.00 | 5.00 |
| **1351** | A198 | 20d | multi, vert. | 5.00 | 5.00 |
| **1351A** | A198 | 20d | multi | 5.00 | 5.00 |
| **1351B** | A198 | 20d | multi, vert. | 5.00 | 5.00 |

Miniature Sheets

Louvre Museum, Bicent. — A199

Details from paintings, by Jacques-Louis David (1748-1825): Nos. 1352a-b, Oath of the Horatii (diff. details). c, The Love of Paris & Helen. d, Rape of the Sabine Women. e, Leonidas of Thermopylae. f-h, Napoleon Crowning Josephine (left, center, right).

Details from paintings, by Antoine (c. 1588-1648) and Louis (1593-1648) Le Nain: No. 1353a, Inside Home of Peasants. b-c, The Tobacco Smokers (diff. details). d, The Cart. e, Peasants' Meal. f-g, Interior Portraits (diff. details). h, The Forge.

Details or entire paintings, by Leonardo Da Vinci: No. 1354a, St. John the Baptist. b, Virgin of the Rocks. c, Bacchus. d, Woman from the Court of Milan. e, The Virgin of the Rocks (detail). f, Mona Lisa. g, Mona Lisa (detail of hands). h, Two Horsemen, Study of the Horse.

No. 1355, Allegory of Victory, by Mathieu Le Nain (1607-1677). No. 1356, The Artist and Her Daughter, by Elisabeth Vigee-Lebrun (1755-1842).

**1993, Jan. 7 Litho. *Perf. 12***

**1352** A199 3d Sheet of 8, #a.-h. 7.50 7.50
**1353** A199 3d Sheet of 8, #a.-h. 7.50 7.50
**1354** A199 3d Sheet of 8, #a.-h. 7.50 7.50

**Souvenir Sheets**

***Perf. 14½***

**1355** A199 20d multicolored 8.25 8.25
**1356** A199 20d multicolored 8.25 8.25

Nos. 1355-1356 each contain one 55x88mm stamp.

Miniature Sheet

Animals of West Africa — A200

No. 1358: a, Giraffe. b, Baboon. c, Caracal. d, Large-spotted genet. e, Bushbuck. f, Red-fronted gazelle. g, Red-flanked duiker. h, Cape buffalo. i, African civet. j, Side-striped jackal. k, Ratel. l, Striped polecat.

No. 1359: a, Vervet. b, Blackish-green guenon. c, Long-tailed pangolin. d, Leopard. e, Elephant. f, Hunting dog. g, Spotted hyena. h, Lion. i, Hippopotamus. j, Nile crocodile. k, Aardvark. l, Warthog.

**1993, Apr. 5 Litho. *Perf. 14***

**1358** A200 2d Sheet of 12, #a.-l. 10.00 10.00
**1359** A200 5d Sheet of 12, #a.-l. 14.00 14.00

**Souvenir Sheet**

**1360** A200 20d like #1359b 8.50 8.50

No. 1360 printed in continuous design with black frameline around stamp. A number has been reserved for an additional value in this set.

Long-Tailed Pangolin — A201

Pangolin in various positions on tree limb.

**1993, Apr. 5**

**1362** A201 1.25d multicolored .70 .70
**1363** A201 1.50d multicolored .80 .80
**1364** A201 2d multicolored 1.00 1.00
**1365** A201 5d multicolored 2.50 2.50
*Nos. 1362-1365 (4)* 5.00 5.00

**Souvenir Sheet**

**1366** A201 20d like #1363 7.50 7.50

World Wildlife Federation.

Birds
A202 A203

Designs: 1.25d, Osprey. 1.50d, Egyptian vulture, horiz. 2d, Martial eagle. 3d, Ruppell's griffon vulture, horiz. 5d, Auger buzzard. 8d, Greater kestrel. 10d, Secretary bird. 15d, Bateleur eagle, horiz.

No. 1375a, Rose-ringed parakeet. b, Variable sunbird. c, Red-billed hornbill. d, Red-billed fire-finch. e, Common go-away bird. f, Crimson-breasted shrike. g, Gray-headed bush-shrike. h, Nicator. i, Egyptian plover. j, Congo peacock. k, Greater painted snipe. l, Crowned crane.

#1376, Verreaux's eagle. #1377, Tawny owl.

**1993, Apr. 15 Litho. *Perf. 14***

**1367** A202 1.25d multicolored .80 .80
**1368** A202 1.50d multicolored 1.00 1.00
**1369** A202 2d multicolored 1.20 1.20
**1370** A202 3d multicolored 1.60 1.60
**1371** A202 5d multicolored 1.75 1.75
**1372** A202 8d multicolored 2.40 2.40
**1373** A202 10d multicolored 2.40 2.40
**1374** A202 15d multicolored 3.50 3.50
*Nos. 1367-1374 (8)* 14.65 14.65
**1375** A203 2d Sheet of 12, #a.-l. 20.00 20.00

**Souvenir Sheets**

**1376** A202 20d multicolored 8.50 8.50
**1377** A202 20d multicolored 8.50 8.50

Nos. 1376-1377 each contain 1 56x42mm stamp.

Aviation Anniversaries — A204

Designs: No. 1379, Guyot balloon, 1785, vert. No. 1380, Dr. Hugo Eckener, zeppelin LZ3 in flight. No. 1381, Sopwith Snipe. No. 1382, Eckener, LZ3 moored to ground. 8d, Eckener, Graf Zeppelin. 10d, Balloon, Comte D'Artois, 1785, vert. 15d, Royal Aircraft Factory S.E.5. No. 1386, Avro 504K. No. 1387, Eckener, LZ3 in flight, diff. No. 1388, Blanchard's flying ship, 1785, vert.

**1993, May Litho. *Perf. 14***

**1379** A204 2d multicolored .70 .70
**1380** A204 2d multicolored .70 .70
**1381** A204 5d multicolored 1.25 1.25
**1382** A204 5d multicolored 1.25 1.25
**1383** A204 8d multicolored 2.00 2.00
**1384** A204 10d multicolored 2.25 2.25
**1385** A204 15d multicolored 3.00 3.00
*Nos. 1379-1385 (7)* 11.15 11.15

**Souvenir Sheets**

**1386** A204 20d multicolored 7.50 7.50
**1387** A204 20d multicolored 7.50 7.50
**1388** A204 20d multicolored 7.50 7.50

Dr. Hugo Eckener, 125th birth anniv. (Nos. 1380, 1382, 1383, 1387). Royal Air Force, 75th anniv. (Nos. 1381, 1385, 1386).

Nos. 1379, 1384, 1388 are airmail.

Miniature Sheet

Coronation of Queen Elizabeth II, 40th Anniv. — A205

Designs: a, 2d, Official coronation photograph. b, 5d, Orb and Scepter. c, 8d, Winston Churchill. d, 10d, Queen during Trooping of the Color.

20d, Portrait, by Joe King, 1972.

**1993, June 2 *Perf. 13½x14***

**1389** A205 Sheet of 8, 2 each #a.-d. 16.00 16.00

**Souvenir Sheet**

***Perf. 14***

**1390** A205 20d multicolored 8.50 8.50

No. 1390 contains one 28x42mm stamp.

Miniature Sheet

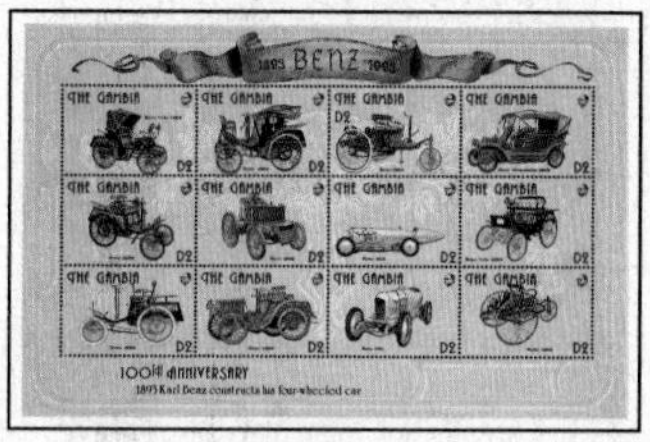


A206

No. 1391 — Benz Automobiles: a, 1894 Benz Velo. b, 1894 Benz. c, 1885 Benz. d, 1905 Benz Mannheim. e, 1892 Benz. f, 1900 Benz, blue. g, 1911 Benz. h, 1893 Benz Velo. i, 1900 Benz, black. j, 1900 Benz, red. k, 1911 Benz, front view. l, 1885 Benz, rear view.

No. 1393, 20d, 1900 Benz, diff.

No. 1392 — Ford automobiles: a, Henry Ford, age 30, 1910 Model T. b, 1896, green seat. c, Henry Ford with Barney Oldfield and 1902 racing car, 999. d, 1896, Henry Ford with bicycle. e, 1903 Model A. f, 1908 Model T, top down. g, 1908 Model T, top up. h, 1906 Model K. i, 1931 Model A. j, 1906 Model A. k, 1906 Model N. l, 1905 Model F.

No. 1393, 1900 Benz, diff. No. 1394, 1896 Ford with red seat.

**1993, June 7 *Perf. 14***

**1391** A206 2d Sheet of 12, #a.-l. 8.00 8.00
**1392** A206 2d Sheet of 12, #a.-l. 8.00 8.00

**Souvenir Sheets**

**1393** A206 20d multicolored 6.50 6.50
**1394** A206 20d multicolored 6.50 6.50

1st Benz 4-wheel automobile, cent. (Nos. 1391, 1393).

1st engine by Henry Ford, cent. (Nos. 1392, 1394).

Miniature Sheets

Entertainers — A207

No. 1395: a, Buddy Holly. b, Otis Redding. c, Bill Haley. d, Dinah Washington. e, Musical instruments. f, Ritchie Valens. g, Clyde McPhatter. h, Elvis Presley.

No. 1396: a-i, Various pictures of Madonna.

No. 1397: a-i, Various pictures of Elvis Presley.

No. 1398: a-i, Various pictures of Marilyn Monroe.

**1993, July 26 Litho. *Perf. 14***

**1395** A207 3d Sheet of 8, #a.-h. 12.00 12.00
**1396** A207 3d Sheet of 9, #a.-i. 12.00 12.00
**1397** A207 3d Sheet of 9, #a,-i. 12.00 12.00
**1398** A207 3d Sheet of 9, #a.-i. 12.00 12.00
*Nos. 1395-1398 (4)* 48.00 48.00

Cats and Dogs A208

No. 1399 — Cats, Siamese. b, Colorpoint longhair. c, Burmese. d, Birman. e, Snowshoe. f, Tonkinese. g, Foreign shorthair. h, Balinese. i, Oriental shorthair. j, Foreign shorthair, diff. k, Colorpoint longhair, diff. l, Colorpoint longhair, diff.

Dogs: No. 1400a, Shih tzu. b, Skye terrier. c, Berner laufhund. d, Boxer. e, Welsh corgi (Queen Elizabeth II). f, Dumfrieshire. g, Lurcher. h, Welsh corgi (Princess Anne). i, Pekinese. j, Papillon. k, Otterhound. l, Pug.

No. 1401, Colorpoint shorthair, vert. No. 1402, Burmese, vert. No. 1403, Long-haired dachshund. No. 1404, Cairn terrier.

**1993, Sept. 13 Litho. *Perf. 14***

**1399** A208 2d Sheet of 12, #a.-l. 15.00 15.00
**1400** A208 2d Sheet of 12, #a.-i. 14.00 14.00

**Souvenir Sheets**

**1401** A208 20d multicolored 7.00 7.00
**1402** A208 20d multicolored 7.00 7.00
**1403** A208 20d multicolored 7.00 7.00
**1404** A208 20d multicolored 7.00 7.00

Taipei '93 — A209

Designs: No. 1405, Fawang Si Pagoda, Song Shan Mt., Henan. No. 1406, Wanshoubao Pagoda, Shashi. No. 1407, Red Pavilion, Shibaozhai. No. 1408, Songyue Si Pagoda, Song Shan Mt., Henan. No. 1409, Bond Center, Hong Kong. No. 1410, Tianning Si Pagoda, Beijing. No. 1411, Xuanzhuang Pagoda, Xian, Shenxi. No. 1412, Forbidden City, Beijing.

No. 1413 — Tang Dynasty funerary objects: a, Camel. b, Horse and female rider. c, Camel, diff. d, Yellow-glazed horse. e, Camel, diff. f, Horse with saddle.

No. 1414 — Pottery: a, Vase. b, Small wine cup. c, Fahua type Mei-ping vase. d, Urn vase, export ware. e, Tureen. f, Lidded Potiche.

No. 1415, Standing Buddhas,Hallway of Upper Huayan Si Temple, Datong, horiz. No. 1416, Seated Buddha, Main Hall, Shanhua Si Temple, Datong.

**1993, Sept. 27 Litho. *Perf. 14***

**1405** A209 20b multicolored .25 .25
**1406** A209 20b multicolored .25 .25
**1407** A209 2d multicolored .80 .80
**1408** A209 2d multicolored .80 .80
**1409** A209 5d multicolored 1.75 1.75
**1410** A209 5d multicolored 1.75 1.75
**1411** A209 15d multicolored 3.50 3.50
**1412** A209 15d multicolored 3.50 3.50
*Nos. 1405-1412 (8)* 12.60 12.60

**Miniature Sheets**

**1413** A209 5d Sheet of 6, #a.-f. 15.00 15.00
**1414** A209 5d Sheet of 6, #a.-f. 15.00 15.00

**Souvenir Sheets**

**1415** A209 18d multicolored 6.00 6.00
**1416** A209 18d multicolored 6.00 6.00

**With Bangkok '93 Emblem**

No. 1417, Sanctuary of Prasat Phanom Wan. No. 1418, Lai Kham Vihan, Chiang Mai. No. 1419, Spirit Shrine, Bangkok. No. 1420, Walking Buddha, Wat Phra Si Ratana Mahathat. No. 1421, Buddha, Sukhothai's Wat Mahathat. No. 1422, Gopura of Prasat Phanom Rung. No. 1423, Prang of Prasat Hin Phimai. No. 1424, Slender Chedis, Wat Yai Chai, Mongkon.

No. 1425 — Thai painting: a, Early Fruit Stand. b, Scene in Chinese Style, Wat Bovornivet. c, Buddha Descends from Tauatimsa. d, Sang Thong Tales, Lai Kham Vihan. e, The Damned in Hell, Wah Suthat. f, King Sanjaya Travels on Elephant, Wat Suwannaram.

No. 1426 — Thai Buddha sculpture: a, U Thong C, 14th-15th cent. b, Adorned Seated, 17th cent. c, Phra Chai, 19th cent. d, Bronze, 14th cent. e, U Thong A, bronze. f, Crowned, 14th-15th cent.

No. 1427, Ceramics, horiz. No. 1428, Character in Khon, dance drama.

**1993**

**1417** A209 20b multicolored .25 .25
**1418** A209 20b multicolored .25 .25
**1419** A209 2d multicolored .80 .80
**1420** A209 2d multicolored .80 .80
**1421** A209 5d multicolored 1.75 1.75
**1422** A209 5d multicolored 1.75 1.75

| | | | | | |
|---|---|---|---|---|---|
| **1423** | A209 | 15d multicolored | | 3.50 | 3.50 |
| **1424** | A209 | 15d multicolored | | 3.50 | 3.50 |
| | | *Nos. 1417-1424 (8)* | | 12.60 | 12.60 |

**Miniature Sheets**

| | | | | |
|---|---|---|---|---|
| **1425** | A209 | 5d Sheet of 6, #a.-f. | 15.00 | 15.00 |
| **1426** | A209 | 5d Sheet of 6, #a.-f. | 15.00 | 15.00 |

**Souvenir Sheets**

| | | | | |
|---|---|---|---|---|
| **1427** | A209 | 18d multicolored | 6.00 | 6.00 |
| **1428** | A209 | 18d multicolored | 6.00 | 6.00 |

### With Indopex '93 Emblem

Designs: No. 1429, Pura Taman Ayun (garden temple), Mengwi, Bali. No. 1430, Natl. monument with statue of Prince Diponegoro, Jakarta. No. 1431, Candi Jawi, East Java. No. 1432, Guardian at Singosari Palace, East Java. No. 1433, Monument of Irian Jaya, (liberation), Jakarta. No. 1434, Central Temple, Prambanan complex, Lara Djonggrang. No. 1435, "Date of the Year Temple," Panataran complex, East Java. No. 1436, Brahma & Siva Temples, Loro Jonggrang, Java.

No. 1437 — Masks: a, Telek Luh. b, Jero Gde. c, Barong Macan. d, Monkey. e, Mata Gde. f, Jauk Kras.

No. 1438 — Paintings: a, Tree Mask, Soedibio, 1978. b, Dry Lizard, Hendra Gunawan, 1977. c, The Corn Eater, Sudjana Kerton, 1988. d, Night Watchman, Djoko Pekik, 1988. e, Hunger, Kerton, 1984. f, Arje Player, Soedjojono, 1971.

No. 1439, Stone carving, Brahma & Gods, Borobudur, Java, horiz. No. 1440, Effigies of the Dead, Torajaland, horiz.

**1993, Sept. 27 Litho. *Perf. 14***

| | | | | |
|---|---|---|---|---|
| **1429** | A209 | 20b multicolored | .25 | .25 |
| **1430** | A209 | 20b multicolored | .25 | .25 |
| **1431** | A209 | 2d multicolored | .80 | .80 |
| **1432** | A209 | 2d multicolored | .80 | .80 |
| **1433** | A209 | 5d multicolored | 1.75 | 1.75 |
| **1434** | A209 | 5d multicolored | 1.75 | 1.75 |
| **1435** | A209 | 15d multicolored | 3.50 | 3.50 |
| **1436** | A209 | 15d multicolored | 3.50 | 3.50 |
| | | *Nos. 1429-1436 (8)* | 12.60 | 12.60 |

**Miniature Sheets**

| | | | | |
|---|---|---|---|---|
| **1437** | A209 | 5d Sheet of 6, #a.-f. | 14.00 | 14.00 |
| **1438** | A209 | 5d Sheet of 6, #a.-f. | 14.00 | 14.00 |

**Souvenir Sheets**

| | | | | |
|---|---|---|---|---|
| **1439** | A209 | 18d multicolored | 6.00 | 6.00 |
| **1440** | A209 | 18d multicolored | 6.00 | 6.00 |

Miniature Sheet

Casey at the Bat — A210

Nos. 1441-1443: Characters and scenes from Disney's animated film Casey at the Bat.

**1993, Oct. 25 Litho. *Perf. 14x13½***

| | | | | |
|---|---|---|---|---|
| **1441** | A210 | 2d Sheet of 9, #a.-i. | 12.00 | 12.00 |

**Souvenir Sheets**

| | | | | |
|---|---|---|---|---|
| **1442** | A210 | 20d multicolored | 7.50 | 7.50 |

***Perf. 13½x14***

| | | | | |
|---|---|---|---|---|
| **1443** | A210 | 20d multi, vert. | 7.50 | 7.50 |

Picasso — A211

Paintings: 2d, Woman with a Comb, 1906. 5d, The Mirror, 1932. 7d, Woman on a Pillow, 1969. 18d, The Three Dancers, 1925.

**1993, Oct. 7 Litho. *Perf. 14***

| | | | | |
|---|---|---|---|---|
| **1444-1446** | A211 | Set of 3 | 4.50 | 4.50 |

**Souvenir Sheet**

| | | | | |
|---|---|---|---|---|
| **1447** | A211 | 18d multicolored | 6.00 | 6.00 |

Copernicus A212

5d, Early astronomical instrument. 10d, Telescope.

**1993, Oct. 7 *Perf. 14***

| | | | | |
|---|---|---|---|---|
| **1448-1449** | A212 | Set of 2 | 4.50 | 4.50 |

**Souvenir Sheet**

***Perf. 12x13***

| | | | | |
|---|---|---|---|---|
| **1450** | A212 | 18d Copernicus | 6.00 | 6.00 |

Polska '93 A213

Paintings: 2d, Pont-Neuf, Paris, by Rudzka-Cybisowa, 1932. No. 1452, 10d, Honegger's Liturgical Symphony, by Bogusz, 1973. No. 1453, 10d, Niedzica castle. 18d, When You Enter Here, Whisper My Name Soundlessly, by Waniek, 1973.

**1993, Oct. 7 *Perf. 14***

| | | | | |
|---|---|---|---|---|
| **1451-1453** | A213 | Set of 3 | 6.75 | 6.75 |

**Souvenir Sheet**

| | | | | |
|---|---|---|---|---|
| **1454** | A213 | 18d multicolored | 6.00 | 6.00 |

1994 World Cup Soccer Championships, US — A214

Players, country: 1.25d, Hannich, Hungary; Stopyra, France. 1.50d, Labd, Morocco; Lineker, England. 2d, Segota, Canada; Morozov, Russia. 3d, Roger Milla, Cameroun. 5d, Rodax, Australia; Weiss, Czech Republic. 10d, Claesen, Belgium; Bossis & Amoros, France. 12d, Candida, Brazil; Ramirez, Costa Rica. 15d, Silva, Brazil; Platini, France. No. 1463, Muller, Brazil; McDonald, Ireland, horiz. No. 1463A, Buchwald and Matthaeus, Germany; Maradona, Argentina, horiz.

**1993, Nov. 22 *Perf. 13½x14***

| | | | | |
|---|---|---|---|---|
| **1455** | A214 | 1.25d multi | .60 | .60 |
| **1456** | A214 | 1.50d multi | .65 | .65 |
| **1457** | A214 | 2d multi | .90 | .90 |
| **1458** | A214 | 3d multi | 1.60 | 1.60 |
| **1459** | A214 | 5d multi | 2.25 | 2.25 |
| **1460** | A214 | 10d multi | 3.25 | 3.25 |
| **1461** | A214 | 12d multi | 3.50 | 3.50 |
| **1462** | A214 | 15d multi | 4.50 | 4.50 |
| | | *Nos. 1455-1462 (8)* | 17.25 | 17.25 |

**Souvenir Sheets**

***Perf. 13***

| | | | | |
|---|---|---|---|---|
| **1463** | A214 | 25d multi | 8.00 | 8.00 |
| **1463A** | A214 | 25d multi | 8.00 | 8.00 |

Christmas A215

Designs: No. 1464, 25b, No. 1467, 2d, No. 1471, 15d, Details or entire painting, Adoration of the Magi, by Rubens.

Details or entire woodcut by Durer: No. 1465, 1d, Holy Family with Joachim & Anna. No. 1466, 1.50d, The Annunciation, Life of the Virgin. No. 1468, 2d, The Virgin Mary Worshipped by Albrecht Bonstetten. No. 1469, 7d, Virgin on a Throne, Crowned by an Angel. No. 1470, 10d, The Holy Family with Two Angels in a Portico (detail).

No. 1472, 20d, Adoration of the Magi, by Rubens. No. 1473, 20d, The Holy Family with Two Angels in a Portico, (entire), by Durer, horiz.

**1993, Dec. 1 *Perf. 13½x14, 14x13½***

| | | | | |
|---|---|---|---|---|
| **1464-1471** | A215 | Set of 8 | 14.00 | 14.00 |

**Souvenir Sheets**

| | | | | |
|---|---|---|---|---|
| **1472-1473** | A215 | Set of 2 | 12.00 | 12.00 |

Fine Art — A216

Paintings by Rembrandt: 50b, A Man in a Cap. No. 1476, Man with a Gold Helmet. 7d, A Franciscan Monk. 15d, The Apostle Paul. 20d, Dr. Tulp Demonstrating the Anatomy of the Arm, horiz.

Paintings by Matisse: 1.50d, Portrait of Pierre Matisse. No. 1477, Portrait of Auguste Pellerin (II). 5d, Andre Derain. 12d, The Young Sailor (II). No. 1483, Pianist and Checker Players, horiz.

**1993, Dec. 15 *Perf. 13½x14***

| | | | | |
|---|---|---|---|---|
| **1474** | A216 | 50b multicolored | .65 | .65 |
| **1475** | A216 | 1.50d multicolored | 1.00 | 1.00 |
| **1476** | A216 | 2d multicolored | 1.10 | 1.10 |
| **1477** | A216 | 2d multicolored | 1.10 | 1.10 |
| **1478** | A216 | 5d multicolored | 2.25 | 2.25 |
| **1479** | A216 | 7d multicolored | 3.00 | 3.00 |
| **1480** | A216 | 12d multicolored | 3.50 | 3.50 |
| **1481** | A216 | 15d multicolored | 4.50 | 4.50 |
| | | *Nos. 1474-1481 (8)* | 17.10 | 17.10 |

**Souvenir Sheets**

***Perf. 14x13½***

| | | | | |
|---|---|---|---|---|
| **1482** | A216 | 20d multicolored | 7.50 | 7.50 |
| **1483** | A216 | 20d multicolored | 7.50 | 7.50 |

Winter Sports A217

Disney characters portraying sports: 50b, Ski ballet. 75b, Pairs figure skating. 1d, Speed skating. 1.25d, Biathlon. 4d, 4-Man bobsled. 5d, Luge. 7d, Figure skating. 10d, Downhill skiing. 15d, Ice hockey.

No. 1493, 20d, Cross country skiing. No. 1494, 20d, Mogul skiing.

**1993, Dec. 20 *Perf. 13½x14***

| | | | | |
|---|---|---|---|---|
| **1484-1492** | A217 | Set of 9 | 16.00 | 16.00 |

**Souvenir Sheets**

| | | | | |
|---|---|---|---|---|
| **1493-1494** | A217 | 20d Set of 2 | 13.50 | 13.50 |

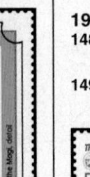

A218

Hong Kong '94 — A219

Stamps, painting, Spring Garden-1846, by M. Bruce: No. 1495, Hong Kong #357, left detail. No. 1496, Right detail, #1000.

No. 1497 — Museum of Qin Figures, Shaanxi Province, Tomb of First Emperor: a, Qin warriors, horses. b, Warrior in battle dress. c, Armor clad warrior. d, Chariot driver. e, Dog. f, Qin warriors.

No. 1498, Show emblem, Hong Kong #253, vert.

**1994, Feb. 18 Litho. *Perf. 14***

| | | | | |
|---|---|---|---|---|
| **1495** | A218 | 1.50d multicolored | .80 | .40 |
| **1496** | A218 | 1.50d multicolored | .80 | .40 |
| *a.* | | Pair, #1495-1496 | 2.00 | 1.50 |
| **1497** | A219 | 1.50d Sheet of 6, #a.-f. | 5.00 | 5.00 |

**Souvenir Sheet**

| | | | | |
|---|---|---|---|---|
| **1498** | A218 | 20d multicolored | 5.75 | 5.75 |

Nos. 1495-1496 issued in sheets of 5 pairs. No. 1496a is a continuous design.

New Year 1994 (Year of the Dog) (Nos. 1497e, #1498).

New Year 1994 (Year of the Dog) A220

Disney characters: 25b, Pluto the Racer. 50b, Fifi. 75b, Pluto, Jr. 1.25d, Goofy and Bowser. 1.50d, Butch. 2d, Toliver. 3d, Ronnie. 5d, Primo. 8d, Pluto's kid brother. 10d, Army mascot. 12d, Pluto and Dinah's pups. 18d, Bent Tail, Junior.

No. 1511, Pluto, Dinah. No. 1512, Eega Beeva, Dog Pflip, Goofy, horiz. No. 1513, Dinah's pups, Pluto.

**1994, Apr. 11 Litho. *Perf. 13½x14***

| | | | | |
|---|---|---|---|---|
| **1499-1510** | A220 | Set of 12 | 22.50 | 22.50 |

**Souvenir Sheets**

| | | | | |
|---|---|---|---|---|
| **1511** | A220 | 20d multicolored | 5.00 | 5.00 |

***Perf. 14x13½, 13½x14***

| | | | | |
|---|---|---|---|---|
| **1512** | A220 | 20d multicolored | 5.00 | 5.00 |
| **1513** | A220 | 20d multicolored | 5.00 | 5.00 |

Orchids A221

Designs: 1d, Oeceoclades maculata. 1.25d, Angraecum distichum. 2d, Plectrelminthus caudatus. 5d, Tridactyle tridactylites. 8d, Bulbophyllum lepidum. 10d, Angraecum eburneum. 12d, Eulophia guineensis. 15d, Angraecum eichleranum.

No. 1522, Ancistrochilus rothschildianus. No. 1523, Vanilla imperialis.

**1994, May 1** *Perf. 14*

| | | | | | |
|---|---|---|---|---|---|
| **1514** | A221 | 1d | multicolored | .30 | .30 |
| **1515** | A221 | 1.25d | multicolored | .30 | .30 |
| **1516** | A221 | 2d | multicolored | .50 | .50 |
| **1517** | A221 | 5d | multicolored | 1.25 | 1.25 |
| **1518** | A221 | 8d | multicolored | 2.10 | 2.10 |
| **1519** | A221 | 10d | multicolored | 2.50 | 2.50 |
| **1520** | A221 | 12d | multicolored | 3.00 | 3.00 |
| **1521** | A221 | 15d | multicolored | 3.75 | 3.75 |
| | *Nos. 1514-1521 (8)* | | | 13.70 | 13.70 |

**Souvenir Sheets**

| | | | | | |
|---|---|---|---|---|---|
| **1522** | A221 | 25d | multicolored | 7.00 | 7.00 |
| **1523** | A221 | 25d | multicolored | 7.00 | 7.00 |

Easter A222

Disney characters celebrate Easter: No. 1524, 25b, No. 1527, 4d, No. 1529, 8d, No. 1531, 12d, Ludwig von Drake. No. 1525, 50b, Minnie Mouse, Daisy Duck. No. 1526, 3d, Mickey Mouse. No. 1528, 5d, Donald Duck. No. 1530, 10d, Goofy.

No. 1532, 20d, Von Drake. No. 1533, 20d, Mickey, Minnie.

**1994, Apr. 11** **Litho.** *Perf. 13½x14*

| | | | | |
|---|---|---|---|---|
| **1524-1531** | A222 | Set of 8 | 18.00 | 18.00 |

**Souvenir Sheets**

| | | | | |
|---|---|---|---|---|
| **1532-1533** | A222 | Set of 2 | 14.00 | 14.00 |

Sierra Club, Cent. A223

No. 1534, 5d — Various views of: a-b, Prince William Sound. c-d, The Serengeti. e-f, Ross Island.

No. 1535, 5d: a-c, Briksdal Fjord, vert. d-f, Yosemite, vert.

No. 1536, 5d: a-b, Tibetan Plateau, vert. c-d, Yellowstone, vert. e, Ross Island, vert. f, The Serengeti, vert. g, Mount Erebus, vert. h, Ansel Adams Wilderness, vert.

No. 1537, 5d: a-b, Ansel Adams Wilderness. c-d, Mount Erebus. e, Prince William Sound. f, Yellowstone. g, Tibetan Plateau. h, Sierra Club emblem.

**1994, Apr. 25** *Perf. 14*

**Miniature Sheets of 6, #a-f**

| | | | | |
|---|---|---|---|---|
| **1534-1535** | A223 | Set of 2 | 22.50 | 22.50 |

**Miniature Sheets of 8, #a-h**

| | | | | |
|---|---|---|---|---|
| **1536-1537** | A223 | Set of 2 | 27.50 | 27.50 |

Paintings of Cats A224

No. 1538, 5d: a, The Arena, by Harold Weston. b, Cat Killing a Bird, by Picasso. c, Cat and Butterfly, by Hokusai. d, Winter: Cat on a Cushion, by Steinlen. e, Rattown Tigers, by Prang. f, Cat on the Floor, by Steinlen. g, Cat and Kittens. h, Cats Looking Over a Fence, by Prang. i, Little White Kittens into Mischief, by Ives. j, Cat Bathing, by Hiroshige. k, Playtime, by Tuck. l, Summer: Cat on a Balustrade, by Steinlen.

No. 1539, 5d, vert.: a, Girl with a Kitten, by Perronneau. b, Still Life with Cat and Fish, by Chardin. c, Tinkle a Cat. d, Naughty Puss! e, Cats, by Steinlen. f, Girl in Red with Cat and Dog, by Phillips. g, Cat, Butterfly and Begonia, by Haronobu. h, Cat and Kitten, by Higgins. i, Woman with a Cat, by Renoir. j, Minnie from Outskirts of Village, by Thrall. k, The Fisher, by Tuck. l, Artist and His Family, by Vaenius.

No. 1540, 20d, The Morning Rising, by Lepicie. No. 1541, 20d, The Graham Children, by Hogarth, vert.

**1994, July 11** **Litho.** *Perf. 14*

**Sheets of 12, #a-l**

| | | | | |
|---|---|---|---|---|
| **1538-1539** | A224 | Set of 2 | 47.50 | 47.50 |

**Souvenir Sheets**

| | | | | |
|---|---|---|---|---|
| **1540-1541** | A224 | Set of 2 | 14.00 | 14.00 |

Monkeys — A225

Designs: 1d, Patas. 1.50d, Collared mangabey. 2d, Black and white colobus. 5d, Mona. 8d, Kirk's colobus. 10d, Vervet. 12d, Red colobus. 15d, Guinea baboon.

Heads of: No. 1550, 25d, Collared mangabey. No. 1551, 25d, Guinea baboon.

**1994, Aug. 1** **Litho.** *Perf. 14*

| | | | | |
|---|---|---|---|---|
| **1542-1549** | A225 | Set of 8 | 17.00 | 17.00 |

**Souvenir Sheets**

| | | | | |
|---|---|---|---|---|
| **1550-1551** | A225 | 25d Set of 2 | 18.00 | 18.00 |

D-Day, 50th Anniv. A226

Designs: 50b, Free Dutch sloop Soema joins attack. 75b, HMS Belfast fires on beach defenses. 1d, USS Texas hits Point Du Hoc. 2d, Free French cruiser George Leygues.

20d, HMS Ramillies.

**1994, Aug. 16**

| | | | | |
|---|---|---|---|---|
| **1552-1555** | A226 | Set of 4 | 4.00 | 4.00 |

**Souvenir Sheet**

| | | | | |
|---|---|---|---|---|
| **1556** | A226 | 20d multicolored | 6.50 | 6.50 |

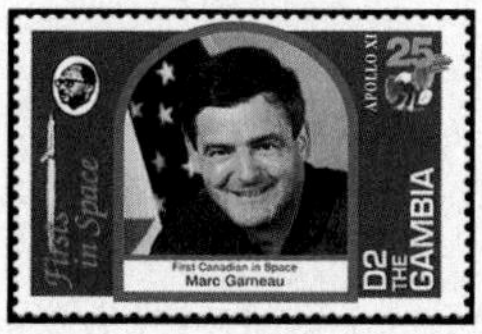

First Manned Moon Landing, 25th Anniv. A227

No. 1557: a, Yuri Gagarin. b, Valentina Tereshkova. c, Ham (chimpanzee). d, Alexei Leonov. e, Neil Armstrong. f, Svetlana Y. Savitskaya. g. Marc Garneau. h, Vladimir Komarov. i, Ulf Merbold.

30d, Neil Armstrong, Edwin "Buzz" Aldrin, Michael Collins at press conference.

**1994, Aug. 16**

| | | | | |
|---|---|---|---|---|
| **1557** | A227 | 2d Sheet of 9, #a.-i. | 8.50 | 8.50 |

**Souvenir Sheet**

| | | | | |
|---|---|---|---|---|
| **1558** | A227 | 30d multicolored | 10.00 | 10.00 |

A228

PHILAKOREA '94 — A229

Designs: 50b, Kungnakchon Hall, Naejangsa. 2d, Kettle of Popchusa. 3d, Pomun Tourist Resort.

Paper screen panels, episode from Sanguozhi, 18th cent. Choson Dynasty: a, Warriors on horseback. b, Soldiers atop fort. c, Shooting with bows and arrows. d, Bowing before horse & rider. e, Fight on horseback. f, h, Charging on horses. g, Trudging through valley. i, j, Living peacefully.

20d, Traditional tombstone guardian, Taenung, vert.

**1994, Aug. 16** *Perf. 14, 13½ (#1562)*

| | | | | |
|---|---|---|---|---|
| **1559-1561** | A228 | Set of 3 | 2.00 | 2.00 |
| **1562** | A229 | 1d Sheet of 10, #a.-j. | 6.00 | 6.00 |

**Souvenir Sheet**

| | | | | |
|---|---|---|---|---|
| **1563** | A228 | 20d multicolored | 7.50 | 7.50 |

A230

Intl. Olympic Committee, Cent. — A231

Designs: 1.50d, Daley Thompson, Great Britain, decathalon, 1980, 1984. 5d, Heide Marie Rosendohl, Germany, long jump, 1972.

20d, Team Sweden, ice hockey, 1994.

**1994, Aug. 16** *Perf. 14*

| | | | | | |
|---|---|---|---|---|---|
| **1564** | A230 | 1.50d | multicolored | .60 | .60 |
| **1565** | A230 | 5d | multicolored | 1.75 | 1.75 |

**Souvenir Sheet**

| | | | | |
|---|---|---|---|---|
| **1566** | A231 | 20d multicolored | 7.25 | 7.25 |

Butterflies A232

Designs: 1d, Mylothris rhodope. 1.25d, Iolaphilus menas. 2d, Neptis nemetes. 5d, Antanartia delius. 8d, Acraea caecilia. 10d, Papilio nireus. 12d, Pipilio menestheus. 15d, Iolaphilus julus.

No. 1575, 25d, Colotis evippe. No. 1576, 25d, Bematistes epaea.

**1994, Aug. 18** *Perf. 14*

| | | | | |
|---|---|---|---|---|
| **1567-1574** | A232 | Set of 8 | 16.00 | 16.00 |

**Souvenir Sheets**

| | | | | |
|---|---|---|---|---|
| **1575-1576** | A232 | Set of 2 | 16.00 | 16.00 |

1994 World Cup Soccer Championships, US — A233

Designs: 50b, Bobby Charlton, England. 75b, Ferenc Puskas, Hungary. 1d, Paolo Rossi, Italy. 2d, Biri Biri, Gambian playing for Spain. 3d, Diego Maradona, Argentina. 8d, Johan Cruyff, Netherlands. 10d, Franz Beckenbauer, Germany. 15d, Thomas Dooley, US.

No. 1585, 25d, Pele, Brazil. No. 1586, 25d, Gordon Banks, England.

**1994, Sept. 1**

| | | | | |
|---|---|---|---|---|
| **1577-1584** | A233 | Set of 8 | 13.50 | 13.50 |

**Souvenir Sheets**

| | | | | |
|---|---|---|---|---|
| **1585-1586** | A233 | Set of 2 | 16.00 | 16.00 |

Mushrooms A234

No. 1587, 5d: a, Agaricus campestris. b, Lepista nuda. c, Podaxis pistillaris. d, Oudemansiella radicata. e, Schizophyllum commune. f, Chlorophyllum molybdites. g, Hypholoma fasciculare. h, Mycena pura. i, Ganoderma lucidum.

No. 1588, 5d: a, Suillus luteus. b, Bolbitius vitellinus. c, Clitocybe nebularis. d, Omphalotus olearius. e, Auricularia auricula. f, Macrolepiota rhacodes. g, Volvariella volvacea. h, Psilocybe coprophila. i, Suillus granulatus.

No. 1589, 20d, Cyathus striatus. No. 1590, 20d, Leucoagaricus naucina.

**1994, Sept. 30**

**Sheets of 9, #a-i**

| | | | | |
|---|---|---|---|---|
| **1587-1588** | A234 | Set of 2 | 24.00 | 24.00 |

**Souvenir Sheets**

| | | | | |
|---|---|---|---|---|
| **1589-1590** | A234 | Set of 2 | 15.00 | 15.00 |

Christmas A235

French paintings: 50b, Expectant Madonna with St. Joseph, by unknown artist. 75b, Rest of the Holy Family, by Louis Le Nain. 1d, Rest on the Flight into Egypt, by Antoine Watteau. No. 1594, 2d, Noon, by Claude Lorrain. No. 1595, 2d, Rest on the Flight into Egypt, by Francois Boucher. No. 1596, 2d, Rest on the Flight into Egypt, by Jean-Honore Fragonard. 10d, The Holy Family, by Nicolas Poussin. 12d, Mystical Marriage of St. Catherine, by Pierre-Francois Mignard.

No. 1599, 25d, The Nativity by Torchlight, by Louis Le Nain. No. 1600, 25d, Adoration of the Shepherds, by Mathieu Le Nain.

**1994, Dec. 5** **Litho.** *Perf. 13½x14*

| | | | | |
|---|---|---|---|---|
| **1591-1598** | A235 | Set of 8 | 12.00 | 12.00 |

**Souvenir Sheets**

| | | | | |
|---|---|---|---|---|
| **1599-1600** | A235 | Set of 2 | 15.00 | 15.00 |

Marilyn Monroe (1926-62), Actress — A236

No. 1601: a-i, Various portraits.
No. 1602, 25d, Wearing red dress. No. 1603, 25d, Wearing long, dangling earrings.

**1995, Jan. 8 Litho. *Perf. 14***

| | | | | |
|---|---|---|---|---|
| **1601** | A236 | 4d Sheet of 9, #a.-i. | 11.00 | 11.00 |

**Souvenir Sheets**

| | | | | |
|---|---|---|---|---|
| **1602-1603** | A236 | Set of 2 | 12.00 | 12.00 |

Elvis Presley (1935-77), Entertainer A237

No. 1604: a, As child. b, Singing, later years. c, With mother. d, With wife, Priscilla. e, With gold medallion. f, Wearing army uniform. g, Singing, younger years. h, Wearing hat. i, With daughter, Lisa Marie.

**1995, Jan. 8**

| | | | | |
|---|---|---|---|---|
| **1604** | A237 | 4d Sheet of 9, #a.-i. | 10.50 | 10.50 |

Dinosaurs A238

No. 1605: a, Pteranodon. b, Archaeopteryx. c, Rhamphorhynchus. d, Ornithomimus. e, Stegosaurus. f, Heterodontosaurus. g, Lystrosaurus. h, Euoplocephalus. i, Coelophysis. j, Staurilosaurus. k, Giantoperis. l, Diarthrognathus.
No. 1606: a, Archaeopteryx, diff. b, Vangehuanosaurus. c, Ceolophysis, diff. d, Plateosaurus. e, Baryonyx. f, Ornitholestes. g, Dryosaurus. h, Estemmenosuchus. i, Macroplata. j, Shonisaurus. k, Muraeonosaurus. l, Archelon.
20d, Bactrosaurus. 22d, Tyrannosaurus, vert. No. 1609, 25d, Triceratops, vert. No. 1610, 25d, Spinosaurus.

**1995 Litho. *Perf. 14***

| | | | | |
|---|---|---|---|---|
| **1605** | A238 | 2d Sheet of 12, #a.-l. | 10.00 | 10.00 |
| **1606** | A238 | 3d Sheet of 12, #a.-l. | 10.00 | 10.00 |

**Souvenir Sheets**

| | | | | |
|---|---|---|---|---|
| **1607** | A238 | 20d multi | 7.00 | 7.00 |
| **1608** | A238 | 22d multi | 7.00 | 7.00 |
| **1609-1610** | A238 | Set of 2 | 14.00 | 14.00 |

New Year 1995 (Year of the Boar) — A239

No. 1611: Stylized boars with Chinese inscriptions in: a, Green. b, Blue violet. c, White. d, Black.
10d, Three boars.

**1995, May 4 *Perf. 14½***

| | | | | |
|---|---|---|---|---|
| **1611** | A239 | 3d Sheet of 4, #a.-d. | 3.50 | 3.50 |

**Souvenir Sheet**

| | | | | |
|---|---|---|---|---|
| **1612** | A239 | 10d multicolored | 3.50 | 3.50 |

Water Birds A240

Designs: 2d, Great white egret. 8d, Hammerkop. 10d, Shoveler. 12d, Crowned crane.
No. 1617: a, Pintail. b, Fulvous tree duck (a). c, Garganey. d, White-faced tree duck. e, White-backed duck. f, Egyptian goose. g, Pigmy goose. h, Little bittern (k). i, Redshank. j, Ringed plover. k, Black-winged stilt. l, Squacco heron (k).
No. 1618, 25d, Ferruginous duck. No. 1619, 25d, Moorhen.

**1995, May 8 *Perf. 14***

| | | | | |
|---|---|---|---|---|
| **1613-1616** | A240 | Set of 4 | 10.00 | 10.00 |
| **1617** | A240 | 3d Sheet of 12, #a.-l. | 11.00 | 11.00 |

**Souvenir Sheets**

| | | | | |
|---|---|---|---|---|
| **1618-1619** | A240 | Set of 2 | 15.00 | 15.00 |

ECOWAS — A241

Designs: 2d, Free movement of people in Gambia. 5d, Captain Yaya AJJ Jammeh, Chairman of Arm Force Provisional Ruling Council, Head of State.

**1995, May 30 Litho. *Perf. 14***

| | | | | |
|---|---|---|---|---|
| **1620** | A241 | 2d multicolored | .55 | .55 |
| **1621** | A241 | 5d multicolored | 1.40 | 1.40 |

Marine Life A242

No. 1622, vert: a, Multicolored parrot fish. b, Sparisoma viride. c, Queen parrot fish. d, Bicolor parrot fish.
No. 1623: a, Leatherback turtle. b, Tiger shark. c, Surgeon fish. d, Emperor angelfish. e, Blue parro fish. f, Triggerfish. g, Sea horse. h, Lionfish. i, Moray eel. j, Red fin butterflyfish. k, Octopus. l, Ray.
No. 1624, 25d, Holacanthus ciliaris. No. 1625, 25d, Angelichthys isabelita.

**1995, June 20**

| | | | | |
|---|---|---|---|---|
| **1622** | A242 | 8d Strip of 4, #a.-d. | 10.00 | 10.00 |
| **1623** | A242 | 3d Sheet of 12, #a.-l. | 10.00 | 10.00 |

**Souvenir Sheets**

| | | | | |
|---|---|---|---|---|
| **1624-1625** | A242 | Set of 2 | 19.00 | 19.00 |

UN, 50th Anniv. — A243

No. 1626: a, 3d, Girls. b, 5d, Woman helping girl at blackboard. c, 8d, Girl writing on blackboard.
25d, Nurse holding baby on scales.

**1995, July 6**

| | | | | |
|---|---|---|---|---|
| **1626** | A243 | Strip of 3, #a.-c. | 3.50 | 3.50 |

**Souvenir Sheet**

| | | | | |
|---|---|---|---|---|
| **1627** | A243 | 25d multicolored | 6.50 | 6.50 |

World War II Motion Pictures A244

No. 1628 — Movie stars: a, Peter Lawford. b, Gene Tierney, Dana Andrews. c, Groucho, Gummo Marx. d, James Stewart. e, Chico, Harpo Marx. f, Tyrone Power. g, Cary Grant, Ingrid Bergman. h, Veronica Lake.
Motion pictures: No. 1629, 25d, A Lady Fights Back. No. 1630, 25d, Desert Victory.

**1995, July 6**

| | | | | |
|---|---|---|---|---|
| **1628** | A244 | 3d Sheet of 8, #a.-h. + label | 11.00 | 11.00 |

**Souvenir Sheets**

| | | | | |
|---|---|---|---|---|
| **1629-1630** | A244 | Set of 2 | 13.50 | 13.50 |

VJ Day, 50th Anniv. A245

No. 1631: a, Fairey Firefly. b, Fairey Barracuda II. c, Vickers Supermarine Seafire II. d, HMS Repulse. e, HMS Illustrious. f, HMS Exeter.
25d, Bomber being shot down by 3-stack cruiser.

**1995, Aug. 1**

| | | | | |
|---|---|---|---|---|
| **1631** | A245 | 5d Sheet of 6, #a.-f. + label | 10.00 | 10.00 |

**Souvenir Sheet**

| | | | | |
|---|---|---|---|---|
| **1632** | A245 | 25d multicolored | 8.00 | 8.00 |

A246

A247

Carrying sacks of grain: No. 1633a, 3d, Woman in pink. b, 5d, Two people. c, 8d, Man.
25d, Fisherman with net.

**1995, Aug. 1 Litho. *Perf. 14***

| | | | | |
|---|---|---|---|---|
| **1633** | A246 | Strip of 3, #a.-c. | 3.75 | 3.75 |

**Souvenir Sheet**

| | | | | |
|---|---|---|---|---|
| **1634** | A246 | 25d multicolored | 6.50 | 6.50 |

FAO, 50th Anniv. No. 1633 is a continuous design.

**1995, Aug. 1**

Nobel Prize Winners: 2d, Kenichi Fukui, chemistry, 1981. 3d, Gustav Stresemann, peace, 1929. 5d, Thomas Mann, literature, 1929. 8d, Albert Schweitzer, peace, 1952. 12d, Leo Esaki, physics, 1973. 15d, Lech Walsea, peace, 1983.
No. 1635: a, Marie Curie, chemistry, 1911. b, Adolf Butenandt, chemistry, 1939. c, Tonegawa Susumu, medicine, 1987. d, Nelly Sachs, literature, 1966. e, Kawabata Yasunari, literature, 1968. f, Yukawa Hideki, physics, 1949. g, Paul Ehrlich, medicine, 1908. h, Sato Eisaku, peace, 1974. i, Carl von Ossietzky, peace, 1935.
25d, Willy Brandt, peace, 1971.

| | | | | |
|---|---|---|---|---|
| **1634A-1634F** | A247 | Set of 6 | 10.00 | 10.00 |
| **1635** | A247 | 5d Sheet of 9, #a.-i. | 11.00 | 11.00 |

**Souvenir Sheet**

| | | | | |
|---|---|---|---|---|
| **1636** | A247 | 25d multicolored | 7.00 | 7.00 |

Rotary Intl., 90th Anniv. A248

Designs: 15d, Paul Haris, Rotary emblem. 20d, Natl. flag, Rotary emblem.

**1995, Aug. 1**

| | | | | |
|---|---|---|---|---|
| **1637** | A248 | 15d multicolored | 3.25 | 3.25 |

**Souvenir Sheet**

| | | | | |
|---|---|---|---|---|
| **1638** | A248 | 20d multicolored | 5.25 | 5.25 |

**Miniature Sheets of 3**

1995 Boy Scout Jamboree, Holland — A249

No. 1639 — How to tie the lariat: a, First step. b, Second step. c, Completed.
No. 1640 — How to tie bowline: a, 12d, First step. b, 10d, Second step. c, 5d, Completed.
No. 1641, 25d, Bowline used to lift injured scout. No. 1642, 25d, Hitch used in lifesaving lift.

**1995, Aug. 1**

| | | | | |
|---|---|---|---|---|
| **1639** | A249 | 2d Sheet of 3, #a.-c. | 1.75 | 1.75 |
| **1640** | A249 | Sheet of 3, #a.-c. | 8.00 | 8.00 |

**Souvenir Sheets**

| | | | | |
|---|---|---|---|---|
| **1641-1642** | A249 | Set of 2 | 12.00 | 12.00 |

Queen Mother, 95th Birthday A250

No. 1643: a, Drawing. b, Bright blue hat, dress. c, Formal portrait. d, Green hat, dress.
25d, Pale blue & white dress, blue hat.

**1995, Aug. 1 *Perf. 13½14***

| | | | | |
|---|---|---|---|---|
| **1643** | A250 | 5d Strip or block of 4, #a.-d. | 4.50 | 4.50 |

**Souvenir Sheet**

| | | | | |
|---|---|---|---|---|
| **1644** | A250 | 25d multicolored | 5.50 | 5.50 |

No. 1643 was issued in sheets of 8 stamps.
Nos. 1643-1644 exist with black frame and overprint in sheet margin "In Memoriam 1900-2002" in one or two lines.

1996 Summer Olympics, Atlanta A251

Designs: 1d, Bruce Jenner, US, decathlon. 1.25d, Greg Louganis, US, diving. 1.50d, Michael Gross, Germany 50-meter butterfly. 2d, Vasily Alexeev, USSR, weight lifting. 3d, Patrick Ewing, US, Juan Antonio Corbalan, Spain, basketball. 5d, Men's volleyball, US v. Brazil. 10d, John Svenden, West Germany, Armando Fernandez, US, water polo. 15d, Pertti Karppinen, Finland, single sculls.
No. 1653, vert: a, Stefano Cerioni, Italy, fencing. b, Alberto Covo, Italy, 10,000-meter run. c, Mary Lou Retton, US, women's gymnastics. d, Vladimir Artemov, USSR, men's gymnastics. e, Florence Griffith-Joyner, US, 400-meter relay. f, Brazil, soccer. g, Nelson Valis, US, 1000-meter sprint cycling. h, Cheryl Miller, US, women's basketball.
No. 1654, 25d, Karen Stives, US, equestrian. No. 1655, 25d, Edwin Moses, US, 400-meter hurdles, vert.

**1995, Aug. 17**
**1645-1652** A251 Set of 8 10.00 10.00
**1653** A251 3d Sheet of 8, #a.-h. 6.50 6.50

**Souvenir Sheets**

**1654-1655** A251 Set of 2 14.00 14.00

Volleyball, cent. (No. 1650).

Rotary, Intl., 90th Anniv., 1995 Boy Scout Jamboree, Holland — A252

Designs: 2d, Gambia Rotary contributing to education. No. 1657, 5d, Wood Badge course, Yundum, 1980. No. 1658, 5d, M.J.E. Sambou, organizing scout commissioner, vert.

**1995, Sept. 5**
**1656-1658** A252 Set of 3 3.50 3.50

Flowers — A253

Designs: 2d, Zantedeschia rehmannii. 5d, Euadenia eminens. 10d, Passiflora vitifolia. 15d, Dietes grandiflora.

No. 1663, 3d: a, Canarina abyssinica. b, Nerine bowdenii. c, Zantedeschia aethiopica. d, Aframomum sceptrum. e, Schotia brachypetala. f, Catharanthus roseus. g, Protea grandiceps. h, Plumbago capensis. i, Uncarina grandidieri.

No. 1664, 3d: a, Kigelia africana. b, Hibiscus schizopetalus. c, Dombeya mastersii. d, Agapanthus orientalis. e, Strelitzia reginae. f, Spathodea campanulata. g, Rhodolaena bakeriana. h, Gazania rigens. i, Ixianthes retzioides.

No. 1665, 25d, Eulophia quartiniana. No. 1666, 25d, Gloriosa simplex.

**1995, Oct. 2 Litho. *Perf. 14***
**1659-1662** A253 Set of 4 8.00 8.00

**Sheets of 9, #a-i**

**1663-1664** A253 Set of 2 14.50 14.50

**Souvenir Sheets**

**1665-1666** A253 Set of 2 15.00 15.00

SOS Children's Villages A254

Designs: No. 1667, 2d, Children playing near houses. No. 1668, 2d, Aid worker with child, vert. 5d, Children.

**1995, Oct. 9 Litho. *Perf. 14***
**1667-1669** A254 Set of 3 2.50 2.50

Entertainers A255

No. 1670: a, Roy Orbison. b, Mick Jagger. c, Bruce Springsteen. d, Jimi Hendrix. e, Bill Haley. f, Gene Vincent. g, Buddy Holly. h, Jerry Lee Lewis. i, Chuck Berry.

No. 1671: a-i, Various pictures of James Dean.

No. 1672, 25d, James Dean. No. 1673, 25d, Elvis Presley.

**1995, Dec. 1 Litho. *Perf. 13½x14***
**1670** A255 3d Sheet of 9, #a.-i. 9.50 9.50
**1671** A255 3d Sheet of 9, #a.-i. 8.50 8.50

**Souvenir Sheets**

**1672-1673** A255 Set of 2 17.50 17.50

Motion pictures, cent. (Nos. 1671-1672).

Christmas A256

Details or entire paintings: 75b, Madonna of the, Valley. 1d, Madonna, by Giotto. 2d, The Flight into Egypt, by Luca Giordano. 5d, The Epiphany, by Bondone. 8d, Virgin & Child, by Burgkmair. 12d, Madonna, by Bellini.

No. 1680, 25d, Mother and Child, by Rubens. No. 1681, 25d, The Christ, by Carpaccio.

**1995, Dec. 18**
**1674-1679** A256 Set of 6 10.00 10.00

**Souvenir Sheets**

**1680-1681** A256 Set of 2 16.00 16.00

Banjul Intl. Airport A257

Denominations: 1d, 2d, 3d, 5d.

**1995, Dec. 21 Litho. *Perf. 14***
**1682-1685** A257 Set of 4 3.50 3.50

UPU, 121st Anniv. — A258

Denominations: 1d, 2d, 3d, 7d.

**1995, Dec. 21**
**1686-1689** A258 Set of 4 3.50 3.50

Marine Life A259

Designs: 2d, Commerson's dolphin. 5d, Narwhal. 8d, True's beaked whale. 10d, Rough-toothed dolphin.

No. 1694, 3d — Dolphins:a, Northern rightwhale. b, Spotted. c, Common. d, Pacific white-sided. e, Atlantic humpbacked. f, Atlantic white-sided. g, White-beaked. h, Striped. i, Risso's.

No. 1695, 3d — Whales: a, Bryde's. b, Sperm. c, Humpback. d, Sei. e, Blue. f, Gray. g, Fin. h, Killer. i, Right.

No. 1696, 25d, Beluga, clymene dolphin. No. 1697, 25d, Bowhead whale, dall's porpoise, blue shark.

**1995, Dec. 22**
**1690-1693** A259 Set of 4 6.25 6.25

**Sheets of 9, #a-i**

**1694-1695** A259 Set of 2 13.00 13.00

**Souvenir Sheets**

**1696-1697** A259 Set of 2 14.00 14.00

Cowboys and American Indians — A260

Disney characters portraying Amerian Indians or in western scenes: 15b, Pete, Seminole. 20b, Donald, Chinook. 25b, Huey, Dewey, Louie, Blackfoot. 30b, Sharp shooter Minnie. 40b, Bull-riding Donald. 50b, Cattle-branding Mickey. 2d, Donald, Tlingit. 3d, Bronco-busting Mickey. 12d, Trick-roping Grandma Duck. No. 1707, 15d, Goofy the ranch hand. No. 1708, 15d, Mickey, Pomo. 20d, Minnie, Goofy, Navaho.

No. 1710, 25d, Minnie, Massachusetts Tribe. No. 1711, 25d, Pluto singing, vert. No. 1712, 25d, Donald with rope around neck, vert. No. 1712, 25d, Minnie, Shoshoni, vert.

**1995, Dec. 22 *Perf. 14x13½***
**1698-1709** A260 Set of 12 20.00 20.00

**Souvenir Sheets**

**1710-1713** A260 Set of 4 30.00 30.00

New Year 1996 (Year of the Rat) — A261

No. 1714 — Various stylized rats: a, 63b. b, 75b. c, 1.50d. d, 4d.

No. 1715a, Like #1714a. b, Like #1714d. c, Like #1714c. d, Like #1714b.

No. 1716, Two rats.

**1996, Jan. 2 *Perf. 14½***
**1714** A261 Strip of 4, #a.-d. 1.25 1.25
**1715** A261 3d Sheet of 4, #a.-d. 2.50 2.50

**Souvenir Sheet**

**1716** A261 10d multicolored 4.50 4.50

No. 1714 issued in sheets of 16 stamps.

Paintings from Metropolitan Museum of Art — A262

No. 1717, 4d: a, Don Tiburcio Pérez y Cuervo, by Goya. b, Jean Antoine Moltedo, by J.A.D. Ingres. c, The Letter, by Corot. d, General Etienne Maurice Gerard, by J.L. David. e, Portrait of the Artist, by Van Gogh. f, Joseph Henri Altés, by Degas. g, Princess de Broglie, by Ingres. h, Lady at the Table, by Cassatt.

No. 1718, 4d: a, Broken Eggs, by Greuze. b, Johann Joachim Winckelmann, by Mengs. c, Col. George K.H. Coussmaker, by Reynolds. d, Self Portrait with Pupils, by Labille-Guiard. e, Courtesan Holding a Fan, by Utamaro. f, The Woodgatherers, by Gainsborough. g, Mr. Grace D. Elliott, by Gainsborough. h, The Drummond Children, by Raeburn.

No. 1719, 4d: a, Sunflowers, by Monet. b, Still Life with Pansies, by Fantin-Latour. c, Parisians Enjoying the Park, by Monet. d, La Mére Larchevêque, by Pissarro. e, Rue de L'Epicerie, Rouen, by Pissarro. f, The Abduction of Rebecca, by Delacroix. g, Daughter, Abraham-Ben-Chimol, by Delacroix. h, Christ on Lake of Gennesaret, by Delacroix.

No. 1720, 4d: a, Henry Frederick, Prince of Wales, by Peake. b, Saints Peter, Martha, Mary & Leonard, by Correggio. c, Marriage Feast at Cana, by Juan de Flandes. d, Portrait of one of Wedigh Family, by Holbein. e, Guillaume Budé, by Clouet. f, Portrait of a Cardinal, by El Greco. g, St. Jerome as a Cardinal, by El Greco. h, Portrait of a Man, by Titian.

No. 1721, 25d, The Harvesters, by Bruegel. No. 1722, 25d, The Creation of the World and the Expulsion from Paradise, by Giovanni de Paolo. No. 1723, 25d, Henry IV at the Battle of Ivry, by Rubens. No. 1724, 25d, The Israelites Gathering Manna in the Desert, by Rubens.

**1996, Jan. 29 Litho. *Perf. 13½x14***

**Sheets of 8, #a-h**

**1717-1720** A262 Set of 4 35.00 35.00

**Souvenir Sheets**

***Perf. 14***

**1721-1724** A262 Set of 4 26.00 26.00

Nos. 1721-1724 each contain one 85x57mm stamp.

No. 1723 is actually in the Uffizi Gallery in Florence; No. 1724 in the Los Angeles County Museum of Art.

Traditional Fire Dance A263

Designs: 1d, Blowing fire from mouth, vert. 2d, Like 1d, diff. 3d, Holding sticks of fire at leg, vert. 7d, Holding out two sticks of fire.

**1996, Jan. 29 Litho. *Perf. 14***
**1725-1728** A263 Set of 4 3.50 3.50

Disney Characters Performing Good Deeds — A264

Designs: 1d, Community blood drive. 4d, Adopt-a-pet. 5d, Christmas giving for the needy. 10d, Teaching outdoor skills. 15d, Teaching reading. 20d, Volunteer fire fighters.

No. 1735, 25d, Highway volunteers. No. 1736, 25d, Counting whales.

**1996, Apr. 12 Litho. *Perf. 13½x14***
**1729-1734** A264 Set of 6 14.00 12.00

**Souvenir Sheets**

**1735-1736** A264 Set of 2 13.00 11.00

Bruce Lee (1940-73), Martial Arts Expert — A265

No. 1737: Various portraits. 25d, In fighting stance.

**1996, Apr. 1 Litho. *Perf. 14***
**1737** A265 3d Sheet of 9, #a.-i. 7.00 7.00

**Souvenir Sheet**

**1738** A265 25d multicolored 5.75 5.75

China '96, 9th Asian Intl. Philatelic Exhibition (No. 1737).

African Wildlife A266

15d, African civet.

No. 1740: a, Roan antelope. b, Lesser bush baby. c, Leopard. d, Guinea forest red colobus. e, Kob. f, Common eland.

No. 1741: a, African buffalo. b, Topi. c, Vervet. d, Hippopotamus. e, Waterbuck. f, Senegal chameleon. g, Western green mamba. h, Slender snouted crocodile (i). i, Adanson's mud turtle.

No. 1742, 25d, Lion. No. 1743, 25d, Chimpanzee.

**1996, Apr. 15 Litho. *Perf. 14***

**1739** A266 15d multicolored 3.25 3.25
**1740** A266 3d Block of 6, #a.-f. 4.00 4.00
**1741** A266 4d Sheet of 9, #a.-i. 6.75 6.75

**Souvenir Sheets**

**1742-1743** A266 Set of 2 12.00 12.00

No. 1740 issued in sheets of 12 stamps.

Queen Elizabeth II, 70th Birthday A267

No. 1744: a, Portrait wearing blue dress. b, Wearing white dress, crown. c, Younger picture, crown.

25d, Buckingham Palace, horiz.

**1996, May 9 Litho. *Perf. 13½x14***

**1744** A267 8d Strip of 3, #a.-c. 4.75 4.75

**Souvenir Sheet**

***Perf. 14x13½***

**1745** A267 25d multicolored 5.50 5.50

No. 1744 was issued in sheets of 9 stamps with each strip in a different order.

Classic Cars and Fire Engines A268

No. 1746, 4d — Classic cars: a, 1912 Fiat Tipo 510, Italy. b, 1936 Toyota Model 4B Phaeton, Japan. c, 1924 NAG C4B, Germany. d, 1903 Cadillac, US. e, 1925 Bentley, Great Britain. f, 1909 Renault Model AX, France.

No. 1747, 4d — Fire engines: a, 1850 Pumper Hose Cart, US. b, 1891 Steam Fire Engine, US. c, 1864 Lausitzer, Germany. d, 1902 Chemical Engine, Great Britain. e, 1904 Motor Fire Engine, Great Britain. f, 1860 Colonia No. 5, Germany.

No. 1748, 25d, 1917 Mitsubishi Model A, Japan. No. 1749, 25d, 1865 Amoskeag steamer, US.

**1996, May 27 *Perf. 14***

**Sheets of 6, #a-f**

**1746-1747** A268 Set of 2 11.00 11.00

**Souvenir Sheets**

**1748-1749** A268 Set of 2 12.00 12.00

Euro '96, 1996 European Soccer Championships, England — A269

Team pictures: No. 1750, 2d, Bulgaria. No. 1751, 2d, Croatia. No. 1752, 2d, Czech Republic. No. 1753, 2d, Denmark. No. 1754, 2d, England. No. 1755, 2d, France. No. 1756, 2d, Germany. No. 1757, 2d, Holland. No. 1758, 2d, Italy. No. 1759, 2d, Portugal. No. 1760, 2d, Romania. No. 1761, 2d, Russia. No. 1762, 2d, Scotland. No. 1763, 2d, Spain. No. 1764, 2d, Switzerland. No. 1765, 2d, Turkey.

No. 1766, 25d, Hristo Stoitchkov, Bulgaria, vert. No. 1767, 25d, Davor Suker, Croatia, vert. No. 1768, 25d, Pavel Hapal, Czech Republic. No. 1769, 25d, 1992 Denmark team, European championship winners. No. 1770, 25d, Bryan Robson, England, vert. No. 1771, 25d, 1984 Championship cup won by French team, vert. No. 1772, 25d, Jüegen Klinsmann, Germany. No. 1773, 25d, Ruud Gullit, Holland, vert. No. 1774, 25d, Roberto Baggio, Italy, vert. No. 1775, 25d, Eusebio, Portugal, vert. No. 1776, 25d, Gheorge Hagi, Romania, vert. No. 1777, 25d, Oleg Salenko, Russia, vert.No. 1778, 25d, Gary McAllister, Scotland, vert. No. 1779, 25d, Juan Goikoetxea, Spain, vert. No. 1780, 25d, Christophe Ohrel, Switzerland, vert. No. 1781, 25d, Hami Mandirali, Turkey, vert.

**1996, June 8 Litho. *Perf. 14***

**1750-1765** A269 Set of 16 11.50 11.50

**Souvenir Sheets**

**1766-1781** A269 Set of 16 100.00 100.00

Nos. 1750-1765 each exist in miniature sheets of 8 + 1 label.

See Nos. 1808-1819.

1996 Summer Olympic Games, Atlanta — A270

1912 Olympics, Stockholm: 1d, Ray Ewry, standing high jump. 2d, Fanny Durack, freestyle swimming. 5d, Stadium, scenes in Stocholm. 10d, Jim Thorpe, decathlon, pentathlon.

No. 1786, 3d — Winners in past Olympics: a, Japanese volleyball team, 1964. b, Li Neng, floor exercises, 1984. c, Sergei Bubka, pole vault, 1988. d, Nadia Comaneci, all around gymnastics, 1976. e, Edwin Moses, 400-meter hurdles, 1984. f, Vitaly Shcherbo, all around gymnastics, 1992. g, Evelyn Ashford, 100-meters, 1984. h, Muhammad Ali, light heavyweight boxing, 1960. i, Carl Lewis, C. Smith, 400-meters relay, 1984.

No. 1787, 3d — 1992 Olympians: a, Fu Mingxia, platform diving. b, Heike Henkel, high jump. c, Spanish soccer team. d, Jackie Joyner-Kersee, heptathlon. e, Tatiana Gutsu, all around gymnastics. f, Michael Johnson, 400-meters. g, Lin Li, 200-meter individual medley. h, Gail Devers, 100-meters. i, Mike Powell, long jump.

No. 1788, 25d, Michael Gross, swimming, 1984, 1988, horiz. No. 1789, 25d, Ulrike Meyfarth, high jump, 1972, 1984.

**1996, July 18 Litho. *Perf. 14***

**1782-1785** A270 Set of 4 3.25 3.25

**Sheets of 9, #a-i**

**1786-1787** A270 Set of 2 9.00 9.00

**Souvenir Sheets**

**1788-1789** A270 Set of 2 10.00 10.00

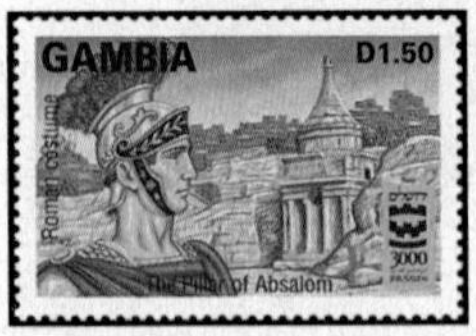


Jerusalem, 3000th Anniv. — A271

Designs: 1.50d, Roman costume, Pillar of Absalem. 2d, Turkish costume, Gate of Mercy. 3d, Greek costume, Church of the Holy Sepulcher. 10d, Western Wall of the Temple Mount, Hasidic costume.

25d, Emblem, King David Tower, vert.

**1996, July 25**

**1790-1793** A271 Set of 4 3.75 3.75

**Souvenir Sheet**

**1794** A271 25d multicolored 5.50 5.50

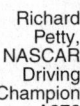

Radio, Cent. A272

Designs: 1d, Glenn Miller. 4d, Louis Armstrong. 5d, Nat King Cole. 10d, Andrews Sisters.

25d, Harry S Truman.

**1996, July 25 *Perf. 13½x14***

**1795-1798** A272 Set of 4 5.00 5.00

**Souvenir Sheet**

**1799** A272 25d multicolored 5.50 5.50

UNICEF, 50th Anniv. — A273

Designs: 63b, Boy holding shoes. 3d, Girl receiving vaccination. 8d, Boy with soup ladle. 10d, Girl with blanket.

25d, Boy receiving vaccination, horiz.

**1996, July 25 *Perf. 14***

**1800-1803** A273 Set of 4 4.25 4.25

**Souvenir Sheet**

**1804** A273 25d multicolored 5.00 5.00

A274

A275

No. 1805: a, John F. Kennedy. b, Jacqueline Kennedy Onassis. c, Willy Brandt. d, Marilyn Monroe. e, Mao Tse Tung. f, Sung Ching Ling. g, Charles de Gaulle. h, Marlene Dietrich.

Nos. 1806-1807: Various portraits of Jacqueline Kennedy Onassis (1929-94).

**1996, Aug. 22**

**1805** A274 5d Sheet of 8, #a.-h. 9.50 9.50
**1806** A275 5d Sheet of 9, #a.-i. 11.00 11.00

**Souvenir Sheet**

**1807** A274 25d multicolored 5.75 5.75

**Nos. 1751-1752, 1754, 1756, 1758, 1761, 1767-1768, 1770, 1772, 1774, 1777 With Added Inscriptions**

**1996, Aug. 26**

**1808-1813** A269 Set of 6 3.25 3.25

**Souvenir Sheets**

**1814-1819** A269 Set of 6 32.50 32.50

Nos. 1808-1813, each of which are 2d stamps, were issued in sheets of 8 + 1 label. Inscriptions on Nos. 1808-1813 and in sheet margins of Nos. 1814-1819, each of which are 25d stamps, show date of game, teams competing, and final score. Margin of the miniature sheets show additional information about individual games, and name of Germany as winner.

Team or team player shown as follows: Croatia (Nos. 1808, 1814), Czech Republic (Nos. 1809, 1815), England (Nos. 1810, 1816), Germany (Nos. 1811, 1817), Italy (Nos. 1812, 1818), Russia (Nos. 1813, 1819).

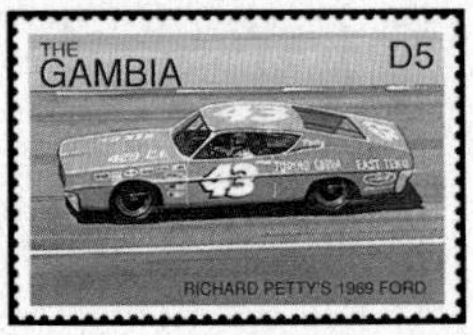


Richard Petty, NASCAR Driving Champion A276

No. 1820: a, 1969 Ford. b, Richard Petty. c, 1978 Dodge Magnum. d, 1987 Pontiac. e, 1989 Pontiac. f, 1975 Dodge Daytona.

25d, 1972 Plymouth.

**1996, Aug. 27**

**1820** A276 5d Sheet of 6, #a.-f. 7.25 7.25

**Souvenir Sheet**

**1821** A276 25d multicolored 5.00 5.00

No. 1821 contains one 85x28mm stamp.

Elvis Presley's 1st "Hit" Year, 40th Anniv. A277

Designs: Various portraits.

**1996, Sept. 8 Litho. *Perf. 13½x14***

**1822** A277 5d Sheet of 6, #a.-f. 7.25 7.25

Supermarine S6B's Schneider Trophy Victory, 65th Anniv. — A278

No. 1823 — Spitfire aircraft: a, PR XIX, Royal Swedish Air Force. b, MK VB, US Army Air. c, MK VC, French Air Force. d, MK VB, Soviet Air Force. e, MK IXE, Netherlands East Indies Air Force. f, MK IXE, Israeli Defense Force. g, MK VIII, Royal Australian Air Force. h, MK VB, Turkish Air Force. i, PR XI, Royal Danish Air Force.

No. 1823J: k, K5054, first prototype aircraft. l, K9787, first production aircraft. m, MK 1A, "Battle of Britain." n, LF MK IXE, D-Day invasion markings. o, MK XII, first "Griffon" engined model. p, MK XIVC, SEAC markings. q, PR XIX, Royal Swedish Air Force. r, PR MK XIX. s, FMK 22/24 final variant.

No. 1824, The Supermarine S.6B S1595. No. 1824A, Supermarine S.6B S1595 seaplane.

**1996, Sept. 13 Litho. *Perf. 14***

**1823** A278 4d Sheet of 9, #a.-i. 8.50 8.50
**1823J** A278 4d Sheet of 9, #k.-s. 8.50 8.50

**Souvenir Sheets**

**1824** A278 25d multicolored 6.00 6.00
**1824A** A278 25d multicolored 6.00 6.00

Bob Dylan, Singer — A279

**1996, Sept. 8 Litho. *Perf. 14***

**1825** A279 5d multicolored 1.60 1.60

Issued in sheets of 16.

Birds — A280

Designs: 50b, Egyptian plover. 63b, Painted snipe. 75b, Golden-breasted bunting. 1d, Bateleur. 1.50d, Didric cuckoo. 2d, European turtle dove. 3d, Village weaver. 4d, European roller. 5d, Cut-throat. 10d, Hoopoe. 15d, White-faced scops-owl. 20d, Narina trogan. 25d, Pied kingfisher. 30d, Common kestrel.

**1996, Oct. 22 Litho. *Perf. 14***

| | | | | | |
|---|---|---|---|---|---|
| **1826** | A280 | 50b | multicolored | .25 | .25 |
| **1827** | A280 | 63b | multicolored | .25 | .25 |
| **1828** | A280 | 75b | multicolored | .25 | .25 |
| **1829** | A280 | 1d | multicolored | .25 | .25 |
| **1830** | A280 | 1.50d | multicolored | .30 | .30 |
| **1831** | A280 | 2d | multicolored | .45 | .45 |
| **1832** | A280 | 3d | multicolored | .65 | .65 |
| **1833** | A280 | 4d | multicolored | .90 | .90 |
| **1834** | A280 | 5d | multicolored | 1.10 | 1.10 |
| **1835** | A280 | 10d | multicolored | 2.25 | 2.25 |
| **1836** | A280 | 15d | multicolored | 3.25 | 3.25 |
| **1837** | A280 | 20d | multicolored | 4.50 | 4.50 |
| **1838** | A280 | 25d | multicolored | 5.50 | 5.50 |
| **1839** | A280 | 30d | multicolored | 6.50 | 6.50 |
| | *Nos. 1826-1839 (14)* | | | 26.40 | 26.40 |

See Nos. 1898-1900.

Christmas A281

Details of painting, Assumption of the Madonna, by Titian: 1d, Watching assumption, cherub, clouds. 1.50d, Cherubs. 2d, Cherub. 3d, Cherub holding up cloud, outstretched arms below. 10d, People watching assumption. 15d, Cherubs pointing.

No. 1846, 25d, Madonna and Child with Two Angels, by Filippo Lippi, horiz. No. 1847, 25d, Virgin and Child with Infant St. John, by Raphael.

**1996, Nov. 18 *Perf. 13½x14***

**1840-1845** A281 Set of 6 6.75 6.75

**Souvenir Sheets**

**1846-1847** A281 Set of 2 10.00 10.00

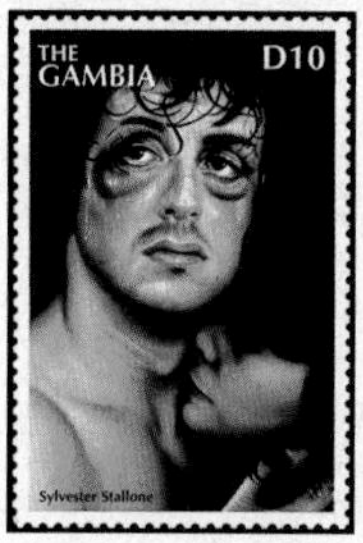

Sylvester Stallone in Movie, "Rocky" — A282

**1996, Nov. 21 Litho. *Perf. 14***

**1848** A282 10d multicolored 2.00 2.00

Issued in sheets of 3.

Development Projects — A283

Designs: No. 1849, 63b, No. 1852, 2d, Arch 22, vert. 1d, Tractor, rice development project. 1.50d, Worker in rice paddy, vert. 3d, Banjul Intl. Airport Terminal Building. 5d, Chamoi Bridge. 20d, Workers in rice paddy. 25d, Statue in front of Arch 22, vert.

**1996 Litho. *Perf. 14***

**1849-1854** A283 Set of 6 2.75 2.75

**Souvenir Sheets**

| | | | | | |
|---|---|---|---|---|---|
| **1855** | A283 | 20d | multicolored | 4.00 | 4.00 |
| **1856** | A283 | 25d | multicolored | 5.00 | 5.00 |

New Year 1997 (Year of the Ox) — A284

Nos. 1857-1858 — Various stylized oxen, background color: a, 63b, orange. b, 75b, purple. c, 1.50d, blue green. d, 4d, yellow orange. All stamps in No. 1858 are 3d.

10d, Ox with baby lying on its back.

**1997, Jan. 16 *Perf. 15***

**1857** A284 Strip of 4, #a.-d. 1.50 1.50
**1858** A284 3d Sheet of 4, #a.-d. 2.75 2.75

**Souvenir Sheet**

***Perf. 14***

**1859** A284 10d multicolored 3.00 3.00

No. 1859 contains one 43x29mm stamp.

Mickey's Journey to the West — A285

Nos. 1860-1861: a-f, Scenes from Disney's "Monkey King."

No. 1862, Donald, Mickey, vert. No. 1863, Wu-Kong Sun (The Monkey King), monkeys, Mickey. No. 1864, Mickey, Intelligent Tortoise, Master San Tang. No. 1865, Mickey, Minnie obtaining Buddhist scriptures.

**1997, Jan. 28 *Perf. 14x13½***

| | | | | | |
|---|---|---|---|---|---|
| **1860** | A285 | 2d Sheet of 6, #a.-f. | | 5.50 | 5.50 |
| *g.* | | No. 1860 overprinted | | 5.50 | 5.50 |
| **1861** | A285 | 3d Sheet of 6, #a.-f. | | 6.25 | 6.25 |
| *g.* | | No. 1861 overprinted | | 7.00 | 7.00 |

**Souvenir Sheets**

| | | | | |
|---|---|---|---|---|
| **1862** | A285 | 5d multi | 4.75 | 4.75 |
| *a.* | | With marginal overprint | 5.00 | 5.00 |
| **1863** | A285 | 10d multi | 4.75 | 4.75 |
| *a.* | | With marginal overprint | 5.00 | 5.00 |
| **1864** | A285 | 10d multi | 4.75 | 4.75 |
| *a.* | | With marginal overprint | 5.00 | 5.00 |
| **1865** | A285 | 15d multi | 4.75 | 4.75 |
| *a.* | | With marginal overprint | 5.00 | 5.00 |

Nos. 1860g, 1861g are overprinted in red in sheet margin: "70TH ANNIVERSARY OF MICKEY & MINNIE," and in black with "Happy Birthday," Mickey Mouse, and "1998" in emblem. Nos. 1862a, 1863a, 1864a, 1865a are overprinted in black in sheet margin with just "Happy Birthday" emblem.

Souvenir Sheet

Deng Xiaoping — A286

No. 1867, Like No. 1866.

**1996, May 13 Litho. *Perf. 13***

**1866** A286 5d shown 5.25 5.25

**Litho. & Embossed**

***Die Cut Perf. 9***

**Size: 95x56mm**

**1867** A286 300d gold

China '96. Nos. 1866-1867 were not available until March 1997.

Jackie Chan, Action Film Actor — A287

A287a

Various portraits.

**1997, Feb. 12 *Perf. 14***

**1868** A287 4d Sheet of 8, #a.-h. 8.00 8.00

**Souvenir Sheet**

**1869** A287 25d multi, horiz. 7.00 7.00

**Litho. & Embossed**

***Die Cut Perf. 9***

**Without Gum**

**1869A** A287a 300d gold & multi

Endangered Species — A288

No. 1870, 1.50d: a, Clouded leopard. b, Audouin's gull. c, Leatherback turtle. d, White-eared pheasant. e, Kakapo. f, Right whale. g, Black-footed ferret. h, Dwarf lemur. i, Peacock pheasant. j, Brown hyena. k, Cougar. l, Gharial. m, Monk seal. n, Mountain gorilla. o, Blyth's tragopan. p, Malayan tapir. q, Black rhinoceros. r, Polar bear. s, Red colobus. t, Tiger.

No. 1871, 1.50d: a, Arabian oryx. b, Baiji. c, Ruffed lemur. d, California condor. e, Blue-headed quail-dove. f, Numbat. g, Congo peacock. h, White uakari. i, Eskimo curlew. j, Gouldian finch. k, Coelacanth. l, Toucan barbet. m, Snow leopard. n, Queen Alexandra's birdwing. o, Dalmatian pelican. p, Chaco tortoise. q, Medong catfish. r, Helmeted hornbill. s, White-eyed river martin. t, Fluminense swallowtail.

No. 1872, 25d, Giant panda. No. 1873, 25d, Humpback whale. No. 1874, 25d, Japanese crane.

**1997, Feb. 24**

**Sheets of 20, #a-t**

**1870-1871** A288 Set of 2 14.00 14.00

**Souvenir Sheets**

**1872-1874** A288 Set of 3 17.00 17.00

Hong Kong '97 (Nos. 1870-1871).

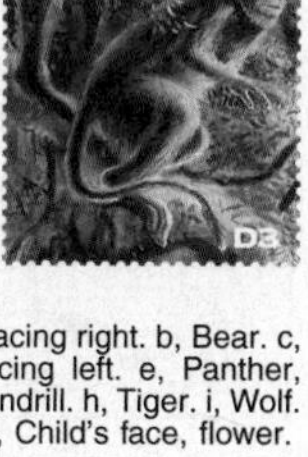

Jungle Book — A289

No. 1875: a, Monkey facing right. b, Bear. c, Elephant. d, Monkey facing left. e, Panther, butterfly. f, Buffalo. g, Mandrill. h, Tiger. i, Wolf. j, Cobra. k, Mongoose. l, Child's face, flower.

**1997**

**1875** A289 3d Sheet of 12, #a.-l. 8.25 8.25

Mushrooms — A290

Designs: 1d, Polyporus squamosus. 3d, Armillaria tabescens. 5d, Collybia velutipes. 10d, Sarcoscypha coccinea.

No. 1880, vert: a, Amanita caesarea. b, Lepiota procera. c, Hygophorus psittacinus. d, Russula xerampelina. e, Laccaria amethystina. f, Coprinus micaceus. g, Boletus edulis. h, Morchella esculenta. i, Otidea auricula.

25d, Volvariella bombycina.

**1997, Mar. 10 Litho. *Perf. 14***

**1876-1879** A290 Set of 4 4.50 4.50
**1880** A290 4d Sheet of 9, #a.-i. 7.75 7.75

**Souvenir Sheet**

**1881** A290 25d multicolored 7.00 7.00

UNESCO, 50th Anniv. — A291

World Heritage sites: 1d, Horyu-Ji, Japan. 2d, Great Wall, China. 3d, City of Ayutthaya, Thailand. 4d, Ascension Convent, Santa Maria, Philippines. 10d, Dragons, Komodo Natl. Park, Indonesia. 15d, Timbuktu, Mali.

No. 1888, 4d, vert. — Various sites in Japan: a, g, h. Kyoto. b, Himeji-Jo. c, d, Horyu-Ji. e, f, Yakushma.

No. 1889, 4d, vert. — Various sites in China: a, b, c, Mogao Caves. d, e, Great Wall. f, g, h, Imperial Palace.

No. 1890, 4d, vert. — Various sites: a, Mt. Nimba Strict Nature Reserve, Guinea. b, Banc D'Argun Natl. Park, Mauritania. c, Marrakesh, Morocco. d, Ichkeul Natl. Park, Tunisia. e, Mali. f, Salonga Natl. Park, Zaire. g, Timgad, Algeria. h, Benin.

No. 1891, 5d — Various sites in Germany: a, b, c, Bamberg. d, e, Maulbronn.

No. 1892, 5d — Various sites in Greece: a, d, e, Ruins in Delphi. b, c, City of Rhodes.

No. 1893, 5d — Various sites in Japan: a, b, Shirakami-Sanchi. c, d, e, Himeji-Jo.

No. 1894, 25d, Cloisters, Santa Maria de Alcobaca, Portugal, No. 1895, 25d, Kyoto, Japan. No. 1896, 25d, Ruins of Kilwa Kisiwani, Tanzania. No. 1897, 25d, Plitvice Lakes Natl. Park, Croatia.

**1997, Mar. 24**

**1882-1887** A291 Set of 6 7.25 7.25

**Sheets of 8, #a-h, + Label**

**1888-1890** A291 Set of 3 20.00 20.00

**Sheets of 5, #a-e, + Label**

**1891-1893** A291 Set of 3 15.50 15.50

**Souvenir Sheets**

**1894-1897** A291 Set of 4 20.00 20.00

**Bird Type of 1996**

Designs: 40d, Temminck's courser. 50d, European bee-eater. 100d, Green-winged teal.

**1997, Mar. 25 Litho. *Perf. 14***

| | | | | | |
|---|---|---|---|---|---|
| **1898** | A280 | 40d | multicolored | 8.00 | 8.00 |
| **1899** | A280 | 50d | multicolored | 10.00 | 10.00 |
| **1900** | A280 | 100d | multicolored | 20.00 | 20.00 |
| | *Nos. 1898-1900 (3)* | | | 38.00 | 38.00 |

Disney's 101 Dalmatians — A293

No. 190, vert.1: a, Dipstick. b, Fidget. c, Jewel. d, Lucky. e, Two-Tone. f, Wizzer.

No. 1902: a-i, Various "Playful Puppies."

No. 1903: a-i, Various "Mischievous puppies."
No. 1904, 25d, Hiding under sheep. No. 1905, 25d, Cruella. No. 1906, 25d, Looking at picture. No. 1907, 25d, Distributing mail, vert. No. 1908, 25d, Into paint. No. 1909, 25d, Playing video game.

**1997, May 1** *Perf. 13½x14, 14x13½*

**1901** A293 50b Sheet of 6, #a.-f. 2.50 2.50
**1902** A293 2d Sheet of 9, #a.-i. 4.50 4.50
**1903** A293 3d Sheet of 9, #a.-i. 7.00 7.00

**Souvenir Sheets**

**1904-1909** A293 Set of 6 42.50 42.50

Minnie Thru the Years — A294

No. 1910 — Minnie in various scenes dated: a, 1928. b, 1933. c, 1934. d, 1937. e, 1938. f, 1941. g, 1950. h, 1990. i, 1997.
25d, 1987.

**1997, May 1** *Perf. 13½x14*

**1910** A294 4d Sheet of 9, #a.-i. 11.00 11.00

**Souvenir Sheet**

**1911** A294 25d multicolored 9.00 9.00

Juventus (World Club Soccer Champions), Cent. — A295

No. 1912: a, Juventus, 1897. b, Player from early years, emblems. c, Giampiero Boniperti. d, Roberto Bettega. e, European/ South American Cup, 1996. f, Drawing in celebration of cent.

**1997, May 9** **Litho.** *Perf. 14x13½*

**1912** A295 5d Sheet of 6, #a.-f. 5.75 5.75

Queen Elizabeth II, Prince Philip, 50th Wedding Anniv. A296

No. 1913: a, Queen. b, Royal Arms. c, Queen, Prince Philip. d, Queen holding flowers, Prince saluting. e, Royal Yacht Britannia. f, Prince Philip.
20d, Queen in red hat.

**1997, May 20** *Perf. 14*

**1913** A296 4d Sheet of 6, #a.-f. 4.75 4.75

**Souvenir Sheet**

**1914** A296 20d multicolored 4.00 4.00

Paul P. Harris (1868-1947), Founder of Rotary Intl. — A297

Rotary emblem, portrait of Harris and: 10d, Tree of friendship planted by Sydney W. Pascall, Rotary Pres. 1931-32.
25d, Emblem, preserve planet earth.

**1997, May 20** **Litho.** *Perf. 14*

**1915** A297 10d multicolored 1.75 1.75

**Souvenir Sheet**

**1916** A297 25d multicolored 4.75 4.75

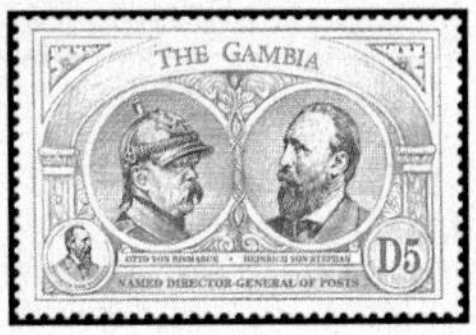


Heinrich von Stephan (1831-97), Founder of UPU A298

No. 1917 — Portrait of von Stephan and: a, Otto von Bismarck. b, UPU emblem. c, Two-horse team and wagon, Boston, 1900.
25d, Hamburg-Lübeck postilion, 1828.

**1997, May 20**

**1917** A298 5d Sheet of 3, #a.-c. 3.00 3.00

**Souvenir Sheet**

**1918** A298 25d multicolored 5.25 5.25

PACIFIC 97.

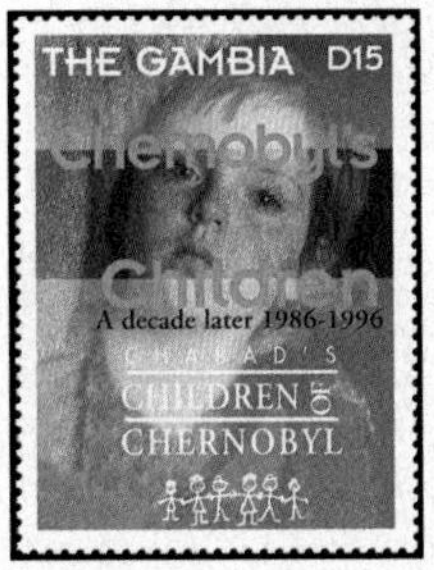


Chernobyl Disaster, 10th Anniv. A299

Designs: No. 1919, Chabad's Children of Chernobyl. No. 1920, UNESCO.

**1997, May 20** **Litho.** *Perf. 13½x14*

**1919** A299 15d multicolored 2.75 2.75
**1920** A299 15d multicolored 2.75 2.75

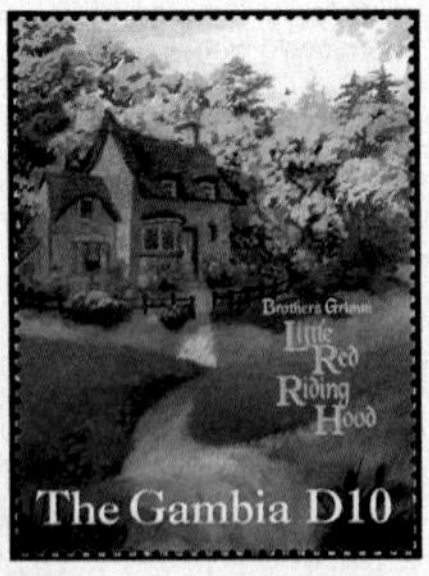


Grimm's Fairy Tales A300

Mother Goose — A301

No. 1921 — Scenes from "Little Red Riding Hood": a, Grandmother's house. b, Little Red Riding Hood. c, Wolf.
No. 1922, Little Red Riding Hood, wolf, horiz. No. 1923, Girl seated on chair from "I'll Tell You a Story."

**1997, May 20** *Perf. 13½x14*

**1921** A300 10d Sheet of 3, #a.-c. 5.50 5.50

**Souvenir Sheets**

*Perf. 14x13½*

**1922** A300 10d multicolored 4.00 4.00

*Perf. 14*

**1923** A301 25d multicolored 4.75 4.75

Paintings, by Hiroshige (1797-1858) A302

No. 1924, 4d: a, Morning Glory and Cricket. b, Dragonfly and Begonia. c, Two Ducks Swimming among Reeds. d, A Black-Naped Oriole Perched on a Stem of Rose Mallow. e, A Pheasant on a Snow-covered Pine. f, A Cuckoo Flying through the Rain.
No. 1925, 4d: a, An Egret among Rushes. b, Peacock and Peonies. c, Three Wild Geese Flying across the Moon. d, A Cock in the Snow. e, A Pheasant and Bracken. f, Peonies.
No. 1926, 4d: a, Sparrow and Bamboo. b, Mandarin Ducks on an Icy Pond with Brown Leaves Falling. c, Blossoming Plum Tree. d, Java Sparrow and Magnolia. e, Chinese Bellflowers and Miscanthus. f, A Small Black Bird Clinging to a Tendril of Ivy.
No. 1927, 5d: a, Sparrows and Camellia in Snow. b, Parrot on a Branch of Pine. c, A Long-tailed Blue Bird on a Branch of Flowering Plum. d, Sparrow and Bamboo. e, Bird in a Tree. f, A Wild Duck Swimming beneath Snow-laden Reeds.
No. 1928, 5d: a, Kingfisher above a Yellow-flowered Water Plant. b, Wagtail and Roses. c, A Mandarin Duck on a Snowy Bank. d, A Japanese White-eye on a Persimmon Branch. e, Sparrows and Camellia in Snow. f, Kingfisher and Moon above a Yellow-flowered Water Plant.
No. 1929, 5d: a, Sparrow and Bamboo. b, Birds Flying over Waves. c, Blossoming Plum Tree with Full Moon. d, Kingfisher and Iris. e, A Blue-and-white Flycatcher on a Hibiscus Flower. f, Mandarin Ducks in Snowfall.
Unidentified paintings of: No. 1930, 25d, Falcon on perch. No. 1931, 25d, Two birds seated on branch. No. 1932, 25d, Kingfisher above Iris. No. 1933, 25d, Like #1925c. No. 1934, 25d, Bird on grapevine. No. 1935, 25d, Small bird in flowering tree.

**1997, May 20** *Perf. 14*

**Sheets of 6, #a-f**

**1924-1926** A302 Set of 3 15.00 15.00
**1927-1929** A302 Set of 3 19.00 19.00

**Souvenir Sheets**

**1930-1935** A302 Set of 6 33.00 33.00

Return of Hong Kong & Macao to China — A303

No. 1936: a, Signing of joint declaration on question of Macao, 1987. b, Deng Xiaoping sharing toast with Portugal's Prime Minister Anibal Cavaco Silva after signing declaration. c, Deng Xiaoping, Britain's Prime Minister Margaret Thatcher sharing toast after signing Sino-British Declaration, 1984. d, Signing of the Sino-British Joint Declaration on question of Hong Kong, 1984.
No. 1937: a, Sir Henry Pottinger, 1st governor of Hong Kong, 1841-44, Hong Kong Island ceded to Britain, 1843. b, Sir Hercules Robinson, governor 1859-65, Kowloon ceded to Britain, 1860. c, Sir Henry Blake, governor 1898-1903, New Territories leased to Britain, 1899.

No. 1938: a, Ships in harbor, Sir Henry Pottinger. b, Suspension bridge, Chris Patten, governor of Hong Kong, 1992-1997. c, Skyline at night, C.H. Tung, first Chinese chief executive, 1997.
No. 1939: a, Signing of Treaty of Nanking, 1842. b, Signing of Japanese surrender document, 1945. c, Signing of Sino-British Joint Declaration on question of Hong Kong, 1984, diff.

**1997, July 1**

**1936** A303 3d Sheet of 4, #a.-d. 2.75 2.75
**1937** A303 4d Sheet of 3, #a.-c. 2.75 2.75
**1938** A303 5d Sheet of 3, #a.-c. 3.00 3.00
**1939** A303 6d Sheet of 3, #a.-c. 3.50 3.50

Wonders of the World — A304

Designs: 63b, Great Mosque at Samarra, Iraq, vert. (24x38mm). 75b, Moai stone faces, Easter Island. 1d, Golden Gate Bridge, San Francisco. 1.50d, Statue of Liberty, New York, vert. (24x38mm). 2d, Parthenon, Greece. 3d, Pyramid of the Sun, Teotihuacán, Mexico.
No. 1946, 5d: a, Rock of Gibraltar. b, St. Peter's Basilica, Vatican City. c, Santa Sophia, Istanbul. d, Gateway Arch, St. Louis. e, Great Wall of China. f, Carcassonne, France.
No. 1947, 5d: a, Stonehenge, England. b, Hughes HK-1 Hercules "Spruce Goose" airplane. c, Hoverspeed catamaran, Great Britain. d, Jet powered "Thrust 2." e, Djoser Step Pyramid, Egypt. f, Mallard steam locomotive.
No. 1948, 25d, Grand Canyon of the Colorado River, Arizona. No. 1949, 25d, Mt. Everest, Nepal. No. 1950, 25d, Washington Monument, Washington, DC.

**1997, July 15**

**1940-1945** A304 Set of 6 3.75 3.75

**Sheets of 6, #a-f**

**1946-1947** A304 Set of 2 12.50 12.50

**Souvenir Sheets**

**1948-1950** A304 Set of 3 15.00 15.00

1993 Winter Olympics, Nagano A305

Designs: 5d, Downhill skiing. 10d, Luge. 15d, Speed skating. 20d, Ice hockey.
No. 1955, 5d: a, Luge, diff. b, Ice hockey (goalie). c, 4-man bobsled. d, Ski jumping. e, Curling. f, Women's figure skating. g, Speed skating, diff. h, Biathlon. i, Downhill skiing, diff.
No. 1956, 5d, vert: a, 2-man bobsled. b, Free-style skiing. c, Speed skating, diff. d, Downhill skiing, diff. e, Women's figure skating, diff. f, Slalom skiing. g, Pairs figure skating. h, Cross-country skiing. i, Ski jumping, diff.
No. 1957, 25d, Female figure skater, vert. No. 1958, 25d, 2-man bobsled, diff.

**1997, July 21** **Litho.** *Perf. 14*

**1951-1954** A305 Set of 4 10.00 10.00

**Sheets of 9, #a-i**

**1955-1956** A305 Set of 2 19.00 19.00

**Souvenir Sheets**

**1957-1958** A305 Set of 2 11.00 11.00

Cats A306

Designs: 63b, Scottish fold. 1.50d, American curl. 2d, British bi-color. 3d, Devon rex. 6d, Silver tabby 20d, Abyssinian.
No. 1965: a, Burmilla. b, Blue Burmese. c, Korat. d, British tabby. e, Foreign white. f, Somali.
No. 1966, 25d, Cornish rex. No. 1967, 25d, Siamese.

**1997, Aug. 12**

**1959-1964** A306 Set of 6 8.25 8.25
**1965** A306 5d Sheet of 6, #a.-f. 7.50 7.50

**Souvenir Sheets**

**1966-1967** A306 Set of 2 11.50 11.50

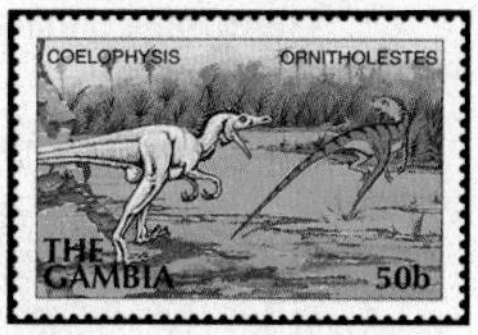


Dinosaurs A307

Designs: 50b, Coelophysis, ornitholestes. 63b, Spinosaurus. 75b, Kentrosaurus. 1d, Ceratosaurus. 1.50d, Stygimoloch. 2d, Troodon. 3d, Velociraptor. 4d, Triceratops. 5d, Protoceratops. 10d, Ornithomimus. 15d, Stegosaurus. 20d, Ankylosaurus saichania.

No. 1980, 4d: a, Anurognathus. b, Pteranodon. c, Pterosaurus. d, Saltasaurus. e, Agathaumus. f, Stegosaurus. g, Albertosaurus libratus. h, 4 Lesothosaurus. i, 7 Lesothosaurus.

No. 1981, 4d: a, Tarbosaurus bataar. b, Brachiosaurus. c, Styracosasaurus. d, Baryonyx. e, Coelophysis. f, Carnotaurus. g, Compsognathus longipes. h, Compsognathus-elegant jaw. i, Stenonychosaurus.

No. 1982, 25d, Deinonychus. No. 1983, 25d, Seismosaurus.

**1997, June 23 Litho. *Perf. 14***

**1968-1979** A307 Set of 12 17.50 17.50

**Sheets of 9, #a-i**

**1980-1981** A307 Set of 2 13.50 13.50

**Souvenir Sheets**

**1982-1983** A307 Set of 2 13.00 13.00

No. 1982 contains one 50x38mm stamp. No. 1983 contains one 89x28mm stamp.

Dogs A308

Designs: 75b, Dalmatian. 1d, Rottweiler. 3d, Newfoundland. 4d, Great Dane. 10d, Old English sheepdog. 15d, Queensland heeler.

No. 1990: a, Akita. b, Welsh corgi. c, German shepherd. d, St. Bernard. e, Bullmastiff. f, Malamute.

No. 1991, 25d, Doberman pinscher. No. 1992, 25d, Boxer.

**1997, Aug. 12**

**1984-1989** A308 Set of 6 8.25 8.25
**1990** A308 5d Sheet of 6, #a.-f. 7.50 7.50

**Souvenir Sheets**

**1991-1992** A308 Set of 2 11.50 11.50

1998 World Cup Soccer Championships, France — A309

Winning teams: 1d, Uruguay, 1950. 1.50d, W. Germany, 1954. 2d, Brazil, 1970. 3d, Brazil, 1962. 5d, Italy, 1938. 10d, Uruguay, 1930.

No. 1999, 4d: a, Brazil, 1994. b, Argentina, 1986. c, Brazil, 1970. d, Italy, 1934. e, Uruguay, 1958. f, England, 1966. g, Brazil, 1962. h, W. Germany, 1990.

No. 2000, 4d: a, Mario Kempes, Argentina, 1978. b, Ademir, Brazil, 1950. c. Muller, W. Germany, 1970. d, Lineker, England, 1986. e, Eusebio, Portugal, 1966. f, Schillaci, Italy, 1990. g, Lata, Poland, 1974. h, Rossi, Italy, 1982.

No. 2001, 4d, vert: a, Kinkladze, Georgia. b, Shearer, England. c, Dani, Portugal. d, Weah, Liberia. e, Ravanelli, Italy. f, Raducioiu, Romania. g, Peter Schmeichel, Denmark. h, Bergkamp, Holland.

No. 2002, 4d, vert: a, Moore, England, 1966. b, Fritzwalter, W. Germany, 1954. c, Beckenbauer, W. Germany, 1974. d, Zoff, Italy, 1982. e, Maradona, Argentina, 1986. f, Passarella, Argentina, 1978. g, Matthäus, W. Germany, 1990. h, Dunga, Brazil, 1994.

No. 2003, 25d, Pele, Brazil. No. 2004, 25d, Eusebio, Portugal. No. 2005, 25d, Juninho, Brazil. No. 2006, 25d, Philippe Albert, Belgium.

**1997, Sept. 4 *Perf. 14x13½, 13½x14***

**1993-1998** A309 Set of 6 4.00 4.00

**Sheets of 8, #a-h, + Label**

**1999-2002** A309 Set of 4 27.50 27.50

**Souvenir Sheets**

**2003-2006** A309 Set of 4 22.50 22.50

Sea Birds A310

Designs: 5d, Red-legged cormorant. 10d, Roseate tern. 15d, Blue-footed booby. 20d, Sanderling.

No. 2011: a, Brown pelican. b, Galapagos penguin. c, Red billed tropic bird. d, Little tern. e, Dunlin. f, Kittiwake. g, Atlantic puffin. h, Wandering albatross. i, Masked booby. j, Glaucous winged gull. k, Artic tern. l, Piping plover.

No. 2012, 23d, Osprey. No. 2013, 23d, Long-tailed skua.

**1997, Aug. 4 Litho. *Perf. 14***

**2007-2010** A310 Set of 4 10.00 10.00
**2011** A310 3d Sheet of 12, #a.-l. 9.00 9.00

**Souvenir Sheets**

**2012-2013** A310 Set of 2 9.00 9.00

A311

Diana, Princess of Wales (1961-97) — A312

Various portraits.

**1997, Nov. 26 Litho. *Perf. 14***

**2014** A311 10d Sheet of 4, #a.-d. 8.00 8.00

**Souvenir Sheet**

**2015** A312 25d multicolored 5.25 5.25

Christmas A313

Entire paintings or details: 1d, Angel, by Rembrandt. 1.50d, Initiation into the Rites of Dionysus, in Villa dei Misteri, Pompeii. 2d, Pair of Erotes with Purple Cloaks. 3d, The Ecstasy of Saint Teresa, by Gianlorenzo Bernini (carving). 5d, Annunciation, by Mathias Grunewald. 10d, Angel Playing the Organ, by Stefan Lochner.

No. 2022, 25d, The Rest on the Flight into Egypt, by Caravaggio. No. 2023, 25d, Education of Cupid, by Titian.

**1997, Dec. 8**

**2016-2021** A313 Set of 6 7.75 7.75

**Souvenir Sheets**

**2022-2023** A313 Set of 2 9.50 9.50

New Year 1998 (Year of the Tiger) — A314

No. 2024 — Various stylized tigers with: a, Yellow brown background. b, Purple background. c, Brown background. d, Orange background.

10d, Tiger, landscape.

**1998, Jan. 5 Litho. *Perf. 14½***

**2024** A314 3d Sheet of 4, #a.-d. 2.75 2.75

**Souvenir Sheet**

***Perf. 14***

**2025** A314 10d multicolored 2.75 2.75

No. 2025 contains one 38x24mm stamp.

Trains A315

No. 2026, 5d: a, Electric Train, Scotland. b, Beaconsfield, China. c, TGV, France. d, People Mover, England. e, ICE train, Germany. f, Montmartre Funicular, France.

No. 2027, 5d: a, SD70 Burlington Northern, US. b, Mallard, England. c, Baldwin 4-8-0, Peru. d, Sweden Rail. e, Rack Train, Amberawa-Java. f, Beyer-Peacock, Pakistan.

No. 2028, 25d, Monorail, England. No. 2029, 25d, Southern Pacific, US.

**1998, May 19 Litho. *Perf. 14***

**Sheets of 6, #a-f**

**2026-2027** A315 Set of 2 13.00 13.00

**Souvenir Sheets**

**2028-2029** A315 Set of 2 9.50 9.50

Flowers A316

Designs, vert: 75b, Daffodil. 1.50d, Transvaal daisy. 3d, Torchlily. 4d, Ancistrochilus rothschildianus. 10d, Polystachya vulcanica. 15d, Gladiolus.

No. 2036: a, Adenium multiflorum. b, Huernia namaquensis. c, Gloriosa superba. d, Strelitzia reginae. e, Passiflora mollissima. f, Bauhinia variegata.

No. 2037, 25d, Aerangis rhodosticta, vert. No. 2038, 25d, Ansella gigantea, vert.

**1998, June 2 Litho. *Perf. 14***

**2030-2035** A316 Set of 6 8.00 8.00
**2036** A316 5d Sheet of 6, #a.-f. 7.00 7.00

**Souvenir Sheets**

**2037-2038** A316 Set of 2 11.00 11.00

Historical Aircraft A317

No. 2039, 5d: a, Short Type 38, 1913. b, Fokker F.VII B 3m, 1925. c, Junkers F-13, 1919. d, Pitcairn "Mailwing," 1927. e, Douglas, 1920. f, Curtiss "Condor," 1934.

No. 2040, 5d: a, Wright Brothers, 1903. b, Curtiss, 1910. c, Farman, 1907. d, Bristol, 1911. e, Antoinette, 1908. f, Sopwith "Bat Boat," 1912.

No. 2041, 25d, Albatross, 1913. No. 2042, 25d, Boeing 247, 1932.

**1998, June 10 Sheets of 6, #a-f**

**2039-2040** A317 Set of 2 14.00 14.00

**Souvenir Sheets**

**2041-2042** A317 Set of 2 11.00 11.00

Nos. 2041-2042 each contain one 85x28mm stamp.

Disney's "Mulan" A318

Characters from the animated movie — No. 2043: a, Mulan. b, Mushu. c, Little Brother. d, Cri-Kee. e, Grandmother Fa. f, Fa Li. g, Fa Zhou. h, Mulan and Khan.

No. 2044: a, Mulan riding Khan. b, Shang. c, Chi Fu. d, Chien-Po. e, Yao. f, Ling. g, Shan-Yu. h, Mulan, Shang & Mushu.

No. 2045, 25d, Mulan. No. 2046, 25d, Mulan riding Khan, diff. No. 2047, 25d, Mulan jumping in air. No. 2048, 25d, Mulan looking at Shang (in margin).

**1998, July 1 Litho. *Perf. 13½x14***

**2043** A318 4d Sheet of 8, #a.-h. 10.00 10.00
**2044** A318 5d Sheet of 8, #a.-h. 10.50 10.50

**Souvenir Sheets**

**2045-2048** A318 Set of 4 27.50 27.50

Ferrari Automobiles — A318a

No. 2048A: c, 365 GTB/4. d, Daytona. e, 1966 275 GTB.

25d, 365 GTB/4, diff.

**1998, Oct. 29 Litho. *Perf. 14***

**2048A** A318a 10d Sheet of 3, #c-e 5.25 5.25

**Souvenir Sheet**

***Perf. 13¾x14¼***

**2048B** A318a 25d multi 4.50 4.50

No. 2048A contains three 39x25mm stamps.

Famous People — A319

Sinking of the Titanic — A320

No. 2049, 4d — Jazz musicians: a, Sidney Bechet (1897-1959). b, Bechet playing clarinet. c, "Duke" Ellington conducting band. d, Ellington (1899-1974). e, Louis Armstrong (1900-71). f, Armstrong playing trumpet. g, Charlie "Bird" Parker playing saxophone. h, Parker (1920-55).

No. 2050, 4d — 2:49 PM 12/6/2007 Composers: a, Cole Porter (1893-1964). b, "Born to Dance," by Porter. c, "Porgy and Bess," by George Gershwin. d, Gershwin (1898-1937). e, Richard Rodgers (1902-79) & Oscar Hammerstein II (1895-1960). f, "The King and I," by Rodgers & Hammerstein. g, "West Side Story," by Leonard Bernstein. h, Bernstein (1918-90).

No. 2051, 25d, Ella Fitzgerald (1917-96). No. 2052, 25d, Irving Berlin (1888-1989), "Oh How I Hate to Get Up in the Morning."

**1998, Oct. 12 Litho. *Perf. 14***

**Sheets of 8, #a-h**

**2049-2050** A319 Set of 2 14.00 14.00

**Souvenir Sheets**

**2051-2052** A319 Set of 2 13.00 13.00

Nos. 2049b-2049c, 2049f-2049g, 2050b-2050c, 2050f-2050g are 53x38mm.

**1998, Oct. 25**

No. 2053: a, Capt. Edward J. Smith. b, Molly Brown. c, News of the disaster breaks. d, Benjamin Guggenheim. e, Isidor Strauss. f, Ida Strauss.

No. 2054, 25d, Picture of ship on postcard. No. 2055, 25d, Ship sinking. No. 2056, 25d, Remains of ship lying on bottom of ocean years later.

**2053** A320 5d Sheet of 6, #a.-f. 7.75 7.75

**Souvenir Sheets**

**2054-2056** A320 Set of 3 18.00 18.00

Diana, Princess of Wales (1961-97) A321

**1998, Oct. 29 *Perf. 14½x14***

**2057** A321 10d multicolored 1.75 1.75

Issued in sheets of 6.

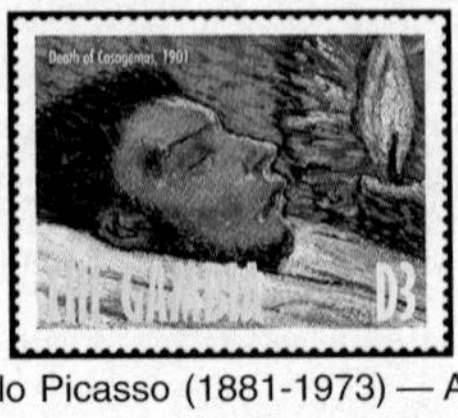


Pablo Picasso (1881-1973) — A322

Paintings: 3d, Death of Casagemas, 1901. 5d, Seated Woman, 1920, vert. 10d, Mother and Child, 1907, vert.

25d, Child Playing with a Toy Truck, 1953, vert.

**1998, Oct. 29 *Perf. 14½***

**2058-2060** A322 Set of 3 3.25 3.25

**Souvenir Sheet**

**2061** A322 25d multicolored 4.50 4.50

A323

A324

No. 2062 — Mahatma Gandhi (1869-1948) : a, Age 62, 1932. b, Age 60, 1930, with Sarojini Naidu. c, Age 61, 1931, spinning yarn. d, Age 47, 1916.

25d, Age 61, 1931.

**1998, Oct. 29 *Perf. 14***

**2062** A323 10d Sheet of 4, #a.-d. 7.50 7.50

**Souvenir Sheet**

**2063** A323 25d multicolored 5.00 5.00

Nos. 2062b-2062c are 53x39mm.

**1998**

Ships: 2d, Chinese Junk. 3d, HMS Victory. 10d, County Class Destroyer. 15d, Viking Longboat.

No. 2068, 5d, horiz: a, HMS Dreadnought. b, Truxton Class Cruiser. c, Queen Mary. d, Canberra. e, Queen Elizabeth. f, Queen Elizabeth 2.

No. 2069, 5d: a, Santa Maria. b, Mary Rose. c, Mayflower. d, Ark Royal. e, HMS Beagle. f, HMS Bounty.

No. 2070, 25d, Cutty Sark. No. 2071, 25d, Sovereign of the Seas.

**2064-2067** A324 Set of 4 5.50 5.50

**Sheets of 6, #a-f**

**2068-2069** A324 Set of 2 11.00 11.00

**Souvenir Sheets**

**2070-2071** A324 Set of 2 9.00 9.00

No. 2070 contains one 42x56mm stamp; No. 2071, one 56x42mm stamp.

1998 World Scouting Jamboree, Chile — A325

No. 2072: a, Scout handclasp. b, Small boat sailing. c, Scout salute.

No. 2073, Lord Robert Baden-Powell.

**1998, Oct. 29 Litho. *Perf. 14***

**2072** A325 10d Sheet of 3, #a.-c. 5.50 5.50

**Souvenir Sheet**

**2073** A325 25d multicolored 4.50 4.50

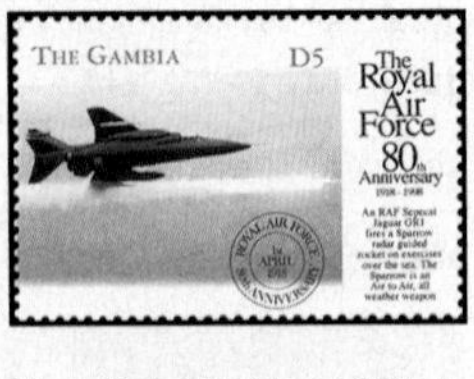


Royal Air Force, 80th Anniv. A326

No. 2074, 5d: a, Sepecat Jaguar GR1. b, BAe Harrier GR7. c, Panavia Tornado GR1 firing Sidewinder AIM 9-L missle. d, Panavia Tornado GR1 on afterburner.

No. 2075, 5d: a, Sepecat Jaguar GR1A in low visibility gray finish. b, Panavia Tornado GR1A. c, Sepecat Jaguar GR1A in Bosnia theater camouflage finish. d, BAe Hawk 200.

No. 2076, 7d: a, Panavia Tornado GR1 flying left. b, BAe Hawk TIA. c, Sepecat Jaguar GR1A. d, Panavia Tornado GR1 flying right.

No. 2077, 20d, Eurofighters. No. 2078, 25d, Biplane, hawk's head. No. 2079, 25d, Lightning, Eurofighter. No. 2080, 25d, Biplane, hawk in flight. No. 2081, 25d, Lancaster, Eurofighter. No. 2082, 25d, Biplane, hawk perched.

**1998, Oct. 29 Sheets of 4, #a-d**

**2074-2076** A326 Set of 3 12.50 12.50

**Souvenir Sheets**

**2077-2082** A326 Set of 6 27.50 27.50

Paintings by Eugène Delacroix (1798-1863) — A327

No. 2083, 4d: a, Mule Drivers from Tetuan. b, Encampment of Arab Mule Drivers. c, An Orange Seller. d, The Banks of the River. e, View of Tangier from the Seashore. f, Arab Horses Fighting in a Stable. g, Horses at the Trough. h, The Combat of the Giaour and Hassan.

No. 2084, 4d, vert: a, Moroccan from Tangier Standing. b, A Man of Tangier. c, Young Arab Standing with a Rifle. d, Moroccan Chieftan. e, Jewish Bride of Tangiers. f, Seated Jewess from Morocco. g, A seated Arab. h, Young Arab Seated by a Wall.

No. 2085, 4d: a, Turk Seated on a Sofa Smoking. b, View of Tangier from North African and Spanish Album. c, The Spanish Coast at Salobrena from North African and Spanish Album. d, The Aissaouas. e, Sea View from the Heights of Dieppe. f, An Arab Fantasy. g, Arab Comic Fantasy. h, An Arab Camp at Night.

Details: No. 2086, 25d, Self-portrait, vert. No. 2087, 25d, Two Women of Algiers in Their Apartment. No. 2088, 25d, Massacre of Chios.

**1998, Oct. 29 Sheets of 8, #a-h**

**2083-2085** A327 Set of 3 18.50 18.50

**Souvenir Sheets**

**2086-2088** A327 Set of 3 14.00 14.00

Christmas — A328

Designs: 1d, Beagle in sock. 2d, Giraffe, wreath. 3d, Rainbow bee eater, ribbon, ornament. 4d, Adult deer. 5d, Fawn. 10d, Irish red and white setter in package.

No. 2095, 25d, Brown classic tabby kitten. No. 2096, 25d, Basset hound, rough collie.

**1998, Nov. 23**

**2089-2094** A328 Set of 6 5.00 5.00

**Souvenir Sheets**

**2095-2096** A328 Set of 2 10.00 10.00

New Year 1999 (Year of the Rabbit) — A329

No. 2097 — Stylized rabbits, background color: a, Olive brown. b, Green blue. c, Red brown. d, Pale orange.

**1999, Jan. 4 Litho. *Perf. 14½***

**2097** A329 3d Sheet of 4, #a.-d. 2.40 2.40

**Souvenir Sheet**

**2098** A329 10d multicolored 2.00 2.00

No. 2098 contains one 39x24mm stamp.

Disney's Jungle Book A330

No. 2099: a, Mowgli, King Louie (bear). b, Mowgli, snake, c, Flunky Monkey. d, Monkey singing. e, Girl. f, Mowgli, Flunky Monkey. g, Mowgli, buzzards. h, Shere Khan (tiger).

No. 2100, 25d, Baby elephant, horiz. No. 2101, 25d, King Louie, horiz.

**1999, Mar. 11 Litho. *Perf. 13½x14***

**2099** A330 5d Sheet of 8, #a.-h. 10.00 10.00

**Souvenir Sheets**

**2100-2101** A330 Set of 2 10.00 10.00

Australia '99, World Stamp Expo A331

No. 2102, 6d — African butterflies: a, Golden piper. b, Citrus swallowtail. c, Azure hairstreak. d, Two-tailed pasha. e, Blue pansy. f, African leaf butterfly.

No. 2103, 6d: a, Plain tiger. b, Blue swallowtail. c, Papilio mnesheus. d, Common opal. e, Forest green. f, Boisduval's false acraea.

No. 2104, 25d, Pirate butterfly, vert. No. 2105, 25d, Two-tailed pasha, vert.

**1999, Apr. 12 Litho. *Perf. 14***

**Sheets of 6, #a-f**

**2102-2103** A331 Set of 2 12.00 12.00

**Souvenir Sheets**

**2104-2105** A331 Set of 2 9.00 9.00

Wedding of Prince Edward and Sophie Rhys-Jones A332

No. 2106 — Various portraits of couple showing Sophie with: a, Blue collar. b, Long hair. c, Red collar.

25d, Couple, horiz.

**1999, June 19 Litho. *Perf. 13½***

**2106** A332 10d Sheet of 3, #a.-c. 5.00 5.00

**Souvenir Sheet**

**2107** A332 25d multicolored 4.50 4.50

IBRA '99, World Philatelic Exhibition, Nuremberg — A333

Exhibition emblem, Adler 2-3-2 steam engine and: 4d, Samoa #104d. 5d, Samoa #55.

Emblem, sailing ship Friedrech August and: 10d, Samoa #64, #65. 15d, Samoa #67.

25d, Cover with Samoa #67 (part), 68.

**1999, July 6 *Perf. 14x14¼***

**2108-2111** A333 Set of 4 6.25 6.25

**Souvenir Sheet**

**2112** A333 25d multicolored 4.50 4.50

No. 2112 contains one 60x40mm stamp.

Apollo 11 Moon Landing, 30th Anniv. — A334

No. 2113: a, Bell X-14A VTOL aircraft. b, Lunar landing practice rig. c, Early prototype lander. d, Zero gravity training. e, Jet pack training. f, Lunar lander pilot training.

No. 2114, 25d, Apollo 11 Eagle, horiz. No. 2115, 25d, Apollo 11 splash down, horiz.

**1999, July 6** ***Perf. 14***

**2113** A334 6d Sheet of 6, #a.-f. 6.50 6.50

**Souvenir Sheets**

**2114-2115** A334 Set of 2 10.00 10.00

Souvenir Sheets

PhilexFrance '99, World Philatelic Exhibition — A335

Early railroads: No. 2116, 25d, Road-railer carriage. No. 2117, 25d, 2-2-2 Passenger locomotive, 1846.

**1999, July 6** ***Perf. 13¾***

**2116-2117** A335 Set of 2 9.00 9.00

Roots Homecoming Festival — A336

Designs: 1d, Cannon, Freedom Post, Juffureh. 2d, Fort Bullen, Barra. 3d, James Fort Island.

**1999, June 21** **Litho.** ***Perf. 14***

**2118-2120** A336 Set of 3 1.00 1.00

UN Rights of the Child, 10th Anniv. — A337

No. 2121 — Children: a, With head down on table. b, Drinking from cup. c, Drawing on paper.

25d, Child smiling under umbrella.

**1999, July 6**

**2121** A337 10d Sheet of 3, #a.-c. 5.25 5.25

**Souvenir Sheet**

**2122** A337 25d multicolored 4.50 4.50

Johann Wolfgang von Goethe (1749-1832), Poet — A338

No. 2123: a, Faust quaffs the spirit's nectar. b, Portraits of Goethe and Friedrich von Schiller (1759-1805). c, Faust contemplates mortality.

25d, Portrait of Goethe, vert.

**1999, July 6**

**2123** A338 15d Sheet of 3, #a.-c. 8.00 8.00

**Souvenir Sheet**

**2124** A338 25d multicolored 4.50 4.50

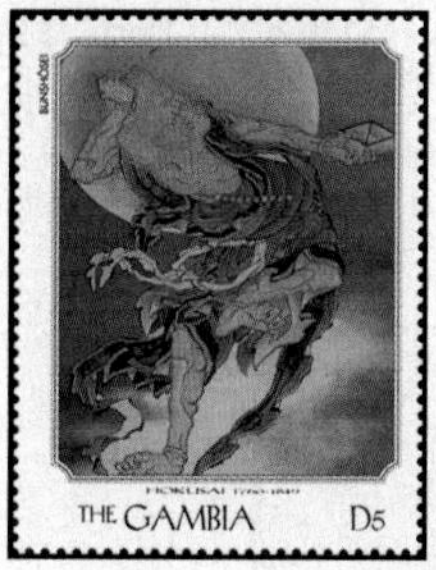


Paintings by Hokusai (1760-1849) A339

No. 2125, 5d — Details or entire paintings: a, Bunshosei. b, Overthrower of Castles, Overthrower of Nations. c, Bee on Wild Rose. d, Sei Shonagon. e, Kuan-Yu. f, The Fifth Month.

No. 2126, 5d: a, Exotic Beauty. b, Wind (2 people). c, Dancing Monkey. d, Lady and Maiden on an Outing. e, Wind (3 people). f, Courtesan with Fan.

No. 2127, 25d, People on the Balcony of Sazaido. No. 2128, 25d, Caocao before the Battle of Chibi.

**1999, July 6** ***Perf. 13¾***

**Sheets of 6, #a-f**

**2125-2126** A339 Set of 2 11.00 11.00

**Souvenir Sheets**

**2127-2128** A339 Set of 2 9.00 9.00

Sea Birds A340

Designs: 2d, American oystercatcher. 3d, Blue-footed booby. 10d, Western gull. 15d, Brown pelican.

No. 2133, 4d: a, Atlantic puffin. b, Red-tailed tropicbird. c, Reddish egret. d, Laughing gull. e, Great white egret. f, Northern gannet. g, Forster's tern. h, Great cormorant. i, Razor bill.

No. 2134, 4d: a, Adélie penguin. b, Black skimmer. c, Erect-crested penguin. d, Heerman's gull. e, Glaucous-winged gull. f, Layson albatross. g, White pelican. h, Tufted puffin. i, Black guillemot.

No. 2135: a, Razor bill. b, Shelduck. c, Sandwich tern. d, Arctic skua. e, Gannet. f, Common gull.

No. 2136, 25d, Pelicans. No. 2137, 25d, California gull. No. 2138, 25d, Gentoo penguin.

**1999, Aug. 1** ***Perf. 14***

**2129-2132** A340 Set of 4 5.50 5.50

**Sheets of 9, #a-i**

**2133-2134** A340 Set of 2 14.50 14.50

**2135** A340 5d Sheet of 6, #a.-f. 9.75 9.75

**Souvenir Sheets**

**2136-2138** A340 Set of 3 15.00 15.00

Nos. 2135-2138 have continuous designs.

Prehistoric Amimals — A341

No. 2139, 3d: a, Diatryma. b, Pteranodon. c, Stegodon. d, Icaronycteris. e, Archaeopteryx. f, Chasmatosaurus. g, Tytthostonyx. h, Hyaenodon. i, Uintatherium. j, Hesperocyon. k, Ambelodon. l, Indricotherium.

No. 2140, 3d: a, Carnotaurus. b, Quetzalcoatlus. c, Peteinosaurus. d, Prenocephale. e, Hesperornis. f, Coelophysis. g, Camptosaurus. h, Panderichthys. i, Garudimimus. j, Cacops. k, Ichthyostega. l, Scutellosaurus.

No. 2141, 25d, Lepisosteus. No. 2142, 25d, Sabertooth cat. No. 2143, 25d, Deinonychus. No. 2144, 25d, Microceratops.

**1999, Aug. 1** **Sheets of 12, #a-l**

**2139-2140** A341 Set of 2 12.00 12.00

**Souvenir Sheets**

**2141-2144** A341 Set of 4 19.00 19.00

Queen Mother, 100th Birthday (in 2000) — A342

No. 2145: a, Duchess of York, Princess Elizabeth, 1928. b, Lady Elizabeth Bowles-Lyon, 1923. c, Queen Elizabeth, 1946. d, Queen Mother, Prince Harry.

25d, Queen Mother celebrating 89th birthday, 1989.

**1999, Aug. 4**

**2145** A342 10d Sheet of 4, #a.-d. + label 7.00 7.00

**Souvenir Sheet**

***Perf. 13¾***

**2146** A342 25d multicolored 5.00 5.00

No. 2146 contains one 38x51mm stamp. Margins of sheets are embossed.

See Nos. 2555-2556.

Orchids — A343

Designs: 2d, Sophrocattleya. 3d, Cattleya. 4d, Brassolaeliocattleya. 5d, Brassoepidendrum. 10d, Sophrolaeliocattleya. 15d, Iwanagaara.

No. 2153, 6d: a, Brassolaeliocattleya (yellow). b, Cattleytonia. c, Laeliocattleya (yellow). d, Miltonia. e, Cattleya forbesii. f, Odontoglossum cervantesii.

No. 2154, 6d: a, Lycaste macrobulbon. b, Laeliocattleya (red). c, Brassocattleya (pink). d, Cattleya, diff. e, Brassocattleya (speckled). f, Brassolaeliocattleya (yellow & red).

No. 2155, 25d, Unnamed. No. 2156, 25d, Brassolaeliocattleya (white & red).

**1999, Aug. 1** **Litho.** ***Perf. 14***

**2147-2152** A343 Set of 6 7.25 7.25

**Sheets of 6, #a-f**

**2153-2154** A343 Set of 2 14.00 14.00

**Souvenir Sheets**

**2155-2156** A343 Set of 2 10.00 10.00

Marine Fauna A344

Designs: 1d, Sea gull. 1.50d, Portuguese man-of-war. 5d, Walrus. 10d, Manatee.

No. 2161, 3d: a, Anglefish. b, Leafy sea dragon. c, Hawksbill turtle. d, Mandarin fish. e, Candy cane sea star. f, Plate coral. g. Butterflyfish. h, Coral polyp. i, Hermit crab. j, Strawberry shrimp. k, Giant blue clam. l, Sea cucumber.

No. 2162, 3d: a, Whale shark. b, Gray reef shark. c, New ZEngland octopus. d, Puffer fish. e, Lionfish. f, Squid. g, Chambered nautilus. h, Clown fish. i, Moray eel. j, Spiny lobster. k, Sotted ray. l, Clown anemone.

25d, Common dolphin.

**1999, Aug. 1**

**2157-2160** A344 Set of 4 3.50 3.50

**Sheets of 12, #a-l**

**2161-2162** A344 Set of 2 13.00 13.00

**2163** A343 25d multicolored 5.00 5.00

Galapagos Islands Marine Fauna — A345

No. 2164: a, Swallow-tailed gull. b, Frigate bird. c, Red-footed booby. d, Galapagos hawk. e, Great blue heron. f, Masked booby. g, Bottlenose dolphins. h, Black grunts. i, Surgeonfish. j, Stingray. k, Pilot whales. l, Pacific green sea turtle. m, Shark. n, Sea lion. o, Marine iguana. p, Pacific manta ray. q, Moorish idol. r, Galapagos penguin. s, Silver grunts. t, Sea urchin. u, Wrasse. v, Almaco amberjack. w, Blue-chin parrotfish. x, Yellow sea urchin. y, Lobster. z, Grouper. aa, Scorpionfish. ab, Squirrelfish. ac, Octopus. ad, King angelfish. ae, Horned shark. af, Galapagos hogfish. ag, Puffer fish. ah, Moray eel. ai, Orange tube corals. aj, Whitestripe chromis. ak, Longnose hawkfish. al, Sea cucumber, am, Spotted hawkfish. an, Zebra moray eel.

25d, Emperor penguins.

**1999, Aug. 1**

**2164** A345 1.50d Sheet of 40, #a.-an. 14.00 14.00

**Souvenir Sheet**

**2165** A345 25d multicolored 5.00 5.00

Souvenir Sheet

1999 Return of Macao to People's Republic of China — A346

No. 2166: a, Temple of A-ma. b, Border gate. c, Ruins of St. Paul's Cathedral.

**1999, Aug. 20** **Litho.** ***Perf. 14***

**2166** A346 7d Sheet of 3, #a-c 4.00 4.00

Space Exploration A347

Designs: 1d, Telstar I, horiz. 1.50d, Skylab. 2d, Mars 3 orbiter and lander. 3d, COBE. 10d, Astronaut Bruce McCandless. 15d, Apollo 13.

No. 2173, 6d: a, German V-2 rocket. b, Delta Straight 8. c, Ariane 4. d, Mercury on Atlas rocket. e, Saturn 1B. f, Cassini.

No. 2174, 6d, horiz.: a, Mariner 4. b, Viking Mars orbiter and lander. c, Giotto. d, Luna 9. e, Voyager. f, Galileo.

No. 2175, 6d, horiz.: a, Soviet Vostok 1. b, Apollo command and service modules. c, Mecury capsule. d, Apollo 16 lunar module. e, Gemini 8. f, Soviet Soyuz.

No. 2176, 25d, Apollo-Soyuz, horiz. No. 2177, 25d, Mars Pathfinder, horiz.

**1999**

**2167-2172** A347 Set of 6 6.00 6.00

**Sheets of 6, #a-f**

**2173-2175** A347 Set of 3 18.50 18.50

**2176-2177** A347 Set of 2 9.50 9.50

Nos. 2176-2177 each contain one 57x43mm stamp.

John F. Kennedy, Jr. (1960-99) A348

No. 2178: a, In 1961. b, In 1970s. c, In 1997.

**1999, Dec. 7**

**2178** A348 15d Sheet of 3, #a.-c. 7.25 7.25

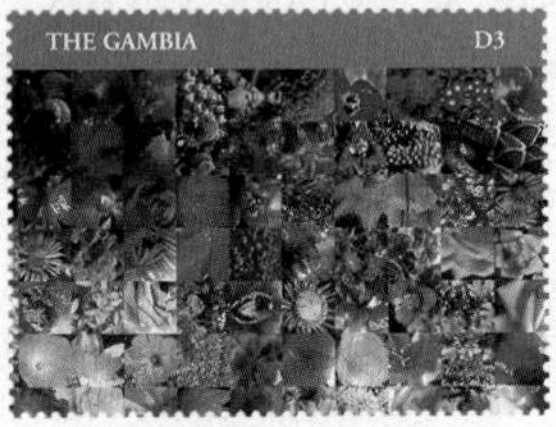


Flowers — A349

Various flower photographs making up a photomosaic of Princess Diana.

**1999, Dec. 31 Litho. *Perf. 13¾***

**2179** A349 3d Sheet of 8, #a.-h. 5.00 5.00

See No. 2290.

Millennium A350

No. 2180, 3d — Highlights of 1450-1500: a, Da Vinci designs 1st flying machine. b, Gutenberg prints the Bible. c, 1st book in color printed. d, Ivan III becomes Grand Prince of Moscow. e, Ottomans capture Constantinople. f, Ming emperors rebuild Great Wall of China. g, Lorenzo de Medici begins rule in Florence. h, Henry VII becomes first Tudor king of England. i, Vasco da Gama sails to India. j, Aragon and Castile unite. k, Birth of Desiderius Erasmus. l, Cabot explores No. America. m, Henry VI wages War of the Roses. n, Bartholomeu Dias discovers Cape of Good Hope. o, Matthias Corvinus (Hunyadi) becomes king of Hungary. p, Columbus sails to America (60x40mm). q, Girolamo Savonarola burned at stake.

No. 2181, 3d — Highlights of 1900-1910: a, Max Planck develops quantum theory. b, Graf Ferdinand von Zeppelin constructs first airship. c, Marconi sends 1st transatlantic message. d, Queen Victoria dies. e, 1st Nobel Prize. f, Boer War ends. g, Wright Brothers' 1st flight. h, 1st teddy bears made in Germany. i, Work begins on Panama Canal. j, Einstein develops theory of relativity. k, 1905 revolution in Russia. l, San Francisco earthquake. m, Color photography developed by Louis Lumière. n, Picasso paints "Les Demoiselles d'Avignon." o, Peary reaches North Pole. p, Model T appears (60x40mm). q, 1st kibbutz founded in Holy Land.

**2000, Feb. 1 *Perf. 12¾x12½***

**Sheets of 17, #a-q**

**2180-2181** A350 Set of 2 21.00 21.00

Inscriptions are misspelled on several stamps on No. 2181.

New Year 2000 (Year of the Dragon) A351

No. 2182 — Various dragons and Chinese characters with background colors: a, Blue green. b, Brownish gray. c, Red orange (purple dragon). d, Orange.

15d, Dull orange.

**2000, Feb. 5 *Perf. 14x14½***

**2182** A351 5d Sheet of 4, #a.-d. 4.25 4.25

**Souvenir Sheet**

***Perf. 14***

**2183** A351 15d multi 3.00 3.00

No. 2183 contains one 42x28mm stamp.

African Wildlife A352

Designs: 50b, Indri. 75b, Nubian ibex. 1d, Grevy's zebra, vert. 2d, Bongo, vert. 3d, White rhinoceros. 4d, Lesser galago. 5d, Okapi, vert. 10d, Mhorr gazelle, vert.

No. 2192, 5d: a, Giant sable antelope. b, Greater kudu. c, Somali wild ass. d, Dorcas gazelle. e, Addax. f, Pelzeln's gazelle.

No. 2193, 6d: a, Cheetah. b, Chimpanzee. c, Angwantibo. d, Black rhinoceros. e, Bontebok. f, Giant eland.

No. 2194, 7d: a, Mountain gorilla. b, Black-faced impala. c, Crowned lemur. d, Long-tailed ground roller. e, Brown hyena. f, Mountain zebra.

No. 2195, 7d: a, Sacred ibis. b, Mauritius kestrel. c, Barbary leopard. d, Radiated tortoise. e, Pygmy hippopotamus. f, Bald ibis.

No. 2196, 25d, Aye-aye. No. 2197, 25d, Black lechwe, vert. No. 2198, 25d, Nile crocodile. No. 2199, 25d, African elephant.

**2000, Feb. 18 *Perf. 14***

**2184-2191** A352 4.50 4.50

**Sheets of 6, #a.-f.**

**2192-2195** A352 Set of 4 29.00 29.00

**Souvenir Sheets**

**2196-2199** A352 Set of 4 23.00 23.00

AmeriStamp Expo, Portland, Ore. (No. 2194).

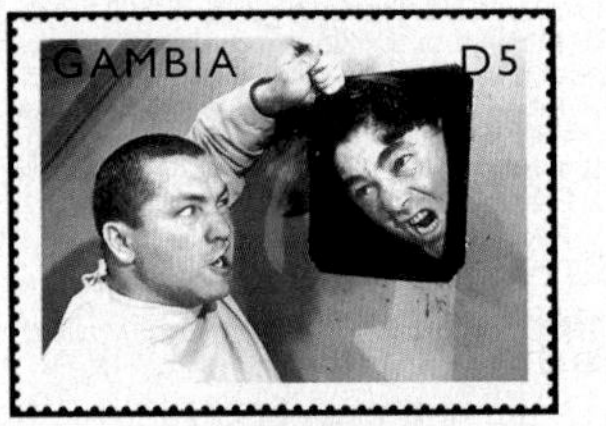


The Three Stooges — A353

No. 2200: a, Curly pulling Moe's hair. b, Curly caught in wringer. c, Curly, Moe with drill. d, Moe pulling Larry's hair. e, Moe. f, Moe sticking finger in Curly's nose. g, Stooges pointing. h, Skull biting Curly's nose. i, Shemp.

No. 2201, 25d, Larry with crown. No. 2202, 25d, Curly on telephone, vert.

**2000, Jan. 14 Litho. *Perf. 13¼***

**2200** A353 5d Sheet of 9, #a.-i. 10.50 10.50

**Souvenir Sheets**

**2201-2202** A353 Set of 2 9.50 9.50

See Nos. 2446-2448.

I Love Lucy — A354

No. 2203: a, Lucy on sofa. b, Lucy, Ricky. c, Fred, Lucy, and Ethel. d, Lucy standing. e, Lucy, Ricky embracing. f, Lucy looking in mirror. g, Lucy with fists clenched. h, Lucy, Ricky on sofa. i, Lucy and Ethel.

No. 2204, 25d, Lucy, Ricky embracing, vert. No. 2205, 25d, Lucy looking in mirror, vert.

**2000, Jan. 14 Litho. *Perf. 13¼***

**2203** A354 5d Sheet of 9, #a.-i. 10.50 10.50

**Souvenir Sheets**

**2204-2205** A354 Set of 2 9.50 9.50

See Nos. 2440-2442, 2449-2451.

Betty Boop A355

No. 2206: a, In green and yellow outfit. b, In red dress. c, In red shirt and blue jeans. d, In green and brown outfit. e, Seated in chair. f, In orange shirt and blue jeans. g, In fur coat. h, In pink dress. i, With dumbbell and water bottle.

No. 2207, 25d, In yellow flowered dress. No. 2208, 25d, In bathtub.

**2000, Jan. 14 Litho. *Perf. 13¼***

**2206** A355 5d Sheet of 9, #a.-i. 10.50 10.50

**Souvenir Sheets**

**2207-2208** A355 Set of 2 9.50 9.50

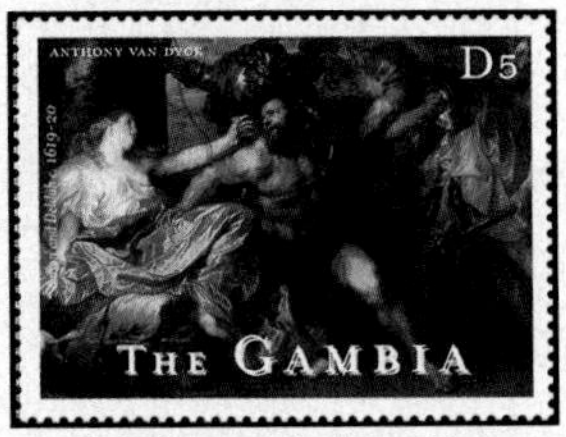


Paintings of Anthony Van Dyck — A356

No. 2209: a, Samson and Delilah, c. 1619-20. b, Samson and Delilah sketch, 1618-20. c, Samson and Delilah, c. 1628-30.

No. 2210, 5d: a, The Adoration of the Shepherds. b, The Rest on the Flight to Egypt, The Virgin of the Partridges. c, Suffer the Little Children to Come Unto Me. d, Christ and the Moneychangers. e, Feast at the House of Simon the Pharisee. f, The Lamentation Over the Dead Christ.

No. 2211, 5d, vert.: a, Anton Giulo Brignole-Sale. b, Paolina Adorno Brignole-Sale. c, Battina Balbi Durazzo. d, Portrait of a Man of the Cattaneo Family. e, Portrait of a Woman. f, Elena Grimaldi Cattaneo.

No. 2212, 5d, vert.: a, A Genoese Senator. b, A Seated Gentlewoman. c, The Senator's Wife. d, A Genoese Lady, The Marchesa Balbi. e, Polyxena Spinola, Marchesa de Legones. f, Agostino Pallavicini.

No. 2213, 5d, vert.: a, Prince Rupert of the Palatinate. b, William II of Nassau and Orange. c, Prince Charles Louis of the Palatinate. d, Prince Rupert, Count Palatine. e, The Princess Mary. f, Prince Charles Louis, Count Palatine.

No. 2214, 5d, vert.: a, Sir George Villiers and Lady Katherine Manners as Adonis and Venus. b, Lady Mary Villiers with Lord Arran. c, Rachel de Ruvigny, Countess Southampton as Fortune. d, Venus at Forge of Vulcan. e, Daedalus and Icarus. f, The Clipping of Cupid's Wing.

No. 2215, 25d, A Man with His Son. No. 2216, 25d, Prince Charles Louis, Elector Palatine and His Brother, Prince Rupert of the Palatinate, vert. No. 2217, 25d, Venetia, Lady Digby, as Prudence, vert. No. 2218, 25d, Drunken Silenus, vert. No. 2219, 25d, Portrait of a Genoese Lady, vert. No. 2220, 25d, Charles II as Prince of Wales, vert. No. 2221, 25d, William II, Prince of Orange, and His Bride, Mary, Princess Royal of England, vert. No. 2222, 25d, The Three Eldest Children of Charles I, vert.

**2000, May 1 *Perf. 13¾***

**2209** A356 5d Sheet of 3, #a.-c. 2.75 2.75

**Sheets of 6, #a.-f.**

**2210-2214** A356 Set of 5 27.50 27.50

**Souvenir Sheets**

**2215-2222** A356 Set of 8 42.50 42.50

Papal Visits — A357

No. 2223, 6d — 1991-92 Visits: a, Portugal. b, Poland. c, Hungary. d, Brazil. e, Senegal. f, Gambia. g, Guinea. h, Angola. i, Sao Tomé. j, Dominican Republic.

No. 2224, 6d — 1993 Visits: a, Benin. b, Uganda. c, Sudan. d, Albania. e, Spain. f, Jamaica. g, Mexico. h, United States. i, Lithuania. j, Latvia.

No. 2225, 6d — 1993-95 Visits: a, Estonia. b, Croatia. c, Philippines. d, Papua New Guinea. e, Australia. f, Sri Lanka. g, Czech Republic. h, Belgium. i, Slovakia. j, Cameroon.

No. 2226, 6d — 1995-96 Visits: a, South Africa. b, Kenya. c, United States. d, United Nations. e, Guatemala. f, Nicaragua. g, El Salvador. h, Venezuela. i, Tunisia. j, Slovenia.

No. 2227, 6d — 1996-98 Visits: a, Germany. b, Hungary. c, France, 1996. d, Bosnia. e, Czech Republic. f, Lebanon. g, Poland. h, France, 1997. i, Brazil. j, Cuba.

No. 2228, 6d — 1998-99 Visits: a, Nigeria. b, Austria. c, Croatia. d, Mexico. e, United States. f, Romania. g, Poland. h, Slovenia. i, India. j, Georgia.

No. 2229, 25d, Pope rekindles Eternal Flame. No. 2230, 25d, Pope blesses Holy Land. No. 2231, 25d, Pope places prayer on Western Wall. No. 2232, 25d, Pope assisted by Israeli president and prime minister. No. 2233, 25d, Pope prays at Western Wall. No. 2234, 25d, Pope receives Bible from chief rabbis. No. 2235, 25d, Pope touches bowl of soil. No. 2236, 25d, Pope at Yad Vashem, horiz.

**2000, May 15 Litho. *Perf. 13¾***

**Sheets of 10, #a.-j, + 2 labels**

**2223-2228** A357 Set of 6 57.50 57.50

**Souvenir Sheets**

***Perf. 14½x14¾, 14¾x14½ (#2236)***

**2229-2236** A357 Set of 8 33.00 33.00

Stamps from Nos. 2223-2228 are 28x47mm.

Mushrooms A358

Designs: 4d, Morel. 5d, Chanterelle. 15d, Knight cap. 20d, Spindle.

No. 2241, 7d: a, Yellow parasol. b, Mottle-gill. c, Poplar field cap. d, Caesar's. e, Flame shield-cap. f, Lilac bonnet.

No. 2242, 7d: a, Common puffball. b, Earth star. c, Silky volvar. d, Stump puffball. e, Spindle-stemmed bolete. f, Fox-orange cort.

No. 2243, 25d, Red-stemmed tough shank. No. 2244, 25d, St. George's.

**2000, May 15 *Perf. 14***

**2237-2240** A358 Set of 4 7.75 7.75

**Sheets of 6, #a.-f.**

**2241-2242** A358 Set of 2 15.00 15.00

**Souvenir Sheets**

**2243-2244** A358 Set of 2 9.00 9.00

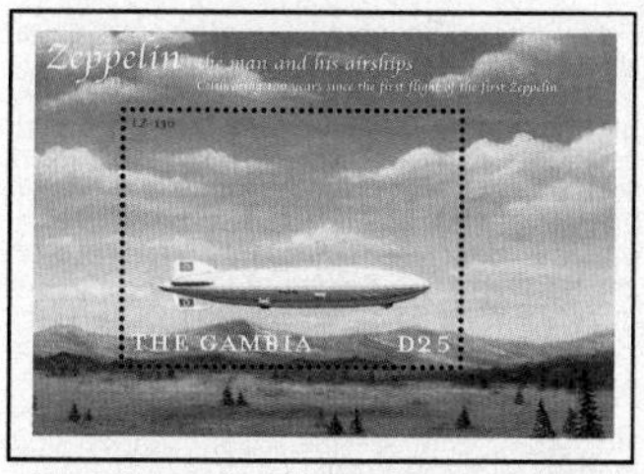


First Zeppelin Flight, Cent. — A359

No. 2245: a, LZ-10. b. LZ-127. c, LZ-129. 25d, LZ-130.

**2000, May 1 Litho. *Perf. 14***
**2245** A359 15d Sheet of 3, #a-c 7.25 7.25

**Souvenir Sheet**

**2246** A359 25d multi 4.25 4.25

No. 2246 contains one 50x38mm stamp.

Prince William, 18th Birthday — A360

No. 2247: a, As child. b, In sweater. c, In suit, with flowers. d, In suit.
25d, With Prince Harry.

**2000, May 1 *Perf. 14***
**2247** A360 7d Sheet of 4, #a-d 4.75 4.75

**Souvenir Sheet**
***Perf. 13¾***

**2248** A360 25d multi 4.25 4.25

No. 2248 contains one 38x50mm stamp.

Berlin Film Festival, 50th Anniv. — A361

No. 2249: a, Pane. Amore e Fantasia. b, Richard III. c, Smultronstället (Wild Strawberries). d, The Defiant Ones. e, The Living Desert. f, A Bout de Souffle.
25d, Twelve Angry Men.

**2000, May 1 *Perf. 14***
**2249** A361 7d Sheet of 6, #a-f 6.75 6.75

**Souvenir Sheet**

**2250** A361 25d multi 4.25 4.25

Apollo-Soyuz Mission, 25th Anniv. — A362

No. 2251: a, Donald K. Slayton. b, Thomas P. Stafford. c, Vance D. Brand.
25d, Diagram of docked spacecraft.

**2000, May 1**
**2251** A362 15d Sheet of 3, #a-c 7.75 7.75

**Souvenir Sheet**

**2252** A362 25d multi 4.50 4.50

Souvenir Sheet

2000 Summer Olympics, Sydney — A363

No. 2253: a, Paavo Nurmi. b, Basketball. c, Panathenian Stadium, Athens and Greek flag. d, Ancient Greek chariot racing.

**2000, May 1**
**2253** A363 6d Sheet of 4, #a-d 4.00 4.00

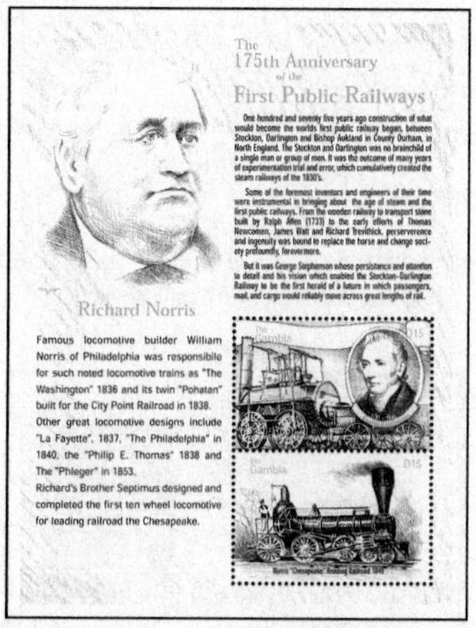


Public Railways, 175th Anniv. — A364

No. 2254: a, Locomotion No. 1, George Stephenson. b, Chesapeake.

**2000, May 1**
**2254** A364 15d Sheet of 2, #a-b 5.00 5.00

Souvenir Sheet

Johann Sebastian Bach (1685-1750) — A365

**2000, May 1**
**2255** A365 25d multi 4.25 4.25

Popes — A366

No. 2256, 7d: a, Pope Felix IV, 526-30. b, Gelasius I, 492-96. c, Gregory I, 590-604. d, Gregory IX, 1227-41. e, Gregory XII, 1406-15. f, Honorius III, 1216-27.

No. 2257, 7d: a, Gregory XIII, 1572-85. b, Urban II, 1088-99. c, Sixtus I, 115-125. d, Pius IX, 1846-78. e, Pius IV, 1559-65. f, Paschal I, 817-24.

No. 2258, 7d: a, Alexander VII, 1655-67. b, Benedict XI, 1303-04. c, Calixtus III, 1455-58. d, Celestine V, 1294. e, Clement IX, 1667-69. f, Fabian, 236-50.

No. 2259, 25d, Peter, 33-64. No. 2260, 25d, Damasus I, 366-384. No. 2261, 25d, John I, 523-526.

**2000, July 26 Litho. *Perf. 13¾***
**Sheets of 6, #a-f**

**2256-2258** A366 Set of 3 19.00 19.00

**Souvenir Sheets**

**2259-2261** A366 Set of 3 12.00 12.00

Butterflies — A367

Designs: 1.50d, Amphicalia tigris. 2d, Myrina silenus. 3d, Chrysiridia madagascarensis. 5d, Papilionidae. 10d, Dasiothia medea.

**2000, Aug. 7 *Perf. 14¾x14***

| | | | | |
|---|---|---|---|---|
| **2262** A367 | 1.50d multi | .25 | .25 |
| **2263** A367 | 2d multi | .35 | .35 |
| **2264** A367 | 3d multi | .50 | .50 |
| **2265** A367 | 5d multi | .80 | .80 |
| **2266** A367 | 10d multi | 1.60 | 1.60 |
| | *Nos. 2262-2266 (5)* | 3.50 | 3.50 |

Nos. 2264-2266 exist dated 2003.
See Nos. 2436-2439, 2452-2452B, 2699.

Souvenir Sheet

Albert Einstein (1879-1955) — A368

**2000, May 1 Litho. *Perf. 14¼***
**2267** A368 25d multi 3.75 3.75

Space — A369

No. 2268, 7d: a, Uhuru. b, Rosat. c, I.U.E. d, Astro E. e, Exosat. f, Chandra.

No. 2269, 7d, vert.: a, Helios. b, Solar Max. c, SOHO. d, O.S.O. e, Special rocket launch. f, I.M.P.

No. 2270, 25d, XMM. No. 2271, 25d, Cassini Huygens.

**2000, May 1 *Perf. 14***
**Sheets of 6, #a-f**

**2268-2269** A369 Set of 2 12.50 12.50

**Souvenir Sheets**

**2270-2271** A369 Set of 2 7.50 7.50

The Stamp Show 2000, London; World Stamp Expo 2000, Anaheim.

Monarchs — A370

No. 2272: a, Charles I of Great Britain, 1625-49. b, Clovis III, king of the Franks (691-95).

No. 2273, 7d: a, Charles II of France, 885-887. b, Catherine de Medici of France, 1547-59. c, Boris Godunov of Russia, 1598-1605. d, Basil III of Russia, 1505-33. e, Anne of Great Britain, 1702-14. f, Charles IX of France, 1560-74.

No. 2274, 7d: a, James IV of Scotland, 1488-1513. b, James V of Scotland, 1513-42. c, James VI of Scotland, 1567-1625. d, Mary of Scotland, 1542-67. e, Mary of Great Britain, 1689-94. f, Elizabeth II, of Great Britain, 1952-present.

No. 2275, 25d, James Francis Edward Stuart. No. 2276, 25d, James IV of Scotland. No. 2277, 25d, Bahadur Shah of India, 1837-57.

**2000, July 26 *Perf. 13¾***
**2272** A370 7d Sheet of 2, #a-b 1.90 1.90

**Sheets of 6, #a-f**

**2273-2274** A370 Set of 2 11.50 11.50

**Souvenir Sheets**

**2275-2277** A370 Set of 3 10.00 10.00

Puppies — A371

Designs: 1d, West Highland terrier. 1.50d, Bernese mountain dog. 3d, Yorkshire terrier. 4d, West Highland terrrier, diff. 10d, Chow chow. 15d, Poodle.

No. 2284: a, Border collie (brown and white). b, Border collie (black, brown and white). c, Yorkshire terrier. d, German shepherd. e, Beagle. f, Spaniel.

**2000, Aug. 7** *Perf. 14¼*

**2278-2283** A371 Set of 6 5.25 5.25
**2284** A371 7d Sheet of 6, #a-f 6.25 6.25

**Souvenir Sheet**

**2285** A371 25d Boxer 3.50 3.50

The Stamp Show 2000, London (Nos. 2284-2285).

Cats — A372

No. 2286, 4d: a, Egyptian mau. b, Singapura. c, American shorthair. d, Cornish rex. e, Birman. f, Scottish fold. g, Turkish angora. h, Turkish van.

No. 2287, 5d: a, Ragdoll. b, Bombay. c, Korat. d, Somali. e, British shorthair. f, American curl. g, Maine coon cat. h, Like No. 2286h.

No. 2288, 25d, Cat and kitten. No. 2289, 25d, Cat.

**2000, Aug. 7** **Sheets of 8, #a-h**

**2286-2287** A372 Set of 2 10.50 10.50

**Souvenir Sheets**

**2288-2289** A372 Set of 2 7.50 7.50

The Stamp Show 2000, London.

**Flower Photomosaic Type of 1999 and**

Queen Mother, 100th Birthday — A373

Designs: No. 2090, Various flower photographs making up a photomosaic of the Queen Mother. No. 2290I: Various photos of religious scenes making up a photomosaic of Pope John Paul II.

**2000, Aug. 7** **Litho.** *Perf. 13¾*

**2290** A349 5d Sheet of 8, #a-h 5.50 5.50
**2290I** A349 6d Sheet of 8, #j-q 7.00 7.00

**Litho. & Embossed**
**Without Gum**
***Die Cut 9x8¾***

**2291** A373 85d multi

Issued: Nos. 2290, 2291 8/7. No. 2290I, 8/8.

European Soccer Championships — A374

No. 2292, horiz. — Czech Republic: a, Nedved. b, Team photo. c, Maier. d, Antonin Panenka. e, Selessin Stadium, Liege. f, Patrik Berger.

No. 2293, horiz. — England: a, Alan Shearer. b, Team photo. c, David Seaman. d, Sol Campbell. e, Philips Stadium, Eindhoven. f, Southgate.

No. 2294, horiz. — Norway: a, Leonardsen. b, Team photo. c, Mykland. d, Solbakken. e, Rekdal.

No. 2295, horiz. — Slovenia: a, Aleksander Knavs. b, Team photo. c, Zlatko Zahovic. d, Ales Ceh. e, Stade Communal, Charleroi. f, Miran Pavlin.

No. 2296, horiz. — Sweden: a, Ljungberg. b, Team photo. c, Andersson. d, Nilsson. e, Schwarz.

No. 2297, horiz. — Turkey: a, Yalcin. b, Team photo. c, Buruk. d, Erdem. e, King Baudouin Stadium. f, Korkut.

No. 2298, 25d, Czech Republic coach, Jozef Chovanec. No. 2299, 25d, England coach Kevin Keegan. No. 2300, 25d, Norway coach Nils-Johan Semb. No. 2301, 25d, Slovenia coach Srecko Katanec. No. 2302, 25d, Sweden coaches, Söderberg and Lagerbäck. No. 2303, 25d, Turkey coach Mustafa Denizli.

**2000, Aug. 7** **Litho.** *Perf. 13¾*

**2292** A374 7d Sheet of 6, #a-f 5.75 5.75
**2293** A374 7d Sheet of 6, #a-f 5.75 5.75
**2294** A374 7d Sheet of 6, #a-e, 2292e 5.75 5.75
**2295** A374 7d Sheet of 6, #a-f 5.75 5.75
**2296** A374 7d Sheet of 6, #a-e, 2293e 5.75 5.75
**2297** A374 7d Sheet of 6, #a-f 5.75 5.75
*Nos. 2292-2297 (6)* 34.50 34.50

**Souvenir Sheets**

**2298-2303** A374 Set of 6 20.00 20.00

Paintings of Birds — A375

Designs: 1.50d, A White Pheasant and Other Fowl in a Classical Landscape, by Abraham Bisschop. 3d, Salmon-crested Cockatoo, by Bartolomeo Bimbi. 4d, A Great Bustard Cock and Other Birds, by Ludger Tom Ring. 15d, A Great Black-backed Gull and Other Birds, by Jokob Bogdani.

No. 2308, 5d: a, Peacocks, Hens and Mouse, by Tobias Stranover. b, Lady in a Red Jacket Feeding a Parrot, by Frans van Mieris. c, Birds by a Pool, by Melchior de Hondecoeter. d, Ganymede and the Eagle, by Peter Paul Rubens. e, Leda and the Swan, by Cesare de Sesto. f, Ducks and Ducklings at the Foot of a Tree in a Mediterranean Landscape, by Adriaen van Oolen. g, Portrait of the Falconer Robert Cheseman Carrying a Hooded Falcon, by Hans Holbein. h, A Golden Pheasant on a Stone Plinth, with Other Birds, by Jacobus Vonck.

No. 2309, 5d, horiz.: a, Still Life of Birds, by Caravaggio (hanging dead birds, basket). b, Turkeys with Young and Rock Doves, by Johan Wenzel Peter. c, The Threatened Swan, by Jan Asselyn. d, Still Life of Fruit and Birds in a Landscape, by Jakab Bogdany. e, Mobbing the Owl, by Tobias Stranover (owl at right, other birds). f, A Concert of Birds, by Hondecoeter (owl, cockatoo at center). g, Owls and Young Ones, by William Tomkins. h, Birds by a Stream, by Jean Baptiste Oudry.

No. 2310, 25d, The King Eagle Pursued to the Sun, by Philip Reinagle. No. 2311, 25d, Still Life of Birds, by Georg Flegl, horiz.

**2000, Oct. 2** *Perf. 13½*

**2304-2307** A375 Set of 4 3.50 3.50

**Sheets of 8, #a-h**

**2308-2309** A375 Set of 2 12.00 12.00

**Souvenir Sheets**

**2310-2311** A375 Set of 2 7.50 7.50

Descriptions of paintings are in margins on Nos. 2308-2311.

Paintings from the Prado — A376

No. 2312, 6d: a, The Madonna of the Fish, by Raphael. b, The Holy Family with a Lamb, by Raphael. c, The Madonna of the Stair, by Andrea del Sarto. d, Moneychanger from The Moneychanger and his Wife, by Marinus van Reymerswaele. e, Madonna and Child by Jan Gossaert. f, Wife from The Moneychanger and his Wife.

No. 2313, 6d: a, Bearded man from St. Benedict's Supper, by Juan Andres Ricci. b, Our Lady of the Immaculate Conception, by Francisco de Zurbarán. c, Monk with candle from St. Benedict's Supper. d, The Penitient Magdalen, by José de Ribera. e, Christ as Man of Sorrows, by Antonion de Pereda. f, St. Jerome, by Pereda.

No. 2314, 6d: a, Children with a Shell, by Bartolomé Esteban Murillo. b, Our Lady of the Immaculate Conception, by Murillo. c, The Good Shepherd, by Murillo. d, Woman with red headdress from The Parasol, by Francisco de Goya. e, A Rural Gift, by Ramon Bayeu. f, Woman with blue headdress from The Parasol.

No. 2315, 6d: a, Queen Isabella Farnese, by Jean Ranc. b, Young Woman Seen from the Back, by Jean-Baptiste Greuze. c, Charles III as a Child, by Ranc. d, James Bourdieu, by Sir Joshua Reynolds. e, Dr. Isaac Henrique Sequeira, by Thomas Gainsborough. f, Portrait of a Clergyman, by Reynolds.

No. 2316, 6d: a, Portrait of a Young Woman, by Zacarias González Velázquez. b, The Painter Francisco de Goya, by Vicente Lopez Portaña. c, Portrait of a Girl, by Rafael Tejeo Diaz. d, Mary, from The Nativity, by Federico Barocci. e, Madonna and Child with St. John, by Correggio. f, Jesus, from The Nativity.

No. 2317, 6d: a, St. Andrew, by Francisco Rizi. b, Christ Crucified, by Diego Velázquez. c, St. Onuphrius, by Francisco Collantes. d, Charles II, by Juan Carreño de Miranda. e, St. Sebastian, by Carreño de Miranda. f, Peter Ivanovich Potemkin, by Carreño de Miranda.

No. 2318, 25d, The Defense of Cádiz Against the English, by Zurbarán. No. 2319, 25d, The Surrender of Juliers, by Jusepe Leonardo. No. 2320, 25d, The Holy Family with a Bird, by Murillo. No. 2321, 25d, Danäe, by Titian, horiz. No. 2322, 25d, Venus and Adonis, by Paolo Veronese, horiz. No. 2323, 25d, Jacob's Dream, by Ribera.

**2000, Oct. 6** *Perf. 12x12¼, 12¼x12*

**Sheets of 6, #a-f**

**2312-2317** A376 Set of 6 29.00 29.00

**Souvenir Sheets**

**2318-2323** A376 Set of 6 20.00 20.00

Espana 2000, Intl. Philatelic Exhibition.

Battle of Britain, 60th Anniv. — A377

No. 2324, 5d, horiz.: a, Hurricane downing German BF109. b, Spitfire over River Thames. c, Flight Lt. Denys E. Gilliam attacking German Dornier 217 planes. d, Hurricanes heading to intercept Luftwaffe bombers. e, Hurricanes returning to Croydon. f, G.A. Langley in combat with BF109. g, Bristol Blenheim IV over English Channel. h, Spitfires taking off from Hornchurch.

No. 2325, 5d, horiz.: a, Plane from 29th Blenheim Squadron heading to Norwegian coast. b, Luftwaffe pilot Helmut Wick downs RAF pilot John Cock. c, Spitfire downs Dornier 217 off Dover. d, Bristol Beaufighter IIF on patrol. e, Bolton-Paul Defiants intercept Luftwaffe bombers. f, Spitfire in dogfite with German Stuka JU-87 divebomber. g, Spitfire and Hurricane fly over London and River Thames. h, Gloster Gladiator.

No. 2326, 25d, Group Captain Frank Carey. No. 2327, 25d, German Commander Adolf Joseph Ferdinand Galland.

**2000, Oct. 16** *Perf. 14*

**Sheets of 8, #a-h**

**2324-2325** A377 Set of 2 11.00 11.00

**Souvenir Sheets**

**2326-2327** A377 Set of 2 7.00 7.00

Composers — A378

No. 2328, 7d: a, Antonio Vivaldi. b, Giacomo Puccini. c, Franz Joseph Haydn. d, Leopold Stokowski. e, Felix Mendelssohn. f, Gaetano Donizetti.

No. 2329, 7d: a, Witold Lutoslawski. b, William Sterndale Bennett. c, Wolfgang Amadeus Mozart. d, Ludwig van Beethoven. e, Sergei Rachmaninoff. f, Peter Ilich Tchaikovsky.

No. 2330, 25d, Manuel de Falla. No. 2331, 25d, Fréderic Chopin.

**2000, Oct. 2** **Litho.** *Perf. 13¾x13¼*

**Sheets of 6, #a-f**

**2328-2329** A378 Set of 2 11.50 11.50

**Souvenir Sheets**

**2330-2331** A378 Set of 2 7.00 7.00

Transportation of the Future — A379

No. 2332 — Automobiles: b, Mazda RX-Evolv. c, Isuzu Kai. d, Ford 021C. e, Pontiac GTO. f, Chevrolet CERV III. g, Toyota Will VI.

No. 2333 — Aircraft: a, Blended wing body, BWB-1. b, Boeing 767-400 ERX. c, Lockheed concept. d, Boeing X. e, American National Aerospace plane X-30 concept. f, Hotol taking off from Russian AN-225.

No. 2334 — Trains: a, Maglev train MLU-002. b, Magnetic rail car. c, Monorail above ground concept. d, Seattle Monorail. e, Monorail above cabin concept. f, Monorail concept.

No. 2335 — Watercraft: h, Pendolare concept boat. i, Planesail boat. j, Airfoil concept. k, Ferry Sea Coaster concept. l, Shinaitoku Matu new sail technology. m, Supersport luxury yacht concept.

No. 2335G, 25d, Nautic Air 400 concept. No. 2335H, 25d, Maglev train. No. 2334I, 25d, Honda Sprocket concept. No. 2335J, 25d, Triton, US Coast Guard concept.

**2000, Oct. 2** *Perf. 14*

**Sheets of 6, #a-f**

**2332** A379 7d Sheet of 6, #b-g 5.75 5.75
**2333** A379 7d Sheet of 6, #a-f 5.75 5.75
**2334** A379 8d Sheet of 6, #a-f 6.00 6.00
**2335** A379 8d Sheet of 6, #h-m 7.00 7.00

**Souvenir Sheets**

**2335G-2335J** A379 Set of 4 14.00 14.00

Nos. 2335 and 2335A contain one 56x41mm stamp.

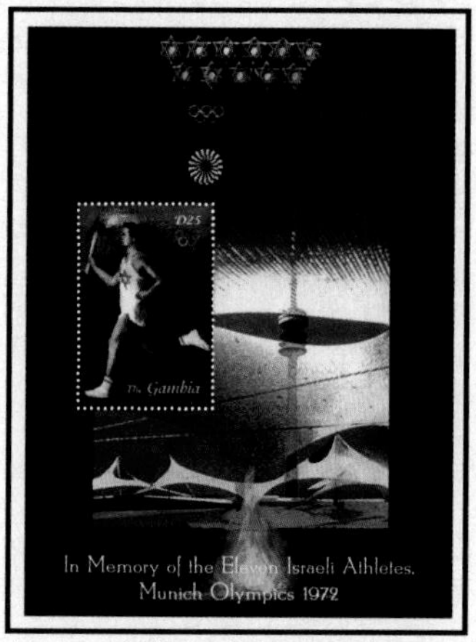


Massacre of Israeli Olympic Athletes, 1972 — A380

No. 2336, horiz.: a, Moshe Weinberg. b, Eliezer Halffin. c, Mark Slavin. d, Ze'ev Friedman. e, Joseph Romano. f, Kahat Shor. g, David Berger. h, Joseph Gottfreund. i, Andrei Schpitzer. j, Amitsur Shapira. k, Yaakov Springer. l, Olympic poster.

**2000, Nov. 9**

**2336** A380 4d Sheet of 12, #a-l 6.75 6.75

**Souvenir Sheet**

**2337** A380 25d Torchbearer 3.75 3.75

Ships A381

Designs: 5d, Spanish Armada. 10d, Brazilian river gunboat Colombo. 15d, Russian Navy mine carrier Jenissel. 20d, Japanese battleship Yamato.

No. 2342, 7d: a, British first-rate battleship, 18th cent. b, Spanish galleon, 16th cent. c, Russian four-masted barque, 20th cent. d, Henri Grace à Dieu with flag on stern, 16th cent. e, Frontispiece of John Dee's Arte of Navigation, 16th cent. f, British ironclad, 19th cent.

No. 2343, 7d: a, Chinese junk, 18th cent. b, Two-masted cog, 15th cent. c, Henri Grace à Dieu, no flag on stern, 16th cent. d, St. Brendan and monks at sea, 6th cent. e, Figurehead. f, British carrack, 16th cent.

No. 2344, 25d, Challenger, 19th cent. No. 2345, 25d, Golden Hind, 16th cent.

**2000, Oct. 2** **Litho.** *Perf. 14*

**2338-2341** A381 Set of 4 6.75 6.75

**Sheets of 6, #a-f**

**2342-2343** A381 Set of 2 11.00 11.00

**Souvenir Sheets**

**2344-2345** A381 Set of 2 6.75 6.75

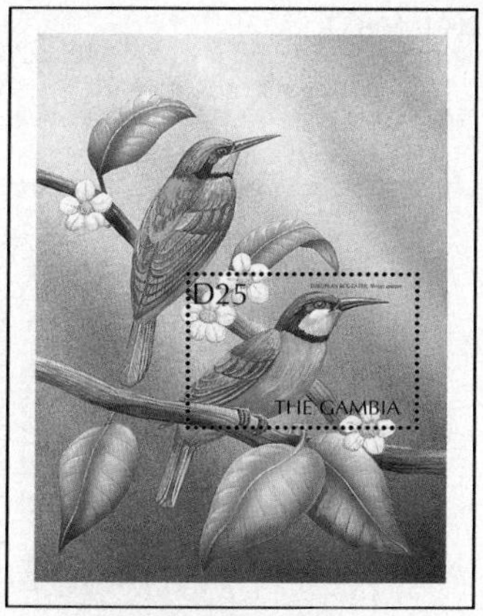


Birds — A382

No. 2346, 7d, vert.: a, Pied flycatcher. b, Blackcap. c, Stonechat. d, Nightingale. e, Black-headed tchagra. f, Yellow wagtail.

No. 2347, 7d, vert.: a, Gray parrot. b, Great spotted cuckoo. c, Bar-tailed trogon. d, African hobby. e, Green turaco. f, Trumpeter hornbill.

No. 2348, 7d, vert.: a, Yellow-rumped tinkerbird. b, Greater honeyguide. c, Hoopoe. d, European roller. e, Carmine bee-eater. f, White-throated bee-eater.

No. 2349, 25d, European bee-eater. No. 2350, 25d, Bateleur. No. 2351, 25d, Secretary bird.

**2000, Oct. 2** *Perf. 13¾x13¼*

**Sheets of 6, #a-f**

**2346-2348** A382 Set of 3 17.50 17.50

**Souvenir Sheets**

**2349-2351** A382 Set of 3 10.50 10.50

Ferrari Automobiles — A383

Designs: 4d, 3335P. 5d, 5125. 10d, 312P. 25d, 330P4.

**2000, Nov. 15** *Perf. 14*

**2352-2355** A383 Set of 4 5.75 5.75

12th Classic Automobile Marathon — A384

No. 2356, 5d: a, Morgan. b, Rover. c, Marmon. d, Rolls Royce Silver Cloud. e, Rolls Royce Phantom. f, Mercedes 680S. g, Mercedes 74. h, Invicta.

No. 2357, 5d: a, Allard. b, Ford coupe. c, Citroen Pilot. d, Packard (white). e, Austin A90. f, Bentley. g, Packard (red). h, Aston Martin.

No. 2358, 25d, Cadillac. No. 2359, 25d, Morris Minor.

**2000, Nov. 15** **Sheets of 8, #a-h**

**2356-2357** A384 Set of 2 10.50 10.50

**Souvenir Sheets**

**2358-2359** A384 Set of 2 6.75 6.75

Queen Mother, 100th Birthday — A385

**2000, Aug. 7** **Litho.** *Perf. 14*

**2360** A385 7d multi .90 .90

Printed in sheets of 6.

The Horse in Art A386

Designs: 4d, At Full Stretch, by John Skeaping. 5d, The Burton, by Lionel Edwards. 10d, A Game of Polo, by Li Lin. 15d, St. George and the Dragon, by Raphael, vert.

No. 2365, 7d: a, Horses Emerging From the Sea, by Eugène Delacroix. b, The Ninth Duke of Marlborough on a Grey Horse, by Sir Alfred Munnings. c, Ovid in Exile Amongst the Scythians, by Delacroix. d, Early Morning Gallop, by Skeaping. e, Mare and Foal, by Munnings. f, Detail from Three-a-side Polo at Simla, by Edwards.

No. 2366, 7d, vert.: a, A Lady Hawking, by E. J. H. Vernet. b, Captain Robert Orme, by Sir Joshua Reynolds. c, Napoleon Crossing the Alps, by Jacques-Louis David. d, Nobby Gray, by Munnings. e, Amateur Jockeys Near a Carriage, by Edgar Degas. f, Detail from Three-a-side Polo at Simla, diff.

No. 2367, 25d, The Reckoning, by George Morland. No. 2368, 25d, One of the Family, by Frederic G. Cotman.

**2000, Oct. 2**

**2361-2364** A386 Set of 4 4.75 4.75

**Sheets of 6, #a-f**

**2365-2366** A386 Set of 2 11.00 11.00

**Souvenir Sheets**

**2367-2368** A386 Set of 2 6.75 6.75

New Year 2001 (Year of the Snake) — A387

No. 2369: a, Vermilion background. b, Purple background. c, Dark blue background. d, Light green background.

**2001, Jan. 2**

**2369** A387 4d Sheet of 4, #a-d 2.40 2.40

**Souvenir Sheet**

**2370** A387 15d Snake 2.25 2.25

Rijksmuseum, Amsterdam, Bicent. (in 2000) — A388

No. 2371, 7d, vert.: a, Vessels in a Strong wind, by Jan Porcellis. b, Seascape in the Morning, by Simon de Vlieger. c, Travelers at a Country Inn, by Isaack van Ostade. d, Orpheus with Animals in a Landscape, by Aelbert Cuyp. e, Italian With a Mountain Plateau, by Cornelis van Poelenburch. f, Boatmen and hill from Boatman Moored on a Lake Shore, by Adam Pynacker.

No. 2372, 7d, vert.: a, Cow, boatmen and sailboat from Boatmen Moored on a Lake Shore. b, The Ford in the River, by Jan Baptist Weenix. c, Two Horses Near a Gate in a Meadow, by Paulus Potter. d, Cows and Sheep at a Stream, by Karel Dujardin. e, Violin player from The Duet, by Cornelis Saftleven. f, Lute player from The Duet.

No. 2373, 7d, vert.: a, Teapot from Still Life With Turkey Pie, by Pieter Claesz. b, Bouquet of Flowers in a Vase, by Ambrosius Bosschaert. c, Vase from Still Life With Flowers, Fruit and Shells, by Balthasar van der Ast. d, Flowers and fruit from Still Life With Flowers, Fruit and Shells. e, Tulips in a Vase, by Hans Boulenger. f, Laid Table With Cheese and Fruit, by Floris van Dijck.

No. 2374, 7d, vert.: a, Turkey, from Still Life With Turkey Pie. b, Still Life With Gilt Goblet, by Willem Claesz Heda. c, Still Life With Lobster and Nautilus Cup, by Jan Davidsz de Heem. d, Bacchanal, by Moses van Uyttenbroeck. e, The Anatomy Lesson of Dr. Nicolaes Tulp, by Rembrandt. f, Johannes Lutma, by Jacob Backer.

No. 2375, 7d, vert.: a, The Meagre Company, by Frans Hals and Pieter Codde. b, The Twins Clara and Aelbert de Bray, by Salomon de Bray. c, Self-portrait, by Ferdinand Bol. d, Ambulatory of the New Church in Delft, with the Tomb of Willem the Silent, by Gerard Houckgeest. e, View of the Tomb of Willem in the New Church in Delft, by Emanuel de Witte. f, Mountainous Landscape, by Hercules Segers.

No. 2376, 7d, vert.: a, Lute player from Gallant Company by Codde. b, Men and archway from Gallant Company. c, Man on bended knee from The Marriage of Willem van Loon and Margaretha Bas, by Jan Miense Molenaer. d, Crowd from The Marriage of Willen van Loon and Margaretha Bas. e, Woman in black robe from The Marriage of Willem van Loon and Margaretha Bas. f, Johanna Le Maire, by Nicolaes Eliasz Pickenoy.

No. 2377, 25d, The Fall of Man, by Cornelis van Haarlem. No. 2378, 25d, The Art Gallery of Jan Gildemeester Jansz, by Jan Ekels II. No. 2379, 25d, View of the Nieuwe Kerk and the Rear of the Town Hall in Amsterdam, by Isaak Outwater. No. 2380, 25d, The Spendthrift, by Cornelis Troost. No. 2381, 25d, Morning Ride on the Beach, by Anton Mauve. No. 2382, 25d, Meadow Landscape With Cattle, by Willen Roelofs.

**2001, Jan. 15** *Perf. 13¾*

**Sheets of 6, #a-f**

**2371-2376** A388 Set of 6 32.50 32.50

**Souvenir Sheets**

**2377-2382** A388 Set of 6 21.00 21.00

The Wizard of Oz, Cent. (in 2000) — A389

No. 2383, 7d: a, Witch of the North. b, Poppies. c, Dorothy's house. d, Witch of the East. e, Dorothy. f, The Wizard.

No. 2384, 7d: a, Witch's wolf. b, Witch's forest. c, Witch's monkeys. d, Dorothy in poppies. e, Queen Mouse. f, Witch and evil bees.

No. 2385, 7d: a, Cowardly Lion. b, Land of Oz. c, Tin Man. d, Scarecrow. e, Toto. f, Munchkins.

No. 2386, 27d, Green Maiden. No. 2387, 27d, Gate keeper. No. 2388, 27d, Dorothy at crossroads, horiz.

**2001, Jan. 30** **Sheets of 6, #a-f**

**2383-2385** A389 Set of 3 16.50 16.50

**Souvenir Sheets**

**2386-2388** A389 Set of 3 11.00 11.00

History of the Theater — A390

No. 2389, 6d: a, Terra cotta statue. b, Tragic masks of King Priam. c, Euripides. d, Terra cotta statues of actors portraying drunks. e, Scene from Chinese play. f, Indian actors. g, Scene from Noh play, Japan. h, Scene from Clytemnestra.

No. 2390, 6d: a, William Shakespeare. b, Johann Wolfgang von Goethe. c, Moliere. d, Henrik Ibsen. e, George Bernard Shaw. f, Anton Chekhov. g, Sholom Aleichem. h, Tennessee Williams.

No. 2391, 25d, Sarah Bernhardt, vert. No. 2392, 25d, John Barrymore, vert.

**2001, Jan. 30** ***Perf. 14***

**Sheets of 8, #a-h**

**2389-2390** A390 Set of 2 13.00 13.00

**Souvenir Sheet**

**2391-2392** A390 Set of 2 6.75 6.75

Pokémon — A391

No. 2393: a, Beedrill. b, Arbok. c, Machop. d, Vileplume. e, Clefairy. f, Poliwhirl.

**2001, Feb. 1** ***Perf. 13¾***

**2393** A391 7d Sheet of 6, #a-f 5.50 5.50

**Souvenir Sheet**

**2394** A391 25d Articuno 3.00 3.00

Orchids — A392

Designs: 1.50d, Encyclia alata. 2d, Dendrobium lasiantherum. 3d, Cymbidiella pardalina. No. 2398, 4d, Cymbidium lowianum. 5d, Cypripedium irapeanum. 15d, Doritas pulcherrima.

No. 2401: a, Epidendrum pseudepidendrum. b, Eriopsis biloba. c, Masdevallia coccinea. d, Odontoglossum lindleyanum. e, Oerstedella wallisii. f, Paphiopedilum acmodontum. g, Laelia rubescens. h, Huntleya wallisii. i, Lycaste longiscapa. j, Maxillaria variabilis. k, Mexicoa ghiesbrechtiana. l, Miltoniopsis phalaenopsis.

No. 2402: a, Sobralia candida. b, Phragmipedium basseae. c, Phaius tankervilleae. d, Vanda rothchildiana. e, Telipogon pulchera. f, Rossioglossum insleayi.

No. 2403, 25d, Chaubardia heteroclita. No. 2404, 25d, Cychnoches loddigesii. No. 2405, 25d, Cattleya dowiana.

**2001, Feb. 1** **Litho.** ***Perf. 14***

**2395-2400** A392 Set of 6 6.00 6.00

**2401** A392 4d Sheet of 12, #a-l 9.25 9.25

**2402** A392 7d Sheet of 6, #a-f 8.25 8.25

**Souvenir Sheets**

**2403-2405** A392 Set of 3 15.00 15.00

Hong Kong 2001 Stamp Exhibition (Nos. 2401-2405).

Medicinal Plants — A393

Designs: 3d, Pokeweed. 5d, Bay laurel. 10d, Coltsfoot. 15d, Marshmallow.

No. 2410, 8d, vert.: a, Restharrow. b, White willow. c, Sweet serge. d, Passion flower. e, Rosemary. f, Pepper.

No. 2411, 8d, vert.: a, Succory. b, Dandelion. c, Garlic. d, Hemp agrimony. e, Star thistle. f, Cypress.

No. 2412, 25d, Arbutus, vert. No. 2413, 25d, Olive, vert.

**2001, Mar. 1**

**2406-2409** A393 Set of 4 5.75 5.75

**Sheets of 6, #a-f**

**2410-2411** A393 Set of 2 18.00 18.00

**Souvenir Sheets**

**2412-2413** A393 Set of 2 9.00 9.00

Japanese Art — A394

Designs: 1d, Mount Fuji and Tea Fields, by Matsuoka Eikyu. 2d, One heron from Herons and Flowers, by Okamoto Shuki. No. 2416, 3d, Two herons from Herons and Flowers. No. 2417, 3d, The Realm of Gods in Yingzhou, by Tomioka Tessai. No. 2418, 4d, Peach Blossom Spring in Wuling, by Tessai. No. 2419, 4d, Egret, by Takeuchi Seiho. No. 2420, 5d, Spring Colors of the Lake and Mountains, by Shoda Gyokan. No. 2421, 5d, Sparrows, by Seiho. No. 2422, 10d, Red Lotus and White Goose, by Goun Saku. No. 2423, 10d, Portrait of Ushiwakamaru, by Kano Osanobu. 15d, Woman Selling Flowers, by Ito Shoha. 20d, The Sound of the Ocean, by Matsumoto Ichiyo.

No. 2426, 5d — Birds and Flowers of the Twelve Months, by Sakai Hoitsu: a, Red and white flowers, bird on branch. b, Yellow flowers, bird flying. c, White flowers, bird on branch. d, Blue flowers. e, Sun, white and blue flowers. f, Red and white flowers.

No. 2427, 5d — Birds and Flowers of the Twelve Months, by Hoitsu: a, Insect in sky, red pink and white flowers. b, Blue irises. c, Red, white light blue flowers. d, Fruit on tree. e, Bird standing in water. f, Snow-covered tree.

No. 2428, 7d — Birds and Flowers, by Soga Chokuan: a, White flowers. b, Rooster at R. c, Roosters at L, red flower at R. d, Rooster at R, white flowers. e, Birds in sky. f, Roosters at L and R, white and red flowers. g, Roosters at L and R. Rooster at L, tree and red flowers.

No. 2429, 7d — The Four Accomplishments, by Kaiho Yusho: a, Table. b, Two people near tree. c, Rock and hill. d, Two people. e, Rock and tree. f, One person. g, Three people. h, Three people, table.

No. 2430 — Book of Lacquer Paintings, by Shibata Zeshin: a, Flower. b, Birds. c, Butterfly on flower. d, Lobster.

No. 2431, 30d, Untitled painting (Yanagibashi at Ryogoku), by Utagawa Kuniyoshi, horiz. No. 2432, 30d, Poppies, by Tsuchida Bakusen, horiz. No. 2433, 30d, Poppies and Morning Glories, by Yamaguchi Soken, horiz. No. 2434, 30d, Deep Pool, by Nishimura Goun, horiz. No. 2435, 30d, Spring Farming Near a Riverside Village, by Mori Getsujo, horiz.

**2001, Apr. 17**

**2414-2425** A394 Set of 12 15.00 15.00

**Sheets of 6, #a-f**

**2426-2427** A394 Set of 2 10.50 10.50

**Sheets of 8, #a-h**

**2428-2429** A394 Set of 2 21.00 21.00

**2430** A394 10d Sheet of 4, #a-d 7.00 7.00

**Imperf.**

**Size: 118x88mm**

**2431-2435** A394 Set of 5 27.50 27.50

Nos. 2428-2430 contain 28x42mm stamps. Phila Nippon '01, Japan.

**Butterflies Type of 2000**

Designs: 7d, Salamis temora. 8d, Cyrestus camillus. 20d, Papilio demodocus. 25d, Danaus chrysippus.

**2001** ***Perf. 14¾x14***

**2436-2439** A367 Set of 4 11.50 11.50

No. 2439 exists dated 2003.

**I Love Lucy Type of 2000**

No. 2440: a, Lucy singing. b, Lucy with tambourine. c, Lucy with Ricky and Ethel. d, Lucy. e, Ethel and Ricky at piano. f, Ethel and Ricky on bench. g, Lucy at typewriter. h, Ethel singing. i, Lucy on bench.

No. 2441, 25d, Like No. 2440a, vert. No. 2442, 25d, Like No. 2440d, vert.

**2001** ***Perf. 13¾***

**2440** A354 5d Sheet of 9, #a-i 8.25 8.25

**Souvenir Sheets**

**2441-2442** A354 Set of 2 9.00 9.00

Horses — A395

No. 2443, 7d, Head of: a, Akhal-Teke. b, Palomino. c, Kladruber. d, Paint Horse. e, Pinto. f, Kabardin.

No. 2444, 7d, horiz: a, Akhal-Teke. b, Kladruber. c, Palomino. d, Pinto. e, Paint Horse. f, Kabardin.

**2001** **Litho.** ***Perf. 14***

**Sheets of 6, #a-f**

**2443-2444** A395 Set of 2 10.50 10.50

**Souvenir Sheet**

**2445** A395 25d Palomino 3.00 3.00

**Three Stooges Type of 2000**

No. 2446: a, Shemp as angel. b, Larry, Moe, Shemp, wearing feathered hats. c, Moe, Shemp and Larry wearing hospital uniforms. d, Larry with hammer, Shemp with gun, Moe. e, Moe, Larry, Shemp with woman. f, Moe and Shemp wearing tams. g, Moe, Larry, wagon wheel. h, Shemp, Moe, Larry in bus driver uniforms. i, Shemp hitting Larry and Moe.

No. 2447, 25d, Curly with telephone, skull, vert. No. 2448, 25d, Shemp on Moe's back, vert.

**2001** ***Perf. 13¾***

**2446** A353 5d Sheet of 9, #a-i 5.75 5.75

**Souvenir Sheets**

**2447-2448** A353 Set of 2 6.50 6.50

**I Love Lucy Type of 2000**

No. 2449 : a, Lucy crawling on building ledge. b, Lucy standing against wall, arms outstretched. c, Lucy in apartment. d, Lucy reclining on ledge. e, Lucy with hand on forehead. f, Lucy reclining against wall. g, Ricky, bound and gagged Lucy. h, Lucy on sofa. i, Lucy, robber.

No. 2450, 25d, Lucy, robber, vert. No. 2451, 25d, Bound and gagged Lucy, seated Ethel, vert.

**2001**

**2449** A354 5d Sheet of 9, #a-i 5.75 5.75

**Souvenir Sheets**

**2450-2451** A354 Set of 2 6.50 6.50

**Butterfly Type of 2000**

**2001** ***Perf. 14¾x14***

**2452** A367 50d Coeliades forestan 7.00 7.00

**2452A** A367 75d Ornithoptera alexandrae 10.00 10.00

**2452B** A367 100d Morpho cypris 14.00 14.00

Queen Victoria (1819-1901) — A396

No. 2453, horiz.: a, Reading speech from throne. b, Benjamin Disraeli. c, Riding in procession from Parliament.

**2001, Apr. 26** ***Perf. 14***
**2453** A396 15d Sheet of 3, #a-c 5.75 5.75

**Souvenir Sheet**

**2454** A396 25d Portrait 3.25 3.25

Queen Elizabeth II, 75th Birthday — A397

No. 2456: a, In uniform. b, In pink hat. c, Wearing crown, facing R. d, Wearing crown, facing L.

**2001, Apr. 26** ***Perf. 14***
**2455** A397 15d Sheet of 4, #a-d 7.75 7.75

**Souvenir Sheet**

**2456** A397 25d In wedding dress 3.25 3.25

Flowers — A398

Designs: 1d, Disa unifloria. 4d, Monodora myristica. 6d, Clappertonia ficifolia. 20d, Calanthe rosea.

No. 2461, 7d: a, Vanilla planifolia. b, Strelitzia reginae. c, Gladiolus cardinalis. d, Arctotis venusta. e, Protea obtusifolia. f, Geissorhiza rochensis.

No. 2462, 7d: a, Canarina abyssinica. b, Amorphophallus abyssinicus. c, Calanthe rosea, diff. d, Gloriosa simplex. e, Clappertonia ficifolia, diff. f, Ansellia gigantea.

No. 2463, 25d, Arctoris venusta, diff. No. 2464, 25d, Geissorhiza rochensis, horiz.

**2001, Mar. 1** **Litho.** ***Perf. 14***
**2457-2460** A398 Set of 4 4.75 4.75

**Sheets of 6, #a-f**

**2461-2462** A398 Set of 2 12.50 12.50

**Souvenir Sheets**

**2463-2464** A398 Set of 2 7.50 7.50

Photomosaic of Queen Elizabeth II — A399

**2001, Apr. 26**
**2465** A399 8d multi 1.00 1.00

Printed in sheets of 8, with and without marginal inscription "In Celebration of the 50th Anniversary of H. M. Queen Elizabeth II's Accession to the Throne.'

Marlene Dietrich — A400

No. 2466: a, With head on forearm. b, With bare shoulder. c, With arms crossed. d, Wearing hat.

**2001, Apr. 26** ***Perf. 13¾***
**2466** A400 10d Sheet of 4, #a-d 5.25 5.25

Mao Zedong (1893-1976) — A401

No. 2467: a, In 1935. b, In 1949. c, In 1951. 25d, In 1928.

**2001, Apr. 26** ***Perf. 14***
**2467** A401 15d Sheet of 3, #a-c 5.75 5.75

**Souvenir Sheet**

**2468** A401 25d multi 3.25 3.25

Giuseppe Verdi (1813-1901), Opera Composer — A402

No. 2469: a, Verdi with gray hair. b, Score and perfromers from La Traviata. c, Score and performer from Aida. d, Verdi with brown hair.

25d, Verdi and scores of Don Carlos and Rigoletto.

**2001, Apr. 26**
**2469** A402 10d Sheet of 4, #a-d 5.25 5.25

**Souvenir Sheet**

**2470** A402 25d multi 3.25 3.25

Monet Paintings — A403

No. 2471, horiz.: a, Madame Monet on the Sofa. b, The Picnic. c, The Luncheon. d, Jean Monet on His Mechanical Horse.

25d, La Japonaise.

**2001, Apr. 26** ***Perf. 13¾***
**2471** A403 10d Sheet of 4, #a-d 5.25 5.25

**Souvenir Sheet**

**2472** A403 25d multi 3.25 3.25

Toulouse-Lautrec Paintings — A404

No. 2473: a, At Le Rat Mort. b, The Milliner. c, Messaline.

25d, Napoleon.

**2001, Apr. 26**
**2473** A404 7d Sheet of 3, #a-c 2.75 2.75

**Souvenir Sheet**

**2474** A404 25d multi 3.25 3.25

Orchids — A405

Designs: 3d, Orchis morio. 4d, Fulophia speciosa. 5d, Angraecum leonis. 15d, Oeceoclades maculata.

No. 2479, 8d: a, Ceratostylis retisquama. b, Rangaeris rhipsalisocia. c, Phaius hybrid. d, Disa hybrid. e, Disa uniflora. f, Angraecum leonis.

No. 2480, 8d, horiz.: a, Satyrium erectum. b, Aeranthes grandiose. c, Aerangis somasticta. d, Polystachya bella. e, Eulophia guineensis. f, Disa blackii.

No. 2482, 25d, Disa kirstenbosch pride.

**2001, June 15** ***Perf. 14***
**2475-2478** A405 Set of 4 4.00 4.00

**Sheets of 6, #a-f**

**2479-2480** A405 Set of 2 13.00 13.00

**Souvenir Sheets**

**2482** A405 multi 3.50 3.50

Belgica 2001 Intl. Stamp Exhibition, Brussels (Nos. 2479-2480).

A 25d souvenir sheet, similar to No. 2482, depicting Aerangis curnowiana, was prepared but not issued.

SOS Children's Village A406

**2001, July 2**
**2483** A406 10d multi 1.25 1.25

Flora & Fauna A407

Designs: 2d, Hoopoe. 3d, Great spotted cuckoo. 4d, Plain tiger butterfly. 5d, Zebra duiker. 10d, Sooty managbey. 20d, Greater kudu.

No. 2490, 8d: a, Hippopotamus. b, Elephant. c, Parusta simplex. d, Gray heron. e, Charaxes imperialis. f, Gloriosa simplex.

No. 2491, 8d: a, Alpine swift. b, Blotched genet. c, Thomas' galago. d, Carmine bee-eater. e, Tree pangolin. f, Campbell's monkey.

No. 2492, 8d: a, Gray parrot. b, Rachel's weaver. c, European bee-eater. d, River kingfisher. e, Red river hog. f, Bushbuck.

No. 2493, 8d: a, Blue diadem butterfly. b, Fire-footed rope squirrel. c, Clappertonia ficifolia. d, Costus spectabilis. e, African migrant butterfly. f, Giant African snail.

No. 2494, 25d, Long-tailed pangolin, vert. No. 2495, 25d, Eurasian kestrel, vert.

**2001, July 16**
**2484-2489** A407 Set of 6 6.00 6.00

**Sheets of 6, #a-f**

**2490-2493** A407 Set of 4 26.00 26.00

**Souvenir Sheets**

**2494-2495** A407 Set of 2 7.00 7.00

A408

Ducks and Geese — A409

Designs: 2d, Blue-winged teal. No. 2497, 3d, Red-crested pochard. No. 2498, 4d, Falcated teal. No. 2499, 5d, Mandarin duck. No. 2500, 10d, King eider. 15d, Hooded merganser.

No. 2502, 3d, Wood duck. No. 2503, 4d, Mallard. No. 2504, 5d, Barrow's goldeneye. No. 2505, 10d, Bufflehead.

No. 2506, 7d, horiz.: a, Barrow's goldeneye. b, Harlequin duck. c, Pintail. d, Black-bellied whistling duck. e, Cinnamon teal. f, Surf scoter.

No. 2507, 7d, horiz.: a, Black scoter. b, Black duck. c, Green-winged teal. d, Bufflehead. e, Red-breasted merganser. f, Fulvous whistling duck.

No. 2508, 8d: a, European wigeon. b, Mallard. c, Garganey. d, Pintail, diff. e, Shoveler. f, Green-winged teal.

No. 2509, 8d: a, Black duck. b, Bufflehead. c, Cinnamon teal, diff. d, Goldeneye. e, Ruddy shelduck. f, Ferruginous duck.

No. 2510, 8d: a, Masked duck. b, Old squaw. c, Ring-necked duck. d, Harlequin duck, diff. e, Redhead. f, Canvasback.

No. 2511, 25d, American wigeon. No. 2512, 25d, Wood duck. No. 2513, 25d, Baikal teal.
No. 2514, 25d, Green-winged teal, horiz. No. 2515, 25d, Canada geese, horiz.

**2001, July 16**

| | | | | |
|---|---|---|---|---|
| **2496-2501** | A408 | Set of 6 | 5.25 | 5.25 |
| **2502-2505** | A409 | Set of 4 | 3.00 | 3.00 |

**Sheets of 6, #a-f**

| | | | | |
|---|---|---|---|---|
| **2506-2507** | A409 | Set of 2 | 11.00 | 11.00 |
| **2508-2510** | A408 | Set of 3 | 19.00 | 19.00 |

**Souvenir Sheets**

| | | | | |
|---|---|---|---|---|
| **2511-2513** | A408 | Set of 3 | 9.25 | 9.25 |
| **2514-2515** | A409 | Set of 2 | 6.25 | 6.25 |

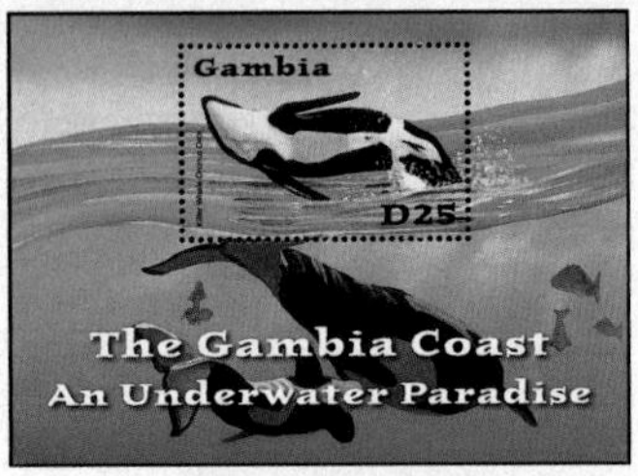


Cetaceans — A410

No. 2516, 7d: a, Killer whale (denomination at UR). b, Sperm whale (denomination at UR). c, Strap-toothed whale. d, Humpback whale. e, Southern right whale. f, Beluga.
No. 2517, 7d: a, Killer whale (denomination at LR). b, Sperm whale (denomination at LR). c, Narwhal. d, Gray whale. e, Blue whale. f, Northern right whale.
No. 2518, 25d, Killer whale. No. 2519, 25d, Humpback whale.

**2001, July 16 — Sheets of 6, #a-f**

| | | | | |
|---|---|---|---|---|
| **2516-2517** | A410 | Set of 2 | 11.00 | 11.00 |

**Souvenir Sheets**

| | | | | |
|---|---|---|---|---|
| **2518-2519** | A410 | Set of 2 | 6.50 | 6.50 |

A411

Trains A412

Designs: 2d, Rheingold Express. No. 2521, 10d, Amtrak train. No. 2522, 15d, The Blue Train. 20d, Cisalpino.
4d, Eurostar. No. 2525, 7d, Mallard. No. 2526, 10d, Rocket. No. 2527, TGV.
No. 2528, 7d: a, Eurostar, diff. b, Flying Hamburger. c, Coast Starlight. d, Tres Grande Vitesse. e, Golden Arrow. f, Shinkanzen "Max."
No. 2529, 7d: a, Siliguri to Darjeeling, India train. b, California Zephyr. c, Flying Scotsman. d, Trans-Siberian Express. e, Indian-Pacific. f, Thunersee.
No. 2530, 8d: a, Le Shuttle. b, Nord Express. c, 2-6-0, Switzerland. d, Duchess. e, Balkan Express. f, Class 44 2-10-0, Germany.
No. 2531, 8d: a, 7029 Clun Castle. b, Puffing Billy. c, ICE Electric. d, 4-4-2 S, Belgium. e, 2-8-2, Germany. f, PLM Coupe-Vents.
No. 2532, 25d, Cape Town to Victoria Falls train. No. 2533, 25d, The Southerner.
No. 2534, 25d, Stanier Class 5 4-6-0. No. 2535, 25d, Flying Scotsman, diff.

**2001, July 31** ***Perf. 14***

| | | | | |
|---|---|---|---|---|
| **2520-2523** | A411 | Set of 4 | 5.75 | 5.75 |
| **2524-2527** | A412 | Set of 4 | 4.50 | 4.50 |

**Sheets of 6, #a-f**

| | | | | |
|---|---|---|---|---|
| **2528-2529** | A411 | Set of 2 | 10.00 | 10.00 |
| **2530-2531** | A412 | Set of 2 | 12.00 | 12.00 |

**Souvenir Sheets**

| | | | | |
|---|---|---|---|---|
| **2532-2533** | A411 | Set of 2 | 6.00 | 6.00 |
| **2534-2535** | A412 | Set of 2 | 6.00 | 6.00 |

British Royal Navy — A413

Designs: 3d, St. Andrew, 1600s. 4d, Fleet maneuvers, 1914. 10d, HMS Illustrious, 1899. 15d, Battle of North Foreland, 1666.
No. 2540, 7d, horiz.: a, Mary Rose, 1512. b, Attack off Quebec, 1759. c, Armada campaign, 1588. d, Battle of Scheveningen, 1653. e, Blanche captures La Pique, 1795. f, Embarkation at Dover, 1520.
No. 2541, 7d, horiz. — Battles: a, Quiberon Bay, 1759. b, Barfleur, 1692. c, Nile, 1798. d, Trafalgar, 1805. e, Jutland, 1916. f, Camperdown, 1797.
No. 2542, 7d, horiz.: a, Battle of Navarino, 1827. b, Sinking of Eurydice, 1878. c, HMS Pantaloon captures Borboleta, 1845. d, Dardanelles, 1915. e, HMS Pickle captures Bolodora, 1829. f, HMS Invincible and Inflexible, Battle of the Falklands, 1914.
No. 2543, 25d, Ark Royal, 1582, horiz. No. 2544, 25d, Sovereign of the Seas, 1637, horiz.

**2001, Sept. 6** **Litho.**

| | | | | |
|---|---|---|---|---|
| **2536-2539** | A413 | Set of 4 | 4.00 | 4.00 |

**Sheets of 6, #a-f**

| | | | | |
|---|---|---|---|---|
| **2540-2542** | A413 | Set of 3 | 16.00 | 16.00 |

**Souvenir Sheets**

| | | | | |
|---|---|---|---|---|
| **2543-2544** | A413 | Set of 2 | 6.00 | 6.00 |

2002 World Cup Soccer Championships, Japan and Korea — A414

Jules Rimet Trophy and: 2d, Netherlands flag and player. 3d, Argentina flag and player. 4d, Ibaraki Kashima Stadium, Japan, horiz. 5d, George Best and Northern Ireland flag. 10d, Dino Zoff and Italian flag. 15d, Poster for 1938 tournament, France.
25d, Pat Bonner making save for Ireland.

**2001, Sept. 6**

| | | | | |
|---|---|---|---|---|
| **2545-2550** | A414 | Set of 6 | 4.75 | 4.75 |

**Souvenir Sheet**

| | | | | |
|---|---|---|---|---|
| **2551** | A414 | 25d multi | 3.00 | 3.00 |

No. 2551 contains one 56x42mm stamp.

European Royalty — A415

No. 2552: a, King Harald V, Queen Sonja, Norway. b, Queen Margrethe II, Denmark. c, King Carl XVI Gustaf and Queen Silvia, Sweden. d, King Juan Carlos, Queen Sofia, Spain. e, Queen Beatrix, Netherlands. f, King Albert II, Queen Paola, Belgium.
No. 2553, 25d, Crown Prince Haakon, Princess Mette-Marit, Norway. No. 2554, 25d, King Juan Carlos, Spain, vert.

***Perf. 14¼x14½, 14½x14¼***

**2001, Nov. 15**

| | | | | |
|---|---|---|---|---|
| **2552** | A415 | 7d Sheet of 6, #a-f | 5.00 | 5.00 |

**Souvenir Sheets**

| | | | | |
|---|---|---|---|---|
| **2553-2554** | A415 | Set of 2 | 5.75 | 5.75 |

**Queen Mother Type of 1999**

No. 2555: a, Duchess of York, Princess Elizabeth, 1928. b, Lady Elizabeth Bowes-Lyon, 1923. c, Queen Elizabeth, 1946. d, Queen Mother, Prince Harry.
40d, Queen Mother celebrating 89th birthday, 1989.

**2001, Dec. 13** ***Perf. 14***

| | | | | |
|---|---|---|---|---|
| **2555** | A342 | 15d Sheet of 4, #a-d + label | 7.25 | 7.25 |

**Souvenir Sheet**

***Perf. 13¾***

| | | | | |
|---|---|---|---|---|
| **2556** | A342 | 40d multi | 4.50 | 4.50 |

No. 2556 contains one 38x50mm stamp.

Oriental Actors and Actresses — A416

No. 2557, 15d: a, Alex Fong. b, William So. c, Flora Chan. d, Rain Li.
No. 2558, 15d — Kelly Chen: a, Close-up. b, As child, with cherry. c, On swing. d, As child, with hand above eyes.
No. 2559, 15d — Jacky Cheung: a, At L, laughing, looking to R. b, Looking forward, mouth open. c, At R, laughing, looking L. d, Looking forward, mouth closed.
No. 2560, 15d — Andy Hui, and Chinese characters at: a, L (pink suit). b, R (yellow suit). c, L (yellow suit). d, R (pink suit).
No. 2561, 15d — Miriam Yeung, with roses and petals at: a, LR. b, LL. c, UR. d, UL.

**2001, Nov. 5 Litho.** ***Perf. 13¾x13¼***

**Sheets of 4, #a-d**

| | | | | |
|---|---|---|---|---|
| **2557-2561** | A416 | Set of 5 | 35.00 | 35.00 |

New Year 2002 (Year of the Horse) — A417

No. 2562 — Denomination at: a, UR. b, UL. c, LR. d, LL.
20d, African zebra.

**2001, Dec. 26** ***Perf. 13***

| | | | | |
|---|---|---|---|---|
| **2562** | A417 | 6d Miniature sheet of 4, #a-d | 3.00 | 3.00 |

**Souvenir Sheet**

***Perf. 12½x13***

| | | | | |
|---|---|---|---|---|
| **2563** | A417 | 20d multi | 2.25 | 2.25 |

No. 2563 contains one 68x31mm triangular stamp.

Jacqueline Kennedy Onassis (1929-94) — A418

No. 2564: a, As baby. b, At age 6. c, Engagement to J.F.K. d, In wedding gown, 1955. e, In 1960. f, In 1980.
30d, At wedding to Aristotle Onassis.

**2002, Jan. 24** ***Perf. 14***

| | | | | |
|---|---|---|---|---|
| **2564** | A418 | 7d Sheet of 6, #a-f | 5.00 | 5.00 |

**Souvenir Sheet**

| | | | | |
|---|---|---|---|---|
| **2565** | A418 | 30d multi | 3.75 | 3.75 |

Princess Diana (1961-97) — A419

No. 2566 — Diana and: a, Coral rose. b, White rose. c, Yellow rose. d, Purple rose.
40d, Portrait.

**2002, Jan. 24**

| | | | | |
|---|---|---|---|---|
| **2566** | A419 | 15d Sheet of 4, #a-d | 7.25 | 7.25 |

**Souvenir Sheet**

| | | | | |
|---|---|---|---|---|
| **2567** | A419 | 40d multi | 4.75 | 4.75 |

Moths A420

Designs: 2d, Tiger moth. 3d, Hawk moth. No. 2570, 10d, Pericopid moth. 15d, Spurge hawk.
No. 2572, 10d (50x38mm): a, Sloane's urania. b, Saturniid moth. c, Black witch moth. d, Burnet moth on plant. e, Day-flying moth. f, Lime hawk moth.
No. 2573, 10d (50x38mm): a, Emperor moth. b, Millar's tiger. c, Hawk moth, diff. d, Phrygionis privignara. e, Burnet moth, waterfall. f, Urania leilus.
No. 2574, 40d, Emerald moth. No. 2575, 40d, Red under-wing moth, vert.

***Perf. 14, 13¾ (#2572-2573)***

**2002, Jan. 24**

| | | | | |
|---|---|---|---|---|
| **2568-2571** | A420 | Set of 4 | 4.00 | 4.00 |

**Sheets of 6, #a-f**

| | | | | |
|---|---|---|---|---|
| **2572-2573** | A420 | Set of 2 | 15.00 | 15.00 |

**Souvenir Sheets**

| | | | | |
|---|---|---|---|---|
| **2574-2575** | A420 | Set of 2 | 10.00 | 10.00 |

United We Stand — A421

**2002, Feb. 6** ***Perf. 13¾x13¼***

| | | | | |
|---|---|---|---|---|
| **2576** | A421 | 20d multi | 2.25 | 2.25 |

Issued in sheets of 4.

Reign of Queen Elizabeth II, 50th Anniv. — A422

No. 2577: a, With beige hat. b, With red hat. c, With blue hat. d, Near vehicle.
40d, Wearing uniform.

**2002, Feb. 6** ***Perf. 14½***

| | | | | |
|---|---|---|---|---|
| **2577** | A422 | 15d Sheet of 4, #a-d | 7.00 | 7.00 |

**Souvenir Sheet**

| | | | | |
|---|---|---|---|---|
| **2578** | A422 | 40d multi | 4.50 | 4.50 |

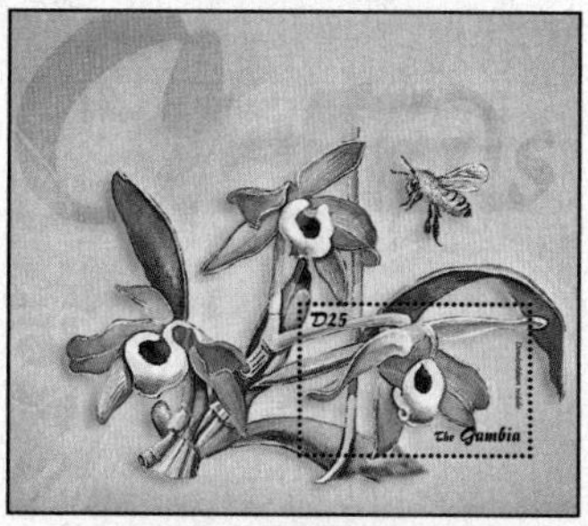


A423

Orchids — A424

No. 2579, vert.: a, Machu piechu. b, Masdevallia copper angel. c, Masdevallia hirtzi. d, Tuakau canoy.

No. 2580: a, Eriopsis sceptrum. b, Sarcanthopsis muellem. c, Bougainville white. d, Telipogon klotzchianus.

No. 2581, 7d: a, Richard Mueller. b, Colmanara wildcat. c, Cycnoches chlorochilon. d, Vanda coerylea. e, Disa blackii. f, Unnamed.

No. 2582, 7d: a, Seagulls beaulu queen. b, Hazel Boyd. c, Costa Rica. d, Dendrobium infudibulum. e, Disa hybrid. f, Chysis.

No. 2583, 6d, horiz.: a, Spathoglottis portusfinschii. b, Dendrobium macrophyllum. c, Grammaneis ellisii. d, Stanhopea wardii. e, Dendrobium nindi. f, Dendrobium williamsianum.

No. 2584, 7d: a, Seutieama steeli. b, Dendrobium inaequale. c, Dendrobium lasiathera. d, Calypso bulbosa. e, Vanda hindsii. f, Dendrobium violaceoflavens.

No. 2585, 8d, horiz.: a, Phaleonopsis rosenstomii. b, Cypripedium guttatum. c, Cypripedium reginae. d, Dendrobium engae. e, Diplocaulobium hydrophilum. f, Dendrobium cuthbertsonii.

No. 2586, 25d, Dendrobium nobile. No. 2587, 25d, Ancidium alliance, vert.

No. 2588, 25d, Menadenium labiosum. No. 2589, 25d, Dendrobium spectabile. No. 2590, 25d, Dendrobium canaliculatum, horiz.

**2001, June 15** **Litho.** ***Perf. 14***

| | | | | |
|---|---|---|---|---|
| **2579** | A423 | 7d Sheet of 4, #a-d | 2.75 | 2.75 |
| **2580** | A424 | 10d Sheet of 4, #a-d | 4.00 | 4.00 |

**Sheets of 6, #a-f**

| | | | | |
|---|---|---|---|---|
| **2581-2582** | A423 | Set of 2 | 8.50 | 8.50 |
| **2583-2585** | A424 | Set of 3 | 12.50 | 12.50 |

**Souvenir Sheets**

| | | | | |
|---|---|---|---|---|
| **2586-2587** | A423 | Set of 2 | 5.00 | 5.00 |
| **2588-2590** | A424 | Set of 3 | 7.50 | 7.50 |

Nos. 2579-2590 were not available until 2002. Belgica 2001 Intl. Stamp Exhibition (No. 2579).

Wildlife A425

Designs: 2d, Martial eagle. 4d, Lion. 5d, Aardvark. 10d, Lion cub, vert.

No. 2595, 7d: a, Lion cub. b, Water buffalo. c, Topi. d, Hyena. e, Secretary bird. f, Genet.

No. 2596, 7d: a, Reedbuck. b, Hippopotamus. c, Waterbuck and malachite kingfisher. d, Hoopoe. e, White pelican. f, Waterbuck.

No. 2597, 25d, Hippopotamus. No. 2598, 25d, Crocodile.

**2001, July 16**

| | | | | |
|---|---|---|---|---|
| **2591-2594** | A425 | Set of 4 | 2.10 | 2.10 |

**Sheets of 6, #a-f**

| | | | | |
|---|---|---|---|---|
| **2595-2596** | A425 | Set of 2 | 8.50 | 8.50 |

**Souvenir Sheets**

| | | | | |
|---|---|---|---|---|
| **2597-2598** | A425 | Set of 2 | 5.00 | 5.00 |

Nos. 2591-2598 were not available until 2002.

Pres. Theodore Roosevelt (1858-1919) — A426

No. 2599: a, Wearing hat and uniform. b, Close-up. c, With hand on chair. d, Wearing hat and neckerchief.
40d, Close-up, diff.

**2002, Jan. 24**

| | | | | |
|---|---|---|---|---|
| **2599** | A426 | 15d Sheet of 4, #a-d | 7.25 | 7.25 |

**Souvenir Sheet**

| | | | | |
|---|---|---|---|---|
| **2600** | A426 | 40d multi | 5.00 | 5.00 |

Betty Boop — A427

No. 2602, 40d, With gray ribbon in hair, horiz. No. 2603, 40d, With ice cream sundae.

**2002, Feb. 13** ***Perf. 13¾***

| | | | | |
|---|---|---|---|---|
| **2601** | A427 | 7d shown | .80 | .80 |

**Souvenir Sheets**

| | | | | |
|---|---|---|---|---|
| **2602-2603** | A427 | Set of 2 | 9.50 | 9.50 |

No. 2601 was issued in sheets of 9.

Shirley Temple in "Little Miss Broadway" — A428

No. 2604, horiz.: a, With man and old woman. b, Close-up. c, Waving. d, Holding man's tie. e, At hotel desk with men. f, Woman watching Temple point to tooth.

No. 2605: a, Dancing with young man. b, Dancing with old man with hat. c, Sitting with boy. d, Holding hands with old man.
30d, Wearing tiara and dancing with young man.

**2002, Feb. 13**

| | | | | |
|---|---|---|---|---|
| **2604** | A428 | 8d Sheet of 6, #a-f | 5.50 | 5.50 |
| **2605** | A428 | 10d Sheet of 4, #a-d | 4.75 | 4.75 |

**Souvenir Sheet**

| | | | | |
|---|---|---|---|---|
| **2606** | A428 | 30d multi | 3.75 | 3.75 |

2002 Winter Olympics, Salt Lake City — A429

Designs: No. 2607, 20d, Curling. No. 2608, 20d, Ski jumping.

**2002, Mar. 18** ***Perf. 14***

| | | | | |
|---|---|---|---|---|
| **2607-2608** | A429 | Set of 2 | 4.75 | 4.75 |
| *a.* | | Souvenir sheet, #2607-2608 | 4.75 | 4.75 |

Chiune Sugihara, Japanese Diplomat Who Saved Jews in World War II — A430

**2002, Apr. 29** ***Perf. 13½x13¼***

| | | | | |
|---|---|---|---|---|
| **2609** | A430 | 10d multi | 1.10 | 1.10 |

Printed in sheets of 4.

Intl. Year of Mountains — A431

No. 2610: a, Winkler Tower, Italy. b, Mt. Huanstan Chico, Peru. c, Hodaka Mountains, Japan. d, Mustagh Ata, Kashmir.
40d, Mt. Myoko, Japan.

**2002, July 1** ***Perf. 13¼x13½***

| | | | | |
|---|---|---|---|---|
| **2610** | A431 | 15d Sheet of 4, #a-d | 6.75 | 6.75 |

**Souvenir Sheet**

| | | | | |
|---|---|---|---|---|
| **2611** | A431 | 40d multi | 4.50 | 4.50 |

2002 World Cup Soccer Championships, Japan and Korea — A432

Players, dates and locations of matches — No. 2612, 9d: a, France v. Senegal. b, Uruguay v. Denmark. c, France v. Uruguay. d, Denmark v. Senegal. e, Denmark v. France. f, Senegal v. Uruguay.

No. 2613, 9d: a, Paraguay v. South Africa. b, Spain v. Slovenia. c, Spain v. Paraguay. d, South Africa v. Slovenia. e, South Africa v. Spain. f, Slovenia v. Paraguay.

No. 2614, 9d: a, Brazil v. Turkey. b, China v. Costa Rica. c, Brazil v. China. d, Costa Rica v. Turkey. e, Costa Rica v. Brazil. f, Turkey v. China.

No. 2615, 9d: a, South Korea v. Poland. b, US v. Portugal. c, South Korea v. US. d, Portugal v. Poland. e, Portugal v. South Korea. f, Poland v. US.

No. 2616, 9d: a, Germany v. Saudi Arabia. b, Ireland v. Cameroun. c, Germany v. Ireland. d, Cameroun v. Saudi Arabia. e, Cameroun v. Germany. f, Saudi Arabia v. Ireland.

No. 2617, 9d: a, England v. Sweden. b, Argentina v. Nigeria. c, Sweden v. Nigeria. d, Argentina v. England. e, Sweden v. Argentina. f, Nigeria v. England.

No. 2618, 9d: a, Croatia v. Mexico. b, Italy v. Ecuador. c, Italy v. Croatia. d, Mexico v. Ecuador. e, Mexico v. Italy. f, Ecuador v. Croatia.

No. 2619, 9d: a, Japan v. Belgium. b, Russia v. Tunisia. c, Japan v. Russia. d, Tunisia v. Belgium. e, Tunisia v. Japan. f, Belgium v. Russia.

Stadia and dates of matches between — No. 2620, 20d: a, France v. Senegal. b, Uruguay v. Denmark.

No. 2621, 20d: a, France v. Uruguay. b, Denmark v. Senegal.

No. 2622, 20d: a, Denmark v. France. b, Senegal v. Uruguay.

No. 2623, 20d: a, Paraguay v. South Africa. b, Spain v. Slovenia.

No. 2624, 20d: a, Spain v. Paraguay. b, South Africa v. Slovenia.

No. 2625, 20d, a, South Africa v. Spain. b, Slovenia v. Paraguay.

No. 2626, 20d: a, Brazil v. Turkey. b, China v. Costa Rica.

No. 2627, 20d: a, Brazil v. China. b, Costa Rica v. Turkey.

No. 2628, 20d: a, Costa Rica v. Brazil. b, Turkey v. China.

No. 2629, 20d: a, South Korea v. Poland. b, US v. Portugal.

No. 2630, 20d: a, South Korea v. US. b, Portugal v. Poland.

No. 2631, 20d: a, Portugal v. South Korea. b, Poland v. US.

No. 2632, 20d: a, Germany v. Saudi Arabia. b, Ireland v. Cameroun.

No. 2633, 20d: a, Germany v. Ireland. b, Cameroun v. Saudi Arabia.

No. 2634, 20d: a, Cameroun v. Germany. b, Saudi Arabia v. Ireland.

No. 2635, 20d: a, England v. Sweden. b, Argentina v. Nigeria.
No. 2636, 20d: a, Sweden v. Nigeria. b, Argentina v. England.
No. 2637, 20d: a, Sweden v. Argentina. b, Nigeria v. England.
No. 2638, 20d: a, Croatia v. Mexico. b, Italy v. Ecuador.
No. 2639, 20d: a, Italy v. Croatia. b, Mexico v. Ecuador.
No. 2640, 20d: a, Mexico v. Italy. b, Ecuador v. Croatia.
No. 2641, 20d: a, Japan v. Belgium. b, Russia v. Tunisia.
No. 2642, 20d: a, Japan v. Russia. b, Tunisia v. Belgium.
No. 2643, 20d: a, Tunisia v. Japan. b, Belgium v. Russia.

**2002, July 1** ***Perf. 13¼***

**Sheets of 6, #a-f**

**2612-2619** A432 Set of 8 47.50 47.50

**Souvenir Sheets**

**2620-2643** A432 Set of 24 100.00 100.00

See Nos. 2654-2656 for sheets with match results.

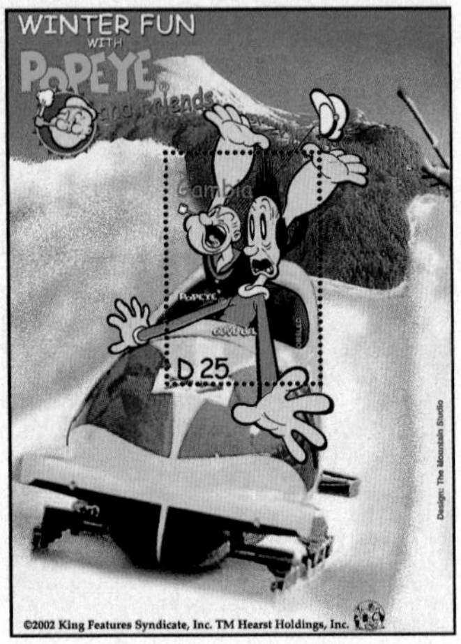


Popeye — A433

No. 2644, 10d: a, Popeye on cross-country skis. b, Popeye ski jumping. c, Popeye slalom-ing. d, Popeye snowboarding.
No. 2645, 10d: a, Swee'Pea on sled. b, Olive Oyl on skis. c, Brutus. d, Wimpy on ice skates.
No. 2646, 25d, Popeye and Olive in bob-sled. No. 2647, 25d, Brutus playing hockey. No. 2648, 25d, Olive on ice skates. No. 2649, 25d, Popeye speed skating, horiz.

**2002, June 17** **Litho.** ***Perf. 14***

**Sheets of 6, #a-f**

**2644-2645** A433 Set of 2 9.00 9.00

**Souvenir Sheets**

**2646-2649** A433 Set of 4 11.50 11.50

20th World Scout Jamboree, Thailand — A434

No. 2650: a, Scout with bugle. b, Scout making fire. c, Scout fishing.
40d, Scout tying knot.

**2002, July 1** ***Perf. 13½x13¼***

**2650** A434 15d Sheet of 3, #a-c 5.00 5.00

**Souvenir Sheet**

**2651** A434 40d multi 4.50 4.50

Intl. Year of Ecotourism — A435

No. 2652: a, Bird-of-Paradise flower. b, Goliath heron. c, Baobab tree. d, Roan antelope. e, Red tip butterfly. f, Egyptian cobra.
No. 2653, Yellow-billed stork.

**2002, July 1**

**2652** A435 9d Sheet of 6, #a-d 6.00 6.00

**Souvenir Sheet**

**2653** A435 9d multi .90 .90

**Nos. 2616, 2617 and 2619 Redrawn With Match Scores**

No. 2654, 9d: a, Germany 8, Saudi Arabia 0. b, Ireland 1, Cameroun 1. c, Germany 1, Ireland 1. d, Cameroun 1, Saudi Arabia 0. e, Cameroun 0, Germany 2. f, Saudi Arabia 0, Ireland 3
No. 2655, 9d: a, England 1, Sweden 1. b, Argentina 1, Nigeria 0. c, Sweden 2, Nigeria 1. d, Argentina 0, England 1. e, Sweden 1, Argentina 1. f, Nigeria 0, England 0.
No. 2656, 9d: a, Japan 2, Belgium 2. b, Russia 2, Tunisia 0. c, Japan 1, Russia 0. d, Tunisia 1, Belgium 1. e, Japan 2, Tunisia 0. f, Belgium 3, Russia 2.

**2002, July 15** ***Perf. 13¼***

**Sheets of 6, #a-f**

**2654-2656** A432 Set of 3 18.00 18.00

Elvis Presley (1935-77) A436

**2002, Aug. 19** ***Perf. 13½x13¾***

**2657** A436 5d multi .50 .50

Things from the Netherlands — A437

Netherlands Lighthouses — A438

Netherlands Postage Stamps, 150th Anniv. — A439

Women's Traditional Costumes of the Netherlands — A440

No. 2658: a, Farm. b, Porcelain. c, Building. d, Ice skaters. e, Cheese, flowers and wooden shoes. f, Prince Willem-Alexander and his bride.
No. 2659: a, Den Helder. b, Terschelling. c, Maasvlakte. d, Ijmuiden. e, Westkapelle. f, Breskens.
No. 2660: a, Netherlands #1. b, Netherlands #B72. c, Netherlands #279. d, Netherlands #586. e, Netherlands #620. f, Netherlands #1108a.
No. 2661: a, Woman from Friesland (plaid headdress). b, Back of woman from Utrecht. c, Woman and child from Noord-Holland.

**2002, Aug. 30** ***Perf. 13½x13¼***

**2658** A437 10d Sheet of 6, #a-f 6.25 6.25
**2659** A438 10d Sheet of 6, #a-f 6.25 6.25

***Perf. 13¼x13½***

**2660** A439 10d Sheet of 6, #a-f 6.25 6.25

***Perf. 13¼***

**2661** A440 20d Sheet of 3, #a-c 6.25 6.25

Amphilex 2002 Intl. Stamp Exhibition, Amsterdam.

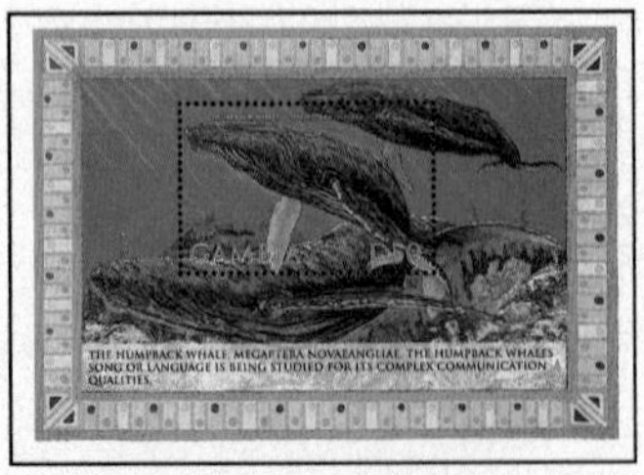

Marine Mammals and Flowers — A441

No. 2662, 10d: a, Blue whale. b, Pan-tropical spotted dolphin. c, Killer whale. d, Minke whale. e, Sperm whale. f, Pilot whale.

No. 2663, 10d: a, Juba-jamba. b, Devil's tongue. c, Rattle box. d, Vernonia purpurea. e, Seaside purslane. f, Fireball lily.
No. 2664, 50d, Humpback whale. No. 2665, 50d, Cape weed, swamp arum, vert.

**2002, Sept. 23** ***Perf. 14***

**Sheets of 6, #a-f**

**2662-2663** A441 Set of 2 11.50 11.50

**Souvenir Sheets**

**2664-2665** A441 Set of 2 10.00 10.00

See Nos. 2763-2764.

A442

Teddy Bears, Cent. — A443

No. 2666: a, Bear with green feathered cap. b, Bear with beer stein. c, Bear with flower bouquet. d, Bear with mountain hat.
No. 2667 — Color of denomination and country name: a, White. b, Red violet. c, Blue violet. d, Green.

**2002, Oct. 21** ***Perf. 14***

**2666** A442 15d Sheet of 4, #a-d 6.00 6.00

***Perf. 14¼***

**2667** A443 15d Sheet of 4, #a-d 6.00 6.00

Christmas — A444

Designs: 3d, Madonna of Loreto, by Perugino. 5d, Madonna della Consolazione, by Perugino. 7d, Adoration of the Shepherds, by Perugino. 15d, Transfiguration of Christ, by Giovanni Bellini. 35d, Adoration of the Magi, by Perugino.
45d, Christ Blessing, by Bellini.

**2002, Nov. 4** ***Perf. 14***

**2668-2672** A444 Set of 5 6.00 6.00

**Souvenir Sheet**

**2673** A444 45d multi 4.25 4.25

Princess Diana (1961-97) — A445

No. 2674, 15d — With red panel at bottom: a, As child. b, Wearing tiara. c, Holding baby. d, With children.

No. 2675, 15d: a, Wearing red hat. b, Wearing red and white hat. c, Wearing white gown. d, Wearing black gown and choker.

**2002, Nov. 18**

**Sheets of 4, #a-d**

**2674-2675** A445 Set of 2 10.50 10.50

Souvenir Sheet

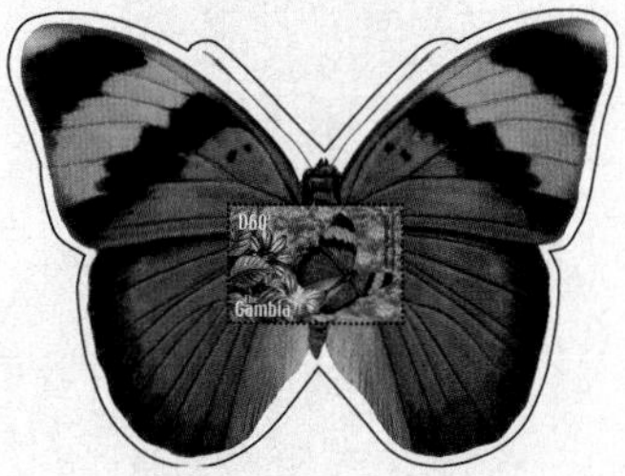


Gold-banded Forester Butterfly — A446

**2002 Litho. *Perf. 14***

**2676** A446 60d multi 5.75 5.75

Birds — A447

No. 2677: a, Black-crowned crane. b, Barn owl. c, African pygmy kingfisher. d, Audouin's gull. e, Royal tern. f, Blue-bellied roller.

**2002**

**2677** A447 7d Sheet of 6, #a-f 4.25 4.25

Pres. John F. Kennedy (1917-63) — A448

No. 2678, 15d: a, With daughter Caroline. b, At typewriter. c, At wedding to Jacqueline. d, With Jacqueline.

No. 2679, 15d, vert: a, In naval uniform. b, As child. c, Wearing shirt with open collar. d, At microphone.

**2002, Nov. 8 Sheets of 4, #a-d**

**2678-2679** A448 Set of 2 11.00 11.00

A449

Trains A450

Designs: 2d, Paris, Lyon & Mediterranean Railway. 3d, Zugspitz rack train, Germany. No. 2682, 10d, Austrian State Railway Class 210. 15d, State Railway of Saxony.

4d, 1922 Great Britain Class A1 4-6-2. 5d, 1957 Tee four car train. No. 2686, 7d, 1928 German Rheingold Mitropa car. 8d, 1900 German Gerda 4-4-0.

No. 2688, 7d: a, French Natl. Railway Series 68. b, French Natl. Railway Mistral. c, Prussian State Railway. d, Austrian Southern Railway. e, Paris-Orleans Railway. f, German Federal Railway E10.

No. 2689, 7d: a, Royal Prussian Union Railway. b, Austrian Federal Railway. c, German Rugen steam locomotive. d, Rh B Ge 2/4 electric locomotive. e, Panoramic Express, Switzerland. f, Brunig steam engine, Swiss Natl. Railway.

No. 2690, 10d: a, 1813 Puffing Billy, Great Britain. b, Adler, Germany, 1836. c, 1906 German 4-6-0. d, Class 132 Co-Co, Germany.

No. 2691, 10d: a, 1832 Brother Jonathan 4-2-0, US. b, Medoc Class 2-4-0, Germany and Switzerland, 1857. c, 1908 German Class S 3/6 4-6-2. d, 1959 German Class VT 11.5.

No. 2692, 10d: a, 1843 Beuth 2-2-2, Germany. b, 1852 Crampton 4-2-0, France. c, 1932 Sut 877 Flying Hamburger, Germany. d, 1970 Class 103.1 Co-Co, Germany.

No. 2693, 25d, German Federal Railway V200. No. 2694, 25d, German Federal Railway Trans-Europe Express.

No. 2695, 25d, 1953 VT10.5, Germany. No. 2696, 25d,1973 Class ET 403 four-car electric, Germany.

**2002**

| | | | | |
|---|---|---|---|---|
| **2680-2683** | A449 | Set of 4 | 2.50 | 2.50 |
| **2684-2687** | A450 | Set of 4 | 2.25 | 2.25 |

**Sheets of 6, #a-f**

**2688-2689** A449 Set of 2 7.75 7.75

**Sheets of 4, #a-d**

**2690-2692** A450 Set of 3 11.00 11.00

**Souvenir Sheets**

| | | | | |
|---|---|---|---|---|
| **2693-2694** | A449 | Set of 2 | 4.75 | 4.75 |
| **2695-2696** | A450 | Set of 2 | 4.75 | 4.75 |

Charles A. Lindbergh (1902-74), Aviator — A451

No. 2697, 15d: a, As child, with dog. b, As young man, brown violet background. c, With aviator goggles. d, Anne Morrow Lindbergh.

No. 2698, 15d: a, As child. b, As young man, blue background. c, Wearing uniform. d, Wearing suit and tie.

**2002, Nov. 18 Litho. *Perf. 14***

**Sheets of 4, #a-d**

**2697-2698** A451 Set of 2 11.00 11.00

**Butterfly Type of 2000**

Designs: 4d, Amphicalia tigris.

**2003, Jan. 14 *Perf. 14¾x14***

**2699** A367 4d multi .40 .40

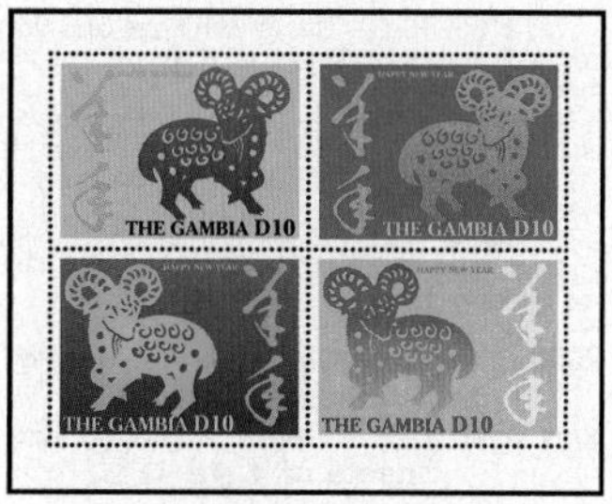


New Year 2003 (Year of the Ram) — A452

No. 2697: a, Tan background, brown ram. b, Purple background. c, Brown background, orange ram. d, Orange background, purple and red ram.

**2003, Jan. 27 *Perf. 13¾***

**2701** A452 10d Sheet of 4, #a-d 3.50 3.50

A453

Coronation of Queen Elizabeth II, 50th Anniv. — A454

No. 2702: a, Wearing tiara. b, Wearing blue hat. c, Wearing cape and hat.

**2003 Litho. *Perf. 14***

**2702** A453 20d Sheet of 3, #a-c 5.50 5.50

**Souvenir Sheet**

**2703** A453 45d shown 4.25 4.25

**Miniature Sheet**

**Litho. & Embossed**

***Perf. 13¼x13***

**2704** A454 130d shown 10.50 10.50

Issued: Nos. 2702-2703, 5/13; 130d, 2/24.

Art by Yoshitoshi Taiso (1839-92) A455

Designs: 5d, Concubine Washing Her Hands Under an Ornate Faucet. 10d, Housewife in an Inner Chamber Fanning a Fire. 15d, Geisha Catching a Firefly. 25d, A Young Geisha Dressed as an Elegant Young Man While Taking Part in the Niwaka Celebration.

No. 2709: a, Music Teacher Playing on a Samisen. b, An "Okamisan," or Proprietress of a Tea House, at Work. c, A City Merchant's Widow Absorbed in a Novelette. d, Busy Young Waitress Preoccupied With Her Responsibilities.

45d, A "Saikun," or Wife of a Government Official, Lighting an Oil Lamp.

**2003, Mar. 10 Litho. *Perf. 14¼***

| | | | | |
|---|---|---|---|---|
| **2705-2708** | A455 | Set of 4 | 4.75 | 4.75 |
| **2709** | A455 | 20d Sheet of 4, #a-d | 6.50 | 6.50 |

**Souvenir Sheet**

**2710** A455 45d multi 4.00 4.00

Paintings by the Cranachs A456

Paintings by Lucas Cranach the Elder (1472-1553) or Lucas Cranach the Younger (1515-86) (Y): 5d, Portrait of Johannes Scheyring. 7d, Rudolph Agricola. 10d, Portrait Head of a Gentleman (Y). 20d, Hans von Lindau (Y).

No. 2715: a, Margravine Elizabeth von Ansbach (Y). b, Elector Joachim II of Brandenburg (Y). c, Portrait of a Nobleman (Y). d, Portrait of a Noblewoman (Y).

40d, The Ill-matched Couple.

**2003, Mar. 10**

| | | | | |
|---|---|---|---|---|
| **2711-2714** | A456 | Set of 4 | 3.50 | 3.50 |
| **2715** | A456 | 15d Sheet of 4, #a-d | 5.00 | 5.00 |

**Souvenir Sheet**

**2716** A456 40d multi 3.25 3.25

Paintings by Wassily Kandinsky (1866-1944) — A457

Designs: 2d, Composition X. 4d, Arrow Towards the Circle. 5d, Yellow-Red-Blue. 7d, Accompanied Middle. 10d, In Blue. 20d, Round and Pointed.

No. 2723, vert.: a, Picture with Archer. b, Light. c, Picture in the Picture. d, White Stroke.

No. 2724, 45d, Improvisation XIX. No. 2725, 45d, On the Points.

**2003, Mar. 10 *Perf. 14¼***

| | | | | |
|---|---|---|---|---|
| **2717-2722** | A457 | Set of 6 | 4.25 | 4.25 |
| **2723** | A457 | 15d Sheet of 4, #a-d | 5.00 | 5.00 |

**Size: 97x78mm**

***Imperf***

**2724-2725** A457 Set of 2 7.50 7.50

A458

Astronauts Killed In Space Shuttle Columbia Accident — A459

No. 2726, 15d — Michael P. Anderson: a, Columbia crew, brown background, country name at UL. b, Anderson and jet. c, Shuttle lifting off. d, Shuttle in orbit, Space Station.
No. 2727, 15d — Kalpana Chawla: a, Like No. 2726a, country name at LL. b, Shuttle being transported by jet. c, Shuttle glowing in re-entry. d, Chawla, astronaut spacewalking.
No. 2728, 15d — Laurel Blair Salton Clark: a, Like No. 2727a, green and red background. b, Shuttle in orbit, moon in background. c, Shuttle on launch pad. d, Clark and jet.
No. 2729, 15d — Ilan Ramon: a, Columbia crew, purple and yellow background. b, Ramon in jet. c, Shuttle with engines firing at launch pad. d, Shuttle in orbit.
No. 2730: a, Mission Specialist David M. Brown. b, Commander Rick D. Husband. c, Mission Specialist 4 Laurel Blair Salton Clark. d, Mission Specialist 4 Kalpana Chawla. e, Payload Commander, Michael P. Anderson. f, Pilot William C. McCool. g, Payload Specialist 4 Ilan Ramon.

**2003, Apr. 7** *Perf. 14¼*

**Sheets of 4, #a-d**

**2726-2729** A458 Set of 4 21.00 21.00

**Souvenir Sheet**

**2730** A459 10d Sheet of 7, #a-g 6.00 6.00

A460

Teddy Bears — A461

No. 2732, 15d — Bears with flags and soccer uniforms of: a, England. b, Brazil. c, Germany. d, Spain.
No. 2733, 15d — Bears with soocer uniforms of German teams: a, Schalke 04. b, FC Bayern Munich. c, Bayer Leaerkusen. d, Hertha Berlin.
No. 2734, 45d, FC Bayern Munich, white uniform. No. 2735, 45d, FC Bayern Munich red uniform, horiz.

**2003 Embroidered** *Imperf.*

**Self-Adhesive (#2731)**

**2731** A460 150d shown 14.00 14.00

**Sheets of 4, #a-d**

**Litho.**

*Perf. 13¼*

**2732-2733** A461 Set of 2 11.00 11.00

**Souvenir Sheets**

**2734-2735** A461 Set of 2 8.25 8.25

Issued: No. 2731, Apr.; Nos. 2732-2735, 7/1.
No. 2731 was issued in sheets of 4.

Prince William, 21st Birthday — A462

No. 2736: a, Wearing suit, no tie. b, Wearing suit and tie. c, Wearing blue shirt, no suit.
45d, Wearing polo uniform.

**2003, May 13 Litho.** *Perf. 14*

**2736** A462 20d Sheet of 3, #a-c 5.50 5.50

**Souvenir Sheet**

**2737** A462 45d multi 4.25 4.25

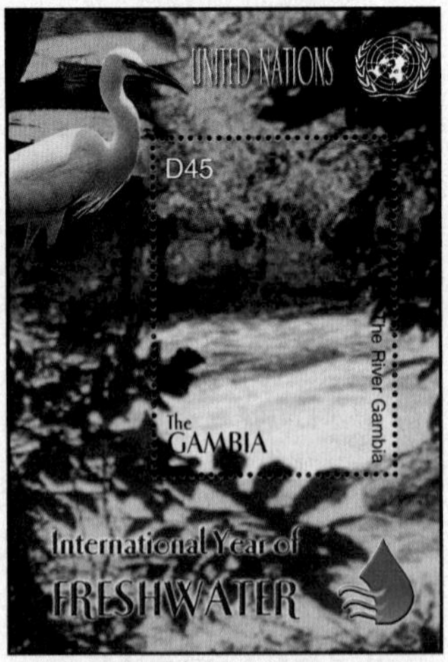


Intl. Year of Fresh Water — A463

No. 2738 — Gambia River: a, Foliage at top. b, Foliage at top, silhouette of far shore at center. c, Trees at right.
45d, Gambia River rapids.

**2003, July 1** *Perf. 13¼*

**2738** A463 20d Sheet of 3, #a-c 5.50 5.50

**Souvenir Sheet**

**2739** A463 45d multi 4.25 4.25

Tour de France Bicycle Race, Cent. — A464

No. 2740, 15d: a, Henri Pelissier, 1923. b, Ottavio Bottecchia, 1924. c, Bottecchia, 1925. d, Lucien Buysse, 1926.
No. 2741, 15d: a, Nicholas Frantz, 1927. b, Frantz, 1928. c, Maurice de Waele, 1929. d, André Leducq, 1930.
No. 2742, 15d: a, Antonin Magne, 1931. b, Leducq, 1932. c, Georges Speicher, 1933. d, Magne, 1934.

**2003, July 1** *Perf. 13¼*

**Sheets of 4, #a-d**

**2740-2742** A464 Set of 3 17.00 17.00

General Motors Automobiles — A465

No. 2743, 15d — Cadillacs: a, 1937 Series 60. b, 1927 La Salle. c, 1930 V-16. d, 1931 V-16 Convertible.
No. 2744, 15d — Corvettes: a, 1960 Shark. b, 1964 Sting Ray Convertible. c, 1956 Convertible. d, 1967.
No. 2745, 45d, 1954 Cadillac Eldorado. No. 2746, 45d, 1964 Corvette Sting Ray.

**2003, July 1** *Perf. 13¼x13½*

**Sheets of 4, #a-d**

**2743-2744** A465 Set of 2 11.00 11.00

**Souvenir Sheets**

**2745-2746** A465 Set of 2 8.25 8.25

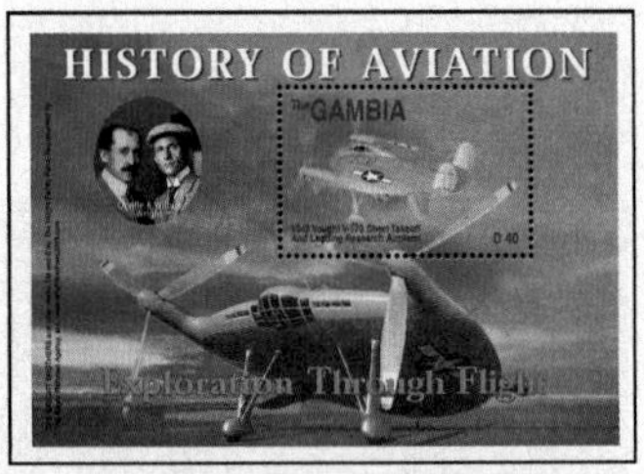


History of Aviation — A466

No. 2747, 15d: a, First powered flight by Wright Brothers, 1903. b, Goupy I, first full-size triplane, 1908. c, Deutschland LZ-7, first commercial airship, 1909. d, Lt. Col. Richard Byrd's flight over North Pole, 1926.
No. 2748, 15d: a, Granville Gee Bee, world speed record, 1932. b, Boeing 247D with all-metal construction retractable landing gear, 1933. c, Douglas DC-3, 1935. d, Amelia Earhart's solo flight from Hawaii to California, 1935.
No. 2749, 15d: a, First solar powered flight, by MacCready Solar Challenger, 1981. b, Voyager 2 space probe explores Saturn, 1981. c, Space Shuttle Columbia, 1981. d, First non-stop non-refueled around the world flight, by Voyager, 1986.
No. 2750, 40d, Vought V-173 Short Takeoff and Landing research airplane, 1942. No. 2751, 40d, Pioneer 10 space probe, 1972. No. 2752, 40d, AD-1 scissors-wing SST, 1979.

**2003, July 14** *Perf. 14*

**Sheets of 4, #a-d**

**2747-2749** A466 Set of 3 17.00 17.00

**Souvenir Sheets**

**2750-2752** A466 Set of 3 11.00 11.00

Ferrari Race Cars — A467

Designs: 2d, 126 C2. 3d, 312 T2. 5d, 312 T4. 7d, 126 C3. 10d, F399. 15d, F1-2000. 20d, F2001. 25d, F2002.

**2003, July 28** *Perf. 14¼*

**2753-2760** A467 Set of 8 6.50 6.50

Circus Performers — A468

No. 2761, 15d: a, Francesco Caroli. b, Lou Jacobs. c, Frankie Saluto. d, Gingernut.
No. 2762, 15d: a, Evgeny Maranogli. b, Saby. c, Colonel Joe. d, Puma.

**2003, Sept. 1** *Perf. 14*

**Sheets of 4, #a-d**

**2761-2762** A468 Set of 2 10.00 10.00

**Marine Mammals and Flowers Type of 2002**

No. 2763 — Insects and flowers: a, Colored shield-backed bug, Waltheria indica. b, Dragonfly, Red mangrove. c, Cotton stainer bug, Baissea multiflora. d, Harpagomantis. Mimosa pigra. e, Katydid, Coia cordifolia. f, African grasshopper, Urena labata.
50d, Giant swallowtail butterfly, Ipomoea cairica.

**2003** *Perf. 14*

**2763** A441 10d Sheet of 6, #a-f 4.50 4.50

**Souvenir Sheet**

**2764** A441 50d multi 4.00 4.00

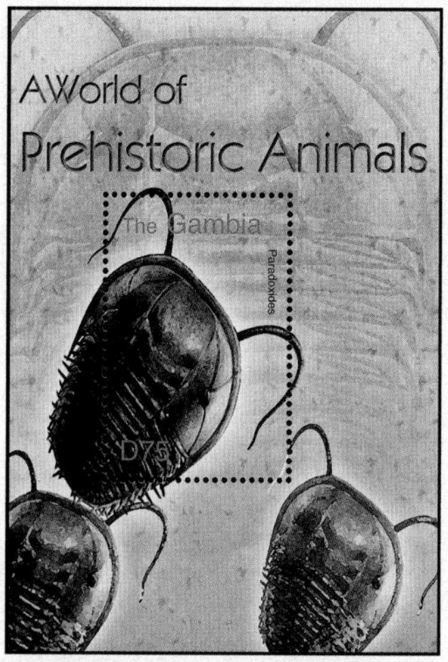


Prehistoric Animals — A469

No. 2765, 30d: a, Peteinosaurus. b, Pachycephalosaurus. c, Ichthyosaur. d, Anomalocaris.
No. 2766, 30d, horiz.: a, Criorhynchus. b, Seismosaurus. c, Triceratops. d, Stegosaurus.
No. 2767, 75d, Paradoxides. No. 2768, 75d, Edmontosaurus, horiz.

**2003, Nov. 4 Litho. *Perf. 14***

**Sheets of 4, #a-d**

**2765-2766** A469 Set of 2 17.00 17.00

**Souvenir Sheets**

**2767-2768** A469 Set of 2 10.50 10.50

Christmas A470

Paintings: 3d, Madonna of the Grand Duke, by Raphael. 5d, Madonna della Impannata, by Raphael. 7d, Adoration of the Magi, by Filippo Lippi. 60d, Adoration in the Woods, by Lippi.
75d, Madonna del Carmelo, by Giambattista Tiepolo.

**2003, Nov. 17 *Perf. 14¼***

**2769-2772** A470 Set of 4 5.50 5.50

**Souvenir Sheet**

**2773** A470 75d multi 5.50 5.50

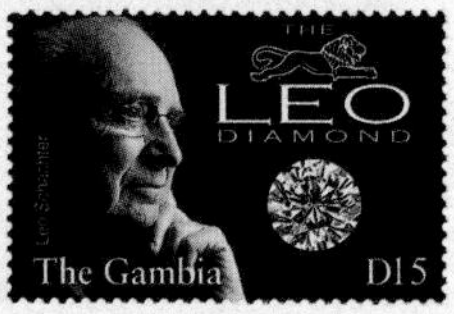


Leo Diamond A471

**2003, Nov. 18 *Perf. 13¼x13½***

**2774** A471 15d multi 1.10 1.10

**Souvenir Sheet**

**2775** A471 60d multi 4.50 4.50

No. 2774 issued in sheets of six.

Pearls — A472

No. 2776: a, South Sea pearls. b, Mabe pearls. c, Pinctada maxima. d, Australian pearls. e, Pearls on ocean floor. f, South Sea white pearls.
60d, Champagne pearls.

**2003, Nov. 18**

**2776** A472 15d Sheet of 6, #a-f 6.50 6.50

**Souvenir Sheet**

**2777** A472 60d multi 4.50 4.50

James Cagney (1899-1986) — A473

No. 2778: a, With solid tie. b, With hat. c, With gun. d, With lapel handkerchief. e, With plaid tie. f, With woman.

**2003 *Perf. 14***

**2778** A473 10d Sheet of 6, #a-d 4.50 4.50

Clark Gable (1901-60) — A474

No. 2779: a, Wearing tuxedo and bow tie, hand showing. b, Wearing suit and tie, no mustache, no hand showing. c, Wearing tuxedo and bow tie, no hand showing. d, Wearing suit and tie, hand showing. e, Wearing suit and solid tie, with mustache. f, Wearing suit and striped tie, with mustache.

**2003**

**2779** A474 10d Sheet of 6, #a-f 4.50 4.50

Diamonds — A475

No. 2780: a, Rough diamonds. b, Yellow diamonds. c, Pink diamonds. d, Blue diamonds. e, White diamonds. f, Green diamonds.
75d, Champagne diamonds.

***Perf. 13¼x13½***

**2003, Nov. 18 Litho.**

**2780** A475 20d Sheet of 6, #a-f 8.00 8.00

**Souvenir Sheet**

**2781** A475 75d multi 5.00 5.00

Minerals — A476

No. 2782: a, Stilbite. b, Smoky quartz. c, Lapis lazuli. d, Amethyst. e, Black opals. f, Rubies.
60d, Quartz.

**2003, Nov. 18**

**2782** A476 15d Sheet of 6, #a-f 6.00 6.00

**Souvenir Sheet**

**2783** A476 60d multi 4.00 4.00

New Year 2004 (Year of the Monkey) — A477

No. 2784: a, Monkey with white and brown face, white ears. b, Monkey with white and blue gray face. c, Monkey with white and brown face. d, Monkey with orange and white face.

**2004, Jan. 5 *Perf. 13¼***

**2784** A477 15d Sheet of 4, #a-d 4.50 4.50

Paintings by Xu Beihong (1895-1953) — A478

No. 2785, vert.: a, Four Magpies. b, Cormorants. c, Under the Banyan Tree. d, Citrus Tree. e, Double Happiness. f, Rooster in Bamboo Garden.
No. 2786: a, Bird on the Kapok Tree. b, Twin Pines.

**2004, Jan. 21 Litho. *Perf. 13½x13¼***

**2785** A478 10d Sheet of 6, #a-f 4.00 4.00

***Perf. 13¼***

**2786** A478 25d Sheet of 2, #a-b 3.50 3.50

2004 Hong Kong Stamp Expo. No. 2785 contains six 28x42mm stamps.

FIFA (Fédération Internationale de Football Association), Cent. — A479

FIFA cups: No. 2787, 10d, World Cup. No. 2788, 10d, Jules Rimet Cup. No. 2789, 10d, Women's World Cup. No. 2790, 10d, Under 17 World Championship Cup. No. 2791, 10d, Under 19 Women's World Championship Cup. No. 2792, 10d, Club World Championship Cup. No. 2793, 10d, Confederations Cup. No. 2794, 10d, World Youth Championship Cup. No. 2795, 10d, Fustal (Indoor Soccer) World Championship Cup.

**2004, Feb. 16 *Perf. 13¼***

**2787-2795** A479 Set of 9 6.25 6.25

Arthur and Friends — A480

No. 2796 — Characters reading: a, Brain. b, Sue Ellen. c, Buster. d, Francine. e, Muffy. f, Binky.
No. 2797, 30d: a, Brain playing clarinet. b, Francine playing banjo. c, Buster playing flute. d, Sue Ellen playing violin.
No. 2798, 30d: a, Brain playing bass. b, Francine playing drum. c, Buster playing tuba. d, Sue Ellen playing saxophone.

**2004, Feb. 16**

**2796** A480 20d Sheet of 6, #a-f 8.25 8.25

**Sheets of 4, #a-d**

**2797-2798** A480 Set of 2 16.50 16.50

Concorde and Queen Elizabeth 2 — A481

Concorde — A482

No. 2800, 25d — Concorde 216 G-BOAF and: a, British flag, with dots of blue at UR. b, British flag, no dots at UR, c, Clouds.

No. 2801, 25d — Concorde 216 G-BOAF and: a, Statue of Liberty. b, Field of US flag. c, Stripes of US flag.

No. 2802, 25d — Concorde 213 F-BTSD and: a, Top of Eiffel Tower. b, French flag, middle part of Eiffel Tower. c, French flag, first and second landings of Eiffel Tower.

**2004, Feb. 17** ***Perf. 14***

**2799** A481 60d multi 4.25 4.25

**Sheets of 3, #a-c**

***Perf. 13¼x13½***

**2800-2802** A482 Set of 3 15.50 15.50

Paintings in the Hermitage, St. Petersburg, Russia — A483

No. 2803, vert.: a, Portrait of a Gentleman, by Domenico Capriolo. b, Sybil, by Dosso Dossi. c, A Woman in a Turban, by Anne-Louis Girodet-Trioson. d, Portrait of a Gentleman, by Ambrosius Holbein.

75d, Husband and Wife, by Lorenzo Lotto.

**2004, Feb. 17** ***Perf. 13¼***

**2803** A483 30d Sheet of 4, #a-d 8.25 8.25

***Imperf***

**2804** A483 75d multi 5.25 5.25

St. Petersburg, 300th anniv. No. 2803 contains four 37x50mm stamps.

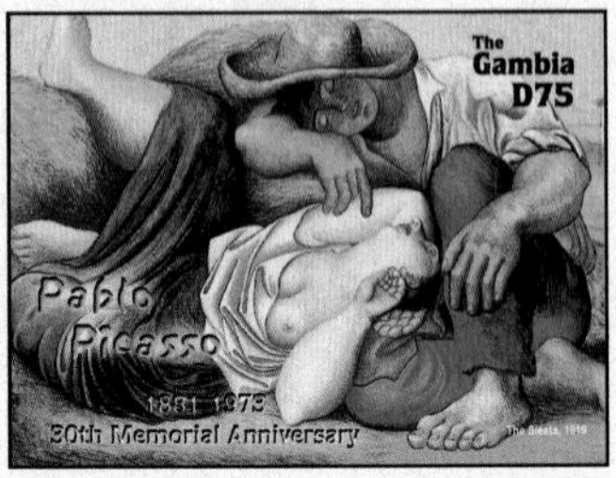


Paintings by Pablo Picasso — A484

No. 2805, vert.: a, Girl in Chemise. b, Portrait of Jacinto Salvadó as Harlequin. c, Tumblers. d, Woman with a Crow.

75d, The Siesta.

**2004, Feb. 17** ***Perf. 13¼***

**2805** A484 30d Sheet of 4, #a-d 8.25 8.25

***Imperf***

**2806** A484 75d multi 5.25 5.25

No. 2805 contains four 37x50mm stamps.

Paintings by Norman Rockwell — A485

No. 2807: a, Detail of 1957 Saturday Evening Post Illustration. b, Girl at Mirror. c, After the Prom. d, The Prom Dress.

75d, Losing the Game.

**2004, Feb. 17** ***Perf. 13¼***

**2807** A485 30d Sheet of 4, #a-d 8.25 8.25

**Souvenir Sheet**

**2808** A485 75d multi 5.25 5.25

Paintings by Kunichika Toyohara (1835-1900) A486

Designs: 10d, The Actor Kikugoro Onoe V as Moronao with the Late Sojuro Nakamura I as Hangan Enya. 15d, The Actor Kikugoro Onoe V as Kunimoto Shinohara with Danjuro Ichikawa IX as Takamori. 20d, The Actor Kikugoro Onoe V as Kansuke Yamamoto with Sadanji Ichikawa I as Daizo Ushikubo. 35d, The Actor Kikugoro Onoe V as the Ghost Seigen with Fukusuke Nakamura IV as Sakurahime.

No. 2813: a, The Actor Sadanji Ichikawa I as the Fishmonger Fukashichi. b, The Actor Sadanji Ichikawa I as Umeomaru. c, The Actor Kuzo Ichikawa III as Shihei Fujiwara. d, The Actor Shikan Nakamura IV as Motome.

75d, The Actor Udanji Ichikawa as Saihei Koya (Ozawa Keifu Tomofusa), horiz.

**2004, Feb. 17**

**2809-2812** A486 Set of 4 5.50 5.50

**2813** A486 30d Sheet of 4, #a-d 8.25 8.25

**Souvenir Sheet**

**2814** A486 75d multi 5.25 5.25

Sharks — A487

No. 2815: a, Lemon shark. b, Nurse shark. c, Leopard shark. d, Starry smoothhound sharks.

75d, Basking shark.

**2004, Mar. 8** ***Perf. 13¼x13½***

**2815** A487 30d Sheet of 4, #a-d 8.25 8.25

**Souvenir Sheet**

**2816** A487 75d multi 5.25 5.25

Cats — A488

No. 2817, vert.: a, Black and white bicolor American shorthair. b, Brown and white Sphinx. c, Copper-eyed white Persian. d, Blue mackerel tabby Oriental longhair.

75d, Copper-eyed cameo Persian.

**2004, Mar. 8** ***Perf. 13½x13¼***

**2817** A488 30d Sheet of 4, #a-d 7.75 7.75

**Souvenir Sheet**

***Perf. 13¼x13½***

**2818** A488 75d multi 5.00 5.00

Dogs — A489

No. 2819, vert.: a, Bracco. b, Shih tzu. c, Boston terrier. d, Chihuahua.

75d, Borzoi.

**2004, Mar. 8** ***Perf. 13½x13¼***

**2819** A489 30d Sheet of 4, #a-d 7.75 7.75

**Souvenir Sheet**

***Perf. 13¼x13½***

**2820** A489 75d multi 5.00 5.00

Mushrooms — A490

No. 2821, 30d: a, Hydrocybe conica. b, Laccaria fraterna. c, Gomphus clavatus. d, Hydrocybe psittacina.

No. 2822, 30d, horiz.: a, Steel blue entoloma. b, Caged stinkhorn. c, Flowerpot depiota. d, Singeri dodge.

75d, Russula sanguinea.

***Perf. 13½x13¼, 13¼x13½***

**2004, Mar. 8** **Sheets of 4, #a-d**

**2821-2822** A490 Set of 2 16.00 16.00

**Souvenir Sheet**

**2823** A490 75d multi 5.00 5.00

Orchid Cacti — A491

No. 2824, 30d: a, Echinocerus. b, Harrisia. c, Stapelia. d, Matucana.

No. 2825, 30d: a, Epiphyllum crenatum. b, Isopogon latifolius. c, Banksia ericifolia. d, Echinopsis.

75d, Epiphyllum.

**2004, Mar. 8** ***Perf. 13¼x13½***

**Sheets of 4, #a-d**

**2824-2825** A491 Set of 2 16.50 16.50

**Souvenir Sheet**

**2826** A491 75d multi 5.25 5.25

European Soccer Championships, Portugal — A492

No. 2827 — Teams from: a, Bulgaria. b, Croatia. c, Czech Republic. d, Denmark. e, England. f, France. g, Germany. h, Greece. i, Italy. j, Latvia. k, Netherlands. l, Portugal (no country name). m, Russia. n, Spain. o, Sweden. p, Switzerland.

No. 2828, vert.: a, Angelo Domenghini. b, Dragan Dzajic. c, Luigi Riva. d, Stadio Olimpico.

65d, 1968 champions, Italy.

***Perf. 13¼, 13½x13¼ (#2828)***

**2004, Mar. 26**

**2827** A492 6d Sheet of 16, #a-p 6.75 6.75

**2828** A492 25d Sheet of 4, #a-d 7.00 7.00

**Souvenir Sheet**

**2829** A492 65d multi 4.50 4.50

No. 2828 contains four 28x42mm stamps.

2004 Summer Olympics, Athens — A493

Designs: 10d, Swimming. 15d, Henri de Baillet-Latour (1876-1942), Intl. Olympic Committee President, vert. 20d, Gold medal of 1896 Olympics, vert. 30d, Pentathlon.

**2004, Apr. 19** ***Perf. 13¼***

**2830-2833** A493 Set of 4 5.25 5.25

Trains, Bridges, Tunnels and Stations — A494

No. 2834, 12d: a, Mallard locomotive. b, North British 4-8-2T locomotive. c, Russian P36 4-8-4 locomotive. d, Forth Rail Bridge. e, Lune Viaduct. f, Lambley Viaduct. g, Alston Arches Viaduct. h, Royal Albert Bridge. i, Blackfriar's Bridge.

No. 2835, 12d: a, City of Truro train. b, Sharp Stewart 4-4-0 locomotive. c, Indian Railways WT Class locomotive. d, Charing Cross Station. e, Linlithgow Station. f, Hellifield Station. g, Kings Cross Station. h, Paddington Station. i, Victoria Station.

No. 2836, 12d: a, Virgin Pendolino train. b, Mountain Class Garratt locomotive. c, 2-8-8-4 No. 227 locomotive. d, Kilsby Tunnel. e, Box Tunnel. f, Willersley Tunnel. g, Stansted Airport Tunnel. h, Clayton Tunnel. i, Severn Tunnel.

No. 2837, 65d, West Highland Line train. No. 2838, 65d, Darjeeling-Himalaya train. No. 2839, 65d, Eurostar.

**2004, Apr. 19** *Perf. 13¼x13½*

**Sheets of 9, #a-i**

**2834-2836** A494 Set of 3 22.50 22.50

**Souvenir Sheets**

**2837-2839** A494 Set of 3 13.50 13.50

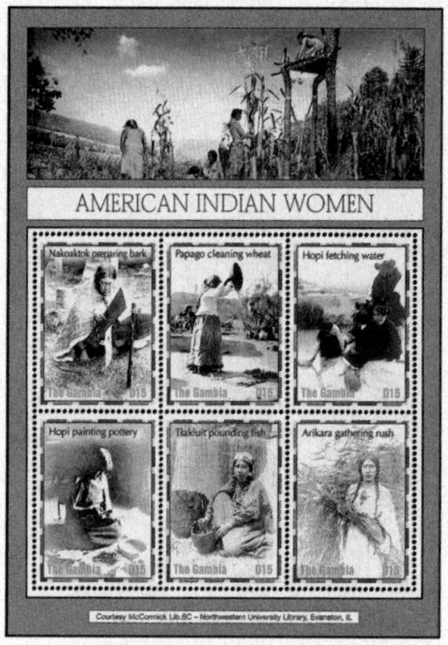


American Indians — A495

No. 2840: a, Nakoaktok preparing bark. b, Papago cleaning wheat. c, Hopi fetching water. d, Hopi painting pottery. e, Tlakluit pounding fish. f, Arikara gathering rush.

No. 2841, horiz.: a, Apsaroke Indians and teepee. b, Pigean Indians. c, Apsaroke Indians. d, Sioux chiefs.

**2004, May 3** *Perf. 14¼x14¾*

**2840** A495 15d Sheet of 6, #a-f 6.25 6.25

*Perf. 13¾*

**2841** A495 30d Sheet of 4, #a-d 8.25 8.25

No. 2841 contains four 38x30mm stamps.

History of Aviation — A496

No. 2842: a, Leonardo da Vinci. b, Count Ferdinand von Zeppelin. c, William E. Boeing. d, Capt. John Cunningham. e, Capt. Edwin C. Musick. f, Capt. Jock Lowe. g, William Lear. h, Jenny Murray.

60d, Mars Rover mission.

**2004, May 3** *Perf. 14*

**2842** A496 12d Sheet of 8, #a-h 6.75 6.75

**Souvenir Sheet**

**2843** A496 60d multi 4.25 4.25

A497

Marilyn Monroe (1926-62) — A498

No. 2844: a, Wearing necklace. b, No necklace.

No. 2845 — Background color: a, Orange. b, Green. c, Bright lilac rose. d, Bright yellow. e, Bright blue. f, Bright red. g, Dull blue. h, Bright yellow green. i, Blue green. j, Yellow. k, Red orange. l, Purple. m, Red lilac. n, Light blue. o, Dark blue. p, Rose pink.

No. 2846 — Black background and: a, Hand on face. b, Wearing necklace. c, Wearng red dress. d, Wearing blouse with collar.

**2004, May 3** *Perf. 14*

**2844** A497 25d Pair, #a-b 3.50 3.50
**2845** A498 7d Sheet of 16, #a-p 7.75 7.75
**2846** A498 25d Sheet of 4, #a-d 7.00 7.00

No. 2844 was printed in sheets containing two pairs.

D-Day, 60th Anniv. A499

Designs: 7d, Jim Wallwork, 6th Airborne Division. 10d, Major Gen. Richard Gale. 15d, Winston Churchill. 30d, J.K. "Paddy" Byrne, 197th Typhoon Squadron.

No. 2851, 25d: a, Bombers over coast of Normandy. b, RAF Mitchell bomber dropping bombs. c, British Horsa gliders behind enemy lines. d, Paratroopers dropping into Normandy.

No. 2852, 25d: a, British paratroopers prepare for mission. b, British paratroopers secure Pegasus Bridge. c, American paratroopers drop into Sainte-Mère-Eglise area. d, American paratroopers enter town of Sainte-Mère-Eglise.

No. 2853, 60d, RAF bombers under construction. No. 2854, 60d, Troops disembarking from landing craft.

**2004, May 3** **Litho.**

**2847-2850** A499 Set of 4 + labels 4.25 4.25

**Sheets of 4, #a-d**

**2851-2852** A499 Set of 2 14.00 14.00

**Souvenir Sheets**

**2853-2854** A499 Set of 2 8.25 8.25

Election of Pope John Paul II, 25th Anniv. (in 2003) — A500

No. 2855 — Pope in: a, 1988. b, 1989. c, 1990. d, 1991. e, 1992. f, 1993. g, 1994. h, 1995. i, 1996. j, 1997. k, 1998. l, 1999. m, 2000. n, 2001. o, 2002.

No. 2856 — Pope in: a, 1978. b, 1979. c, 1980. d, 1981. e, 1982. f, 1983. g, 1984. h, 1985. i, 1986. j, 1987.

**2004, May 13** *Perf. 13½x13¼*

**2855** A500 7d Sheet of 15, #a-o 7.25 7.25
**2856** A500 10d Sheet of 10, #a-j 6.75 6.75

American Lighthouses A501

Designs: 25d, Tybee Island, Georgia. 30d, Old Cape Henry, Virginia. 35d, Morris Island, South Carolina. 40d, Hillsboro Inlet, Florida. 50d, Cape Lookout, North Carolina.

**2004, May 27** *Perf. 14¾x14¼*

**2857-2861** A501 Set of 5 12.50 12.50

See Nos. 2911A-2911G.

Gambian postal authorities have declared the following items as "illegal:"

Sheet of nine 25d stamps: Oceans;

Sheets of six 25d stamps: Birds of Prey with Rotary emblem, Orchids with Rotary emblem, New Cinema, Vincent van Gogh Paintings, Monuments of Egypt, Fire Engines;

Sheets of four 25d stamps: Pope John Paul II, Nude Art, Great Composers, Lighthouses with Rotary emblem, Aircraft with Rotary emblem, Actresses, Pin-up Art;

Sheet of three 25d stamps: Polar Birds with Rotary emblem;

Sheets of two 25d stamps: Prehistoric World, Chinese New Year, Looney Tunes, Games and Sports.

Paintings by Joan Miró A502

Designs: 20d, Woman, 1934, pastel on paper. 25d, Woman, 1934, pastel and pencil on emery paper. 35d, Self-portrait. No. 2865, 75d, Man with Pipe.

No. 2866: a, Portrait IV. b, Seated Woman. c, Painting on Ingres Paper. d, Portrait II.

No. 2867, 75d, Composition with Personages in the Burning Forest, horiz. No. 2868, 75d, Bird, horiz.

**2004, Feb. 17** **Litho.** *Perf. 13¼*

**2862-2865** A502 Set of 4 11.00 11.00

**2866** A502 30d Sheet of 4, #a-d 8.25 8.25

**Size: 100x80mm**

***Imperf***

**2867-2868** A502 Set of 2 10.50 10.50

Souvenir Sheet

Deng Xiaoping (1904-97), Chinese Leader — A503

**2004, May 3** *Perf. 13½*

**2869** A503 75d multi 5.25 5.25

Miniature Sheet

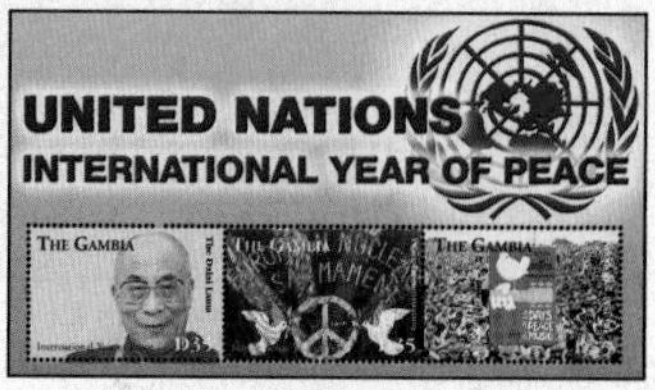


Intl. Year of Peace — A504

No. 2870: a, Dalai Lama. b, European nuclear disarmament banner. c, Woodstock music festival.

**2004, May 3** *Perf. 14*

**2870** A504 35d Sheet of 3, #a-c 7.25 7.25

Miniature Sheet

Rare and Famous Postage Stamps — A505

No. 2871: a, British Guiana #13. b, Great Britain #1. c, United States #85A. d, United States #C3a. e, United States #1.

**2004, June 24** *Perf. 13*

**2871** A505 20d Sheet of 5, #a-e, + label 6.75 6.75

Flowers — A506

Designs: 1d, Babiana rubrocyanaea. 2d, Protea. 3d, Lithops bromfieldii. 5d, Saintpaulia ionantha. 6d, Monopsis lutea. 7d, Dudleya lanceolata. 9d, Euphorbia punicea. 10d, Oxalis violacea. 25d, Helichrysum bracteatum. 50d, Senecio obovatus. 75d, Mesembryanthemum acinaciforme. 100d, Montbretia crocosmiiflora. 200d, Gladiolus colvillei.

**2004, July 1** *Perf. 14¾x14*

| | | | | |
|---|---|---|---|---|
| **2872** | A506 | 1d multi | .25 | .25 |
| **2873** | A506 | 2d multi | .25 | .25 |
| **2874** | A506 | 3d multi | .25 | .25 |
| **2875** | A506 | 5d multi | .35 | .35 |
| **2876** | A506 | 6d multi | .40 | .40 |
| **2877** | A506 | 7d multi | .50 | .50 |
| **2878** | A506 | 9d multi | .60 | .60 |
| **2879** | A506 | 10d multi | .70 | .70 |
| **2880** | A506 | 25d multi | 1.75 | 1.75 |
| **2881** | A506 | 50d multi | 3.50 | 3.50 |
| **2882** | A506 | 75d multi | 5.00 | 5.00 |

**2883** A506 100d multi 6.75 6.75
**2884** A506 200d multi 13.50 13.50
*Nos. 2872-2884 (13)* 33.80 33.80

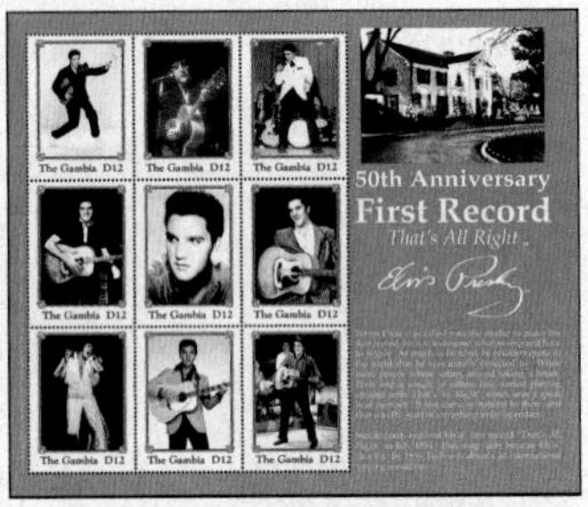


A507

First Elvis Presley Record, 50th Anniv. — A508

Various portraits of Elvis Presley.

**2004, Aug. 2** ***Perf. 13¼***
**2885** A507 12d Sheet of 9, #a-i 7.50 7.50
**2886** A508 12d Sheet of 9, #a-i 7.50 7.50

Miniature Sheet

George Herman "Babe" Ruth (1895-1948), Baseball Player — A509

No. 2887: a, Swinging, legs spread apart. b, Standing. c, Swinging, legs together. d, Holding bat.

**2004, Sept. 3** ***Perf. 13½***
**2887** A509 25d Sheet of 4, #a-d 6.75 6.75

Pres. Ronald Reagan (1911-2004) — A510

No. 2888: a, With wife, Nancy and Pope John Paul II. b, With Israeli Prime Minister Shimon Peres.
No. 2889: a, With window in background. b, Before microphones. c, Holding glass.

**2004, Oct. 13**
**2888** A510 15d Pair, #a-b 2.10 2.10
**2889** A510 15d Vert. strip of 3, #a-c 3.25 3.25

No. 2888 was printed in sheets of three pairs. No. 2889 was printed in sheets of two strips.

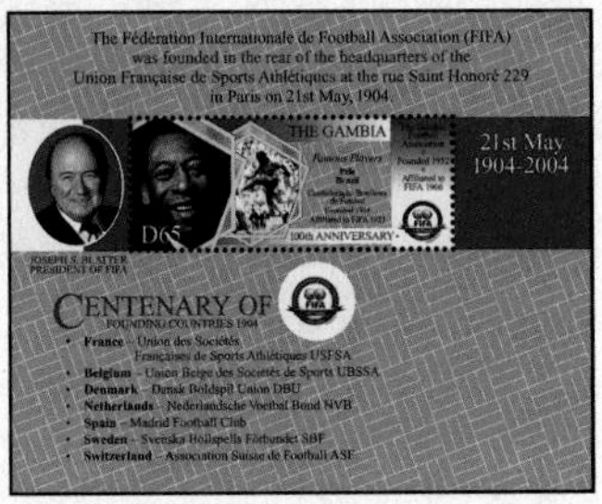


FIFA (Fédération Internationale de Football Association), Cent. — A511

No. 2890: a, Dixie Dean. b, Ruud Gullit. c, Karl-Heinz Rummenigge. d, Luis Enrique Martinez.
65d, Pele.

**2004, Oct. 27** ***Perf. 12¾x12½***
**2890** A511 25d Sheet of 4, #a-d 7.00 7.00

**Souvenir Sheet**

**2891** A511 65d multi 4.50 4.50

National Basketball Association Players — A512

Designs: No. 2892, 10d, Darko Milicic, Detroit Pistons. No. 2893, 10d, Chris Kaman, Los Angeles Clippers. No. 2894, 10d, Andrei Kirilenko, Utah Jazz. No. 2895, 10d, T. J. Ford, Milwaukee Bucks.

**2004** ***Perf. 14***
**2892-2895** A512 Set of 4 2.75 2.75

Issued: No. 2892, 11/2; Nos. 2893-2894, 11/3; No. 2895, 11/6. Each stamp printed in sheets of 12.
See Nos. 2916-2917.

Ocean Liners — A513

Designs: 7d, Bremen. 10d, RMS Queen Mary. 15d, Queen Mary II. 20d, RMS Queen Elizabeth 2. 25d, Britannic. 35d, RMS Majestic.
90d, RMS Aquitania.

**2004, Nov. 5** ***Perf. 14¼***
**2896-2901** A513 Set of 6 7.75 7.75

**Souvenir Sheet**

**2902** A513 90d multi 6.25 6.25

Miniature Sheet

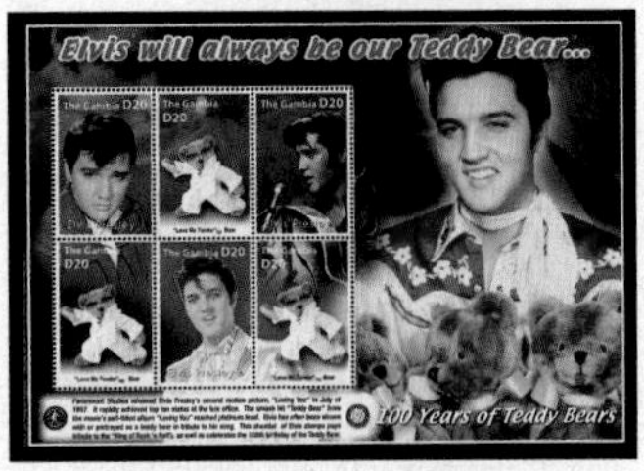


Elvis Presley and Teddy Bears — A514

No. 2903: a, Presley in dark red suit. b, Teddy bear, plaid sleeve in background. c, Presley with guitar. d, Teddy bear, dark red suit in background. e, Presley in pink suit and tie. f, Teddy bear, guitar in background.

**2004, Nov. 29** ***Perf. 14***
**2903** A514 20d Sheet of 6, #a-f 8.25 8.25

Christmas A515

Designs: 7d, Greek Madonna, by Giovanni Bellini. 10d, Madonna in the Church, by Jan van Eyck. 20d, Conestabile Madonna, by Raphael. 25d, Madonna and Child, by Sandro Botticelli.
65d, Madonna and Child with Chancellor Rolin, by van Eyck.

**2004, Dec. 13** ***Perf. 12***
**2904-2907** A515 Set of 4 4.25 4.25

**Souvenir Sheet**

**2908** A515 65d multi 4.50 4.50

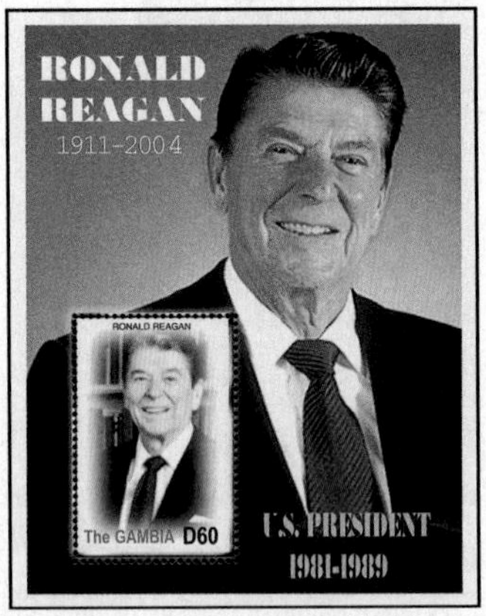


Pres. Ronald Reagan (1911-2004) — A516

No. 2909, 25d: a, With Margaret Thatcher, 1986. b, With Pope John Paul II, 1982. c, Signing Missing Children's Act and Victim Witness Protection Act, 1992. d, With wife, Nancy, 1987.
No. 2910, 25d, horiz.: a, First Family, 1982. b, Signing treaty with Mikhail Gorbachev, 1987. c, Assassination attempt, 1981. d, With Deng Xiaoping, 1984.
60d, Portrait.

**2004, Oct. 13** **Litho.** ***Perf. 14***

**Sheets of 4, #a-d**

**2909-2910** A516 Set of 2 14.00 14.00

**Souvenir Sheet**

**2911** A516 60d multi 4.25 4.25

**Lighthouse Type of 2004**

Designs: 5d, Isla de Flores Lighthouse, Uruguay. 7d, Punta Brava Lighthouse, Uruguay. 15d, Boston Lighthouse, US. No. 2911D, 20d, Cabo Polonio Lighthouse, Uruguay. No. 2911E, 20d, Bass Harbor Head Lighthouse, US. 45d, Punta del Este Lighthouse, Uruguay. 60d, Portland Head Lighthouse, US.

**2004** **Litho.** ***Perf. 14¾x14***
**2911A-2911G** A501 Set of 7 12.00 12.00

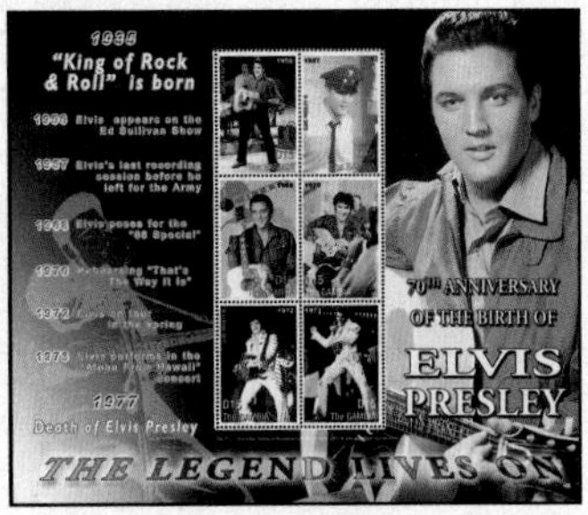


Elvis Presley (1935-77) — A517

No. 2912, 15d: a, Standing, with guitar, 1956. b, Wearing army hat, 1957. c, Holding guitar, 1968. d, Holding guitar, 1970. e, Playing guitar, 1972. f, Singing, 1973.
No. 2913, 15d: a, Seated, with guitar, 1956. b, With guitar, 1958. c, Playing guitar, 1964. d, Playing drums, 1966. e, On horse, 1968. f, Playing guitar, 1969.

**2005, Jan. 8** **Sheets of 6, #a-f**
**2912-2913** A517 Set of 2 12.50 12.50

New Year 2005 (Year of the Rooster) A518

Paintings by Xu Beihong: 10d, Rooster. 40d, Black Rooster, horiz.

**2005, Jan.** ***Perf. 11½***
**2914** A518 10d multi .70 .70

**Souvenir Sheet**

**2915** A518 40d multi 2.75 2.75

No. 2914 printed in sheets of 4. No. 2915 contains one 46x36mm stamp.

**Basketball Players Type of 2004**

Designs: No. 2916, 25d, Steve Nash, Dallas Mavericks. No. 2917, 25d, Shaquille O'Neal, Los Angeles Lakers.

**2005, Feb. 10** ***Perf. 14***
**2916-2917** A512 Set of 2 3.50 3.50

Both players were on different teams when stamps were released.

Intl. Year of Rice (in 2004) — A519

No. 2918, vert.: a, Rice terraces. b, Woman holding rice plants. c, Two people holding rice plants.
60d, Rice farmers.

**2005, Feb. 10**
**2918** A519 30d Sheet of 3, #a-c 6.25 6.25

**Souvenir Sheet**

**2919** A519 60d multi 4.25 4.25

Butterflies — A520

Designs: 1d, Belenois solilucis. 2d, Colotis evippe. 3d, Acraea cepheus. 5d, Bebearia senegalensis. 6d, Danaus chrysippus. 7d, Papilio dardanus. 10d, Graphium agamedes. 15d, Papilio hesperus. 25d, Charaxes boueti. 30d, Cymothoe egesta. 50d, Amauris albimaculata. 75d, Charaxes lucretius. 100d, Papilio zalmoxis. 200d, Papilio antimachus.

***Perf. 13¼x13½, 14¾x14¼ (7d, 30d)***

**2005, Apr. 4**

| | | | | | |
|---|---|---|---|---|---|
| **2920** | A520 | 1d | multi | .25 | .25 |
| **2921** | A520 | 2d | multi | .25 | .25 |
| **2922** | A520 | 3d | multi | .25 | .25 |
| **2923** | A520 | 5d | multi | .35 | .35 |
| **2924** | A520 | 6d | multi | .40 | .40 |
| **2924A** | A520 | 7d | multi | .50 | .50 |
| **2925** | A520 | 10d | multi | .70 | .70 |
| **2926** | A520 | 15d | multi | 1.00 | 1.00 |
| **2927** | A520 | 25d | multi | 1.75 | 1.75 |
| **2927A** | A520 | 30d | multi | 2.10 | 2.10 |
| **2928** | A520 | 50d | multi | 3.50 | 3.50 |
| **2929** | A520 | 75d | multi | 5.25 | 5.25 |
| **2929A** | A520 | 100d | multi | 7.00 | 7.00 |
| **2929B** | A520 | 200d | multi | 14.00 | 14.00 |
| | *Nos. 2920-2929B (14)* | | | 37.30 | 37.30 |

Battle of Trafalgar, Bicent. — A521

Designs: 5d, Santisima Trinidad. 10d, Victory firing at French flagship Bucentaure, horiz. 15d, Lord Horatio Nelson. 30d, French sailors from the Redoubtable boarding Victory.
60d, Vice-admiral Horatio Nelson.

**2005, Apr. 4** ***Perf. 14***
**2930-2933** A521 Set of 4 4.25 4.25

**Souvenir Sheet**

**2934** A521 60d multi 4.25 4.25

Souvenir Sheet

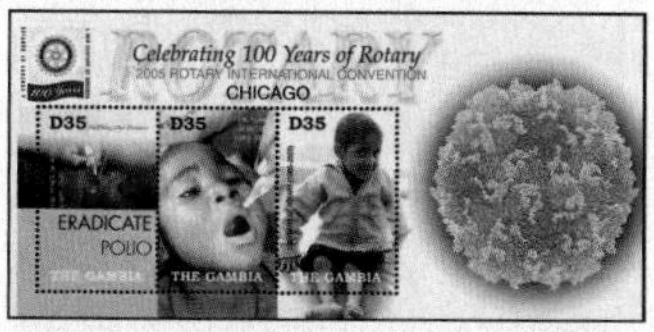


Rotary International, Cent. — A522

No. 2935: a, "Eradicate Polio," child receiving polio vaccine. b, Child receiving polio vaccine, diff. c, Child seated.

**2005, Apr. 4**
**2935** A522 35d Sheet of 3, #a-c 7.25 7.25

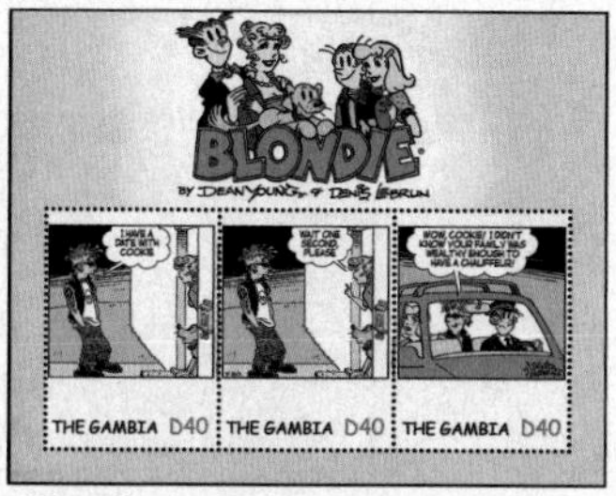


Blondie, by Dean Young and Denis LeBrun — A523

No. 2936, 40d: a, "I have a date with Cookie." b, "Wait one second, please." c, "Wow, Cookie! I didn't know your family was wealth enough to have a chauffeur!"
No. 2937, 40d: a, "Listen up, everybody. . ." b, "Then after he leaves you can get back to normal." c, "I want to see this place humming with activity and enthusiasm!"

**2005, Apr. 4** ***Perf. 13¼***
**Sheets of 3, #a-c**
**2936-2937** A523 Set of 2 17.00 17.00

World Cup Soccer Championships, 75th Anniv. — A524

No. 2938 — Brazilian flag and scenes from 1950 World Cup: a, 1950 Uruguay team. b, Goal from Uruguay-Brazil championship game. c, Maracaná Municipal Stadium, Brazil. d, Alcide Edgardo Ghiggia.
60d, 1950 Uruguay team, diff.

**2005, Apr. 4** ***Perf. 14¼***
**2938** A524 25d Sheet of 4, #a-d 7.00 7.00

**Souvenir Sheet**

**2939** A524 60d multi 4.25 4.25

African Fauna — A525

No. 2940, 25d: a, African fish eagle. b, Hummingbird hawkmoth. c, Nile crocodile. d, Blue wildebeest.
No. 2941, 25d: a, Bateleur eagle. b, Green mamba. c, Chimpanzee. d, Yellow pansy butterfly.
No. 2942, 25d: a, Jackass penguins. b, Leatherback turtle. c, Scaevola thunbergii. d, Cancrid crab.
No. 2943, 25d: a, Mediterranean monk seal. b, Horned boxfish. c, Scorpion fish. d, Cnidarians.
No. 2944, Burchell's zebra. No. 2945, 65d, Greater galago. No. 2946, 65d, Bottlenose dolphin, vert. No. 2947, 65d, Gerbera daisies, vert.

**2005, Apr. 4** ***Perf. 13¼x13½***
**Sheets of 4, #a-d**
**2940-2943** A525 Set of 4 28.00 28.00

**Souvenir Sheets**

**2944-2947** A525 Set of 4 18.00 18.00

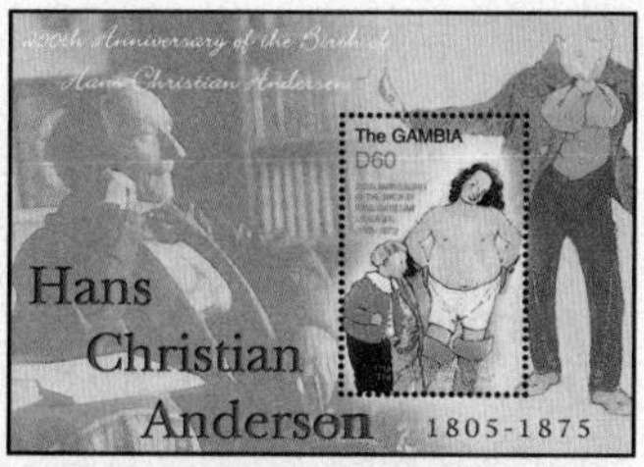


Hans Christian Andersen (1805-75), Author — A526

No. 2942, horiz.: a, The Ugly Duckling. b, The Little Match Girl. c, The Rose Tree Regiment.
60d, The Emperor's New Clothes.

**2005, Apr. 4** ***Perf. 14***
**2948** A526 35d Sheet of 3, #a-c 7.25 7.25

**Souvenir Sheet**

**2949** A526 60d multi 4.25 4.25

Wedding of Prince Charles and Camilla Parker Bowles — A527

Various photos of couple with oval color of: No. 2950, 2d, Brown. No. 2951, 2d, Purple. No. 2952, 2d, Red brown.

**2005, Apr. 9** ***Perf. 13½***
**2950-2952** A527 Set of 3 .45 .45

Each stamp printed in sheets of 4.

Friedrich von Schiller (1759-1805), Writer — A528

No. 2953: a, Statue of Schiller. b, Painting of Schiller. c, Bust of Schiller.
60d, Cameo of Schiller.

**2005, Apr. 4** **Litho.** ***Perf. 14***
**2953** A528 35d Sheet of 3, #a-c 7.25 7.25

**Souvenir Sheet**

**2954** A528 60d multi 4.25 4.25

Miniature Sheet

End of World War II, 60th Anniv. — A529

No. 2955 — Prince Bernhard of the Netherlands: a, And Prime Minister Pieter Gerbrandy. b, And Queen Wilhelmina. c, And Generals Bernard Montgomery and Hendrik Kruls. d, And people of Nimwegen. e, At German surrender. f, Returning home with family.

**2005, Apr. 14** **Litho.** ***Perf. 12¾***
**2955** A529 12d Sheet of 6, #a-f 5.00 5.00

End of World War II, 60th Anniv. — A530

No. 2956, 20d — Dunkirk: a, Germans advance across France. b, Anthony C. Bartley. c, Ships and boats. d, Rescued soldiers.
No. 2957, 20d — D-Day: a, Allied troops hit the beaches of Normandy. b, Germans blast Sword Beach. c, Allied troops advance inland. d, Germans begin to surrender.
No. 2958, 80d, Operation Dynamo. No. 2959, 80d, Royal Navy lands on Gold Beach.

**2005, May 9** ***Perf. 13¼x13½***
**Sheets of 4, #a-d**
**2956-2957** A530 Set of 2 11.50 11.50

**Souvenir Sheets**

**2958-2959** A530 Set of 2 11.50 11.50

Souvenir Sheet

Expo 2005, Aichi, Japan — A531

No. 2960: a, Mt. Kilimanjaro. b, Lion. c, Splitting of the Red Sea. d, Astronaut on Moon.

**2005, May 16** ***Perf. 12***
**2960** A531 15d Sheet of 4, #a-d 4.25 4.25

Pope John Paul II (1920-2005) and Mother Teresa (1910-97) — A532

**2005, June 1** ***Perf. 14***
**2961** A532 30d multi 2.10 2.10

Printed in sheets of 6.

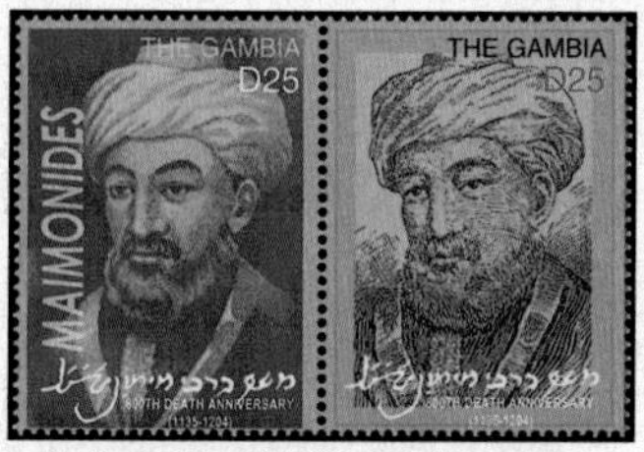


Maimonides (1135-1204) — A533

No. 2962: a, Denomination in white. b, Denomination in red.

**2005, July 12** ***Perf. 12***
**2962** A533 25d Pair, #a-b 3.75 3.75

Printed in sheets of 2 pairs.

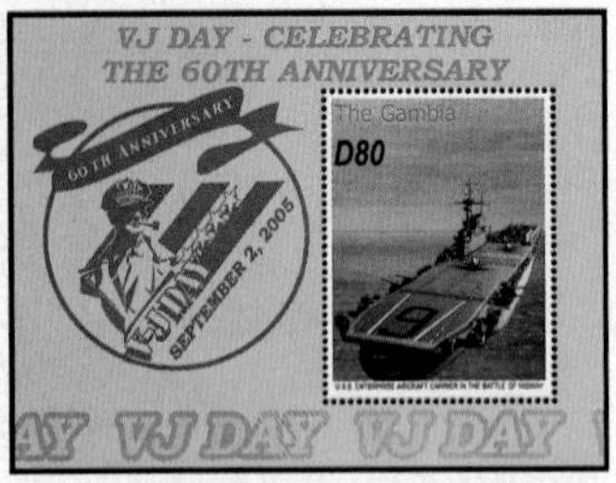


VJ Day, 60th Anniv. — A534

No. 2963, horiz. — Paintings by Jean Masterly: a, B-29 Flies Over the Missouri. b, Enola Gay Over Hiroshima. c, Dogfight Over the Pacific. d, Hellcat Fury Engages the Enemy.
80d, USS Enterprise Aircraft Carrier in the Battle of Midway.

**2005, July 12** ***Perf. 12¾***
**2963** A534 25d Sheet of 4, #a-d 7.25 7.25

**Souvenir Sheet**

**2964** A534 80d multi 5.75 5.75

No. 2963 contains four 40x31mm stamps.

Jules Verne (1828-1905), Writer — A535

No. 2965, horiz.: a, Hungary #C287. b, Monaco #1100. c, France #770.
80d, Scene from "From the Earth to the Moon."

**2005, July 12**
**2965** A535 35d Sheet of 3, #a-c 7.75 7.75

**Souvenir Sheet**

**2966** A535 80d multi 5.75 5.75

**Souvenir Sheet**

Albert Einstein (1879-1955), Physicist — A536

No. 2967: a, Einstein, country name in red. b, Einstein, country name in white. c, Israel #117.

**2005, July 28**
**2967** A536 35d Sheet of 3, #a-c 7.75 7.75

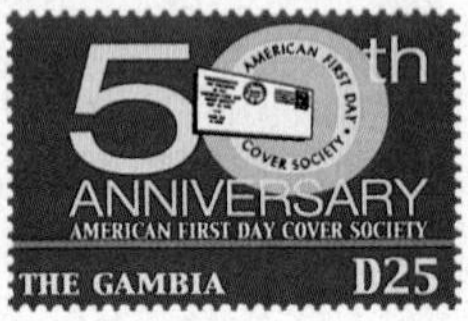


American First Day Cover Society, 50th Anniv. A537

**2005, July 29**
**2968** A537 25d multi 1.90 1.90

**Souvenir Sheet**

Taipei 2005 Stamp Exhibition — A538

No. 2969: a, Presidential Palace, Taipei. b, Chiang Kai-Shek Memorial, Taipei. c, Queen's Head, Yehliu. d, National Palace Museum, Taipei.

**2005, Aug. 19** ***Perf. 14***
**2969** A538 35d Sheet of 4, #a-d 10.00 10.00

First Europa Stamps, 50th Anniv. (in 2006) A539

Designs: 35d, Mailman, Luxembourg #318. 40d, Stars, "50," France #806. 50d, Map of Europe, France #805.

**2005, Oct. 20**
**2970-2972** A539 Set of 3 9.00 9.00
*2972a* Souvenir sheet, #2970-2972 + label 9.00 9.00

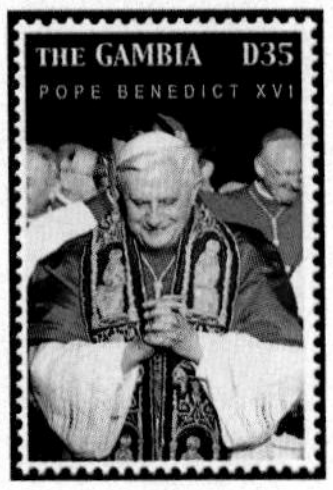


Election of Pope Benedict XVI — A540

**2005, Nov. 15** ***Perf. 13½***
**2973** A540 35d multi 2.50 2.50

Printed in sheets of 4.

Pope John Paul II (1920-2005) A541

Pope John Paul II: No. 2974, 40d, Looking right. No. 2975, 40d, With arm raised. No. 2976, 40d, With hand to face. No. 2977, 40d, Praying with four men at side. No. 2978, 40d, Surrounded by praying clergymen. No. 2979, With praying hands of other people. No. 2980, 40d, Wearing miter, with crowd. No. 2981, 40d, Praying at church. No. 2982, 40d, With arms outstretched at church. No. 2983, 40d, Praying with rosary. No. 2984, 40d, Holding crucifix, round globe. No. 2985, 40d, Holding crucifix, oval world map. No. 2986, 40d, Holding crucifix, and at doorway. No. 2987, 40d, With crucifix at side of face. No. 2988, 40d, Holding crucifix in front of his face. No. 2989, 40d, Holding crucifix, with other arm raised. No. 2990, 40d, With crucifix, Papal arms. No. 2991, 40d, With Good Shepherd. No. 2992, 40d, Holding child. No. 2993, 40d, With UN emblem. No. 2994, 40d, Being assisted.
No. 2995, 80d, Bowing with crucifix. No. 2996, 80d, Wearing miter in front of church. No. 2997, 80d, With kneeling bishop. No. 2998, 80d, Holding microphone. No. 2999, 80d, With raised hands, Papal arms. No. 3000, 80d, With Virgin Mary.

**Embossed on Metal**

**2005** ***Die Cut Perf. 12½***

**Self-Adhesive**

**Silver-Colored Metal**

**2974-2994** A541 Set of 21 60.00 60.00

**Gold-Colored Metal**

**2995-3000** A541 Set of 6 35.00 35.00

**Miniature Sheet**

American Indian Chiefs — A542

No. 3001: a, Hiawatha. b, Chief Joseph. c, Sitting Bull. d, Red Cloud. e, Powhatan. f, Sequoyah. g, Crazy Horse. h, Cochise. i, Geronimo. j, Tecumseh.

**2005, Nov. 15** **Litho.** ***Perf. 13½***
**3001** A542 12d Sheet of 10, #a-j 8.50 8.50

Christmas — A543

Designs: 7d, The Annunciation, by Lorenzo di Credi. 10d, The Holy Family, by di Credi. 25d, The Adoration of the Magi, by Filippo Lippi. 30d, Marriage of St. Catherine, by Lippi. 65d, The Annunciation, by Fra Angelico.

**2005, Dec. 19** ***Perf. 13½x¼***
**3002-3005** A543 Set of 4 5.00 5.00

**Souvenir Sheet**

**3006** A543 65d multi 4.50 4.50

New Year 2006 (Year of the Dog) A544

**2006, Jan. 3** ***Perf. 13¼***
**3007** A544 15d multi 1.10 1.10

Printed in sheets of 4.

Elvis Presley (1935-77) — A545

***Serpentine Die Cut 7¾***

**2006, Jan. 24** **Litho. & Embossed**
**3008** A545 200d multi 14.50 14.50

Children's Drawings — A546

No. 3009, 25d — Cats: a, Kitty, by Raquel Bobolia. b, Jaguar, by Megan Albe. c, Quazy Jaguar, by Nick Abrams. d, Chelsy Cheetah, by Carly Bowerman.

No. 3010, 25d — Reptiles: a, Stripey, by Christopher Bowerman. b, Sea Turtle, by Tyler Overton. c, Hungry Lizard, by Jessica Shutt. d, Frogs, by Elyse Bobczynski.
No. 3011, 25d — Flowers: a, Three Flowers, by Lauren Van Way. b, Blossoms, by Michelle Malachowsky. c, Flower Pot, by Van Way. d, Red Flower Pot, by Anne Wilks.

**2006, Jan. 24** **Litho.** ***Perf. 13¼***

**Sheets of 4, #a-d**

**3009-3011** A546 Set of 3 22.00 22.00

Queen Elizabeth II, 80th Birthday — A547

No. 3012: a, Wearing military uniform. b, At coronation. c, On Time Magazine cover. d, Wearing wedding gown.
65d, Wearing robe and crown.

**2006, Feb. 27** ***Perf. 13¼***
**3012** A547 30d Sheet of 4, #a-d 8.50 8.50

**Souvenir Sheet**

***Perf. 12***

**3013** A547 65d multi 4.75 4.75

Worldwide Fund for Nature (WWF) — A548

No. 3014 — Black-crowned crane: a, Head. b, Standing on one leg. c, Birds in wild. d, Chick.

**2006, Feb. 27** ***Perf. 12¾***
**3014** A548 30d Block or strip of 4, #a-d 8.25 8.25
*e.* Souvenir sheet, 2 each #3014a-3014d 16.50 16.50

2006 Winter Olympics, Turin A549

Designs: No. 3015, Norway #1048. No. 3015A, Poster for 1992 Albertville Winter Olympics. 15d, Norway #1047. No. 3017,

Poster for 2002 Salt Lake City Winter Olympics. No. 3017A, France #B611, horiz. 25d, Poster for 1994 Lillehammer Winter Olympics.

**2006, Mar. 23** ***Perf. 13¼***

**3015** A549 10d multicolored .75 .75
**3015A** A549 10d multicolored .75 .75
**3016** A549 15d multicolored 1.10 1.10
**3017** A549 20d multicolored 1.40 1.40
**3017A** A549 20d multicolored 1.40 1.40
**3018** A549 25d multicolored 1.75 1.75
*Nos. 3015-3018 (6)* 7.15 7.15

Marilyn Monroe (1926-62), Actress — A550

**2006, Apr. 6**

**3019** A550 30d multi 2.10 2.10

Printed in sheets of 4.

Dr. Martin Luther King, Jr. (1929-68), Civil Rights Activist — A551

**2006, May 27** ***Perf. 11½x12***

**3020** A551 40d multi 3.00 3.00

Printed in sheets of 3.

Miniature Sheet

American Philatelic Society, 120th Anniv. — A552

No. 3021 — United States stamps: a, #1120. b, #E14. c, #114. d, #C3. e, #894. f, #E2. g, #294. h, #Q2.

**2006, May 27** ***Perf. 13¼***

**3021** A552 17d Sheet of 8, #a-h 9.75 9.75

Washington 2006 World Philatelic Exhibition.

Souvenir Sheet

Ludwig Durr (1878-1956), Engineer, and Zeppelins — A553

No. 3022 — Durr and: a, Zeppelin NT. b, Zeppelin ZR-3 (U.S.S. Los Angeles). c, Zeppelin ZRS (U.S.S. Macon)

**2006, June 22** ***Perf. 12¾***

**3022** A553 40d Sheet of 3, #a-c 8.75 8.75

Souvenir Sheet

Wolfgang Amadeus Mozart (1756-91), Composer — A554

No. 3023: a, Mozart's Memorial, Vienna. b, Portrait of Mozart, by Barbara Kraft. c, Portrait of Mozart by unknown artist. d, Mozart family graves, Salzburg.

**2006, June 22**

**3023** A554 30d Sheet of 4, #a-d 8.75 8.75

Rembrandt (1606-69), Painter A555

Details from paintings: 10d, Jacob Blessing the Sons of Joseph. 12d, Jacob Blessing the Sons of Joseph, diff. 15d, Jacob Blessing the Sons of Joseph, diff. No. 3027, 25d, Jacob Wrestling with the Angel.

No. 3028, 25d — The Staalmeesters: a, Man wearing hat, leaning to right, "Rembrandt" in white. b, Man wearing hat, "Rembrandt" in white. c, Man without hat. d, Man wearing hat, "Rembrandt" in black.

No. 3029, 25d: a, Young Girl at Open Half-Door. b, Self-portrait, 1632-39. c, Self-portrait, 1640. d, Portrait of a Young Woman.

No. 3030, 25d — A Married Couple with Their Children: a, Man. b, Child, "Rembrandt" in white. c, Child, "Rembrandt" in black. d, Woman.

No. 3031, 65d — A Polish Nobleman. No. 3032, 65d, The Knight with the Falcon. No. 3033, 65d, A Young Woman in Fancy Dress. No. 3034, 65d, Portrait of a Lady with a Lap Dog.

**2006, Aug. 23** **Litho.** ***Perf. 14¼***

**3024-3027** A555 Set of 4 4.50 4.50

**Sheets of 4, #a-d**

**3028-3030** A555 Set of 3 22.00 22.00

***Imperf***

**Size: 76x106mm**

**3031-3034** A555 Set of 4 18.50 18.50

Queen Juliana of the Netherlands A556

**2006, July 24** **Litho.** ***Perf. 13¼***

**3035** A556 15d multi 1.10 1.10

Printed in sheets of 6.

Princess Maxima of the Netherlands — A557

No. 3036: a, Head. b, Head and torso.

**2006, Dec. 6**

**3036** A557 30d Pair, #a-b 4.50 4.50

Printed in sheets containing 3 of each stamp.

Christmas — A558

Designs: No. 3037, 25d, Gingerbread man. 30d, Christmas tree. 45d, Bell. 50d, Mittens.

No. 3041: a, 15d, Gingerbread man. b, 18d, Christmas tree. c, 25d, Bell.

**2006, Dec. 8** ***Perf. 14***

**3037-3040** A558 Set of 4 11.00 11.00

**Souvenir Sheet**

**3041** A558 Sheet of 4, #3041a-3041c, 3040 7.75 7.75

Miniature Sheet

2006 World Cup Soccer Championships, Germany — A559

No. 3042 — World Cup and soccer ball with flag of: a, 10d, Australia. b, 20d, Germany. c, 25d, Sweden. d, 30d, Brazil.

**2006, Dec. 20** ***Perf. 13¼***

**3042** A559 Sheet of 4, #a-d 6.25 6.25

Concorde A560

No. 3043, 15d: a, Concorde arriving at Filton. b, Concorde G-BOAF in flight.

No. 3044, 15d: a, Concorde taking off from Toulouse. b, Concorde test pilot Andre Turcat.

**2006, Dec. 20** ***Perf. 13¼x13½***

**Pairs, #a-b**

**3043-3044** A560 Set of 2 4.50 4.50

Nos. 3043-3044 were each printed in sheets containing three pairs.

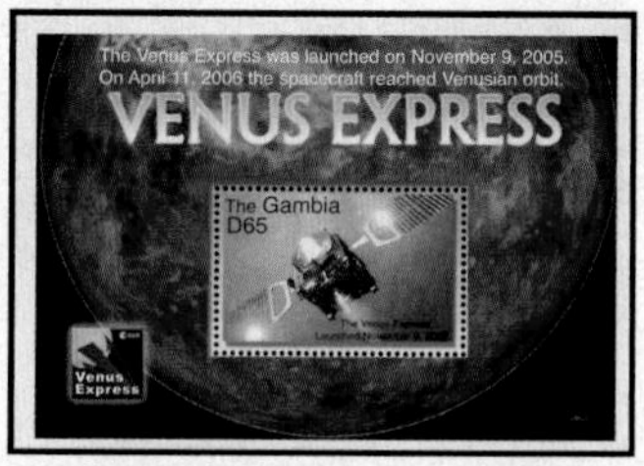


Space Achievements — A561

No. 3045, 20d — Various views of Mars Reconnaissance Orbiter.

No. 3046, 20d — Space Shuttle Columbia: a, Columbia attached to rocket boosters in flight. b, Lift-off of Columbia. c, Shuttle mission simulator. d, Mission control. e, Capt. John W. Young. f, Capt. Robert L. Crippen.

No. 3047, 25d — Giotto Comet Probe: a, Halley's Comet. b, Giotto Comet Probe, green and orange lines. c, Giotto Comet Probe. d, Comet and Giotto Comet Probe.

No. 3048, 25d — Viking 1: a, Viking 1 in flight. b, Viking 1 on Mars, text in black, denomination at UL. c, Viking 1 on Mars, text in black, denomination at UR. d, Viking 1 on Mars, "Viking 1" in white.

No. 3049, 65d, Venus Express. No. 3050, 65d, Hayabusa spacecraft. No. 3051, 65d, Luna 9, vert. No. 3052, 65d, Space Shuttle Discovery returns to space, vert.

**2006, Dec. 20** ***Perf. 14***

**Sheets of 6, #a-f**

**3045-3046** A561 Set of 2 17.50 17.50

**Sheets of 4, #a-d**

**3047-3048** A561 Set of 2 14.50 14.50

**Souvenir Sheets**

**3049-3052** A561 Set of 4 19.00 19.00

New Year 2007 (Year of the Pig) A562

**2007, Feb. 15** ***Perf. 13x13½***

**3053** A562 20d multi 1.50 1.50

Printed in sheets of 4.

Scouting, Cent. A563

Knot in: 30d, Green. 65d, Orange.

**2007, Feb. 15** ***Perf. 13¼***

**3054** A563 30d multi 2.25 2.25

**Souvenir Sheet**

**3055** A563 65d multi 4.75 4.75

No. 3054 printed in sheets of 4.

### Miniature Sheets

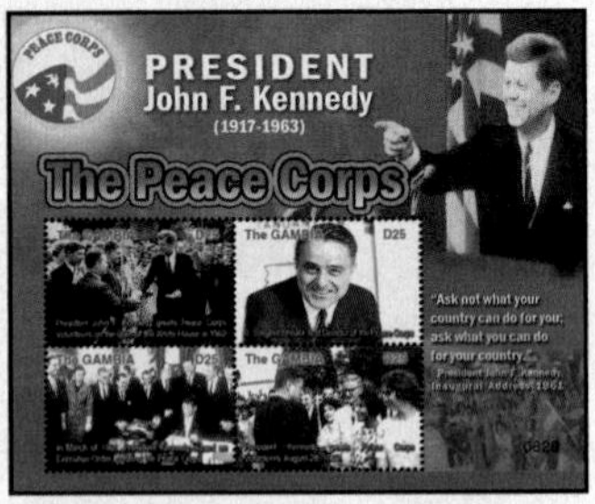


Programs of Pres. John F. Kennedy — A564

No. 3056, 25d — Peace Corps: a, Kennedy greeting Peace Corps volunteers at White House. b, R. Sargent Shriver, first director of Peace Corps. c, Kennedy signing executive order creating Peace Corps. d, Kennedy greeting Peace Corps volunteers.

No. 3057, 25d — Alliance for Progress: a, Kennedy in rocking chair. b, Kennedy and Cabinet. c, Volunteer Ida Shoatz in Peru. d, Kennedy speaking at University of Michigan.

**2007, Feb. 15** ***Perf. 12¾***

**Sheets of 4, #a-d**

**3056-3057** A564 Set of 2 14.50 14.50

Betty Boop — A565

No. 3058 — Betty Boop: a, With hands at side. b, Holding flowers. c, With dog biting swimsuit. d, Wearing long red dress. e, With hands clasped. f, Holding top hat and cane.

No. 3059 — Betty Boop in: a, Red. b, Purple.

**2007, Feb. 15** **Litho.**

**3058** A565 15d Sheet of 6, #a-f 6.50 6.50

**Souvenir Sheet**

**3059** A565 40d Sheet of 2, #a-b 6.00 6.00

Pope Benedict XVI — A566

**2007, May 1** ***Perf. 13¼***

**3060** A566 12d multi .90 .90

Printed in sheets of 8.

Intl. Polar Year — A567

No. 3061 — Penguin: a, At bongo drums. b, With lei and grass skirt. c, At drum set. d, With purple guitar. e, At microphone. f, With yellow and orange guitar.

65d, Penguin in chair at table.

**2007, May 1** **Litho.**

**3061** A567 15d Sheet of 6, #a-f 6.75 6.75

**Souvenir Sheet**

**3062** A567 65d multi 4.75 4.75

Wedding of Queen Elizabeth II and Prince Philip, 60th Anniv. — A568

No. 3063, vert. — Photos of Queen and Prince: a, On wedding day, gray brown frame. b, As older couple, gray brown frame. c, As older couple, pink frame. d, On wedding day, pink frame. e, On wedding day, blue gray frame. f, As older couple, blue gray frame.

65d, Queen and Prince, diff.

**2007, May 1**

**3063** A568 15d Sheet of 6, #a-f 6.75 6.75

**Souvenir Sheet**

**3064** A568 65d multi 4.75 4.75

Princess Diana (1961-97) — A569

No. 3065, vert. — Diana wearing: a, Tiara, close-up. b, Light blue dress, close-up. c, Maroon dress, close-up. d, Tiara, from distance. e, Light blue dress, from distance. f, Maroon dress, from distance.

No. 3066, vert. — Diana wearing: a, Blue and white hat. b, Lilac and purple hat. c, Black dress. d, Red and white hat.

65d, Painting of Diana.

**2007, May 1**

**3065** A569 15d Sheet of 6, #a-f 6.75 6.75

**3066** A569 25d Sheet of 4, #a-d 7.50 7.50

**Souvenir Sheet**

**3067** A569 65d multi 4.75 4.75

1986 Halley's Comet Merchandising Emblem — A570

No. 3068: a, Light olive green frame. b, Light blue frame. c, Violet black frame. d, Brown frame.

65d, Black background.

**2007, June 20** ***Perf. 13¼***

**3068** A570 20d Sheet of 4, #a-d 6.00 6.00

**Souvenir Sheet**

**3069** A570 65d black 5.00 5.00

Ferrari Automobiles, 60th Anniv. — A571

No. 3070: a, 1970 512 S. b, 1996 F 310. c, 1950 195 S. d, 1965 275 P2. e, 1980 Mondial 8. f, 1975 312 T. g, 1952 500 F2. h, 1986 GTB Turbo.

**2007, June 20** ***Perf. 13½x13¼***

**3070** A571 12d Sheet of 8, #a-h 7.25 7.25

Paintings by Qi Baishi (1864-1957) — A572

No. 3071: a, Autumn Leaves and Magpie. b, Camellias. c, Pomegranates. d, Mynahs and Amaranthus.

65d, Magpie and Plum Blossoms.

**2007, July 16** ***Perf. 12½***

**3071** A572 25d Sheet of 4, #a-d 8.25 8.25

**Souvenir Sheet**

***Perf. 11¼x11½***

**3072** A572 65d multi 5.50 5.50

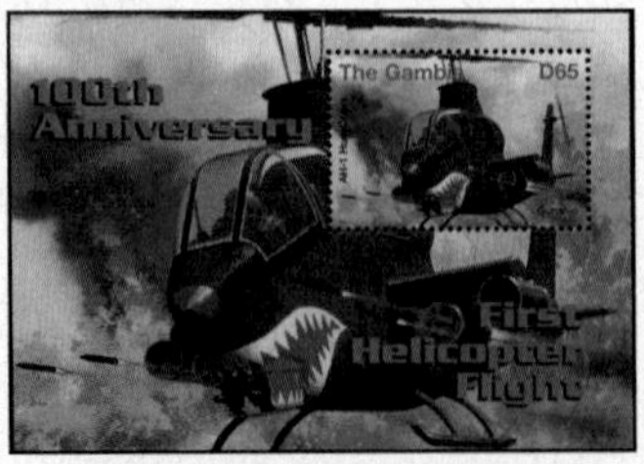


First Helicopter Flight, Cent. — A573

No. 3073: a, UH-1B/C. b, S-65/RH-53B. c, UH-1. d, BK 117. e, Autogyro. f, AS-61.

65d, AH-1 Huey Cobra.

**2007, July 16** ***Perf. 13¼***

**3073** A573 15d Sheet of 6, #a-f 7.50 7.50

**Souvenir Sheet**

**3074** A573 65d multi 5.50 5.50

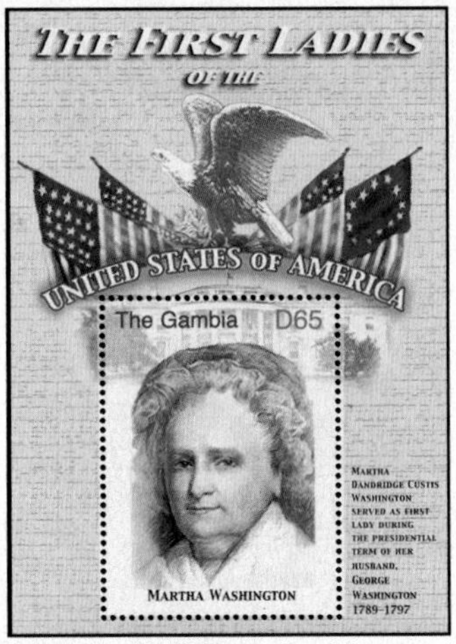


Wives of United States Presidents and First Ladies — A574

No. 3075: a, Martha Washington. b, Abigail Adams. c, Dolley Madison. d, Elizabeth Monroe. e, Louisa Adams. f, Emily Donelson. g, Angelica Van Buren. h, Anna Harrison. i, Letitia Tyler. j, Julia Tyler. k, Sarah Polk. l, Margaret Taylor. m, Abigail Fillmore. n, Jane Pierce. o, Eagle, flags, White House.

No. 3076: a, Harriet Johnston. b, Mary Lincoln. c, Eliza Johnson. d, Julia Grant. e, Lucy Hayes. f, Lucretia Garfield. g, Mary Arthur McElroy. h, Frances Cleveland. i, Caroline Harrison. j, Ida McKinley. k, Edith Roosevelt. l, Helen Taft. m, Ellen Wilson. n, Edith Wilson.

No. 3077: a, Florence Harding. b, Grace Coolidge. c, Lou Hoover. d, Eleanor Roosevelt. e, Bess Truman. f, Mamie Eisenhower. g, Jacqueline Kennedy. h, Lady Bird Johnson. i, Pat Nixon. j, Betty Ford. k, Rosalynn Carter. l, Nancy Reagan. m, Barbara Bush. n, Hillary Clinton. o, Laura Bush.

No. 3078, 65d, Martha Washington. No. 3079, 65d, Abigail Adams. No. 3080, 65d, Martha Jefferson. No. 3081, 65d, Martha Washington Jefferson Randolph. No. 3082, 65d, Dolley Madison. No. 3083, 65d, Elizabeth Monroe. No. 3084, 65d, Louisa Adams. No. 3085, 65d, Rachael Jackson. No. 3086, 65d, Emily Donelson. No. 3087, 65d, Hannah Van Buren. No. 3088, 65d, Angelica Van Buren. No. 3089, 65d, Anna Harrison. No. 3090, 65d, Letitia Tyler. No. 3091, 65d, Priscilla Tyler. No. 3092, 65d, Julia Tyler. No. 3093, 65d, Sarah Polk. No. 3094, 65d, Margaret Taylor. No. 3095, 65d, Mary Taylor. No. 3096, 65d, Abigail Fillmore. No. 3097, 65d, Jane Pierce. No. 3098, 65d, Harriet Johnston. No. 3099, 65d, Mary Lincoln. No. 3100, 65d, Eliza Johnson. No. 3101, 65d, Julia Grant. No. 3102, 65d, Lucy Hayes. No. 3103, 65d, Lucretia Garfield. No. 3104, 65d, Ellen Arthur. No. 3105, 65d, Mary Arthur McElroy. No. 3106, 65d, Frances Cleveland. No. 3107, 65d, Caroline Harrison. No. 3108, 65d, Mary Lord Harrison. No. 3109, 65d, Ida McKinley. No. 3110, 65d, Edith Roosevelt. No. 3111, 65d, Helen Taft. No. 3112, 65d, Ellen Wilson. No. 3113, 65d, Edith Wilson. No. 3114, 65d, Florence Harding. No. 3115, 65d, Grace Coolidge. No. 3116, 65d, Lou Hoover. No. 3117, 65d, Eleanor Roosevelt. No. 3118, 65d, Bess Truman. No. 3119, 65d, Mamie Eisenhower. No. 3120, 65d, Jacqueline Kennedy. No. 3121, 65d, Lady Bird Johnson. No. 3122, 65d, Pat Nixon. No. 3123, 65d, Betty Ford. No. 3124, 65d, Rosalynn Carter. No. 3125, 65d, Nancy Reagan. No. 3126, 65d, Barbara Bush. No. 3127, 65d, Hillary Clinton. No. 3128, 65d, Laura Bush.

**2007** ***Perf. 13¼***

**3075** A574 10d Sheet of 15, #a-o 12.50 12.50

**3076** A574 10d Sheet of 15, #a-n, 3075o 12.50 12.50

**3077** A574 10d Sheet of 15, #a-o 12.50 12.50

*Nos. 3075-3077 (3)* 37.50 37.50

**Souvenir Sheets**

**3078-3128** A574 Set of 51 350.00 350.00

*3078a* Perf. 14¼ 6.75 6.75

Issued: Nos. 3075-3077, 7/31. Nos. 3078-3128, 10/24. Nos. 3075-3077 each contain fifteen 25x37mm stamps.

No. 3078a was not issued in a souvenir sheet.

See No. 3293.

Miniature Sheet

Pres. Gerald R. Ford (1913-2006) — A575

No. 3129 — Ford: a, With wife, Betty. b, At Presidential inauguration ceremony. c, With Betty, Pres. Richard Nixon and Pat Nixon. d, At 90th birthday celebration.

**2007, Aug. 9 Litho. *Perf. 13¼***
**3129** A575 25d Sheet of 4, #a-d 8.25 8.25

Miniature Sheet

Elvis Presley (1935-77) — A576

No. 3130 — Presley, guitar and background color of: a, Green. b, Tan. c, Orange. d, Black (white suit). e, Brown. f, Black (black jacket).

**2007, Sept. 6**
**3130** A576 15d Sheet of 6, #a-f 7.75 7.75

Miniature Sheets

Intl. Holocaust Remembrance Day — A577

No. 3131, 14d — United Nations diplomats and delegates: a, Ronaldo Mota Sardenberg, Brazil. b, Alisher Vohidov, Uzbekistan. c, Martin Belinga-Eboutou, Cameroun. d, Fernand Poukre-Kono, Central African Republic. e, Heraldo Muñoz, Chile. f, Wang Guangya, China. g, Elbio O. Rosselli, Uruguay. h, Shashi Tharoor, Undersecretary General.

No. 3132, 14d: a, Basile Ikouebe, Republic of the Congo. b, Saul Weisleder, Costa Rica. c, Alcicle Djedje, Ivory Coast. d, Andreas D. Mavroiannis, Cyprus. e, Martin Palous, Czech Republic. f, Atoki Ileka, Democratic Republic of the Congo. g, Crispin S. Gregoire, Dominica. h, Parfait Onanga-Anyanga, Ambassador and Special Advisor of the 61st UN General Assembly.

No. 3133, 14d: a, Hoya Rashed Al-Khalifa, President of 61st UN General Assembly. b, Denis Dangue Rewaka, Gabon. c, Crispin Grey-Johnson, Gambia. d, Irakli Alasania, Georgia. e, Nana Effah-Apenteng, Ghana. f, Adamantios Vassilakis, Greece. g, Jorge Skinner-Klee Arenales, Guatemala. h, Jean-Maurice Ripert, France.

No. 3134, 14d: a, Hilari G. Davide, Jr., Philippines. b, Andrzej Towpik, Poland. c, Joao Manuel Guerra Salgueiro, Portugal. d, Alexei Tulbure, Moldova. e, Mihnea I. Motoc, Romania. f, Vitaly I. Churkin, Russia. g, Joseph Nsengimana, Rwanda. h, Augustine P. Mahiga, Tanzania.

**2007, Nov. 28 Litho. *Perf. 13½***
**Sheets of 8, #a-h**
**3131-3134** A577 Set of 4 41.00 41.00

2008 Summer Olympics, Beijing — A578

***Die Cut Perf. 8½x8¼***
**2007, Nov. 29 Litho. & Embossed**
**Without Gum**
**3135** A578 40d multi 3.75 3.75

Christmas A579

Designs: 25d, Girl at manger scene. 30d, Children eating holiday dishes. 45d, Boy with Madonna and Child sculptures. 50d, Christmas celebrations with music.

**2007, Dec. 3 Litho. *Perf. 12***
**3136-3139** A579 Set of 4 14.00 14.00

Souvenir Sheet

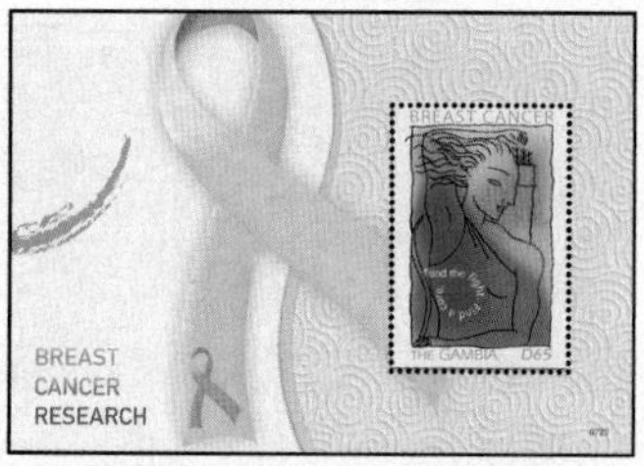


Breast Cancer Prevention — A580

**2007, Dec. 10 *Perf. 14***
**3140** A580 65d multi 6.00 6.00

America's Cup Yacht Races A581

No. 3141 — Various yachts with wide panels in: a, Blue. b, Yellow orange. c, Red. d, Orange.

**2007, Dec. 28 *Perf. 13¼***

| | | | |
|---|---|---|---|
| **3141** | Strip of 4 | 6.75 | 6.75 |
| *a.* | A581 10d multi | .85 | .85 |
| *b.* | A581 15d multi | 1.40 | 1.40 |
| *c.* | A581 20d multi | 1.75 | 1.75 |
| *d.* | A581 30d multi | 2.75 | 2.75 |

Miniature Sheet

National Basketball Association Players — A582

No. 3142: a, Carmelo Anthony, Denver Nuggets. b, Kobe Bryant, Los Angeles Lakers. c, Vince Carter, New Jersey Nets. d, Allen Iverson, Denver Nuggets. e, LeBron James, Cleveland Cavaliers. f, Yao Ming, Houston Rockets. g, Steve Nash, Phoenix Suns. h, Shaquille O'Neal, Miami Heat. i, Dwayne Wade, Miami Heat.

**2007, Dec. 28 *Perf. 13¼***
**3142** A582 10d Sheet of 9, #a-i 8.25 8.25

Hummer Vehicles — A583

No. 3143: a, H2 on road, denomination in white. b, H2 on road, denomination in black. c, H2, white background. d, H2 on rocks. 65d, H2 SUT.

**2007, Dec. 28 *Perf. 13½***
**3143** A583 25d Sheet of 4, #a-d 9.00 9.00

**Souvenir Sheet**

**3144** A583 65d multi 6.00 6.00

New Year 2008 (Year of the Rat) A584

**2008, Jan. 28 Litho. *Perf. 12***
**3145** A584 30d multi 2.75 2.75

Printed in sheets of 4.

2008 Taipei Intl. Stamp Exhibition — A585

No. 3146, horiz. — Taipei landmarks: a, Temple and garden. b, Dr. Sun Yat-sen Memorial Hall. c, Natl. Opera House. d, Temple. 45d, Lover's Bridge, Tamsui.

**2008, Apr. 11 *Perf. 13¼***
**3146** A585 12d Sheet of 4, #a-d 5.00 5.00

**Souvenir Sheet**

***Perf. 13¼x13½***

**3147** A585 45d multi 4.50 4.50

No. 3146 contains four 42x28mm stamps.

Pioneer Satellites — A586

No. 3148: a, Pioneer 1 in orbit, Moon in background. b, Pioneer 1 in nose cone. c, Pioneer 1.

No. 3149, horiz.: a, Technicians and Pioneer 3. b, Pioneer 3 in orbit. c, Pioneer 3 on launch pad.

No. 3150: a, Pioneer 1 on launch pad. b, Pioneer 1 in orbit, diff.

No. 3151: a, Pioneer 3. b, Pioneer 3 in orbit, Moon in background.

No. 3152, Pioneer 1, horiz. No. 3153, Pioneer 3, horiz.

**2008, Apr. 11 *Perf. 13¼***

| | | | | |
|---|---|---|---|---|
| **3148** | A586 | 15d Horiz. strip of 3, #a-c | 4.50 | 4.50 |
| **3149** | A586 | 15d Vert. strip of 3, #a-c | 4.50 | 4.50 |
| **3150** | A586 | 20d Pair, #a-b | 4.00 | 4.00 |
| **3151** | A586 | 20d Pair, #a-b | 4.00 | 4.00 |

**Souvenir Sheets**

**3152** A586 65d multi 6.50 6.50

***Perf. 13¼x13½***

**3153** A586 65d multi 6.50 6.50

No. 3153 contains one 51x38mm stamp. Nos. 3148-3151 were issued in sheets containing two strips or pairs.

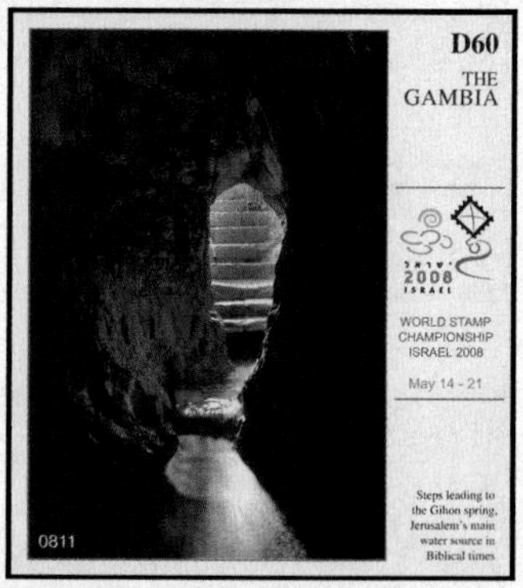


2008 World Stamp Championship, Israel — A587

**2008, May 14 *Imperf.***
**3154** A587 60d multi 5.75 5.75

Miniature Sheet

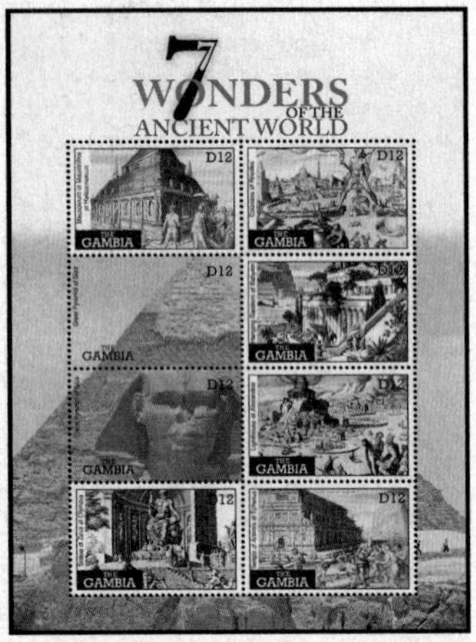


Seven Wonders of the Ancient World — A588

No. 3155: a, Mausoleum of Maussollos, Halicarnassus. b, Colossus of Rhodes. c, Tip of Giant Pyramid, Giza. d, Hanging Gardens of Babylon. e, Sphinx and Giant Pyramid. f, Lighthouse of Alexandria. g, Statue of Zeus, Olympia. h, Temple of Artemis, Ephesus.

**2008, May 16** ***Perf. 13¼***
**3155** A588 12d Sheet of 8, #a-h 9.25 9.25

Miniature Sheet

Elvis Presley (1935-77) — A589

No. 3156 — Presley: a, Wearing striped jacket. b, With acoustic guitar. c, With arms on knee. d, With electric guitar.

**2008, May 16**
**3156** A589 25d Sheet of 4, #a-d 9.50 9.50

Miniature Sheet

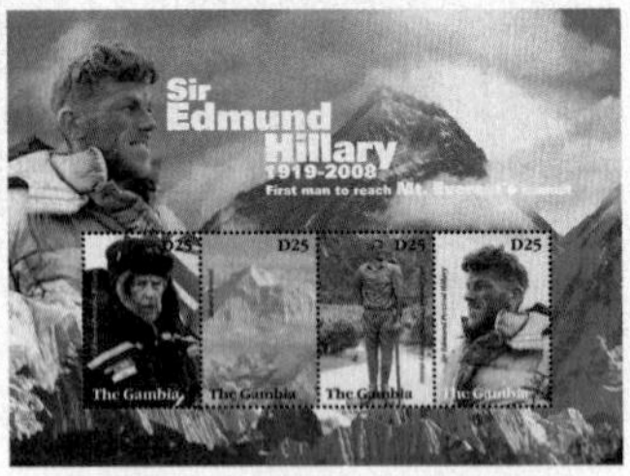


Sir Edmund Hillary (1919-2008), Mountaineer — A590

No. 3157: a, Hillary and flag. b, Mt. Everest. c, Statue of Hillary. d, Hillary as young man.

**2008, May 16**
**3157** A590 25d Sheet of 4, #a-d 9.50 9.50

Miniature Sheet

2008 Summer Olympics, Beijing — A591

No. 3158: a, Suzanne Lenglen, 1920 Tennis gold medalist. b, Duke Kahanamoku, 1920 Swimming gold medalist. c, Nedo Nadi, 1920 Fencing gold medalist. d, Olympic rings and text "Olympex 2008."

**2008, May 28** ***Perf. 12***
**3158** A591 10d Sheet of 4, #a-d 4.00 4.00

Visit of Pope Benedict XVI to United States — A592

**2008, June 12** ***Perf. 13¼***
**3159** A592 25d multi 2.40 2.40

Printed in sheets of 4.

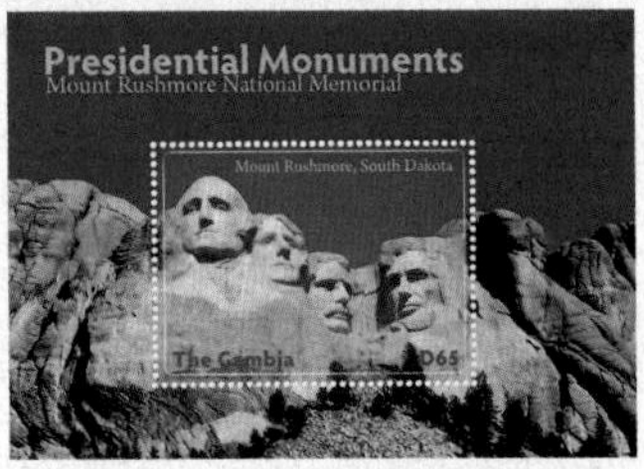


United States Landmarks — A593

No. 3160, vert.: a, Grant's Tomb, New York. b, Jefferson Memorial, Washington, DC. c, Kennedy Eternal Flame, Arlington, Virginia. d, Capitol, Washington, DC. e, Lincoln Memorial, Washington, DC. f, Washington Monument, Washington, DC.

65d, Mount Rushmore, South Dakota.

**2008, June 12**
**3160** A593 15d Sheet of 6, #a-f 8.50 8.50

**Souvenir Sheet**

**3161** A593 65d multi 6.25 6.25

Muhammad Ali, Boxer — A594

No. 3162, 25d — Ali : a, With white trunks, fists in front of chest. b, Seated. c, With white trunks, arm extended. d, Wearing drawstring shorts.

No. 3163, 25d, horiz. — Ali: a, Behind microphone. b, With hand on chin. c, With fist raised. d, Running.

No. 3164, 65d, Head of Ali in color. No. 3165, 65d, Head of Ali in black and white.

**2008, July 21** ***Perf. 11½***

**Sheets of 4, #a-d**

**3162-3163** A594 Set of 2 19.00 19.00

**Souvenir Sheets**

***Perf. 13¼***

**3164-3165** A594 Set of 2 12.50 12.50

No. 3162 contains four 30x40mm stamps. No. 3163 contains four 40x30mm stamps.

Gambia Coat of Arms — A595

**2008, Sept. 15 Litho.** ***Perf. 14x15***
**3166** A595 40d blk & mar + label 3.50 3.50

Printed in sheets of 8 stamps + 8 labels.

Miniature Sheet

Marilyn Monroe (1926-62), Actress — A596

No. 3167 — Monroe: a, Facing forward, eyes open. b, Facing left. c, Facing right. d, Facing forward, eyes shut.

**2008, Sept. 22** ***Perf. 13¼***
**3167** A596 25d Sheet of 4, #a-d 8.50 8.50

Miniature Sheets

A597

End of World War I, 90th Anniv. — A598

No. 3168: a, Generals talking. b, Soldier and trench. c, Pilot. d, Pilot and propeller. e, Soldier wearing helmet. f, Officers standing in row.

No. 3169: a, Soldiers at air field. b, Tanks. c, Two soldiers. d, Soldiers at cannon.

**2008, Nov. 11 Litho.** ***Perf. 11½x12***
**3168** A597 15d Sheet of 6, #a-f 6.75 6.75
**3169** A598 25d Sheet of 4, #a-d 7.50 7.50

Miniature Sheet

Prince Charles, 60th Birthday — A599

No. 3170: a, Wearing black suit. b, Wearing top hat. c, Wearing gray suit. d, Wearing military uniform.

**2008, Nov. 14** ***Perf. 11¼x11½***
**3170** A599 25d Sheet of 4, #a-d 7.50 7.50

Christmas A600

Designs: 25d, Map of West Africa, ribbon and bow. 30d, Red, blue and green bows. 45d, Woman carrying gift on head, flag, vert. 50d, Gifts, flag.

**2008, Dec. 1** ***Perf. 14¾x14, 14x14¾***
**3171-3174** A600 Set of 4 11.50 11.50

Miniature Sheet

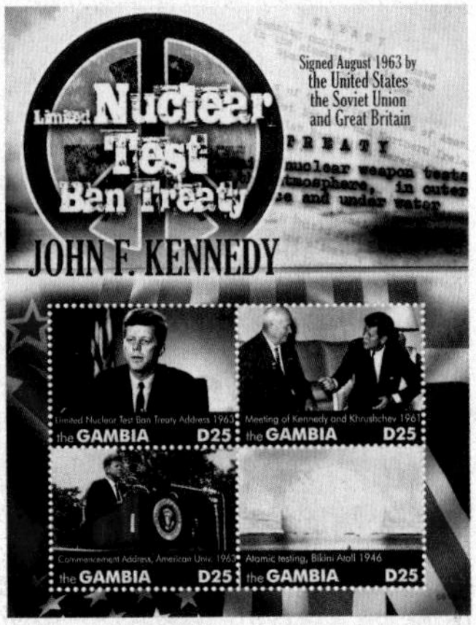


Signing of Limited Nuclear Test Ban Treaty — A601

No. 3175: a, Pres. John F. Kennedy. b, Kennedy and Soviet Premier Nikita Khrushchev. c, Kennedy at American University commencement. d, Atomic bomb test, Bikini Atoll, 1946.

**2008, Dec. 4** ***Perf. 11½x12***
**3175** A601 25d Sheet of 4, #a-d 7.50 7.50

Miniature Sheet

Pres. Abraham Lincoln (1809-65) — A602

No. 3176: a, Lincoln with son, Tad. b, Lincoln wih beard in profile. c, Lincoln without beard. d, Lincoln with beard.

**2008, Dec. 4** ***Perf. 13¼***
**3176** A602 25d Sheet of 4, #a-d 7.50 7.50

A603

A604

A605

Flowers — A606

No. 3177: a, Calotropis procera. b, Calliandra surinamensis. c, Plumeria alba. d, Quisqualis indica.

No. 3178: a, Adansonia digitata. b, Commelina benghalensis. c, Heliconia psittacorum. d, Tabebuia rosea.

**2008, Dec. 31** ***Perf. 12½***

**3177** A603 25d Sheet of 4, #a-d 7.50 7.50

***Perf. 12***

**3178** A604 25d Sheet of 4, #a-d 7.50 7.50

**Souvenir Sheets**

**3179** A605 65d multi 5.00 5.00

**3180** A606 65d multi 5.00 5.00

New Year 2009 (Year of the Ox) A607

**2009, Jan. 5** ***Perf. 12***

**3181** A607 25d multi 1.90 1.90

Printed in sheets of 4.

Inauguration of US Pres. Barack Obama — A608

No. 3183: a, Pres. Obama. b, Vice-president Joseph Biden.

**2009, Jan. 20** ***Perf. 14x14¾***

**3182** A608 16d shown 1.25 1.25

**Souvenir Sheet**

**3183** A608 60d Sheet of 2, #a-b 9.00 9.00

No. 3182 was printed in sheets of 9.

Miniature Sheet

Pope John Paul II (1920-2005) — A609

No. 3184 — Pope John Paul II at: a, Inaugural Mass, 1978. b, United Nations, 1979. c, Warsaw, 1983. d, Denver, Colorado, 1993.

**2009, Feb. 4** ***Perf. 13¼***

**3184** A609 25d Sheet of 4, #a-d 7.75 7.75

A610

A611

A612

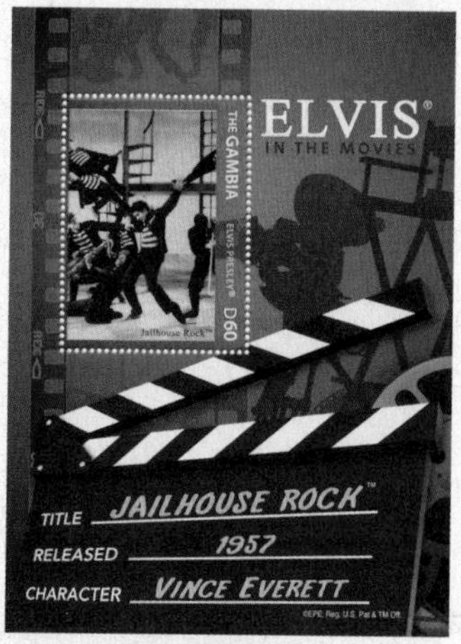


A613

Elvis Presley (1935-77) — A614

No. 3185 — Presley wearing: a, Black suit and tie, white shirt. b, Black suit and shirt, no tie. c, Red sweater. d, Brown shirt and gray tie. e, Blue shirt. f, Gray sweater and white shirt.

**2009** ***Perf. 13¼***

**3185** A610 20d Sheet of 6, #a-f 9.00 9.00

**Souvenir Sheets**

**3186** A611 60d multi 4.75 4.75

**3187** A612 60d multi 4.75 4.75

**3188** A613 60d multi 4.75 4.75

**3189** A614 60d multi 4.75 4.75

Issued: No. 3185, 4/30; others, 2/25.

Miniature Sheet

Jet Li One Foundation — A615

No. 3190: a, Education. b, Jet Li. c, Poverty. d, Health. e, Environment. f, Disaster relief.

**2009, Apr. 1** ***Perf. 12¾***

**3190** A615 40d Sheet of 6, #a-f 18.00 18.00

Souvenir Sheet

Great Wall of China — A616

**2009, Apr. 10** ***Perf. 12***

**3191** A616 80d multi 6.00 6.00

China 2009 Intl. Philatelic Exhibition.

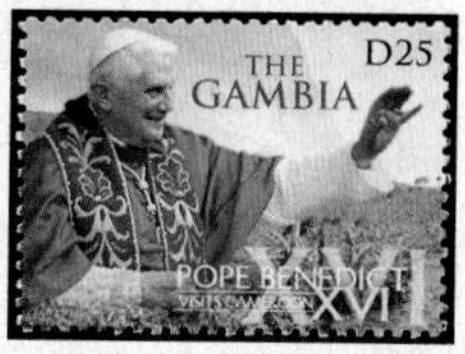


Visit to Cameroun of Pope Benedict XVI A617

**2009, Apr. 30** ***Perf. 11½x11¼***

**3192** A617 25d multi 1.90 1.90

Printed in sheets of 4.

Miniature Sheet

Whistle-stop Inaugural Journeys of US Presidents Abraham Lincoln and Barack Obama — A618

No. 3193: a, Inaugural speech of Pres. Obama. b, Inaugural speech of Pres. Lincoln. c, Lincoln, map of train route. d, Pres. Obama and Vice-president Joseph Biden on train in Wilmington, Delaware.

**2009, Apr. 30** ***Perf. 14¾x14***

**3193** A618 25d Sheet of 4, #a-d 7.50 7.50

American Military Aviation, Cent. — A619

No. 3194, horiz.: a, B-17 and P-51 Escort. b, Doolittle's B-25. c, B-24. d, P-47D. e, F-86F. f, AT-6. g, F-80. h, F-15. i, T-38 and F-117.
80d, P-38 and ME-262.

**2009, June 12** ***Perf. 11½x11¼***
**3194** A619 15d Sheet of 9, #a-i 10.50 10.50

**Souvenir Sheet**
***Perf. 13¼***
**3195** A619 80d multi 6.00 6.00

No. 3194 contains nine 40x30mm stamps. National Topical Stamp Show, Dayton, Ohio.

Miniature Sheets

Michael Jackson (1958-2009), Singer — A620

No. 3196: a, 20d, Holding microphone. b, 20d, Wearing white jacket and hat. c, 30d, As "b." d, 30d, As "a."
No. 3197, horiz.: a, 20d, Wearing black jacket and hat. b, 20d, Wearing white jacket. c, 30d, As "a." d, 30d, As "b."

***Perf. 12x11½, 11½ (#3197)***
**2009, July 7** **Litho.**
**Sheets of 4, #a-d**
**3196-3197** A620 Set of 2 15.00 15.00

Miniature Sheet

First Man on the Moon, 40th Anniv. — A621

No. 3198: a, Obverse and reverse of US Susan B. Anthony dollar coin. b, Apollo 11 Lunar Module. c, Neil Armstrong. d, Apollo 11. e, Statue of Armstrong. f, Apollo 11 Command Module.

**2009, July 20** ***Perf. 13¼***
**3198** A621 20d Sheet of 6, #a-f 9.00 9.00

Miniature Sheets

Dogs — A622

No. 3199, 25d — Pembroke Welsh corgi: a, Jumping. b, Sitting in leaves. c, Sitting in front of flower basket. d, Sitting on lawn.
No. 3200, 25d — West Highland white terrier and: a, Upright basket. b, Beach ball. c, Gift boxes. d, Yellow flowers and basket on side.

**2009, Aug. 29** ***Perf. 12***
**Sheets of 4, #a-d**
**3199-3200** A622 Set of 2 15.00 15.00

Birds A623

Designs: 15d, Hamerkop. 20d, Pied kingfisher. No. 3203, 25d, Black-capped babbler. No. 3204, 40d, African darter.
No. 3205, 25d, vert.: a, Malachite kingfisher. b, Common bulbul. c, Black-crowned night heron. d, Wire-tailed swallow.
No. 3206, 40d: a, Sacred ibis. b, Little grebe.

**2009, Aug. 29** ***Perf. 11½***
**3201-3204** A623 Set of 4 7.50 7.50
**3205** A623 25d Sheet of 4, #a-d 7.50 7.50

**Souvenir Sheet**
**3206** A623 40d Sheet of 2, #a-b 6.00 6.00

Miniature Sheet

Teenage Mutant Ninja Turtles, 25th Anniv. — A624

No. 3207: a, Raphael. b, Leonardo. c, Michelangelo. d, Donatello.

**2009, Aug. 29** ***Perf. 13¼***
**3207** A624 25d Sheet of 4, #a-d 7.50 7.50

Pres. Barack Obama and Queen Elizabeth II — A625

No. 3208, horiz.: a, Pres. Obama. b, Queen Elizabeth II. c, Michelle Obama.
80d, Pres. Obama and Queen Elizabeth II at G20 World Leader Reception.

**2009, Aug. 29** ***Perf. 11½x12***
**3208** A625 25d Sheet of 3, #a-c 5.75 5.75

**Souvenir Sheet**
***Perf. 11½***
**3209** A625 80d multi 6.00 6.00

Pres. Barack Obama in Germany — A626

No. 3210: a, Obama, Bishop Jochen Bohl, German Chancellor Angela Merkel. b, Obama. c, Merkel. d, Obama and Merkel.
65d, Obama, Merkel, Elie Wiesel and Bertrand Herz at Buchenwald Concentration Camp.

**2009, Oct. 22** ***Perf. 11½***
**3210** A626 25d Sheet of 4, #a-d 7.50 7.50

**Souvenir Sheet**
***Perf. 13¼***
**3211** A626 65d multi 4.75 4.75

No. 3210 contains four 30x40mm stamps.

Methodist Church Conference — A627

Cross and map of: 25d, The Gambia. 35d, Africa, vert.

**2009** ***Perf. 11½***
**3212-3213** A627 Set of 2 4.50 4.50

Miniature Sheet

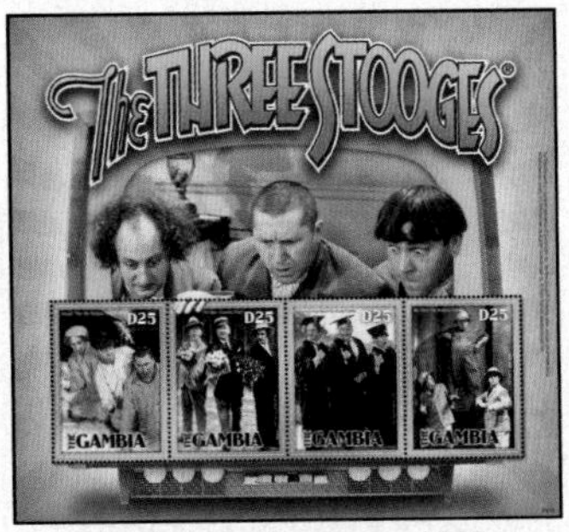


The Three Stooges — A628

No. 3214 — Scenes from: a, Rockin' Thru the Rockies. b, The Sitter Downers. c, Violent is the Word for Curly. d, We Want Our Mummy.

**2009** ***Perf. 13¼***
**3214** A628 25d Sheet of 4, #a-d 7.50 7.50

Miniature Sheet

Pres. Barack Obama, 2009 Nobel Peace Laureate — A629

No. 3215 — Pres. Obama with: a, Microphones at LR. b, Microphones at LL. c, Foliage at right. d, Flag at right.

**2009, Dec. 30** **Litho.** ***Perf. 13x13¼***
**3215** A629 25d Sheet of 4, #a-d 7.50 7.50

Mushrooms A630

Designs: 10d, Panaeolus bispora. No. 3217, 15d, Panaeolus tropicalis. 25d, Psilocybe mairei. 30d, Gymnopilus aeruginosus.
No. 3220, 15d, horiz.: a, Panaeolus retirugis. b, Gymnopilus junionius. c, Psilocybe natalensis. d, Panaeolus africanus. e, Panaeolus cinctulus. f, Panaeolus subbalteatus.

**2009, Dec. 30** ***Perf. 14x14¾***
**3216-3219** A630 Set of 4 6.00 6.00

***Perf. 14¾x14***
**3220** A630 15d Sheet of 6, #a-f 6.75 6.75

Butterflies A631

Designs: 10d, Elegant acraea. No. 3222, 15d, Bamboo charaxes. 25d, Green-veined charaxes. 30d, Pink acraea.
No. 3225, 15d, horiz.: a, Abadima acraea. b, African common white. c, Cream-bordered charaxes. d, African caper white. e, Large spotted acraea. f, Tiny orange tip.

**2009, Dec. 30** ***Perf. 14x14¾***
**3221-3224** A631 Set of 4 6.00 6.00

***Perf. 14¾x14***
**3225** A631 15d Sheet of 6, #a-f 6.75 6.75

Christmas — A632

Designs: 10d, Map of Africa with stocking cap. 15d, Cane-shaped cookies. 25d, Christmas light display. 30d, Candle and poinsettia.

**2009, Dec. 30** ***Perf. 14x14¾***
**3226-3229** A632 Set of 4 6.00 6.00

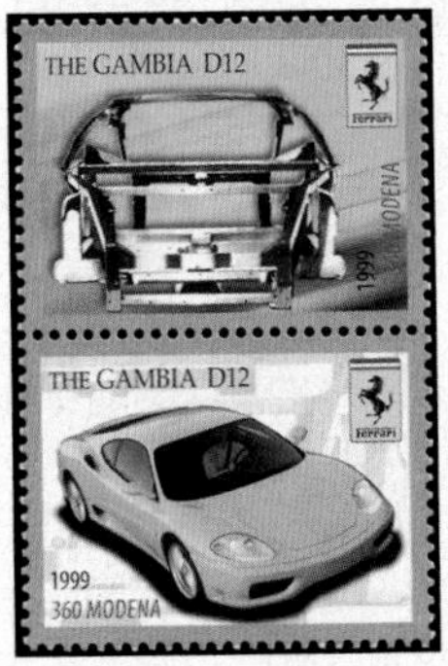


Ferraris and Their Parts A633

No. 3230, 12d: a, Chassis of 1999 360 Modena. b, 1999 360 Modena.
No. 3231, 12d: a, Engine and drive train of 2003 F2003-GA. b, 2003 F2003-GA.
No.3232, 12d: a, Convertible roof of 2005 Superamerica. b, 2005 Superamerica.
No. 3233, 12d: a, Engine of 2008 California. b, 2008 California.

**2010, Feb. 24** ***Perf. 12***
**Vert. Pairs, #a-b**
**3230-3233** A633 Set of 4 7.25 7.25

Whales and Dolphins A634

Designs: 10d, Common dolphin. 15d, Pygmy killer whale. No. 3236, 25d, Short-finned pilot whale. 30d, Clymene dolphin.
No. 3228, 25d: a, Southern bottlenose whale. b, Fraser's dolphin. c, Atlantic hump-backed dolphin. d, Ginkgo-toothed beaked whale.

No. 3239, 35d: a, Blainville's beaked whalen. b, Atlantic spotted dolphin.

**2010, Feb. 24** ***Perf. 11½x11¼***

**3234-3237** A634 Set of 4 6.00 6.00

***Perf. 11½x12***

**3238** A634 25d Sheet of 4, #a-d 7.50 7.50

**Souvenir Sheet**

***Perf. 11½x11¼***

**3239** A634 35d Sheet of 2, #a-b 5.25 5.25

Miniature Sheet

Charles Darwin (1809-82), Naturalist — A635

No. 3240 — Birds: a, Warbler finch. b, Common cactus finch. c, Large cactus finch. d, Small ground finch.

**2010, Feb. 24** ***Perf. 13¼***

**3240** A635 25d Sheet of 4, #a-d 7.50 7.50

Miniature Sheet

Pres. John F. Kennedy (1917-63) — A636

No. 3241 — Kennedy: a, Curtainin background at left. b, At inauguration ceremony. c, With flag in background at right. d, With family.

**2010, Apr. 15** ***Perf. 12x11½***

**3241** A636 30d Sheet of 4, #a-d 9.00 9.00

Miniature Sheets

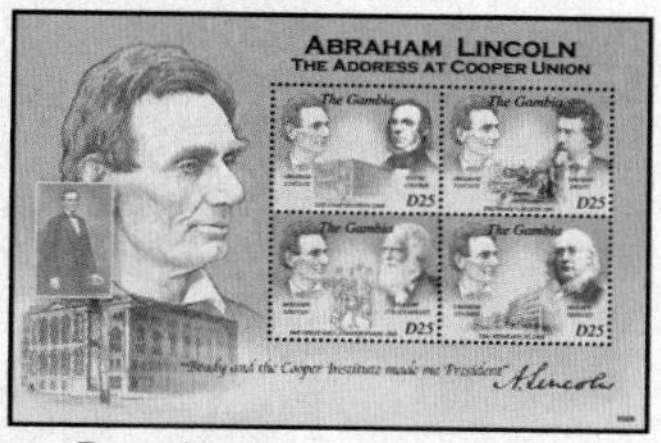


Pres. Abraham Lincoln (1809-65) — A637

No. 3242, 25d — Lincoln and: a, Peter Cooper, Cooper Union. b, Mathew Brady, Brady Gallery. c, William Cullen Bryant, Great Hall, Cooper Union. d, Horace Greeley, Astor House.

No. 3243, 25d — Lincoln and: a, Brady, photograph of Lincoln by Brady. b, Alexander Gardner, photographs of Lincoln by Gardner. c, Victor David Brenner, Lincoln cent, Pres. Theodore Roosevelt. d, Daniel Chester French, statue of Lincoln in Lincoln Memorial.

**2010, Apr. 15** ***Perf. 11½x12***

**Sheets of 4, #a-d**

**3242-3243** A637 Set of 2 15.00 15.00

Miniature Sheets

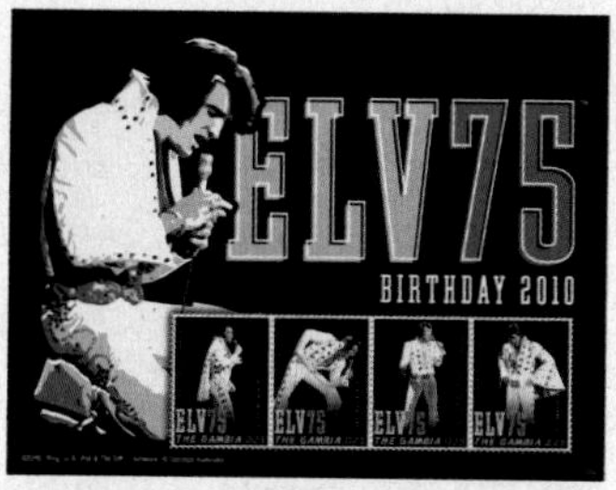


A638

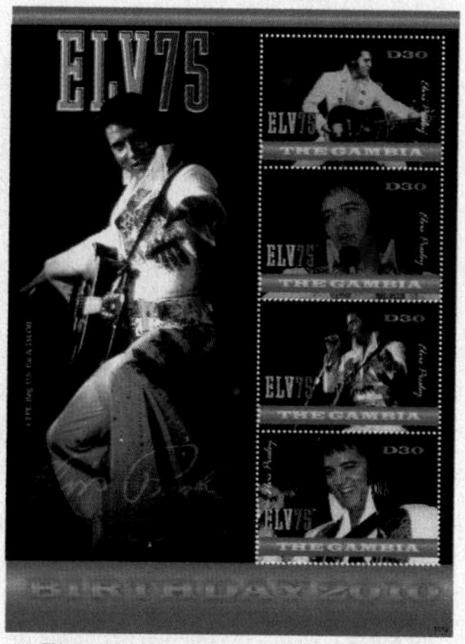


Elvis Presley (1935-77) — A639

No. 3244 — Presley: a, Holding microphone, facing right, cape and microphone cord visible. b, Holding microphone, leaning. c, Holding microphone, no cord visible. d, Standing with arms akimbo.

No. 3245 — Presley: a, With guitar. b, With microphone near mouth. c, With guitar, pointing, and holding microphone on stand. d, Holding microphone on stand, with guitar strap on shoulder.

**2010, Apr. 15** ***Perf. 11¼x11½***

**3244** A638 25d Sheet of 4, #a-d 7.50 7.50

***Perf. 13¼***

**3245** A639 30d Sheet of 4, #a-d 9.00 9.00

2010 World Cup Soccer Championships, South Africa — A640

Soccer ball with flag of participating nations: No. 3246, 20d, Algeria. No. 3247, 20d, Argentina. No. 3248, 20d, Australia. No. 3249, 20d, Brazil. No. 3250, 20d, Cameroon. No. 3251, 20d, Chile. No. 3252, 20d, Denmark. No. 3253, 20d, England. No. 3254, 20d, France. No. 3255, 20d, Germany. No. 3256, 20d, Ghana. No. 3257, 20d, Greece. No. 3258, 20d, Honduras. No. 3259, 20d, Italy. No. 3260, 20d, Ivory Coast (Côte d'Ivoire). No. 3261, 20d, Japan. No. 3262, 20d, Korea DPR (North Korea). No. 3263, 20d, Korea Republic (South Korea). No. 3264, 20d, Mexico. No. 3265, 20d, Netherlands. No. 3266, 20d, New Zealand. No. 3267, 20d, Nigeria. No. 3268, 20d, Paraguay. No. 3269, 20d, Portugal. No. 3270, 20d, Serbia. No. 3271, 20d, Slovakia. No. 3272, 20d, Slovenia. No. 3273, 20d, South Africa. No. 3274, 20d, Spain. No. 3275, 20d, Switzerland. No. 3276, 20d, United States. No. 3277, 20d, Uruguay.

**2010, May 24** ***Perf. 14x14¾***

**3246-3277** A640 Set of 32 45.00 45.00

Nos. 3246-3277 each were printed in sheets of 6.

Traditional Musical Instruments A641

Designs: 2d, 25d, Wollof tabala. 3d, 30d, Jola bugarab. 5d, 35d, Fula rilty. 6d, 50d, Mandinka kontingo. 7d, 65d, Mandinka bolongbato. 10d, 100d, Mandinka kora. 15d, 200d, Mandinka kora, diff. 18d, Mandinka balafongo, horiz.

***Perf. 11¼x11½, 11½x11¼***

**2010, June 8**

| | | | | |
|---|---|---|---|---|
| **3278** | A641 | 2d multi | .25 | .25 |
| **3279** | A641 | 3d multi | .25 | .25 |
| **3280** | A641 | 5d multi | .35 | .35 |
| **3281** | A641 | 6d multi | .40 | .40 |
| **3282** | A641 | 7d multi | .50 | .50 |
| **3283** | A641 | 10d multi | .70 | .70 |
| **3284** | A641 | 15d multi | 1.00 | 1.00 |
| **3285** | A641 | 18d multi | 1.25 | 1.25 |
| **3286** | A641 | 25d multi | 1.75 | 1.75 |
| **3287** | A641 | 30d multi | 2.00 | 2.00 |
| **3288** | A641 | 35d multi | 2.40 | 2.40 |
| **3289** | A641 | 50d multi | 3.50 | 3.50 |
| **3290** | A641 | 65d multi | 4.50 | 4.50 |
| **3291** | A641 | 100d multi | 6.75 | 6.75 |
| **3292** | A641 | 200d multi | 13.50 | 13.50 |
| | *Nos. 3278-3292 (15)* | | 39.10 | 39.10 |

**US First Ladies Type of 2007**

Souvenir Sheet

No. 3293, Michelle Obama.

**2010, June 8** ***Perf. 13¼***

**3293** A574 65d multi 4.50 4.50

Miniature Sheet

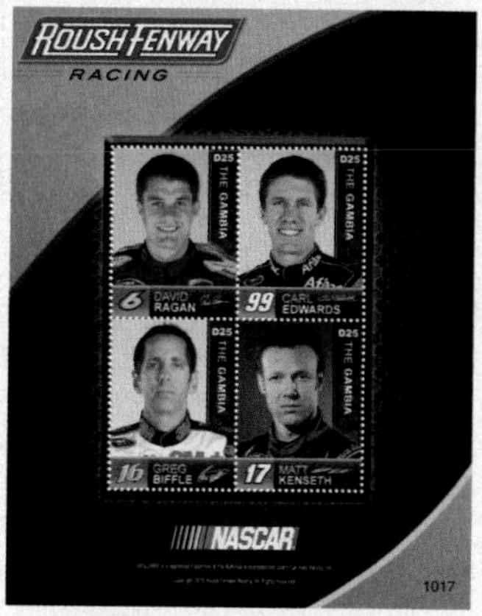


NASCAR Drivers — A642

No. 3294: a, David Ragan. b, Carl Edwards. c, Greg Biffle. d, Matt Kenseth.

**2010, June 8** ***Perf. 13¼x13***

**3294** A642 25d Sheet of 4, #a-d 6.75 6.75

Souvenir Sheet

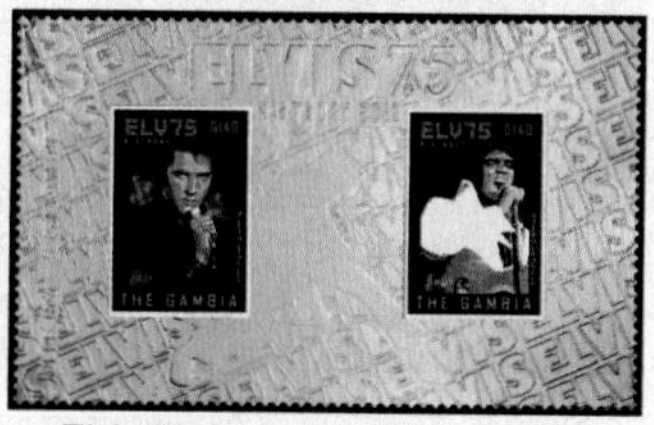


Elvis Presley (1935-77) — A643

No. 3295 — Presley wearing: a, Black jacket. b, White jacket.

**2010, June 11** ***Imperf.***

**3295** A643 140d Sheet of 2, #a-b 19.00 19.00

Miniature Sheet

Elvis Presley (1935-77) — A644

No. 3296 — Presley wearing: a, Checked shirt. b, Jacket and tie. c, Sweater. d, White shirt with open collar.

**2010, Apr. 15** **Litho.** ***Perf. 13¼***

**3296** A644 30d Sheet of 4, #a-d 9.00 9.00

Lech Kaczynski (1949-2010), President of Poland — A645

**2010, July 14** ***Perf. 12x11½***

**3297** A645 30d multi 2.25 2.25

Printed in sheets of 4.

Miniature Sheet

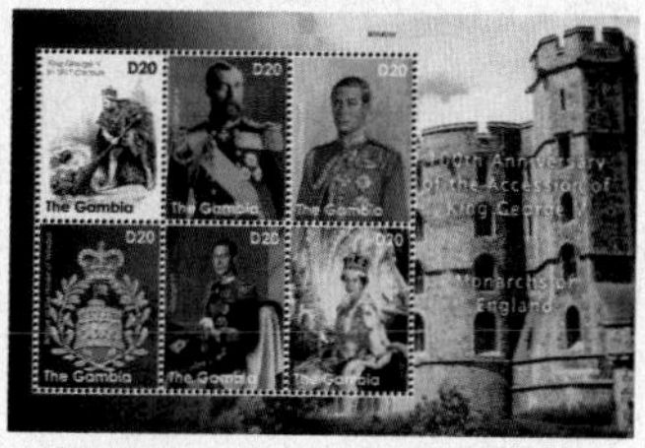


Accession to the Throne by King George V, Cent. — A646

No. 3298: a, 1917 cartoon of King George V. b, King George V. c, King Edward VIII. d, Badge of the House of Windsor. e, King George VI. f, Queen Elizabeth II.

**2010, July 14** **Litho.** ***Perf. 11¼x11½***

**3298** A646 20d Sheet of 6, #a-f 8.75 8.75

Visit of Pope Benedict XVI to Malta A647

Pope Benedict XVI wearing: No. 3299, 30d, Miter. No. 3300, 30d, Zucchetto.

**2010, Aug. 26** ***Perf. 13¼***

**3299-3300** A647 Set of 2 4.25 4.25

Nos. 3299-3300 each were printed in sheets of 5.

Miniature Sheet

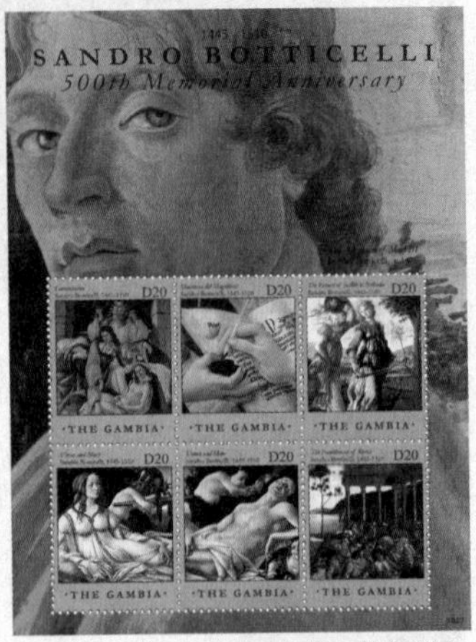


Paintings by Sandro Botticelli (1445-1510) — A648

No. 3301: a, Lamentation. b, Madonna del Magnificat. c, The Return of Judith to Bethulia. d, Venus from Venus and Mars. e, Mars from Venus and Mars. f, The Punishment of Korah.

**2010, Aug. 26** ***Perf. 11¼x11½***

**3301** A648 20d Sheet of 6, #a-f 8.25 8.25

Miniature Sheets

Mother Teresa (1910-97), Humanitarian — A649

No. 3302, 30d — Mother Teresa at left, Princess Diana at right, with: a, Princess Diana bending to talk to Mother Teresa. b, Princess Diana with hands clasped at waist and Mother Teresa with hands clasped below chin. c, Mother Teresa and Princess Diana holding hands, Mother Teresa's arm at side. d, Mother Teresa and Princess Diana holding hands, Mother Teresa's arm extended.

No. 3303, 30d — Mother Teresa with: a, Pres. Ronald Reagan. b, Archbishop Desmond Tutu. c, Pope John Paul II. d, Queen Elizabeth II.

**2010, Aug. 26** ***Perf. 11½x12***

**Sheets of 4, #a-d**

**3302-3303** A649 Set of 2 16.50 16.50

Robert Schumann (1810-56), Composer — A650

No. 3304, horiz. — Schumann and: a, Birthplace. b, His wife, Clara. c, Schumann Monument, Zwickau, Germany. d, Grave marker, Bonn, Germany.

65d, Robert and Clara Schumann.

**2010, Aug. 26** ***Perf. 11½x12***

**3304** A650 30d Sheet of 4, #a-d 8.25 8.25

**Souvenir Sheet**

***Perf. 11¼x11½***

**3305** A650 65d multi 4.50 4.50

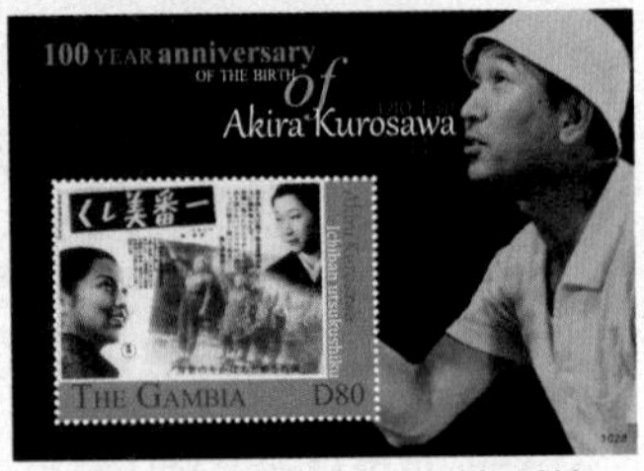


Posters for Films Directed by Akira Kurosawa (1910-98) — A651

No. 3306, 30d, vert.: a, Nora Inu (Stray Dog). b, Zoku Sugata Sanshiro (Sanshiro Sugata Part II). c, Shichinin no Samurai (Seven Samurai). d, Shizukanaru Ketto (The Quiet Duel).

No. 3307, 30d, vert.: a, Donzoko (The Lower Depths). b, Hakuchi (The Idiot). c, Ikimono no Kiroku (I Live in Fear). d, Ikiru.

80d, Ichiban Utsukushiku (The Most Beautiful).

**2010, Aug. 26** ***Perf. 13¼***

**Sheets of 4, #a-d**

**3306-3307** A651 Set of 2 16.50 16.50

**Souvenir Sheet**

**3308** A651 80d multi 5.50 5.50

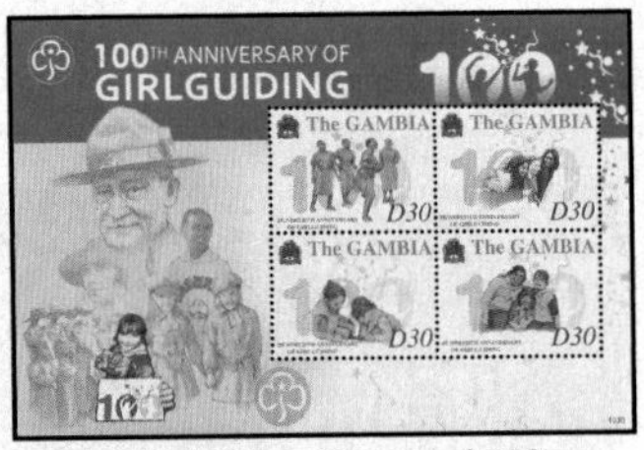


Girl Guides, Cent. — A652

No. 3309 — Girl Guides emblem, centenary emblem and: a, Four Girl Guides in green uniforms. b, Four Girl Guides not wearing uniforms. c, Two Girl Guides. d, Three Girl Guides.

80d, Two Girl Guides with backpacks, vert.

**2010, Oct. 15** ***Perf. 11½x12***

**3309** A652 30d Sheet of 4, #a-d 8.50 8.50

**Souvenir Sheet**

***Perf. 11¼x11½***

**3310** A652 80d multi 5.75 5.75

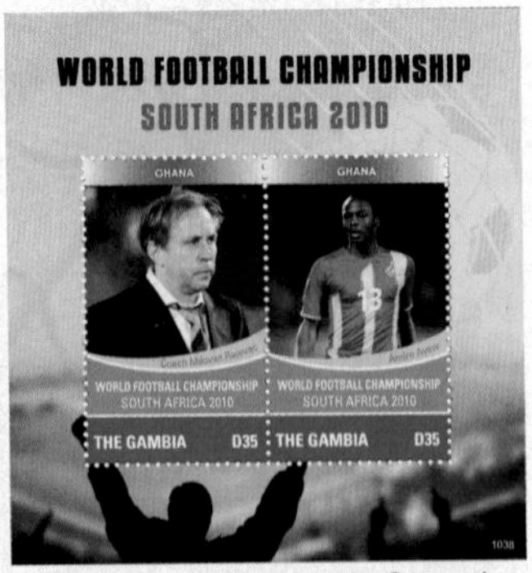


Players and Coaches in Second Round Matches of 2010 World Cup Soccer Championships — A653

No. 3311, 15d — United States vs. Ghana: a, Jay Demerit. b, Asamoah Gyan. c, Robbie Findley. d, Samuel Inkoom. e, Ricardo Clark. f, Stephen Appiah.

No. 3312, 15d — Uruguay vs. South Korea: a, Fernando Musiera. b, Lee Chung-Yong. c, Jorge Fucile. d, Cha Du-Ri. e, Maximiliano Pereira. f, Park Chu-Young.

No. 3313, 15d — Argentina vs. Mexico: a, Gabriel Heinze. b, Efrain Juarez. c, Carlos Tevez. d, Carlos Salcido. e, Lionel Messi. f, Andres Guardado.

No. 3314, 15d — Germany vs. England: a, Sami Khedira. b, Steven Gerrard. c, Philipp Lahm. d, Joe Cole. e, Lukas Podolski. f, Ashley Cole.

No. 3315, 35d — Ghana: a, Coach Milovan Rajevac. b, Andre Ayew.

No. 3316, 35d — Uruguay: a, Coach Oscar Tabarez. b, Diego Forlan.

No. 3317, 35d — Argentina: a, Coach Diego Maradona. b, Nicolas Otramendi.

No. 3318, 35d — Germany: a, Coach Joachim Loew. b, Thomas Mueller.

**2010, Oct. 15** ***Perf. 12***

**Sheets of 6, #a-f**

**3311-3314** A653 Set of 4 26.00 26.00

**Souvenir Sheets of 2, #a-b**

**3315-3318** A653 Set of 4 20.00 20.00

Miniature Sheets

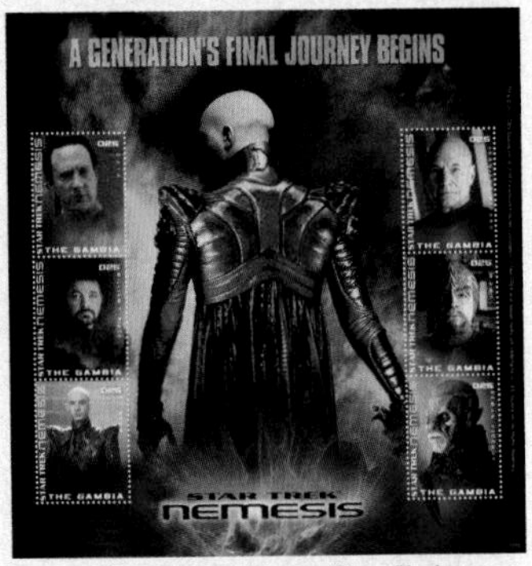


Characters From Star Trek Movies — A654

No. 3319, 25d — Characters from *Star Trek: Nemesis*: a, Lt. Commander Data. b, Capt. Jean-Luc Picard. c, Commander William T. Riker. d, Lt. Commander Worf. e, Praetor Shinzon. f, Reman Viceroy Vkruk.

No. 3320, 25d, horiz. — Characters from *Star Trek: First Contact*: a, Worf. b, Riker and Picard. c, Data and Borg Queen. d, Dr. Zefram Cochrane. e, Lt. Commander Geordi La Forge. f, Picard and Dr. Beverly Crusher.

**2010, Nov. 5** **Litho.** ***Perf. 12***

**Sheets of 6, #a-f**

**3319-3320** A654 Set of 2 21.00 21.00

Christmas A655

Paintings: 15d, Madonna with Child, by Carlo Crivelli. 25d, Nativity, Birth of Jesus, by Giotto di Bondone. 30d, The Journey of the Magi, by Stefano di Giovanni. 40d, Nativity, by Bernardo Daddi.

**2010, Dec. 25**

**3321-3324** A655 Set of 4 7.75 7.75

Souvenir Sheets

A656

Designs: No. 3325: a, Pope Leo XIII (1810-1903). b, Coat of arms of Pope Leo XIII. No. 3325C: d, St. Pius X (1835-1914). e, Arms of St. Pius X.

**2010, Dec. 25** **Litho.** ***Imperf.***

**Without Gum**

**3325** A656 100d Sheet of 2, #a-b 14.50 14.50

**3325C** A656 100d Sheet of 2, #a-b 14.50 14.50

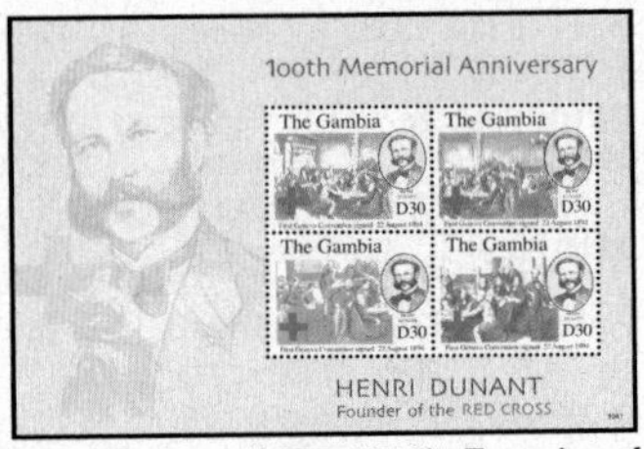


Henri Dunant (1828-1910), Founder of Red Cross — A657

No. 3326 — Red Cross, depictions of First Geneval Convention negotiations and portrait of Dunant in: a, Green blue. b, Brown. c, Purple. d, Blue.

65d, Portrait of Dunant, portraits of 1863 members of International Committee of the Red Cross.

**2010, Dec. 30** ***Perf. 12***

**3326** A657 30d Sheet of 4, #a-d 8.50 8.50

**Souvenir Sheet**

**3327** A657 65d multi 4.75 4.75

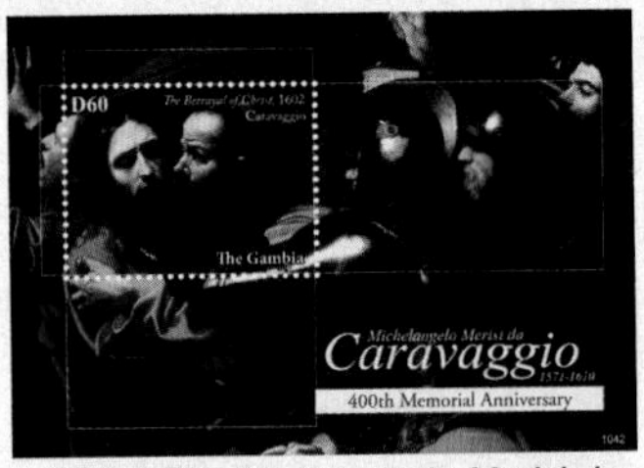


Paintings by Michelangelo Merisi da Caravaggio (1573-1610) — A658

No. 3328, vert.: a, The Seven Works of Mercy. b, The Conversion on the Way to Damascus. c, Alof de Wignacourt. d, David and Goliath. e, The Death of the Virgin. f, The Raising of Lazarus.

60d, The Betrayal of Christ.

**2010, Dec. 30**

**3328** A658 20d Sheet of 6, #a-f 8.50 8.50

**Souvenir Sheet**

**3329** A658 60d multi 4.25 4.25

Pres. John F. Kennedy (1917-63) A659

No. 3330, 30d — Pres. Kennedy and wife, Jacqueline: a, Standing. b, Sitting in limousine.

No. 3331, 30d — Pres. Kennedy and: a, Jacqueline, watching America's Cup race. b, Daughter Caroline.

No. 3332, 60d, Pres. Kennedy standing in limousine. No. 3333, 60d, With Jacqueline, leaving Air Force One, horiz.

**2010, Dec. 30** ***Perf. 12***

**Vert. Pairs, #a-b**

**3330-3331** A659 Set of 2 8.50 8.50

**Souvenir Sheets**

**3332-3333** A659 Set of 2 11.50 11.50

Nos. 3330-3331 each were printed in sheets containing two pairs.

A660

No. 3334, 30d — Denomination in black, Princess Diana wearing: a, Red hat. b, Black hat. c, White dress. d, Hooded raincoat.

No. 3335, 30d — Denomination in white, Princess Diana wearing: a, Tiara. b, Black hat with veil. c, Red hat. d, Black hat with bow.

80d, Princess Diana wearing white dress.

**2010, Dec. 30** **Litho.**

**Sheets of 4, #a-d**

**3334-3335** A660 Set of 2 17.00 17.00

**Souvenir Sheet**

**3336** A660 80d multi 5.75 5.75

Bengal Tiger — A661

No. 3337, vert. — Tiger with: a, Paws visible. b, Paws not shown.

***Perf. 13 Syncopated***

**2011, Feb. 8** **Litho.**

**3337** A661 30d Sheet of 4, 2 each #a-b 9.00 9.00

**Souvenir Sheet**

***Perf. 12***

**3338** A661 120d shown 9.00 9.00

Indipex 2011 World Philatelic Exhibition, New Delhi.

Miniature Sheets

A662

Princess Diana (1961-97) — A663

No. 3339 — Princess Diana wearing: a, Black dress. b, Red and white polka dot dress. c, Red and black plaid blouse. d, Black dress and hat.

No. 3340 — Princess Diana wearing: a, Black dress and necklace. b, Red dress and tiara. c, Tiara and necklace. d, Black dress and headband.

**2011, Feb. 8** ***Perf. 12***

**3339** A662 30d Sheet of 4, #a-d 9.00 9.00

**3340** A663 30d Sheet of 4, #a-d 9.00 9.00

Engagement of Prince William and Catherine Middleton A664

Designs: No. 3341, Couple. No. 3343, Couple, horiz.

No. 3342: a, Middleton. b, Prince William.

No. 3344, horiz.: a, Prince William. b, Middleton.

**2011, Feb. 8** ***Perf. 13 Syncopated***

**3341** A664 30d multi 2.25 2.25

**3342** A664 30d Horiz. pair, #a-b 4.50 4.50

***Perf. 12***

**3343** A664 40d multi 3.00 3.00

**Souvenir Sheet**

**3344** A664 40d Sheet of 2, #a-d 6.00 6.00

No. 3341 was printed in sheets of 4. No. 3342 was printed in sheets containing two pairs. No. 3343 was printed in sheets of 2.

Miniature Sheets

U.S. Civil War Battles, 150th Anniv. — A665

No. 3345, 30d — Eagle, shield, Union and Confederate flags, Brigadier General Daniel Ruggles and Commander James Harmon Ward from Battle of Aquia Creek, May 29, 1861, and: a, Union vessels Pawnee and Thomas Freeborn. b, USS Thomas Freeborn at Mathias Point. c, Sighting a gun aboard the USS Thomas Freeborn. d, Attack on the Confederate batteries.

No. 3346, 30d — Eagle, shield, Union and Confederate flags, Colonel John B. Magruder and Brigadier General Ebenezer W. Peirce from Battle of Big Bethel, June 10, 1861, and: a, Fort Monroe wounded. b, Rodman gun battery at Fort Monroe. c, New York 5th Regiment (Duryee's Zouaves). d, New York 5th Regiment's charge on Big Bethel.

No. 3347, 30d — Eagle, shield, Union and Confederate flags, Colonel John S. Marmaduke and Brigadier General Nathaniel Lyon from Battle of Boonville, June 17, 1861, and: a, St. Louis riot. b, General Lyon departing Boonville. c, Battle scene. d, Confederates retreat from Union forces.

No. 3348, 30d — Eagle, shield, Union and Confederate flags, Colonel Stonewall Jackson and Major General Robert Patterson from Battle of Hoke's Run, July 2, 1861, and: a, General Patterson's division crossing the Potomac. b, Union soldiers skirmish at Hoke's Run. c, Union scout at Shenandoah Valley. d, Union forces advance near Martinsburg.

No. 3349, 30d — Eagle, shield, Union and Confederate flags, Governor Claiborne Fox Jackson and Colonel Franz Sigel from Battle of Carthage, July 5, 1861, and: a, The Wide Wakes Demonstration. b, Colonel Sigel at the Missouri River. c, Battle scene. d, Union forces retreat to Sarcoxie.

**2011, Feb. 8** ***Perf. 13 Syncopated***

**Sheets of 4, #a-d**

**3345-3349** A665 Set of 5 45.00 45.00

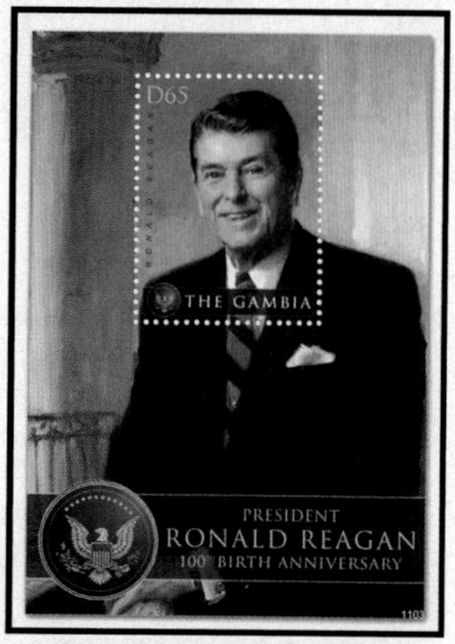


Pres. Ronald Reagan (1911-2004) — A666

No. 3350, horiz. — Pres. Reagan and: a, Flags. b, Wife, Nancy. c, Helicopter. d, Horse.

**2011, Feb. 8** ***Perf. 12***

**3350** A666 30d Sheet of 4, #a-d 9.00 9.00

**Souvenir Sheet**

**3351** A666 65d shown 5.00 5.00

Miniature Sheet

Jewish South African Anti-Apartheid Leaders — A667

No. 3352: a, Hilda Bernstein (1915-2006). b, Lionel "Rusty" Bernstein (1920-2002). c, Ruth First (1925-82). d, Ronald Segal (1932-2008).

**2011, Mar. 1** **Litho.**

**3352** A667 25d Sheet of 4, #a-d 7.25 7.25

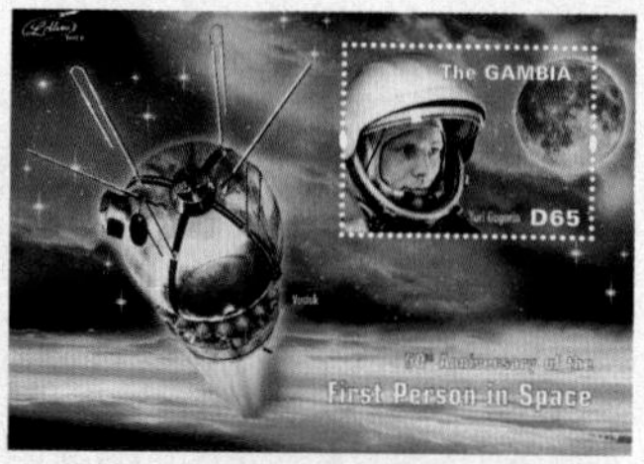


First Man in Space, 50th Anniv. — A668

No. 3353, 30d: a, Raising to vertical of Vostok rocket. b, Tracking ship Yuri Gagarin. c, U.S. astronaut John Glenn. d, Monument to Conquerors of Space, Moscow.

No. 3354, 30d, vert.: a, Yuri Gagarin, first man in space. b, U.S. astronaut Scott Carpenter. c, Vostok spaceship. d, Titanium statue.

No. 3355, 65d, Gagarin and Moon. No. 3356, 65d, Gagarin.

**2011, Mar. 29** ***Perf. 12***

**Sheets of 4, #a-d**

**3353-3354** A668 Set of 2 17.50 17.50

**Souvenir Sheets**

***Perf. 13 Syncopated***

**3355-3356** A668 Set of 2 9.50 9.50

Souvenir Sheets

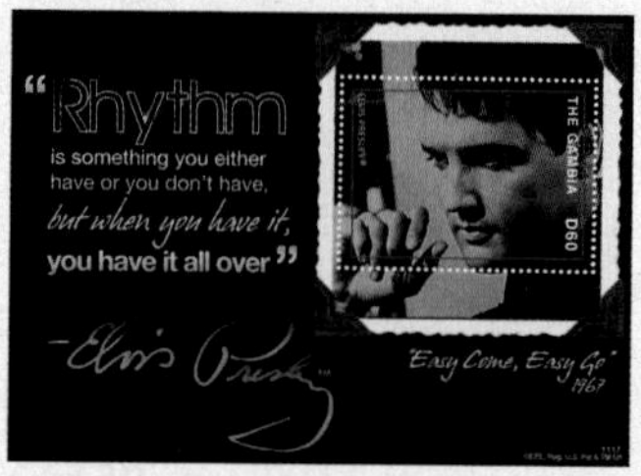


A669

A670

A671

Elvis Presley (1935-77) — A672

**2011, Mar. 29** ***Perf. 12¾***

**3357** A669 60d multi 4.50 4.50

**3358** A670 60d multi 4.50 4.50

**3359** A671 60d multi 4.50 4.50

**3360** A672 60d multi 4.50 4.50

*Nos. 3357-3360 (4)* 18.00 18.00

Wedding of Prince William and Catherine Middleton
A673

Designs: No. 3361, Couple.
No. 3362: a, Prince William. b, Middleton.
65d, Couple, diff.

**2011, Apr. 29** *Perf. 12*

**3361** A673 30d multi 2.25 2.25
**3362** A673 30d Sheet of 4, 2 each #a-b 8.75 8.75

**Souvenir Sheet**

**3363** A673 65d multi 4.75 4.75

No. 3361 was printed in sheets of 4.

Miniature Sheet

Discovery of Machu Picchu by Hiram Bingham, Cent. — A674

No. 3364: a, Aerial view of Machu Picchu. b, Stonework. c, Stone buildings as seen through hole in wall. d, Bingham.

**2011, May 16** ***Perf. 13 Syncopated***

**3364** A674 30d Sheet of 4, #a-d 8.75 8.75

Beatification of Pope John Paul II — A675

No. 3365: a, Pope John Paul II greeting crowd. b, Pope John Paul II in procession, Sister Marie Simon Pierre. c, Pope John Paul II at Midnight mass. d, Crowd in St. Peter's Square honoring Pope John Paul II.
60d, Pope John Paul II and Mother Teresa.

**2011, May 16** ***Perf. 13 Syncopated***

**3365** A675 30d Sheet of 4, #a-d 8.75 8.75

**Souvenir Sheet**

***Perf. 12¾***

**3366** A675 60d multi 4.25 4.25

No. 3366 contains one 50x38mm stamp.

Cats — A676

No. 3367: a, Munchkin. b, Ragamuffin. c, Chinchilla. d, Burman.
70d, Turkish Van.

**2011, May 16** ***Perf. 13 Syncopated***

**3367** A676 30d Sheet of 4, #a-d 8.75 8.75

**Souvenir Sheet**

***Perf. 12***

**3368** A676 70d multi 5.00 5.00

A677

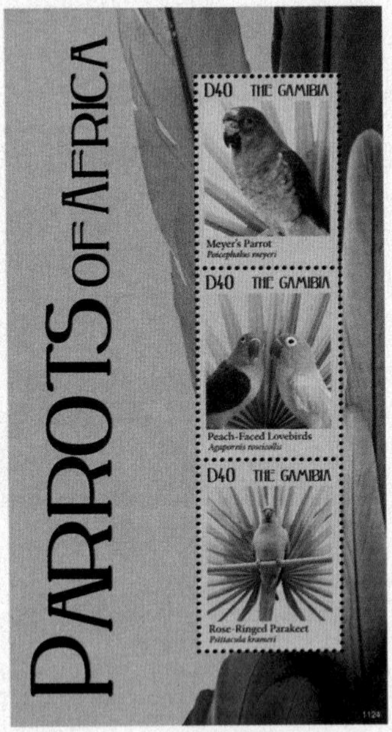


A678

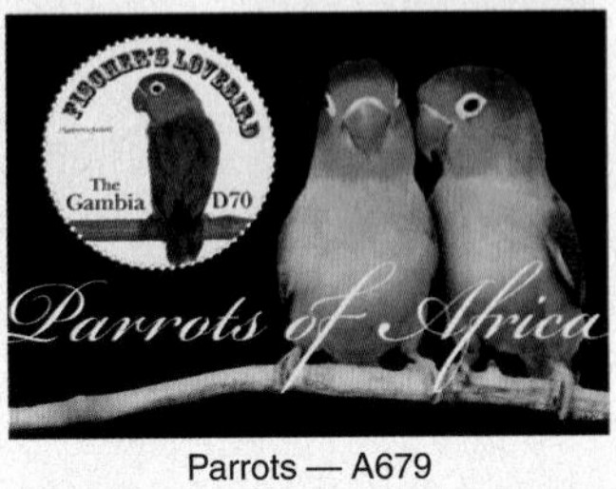


Parrots — A679

No. 3369: a, Masked lovebird. b, Madagascar lovebird. c, Red-fronted macaw. d, Senegal parrot.
No. 3370: a, Meyer's parrot. b, Peach-faced lovebirds. c, Rose-ringed parakeet.
No. 3371, 70d, Fischer's lovebird. No. 3372, 70d, African gray parrot.

**2011, May 16** ***Perf. 13 Syncopated***

**3369** A677 30d Sheet of 4, #a-d 8.75 8.75
**3370** A678 40d Sheet of 3, #a-c 8.75 8.75

**Souvenir Sheets**

***Perf.***

**3371-3372** A679 Set of 2 10.00 10.00

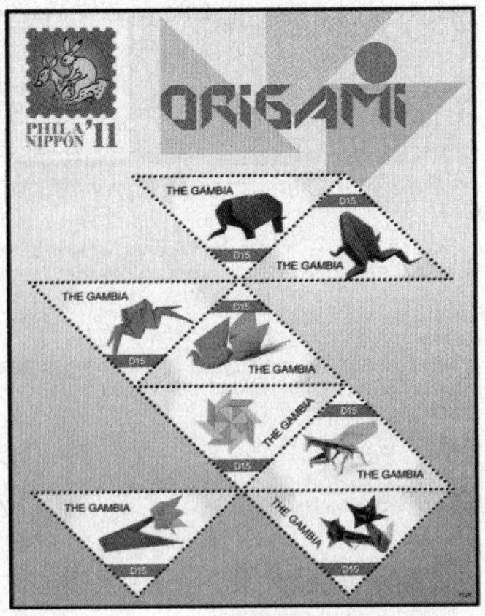


A680

PhilaNippon '11, Yokohama — A681

No. 3373 — Origami: a, Brown elephant. b, Green frog. c, Red crab. d, Bright pink and blue cranes. e, Yellow and orange pinwheel. f, Light green praying mantis. g, Orange flower. h, Purple flowers.
No. 3374: a, Two cherry blossoms. b, Cherry blossom petals. c, Three cherry blossoms.
No. 3375, Crane. No. 3376, Cherry blossom and bud.

***Perf. 12. Perf. (A681)***

**2011, May 16** **Litho.**

**3373** A680 15d Sheet of 8, #a-h 8.75 8.75
**3374** A681 40d Sheet of 3, #a-c 8.75 8.75

**Souvenir Sheets**

**3375** A680 65d multi 4.75 4.75
**3376** A681 65d multi 4.75 4.75

Jane Goodall Institute, Gombe, Tanzania, 50th Anniv. — A682

No. 3377: a, Jane Goodall. b, Baby chimpanzee hanging from tree. c, Head of chimpanzee. d, Goodall and chimpanzee.
No. 3378, horiz.: a, Goodall looking at hills through binoculars. b, Chimpanzee. c, Goodall, diff.
No. 3379, horiz.: a, Baby chimpanzee pointing. b, Goodall holding binoculars. c, Chimpanzee in tree.
80d, Adult and juvenile chimpanzee.

***Perf. 13¼x13, 12 (#3378-3379)***

**2011, May 26**

**3377** A682 30d Sheet of 4, #a-d 8.75 8.75
**3378** A682 35d Sheet of 3, #a-c 7.50 7.50
**3379** A682 35d Sheet of 3. #a-c 7.50 7.50
*Nos. 3377-3379 (3)* 23.75 23.75

**Souvenir Sheet**

**3380** A682 80d multi 5.75 5.75

Worldwide Fund for Nature (WWF) — A683

No. 3381 — Yellow-billed storks: a, Two birds in flight. b, Two birds in water. c, One bird landing, heads of two birds. d, Three birds in water.

**2011, June 30** ***Perf. 12¾***

**3381** Horiz. strip of 4 5.75 5.75
*a.-d.* A683 20d Any single 1.40 1.40
*e.* Souvenir sheet of 8, 2 each #3381a-3381d 11.50 11.50

A684

Pres. John F. Kennedy (1917-63) — A685

No. 3382 — Kennedy: a, At microphone, pointing. b, At microphone. c, At microphone, with arms extended. d, In front of White House.

**2011, July 6** ***Perf. 12***

**3382** A684 30d Sheet of 4, #a-d 8.25 8.25

**Souvenir Sheet**

***Perf. 12¾x12½***

**3383** A685 60d multi 4.25 4.25

Visit of U.S. Pres. Barack Obama to the United Kingdom — A686

No. 3384, 30d: a, Pres. Barack Obama. b, First Lady Michelle Obama. c, Prince William. d, Catherine, Duchess of Cambridge.
No. 3385, 30d, horiz. — Obamas with: a, Queen Elizabeth II and Prince Philip. b, John Hall, Dean of Westminster Abbey. c, Prince William and Catherine, Duchess of Cambridge. d, Prime Minister David Cameron and his wife, Samantha.
No. 3386: a, Cameron. b, Pres. Obama.
65d, Queen Elizabeth II and Pres. Obama, horiz.

**2011, July 25** ***Perf. 12, 12½ (#3387)***

**Sheets of 4, #a-d**

**3384-3385** A686 Set of 2 18.50 18.50

**3386** A686 35d Sheet of 2, #a-d 5.50 5.50

**Souvenir Sheet**

**3387** A686 65d multi 5.00 5.00

No. 3387 contains one 51x38mm stamp.

British Royalty — A687

Designs: No. 3388, 30d, King George V (1865-1936). No. 3389, 30d, King George VI (1895-1952). No. 3390, 30d, Queen Elizabeth II. No. 3391, 30d, Prince Philip.

**2011, Oct. 11** ***Perf. 13¼x13***

**3388-3391** A687 Set of 4 8.00 8.00

Nos. 3388-3391 each were printed in sheets of 4.

Miniature Sheet

Sept. 11, 2001 Terrorist Attacks, 10th Anniv. — A688

No. 3392 — Color of stripe at upper left corner: a, Dark blue. b, Orange. c, Red violet. d, Green.

**2011, Oct. 11**

**3392** A688 30d Sheet of 4, #a-d 8.00 8.00

Miniature Sheet

Inter Milan Soccer Team — A689

No. 3393 — Team emblem and photos: a, Italian League, 1963. b, UEFA Champions League, 1963-64. c, Italian League, 1965. d, UEFA Champions League, 1964-65. e, Italian Super Cup, 2010. f, Intercontinental Cup, 1964. g, Intercontinental Cup, 1965. h, UEFA Cup, 1998. i, FIFA Club World Cup, 2010.

**2011, Oct. 11** ***Perf. 12½***

**3393** A689 12d Sheet of 9, #a-i 7.25 7.25

Miniature Sheets

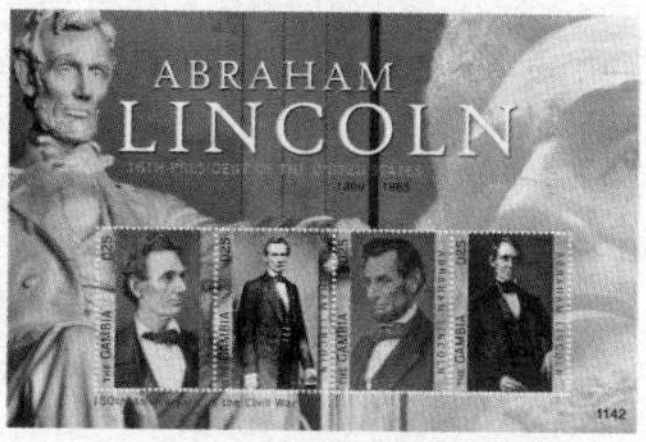


A690

Pres. Abraham Lincoln (1809-65) — A691

No. 3394 — Lincoln: a, Facing right. b, Standing, with hand on book. c, Facing left. d, Standing, with both arms bent.

No. 3395 — Lincoln: a, Seated, name in brown. b, Standing, name in brown. c, Seated, name in tan. d, Standing, name in tan.

**2011, Oct. 11** ***Perf. 13¼x13***

**3394** A690 25d Sheet of 4, #a-d 6.75 6.75
**3395** A691 25d Sheet of 4, #a-d 6.75 6.75

Birds — A692

No. 3396, 16d: a, Bald eagle. b, European bee-eater. c, Keel-billed toucan. d, Red-crowned crane. e, Emperor penguin. f, Australian pelican.

No. 3397, 16d: a, African gray parrot. b, African darter. c, African fish eagle. d, African penguin. e, Reed cormorant. f, Spotted eagle-owl.

No. 3398, 80d, Lesser flamingo. No. 3399, 80d, African gray hornbill.

**2011, Oct. 11** ***Perf. 13x12¾***

**Sheets of 6, #a-f, + label**

**3396-3397** A692 Set of 2 13.00 13.00

**Souvenir Sheets**

***Perf. 13x13¼***

**3398-3399** A692 Set of 2 10.50 10.50

Orchids — A693

No. 3400: a, Cephalanthera rubra. b, Aerangis biloba. c, Angreacum angustum. d, Ancistrochilus thomsonianus. e, Aerangis luteoalba. f, Polystacha carnosa.

No. 3401, vert.: a, Ansellia africana. b, Bulbophyllum falcatum. c, Angraecopsis ischnopus. d, Angraecum moandense.

No. 3402, 80d, Ancistrochilus rothschildianus. No. 3403, 80d, Bulbophyllum cochleatum, vert.

**2011, Oct. 11** ***Perf. 13 Syncopated***

**3400** A693 20d Sheet of 6, #a-f 8.00 8.00
**3401** A693 30d Sheet of 4, #a-d 8.00 8.00

**Souvenir Sheets**

**3402-3403** A693 Set of 2 10.50 10.50

Statue of Liberty, 125th Anniv. (in 2011) — A694

No. 3404: a, Frederic Auguste Bartholdi, sculptor of Statue of Liberty. b, Statue's torch under construction. c, Statue's head under construction. d, Statue.

70d, Statue, diff.

**2012, Feb. 24** ***Perf. 13 Syncopated***

**3404** A694 30d Sheet of 4, #a-d 8.00 8.00

**Souvenir Sheet**

**3405** A694 70d multi 4.75 4.75

Visit of Pope Benedict XVI to Germany — A695

No. 3406 — Pope Benedict XVI: a, Waving at Brandenburg Gate. b, Holding censer. c, Facing left, with Berlin skyline in background.

90d, Pope Benedict XVI wearing miter.

**2012, Feb. 24** ***Perf. 12***

**3406** A695 30d Sheet of 3, #a-c 6.00 6.00

**Souvenir Sheet**

**3407** A695 90d multi 6.00 6.00

Puppies — A696

No. 3408: a, Toy poodle. b, Yorkshire terrier. c, Beagle.

No. 3409: a, Rottweiler. b, Chihuahua. c, Golden retriever. d, German shepherd.

No. 3410, 100d, Maltese. No. 3411, 100d, Pomeranian.

**2012, Feb. 29**

**3408** A696 40d Sheet of 3, #a-c 8.00 8.00
**3409** A696 40d Sheet of 4, #a-d 11.00 11.00

**Souvenir Sheets**

**3410-3411** A696 Set of 2 13.50 13.50

Christmas 2011 A697

Paintings: 15d, Adoration of the Shepherds, by Gerard van Honthorst. 25d, Adoraton of the Shepherds, by Agnolo Bronzino. 30d, The Adoration of the Magi, by Peter Paul Rubens. 40d, The Journey of the Magi, by James Jacques Joseph Tissot.

**2012, Mar. 3** ***Perf. 14***

**3412-3415** A697 Set of 4 7.50 7.50

Sinking of the Titanic, Cent. — A698

No. 3416: a, Staircase. b, Lifeboat. c, Parlor. 100d, Titanic.

**2012, Mar. 2** ***Perf. 12***

**3416** A698 45d Sheet of 3, #a-c 9.00 9.00

**Souvenir Sheet**

**3417** A698 100d multi 6.75 6.75

Miniature Sheet

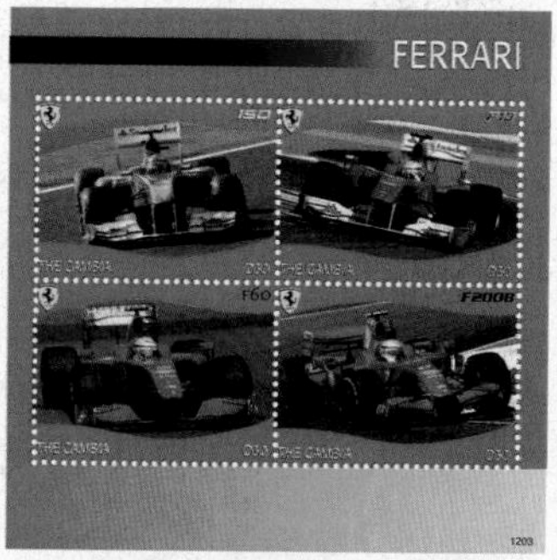


Ferrari Race Cars — A699

No. 3418: a, 150 Italia. b, F10. c, F60. d, F2008.

**2012, Mar. 13** ***Perf. 12***

**3418** A699 30d Sheet of 4, #a-d 8.25 8.25

Souvenir Sheets

Bishop Hannah C. Faal-Heim, Gambian Methodist Presiding Bishop — A700

Bishop Faal-Heim, cross and: 15d, Map of Gambia. 25d, Church. 35d, Emblem of Gambian Methodist Church. 50d, Bishop Emeritus Peter Stephens.

**2012, Feb. 2** ***Perf. 13x13¼***

**3419-3422** A700 Set of 4 8.25 8.25

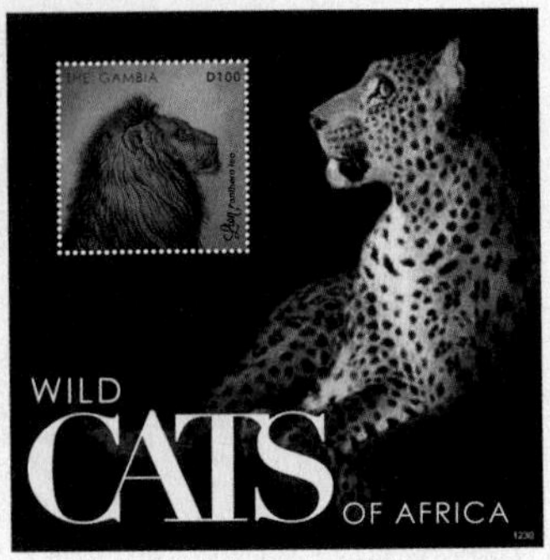


Wild Cats — A701

No. 3423: a, Caracal. b, Cheetah. c, Jungle cat.
100d, Lion.

**2012, May 16** ***Perf. 13¾***
**3423** A701 40d Sheet of 3, #a-c 7.75 7.75

**Souvenir Sheet**

**3424** A701 100d multi 6.50 6.50

British Monarchs A702

Designs: No. 3425, 20d, King William I. No. 3426, 20d, King Henry II. No. 3427, 20d, King Henry IV. No. 3428, 20d, King Henry VI. No. 3429, 20d, King Richard III. No. 3430, 20d, Queen Elizabeth I. No. 3431, 20d, King James I. No. 3432, 20d, King Edward VII.

**2012, June 27** ***Perf. 13¼x13***
**3425-3432** A702 Set of 8 10.50 10.50

Nos. 3425-3432 each were printed in sheets of 8 + central label.

Miniature Sheet

2012 Summer Olympics, London — A703

No. 3433: a, High jump. b, Gymnastics. c, Uneven bars. d, Long jump.

**2012, June 27** ***Perf. 14***
**3433** A703 25d Sheet of 4, #a-d 6.50 6.50

Pres. Yahya A. J. J. Jammeh — A704

Gambian Second Republic, 18th Anniv. — A705

No. 3435: a, 25d, Women empowerment of the Second Republic. b, 35d, Fort Bullen Historic Monument. c, 35d, Cultural masquerade, The Kumpo. d, 50d, Back to the land.
75d, Pres. Jammeh, diff.

**2012, July 22** ***Perf. 14***
**3434** A704 150d shown 9.75 9.75

***Perf. 12***

**3435** A705 Sheet of 4, #a-d 9.50 9.50

**Souvenir Sheet**

**3436** A704 75d multi 5.00 5.00

Miniature Sheet

Reign Of Queen Elizabeth II, 60th Anniv. — A706

No. 3437 — Photographs of Queen Elizabeth II from: a, 1937. b, 1946. c, 1953. d, 1952. e, 1962. f, 2004.

**2012, July 31** ***Perf. 13 Syncopated***
**3437** A706 30d Sheet of 6, #a-f 11.50 11.50

Whales — A707

No. 3438: a, Humpback whale. b, Bryde's whale. c, Southern right whale. d, Blue whale. e, Killer whale. f, Sperm whale.
100d, Minke whale.

**2012, Aug. 2** ***Perf. 14***
**3438** A707 30d Sheet of 6, #a-f 11.50 11.50

**Souvenir Sheet**

***Perf. 12***

**3439** A707 100d multi 6.50 6.50

Drafting of the Emancipation Proclamation by Pres. Abraham Lincoln, 150th Anniv. — A708

No. 3440: a, Drawing of Lincoln seated at desk. b, Text of preliminary draft of the Emancipation Proclamation. c, Drawing of Lincoln writing the Emancipation Proclamation, d, First reading of the Emancipation Proclamation.
100d, Lincoln writing, vert.

**2012, Aug. 2** ***Perf. 13 Syncopated***
**3440** A708 40d Sheet of 4, #a-d 10.50 10.50

**Souvenir Sheet**

**3441** A708 100d multi 6.50 6.50

Premiere of *The Three Stooges The Movie* — A709

No. 3442: a, Moe grabbing heads of Larry and Curly, denomination in purple. b, Stooges on bicycle. c, Moe grabbing heads of Larry and Curly, denomination in orange. d, Stooges standing.
100d, Silhouette of Stooges, vert.

**2012, Aug. 2** ***Perf. 12¾***
**3442** A709 40d Sheet of 4, #a-d 10.50 10.50

**Souvenir Sheet**

**3443** A709 100d multi 6.50 6.50

Souvenir Sheets

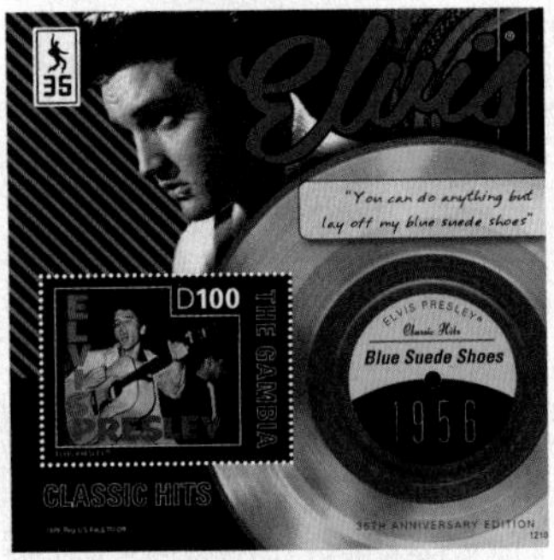


Record Covers of Elvis Presley — A710

Record: No. 3444, 100d, Elvis Presley. No. 3445, 100d, All Shook Up and That's When Your Heartaches Begin. No. 3446, 100d, 50,000,000 Elvis Fans Can't Be Wrong. No. 3447, 100d, A Big Hunk O'Love and My Wish Came True. No. 3448, 100d, (You're the) Devil in Disguise and Please Don't Drag That String Around.

**2012, Aug. 2** ***Perf. 12¾***
**3444-3448** A710 Set of 5 32.50 32.50

## GEORGIA

'jor-jə

LOCATION — South of Russia, bordering on the Black Sea and occupying the entire western part of Transcaucasia
GOVT. — Republic
AREA — 26,900 sq. mi.
POP. — 5,066,499 (1999 est.)
CAPITAL — Tbilisi (Tiflis)

Georgia was formerly a province of the Russian Empire and later a part of the Transcaucasian Federation of Soviet Republics. Stamps of Georgia were replaced in 1923 by those of Transcaucasian Federated Republics.

On Mar. 1, 1994, Georgia joined the Commonwealth of Independent States.

100 Kopecks = 1 Ruble
100 Kopecks = 1 Coupon (1993)
100 Tetri = 1 Lari (Sept. 25, 1995)

**Catalogue values for unused stamps in this country are for Never Hinged items, beginning with Scott 75 in the regular postage section, and Scott B10 in the semi-postal section.**

Tiflis

A 6k local stamp, imperforate and embossed without color on white paper, was issued in November, 1857, at Tiflis by authority of the viceroy. The square design shows a coat of arms.

**National Republic**

St. George
A1 A2

**1919 Litho. Unwmk.** ***Perf. 11½***

| | | | | |
|---|---|---|---|---|
| 1 | A1 | 10k blue | .80 | .80 |
| 2 | A1 | 40k red orange | .80 | .80 |
| *a.* | | Tête bêche pair | 50.00 | 50.00 |
| 3 | A1 | 50k emerald | .80 | .80 |
| 4 | A1 | 60k red | .80 | .80 |
| 5 | A1 | 70k claret | .80 | *.80* |
| 6 | A2 | 1r orange brown | .80 | *.80* |
| | | *Nos. 1-6 (6)* | 4.80 | 4.80 |

***Imperf***

| | | | | |
|---|---|---|---|---|
| 7 | A1 | 10k blue | .80 | .80 |
| 8 | A1 | 40k red orange | .80 | .80 |
| *a.* | | Tête bêche pair | 50.00 | 50.00 |
| 9 | A1 | 50k emerald | .80 | .80 |
| 10 | A1 | 60k red | .80 | .80 |
| 11 | A1 | 70k claret | .80 | *.80* |
| 12 | A2 | 1r orange brown | .80 | *.80* |
| | | *Nos. 7-12 (6)* | 4.80 | 4.80 |

Queen Thamar — A3

**1920** ***Perf. 11½***

| | | | | |
|---|---|---|---|---|
| 13 | A3 | 2r red brown | .65 | 1.00 |
| 14 | A3 | 3r gray blue | .65 | 1.00 |
| 15 | A3 | 5r orange | .65 | 1.00 |
| | | *Nos. 13-15 (3)* | 1.95 | 3.00 |

***Imperf***

| | | | | |
|---|---|---|---|---|
| 16 | A3 | 2r red brown | .65 | 1.00 |
| 17 | A3 | 3r gray blue | .65 | 1.00 |
| 18 | A3 | 5r orange | .65 | 1.00 |
| | | *Nos. 16-18 (3)* | 1.95 | 3.00 |

Nos. 1-18 with parts of design inverted, sideways or omitted are fraudulent varieties.

Overprints meaning "Day of the National Guard, 12, 12, 1920" (5 lines) and "Recognition of Independence, 27, 1, 1921" (4 lines) were applied, probably in Italy, to remainders taken by government officials who fled when Russian forces occupied Georgia.

"Constantinople" and new values were unofficially surcharged on stamps of 1919-20 by a consul in Turkey.

**Soviet Socialist Republic**

Soldier with Flag — A5 Peasant Sowing Grain — A6

Industry and Agriculture — A7

**1922 Unwmk. *Perf. 11½***

| | | | | |
|---|---|---|---|---|
| **26** | A5 500r rose | 8.00 | 3.25 |
| **27** | A6 1000r bister brown | 8.00 | 3.25 |
| **28** | A7 2000r slate | 11.50 | 6.00 |
| **29** | A7 3000r brown | 11.50 | 6.00 |
| **30** | A7 5000r green | 11.50 | 6.00 |
| | *Nos. 26-30 (5)* | 50.50 | 24.50 |

Forgeries exist of Nos. 26-30.

Nos. 26 to 30 exist imperforate but were not so issued. Value for set, $100.

**Nos. 26-30 Handstamped with New Values in Violet**

**1923**

| | | | |
|---|---|---|---|
| **36** | A6 10,000r on 1000r | 6.50 | *6.50* |
| *a.* | Black surcharge | 20.00 | *25.00* |
| *b.* | 20,000r on 1000r | 200.00 | |
| **37** | A7 15,000r on 2000r, blk surch. | 7.75 | *8.50* |
| *a.* | Violet surcharge | 30.00 | 30.00 |
| **38** | A5 20,000r on 500r | 7.75 | *8.50* |
| *a.* | Black surcharge | 15.00 | 7.50 |
| **39** | A7 40,000r on 5000r | 5.50 | 5.50 |
| *a.* | Black surcharge | 15.00 | *15.00* |
| **40** | A7 80,000r on 3000r | 7.75 | *8.50* |
| *a.* | Black surcharge | 15.00 | *17.50* |
| | *Nos. 36-40 (5)* | 35.25 | *37.50* |

There were two types of the handstamped surcharges, with the numerals 5½mm and 6½mm high. The impressions are often too indistinct to measure or even to distinguish the numerals.

Double and inverted surcharges exist, as is usual with handstamps.

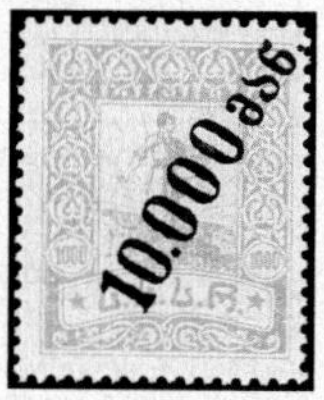

Surcharged in Black

| | | | |
|---|---|---|---|
| **43** | A6 10,000r on 1000r | 7.50 | 7.50 |
| **44** | A7 15,000r on 2000r | 5.00 | 5.00 |
| **45** | A5 20,000r on 500r | 2.50 | 2.50 |
| **46** | A7 40,000r on 5000r | 5.00 | 5.00 |
| **47** | A7 80,000r on 3000r | 5.00 | 5.00 |
| | *Nos. 43-47 (5)* | 25.00 | *25.00* |

Nos. 43, 45, 46 and 47 exist imperforate but were not so issued. Value $25 each.

Russian Stamps of 1909-18 Handstamp Surcharged

Type I — Surcharge 20x5½mm.
Type II — Surcharge 22x7¼mm.

**1923 *Perf. 14½x15***

| | | | |
|---|---|---|---|
| **48** | A14 10,000r on 7k lt bl | 150.00 | 150.00 |
| **49** | A11 15,000r on 15k red brn & bl (I) | 15.00 | 15.00 |
| *a.* | Type II | 10.00 | 10.00 |

**Type I Surcharge Handstamped on Armenia No. 141**

| | | | |
|---|---|---|---|
| **50** | A11 15,000r on 5r on 15k red brn & bl | 200.00 | *500.00* |
| *a.* | Type II | | |
| | *Nos. 48-50 (3)* | 365.00 | *665.00* |

Russian Stamps and Types of 1909-18 Surcharged in Dark Blue or Black

**1923 *Perf. 11½, 14½x15***

| | | | |
|---|---|---|---|
| **51** | A14 75,000r on 1k org | 3.00 | *4.25* |
| *a.* | Imperf. | 150.00 | *150.00* |
| **52** | A14 200,000r on 5k cl | 4.00 | *5.00* |
| **53** | A8 300,000r on 20k bl & car (Bk) | 4.00 | *5.00* |
| *a.* | Dark blue surcharge | 70.00 | *100.00* |
| **54** | A14 350,000r on 3k red | 7.00 | *8.00* |
| *a.* | Imperf. | 7.00 | *7.25* |

***Imperf***

| | | | |
|---|---|---|---|
| **55** | A14 700,000r on 2k grn | 7.00 | *10.00* |
| *a.* | Perf. 14½x15 | 27.50 | *32.50* |
| | *Nos. 51-55 (5)* | 25.00 | *32.25* |

**Catalogue values for unused stamps in this section, from this point to the end of the section, are for Never Hinged items.**

**Republic**

Admission to UN, 1st Anniv. A20

Map, flag, UN emblem.

**1993, July 31 Litho. *Perf. 13¼***

| | | | |
|---|---|---|---|
| **73** | A20 25r green & multi | .75 | .75 |
| **74** | A20 50r brown & multi | 1.10 | 1.10 |
| **75** | A20 100r violet & multi | 1.75 | 1.75 |
| *a.* | Souvenir sheet of 3, #73-75 + label | 4.00 | 4.00 |
| | *Nos. 73-75 (3)* | 3.60 | 3.60 |

For overprint, see Nos. 327-328.

Natl. Arms, Flag — A21

Fresco, 18th Cent. — A22

Apostle Simon, 11th Cent. — A23

Three Women, by Lado Gudiashvili A24

**1993, Oct. 11 Photo. *Perf. 12x11½***

| | | | |
|---|---|---|---|
| **76** | A21 50k multicolored | .50 | .50 |

**Litho.**

***Perf. 12x12½***

| | | | |
|---|---|---|---|
| **77** | A22 50k multicolored | 1.10 | 1.10 |
| **78** | A23 1c multicolored | .90 | .90 |
| **79** | A24 1c multicolored | 1.40 | 1.40 |
| | *Nos. 76-79 (4)* | 3.90 | 3.90 |

Nos. 76, 78-79 dated 1992.

For surcharges see Nos. 80-83, 93-95, 404, 458.

Surcharged in Claret, Black, or Blue

**1994, May 31 Photo. *Perf. 12x11½***

| | | | |
|---|---|---|---|
| **80** | A21 5000c on 50k #76 (C) | .45 | .45 |

**Litho.**

***Perf. 12x12½***

| | | | |
|---|---|---|---|
| **81** | A22 5000c on 50k #77 (Blk) | .45 | .45 |
| **82** | A23 10,000c on 1c #78 (Bl) | .65 | .65 |
| **83** | A24 10,000c on 1c #79 (C) | .65 | .65 |
| | *Nos. 80-83 (4)* | 2.20 | 2.20 |

Size and location of surcharge varies.

Places of Worship — A25

30c, Mtskheta Church. 40c, Gelati Church. 50c, Nikortsminda Church. 60c, Ikorta Church. 70c, Samtavisi Church. 80c, Bolnisi Zion Synagogue. 90c, Gremi Citadel Church.

**1993, Oct. 11 Litho. *Perf. 13½***

| | | | |
|---|---|---|---|
| **84** | A25 30c blue | .45 | .45 |
| **85** | A25 40c red brown | .55 | .55 |
| **86** | A25 50c olive brown | .65 | .65 |
| **87** | A25 60c rose carmine | .85 | .85 |
| **88** | A25 70c rose lake | .95 | .95 |
| **89** | A25 80c green | 1.10 | 1.10 |
| **90** | A25 90c slate | 1.25 | 1.25 |
| | *Nos. 84-90 (7)* | 5.80 | 5.80 |

See Nos. 111-120.

Niko Nikoladze (1843-1928) — A26

**1994, May 31 Litho. *Perf. 13½***

| | | | |
|---|---|---|---|
| **91** | A26 150c black & gold | 1.10 | 1.10 |

UPU, 120th Anniv. A27

**1994, May 30**

| | | | |
|---|---|---|---|
| **92** | A27 200c multicolored | 1.10 | 1.10 |

Nos. 77-79 Surcharged in Green or Red

**1994 Litho. *Perf. 12x12½***

| | | | |
|---|---|---|---|
| **93** | A22 200c on 50k #77 | .50 | .50 |
| **94** | A23 300c on 1c #78 (R) | .55 | .55 |
| **95** | A24 500c on 1c #79 | 1.25 | 1.25 |
| | *Nos. 93-95 (3)* | 2.30 | 2.30 |

Set exists with inverted surcharges. Value $10.

A27a

**1994, Oct. 9 Litho. *Perf. 14***

| | | | |
|---|---|---|---|
| **95A** | A27a 100c shown | 2.75 | 2.75 |
| **95B** | A27a 200c Monument | 5.00 | 5.00 |

All Georgian Congress.

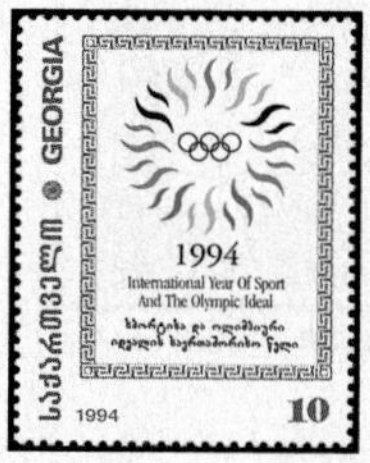


A28

Georgia Natl. Olympic Committee: 10c, Intl. year of sport & Olympic ideal. 15c, Olympic congress, cent. 20c, Intl. Olympic Committee, cent. 25c, Olympic truce.

**1995, Mar. 28 Litho. *Perf. 14½***

| | | | |
|---|---|---|---|
| **96-99** | A28 Set of 4 | 5.50 | 5.50 |

Dated 1994.

Paintings by Niko Piromanashvili (1862-1918) — A29

No. 100, Three Princes Carousing on the Grass. No. 101, Still life. No. 102, Georgian Woman with a Tambourine, vert. No. 103, Bear on a Moonlit Night, vert. No. 104, Woman with a Tankard of Beer, vert. No. 105, Deer, vert. No. 106, Fisherman, vert. No. 107, Giraffe, vert. No. 108, Boy on a Donkey, vert. No. 109, Brooder with Chicks.

No. 110, Family Picnicking.

**1995, Mar. 29 Litho. *Perf. 14***

| | | | |
|---|---|---|---|
| **100-109** | A29 20c Set of 10 | 11.50 | 11.50 |

**Souvenir Sheet**

| | | | |
|---|---|---|---|
| **110** | A29 100c multicolored | 6.25 | 6.25 |

**Churches Type of 1993**

10c

20c

400c

1c, No. 120, Metechi, 1278-1289. 2c, No. 117, Alaverdi, 11th cent. 3c, No. 116, Dranda,

8th cent. No. 114, Sveti-Zchoveli, 1010-1019. No. 115, Kumurdo, 964. No. 118, Anauri, 17th cent. No. 119, Bitschvinta, 10th cent.

**Size: 25½x39mm**

| **1995** | **Litho.** | ***Perf. 14*** | |
|---|---|---|---|
| **111** A25 | 1c black & violet | 1.60 | 1.60 |
| **112** A25 | 2c black & sepia | 1.60 | 1.60 |
| **113** A25 | 3c black & red brn | 1.60 | 1.60 |
| **114** A25 | 10c black & violet | 1.60 | 1.60 |
| **115** A25 | 10c black & sepia | 1.60 | 1.60 |
| **116** A25 | 10c black & grn blue | 1.60 | 1.60 |
| **117** A25 | 20c black & slate | 1.60 | 1.60 |
| **118** A25 | 20c black & olive grn | 1.60 | 1.60 |
| **119** A25 | 400c black & org brn | 1.60 | 1.60 |
| **120** A25 | 400c black & red brn | 1.60 | 1.60 |
| | *Nos. 111-120 (10)* | 16.00 | 16.00 |

Paolo Iashvili (1894-1937) — A30

| **1995, Apr. 1** | | | |
|---|---|---|---|
| **125** A30 | 300c multicolored | 1.25 | 1.25 |

Prehistoric Animals — A31

No. 126, Brontosaurus. No. 127, Saurolophus. No. 128, Scolosaurus. No. 129, Triceratops. No. 130, Parasaurolophus. No. 131, Ceratosaurus. No. 132, Deinonichus. No. 133, Tyrannosaurus. No. 134, Stegosaurus.

No. 135: a, Pterodactylus (d). b, Rhamphophynghus (c, e). c, Pteranodon. d, Spinosaurus. e, Tyrannosaurus (f, h, i). f, Velociraptor. g, Monoklonius. h, Ornithomimus. i, Mastodon.

100c, Deinonychus.

| **1995** | **Litho.** | ***Perf. 14*** | |
|---|---|---|---|
| **126-134** A31 | 15c Set of 9 | 6.25 | 6.25 |

**Miniature Sheet of 9**

| | | | |
|---|---|---|---|
| **135** A31 | 15c #a.-i. | 7.25 | 7.25 |

**Souvenir Sheet**

| | | | |
|---|---|---|---|
| **136** A31 | 100c multicolored | 5.25 | 5.25 |

Issued: Nos. 126-134, 5/12.

UNESCO World Heritage Sites A32

100c, Bagrati Cathedral. 500c, Jvari of Mtskhetha.

| **1995, Aug. 30** | **Litho.** | ***Perf. 14*** | |
|---|---|---|---|
| **137** A32 | 100c multi | 1.25 | 1.25 |

**Souvenir Sheet**

| | | | |
|---|---|---|---|
| **138** A32 | 500c multi, vert. | 6.50 | 6.50 |

Miniature Sheet

Wildlife Painting A33

Design: Nos. a.-p., Various animals and birds.

| **1995, Aug. 4** | | | |
|---|---|---|---|
| **139** A33 | 15c Sheet of 16, #a.-p. | 9.75 | 9.75 |

Miniature Sheets

Birds — A34

Designs: Each 15t: Nos. 140a-140p, Various songbirds. Nos. 141a-141p, Various raptors.

Each 100t: No. 142, Songbird. No. 143, Owl.

| **1996, Feb. 26** | **Litho.** | ***Perf. 14*** | |
|---|---|---|---|
| **140-141** A34 | Set of 2 | *22.50* | *22.50* |

**Souvenir Sheets**

| | | | |
|---|---|---|---|
| **142-143** A34 | Set of 2 | *12.50* | *12.50* |

Miniature Sheet

Fauna and Flora — A35

a, Stork's head. b, Stork's body (a, f), berries. c, Snake (d, g, h). d, Moth. e, Lizard. f, Songbirds. g, Insect, flowers. h, Bee on flower. i, Butterfly, flower. j, Frog, lily (f). k, Snail. l, Turtle (p). m. Lobster. n, Sea plant, eel (o). o, Fish. p, Salamander.

| **1996, Mar. 14** | **Litho.** | ***Perf. 14*** | |
|---|---|---|---|
| **144** A35 | 10t Sheet of 16, #a.-p. | 12.00 | 12.00 |

Dinosaurs — A36

| **1996, Apr. 24** | **Litho.** | ***Perf. 14*** | |
|---|---|---|---|
| **145** A36 | 10t Sheet of 9, #a.-i. | 7.50 | 7.50 |

Intl. Olympic Committee, Cent. — A37

Georgian Olympians, landmarks from earlier Summer Olympic Games: 1t, Helsinki, 1952. 2t, Melbourne, 1956. 3t, Rome, 1960. 4t, Tokyo, 1964. 5t, Mexico City, 1968. 6t, Munich, 1972. 7t, Montreal, 1976. 8t, Moscow, 1980. 9t, Seoul, 1988. 10t, Barcelona, 1992.

Early Greek: 50t, Wrestlers. 70t, Runner.

| **1996, Aug. 16** | **Litho.** | ***Perf. 14*** | |
|---|---|---|---|
| **146-155** A37 | Set of 10 | 8.25 | 8.25 |

**Souvenir Sheets**

| | | | |
|---|---|---|---|
| **156** A37 | 50t multicolored | 7.50 | 7.50 |
| **157** A37 | 70t multicolored | 8.75 | 8.75 |

Olymphilex '96 (No. 157).

Paintings — A38

Designs: 10t, Citizens of Paris, by Lado Gudiashvili. 20t, Abstract, by Wassily Kandinsky. 30t, Still Life, by David Kakabadze. 50t, Three Painters, by Shalva Kikodze.

80t, Portrait of Niko Pirosmani, by Pablo Picasso.

| **1996, Aug. 2** | **Litho.** | ***Perf. 14*** | |
|---|---|---|---|
| **158** A38 | 10t multicolored | .40 | .40 |
| **159** A38 | 20t multicolored | .70 | .70 |
| **160** A38 | 30t multicolored | 1.00 | 1.00 |
| **161** A38 | 50t multicolored | 1.40 | 1.40 |

**Size: 72x90mm**

***Imperf***

| | | | |
|---|---|---|---|
| **162** A38 | 80t multicolored | 3.00 | 3.00 |
| | *Nos. 158-162 (5)* | 6.50 | 6.50 |

A39

| **1996, Dec. 25** | **Litho.** | ***Perf. 13x14*** | |
|---|---|---|---|
| **163** A39 | 30t Anton I (1720-88) | 1.25 | 1.25 |

Ivan Javakhishvili (1876-1940), Writer — A40

| **1997, Mar. 6** | | ***Perf. 14*** | |
|---|---|---|---|
| **164** A40 | 50t multicolored | 1.50 | 1.50 |

UN, 50th Anniv. A41

| **1997, Mar. 5** | **Litho.** | ***Perf. 14*** | |
|---|---|---|---|
| **165** A41 | 30t purple & blue | 1.50 | 1.50 |
| **166** A41 | 125t red & blue | 4.00 | 4.00 |

Dogs — A42

Designs: 10t, Rottweiler. 30t, Gordon setter. 50t, St. Bernard. 60t, English bulldog. 70t, Caucasian sheep dog.

125t, Caucasian sheep dog, diff.

| **1997, June 2** | **Litho.** | ***Perf. 14*** | |
|---|---|---|---|
| **167** A42 | 10t multicolored | .35 | .35 |
| **168** A42 | 30t multicolored | .85 | .85 |
| **169** A42 | 50t multicolored | 1.40 | 1.40 |
| **170** A42 | 60t multicolored | 1.60 | 1.60 |
| **171** A42 | 70t multicolored | 2.00 | 2.00 |
| *a.* | Sheet of 6, #167-172 | 9.50 | |
| | *Nos. 167-171 (5)* | 6.20 | 6.20 |

**Souvenir Sheet**

| | | | |
|---|---|---|---|
| **172** A42 | 125t multicolored | 3.75 | 3.75 |

No. 171a contains stamp from No. 172 without the continuous design. Issued: 2/27/98.

Animated Film Characters — A43

Designs: a, 20t, Two mice talking. b, 30t, Man in bed. c, 40t, Balloons, bear, girl on cloud. d, 50t, Animals dancing, tree. e, 60t, Duck dressed as woman, tree.

| **1997, July 15** | **Litho.** | ***Perf. 14*** | |
|---|---|---|---|
| **173** A43 | Strip of 5, #a.-e. | 9.00 | 9.00 |

Georgian Women's Team, Winners of 1996 World Chess Olympiad — A44

No. 174: a, Maia Chiburdanidze, Nona Gaprindashvili, Nana Ioseliani, Nino Gurieli, 1992 winners. b, Chiburdanidze, Ioseliani, Ketevan Arakhamia, Gurieli, 1994 winners. c, Chiburdanidze, Ioseliani, Arakhamia, Gurieli, 1996 winners.

No. 175: a, 20t, Vice-Champion Nana Alexandria, 1975, 1981. b, 40t, Chiburdanidze, 1978, 1981 (Vice-Champion), 1984, 1986, 1991. c, 20t, Ioseliani, 1988, 1993. d, 50t, Gaprindashvili, 1962, 1965, 1969, 1972, 1975 (Vice-Champion).

| **1997, July 21** | **Litho.** | ***Imperf.*** | |
|---|---|---|---|
| **174** A44 | 30t Sheet of 3, #a.-d.+ label | 3.00 | 3.00 |
| **175** A44 | Sheet of 4, #a.-d. | 4.00 | 4.00 |

Nos. 174-175 have simulated perforations.

A45

1998 Winter Olympic Games, Nagano A46

Stylized skier — No. 176: a, 20t. b, 30t. c, 40t. d, 50t.

Early hand-made winter apparel, equipment — No. 177: a, 20t, Snow shoe, hat, gloves. b, 30t, Scarf, snow shoe. c, 40t, Sled, gloves. d, 50t, Scarf, snow shoe.

No. 178, Stylized skier, diff. No. 179, Man's feet with snow shoes.

| **1998, Feb. 8** | **Litho.** | ***Perf. 14*** | |
|---|---|---|---|
| **176** A45 | Sheet of 4, #a.-d. | 4.00 | 4.00 |
| **177** A46 | Sheet of 4, #a.-d. | 4.00 | 4.00 |

**Souvenir Sheets**

| | | | |
|---|---|---|---|
| **178** A45 | 70t multicolored | 2.75 | 2.75 |
| **179** A46 | 70t multicolored | 2.75 | 2.75 |

Moscow '97 — A47

Tiflis local postage stamp of 1857.

**1997, Oct. 17 Litho. *Perf. 13x14***
**180** A47 80t multicolored 2.25 2.25

### Souvenir Sheet

**181** A47 1 l multicolored 3.00 3.00

Prince Vakhushti Bagrationi (1696-1758) — A48

40t, Map of Georgia, 1745, portrait. 80t, Portrait.

**1997, Oct. 9**
**182** A48 40t multi 1.00 1.00
**183** A48 80t multi, vert. 2.25 2.25

World Delphic Congress — A49

40t, Symbols of education, art & music, 1st World Junior Delphics. 80t, Building on mountaintop, 2nd World Delphic Cong.

**1997, Nov. 24 Litho. *Perf. 14***
**184** A49 40t multicolored 1.10 1.10
**185** A49 80t multicolored 2.10 2.10

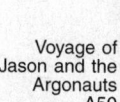

Voyage of Jason and the Argonauts A50

Plate and Vase Paintings: a, 30t, Greek galley from Rhodes, terracotta plate, 700-650BC. b, 40t, Preparation for Battle, vase painting, 460BC. c, 50t, Boreades, Phineus & Harpy, vase painting, 6th cent. d, 60t, Punishment of King Amicus, vase painting, 420-400BC. e, 70t, Argonauts in Colchis, vase painting, 4th cent. BC. f, 80t, The Dragon Vomiting Jason, vase painting, 490-485BC.

**1998, June 23 Litho. *Perf. 13x13½***
**186** A50 Sheet of 6, #a.-f. 9.25 9.25

Independence, 80th Anniv. — A51

**1998, Dec. 25 Litho. *Perf. 14***
**187** A51 80t multicolored 2.50 2.50

Horses A52

Various breeds.

**1998, Dec. 22**
**188** A52 10t multicolored .55 .55
**189** A52 40t multicolored 1.60 1.60
**190** A52 70t multicolored 2.75 2.75
**191** A52 80t multicolored 3.25 3.25
*Nos. 188-191 (4)* 8.15 8.15

### Souvenir Sheet
### *Imperf*

**192** A52 100t multicolored 4.50 4.50

No. 192 has simulated perfs.

Locomotives — A53

Various locomotives built at Tbilisi Locomotives Works.

**1998, Dec. 24**
**193** A53 10t multicolored .40 .40
**194** A53 30t multicolored 1.10 1.10
**195** A53 40t multicolored 1.40 1.40
**196** A53 50t multicolored 1.60 1.60
**197** A53 80t multicolored 2.75 2.75
*Nos. 193-197 (5)* 7.25 7.25

### Souvenir Sheet

**198** A53 100t multicolored 4.00 4.00

Europa A54

**1998, Dec. 31 Litho. *Perf. 13x12¾***
**199** A54 (80t) Berikaoba *1.60 1.60*
**200** A54 (100t) Chiakokonoba *2.10 2.10*

Wildlife A55

10t, Vormela peregusna guld. 40t, Hyaena hyaena. 80t, Ursus arctos syriacus. 100t, Capra aegagrus erxleber.

**1999, Feb. Litho. *Perf. 14x13½***
**201** A55 10t multicolored .40 .40
**202** A55 40t multicolored 1.25 1.25
**203** A55 80t multicolored 2.50 2.50
*Nos. 201-203 (3)* 4.15 4.15

### Souvenir Sheet
### *Imperf*

**204** A55 100t multicolored 3.25 3.25

Dated 1998. No. 204 has simulated perfs.

Ancient and Modern Bridges of Tbilisi A56

Bridges: a, 10t, Michael. b, 40t, Saarbruken. c, 50t, N. Baratashvili. d, 60t, Mukhrani. e, 70t, Avlabari. f, 80t, Metekhi.

**1999, Feb. *Perf. 13½x14***
**205** A56 Sheet of 6, #a.-f. 12.00 12.00

Mustela Lutreola, Worldwide Fund for Wildlife A57

**1999, Apr. 27 Litho. *Perf. 13x12¾***
**206** A57 (10t) Standing in water *1.75 1.75*
**207** A57 (20t) Feeding *1.75 1.75*
**208** A57 (30t) Two standing *1.75 1.75*
**209** A57 (60t) In burrow *1.75 1.75*
*b.* Strip of 4, #206-209 14.00 14.00

Nos. 206-209 were issued in sheets of 10 of each denomination and as se-tenant blocks of 4 in sheets of 20. The stamps from the se-tenant sheets have thicker lettering in the country and Latin names. Singles from the se-tenant sheets of 20 and from the individual sheetlets of 10 are of equal value.

Europa — A58

(80t), Batsara-Babaneury Reserve. (100t), Lagodekhy Reserve.

**1999, Apr. 28 Litho. *Perf. 12¾x13***
**210** A58 (80t) multi *2.50 2.50*
**211** A58 (100t) multi *3.00 3.00*

Council of Europe, 50th Anniv. — A59

**1999, Nov. Litho. *Perf. 12¾***
**212** A59 50t shown *1.45 1.45*
**213** A59 80t Latin letters *2.00 2.00*

Georgian Olympic Committee, 10th Anniv. A60

**1999, Nov. *Perf. 13¾***
**214** A60 20t multi .90 .90
**215** A60 50t multi 2.00 2.00

Butterflies A61

Designs: 10t, Iphiclides podalirius. 20t, Parnassius apollo. 50t, Colias aurorina herrich-schaffer. 80t, Tomares romanovi.

**1999, Nov.**
**216** A61 10t multi .50 .50
**217** A61 20t multi .85 .85
**218** A61 50t multi 1.60 1.60
**219** A61 80t multi 3.50 3.50
*Nos. 216-219 (4)* 6.45 6.45

UPU, 125th Anniv. — A62

**1999, Nov. *Perf. 13¼x13½***
**220** A62 20t shown .75 .75
**221** A62 80t Letter writer 2.75 2.75

Trucks A63

**1999, Dec. *Perf. 13¾***

### Color of Truck

**222** A63 20t green .65 .65
**223** A63 40t red & yellow 1.25 1.25
**224** A63 50t blue & white 1.60 1.60
**225** A63 80t red & white 2.50 2.50
*Nos. 222-225 (4)* 6.00 6.00

### Souvenir Sheet

**226** A63 100t red 4.25 4.25

Souvenir Sheet

Svaneti, World Heritage Site — A64

**1999, Dec. *Perf. 12¾***
**227** A64 100t multi 3.50 3.50

### Europa, 2000
Common Design Type

Denominations: 80t, 100t.

**2000, Mar. 31 Litho. *Perf. 12¾x13***
**228-229** CD17 Set of 2 *9.00 9.00*

Scenes from "The Knight in a Tiger's Skin," by Shota Rustaveli A65

Denominations: 10t, 20t, 30t, 50t, 60t.

**2000, May 8 *Perf. 14¼x13¾***
**230-234** A65 Set of 5 5.50 5.50

### Souvenir Sheet

**235** A65 80t multi + label 4.25 4.25

Nos. 230-235 also issued imperf. Value, set $10.

Christianity, 2000th Anniv. — A66

Icons: 20t, St. Nino the Preacher. 50t, The Savior. 80t, The Virgin Hodigitria.

**2000, May 10** ***Perf. 13¾***
**236-238** A66 Set of 3 *5.50 5.50*

Souvenir Sheet

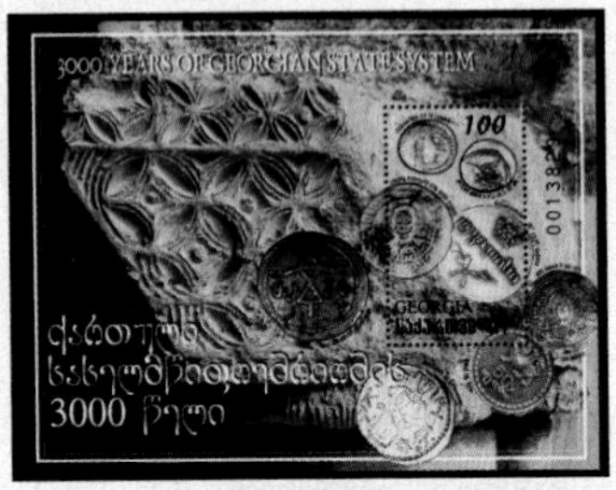


Georgian State System, 3000th Anniv. — A67

**2000, May 11** ***Perf. 13***
**239** A67 100t multi *4.50 4.50*

Fish — A68

Various fish: 10t, 20t, 30t, 50t, 80t.

**2000, May 12** ***Perf. 13¾x13¼***
**240-244** A68 Set of 5 7.25 7.25

David Saradjishvili (1848-1911), Brandy Maker A69

**2000, Sept. 20 Litho.** ***Perf. 14¼x14***
**245** A69 80t multi 2.25 2.25

2000 Summer Olympics, Sydney — A70

No. 246: a, 20t, Runner at left. b, 50t, Runner at center. c, 80t, Runner at right.

**2000 Sept. 20** ***Perf. 13¾***
**246** A70 Strip of 3, #a-c 6.00 6.00

Millennium — A71

No. 247: a, 20t, "1999." b, 50t, "2000." c, 80t, "2001."

**2000, Sept. 20**
**247** A71 Strip of 3, #a-c *6.50 6.50*

Joint Georgia-Russia Space Reflector Project — A72

Designs: 20t, Astronauts at work. 80t, Reflector.

**2000, Dec. 11 Litho.** ***Perf. 13¾***
**248-249** A72 Set of 2 4.00 4.00

Human Rights in Europe, 50th Anniv. A73

Denomination colors: 50t, Orange brown. 80t, Blue.

**2000, Dec. 12** ***Perf. 14¼x14***
**250-251** A73 Set of 2 3.75 3.75

Mushrooms A74

Designs: 10t, Cantharellus cibarius. 20t, Agaricus campestris. 30t, Armillariella mella. 50t, Russula adusta. 80t, Cortinarus violaceus.

**2000, Dec. 14** ***Perf. 13¼x13½***
**252-256** A74 Set of 5 7.75 7.75

UN High Commissioner for Refugees, 50th Anniv. — A75

**2000, Dec. 14** ***Perf. 13½x14***
**257** A75 50t multi 1.50 1.50

**Houses of Worship Type of 1993**

Unidentified buildings. Colors: 10t, Brown. 50t, Blue.

**Size: 24x32mm**

**2000, Dec. 18** ***Perf. 13¼x13***
**258-259** A25 Set of 2 2.25 2.25

Writers — A76

Designs: 30t, Alexander Kazbegi (1848-93). 40t, Jakob Gogebashvili (1840-1912). 50t, Vadja Pshavela (1861-1915). 70t, Akaki Tsereteli (1840-1915). 80t, Ilia Chavchavadze (1837-1907).

**2000, Dec. 19** ***Perf. 13¼x13¾***
**260-264** A76 Set of 5 6.50 6.50

Alexander Kartveli (1896-1977), Aircraft Designer — A77

Designs: 10t, P-47D Thunderbolt. 20t, F-84. 80t, F-105D Thunderchief.

**2000, Dec. 20** ***Perf. 13¾x14***
**265-267** A77 Set of 3 4.00 4.00

**Souvenir Sheet**

***Perf. 13***

**268** A77 100t Portrait, vert. 3.50 3.50

Fire Fighting Service, 175th Anniv. — A78

**2000, Dec. 24** ***Perf. 13¾x14***
**269** A78 50t multi 2.25 2.25

Europa — A79

Designs: 40t, Ritsa Lake. 80t, Borjomi Park.

**2001, Sept. 10 Litho.** ***Perf. 12½x13***
**270-271** A79 Set of 2 *5.75 5.75*
*a.* Booklet pane, 2 each #270-271, perf. 12½x13 on 3 sides *11.00*
Booklet, #271a *12.00*

Great Silk Route A80

**2001, Sept. 20** ***Perf. 13x12½***
**272** A80 20t shown .75 .75

**Souvenir Sheet**

**273** A80 80t Like 20t, no emblem 3.00 3.00

Kutaisi Synagogue — A81

**2001, Sept. 13 Litho.** ***Perf. 13x14***
**274** A81 140t multi 4.50 4.50

First Europe-Asia Chess Match — A82

**2001, Sept. 18 Litho.** ***Perf. 13¾***
**275** A82 1 l multi 4.50 4.50

Poets — A83

No. 276: a, Taras Shevchenko (1814-61), Ukrainian poet. b, Akaki Tsereteli (1840-1915), Georgian poet.

**2001, Dec. 19** ***Perf. 13***
**276** A83 50t Horiz. pair, #a-b 3.75 3.75

See Ukraine No. 445.

Georgian National Ballet — A84

Designs: 30t, Dancers Iliko Sukhishvili (1907-85) and Nino Ramishvili (1910-2000), sketch for dance "Mtiuluri." 50t, Dancers, sketch for dance "Samaya." 80t, Sukhishvili, Ramishvili, and sketch for dance "Jeirani."

**2002, Feb. 11** ***Perf. 13½x13¼***
**277-279** A84 Set of 3 5.25 5.25

Port of Poti, 140th Anniv. — A85

No. 280: a, Map, ship (black and white photograph). b, Mobile container crane, containers. c, Ship and tugboat, cargo hauler. d, Cargo hauler, small boat, container crane lifting container (black and white photograph). e, Ship, cargo hauler (black and white photograph). f, Cargo hauler, large ship.

**2002, Feb. 11** ***Perf. 13¼x13½***
**280** A85 30t Sheet of 6, #a-f 6.00 6.00

A86

Ashot Kurapalatl Opiza — A87

**2002, Feb. 11** ***Perf. 13¼x13½***
**281** A86 100t blue 2.50 2.50

***Perf. 13¼***

**282** A87 5 l brown 9.50 9.50

Europa — A88

Designs: 40t, Georgian Circus. 80t, Tbilisi Circus.

**2002, Mar. 22** ***Perf. 13½x13¼***
**283-284** A88 Set of 2 *3.75 3.75*
*a.* Booklet pane, 2 each #283-284, perf. 13½x13¼ on 3 sides *8.75*
Booklet, #284a *9.75*

Convention on Status of Refugees, 50th Anniv. — A89

**2002, May 15** **Litho.** ***Perf. 13¼***
**285** A89 50t multi 1.25 1.25

Dinamo Tbilisi, Winner of 1981 European Soccer Cup — A90

**2002, Sept. 23** ***Perf. 13¾***
**286** A90 20t multi 3.50 3.50

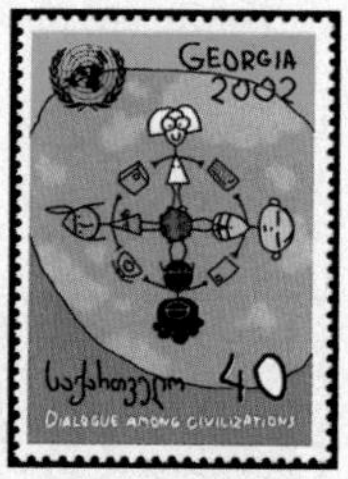

Year of Dialogue Among Civilizations A91

**2002, Sept. 23** ***Perf. 13x13¾***
**287** A91 40t multi 1.75 1.75

Intl. Federation of Stamp Dealers Associations, 50th Anniv. — A92

**2002, Sept. 23** ***Perf. 13¼x13***
**288** A92 100t No. 12 3.00 3.00

Fighter Aircraft A93

Designs: 30t, SU-25 Scorpio. 80t, MiG 21U.

**2002, Sept. 23** ***Perf. 13¾x13***
**289-290** A93 Set of 2 3.25 3.25

Traditional Costumes A94

Men and women in various costumes: 20t, 30t, 50t.

**2002, Sept. 23** ***Perf. 13¾***
**291-293** A94 Set of 3 4.00 4.00

Church Murals A95

Murals from: 10t, 14th cent., vert. 30t, 16th-17th cent. 80t, 18th cent., vert.

***Perf. 13½x13, 13x13½***

**2002, Sept. 23**
**294-296** A95 Set of 3 5.25 5.25

Pectoral Crosses A96

Designs: 10t, Crucifixion, 10th cent. 20t, Cross from Martvili, 7th-9th cent. 50t, Cross from Martvili, 10th cent. 80t, Cross of King Tamari, 12th cent.

**2002, Sept. 23** ***Perf. 14¼x14***
**297-300** A96 Set of 4 6.00 6.00

Flowers — A97

Designs: 20t, Bellflower. 30t, Caucasia rhododendron. 50t, Anemone. 80t, Marsh marigold.

**2003, Sept. 23** ***Perf. 13x13¾***
**301-304** A97 Set of 4 6.00 6.00

Souvenir Sheet

Alexandre Dumas (Père) (1802-70), French Novelist — A98

**2002, Sept. 23** ***Perf. 14x13¾***
**305** A98 120t multi 4.25 4.25

Europa — A99

Poster art: 40t, Three men and donkey. 80t, Four people.

**2003, Mar. 10** ***Perf. 13½x13¼***
**306-307** A99 Set of 2 *4.50 4.50*
*307a* Booklet pane, 2 each #306-307, perf. 13½x13¼ on 3 sides 8.75 —
Complete booklet, #307a 9.75

Souvenir Sheet

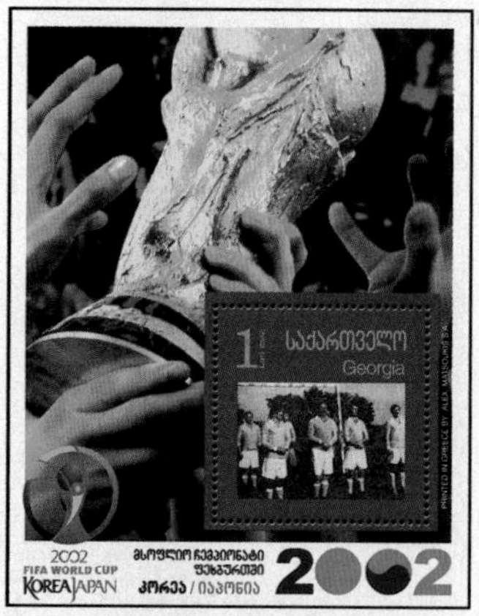

2002 World Cup Soccer Championships, Japan and Korea — A100

**2003, Apr. 25** ***Perf. 13¾***
**308** A100 1 l multi 3.25 3.25

Souvenir Sheet

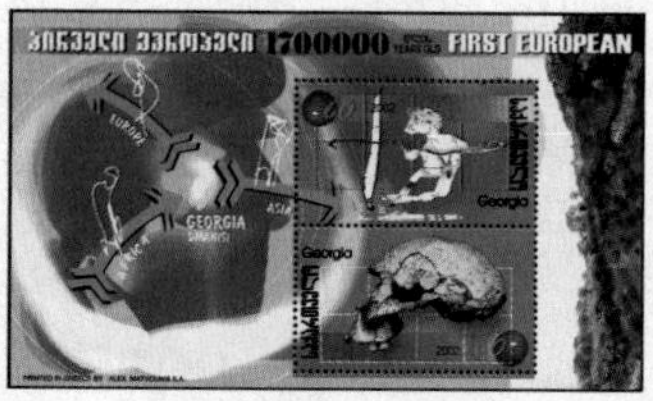

Paleontology — A101

No. 309: a, Stylized drawing of ancient European man. b, Skull.

**2003, Apr. 25** ***Perf. 12¾***
**309** A101 60t Sheet of 2, #a-b 5.00 5.00

Margin of No. 309 has "1700000 YEARS OLD" overprinted in red brown on silver oval that is an overprint over an inscription that reads "17000000 YEARS OLD". Examples exist without the red brown overprint.

Youth — A102

**2003, June 20** **Litho.** ***Perf. 14x14¼***
**310** A102 50t multi 1.50 1.50

Women for Peace A103

**2003, June 20** ***Perf. 13¾x13***
**311** A103 50t multi 1.50 1.50

Zoo Animals — A104

Minerals — A105

Animals at Tbilisi Zoo: 20t, Elephant. 30t, Wolf. 40t, Ostrich. 50t, Bear.

**2003, Aug. 25** ***Perf. 14x13¾***
**312-315** A104 Set of 4 4.75 4.75
*315a* Miniature sheet, 2 each #312-315 12.00 12.00

No. 315a was sold in a booklet cover but unattached, and is comprised of two tete-beche blocks of Nos. 312-315.

**2003, Aug. 25** ***Perf. 13¼x13***

Minerals: 10t, Rock crystal. 20t, Agate with amethyst. 30t, Orpiment rose. 50t, Realgar with orpiment.

**316-319** A105 Set of 4 3.75 3.75
*319a* Miniature sheet, 2 each #316-319 9.00 9.00

No. 319a was sold in a booklet cover but unattached, and is composed of two tete-beche blocks of Nos. 316-319.

Fruit — A106

Designs: 10t, Prunus spinosa. 20t, Laurocerasus officinalis. 30t, Cydonia oblonga. 50t, Punica granatum. 80t, Pyrus caucasica.

**2003, Aug. 25** ***Perf. 14x13¾***
**320-324** A106 Set of 5 6.00 6.00

Souvenir Sheet

Old Tbilisi, by Elene Akhvlediani (1901-75) — A107

**2003, Aug. 25**

**325** A107 80t multi 3.00 3.00

Souvenir Sheet

Self-portrait, by Vincent van Gogh (1853-90) — A108

**2003, Aug. 25** ***Perf. 13x12¾***

**326** A108 100t multi 4.00 4.00

**Nos. 73, 75a Overprinted**

**2003, Oct. 6** **Litho.** ***Perf. 13¼***

**327** A20 25t green & multi .85 .85

**Souvenir Sheet**

**328** Sheet, #327, 328a, 328b 6.00 6.00
*a.* A20 50t brown & multi 1.60 1.60
*b.* A20 100t violet & multi 3.50 3.50

First postage stamps, 10th anniv.

Intl. Association of Academies of Science, 10th Anniv. — A109

**2003, Nov. 28** ***Perf. 13¾x13¼***

**329** A109 30t multi 1.10 1.10

East-West Energy Corridor — A110

**2003, Nov. 28** ***Perf. 13¼x13¾***

**330** A110 80t multi 2.50 2.50

Tourism — A111

Designs: 10t, Skiers, Bakuriani. 20t, Caves, Vardzia. 30t, Harbor, Batum. 50t, Lake Ritsa.

**2003, Nov. 28** ***Perf. 13¾x13¼***

**331-334** A111 Set of 4 3.50 3.50
*334a* Booklet pane, 2 each #331-334 7.00 —
Complete booket, #334a 7.50

No. 334a is composed of two tete-beche blocks of Nos. 331-334.

Grapes A112

Designs: 10t, Aladasturi. 20t, Rkhatsiteli. 30t, Ojaleshi. 50t, Goruli Mtsvane. 80t, Aleksandrouli (Khvanchkhara).

**2003, Nov. 28**

**335-339** A112 Set of 5 7.00 7.00

Europa A113

Designs: 40t, Merry Christmas. 80t, Happy Easter.

**2004, Jan. 28** **Litho.** ***Perf. 13¼x13½***

**340-341** A113 Set of 2 *5.00 5.00*
*341a* Booklet pane, 4 each #340-341, perf. 13¼x13½ on 2 or 3 sides *17.50* —
Complete booklet, #341a *20.00*

Georgi Tsereteli (1904-73), Director of Institute of Oriental Studies A114

**2004, Nov. 5** **Litho.** ***Perf. 13¼x13¾***

**342** A114 30t multi 1.10 1.10

Souvenir Sheet

Rose Revolution, 1st Anniv. — A115

No. 343: a, Crowd with flags. b, Protestors with flag sprayed with water.

**2004, Nov. 5** ***Perf. 13¼x13***

**343** A115 50t Sheet of 2, #a-b 3.75 3.75

FIFA (Fédération Internationale de Football Association), Cent. — A116

Caricatures of soccer players: 20t, Boris Paichadze. 30t, Avtandil Gogoberidze. 50t, Mikheil Meskhi. 80t, David Kipiani.

**2004, Nov. 5** ***Perf. 13¾x13¼***

**344-347** A116 Set of 4 5.50 5.50

2004 Summer Olympics, Athens — A117

Sculptures of athletes by: 20t, B. Skhulukhia. 30t, V. Cherkezishvili. 50t, N. Jikia. 80t, L. Vardosanidze.

**2004, Nov. 5** ***Perf. 13¼x13¾***

**348-351** A117 Set of 4 5.50 5.50

Ancient Jewelry — A118

Designs: 20t, Belt and buckle, 3rd-4th cent. 30t, Necklace and belt buckle, 3rd-4th cent. 40t, Necklace and pins, 2000-1500 B.C. 80t, Necklace, 5th cent. B.C., double-voluted pins, 3rd millennium B.C.

**2004, Nov. 5**

**352-355** A118 Set of 4 5.00 5.00

UNESCO World Heritage Sites A119

Designs: 20t, Ushguli. 30t, Bagrati. 50t, Gelati. 60t, Samtavro. 70t, Svetitskhoveli. 80t, Jvari.

**2004, Nov. 5** **Litho.** ***Perf. 14x13¼***

**356-361** A119 Set of 6 *9.50 9.50*

Flag of Georgia A120

**2005, Feb. 11** **Litho.** ***Perf. 14x13¼***

**362** A120 50t multi 1.75 1.75

Europa — A121

Loaves of bread and: 20t, Girl. 80t, Bakers.

**2005, May 27** ***Perf. 14x13¾***

**363** A121 20t multi *1.25 1.25*
**364** A121 80t multi *4.75 4.75*

**Booklet Stamps**

**Size: 29x41mm**

***Perf. 13¾ on 2, 3 or 4 Sides***

**365** A121 20t multi *1.25 1.25*
**366** A121 80t multi *4.75 4.75*
*a.* Booklet pane, 2 each #365-366 *12.50* —
*b.* Booklet pane, 3 each #365-366 *19.00* —
Complete booklet, #366a, 366b *32.50*

For overprints see Nos. 402-403.

Rabbi Abraam Khvoles — A122

**2005, June 1** ***Perf. 12***

**367** A122 1 l multi 3.00 3.00

2008 Summer Olympics, Beijing A123

**2005, Dec. 28** **Litho.** ***Perf. 12***

**368** A123 80t multi 2.40 2.40

2006 World Cup Soccer Championships, Germany — A124

**2005, Dec. 28**

**369** A124 100t multi 3.00 3.00

Georgian Ballet — A125

Designs: 40t, V. Tsiguadze. 50t, V. Chabukiani.

**2005, Dec. 28**

**370-371** A125 Set of 2 3.00 3.00

Orchids — A126

Designs: 20t, Dactylorhiza euxina. 40t, Dactylorhiza iberica. 50t, Oprys caucasica. 80t, Orchis caucasica.

**2005, Dec. 28**

**372-375** A126 Set of 4 6.00 6.00

Theaters — A127

Designs: No. 376, 30t, Georgian Drama Theater, Batumi. No. 377, 30t, Georgian Drama Theater, Kutaisi. No. 378, 30t, Abkhazian Drama Theater, Sukhumi. No. 379, 30t, Georgian Academic Theater, Tbilisi. No. 380, 30t, Georgian Drama Theater, Tbilisi. No. 381, 30t, Georgian Opera and Ballet Theater, Tbilisi. No. 382, 30t, Armenian Drama Theater, Tbilisi. No. 383, 30t, Ossetian Drama Theater, Tskhinvali.

**2005, Dec. 28**
**376-383** A127 Set of 8 6.50 6.50

2006 Winter Olympics, Turin A128

Designs: 10t, Speed skating. 20t, Biathlon. 30t, Ski jumping. 40t, Figure skating. 80t, Downhill skiing.

**2005, Dec. 29**
**384-388** A128 Set of 5 5.00 5.00

Souvenir Sheet

Tbilisi Funicular, Cent. — A129

**2005, Dec. 30**
**389** A129 100t multi 3.00 3.00

Europa Stamps, 50th Anniv. A130

Designs: 10t, Various Georgian Europa stamps. 20t, Person inserting postcard in mail slot. 30t, France #805, Germany #748, magnifying glass, newspaper. 40t, Earth in ripped newspaper wrapper.

No. 394, 80t, Like 10t. No. 395, 80t, Like 20t. No. 396, 80t, Like 30t. No. 397, 80t, Like 40t.

**2006, Jan. 30** ***Perf. 12¾x13***
**390-393** A130 Set of 4 *3.75 3.75*

**Souvenir Sheets**

**394-397** A130 Set of 4 *12.50 12.50*

Europa — A131

Stars and: 20t, People holding flags. 80t, Earth, Georgian flag.

***Perf. 13½x13¼***

**2006, June 30** **Litho.**
**398-399** A131 Set of 2 *4.50 4.50*
*399a* Booklet pane, 4 each #398-399, perf. 13½x13¼ on 3 sides *22.00* —
Complete booklet, #399a *23.00*

No. 399a contains two tete-beche pairs of Nos. 398-399.

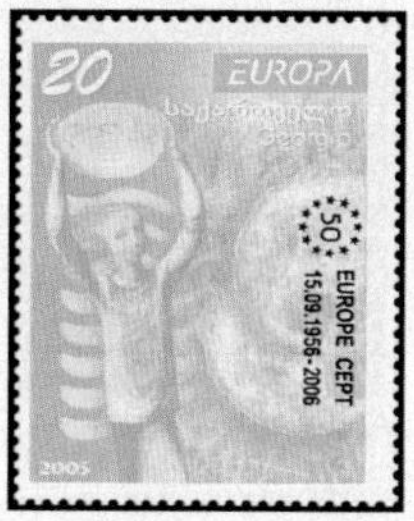
Nos. 365-366 Overprinted

***Perf. 13¾ on 2, 3 or 4 Sides***

**2006, Oct. 23** **Litho.**
**402** A121 20t multi *.90 .90*
**403** A121 80t multi *3.75 3.75*
***a.*** Sheet of 4, 2 each #402-403 *9.50 9.50*
***b.*** Sheet of 6, 3 each #402-403 *14.50 14.50*

Europa stamps, 50th anniv. Nos. 403a and 403b are Nos. 366a and 366b removed from the booklet and overprinted on the stamps and margin.

No. 79 Surcharged in Gray and Silver

**Method and Perf. As Before**

**2006, Nov. 2**
**404** A24 10t on 1c #79 .40 .40

Nikola Tesla (1856-1943), Electrical Engineer, and Wireless Transmission Tower — A132

**2006, Nov. 15** **Litho.** ***Perf. 12x12¼***
**405** A132 50t multi 1.50 1.50

Souvenir Sheet

Georgian Wild West Show Horsemen — A133

**2007, Jan. 25** **Litho.** ***Perf. 12¼***
**406** A133 100t multi 3.50 3.50

Tbilisi State University, Cent. A134

**2007, Jan. 25** **Litho.** ***Perf. 12¼x12***
**407** A134 40t multi 1.10 1.10

Prince David Guramishvili (1705-92), Poet A135

**2007, July 11** ***Perf. 13¾x13¼***
**408** A135 50t multi 1.40 1.40

2006 Chess Olympics, Turin A136

**2007, July 11**
**409** A136 200t multi 5.50 5.50

Famous Men A137

Designs: No. 410, Rembrandt (1606-69), painter. No. 411, Wolfgang Amadeus Mozart (1756-91), composer.

**2007, July 11** ***Perf. 13¾x13¼***
**410** A137 100t multi 2.75 2.75

***Perf. 13¾x14***
**Size: 39x27mm**

**411** A137 100t multi 2.75 2.75

Worldwide Fund for Nature (WWF) — A138

Aquila clanga: 30t, In flight. 40t, On branch. 50t, With prey. 60t, Head.

**2007, July 11** ***Perf. 13¼x13¾***
**412-415** A138 Set of 4 5.50 5.50

Eagles — A139

Designs: 10t, Aquila rapax. 30t, Haliaeetus albicilla. 50t, Circaetus gallicus. 70t, Aquila chryaetus.

**2007, July 11**
**416-419** A139 Set of 4 4.50 4.50

Georgian Military A140

Designs: 20t, Tanks. 30t, Soldiers. 40t, Ship. 50t, Helicopters.

**2007, July 11** ***Perf. 14¼x14***
**420-423** A140 Set of 4 3.75 3.75

Ancient Ships A141

Various ships: 20t, 30t, 50t, 70t.

**2007, July 11**
**424-427** A141 Set of 4 4.75 4.75

Souvenir Sheets

Guns from National Museum — A142

Sculpture from National Museum — A143

No. 428 — Various guns with background color of: a, Yellow. b, Buff. c, Light blue. d, Light green.

**2007, July 11** ***Perf. 13x13¼***
**428** A142 50t Sheet of 4, #a-d 5.00 5.00
**429** A143 100t multi 2.75 2.75

Souvenir Sheet

Magician, Cards and Dove — A144

*Perf. 13¼x13¾*

**2008, Mar. 14** **Litho.**

**430** A144 1 l multi 3.50 3.50

Europa — A145

Designs: 90t, Scouts in boat and near tent. 1 l, Scouts around campfire.

**2008, Mar. 14** ***Perf. 14x13¾***

**431-432** A145 Set of 2 6.75 6.75

*432a* Booklet pane, 4 each #431-432 *27.00* —

Complete booklet, #432a *27.00*

Scouting, cent. (in 2007). No. 432a contains two tete-beche pairs of Nos. 431-432.

Diplomatic Relations Between Georgia and Japan, 15th Anniv. (in 2007) — A146

**2008, Mar. 14** **Litho.** ***Perf. 13¾***

**433** A146 1 l multi 3.50 3.50

Dated 2007.

Mountains A147

Designs: 20t, Mt. Ushba. 30t, Mt. Ushba, diff. 50t, Mt. Kazbeg. 70t, Mt. Shkhara.

**2008** **Litho.** ***Perf. 13¼x13¾***

**434-437** A147 Set of 4 6.25 6.25

Issued: 30t, 6/1; others, 3/14. Bottom panel with mountain name on No. 435 was overprinted in silver and black to correct inscription. No. 435 was not issued without overprint.

King David IV (1073-1125) A148

**2008, Dec. 5** **Litho.** ***Perf. 13¾x14¼***

**438** A148 50t multi 1.75 1.75

Europa A149

Dove and: 90t, Georgia #398, cover with Georgia #213. 1 l, Letter, pencil, eyeglasses, Georgia #399.

**2008, Dec. 5** ***Perf. 13¾x14***

**439-440** A149 Set of 2 *7.00 7.00*

*440a* Booklet pane of 8, 4 each #439-440, perf. 13¾x13¼ on 3 sides *28.00*

No. 440a was sold with but not attached to a booklet cover.

2008 Summer Olympics, Beijing A150

Designs: 10t, Shooting. 30t, Wrestling. 60t, Weight lifting. 80t, Judo.

**2008, Dec. 5** ***Perf. 14¼x14***

**441-444** A150 Set of 4 6.75 6.75

Prince Sulkhan-Saba Orbeliani (1658-1725), Monk — A151

**2009, Mar. 20** ***Perf. 13¼***

**445** A151 60t multi 1.75 1.75

Kakutsa Cholokhashvili (1888-1930), Military Leader — A152

**2009, Mar. 20**

**446** A152 80t multi 2.10 2.10

Port of Poti, 150th Anniv. A153

**2009, Mar. 20**

**447** A153 1 l multi 2.75 2.75

Grape Varieties A154

Designs: 10t, Chkhaveri. 20t, Aleksandrouli. 30t, Rkatsiteli. 40t, Ojaleshi. 50t, Tsolikouri. 70t, Tavkveri. 90t, Saperavi.

**2009, Mar. 20**

**448-454** A154 Set of 7 7.25 7.25

Souvenir Sheet

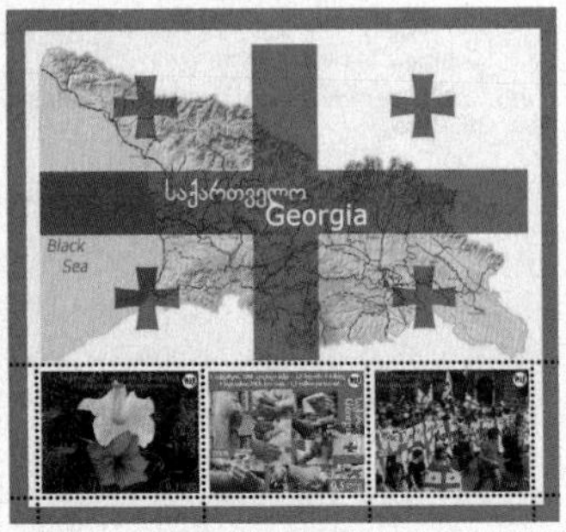


Anti-war Movement in Georgia — A155

No. 455: a, 30t, Flowers. b, 50t, Hands, Georgian flags. c, 70t, Demonstrators.

**2009, Mar. 20**

**455** A155 Sheet of 3, #a-c 4.50 4.50

European Court of Human Rights, 50th Anniv. A156

Council of Europe, 60th Anniv. A157

**2009, Aug. 10** **Litho.** ***Perf. 13¼***

**456** A156 1 l multi 2.50 2.50

**457** A157 2 l multi 5.00 5.00

**No. 79 Surcharged in Gold and Black**

**Method and Perf. As Before**

**2010, Sept. 9**

**458** A24 1 l on 1c #79 2.50 2.50

Georgian National Rugby Team, 2009 European Champions A158

**2010, Oct. 15** **Litho.** ***Perf. 13¼***

**459** A158 5 l multi *9.00 9.00*

Nodar Kumaritashvili (1988-2010), Luger Killed in Winter Olympics Practice Accident — A159

**2010, Oct. 15** ***Perf. 13¼x13½***

**460** A159 5 l multi *9.00 9.00*

Georgian Women's Chess Team, Four-time Chess Olympics Champion — A160

**2010, Oct. 15** ***Perf. 13¼***

**461** A160 7 l multi *12.00 12.00*

Flowers — A161

**2010, Oct. 15** ***Perf. 14x14¼***

**462** A161 1 l Iris *1.50 1.50*

**463** A161 1.20 l Lilium *1.75 1.75*

**464** A161 2 l Viola *3.00 3.00*

**465** A161 3 l Colchicum *4.50 4.50*

*Nos. 462-465 (4)* *10.75 10.75*

Birds A162

Designs: 20t, Grus grus. 40t, Perdix perdix. 50t, Tetraogallus caspius. 60t, Lyrurus mlokosiewiczi. 1 l, Tetrax tetrax.

**2010, Oct. 15** ***Perf. 13¼***

**466-470** A162 Set of 5 *6.00 6.00*

Latin names on 40t, 60t and 1 l are misspelled.

Souvenir Sheet

David Gareji Monastery Complex — A163

No. 471: a, Monastery complex. b, Frescoes on walls.

**2010, Oct. 15** **Litho.**

**471** A163 60t Sheet of 2, #a-b *2.75 2.75*

Souvenir Sheet

Georgian Alphabet — A164

No. 472 — Columns of letters and: a, Numerals 1-40. b, Numerals 50-700. c, Numerals 800-10,000.

**2010, Oct. 15** *Perf. 13¼*

| | | | | |
|---|---|---|---|---|
| **472** | A164 | 40t Sheet of 3, #a-c | *2.75* | *2.75* |

Europa — A165

Planets and: 2 l, Orbital diagram. 3 , Pectoral of priestess depicting Sun.

**2010, Oct. 15** *Perf. 13½x13¼*

| | | | | |
|---|---|---|---|---|
| **473-474** | A165 | Set of 2 | 10.00 | 10.00 |
| *474a* | | Souvenir sheet of 2, #473-474 | 10.00 | 10.00 |
| *474b* | | Booklet pane of 8, 4 each #473-474 | 40.00 | — |

Intl. Year of Astronomy. No. 474b was sold with, but unattached to, a booklet cover.

Flowers — A166

**2012, Apr. 11** *Perf. 13¼*

| | | | | |
|---|---|---|---|---|
| **475** | A166 | 10t Daisy | .25 | .25 |
| **476** | A166 | 25t Carnation | .60 | .60 |
| **477** | A166 | 50t Rose | 1.25 | 1.25 |
| **478** | A166 | 1 l Lilac | 2.40 | 2.40 |
| | | *Nos. 475-478 (4)* | 4.50 | 4.50 |

Dated 2011.

Souvenir Sheet

Georgian Illuminated Manuscripts — A167

No. 479 — Various manuscripts: a, 1 l. b, 1.50 l. c, 2.50 l.

**2012, Apr. 11**

| | | | | |
|---|---|---|---|---|
| **479** | A167 | Sheet of 3, #a-c | 12.50 | 12.50 |

Dated 2011.

Past Olympic Champions of Georgia — A168

Georgian flag, Olympic rings, list of winners and: 1.50 l, Parthenon, Athens. 2.50 l, Temple of Heaven, Beijing.

**2012, Apr. 11** *Perf. 12¾x13¼*

| | | | | |
|---|---|---|---|---|
| **480-481** | A168 | Set of 2 | 10.00 | 10.00 |

United Nations High Commissioner for Refugees, 60th Anniv. (in 2011) — A169

**2012, Apr. 11** *Perf. 13¼*

| | | | | |
|---|---|---|---|---|
| **482** | A169 | 4 l multi | 10.00 | 10.00 |

## SEMI-POSTAL STAMPS

**Surcharge in Red or Black**

SP1

SP2

SP3

SP4

**1922** **Unwmk.** *Perf. 11½*

| | | | | |
|---|---|---|---|---|
| **B1** | SP1 | 1000r on 50r vio (R) | .75 | *3.00* |
| **B2** | SP2 | 3000r on 100r brn red | .75 | *3.00* |
| **B3** | SP3 | 5000r on 250r gray grn | .75 | *3.00* |
| **B4** | SP4 | 10,000r on 25r blue (R) | .75 | *3.00* |
| | | *Nos. B1-B4 (4)* | 3.00 | *12.00* |

Nos. B1-B4 exist imperf but were not so issued. Value slightly more than perforated examples.

Georgian Natl. Olympic Committee SP10

**1994, May 27** **Litho.** *Perf. 13½*

| | | | | |
|---|---|---|---|---|
| **B10** | SP10 | 100c +50c multi | 1.10 | 1.10 |

UNICEF, 50th Anniv. SP11

Children's paintings: 20t+5t, People on ladder above rainbow, vert. 30t+10t, Animal character.

*Perf. 13x14, 14x13*

**1996, Dec. 20** **Litho.**

| | | | | |
|---|---|---|---|---|
| **B11** | SP11 | 20t +5t multi | 1.40 | 1.40 |
| **B12** | SP11 | 30t +10t multi | 1.90 | 1.90 |

In Remembrance of Sept. 11, 2001 Terrorist Attacks — SP12

**2001, Dec. 31** **Litho.** *Perf. 13x13¼*

| | | | | |
|---|---|---|---|---|
| **B13** | SP12 | 30t +10t multi | 1.60 | 1.60 |

**Souvenir Sheet**

| | | | | |
|---|---|---|---|---|
| **B14** | SP12 | 120t +10t multi | 5.50 | 5.50 |

# GERMAN EAST AFRICA

'jər-mən 'ēst 'a-fri-kə

LOCATION — In East Africa, bordering on the Indian Ocean
GOVT. — German Colony
AREA — 384,180 sq. mi.
POP. — 7,680,132 (1913)
CAPITAL — Dar-es Salaam

Following World War I, the greater part of this German Colonial possession was mandated to Great Britain. The British ceded to the Belgians the provinces of Ruanda and Urundi (Belgian East Africa). The Kionga triangle was awarded to the Portuguese and became part of the Mozambique Colony. The remaining area became the British Mandated Territory of Tanganyika.

64 Pesa = 1 Rupee
100 Heller = 1 Rupee (1905)
100 Centimes = 1 Franc (1916)
12 Pence = 1 Shilling (1916)
100 Cents = 1 Rupee (1917)
12 Pence = 1 Shilling 100 Cents = 1 Rupee (1917)

**Stamps of Germany surcharged in Black**

Nos. 1-5

Nos. 6-10

**1893** **Unwmk.** *Perf. 13½x14½*

**Surcharge 15¼mm long**

| | | | | |
|---|---|---|---|---|
| **1** | A9 | 2pes on 3pf brown | 45.00 | *57.50* |
| **2** | A9 | 3pes on 5pf green | 52.50 | *57.50* |
| **3** | A10 | 5pes on 10pf car | 45.00 | 29.00 |

**Surcharge 16¼mm long**

| | | | | |
|---|---|---|---|---|
| **4** | A10 | 10pes on 20pf ultra | 32.50 | 16.00 |

**Surcharge 16¾mm long**

| | | | | |
|---|---|---|---|---|
| **5** | A10 | 25pes on 50pf red brn | 45.00 | 32.50 |
| | | *Nos. 1-5 (5)* | 220.00 | 192.50 |

The surcharge also comes 16¾mm on No. 1; 14¼ or 16¼mm on Nos. 2-3; 17½mm on No. 5. See the *Scott Classic Catalogue* for listings of these spacings.

**1896**

| | | | | |
|---|---|---|---|---|
| **6** | A9 | 2pes on 3pf dk brn | 2.10 | *37.50* |
| *a.* | | 2pes on 3pf light brown | 28.00 | *45.00* |
| *b.* | | 2pes on 3pf grayish brown | 11.50 | 11.50 |
| *c.* | | 2pes on 3pf reddish brown | 105.00 | *200.00* |
| **7** | A9 | 3pes on 5pf green | 2.50 | *4.50* |
| **8** | A10 | 5pes on 10pf car | 4.75 | 4.50 |
| **9** | A10 | 10pes on 20pf ultra | 5.25 | 5.25 |
| **10** | A10 | 25pes on 50pf red brn | 23.00 | *28.00* |
| | | *Nos. 6-10 (5)* | 37.60 | *79.75* |

A5

Kaiser's Yacht "Hohenzollern" — A6

**1900** **Typo.** *Perf. 14*

| | | | | |
|---|---|---|---|---|
| **11** | A5 | 2p brown | 2.75 | 1.60 |
| **12** | A5 | 3p green | 2.75 | 2.00 |
| **13** | A5 | 5p carmine | 3.25 | 2.50 |
| **14** | A5 | 10p ultra | 5.25 | 5.00 |
| **15** | A5 | 20p org & blk, *sal* | 5.25 | *6.50* |
| **16** | A5 | 20p lake & blk | 7.50 | *15.00* |
| **17** | A5 | 25p pur & blk, *sal* | 7.50 | *15.00* |
| **18** | A5 | 40p lake & blk, *rose* | 9.00 | *23.00* |

**Engr.**

*Perf. 14½x14*

| | | | | |
|---|---|---|---|---|
| **19** | A6 | 1r claret | 20.00 | *57.50* |
| **20** | A6 | 2r yel green | 10.00 | *90.00* |
| **21a** | A6 | 3r red & slate | 120.00 | *200.00* |
| | | *Nos. 11-21a (11)* | 193.25 | *418.10* |

**Value in Heller**

**1905** **Typo.** *Perf. 14*

| | | | | |
|---|---|---|---|---|
| **22** | A5 | 2½h brown | 4.00 | 1.75 |
| **23** | A5 | 4h dk olive green | 16.50 | 5.75 |
| *a.* | | 4h green | 15.00 | 2.00 |
| *b.* | | 4h dark yellowish green | 29.00 | *20.00* |
| **24** | A5 | 7½h carmine | 15.00 | 1.60 |
| **25** | A5 | 15h ultra | 24.00 | 6.00 |
| *a.* | | 15h violet blue | 50.00 | 16.00 |
| **26** | A5 | 20h org & blk, *yel* | 15.00 | *16.00* |
| **27** | A5 | 30h lake & blk | 15.00 | 6.00 |
| **28** | A5 | 45h pur & blk | 29.00 | *37.50* |
| **29** | A5 | 60h lake & blk, *rose* | 37.50 | *100.00* |
| | | *Nos. 22-29 (8)* | 156.00 | *174.60* |

**1905-16** **Wmk. Lozenges (125)**

| | | | | |
|---|---|---|---|---|
| **31** | A5 | 2½h brn ('06) | 1.00 | 1.00 |
| **32** | A5 | 4h grn ('06) | 1.00 | .65 |
| *b.* | | Booklet pane of 4 + 2 labels | 45.00 | |
| *c.* | | Booklet pane of 5 + label | 400.00 | |
| **33** | A5 | 7½h car ('06) | 1.10 | *1.60* |
| *b.* | | Booklet pane of 4 + 2 labels | 45.00 | |
| *c.* | | Booklet pane of 5 + label | 400.00 | |
| **34** | A5 | 15h dk blue ('08) | 2.25 | 1.50 |
| **35** | A5 | 20h org & blk, *yel* ('11) | 2.50 | *20.00* |
| **36** | A5 | 30h lake & blk ('09) | 2.60 | *8.25* |
| **37** | A5 | 45h pur & blk ('06) | 5.75 | *57.50* |
| **38** | A5 | 60h lake & blk, *rose* | 30.00 | *200.00* |

**Engr.**

*Perf. 14½x14*

| | | | | |
|---|---|---|---|---|
| **39** | A6 | 1r red ('16) | 15.00 | *25,000.* |
| **40** | A6 | 2r yel grn | 50.00 | |
| **41** | A6 | 3r car & sl ('08) | 50.00 | *250.00* |
| *a.* | | 3r red & blackish green ('08) | 160.00 | *400.00* |
| | | *Nos. 31-41 (11)* | 161.20 | 25,540. |

No. 40 was never placed in use.

The frame of No. 41a fluoresces bright orange under ultra-violet light.

Forged cancellations are found on #35-39, 41.

In early 1916, German East African authorities ordered supplies of provisional stamps, printed by the press of the Evangelical Mission in Wuga. Three values in denominations most urgently needed were produced in March, but before they could be issued, new stocks of regular stamps were received from Germany. To prevent their capture by the British, the provisionals were buried until 1922, when they were retrieved by the German government and sold at auction. Because of their long storage in the tropical climate, 90-95% of the stamps were destroyed and those surviving are usually brittle and somewhat faded.

Values: 2½h violet brown, $57.50; 7½h, carmine, $25; 1r pink, $1,400.

## OCCUPATION STAMPS

### Issued Under Belgian Occupation

**Stamps of Belgian Congo, 1915, Handstamped "RUANDA" in Black, Blue or Red Violet**

**1916 Unwmk. *Perf. 13½ to 15***

| | | | | |
|---|---|---|---|---|
| **N1** | A29 | 5c green & blk | 65.00 | |
| **N2** | A30 | 10c carmine & blk | 65.00 | |
| **N3** | A21 | 15c blue grn & blk | 125.00 | |
| **N4** | A31 | 25c blue & blk | 65.00 | |
| **N5** | A23 | 40c brown red & blk | 65.00 | |
| **N6** | A24 | 50c brown lake & blk | 75.00 | |
| **N7** | A25 | 1fr olive bis & blk | 250.00 | |
| **N8** | A27 | 5fr ocher & blk | *3,000.* | |
| | | *Nos. N1-N7 (7)* | 710.00 | |

**Stamps of Belgian Congo, 1915, Handstamped "URUNDI" in Black, Blue or Red Violet**

| | | | | |
|---|---|---|---|---|
| **N9** | A29 | 5c green & blk | 65.00 | |
| **N10** | A30 | 10c carmine & blk | 65.00 | |
| **N11** | A21 | 15c bl grn & blk | 125.00 | |
| **N12** | A31 | 25c blue & blk | 65.00 | |
| **N13** | A23 | 40c brn red & blk | 65.00 | |
| **N14** | A24 | 50c brn lake & blk | 75.00 | |
| **N15** | A25 | 1fr ol bis & blk | 250.00 | |
| **N16** | A27 | 5fr ocher & blk | *3,000.* | |
| | | *Nos. N9-N15 (7)* | 710.00 | |

Stamps of Belgian Congo overprinted "Karema," "Kigoma" and "Tabora" were not officially authorized.

Nos. N1-N16 exist with forged overprint.

Stamps of Belgian Congo, 1915, Ovptd. in Dark Blue

**1916 *Perf. 12½ to 15***

| | | | | |
|---|---|---|---|---|
| **N17** | A29 | 5c green & blk | 1.00 | .30 |
| *b.* | | Inverted overprint | 200.00 | — |
| **N18** | A30 | 10c carmine & blk | 1.25 | .50 |
| **N19** | A21 | 15c bl grn & blk | 1.00 | .30 |
| **N20** | A31 | 25c blue & blk | 6.50 | 1.75 |
| **N21** | A23 | 40c brn red & blk | 14.00 | 6.00 |
| **N22** | A24 | 50c brn lake & blk | 17.50 | 6.00 |
| **N23** | A25 | 1fr olive bis & blk | 3.00 | .75 |
| **N24** | A27 | 5fr ocher & blk | 3.50 | 1.75 |
| | | *Nos. N17-N24 (8)* | 47.75 | 17.35 |

Nos. N17-N18, N20-N22 Surcharged in Black or Red

**1922**

| | | | | |
|---|---|---|---|---|
| **N25** | A24 | 5c on 50c brn lake & blk | .75 | .45 |
| **N26** | A29 | 10c on 5c grn & blk (R) | .75 | .40 |
| **N27** | A23 | 25c on 40c brn red & blk (R) | 3.75 | 2.00 |
| **N28** | A30 | 30c on 10c car & blk | .75 | .30 |
| **N29** | A31 | 50c on 25c bl & blk (R) | .75 | .30 |
| | | *Nos. N25-N29 (5)* | 6.75 | 3.45 |

No. N25 has the surcharge at each side.

### ISSUED UNDER BRITISH OCCUPATION

Stamps of Nyasaland Protectorate, 1913-15 Overprinted

**1916 Wmk. 3 *Perf. 14***

| | | | | |
|---|---|---|---|---|
| **N101** | A3 | ½p green | 1.75 | *9.50* |
| *a.* | | Double overprint (R & Bk) | | |
| **N102** | A3 | 1p carmine | 1.75 | *3.75* |
| **N103** | A3 | 3p violet, *yel* | 18.00 | 18.00 |
| *a.* | | Double overprint | | *26,000.* |
| **N104** | A3 | 4p scar & blk, *yel* | 42.00 | 42.00 |
| **N105** | A3 | 1sh black, *green* | 55.00 | *60.00* |
| | | *Nos. N101-N105 (5)* | 118.50 | *133.25* |

"N.F." stands for "Nyasaland Force."

Stamps of East Africa and Uganda, 1912-14, Overprinted in Black or Red

**1917**

| | | | | |
|---|---|---|---|---|
| **N106** | A3 | 1c black (R) | .25 | *.95* |
| **N107** | A3 | 3c blue green | .25 | .25 |
| **N108** | A3 | 6c carmine | .25 | .25 |
| **N109** | A3 | 10c brown orange | .60 | *.70* |
| **N110** | A3 | 12c gray | .60 | *2.50* |
| **N111** | A3 | 15c ultramarine | 1.50 | *3.50* |
| **N112** | A3 | 25c scar & blk, *yel* | .90 | *4.00* |
| **N113** | A3 | 50c violet & blk | 1.50 | *3.75* |
| **N114** | A3 | 75c blk, *bl grn,* olive back (R) | 1.20 | *5.25* |
| *a.* | | 75c black, *emerald* (R) | 3.75 | *52.50* |

Overprinted

| | | | | |
|---|---|---|---|---|
| **N115** | A4 | 1r blk, *green*(R) | 4.25 | *8.00* |
| *a.* | | 1r black, *emerald* (R) | 9.50 | *65.00* |
| **N116** | A4 | 2r blk & red, *bl* | 13.00 | *55.00* |
| **N117** | A4 | 3r gray grn & vio | 15.00 | *95.00* |
| **N118** | A4 | 4r grn & red, *yel* | 22.50 | *105.00* |
| **N119** | A4 | 5r dl vio & ultra | 45.00 | *110.00* |
| **N120** | A4 | 10r grn & red, *grn* | 120.00 | *375.00* |
| *a.* | | 10r grn & red, *emerald* | 130.00 | *450.00* |
| **N121** | A3 | 20r vio & blk, *red* | 250.00 | *500.00* |
| **N122** | A3 | 50r gray grn & red | 600.00 | *950.00* |
| | | *Nos. N106-N120 (15)* | 226.80 | *769.15* |

See Tanganyika for "G.E.A." overprints on stamps inscribed "East Africa and Uganda Protectorates" with watermark 4.

## SEMI-POSTAL STAMPS

### Issued under Belgian Occupation

Semi-Postal Stamps of Belgian Congo, 1918, Overprinted

**1918 Unwmk. *Perf. 14, 15***

| | | | | |
|---|---|---|---|---|
| **NB1** | A29 | 5c + 10c grn & bl | .50 | .50 |
| **NB2** | A30 | 10c + 15c car & bl | .80 | .50 |
| **NB3** | A21 | 15c + 20c bl grn & bl | 1.00 | .50 |
| **NB4** | A31 | 25c + 25c dp & pale bl | 1.50 | .50 |
| **NB5** | A23 | 40c + 40c brn red & bl | 1.00 | .75 |
| **NB6** | A24 | 50c + 50c brn lake & bl | 1.50 | 1.00 |
| **NB7** | A25 | 1fr + 1fr ol bis & bl | 2.75 | 2.75 |
| **NB8** | A27 | 5fr + 5fr ocher & bl | 9.50 | 8.50 |
| **NB9** | A28 | 10fr + 10fr grn & bl | 70.00 | 70.00 |
| | | *Nos. NB1-NB9 (9)* | 88.55 | 85.00 |

The letters "A.O." are the initials of "Afrique Orientale" (East Africa).

# GERMAN NEW GUINEA

ˈjər-mən ˈnü ˈgi-nē

LOCATION — A group of islands in the west Pacific Ocean, including a part of New Guinea and adjacent islands of the Bismarck Archipelago.
GOVT. — German Protectorate
AREA — 93,000 sq. mi.
POP. — 601,427 (1913)
CAPITAL — Herbertshohe (later Kokopo)

The islands were occupied by Australian troops during World War I and renamed "New Britain." By covenant of the League of Nations they were made a mandated territory of Australia in 1920. The old name of "New Guinea" has since been restored. Postage stamps were issued under all regimes. For other listings see New Britain (1914-15), North West Pacific Islands (1915-22) and New Guinea in Vol. 4.



100 Pfennig = 1 Mark

Stamps of Germany Overprinted in Black

**1897-99 Unwmk. *Perf. 13½x14½***

| | | | | |
|---|---|---|---|---|
| **1** | A9 | 3pf brown | 8.25 | *11.00* |
| *a.* | | 3pf reddish brown ('99) | 115.00 | *200.00* |
| *b.* | | 3pf yellow brown ('99) | 31.00 | *57.50* |
| **2** | A9 | 5pf green | 4.00 | *5.75* |
| **3** | A10 | 10pf carmine | 6.50 | *9.00* |
| **4** | A10 | 20pf ultra | 9.00 | *14.00* |
| **5** | A10 | 25pf orange ('98) | 29.00 | *52.50* |
| *a.* | | Inverted overprint | *2,750.* | |
| **6** | A10 | 50pf red brown | 32.50 | *50.00* |
| | | *Nos. 1-6 (6)* | 89.25 | *142.25* |

Kaiser's Yacht "Hohenzollern"
A3 A4

**1901 Typo. *Perf. 14***

| | | | | |
|---|---|---|---|---|
| **7** | A3 | 3pf brown | 1.25 | 1.25 |
| **8** | A3 | 5pf green | 7.50 | 1.25 |
| **9** | A3 | 10pf carmine | 25.00 | 3.25 |
| **10** | A3 | 20pf ultra | 1.50 | *3.25* |
| **11** | A3 | 25pf org & blk, *yel* | 1.75 | *16.00* |
| **12** | A3 | 30pf org & blk, *sal* | 1.75 | *20.00* |
| **13** | A3 | 40pf lake & blk | 1.75 | *23.00* |
| **14** | A3 | 50pf pur & blk, *sal* | 2.00 | *20.00* |
| **15** | A3 | 80pf lake & blk, *rose* | 3.75 | *27.50* |

**Engr.**

***Perf. 14½x14***

| | | | | |
|---|---|---|---|---|
| **16** | A4 | 1m carmine | 8.00 | *52.50* |
| **17** | A4 | 2m blue | 8.00 | *77.50* |
| **18** | A4 | 3m blk vio | 11.00 | *150.00* |
| **19** | A4 | 5m slate & car | 190.00 | *500.00* |
| | | *Nos. 7-19 (13)* | 263.25 | *895.50* |

Fake cancellations exist on Nos. 10-19.

The stamps of German New Guinea overprinted 'G.R.I.' and new values in British currency were all used in New Britain and are listed under that country as Nos. 1-29C, O1-2.

A5

A6

**Wmk. Lozenges (125)**

**1914-19 Typo. *Perf. 14***

| | | | | |
|---|---|---|---|---|
| **20** | A3 | 3pf brown ('19) | .80 | |
| **21** | A5 | 5pf green | 1.60 | |
| **22** | A5 | 10pf carmine | 1.60 | |

**Engr.**

***Perf. 14½x14***

| | | | | |
|---|---|---|---|---|
| **23** | A6 | 5m slate & carmine | 32.50 | |
| | | *Nos. 20-23 (4)* | 36.50 | |

Nos. 20-23 were never placed in use.

Nos. 21-23 have "NEUGUINEA" as one word without a hyphen.

## GERMAN SOUTH WEST AFRICA

'jər-mən 'sauth 'west 'a-fri-kə

LOCATION — In southwest Africa, bordering on the South Atlantic
GOVT. — German Colony
AREA — 322,450 sq. mi. (1913)
POP. — 94,372 (1913)
CAPITAL — Windhoek

The Colony was occupied by South African troops during World War I and in 1920 was mandated to the Union of South Africa by the League of Nations. See South West Africa in Vol. 6.

100 Pfennig = 1 Mark

Stamps of Germany Overprinted

**1897 Unwmk. *Perf. 13½x14½***

| | | | | |
|---|---|---|---|---|
| 1 | A9 | 3pf dark brown | 8.25 | *12.00* |
| *a.* | | 3pf yellow brown | 50.00 | *2,800.* |
| 2 | A9 | 5pf green | 4.50 | 4.75 |
| 3 | A10 | 10pf carmine | 21.00 | 20.00 |
| 4 | A10 | 20pf ultra | 5.75 | 5.25 |
| 5 | A10 | 25pf orange | 225.00 | *29,000.* |
| 6 | A10 | 50pf red brown | 225.00 | *29,000.* |
| | | *Nos. 1-4 (4)* | 39.50 | 42.00 |

Nos. 5 and 6 were prepared for issue but were not sent to the Colony.

Overprinted in Black on 2 lines

**1899**

| | | | | |
|---|---|---|---|---|
| 7 | A9 | 3pf dark brown | 4.00 | *12.00* |
| *a.* | | 3pf reddish brown | 52.50 | *160.00* |
| *b.* | | 3pf yellow brown | 7.00 | *12.00* |
| 8 | A9 | 5pf green | 3.25 | 3.25 |
| 9 | A10 | 10pf carmine | 3.25 | 4.00 |
| 10 | A10 | 20pf ultra | 11.50 | *15.00* |
| 11 | A10 | 25pf orange | 350.00 | 400.00 |
| 12 | A10 | 50pf red brown | 12.00 | 12.00 |

Kaiser's Yacht "Hohenzollern"
A3 A4

**1900 Typo. *Perf. 14***

| | | | | |
|---|---|---|---|---|
| 13 | A3 | 3pf brown | 4.00 | 1.60 |
| 14 | A3 | 5pf green | 20.00 | 1.60 |
| 15 | A3 | 10pf carmine | 14.00 | .80 |
| 16 | A3 | 20pf ultra | 30.00 | 1.50 |
| 17 | A3 | 25pf org & blk, *yel* | 1.50 | *5.50* |
| 18 | A3 | 30pf org & blk, *sal* | 72.50 | 2.75 |
| 19 | A3 | 40pf lake & blk | 1.75 | *3.25* |
| 20 | A3 | 50pf pur & blk, *sal* | 2.10 | 2.10 |
| 21 | A3 | 80pf lake & blk, *rose* | 2.10 | *9.00* |

**Engr.**
***Perf. 14½x14***

| | | | | |
|---|---|---|---|---|
| 22 | A4 | 1m carmine | 110.00 | 30.00 |
| 23 | A4 | 2m blue | 30.00 | *37.50* |
| 24 | A4 | 3m blk vio | 32.50 | *50.00* |
| 25 | A4 | 5m slate & car | 200.00 | 160.00 |
| | | *Nos. 13-25 (13)* | 520.45 | *305.60* |

**Wmk. Lozenges (125)**

**1906-19 Typo. *Perf. 14***

| | | | | |
|---|---|---|---|---|
| 26 | A3 | 3pf dk brn ('07) | .80 | *3.75* |
| 27 | A3 | 5pf green | .80 | *1.40* |
| *b.* | | Bklt. pane of 6 (2 #27, 4 #28) | 40.00 | |
| *c.* | | Booklet pane of 5 + label | *160.00* | |
| 28 | A3 | 10pf lt rose | 1.00 | *1.40* |
| *b.* | | Booklet pane of 5 + label | *400.00* | |
| 29 | A3 | 20pf ultra ('11) | 1.00 | *3.75* |
| 30 | A3 | 30pf org & blk, *pale yellow* ('11) | 16.00 | *52.50* |

**Engr.**
***Perf. 14½x14***

| | | | | |
|---|---|---|---|---|
| 31 | A4 | 1m carmine ('12) | 12.50 | *75.00* |
| 32 | A4 | 2m blue ('11) | 12.50 | *75.00* |
| 33 | A4 | 3m blk vio ('19) | 14.00 | |
| *a.* | | 3m gray violet | 40.00 | |
| 34 | A4 | 5m slate & car | 36.00 | *300.00* |
| *a.* | | 5m slate & rose red | 100.00 | |
| | | *Nos. 26-34 (9)* | 94.60 | 512.80 |

Nos. 33, 33a, 34a were never placed in use.
Forged cancellations are found on #30-32, 34.

## GERMAN STATES

'jər-mən 'stāts

**Watermarks**

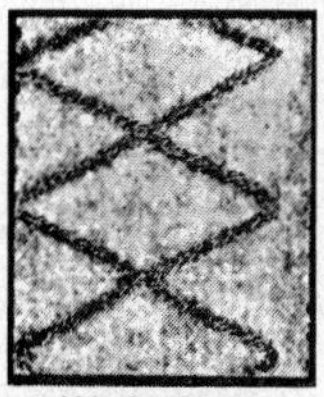

Wmk. 92 — 17mm wide

Wmk. 93 — 14mm wide

Wmk. 94 — Horiz. Wavy Lines Wide Apart

Wmk. 95v — Vert. Wavy Lines Close Together

Wmk. 95h — Horiz. Wavy Lines Close Together

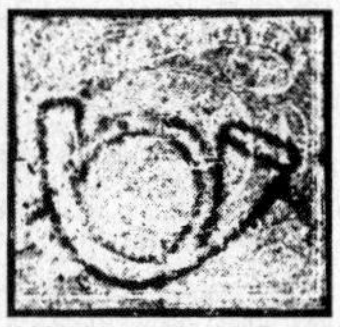

Wmk. 102 — Post Horn

Wmk. 116 — Crosses and Circles

Wmk. 128 — Wavy Lines

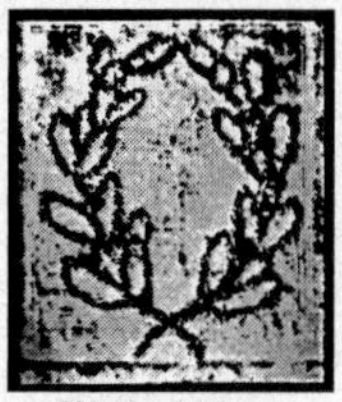

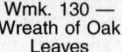

Wmk. 130 — Wreath of Oak Leaves

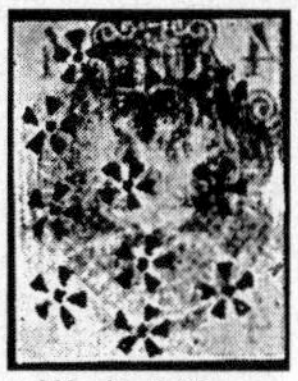

Wmk. 148 — Small Flowers

Wmk. 162 — Laurel Wreath

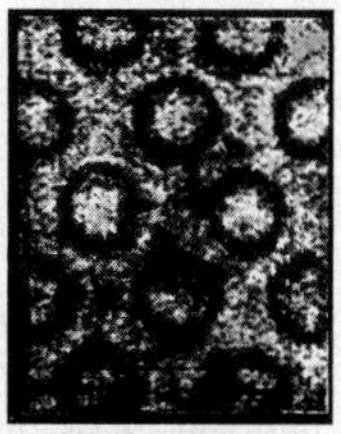

Wmk. 192 — Circles

## BADEN

LOCATION — In southwestern Germany
GOVT. — Former Grand Duchy
AREA — 5,817 sq. mi.
POP. — 1,432,000 (1864)
CAPITAL — Karlsruhe (Principal city)

Baden was a member of the German Confederation. In 1870 it became part of the German Empire.

60 Kreuzer = 1 Gulden

Values for unused stamps are for examples with original gum as defined in the catalogue introduction except for Nos. 1-9 which are valued without gum. Very fine examples of Nos. 1-9 will have one or two margins touching the framelines due to the very narrow spacing of the stamps on the plates. Stamps with margins clear of the framelines on all four sides are scarce and sell for considerably more.

A1

**1851-52 Unwmk. Typo. *Imperf.***

| | | | | |
|---|---|---|---|---|
| 1 | A1 | 1kr blk, *dk buff* | 275.00 | 250.00 |
| 2 | A1 | 3kr blk, *yellow* | 140.00 | 16.00 |
| 3 | A1 | 6kr blk, *yel grn* | 440.00 | 45.00 |
| 4 | A1 | 9kr blk, *lil rose* | 90.00 | 24.00 |
| | | *Nos. 1-4 (4)* | 945.00 | 335.00 |

**Thin Paper (First Printing, 1851)**

| | | | | |
|---|---|---|---|---|
| *1a* | A1 | 1kr black, *buff* | 2,000. | 800.00 |
| *2a* | A1 | 3kr black, *orange* | 675.00 | 35.00 |
| *3a* | A1 | 6kr black, *blue green* | 2,250. | 90.00 |
| *4a* | A1 | 9kr black, *deep rose* | 2,800. | 160.00 |

No. 4b

| | | | | |
|---|---|---|---|---|
| *4b* | A1 | 9kr black, *bl grn* (error) | | 1,300,000. |

**1853-58**

| | | | | |
|---|---|---|---|---|
| 6 | A1 | 1kr black | 160.00 | 27.50 |
| *a.* | | Tête bêche gutter pair | | *40,000.* |
| 7 | A1 | 3kr black, *green* | 160.00 | 14.00 |
| 8 | A1 | 3kr black, *bl* ('58) | 675.00 | 30.00 |
| *a.* | | Printed on both sides | | |
| 9 | A1 | 6kr black, *yellow* | 250.00 | 27.50 |
| | | *Nos. 6-9 (4)* | 1,245. | 99.00 |

*Reissues (1865) of Nos. 1, 2, 3, 6, 7 and 8 exist on thick paper and No. 9 on thin paper; the color of the last is brighter than that of the original.*

Coat of Arms
A2 A3

**1860-62 *Perf. 13½***

| | | | | |
|---|---|---|---|---|
| 10 | A2 | 1kr black | 80.00 | 30.00 |
| 12 | A2 | 3kr ultra ('61) | 90.00 | 20.00 |
| *a.* | | 3kr Prussian blue | 290.00 | 50.00 |
| 13 | A2 | 6kr red org ('61) | 100.00 | 72.50 |
| *a.* | | 6kr yellow orange ('62) | 175.00 | 80.00 |
| 14 | A2 | 9kr rose ('61) | 250.00 | 190.00 |
| | | *Nos. 10-14 (4)* | 520.00 | 312.50 |

Examples of Nos. 10-14 and 18 with all perforations intact sell for considerably more.

**1862 *Perf. 10***

| | | | | |
|---|---|---|---|---|
| 15 | A2 | 1kr black | 65.00 | 80.00 |
| *a.* | | 1kr silver gray | | *6,600.* |
| 16 | A2 | 6kr Prus bl ('62) | 140.00 | 72.50 |
| 17 | A2 | 9kr brown | 90.00 | 72.50 |
| *a.* | | 9kr dark brown | 350.00 | 275.00 |

***Perf. 13½***

| | | | | |
|---|---|---|---|---|
| 18 | A3 | 3kr rose | 2,500. | 375.00 |

**1862-65 *Perf. 10***

| | | | | |
|---|---|---|---|---|
| 19 | A3 | 1kr black ('64) | 50.00 | 15.00 |
| *a.* | | 1kr silver gray | | *2,250.* |
| 20 | A3 | 3kr rose | 50.00 | 4.00 |
| *a.* | | Imperf. | *100,000.* | *40,000.* |
| 22 | A3 | 6kr ultra ('65) | 11.00 | *25.00* |
| *a.* | | 6kr Prussian blue ('64) | *575.00* | 65.00 |
| 23 | A3 | 9kr brn ('64) | 16.00 | 30.00 |
| *a.* | | 9kr bister | 375.00 | 90.00 |
| *b.* | | Printed on both sides | | *6,500.* |
| 24 | A3 | 18kr green | 400.00 | 575.00 |
| 25 | A3 | 30kr deep orange | 32.50 | *2,250.* |
| *a.* | | 30kr yellow orange | 140.00 | *2,400.* |

Forged cancellations are known on #25.

A4

**1868**

| | | | | |
|---|---|---|---|---|
| 26 | A4 | 1kr green | 4.00 | *9.00* |
| 27 | A4 | 3kr rose | 2.50 | 4.00 |
| 28 | A4 | 7kr dull blue | 20.00 | *35.00* |
| *a.* | | 7kr sky blue | 42.50 | *92.50* |
| | | *Nos. 26-28 (3)* | 26.50 | 48.00 |

Forged cancellations are known on #28a.
The postage stamps of Baden were superseded by those of the German Empire on Jan. 1, 1872, but Official stamps were used during the year 1905.

**Stamps of the Baden sector of the French Occupation Zone of Germany, issued in 1947-49, are listed under Germany, Occupation Issues.**

### RURAL POSTAGE DUE STAMPS

RU1

**1862 Unwmk. *Perf. 10***
**Thin Paper**

| | | | | |
|---|---|---|---|---|
| LJ1 | RU1 | 1kr blk, *yellow* | 5.00 | *325.00* |
| *a.* | | Thick paper | 140.00 | *600.00* |
| LJ2 | RU1 | 3kr blk, *yellow* | 2.75 | *125.00* |
| *a.* | | Thick paper | 110.00 | *400.00* |
| LJ3 | RU1 | 12kr blk, *yellow* | 35.00 | *20,000.* |
| *a.* | | Half used as 6kr on cover | | *25,000.* |

*b.* Quarter used as 3kr on cover —
*Nos. LJ1-LJ3 (3)* 42.75 20,450.

On #LJ3, "LAND-POST" is a straight line. Paper of #LJ1a, LJ2a is darker yellow. Forged cancellations abound on #LJ1-LJ3.

**OFFICIAL STAMPS**

**See Germany Nos. OL16-OL21.**

## BAVARIA

LOCATION — In southern Germany
GOVT. — Kingdom
AREA — 30,562 sq. mi. (1920)
POP. — 7,150,146 (1919)
CAPITAL — Munich

Bavaria was a member of the German Confederation and became part of the German Empire in 1870. After World War I, it declared itself a republic. It lost its postal autonomy on Mar. 31, 1920.

60 Kreuzer = 1 Gulden
100 Pfennig = 1 Mark (1874)

Values for unused stamps are for examples with original gum as defined in the catalogue introduction. Unused examples of the 1849-78 issues without gum sell for about 50-60% of the figures quoted.

A1

Broken Circle — A1a

**1849 Unwmk. Typo. *Imperf.***
1 A1 1kr black 1,000. *2,000.*
*a.* deep black 2,800. *2,900.*
*b.* Tête bêche pair *125,000.*

**With Silk Thread**
2 A1a 3kr blue 60.00 3.50
*a.* 3kr greenish blue 60.00 3.50
*b.* 3kr deep blue 60.00 3.50
3 A1a 6kr brown *7,000.* 240.00

No. 1 exists with silk thread, from a single proof sheet, value about $4,000.

Complete circle — A2

Coat of Arms — A3

**1850-58 With Silk Thread**
4 A2 1kr pink 95.00 22.50
5 A2 6kr brown 50.00 6.50
*a.* Half used as 3kr on cover *16,000.*
6 A2 9kr yellow green 65.00 16.00
*a.* 9kr blue green ('53) *11,000.* 150.00
7 A2 12kr red ('58) 150.00 *140.00*
8 A2 18kr yel ('54) 140.00 *190.00*
*Nos. 4-8 (5)* 500.00 375.00

**1862**
9 A2 1kr yellow 70.00 20.00
10 A1a 3kr rose 140.00 3.50
*a.* 3kr carmine 52.50 5.25
11 A2 6kr blue 70.00 12.00
*a.* 6kr ultra *2,400.* *9,000.*
*b.* Half used as 3kr on cover *10,000.*
12 A2 9kr bister 110.00 16.00
13 A2 12kr yel grn 95.00 65.00
*a.* Half used as 6kr on cover *32,000.*
14 A2 18kr ver red 875.00 140.00
*a.* 18kr pale red 190.00 *450.00*
*Nos. 9-14 (6)* 1,360. 256.50

No. 11a was not put in use.

**1867-68 Embossed**
15 A3 1kr yel grn 75.00 12.00
*a.* 1kr dark blue green 300.00 52.50
16 A3 3kr rose 70.00 2.40
*a.* Printed on both sides *5,000.*
17 A3 6kr ultra 45.00 19.00
*a.* Half used as 3kr on cover *75,000.*
18 A3 6kr bis ('68) 80.00 50.00
*a.* Half used as 3kr on cover *32,000.*
19 A3 7kr ultra ('68) 400.00 16.00
20 A3 9kr bister 45.00 35.00
21 A3 12kr lilac 350.00 95.00
22 A3 18kr red 140.00 175.00
*Nos. 15-22 (8)* 1,205. 404.40

The paper of the 1867-68 issues often shows ribbed or laid lines.

**1870-72 Wmk. 92 *Perf. 11½***
**Without Silk Thread**
23 A3 1kr green 11.00 1.60
24 A3 3kr rose 24.00 1.25
25 A3 6kr bister 30.00 27.50
26 A3 7kr ultra 3.50 *4.50*
*a.* 7kr Prussian blue 19.00 11.00
27 A3 9kr pale brn ('72) 4.50 4.00
28 A3 10kr yellow 5.50 *13.50*
29 A3 12kr lilac 1,200. *4,800.*
30 A3 18kr dull brick red 12.00 *14.50*
*b.* 18kr dark brick red 225.00 62.50

The paper of the 1870-75 issues frequently appears to be laid with the lines either close or wide apart.
See Nos. 33-37.
*Reprints exist.*

**Wmk. 93**
*23a* A3 1kr green 100.00 9.50
*24a* A3 3kr rose 95.00 2.40
*25a* A3 6kr bister 175.00 70.00
*26b* A3 7kr ultra 140.00 35.00
*27a* A3 9kr pale brown 290.00 *475.00*
*28a* A3 10kr yellow 240.00 *360.00*
*29a* A3 12kr lilac 360.00 *1,125.*
*30a* A3 18kr dull brick red 300.00 190.00
*c.* 18kr dark brick red 400.00 225.00

A4

A5

**1874-75 Wmk. 92 *Imperf.***
31 A4 1m violet 640.00 80.00

***Perf. 11½***
32 A4 1m violet ('75) 200.00 50.00

See Nos. 46-47, 54-57, 73-76.

**1875 Wmk. 94**
33 A3 1kr green .80 *24.00*
34 A3 3kr rose .80 *8.00*
35 A3 7kr ultra 5.25 *275.00*
36 A3 10kr yellow 30.00 *250.00*
37 A3 18kr red 24.00 *60.00*
*Nos. 33-37 (5)* 60.85 617.00

**1876-78 Embossed *Perf. 11½***
38 A5 3pf lt grn 35.00 1.60
39 A5 5pf dk grn 90.00 13.00
40 A5 5pf lilac ('78) 160.00 20.00
41 A5 10pf rose 190.00 1.25
42 A5 20pf ultra 190.00 3.25
43 A5 25pf yel brn 175.00 6.50
44 A5 50pf scarlet 55.00 7.25
45 A5 50pf brn ('78) 800.00 27.50
46 A4 1m violet 1,900. 90.00
47 A4 2m orange 24.00 9.50

The paper of the 1876-78 issue often shows ribbed lines.
See Nos. 48-53, 58-72. For overprints and surcharge see Nos. 237, O1-O5.

**1881-1906 Wmk. 95v *Perf. 11½***
48 A5 3pf green 12.00 .80
*a.* Imperf. 400.00 *2,000.*
49 A5 5pf lilac 17.50 1.25
50 A5 10pf carmine 12.50 .65
*a.* Imperf. *400.00* 2,000.
51 A5 20pf ultramarine 13.00 .80
52 A5 25pf yellow brown 125.00 3.50
53 A5 50pf deep brown 145.00 3.25
54 A4 1m rose lil ('00) 225.00 1.40
*a.* 1m brownish lilac, toned paper 62.50 3.00
55 A4 2m orange ('01) 5.50 *8.00*
*a.* Toned paper ('90) 90.00 13.00
56 A4 3m olive gray ('00) 24.00 *30.00*
*a.* White paper ('06) 175.00 *500.00*
57 A4 5m yellow green ('00) 24.00 *30.00*
*a.* White paper ('06) 150.00 *375.00*
*Nos. 48-57 (10)* 603.50 79.65

Nos. 54-55 are on white paper. Nos. 56-57 are on toned paper. A 2m lilac was not regularly issued.

**1888-1900 Wmk. 95h *Perf. 14½***
58 A5 2pf gray ('00) 2.40 .55
59 A5 3pf green 9.25 2.10
60 A5 3pf brown ('00) .30 *.65*
61 A5 5pf lilac 24.00 5.50
62 A5 5pf dk grn ('00) .30 *.65*
63 A5 10pf carmine .40 *.80*
64 A5 20pf ultra .40 *.80*
65 A5 25pf yel brn 32.50 6.75
66 A5 25pf orange ('00) .60 *1.10*
67 A5 30pf ol grn ('00) .80 *1.40*
68 A5 40pf yellow ('00) .80 *1.10*
69 A5 50pf dp brn 60.00 6.75
70 A5 50pf maroon ('00) .50 *1.60*
71 A5 80pf lilac ('00) 3.25 *4.00*
*Nos. 58-71 (14)* 193.00 33.75

Nos. 59, 61, 65, 69 and 70 are on toned paper; Nos. 67-68 on white.

**1888-99 Toned Paper**
*58a* A5 2pf gray ('99) 12.00 5.25
*60a* A5 3pf dk ocher brn ('90) 9.25 .40
*62a* A5 5pf dk green ('90) 10.00 .65
*63a* A5 10pf car red 6.75 .80
*b.* Imperf. 72.50 *175.00*
*64a* A5 20pf ultra 10.00 1.25
*66a* A5 25pf org ('90) 16.50 1.60
*70a* A5 50pf mar ('90) 47.50 2.40
*71a* A5 80pf lilac ('99) 32.50 12.00

**1911, Jan. 23 Wmk. 95v**
72 A5 5pf dark green .65 *13.50*

**1911, Jan. Wmk. 95h *Perf. 11½***
73 A4 1m rose lilac 4.00 *27.50*
74 A4 2m orange 17.00 *37.50*
75 A4 3m olive gray 17.00 *57.50*
76 A4 5m pale yel grn 17.00 *57.50*
*Nos. 73-76 (4)* 55.00 180.00

See note after No. 91 concerning used values.

A6

A7

A8

Prince Regent Luitpold

***Perf. 14x14½***
**1911 Wmk. 95h Litho.**
77 A6 3pf brn, *gray brn* .30 .30
*a.* "911" for "1911" *325.00* *325.00*
78 A6 5pf dk grn, *grn* .30 .30
*a.* Tête bêche pair 4.50 *10.50*
*b.* Booklet pane of 4 + 2 labels 100.00 *150.00*
*c.* Bklt. pane of 5 + label 225.00 *375.00*
*d.* Bklt. pane of 6 35.00
79 A6 10pf scar, *buff* .30 .30
*a.* Tête bêche pair 5.75 *62.50*
*b.* "911" for "1911" 15.00 15.00
*d.* Booklet pane of 5 + label 65.00 30.00
80 A6 20pf dp bl, *bl* 2.00 .75
81 A6 25pf vio brn, *buff* 3.25 1.25

***Perf. 11½***
**Wmk. 95v**
82 A7 30pf org buff, *buff* 2.00 1.25
83 A7 40pf ol grn, *buff* 3.25 1.25
84 A7 50pf cl, *gray brn* 3.25 *3.25*
84A A7 60pf dk grn, *buff* 3.25 *3.25*
85 A7 80pf vio, *gray brn* 7.00 *10.00*
86 A8 1m brn, *gray brn* 3.25 *4.00*
87 A8 2m dk grn, *grn* 4.75 *12.00*
88 A8 3m lake, *buff* 13.00 *55.00*
89 A8 5m dk bl, *buff* 13.00 *45.00*
90 A8 10m org, *yel* 25.00 *65.00*
91 A8 20m blk brn, *yel* 25.00 *32.50*
*Nos. 77-91 (16)* 128.90 *235.40*

90th birthday of Prince Regent Luitpold.
All values exist in 2 types except No. 84A.
Nos. 77-84, 85-91 exist imperf.
**Used values:** Nos. 73-76 and 77-91 often were canceled en masse for accounting purposes. These cancels are perfectly clear, and used values are for stamps canceled thus. Postally used examples are worth about twice as much.

Prince Regent Luitpold — A9

**1911, June 10 Unwmk.**
92 A9 5pf grn, yel & blk .80 *1.40*
*b.* Horiz. pair, imperf. btwn. 140.00 *225.00*
93 A9 10pf rose, yel & blk 1.25 *2.40*
*b.* Pair, imperf. between 140.00 *225.00*

Silver Jubilee of Prince Regent Luitpold.

Used values of Nos. 94-275, B1-B3 are for postally used stamps. Canceled-to-order stamps, which abound, sell for same prices as unused.

A10

A11

King Ludwig III
A12

A13

***Perf. 14x14½***
**1914-20 Wmk. 95h Photo.**
94 A10 2pf gray ('18) .25 *2.00*
95 A10 3pf brown .25 *2.00*
96 A10 5pf yellow grn 1.10 *2.00*
*a.* 5pf dark green 1.10 *2.00*
*b.* Tête bêche pair 3.50 *16.50*
*c.* Booklet pane of 5 + 1 label 16.00 *60.00*
97 A10 7½pf dp green ('16) .25 *2.00*
*a.* Tête bêche pair 2.40 *11.00*
*b.* Booklet pane of 6 16.00
98 A10 10pf vermilion 1.40 *2.00*
*a.* Tête bêche pair 3.50 *16.50*
*b.* Booklet pane of 5 + 1 label 16.00 *60.00*
99 A10 10pf car rose ('16) .25 *2.00*
100 A10 15pf ver ('16) .25 *2.00*
*a.* Tête bêche pair 2.40 *11.00*
*b.* Booklet pane of 5 + 1 label 6.75 *24.00*
101 A10 15pf car ('20) 1.50 *27.50*
102 A10 20pf blue .25 *2.00*
103 A10 25pf gray .25 *2.00*
104 A10 30pf orange 1.25 *2.00*
105 A10 40pf olive grn .25 *2.00*
106 A10 50pf red brn .25 *2.00*
107 A10 60pf blue grn .80 *2.00*
108 A10 80pf violet .25 *2.00*

***Perf. 11½***
**Wmk. 95v**
109 A11 1m brown .25 *2.00*
110 A11 2m violet .25 *2.75*
111 A11 3m scarlet .40 *5.50*

**Wmk. 95h**
112 A12 5m deep blue .55 *20.00*
113 A12 10m yellow grn 1.75 *55.00*
114 A12 20m brown 3.25 *100.00*
*Nos. 94-114 (21)* 15.00 *240.75*

**No. 94 Surcharged**

**1916 Wmk. 95h *Perf. 14x14½***
115 A13 2½pf on 2pf gray .25 *2.00*
*a.* Double surcharge

**Ludwig III Types of 1914-20**

**1916-20 *Imperf.***
117 A10 2pf gray .25 *13.50*
118 A10 3pf brown .25 *14.50*
119 A10 5pf pale yel grn .25 *14.50*
120 A10 7½pf dp green .25 *14.50*
*a.* Tête bêche pair 3.25 *25.00*
121 A10 10pf car rose .25 *14.50*
122 A10 15pf vermilion .25 *14.50*
*a.* Tête bêche pair 3.25 *25.00*
123 A10 20pf blue .25 *14.50*
124 A10 25pf gray .25 *14.50*
125 A10 30pf orange .25 *14.50*
126 A10 40pf olive grn .25 *14.50*
127 A10 50pf red brown .25 *14.50*
128 A10 60pf dark green .25 *16.00*
129 A10 80pf violet .25 *16.00*
130 A11 1m brown .35 *16.00*
131 A11 2m violet .35 *20.00*
132 A11 3m scarlet .50 *27.50*
133 A12 5m deep blue .95 *45.00*
134 A12 10m yellow green 1.60 *65.00*
135 A12 20m brown 2.25 *110.00*
*Nos. 117-135 (19)* 9.25 474.00

**Stamps and Type of 1914-20 Overprinted**

a

b

**Wmk. 95h or 95v**

**1919** ***Perf. 14x14½***

**Overprint "a"**

| | | | | |
|---|---|---|---|---|
| **136** | A10 | 3pf brown | .25 | *2.00* |
| **137** | A10 | 5pf yellow grn | .25 | *2.00* |
| **138** | A10 | 7½pf deep green | .25 | *2.00* |
| **139** | A10 | 10pf car rose | .25 | *2.00* |
| **140** | A10 | 15pf vermilion | .25 | *2.00* |
| **141** | A10 | 20pf blue | .25 | *2.00* |
| **142** | A10 | 25pf gray | .25 | *2.00* |
| **143** | A10 | 30pf orange | .25 | *2.00* |
| **144** | A10 | 35pf orange | .25 | *2.50* |
| *a.* | | Without overprint | 100.00 | |
| **145** | A10 | 40pf olive grn | .25 | *2.00* |
| **146** | A10 | 50pf red brown | .25 | *2.00* |
| **147** | A10 | 60pf dark green | .25 | *2.00* |
| **148** | A10 | 75pf red brown | .25 | *2.00* |
| *a.* | | Without overprint | 22.50 | *225.00* |
| **149** | A10 | 80pf violet | .25 | *2.00* |

***Perf. 11½***

**Overprint "a"**

| | | | | |
|---|---|---|---|---|
| **150** | A11 | 1m brown | .25 | *2.00* |
| **151** | A11 | 2m violet | .25 | *2.00* |
| **152** | A11 | 3m scarlet | .40 | *4.75* |

**Overprint "b"**

| | | | | |
|---|---|---|---|---|
| **153** | A12 | 5m deep blue | .90 | *12.00* |
| **154** | A12 | 10m yellow green | .95 | *50.00* |
| **155** | A12 | 20m dk brown | 2.50 | *50.00* |
| | | *Nos. 136-155 (20)* | 8.75 | 149.25 |

Inverted overprints exist on Nos. 137-143, 145-147, 149. Value, each $15.

Double overprints exist on Nos. 137, 139, 143, 145, 150. Values, $30-$75.

***Imperf***

**Overprint "a"**

| | | | | |
|---|---|---|---|---|
| **156** | A10 | 3pf brown | .25 | *20.00* |
| **157** | A10 | 5pf pale yel grn | .25 | *20.00* |
| **158** | A10 | 7½pf dp green | .25 | *20.00* |
| **159** | A10 | 10pf car rose | .25 | *20.00* |
| **160** | A10 | 15pf vermilion | .25 | *20.00* |
| **161** | A10 | 20pf blue | .25 | *20.00* |
| **162** | A10 | 25pf gray | .25 | *20.00* |
| **163** | A10 | 30pf orange | .25 | *20.00* |
| **164** | A10 | 35pf orange | .25 | *20.00* |
| *a.* | | Without overprint | 13.00 | |
| **165** | A10 | 40pf olive grn | .25 | *20.00* |
| **166** | A10 | 50pf red brown | .25 | *20.00* |
| **167** | A10 | 60pf dk green | .25 | *20.00* |
| **168** | A10 | 75pf red brown | .25 | *20.00* |
| *a.* | | Without overprint | 190.00 | |
| **169** | A10 | 80pf violet | .25 | *20.00* |
| **170** | A11 | 1m brown | .25 | *24.00* |
| **171** | A11 | 2m violet | .50 | *27.50* |
| **172** | A11 | 3m scarlet | .70 | *45.00* |

**Overprint "b"**

| | | | | |
|---|---|---|---|---|
| **173** | A12 | 5m deep blue | .95 | *55.00* |
| **174** | A12 | 10m yellow grn | 1.40 | *80.00* |
| **175** | A12 | 20m brown | 2.75 | *80.00* |
| | | *Nos. 156-175 (20)* | 10.05 | 591.50 |

Stamps of Germany 1906-19 Overprinted

**1919** **Wmk. 125** ***Perf. 14, 14½***

| | | | | |
|---|---|---|---|---|
| **176** | A22 | 2½pf gray | .25 | *2.00* |
| **177** | A16 | 3pf brown | .25 | *2.00* |
| **178** | A16 | 5pf green | .25 | *2.00* |
| **179** | A22 | 7½pf orange | .25 | *2.00* |
| **180** | A16 | 10pf carmine | .25 | *2.00* |
| **181** | A22 | 15pf dk violet | .25 | *2.00* |
| *a.* | | Double overprint | 375.00 | *1,050.* |
| **182** | A16 | 20pf ultra | .25 | *2.00* |
| **183** | A16 | 25pf org & blk, *yel* | .25 | *2.00* |
| **184** | A22 | 35pf red brown | .25 | *2.00* |
| **185** | A16 | 40pf lake & blk | .40 | *2.00* |
| **186** | A16 | 75pf green & blk | .55 | *2.40* |
| **187** | A16 | 80pf lake & blk, *rose* | .55 | *3.25* |
| **188** | A17 | 1m car rose | 1.25 | *4.75* |
| **189** | A21 | 2m dull blue | 1.60 | *11.00* |
| **190** | A19 | 3m gray violet | 1.60 | *13.00* |
| **191** | A20 | 5m slate & car | 1.60 | *13.00* |
| *a.* | | Inverted overprint | *3,575.* | |
| | | *Nos. 176-191 (16)* | 9.80 | 67.40 |

**Bavarian Stamps of 1914-16 Overprinted**

c

d

**Wmk. 95h or 95v**

**1919-20** ***Perf. 14x14½***

**Overprint "c"**

| | | | | |
|---|---|---|---|---|
| **193** | A10 | 3pf brown | .25 | *2.00* |
| **194** | A10 | 5pf yellow grn | .25 | *2.00* |
| **195** | A10 | 7½pf dp green | .25 | *16.00* |
| **196** | A10 | 10pf car rose | .25 | *2.00* |
| **197** | A10 | 15pf vermilion | .25 | *2.00* |
| **198** | A10 | 20pf blue | .25 | *2.00* |
| **199** | A10 | 25pf gray | .25 | *2.00* |
| **200** | A10 | 30pf orange | .25 | *2.00* |
| **201** | A10 | 40pf olive grn | .25 | *14.50* |
| **202** | A10 | 50pf red brown | .25 | *2.00* |
| **203** | A10 | 60pf dk green | .25 | *14.50* |
| **204** | A10 | 75pf olive bister | .40 | *14.50* |
| **205** | A10 | 80pf violet | .25 | *3.50* |

***Perf. 11½***

**Overprint "c"**

| | | | | |
|---|---|---|---|---|
| **206** | A11 | 1m brown | .25 | *3.50* |
| **207** | A11 | 2m violet | .25 | *4.25* |
| **208** | A11 | 3m scarlet | .35 | *6.00* |

**Overprint "d"**

| | | | | |
|---|---|---|---|---|
| **209** | A12 | 5m deep blue | 1.10 | *17.50* |
| **210** | A12 | 10m yellow grn | 2.00 | *35.00* |
| **211** | A12 | 20m dk brown | 2.40 | *60.00* |
| | | *Nos. 193-211 (19)* | 9.75 | 205.25 |

***Imperf***

**Overprint "c"**

| | | | | |
|---|---|---|---|---|
| **212** | A10 | 3pf brown | .25 | *12.00* |
| **213** | A10 | 5pf pale yel grn | .25 | *12.00* |
| **214** | A10 | 7½pf deep green | .25 | *22.50* |
| **215** | A10 | 10pf car rose | .25 | *12.00* |
| **216** | A10 | 15pf vermilion | .25 | *12.00* |
| **217** | A10 | 20pf blue | .25 | *12.00* |
| *a.* | | Double overprint | 50.00 | |
| **218** | A10 | 25pf gray | .25 | *12.00* |
| **219** | A10 | 30pf orange | .25 | *13.50* |
| **220** | A10 | 40pf olive grn | .25 | *14.50* |
| **221** | A10 | 50pf red brn | .25 | *14.50* |
| **222** | A10 | 60pf dk green | .25 | *14.50* |
| **223** | A10 | 75pf olive bis | .25 | *35.00* |
| *a.* | | Without overprint | 5.00 | |
| **224** | A10 | 80pf violet | .25 | *14.50* |
| **225** | A11 | 1m brown | .25 | *22.50* |
| **226** | A11 | 2m violet | .25 | *22.50* |
| **227** | A11 | 3m scarlet | .65 | *27.50* |

**Overprint "d"**

| | | | | |
|---|---|---|---|---|
| **228** | A12 | 5m deep blue | 1.10 | *40.00* |
| **229** | A12 | 10m yellow grn | 2.00 | *70.00* |
| **230** | A12 | 20m brown | 2.40 | *110.00* |
| | | *Nos. 212-230 (19)* | 9.90 | 493.50 |

Ludwig Type of 1914, Printed in Various Colors and Surcharged

**1919** ***Perf. 11½***

| | | | | |
|---|---|---|---|---|
| **231** | A11 | 1.25m on 1m yel grn | .25 | *2.40* |
| **232** | A11 | 1.50m on 1m orange | .25 | *3.25* |
| **233** | A11 | 2.50m on 1m gray | .35 | *6.50* |
| | | *Nos. 231-233 (3)* | .85 | 12.15 |

**1920** ***Imperf.***

| | | | | |
|---|---|---|---|---|
| **234** | A11 | 1.25m on 1m yel grn | .25 | *35.00* |
| *a.* | | Without surcharge | 325.00 | |
| **235** | A11 | 1.50m on 1m org | .25 | *35.00* |
| *a.* | | Without surcharge | 6.50 | |
| **236** | A11 | 2.50m on 1m gray | .35 | *35.00* |
| *a.* | | Without surcharge | 6.50 | |
| | | *Nos. 234-236 (3)* | .85 | 105.00 |

No. 60 Surcharged in Dark Blue

**1920** ***Perf. 14½***

| | | | | |
|---|---|---|---|---|
| **237** | A5 | 20pf on 3pf brown | .25 | *1.25* |
| *a.* | | Inverted surcharge | 6.50 | *26.00* |
| *b.* | | Double surcharge | 80.00 | *190.00* |

Plowman
A14

"Electricity" Harnessing Light to a Water Wheel
A15

Sower — A16

Madonna and Child — A17

von Kaulbach's "Genius" — A18

TWENTY PFENNIG
Type I — Foot of "2" turns downward.
Type II — Foot of "2" turns upward.

***Perf. 14x14½***

**1920** **Wmk. 95h** **Typo.**

| | | | | |
|---|---|---|---|---|
| **238** | A14 | 5pf yellow grn | .25 | *2.40* |
| **239** | A14 | 10pf orange | .25 | *2.40* |
| **240** | A14 | 15pf carmine | .25 | *2.40* |
| **241** | A15 | 20pf violet (I) | .25 | *2.40* |
| *a.* | | 20pf violet (II) | 8.00 | *1,150.* |
| **242** | A15 | 30pf dp blue | .25 | *3.25* |
| **243** | A15 | 40pf brown | .25 | *2.40* |
| **244** | A16 | 50pf vermilion | .25 | *2.40* |
| **245** | A16 | 60pf blue green | .25 | *2.40* |
| **246** | A16 | 75pf lilac rose | .25 | *2.40* |

***Perf. 12x11½***

**Wmk. 95v**

| | | | | |
|---|---|---|---|---|
| **247** | A17 | 1m car & gray | .35 | *2.40* |
| **248** | A17 | 1¼m ultra & ol bis | .25 | *2.40* |
| **249** | A17 | 1½m dk grn & gray | .25 | *3.25* |
| **250** | A17 | 2½m blk & gray | .25 | *32.50* |

***Perf. 11½x12***

**Wmk. 95h**

| | | | | |
|---|---|---|---|---|
| **251** | A18 | 3m pale blue | .55 | *14.50* |
| **252** | A18 | 5m orange | .55 | *14.50* |
| **253** | A18 | 10m deep green | .95 | *25.00* |
| **254** | A18 | 20m black | 1.40 | *32.50* |
| | | *Nos. 238-254 (17)* | 6.80 | 149.50 |

**Imperf. Pairs**

| | | | | |
|---|---|---|---|---|
| *238a* | A14 | 5pf yellow grn | 55.00 | *350.00* |
| *239a* | A14 | 10pf orange | 125.00 | |
| *241b* | A15 | 20pf violet (I) | 55.00 | |
| *243a* | A15 | 40pf brown | 110.00 | |
| *244a* | A16 | 50pf vermilion | 32.50 | |
| *245a* | A16 | 60pf blue green | 37.50 | |
| *246a* | A16 | 75pf lilac rose | 37.50 | |
| *247a* | A17 | 1m car & gray | 6.50 | *26.00* |
| *248a* | A17 | 1¼m ultra & ol bis | 6.50 | *26.00* |
| *249a* | A17 | 1½m dk grn & gray | 6.50 | *26.00* |
| *250a* | A17 | 2½m blk & gray | 11.50 | *80.00* |
| *251a* | A18 | 3m pale blue | 11.50 | *65.00* |
| *252a* | A18 | 5m orange | 11.50 | *65.00* |
| *253a* | A18 | 10m deep green | 11.50 | *65.00* |
| *254a* | A18 | 20m black | 11.50 | *65.00* |

***Perf. 12x11½***

**1920** **Litho.** **Wmk. 95v**

| | | | | |
|---|---|---|---|---|
| **255** | A17 | 2½m black & gray | .50 | *65.00* |

On No. 255 the background dots are small, hazy and irregularly spaced. On No. 250 they are large, clear, round, white and regularly spaced in rows. The backs of the typo. stamps usually show a raised impression of parts of the design.

Stamps and Types of Preceding Issue Overprinted

**1920**

| | | | | |
|---|---|---|---|---|
| **256** | A14 | 5pf yellow green | .25 | *1.60* |
| *a.* | | Inverted overprint | 30.00 | |
| *b.* | | Imperf., pair | 37.50 | *375.00* |
| **257** | A14 | 10pf orange | .25 | *1.60* |
| *a.* | | Imperf., pair | 37.50 | *375.00* |
| *b.* | | Inverted overprint | 30.00 | *600.00* |
| **258** | A14 | 15pf carmine | .25 | *1.60* |
| *a.* | | Inverted overprint | 30.00 | |
| **259** | A15 | 20pf violet | .25 | *1.60* |
| *a.* | | Inverted overprint | 30.00 | *750.00* |
| *b.* | | Double overprint | 13.00 | |
| *c.* | | Imperf., pair | 50.00 | |
| **260** | A15 | 30pf deep blue | .25 | *1.60* |
| *a.* | | Inverted overprint | 30.00 | |
| *b.* | | Imperf., pair | 50.00 | *375.00* |
| **261** | A15 | 40pf brown | .25 | *1.60* |
| *a.* | | Inverted overprint | 30.00 | *750.00* |
| *b.* | | Imperf., pair | 50.00 | |
| **262** | A16 | 50pf vermilion | .25 | *2.40* |
| *a.* | | Inverted overprint | 30.00 | *900.00* |
| **263** | A16 | 60pf blue green | .50 | *1.40* |
| **264** | A16 | 75pf lilac rose | .40 | *5.25* |
| *a.* | | Inverted overprint | 30.00 | |
| **265** | A16 | 80pf dark blue | .40 | *2.75* |
| *a.* | | Without overprint | *100.00* | |
| *b.* | | Imperf., pair | 50.00 | |

Overprinted in Black or Red

| | | | | |
|---|---|---|---|---|
| **266** | A17 | 1m car & gray | .50 | *2.75* |
| *a.* | | Imperf., pair | 50.00 | *375.00* |
| *b.* | | Inverted overprint | 52.50 | |
| **267** | A17 | 1¼m ultra & ol bis | .50 | *2.75* |
| *a.* | | Imperf., pair | 47.50 | |
| **268** | A17 | 1½m dk grn & gray | .50 | *3.50* |
| *a.* | | Imperf., pair | 47.50 | |
| **269** | A17 | 2m vio & ol bis | .80 | *4.00* |
| *a.* | | Without overprint | 32.50 | |
| *b.* | | Imperf., pair | 50.00 | |
| **270** | A17 | 2½m (#250) (R) | .25 | *2.75* |
| *c.* | | Imperf., pair | 50.00 | |
| **270A** | A17 | 2½m (#255) (R) | .95 | *95.00* |
| *b.* | | Imperf., pair | 50.00 | |

Nos. 251-254 Overprinted

| | | | | |
|---|---|---|---|---|
| **271** | A18 | 3m pale blue | 2.75 | *8.75* |
| **272** | A18 | 4m dull red | 3.25 | *10.00* |
| *a.* | | Without overprint | 47.50 | |
| **273** | A18 | 5m orange | 2.75 | *6.50* |
| **274** | A18 | 10m dp green | 3.25 | *16.00* |
| **275** | A18 | 20m black | 6.00 | *13.00* |
| | | *Nos. 256-275 (21)* | 24.55 | 186.40 |

Nos. 256-275 were available for postage through all Germany, but were used almost exclusively in Bavaria.

**SEMI-POSTAL STAMPS**

Regular Issue of 1914-20 Surcharged in Black

**1919** **Wmk. 95h** ***Perf. 14x14½***

| | | | | |
|---|---|---|---|---|
| **B1** | A10 | 10pf + 5pf car rose | .40 | *2.00* |
| *a.* | | Inverted surcharge | 26.00 | *65.00* |
| *b.* | | Surcharge on back | 50.00 | |
| *c.* | | Imperf., pair | 325.00 | |
| **B2** | A10 | 15pf + 5pf ver | .40 | *2.00* |
| *a.* | | Inverted surcharge | 26.00 | *65.00* |
| *b.* | | Imperf., pair | *190.00* | |
| **B3** | A10 | 20pf + 5pf blue | .40 | *2.40* |
| *a.* | | Inverted surcharge | 26.00 | *65.00* |
| *b.* | | Imperf., pair | *375.00* | |
| | | *Nos. B1-B3 (3)* | 1.20 | 6.40 |

Surtax was for wounded war veterans.

## POSTAGE DUE STAMPS

D1

D2

### With Silk Thread

**1862 Typeset Unwmk. *Imperf.***

J1 D1 3kr black 125.00 *325.00*
a. "Empfange" 375.00 *1,000.*

### Without Silk Thread

**1870 Typo. Wmk. 93 *Perf. 11½***

J2 D1 1kr black 12.00 *800.00*
a. Wmk. 92 55.00 *1,750.*
J3 D1 3kr black 12.00 *475.00*
a. Wmk. 92 55.00 *960.00*

### Type of 1876 Regular Issue Overprinted in Red "Vom Empfänger zahlbar"

**1876 Wmk. 94**

J4 D2 3pf gray 16.00 *40.00*
J5 D2 5pf gray 10.00 *17.00*
J6 D2 10pf gray 3.25 1.25
a. Vert. half used as 5pf on cover *2,800.*
*Nos. J4-J6 (3)* 29.25 *58.25*

**1883 Wmk. 95v**

J7 D2 3pf gray 90.00 *100.00*
J8 D2 5pf gray 55.00 *70.00*
J9 D2 10pf gray 2.40 .80
a. "Empfanper" 140.00 140.00
b. "zahlhar" 80.00 80.00
c. Imperf. 95.00
*Nos. J7-J9 (3)* 147.40 *170.80*

**1895-1903 Wmk. 95h *Perf. 14½***

J10 D2 2pf gray .80 *2.40*
J11 D2 3pf gray ('03) .80 *2.50*
J12 D2 5pf gray ('03) 1.00 *1.75*
J13 D2 10pf gray ('03) .60 *.90*
*Nos. J10-J13 (4)* 3.20 *7.55*

**1888 Rose-toned Paper**

*J10a* D2 2pf gray 2.00 *4.75*
*J11a* D2 3pf gray 2.60 2.40
b. Inverted overprint 2,200.
*J12a* D2 5pf gray 2.60 2.60
*J13a* D2 10pf gray 2.60 1.25
b. As "a," double overprint *2,200.*
*Nos. J10a-J13a (4)* 9.80 11.00

No. J13b was used at Pirmasens.

### Surcharged in Red in Each Corner

**1895**

J14 D2 2pf on 3pf gray *150,000.*

Six used examples of No. J14 exist, all used in Aichach. There are two covers (each bearing two examples) and two loose stamps.

## OFFICIAL STAMPS

Nos. 77-81, 84, 95-96, 98-99, 102 perforated with a large E were issued for official use in 1912-16.

Regular Issue of 1888-1900 Overprinted

**1908 Wmk. 95h *Perf. 14½***

O1 A5 3pf dk brown (R) .75 *3.25*
O2 A5 5pf dk green (R) .25 .40
O3 A5 10pf carmine (G) .25 .40
O4 A5 20pf ultra (R) .50 .80
O5 A5 50pf maroon 4.50 *7.25*
*Nos. O1-O5 (5)* 6.25 *12.10*

Nos. O1-O5 were issued for the use of railway officials. "E" stands for "Eisenbahn."

Coat of Arms — O1

**1916-17 Typo. *Perf. 11½***

O6 O1 3pf bister brn .25 *.80*
O7 O1 5pf yellow grn .25 *.80*
O8 O1 7½pf grn, *grn* .25 *.50*
O9 O1 7½pf grn ('17) .25 *.80*
O10 O1 10pf deep rose .25 *.65*
O11 O1 15pf red, *buff* .30 *.50*
O12 O1 15pf red ('17) .25 *.80*
O13 O1 20pf dp bl, *bl* 2.00 *2.00*
O14 O1 20pf dp blue ('17) .25 *.65*
O15 O1 25pf gray .25 *.65*
O16 O1 30pf orange .25 *.65*
O17 O1 60pf dark green .25 *1.25*
O18 O1 1m dl vio, *gray* .95 *2.75*
O19 O1 1m maroon ('17) 2.75 *475.00*
*Nos. O6-O19 (14)* 8.50 487.80

Used values of Nos. O6-O69 are for postally used stamps. Canceled-to-order stamps, which abound, sell for same prices as unused.

Official Stamps and Type of 1916-17 Overprinted

**1918**

O20 O1 3pf bister brn .25 *13.50*
O21 O1 5pf yellow green .25 *2.00*
O22 O1 7½pf gray green .25 *13.00*
O23 O1 10pf deep rose .25 *2.25*
O24 O1 15pf red .25 *2.25*
O25 O1 20pf blue .25 *2.25*
O26 O1 25pf gray .25 *2.25*
O27 O1 30pf orange .25 *2.25*
O28 O1 35pf orange .25 *2.25*
O29 O1 50pf olive gray .25 *2.50*
O30 O1 60pf dark green .30 *13.50*
O31 O1 75pf red brown .35 *3.50*
O32 O1 1m dl vio, *gray* 1.10 *14.50*
O33 O1 1m maroon 4.00 *375.00*
*Nos. O20-O33 (14)* 8.25 451.00

O2

O3

O4

**1920 Typo. *Perf. 14x14½***

O34 O2 5pf yellow grn .25 *6.50*
O35 O2 10pf orange .25 *6.50*
O36 O2 15pf carmine .25 *6.50*
O37 O2 20pf violet .25 *6.50*
O38 O2 30pf dark blue .25 *7.25*
O39 O2 40pf bister .25 *7.25*

***Perf. 14½x14***

**Wmk. 95v**

O40 O3 50pf vermilion .25 *22.50*
O41 O3 60pf blue green .25 *9.50*
O42 O3 70pf dk violet .25 *27.50*
a. Imperf., pair 26.00
O43 O3 75pf deep rose .25 *35.00*
O44 O3 80pf dull blue .25 *35.00*
O45 O3 90pf olive green .25 *55.00*
O46 O4 1m dark brown .25 *50.00*
a. Imperf., pair 72.50
O47 O4 1¼m green .25 *65.00*
O48 O4 1½m vermilion .25 *65.00*
a. Imperf. pair 25.00
O49 O4 2½m deep blue .25 *70.00*
a. Imperf. pair 72.50
O50 O4 3m dark red .25 *100.00*
a. Imperf. pair 20.00
O51 O4 5m black 1.50 *125.00*
a. Imperf., pair 72.50
*Nos. O34-O51 (18)* 5.75 700.00

Stamps of Preceding Issue Overprinted

**1920, Apr. 1**

O52 O2 5pf yellow green .25 *3.25*
a. Imperf., pair 26.00
O53 O2 10pf orange .25 *1.90*
O54 O2 15pf carmine .25 *2.00*
O55 O2 20pf violet .25 *1.60*
O56 O2 30pf dark blue .25 *1.60*
O57 O2 40pf bister .25 *1.60*
O58 O3 50pf vermilion .25 *2.00*
a. Imperf., pair 26.00
O59 O3 60pf blue green .25 *1.60*
O60 O3 70pf dark violet 2.00 *2.75*
O61 O3 75pf deep rose .35 *1.40*
O62 O3 80pf dull blue .25 *1.40*
O63 O3 90pf olive green 1.60 *3.50*

### Similar Ovpt., Words 8mm apart

O64 O4 1m dark brown .25 *2.00*
a. Imperf., pair 26.00
O65 O4 1¼m green .25 *2.00*
O66 O4 1½m vermilion .25 *2.00*
O67 O4 2½m deep blue .25 *2.00*
a. Imperf., pair 37.50
O68 O4 3m dark red .25 *2.00*
O69 O4 5m black 8.75 *25.00*
*Nos. O52-O69 (18)* 16.20 59.60

Nos. O52-O69 could be used in all parts of Germany, but were almost exclusively used in Bavaria.

## BERGEDORF

LOCATION — A town in northern Germany.
POP. — 2,989 (1861)

Originally Bergedorf belonged jointly to the Free City of Hamburg and the Free City of Lübeck. In 1867 it was purchased by Hamburg.

16 Schillings = 1 Mark

Values for unused stamps are for examples with original gum as defined in the catalogue introduction. Copies without gum sell for about 40% of the figures quoted. Values for used stamps are for examples canceled with parallel bars. Copies bearing dated town postmarks sell for more.

Combined Arms of Lübeck and Hamburg
A1 A2 A3

A4

A5

**1861-67 Unwmk. Litho. *Imperf.***

1 A1 ½s blk, *pale bl* 45.00 *725.00*
a. ½s black, *blue* ('67) 125.00 *4,750.*
2 A3 1s blk, *white* 45.00 *375.00*
a. Tête bêche pair, vert. 225.00
b. Tête bêche pair, horiz. 300.00
3 A4 1½s blk, *yellow* 20.00 *1,350.*
a. Tête bêche pair *125.00*
4 A2 3s blue, *pink* 25.00 *2,000.*
5 A5 4s blk, *brown* 25.00 *2,250.*
*Nos. 1-5 (5)* 160.00 6,700.

Full margins Nos. 1-3 = 1½mm; No. 4 = ¾mm; No. 5 = 1mm. There are vertical dividing lines between stamps.

Counterfeit cancellations are plentiful.

No. 3 exists in a tête bêche gutter pair. Value, unused $310.

The ½s on violet and 3s on rose, listed previously, as well as 1s and 1½s on thick paper and 4s on light rose brown, come from proof sheets and were never placed in use. A 1½ "SCHILLINGE" (instead of SCHILLING) also exists only as a proof.

### REPRINTS

½ SCHILLING
*There is a dot in the upper part of the right branch of "N" of "EIN." The upper part of the shield is blank or almost blank. The horizontal bar of "H" in "HALBER" is generally defective.*

1 SCHILLING
*The "1" in the corners is generally with foot. The central horizontal bar of the "E" of "EIN" is separated from the vertical branch by a black line. The "A" of "POSTMARKE" has the horizontal bar incomplete or missing. The horizontal bar of the "H" of "SCHILLING" is separated from the vertical branches by a dark line at each side, sometimes the bar is missing.*

1½ SCHILLINGE
*There is a small triangle under the right side of the tower, exactly over the "R" of "POSTMARKE."*

3 SCHILLINGE
*The head of the eagle is not shaded. The horizontal bar of the second "E" of "BERGEDORF" is separated from the vertical branch by a thin line. There is generally a colored dot in the lower half of the "S" of "POSTMARKE."*

4 SCHILLINGE
*The upper part of the shield is blank or has two or three small dashes. In most of the reprints there is a diagonal dash across the wavy lines of the groundwork at the right of "I" and "E" of "VIER."*

*Reprints, value $1 each.*

These stamps were superseded by those of the North German Confederation in 1868.

## BREMEN

LOCATION — In northwestern Germany
AREA — 99 sq. mi.
POP. — 122,402 (1871)

Bremen was a Free City and member of the German Confederation. In 1870 it became part of the German Empire.

22 Grote = 10 Silbergroschen.

Values for unused stamps are for examples with original gum as defined in the catalogue introduction. Stamps without gum sell for about 50-60% the figures quoted.

Coat of Arms — A1

I

II

III

Type I. The central part of the scroll below the word Bremen is crossed by one vertical line.

Type II. The center of the scroll is crossed by two vertical lines.

Type III. The center of the scroll is crossed by three vertical lines.

**1855 Unwmk. Litho. *Imperf.***

**Horizontally Laid Paper**

1 A1 3gr black, *blue* 200.00 *290.00*

**Vertically Laid Paper**

1A A1 3gr black, *blue* 350.00 *550.00*

No. 1 can be found with parts of a papermaker's watermark, consisting of lilies. Value: unused $650; unused, no gum, $375; used $950.

See Nos. 9-10.

A2

A3

### FIVE GROTE

Type I. The shading at the left of the ribbon containing "funf Grote" runs downward from the shield.

Type II. The shading at the left of the ribbon containing "funf Grote" runs upward.

**1856-60 Wove Paper**

2 A2 5gr blk, *rose* 150.00 *300.00*
a. Printed on both sides 4,000.
b. "Marken" (not issued) 12.00
3 A2 7gr blk, *yel* ('60) 240.00 *725.00*
4 A3 5sgr green ('59) 275.00 *300.00*
a. Chalky paper 50.00 *1,500.*
b. 5sgr yellow green 125.00 *300.00*

See Nos. 6, 8, 12-13, 15.

A4

A5

**1861-63** ***Serpentine Roulette***

5 A4 2gr orange ('63) 400.00 *2,000.*
a. 2gr red orange 700.00 *3,000.*
b. Chalky paper 350.00 *2,800.*
c. as "a," chalky paper 700.00 *4,000.*
6 A2 5gr blk, *rose* ('62) 200.00 *175.00*
a. Horiz. pair, imperf between —
7 A5 10gr black 700.00 *850.00*
8 A3 5sgr yellow green ('63) 1,100. 175.00
a. Chalky paper 600.00 425.00
b. 5sgr green 925.00 210.00

See Nos. 11, 14.

**1863**

**Horizontally (H) or Vertically (V) Laid Paper**

9 A1 3gr blk, *blue* (V) 650.00 725.00
a. 3gr black, *blue* (H) 2,250. *4,000.*

**1866-67** ***Perf. 13***

10 A1 3gr black, *blue* 80.00 *325.00*

**Wove Paper**

11 A4 2gr orange 95.00 *325.00*
a. 2gr red orange 275.00 *500.00*
b. Horiz. pair, imperf. btwn. 2,800.
12 A2 5gr blk, *rose* 125.00 *325.00*
a. Horiz. pair, imperf. btwn. 1,250. —
13 A2 7gr blk, *yel* ('67) 150.00 *4,500.*
14 A5 10gr black ('67) 190.00 *1,125.*
15 A3 5sgr green 140.00 *3,750.*
a. 5sgr yellow green 450.00 175.00
b. As "a," chalky paper 450.00 275.00

The stamps of Bremen were superseded by those of the North German Confederation on Jan. 1, 1868.

## BRUNSWICK

LOCATION — In northern Germany
GOVT. — Former duchy
AREA — 1,417 sq. mi.
POP. — 349,367 (1880)
CAPITAL — Brunswick

Brunswick was a member of the German Confederation and, in 1870 became part of the German Empire.

12 Pfennigs = 1 Gutegroschen
30 Silbergroschen (Groschen) = 24 Gutegroschen = 1 Thaler

Values for unused stamps are for examples with original gum as defined in the catalogue introduction except for Nos. 1-3 which are valued without gum. Nos. 1-3 with original gum sell for much higher prices, and Nos. 4-26 without gum sell for about 50-60% of the figures quoted.

The "Leaping Saxon Horse" — A1

The ½gr has white denomination and "Gr" in right oval.

**1852 Unwmk. Typo.** ***Imperf.***

1 A1 1sgr rose 2,000. 300.00
2 A1 2sgr blue 1,450. 250.00
a. Half used as 1sgr on cover —
3 A1 3sgr vermilion 1,450. 250.00

See Nos. 4-11, 13-22.

**1853-63** **Wmk. 102**

4 A1 ¼ggr blk, *brn* ('56) 800.00 250.00
5 A1 ⅓sgr black ('56) 140.00 325.00
6 A1 ½gr blk, *grn* ('63) 25.00 *240.00*
7 A1 1sgr blk, *orange* 400.00 55.00
a. 1sgr black, *orange buff* 400.00 57.50
8 A1 1sgr blk, *yel* ('61) 400.00 50.00
a. Diagonal half used as ½sgr on cover *18,000.*
9 A1 2sgr blk, *blue* 325.00 65.00
a. Diagonal half used as 1sgr on cover *9,600.*
b. Vertical half used as 1sgr on cover *18,000.*
10 A1 3sgr blk, *rose* 475.00 72.50
11 A1 3sgr rose ('62) 600.00 200.00

A3

A4

**1857**

12 A3 Four ¼ggr blk, *brn* ('57) 40.00 95.00
a. Four ¼ggr blk, *yel brown* — 210.00

The bister on white paper was not issued. Value $6.

**1864** ***Serpentine Roulette 16***

13 A1 ⅓sgr black 475.00 *2,250.*
14 A1 ½gr blk, *green* 190.00 *3,000.*
15 A1 1sgr blk, *yellow* *2,850.* *1,425.*
16 A1 1sgr yellow 400.00 145.00
17 A1 2sgr blk, *blue* 400.00 340.00
a. Half used as 1sgr on cover *12,000.*
18 A1 3sgr rose 800.00 525.00

***Rouletted 12***

20 A1 1sgr blk, *yellow* *11,000.*
21 A1 1sgr yellow 600.00 325.00
22 A1 3sgr rose — 2,500.

Nos. 13, 16, 18, 21-22 are on white paper. Faked roulettes of Nos. 13-22 exist.

***Serpentine Roulette***

**1865 Embossed Unwmk.**

23 A4 ⅓gr black 27.50 *350.00*
24 A4 1gr carmine 2.50 *50.00*
25 A4 2gr ultra 8.75 *125.00*
a. 2gr gray blue 8.75 *125.00*
c. Half used as 1sgr on cover *20,000.*
26 A4 3gr brown 7.25 *160.00*
*Nos. 23-26 (4)* 46.00 685.00

Faked cancellations of Nos. 5-26 exist.

**Imperf., Pairs**

*23a* A4 ⅓gr 110.00
*24a* A4 1gr 32.50
*25b* A4 2gr 92.50
*26a* A4 3gr 110.00

Stamps of Brunswick were superseded by those of the North German Confederation on Jan. 1, 1868.

## HAMBURG

LOCATION — Northern Germany
GOVT. — A former Free City
AREA — 160 sq. mi.
POP. — 453,869 (1880)
CAPITAL — Hamburg

Hamburg was a member of the German Confederation and became part of the German Empire in 1870.

16 Schillings = 1 Mark

Values for unused stamps are for examples with original gum as defined in the catalogue introduction. Stamps without gum sell for about 50-60% of the figures quoted.

Value Numeral on Arms — A1

**1859 Typo. Wmk. 128** ***Imperf.***

1 A1 ½s black 125.00 *600.00*
2 A1 1s brown 125.00 *95.00*
3 A1 2s red 125.00 *100.00*
4 A1 3s blue 125.00 *125.00*
5 A1 4s yellow green 50.00 *1,450.*
a. 4s green 125.00 *1,300.*
b. Double impression —
6 A1 7s orange 100.00 40.00
7 A1 9s yellow 200.00 *2,000.*

See Nos. 13-21.

A2

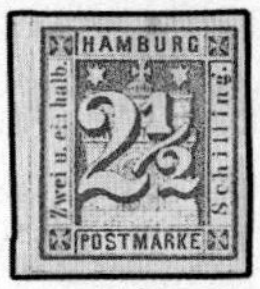
A3

**1864** **Litho.**

9 A2 1¼s gray 90.00 80.00
a. 1¼s lilac 150.00 85.00
b. 1¼s red lilac 125.00 72.50
c. 1¼s blue 425.00 *850.00*
d. 1¼s greenish gray 110.00 *200.00*
12 A3 2½s green 140.00 *140.00*

See Nos. 22-23.

*The 1¼s and 2½s have been reprinted on watermarked and unwatermarked paper.*

**1864-65 Typo.** ***Perf. 13½***

13 A1 ½s black 6.50 *12.00*
a. Horiz. pair, imperf between 72.50
14 A1 1s brown 13.00 *17.50*
a. Half used as ½s on cover *16,000.*
b. Horiz. pair, imperf between 450.00 *650.00*
15 A1 2s red 16.00 *20.00*
17 A1 3s ultra 40.00 40.00
a. Imperf., pair 140.00
b. Horiz. pair, imperf. vert. —
c. 3s blue 42.50 29.00
18 A1 4s green 10.00 20.00
19 A1 7s orange 160.00 125.00
20 A1 7s vio ('65) 11.50 16.00
a. Imperf, pair 275.00
21 A1 9s yellow 25.00 *2,000.*
a. Vert. pair, imperf btwn. 400.00

**Litho.**

22 A2 1¼s lilac 95.00 12.00
a. 1¼s red lilac 95.00 12.00
b. 1¼s violet 95.00 12.00
23 A3 2½s yel grn, blurred printing 125.00 35.00
a. 2½s blue green 125.00 35.00

*The 1¼s has been reprinted on watermarked and unwatermarked paper; the 2½s on unwatermarked paper.*

A4

A5

***Rouletted 10***

**1866 Unwmk. Embossed**

24 A4 1¼s violet 40.00 35.00
a. 1¼s red violet 72.50 72.50
25 A5 1½s rose 9.50 *125.00*

**REPRINTS**

*1¼s: The rosettes between the words of the inscription have a well-defined open circle in the center of the originals, while in the reprints this circle is filled up.*

*In the upper part of the top of the "g" of "Schilling", there is a thin vertical line which is missing in the reprints.*

*The two lower lines of the triangle in the upper left corner are of different thicknesses in the originals while in the reprints they are of equal thickness.*

*The labels at the right and left containing the inscriptions are 2¾mm in width in the originals while they are 2½mm in reprints.*

*1½s: The originals are printed on thinner paper than the reprints. This is easily seen by turning the stamps over, when on the originals the color and impression will clearly show through, which is not the case in the reprints.*

*The vertical stroke of the upper part of the "g" in Schilling is very short on the originals, scarcely crossing the top line, while in the reprints it almost touches the center of the "g."*

*The lower part of the "g" of Schilling in the originals, barely touches the inner line of the frame, in some stamps it does not touch it at all, while in the reprints the whole stroke runs into the inner line of the frame.*

A6

**1867 Typo. Wmk. 128** ***Perf. 13½***

26 A6 2½s dull green 12.50 *80.00*
a. 2½s dark green 65.00 *100.00*
b. Imperf., pair 225.00
c. Horiz. pair, imperf between 92.50

Forged cancellations exist on almost all stamps of Hamburg, especially on Nos. 4, 7, 21 and 25.

Nos. 1-23 and 26 exist without watermark, but they come from the same sheets as the watermarked stamps.

The stamps of Hamburg were superseded by those of the North German Confederation on Jan. 1, 1868.

## HANOVER

LOCATION — Northern Germany
GOVT. — A former Kingdom
AREA — 14,893 sq. mi.
POP. — 3,191,000
CAPITAL — Hanover

Hanover was a member of the German Confederation and became in 1866 a province of Prussia.

10 Pfennigs = 1 Groschen
24 Gute Groschen = 1 Thaler
30 Silbergroschen = 1 Thaler (1858)

Values for unused stamps are for examples with original gum as defined in the catalogue introduction. Examples without gum sell for about 50-60% of the figures quoted.

Coat of Arms
A1 A2

**Wmk. Square Frame**

**1850 Rose Gum Typo.** ***Imperf.***

1 A1 1g g blk, *gray bl* 4,000. 60.00

See Nos. 2, 11.

*The reprints have white gum and no watermark.*

**1851-55** **Wmk. 130**

2 A1 1g g blk, *gray grn* 95.00 9.00
a. 1g g black, *yellow green* 950.00 32.50
3 A2 1/30th blk, *salmon* 125.00 50.00
a. 1/30th black, *crimson* ('55) 125.00 50.00
b. Bisect on cover —
5 A2 1/15th blk, *gray bl* 190.00 80.00
a. Bisect on cover —
6 A2 1/10th blk, *yellow* 240.00 70.00
a. 1/10th black, *orange* 240.00 65.00
*Nos. 2-6 (4)* 650.00 209.00

Bisects Nos. 3b, 5a, 12a and 13a were used for ½g.

See Nos. 8, 12-13.

*The 1/10th has been reprinted on unwatermarked paper, with white gum.*

Crown and Numeral — A3

**1853** **Wmk. 130**

7 A3 3pf rose 475.00 325.00

See Nos. 9, 16-17, 25.

*The reprints of No. 7 have white gum.*

**Fine Network in Second Color**

**1855** **Unwmk.**

8 A2 1/10th blk & org 240.00 160.00
a. 1/10th black & yellow 400.00 240.00

No. 8 with olive yellow network and other values with fine network are essays.

**Large Network in Second Color**

**1856-57**

9 A3 3pf rose & blk 325.00 275.00
a. 3pf rose & gray 425.00 360.00

| | | | | |
|---|---|---|---|---|
| 11 | A1 | 1g g blk & grn | 80.00 | 12.00 |
| 12 | A2 | 1/30th blk & rose | 160.00 | 32.50 |
| *a.* | | Bisect on cover | | *13,500.* |
| 13 | A2 | 1/15th blk & bl | 125.00 | 72.50 |
| *a.* | | Bisect on cover | | *12,000.* |
| 14 | A2 | 1/10th blk & org ('57) | 800.00 | 55.00 |

*The reprints have white gum, and the network does not cover all the outer margin.*

**1859-63 Without Network**

| | | | | |
|---|---|---|---|---|
| 16 | A3 | 3pf pink | 140.00 | *100.00* |
| *a.* | | 3pf carmine rose | 80.00 | *90.00* |
| 17 | A3 | 3pf grn (Drei Zehntel) ('63) | 400.00 | *950.00* |

Examples of No. 25 with rouletting trimmed off are sometimes offered as No. 17. Minimum size of No. 17 acknowledged as genuine: 21½x24½mm.

*The reprints of No. 16 have pink gum instead of red; the extremities of the banderol point downward instead of outward.*

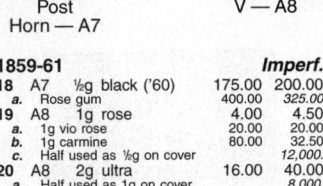

Crown and Post Horn — A7

King George V — A8

**1859-61** ***Imperf.***

| | | | | |
|---|---|---|---|---|
| 18 | A7 | ½g black ('60) | 175.00 | 200.00 |
| *a.* | | Rose gum | 400.00 | *325.00* |
| 19 | A8 | 1g rose | 4.00 | 4.50 |
| *a.* | | 1g vio rose | 20.00 | 20.00 |
| *b.* | | 1g carmine | 80.00 | 32.50 |
| *c.* | | Half used as ½g on cover | | *12,000.* |
| 20 | A8 | 2g ultra | 16.00 | 40.00 |
| *a.* | | Half used as 1g on cover | | *8,000.* |
| 22 | A8 | 3g yellow | 260.00 | 60.00 |
| *a.* | | 3g orange yellow | 160.00 | 120.00 |
| 23 | A8 | 3g brown ('61) | 27.50 | 50.00 |
| *a.* | | One third used as 1g on cover | | — |
| 24 | A8 | 10g green ('61) | 240.00 | 875.00 |

*Reprints of ½g are on thick toned paper with yellowish gum. Originals are on white paper with rose or white gum. Reprints exist tête bêche.*

*Reprints of 3g yellow and 3g brown have white or pinkish gum. Originals have rose or orange gum.*

**1864 White Gum** ***Perce en Arc 16***

| | | | | |
|---|---|---|---|---|
| 25 | A3 | 3pf grn (Drei Zehntel) | 30.00 | 60.00 |
| 26 | A7 | ½g black | 275.00 | 275.00 |
| 27 | A8 | 1g rose | 12.00 | 8.00 |
| 28 | A8 | 2g ultra | 125.00 | 60.00 |
| *a.* | | Half used as 1g on cover | | 16,000. |
| 29 | A8 | 3g brown | 70.00 | 70.00 |
| | | *Nos. 25-29 (5)* | 512.00 | 473.00 |

*Reprints of 3g are percé en arc 13½.*

**Rose Gum**

| | | | | |
|---|---|---|---|---|
| *25a* | A3 | 3pf green | 80.00 | 80.00 |
| *26a* | A7 | ½g black | 475.00 | 450.00 |
| *27a* | A8 | 1g rose | 40.00 | 25.00 |
| *29a* | A8 | 3g brown | *1,200.* | *1,200.* |

Used examples of Nos. 25a-29a retain the rose color on the reverse after the gum has been removed.

The stamps of Prussia superseded those of Hanover on Oct. 1, 1866.

## LUBECK

LOCATION — Situated on an arm of the Baltic Sea between the former German States of Holstein and Mecklenburg.
GOVT. — Former Free City and State
AREA — 115 sq. mi.
POP. — 136,413
CAPITAL — Lubeck

Lubeck was a member of the German Confederation and became part of the German Empire in 1870.

16 Schillings = 1 Mark

Values for Nos. 1-7 unused are for stamps without gum. Nos. 6 and 7 with gum sell for about twice the figures quoted. Values for Nos. 8-14 unused are for examples with original gum as defined in the catalogue introduction. Nos. 8-14 without gum sell for about 50-60% of the figures quoted.

Coat of Arms — A1

**1859 Litho. Wmk. 148** ***Imperf.***

| | | | | |
|---|---|---|---|---|
| 1 | A1 | ½g gray lilac | 475.00 | *2,000.* |
| 2 | A1 | 1s orange | 475.00 | *2,000.* |
| 3 | A1 | 2s brown | 25.00 | *240.00* |
| *a.* | | Value in words reads "ZWEI EIN HALB" | 400.00 | *7,200.* |
| 4 | A1 | 2½s rose | 50.00 | *800.00* |
| 5 | A1 | 4s green | 25.00 | *600.00* |

*The 1872 reprints of the 1859 issue are unwatermarked and printed in bright colors. Values: unused, $240 each; never hinged, $550 each.*

**1862 Unwmk.**

| | | | | |
|---|---|---|---|---|
| 6 | A1 | ½s lilac | 17.50 | *1,600.* |
| 7 | A1 | 1s yellow orange | 27.50 | *1,600.* |

A2

A3

**1863** ***Rouletted 11½***

**Eagle embossed**

| | | | | |
|---|---|---|---|---|
| 8 | A2 | ½s green | 50.00 | *72.50* |
| 9 | A2 | 1s orange | 125.00 | *160.00* |
| *a.* | | Rouletted 10 | 200.00 | *475.00* |
| 10 | A2 | 2s rose | 27.50 | *65.00* |
| 11 | A2 | 2½s ultra | 125.00 | *400.00* |
| 12 | A2 | 4s bister | 55.00 | *100.00* |
| | | *Nos. 8-12 (5)* | 382.50 | *797.50* |

*The 1872 reprints are imperforate and without embossing. Values: unused, $120 each; never hinged, $225 each.*

**1864 Litho.** ***Imperf.***

| | | | | |
|---|---|---|---|---|
| 13 | A3 | 1¼s dark brown | 40.00 | *72.50* |
| *a.* | | 1¼s reddish brown | 32.50 | *125.00* |

A4

**1865** ***Rouletted 11½***

**Eagle embossed**

| | | | | |
|---|---|---|---|---|
| 14 | A4 | 1½s red lilac | 30.00 | *80.00* |

*The 1872 reprints are imperforate and without embossing. Values: unused, $120; never hinged, $225.*

Counterfeit cancellations are found on Nos. 1-14.

The stamps of Lübeck were superseded by those of the North German Confederation on Jan. 1, 1868.

## MECKLENBURG-SCHWERIN

LOCATION — In northern Germany, bordering on the Baltic Sea.
GOVT. — Grand Duchy
AREA — 5,065 sq. mi. (approx.)
POP. — 674,000 (approx.)
CAPITAL — Schwerin

Mecklenburg-Schwerin was a member of the German Confederation and became part of the German Empire in 1870.

48 Schillings = 1 Thaler

Values for unused stamps are for examples with original gum as defined in the catalogue introduction. Examples without gum sell for about 70% of the figures quoted.

Coat of Arms

A1 A2

**1856 Unwmk. Typo.** ***Imperf.***

| | | | | |
|---|---|---|---|---|
| 1 | A1 | Four ¼s red | 140.00 | 125.00 |
| *a.* | | ¼s red | 14.50 | 12.00 |
| 2 | A2 | 3s yellow | 82.50 | 50.00 |
| 3 | A2 | 5s blue | 225.00 | 275.00 |
| | | *Nos. 1-3 (3)* | 447.50 | 450.00 |

See Nos. 4, 6-8.

A3

**1864-67** ***Rouletted 11½***

| | | | | |
|---|---|---|---|---|
| 4 | A1 | Four ¼s red | *2,800.* | *1,750.* |
| *a.* | | ¼s red | 175.00 | 240.00 |
| 5 | A3 | Four ¼s red | 65.00 | 50.00 |
| *a.* | | ¼s red | 9.50 | 9.50 |
| 6 | A2 | 2s gray lil ('67) | 140.00 | *1,600.* |
| *a.* | | 2s red violet ('66) | 240.00 | 240.00 |
| 7 | A2 | 3s org yel, wide margin ('67) | 40.00 | *300.00* |
| *a.* | | Narrow margin ('65) | 160.00 | 125.00 |
| 8 | A2 | 5s bister brn | 160.00 | *240.00* |
| *a.* | | Thick paper | 240.00 | *340.00* |

The overall size of #7, including margin, is 24½x24½mm. That of #7a is 23½x23mm.

The bister on white paper was not issued. Value $12.

Counterfeit cancellations exist on those stamps valued higher used than unused.

These stamps were superseded by those of the North German Confederation on Jan. 1, 1868.

## MECKLENBURG-STRELITZ

LOCATION — In northern Germany, divided by Mecklenburg-Schwerin
GOVT. — Grand Duchy
AREA — 1,131 sq. mi.
POP. — 106,347
CAPITAL — Neustrelitz

Mecklenburg-Strelitz was a member of the German Confederation and became part of the German Empire in 1870.

30 Silbergroschen = 48 Schillings = 1 Thaler

Values for unused stamps are for examples with original gum as defined in the catalogue introduction. Examples without gum sell for about 50% of the figures quoted.

Coat of Arms

A1 A2

***Rouletted 11½***

**1864 Unwmk. Embossed**

| | | | | |
|---|---|---|---|---|
| 1 | A1 | ¼sg orange | 175.00 | *2,400.* |
| *a.* | | ¼sg yellow orange | 340.00 | *4,000.* |
| 2 | A1 | ⅓sg green | 80.00 | *1,350.* |
| *a.* | | ⅓sg dark green | 140.00 | *2,400.* |
| 3 | A1 | 1sch violet | 275.00 | *3,200.* |
| 4 | A2 | 1sg rose | 140.00 | 190.00 |
| 5 | A2 | 2sg ultra | 40.00 | *800.00* |
| 6 | A2 | 3sg bister | 32.50 | *1,275.* |

Counterfeit cancellations abound.

These stamps were superseded by those of the North German Confederation in 1868.

## OLDENBURG

LOCATION — In northwestern Germany, bordering on the North Sea.
GOVT. — Grand Duchy
AREA — 2,482 sq. mi.
POP. — 483,042 (1910)
CAPITAL — Oldenburg

Oldenburg was a member of the German Confederation and became part of the German Empire in 1870.

30 Silbergroschen = 1 Thaler
30 Groschen = 1 Thaler

Values for unused stamps are for examples with original gum as defined in the catalogue introduction. Examples without gum sell for about 50% of the figures quoted.

A1

A2

**1852-55 Unwmk. Litho.** ***Imperf.***

| | | | | |
|---|---|---|---|---|
| 1 | A1 | 1/30th blk, *blue* | 350.00 | 27.50 |
| 2 | A1 | 1/15th blk, *rose* | 800.00 | 80.00 |
| 3 | A1 | 1/10th blk, *yellow* | 800.00 | 95.00 |
| 4 | A2 | ⅓sgr blk, *grn* ('55) | 1,275. | 1,100. |

There are three types of Nos. 1 and 2.

A3

A4

**1859**

| | | | | |
|---|---|---|---|---|
| 5 | A3 | ⅓g blk, *green* | 2,400. | *2,900.* |
| 6 | A3 | 1g blk, *blue* | 725.00 | 45.00 |
| 7 | A3 | 2g blk, *rose* | 950.00 | 600.00 |
| 8 | A3 | 3g blk, *yellow* | 950.00 | 600.00 |
| *a.* | | "OLBENBURG" | 1,600. | 1,200. |

See Nos. 10, 13-15.

**1861**

| | | | | |
|---|---|---|---|---|
| 9 | A4 | ¼g orange | 300.00 | *3,600.* |
| 10 | A3 | ⅓g green | 475.00 | *875.00* |
| *a.* | | ⅓g bluish green | 475.00 | *875.00* |
| *b.* | | ⅓g moss green | 1,600. | *2,800.* |
| *c.* | | "OLDEIBURG" | *800.00* | *1,450.* |
| *d.* | | "Dritto" | *800.00* | *1,450.* |
| *e.* | | "Drittd" | *800.00* | *1,450.* |
| *f.* | | Printed on both sides | | *5,000.* |
| 12 | A4 | ½g redsh brn | 400.00 | 525.00 |
| *a.* | | ½g dark brown | 400.00 | 525.00 |
| 13 | A3 | 1g blue | 240.00 | 160.00 |
| *a.* | | 1g gray blue | 475.00 | 250.00 |
| *b.* | | Printed on both sides | | *3,750.* |
| 14 | A3 | 2g red | 450.00 | 450.00 |
| 15 | A3 | 3g yellow | 450.00 | 450.00 |
| *a.* | | "OLDEIBURG" | *800.00* | *875.00* |
| *b.* | | Printed on both sides | | *5,000.* |

Forged cancellations are found on Nos. 9, 10, 12 and their minor varieties.

Coat of Arms — A5

**1862 Embossed** ***Rouletted 11½***

| | | | | |
|---|---|---|---|---|
| 16 | A5 | ⅓g green | 200.00 | 190.00 |
| 17 | A5 | ½g orange | 200.00 | 95.00 |
| *a.* | | ½g orange red | 250.00 | 150.00 |
| 18 | A5 | 1g rose | 75.00 | 16.00 |
| 19 | A5 | 2g ultra | 200.00 | 50.00 |
| 20 | A5 | 3g bister | 210.00 | 52.50 |

**1867** ***Rouletted 10***

| | | | | |
|---|---|---|---|---|
| 21 | A5 | ⅓g green | 32.50 | *725.00* |
| 22 | A5 | ½g orange | 32.50 | *360.00* |
| 23 | A5 | 1g rose | 20.00 | *55.00* |
| *a.* | | Half used as ½g on cover | | — |
| 24 | A5 | 2g ultra | 20.00 | *475.00* |
| 25 | A5 | 3g bister | 45.00 | *400.00* |
| | | *Nos. 21-25 (5)* | 150.00 | *2,015.* |

Forged cancellations are found on #21-25.

The stamps of Oldenburg were replaced by those of the North German Confederation on Jan. 1, 1868.

## PRUSSIA

LOCATION — The greater part of northern Germany.
GOVT. — Independent Kingdom
AREA — 134,650 sq. mi.
POP. — 40,165,219 (1910)
CAPITAL — Berlin

Prussia was a member of the German Confederation and became part of the German Empire in 1870.

12 Pfennigs = 1 Silbergroschen
60 Kreuzer = 1 Gulden (1867)

Values for unused stamps are for examples with original gum as defined in the catalogue introduction. Examples without gum sell for about 50% of the figures quoted.

King Frederick William IV
A1 A2

**1850-56 Engr. Wmk. 162 *Imperf.***
**Background of Crossed Lines**

1 A1 4pf yel grn ('56) 110.00 72.50
a. 4pf dark green 160.00 125.00
2 A1 6pf (½sg) red org 90.00 52.50
3 A2 1sg black, *rose* 80.00 12.00
a. 1sg black, *bright red* *18,750.* 400.00
4 A2 2sg black, *blue* 110.00 16.00
b. Half used as 1sg on cover —
5 A2 3sg black, *yellow* 110.00 16.00
a. 3sg black, *orange buff* 390.00 37.50
*Nos. 1-5 (5)* 500.00 169.00

See Nos. 10-13.

*Reprints exist on watermarked and unwatermarked paper.*

A3

A4

**Solid Background**

**1857 Typo. Unwmk.**

6 A3 1sg rose 325.00 35.00
a. 1sg carmine rose 360.00 50.00
7 A3 2sg blue 1,280. 90.00
a. 2sg dark blue 1,795. 125.00
b. Half used as 1sg on cover —
8 A3 3sg orange 160.00 40.00
a. 3sg yellow 1,625. 100.00
b. 3sg deep orange 800.00 125.00
*Nos. 6-8 (3)* 1,765. 165.00

*The reprints of Nos. 6-8 have a period instead of a colon after "SILBERGR."*

**Background of Crossed Lines**

**1858-60 Typo.**

9 A4 4pf green 72.50 35.00

**Engr.**

10 A1 6pf (½sg) org ('59) 190.00 160.00
a. 6pf (½sg) brick red 290.00 200.00

**Typo.**

11 A2 1sg rose 32.50 4.00
12 A2 2sg blue 110.00 17.50
a. 2sg dark blue 160.00 42.50
b. Half used as 1sg on cover —
13 A2 3sg orange 95.00 16.00
a. 3sg yellow 140.00 17.50
*Nos. 9-13 (5)* 500.00 232.50

Coat of Arms
A6 A7

**1861-67 Embossed *Rouletted 11½***

14 A6 3pf red lilac ('67) 27.50 45.00
a. 3pf red violet ('65) 340.00 275.00
15 A6 4pf yellow green 12.00 12.00
a. 4pf green 42.50 55.00
16 A6 6pf orange 12.00 14.50
a. 6pf vermilion 125.00 67.50
17 A7 1sg rose 3.25 1.60
18 A7 2sg ultra 12.00 1.60
a. 2sg blue 425.00 30.00
20 A7 3sg bister 8.75 2.00
a. 3sg gray brown ('65) — 30.00
*Nos. 14-20 (6)* 75.50 76.70

A8

A9

**Typographed in Reverse on Paper Resembling Goldbeater's Skin**

**1866 *Rouletted 10***

21 A8 10sg rose 95.00 *105.00*
22 A9 30sg blue 110.00 *225.00*

Perfect examples of Nos. 21-22 are extremely rare.

A10

**1867 Embossed *Rouletted 16***

23 A10 1kr green 25.00 *45.00*
24 A10 2kr orange 40.00 *95.00*
25 A10 3kr rose 20.00 *27.50*
26 A10 6kr ultra 20.00 *45.00*
27 A10 9kr bister brown 25.00 *47.50*
*Nos. 23-27 (5)* 130.00 *260.00*

Imperforate stamps of the above sets are proofs.

The stamps of Prussia were superseded by those of the North German Confederation on Jan. 1, 1868.

OFFICIAL STAMPS
See Germany Nos. OL1-OL15.

## SAXONY

LOCATION — In central Germany
GOVT. — Kingdom
AREA — 5,787 sq. mi.
POP. — 2,500,000 (approx.)
CAPITAL — Dresden

Saxony was a member of the German Confederation and became a part of the German Empire in 1870.

10 Pfennigs = 1 Neu-Groschen
30 Neu-Groschen = 1 Thaler

Values for unused stamps are for examples with original gum as defined in the catalogue introduction. Examples without gum sell for about 50-60% of the figures quoted.

A1

**1850 Unwmk. Typo. *Imperf.***

1 A1 3pf brick red *7,200.* *7,200.*
a. 3pf cherry red *11,200.* *13,600.*
b. 3pf brown red *11,200.* *11,575.*

There are vertical dividing lines between stamps.

Coat of Arms — A2

Frederick Augustus II — A3

**1851**

2 A2 3pf green 125.00 95.00
a. 3pf yellow green 1,600. 600.00

Nos. 2 and 2a are valued with the margin just touching the design in one or two places. Stamps with margins all around sell for considerably more.

Stamps with very fine impressions, from the first printing, command substantial premiums.

**1851-52 Engr.**

3 A3 ½ng black, *gray* 72.50 12.00
a. ½ng black, *pale blue* (error) *19,000.*
5 A3 1ng black, *rose* 95.00 9.50
6 A3 2ng black, *pale bl* 250.00 65.00
7 A3 2ng blk, *dk bl* ('52) 725.00 55.00
8 A3 3ng black, *yellow* 160.00 25.00
*Nos. 3-8 (5)* 1,302. 166.50

The error No. 3a occurred when paper meant for printing No. 6 was inadvertently placed in the stack of paper for printing No. 3.

King John I — A4

**1855-60**

9 A4 ½ng black, *gray* 9.50 4.00
a. "11/22" at left or right — —
10 A4 1ng black, *rose* 9.50 4.00
11 A4 2ng black, *dark blue* 20.00 16.00
a. 2ng black, *blue* 72.50 47.50
12 A4 3ng black, *yellow* 21.00 12.00
13 A4 5ng ver ('56) 90.00 55.00
a. 5ng orange brown ('60) 225.00 *300.00*
b. 5ng deep brown ('57) *650.00* 175.00
14 A4 10ng milky blue ('56) 225.00 225.00

A5

A6

**Typo.; Arms Embossed**

**1863 *Perf. 13***

15 A5 3pf blue green 2.00 *40.00*
a. 3pf yellow green 95.00 *125.00*
16 A5 ½ng orange 2.00 *2.75*
a. ½ng red orange 22.50 4.50
17 A6 1ng rose 1.25 2.40
a. Vert. pair, imperf. between *225.00*
b. Horiz. pair, imperf. between *375.00*
18 A6 2ng blue 2.75 6.50
a. 2ng dark blue 11.00 25.00
19 A6 3ng red brown 4.00 8.75
a. 3ng bister brown 22.50 7.25
20 A6 5ng dull violet 30.00 *47.50*
a. 5ng gray violet 10.00 *450.00*
b. 5ng gray blue 30.00 *72.50*
c. 5ng slate 22.50 *250.00*

The stamps of Saxony were superseded on Jan. 1, 1868, by those of the North German Confederation.

## SCHLESWIG-HOLSTEIN

LOCATION — In northern Germany.
GOVT. — Duchies
AREA — 7,338 sq. mi.
POP. — 1,519,000 (approx.)
CAPITAL — Schleswig

Schleswig-Holstein was an autonomous territory from 1848 to 1851 when it came under Danish rule. In 1864, it was occupied by Prussia and Austria, and in 1866 it became a province of Prussia.

16 Schillings = 1 Mark

Values for unused stamps are for examples with original gum as defined in the catalogue introduction. Stamps without gum sell for about 50% of the figures quoted.

Coat of Arms — A1

**Typographed; Arms Embossed**
**1850 Unwmk. *Imperf.***
**With Silk Threads**

1 A1 1s dl bl & grnsh bl 325.00 *5,600.*
a. 1s Prussian blue 725.00
2 A1 2s rose & pink 560.00 *5,325.*
a. 2s deep pink & rose 725.00
b. Double embossing *3,100.*

Forged cancellations are found on Nos. 1-2, 5-7, 9, 16 and 19.

A2

A3

**1865 Typo. *Rouletted 11½***

3 A2 ½s rose 35.00 *45.00*
4 A2 1¼s green 17.50 *20.00*
5 A3 1⅓s red lilac 45.00 *125.00*
6 A2 2s ultra 50.00 *240.00*
7 A3 4s bister 65.00 *1,300.*
*Nos. 3-7 (5)* 212.50 1,730.

**Schleswig**

A4

A5

**1864 Typo. *Rouletted 11½***

8 A4 1¼s green 40.00 18.50
9 A4 4s carmine 87.50 *450.00*

**1865 *Rouletted 10, 11½***

10 A4 ½s green 32.50 *55.00*
11 A4 1¼s red lilac 55.00 25.00
a. 1¼s gray lilac ('67) 255.00 47.50
b. Half of #11a used as ½s on cover *32,000.*
12 A5 1⅓s rose 27.50 *60.00*
13 A4 2s ultra 27.50 *60.00*
14 A4 4s bister 32.50 *80.00*
*Nos. 10-14 (5)* 175.00 *280.00*

**Holstein**

A6

Type I — Small lettering in frame. Wavy lines in spandrels close together.
Type II — Small lettering in frame. Wavy lines wider apart.
Type III — Larger lettering in frame and no periods after "H R Z G." Wavy lines as II.

**1864 Litho. *Imperf.***

15 A6 1¼s bl & gray, I 52.50 *55.00*
a. Half used as ½s on cover *9,500.*
16 A6 1¼s bl & gray, II 800.00 *2,400.*
a. Half used as ½s on cover *24,000.*
17 A6 1¼s bl & gray, III 45.00 *55.00*
a. Half used as ½s on cover *8,000.*

A7

**1864 Typo. *Rouletted 8***

18 A7 1¼s blue & rose 40.00 20.00
a. Half used as ½s on cover *2,000.*

A8

**1865** *Rouletted 8*

| | | | | |
|---|---|---|---|---|
| 19 | A8 | ½s green | 65.00 | 95.00 |
| 20 | A8 | 1 ¼s red lilac | 47.50 | 25.00 |
| 21 | A8 | 2s blue | 52.50 | 47.50 |
| | | *Nos. 19-21 (3)* | 165.00 | 167.50 |

A9

A10

**1865-66** *Rouletted 7 and 8*

| | | | | |
|---|---|---|---|---|
| 22 | A9 | 1 ¼s red lilac ('66) | 72.50 | 25.00 |
| a. | | Half used as ½s on cover | | 24,000. |
| 23 | A10 | 1 ⅓s carmine | 60.00 | 45.00 |
| 24 | A9 | 2s blue ('66) | 145.00 | 160.00 |
| 25 | A10 | 4s bister | 55.00 | 80.00 |
| | | *Nos. 22-25 (4)* | 332.50 | 310.00 |

These stamps were superseded by those of North German Confederation on Jan. 1, 1868.

## THURN AND TAXIS

A princely house which, prior to the formation of the German Empire, enjoyed the privilege of a postal monopoly. These stamps were superseded on July 1, 1867, by those of Prussia, followed by those of the North German Postal District on Jan. 1, 1868, and later by stamps of the German Empire on Jan. 1, 1872.

Values are for stamps with four complete margins just clear of the framelines. Stamps with margins just touching the framelines on one or two sides are worth approximately 60% of the values quoted. Stamps with four large margins are rare and command premiums of up to 500% over the values quoted.

Values for unused stamps are for examples with original gum as defined in the catalogue introduction. Stamps without gum sell for about 50% of the figures quoted.

### NORTHERN DISTRICT

30 Silbergroschen or Groschen = 1 Thaler

A1

A2

**1852-58** **Unwmk.** **Typo.** *Imperf.*

| | | | | |
|---|---|---|---|---|
| 1 | A1 | ¼sgr blk, *red brn* ('54) | 265.00 | 60.00 |
| 2 | A1 | ⅓sgr blk, *buff* ('58) | 125.00 | 250.00 |
| 3 | A1 | ½sgr blk, *green* | 725.00 | 40.00 |
| 4 | A1 | 1sgr blk, *dk bl* | 1,325. | 140.00 |
| 5 | A1 | 1sgr blk, *lt bl* ('53) | 800.00 | 22.50 |
| 6 | A1 | 2sgr blk, *rose* | 850.00 | 32.50 |
| a. | | Half used as 1sgr on cover | | 10,000. |
| 7 | A1 | 3sgr blk, *brownish yellow* | 1,000. | 30.00 |
| a. | | 3sgr blk, *pale orange yellow* | 1,000. | 80.00 |

*Reprints of Nos. 1-12, 15-20, 23-24, were made in 1910. They have "ND" in script on the back. Value, $6.50 each.*

**1859-60**

| | | | | |
|---|---|---|---|---|
| 8 | A1 | ¼sgr red ('60) | 67.50 | 67.50 |
| 9 | A1 | ½gr green | 300.00 | 95.00 |
| 10 | A1 | 1sgr blue | 300.00 | 45.00 |
| 11 | A1 | 2sgr rose ('60) | 145.00 | 80.00 |
| 12 | A1 | 3sgr red brn ('60) | 145.00 | 110.00 |
| 13 | A2 | 5sgr lilac | 275.00 | 400.00 |
| 14 | A2 | 10sgr orange | 2.75 | 875.00 |

Excellent forged cancellations exist on Nos. 13 and 14. For reprints, see note after No. 7.

**1862-63**

| | | | | |
|---|---|---|---|---|
| 15 | A1 | ¼sgr black ('63) | 35.00 | 75.00 |
| 16 | A1 | ⅓sgr green ('63) | 50.00 | 250.00 |
| 17 | A1 | ½sgr org yel | 100.00 | 47.50 |
| 18 | A1 | 1sgr rose ('63) | 67.50 | 27.50 |
| 19 | A1 | 2sgr blue ('63) | 60.00 | 100.00 |
| 20 | A1 | 3sgr bister ('63) | 27.50 | 55.00 |
| | | *Nos. 15-20 (6)* | 340.00 | 555.00 |

For reprints, see note after No. 7.

**1865** *Rouletted*

| | | | | |
|---|---|---|---|---|
| 21 | A1 | ¼sgr black | 7.50 | 400.00 |
| 22 | A1 | ⅓sgr green | 11.00 | 240.00 |
| 23 | A1 | ½sgr yellow | 22.50 | 37.50 |
| 24 | A1 | 1sgr rose | 25.00 | 25.00 |
| 25 | A1 | 2sgr blue | 1.50 | 67.50 |
| 26 | A1 | 3sgr bister | 2.75 | 27.50 |
| | | *Nos. 21-26 (6)* | 70.25 | 797.50 |

For reprints, see note after No. 7.

**1866** *Rouletted in Colored Lines*

| | | | | |
|---|---|---|---|---|
| 27 | A1 | ¼sgr black | 2.00 | 1,250. |
| 28 | A1 | ⅓sgr green | 2.00 | 600.00 |
| 29 | A1 | ½sgr yellow | 2.00 | 120.00 |
| 30 | A1 | 1sgr rose | 1.50 | 60.00 |
| a. | | Horizontal pair without rouletting between | 150.00 | 1,500. |
| b. | | Half used as ½sgr on cover | | 52,500. |
| 31 | A1 | 2sgr blue | 1.50 | 600.00 |
| 32 | A1 | 3sgr bister | 1.50 | 150.00 |
| | | *Nos. 27-32 (6)* | 10.50 | 2,780. |

Forged cancellations on Nos. 2, 13-14, 15-16, 21-22, 25-32 are plentiful.

### SOUTHERN DISTRICT

60 Kreuzer = 1 Gulden

A1

A2

**1852-53** **Unwmk.** *Imperf.*

| | | | | |
|---|---|---|---|---|
| 42 | A1 | 1kr blk, *lt grn* | 240.00 | 15.00 |
| 43 | A1 | 3kr blk, *dk bl* | 925.00 | 50.00 |
| 44 | A1 | 3kr blk, *bl* ('53) | 800.00 | 20.00 |
| 45 | A1 | 6kr blk, *rose* | 800.00 | 11.00 |
| 46 | A1 | 9kr blk, *brnish yell* | 875.00 | 17.50 |
| a. | | 9kr blk, *pale orange yellow* | 750.00 | 45.00 |

*Reprints of Nos. 42-50, 53-56 were made in 1910. Each has "ND" in script on the back. Value, each $6.50.*

**1859**

| | | | | |
|---|---|---|---|---|
| 47 | A1 | 1kr green | 25.00 | 10.00 |
| 48 | A1 | 3kr blue | 560.00 | 25.00 |
| 49 | A1 | 6kr rose | 560.00 | 67.50 |
| 50 | A1 | 9kr yellow | 560.00 | 67.50 |
| 51 | A2 | 15kr lilac | 2.75 | 175.00 |
| 52 | A2 | 30kr orange | 2.75 | 475.00 |

Forged cancellations exist on Nos. 51 and 52. For reprints, see note after No. 46.

**1862**

| | | | | |
|---|---|---|---|---|
| 53 | A1 | 3kr rose | 13.50 | 30.00 |
| 54 | A1 | 6kr blue | 13.50 | 30.00 |
| 55 | A1 | 9kr bister | 13.50 | 35.00 |
| | | *Nos. 53-55 (3)* | 40.50 | 95.00 |

For reprints, see note after No. 46.

**1865** *Rouletted*

| | | | | |
|---|---|---|---|---|
| 56 | A1 | 1kr green | 12.50 | 13.50 |
| 57 | A1 | 3kr rose | 18.50 | 7.50 |
| 58 | A1 | 6kr blue | 1.50 | 20.00 |
| 59 | A1 | 9kr bister | 2.25 | 22.50 |
| | | *Nos. 56-59 (4)* | 34.75 | 63.50 |

For reprint of No. 56, see note after No. 46.

**1866** *Rouletted in Colored Lines*

| | | | | |
|---|---|---|---|---|
| 60 | A1 | 1kr green | 1.50 | 22.50 |
| 61 | A1 | 3kr rose | 1.50 | 20.00 |
| 62 | A1 | 6kr blue | 1.50 | 37.50 |
| 63 | A1 | 9kr bister | 1.50 | 32.50 |
| | | *Nos. 60-63 (4)* | 6.00 | 112.50 |

Forged cancellations exist on Nos. 51-52, 58-63.

The Thurn & Taxis Stamps, Northern and Southern Districts, were replaced on July 1, 1867, by those of Prussia.

## WURTTEMBERG

LOCATION — In southern Germany
GOVT. — Kingdom
AREA — 7,530 sq. mi.
POP. — 2,580,000 (approx.)
CAPITAL — Stuttgart

Württemberg was a member of the German Confederation and became a part of the German Empire in 1870. It gave up its postal autonomy on March 31, 1902, but official stamps were issued until 1923.

16 Kreuzer = 1 Gulden
100 Pfennigs = 1 Mark (1875)

Values for unused stamps are for examples with original gum as defined in the catalogue introduction. Unused stamps without gum of Nos. 1-46 sell for about 60-70% of the figures quoted. Unused stamps without gum of Nos. 47-54 sell for about 50% of the figures quoted.

A1

A1a

**1851-52** **Unwmk.** **Typo.** *Imperf.*

| | | | | |
|---|---|---|---|---|
| 1 | A1 | 1kr blk, *buff* | 1,125. | 95.00 |
| a. | | 1kr black, *straw* | 3,500. | 500.00 |
| 2 | A1 | 3kr blk, *yellow* | 275.00 | 7.25 |
| a. | | 3kr black, *orange* | 3,000. | 300.00 |
| 4 | A1 | 6kr blk, *yel grn* | 1,450. | 32.50 |
| a. | | 6kr black, *blue green* | 2,600. | 50.00 |
| 5 | A1 | 9kr blk, *rose* | 4,800. | 32.50 |
| 6 | A1a | 18kr blk, *dl vio* ('52) | 1,450. | 725.00 |

*On the "reprints" the letters of "Württemberg" are smaller, especially the first "e"; the right branch of the "r's" of Württemberg runs upward in the reprints and downward in the originals.*

Coat of Arms — A2

**With Orange Silk Threads**

**Typographed and Embossed**

**1857**

| | | | | |
|---|---|---|---|---|
| 7 | A2 | 1kr yel brn | 800.00 | 80.00 |
| a. | | 1kr dark brown | 1,100. | 225.00 |
| 9 | A2 | 3kr yel org | 400.00 | 11.00 |
| 10 | A2 | 6kr green | 800.00 | 65.00 |
| 11 | A2 | 9kr car rose | 1,925. | 70.00 |
| 12 | A2 | 18kr blue | 3,350. | 1,350. |

Very fine examples of Nos. 7-12 with have one or two margins touching, but not cutting, the frameline.

See Nos. 13-46, 53.

*The reprints have red or yellow silk threads and are printed 2mm apart, while the originals are ¾mm apart.*

**1859** **Without Silk Threads**

| | | | | |
|---|---|---|---|---|
| 13 | A2 | 1kr brown | 650.00 | 100.00 |
| a. | | 1kr dark brown | 2,000. | 725.00 |
| 15 | A2 | 3kr yel org | 275.00 | 13.00 |
| 16 | A2 | 6kr green | 9,600. | 125.00 |
| 17 | A2 | 9kr car rose | 1,275. | 70.00 |
| 18 | A2 | 18kr dark blue | 2,900. | 1,700. |

*The colors of the reprints are brighter; they are also printed 2mm apart instead of 1¼mm.*

**1860** *Perf. 13½*

| | | | | |
|---|---|---|---|---|
| 19 | A2 | 1kr brown | 1,125. | 125.00 |
| 20 | A2 | 3kr yel org | 325.00 | 9.50 |
| 21 | A2 | 6kr green | 3,000. | 110.00 |
| 22 | A2 | 9kr carmine | 1,200. | 125.00 |

**1861** **Thin Paper**

| | | | | |
|---|---|---|---|---|
| 23 | A2 | 1kr brown | 950.00 | 250.00 |
| a. | | 1kr black brown | 950.00 | 250.00 |
| 25 | A2 | 3kr yel org | 200.00 | 65.00 |
| 26 | A2 | 6kr green | 400.00 | 110.00 |
| 27 | A2 | 9kr rose | 1,275. | 300.00 |
| a. | | 9kr claret | 1,160. | 325.00 |
| 29 | A2 | 18kr dark blue | 3,000. | 2,250. |

Examples of Nos. 23-29 with all perforations intact sell for considerably more.

**1862** *Perf. 10*

| | | | | |
|---|---|---|---|---|
| 30 | A2 | 1kr blk brn | 650.00 | 440.00 |
| 31 | A2 | 3kr yel org | 800.00 | 47.50 |
| 32 | A2 | 6kr green | 525.00 | 200.00 |
| 33 | A2 | 9kr claret | 4,000. | 800.00 |

**1863**

| | | | | |
|---|---|---|---|---|
| 34 | A2 | 1kr yel grn | 45.00 | 13.50 |
| a. | | 1kr green | 400.00 | 95.00 |
| 36 | A2 | 3kr rose | 325.00 | 4.75 |
| a. | | 3kr dark claret | 1,600. | 275.00 |
| 37 | A2 | 6kr blue | 160.00 | 52.50 |
| 39 | A2 | 9kr yel brn | 750.00 | 160.00 |
| a. | | 9kr red brown | 260.00 | 52.50 |
| b. | | 9kr black brown | 1,200. | 190.00 |
| 40 | A2 | 18kr orange | 1,200. | 400.00 |

**1865-68** *Rouletted 10*

| | | | | |
|---|---|---|---|---|
| 41 | A2 | 1kr yel grn | 45.00 | 12.00 |
| a. | | 1kr dark green | 575.00 | 300.00 |
| 42 | A2 | 3kr rose | 45.00 | 3.25 |
| a. | | 3kr claret | 1,900. | 2,250. |
| 43 | A2 | 6kr blue | 275.00 | 52.50 |
| 44 | A2 | 7kr slate bl ('68) | 960.00 | 125.00 |
| 45 | A2 | 9kr bis brn | 1,500. | 110.00 |
| a. | | 9kr red brown | 1,150. | 100.00 |
| 46 | A2 | 18kr orange ('67) | 1,750. | 1,000. |

A3

**1869-73** **Typo. & Embossed**

| | | | | |
|---|---|---|---|---|
| 47 | A3 | 1kr yel grn | 32.50 | 2.40 |
| 48 | A3 | 2kr orange | 175.00 | 140.00 |
| 49 | A3 | 3kr rose | 16.00 | 1.60 |
| 50 | A3 | 7kr blue | 67.50 | 17.50 |
| 51 | A3 | 9kr lt brn ('73) | 80.00 | 40.00 |
| 52 | A3 | 14kr orange | 88.00 | 45.00 |
| a. | | 14kr lemon yellow | 1,500. | 1,500. |
| | | *Nos. 47-52 (6)* | 459.00 | 246.50 |

See No. 54.

**1873** *Imperf.*

| | | | | |
|---|---|---|---|---|
| 53 | A2 | 70kr red violet | 1,750. | 4,000. |
| a. | | 70kr violet | 2,900. | 5,250. |

Nos. 53 and 53a have single or double lines of fine black dots printed in the gutters between the stamps.

**1874** *Perf. 11½x11*

| | | | | |
|---|---|---|---|---|
| 54 | A3 | 1kr yellow green | 110.00 | 40.00 |

A4

A5

**1875-1900** **Typo.**

| | | | | |
|---|---|---|---|---|
| 55 | A4 | 2pf sl gray ('93) | 2.00 | .95 |
| 56 | A4 | 3pf green | 20.00 | 1.60 |
| 57 | A4 | 3pf brn ('90) | .80 | .55 |
| a. | | Imperf., pair | 125.00 | |
| 58 | A4 | 5pf violet | 9.50 | .80 |
| 59 | A4 | 5pf grn ('90) | 1.60 | .55 |
| a. | | 5pf blue green | 300.00 | 24.00 |
| b. | | Imperf., pair | 125.00 | |
| 60 | A4 | 10pf carmine | 1.25 | .80 |
| a. | | 10pf rose | 80.00 | 1.25 |
| b. | | Imperf., pair | 80.00 | |
| 61 | A4 | 20pf ultra | 1.25 | .80 |
| a. | | 20pf dull blue | 1.25 | .80 |
| b. | | Imperf., pair | 125.00 | |
| 62 | A4 | 25pf red brn | 125.00 | 9.50 |
| 63 | A4 | 25pf org ('90) | 2.75 | 1.60 |
| a. | | Imperf., pair | 125.00 | |
| 64 | A5 | 30pf org & blk ('00) | 3.25 | 4.75 |
| 65 | A5 | 40pf dp rose & blk ('00) | 4.00 | 5.50 |
| 66 | A4 | 50pf gray | 725.00 | 40.00 |
| 67 | A4 | 50pf gray grn | 65.00 | 6.50 |
| 68 | A4 | 50pf pur brn ('90) | 2.75 | .95 |
| a. | | 50pf red brown | 640.00 | 65.00 |
| b. | | Imperf., pair | 125.00 | |
| 69 | A4 | 2m yellow | 800.00 | 260.00 |
| 70 | A4 | 2m ver, *buff* ('79) | 2,800. | 125.00 |
| 71 | A5 | 2m org & blk ('86) | 8.00 | 9.50 |
| | | Telegraph cancel | | 3.00 |
| a. | | 2m yellow & black | 450.00 | 47.50 |
| b. | | Imperf., pair | 125.00 | |
| 72 | A5 | 5m bl & blk ('81) | 45.00 | 160.00 |
| | | Telegraph cancel | | 72.50 |
| a. | | Double impression of figure of value | 200.00 | |

No. 70 has "Unverkauflich" (not for sale) printed on its back to remind postal clerks that it, like No. 69, was for their use and not to be sold to the public.

The regular postage stamps of Württemberg were superseded by those of the German Empire in 1902. Official stamps were in use until 1923.

## WURTTEMBERG OFFICIAL STAMPS

### For the Communal Authorities

O1

*Perf. 11½x11*

**1875-1900 Typo. Unwmk.**

| | | | | |
|---|---|---|---|---|
| **O1** | O1 | 2pf sl gray ('00) | 2.40 | 1.60 |
| **O2** | O1 | 3pf brn ('96) | 2.40 | 1.60 |
| **O3** | O1 | 5pf violet | 45.00 | 2.40 |
| *a.* | | Imperf., pair | | *4,000.* |
| **O4** | O1 | 5pf bl grn ('90) | 1.60 | 1.45 |
| *a.* | | Imperf., pair | 47.50 | |
| **O5** | O1 | 10pf rose | 9.50 | 2.25 |
| *a.* | | Imperf., pair | 82.50 | |
| **O6** | O1 | 25pf org ('00) | 25.00 | 8.00 |
| | | *Nos. O1-O6 (6)* | 85.90 | 17.30 |

See Nos. O12-O32. For overprints and surcharges see Nos. O7-O11, O40-O52, O59-O93.

Used Values
When italicized, used values for Nos. O7-O183 are for favor-canceled stamps. Postally used stamps command a premium.

Stamps of Previous Issues Overprinted in Black

**1906, Jan. 30**

| | | | | |
|---|---|---|---|---|
| **O7** | O1 | 2pf slate gray | 45.00 | 80.00 |
| **O8** | O1 | 3pf dk brown | 14.00 | 10.00 |
| **O9** | O1 | 5pf green | 4.75 | 5.50 |
| **O10** | O1 | 10pf deep rose | 4.75 | 5.25 |
| **O11** | O1 | 25pf orange | 55.00 | 75.00 |
| | | *Nos. O7-O11 (5)* | 123.50 | 175.75 |
| | | Set, C.T.O. | | 40.00 |

Centenary of Kingdom of Württemberg.
Nos. O7-O11 also exist imperf but it is doubtful if they were ever issued in that condition.

**1906-21 Wmk. 116**

| | | | | |
|---|---|---|---|---|
| **O12** | O1 | 2pf slate gray | 4.00 | *.40* |
| **O13** | O1 | 2½pf gray blk ('16) | .80 | *.25* |
| **O14** | O1 | 3pf dk brown | .95 | *.40* |
| **O15** | O1 | 5pf green | .80 | *.40* |
| **O16** | O1 | 7½pf orange ('16) | .80 | *.25* |
| **O17** | O1 | 10pf dp rose | .80 | *.40* |
| **O18** | O1 | 10pf orange ('21) | .30 | *.25* |
| **O19** | O1 | 15pf yellow brn ('16) | 2.00 | *.25* |
| **O20** | O1 | 15pf purple ('17) | 1.25 | *.25* |
| **O21** | O1 | 20pf dp ultra ('11) | 1.60 | *.40* |
| **O22** | O1 | 20pf dp green ('21) | .30 | *.25* |
| **O23** | O1 | 25pf orange | .95 | *.40* |
| **O24** | O1 | 25pf brn & blk ('17) | 1.25 | *.25* |
| **O25** | O1 | 35pf brown ('19) | 1.60 | *.95* |
| **O26** | O1 | 40pf rose red ('21) | .30 | *.25* |
| **O27** | O1 | 50pf rose lake ('11) | 14.50 | *.40* |
| **O28** | O1 | 50pf vio brn ('21) | .30 | *.25* |
| **O29** | O1 | 60pf olive grn ('21) | .55 | *.25* |
| **O30** | O1 | 1.25m emerald ('21) | .30 | *.25* |
| **O31** | O1 | 2m gray ('21) | .80 | *.25* |
| **O32** | O1 | 3m brown ('21) | .50 | *.25* |
| | | *Nos. O12-O32 (21)* | 34.65 | *7.00* |

No. O24 contains solid black numerals.
Nos. O12-O32 exist imperf. Value, each pair, $6.50-$17.50.

O3

*Perf. 14½x14*

**1916, Oct. 6 Typo. Unwmk.**

| | | | | |
|---|---|---|---|---|
| **O33** | O3 | 2½pf slate | 1.60 | *1.25* |
| **O34** | O3 | 7½pf orange | 1.25 | *1.25* |
| **O35** | O3 | 10pf car rose | 1.25 | *1.25* |
| **O36** | O3 | 15pf yellow brn | 1.25 | *1.25* |
| **O37** | O3 | 20pf blue | 1.25 | *1.25* |
| **O38** | O3 | 25pf gray blk | 4.00 | *1.25* |
| **O39** | O3 | 50pf red brown | 8.00 | *1.25* |
| | | *Nos. O33-O39 (7)* | 18.60 | *8.75* |

25th year of the reign of King Wilhelm II.

Stamps of 1900-06 Surcharged

*Perf. 11½x11*

**1916, Sept. 10 Wmk. 116**

| | | | | |
|---|---|---|---|---|
| **O40** | O1 | 25pf on 25pf orange | 4.00 | *.95* |
| *a.* | | Without wmk. | 32.50 | |

No. O13 Surcharged in Blue

**1919 Wmk. 116**

| | | | | |
|---|---|---|---|---|
| **O42** | O1 | 2pf on 2½pf gray blk | .80 | *.55* |

Official Stamps of 1906-19 Overprinted

**1919**

| | | | | |
|---|---|---|---|---|
| **O43** | O1 | 2½pf gray blk | .40 | *.55* |
| **O44** | O1 | 3pf dk brown | 12.00 | *.55* |
| **O45** | O1 | 5pf green | .35 | *.55* |
| **O46** | O1 | 7½pf orange | 1.00 | *.55* |
| **O47** | O1 | 10pf rose | .35 | *.55* |
| **O48** | O1 | 15pf purple | .35 | *.55* |
| **O49** | O1 | 20pf ultra | .35 | *.55* |
| **O50** | O1 | 25pf brown & blk | .40 | *.55* |
| **O51** | O1 | 35pf brown | 4.00 | *.55* |
| **O52** | O1 | 50pf red brown | 5.50 | *.55* |
| | | *Nos. O43-O52 (10)* | 24.70 | *5.50* |

Stag — O4

**Wmk. 192**

**1920, Mar. 19 Litho. *Perf. 14½***

| | | | | |
|---|---|---|---|---|
| **O53** | O4 | 10pf maroon | 1.45 | *1.25* |
| **O54** | O4 | 15pf brown | 1.45 | *1.25* |
| **O55** | O4 | 20pf indigo | 1.45 | *1.25* |
| **O56** | O4 | 30pf deep green | 1.45 | *1.25* |
| **O57** | O4 | 50pf yellow | 1.60 | *1.25* |
| **O58** | O4 | 75pf bister | 3.25 | *1.25* |
| | | *Nos. O53-O58 (6)* | 10.65 | *7.50* |

Official Stamps of 1906-19 Overprinted

*Perf. 11½x11*

**1920, Apr. 1 Wmk. 116**

| | | | | |
|---|---|---|---|---|
| **O59** | O1 | 5pf green | 4.00 | 10.00 |
| **O60** | O1 | 10pf deep rose | 2.40 | 4.75 |
| **O61** | O1 | 15pf dp violet | 2.40 | 5.25 |
| **O62** | O1 | 20pf ultra | 4.00 | 8.75 |
| *a.* | | Wmk. 192 | 4.75 | 8.75 |
| **O63** | O1 | 50pf red brown | 4.75 | 17.50 |
| | | *Nos. O59-O63 (5)* | 17.55 | 46.25 |

Nos. O59 to O63 were available for official postage throughout all Germany but were used almost exclusively in Württemberg.

Stamps of 1917-21 Surcharged in Black, Red or Blue

**1923**

| | | | | |
|---|---|---|---|---|
| **O64** | O1 | 5m on 10pf orange | .25 | *.55* |
| **O65** | O1 | 10m on 15pf dp violet | .25 | *.55* |
| **O66** | O1 | 12m on 40pf rose red | .25 | *.55* |
| **O67** | O1 | 20m on 10pf orange | .80 | *.55* |
| **O68** | O1 | 25m on 20pf green | .25 | *.55* |
| **O69** | O1 | 40m on 20pf green | .25 | *.55* |
| **O70** | O1 | 50m on 60pf olive grn | .25 | *.55* |

Surcharged

| | | | | |
|---|---|---|---|---|
| **O71** | O1 | 60m on 1.25m emerald | .25 | *.55* |
| **O72** | O1 | 100m on 40pf rose red | .25 | *.55* |
| **O73** | O1 | 200m on 2m gray (R) | .25 | *.55* |
| **O74** | O1 | 300m on 50pf red brn (Bl) | .25 | *.55* |
| **O75** | O1 | 400m on 3m brn (Bl) | .25 | *.55* |
| **O76** | O1 | 1000m on 60pf ol grn | .25 | *.55* |
| **O77** | O1 | 2000m on 1.25m emerald | .25 | *.55* |
| | | *Nos. O64-O77 (14)* | 4.05 | *7.70* |

Abbreviations:
Th = (Tausend) Thousand
Mil = (Million) Million
Mlrd = (Milliarde) Billion

Surcharged

**1923**

| | | | | |
|---|---|---|---|---|
| **O78** | O1 | 5th m on 10pf orange | .25 | *.50* |
| **O79** | O1 | 20th m on 40pf rose red | .25 | *.50* |
| **O80** | O1 | 50th m on 15pf violet | .80 | *.50* |
| **O81** | O1 | 75th m on 2m gray | 1.60 | *.50* |
| **O82** | O1 | 100th m on 20pf green | .25 | *.50* |
| **O83** | O1 | 250th m on 3m brown | .25 | *.50* |

Surcharged

| | | | | |
|---|---|---|---|---|
| **O84** | O1 | 1mil m on 60pf ol grn | 1.25 | *.50* |
| **O85** | O1 | 2mil m on 50pf red brn | .25 | *.50* |
| **O86** | O1 | 5mil m on 1.25m emer | .25 | *.50* |

Surcharged

| | | | | |
|---|---|---|---|---|
| **O87** | O1 | 4 mlrd m on 50pf red brn | 3.25 | *.50* |
| **O88** | O1 | 10 mlrd m on 3m brn | 3.25 | *.50* |
| | | *Nos. O78-O88 (11)* | 11.65 | *5.50* |

No. O23 Surcharged in Rentenpfennig as

**1923, Dec.**

| | | | | |
|---|---|---|---|---|
| **O89** | O1 | 3pf on 25pf orange | .50 | *.35* |
| **O90** | O1 | 5pf on 25pf orange | .50 | *.35* |
| **O91** | O1 | 10pf on 25pf orange | .40 | *.35* |
| **O92** | O1 | 20pf on 25pf orange | .40 | *.35* |
| **O93** | O1 | 50pf on 25pf orange | .65 | *.35* |
| | | *Nos. O89-O93 (5)* | 2.45 | *1.75* |

### For the State Authorities

O6

*Perf. 11½x11*

**1881-1902 Typo. Unwmk.**

| | | | | |
|---|---|---|---|---|
| **O94** | O6 | 2pf sl gray ('96) | 1.60 | 1.60 |
| **O95** | O6 | 3pf green | 25.00 | 4.50 |
| **O96** | O6 | 3pf dk brown ('90) | 1.60 | .80 |
| **O97** | O6 | 5pf violet | 8.00 | 1.90 |
| **O98** | O6 | 5pf green ('90) | 2.40 | .80 |
| **O99** | O6 | 10pf rose | 8.00 | 1.90 |
| **O100** | O6 | 20pf ultra | 1.00 | 1.60 |
| **O101** | O6 | 25pf brown | 35.00 | 6.50 |
| **O102** | O6 | 25pf orange ('90) | 5.25 | 1.40 |
| **O103** | O6 | 30pf org & blk ('02) | 2.00 | 2.75 |
| **O104** | O6 | 40pf dp rose & blk ('02) | 2.00 | 2.75 |
| **O105** | O6 | 50pf gray grn | 7.00 | 8.75 |
| **O106** | O6 | 50pf maroon ('91) | 1.60 | 4.00 |
| *a.* | | 50pf red brown ('90) | 240.00 | *1,750.* |
| **O107** | O6 | 1m yellow | 72.50 | 200.00 |
| **O108** | O6 | 1m violet ('90) | 6.25 | 16.00 |
| | | *Nos. O94-O108 (15)* | 179.20 | *255.25* |

See #O119-O135. For overprints & surcharges see #O109-O118, O146-O164, O176-O183.

Overprinted in Black

**1906**

| | | | | |
|---|---|---|---|---|
| **O109** | O6 | 2pf slate gray | 27.50 | *5.25* |
| **O110** | O6 | 3pf dk brown | 5.25 | *5.25* |
| **O111** | O6 | 5pf green | 4.75 | *5.25* |
| **O112** | O6 | 10pf dp rose | 4.50 | *5.25* |
| **O113** | O6 | 20pf ultra | 4.75 | *5.25* |
| **O114** | O6 | 25pf orange | 11.00 | *5.25* |
| **O115** | O6 | 30pf org & blk | 9.50 | *5.25* |
| **O116** | O6 | 40pf dp rose & blk | 32.50 | *5.25* |
| **O117** | O6 | 50pf red brown | 32.50 | *5.25* |
| **O118** | O6 | 1m purple | 65.00 | *5.25* |
| | | *Nos. O109-O118 (10)* | 197.25 | 52.50 |

Cent. of the kingdom of Wüttemberg.
Nos. O109 to O118 are also found imperforate, but it is doubtful if they were ever issued in that condition.

**1906-19 Wmk. 116**

| | | | | |
|---|---|---|---|---|
| **O119** | O6 | 2pf slate gray | .50 | *.25* |
| **O120** | O6 | 2½pf gray blk ('16) | .50 | *.25* |
| **O121** | O6 | 3pf dk brown | .50 | *.25* |
| **O122** | O6 | 5pf green | .50 | *.25* |
| **O123** | O6 | 7½pf orange ('16) | .55 | *.25* |
| **O124** | O6 | 10pf deep rose | .50 | *.25* |
| **O125** | O6 | 15pf yel brn ('16) | .55 | *.25* |
| **O126** | O6 | 15pf purple ('17) | 1.25 | *.30* |
| **O127** | O6 | 20pf ultra | .65 | *.25* |
| **O128** | O6 | 25pf orange | .50 | *.25* |
| **O129** | O6 | 25pf brn & blk ('17) | .40 | *.25* |
| **O130** | O6 | 30pf org & blk | .50 | *.25* |
| **O131** | O6 | 35pf brown ('19) | 1.60 | *3.25* |
| **O132** | O6 | 40pf dp rose & blk | .50 | *.25* |
| **O133** | O6 | 50pf red brown | .65 | *.25* |
| **O134** | O6 | 1m purple | 2.40 | *.25* |
| **O135** | O6 | 1m sl & blk ('17) | 2.40 | *.65* |
| | | *Nos. O119-O135 (17)* | 14.45 | *7.70* |

King Wilhelm II — O8

**1916 Unwmk. Typo. *Perf. 14***

| | | | | |
|---|---|---|---|---|
| **O136** | O8 | 2½pf slate | .80 | *.60* |
| **O137** | O8 | 7½pf orange | .80 | *.60* |
| **O138** | O8 | 10pf carmine | .80 | *.60* |
| **O139** | O8 | 15pf yellow brn | .80 | *.60* |
| **O140** | O8 | 20pf blue | .80 | *.60* |
| **O141** | O8 | 25pf gray blk | 1.60 | *.60* |
| **O142** | O8 | 30pf green | 1.60 | *.60* |
| **O143** | O8 | 40pf claret | 2.40 | *.60* |
| **O144** | O8 | 50pf red brn | 3.25 | *.60* |
| **O145** | O8 | 1m violet | 3.25 | *.60* |
| | | *Nos. O136-O145 (10)* | 16.10 | *6.00* |

25th year of the reign of King Wilhelm II.

Stamps of 1890-1906 Surcharged

**1916-19 Wmk. 116 *Perf. 11½x11***

| | | | | |
|---|---|---|---|---|
| **O146** | O6 | 25pf on 25pf orange | 3.00 | *.80* |
| *a.* | | Without watermark | 35.00 | 14,400. |
| **O147** | O6 | 50pf on 50pf red brn | 1.60 | *1.10* |
| *a.* | | Inverted surcharge | 32.50 | |

Beware of fake cancels on No. O146a.

No. O120 Surcharged in Blue

**1919** **Wmk. 116**

| | | | | |
|---|---|---|---|---|
| **O149** | O6 | 2pf on 2½pf gray blk | 1.45 | *1.60* |

Official Stamps of 1890-1919 Overprinted

**1919**

| | | | | |
|---|---|---|---|---|
| **O150** | O6 | 2½pf gray blk | .55 | *.40* |
| **O151** | O6 | 3pf dk brown | 7.25 | *.80* |
| *a.* | | Without watermark | 52.50 | |
| **O152** | O6 | 5pf green | .40 | *.40* |
| **O153** | O6 | 7½pf orange | .40 | *.40* |
| **O154** | O6 | 10pf rose | .40 | *.40* |
| **O155** | O6 | 15pf purple | .40 | *.40* |
| **O156** | O6 | 20pf ultra | .40 | *.40* |
| **O157** | O6 | 25pf brn & blk | .40 | *.40* |
| *a.* | | Inverted overprint | 82.50 | *160.00* |
| **O158** | O6 | 30pf org & blk | .80 | *.40* |
| *a.* | | Inverted overprint | 225.00 | *350.00* |
| **O159** | O6 | 35pf brown | .55 | *.40* |
| **O160** | O6 | 40pf rose & blk | .55 | *.40* |
| **O161** | O6 | 50pf claret | .80 | *.65* |
| **O162** | O6 | 1m slate & blk | .80 | *.80* |
| | | *Nos. O150-O162 (13)* | 13.70 | *6.25* |

Nos. O151, O151a Surcharged in Carmine

**1920** **Wmk. 116**

| | | | | |
|---|---|---|---|---|
| **O164** | O6 | 75pf on 3pf dk brn | 1.25 | *1.25* |
| *a.* | | Without watermark | 80.00 | *20.00* |

View of Stuttgart
O9

10pf, 50pf, 2.50m, 3m, View of Stuttgart. 15pf, 75pf, View of Ulm. 20pf, 1m, View of Tubingen. 30pf, 1.25m, View of Ellwangen.

**Wmk. 192**

**1920, Mar. 25** **Typo.** ***Perf. 14½***

| | | | | |
|---|---|---|---|---|
| **O166** | O9 | 10pf maroon | .55 | *1.00* |
| **O167** | O9 | 15pf brown | .55 | *1.00* |
| **O168** | O9 | 20pf indigo | .55 | *1.00* |
| **O169** | O9 | 30pf blue grn | .55 | *1.00* |
| **O170** | O9 | 50pf yellow | .55 | *1.00* |
| **O171** | O9 | 75pf bister | .55 | *1.00* |
| **O172** | O9 | 1m orange red | .80 | *1.00* |
| **O173** | O9 | 1.25m dp violet | .80 | *1.00* |
| **O174** | O9 | 2.50m dark ultra | 2.00 | *1.00* |
| **O175** | O9 | 3m yellow grn | 2.40 | *1.00* |
| | | *Nos. O166-O175 (10)* | 9.30 | *10.00* |

Official Stamps of 1906-19 Overprinted

**1920** **Wmk. 116** ***Perf. 11½x11***

| | | | | |
|---|---|---|---|---|
| **O176** | O6 | 5pf green | 2.40 | *3.25* |
| **O177** | O6 | 10pf deep rose | 1.60 | *2.75* |
| **O178** | O6 | 15pf purple | 1.60 | *2.75* |
| **O179** | O6 | 20pf ultra | 1.60 | *1.25* |
| *a.* | | Wmk. 192 | 125.00 | *275.00* |
| **O180** | O6 | 30pf orange & blk | 1.60 | *3.25* |
| **O181** | O6 | 40pf dp rose & blk | 1.60 | *2.75* |
| **O182** | O6 | 50pf red brown | 1.60 | *3.25* |
| **O183** | O6 | 1m slate & blk | 2.40 | *7.00* |
| | | *Nos. O176-O183 (8)* | 14.40 | *26.25* |

The note after No. O63 will also apply to Nos. O176-O183.

## NORTH GERMAN CONFEDERATION

Northern District
30 Groschen = 1 Thaler
Southern District
60 Kreuzer = 1 Gulden
Hamburg
16 Schillings = 1 Mark

Values for unused stamps are for examples with original gum as defined in the catalogue introduction. Stamps without gum sell for about 50% of the figures quoted.

A1

A2

***Rouletted 8½ to 10, 11 to 12½ and Compound***

**1868** **Typo.** **Unwmk.**

| | | | | |
|---|---|---|---|---|
| **1** | A1 | ¼gr violet | 25.00 | 15.00 |
| **2** | A1 | ⅓gr green | 30.00 | 4.00 |
| **3** | A1 | ½gr orange | 30.00 | 2.50 |
| **4** | A1 | 1gr rose | 20.00 | 1.60 |
| *b.* | | Half used as ½gr on cover | | — |
| **5** | A1 | 2gr ultra | 80.00 | 3.25 |
| **6** | A1 | 5gr bister | 80.00 | 9.50 |
| **7** | A2 | 1kr green | 35.00 | 8.00 |
| **8** | A2 | 2kr orange | 55.00 | 55.00 |
| **9** | A2 | 3kr rose | 35.00 | 3.25 |
| **10** | A2 | 7kr ultra | 160.00 | 11.00 |
| **11** | A2 | 18kr bister | 35.00 | 65.00 |
| | | *Nos. 1-11 (11)* | 585.00 | 178.10 |

See Nos. 13-23.

**Imperf**

| | | | | |
|---|---|---|---|---|
| *1a* | A1 | ¼gr red lilac | 200.00 | — |
| *2a* | A1 | ⅓gr green | 95.00 | — |
| *3a* | A1 | ½gr orange | 140.00 | — |
| *4a* | A1 | 1gr rose | 80.00 | — |
| *5a* | A1 | 2gr ultra | 275.00 | — |
| *6a* | A1 | 5gr bister | 275.00 | — |
| *7a* | A2 | 1kr green | 72.50 | *125.00* |
| *8a* | A2 | 2kr orange | 200.00 | 95.00 |
| *9a* | A2 | 3kr rose | 80.00 | 100.00 |
| *10a* | A2 | 7kr ultra | 350.00 | *675.00* |
| *11a* | A2 | 18kr bister | 350.00 | *675.00* |

A3

**1868**

| | | | | |
|---|---|---|---|---|
| **12** | A3 | (½s) lilac brown | 110.00 | 55.00 |
| *d.* | | Imperf | 225.00 | |

See No. 24.

**1869** ***Perf. 13½x14***

| | | | | |
|---|---|---|---|---|
| **13** | A1 | ¼gr lilac | 14.50 | 16.00 |
| *a.* | | ¼gr red violet | 25.00 | 20.00 |
| **14** | A1 | ⅓gr green | 5.25 | 2.75 |
| **15** | A1 | ½gr orange | 5.25 | 2.75 |
| **16** | A1 | 1gr rose | 4.00 | 1.60 |
| **17** | A1 | 2gr ultra | 7.25 | 2.00 |
| **18** | A1 | 5gr bister | 8.75 | 10.00 |
| **19** | A2 | 1kr green | 12.75 | 10.00 |
| **20** | A2 | 2kr orange | 40.00 | *110.00* |
| **21** | A2 | 3kr rose | 7.25 | 3.25 |
| **22** | A2 | 7kr ultra | 11.00 | 12.00 |
| **23** | A2 | 18kr bister | 150.00 | *1,750.* |
| | | *Nos. 13-23 (11)* | 266.00 | 1,920. |

Counterfeit cancels exist on No. 23.

**1869**

| | | | | |
|---|---|---|---|---|
| **24** | A3 | (½s) dull violet brown | 4.75 | 8.75 |

A4

A5

***Perf. 14x13½***

| | | | | |
|---|---|---|---|---|
| **25** | A4 | 10gr gray | 325.00 | 400.00 |
| | | Pen cancellation | | 200.00 |
| **26** | A5 | 30gr blue | 240.00 | *960.00* |
| | | Pen cancellation | | *400.00* |

Counterfeit cancels exist on No. 26.

See Germany designs A2, A3 and A8 for similar stamps.

### OFFICIAL STAMPS

O1

**1870** **Unwmk.** **Typo.** ***Perf. 14½x14***

| | | | | |
|---|---|---|---|---|
| **O1** | O1 | ¼gr black & buff | 27.50 | *45.00* |
| **O2** | O1 | ⅓gr black & buff | 9.50 | *20.00* |
| **O3** | O1 | ½gr black & buff | 2.75 | *4.00* |
| **O4** | O1 | 1gr black & buff | 2.75 | 2.00 |
| **O5** | O1 | 2gr black & buff | 7.25 | 4.75 |
| **O6** | O1 | 1kr black & gray | 32.50 | *250.00* |
| **O7** | O1 | 2kr black & gray | 80.00 | *1,250.* |
| **O8** | O1 | 3kr black & gray | 25.00 | *47.50* |
| **O9** | O1 | 7kr black & gray | 45.00 | *275.00* |
| | | *Nos. O1-O9 (9)* | 232.25 | 1,898. |

Counterfeit cancels exist on Nos. O6-O9.

The stamps of the North German Confederation were replaced by those of the German Empire on Jan. 1, 1872.

# GERMANY

ˈjər-mə-nē

LOCATION — In northern Europe bordering on the Baltic and North Seas
AREA — 182,104 sq. mi. (until 1945)
POP. — 67,032,242 (1946)
CAPITAL — Berlin

In 1949 the Russian occupied areas became a separate country, the German Democratic Republic. The country was reunified Oct. 3, 1990.

30 Silbergroschen or Groschen = 1 Thaler
60 Kreuzer = 1 Gulden
100 Pfennigs = 1 Mark (1875)
100 Pfennigs = 1 Deutsche Mark (1948)
100 Cents = 1 Euro (2002)

**Catalogue values for unused stamps in this country are for Never Hinged items, beginning with Scott 722 in the regular postage section, Scott B338 in the semi-postal section, Scott C61 in the airpost section, Scott 9N103 in the Berlin regular postage section and Scott 9NB12 in the Berlin semi-postal section.**

### Watermarks

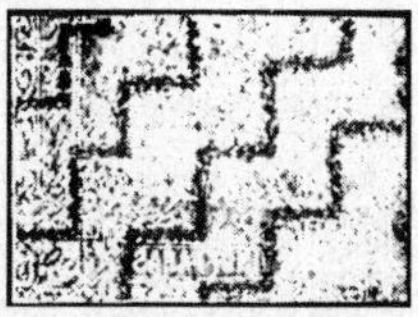
Wmk. 48 — Diagonal Zigzag Lines

Wmk. 116 — Crosses and Circles

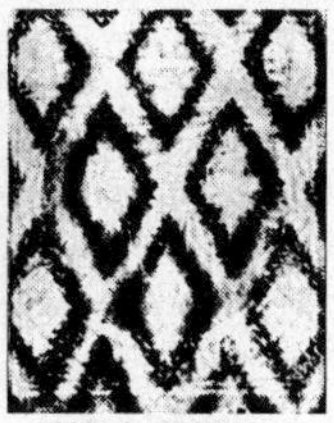
Wmk. 125 — Lozenges

Wmk. 126 — Network

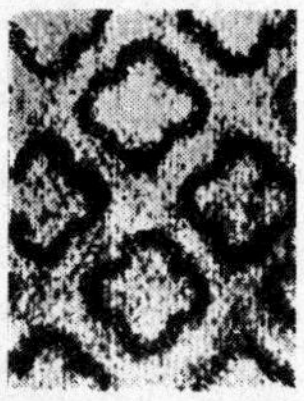
Wmk. 127 — Quatrefoils

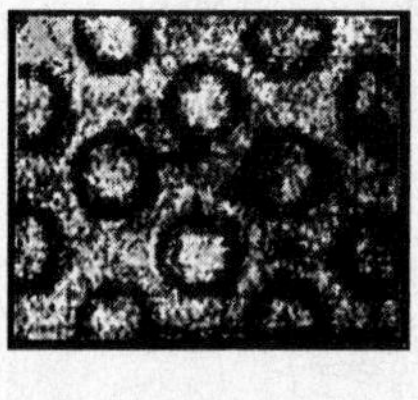
Wmk. 192 — Circles

Wmk. 223 — Eagle

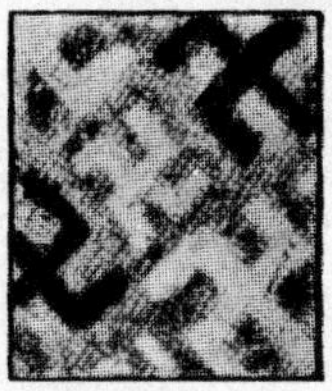
Wmk. 237 — Swastikas

Wmk. 241 — Cross

Wmk. 284 — "DEUTSCHE POST" Multiple

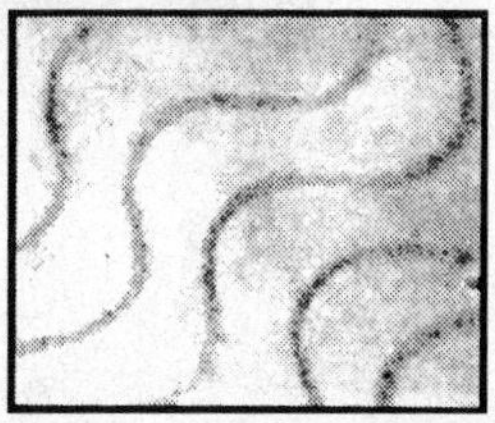
Wmk. 285 — Marbleized Pattern

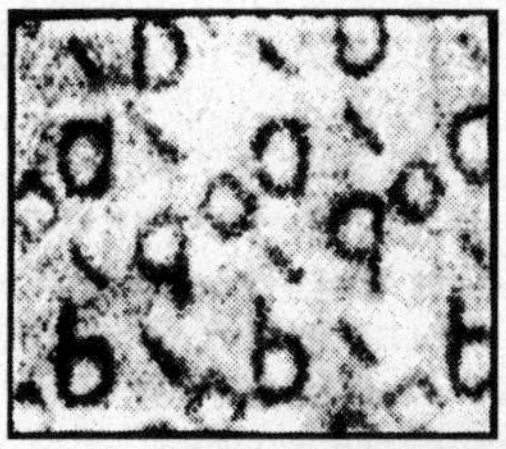
Wmk. 286 — D P Multiple

Wmk. 292 — Flowers, Multiple

Wmk. 295 — B P and Zigzag Lines

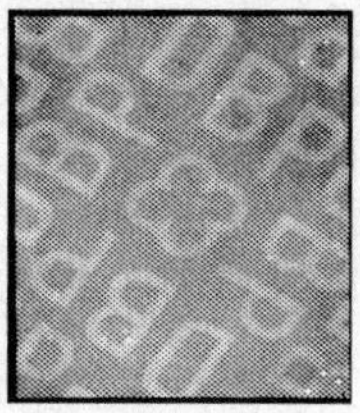
Wmk. 304 — DBP and Rosettes Multiple

### Empire

Values for unused stamps are for examples with original gum as defined in the catalogue introduction. Any exceptions are specifically mentioned.

Imperial Eagle — A1

**Typographed, Center Embossed**

**1872 Unwmk. *Perf. 13½x14½***

**Eagle with small shield**

| | | | | |
|---|---|---|---|---|
| **1** | A1 | ¼gr violet | 190.00 | 87.50 |
| **2** | A1 | ⅓gr green | 450.00 | 37.50 |
| ***a.*** | | Imperf. | | — |
| **3** | A1 | ½gr red orange | 950.00 | 37.50 |
| ***a.*** | | ½gr orange yellow | 1,100. | 45.00 |
| **4** | A1 | 1gr rose | 300.00 | 5.25 |
| ***a.*** | | Imperf. | | — |
| ***b.*** | | Half used as ½gr on cover | | *47,500.* |
| **5** | A1 | 2gr ultra | 1,600. | 14.50 |
| ***a.*** | | Imperf. | | *8,750.* |
| **6** | A1 | 5gr bister | 875.00 | 87.50 |
| ***a.*** | | Imperf. | | *10,000.* |
| **7** | A1 | 1kr green | 650.00 | 52.50 |
| **8** | A1 | 2kr orange | 37.50 | *160.00* |
| ***a.*** | | 2kr red orange | 600.00 | 300.00 |
| **9** | A1 | 3kr rose | 1,750. | 12.50 |
| **10** | A1 | 7kr ultra | 2,350. | 87.50 |
| **11** | A1 | 18kr bister | 475.00 | 375.00 |

Values for imperforates are for copies postmarked at Leipzig (⅓gr), Coblenz (1gr), Hoengen (2gr) and Leutersdorf (5gr).

A2

A3

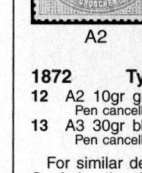

**1872 Typo. *Perf. 14½x13½***

| | | | | |
|---|---|---|---|---|
| **12** | A2 | 10gr gray | 52.50 | *2,400.* |
| | | Pen cancellation | | 150.00 |
| **13** | A3 | 30gr blue | 105.00 | *2,500.* |
| | | Pen cancellation | | *525.00* |

For similar designs see A8, North German Confederation A4, A5.

A4

A5

**Center Embossed**

**1872 *Perf. 13½x14½***

**Eagle with large shield**

| | | | | |
|---|---|---|---|---|
| **14** | A4 | ¼gr violet | 72.50 | 95.00 |
| **15** | A4 | ⅓gr yellow green | 32.50 | 14.50 |
| ***a.*** | | ⅓gr blue green | 125.00 | 110.00 |
| **16** | A4 | ½gr orange | 37.50 | 8.00 |
| ***a.*** | | Imperf. | | |
| **17** | A4 | 1gr rose | 42.50 | 1.90 |
| ***a.*** | | Imperf. | | *16,000.* |
| ***b.*** | | Half used as ½gr on cover | | *50,000.* |
| **18** | A4 | 2gr ultra | 19.00 | 4.25 |
| **19** | A4 | 2½gr orange brn | 1,800. | 55.00 |
| ***a.*** | | 2½gr lilac brown | *4,750.* | 375.00 |
| **20** | A4 | 5gr bister | 29.00 | 29.00 |
| ***a.*** | | Imperf. | | *6,500.* |
| **21** | A4 | 1kr yel grn | 32.50 | 25.00 |
| ***a.*** | | 1kr blue green | 365.00 | 440.00 |
| **22** | A4 | 2kr orange | 475.00 | *2,350.* |
| **23** | A4 | 3kr rose | 22.50 | 5.00 |
| **24** | A4 | 7kr ultra | 30.00 | *67.50* |
| **25** | A4 | 9kr red brown | 440.00 | 400.00 |
| ***a.*** | | 9kr lilac brown | 1,400. | 450.00 |
| **26** | A4 | 18kr bister | 35.00 | *2,000.* |

Values for Nos. 17a and 20a are for copies postmarked at Potsdam (1gr), Damgarten or Anklam (5gr).

Nos. 14-26 with embossing inverted are fraudulent.

**1874 Brown Surcharge**

| | | | | |
|---|---|---|---|---|
| **27** | A5 | 2½gr on 2½gr brn | 37.50 | 40.00 |
| **28** | A5 | 9kr on 9kr brown | 65.00 | *450.00* |

A6

A7

**"Pfennige"**

**1875-77 Typo.**

| | | | | |
|---|---|---|---|---|
| **29** | A6 | 3pf blue green | 55.00 | 5.25 |
| **30** | A6 | 5pf violet | 97.50 | 3.75 |

**Center Embossed**

| | | | | |
|---|---|---|---|---|
| **31** | A7 | 10pf rose | 40.00 | 1.50 |
| **32** | A7 | 20pf ultra | 450.00 | 1.50 |
| **33** | A7 | 25pf red brown | 475.00 | 18.00 |
| **34** | A7 | 50pf gray | 1,500. | 11.00 |
| **35** | A7 | 50pf ol gray ('77) | 1,650. | 12.50 |
| | | *Nos. 29-35 (7)* | 4,267. | 53.50 |

See Nos. 37-42. For surcharges see Offices in Turkey Nos. 1-6.

A8

**1875-90 Typo. *Perf. 14½x13½***

36 A8 2m brownish pur ('90) 65.00 3.50
a. 2m purple ('75) 375.00 125.00
b. 2m dull vio pur ('89) 1,500. 60.00

No. 36a used is valued as a stamp with cds cancel dated between Jan. 1875 and November 17, 1884.

**Types of 1875-77, "Pfennig" without final "e"**

**1880-83 *Perf. 13½x14½***

37 A6 3pf yel green 3.00 1.25
a. Imperf. —
38 A6 5pf violet 1.50 1.25

**Center Embossed**

39 A7 10pf red 8.00 1.25
a. Imperf. *325.00*
40 A7 20pf brt ultra 6.00 1.25
41 A7 25pf dull rose brn 15.00 5.25
a. 25pf red brown, thick paper 190.00 6.00
42 A7 50pf dp grayish ol grn 7.50 1.25
a. 50pf olive green 210.00 1.25
*Nos. 37-42 (6)* 41.00 11.50

Values for Nos. 37-42 are for stamps on thin paper. Those on thick paper sell for considerably more.

A9

A10

**1889-1900 *Perf. 13½x14½***

45 A9 2pf gray ('00) .50 *.75*
a. "REIGHSPOST" 55.00 *140.00*
Never hinged 190.00
46 A9 3pf brown 2.25 1.10
a. 3pf yellow brown 9.00 3.75
b. Imperf. 600.00 —
Never hinged 1,800.
c. 3pf reddish brown 110.00 8.00
47 A9 5pf blue green 1.40 1.10
48 A10 10pf carmine 1.75 1.10
a. Imperf. 225.00
Never hinged 650.00
49 A10 20pf ultra 7.50 1.10
a. 20pf Prus blue 2,250. 110.00
50 A10 25pf orange ('90) 30.00 1.50
a. Imperf. 190.00
Never hinged 625.00
51 A10 50pf chocolate 26.00 1.10
a. 50pf copper brown 375.00 9.75
b. Imperf. 325.00
Never hinged 425.00
*Nos. 45-51 (7)* 69.40 7.75
Set, never hinged 320.00

For surcharges and overprints see Offices in China Nos. 1-6, 16, Offices in Morocco 1-6, Offices in Turkey 8-12.

Germania — A11

**1900, Jan. 1 *Perf. 14***

52 A11 2pf gray .85 .50
a. Imperf. 350.00
Never hinged 1,600.
53 A11 3pf brown .85 1.00
a. Imperf. 350.00
Never hinged 1,600.
54 A11 5pf green 1.60 .60
55 A11 10pf carmine 2.40 .75
a. Imperf. 60.00
Never hinged 160.00
56 A11 20pf ultra 8.00 .60
57 A11 25pf orange & blk, *yel* 14.50 4.50
58 A11 30pf orange & blk, *sal* 18.50 .85
59 A11 40pf lake & black 22.50 1.25
60 A11 50pf pur & blk, *sal* 22.50 1.00
61 A11 80pf lake & blk, *rose* 37.50 2.25
*Nos. 52-61 (10)* 129.20 13.30
Set, never hinged 795.00

Early printings of Nos. 57-61 had "REICHSPOST" in taller and thicker letters than on the ordinary stamps.

For surcharges see Nos. 65B, Offices in China 17-32, Offices in Morocco 7-15, 32A, Offices in Turkey 13-20, 25-27.

**"REICHSPOST" Larger**

*57a A11 25pf 1,900. 7,200.*
*58a A11 30pf 1,900. 4,800.*
*59a A11 40pf 1,900. 4,800.*
*60a A11 50pf 1,900. 7,200.*
*61a A11 80pf 1,900. 7,200.*

General Post Office in Berlin — A12

"Union of North and South Germany" A13

Unveiling Kaiser Wilhelm I Memorial, Berlin — A14

Wilhelm II Speaking at Empire's 25th Anniversary Celebration A15

Type I

Type II

Two types of 5m:
I — "5" is thick; "M" has slight serifs.
II — "5" thinner; "M" has distinct serifs.

**Engr. *Perf. 14½x14***

62 A12 1m carmine rose 110.00 2.75
Never hinged 450.00
a. Imperf. *2,600.*
63 A13 2m gray blue 75.00 6.75
Never hinged 450.00
64 A14 3m black violet 110.00 50.00
Never hinged 650.00
65 A15 5m slate & car, I 1,350. 2,250.
Never hinged 4,800.
d. Red and white retouched 350.00 *400.00*
Never hinged 1,450.
e. White only retouched 640.00 *640.00*
Never hinged 1,750.
65A A15 5m slate & car, II 350.00 *400.00*
Never hinged 1,450.

Nos. 62-65 exist perf. 11½.

The vignette and frame of No. 65 usually did not align perfectly during printing. Red paint was used to retouch the vignette and/or white paint was used to retouch the inner frame.

No. 62a is without gum.

For surcharges see Offices in China Nos. 33-36A, Offices in Morocco 16-19A, Offices in Turkey 21-24B, 28-30.

**Half of No. 54 Handstamp Surcharged in Violet**

**3PF**

**1901 *Perf. 14***

65B A11 3pf on half of 5pf *9,750. 7,500.*
Never hinged *26,500.*

This provisional was produced aboard the German cruiser Vineta. The purser, with the ship commander's approval, surcharged and bisected 300 5pf stamps so the ship's post office could meet the need for a 3pf (printed matter rate). The crew wanted to send home U.S. newspapers reporting celebrations of the Kaiser's birthday.

Forgeries exist and improper usages as well.

A16

**1902 Typo.**

65C A16 2pf gray 1.50 .60
66 A16 3pf brown .75 *1.00*
a. "DFUTSCHES" 9.75 *40.00*
67 A16 5pf green 2.25 1.00
68 A16 10pf carmine 7.25 1.00
69 A16 20pf ultra 30.00 1.00
70 A16 25pf org & blk, *yel* 45.00 2.10
71 A16 30pf org & blk, *sal* 52.50 .60
72 A16 40pf lake & blk 67.50 1.00
73 A16 50pf pur & blk, *buff* 67.50 1.10
74 A16 80pf lake & blk, *rose* 150.00 2.75
*Nos. 65C-74 (10)* 424.25 12.15
Set, never hinged 1,900.

Nos. 65C-74 exist imperf. Value, set $2,000.

See Nos. 80-91, 118-119, 121-132, 169, 174, 210. For surcharges see Nos. 133-136, B1, Offices in China 37-42, 47-52, Offices in Morocco 20-28, 33-41, 45-53, Offices in Turkey 31-38, 43-50, 55-59.

A17

A18

A19

A20

***Perf. 14¼-14½ (26x17 holes)***

**Engr.**

75 A17 1m carmine rose 240.00 2.75
a. Imperf. 900.00 —
76 A18 2m gray blue 82.50 97.50
77 A19 3m black violet 225.00 18.00
a. Imperf. 900.00 —
78 A20 5m slate & car 210.00 18.00
a. Imperf. 900.00 —

See Nos. 92, 94-95, 102, 111-113. For surcharges see Nos. 115-116, Offices in China 43, 45-46, 53, 55-56, Offices in Morocco 29, 31-32, 42, 44, 54, 56-57, Offices in Turkey 39, 41-42, 51, 53-54.

A21

79 A21 2m gray blue 120.00 5.00
a. Imperf. 900.00 —
Never hinged 2,600.
*Nos. 75-79 (5)* 877.50 141.25
Set, never hinged 3,125.

See Nos. 93, 114. For surcharges see Nos. 117, Offices in China 44, 54, Offices in Morocco 30, 43, 55, Offices in Turkey 40, 52.

**1905-19 Typo. Wmk. 125 *Perf. 14***

80 A16 2pf gray ('05) 1.60 2.60
81 A16 3pf brown ('15) .60 *1.40*
82 A16 5pf green (shades) .60 *1.40*
b. Bklt. pane of 5 + label ('11) 250.00 500.00
Never hinged 500.00
c. Bklt. pane of 4 + 2 labels ('10) 400.00 800.00
Never hinged 800.00
d. Bklt. pane of 2 + 4 labels ('12) 250.00 500.00
Never hinged 500.00
e. Bklt. pane, #82 + 5 #83 ('17) 75.00 190.00
Never hinged 190.00
f. Bklt. pane, 2 #82 + 4 #83 ('20) 21.00 50.00
Never hinged 50.00
g. Bklt. pane, 4 #82 + 2 #83 ('19) 21.00 50.00
Never hinged 50.00
83 A16 10pf red .60 *1.40*
b. Bklt. pane of 5 + label ('10) 325.00 650.00
Never hinged 650.00
c. Bklt. pane of 4 + 2 labels ('12) 300.00 625.00
Never hinged 625.00
d. 10pf carmine red 2.00 1.50
84 A16 20pf blue vio ('18) .75 1.40
a. 20pf light blue 13.00 3.75
Never hinged 52.50
b. 20pf ultramarine 8.00 1.50
Never hinged 42.50
c. Imperf. 625.00 *2,750.*
Never hinged 1,750.
d. Half used as 10pf on cover 700.00
85 A16 25pf org & blk, *yel* .60 *1.40*
86 A16 30pf org & blk, *buff* .60 *1.40*
a. 30pf org & blk, *cr* 26.00 *90.00*
87 A16 40pf lake & black 1.00 *1.40*
88 A16 50pf pur & blk, *buff* .60 *1.40*

89 A16 60pf magenta 1.50 1.40
a. 60pf red violet 22.50 13.50
90 A16 75pf green & blk ('19) .25 *2.25*
91 A16 80pf lake & blk, *rose* 1.10 *1.90*

***Perf. 14½ (25x17 holes)***

**Engr.**

92 A17 1m car rose 2.25 2.25
93 A21 2m brt blue 5.25 4.75
a. 2m gray blue ('16) 42.50 *52.50*
94 A19 3m violet gray 2.25 *4.25*
b. 3m blk violet 11.50 26.00
95 A20 5m slate & car 1.90 *4.75*
a. Center inverted *45,000. 65,000.*
*Nos. 80-95 (16)* 21.45 35.35
Set, Never Hinged 52.50

Pre-war printings of Nos. 80-91 have brighter colors and white instead of yellow gum. They sell for considerably more than the wartime printings which are valued here. No. 80 exists only from a pre-war printing.

Nos. 92-95 exist only from a wartime printing. The 1m-5m also exist perf 14¼-14¾ (26x17 holes) in both pre-war and wartime printings. Both of these printings are much more expensive than Nos. 92-95. See the *Scott Classic Specialized Catalogue* for detailed listings.

Labels in No. 82c contain an "X." The version with advertising is worth 3 times as much. No. 82f has three 10pf stamps in the top row. The version with 3 on the bottom row is worth 4 times as much.

No. 84d was used at Field Post Office No. 107 in 1915, and at Field Post Office No. 766 during 1917.

Surcharged and overprinted stamps of designs A16-A22 are listed under Allenstein, Belgium, Danzig, France, Latvia, Lithuania, Marienwerder, Memel, Poland, Romania, Saar and Upper Silesia.

A22

**1916-19 Typo.**

96 A22 2pf lt gray ('18) .25 *3.25*
97 A22 2½pf lt gray .25 *1.90*
98 A22 7½pf red orange .30 2.25
b. Bklt. pane, 4 #98 + 2 #100 110.00 275.00
Never hinged 275.00
c. Bklt. pane, 2 #98 + 4 #99 125.00 300.00
Never hinged 300.00
d. Bklt. pane, 2 #98 + 4 #100 110.00 275.00
Never hinged 275.00
e. Bklt. pane, 2 #82 + 4 #98 37.50 90.00
Never hinged 90.00
f. 7½pf yellow orange 3.25 2.25
99 A22 15pf yellow brown 3.00 2.25
100 A22 15pf dk violet ('17) .25 *1.90*
b. Bklt. pane, 4 #82 + 2 #100 110.00 275.00
Never hinged 275.00
c. Bklt. pane, 2 #83 + 4 #100 82.50 210.00
Never hinged 210.00
101 A22 35pf red brown ('19) .25 *2.25*
*Nos. 96-101 (6)* 4.30 *13.80*
Set, never hinged 13.50

See No. 120. For surcharge see No. B2.

Nos. 98e and 100c have the 2 stamps first in the bottom row.

**Type of 1902**

**1920 Engr. Wmk. 192 *Perf. 14½***

102 A19 3m black violet 1,875. *3,750.*
Never hinged 4,500.

**Republic**
**National Assembly Issue**

A23

A24

Rebuilding Germany — A25

Designs: A23, Live Stump of Tree Symbolizing that Germany will Survive her Difficulties. A24, New Shoots from Oak Stump Symbolical of New Government.

***Perf. 13x13½***

**1919-20 Unwmk. Typo.**

105 A23 10pf carmine rose .25 1.50
106 A24 15pf choc & blue .25 1.50
107 A25 25pf green & red .25 1.50
108 A25 30pf red vio & red ('20) .25 1.50
*Nos. 105-108 (4)* 1.00 *6.00*
Set, never hinged 2.65

**Types of 1902**
***Perf. 15x14½***

**1920 Wmk. 125 Offset**

111 A17 1m red 2.00 *2.50*
a. Double impression 120.00 *600.00*
112 A17 1.25m green 1.60 *1.90*
a. Double impression 1,200.
113 A17 1.50m yellow brown .50 *1.90*
c. As "a," double impression 100.00 *725.00*
114 A21 2.50m lilac rose .50 *2.50*
a. 2.50m magenta 1.50 *12.00*
b. 2.50m brown lilac .60 *2.75*
c. Double impression 100.00 *725.00*
d. As "a," double impression 650.00
e. As "b," double impression 650.00
*Nos. 111-114 (4)* 4.60 *8.80*
Set, never hinged 14.00

Nos. 111, 112 and 113 differ from the illustration in many minor respects. The numerals of Nos. 75 and 92 are outlined, with shaded background. Those of No. 111 are plain, with solid background and flags have been added to the top of the building, at right and left.

Types of 1902 Surcharged

**1920 Engr. *Perf. 14½***

115 A17 1.25m on 1m green .40 *6.00*
116 A17 1.50m on 1m org brn .40 *7.25*
117 A21 2.50m on 2m lilac rose 8.75 *200.00*
*Nos. 115-117 (3)* 9.55 *213.25*
Set, never hinged 25.00

**Germania Types of 1902-16**

**1920 Typo. *Perf. 14, 14½***

118 A16 5pf brown .25 *2.00*
119 A16 10pf orange .25 *1.50*
a. Tête bêche pair .90 *5.75*
Never hinged 2.25
d. Bklt. pane, 4 #119 + 2 #123 2.40 13.00
Never hinged 6.00
120 A22 15pf violet brn .25 *1.90*
a. Imperf. 67.50
Never hinged 190.00
c. Bklt. pane, 4 #84 + 2 #120 7.25 17.00
Never hinged 17.00
121 A16 20pf green .25 *2.25*
a. Imperf. *1,200.*
123 A16 30pf dull blue .25 *2.50*
a. Tête bêche pair .90 *6.75*
Never hinged 2.25
d. Bklt. pane, 2 #123 + 4 #124 2.40 13.00
Never hinged 6.00
124 A16 40pf carmine rose .25 *1.90*
a. Tête bêche pair .90 *6.75*
Never hinged 2.25
b. Imperf. 150.00 900.00
Never hinged 375.00
d. Bklt. pane, 2 #124 + 4 #126 4.50 42.50
Never hinged 11.50
125 A16 50pf red lilac .60 *1.90*
126 A16 60pf olive green .25 *1.60*
a. Tête bêche pair .70 *9.75*
Never hinged 1.75
c. Imperf. 160.00
Never hinged 425.00
127 A16 75pf red violet .60 *1.90*
128 A16 80pf blue violet .25 *2.25*
a. Imperf. 190.00
Never hinged 450.00
129 A16 1m violet & grn .25 *2.25*
a. Imperf. 77.50
Never hinged 190.00
130 A16 1¼m ver & mag .25 *1.90*
131 A16 2m carmine & bl .60 *1.50*
132 A16 4m black & rose .25 *2.25*
*Nos. 118-132 (14)* 4.55 *27.60*
Set, never hinged 10.50

**Stamps of 1920 Surcharged**

No. 133

No. 135

Nos. 134, 136

**1921, Aug.**

133 A16 1.60m on 5pf .25 *2.25*
134 A16 3m on 1¼m .25 *2.25*
135 A16 5m on 75pf (G) .25 *2.25*
136 A16 10m on 75pf .40 *2.25*
*Nos. 133-136 (4)* 1.15 *9.00*
Set, never hinged 3.50

In 1920 the current stamps of Bavaria were overprinted "Deutsches Reich". These stamps were available for postage throughout Germany, but because they were used almost exclusively in Bavaria, they are listed among the issues of that state.

A26

Iron Workers
A27

Miners
A28

Farmers
A29

Post Horn
A30

Numeral of Value — A31

Plowing
A32

**Wmk. Lozenges (125)**

**1921 Typo. *Perf. 14***

137 A26 5pf claret .25 *1.75*
138 A26 10pf olive green .25 *1.90*
a. Tête bêche pair .85 *21.00*
Never hinged 2.10
b. Bklt. pane, 5 #138 + 1 #141 4.50 60.00
Never hinged 11.50
139 A26 15pf grnsh blue .25 *1.60*
140 A26 25pf dark brown .25 *1.60*
141 A26 30pf blue green .25 *1.60*
a. Tête bêche pair .70 *19.00*
Never hinged 1.75
b. Bklt. pane, 2 #124 + 4 #141 5.00 42.50
Never hinged 12.00
142 A26 40pf red orange .25 *1.40*
143 A26 50pf violet .30 *1.60*
144 A27 60pf red violet .25 *1.40*
145 A27 80pf carmine rose .25 *5.25*
146 A28 100pf yellow grn .30 *1.90*
147 A28 120pf ultra .25 *1.60*
148 A29 150pf orange .25 *1.90*
149 A29 160pf slate grn .25 *8.25*
150 A30 2m dp vio & rose .40 *3.50*
151 A30 3m red & yel .40 *15.00*
152 A30 4m dp grn & yel grn .25 *3.50*

**Engr.**

153 A31 5m orange .30 *2.25*
154 A31 10m carmine rose .50 *2.50*
155 A32 20m indigo & grn 1.10 *2.75*
a. Green background inverted 190.00 *900.00*
Never hinged 675.00
*Nos. 137-155 (19)* 6.30 *61.25*
Set, never hinged 16.00

See Nos. 156-209, 211, 222-223, 225, 227. For surcharges and overprints see Nos. 241-245, 247-248, 261-262, 273-276, B6-B7, O24.

**1922 Litho. *Perf. 14½x14***

156 A31 100m brown vio, *buff* .25 *1.40*
157 A31 200m rose, *buff* .25 *1.40*
158 A31 300m green, *buff* .25 *1.40*
159 A31 400m bis brn, *buff* .50 *2.25*
160 A31 500m orange, *buff* .25 *1.40*
*Nos. 156-160 (5)* 1.50 *7.85*
Set, never hinged 3.40

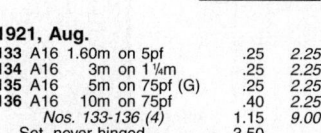

**Postally Used vs. CTO**

Values quoted for canceled stamps of the 1921-1923 issues are for postally used stamps. These bring higher prices than the plentiful canceled-to-order stamps made by applying genuine handstamps to remainders. C.T.O. examples sell for about the same price as unused stamps. Certification of postal usage by competent authorities is necessary.

*Perf. 14, 14½*

**1921-22 Typo. Wmk. 126**

**161** A26 5pf claret .75 *200.00*
**162** A26 10pf olive grn 6.75 *175.00*
**163** A26 15pf grnsh blue .55 *210.00*
**164** A26 25pf dark brown .25 *3.00*
**165** A26 30pf blue green .85 *300.00*
**166** A26 40pf red orange .25 *3.75*
**167** A26 50pf violet ('21) .25 *1.50*
**168** A27 60pf red violet .25 *20.00*
**169** A16 75pf red violet .35 *2.25*
**170** A26 75pf deep ultra .25 *3.00*
**171** A27 80pf car rose .40 *55.00*
**172** A28 100pf olive green .25 *1.50*
*a.* Imperf. 60.00 1,500.
Never hinged 150.00
**173** A28 120pf ultra .70 *110.00*
**174** A16 1¼m ver & mag .25 *1.50*
**175** A29 150pf orange .25 *1.40*
*a.* Imperf. 37.50
Never hinged 110.00
**176** A29 160pf slate green .70 *160.00*
**177** A30 2m violet & rose .25 *1.40*
**178** A30 3m red & yel ('21) .25 *1.40*
*a.* Imperf. 37.50 *375.00*
Never hinged 110.00
**179** A30 4m dp grn & yel grn .25 *1.40*
**180** A30 5m org & yel .30 *1.90*
*a.* Imperf. 140.00
**181** A30 10m car & pale rose .30 *1.50*
*a.* Pale rose (background) omitted 45.00 *975.00*
**182** A30 20m violet & org .25 *2.50*
**183** A30 30m brown & yel .25 *1.50*
**184** A30 50m dk grn & vio .25 *1.50*
*Nos. 161-184 (24)* 15.15 *1,261.*
Set, never hinged 37.50

**1922-23**

SIX MARKS:
Type I — Numerals upright.
Type II — Numerals leaning toward the right and slightly thinner.

EIGHT MARKS:
Type I — Numerals 2½mm wide with thick strokes.
Type II — Numerals 2mm wide with thinner strokes.

**185** A30 2m blue violet .25 *1.50*
*a.* Imperf. 140.00
**186** A30 3m red .25 *1.50*
**187** A30 4m dark green .25 *1.50*
*a.* Imperf. 30.00
*b.* 4m deep blue green 1.50 5.25
**188** A30 5m orange .25 *1.50*
*a.* Imperf. 110.00
**189** A30 6m dark blue (II) .25 *1.50*
*a.* Type I .25 *1.90*
*b.* Imperf. 110.00
**190** A30 8m olive green (I) .25 *1.50*
*a.* Type II .40 *37.50*
**191** A30 20m dk violet ('23) .25 *1.50*
**192** A30 30m pur brn ('23) .25 *7.25*
**193** A30 40m lt green .25 *1.90*

**Engr.**

**194** A31 5m orange .25 *1.50*
*a.* Imperf. 140.00 2,100.
**195** A31 10m carmine rose .55 *2.25*
**196** A32 20m indigo & grn .25 *3.50*
*a.* Imperf. 175.00 2,100.
*b.* Green background inverted 32.50 *675.00*
*Nos. 185-196 (12)* 3.30 *26.90*
Set, never hinged 8.85

**1922-23 Litho. *Perf. 14½x14***

**198** A31 50m indigo .25 *1.50*
**199** A31 100m brn vio, *buff* ('23) .25 *1.40*
**200** A31 200m rose, *buff* ('23) .25 *1.90*
**201** A31 300m grn, *buff* ('23) .25 *1.50*
**202** A31 400m bis brn, *buff* ('23) .25 *1.50*
**203** A31 500m org, *buff* ('23) .25 *1.50*
**204** A31 1000m gray ('23) .25 *1.50*
**205** A31 2000m bl ('23) .35 *1.90*
**206** A31 3000m brn ('23) .25 *2.75*
**207** A31 4000m vio ('23) .25 *1.50*
*a.* Imperf. 37.50 *190.00*
Never hinged 110.00

**208** A31 5000m gray grn ('23) .30 *1.50*
*a.* Imperf. 52.50 *225.00*
Never hinged 150.00
**209** A31 100,000m ver ('23) .25 *1.40*
*a.* Imperf. 52.50 225.00
Never hinged 150.00
*Nos. 198-209 (12)* 3.15 *19.85*
Set, never hinged 5.35

**1920-22 Wmk. 127 Typo.**

**210** A16 1¼m ver & mag 450.00 *975.00*
Never hinged 1,350.
**211** A30 50m grn & vio ('22) 2.25 *825.00*
Never hinged 5.25

Wmk. 127 was intended for use only in printing revenue stamps.

Arms of Munich — A33

**Wmk. Network (126)**

**1922, Apr. 22 Typo. *Perf. 13x13½***

**212** A33 1¼m claret .25 *1.90*
**213** A33 2m dark violet .25 *1.90*
**214** A33 3m vermilion .25 *1.90*
**215** A33 4m deep blue .25 *1.90*

**Wmk. Lozenges (125)**

**216** A33 10m brown, *buff* .55 *2.75*
**217** A33 20m lilac rose, *pink* 3.25 *11.50*
*Nos. 212-217 (6)* 4.80 *21.85*
Set, never hinged 14.70

Munich Industrial Fair.

**Type of 1921 and**

Miners — A34

A35

**1922-23 Wmk. 126 *Perf. 14***

**221** A34 5m orange .25 *13.00*
**222** A29 10m dull blue ('22) .25 *1.50*
**223** A29 12m vermilion ('22) .25 *1.50*
**224** A34 20m red lilac .25 *1.50*
**225** A29 25m olive brown .25 *1.50*
**226** A34 30m olive green .25 *2.25*
**227** A29 40m green .25 *1.50*
**228** A34 50m grnsh blue .35 *125.00*
**229** A35 100m violet .25 *1.50*
**230** A35 200m carmine rose .25 *1.50*
**231** A35 300m green .25 *1.40*
**232** A35 400m dark brown .25 *5.75*
**233** A35 500m red orange .25 *6.50*
**234** A35 1000m slate .25 *1.40*
*Nos. 221-234 (14)* 3.60 *165.80*
Set, never hinged 7.00

The 50m was issued only in vertical coils.
Nos. 222-223 exist imperf.
For surcharges and overprints see Nos. 246, 249-260, 263-271, 277, 310, B5, O22-O23, O25-O28.

Wartburg Castle — A36

Cathedral of Cologne — A37

**1923 Engr.**

**237** A36 5000m deep blue .30 *3.25*
*a.* Imperf. 300.00 *1,100.*
Never hinged 750.00
**238** A37 10,000m brn ol .30 *4.00*
Set, never hinged 1.80

Abbreviations:
Th = (Tausend) Thousand
Mil = (Million) Million
Mlrd = (Milliarde) Billion

A38

**1923 Typo.**

**238A** A38 5th m grnsh blue .25 *17.00*
*b.* Imperf. 90.00
Never hinged 240.00
**239** A38 50th m bister .25 *1.50*
*a.* Imperf. 22.50 *3,750.*
Never hinged 60.00
**240** A38 75th m dark violet .25 *11.00*
*Nos. 238A-240 (3)* .75 29.50
Set, never hinged 1.10

For surcharges see Nos. 272, 278.

**Stamps and Types of 1922-23 Surcharged in Black, Blue, Green or Brown**

No. 241

No. 243

No. 246

No. 253

No. 269

**Wmk. Lozenges (125)**

**1923 *Perf. 14***

**241** A26 8th m on 30pf .25 *1.50*
*a.* "8" inverted 21.00 *325.00*
Never hinged 60.00

**Wmk. Network (126)**

**242** A26 5th m on 40pf .25 *1.60*
**242A** A26 8th m on 30pf 16.00 *6,000.*
**243** A29 15th m on 40m .25 *1.50*
**244** A29 20th m on 12m .25 *1.50*
*a.* Inverted surcharge 110.00 *1,000.*
**245** A29 20th m on 25m .25 *2.25*
**246** A35 20th m on 200m .25 *2.25*
*a.* Inverted surcharge 57.50 750.00
Never hinged 150.00
**247** A29 25th m on 25m .25 *14.50*
**248** A29 30th m on 10m dp bl .25 *1.40*
*a.* Inverted surcharge 67.50
Never hinged 175.00
**249** A35 30th m on 200m pale bl (Bl) .25 *1.50*
*a.* Without surcharge 110.00
Never hinged 225.00
**250** A35 75th m on 300m yel grn .25 *14.50*
*a.* Imperf. 45.00
Never hinged 125.00
**251** A35 75th m on 400m yel grn .25 *1.50*

**252** A35 75th m on 1000m yel grn .25 *1.90*
*a.* Without surcharge 110.00
Never hinged 225.00
**253** A35 100th m on 100m .25 *2.25*
*a.* Double surcharge 37.50 *450.00*
Never hinged 97.50
*b.* Inverted surcharge 14.50
Never hinged 37.50
**254** A35 100th m on 400m bluish grn (G) .25 *1.40*
*a.* Imperf. 50.00 525.00
Never hinged 110.00
*b.* Without surcharge 110.00
Never hinged 225.00
**255** A35 125th m on 1000m sal .25 *1.90*
**256** A35 250th m on 200m .25 *5.25*
*a.* Inverted surcharge 35.00
Never hinged 90.00
*b.* Double surcharge 52.50
Never hinged 140.00
**257** A35 250th m on 300m dp grn .25 *17.00*
*a.* Inverted surcharge 35.00
Never hinged 90.00
**258** A35 250th m on 400m .25 *19.00*
*a.* Inverted surcharge 26.00
Never hinged 75.00
**259** A35 250th m on 500m pink .25 *1.50*
*a.* Imperf. 52.50 *675.00*
Never hinged 125.00
**260** A35 250th m on 500m red org .25 *19.00*
*a.* Double surcharge 30.00 *975.00*
Never hinged 75.00
*b.* Inverted surcharge 30.00
Never hinged 82.50
**261** A26 800th m on 5pf lt grn (G) .25 *4.25*
*a.* Imperf. 35.00 *150.00*
Never hinged 90.00
**262** A26 800th m on 10pf lt grn (G) .25 *5.00*
*a.* Imperf. 30.00
Never hinged 90.00
**263** A35 800th m on 200m .25 *75.00*
*a.* Double surcharge 75.00 *975.00*
Never hinged 190.00
*b.* Inverted surcharge 37.50
Never hinged 110.00
**264** A35 800th m on 300m lt grn (G) .25 *5.00*
*a.* Black surcharge 47.50
**265** A35 800th m on 400m dk brn .25 *14.50*
*a.* Inverted surcharge 42.50
Never hinged 110.00
*b.* Double surcharge 75.00
Never hinged 190.00
**266** A35 800th m on 400m lt grn (G) .25 *3.75*
**267** A35 800th m on 500m lt grn (G) .25 *1,500.*
*a.* 800th m on 500m red org (Bk) 37.50
**268** A35 800th m on 1000m lt grn (G) .25 *1.50*
**269** A35 2mil m on 200m rose red .25 *2.25*
*b.* 2mil m on 200m car rose (#230) *1,500.*
Never hinged 3,400.
**270** A35 2mil m on 300m dp grn .25 *2.25*
*a.* Inverted surcharge 42.50
Never hinged 110.00
*b.* Double surcharge 75.00
Never hinged 190.00
**271** A35 2mil m on 500m dl rose .25 *6.50*
**272** A38 2mil m on 5th m dl rose .25 *1.50*
*b.* Imperf. 42.50 *125.00*

Nos. 264a, 267a were not put in use.

***Serrate Roulette 13½***

**273** A26 400th m on 15pf bis (Br) .25 *4.50*
*a.* Imperf. 52.50 275.00
Never hinged 125.00
**274** A26 400th m on 25pf bis (Br) .25 *4.50*
*a.* Imperf. 90.00 *275.00*
Never hinged 225.00
**275** A26 400th m on 30pf bis (Br) .25 *4.50*
*a.* Imperf. 45.00
Never hinged 110.00
*b.* Double surcharge 90.00
Never hinged 175.00
**276** A26 400th m on 40pf bis (Br) .25 *4.50*
*a.* Imperf. 45.00 —
Never hinged 110.00
*b.* Double surcharge 90.00
Never hinged 175.00

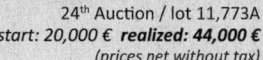

**277** A35 2mil m on 200m rose red .45 *150.00*
**278** A38 2mil m on 5th m dull rose .25 *9.00*
*Nos. 241-278 (39)* 25.70 *7,911.*
Set, never hinged 51.00

Nos. 272-276 exist without surcharge. Value each, $150 unused, $375 never hinged.

A39

A39a

The stamps of types A39 and A39a usually have the value darker than the rest of the design.

**1923** **Wmk. 126** ***Perf. 14***

**280** A39 500th m brown .25 *2.75*
**281** A39 1mil m grnsh bl .25 *1.60*
*a.* Imperf. 52.50 *350.00*
Never hinged 110.00
**282** A39 2mil m dull vio .25 *20.00*
**284** A39 4mil m yel grn .25 1.50
*a.* Value double 57.50
Never hinged 140.00
*b.* Imperf. 42.50
Never hinged 97.50
**285** A39 5mil m rose .25 *1.50*
**286** A39 10mil m red .25 1.50
*a.* Value double 50.00 *3,750.*
Never hinged 125.00
**287** A39 20mil m ultra .25 *1.90*
**288** A39 30mil m red brn .25 *9.25*
**289** A39 50mil m dull ol grn .25 *1.90*
*a.* Imperf. 52.50 *350.00*
Never hinged 125.00
*b.* Value inverted 45.00
Never hinged 120.00
**290** A39 100mil m gray .25 *1.50*
**291** A39 200mil m bis brn .25 *1.50*
*a.* Imperf. 42.50
Never hinged 97.50
**293** A39 500mil m ol grn .25 *1.40*
**294** A39a 1mlrd m choc .30 *1.90*
**295** A39a 2mlrd m pale brn & grn .25 *1.90*
**296** A39a 5mlrd m yellow & brn .25 *1.50*
**297** A39a 10mlrd m ap grn & grn .25 *1.50*
*a.* Imperf. 45.00 *275.00*
Never hinged 110.00
**298** A39a 20mlrd m bluish grn & brn .25 *1.90*
**299** A39a 50mlrd m bl & dp bl .25 *35.00*
*Nos. 280-299 (18)* 4.55 *90.00*
Set, never hinged 11.50

The variety "value omitted" exists on Nos. 280-281, 284-287, 290-291, 293-294, 296 and 298-299. Values $37.50 to $100 hinged, $75 to $190 never hinged.

See Nos. 301-309. For surcharges and overprints see Nos. 311-321, O40-O46.

***Serrate Roulette 13½***

**301** A39 10mil m red .55 *45.00*
**302** A39 20mil m ultra .55 *300.00*
**303** A39 50mil m dull grn .55 *6.00*
**304** A39 200mil m bis brn .55 *11.50*
**305** A39a 1mlrd m choc .55 *7.50*
**306** A39a 2mlrd m pale brn & grn .55 *3.50*
**307** A39a 5mlrd m yel & brn .75 *2.25*
**308** A39a 20mlrd m bluish grn & brn .75 *11.00*
**309** A39a 50mlrd m bl & dp bl 1.90 *675.00*
*Nos. 301-309 (9)* 6.70 *1,061.*
Set, never hinged 18.50

**Stamps and Types of 1923 Surcharged with New Values**

**1923** ***Perf. 14***

**Design Type A35**

**310** 1mlrd m on 100m vio .25 *29.00*
*a.* Inverted surcharge 110.00
Never hinged 300.00
*b.* Deep reddish purple 60.00 *3,600.*
Never hinged 150.00

**Design Type A39**

**311** 5mlrd m on 2mil m .25 *125.00*
*a.* Inverted surcharge 19.00
Never hinged 57.50
*b.* Double surcharge 45.00
Never hinged 110.00
**312** 5mlrd m on 4mil m .25 *22.50*
*a.* Inverted surcharge 37.50 *1,200.*
Never hinged 110.00
*b.* Double surcharge 37.50
Never hinged 97.50
**313** 5mlrd m on 10mil m .25 *2.75*
*a.* Inverted surcharge 19.00 *1,100.*
Never hinged 57.50
*b.* Double surcharge 37.50
Never hinged 97.50
**314** 10mlrd m on 20mil m .25 *4.50*
*a.* Double surcharge 45.00
Never hinged 125.00
*b.* Inverted surcharge 26.00
Never hinged 75.00
**315** 10mlrd m on 50mil m .25 *4.50*
*a.* Inverted surcharge 19.00 *900.00*
Never hinged 57.50
*b.* Double surcharge 45.00
Never hinged 125.00
**316** 10mlrd m on 100mil m .25 *7.50*
*a.* Inverted surcharge 26.00 *1,500.*
Never hinged 75.00
*b.* Double surcharge 45.00
Never hinged 125.00
*Nos. 310-316 (7)* 1.75 *195.75*
Set, never hinged 5.00

No. 310b was issued in Bavaria only and is known as the Hitler provisional. Excellent forgeries exist.

***Serrate Roulette 13½***

**Design Type A39**

**319** 5mlrd m on 10mil m 1.90 *190.00*
*a.* Inverted surcharge 26.00 *1,100.*
Never hinged 67.50
*b.* Double surcharge 45.00
Never hinged 110.00
**320** 10mlrd m on 20mil m 5.00 *110.00*
**321** 10mlrd m on 50mil m 1.90 *37.50*
*a.* Inverted surcharge 26.00 *1,100.*
Never hinged 67.50
*Nos. 319-321 (3)* 8.80 *337.50*
Set, never hinged 22.50

A40

German Eagle — A41

**1923** ***Perf. 14***

**323** A40 3pf brown .35 .25
**324** A40 5pf dark green .35 .25
**325** A40 10pf carmine .35 .25
**326** A40 20pf deep ultra .95 .35
**327** A40 50pf orange 2.75 1.00
**328** A40 100pf brn vio 8.25 1.10
*Nos. 323-328 (6)* 13.00 3.20
Set, never hinged 80.00

For overprints see Nos. O47-O52.

**Imperf**

| | | | | |
|---|---|---|---|---|
| *323a* | A40 | 3pf | 125.00 | *275.00* |
| *324a* | A40 | 5pf | 110.00 | — |
| *325a* | A40 | 10pf | 110.00 | 190.00 |
| *326a* | A40 | 20pf | 140.00 | *225.00* |
| *327a* | A40 | 50pf | 800.00 | — |
| *328a* | A40 | 100pf | 175.00 | — |
| *Nos. 323a-328a (6)* | | | 1,460. | *690.00* |
| Set, never hinged | | | 3,100. | |

**Value Omitted**

| | | | | |
|---|---|---|---|---|
| *323b* | A40 | 3pf | 160.00 | *300.00* |
| *324b* | A40 | 5pf | 160.00 | *300.00* |
| *325b* | A40 | 10pf | 160.00 | |
| *326b* | A40 | 20pf | 160.00 | |
| *327b* | A40 | 50pf | 160.00 | |
| *328b* | A40 | 100pf | 160.00 | |
| *Nos. 323b-328b (6)* | | | 960.00 | |
| Set, never hinged | | | 2,250. | |

**1924** **Wmk. 126**

**330** A41 3pf lt brown .30 .35
**331** A41 5pf lt green .30 .35
**332** A41 10pf vermilion .35 .35
**333** A41 20pf dull blue 1.90 .35
**334** A41 30pf rose lilac 1.90 .45
**335** A41 40pf olive green 13.00 .75
**336** A41 50pf orange 13.50 1.10
*Nos. 330-336 (7)* 31.25 3.70
Set, never hinged 275.00

The values above 5pf have "Pf" in the upper right corner.
For overprints see Nos. O53-O61.

**Imperf.**

| | | | | |
|---|---|---|---|---|
| *330a* | A41 | 3pf | 140.00 | *375.00* |
| *331a* | A41 | 5pf | 175.00 | *375.00* |
| *332a* | A41 | 10pf | 225.00 | |
| *333a* | A41 | 20pf | 160.00 | |
| *334a* | A41 | 30pf | 160.00 | |
| *335a* | A41 | 40pf | 190.00 | |
| *Nos. 330a-335a (6)* | | | 1,050. | |
| Set, never hinged | | | 2,475. | |

Rheinstein Castle — A43

View of Cologne A44

Marienburg Castle — A45

**1924** **Engr.** **Wmk. 126**

**337** A43 1m green 10.50 2.25
**338** A44 2m blue 18.00 2.00
**339** A45 3m claret 21.00 5.25
*Nos. 337-339 (3)* 49.50 9.50
Set, never hinged 153.75

See No. 387.

Dr. Heinrich von Stephan
A46 A47

**1924-28** **Typo.**

**340** A46 10pf dark green .55 .30
*a.* Imperf 325.00
**341** A46 20pf dark blue 1.25 .60
**342** A47 60pf red brown 3.75 .75
*a.* Chalky paper ('28) 21.00 13.50
**343** A47 80pf slate 9.75 1.50
*Nos. 340-343 (4)* 15.30 3.15
Set, never hinged 77.75

Universal Postal Union, 50th anniversary.

Traffic Wheel — A48

German Eagle Watching Rhine Valley — A49

**1925, May 30** ***Perf. 13½x13***

**345** A48 5pf deep green 3.00 5.25
**346** A48 10pf vermilion 3.75 9.75
Set, never hinged 38.00

German Traffic Exhibition, Munich, May 30-Oct. 11, 1925.

**1925** ***Perf. 14***

**347** A49 5pf green .45 .35
**348** A49 10pf vermilion 1.10 .35
**349** A49 20pf deep blue 4.50 1.00
*Nos. 347-349 (3)* 6.05 1.70
Set, never hinged 35.00

1000 years' union of the Rhineland with Germany.

Speyer Cathedral A50

**1925, Sept. 11** **Engr.**

**350** A50 5m dull green 32.50 14.50
Never hinged 125.00

Johann Wolfgang von Goethe — A51

Designs: 3pf, 25pf, Goethe. 5pf, Friedrich von Schiller. 8pf, 20pf, Ludwig van Beethoven. 10pf, Frederick the Great. 15pf, Immanuel Kant. 30pf, Gotthold Ephraim Lessing. 40pf, Gottfried Wilhelm Leibnitz. 50pf, Johann Sebastian Bach. 80pf, Albrecht Durer.

**1926-27** **Typo.** ***Perf. 14***

**351** A51 3pf olive brown 1.25 .30
**352** A51 3pf bister ('27) 1.25 .30
**353** A51 5pf dark green 1.25 .30
*b.* 5pf light green ('27) 1.10 .30
Never hinged 9.50
**354** A51 8pf blue grn ('27) 1.60 .30
**355** A51 10pf carmine 1.60 .30
**356** A51 15pf vermilion 2.40 .30
*a.* Booklet pane of 8 + 2 labels 275.00
Never hinged 675.00
**357** A51 20pf myrtle grn 11.00 1.10
**358** A51 25pf blue 3.50 .90
**359** A51 30pf olive grn 6.50 .50
**360** A51 40pf dp violet 12.00 .55
**361** A51 50pf brown 15.00 7.50
**362** A51 80pf chocolate 30.00 4.75
*Nos. 351-362 (12)* 87.35 17.10
Set, never hinged 930.00

Nos. 351-354, 356 and 357 exist imperf. See *Scott Classic Specialized Catalogue of Stamps & Covers* for detailed listing.

Nos. 354, 356 and 358 Overprinted

**1927, Oct. 10**

**363** A51 8pf blue green 17.00 *62.50*
**364** A51 15pf vermilion 17.00 *62.50*
**365** A51 25pf blue 17.00 *62.50*
*Nos. 363-365 (3)* 51.00 *187.50*
Set, never hinged 180.00

"I.A.A." stands for "Internationales Arbeitsamt," (Intl. Labor Bureau), an agency of the League of Nations. Issued in connection with a meeting of the I.A.A. in Berlin, Oct. 10-15, 1927, they were on sale to the public.

Pres. Friedrich Ebert A60

Pres. Paul von Hindenburg A61

**1928-32** **Typo.** ***Perf. 14***

**366** A60 3pf bister .25 .60
**367** A61 4pf lt blue ('31) .75 1.25
*a.* Tête bêche pair 4.75 9.00
Never hinged 9.00
*b.* Bklt. pane of 9 + label 35.00 90.00
Never hinged 90.00
**368** A61 5pf lt green .40 .60
*a.* Tête bêche pair 4.25 9.00
Never hinged 9.00
*b.* Imperf. 125.00
Never hinged 250.00
*c.* Bklt. pane of 6 + 4 labels 22.50 60.00
Never hinged 60.00
*d.* Bklt. pane, 4 #368 + 6 #369 35.00 90.00
Never hinged 90.00
**369** A60 6pf lt olive grn ('32) .75 .65
*a.* Bklt. pane, 2 #369 + 8 #373 55.00 135.00
Never hinged 135.00
**370** A60 8pf dark green .25 .60
*a.* Tête bêche pair 3.75 7.50
Never hinged 7.50
**371** A60 10pf vermilion 2.00 2.25
**372** A60 10pf red violet ('30) .95 .75
**373** A61 12pf orange ('32) 1.10 .65
*a.* Tête bêche pair 11.00 22.50
Never hinged 22.50
**374** A61 15pf car rose .60 .60
*a.* Tête bêche pair 7.75 15.00
Never hinged 30.00
*b.* Bklt. pane 6 + 4 labels 27.50 67.50
Never hinged 67.50
**375** A60 20pf Prus green 6.25 3.75
*a.* Imperf. 300.00
Never hinged 600.00
**376** A60 20pf gray ('30) 6.00 .75
**377** A61 25pf blue 7.50 .90
**378** A60 30pf olive green 5.00 .90
**379** A61 40pf violet 13.00 .90
**380** A60 45pf orange 9.00 3.00
**381** A61 50pf brown 9.00 2.50
**382** A60 60pf orange brn 11.50 3.00
**383** A61 80pf chocolate 21.00 6.75
**384** A61 80pf yel bis ('30) 9.00 2.25
*Nos. 366-384 (19)* 104.30 32.65
Set, never hinged 1,080.

Stamps of 1928 Overprinted

**1930, June 30**

**385** A60 8pf dark green 1.10 .90
**386** A61 15pf carmine rose 1.10 .90
Set, never hinged 15.00

Issued in commemoration of the final evacuation of the Rhineland by the Allied forces.

View of Cologne A63

**1930 Engr. Wmk. 126**
**Inscribed: "Reichsmark"**

**387** A63 2m dark blue 29.00 14.00
Never hinged 100.00

A type of design A43 in green exists with "Reichsmark" instead of "Mark." It was not issued, though some examples are known in private hands. Value $15,000.

Pres. von Hindenburg A64

Frederick the Great A65

**1932, Oct. 1 Typo. Wmk. 126**

**391** A64 4pf blue .55 .60
**392** A64 5pf brt green .75 .60
**393** A64 12pf dp orange 4.50 .60
**394** A64 15pf dk red 3.75 *9.75*
**395** A64 25pf ultra 1.10 .75
**396** A64 40pf violet 18.00 1.50
**397** A64 50pf dk brown 6.00 *11.00*
*Nos. 391-397 (7)* 34.65 24.80
Set, never hinged 129.00

85th birthday of von Hindenburg.
See Nos. 401-431, 436-441. For surcharges and overprints see France N27-N58, Luxembourg N1-N16 and Poland N17-N29.

**1933, Apr. 12 Photo.**

**398** A65 6pf dk green .60 .90
*a.* Tête bêche pair 5.25 13.50
Never hinged 10.50
**399** A65 12pf carmine .60 .90
*a.* Tête bêche pair 5.25 13.50
Never hinged 10.50
*b.* Bklt. pane of 5 + label 19.00 45.00
Never hinged 45.00
**400** A65 25pf ultra 37.50 21.00
*Nos. 398-400 (3)* 38.70 22.80
Set, never hinged 249.00

Celebration of Potsdam Day.

**Hindenburg Type of 1932**

**1933 Typo.**

**401** A64 3pf olive bister 13.50 .75
**402** A64 4pf dull blue 3.75 .75
**403** A64 6pf dk green 1.90 .75
**404** A64 8pf dp orange 6.00 .75
*a.* Bklt. pane, 3 #404 + 5 #406 75.00 *180.00*
Never hinged 180.00
*b.* Open "D" 19.00 3.75
Never hinged 37.50
**405** A64 10pf chocolate 3.75 .75
**406** A64 12pf dp carmine 2.25 .75
*a.* Bklt. pane, 4 #392 + 4 #406 40.00 *97.50*
Never hinged 97.50
**407** A64 15pf maroon 5.25 *26.00*
**408** A64 20pf brt blue 6.75 1.50
**409** A64 30pf olive grn 6.75 1.40
**410** A64 40pf red violet 27.50 2.75
**411** A64 50pf dk grn & blk 15.00 2.25
**412** A64 60pf claret & blk 27.50 .95
**413** A64 80pf dk blue & blk 9.00 1.10
**414** A64 100pf orange & blk 24.00 12.50
*Nos. 401-414 (14)* 152.90 *52.95*
Set, never hinged 900.00

**Hindenburg Type of 1932**

**1933-36 Wmk. 237 *Perf. 14***

**415** A64 1pf black .25 .35
*a.* Bklt. pane, 4 #415, 3 #417, label 4.00 *10.50*
Never hinged 10.50
*b.* Bklt. pane, 3 #415, 3 #416 + 2 #418 6.00 *15.00*
Never hinged 15.00
*c.* Bklt. pane, 2 #415, 5 #420, label 9.00 *22.50*
Never hinged 22.50
*d.* Bklt. pane, 4 #415 + 4 #422 3.25 *7.50*
Never hinged 7.50
**416** A64 3pf olive bis ('34) .25 .35
*a.* Bklt. pane, 4 #416 + 4 #418 3.00 *7.50*
Never hinged 7.50
*b.* Bklt. pane, 4 #416 + 4 #419 3.00 *7.50*
Never hinged 7.50
*c.* Bklt. pane, 6 #416, 1 #422, label 2.50 *6.00*
Never hinged 6.00
**417** A64 4pf dull blue ('34) .25 .35
*a.* Bklt. pane, 3 #417, 4 #422, label 7.50 *19.00*
Never hinged 19.00
**418** A64 5pf brt green ('34) .25 .35
*a.* Bklt. pane, 2 #418, 5 #419, label 5.25 *13.50*
Never hinged 13.50
*b.* Bklt. pane, 2 #418, 3 #419 + 3 #420 4.50 *11.00*
Never hinged 11.00
*c.* Bklt. pane, 4 #418 + 4 #420 5.25 *13.50*
Never hinged 13.50
**419** A64 6pf dk green ('34) .25 .35
*b.* Bklt. pane of 7 + label 9.00 *22.50*
Never hinged 22.50
*c.* Bklt. pane, 1 #419, 6 #422, label 25.00 *67.50*
Never hinged 67.50
**420** A64 8pf dp orange ('34) .25 .35
*a.* Bklt. pane, 3 #420, 4 #422, label 5.25 *13.50*
Never hinged 13.50
*b.* Open "D" 4.50 4.50
Never hinged 13.00
**421** A64 10pf choc ('34) .25 .35
**422** A64 12pf dp car ('34) .25 .35
*a.* Bklt. pane of 7 + label 9.00 *22.50*
Never hinged 22.50
**423** A64 15pf maroon ('34) .30 .35
**424** A64 20pf brt blue ('34) .45 .35
**425** A64 25pf ultra ('34) .45 .35
**426** A64 30pf olive grn ('34) .75 .35
**427** A64 40pf red violet ('34) .75 .35
**428** A64 50pf dk grn & blk ('34) 3.00 .35
**429** A64 60pf claret & blk ('34) .75 .35
**430** A64 80pf dk bl & blk ('36) 2.25 1.25
**431** A64 100pf orange & blk ('34) 3.00 1.10
*Nos. 415-431 (17)* 13.70 7.60
Set, never hinged 100.00

Karl Peters — A66

Designs: 3pf, Franz Adolf E. Lüderitz. 6pf, Dr. Gustav Nachtigal. 12pf, Karl Peters. 25pf, Hermann von Wissmann.

**1934, June 30 *Perf. 13x13½***

**432** A66 3pf brown & choc 2.25 *6.00*
**433** A66 6pf dk grn & choc 1.10 1.50
**434** A66 12pf dk car & choc 1.75 1.50
**435** A66 25pf brt blue & choc 9.00 *20.00*
*Nos. 432-435 (4)* 14.10 29.00
Set, never hinged 149.00

Issued in remembrance of the lost colonies of Germany.

**Hindenburg Memorial Issue**
**Type of 1932**
**With Black Border**

**1934, Sept. 4 *Perf. 14***

**436** A64 3pf olive bister .75 .45
**437** A64 5pf brt green .75 .55
**438** A64 6pf dk green 1.40 .45
**439** A64 8pf vermilion 2.25 .45
**440** A64 12pf deep carmine 2.25 .45
**441** A64 25pf ultra 6.75 *8.25*
*Nos. 436-441 (6)* 14.15 10.60
Set, never hinged 120.00

Swastika, Sun and Nuremberg Castle — A70

**1934, Sept. 1 Photo.**

**442** A70 6pf dark green 3.00 .60
**443** A70 12pf dark carmine 3.75 .60
Set, never hinged 63.50

Nazi Congress at Nuremberg.
Imperfs exist. Value never hinged, each $750.

Allegory "Saar Belongs to Germany" A71

German Eagle A72

**1934, Aug. 26 Typo. Wmk. 237**

**444** A71 6pf dark green 3.00 .60
**445** A72 12pf dark carmine 3.25 .60
Set, never hinged 63.50

Issued to mark the Saar Plebiscite.

Friedrich von Schiller A73

Germania Welcoming Home the Saar A74

**1934, Nov. 5**

**446** A73 6pf green 2.50 .60
**447** A73 12pf carmine 4.50 .60
Set, never hinged 82.50

175th anniv. of the birth of von Schiller.

**1935, Jan. 16 Photo.**

**448** A74 3pf brown .35 1.10
**449** A74 6pf dark green .35 .75
**450** A74 12pf lake 1.75 .75
**451** A74 25pf dark blue 7.25 8.25
*Nos. 448-451 (4)* 9.70 10.85
Set, never hinged 92.50

Return of the Saar to Germany.

German Soldier A75

Wreath and Swastika A76

**1935, Mar. 15**

**452** A75 6pf dark green .75 1.50
**453** A75 12pf copper red .75 1.50
Set, never hinged 15.75

Issued to commemorate War Heroes' Day.

**1935, Apr. 26 Unwmk.**

**454** A76 6pf dark green .75 1.40
**455** A76 12pf crimson .90 1.40
Set, never hinged 18.50

Young Workers' Professional Competitions.

Heinrich Schütz — A77

"The Eagle" — A80

**Wmk. Swastikas (237)**

**1935, June 21 Engr. *Perf. 14***

**456** A77 6pf shown .45 .50
**457** A77 12pf Bach .65 .50
**458** A77 25pf Handel 1.10 .90
*Nos. 456-458 (3)* 2.20 1.90
Set, never hinged 24.00

Schutz-Bach-Handel celebration.

**1935, July 10 *Perf. 14***

Designs: 12pf, Modern express train. 25pf, "The Hamburg Flyer." 40pf, Streamlined locomotive.

**459** A80 6pf dark green .90 .60
**460** A80 12pf copper red .90 .60
**461** A80 25pf ultra 5.00 1.75
**462** A80 40pf red violet 8.25 1.75
*Nos. 459-462 (4)* 15.05 4.70
Set, never hinged 102.00

Centenary of railroad in Germany.
Exist imperf. Values: Nos. 459-460, $900 each; Nos. 461-462, $1,100 each.

Bugler of Hitler Youth Movement A84

Eagle and Swastika over Nuremberg A85

**1935, July 25 Photo.**

**463** A84 6pf deep green 1.10 2.25
**464** A84 15pf brown lake 1.50 2.50
Set, never hinged 18.75

Hitler Youth Meeting.

**1935, Aug. 30 Engr.**

**465** A85 6pf gray green .75 .35
**466** A85 12pf dark carmine 1.90 .35
Set, never hinged 15.00

1935 Nazi Congress at Nuremberg.

Nazi Flag Bearer and Feldherrnhalle at Munich — A86

Airplane — A87

**1935, Nov. 5 Photo. *Perf. 13½***

**467** A86 3pf brown .30 .60
**468** A86 12pf dark carmine .45 .60
Set, never hinged 11.25

12th anniv. of the 1st Hitler "Putsch" at Munich, Nov. 9, 1923.

**1936, Jan. 6**

**469** A87 40pf sapphire 6.40 3.25
Never hinged 45.00

10th anniv. of the Lufthansa air service.

Gottlieb Daimler — A88

Carl Benz — A89

**1936, Feb. 15 *Perf. 14***

**470** A88 6pf dark green .50 .75
**471** A89 12pf copper red .50 .75
Set, never hinged 12.00

The 50th anniv. of the automobile; Intl. Automobile and Motorcycle Show, Berlin.

Otto von Guericke A90

Symbolical of Municipalities A91

**1936, May 4**

**472** A90 6pf dark green .30 .45
Never hinged 1.20

250th anniv. of the death of the German inventor, Otto von Guericke, May 11, 1686.

**1936, June 3**

**473** A91 3pf dark brown .65 .30
**474** A91 5pf deep green .65 .30
**475** A91 12pf lake 1.00 .50
**476** A91 25pf dark ultra 1.60 1.00
*Nos. 473-476 (4)* 3.90 2.10
Set, never hinged 15.00

6th Intl. Cong. of Municipalities, June 7-13.

Allegory of Recreation Congress A92

Salute to Swastika A93

**1936, June 30**

**477** A92 6pf dark green .35 .50
**478** A92 15pf deep claret .55 .95
Set, never hinged 13.50

World Congress for Vacation and Recreation held at Hamburg.

**1936, Sept. 3** *Perf. 14*

**479** A93 6pf deep green .45 .50
**480** A93 12pf copper red .55 1.00
Set, never hinged 14.00

The 1936 Nazi Congress.

Shield Bearer — A94

German and Austrian Carrying Nazi Flag — A95

**1937, Mar. 3 Engr. Unwmk.**

**481** A94 3pf brown .55 .30
**482** A94 6pf green .55 .30
**483** A94 12pf carmine 1.25 .60
*Nos. 481-483 (3)* 2.35 1.20
Set, never hinged 12.00

The Reich's Air Protection League.

**Wmk. Swastikas (237)**

**1938, Apr. 8 Photo.** *Perf. 14x13½*

**Size: 23x28mm**

**484** A95 6pf dark green .80 .65
Never hinged 2.00

**Unwmk.** *Perf. 12½*

**Size: 21½x26mm**

**485** A95 6pf deep green .80 1.40
Never hinged 2.00

Union of Austria and Germany.

Cathedral Island A96

Hermann Goering Stadium A97

Town Hall, Breslau — A98

Centennial Hall, Breslau — A99

**1938, June 21 Engr.** *Perf. 14*

**486** A96 3pf dark brown .50 .55
**487** A97 6pf deep green .50 .55
**488** A98 12pf copper red .75 .55
**489** A99 15pf violet brown 1.50 .80
*Nos. 486-489 (4)* 3.25 2.45
Set, never hinged 13.00

16th German Gymnastic and Sports Festival held at Breslau, July 23-31, 1938.

Nazi Emblem — A100

**1939, Apr. 4 Photo. Wmk. 237**

**490** A100 6pf dark green 1.90 4.00
**491** A100 12pf deep carmine 2.50 4.00
Set, never hinged 20.00

Young Workers' Professional Competitions.

St. Mary's Church — A101

The Krantor, Danzig — A102

**1939, Sept. 18**

**492** A101 6pf dark green .45 .80
**493** A102 12pf orange red .65 .80
Set, never hinged 4.00

Unification of Danzig with the Reich.

Johannes Gutenberg and Library at Leipzig — A103

Designs: 6pf, "High House," Leipzig. 12pf, Old Town Hall, Leipzig. 25pf, View of Leipzig Fair.

Inscribed "Leipziger Messe"

*Perf. 10½*

**1940, Mar. 3 Photo. Unwmk.**

**494** A103 3pf dark brown .45 .50
**495** A103 6pf dk gray green .45 .50
**496** A103 12pf henna brown .45 .50
**497** A103 25pf ultra 1.10 1.25
*Nos. 494-497 (4)* 2.45 2.75
Set, never hinged 8.00

Leipzig Fair.

House of Nations, Leipzig — A107

6pf, Concert Hall, Leipzig. 12pf, Leipzig Fair Office. 25pf, Railroad Terminal, Leipzig.

**Inscribed: "Reichsmesse Leipzig, 1941"**

**1941, Mar. 1** *Perf. 14x13½*

**498** A107 3pf brown .25 1.00
**499** A107 6pf green .25 1.00
**500** A107 12pf dark red .35 1.25
**501** A107 25pf bright blue .80 1.60
*Nos. 498-501 (4)* 1.65 4.85
Set, never hinged 10.00

Leipzig Fair.

Fashion Allegory — A111

Vienna Fair Hall — A112

"Burgtheater" A113

Monument to Prince Eugene A114

**1941, Mar. 8** *Perf. 13½x14*

**502** A111 3pf dark red brown .40 .55
**503** A112 6pf brt blue grn .40 .55
**504** A113 12pf scarlet .40 .65
**505** A114 25pf bright blue 1.10 1.60
*Nos. 502-505 (4)* 2.30 3.35
Set, never hinged 10.00

Vienna Fair.

A115

Adolf Hitler — A116

**1941-44 Typo.** *Perf. 14*

**Size: 18½x22½mm**

**506** A115 1pf gray black .25 .30
a. Bklt. pane, 4 #506 + 4 #509 1.10 *2.50*
Never hinged 2.50
**507** A115 3pf lt brown .25 .30
a. Bklt. pane, 6 #507 + 2 #510 1.20 *3.00*
Never hinged 3.00
**508** A115 4pf slate .25 .30
a. Bklt. pane, 4 #508, 2 #511 + 2 labels 1.00 *2.50*
Never hinged 2.50
**509** A115 5pf dp yellow grn .25 .30
**510** A115 6pf purple .25 .30
a. Bklt. pane of 7 + label 7.75 *19.00*
Never hinged 19.00
**511** A115 8pf red .25 .30
**511A** A115 10pf dk brown ('42) .25 .45
**511B** A115 12pf carmine ('42) .25 .45

**Engr.**

**512** A115 10pf dark brown .35 .30
**513** A115 12pf brt carmine .35 .30
a. Bklt. pane of 6 + 2 labels 3.25 *7.50*
Never hinged 7.50
**514** A115 15pf brown lake .25 .35
**515** A115 16pf peacock green .25 1.50
**516** A115 20pf blue .25 .35
**517** A115 24pf orange brown .25 1.50

**Size: 21½x26mm**

**518** A115 25pf brt ultra .25 .45
**519** A115 30pf olive green .25 .45
**520** A115 40pf brt red vio .25 .45
**521** A115 50pf myrtle green .25 .45
**522** A115 60pf dk red brown .25 .45
**523** A115 80pf indigo .25 .45
**524** A116 1m dk slate grn ('44) .40 5.25
a. Perf. 12½ ('42) 1.25 6.00
**525** A116 2m violet ('44) .90 5.25
a. Perf. 12½ ('42) 1.40 6.00

*Perf. 12½*

**526** A116 3m cop red ('42) 1.25 15.00
a. Perf. 14 ('44) 2.00 9.00
**527** A116 5m dark blue ('42) 2.25 47.50
a. Perf. 14 ('44) 3.50 13.00
*Nos. 506-527 (24)* 10.00 82.70
Set, #506-527, never hinged 23.00
Set, #524a-527a, never hinged 40.00

Nos. 507, 510, 511, 511A, 511B, 520, 524-526 exist imperf.

For surcharge see No. MQ3. For overprints see Russia Nos. N9-N48.

Storm Trooper Emblem A117

Adolf Hitler A118

**1942, Aug. 8 Photo.** *Perf. 14*

**528** A117 6pf purple .25 .75
Never hinged .75

War Effort Day of the Storm Troopers.

**1944 Engr.**

**529** A118 42pf bright green .25 2.00
Never hinged .30

Exists imperf. Value $375.

A119

**1946 Typo. Wmk. 284** *Perf. 14*

**Size: 18x22mm**

**530** A119 1pf black .25 *3.00*
**531** A119 2pf black .25 .25
**532** A119 3pf yellow brn .25 *3.25*
**533** A119 4pf slate .25 *4.50*
**534** A119 5pf yellow grn .25 *.60*
**535** A119 6pf purple .25 .25
**536** A119 8pf dp ver .25 .25
**537** A119 10pf chocolate .25 .25
**538** A119 12pf bright red .25 .25
**539** A119 12pf slate gray .25 .25
a. Bklt. pane, 5 #539 + 3 #542 9.00 *90.00*
Never hinged 18.00
**540** A119 15pf violet brn .25 *6.75*
**541** A119 15pf lt yel grn .25 .25
**542** A119 16pf slate green .25 .25
**543** A119 20pf lt blue .25 .25
**544** A119 24pf orange brn .25 .25
**545** A119 25pf brt ultra .25 *6.00*
**546** A119 25pf orange yel .25 *1.20*
**547** A119 30pf olive .25 .25
**548** A119 40pf red violet .25 .25
**549** A119 42pf emerald .75 *30.00*
**550** A119 45pf brt red .25 *.30*
**551** A119 50pf dk ol grn .25 .25
**552** A119 60pf brown red .25 .25
**553** A119 75pf deep ultra .25 .25
**554** A119 80pf dark blue .25 .25
**555** A119 84pf emerald .25 .25

**Size: 24½x29½mm**

**556** A119 1m olive green .25 .25
*Nos. 530-556 (27)* *60.10*
Set, never hinged 5.25

Imperf. examples of Nos. 543, 544 and 548 are usually from the souvenir sheet No. B295. Most other denominations exist imperf.

For overprints see Nos. 585A-599, 9N64, 10N17-10N21.

Planting Olive A120

Sower A121

Laborer
A122

Reaping
Wheat
A123

Germany
Reaching for
Peace — A124

Heinrich von
Stephan — A125

| | | | | | |
|---|---|---|---|---|---|
| **1947-48** | | | | | ***Perf. 14*** |
| **557** | A120 | 2pf | brown blk | .25 | .35 |
| **558** | A120 | 6pf | purple | .25 | .25 |
| **559** | A121 | 8pf | red | .25 | .35 |
| **560** | A121 | 10pf | yel grn ('48) | .25 | .35 |
| **561** | A122 | 12pf | gray | .25 | .25 |
| **562** | A120 | 15pf | choc ('48) | .25 | *3.75* |
| **563** | A123 | 16pf | dk bl grn | .25 | .35 |
| **564** | A121 | 20pf | blue | .25 | *1.10* |
| **565** | A123 | 24pf | brown org | .25 | .35 |
| **566** | A120 | 25pf | orange yel | .25 | *1.10* |
| **567** | A122 | 30pf | red ('48) | .25 | *3.00* |
| **568** | A121 | 40pf | red vio | .25 | .35 |
| **569** | A123 | 50pf | ultra ('48) | .25 | *2.00* |
| **571** | A122 | 60pf | red brn ('48) | .25 | .75 |
| *a.* | | 60pf | brown red | .25 | .35 |
| **572** | A122 | 80pf | dark blue | .25 | *1.10* |
| **573** | A123 | 84pf | emerald | .25 | *1.90* |
| | | | **Engr.** | | |
| **574** | A124 | 1m | olive | .25 | .35 |
| **575** | A124 | 2m | dk brown vio | .25 | *1.10* |
| **576** | A124 | 3m | copper red | .25 | *10.00* |
| **577** | A124 | 5m | dk blue ('48) | .75 | *40.00* |
| | | | *Nos. 557-577 (20)* | | *68.75* |
| | | | Set, never hinged | 5.25 | |

Used examples of Nos. 576-577 with expertized postal cancellations sell for much more.

For overprints see Nos. 600-633, 9N1-9N34, 9N65-9N67, 10N1-10N16.

| | | | | | |
|---|---|---|---|---|---|
| **1947, May 15** | | | | | **Litho.** |
| **578** | A125 | 24pf | orange brown | .25 | *1.50* |
| **579** | A125 | 75pf | dark blue | .25 | *1.50* |
| | | | Set, never hinged | .45 | |

50th anniv. of the death of Heinrich von Stephan, 1st postmaster general of the German Empire.

## Leipzig Fair Issues

Type of Semi-Postal Stamp of 1947

12pf, Maximilian I granting charter, 1497. 75pf, Estimating and collecting taxes, 1365.

***Perf. 13½x13***

| | | | | | |
|---|---|---|---|---|---|
| **1947, Sept. 2** | | **Litho.** | | | **Wmk. 284** |
| **580** | SP252 | 12pf | carmine | .25 | 1.90 |
| **581** | SP252 | 75pf | dk vio blue | .25 | 2.50 |
| | | | Set, never hinged | .45 | |

## Type of Semi-Postal Stamp of 1947, Dated 1948

50pf, Merchants at customs barrier, 1388. 84pf, Arranging stocks of merchandise, 1433.

| | | | | | |
|---|---|---|---|---|---|
| **1948, Mar. 2** | | | | | **Engr.** |
| **582** | SP252 | 50pf | deep blue | .25 | 1.50 |
| **583** | SP252 | 84pf | green | .25 | 2.25 |
| | | | Set, never hinged | .45 | |

Exist imperf. Value, each, $450.

## Hanover Fair Issue

Weighing
Goods for
Export — A126

| | | | | | |
|---|---|---|---|---|---|
| **1948, May 22** | | **Typo.** | | | ***Perf. 14*** |
| **584** | A126 | 24pf | deep carmine | .25 | 1.50 |
| **585** | A126 | 50pf | ultra | .25 | 2.25 |
| *c.* | | | Pair, #584-585 | 2.10 | 15.00 |
| | | | Pair, never hinged | 5.50 | |
| | | | Set, never hinged | .45 | |

## For Use in the United States and British Zones
## Stamps of Germany 1946-47 Overprinted in Black

a

b

### Overprint Type "a" on 1946 Numeral Issue

| | | | | | |
|---|---|---|---|---|---|
| **1948** | | **Wmk. 284** | | | ***Perf. 14*** |
| **585A** | A119 | 2pf | black | 2.25 | *32.50* |
| **585B** | A119 | 8pf | dp ver | 5.25 | *62.50* |
| **586** | A119 | 10pf | chocolate | .30 | *4.75* |
| **586A** | A119 | 12pf | bright red | 3.75 | *52.50* |
| **586B** | A119 | 12pf | slate gray | 67.50 | *550.00* |
| **586C** | A119 | 15pf | violet brn | 3.75 | *52.50* |
| **587** | A119 | 15pf | lt yel grn | 1.25 | *16.00* |
| **587A** | A119 | 16pf | slate green | 21.00 | *200.00* |
| **587B** | A119 | 24pf | orange brn | 37.50 | *210.00* |
| **587C** | A119 | 25pf | brt ultra | 7.50 | *62.50* |
| **588** | A119 | 25pf | orange yel | .60 | *8.25* |
| **589** | A119 | 30pf | olive | .60 | *8.25* |
| **589A** | A119 | 40pf | red violet | 27.50 | *210.00* |
| **590** | A119 | 45pf | brt red | .90 | *8.25* |
| **591** | A119 | 50pf | dk olive grn | .90 | *8.25* |
| **592** | A119 | 75pf | dp ultra | 2.25 | *24.00* |
| **593** | A119 | 84pf | emerald | 2.25 | *24.00* |
| | | | *Nos. 585A-593 (17)* | 185.05 | |
| | | | Set, never hinged | 375.00 | |

### Same, Overprinted Type "b"

| | | | | | |
|---|---|---|---|---|---|
| **593A** | A119 | 2pf | black | 10.50 | *67.50* |
| **593B** | A119 | 8pf | dp ver | 18.00 | *140.00* |
| **593C** | A119 | 10pf | chocolate | 16.50 | *140.00* |
| **593D** | A119 | 12pf | bright red | 5.25 | *67.50* |
| **593E** | A119 | 12pf | slate gray | 140.00 | *1,000.* |
| **593F** | A119 | 15pf | violet brown | 5.25 | *47.50* |
| **594** | A119 | 15pf | lt yel grn | .35 | *8.25* |
| **594A** | A119 | 16pf | slate grn | 20.00 | *160.00* |
| **594B** | A119 | 24pf | org brn | 21.00 | *210.00* |
| **594C** | A119 | 25pf | brt ultra | 6.00 | *62.50* |
| **594D** | A119 | 25pf | orange yel | 19.00 | *200.00* |
| **595** | A119 | 30pf | olive | .60 | *6.75* |
| **595A** | A119 | 40pf | red violet | 27.50 | *250.00* |
| **596** | A119 | 45pf | bright red | 1.25 | *12.00* |
| **597** | A119 | 50pf | dk ol grn | 1.25 | *12.00* |
| **598** | A119 | 75pf | dp ultra | 1.40 | *12.00* |
| **599** | A119 | 84pf | emerald | 1.40 | *13.00* |
| | | | *Nos. 593A-599 (17)* | 295.25 | |
| | | | Set, never hinged | 600.00 | |

Nine other denominations of type A119 (1, 3, 4, 5, 6, 20, 42, 60 and 80pf) were also overprinted with types "a" and "b." These overprints were not authorized, but the stamps were sold at post offices and tolerated for postal use. Forgeries exist.

The overprints on Nos. 585A-599 have been extensively counterfeited.

### Overprint Type "a" on Stamps and Types of 1947 Pictorial Issue

| | | | | | |
|---|---|---|---|---|---|
| **600** | A120 | 2pf | brown black | .25 | *.45* |
| **601** | A120 | 6pf | purple | .25 | *.45* |
| **602** | A121 | 8pf | dp vermilion | .25 | *.45* |
| **603** | A121 | 10pf | yellow green | .25 | .45 |
| **604** | A122 | 12pf | slate gray | .25 | .45 |
| **605** | A120 | 15pf | chocolate | 3.00 | *15.00* |
| **606** | A123 | 16pf | dk blue green | .60 | *2.25* |
| **607** | A121 | 20pf | blue | .25 | *.90* |
| **608** | A123 | 24pf | brown orange | .25 | *.45* |
| **609** | A120 | 25pf | orange yellow | .25 | *.45* |
| **610** | A122 | 30pf | red | 1.10 | *4.50* |
| **611** | A121 | 40pf | red violet | .30 | *1.10* |
| **612** | A123 | 50pf | ultra | .35 | *.90* |
| **614** | A122 | 60pf | red brown | .35 | *.90* |
| *a.* | | 60pf | brown red | 22.50 | *225.00* |
| | | | Never hinged | 60.00 | |
| **615** | A122 | 80pf | dark blue | .60 | *2.25* |
| **616** | A123 | 84pf | emerald | 1.90 | *6.00* |
| | | | *Nos. 600-616 (16)* | 10.20 | *36.95* |
| | | | Set, never hinged | 22.50 | |

### Same, Overprinted Type "b"

| | | | | | |
|---|---|---|---|---|---|
| **617** | A120 | 2pf | brown black | .35 | *1.40* |
| **618** | A120 | 6pf | purple | .35 | *1.40* |
| **619** | A121 | 8pf | red | .35 | *1.40* |
| **620** | A121 | 10pf | yellow green | .25 | *.45* |
| **621** | A122 | 12pf | gray | .35 | *1.50* |
| **622** | A120 | 15pf | chocolate | .25 | *.65* |
| **623** | A123 | 16pf | dk blue green | .65 | *2.25* |
| **624** | A121 | 20pf | blue | .25 | *.45* |
| **625** | A123 | 24pf | brown orange | .30 | *1.50* |
| **626** | A120 | 25pf | orange yel | 3.50 | *15.00* |
| **627** | A122 | 30pf | red | .25 | *.65* |
| **628** | A121 | 40pf | red violet | .25 | *.60* |
| **629** | A123 | 50pf | ultra | .25 | *.60* |
| **631** | A122 | 60pf | red brown | .25 | *.65* |
| *a.* | | 60pf | brown red | 1.10 | *3.75* |
| | | | Never hinged | 2.25 | |
| **632** | A122 | 80pf | dark blue | .25 | *.65* |
| **633** | A123 | 84pf | emerald | .45 | *1.40* |
| | | | *Nos. 617-633 (16)* | 8.30 | *30.55* |
| | | | Set, never hinged | 18.00 | |

Most of Nos. 585A-633 exist with inverted and double overprints.

Frankfurt
Town Hall
A127

Our Lady's
Church,
Munich
A128

Cologne
Cathedral
A129

Brandenburg
Gate, Berlin
A130

Holsten Gate,
Lübeck — A131

Two types of mark values:
Type I — Four horiz. lines in stairs.
Type II — Seven horizontal lines.

***Perf. 11½x11, 11***

| | | | | | |
|---|---|---|---|---|---|
| **1948-51** | | **Litho.** | | | **Wmk. 286** |
| **634** | A127 | 2pf | black | .25 | *.45* |
| *a.* | | | Perf. 14 | 1.10 | *4.75* |
| **635** | A128 | 4pf | orange brown | .25 | *.45* |
| *a.* | | | Perf. 14 | 2.75 | .90 |
| **636** | A129 | 5pf | blue | .25 | *.45* |
| *a.* | | | Perf. 14 | .75 | .45 |
| **637** | A128 | 6pf | orange brown | .25 | *.60* |
| **638** | A128 | 6pf | orange | .25 | *.45* |
| *a.* | | | Perf. 14 | 6.00 | 4.50 |
| **639** | A127 | 8pf | orange yel | .25 | *.45* |
| **640** | A128 | 8pf | dk slate blue | .25 | *.45* |
| **641** | A129 | 10pf | green | .25 | *.45* |
| *a.* | | | Perf. 14 | .75 | .45 |
| **642** | A128 | 15pf | orange | .90 | *4.50* |
| **643** | A127 | 15pf | violet | .50 | .45 |
| *a.* | | | Perf. 14 | 4.50 | .45 |
| **644** | A127 | 16pf | bluish green | .30 | *.60* |
| **645** | A127 | 20pf | blue | .45 | *3.00* |
| **646** | A130 | 20pf | carmine | .30 | *.60* |
| *a.* | | | Perf. 14 | 1.90 | .45 |
| **647** | A130 | 24pf | carmine | .25 | *.45* |
| **648** | A129 | 25pf | vermilion | .45 | *.45* |
| *a.* | | | Perf. 14 | 27.50 | *160.00* |
| **649** | A130 | 30pf | blue | .60 | .45 |
| *a.* | | | Perf. 14 | 11.00 | .45 |
| **650** | A128 | 30pf | scarlet | 1.10 | *5.25* |
| **651** | A129 | 40pf | rose lilac | .75 | .45 |
| *a.* | | | Perf. 14 | 7.50 | .45 |
| **652** | A130 | 50pf | ultra | .60 | *1.90* |
| **653** | A128 | 50pf | bluish green | .75 | .45 |
| *a.* | | | Perf. 14 | 67.50 | .45 |
| **654** | A129 | 60pf | violet brn | 30.00 | .45 |
| *a.* | | | Perf. 14 | 1.10 | .45 |
| **655** | A130 | 80pf | red violet | 1.25 | .45 |
| *a.* | | | Perf. 14 | 45.00 | .45 |
| **656** | A128 | 84pf | rose violet | .75 | 6.00 |
| **657** | A129 | 90pf | rose lilac | 1.25 | .45 |
| *a.* | | | Perf. 14 | 65.00 | .50 |
| | | | ***Perf. 11, 11x11½*** | | |
| **658** | A131 | 1m | yellow grn (I) | 15.00 | .60 |
| *a.* | | | Perf. 14 (II) ('51) | 60.00 | .45 |
| *b.* | | | Perf. 11 (II) | 19.00 | .45 |
| **659** | A131 | 2m | violet (I) | 13.50 | .60 |
| *a.* | | | Type II | 22.50 | .45 |
| **660** | A131 | 3m | car rose (I) | 15.00 | 2.50 |
| *a.* | | | Type II | 75.00 | 1.00 |
| **661** | A131 | 5m | blue (I) | 22.50 | 21.00 |
| *a.* | | | Type II | 90.00 | 3.25 |
| | | | *Nos. 634-661 (28)* | 108.20 | 54.35 |
| | | | Set, never hinged | 260.00 | |
| | | | Set, 634a-658a, never hinged | 550.00 | |
| | | | Set, 658b-661a, never hinged | 375.00 | |

Imperforates of many values exist.

Specialists collect Nos. 634-661 with watermark in four positions: upright, D's facing left; upright, D's facing right; sideways, D's facing up; sideways, D's facing down.

Two types of perforation: line and comb. Nos. 634-657 are found both perf. 11 and 11½x11.

Herman Hildebrant
Wedigh — A132

**Wmk. 116**

| | | | | | |
|---|---|---|---|---|---|
| **1949, Apr. 22** | | **Engr.** | | | ***Perf. 14*** |
| **662** | A132 | 10pf | green | 1.10 | *2.25* |
| **663** | A132 | 20pf | carmine rose | 1.10 | *2.25* |
| **664** | A132 | 30pf | blue | 1.50 | 3.00 |
| *a.* | | | Sheet of 3, #662-664 | 32.50 | *180.00* |
| | | | Sheet, never hinged | 82.50 | |
| | | | *Nos. 662-664 (3)* | 3.70 | 7.50 |
| | | | Set, never hinged | 8.50 | |

Hanover Export Fair, 1949.
No. 664a sold for 1 mark.

## Federal Republic

AREA — 95,520 sq. mi.
POP. — 62,040,000 (1974 est.)
CAPITAL — Bonn

"Reconstruction"
A133

Bavaria Stamp
A134

| | | | | | |
|---|---|---|---|---|---|
| **1949, Sept. 7** | | **Litho.** | | | **Wmk. 286** |
| **665** | A133 | 10pf | blue green | 15.00 | *21.00* |
| **666** | A133 | 20pf | rose carmine | 17.50 | *24.00* |
| | | | Set, never hinged | 90.00 | |

Opening of the first Federal Assembly.
Exist imperf. Value, each $475.

**Wmk. 285**

| | | | | | |
|---|---|---|---|---|---|
| **1949, Sept. 30** | | **Litho.** | | | ***Perf. 14*** |

Design: 30pf, Bavaria 6kr.

| | | | | | |
|---|---|---|---|---|---|
| **667** | A134 | 20pf | red & dull blue | 19.00 | *37.50* |
| **668** | A134 | 30pf | dull blue & choc | 32.50 | *60.00* |
| | | | Set, never hinged | 90.00 | |

Cent. of German postage stamps. See No. B309.

Heinrich von Stephan, General Post Office and Guild House, Bern
A135

| | | | | | |
|---|---|---|---|---|---|
| **1949, Oct. 9** | | | | | **Wmk. 286** |
| **669** | A135 | 30pf | ultra | 21.00 | *37.50* |
| | | | Never hinged | 60.00 | |

75th anniv. of the UPU.

Numeral and Post
Horn — A136

| | | | | | |
|---|---|---|---|---|---|
| **1951-52** | | **Typo.** | | | **Wmk. 295** |
| **670** | A136 | 2pf | yellow grn | .35 | .95 |
| **671** | A136 | 4pf | yellow brn | .35 | .30 |
| *a.* | | | Booklet pane, 3 #671 + 3 #673 + 4 #677 | 110.00 | 450.00 |
| | | | Never hinged | 450.00 | |
| **672** | A136 | 5pf | dp rose vio | 1.90 | .30 |
| **673** | A136 | 6pf | orange | 4.50 | 3.00 |
| **674** | A136 | 8pf | gray | 5.25 | 7.50 |
| **675** | A136 | 10pf | dk green | .75 | .30 |
| *a.* | | | Booklet pane, 4 #675 + 5 #677 + label | 110.00 | 450.00 |
| | | | Never hinged | 450.00 | |
| **676** | A136 | 15pf | purple | 10.00 | .95 |
| **677** | A136 | 20pf | carmine | .75 | .30 |
| **678** | A136 | 25pf | dk rose lake | 22.50 | 4.75 |

**Engr.**

**Size: 20x24½mm**

**679** A136 30pf blue 13.00 .45
**680** A136 40pf rose lilac ('52) 32.50 .45
**681** A136 50pf blue gray ('52) 45.00 .45
**682** A136 60pf brown ('52) 32.50 .45
**683** A136 70pf dp yel ('52) 135.00 14.00
**684** A136 80pf carmine ('52) 150.00 1.90
**685** A136 90pf yel grn ('52) 150.00 2.25
*Nos. 670-685 (16)* 604.35 38.30
Set, never hinged 1,875.

Imperfs. exist of #671, 673, 675, 681 & 684.

W. K. Roentgen A137

Mona Lisa A138

**1951, Dec. 10**

**686** A137 30pf blue 30.00 18.00
Never hinged 72.50

50th anniv. of the awarding of the Nobel prize in physics to Wilhelm K. Roentgen.

**Wmk. 285**

**1952, Apr. 15 Litho. *Perf. 13½***

**687** A138 5pf multicolored .75 *1.10*
Never hinged 2.00

500th anniv. of the birth of Leonardo da Vinci.

N. A. Otto — A139

Martin Luther — A140

**Wmk. 295**

**1952, July 25 Engr. *Perf. 14***

**688** A139 30pf deep blue 15.00 15.00
Never hinged 29.00

75th anniv. of the four-cycle gas engine.

**1952, July 25**

**689** A140 10pf green 4.00 *4.75*
Never hinged 13.50

Issued to publicize the Lutheran World Federation Assembly, Hanover, 1952.

Freighter Off Heligoland A141

Carl Schurz A142

**1952, Sept. 6**

**690** A141 20pf red 6.25 5.75
Never hinged 15.00

Return of Heligoland, Mar. 1, 1952.

**Wmk. 285**

**1952, Sept. 17 Litho. *Perf. 13½***

**691** A142 20pf blue, blk & brn org 6.25 *7.50*
Never hinged 19.00

Centenary of Carl Schurz's arrival in America.

Thurn and Taxis Postilion A143

**1952, Oct. 25**

**692** A143 10pf multicolored 3.00 2.00
Never hinged 7.50

1st Thurn and Taxis stamp, cent.

Philipp Reis — A144

**1952, Oct. 27 Photo. *Perf. 14***

**693** A144 30pf blue 18.00 15.00
Never hinged 45.00

75 years of telephone service in Germany.

"Prevent Traffic Accidents" — A145

**1953, Mar. 30 Litho. Wmk. 285**

**694** A145 20pf blk, red & bl grn 6.25 4.50
Never hinged 16.50

Justus von Liebig — A146

Red Cross and Compass — A147

**1953, May 12 Engr. Wmk. 295**

**695** A146 30pf dark blue 14.50 *22.50*
Never hinged 45.00

150th anniv. of the birth of Justus von Liebig, chemist.

***Perf. 14x13½***

**1953, May 8 Litho. Wmk. 285**

**696** A147 10pf dp ol grn & red 4.50 *6.75*
Never hinged 20.00

125th anniv. of the birth of Henri Dunant, founder of the Red Cross.

War Prisoner and Barbed Wire — A148

Train and Hand Signal — A149

**Typographed and Embossed**

**1953, May 9 Unwmk. *Perf. 14***

**697** A148 10pf gray & black 1.90 .35
Never hinged 6.00

Issued in memory of the prisoners of war.

**Wmk. 295**

**1953, June 20 Engr. *Perf. 14***

Designs: 10pf, Pigeon and planes. 20pf, Automobiles and traffic signal. 30pf, Ship, barges and buoy.

**698** A149 4pf brown 2.25 *3.75*
**699** A149 10pf deep green 4.50 *6.00*
**700** A149 20pf red 5.75 *9.75*
**701** A149 30pf deep ultra 17.50 *22.50*
*Nos. 698-701 (4)* 30.00 42.00
Set, never hinged 77.50

Exhibition of Transport and Communications, Munich, 1953.

Pres. Theodor Heuss — A150

**1954-60 Typo. *Perf. 14***

**Size: 18½x22mm**

**702** A150 2pf citron .25 .25
*a.* Booklet pane, 5 #702, 4 #704 + label ('55) 22.50 110.00
Never hinged 42.50
*b.* Booklet pane, 3 #702, 6 #704 + label ('56) 3.75 60.00
Never hinged 7.50
*c.* Booklet pane, 3 #702, 1 #707, 5 #708 + label ('56) 7.50 75.00
Never hinged 16.50
**703** A150 4pf orange brn .25 .25
**704** A150 5pf rose lilac .25 .25
*a.* Booklet pane, 2 #704, 7 #708 + label ('55) 22.50 110.00
Never hinged 42.50
**705** A150 6pf lt brown .25 .75
**706** A150 7pf bluish green .25 .30
**707** A150 8pf gray .25 .60
**708** A150 10pf green .25 .25
*a.* Booklet pane, 4 #708, 5 #710 + label ('55) 22.50 110.00
Never hinged 42.50
**709** A150 15pf ultra .25 .45
**710** A150 20pf dk car rose .25 .25
**711** A150 25pf red brown .30 .60

**Engr.**

**Size: 19½x24mm**

**712** A150 30pf blue 4.50 4.50
**713** A150 40pf red violet 1.90 .30
**714** A150 50pf gray 67.50 .45
**715** A150 60pf red brown 15.00 .60
**716** A150 70pf olive 4.50 1.90
**717** A150 80pf deep rose .75 4.50
**718** A150 90pf deep green 4.50 2.25

**Size: 24½x29½mm**

**719** A150 1m olive green .50 .30
**720** A150 2m lt vio blue .75 1.10
**721** A150 3m deep plum 1.90 2.25
*Nos. 702-721 (20)* 104.35 22.10
Set, never hinged 275.00

Coils and sheets of 100 were issued of the 5, 7, 10, 15, 20, 25, 40 and 70pf. Every fifth coil stamp has a control number on the back.

Printings of Nos. 704, 706, 708-711 and 708b were made on fluorescent paper beginning in 1960.

Nos. 702, 709, 714 exist imperf. Value about $425 each.

See Nos. 737Ab, 755-761.

**Catalogue values for unused stamps in this section, from this point to the end of the section, are for Never Hinged items.**

Paul Ehrlich and Emil von Behring — A151

**Wmk. 285**

**1954, Mar. 13 Litho. *Perf. 13½***

**722** A151 10pf dark green 11.00 3.75

Centenary of the births of Paul Ehrlich and Emil von Behring, medical researchers.

Exists imperf. Value $1,000.

15th Century Printer — A152

**1954, May 5 Typo. Wmk. 295**

**723** A152 4pf chocolate 1.10 .60

500th anniversary of the publication of Gutenberg's 42-line Bible. Design from woodcut by Jost Amman.

Bishop's Miter and Sword — A153

Carl F. Gauss — A154

**Engraved; Center Embossed**

**1954, June 5 Unwmk. *Perf. 13½x14***

**724** A153 20pf gray & red 8.00 4.50

Martyrdom of Saint Boniface, 1200th anniv.

**Wmk. 295**

**1955, Feb. 23 Engr. *Perf. 14***

**725** A154 10pf deep green 5.00 .60

Cent. of the death of Carl Friedrich Gauss, mathematician.

A155

A156

**Wmk. 304**

**1955, May 7 Litho. *Perf. 13½***

**726** A155 10pf green 5.00 1.50

Cent. of the birth of Oskar von Miller, electrical engineer.

**Engraved and Embossed**

**1955, May 9 Unwmk. *Perf. 13½x14***

**727** A156 40pf blue 16.50 5.50

Friedrich von Schiller, poet, 150th death anniv.

1906 Automobile A157

**Wmk. 304**

**1955, June 1 Typo. *Perf. 13½***

**728** A157 20pf red & black 10.50 5.00

German postal motor-bus service, 50th anniv.

Arms of Baden-Württemberg A158

Globe and Atomic Symbol A159

*Perf. 13x13½*

**1955, June 15 Litho. Wmk. 295**

**729** A158 7pf lemon, blk & brn red 4.00 4.50

**730** A158 10pf lemon, blk & grn 6.50 6.50

*a.* Value omitted *475.00 450.00*

Baden-Wurttemberg Exhibition, Stuttgart, 1955.

**1955, June 24 Photo. *Perf. 13½x14***

**731** A159 20pf rose brown 10.50 1.10

Issued to encourage scientific research.

Orb and Symbols of Battle — A160

**Photogravure and Embossed**

*Perf. 14x13½*

**1955, Aug. 10 Unwmk.**

**732** A160 20pf red lilac 9.00 3.75

Issued in honor of Augsburg and the millenium of the Battle on the Lechfeld.

Family in Flight — A161

**1955, Aug. 2 Engr. Wmk. 304**

**733** A161 20pf brown lake 3.75 .50

Ten years of German expatriation. See No. 930.

Railroad Signal, Tracks — A162

*Perf. 13½x14*

**1955, Oct. 5 Litho. Wmk. 304**

**734** A162 20pf red & black 10.00 2.50

European Timetable conf. at Wiesbaden, Oct. 5-15, 1955.

A163

Stifter monument and sylized Trees.

**1955, Oct. 22 Engr.**

**735** A163 10pf dark green 3.75 2.50

150th anniv. of the birth of Adalbert Stifter, poet.

A164

**Lithographed and Embossed**

*Perf. 14x13½*

**1955, Oct. 24 Unwmk.**

**736** A164 10pf UN emblem 3.75 4.50

United Nations Day, Oct. 24, 1955.

Numeral A165

Numeral and Signature A166

**1955-58 Wmk. 304 Typo. *Perf. 14***

**737** A165 1pf gray .25 .25

**Wmk. 295**

**737A** A165 1pf gray ('58) 7.75 *19.00*

*b.* Bklt. pane of 10 (#707, 2 each #737A, #704, #708, 3 #710) 22.50 52.50

No. 737A was issued only in the booklet pane, No. 737b. No. 737 was issued on fluorescent paper in 1963.

**1956, Jan. 7 Engr. Wmk. 304**

**738** A166 20pf dark red 6.75 2.75

125th anniv. of the birth of Heinrich von Stephan, co-founder of the UPU.

Clavichord A167

**1956, Jan. 27 Litho.**

**739** A167 10pf dull lilac .75 .35

200th anniv. of the birth of Wolfgang Amadeus Mozart, composer.

Heinrich Heine, Poet, Death Cent. — A168

*Perf. 13x13½*

**1956, Feb. 17 Wmk. 295**

**740** A168 10pf ol grn & blk 2.75 3.00

Old Buildings, Lüneburg A169

**Wmk. 304**

**1956, May 2 Engr. *Perf. 14***

**741** A169 20pf dull red 7.50 8.25

Millenary of Lüneburg.

Olympic Rings A170

Robert Schumann A171

**1956, June 9 *Perf. 13½x14***

**742** A170 10pf slate green .80 .60

Issued to publicize the Olympic year, 1956.

**1956, July 28 Litho. Unwmk.**

**743** A171 10pf citron, blk & red .65 .45

Schumann, composer, death cent.

Synod Emblem — A172

Thomas Mann — A173

*Perf. 13½x13*

**1956, Aug. 8 Wmk. 304**

**744** A172 10pf green 3.50 3.75

**745** A172 20pf brown carmine 4.00 5.25

Meeting of German Protestants (Evangelical Synod), Frankfurt-on-Main, Aug. 8-12.

**1956, Aug. 11 Engr. *Perf. 13½x14***

**746** A173 20pf pale rose vio 3.00 2.10

1st anniv. of the death of Thomas Mann, novelist.

Maria Laach Abbey — A174

"Rebuilding Europe" — A175

**1956, Aug. 24 Photo. *Perf. 13x13½***

**747** A174 20pf brn lake & gray 2.25 2.00

800th anniv. of the dedication of the Maria Laach Abbey.

**Europa Issue, 1956**

**1956, Sept. 15 Engr. *Perf. 14***

**748** A175 10pf green *1.00* *.25*

**749** A175 40pf blue *6.00* *.95*

Issued to symbolize the cooperation among the six countries comprising the Coal and Steel Community.

Plan of Cologne Cathedral and Hand — A176

**1956, Aug. 29 Litho. *Perf. 13x13½***

**750** A176 10pf gray grn & red brn 2.75 2.50

77th meeting of German Catholics, Cologne, Aug. 29.

Map of the World and Policeman's Hand — A177

**1956, Sept. 1 *Perf. 13½x13***

**751** A177 20pf red org, grn & blk 3.00 2.50

Issued on the occasion of the International Police Show, Essen, Sept. 1-23.

Pigeon Holding Letter — A178

**1956, Oct. 27 Engr. *Perf. 14***

**752** A178 10pf green 1.50 .65

Issued to publicize the Day of the Stamp.

Cemetery Crosses — A179

**1956, Nov. 17 *Perf. 14x13½***

**753** A179 10pf slate 1.50 .65

Issued to commemorate the people of Germany who died during WWII and to promote the Society for the Care of Military Cemeteries.

Saar Coat of Arms — A180

**1957, Jan. 2 Litho. *Perf. 13x13½***

**754** A180 10pf bluish grn & brn .45 .45

Return of the Saar to Germany. See Saar #262.

**Heuss Type of 1954**

**1956-57 Wmk. 304 Engr. *Perf. 14***

**Size: 18½x22mm**

**755** A150 30pf slate green .40 .60

**756** A150 40pf lt ultra 1.90 .30

**757** A150 50pf olive .95 .30

**758** A150 60pf lt brown 3.25 .45

**759** A150 70pf violet 10.00 .45

**760** A150 80pf red orange 5.25 1.90

**761** A150 90pf bluish green 16.50 .95

*Nos. 755-761 (7)* 38.25 4.95

Nos. 755-756 were printed on both ordinary and fluorescent paper; Nos. 757-761 only on ordinary paper. Issue dates: 40pf, 1956. Others, 1957.

The 40pf and 70pf were also issued in coils. Every fifth coil stamp has control number on back.

Heinrich Hertz — A181

**1957, Feb. 22 Litho. *Perf. 14***

**762** A181 10pf lt green & blk 1.25 .50

Heinrich Hertz, physicist, birth cent.

Paul Gerhardt — A182

**1957, May 18 Engr.**

**763** A182 20pf carmine lake .50 .50

350th anniv. of the birth of Paul Gerhardt, Lutheran clergyman and hymn writer.

Tulip and Post Horn — A183

**1957, June 8**
**764** A183 20pf red orange .50 .50

Flora & Philately Exhib., Cologne, June 8-10.

Arms of Aschaffenburg, 1332 — A184

***Perf. 13x13½***
**1957, June 15** **Wmk. 304**
**765** A184 20pf dp salmon & blk .50 .50

1000th anniv. of the founding of the Abbey and town of Aschaffenburg.

Scholars (Sapiens Manuscript) A185

**1957, June 24** ***Perf. 13½x13***
**766** A185 10pf blk, bl grn & red org .40 .40

Founding of Freiburg University, 500th anniv.

Modern Passenger Freighter — A186

**1957, June 25** ***Perf. 13½x14***
**767** A186 15pf brt blue, blk & red 1.10 1.00

Merchant Marine Day, June 25.

Liebig Laboratory A187

**1957, July 3** **Engr.** ***Perf. 14x13½***
**768** A187 10pf dark green .40 .40

350th anniv. of the Justus Liebig School at Ludwig University, Giessen.

Albert Ballin — A188

***Perf. 13½x14***
**1957, Aug. 15** **Litho.** **Wmk. 304**
**769** A188 20pf dk car rose & blk 1.25 .45

Cent. of the birth of Albert Ballin, founder of the Hamburg-America Steamship Line.

Television Screen — A189

**1957, Aug. 23** **Engr.** ***Perf. 14x13½***
**770** A189 10pf blue vio & grn .40 .40

Issued to publicize the television industry.

**Europa Issue, 1957**

"United Europe" A190

**Lithographed; Tree Embossed**
**1957-58** **Unwmk.** ***Perf. 14x13½***
**771** A190 10pf yel grn & lt bl .35 .25
*a.* Imperf. *300.00 300.00*
**772** A190 40pf dk bl & lt bl *3.75 .35*

**Wmk. 304**
**772A** A190 10pf yel grn & lt bl *5.50 8.25*
*Nos. 771-772A (3)* 9.60 8.85

A united Europe for peace and prosperity.
Issued: #771-772, 9/16; #772A, 8/1958.

Water Lily — A191

European Robin — A192

**Wmk. 304**
**1957, Oct. 4** **Litho.** ***Perf. 14***
**773** A191 10pf yel grn & org yel .35 .45
**774** A192 20pf multicolored .55 .45

Protection of wild animals and plants.

Carrier Pigeons — A193

**1957, Oct. 5**
**775** A193 20pf dp car & blk .85 .50

Intl. Letter Writing Week, Oct. 6-12.

Baron vom Stein — A194

**1957, Oct. 26** **Engr.** ***Perf. 13½x14***
**776** A194 20pf red 1.50 .60

200th anniv. of the birth of Baron Heinrich Friedrich vom und zum Stein, Prussian statesman.

Leo Baeck — A195

Landschaft Building, Stuttgart — A196

**1957, Nov. 2**
**777** A195 20pf dark red 1.50 .60

1st anniv. of the death of Rabbi Leo Baeck of Berlin.

***Perf. 13x13½***
**1957, Nov. 16** **Litho.** **Wmk. 304**
**778** A196 10pf dk grn & yel grn .80 .50

500th anniversary of the Wurttemberg Landtag (Assembly).

Coach — A197

**1957, Nov. 26** **Engr.** ***Perf. 14***
**779** A197 10pf olive green .75 .50

Centenary of the death of Joseph V. Eichendorff, poet.

"Max and Moritz" — A198

Design: 20pf, Wilhelm Busch.

**1958, Jan. 9** **Litho.** ***Perf. 13½x13***
**780** A198 10pf lt ol grn & blk .25 .25
**781** A198 20pf red & black .75 .60

50th anniv. of the death of Wilhelm Busch, humorist.

"Prevent Forest Fires" — A199

**1958, Mar. 5** ***Perf. 14***
**782** A199 20pf brt red & blk .65 .50

Rudolf Diesel A200

**1958, Mar. 18** **Engr.** ***Perf. 14***
**783** A200 10pf dk blue grn .40 .40

Centenary of the birth of Rudolf Diesel, inventor.

Giraffe and Lion — A201

***Perf. 13x13½***
**1958, May 7** **Litho.** **Wmk. 304**
**784** A201 10pf brt yel grn & blk .50 .40

Zoo at Frankfort on the Main, cent.
Exists imperf. Value $225.

View of Old Munich — A202

**1958, May 22** **Engr.** ***Perf. 14x13½***
**785** A202 20pf dark red .50 .40

800th anniversary of Munich.

Market Cross, Trier — A203

**1958, June 3**
**786** A203 20pf dark red & black .50 .40

Millennium of the market of Trier (Treves).

Heraldic Eagle 5m Coin — A204

**1958, June 20** **Litho.** ***Perf. 13x13½***
**787** A204 20pf red & black .60 1.40

10th anniv. of the German currency reform.
Exists imperf. Value $300.

Turner Emblem and Oak Leaf A205

Schulze-Delitzsch A206

***Perf. 13½x14***
**1958, July 21** **Wmk. 304**
**788** A205 10pf gray, blk & dl grn .35 .45

150 years of German Turners and on the occasion of the 1958 Turner festival.

**1958, Aug. 29** **Engr.** ***Perf. 13½x14***
**789** A206 10pf yellow green .45 .35

150th anniv. of the birth of Hermann Schulze-Delitzsch, founder of German trade organizations.

---

Common Design Types pictured following the introduction.

---

**Europa Issue, 1958**
Common Design Type

**1958, Sept. 13** **Litho.**
**Size: 24½x30mm**
**790** CD1 10pf yel grn & blue *.35* .25
**791** CD1 40pf lt blue & red *3.00* .35

Nicolaus Cusanus (Nikolaus Krebs) A207

Pres. Theodor Heuss A208

**1958, Dec. 3 Litho. *Perf. 14x13½***

**792** A207 20pf dk car rose & blk .45 .35

500th anniv. of the Cusanus Hospice at Kues, founded by Cardinal Nicolaus (1401-64).

Exists imperf. Value $300.

**1959 Wmk. 304 *Perf. 14***

**793** A208 7pf blue green .25 .25
**794** A208 10pf green .40 .25
**795** A208 20pf dk car rose .40 .25

**Engr.**

**796** A208 40pf blue 12.00 .90
**797** A208 70pf deep purple 3.50 .75
*Nos. 793-797 (5)* 16.55 2.40

Nos. 793-795 were issued in sheets of 100 and in coils. Every fifth coil stamp has a control number on the back.

An experimental booklet containing one pane of 10 of No. 794 was sold at Darmstadt in 1960. Value $750.

Jakob Fugger — A209

**1959, Mar. 6 *Perf. 13x13½***

**798** A209 20pf dk red & black .40 .45

500th anniversary of the birth of Jakob Fugger the Rich, businessman and banker.

Adam Riese — A210

**1959, Mar. 28 *Perf. 13½x13***

**799** A210 10pf ol grn & blk .40 .45

Adam Riese (c. 1492-1559), arithmetic teacher, 400th death anniversary.

Alexander von Humboldt — A211

**1959, May 6 Engr. *Perf. 13½x14***

**800** A211 40pf blue 1.60 1.25

Alexander von Humboldt (1769-1859), naturalist and geographer, death centenary.

Buildings, Buxtehude A212

**1959, June 20 Litho. *Perf. 14***

**801** A212 20pf lt blue, ver & blk .40 .40

Millennium of town of Buxtehude.

Holy Coat of Trier — A213

**Lithographed; Coat Embossed**

**1959, July 18 Wmk. 304 *Perf. 14***

**802** A213 20pf dull cl, buff & blk .40 .40

Showing of the seamless robe of Christ at the Cathedral of Trier, July 19-Sept. 20.

Synod Emblem — A214

**1959, Aug. 12 Litho.**

**803** A214 10pf grn, brt vio & blk .30 .30

Meeting of German Protestants (Evangelical Synod), Munich, Aug. 12-16.

Souvenir Sheet

A215

Portraits: 10pf, George Friedrich Handel. 15pf, Louis Spohr. 20pf, Ludwig van Beethoven. 25pf, Joseph Haydn. 40pf, Felix Mendelssohn-Bartholdy.

***Perf. 14x13½***

**1959, Sept. 8 Engr. Wmk. 304**

**804** A215 Sheet of 5 24.00 *50.00*
*a.* 10pf deep green 3.00 *5.50*
*b.* 15pf blue 3.00 *5.50*
*c.* 20pf dark carmine 3.00 *3.75*
*d.* 25pf brown 3.00 *7.50*
*e.* 40pf dark blue 3.00 *5.50*

Opening of Beethoven Hall in Bonn and to honor various anniversaries of German composers.

**Europa Issue, 1959**

Common Design Type

**1959, Sept. 19 Litho. *Perf. 13½x14***

**Size: 24x29½mm**

**805** CD2 10pf olive green .30 .25
**806** CD2 40pf dark blue *1.60* *.40*

Uprooted Oak Emblem — A216

**1960, Apr. 7 *Perf. 13½x13***

**807** A216 10pf grn, blk & lil .25 .25
**808** A216 40pf bl, blk & org 2.10 2.10

World Refugee Year, 7/1/59-6/30/60.

Philipp Melanchthon A217

**1960, Apr. 19 *Perf. 13½x14***

**809** A217 20pf dk car rose & blk 1.25 1.10

400th anniversary of the death of Philipp Melanchthon, co-worker of Martin Luther in the German Reformation.

Symbols of Christ's Sufferings A218

**1960, May 17 *Perf. 14x13½***

**810** A218 10pf Prus grn, gray & ocher .30 .30

1960 Passion Play, Oberammergau, Bavaria.

Dove, Chalice and Crucifix — A219

**1960, July 30 Engr. *Perf. 14x13½***

**811** A219 10pf dull green .55 .45
**812** A219 20pf maroon .75 .75

37th Eucharistic World Congress, Munich.

Wrestlers and Olympic Rings — A220

Sport scenes from Greek urns: 10pf, Sprinters. 20pf, Discus and Javelin throwers. 40pf, Chariot race.

**1960, Aug. 8 Wmk. 304**

**813** A220 7pf red brown .25 .25
**814** A220 10pf olive green .40 .25
**815** A220 20pf vermilion .40 .25
**816** A220 40pf dark blue 1.25 1.25
*Nos. 813-816 (4)* 2.30 2.00

17th Olympic Games, Rome, 8/25-9/11.

Hildesheim Cathedral, Miters, Cross and Crosier — A221

**1960, Sept. 6 Engr. *Perf. 13½x14***

**817** A221 20pf claret .75 .45

St. Bernward (960-1022) and St. Godehard (960-1038), bishops.

**Europa Issue, 1960**

Common Design Type

**1960, Sept. 19 Wmk. 304**

**Size: 30x25mm**

**818** CD3 10pf ol grn & yel grn .25 .25
**819** CD3 20pf brt red & lt red *.75* .25
**820** CD3 40pf bl & lt bl *1.25* *.75*
*Nos. 818-820 (3)* 2.25 1.25

George C. Marshall A222

Steam Locomotive A223

**1960, Oct. 15 Litho. *Perf. 13x13½***

**821** A222 40pf dp blue & blk 2.50 2.10

Issued to honor George C. Marshall, US general and statesman.

**1960, Dec. 7 *Perf. 13½x14***

**822** A223 10pf ol bis & blk .30 .35

125th anniversary of German railroads.

St. George — A224

**Wmk. 304**

**1961, Apr. 23 Engr. *Perf. 14***

**823** A224 10pf green .25 .30

Honoring Boy Scouts of the world on St. George's Day (patron saint of Boy Scouts).

Albrecht Dürer — A225

Portraits: 5pf, Albertus Magnus. 7pf, St. Elizabeth of Thuringia. 8pf, Johann Gutenberg. 15pf, Martin Luther. 20pf, Johann Sebastian Bach. 25pf, Balthasar Neumann. 30pf, Immanuel Kant. 40pf, Gotthold Ephraim Lessing. 50pf, Johann Wolfgang von Goethe. 60pf, Friedrich von Schiller. 70pf, Ludwig van Beethoven. 80pf, Heinrich von Kleist. 90pf, Prof. Franz Oppenheimer. 1m, Annette von Droste-Hülshoff. 2m, Gerhart Hauptmann.

**1961-64 Typo. *Perf. 14***

**Fluorescent or Ordinary Paper**

**824** A225 5pf olive .25 .25
*b.* Tête bêche pair ('63) .50 .90
**825** A225 7pf dark bister .25 .25
**826** A225 8pf lilac .25 .35
**827** A225 10pf olive green .25 .25
*b.* Tête bêche pair .50 1.50
**828** A225 15pf blue .35 .75
*b.* Tête bêche pair ('63) .90 2.10
**829** A225 20pf dk red .35 .30
*b.* Tête bêche pair ('63) .60 1.90
**830** A225 25pf orange brn .25 .25

**Engr.**

**831** A225 30pf gray .25 .25
**832** A225 40pf blue .25 .25
**833** A225 50pf red brown .35 .25
**834** A225 60pf dk car rose ('62) .35 .25
**835** A225 70pf grnsh black .25 .25
*a.* 70pf deep green .60 .25
**836** A225 80pf brown .40 .40
**837** A225 90pf yel ol ('64) .35 .30
**838** A225 1m violet blue .50 .25
**839** A225 2m yel grn ('62) 3.00 .50
*Nos. 824-839 (16)* 7.65 5.10

Nos. 824-825, 827-830, 832, 834-835, 835a were issued in coils as well as in sheets. Every fifth coil stamp has a black control number on the back.

Nos. 824-839, including booklet panes and tête bêche pairs, were printed on fluorescent paper. Nos. 824-829 and 832 were also printed on ordinary paper.

Gottlieb Daimler's Car of 1886 and Signature A226

Design: 20pf, Carl Benz's 3-wheel car of 1886 and signature.

**1961, July 3** **Litho.**
**840** A226 10pf green & blk .25 .25
**841** A226 20pf brick red & blk .35 .30

75 years of motorized traffic.

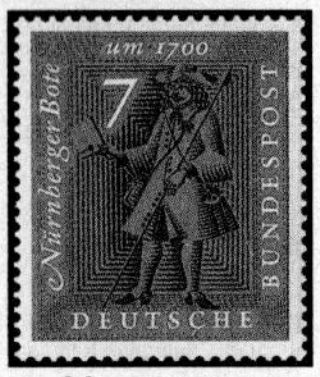


Messenger, Nuremberg, 18th Century — A227

Cathedral, Speyer — A228

**Photogravure and Engraved**

**1961, Aug. 31** **Wmk. 304** ***Perf. 14***
**842** A227 7pf brown red & blk .25 .30

Issued to publicize the exhibition "The Letter in Five Centuries," Nuremberg.

**1961, Sept. 2** **Engr.**
**843** A228 20pf vermilion .30 .45

900th anniversary of Speyer Cathedral.

**Europa Issue, 1961**

Common Design Type

**1961, Sept. 18** **Litho.**
**Size: 28½x18½mm**
**844** CD4 10pf olive green .25 .25
**845** CD4 40pf violet blue *.35 .50*

No. 844 was printed on both ordinary and fluorescent paper.

Reis Telephone A229

**Wmk. 304**

**1961, Oct. 26** **Engr.** ***Perf. 14***
**846** A229 10pf green .30 .35

Cent. of the demonstration of the 1st telephone by Philipp Reis.

Wilhelm Emanuel von Ketteler — A230

**1961, Dec. 22** **Litho.**
**847** A230 10pf olive grn & blk .30 .35

Sesquicentennial of the birth of von Ketteler, Bishop of Mainz and pioneer in social development.

Fluorescent Paper

was introduced for all stamps, starting with No. 848. Of the stamps before No. 848, those issued on both ordinary and fluorescent paper include Nos. 704, 706, 708-711, 737, 755-756, 824-829, 832, 844. Those issued only on fluorescent paper (up to No. 848) include Nos. 708b, 830-831, 833-839 and 842.

Drusus Stone and Old View of Mainz — A231

**1962, May 10** **Engr.** **Wmk. 304**
**848** A231 20pf deep claret .30 .35

The 2000th anniversary of Mainz.

Notes and Tuning Fork — A232

**1962, July 12** **Litho.** ***Perf. 14***
**849** A232 20pf red & black .30 .45

Issued to show appreciation of choral singing. The music is from the choral movement for three voices "In dulci jubilo" from "Musae Sioniae" by Michael Praetorius.

"Faith, Thanksgiving, Service" A233

**1962, Aug. 22** **Engr.** **Unwmk.**
**850** A233 20pf magenta .30 .45

79th meeting of German Catholics, Hanover, Aug. 22-29.

Open Bible, Chrismon and Chalice — A234

**1962, Sept. 11** **Litho.** **Wmk. 304**
**851** A234 20pf vermilion & blk .30 .45

Württemberg Bible Society, 150th anniv.

**Europa Issue, 1962**

Common Design Type

**1962, Sept. 17** **Engr.**
**Size: 28x23mm**
**852** CD5 10pf green .25 .25
**853** CD5 40pf blue *.40 .35*

"Bread for the World" — A235

**Lithographed and Embossed**

**1962, Nov. 23** ***Perf. 14***
**854** A235 20pf brown red & blk .30 .45

Issued in connection with the Advent Collection of the Protestant Church in Germany.

Mother and Child Receiving Gift Parcel — A236

**1963, Feb. 9** **Engr.**
**855** A236 20pf dark carmine .25 .35

Issued to express gratitude to the American organizations, CRALOG (Council of Relief Agencies Licensed to Operate in Germany) and CARE (Cooperative for American Remittances to Everywhere), for help during 1946-1962.

Globe, Cross, Seeds and Stalks of Wheat — A237

**Lithographed and Engraved**

**1963, Feb. 27** **Wmk. 304** ***Perf. 14***
**856** A237 20pf gray, blk & red .25 .35

German Catholic "Misereor" (I have compassion) campaign against hunger and illness.

Checkered Lily — A238

Flowers: 15pf, Lady's slipper. 20pf, Columbine. 40pf, Beach thistle.

**1963, Apr. 28** **Litho.** **Unwmk.**
**857** A238 10pf multicolored .25 .25
**858** A238 15pf multicolored .25 .25
**859** A238 20pf multicolored .25 .25
**860** A238 40pf multicolored .35 .35
*Nos. 857-860 (4)* 1.10 1.10

Flora and Philately Exhibition, Hamburg.

Heidelberg Catechism A239

**1963, May 2** **Litho. & Engr.**
**861** A239 20pf dp org, brn org & blk .30 .35

400th anniv. of the Heidelberg Catechism, containing the doctrine of the reformed church.

Cross of Golgotha, Darkened Sun and Moon — A240

**1963, May 4** **Litho.** **Wmk. 304**
**862** A240 10pf grn, dp car, blk & vio .25 .30

Consecration of the Regina Martyrum Church, Berlin-Plötzensee, in memory of the victims of Nazism.

Arms of 18 Participating Countries, Paris Conference, 1863 — A241

**1963, May 7** **Engr.**
**863** A241 40pf violet blue .40 .50

1st Intl. Postal Conf., Paris, 1863, cent.

Map Showing New Railroad Link, German and Danish Flags — A242

**1963, May 14** **Litho.** **Unwmk.**
**864** A242 20pf multi .30 .30

Inauguration of the "Bird Flight Line" railroad link between Germany and Denmark.

Cross — A243

**Lithographed and Embossed**

**1963, May 24** **Unwmk.** ***Perf. 14***
**865** A243 20pf magenta, red & yel .25 .30

Cent. of the founding of the Intl. Red Cross in connection with the German Red Cross cent. celebrations, Munster, May 24-26.

Synod Emblem and Crown of Barbed Wire — A244

***Perf. 13½x13***

**1963, July 24** **Litho.** **Wmk. 304**
**866** A244 20pf dp orange & blk .30 .35

Meeting of German Protestants (Evangelical Synod), Dortmund, July 24-28.

**Europa Issue, 1963**

Common Design Type

**1963, Sept. 14** **Engr.** ***Perf. 14***
**Size: 28x23½mm**
**867** CD6 15pf green .25 .30
**868** CD6 20pf red .25 .25

Old Town Hall, Hanover A245

State Capitals: #870, Hamburg harbor, 775th anniv. #871, North Ferry pier, Kiel. #872, National Theater, Munich. #873, Fountain & building, Wiesbaden. #874, Reichstag Building,Berlin. #875, Gutenberg Museum, Mainz. #876, Jan Wellem (Johann Wilhelm II, 1658-1716) statue, Dusseldorf. #877, City Hall, Bonn. #878, City Hall, Bremen. #879, View of Stuttgart. #879A, Ludwig's Church, Saarbrucken.

***Perf. 14, 13½x13 (#873, 876, 877)***

**1964-65** **Litho.** **Unwmk.**
**869** A245 20pf gray, blk & red .25 .30
**870** A245 20pf multicolored .25 .30
**871** A245 20pf multicolored .25 .30
**872** A245 20pf multicolored .25 .30
**873** A245 20pf multicolored .25 .30
**874** A245 20pf blue, blk, & grn .25 .30
**875** A245 20pf multicolored .25 .30
**876** A245 20pf multicolored .25 .30
**877** A245 20pf multi ('65) .25 .30
**878** A245 20pf multi ('65) .25 .30
**879** A245 20pf multi ('65) .25 .30
**879A** A245 20pf multi ('65) .25 .30
*Nos. 869-879A (12)* 3.00 3.60

View of Ottobeuren Abbey — A246

**Lithographed and Engraved**

**1964, May 29** ***Perf. 14***
**880** A246 20pf pink, red & blk .25 .30

Ottobeuren Benedictine Abbey, 1200th anniv.

Pres. Heinrich Lübke — A247

**1964, July 1** **Litho.** ***Perf. 14***

**881** A247 20pf carmine .25 .25
**882** A247 40pf ultra .25 .30

Lübke's re-election. See Nos. 974-975.

Sophie Scholl — A248

Designs: No. 884, Ludwig Beck. No. 885, Dietrich Bonhoeffer. No. 886, Alfred Delp. No. 887, Karl Friedrich Goerdeler. No. 888, Wilhelm Leuschner. No. 889, Count James von Moltke. No. 890, Count Claus Schenk von Stauffenberg.

**1964, July 20** **Litho. & Engr.**

**883** A248 20pf blue gray & blk .60 1.10
**884** A248 20pf blue gray & blk .60 1.10
**885** A248 20pf blue gray & blk .60 1.10
**886** A248 20pf blue gray & blk .60 1.10
**887** A248 20pf blue gray & blk .60 1.10
**888** A248 20pf blue gray & blk .60 1.10
**889** A248 20pf blue gray & blk .60 1.10
**890** A248 20pf blue gray & blk .60 1.10
*Nos. 883-890 (8)* 4.80 8.80

Issued to honor the German resistance to the Nazis, 1943-45. Printed in sheet of eight, containing one each of Nos. 883-890, se-tenant. Size: 148x105mm. The stamps were valid; the sheet was not, though widely used.

John Calvin — A249

Benzene Ring, Kekulé's Formula — A250

**1964, Aug. 3** **Litho.** ***Perf. 14***

**891** A249 20pf red & black .25 .30

Issued to honor the meeting of the International Union of the Reformed Churches in Germany, Frankfort on the Main, Aug. 3-13.

**1964, Aug. 14** **Unwmk.** ***Perf. 14***

Designs: 15pf, Cerenkov radiation, reactor in operation. 20pf, German gas engine.

**892** A250 10pf dk brn, brt grn & blk .25 .25
**893** A250 15pf brt grn, ultra & blk .25 .25
**894** A250 20pf red, grn & blk .25 .25
*Nos. 892-894 (3)* .75 .75

Progress in science and technology: 10pf, centenary of benzene formula by August Friedrich Kekulé; 15pf, 25 years of nuclear fission, Hahn and Strassmann; 20pf, centenary of German internal combustion engine, Nikolaus August Otto and Eugen Langen.

Ferdinand Lasalle — A251

**1964, Aug. 31** **Litho.**

**895** A251 20pf slate bl & blk .25 .30

Cent. of the death of Ferdinand Lasalle, a founder of the German Labor Movement.

Radiating Sun — A252

**1964, Sept. 2** **Engr.** **Wmk. 304**

**896** A252 20pf gray & red .25 .30

80th meeting of German Catholics, Stuttgart, Sept. 2-6. The inscription from Romans 12:2: ". . . be ye transformed through the renewing of your mind."

### Europa Issue, 1964

Common Design Type

**1964, Sept. 14** **Litho.** **Unwmk.**

**Size: 23x29mm**

**897** CD7 15pf yellow grn & lil .25 .25
**898** CD7 20pf rose & lilac .25 .25

Judo — A253

**1964, Oct. 10**

**899** A253 20pf multicolored .25 .30

18th Olympic Games, Tokyo, Oct. 10-25.

Prussian Eagle — A254

**Lithographed and Embossed**

**1964, Oct. 30** **Unwmk.** ***Perf. 14***

**900** A254 20pf brown org & blk .25 .30

250 years of the Court of Accounts in Germany, founded as the Royal Prussian Upper Chamber of Accounts.

John F. Kennedy (1917-63) A255

Castle Gate, Ellwangen A256

**1964, Nov. 21** **Engr.** **Wmk. 304**

**901** A255 40pf dark blue .30 .30

**1964-66** **Typo.** **Unwmk.**

Designs: (German buildings through 12 centuries): 10pf, Wall pavilion, Zwinger, Dresden. 15pf, Tegel Castle, Berlin. 20pf, Portico, Lorsch. 40pf, Trifels Fortress, Palatinate. 60pf, Treptow Gate, Neubrandenburg. 70pf, Osthofen Gate, Soest. 80pf, Elling Gate, Weissenburg.

**903** A256 10pf brown ('65) .25 .25
**904** A256 15pf dk green ('65) .25 .25
*b.* Tête bêche pair ('65) 1.10 1.25
**905** A256 20pf brown red ('65) .25 .25
*b.* Tête bêche pair ('66) 1.10 1.50

**Engr.**

**908** A256 40pf violet bl ('65) .25 .25
**909** A256 50pf olive bister .40 .25
**910** A256 60pf rose red .95 .35
**911** A256 70pf dark green ('65) 1.25 .35
**912** A256 80pf chocolate .95 .35
*Nos. 903-912 (8)* 4.55 2.30

Nos. 903-905, 908, 910-912 were issued in sheets of 100 and in coils. Every fifth coil stamp has a black control number on the back.

Illustrations from the Works of Matthias Claudius A257

**1965, Jan. 21** **Engr.** ***Perf. 14***

**917** A257 20pf black & red .25 .30

150th anniv. of the death of Matthias Claudius, poet and editor of the "Wandsbecker Bothe." Exists imperf. Value $225.

Otto von Bismarck by Franz von Lenbach — A258

**1965, Apr. 1** **Litho.** ***Perf. 14***

**918** A258 20pf black & dull red .25 .30

Prince Otto von Bismarck (1815-1898), Prussian statesman and 1st chancellor of the German Empire.

Exists imperf. Value $750.

Jet Plane and Space Capsule — A259

Designs: 5pf, Traffic lights and signs. 10pf, Communications satellite and ground station. 15pf, Old and new post buses. 20pf, Semaphore telegraph and telecommunication tower. 40pf, Old and new railroad engines. 70pf, Sailing ship and ocean liner.

**1965**

**919** A259 5pf gray & multi .25 .30
**920** A259 10pf multicolored .25 .30
**921** A259 15pf multicolored .25 .30
**922** A259 20pf maroon & multi .25 .30
**923** A259 40pf dk blue & multi .25 .30
**924** A259 60pf dull vio, yel & lt bl .25 .30
**925** A259 70pf multicolored .30 .30
*Nos. 919-925 (7)* 1.80 2.10

Intl. Transport and Communications Exhib., Munich, June 25-Oct. 30. No. 924 also for the 10th anniv. of the reopening of air service by Lufthansa. Issued: 60pf, 4/1; others, 6/25.

No. 919 exists imperf. Value $225.

Bouquet of Flowers — A260

**1965, May 1** **Litho.**

**926** A260 15pf multicolored .25 .25

75th anniv. of May Day celebration in Germany.

ITU Emblem — A261

**1965, May 17** **Unwmk.** ***Perf. 14***

**927** A261 40pf dp blue & blk .30 .35

Cent. of the ITU.

Adolph Kolping — A262

**1965, May 26** **Typo.**

**928** A262 20pf black, gray & red .25 .30

Kolping (1813-65). founder of the Catholic Unions of Journeymen, the Kolpingwork.

Rescue Ship — A263

**1965, May 29** **Litho. & Engr.**

**929** A263 20pf red & black .25 .30

Cent. of the German Sea Rescue Service.

**Type of 1955 Dated "1945-1965"**

***Perf. 14x13½***

**1965, July 28** **Engr.** **Wmk. 304**

**930** A161 20pf gray .25 .30

20 years of German expatriation.

Synod Emblem and Labyrinth — A264

**Lithographed and Engraved**

***Perf. 13½x14***

**1965, July 28** **Unwmk.**

**931** A264 20pf dp bl, grnsh bl & blk .25 .30

12th meeting of German Protestants (Evangelical Synod), Cologne, July 28-Aug. 1.

Waves and Stuttgart Television Tower — A265

**1965, July 28** **Litho.** ***Perf. 13½x13***

**932** A265 20pf dp bl, blk & brt pink .25 .30

Issued to publicize the German Radio Exhibition, Stuttgart, Aug. 27-Sept. 5.

Stamps of Thurn and Taxis, 1852-59 A266

**1965, Aug. 28** ***Perf. 14***

**933** A266 20pf multicolored .25 .30

125th anniv. of the introduction of postage stamps in Great Britain.

### Europa Issue, 1965

Common Design Type

***Perf. 14x13½***

**1965, Sept. 27** **Engr.** **Wmk. 304**

**Size: 28x23mm**

**934** CD8 15pf green .25 .25
**935** CD8 20pf dull red .25 .25

Nordertor, Flensburg
A267

Brandenburg Gate
A268

Designs: 5pf, Berlin Gate, Stettin. 10pf, Wall Pavilion, Zwinger, Dresden. 20pf, Portico, Lorsch. 40pf, Trifels Fortress, Palatinate. 50pf, Castle Gate, Ellwangen. 60pf, Treptow Gate, Neubrandenburg. 70pf, Osthofen Gate, Soest. 80pf, Elling Gate, Weissenburg. 90pf, Zschocke Ladies' Home, Königsberg. 1m, Melanchthon House, Wittenberg. 1.10m, Trinity Hospital, Hildesheim. 1.30m, Tegel Castle, Berlin. 2m, Löwenberg, Town Hall, interior view.

**1966-69 Unwmk. Engr. *Perf. 14***

| | | | | | |
|---|---|---|---|---|---|
| **936** | A267 | 5pf | olive | .25 | .25 |
| **937** | A267 | 10pf | dk brn ('67) | .25 | .25 |
| **939** | A267 | 20pf | dk grn ('67) | .25 | .25 |
| **940** | A267 | 30pf | yellow green | .25 | .25 |
| **941** | A267 | 30pf | red ('67) | .25 | .25 |
| **942** | A267 | 40pf | olive bis ('67) | .30 | .30 |
| **943** | A267 | 50pf | blue ('67) | .40 | .25 |
| **944** | A267 | 60pf | dp org ('67) | 2.50 | 1.50 |
| **945** | A267 | 70pf | slate grn ('67) | 1.10 | .25 |
| **946** | A267 | 80pf | red brown ('67) | 2.10 | 1.50 |
| **947** | A267 | 90pf | black | .75 | .30 |
| **948** | A267 | 1m | dull blue | .75 | .25 |
| **949** | A267 | 1.10m | red brown | .75 | .35 |
| **950** | A267 | 1.30m | green ('69) | 2.10 | 1.40 |
| **951** | A267 | 2m | purple | 2.10 | .60 |
| | | | *Nos. 936-951 (15)* | 14.10 | 7.95 |

**1966-68 Typo. *Perf. 14***

| | | | | | |
|---|---|---|---|---|---|
| **952** | A268 | 10pf | chocolate | .25 | .25 |
| *a.* | | | Bklt. pane, 4 #952, 2 #953, 4 #954 ('67) | 3.75 | 15.00 |
| *b.* | | | Tête bêche pair | .65 | .75 |
| *c.* | | | Bklt. pane, 2 #952, 4 #953 | 2.25 | 7.50 |
| **953** | A268 | 20pf | deep green | .30 | .25 |
| *a.* | | | Tête bêche pair ('68) | .90 | 1.25 |
| *b.* | | | Bklt. pane, 2 #953, 2 #954 | 1.50 | 6.00 |
| **954** | A268 | 30pf | red | .30 | .25 |
| *a.* | | | Tête bêche pair ('68) | .95 | 1.40 |
| **955** | A268 | 50pf | dark blue | 1.25 | .35 |
| **956** | A268 | 100pf | dark blue ('67) | 9.75 | .60 |
| | | | *Nos. 952-956 (5)* | 11.85 | 1.70 |

Nos. 952-956 were issued in sheets of 100 and in coils. Every fifth coil stamp has a black control number on the back.

Nathan Söderblom
A269

Cardinal von Galen
A270

**1966, Jan. 15 Litho. *Perf. 13x13½***
**959** A269 20pf dull lilac & blk .25 .30

Soderblom (1866-1931),Swedish Protestant theologian, who worked for the union of Christian churches and received 1930 Nobel Peace Prize.

**1966, Mar. 22 Litho. *Perf. 14***
**960** A270 20pf dp lil rose, sal pink & blk .25 .30

Clemens August Cardinal Count von Galen (1878-1946), anti-Nazi Bishop of Munster.

"The Miraculous Draught" — A271

G. W. Leibniz — A272

**1966, July 13 Litho. *Perf. 14***
**961** A271 30pf dp orange & blk .25 .30

81st meeting of German Catholics, Bamberg, July 13-17.

**1966, Aug. 24 Unwmk. *Perf. 14***
**962** A272 30pf rose car, pink & blk .25 .30

Gottfried Wilhelm Leibniz (1646-1716), philosopher and mathematician.

**Europa Issue, 1966**
Common Design Type

**1966, Sept. 24 *Perf. 14***
**Size: 23x28½mm**

| | | | | | |
|---|---|---|---|---|---|
| **963** | CD9 | 20pf | multicolored | *.25* | *.30* |
| **964** | CD9 | 30pf | multicolored | .25 | .25 |

Diagram of Three-Phase Transmission
A273

UNICEF Emblem
A274

**1966, Sept. 28 Litho.**

| | | | | | |
|---|---|---|---|---|---|
| **965** | A273 | 20pf | shown | .25 | .25 |
| **966** | A273 | 30pf | Dynamo | .25 | .25 |

Progress in science and technology: 20pf, 75th anniv. of three-phase power transmission; 30pf, cent.y of discovery by Werner von Siemens of the dynamoelectric principle.

**1966, Oct. 24 Litho. *Perf. 14***
**967** A274 30pf red, blk & gray .25 .30

Awarding of the 1965 Nobel Peace Prize to UNICEF.

Werner von Siemens (1816-92), Electrical Engineer and Inventor — A275

**1966, Dec. 13 Engr. *Perf. 14***
**968** A275 30pf maroon .25 .30

**Europa Issue, 1967**
Common Design type

**1967, May 2 Photo. *Perf. 14***
**Size: 23x28mm**

| | | | | | |
|---|---|---|---|---|---|
| **969** | CD10 | 20pf | multi | .30 | .30 |
| **970** | CD10 | 30pf | multi | .25 | .25 |

Franz von Taxis — A276

"Peace Is Among Us" — A277

**Lithographed and Engraved**
**1967, June 3 *Perf. 14***
**971** A276 30pf dp orange & blk .25 .30

450th anniv. of the death of Franz von Taxis, founder of the Taxis (Thurn and Taxis) postal system.

**1967, June 21**
**972** A277 30pf brt pink & blk .25 .30

13th meeting of German Protestants (Evangelical Synod), Hanover, June 21-25.

Friedrich von Bodelschwingh
A278

***Perf. 13½x13***
**1967, July 1 Litho. Unwmk.**
**973** A278 30pf redsh brown & blk .25 .30

Cent. of Bethel Institution (for the incurable). Friedrich von Bodelschwingh (1877-1946), manager of Bethel (1910-46) & son of the founder.

**Lübke Type of 1964**

**1967, Oct. 14 Litho. *Perf. 14***

| | | | | | |
|---|---|---|---|---|---|
| **974** | A247 | 30pf | carmine | .25 | .30 |
| **975** | A247 | 50pf | ultra | .35 | .35 |

Re-election of President Heinrich Lübke.

The Wartburg, Eisenach
A279

**1967, Oct. 31 Engr. *Perf. 14***
**976** A279 30pf red .30 .35

450th anniversary of the Reformation.

Cross and Map of South America — A280

Koenig Printing Press — A281

**1967, Nov. 17 Photo. *Perf. 14***
**977** A280 30pf multicolored .25 .30

"Adveniat," aid movement of German Catholics for the Latin American church.

**1968, Jan. 12 Litho. *Perf. 14***

Designs: 20pf, Zinc sulfide and lead sulfide crystals. 30pf, Schematic diagram of a microscope.

| | | | | | |
|---|---|---|---|---|---|
| **978** | A281 | 10pf | multicolored | .25 | .25 |
| **979** | A281 | 20pf | multicolored | .25 | .25 |
| **980** | A281 | 30pf | multicolored | .25 | .25 |
| | | | *Nos. 978-980 (3)* | .75 | .75 |

Progress in science and technology: 10pf, 150th anniv. of the Koenig printing press; 20pf, 1000th anniv. of mining in the Harz Mountains; 30pf, cent. of scientific microscope construction.

Symbols of Various Crafts
A282

**1968, Mar. 8 Litho. *Perf. 14***
**981** A282 30pf multicolored .30 .35

Traditions and progress of the crafts.
Exists imperf. Value $250.

Souvenir Sheet

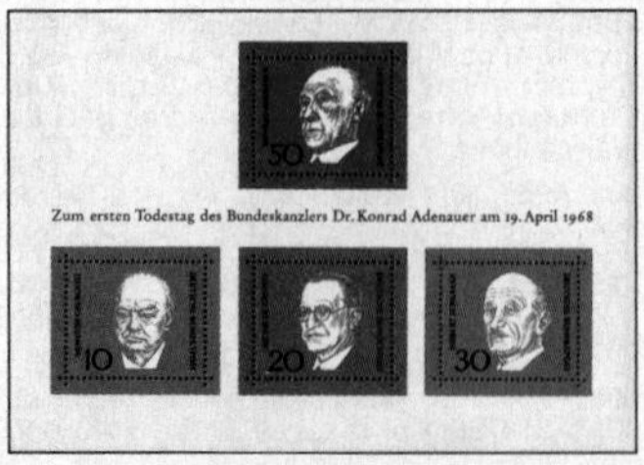

Adenauer, Churchill, de Gasperi and Schuman — A283

Portraits: 10pf, Winston S. Churchill. 20pf, Alcide de Gasperi. 30pf, Robert Schuman. 50pf, Konrad Adenauer.

**1968, Apr. 19 Litho. *Perf. 14***
**Black Inscriptions**

| | | | | |
|---|---|---|---|---|
| **982** | A283 | Sheet of 4 | 2.25 | 2.25 |
| *a.* | | 10pf dark red brown | .50 | .30 |
| *b.* | | 20pf green | .50 | .35 |
| *c.* | | 30pf dark red | .50 | .50 |
| *d.* | | 50pf bright blue | .50 | .75 |

1st anniv. of the death of Konrad Adenauer (1876-1967), chancellor of West Germany (1949-63), and honoring leaders in building a united Europe.

**Europa Issue, 1968**
Common Design Type

**1968, Apr. 29 Photo.**
**Size: 29x24½mm**

| | | | | | |
|---|---|---|---|---|---|
| **983** | CD11 | 20pf | green, yel & brn | *.25* | *.30* |
| **984** | CD11 | 30pf | car, yel & brn | .25 | .25 |

Karl Marx (1818-83)
A284

**Lithographed and Engraved**
**1968, Apr. 29 *Perf. 14***
**985** A284 30pf red, black & gray .25 .30

Pierre de Coubertin — A285

**1968, June 6 Unwmk. *Perf. 14***
**986** A285 30pf lilac & dk pur .30 .30
*Nos. 986,B434-B437 (5)* 2.20 2.30

19th Olympic Games, Mexico City, 10/12-27.

Opening Bars, "Die Meistersinger von Nurnberg," by Wagner — A286

**Lithographed and Photogravure**
**1968, June 21**
**987** A286 30pf gray, blk & fawn .25 .30

Cent. of the 1st performance of Richard Wagner's "Die Meistersinger von Nurnberg."

Konrad Adenauer (1876-1967)
A287

**1968, July 19 Litho. *Perf. 14***
**988** A287 30pf dp orange & blk .30 .30

Cross and Dove in Center of Universe
A288

**1968, July 19 Litho. & Engr.**
**989** A288 20pf brt grn, bl blk & yel .25 .30

Issued to publicize the 82nd meeting of German Catholics, Essen, Sept. 4-8.

North German Confederation Nos. 4 and 10 — A289

**1968, Sept. 5** **Engr.** ***Perf. 14***
**990** A289 30pf cop red, gray vio & blk .25 .30

Cent. of the stamps of the North German Confederation.

Arrows Symbolizing Determination A290

Human Rights Flame A291

**1968, Sept. 26** **Photo.** ***Perf. 14***
**991** A290 30pf multi .25 .30

Centenary of the German trade unions.

**1968, Dec. 10** **Photo.** ***Perf. 14***
**992** A291 30pf multicolored .25 .30

International Human Rights Year.

Junkers 52 A292

Design: 30pf, Boeing 707.

**1969, Feb. 6** **Litho.** ***Perf. 14***
**993** A292 20pf green & multi .40 .25
**994** A292 30pf red & multi .60 .25

50th anniv. of German airmail service.

Five-pointed Star — A293

**1969, Apr. 28** **Litho.** ***Perf. 13½x13***
**995** A293 30pf red & multi .45 .30

50th anniv. of the ILO.

**Europa Issue, 1969**
Common Design Type

**1969, Apr. 28** **Photo.** ***Perf. 14***
**Size: 29x23mm**
**996** CD12 20pf green, blue & yel .30 .25
**997** CD12 30pf red brn, yel & blk .35 .25

Heraldic Eagles of Federal and Weimar Republics A294

**1969, May 23** **Photo.** ***Perf. 14***
**998** A294 30pf red, black & gold .90 .45

German Basic Law, 20th anniv., and the proclamation of the Weimar Constitution, 50th anniv.

Crosses — A295

**1969, June 4** **Litho. & Engr.**
**999** A295 30pf dk violet bl & cream .45 .30

German War Graves Commission, 50th anniv.

Seashore A296

**1969, June 4** ***Perf. 14***
**1000** A296 10pf shown .25 .25
**1001** A296 20pf Foothills .60 .35
**1002** A296 30pf Mountains .30 .25
**1003** A296 50pf Riverbed .90 .50
*Nos. 1000-1003 (4)* 2.05 1.35

Issued to publicize Nature Protection.

"Hungry for Justice" — A297

**1969, July 7** **Litho.** ***Perf. 14***
**1004** A297 30pf multicolored .45 .30

14th meeting of German Protestants (Evangelical Synod), Stuttgart, July 16-20.

Electromagnetic Field — A298

**1969, Aug. 11** **Litho.** ***Perf. 14***
**1005** A298 30pf red & multi .45 .30

Issued to publicize the German Radio Exhibition, Stuttgart, Aug. 29-Sept. 7.

Maltese Cross — A299

**1969, Aug. 11** ***Perf. 13x13½***
**1006** A299 30pf red & black .45 .30

Maltese Relief Service, founded 1955, world-wide activities in social services, first aid and disaster assistance.

Souvenir Sheet

Marie Juchacz, Marie-Elisabeth Lüders and Helene Weber — A300

**1969, Aug. 11** **Engr.** ***Perf. 14***
**1007** A300 Sheet of 3 .90 .65
*a.* 10pf olive .25 .25
*b.* 20pf dark green .25 .25
*c.* 30pf lake .25 .25

50th anniv. of universal women's suffrage. Marie Juchacz (1879-1956), Marie-Elisabeth Lüders (1878-1966) and Helene Weber (1881-1962) were members of the German Reichstag.

Bavaria No. 16 — A301

**1969, Sept. 4** **Litho. & Embossed**
**1008** A301 30pf gray & rose .45 .30

23rd meeting of the Federation of German Philatelists, Sept. 6, the 70th Philatelists' Day, Sept. 7, and the phil. exhib. "120 Years of Bavarian Stamps" in Garmish-Partenkirchen, Sept. 4-7.

Brine Pipe Line — A302

**1969, Sept. 4** **Litho.** ***Perf. 13½x13***
**1009** A302 20pf multicolored .45 .30

350th anniversary of the Brine Pipe Line from Traunstein to Bad Reichenhall.

Rothenburg ob der Tauber — A303

**Lithographed and Engraved**
**1969, Sept. 4** ***Perf. 14***
**1010** A303 30pf dark red & blk .45 .30

See #1047-1049, 1067-1069A, 1106-1110.

Pope John XXIII (1881-1963) A304

Mahatma Gandhi (1869-1948) A305

**1969, Oct. 2** **Engr.** ***Perf. 13½x14***
**1011** A304 30pf dark red .35 .30

**1969, Oct. 2** **Litho.**
**1012** A305 20pf yellow grn & blk .30 .30

Ernst Moritz Arndt A306

Ludwig van Beethoven A307

**1969, Nov. 13** **Litho. & Engr.**
**1013** A306 30pf gray & maroon .35 .30

Arndt (1769-1860), historian, poet and member of German National Assembly.

**1970, Mar. 20** ***Perf. 13½x14***

Portraits: 20pf, Georg Wilhelm Hegel (1770-1831), philosopher. 30pf, Friedrich Hölderlin (1770-1843), poet.

**1014** A307 10pf pale vio & blk .75 .25
**1015** A307 20pf olive & blk .35 .25
**1016** A307 30pf rose & blk .35 .25
*Nos. 1014-1016 (3)* 1.45 .75

Saar No. 171 A308

**1970, Apr. 29** **Photo.** ***Perf. 14x13½***
**1017** A308 30pf blk, red & gray grn .35 .30

Issued to publicize the SABRIA National Stamp Exhibition, Saarbrucken, Apr. 29-May 4. No. 1017 was issued Apr. 29 at the SABRIA post office in Saarbrucken, on May 4 throughout Germany.

**Europa Issue, 1970**
Common Design Type

**1970, May 4** **Engr.** ***Perf. 14x13½***
**Size: 28x23mm**
**1018** CD13 20pf green .30 .25
**1019** CD13 30pf red .35 .25

Münchhausen on His Severed Horse — A309

**1970, May 11** **Litho.** ***Perf. 13½x13***
**1020** A309 20pf multicolored .35 .30

Soldier and storyteller Count Hieronymus C. F. von Münchhausen (1720-97).

Seagoing Vessel and Underpass A310

**1970, June 18 Litho. *Perf. 14***

**1021** A310 20pf multicolored .35 .30

North Sea-Baltic Sea Canal, 75th anniv.

Nurse Assisting Elderly Woman — A311

5pf, Welder (industrial protection). 10pf, Mountain climbers (rescuer bringing down casualty). 30pf, Fireman. 50pf, Stretcher bearer, casualty & ambulance. 70pf, Rescuer & drowning boy.

**1970 Photo.**

**1022** A311 5pf dull blue & multi .25 .25
**1023** A311 10pf brown & multi .25 .25
**1024** A311 20pf green & multi .30 .25
**1025** A311 30pf red & multi .75 .25
**1026** A311 50pf blue & multi .75 .35
**1027** A311 70pf green & multi .90 .75
*Nos. 1022-1027 (6)* 3.20 2.10

Honoring various voluntary services.
Issued: 20pf, 30pf, 6/18; others, 9/21.

Pres. Gustav Heinemann A312

Cross Seen through Glass A313

**1970-73 Engr. *Perf. 14***

**1028** A312 5pf dark gray .25 .25
**1029** A312 10pf brown .25 .25
**1030** A312 20pf green .25 .25
**1030A** A312 25pf dp yellow grn .30 .25
**1031** A312 30pf red brown .30 .25
**1032** A312 40pf brown org .30 .25
**1033** A312 50pf dark blue 1.40 .25
**1034** A312 60pf blue .50 .25
**1035** A312 70pf dark brown .65 .30
**1036** A312 80pf slate grn .65 .30
**1037** A312 90pf magenta 1.25 1.10
**1038** A312 1m olive .90 .30
**1038A** A312 110pf olive gray 1.00 .60
**1039** A312 120pf ocher 1.10 .75
**1040** A312 130pf ocher 1.25 .75
**1040A** A312 140pf dk blue grn 1.40 .90
**1041** A312 150pf purple 1.40 .60
**1042** A312 160pf orange 2.00 1.00
**1042A** A312 170pf orange 1.60 .60
**1043** A312 190pf deep claret 2.25 .75
**1044** A312 2m deep violet 1.75 .35
*Nos. 1028-1044 (21)* 20.75 10.30

Issued: 5pf, 1m, 7/23/70; 10, 20pf, 10/23/70; 30, 90pf, 2m, 1/7/71; 40, 50, 70, 80pf, 4/8/71; 60pf, 6/25/71; 25pf, 8/27/71; 120, 160pf, 3/8/72; 130pf, 6/20/72; 150pf, 7/5/72; 170pf, 9/11/72; 110, 140, 190pf, 1/16/73.

**1970, Aug. 25 Litho.**

**1045** A313 20pf emerald & yellow .30 .25

Issued to publicize the world mission of Catholic missionaries who bring the Gospel to all peoples.

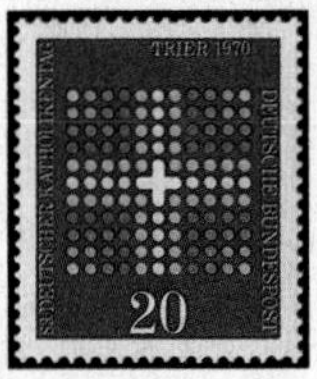

Cross — A314

**1970, Sept. 4 *Perf. 13x13½***

**1046** A314 20pf multicolored .30 .30

Issued to publicize the 83rd meeting of German Catholics, Trier, Sept. 9-13.

**Town Type of 1969**

Designs: No. 1047, View of Cochem and Moselle River. No. 1048, Cathedral and view of Freiburg im Breisgau. No. 1049, View of Oberammergau.

**1970 Litho. *Perf. 14***

**1047** A303 20pf apple grn & blk .45 .30
**1048** A303 20pf green & dk brn .45 .30
**1049** A303 30pf dp orange & blk .45 .30
*Nos. 1047-1049 (3)* 1.35 .90

Issued: #1047, 9/21; #1048, 11/4; #1049, 5/11.

Comenius — A315

**1970, Nov. 12 *Perf. 13½x14***

**1050** A315 30pf dark red & blk .45 .30

John Amos Comenius (1592-1670), theologian and educator.

Friedrich Engels — A316

**1970, Nov. 27 Litho. *Perf. 14***

**1051** A316 50pf red & vio blue 1.40 .75

Engels (1820-95), socialist, collaborator with Marx.

Imperial Eagle, 1872 — A317

**1971, Jan. 18 Litho. *Perf. 13½x14***

**1052** A317 30pf multicolored 1.40 .30

Centenary of the German Empire.

Friedrich Ebert (Germany No. 378) — A318

**1971, Jan. 18 *Perf. 13***

**1053** A318 30pf red brn, ol & blk 1.40 .30

Ebert (1871-1925), 1st Pres. of the German Republic.

Molecule Diagram Textile Pattern — A319

**1971, Feb. 18 Litho. *Perf. 13½x13***

**1054** A319 20pf brt grn, red & blk .30 .25

Synthetic textile fiber research, 125th anniversary.

School Crossing — A320

Traffic Signs: 20pf, Proceed with caution. 30pf, Stop. 50pf, Pedestrian crossing.

**1971, Feb. 18 *Perf. 14***

**1055** A320 10pf black, ultra & red .25 .25
**1056** A320 20pf black, red & grn .30 .25
**1057** A320 30pf black, gray & red .45 .25
**1058** A320 50pf black, ultra & red .75 .45
*Nos. 1055-1058 (4)* 1.75 1.20

New traffic rules, effective Mar. 1, 1971.

Signal to Pass — A321

Traffic Signs: 10pf, Warning signal. 20pf, Drive at right. 30pf, "Observe pedestrian crossings."

**1971, Apr. 16 Photo. *Perf. 14***

**1059** A321 5pf blue, blk & car .25 .25
**1060** A321 10pf multicolored .25 .25
**1061** A321 20pf brt grn, blk & car .35 .25
**1062** A321 30pf carmine & multi .65 .25
*Nos. 1059-1062 (4)* 1.50 1.00

New traffic rules, effective Mar. 1, 1971.

Luther Facing Charles V, Woodcut by Rabus — A322

**1971, Mar. 18 *Perf. 14***

**1063** A322 30pf red & black .60 .30

450th anniversary of the Diet of Worms.

**Europa Issue, 1971**
Common Design Type

**1971, May 3 Photo. *Perf. 14***
**Size: 28½x23mm**

**1064** CD14 20pf green, gold & blk .30 .25
**1065** CD14 30pf dp car, gold & blk .30 .25

Thomas à Kempis — A323

**1971, May 3 Engr.**

**1066** A323 30pf red & black .50 .30

500th anniversary of the death of Thomas à Kempis (1379-1471), Augustinian monk, author of "The Imitation of Christ."

**Town Type of 1969**

20pf, View of Goslar. #1068, View of Nuremberg. #1069, Heligoland. 40pf, Heidelberg.

**1971-72 Litho. & Engr. *Perf. 14***

**1067** A303 20pf brt green & blk .45 .35
**1068** A303 30pf vermilion & blk .45 .30
**1069** A303 30pf lt grn & blk ('72) .45 .25
**1069A** A303 40pf orange & blk ('72) .50 .25
*Nos. 1067-1069A (4)* 1.85 1.15

Issued: 20pf, 9/15; #1068, 5/21; #1069, 1069A, 10/20.

Dürer's Signature A324

**1971, May 21 Engr.**

**1070** A324 30pf copper red & blk 1.25 .30

500th anniversary of the birth of Albrecht Dürer (1471-1528), painter and engraver.

Congress Emblem — A325

**1971, May 28 Litho. *Perf. 13½x13***

**1071** A325 30pf red, orange & blk .45 .30

Ecumenical Meeting at Pentecost of the German Evangelical and Catholic Churches, Augsburg, June 2-5.

Illustration from New Astronomy, by Kepler — A326

**1971, June 25 Photo. *Perf. 14***

**1072** A326 30pf brt car, gold & blk .50 .30

Johannes Kepler (1571-1630), astronomer.

Dante Alighieri — A327

"Matches Cause Fires" — A328

**1971, Sept. 3 Engr. *Perf. 14***

**1073** A327 10pf black .25 .25

650th anniversary of the death of Dante Alighieri (1265-1321), poet.

**1971-74 Typo. *Perf. 14***

Designs: 10pf, Broken ladder. 20pf, Hand and circular saw. 25pf, "Alcohol and automobile." 30pf, Safety helmets prevent injury. 40pf, Defective plug. 50pf, Nail sticking from board. 60pf, 70pf, Traffic safety (ball rolling before car). 1m, Hoisted cargo. 1.50m, Fenced-in open manhole.

**1074** A328 5pf orange .25 .25
*a.* Bklt. pane, 2 each #1074, 1077-1079 ('74) 5.25 11.00
**1075** A328 10pf dark brown .25 .25
*a.* Bklt. pane, 4 #1075, 2 #1078 3.00 3.00
*b.* Bklt. pane, 2 each #1075-1076, 1078-1079 ('75) 5.25 11.00
*c.* Bklt. pane, 2 each #1079, 1075, 1078, 1076 13.50 16.50

| | | | | | |
|---|---|---|---|---|---|
| **1076** | A328 | 20pf purple | .30 | .25 |
| **1077** | A328 | 25pf green | .40 | .25 |
| **1078** | A328 | 30pf dark red | .35 | .25 |
| **1079** | A328 | 40pf rose claret | .35 | .25 |
| **1080** | A328 | 50pf Prus blue | 1.90 | .25 |
| **1081** | A328 | 60pf violet blue | 1.10 | .45 |
| **1082** | A328 | 70pf green & vio bl | 1.10 | .30 |
| **1083** | A328 | 100pf olive | 1.60 | .25 |
| **1085** | A328 | 150pf red brown | 5.00 | 1.10 |
| | | *Nos. 1074-1085 (11)* | 12.60 | 3.85 |

Accident prevention.

Issued in sheets of 100 and in coils. Every fifth coil stamp has a control number on the back.

Issued: 25pf, 60pf, 9/10; 5pf, 10/29; 10pf, 30pf, 3/8/72; 40pf, 6/20/72; 20pf, 100pf, 7/5/72; 150pf, 9/11/72; 50pf, 1/16/73; 70pf, 6/5/73.

Deaconesses A329

**1972, Jan. 20 Litho. *Perf. 13x13½***

**1087** A329 25pf green, blk & gray .45 .30

Wilhelm Löhe (1808-1872), founder of the Deaconesses Training Institute at Neuendettelsau.

Senefelder's Lithography Press — A330

**1972, Apr. 14 Litho. *Perf. 13½x13***

**1088** A330 25pf multicolored .45 .30

175th anniv. of the invention of the lithographic printing process by Alois Senefelder in 1796.

### Europa Issue 1972

Common Design Type

**1972, May 2 Photo. *Perf. 13½x14***

**Size: 23x29mm**

**1089** CD15 25pf yel grn, dk bl & yel .35 .25

**1090** CD15 30pf pale rose, dk & lt bl .50 .25

Lucas Cranach, by Dürer A331

Archer in Wheelchair A332

**Lithographed and Engraved**

**1972, May 18 *Perf. 14***

**1091** A331 25pf green, buff & blk .50 .30

Cranach (1472-1553), painter and engraver.

**1972, July 18 Litho. *Perf. 14***

**1092** A332 40pf yel, blk & red brn .60 .30

21st Stoke-Mandeville Games for the Paralyzed, Heidelberg, Aug. 1-10.

Kurt Schumacher A333

**1972, Aug. 18 Litho. & Engr.**

**1093** A333 40pf red & black 1.25 .30

Schumacher (1895-1952), 1st chairman of the German Social Democratic Party.

Post Horn and Decree — A334

**1972, Aug. 18 Photo.**

**1094** A334 40pf gold, car & blk .80 .30

Centenary of the German Postal Museum, Berlin. Design shows page from Heinrich von Stephan's decree establishing the museum.

Open Book — A335

**1972, Sept. 11 Photo. *Perf. 13x13½***

**1095** A335 40pf red & multi .60 .30

International Book Year 1972.

Music by Heinrich Schütz — A336

**Lithographed and Engraved**

**1972, Sept. 29 *Perf. 14***

**1096** A336 40pf multicolored .75 .30

300th anniversary of the death of Heinrich Schütz (1585-1672), composer.

Carnival Dancers A337

**1972, Nov. 10 Litho. *Perf. 14***

**1097** A337 40pf red & multi .90 .30

Cologne Carnival sesquicentennial.

Heinrich Heine (1797-1856), Poet — A338

**1972, Dec. 13 Litho. *Perf. 14***

**1098** A338 40pf rose, blk & red .90 .30

"Bread for the World" A339

**1972, Dec. 13 Photo. *Perf. 14***

**1099** A339 30pf green & red .45 .45

14th "Bread for the World-Developing Peace" campaign of the Protestant Church in Germany.

Würzburg Cathedral, 13th Century Seal — A340

**1972, Dec. 13 Litho.**

**1100** A340 40pf dp car, lil rose & blk .50 .30

Synod 72, meeting of Catholic bishoprics, Würzburg.

Colors of France and Germany Interlaced — A340a

**1973, Jan. 22 Litho. *Perf. 14***

**Size: 51x28mm**

**1101** A340a 40pf multicolored 1.25 .30

10th anniversary of the Franco-German Cooperation Treaty.

Meteorological Map — A341

**1973, Feb. 19 Litho. *Perf. 14***

**1102** A341 30pf multicolored .35 .30

Cent. of intl. meteorological cooperation.

Radio Tower and "Interpol" A342

**1973, Feb. 19 *Perf. 13½x13***

**1103** A342 40pf blk & red .45 .30

50th anniversary of International Criminal Police Organization (INTERPOL).

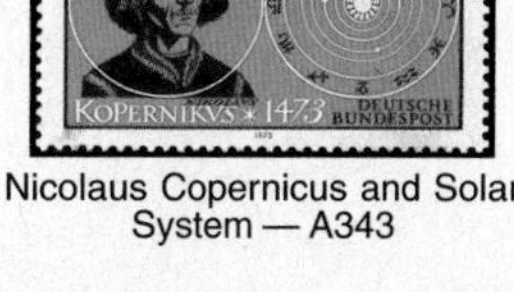

Nicolaus Copernicus and Solar System — A343

**1973, Feb. 19 *Perf. 14***

**1104** A343 40pf blk & red 1.25 .30

Festival Poster — A344

**1973, Mar. 15 Photo. *Perf. 14***

**1105** A344 40pf multicolored .45 .30

German Turner Festival, Stuttgart, 6/12-17.

### Town Type of 1969

Designs: 30pf, Saarbrücken. No. 1107, Ship in Hamburg Harbor. No. 1108, Rüdesheim. No. 1109, Aachen. No. 1110, Ships, Bremen Harbor.

**1973 Lithographed and Engraved**

| | | | | | |
|---|---|---|---|---|---|
| **1106** | A303 | 30pf yel grn & blk | .60 | .25 |
| **1107** | A303 | 40pf red & blk | .90 | .25 |
| **1108** | A303 | 40pf org & blk | .75 | .25 |
| **1109** | A303 | 40pf brn red & blk | .60 | .25 |
| **1110** | A303 | 40pf red & blk | .60 | .25 |
| | | *Nos. 1106-1110 (5)* | 3.45 | 1.25 |

Issued: #1107-1108, 3/15; others 10/19.

### Europa Issue 1973

Common Design Type

**1973, Apr. 30 Photo. *Perf. 13½x14***

**Size: 38½x21mm**

**1114** CD16 30pf grn, lt grn & yel .35 .25

**1115** CD16 40pf dp mag, lil & yel .50 .25

Maximilian Kolbe — A345

**1973, May 25 Litho. *Perf. 14***

**1116** A345 40pf red, blk & brn .50 .30

Maximilian Kolbe (1894-1941), Polish priest who died in Auschwitz and was beatified in 1971.

"R" for Roswitha — A346

"Not by Bread Alone" — A347

**1973, May 25**

**1117** A346 40pf red, blk & yel .50 .30

Millenary of the death of Roswitha of Gandersheim, Germany's first poetess.

**1973, May 25 Photo.**

**1118** A347 30pf multicolored .35 .25

15th meeting of German Protestants (Evangelical Synod), Dusseldorf, June 27-July 1.

Environment Emblem and "Waste" — A348

30pf, "Water." 40pf, "Noise." 70pf, "Air."

**1973, June 5 Litho.**

| | | | | |
|---|---|---|---|---|
| **1119** | A348 25pf multicolored | | .35 | .25 |
| **1120** | A348 30pf multicolored | | .40 | .25 |
| **1121** | A348 40pf org & multi | | .75 | .25 |
| **1122** | A348 70pf ultra & multi | | 1.25 | .65 |
| | *Nos. 1119-1122 (4)* | | 2.75 | 1.40 |

International environment protection and Environment Day, June 5.

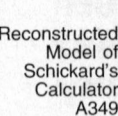

Reconstructed Model of Schickard's Calculator A349

**1973, June 12**

**1123** A349 40pf org & multi .45 .40

350th anniv. of the calculator built by Prof. Wilhelm Shickard, University of Tubingen.

Otto Wels (1873-1939), Leader of German Social Democratic Party — A350

**1973, Sept. 14 Litho. *Perf. 14***

**1124** A350 40pf magenta & lilac .50 .30

Lubeck Cathedral — A351

**1973, Sept. 14 Litho. & Engr.**

**1125** A351 40pf blk & multi .90 .30

800th anniversary of Lubeck Cathedral.

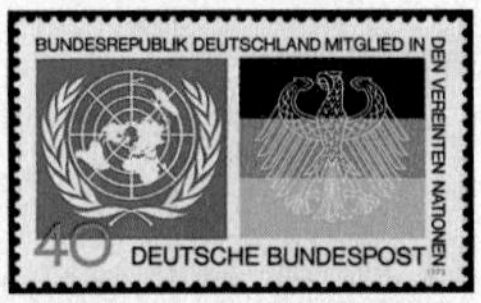


Emblems from UN and German Flags A352

**1973, Sept. 21 Litho.**

**1126** A352 40pf multicolored 1.25 .30

Germany's admission to the UN.

Radio and Speaker, 1923 — A353

**1973, Oct. 19 Photo. *Perf. 14***

**1127** A353 30pf brt grn & multi .35 .25

50 years of German broadcasting.

Luise Otto-Peters A354

**1974, Jan. 15 Litho. & Engr.**

| | | | |
|---|---|---|---|
| **1128** | A354 40pf shown | .60 | .45 |
| **1129** | A354 40pf Helene Lange | .60 | .45 |
| **1130** | A354 40pf Gertrud Bäumer | .60 | .45 |
| **1131** | A354 40pf Rosa Luxemburg | .60 | .45 |
| | *Nos. 1128-1131 (4)* | 2.40 | 1.80 |

Honoring German women writers and leaders in political and women's movements.

Drop of Blood and Police Car Light A355

**1974, Feb. 15 Photo. *Perf. 14***

**1132** A355 40pf carmine & ultra .80 .30

Blood donor service in conjunction with accident emergency service.

Handicapped People — A356

**1974, Feb. 15 Litho. *Perf. 14***

**1133** A356 40pf red & blk .80 .30

Rehabilitation of the handicapped.

Thomas Aquinas Teaching A357

**1974, Feb. 15**

**1134** A357 40pf blk & red .50 .30

St. Thomas Aquinas (1225-1274), scholastic philosopher.

Girls under Trees, by August Macke — A358

Paintings: No. 1135, Deer in Red, by Franz Marc. 40pf, Portrait in Blue, by Alexej von Jawlensky, vert. 50pf, Pechstein (man) Asleep, by Erich Heckel, vert. 70pf, "Big Still-life," by Max Beckmann. 120pf, Old Farmer, by Ernst Ludwig Kirchner, vert.

**1974 Photo.**

| | | | |
|---|---|---|---|
| **1135** | A358 30pf multicolored | .50 | .25 |
| **1136** | A358 30pf multicolored | .60 | .25 |
| **1137** | A358 40pf multicolored | .60 | .25 |
| **1138** | A358 50pf multicolored | .65 | .25 |
| **1139** | A358 70pf multicolored | .90 | .75 |
| **1140** | A358 120pf multicolored | 1.75 | 1.50 |
| | *Nos. 1135-1140 (6)* | 5.00 | 3.25 |

German expressionist painters.

Issued: #1135, 1137, Feb. 15; #1136, 1138, Aug. 16; #1139-1140, Oct. 29.

Young Man, by Lehmbruck A359

Immanuel Kant A360

Europa: 40pf, Kneeling Woman, by Wilhelm Lehmbruck.

**1974, Apr. 17 Litho. *Perf. 14***

**1141** A359 30pf multicolored .35 .25

**1142** A359 40pf multicolored .50 .25

**1974 Litho. and Engr. *Perf. 14***

**1143** A360 40pf Klopstock .50 .25

**Engr.**

**1144** A360 90pf shown 1.90 .45

Friedrich Gottlieb Klopstock (1724-1803), poet, and Immanuel Kant (1724-1804), philosopher.

Issue dates: 40pf, May 15; 90pf, Apr. 17.

Souvenir Sheet

Federal Eagle and Flag — A361

**1974, May 15 Litho. & Embossed**

**1145** A361 40pf gray & multi 1.25 1.90

Federal Republic of Germany, 25th anniv.

Soccer and Games Emblem A362

Design: 40pf, Three soccer players.

**1974, May 15 Litho.**

**1146** A362 30pf grn & multi .80 .25

**1147** A362 40pf org & multi 1.60 .25

World Cup Soccer Championship, Munich, June 13-July 7.

Crowned Cross Emblem of Diaconate A363

Landscape A364

**1974, May 15**

**1148** A363 40pf multicolored .45 .30

125th anniversary of the Diaconal Association of the German Protestant Church.

**1974, May 15**

**1149** A364 30pf multicolored .35 .30

To promote hiking and youth hostels.

Broken Bars of Prison Window — A365

**1974, July 16 Litho. *Perf. 14x13½***

**1150** A365 70pf violet bl & blk .95 .45

"Amnesty International," an organization for the protection of the rights of political, non-violent, prisoners.

Hans Holbein, Self-portrait A366

**Lithographed and Engraved**

**1974, July 16 *Perf. 13½x14***

**1151** A366 50pf multicolored .75 .30

Hans Holbein the Elder (c. 1470-1524), painter.

Man and Woman Looking at Moon, by Friedrich — A367

**1974, Aug. 16 Photo. *Perf. 14***

**1152** A367 50pf multicolored .95 .30

Caspar David Friedrich (1774-1840), German Romantic painter.

Swiss and German 19th Century Mail Boxes — A368

**1974, Oct. 29 Litho. *Perf. 14***

| | | | | |
|---|---|---|---|---|
| **1153** | A368 | 50pf red & multi | 1.25 | .35 |

Centenary of Universal Postal Union.

Mothers and Foundation Emblem — A369

**1975, Jan. 15 Litho. *Perf. 13***

| | | | | |
|---|---|---|---|---|
| **1154** | A369 | 50pf multicolored | .65 | .30 |

Convalescent Mothers' Foundation, 25th anniversary.

Annette Kolb (1875-1967), Writer — A370

German women writers: 40pf, Ricarda Huch (1864-1947), writer. 50pf, Else Lasker-Schüler (1869-1945), poetess. 70pf, Gertrud von Le Fort (1876-1971), writer.

**Lithographed and Engraved**

**1975, Jan. 15 *Perf. 14***

| | | | | |
|---|---|---|---|---|
| **1155** | A370 | 30pf brown & multi | .60 | .30 |
| **1156** | A370 | 40pf multicolored | .50 | .30 |
| **1157** | A370 | 50pf claret & multi | .50 | .30 |
| **1158** | A370 | 70pf blue & multi | .90 | .90 |
| | | *Nos. 1155-1158 (4)* | 2.50 | 1.80 |

Dr. Albert Schweitzer — A371

Design: 40pf, Hans Böckler.

**1975 Engr.**

| | | | | |
|---|---|---|---|---|
| **1159** | A371 | 40pf grn & blk | .65 | .30 |
| **1160** | A371 | 70pf bl & blk | 1.90 | .75 |

Böckler (1875-1951), German Workers' Union leader, and of Dr. Albert Schweitzer (1875-1965), medical missionary. Issued: 40pf, Feb. 14; 70pf, Jan. 15.

Head, by Michelangelo A372

Plan of St. Peter's, Rome A373

**1975, Feb. 14 Photo. *Perf. 14***

| | | | | |
|---|---|---|---|---|
| **1161** | A372 | 70pf vio bl & blk | 1.40 | 1.25 |

Michelangelo Buonarroti (1475-1564), Italian sculptor, painter and architect.

**1975, Feb. 14**

| | | | | |
|---|---|---|---|---|
| **1162** | A373 | 50pf red & multi | .65 | .30 |

Holy Year 1975, the "Year of Reconciliation."

Ice Hockey A374

**1975, Feb. 14 Litho. *Perf. 14***

| | | | | |
|---|---|---|---|---|
| **1163** | A374 | 50pf bl & multi | .95 | .30 |

Ice Hockey World Championship, Munich and Düsseldorf, Apr. 3-19.

Concentric Group, by Oskar Schlemmer — A375

Europa: 50pf, Bauhaus Staircase, painting by Oskar Schlemmer (1888-1943) and CEPT emblem.

**1975, Apr. 15 Litho. & Engr.**

| | | | | |
|---|---|---|---|---|
| **1164** | A375 | 40pf gray & multi | *.45* | .25 |
| **1165** | A375 | 50pf gray & multi | *.70* | .25 |

Eduard Mörike, Weather Vane, Quill and Signature A376

**1975, May 15**

| | | | | |
|---|---|---|---|---|
| **1166** | A376 | 40pf multicolored | .40 | .25 |

Eduard Mörike (1804-75), pastor and poet.

Joust, from Jousting Book of William IV A377

**1975, May 15 Photo. *Perf. 14***

| | | | | |
|---|---|---|---|---|
| **1167** | A377 | 50pf multicolored | .90 | .30 |

500th anniv. of the Wedding of Landshut, (last Duke of Landshut married the daughter of King of Poland, now a yearly local festival).

Cathedral of Mainz A378

**1975, May 15 Litho. & Engr.**

| | | | | |
|---|---|---|---|---|
| **1168** | A378 | 40pf multicolored | .90 | .30 |

Millennium of the Cathedral of Mainz.

View of Neuss, Woodcut A379

Satellite A380

**1975, May 15**

| | | | | |
|---|---|---|---|---|
| **1169** | A379 | 50pf multicolored | .60 | .30 |

500th anniv. of the unsuccessful siege of Neuss by Duke Charles the Bold of Burgundy.

**1975-82 Engr. *Perf. 14***

| | | | | |
|---|---|---|---|---|
| **1170** | A380 | 5pf Shown | .25 | .25 |
| **1171** | A380 | 10pf Electric train | .25 | .25 |
| **1172** | A380 | 20pf Old Weser lighthouse | .25 | .25 |
| **1173** | A380 | 30pf Rescue helicopter | .25 | .25 |
| **1174** | A380 | 40pf Space shuttle | .30 | .25 |
| **1175** | A380 | 50pf Radar station | .40 | .25 |
| **1176** | A380 | 60pf X-ray machine | .50 | .25 |
| **1177** | A380 | 70pf Shipbuilding | .60 | .25 |
| **1178** | A380 | 80pf Tractor | .65 | .25 |
| **1179** | A380 | 100pf Bituminous coal excavator | .75 | .25 |
| **1180** | A380 | 110pf Color TV camera | 1.50 | .60 |
| **1181** | A380 | 120pf Chemical plant | .95 | .30 |
| **1182** | A380 | 130pf Brewery | 1.90 | .60 |
| **1183** | A380 | 140pf Heating plant, Licterfelde | 1.10 | .40 |
| **1184** | A380 | 150pf Power shovel | 2.40 | .75 |
| **1185** | A380 | 160pf Blast furnace | 1.50 | .60 |
| **1186** | A380 | 180pf Payloader | 1.90 | .75 |
| **1187** | A380 | 190pf As #1184 | 2.25 | .60 |
| **1188** | A380 | 200pf Oil drilling | 1.60 | .30 |
| **1189** | A380 | 230pf Frankfurt Airport | 2.75 | .90 |
| **1190** | A380 | 250pf Airport | 3.25 | 1.40 |
| **1191** | A380 | 300pf Electro. RR | 3.75 | 1.40 |
| **1192** | A380 | 500pf Effelsberg radio telescope | 4.00 | 1.10 |
| | | *Nos. 1170-1192 (23)* | 33.05 | 12.20 |

Issued: 40, 50, 100pf, 5/15; 10, 30, 70pf, 8/14; 80, 120, 160pf, 10/15; 5, 140, 200pf, 11/14; 20, 500pf, 2/17/76; 60pf, 11/16/78; 230pf, 5/17/79; 150, 180pf, 7/12/79; 110, 130, 300pf, 6/16/82; 190, 250pf, 7/15/82.

Market and Town Hall, Alsfeld A381

#1197, Plönlein Corner, Siebers Tower and Kobolzeller Gate, Rothenburg. #1198, Town Hall (Steipe), Trier. #1199, View of Xanten.

**1975, July 15 Litho. & Engr.**

| | | | | |
|---|---|---|---|---|
| **1196** | A381 | 50pf multicolored | .75 | .50 |
| **1197** | A381 | 50pf multicolored | .75 | .50 |
| **1198** | A381 | 50pf multicolored | .75 | .50 |
| **1199** | A381 | 50pf multicolored | .75 | .50 |
| | | *Nos. 1196-1199 (4)* | 3.00 | 2.00 |

European Architectural Heritage Year.

Three Stages of Drug Addiction A382

**1975, Aug. 14 Photo. *Perf. 14***

| | | | | |
|---|---|---|---|---|
| **1200** | A382 | 40pf multicolored | .40 | .30 |

Fight against drug abuse.

Matthias Erzberger A383

**1975, Aug. 14 Engr.**

| | | | | |
|---|---|---|---|---|
| **1201** | A383 | 50pf red & black | .60 | .30 |

Erzberger (1875-1921), statesman, signer of Compiègne Armistice (1918) at end of World War I.

Sign of Royal Prussian Post, 1776 — A384

**1975, Aug. 14 Litho.**

| | | | | |
|---|---|---|---|---|
| **1202** | A384 | 10pf blue & multi | .35 | .25 |

Stamp Day, 1975, and 76th German Philatelists' Day, Sept. 21.

Souvenir Sheet

Gustav Stresemann, Ludwig Quidde, Carl von Ossietzky — A385

**1975, Nov. 14 Engr. *Perf. 14***

| | | | |
|---|---|---|---|
| **1203** A385 | Sheet of 3 | 1.90 | 1.90 |
| ***a.-c.*** | 50pf, single stamp | .60 | .50 |

German winners of Nobel Peace Prize. No. 1203 has litho. marginal inscription.

Olympic Rings, Symbolic Mountains A386

**1976, Jan. 5 Litho. & Engr.**

| | | | | |
|---|---|---|---|---|
| **1204** | A386 | 50pf red & multi | .90 | .30 |

12th Winter Olympic Games, Innsbruck, Austria, Feb. 4-15.

Konrad Adenauer — A387

**1976, Jan. 5 Engr.**

| | | | | |
|---|---|---|---|---|
| **1205** | A387 | 50pf dark slate green | 1.75 | .30 |

Konrad Adenauer (1876-1967), Chancellor (1949-63).

Books by Hans Sachs — A388

**1976, Jan. 5 Litho.**

| | | | | |
|---|---|---|---|---|
| **1206** | A388 | 40pf multicolored | .60 | .30 |

Hans Sachs (1494-1576), poet (meistersinger), 400th death anniversary.

Junkers F 13, 1926 — A389

**1976, Jan. 5**

**1207** A389 50pf multicolored .90 .30

Lufthansa, 50th anniversary.

German Eagle — A390

**1976, Feb. 17 Photo. *Perf. 14***

**1208** A390 50pf red, blk & gold .75 .30

Federal Constitutional Court, 25th anniv.

"EG" A391

**1976, Apr. 6 Photo. *Perf. 14***

**1209** A391 40pf red & multi .75 .30

European Coal and Steel Community, 25th anniversary.

Wuppertal Suspension Train — A392

**1976, Apr. 6 Litho.**

**1210** A392 50pf multicolored .75 .30

Wuppertal suspension railroad, 75th anniv.

Girl Selling Trinkets and Prints — A393

Europa: 50pf, Boy selling copperplate prints, and CEPT emblem. Ludwigsburg china figurines, c. 1765.

**1976, May 13 Photo.**

**1211** A393 40pf olive & multi *.40* .25
**1212** A393 50pf scarlet & multi *.60* .25

Dr. Carl Sonnenschein A394

**1976, May 13 Litho.**

**1213** A394 50pf carmine & multi .60 .30

Sonnenschein (1876-1929), Roman Catholic clergyman and social reformer.

Weber Conducting "Freischutz" in Covent Garden — A395

**1976, May 13**

**1214** A395 50pf red brown & blk .75 .30

Carl Maria von Weber (1786-1826), composer, 150th death anniversary.

Hymn, by Paul Gerhardt A396

**1976, May 13 Engr. & Litho.**

**1215** A396 40pf multicolored .40 .25

Gerhardt (1607-76), Lutheran hymn writer.

Carl Schurz, American Flag, Capitol A397

**1976, May 13 Litho.**

**1216** A397 70pf multicolored .95 .35

American Bicentennial.

Modern Stage A398

**1976, July 14 Litho. *Perf. 14***

**1217** A398 50pf multicolored 1.25 .30

Bayreuth Festival, centenary.

Bronze Ritual Chariot c. 1000 B.C. A399

Archaeological Treasures: 40pf, Celtic gold vessel, 5th-4th centuries B.C. 50pf, Celtic silver torque, 2nd-1st centuries B.C. 120pf, Roman cup with masks, 1st century A.D.

**1976, July 14**

**1218** A399 30pf multicolored .35 .30
**1219** A399 40pf multicolored .50 .30
**1220** A399 50pf multicolored .75 .45
**1221** A399 120pf multicolored 1.60 1.60
*Nos. 1218-1221 (4)* 3.20 2.65

Golden Plover A400

"Simplicissimus Teutsch" A401

**1976, Aug. 17**

**1222** A400 50pf multicolored 1.00 .30

Protection of birds.

**1976, Aug. 17**

**1223** A401 40pf multicolored 1.00 .30

Johann Jacob Christoph von Grimmelshausen, 300th birth anniversary; author of the "Adventures of Simplicissimus Teutsch."

Imperial Post Emblem, Höchst am Main, 18th Cent. — A402

Caroline Neuber as Medea — A403

**1976, Oct. 14 Litho. *Perf. 14***

**1224** A402 10pf brown & multi .30 .25

Stamp Day.

**1976, Nov. 16 Photo.**

German Actresses: 40pf, Sophie Schröder (1781-1868) as Sappho. 50pf, Louise Dumont (1862-1932) as Hedda Gabler. 70pf, Hermine Körner (1878-1960) as Lady Macbeth.

**1225** A403 30pf multicolored .40 .25
**1226** A403 40pf multicolored .40 .25
**1227** A403 50pf multicolored .60 .30
**1228** A403 70pf multicolored 1.00 .90
*Nos. 1225-1228 (4)* 2.40 1.70

Palais de l'Europe, Strasbourg — A404

**1977, Jan. 13 Engr. *Perf. 14***

**1229** A404 140pf green & blk 1.60 .50

Inauguration of the new Council of Europe Headquarters, Jan. 28.

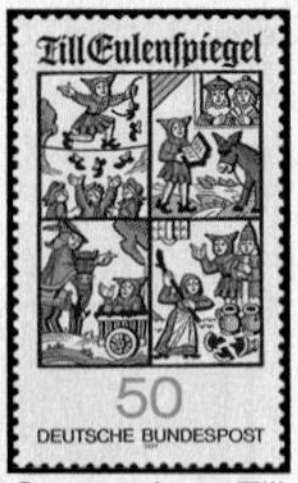


Scenes from Till Eulenspiegel A405

Pfaueninsel Castle A406

**1977, Jan. 13 Litho.**

**1230** A405 50pf multicolored .50 .30

Till Eulenspiegel (d. 1350), roguish fool and hero, his adventures reported in book of same name.

**1977-79 Typo. *Perf. 14***

**1231** A406 10pf Glucksburg .25 .25
*a.* Bklt. pane, 4 #1231, 2 each #1234, 1236 4.00 6.75
*b.* Bklt. pane, 4 #1231, 2 #1234, 2 #1310 2.50 3.00
*c.* Bklt. pane, 4 #1231, 2 #1310, 2 #1312 6.00 6.25
*d.* Bklt. pane, 2 each #1231, 1234, 1310-1311 9.00 13.50
**1232** A406 20pf Shown .25 .25
**1233** A406 25pf Gemen .35 .25
**1234** A406 30pf Ludwigstein .30 .25
**1235** A406 40pf Eltz .50 .25
**1236** A406 50pf Neuschwanstein .55 .25
**1237** A406 60pf Marksburg .75 .25
**1238** A406 70pf Mespelbrunn .75 .25
**1239** A406 90pf Vischerenburg 1.10 .35
**1240** A406 190pf Pfaueninsel 1.90 .75
**1240A** A406 200pf Burresheim 2.25 .75
**1241** A406 210pf Schwanenburg 3.00 1.10
**1242** A406 230pf Lichtenberg 3.00 1.10
*Nos. 1231-1242 (13)* 14.95 6.05

See Nos. 1308-1315.

Issued in sheets of 100 and in coils. Every fifth coil stamp has control number on the back.

Issued: 60, 200pf, 1/13; 40, 190pf, 2/16; 10, 30pf, 4/14; 50, 70pf, 5/17; 230pf, 11/16/78; 25, 90pf, 1/11/79; 20, 210pf, 2/14/79.

### Souvenir Sheet

German Art Nouveau — A407

Designs: 30pf, Floral ornament. 70pf, Athena, poster by Franz von Stuck. 90pf, Chair, c. 1902.

**1977, Feb. 16 Litho. *Perf. 14***

**1243** A407 Sheet of 3 2.00 1.50
*a.* 30pf multicolored .30 .25
*b.* 70pf multicolored .55 .50
*c.* 90pf multicolored .90 .70

1st German Art Nouveau Exhib., 75th anniv.

Jean Monnet A408

**1977, Feb. 16**

**1244** A408 50pf black & yellow .60 .30

Jean Monnet (1888-1979), French proponent of unification of Europe, became first Honorary Citizen of Europe in Apr. 1976.

Flower Show Emblem A409

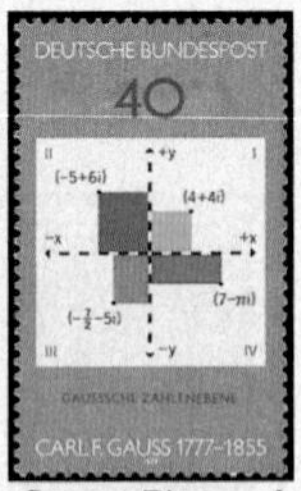


Gauss Plane of Complex Numbers A410

**1977, Apr. 14**

**1245** A409 50pf green & multi .80 .30

25th Federal Horticultural Show, Stuttgart, Apr. 29-Oct. 23.

**1977, Apr. 14**

**1246** A410 40pf silver & multi 1.25 .30

Carl Friedrich Gauss (1777-1855), mathematician, 200th birth anniversary.

Barbarossa Head, Cappenberg Reliquary — A411

**1977, Apr. 14**
**1247** A411 40pf multicolored 1.25 .30

Staufer Year 1977. "Time of the Hohenstaufen" Exhibition, Stuttgart, Mar. 25-June 5, in connection with the 25th anniversary of Baden-Wurttemberg.

Rhön Highway A412

Europa: 50pf, Rhine, Siebengebirge and train.

**1977, May 7** **Litho. & Engr.**
**1248** A412 40pf brt green & blk *.70 .25*
**1249** A412 50pf brt red & blk *.70 .25*

Rubens, Self-portrait A413

Ulm Cathedral A414

**1977, May 17** **Engr.**
**1250** A413 30pf brown black .80 .30

Peter Paul Rubens (1577-1640), Flemish painter, 400th birth anniversary.

**1977, May 17** **Litho. & Engr.**
**1251** A414 40pf blue & sepia .50 .30

600th anniversary of Ulm Cathedral.

Madonna, Oldest Rector's Seal A415

Landgrave Philipp, Great Seal of University A416

**1977, May 17** **Photo.**
**1252** A415 50pf indigo & org red .75 .30
**1253** A416 50pf indigo & org red .75 .30

Mainz University, 500th anniv. (No. 1252); Marburg University, 450th anniv. (No. 1253).

Morning, by Runge — A417

**1977, July 13** **Litho.** ***Perf. 14***
**1254** A417 60pf blue & multi .75 .35

Philipp Otto Runge (1777-1810), painter.

Bishop Ketteler's Coat of Arms — A418

**1977, July 13**
**1255** A418 50pf multicolored .60 .30

Wilhelm Emmanuel von Ketteler (1811-1877), Bishop of Mainz, Reichstag member and social reformer, death centenary.

Fritz von Bodelschwingh A419

**1977, July 13** **Litho. & Engr.**
**1256** A419 50pf multicolored .75 .30

Pastor Fritz von Bodelschwingh (1877-1946), manager of Bethel Institute (for the incurable sick), birth centenary.

Jesus as Teacher, Great Seal of University — A420

**1977, Aug. 16** **Photo.**
**1257** A420 50pf multicolored .90 .30

Tübingen University, 500th anniversary.

Golden Hat, Schifferstadt, Bronze Age — A421

Archaeological heritage: 120pf, Gilt helmet, from Prince's Tomb, Krefeld-Gellep. 200pf, Bronze Centaur's head, Schwarzenacker.

**1977, Aug. 16** **Litho.**

| | | | | |
|---|---|---|---|---|
| **1258** A421 | 30pf | multicolored | .40 | .30 |
| **1259** A421 | 120pf | multicolored | 1.50 | 1.10 |
| **1260** A421 | 200pf | multicolored | 2.00 | 1.60 |
| | *Nos. 1258-1260 (3)* | | 3.90 | 3.00 |

Telephone Operator and Switchboard, 1881 — A422

**1977, Oct. 13** **Litho.** ***Perf. 14***
**1261** A422 50pf multicolored 1.00 .30

German telephone centenary.

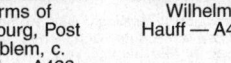

Arms of Hamburg, Post Emblem, c. 1861 — A423

Wilhelm Hauff — A424

**1977, Oct. 13**
**1262** A423 10pf multicolored .35 .25

Stamp Day.

**1977, Nov. 10** **Photo.** ***Perf. 14***
**1263** A424 40pf multicolored .40 .25

Wilhelm Hauff (1802-1827), writer and fabulist, 150th death anniversary.

Traveling Surgeon A425

Book Cover, by Alexander Schröder A426

**1977, Nov. 10** **Litho.**
**1264** A425 50pf multicolored .75 .30

Dr. Johann Andreas Eisenbarth (1663-1727), traveling surgeon and adventurer.

**1978, Jan. 12** **Litho.** ***Perf. 14***
**1265** A426 50pf multicolored .60 .30

Rudolf Alexander Schröder (1878-1962), writer, designer, Lutheran minister.

"Refugees" — A427

**1978, Jan. 12** **Photo.**
**1266** A427 50pf multicolored .60 .30

Friedland Aid Society for displaced Germans, 20th anniversary.

Souvenir Sheet

Gerhart Hauptmann, Hermann Hesse, Thomas Mann — A428

**1978, Feb. 16** **Litho.** ***Perf. 14***

| | | | |
|---|---|---|---|
| **1267** A428 | Sheet of 3 | 1.75 | 1.40 |
| *a.* | 30pf multicolored | .35 | .25 |
| *b.* | 50pf multicolored | .50 | .30 |
| *c.* | 70pf multicolored | .70 | .50 |

German winners of Nobel Literature Prize.

Martin Buber (1878-1965), Writer and Philosopher A429

**1978, Feb. 16**
**1268** A429 50pf multicolored .60 .30

Museum Tower and Observatory — A430

**1978, Apr. 13** **Litho.** ***Perf. 14***
**1269** A430 50pf multicolored .60 .30

German Museum for Natural Sciences and Technology, Munich, 75th anniversary.

Old City Halls A431

Europa: 40pf, Bamberg. 50pf, Regensburg. 70pf, Esslingen on Neckar.

**Lithographed and Engraved**

**1978, May 22** ***Perf. 14***

| | | | | |
|---|---|---|---|---|
| **1270** A431 | 40pf | multicolored | *.50* | .25 |
| **1271** A431 | 50pf | multicolored | *.85* | .25 |
| **1272** A431 | 70pf | multicolored | *.95* | *.45* |
| | *Nos. 1270-1272 (3)* | | 2.30 | .95 |

Pied Piper of Hamelin A432

**1978, May 22** **Litho.**
**1273** A432 50pf multicolored .75 .30

The Pied Piper led 130 children of Hamelin away never to be seen again.

Janusz Korczak — A433

Fossil Bat — A434

**1978, July 13** **Litho.** ***Perf. 14***
**1274** A433 90pf multicolored 1.00 .50

Dr. Janusz Korczak (1878-1942), physician, educator, proponent of children's rights.

**1978, July 13**

200pf, Eohippus (primitive horse), horiz.

**1275** A434 80pf multicolored 1.40 1.40
**1276** A434 200pf multicolored 1.50 1.50

Archaeological heritage from Messel open-cast mine, c. 50 million years old.

Parliament, Bonn — A435

**1978, Aug. 17** **Litho.** ***Perf. 14***
**1277** A435 70pf multicolored 1.10 .35

65th Interparliamentary Conf., Bonn, Sept. 3-14.

A436

Rose Window, Freiburg Cathedral.

**1978, Aug. 17**
**1278** A436 40pf multicolored .40 .30

85th Congress of German Catholics, Freiburg, Sept. 13-17.

A437

Brentano as Butterfly, by Luise Duttenhofer.

**1978, Aug. 17**
**1279** A437 30pf multicolored .40 .30

Clemens Brentano (1778-1842), poet.

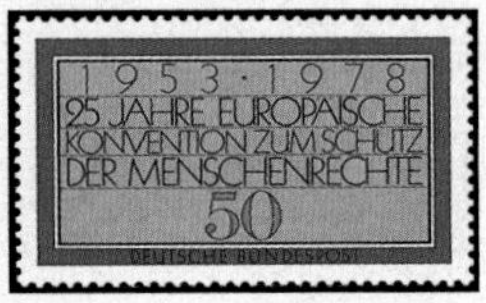


A438

**1978, Aug. 17**
**1280** A438 50pf multicolored .75 .30

European Human Rights Convention, 25th anniversary.

Baden Posthouse Sign, c. 1825 — A439

Saxony No. 1 with "World Philatelic Movement" Cancel — A440

**1978, Oct. 12** **Litho.** ***Perf. 14***
**1281** A439 40pf multicolored .40 .25
**1282** A440 50pf multicolored .40 .25
*a.* Pair, #1281-1282 1.10 1.25

Stamp Day and German Philatelists' Meeting, Frankfurt am Main, Oct. 12-15.

Easter at Walchensee, by Lovis Corinth — A441

Impressionist Paintings: 70pf, Horseman on Shore, by Max Liebermann, vert. 120pf, Lady with Cat, by Max Slevogt, vert.

**1978, Nov. 16** **Photo.** ***Perf. 14***
**1283** A441 50pf multicolored .55 .45
**1284** A441 70pf multicolored .85 .60
**1285** A441 120pf multicolored 1.50 1.40
*Nos. 1283-1285 (3)* 2.90 2.45

Child and Building A442

**1979, Jan. 11** **Photo.**
**1286** A442 60pf black & rose .90 .30

International Year of the Child and 20th anniv. of Declaration of Children's Rights.

Agnes Miegel — A443

Film — A444

**1979, Feb. 14** **Photo.** ***Perf. 14***
**1287** A443 60pf multicolored .60 .30

Agnes Miegel (1879-1964), poet.

**1979, Feb. 14** **Litho.**
**1288** A444 50pf black & green .75 .30

25th German Short-Film Festival, Oberhausen, Apr. 23-28.

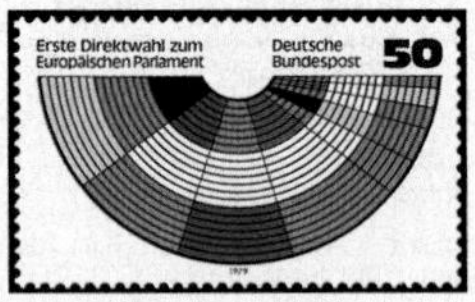


Parliament Benches in Flag Colors of Members — A445

**1979, Feb. 14**
**1289** A445 50pf multicolored .90 .30

European Parliament, first direct elections, June 7-10, 1979.

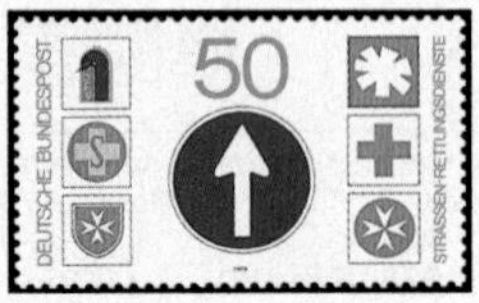


Emblems of Road Rescue Services A446

**1979, Feb. 14**
**1290** A446 50pf multicolored .75 .30

A447

Europa: 50pf, Telegraph office, 1863. 60pf, Post Office window, 1854.

**1979, May 17** **Litho.** ***Perf. 14***
**1291** A447 50pf multicolored *.60* .25
**1292** A447 60pf multicolored *.75* .25

A448

**1979, May 17** **Photo.**
**1293** A448 60pf red & black .85 .30

Anne Frank (1929-45), author, Nazi victim.

First Electric Train, 1879 Berlin Exhibition A449

**1979, May 17** **Litho.**
**1294** A449 60pf multicolored .90 .30

Intl. Transportation Exhib., Hamburg.

Hand Setting Radio Dial A450

**1979, July 12** **Litho.** ***Perf. 14***
**1295** A450 60pf multicolored .85 .30

World Administrative Radio Conference, Geneva, Sept. 24-Dec. 1.

Moses Receiving Tablets of the Law, by Lucas Cranach — A451

**1979, July 12** **Litho. & Engr.**
**1296** A451 50pf black & blue grn .90 .30

450th anniv. of Martin Luther's Catechism.

Cross and Charlemagne's Emblem — A452

**1979, July 12** **Litho. & Embossed**
**1297** A452 50pf multicolored .60 .30

1979 pilgrimage to Aachen.

Hildegard von Bingen with Manuscript A453

**1979, Aug. 9** **Litho.**
**1298** A453 110pf multicolored 1.10 .50

Hildegard von Bingen, Benedictine nun, mystic and writer, 800th death anniversary.

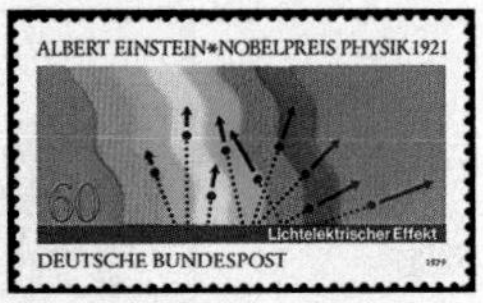


Diagram of Einstein's Photoelectric Effect — A454

Designs: No. 1300, Otto Hahn's diagram of the splitting of the uranium nucleus. No. 1301, Max von Laue's atom arrangement in crystals.

**1979, Aug. 9** **Photo.**
**1299** A454 60pf multicolored .75 .35
**1300** A454 60pf multicolored 1.50 .35
**1301** A454 60pf multicolored .75 .35
*Nos. 1299-1301 (3)* 3.00 1.05

Birth centenaries of German Nobel Prize winners: Albert Einstein, physics, 1921; Otto Hahn, chemistry, 1944; Max von Laue, physics, 1914.

Pilot on Board — A455

**Lithographed and Engraved**

**1979, Oct. 11** ***Perf. 14***
**1302** A455 60pf multicolored .60 .30

Three centuries of pilots' regulations.

Birds in Garden, by Paul Klee — A456

**1979, Nov. 14** **Photo.**
**1303** A456 90pf multicolored .90 .50

Paul Klee (1879-1940), Swiss artist.

Mephistopheles and Faust — A457

**1979, Nov. 14** **Litho.**
**1304** A457 60pf multicolored 1.10 .30

Doctor Johannes Faust.

Energy Conservation A458

**1979, Nov. 14** ***Perf. 13x13½***
**1305** A458 40pf multicolored .60 .30

**Castle Type A406 of 1977-79**

**1979-82** **Typo.** ***Perf. 14***
**1308** 35pf Lichtenstein .50 .30
**1309** 40pf Wolfsburg .45 .25
**1310** 50pf Inzlingen .60 .25
**1311** 60pf Rheydt .65 .30
**1312** 80pf Wilhelmsthal .95 .25
**1313** 120pf Charlottenburg 1.50 .50
**1314** 280pf Ahrensburg 3.25 .50
**1315** 300pf Herrenhausen 3.75 .35
*Nos. 1308-1315 (8)* 11.65 2.70

Issued: 60pf, 11/14; 40pf, 50pf, 2/14/80; 35pf, 80pf, 300pf, 6/16/82; 120pf, 280pf, 7/15/82.

Iphigenia, by Anselm Feuerbach — A459

**1980, Jan. 10** **Litho.**
**1321** A459 50pf multicolored 1.00 .30

Anselm Feuerbach (1829-1880), historical and portrait painter.

Flags of NATO and Members A460

**1980, Jan. 10**
**1322** A460 100pf multicolored 1.60 .75

Germany's membership in NATO, 25th anniv.

Osnabruck, 1,200th Anniversary — A461

**1980, Jan. 10** **Litho. & Engr.**
**1323** A461 60pf multicolored .75 .30

Götz von Berlichingen, Painting on Glass — A462

**1980, Jan. 10** **Litho.**
**1324** A462 60pf multicolored .75 .30

Götz von Berlichingen (1480-1562), knight.

Duden Dictionary, Old and New Editions — A463

**1980, Jan. 14**
**1325** A463 60pf multicolored .75 .30

Konrad Duden's German Language Dictionary, centenary of publication.

German Association for Public and Private Social Welfare Centenary — A464

**1980, Apr. 10**
**1326** A464 60pf multicolored .75 .30

A465

Emperor Frederick I (Barbarossa) and Sons, Welf Chronicles, 12th century.

**1980, Apr. 10**
**1327** A465 60pf multicolored 1.00 .30

Imperial Diet of Geinhausen, 800th anniv.

A466

Europa: 50pf, Albertus Magnus (1193-1280), saint and doctor of the Church. 60pf, Gottfried Wilhelm Leibniz (1646-1716), philosopher.

**1980, May 8** **Litho.** ***Perf. 14***
**1328** A466 50pf multicolored *.75 .25*
**1329** A466 60pf multicolored *.75 .25*

Confession of Augsburg, Engraving, 1630 — A467

**1980, May 8**
**1330** A467 50pf multicolored .60 .30

Reading of Confession of Augsburg to Charles V (first official creed of Lutheran Church), 450th anniversary.

Nature Preserves A468

**1980, May 8** **Photo.**
**1331** A468 40pf multicolored 1.00 .30

Oscillogram Pulses and Ear — A469

**Lithographed and Embossed**

**1980, July 10** ***Perf. 14***
**1332** A469 90pf multicolored 1.10 .35

16th Intl. Cong. for the Training and Education of the Hard of Hearing, Hamburg, 8/4-8.

Book of Daily Bible Readings, Title Page, 1731 A470

**1980, July 10** **Litho.**
**1333** A470 50pf multicolored .60 .30

Moravian Brethren's Book of Daily Bible Readings, 250th edition.

St. Benedict of Nursia, 1500th Birth Anniv. — A471

**1980, July 10** ***Perf. 13x13½***
**1334** A471 50pf multicolored .60 .30

Helping Hand — A472

**1980, Aug. 14** **Litho. & Engr.**
**1335** A472 60pf multicolored .75 .30

Dr. Friedrich Joseph Haass (1780-1853), physician and philanthropist.

Marie von Ebner-Eschenbach (1830-1916), Writer — A473

**1980, Aug. 14** **Photo.**
**1336** A473 60pf multicolored .75 .30

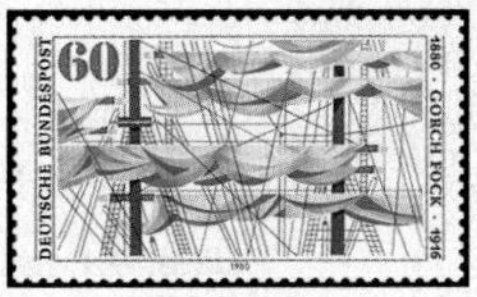


Ship's Rigging A474

**1980, Aug. 14** **Litho.**
**1337** A474 60pf multicolored 1.50 .30

Gorch Fock (pen name of Johan Kinau) (1880-1916), poet and dramatist.

Hoeing, Pressing Grapes, Wine Cellar, 14th Century Woodcuts A475

**1980, Oct. 9** **Litho.** ***Perf. 14***
**1338** A475 50pf multicolored .75 .30

Wine production in Central Europe, 2000th anniversary.

Setting Final Stone in South Tower, Cologne Cathedral — A476

**1980, Oct. 9**
**1339** A476 60pf multicolored 1.50 .30

Completion of Cologne Cathedral, cent.

Landscape with Fir Trees, by Altdorfer — A477

**Lithographed and Engraved**

**1980, Nov. 13** ***Perf. 14***
**1340** A477 40pf multicolored .60 .30

Albrecht Altdorfer (1480-1538), painter and engraver.

Elly Heuss-Knapp A478

**1981, Jan. 15** **Photo.**
**1341** A478 60pf multicolored .75 .30

Elly Heuss-Knapp (1881-1951), founded Elly Heuss-Knapp Foundation (Rest and Recuperation for Mothers).

International Year of the Disabled — A479

**1981, Jan. 15** **Litho.**
**1342** A479 60pf multicolored .75 .30

European Urban Renaissance — A480

**1981, Jan. 15** **Litho. & Engr.**
**1343** A480 60pf multicolored .85 .30

Georg Philipp Telemann, Title Page of "Singet dem Herrn" Cantata — A481

**1981, Feb. 12** **Photo.**
**1344** A481 60pf multicolored .75 .30

Georg Telemann (1681-1767), composer.

Foreign Guest Worker Integration — A482

**1981, Feb. 12** **Litho.**
**1345** A482 50pf multicolored .85 .30

Preservation of the Environment A483

**1981, Feb. 12**
**1346** A483 60pf multicolored 1.25 .30

European Patent Office Centenary
A484

**1981, Feb. 12**
**1347** A484 60pf multicolored .75 .30

A485

**1981, Feb. 12** ***Perf. 13x13½***
**1348** A485 40pf Chest scintigram .60 .30

Early examination for the prevention of cancer.

A486

50pf, South German couple dancing in regional costumes. 60pf, Northern couple.

**1981, May 7** **Litho.** ***Perf. 14***
**1349** A486 50pf multicolored *.60* .25
**1350** A486 60pf multicolored *.70* .25

Europa.

19th German Protestant Convention, Hamburg, June 17-21 — A487

**1981, May 7** **Photo.**
**1351** A487 50pf multicolored .75 .30

A488

**1981, May 7** **Litho.**
**1352** A488 60pf Altar figures .75 .30

Tilman Riemenschneider (1460-1531), sculptor, 450th death anniversary.

A489

**1981, July 16** **Litho.** ***Perf. 14***
**1353** A489 110pf multicolored 1.60 .50

Georg von Neumayer polar research station.

Energy Conservation Research — A490

**1981, July 16**
**1354** A490 50pf Solar generator .95 .30

Wildlife Protection
A491

**1981, July 16**
**1355** A491 60pf Baby coot 1.25 .30

Cooperation in Third World Development — A492

**1981, July 16**
**1356** A492 90pf multicolored 1.25 .45

Wilhelm Raabe (1831-1910), Poet — A493

**1981, Aug. 13** **Litho. & Engr.**
**1357** A493 50pf dk green & green .75 .30

Statement of Constitutional Freedom (Fundamental Concept of Democracy) — A494

**1981, Aug. 13** **Litho.** ***Perf. 14***
**1358** A494 40pf shown .85 .25
**1359** A494 50pf Separation of powers .85 .25
**1360** A494 60pf Sovereignty of the people 1.25 .25
*Nos. 1358-1360 (3)* 2.95 .75

A495

People by Mailcoach, lithograph, 1855.

**1981, Oct. 8** **Litho.**
**1361** A495 60pf multicolored 1.25 .30

Stamp Day, Oct. 25.

A496

**1981, Nov. 12** **Litho.** ***Perf. 14***
**1362** A496 100pf multicolored 1.40 .45

Antarctic Treaty, 20th anniv.

St. Elizabeth of Thuringia, 750th Anniv. of Death — A497

**1981, Nov. 12**
**1363** A497 50pf multicolored 1.00 .30

Karl von Clausewitz, by W. Wach — A498

**1981, Nov. 12** **Photo.**
**1364** A498 60pf multicolored 1.00 .30

Prussian general and writer, (1780-1831).

Social Insurance Centenary — A499

**1981, Nov. 12**
**1365** A499 60pf multicolored .85 .30

Pear-shaped Pot with Lid, 1715 — A500

**1982, Jan. 13** **Litho.**
**1366** A500 60pf multicolored .85 .30

Johann Friedrich Bottger (1682-1719), originator of Dresden china, 300th birth anniv.

Energy Conservation — A501

**1982, Jan. 13**
**1367** A501 60pf multicolored .85 .30

A502

Illustration from The Town Band of Bremen (folktale).

**1982, Jan. 13**
**1368** A502 40pf red & black .60 .30

A503

**1982, Feb. 18** **Photo.**
**1369** A503 60pf multicolored 2.25 .30

Johann Wolfgang von Goethe (1749-1832), by Georg Melchior Kraus, 1776.

Robert Koch (1843-1910), Discoverer of Tubercle Bacillus, (1882) — A504

**1982, Feb. 18**
**1370** A504 50pf multicolored 2.50 .30

Die Fromme Helene, by Wilhelm Busch (1832-1908)
A505

**1982, Apr. 15** **Litho.** ***Perf. 13½x14***
**1371** A505 50pf multicolored 1.00 .30

Europa 1982
A506

**1982, May 5** **Litho.** ***Perf. 14***
**1372** A506 50pf Hambach Meeting sesquicentennial *.90* *.25*
**1373** A506 60pf Treaties of Rome, 1957-1982 *1.10* *.25*

Kiel Regatta Week Centenary — A507

**1982, May 5**
**1374** A507 60pf multicolored 1.00 .30

Young Men's Christian Assoc. (YMCA) Centenary — A508

**1982, May 5**
**1375** A508 50pf multicolored .75 .30

"Don't Drink and Drive" A509

**1982, July 15** **Photo.**
**1376** A509 80pf red & black 1.00 .30

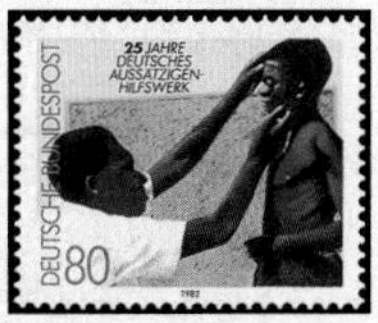


25th Anniv. of German Lepers' Org. — A510

**1982, July 15** **Photo.**
**1377** A510 80pf multicolored 1.00 .30

Prevent Water Pollution A511

**1982, July 15**
**1378** A511 120pf multicolored 2.50 .35

Urea Model and Synthesis Formula A512

**1982, Aug. 12** **Photo.**
**1379** A512 50pf multicolored .90 .30

Friedrich Wohler (1800-1882), chemist, discoverer of organic chemistry.

St. Francis Preaching to the Birds, by Giotto — A513

**1982, Aug. 12** **Litho.**
**1380** A513 60pf multicolored .90 .30

800th birth anniv. of St. Francis of Assisi and 87th German Catholics Cong., Dusseldorf, 9/1-5.

James Franck, Max Born — A514

**1982, Aug. 12** **Litho. & Engr.**
**1381** A514 80pf multicolored 1.25 .30

James Franck (1882-1964) and Max Born (1882-1970), Nobel Prize physicists, developed quantum theory.

Stamp Day, Oct. 24 A515

**1982, Oct. 14** **Photo.** ***Perf. 14***
**1382** A515 80pf Poster 1.40 .30

400th Anniv. of the Gregorian Calendar — A516

Design: Calendar illumination, by Johannes Rasch, 1586.

**1982, Oct. 14** **Litho.**
**1383** A516 60pf multicolored .90 .30

A517

Presidents: a, Theodor Heuss, 1949-59. b, Heinrich Lubke, 1959-69. c, Gustav Heinemann, 1969-74. d, Walter Scheel, 1974-79. e, Karl Carstens, 1979-84.

**1982, Nov. 10**
**1384** Sheet of 5 5.00 4.50
***a.-e.*** A517 80pf, single stamp .75 .75

A518

**1983, Jan. 13** **Litho.** ***Perf. 14***
**1385** A518 80pf gray & black 1.50 .45

Edith Stein (d. 1942), philospher and Carmelite Nun.

Persecution and Resistance, 1933-1945 — A519

**1983, Jan. 13**
**1386** A519 80pf multicolored 1.50 .45

Light Space Modulator, 1930 — A520

Walter Gropius (1883-1969), Founder of Bauhaus Architecture: 60pf, Sanctuary, zinc lithograph, 1942. 80pf, Bauhaus Archives, Berlin, 1979.

**1983, Feb. 8**
**1387** A520 50pf multicolored .75 .30
**1388** A520 60pf multicolored 1.10 .30
**1389** A520 80pf multicolored 1.25 .30
*Nos. 1387-1389 (3)* 3.10 .90

Federahannes, Swabian-Alemannic Carnival — A521

**1983, Feb. 8**
**1390** A521 60pf multicolored 1.00 .30

4th Intl. Horticultural Show, Munich, Apr. 28-Oct. 9 — A522

**1983, Apr. 12** **Litho.** ***Perf. 14***
**1391** A522 60pf multicolored 1.00 .30

Europa 1983 A523

Discoveries: 60pf, Printing press by Johannes Guttenburg. 80pf, Electromagnetic waves by Heinrich Hertz.

**1983, May 5** **Litho.** ***Perf. 14***
**1392** A523 60pf Movable type *1.90* *.35*
**1393** A523 80pf Resonant circuit, electric flux lines *1.10* *.35*

Johannes Brahms (1833-1897), Composer A524

**1983, May 5** **Photo.**
**1394** A524 80pf multicolored 1.50 .45

Franz Kafka (1883-1924), Writer — A525

**1983, May 5**
**1395** A525 80pf Signature, Tyn Church, Prague 1.50 .45

Beer Pureness Law, 450th Anniv. A526

**1983, May 5** **Litho.**
**1396** A526 80pf Brewers, engraving, 1677 1.50 .45

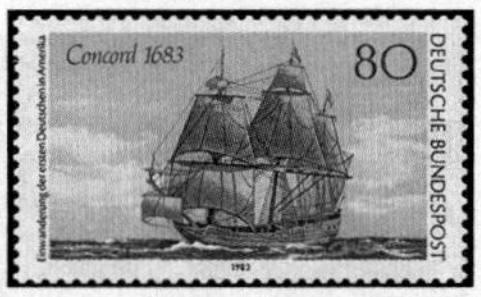


300th Anniv. of Immigration to US — A527

**1983, May 5** **Litho. & Engr.**
**1397** A527 80pf Concord 1.60 .45

See US No. 2040.

Children and Road Safety A528

**1983, July 14** **Litho.** ***Perf. 14***
**1398** A528 80pf multicolored 1.50 .45

50th Intl. Auto Show, Frankfurt, Sept. 15-25 A529

**1983, July 14**
**1399** A529 60pf multicolored .75 .30

Otto Warburg — A530

**1983, Aug. 11** **Photo.** ***Perf. 14***
**1400** A530 50pf multicolored .90 .45

Warburg (1883-1970), pioneer of modern biochemistry, 1931 Nobel prize winner in medicine.

Christoph Martin Wieland (1733-1813), Poet — A531

**1983, Aug. 11** **Litho.**
**1401** A531 80pf multicolored 1.25 .45

10th Anniv. of UN Membership — A532

**1983, Aug. 11** **Photo.**
**1402** A532 80pf multicolored 1.60 .45

Rauhe Haus Orphanage Sesquicentennial — A533

**1983, Aug. 11** **Litho.**
**1403** A533 80pf multicolored 1.25 .45

Survey and Measuring Maps — A534

**1983, Aug. 11**
**1404** A534 120pf multicolored 1.60 .50

Intl. Union of Geodesy and Geophysics Gen. Assembly, Hamburg, Aug. 15-26.

Stamp Day — A535

**1983, Oct. 13** **Litho.** ***Perf. 13½***
**1405** A535 80pf Postrider 1.40 .45

Martin Luther (1483-1546) A536

**1983, Oct. 13** ***Perf. 14***

**1406** A536 80pf Engraving by G. Konig 2.25 .45

Customs Union Sesquicentennial — A537

**1983, Nov. 10**

**1407** A537 60pf multicolored 1.60 .30

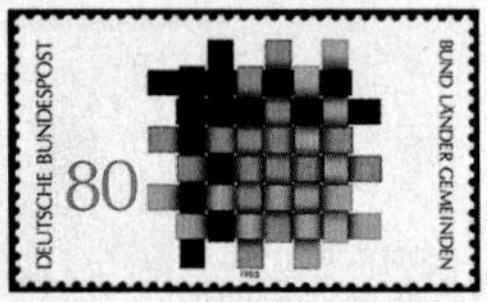


Territorial Authorities (Federation, Land, Communities) — A538

**1983, Nov. 10** **Litho.**

**1408** A538 80pf multicolored 1.60 .45

Trier, 2000th Anniv. A539

**1984, Jan. 12** **Litho. & Engr.**

**1409** A539 80pf Black Gate, 175 A.D. 1.60 .45

Philipp Reis (1834-1874) Physicist and Inventor — A540

**1984, Jan. 12** **Litho.**

**1410** A540 80pf multicolored 1.60 .45

Gregor Mendel (1822-1884), Basic Laws of Heredity — A541

**1984, Jan. 12** **Litho.**

**1411** A541 50pf multicolored 1.00 .30

500th Anniv. of Michelstadt Town Hall — A542

**1984, Feb. 16** **Litho.**

**1412** A542 60pf multicolored 1.00 .30

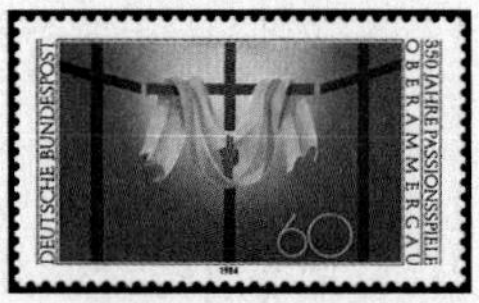


350th Anniv. of Oberammergau Passion Play — A543

**1984, Feb. 16** **Photo.**

**1413** A543 60pf multicolored 1.00 .30

Second Election of Parliament, June 17 — A544

**1984, Apr. 12** **Litho.** ***Perf. 13½***

**1414** A544 80pf multicolored 1.75 .50

Europa (1959-1984) A545

**1984, May 8** **Photo.** ***Perf. 14***

**1415** A545 60pf multicolored *1.25* *.35*

**1416** A545 80pf multicolored *1.25* *.35*

A546

**1984, May 8** **Engr.**

**1417** A546 60pf multicolored .75 .30

Nursery Rhyme Illustration, by Ludwig Richter (1803-84).

A547

**1984, May 8**

**1418** A547 80pf Statue, 1693 1.25 .45

St. Norbert von Xanten (1080-1134).

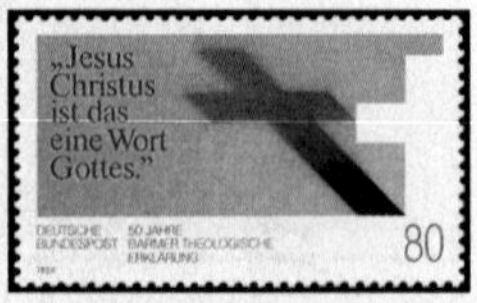


Barmer Theological Declaration, 50th Anniv. — A548

**1984, May 8** **Litho.**

**1419** A548 80pf Cross, text 1.25 .45

Souvenir Sheet

1984 UPU Congress — A549

**1984, June 19** **Litho.** ***Perf. 14***

**1420** Sheet of 3 3.50 2.75

*a.* A549 60pf Letter sorting, 19th cent. .60 .50

*b.* A549 80pf Scanner .90 .75

*c.* A549 120pf H. von Stephan, founder 1.50 1.40

City of Neuss Bimillenium A550

**1984, June 19** **Litho. & Engr.**

**1421** A550 80pf Tomb of Oclatius 1.25 .45

Friedrich Wilhelm Bessel (1784-1846), Astronomer A551

**1984, June 19**

**1422** A551 80pf Bessel function diagram 1.25 .45

88th German Catholic Convention, Munich, July 4-8 — A552

**1984, June 19** **Photo.**

**1423** A552 60pf Pope Pius XII 1.00 .30

Town Hall, Duderstadt — A553

**1984, Aug. 21** **Litho.** ***Perf. 14***

**1424** A553 60pf multicolored .90 .30

Medieval Document, Computer — A554

**1984, Aug. 21**

**1425** A554 70pf multicolored 1.25 .45

10th Intl. Archives Congress, Bonn.

German Electron Synchrotron (DESY) Research Center, Hamburg — A555

**1984, Aug. 21** **Photo.**

**1426** A555 80pf multicolored 1.60 .45

Schleswig-Holstein Canal Bicentenary — A556

**1984, Aug. 21** **Litho.**

**1427** A556 80pf Knoop lock 1.50 .45

Stamp Day A557

**1984, Oct. 18** **Litho.** ***Perf. 14***

**1428** A557 80pf Imperial Taxis Posthouse, Augsburg 1.60 .45

Anti-smoking Campaign — A558

**1984, Nov. 8** **Litho.**

**1429** A558 60pf Match, text 1.00 .30

Equal Rights for Men and Women — A559

**1984, Nov. 8**

**1430** A559 80pf Male & female symbols 1.50 .45

Peace and Understanding — A560

**1984, Nov. 8**

**1431** A560 80pf Text 1.25 .45

Augsburg, 2000th Anniv. — A561

**1985, Jan. 10** **Litho.**

**1432** A561 80pf Roman Emperor Augustus, Augsburg buildings 1.50 .35

Philipp Jakob Spener, Religious Leader (1635-1705) A562

**1985, Jan. 10** **Litho.**
**1433** A562 80pf multicolored 1.25 .45

Deutches Wortebuch — A563

**1985, Jan. 10** **Litho.**
**1434** A563 80pf Bros. Grimm, text 1.60 .45

Romano Guardini, Theologist (1885-1968) A564

**1985, Jan. 10** **Litho.**
**1435** A564 80pf multicolored 1.25 .45

Market and Coinage Rights in Verden, 1000th Anniv. A565

**1985, Feb. 21** **Litho.**
**1436** A565 60pf multicolored 1.60 .30

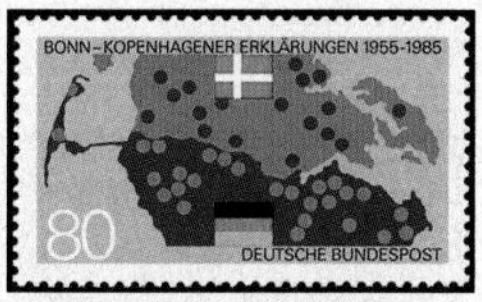


German-Danish Border Areas and Flags — A566

**1985, Feb. 21** **Litho.**
**1437** A566 80pf multicolored 1.75 .60

Bonn-Copenhagen declarations on mutual minorities, 30th anniv.

Johann Peter Hebel (1760-1826), Poet — A567

**1985, Apr. 16** **Litho.**
**1438** A567 80pf multicolored 1.25 .45

Egon Erwin Kisch (1885-1948), Journalist A568

**1985, Apr. 16** **Litho.**
**1439** A568 60pf Kisch using telephone 1.00 .30

Europa 1985 — A569

European Music Year: 60pf, Georg Friedrich Handel. 80pf, Johann Sebastian Bach.

**1985, May 7** **Photo.**
**1440** A569 60pf Portrait of Handel *1.50 .35*
**1441** A569 80pf Portrait of Bach *1.50 .35*

Dominikus Zimmermann (1685-1766), Architect — A570

**1985, May 7** **Photo.**
**1442** A570 70pf Stucco column 1.10 .45

St. George's Cathedral, 750th Anniv. — A571

**1985, May 7** **Litho.** ***Perf. 14***
**1443** A571 60pf Cathedral, Limburg .90 .45

Father Josef Kentenich (1885-1968) — A572

**1985, May 7** **Litho.**
**1444** A572 80pf Portrait 1.25 .45

Forest Conservation A573

**1985, July 16** **Litho.** ***Perf. 14***
**1445** A573 80pf Clock, forest 1.75 .45

Intl. Youth Year A574

**1985, July 16** ***Perf. 14***
**1446** A574 60pf Scouts, scouting and IYY emblems 1.00 .45

30th World Scouting Conf., Munich, 7/15-19.

Frankfurt Stock Exchange, 400th Anniv. — A575

Design: Bourse, est. 1879, and Frankfurt Eagle, the exchange emblem.

**1985, Aug. 13** ***Perf. 14x14½***
**1447** A575 80pf multicolored 1.50 .45

The Sunday Walk, by Carl Spitzweg (1808-85) A576

**1985, Aug. 13**
**1448** A576 60pf multicolored 1.60 .45

Fritz Reuter (1810-1874), Dialect Author — A577

**1985, Oct. 15** **Litho.** ***Perf. 14***
**1449** A577 80pf Portrait, manuscript 1.75 .45

Departure of the 1st Train from Nuremberg to Furth, 1835 — A578

**1985, Nov. 12** **Litho.** ***Perf. 14x14½***
**1450** A578 80pf Adler locomotive 1.75 .45

Founder Johannes Scharrer (1785-1844), German Railways 150th anniv.

Reintegration of German World War II Refugees, 40th Anniv. — A579

**1985, Nov. 12** ***Perf. 14***
**1451** A579 80pf multicolored 1.75 .45

Natl. Armed Forces, 30th Anniv. A580

**1985, Nov. 12** ***Perf. 14x14½***
**1452** A580 80pf Iron Cross, natl. colors 2.50 .45

Benz Tricycle, Saloon Car, 1912, and Modern Automobile — A581

**1986, Jan. 16** **Litho.** ***Perf. 14***
**1453** A581 80pf multicolored 1.75 .45

Automobile cent.

Bad Hersfeld, 1250th Anniv. A582

**1986, Feb. 13** **Litho.** ***Perf. 14***
**1454** A582 60pf multicolored 1.25 .45

Bach Contata, Detail, by Oskar Kokoschka (1886-1980) A583

**1986, Feb. 13**
**1455** A583 80pf Self portrait 1.25 .45

Halley's Comet A584

**1986, Feb. 13**
**1456** A584 80pf multicolored 1.75 .50

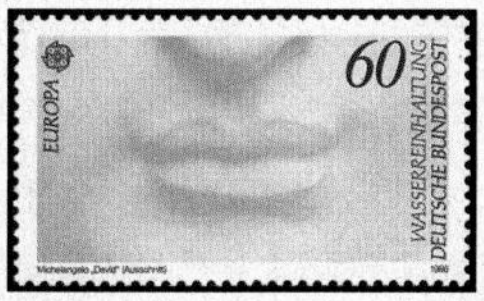


Europa 1986 A585

Details from Michelangelo's David: 60pf, Mouth (pure water). 80pf, Nose, (pure air).

**1986, May 5** **Photo.** ***Perf. 14***
**1457** A585 60pf multicolored *1.25 .35*
**1458** A585 80pf multicolored *1.25 .35*

St. Johannis Monastery, Walsrode — A586

**1986, May 5** **Litho. & Engr.**
**1459** A586 60pf multicolored 1.25 .45

Monastery millennium and town of Walsrode, 603rd anniv.

King Ludwig II of Bavaria (1845-1886), Neuschwanstein Castle — A587

**1986, May 5** **Litho.**
**1460** A587 60pf multicolored 2.10 .45

Karl Barth (1886-1968), Protestant Theologian A588

**1986, May 5** **Engr.**
**1461** A588 80pf blk, dk red & red lil 1.40 .45

Religion, Science, Friendship and Fatherland — A589

**1986, May 5** **Litho.**
**1462** A589 80pf multicolored 1.40 .45

Union of German Catholic Students, 100th assembly, Frankfurt, June 12-15.

Carl Maria von Weber (1786-1826), Mass in E-flat Major — A590

**1986, June 20** **Litho.** ***Perf. 14***
**1463** A590 80pf multicolored 1.75 .45

Franz Liszt and Signature A591

**1986, June 20**
**1464** A591 80pf dk blue & dk org 1.75 .45

Intl. Peace Year A592

**1986, June 20**
**1465** A592 80pf multicolored 1.60 .45

Souvenir Sheet

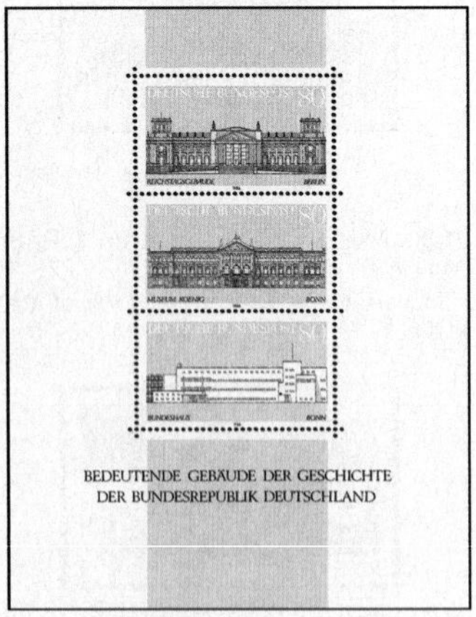


Reichstag, Berlin — A593

Historic buildings: b, Koening Museum, Bonn. c, Parliament, Bonn.

**1986, June 20**
**1466** Sheet of 3 3.75 3.25
***a.-c.*** A593 80pf, any single 1.00 1.00

European Satellite Technology — A594

Design: TV-SAT/TDF-1 over Europe.

**1986, June 20**
**1467** A594 80pf multicolored 1.90 .50

Augsburg Cathedral Stained Glass Window A595

**1986, Aug. 14** ***Perf. 14***
**1468** A595 80pf multicolored 1.90 .45

Monuments protection.

King Frederick the Great (1712-1786) A596

**1986, Aug. 14**
**1469** A596 80pf multicolored 2.50 .45

German Skat Congress, Cent. — A597

**1986, Aug. 14**
**1470** A597 80pf Tournament card 1.75 .45

Organization for Economic Cooperation and Development, 25th Anniv. — A598

**1986, Aug. 14**
**1471** A598 80pf multicolored 1.40 .45

Heidelberg University, 600th Anniv. — A599

**1986, Oct. 16** **Litho.**
**1472** A599 80pf multicolored 1.60 .45

Stagecoach, Stamps from 1975-1984 — A600

**1986, Oct. 16**
**1473** A600 80pf multicolored 1.60 .45

Stamp Day, 50th Anniv.

A601

**1986, Nov. 13** **Litho.** ***Perf. 14***
**1474** A601 70pf multicolored 1.00 .45

Mary Wigman (1886-1973), dancer.

A602

Famous Women: 5pf, Emma Ihrer (1857-1911), politician, labor leader. 10pf, Paula Modersohn-Becker (1876-1907), painter. 20pf, Cilly Aussem (1909-63), tennis champion. 30pf, Kathe Kollwitz (1867-1945), painter, graphic artist. 40pf, Maria Sibylla Merian (1647-1717), naturalist, painter. 50pf, Christine Teusch (1888-1968), minister of education and cultural affairs. 60pf, Dorothea Erxleben (1715-62), physician. 70pf, Elisabet Boehm (1859-1943), social organizer. 80pf, Clara Schumann (1819-96), pianist, composer. 100pf, Therese Giehse (1898-1975), actress. 120pf, Elisabeth Selbert (1896-1986), politician. 130pf, Lise Meitner (1878-1968), physicist. 140pf, Cecile Vogt (1875-1962), neurologist. 150pf, Sophie Scholl (1921-43), member of anti-Nazi resistance. 170pf, Hannah Arendt (1906-75), American political scientist. 180pf, Lotte Lehmann (1888-1976), soprano. 200pf, Bertha von Suttner (1843-1914), 1905 Nobel Peace Prize winner. 240pf, Mathilde Franziska Anneke, (1817-84), American author. 250pf, Queen Louise of Prussia (1776-1810). 300pf, Fanny Hensel (1805-47), composer-conductor. 350pf, Hedwig Dransfeld (1871-1925), women's rights activist. 500pf, Alice Salomon (1872-1948), feminist and social activist.

**1986-91** **Engr.** ***Perf. 14***

| | | | | | |
|---|---|---|---|---|---|
| **1475** | A602 | 5pf | multi | .25 | .25 |
| **1476** | A602 | 10pf | multi | .25 | .25 |
| **1477** | A602 | 20pf | multi | .75 | .35 |
| **1478** | A602 | 30pf | multi | .35 | .30 |
| **1479** | A602 | 40pf | multi | .75 | .25 |
| **1480** | A602 | 50pf | multi | .75 | .25 |
| **1481** | A602 | 60pf | multi | .90 | .25 |
| **1482** | A602 | 70pf | multi | 1.10 | .60 |
| **1483** | A602 | 80pf | multi | .90 | .25 |
| **1484** | A602 | 100pf | multi | 1.10 | .35 |
| **1485** | A602 | 120pf | multi | 1.50 | .90 |
| **1486** | A602 | 130pf | multi | 2.25 | .75 |
| **1487** | A602 | 140pf | multi | 2.60 | 1.40 |
| **1488** | A602 | 150pf | multi | 3.00 | 1.40 |
| **1489** | A602 | 170pf | multi | 1.90 | 1.10 |
| **1490** | A602 | 180pf | multi | 2.25 | 1.10 |
| **1491** | A602 | 200pf | multi | 1.90 | .75 |
| **1492** | A602 | 240pf | multi | 2.60 | 1.90 |
| **1493** | A602 | 250pf | multi | 3.75 | 1.90 |
| **1493A** | A602 | 300pf | multi | 2.25 | 1.10 |
| **1494** | A602 | 350pf | multi | 4.00 | 2.25 |
| **1494A** | A602 | 500pf | multi | 5.00 | 3.00 |
| | *Nos. 1475-1494A (22)* | | | 40.10 | 20.65 |

Issued: 50pf, 80pf, 11/18; 40pf, 60pf, 9/17/87; 120pf, 11/7/87; 10pf, 4/14/88; 20pf, 130pf, 5/5/88; 100pf, 170pf, 240pf, 350pf, 11/10/88; 500pf, 1/12/89; 5pf, 2/9/89; 180pf, 250pf, 7/13/89; 140pf, 300pf, 8/10/89; 30pf, 70pf, 1/8/91; 150pf, 200pf, 2/14/91.

See #1723/1735, 2185-2188, Berlin #9N516-9N532.

Advent Collection for Church Projects in Latin America, 25th Anniv. A603

**1986, Nov. 13** **Litho.** ***Perf. 14***
**1495** A603 80pf multicolored 1.00 .45

Berlin, 750th Anniv. — A604

**1987, Jan. 15** **Litho.**
**1496** A604 80pf multicolored 2.00 .60

Archbishop's Residence at Wurzburg, 1719-44 A605

**1987, Jan. 15** **Photo.**
**1497** A605 80pf multicolored 1.50 .45

Balthasar Neumann (1687-1753), Baroque architect.

Ludwig Erhard (1897-1977), Economist, Chancellor 1963-66 A606

**1987, Jan. 15**
**1498** A606 80pf multicolored 1.75 .35

1987 Census — A607

**1987, Jan. 15** **Litho.**
**1499** A607 80pf Federal Eagle 1.60 .45

Clemenswerth Hunting Castle, 250th Anniv. — A608

**1987, Feb. 12** **Litho.**
**1500** A608 60pf multicolored 1.25 .45

Joseph von Fraunhofer (1787-1826), Optician, Physicist — A609

**1987, Feb. 12** **Litho. & Engr.**
**1501** A609 80pf Light spectrum diagram 1.25 .45

Karl May (1842-1912), Novelist — A610

**1987, Feb. 12** **Photo.**
**1502** A610 80pf Apache Chief Winnetou 1.40 .45

Papal Arms, Madonna and Child, Buildings in Kevelaer — A611

**1987, Apr. 9** **Litho.**
**1503** A611 80pf multicolored 1.60 .45

State visit of Pope John Paul II, Apr. 30-May 4; 17th Marian and 10th Mariological World Congress, Kevelaer, Sept. 11-20.

German Choral Soc., 125th Anniv. A612

**1987, Apr. 9**
**1504** A612 80pf multicolored 1.40 .45

Europa 1987 A613

Modern architecture: 60pf, German Pavilion, designed by Ludwig Mies van der Rohe, 1928 World's Fair, Barcelona. 80pf, Kohlbrand Bridge, 1974, Hamburg, designed by Thyssen Engineering.

**1987, May 5** **Litho.**
**1505** A613 60pf multicolored *1.25* *.35*
**1506** A613 80pf multicolored *1.50* *.35*

Organ Pipes, Signature A614

**1987, May 5**
**1507** A614 80pf multicolored 1.00 .45

Dietrich Buxtehude (c. 1637-1707), composer.

Wilhelm Kaisen (1887-1979), Bremen City Senate President — A615

**1987, May 5**
**1508** A615 80pf multicolored 1.40 .45

Johann Albrecht Bengel (1687-1752), Lutheran Theologian — A616

**1987, May 5** **Photo.** ***Perf. 14***
**1509** A616 80pf multicolored 1.25 .45

Kurt Schwitters (1887-1948), Artist — A617

**1987, May 5** **Litho.**
**1510** A617 80pf multicolored 1.25 .45

Rotary Intl. Convention, Munich, June 7-10 — A618

**1987, May 5** **Photo.**
**1511** A618 70pf multicolored 1.40 .45

Dulmen's Wild Horses, Merfelder Bruch Nature Reserve A619

**1987, May 5**
**1512** A619 60pf multicolored 1.60 .45

European Environmental Conservation Year.

Bishopric of Bremen, 1200th Anniv. A620

Design: Charlemagne, Bremen Cathedral, city arms, Bishop Willehad.

**1987, July 16** **Litho.** ***Perf. 14***
**1513** A620 80pf multicolored 1.25 .45

7th European Rifleman's Festival, Lippstadt, Sept. 12-13 — A621

**1987, Aug. 20** **Litho.** ***Perf. 14***
**1514** A621 80pf multicolored 1.25 .45

Stamp Day — A622

**1987, Oct. 15** **Litho.**
**1515** A622 80pf Postmen, 1897 1.25 .85

Historic Sites and Objects — A623

Designs: 5pf, Brunswick Lion. 10pf, Frankfurt Airport. 20pf, No. 1526, Queen Nefertiti of Egypt, bust, Egyptian Museum, Berlin. 30pf, Corner tower, Celle Castle, 14th cent. 33pf, 120pf, Schleswig Cathedral. 38pf, 280pf, Statue of Roland, Bremen. 40pf, Chile House, Hamburg. 41pf, 170pf, Russian church, Wiesbaden. 45pf, Rastatt Castle. 50pf, Filigree tracery on spires, Freiburg Cathedral. 60pf, Bavaria Munich, bronze statue above the Theresienwiese, Hall of Fame. No. 1527, Heligoland. 80pf, Entrance to Zollern II coal mine, Dortmund. 90pf, 140pf, Bronze flagon from Reinheim. 100pf, Altotting Chapel, Bavaria. 200pf, Magdeburg Cathedral. 300pf, Hambach Castle. 350pf, Externsteine Bridge near Horn-Bad Meinberg. 400pf, Opera House, Dresden. 450pf, New Gate, Neubrandenburg. 500pf, State Theatre, Cottbus. 700pf, German Theater, Berlin.

**1987-96** **Typo.** ***Perf. 14***

| | | | | | |
|---|---|---|---|---|---|
| **1515A** | A623 | 5pf multi | .25 | .25 |
| **1516** | A623 | 10pf multi | .25 | .25 |
| **1517** | A623 | 20pf multi | .30 | .25 |
| **1518** | A623 | 30pf multi | .50 | .25 |
| **1519** | A623 | 33pf tmulti | .45 | .30 |
| **1520** | A623 | 38pf multi | .75 | .45 |
| **1521** | A623 | 40pf multi | .30 | .30 |
| **1522** | A623 | 41pf multi | .50 | .35 |
| **1523** | A623 | 45pf multi | .45 | .35 |
| **1524** | A623 | 50pf multi | .50 | .25 |
| **1525** | A623 | 60pf multi | .75 | .25 |
| **1526** | A623 | 70pf multi | .70 | .25 |
| **1527** | A623 | 70pf multi | .45 | .30 |
| **1528** | A623 | 80pf multi | .75 | .25 |
| *a.* | | Bklt. pane, 4 10pf, 2 50pf, 2 80pf ('89) | 3.75 | 4.00 |
| *b.* | | Bklt. pane, 2 each 20pf, 80pf | 4.00 | 5.50 |
| **1529** | A623 | 90pf multi | 1.25 | 1.50 |
| **1530** | A623 | 100pf multi | 1.50 | .30 |
| *a.* | | Bklt. pane, 2 each 10, 60, 80, 100pf | 7.50 | 9.00 |
| *b.* | | Bklt. pane, 2 each 20, 50, 80, 100pf | 5.75 | 9.75 |
| *c.* | | Booklet pane, 10 #1530 | 19.00 | 16.00 |
| | | Complete booklet, #1530c | 22.50 | |
| *d.* | | Booklet pane, 4 #1516, 2 each #1524, 1528, 1530 | 6.00 | 7.50 |
| | | Complete booklet, #1530d | 7.00 | |
| **1531** | A623 | 120pf multi | 1.50 | .50 |
| **1532** | A623 | 140pf multi | 1.75 | .60 |
| **1533** | A623 | 170pf multi | 2.50 | .75 |
| **1534** | A623 | 200pf lmulti | 2.25 | .65 |
| **1535** | A623 | 280pf multi | 3.75 | 1.90 |
| **1536** | A623 | 300pf multi | 2.60 | .45 |
| **1537** | A623 | 350pf multi | 3.00 | .60 |
| **1538** | A623 | 400pf multi | 3.75 | .60 |
| **1539** | A623 | 450pf multi | 5.00 | .50 |
| **1540** | A623 | 500pf multi | 5.00 | 1.40 |
| **1540A** | A623 | 700pf multi | 8.00 | 3.00 |
| | | *Nos. 1515A-1540A (27)* | 48.75 | 16.80 |

Issued: 30, 50, 60, 80pf, 11/6/87; 10, 300pf, 1/14/88; 120pf, #1526, 7/14/88; 40, 90, 280pf, 8/11/88; 20, 33, 38, 140pf, 1/12/89; 100, 350pf, 2/9/89; 5pf, 2/15/90; 45p, #1527, 6/21/90; 170pf, 6/4/91; 400pf, 10/10/91; 450pf, 8/13/92; 200pf, 4/15/93; 500pf, 6/17/93; 41pf, 8/12/93; 700pf, 9/16/93; #1530b, 11/9/94; #1530d, 8/14/96.

See #1655-1663, 1838-60, 2199-2216, Berlin #9N543-9N557.

Christoph Willibald Gluck (1714-1787), Composer, and Score from the Opera Armide — A624

**1987, Nov. 6** ***Perf. 14***
**1541** A624 60pf car lake & dk gray 1.00 .35

Gerhart Hauptmann (1862-1946), Playwright — A625

**1987, Nov. 6** **Litho.**
**1542** A625 80pf black & brick red 1.50 .45

German Agro Action Organization, 125th Anniv. — A626

**1987, Nov. 6** **Photo.**
**1543** A626 80pf Rice field 1.50 .45

Mainz Carnival, 150th Anniv. — A627

**1988, Jan. 14** **Litho.** ***Perf. 14***
**1544** A627 60pf Jester 1.00 .45

Jacob Kaiser (1888-1961), Labor Leader — A628

**1988, Jan. 14** **Litho. & Engr.**
**1545** A628 80pf black 1.00 .45

Franco-German Cooperation Treaty, 25th Anniv. — A629

**1988, Jan. 14**
**1546** A629 80pf Adenauer, De Gaulle 1.60 .60

See France No. 2086.

Beatification of Edith Stein and Rupert Mayer by Pope John Paul II in 1987 — A630

**1988, Jan. 14** **Photo.**
**1547** A630 80pf brown, blk & ver 1.25 .45

A631

Woodcut (detail) by Ludwig Richter.

**1988, Feb. 18** **Litho.**
**1548** A631 60pf multicolored 1.25 .45

Woodcut inspired by poem Solitude of the Green Woods, by Baron Joseph von Eichendorff (1788-1857).

A632

**1988, Feb. 18** **Photo.**
**1549** A632 80pf dk red & brn blk 1.50 .45

Arthur Schopenhauer (1788-1860), philosopher.

Friedrich Wilhelm Raiffeisen (1818-1888), Economist — A633

**1988, Feb. 18** **Litho.**
**1550** A633 80pf black & brt yel grn 1.60 .45

The German Raiffeisen Assoc., an agricultural cooperative credit soc., was founded by Raiffeisen.

Ulrich Reichsritter von Hutten (1488-1523), Humanist — A634

Design: Detail from an engraving published with Hutten's *Conquestiones.*

**1988, Apr. 14** **Litho. & Engr.**
**1551** A634 80pf multicolored 1.25 .50

Europa 1988 A635

Transport and communication: 60pf, Airbus A320. 80pf, Integrated Services Digital Network (ISDN) system.

**1988, May 5** **Litho.**
**1552** A635 60pf multicolored *1.00* *.35*
**1553** A635 80pf multicolored *1.00* *.35*

City of Dusseldorf, 700th Anniv. — A636

**1988, May 5**
**1554** A636 60pf multicolored 1.25 .45

Cologne University, 600th Anniv. — A637

**1988, May 5**
**1555** A637 80pf multicolored 1.25 .45

Jean Monnet (1888-1979), French Statesman A638

**1988, May 5**
**1556** A638 80pf multicolored 1.25 .45

Theodor Storm (1817-1888), Poet, Novelist — A639

**1988, May 5**
**1557** A639 80pf multicolored 1.25 .45

German Volunteer Service, 25th Anniv. — A640

**1988, May 5**
**1558** A640 80pf multicolored 1.25 .45

Town of Meersburg, Millennium — A641

**1988, July 14** **Litho.** ***Perf. 14***
**1559** A641 60pf multicolored .90 .45

Leopold Gmelin (1788-1853), Chemist A642

**1988, July 14** **Litho. & Engr.**
**1560** A642 80pf multicolored 1.00 .45

Vernier Scale as a Symbol of Precision and Quality — A643

**1988, July 14** **Litho.**
**1561** A643 140pf multicolored 1.90 .90

Made in Germany.

August Bebel (1840-1913), Founder of the Social Democratic Party — A644

**1988, Aug. 11** **Photo.**
**1562** A644 80pf multicolored 1.40 .45

Intl. Red Cross, 125th Anniv. — A645

**1988, Oct. 13** **Litho. & Engr.**
**1563** A645 80pf scarlet & black 1.40 .45

Stamp Day — A646

**1988, Oct. 13** **Litho.**
**1564** A646 20pf Carrier pigeon .60 .35

1st Nazi Pogrom, Nov. 9, 1938 A647

Star, "Remembering is the secret of redemption," & burning synagogue in Baden-Baden.

**1988, Oct. 13** **Photo.**
**1565** A647 80pf dull pale pur & blk 1.00 .45

Postage Stamps for Bethel, Cent. A648

**1988, Nov. 10** **Litho.**
**1566** A648 60pf multicolored 1.10 .45

The Postage Stamps for Bethel program was founded by Pastor Friedrich V. Bodelschwingh to employ disabled residents of Bethel.

Samaritan Association of Workers (ASB) Rescue Service, Cent. — A649

**1988, Nov. 10**
**1567** A649 80pf multicolored 1.10 .45

Bonn Bimillennium — A650

**1989, Jan. 12** **Litho.**
**1568** A650 80pf multicolored 1.50 .65

Bonn as capital of the federal republic, 40th anniv.

*Bluxao I,* 1955, by Willi Baumeister (1889-1955) — A651

**1989, Jan. 12**
**1569** A651 60pf multicolored 1.00 .45

Misereor and Brot fur die Welt, 30th Annivs. A652

**1989, Jan. 12** **Photo.**
**1570** A652 80pf Barren and verdant soil 1.10 .45

Church organizations helping Third World nations to become self-sufficient in food production.

*Cats in the Attic,* Woodcut by Gerhard Marcks (1889-1981) — A653

**1989, Feb. 9** **Litho.** ***Perf. 14***
**1571** A653 60pf multicolored 1.00 .45

European Parliament 3rd Elections, June 18 — A654

Flags of member nations.

**1989, Apr. 20** **Litho.**
**1572** A654 100pf multicolored 1.90 .90

Europa 1989 A655

**1989, May 5**
**1573** A655 60pf Kites *1.00* *.30*
**1574** A655 100pf Puppets *1.50* *.35*

Hamburg Harbor, 800th Anniv. A656

**1989, May 5**
**1575** A656 60pf multicolored 1.40 .45

Cosmas Damian Asam (1686-1739), Painter, Architect A657

**1989, May 5** **Litho. & Engr.**
**1576** A657 60pf Fresco .75 .45

Federal Republic of Germany, 40th Anniv. — A658

**1989, May 5** **Photo.**
**1577** A658 100pf Natl. crest, flag, presidents' signatures 1.75 .65

Council of Europe, 40th Anniv. — A659

**1989, May 5** ***Perf. 14***
**1578** A659 100pf Parliamentary Assembly, stars 1.60 .75

Franz Xaver Gabelsberger (1789-1849), Inventor of a German Shorthand — A660

**1989, May 5** **Litho.**
**1579** A660 100pf multicolored 1.60 .60

Sts. Kilian, Colman and Totnan (d. 689), Martyred Missionaries, and Clover — A661

**1989, June 15** **Litho.**
**1580** A661 100pf multicolored 1.50 .60

See Ireland No. 748.

Friedrich Silcher (1789-1860), Composer, and *Lorelai* Score — A662

**1989, June 15**
**1581** A662 80pf multicolored 1.00 .45

Social Security Pension Insurance, Cent. — A663

**1989, June 15**
**1582** A663 100pf dull ultra, bl & ver 1.50 .50

Friedrich List (1789-1846), Economist — A664

**1989, July 13** **Engr.** ***Perf. 14***
**1583** A664 170pf black & dark red 2.25 .90

*Summer Evening,* 1905, by Heinrich Vogler — A665

**1989, July 13** **Litho.**
**1584** A665 60pf multicolored .85 .45

Worpswede Artists' Village, cent.

A666

**1989, July 13** **Photo.**
**1585** A666 100pf slate grn, blk & gray 1.10 .50

Reverend Paul Schneider (d. 1939), martyr of Buchenwald concentration camp.

A667

**1989, Aug. 10** **Litho.**
**1586** A667 60pf multicolored 1.25 .45

Frankfurt Cathedral, 750th anniv.

Child Welfare A668

**1989, Aug. 10** ***Perf. 14***
**1587** A668 100pf multicolored 1.40 .50

Trade Union of the Mining and Power Industries, Cent. — A669

**1989, Aug. 10** ***Perf. 14***
**1588** A669 100pf multicolored 1.25 .50

Reinhold Maier (1889-1971), Politician A670

**1989, Oct. 12** **Litho.**
**1589** A670 100pf multicolored 1.40 .50

Restoration of St. James Church Organ, Constructed by Arp Schnitger, 1689 — A671

**1989, Nov. 16**
**1590** A671 60pf multicolored 1.25 .45

Speyer, 2000th Anniv. A672

**1990, Jan. 12** **Litho.** ***Perf. 14x14½***
**1591** A672 60pf multicolored 1.25 .45

A673

Design: *The Young Post Rider,* an Engraving by Albrecht Durer.

**Litho. & Engr.**

**1990, Jan. 12** ***Perf. 14***
**1592** A673 100pf buff, vio brn & gray 2.00 .60

Postal communications in Europe, 500th anniv. See Austria No. 1486, Belgium No. 1332, Berlin 9N584, and DDR No. 2791.

A674

**1990, Jan. 12** **Litho.**
**1593** A674 100pf multicolored 1.25 .60

Riesling Vineyards, 500th anniv.

Addition of Lubeck to the UNESCO World Heritage List, 1987 A675

**1990, Jan. 12** **Litho. & Engr.**
**1594** A675 100pf multicolored 1.25 .60

Seal of Col. Spittler, 1400, and Teutonic Order Heraldic Emblem A676

**1990, Feb. 15** **Litho.**
**1595** A676 100pf multicolored 1.50 .60

Teutonic Order, 800th anniv.

Seal of Frederick II and Galleria Reception Hall at the Frankfurt Fair A677

**1990, Feb. 15**
**1596** A677 100pf multicolored 1.50 .60

Granting of fair privileges to Frankfurt by Frederick II, 750th anniv.

Youth Science and Technology Competition, 25th Anniv. — A678

**1990, Feb. 15**
**1597** A678 100pf multicolored 1.50 .60

Nature and Environmental Protection — A679

**1990, Feb. 15**
**1598** A679 100pf North Sea 1.60 .60

Labor Day, Cent. A680

**1990, Apr. 19** **Photo.** ***Perf. 14***
**1599** A680 100pf dark red & blk 1.25 .60

German Assoc. of Housewives, 75th Anniv. — A681

**1990, Apr. 19** **Litho.**
**1600** A681 100pf multicolored 1.25 .60

Europa A682

Post offices in Frankfurt am Main: 60pf, Thurn and Taxis Palace. 100pf, Modern Giro office.

**1990, May 3** **Litho.**
**1601** A682 60pf multicolored *1.10* *.50*
**1602** A682 100pf multicolored *1.50* *.50*

German Students' Fraternity, 175th Anniv. — A683

**1990, May 3** **Litho. & Engr.**
**1603** A683 100pf multicolored 1.60 .60

Intl. Telecommunication Union, 125th Anniv. — A684

**1990, May 3** **Litho.**
**1604** A684 100pf multicolored 1.25 .60

German Life Boat Institution, 125th Anniv. — A685

**1990, May 3**
**1605** A685 60pf multicolored 1.25 .50

Wilhelm Leuschner (1890-1944), Politician A686

**1990, May 3** **Litho. & Engr.**
**1606** A686 100pf lt gray violet 1.50 .60

Rummelsberg Diaconal Institution, Cent. — A687

**1990, May 3** **Litho.**
**1607** A687 100pf multicolored 1.25 .60

Charter of German Expellees, 40th Anniv. — A688

**1990, June 21** **Photo.**
**1608** A688 100pf multicolored 1.50 .50

Intl. Chamber of Commerce, 30th Universal Congress — A689

**1990, June 21** **Litho.**
**1609** A689 80pf multicolored 1.25 .75

Matthias Claudius (1740-1815), Writer — A691

**1990, Aug. 9** **Litho.**
**1611** A691 100pf multicolored 1.40 .45

**Reunified Germany**
AREA — 137,179 sq. mi.
POP. — 82,087,361 (1999 est.)
CAPITAL — Berlin

German Reunification — A692

**1990, Oct. 3** **Litho.** ***Perf. 14***
**1612** A692 50pf black, red & yel 1.10 .35
**1613** A692 100pf black, red & yel 1.50 .50

First Postage Stamps, 150th Anniv. — A693

**1990, Oct. 11** **Litho.**
**1614** A693 100pf multicolored 1.40 .45

Heinrich Schliemann (1822-1890), Archaeologist — A694

**1990, Oct. 11**
**1615** A694 60pf multicolored 1.25 .45

See Greece No. 1705.

Kathe Dorsch (1912-1957), Actress — A695

**1990, Nov. 6** **Photo.**
**1616** A695 100pf red & violet 1.40 .60

Opening of Berlin Wall, 1st Anniv. — A696

**1990, Nov. 6** **Photo.** ***Perf. 14***
**1617** A696 50pf shown 1.10 .70
**1618** A696 100pf Brandenburg Gate 1.50 .70

**Souvenir Sheet**

**1619** Sheet of 2 3.00 3.25
*a.* A696 50pf like No. 1617 1.10 .90
*b.* A696 100pf like No. 1618 1.50 1.10

Rainbow continuous on stamps from #1619.

Pharmacy Profession, 750th Anniv. — A697

**1991, Jan. 8** **Litho.**
**1620** A697 100pf multicolored 1.50 .60

Hanover, 750th Anniv. — A698

**1991, Jan. 8**
**1621** A698 60pf multicolored 1.25 .45

Brandenburg Gate, Bicentennial — A699

**1991, Jan. 8** **Litho. & Engr.**
**1622** A699 100pf gray, dk bl & red 1.75 .45

A700

**1991, Jan. 8** **Photo.**
**1623** A700 60pf multicolored 1.00 .45

Erich Buchholz (1891-1972), painter and architect.

A701

**1991, Jan. 8** **Litho.**
**1624** A701 100pf multicolored 1.25 .60

Walter Eucken (1891-1950), economist.

25th Intl. Tourism Exchange, Berlin — A702

**1991, Jan. 8**
**1625** A702 100pf multicolored 1.40 .45

Souvenir Sheet

World Bobsled Championships, Altenberg — A703

**1991, Jan. 8** ***Perf. 12½x13***
**1626** A703 100pf multicolored 1.75 2.00

Friedrich Spee von Langenfeld (1591-1635), Poet — A704

**1991, Feb. 14** **Litho.** ***Perf. 14***
**1627** A704 100pf multicolored 1.40 .45

A705

**1991, Feb. 14**
**1628** A705 100pf multicolored 1.40 .45

Ludwig Windthorst (1812-1891), politician.

A706

**1991, Mar. 12**
**1629** A706 60pf multicolored 1.00 .45

Jan von Werth (1591-1652), general.

Flowers A707

**1991, Mar. 12** ***Perf. 13***
**1630** A707 30pf Schweizer mannschild .40 .30
**1631** A707 50pf Wulfens primel (primula) .55 .50
**1632** A707 80pf Sommerenzian (gentian) .90 .35
**1633** A707 100pf Preiselbeere (cranberry) 1.25 .35
**1634** A707 350pf Alpenedelweiss 4.00 3.00
*Nos. 1630-1634 (5)* 7.10 4.50

Battle of Legnica, 750th Anniv. A708

**Litho. & Engr.**

**1991, Apr. 9** *Perf. 14*

**1635** A708 100pf multicolored 1.50 .90

See Poland No. 3019.

Choral Singing Academy of Berlin, Bicent. A709

**1991, Apr. 9**

**1636** A709 100pf multicolored 1.40 .60

Lette Foundation, 125th Anniv. — A710

**1991, Apr. 9** **Photo.**

**1637** A710 100pf multicolored 1.40 .45

Historic Aircraft A711

**1991, Apr. 9**

**1638** A711 30pf Junkers F13, 1930 .35 .35
**1639** A711 50pf Grade Eindecker, 1909 .55 .30
**1640** A711 100pf Fokker FIII, 1922 1.50 .35
**1641** A711 165pf Graf Zeppelin LZ 127, 1928 2.25 2.00
*Nos. 1638-1641 (4)* 4.65 3.00

Europa A712

Satellites: 60pf, ERS-1. 100pf, Copernicus.

**1991, May 2** **Litho.** *Perf. 14*

**1642** A712 60pf multicolored *1.10 .45*
**1643** A712 100pf multicolored *2.00 .45*

Town Charters, 700th Anniv. — A713

Design: Arms of Bernkastel, Mayen, Montabaur, Saarburg, Welschbillig, and Wittlich.

**1991, May 2**

**1644** A713 60pf multicolored 1.00 .45

Max Reger (1873-1916), Composer — A714

**1991, May 2**

**1645** A714 100pf multicolored 1.50 .45

Inter-City Express Railway A715

**1991, May 2**

**1646** A715 60pf multicolored 1.00 .45

18th World Gas Congress, Berlin — A716

Designs: 60pf, Wilhelm August Lampadius (1772-1842), chemist. 100pf, Gas street lamp.

**1991, June 4** **Litho.** *Perf. 13x12½*

**1647** A716 60pf lt blue & black .75 .30
**1648** A716 100pf lt blue & black 1.10 .45
*a.* Pair, #1647-1648 + label 2.40 2.40

Sea Birds — A717

Designs: 60pf, Kampflaufer, Philomachus pugnax. 80pf, Zwergseeschwalbe, Sterna albifrons. 100pf, Ringelgans, Branta bernicla. 140pf, Seeadler, Haliaeetus albicilla.

**1991, June 4** **Litho.** *Perf. 14*

**1649** A717 60pf multicolored .75 .45
**1650** A717 80pf multicolored 1.10 .75
**1651** A717 100of multicolored 1.10 .75
**1652** A717 140pf multicolored 2.10 1.50
*Nos. 1649-1652 (4)* 5.05 3.45

Paul Wallot (1841-1912), Architect — A718

**Litho. & Engr.**

**1991, June 4** *Perf. 14*

**1653** A718 100pf multicolored 1.50 .45

**Historic Sites Type of 1987**

Designs: No. 1655, Frankfurt Airport. No. 1656, Wernigerode Town Hall. 60pf, Munich, Bavaria. 80pf, Zech Zollern II Dortmund. No. 1663, Wallfahrtskapelle Alloting. No. 1664, Schwerin Castle. 110pf, Regensburg Stone Bridge.

***Die Cut perf 10¼x10¾ on 3 sides (#1656, 1664, 1666), Die Cut Imperf***

**1991-2001** **Litho.**

**Self-Adhesive**

**1655** A623 10pf multi 1.00 1.40
**1656** A623 10pf multi 2.25 1.90
**1659** A623 60pf multi 1.00 1.40
**1661** A623 80pf multi 1.00 1.00
**1663** A623 100pf multi 1.25 1.25
*a.* Bklt. pane, 2 each #1655, 1659, 1661, 1663 8.25 8.25
**1664** A623 100pf multi 2.25 2.25
**1666** A623 110pf multi 2.25 2.25
*a.* Booklet, 2 each #1656, 1664, 8 #1666 25.00 25.00
*Nos. 1655-1666 (7)* 11.00 11.45

Issued: #1655, 1659, 1661, 1663, June 4. Nos. 1656, 1664, 110pf, 5/25/01.

Nos. 1655, 1659, 1661, 1663 issued on peelable paper backing serving as booklet cover.

Dragonflies A719

50pf, #1671, Libellula depressa. #1672, 70pf, Sympetrum sanguineum. #1673, 80pf, Cordulegaster boltonii. #1674, 100pf, Aeshna viridis.

**1991, July 9** **Photo.** *Perf. 14*

**1670** A719 50pf multicolored .65 .30
**1671** A719 60pf multicolored 1.25 .60
**1672** A719 60pf multicolored 1.25 .60
**1673** A719 60pf multicolored 1.25 .60
**1674** A719 60pf multicolored 1.25 .60
*a.* Block of 4, #1671-1674 5.50 5.50
**1675** A719 70pf multicolored 1.00 .75
**1676** A719 80pf multicolored 1.10 .75
**1677** A719 100pf multicolored 1.25 .75
*Nos. 1670-1677 (8)* 9.00 4.95

Traffic Safety A720

**1991, July 9** **Litho.**

**1678** A720 100pf multicolored 1.50 .60

Geneva Convention on Refugees, 40th Anniv. — A721

**1991, July 9**

**1679** A721 100pf blk, gray & pink 1.40 .45

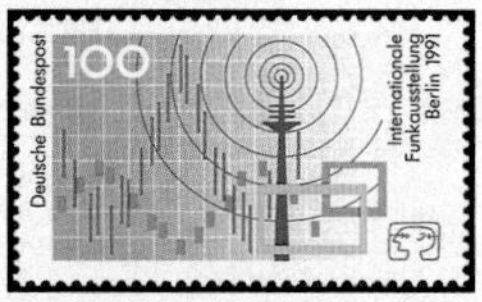


Intl. Radio Exhibition, Berlin — A722

**1991, July 9**

**1680** A722 100pf multicolored 1.40 .45

Reinold von Thadden-Trieglaff (1891-1976), Founder of German Protestant Convention — A723

**1991, Aug. 8** **Litho.** *Perf. 14*

**1681** A723 100pf multicolored 1.40 .45

August Heinrich Hoffman von Fallersleben (1798-1874), Poet and Philologist — A724

**1991, Aug. 8**

**1682** A724 100pf multicolored 1.40 .45

German national anthem, 150th anniv.

3-Phase Energy Transmission, Cent. — A725

**1991, Aug. 8**

**1683** A725 170pf multicolored 2.25 1.10

Rhine-Ruhr Harbor, Duisburg, 275th Anniv. — A726

**1991, Sept. 12** **Litho.** *Perf. 14*

**1684** A726 100pf multicolored 1.40 .45

Souvenir Sheet

Theodor Korner (1791-1813), Poet — A727

**1991, Sept. 12** *Perf. 13x12½*

**1685** A727 Sheet of 2 2.25 2.25
*a.* 60pf Sword and pen 1.10 1.10
*b.* 100pf Portrait 1.10 1.10

Hans Albers (1891-1960), Actor — A728

**1991, Sept. 12** **Photo.** *Perf. 14*

**1686** A728 100pf multicolored 1.75 .45

Postman, Spreewald Region
A729

**1991, Oct. 10 Litho. *Perf. 14***
**1687** A729 100pf multicolored 1.40 .45

Stamp Day.

Bird Monument by Max Ernst — A730

**1991, Oct. 10**
**1688** A730 100pf multicolored 1.40 .45

Sorbian Legends
A731

**1991, Nov. 5 *Perf. 13***
**1689** A731 60pf Fiddler, water sprite .90 .45
**1690** A731 100pf Midday woman, woman from Nochten 1.40 .45

Souvenir Sheet

Wolfgang Amadeus Mozart, Death Bicent. — A732

**1991, Nov. 5 Litho. *Perf. 14***
**1691** A732 100pf multicolored 2.25 2.25

Otto Dix (1891-1969), Painter — A733

Designs: 60pf, Portrait of the Dancer Anita Berber. 100pf, Self-portrait.

**1991, Nov. 5 Photo. *Perf. 14***
**1692** A733 60pf multicolored .75 .45
**1693** A733 100pf multicolored 1.50 .45

Julius Leber (1891-1945), Politician
A734

**1991, Nov. 5 Litho.**
**1694** A734 100pf black & red 1.40 .45

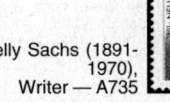

Nelly Sachs (1891-1970), Writer — A735

**1991, Nov. 5**
**1695** A735 100pf violet 1.40 .45

City of Koblenz, 2000th Anniv.
A736

**1992, Jan. 9 *Perf. 13x12½***
**1696** A736 60pf multicolored 1.50 .50

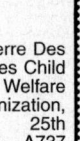

Terre Des Hommes Child Welfare Organization, 25th Anniv. — A737

**1992, Jan. 9 Litho. *Perf. 14***
**1697** A737 100pf multicolored 1.50 .60

Martin Niemoller (1892-1984), Theologian
A738

**1992, Jan. 9**
**1698** A738 100pf multicolored 1.10 .45

Coats of Arms of States of the Federal Republic of Germany
A739

**1992-94 *Perf. 13½***

| | | | | |
|---|---|---|---|---|
| **1699** | 100pf | Baden-Wurttemberg | 1.40 | .65 |
| **1700** | 100pf | Bavaria | 1.40 | .65 |
| **1701** | 100pf | Berlin | 1.40 | .65 |
| **1702** | 100pf | Brandenburg | 1.40 | .65 |
| **1703** | 100pf | Bremen | 1.40 | .65 |
| **1704** | 100pf | Hamburg | 1.40 | .65 |
| **1705** | 100pf | Hesse | 1.40 | .65 |
| **1706** | 100pf | Mecklenburg-Western Pomerania | 1.40 | .65 |
| **1707** | 100pf | Lower Saxony | 1.40 | .65 |
| **1708** | 100pf | North Rhine - Westphalia | 1.40 | .65 |
| **1709** | 100pf | Rhineland-Palatinate | 1.40 | .65 |
| **1710** | 100pf | Saar | 1.40 | .65 |
| **1711** | 100pf | Saxony | 1.40 | .65 |
| **1712** | 100pf | Saxony-Anhalt | 1.40 | .65 |
| **1713** | 100pf | Schleswig-Holstein | 1.40 | .65 |
| **1714** | 100pf | Thuringia | 1.40 | .65 |
| | | *Nos. 1699-1714 (16)* | 22.40 | 10.40 |

See #B818.

Issued: #1699, 1/9/92; #1700, 3/12/92; #1701, 6/11/92; #1702, 7/16/92; #1703, 8/13/92; #1704, 9/10/92; #1705. 3/11/93; #1706, 6/17/93; #1707, 7/15/93; #1708, 8/12/93; #1709, 9/16/93; #1710, 1/13/94; #1711, 3/10/94; #1712, 6/16/94; #1713, 7/14/94; #1714, 9/8/94.

**Famous Women Type of 1986**

80pf, Rahel Varnhagen von Ense (1771-1833), pioneer in women's movement. No. 1724, Elisabeth Schwarzhaupt (1901-86), politician. No. 1725, Louise Henriette of Orange (1627-67), mother of Frederick, King of Prussia. No. 1726, Grethe Weiser (1903-70), actress. No. 1727, Marlene Dietrich (1901-92), actress. No. 1728, Käte Strobel (1907-96), government minister. No. 1729, Marie-Elisabeth Lüders (1878-1966), politician. No. 1730, Marieluise Fleisser (1901-74), writer. No. 1731, Maria Probst (1902-67), politician. No. 1732, Nelly Sachs (1891-1970), writer. 400pf, Charlotte von Stein (1742-1827), confidant of Goethe. 440pf, Gret Palucca (1902-93), dancer. 450pf, Hedwig Courths-Mahler (1867-1950), novelist.

**1992-2000 Engr. *Perf. 14***

| | | | | | |
|---|---|---|---|---|---|
| **1723** | A602 | 80pf | blue & brown | .85 | .45 |
| **1724** | A602 | 100pf | green & org brown | 1.00 | .75 |
| **1725** | A602 | 100pf | violet & bister | .85 | .45 |
| **1726** | A602 | 100pf | ol bis & bl grn | .85 | .75 |
| **1727** | A602 | 110pf | vio & dk brn | 1.00 | .60 |
| **1728** | A602 | 110pf | ol & red brn | .90 | .75 |
| **1729** | A602 | 220pf | grn bl & vio bl | 1.90 | 1.75 |
| **1730** | A602 | 220pf | grn & brn | 1.60 | 1.60 |
| **1731** | A602 | 300pf | deep blue & brown | 2.25 | 1.90 |
| **1732** | A602 | 300pf | brn & vio | 2.10 | 2.10 |
| **1733** | A602 | 400pf | lake & blk | 4.50 | 3.25 |
| **1734** | A602 | 440pf | dp vio & dk car | 4.25 | 5.00 |
| **1735** | A602 | 450pf | brt blue & blue | 5.00 | 3.75 |
| | | | *Nos. 1723-1735 (13)* | 27.05 | 23.10 |

Issued: 400pf, 1/9/92; 450pf, 6/11/92; 80pf, #1725, 10/13/94; #1727, 8/14/97; #1729, 8/28/97; #1724, #1731, 10/16/97; 440pf, 10/8/98; #1726, 1728, 11/9/00; Nos. 1730, 1732, 1/11/01.

Arthur Honegger (1892-1955), Composer
A740

**1992, Feb. 6 Photo. *Perf. 14***
**1736** A740 100pf sepia & black 1.50 .65

Ferdinand von Zeppelin (1838-1917), Airship Builder — A741

**1992, Feb. 6 Litho.**
**1737** A741 165pf multicolored 2.25 1.25

City of Kiel, 750th Anniv.
A742

**1992, Mar. 12**
**1738** A742 60pf multicolored 1.00 .50

Konrad Adenauer
A743

**1992, Mar. 12 Photo.**
**1739** A743 100pf black & dull org 1.75 .50

Ernst Jakob Renz (1815-1892), Circus Director — A744

**1992, Mar. 12 Litho.**
**1740** A744 100pf multicolored 1.40 .50

Berlin Sugar Institute, 125th Anniv.
A745

**1992, Mar. 12 *Perf. 13x12½***
**1741** A745 100pf multicolored 1.40 .65

Johann Adam Schall von Bell (1592-1666), Astronomer and Missionary — A746

**1992, Apr. 9 Litho. *Perf. 13x12½***
**1742** A746 140pf multicolored 2.00 1.00

Erfurt, Capital of Thuringia, 1250th Anniv. — A747

**1992, May 7 Litho. *Perf. 14***
**1743** A747 60pf multicolored 1.00 .50

Discovery of America, 500th Anniv. — A748

Europa: 60pf, Woodcut illustrating letters from Columbus, 1493. 100pf, Rene de Laudonniere and Chief Athore by Jacques le Moyne de Morgues, 1564.

**1992, May 7 *Perf. 13½***
**1744** A748 60pf multicolored *.85 .40*
**1745** A748 100pf multicolored *1.50 .45*

A749

**1992, May 7 *Perf. 13***
**1746** A749 100pf multicolored 1.40 .50

Order of Merit, 150th anniv.

A750

**1992, May 7 Litho. *Perf. 14***
**1747** A750 100pf multicolored 1.40 .60

St. Ludgerus, 1250th birth anniv.

Adam Riese (1492-1559), Mathematician — A751

**1992, May 7**
**1748** A751 100pf multicolored 1.40 .60

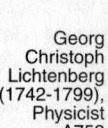

Georg Christoph Lichtenberg (1742-1799), Physicist A752

**1992, June 11 Litho. *Perf. 14***
**1749** A752 100pf multicolored 1.40 .60

20th Century Paintings — A753

Designs: 60pf, Landscape with a Horse, by Franz Marc (1880-1916). 100pf, Fashion Shop, by August Macke (1887-1914). 170pf, Murnau with a Rainbow, by Vassily Kandinsky (1866-1944).

**1992, June 11 Litho. *Perf. 14***
**1750** A753 60pf multicolored .75 .60
**1751** A753 100pf multicolored 1.25 .60
**1752** A753 170pf multicolored 2.00 1.60
*Nos. 1750-1752 (3)* 4.00 2.80

See Nos. 1878-1880.

Leipzig Botanical Garden A754

**1992, July 16 Litho. *Perf. 13x12½***
**1753** A754 60pf multicolored 1.00 .50

Family Living — A755

**1992, July 16 *Perf. 13½***
**1754** A755 100pf multicolored 1.50 .50

17th World Congress on Home Economics, Hanover — A756

**1992, July 16 Photo. *Perf. 14***
**1755** A756 100pf multicolored 1.50 .60

Egid Quirin Asam (1692-1750), Architect and Sculptor — A757

**1992, Aug. 13 Litho. *Perf. 14***
**1756** A757 60pf multicolored 1.00 .50

German State Opera, Berlin, 250th Anniv. A758

**1992, Aug. 13**
**1757** A758 80pf multicolored 1.25 .50

Federation of German Amateur Theaters, Cent. — A759

**1992, Aug. 13**
**1758** A759 100pf multicolored 1.50 .50

Construction of First Globe by Martin Behaim, 500th Anniv. — A760

**1992, Sept. 10 *Perf. 13½***
**1759** A760 60pf multicolored 1.25 .50

Opening of Main-Danube Canal — A761

**1992, Sept. 10 *Perf. 14***
**1760** A761 100pf multicolored 1.25 .50

Werner Bergengruen (1892-1964), Writer — A762

**1992, Sept. 10**
**1761** A762 100pf blk, bl & gray 1.25 .50

Jewelry & Watch Industries in Pforzheim, 225th Anniv. — A763

**1992, Sept. 10**
**1762** A763 100pf multicolored 1.25 .50

Balloon Post — A764

**1992, Oct. 15 Litho. *Perf. 14***
**1763** A764 100pf multicolored 1.50 .60

Stamp Day.

Hugo Distler (1908-1942), Composer A765

**1992, Oct. 15**
**1764** A765 100pf violet & black 1.50 .50

Association of German Plant and Machine Builders, Cent. — A766

**1992, Oct. 15 Litho. & Engr.**
**1765** A766 170pf multicolored 2.00 1.00

Single European Market A767

**1992, Nov. 5 Litho. *Perf. 14***
**1766** A767 100pf multicolored 1.60 .60

Jochen Klepper (1903-1942), Writer — A768

**Litho. & Engr.**
**1992, Nov. 5 *Perf. 14***
**1767** A768 100pf multicolored 1.50 .50

A769

**1992, Nov. 5 Photo.**
**1768** A769 100pf sepia & black 1.50 .50

Werner von Siemens (1816-1892), electrical engineer.

A770

**1992, Nov. 5 Litho.**
**1769** A770 100pf multicolored 1.50 .50

Gebhard Leberecht von Blucher (1742-1819), Commander of Prussian Army.

City of Munster, 1200th Anniv. — A771

**1993, Jan. 14 Litho. *Perf. 14***
**1770** A771 60pf multicolored 1.00 .50

Sir Isaac Newton, Scientist A772

**1993, Jan. 14 Litho. & Engr.**
**1771** A772 100pf multicolored 1.25 .50

North German Naval Observatory, Hamburg, 125th Anniv. — A773

**1993, Jan. 14 Litho. *Perf. 13x12½***
**1772** A773 100pf multicolored 1.25 .50

Health and Safety in Workplace — A774

**1993, Jan. 14 Photo. *Perf. 14***
**1773** A774 100pf blk, yel & bl 1.25 .50

Association of German Electrical Engineers, Cent. — A775

**1993, Jan. 14**
**1774** A775 170pf multicolored 1.90 1.00

Leipzig Gewandhaus Orchestra, 250th Anniv. — A776

**1993, Feb. 11 Litho. *Perf. 13x12½***
**1775** A776 100pf black & gold 1.25 .50

St. John of Nepomuk, 600th Death Anniv. — A777

**1993, Mar. 11**
**1776** A777 100pf multicolored 1.25 .50

New Postal Codes A778

**1993, Mar. 11** ***Perf. 14***

**1777** A778 100pf multicolored 1.50 .50

20th Century German Paintings — A779

Designs: No. 1778, Cafe, by George Grosz (1893-1959). No. 1779, Sea and Sun, by Otto Pankok (1893-1966). No. 1780, Audience, by A. Paul Weber (1893-1980).

**1993, Mar. 11**

| | | | | | |
|---|---|---|---|---|---|
| **1778** | A779 | 100pf multicolored | | 1.25 | .75 |
| **1779** | A779 | 100pf multicolored | | 1.25 | .75 |
| **1780** | A779 | 100pf multicolored | | 1.25 | .75 |
| | | *Nos. 1778-1780 (3)* | | 3.75 | 2.25 |

See Nos. 1863-1865, 1922-1924.

Benedictine Abbeys of Maria Laach and Bursfelde, 900th Anniv. — A780

**Litho. & Engr.**

**1993, Apr. 15** ***Perf. 14***

**1781** A780 80pf multicolored 1.25 .50

5th Intl. Horticultural Show, Stuttgart — A781

**1993, Apr. 15 Litho.** ***Perf. 13x12½***

**1782** A781 100pf multicolored 1.25 .50

Contemporary Art — A782

Europa: 80pf, Storage Place, by Joseph Beuys (1921-1986). 100pf, Homage to the Square, by Joseph Albers (1888-1976).

**1993, May 5 Litho.** ***Perf. 13½x14***

| | | | | |
|---|---|---|---|---|
| **1783** | A782 | 80pf multicolored | *1.25* | .60 |
| **1784** | A782 | 100pf multicolored | *1.25* | .60 |

Dahlwitz Hoppegarten (Hippodrome), Berlin, 125th Anniv. — A783

**1993, May 5 Litho.** ***Perf. 14***

**1785** A783 80pf multicolored 1.00 .60

Lake Constance Steamer Hohentwiel — A784

**1993, May 5** **Photo.**

**1786** A784 100pf multicolored 1.25 .50

See Austria No. 1618, Switzerland No. 931.

Schulpforta School for Boys, 450th Anniv. — A785

**1993, May 5** **Litho.**

**1787** A785 100pf multicolored 1.25 .50

Coburger Convent, 125th Anniv. A786

**1993, May 5** **Litho. & Engr.**

**1788** A786 100pf black, green & red 1.25 .50

City of Potsdam, 1000th Anniv. A787

**1993, June 17 Litho.** ***Perf. 13x12½***

**1789** A787 80pf multicolored 1.25 .50

German UNICEF Committee, 40th Anniv. — A788

**1993, June 17 Litho.** ***Perf. 14***

**1790** A788 100pf multicolored 1.25 .50

Friedrich Holderlin (1770-1843), Writer — A789

**1993, June 17 Photo.** ***Perf. 14***

**1791** A789 100pf multicolored 1.25 .50

Hans Fallada (1893-1947), Novelist — A790

**1993, July 15**

**1792** A790 100pf multicolored 1.25 .50

Scenic Regions in Germany — A791

**1993-96 Litho.** ***Perf. 14***

**Denominations 100pf**

| | | | | |
|---|---|---|---|---|
| **1793** | A791 | Rugen Island | 1.10 | .65 |
| **1794** | A791 | Harz Mountains | 1.10 | .65 |
| **1795** | A791 | Rhon Mountains | 1.10 | .65 |
| **1796** | A791 | Bavarian Alps | 1.10 | .75 |
| **1797** | A791 | Ore Mountains | 1.10 | .75 |
| **1798** | A791 | Main River Valley | 1.10 | .75 |
| **1799** | A791 | Mecklenburg lake district | 1.10 | .75 |
| **1800** | A791 | Franconian Switzerland | 1.00 | .75 |
| **1801** | A791 | Upper Lusatia | 1.00 | .75 |
| **1802** | A791 | Sauerland | 1.00 | .75 |
| **1803** | A791 | Havel River, Berlin | 1.00 | .75 |
| **1804** | A791 | Holstein Switzerland | 1.00 | .75 |
| **1805** | A791 | Saale | 1.00 | .75 |
| **1806** | A791 | Spreewald | 1.00 | .75 |
| **1807** | A791 | Eifel | 1.00 | .75 |
| | | *Nos. 1793-1807 (15)* | 15.70 | 10.95 |

Issued: #1793-1795, 7/15/93; #1796-1799, 7/14/94; #1800-1803, 7/6/95; #1804-1807, 4/11/96.

See #1938, 1974-1976, 2072-2073.

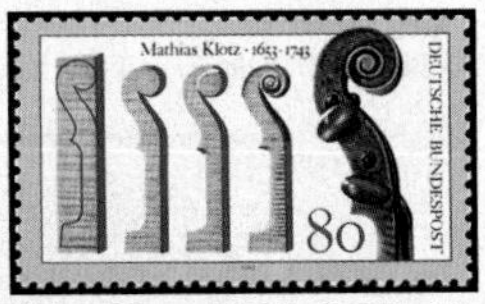


Mathias Klotz (1653-1743), Violin Maker — A792

**1993, Aug. 12 Litho.** ***Perf. 13x12½***

**1808** A792 80pf multicolored 1.00 .45

Heinrich George (1893-1946), Actor — A793

**1993, Aug. 12** ***Perf. 14***

**1809** A793 100pf multicolored 1.25 .50

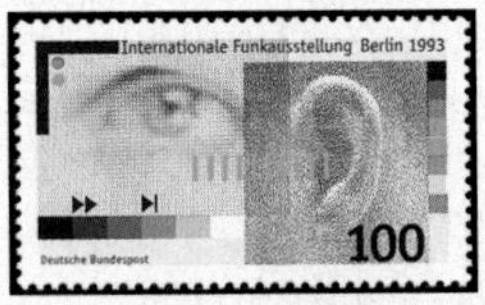


Intl. Radio Exhibition, Berlin — A794

**1993, Aug. 12**

**1810** A794 100pf multicolored 1.25 .50

Hans Leip (1893-1983), Poet and Painter A795

**1993, Sept. 16 Litho.** ***Perf. 13***

**1811** A795 100pf red, black & blue 1.50 .50

Birger Forell (1893-1958), Swedish Priest — A796

**1993, Sept. 16** ***Perf. 14***

**1812** A796 100pf multicolored 1.50 .70

Souvenir Sheet

For the Children — A797

**1993, Sept. 16**

**1813** A797 100pf multicolored 1.50 1.50

Peter I. Tchaikovsky (1840-93), Composer — A798

**1993, Oct. 14**

**1814** A798 80pf multicolored 1.25 .50

Max Reinhardt (1873-1943), Theatrical Director — A799

**1993, Oct. 14**

**1815** A799 100pf buff, black & red 1.50 .50

St. Hedwig of Silesia, 750th Death Anniv. — A800

**1993, Oct. 14**

**1816** A800 100pf multicolored 1.50 .50

See Poland No. 3176.

Paracelsus (1493-1541), Physician, Teacher — A801

**Litho. & Engr.**

**1993, Nov. 10** ***Perf. 14***

**1817** A801 100pf multicolored 1.50 .50

Claudio Monteverdi (1567-1643), Composer — A802

**1993, Nov. 10 Litho. *Perf. 13x12½***
**1818** A802 100pf multicolored 1.50 .50

Willy Brandt (1913-92), Statesman A803

**1993, Nov. 10 *Perf. 14***
**1819** A803 100pf multicolored 1.75 .90

Staade, 1000th Anniv. A804

**Litho. & Engr.**

**1994, Jan. 13. *Perf. 14***
**1820** A804 80pf multicolored 1.00 .50

Intl. Year of the Family A805

**1994, Jan. 13 Litho.**
**1821** A805 100pf multicolored 1.25 .65

Heinrich Hertz (1857-94), Physicist — A806

**1994, Jan. 13 *Perf. 13x12½***
**1822** A806 200pf multicolored 2.25 1.00

Frankfurt Am Main, 1200th Anniv. A807

**1994, Feb. 10**
**1823** A807 80pf multicolored 1.00 .50

Fulda, 1250th Anniv. A808

**1994, Mar. 10 *Perf. 14***
**1824** A808 80pf multicolored 1.00 .50

German Women's Associations, German Women's Council, Cent. — A809

**1994, Mar. 10 *Perf. 13x12½***
**1825** A809 100pf black, red & yellow 1.25 .60

Fourth European Parliamentary Elections — A810

**1994, Mar. 10 *Perf. 14***
**1826** A810 100pf multicolored 1.50 .65

Foreigners in Germany: Living Together — A811

**1994, Mar. 10**
**1827** A811 100pf multicolored 1.25 .65

Church of Our Lady, Munich, 500th Anniv. A812

**1994, Apr. 14 Litho. *Perf. 14***
**1828** A812 100pf multicolored 1.50 .75

Europa A813

Designs: 80pf, Ohm's Law, by Georg Simon Ohm. 100pf, Quantum theory, by Max Planck.

**1994, May 5 Photo.**
**1829** A813 80pf multicolored *1.00 .45*
**1830** A813 100pf multicolored *1.00 .45*

**Souvenir Sheet**

Carl Hagenbeck (1844-1913), Circus Director, Animal Trainer, and Berlin Zoo, 150th Anniv. — A814

Designs: a, Hagenbeck, circus animals, zoo entrance. b, Zoo entrance, animals.

**1994, May 5 Litho.**
**1831** A814 Sheet of 2 3.25 4.00
*a.* 100pf multicolored 1.00 .95
*b.* 200pf multicolored 2.00 2.00

Hans Pfitzner (1869-1949), Composer, Conductor — A815

**1994, May 5**
**1832** A815 100pf multicolored 1.25 .60

Spandau Fortress, 400th Anniv. A816

**1994, June 16 Litho. *Perf. 14***
**1833** A816 80pf multicolored 1.00 .50

Herzogsagmuhle, Social Welfare Organization, Cent. — A817

**1994, June 16 *Perf. 13***
**1834** A817 100pf blue, yel & blk 1.25 .60

Emperor Frederick II (1194-1250) A818

**1994, June 16 *Perf. 13½x14***
**1835** A818 400pf multicolored 4.25 3.25

**Souvenir Sheet**

Attempt to Assassinate Hitler, 50th Anniv. — A819

**1994, July 20 Litho. *Perf. 14***
**1836** A819 100pf multicolored 1.50 1.50

**Historic Sites Type of 1987**

No. 1838, Wernigerode Town Hall. No. 1839, Böttcherstrasse, Bremen. No. 1840, Berus Monument, Uberherrn. No. 1841, Wilhelmshöhe Hillside Park, Kassel. No. 1842, Kirchheim Castle. No. 1843, St. Reinoldi Church, Dortmund. No. 1844, Goethe-Schiller Monument. No. 1845, Schwerin Castle, Weimar. No. 1846, Bellevue Castle, Berlin. No. 1847, EXPO 2000, Hanover. No. 1848, Regensburg Stone Bridge. No. 1849, Brühl's Terrace, Dresden. No. 1850, St. Nikolai Cathedral, Greifswald. No. 1851, Grimma Town Hall. No. 1852, Wartburg Castle, Eisenach. No. 1853, Town hall, Bremen. No. 1854, Cologne Cathedral. No. 1855, Holsten Gate, Lübeck. No. 1856, Heidelberg Castle. No. 1857, Town Hall, Suhl-Heinrichs. No. 1858, Speyer Cathedral. No. 1859, St. Michael's Church, Hamburg. No. 1860, Hildesheim Town Hall.

**1994-2001 Typo. *Perf. 14***
**1838** A623 10pf multi .45 .25
**1839** A623 20pf dk bl & brn org .35 .35
**1840** A623 47pf green & gray .55 .45
**1841** A623 47pf dk grn & gray .45 .45
**1842** A623 50pf vio brn & beige .75 .50
**1843** A623 80pf dull grn & sepia .75 .60
**1844** A623 100pf blue & black .80 .75
*a.* Booklet pane of 10 9.00 9.00
Complete booklet, #1844a 9.00 9.00
**1845** A623 100pf multi 1.10 1.10
**1846** A623 110pf dark gray & buff 1.00 .35
*a.* Booklet pane of 10 11.50 11.50
Complete booklet, #1846a 11.50
**1847** A623 110pf org & bl 1.10 .50
*a.* Booklet pane of 10 13.50 13.50
Complete booklet, #1847a 13.50
**1848** A623 110pf multi 1.10 .75
*a.* Booklet pane of 10 12.50 12.50
Booklet, #1848a 13.50
**1849** A623 220pf grn & blk 1.60 .75
**1850** A623 220pf multi 2.25 1.90
**1851** A623 300pf brn & ind 2.25 2.00
**1852** A623 400pf vio brn & beige 4.50 3.00
**1853** A623 440pf multicolored 4.25 3.25
**1854** A623 440pf blk & gray 5.00 3.25
**1855** A623 510pf red brn & ind 5.00 3.75
**1856** A623 510pf brn & bis brn 5.50 4.25
**1857** A623 550pf multicolored 5.25 2.10
**1858** A623 640pf rose brn & gray bl 6.75 2.25
**1859** A623 690pf blk & grn 7.25 2.50
**1860** A623 720pf dk gray & lil 7.50 5.50
*Nos. 1838-1860 (23)* 65.50 40.55

Issued: 550pf, 8/11/94; 640pf, 8/10/95; 690pf, 6/13/96; 47pf, 7/17/97; #1846, #1849, #1853, 8/14/97: #1844, #1855, 8/28/97; #1847, 9/10/98; 10pf, #1848, 300pf, 9/28/00; #1845, 1/11/01. #1841, 80pf, 4/5/01. 720pf, 7/2/01. #1850, #1854, 8/9/01. 50pf, #1852, 9/5/01. 20pf, #1856, 11/8/01.

Johann Gottfried Herder (1744-1803), Theologian A820

**1994, Aug. 11 Photo. *Perf. 14***
**1862** A820 80pf multicolored 1.00 .50

**Paintings Type of 1993**

Designs: 100pf, Maika, by Christian Schad. 200pf, Landscape, by Erich Heckel. 300pf, Couple Lying on Grass, by Gabriele Munter.

**1994, Aug. 11 Litho. *Perf. 14***
**1863** A779 100pf multicolored 1.00 .60
**1864** A779 200pf multicolored 2.00 1.50
**1865** A779 300pf multicolored 3.00 2.40
*Nos. 1863-1865 (3)* 6.00 4.50

Ethnological Museum, Leipzig, 125th Anniv. — A821

**1994, Sept. 8 Litho. *Perf. 13x12½***
**1866** A821 80pf multicolored 1.00 .50

Hermann von Helmholtz (1821-94), Scientist — A822

**Litho. & Engr.**

**1994, Sept. 8 *Perf. 13½x14***
**1867** A822 100pf multicolored 1.40 .50

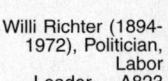

Willi Richter (1894-1972), Politician, Labor Leader — A823

**1994, Sept. 8** **Litho.**

**1868** A823 100pf multicolored 1.25 .50

Souvenir Sheet

For the Children — A824

**1994, Sept. 8** ***Perf. 14***

**1869** A824 100pf multicolored 1.50 1.50

Hans Sachs (1494-1576), Singer & Poet — A825

**1994, Oct. 13** **Engr.** ***Perf. 13½x14***

**1870** A825 100pf olive & maroon 1.25 .60

St. Wolfgang (924-94), Bishop of Regensburg A826

**1994, Oct. 13** **Litho.** ***Perf. 14***

**1871** A826 100pf multicolored 1.25 .60

Mail Delivery, Spreewald Region, c. 1900 — A827

**1994, Oct. 13**

**1872** A827 100pf multicolored 1.25 .60

Stamp Day.

Quedlinburg, 1000th Anniv. — A828

**Litho. & Engr.**

**1994, Nov. 9** ***Perf. 14***

**1873** A828 80pf multicolored 1.00 .50

Opening of the Berlin Wall, 5th Anniv. A829

**1994, Nov. 9** **Litho.** ***Perf. 13x12½***

**1874** A829 100pf black, org & yel 1.25 .60

Natl. Assoc. for Preservation of German Graves Abroad, 75th Anniv. — A830

**1994, Nov. 9** ***Perf. 14***

**1875** A830 100pf black & red 1.25 .60

Theodore Fontane (1819-98), Poet — A831

**1994, Nov. 9** ***Perf. 13½x14***

**1876** A831 100pf multicolored 1.25 .60

Baron Friedrich von Steuben (1730-94) A832

**1994, Nov. 9** ***Perf. 14***

**1877** A832 100pf multicolored 1.25 .60

**Paintings Type of 1992**

Designs: 100pf, The Water Tower in Bremen, by Franz Radziwill. 200pf, Still Life with a Cat, by Georg Schrimpf. 300pf, An Estate in Dangast, by Karl Schmidt-Rottluff.

**1995, Jan. 12** **Litho.** ***Perf. 14***

**1878** A753 100pf multicolored 1.00 .50
**1879** A753 200pf multicolored 2.00 1.50
**1880** A753 300pf multicolored 3.00 2.25
*Nos. 1878-1880 (3)* 6.00 4.25

Province of Gera, 1000th Anniv. — A833

**1995, Jan. 12** ***Perf. 13½x13***

**1881** A833 80pf multicolored .90 .50

Diet of Worms, 500th Anniv. A834

**1995, Jan. 12** ***Perf. 13x12½***

**1882** A834 100pf multicolored 1.00 .60

Frederick William of Brandenburg, the Great Elector (1620-88) A835

**1995, Feb. 9** **Litho.** ***Perf. 14***

**1883** A835 300pf multicolored 3.25 2.10

Conf. of General Convention on Climate, Berlin — A836

**1995, Mar. 9** **Litho.** ***Perf. 14***

**1884** A836 100pf multicolored 1.00 .60

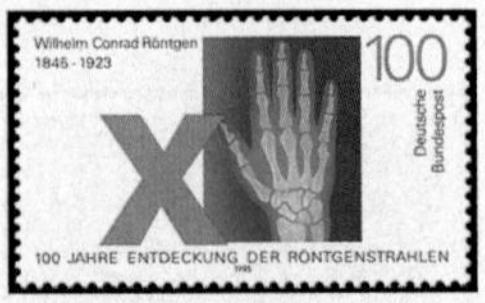


W.K. Roentgen (1845-1923) — A837

**1995, Mar. 9**

**1885** A837 100pf multicolored 1.00 .60

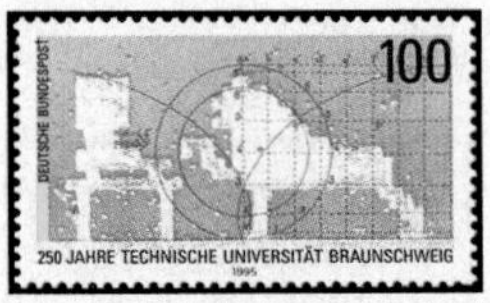


Carolo-Wilhelmina Technical University, Braunschweig, 250th Anniv. — A838

**1995, Mar. 9**

**1886** A838 100pf multicolored 1.00 .60

Former State of Mecklenburg, 1000th Anniv. — A839

**1995, Mar. 9**

**1887** A839 100pf multicolored 1.00 .60

City of Regensburg, 750th Anniv. — A840

**1995, Apr. 6** **Litho.** ***Perf. 14***

**1888** A840 80pf multicolored .90 .50

Freedom of Expression A841

**1995, Apr. 6** **Photo.**

**1889** A841 100pf multicolored 1.00 .60

Dietrich Bonhoeffer (1906-45), Protestant Theologian — A842

**1995, Apr. 6**

**1890** A842 100pf multicolored 1.00 .60

Johann Conrad Schlaun (1695-1773), Architect A843

**1995, Apr. 6** **Litho.** ***Perf. 13***

**1891** A843 200pf multicolored 2.00 1.60

Vincent Conferences in Germany, 150th Anniv. — A844

**1995, May 5** **Litho.** ***Perf. 14***

**1892** A844 100pf multicolored 1.00 .65

Schiller Society, Cent. — A845

**1995, May 5** **Photo.**

**1893** A845 100pf multicolored 1.00 .60

End of World War II, 50th Anniv. — A846

Designs: No. 1894, End of the war. 200pf, Moving towards United Europe.

No. 1896, Liberation of concentration camps. No. 1897: a, Destruction of buildings. b, Refugees.

**1995, May 5** **Litho.** ***Perf. 14***

**1894** A846 100pf red & black *1.00* *.55*
**1895** A846 200pf bl, gray, yel & blk *2.00* *1.00*

**Souvenir Sheets**

**1896** A846 100pf multicolored 1.10 *1.50*
**1897** Sheet of 2 2.25 *2.50*
***a.-b.*** A846 100pf any single 1.10 1.10

Europa (#1894-1895).

Kiel Canal, Cent. — A847

**1995, June 8** **Litho.** ***Perf. 14***

**1898** A847 80pf multicolored .90 .50

UN, 50th Anniv. — A848

**1995, June 8**

**1899** A848 100pf gold, lil & gray 1.00 .60

Radio, Cent. A849

**1995, June 8**
**1900** A849 100pf Marconi, wireless apparatus 1.25 .80

See Ireland Nos. 973-974, Italy 2038-2039, San Marino Nos. 1336-1337, Vatican City Nos. 978-979.

Carl Orff (1895-1982), Composer — A850

**1995, July 6 Litho. *Perf. 13x13½***
**1901** A850 100pf multicolored 1.00 .60

Henry the Lion, Duke of Bavaria (1129-95) A851

**1995, July 6 *Perf. 14***
**1902** A851 400pf multicolored 3.75 3.00

Kaiser Wilhelm Memorial Church, Berlin, Cent. — A852

**1995, Aug. 10 Photo. *Perf. 14***
**1903** A852 100pf multicolored 1.00 .60

Franz Werfel (1890-1945), Author — A853

**1995, Aug. 10 Litho.**
**1904** A853 100pf multicolored 1.00 .60

Franz Josef Strauss (1915-88), Politician A854

**1995, Sept. 6 Photo. *Perf. 14x13½***
**1905** A854 100pf multicolored 1.10 .75

Souvenir Sheet

German Film, Cent. — A855

**1995, Sept. 6 *Perf. 14***
**1906** A855 Sheet of 3 4.00 *4.75*
*a.* 80pf Metropolis .75 .75
*b.* 100pf Little Superman .90 .90
*c.* 200pf The Sky Over Berlin 2.10 2.10

Kurt Schumacher (1895-1952), Politician A856

**1995, Oct. 12 Litho. *Perf. 13***
**1907** A856 100pf multicolored 1.00 .60

Souvenir Sheet

For the Children — A857

**1995, Oct. 12 *Perf. 14***
**1908** A857 100pf multicolored 1.25 *1.50*

Leopold von Ranke (1795-1886), Historian A858

**1995, Nov. 9 Litho. *Perf. 14***
**1909** A858 80pf multicolored .85 .50

Paul Hindemith (1895-1963), Composer A859

**1995, Nov. 9**
**1910** A859 100pf multicolored 1.00 .60

Nobel Prize Fund Established, Cent. — A860

**1995, Nov. 9 Litho. & Engr.**
**1911** A860 100pf Nobel, last will 1.25 .90

See Sweden Nos. 2155-2158.

CARE, 50th Anniv. A861

**1995, Nov. 9 Litho. *Perf. 13x12½***
**1912** A861 100pf multicolored 1.00 .60

Victims of a Divided Germany, 1945-89 A862

**1995, Nov. 9 *Perf. 14***
**1913** A862 100pf Berlin Wall 1.00 .60

Borussia Dortmund, Soccer Champions — A863

**1995, Dec. 6 Photo. *Perf. 14***
**1914** A863 100pf multicolored 1.25 .75

Children's Missionary Work in Germany, Cent. — A864

**1996, Jan. 11 Litho. *Perf. 14***
**1915** A864 100pf multicolored .95 .65

Friedrich von Bodelschwingh (1877-1946), Protestant Theologian A865

**1996, Jan. 11 *Perf. 13½***
**1916** A865 100pf black & red .95 .65

Martin Luther (1483-1546), Theologian A866

**1996, Feb. 8 Litho. *Perf. 14***
**1917** A866 100pf multicolored 1.00 .80

Philipp Franz von Siebold (1796-1866), Physician and Diplomat — A867

**1996, Feb. 17 *Perf. 13x12½***
**1918** A867 100pf multicolored 1.00 .80

Cathedral Square, Halberstadt, 1000th Anniv. — A868

**1996, Mar. 7 Litho. *Perf. 13***
**1919** A868 80pf multicolored .80 .45

August Cardinal Graf von Galen (1878-1946) A869

**1996, Mar. 7 *Perf. 13½***
**1920** A869 100pf bl, gray & bis .95 .60

Giovanni Battista Tiepolo (1696-1770), Painter — A870

**1996, Mar. 7 *Perf. 13***
**1921** A870 200pf multicolored 2.00 1.40

**20th Century German Paintings Type of 1993**

Designs: 100pf, Sitting Female Nude, by Max Pechstein (1881-1955). 200pf, Abstract For Wilhelm Runge, by Georg Muche (1895-1987). 300pf, Still Life with Guitar, Book and Vase, by Helmut Kolle (1899-1931).

**1996, Mar. 7 *Perf. 14***
**1922** A779 100pf multicolored 1.10 .90
**1923** A779 200pf multicolored 2.40 1.75
**1924** A779 300pf multicolored 2.50 2.50
*Nos. 1922-1924 (3)* 6.00 5.15

Souvenir Sheet

For the Children — A871

**1996, Apr. 11 Litho. *Perf. 14***
**1925** A871 100pf Racing messenger 1.10 1.40

Famous Women — A872

Europa: 80pf, Self-portrait, by Paula Modersohn-Becker (1876-1907). 100pf, Self-portrait, by Käthe Kollwitz (1867-1945).

**1996, May 3**
**1926** A872 80pf multicolored *1.00 .35*
**1927** A872 100pf red & black *1.00 .75*

Freising's Right to Hold Markets, 1000th Anniv. A873

**1996, May 3**
**1928** A873 100pf multicolored 1.00 .65

Wolfgang Borchert (1921-47), Writer — A874

**1996, May 3** ***Perf. 13***
**1929** A874 100pf multicolored 1.00 .65

Ruhr Festival, Recklinghausen, 50th Anniv. — A875

**1996, May 3**
**1930** A875 100pf multicolored 1.00 .65

German Theater Assoc., 150th Anniv. — A876

**1996, May 3** **Photo.** ***Perf. 14***
**1931** A876 200pf multicolored 2.00 1.10

Academy of Arts in Berlin, 300th Anniv. A877

**1996, June 13** **Litho.** ***Perf. 13***
**1932** A877 100pf multicolored 1.00 .65

Gottfried Wilhelm Leibniz (1646-1716), Mathematician, Philosopher — A878

**1996, June 13** ***Perf. 14***
**1933** A878 100pf multicolored 1.00 .65

City of Heidelberg, 800th Anniv. — A879

**1996, July 18** **Litho.** ***Perf. 14***
**1934** A879 100pf multicolored 1.00 .65
Complete booklet, 10 #1934 10.00

UNICEF, 50th Anniv. A880

**1996, July 18**
**1935** A880 100pf multicolored 1.00 .65

Ludwig Thoma (1867-1921), Satirist A881

**1996, July 18** ***Perf. 13x13½***
**1936** A881 100pf multicolored 1.00 .65

Souvenir Sheet

German Natl. Parks — A882

**1996, July 18** ***Perf. 14***
**1937** Sheet of 3 6.50 6.50
*a.* A882 100pf Coastal 1.00 1.00
*b.* A882 200pf Mudflat 1.75 1.75
*c.* A882 300pf Sea-inlet 2.75 2.75

**Scenic Regions Type of 1993**

"Gendarmenmarkt," central district of Berlin.

**1996, Aug. 14** **Litho.** ***Perf. 14***
**1938** A791 100pf multicolored 1.00 .65

Assoc. of German Philatelists, 50th Anniv. — A883

**1996, Aug. 14** **Photo.** ***Perf. 14***
**1939** A883 100pf multicolored 1.00 .65

Paul Lincke (1866-1946), Musician, Composer A884

**1996, Aug. 14** **Litho.** ***Perf. 13***
**1940** A884 100pf multicolored 1.00 .65

UNESCO World Cultural Heritage A885

Design: Closed blast furnace, Völklingen.

**1996, Aug. 14** ***Perf. 13½***
**1941** A885 100pf multicolored 1.00 .65

German Civil Code, Cent. — A886

**1996, Aug. 14**
**1942** A886 300pf multicolored 3.00 2.25

Borussia Dortmund, Champion Soccer Club — A887

**1996, Aug. 27**
**1943** A887 100pf multicolored 1.00 .65

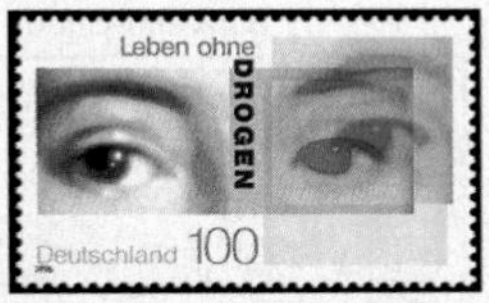


Life Without Drugs A888

**1996, Sept. 12** **Photo.** ***Perf. 14***
**1944** A888 100pf multicolored 1.00 .65

UNESCO World Cultural Heritage A889

Design: Old Town, Bamberg

**1996, Sept. 12** **Litho.** ***Perf. 14***
**1945** A889 100pf multicolored 1.00 .65

Homeopathic Medicine, Bicent. — A890

Samuel Hahnemann (1755-1843), physician.

**1996, Sept. 12** **Litho.** ***Perf. 14***
**1946** A890 400pf multicolored 4.00 3.00

Anton Bruckner (1824-96), Composer A891

**1996, Oct. 9** **Litho.** ***Perf. 13***
**1947** A891 100pf multicolored 1.00 .65

Donaueschingen Music Festival, 75th Anniv. — A892

**1996, Oct. 18** **Litho.** ***Perf. 13½***
**1948** A892 100pf multicolored 1.00 .65

Baron Ferdinand von Mueller (1825-96), Botanist — A893

**Litho. & Engr.**

**1996, Oct. 18** ***Perf. 14***
**1949** A893 100pf multicolored 1.00 .65

See Australia No. 1566.

Carl Zuckmayer (1896-1977), Playwright A894

**1996, Nov. 14** **Litho.** ***Perf. 13***
**1950** A894 100pf red, gray & blue 1.00 .65

Carlo Schmid (1896-1979), Politician, Scholar & Writer — A895

**1996, Dec. 3** **Photo.** ***Perf. 14***
**1951** A895 100pf multicolored 1.00 .65

Franz Schubert (1797-1828), Composer A896

**1997, Jan. 16** **Litho.** ***Perf. 14***
**1952** A896 100pf multicolored 1.00 .65

Sepp Herberger (1897-1977), Soccer Coach — A897

**1997, Jan. 16**
**1953** A897 100pf multicolored 1.00 .65

Traffic Safety for Children A898

**1997, Jan. 16**
**1954** A898 100pf multicolored 1.00 .65

See No. 1979.

Philipp Melanchthon (1497-1560), Protestant Reformer A899

**1997, Feb. 4** **Litho.** ***Perf. 14***
**1955** A899 100pf multicolored 1.00 .65

Cologne Carnival, 175th Anniv. — A900

**1997, Feb. 4**
**1956** A900 100pf multicolored 1.00 .65

Chancellor Ludwig Erhard (1897-1977) A901

**1997, Feb. 4** **Photo.**
**1957** A901 100pf multicolored 1.00 .65

Leipzig Fair, 500th Anniv. A902

**1997, Mar. 6** ***Perf. 13x12½***
**1958** A902 100pf red, sil & blue 1.00 .65

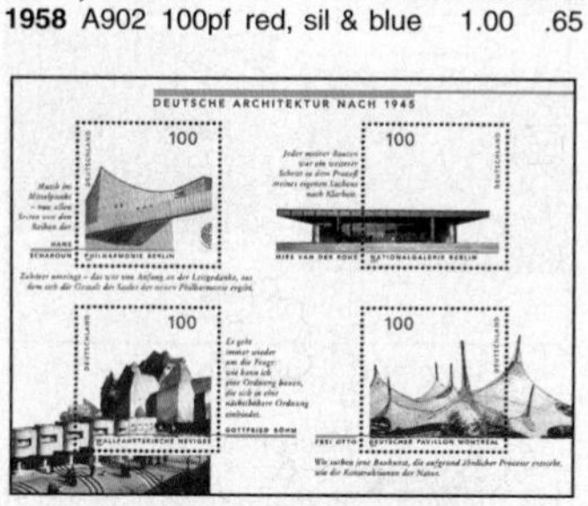


German Architecture after 1945 — A903

Building, architect: a, Berlin Philharmonic, by Hans Scharoun. b, New National Gallery, Berlin, by Ludwig Mies van der Rohe. c, St. Mary, Queen of Peace Church, Neviges, by Gottfried Böhm. d, German Pavilion, 1967 World's Fair, Montreal, by Frei Otto.

**1997, Mar. 6** **Litho.** ***Perf. 14***
**1959** A903 Sheet of 4 4.50 4.50
*a.-d.* 100pf any single 1.00 1.00

City of Straubing, 1100th Anniv. — A904

**1997, Mar. 10** ***Perf. 13x12½***
**1960** A904 100pf multicolored 1.00 .65

Heinrich von Stephan (1831-97) — A905

**1997, Apr. 8** **Litho.** ***Perf. 14***
**1961** A905 100pf multicolored 1.00 .65

Augustusburg and Falkenlust Castles, UNESCO World Heritage Sites — A906

**1997, Apr. 8**
**1962** A906 100pf multicolored 1.00 .65

Idar-Oberstein Gem & Jewelry Industry, 500th Anniv. — A907

**1997, Apr. 8** ***Perf. 13½***
**1963** A907 300pf multicolored 3.25 2.25

St. Adalbert (956-997) — A908

**1997, Apr. 23** **Engr.** ***Perf. 14***
**1964** A908 100pf deep violet 1.00 .65

See Poland #3337, Czech Republic #3012, Hungary #3569, Vatican City #1040.

Stories and Legends A909

Europa: 80pf, Fisherman and his Wife. 100pf, Rübezahl of Riesengebirge (Giant Mountains).

**1997, May 5** **Litho.** ***Perf. 14***
**1965** A909 80pf multicolored *1.00 .60*
**1966** A909 100pf multicolored *1.00 .75*

Sister Cities Movement, 50th Anniv. — A910

**1997, May 5**
**1967** A910 100pf multicolored 1.10 .65

Souvenir Sheet

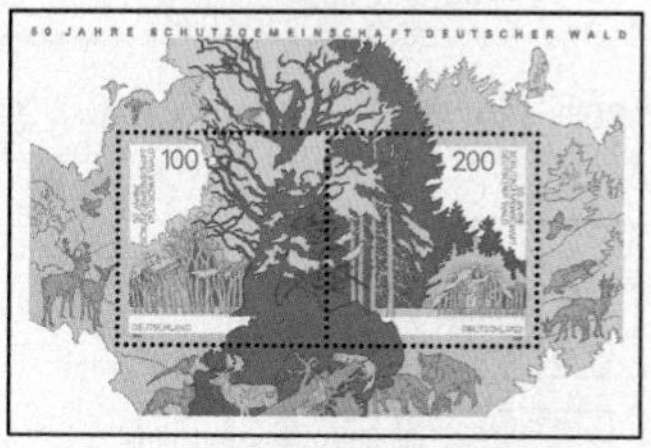


Society for Protection of German Forests, 50th Anniv. — A911

**1997, May 5**
**1968** A911 Sheet of 2 3.25 3.25
*a.* 100pf multicolored 1.10 1.10
*b.* 200pf multicolored 2.00 2.00

Fr. Sebastian Kneipp (1821-97), Hydrotherapist A912

**1997, June 9** ***Perf. 13***
**1969** A912 100pf multicolored 1.00 .65

Marshall Plan, 50th Anniv. A913

**1997, June 9** ***Perf. 13***
**1970** A913 100pf multicolored 1.10 .65

"Documenta" Intl. Exhibition of Modern Art, Kassel — A914

Designs: a, Composition, by Fritz Winter, 1956. b, Mouth No. 15, by Tom Wesselmann, 1968. c, Quathlamba, by Frank Stella, 1964. d, Video sculpture, Beuys/Bois, by Nam June Paik.

**1997, June 20** **Litho.** ***Perf. 14***
**1971** A914 100pf Sheet of 4, #a.-d. 4.25 4.25

Müngsten Bridge, Cent. — A915

**1997, June 20** **Litho.** ***Perf. 13½***
**1972** A915 100pf multicolored 1.00 .65

Souvenir Sheet

For the Children — A916

**1997, July 17** **Photo.** ***Perf. 13½***
**1973** A916 100pf multicolored 1.10 1.40

### Scenic Regions Type of 1993

#1974, Bavarian Forest. #1975, Lüneburg Heath. #1976, North German Moorland.

**1997, Aug. 28** **Litho.** ***Perf. 14***
**1974** A791 110pf multicolored 1.10 .90
**1975** A791 110pf multicolored 1.10 .90
**1976** A791 110pf multicolored 1.10 .90
*Nos. 1974-1976 (3)* 3.30 2.70

Centenary of Rudolf Diesel's Engine A917

**1997, Aug. 28** ***Perf. 13***
**1977** A917 300pf blue & gray 3.00 2.25

Cultivation of Potatoes in Germany, 350th Anniv. — A918

**1997, Sept. 17** **Litho.** ***Perf. 13***
**1978** A918 300pf multicolored 3.00 2.25

### Traffic Safety for Children Type

**1997, Oct. 9** **Litho.** ***Perf. 14***
**1979** A898 10pf like #1954 .25 .25

Felix Mendelssohn-Bartholdy (1809-47), Composer — A919

**1997, Oct. 9** *Perf. 13x13½*
**1980** A919 110pf multicolored 1.10 .75

FC Bayern Munchen, 1997 German Soccer Champions — A920

**1997, Oct. 16** **Photo.** *Perf. 14*
**1981** A920 110pf multicolored 1.10 .75

Third Saar-Lorraine-Luxembourg Summit — A921

**1997, Oct. 16** **Litho.**
**1982** A921 110pf multicolored 1.10 .75

See Luxembourg #972, France #2613.

Charitable Assoc. of the German Catholic Church, Cent. — A922

**1997, Nov. 6** **Photo.** *Perf. 14*
**1983** A922 110pf multicolored 1.10 .75

Heinrich Heine (1797-1856), Poet — A923

**1997, Nov. 6** **Litho.** *Perf. 13*
**1984** A923 110pf multicolored *1.25 .75*

No. 1984 was sold in sheets of 10. It was withdrawn from sale 11/18/97, because runes associated with Nazi Germany were printed on the decorative selvage of the sheet. Value of withdrawn sheet of 10, $35. It was again placed on sale in sheets with runes removed.

Gerhard Tersteegen (1697-1769), Author of Religious Hymns, Booklets — A924

**1997, Nov. 6** *Perf. 14*
**1985** A924 110pf multicolored 1.10 .75

Thomas Dehler (1897-1967), Politician — A925

**1997, Nov. 6**
**1986** A925 110pf multicolored 1.10 .75

Cistercian Monastery Maulbronn, UNESCO World Heritage Site — A926

**1998, Jan. 22** **Litho.** *Perf. 14*
**1987** A926 100pf multicolored 1.10 .75

Glienicke Bridge, Berlin — A927

**1998, Jan. 22**
**1988** A927 110pf multicolored 1.10 .75

City of Nördlingen, 1100th Anniv. — A928

**1998, Jan. 22**
**1989** A928 110pf multicolored 1.10 .75
*a.* Booklet pane of 10 11.50
Complete booklet, #1989a + 20 self-adhesive labels 12.00

Bertolt Brecht (1898-1956), Playwright A929

**1998, Feb. 5**
**1990** A929 110pf multicolored 1.10 .75

Max Planck Society for Advancement of Science, 50th Anniv. — A930

**1998, Feb. 5**
**1991** A930 110pf multicolored 1.10 .75

Town of Bad Frankenhausen, 1000th Anniv. — A931

**1998, Mar. 12** **Litho.** *Perf. 13*
**1992** A931 110pf multicolored 1.10 .75

Peace of Westphalia, End of Thirty Years' War, 350th Anniv. — A932

**1998, Mar. 12** *Perf. 14*
**1993** A932 110pf black & red 1.10 .75

German State Parliament Buildings — A933

Designs: No. 1994, Baden-Württemberg. No. 1995, Bavaria. No. 1996, Chamber of Deputies, Berlin. No. 1997, Brandenburg.

**1998, Mar. 12**
**1994** A933 110pf multicolored 1.25 .75
**1995** A933 110pf multicolored 1.25 .75
**1996** A933 110pf multicolored 1.25 .75
**1997** A933 110pf multicolored 1.25 .75
*Nos. 1994-1997 (4)* 5.00 3.00

See Nos 2027, 2029-2031, 2074-2076, 2113-2116.

Hildegard von Bingen (1098-1179), Christian Mystic — A934

**1998, Apr. 16**
**1998** A934 100pf multicolored 1.00 .75

Cistercian Abbey of St. Marienstern, Panschwitz-Kuckau, 750th Anniv. — A935

**1998, Apr. 16** *Perf. 13x12½*
**1999** A935 110pf multicolored 1.10 .75

Souvenir Sheet

For the Children — A936

**1998, Apr. 16** *Perf. 14*
**2000** A936 110pf multicolored 1.25 1.25

Bayreuth Opera, 250th Anniv. — A937

**1998, Apr. 16** *Perf. 13½*
**2001** A937 300pf multicolored 3.25 2.40

Ernst Jünger (1895-1998), Writer — A938

**1998, Apr. 22** *Perf. 14*
**2002** A938 110pf multicolored 1.10 .75

German Rural Women's Assoc. A939

**1998, May 7** **Litho.** *Perf. 13*
**2003** A939 110pf multicolored 1.10 .75

Europa and German Reunification Day — A940

**1998, May 7** *Perf. 14½x14*
**2004** A940 110pf multicolored 1.10 .75

Souvenir Sheet

German Constitution — A941

Designs: a, Parliamentary Council, Bonn, 1948, convening to draw up constitution. b, Natl. Assembly, St. Paul's Church, Frankfurt, 1848, electing pan-German constitutional Parliament.

**1998, May 7** *Perf. 14*

| | | | |
|---|---|---|---|
| **2005** A941 Sheet of 2 | | 3.50 | 3.50 |
| *a.* | 110pf multicolored | 1.00 | 1.00 |
| *b.* | 220pf multicolored | 2.00 | 2.00 |

Congress of German Catholics, 150th Anniv. — A942

**1998, June 10 Litho.** *Perf. 13x13½*

**2006** A942 110pf multicolored 1.25 .70

Deutsche Mark, 50th Anniv. — A943

**1998, June 19** *Perf. 13*

**2007** A943 110pf multicolored 1.25 .90

German Cultivation of Hops — A944

**1998, July 16 Litho.** *Perf. 13*

**2008** A944 110pf multicolored 1.10 .75

Founding of the European Central Bank, Frankfurt am Main — A945

**1998, July 16 Photo.** *Perf. 14*

**2009** A945 110pf multicolored 1.10 .70

Souvenir Sheet

Saxon Switzerland Natl. Park — A945a

**1998, July 16 Litho.** *Perf. 14*

| | | | |
|---|---|---|---|
| **2009A** A945a Sheet of 2 | | 3.50 | 3.50 |
| *b.* | 110pf multicolored | 1.00 | 1.00 |
| *c.* | 220pf multicolored | 2.00 | 2.00 |

1998 Intl. Congress of Mathematicians, Berlin — A946

**1998, Aug. 20 Photo.** *Perf. 14x13½*

**2010** A946 110pf multicolored 1.10 .75

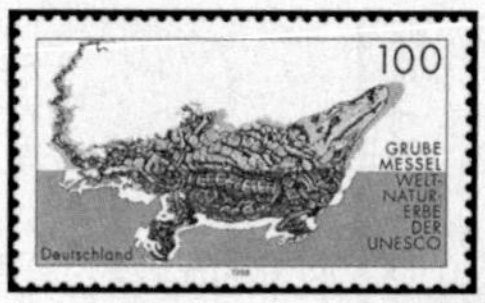


Grube Messel Fossil Beds A947

Würzburg Palace, Germany — A948

UNESCO World Heritage Sites: No. 2013, Puning Temple, Chengde, People's Republic of China.

**1998, Aug. 20 Litho.** *Perf. 13x12½*

**2011** A947 100pf multicolored 1.00 .65

*Perf. 13½x14*

**2012** A948 110pf multicolored 1.10 .70
**2013** A948 110pf multicolored 1.10 .70

See China People's Republic #2887-2888.

Souvenir Sheet

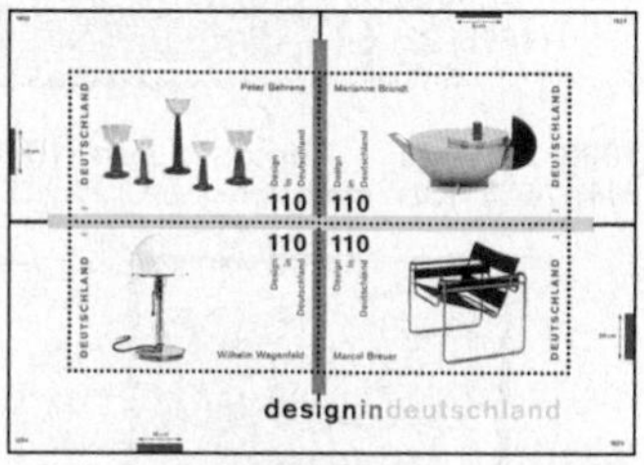


20th Cent. German Design — A949

Designs: a, Glassware, by Peter Behrens, 1910. b, Teapot, by Marianne Brandt, 1924. c, Desk lamp, by Wilhelm Wagenfeld, 1924. d, "Wassily" chair, by Marcel Breuer, 1926.

**1998, Aug. 20** *Perf. 14*

| | | | |
|---|---|---|---|
| **2014** | Sheet of 4 | 4.75 | 4.75 |
| *a.-d.* | A949 110pf any single | 1.10 | 1.10 |

See No. 2051.

Manfred Hausmann (1898-1986), Author — A950

**1998, Sept. 10 Litho.** *Perf. 14*

**2015** A950 110pf multicolored 1.10 .75

A951

**1998, Sept. 10**

**2016** A951 110pf multicolored 1.10 .75

Team 1 FC Kaiserslautern, 1998 German soccer champions.

Prevent Child Abuse — A952

**1998, Sept. 10**

**2017** A952 110pf black & red 1.10 .75

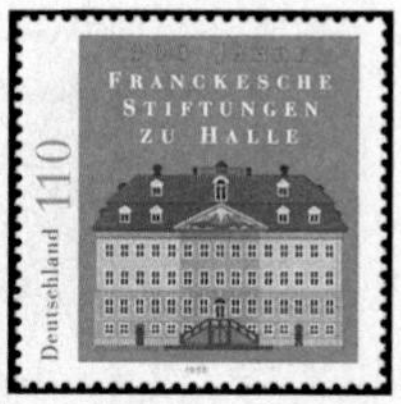


Francke Charitable Institutions, Halle, 300th Anniv. — A953

**1998, Sept. 10** *Perf. 13*

**2018** A953 110pf Building 1.10 .75

Mail Boat, "Hiorten" A954

**1998, Oct. 8 Litho.** *Perf. 14*

**2019** A954 110pf multicolored 1.10 .75

Stamp Day.

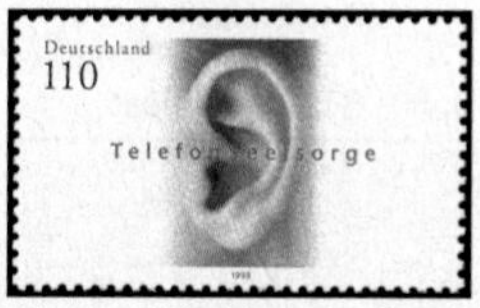


Telephone Help Lines for People in Distress — A955

**1998, Oct. 8** *Perf. 13x12½*

**2020** A955 110pf multicolored 1.10 .75

Günther Ramin (1898-1956), Organist, Choir Leader — A956

**1998, Oct. 8 Photo.** *Perf. 14x14½*

**2021** A956 300pf multicolored 3.00 2.25

Saxony State Orchestra, Dresden, 450th Anniv. — A957

**1998, Nov. 12 Litho.** *Perf. 14*

**2022** A957 300pf multicolored 3.00 2.25

Universal Delcaration of Human Rights, 50th Anniv. — A958

**1998, Nov. 12** *Perf. 13x12½*

**2023** A958 110pf multicolored 1.10 .75

See No. B848.

Weimar, 1999 European City of Culture, 1100th Anniv. — A959

**1999, Jan. 14 Litho.** *Perf. 14*

| | | | |
|---|---|---|---|
| **2024** A959 100pf multicolored | | 1.10 | .80 |
| *a.* | Booklet pane of 10 | 12.50 | 12.50 |
| | Complete booklet, #2024a + 20 labels | 12.50 | |

The self-adhesive labels are part of the booklet cover.

International Year of the Elderly A960

**1999, Jan. 14** *Perf. 13*

**2025** A960 110pf multicolored 1.10 .80

Katharina von Bora (1499-1552), Wife of Martin Luther, from Painting by Lucas Cranach A961

**1999, Jan. 14** *Perf. 14*

**2026** A961 110pf multicolored 1.10 .80

**State Parliaments Type of 1998**

The Hessian Parliament.

**1999, Jan. 14**

**2027** A933 110pf multicolored 1.10 .80

Erich Kästner (1899-1974), Writer — A963

**1999, Feb. 18 Litho.** *Perf. 13*

**2028** A963 300pf multicolored 3.00 2.40

**State Parliaments Type of 1998**

Buildings: No. 2029, Hamburg. No. 2030, Mecklenburg-Western Pomerania. No. 2031, Bremen City Parliament.

**1999 Litho.** *Perf. 14*

| | | | |
|---|---|---|---|
| **2029** A933 110pf multicolored | | 1.10 | .80 |
| **2030** A933 110pf multicolored | | 1.10 | .80 |
| **2031** A933 110pf multicolored | | 1.10 | .80 |
| | *Nos. 2029-2031 (3)* | 3.30 | 2.40 |

Issued: #2029-2030, 3/11; #2031, 4/27.

NATO, 50th Anniv. A963a

**1999, Mar. 11** **Photo.**
**2032** A963a 110pf multicolored 1.10 .80

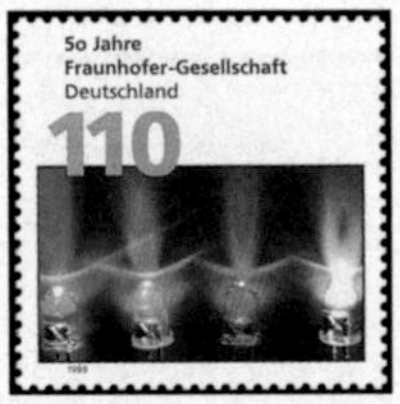


Fraunhofer Society, 50th Anniv. — A964

**1999, Mar. 11** **Litho.** ***Perf. 13***
**2033** A964 110pf multicolored 1.10 .80

Expo 2000, Hanover A965

**1999, Apr. 27**
**2034** A965 110pf multicolored 1.10 .80

See No. 2083.

German Automobile Club, Cent. — A966

**1999, Apr. 27** **Photo.**
**2035** A966 110pf multicolored 1.10 .80

German Cancer Relief Organization, 25th Anniv. — A967

**1999, Apr. 27** **Litho.** ***Perf. 13***
**2036** A967 110pf multicolored 1.10 .80

Knights of St. John of Jerusalem and Knights of Malta, 900th Anniv. — A968

**1999, May 4**
**2037** A968 110pf multicolored 1.10 .80

Berlin Airlift, 1948-49 A969

**1999, May 4** **Photo.** ***Perf. 14***
**2038** A969 110pf multicolored 1.10 .80

Council of Europe, 50th Anniv. — A970

**1999, May 4** **Litho.** ***Perf. 13***
**2039** A970 110pf multicolored 1.10 .80

Souvenir Sheet

Berchtesgaden Natl. Park — A971

**1999, May 4** ***Perf. 14***
**2040** A971 110pf multicolored *1.40* *1.60*

Europa.

Souvenir Sheet

Basic Law, 50th Anniv. — A972

**1999, May 21** **Litho.** ***Perf. 14***
**2041** A972 110pf multicolored 1.25 1.25

Souvenir Sheet

Federal Republic of Germany, 50th Anniv. — A973

Scenes from 1949, 1999: a, Leaders gathering, session of Parliament. b, Child carrying wood, child picking flower. c, Building "The Wall," people walking where "The Wall" has been removed. d, Soldiers, government assembly.

**1999, May 21**
**2042** Sheet of 4 4.50 4.50
***a.-d.*** A973 110pf any single 1.10 1.10

SOS Children's Village, 50th Anniv. — A974

**1999, June 10** **Litho.** ***Perf. 13¾x14***
**2043** A974 110pf multicolored 1.10 .75

Paderborn Bishopric, 1200th Anniv. — A975

**1999, June 10** ***Perf. 14***
**2044** A975 110pf multicolored 1.10 .75

Johann Strauss, the Younger (1825-99) A976

**1999, June 10** **Photo.** ***Perf. 13¾***
**2045** A976 300pf multicolored 3.25 2.25

Dominikus-Ringeisen Institution, Ursberg, 115th Anniv. — A977

**1999, July 15** **Litho.**
**2046** A977 110pf multicolored 1.10 .75

Pres. Gustav Heinemann (1899-1976) A978

**1999, July 15**
**2047** A978 110pf multicolored 1.10 .75

Cultural Foundation of the Federal States — A979

Sculpture: 110pf, Old Woman Smiling, by Ernst Barlach (1870-1938). 220pf, Bust of a Thinker, by Wilhelm Lehmbruck (1881-1919).

**1999, July 15** **Photo.** ***Perf. 14***
**2048** A979 110pf multicolored 1.25 .80
**2049** A979 220pf multicolored 2.10 1.50

First Peace Conference in The Hague, Cent. — A980

**1999, July 15** **Litho.** ***Perf. 13¼x13***
**2050** A980 300pf multicolored 3.25 2.10

**20th Cent. German Design Type of 1998**

Souvenir Sheet

Designs: a, HF1 Television set, by Herbert Hirche, 1958. b, Knife, fork, spoon and teaspoon, by Peter Raacke, 1959. c, Pearl bottle, by Günter Kupetz, 1969. d, "Transrapid," Maglev train, by Alexander Neumeister, 1982.

**1999, Aug. 12** **Litho.** ***Perf. 14***

**Souvenir Sheet**

**2051** Sheet of 4 4.50 4.50
***a.-d.*** A949 110pf any single 1.10 1.10

Johann Wolfgang von Goethe (1749-1832), Poet — A981

**1999, Aug. 12** ***Perf. 13¾***
**2052** A981 110pf multicolored 1.10 .80

Souvenir Sheet

For the Children — A982

**1999, Aug. 12** ***Perf. 13¼***
**2053** A982 110pf multicolored 1.10 1.10

Bayern München, 1999 German Soccer Champions — A983

**1999, Sept. 16** **Litho.** ***Perf. 14***
**2054** A983 110pf multicolored 1.10 .80

Federal Association of German Book Traders Peace Prize, 50th Anniv. — A984

**1999, Sept. 16** **Photo.** ***Perf. 13¾***
**2055** A984 110pf multicolored 1.10 .80

Richard Strauss (1864-1949), Composer A985

**1999, Sept. 16 Litho. *Perf. 13¼***

**2056** A985 300pf multicolored 3.25 2.40

Göltzsch Valley Bridge A986

**1999, Oct. 14 Litho. *Perf. 14***

**2057** A986 110pf multicolored 1.10 .80

German Federation of Trade Unions, 50th Anniv. — A987

**1999, Oct. 14**

**2058** A987 110pf red & black 1.10 .80

Endangered Species A988

**1999, Nov. 4 Litho. *Perf. 13¾***

**2059** A988 100pf Large horse-shoe bat 1.00 .80

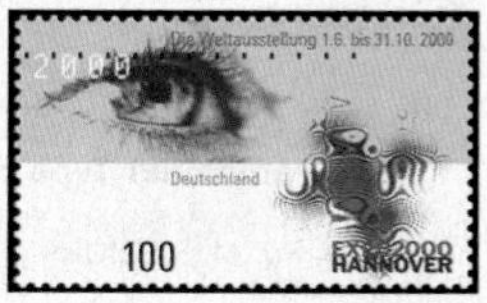


EXPO 2000, Hanover A989

**2000, Jan. 13 Litho. *Perf. 14x14¼***

**2060** A989 100pf multi 1.10 .80

See No. 2094.

Holy Year 2000 — A990

**2000, Jan. 13 *Perf. 13¾***

**2061** A990 110pf multi 1.10 .80

Completion of Aachen Cathedral, 1200th Anniv. — A991

**2000, Jan. 13**

**2062** A991 110pf Charlemagne 1.10 .80

German Soccer Assoc., Cent. — A992

**2000, Jan. 13 Photo.**

**2063** A992 110pf multi 1.10 .80

Value is for stamp with surrounding selvage.

Herbert Wehner (1906-90), Politician A993

**2000, Jan. 13**

**2064** A993 110pf multi 1.10 .80

Albert Schweitzer (1875-1965), Humanitarian A994

**2000, Jan. 13 Litho. *Perf. 14x13¾***

**2065** A994 110pf multi 1.10 .80

Prevention of Violence Against Women — A995

**2000, Jan. 13 *Perf. 14***

**2066** A995 110pf multi 1.10 .80

Berlin Intl. Film Festival, 50th Anniv. A996

**2000, Feb. 17 Litho. *Perf. 14***

**2067** A996 100pf multi 1.00 .80

Johannes Gutenberg (c. 1400-1468) A997

**2000, Feb. 17 *Perf. 13¾***

**2068** A997 110pf red & black 1.10 .80

Friedrich Ebert (1871-1925), President of German Reich — A998

**2000, Feb. 17 Photo.**

**2069** A998 110pf multi 1.25 .80

Düsseldorf Carnival, 175th Anniv. — A999

**2000, Feb. 17 Litho. *Perf. 13x13½***

**2070** A999 110pf multi 1.10 .80

Kurt Weill (1900-50), Composer — A1000

**2000, Feb. 17 *Perf. 14***

**2071** A1000 300pf multi 3.25 2.40

**Scenic Regions Type of 1993**

Design: #2072, Passau. #2073, Saar River bend, Mettlach.

**2000 Litho. *Perf. 13¾x14***

**2072** A791 110pf multi 1.25 .80
**2073** A791 110pf multi 1.25 .80

Issued: No. 2072, 3/16.

**State Parliament Building Type**

#2074, Lower Saxony. #2075, North Rhine-Westphalia. #2076, Rhineland-Palatinate. #2077, Saarland.

**2000 Litho. *Perf. 13¾x14***

**2074** A933 110pf multi 1.10 .80
**2075** A933 110pf multi 1.10 .80
**2076** A933 110pf multi 1.10 .80

***Perf. 14***

**2077** A933 110pf multi 1.10 .80
*Nos. 2074-2077 (4)* 4.40 3.20

Issued: #2074, 3/16; #2075, 4/13; #2076, 8/14; #2077, 11/9.

Pinwheel A1001

**2000, Mar. 16 Litho. *Perf. 13¾***

**2078** A1001 110pf multi 1.25 .80

Souvenir Sheet

Hainich National Park — A1002

**2000, Mar. 16 *Perf. 13¼***

**2079** A1002 110pf multi 1.25 1.25

Blue Wonder Bridge, Dresden A1003

**2000, Apr. 13 Litho. *Perf. 13¼***

**2080** A1003 100pf multi 1.10 .75

**Cultural Foundation Type of 1999**

Designs: 110pf, The Expulsion from Paradise, sculpture by Leonhard Kern. 220pf, Silver table fountain, 1652-53, by Melchior Gelb.

**2000, Apr. 13 *Perf. 14x14¼***

**2081** A979 110pf multi 1.25 .75
**2082** A979 220pf multi 2.10 1.60

**Expo 2000 Type of 1999**

**2000, Apr. 13 *Die Cut Perf. 11***

**Booklet Stamp**

**Self-Adhesive**

**2083** A965 110pf multi 4.00 3.75
*a.* Booklet pane of 10 42.50

No. 2083a is a complete booklet.

Griefswald, 750th Anniv. — A1004

**Litho. & Engr.**

**2000, Apr. 13 *Perf. 14x14¼***

**2084** A1004 110pf multi 1.10 .80

Nikolaus Ludwig von Zinzendorf (1700-60), Religious Leader A1005

**2000, May 12 Photo. *Perf. 13¾***

**2085** A1005 110pf multi 1.10 .75

**Europa, 2000**

Common Design Type

**2000, May 12 Litho. *Perf. 13¾***

**2086** CD17 110pf multi *1.40 .80*

**Booklet Stamp**

**Self-Adhesive**

***Die Cut Perf. 10¾***

**2087** CD17 110pf multi *1.50 1.25*
*a.* Complete booklet of 10 *17.50*

Einkommende Zeitungen, First Daily Newspaper, 350th Anniv. — A1006

**2000, June 8 Litho. *Perf. 13¾x14***

**2088** A1006 110pf multi 1.10 .80

Chambers of Handicrafts in Germany, Cent. — A1007

**2000, June 8 *Perf. 14***

**2089** A1007 300pf gray & org 3.25 2.40

Zugspitze Weather Station, Cent. — A1008

**2000, July 13 Litho.** ***Perf. 13¾x14***
**2090** A1008 100pf multi 1.10 .80

Federal Disaster Relief Organization, 50th Anniv. — A1009

**2000, July 13** ***Perf. 14***
**2091** A1009 110pf multi 1.25 .80

Johann Sebastian Bach (1685-1750) A1010

**2000, July 13** ***Perf. 13¼***
**2092** A1010 110pf multi 1.10 .80

First Zeppelin Flight, Cent. — A1011

**2000, July 13**
**2093** A1011 110pf multi 1.25 .80

### Expo 2000 Type of 2000

110pf, Expo emblem, Earth, fingerprint.

**2000, Aug. 14 Litho.** ***Perf. 14x14¼***
**2094** A989 110pf multi 1.25 .80

Friedrich Nietzsche (1844-1900), Philosopher A1012

**2000, Aug. 14** ***Perf. 13¼***
**2095** A1012 110pf multi 1.25 .80

Ernst Wiechert (1887-1950), Writer A1013

**2000, Aug. 14** ***Perf. 13¾***
**2096** A1013 110pf multi 1.25 .80

"For You" — A1014

**2000, Sept. 14 Litho.** ***Perf. 13x13¼***
**2097** A1014 100pf multi 1.00 .80

Souvenir Sheet

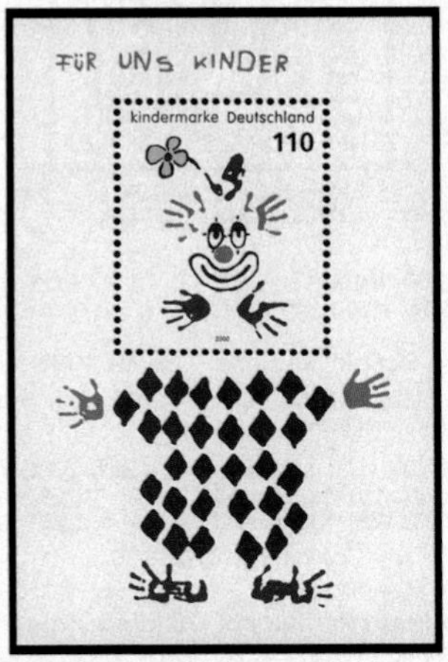


For the Children — A1015

**2000, Sept. 14** ***Perf. 13¾x14***
**2098** A1015 110pf multi 1.25 1.25

Adolph Kolping (1813-65) A1016

**2000, Sept. 14** ***Perf. 13¼***
**2099** A1016 110pf multi 1.25 .80

Kolping Society, 150th anniv.

Federal Court of Justice, 50th Anniv. A1017

**Litho. & Engr.**

**2000, Sept. 14** ***Perf. 14x14¼***
**2100** A1017 110pf multi 1.25 .80

Bernhard Nocht Institute for Tropical Medicine, Cent. — A1018

**2000, Sept. 14 Litho.** ***Perf. 13¾x14***
**2101** A1018 300pf multi 3.25 2.50

Reunification of Germany, 10th Anniv. A1019

**2000, Sept. 28** ***Perf. 13¼***
**2102** A1019 110pf multi 1.10 .80

Stamp Day — A1020

**2000, Oct. 12 Litho.** ***Perf. 13x13¼***
**2103** A1020 110pf multi 1.10 .80

Rainer Maria Rilke (1875-1926), Poet — A1021

**2000, Nov. 9 Litho.** ***Perf. 13¼x13½***
**2104** A1021 110pf multi 1.10 .80

Arnold Bode (1900-77), Artist — A1022

**2000, Nov. 9** ***Perf. 13¼***
**2105** A1022 110pf red & black 1.10 .80

Leonhart Fuchs (1501-66), Botanist A1023

**2001, Jan. 11 Litho.** ***Perf. 13¾***
**2106** A1023 100pf multi 1.25 .70

Kingdom of Prussia, 300th Anniv. A1024

**2001, Jan. 11** ***Perf. 14***
**2107** A1024 110pf multi 1.40 1.00

Association of Disabled War Veterans, 50th Anniv. — A1025

**2001, Jan. 11 Photo.** ***Perf. 14***
**2108** A1025 110pf multi 1.40 1.00

Youth Helpline Federation — A1026

**2001, Jan. 11 Litho.** ***Perf. 13¾x14***
**2109** A1026 110pf multi 1.40 1.00

Albert Lortzing (1801-51), Opera Composer A1027

**2001, Jan. 11** ***Perf. 13¾***
**2110** A1027 110pf multi 1.40 1.00

Martin Bucer (1491-1551), Theologian A1028

**2001, Feb. 8 Litho.** ***Perf. 13¾***
**2111** A1028 110pf multi 1.40 1.00

Johann Heinrich Voss (1751-1826), Translator of Greek Classics A1029

**2001, Feb. 8** ***Perf. 13¼***
**2112** A1029 300pf multi 3.75 2.75

See No. 2157.

### State Parliament Type of 1998

Design: No. 2113, Saxony. No. 2114, Saxony-Anhalt. No. 2115, Schleswig-Holstein. No. 2116, Thuringia.

**2001 Litho.** ***Perf. 13¾x14***
**2113** A933 110pf multi 1.40 1.00
**2114** A933 110pf multi 1.40 1.00
**2115** A933 110pf multi 1.40 1.00
**2116** A933 110pf multi 1.40 1.00
*Nos. 2113-2116 (4)* 5.60 4.00

Issued: No. 2113, 3/8/01. No. 2114, 5/10. No. 2115, 7/12. No. 2116, 9/5.

Erich Ollenhauer (1901-63), Politician — A1030

**2001, Mar. 8 Litho.** ***Perf. 14***
**2117** A1030 110pf multi 1.40 1.00

Karl Arnold (1901-58), Politician A1031

**2001, Mar. 8** ***Perf. 13¼***
**2118** A1031 110pf multi 1.40 1.00

Federal Border Police, 50th Anniv. A1032

**2001, Mar. 8** **Litho.** ***Perf. 13¾***
**2119** A1032 110pf multi 1.40 1.00

Rendsburg Railway Bridge — A1033

**2001, Apr. 5** **Litho.** ***Perf. 14***
**2120** A1033 100pf multi 1.25 .95

Folk Music — A1034

**2001, Apr. 5** ***Perf. 13x13½***
**2121** A1034 110pf multi 1.40 1.00

"Post!" A1035

**2001, Apr. 5** **Photo.** ***Perf. 14***
**2122** A1035 110pf multi 1.40 1.00

Goethe Institute, 50th Anniv. — A1036

**2001, Apr. 5** **Litho.**
**2123** A1036 300pf multi 3.75 2.75

Endangered Species — A1037

Designs: No. 2124, Mountain gorilla. No. 2125, Indian rhinoceros.

**2001, May 10** **Litho.** ***Perf. 14***
**2124** A1037 110pf multi 1.40 1.00
**2125** A1037 110pf multi 1.40 1.00

See Nos. 2132-2133.

Europa A1038

**2001, May 10** ***Perf. 13¾***
**2126** A1038 110pf multi *1.25 1.00*

Werner Egk (1901-83), Composer — A1039

**2001, May 10** ***Perf. 14***
**2127** A1039 110pf multi 1.40 1.00

St. Catherine's Monastery, 750th Anniv., Oceanographic Museum, 50th Anniv. — A1040

**2001, June 13** **Litho.** ***Perf. 13x13¼***
**2128** A1040 110pf multi 1.40 1.00

Catholic Court Church, Dresden, 250th Anniv. A1041

**2001, June 13** ***Perf. 13¼***
**2129** A1041 110pf multi 1.40 1.00

Canzow Village Church A1042

**2001, July 12** **Photo.** ***Perf. 14x14¼***
**2130** A1042 110pf multi 1.40 1.00

Conservation of sacred monuments.

Souvenir Sheet

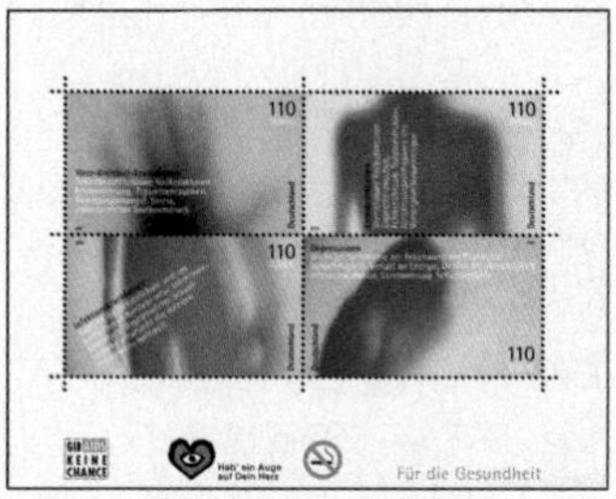


Health — A1043

No. 2131: a, Hand (circulatory diseases). b, Chest (cancer). c, Abdomen (infectious diseases). d, Head (depression).

**2001, July 12** **Litho.** ***Perf. 13x13½***
**2131** A1043 Sheet of 4 5.00 5.00
*a.-d.* 110pf Any single 1.25 1.25

**Endangered Species Type of 2001**
***Die Cut Perf. 11¼x11***
**2001, July 12** **Litho.**
**Booklet Stamps**
**Self-Adhesive**

**2132** A1037 110pf Like #2124 1.40 1.40
**2133** A1037 110pf Like #2125 1.40 1.40
*a.* Booklet, 5 each #2132-2133 20.00

Furth Dragon Lancing Festival A1044

**2001, Aug. 9** **Litho.** ***Perf. 13¼***
**2134** A1044 100pf multi 1.25 .95

Himmelsberg Lime Tree Natural Monument — A1045

**2001** ***Perf. 13¾x14***
**2135** A1045 110pf multi 1.40 1.00

**Booklet Stamp**
**Self-Adhesive**
***Die Cut Perf. 9¾x10½***

**2135A** A1045 110pf multi 2.25 1.10
*b.* Booklet of 20 47.50

Issued: No. 2135, 8/9; No. 2135A, 9/13.

Lifelong Learning A1046

**2001, Aug. 9** ***Perf. 14***
**2136** A1046 110pf multi 1.40 1.00

Federal Constitutional Court, 50th Anniv. — A1047

**2001, Sept. 5**
**2137** A1047 110pf multi 1.40 1.00

First World Congress of Union Network International — A1048

**2001, Sept. 5** ***Perf. 13x13½***
**2138** A1048 110pf multi 1.40 1.00

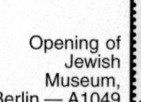

Opening of Jewish Museum, Berlin — A1049

**2001, Sept. 5** **Photo.** ***Perf. 13¾***
**2139** A1049 110pf multi 1.40 1.00

Souvenir Sheet

For Children — A1050

**2001, Sept. 5** **Litho.** ***Perf. 13¾x14***
**2140** A1050 110pf multi 1.40 1.00

"For You" — A1051

**2001, Oct. 11** ***Perf. 13x13¼***
**2141** A1051 110pf multi 1.40 1.00

Werner Heisenberg (1901-76), Physicist A1052

**2001, Nov. 8** **Litho.** ***Perf. 13¾***
**2142** A1052 300pf multi 3.75 2.75

Souvenir Sheet

German Antarctic Expeditions, Cent. — A1053

Expedition vessels: a, Gauss. b, Polarstern.

**2001, Nov. 8** ***Perf. 13¾x14***
**2143** A1053 Sheet of 2, #a-b 3.75 3.75
*a.* 110pf multi 1.25 1.25
*b.* 220pf multi 2.50 2.50

Introduction of the Euro, Jan. 1 — A1054

**2002, Jan. 10** **Litho.** ***Perf. 13¾***
**2144** A1054 56c multi 1.50 .50

**Coil Stamp**
**Perf. 10½**
**Self-Adhesive**

**2144A** A1054 56c multi 3.25 2.40

Hans von Dohnanyi (1902-45), Documenter of Nazi Atrocities A1055

**2002, Jan. 10** **Photo.**
**2145** A1055 56c multi 1.75 1.40
**2145A** A1055 56c multi *900.00* —

No. 2145A has "2002" in upper right corner and colored face and name. Approximately 320 small panes of 10 of No. 2145A were accidentally mixed in with approved stock of No. 2145 and sold over post office counters.

Bautzen, 1000th Anniv. A1056

**2002, Jan. 10** **Litho.** ***Perf. 13¾***
**2146** A1056 56c multi 1.50 .80

***Die Cut Perf. 11***
**Litho.**
**Booklet Stamp**
**Self-Adhesive**

**2146A** A1056 56c multi 2.40 1.90
*b.* Booklet of 10 24.00

More Tolerance — A1057

**2002, Jan. 10** ***Perf. 13¾x14***
**2147** A1057 56c multi 1.50 .80

Adolph Freiherr Knigge (1762-96), Writer — A1058

**2002, Feb. 7** **Litho.** ***Perf. 13¾***
**2148** A1058 56c multi 1.50 .80

Berlin Subway System, Cent. — A1059

**2002, Feb. 7** ***Perf. 13¼***
**2149** A1059 56c multi 1.50 .80

Johann Christoph Schuster's Mechanical Calculator — A1060

**2002, Mar. 7** **Litho.** ***Perf. 14***
**2150** A1060 56c multi 1.50 .80

Cultural Foundation of the Federal States.

Deggendorf, 1000th Anniv. — A1061

**2002, Mar. 7**
**2151** A1061 56c multi 1.50 .80

Ecksberg Foundation for the Mentally Handicapped, 150th Anniv. — A1062

**Litho. & Engr.**
**2002, Apr. 4** ***Perf. 14x13¾***
**2152** A1062 56c multi 1.50 .80

Freemason's Museum, Cent. — A1063

**2002, Apr. 4** **Litho.** ***Perf. 14***
**2153** A1063 56c multi 1.50 .80

Baden-Württemberg, 50th Anniv. — A1064

**2002, Apr. 4** ***Perf. 13¼***
**2154** A1064 56c multi 1.50 .80

"Post" — A1065

**2002, Apr. 4** ***Perf. 13x13½***
**2155** A1065 56c multi 1.50 .80

Federal Employment Services, 50th Anniv. — A1066

**2002, Apr. 4** ***Perf. 14***
**2156** A1066 153c black & red 4.25 2.40

**Voss Type of 2001**
***Die Cut Perf. 10¼***
**2002, Apr. 4** **Litho.**
**Coil Stamp**
**Self-Adhesive**

**2157** A1029 €1.53 multi 4.25 2.75

Dated 2001. No. 2157 was sold only for euro currency.

Europa A1067

**2002** **Litho.** ***Perf. 13¼***
**2158** A1067 56c multi *1.50 .80*

**Self-Adhesive**
**Coil Stamp**
***Die Cut Perf. 10¼***

**2158A** A1067 56c multi *2.40 2.00*

Issued: No. 2158, 5/2; No. 2158A, 7/4.

Garden Kingdom of Dessau-Wörlitz, UNESCO World Heritage Site — A1068

**2002** ***Perf. 13¾x14***
**2159** A1068 56c multi 1.50 .80

**Booklet Stamp**
**Self-Adhesive**
***Die Cut Perf. 10¾***

**2159A** A1068 56c multi 1.50 .80
*b.* Booklet of 20 30.00

Issued: No. 2159, 5/2; No. 2159A, 8/8.

Halle-Wittenberg University, 500th Anniv. — A1069

**2002, May 2** ***Perf. 14***
**2160** A1069 56c multi 1.50 .80

Children's Church, 150th Anniv. A1070

**2002, May 2** ***Perf. 13¼***
**2161** A1070 56c multi 1.50 .80

Souvenir Sheet

Documenta 11 Art Exhibition — A1071

**2002, May 2** ***Perf. 13¾x14***
**2162** A1071 56c multi 1.50 .80

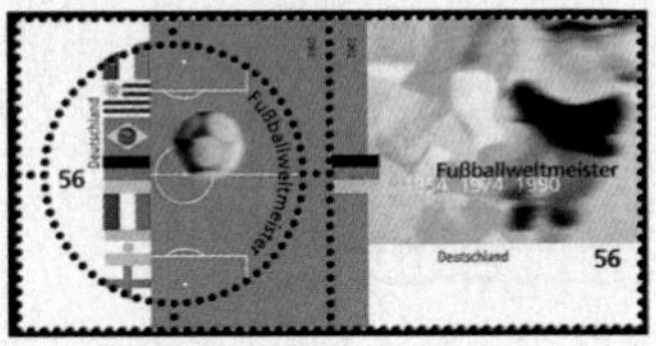


2002 World Cup Soccer Championships, Japan and Korea — A1072

No. 2163: a, Flags, soccer ball and field (28mm diameter). b, Soccer players, years of German championships.

**2002, May 2** ***Perf. 13¾***
**2163** A1072 Horiz. pair 3.00 2.25
*a.-b.* 56c Any single 1.50 .95

See Argentina No. 2184, Brazil No. 2840, France No. 2891, Italy No. 2526 and Uruguay No. 1946.

Albrecht Daniel Thaer (1752-1828), Agronomist — A1073

**2002, May 2** ***Perf. 13x13½***
**2164** A1073 225c multi 6.25 3.50

Yellow Feather in Red, by Ernst Wilhelm Nay (1902-68) — A1074

**2002, June 6** **Litho.** ***Perf. 13¾x14***
**2165** A1074 56c multi 1.50 .80

Endangered Species — A1075

Designs: 51c, Desmoulins whorl snail. 56c, Freshwater pearl mussel.

**2002, June 6** ***Perf. 14x14¼***
**2166** A1075 51c multi 1.40 .80
**2167** A1075 56c multi 1.50 .80

See Czech Republic No. 3173.

World Hunger Help — A1076

**2002, July 4 Litho. *Perf. 13¾x14***
**2168** A1076 51c multi 1.40 .80

Natl. Germanic Museum, 150th Anniv. — A1077

**2002, July 4**
**2169** A1077 56c multi 1.50 .80

Hermann Hesse (1877-1962), Writer — A1078

**2002, July 4 *Perf. 14***
**2170** A1078 56c multi 1.50 .80

Souvenir Sheet

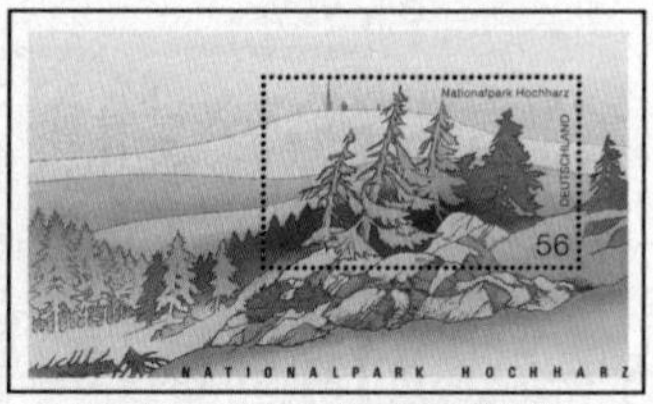

Hochharz Natl. Park — A1079

**2002, July 4 *Perf. 13¾x14***
**2171** A1079 56c multi 1.60 1.00

Josef Felder (1900-2000), Politician, Journalist A1080

**2002, Aug. 8 Litho. *Perf. 13***
**2172** A1080 56c multi 1.50 .80

Volunteer Fire Brigades A1081

**2002, Aug. 8 *Perf. 14***
**2173** A1081 56c multi 1.50 .80

Museum Island, Berlin, UNESCO World Heritage Site A1082

**Litho. & Engr.**
**2002, Aug. 8 *Perf. 13¾x14***
**2174** A1082 56c blk & Prus blue 1.50 .80

Communications Museum, Berlin — A1083

**2002, Aug. 8 Litho. *Perf. 14***
**2175** A1083 153c multi 4.25 2.40

Foundation Walls of Roman Villa Bathhouse, Wurmlingen — A1084

**2002, Sept. 5 Litho. *Perf. 13¾x14***
**2176** A1084 51c multi 1.40 .70

Rotes Elisabeth-Ufer, by Ernst Ludwig Kirchner (1880-1938) — A1085

**2002, Sept. 5**
**2177** A1085 112c multi 3.25 1.60

Souvenir Sheet

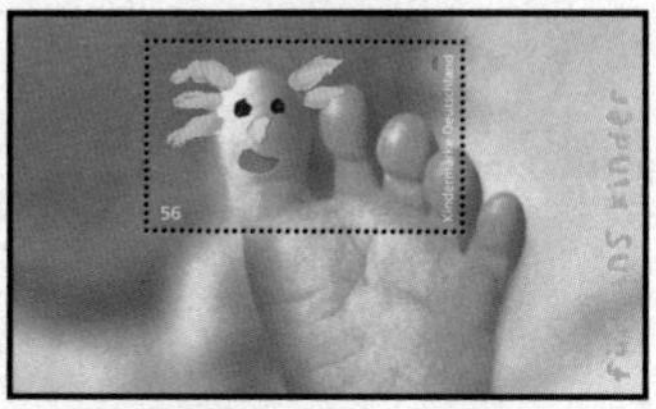

For Children — A1086

**2002, Sept. 5 *Perf. 13x13½***
**2178** A1086 56c multi 1.50 1.00

Heinrich von Kleist (1777-1811), Writer — A1087

**2002, Oct. 10 Litho. *Perf. 13***
**2179** A1087 56c multi 1.50 .80

Eugen Jochum (1902-87), Conductor A1088

**2002, Oct. 10 *Perf. 14x14¼***
**2180** A1088 56c multi 1.50 .80

Otto von Guericke (1602-86), Physicist — A1089

**2002, Oct. 10 *Perf. 14***
**2181** A1089 153c multi 4.25 2.25

Federal Agency for Civic Education, 50th Anniv. A1090

**2002, Nov. 7 Litho. *Perf. 13¼***
**2182** A1090 56c blk, red & org 1.50 .80

German Television, 50th Anniv. — A1091

**2002, Nov. 7 *Perf. 14***
**2183** A1091 56c multi 1.50 .80

Halle Market Church, by Lyonel Feininger (1871-1956) — A1092

**2002, Dec. 5 Litho. *Perf. 13¾x14***
**2184** A1092 55c multi 1.50 .80

### Famous Women Type of 1986 With Euro Denominations Only

Designs: 45c, Annette von Droste-Hülshoff (1797-1848), poet. 55c, Hildegard Knef (1925-2002), actress. €1, Marie Juchacz (1879-1956), politician. €1.44, Esther von Kirchbach (1894-1946), writer.

**2002-03 Engr. *Perf. 14***
**2185** A602 45c ol grn & Prus bl 1.25 .65
**2186** A602 55c car & blk 1.50 .80
**2187** A602 €1 dk bl & claret 2.75 1.40
**2188** A602 €1.44 dk bl & ocher 4.00 2.10
*Nos. 2185-2188 (4)* 9.50 4.95

Issued: 45c, 55c, €1.44, 12/27/02; €1, 1/16/03.

### Historic Sites Type of 1987 With Euro Denominations Only

Designs: 25c, Prince's Residence, Arolsen. 40c, Bach Statue, Leipzig.44c, Berlin Philharmonic Hall. 45c, Tönninger Packhaus (Warehouse, Tönning). 55c, Old Opera House, Frankfurt. €1, Porta Nigra, Trier. €1.44, Birthplace of Ludwig van Beethoven, Bonn. €1.60, Bauhaus, Dessau. €1.80, Stuttgart Staatsgalerie. €2, Equestrian statue, Bamberg. €2.20, Monument to Theodor Fontane, Neuruppin. €2.60, Barque "Seute Deern," Bremerhaven. €4.10, Gabled houses, Wismar.

**2002-04 Litho. *Perf. 14***
**2199** A623 5c olive & turq .25 .25
**2200** A623 25c multi .70 .35
**2201** A623 40c pur & grn 1.10 .60
**2202** A623 44c blk & yel 1.25 .60
**2203** A623 45c gray blk & brick red 1.25 .60
**2204** A623 55c blk & yel 1.50 .75
**2205** A623 €1 blk & greenish gray 2.75 1.40
**2206** A623 €1.44 gray grn & pink 4.00 2.00
**2207** A623 €1.60 slate & org 4.50 2.25
**2208** A623 €1.80 dull grn & brn 5.00 2.50
**2209** A623 €2 brn blk & lake 5.50 2.75
**2210** A623 €2.20 blue blk & gray bl 6.25 3.50
**2211** A623 €2.60 blue & red 7.25 3.75
**2212** A623 €4.10 bl grn & red vio 11.50 6.00

**Coil Stamps**
**Self-Adhesive**
***Die Cut Perf. 10¼x11***
**Photo.**
**2213** A623 €1.44 gray grn & pink 4.00 2.00
**Litho.**
**2214** A623 55c blk & yel 2.00 1.00

**Booklet Stamps**
***Die Cut Perf. 10¼x11 on 3 Sides***
**2215** A623 45c gray blk & brick red 1.60 .80
**2216** A623 55c blk & yel 2.00 1.00
*a.* Booklet 4 #2215, 8 #2216 20.00
*Nos. 2199-2216 (18)* 62.40 32.10

Issued: 44c, 45c, 55c, €1, €1.60, 12/27/02; €1.44, €2.20, 1/16/03; €1.80, €2, 2/13/03; €2.60, €4.10, 3/6/03; No. 2213, June 2003. 25c, 40c, 1/8/04; 5c, 2/5/04.

Kronach, 1000th Anniv. — A1093

**2003, Jan. 16 Litho. *Perf. 14***
**2222** A1093 45c multi 1.25 .65

Georg Elser (1903-45), Failed Assassin of Hitler — A1094

**2003, Jan. 16 *Perf. 13¼***
**2223** A1094 55c multi 1.50 .80

Treaty for German-French Cooperation, 40th Anniv. A1095

**2003, Jan. 16 *Perf. 13¾***
**2224** A1095 55c multi 1.50 .80

Bible Year A1096

**2003, Jan. 16 *Perf. 14x14¼***
**2225** A1096 55c multi 1.50 .80

Proun 30t, by El Lissitzky (1890-1941) — A1097

**2003, Jan. 16**
**2226** A1097 144c multi 4.00 2.10

Cultural Foundation of the Federal States.

Rose A1098

**2003, Feb. 13 Litho. *Perf. 14***

2227 A1098 55c multi 1.50 .80

**Booklet Stamp**

**Self-Adhesive**

***Die Cut Perf. 10x10¼***

2228 A1098 55c multi 1.50 .80
*a.* Booklet pane of 10 15.00

Junger Argentinier, by Max Beckmann — A1099

Composition, by Adolf Hölzel — A1100

**2003, Feb. 13 *Perf. 13¾x14***

2229 A1099 55c multi 1.50 .80
2230 A1100 100c multi 2.75 1.40

Souvenir Sheet

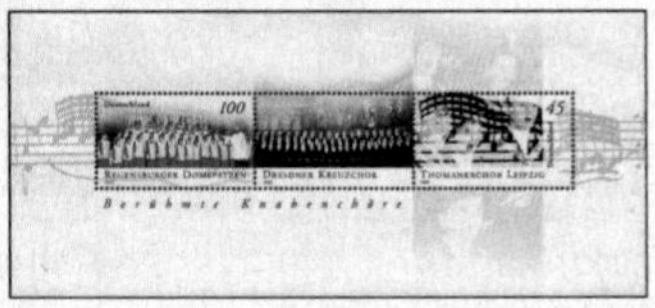

Boys' Choirs — A1101

No. 2231: a, Thomanerchor Leipzig. b, Dredner Kreuzchor. c, Regensburger Domspatzen.

**2003, Feb. 13 *Perf. 14x14¼***

2231 A1101 Sheet of 3 5.50 3.25
*a.* 45c multi 1.25 .80
*b.* 55c multi 1.50 .80
*c.* 100c multi 2.75 1.40

Cologne Cathedral, UNESCO World Heritage Site — A1102

**2003, Mar. 6 *Perf. 13¼***

2232 A1102 55c multi 1.50 .80

**Self-Adhesive**

**Coil Stamp**

***Die Cut Perf. 10¼***

2233 A1102 55c multi 1.50 .80

Intl. Horticultural Exhibition 2003, Rostock A1103

**2003, Apr. 10 Litho. *Perf. 13¼***

2234 A1103 45c multi 1.25 .70

German Museum, Munich, Cent. A1104

**2003, Apr. 10 Photo. *Perf. 14x14¼***

2235 A1104 55c multi 1.50 .80

Deutsche Welle Radio, 50th Anniv. — A1105

**2003, Apr. 10 Litho. *Perf. 14***

2236 A1105 55c multi 1.50 .80

German Society for the Protection of Children, 50th Anniv. A1106

**2003, Apr. 10 *Perf. 13¼***

2237 A1106 55c multi 1.50 .80

Reinhold Schneider (1903-58), Writer — A1107

**2003, May 8 Litho. *Perf. 13¼***

2238 A1107 55c multi 1.50 .80

Ecumenical Church Conference, Berlin — A1108

**2003, May 8 *Perf. 14***

2239 A1108 55c multi 1.50 .80

Justus von Liebig (1803-73), Chemist — A1109

**2003, May 8**

2240 A1109 55c multi 1.50 .80

German General Automobile Club, Cent. — A1110

**2003, May 8 *Perf. 13¼x13½***

2241 A1110 55c multi 1.50 .80

Europa — A1111

**2003, May 8**

2242 A1111 55c multi *1.50 .80*

Hans Jonas (1903-93), Philosopher — A1112

**2003, May 8 *Perf. 13¾x14***

2243 A1112 220c multi 6.25 3.25

Five Digit Postal Codes, 10th Anniv. A1113

**2003, June 12 Litho. *Perf. 14***

2244 A1113 55c multi 1.50 .80

Salzach River Bridge, Laufen, Germany - Oberndorf, Austria, Cent. — A1114

**2003, June 12**

2245 A1114 55c multi 1.50 .80

**Booklet Stamp**

**Self-Adhesive**

2245A A1114 55c multi 1.50 .80
*b.* Booklet pane of 20 30.00

See Austria No. 1922.

Souvenir Sheet

Unteres Odertal National Park — A1115

**2003, June 12 *Perf. 13x13½***

2246 A1115 55c multi 1.50 1.00

German Music Council, 50th Anniv. A1116

**2003, June 12 *Perf. 14***

2247 A1116 144c multi 4.00 2.10

**Self-Adhesive**

**Booklet Stamp**

***Die Cut Perf. 11¼x11***

2247A A1116 144c multi 4.00 2.10
*b.* Booklet pane of 10 40.00

Issued: No. 2247, 6/12/03; No. 2247A, 1/8/04.

Scenic Regions in Germany — A1117

**2003 Litho. *Perf. 13x13½***

2248 A1117 55c Ruhr Region 1.50 .80

Issued: No. 2248, 7/10. This is an expanding set. Numbers have been reserved for additional items.

Andreas Hermes (1878-1964), Politician — A1118

**2003, July 10 Photo. *Perf. 14x14¼***

2258 A1118 55c multi 1.50 .80

Petrified Forest, Chemnitz A1119

**2003, Aug. 7 Litho. *Perf. 13¼***

2259 A1119 144c multi 4.00 2.10

**City Views**

Market, Munich A1120

Buildings in Old City, Görlitz — A1121

**2003, Aug. 7 Litho. *Perf. 13¼***

2260 A1120 45c multi 1.25 .65

***Perf. 13x13½***

2261 A1121 55c multi 1.50 .80

**Self-Adhesive**

**Booklet Stamp**

***Die Cut Perf. 11x 10¾***

2261A A1120 45c multi 1.40 .55
*b.* Booklet pane of 10 14.00

Issued: Nos. 2260, 2261, 8/7/03; No. 2261A, 1/8/04.

Theodor W. Adorno (1903-69), Philosopher — A1122

**2003, Sept. 11 *Perf. 14***

2262 A1122 55c multi 1.50 .80

Bietigheim Enzviadukt, 150th Anniv. — A1123

**2003, Sept. 11** ***Perf. 13x13½***
**2263** A1123 55c multi 1.50 .80

Souvenir Sheet

For Children — A1124

**2003, Sept. 11** ***Perf. 13¾x14***
**2264** A1124 55c multi 1.50 .80

Mailbox A1125

**2003, Oct. 9** **Litho.** ***Perf. 13¼***
**2265** A1125 55c multi 1.50 .80

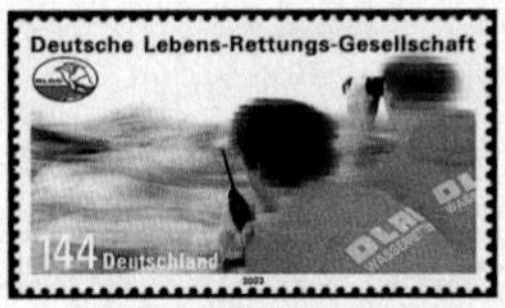

German Lifesaving Association — A1126

**2003, Oct. 9** ***Perf. 13¾***
**2266** A1126 144c multi 4.00 2.10

Opera House, Dresden, by Gottfried Semper (1803-79), Architect — A1127

**2003, Nov. 13** **Litho.** ***Perf. 13x13½***
**2267** A1127 55c multi 1.50 .80

German Catholic Women's Organization, Cent. — A1128

**2003, Nov. 13** ***Perf. 14***
**2268** A1128 55c multi 1.50 .80

Ratification of Maastricht Treaty, 10th Anniv. — A1129

**2003, Nov. 13**
**2269** A1129 55c multi 1.50 .80

Landshut, 800th Anniv. — A1130

**2004, Jan. 8** **Litho.** ***Perf. 14***
**2270** A1130 45c multi 1.25 .65

Schleswig, 1200th Anniv. A1131

**2004, Jan. 8** ***Perf. 13¼***
**2271** A1131 55c multi 1.50 .80

Arnstadt, 1300th Anniv. A1132

**2004, Feb. 5** **Litho.** ***Perf. 13¼***
**2272** A1132 55c multi 1.50 .80

Greetings — A1133

**2004, Feb. 5** ***Perf. 14***
**2273** A1133 55c multi 1.50 .80

Joseph Schmidt (1904-42), Singer — A1134

**2004, Mar. 11** **Litho.** ***Perf. 14***
**2274** A1134 55c multi 1.50 .80

Paul Ehrlich (1854-1915) and Emil von Behring (1854-1917), Physicians — A1135

**2004, Mar. 11**
**2275** A1135 144c multi 4.00 2.10

Souvenir Sheet

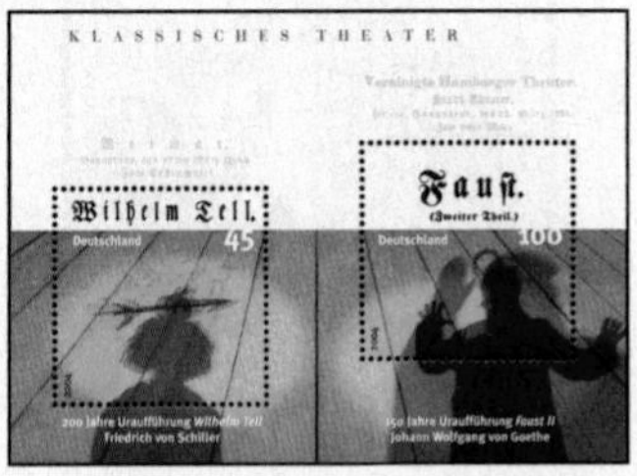

Classical Theater — A1136

No. 2276: a, Premiere of *William Tell,* by Friedrich von Schiller, bicent. b, Premiere of *Faust,* by Johann Wolfgang von Goethe, 150th anniv.

**2004, Mar. 11** ***Perf. 13¾***
**2276** A1136 Sheet of 2 4.00 2.10
*a.* 45c multi 1.25 .65
*b.* 100c multi 2.75 1.40

Bauhaus World Heritage Sites, Weimar and Dessau — A1137

**2004, Apr. 7** **Litho.** ***Perf. 14***
**2277** A1137 55c multi 1.50 .80

White Stork A1138

**2004, Apr. 7**
**2278** A1138 55c multi 1.50 .80

Kurt Georg Kiesinger (1904-88), Chancellor A1139

**2004, Apr. 7** ***Perf. 13¾***
**2279** A1139 55c multi 1.50 .80

Electric Light Bulb of Heinrich Göbel, 150th Anniv. A1140

**2004, Apr. 7**
**2280** A1140 220c red & blue 6.25 3.25

Europa A1141

**2004, May 6** **Litho.** ***Perf. 13¼***
**2281** A1141 45c multi *1.25 .65*

Expansion of the European Union A1142

**2004, May 6**
**2282** A1142 55c multi 1.50 .80

St. Boniface of Mainz (c. 675-754) A1143

**2004, May 6** ***Perf. 13¾***
**2283** A1143 55c multi 1.50 .80

Reinhard Schwarz-Schilling (1904-85), Composer — A1144

**2004, May 6** ***Perf. 14***
**2284** A1144 55c multi 1.50 .80

Ludwigsburg Castle, 300th Anniv. — A1145

**2004, May 6**
**2285** A1145 144c multi 4.00 2.10

Wattenmeer National Park — A1146

**2004, June 3** **Litho.** ***Perf. 13***
**2286** A1146 55c multi 1.50 .80

German - Russian Youth Meeting A1147

**2004, June 3** ***Perf. 13¾***
**2287** A1147 55c multi 1.50 .80

See Russia No. 6845.

Transatlantic Speed Record-Breaking Voyage of the Steamship "Bremen," 75th Anniv. — A1148

**2004, July 8** **Litho.** ***Perf. 14***
**2288** A1148 55c multi 1.50 .80

**Booklet Stamp**
**Self-Adhesive**
***Die Cut Perf. 14***

**2288A** A1148 55c multi 1.50 .80
*b.* Booklet pane of 20 30.00

Ludwig Feuerbach (1804-72), Philosopher A1149

**2004, July 8** ***Perf. 13¾***
**2289** A1149 144c multi 4.00 2.10

Lighthouses A1150

**2004, July 8**
**2290** A1150 45c Griefswalder Oie 1.25 .65
**2291** A1150 55c Roter Sand 1.50 .80

***Die Cut Perf. 10¼***
**Coil Stamp**
**Self-Adhesive**

**2291A** A1150 55c Roter Sand 1.50 .80

See Nos. 2344-2345B, 2390-2391, 2447-2448, 2491-2494, 2537-2538, 2574-2575, 2629-2632, 2673, 2680-2681.

Memorial Church, Speyer, Cent. A1151

**2004, Aug. 12** **Litho.** ***Perf. 13¾***
**2292** A1151 55c multi 1.50 .80

Camellia — A1152

**2004, Aug. 12** ***Perf. 14***
**2293** A1152 55c multi 1.50 .80

**Booklet Stamp**
**Self-Adhesive**
***Die Cut Perf. 10x10¼***

**2294** A1152 55c multi 1.50 .80
*a.* Booklet pane, 5 each #2228, 2294 15.00

Engelbert Humperdinck (1854-1921), Composer — A1153

**2004, Sept. 9** **Litho.** ***Perf. 14***
**2295** A1153 45c multi 1.25 .65

Eduard Mörike (1804-75), Poet — A1154

**2004, Sept. 9**
**2296** A1154 55c multi 1.50 .80

For Children A1155

**2004, Sept. 9** ***Perf. 13¾***
**2297** A1155 55c multi 1.50 .80

Egon Eiermann (1904-70), Architect — A1156

**2004, Sept. 9** ***Perf. 14***
**2298** A1156 100c multi 2.75 1.40

Federal Social Court, 50th Anniv. A1157

**Litho. & Embossed**

**2004, Sept. 9** ***Perf. 13¾***
**2299** A1157 144c multi 4.00 2.10

Dornier Do X A1158

**2004, Oct. 7** **Litho.** ***Perf. 14***
**2300** A1158 55c multi 1.50 .80

Stamp Day.

Winter Scene A1159

**2004, Nov. 4**
**2301** A1159 55c multi 1.50 .80

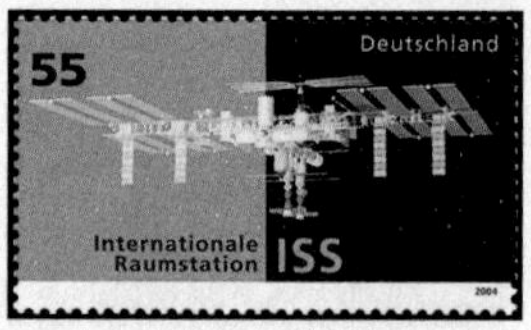

International Space Station — A1160

**2004, Nov. 4**
**2302** A1160 55c multi 1.50 .80

The Secret, by Felix Nussbaum (1904-44) — A1161

**2004, Nov. 4**
**2303** A1161 55c multi 1.50 .80

Forchheim, 1200th Anniv. A1162

**2005, Jan. 3** **Litho.** ***Perf. 13¼***
**2304** A1162 45c multi 1.25 .65

Adoration of the Magi, St. Clara's Church, Cologne A1163

**2005, Jan. 3**
**2305** A1163 55c multi 1.50 .80

See No. 2509.

Sculpture of Celtic Prince Found in Glauberg A1164

**2005, Jan. 3** ***Perf. 13¾***
**2306** A1164 144c multi 4.00 2.10

Flowers — A1165

Designs: 5c, Krokus (crocus). 10c, Tulpe (tulip). 20c, Tagetes (marigold). 25c, Malve (mallow). 35c, Dahlie (dahlia). 40c, Leberblümchen (hepatica). 45c, Margerite (daisy). 50c, Aster. 55c, Klatschmohn (red poppy). 65c, Sonnenhut (rudbeckia). 70c, Kartaüsernelke (clusterhead pink). 90c, Narzisse (narcissus). 95c, Sonnenblume (sunflower). 100c, Trănendes herz (Bleeding heart). 145c, Schwertlilie (iris). 220c, Edelweiss. 390c, Feuerlilie (tiger lily). 430c, Rittersporn (larkspur).

**2005-06** **Litho.** ***Perf. 14***

| | | | | |
|---|---|---|---|---|
| **2307** | A1165 | 5c multi | .25 | .25 |
| **2308** | A1165 | 10c multi | .30 | .25 |
| **2309** | A1165 | 20c multi | .55 | .30 |
| *a.* | Miniature sheet, 4 each #2307-2308, 2 each #2309 | | 2.75 | 2.75 |
| **2310** | A1165 | 25c multi | .70 | .40 |
| **2311** | A1165 | 35c multi | 1.00 | .50 |
| **2312** | A1165 | 40c multi | 1.10 | .55 |
| **2313** | A1165 | 45c multi | 1.25 | .65 |
| **2314** | A1165 | 50c multi | 1.40 | .70 |
| **2315** | A1165 | 55c multi | 1.50 | .80 |
| **2316** | A1165 | 65c multi | 1.75 | .90 |
| **2317** | A1165 | 70c multi | 2.00 | .95 |
| **2318** | A1165 | 90c multi | 2.50 | 1.25 |
| **2319** | A1165 | 95c multi | 2.75 | 1.40 |
| **2320** | A1165 | 100c multi | 2.75 | 1.40 |
| **2321** | A1165 | 145c multi | 4.00 | 2.10 |
| **2322** | A1165 | 220c multi | 6.25 | 3.00 |
| **2323** | A1165 | 390c multi | 11.00 | 5.50 |
| **2324** | A1165 | 430c multi | 12.00 | 6.25 |
| | *Nos. 2307-2324 (18)* | | 53.05 | 27.15 |

**Coil Stamp**
**Self-Adhesive**
***Die Cut Perf. 10¼x10***

| | | | | |
|---|---|---|---|---|
| **2325** | A1165 | 25c multi | .70 | .40 |
| **2326** | A1165 | 35c multi | 1.00 | .55 |
| **2326A** | A1165 | 55c multi | 1.50 | .80 |
| **2326B** | A1165 | 90c multi | 2.50 | 1.40 |
| *a.* | Booklet pane of 10 | | 25.00 | |

Issued: 95c, 430c, 1/3. 45c, 4/7. #2310, 50c, 6/2. 20c, #2315, 7/7. 5c, 8/11.10c, 40c, 9/8; #2326A, 7/7. #2325, 35c, 90c, 145c, 1/2/06. 65c, 3/2/06. 70c, 220c, 4/13/06. 390c, 5/4/06. 100c, 7/13/06. #2309a, 3/1/07.

See Nos. 2405-2422.

Advertising Pillars, 150th Anniv. A1166

**2005, Feb. 10** **Litho.** ***Perf. 13¾***
**2327** A1166 55c multi 1.50 .80

Berlin Cathedral, Cent. A1167

**2005, Feb. 10** ***Perf. 13***
**2328** A1167 95c multi 2.75 1.40

**Booklet Stamp**
**Self-Adhesive**
***Die Cut Perf. 11***

**2329** A1167 95c multi 2.75 1.40
*a.* Booklet pane of 10 27.50

Bonn-Copenhagen Declaration, 50th Anniv. — A1168

**2005, Mar. 3** ***Perf. 14***
**2330** A1168 55c multi 1.50 .80

See Denmark No. 1322.

Resumption of Regulated Civil Aviation, 50th Anniv. — A1169

**2005, Mar. 3**
**2331** A1169 155c multi 4.25 2.25

Postal Workers A1170

Designs: No. 2332, Postman on bicycle. No. 2333, Postman on snowy hillside.

**2005, Mar. 3** ***Perf. 13¾***
**2332** A1170 55c multi 1.50 .80
**2333** A1170 55c multi 1.50 .80

See Nos. 2348-2349.

Mittelland Canal, Cent. — A1171

**2005, Apr. 7** **Litho.** ***Perf. 14***
**2334** A1171 45c multi 1.25 .80

Bavarian Forest National Park — A1172

**2005, Apr. 7** ***Perf. 13¾***
**2335** A1172 55c multi 1.50 .80

Hans Christian Andersen (1805-75), Author — A1173

**2005, Apr. 7** ***Perf. 14***
**2336** A1173 144c multi 4.00 2.10

**Coil Stamp**
**Self-Adhesive**
***Die Cut Perf. 10¼***

**2336A** A1173 144c multi 4.00 2.10

Founding of Die Brücke Expressionist Group, Cent. A1174

**2005, May 12** **Litho.** ***Perf. 13¾***
**2337** A1174 55c buff, blk & red 1.50 .80

Paris Treaty, 50th Anniv. A1175

**2005, May 12**
**2338** A1175 55c black & red 1.50 .80

Friedrich von Schiller Year — A1176

**2005, May 12** ***Perf. 14***
**2339** A1176 55c multi 1.50 .80

Pope John Paul II (1920-2005) — A1177

**2005, May 12**
**2340** A1177 55c multi 1.50 .80

Europa A1178

**2005, May 12**
**2341** A1178 55c multi *1.50* *.80*

Sixth Congress of European Organization of Supreme Audit Institutions, Bonn A1179

**2005, June 2** **Litho.** ***Perf. 13¾***
**2342** A1179 55c multi 1.50 .80

20th World Youth Day A1180

**2005, June 2** ***Perf. 14***
**2343** A1180 55c multi 1.50 .80

See Vatican City No. 1298.

**Lighthouse Type of 2004**

Designs: Nos. 2344, 2345B, Brunsbüttel, Jetty 1. No. 2345A, Griefswalde Oie. 55c, Westerheversand.

**2005, July 7** **Litho.** ***Perf. 13¾***
**2344** A1150 45c multi 1.25 .65
**2345** A1150 55c multi 1.50 .80

**Booklet Stamps**
**Self-Adhesive**
***Die Cut Perf. 10¾***

**2345A** A1150 45c multi 1.25 .65
**2345B** A1150 45c multi 1.25 .65
*c.* Booklet pane, 5 each #2345A-2345B 12.50

Albert Einstein's Theory of Relativity, Cent. — A1181

**2005, July 7** ***Perf. 14***
**2346** A1181 55c multi 1.50 .80

Souvenir Sheet

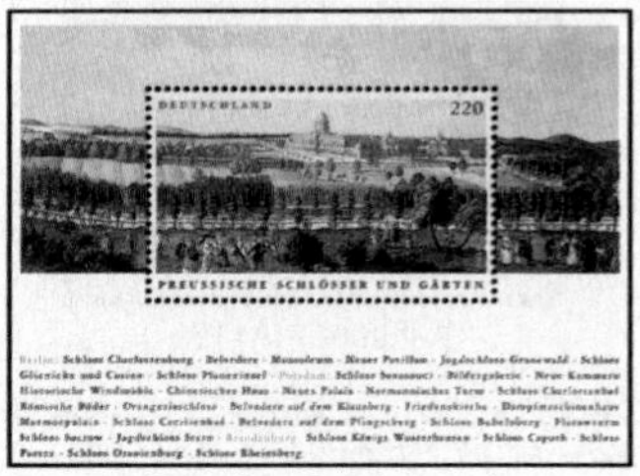


Prussian Castles and Gardens — A1182

**2005, July 7** ***Perf. 13x13½***
**2347** A1182 220c multi 6.25 3.25

**Self-Adhesive**
**Booklet Stamp**
***Die Cut Perf. 11***

**2347A** A1182 220c multi 6.25 3.25
*b.* Booklet pane of 10 57.50 —

Issued: #2347, 7/7. #2347A, 11/3.

**Postal Workers Type of 2005**

Designs: No. 2348, Postman on punt. No. 2349, Postman with handcart.

**2005, Aug. 11** **Litho.** ***Perf. 13¾***
**2348** A1170 55c multi 1.50 .80
**2349** A1170 55c multi 1.50 .80

German Friends of Nature, Cent. A1183

**2005, Aug. 11** ***Perf. 13¼***
**2350** A1183 144c multi 4.00 2.10

Magdeburg, 1200th Anniv. — A1184

**2005, Sept. 8** **Litho.** ***Perf. 14***
**2351** A1184 55c multi 1.50 .80

For Children — A1185

**2005, Sept. 8**
**2352** A1185 55c multi 1.50 .80

Peace of Augsburg, 450th Anniv. A1186

**2005, Sept. 8** ***Perf. 13¾***
**2353** A1186 55c multi 1.50 .80

See No. 2508.

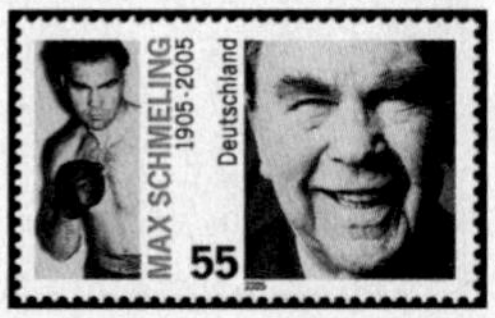


Max Schmeling (1905-2005), Boxer — A1187

**2005, Sept. 8** ***Perf. 14***
**2354** A1187 55c multi 1.50 .80

Dedication of Rebuilt Church of Our Lady, Dresden — A1188

**2005, Oct. 13** **Litho.** ***Perf. 14***
**2355** A1188 55c multi 1.50 .80

Adalbert Stifter (1805-68), Writer A1189

**2005, Oct. 13** ***Perf. 13¾***
**2356** A1189 95c multi 2.75 1.40

St. Leonhard's Day Procession, Bad Tölz — A1190

**2005, Nov. 3** **Litho.** ***Perf. 13¼***
**2357** A1190 45c multi 1.25 .65

Federal Armed Forces, 50th Anniv. A1191

**2005, Nov. 3** ***Perf. 13¾***
**2358** A1191 55c multi 1.50 .80

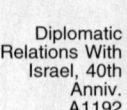

Diplomatic Relations With Israel, 40th Anniv. A1192

**2005, Nov. 3**

**2359** A1192 55c multi 1.50 .80

See Israel No. 1619.

Awarding of Nobel Peace Prize to Bertha von Suttner, Cent. — A1193

**2005, Nov. 3** ***Perf. 14***

**2360** A1193 55c multi 1.50 .80

Awarding of Nobel Physiology or Medicine Prize to Robert Koch, Cent. — A1194

**2005, Nov. 3** ***Perf. 13¼***

**2361** A1194 144c multi 4.00 2.10

Halle, 1200th Anniv. A1195

**2006, Jan. 2** **Litho.** ***Perf. 14***

**2362** A1195 45c multi 1.25 .65

Winter A1196

**2006, Jan. 2** **Litho.** ***Perf. 14***

**2363** A1196 55c multi 1.50 .80

See No. 2400.

Spring A1197

**2006, Apr. 13** **Litho.** ***Perf. 14***

**2364** A1197 55c multi 1.50 .80

See No. 2397.

Summer — A1198

**2006, July 13** **Litho.** ***Perf. 14***

**2365** A1198 55c multi 1.50 .80

See No. 2398.

Autumn — A1199

**2006, Oct. 5** **Litho.** ***Perf. 14***

**2366** A1199 55c multi 1.50 .80

See No. 2399.

Wolfgang Amadeus Mozart (1756-91), Composer A1200

**2006, Jan. 2** **Litho.** ***Perf. 13¼***

**2367** A1200 55c multi 1.50 .80

Golden Bull of Emperor Charles IV — A1201

**2006, Jan. 2** ***Perf. 14***

**2368** A1201 145c multi 4.00 2.10

**Self-Adhesive**

**Booklet Stamp**

***Die Cut Perf. 10***

**2369** A1201 145c multi 4.00 2.10

*a.* Booklet pane of 10 40.00

St. Michael's Church, Schwäbisch Hall, 850th Anniv. — A1202

**2006, Feb. 9** **Litho.** ***Perf. 14***

**2370** A1202 55c multi 1.50 .80

Frisian Council, 50th Anniv. A1203

**2006, Feb. 9**

**2371** A1203 90c multi 2.50 1.40

Ingolstadt, 1200th Anniv. A1204

**2006, Mar. 2** **Litho.** ***Perf. 13¼***

**2372** A1204 55c multi 1.50 .80

Karl Friedrich Schinkel (1781-1841), Architect — A1205

**2006** ***Perf. 14***

**2373** A1205 55c multi 1.50 .80

**Coil Stamp**

**Self-Adhesive**

***Die Cut Perf. 10x10¼***

**2373A** A1205 55c multi 1.50 .80

Issued: No. 2373, 3/2. No. 2373A, 7/13.

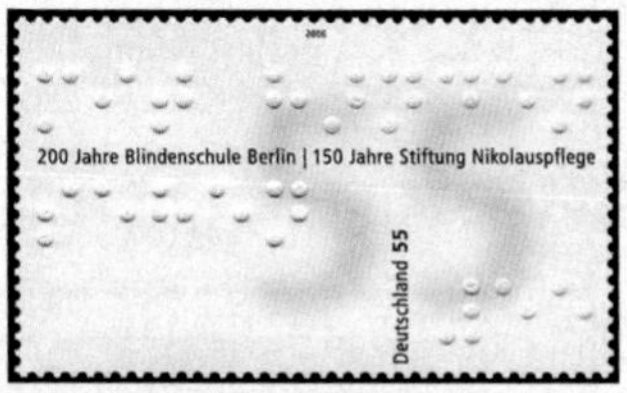


Care for the Blind — A1206

**Litho. & Embossed**

**2006, Mar. 2** ***Perf. 13x13½***

**2374** A1206 55c black & gray 1.50 .80

Berlin School for the Blind, 200th Anniv., Nikolaus Care Foundation, 150th Anniv.

Pres. Johannes Rau (1931-2006) — A1207

**2006, Mar. 2** **Litho.** ***Perf. 14***

**2375** A1207 55c multi 1.50 .80

Viadrina Universtiy, Frankfurt an der Oder, 500th Anniv. A1208

**Litho. & Embossed**

**2006, Apr. 13** ***Perf. 13¾***

**2376** A1208 55c multi 1.50 .80

Self-Portrait in Fur Coat, by Albrecht Dürer A1209

**2006, Apr. 13** **Litho.**

**2377** A1209 145c multi 4.00 2.10

Upper Middle Rhine Valley UNESCO World Heritage Site — A1210

**2006, May 4** **Litho.** ***Perf. 13¾***

**2378** A1210 55c multi 1.50 .80

**Self-Adhesive**

**Booklet Stamp**

***Die Cut Perf. 11***

**2379** A1210 55c multi 1.50 .80

*a.* Booklet pane of 10 15.00

Europa A1211

**2006, May 4** ***Perf. 14***

**2380** A1211 55c multi 1.50 .80

Gerd Bucerius (1906-95), Publisher and Politician — A1212

**2006, May 4**

**2381** A1212 85c multi 2.40 1.25

Stefan Andres (1906-70), Writer — A1213

**2006, June 8**

**2382** A1213 55c multi 1.50 .80

John Augustus Roebling (1806-69), Bridge Designer — A1214

**2006, June 8** ***Perf. 14***

**2383** A1214 145c multi 4.00 2.10

**Self-Adhesive**

**Coil Stamp**

***Die Cut Perf. 11***

**2384** A1214 145c multi 4.00 2.10

Standardized Motor Vehicle Identification, Cent. — A1215

**2006, July 13** **Litho.** ***Perf. 14***

**2385** A1215 45c multi 1.25 .65

Burghausen Castle, Burghausen — A1216

**2006, July 13**
**2386** A1216 55c multi 1.50 .80

Saskia van Uylenburgh, by Rembrandt (1606-69) A1217

**2006, July 13** ***Perf. 13¾***
**2387** A1217 70c multi 2.00 1.00

See Netherlands No. 1253. The design of No. 2387 was reproduced without the permission of the German authorities in a Netherlands booklet pane that also contains a similar Netherlands stamp.

Discovery of Neanderthal Man Bones, 150th Anniv. — A1218

**2006, Aug. 10** **Litho.** ***Perf. 14***
**2388** A1218 220c multi 6.00 3.25

Souvenir Sheet

Black Forest — A1219

**2006, Aug. 10** ***Perf. 13¾***
**2389** A1219 55c multi 1.50 .80

**Lighthouses Type of 2004**

Designs: 45c, Neuland. 55c, Hohe Weg.

**2006, Aug. 10** ***Perf. 13¾***
**2390** A1150 45c multi 1.25 .65
**2391** A1150 55c multi 1.50 .80

"Captain of Köpenick" A1220

**2006, Sept. 7** **Litho.** ***Perf. 13¼***
**2392** A1220 55c multi 1.50 .80

Theft of town funds and arrest of mayor in Köpenick by petty thief Friedrich Wilhelm Voigt, who masqueraded as an army officer, cent.

For Children A1221

**2006, Sept. 7**
**2393** A1221 55c multi 1.50 .80

Hanseatic League, 650th Anniv. — A1222

**Litho. & Engr.**

**2006, Sept. 7** ***Perf. 14***
**2394** A1222 70c multi 2.00 1.00

See Sweden No. 2541

Stamp Day A1223

**2006, Oct. 5** **Litho.** ***Perf. 14***
**2395** A1223 55c multi 1.50 .80

Hannah Arendt (1906-75), Political Scientist — A1224

**2006, Oct. 5** ***Perf. 13¾x14***
**2396** A1224 145c multi 4.00 2.10

**Seasons Types of 2006**

***Die Cut Perf. 14***

**2006, Nov. 9** **Litho.**

**Booklet Stamps**

**Self-Adhesive**

**2397** A1197 55c Spring 1.50 .80
**2398** A1198 55c Summer 1.50 .80
**2399** A1199 55c Autumn 1.50 .80
**2400** A1196 55c Winter 1.50 .80
*a.* Booklet pane, 5 each #2397-2400 30.00

Eugen Bolz (1881-1945), Politician A1225

**2006, Nov. 9** ***Perf. 13¾***
**2401** A1225 45c multi 1.25 .65

Joseph Cardinal Höffner (1906-87) A1226

**2006, Nov. 9** ***Perf. 13¼***
**2402** A1226 55c multi 1.50 .80

Werner Forssmann (1904-79), 1956 Physiology or Medicine Nobel Laureate — A1227

**2006, Nov. 9** ***Perf. 14***
**2403** A1227 90c multi 2.50 1.40

**Flowers Type of 2005**

Designs: 25c, Gartennelke (carnation). 45c, Maiglöckchen (lily of the valley). 55c, Gartenrose (rose). 58c, Kuhschelle (pasque flower). 65c, Sonnenhut (rudbeckia). 70c, Kartäusernelke (clusterhead pink). 75c, Ballonblume (balloon flower). 200c, Goldmohn (California poppy). 240c, Prachtkerze (white gaura). 410c, Frauenschuh (lady's slipper). 500c, Enzian (gentian).

**2006-11** **Litho.** ***Perf. 14***
**2405** A1165 25c multi .70 .35
**2406** A1165 45c multi 1.25 .60
**2407** A1165 55c multi 1.75 .85
**2407A** A1165 58c multi 1.50 .75
**2408** A1165 75c multi 2.00 1.00
**2416** A1165 200c multi 5.50 2.75
**2416A** A1165 240c multi 6.25 3.25
**2417** A1165 410c multi 12.00 6.00
**2418** A1165 500c multi 14.00 7.00
*Nos. 2405-2418 (7)* 37.20 18.55

**Coil Stamps**

**Self-Adhesive**

***Die Cut Perf. 10¼x10***

**2419** A1165 25c multi .70 .35
**2420** A1165 55c multi 1.75 .85
*a.* Booklet pane of 10 17.50

**Booklet Stamps**

**2420B** A1165 45c multi 1.25 .65
*c.* Booklet pane of 10 12.50
**2421** A1165 65c multi 1.75 .85
*a.* Booklet pane of 5 + 5 etiquettes 8.75
**2422** A1165 70c multi 1.90 .95
*a.* Booklet pane of 5 + 5 etiquettes 9.50
*b.* Booklet pane of 10 19.00

Issued: 200c, 11/9/06; 55c, 6/12/08. 25c, 10/9/08. No. 2419, 10/9/08; No. 2420, 6/12/08, No. 2420a, 3/11/10; Nos. 2421-2422, 1/2/09. No. 2417, 1/2/10. 45c, 5/6/10; No. 2422b, 6/10/2010; 75c, 1/3/11; No. 2420B, 3/1/11, 500c, 7/7/11. 58c, 240c, 12/6/12.

Fürth, 1000th Anniv. A1228

**2007, Jan. 2** **Litho.** ***Perf. 13¼***
**2424** A1228 45c multi 1.25 .65

**Booklet Stamp**

**Self-Adhesive**

***Die Cut Perf. 11***

**2425** A1228 45c multi 1.25 .65
*a.* Booklet pane of 10 12.50

Germany, 2007 President of the European Union A1229

**Litho. & Embossed**

**2007, Jan. 2** ***Perf. 13¾***
**2426** A1229 55c multi 1.50 .80

Bamberg Bishopric, 1000th Anniv. A1230

**2007, Jan. 2** **Litho.** ***Perf. 13¼***
**2427** A1230 55c multi 1.50 .80

Admission of Saarland into Federal Republic, 50th Anniv. — A1231

**2007, Jan. 2** ***Perf. 14***
**2428** A1231 55c multi 1.50 .80

**Booklet Stamp**

**Self-Adhesive**

***Die Cut Perf. 10x10¼***

**2428A** A1231 55c multi 1.50 .80
*b.* Booklet pane of 10 15.00

Wankel Rotary Engine, 50th Anniv. — A1232

**2007, Jan. 2**
**2429** A1232 145c multi 4.00 2.10

Johann Christian Senckenberg (1707-72), Founder of Hospital, Frankfurt am Main — A1233

**2007, Feb. 8** **Litho.** ***Perf. 14***
**2430** A1233 90c multi 2.50 1.40

Munich Jewish Center A1234

**2007, Mar. 1** **Litho.** ***Perf. 14***
**2431** A1234 55c multi 1.50 .80

Paul Gerhardt (1607-76), Hymn Writer — A1235

**2007, Mar. 1**
**2432** A1235 55c multi 1.50 .80

The Unearthing of the Cross, by Adam Elsheimer A1236

**2007, Mar. 1** ***Perf. 13¼***
**2433** A1236 55c multi 1.50 .80

Rome Treaty, 50th Anniv. A1237

**2007, Mar. 1** ***Perf. 13¾***
**2434** A1237 55c multi 1.50 .80

Leaders of Anti-Nazi Resistance Movement — A1238

**2007, Mar. 1** ***Perf. 13¾x14***
**2435** A1238 55c multi 1.50 .80

Claus Schenk Graf von Stauffenberg (1907-44), Hitler assassination plotter, and Helmuth James Graf von Moltke (1907-45), founding member of Kreisau Circle resistance group.

Pope Benedict XVI, 80th Birthday — A1239

**2007, Apr. 12** **Litho.** ***Perf. 14***
**2436** A1239 55c multi 1.50 .80

Letter Writing A1240

**2007, Apr. 12** ***Perf. 13¾***
**2437** A1240 55c Boy writing letter 1.50 .80
**2438** A1240 55c Boy mailing letter 1.50 .80

See Nos. 2454-2455.

Publication of World Map of Martin Waldseemuller, 500th Anniv. — A1241

**Litho. & Engr.**

**2007, Apr. 12** ***Perf. 14***
**2439** A1241 220c multi 6.00 3.25

Europa A1242

**2007, May 3** **Litho.** ***Perf. 14***
**2440** A1242 45c multi 1.25 .65

Scouting, cent.

Bellevue Palace, Presidential Residence — A1243

**2007, May 3**
**2441** A1243 55c multi 1.50 .80

**Coil Stamp**
**Self-Adhesive**
***Die Cut Perf. 10x10¼***

**2441A** A1243 55c multi 1.50 .80

Moyland Castle, 700th Anniv. — A1244

**2007, May 3**
**2442** A1244 85c multi 2.40 1.25

Hambacher Fest, 175th Anniv. — A1245

**2007, May 3** ***Perf. 14***
**2443** A1245 145c multi 4.00 2.00

**Booklet Stamp**
**Self-Adhesive**
***Die Cut Perf. 10x10¼***

**2444** A1245 145c multi 4.00 2.00
*a.* Booklet pane of 10 40.00

Karl Valentin (1882-1948), Writer A1246

**2007, June 14** **Litho.** ***Perf. 13¾***
**2445** A1246 45c multi 1.25 .65

Paul Klinger (1907-71), Film Actor A1247

**2007, June 14**
**2446** A1247 55c multi 1.50 .80

**Lighthouses Type of 2004**

Designs: 45c, Bremerhaven Oberfeuer. 55c, Hörnum.

**2007, July 12** ***Perf. 13¾***
**2447** A1150 45c multi 1.25 .65
**2448** A1150 55c multi 1.50 .80

UNESCO World Heritage Sites — A1248

Designs: 65c, Historic Center of Riga, Latvia. 70c, Historic Centers of Straslund and Wismar, Germany.

**2007, July 12** ***Perf. 14***
**2449** A1248 65c multi 1.90 .95
**2450** A1248 70c multi 2.00 1.00

See Latvia Nos. 679-680.

Saale Valley Dam and Lake Bleiloch, 75th Anniv. — A1249

**2007, Aug. 9** **Litho.** ***Perf. 14***
**2451** A1249 55c multi 1.50 .80

German Federal Bank, 50th Anniv. A1250

**2007, Aug. 9**
**2452** A1250 55c multi 1.50 .80

Kaiser Wilhelm Bridge, Wilhelmshaven, Cent. — A1251

**2007, Aug. 9** **Litho. & Engr.**
**2453** A1251 145c multi 4.00 2.00

**Letter Writing Type of 2007**

Designs: No. 2454, Postman delivering letter to woman. No. 2455, Woman reading letter.

**2007, Sept. 20** **Litho.** ***Perf. 13¾***
**2454** A1240 55c multi 1.60 .80
**2455** A1240 55c multi 1.60 .80

For Children — A1252

**2007, Sept. 20** ***Perf. 14***
**2456** A1252 55c multi 1.60 .80

Science Advisory Committee, 50th Anniv. — A1253

**2007, Sept. 20**
**2457** A1253 90c multi 2.60 1.40

German Work Federation (Architecture Group), Cent. A1254

**2007, Oct. 11** **Litho.** ***Perf. 13¼***
**2458** A1254 55c multi 1.60 .80

**Souvenir Sheet**

Frontiers of the Roman Empire UNESCO World Heritage Site — A1255

**2007, Oct. 11** ***Perf. 14***
**2459** A1255 55c multi 1.60 .80

Heinrich Friedrich Carl Freiherr vom und zum Stein (1757-1831), Prussian Statesman — A1256

**2007, Oct. 11** ***Perf. 13¾x14***
**2460** A1256 145c multi 4.00 2.10

St. Elizabeth of Hungary (1207-31) A1257

**2007, Nov. 8** **Litho.** ***Perf. 13¾***
**2461** A1257 55c multi 1.60 .80

Astrid Lindgren (1907-2002), Writer — A1258

**Litho. & Engr.**

**2007, Nov. 8** ***Perf. 13¾x14***

**2462** A1258 100c multi 2.75 1.40

See Sweden No. 2572.

Brandenburg Gate, Designed by Carl Gotthard Langhans (1732-1808) — A1259

**2007, Dec. 27** **Litho.** ***Perf. 14***

**2463** A1259 55c multi 1.60 .80

**Self-Adhesive**

**Booklet Stamp**

***Die Cut Perf. 10x10¼***

**2464** A1259 55c multi 1.60 .80
***a.*** Booklet pane of 10 16.00

Reichenau Monastic Island UNESCO World Heritage Site — A1260

**2008, Jan. 2** **Litho.** ***Perf. 13***

**2465** A1260 45c multi 1.40 .70

**Booklet Stamp**

**Self-Adhesive**

***Die Cut Perf. 10¾***

**2466** A1260 45c multi 1.40 .70
***a.*** Booklet pane of 10 14.00

Heinrich Zille (1858-1929), Illustrator A1261

**2008, Jan. 2** ***Perf. 13¾***

**2467** A1261 55c multi 1.60 .80

Federal Cartel Office, 50th Anniv. A1262

**2008** ***Perf. 14***

**2468** A1262 90c multi 2.50 1.40

**Booklet Stamp**

**Self-Adhesive**

***Die Cut Perf. 11¼x11***

**2468A** A1262 90c multi 3.00 1.50
***b.*** Booklet pane of 10 30.00

Issued: No. 2468, 1/2; No. 2468A, 3/13.

Eichstätt, 1100th Anniv. A1263

**2008, Jan. 2** ***Perf. 13¾***

**2469** A1263 145c multi 4.00 2.10

**Coil Stamp**

**Self-Adhesive**

***Die Cut Perf. 10¼***

**2469A** A1263 145c multi 4.25 2.10

Wenzel Jamnitzer (1508-85), Goldsmith — A1264

**2008, Jan. 2** ***Perf. 13¾x14***

**2470** A1264 220c multi 6.00 3.25

"Congratulations" — A1265

"All the Best" A1266

**2008, Feb. 7** ***Perf. 14***

**2471** A1265 55c multi 1.60 .80
**2472** A1266 55c multi 1.60 .80

See Nos. 2487-2488.

Carl Spitzweg (1808-85), Painter A1267

**2008, Feb. 7** **Litho.** ***Perf. 13¾***

**2473** A1267 55c multi 1.60 .80

**Coil Stamp**

**Self-Adhesive**

***Die Cut Perf. 10¼***

**2474** A1267 55c multi 1.60 .80

Village Church, Bochum-Stiepel, 1000th Anniv. — A1268

**2008, Feb. 7** **Litho.** ***Perf. 13¾***

**2475** A1268 145c multi 4.00 2.10

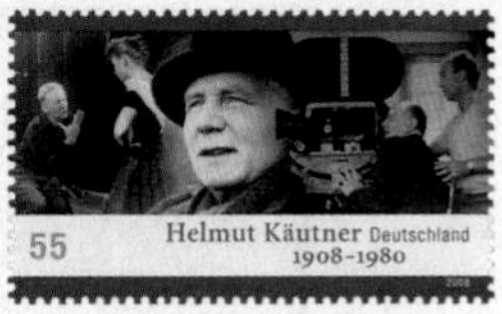


Helmut Käutner (1908-80), Film Director — A1269

**2008, Mar. 13** **Litho.** ***Perf. 14***

**2476** A1269 55c multi 1.75 .85

Frankfurt Zoo, 150th Anniv. A1270

**2008, Mar. 13** ***Perf. 13¼***

**2477** A1270 65c multi 2.10 1.10

Seebach Bird Sanctuary, Cent. — A1271

**2008, Apr. 10** **Litho.** ***Perf. 14***

**2478** A1271 45c multi 1.50 .75

Johann Hinrich Wichern (1808-81), Theologian — A1272

**2008, Apr. 10**

**2479** A1272 55c multi 1.75 .85

Max Planck (1858-1947), Physicist A1273

**2008, Apr. 10** ***Perf. 13¾***

**2480** A1273 55c multi 1.75 .85

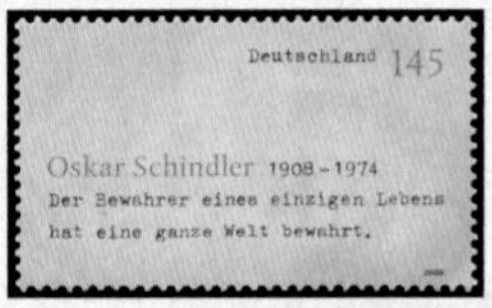


Oskar Schindler (1908-74), Industrialist Who Saved Jews From Holocaust — A1274

**2008, Apr. 10** ***Perf. 14x14¼***

**2481** A1274 145c multi 4.75 2.40

First International Match of German Soccer Team, Cent. A1275

**2008, Apr. 10** ***Perf. 13¾***

**2482** A1275 170c multi 5.50 2.75

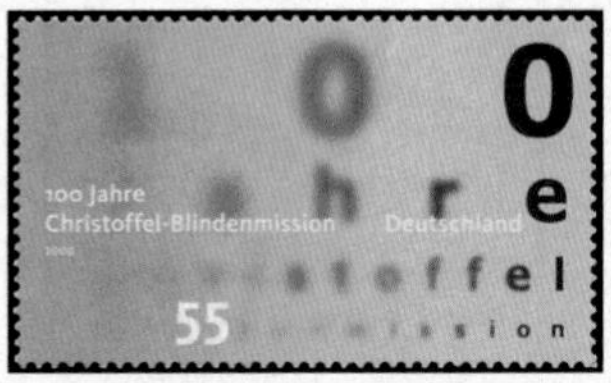


Christoffel Blind Mission, Cent. — A1276

**2008, May 8** **Litho.** ***Perf. 13x13½***

**2483** A1276 55c multi 1.75 .85

**Greetings Types of 2008 and**

"Kind Regards" — A1277

"Thank You" A1278

**2008, May 8** ***Perf. 14***

**2484** A1277 55c multi 1.75 .85
**2485** A1278 55c multi 1.75 .85

**Booklet Stamps**

**Self-Adhesive**

***Die Cut Perf. 14***

**2486** A1277 55c multi 1.75 .85
**2487** A1265 55c multi 1.75 .85
**2488** A1266 55c multi 1.75 .85
**2489** A1278 55c multi 1.75 .85
***a.*** Booklet pane of 20, 5 each #2486-2489 35.00
*Nos. 2486-2489 (4)* 7.00 3.40

Europa (#2484, 2486).

Honorary Offices — A1279

**2008, June 12** **Litho.** ***Perf. 14***

**2490** A1279 55c multi 1.75 .85

**Lighthouses Type of 2004**

Designs: No. 2491, 45c, Warnemünde. Nos. 2492, 2494, 55c, Amrum. No. 2493, 55c, Hörnum.

**2008, July 3** **Litho.** ***Perf. 13¾***

**2491** A1150 45c multi 1.40 .70
**2492** A1150 55c multi 1.75 .85

**Booklet Stamps**

**Self-Adhesive**

***Die Cut Perf. 11***

**2493** A1150 55c multi 1.75 .85
**2494** A1150 55c multi 1.75 .85
***a.*** Booklet pane of 10, 5 each #2493-2494 17.50

See No. 2632 for self-adhesive version of 45c.

Drachenfels Railway, 125th Anniv. — A1280

**2008, July 3** *Perf. 14*
**2495** A1280 45c multi 1.40 .70

Franz Kafka (1883-1924), Writer — A1281

**2008, July 3**
**2496** A1281 55c black 1.75 .85

Self-portrait With Model, by Lovis Corinth (1858-1925) — A1282

**2008, July 3** *Perf. 13x13½*
**2497** A1282 145c multi 4.75 2.40

Training Ship Gorch Fock, 50th Anniv. A1283

**2008, Aug. 7** **Litho.** *Perf. 13¼*
**2498** A1283 55c multi 1.75 .85

Joachim Ringelnatz (1883-1934), Writer and Painter A1284

**2008, Aug. 7** *Perf. 13¾*
**2499** A1284 85c pur & black 2.60 1.40

Hermann Schulze-Delitzsch (1808-83), Economist — A1285

**2008, Aug. 7** *Perf. 14*
**2500** A1285 90c multi 2.75 1.40

Stamp Day — A1286

**2008, Sept. 4** **Litho.** *Perf. 13¼*
**2501** A1286 55c multi 1.60 .80

For Children A1287

**2008, Sept. 4** *Perf. 14*
**2502** A1287 55c multi 1.60 .80

Old Rhine Bridge, Bad Sackingen, Germany - Stein, Switzerland — A1288

**2008, Sept. 4**
**2503** A1288 70c multi 2.00 1.00

See Switzerland No. 1319.

Gallimarkt (Livestock Market) of Leer, 500th Anniv. — A1289

**2008, Oct. 9** **Litho.** *Perf. 14*
**2504** A1289 45c multi 1.25 .60

Nebra Sky Disk A1290

**2008, Oct. 9**
**2505** A1290 55c multi 1.50 .75

Lorenz Werthmann (1858-1921), Founder of Caritas Charity A1291

**2008, Oct. 9** *Perf. 13¾*
**2506** A1291 55c multi 1.50 .75

First Powered Flight Over Germany, by Hans Grade, Cent. — A1292

**2008, Oct. 9** *Perf. 14*
**2507** A1292 145c multi 4.00 2.00

**Peace of Augsburg and Adoration of the Magi Types of 2005**

***Die Cut Perf. 11¼***

**2008, Nov. 1** **Litho.**

**Booklet Stamps**

**Self-Adhesive**

**2508** A1186 55c multi 1.40 .70
**2509** A1163 55c multi 1.40 .70
*a.* Booklet pane of 10, 5 each #2508-2509 14.00

Lebenshilfe (Organization for the Mentally Handicapped), 50th Anniv. — A1293

**2008, Nov. 13** *Perf. 14*
**2510** A1293 55c multi 1.40 .70

A Heart for Children Charity, 30th Anniv. A1294

**2008, Nov. 13** *Perf. 13¼*
**2511** A1294 55c black & red 1.40 .70

Nils Holgersson on Goose A1295

**2008, Nov. 13** *Perf. 13¾*
**2512** A1295 100c multi 2.60 1.25

Selma Lagerlöf (1858-1940), author of *Nils Holgersson's Wonderful Journey Through Sweden.*

Frankenberg City Hall, 500th Anniv. A1296

**2009, Jan. 2** **Litho.** *Perf. 13¾*
**2513** A1296 45c multi 1.25 .60

**Booklet Stamp**

**Self-Adhesive**

***Die Cut Perf. 10¾***

**2514** A1296 45c multi 1.25 .60
*a.* Booklet pane of 10 12.50

Misereor and Bread for the World Charities, 50th Anniv. — A1297

**2009, Jan. 2** *Perf. 14*
**2515** A1297 55c multi 1.50 .75

Tangermünde, 1000th Anniv. — A1298

**2009, Jan. 2**
**2516** A1298 90c multi 2.40 1.25

Pres. Theodor Heuss (1884-1963) A1299

**2009, Jan. 2** *Perf. 13¾*
**2517** A1299 145c multi 4.00 2.00

Heinz Erhardt (1909-79), Comedian A1300

**2009, Feb. 12** **Litho.** *Perf. 13¾*
**2518** A1300 55c multi 1.40 .70

Felix Mendelssohn Bartholdy (1809-47), Composer A1301

**2009, Feb. 12** *Perf. 13¼*
**2519** A1301 65c multi 1.75 .85

Munich Propylaea, by Architect Leo von Klenze (1784-1864) A1302

**2009, Feb. 12** *Perf. 13¾*
**2520** A1302 70c multi 1.90 .95

Der Feuervogel (Firebird), Woodcut by Helmut Andreas Paul Grieshaber (1909-81) A1303

**2009, Feb. 12** *Perf. 13¼*
**2521** A1303 165c multi 4.25 2.10

Golo Mann (1909-94), Historian A1304

**2009, Mar. 12 Litho. *Perf. 13¾***
**2522** A1304 45c multi 1.25 .60

1889 Daimler Automobile A1305

**2009, Mar. 12 *Perf. 13¾x14***
**2523** A1305 170c multi 4.75 2.40

Gottlieb Daimler (1834-1900), automobile engineer and manufacturer.

The Post — A1306

Designs: No. 2524, Hand affixing stamp on letter. No. 2525, Postal clerk serving customer. No. 2526, Postal truck. No. 2527, Postman carrying mail.

**2009 *Perf. 13***
**2524** A1306 55c multi 1.50 .75
**2525** A1306 55c multi 1.50 .75
**2526** A1306 55c multi 1.50 .75
**2527** A1306 55c multi 1.50 .75

Issued: Nos. 2524-2525, 3/12. Nos. 2526-2527, 5/7.

Bernhard Grzimek (1909-87), Zoologist A1307

**2009, Apr. 9**
**2528** A1307 55c multi 1.50 .75

Europa A1308

**2009, May 7 *Perf. 14***
**2529** A1308 55c multi 1.50 .75

Intl. Year of Astronomy.

Luther Memorials in Eisleben and Wittenberg UNESCO World Heritage Sites — A1309

**2009, May 7 *Perf. 13¾x14***
**2530** A1309 145c multi 4.00 2.00

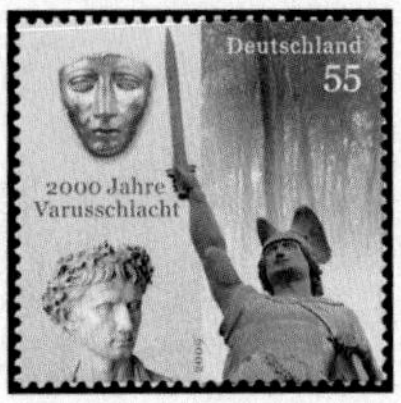


Battle of the Teutoberg Forset, 2000th Anniv. A1310

**2009, June 4 *Perf. 13¼***
**2531** A1310 55c multi 1.60 .80

**Booklet Stamp**
**Self-Adhesive**
***Serpentine Die Cut 10¾***

**2532** A1310 55c multi 1.60 .80
*a.* Booklet pane of 20 32.50

Frankfurt Intl. Aeronautical Exposition, Cent. A1311

**2009, June 4 *Perf. 13¾***
**2533** A1311 55c multi 1.60 .80

**Coil Stamp**
**Self-Adhesive**
***Die Cut Perf. 10¼***

**2534** A1311 55c multi 1.60 .80

Heinrich Hoffmann (1809-94), Writer — A1312

**2009, June 4 *Perf. 13¼***
**2535** A1312 85c multi 2.40 1.25

Souvenir Sheet

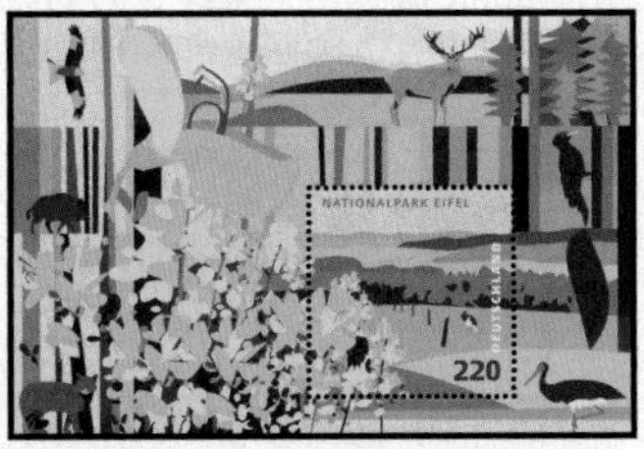


Eifel National Park — A1313

**2009, June 4 *Perf. 13¾***
**2536** A1313 220c multi 6.25 3.25

**Lighthouses Type of 2004**

Designs: 45c, Norderney. 55c, Dornbusch.

**2009, July 2**
**2537** A1150 45c multi 1.25 .65
**2538** A1150 55c multi 1.60 .80

See No. 2631 for self-adhesive version of 45c.

Leipzig University, 600th Anniv. — A1314

**2009, July 2 *Perf. 14***
**2539** A1314 55c multi 1.60 .80

**Booklet Stamp**
**Self-Adhesive**
**Size: 39x22mm**
***Die Cut Perf. 10***

**2540** A1314 55c multi 1.60 .80
*a.* Booklet pane of 10 16.00

John Calvin (1509-64), Theologian and Religious Reformer A1315

**2009, July 2 *Perf. 13¼***
**2541** A1315 70c black 2.00 1.00

Rail Ferry From Sassnitz to Trelleborg, Sweden, Cent. — A1316

**2009, July 2 *Perf. 13¾x14***
**2542** A1316 145c multi 4.25 2.10

Youth Hostels in Germany, Cent. — A1317

**2009, Aug. 13 *Perf. 14***
**2543** A1317 55c multi 1.60 .80

Consecration of Mainz Cathedral, 1000th Anniv. A1318

**2009, Aug. 13 *Perf. 13¾***
**2544** A1318 90c multi 2.60 1.40

Souvenir Sheet

Historical Motor Sports — A1319

**2009, Aug. 13 *Perf. 14***
**2545** A1319 85c multi 2.40 1.25

For Children — A1320

**2009, Sept. 3**
**2546** A1320 55c multi 1.60 .80

People Waving German Flags — A1321

**2009, Sept. 3**
**2547** A1321 55c multi 1.60 .80

Opening of Border Between Austria and Hungary, 20th Anniv. A1322

**2009, Sept. 3 *Perf. 13¾***
**2548** A1322 70c multi 2.00 1.00

See Austria No. 2219, Hungary No. 4136.

Souvenir Sheet

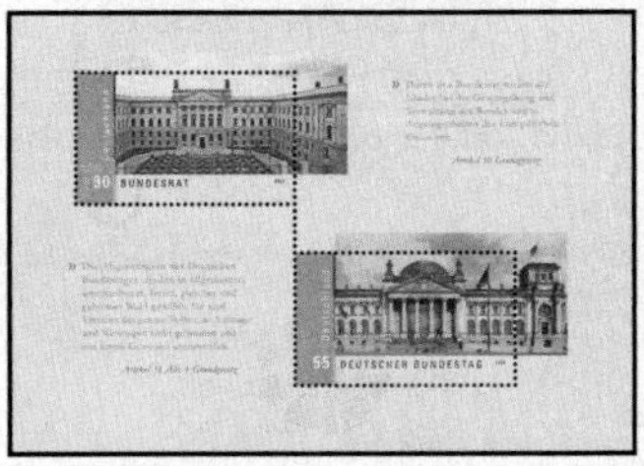


Federal Government Buildings, Berlin — A1323

**2009, Sept. 3 *Perf. 14***
**2549** A1323 Sheet of 2 4.25 2.10
*a.* 55c Bundestag 1.60 .80
*b.* 90c Bundesrat 2.60 1.25

Still Life with Cheese and Cherries, by Georg Flegel A1324

**2009, Oct. 8 *Perf. 13¼***
**2550** A1324 45c multi 1.40 .70

Crowd at St. Nicholas' Church, Leipzig A1325

**2009, Oct. 8**
**2551** A1325 55c multi 1.60 .80

Peaceful political protest in East Germany, 20th anniv.

Marion Gräfin Dönhoff (1909-2002), Journalist — A1326

**2009, Nov. 12 *Perf. 14***
**2552** A1326 55c multi 1.75 .85

Badger
A1327

**2009, Nov. 12** *Perf. 13¾*
**2553** A1327 55c multi 1.75 .85

Friedrich von Schiller (1759-1805), Writer
A1328

**2009, Nov. 12**
**2554** A1328 145c multi 4.50 2.25

Berlin Natural History Museum, 200th Anniv. — A1329

**2010, Jan. 2** **Litho.** *Perf. 13½x13¾*
**2555** A1329 45c multi 1.40 .70

**Booklet Stamp**
**Self-Adhesive**
***Die Cut Perf. 10***

**2556** A1329 45c multi 1.40 .70
*a.* Booklet pane of 10 14.00

Ruhr Valley, 2010 European Cultural Capital — A1330

**2010, Jan. 2** *Perf. 13½x13¾*
**2557** A1330 55c multi 1.60 .80

Limburg an der Lahn, 1100th Anniv.
A1331

**2010, Jan. 2** *Perf. 13½x13¾*
**2558** A1331 145c multi 4.25 2.10

**Booklet Stamp**
**Self-Adhesive**
***Die Cut Perf. 10***

**2559** A1331 145c multi 4.25 2.10
*a.* Booklet pane of 10 42.50

St. Michael's Church, Hildesheim UNESCO World Heritage Site — A1332

**2010, Jan. 2** *Perf. 13¼*
**2560** A1332 220c multi 6.25 3.00

**Booklet Stamp**
**Self-Adhesive**
***Die Cut Perf. 10¾***

**2561** A1332 220c multi 6.25 3.00
*a.* Booklet pane of 10 62.50

Mensch Argere Dich Nicht Board Game
A1333

*Perf. 13½x13¾*

**2010, Feb. 11** **Litho.**
**2562** A1333 55c multi 1.50 .75

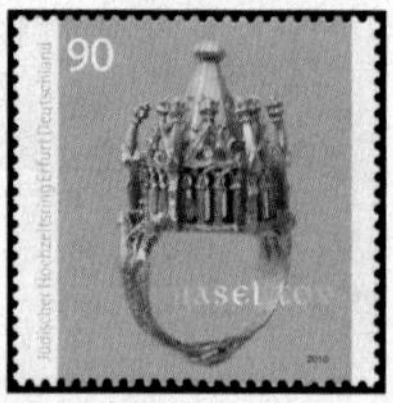


Jewish Wedding Ring — A1334

**2010, Feb. 11** *Perf. 13¼*
**2563** A1334 90c multi 2.50 1.25

Ariadne Abandoned by Theseus, by Angelica Kauffmann (1741-1807)
A1335

**2010, Mar. 11** **Litho.** *Perf. 13¾*
**2564** A1335 260c multi 7.00 3.50

Greetings — A1336

**2010** **Litho.** *Perf. 13¾*
**2565** A1336 55c Rainbow 1.50 .75
**2566** A1336 55c Ship 1.50 .75
**2567** A1336 55c Dove 1.50 .75
**2568** A1336 55c Angel with heart 1.50 .75
*Nos. 2565-2568 (4)* 6.00 3.00

Issued: Nos. 2565-2566, 3/11; Nos. 2567-2568, 4/8. See Nos. 2596-2597, 2605-2606.

Souvenir Sheet

Heligoland Bird Station, Cent. — A1337

**2010, Apr. 8** *Perf. 14*
**2569** A1337 145c multi 4.00 2.00

**Coil Stamp**
***Die Cut Perf. 11***
**Self-Adhesive**

**2570** A1337 145c multi 4.00 2.00

Robert Schumann (1810-56), Composer — A1338

**2010, May 6** **Litho.** *Perf. 13½x13¾*
**2571** A1338 55c multi 1.40 .70

Bee on Flower
A1339

**2010, May 6** *Perf. 13¾*
**2572** A1339 55c multi 1.40 .70

**Self-Adhesive**
***Die Cut Perf. 10¼***

**2572A** A1339 55c multi 1.40 .70
*2572Ab* Booklet pane of 10 14.00

Issued: No. 2572Ab, 7/2/12.

Europa
A1340

**2010, May 6** *Perf. 13¼*
**2573** A1340 55c multi 1.40 .70

**Lighthouses Type of 2004**

Designs: 45c, Neuwerk. 55c, Falshöft.

**2010, June 10** **Litho.** *Perf. 13¾*
**2574** A1150 45c multi 1.10 .55
**2575** A1150 55c multi 1.40 .70

Konrad Zuse (1910-95), Computer Engineer — A1341

**2010, June 10** *Perf. 13½x13¾*
**2576** A1341 55c multi 1.40 .70

Porcelain Manufacturing in Germany, 300th Anniv. — A1342

**2010, July 1** **Litho.** *Perf. 13½x13¾*
**2577** A1342 55c multi 1.40 .70

**Booklet Stamp**
**Self-Adhesive**
***Die Cut Perf. 9¾x10***

**2577A** A1342 55c multi 1.40 .70
*b.* Booklet pane of 20 28.00

Four-seat Mail Coach, 1858 — A1343

**2010, July 1** *Perf. 13¾*
**2578** A1343 145c multi 3.75 1.90

Andrea Doria
A1344

Pankow Special Train
A1345

**2010, July 1** *Perf. 13½x13¾*
**2579** A1344 45c multi 1.10 .55
**2580** A1345 55c multi 1.40 .70

**Booklet Stamps**
**Self-Adhesive**
***Die Cut Perf. 10***

**2581** A1344 45c multi 1.10 .55
*a.* Booklet pane of 10 11.00
**2582** A1345 55c multi 1.40 .70
*a.* Booklet pane of 10 14.00

Drawings on stamps are subjects of songs by the stamp designer, Udo Lindenberg.

Elly Beinhorn (1907-2007), Pilot — A1346

*Perf. 13½x13¾*

**2010, Aug. 12** **Litho.**
**2583** A1346 55c multi 1.50 .75

Mother Teresa (1910-97), Humanitarian
A1347

**2010, Aug. 12** *Perf. 13¼*
**2584** A1347 70c multi 1.90 .95

Jorge Luis Borges (1899-1986), Writer — A1348

**2010, Aug. 12** *Perf. 13¾x13½*
**2585** A1348 170c multi 4.50 2.25

2010 Frankfurt Book Fair. See Argentina No. 2585.

For Children
A1349

**2010, Sept. 9** **Litho.** *Perf. 13¾*
**2586** A1349 55c multi 1.40 .70

Octoberfest, 200th Anniv. A1350

**2010, Sept. 9** ***Perf. 13¼***
**2587** A1350 55c multi 1.40 .70

Stamp Day — A1351

**2010, Sept. 9**
**2588** A1351 55c multi 1.40 .70

Reunification of Germany, 20th Anniv. A1352

**2010, Sept. 9** **Litho.** ***Perf. 13¾***
**2589** A1352 55c multi 1.40 .70

**Coil Stamp**
**Self-Adhesive**
***Die Cut Perf. 10¼***

**2590** A1352 55c multi 1.50 .75

St. John's Foundation, 150th Anniv. A1353

**2010, Sept. 9** **Litho.** ***Perf. 13¾***
**2591** A1353 90c multi 2.40 1.25

Old Buildings A1354

Buildings in: 45c, Eppingen, 1582. 55c, Trebel-Dänsche, 1734.

**2010, Oct. 7** **Litho.** ***Perf. 13¾***
**2592** A1354 45c multi 1.25 .65
**2593** A1354 55c multi 1.60 .80

See Nos. 2617-2618, 2669, 2702.

Thanksgiving A1355

**2010, Oct. 7**
**2594** A1355 55c multi 1.60 .80

Friedrich Loeffler (1852-1915), Bacteriologist, Virus and Microscope — A1356

**2010, Oct. 7** ***Perf. 13½x13¾***
**2595** A1356 85c multi 2.40 1.25

Friedrich Loeffler Institute, Cent.

**Greetings Type of 2010**
***Die Cut Perf. 10***

**2010, Nov. 11** **Litho.**

**Booklet Stamps**
**Self-Adhesive**

**2596** A1336 55c Dove 1.50 .75
**2597** A1336 55c Angel with heart 1.50 .75
*a.* Booklet pane of 10, 5 each #2596-2597 15.00

Railroads in Germany, 175th Anniv. A1357

**Litho. & Engr.**

**2010, Nov. 11** ***Perf. 13¾***
**2598** A1357 55c multi 1.50 .75

2010 World Alpine Skiing Championships, Garmisch-Partenkirchen — A1358

***Perf. 13½x13¾***

**2010, Nov. 11** **Litho.**
**2599** A1358 55c multi 1.50 .75

Fritz Reuter (1810-74), Writer A1359

**2010, Nov. 11** ***Perf. 13¼***
**2600** A1359 100c multi 2.75 1.40

German Miners' Guild, 750th Anniv. A1360

**2010, Nov. 11** ***Perf. 13½x13¾***
**2601** A1360 145c black & red 4.00 2.00

Glider Flights from Wasserkuppe, Cent. — A1361

**2011, Jan. 3** **Litho.** ***Perf. 13½x13¾***
**2602** A1361 45c multi 1.25 .60

The Wanderer Above the Mists, by Caspar David Friedrich A1362

**2011** ***Perf. 13¾***
**2603** A1362 55c multi 1.50 .75

**Coil Stamp**
**Self-Adhesive**
***Die Cut Perf. 10¼***

**2603A** A1362 55c multi 1.60 .80

Issued: No. 2603, 1/3; No. 2603A, 5/5.

Kellerwald-Edersee National Park — A1363

**2011** ***Perf. 13½x13¾***
**2604** A1363 145c multi 4.00 2.00

**Booklet Stamp**
**Self-Adhesive**
***Die Cut Perf. 10***

**2604A** A1363 145c multi 4.00 2.00
*b.* Booklet pane of 10 40.00

Issued: No. 2604, 1/3; No. 2604A, 4/7.

**Greetings Type of 2010**
***Die Cut Perf. 10***

**2011, Feb. 3** **Litho.**

**Booklet Stamps**
**Self-Adhesive**

**2605** A1336 55c Ship 1.50 .75
**2606** A1336 55c Rainbow 1.50 .75
*a.* Booklet pane of 10, 5 each #2605-2606 15.00

Franz Liszt (1811-86), Composer — A1364

**2011, Feb. 3** ***Perf. 13½x13¾***
**2607** A1364 55c multi 1.50 .75

Werra Valley View of Ludwigstein Castle and Ruins of Hanstein Castle — A1365

**2011, Feb. 3** ***Perf. 13½x13¾***
**2608** A1365 90c multi 2.50 1.25

**Booklet Stamp**
**Self-Adhesive**
***Die Cut Perf. 9¾***

**2609** A1365 90c multi 2.50 1.25
*a.* Booklet pane of 10 25.00

UNESCO World Heritage Sites — A1366

Designs: 55c, Historic Monuments of Ancient Nara, Japan. 75c, Old Town, Regensburg, Germany.

**2011, Feb. 3** ***Perf. 13½x13¾***
**2610** A1366 55c multi 1.50 .75
**2611** A1366 75c multi 2.10 1.10

**Booklet Stamp**
**Self-Adhesive**
***Die Cut Perf. 10***

**2612** A1366 75c multi 2.10 1.10
*a.* Booklet pane of 10 21.00

See Japan No. 3301.

The Four Elements — A1367

Designs: No. 2613, Earth (sand dune). No. 2614, Wind (bird and clouds). No. 2615, Fire (volcano). No. 2616, Water (droplets on leaf).

**2011, Mar. 3** ***Perf. 13½x13¾***
**2613** A1367 55c multi 1.60 .80
**2614** A1367 55c multi 1.60 .80
**2615** A1367 55c multi 1.60 .80
**2616** A1367 55c multi 1.60 .80
*Nos. 2613-2616 (4)* 6.40 3.20

**Old Buildings Type of 2010**

Buildings in: 45c, Alsfeld, 1512-16. 55c, Hartenstein, Saxony, 1625.

**2011, Apr. 7** **Litho.** ***Perf. 13¾***
**2617** A1354 45c multi 1.25 .65
**2618** A1354 55c multi 1.60 .80

Europa A1368

**2011, May 5** **Litho.** ***Perf. 13½x13¾***
**2619** A1368 55c multi 1.60 .80

Intl. Year of Forests.

Automobiles, 125th Anniv. — A1369

**2011, May 5**
**2620** A1369 55c multi 1.60 .80

Wallraf-Richartz Museum, Cologne, 150th Anniv. — A1370

**2011, May 5** ***Perf. 13¾***
**2621** A1370 85c multi 2.50 1.25

German Chamber of Commerce and Industry, 150th Anniv. — A1371

**2011, May 5** ***Perf. 13½x13¾***
**2622** A1371 145c multi 4.25 2.10

National Insurance System, Cent. — A1372

**2011, May 5**
**2623** A1372 205c multi 6.00 3.00

Mecklenburg "Molli" Rail Line, 125th Anniv. — A1373

**2011, June 9**
**2624** A1373 45c multi 1.40 .70

Amnesty International, 50th Anniv. — A1374

**2011, June 9**
**2625** A1374 55c multi 1.60 .80

Berlin Open-Air Gymnasium of Friedrich Ludwig Jahn, 200th Anniv. — A1375

**Litho. & Engr.**

**2011, June 9** ***Perf. 12¾***
**2626** A1375 165c multi 5.00 2.50

Souvenir Sheet

Steam Navigation in Saxony, 175th Anniv. — A1376

**2011, June 9** **Litho.** ***Perf. 13¼***
**2627** A1376 220c multi 6.50 3.25

**Booklet Stamp**
**Self-Adhesive**

***Die Cut Perf. 10¾***

**2628** A1376 220c multi 6.50 3.25
*a.* Booklet pane of 10 65.00

**Lighthouses Type of 2004**

Designs: 55c, Arngast. 90c, Dahmeshöved. No. 2631, Norderney. No. 2632, Warnemünde.

**2011** **Litho.** ***Perf. 13¾***
**2629** A1150 55c multi 1.60 .80
**2630** A1150 90c multi 2.60 1.25

**Booklet Stamps**
**Self-Adhesive**

***Die Cut Perf. 10¾***

**2631** A1150 45c multi 1.25 .65
**2632** A1150 45c multi 1.25 .65
*a.* Booklet pane of 10, 5 each #2631-2632 12.50

Issued: Nos. 2629-2630, 7/7; Nos. 2631-2632, 7/1.

First Publishing of Till Eulenspiegel Folk Tales, 500th Anniv. — A1377

**2011, July 7** ***Perf. 13¼***
**2633** A1377 55c multi 1.60 .80

German Shooting Federation, 150th Anniv. A1378

**2011, July 7** ***Perf. 13¾***
**2634** A1378 145c multi 4.25 2.10

Discovery of Archaeopteryx Fossil, 150th Anniv. A1379

**2011, Aug. 11**
**2635** A1379 55c multi 1.60 .80

Elbe River Tunnel, Hamburg, Cent. — A1380

**2011, Sept. 15** ***Perf. 13½x13¾***
**2636** A1380 55c blue & black 1.50 .75

For Children A1381

**2011, Sept. 15** ***Perf. 13¾***
**2637** A1381 55c multi 1.50 .75

Biertan Church Castle UNESCO World Heritage Site, Romania A1382

**2011, Sept. 15** ***Perf. 13¼***
**2638** A1382 75c multi 2.10 1.10

See Romania No. 5299.

Calla Lily — A1383

**2011, Oct. 13**
**2639** A1383 55c multi 1.50 .75

German Innovations and Inventions — A1384

Designs: 45c, Thermos bottle, currywurst, two-part teabag. 55c, Emil Berliner's gramophone, reel-to-reel tape recorder, mp3.

**2011, Oct. 3** ***Perf. 13½x13¾***
**2640** A1384 45c multi 1.25 .60
**2641** A1384 55c multi 1.50 .75

Pinakothek Art Museum, Munich, 175th Anniv. — A1385

**2011, Oct. 13**
**2642** A1385 145c multi 4.00 2.00

Adveniat Charity, 50th Anniv. A1386

**2011, Nov. 10** ***Perf. 13½x13¾***
**2643** A1386 55c multi 1.50 .75

Kaiser Wilhelm Memorial Church, Berlin, 50th Anniv. A1387

**2011, Nov. 10** ***Perf. 13¼***
**2644** A1387 55c multi 1.50 .75

Emil Wiechert (1861-1928), Geophysicist A1388

**2011, Nov. 10** ***Perf. 13¾***
**2645** A1388 90c multi 2.50 1.25

Skiers in Winter A1389

**2012, Jan. 2** ***Perf. 13½x13¾***
**2646** A1389 45c multi 1.25 .60

King Frederick II (the Great) of Prussia (1712-86) A1390

**2012, Jan. 2** ***Perf. 13***
**2647** A1390 55c multi 1.50 .75

Jasmund National Park — A1391

**2012, Jan. 2** ***Perf. 13½x13¾***
**2648** A1391 55c multi 1.50 .75

**Booklet Stamp**
**Self-Adhesive**
**Size: 39x23mm**

***Die Cut Perf. 10***

**2649** A1391 55c multi 1.50 .75
*a.* Booklet pane of 10 15.00

Spectrum of Sun with Frauenhofer Lines — A1392

**2012** ***Perf. 13½x13¾***
**2650** A1392 90c multi 2.40 1.25

**Booklet Stamp**
**Self-Adhesive**
**Size:39x23mm**
***Die Cut Perf. 10***

**2651** A1392 90c multi 2.40 1.25
*a.* Booklet pane of 10 24.00

Joseph von Fraunhofer (1787-1826), physicist. Issued: No. 2650, 1/2; No. 2651, 4/12.

Zwinger, Dresden, Designed by Matthäus Daniel Pöppelmann (1662-1736), Architect — A1393

**2012** ***Perf. 13½x13¾***
**2652** A1393 145c multi 3.75 1.90

**Booklet Stamp**
**Self-Adhesive**
**Size: 39x23mm**
***Die Cut Perf. 10***

**2653** A1393 145c multi 3.75 1.90
*a.* Booklet pane of 10 37.50

Issued: No. 2652, 1/2; No. 2653, 2/9.

Harz Mountains Narrow-Gauge Railway, 125th Anniv. — A1394

**2012, Feb. 9** ***Perf. 13½x13¾***
**2654** A1394 45c multi 1.25 .60

**Booklet Stamp**
**Self-Adhesive**
**Size: 39x23mm**
***Die Cut Perf. 10***

**2655** A1394 45c multi 1.25 .60
*a.* Booklet pane of 10 12.50

Biathlon World Championships, Ruhpolding — A1395

**2012, Feb. 9** ***Perf. 13½x13¾***
**2656** A1395 55c multi 1.50 .75

Blue Horse I, by Franz Marc A1396

**2012, Feb. 9** **Litho.** ***Perf. 13¾***
**2657** A1396 145c multi 4.00 2.00

Der Blaue Reiter (Blue Rider) art movement, cent.

Reintroduction of Endangered Animals into Native Habitats — A1397

Designs: Nos. 2658, 2660, Lynx (luchs). Nos. 2659, 2661, Elk (elch).

**2012** ***Perf. 13½x13¾***
**2658** A1397 55c multi 1.50 .75
**2659** A1397 55c multi 1.50 .75

**Booklet Stamps**
**Self-Adhesive**
**Size: 39x23mm**
***Die Cut Perf. 10***

**2660** A1397 55c multi 1.50 .75
**2661** A1397 55c multi 1.50 .75
*a.* Booklet pane of 20, 10 each #2660-2661 30.00

Issued: Nos. 2658-2659, 2/9; Nos. 2660-2661, 3/1.

Tree in Spring A1398

**2012, Mar. 1** ***Perf. 13½x13¾***
**2662** A1398 55c multi 1.50 .75

**Booklet Stamp**
**Self-Adhesive**
**Size: 39x23mm**
***Die Cut Perf. 10***

**2663** A1398 55c multi 1.50 .75
*a.* Booklet pane of 10 15.00

Trees at Dusk A1399

**2012, Mar. 1** ***Perf. 13½x13¾***
**2664** A1399 55c multi 1.50 .75

Gerardus Mercator (1512-94), Cartographer A1400

**2012, Mar. 1** ***Perf. 13¼***
**2665** A1400 220c multi 6.00 3.00

Souvenir Sheet

Sistine Madonna, by Raphael, 500th Anniv. — A1401

**2012, Mar. 1** ***Perf. 13¾***
**2666** A1401 55c multi 1.50 .75

See Vatican City Nos. 1496, 1498.

Welthungerhilfe (World Hunger Help) Charity, 50th Anniv. — A1402

**2012, Apr. 12** **Litho.** ***Perf. 13¼***
**2667** A1402 55c multi 1.50 .75

Axel Springer (1912-85), Journalist and Publisher A1403

**2012, Apr. 12** ***Perf. 13¾***
**2668** A1403 55c multi 1.50 .75

**Old Buildings Type of 2010**

Design: Building in Bad Münstereifel, 1644-64.

**2012, May 2** ***Perf. 13¾***
**2669** A1354 165c multi 4.50 2.25

Soccer Fans with German Flags A1404

**2012, May 2** ***Perf. 13¾***
**2670** A1404 55c multi 1.50 .75

**Booklet Stamp**
**Self-Adhesive**
***Die Cut Perf. 11***

**2671** A1404 55c multi 1.50 .75
*a.* Booklet pane of 10 + 5 stickers 15.00

Johann Gottlieb Fichte (1762-1814), Philosopher A1405

**2012, May 2** ***Perf. 13¾***
**2672** A1405 70c multi 1.90 .95

**Lighthouse Type of 2004**

**2012, May 2** ***Die Cut Perf. 10¼***

**Coil Stamp**
**Self-Adhesive**

**2673** A1150 55c Arngast 1.50 .75

Europa A1406

**2012, May 2** ***Perf. 13½x13¾***
**2674** A1406 55c multi 1.50 .75

Grimm's Fairy Tales, 200th Anniv. A1407

**2012, June 14** ***Perf. 13¾***
**2675** A1407 55c multi 1.40 .70

Pfälzer Hutte Mountain Lodge, Liechtenstein — A1408

***Perf. 13½x13¾***

**2012, June 14** **Litho.**
**2677** A1408 75c multi 1.90 .95

See Liechtenstein No. 1542.

German Choir Association, 150th Anniv. A1409

**2012, June 14** ***Perf. 13¼***
**2678** A1409 85c multi 2.10 1.10

Balcony Room, by Adolph Menzel A1410

**2012, June 14** ***Perf. 13¾***
**2679** A1410 260c multi 6.50 3.25

**Lighthouses Type of 2012**

Designs: 45c, Little Borkum Lighthouse (Kleiner Leuchtturm Borkum). 55c, Arkona.

**2012, July 12**
**2680** A1150 45c multi 1.10 .55
**2681** A1150 55c multi 1.40 .70

Apartment Intercom with Names of Different Nationalities — A1411

**2012, July 12** ***Perf. 13½x13¾***
**2682** A1411 55c multi 1.40 .70

Muskauer Park UNESCO World Heritage Site, Germany and Poland — A1412

**2012, July 12**
**2683** A1412 90c multi 2.25 1.10
See Poland No. 4050.

Animals From Shelters A1413

**2012, July 12**
**2684** A1413 145c multi 3.75 1.90

King Otto the Great (912-73) A1414

**2012, Aug. 9** *Perf. 13¾*
**2685** A1414 45c multi 1.25 .60

Gäubodenvolksfest (Folk Festival), Straubing, 200th Anniv. — A1415

**2012, Aug. 9** *Perf. 13½x13¾*
**2686** A1415 55c multi 1.40 .70

Mittenwald Railroad, Cent. — A1416

**2012, Aug. 9**
**2687** A1416 75c multi 2.00 1.00

Valley in Autumn A1417

**2012, Sept. 13**
**2688** A1417 55c multi 1.50 .75

Stamp Day A1418

**2012, Sept. 13**
**2689** A1418 55c multi 1.50 .75
First official airmail flight in Germany, cent.

National Library, Cent. A1419

**2012, Sept. 13**
**2690** A1419 55c multi 1.50 .75

For Children A1420

**2012, Sept. 13**
**2691** A1420 55c multi 1.50 .75

German Bible Association, Cent. — A1421

**2012, Sept. 13**
**2692** A1421 85c multi 2.25 1.10

Second Vatican Council, 50th Anniv. A1422

**2012, Oct. 11** *Perf. 13¾*
**2693** A1422 45c multi 1.25 .60

Chancellor Helmut Kohl, Honorary Citizen of Europe A1423

**2012, Oct. 11**
**2694** A1423 55c multi 1.40 .70

Castles in Gleichen, Mühlburg and Wachsenburg — A1424

**2012, Oct. 11**
**2695** A1424 55c multi 1.40 .70

Domowina (Society of Sorbs and Wends), Cent. — A1425

**2012, Oct. 11**
**2696** A1425 145c multi 3.75 1.90

Numeral — A1426

**2012, Nov. 2** *Perf. 14x13½*
**2697** A1426 3c multi .25 .25

**Self-Adhesive**
***Die Cut Perf. 9¾***

**2698** A1426 3c multi .25 .25

Protest of the Göttingen Seven, 175th Anniv. A1427

**2012, Nov. 2** *Perf. 13¾*
**2699** A1427 55c multi 1.40 .70

Gerhart Hauptmann (1862-1946), 1912 Nobel Literature Laureate — A1428

**2012, Nov. 2**
**2700** A1428 55c multi 1.40 .70

Sistine Madonna, by Raphael, 500th Anniv. A1429

**2012, Nov. 2** *Die Cut Perf. 11*

**Booklet Stamp**
**Self-Adhesive**

**2701** A1429 55c multi 1.40 .70
*a.* Booklet pane of 10 + 4 stickers 14.00

**Old Buildings Type of 2010**

Design: Building in Dinkelbühl, 1600.

**2012, Dec. 6** *Perf. 13¾*
**2702** A1354 58c multi 1.50 .75

Elysée Treaty, 50th Anniv. A1430

**2013, Jan. 2** *Perf. 13½x13¾*
**2703** A1430 75c multi 2.00 1.00
See France No.

Museum Treasures A1431

Designs: 58c, Bust of Queen Nefertiti, from Neues Museum, Berlin. 145c, Ishtar Gate, from Pergamon Museum, Berlin.

**2013, Jan. 2** ***Perf. 14x13¾***

**2704** A1431 58c multi 1.60 .80
**2705** A1431 145c multi 4.00 2.00

Castles and Palaces A1432

Designs: 45c, Glücksburd Castle (Schloss Glücksburg). 58c, Nuremberg Castle (Kaiserburg Nürnberg).

**2013, Jan. 2** ***Perf. 13½x13¾***

**2706** A1432 45c multi 1.25 .60
**2707** A1432 58c multi 1.60 .80

**Booklet Stamp**
**Self-Adhesive**
**Size: 39x23mm**
***Die Cut Perf. 10***

**2708** A1432 58c multi 1.60 .80
*a.* Booklet pane of 10 16.00

The Bleaching, by Max Liebermann (1847-1935) A1433

**2013, Jan. 2** ***Perf. 13¼***

**2709** A1433 240c multi 6.50 3.25

**Booklet Stamp**
**Self-Adhesive**
***Die Cut Perf. 11***

**2710** A1433 240c multi 6.50 3.25
*a.* Booklet pane of 10 65.00

---

## SEMI-POSTAL STAMPS

### Issues of the Republic

Nos. 83, 83d, 100, 100a, 100d Surcharged

**1919, May 1** **Wmk. 125** ***Perf. 14***

**B1** A16 10pf + 5pf on #83d .45 *4.50*
**B2** A22 15pf + 5pf on #100 .45 *4.50*
Set, never hinged 2.75

The surtax was for the war wounded.

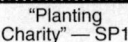

"Planting Charity" — SP1

Feeding the Hungry — SP2

**1922, Dec. 11** **Litho.** **Wmk. 126**

**B3** SP1 6m + 4m ultra & brn .25 *22.50*
**B4** SP1 12m + 8m red org & bl gray .25 *22.50*
Set, never hinged 1.50

Nos. 221, 225 and 196 Surcharged

**1923, Feb. 19**

**B5** A34 5m + 100m .25 *9.00*
**B6** A29 25m + 500m .25 *22.50*
*a.* Inverted surcharge 95.00
Never hinged 190.00
**B7** A32 20m + 1000m 2.10 *87.50*
*a.* Inverted surcharge 975.00 *3,750.*
Never hinged 2,100.
*b.* Green background inverted 260.00 1,200.
Never hinged 400.00
*Nos. B5-B7 (3)* 2.60 *119.00*
Set, never hinged 5.50

Note following No. 160 applies to #B1-B7.

**1924, Feb. 25** **Typo.** ***Perf. 14½x15***

Designs: 10pf+30pf, Giving drink to the thirsty. 20pf+60pf, Clothing the naked. 50pf+1.50m, Healing the sick.

**B8** SP2 5pf + 15pf dk grn 1.10 *2.60*
**B9** SP2 10pf + 30pf ver 1.10 *2.60*
**B10** SP2 20pf + 60pf dk blue 6.00 *7.50*
**B11** SP2 50pf + 1.50m red brn 22.50 *60.00*
*Nos. B8-B11 (4)* 30.70 *72.70*
Set, never hinged 126.00

The surtax was used for emergency aid. See No. B58.

Prussia — SP6

**1925, Dec. 15** ***Perf. 14***

**Inscribed: "1925"**

**B12** SP6 5pf + 5pf shown .50 *1.90*
**B13** SP6 10pf + 10pf Bavaria 1.90 *1.90*
**B14** SP6 20pf + 20pf Saxony 9.00 *13.50*
*a.* Bklt. pane of 2 + 2 labels 190.00 600.00
Never hinged 500.00
*Nos. B12-B14 (3)* 11.40 *17.30*
Set, never hinged 33.40

**1926, Dec. 1** **Inscribed: "1926"**

**B15** SP6 5pf + 5pf Wurttemberg 1.00 *2.25*
**B16** SP6 10pf + 10pf Baden 1.75 *3.00*
*a.* Bklt. pane of 6 + 2 labels 77.50 190.00
Never hinged 190.00
**B17** SP6 25pf + 25pf Thuringia 11.00 *19.00*
**B18** SP6 50pf + 50pf Hesse 40.00 *95.00*
*Nos. B15-B18 (4)* 53.75 *119.25*
Set, never hinged 170.00

See Nos. B23-B32.

Pres. Paul von Hindenburg — SP13

**1927, Sept. 26** **Photo.**

**B19** SP13 8pf dark green 1.25 *2.50*
*a.* Bklt. pane, 4 #B19, 3 #B20 + label 45.00 110.00
Never hinged 110.00
**B20** SP13 15pf scarlet 1.90 *2.25*
**B21** SP13 25pf deep blue 9.00 *21.00*
**B22** SP13 50pf bister brown 11.25 *24.00*
*Nos. B19-B22 (4)* 23.40 *49.75*
Set, never hinged 81.00

80th birthday of Pres. Hindenburg. The stamps were sold at double face value. The surtax was given to a fund for War Invalids.

**Arms Type of 1925**

Design: 8pf+7pf, Mecklenberg-Schwerin.

**1928, Nov. 15** **Typo.**

**Design Type SP6**
**Inscribed: "1928"**

**B23** 5pf + 5pf Hamburg .50 *3.75*
**B24** 8pf + 7pf multi .50 *3.75*
*a.* Bklt. pane, 4 #B24, 3 #B25 + label 110.00 275.00
Never hinged 275.00
**B25** 15pf + 15pf Oldenburg .75 *3.75*
**B26** 25pf + 25pf Brunswick 9.00 *47.50*
**B27** 50pf + 50pf Anhalt 45.00 *90.00*
*Nos. B23-B27 (5)* 55.75 *148.75*
Set, never hinged 178.00

**1929, Nov. 4**

Coats of Arms: 8pf+4pf, Lippe-Detmold. 25pf+10pf, Mecklenburg-Strelitz. 50pf+40pf, Schaumburg-Lippe.

**Inscribed: "1929"**

**B28** SP6 5pf + 2pf Bremen .75 *1.50*
*a.* Bklt. pane of 6 + 2 labels 12.50 32.50
Never hinged 32.50
**B29** SP6 8pf + 4pf multi 1.40 *1.50*
*a.* Bklt. pane, 4 #B29, 3 #B30 + label 40.00 100.00
Never hinged 100.00
**B30** SP6 15pf + 5pf Lubeck 1.50 1.50
**B31** SP6 25pf + 10pf multi 11.00 *45.00*
**B32** SP6 50pf + 40pf choc, ocher & red 40.00 *90.00*
*a.* "PE" for "PF" 150.00 400.00
Never hinged 450.00
*Nos. B28-B32 (5)* 54.65 *139.50*
Set, never hinged 180.00

Cathedral of Aachen — SP24

Brandenburg Gate, Berlin — SP25

Castle of Marienwerder SP26

Statue of St. Kilian and Marienburg Fortress at Würzburg SP27

**Souvenir Sheet**

**Wmk. 223**

**1930, Sept. 12** **Engr.** ***Perf. 14***

**B33** Sheet of 4 375.00 *1,500.*
Never hinged 1,200.
*a.* SP24 8pf + 4pf dark green 26.00 *90.00*
Never hinged 67.50
*b.* SP25 15pf + 5pf carmine 26.00 *90.00*
Never hinged 67.50
*c.* SP26 25pf + 10p dark blue 26.00 *90.00*
Never hinged 67.50
*d.* SP27 50pf + 40pf dark brown 26.00 *90.00*
Never hinged 67.50

Intl. Phil. Exhib., Berlin, Sept. 12-21, 1930.

No. B33 is watermarked Eagle on each stamp and "IPOSTA"-"1930" in the margins. Size: approximately 105x150. Each holder of an admission ticket was entitled to purchase one sheet. The ticket cost 1m and the sheet 1.70m (face value 98pf, charity 59pf, special paper 13pf).

The margin of the souvenir sheet is ungummed.

**Types of International Philatelic Exhibition Issue**

**1930, Nov. 1** **Wmk. 126**

**B34** SP24 8 + 4pf dp green .75 .75
*a.* Bklt. pane of 7 + label 19.00 50.00
Never hinged 50.00
*b.* Bklt. pane, 3 #B34, 4 #B35 + label 25.00 60.00
Never hinged 60.00
**B35** SP25 15 + 5pf car .75 *1.10*
**B36** SP26 25 + 10pf dk blue 9.00 *22.50*
**B37** SP27 50 + 40pf dp brn 21.00 *82.50*
*Nos. B34-B37 (4)* 31.50 *106.85*
Set, never hinged 105.00

The surtax was for charity.

The Zwinger at Dresden SP28

Breslau City Hall SP29

Heidelberg Castle SP30

Holsten Gate, Lübeck SP31

**1931, Nov. 1**

**B38** SP28 8 + 4pf dk grn .60 *1.00*
*a.* Bklt. pane of 7 + label 15.00 35.00
Never hinged 40.00
*b.* Bklt. pane, 3 #B38, 4 #B39 + label 25.00 57.50
Never hinged 57.50
**B39** SP29 15 + 5pf carmine .60 *1.00*
**B40** SP30 25 + 10pf dk blue 7.50 *22.50*
**B41** SP31 50 + 40pf dp brown 32.50 *75.00*
*Nos. B38-B41 (4)* 41.20 *99.50*
Set, never hinged 165.00

The surtax was for charity.

Nos. B38-B39 Surcharged

**1932, Feb. 2**

**B42** SP28 6 + 4pf on 8+4pf 4.50 *9.75*
**B43** SP29 12 + 3pf on 15+5pf 5.00 *11.00*
Set, never hinged 41.50

Wartburg Castle — SP32

Stolzenfels Castle — SP33

Nuremberg Castle — SP34

Lichtenstein Castle — SP35

Marburg Castle — SP36

**1932, Nov. 1** **Engr.**

**B44** SP32 4 + 2pf lt blue .90 .50
*a.* Bklt. pane, 5 #B44, 5 #B45 11.00 27.50
Never hinged 27.50
**B45** SP33 6 + 4pf olive grn .90 .50
**B46** SP34 12 + 3pf lt red .90 1.00
*b.* Bklt. pane of 8 + 2 labels 11.00 27.50
Never hinged 27.50
**B47** SP35 25 + 10pf dp blue 7.50 *17.00*
**B48** SP36 40 + 40pf brn vio 27.50 *60.00*
*Nos. B44-B48 (5)* 37.70 *79.00*
Set, never hinged 140.25

The surtax was for charity.

"Tannhäuser" SP37

Designs: 4pf+2pf, "Der Fliegende Hollander." 5pf+2pf, "Das Rheingold." 6pf+4pf, "Die Meistersinger." 8pf+4pf, "Die Walkure." 12pf+3pf, "Siegfried." 20pf+10pf, "Tristan und

Isolde." 25pf+15pf, "Lohengrin." 40pf+35pf, "Parsifal."

**Wmk. Swastikas (237)**

**1933, Nov. 1** *Perf. 13½x13*

| | | | | |
|---|---|---|---|---|
| **B49** | SP37 | 3 + 2pf bis brn | 4.50 | *5.50* |
| **B50** | SP37 | 4 + 2pf dk blue | 1.90 | *2.25* |
| *b.* | | Bklt. pane, 5 #B50, 5 #B52 | 65.00 | 160.00 |
| | | Never hinged | 160.00 | |
| **B51** | SP37 | 5 + 2pf brt grn | 6.00 | *6.75* |
| **B52** | SP37 | 6 + 4pf gray grn | 1.50 | *2.25* |
| **B53** | SP37 | 8 + 4pf dp org | 3.75 | 3.75 |
| *b.* | | Bklt. pane, 5 #B53, 4 #B54 + label | 77.50 | 190.00 |
| | | Never hinged | 190.00 | |
| **B54** | SP37 | 12 + 3pf brn red | 3.25 | 2.60 |
| **B55** | SP37 | 20 + 10pf blue | 150.00 | *190.00* |
| **B56** | SP37 | 25 + 15pf ultra | 24.00 | *37.50* |
| **B57** | SP37 | 40 + 35pf mag | 110.00 | *125.00* |
| | | *Nos. B49-B57 (9)* | 304.90 | 375.60 |
| | | Set, never hinged | 2,205. | |

***Perf. 13½x14***

| | | | | |
|---|---|---|---|---|
| *B50a* | SP37 | 4 + 2pf dark blue | 1.90 | *3.00* |
| *B52a* | SP37 | 6 + 4pf gray grn | 1.50 | *4.75* |
| *B53a* | SP37 | 8 + 4pf dp org | 3.25 | *4.00* |
| *B54a* | SP37 | 12 + 3pf brn red | 3.25 | *6.25* |
| *B55a* | SP37 | 20 + 10pf blue | 110.00 | 97.50 |
| | | *Nos. B50a-B55a (5)* | 119.90 | 115.50 |
| | | Set, never hinged | 765.00 | |

**Types of Semi-Postal Stamps of 1924 Issue Overprinted**

**Souvenir Sheet**

**1933, Nov. 29** **Typo.** *Perf. 14½*

| | | | |
|---|---|---|---|
| **B58** | Sheet of 4 | 1,350. | *9,750.* |
| | Never hinged | 5,250. | |
| *a.* | SP2 5 + 15pf dark green | 75.00 | *300.00* |
| *b.* | SP2 10 + 30pf vermilion | 75.00 | *300.00* |
| *c.* | SP2 20 + 60pf dark blue | 75.00 | *300.00* |
| *d.* | SP2 50pf + 1.50m dk brown | 75.00 | *300.00* |
| | Any single, never hinged | 190.00 | |

The Swastika watermark covers the four stamps and above them appears a further watermark "10 Jahre Deutsche Nothilfe" and "1923-1933" below. Sheet size: 208x148mm.

The margin of the souvenir sheet is ungummed.

Businessman
SP46

Judge
SP54

Designs: 4pf+2pf, Blacksmith. 5pf+2pf, Mason. 6pf+4f, Miner. 8pf+4pf, Architect. 12pf+3pf, Farmer. 20pf+10pf, Agricultural Chemist. 25pf+15pf, Sculptor.

**1934, Nov. 5** **Engr.** *Perf. 13x13½*

| | | | | |
|---|---|---|---|---|
| **B59** | SP46 | 3 + 2pf brown | .75 | *1.50* |
| **B60** | SP46 | 4 + 2pf black | .75 | *1.50* |
| *a.* | | Bklt. pane, 5 #B60, 5 #B62 | 18.00 | 45.00 |
| | | Never hinged | 45.00 | |
| **B61** | SP46 | 5 + 2pf green | 6.00 | *7.50* |
| **B62** | SP46 | 6 + 4pf dull grn | .45 | *.50* |
| **B63** | SP46 | 8 + 4pf org brn | .75 | *1.90* |
| *a.* | | Bklt. pane, 5 #B63, 4 #B64 + label | 30.00 | 75.00 |
| | | Never hinged | 75.00 | |
| **B64** | SP46 | 12 + 3pf hn brn | .45 | *.50* |
| **B65** | SP46 | 20 + 10pf Prus bl | 15.00 | *21.00* |
| **B66** | SP46 | 25 + 15pf ultra | 15.00 | *21.00* |
| **B67** | SP54 | 40 + 35pf plum | 45.00 | *67.50* |
| | | *Nos. B59-B67 (9)* | 84.15 | *122.90* |
| | | Set, never hinged | 420.00 | |

Souvenir Sheet

SP55

**1935, June 23** **Wmk. 241** *Perf. 14*

| | | | | |
|---|---|---|---|---|
| **B68** | SP55 | Sheet of 4 | 825.00 | 700.00 |
| *a.* | | 3pf red brown | 32.50 | 37.50 |
| *b.* | | 6pf dark green | 32.50 | 37.50 |
| *c.* | | 12pf dark carmine | 32.50 | 37.50 |
| *d.* | | 25pf dark blue | 32.50 | 37.50 |

Watermarked cross on each stamp and "OSTROPA 1935" in the margins of the sheet. Size: 148x104mm. 1.70m was the price of a ticket of admission to the Intl. Exhib., Königsberg, June 23-July 3, 1935.

Because the gum on No. B68 contains sulphuric acid and tends to damage the sheet, most collectors prefer to remove it. **Catalogue unused values are for sheet and singles without gum.**

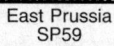

East Prussia
SP59

Skating
SP69

Designs (Costumes of Various Sections of Germany): 4pf+3pf, Silesia. 5pf+3pf, Rhineland. 6pf+4pf, Lower Saxony. 8pf+4pf, Brandenburg. 12pf+6pf, Black Forest. 15pf+10pf, Hesse. 25pf+15pf, Upper Bavaria. 30pf+20pf, Friesland. 40pf+35pf, Franconia.

**Wmk. Swastikas (237)**

**1935, Oct. 4** *Perf. 14x13½*

| | | | | |
|---|---|---|---|---|
| **B69** | SP59 | 3 + 2pf dk brown | .30 | *.35* |
| *a.* | | Bklt. pane, 4 #B69, 5 #B74 + label | 15.00 | 37.50 |
| | | Never hinged | 37.50 | |
| **B70** | SP59 | 4 + 3pf gray | 1.20 | *1.50* |
| **B71** | SP59 | 5 + 3pf emerald | .30 | *1.00* |
| *a.* | | Bklt. pane, 5 #B71, 5 #B72 | 4.75 | 11.00 |
| | | Never hinged | 11.00 | |
| **B72** | SP59 | 6 + 4pf dk green | .25 | *.35* |
| **B73** | SP59 | 8 + 4pf yel brn | 1.75 | 1.50 |
| **B74** | SP59 | 12 + 6pf dk car | .25 | *.35* |
| **B75** | SP59 | 15 + 10pf red brn | 4.25 | *5.50* |
| **B76** | SP59 | 25 + 15pf ultra | 7.50 | 6.00 |
| **B77** | SP59 | 30 + 20pf olive brn | 9.00 | *19.50* |
| **B78** | SP59 | 40 + 35p plum | 8.25 | *14.00* |
| | | *Nos. B69-B78 (10)* | 33.05 | *50.05* |
| | | Set, never hinged | 160.00 | |

**1935, Nov. 25** *Perf. 13½*

12+6pf, Ski jump. 25+15pf, Bobsledding.

| | | | | |
|---|---|---|---|---|
| **B79** | SP69 | 6 + 4pf green | .70 | *1.40* |
| **B80** | SP69 | 12 + 6pf carmine | 1.40 | 1.20 |
| **B81** | SP69 | 25 + 15pf ultra | 6.00 | *7.50* |
| | | *Nos. B79-B81 (3)* | 8.10 | 10.10 |
| | | Set, never hinged | 51.00 | |

Winter Olympic Games held in Bavaria, Feb. 6-16, 1936.

**1936, May 8**

Designs: 3pf+2pf, Horizontal bar. 4pf+3pf, Diving. 6pf+4pf, Soccer. 8pf+4pf, Throwing javelin. 12pf+6pf, Torch runner. 15pf+10pf, Fencing. 25pf+15pf, Sculling. 40pf+35pf, Equestrian.

| | | | | |
|---|---|---|---|---|
| **B82** | SP69 | 3 + 2pf brown | .30 | *.45* |
| *a.* | | Bklt. pane, 5 #B82, 5 #B86 | 8.00 | 20.00 |
| | | Never hinged | 20.00 | |
| **B83** | SP69 | 4 + 3pf indigo | .25 | *.75* |
| *a.* | | Bklt. pane, 5 #B83, 5 #B84 | 8.00 | 20.00 |
| | | Never hinged | 20.00 | |
| **B84** | SP69 | 6 + 4pf green | .25 | *.45* |
| **B85** | SP69 | 8 + 4pf red org | 3.00 | 1.25 |
| **B86** | SP69 | 12 + 6pf carmine | .30 | *.45* |
| **B87** | SP69 | 15 + 10pf brn vio | 5.00 | 3.00 |
| **B88** | SP69 | 25 + 15pf ultra | 3.00 | *3.75* |
| **B89** | SP69 | 40 + 35pf violet | 5.25 | *7.50* |
| | | *Nos. B82-B89 (8)* | 17.35 | *17.60* |
| | | Set, never hinged | 110.00 | |

Summer Olympic Games, Berlin, 8/1-16/36.
See Nos. B91-B92.

Souvenir Sheet

Horse Race — SP80

**1936, June 22** **Wmk. 237** *Perf. 14*

| | | | | |
|---|---|---|---|---|
| **B90** | SP80 | 42pf brown | 7.50 | *13.50* |
| | | Never hinged | 24.00 | |

A surtax of 1.08m was to provide a 100,000m sweepstakes prize. Wmk. 237 appears on the stamp, with "Munchen Riem 1936" watermarked on sheet margin.

For overprint see No. B105.

**Types of 1936**

**Souvenir Sheets**

**1936, Aug. 1** *Perf. 14x13½*

| | | | | |
|---|---|---|---|---|
| **B91** | SP69 | Sheet of 4 | 30.00 | *47.50* |
| **B92** | SP69 | Sheet of 4 | 30.00 | *47.50* |
| | | Set, never hinged | 180.00 | |

11th Olympic Games, Berlin. No. B91 contains Nos. B82-B84, B89. No. B92 contains Nos. B85-B88.

Wmk. 237 appears on each stamp with "XI Olympische Spiele-Berlin 1936" watermarked on sheet margin. Sold for 1m each.

Frontier Highway, Munich — SP81

Designs: 4pf+3pf, Ministry of Aviation. 5pf+3pf, Nuremberg Memorial. 6pf+4pf, Bridge over the Saale, Saxony. 8pf+4pf, Germany Hall, Berlin. 12pf+6pf, German Alpine highway. 15pf+10pf, Fuhrer House, Munich. 25pf+15pf, Bridge over the Mangfall. 40pf+35pf, Museum of German Art, Munich.

***Perf. 13½x14***

**1936, Sept. 21** **Unwmk.**

| | | | | |
|---|---|---|---|---|
| **B93** | SP81 | 3pf + 2pf blk brn | .25 | *.35* |
| *a.* | | Bklt. pane, 4 #B93 + 5 #B98 + label | 10.00 | 24.00 |
| | | Never hinged | 24.00 | |
| **B94** | SP81 | 4pf + 3pf black | .25 | *.55* |
| **B95** | SP81 | 5pf + 3pf brt grn | .25 | *.35* |
| *a.* | | Bklt. pane, 5 #B95, 5 #B96) | 3.75 | 9.75 |
| | | Never hinged | 9.75 | |
| **B96** | SP81 | 6pf + 4pf dk grn | .25 | *.35* |
| **B97** | SP81 | 8pf + 4pf brown | .80 | *1.25* |
| **B98** | SP81 | 12pf + 6pf brn car | .25 | *.35* |
| **B99** | SP81 | 15pf + 10pf vio brn | 2.75 | *3.25* |
| **B100** | SP81 | 25pf + 15pf indigo | 1.90 | *3.75* |
| **B101** | SP81 | 40pf + 35pf rose vio | 3.00 | *5.50* |
| | | *Nos. B93-B101 (9)* | 9.70 | *15.70* |
| | | Set, never hinged | 62.50 | |

Souvenir Sheets

Adolf Hitler — SP90

**Wmk. 237**

**1937, Apr. 5** **Photo.** *Perf. 14*

| | | | | |
|---|---|---|---|---|
| **B102** | SP90 | Sheet of 4 | 18.00 | 12.00 |
| | | Never hinged | 52.50 | |
| *a.* | | 6pf dark green | 1.10 | *1.50* |
| | | Never hinged | 4.00 | |

48th birthday of Adolf Hitler. Sold for 1m.
See #B103-B104. For overprint see #B106.

**1937, Apr. 16** *Imperf.*

| | | | | |
|---|---|---|---|---|
| **B103** | SP90 | Sheet of 4 | 37.50 | 22.50 |
| | | Never hinged | 165.00 | |
| *a.* | | 6pf dark green | 2.25 | 3.00 |
| | | Never hinged | 7.50 | |

German Natl. Phil. Exhib., Berlin, June 16-18, 1937 and the Phil. Exhib. of the Stamp Collectors Group of the Strength Through Joy Organization at Hamburg, Apr. 17-20, 1937. Sold at the Exhib. post offices for 1.50m.

**No. B102 with Marginal Inscriptions**

***Perf. 14 and Rouletted***

**1937, June 10** **Wmk. 237**

| | | | | |
|---|---|---|---|---|
| **B104** | SP90 | Sheet of 4 | 37.50 | *67.50* |
| | | Never hinged | 240.00 | |
| *a.* | | 6pf dark grn + 25pf label | 3.00 | 6.75 |
| | | Never hinged | 9.75 | |

No. B104 inscribed in the margin beside each stamp "25 Rpf. einschliesslich Kulturspende" in three lines.

The sheets were rouletted to allow for separation of each stamp with its component label. Sold at the post office as individual stamps with labels attached or in complete sheets.

Souvenir Sheet No. B90 Overprinted in Red

**1937, Aug. 1** *Perf. 14*

| | | | | |
|---|---|---|---|---|
| **B105** | SP80 | 42pf brown | 60.00 | *97.50* |
| | | Never hinged | 150.00 | |

4th running of the "Brown Ribbon" horse race at the Munich-Riem Race Course, Aug. 1, 1937.

Souvenir Sheet No. B104 Overprinted in Black on Each Stamp

***Perf. 14 and Rouletted***

**1937, Sept. 3** **Wmk. 237**

| | | | | |
|---|---|---|---|---|
| **B106** | SP90 | Sheet of 4 | 75.00 | 45.00 |
| | | Never hinged | 250.00 | |
| *a.* | | 6pf dark grn + 25pf label | 4.50 | 5.50 |
| | | Never hinged | 13.50 | |

1937 Nazi Congress at Nuremburg.

Lifeboat — SP91

Designs: 4pf+3pf, Lightship "Elbe I." 5pf+3pf, Fishing smacks. 6pf+4pf, Steamer. 8pf+4pf, Sailing vessel. 12pf+6pf, The "Tannenberg." 15pf+10pf, Sea-Train "Schwerin." 25pf+15pf, S. S. Hamburg. 40pf+35pf, S. S. Bremen.

***Perf. 13½***

**1937, Nov. 4** **Engr.** **Unwmk.**

| | | | | |
|---|---|---|---|---|
| **B107** | SP91 | 3pf + 2pf dk brwn | .25 | .35 |
| *a.* | | Bklt. pane, 4 #B107 + 5 #B112 + label | 25.00 | |
| | | Never hinged | 47.50 | |
| **B108** | SP91 | 4pf + 3pf black | 1.00 | *1.10* |
| **B109** | SP91 | 5pf + 3pf yel grn | .25 | *.35* |
| *a.* | | Bklt. pane, 5 #B109, 5 #B110 | 14.00 | |
| | | Never hinged | 24.00 | |
| **B110** | SP91 | 6pf + 4pf bl grn | .25 | *.35* |
| **B111** | SP91 | 8pf + 4pf orange | .60 | *1.25* |
| **B112** | SP91 | 12pf + 6pf car lake | .25 | .35 |
| **B113** | SP91 | 15pf + 10pf vio brn | 1.25 | *3.75* |
| **B114** | SP91 | 25pf + 15pf ultra | 3.00 | *3.75* |
| **B115** | SP91 | 40pf + 35pf red vio | 5.00 | *7.50* |
| | | *Nos. B107-B115 (9)* | 11.85 | *18.75* |
| | | Set, never hinged | 83.55 | |

No. B115 actually pictures the S.S. Europa.

Youth Carrying Torch and Laurel — SP100

Adolf Hitler — SP101

**Wmk. 237**

**1938, Jan. 28 Photo. *Perf. 14***

**B116** SP100 6 + 4pf dk green .90 *1.90*
**B117** SP100 12 + 8pf brt car .90 *1.90*
Set, never hinged 15.00

Assumption of power by the Nazis, 5th anniv.

**1938, Apr. 13 Engr. Unwmk.**

**B118** SP101 12 + 38pf copper red 1.90 2.25
Never hinged 9.75

Hitler's 49th birthday.

Horsewoman SP102

**1938, July 20**

**B119** SP102 42 + 108pf dp brn 21.00 *45.00*
Never hinged 125.00

5th "Brown Ribbon" at Munich.

Adolf Hitler SP103

Theater at Saarbrücken SP104

**1938, Sept. 1**

**B120** SP103 6 + 19pf deep grn 2.25 *4.00*
Never hinged 15.00

1938 Nazi Congress at Nuremberg. The surtax was for Hitler's National Culture Fund.

**1938, Oct. 9 Photo. Wmk. 237**

**B121** SP104 6 + 4pf blue grn .90 *1.90*
**B122** SP104 12 + 8pf dk car 1.90 *2.60*
Set, never hinged 20.00

Inauguration of the theater of the District of Saarpfalz at Saarbrücken. The surtax was for Hitler's National Culture Fund.

Castle of Forchtenstein SP105

Designs (scenes in Austria and various flowers): 4pf+3pf, Flexenstrasse in Vorarlberg. 5pf+3pf, Zell am See, Salzburg. 6pf+4pf, Grossglockner. 8pf+4pf, Ruins of Aggstein. 12pf+6pf, Prince Eugene Monument, Vienna. 15pf+10pf, Erzberg. 25pf+15pf, Hall, Tyrol. 40pf+35pf, Braunau.

**Unwmk.**

**1938, Nov. 18 Engr. *Perf. 14***

**B123** SP105 3 + 2pf olive brn .25 *.45*
*a.* Bklt. pane, 4 #B123, 5 #B128 + label 9.25 24.00
Never hinged 24.00
**B124** SP105 4 + 3pf indigo 1.60 1.25
**B125** SP105 5 + 3pf emerald .25 *.45*
*a.* Bklt. pane, 5 #B125, 5 #B126 3.25 7.50
Never hinged 7.50
**B126** SP105 6 + 4pf dk grn .25 .35
**B127** SP105 8 + 4pf red org 1.60 1.25
**B128** SP105 12 + 6pf dk car .25 *.45*
**B129** SP105 15 + 10pf dp cl 3.00 *4.50*
**B130** SP105 25 + 15pf dk blue 2.50 *4.50*
**B131** SP105 40 + 35pf plum 6.00 *7.50*
*Nos. B123-B131 (9)* 15.70 *20.70*
Set, never hinged 76.00

The surtax was for "Winter Help."

Sudeten Couple — SP114

**1938, Dec. 2 Photo. Wmk. 237**

**B132** SP114 6 + 4pf blue grn 1.10 *3.00*
**B133** SP114 12 + 8pf dk car 2.25 *3.00*
Set, never hinged 30.00

Annexation of the Sudeten Territory. The surtax was for Hitler's National Culture Fund.

Early Types of Automobiles SP115

Designs: 12pf+8pf, Racing cars. 25pf+10pf, Modern automobile.

**1939**

**B134** SP115 6 + 4pf dk grn 3.50 3.50
**B135** SP115 12 + 8pf brt car 3.50 3.50
**B136** SP115 25 + 10pf dp blue 5.75 *6.00*
*Nos. B134-B136 (3)* 12.75 13.00
Set, never hinged 82.50

Berlin Automobile and Motorcycle Exhibition. The surtax was for Hitler's National Culture Fund. For overprints see #B141-B143.

Adolf Hitler SP118

Exhibition Building SP119

**Unwmk.**

**1939, Apr. 13 Engr. *Perf. 14***

**B137** SP118 12 + 38pf carmine 1.50 *4.50*
Never hinged 8.25

Hitler's 50th birthday. The surtax was for Hitler's National Culture Fund.

**1939, Apr. 22 Photo. *Perf. 12½***

**B138** SP119 6 + 4pf dk green 1.00 *3.00*
**B139** SP119 15 + 5pf dp plum 1.00 *3.00*
Set, never hinged 12.75

Horticultural Exhib. held at Stuttgart. Surtax for Hitler's National Culture Fund.

Adolf Hitler — SP120

***Perf. 14x13½***

**1939, Apr. 28 Wmk. 237**

**B140** SP120 6 + 19pf black brn 2.25 *5.00*
Never hinged 12.00

Day of National Labor. The surtax was for Hitler's National Culture Fund.
See No. B147.

Nos. B134-B136 Overprinted in Black

**1939, May 18 *Perf. 14***

**B141** SP115 6 + 4pf dk green 18.00 *26.00*
**B142** SP115 12 + 8pf brt car 18.00 *26.00*
**B143** SP115 25 + 10pf dp blue 18.00 *26.00*
*Nos. B141-B143 (3)* 54.00 *78.00*
Set, never hinged 210.00

Nurburgring Auto Races, 5/21, 7/23/39.

Racehorse "Investment" and Jockey SP121

**1939, June 18 Engr. Unwmk.**

**B144** SP121 25 + 50pf ultra 15.00 15.00
Never hinged 60.00

70th anniv. of the German Derby. The surtax was divided between Hitler's National Culture Fund and the race promoters.

Man Holding Rearing Horse — SP122

**1939, July 12**

**B145** SP122 42 + 108pf dp brown 15.00 *24.00*
Never hinged 60.00

6th "Brown Ribbon" at Munich.

"Venetian Woman" by Albrecht Dürer — SP123

**1939, July 12 Photo. Wmk. 237**

**B146** SP123 6 + 19pf dk grn 5.25 *9.75*
Never hinged 26.00

Day of German Art. The surtax was used for Hitler's National Culture Fund.

**Hitler Type of 1939**
**Inscribed "Reichsparteitag 1939"**

**1939, Aug. 25 *Perf. 14x13½***

**B147** SP120 6 + 19pf blk brn 3.50 *9.00*
Never hinged 18.00

1939 Nazi Congress at Nuremberg.

Meeting in German Hall, Berlin SP124

Designs: 4pf+3pf, Meeting of postal and telegraph employees. 5pf+3pf, Professional competitions. 6pf+4pf, 6pf+9pf, Professional camp. 8pf+4pf, 8pf+12pf, Gold flag competitions. 10pf+5pf, Awarding prizes. 12&f+6pf, 12pf+18pf, Automobile race. 15pf+10pf, Sports. 16pf+10pf, 16pf+24pf, Postal police. 20pf+10pf, 20pf+30pf, Glider workshops. 24pf+10pf, 24pf+36pf, Mail coach. 25pf+15pf, Convalescent home, Konigstein.

***Perf. 13½x14***

**1939-41 Unwmk. Photo.**

**B148** 3 + 2pf bister brn 2.25 *5.25*
**B149** 4 + 3pf slate blue 2.00 *5.25*
**B150** 5 + 3pf brt bl grn .55 *1.50*
**B151** 6 + 4pf myrtle grn .70 *1.50*
**B151A** 6 + 9pf dk grn ('41) .70 *2.25*
**B152** 8 + 4pf dp org .70 *1.50*
**B152A** 8 + 12pf hn brn ('41) 1.00 *1.50*
**B153** 10 + 5pf dk brown .70 *2.00*
**B154** 12 + 6pf rose brown .85 *2.00*
**B154A** 12 + 18pf dk car rose ('41) 1.00 *1.90*
**B155** 15 + 10pf dp red lilac .70 *2.25*
**B156** 16 + 10pf slate grn .70 *2.25*
**B156A** 16 + 24pf black ('41) 1.00 *3.75*
**B157** 20 + 10pf ultra .70 *2.00*
**B157A** 20 + 30pf ultra ('41) 1.50 *3.75*
**B158** 24 + 10pf ol grn 2.00 *3.75*
**B158A** 24 + 36pf pur ('41) 3.50 *11.25*
**B159** 25 + 15pf dk blue 1.80 *3.00*
*Nos. B148-B159 (18)* 22.35 *56.65*
Set, never hinged 120.00

The surtax was used for Hitler's National Culture Fund and the Postal Employees' Fund.
See Nos. B273, B275-B277.

Elbogen Castle — SP136

Buildings: 4pf+3pf, Drachenfels on the Rhine. 5pf+3pf, Kaiserpfalz at Goslar. 6pf+4pf, Clocktower at Graz. 8pf+4pf, Town Hall, Frankfurt. 12pf+6pf, Guild House, Klagenfurt. 15pf+10pf, Ruins of Schreckenstein Castle. 25pf+15pf, Fortress of Salzburg. 40pf+35pf, Castle of Hohentwiel.

**1939 Unwmk. Engr. *Perf. 14***

**B160** SP136 3 + 2pf dk brn .25 *.45*
*a.* Bklt. pane, 4 #B160, 5 #B165 + label 9.25 24.00
**B161** SP136 4 + 3pf gray blk 1.75 *1.90*
**B162** SP136 5 + 3pf emerald .30 *.50*
*a.* Bklt. pane, 5 #B162, 5 #B163 4.00 9.75
**B163** SP136 6 + 4pf slate grn .25 *.35*
**B164** SP136 8 + 4pf red org 1.40 *1.60*
**B165** SP136 12 + 6pf dk car .30 *.75*
**B166** SP136 15 + 10pf brn vio 2.25 *4.50*
**B167** SP136 25 + 15pf ultra 1.75 *4.50*
**B168** SP136 40 + 35pf rose vio 2.40 *6.00*
*Nos. B160-B168 (9)* 10.65 *20.55*
Set, never hinged 47.50

Hall of Honor at Chancellery, Berlin — SP145

**1940, Mar. 28**

**B169** SP145 24 + 76pf dk grn 6.00 *17.00*
Never hinged 27.50

2nd National Stamp Exposition, Berlin.

Child Greeting Hitler — SP146

***Perf. 14x13½***

**1940, Apr. 10 Photo. Wmk. 237**

**B170** SP146 12 + 38pf cop red 1.50 *6.00*
Never hinged 12.00

51st birthday of Adolf Hitler.

Armed Warrior SP147

Horseman SP148

**1940, Apr. 30 Unwmk. *Perf. 14***

**B171** SP147 6 + 4pf sl grn & lt grn .30 *1.25*
Never hinged 1.40

Issued to commemorate May Day.

***Perf. 14x13½***

**1940, June 22 Wmk. 237**

**B172** SP148 25 + 100pf dp ultra 3.50 *11.00*
Never hinged 20.00

Blue Ribbon race, Hamburg, June 30, 1940. Surtax for Hitler's National Culture Fund.

Chariot
SP149

**Unwmk.**

**1940, July 20 Engr. *Perf. 14***
**B173** SP149 42 + 108pf brown 22.50 *26.00*
Never hinged 90.00

7th "Brown Ribbon" at Munich.
The surtax was for Hitler's National Culture Fund and the promoters of the race.

View of
Malmedy
SP150

Design: 12pf+8pf, View of Eupen.

***Perf. 14x13½***

**1940, July 25 Photo. Wmk. 237**
**B174** SP150 6 + 4pf dk green .65 *2.90*
**B175** SP150 12 + 8pf org red .65 *2.90*
Set, never hinged 9.50

Issued on the occasion of the reunion of Eupen-Malmedy with the Reich.

Rocky Cliffs of
Heligoland
SP152

**1940, Aug. 9 Unwmk.**
**B176** SP152 6 + 94pf brt bl grn & red org 4.00 *11.00*
Never hinged 22.50

Heligoland's 50th year as part of Germany.

Artushof in
Danzig — SP153

Buildings: 4pf+3pf, Town Hall, Thorn. 5pf+3pf, Castle at Kaub. 6pf+4pf, City Theater, Poznan. 8pf+4pf, Castle at Heidelberg. 12pf+6pf, Porta Nigra Trier. 15pf+10pf, New German Theater, Prague. 25pf+15pf, Town Hall, Bremen. 40pf+35pf, Town Hall, Munster.

**1940, Nov. 5 Engr. *Perf. 14***
**B177** SP153 3 + 2pf dk brn .25 *.45*
a. Bklt. pane, 4 #B177 + 5 #B182 + label 7.50 19.00
Never hinged 19.00
**B178** SP153 4 + 3pf bluish blk .65 *.80*
**B179** SP153 5 + 3pf yel grn .25 *.50*
a. Bklt. pane, 5 #B179, 5 #B180 3.75 9.25
Never hinged 9.25
**B180** SP153 6 + 4pf dk grn .25 *.45*
**B181** SP153 8 + 4pf dp org 1.00 .80
**B182** SP153 12 + 6pf carmine .25 *.45*
**B183** SP153 15 + 10pf dk vio brn 1.00 *2.60*
**B184** SP153 25 + 15pf dp ultra 1.40 *2.60*
**B185** SP153 40 + 35pf red lil 2.50 *6.00*
*Nos. B177-B185 (9)* 7.55 *14.65*
Set, never hinged 35.00

von
Behring — SP162

**1940, Nov. 26 Photo.**
**B186** SP162 6 + 4pf dp green .45 *2.25*
**B187** SP162 25 + 10pf brt ultra .90 *2.25*
Set, never hinged 11.00

Dr. Emil von Behring (1854-1917), bacteriologist.

Postilion — SP163

**1941, Jan. 12 *Perf. 14x13½***
**B188** SP163 6 +24pf dp green 1.25 *3.25*
Never hinged 5.25

Postage Stamp Day. The surtax was for Hitler's National Culture Fund.

Benito
Mussolini
and Adolf
Hitler
SP164

***Perf. 13½x14***

**1941, Jan. 30 Wmk. 237**
**B189** SP164 12 + 38pf rose brn 1.25 *4.50*
Never hinged 6.75

Issued as propaganda for the Rome-Berlin Axis. The surtax was for Hitler's National Culture Fund.

Adolf Race
Hitler — SP165 Horse — SP166

**1941, Apr. 17 *Perf. 14x13½***
**B190** SP165 12 + 38pf dk red 1.25 *3.25*
Never hinged 8.00

52nd birthday of Adolf Hitler. The surtax was for Hitler's National Culture Fund.

***Perf. 13½x14***

**1941, June 20 Engr. Unwmk.**
**B191** SP166 25 + 100pf sapphire 2.75 *7.50*
Never hinged 13.00

Issued in commemoration of the Blue Ribbon race held at Hamburg, June 29, 1941.

Amazons
SP167

**1941, July 20 *Perf. 14***
**B192** SP167 42 + 108pf brown 2.00 *5.25*
Never hinged 9.50

8th "Brown Ribbon" at Munich.

Brandenburg
Gate,
Berlin — SP168

**1941, Sept. 9**
**B193** SP168 25 + 50pf dp ultra 2.75 *7.25*
Never hinged 11.00

Issued in honor of the Berlin races.

Marburg Veldes
SP169 SP170

Pettau — SP171 Triglav — SP172

**1941, Sept. 29 Photo.**
**B194** SP169 3 + 7pf brown .70 *2.00*
**B195** SP170 6 + 9pf purple .55 *2.00*
**B196** SP171 12 + 13pf rose brn .70 *2.40*
**B197** SP172 25 + 15pf dk blue 1.40 *1.75*
*Nos. B194-B197 (4)* 3.35 *8.15*
Set, never hinged 16.00

Annexation of Styria and Carinthia.

View from
Belvedere Palace,
Vienna — SP173

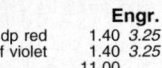

Belvedere
Gardens,
Vienna
SP174

**1941, Sept. 16 Engr.**
**B198** SP173 12 + 8pf dp red 1.40 *3.25*
**B199** SP174 15 + 10pf violet 1.40 *3.25*
Set, never hinged 11.00

Issued to commemorate the Vienna Fair.

Mozart — SP175

**1941, Nov. 28**
**B200** SP175 6 + 4pf dk rose vio .25 *.60*
Never hinged .75

Wolfgang Amadeus Mozart (1756-91).

Philatelist
SP176

**1942, Jan. 11 Photo.**
**B201** SP176 6 + 24pf dp purple .50 *2.75*
Never hinged 3.00

To commemorate Stamp Day.

Soldier's
Head — SP177

**1942, Mar. 10 *Perf. 14x13½***
**B202** SP177 12 + 38pf slate blk .30 *1.50*
Never hinged 1.60

To commemorate Hero Memorial Day.

Adolf
Hitler — SP178

**1942, Apr. 13**
**B203** SP178 12 + 38pf lake 1.50 *6.00*
Never hinged 11.00

To commemorate Hitler's 53rd birthday.

Racing Three-
year-old
SP179

**1942, June 16 Engr. *Perf. 14***
**B204** SP179 25 + 100pf dk bl 4.50 *11.00*
Never hinged 16.50

73rd Hamburg Derby.

Race Horses
SP180

**1942, July 14**
**B205** SP180 42 + 108pf brown 1.50 *5.25*
Never hinged 7.50

9th "Brown Ribbon" at Munich.

Lüneburg Lion
and Nuremberg
Betrothal
Cup — SP181

**1942, Aug. 8 Photo. *Perf. 14x13½***
**B206** SP181 6 + 4pf copper red .25 *1.50*
**B207** SP181 12 + 88pf green .50 *2.25*
Set, never hinged 3.00

10th anniv. of the German Goldsmiths' Society and the 1st Goldsmiths' Day in Germany.

Henlein Monument,
Nuremberg — SP182

**1942, Aug. 29 *Perf. 14***
**B208** SP182 6 + 24pf rose vio .45 *1.50*
Never hinged 1.60

400th anniversary of the death of Peter Henlein, inventor of the pocket watch.

Postilion and
Map of
Europe
SP183

Postilion and Globe — SP184

Postilion SP185

***Perf. 13½x14, 14x13½***

**1942, Oct. 12** **Photo.**

**B209** SP183 3 + 7pf dull blue .25 *1.50*

**Engr.**

**B210** SP184 6 + 14pf ultra & dp brn .35 *1.50*
**B211** SP185 12 + 38pf rose red & dp brn .50 *2.50*
*Nos. B209-B211 (3)* 1.10 *5.50*
Set, never hinged 3.75

European Postal Congress, Vienna.

Nos. B209 to B211 Overprinted in Black

**1942, Oct. 19**

**B212** SP183 3 + 7pf .65 *2.50*
**B213** SP184 6 + 14pf .65 *2.50*
**B214** SP185 12 + 38pf .90 *4.50*
*Nos. B212-B214 (3)* 2.20 *9.50*
Set, never hinged 7.50

To commemorate the signing of the European postal-telegraph agreement at Vienna.

Mail Coach SP186

**1943, Jan. 10** **Engr.**

**B215** SP186 6 + 24pf gray, brn & yel .25 *.90*
Never hinged .75

To commemorate Stamp Day. The surtax went to Hitler's National Culture Fund.

Brandenburg Gate SP187

Nazi Emblem SP188

**1943, Jan. 26** **Photo.**

**B216** SP187 54 + 96pf cop red .45 *2.25*
Never hinged 1.90

10th anniversary of the assumption of power by the Nazis.

**1943, Jan. 26**

**B217** SP188 3 + 2pf olive bister .25 *.90*
Never hinged .60

Used to secure special philatelic cancellations.

Submarine SP189

Designs: 4pf+3pf, Schutz-Staffel Troops. 5pf+4pf, Motorized marksmen. 6pf+9pf, Signal Corps. 8pf+7pf, Engineer Corps. 12pf+8pf, Grenade assault. 15pf+10pf, Heavy artillery. 20pf+14pf, Anti-aircraft units in action. 25pf+15pf, Dive bombers. 30pf+30pf, Paratroops. 40pf+40pf, Tank. 50pf+50pf, Speed boat.

**1943, Mar. 21** **Engr.**

**B218** SP189 3 + 2pf dk brn .35 *1.25*
**B219** SP189 4 + 3pf brown .35 *1.25*
**B220** SP189 5 + 4pf dk grn .35 *1.25*
**B221** SP189 6 + 9pf dp violet .35 *1.25*
**B222** SP189 8 + 7pf brn org .35 *1.25*
**B223** SP189 12 + 8pf car lake .35 *1.25*
**B224** SP189 15 + 10pf vio brn .35 *1.25*
**B225** SP189 20 + 14pf slate bl .35 *1.25*
**B226** SP189 25 + 15pf indigo .35 *1.25*
**B227** SP189 30 + 30pf green .55 *1.90*
**B228** SP189 40 + 40pf red lil .55 *1.90*
**B229** SP189 50 50pf grnsh blk .80 *3.00*
*Nos. B218-B229 (12)* 5.05 *18.05*
Set, never hinged 17.00

Army Day and Hero Memorial Day.
Nos. B220 and B224 exist imperf. Value, each $75.

Nazi Flag and Children SP201

**1943, Mar. 26** **Photo.**

**B230** SP201 6 + 4pf dk green .25 *.90*
Never hinged .85

To commemorate the Day of Youth Obligation when all German boys and girls had to take an oath of allegiance to Hitler.

Adolf Hitler SP202

**1943, Apr. 13**

**B231** SP202 3 + 7pf brown blk .45 *1.50*
**B232** SP202 6 + 14pf dk grn .45 *1.50*
**B233** SP202 8 + 22pf dk chlky bl .45 *1.50*
**B234** SP202 12 + 38pf cop red .45 *1.50*
**B235** SP202 24 + 76pf vio brn .95 *3.50*
**B236** SP202 40 + 160pf dk ol grn .95 *3.50*
*Nos. B231-B236 (6)* 3.70 *13.00*
Set, never hinged 9.75

Hitler's 54th birthday. No. B231 exists imperf. Value $100.

Reich Labor Service Corpsmen
SP203 SP204

Designs: 6pf+14pf, Corpsman chopping. 12pf+18pf, Corpsman with implements.

**1943, June 26** **Engr.**

**B237** SP203 3 + 7pf bis brn .25 *.75*
**B238** SP204 5 + 10pf pale ol grn .25 *.50*
**B239** SP204 6 + 14pf dp blue .25 *.50*
**B240** SP204 12 + 18pf dk red .35 *1.40*
*Nos. B237-B240 (4)* 1.10 *3.15*
Set, never hinged 2.40

Anniversary of Reich Labor Service.
Nos. B237-B238, B240 exist imperf. Values: Nos. B237-B238, $45 each; No. B240, $60.

Rosegger's Birthplace, Upper Styria — SP207

Peter Rosegger SP208

***Perf. 13½x14, 14x13½***

**1943, July 27** **Photo.**

**B241** SP207 6 + 4pf green .25 *.90*
**B242** SP208 12 + 8pf copper red .25 *.90*
Set, never hinged 1.50

Centenary of the birth of Peter Rosegger, Austrian writer.

Hunter SP209

**1943, July 27** **Engr.**

**B243** SP209 42 + 108pf brown .25 *1.25*
Never hinged .90

10th "Brown Ribbon" at Munich.
No. B243 exists imperf. Value $200.

Race Horse — SP210

**1943, Aug. 14**

**B244** SP210 6 + 4pf vio blk .25 *1.25*
**B245** SP210 12 + 88pf dk car .25 *1.25*
Set, never hinged 1.60

Grand Prize of the Freudenau, the Vienna race track, Aug. 15, 1943.

Mother and Children — SP211

**1943, Sept. 1**

**B246** SP211 12 + 38pf dark red .25 *1.25*
Never hinged .80

10th anniversary of Winter Relief.

St. George in Gold — SP212

**1943, Oct. 1**

**B247** SP212 6 + 4pf dk ol grn .25 *.75*
**B248** SP212 12 + 88pf vio brn .25 *1.10*
Set, never hinged 1.10

German Goldsmiths' Society.

Ancient Lübeck — SP213

**1943, Oct. 24** **Photo.**

**B249** SP213 12 + 8pf copper red .25 *1.10*
Never hinged .65

Hanseatic town of Lubeck, 800th anniv.
No. B249 exists imperf. Value, $110.

"And Despite All, You Were Victorious" SP214

**1943, Nov. 5**

**B250** SP214 24 + 26pf henna .25 *1.10*
Never hinged .80

20th anniv. of the Nazis' Munich beer-hall putsch and to honor those who died for the Nazi movement. No. B250 exists imperf; value, $100.

Dr. Robert Koch — SP215

**1944, Jan. 25 Engr. Unwmk.**

**B251** SP215 12 + 38pf sepia .25 *1.10*
Never hinged .75

Centenary of the birth of the bacteriologist, Robert Koch (1843-1910).

Hitler and Nazi Emblems SP216

**1944, Jan. 29 Photo.**

**B252** SP216 54 + 96pf yel brn .25 *1.25*
Never hinged .80

Assumption of power by the Nazis, 11th anniv.

Airport Scene — SP217

Seaplane SP218

Plane Seen from Above — SP219

***Perf. 14x13½, 13½x14***

**1944, Feb. 11 Photo. Unwmk.**

**B252A** SP217 6 + 4pf dk grn .25 *1.10*
**B252B** SP218 12 + 8pf maroon .25 *1.10*
**B252C** SP219 42 + 108pf dp slate bl .30 *2.25*
*Nos. B252A-B252C (3)* .80 *4.45*
Set, never hinged 2.40

25th anniv. of German air mail. The surtax was for the National Culture Fund.

Infant's Crib — SP220

6pf+4pf, Public nurse. 12pf+8pf, "Mother & Child" clinic. 15pf+10pf, Expectant mothers.

**1944, Mar. 2**

**B253** SP220 3 + 2pf dk brn .25 *.50*
**B254** SP220 6 + 4pf dk grn .25 *.50*
**B255** SP220 12 + 8pf dp car .25 *.50*
**B256** SP220 15 + 10pf vio brn .25 *.65*
*Nos. B253-B256 (4)* 1.00 *2.15*
Set, never hinged 1.25

10th anniv. of "Mother and Child" aid.

Assault Boat — SP221

Designs: 4pf+3pf, Chain-wheel vehicle. 5pf+3pf, Paratroops. 6pf+4pf, Submarine officer. 8pf+4pf, Schutz-Staffel grenade throwers. 10pf+5pf, Searchlight. 12pf+6pf, Infantry. 15pf+10pf, Self-propelled gun. 16pf+10pf, Speed boat. 20pf+10pf, Sea raider. 24pf+10pf, Railway artillery. 25pf+15pf, Rockets. 30pf+20pf, Mountain trooper.

**Inscribed: "Grossdeutsches Reich"**

**1944, Mar. 11**

**B257** SP221 3 + 2pf yel brn .25 *1.25*
**B258** SP221 4 + 3pf royal bl .25 *.70*
**B259** SP221 5 + 3pf dp yel grn .25 *.60*
**B260** SP221 6 + 4pf dp vio .25 *.60*
**B261** SP221 8 + 4pf org ver .25 *.70*
**B262** SP221 10 + 5pf chocolate .25 *.60*
**B263** SP221 12 + 6pf carmine .25 *.60*
**B264** SP221 15 + 10pf dp claret .25 *.70*
**B265** SP221 16 + 10pf dk bl grn .25 *1.25*
**B266** SP221 20 + 10pf brt bl .25 *1.50*
**B267** SP221 24 + 10pf dl org brn .25 *1.50*
**B268** SP221 25 + 15pf vio bl .80 *4.00*
**B269** SP221 30 + 20pf olive grn .80 *4.00*
*Nos. B257-B269 (13)* 4.35 *18.00*
Set, never hinged 14.00

To commemorate Hero Memorial Day.

Flora Statue in Fulda's Schloss Garden — SP234

**1944, Mar. 11**

**B270** SP234 12 + 38pf dp brown .25 *.90*
Never hinged .60

1,200th anniversary of town of Fulda.

Adolf Hitler — SP235

**1944, Apr. 14 Engr. Unwmk.**

**B271** SP235 54 + 96pf rose car .30 *1.75*
Never hinged 1.25

To commemorate Hitler's 55th birthday.

**Type of 1939-41 and**

Woman Mail Carrier SP236

Field Post in the East — SP237

Designs: 8pf+12pf, Mail coach. 16pf+24pf, Automobile race. 20pf+30pf, Postal police. 24pf+36pf, Glider workshops.

**1944, May 3 Photo.**

**Designs measure 29½x24½mm**

**B272** SP236 6 + 9pf vio bl .25 *.75*
**B273** SP124 8 + 12pf gray blk .25 *.75*
**B274** SP237 12 + 18pf dp plum .25 *.75*
**B275** SP124 16 + 24pf dk grn .25 *.75*
**B276** SP124 20 + 30pf blue .25 *1.40*
**B277** SP124 24 + 36pf dk pur .25 *1.40*
*Nos. B272-B277 (6)* 1.50 *5.80*
Set, never hinged 2.50

Surtax for the Postal Employees' Fund.

Soldier and Tirolese Rifleman — SP238

**1944, July**

**B278** SP238 6 + 4pf dp grn .25 *.80*
**B279** SP238 12 + 8pf brn lake .25 *.80*
Set, never hinged .75

7th National Shooting Matches at Innsbruck.

Albert I, Duke of Prussia — SP239

**1944, July**

**B280** SP239 6 + 4pf dk bl grn .25 *1.25*
Never hinged .75

400th anniv. of Albert University, Königsberg.

Labor Corps Girl SP240

Labor Corpsman SP241

**1944, June Engr.**

**B281** SP240 6 + 4pf green .25 *.60*
**B282** SP241 12 + 8pf carmine .25 *.65*
Set, never hinged .80

Issued to honor an exhibit of the Reich Labor Service.

Race Horse and Foal — SP242

**1944, July 23 *Perf. 14x13½***

**B283** SP242 42 + 108pf brown .25 *2.00*
Never hinged 1.10

11th "Brown Ribbon" at Munich.

Race Horse's Head in Oak Wreath — SP243

**1944, Aug. Photo. *Perf. 14***

**B284** SP243 6 + 4pf Prus green .25 *1.10*
**B285** SP243 12 + 88pf car lake .25 *1.10*
Set, never hinged 1.10

Vienna Grand Prize Race.

Nautilus Cup in Green Vault, Dresden — SP244

**1944, Sept. 11**

**B286** SP244 6 + 4pf dk green .25 *1.10*
**B287** SP244 12 + 88pf car brn .25 *1.10*
Set, never hinged 1.10

German Goldsmiths' Society.
No. B287 exists imperf. Value $175.

Post Horn and Letter — SP245

**1944, Oct. 2**

**B288** SP245 6 + 24pf dk green .25 *1.25*
Never hinged .65

To commemorate Stamp Day.

Eagle and Serpent — SP246

**1944, Nov. 9**

**B289** SP246 12 + 8pf rose red .25 *1.25*
Never hinged .75

21st anniv. of the Munich putsch.

Count Anton Günther — SP247

**1945, Jan. 6 Typo. *Perf. 13½x14***

**B290** SP247 6 + 14pf brown vio .25 *1.25*
Never hinged .75

600th anniv. of municipal law in Oldenburg. Exists imperf. Value, $75.

People's Army — SP248

**1945, Feb. Photo. *Perf. 14x13½***

**B291** SP248 12 + 8pf rose car .30 *2.25*
Never hinged 1.25

Proclamation of the People's Army (Volkssturm) in East Prussia to fight the Russians.

Elite Storm Trooper (S. S.) — SP249

Storm Trooper (S. A.) — SP250

**1945, Apr. 21** ***Perf. 13½x14***

**B292** SP249 12 + 38pf brt car 7.50 *900.00*
**B293** SP250 12 + 38pf brt car 7.50 *900.00*
Set, never hinged 65.00

12th anniv. of the assumption of power by the Nazis. Nos. B292-B293 were on sale in Berlin briefly before the collapse of that city.
Exist imperf unused. Value same as perf.
Forged cancels abound. Certificates of authenticity mandatory for used examples.

Souvenir Sheets

SP251

**Wmk. 284**

**1946, Dec. 8** **Typo.** ***Perf. 14***

**B294** SP251 Sheet of 3 19.00 *140.00*
Never hinged 45.00

***Imperf***

**B295** SP251 Sheet of 3 19.00 *175.00*
Never hinged 45.00
*a.* A119 20pf light blue 3.75 *19.00*
*b.* A119 24pf orange brown 3.75 *19.00*
*c.* A119 40pf red violet 3.75 *19.00*

No. B294 contains Nos. 543, 544 and 548.
Nos. B294-B295 sold for 5m each. Surtax for refugees and the aged.

Leipzig Proclaimed Market Place, 1160 — SP252

Design: 60pf+40pf, Foreign merchants displaying their wares, 1268.

**Wmk. 48**

**1947, Mar. 5** **Engr.** ***Perf. 13***

**B296** SP252 24 +26pf chestnut brn .25 *4.75*
**B297** SP252 60 + 40pf dp vio blue .25 *4.75*
Set, never hinged 1.50

1947 Leipzig Fairs.
No. B296 exists imperf. Value $150.
See Nos. 580-583, 10NB1-10NB2, 10NB4-10NB5, 10NB12-10NB13 and German Democratic Republic Nos. B15-B16.

Madonna SP254

Cathedral Towers SP255

Designs: 12pf+8pf, Three Kings. 24pf+16pf, Cologne Cathedral.

**Wmk. 286**

**1948, Aug. 15** **Typo.** ***Perf. 11***

**B298** SP254 6 + 4pf org brn .30 *.75*
*a.* "1948-1248" 4.75 *19.00*
Never hinged 11.50
**B299** SP254 12 + 8pf grnsh blue .70 *1.90*
*a.* "1948-1948" 6.25 *22.50*
Never hinged 15.00
**B300** SP254 24 + 16pf car 1.40 *3.50*
**B301** SP255 50 + 50pf blue 3.25 *9.00*
*Nos. B298-B301 (4)* 5.65 *15.15*
Set, never hinged 10.50

700th anniv. of the laying of the cornerstone of Cologne Cathedral. The surtax was to aid in its reconstruction.

Specialists collect Nos. B298-B301 with watermark in four positions: upright, D's facing left; upright, D's facing right; sideways, D's facing up; sideways, D's facing down. Two types of perforation: line and comb.

Brandenburg Gate, Berlin SP256

Bicycle Racers SP257

***Perf. 10½x11½, 11***

**1948, Dec.** **Litho.**

**B302** SP256 10 + 5pf green 3.00 *7.50*
**B303** SP256 20 + 10pf rose car 3.00 *7.50*
Set, never hinged 11.50

The surtax was for aid to Berlin.

**Wmk. 116**

**1949, May 15** **Engr.** ***Perf. 14***

**B304** SP257 10 + 5pf green 1.90 *6.00*
**B305** SP257 20 + 10pf brn org 4.50 *16.50*
Set, never hinged 16.50

1949 Bicycle Tour of Germany.

Goethe at Rome — SP258

Goethe — SP259

30pf+15pf, Goethe portrait facing left.

**1949, Aug. 15**

**B306** SP258 10 + 5pf green .90 *3.00*
**B307** SP259 20 + 10pf red 1.40 *5.25*
**B308** SP259 30 + 15pf blue 7.50 *24.00*
*Nos. B306-B308 (3)* 9.80 *32.25*
Set, never hinged 32.50

Bicentenary of the birth of Johann Wolfgang von Goethe.
The surtax was for the reconstruction of Goethe House, Frankfurt-on-Main.

**Federal Republic**

Bavaria Stamp of 1849 SP260

St. Elisabeth SP261

**1949, Sept. 30** **Litho.** **Wmk. 285**

**B309** SP260 10 + 2pf grn & blk 7.25 *22.50*
Never hinged 13.00

Centenary of German postage stamps.

**1949, Dec. 14** **Engr.** **Wmk. 286**

Designs: 10pf+5pf, Paracelsus. 20pf+10pf, F. W. A. Froebel. 30pf+15pf, J. H. Wichern.

**B310** SP261 8 + 2pf brn vio 8.50 *22.50*
**B311** SP261 10 + 5pf yel grn 6.25 *11.50*
**B312** SP261 20 + 10pf red 6.25 *11.50*
**B313** SP261 30 + 15pf vio bl 32.50 *100.00*
*Nos. B310-B313 (4)* 53.50 *145.50*
Set, never hinged 125.00

The surtax was for welfare organizations.

Seal of Johann Sebastian Bach — SP262

**1950, July 28** ***Perf. 14***

**B314** SP262 10 + 2pf dk grn 22.50 *42.50*
**B315** SP262 20 + 3pf dk car 26.00 *50.00*
Set, never hinged 120.00

Bicentenary of the death of Bach.

Frescoes from Marienkirche SP263

**1951, Aug. 30** **Photo.** **Wmk. 286**

**Center in Gray**

**B316** SP263 10 + 5pf green 27.50 *67.50*
**B317** SP263 20 + 5pf brn lake 32.50 *75.00*
Set, never hinged 180.00

Construction of Marienkirche, Lübeck, 700th anniv.
The surtax aided in its reconstruction.

Stamps Under Magnifying Glass — SP264

St. Vincent de Paul — SP265

**Wmk. 295**

**1951, Sept. 14** **Typo.** ***Perf. 14***

**B318** SP264 10 + 2pf multi 15.00 *45.00*
**B319** SP264 20 + 3pf multi 15.00 *45.00*
Set, never hinged 82.50

Natl. Philatelic Exposition, Wuppertal, 1951.

**1951, Oct. 23** **Engr.**

Portraits: 10pf+3pf, Friedrich von Bodelschwingh. 20pf+5pf, Elsa Brandstrom. 30pf+10pf, Johann Heinrich Pestalozzi.

**B320** SP265 4 + 2pf brown 4.25 *9.00*
**B321** SP265 10 + 3pf green 6.25 *7.50*
**B322** SP265 20 + 5pf rose red 6.25 *7.50*
**B323** SP265 30 + 10pf dp blue 47.50 *110.00*
*Nos. B320-B323 (4)* 64.25 *134.00*
Set, never hinged 130.00

The surtax was for charitable purposes.

Nuremberg Madonna SP266

Boy Hikers and Youth Hostel SP267

**1952, Aug. 9**

**B324** SP266 10 + 5pf green 7.50 *18.00*
Never hinged 15.00

Centenary of the founding of the Germanic National Museum, Nuremberg. The surtax was for the museum.

**1952, Sept. 17** ***Perf. 13½x14***

Design: 20pf+3pf, Girls and Hostel.

**B325** SP267 10 + 2pf green 9.25 *20.00*
**B326** SP267 20 + 3pf dp car 9.25 *20.00*
Set, never hinged 37.50

The surtax was to aid the youth program of the Federal Republic.

Elizabeth Fry SP268

Owl and Cogwheel SP269

10pf+5pf, Dr. Carl Sonnenschein. 20pf+10pf, Theodor Fliedner. 30pf+10pf, Henri Dunant.

**1952, Oct. 1**

**B327** SP268 4 + 2pf org brn 3.25 *6.00*
**B328** SP268 10 + 5pf green 3.25 *6.00*
**B329** SP268 20 + 10pf brn car 6.75 *12.00*
**B330** SP268 30 + 10pf dp blue 35.00 *82.50*
*Nos. B327-B330 (4)* 48.25 *106.50*
Set, never hinged 120.00

The surtax was for welfare organizations.

**1953, May 7** **Wmk. 295** ***Perf. 14***

**B331** SP269 10 + 5pf dp grn 13.00 *30.00*
Never hinged 27.50

50th anniv. of the founding of the German Museum in Munich.

Thurn and Taxis Palace Gate — SP270

August Hermann Francke — SP271

Design: 20pf+3pf, Telecommunications Bldg., Frankfurt-on-Main.

**Wmk. 285**

**1953, July 29** **Litho.** ***Perf. 13½***

**B332** SP270 10 + 2pf yel grn, bl & fawn 8.25 *25.00*
**B333** SP270 20 + 3pf fawn, blk & gray 8.25 *25.00*
Set, never hinged 47.50

The surtax was for the International Stamp Exhibition, Frankfurt-on-Main, 1953.

**Wmk. 295**

**1953, Nov. 2** **Engr.** ***Perf. 14***

Designs: 10pf+5pf, Sebastian Kneipp. 20pf+10pf, Dr. Johann Christian Senckenberg. 30pf+10pf, Fridtjof Nansen.

**B334** SP271 4 + 2pf choc 1.75 *7.50*
**B335** SP271 10 + 5pf bl grn 3.00 *7.50*
**B336** SP271 20 + 10pf red 5.00 *11.00*
**B337** SP271 30 + 10pf blue 20.00 *67.50*
*Nos. B334-B337 (4)* 29.75 *93.50*
Set, never hinged 77.50

The surtax was for welfare organizations.

**Catalogue values for unused stamps in this section, from this point to the end of the section, are for Never Hinged items.**

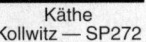

Käthe Kollwitz — SP272

Carrier Pigeon and Magnifying Glass — SP273

Portraits: 10pf+5pf, Lorenz Werthmann. 20pf+10pf, Johann Friedrich Oberlin. 40pf+10pf, Bertha Pappenheim.

**1954, Dec. 28** *Perf. 13½x14*

**B338** SP272 7pf + 3pf brown 3.00 3.00
**B339** SP272 10pf + 5pf green 1.50 1.50
**B340** SP272 20pf + 10pf red 7.50 4.50
**B341** SP272 40pf + 10pf blue 32.50 *40.00*
*Nos. B338-B341 (4)* 44.50 *49.00*

The surtax was for welfare organizations.

**1955, Sept. 14 Wmk. 304** *Perf. 14*

20pf+3pf, Post horn and stamp tongs.

**B342** SP273 10pf + 2pf green 4.50 *5.75*
**B343** SP273 20pf + 3pf red 10.50 *13.50*

WESTROPA, 1955, philatelic exhibition at Dusseldorf. The surtax aided the Society of German Philatelists.

Amalie Sieveking — SP274

Portraits: 10pf+5pf, Adolph Kolping. 20pf+10pf, Dr. Samuel Hahnemann. 40pf+10pf, Florence Nightingale.

**1955, Nov. 15 Photo. & Litho.**

**B344** SP274 7 + 3pf olive bis 3.00 3.00
**B345** SP274 10 + 5pf dk green 2.25 1.50
**B346** SP274 20 + 10pf red org 2.25 1.50
**B347** SP274 40 + 10pf grnsh blue 30.00 *37.50*
*Nos. B344-B347 (4)* 37.50 *43.50*

Surtax for independent welfare organizations.

Boy and Geometrical Designs SP275

Design: 10pf+5pf, Girl playing flute.

**Unwmk.**

**1956, July 21 Litho.** *Perf. 14*

**B348** SP275 7pf + 3pf multi 1.90 *3.00*
**B349** SP275 10pf + 5pf multi 6.50 *7.50*

The surtax was for the Youth Hostel Organization.

The Midwife SP276

10+5pf, Ignaz Philipp Semmelweis. 20+10pf, The mother. 40+10pf, The children's nurse.

**1956, Oct. 1 Photo.**

**Design and Inscription in Black**

**B350** SP276 7pf + 3pf org brn 1.50 *2.25*
**B351** SP276 10pf + 5pf green 1.10 .75
**B352** SP276 20pf + 10pf brt red 1.10 .75
**B353** SP276 40pf + 10pf brt blue 15.00 15.00
*Nos. B350-B353 (4)* 18.70 *18.75*

Issued to honor Ignaz Philipp Semmelweis, the discoverer of the cause of puerperal fever. Surtax for independent welfare organizations.

Children Leaving SP277

Design: 20pf+10pf, Child arriving.

**1957, Feb. 1 Litho.** *Perf. 13½x13*

**B354** SP277 10pf + 5pf gray grn & red org 1.10 *1.90*
**B355** SP277 20pf + 10pf red org & lt bl 2.75 *3.75*

The surtax was for vacations for the children of Berlin.

Young Miner — SP278

10+5pf, Miner with drill. 20+10pf, Miner & conveyor. 40+10pf, Miner & coal elevator.

**1957, Oct. 1 Wmk. 304** *Perf. 14*

**B356** SP278 7pf + 3pf bis brn & blk 1.10 *1.50*
**B357** SP278 10pf + 5pf blk & yel grn .75 .75
**B358** SP278 20pf + 10pf black & red 1.10 .75
**B359** SP278 40pf + 10pf black & blue 16.50 *18.00*
*Nos. B356-B359 (4)* 19.45 *21.00*

Surtax for independent welfare organizations.

"A Hunter from the Palatinate." SP279

10pf + 5pf, "The Fox who Stole the Goose"

**1958, Apr. 1 Litho.**

**B360** SP279 10pf + 5pf brn red, grn & blk 1.50 *1.90*
**B361** SP279 20pf + 10pf multi 3.00 *3.50*

The surtax was to finance young peoples' study trips to Berlin.

Friedrich Wilhelm Raiffeisen SP280

Dairy Maid SP281

Designs: 20pf+10pf, Girl picking grapes. 40pf+10pf, Farmer with pitchfork.

**1958, Oct. 1 Wmk. 304** *Perf. 14*

**B362** SP280 7pf + 3pf gldn brn & dk brn .45 .45
**B363** SP281 10pf + 5pf grn, red & yel .45 .45
**B364** SP281 20pf + 10pf red, yel & bl .45 .45
**B365** SP281 40pf + 10pf blue & ocher 6.00 *7.25*
*Nos. B362-B365 (4)* 7.35 *8.60*

Surtax for independent welfare organizations.

Stamp of Hamburg, 1859 — SP282

Design: 20pf+10pf, Stamp of Lübeck, 1859.

**1959 Engr. Wmk. 304**

**B366** SP282 10pf + 5pf yel green & brown .25 *.60*
*a.* 10pf + 5pf green & brown .75 *2.10*
**B367** SP282 20pf + 10pf red org & red brn .25 *.65*
*a.* 20pf + 10pf maroon & red brown 1.10 *2.10*

"Interposta" Philatelic Exhibition, Hamburg, May 22-31, 1959 for the cent. of the 1st stamps of Hamburg and Lübeck.

The surtax on #B366, B367 was for vacations for the children of Berlin.

Issued: #B366-B367, 8/22; #B366a-B367a, 5/22.

Girl Giving Bread to Beggar SP283

Jacob and Wilhelm Grimm SP284

Designs (from "Star Dollars" fairy tale): 10pf+5pf, Girl giving coat to boy, 20pf+10pf, Star-Money from Heaven.

**1959, Oct. 1 Litho.** *Perf. 14*

**B368** SP283 7pf + 3pf brown & yel .25 *.35*
**B369** SP283 10pf + 5pf green & yel .25 *.35*
**B370** SP283 20pf + 10pf brick red & yel .30 *.35*
**B371** SP284 40pf + 10pf bl, blk, ocher & emer 3.00 *4.50*
*Nos. B368-B371 (4)* 3.80 *5.55*

Surtax for independent welfare organizations.

Little Red Riding Hood and the Wolf — SP285

Various Scenes from Little Red Riding Hood.

**1960, Oct. 1 Wmk. 304** *Perf. 14*

**B372** SP285 7pf + 3pf brn ol, red & blk .45 .45
**B373** SP285 10pf + 5pf grn, red & blk .45 .35
**B374** SP285 20pf + 10pf brick red, emer & blk .45 .35
**B375** SP285 40pf + 20pf brt bl, red & blk 2.25 *3.75*
*Nos. B372-B375 (4)* 3.60 *4.90*

Surtax for independent welfare organizations.

**1961, Oct. 2**

Various Scenes from Hansel and Gretel.

**B376** SP285 7pf + 3pf multi .25 *.30*
**B377** SP285 10pf + 5pf multi .25 *.30*
**B378** SP285 20pf + 10pf multi .25 *.30*
**B379** SP285 40pf + 20pf multi 1.00 *1.75*
*Nos. B376-B379 (4)* 1.75 *2.65*

Surtax for independent welfare organizations.

See B384-B387, B392-B395, B400-B403.

---

Fluorescent Paper was introduced for semipostal stamps, starting with No. B380.

---

Apollo — SP286

10pf+5pf, Camberwell beauty. 20pf+10pf, Tortoise-shell. 40pf+20pf, Tiger swallowtail.

**Wmk. 304**

**1962, May 25 Litho.** *Perf. 14*

**Butterflies in Natural Colors, Black Inscriptions**

**B380** SP286 7pf + 3pf bis brn .35 *.60*
**B381** SP286 10pf + 5pf brt green .35 *.60*
**B382** SP286 20pf + 10pf dp crim .75 *1.10*
**B383** SP286 40pf + 20pf brt blue 1.10 *1.90*
*Nos. B380-B383 (4)* 2.55 *4.20*

Issued for the benefit of young people.

Nos. B381-B383 exist without watermark. Value, each $900 unused, $975 used.

**Fairy Tale Type of 1960**

Scenes from Snow White (Schneewittchen).

**1962, Oct. 10** *Perf. 14*

**B384** SP285 7pf + 3pf multi .25 *.25*
**B385** SP285 10pf + 5pf multi .25 *.25*
**B386** SP285 20pf + 10pf multi .25 *.25*
**B387** SP285 40pf + 20pf multi .80 *1.25*
*Nos. B384-B387 (4)* 1.55 *2.00*

Surtax for independent welfare organizations.

Hoopoe — SP287

Birds: 15pf+5pf, European golden oriole. 20pf+10pf, Bullfinch. 40pf+20pf, European kingfisher.

**1963, June 12 Unwmk.** *Perf. 14*

**B388** SP287 10pf + 5pf multi .45 *.60*
**B389** SP287 15pf + 5pf multi .35 *.60*
**B390** SP287 20pf + 10pf multi .35 *.60*
**B391** SP287 40pf + 20pf multi 1.60 *2.40*
*Nos. B388-B391 (4)* 2.75 *4.20*

Issued for the benefit of young people.

**Fairy Tale Type of 1960**

Various Scenes from the Grimm Brothers' "The Wolf and the Seven Kids."

**1963, Sept. 23 Litho.**

**B392** SP285 10pf + 5pf multi .25 *.25*
**B393** SP285 15pf + 5pf multi .25 *.25*
**B394** SP285 20pf + 10pf multi .25 *.25*
**B395** SP285 40pf + 20pf multi .60 *1.10*
*Nos. B392-B395 (4)* 1.35 *1.85*

Surtax for independent welfare organizations.

Herring SP288

Fish: 15pf+5pf, Rosefish. 20pf+10pf, Carp. 40pf+20pf, Cod.

**1964, Apr. 10 Unwmk.** *Perf. 14*

**B396** SP288 10pf + 5pf multi .25 *.30*
**B397** SP288 15pf + 5pf multi .25 *.30*
**B398** SP288 20pf + 10pf multi .35 *.45*
**B399** SP288 40pf + 20pf multi .95 *1.90*
*Nos. B396-B399 (4)* 1.80 *2.95*

Issued for the benefit of young people.

**Fairy Tale Type of 1960**

Various Scenes from Sleeping Beauty (Dornroschen).

**1964, Oct. 6 Litho. *Perf. 14***
**B400** SP285 10pf + 5pf multi .25 *.25*
**B401** SP285 15pf + 5pf multi .25 *.25*
**B402** SP285 20pf + 10pf multi .25 *.25*
**B403** SP285 40pf + 20pf multi .35 *.90*
*Nos. B400-B403 (4)* 1.10 *1.65*

Surtax for independent welfare organizations.

Woodcock SP289

Birds: 15pf+5pf, Ring-necked pheasant. 20pf+10pf, Black grouse. 40pf+20pf, Capercaillie.

**1965, Apr. 1 Unwmk. *Perf. 14***
**B404** SP289 10pf + 5pf multi .25 *.30*
**B405** SP289 15pf + 5pf multi .25 *.30*
**B406** SP289 20pf + 10pf multi .25 *.30*
**B407** SP289 40pf + 20pf multi .30 *.90*
*Nos. B404-B407 (4)* 1.05 *1.80*

Issued for the benefit of young people.

Cinderella Feeding Pigeons SP290

Various Scenes from Cinderella.

**1965, Oct. 6 Litho. *Perf. 14***
**B408** SP290 10pf + 5pf multi .25 *.25*
**B409** SP290 15pf + 5pf multi .25 *.25*
**B410** SP290 20pf + 10pf multi .25 *.25*
**B411** SP290 40pf + 20pf multi .45 *.65*
*Nos. B408-B411 (4)* 1.20 *1.40*

Surtax for independent welfare organizations. See Nos. B418-B421, B426-B429.

Roe Deer — SP291

Designs: 20pf+10pf, Chamois. 30pf+15pf, Fallow deer. 50pf+25pf, Red deer.

**1966, Apr. 22 Litho. *Perf. 14***
**B412** SP291 10pf + 5pf multi .25 .25
**B413** SP291 20pf + 10pf multi .25 .25
**B414** SP291 30pf + 15pf multi .25 *.30*
**B415** SP291 50pf + 25pf multi .60 *.90*
*Nos. B412-B415 (4)* 1.35 *1.70*

Issued for the benefit of young people. See Nos. B422-B425.

Prussian Letter Carrier — SP292

Design: 30pf+15pf, Bavarian mail coach.

**1966 Litho. *Perf. 14***
**B416** SP292 30pf + 15pf multi .35 *.65*
**B417** SP292 50pf + 25pf multi .50 *.65*

Meeting of the Federation Internationale de Philatélie (FIP), Munich, Sept. 26-29, and stamp exhibition, Municipal Museum, Sept. 24-Oct. 1. The surcharge was for the Foundation for the Promotion of Philately and Postal History.
Issued: #B416, 9/24; #B417, 7/13.

### Fairy Tale Type of 1965

Various Scenes from The Princess and the Frog.

**1966, Oct. 5 Litho. *Perf. 14***
**B418** SP290 10pf + 5pf multi .25 *.25*
**B419** SP290 20pf + 10pf multi .25 *.25*
**B420** SP290 30pf + 15pf multi .25 *.25*
**B421** SP290 50pf + 25pf multi .45 *.90*
*Nos. B418-B421 (4)* 1.20 *1.65*

Surtax for independent welfare organizations.

### Animal Type of 1966

10pf+5pf, Rabbit. 20pf+10pf, Ermine. 30pf+15pf, Hamster. 50pf+25pf, Red fox.

**1967, Apr. 4 Litho. *Perf. 14***
**B422** SP291 10pf + 5pf multi .25 *.30*
**B423** SP291 20pf + 10pf multi .25 *.30*
**B424** SP291 30pf + 15pf multi .45 *.60*
**B425** SP291 50pf + 25pf multi .95 *1.50*
*Nos. B422-B425 (4)* 1.90 *2.70*

Issued for the benefit of young people.

### Fairy Tale Type of 1965

Various Scenes from Frau Holle.

**1967, Oct. 3 Litho. *Perf. 14***
**B426** SP290 10pf + 5pf multi .25 *.25*
**B427** SP290 20pf + 10pf multi .25 *.25*
**B428** SP290 30pf + 15pf multi .25 *.25*
**B429** SP290 50pf + 25pf multi .60 *1.10*
*Nos. B426-B429 (4)* 1.35 *1.85*

Surtax for independent welfare organizations.

Wildcat SP293

Animals: 20pf+10pf, Otter. 30pf+15pf, Badger. 50pf+25pf, Beaver.

**1968, Feb. 2 Photo. Unwmk.**
**B430** SP293 10pf + 5pf multi .25 *.45*
**B431** SP293 20pf + 15pf multi .35 *.75*
**B432** SP293 30pf + 15pf multi .50 *1.00*
**B433** SP293 50pf + 25pf multi 1.90 *3.00*
*Nos. B430-B433 (4)* 3.00 *5.20*

The surtax was for the benefit of young people.

### Olympic Games Type of Regular Issue

10pf+5pf, Karl-Friedrich Freiherr von Langen, equestrian. 20pf+10pf, Rudolf Harbig, runner. 30pf+15pf, Helene Mayer, fencer. 50pf+25pf, Carl Diem, sports organizer.

### Lithographed and Engraved

**1968, June 6 Unwmk. *Perf. 14***
**B434** A285 10 + 5pf olive & dk brn .30 .30
**B435** A285 20 + 10pf dp emer & dk grn .30 .30
**B436** A285 30 + 15pf dp rose & dk red .50 .50
**B437** A285 50 + 25pf brt bl & dk bl .80 *.90*
*Nos. B434-B437 (4)* 1.90 2.00

The surtax was for the Foundation for the Promotion of the 1972 Olympic Games in Munich.

Doll, c. 1878 — SP294

Various 19th Cent. Dolls. #B438-B440 are from Germanic Natl. Museum, Nuremberg; #B441 is from Altona Museum, Hamburg.

**1968, Oct. 3 Litho. *Perf. 14***
**B438** SP294 10pf + 5pf multi .25 *.25*
**B439** SP294 20pf + 10pf multi .25 *.25*
**B440** SP294 30pf + 15pf multi .25 *.25*
**B441** SP294 50pf + 25pf multi .60 *.90*
*Nos. B438-B441 (4)* 1.35 *1.65*

Surtax for independent welfare organizations.

Pony — SP295

Horses: 20pf+10pf, Work horse. 30pf+15pf, Hotblood. 50pf+25pf, Thoroughbred.

**1969, Feb. 6 Litho. *Perf. 14***
**B442** SP295 10pf + 5pf multi .30 *.45*
**B443** SP295 20pf + 10pf multi .30 *.45*
**B444** SP295 30pf + 15pf multi .50 *.75*
**B445** SP295 50pf + 25pf multi 1.60 1.50
*Nos. B442-B445 (4)* 2.70 *3.15*

Surtax for the benefit of young people.

SP296

SP297

Olympic Rings and: 10pf+5pf, Track. 20pf+10pf, Hockey. 30pf+15pf, Archery. 50pf+25pf, Sailing.

**1969, June 4 Photo. *Perf. 14***
**B446** SP296 10pf + 5pf dk brn & lem .25 .25
**B447** SP296 20pf + 10pf bl grn & emer .35 .30
**B448** SP296 30pf + 15pf mag & dp lil rose .50 .45
**B449** SP296 50pf + 25pf dp bl & brt bl 1.10 .90
*Nos. B446-B449 (4)* 2.20 1.90

1972 Olympic Games in Munich. The surtax was for the German Olympic Committee.

**1969, Oct. 2 Litho. *Perf. 13½x14***

Tin Toys: 10pf+5pf, Locomotive. 20pf+10pf, Gardener. 30pf+15pf, Bird seller. 50pf+25pf, Knight on horseback.

**B450** SP297 10pf + 5pf multi .25 .25
**B451** SP297 20pf + 10pf multi .25 .25
**B452** SP297 30pf + 15pf multi .30 .30
**B453** SP297 50pf + 25pf multi .85 *1.10*
*Nos. B450-B453 (4)* 1.65 1.90

Surtax for independent welfare organizations.

### Tin Toy Type of 1969 Inscribed: "Weihnachtsmarke 1969"

Christmas: 10pf+5pf, Jesus in Manger.

**1969, Nov. 13 *Perf. 13½x14***
**B454** SP297 10pf + 5pf multi .30 .30

Heinrich von Rugge — SP298

Minnesingers: 20pf+10pf, Wolfram von Eschenbach. 30pf+15pf, Walther von Metz. 50pf+25pf, Walther von der Vogelweide.

**1970, Feb. 5 Photo. *Perf. 13½x14***
**B455** SP298 10pf + 5pf multi .35 .30
**B456** SP298 20pf + 10pf multi .60 .35
**B457** SP298 30pf + 15pf multi .75 .60
**B458** SP298 50pf + 25pf multi 1.60 1.50
*Nos. B455-B458 (4)* 3.30 2.75

Surtax was for benefit of young people.

Residenz (Palace), Munich SP299

Munich Buildings: 20pf+10pf, Propylaea. 30pf+15pf, Glyptothek. 50pf+25pf, Bavaria Statue and Colonnade.

**1970, June 5 Engr. *Perf. 14***
**B459** SP299 10pf + 5pf olive bis .25 .25
**B460** SP299 20pf + 10pf dk bl grn .45 .30
**B461** SP299 30pf + 15pf carmine .60 .45
**B462** SP299 50pf + 25pf dk blue 1.00 .90
*Nos. B459-B462 (4)* 2.30 1.90

The surtax was for the Foundation for the Promotion of the 1972 Olympic Games in Munich.

Jester — SP300

King Caspar — SP301

Puppets: 20pf+10pf, "Hanswurst." 30pf+15pf, Clown. 50pf+25pf, Harlequin.

**1970, Oct. 6 Litho. *Perf. 13½x14***
**B463** SP300 10pf + 5pf multi .25 .25
**B464** SP300 20pf + 10pf multi .25 *.30*
**B465** SP300 30pf + 15pf multi .35 .35
**B466** SP300 50pf + 25pf multi .90 *.95*
*Nos. B463-B466 (4)* 1.75 *1.85*

Surtax for independent welfare organizations.

**1970, Nov. 12**

Christmas: 10pf+5pf, Rococo Angel, from Ursuline Sisters' Convent, Innsbruck.

**B467** SP300 10pf + 5pf multi .30 .25

**1971, Feb. 5 Litho. *Perf. 14***

Children's Drawings: 20pf+10pf, Flea. 30pf+15pf, Puss-in-Boots. 50pf+25pf, Snake.

**B468** SP301 10pf + 5pf multi .30 .30
**B469** SP301 20pf + 10pf multi .35 .35
**B470** SP301 30pf + 15pf multi .60 .60
**B471** SP301 50pf + 25pf multi 1.00 1.00
*Nos. B468-B471 (4)* 2.25 2.25

Surtax for the benefit of young people.

Ski Jump — SP302

Women Churning Butter — SP303

20pf+10pf, Figure skating. 30pf+15pf, Downhill skiing. 50pf+25pf, Ice hockey.

### "1971" at Lower Right

**1971, June 4 Litho. *Perf. 14***
**B472** SP302 10pf + 5pf brn org & blk .25 .25
**B473** SP302 20pf + 10pf green & blk .45 .30
**B474** SP302 30pf + 15pf rose red & blk .60 .60
**B475** SP302 50pf + 25pf blue & blk 1.50 1.50
*a.* Souvenir sheet of 4 3.00 2.50
*b.* 10pf + 5pf brown org & blk .25 .25
*c.* 20pf + 10pf green & black .45 .30
*d.* 30pf + 15pf rose red & black .80 .60
*e.* 50pf + 25pf blue & black 1.50 1.25
*Nos. B472-B475 (4)* 2.80 2.65

Olympic Games 1972.
#B475a contains #B475b-B475e which lack the small date ("1971") at lower right.

**1971, Oct. 5 Litho. *Perf. 14***

Wooden Toys: 25pf+10pf, Horseback rider. 30pf+15pf, Nutcracker. 60pf+30pf, Dovecot.

**B476** SP303 20pf + 10pf multi .25 .25
**B477** SP303 25pf + 10pf multi .25 .25
**B478** SP303 30pf + 15pf multi .45 .45
**B479** SP303 60pf + 30pf multi 1.25 1.25
*Nos. B476-B479 (4)* 2.20 2.20

Surtax for independent welfare organizations.

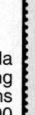

**1971, Nov. 11**

Christmas: Christmas angel with lights.

**B480** SP303 20pf + 10pf multi .45 .35

Ducks Crossing Road — SP304

Designs: 25pf+10pf, Hunter chasing deer and rabbits. 30pf+15pf, Girl protecting birds from cat. 60pf+30pf, Boy annoying swans.

**1972, Feb. 4 Litho. *Perf. 14***

**B481** SP304 20pf + 10pf multi .50 .45
**B482** SP304 25pf + 10pf multi .40 .30
**B483** SP304 30pf + 15pf multi .75 .75
**B484** SP304 60pf + 30pf multi 1.50 1.50
*Nos. B481-B484 (4)* 3.15 3.00

Animal protection. Surtax for the benefit of young people.

Olympic Rings and Wrestling — SP305

25pf+10pf, Sailing. 30pf+15pf, Gymnastics. 60pf+30pf, Swimming.

**1972, June 5 Photo. *Perf. 14***

**B485** SP305 20pf + 10pf multi .45 .35
**B486** SP305 25pf + 10pf multi .45 .35
**B487** SP305 30pf + 15pf multi .45 .35
**B488** SP305 60pf + 30pf multi 1.60 1.50
*Nos. B485-B488 (4)* 2.95 2.55

20th Olympic Games, Munich, Aug. 26 Sept. 10. See No. B490.

Souvenir Sheet

Olympic Games Site, Munich — SP306

**1972, July 5 Litho. *Perf. 14***

**B489** SP306 Sheet of 4 5.00 5.00
*a.* 25pf + 10pf Gymnastics stadium 1.10 1.10
*b.* 30pf + 15pf Soccer stadium 1.10 1.10
*c.* 40pf + 20pf Tent and lake 1.10 1.10
*d.* 70pf + 35pf Television tower, vert. 1.10 1.10

20th Olympic Games, Munich. Surcharge was for the Foundation for the Promotion of the Munich Olympic Games.

**Olympic Games Type of 1972**
Souvenir Sheet

**1972, Aug. 18 Litho. *Perf. 14***

**B490** Sheet of 4 4.50 4.50
*a.* SP305 25pf + 5pf Long jump, women's .45 .45
*b.* SP305 30pf + 10pf Basketball 1.25 1.25
*c.* SP305 40pf + 10pf Discus, women's 1.60 1.60
*d.* SP305 70pf + 10pf Canoeing .80 .80
*e.* Bklt. pane of 4, #B490a-B490d 8.00 8.00

20th Olympic Games, Munich.

Knight — SP307

**1972, Oct. 5**

**B491** SP307 25pf + 10pf shown .30 .30
**B492** SP307 30pf + 15pf Rook .30 .25
**B493** SP307 40pf + 20pf Queen .50 .25
**B494** SP307 70pf + 35pf King 1.90 1.75
*Nos. B491-B494 (4)* 3.00 2.55

19th cent. chess pieces made by Faience Works, Gien, France; now in Hamburg Museum. Surtax for independent welfare organizations.

Adoration of the Kings — SP308

**1972, Nov. 10 Litho.**

**B495** SP308 30pf + 15pf multi .65 .45

Christmas 1972.

Osprey SP309

Hesse-Kassel SP310

Birds of Prey: 30pf+15pf, Buzzard. 40pf+20pf, Red kite. 70pf+35pf, Montagu's harrier.

**1973, Feb. 6 Photo. *Perf. 14***

**B496** SP309 25pf + 10pf multi .90 .75
**B497** SP309 30pf + 15pf multi 1.10 .90
**B498** SP309 40pf + 20pf multi 1.50 1.40
**B499** SP309 70pf + 35pf multi 3.50 3.50
*Nos. B496-B499 (4)* 7.00 6.55

Surtax was for benefit of young people.

**1973, Apr. 5 Litho. *Perf. 14***

Posthouse Signs: No. B501, Prussia. No. B502a, Württemberg. No. B502b, Bavaria.

**B500** SP310 40pf + 20pf multi .65 .65
**B501** SP310 70pf + 35pf multi 1.25 1.25

**Souvenir Sheet**

**B502** Sheet of 2 4.25 4.25
*a.* SP310 40pf + 20pf multi .90 .90
*b.* SP310 70pf + 35pf multi 1.50 1.50

IBRA München 1973 International Philatelic Exhibition, Munich, May 11-20. No. B502 sold for 2.20 mark.

French Horn, 19th Century — SP311

Christmas Star — SP312

Musical Instruments: 30pf+15pf, Pedal piano, 18th century. 40pf+20pf, Violin, 18th century. 70pf+35pf, Pedal harp, 18th century.

**1973, Oct. 5 Litho. *Perf. 14***

**B503** SP311 25pf + 10pf multi .50 .30
**B504** SP311 30pf + 15pf multi .60 .30
**B505** SP311 40pf + 20pf multi .75 .45
**B506** SP311 70pf + 35pf multi 1.90 1.50
*Nos. B503-B506 (4)* 3.75 2.55

Surtax was for independent welfare organizations.

**1973, Nov. 9 Litho. & Engr.**

**B507** SP312 30pf + 15pf multi .60 .45

Christmas 1973.

Young Builder — SP313

30+15pf, Girl in national costume. 40+20pf, Boy studying. 70+35pf, Girl with microscope.

**1974, Apr. 17 Photo. *Perf. 14***

**B508** SP313 25pf + 10pf multi .50 .45
**B509** SP313 30pf + 15pf multi .90 .75
**B510** SP313 40pf + 20pf multi 1.50 1.40
**B511** SP313 70pf + 35pf multi 2.75 2.25
*Nos. B508-B511 (4)* 5.65 4.85

Surtax was for benefit of young people.

Campion — SP314

Flowers: 40pf+20pf, Foxglove. 50pf+25pf, Mallow. 70pf+35pf, Bellflower.

**1974, Oct. 15 Litho. *Perf. 14***

**B512** SP314 30pf + 15pf multi .30 .30
**B513** SP314 40pf + 20pf multi .40 .30
**B514** SP314 50pf + 25pf multi .45 .40
**B515** SP314 70pf + 35pf multi 1.25 1.25
*Nos. B512-B515 (4)* 2.40 2.25

Surtax was for independent welfare organizations.

**1974, Oct. 29**

Christmas: 40pf+20pf, Advent decoration.

**B516** SP314 40pf + 20pf multi .75 .50

Diesel Locomotive Class 218 — SP315

Locomotives: 40pf+20pf, Electric engine Class 103. 50pf+25pf, Electric rail motor train Class 403. 70pf+35pf, Magnetic suspension train "Transrapid" (model).

**1975, Apr. 15 Litho. *Perf. 14***

**B517** SP315 30pf + 15pf multi .45 .40
**B518** SP315 40pf + 20pf multi .70 .60
**B519** SP315 50pf + 25pf multi .95 .90
**B520** SP315 70pf + 35pf multi 1.60 1.50
*Nos. B517-B520 (4)* 3.70 3.40

Surtax was for benefit of young people.

Edelweiss — SP316

Alpine Flowers: 40pf+20pf, Trollflower. 50pf+25pf, Alpine rose. 70pf+35pf, Pasqueflower.

**1975, Oct. 15 Litho. *Perf. 14***

**B521** SP316 30pf + 15pf multi .35 .30
**B522** SP316 40pf + 20pf multi .35 .30
**B523** SP316 50pf + 25pf multi .60 .45
**B524** SP316 70pf + 35pf multi 1.40 1.40
*Nos. B521-B524 (4)* 2.70 2.45

Surtax was for independent welfare organizations.

**1975, Nov. 14**

Christmas: Snow rose.

**B525** SP316 40pf + 20pf multi .75 .75

Basketball SP317

Designs: 40pf+20pf, Rowing. 50pf+25pf, Gymnastics, women's. 70pf+35pf, Volleyball.

**1976, Apr. 6 Litho. *Perf. 14***

**B526** SP317 30pf + 15pf multi .45 .35
**B527** SP317 40pf + 20pf multi .80 .60
**B528** SP317 50pf + 25pf multi 1.00 .90
**B529** SP317 70pf + 35pf multi 1.40 1.25
*Nos. B526-B529 (4)* 3.65 3.10

Youth training for Olympic Games. Surtax was for benefit of young people.

Swimmer and Olympic Rings — SP318

30pf+15pf, Hockey. 50pf+25pf, High jump. 70pf+35pf, Rowing, coxed four.

**1976, Apr. 6**

**B530** SP318 40pf + 20pf multi .75 .45
**B531** SP318 50pf + 25pf multi 1.00 .75

**Souvenir Sheet**

**B532** Sheet of 2 2.00 2.00
*a.* SP318 30pf + 15pf multi .75 .50
*b.* SP318 70pf + 35pf multi 1.00 .85

21st Olympic Games, Montreal, Canada, July 17-Aug. 1. The surtax was for the German Sports Aid Foundation.

Phlox SP319

Flowers: 40pf+20pf, Marigolds. 50pf+25pf, Dahlias. 70pf+35pf, Pansies.

**1976, Oct. 14 Litho. *Perf. 14***

**B533** SP319 30pf + 15pf multi .45 .35
**B534** SP319 40pf + 20pf multi .60 .50
**B535** SP319 50pf + 25pf multi .65 .60
**B536** SP319 70pf + 35pf multi 1.10 1.10
*Nos. B533-B536 (4)* 2.80 2.55

Surtax was for independent welfare organizations.

Souvenir Sheet

Nativity, Window, Frauenkirche, Esslingen — SP320

**1976, Nov. 16** **Litho. & Engr.**
**B537** SP320 50pf + 25pf multi .90 .75

Christmas 1976.

Wapen von Hamburg, c. 1730 SP321

Historic Ships: 40pf+20pf, Preussen, 5-master, 1902. 50pf+25pf, Bremen, 1929. 70pf+35pf, Freighter Sturmfels, 1972.

**1977, Apr. 14** **Litho.** ***Perf. 14***
**B538** SP321 30pf + 15pf multi .50 .50
**B539** SP321 40pf + 20pf multi .65 .60
**B540** SP321 50pf + 25pf multi .90 .80
**B541** SP321 70pf + 35pf multi 1.25 1.25
*Nos. B538-B541 (4)* 3.30 3.15

Surtax was for benefit of young people.

Caraway — SP322

Meadow Flowers: 40pf+20pf, Dandelion. 50pf+25pf, Red clover. 70pf+35pf, Meadow sage.

**1977, Oct. 13** **Litho.** ***Perf. 14***
**B542** SP322 30pf + 15pf multi .35 .30
**B543** SP322 40pf + 20pf multi .45 .35
**B544** SP322 50pf + 25pf multi .50 .45
**B545** SP322 70pf + 35pf multi 1.00 *1.10*
*Nos. B542-B545 (4)* 2.30 *2.20*

Surtax was for independent welfare organizations.
See Nos. B553-B556.

Souvenir Sheet

King Caspar Offering Gold, Window, St. Gereon's, Cologne — SP323

**1977, Nov. 10**
**B546** SP323 50pf + 25pf multi .80 .75

Christmas 1977.

Giant Slalom SP324

Design: No. B548, Steeplechase.

**1978** **Litho.** ***Perf. 14***
**B547** SP324 50pf + 25pf multi 1.40 1.10
**B548** SP324 70pf + 35pf multi 3.00 2.75

Issued: #B547, Jan. 12, #B548, Apr. 13.
Surtax was for the German Sports Foundation.

Balloon Ascent, Oktoberfest, Munich, 1820 — SP325

Designs: 40pf+20pf, Airship LZ 1, 1900. 50pf+25pf, Bleriot monoplane, 1909. 70pf+35pf, Grade monoplane, 1909.

**1978, Apr. 13** **Litho.** ***Perf. 14***
**B549** SP325 30pf + 15pf multi .50 .45
**B550** SP325 40pf + 20pf multi .70 .60
**B551** SP325 50pf + 25pf multi .90 .80
**B552** SP325 70pf + 35pf multi 1.10 1.10
*Nos. B549-B552 (4)* 3.20 2.95

Surtax was for benefit of young people.

## Flower Type of 1977

Woodland Flowers: 30pf+15pf, Arum. 40pf+20pf, Weaselsnout. 50pf+25pf, Turk's-cap lily. 70pf+35pf, Liverwort.

**1978, Oct. 12** **Litho.** ***Perf. 14***
**B553** SP322 30pf + 15pf multi .35 .30
**B554** SP322 40pf + 20pf multi .50 .40
**B555** SP322 50pf + 25pf multi .75 .65
**B556** SP322 70pf + 35pf multi 1.00 1.00
*Nos. B553-B556 (4)* 2.60 2.35

Surtax was for independent welfare organizations.

Souvenir Sheet

Christ Child, Window, Frauenkirche, Munich — SP326

**1978, Nov. 16** **Litho.** ***Perf. 14***
**B557** SP326 50pf + 25pf multi .75 .75

Christmas 1978.

Dornier Wal, 1922 SP327

Airplanes: 50pf+25pf, Heinkel HE70, 1932. 60pf+30pf, Junkers W33 Bremen, 1928. 90pf+45pf, Focke-Wulf FW61, 1936.

**1979, Apr. 5** **Litho.** ***Perf. 14***
**B558** SP327 40pf + 20pf multi .50 .50
**B559** SP327 50pf + 25pf multi .75 .75
**B560** SP327 60pf + 30pf multi .90 .90
**B561** SP327 90pf + 45pf multi 1.25 1.25
*Nos. B558-B561 (4)* 3.40 3.40

Surtax was for benefit of young people.
See Nos. B570-B573.

Handball SP328

Design: 90pf+45pf, Canoeing.

**1979, Apr. 5**
**B562** SP328 60pf + 30pf multi .90 .80
**B563** SP328 90pf + 45pf multi 1.40 1.25

Surtax was for German Sports Foundation.

Post House Sign, Altheim, Saar, 1754 — SP329

**1979, Oct. 11** **Litho.** ***Perf. 14***
**B564** SP329 60pf + 30pf multi 1.10 1.10

Stamp Day. Surtax was for Foundation of Promotion of Philately and Postal History.
Issued in sheet of 10.

Red Beech SP330

Woodland Plants: 50pf+25pf, English oak. 60pf+30pf, Hawthorn. 90pf+45pf, Mountain pine.

**1979, Oct. 11** **Litho.** ***Perf. 14***
**B565** SP330 40pf + 20pf multi .45 .45
**B566** SP330 50pf + 25pf multi .60 .60
**B567** SP330 60pf + 30pf multi .70 .70
**B568** SP330 90pf + 45pf multi 1.25 1.25
*Nos. B565-B568 (4)* 3.00 3.00

Surtax was for independent welfare organizations.

Nativity, Medieval Manuscript SP331

**1979, Nov. 14** **Litho.** ***Perf. 13½***
**B569** SP331 60pf + 30pf multi .90 .90

Christmas 1979.

## Aviation Type of 1979

40+20pf, FS 24 Phoenix, 1957. 50+25pf, Lockheed Super Constellation, 1950. 60+30pf, Airbus A300, 1972. 90+45pf, Boeing 747, 1969.

**1980, Apr. 10** **Litho.** ***Perf. 14***
**B570** SP327 40 + 20pf multi .35 .35
**B571** SP327 50 + 25pf multi .60 .60
**B572** SP327 60 + 30pf multi .80 .80
**B573** SP327 90 + 45pf multi 1.25 1.25
*Nos. B570-B573 (4)* 3.00 3.00

Surtax was for benefit of young people.

Soccer SP332

Designs: 60pf+30pf, Equestrian. 90pf+45pf, Cross-country skiing.

**1980, May 8** **Photo.** ***Perf. 14***
**B574** SP332 50 + 25pf multi .50 .45
**B575** SP332 60 + 30pf multi .75 .60
**B576** SP332 90 + 45pf multi 1.40 1.40
*Nos. B574-B576 (3)* 2.65 2.45

Surtax was for German Sports Foundation.

Ceratocephalus — SP333

Wildflowers: 50pf+25pf, Climbing meadow pea. 60pf+30pf, Corn cockle. 90pf+45pf, Grape hyacinth.

**1980, Oct. 9** **Litho.** ***Perf. 14***
**B577** SP333 40 + 20pf multi .50 .45
**B578** SP333 50 + 25pf multi .65 .60
**B579** SP333 60 + 30pf multi .75 .75
**B580** SP333 90 + 45pf multi 1.25 1.25
*Nos. B577-B580 (4)* 3.15 3.05

Surtax was for independent welfare organizations.

Post House Sign, 1754, Altheim, Saar — SP334

**1980, Nov. 13** **Litho.** ***Perf. 14***
**B581** SP334 60 + 30pf multi .75 .65

49th FIP Congress (Federation Internationale de Philatelie), Essen, Nov. 12-13.

Nativity, Altomunster Manuscript, 12th Century SP335

**1980, Nov. 13** *Perf. 14x13½*

**B582** SP335 60 + 30pf multi 1.00 .90

Christmas 1980.

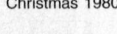

Borda Circle, 1800 — SP336

Historic Optical Instruments: 50pf+25pf, Reflecting telescope, 1770. 60pf+30pf, Binocular microscope, 1860. 90pf+45pf, Octant, 1775.

**1981, Apr. 10** **Litho.** *Perf. 13½*

| | | | |
|---|---|---|---|
| **B583** | SP336 40 + 20pf multi | .50 | .35 |
| **B584** | SP336 50 + 25pf multi | .90 | .75 |
| **B585** | SP336 60 + 30pf multi | .90 | .75 |
| **B586** | SP336 90 + 45pf multi | 1.25 | 1.25 |
| | *Nos. B583-B586 (4)* | 3.55 | 3.10 |

Surtax was for benefit of young people.

Rowing SP337

**1981, Apr. 10** *Perf. 14*

| | | | |
|---|---|---|---|
| **B587** | SP337 60 + 30pf shown | .90 | .75 |
| **B588** | SP337 90 + 45pf Gliding | 1.40 | 1.25 |

Surtax was for the German Sports Foundation.

Water Nut — SP338

Endangered Species: 50pf+25pf, Floating heart. 60pf+30pf, Water gillyflower. 90pf+45pf, Water lobelia.

**1981, Oct. 8** **Litho.**

| | | | |
|---|---|---|---|
| **B589** | SP338 40 + 20pf multi | .45 | .35 |
| **B590** | SP338 50 + 25pf multi | .60 | .50 |
| **B591** | SP338 60 + 30pf multi | .75 | .75 |
| **B592** | SP338 90 + 45pf multi | 1.40 | 1.40 |
| | *Nos. B589-B592 (4)* | 3.20 | 3.00 |

Surtax was for independent welfare organizations.

Nativity, 19th Cent. Painting SP339

**1981, Nov. 12** **Litho.**

**B593** SP339 60 + 30pf multi 1.00 .85

Christmas 1981.

Antique Cars SP340

Designs: 40+20pf, Benz, 1886. 50+25pf, Mercedes, 1913. 60+30pf, Hanomag, 1925. 90+45pf, Opel Olympia, 1937.

**1982, Apr. 15** **Litho.**

| | | | |
|---|---|---|---|
| **B594** | SP340 40 + 20pf multi | .50 | .45 |
| **B595** | SP340 50 + 25pf multi | .65 | .60 |
| **B596** | SP340 60 + 30pf multi | .90 | .75 |
| **B597** | SP340 90 + 45pf multi | 1.50 | 1.60 |
| | *Nos. B594-B597 (4)* | 3.55 | 3.40 |

Surtax was for benefit of young people.

Jogging SP341

**1982, Apr. 15** **Litho.**

| | | | |
|---|---|---|---|
| **B598** | SP341 60 + 30pf shown | .90 | .80 |
| **B599** | SP341 90 + 45pf Archery | 1.40 | 1.25 |

Surtax was for the German Sports Foundation.

Tea-rose Hybrid — SP342

60+30pf, Floribunda. 80f+40pf, Bourbon rose. 120+60pf, Polyantha hybrid.

**1982, Oct. 14** **Litho.** *Perf. 14*

| | | | |
|---|---|---|---|
| **B600** | SP342 50 + 20pf multi | .50 | .45 |
| **B601** | SP342 60 + 30pf multi | .65 | .60 |
| **B602** | SP342 80 + 40pf multi | 1.10 | 1.00 |
| **B603** | SP342 120 + 60pf multi | 1.50 | 1.50 |
| | *Nos. B600-B603 (4)* | 3.75 | 3.55 |

Surtax was for independent welfare organizations.

Christmas SP343

Designs: Nativity, Oak altar, St. Peter's Church, Hamburg, 1380.

**1982, Nov. 10**

**B604** SP343 80 + 40pf multi 1.50 1.00

Historic Motorcycles — SP344

Designs: 50pf+20pf, Daimler-Mayback, 1885. 60pf+30pf, NSU, 1901. 80pf+40pf, Megola-Sport, 1922. 120pf+60pf, BMW, 1936.

**1983, Apr. 12** **Litho.** *Perf. 14*

| | | | |
|---|---|---|---|
| **B605** | SP344 50 + 20pf multi | .50 | .45 |
| **B606** | SP344 60 + 30pf multi | .65 | .60 |
| **B607** | SP344 80 + 40pf multi | 1.25 | 1.10 |
| **B608** | SP344 120 + 60pf multi | 1.75 | 1.60 |
| | *Nos. B605-B608 (4)* | 4.15 | 3.75 |

Surtax was for benefit of young people.

1983 Sports Championships — SP345

80+40pf, Gymnastics Festival. 120+60pf, Modern Pentathlon World Championships.

**1983, Apr. 12**

| | | | |
|---|---|---|---|
| **B609** | SP345 80 + 40pf multi | 1.10 | .95 |
| **B610** | SP345 120 + 60pf multi | 1.75 | 1.60 |

Surtax was for German Sports Foundation.

Swiss Androsace SP346

60+30pf, Krain groundsel. 80+40pf, Fleischer's willow herb. 120+60pf, Alpine sow-thistle.

**1983, Oct. 13** **Litho.** *Perf. 14*

| | | | |
|---|---|---|---|
| **B611** | SP346 50 + 20pf multi | .50 | .45 |
| **B612** | SP346 60 + 30pf multi | .65 | .60 |
| **B613** | SP346 80 + 40pf multi | 1.25 | 1.10 |
| **B614** | SP346 120 + 60pf multi | 1.75 | 1.60 |
| | *Nos. B611-B614 (4)* | 4.15 | 3.75 |

Surtax was for welfare organizations.

Christmas SP347

**1983, Nov. 10** **Litho.**

**B615** SP347 80 + 40pf Carolers 1.60 1.25

Surtax was for free welfare work.

Insects — SP348

Designs: 50pf+20pf, Trichodes apoarius. 60pf+30pf, Vanessa atalanta. 80pf+40pf, Apis mellifera. 120pf+60pf, Chrysotoxum festivum.

**1984, Apr. 12** **Litho.**

| | | | |
|---|---|---|---|
| **B616** | SP348 50 + 20pf multi | .60 | .50 |
| **B617** | SP348 60 + 30pf multi | 1.10 | 1.00 |
| **B618** | SP348 80 + 40pf multi | 1.50 | 1.40 |
| **B619** | SP348 120 + 60pf multi | 2.10 | 2.10 |
| | *Nos. B616-B619 (4)* | 5.30 | 5.00 |

Surtax was for German Youth Stamp Foundation.

Women's Discus SP349

Olympic Sports: 80pf+40pf, Rhythmic gymnastics. 120pf+60pf, Wind surfing.

**1984, Apr. 12**

| | | | |
|---|---|---|---|
| **B620** | SP349 60 + 30pf multi | 1.00 | .75 |
| **B621** | SP349 80 + 40pf multi | 1.40 | 1.25 |
| **B622** | SP349 120 + 60pf multi | 2.75 | 2.50 |
| | *Nos. B620-B622 (3)* | 5.15 | 4.50 |

Surtax was for German Sports Foundation.

Orchids SP350

Designs: 50pf+20pf, Aceras anthropophorum. 60pf+30pf, Orchis ustulata. 80pf+40pf, Limodorum abortivum. 120+60pf, Dactylorhiza sambucina.

**1984, Oct. 18** **Litho.** *Perf. 14*

| | | | |
|---|---|---|---|
| **B623** | SP350 50 + 20pf multi | .75 | .65 |
| **B624** | SP350 60 + 30pf multi | .75 | .65 |
| **B625** | SP350 80 + 40pf multi | 1.10 | 1.00 |
| **B626** | SP350 120 + 60pf multi | 2.25 | 2.25 |
| | *Nos. B623-B626 (4)* | 4.85 | 4.55 |

Surtax was for welfare organizations.

Christmas 1984 — SP351

**1984, Nov. 8** **Litho.**

**B627** SP351 80pf + 40pf St. Martin 1.40 1.25

Surtax was for welfare organizations.

Bowling SP352

**1985, Feb. 21** **Photo.**

| | | | |
|---|---|---|---|
| **B628** | SP352 80pf + 40pf multi | 1.25 | 1.00 |
| **B629** | SP352 120pf + 60pf Kayaking | 2.00 | 1.75 |

Surtax was for German Sports Foundation.

Antique Bicycles SP353

50pf+20pf, Draisienne, 1817. 60pf+30pf, NSU Germania, 1886. 80pf+40pf, Cross-frame, 1887. 120pf+60pf, Adler tricycle, 1888.

**1985, Apr. 16** **Litho.**

| | | | |
|---|---|---|---|
| **B630** | SP353 50pf + 20pf multi | .75 | .75 |
| **B631** | SP353 60pf + 30pf multi | .90 | .90 |
| **B632** | SP353 80pf + 40pf multi | 1.25 | 1.25 |
| **B633** | SP353 120pf + 60pf multi | 2.40 | 2.40 |
| | *Nos. B630-B633 (4)* | 5.30 | 5.30 |

Surtax was for benefit of young people. Each stamp shows the Intl. Youth Year emblem.

MOPHILA '85, Hamburg, Sept. 11-15 SP354

**1985, Aug. 13** **Litho.** *Perf. 14x14½*

| | | | |
|---|---|---|---|
| **B634** | SP354 60 + 20pf Coach-man, horses | 2.25 | 1.90 |
| **B635** | SP354 80 + 20pf Stage-coach | 2.25 | 1.90 |
| *a.* | Pair, #B634-B635 | 6.00 | 5.25 |

Surtax for the benefit of the Philatelic & Postal History Foundation. No. B635a has continuous design.

SP355

Various ornamental borders, medieval prayer book, Prussian State Library, Berlin.

**1985, Oct. 15 Litho. *Perf. 14***

**B636** SP355 50pf + 20pf multi .70 .60
**B637** SP355 60pf + 30pf multi .85 .75
**B638** SP355 80pf + 40pf multi 1.10 1.00
**B639** SP355 120pf + 60pf multi 1.90 1.90
*Nos. B636-B639 (4)* 4.55 4.25

Surtax for welfare organizations.

Christmas 1985 — SP356

Woodcut: The Birth of Christ, by Hans Baldung Grien (1485-1545), Freiburg Cathedral High Altar.

**1985, Nov. 12 Litho. *Perf. 14***

**B640** SP356 80pf + 40pf multi 1.40 1.40

Surtax for welfare organizations.

European World Sports Championships — SP357

**1986, Feb. 13 Litho. *Perf. 14***

**B641** SP357 80 + 40pf Running 1.50 1.50
**B642** SP357 120 + 55pf Bobsledding 2.25 2.25

Surtax for the Natl. Sports Promotion Foundation.

Vocational Training — SP358

**1986, Apr. 10**

**B643** SP358 50 + 25pf Optician 1.00 .90
**B644** SP358 60 + 30pf Mason 1.10 1.00
**B645** SP358 70 + 35pf Beautician 1.40 1.25
**B646** SP358 80 + 40pf Baker 1.90 1.75
*Nos. B643-B646 (4)* 5.40 4.90

Surtax for German Youth Stamp Foundation.

Glassware in German Museums — SP359

**1986, Oct. 16 Litho.**

**B647** SP359 50 + 25pf Ornamental flask, c. 300 .70 .60
**B648** SP359 60 + 30pf Goblet, c. 1650 .90 .80
**B649** SP359 70 + 35pf Imperial eagle tankard, c. 1662 1.00 .90
**B650** SP359 80 + 40pf Engraved goblet, c. 1720 1.25 1.10
*Nos. B647-B650 (4)* 3.85 3.40

Surtax for public welfare organizations.

Christmas SP360

Adoration of the Infant Jesus, Ortenberg Altarpiece, c. 1430, Hesse Museum, Darmstadt.

**1986, Nov. 13 Litho. *Perf. 14***

**B651** SP360 80 + 40pf multi 1.40 1.25

Surtax for public welfare organizations.

World Championships — SP361

**1987, Feb. 12 Litho.**

**B652** SP361 80 + 40pf Sailing 1.25 1.25
**B653** SP361 120 + 55pf Cross-country skiing 2.10 2.10

Surtax for the benefit of the national Sports Promotion Foundation.

Youth in Industry SP362

**1987, Apr. 9 Litho.**

**B654** SP362 50 + 25pf Plumber 1.10 1.10
**B655** SP362 60 + 30pf Dental technician 1.40 1.40
**B656** SP362 70 + 35pf Butcher 1.50 1.50
**B657** SP362 80 + 40pf Bookbinder 2.00 2.00
*Nos. B654-B657 (4)* 6.00 6.00

Surtax for youth organizations.

Gold and Silver Artifacts SP363

**1987, Oct. 15**

**B658** SP363 50 + 25pf Roman bracelet, 4th cent. 1.10 1.10
**B659** SP363 60 + 30pf Gothic buckle, 6th cent. 1.10 1.10
**B660** SP363 70 + 35pf Merovingian disk fibula, 7th cent. 1.10 1.10
**B661** SP363 80 + 40pf Purse-shaped reliquary, 8th cent. 1.50 1.50
*Nos. B658-B661 (4)* 4.80 4.80

Surtax for welfare organizations sponsoring free museum exhibitions.

Christmas SP364

Illustration from Book of Psalms, 13th cent., Bavarian Natl. Museum: Birth of Christ.

**1987, Nov. 6**

**B662** SP364 80 + 40pf multi 1.50 1.25

Surtax for public welfare organizations.

Sports SP365

**1988, Feb. 18 Litho.**

**B663** SP365 60 + 30pf Soccer 1.10 1.10
**B664** SP365 80 + 40pf Tennis 1.90 1.90
**B665** SP365 120 + 55pf Diving 2.25 2.25
*Nos. B663-B665 (3)* 5.25 5.25

Surtax for Stiftung Deutsche Sporthilfe, a foundation for the promotion of sports in Germany.

Rock Stars SP366

#B666, Buddy Holly (1936-59). #B667, Elvis Presley (1935-77). #B668, Jim Morrison (1943-71). #B669, John Lennon (1940-80).

**1988, Apr. 14 Litho. *Perf. 14***

**B666** SP366 50 + 25pf multi 1.10 1.10
**B667** SP366 60 + 30pf multi 2.75 2.75
**B668** SP366 70 + 35pf multi 1.50 1.50
**B669** SP366 80 + 40pf multi 2.40 2.40
*Nos. B666-B669 (4)* 7.75 7.75

Surtax for German Youth Stamp Foundation.

Gold and Rock Crystal Reliquary, c. 1200, Schnutgen Museum, Cologne SP367

Gold and silver artifacts: No. B671, Bust of Charlemagne, 14th cent., Aachen cathedral. No. B672, Crown of Otto III, 10th cent., Essen cathedral. No. B673, Flower bouquet, c. 1620, Schmuck Museum, Pforzheim.

**1988, Oct. 13 Litho.**

**B670** SP367 50 + 25pf multi .60 .60
**B671** SP367 60 + 30pf multi .95 .95
**B672** SP367 70 + 35pf multi .95 .95
**B673** SP367 80 + 40pf multi 1.40 1.40
*Nos. B670-B673 (4)* 3.90 3.90

Surtax for welfare organizations.

Christmas SP368

Illumination from *The Gospel Book of Henry the Lion,* Helmarshausen, 1188, Prussian Cultural Museum, Bavaria: Adoration of the Magi.

**1988, Nov. 10 Litho.**

**B674** SP368 80 + 40pf multi 1.40 1.25

Surtax for public welfare organizations.

World Championship Sporting Events Hosted by Germany — SP369

**1989, Feb. 9 Litho.**

**B675** SP369 100pf + 50pf Table tennis 2.00 2.00
**B676** SP369 140pf + 60pf Gymnastics 3.00 3.00

Surtax for the Natl. Sports Promotion Foundation.

IPHLA Philatelic Literature Exhibition, Frankfurt, Apr. 19-23 — SP370

**1989, Apr. 20 Litho.**

**B677** SP370 100 + 50pf multi 2.75 2.75

Surtax benefited the Foundation for the Promotion of Philately and Postal History.

Circus SP371

**1989, Apr. 20**

**B678** SP371 60 + 30pf Elephants 1.75 1.75
**B679** SP371 70 + 30pf Bareback rider 2.10 2.10
**B680** SP371 80 + 35pf Clown 3.00 3.00
**B681** SP371 100 + 50pf Caravans, big top 4.50 4.50
*Nos. B678-B681 (4)* 11.35 11.35

Surtax for natl. youth welfare organizations.

Mounted Courier of Thurn and Taxis, 18th Cent. SP372

History of mail carrying: No. B683, Hamburg postal service messenger, 1808. No. B684, Bavarian mail coach, c. 1900.

**1989, Oct. 12 Litho.**

**B682** SP372 60 + 30pf multi 1.10 1.10
**B683** SP372 80 + 35pf multi 1.90 1.90
**B684** SP372 100 + 50pf multi 2.50 2.50
*Nos. B682-B684 (3)* 5.50 5.50

Surtax for the benefit of Free Welfare Work.

Christmas SP373

Wood carvings by Veit Stoss in St. Lawrence's Church, Nuremburg, 1517-18.

**1989, Nov. 16 Litho.**

**B685** SP373 60 + 30pf Angel 1.25 1.10
**B686** SP373 100 + 50pf Adoration of the Kings 1.60 1.50

Surtax for benefit of the Federal Working Assoc. of Free Welfare Work.

Popular Sports SP374

**1990, Feb. 15 Litho.**

**B687** SP374 100 + 50pf Handball 2.50 2.50
**B688** SP374 140 + 60pf Physical fitness 3.00 3.00

Surtax for the Natl. Sports Promotion Foundation.

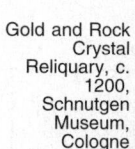

*Max and Moritz, by Wilhelm Busch, 125th Anniv.* SP375

**1990, Apr. 19** **Litho.**

| | | | | |
|---|---|---|---|---|
| **B689** SP375 | 60 + 30pf Widow Bolte | | .80 | .80 |
| **B690** SP375 | 70 + 30pf Max | | 1.25 | 1.25 |
| **B691** SP375 | 80 + 35pf Max and Moritz | | 1.60 | 1.60 |
| **B692** SP375 | 100 + 50pf Max and Moritz, diff. | | 2.00 | 2.00 |
| | *Nos. B689-B692 (4)* | | 5.65 | 5.65 |

Surcharge for the German Youth Stamp Foundation.

Souvenir Sheet

Dusseldorf '90 — SP376

**1990, June 21** **Litho.**

| | | | |
|---|---|---|---|
| **B693** SP376 | Sheet of 6 | 17.00 | *19.00* |
| *a.* | 100pf + 50pf multi | 2.75 | 2.75 |

Surtax for the Foundation for Promotion of Philately and Postal History. 10th Intl. Philatelic Exhibition of Youth and 11th Natl. Philatelic Exhibition of Youth.

Post and Telecommunications — SP377

Designs: 60pf+30pf, Postal vehicle, 1900. 80pf+35pf, Telephone exchange, 1890. 100pf+50pf, Post office, 1900.

**1990, Sept. 27** **Litho.** ***Perf. 13½x14***

| | | | |
|---|---|---|---|
| **B694** SP377 | 60pf + 30pf multi | .90 | .90 |
| **B695** SP377 | 80pf + 35pf multi | 1.40 | 1.40 |
| **B696** SP377 | 100pf + 50pf multi | 2.00 | 2.00 |
| | *Nos. B694-B696 (3)* | 4.30 | 4.30 |

Surtax for welfare organizations.

Christmas SP378

**1990, Nov. 6** **Litho.** ***Perf. 14***

| | | | |
|---|---|---|---|
| **B697** SP378 | 50pf + 20pf shown | .90 | .90 |
| **B698** SP378 | 60pf + 30pf Smoking manikin | 1.00 | 1.00 |
| **B699** SP378 | 70pf + 30pf Nutcracker | 1.40 | 1.40 |
| **B700** SP378 | 100pf + 50pf Angel, diff. | 2.25 | 2.25 |
| | *Nos. B697-B700 (4)* | 5.55 | 5.55 |

Surtax for welfare organizations.

Sports SP379

**1991, Feb. 14** **Litho.** ***Perf. 14***

| | | | |
|---|---|---|---|
| **B701** SP379 | 70 +30pf Weight lifting | 1.50 | 1.50 |
| **B702** SP379 | 100 +50pf Cycling | 1.50 | 1.50 |
| **B703** SP379 | 140 +60pf Basketball | 2.25 | 2.25 |
| **B704** SP379 | 170 +80pf Wrestling | 2.25 | 2.25 |
| | *Nos. B701-B704 (4)* | 7.50 | 7.50 |

Surtax for the Foundation for the Promotion of Sports.

Endangered Butterflies SP380

#B705, Alpen gelbling, alpine sulphur. #B706, Grosser eisvogel, Viceroy. #B707, Grosser schillerfalter, purple emperor. #B708, Blauschillernder beuerfalter, bluish copper. #B709,Schwalben-schwanz, swallowtail. #B710, Alpen apollo, alpine apollo. #B711, Hochmoor gelbling, moor sulphur. #B712, Grosser feuerfalter, large copper.

**1991, Apr. 9** **Litho.** ***Perf. 13½***

| | | | |
|---|---|---|---|
| **B705** SP380 | 30 +15pf multi | .50 | .50 |
| **B706** SP380 | 50 +25pf multi | .60 | .60 |
| **B707** SP380 | 60 +30pf multi | 1.10 | 1.10 |
| **B708** SP380 | 70 +30pf multi | 1.25 | 1.25 |
| **B709** SP380 | 80 +35pf multi | 1.50 | 1.50 |
| **B710** SP380 | 90 +45pf multi | 2.00 | 2.00 |
| **B711** SP380 | 100 +50pf multi | 2.50 | 2.50 |
| **B712** SP380 | 140 +60pf multi | 3.00 | 3.00 |
| | *Nos. B705-B712 (8)* | 12.45 | 12.45 |

Surtax for German Youth Stamp Foundation. See Nos. B728-B732.

Souvenir Sheet

Otto Lilienthal's First Glider Flight, Cent. — SP381

**1991, July 9** **Litho.** ***Perf. 14***

| | | | |
|---|---|---|---|
| **B713** SP381 | 100pf +50pf multi | 3.00 | 3.00 |

Surtax benefited Foundation of Philately and Postal History.

Post Offices SP382

30pf+15pf, Bethel. 60pf+30pf, Budingen postal station. 70pf+30pf, Stralsund. 80pf+35pf, Lauscha. 100pf+50pf, Bonn. 140pf+60pf, Weilburg.

**1991, Oct. 10** **Litho.** ***Perf. 14***

| | | | |
|---|---|---|---|
| **B714** SP382 | 30pf +15pf multi | .50 | .50 |
| **B715** SP382 | 60pf +30pf multi | 1.00 | 1.00 |
| **B716** SP382 | 70pf +30pf multi | 1.25 | 1.25 |
| **B717** SP382 | 80pf +35pf multi | 1.50 | 1.50 |
| **B718** SP382 | 100pf +50pf multi | 2.00 | 2.00 |
| **B719** SP382 | 140pf +60pf multi | 2.50 | 2.50 |
| | *Nos. B714-B719 (6)* | 8.75 | 8.75 |

Christmas SP383

Paintings by Martin Schongauer (c. 1450-1491): 60pf+30pf, Angel of the Annunciation. 70pf+30pf, The Annunciation. 80pf+35pf, Angel. 100pf+50pf, Nativity.

**1991, Nov. 5** **Litho.** ***Perf. 14***

| | | | |
|---|---|---|---|
| **B720** SP383 | 60pf +30pf multi | 1.00 | 1.00 |
| **B721** SP383 | 70pf +30pf multi | 1.25 | 1.25 |
| **B722** SP383 | 80pf +35pf multi | 2.25 | 2.25 |
| **B723** SP383 | 100pf +50pf multi | 3.00 | 3.00 |
| | *Nos. B720-B723 (4)* | 7.50 | 7.50 |

Surtax for Federal Working Association of Free Welfare Work.

Olympic Sports SP384

**1992, Feb. 6** **Litho.** ***Perf. 14***

| | | | |
|---|---|---|---|
| **B724** SP384 | 60pf +30pf Women's fencing | .90 | .90 |
| **B725** SP384 | 80pf +40pf Rowing coxed eights | 1.10 | 1.10 |
| **B726** SP384 | 100pf +50pf Dressage | 2.25 | 2.25 |
| **B727** SP384 | 170pf +80pf Men's slalom skiing | 3.50 | 3.50 |
| | *Nos. B724-B727 (4)* | 7.75 | 7.75 |

**Endangered Butterfly Type of 1991**

60+30pf, Purpurbar. 70+30pf, Labkraut schwarmer. 80+40pf, Silbermonch. 100+50pf, Schwarzer bar. 170+80pf, Rauschbeerenfleckenspanner.

**1992, Apr. 9** **Litho.** ***Perf. 13½***

| | | | |
|---|---|---|---|
| **B728** SP380 | 60pf +30pf multi | 1.50 | 1.50 |
| **B729** SP380 | 70pf +30pf multi | 1.75 | 1.75 |
| **B730** SP380 | 80pf +40pf multi | 2.25 | 2.25 |
| **B731** SP380 | 100pf +50pf multi | 2.50 | 2.50 |
| **B732** SP380 | 170pf +80pf multi | 2.75 | 2.75 |
| | *Nos. B728-B732 (5)* | 10.75 | 10.75 |

Surtax for German Youth Stamp Foundation.

Preservation of Tropical Rain Forests SP385

**1992, June 11** **Litho.** ***Perf. 13***

| | | | |
|---|---|---|---|
| **B733** SP385 | 100pf +50pf multi | 1.75 | 1.75 |

Antique Clocks SP386

Antique clocks: 60pf+30pf, Turret, c. 1400. 70pf+30pf, Astronomical geographical mantelpiece, 1738. 80pf+40pf, Fluted, c. 1790. 100fpf+50pf, Figurine, c. 1580. 170pf+80pf, Table, c. 1550.

**1992, Oct. 15** **Litho.** ***Perf. 14***

| | | | |
|---|---|---|---|
| **B734** SP386 | 60pf +30pf multi | 1.10 | 1.10 |
| **B735** SP386 | 70pf +30pf multi | 1.40 | 1.40 |
| **B736** SP386 | 80pf +40pf multi | 1.40 | 1.40 |
| **B737** SP386 | 100pf +50pf multi | 1.75 | 1.75 |
| **B738** SP386 | 170pf +80pf multi | 2.50 | 2.50 |
| | *Nos. B734-B738 (5)* | 8.15 | 8.15 |

Surtax for welfare organizations.

Christmas SP387

Carvings from Church of St. Anne, Annaberg-Buchholz, by Franz Maidburg: 60pf + 30pf, Adoration of the Magi. 100pf + 50pf, The Nativity.

**1992, Nov. 5**

| | | | |
|---|---|---|---|
| **B739** SP387 | 60pf +30pf multi | 1.00 | .90 |
| **B740** SP387 | 100pf +50pf multi | 1.75 | 1.50 |

Surtax for benefit of free welfare work.

Sports SP388

Designs: 60pf+30pf, Olympic ski jump, Garmisch-Partenkirchen. 80pf+40pf, Olympic Park, Munich. 100pf+50pf, Olympic Stadium, Berlin. 170pf+80pf, Olympic harbor, Kiel.

**1993, Feb. 11** **Litho.** ***Perf. 13½***

| | | | |
|---|---|---|---|
| **B741** SP388 | 60pf +30pf multi | 1.50 | 1.50 |
| **B742** SP388 | 80pf +40pf multi | 2.00 | 2.00 |
| **B743** SP388 | 100pf +50pf multi | 2.50 | 2.50 |
| **B744** SP388 | 170pf +80pf multi | 3.00 | 3.00 |
| | *Nos. B741-B744 (4)* | 9.00 | 9.00 |

Surtax for Natl. Sports Promotion Foundation.

Beetles SP389

Designs: No. B745, Alpenbock (Alpine sawyer). No. B746, Rosenkafer (rose chafer). No. B747, Hirschkafer (stag beetle). No. B748, Sandlaufkafer (tiger beetle). 200pf + 50pf, Maikafer (cockchafer).

**1993, Apr. 15** **Litho.** ***Perf. 14***

| | | | |
|---|---|---|---|
| **B745** SP389 | 80pf +40pf multi | 1.60 | 1.60 |
| **B746** SP389 | 80pf +40pf multi | 1.60 | 1.60 |
| **B747** SP389 | 100pf +50pf multi | 2.00 | 2.00 |
| **B748** SP389 | 100pf +50pf multi | 2.00 | 2.00 |
| **B749** SP389 | 200pf +50pf multi | 3.25 | 3.25 |
| | *Nos. B745-B749 (5)* | 10.45 | 10.45 |

Surtax for German Youth Stamp Foundation.

Stamp Day — SP390

**1993, Sept. 16** **Litho.** ***Perf. 13½x14***

| | | | |
|---|---|---|---|
| **B750** SP390 | 100pf +50pf multi | 1.60 | 1.60 |

Surtax for the Foundation for Promotion of Philately and Postal History.

Traditional Costumes SP391

Costumes from: No. B751, Rugen, Mecklenburg, Western Pomerania. No. B752, Fohr, Schleswig-Holstein. No. B753, Schwalm, Hesse. No. B754, Oberndorf, Bavaria. 200pf + 40pf, Ernstroda, Thuringia.

**1993, Oct. 14** ***Perf. 14***

| | | | | |
|---|---|---|---|---|
| **B751** | SP391 | 80pf +40pf multi | 1.50 | 1.50 |
| **B752** | SP391 | 80pf +40pf multi | 1.50 | 1.50 |
| **B753** | SP391 | 100pf +50pf multi | 1.75 | 1.75 |
| **B754** | SP391 | 100pf +50pf multi | 1.75 | 1.75 |
| **B755** | SP391 | 200pf +40pf multi | 3.00 | 3.00 |
| | | *Nos. B751-B755 (5)* | 9.50 | 9.50 |

Surtax for welfare organizations. See Nos. B768-B772.

Christmas SP392

Wings of high altar in choir of Blaubeuren Monastery: 80pf+40pf, Adoraration of Magi. 100pf+50pf, Nativity.

**1993, Nov. 10** **Litho.** ***Perf. 14***

| | | | | |
|---|---|---|---|---|
| **B756** | SP392 | 80pf +40pf multi | 1.00 | .90 |
| **B757** | SP392 | 100pf +50pf multi | 1.90 | 1.75 |

Surtax for welfare organizations.

Figure Skating SP393

Sports: #B759, Olympic Flame. #B760, Soccer ball, World Cup Trophy. 200pf+80pf, Skiier.

**1994, Feb. 10** **Litho.** ***Perf. 14x13½***

| | | | | |
|---|---|---|---|---|
| **B758** | SP393 | 80pf +40pf multi | 1.40 | 1.40 |
| **B759** | SP393 | 100pf +50pf multi | 1.60 | 1.60 |
| **B760** | SP393 | 100pf +50pf multi | 1.60 | 1.60 |
| **B761** | SP393 | 200pf +80pf multi | 2.75 | 2.75 |
| | | *Nos. B758-B761 (4)* | 7.35 | 7.35 |

1994 Winter Olympics, Lillehammer (#B758). Intl. Olympic Committee, Cent. (#B759). 1994 World Cup Soccer Championships, US (#B760). 1994 Paralympics, Lillehammer (#B761).

Heinrich Hoffmann (1809-94), Physician, Writer of Children's Books SP394

Characters from "Slovenly Peter:" No. B762, Little Pauline. No. B763, Johnny Head-in-the-air. No. B764, Slovenly Peter. No. B765, Naughty Frederick. 200pf+80pf, The Fidget.

**1994, Apr. 14** **Litho.** ***Perf. 13½***

| | | | | |
|---|---|---|---|---|
| **B762** | SP394 | 80pf +40pf multi | 1.25 | 1.25 |
| **B763** | SP394 | 80pf +40pf multi | 1.25 | 1.25 |
| **B764** | SP394 | 100pf +50pf multi | 1.50 | 1.50 |
| **B765** | SP394 | 100pf +50pf multi | 1.50 | 1.50 |
| **B766** | SP394 | 200pf +80pf multi | 2.75 | 2.75 |
| | | *Nos. B762-B766 (5)* | 8.25 | 8.25 |

Surtax for German Youth Stamp Foundation.

Environmental Protection SP395

**1994, June 16** **Litho.** ***Perf. 13***

| | | | | |
|---|---|---|---|---|
| **B767** | SP395 | 100pf +50pf blk & grn | 1.60 | 1.60 |

**Traditional Costume Type 1993**

Costumes from: No. B768, Buckeburg. No. B769, Halle an der Saale. No. B770, Hoyerswerda. No. B771, Minden. 200pf+70pf, Betzingen.

**1994, Oct. 13** **Litho.** ***Perf. 13½***

| | | | | |
|---|---|---|---|---|
| **B768** | SP391 | 80pf +40pf multi | 1.25 | 1.25 |
| **B769** | SP391 | 80pf +40pf multi | 1.25 | 1.25 |
| **B770** | SP391 | 100pf +50pf multi | 1.75 | 1.75 |
| **B771** | SP391 | 100pf +50pf multi | 1.75 | 1.75 |
| **B772** | SP391 | 200pf +70pf multi | 2.75 | 2.75 |
| | | *Nos. B768-B772 (5)* | 8.75 | 8.75 |

Surtax for welfare organizations.

Christmas SP396

Paintings by Hans Memling: 80pf+40pf, Adoration of the Magi. 100pf+50pf, Nativity Scene.

**1994, Nov. 9** **Litho.** ***Perf. 13½***

| | | | | |
|---|---|---|---|---|
| **B773** | SP396 | 80pf +40pf multi | 1.25 | 1.10 |
| **B774** | SP396 | 100pf +50pf multi | 1.75 | 1.60 |

Sports SP397

**1995, Feb. 9** **Photo.** ***Perf. 13½***

| | | | | |
|---|---|---|---|---|
| **B775** | SP397 | 80pf +40pf Rowing | 1.25 | 1.25 |
| **B776** | SP397 | 100pf +50pf Gymnastics | 1.50 | 1.50 |
| **B777** | SP397 | 100pf +50pf Boxing | 1.50 | 1.50 |
| **B778** | SP397 | 200pf +80pf Volleyball | 3.00 | 3.00 |
| | | *Nos. B775-B778 (4)* | 7.25 | 7.25 |

World Kayaking Championships, Duisburg (#B775). Intl. Gymnastics Festival, Berlin (#B776). World Amateur Boxing Championships, Berlin (#B777). Volleyball, cent. (#B778).

Dogs SP398

#B779, Munsterlander. #B780, Schnauzer. #B781, German shepherd. #B782, Wire haired dachshund. 200pf+80pf, Wolf spitz.

**1995, June 8** **Litho.** ***Perf. 13½***

| | | | | |
|---|---|---|---|---|
| **B779** | SP398 | 80pf +40pf multi | 1.25 | 1.25 |
| **B780** | SP398 | 80pf +40pf multi | 1.25 | 1.25 |
| **B781** | SP398 | 100pf +50pf multi | 1.60 | 1.60 |
| **B782** | SP398 | 100pf +50pf multi | 1.60 | 1.60 |
| **B783** | SP398 | 200pf +80pf multi | 2.75 | 2.75 |
| | | *Nos. B779-B783 (5)* | 8.45 | 8.45 |

Surtax for benefit of German Youth Stamp Foundation.
See Nos. B792-B796.

Stamp Day — SP399

**1995, Sept. 6** **Litho.** ***Perf. 13***

| | | | | |
|---|---|---|---|---|
| **B784** | SP399 | 200pf +100pf multi | 3.00 | 3.00 |

Surtax for Foundation for Promotion of Philately and Postal History.

Farmhouses — SP400

#B785, Eifel region. #B786, Saxony. #B787, Lower Germany. #B788, Upper Bavaria. 200pf+70pf, Mecklenburg.

**1995, Oct. 12** **Litho.** ***Perf. 14***

| | | | | |
|---|---|---|---|---|
| **B785** | SP400 | 80pf +40pf multi | 1.25 | 1.25 |
| **B786** | SP400 | 80pf +40pf multi | 1.25 | 1.25 |
| **B787** | SP400 | 100pf +50pf multi | 1.60 | 1.60 |
| **B788** | SP400 | 100pf +50pf multi | 1.60 | 1.60 |
| **B789** | SP400 | 200pf +70pf multi | 2.75 | 2.75 |
| | | *Nos. B785-B789 (5)* | 8.45 | 8.45 |

Surtax for welfare organizations.
See Nos. B802-B806.

Christmas SP401

Stained glass windows, Augsburg Cathedral: 80pf+40pf, Annunciation. 100pf+50pf, Nativity.

**1995, Nov. 9** **Litho.** ***Perf. 14***

| | | | | |
|---|---|---|---|---|
| **B790** | SP401 | 80pf +40pf multi | 1.25 | 1.10 |
| **B791** | SP401 | 100pf +50pf multi | 1.75 | 1.60 |

Surtax for welfare organizations.

**Dog Type of 1995**

#B792, Borzoi. #B793, Chow chow. #B794, St. Bernard. #B795, Collie. 200pf+80pf, Briard.

**1996, Feb. 8** **Litho.** ***Perf. 13½***

| | | | | |
|---|---|---|---|---|
| **B792** | SP398 | 80pf +40pf multi | 1.25 | 1.25 |
| **B793** | SP398 | 80pf +40pf multi | 1.25 | 1.25 |
| **B794** | SP398 | 100pf +50pf multi | 1.60 | 1.60 |
| **B795** | SP398 | 100pf +50pf multi | 1.60 | 1.60 |
| **B796** | SP398 | 200pf +80pf multi | 2.50 | 2.50 |
| | | *Nos. B792-B796 (5)* | 8.20 | 8.20 |

Surtax for benefit of German Youth Stamp Foundation.

Modern Olympic Games, Cent. SP402

Olympic champions: 80pf+40pf, Carl Schuhmann (1869-1946), pommel horse. No. B798, Annie Hübler Horn (1885-1976), pairs figure skating. No. B799, Josef Neckermann (1912-92), equestrian. 200pf+80pf, Alfred Flatow (1869-1942), Gustav Felix Flatow (1875-1945), gymnastics.

**1996, June 13** **Photo.** ***Perf. 13½***

| | | | | |
|---|---|---|---|---|
| **B797** | SP402 | 80pf +40pf multi | 1.25 | 1.25 |
| **B798** | SP402 | 100pf +50pf multi | 1.60 | 1.60 |
| **B799** | SP402 | 100pf +50pf multi | 1.60 | 1.60 |
| **B800** | SP402 | 200pf +80pf multi | 2.75 | 2.75 |
| | | *Nos. B797-B800 (4)* | 7.20 | 7.20 |

Preservation of Tropical Habitats — SP403

**1996, July 18** **Photo.** ***Perf. 14***

| | | | | |
|---|---|---|---|---|
| **B801** | SP403 | 100pf +50pf multi | 1.50 | 1.50 |

**Farmhouse Type of 1995**

Location: No. B802, Spree Forest. No. B803, Thuringia. No. B804, Black Forest. No. B805, Westphalia. 200pf+70pf, Schleswig-Holstein.

**1996, Oct. 9** **Litho.** ***Perf. 14***

| | | | | |
|---|---|---|---|---|
| **B802** | SP400 | 80pf +40pf multi | 1.25 | 1.25 |
| **B803** | SP400 | 80pf +40pf multi | 1.25 | 1.25 |
| **B804** | SP400 | 100pf +50pf multi | 1.50 | 1.50 |
| **B805** | SP400 | 100pf +50pf multi | 1.50 | 1.50 |
| **B806** | SP400 | 200pf +70pf multi | 2.50 | 2.50 |
| | | *Nos. B802-B806 (5)* | 8.00 | 8.00 |

Christmas SP404

Illuminated pages from Henry II's book of pericopes (Gospels), 11th cent.: 80pf+40pf, Adoration of the Magi. 100pf+50pf, Nativity.

**1996, Nov. 14** **Litho.** ***Perf. 14***

| | | | | |
|---|---|---|---|---|
| **B807** | SP404 | 80pf +40pf multi | 1.25 | 1.10 |
| **B808** | SP404 | 100pf +50pf multi | 1.50 | 1.40 |

Surtax for welfare organizations.

Sports SP405

**1997, Feb. 4** **Litho.** ***Perf. 14x13½***

| | | | | |
|---|---|---|---|---|
| **B809** | SP405 | 80pf +40pf Aerobics | 1.25 | 1.25 |
| **B810** | SP405 | 100pf +50pf Inline skating | 1.60 | 1.60 |
| **B811** | SP405 | 100pf +50pf Streetball | 1.60 | 1.60 |
| **B812** | SP405 | 200pf +80pf Free climbing | 2.50 | 2.50 |
| | | *Nos. B809-B812 (4)* | 6.95 | 6.95 |

Horses SP406

**1997, June 9** **Litho.** ***Perf. 14***

| | | | | |
|---|---|---|---|---|
| **B813** | SP406 | 80pf + 40pf Rhe-no-German draft | 1.25 | 1.25 |
| **B814** | SP406 | 80pf + 40pf Shetland pony | 1.25 | 1.25 |
| **B815** | SP406 | 100pf + 50pf Friesian | 1.50 | 1.50 |
| **B816** | SP406 | 100pf + 50pf Haflinger | 1.50 | 1.50 |
| **B817** | SP406 | 200pf + 80pf Hanoverian | 3.00 | 3.00 |
| | | *Nos. B813-B817 (5)* | 8.50 | 8.50 |

**Arms Type of 1992 Redrawn and Inscribed "Hochwasserhilfe 1997" and "DEUTSCHLAND"**

**1997, Aug. 19 Litho. *Perf. 13½***

**B818** A739 110pf +90pf like #1702 2.00 2.00

Souvenir Sheet

Stamp Day — SP407

**1997, Sept. 17 Litho. *Perf. 14***

**B819** SP407 440pf +220pf multi 6.75 6.75

Mills — SP408

Designs: 100pf+50pf, Black Forest. No. B821, Hesse. No. B822, Windmill, lower Rhine. No. B823, Scoop windmill, Schleswig-Holstein. 220pf+80pf, Dutch windmill.

**1997, Oct. 9 Litho. *Perf. 13½x14***

**Background Color**

**B820** SP408 100pf +50pf grn 1.75 1.75
**B821** SP409 110pf +50pf brn 1.75 1.75
**B822** SP408 110pf +50pf blue 1.75 1.75
**B823** SP408 110pf +50pf yel 1.75 1.75
**B824** SP408 220pf +80pf pink 3.00 3.00
*Nos. B820-B824 (5)* 10.00 10.00

Christmas SP409

**1997, Nov. 6 Litho. *Perf. 14***

**B825** SP409 100pf +50pf Magi 1.40 1.25
**B826** SP409 110pf +50pf Nativity 1.60 1.50

Surtax for Federal Assoc. of Free Welfare Work in Bonn.

Sports SP410

1998 Sporting events: 100pf+50pf, World Cup Soccer Championships, France. No. B828, Winter Olympic Games, Nagano. No. B829, Rowing Championships, Cologne. 300pf+100pf, Winter Paralympics, Nagano.

**1998, Feb. 5 Photo. *Perf. 14***

**B827** SP410 100pf +50pf multi 1.50 1.50
**B828** SP410 110pf +50pf multi 1.75 1.75
**B829** SP410 110pf +50pf multi 1.75 1.75
**B830** SP410 300pf +100pf multi 4.25 4.25
*Nos. B827-B830 (4)* 9.25 9.25

Environmental Protection — SP411

**1998, May 7 Litho. *Perf. 14***

**B831** SP411 110pf +50pf multi 1.60 1.60

See No. B831.

Cartoon Figures SP412

#B832, Mouse, Little Yellow Duck, Elephant. #833, Sandman. #834, Maja the Bee. #835, Captain Bluebear. #836, Pumuckl.

**1998, June 10 Litho. *Perf. 14***

**B832** SP412 100pf +50pf multi 1.50 1.50
**B833** SP412 100pf +50pf multi 1.50 1.50
**B834** SP412 110pf +50pf multi 1.75 1.75
**B835** SP412 110pf +50pf multi 1.75 1.75
**B836** SP412 220pf +80pf multi 3.50 3.50
*Nos. B832-B836 (5)* 10.00 10.00

Surtax for the German Youth Stamp Foundation.

Welfare Stamps SP413

Birds: 100pf+50pf, Hen-harrier. No. B838, Great bustard. No. B839, White-eyed duck. No. B840, Sedge warbler. 220pf+80pf, Woodchat shrike.

**1998, Oct. 8 Litho. *Perf. 14***

**Background Colors**

**B837** SP413 100pf +50pf tan 1.50 1.50
**B838** SP413 110pf +50pf gray grn 1.75 1.75
**B839** SP413 110pf +50pf gray blue 1.75 1.75
**B840** SP413 110pf +50pf blue grn 1.75 1.75
**B841** SP413 220pf +80pf lilac 3.50 3.50
*Nos. B837-B841 (5)* 10.25 10.25

Christmas SP414

**1998, Nov. 12**

**B842** SP414 100pf +50pf Shepherds 1.50 1.40
**B843** SP414 110pf +50pf Holy Child 1.75 1.60

Racing Sports SP415

**1999, Feb. 18 Photo. *Perf. 14***

**B844** SP415 100pf +50pf Bicycles 1.75 1.75
**B845** SP415 110pf +50pf Cars 1.75 1.75
**B846** SP415 110pf +50pf Horses 1.75 1.75
**B847** SP415 300pf +100pf Motorcycles 3.75 3.75
*Nos. B844-B847 (4)* 9.00 9.00

**Declaration of Human Rights Type of 1998 Inscribed "KOSOVO-HILFE 1999"**

**1999, Apr. 27 Litho. *Perf. 14***

**B848** A958 110pf +100pf multi 2.25 2.25

Surtax for aid to refugees from Kosovo.

Souvenir Sheet

IBRA '99, Intl. Stamp Exhibition, Nuremberg — SP416

Design: Bavaria #1 & Saxony #1.

**1999, Apr. 27 *Perf. 13½***

**B849** SP416 300pf +110pf multi 4.50 4.50

German postage stamps, 150th anniv.

Cartoons SP417

#B850, The Little Polar Bear. #B851, Rudi the Crow. #B852, Mecki (hedgehog). #B853, Twipsy, mascot of Expo 2000, Hanover. 220pf+80pf, Tabaluga (green dragon).

**1999, June 10 Litho. *Perf. 13¾***

**B850** SP417 100pf +50pf multi 1.75 1.75
**B851** SP417 100pf +50pf multi 1.75 1.75
**B852** SP417 110pf +50pf multi 2.00 2.00
**B853** SP417 110pf +50pf multi 2.00 2.00
**B854** SP417 220pf +80pf multi 2.50 2.50
*Nos. B850-B854 (5)* 10.00 10.00

Surtax for the German Youth Stamp Foundation.

The Cosmos — SP418

#B855, Andromeda galaxy. #B856, Cygnus constellation. #B857, X-ray image of exploding star. #B858, Collision of Comet Shoemaker-Levy 9 and Jupiter. 300pf + 100pf, Gamma ray image of entire sky, satellite.

**1999, Oct. 14 Litho. *Perf. 14***

**B855** SP418 100pf +50pf multi 1.50 1.50
**B856** SP418 100pf +50pf multi 1.50 1.50
**B857** SP418 110pf +50pf multi 1.75 1.75
**B858** SP418 110pf +50pf multi 1.75 1.75
**B859** SP418 300pf +100pf multi 3.50 3.50
*Nos. B855-B859 (5)* 10.00 10.00

Surtax for the Federal Association of Free Welfare Work. Nos. B858-B859 have a holographic image. Soaking in water may affect hologram.

Christmas SP419

**1999, Nov. 4 Litho. *Perf. 13¾***

**B860** SP419 100pf +50pf Angel 1.60 1.40
**B861** SP419 110pf +50pf Manger 1.75 1.50

Sports — SP420

Ancient art and: 100pf + 50pf, Swimmer. No. B863, Gymnast. No. B864, Sprinters. 300pf + 100pf, Hands.

**2000, Feb. 17 Litho. *Perf. 13¾x14***

**B862** SP420 100pf + 50pf multi 1.60 1.60
**B863** SP420 110pf + 50pf multi 1.75 1.75
**B864** SP420 110pf + 50pf multi 1.75 1.75
**B865** SP420 300pf + 100pf multi 4.25 4.25
*Nos. B862-B865 (4)* 9.35 9.35

Surtax was for German Sports Federation.

Environmental Protection — SP421

**2000, May 12 Litho. *Perf. 13¾x14***

**B866** SP421 110pf +50pf multi 1.75 1.75

Expo 2000, Hanover — SP422

#B867, 4 backpackers. #B868, Crowd. #B869, Map of Africa, words "see, come, hear, feel." #B870, Eye. #B871, Abstract with Chinese characters. #B872, Abstract.

**2000, June 8 Litho. *Perf. 13¾x14***

**B867** SP422 100pf +50pf multi 1.50 1.50
**B868** SP422 100pf +50pf multi 1.50 1.50
**B869** SP422 110pf +50pf multi 1.60 1.60
**B870** SP422 110pf +50pf multi 1.60 1.60
**B871** SP422 110pf +50pf multi 1.60 1.60
**B872** SP422 300pf +100pf multi 4.25 4.25
*Nos. B867-B872 (6)* 12.05 12.05

Surtax for German Youth Stamp Foundation.

Actors and Actresses — SP423

#B873, Curd Jürgens (1915-82). #B874, Lilli Palmer (1914-86). #B875, Heinz Rühmann (1902-94). #B876, Romy Schneider (1938-82). #B877, Gert Fröbe (1913-88).

**2000, Oct. 12 Litho. *Perf. 14***

**B873** SP423 100pf +50pf multi 1.50 1.50
**B874** SP423 100pf +50pf multi 1.50 1.50
**B875** SP423 110pf +50pf multi 1.75 1.75
**B876** SP423 110pf +50pf multi 1.75 1.75

**B877** SP423 300pf +100pf multi 4.00 4.00
*Nos. B873-B877 (5)* 10.50 10.50

Surtax was for Federal Association of Welfare Work.

Christmas SP424

Designs: 100pf+50pf, Birth of Christ, by Conrad von Soest. 110pf+50pf, Nativity scene.

**2000, Nov. 9 Litho. *Perf. 13¾***
**B878** SP424 100pf +50pf multi 1.50 1.40
**B879** SP424 110pf +50pf multi 1.75 1.60

Surtax for the Federal Association of Voluntary Welfare Work.
See Spain Nos. 3071-3072.

Sports — SP425

Designs: 100pf+50pf, Sports for schools. No. B881, Sports for the disabled. No. B882, Popular and leisure sports. 300pf+100pf, Sports for senior citizens.

**2001, Feb. 8 Litho. *Perf. 13¾x14***
**B880** SP425 100pf +50pf multi 1.90 1.90
**B881** SP425 110pf +50pf multi 2.00 2.00
**B882** SP425 110pf +50pf multi 2.00 2.00
**B883** SP425 300pf +100pf multi 4.75 4.75
*Nos. B880-B883 (4)* 10.65 10.65

Surtax for German Sports Federation.

Wuppertal Suspension Railway — SP426

**2001, Mar. 8**
**B884** SP426 110pf +50pf multi 2.00 2.00

Surtax for the Foundation for Promotion of Philately and Postal History.

Characters from Children's Stories SP427

Designs: No. B885, Pinocchio. No. B886, Pippi Longstockings. No. B887, Jim Knopf. No. B888, Heidi. 300pf +100pf, Tom Sawyer and Huckleberry Finn.

**2001, June 13 Litho. *Perf. 13¾***
**B885** SP427 100pf +50pf multi 1.90 1.90
**B886** SP427 100pf +50pf multi 1.90 1.90
**B887** SP427 110pf +50pf multi 2.00 2.00
**B888** SP427 110pf +50pf multi 2.00 2.00
**B889** SP427 300pf +100pf multi 4.75 4.75
*Nos. B885-B889 (5)* 12.55 12.55

Surtax for the German Youth Stamp Foundation.

Film Stars SP428

Designs: No. B890, Marilyn Monroe. No. B891, Charlie Chaplin. No. B892, Film reel. No. B893, Greta Garbo. 300pf+100pf, Jean Gabin.

**2001, Oct. 11 Litho. *Perf. 14***
**B890** SP428 100pf +50pf multi 1.90 1.90
*a.* Perf. 13x13¼x13½x13¼ 1.90 1.90
**B891** SP428 100pf +50pf multi 1.90 1.90
*a.* Perf. 13½x13¼ 1.90 1.90
**B892** SP428 110pf +50pf multi 2.00 2.00
*a.* Perf. 13½x13¼ 2.00 2.00
**B893** SP428 110pf +50pf multi 2.00 2.00
*a.* Perf. 13x13¼ 2.00 2.00
**B894** SP428 300pf +100pf multi 4.75 4.75
*a.* Perf. 13x13¼ 4.75 4.75
*b.* Booklet pane, #B890a-B894a 11.50 11.50
Booklet, #B894b 11.50
*Nos. B890-B894 (5)* 12.55 12.55

Surtax for the Federal Association of Voluntary Welfare Work.

---

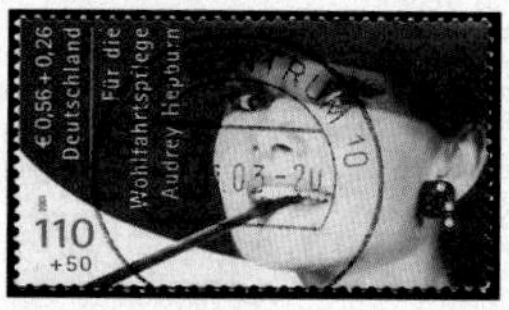

A stamp picturing Audrey Hepburn originally was to have been included in this set but was withdrawn. It was never officially issued, nor were any examples sold over post office counters. However, 30 examples from the original printing were not recovered and destroyed as ordered by the post office. Four of the stamps have been found used on German mail.

---

Christmas SP429

Designs: 100pf+50pf, Madonna and Child, by Alfredo Roldán. 110pf+50pf, Adoration of the Shepherds, by José de Ribera.

**2001, Nov. 8 Litho. *Perf. 13¼***
**B895** SP429 100pf +50pf multi 1.90 1.90
**B896** SP429 110pf +50pf multi 2.00 2.00
*a.* Souvenir sheet (see footnote) 5.50 5.50

No. B896a contains Nos. B895-B896 and lithographed and perf. 13¼ examples of Spain Nos. 3123-3124. No. B896a sold for 4.45m.
See Spain Nos. 3123-3124.

Intl. Year of Mountains — SP430

**2002, Jan. 10 Litho. *Perf. 14***
**B897** SP430 56c +26c multi 2.00 2.00

Winter Olympic Sports — SP431

Designs: 51c+26c, Biathlon. No. B899, 56c+26c, Ski jumping. No. B900, 56c+26c, Speed skating. 153c+51c, Luge.

**2002, Feb. 7 Litho. *Perf. 13¾x14***
**B898** SP431 51c +26c multi 1.90 1.90
**B899** SP431 56c +26c multi 2.00 2.00
**B900** SP431 56c +26c multi 2.00 2.00
**B901** SP431 153c +51c multi 4.75 4.75
*a.* Booklet pane, #B898-B901 10.50 10.50
Booklet, #B901a 10.50
*Nos. B898-B901 (4)* 10.65 10.65

Surtax for German Sports Promotion Foundation.

Toys and Games SP432

Designs: No. B902, Chess pieces. No. B903, Toy truck. No. B904, Doll. No. B905, Teddy bear. 153c+51c, Toy train.

**2002, June 6 Litho. *Perf. 13¾***
**B902** SP432 51c +26c multi 1.90 1.90
**B903** SP432 51c +26c multi 1.90 1.90
**B904** SP432 56c +26c multi 2.00 2.00
**B905** SP432 56c +26c multi 2.00 2.00
**B906** SP432 153c +51c multi 4.75 4.75
*Nos. B902-B906 (5)* 12.55 12.55

Surtax for German Youth Stamp Foundation.

### Environmental Protection Type of 1998 Inscribed "Hochwasserhilfe 2002"

**2002, Aug. 30 Litho. *Perf. 13x13½***
**B907** SP411 56c +44c multi 2.40 2.40

Surtax for flood victims relief.

Christmas SP433

Details from paintings by Rogier van der Weyden: 51c+26c, Annunciation to the Virgin. 56c+26c, Miraflores Altarpiece.

**2002, Nov. 7 Litho. *Perf. 13¾***
**B908** SP433 51c +26c multi 2.00 2.00
**B909** SP433 56c +26c multi 2.00 2.00

Surtax for Federal Working Party on Independent Welfare.

Automobiles — SP434

Designs: 45c+20c, 1960 BMW Isetta 300. No. B911, 55c+25c, 1961 VEB Sachsenring Trabant P50. No. B912, 55c+25c, 1949 Volkswagen Beetle. No. B913, 55c+25c, 1954 Mercedes-Benz 300 SL. 144c+56c, 1957 Borgward Isabella Coupe.

**2002, Dec. 5 Litho. *Perf. 14***
**B910** SP434 45c +20c multi 1.60 1.60
**B911** SP434 55c +25c multi 1.90 1.90
**B912** SP434 55c +25c multi 1.90 1.90
**B913** SP434 55c +25c multi 1.90 1.90
**B914** SP434 144c +56c multi 5.00 5.00
*Nos. B910-B914 (5)* 12.30 12.30

Surtax for Federal Working Party on Independent Welfare.
See Nos. B923-B927.

2006 World Cup Soccer Championships, Germany — SP435

Designs: 45c+20c, Player kicking ball. No. B916, Player heading ball. No. B917, Four children playing soccer. No. B918, Fan celebrating. 144c+56c, Child and adult playing soccer.

**2003, Mar. 6 Litho. *Perf. 13x13½***
**B915** SP435 45c +20c multi 1.40 1.40
**B916** SP435 55c +25c multi 1.75 1.75
**B917** SP435 55c +25c multi 1.75 1.75
**B918** SP435 55c +25c multi 1.75 1.75
**B919** SP435 144c +56c multi 4.50 4.50
*Nos. B915-B919 (5)* 11.15 11.15

Surtax for German Sports Promotion Foundation.

First East-to-West Non-Stop Transatlantic Flight, 75th Anniv. SP436

**2003, Apr. 10 *Perf. 13¾***
**B920** SP436 144c +56c multi 4.25 4.25

Surtax for German Organization for the Enhancement of Philately and Postal History.

June 17, 1953 Uprising in East Germany, 50th Anniv. SP437

**2003, June 12 Photo. *Perf. 14x14¼***
**B921** SP437 55c +25c multi 1.90 1.90

Souvenir Sheet

Father and Son, Cartoons by Ehrich Ohser — SP438

No. B922: a, Father and son running in same direction. b, Father and son falling. c, Son running, father seated. d, Father and son running in different directions. e, Father and son with arms extended.

**2003, July 10 Litho. *Perf. 13x13½***

| | | | | |
|---|---|---|---|---|
| **B922** | SP438 | Sheet of 5 | 11.50 | 11.50 |
| *a.* | | 45c +20c multi | 1.50 | 1.50 |
| *b.-d.* | | 55c +25c any single | 1.75 | 1.75 |
| *e.* | | 144c +56c multi | 4.50 | 4.50 |

### Automobile Type of 2002

Designs: 45c+20c, Wartburg 311 Coupe. No. B924, Olympia Rekord P1. No. B925, 356 B Coupe. No. 926, 55c+25c, Taunus 17 M P3. 144c+56c, Auto Union 1000 S.

**2003, Oct. 9 Litho. *Perf. 14***

| | | | | |
|---|---|---|---|---|
| **B923** | SP434 | 45c +20c multi | 1.50 | 1.50 |
| **B924** | SP434 | 55c +25c multi | 1.90 | 1.90 |
| **B925** | SP434 | 55c +25c multi | 1.90 | 1.90 |
| **B926** | SP434 | 55c +25c multi | 1.90 | 1.90 |
| **B927** | SP434 | 144c +56c multi | 4.50 | 4.50 |
| | | *Nos. B923-B927 (5)* | 11.70 | 11.70 |

Christmas SP439

Designs: 45c+20c, Adoration of the Shepherds. 55c+25c, Holy Family.

**2003, Nov. 13 Litho. *Perf. 13¾***

| | | | | |
|---|---|---|---|---|
| **B928** | SP439 | 45c +20c multi | 1.50 | 1.50 |
| **B929** | SP439 | 55c +25c multi | 1.90 | 1.90 |

Wind Energy SP440

**2004, Jan. 8 Litho. *Perf. 13¾***

| | | | | |
|---|---|---|---|---|
| **B930** | SP440 | 55c +25c multi | 2.10 | 2.10 |

Sporting Events and Anniversaries — SP441

Designs: 45c+20c, European Soccer Championships, June 12-July 4, 2004. No. B932, Summer Olympic Games, Athens, Greece. No. B933, Paralympics, Athens, Greece. No. B934, First German World Cup Championship, 50th anniv. 144c+56c, FIFA (Fédération Internationale de Football Association), cent.

**2004, Feb. 5 Litho. *Perf. 13x13½***

| | | | | |
|---|---|---|---|---|
| **B931** | SP441 | 45c +20c multi | 1.75 | 1.75 |
| **B932** | SP441 | 55c +25c multi | 2.10 | 2.10 |
| **B933** | SP441 | 55c +25c multi | 2.10 | 2.10 |
| **B934** | SP441 | 55c +25c multi | 2.10 | 2.10 |
| **B935** | SP441 | 144c +56c multi | 5.25 | 5.25 |
| | | *Nos. B931-B935 (5)* | 13.30 | 13.30 |

Cats — SP442

Designs: 45c+20c, Two cats playing with ball of string. No. B937, Cat, two kittens playing with ball. No. B938, Kitten on cat. No. B939, Cat licking paw. 144c+56c, Two cats sleeping.

**2004, June 3 Litho. *Perf. 13¾x14***

| | | | | |
|---|---|---|---|---|
| **B936** | SP442 | 45c +20c multi | 1.60 | 1.60 |
| **B937** | SP442 | 55c +25c multi | 1.90 | 1.90 |
| **B938** | SP442 | 55c +25c multi | 1.90 | 1.90 |
| **B939** | SP442 | 55c +25c multi | 1.90 | 1.90 |
| **B940** | SP442 | 144c +56c multi | 4.75 | 4.75 |
| | | *Nos. B936-B940 (5)* | 12.05 | 12.05 |

Landscapes — SP443

Designs: 45c+20c, Iceberg and pack ice. No. B942, Mountains and clouds. No. B943, Islands. No. B944, Sand dunes. 144c+56c, Tree tops.

**2004, Oct. 7 Litho. *Perf. 14***

| | | | | |
|---|---|---|---|---|
| **B941** | SP443 | 45c +20c multi | 1.60 | 1.60 |
| **B942** | SP443 | 55c +25c multi | 2.00 | 2.00 |
| **B943** | SP443 | 55c +25c multi | 2.00 | 2.00 |
| **B944** | SP443 | 55c +25c multi | 2.00 | 2.00 |
| **B945** | SP443 | 144c +56c multi | 5.00 | 5.00 |
| | | *Nos. B941-B945 (5)* | 12.60 | 12.60 |

Christmas SP444

Paintings by Peter Paul Rubens: 45c+20c, The Flight Into Egypt. 55c+25c, Adoration of the Magi.

**2004, Nov. 4 *Perf. 13¾***

| | | | | |
|---|---|---|---|---|
| **B946** | SP444 | 45c +20c multi | 1.75 | 1.75 |
| **B947** | SP444 | 55c +25c multi | 2.10 | 2.10 |

See Belgium Nos. 2051-2053.

Sports — SP445

Designs: 45c+20c, Soccer fans, mascot of 2006 World Cup Soccer Championships. No. B949, Soccer players, soccer ball globe. No. B950, Gymnasts, Brandenburg Gate, Berlin. No. B951, Ski jumper and ski jump. 144c+56c, Fencers, Leipzig Arena.

**2005, Feb. 10 Litho. *Perf. 13¾x14***

| | | | | |
|---|---|---|---|---|
| **B948** | SP445 | 45c +20c multi | 1.75 | 1.75 |
| **B949** | SP445 | 55c +25c multi | 2.10 | 2.10 |
| **B950** | SP445 | 55c +25c multi | 2.10 | 2.10 |
| **B951** | SP445 | 55c +25c multi | 2.10 | 2.10 |
| **B952** | SP445 | 144c +56c multi | 5.25 | 5.25 |
| | | *Nos. B948-B952 (5)* | 13.30 | 13.30 |

2006 World Cup Soccer Championships (Nos. B948-B949), Intl. Gymnastics Exhibition, Berlin (No. B950), Nordic Skiing World Championships, Oberstdorf (No. B951), Fencing World Championships, Leipzig (No. B952).

Stamp Day SP446

**2005, May 12 Litho. *Perf. 14***

| | | | | |
|---|---|---|---|---|
| **B953** | SP446 | 55c +25c multi | 2.10 | 2.10 |

Sailing Ships — SP447

Designs: 45c+20c, Greif. No. B955, Rickmer Rickmers. No. B956, Passat. No. B957, Grossherzogin Elisabeth. 144c+56c, Deutschland.

**2005, June 2 Litho. *Perf. 13¾x14***

| | | | | |
|---|---|---|---|---|
| **B954** | SP447 | 45c +20c multi | 1.60 | 1.60 |
| **B955** | SP447 | 55c +25c multi | 2.00 | 2.00 |
| **B956** | SP447 | 55c +25c multi | 2.00 | 2.00 |
| **B957** | SP447 | 55c +25c multi | 2.00 | 2.00 |
| **B958** | SP447 | 144c +56c multi | 5.00 | 5.00 |
| | | *Nos. B954-B958 (5)* | 12.60 | 12.60 |

Christmas SP448

Paintings by Stefan Lochner: 45c+20c, Adoration of the Child. 55c+25c, Madonna and Child in Rose Garden.

**2005, Nov. 3 Litho. *Perf. 13¾***

| | | | | |
|---|---|---|---|---|
| **B959** | SP448 | 45c +20c multi | 1.60 | 1.60 |
| **B960** | SP448 | 55c +25c multi | 1.90 | 1.90 |

Butterflies — SP449

Designs: 45c+20c, Zitronenfalter. No. B962, Russischer Bär. Nos. B963, B965, Tagpfauenauge. 145c+55c, Weisser Waldportier.

**2005, Dec. 1 Litho. *Perf. 14***

| | | | | |
|---|---|---|---|---|
| **B961** | SP449 | 45c +20c multi | 1.60 | 1.60 |
| **B962** | SP449 | 55c +25c multi | 1.90 | 1.90 |
| **B963** | SP449 | 55c +25c multi | 1.90 | 1.90 |
| **B964** | SP449 | 145c +55c multi | 4.75 | 4.75 |
| | | *Nos. B961-B964 (4)* | 10.15 | 10.15 |

### Self-Adhesive
### Booklet Stamp
### *Die Cut Perf. 11*

| | | | | |
|---|---|---|---|---|
| **B965** | SP449 | 55c +25c multi | 2.25 | 2.25 |
| *a.* | | Booklet pane of 10 | 22.50 | |

Protection of the Ozone Layer — SP450

**2006, Jan. 2 *Perf. 14***

| | | | | |
|---|---|---|---|---|
| **B966** | SP450 | 55c +25c multi | 2.50 | 2.50 |

Sports — SP451

Designs: 45c+20c, Crowd waving German flags, stadium lights. No. B968, Stadium exterior, blurred athlete. No. B969, Stadium interior, players holding World Cup. No. B970, Horse and rider, rider's leg. 145c+55c, Emblem of 2006 World Cup Soccer Championships, blurred picture of soccer player kicking ball.

**2006, Feb. 9 Litho. *Perf. 13x13½***

| | | | | |
|---|---|---|---|---|
| **B967** | SP451 | 45c +20c multi | 1.60 | 1.60 |
| **B968** | SP451 | 55c +25c multi | 1.90 | 1.90 |
| **B969** | SP451 | 55c +25c multi | 1.90 | 1.90 |
| **B970** | SP451 | 55c +25c multi | 1.90 | 1.90 |
| **B971** | SP451 | 145c +55c multi | 4.75 | 4.75 |
| *a.* | | Souvenir sheet, #B967-B969, B971 | 12.00 | 12.00 |
| | | *Nos. B967-B971 (5)* | 12.05 | 12.05 |

2006 World Cup Soccer Championships (Nos. B967-B969, B971), World Equestrian Championships, Aachen (No. B970).

No. B971a issued 5/4.

Mammals — SP452

Designs: 45c+20c, Pine marten. No. B973, Doe and fawn. No. B974, Hares. No. B975, Squirrel. 145c+55c, Wild pig and piglets.

**2006, June 8 Litho. *Perf. 14***

| | | | | |
|---|---|---|---|---|
| **B972** | SP452 | 45c +20c multi | 1.75 | 1.75 |
| **B973** | SP452 | 55c +25c multi | 2.10 | 2.10 |
| **B974** | SP452 | 55c +25c multi | 2.10 | 2.10 |
| **B975** | SP452 | 55c +25c multi | 2.10 | 2.10 |
| **B976** | SP452 | 145c +55c multi | 5.25 | 5.25 |
| | | *Nos. B972-B976 (5)* | 13.30 | 13.30 |

Surtax for the German Youth Stamp Foundation.

Trains — SP453

Designs: 45c+20c, Fliegender Hamburger (VT 877). No. B978, Trans Europ Express (VT 11.5). Nos. B979, B981, InterCityExpress (ET403). 145c+55c, Henschel-Wegmann train (61 001).

**2006, Oct. 5 Litho. *Perf. 13¾x14***

| | | | | |
|---|---|---|---|---|
| **B977** | SP453 | 45c +20c multi | 1.75 | 1.75 |
| **B978** | SP453 | 55c +25c multi | 2.00 | 2.00 |
| **B979** | SP453 | 55c +25c multi | 2.00 | 2.00 |
| **B980** | SP453 | 145c +55c multi | 5.00 | 5.00 |
| | | *Nos. B977-B980 (4)* | 10.75 | 10.75 |

### Booklet Stamp
### Self-Adhesive
### *Die Cut Perf. 11*

| | | | | |
|---|---|---|---|---|
| **B981** | SP453 | 55c +25c multi | 2.50 | 2.50 |
| *a.* | | Booklet pane of 10 | 25.00 | |

Christmas — SP454

15th Cent. altarpiece art by Meister Francke: 45c+20c, Nativity. 55c+25c, Adoration of the Magi.

**2006, Nov. 9 Litho. *Perf. 14***

| | | | | |
|---|---|---|---|---|
| **B982** | SP454 | 45c +20c multi | 1.75 | 1.75 |
| **B983** | SP454 | 55c +25c multi | 2.00 | 2.00 |

SP455

Designs: 45c+20c, Canoe World Championships. No. B985, Handball World Championships. No. B986, Gymnastics World Championships. 145c+55c, Modern Pentathlon World Championships.

**2007 Litho. *Perf. 13x13½***

| | | | | |
|---|---|---|---|---|
| **B984** | SP455 | 45c +20c multi | 1.75 | 1.75 |
| **B985** | SP455 | 55c +25c multi | 2.10 | 2.10 |
| **B986** | SP455 | 55c +25c multi | 2.10 | 2.10 |
| **B987** | SP455 | 145c +55c multi | 5.25 | 5.25 |
| *a.* | | Souvenir sheet, #B984-B987 | 12.00 | 12.00 |
| | | *Nos. B985-B987 (3)* | 9.45 | 9.45 |

Issued: B985, 1/2. B984, B986-B987, 2/8. B987a, 5/3.

Souvenir Sheet

Graf Zeppelin and Itinerary of Flight to South America — SP456

**Litho. & Engr.**

**2007, Mar. 1 *Perf. 14x14¼***

| | | | | |
|---|---|---|---|---|
| **B988** | SP456 | 170c +70c multi | 6.50 | 6.50 |

Stamp Day.

Souvenir Sheet

Hans Huckelbein, der Unglücksrabe, by Wilhelm Busch — SP457

No. B989: a, Bird eating berry jam. b, Bird standing in jam. c, Bird tipping pan of jam. d, Bird dirtying clean laundry.

**2007, June 14 Litho. *Perf. 13¼***

| | | | | |
|---|---|---|---|---|
| **B989** | SP457 | Sheet of 4 | 12.00 | 12.00 |
| *a.* | | 45c +20c multi | 1.75 | 1.75 |
| *b.-c.* | | 55c +25c either single | 2.10 | 2.10 |
| *d.* | | 145c +55c multi | 5.50 | 5.50 |

Christmas SP458

Designs: 45c+20c, Magi. 55c+25c, Madonna and Child, donkey and bull.

**2007, Nov. 8 Litho. *Perf. 13¼***

| | | | | |
|---|---|---|---|---|
| **B990** | SP458 | 45c +20c multi | 1.90 | 1.90 |
| **B991** | SP458 | 55c +25c multi | 2.40 | 2.40 |

Adult and Juvenile Animals — SP459

Designs: 45c+20c, Guinea pigs. Nos. B993, B996, Horses. No. B994, Dogs. 145c+55c, Rabbits.

**2007, Dec. 27 Photo. *Perf. 13¾x14***

| | | | | |
|---|---|---|---|---|
| **B992** | SP459 | 45c +20c multi | 1.90 | 1.90 |
| **B993** | SP459 | 55c +25c multi | 2.40 | 2.40 |
| **B994** | SP459 | 55c +25c multi | 2.40 | 2.40 |
| **B995** | SP459 | 145c +55c multi | 6.00 | 6.00 |
| | | *Nos. B992-B995 (4)* | 12.70 | 12.70 |

**Self-Adhesive**

**Booklet Stamp**

***Die Cut Perf. 11***

| | | | | |
|---|---|---|---|---|
| **B996** | SP459 | 55c +25c multi | 2.50 | 2.50 |
| *a.* | | Booklet pane of 10 | 25.00 | |

Sports Championships — SP460

Designs: 45c+20c, World Gliding Championships, Berlin. No. B998, Chess Olympiad, Dresden. No. B999, European Soccer Championships, Austria and Switzerland. 145c+55c, 2008 Summer Olympics, Beijing.

***Perf. 13¼x13½***

**2008, Mar. 13 Litho.**

| | | | | |
|---|---|---|---|---|
| **B997** | SP460 | 45c +20c multi | 2.10 | 2.10 |
| **B998** | SP460 | 55c +25c multi | 2.50 | 2.50 |
| **B999** | SP460 | 55c +25c multi | 2.50 | 2.50 |
| **B1000** | SP460 | 145c +55c multi | 6.25 | 6.25 |
| | | *Nos. B997-B1000 (4)* | 13.35 | 13.35 |

Knut, Polar Bear Cub in Berlin Zoo SP461

**2008, Apr. 10 Litho. *Perf. 14***

| | | | | |
|---|---|---|---|---|
| **B1001** | SP461 | 55c +25c multi | 2.60 | 2.60 |

Aircraft — SP462

Designs: 45c+20c, Dornier Do J Wal. No. B1003, Junkers Ju 52. Nos. B1004, B1006, Airbus A380. 145c+55c, Messerschmitt-Bölkow-Blohm BO 105 helicopter.

**2008, June 12 Litho. *Perf. 14***

| | | | | |
|---|---|---|---|---|
| **B1002** | SP462 | 45c +20c multi | 2.00 | 2.00 |
| **B1003** | SP462 | 55c +25c multi | 2.50 | 2.50 |
| **B1004** | SP462 | 55c +25c multi | 2.50 | 2.50 |
| **B1005** | SP462 | 145c +55c multi | 6.25 | 6.25 |
| | | *Nos. B1002-B1005 (4)* | 13.25 | 13.25 |

**Self-Adhesive**

***Die Cut Perf. 11***

| | | | | |
|---|---|---|---|---|
| **B1006** | SP462 | 55c +25c multi | 2.50 | 2.50 |
| *a.* | | Booklet pane of 10 | 25.00 | |

Miniature Sheet

Dinosaurs — SP463

No. B1007: a, Triceratops. b, Diplodocus. c, Tyrannosaurus rex. d, Plateosaurus.

**2008, Sept. 4 Litho. *Perf. 13x13½***

| | | | | |
|---|---|---|---|---|
| **B1007** | SP463 | Sheet of 4 | 12.50 | 12.50 |
| *a.* | | 45c +20c multi | 1.90 | 1.90 |
| *b.-c.* | | 55c +25c Either single | 2.40 | 2.40 |
| *d.* | | 145c +55c multi | 5.75 | 5.75 |

Christmas SP464

Designs: 45c+20c, Nativity, by Albrecht Dürer. 55c+25c, Adoration of the Magi, by Raphael, horiz.

**2008, Nov. 13 Litho. *Perf. 14***

| | | | | |
|---|---|---|---|---|
| **B1008** | SP464 | 45c +20c multi | 1.75 | 1.75 |
| **B1009** | SP464 | 55c +25c multi | 2.10 | 2.10 |

See Vatican City Nos. 1399-1401.

Atmospheric Phenomena — SP465

Designs: 45c+20c, Rainbow. Nos. B1011, B1014, Clouds. No. B1012, Aurora borealis. 145c+55c, Lightning.

**2009, Jan. 2 Litho. *Perf. 14***

| | | | | |
|---|---|---|---|---|
| **B1010** | SP465 | 45c +20c multi | 1.75 | 1.75 |
| **B1011** | SP465 | 55c +25c multi | 2.25 | 2.25 |
| **B1012** | SP465 | 55c +25c multi | 2.25 | 2.25 |
| **B1013** | SP465 | 145c +55c multi | 5.50 | 5.50 |
| | | *Nos. B1010-B1013 (4)* | 11.75 | 11.75 |

**Booklet Stamp**

**Self-Adhesive**

***Die Cut Perf. 11***

| | | | | |
|---|---|---|---|---|
| **B1014** | SP465 | 55c +25c multi | 2.25 | 2.25 |
| *a.* | | Booklet pane of 10 | 22.50 | |

2009 World Track and Field Championships, Berlin — SP466

Designs: 45c+20c, Hurdles. No. B1016, Pole vault. No. B1017, Runners. 145c+55c, Discus.

**2009, Apr. 9 *Perf. 13x13½***

| | | | | |
|---|---|---|---|---|
| **B1015** | SP466 | 45c +20c multi | 1.75 | 1.75 |
| **B1016** | SP466 | 55c +25c multi | 2.10 | 2.10 |
| *a.* | | Booklet pane of 8, 4 each #B1015-B1016 | 15.50 | |
| | | Complete booklet, #B1016a | 15.50 | |
| **B1017** | SP466 | 55c +25c multi | 2.10 | 2.10 |
| **B1018** | SP466 | 145c +55c multi | 5.25 | 5.25 |
| | | *Nos. B1015-B1018 (4)* | 11.20 | 11.20 |

Stamp Day — SP467

**2009, May 7 *Perf. 13¾ Syncopated***

| | | | | |
|---|---|---|---|---|
| **B1019** | SP467 | 55c +25c multi | 2.25 | 2.25 |

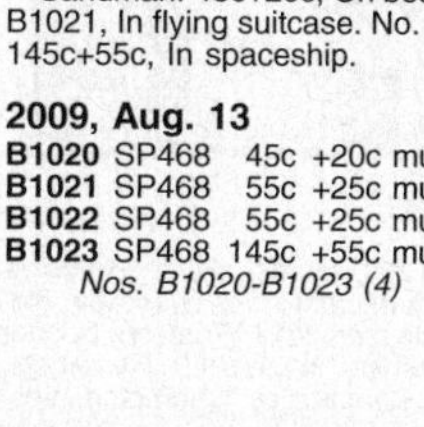

"Our Sandman" Children's Television Show, 50th Anniv. SP468

Sandman: 45c+20c, On beach with boy. No. B1021, In flying suitcase. No. B1022, On train. 145c+55c, In spaceship.

**2009, Aug. 13 *Perf. 13¼***

| | | | | |
|---|---|---|---|---|
| **B1020** | SP468 | 45c +20c multi | 1.90 | 1.90 |
| **B1021** | SP468 | 55c +25c multi | 2.25 | 2.25 |
| **B1022** | SP468 | 55c +25c multi | 2.25 | 2.25 |
| **B1023** | SP468 | 145c +55c multi | 5.75 | 5.75 |
| | | *Nos. B1020-B1023 (4)* | 12.15 | 12.15 |

Christmas — SP469

Illuminated manuscripts depicting: 45c+20c, Adoration of the Magi. 55c+25c, Nativity.

**2009, Nov. 12 *Perf. 14***

| | | | | |
|---|---|---|---|---|
| **B1024** | SP469 | 45c +20c multi | 2.00 | 2.00 |
| **B1025** | SP469 | 55c +25c multi | 2.40 | 2.40 |

Fruit — SP470

Blossom and fruit (whole and halved): 45c+20c, Apple (Malus domestica). No. B1027, Lemon (Citrus limon). Nos. B1028, B1030, Strawberry (Fragaria ananassa). 145c+55c, Blueberry (vaccinium myrtillus).

**2010, Jan. 2 Litho. *Perf. 14***

| | | | | |
|---|---|---|---|---|
| **B1026** | SP470 | 45c +20c multi | 1.90 | 1.90 |
| **B1027** | SP470 | 55c +25c multi | 2.40 | 2.40 |
| **B1028** | SP470 | 55c +25c multi | 2.40 | 2.40 |
| **B1029** | SP470 | 145c +55c multi | 5.75 | 5.75 |
| | | *Nos. B1026-B1029 (4)* | 12.45 | 12.45 |

**Self-Adhesive**

***Die Cut Perf. 10¾***

| | | | | |
|---|---|---|---|---|
| **B1030** | SP470 | 55c +25c multi | 2.40 | 2.40 |
| *a.* | | Booklet pane of 10 | 24.00 | |

Nos. B1026-B1030 have a scratch-and-sniff coating on the whole and halved fruit parts of the vignette having the scent of the fruit shown.

Athletes — SP471

Designs: 45c+20c, Skier at Winter Paralympics, Vancouver. No B1032, Skier at 2010 Winter Olympics, Vancouver. Designs: No. B1033, Soccer players, 2010 World Cup Soccer Championships, South Africa. 145c+55c, Ice hockey players, 2010 World Ice Hockey Championships, Germany.

**2010 Litho. *Perf. 14***

| | | | | |
|---|---|---|---|---|
| **B1031** | SP471 | 45c +20c multi | 1.75 | 1.75 |
| **B1032** | SP471 | 55c +25c multi | 2.25 | 2.25 |
| **B1033** | SP471 | 55c +25c multi | 2.25 | 2.25 |
| **B1034** | SP471 | 145c+55c multi | 5.50 | 5.50 |

Issued: Nos. B1031-B1032, 2/11. Nos. B1033-B1034, 4/8.

Protection of the Seas — SP472

**2010, May 6 Litho. *Perf. 13x13½***

| | | | | |
|---|---|---|---|---|
| **B1035** | SP472 | 55c +25c multi | 2.10 | 2.10 |

Steamers — SP473

Designs: 45c+20c, Deutschland. No. B1037, Aller. No. B1038, Imperator. 145c+55c, Columbus.

**2010, Aug. 12 Litho. *Perf. 13x13¼***

**B1036** SP473 45c +20c multi 1.75 1.75
**B1037** SP473 55c +25c multi 2.10 2.10
**B1038** SP473 55c +25c multi 2.10 2.10
**B1039** SP473 145c +55c multi 5.50 5.50
*Nos. B1036-B1039 (4)* 11.45 11.45

Christmas — SP474

Creche figures: 45c+20c, Nativity. 55c+25c, Adoration of the Magi.

**2010, Nov. 11 Litho. *Perf. 13x13½***

**B1040** SP474 45c +20c multi 1.75 1.75
**B1041** SP474 55c +25c multi 2.25 2.25

Cartoons by Loriot (Bernhard-Viktor von Bülow) — SP475

Designs: 45c+20c, Two men and talking dog. Nos. B1043, B1046, Two men at racetrack fence. No. B1044, Two naked men standing in bathtub. 145c+55c, Man and woman at breakfast table.

**2011, Jan. 3 Litho. *Perf. 13¾x14***

**B1042** SP475 45c +20c multi 1.75 1.75
**B1043** SP475 55c +25c multi 2.25 2.25
**B1044** SP475 55c +25c multi 2.25 2.25
**B1045** SP475 145c +55c multi 5.50 5.50
*Nos. B1042-B1045 (4)* 11.75 11.75

**Booklet Stamp**
**Self-Adhesive**
***Die Cut Perf. 11***

**B1046** SP475 55c +25c multi 2.25 2.25
*a.* Booklet pane of 10 22.50

Athletes — SP476

Designs: 45c+20c, Goalie, 2011 Women's Soccer World Championships, Germany. No. B1048, Soccer players, 2011 Women's Soccer World Championships. No. B1049, Gymnasts, 2011 European Gymnastics Championships, Berlin. 145c+55c, Field hockey players, 2011 Men's European Field Hockey Championships, Mönchengladbach.

**2011, Apr. 7 *Perf. 13¼x13½***

**B1047** SP476 45c +20c multi 1.90 1.90
**B1048** SP476 55c +25c multi 2.25 2.25
*a.* Booklet pane of 8, 4 each #B1047-B1048 17.00 —
Complete booklet, #B1048a 17.00
**B1049** SP476 55c +25c multi 2.25 2.25
**B1050** SP476 145c +55c multi 5.75 5.75
*Nos. B1047-B1050 (4)* 12.15 12.15

Issued: No. B1048a, 6/9.

Stamp Day, 75th Anniv. SP477

**2011, Aug. 11 *Perf. 13½x13¾***

**B1051** SP477 55c +25c multi 2.40 2.40

Astronomy — SP478

Designs: 45c+20c, Horeshead Nebula. No. B1053, Earth, Saturn, other planets, half of Sun. No. B1054, Jupiter, other planets, half of Sun. 145c+55c, Pleiades.

**2011, Aug. 11 *Perf. 14***

**B1052** SP478 45c +20c multi 1.90 1.90
**B1053** SP478 55c +25c multi 2.40 2.40
**B1054** SP478 55c +25c multi 2.40 2.40
*a.* Horiz. pair, #B1053-B1054 4.80 4.80
**B1055** SP478 145c +55c multi 5.75 5.75
*Nos. B1052-B1055 (4)* 12.45 12.45

Christmas — SP479

Stained-glass windows depicting: 45c+20c, St. Martin. 55c+25c, St. Nicholas.

**2011, Nov. 10 Litho. *Perf. 13x13½***

**B1056** SP479 45c+20c multi 1.75 1.75
**B1057** SP479 55c+25c multi 2.25 2.25

Gems — SP480

Designs: 55c+25c, Ruby. 90c+40c, Emerald. 145c+55c, Sapphire.

**2012, Jan. 2 *Perf. 13¼x13½***

**B1058** SP480 55c +25c multi 2.10 2.10
**B1059** SP480 90c +40c multi 3.50 3.50
**B1060** SP480 145c +55c multi 5.25 5.25
*Nos. B1058-B1060 (3)* 10.85 10.85

**Booklet Stamp**
**Self-Adhesive**
***Die Cut Perf. 11***

**B1061** SP480 55c +25c multi 2.10 2.10
*a.* Booklet pane of 10 21.00

Sports — SP481

Designs: 55c+25c, 2012 European Soccer Championships, Poland and Ukraine. 90c+40c, 2012 Summer Olympics, London. 145c+55c, 2012 World Team Table Tennis Championships, Dortmund.

**2012, Apr. 12 *Perf. 13¼x13½***

**B1062** SP481 55c +25c multi 2.10 2.10
**B1063** SP481 90c +40c multi 3.50 3.50
**B1064** SP481 145c +55c multi 5.25 5.25
*Nos. B1062-B1064 (3)* 10.85 10.85

"Waste is Raw Material" SP482

**2012, May 2 Litho. *Perf. 13¾***

**B1065** SP482 55c +25c multi 2.10 2.10

Historical Locomotives — SP483

Designs: 55c+25c, S3/6. 90c+40c, PTL 2/2. 145c+55c, Leopold Friedrich.

**2012, Aug. 9 *Perf. 13¾x14***

**B1066** SP483 55c +25c multi 2.10 2.10
**B1067** SP483 90c +40c multi 3.50 3.50
**B1068** SP483 145c +55c multi 5.25 5.25
*Nos. B1066-B1068 (3)* 10.85 10.85

## AIR POST STAMPS

### Issues of the Republic

Post Horn with Wings — AP1

Biplane AP2

***Perf. 15x14½***

**1919, Nov. 10 Typo. Unwmk.**

**C1** AP1 10pf orange .25 *2.50*
**C2** AP2 40pf dark green .25 *3.00*
*a.* Imperf. 1,875.
Set, never hinged 1.30

No. C2a is ungummed.

Carrier Pigeon — AP3

**1922-23 Wmk. 126 *Perf. 14, 14½***

**Size: 19x23mm**

| | | | | |
|---|---|---|---|---|
| **C3** | AP3 | 25(pf) chocolate | .45 | *18.00* |
| **C4** | AP3 | 40(pf) orange | .35 | *24.00* |
| **C5** | AP3 | 50(pf) violet | .25 | *8.25* |
| **C6** | AP3 | 60(pf) carmine | .50 | *20.00* |
| **C7** | AP3 | 80(pf) blue grn | .35 | *20.00* |

***Perf. 13x13½***

**Size: 22x28mm**

| | | | | |
|---|---|---|---|---|
| **C8** | AP3 | 1m dk grn & pale grn | .25 | *3.75* |
| **C9** | AP3 | 2m lake & gray | .25 | *3.75* |
| **C10** | AP3 | 3m dk blue & gray | .25 | *4.50* |
| **C11** | AP3 | 5m red org & yel | .25 | *3.75* |
| **C12** | AP3 | 10m vio & rose ('23) | .25 | *10.50* |
| **C13** | AP3 | 25m brn & yel ('23) | .25 | *8.50* |
| **C14** | AP3 | 100m ol grn & rose ('23) | .25 | *7.25* |
| | | *Nos. C3-C14 (12)* | 3.65 | *132.25* |
| | | Set, never hinged | 11.50 | |

**1923**

| | | | | |
|---|---|---|---|---|
| **C15** | AP3 | 5m vermilion | .25 | *45.00* |
| **C16** | AP3 | 10m violet | .25 | *10.50* |
| **C17** | AP3 | 25m dark brown | .25 | *10.50* |
| **C18** | AP3 | 100m olive grn | .25 | *11.00* |
| **C19** | AP3 | 200m deep blue | .25 | *32.50* |
| *a.* | | Imperf. | 60.00 | |
| | | *Nos. C15-C19 (5)* | 1.25 | 109.50 |
| | | Set, never hinged | 2.25 | |

Issued: #C15-C18, June 1. #C19, July 25.
Note following #160 applies to #C1-C19.

**1924, Jan. 11 *Perf. 14***

**Size: 19x23mm**

| | | | | |
|---|---|---|---|---|
| **C20** | AP3 | 5(pf) yellow grn | 1.25 | *2.25* |
| **C21** | AP3 | 10(pf) carmine | 1.25 | *1.90* |
| **C22** | AP3 | 20(pf) violet blue | 6.75 | 5.25 |
| **C23** | AP3 | 50(pf) orange | 11.00 | *24.00* |
| **C24** | AP3 | 100(pf) dull violet | 30.00 | *55.00* |
| **C25** | AP3 | 200(pf) grnsh blue | 55.00 | *75.00* |
| **C26** | AP3 | 300(pf) gray | 97.50 | 100.00 |
| *a.* | | Imperf. | *1,425.* | |
| | | *Nos. C20-C26 (7)* | 202.75 | *263.40* |
| | | Set, never hinged | 1,130. | |

German Eagle — AP4

**1926-27**

| | | | | |
|---|---|---|---|---|
| **C27** | AP4 | 5pf green | 1.10 | *1.10* |
| **C28** | AP4 | 10pf rose red | 1.90 | *1.10* |
| *b.* | | Tête bêche pair | 92.50 | 200.00 |
| | | Never hinged | 200.00 | |
| *d.* | | Bklt. pane 10 (6 No. C28 + 4 No. C29) | 55.00 | 150.00 |
| | | Never hinged | 150.00 | |
| **C29** | AP4 | 15pf lilac rose ('27) | 1.90 | 1.90 |
| *a.* | | Double impression | *1,375.* | |
| **C30** | AP4 | 20pf dull blue | 1.90 | *1.90* |
| *a.* | | Tête bêche pair | 92.50 | 200.00 |
| | | Never hinged | 200.00 | |
| *b.* | | Bklt. pane 4 (4 No. C30 + 6 labels) | 62.50 | 150.00 |
| | | Never hinged | 150.00 | |
| *c.* | | Bklt. pane 5 (5 No. C30 + 5 labels) | 200.00 | 500.00 |
| | | Never hinged | 500.00 | |
| **C31** | AP4 | 50pf brown org | 18.00 | 5.25 |
| **C32** | AP4 | 1m black & salmon | 18.00 | 6.00 |
| **C33** | AP4 | 2m black & blue | 18.00 | *22.50* |
| **C34** | AP4 | 3m black & ol grn | 52.50 | *90.00* |
| | | *Nos. C27-C34 (8)* | 113.30 | *129.75* |
| | | Set, never hinged | 935.00 | |

"Graf Zeppelin" Crossing Ocean — AP5

**1928-31 Photo.**

| | | | | |
|---|---|---|---|---|
| **C35** | AP5 | 1m carmine ('31) | 25.00 | *32.50* |
| **C36** | AP5 | 2m ultra | 37.50 | *52.50* |
| **C37** | AP5 | 4m black brown | 27.50 | *35.00* |
| | | *Nos. C35-C37 (3)* | 90.00 | *120.00* |
| | | Set, never hinged | 400.00 | |

Issued: 2m, 4m, Sept. 20. 1m, May 8.
For overprints see Nos. C40-C45.

AP6

**1930, Apr. 19 Wmk. 126**

| | | | | |
|---|---|---|---|---|
| **C38** | AP6 | 2m ultra | 240.00 | *300.00* |
| **C39** | AP6 | 4m black brown | 240.00 | *300.00* |
| | | Set, never hinged | 2,625. | |

First flight of Graf Zeppelin to South America. Nos. C38-C39 exist with watermark vertical or horizontal.

Counterfeits exist of Nos. C38-C45.

Nos. C35-C37 Overprinted in Brown

**1931, July 15**

| | | | | |
|---|---|---|---|---|
| **C40** | AP5 | 1m carmine | 110.00 | 110.00 |
| **C41** | AP5 | 2m ultra | 160.00 | *200.00* |
| **C42** | AP5 | 4m black brown | 400.00 | *675.00* |
| | | *Nos. C40-C42 (3)* | 670.00 | *985.00* |
| | | Set, never hinged | 3,050. | |

Polar flight of Graf Zeppelin.

Nos. C35-C37 Overprinted

**1933, Sept. 25**

| | | | | |
|---|---|---|---|---|
| **C43** | AP5 | 1m carmine | 750.00 | *375.00* |
| **C44** | AP5 | 2m ultra | 75.00 | *190.00* |
| **C45** | AP5 | 4m black brown | 75.00 | *190.00* |
| | | *Nos. C43-C45 (3)* | 900.00 | *755.00* |
| | | Set, never hinged | 3,000. | |

Graf Zeppelin flight to Century of Progress International Exhibition, Chicago.

Swastika Sun, Globe and Eagle — AP7

Otto Lilienthal — AP8

Design: 3m, Count Ferdinand von Zeppelin.

***Perf. 14, 13½x13***

**1934, Jan. 21 Typo. Wmk. 237**

| | | | | |
|---|---|---|---|---|
| **C46** | AP7 | 5(pf) brt green | 1.10 | .90 |
| **C47** | AP7 | 10(pf) brt carmine | 1.10 | .90 |
| **C48** | AP7 | 15(pf) ultra | 1.80 | 1.25 |
| **C49** | AP7 | 20(pf) dull blue | 3.25 | 1.60 |
| **C50** | AP7 | 25(pf) brown | 3.50 | 1.90 |
| **C51** | AP7 | 40(pf) red violet | 6.75 | 1.10 |
| **C52** | AP7 | 50(pf) dk green | 12.00 | .90 |
| **C53** | AP7 | 80(pf) orange yel | 3.75 | 3.75 |
| **C54** | AP7 | 100(pf) black | 7.50 | 2.75 |
| **C55** | AP8 | 2m green & blk | 16.50 | *19.00* |
| **C56** | AP8 | 3m blue & blk | 30.00 | *42.50* |
| | | *Nos. C46-C56 (11)* | 87.25 | 76.55 |
| | | Set, never hinged | 535.00 | |

"Hindenburg" — AP10

***Perf. 14, 14½x14***

**1936, Mar. 16 Engr.**

| | | | | |
|---|---|---|---|---|
| **C57** | AP10 | 50pf dark blue | 18.00 | .75 |
| **C58** | AP10 | 75pf dull green | 19.00 | 1.10 |

The note concerning gum after No. B68 also applies to Nos. C57-C58.

**Unused values are for stamps without gum.**

Count Zeppelin — AP11

Airship Gondola — AP12

**1938, July 5 Unwmk. *Perf. 13½***

| | | | | |
|---|---|---|---|---|
| **C59** | AP11 | 25pf dull blue | 2.25 | 1.50 |
| **C60** | AP12 | 50pf green | 3.50 | 1.50 |
| | | Set, never hinged | 42.00 | |

Count Ferdinand von Zeppelin (1838-1917), airship inventor and builder.

**Catalogue values for unused stamps in this section, from this point to the end of the section, are for Never Hinged items.**

**Federal Republic**

Lufthansa Emblem AP13

***Perf. 13½x13***

**1955, Mar. 31 Litho. Wmk. 295**

| | | | | |
|---|---|---|---|---|
| **C61** | AP13 | 5pf lilac rose & blk | 1.00 | .75 |
| **C62** | AP13 | 10pf green & blk | 1.25 | 1.25 |
| **C63** | AP13 | 15pf blue & blk | 7.50 | 5.75 |
| **C64** | AP13 | 20pf red & blk | 21.00 | 7.50 |
| | | *Nos. C61-C64 (4)* | 30.75 | 15.25 |

Re-opening of German air service, Apr. 1.

**MILITARY AIR POST STAMP**

Junkers 52 Transport MAP1

**1942 Unwmk. Typo. *Perf. 13½***

| | | | | |
|---|---|---|---|---|
| **MC1** | MAP1 | ultramarine | .25 | *.30* |
| | | Never hinged | .45 | |
| *a.* | | Rouletted | .25 | *.60* |
| | | Never hinged | .45 | |

**MILITARY PARCEL POST STAMPS**

Nazi Emblem — MPP1

**1942 Unwmk. Typo. *Perf. 13½***

**Size: 28x23mm**

| | | | | |
|---|---|---|---|---|
| **MQ1** | MPP1 | red brown | .25 | *.45* |
| | | Never hinged | .45 | |
| *a.* | | Rouletted | .25 | *.45* |
| | | Never hinged | .45 | |

**1944 Size: 22½x18mm *Perf. 14***

| | | | | |
|---|---|---|---|---|
| **MQ2** | MPP1 | bright green | .45 | *2.25* |
| | | Never hinged | 1.10 | |

No. 520 Overprinted in Black

**1944 Engr.**

| | | | | |
|---|---|---|---|---|
| **MQ3** | A115 | on 40pf brt red vio | .45 | *3.50* |
| | | Never hinged | 1.10 | |

Forged surcharges exist.

Used values for Nos. MQ1-MQ3 are for CTO examples. Postally used stamps are scarce and sell for much more.

**OFFICIAL STAMPS**

**Issues of the Republic**

In 1920 the Official Stamps of Bavaria and Wurttemberg then current were overprinted "Deutsches Reich" and made available for official use in all parts of Germany. They were, however, used almost exclusively in the two states where they originated and we have listed them among the issues of those states.

O1

O2

O3

O4

O5

O6

O7

O8

O9

O10

O11

O12

**1920-21 Typo. Wmk. 125 *Perf. 14***

| | | | | |
|---|---|---|---|---|
| **O1** | O1 | 5pf deep green | .90 | *13.50* |
| **O2** | O2 | 10pf car rose | .25 | 1.60 |
| **O3** | O2 | 10pf orange ('21) | .50 | *450.00* |
| **O4** | O3 | 15pf violet brn | .25 | 2.25 |
| *a.* | | Imperf. ('21) | *750.00* | *750.00* |
| **O5** | O4 | 20pf deep ultra | .25 | 1.90 |
| **O6** | O5 | 30pf org, *buff* | .25 | 1.90 |
| **O7** | O6 | 40pf carmine | .25 | 1.90 |
| **O8** | O7 | 50pf violet, *buff* | .25 | 1.90 |
| **O9** | O8 | 60pf red brown ('21) | .25 | 1.90 |
| **O10** | O9 | 1m red, *buff* | .25 | 1.90 |
| **O11** | O10 | 1.25m dk bl, *yel* | .25 | 2.25 |
| **O12** | O11 | 2m dark blue | 4.25 | 3.00 |
| **O13** | O12 | 5m brown, *yel* | .25 | 3.00 |
| | | *Nos. O1-O13 (13)* | 8.15 | *487.00* |
| | | Set, never hinged | 34.00 | |

The value of No. O4a is for a stamp postmarked at Bautzen.

See No. O15. For surcharges see Nos. O29-O33, O35-O36, O38.

Postally Used vs. CTO
Values quoted for canceled examples of Nos. O1-O46 are for postally used stamps. See note after No. 160.

O13

O14

O15

**Wmk. 126, 125 (#O16-O17)**

**1922-23**

| | | | | |
|---|---|---|---|---|
| **O14** | O13 | 75pf dark blue | .25 | *7.50* |
| **O15** | O11 | 2m dark blue | .25 | *1.50* |
| *a.* | | Imperf. | 97.50 | |
| **O16** | O14 | 3m brown, *rose* | .25 | *1.50* |
| **O17** | O15 | 10m dk grn, *rose* | .25 | *1.50* |
| **O18** | O15 | 10m dk grn, *rose* | .25 | *9.00* |
| **O19** | O15 | 20m dk bl, *rose* | .25 | *1.50* |
| **O20** | O15 | 50m vio, *rose* | .25 | *1.50* |
| *a.* | | Imperf | 97.50 | |
| **O21** | O15 | 100m rose red, *rose* | .25 | *1.50* |
| *a.* | | Imperf | 110.00 | *750.00* |
| | | *Nos. O14-O21 (8)* | 2.00 | *25.50* |
| | | Set, never hinged | 4.50 | |

Issue date: #O18-O21, 1923.
Nos. O20-O21 exist imperf.
For surcharges see Nos. O34, O37, O39.

Regular Issue of 1923 Overprinted — a

**1923**

| | | | | |
|---|---|---|---|---|
| **O22** | A34 | 20m red lilac | .30 | *7.50* |
| **O23** | A34 | 30m olive grn | .25 | *32.50* |
| **O24** | A29 | 40m green | .25 | *3.00* |
| **O25** | A35 | 200m car rose | .25 | *1.50* |
| **O26** | A35 | 300m green | .25 | *1.50* |
| **O27** | A35 | 400m dk brn | .25 | *1.50* |
| **O28** | A35 | 500m red orange | .25 | *1.50* |
| | | *Nos. O22-O28 (7)* | 1.80 | *49.00* |
| | | Set, never hinged | 4.50 | |

**Official Stamps of 1920-23 Surcharged with New Values**

Abbreviations:
Th=(Tausend) Thousand
Mil=(Million) Million
Mlrd=(Milliarde) Billion

**1923** **Wmk. 125**

| | | | | |
|---|---|---|---|---|
| **O29** | O12 | 5th m on 5m | .25 | *3.00* |
| *a.* | | Inverted surcharge | 50.00 | |
| | | Never hinged | 110.00 | |
| **O30** | O5 | 20th m on 30pf | .25 | *3.00* |
| *a.* | | Inverted surcharge | 55.00 | |
| | | Never hinged | 125.00 | |
| *b.* | | Imperf. | 60.00 | |
| **O31** | O3 | 100th m on 15pf | .25 | *3.00* |
| *a.* | | Imperf. | 60.00 | |
| | | Never hinged | 150.00 | |
| *b.* | | Inverted surcharge | 50.00 | |
| | | Never hinged | 110.00 | |
| **O32** | O2 | 250th m on 10pf car rose | .25 | *3.00* |
| *a.* | | Double surcharge | 37.50 | |
| | | Never hinged | 90.00 | |
| **O33** | O5 | 800th m on 30pf | .60 | *300.00* |

**Official Stamps and Types of 1920-23 Surcharged with New Values**

**Wmk. 126**

| | | | | |
|---|---|---|---|---|
| **O34** | O15 | 75th m on 50m | .25 | *3.00* |
| *a.* | | Inverted surcharge | 50.00 | |
| | | Never hinged | 110.00 | |
| **O35** | O3 | 400th m on 15pf brn | .25 | *27.50* |
| **O36** | O5 | 800th m on 30pf org, *buff* | .25 | *4.50* |
| **O37** | O13 | 1 mil m on 75pf | .25 | *37.50* |
| **O38** | O2 | 2 mil m on 10pf car rose | .30 | *3.75* |
| *a.* | | Imperf. | 90.00 | |
| | | Never hinged | 210.00 | |
| **O39** | O15 | 5 mil m on 100m | .25 | *5.75* |
| | | *Nos. O29-O39 (11)* | 3.15 | *394.00* |
| | | Set, never hinged | 5.90 | |

The 10, 15 and 30 pfennig are not known with this watermark and without surcharge.

**#290-291, 295-299 Overprinted Type "a"**

**1923**

| | | | | |
|---|---|---|---|---|
| **O40** | A39 | 100 mil m | .25 | *150.00* |
| **O41** | A39 | 200 mil m | .25 | *150.00* |
| **O42** | A39a | 2 mlrd m | .25 | *110.00* |
| **O43** | A39a | 5 mlrd m | .25 | *82.50* |
| **O44** | A39a | 10 mlrd m | 3.00 | *140.00* |
| **O45** | A39a | 20 mlrd m | 3.75 | *150.00* |
| **O46** | A39a | 50 mlrd m | 1.90 | *200.00* |
| | | *Nos. O40-O46 (7)* | 9.65 | *982.50* |
| | | Set, never hinged | 32.50 | |

**Same Overprint on Nos, 323-328, Values in Rentenpfennig**

**1923**

| | | | | |
|---|---|---|---|---|
| **O47** | A40 | 3pf brown | .25 | *.75* |
| **O48** | A40 | 5pf dk green | .25 | *.75* |
| *a.* | | Inverted overprint | 92.50 | 175.00 |
| | | Never hinged | 175.00 | |
| **O49** | A40 | 10pf carmine | .25 | *.75* |
| *a.* | | Inverted overprint | 80.00 | 175.00 |
| | | Never hinged | 150.00 | |
| *b.* | | Imperf. | 60.00 | |
| | | Never hinged | 150.00 | |
| **O50** | A40 | 20pf dp ultra | .60 | *1.10* |
| **O51** | A40 | 50pf orange | .60 | *1.50* |
| **O52** | A40 | 100pf brown vio | 3.75 | *7.50* |
| | | *Nos. O47-O52 (6)* | 5.70 | *12.35* |
| | | Set, never hinged | 26.25 | |

**Same Overprint On Issues of 1924**

**1924**

| | | | | |
|---|---|---|---|---|
| **O53** | A41 | 3pf lt brown | .35 | *2.25* |
| *a.* | | Inverted overprint | 60.00 | 300.00 |
| | | Never hinged | 300.00 | |
| **O54** | A41 | 5pf lt green | .25 | *.75* |
| *a.* | | Imperf. | 75.00 | |
| | | Never hinged | 225.00 | |
| *b.* | | Inverted overprint | 110.00 | |
| | | Never hinged | 300.00 | |
| **O55** | A41 | 10pf vermilion | .25 | *.75* |
| **O56** | A41 | 20pf blue | .25 | *.75* |
| **O57** | A41 | 30pf rose lilac | .75 | *.75* |
| **O58** | A41 | 40pf olive green | .75 | *.75* |
| **O59** | A41 | 50pf orange | 6.75 | 3.75 |
| **O60** | A47 | 60pf red brown | 1.50 | *3.75* |
| **O61** | A47 | 80pf slate | 6.75 | *32.50* |
| | | *Nos. O53-O61 (9)* | 17.60 | *46.00* |
| | | Set, never hinged | 60.00 | |

O16

**1927-33** ***Perf. 14***

| | | | | |
|---|---|---|---|---|
| **O62** | O16 | 3pf bister | .30 | *.75* |
| **O63** | O16 | 4pf lt bl ('31) | .50 | *.90* |
| **O64** | O16 | 4pf blue ('33) | 6.75 | *13.50* |
| **O65** | O16 | 5pf green | .25 | *.75* |
| **O66** | O16 | 6pf pale ol grn ('32) | .75 | *.90* |
| **O67** | O16 | 8pf dk grn | .30 | *.75* |
| **O68** | O16 | 10pf carmine | 7.50 | 6.00 |
| **O69** | O16 | 10pf ver ('29), wmk. upright | 15.00 | *19.00* |
| **O70** | O16 | 10pf red vio ('30) | .45 | *.90* |
| *a.* | | Imperf. | 150.00 | |
| | | Never hinged | 375.00 | |
| **O71** | O16 | 10pf choc ('33) | 3.00 | *9.00* |
| **O72** | O16 | 12pf org ('32) | .50 | *.90* |
| **O73** | O16 | 15pf vermilion | 1.75 | .90 |
| **O74** | O16 | 15pf car ('29) | .45 | *.90* |
| **O75** | O16 | 20pf Prus grn, wmk. upright | 7.50 | 3.00 |
| **O76** | O16 | 20pf gray ('30), wmk. upright | 2.25 | 1.10 |
| **O77** | O16 | 30pf olive grn | .90 | .90 |
| **O78** | O16 | 40pf violet, wmk upright | .75 | *.90* |
| **O79** | O16 | 60pf red brn ('28) | 1.10 | *1.90* |
| | | *Nos. O62-O79 (18)* | 50.00 | 62.95 |
| | | Set, never hinged | 275.00 | |

Swastika — O17

**1934, Jan. 18** **Wmk. 237**

| | | | | |
|---|---|---|---|---|
| **O80** | O17 | 3pf bister | .75 | *1.10* |
| **O81** | O17 | 4pf dull blue | .30 | *.90* |
| **O82** | O17 | 5pf brt green | .25 | *1.10* |
| **O83** | O17 | 6pf dk green | .25 | *.90* |
| *a.* | | Imperf. | 150.00 | |
| | | Never hinged | 375.00 | |
| **O84** | O17 | 8pf vermilion | 2.25 | .90 |
| **O85** | O17 | 10pf chocolate | .30 | *7.50* |
| **O86** | O17 | 12pf brt carmine | 2.25 | 1.50 |
| *a.* | | Unwmkd. | 5.00 | *7.00* |
| **O87** | O17 | 15pf claret | .90 | *9.00* |
| **O88** | O17 | 20pf light blue | .45 | *1.50* |
| **O89** | O17 | 30pf olive grn | .90 | *1.50* |
| **O90** | O17 | 40pf red violet | .90 | *1.50* |
| **O91** | O17 | 50pf orange yel | 1.40 | *3.75* |
| | | *Nos. O80-O91 (12)* | 10.90 | *31.15* |
| | | Set, never hinged | 40.00 | |

**1942** **Unwmk.** ***Perf. 14***

| | | | | |
|---|---|---|---|---|
| **O92** | O17 | 3pf bister brn | .30 | *.65* |
| **O93** | O17 | 4pf dull blue | .30 | *.65* |
| **O94** | O17 | 5pf deep olive | .30 | *3.00* |
| **O95** | O17 | 6pf deep violet | .30 | *.65* |
| **O96** | O17 | 8pf vermilion | .30 | *.65* |
| **O97** | O17 | 10pf chocolate | .30 | *.60* |
| **O98** | O17 | 12pf rose car | .30 | *1.25* |
| *a.* | | Wmk. 237 | 1.50 | *13.50* |
| **O99** | O17 | 15pf brown car | 2.40 | *12.00* |
| **O100** | O17 | 20pf light blue | .30 | *1.30* |
| **O101** | O17 | 30pf olive grn | .30 | *1.30* |
| **O102** | O17 | 40pf red violet | .30 | *1.30* |
| **O103** | O17 | 50pf dk green | 2.25 | *7.25* |
| | | *Nos. O92-O103 (12)* | 7.65 | *30.60* |
| | | Set, never hinged | 35.00 | |

**LOCAL OFFICIAL STAMPS**

**For Use in Prussia**

("Nr. 21" refers to the district of Prussia) — LO1

**1903** **Unwmk.** **Typo.** ***Perf. 14, 14½***

| | | | | |
|---|---|---|---|---|
| **OL1** | LO1 | 2pf slate | .90 | *3.75* |
| **OL2** | LO1 | 3pf bister brn | .90 | *3.75* |
| **OL3** | LO1 | 5pf green | .30 | *.50* |
| **OL4** | LO1 | 10pf carmine | .30 | *.50* |
| **OL5** | LO1 | 20pf ultra | .30 | *.50* |
| **OL6** | LO1 | 25pf org & blk, *yel* | .30 | *1.60* |
| **OL7** | LO1 | 40pf lake & blk | .35 | *1.90* |
| **OL8** | LO1 | 50pf pur & blk, *sal* | .35 | *1.90* |
| | | *Nos. OL1-OL8 (8)* | 3.70 | *14.40* |
| | | Set, never hinged | 11.65 | |

LO2

LO3

LO4

LO5

LO6

LO7

LO8

**1920** **Typo.** **Wmk. 125** ***Perf. 14***

| | | | | |
|---|---|---|---|---|
| **OL9** | LO2 | 5pf green | .25 | *3.00* |
| **OL10** | LO3 | 10pf carmine | .70 | *1.50* |
| **OL11** | LO4 | 15pf vio brn | .25 | *1.50* |
| **OL12** | LO5 | 20pf dp ultra | .25 | *1.40* |
| **OL13** | LO6 | 30pf org, *buff* | .25 | *1.40* |
| **OL14** | LO7 | 50pf brn lil, *buff* | .30 | *1.50* |
| **OL15** | LO8 | 1m red, *buff* | 8.25 | *3.75* |
| | | *Nos. OL9-OL15 (7)* | 10.25 | *14.05* |
| | | Set, never hinged | 35.00 | |

**For Use in Baden**

LO9

**1905** **Unwmk.** **Typo.** ***Perf. 14, 14½***

| | | | | |
|---|---|---|---|---|
| **OL16** | LO9 | 2pf gray blue | 52.50 | *75.00* |
| **OL17** | LO9 | 3pf brown | 6.00 | *10.50* |
| **OL18** | LO9 | 5pf green | 4.25 | *7.50* |
| **OL19** | LO9 | 10pf rose | .75 | *2.10* |
| **OL20** | LO9 | 20pf blue | 1.50 | *3.00* |
| **OL21** | LO9 | 25pf org & blk, *yel* | 35.00 | *52.50* |
| | | *Nos. OL16-OL21 (6)* | 100.00 | *150.60* |
| | | Set, never hinged | 883.00 | |

**NEWSPAPER STAMPS**

Newsboy and Globe — N1

**Wmk. Swastikas (237)**

**1939, Nov. 1** **Photo.** ***Perf. 14***

| | | | | |
|---|---|---|---|---|
| **P1** | N1 | 5pf green | .60 | *5.25* |
| **P2** | N1 | 10pf red brown | .60 | *5.25* |
| | | Set, never hinged | 4.50 | |

**POSTAL TAX STAMPS**

On November 28, 1948, the "Notopfer Berlin" ("Berlin emergency levy") was enacted by the West German authorities to raise funds to subsidize civilian operations in West Berlin. Part of this levy was a 2pf surtax on virtually all types of internal mail in West Germany, except that of the military governments and foreign consulates and surface mail to Berlin. Initially applied to the Bizone (American and British administration), this levy was later extended to the French zone of occupation, and was continued by the Federal Republic of Germany after its formation in Sept. 1949.

From Dec. 1, 1948, until the expiration of the levy on March 31, 1956, most mail was required to carry one of the "Notopfer" tax stamps.

PT1

**1948** **Wmk. 286** **Typo.**

***Imperf***

| | | | | |
|---|---|---|---|---|
| **RA1** | PT1 | 2pf dk blue | .25 | .25 |
| | | Never hinged | .55 | |

***Compound Perf 12 and 14***

| | | | | |
|---|---|---|---|---|
| **RA2** | PT1 | 2pf dk blue | .30 | .30 |
| | | Never hinged | 1.25 | |

No. RA2 also exists perf 9-10, 11, 11¼x11, 11½, compund 11½ and 12, 12x11½, 13½x11½ and rouletted, some of which were produced by local post offices or by private parties.

Issued: RA1, 12/1; RA2, 12/15.

Illustration PT1 actual size.

**1948-50** **Wmk. 285** **Typo.**

***Imperf***

| | | | | |
|---|---|---|---|---|
| **RA3** | PT1 | 2pf dk blue | 15.00 | 1.50 |
| | | Never hinged | 50.00 | |

***Compound Perf 12 and 14***

| | | | | |
|---|---|---|---|---|
| **RA4** | PT1 | 2pf dk blue ('49) | .60 | .25 |
| | | Never hinged | 2.25 | |

No. RA4 also exists perf 9½, 11, 11¼x11, 11½, 12, 12x11, 12x13½, 12¼ and rouletted, some of which were produced by local post offices or by private parties.

**Wmk. 285**

**1950, June 10 Litho.** ***Perf. 14***

**RA5** PT1 2pf dk blue .25 .25
Never hinged .45

**1955, Aug. 8** **Wmk. 295**

**RA6** PT1 2pf dk blue .25 .25
Never hinged .45

## FRANCHISE STAMPS

**For use by the National Socialist German Workers' Party**

Party Emblem — F1

**1938 Typo. Wmk. 237** ***Perf. 14***

| | | | | |
|---|---|---|---|---|
| **S1** | F1 | 1pf black | .70 | *3.00* |
| **S2** | F1 | 3pf bister | .70 | *1.90* |
| **S3** | F1 | 4pf dull blue | .70 | *1.50* |
| **S4** | F1 | 5pf brt green | .40 | *1.50* |
| **S5** | F1 | 6pf dk green | .40 | *1.50* |
| **S6** | F1 | 8pf vermilion | 2.75 | 1.50 |
| **S7** | F1 | 12pf brt car | 4.50 | 1.50 |
| **S8** | F1 | 16pf gray | .65 | *9.00* |
| **S9** | F1 | 24pf citron | 1.00 | *4.75* |
| **S10** | F1 | 30pf olive | 1.00 | *7.50* |
| **S11** | F1 | 40pf red violet | 1.00 | *11.00* |
| | | *Nos. S1-S11 (11)* | 13.80 | *44.65* |
| | | Set, never hinged | 120.00 | |

**1942** **Unwmk.**

| | | | | |
|---|---|---|---|---|
| **S12** | F1 | 1pf gray blk | .70 | *3.50* |
| **S13** | F1 | 3pf bister brn | .30 | *.55* |
| **S14** | F1 | 4pf dk gray blue | .30 | *.55* |
| **S15** | F1 | 5pf gray green | .30 | *3.50* |
| **S16** | F1 | 6pf violet | .30 | *.55* |
| **S17** | F1 | 8pf deep orange | .30 | *.55* |
| *a.* | | Imperf. | 95.00 | |
| | | Never hinged | 190.00 | |
| **S18** | F1 | 12pf carmine | .30 | *.55* |
| **S19** | F1 | 16pf blue green | 3.25 | *16.00* |
| **S20** | F1 | 24pf yellow brn | .50 | *1.00* |
| **S21** | F1 | 30pf dp olive grn | .50 | *1.75* |
| **S22** | F1 | 40pf light rose vio | .55 | *2.25* |
| | | *Nos. S12-S22 (11)* | 7.30 | *30.75* |
| | | Set, never hinged | 25.00 | |

# GERMAN OCCUPATION STAMPS

100 Centimes = 1 Franc
100 Pfennig = 1 Mark

**Issued under Belgian Occupation**

Belgian Stamps of 1915-1920 Overprinted

***Perf. 11½, 14, 14½***

**1919-21** **Unwmk.**

| | | | | |
|---|---|---|---|---|
| **1N1** | A46 | 1c orange | .30 | *.60* |
| **1N2** | A46 | 2c chocolate | .30 | *.60* |
| **1N3** | A46 | 3c gray blk ('21) | .30 | *1.90* |
| **1N4** | A46 | 5c green | .60 | *1.10* |
| **1N5** | A46 | 10c carmine | 1.25 | *1.90* |
| **1N6** | A46 | 15c purple | .60 | *1.10* |
| **1N7** | A46 | 20c red violet | .90 | *1.25* |
| **1N8** | A46 | 25c blue | 1.10 | *1.50* |
| **1N9** | A54 | 25c dp blue ('21) | 3.75 | *11.00* |

Belgian Stamps of 1915-1920 Overprinted

| | | | | |
|---|---|---|---|---|
| **1N10** | A47 | 35c brn org & blk | 1.10 | *1.25* |
| **1N11** | A48 | 40c green & blk | 1.10 | *2.25* |
| **1N12** | A49 | 50c car rose & blk | 5.50 | *10.00* |
| **1N13** | A56 | 65c cl & blk ('21) | 3.00 | *11.00* |
| **1N14** | A50 | 1fr violet | 21.00 | 19.00 |
| **1N15** | A51 | 2fr slate | 35.00 | *45.00* |
| **1N16** | A52 | 5fr deep blue | 8.25 | *11.00* |
| **1N17** | A53 | 10fr brown | 55.00 | 60.00 |
| | | On cover | | — |
| | | *Nos. 1N1-1N17 (17)* | 139.05 | *180.45* |
| | | Set, never hinged | 450.00 | |

Nos. 1N1-1N17 were valid for postage until April 30, 1931, nearly one year after the Belgians and other occupation forces evacuated the Rhineland. Mixed frankings with Belgian stamps were permitted. The values for used stamps are for stamps with cancels from the Belgian military post offices in occupied Germany.

Nos. 1N14-1N17 exist with two overprint types: spacing between "Allemagne" and "Duitshland" 2mm (1919) and 1mm (1920).

**Belgian Stamps of 1915 Surcharged**

Nos. 1N18-1N22

Nos. 1N23-1N24

**Black Surcharge**

**1920**

| | | | | |
|---|---|---|---|---|
| **1N18** | A46 | 5pf on 5c green | .40 | .35 |
| **1N19** | A46 | 10pf on 10c car | .50 | .45 |
| **1N20** | A46 | 15pf on 15c pur | .70 | .70 |
| **1N21** | A46 | 20pf on 20c red vio | .70 | *1.00* |
| **1N22** | A46 | 30pf on 25c blue | 1.10 | *1.25* |

**Red Surcharge**

| | | | | |
|---|---|---|---|---|
| **1N23** | A49 | 75pf on 50c car rose & blk | 15.00 | 19.00 |
| **1N24** | A50 | 1m25pf on 1fr violet | 21.00 | 21.00 |
| | | *Nos. 1N18-1N24 (7)* | 39.40 | *43.75* |
| | | Set, never hinged | 135.00 | |

**EUPEN ISSUE**

**Belgian Stamps of 1915-20 Overprinted**

Nos. 1N25-1N36

Nos. 1N37-1N41

**1920-21** ***Perf. 11½, 14, 14½***

| | | | | |
|---|---|---|---|---|
| **1N25** | A46 | 1c orange | .30 | *.40* |
| | | Never hinged | .75 | |
| **1N26** | A46 | 2c chocolate | .30 | *.40* |
| **1N27** | A46 | 3c gray blk ('21) | .45 | *1.40* |
| **1N28** | A46 | 5c green | .45 | *.90* |
| **1N29** | A46 | 10c carmine | .75 | *1.25* |
| **1N30** | A46 | 15c purple | 1.10 | *1.25* |
| **1N31** | A46 | 20c red violet | 1.25 | *1.40* |
| **1N32** | A46 | 25c blue | 1.10 | *1.90* |
| **1N33** | A54 | 25c dp blue ('21) | 3.50 | *9.50* |
| **1N34** | A47 | 35c brn org & blk | 1.40 | *1.90* |
| **1N35** | A48 | 40c green & blk | 1.75 | *2.25* |
| **1N36** | 49 | 50c car rose & blk | 5.00 | *7.25* |
| **1N37** | A56 | 65c cl & blk ('21) | 2.75 | *11.00* |
| **1N38** | A50 | 1fr violet | 20.00 | 19.00 |
| **1N39** | A51 | 2fr slate | 32.50 | 30.00 |
| **1N40** | A52 | 5fr deep blue | 10.50 | *11.00* |
| **1N41** | A53 | 10fr brown | 45.00 | *50.00* |
| | | *Nos. 1N25-1N41 (17)* | 128.10 | *150.80* |
| | | Set, never hinged | 325.00 | |

**MALMEDY ISSUE**

**Belgian Stamps of 1915-20 Overprinted**

Nos. 1N42-1N50

Nos. 1N51-1N53

Nos. 1N54-1N58

**1920-21**

| | | | | |
|---|---|---|---|---|
| **1N42** | A46 | 1c orange | .25 | *.40* |
| **1N43** | A46 | 2c chocolate | .25 | *.40* |
| **1N44** | A46 | 3c gray blk ('21) | .35 | *1.60* |
| **1N45** | A46 | 5c green | .45 | *.90* |
| **1N46** | A46 | 10c carmine | .70 | *1.25* |
| **1N47** | A46 | 15c purple | 1.10 | *1.40* |
| **1N48** | A46 | 20c red violet | 1.50 | *1.90* |
| **1N49** | A46 | 25c blue | 1.25 | *1.90* |
| **1N50** | A54 | 25c dp blue ('21) | 3.50 | *8.75* |
| **1N51** | A47 | 35c brn org & blk | 1.25 | *2.25* |
| **1N52** | A48 | 40c green & blk | 1.50 | 2.25 |
| **1N53** | A49 | 50c car rose & blk | 6.00 | *7.25* |
| **1N54** | A56 | 65c cl & blk ('21) | 2.75 | *11.00* |
| **1N55** | A50 | 1fr violet | 20.00 | 17.00 |
| **1N56** | A51 | 2fr slate | 32.50 | 30.00 |
| **1N57** | A52 | 5fr deep blue | 10.50 | *17.00* |
| **1N58** | A53 | 10fr brown | 45.00 | *55.00* |
| | | *Nos. 1N42-1N58 (17)* | 128.85 | *160.25* |
| | | Set, never hinged | 325.00 | |

**OCCUPATION POSTAGE DUE STAMPS**

Belgian Postage Due Stamps of 1919-20, Overprinted

**1920 Unwmk.** ***Perf. 14½***

| | | | | |
|---|---|---|---|---|
| **1NJ1** | D3 | 5c green | .75 | *1.10* |
| **1NJ2** | D3 | 10c carmine | 1.50 | *1.90* |
| **1NJ3** | D3 | 20c gray green | 3.00 | *4.50* |
| **1NJ4** | D3 | 30c bright blue | 3.00 | *4.50* |
| **1NJ5** | D3 | 50c gray | 15.00 | *15.00* |
| | | *Nos. 1NJ1-1NJ5 (5)* | 23.25 | *27.00* |
| | | Set, never hinged | 57.50 | |

Belgian Postage Due Stamps of 1919-20, Overprinted

**Unwmk.**

| | | | | |
|---|---|---|---|---|
| **1NJ6** | D3 | 5c green | 1.50 | 1.10 |
| **1NJ7** | D3 | 10c carmine | 3.00 | 1.90 |
| *a.* | | Inverted overprint | 100.00 | 90.00 |
| **1NJ8** | D3 | 20c gray green | 10.50 | *11.50* |
| **1NJ9** | D3 | 30c bright blue | 6.00 | *8.50* |
| **1NJ10** | D3 | 50c gray | 12.00 | 11.00 |
| | | *Nos. 1NJ6-1NJ10 (5)* | 33.00 | *34.00* |
| | | Set, never hinged | 82.50 | |

Nos. 1NJ1-1NJ10 were valid for postage until April 30, 1931, nearly one year after the Belgians and other occupation forces evacuated the Rhineland. Mixed frankings with Belgian stamps were permitted. The values for used stamps are for stamps with cancels from the Belgian military post offices in occupied Germany.

**A. M. G. ISSUE**

**Issued jointly by the Allied Military Government of the US and Great Britain, for civilian use in areas under Allied occupation.**

OS1

Type I. Thick paper, white gum.
Type II. Medium paper, yellow gum.
Type III. Medium paper, white gum.

***Perf. 11, 11½ and Compound***

**1945-46 Litho. Unwmk.**

**Type III, Brunswick Printing**

**Size: 19-19½x22-22½mm**

| | | | | |
|---|---|---|---|---|
| **3N1** | OS1 | 1pf slate gray | .25 | *5.00* |
| **3N2** | OS1 | 3pf dull lilac | .25 | *1.10* |
| **3N3** | OS1 | 4pf lt gray | .25 | *1.50* |
| **3N4** | OS1 | 5pf emerald | .25 | *4.00* |
| **3N5** | OS1 | 6pf yellow | .25 | *1.10* |
| **3N6** | OS1 | 8pf orange | 2.00 | *37.50* |
| **3N7** | OS1 | 10pf yel brn | .25 | *1.50* |
| **3N8** | OS1 | 12pf rose vio | .25 | *.90* |
| **3N9** | OS1 | 15pf rose car | .25 | *3.00* |
| **3N10** | OS1 | 16pf dp Prus grn | .25 | *13.50* |
| **3N11** | OS1 | 20pf blue | .25 | *3.00* |
| **3N12** | OS1 | 24pf chocolate | .25 | *13.50* |
| **3N13** | OS1 | 25pf brt ultra | .25 | *13.50* |

**Size: 21½x25mm**

| | | | | |
|---|---|---|---|---|
| **3N14** | OS1 | 30pf olive | .25 | *1.90* |
| **3N15** | OS1 | 40pf dp mag | .25 | *2.50* |
| **3N16** | OS1 | 42pf green | .25 | *2.25* |
| **3N17** | OS1 | 50pf slate grn | .25 | *15.00* |
| **3N18** | OS1 | 60pf vio brn | .50 | *19.00* |
| **3N19** | OS1 | 80pf bl blk | 17.50 | *300.00* |

**Size: 25x29½mm**

| | | | | |
|---|---|---|---|---|
| **3N20** | OS1 | 1m dk ol grn ('46) | 2.50 | *500.00* |
| | | *Nos. 3N1-3N20 (20)* | 26.50 | *939.75* |
| | | Set, never hinged | 65.00 | |

Most of Nos. 3N1-3N20 exist imperforate and part-perforate.

**Type I, Washington Printing**

**Size: 19-19½x22-22½mm**

***Perf. 11***

| | | | | |
|---|---|---|---|---|
| *3N2a* | OS1 | 3pf lilac | .25 | *1.90* |
| *3N3a* | OS1 | 4pf light gray | .25 | *1.50* |
| *3N4a* | OS1 | 5pf emerald | .25 | *.35* |
| *3N5a* | OS1 | 6pf yellow | .25 | *.35* |
| *3N6a* | OS1 | 8pf deep orange | .25 | *.35* |
| *3N7a* | OS1 | 10pf brown | .25 | *.35* |
| *3N8a* | OS1 | 12pf rose violet | .25 | *.35* |
| *3N9a* | OS1 | 15pf cerise | .25 | *1.50* |
| *3N13a* | OS1 | 25pf bright ultra | .25 | *1.50* |
| | | *Nos. 3N2a-3N13a (9)* | 2.25 | *8.15* |
| | | Set, never hinged | 2.50 | |

**Type II, London Printing**

**Size: 19-19½x22-22½mm**

***Perf. 14, 14½ and Compound***

**Photo.**

| | | | | |
|---|---|---|---|---|
| *3N2b* | OS1 | 3pf lilac | .25 | *.60* |
| *3N3b* | OS1 | 4pf light gray | .25 | *.60* |
| *3N4b* | OS1 | 5pf deep emerald | .25 | *15.00* |
| *3N5b* | OS1 | 6pf orange yellow | .25 | *.60* |
| *3N6b* | OS1 | 8pf dark orange | .25 | *3.75* |
| *3N8b* | OS1 | 12pf rose violet | .25 | *.60* |
| | | *Nos. 3N2b-3N8b (6)* | 1.50 | *21.15* |
| | | Set, never hinged | 2.00 | |

**ISSUED UNDER FRENCH OCCUPATION**

**Coats of Arms**

Rhine Province OS3

Palatinate District OS4

Saarland OS5

Württemberg OS6

Baden
OS7

Johann Wolfgang von Goethe
OS8

Friedrich von Schiller — OS9

Heinrich Heine — OS10

*Perf. 14x13½*

| 1945-46 | | Unwmk. | Typo. | |
|---|---|---|---|---|
| **4N1** | OS3 | 1pf blk, grn & lem | .25 | .25 |
| **4N2** | OS4 | 3pf dk red, blk & dl yel | .25 | .25 |
| **4N3** | OS6 | 5pf brn, blk & org yel | .25 | .25 |
| **4N4** | OS7 | 8pf brn, yel & red | .25 | .25 |
| **4N5** | OS3 | 10pf brn, grn & lem | 6.50 | *57.50* |
| **4N6** | OS4 | 12pf red, blk & org yel | .25 | .25 |
| **4N7** | OS5 | 15pf blk, ultra & red ('46) | .25 | .25 |
| **4N8** | OS6 | 20pf red, org yel & blk | .25 | .25 |
| **4N9** | OS5 | 24pf blk, dp ultra & red ('46) | .25 | .25 |
| **4N10** | OS7 | 30pf blk, org yel & red | .25 | .25 |

*Perf. 13*

**Engr.**

| | | | | |
|---|---|---|---|---|
| **4N11** | OS8 | 1m lilac brn | .70 | *18.00* |
| **4N12** | OS9 | 2m dp bl ('46) | .45 | *52.50* |
| **4N13** | OS10 | 5m dl red brn ('46) | .55 | *67.50* |
| | | *Nos. 4N1-4N13 (13)* | 10.45 | *197.75* |
| | | Set, never hinged | 20.00 | |

Exist imperf. Value for set of 13, $475 mint never hinged.

## BADEN

Johann Peter Hebel
OS1

Girl of Constance
OS2

Hans Baldung Grien — OS3

Rastatt Castle — OS4

Black Forest Scene
OS5

Cathedral of Freiburg — OS6

| 1947 | | Unwmk. Photo. | *Perf. 14* | |
|---|---|---|---|---|
| **5N1** | OS1 | 2pf gray | .25 | .30 |
| **5N2** | OS2 | 3pf brown | .25 | .30 |
| **5N3** | OS3 | 10pf slate blue | .25 | .30 |
| **5N4** | OS1 | 12pf dk green | .25 | .30 |
| **5N5** | OS2 | 15pf purple | .25 | .35 |
| **5N6** | OS4 | 16pf olive green | .25 | *1.50* |
| **5N7** | OS3 | 20pf blue | .25 | .35 |
| **5N8** | OS4 | 24pf crimson | .25 | .30 |
| **5N9** | OS2 | 45pf cerise | .25 | *.90* |
| **5N10** | OS1 | 60pf deep orange | .25 | .30 |
| **5N11** | OS3 | 75pf brt blue | .25 | *1.90* |
| **5N12** | OS5 | 84pf blue green | .25 | *1.90* |
| **5N13** | OS6 | 1m dark brown | .25 | *.75* |
| | | *Nos. 5N1-5N13 (13)* | | *9.45* |
| | | Set, never hinged | 2.25 | |

Festival Headdress
OS7

Grand Duchess Stephanie
OS8

| 1948 | | | | |
|---|---|---|---|---|
| **5N14** | OS1 | 2pf dp orange | .25 | .30 |
| **5N15** | OS2 | 6pf violet brn | .25 | .30 |
| **5N16** | OS7 | 8pf blue green | .25 | *1.10* |
| **5N17** | OS3 | 10pf dark brown | .25 | .30 |
| **5N18** | OS1 | 12pf crimson | .25 | .30 |
| **5N19** | OS2 | 15pf blue | .25 | *.60* |
| **5N20** | OS4 | 16dpf violet | .35 | *1.90* |
| **5N21** | OS3 | 20dpf brown | 1.50 | .95 |
| **5N22** | OS4 | 24pf dark green | .25 | .30 |
| **5N23** | OS7 | 30pf cerise | .55 | 1.10 |
| **5N24** | OS8 | 50pf brt blue | .55 | .30 |
| **5N25** | OS1 | 60dpf gray | 1.90 | .60 |
| **5N26** | OS5 | 84dpf rose brn | 2.75 | *4.50* |
| **5N27** | OS6 | 1dm brt blue | 2.75 | *4.50* |
| | | *Nos. 5N14-5N27 (14)* | 12.10 | *17.05* |
| | | Set, never hinged | 26.50 | |

**Without "PF"**

| 1948-49 | | | | |
|---|---|---|---|---|
| **5N28** | OS1 | 2(pf) dp orange | .35 | *.55* |
| **5N29** | OS4 | 4(pf) violet | .25 | *.45* |
| **5N30** | OS2 | 5(pf) blue | .35 | *.60* |
| **5N31** | OS2 | 6(pf) violet brn | 11.50 | *13.50* |
| **5N32** | OS7 | 8(pf) rose brn | .35 | *1.00* |
| **5N33** | OS3 | 10(pf) dark green | 1.60 | .55 |
| **5N37** | OS3 | 20(pf) cerise | .65 | .35 |
| **5N38** | OS4 | 40(pf) brown | 30.00 | *75.00* |
| **5N39** | OS1 | 80(pf) red | 3.75 | *6.00* |
| **5N40** | OS5 | 90(pf) rose brn | 29.00 | *75.00* |
| | | *Nos. 5N28-5N40 (10)* | 77.80 | *173.00* |
| | | Set, never hinged | 150.00 | |

Constance Cathedral and Insel Hotel — OS9

Type I. Frameline thick and straight. Inscriptions thick. Shading dark. Upper part of "B" narrow.

Type II. Frameline thin and zigzag. Inscriptions fine. Shading light. Upper part of "B" wide.

**1949, June 22**

| | | | | |
|---|---|---|---|---|
| **5N41** | OS9 | 30pf dark blue (I) | 9.00 | *65.00* |
| | | Never hinged | 20.00 | |
| | *a.* | Type II | *250.00* | *1,450.* |
| | | Never hinged | 475.00 | |

Issued to publicize the International Engineering Congress, Constance, 1949.

Conradin Kreutzer — OS10

**1949, Aug. 27**

| | | | | |
|---|---|---|---|---|
| **5N42** | OS10 | 10pf dark green | 1.50 | *11.00* |
| | | Never hinged | 3.00 | |

Conradin Kreutzer (1780-1849), composer.

Stagecoach — OS11

Design: 20pf, Post bus, trailer and plane.

**1949, Sept. 17**

| | | | | |
|---|---|---|---|---|
| **5N43** | OS11 | 10pf green | 2.25 | *10.50* |
| **5N44** | OS11 | 20pf red brown | 2.25 | *10.50* |
| | | Set, never hinged | 10.00 | |

Centenary of German postage stamps.

Globe, Olive Branch and Post Horn — OS12

**1949, Oct. 4**

| | | | | |
|---|---|---|---|---|
| **5N45** | OS12 | 20pf dark red | 2.75 | *10.50* |
| **5N46** | OS12 | 30pf deep blue | 2.75 | *9.00* |
| | | Set, never hinged | 10.00 | |

75th anniv. of the UPU.

## OCCUPATION SEMI-POSTAL STAMPS

Arms of Baden
OSP1

Cornhouse, Freiburg
OSP2

*Perf. 13½x14*

**1949, Feb. 25 Photo. Unwmk.**

**Cross in Red**

| | | | | |
|---|---|---|---|---|
| **5NB1** | OSP1 | 10 + 20pf green | 8.50 | *75.00* |
| **5NB2** | OSP1 | 20 + 40pf lilac | 8.50 | *75.00* |
| **5NB3** | OSP1 | 30 + 60pf blue | 8.50 | *75.00* |
| **5NB4** | OSP1 | 40 + 80pf gray | 8.50 | *75.00* |
| | *a.* | Sheet of 4, #5NB1-5NB4, imperf. | 110.00 | *1,350.* |
| | | *Nos. 5NB1-5NB4 (4)* | 34.00 | *300.00* |
| | | Set, never hinged | 75.00 | |

The surtax was for the Red Cross.

No. 5NB4a measures 90x101mm. and has no gum.

**1949, Feb. 24** *Perf. 14*

10pf+20pf, Cathedral tower. 20pf+30pf, Trumpeting angel. 30pf+50pf, Fish pool.

| | | | | |
|---|---|---|---|---|
| **5NB5** | OSP2 | 4 + 16pf dk vio | 5.25 | *35.00* |
| **5NB6** | OSP2 | 10 + 20pf dk grn | 5.25 | *35.00* |
| **5NB7** | OSP2 | 20 + 30pf car | 5.25 | *35.00* |
| **5NB8** | OSP2 | 30 + 50pf blue | 6.75 | *45.00* |
| | *a.* | Sheet of 4, #5NB5-5NB8 | 26.00 | *210.00* |
| | | Never hinged | 52.50 | |
| | *b.* | As "a," imperf. | 26.00 | *210.00* |
| | | Never hinged | 52.50 | |
| | | *Nos. 5NB5-5NB8 (4)* | 22.50 | *150.00* |
| | | Set, never hinged | 55.00 | |

The surtax was for the reconstruction of historical monuments in Freiburg.

Carl Schurz at Rastatt
OSP3

Goethe
OSP4

**1949, Aug. 23**

| | | | | |
|---|---|---|---|---|
| **5NB9** | OSP3 | 10 + 5pf green | 4.75 | *29.00* |
| **5NB10** | OSP3 | 20 + 10pf cer | 4.75 | *29.00* |
| **5NB11** | OSP3 | 30 + 15pf blue | 5.50 | *29.00* |
| | | *Nos. 5NB9-5NB11 (3)* | 15.00 | *87.00* |
| | | Set, never hinged | 29.00 | |

Centenary of the surrender of Rastatt.

**1949, Aug. 12**

Various Portraits.

| | | | | |
|---|---|---|---|---|
| **5NB12** | OSP4 | 10 + 5pf green | 3.50 | *19.00* |
| **5NB13** | OSP4 | 20 + 10pf cer | 3.50 | *19.00* |
| **5NB14** | OSP4 | 30 + 15pf blue | 5.25 | *45.00* |
| | | *Nos. 5NB12-5NB14 (3)* | 12.25 | *83.00* |
| | | Set, never hinged | 26.00 | |

Johann Wolfgang von Goethe (1749-1832).

## RHINE PALATINATE

Beethoven
OS1

Wilhelm E. F. von Ketteler
OS2

Girl Carrying Grapes
OS3

Porta Nigra, Trier
OS4

Karl Marx
OS5

"Devil's Table", Near Pirmasens
OS6

Street Corner, St. Martin
OS7

Cathedral of Worms
OS8

Cathedral of Mainz
OS9

Statue of Johann Gutenberg
OS10

Gutenfels and Pfalzgrafenstein Castles on Rhine — OS11

Statue of Charlemagne OS12

**1947-48 Unwmk. Photo. *Perf. 14***

| | | | | |
|---|---|---|---|---|
| **6N1** | OS1 | 2pf gray | .25 | .30 |
| **6N2** | OS2 | 3pf dk brown | .25 | .30 |
| **6N3** | OS3 | 10pf slate blue | .25 | .30 |
| **6N4** | OS4 | 12pf green | .25 | .30 |
| **6N5** | OS5 | 15pf purple | .25 | .30 |
| **6N6** | OS6 | 16pf lt ol grn | .25 | *1.10* |
| **6N7** | OS7 | 20pf brt blue | .25 | .30 |
| **6N8** | OS8 | 24pf crimson | .25 | .30 |
| **6N9** | OS10 | 30pf cerise ('48) | .25 | *2.25* |
| **6N10** | OS9 | 45pf cerise | .25 | *.60* |
| **6N11** | OS9 | 50pf blue ('48) | .25 | *2.25* |
| **6N12** | OS1 | 60pf dp orange | .25 | .30 |
| **6N13** | OS10 | 75pf blue | .25 | *.60* |
| **6N14** | OS11 | 84pf green | .25 | *1.40* |
| **6N15** | OS12 | 1m brown | .25 | *.75* |
| | | *Nos. 6N1-6N15 (15)* | | *11.35* |
| | | Set, never hinged | 3.50 | |

Exist imperf. Value for set, $525 mint never hinged.

**1948**

| | | | | |
|---|---|---|---|---|
| **6N16** | OS1 | 2pf dp orange | .25 | .30 |
| **6N17** | OS2 | 6pf violet brn | .25 | .30 |
| **6N18** | OS4 | 8dpf blue green | .25 | *1.10* |
| **6N19** | OS3 | 10pf dk brown | .25 | .30 |
| **6N20** | OS4 | 12pf crim rose | .25 | .30 |
| **6N21** | OS5 | 15pf blue | .60 | *.60* |
| **6N22** | OS6 | 16dpf dk violet | .30 | *1.40* |
| **6N23** | OS7 | 20dpf brown | 1.40 | .60 |
| **6N24** | OS8 | 24pf green | .25 | .30 |
| **6N25** | OS9 | 30pf cerise | .45 | .35 |
| **6N26** | OS10 | 50pf brt blue | .75 | .35 |
| **6N27** | OS1 | 60dpf gray | 3.75 | .35 |
| **6N28** | OS11 | 84dpf rose brown | 1.90 | *5.50* |
| **6N29** | OS12 | 1dm brt blue | 3.00 | *5.75* |
| | | *Nos. 6N16-6N29 (14)* | 13.65 | *17.50* |
| | | Set, never hinged | 26.00 | |

Exist imperf. Value for set, $500 mint never hinged.

**Types of 1947 Without "PF"**

**1948-49**

| | | | | |
|---|---|---|---|---|
| **6N30** | OS1 | 2(pf) dp org | .30 | .35 |
| **6N31** | OS6 | 4(pf) vio ('49) | .30 | .35 |
| **6N32** | OS5 | 5(pf) blue ('49) | .35 | *.60* |
| **6N33** | OS2 | 6(pf) vio brn | 13.50 | 15.00 |
| **6N33A** | OS4 | 8(pf) rose brn ('49) | 30.00 | *375.00* |
| **6N34** | OS3 | 10(pf) dk grn | .35 | .35 |
| *a.* | | Imperf. | 55.00 | 190.00 |
| | | Never hinged | 110.00 | |
| **6N35** | OS7 | 20(pf) cerise | .35 | .35 |
| **6N36** | OS8 | 40(pf) brn ('49) | 1.40 | *3.75* |
| **6N37** | OS4 | 80(pf) red ('49) | 1.50 | *5.00* |
| **6N38** | OS11 | 90(pf) rose brn ('49) | 2.25 | *15.00* |
| | | *Nos. 6N30-6N38 (10)* | 50.30 | *415.75* |
| | | Set, never hinged | 110.00 | |

**Type of Baden, 1949**

Designs as in Baden.

**1949, Sept. 17**

| | | | | |
|---|---|---|---|---|
| **6N39** | OS11 | 10pf green | 4.25 | *19.00* |
| **6N40** | OS11 | 20pf red brown | 4.25 | *19.00* |
| | | Set, never hinged | 16.50 | |

**UPU Type of Baden, 1949**

**1949, Oct. 4**

| | | | | |
|---|---|---|---|---|
| **6N41** | OS12 | 20pf dark red | 3.00 | *11.50* |
| **6N42** | OS12 | 30pf deep blue | 3.00 | *9.75* |
| | | Set, never hinged | 10.50 | |

---

**OCCUPATION SEMI-POSTAL STAMPS**

St. Martin — OSP1

Design: 30pf+50pf, St. Christopher.

**1948 Unwmk. Photo. *Perf. 14***

| | | | | |
|---|---|---|---|---|
| **6NB1** | OSP1 | 20pf + 30pf dp cl | .60 | *57.50* |
| **6NB2** | OSP1 | 30pf + 50pf dp bl | .60 | *57.50* |
| | | Set, never hinged | 3.00 | |

The surtax was to aid victims of an explosion at Ludwigshafen.

**Type of Baden, 1949, Showing Arms of Rhine Palatinate**

**1949, Feb. 25 *Perf. 13½x14***

**Cross in Red**

| | | | | |
|---|---|---|---|---|
| **6NB3** | OSP1 | 10pf + 20pf grn | 7.75 | *82.50* |
| **6NB4** | OSP1 | 20pf + 40pf lil | 7.75 | *82.50* |
| **6NB5** | OSP1 | 30pf + 60pf bl | 7.75 | *82.50* |
| **6NB6** | OSP1 | 40pf + 80pf gray | 7.75 | *82.50* |
| *a.* | | Sheet of 4, #6NB3-6NB6, imperf. | 82.50 | *1,050.* |
| | | *Nos. 6NB3-6NB6 (4)* | 31.00 | *330.00* |
| | | Set, never hinged | 65.00 | |

The surtax was for the Red Cross.
#6NB6a measures 90x100mm and has no gum.

**Goethe Type of Baden, 1949**

Various Portraits.

**1949, Aug. 12**

| | | | | |
|---|---|---|---|---|
| **6NB7** | OSP4 | 10pf + 5pf green | 2.25 | *18.00* |
| **6NB8** | OSP4 | 20pf + 10pf cerise | 2.25 | *18.00* |
| **6NB9** | OSP4 | 30pf + 15pf blue | 4.50 | *42.50* |
| | | *Nos. 6NB7-6NB9 (3)* | 9.00 | *78.50* |
| | | Set, never hinged | 22.50 | |

---

**WURTTEMBERG**

Friedrich von Schiller OS1

Castle of Bebenhausen OS2

Friedrich Hölderlin OS3

Town Gate of Wangen (Allgäu) OS4

Lichtenstein Castle — OS5

Zwiefalten Church — OS6

**1947-48 Unwmk. Photo. *Perf. 14***

| | | | | |
|---|---|---|---|---|
| **8N1** | OS1 | 2pf gray ('48) | .25 | *.60* |
| **8N2** | OS3 | 3pf brown ('48) | .25 | .30 |
| **8N3** | OS4 | 10pf slate bl ('48) | .25 | *.35* |
| **8N4** | OS1 | 12pf dk green | .25 | .25 |
| **8N5** | OS3 | 15pf purple ('48) | .25 | *.45* |
| **8N6** | OS2 | 16pf ol grn ('48) | .25 | *1.00* |
| **8N7** | OS4 | 20pf blue ('48) | .25 | *1.00* |
| **8N8** | OS2 | 24pf crimson | .25 | .30 |
| **8N9** | OS3 | 45pf cerise | .25 | *1.00* |
| **8N10** | OS1 | 60pf dp org ('48) | .25 | .75 |
| **8N11** | OS4 | 75pf brt blue | .25 | *1.10* |
| **8N12** | OS5 | 84pf blue grn | .25 | *1.40* |
| **8N13** | OS6 | 1m dk brown | .25 | *1.10* |
| | | *Nos. 8N1-8N13 (13)* | | *9.60* |
| | | Set, never hinged | 2.25 | |

Nos. 8N4 and 8N10 exist imperf. Value, each $37.50, mint never hinged.

Waldsee OS7

Ludwig Uhland OS8

**1948**

| | | | | |
|---|---|---|---|---|
| **8N14** | OS1 | 2pf dp orange | .25 | *.35* |
| **8N15** | OS3 | 6pf violet brn | .25 | .30 |
| **8N16** | OS7 | 8dpf blue grn | .35 | *1.75* |
| **8N17** | OS4 | 10pf dk brown | .25 | *.35* |
| **8N18** | OS1 | 12pf crimson | .25 | .30 |
| **8N19** | OS3 | 15pf blue | .30 | *.35* |
| **8N20** | OS2 | 16dpf dk violet | .35 | *1.60* |
| **8N21** | OS4 | 20dpf brown | .75 | .75 |
| **8N22** | OS2 | 24pf dk green | .45 | *.60* |
| **8N23** | OS7 | 30pf cerise | .60 | .60 |
| **8N24** | OS8 | 50pf dull blue | .95 | *.60* |
| **8N25** | OS1 | 60dpf gray | 5.75 | .60 |
| **8N26** | OS5 | 84dpf rose brn | 1.50 | 3.75 |
| **8N27** | OS6 | 1dm brt blue | 1.50 | 3.75 |
| | | *Nos. 8N14-8N27 (14)* | 13.50 | 15.65 |
| | | Set, never hinged | 26.00 | |

Nos. 8N14, 8N17, 8N22-8N23 exist imperf. Value, each $35, mint never hinged.

**Without "PF"**

**1948-49**

| | | | | |
|---|---|---|---|---|
| **8N28** | OS1 | 2(pf) dp orange | .35 | *.60* |
| **8N29** | OS2 | 4(pf) violet | 1.10 | .35 |
| **8N30** | OS3 | 5(pf) blue | 3.00 | 2.25 |
| **8N31** | OS3 | 6(pf) vio brown | 3.00 | *5.75* |
| **8N32** | OS7 | 8(pf) rose brn | 3.00 | 2.25 |
| **8N33** | OS4 | 10(pf) dk green | 3.00 | .35 |
| **8N34** | OS4 | 20(pf) cerise | 3.00 | .35 |
| **8N35** | OS2 | 40(pf) brown | 9.75 | *37.50* |
| **8N36** | OS1 | 80(pf) red | 19.00 | *37.50* |
| **8N37** | OS5 | 90(pf) rose brn | 30.00 | *97.50* |
| | | *Nos. 8N28-8N37 (10)* | 75.20 | *184.40* |
| | | Set, never hinged | 150.00 | |

Nos. 8N29 and 8N31 exist imperf. Value, respectively $75 and $57.50, mint never hinged.

**Type of Baden, 1949**

Designs as in Baden.

**1949, Sept. 17**

| | | | | |
|---|---|---|---|---|
| **8N38** | OS11 | 10pf green | 3.50 | *12.00* |
| **8N39** | OS11 | 20pf red brown | 3.50 | *12.00* |
| | | Set, never hinged | 11.50 | |

**UPU Type of Baden, 1949**

**1949, Oct. 4**

| | | | | |
|---|---|---|---|---|
| **8N40** | OS12 | 20pf dark red | 2.25 | *9.75* |
| **8N41** | OS12 | 30pf deep blue | 2.25 | *9.00* |
| | | Set, never hinged | 9.75 | |

---

**OCCUPATION SEMI-POSTAL STAMPS**

**Type of Baden, 1949**

Design: Arms of Württemberg.

***Perf. 13½x14***

**1949, Feb. 25 Photo. Unwmk.**

**Cross in Red**

| | | | | |
|---|---|---|---|---|
| **8NB1** | OSP1 | 10 + 20pf grn | 16.00 | *90.00* |
| **8NB2** | OSP1 | 20 + 40pf lilac | 16.00 | *90.00* |
| **8NB3** | OSP1 | 30 + 60pf blue | 16.00 | *90.00* |
| **8NB4** | OSP1 | 40 + 80pf gray | 16.00 | *90.00* |
| *a.* | | Sheet of 4, imperf. | 110.00 | *1,350.* |
| | | *Nos. 8NB1-8NB4 (4)* | 64.00 | *360.00* |
| | | Set, never hinged | 120.00 | |

The surtax was for the Red Cross.
No. 8NB4a measures 90x100mm and contains one each of Nos. 8NB1 to 8NB4, with red inscription in upper margin and no gum.

View of Isny OSP1

Design: 20pf+6pf, Skier and village.

**Wmk. 116**

**1949, Feb. 11 Typo. *Perf. 14***

| | | | | |
|---|---|---|---|---|
| **8NB5** | OSP1 | 10 + 4pf dull green | 2.75 | *22.50* |
| **8NB6** | OSP1 | 20 + 6pf red brown | 2.75 | *22.50* |
| | | Set, never hinged | 15.00 | |

Issued to commemorate the 1948-49 German Ski Championship at Isny im Allgau.

Gustav Werner — OSP2

**1949, Sept. 4**

| | | | | |
|---|---|---|---|---|
| **8NB7** | OSP2 | 10 + 5pf bl grn | 2.25 | *12.00* |
| **8NB8** | OSP2 | 20 + 10pf claret | 2.25 | *12.00* |
| | | Set, never hinged | 9.75 | |

Cent. of the founding of Gustav Werner's "Christianity in Action" and "House of Brotherhood."

**Goethe Type of Baden, 1949**

Various Portraits.

**1949, Aug. 12**

| | | | | |
|---|---|---|---|---|
| **8NB9** | OSP4 | 10 + 5pf green | 3.75 | *19.00* |
| **8NB10** | OSP4 | 20 + 10pf cerise | 5.50 | *26.00* |
| **8NB11** | OSP4 | 30 + 15pf blue | 5.50 | *37.50* |
| | | *Nos. 8NB9-8NB11 (3)* | 14.75 | *82.50* |
| | | Set, never hinged | 26.00 | |

---

**OCCUPATION POSTAL TAX STAMPS**

**Wohnungsbau Issues**

During July 1-December 31, 1949, a postal tax was levied on most categories of mail, with proceeds going to the 'Social Housing' (*Socialen Wohnungsbau*) program, which provided interest-free loans for housing construction and renovation intended to provide housing for economically-disadvantaged families.

**Germany Nos. RA1, RA2, RA4 Overprinted in Red**

Illustration actual size.

**Overprint 18.7mm wide**

**Wmk. 286**

**1949, July 1 Typo. *Imperf.***

| | | | | |
|---|---|---|---|---|
| **8NRA1** | PT1 | 2pf dk blue | 225.00 | *425.00* |
| | | Never hinged | 550.00 | |

***Compound Perf 12, 14***

| | | | | |
|---|---|---|---|---|
| **8NRA2** | PT1 | 2pf dk blue | 15.00 | 2.75 |
| | | Never hinged | 37.50 | |

**Overprint 16.5 mm wide**

**1949, July 22 Wmk. 285 *Perf. 12¼***

| | | | | |
|---|---|---|---|---|
| **8NRA3** | PT1 | 2pf dk blue | 3.75 | 1.75 |
| | | Never hinged | 9.00 | |

OSPT1

**1949 *Perf. 12¼***

| | | | | |
|---|---|---|---|---|
| **8NRA4** | OSPT1 | 2pf yellow | .25 | *1.00* |
| | | Never hinged | .50 | |
| *a.* | | 2pf yellow orange | 13.50 | *15.00* |

Never hinged 30.00
*b.* 2pf orange .25 1.00
Never hinged .50

Issued: No. 4a, 8/19; No. 4, 8/22. No. 4b, 8/25. No. 4c, 10/4.
Illustration OSPT1 actual size.

## BERLIN

### Issued for Use in the American, British and French Occupation Sectors of Berlin

Germany Nos. 557-569, 571-573 Overprinted Diagonally in Black — a

**Wmk. 284**

**1948, Sept. 1 Typo. *Perf. 14***

| | | | | |
|---|---|---|---|---|
| **9N1** | A120 | 2pf brown blk | .45 | *4.50* |
| **9N2** | A120 | 6pf purple | .30 | *4.50* |
| **9N3** | A121 | 8pf red | .30 | *4.50* |
| **9N4** | A121 | 10pf yellow grn | .25 | 1.10 |
| **9N5** | A122 | 12pf gray | .25 | 1.10 |
| **9N6** | A120 | 15pf chocolate | 4.75 | *67.50* |
| **9N7** | A123 | 16pf dk blue grn | .35 | *1.60* |
| **9N8** | A121 | 20pf blue | 2.25 | *6.75* |
| **9N9** | A123 | 24pf brown org | .25 | *.45* |
| **9N10** | A120 | 25pf orange yel | 6.75 | *52.50* |
| **9N11** | A122 | 30pf red | 1.00 | *7.50* |
| **9N12** | A121 | 40pf red violet | 1.10 | *7.50* |
| **9N13** | A123 | 50pf ultra | 2.50 | *30.00* |
| **9N14** | A122 | 60pf red brown | .75 | *.45* |
| **9N15** | A122 | 80pf dark blue | 2.00 | *26.00* |
| **9N16** | A123 | 84pf emerald | 5.25 | *97.50* |

Germany Nos. 574-577 Overprinted Diagonally in Black — b

**Engr.**

| | | | | |
|---|---|---|---|---|
| **9N17** | A124 | 1m olive | 20.00 | *150.00* |
| **9N18** | A124 | 2m dk brown vio | 22.50 | *475.00* |
| **9N19** | A124 | 3m copper red | 26.00 | *675.00* |
| **9N20** | A124 | 5m dark blue | 30.00 | *675.00* |
| | | *Nos. 9N1-9N20 (20)* | 127.00 | 2,288. |
| | | Set, never hinged | 350.00 | |

Forged overprints and cancellations are found on Nos. 9N1-9N20.

### Stamps of Germany 1947-48 with "a" Overprint in Red

**1948-49 Wmk. 284 Typo. *Perf. 14***

| | | | | |
|---|---|---|---|---|
| **9N21** | A120 | 2pf brn blk ('49) | .75 | *1.90* |
| **9N22** | A120 | 6pf purple ('49) | 4.50 | 1.90 |
| **9N23** | A121 | 8pf red ('49) | 19.00 | 4.50 |
| **9N24** | A121 | 10pf yellow grn | .75 | .60 |
| **9N25** | A120 | 15pf chocolate | 1.60 | 1.90 |
| **9N26** | A121 | 20pf blue | .75 | .75 |
| **9N27** | A120 | 25pf org yel ('49) | 32.50 | 45.00 |
| **9N28** | A122 | 30pf red ('49) | 30.00 | 4.75 |
| **9N29** | A121 | 40pf red vio ('49) | 30.00 | 13.50 |
| **9N30** | A123 | 50pf ultra ('49) | 30.00 | 7.50 |
| **9N31** | A122 | 60pf red brown | 3.75 | .60 |
| **9N32** | A122 | 80pf dk bl ('49) | 42.50 | 9.00 |

### With "b" Overprint in Red

**Engr.**

| | | | | |
|---|---|---|---|---|
| **9N33** | A124 | 1m olive | 225.00 | *450.00* |
| **9N34** | A124 | 2m dk brn vio | 100.00 | *225.00* |
| | | *Nos. 9N21-9N34 (14)* | 521.10 | *766.90* |
| | | Set, never hinged | 1,300. | |

Forgeries exist of the overprints on Nos. 9N21-9N34. No. 9N33 exists imperf.

A1

Statue of Heinrich von Stephan — A2

**1949, Apr. 9 Litho. *Perf. 14***

| | | | | |
|---|---|---|---|---|
| **9N35** | A1 | 12pf gray | 5.75 | *9.00* |
| **9N36** | A1 | 16pf blue green | 11.00 | *19.00* |
| **9N37** | A1 | 24pf orange brn | 7.50 | .75 |
| **9N38** | A1 | 50pf brown olive | 55.00 | 45.00 |
| **9N39** | A1 | 60pf brown red | 65.00 | 37.50 |
| **9N40** | A2 | 1m olive | 30.00 | *140.00* |
| **9N41** | A2 | 2m brown violet | 37.50 | *90.00* |
| | | *Nos. 9N35-9N41 (7)* | 211.75 | *341.25* |
| | | Set, never hinged | 750.00 | |

75th anniv. of the UPU.

Brandenburg Gate, Berlin — A3

Tempelhof Airport — A4

Designs: 4pf, 8pf, 40pf, Schoeneberg, Rudolf Wilde Square. 5pf, 25pf, 5m, Tegel Castle. 6pf, 50pf, Reichstag Building. 10pf, 30pf, Cloisters, Kleist Park. 15pf, Tempelhof Airport. 20pf, 80pf, 90pf, Polytechnic College, Charlottenburg. 60pf, National Gallery. 2m, Gendarmen Square. 3m, Brandenburg Gate.

**1949 Typo. Wmk. 284**
**Size: 22x18mm**

| | | | | |
|---|---|---|---|---|
| **9N42** | A3 | 1pf black | .25 | .35 |
| | *a.* | Bklt. pane 5 + label | 9.00 | *22.50* |
| | | Never hinged | 22.50 | |
| | *b.* | Tête bêche | .35 | *1.25* |
| | | Never hinged | 1.00 | |
| **9N43** | A3 | 4pf yellow brn | .25 | .35 |
| | *a.* | Bklt. pane 5 + label | 9.00 | *22.50* |
| | | Never hinged | 22.50 | |
| | *b.* | Tête bêche | .95 | *2.40* |
| | | Never hinged | 1.90 | |
| **9N44** | A3 | 5pf blue green | .25 | .35 |
| **9N45** | A3 | 6pf red violet | .35 | *1.50* |
| **9N46** | A3 | 8pf red orange | .35 | *1.50* |
| **9N47** | A3 | 10pf yellow grn | .35 | .35 |
| | *a.* | Bklt. pane 5 + label | 65.00 | *175.00* |
| | | Never hinged | 140.00 | |
| **9N48** | A4 | 15pf chocolate | 3.75 | .90 |
| **9N49** | A3 | 20pf red | 1.50 | .35 |
| | *a.* | Bklt. pane 5 + label | 65.00 | *175.00* |
| | | Never hinged | 140.00 | |
| **9N50** | A3 | 25pf orange | 7.50 | 1.10 |
| **9N51** | A3 | 30pf violet bl | 3.50 | 1.25 |
| | *a.* | Imperf. | *675.00* | |
| | | Never hinged | 1,350. | |
| **9N52** | A3 | 40pf lake | 4.50 | 1.10 |
| **9N53** | A3 | 50pf olive | 4.50 | .35 |
| **9N54** | A3 | 60pf red brown | 15.00 | .35 |
| **9N55** | A3 | 80pf dark blue | 3.00 | 1.10 |
| **9N56** | A3 | 90pf emerald | 3.00 | 1.50 |

**Engr.**
**Size: 29¼-29¾x24-24½mm**

| | | | | |
|---|---|---|---|---|
| **9N57** | A4 | 1m olive | 5.50 | 1.10 |
| **9N58** | A4 | 2m brown vio | 15.00 | 1.50 |
| **9N59** | A4 | 3m henna brn | 67.50 | 15.00 |
| **9N60** | A4 | 5m deep blue | 45.00 | 15.00 |
| | | *Nos. 9N42-9N60 (19)* | 181.05 | 45.00 |
| | | Set, never hinged | 700.00 | |

See Nos. 9N101-9N102, 9N108-9N110.

Goethe and "Iphigenie" — A5

Designs (Goethe and scenes from his works): 20pf, "Reineke Fuchs." 30pf, "Faust."

**1949, July 29 Litho. *Perf. 14***

| | | | | |
|---|---|---|---|---|
| **9N61** | A5 | 10pf green | 42.50 | *65.00* |
| **9N62** | A5 | 20pf carmine | 42.50 | *75.00* |
| **9N63** | A5 | 30pf ultra | 7.50 | *50.00* |
| | | *Nos. 9N61-9N63 (3)* | 92.50 | *190.00* |
| | | Set, never hinged | 300.00 | |

Bicentenary of the birth of Johann Wolfgang von Goethe.

### Germany Nos. 550, 565, 572 and 576 Surcharged "BERLIN" and New Value in Dark Green

**1949, Aug. 1 Typo.**

| | | | | |
|---|---|---|---|---|
| **9N64** | A119 | 5pf on 45pf | 1.10 | .35 |
| **9N65** | A123 | 10pf on 24pf | 3.25 | .35 |
| **9N66** | A122 | 20pf on 80pf | 19.00 | 16.50 |

**Engr.**

| | | | | |
|---|---|---|---|---|
| **9N67** | A124 | 1m on 3m | 45.00 | 17.00 |
| | | *Nos. 9N64-9N67 (4)* | 68.35 | 34.20 |
| | | Set, never hinged | 250.00 | |

Statue of Atlas, New York — A6

**1950, Oct. 1 Engr. Wmk. 116**

| | | | | |
|---|---|---|---|---|
| **9N68** | A6 | 20pf dk carmine | 35.00 | 40.00 |
| | | Never hinged | 90.00 | |

European Recovery Plan.

Albert Lortzing — A7

Freedom Bell, Berlin — A8

**1951, Apr. 22**

| | | | | |
|---|---|---|---|---|
| **9N69** | A7 | 20pf red brown | 20.00 | *52.50* |
| | | Never hinged | 52.50 | |

Centenary of the death of Albert Lortzing, composer.

**1951 *Perf. 14***

| | | | | |
|---|---|---|---|---|
| **9N70** | A8 | 5pf chocolate | .75 | *7.50* |
| **9N71** | A8 | 10pf deep green | 3.75 | *22.50* |
| **9N72** | A8 | 20pf rose red | 2.25 | *19.00* |
| **9N73** | A8 | 30pf blue | 19.00 | *67.50* |
| **9N74** | A8 | 40pf rose violet | 5.50 | *37.50* |
| | | *Nos. 9N70-9N74 (5)* | 31.25 | *154.00* |
| | | Set, never hinged | 87.50 | |

### Re-engraved

**1951-52**

| | | | | |
|---|---|---|---|---|
| **9N75** | A8 | 5pf olive bis ('52) | .75 | *1.90* |
| **9N76** | A8 | 10pf yellow grn | 2.25 | *3.75* |
| **9N77** | A8 | 20pf brt red | 10.50 | *16.50* |
| **9N78** | A8 | 30pf blue ('52) | 24.00 | *50.00* |
| **9N79** | A8 | 40pf dp car ('52) | 10.50 | *15.00* |
| | | *Nos. 9N75-9N79 (5)* | 48.00 | *87.15* |
| | | Set, never hinged | 110.00 | |

Bell clapper moved from left to right. Imprint "L. Schnell" in lower margin.
No. 9N76 exists imperf. Value, $575 unused, $1,100 mint never hinged.
See Nos. 9N94-9N98.

Ludwig van Beethoven — A9

Olympic Symbols — A10

**1952, Mar. 26 Engr. Unwmk.**

| | | | | |
|---|---|---|---|---|
| **9N80** | A9 | 30pf blue | 16.00 | *30.00* |
| | | Never hinged | 42.50 | |

125th anniversary of the death of Ludwig van Beethoven.

**1952, June 20 Litho. Wmk. 116**

| | | | | |
|---|---|---|---|---|
| **9N81** | A10 | 4pf yellow brown | .35 | *1.90* |
| **9N82** | A10 | 10pf green | 3.75 | *15.00* |
| **9N83** | A10 | 20pf rose red | 6.75 | *26.00* |
| | | *Nos. 9N81-9N83 (3)* | 10.85 | *42.90* |
| | | Set, never hinged | 27.50 | |

Pre-Olympic Festival Day, June 20, 1952.

Carl Friedrich Zelter — A11

Portraits: 5pf, Otto Lilienthal. 6pf, Walter Rathenau. 8pf, Theodor Fontane. 10pf, Adolph von Menzel. 15pf, Rudolf Virchow. 20pf, Werner von Siemens. 25pf, Karl Friedrich Schinkel. 30pf, Max Planck. 40pf, Wilhelm von Humboldt.

**1952-53 Engr. Wmk. 284**

| | | | | |
|---|---|---|---|---|
| **9N84** | A11 | 4pf brown | .25 | .55 |
| **9N85** | A11 | 5pf dp blue ('53) | .35 | .55 |
| **9N86** | A11 | 6pf choc ('53) | 2.00 | *9.75* |
| **9N87** | A11 | 8pf henna brn ('53) | .75 | *2.25* |
| **9N88** | A11 | 10pf deep green | 1.10 | .55 |
| **9N89** | A11 | 15pf purple ('53) | 5.25 | *15.00* |
| **9N90** | A11 | 20pf brown red | .75 | .75 |
| **9N91** | A11 | 25pf dp olive ('53) | 16.00 | 6.75 |
| **9N92** | A11 | 30pf brn vio ('53) | 5.50 | *9.75* |
| **9N93** | A11 | 40pf black ('53) | 6.75 | 3.00 |
| | | *Nos. 9N84-9N93 (10)* | 38.70 | 48.90 |
| | | Set, never hinged | 140.00 | |

### Bell Type of 1951-1952 Second Re-engraving

**1953 Wmk. 284 *Perf. 14***

| | | | | |
|---|---|---|---|---|
| **9N94** | A8 | 5pf brown | .35 | *1.00* |
| **9N95** | A8 | 10pf deep green | 1.10 | *1.50* |
| **9N96** | A8 | 20pf brt red | 3.00 | 3.00 |
| **9N97** | A8 | 30pf blue | 5.00 | *12.00* |
| **9N98** | A8 | 40pf rose violet | 21.00 | *37.50* |
| | | *Nos. 9N94-9N98 (5)* | 30.45 | *55.00* |
| | | Set, never hinged | 77.50 | |

Bell clapper hangs straight down. Marginal imprint omitted.
For overprint & surcharge see #9N106, 9NB17.

Arms Breaking Chains — A12

Design: 30pf, Brandenburg Gate.

**1953, Aug. 17 Typo.**

| | | | | |
|---|---|---|---|---|
| **9N99** | A12 | 20pf black | 1.25 | *1.50* |
| **9N100** | A12 | 30pf dp carmine | 9.00 | *30.00* |
| | | Set, never hinged | 37.50 | |

Strike of East German workers, 6/17/53.

### Similar to Type of 1949

Designs: 4pf, Exposition halls. 20pf, Olympic Stadium, Berlin.

**1953-54 Wmk. 284 *Perf. 14***

| | | | | |
|---|---|---|---|---|
| **9N101** | A3 | 4pf yellow brn ('54) | 1.75 | *5.00* |
| **9N102** | A3 | 20pf red | 22.50 | 2.50 |
| | | Set, never hinged | 70.00 | |

**Catalogue values for unused stamps in this section, from this point to the end of the section, are for Never Hinged items.**

Allied Council Building — A13

**1954, Jan. 25 Litho.**

| | | | | |
|---|---|---|---|---|
| **9N103** | A13 | 20pf red | 8.25 | 4.50 |

Four Power Conference, Berlin, 1954.

Prof. Ernst Reuter (1889-1953), Mayor of Berlin (1948-53) A14

**1954, Jan. 18 Engr. Wmk. 284**

| | | | | |
|---|---|---|---|---|
| **9N104** | A14 | 20pf chocolate | 8.25 | 1.90 |

See No. 9N174.

Ottmar Mergenthaler and Linotype — A15

**1954, May 11**
**9N105** A15 10pf dk blue grn 3.25 2.75

Cent. of the birth of Ottmar Mergenthaler.

No. 9N96 Overprinted in Black

**1954, July 17** *Perf. 13½x14*
**9N106** A8 20pf bright red 4.75 *5.25*

Issued to publicize the West German presidential election held in Berlin July 17, 1954.

Germany in Bondage — A16

Richard Strauss — A17

**1954, July 20** **Typo.**
**9N107** A16 20pf car & gray 5.25 5.25

10th anniv. of the attempted assassination of Adolf Hitler.

**Similar to Type of 1949**

Designs: 7pf, Exposition halls. 40pf, Memorial library. 70pf, Hunting lodge, Grunewald.

| **1954** | **Wmk. 284** | *Perf. 14* | |
|---|---|---|---|
| **9N108** | A3 7pf aqua | 5.50 | 1.50 |
| **9N109** | A3 40pf rose lilac | 9.75 | 3.00 |
| **9N110** | A3 70pf olive green | 105.00 | 21.00 |
| | *Nos. 9N108-9N110 (3)* | 120.25 | 25.50 |
| | Set, hinged | 50.00 | |

**1954, Sept. 18** **Engr.**
**9N111** A17 40pf violet blue 11.00 3.75

5th anniv. of the death of Richard Strauss, composer.

Early Forge — A18

**1954, Sept. 25**
**9N112** A18 20pf reddish brown 7.50 1.90

Centenary of the death of August Borsig, industrial leader.

M. S. Berlin and Arms of Berlin — A19

**1955, Mar. 12** **Wmk. 284**
**9N113** A19 10pf Prus green 1.10 .75
**9N114** A19 25pf violet blue 7.25 4.25

Issued to publicize the resumption of shipping under West German ownership.

Wilhelm Furtwängler — A20

*Perf. 13½x14*

**1955, Sept. 17** **Unwmk.**
**9N115** A20 40pf ultra 21.00 21.00

Issued to honor the conductor Wilhelm Furtwangler and to publicize the Berlin Music Festival, September 1955.

Arms of Berlin
A21 A22

**1955, Oct. 17** **Litho.** **Wmk. 304**
**9N116** A21 10pf red, org yel & blk .35 *.75*
**9N117** A21 20pf red, org yel & blk 5.25 *9.00*

Meeting of the German Bundestag in Berlin, Oct. 17-22, 1955.

**1956, Mar. 16**
**9N118** A22 10pf red, ocher & blk 1.10 .75
**9N119** A22 25pf red, ocher & blk 4.50 4.50

Meeting of the German Bundesrat in Berlin Mar. 16, 1956.

Radio Station, Berlin (A23 has no top inscription. A24 has top inscription.)
A23 A24

Free University
A25

Monument of the Great Elector Frederick William
A26

Designs: 1pf, 3pf, Brandenburg Gate. 5pf, General Post Office. 8pf, City Hall, Neukölln. 10pf, Kaiser Wilhelm Memorial Church. 15pf, Airlift memorial. 25pf, Lilienthal Monument. 30pf, Pfaueninsel Castle. 40pf, Charlottenburg Castle. 50pf, Reuter power plant. 60pf, Chamber of Commerce and Industry and Stock Exchange. 70pf, Schiller Theater. 3m, Congress Hall.

**Typo.; Litho. (3pf, #9N122)**

| **1956-63** | | **Wmk. 304** | *Perf. 14* | |
|---|---|---|---|---|
| **9N120** | A25 | 1pf gray ('57) | .25 | .25 |
| **9N120A** | A25 | 3pf brt pur ('63) | .25 | .25 |
| **9N121** | A25 | 5pf rose lil ('57) | .25 | .25 |
| **9N122** | A23 | 7pf blue green | 8.25 | 2.40 |
| **9N123** | A24 | 7pf blue green | .25 | .25 |
| **9N124** | A24 | 8pf gray | .45 | .35 |
| **9N125** | A24 | 8pf red org ('59) | .30 | .30 |
| **9N126** | A24 | 10pf emerald | .25 | .25 |
| **9N127** | A24 | 15pf chlky blue | .45 | .25 |
| **9N128** | A25 | 20pf rose car | .45 | .25 |
| **9N129** | A24 | 25pf dull red brn | .45 | .45 |
| | | **Engr.** | | |
| **9N130** | A24 | 30pf gray grn ('57) | .90 | .90 |
| **9N131** | A25 | 40pf lt ultra ('57) | 9.00 | 7.50 |
| **9N132** | A24 | 50pf olive | .90 | .90 |
| **9N133** | A25 | 60pf lt brn ('57) | .90 | .90 |
| **9N134** | A25 | 70pf violet | 24.00 | 13.50 |
| **9N135** | A26 | 1m olive | 1.90 | 2.25 |

**Size: 29x24½mm**

| | | | | |
|---|---|---|---|---|
| **9N136** | A25 | 3m rose cl ('58) | 5.25 | *22.50* |
| | | *Nos. 9N120-9N136 (18)* | 54.45 | 53.70 |

No. 9N120 exists on both ordinary and fluorescent paper; No. 9N120A on fluorescent paper only; others on ordinary paper.

Engineers' Society Emblem — A27

**1956, May 12** **Engr.** *Perf. 14*
**9N140** A27 10pf dark green 1.90 1.50
**9N141** A27 20pf dark red 4.25 *5.00*

Cent. of Soc. of German Civil Engineers.

Paul Lincke — A28

**1956, Sept. 3**
**9N142** A28 20pf dark red 2.50 2.75

Death of Paul Lincke, composer, 10th anniv.

Radio Station, Berlin-Nikolassee A29

**1956, Sept. 15**
**9N143** A29 25pf brown 6.00 *9.00*

German Industrial Fair, Berlin, Sept. 15-30.

Spandau, 1850 — A30

**1957, Mar. 7**
**9N144** A30 20pf gray ol & brn red .60 .75

725th anniversary of Spandau.

Hansa Model Town and "B" — A31

Designs: 20pf, View of exposition grounds and "B." 40pf, Auditorium and "B."

| **1957** | | **Engr.** | | |
|---|---|---|---|---|
| **9N145** | A31 | 7pf violet brown | .25 | .25 |
| **9N146** | A31 | 20pf carmine | .75 | .75 |
| **9N147** | A31 | 40pf violet blue | 1.90 | 2.25 |
| | | *Nos. 9N145-9N147 (3)* | 2.90 | 3.25 |

Intl. Building Show, Berlin, 7/6-9/29/57.

Friedrich Karl von Savigny, Law Teacher — A32

Uta Statue, Naumburg Cathedral — A33

Portraits: 7pf, Theodor Mommsen, historian. 8pf, Heinrich Zille, painter. 10pf, Ernst Reuter, mayor of Berlin. 15pf, Fritz Haber, chemist. 20pf, Friedrich Schleiermacher, theologian. 25pf, Max Reinhardt, theatrical director. 40pf, Alexander von Humboldt, naturalist and geographer. 50pf, Christian Daniel Rauch, sculptor.

**1957-59** **Wmk. 304** *Perf. 14*

**Portraits in Brown**

| | | | | |
|---|---|---|---|---|
| **9N148** | A32 | 7pf blue grn ('58) | .25 | .25 |
| **9N149** | A32 | 8pf gray ('58) | .25 | .25 |
| **9N150** | A32 | 10pf green ('58) | .25 | .25 |
| **9N151** | A32 | 15pf dark blue | .35 | .75 |
| **9N152** | A32 | 20pf carmine ('58) | .25 | .25 |
| **9N153** | A32 | 25pf magenta | .80 | 1.00 |
| **9N154** | A32 | 30pf olive green | 2.10 | 2.75 |
| **9N155** | A32 | 40pf blue ('59) | .80 | 1.00 |
| **9N156** | A32 | 50pf olive | 4.00 | *6.75* |
| | | *Nos. 9N148-9N156 (9)* | 9.05 | 13.25 |

Issued to honor famous men of Berlin.
See No. 9NB19.

**1957, Aug. 6**
**9N157** A33 25pf brown red .90 1.10

Issued to publicize the annual meeting of the East German Culture Society in Berlin.

"Unity and Justice and Liberty" — A34

Postilion 1897-1925 — A35

**1957, Oct. 15** **Litho.**
**9N158** A34 10pf multicolored .30 *.75*
**9N159** A34 20pf multicolored 2.25 *3.00*

1st meeting of the 3rd German Bundesrat, Berlin, 10/15.

**1957, Oct. 23** **Wmk. 304** *Perf. 14*
**9N160** A35 20pf multicolored .75 .90

Issued for Stamp Day and BEPHILA stamp exhibition, Berlin, Oct. 23-27.

World Veterans' Federation Emblem — A36

**1957, Oct. 28**
**9N161** A36 20pf bl grn, ol grn & yel .90 .75

7th General Assembly of the World Veterans' Federation, Berlin, Oct. 24-Nov. 1.

Christ and the Cosmos — A37

**1958, Aug. 13**

**9N162** A37 10pf lt bl grn & blk .35 .60
**9N163** A37 20pf rose lilac & blk 1.00 1.50

Issued in honor of the 78th German Catholics Meeting, Berlin, Aug. 13-17.

Prof. Otto Suhr (1894-1957), Mayor of Berlin (1955-57) A38

**1958, Aug. 30 Engr. *Perf. 14***

**9N164** A38 20pf rose red 1.10 2.00

**Pres. Heuss Type of Germany, 1959**

**Litho., Engraved (40pf, 70pf)**

**1959**

**9N165** A208 7pf blue green .25 *.35*
**9N166** A208 10pf green .25 *.35*
**9N167** A208 20pf dk car rose .50 .35
**9N168** A208 40pf blue 2.25 *4.50*
**9N169** A208 70pf dull purple 8.25 *10.50*
*Nos. 9N165-9N169 (5)* 11.50 *16.05*

Nos. 9N168-9N169 were issued in sheets of 100 and in coils. Every fifth coil stamp has a control number on the back.

Aerial Bridge to Berlin — A39

**1959, May 12 Engr.**

**9N170** A39 25pf maroon & blk .60 .45

10th anniversary of Berlin Airlift.

Globe and Brandenburg Gate — A40

**1959, June 18 Litho. *Perf. 14***

**9N171** A40 20pf lt blue & red .85 .45

Issued to publicize the 14th International Municipal Congress, Berlin, June 18-23.

Friedrich von Schiller (1759-1805), Poet — A41

**1959, Nov. 10 Engr. Wmk. 304**

**9N172** A41 20pf dull red & brn .35 .45

Dr. Robert Koch (1843-1910), Bacteriologist A42

**1960, May 27 *Perf. 14***

**9N173** A42 20pf rose lake .35 .45

**Mayor Type of 1954**

Portrait: Dr. Walther Carl Rudolf Schreiber, Mayor of Berlin, 1953-54.

**1960, June 30 Wmk. 304 *Perf. 14***

**9N174** A14 20pf brown car .50 .65

Hans Böckler (1875-1951), Labor Leader — A43

**1961, Feb. 16 Litho. *Perf. 14***

**9N175** A43 20pf dk brick red & blk .30 .35

Hans Böckler (1875-1951), labor leader.

**Fluorescent Paper was introduced for all stamps, starting with No. 9N176, and including Nos. 9N120 and 9N120A.**

Albrecht Dürer — A44

Portraits: 5pf, Albertus Magnus. 7pf, St. Elizabeth of Thuringia. 8pf, Johann Gutenberg. 15pf, Martin Luther. 20pf, Johann Sebastian Bach. 25pf, Balthasar Neumann. 30pf, Immanuel Kant. 40pf, Gotthold Ephraim Lessing. 50pf, Johann Wolfgang von Goethe. 60pf, Friedrich von Schiller. 70pf, Ludwig van Beethoven. 80pf, Heinrich von Kleist. 1m, Annette von Droste-Hülshoff. 2m, Gerhart Hauptmann.

**1961-62 Typo. Wmk. 304**

**9N176** A44 5pf olive .25 .25
**9N177** A44 7pf dk bister .25 .35
**9N178** A44 8pf lilac .25 .35
**9N179** A44 10pf olive green .25 .25
*b.* Tête bêche pair 1.10 *2.25*
**9N180** A44 15pf blue .25 .35
**9N181** A44 20pf dark red .25 .25
**9N182** A44 25pf orange brn .25 .35

**Engr.**

**9N183** A44 30pf gray .25 *.50*
**9N184** A44 40pf blue .50 *.95*
**9N185** A44 50pf red brown .35 *.95*
**9N186** A44 60pf dk car rose ('62) .35 *1.10*
**9N187** A44 70pf green .50 *1.10*
**9N188** A44 80pf brown 3.00 *7.50*
**9N189** A44 1m violet blue 1.40 *3.50*
**9N190** A44 2m yel grn ('62) 1.75 *5.00*
*Nos. 9N176-9N190 (15)* 9.85 *22.75*

Nos. 9N176-9N182, 9N184 and 9N187 were issued in sheets and in coils. Every fifth coil stamp has a black control number on the back.

Louise Schroeder A45

**1961, June 3 Engr. *Perf. 14***

**9N192** A45 20pf dark brown .35 .35

Issued to honor Louise Schroeder, acting mayor of Berlin (1947-1948).

Synod Emblem & Kaiser Wilhelm Memorial Church — A46

Design: 10pf, Emblem and St. Mary's Church.

**1961, July 19 Litho. Wmk. 304**

**9N193** A46 10pf green & vio .25 .25
**9N194** A46 20pf rose claret & vio .25 .25

10th meeting of German Protestants (Evangelical Synod), Berlin, July 19-23.

Berlin Bear with Record, TV Set & Radio Tower — A47

**1961, Aug. 3 Engr.**

**9N195** A47 20pf brn red & dk brn .30 .30

German Radio, Television and Phonograph Exhibition, Berlin, Aug. 25-Sept. 3.

Berlin, 1650 — A48

Views of Old Berlin: 10pf, Spree and Waisenbrücke (Orphans' Bridge). 15pf, Mauer Street, 1780. 20pf, Berlin Palace, 1703. 25pf, Potsdam Square, 1825. 40pf, Bellevue Palace, 1800. 50pf, Fischer Bridge, 1830. 60pf, Halle Gate, 1880. 70pf, Parochial Church, 1780. 80pf, University, 1825. 90pf, Opera House, 1780. 1m, Grunewald Lake, 1790.

**1962-63 Wmk. 304 *Perf. 14***

**9N196** A48 7pf dk gray & gldn brn .25 .25
**9N197** A48 10pf grn & dk gray .25 .25
**9N198** A48 15pf bluish gray & dk bl ('63) .25 .25
**9N199** A48 20pf org brn & sep .25 .25
**9N200** A48 25pf ol & gray ('63) .25 .25
**9N201** A48 40pf bluish gray & ultra .25 .40
**9N202** A48 50pf gray & dk brn .40 .40
**9N203** A48 60pf gray & car rose ('63) .45 .45
**9N204** A48 70pf dk gray & lilac .45 .45
**9N205** A48 80pf dk gray & dk red ('63) .60 .70
**9N206** A48 90pf sep & brn org ('63) .75 .75
**9N207** A48 1m ol gray & dp grn .90 1.10
*Nos. 9N196-9N207 (12)* 5.05 5.50

Gelber Hund, 1912, and Boeing 707 — A49

**1962, Sept. 12 Litho.**

**9N208** A49 60pf brt blue & blk .55 .55

50th anniv. of German airmail service.

Berlin Bear and Radio Tower — A50

**1963, July 24 Unwmk. *Perf. 14***

**9N209** A50 20pf bl, vio bl & gray .30 .30

German Radio, Television and Phonograph Exhibition, Berlin, Aug. 30-Sept. 8.

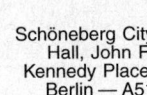

Schöneberg City Hall, John F. Kennedy Place, Berlin — A51

**1964, May 30 Engr. Wmk. 304**

**9N210** A51 20pf dk brn, *cr* .30 .30

700th anniv. of the Schöneberg district of Berlin. The Senate and House of Representatives of West Berlin meet at Schöneberg City Hall.

**Lübke Type of Germany, 1964**

**1964, July 1 Litho. Unwmk.**

**9N211** A247 20pf carmine .25 .25
**9N212** A247 40pf ultra .35 .35

See Nos. 9N263-9N264.

**Capitals Type of Germany**

Design: Reichstag Building, Berlin.

**1964, Sept. 14 Litho. *Perf. 14***

**9N213** A245 20pf blue, blk & grn .35 .35

**Kennedy Type of Germany**

**1964, Nov. 21 Engr. Wmk. 304**

**9N214** A255 40pf dark blue .45 .55

Castle Gate, Ellwangen — A52

Designs (German buildings through 12 centuries): 10pf, Wall pavilion, Zwinger, Dresden. 15pf, Tegel Castle, Berlin. 20pf, Portico, Lorsch. 40pf, Trifels Fortress, Palatinate. 60pf, Treptow Gate, Neubrandenburg. 70pf, Osthofen Gate, Soest. 80pf, Elling Gate, Weissenburg.

**1964-65 Typo. Unwmk.**

**9N215** A52 10pf brown ('65) .25 .25
*b.* Tête bêche pair .45 *2.00*
**9N216** A52 15pf dk green ('65) .25 .25
**9N217** A52 20pf brn red ('65) .25 .25

**Engr.**

**9N218** A52 40pf vio bl ('65) .60 *1.10*
**9N219** A52 50pf olive bis 1.40 *1.50*
**9N220** A52 60pf rose red .95 *1.10*
**9N221** A52 70pf dk green ('65) 1.90 *3.50*
**9N222** A52 80pf chocolate 1.90 1.50
*Nos. 9N215-9N222 (8)* 7.50 *9.45*

Nos. 9N215-9N218, 9N221 were issued in sheets of 100 and in coils. Every fifth coil stamp has a black control number on the back.

Kaiser Wilhelm Memorial Church A53

Nordertor, Flensburg A54

The New Berlin: 15pf, German Opera House, horiz. 20pf, Philharmonic Hall, horiz. 30pf, Jewish Community Center, horiz. 40pf, Regina Martyrum Memorial, horiz. 50pf, Ernst Reuter Square, horiz. 60pf, Europa Center. 70pf, School of Engineering, horiz. 80pf, City Highway. 90pf, Planetarium and observatory, horiz. 1m, Schaeferberg radio tower, Wannsee. 1.10m, University clinic, Steglitz, horiz.

**Engraved and Lithographed**

**1965-66 Unwmk. *Perf. 14***

**9N223** A53 10pf multi .25 .25
**9N224** A53 15pf multi .25 .25
**9N225** A53 20pf multi .25 .25
**9N226** A53 30pf multi ('66) .25 .25
**9N227** A53 40pf multi ('66) .25 .25
**9N228** A53 50pf multi .25 .30
**9N229** A53 60pf multi ('66) .30 .35
**9N230** A53 70pf multi ('66) .45 .45
**9N231** A53 80pf multi .45 .45
**9N232** A53 90pf multi ('66) .55 *.75*

9N233 A53 1m multi ('66) .55 *.90*
9N234 A53 1.10m multi ('66) .55 *.95*
*Nos. 9N223-9N234 (12)* 4.35 5.40

**1966-69 Engr. *Perf. 14***

5pf, Berlin Gate, Stettin. 8pf, Castle, Kaub on the Rhine. 10pf, Wall Pavilion, Zwinger, Dresden. 20pf, Portico, Lorsch. 40pf, Trifels Fortress, Palatinate. 50pf, Castle Gate, Ellwangen. 60pf, Treptow Gate, Neubrandenburg. 70pf, Osthofen Gate, Soest. 80pf, Elling Gate, Weissenburg. 90pf, Zschocke Ladies' Home, Königsberg. 1m, Melanchthon House, Wittenberg. 1.10m, Trinity Hospital, Hildeshelm. 1.30m, Tegel Castle, Berlin. 2m, Löwenberg Town Hall, interior view.

9N235 A54 5pf olive .25 .25
9N236 A54 8pf car rose .25 .25
9N237 A54 10pf dk brn ('67) .25 .25
9N238 A54 20pf dk grn ('67) .25 .25
9N239 A54 30pf yellow grn .25 .25
9N240 A54 30pf red ('67) .25 .25
9N241 A54 40pf ol bis ('67) .55 *.75*
9N242 A54 50pf blue ('67) .35 *.45*
9N243 A54 60pf dp org ('67) 1.50 *1.90*
9N244 A54 70pf sl grn ('67) .75 .75
9N245 A54 80pf red brn ('67) .95 *1.60*
9N246 A54 90pf black .50 *.75*
9N247 A54 1m dull blue .50 *.75*
9N248 A54 1.10m red brn 1.40 1.40
9N249 A54 1.30m green ('69) 2.25 2.25
9N250 A54 2m purple 2.25 1.90
*Nos. 9N235-9N250 (16)* 12.50 14.00

**Brandenburg Gate Type of Germany**

**1966-70 Typo. *Perf. 14***

9N251 A268 10pf chocolate .25 .25
a. Bklt. pane of 10 (4 #9N251, 2 #9N252, 4 #9N253) 6.75 12.00
b. Tête bêche pair .90 1.10
c. Bklt. pane of 6 (4 #9N251, 2 #9N253) ('70) 3.00 *4.50*
9N252 A268 20pf dp green .25 .25
a. Bklt. pane of 4 (2 #9N252, 2 #9N253) ('70) 2.25 *3.00*
9N253 A268 30pf red .25 .25
a. Tête bêche pair 1.10 2.40
9N254 A268 50pf dk blue .55 .35
9N255 A268 100pf dk blue ('67) 4.25 4.25
*Nos. 9N251-9N255 (5)* 5.55 5.35

Nos. 9N251-9N255 were issued in sheets of 100 and in coils. Every fifth coil stamp has a black control number on the back.

A55

A56

Designs: 10pf, Young Man, by Conrat Meit, 1520. 20pf, The Great Elector Friedrich Wilhelm (1640-88), head from monument by Andreas Schlüter. 30pf, The Evangelist Mark, by Tilman Riemenschneider. 50pf, Head of "Victory" from Brandenburg Gate, by Gottfried Schadow, 1793. 1m, Madonna, by Joseph Anton Feuchtmayer. 1.10m, Jesus and John, wood sculpture, anonymous, c. 1320.

**1967 Engr. *Perf. 14***

9N256 A55 10pf sepia & lemon .25 .25
9N257 A55 20pf sl grn & bluish gray .25 .25
9N258 A55 30pf brown & olive .25 .25
9N259 A55 50pf black & gray .35 .35
9N260 A55 1m blue & chlky blue .75 .75

**Size: 22x40mm**

9N261 A55 1.10m brown & buff 1.10 *1.50*
*Nos. 9N256-9N261 (6)* 2.95 3.35

Issued to publicize Berlin art treasures.

**1967, July 19 Litho. and Engr.**

Berlin Radio Tower and Television Screens

9N262 A56 30pf multicolored .30 .35

25th German Radio, Television and Phonograph Exhibition, Berlin, Aug. 25-Sept. 3.

**Lübke Type of Germany, 1964**

**1967, Oct. 14 Litho.**

9N263 A247 30pf carmine .25 .25
9N264 A247 50pf ultra .35 .45

Old Court Building (Berlin Museum) — A57

Turners' Emblem — A58

**1968, Mar. 16 Engr. *Perf. 14***

9N265 A57 30pf black .30 .35

500th anniv. of the Berlin Court of Appeal.

**1968, Apr. 29 Litho. *Perf. 14***

9N266 A58 20pf gray, blk & red .30 .35

Issued to publicize the German Turner Festival, Berlin, May 28-June 3.

Newspaper Vendor by Christian Wilhelm Allers — A59

19th Century Berliners: 5pf, Hack, by Heinrich Zille, horiz. No. 9N269, Horse omnibus, coachman and passengers, 1890, by C. W. Allers. No. 9N270, Cobbler's apprentice, by Franz Kruger. No. 9N271, Cobbler, by Adolph von Menzel. No. 9N272, Blacksmiths, by Paul Meyerheim. No. 9N273, Three Ladies, by Franz Kruger. 50pf, Strollers at Brandenburg Gate, by Christian W. Allers.

**1969 Engr. *Perf. 14***

9N267 A59 5pf black .25 .25
9N268 A59 10pf dp brown .25 .25
9N269 A59 10pf brown .25 .25
9N270 A59 20pf dk olive grn .25 .25
9N271 A59 20pf green .25 .25
9N272 A59 30pf dk red brown .60 .45
9N273 A59 30pf red brown .60 .45
9N274 A59 50pf ultra 1.50 1.75
*Nos. 9N267-9N274 (8)* 3.95 3.90

Souvenir Sheet

Berlin Zoo Animals — A60

Designs: 10pf, Orangutan family. 20pf, White pelicans. 30pf, Gaur and calf. 50pf, Zebra and foal.

**Engraved and Lithographed**

**1969, June 4 *Perf. 14***

9N275 A60 Sheet of 4 1.90 1.90
a. 10pf bister & black .45 .45
b. 20pf light green & black .45 .45
c. 30pf lilac rose & black .45 .45
d. 50pf blue & black .45 .45

125th anniversary of the Berlin Zoo. The sheet was sold with a 20pf surtax for the benefit of the Zoo.

Australian Postman — A61

Joseph Joachim — A62

Designs: 20pf, African telephone operator. 30pf, Middle East telecommunications engineer. 50pf, Loading mail on plane.

**1969, July 21 Litho. *Perf. 14***

9N276 A61 10pf olive & apple grn .25 .25
9N277 A61 20pf dk brn, bis & brn .25 .25
9N278 A61 30pf vio blk & bis .55 .60
9N279 A61 50pf dk blue & blue 1.25 1.25
*Nos. 9N276-9N279 (4)* 2.30 2.35

20th Congress of the Post Office Trade Union Federation, Berlin, July 7-11.

**1969, Sept. 12 Photo. *Perf. 14***

Design: 50pf, Alexander von Humboldt, painting by Joseph Stieler.

9N280 A62 30pf multicolored .55 .45
9N281 A62 50pf multicolored .90 *1.25*

Cent. of the Berlin Music School and honoring its 1st director, Joseph Joachim (1831-1907), violinist, conductor and composer; Alexander von Humboldt (1769-1859), naturalist and explorer.

**1970, Jan. 7**

Theodor Fontane, painting by Hanns Fechner.

9N282 A62 20pf multicolored .35 .30

150th anniv. of the birth of Theodor Fontane (1819-1898), poet and writer.
See No. 9N303.

Film Frame — A63

Symbols of Dance, Theater & Art — A64

**1970, June 18 Photo. *Perf. 14***

9N283 A63 30pf multicolored .45 .55

20th International Film Festival.

**President Heinemann Type of Germany Inscribed "Berlin"**

**1970-73 Engr. *Perf. 14***

9N284 A312 5pf dk gray .25 .25
9N285 A312 8pf olive bis .70 .90
9N286 A312 10pf brown .25 .25
9N286A A312 15pf olive .25 .25
9N287 A312 20pf green .25 .25
9N288 A312 25pf dp yel grn .90 .55
9N289 A312 30pf red brown .95 .55
9N290 A312 40pf brown org .55 .25
9N291 A312 50pf dark blue .55 .25
9N292 A312 60pf blue .90 .55
9N293 A312 70pf dk brown .70 .60
9N294 A312 80pf slate grn .90 .90
9N295 A312 90pf magenta 1.75 2.25
9N296 A312 1m olive .90 .70
9N296A A312 110pf olive gray 1.10 1.10
9N297 A312 120pf ocher 1.10 .90
9N298 A312 130pf ocher 1.60 1.50
9N298A A312 140pf dk blue grn 1.60 1.50
9N299 A312 150pf purple 1.60 .75
9N300 A312 160pf orange 2.25 1.90
9N300A A312 170pf orange 1.60 1.60
9N300B A312 190pf dp claret 1.90 2.75
9N301 A312 2m dp violet 1.90 1.40
*Nos. 9N284-9N301 (23)* 24.45 21.90

Issued: 5pf, 1m, 7/23; 10, 20pf, 10/23; 30, 90pf, 2m, 1/7/71; 8, 40, 50, 70, 80pf, 4/8/71; 60pf, 6/25/71; 25pf, 8/27/71; 120, 160pf, 3/8/72; 15, 130pf, 6/20/72; 150pf, 7/5/72; 170pf, 9/11/72; 110, 140, 190pf, 1/16/73.

**1970, Sept. 4 Litho. *Perf. 13½x14***

9N302 A64 30pf gray & multi .55 .55

20th Berlin Festival Weeks.

**Portrait Type of 1969**

30pf, Leopold von Ranke, by Julius Schrage.

**1970, Oct. 23 Photo. *Perf. 13½x14***

9N303 A62 30pf multicolored .45 .35

175th anniversary of the birth of Leopold von Ranke (1795-1886), historian.

**Imperial Eagle Type of Germany**

**1971, Jan. 18 Litho. *Perf. 13½x14***

9N304 A317 30pf org, red, gray & blk .55 .55

Metropolitan Train, 1932 — A65

5pf, Suburban train, 1925. 10pf, Street cars, 1890. 20pf, Horsedrawn trolley. 50pf, Strect car, 1950. 1m, Subway train, 1971.

**1971 Litho. *Perf. 14***

9N305 A65 5pf multicolored .25 .25
9N306 A65 10pf multicolored .25 .25
9N307 A65 20pf multicolored .25 .25
9N308 A65 30pf multicolored .45 .35
9N309 A65 50pf multicolored 1.60 1.40
9N310 A65 1m multicolored 1.90 1.90
*Nos. 9N305-9N310 (6)* 4.70 4.40

Issued: 30pf, 1m, Jan. 18; others, May 3.

Bagpipe Player, by Dürer — A66

**1971, May 21 Engr. *Perf. 14***

9N311 A66 10pf black & brown .45 .30

500th anniversary of the birth of Albrecht Dürer (1471-1528), painter and engraver.

Score from 2nd Brandenburg Concerto and Bach — A67

**1971, July 14 Litho. *Perf. 14***

9N312 A67 30pf buff, brn & slate .70 .60

250th anniv. of 1st performance of Johann Sebastian Bach's 2nd Brandenburg Concerto.

A68

A69

Telecommunications tower, Berlin.

**1971, July 14 Photo.**

9N313 A68 30pf dk blue, blk & car .75 .60

Intl. Broadcasting Exhibition, Berlin.

**1971, Aug. 27**

9N314 A69 25pf multicolored .55 .40

Hermann von Helmholtz (1821-94), scientist. See Nos. 9N332-9N333, 9N341.

Souvenir Sheet

Racing Cars — A70

**1971, Aug. 27 Litho. *Perf. 14***

9N315 A70 Sheet of 4 1.50 1.50
a. 10pf Opel racer .25 .25
b. 25pf Auto Union racer .25 .25

*c.* 30pf Mercedes-Benz SSKL, 1931 .35 .25
*d.* 60pf Mercedes and Auto Union cars racing on North embankment .60 .60

50th anniversary of Avus Race Track.

### Accident Prevention Type of Germany

5pf, "Matches cause fires." 10pf, Broken ladder. 20pf, Hand & circular saw. 25pf, "Alcohol & automobile." 30pf, Safety helmets prevent injury. 40pf, Defective plug. 50pf, Nail sticking from board. 60pf, 70pf, Traffic safety (ball rolling before car). 100pf, Hoisted cargo. 150pf, Fenced-in open manhole.

**1971-73 Typo. *Perf. 14***

| | | | | |
|---|---|---|---|---|
| **9N316** | A328 | 5pf orange | .25 | .30 |
| **9N317** | A328 | 10pf dk brown | .25 | .25 |
| *a.* | | Bklt. pane, 2 each #9N317-9N318, 9N320-9N321 ('74) | 7.00 | *7.50* |
| **9N318** | A328 | 20pf purple | .25 | .25 |
| **9N319** | A328 | 25pf green | .35 | .60 |
| **9N320** | A328 | 30pf dark red | .35 | .30 |
| **9N321** | A328 | 40pf rose cl | .35 | .40 |
| **9N322** | A328 | 50pf Prus blue | 1.90 | 1.10 |
| **9N323** | A328 | 60pf violet blue | 1.90 | 2.25 |
| **9N323A** | A328 | 70pf green & vio bl | 1.40 | 1.00 |
| **9N324** | A328 | 100pf olive | 1.90 | 1.10 |
| **9N325** | A328 | 150pf red brown | 5.75 | 6.75 |
| | | *Nos. 9N316-9N325 (11)* | 14.65 | 14.30 |

Issued in sheets of 100 and coils. Every fifth coil stamp has a control number on the back.

Issued: 25pf, 60pf, 9/10; 5pf, 10/29; 10pf, 30pf, 3/8/72; 40pf, 6/20/72; 20pf, 100pf, 7/5/72; 150pf, 9/11/72; 50pf, 1/16/73; 70pf, 6/5/73.

Microscope and Metal Slide — A71

Friedrich Gilly, by Gottfried Schadow — A72

**1971, Oct. 26 Photo. *Perf. 14***
**9N326** A71 30pf multicolored .45 .35

Materials Testing Laboratory centenary.

**1972, Feb. 4 Engr. *Perf. 14***
**9N327** A72 30pf black & blue .55 .35

Friedrich Gilly (1772-1800), sculptor.

Grunewaldsee, by Alexander von Riesen — A73

Paintings of Berlin Lakes: 25pf, Wannsee, by Max Liebermann. 30pf, Schlachtensee, by Walter Leistikow.

**1972, Apr. 14 Photo. *Perf. 14***

| | | | | |
|---|---|---|---|---|
| **9N328** | A73 | 10pf blue & multi | .25 | .25 |
| **9N329** | A73 | 25pf green & multi | .55 | .55 |
| **9N330** | A73 | 30pf black & multi | .95 | .60 |
| | | *Nos. 9N328-9N330 (3)* | 1.75 | 1.40 |

A74

A75

**1972, May 18**
**9N331** A74 60pf violet & blk 1.00 1.00

E. T. A. Hoffmann (1776-1822), writer and composer. (Portrait by Wilhelm Hensel.)

### Portrait Type of 1971

Designs: No. 9N332, Max Liebermann (1847-1935), self-portrait. No. 9N333, Karl August, Duke of Hardenberg (1750-1822), Prussian statesman, by J. H. W. Tischbein.

**1972 Photo. *Perf. 14***
**9N332** A69 40pf multicolored .70 .45
**9N333** A69 40pf multicolored .60 .45

Issued: #9N332, July 18; #9N333, Nov. 10.

**1972, Oct. 20 Engr. & Litho.**
**9N334** A75 20pf Stamp-printing press .45 .30

Stamp Day 1972, and for the 5th National Youth Philatelic Exhib., Berlin, Oct. 26-29.

Streetcar, 1907 A76

#9N336, Double-decker bus, 1919. #9N337, Double-decker bus, 1925. #9N338, Electrobus, 1933. #9N339, Double-decker bus, 1970. #9N340, Elongated bus, 1973.

**1973, Apr. 30 Litho. *Perf. 14***

| | | | | |
|---|---|---|---|---|
| **9N335** | A76 | 20pf gray & multi | .35 | .30 |
| **9N336** | A76 | 30pf gray & multi | .75 | .45 |
| **9N337** | A76 | 40pf gray & multi | 1.10 | .70 |

**1973, Sept. 14**

| | | | | |
|---|---|---|---|---|
| **9N338** | A76 | 20pf gray & multi | .35 | .30 |
| **9N339** | A76 | 30pf gray & multi | 1.10 | .45 |
| **9N340** | A76 | 40pf gray & multi | 1.10 | .70 |
| | | *Nos. 9N335-9N340 (6)* | 4.75 | 2.90 |

Public transportation in Berlin.

### Portrait Type of 1971

Design: 40pf, Ludwig Tieck (1773-1853), poet and writer, by Carl Christian Vogel von Vogelstein.

**1973, May 25 Photo. *Perf. 14***
**9N341** A69 40pf multicolored .70 .40

Johann Joachim Quantz (1697-1773), Flutist and Composer — A77

**1973, June 12 Engr. *Perf. 14***
**9N342** A77 40pf black .75 .60

### Souvenir Sheet

50 Years of Broadcasting — A78

**1973, Aug. 23 Litho. *Perf. 14***
**9N343** A78 Sheet of 4 3.75 3.75
*a.* A78 20pf Speaker, set, 1926 .90 .60
*b.* A78 30pf Hans Bredow .90 .90
*c.* A78 40pf Girl, TV, tape recorder .90 .90
*d.* A78 70pf TV camera .90 1.25

50 years of German broadcasting. Sold for 1.80m.

Georg W. von Knobelsdorff A79

**1974, Feb. 15 Engr. *Perf. 14***
**9N344** A79 20pf chocolate .45 .30

275th anniversary of the birth of Georg Wenzelslaus von Knobelsdorff (1699-1753), architect.

Gustav R. Kirchhoff — A80

**1974, Feb. 15 Litho. & Engr.**
**9N345** A80 30pf gray & dk grn .35 .35

Sesquicentennial of the birth of Gustav Robert Kirchhoff (1824-1887), physicist.

Airlift Memorial, Allied Flags — A81

**1974, Apr. 17 Photo. *Perf. 14***
**9N346** A81 90pf multicolored 2.25 1.50

End of the Allied airlift into Berlin, 25th anniv.

Adolf Slaby and Waves — A82

**1974, Apr. 17 Litho. *Perf. 14***
**9N347** A82 40pf black & red .55 .40

125th anniversary of the birth of Adolf Slaby (1849-1913), radio pioneer.

School Seal Showing Athena and Hermes — A83

**1974, July 13 Photo. *Perf. 14***
**9N348** A83 50pf multicolored .70 .45

400th anniversary of the Gray Brothers' School, a secondary Franciscan school.

Berlin-Tegel Airport — A84

### Lithographed and Engraved

**1974, Oct. 15 *Perf. 14***
**9N349** A84 50pf multicolored 1.00 .60

Opening of Berlin-Tegel Airport and Terminal, Nov. 1, 1974.

Venus, by F. E. Meyer, c. 1775 — A85

Gottfried Schadow — A86

Berlin Porcelain: 40pf, "Astronomy," by W. C. Meyer, c. 1772. 50pf, "Justice," by J. G. Müller, c. 1785.

**1974, Oct. 29 Litho. *Perf. 14***

| | | | | |
|---|---|---|---|---|
| **9N350** | A85 | 30pf carmine & multi | .55 | .45 |
| **9N351** | A85 | 40pf carmine & multi | .60 | .55 |
| **9N352** | A85 | 50pf carmine & multi | .70 | .70 |
| | | *Nos. 9N350-9N352 (3)* | 1.85 | 1.70 |

**1975, Jan. 15 Engr. *Perf. 14***
**9N353** A86 50pf maroon .75 .55

Johann Gottfried Schadow (1764-1850), sculptor.

S.S. Princess Charlotte A87

Ships: 40pf, S.S. Siegfried. 50pf, S.S. Sperber. 60pf, M.S. Vaterland. 70pf, M.S. Moby Dick.

**1975, Feb. 14 Litho. *Perf. 14***

| | | | | |
|---|---|---|---|---|
| **9N354** | A87 | 30pf gray & multi | .60 | .30 |
| **9N355** | A87 | 40pf olive & multi | .60 | .30 |
| **9N356** | A87 | 50pf ultra & multi | 1.10 | .70 |
| **9N357** | A87 | 60pf red brn & multi | 1.10 | .70 |
| **9N358** | A87 | 70pf dk blue & multi | 1.50 | 1.40 |
| | | *Nos. 9N354-9N358 (5)* | 4.90 | 3.40 |

Berlin passenger ships

### Industry Type of Germany

**1975-82 Engr. *Perf. 14***

**Design A380**

| | | | | |
|---|---|---|---|---|
| **9N359** | 5pf | Symphonie satellite | .25 | .25 |
| **9N360** | 10pf | Electric train | .25 | .25 |
| **9N361** | 20pf | Old Weser lighthouse | .25 | .25 |
| **9N362** | 30pf | Rescue helicopter | .35 | .25 |
| **9N363** | 40pf | Space shuttle | .50 | .25 |
| **9N364** | 50pf | Radar station | .50 | .25 |
| **9N365** | 60pf | X-ray machine | .80 | .35 |
| **9N366** | 70pf | Shipbuilding | .90 | .45 |
| **9N367** | 80pf | Tractor | .90 | .25 |
| **9N368** | 100pf | Coal excavator | .90 | .45 |
| **9N368A** | 110pf | TV camera | 1.40 | 1.10 |
| **9N369** | 120pf | Chemical plant | 1.25 | .90 |
| **9N369A** | 130pf | Brewery | 2.25 | 1.10 |
| **9N370** | 140pf | Heating plant | 1.25 | 1.25 |
| **9N371** | 150pf | Power shovel | 3.00 | 1.10 |
| **9N372** | 160pf | Blast furnace | 2.90 | 1.25 |
| **9N373** | 180pf | Payloader | 3.00 | 1.90 |
| **9N373A** | 190pf | As #9N371 | 3.00 | 2.10 |
| **9N374** | 200pf | Oil drill platform | 1.60 | .45 |
| **9N375** | 230pf | Frankfurt airport | 2.40 | 1.90 |
| **9N375A** | 250pf | Airport | 4.00 | 2.10 |
| **9N375B** | 300pf | Electric railroad | 4.00 | 2.10 |
| **9N376** | 500pf | Radio telescope | 5.75 | 3.75 |
| | | *Nos. 9N359-9N376 (23)* | 41.40 | 24.00 |

Issued: 40, 50, 100pf, 5/15; 10, 30, 70pf, 8/14; 80, 120, 160pf, 10/15; 5, 140, 200pf, 11/14; 20, 500pf, 2/17/76; 60pf, 11/16/78; 230pf, 5/17/79; 150, 180pf, 7/12/79; 110, 130, 300pf, 6/16/82; 190, 250pf, 7/15/82.

Ferdinand Sauerbruch — A88

**Lithographed and Engraved**

**1975, May 15** ***Perf. 13½x14***
**9N379** A88 50pf dull red & dk brn .75 .55

Ferdinand Sauerbruch (1875-1951) surgeon, birth centenary.

Gymnasts' Emblem — A89

**1975, May 15** **Photo.** ***Perf. 14***
**9N380** A89 40pf green, gold & blk .55 .35

6th Gymnaestrada, Berlin, July 1-5.

Lovis Corinth (1858-1925), Self-portrait, 1900 — A90

**1975, July 15** **Photo.** ***Perf. 14***
**9N381** A90 50pf multicolored .75 .55

**Architecture Type of Germany**

Houses, Naunynstrasse, Berlin-Kreuzberg.

**1975, July 15** **Litho. & Engr.**
**9N382** A381 50pf multicolored .75 .60

European Architectural Heritage Year.

Paul Löbe and Reichstag A92

**1975, Nov. 14** **Engr.** ***Perf. 14***
**9N383** A92 50pf copper red .75 .55

Paul Löbe (1875-1967), president of German Parliament 1920-1932, birth centenary.

Grain — A93

**1976, Jan. 5** **Photo.** ***Perf. 14***
**9N384** A93 70pf green & yellow .75 .60

Green Week International Agricultural Exhibition, Berlin, 50th anniversary.

Hockey A94

**1976, May 13** **Engr.** ***Perf. 14***
**9N385** A94 30pf green .70 .35

Women's World Hockey Championships.

Treble Clef — A95

**1976, May 13** **Photo.**
**9N386** A95 40pf multicolored .75 .45

German Choir Festival.

Berlin Fire Brigade Emblem — A96

**1976, May 13** **Litho.**
**9N387** A96 50pf red & multi 1.25 .75

Berlin Fire Brigade, 125th anniversary.

Sailboat on Havel River — A97

Berlin Views: 40pf, Spandau Castle. 50pf, Tiergarten.

**1976, Nov. 16** **Engr.** ***Perf. 14***
**9N388** A97 30pf blue & blk .55 .35
**9N389** A97 40pf brown & blk .75 .35
**9N390** A97 50pf green & blk .85 .35
*Nos. 9N388-9N390 (3)* 2.15 1.05

See Nos. 9N422-9N424.

**Castle Type of Germany**

10pf, Glücksburg. 20pf, 190pf, Pfaueninsel. 25pf, Gemen. 30pf, Ludwigstein. 40pf, Eltz. 50pf, Neuschwanstein. 60pf, Marksburg. 70pf, Mespelbrunn. 90pf, Vischering. 200pf, Bürresheim. 210pf, Schwanenburg. 230pf, Lichtenberg.

**1977-79** **Typo.** ***Perf. 14***
**9N391** A406 10pf gray blue .25 .25
*a.* Bklt. pane, 4 #9N391, 2 each #9N394, 9N396 8.00 *10.50*
*b.* Bklt. pane, 4 #9N391, 2 #9N394, 2 #9N440 4.00 *6.75*
*c.* Bklt. pane, 4 #9N391, 2 #9N440, 2 #9N442 8.75 *15.00*
*d.* Bklt. pane, 2 each #9N391, 9N394, 9N440-9N441 15.00 *22.50*
**9N392** A406 20pf orange .25 .25
**9N393** A406 25pf crimson .35 .35
**9N394** A406 30pf olive .25 .25
**9N395** A406 40pf blue green .30 .25
**9N396** A406 50pf rose car .55 .25
**9N397** A406 60pf brown .95 .45
**9N398** A406 70pf blue .95 .45
**9N399** A406 90pf dark blue .85 .75
**9N400** A406 190pf red brown 1.40 1.40
**9N401** A406 200pf green 1.40 1.40
**9N402** A406 210pf red brown 2.00 1.50
**9N403** A406 230pf dark green 2.00 1.50
*Nos. 9N391-9N403 (13)* 11.50 9.05

Issued in sheets of 100 and coils. Every fifth coil stamp has a control number on the back.
Issued: 60pf, 200pf, 1/13; 40pf, 190pf, 2/16; 10pf, 20pf, 30pf, 4/14; 50pf, 70pf, 5/17; 230pf, 11/16/78; 25pf, 90pf, 1/11/79; 210pf, 2/14/79.
See Nos. 9N438-9N445.

Eugenie d'Alton, by Rausch — A98

**1977, Jan. 13** **Photo.** ***Perf. 14***
**9N404** A98 50pf violet black .75 .55

Christian Daniel Rausch (1777-1857), sculptor, birth bicentenary.

Eduard Gaertner (1801-77), Painter — A99

**1977, Feb. 16** **Litho. & Engr.**
**9N405** A99 40pf lt grn, grn & blk .55 .35

Fountain, by Georg Kolbe — A100

**1977, Apr. 14** **Photo.** ***Perf. 14***
**9N406** A100 30pf dark olive .55 .35

Georg Kolbe (1877-1947), sculptor.

"Bear each other's burdens" A101

**1977, May 17** **Litho.** ***Perf. 14***
**9N407** A101 40pf green blk & yel .55 .35

17th meeting of German Protestants (Evangelical Synod), Berlin.

Patent Office, Berlin-Kreuzberg — A102

**1977, July 13** **Litho. & Engr.**
**9N408** A102 60pf gray & red 1.50 .65

Centenary of German patent laws.

Telephones, 1905 and 1977 A103

Painting by George Grosz (1893-1959) A104

**1977, July 13** **Litho.**
**9N409** A103 50pf multicolored 1.75 1.00

International Broadcasting Exhibition, Berlin, Aug. 26-Sept. 4, and centenary of telephone in Germany.

**1977, July 13**
**9N410** A104 70pf multicolored .90 .90

15th European Art Exhibition, Berlin, Aug. 14-Oct. 16.

Rhinecanthus Aculeatus — A105

Designs: 30pf, Paddlefish. 40pf, Tortoise. 50pf, Rhinoceros iguana. Designs include statue of iguanodon from Aquarium entrance.

**1977, Aug. 16** **Photo.** ***Perf. 14***
**9N411** A105 20pf multicolored .45 .45
**9N412** A105 30pf multicolored .70 .60
**9N413** A105 40pf multicolored .95 .75
**9N414** A105 50pf multicolored 1.40 .90
*Nos. 9N411-9N414 (4)* 3.50 2.70

25th anniv. of the reopening of Berlin Aquarium.

Walter Kollo (1878-1940), Composer — A106

**1978, Jan. 12** **Engr.** ***Perf. 14***
**9N415** A106 50pf brn, red & dk brn 1.00 .65

Chamber of Commerce Emblem — A107

**1978, Apr. 13** **Engr.** ***Perf. 14***
**9N416** A107 90pf dk blue & red 1.25 1.25

American Chamber of Commerce in Germany, 75th anniversary.

Albrecht von Graefe — A108

**1978, May 22** **Engr.** ***Perf. 14***
**9N417** A108 30pf red brn & blk .55 .35

Dr. von Graefe (1828-70) ophthalmologist.

Friedrich Ludwig Jahn — A109

**1978, July 13** **Engr.** ***Perf. 14***
**9N418** A109 50pf dk carmine .75 .55

Friedrich Ludwig Jahn (1778-1852), founder of organized gymnastics.

Swimmers — A110

**1978, Aug. 17 Litho. *Perf. 14***

**9N419** A110 40pf multicolored 1.00 .80

3rd World Swimming Championships, Berlin, Aug. 18-28.

The Boat, by Karl Hofer — A111

**1978, Oct. 12 Photo. *Perf. 14***

**9N420** A111 50pf multicolored .75 .60

Karl Hofer (1878-1955), painter.

National Library A112

**1978, Nov. 16 Engr. *Perf. 14***

**9N421** A112 90pf red & olive 1.40 .95

Opening of new National Library building.

### Views Type of 1976

Berlin Views: 40pf, Belvedere, Charlottenburg Castle. 50pf, Shell House on Landwehr Canal. 60pf, Village Church, Alt-Lichtenrade.

**1978, Nov. 16**

**9N422** A97 40pf green & blk .60 .35
**9N423** A97 50pf lilac & blk .75 .60
**9N424** A97 60pf brown & blk .90 .70
*Nos. 9N422-9N424 (3)* 2.25 1.65

International Conference Center — A113

### Photogravure and Engraved

**1979, Feb. 14 *Perf. 14***

**9N425** A113 60pf multicolored 1.10 .65

Opening of Intl. Conference Center in Berlin.

A114

A115

**1979, May 17 Litho. *Perf. 14***

**9N426** A114 60pf German eagles 1.40 1.00

Cent. of German Natl. Printing Bureau.

**1979, July 12 Photo. *Perf. 14***

**9N427** A115 60pf TV screen, emblem 1.00 .75

Intl. Broadcasting Exhibition, Berlin.

Target and Arrows A116

**1979, July 12**

**9N428** A116 50pf multicolored .75 .55

World Archery Championships, Berlin.

Moses Mendelssohn A117

**1979, Aug. 9 Engr. *Perf. 14***

**9N429** A117 90pf black 1.25 .75

Mendelssohn (1729-86), philosopher.

Gas Lamp — A118

Historic Street Lanterns: 40pf, Carbon arc lamp. 50pf, Hanging gas lamps. 60pf, 5-armed candelabra.

**1979, Aug. 9 Litho.**

**9N430** A118 10pf multicolored .35 .25
**9N431** A118 40pf multicolored .75 .60
**9N432** A118 50pf multicolored 1.10 .60
**9N433** A118 60pf multicolored 1.10 1.00
*Nos. 9N430-9N433 (4)* 3.30 2.45

300 years of street lighting in Berlin.

Orchid A119

**1979, Aug. 9**

**9N434** A119 50pf multicolored .85 .55

Botanical Gardens, Berlin, 300th anniv.

Berlin Poster Columns, 125th Anniversary A120

### Lithographed and Engraved

**1979, Nov. 14 *Perf. 14***

**9N435** A120 50pf multicolored 1.40 .75

### Castle Type of Germany

**1979-82 Typo. *Perf. 14***

**9N438** A406 35pf Lichtenstein .30 .30
**9N439** A406 40pf Wolfsburg .55 .30
**9N440** A406 50pf Inzlingen .60 .30
**9N441** A406 60pf Rheydt .90 .45
**9N442** A406 80pf Wilhelmsthal .60 .30
**9N443** A406 120pf Charlottenburg 1.00 .90
**9N444** A406 280pf Ahrensburg 3.50 2.25
**9N445** A406 300pf Herrenhausen 3.50 2.25
*Nos. 9N438-9N445 (8)* 10.95 7.05

Issued: 60pf, 11/14; 40pf, 50pf, 2/14/80; 35pf, 80pf, 30pf, 6/16/82; 120pf, 280pf, 7/15/82.

World Map Showing Continental Drift — A121

**1980, Feb. 14 Litho. *Perf. 14***

**9N451** A121 60pf multicolored 1.40 1.00

Alfred Wegener (1880-1930), geophysicist and meteorologist; founded theory of continental drift.

German Catholics Day — A122

Cardinal Count Preysing (1880-1950).

**1980, May 8 Engr. *Perf. 14***

**9N452** A122 50pf blk & car rose .75 .55

Prussian Museum, Berlin, 150th Anniv. — A123

Designs: 40pf, Angel, enamel medallion, 12th cent. 60pf, Monks Reading, oak sculpture, by Ernest Barlach (1870-1938).

**1980, July 10 Litho. *Perf. 14***

**9N453** A123 40pf multicolored .75 .45
**9N454** A123 60pf multicolored 1.00 .60

Von Steuben Leading Troops — A124

**1980, Aug. 14 Litho. *Perf. 14***

**9N455** A124 40pf multicolored 1.00 .55

Friedrich Wilhelm von Steuben (1730-94).

Robert Stolz (1880-1975), Composer A125

**1980, Aug. 14**

**9N456** A125 60pf dk blue & bis 1.00 .75

Lilienthal Memorial — A126

Designs: 50pf, Grosse Neugierde Memorial, 1835. 60pf, Lookout tower, Grunewald Memorial to Kaiser Wilhelm I.

**1980, Nov. 13 Engr. *Perf. 14***

**9N457** A126 40pf dk green & blk .75 .35
**9N458** A126 50pf brown & blk .80 .75
**9N459** A126 60pf dk blue & blk 1.25 .75
*Nos. 9N457-9N459 (3)* 2.80 1.85

Von Gontard and Kleist Park Colonnades, Berlin — A127

**1981, Jan. 15 Litho. *Perf. 14***

**9N460** A127 50pf multicolored .90 .60

Karl Philipp von Gontard (1731-91), architect.

Achim von Arnim (1781-1831), Poet — A128

**1981, Jan. 15 Engr.**

**9N461** A128 60pf dark green .90 .60

Adelbert von Chamisso (1781-1838), Poet — A129

**1981, Jan. 15 Litho.**

**9N462** A129 60pf brn & gldn brn .90 .60

Berlin-Kreuzberg, Liberation Monument, 1813 — A130

**1981, Feb. 12 Engr. *Perf. 14***

**9N463** A130 40pf brown 1.10 .75

Karl Friedrich Schinkel (1781-1841), architect, 400th anniversary of birth.

Arts and Science Medal, Awarded 1842-1933 — A131

**1981, July 16 Litho. *Perf. 14***

**9N464** A131 40pf multicolored .75 .55

"Prussia — an attempt at a balance" exhibition.

Amor and Psyche, by Reinhold Begas (1831-1911) A132

**1981, July 16 Photo.**

**9N465** A132 50pf multicolored .75 .55

Intl. Telecommunications Exhibition — A133

**1981, July 16** **Litho.**

9N466 A133 60pf multicolored 1.25 .75

Peter Beuth (1781-1853), Constitutional Law Expert — A134

**Lithographed and Engraved**

**1981, Nov. 12** ***Perf. 14***

9N467 A134 60pf gold & black .75 .60

Nijinsky, by Georg Kolbe, 1914 — A135

20th Century Sculptures: 60pf, Mother Earth II, by Ernst Barlach, 1920. 90pf, Flora Kneeling, by Richard Scheibe, 1930.

**1981, Nov. 12** **Photo.**

| | | | | | |
|---|---|---|---|---|---|
| 9N468 | A135 | 40pf multicolored | .55 | .35 |
| 9N469 | A135 | 60pf multicolored | .90 | .60 |
| 9N470 | A135 | 90pf multicolored | 1.25 | 1.00 |
| | | *Nos. 9N468-9N470 (3)* | 2.70 | 1.95 |

750th Anniv. of Spandau A136

**Lithographed and Engraved**

**1982, Feb. 18** ***Perf. 14***

9N471 A136 60pf multicolored 1.25 .90

Berlin Philharmonic Centenary — A137

**Lithographed and Embossed**

**1982, Apr. 15** ***Perf. 14***

9N472 A137 60pf multicolored 1.10 .60

Salzburg Emigration to Prussia, 250th Anniv. — A138

**& 1982, May 5** **Litho.** **Engr.**

9N473 A138 50pf multicolored .75 .55

Italian Stone Carriers, by Max Pechstein — A139

80pf, Two Girls Bathing, by Otto Mueller.

**1982, July 15** **Litho.** ***Perf. 14***

| | | | | |
|---|---|---|---|---|
| 9N474 | A139 | 50pf multicolored | .90 | .70 |
| 9N475 | A139 | 80pf multicolored | 1.40 | 1.00 |

Villa Borsig — A140

**1982, Nov. 10** **Engr.** ***Perf. 14***

| | | | | |
|---|---|---|---|---|
| 9N476 | A140 | 50pf shown | 1.10 | .70 |
| 9N477 | A140 | 60pf Sts. Peter and Paul Church | 1.10 | .80 |
| 9N478 | A140 | 80pf Villa von der Heydt | 1.50 | .90 |
| | | *Nos. 9N476-9N478 (3)* | 3.70 | 2.40 |

State Theater, Charlottenburg, 1790 — A141

**1982, Nov. 10** **Litho. & Engr.**

9N479 A141 80pf multicolored 1.60 1.10

Carl Gotthard Langhans (1732-1808), architect.

A142

A142a

Various street pumps and fire hydrants, 1900.

**1983, Jan. 13** **Litho.** ***Perf. 14***

| | | | | |
|---|---|---|---|---|
| 9N480 | A142 | 50pf multi | 1.10 | .75 |
| 9N481 | A142 | 60pf multi | 1.40 | .75 |
| 9N482 | A142 | 80pf multi | 1.60 | 1.25 |
| 9N483 | A142 | 120pf multi | 2.25 | 2.00 |
| | | *Nos. 9N480-9N483 (4)* | 6.35 | 4.75 |

**1983, Feb. 8** **Engr.** ***Perf. 14***

9N484 A142a 80pf dark brown 1.75 1.40

Berlin-Koblenz Telegraph Service sesquicentennial.

Portrait of Barbara Campanini, 1745, by Antoine Pesne (1683-1757) A143

**1983, May 5** **Photo.** ***Perf. 14***

9N485 A143 50pf multicolored .90 .65

Joachim Ringelnatz (1883-1934), Painter and Writer — A144

**1983, July 14** **Litho.** ***Perf. 14***

9N486 A144 50pf Silhouette 1.00 .75

Intl. Radio Exhibition, Sept. 2-11 — A145

**1983, July 14**

9N487 A145 80pf Nipkow's phototelegraphy diagram 1.60 1.25

Ancient Artwork, Berlin Museum A146

30pf, Bust of Queen Cleopatra VII, 69-30 B.C. 50pf, Statue of Egyptian Couple, Giza, 2400 B.C. 60pf, Stone God with Beaded Turban, Mexico, 300 B.C. 80pf, Enamel Plate, 16th cent.

**1984, Jan. 12** **Litho.** ***Perf. 14***

| | | | | |
|---|---|---|---|---|
| 9N488 | A146 | 30pf multicolored | 1.00 | .75 |
| 9N489 | A146 | 50pf multicolored | 1.40 | 1.00 |
| 9N490 | A146 | 60pf multicolored | 1.75 | 1.40 |
| 9N491 | A146 | 80pf multicolored | 2.25 | 1.60 |
| | | *Nos. 9N488-9N491 (4)* | 6.40 | 4.75 |

Electricity Centenary — A147

Design: Allegorical figure holding light bulb (symbol of electric power).

**1984, May 8** **Litho.** ***Perf. 14***

9N492 A147 50pf black & org .90 .65

Conference Emblem — A148

**1984, May 8**

9N493 A148 60pf multicolored 1.10 .75

European Ministers of Culture, 4th Conf.

Erich Klausener (1885-1934), Chairman of Catholic Action — A149

**1984, May 8** **Engr.** ***Perf. 14x13½***

9N494 A149 80pf dark green 1.10 .75

Alfred Brehm (1829-1884), Zoologist — A150

**Lithographed and Engraved**

**1984, Apr. 18** ***Perf. 14***

9N495 A150 80pf Brehm, white stork 1.90 1.25

Ernst Ludwig Heim (1747-1834), Botanist — A151

**1984, Aug. 21** **Engr.** ***Perf. 14***

9N496 A151 50pf brown & blk 1.10 .75

Sunflowers, by Karl Schmidt-Rottluff (1884-1976) A152

**1984, Nov. 8** **Litho.** ***Perf. 14***

9N497 A152 60pf multi 1.10 .75

Bettina von Arnim (1785-1859), Writer — A153

**1985, Feb. 21** **Litho. & Engr.**

9N498 A153 50pf multicolored 1.00 .80

Wilhelm von Humboldt (1767-1835), Statesman A154

**1985, Feb. 21** **Engr.**

9N499 A154 80pf blue, blk & red 1.50 1.25

1985 Berlin Horticultural Show — A155

**1985, Apr. 16** **Litho.** ***Perf. 14***

9N500 A155 80pf Symbolic flower 1.40 1.10

Berlin Bourse, 300th Anniv. A156

**1985, May 7** **Litho. & Engr.**

9N501 A156 50pf multicolored 1.10 .80

Otto Klemperer (1885-1973), Conductor — A157

**1985, May 7** **Engr.**

9N502 A157 60pf dp blue violet 1.40 1.10

Telefunken Camera, 1936 — A158

**1985, July 16 Litho. *Perf. 14***

| | | | | |
|---|---|---|---|---|
| 9N503 | A158 80pf multicolored | | 1.90 | 1.50 |

German Television, 50th anniv., Intl. Telecommunications Exhibition, Berlin.

9th World Gynecological Congress — A159

Design: Emblem of the Intl. Federation for Gynecology and birth aid.

**1985, July 16 Photo. *Perf. 13½x14***

| | | | | |
|---|---|---|---|---|
| 9N504 | A159 60pf pale yel, ap grn & dp grn | | 1.10 | .80 |

Edict of Potsdam, 300th Anniv. A160

**Lithographed and Engraved**

**1985, Oct. 15 *Perf. 14***

| | | | | |
|---|---|---|---|---|
| 9N505 | A160 50pf dk bluish lilac | | .90 | .70 |

Kurt Tucholsky (1890-1935), Novelist, Journalist — A161

**1985, Nov. 12 Litho. *Perf. 14***

| | | | | |
|---|---|---|---|---|
| 9N506 | A161 80pf multi | | 1.75 | 1.10 |

Wilhelm Furtwangler (1886-1954), Composer — A162

Score from Sonata in D Sharp.

**Lithographed and Engraved**

**1986, Jan. 16 *Perf. 14***

| | | | | |
|---|---|---|---|---|
| 9N507 | A162 80pf multi | | 1.90 | 1.60 |

Ludwig Mies van der Rohe (1886-1969), Architect — A163

**1986, Feb. 13**

| | | | | |
|---|---|---|---|---|
| 9N508 | A163 50pf multi | | 1.10 | 1.25 |

New Natl. Gallery, Berlin.

16th European Communities Day — A164

**1986, Apr. 10 Litho. *Perf. 14***

| | | | | |
|---|---|---|---|---|
| 9N509 | A164 60pf Flags | | .95 | 1.00 |

Leopold von Ranke (1795-1886), Historian — A165

Gottfried Benn (1886-1956), Writer and Physician — A166

**1986, May 5 Litho.**

| | | | | |
|---|---|---|---|---|
| 9N510 | A165 80pf brn blk & tan | | 1.75 | 1.40 |

**Engr.**

| | | | | |
|---|---|---|---|---|
| 9N511 | A166 80pf brt blue | | 1.75 | 1.40 |

Portals and Gateways A167

**1986, June 20 Litho. & Engr.**

| | | | | |
|---|---|---|---|---|
| 9N512 | A167 50pf Charlotteburg Gate | | 1.50 | 1.25 |
| 9N513 | A167 60pf Gryphon Gate, Glienicke Castle | | 1.50 | 1.25 |
| 9N514 | A167 80pf Elephant Gate, Berlin Zoo | | 1.75 | 1.75 |
| | *Nos. 9N512-9N514 (3)* | | 4.75 | 4.25 |

King Frederick the Great — A168

Painting: The Flute Concert (detail), by Adolph von Menzel.

**1986, Aug. 14 Litho. *Perf. 14***

| | | | | |
|---|---|---|---|---|
| 9N515 | A168 80pf multicolored | | 1.75 | 1.40 |

**Famous Women Type of Germany**

Designs: 5pf, Emma Ihrer (1857-1911), politician, labor leader. 10pf, Paula Modersohn-Becker (1876-1907), painter. 20pf, Cilly Aussem (1909-63), tennis champion. 40pf, Maria Sibylla Merian. 50pf, Christine Teusch. 60pf, Dorothea Erxleben (1715-62), physician. 80pf, Clara Schumann. 100pf, Therese Giehse (1898-1975), actress. 130pf, Lise Meitner (1878-1968), physicist. 140pf, Cecile Vogt (1875-1962), neurologist. 170pf, Hannah Arendt (1906-75), American political scientist. 180pf, Lotte Lehmann (1888-1976), soprano. 240pf, Mathilde Franziska Anneke, (1817-84), American author. 250pf, Queen Louise of Prussia (1776-1810). 300pf, Fanny Hensel (1805-1847), composer-conductor. 350pf, Hedwig Dransfeld (1871-1925), women's rights activist. 500pf, Alice Salomon (1872-1948), feminist and social activist.

**Type A602**

**1986-89 Engr. *Perf. 14***

| | | | |
|---|---|---|---|
| 9N516 | 5pf bluish gray & org brn | .35 | *1.50* |
| 9N517 | 10pf vio & yel brn | .35 | *1.40* |
| 9N518 | 20pf lake & Prus bl | 1.50 | *3.75* |
| 9N519 | 40pf dp bl & dk lil rose | 1.25 | *3.75* |
| 9N520 | 50pf gray ol & Prus bl | 1.90 | *2.50* |
| 9N521 | 60pf dp vio & grnsh blk | .75 | *3.75* |
| 9N522 | 80pf dk grn & lt red brn | 1.10 | *2.50* |
| 9N523 | 100pf dk red & grnsh blk | 1.50 | 1.50 |
| 9N524 | 130pf Prus bl & dk vio | 3.50 | *11.00* |
| 9N525 | 140pf blk & dk ol bis | 3.75 | *11.00* |
| 9N526 | 170pf gray grn & dk brn | 2.25 | *9.00* |
| 9N527 | 180pf bl & brn vio | 3.50 | *11.00* |
| 9N528 | 240pf Prus bl & yel brn | 3.00 | *13.00* |
| 9N529 | 250pf dp lil rose & dp bl | 7.25 | *21.00* |
| 9N530 | 300pf dk vio & sage grn | 7.50 | *19.00* |
| 9N531 | 350pf gray grn & lake | 5.25 | *15.00* |
| 9N532 | 500pf slate grn & brt ver | 8.25 | *32.50* |
| | *Nos. 9N516-9N532 (17)* | 52.95 | *163.15* |

Issued: 50pf, 80pf, 11/1/86; 40pf, 9/17/87; 10pf, 4/4/88; 20pf, 130pf, 5/5/88; 60pf, 100pf, 170pf, 240pf, 350pf, 11/10/88; 500pf, 1/12/89; 5pf, 2/9/89; 180pf, 250pf, 7/13/89; 140pf, 300pf, 8/10/89.

**Berlin 750th Anniv. Type of Germany**

Designs: a, Berlin, 1650, engraving by Caspar Merian. b, Charlottenburg Castle, c. 1830. c, AEG Company turbine construction building, by architect Walter Behrens, 1909. d, Philharmonic Concert Hall and Chamber Music Rooms on the Kemperplatz, 1987.

**1987, Jan. 15 Litho. *Perf. 14***

| | | | |
|---|---|---|---|
| 9N536 | A604 80pf like #1496 | 1.90 | 1.50 |

**Souvenir Sheet**

***Perf. 14x14½***

| | | | |
|---|---|---|---|
| 9N537 | Sheet of 4 | 4.25 | 4.25 |
| *a.* | A604 40pf multicolored | .90 | .75 |
| *b.* | A604 50pf multicolored | .90 | .75 |
| *c.* | A604 60pf multicolored | .90 | .90 |
| *d.* | A604 80pf multicolored | 1.00 | 1.25 |

No. 9N537 contains four 43x25mm stamps.

Louise Schroeder (1887-1957), Politican — A169

**1987, Feb. 12 Engr. *Perf. 14***

| | | | |
|---|---|---|---|
| 9N538 | A169 50pf sep & dk red | 1.10 | 1.10 |

Settlement of Bohemians at Rixdorf, 250th Anniv. — A170

Bohemian refugees, bas-relief detail from monument to King Friedrich Wilhelm I of Prussia, 1912.

**1987, May 5 Litho. & Engr.**

| | | | |
|---|---|---|---|
| 9N539 | A170 50pf sep & pale gray grn | .80 | .90 |

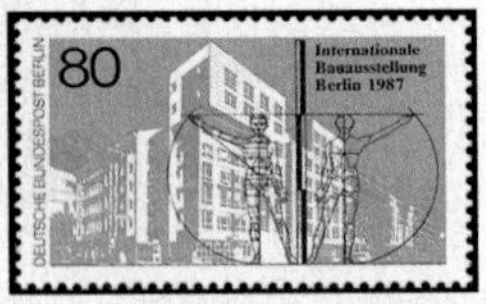


1987 Intl. Architecture Exhibition — A171

**1987, May 5 Litho. *Perf. 14x14½***

| | | | |
|---|---|---|---|
| 9N540 | A171 80pf lt ultra, sil & blk | 1.40 | 1.10 |

14th Int'l. Botanical Congress — A172

**1987, July 16 Litho. *Perf. 14***

| | | | |
|---|---|---|---|
| 9N541 | A172 60pf multicolored | .90 | 1.00 |

Int'l. Radio Exhibition A173

**1987, Aug. 20**

| | | | |
|---|---|---|---|
| 9N542 | A173 80pf Gramophone, compact disc | 1.25 | .95 |

**Historic Sites and Objects Type of Germany**

Designs: 5pf, Brunswick Lion. 10pf, Frankfurt Airport. 20pf, No. 9N550, Queen Nefertiti, bust, Egyptian Museum, Berlin. 30pf, Corner tower, Celle Castle, 14th cent. 40pf, Chile House, Hamburg. 50pf, Filigree tracery on spires, Freiburg Cathedral. 60pf, Bavaria Munich, bronze statue above the Theresienwiese, Hall of Fame. No. 9N551, Heligoland. 80pf, Entrance to Zollern II, coal mine, Dortmund. 100pf, Altotting Chapel, Bavaria. 120pf, Schleswig Cathedral. 140pf, Bronze flagon from Reinheim. 300pf, Hambach Castle. 350pf, Externsteine Bridge near Horn-Bad Meinberg.

**Type A623**

**1987-90 Typo. *Perf. 14***

| | | | |
|---|---|---|---|
| 9N543 | 5pf Prus bl & gray | .30 | *.45* |
| 9N544 | 10pf lt chalky bl & slate bl | .35 | .35 |
| 9N545 | 20pf dull blue & tan | .35 | *.75* |
| 9N546 | 30pf aqua & org brn | .95 | .95 |
| 9N547 | 40pf ultra, dk red brn & org red | 1.25 | *2.10* |
| 9N548 | 50pf ultra & yel brn | 1.50 | 1.10 |
| 9N549 | 60pf cob & pale gray | 1.50 | 1.10 |
| 9N550 | 70pf dull bl & fawn | 1.50 | *2.50* |
| 9N551 | 70pf vio bl & henna brn | 2.10 | *4.50* |
| 9N552 | 80pf cob & pale gray | 1.50 | 1.10 |
| *a.* | Bklt. pane of 8 (4 10pf, 2 50pf, 2 80pf) ('89) | 22.50 | *52.50* |
| 9N553 | 100pf brt bluish grn & olive bis | 1.10 | *1.50* |
| *a.* | Bklt. pane of 8 (2 each 10pf, 60pf, 80pf, 100pf) | 45.00 | *90.00* |
| 9N554 | 120pf brn org & lt grnsh bl | 2.25 | *3.50* |
| 9N555 | 140pf tan & lt grn | 2.25 | *4.25* |
| 9N556 | 300pf dk red brn & tan | 4.50 | 4.50 |
| 9N557 | 350pf brt ultra & ol bis | 4.50 | *7.50* |
| | *Nos. 9N543-9N557 (15)* | 25.90 | 36.15 |

Issued: 30pf, 50pf, 60pf, 80pf, 11/6/87; 10pf, 300pf, 1/14/88; #9N550, 120pf, 7/14/88; 20pf, 140pf, 1/12/89; 100pf, 350pf, 2/9/89; 5pf, 2/15/90; #9N551, 6/21/90.

European Culture — A175

**1988, Jan. 14 Litho. *Perf. 14***

| | | | |
|---|---|---|---|
| 9N568 | A175 80pf Berlin Bear | 1.90 | 1.90 |

Urania Science Museum, Cent. A176

**1988, Feb. 18**

| | | | |
|---|---|---|---|
| 9N569 | A176 50pf multicolored | 1.40 | 1.25 |

A177

Design: Thoroughbred Foal, bronze sculpture by Renee Sintenis (1888-1965).

**1988, Feb. 18**

| | | | |
|---|---|---|---|
| 9N570 | A177 60pf multicolored | .90 | .90 |

A178

Design: The Great Elector with Family in Berlin Castle Gardens.

**1988, May 5** **Litho. & Engr.**
**9N571** A178 50pf multicolored 1.10 1.10

The Great Elector of Brandenburg (d. 1688).

Intl. Monetary Fund and World Bank Congress, Berlin — A179

**1988, Aug. 11** **Litho.**
**9N572** A179 70pf multicolored 1.10 1.00

Berlin-Potsdam Railway, 150th Anniv. — A180

**1988, Oct. 13** **Litho.**
**9N573** A180 10pf multicolored .65 .45

*The Collector*, 1913, by Ernst Barlach (1870-1938) A181

**1988, Oct. 13**
**9N574** A181 40pf multicolored .70 .55

Berlin Airlift, 40th Anniv. — A182

**1989, May 5** **Photo.** ***Perf. 14***
**9N575** A182 60pf multicolored 1.10 1.25

13th Intl. Congress of the Supreme Audit Office, Berlin A183

**1989, May 5** **Litho.**
**9N576** A183 80pf multicolored 1.40 1.40

Ernst Reuter (1889-1953), Mayor of Berlin — A184

**Litho. & Engr.**
**1989, July 13** ***Perf. 14x14½***
**9N577** A184 100pf multicolored 1.90 1.60

Intl. Radio Exhibition, Berlin — A185

**1989, July 13** **Litho.**
**9N578** A185 100pf multicolored 1.60 1.50

Plans of the Zoological Gardens, Berlin, and Designer Peter Joseph Lenne (1789-1866) — A186

**Litho. & Engr.**
**1989, Aug. 10** ***Perf. 14***
**9N579** A186 60pf multicolored 1.50 1.25

Carl von Ossietzky (1889-1938), Awarded Nobel Peace Prize of 1935 — A187

**1989, Aug. 10** **Photo.**
**9N580** A187 100pf multicolored 1.75 1.60

450th Anniv. of the Reformation A188

Design: Nikolai Church, Spandau District.

**1989, Oct. 12** **Litho.**
**9N581** A188 60pf multicolored .95 .85

French Gymnasium, 300th Anniv. — A189

School from 1701 to 1873 and frontispiece of *Leges Gymnasie Gallici*, published in 1689.

**1989, Oct. 12** **Litho. & Engr.**
**9N582** A189 40pf multicolored .95 .85

*Journalists*, 1925, by Hannah Hoch (1889-1978) A190

**1989, Oct. 12** **Litho.** ***Perf. 13½***
**9N583** A190 100pf multicolored 1.90 1.50

**European Postal Service 500th Anniv. Type**
**Litho. & Engr.**

**1990, Jan. 12** ***Perf. 14***
**9N584** A673 100pf *The Young Post Rider* 2.50 2.10

See Austria No. 1486, Belgium No. 1332, Germany No. 1592, and DDR No. 2791.

Public Transportation, 250th Anniv. — A191

**1990, Jan. 12** **Litho.**
**9N585** A191 60pf multicolored 1.90 1.50

Ernst Rudorff (1840-1916), Conservationist — A192

**1990, Jan. 12**
**9N586** A192 60pf multicolored 1.90 1.50

People's Free Theater Organization, Cent. — A193

**1990, Feb. 15** ***Perf. 13½***
**9N587** A193 100pf multicolored 2.00 1.90

Parliament House, 40th Anniv. — A194

**1990, Feb. 15** ***Perf. 14x14½***
**9N588** A194 100pf multicolored 2.75 1.90

Bicent. of the Invention of the Barrel Organ — A195

**1990, May 3** **Litho.** ***Perf. 14***
**9N589** A195 100pf multicolored 2.00 1.75

90th German Catholics Day — A196

**1990, May 3**
**9N590** A196 60pf multicolored 1.75 1.60

German Pharmaceutical Society, Cent. — A197

**1990, Aug. 9** **Litho.** ***Perf. 14***
**9N591** A197 100pf multicolored 3.75 3.00

Adolph Diesterweg (1790-1866), Educator — A198

**1990, Sept. 27**
**9N592** A198 60pf multicolored 2.75 2.75

Stamps for Berlin were discontinued Oct. 3, 1990, when Germany and the German Democratic Republic merged. The stamps remained valid until Dec. 31, 1991.

---

## OCCUPATION SEMI-POSTAL STAMPS

Offering Plate and Berlin Bear — SP1

**Wmk. 284**

**1949, Dec. 1** **Litho.** ***Perf. 14***

| | | | | |
|---|---|---|---|---|
| **9NB1** | SP1 | 10 + 5pf grn | 35.00 | *160.00* |
| **9NB2** | SP1 | 20 + 5pf car | 35.00 | *160.00* |
| **9NB3** | SP1 | 30 + 5pf blue | 37.50 | *225.00* |
| *a.* | | Souv. sheet of 3, #9NB1-9NB3 | 500.00 | *2,100.* |
| | | Never hinged | 900.00 | |
| | | *Nos. 9NB1-9NB3 (3)* | 107.50 | *545.00* |
| | | Set, never hinged | 375.00 | |

The surtax was for Berlin victims of currency devaluation.

Harp and Laurel Branch — SP2

"Singing Angels" — SP3

**1950, Oct. 29** **Engr.** **Wmk. 116**

| | | | | |
|---|---|---|---|---|
| **9NB4** | SP2 | 10 + 5pf grn | 16.00 | *35.00* |
| **9NB5** | SP3 | 30 + 5pf dk sl bl | 32.50 | *90.00* |
| | | Set, never hinged | 140.00 | |

The surtax was to aid in reestablishing the Berlin Philharmonic Orchestra.

Young Stamp Collectors — SP4

Kaiser Wilhelm Memorial Church — SP5

**1951, Oct. 7** ***Perf. 14***

| | | | | |
|---|---|---|---|---|
| **9NB6** | SP4 | 10 + 3pf grn | 10.50 | *30.00* |
| **9NB7** | SP4 | 20 + 2pf brn red | 13.50 | *37.50* |
| | | Set, never hinged | 52.50 | |

Stamp Day, Berlin, Oct. 7, 1951.

**1953, Aug. 9** **Wmk. 284**

Design: 20pf+10pf, 30pf+15pf, Ruins of Kaiser Wilhelm Memorial Church.

**9NB8** SP5 4 + 1pf choc .25 *15.00*
**9NB9** SP5 10 + 5pf green .75 *42.50*
**9NB10** SP5 20 + 10pf car 1.40 *42.50*
**9NB11** SP5 30 + 15pf dp bl 6.00 *97.50*
*Nos. 9NB8-9NB11 (4)* 8.40 *197.50*
Set, never hinged 22.50

The surtax was to aid in reconstructing the church.

**Catalogue values for unused stamps in this section, from this point to the end of the section, are for Never Hinged items.**

Prussian Postilion — SP6

Prussian Field Postilion — SP7

**1954, Aug. 4** **Litho.** **Wmk. 284**
**9NB12** SP6 20 + 10pf multi 15.00 *30.00*

National Stamp Exhibition, Berlin, Aug. 4-8.

***Perf. 13½x14***

**1955, Oct. 27** **Wmk. 304**
**9NB13** SP7 25 + 10pf multi 6.00 *13.50*

The surtax was for the benefit of philately.

St. Otto, Bishop of Bamberg — SP8

Statues: 10pf+5pf, St. Hedwig, Duchess of Silesia. 20pf+10pf, St. Peter.

**1955, Nov. 26** **Engr.** ***Perf. 14***
**9NB14** SP8 7 + 3pf brown .75 *2.75*
**9NB15** SP8 10 + 5pf gray grn 1.40 *3.00*
**9NB16** SP8 20 + 10pf rose lil 1.90 *3.75*
*Nos. 9NB14-9NB16 (3)* 4.05 *9.50*

25th anniv. of the Bishopric of Berlin.
The surtax was for the reconstruction of destroyed churches throughout the bishopric.

Bell Type of 1951 Surcharged

***Perf. 13½x14***

**1956, Aug. 9** **Wmk. 284**
**9NB17** OS8 20pf + 10pf citron 3.75 4.00

The surtax was for help for flood victims.

Postrider of Brandenburg, 1700 — SP9

Ludwig Heck — SP10

**Wmk. 304**

**1956, Oct. 26** **Litho.** ***Perf. 14***
**9NB18** SP9 25pf + 10pf multi 2.50 3.50

The surtax was for the benefit of philately.

**1957, Sept. 7** **Engr.** ***Perf. 13½x14***
**9NB19** SP10 20pf + 10pf red & dk brn .75 .90

Dr. Ludwig Heck, zoologist and long-time director of the Berlin Zoo. The surtax was for the Zoo.

Elly Heuss-Knapp and Relaxing Mothers SP11

**1957, Nov. 30** ***Perf. 14***
**9NB20** SP11 20pf + 10pf dk red 1.40 2.40

The surtax was for welfare work among mothers.

Boy at Window — SP12

Designs: 10pf+5pf, Girl going to school. 20pf+10pf, Girl with flower and mountains. 40pf+20pf, Boy at seashore.

**1960, Sept. 15** **Litho.** **Wmk. 304**
**9NB21** SP12 7pf + 3pf dk brn & brn .25 .30
**9NB22** SP12 10pf + 5pf ol grn & slate grn .25 .30
**9NB23** SP12 20pf + 10pf dk car & brn blk .55 .55
**9NB24** SP12 40pf + 20pf bl & ind 1.25 3.75
*Nos. 9NB21-9NB24 (4)* 2.30 4.90

The surtax was for vacations for the children of Berlin.

**Fluorescent Paper was introduced for semipostal stamps, starting with Nos. 9NB25-9NB28.**

**Fairy Tale Type of 1960**

Various Scenes from Sleeping Beauty.

**1964, Oct. 6** **Unwmk.** ***Perf. 14***
**9NB25** SP285 10pf + 5pf multi .25 .25
**9NB26** SP285 15pf + 5pf multi .25 .25
**9NB27** SP285 20pf + 10pf multi .40 .25
**9NB28** SP285 40pf + 20pf multi .55 .90
*Nos. 9NB25-9NB28 (4)* 1.45 1.65

The surtax was for independent welfare organizations.

Beginning with 9NB25-9NB28 semi-postals are types of Germany inscribed "Berlin" except Nos. 9NB129-9NB131.

**Bird Type of 1965**

Birds: 10pf+5pf, Woodcock. 15pf+5pf, Ring-necked pheasant. 20pf+10pf, Black grouse. 40pf+20pf, Capercaillie.

**1965, Apr. 1** **Litho.** ***Perf. 14***
**9NB29** SP289 10pf + 5pf multi .25 .25
**9NB30** SP289 15pf + 5pf multi .25 .25
**9NB31** SP289 20pf + 10pf multi .25 .25
**9NB32** SP289 40pf + 20pf multi .50 .75
*Nos. 9NB29-9NB32 (4)* 1.25 1.50

Issued for the benefit of young people.

**Fairy Tale Type of 1965**

Various Scenes from Cinderella.

**1965, Oct. 6** **Litho.** ***Perf. 14***
**9NB33** SP290 10pf + 5pf multi .25 .25
**9NB34** SP290 15pf + 5pf multi .25 .25
**9NB35** SP290 20pf + 10pf multi .25 .25
**9NB36** SP290 40pf + 20pf multi .50 .75
*Nos. 9NB33-9NB36 (4)* 1.25 1.50

The surtax was for independent welfare organizations.

**Animal Type of 1966**

10pf+5pf, Roe deer. 20pf+10pf, Chamois. 30pf+15pf, Fallow deer. 50pf+25pf, Red deer.

**1966, Apr. 22** **Litho.** ***Perf. 14***
**9NB37** SP291 10pf + 5pf multi .25 .25
**9NB38** SP291 20pf + 10pf multi .25 .25
**9NB39** SP291 30pf + 15pf multi .25 .25
**9NB40** SP291 50pf + 25pf multi .55 .75
*Nos. 9NB37-9NB40 (4)* 1.30 1.50

Issued for the benefit of young people.

**Fairy Tale Type of 1965**

Various Scenes from The Princess and the Frog.

**1966, Oct. 5** **Litho.** ***Perf. 14***
**9NB41** SP290 10pf + 5pf multi .25 .25
**9NB42** SP290 20pf + 10pf multi .25 .25
**9NB43** SP290 30pf + 15pf multi .35 .25
**9NB44** SP290 50pf + 25pf multi .45 .70
*Nos. 9NB41-9NB44 (4)* 1.30 1.45

Surtax for independent welfare organizations.

**Animal Type of 1966**

10pf+5pf, Rabbit. 20pf+10pf, Ermine. 30pf+15pf, Hamster. 50pf+25pf, Red fox.

**1967, Apr. 4** **Unwmk.**
**9NB45** SP291 10pf + 5pf multi .25 .25
**9NB46** SP291 20pf + 10pf multi .25 .25
**9NB47** SP291 30pf + 15pf multi .35 .30
**9NB48** SP291 50pf + 25pf multi 1.00 1.40
*Nos. 9NB45-9NB48 (4)* 1.85 2.20

Issued for the benefit of young people.

**Fairy Tale Type of 1965**

Various Scenes from Frau Holle.

**1967, Oct. 3** **Litho.** ***Perf. 14***
**9NB49** SP290 10pf + 5pf multi .25 .25
**9NB50** SP290 20pf + 10pf multi .25 .25
**9NB51** SP290 30pf + 15pf multi .25 .35
**9NB52** SP290 50pf + 25pf multi .55 .75
*Nos. 9NB49-9NB52 (4)* 1.30 1.60

The surtax was for independent welfare organizations.

**Animal Type of 1968**

Animals: 10pf+5pf, Wildcat. 20pf+10pf, Otter. 30pf+15pf, Badger. 50pf+25pf, Beaver.

**1968, Feb. 2** **Photo.** ***Perf. 14***
**9NB53** SP293 10pf + 5pf multi .25 .45
**9NB54** SP293 20pf + 10pf multi .30 .45
**9NB55** SP293 30pf + 15pf multi .55 .90
**9NB56** SP293 50pf + 25pf multi 1.60 2.10
*Nos. 9NB53-9NB56 (4)* 2.70 3.90

Surtax for benefit of young people.

**Doll Type of 1968**

Various 19th century dolls in sitting position.

**1968, Oct. 3** **Litho.** ***Perf. 14***
**9NB57** SP294 10pf + 5pf multi .25 .25
**9NB58** SP294 20pf + 10pf multi .25 .25
**9NB59** SP294 30pf + 15pf multi .25 .35
**9NB60** SP294 50pf + 25pf multi .60 .75
*Nos. 9NB57-9NB60 (4)* 1.35 1.60

The surtax was for independent welfare organizations.

**Horse Type of 1969**

Horses: 10pf+5pf, Pony. 20pf+10pf, Work horse. 30pf+15pf, Hotblood. 50pf+25pf, Thoroughbred.

**1969, Feb. 6** **Litho.** ***Perf. 14***
**9NB61** SP295 10pf + 5pf multi .25 .30
**9NB62** SP295 20pf + 10pf multi .30 .55
**9NB63** SP295 30pf + 15pf multi .45 .75
**9NB64** SP295 50pf + 25pf multi 1.25 1.50
*Nos. 9NB61-9NB64 (4)* 2.25 3.10

Surtax for benefit of young people.

**Tin Toy Type of 1969**

Tin Toys: 10pf+5pf, Coach. 20pf+10pf, Woman feeding chickens. 30pf+15pf, Woman grocer. 50pf+25pf, Postilion on horseback.

**1969, Oct. 2** **Litho.** ***Perf. 13½x14***
**9NB65** SP297 10pf + 5pf multi .25 .25
**9NB66** SP297 20pf + 10pf multi .25 .25
**9NB67** SP297 30pf + 15pf multi .35 .35
**9NB68** SP297 50pf + 25pf multi 1.00 1.00
*Nos. 9NB65-9NB68 (4)* 1.85 1.85

The surtax was for independent welfare organizations.

**1969, Nov. 13** **Litho.** ***Perf. 13½x14***

Christmas: 10pf+5pf, The Three Kings.

**9NB69** SP297 10pf + 5pf multi .35 .30

**Minnesinger Type of 1970**

Minnesingers (and their Ladies): 10pf+5pf, Heinrich von Stretlingen. 20pf+10pf, Meinloh von Sevelingen. 30pf+15pf, Burkhart von Hohenfels. 50pf+25pf, Albrecht von Johansdorf.

**1970, Feb. 5** **Photo.** ***Perf. 13½x14***
**9NB70** SP298 10pf + 5pf multi .25 .25
**9NB71** SP298 20pf + 10pf multi .35 .45
**9NB72** SP298 30pf + 15pf multi .55 .60
**9NB73** SP298 50pf + 25pf multi 1.25 1.40
*Nos. 9NB70-9NB73 (4)* 2.40 2.70

Surtax for benefit of young people.

**Puppet Type of 1970**

10pf+5pf, "Kasperl." 20pf+10pf, Polichinelle. 30pf+5pf, Punch. 50pf+25pf, Pulcinella.

**1970, Oct. 6** **Litho.** ***Perf. 13½x14***
**9NB74** SP300 10pf + 5pf multi .25 .25
**9NB75** SP300 20pf + 10pf multi .25 .25
**9NB76** SP300 30pf + 15pf multi .55 .45
**9NB77** SP300 50pf + 25pf multi .90 1.10
*Nos. 9NB74-9NB77 (4)* 1.95 2.05

Surtax for independent welfare organizations.

**1970, Nov. 12**

Christmas: 10pf+5pf, Rococo angel, from Ursuline Sisters' Convent, Innsbruck.

**9NB78** SP300 10pf + 5pf multi .30 .30

**Drawings Type of 1971**

Children's Drawings: 10pf+5pf, Fly. 20pf+10pf, Fish. 30pf+15pf, Porcupine. 50pf+25pf, Cock. All stamps horizontal.

**1971, Feb. 5** **Litho.** ***Perf. 14***
**9NB79** SP301 10pf + 5pf multi .30 .30
**9NB80** SP301 20pf + 10pf multi .30 .30
**9NB81** SP301 30pf + 15pf multi .45 .50
**9NB82** SP301 50pf + 25pf multi 1.25 1.40
*Nos. 9NB79-9NB82 (4)* 2.30 2.50

Surtax for the benefit of young people.

**Wooden Toy Type of 1971**

Wooden Toys: 10pf+5pf, Movable dolls in box. 25pf+10pf, Knight on horseback. 30pf+15pf, Jumping jack. 60pf+30pf, Nurse rocking babies.

**1971, Oct. 5**
**9NB83** SP303 10pf + 5pf multi .25 .25
**9NB84** SP303 25pf + 10pf multi .25 .35
**9NB85** SP303 30pf + 15pf multi .55 .55
**9NB86** SP303 60pf + 30pf multi 1.00 1.10
*Nos. 9NB83-9NB86 (4)* 2.05 2.25

**1971, Nov. 11**

Christmas: Christmas angel with candles.

**9NB87** SP303 10pf + 5pf multi .35 .35

**Animal Protection Type of 1972**

10pf+5pf, Boy trying to rob bird's nest. 25pf+10pf, Girl with kittens to be drowned. 30pf+15pf, Watch dog & man with whip. 60pf+30pf, Hedgehog & deer passing before car at night.

**1972, Feb. 4**
**9NB88** SP304 10pf + 5pf multi .25 .25
**9NB89** SP304 25pf + 10pf multi .30 .30
**9NB90** SP304 30pf + 15pf multi .55 .55
**9NB91** SP304 60pf + 30pf multi 1.25 1.25
*Nos. 9NB88-9NB91 (4)* 2.35 2.35

Surtax for the benefit of young people.

**Chess Type of 1972**

**1972, Oct. 5** **Litho.** ***Perf. 14***
**9NB92** SP307 20pf + 10 Knight .30 .30
**9NB93** SP307 30pf + 15 Rook .45 .45
**9NB94** SP307 40pf + 20 Queen 1.25 1.25
**9NB95** SP307 70pf + 35 King 1.75 1.75
*Nos. 9NB92-9NB95 (4)* 3.75 3.75

Surtax for independent welfare organizations.

**Christmas Type of 1972**

Design: 20pf+10pf, Holy Family.

**1972, Nov. 10** **Litho.** ***Perf. 14***
**9NB96** SP308 20pf + 10pf multi .55 .45

**Bird Type of 1973**

Birds of Prey: 20pf+10pf, Goshawk. 30pf+15pf, Peregrine falcon. 40pf+20pf, Sparrow hawk. 70pf+35pf, Golden eagle.

**1973, Feb. 6 Photo. *Perf. 14***

**9NB97** SP309 20pf + 10pf multi .50 .50
**9NB98** SP309 30pf + 15pf multi .75 .75
**9NB99** SP309 40pf + 20pf multi 1.00 1.00
**9NB100** SP309 70pf + 35pf multi 1.75 1.75
*Nos. 9NB97-9NB100 (4)* 4.00 4.00

Surtax was for benefit of young people.

### Instrument Type of 1973

Musical Instruments: 20+10pf, Hurdygurdy, 17th cent. 30+15pf, Drum, 16th cent. 40+20pf, Archlute, 18th cent. 70+35pf, Organ, 16th cent.

**1973, Oct. 5 Litho. *Perf. 14***

**9NB101** SP311 20pf + 10pf multi .35 .35
**9NB102** SP311 30pf + 15pf multi .75 .75
**9NB103** SP311 40pf + 20pf multi .90 .90
**9NB104** SP311 70pf + 35pf multi 1.25 1.25
*Nos. 9NB101-9NB104 (4)* 3.25 3.25

Surtax was for independent welfare organizations.

### Star Type of 1973

Christmas: 20pf+10pf, Christmas star.

**1973, Nov. 9 Litho. & Engr.**

**9NB105** SP312 20pf + 10pf multi .55 .55

### Youth Type of 1974

Designs: 20pf+10pf, Boy photographing. 30pf+15pf, Boy athlete. 40pf+20pf, Girl violinist. 70pf+35pf, Nurse's aid.

**1974, Apr. 17 Photo. *Perf. 14***

**9NB106** SP313 20pf + 10pf multi .35 .45
**9NB107** SP313 30pf + 15pf multi .40 .45
**9NB108** SP313 40pf + 20pf multi .90 1.00
**9NB109** SP313 70pf + 35pf multi 1.25 1.40
*Nos. 9NB106-9NB109 (4)* 2.90 3.30

Surtax was for benefit of young people.

### Flower Type of 1974

Designs: 30pf+15pf, Spring bouquet. 40pf+20pf, Autumn bouquet. 50pf+25pf, Roses. 70pf+35pf, Winter flowers. All horiz.

**1974, Oct. 15 Litho. *Perf. 14***

**9NB110** SP314 30pf + 15pf multi .40 .40
**9NB111** SP314 40pf + 20pf multi .85 .85
**9NB112** SP314 50pf + 25pf multi .85 .85
**9NB113** SP314 70pf + 35pf multi 1.25 1.25
*Nos. 9NB110-9NB113 (4)* 3.35 3.35

Surtax was for independent welfare organizations.

**1974, Oct. 29**

Christmas: Christmas bouquet, horiz.

**9NB114** SP314 30pf + 15pf multi .75 .85

### Locomotive Type of 1975

Steam Locomotives: 30pf+15pf, Dragon. 40pf+20pf, Class 89 (70-75). 50pf+25pf, Class O50. 70pf+35pf, Class O10.

**1975, Apr. 15 Litho. *Perf. 14***

**9NB115** SP315 30pf + 15pf multi .75 .60
**9NB116** SP315 40pf + 20pf multi .75 .75
**9NB117** SP315 50pf + 25pf multi 1.50 1.25
**9NB118** SP315 70pf + 35pf multi 2.25 2.25
*Nos. 9NB115-9NB118 (4)* 5.25 4.85

Surtax was for benefit of young people.

### Flower Type of 1975

Alpine Flowers: 30pf+15pf, Yellow gentian. 40pf+20pf, Arnica. 50pf+25pf, Cyclamen. 70pf+35pf, Blue gentian.

**1975, Oct. 15 Litho. *Perf. 14***

**9NB119** SP316 30pf + 15pf multi .55 .55
**9NB120** SP316 40pf + 20pf multi .45 .45
**9NB121** SP316 50pf + 25pf multi .60 .60
**9NB122** SP316 70pf + 35pf multi 1.00 1.00
*Nos. 9NB119-9NB122 (4)* 2.60 2.60

Surtax was for independent welfare organizations.

**1975, Nov. 14**

Christmas: 30pf+15pf, Snow heather.

**9NB123** SP316 30pf + 15pf multi .75 .75

### Sports Type of 1976

30+15pf, Shot put, women's. 40+20pf, Hockey. 50+25pf, Handball. 70+35pf, Swimming.

**1976, Apr. 6 Litho. *Perf. 14***

**9NB124** SP317 30pf + 15pf multi .75 .70
**9NB125** SP317 40pf + 20pf multi .75 .70
**9NB126** SP317 50pf + 25pf multi .75 .80
**9NB127** SP317 70pf + 35pf multi 1.50 1.60
*Nos. 9NB124-9NB127 (4)* 3.75 3.80

Youth training for Olympic Games. The surtax was for the benefit of young people.

Iris — SP13

Flowers: 40pf+20pf, Wallflower. 50pf+25pf, Dahlia. 70pf+35pf, Larkspur.

**1976, Oct. 14 Litho. *Perf. 14***

**9NB128** SP13 30pf + 15pf .35 .35
**9NB129** SP13 40pf + 20pf .40 .40
**9NB130** SP13 50pf + 25pf .75 .75
**9NB131** SP13 70pf + 35pf 1.00 1.00
*Nos. 9NB128-9NB131 (4)* 2.50 2.50

Surtax was for independent welfare organizations.

### Christmas Type of 1976

Christmas: 30pf+15pf, Annunciation to the Shepherds, stained-glass window, Frauenkirche, Esslingen.

**1976, Nov. 16 Litho. & Engr.**
**Souvenir Sheet**

**9NB132** SP320 30pf + 15pf multi .75 .65

### Ship Type of 1977

Historic Ships: 30pf+15pf, Bremer Kogge, c. 1380. 40pf+20pf, Helena Sloman, 1850. 50pf+25pf, Passenger ship, Cap Polonio, 1914. 70pf+35pf, Freighter Widar, 1971.

**1977, Apr. 14 Litho. *Perf. 14***

**9NB133** SP321 30pf + 15pf .45 .45
**9NB134** SP321 40pf + 20pf .70 .70
**9NB135** SP321 50pf + 25pf .95 .95
**9NB136** SP321 70pf + 35pf 1.40 1.40
*Nos. 9NB133-9NB136 (4)* 3.50 3.50

Surtax was for benefit of young people.

### Flower Type of 1977

Meadow Flowers: 30pf+15pf, Daisy. 40pf+20pf, Cowslip. 50pf+25pf, Sainfoin. 70pf+35pf, Forget-me-not.

**1977, Oct. 13 Litho. *Perf. 14***

**9NB137** SP322 30pf + 15pf .30 .30
**9NB138** SP322 40pf + 20pf .55 .55
**9NB139** SP322 50pf + 25pf .75 .75
**9NB140** SP322 70pf + 35pf 1.10 1.10
*Nos. 9NB137-9NB140 (4)* 2.70 2.70

Surtax was for independent welfare organizations.
See Nos. 9NB148-9NB151.

### Christmas Type of 1977

30pf+15pf, Virgin and Child, stained-glass window, Sacristy of St. Gereon Basilica, Cologne.

**1977, Nov. 10**
**Souvenir Sheet**

**9NB141** SP323 30pf + 15pf multi .75 .75

### Aviation Type of 1978

Designs: 30pf+15pf, Montgolfier balloon, 1783. 40pf+20pf, Lilienthal's glider, 1891. 50pf+25pf, Wright brothers' plane, 1909. 70pf+35pf, Etrich/Rumpler Taube, 1910.

**1978, Apr. 13 Litho. *Perf. 14***

**9NB142** SP325 30pf + 15pf .35 .45
**9NB143** SP325 40pf + 20pf .55 .60
**9NB144** SP325 50pf + 25pf .70 .75
**9NB145** SP325 70pf + 35pf 1.25 1.25
*Nos. 9NB142-9NB145 (4)* 2.85 3.05

Surtax was for benefit of young people.

### Sports Type of 1978

50+25pf, Bicycling. 70+35pf, Fencing.

**1978, Apr. 13 Litho. *Perf. 14***

**9NB146** SP324 50pf + 25pf .90 .60
**9NB147** SP324 70pf + 35pf 1.25 1.00

Surtax was for German Sports Foundation.

### Flower Type of 1977

Woodland Flowers: 30pf+15pf, Solomon's-seal. 40pf+20pf, Wood primrose. 50pf+25pf, Cephalanthera rubra (orchid). 70pf+35pf, Bugle.

**1978, Oct. 12 Litho. *Perf. 14***

**9NB148** SP322 30pf + 15pf .45 .45
**9NB149** SP322 40pf + 20pf .55 .55
**9NB150** SP322 50pf + 25pf .75 .75
**9NB151** SP322 70pf + 35pf 1.10 1.10
*Nos. 9NB148-9NB151 (4)* 2.85 2.85

Surtax was for independent welfare organizations.

### Christmas Type of 1978

Christmas: 30pf+15pf, Adoration of the Kings, stained glass window, Frauenkirche, Munich.

**1978, Nov. 16 Litho. *Perf. 14***
**Souvenir Sheet**

**9NB152** SP326 30pf + 15pf multi .75 .75

### Aviation Type of 1979

Airplanes: 40pf+20pf, Vampyr, 1921. 50pf+25pf, Junkers JU52/3M, 1932. 60pf+30pf, Messerschmitt BF/ME 108, 1934. 90pf+45pf, Douglas DC3, 1935.

**1979, Apr. 5 Litho. *Perf. 14***

**9NB153** SP327 40pf + 20pf .55 .55
**9NB154** SP327 50pf + 25pf .75 .75
**9NB155** SP327 60pf + 30pf .95 .95
**9NB156** SP327 90pf + 45pf 1.50 1.50
*Nos. 9NB153-9NB156 (4)* 3.75 3.75

Surtax was for benefit of young people.

### Sports Type of 1979

60pf+30pf, Runners. 90pf+45pf, Archers.

**1979, Apr. 5**

**9NB157** SP328 60pf + 30pf .90 .95
**9NB158** SP328 90pf + 45pf 1.25 1.25

Surtax was for German Sports Foundation.

### Plant Type of 1979

Woodland Plants: 40pf+20pf, Larch. 50pf+25pf, Hazelnut. 60pf+30pf, Horse chestnut. 90pf+45pf, Blackthorn.

**1979, Oct. 11 Litho. *Perf. 14***

**9NB159** SP330 40pf + 20pf .60 .45
**9NB160** SP330 50pf + 25pf .75 .70
**9NB161** SP330 60pf + 30pf 1.00 .95
**9NB162** SP330 90pf + 45pf 1.40 1.25
*Nos. 9NB159-9NB162 (4)* 3.75 3.35

Surtax was for independent welfare organizations.

### Christmas Type of 1979

Christmas: Nativity, medieval manuscript, Cistercian Abby, Altenberg.

**1979, Nov. 14 Litho. *Perf. 13½***

**9NB163** SP331 40pf + 20pf multi .90 .75

### Aviation Type of 1979

Designs: 40pf+20pf, Vickers Viscount, 1950. 50pf+25pf, Fokker 27 Friendship, 1955. 60pf+30pf, Sud Aviation Caravelle, 1955. 90pf+45pf, Sikorsky-55, 1949.

**1980, Apr. 10 Litho. *Perf. 14***

**9NB164** SP327 40 + 20pf multi .75 .75
**9NB165** SP327 50 + 25pf multi .80 .80
**9NB166** SP327 60 + 30pf multi 1.00 1.00
**9NB167** SP327 90 + 45pf multi 1.50 1.50
*Nos. 9NB164-9NB167 (4)* 4.05 4.05

Surtax was for benefit of young people.

### Sports Type of 1980

Designs: 50pf+25pf, Javelin. 60pf+30pf, Weight lifting. 90pf+45pf, Water polo.

**1980, May 8 Photo. *Perf. 14***

**9NB168** SP332 50 + 25pf multi .75 .75
**9NB169** SP332 60 + 30pf multi .75 .75
**9NB170** SP332 90 + 45pf multi 1.10 1.10
*Nos. 9NB168-9NB170 (3)* 2.60 2.60

Surtax was for German Sports Foundation.

### Wildflower Type of 1980

Wildflowers: 40pf+20pf, Orlaya. 50pf+25pf, Yellow gagea. 60pf+30pf, Summer pheasant's eye. 90pf+45pf, Small-flowered Venus' looking-glass.

**1980, Oct. 9 Litho. *Perf. 14***

**9NB171** SP333 40 + 20pf multi .80 .80
**9NB172** SP333 50 + 25pf multi .90 .90
**9NB173** SP333 60 + 30pf multi .90 .90
**9NB174** SP333 90 + 45pf multi 1.50 1.50
*Nos. 9NB171-9NB174 (4)* 4.10 4.10

Surtax was for independent welfare organizations.

### Christmas Type of 1980

Christmas: 40pf+20pf, Annunciation to the Shepherds, from Altomunster manuscript, 12th century.

**1980, Nov. 13 Litho. *Perf. 14x13½***

**9NB175** SP335 40 + 20pf multi .90 .80

### Optical Instrument Type of 1981

40pf+20pf, Theodolite, 1810. 50pf+25pf, Equatorial telescope, 1820. 60pf +30pf, Microscope, 1790. 90pf+45pf, Sextant, 1830.

**1981, Apr. 10 Litho. *Perf. 13½***

**9NB176** SP336 40 + 20pf multi .60 .60
**9NB177** SP336 50 + 25pf multi .80 .80
**9NB178** SP336 60 + 30pf multi 1.00 1.00
**9NB179** SP336 90 + 45pf multi 1.60 1.60
*Nos. 9NB176-9NB179 (4)* 4.00 4.00

Surtax for benefit of young people.

### Sports Type of 1981

Designs: 60pf+30pf, Women's gymnastics. 90pf+45pf, Cross-county running.

**1981, Apr. 10 *Perf. 14***

**9NB180** SP337 60 + 30pf multi .90 .75
**9NB181** SP337 90 + 45pf multi 1.40 1.10

Surtax for the German Sports Foundation.

### Plant Type of 1981

40pf+20pf, Common bistort. 50pf+25pf, Pedicularis sceptrum-carolinum. 60pf+30pf, Gladiolus palustris. 90pf+45pf, Iris sibirica.

**1981, Oct. 8 Litho.**

**9NB182** SP338 40 + 20pf multi .75 .75
**9NB183** SP338 50 + 25pf multi .80 .75
**9NB184** SP338 60 + 30pf multi .90 .75
**9NB185** SP338 90 + 45pf multi 1.75 1.50
*Nos. 9NB182-9NB185 (4)* 4.20 3.75

Surtax was for independent welfare organizations.

### Christmas Type of 1981

Adoration of the Kings, 19th cent. painting.

**1981, Nov. 12 Litho.**

**9NB186** SP339 40 + 20pf multi .90 .60

### Antique Car Type of 1982

Designs: 40pf+20pf, Daimler, 1889. 50pf+25pf, Wanderer, 1911. 60pf+30pf, Adler limousine, 1913. 90pf+45pf, DKW-F, 1931.

**1982, Apr. 15 Litho.**

**9NB187** SP340 40 + 20pf multi .75 .75
**9NB188** SP340 50 + 25pf multi .80 .80
**9NB189** SP340 60 + 30pf multi 1.00 1.00
**9NB190** SP340 90 + 45pf multi 1.60 1.60
*Nos. 9NB187-9NB190 (4)* 4.15 4.15

Surtax was for benefit of young people.

### Sports Type of 1982

60pf+30pf, Sprinting. 90pf+45pf, Volleyball.

**1982, Apr. 15 Litho.**

**9NB191** SP341 60 + 30pf multi .95 .75
**9NB192** SP341 90 + 45pf multi 1.40 1.00

Surtax was for the German Sports Foundation.

### Flower Type of 1982

Designs: 50pf+20pf, Floribunda grandiflora. 60pf+30pf, Tea-rose hybrid, diff. 80pf+40pf, Floribunda, diff. 120pf+60pf, Miniature rose.

**1982, Oct. 14 Litho. *Perf. 14***

**9NB193** SP342 50 + 20pf multi 1.00 .90
**9NB194** SP342 60 + 30pf multi 1.10 .90
**9NB195** SP342 80 + 40pf multi 1.50 1.50
**9NB196** SP342 120 + 60pf multi 2.40 2.40
*Nos. 9NB193-9NB196 (4)* 6.00 5.70

Surtax was for independent welfare organizations.

### Christmas Type of 1982

Christmas: Adoration of the Kings, Oak altar, St. Peter's Church, Hamburg, 1380.

**1982, Nov. 10**

**9NB197** SP343 50 + 20pf multi .90 .75

### Motorcycle Type of 1983

Designs: 50pf+20pf, Hildebrand & Wolfmuller, 1894. 60pf+30pf, Wanderer, 1908. 80pf+40pf, DKW-Lomos, 1922. 120pf+60pf, Mars, 1925.

**1983, Apr. 12 Litho.** *Perf. 14*

**9NB198** SP344 50 + 20pf multi .75 .55
**9NB199** SP344 60 + 30pf multi 1.10 .95
**9NB200** SP344 80 + 40pf multi 1.25 .95
**9NB201** SP344 120 + 60pf multi 3.00 2.50
*Nos. 9NB198-9NB201 (4)* 6.10 4.95

Surtax was for benefit of young people.

### Sports Type of 1983

Designs: 80pf+40pf, European Latin American Dance Championship. 120pf+60pf, World Hockey Championship.

**1983, Apr. 12**

**9NB202** SP345 80 + 40pf multi 1.50 1.10
**9NB203** SP345 120 + 60pf multi 2.25 1.90

Surtax was for German Sports Foundation.

### Flower Type of Germany

Designs: 50pf+20pf, Mountain wildflower. 60pf+30pf, Alpine auricula. 80pf+40pf, Little primrose. 120pf+60pf, Einsele's aquilegia.

**1983, Oct. 13 Litho.** *Perf. 14*

**9NB204** SP346 50 + 20pf multi .70 .70
**9NB205** SP346 60 + 30pf multi 1.00 1.00
**9NB206** SP346 80 + 40pf multi 1.75 1.75
**9NB207** SP346 120 + 60pf multi 2.75 2.75
*Nos. 9NB204-9NB207 (4)* 6.20 6.20

Surtax was for welfare organizations.

### Christmas Type of Germany

**1983, Nov. 10 Litho.**

**9NB208** SP347 50 + 20pf Nativity .90 .80

Surtax was for free welfare work.

### Insect Type of 1984

Designs: 50pf+20pf, Trichius fasciatus. 60pf+30pf, Agrumenia carniolioa. 80pf+40pf, Bombus terrestris. 120pf+60pf, Eristalis tenax.

**1984, Apr. 12 Litho.**

**9NB209** SP348 50 + 20pf multi 1.00 .65
**9NB210** SP348 60 + 30pf multi 1.00 .80
**9NB211** SP348 80 + 40pf multi 2.10 1.25
**9NB212** SP348 120 + 60pf multi 2.50 2.50
*Nos. 9NB209-9NB212 (4)* 6.60 5.20

Surtax was for German Youth Stamp Foundation.

### Olympic Type of 1984

Women's Events: 60pf+30pf, Hurdles. 80pf+40pf, Cycling. 120pf+60pf, Kayak.

**1984, Apr. 12**

**9NB213** SP349 60 + 30pf multi 1.50 1.00
**9NB214** SP349 80 + 40pf multi 1.90 1.00
**9NB215** SP349 120 + 60pf multi 2.75 2.75
*Nos. 9NB213-9NB215 (3)* 6.15 4.75

Surtax was for German Sports Foundation.

### Orchid Type of 1984

50+20pf, Listera cordata. 60pf+30pf, Ophrys insectifera. 80pf+40pf, Epipactis palustris. 120pf+60pf, Ophrys coriophora.

**1984, Oct. 18 Litho.** *Perf. 14*

**9NB216** SP350 50 + 20pf multi 1.25 1.10
**9NB217** SP350 60 + 30pf multi 1.75 1.10
**9NB218** SP350 80 + 40pf multi 3.00 2.50
**9NB219** SP350 120 + 60pf multi 4.50 4.00
*Nos. 9NB216-9NB219 (4)* 10.50 8.70

Surtax was for welfare organizations.

### Christmas Type of 1984

**1984, Nov. 8 Litho.**

**9NB220** SP351 50 + 20pf St. Nicholas 1.10 1.10

Surtax was for welfare organizations.

### Sport Type of 1985

**1985, Feb. 21 Photo.**

**9NB221** SP352 80 + 40pf Basketball 1.40 1.40
**9NB222** SP352 120 + 60pf Table Tennis 2.25 2.25

Surtax was for German Sport Foundation.

### Bicycle Type of 1985

50pf+20pf, Bussing bicycle, 1868. 60pf+30pf, Child's tricycle, 1885. 80pf+40pf, Jaray bicycle, 1925. 120pf+60pf, Opel racer, 1925.

**1985, Apr. 16 Litho.**

**9NB223** SP353 50 + 20pf multi 1.10 1.10
**9NB224** SP353 60 + 30pf multi 1.10 1.10
**9NB225** SP353 80 + 40pf multi 1.50 1.50
**9NB226** SP353 120 + 60pf multi 3.50 3.50
*Nos. 9NB223-9NB226 (4)* 7.20 7.20

Surtax was for benefit of young people. Each stamp also shows the International Youth Year emblem.

### Prayer Book Type of 1985

**1985, Oct. 15 Litho.** *Perf. 14*

**9NB227** SP355 50 + 20pf multi 1.10 1.10
**9NB228** SP355 60 + 30pf multi 1.50 1.50
**9NB229** SP355 80 + 40pf multi 1.50 1.50
**9NB230** SP355 120 + 60pf multi 2.25 2.25
*Nos. 9NB227-9NB230 (4)* 6.35 6.35

Surtax for welfare organizations.

### Christmas Type of 1985

Woodcut: Worship of the Kings, Epiphany Altar, Frieburg Cathedral, by Hans Baldung Grien (1485-1545).

**1985, Nov. 12 Litho.** *Perf. 14*

**9NB231** SP356 50 + 20pf multi 1.25 1.00

Surtax for welfare organizations.

### European Sports Championships Type of 1986

**1986, Feb. 13 Litho.** *Perf. 14*

**9NB232** SP357 80 + 40pf Swimming 1.60 1.60
**9NB233** SP357 120 + 55pf Show jumping 2.25 2.25

Surtax for the Natl. Sports Promotion Foundation.

### Vocational Training Type of 1986

**1986, Apr. 10**

**9NB234** SP358 50 + 25pf Glazier 1.10 1.25
**9NB235** SP358 60 + 30pf Mechanic 1.50 1.60
**9NB236** SP358 70 + 35pf Tailor 1.50 1.60
**9NB237** SP358 80 + 40pf Carpenter 1.90 1.90
*Nos. 9NB234-9NB237 (4)* 6.00 6.35

Surtax for German Youth Stamp Foundation.

### Glassware Type of 1986

**1986, Oct. 16 Litho.** *Perf. 13x13½*

**9NB238** SP359 50 + 25pf Cantharus, 1st cent. 1.10 1.10
**9NB239** SP359 60 + 30pf Tumbler, c. 200 1.50 1.50
**9NB240** SP359 70 + 35pf Jug, 3rd cent. 1.50 1.50
**9NB241** SP359 80 + 40pf Diatreta, 4th cent. 1.90 1.90
*Nos. 9NB238-9NB241 (4)* 6.00 6.00

Surtax for public welfare organizations.

### Christmas Type of 1986

Christmas: Adoration of the Magi, Ortenberg Altarpiece, c. 1420.

**1986, Nov. 13 Litho.** *Perf. 14*

**9NB242** SP360 50 + 25pf multi .90 .80

Surtax for public welfare organizations.

### Sports Championships Type of 1987

**1987, Feb. 12 Litho.**

**9NB243** SP361 80 + 40pf Gymnastics 1.50 1.50
**9NB244** SP361 120 + 55pf Judo 2.25 2.25

Surtax for the benefit of the national Sports Promotion Foundation.

### Industry Type of 1987

**1987, Apr. 9 Litho.**

**9NB245** SP362 50 + 25pf Cooper 1.10 1.10
**9NB246** SP362 60 + 30pf Stonemason 1.10 1.10
**9NB247** SP362 70 + 35pf Furrier 1.50 1.50
**9NB248** SP362 80 + 40pf Painter 1.50 1.50
*Nos. 9NB245-9NB248 (4)* 5.20 5.20

Surtax for youth organizations.

### Gold and Silver Artifacts Type of 1987

**1987, Oct. 15**

**9NB249** SP363 50 + 25pf Bonnet ornament, 5th cent. .75 .90
**9NB250** SP363 60 + 30pf Athena plate, 1st cent. B.C. 1.10 1.25
**9NB251** SP363 70 + 35pf Armilla armlet, c. 1180 1.40 1.50
**9NB252** SP363 80 + 40pf Snake bracelet, 300 B.C. 1.60 1.75
*Nos. 9NB249-9NB252 (4)* 4.85 5.40

Surtax for welfare organizations sponsoring free museum exhibitions.

### Christmas Type of 1987

Illustration from Book of Psalms, 13th cent., Bavarian Natl. Museum: Adoration of the Magi.

**1987, Nov. 6**

**9NB253** SP364 50 + 25pf multi .90 .80

Surtax for public welfare ogranizations.

### Sports Type of 1988

**1988, Feb. 18 Litho.**

**9NB254** SP365 60 + 30pf Trapshooting 1.60 1.50
**9NB255** SP365 80 + 40pf Figure skating 1.60 1.50
**9NB256** SP365 120 + 55pf Hammer throw 2.10 2.10
*Nos. 9NB254-9NB256 (3)* 5.30 5.10

### Music Type of 1988

No. 9NB257, Piano terzet. No. 9NB258, Wind quintet. No. 9NB259, Guitar, mandolin, recorder. No. 9NB260, Children's choir.

**1988, Apr. 14 Litho.** *Perf. 14*

**9NB257** SP366 50 +25pf multi 1.25 1.25
**9NB258** SP366 60 +30pf multi 1.60 1.60
**9NB259** SP366 70 +35pf multi 1.60 1.60
**9NB260** SP366 80 +40pf multi 2.50 2.50
*Nos. 9NB257-9NB260 (4)* 6.95 6.95

Surtax for German Youth Stamp Foundation.

### Artifacts Type of 1988

#9NB261, Brooch, c. 1700, Schmuck Jewelry Museum, Pforzheim. #9NB262, Lion, 1540, Kunstgewerbe Museum, Berlin. #9NB263, Lidded goblet, 1536, Kunstgewerbe Museum. #9NB264, Cope clasp, c. 1400, Aachen cathedral.

**1988, Oct. 13 Litho.**

**9NB261** SP367 50 +25pf multi 1.10 *1.25*
**9NB262** SP367 60 +30pf multi 1.25 *1.40*
**9NB263** SP367 70 +35pf multi 1.40 *1.50*
**9NB264** SP367 80 +40pf multi 1.60 1.75
*Nos. 9NB261-9NB264 (4)* 5.35 5.90

Surtax for welfare organizations.

### Christmas Type of 1988

Illumination from *The Gospel Book of Henry the Lion*, Helmarshausen, 1188, Prussian Cultural Museum, Bavaria: Angels announce the birth of Christ to the shepherds.

**1988, Nov. 10 Litho.**

**9NB265** SP368 50 +25pf multi 1.40 1.25

Surtax for public welfare organizations.

### Sports Type of 1989

**1989, Feb. 9 Litho.**

**9NB266** SP369 100 +50pf Volleyball 2.50 2.50
**9NB267** SP369 140 +60pf Hockey 3.25 3.25

Surtax for the Natl. Sports Promotion Foundation.

### Circus Type of 1989

**1989, Apr. 20 Litho.**

**9NB268** SP371 60 +30pf Tamer and tigers 1.60 1.60
**9NB269** SP371 70 +30pf Trapeze artists 2.10 2.10
**9NB270** SP371 80 +35pf Seals 3.00 3.00
**9NB271** SP371 100 +50pf Jugglers 3.25 3.25
*Nos. 9NB268-9NB271 (4)* 9.95 9.95

Surtax for natl. youth welfare organizations.

### Mail Carrying Type of 1989

#9NB272, Messenger, 15th cent. #9NB273, Brandenburg mail wagon, c. 1700. #9NB274, Prussian postal workers, 19th cent.

**1989, Oct. 12 Litho.**

**9NB272** SP372 60 +30pf multi 2.50 2.50
**9NB273** SP372 80 +35pf multi 3.25 3.00
**9NB274** SP372 100 +50pf multi 4.00 4.00
*Nos. 9NB272-9NB274 (3)* 9.75 9.50

Surtax for the benefit of Free Welfare Work.

### Christmas Type of 1989

**1989, Nov. 16 Litho.**

**9NB275** SP373 40 +20pf Angel 1.25 1.25
**9NB276** SP373 60 +30pf Nativity 2.10 2.10

Surtax for the benefit of the Federal Working Assoc. of Free Welfare Work.

### Sports Type of 1990

Designs: No. 9NB277, Water polo. No. 9NB278, Wheelchair basketball.

**1990, Feb. 15 Litho.**

**9NB277** SP374 100 +50pf multi 3.25 3.25
**9NB278** SP374 140 +60pf multi 5.50 *6.25*

Surtax for the Natl. Sports Promotion Foundation.

### Max and Moritz Type of 1990

**1990, Apr. 19 Litho.**

**9NB279** SP375 60 +30pf Max, Moritz 1.60 *1.90*
**9NB280** SP375 70 +30pf Max, Moritz, diff. 2.50 *2.75*
**9NB281** SP375 80 +35pf Moritz 2.50 *2.75*
**9NB282** SP375 100 +50pf Bug, Uncle 2.50 *2.75*
*Nos. 9NB279-9NB282 (4)* 9.10 10.15

Surcharge for the German Youth Stamp Foundation.

### Post and Telecommunications Type

Designs: 60pf + 30pf, Railway mail car, 1900. 80pf + 35pf, Telephone installation, 1900. 100pf + 50pf, Mail truck, 1900.

**1990, Sept. 27 Litho.** *Perf. 13½x14*

**9NB283** SP377 60 +30pf multi 2.10 2.10
**9NB284** SP377 80 +35pf multi 3.00 3.00
**9NB285** SP377 100 +50pf multi 4.00 4.00
*Nos. 9NB283-9NB285 (3)* 9.10 9.10

Surtax for welfare organizations.

## GERMAN OFFICES ABROAD

## OFFICES IN CHINA

100 Pfennings = 1 Mark
100 Cents = 1 Dollar (1905)

Stamps of Germany, 1889-90, Overprinted in Black at 56 degree Angle

| 1898 | Unwmk. | *Perf. 13½x14½* | | |
|---|---|---|---|---|
| 1 | A9 | 3pf dark brown | 5.25 | *5.00* |
| *a.* | | 3pf yellow brown | 12.00 | *12.00* |
| *b.* | | 3pf reddish ocher | 37.50 | *125.00* |
| 2 | A9 | 5pf green | 2.75 | 2.25 |
| 3 | A10 | 10pf carmine | 5.75 | *6.25* |
| 4 | A10 | 20pf ultramarine | 17.00 | 16.50 |
| 5 | A10 | 25pf orange | 32.50 | 30.00 |
| 6 | A10 | 50pf red brown | 16.00 | 12.50 |
| | | *Nos. 1-6 (6)* | 79.25 | 72.50 |

### Overprinted at 45 degree Angle

| | | | | |
|---|---|---|---|---|
| *1c* | A9 | 3pf yellow brown | 125.00 | *23,000.* |
| *1d* | A9 | 3pf reddish ocher | 375.00 | |
| *e.* | | 3pf gray brown | 1,850. | |
| *2a* | A9 | 5pf green | 11.50 | *12.50* |
| *3a* | A10 | 10pf carmine | 30.00 | 10.50 |
| *4a* | A10 | 20pf ultramarine | 13.50 | 10.50 |
| *5a* | A10 | 25pf orange | 50.00 | *60.00* |
| *6a* | A10 | 50pf red brown | 20.00 | 16.50 |

Value for No. 1c used is for a stamp with small 1898 Shanghai cancel. Examples with other cancellations or later Shanghai cancels sell for about half the value quoted.

### Foochow Issue

Nos. 3 and 3a Handstamp Surcharged

| 1900 | | | | |
|---|---|---|---|---|
| 16 | A10 | 5pf on 10pf, #3 | 600.00 | *850.00* |
| *a.* | | On No. 3a | 550.00 | *900.00* |

For similar 5pf surcharges on 10pf carmine, see Tsingtau Issue, Kiauchau.

### Tientsin Issue

German Stamps of 1900 Issue Handstamped

| 1900 | | | | |
|---|---|---|---|---|
| 17 | A11 | 3pf brown | 575.00 | 750.00 |
| 18 | A11 | 5pf green | 375.00 | 350.00 |
| 19 | A11 | 10pf carmine | 900.00 | 850.00 |
| 20 | A11 | 20pf ultra | 750.00 | *900.00* |
| 21 | A11 | 30pf org & blk, *sal* | *6,500.* | *6,500.* |
| 22 | A11 | 50pf pur & blk, *sal* | *29,000.* | *15,000.* |
| 23 | A11 | 80pf lake & blk, *rose* | *4,750.* | *4,500.* |

This handstamp is known inverted and double on most values.
Excellent faked handstamps are plentiful.

### Regular Issue

German Stamps of 1900 Overprinted

A14

A15

| 1901 | | *Perf. 14, 14½* | | |
|---|---|---|---|---|
| | | **Overprinted Horizontally in Black** | | |
| 24 | A11 | 3pf brown | 1.50 | 1.90 |
| *a.* | | 3pf light red brown | 105.00 | *45.00* |
| 25 | A11 | 5pf green | 1.50 | 1.50 |
| 26 | A11 | 10pf carmine | 2.50 | 1.10 |
| 27 | A11 | 20pf ultra | 3.25 | 1.50 |
| 28 | A11 | 25pf org & blk, *yel* | 9.00 | *16.00* |
| 29 | A11 | 30pf org & blk, *sal* | 9.00 | *13.00* |
| 30 | A11 | 40pf lake & blk | 9.00 | 9.00 |
| 31 | A11 | 50pf pur & blk, *sal* | 9.00 | 9.00 |
| 32 | A11 | 80pf lake & blk, *rose* | 11.00 | 11.00 |

### Overprinted in Black or Red

| | | | | |
|---|---|---|---|---|
| 33 | A12 | 1m car rose | 26.00 | *32.50* |
| 34 | A13 | 2m gray blue | 27.50 | *30.00* |
| 35 | A14 | 3m blk vio (R) | 45.00 | *65.00* |
| 36 | A15 | 5m slate & car, I | 1,275. | *2,250.* |
| *b.* | | Red and/or white retouched | 210.00 | *300.00* |
| 36A | A15 | 5m slate & car, II | 210.00 | *300.00* |
| | | *Nos. 24-36A (14)* | 1,639. | *2,741.* |

See note after Germany No. 65A for information on retouches on No. 36. For description of the 5m Type I and Type II, see note above Germany No. 62.

### Surcharged on German Stamps of 1902 in Black or Red

a

b

c

| 1905 | | | | |
|---|---|---|---|---|
| 37 | A16(a) | 1c on 3pf | 2.90 | *3.25* |
| 38 | A16(a) | 2c on 5pf | 2.90 | 1.40 |
| 39 | A16(a) | 4c on 10pf | 5.25 | 1.40 |
| 40 | A16(a) | 10c on 20pf | 2.90 | 1.75 |
| 41 | A16(a) | 20c on 40pf | 20.00 | 7.50 |
| 42 | A16(a) | 40c on 80pf | 32.50 | 13.00 |
| 43 | A17(b) | ½d on 1m (26x17 perf. holes) | 15.00 | *19.00* |
| 44 | A21(b) | 1d on 2m | 17.50 | *21.00* |
| *45a* | A19(c) | 1 ½d 1½d on 3m, 25x16 perf. holes | 15.00 | 45.00 |
| 46 | A20(b) | 2½d on 5m | 110.00 | *300.00* |
| | | *Nos. 37-46 (10)* | 223.95 | *413.30* |

### Surcharged on German Stamps of 1905 in Black or Red

| 1906-13 | | Wmk. 125 | | |
|---|---|---|---|---|
| 47 | A16(a) | 1c on 3pf | .40 | *1.25* |
| 48 | A16(a) | 2c on 5pf | .40 | *1.25* |
| 49 | A16(a) | 4c on 10pf | .40 | *1.50* |
| 50 | A16(a) | 10c on 20pf | .85 | *6.50* |
| 51 | A16(a) | 20c on 40pf | .90 | *3.50* |
| 52 | A16(a) | 40c on 80pf | 1.10 | *50.00* |
| 53 | A17(b) | ½d on 1m | 6.00 | *37.50* |
| 54 | A21(b) | 1d on 2m | 9.00 | *37.50* |
| 55 | A19(c) | 1½d on 3m (R) | 7.50 | *110.00* |
| 56 | A20(b) | 2½d on 5m (26x17 perf. holes) | 29.00 | *67.50* |
| | | *Nos. 47-56 (10)* | 55.55 | *316.50* |

Forged cancellations exist.

## OFFICES IN MOROCCO

100 Centimos = 1 Peseta

Stamps of Germany Surcharged in Black

| 1899 | Unwmk. | *Perf. 13½x14½* | | |
|---|---|---|---|---|
| 1 | A9 | 3c on 3pf dk brn | 3.25 | 2.10 |
| 2 | A9 | 5c on 5pf green | 3.25 | 2.40 |
| 3 | A10 | 10c on 10pf car | 9.00 | 7.50 |
| 4 | A10 | 25c on 20pf ultra | 18.00 | 15.00 |
| 5 | A10 | 30c on 25pf orange | 26.00 | *32.50* |
| 6 | A10 | 60c on 50pf red brn | 22.50 | *37.50* |
| | | *Nos. 1-6 (6)* | 82.00 | 97.00 |

Before Nos. 1-6 were issued, the same six basic stamps of Germany's 1889-1900 issue were overprinted "Marocco" diagonally without the currency-changing surcharge line, but were not issued. Value, $750.

German Stamps of 1900 Surcharged

A12

A13

A14

A15

**Black or Red Surcharge**

| 1900 | | *Perf. 14, 14½* | | |
|---|---|---|---|---|
| 7 | A11 | 3c on 3pf brn | 1.25 | *2.25* |
| 8 | A11 | 5c on 5pf grn | 1.50 | 1.50 |
| 9 | A11 | 10c on 10pf car | 2.00 | 1.50 |
| 10 | A11 | 25c on 20pf ultra | 3.00 | 2.75 |
| 11 | A11 | 30c on 25pf org & blk, *yel* | 9.00 | *15.00* |
| 12 | A11 | 35c on 30pf org & blk, *sal* | 6.75 | 6.25 |
| 13 | A11 | 50c on 40pf lake & blk | 6.75 | 6.25 |
| 14 | A11 | 60c on 50pf pur & blk, *sal* | 14.00 | *32.50* |
| 15 | A11 | 1p on 80pf lake & blk, *rose* | 12.00 | 11.00 |
| 16 | A12 | 1p25c on 1m car rose | 32.50 | *45.00* |
| 17 | A13 | 2p50c on 2m gray bl | 37.50 | *57.50* |
| 18 | A14 | 3p75c on 3m blk vio (R) | 45.00 | *65.00* |
| 19 | A15 | 6p25c on 5m sl & car, type I | 975.00 | *1,325.* |
| *b.* | | Red and/or white retouched | 200.00 | *325.00* |
| 19A | A15 | 6p25c on 5m sl & car, type II | 1,500. | — |
| | | *Nos. 7-19A (14)* | 2,646. | *1,571.* |

See note after Germany No. 65A for information on retouches on No. 19. For description of the 5m Type I and Type II, see note above Germany No. 62.

### New Surcharge Plates

| 1903 | | | | |
|---|---|---|---|---|
| 8D | A11 | 5c on 5pf grn | 70.00 | 11.00 |
| 16D | A12 | 1p25c on 1m car rose | 350.00 | 180.00 |
| 17D | A13 | 2p50c on 2m gray bl | 500.00 | 100.00 |
| 18D | A14 | 3p75c on 3m blk vio (R) | 1,300. | 240.00 |
| 19D | A15 | 6p25c on 5m sl & car, type II | 195.00 | 250.00 |

The 1903 printing Nos. 8D, 16D-18D, 19D differs from Nos. 8, 16-18 and 19A in the "M" and "t" of the surcharge.

### German Stamps of 1902 Surcharged in Black or Red

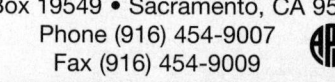

a

b

c

| | | | | |
|---|---|---|---|---|
| **1905** | | | | |
| **20** | A16(a) | 3c on 3pf | 2.75 | 2.75 |
| **21** | A16(a) | 5c on 5pf | 4.75 | 1.10 |
| **22** | A16(a) | 10c on 10pf | 8.25 | 1.10 |
| **23** | A16(a) | 25c on 20pf | 19.00 | 3.00 |
| **24** | A16(a) | 30c on 25pf | 6.75 | 5.50 |
| **25** | A16(a) | 35c on 30pf | 10.00 | 5.50 |
| **26** | A16(a) | 50c on 40pf | 9.50 | 7.75 |
| **27** | A16(a) | 60c on 50pf | 21.00 | 24.00 |
| **28** | A16(a) | 1p on 80pf | 21.00 | 19.00 |
| | | On cover | | 45.00 |
| **29** | A17(b) | 1p25c on 1m | 52.50 | 37.50 |
| **30** | A21(b) | 2p50c on 2m | 95.00 | 150.00 |
| **31** | A19(c) | 3p75c on 3m (R) | 42.50 | 55.00 |
| **32** | A20(b) | 6p25c on 5m | 150.00 | 210.00 |
| | | *Nos. 20-32 (13)* | 443.00 | 522.20 |

### Surcharged on Germany No. 54

| | | | | |
|---|---|---|---|---|
| **32A** | A11(a) | 5c on 5pf | 8.00 | 24.00 |

### German Stamps of 1905 Surcharged

| | | | | |
|---|---|---|---|---|
| **1906-11** | | **Wmk. 125** | | |
| **33** | A16(a) | 3c on 3pf | 8.75 | 2.10 |
| **34** | A16(a) | 5c on 5pf | 6.50 | 1.10 |
| **35** | A16(a) | 10c on 10pf | 6.50 | 1.10 |
| **36** | A16(a) | 25c on 20pf | 16.00 | 7.50 |
| **37** | A16(a) | 30c on 25pf | 19.00 | 11.50 |
| **38** | A16(a) | 35c on 30pf | 16.00 | 9.75 |
| **39** | A16(a) | 50c on 40pf | 32.50 | 150.00 |
| **40** | A16(a) | 60c on 50pf | 25.00 | 17.00 |
| **41** | A16(a) | 1p on 80pf | 125.00 | 275.00 |
| **42** | A17(b) | 1p25c on 1m | 62.50 | 175.00 |
| **43** | A21(b) | 2p50c on 2m | 62.50 | 175.00 |
| **44** | A20(b) | 6p25c on 5m | 125.00 | 325.00 |
| | | *Nos. 33-44 (12)* | 505.25 | 1,150. |

Excellent forgeries exist of No. 41.

### Surcharge Spelled "Marokko" in Black or Red

| | | | | |
|---|---|---|---|---|
| **1911** | | | | |
| **45** | A16(a) | 3c on 3pf | .55 | .75 |
| **46** | A16(a) | 5c on 5pf | .55 | 1.00 |
| **47** | A16(a) | 10c on 10pf | .55 | 1.10 |
| **48** | A16(a) | 25c on 20pf | .65 | 1.40 |
| **49** | A16(a) | 30c on 25pf | 1.50 | 16.00 |
| **50** | A16(a) | 35c on 30pf | 1.50 | 8.75 |
| **51** | A16(a) | 50c on 40pf | 1.25 | 5.25 |
| **52** | A16(a) | 60c on 50pf | 2.40 | 37.50 |
| **53** | A16(a) | 1p on 80pf | 1.60 | 24.00 |
| **54** | A17(b) | 1p25c on 1m | 4.50 | 65.00 |
| **55** | A21(b) | 2p50c on 2m | 6.00 | 47.50 |
| **56** | A19(c) | 3p75c on 3m (R) | 10.50 | 225.00 |
| **57** | A20(b) | 6p25c on 5m | 19.00 | 325.00 |
| | | On cover | | 575.00 |
| | | *Nos. 45-57 (13)* | 50.55 | 758.25 |

Forged cancellations exist.

## OFFICES IN THE TURKISH EMPIRE

Unused values for Nos. 1-6 are for stamps with original gum. Stamps without gum sell for about one-third of the figures quoted.

40 Paras = 1 Piaster

A1

A2

### German Stamps of 1880-83 Surcharged in Black or Blue

| | | | | |
|---|---|---|---|---|
| **1884** | | **Unwmk.** | ***Perf. 13½x14½*** | |
| **1** | A1 | 10pa on 5pf dull vio | 55.00 | 32.50 |
| **2** | A2 | 20pa on 10pf rose | 80.00 | 80.00 |
| **3** | A2 | 1pi on 20pf ultra (Bk) | 65.00 | 5.25 |
| **4** | A2 | 1pi on 20pf ultra (Bl) | 2,250. | 72.50 |
| **5** | A2 | 1¼pi on 25pf brn | 190.00 | 250.00 |
| **6** | A2 | 2½pi on 50pf gray grn | 100.00 | 80.00 |
| *a.* | | 2½pi on 50pf deep olive grn | 275.00 | 210.00 |
| | | *Nos. 1-6 (6)* | 2,740. | 520.25 |

There are two types of the surcharge on the 1¼pi and 2½pi stamps, the difference being in the spacing between the figures and the word "PIASTER."

**Covers:** There are re-issues of these stamps which vary only slightly from the originals in overprint measurements.

### German Stamps of 1889-1900 Surchargd in Black

A3

A4

A5

| | | | | |
|---|---|---|---|---|
| **1889** | | | | |
| **8** | A3 | 10pa on 5pf grn | 3.75 | 4.00 |
| **9** | A4 | 20pa on 10pf car | 8.00 | 2.75 |
| **10** | A4 | 1pi on 20pf ultra | 5.50 | 2.40 |
| **11** | A5 | 1¼pi on 25pf org | 24.00 | 20.00 |
| **12** | A5 | 2½pi on 50pf choc | 37.50 | 24.00 |
| *a.* | | 2½pi on 50pf copper brown | 200.00 | 125.00 |
| | | *Nos. 8-12 (5)* | 78.75 | 53.15 |

### German Stamps of 1900 Surcharged

A11

A12

A13

A14

A15

| | | | | |
|---|---|---|---|---|
| **1900** | | | ***Perf. 14, 14½*** | |
| | | **Black or Red Surcharge** | | |
| **13** | A11 | 10pa on 5pf grn | 1.75 | 1.75 |
| **14** | A11 | 20pa on 10pf car | 2.75 | 2.25 |
| **15** | A11 | 1pi on 20pf ultra | 4.75 | 1.90 |
| **16** | A11 | 1¼pi on 25pf org & blk, *yel* | 6.50 | 4.50 |
| **17** | A11 | 1½pi on 30pf org & blk, *sal* | 6.50 | 4.75 |
| **18** | A11 | 2pi on 40pf lake & blk | 6.50 | 4.75 |
| **19** | A11 | 2½pi on 50pf pur & blk, *sal* | 12.50 | 13.50 |
| **20** | A11 | 4pi on 80pf lake & blk, *rose* | 14.00 | 13.50 |
| **21** | A12 | 5pi on 1m car rose | 40.00 | 40.00 |
| **22** | A13 | 10pi on 2m gray bl | 35.00 | 45.00 |
| **23** | A14 | 15pi on 3m blk vio (R) | 50.00 | 110.00 |
| **24** | A15 | 25pi on 5m sl & car, type I | 640.00 | 1,250. |
| *a.* | | Double surcharge | | 11,000. |
| *d.* | | Red and/or white retouched | 175.00 | 250.00 |
| *e.* | | White only retouched | 290.00 | 500.00 |
| **24B** | A15 | 25pi on 5m sl & car, type II | 290.00 | 500.00 |
| *c.* | | Double surcharge | 9,750. | — |
| | | *Nos. 13-24B (13)* | 1,110. | 1,991. |

See note after Germany #65A for information on retouches on #24. For description of the 5m Type I & Type II, see note above Germany #62.

German Stamps of 1900 Surcharged in Black

| | | | | |
|---|---|---|---|---|
| **1903-05** | | | | |
| **25** | A11 | 10pa on 5pf green | 9.50 | 13.50 |
| | | On cover | | 75.00 |
| **26** | A11 | 20pa on 10pf car | 30.00 | 19.00 |
| **27** | A11 | 1pi on 20pf ultra | 8.75 | 7.25 |

German Stamps of 1900, 1905 Surcharged in Black

| | | | | |
|---|---|---|---|---|
| **28** | A12 | 5pi on 1m car rose | 140.00 | 95.00 |
| **29** | A13 | 10pi on 2m bl ('05) | 160.00 | 275.00 |
| **30** | A15 | 25pi on 5m sl & car | 190.00 | 550.00 |
| *a.* | | Double surcharge | 7,500. | |
| | | *Nos. 25-30 (6)* | 538.25 | 959.75 |

The 1903-05 surcharges may be easily distinguished from those of 1900 by the added bar at the top of the letter "A."

### German Stamps of 1902 Surcharged in Black or Red

a

b

| | | | | |
|---|---|---|---|---|
| **1905** | | | **Unwmk.** | |
| **31** | A16(a) | 10pa on 5pf | 3.50 | 2.50 |
| **32** | A16(a) | 20pa on 10pf | 9.00 | 3.25 |
| **33** | A16(a) | 1pi on 20pf | 19.00 | 2.00 |
| **34** | A16(a) | 1¼pi on 25pf | 9.50 | 8.00 |
| **35** | A16(a) | 1½pi on 30pf | 14.00 | 16.00 |
| **36** | A16(a) | 2pi on 40pf | 22.50 | 16.00 |
| **37** | A16(a) | 2½pi on 50pf | 9.50 | 22.50 |
| **38** | A16(a) | 4pi on 80pf | 27.50 | 17.50 |
| **39** | A17(b) | 5pi on 1m | 47.50 | 45.00 |
| **40** | A21(b) | 10pi on 2m | 40.00 | 47.50 |
| | | On cover | | 110.00 |
| **41** | A19(b) | 15pi on 3m (R) | 47.50 | 55.00 |
| **42** | A20(b) | 25pi on 5m | 240.00 | 550.00 |
| | | *Nos. 31-42 (12)* | 489.50 | 785.25 |

### German Stamps of 1905 Surcharged in Black or Red

| | | | | |
|---|---|---|---|---|
| **1906-12** | | | **Wmk. 125** | |
| **43** | A16(a) | 10pa on 5pf | 2.40 | .90 |
| **44** | A16(a) | 20pa on 10pf | 4.75 | .90 |
| **45** | A16(a) | 1pi on 20pf | 6.50 | .90 |
| **46** | A16(a) | 1¼pi on 25pf | 13.00 | 13.00 |
| **47** | A16(a) | 1½pi on 30pf | 13.00 | 10.00 |
| **48** | A16(a) | 2pi on 40pf | 6.00 | 1.90 |
| **49** | A16(a) | 2½pi on 50pf | 9.50 | 17.50 |
| **50** | A16(a) | 4pi on 80pf | 15.00 | 22.50 |
| **51** | A17(b) | 5pi on 1m | 35.00 | 32.50 |
| **52** | A21(b) | 10pi on 2m | 35.00 | 47.50 |
| **53** | A19(b) | 15pi on 3m (R) | 60.00 | 475.00 |
| **54** | A20(b) | 25pi on 5m | 32.50 | 80.00 |
| | | *Nos. 43-54 (12)* | 232.65 | 702.60 |

German Stamps of 1905 Surcharged Diagonally in Black

| | | | | |
|---|---|---|---|---|
| **1908** | | | | |
| **55** | A16 | 5c on 5pf | 1.60 | 2.75 |
| **56** | A16 | 10c on 10pf | 2.75 | 4.75 |
| **57** | A16 | 25c on 20pf | 6.50 | 25.00 |
| **58** | A16 | 50c on 40pf | 27.50 | 60.00 |
| **59** | A16 | 100c on 80pf | 50.00 | 65.00 |
| | | On cover | | 210.00 |
| | | *Nos. 55-59 (5)* | 88.35 | 157.50 |

Forged cancellations exist on #37, 53-54, 57-59.

# GERMAN DEMOCRATIC REPUBLIC

LOCATION — Eastern Germany
GOVT. — Republic
AREA — 41,659 sq. mi.
POP. — 16,701,500 (1983)
CAPITAL — Berlin (Soviet sector)

100 Pfennigs = 1 Deutsche Mark (East)
100 Pfennigs = 1 Mark of the Deutsche Notenbank (MDN) (1965)
100 Pfennigs = 1 Mark of the National Bank (M) (1969)
100 Pfennigs = 1 Deutsche Mark (West) (1990)

**Catalogue values for unused stamps in this country are for Never Hinged items, beginning with Scott 48 in the regular postage section, Scott B14 in the semi-postal section, Scott C1 in the air-post section, and Scott O1 official section.**

### Watermarks

Watermark 292, see Germany.

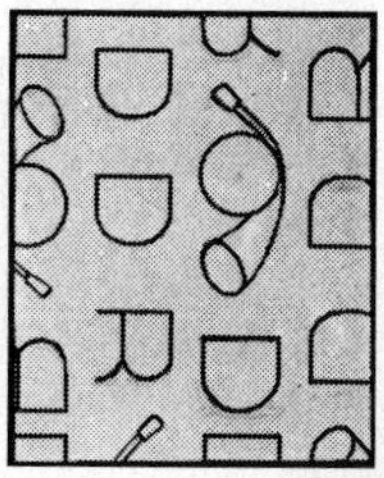

Wmk. 297 — DDR and Post Horn

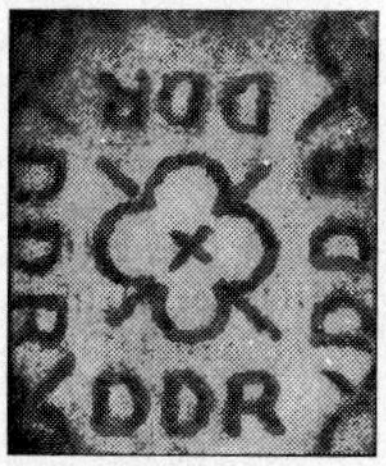

Wmk. 313 — Quatrefoil and DDR

## FOR USE IN ALL PROVINCES IN THE RUSSIAN ZONE

When the mark was revalued in June, 1948, a provisional overprint, consisting of various city and town names and post office or zone numerals, was applied by hand in black, violet or blue at innumerable post offices to their stocks.

Germany Nos. 557 to 573 Overprinted in Black

**1948, July 3 Wmk. 284 *Perf. 14***

| | | | | |
|---|---|---|---|---|
| 10N1 | A120 | 2pf brown blk | .25 | .25 |
| 10N2 | A120 | 6pf purple | .25 | .30 |
| 10N3 | A121 | 8pf red | .25 | .30 |
| 10N4 | A121 | 10pf yellow grn | .25 | .30 |
| 10N5 | A122 | 12pf gray | .25 | .30 |
| 10N6 | A120 | 15pf chocolate | .25 | .30 |
| 10N7 | A123 | 16pf dk blue grn | .25 | .50 |
| 10N8 | A121 | 20pf blue | .25 | .30 |
| 10N9 | A123 | 24pf brown org | .25 | .25 |
| 10N10 | A120 | 25pf orange yel | .25 | .25 |
| 10N11 | A122 | 30pf red | .65 | .30 |
| 10N12 | A121 | 40pf red violet | .25 | .30 |
| 10N13 | A123 | 50pf ultra | .25 | .65 |
| 10N14 | A122 | 60pf red brown | .25 | .65 |
| a. | | 60pf brown red | 30.00 | 125.00 |
| 10N15 | A122 | 80pf dark blue | .80 | .80 |
| 10N16 | A122 | 84pf emerald | .80 | 1.10 |
| | | *Nos. 10N1-10N16 (16)* | 5.50 | 6.85 |
| | | Set, never hinged | 14.00 | |

**Same Overprint on Numeral Stamps of Germany, 1946**

**1948, Sept.**

| | | | | |
|---|---|---|---|---|
| 10N17 | A119 | 5pf yellow grn | .25 | .70 |
| 10N18 | A119 | 30pf olive | .40 | 2.00 |
| 10N19 | A119 | 45pf brt red | .25 | .80 |
| 10N20 | A119 | 75pf deep ultra | .25 | .80 |
| 10N21 | A119 | 84pf emerald | .40 | 1.60 |
| | | *Nos. 10N17-10N21 (5)* | 1.55 | 5.90 |
| | | Set, never hinged | 4.75 | |

Nos 10N1-10N21 all exist with inverted overprint, and majority with double overprint.

**Same Overprint on Berlin-Brandenburg Nos. 11N1-11N7**

**Unwmk.**

**1948, Sept. Litho. *Perf. 14***

| | | | | |
|---|---|---|---|---|
| 10N22 | OS1 | 5pf green | .25 | .80 |
| a. | | Serrate roulette | .25 | .80 |
| 10N23 | OS1 | 6pf violet | .25 | .80 |
| 10N24 | OS1 | 8pf red | .25 | .80 |
| 10N25 | OS1 | 10pf brown | .25 | .80 |
| 10N26 | OS1 | 12pf rose | .25 | 1.20 |
| 10N27 | OS1 | 20pf blue | .25 | 1.20 |
| 10N28 | OS1 | 30pf olive | .25 | 1.20 |
| | | *Nos. 10N22-10N28 (7)* | 1.75 | 6.80 |
| | | Set, never hinged | 3.25 | |

The overprint made #10N22-10N28 valid for postage throughout the Russian Zone.

Gerhard Hauptmann — OS2

Designs: 2pf, 20pf, Käthe Kollwitz. 40pf, Gerhard Hauptmann. 8pf, 50pf, Karl Marx. 10pf, 84pf, August Bebel. 12pf, 30pf, Friedrich Engels. 15pf, 60pf, G. W. F. Hegel. 16pf, 25pf, Rudolf Virchow. 24pf, 80pf, Ernst Thälmann.

***Perf. 13x12½***

**1948 Typo. Wmk. 292**

| | | | | |
|---|---|---|---|---|
| 10N29 | OS2 | 2pf gray | .30 | .80 |
| 10N30 | OS2 | 6pf violet | .30 | .80 |
| 10N31 | OS2 | 8pf red brn | .30 | .80 |
| 10N32 | OS2 | 10pf blue grn | .30 | .80 |
| 10N33 | OS2 | 12pf blue | 1.00 | .80 |
| 10N34 | OS2 | 15pf brown | .40 | 1.60 |
| 10N35 | OS2 | 16pf turquoise | 1.00 | .80 |
| 10N36 | OS2 | 20pf maroon | .40 | 1.00 |
| 10N37 | OS2 | 24pf carmine | .80 | .80 |
| 10N38 | OS2 | 25pf olive grn | .50 | 1.60 |
| 10N39 | OS2 | 30pf red | .80 | 1.60 |
| 10N40 | OS2 | 40pf red violet | 4.75 | 1.60 |
| 10N41 | OS2 | 50pf dk ultra | .40 | 1.60 |
| 10N42 | OS2 | 60pf dull green | 2.40 | 1.60 |
| 10N43 | OS2 | 80pf dark blue | .40 | 1.20 |
| 10N44 | OS2 | 84pf brown lake | .40 | 2.75 |
| | | *Nos. 10N29-10N44 (16)* | 14.45 | 20.15 |
| | | Set, never hinged | 50.00 | |

See German Democratic Republic #122-136.

Karl Liebknecht and Rosa Luxemburg OS3

***Perf. 13½x13***

**1949, Jan. 15 Litho. Wmk. 292**

| | | | | |
|---|---|---|---|---|
| 10N45 | OS3 | 24pf rose | .25 | 1.00 |
| | | Never hinged | .75 | |

30th anniv. of the death of Karl Liebknecht and Rosa Luxemburg, German socialists.

Dove and Laurel — OS4

**1949**

| | | | | |
|---|---|---|---|---|
| 10N46 | OS4 | 24pf carmine rose | .55 | 2.25 |
| | | Never hinged | 1.60 | |

**Overprinted in Black: "3. Deutscher Volkskongress 29.-30. Mai 1949"**

**1949, May 29**

| | | | | |
|---|---|---|---|---|
| 10N47 | OS4 | 24pf carmine rose | .65 | 3.00 |
| | | Never hinged | 2.25 | |

Nos. 10N46 and 10N47 were issued for the 3rd German People's Congress.

## GERMAN DEMOCRATIC REPUBLIC

**Catalogue values for unused stamps in this section, from this point to the end of the section, are for Never Hinged items.**

Canceled to Order

The government stamp agency started in 1949 to sell canceled sets of new issues.

Used values are for CTO's for Nos. 48-2831, except for souvenir sheets, which are valued as postally used.

Pigeon, Letter and Globe A5

**Wmk. Flowers Multiple (292)**

**1949, Oct. 9 Litho. *Perf. 13½***

| | | | | |
|---|---|---|---|---|
| 48 | A5 | 50pf lt blue & dk blue | 8.75 | 9.50 |

75th anniv. of the UPU.

Letter Carriers — A6

Skier — A7

**1949, Oct. 27 *Perf. 13***

| | | | | |
|---|---|---|---|---|
| 49 | A6 | 12pf blue | 6.50 | 8.00 |
| 50 | A6 | 30pf red | 10.00 | 16.00 |

"Day of the International Postal Workers' Trade Union," October 27-29, 1949.

**1950, Mar. 2 *Perf. 13***

| | | | | |
|---|---|---|---|---|
| 51 | A7 | 12pf shown | 5.75 | 4.75 |
| 52 | A7 | 24pf Skater | 7.25 | 6.50 |

1st German Winter Sport Championship Matches, Schierke, 1950.

Globe and Sun — A8

**1950, May 1 Typo.**

| | | | | |
|---|---|---|---|---|
| 53 | A8 | 30pf deep carmine | 16.50 | 14.50 |

60th anniv. of Labor Day.

A9

Pres. Wilhelm Pieck — A10

**1950-51 Wmk. 292 *Perf. 13x12½***

| | | | | |
|---|---|---|---|---|
| 54 | A9 | 12pf dark blue | 17.00 | 2.00 |
| 55 | A9 | 24pf red brown | 24.00 | 1.25 |
| | | ***Perf. 13x13½*** | | |
| 56 | A10 | 1m olive green | 24.00 | 5.75 |
| | | **Litho.** | | |
| 57 | A10 | 2m red brown | 14.00 | 4.75 |
| | | **Engr.** | | |
| 57A | A10 | 5m deep blue ('51) | 6.00 | 1.60 |
| | | *Nos. 54-57A (5)* | 85.00 | 15.35 |

See Nos. 113-117, 120-121.

Leonhard Euler — A11

Miner — A12

Portraits: 5pf, Alexander von Humboldt. 6pf, Theodor Mommsen. 8pf, Wilhelm von Humboldt. 10pf, H. L. F. von Helmholtz. 12pf, Max Planck. 16pf, Jacob Grimm. 20pf, W. H. Nernst. 24pf, Gottfried von Leibnitz. 50pf, Adolf von Harnack.

**Wmk. 292**

**1950, July 10 Litho. *Perf. 12½***

| | | | | |
|---|---|---|---|---|
| 58 | A11 | 1pf gray | 3.50 | 1.60 |
| 59 | A11 | 5pf dp green | 4.25 | 4.00 |
| 60 | A11 | 6pf purple | 8.50 | 4.00 |
| 61 | A11 | 8pf orange brn | 13.00 | 8.00 |
| 62 | A11 | 10pf dk gray grn | 11.50 | 8.00 |
| 63 | A11 | 12pf dk blue | 11.00 | 3.25 |
| 64 | A11 | 16pf Prus blue | 14.50 | 14.50 |
| 65 | A11 | 20pf violet brn | 13.00 | 13.00 |
| 66 | A11 | 24pf red | 14.50 | 3.25 |
| 67 | A11 | 50pf dp ultra | 22.00 | 16.00 |
| | | *Nos. 58-67 (10)* | 115.75 | 75.60 |
| | | Set, hinged | 45.00 | |

250th anniv. of the founding of the Academy of Science, Berlin.

See Nos. 352-354.

**1950, Sept. 1 *Perf. 13***

Design: 24pf, Smelting copper.

| | | | | |
|---|---|---|---|---|
| 68 | A12 | 12pf blue | 4.75 | 6.50 |
| 69 | A12 | 24pf dark red | 7.25 | 7.25 |

750th anniv. of the opening of the Mannsfeld copper mines.

Symbols of a Democratic Vote — A13

**1950, Sept. 28**

| | | | | |
|---|---|---|---|---|
| 70 | A13 | 24pf brown red | 12.00 | 4.00 |

Publicizing the election of Oct. 15, 1950.

Hand Between Dove and Tank — A14

Designs show hand shielding dove from: 8pf, Exploding shell. 12pf, Atomic explosion. 24pf, Cemetery.

**1950, Dec. 15 Litho. *Perf. 13***

**71** A14 6pf violet blue 3.50 2.75
**72** A14 8pf brown 3.50 1.60
**73** A14 12pf blue 5.25 3.50
**74** A14 24pf red 5.25 2.40
*Nos. 71-74 (4)* 17.50 10.25

Issued to publicize the "Fight for Peace."

Tobogganing A15

Design: 24pf, Ski jump.

**1951, Feb. 3 Litho. *Perf. 13***

**76** A15 12pf blue 7.75 6.50
**77** A15 24pf rose 9.75 8.00

Issued to publicize the second Winter Sports Championship Matches at Oberhof.

A16

**1951, Mar. 4 Wmk. 292 *Perf. 13***

**78** A16 24pf rose carmine 15.00 10.00
**79** A16 50pf violet blue 15.00 10.00

Issued to publicize the 1951 Leipzig Fair.

Pres. Wilhelm Pieck and Pres. Boleslaw Bierut Shaking Hands Across Oder-Neisse Frontier — A17

**1951, Apr. 22 *Perf. 13***

**80** A17 24pf scarlet 19.00 16.00
**81** A17 50pf blue 19.00 16.00

Visit of Pres. Boleslaw Bierut of Poland to the Russian Zone of Germany.

Mao Tse-tung A18

Redistribution of Chinese Land — A19

**1951, June 27 *Perf. 13***

**82** A18 12pf dark green 100.00 27.50
**83** A19 24pf deep carmine 125.00 35.00
**84** A18 50pf violet blue 100.00 35.00
*Nos. 82-84 (3)* 325.00 97.50
Set, hinged 150.00

Issued to publicize East Germany's friendship toward Communist China.

Boy Raising Flag A20

5-Year Plan Symbolism A21

Design: 24pf, 50pf, Girls dancing.

**1951, Aug. 3**
**Grayish Paper, Except 30pf**

**85** A20 12pf choc & org brn 10.00 7.00
**86** A20 24pf dk car & yel grn 10.00 4.00
**87** A20 30pf dk bl grn & org brn, *cit* 12.50 8.00
**88** A20 50pf vio bl & dk car 12.50 8.00
*Nos. 85-88 (4)* 45.00 27.00

3rd World Youth Festival, Berlin, 1951.

**1951, Sept. 2 Typo. Wmk. 292**

**89** A21 24pf multicolored 4.00 2.50

East Germany's Five-Year Plan.

Karl Liebknecht — A22

**1951, Oct. 7 Litho. *Perf. 13½x13***

**90** A22 24pf red & blue gray 4.50 2.25

Karl Liebknecht, socialist, 80th birth anniv.

Father and Children with Stamp Collection A23

**1951, Oct. 28 *Perf. 13***

**91** A23 12pf deep blue 5.00 2.75

Stamp Day, Oct. 28, 1951.

Stalin and Wilhelm Pieck A24

Design: 12pf, Pavel Bykov and Erich Wirth.

**1951**

**92** A24 12pf deep blue 4.00 3.50
**93** A24 24pf red 4.75 5.00

Month of East German-Soviet friendship. Issue dates: 12pf, Dec. 15, 24pf, Dec. 1.

Winter Sports Championship Matches, Oberhof, 1952 — A25

Design: 12pf, Skier. 24pf, Ski jump.

**1952, Jan. 12 Wmk. 292**

**94** A25 12pf blue green 4.75 3.25
**95** A25 24pf deep blue 4.75 4.00

Ludwig van Beethoven, 125th Death Anniv. — A26

Design: 12pf, Beethoven full face.

**1952, Mar. 26 *Perf. 13½***

**96** A26 12pf bl gray & vio bl 2.00 .80
**97** A26 24pf gray & red brn 2.75 1.20

See Nos. 100-102.

Cyclists — A27

**1952, May 5 Photo. *Perf. 13x13½***

**98** A27 12pf blue 3.00 1.90

5th International Bicycle Peace Race, Warsaw-Berlin-Prague.

Klement Gottwald — A28

**1952, May 1**

**99** A28 24pf violet blue 2.25 1.75

Friendship between German Democratic Republic and Czechoslovakia.

**Type of 1952**

Portraits: 6pf, G. F. Handel. 8pf, Albert Lortzing. 50pf, C. M. von Weber.

**1952, July 5 Litho. Wmk. 297**

**100** A26 6pf brn buff & choc 2.50 1.25
**101** A26 8pf pink & dp rose pink 2.50 2.25
**102** A26 50pf bl gray & dp bl 2.50 2.50
*Nos. 100-102 (3)* 7.50 6.00

Victor Hugo — A29

Portraits: 20pf, Leonardo da Vinci. 24pf, Nicolai Gogol. 35pf, Avicenna.

**Wmk. 292**
**1952, Aug. 11 Photo. *Perf. 13***

**103** A29 12pf brown 3.25 *3.75*
**104** A29 20pf green 3.25 *3.75*
**105** A29 24pf rose 3.25 *3.75*
**106** A29 35pf blue 4.75 *5.25*
*Nos. 103-106 (4)* 14.50 16.50

Machine, Globe and Dove — A30

**1952, Sept. 7 Wmk. 297 *Perf. 13***

**108** A30 24pf red 2.00 .75
**109** A30 35pf deep blue 2.00 1.50

Issued to publicize the 1952 Leipzig Fair.

Friedrich Ludwig Jahn — A31

**1952, Oct. 15 Litho.**

**110** A31 12pf blue 1.75 1.25

Jahn (1778-1852), introduced gymnastics to Germany, and was a politician.

Halle University — A32

**1952, Oct. 18 Photo.**

**111** A32 24pf green 1.75 1.00

450th anniv. of the founding of Halle University, Wittenberg.

Stamp, Flags, Wreath, Dove and Hammer — A33

**1952, Oct. 26**

**112** A33 24pf red brown 2.25 1.00

Stamp Day, Oct. 26, 1952.

**Pieck Types of 1950**

***Perf. 13x12½***

**1952-53 Wmk. 297 Typo.**

**113** A9 5pf blue green 8.25 2.75
**114** A9 12pf dark blue 21.00 1.50
**115** A9 24pf red brown 20.00 1.25

***Perf. 13x13½***

**116** A10 1m olive green 27.00 16.00

**Litho. *Perf. 13***

**117** A10 2m red brown ('53) 23.00 3.25
*Nos. 113-117 (5)* 99.25 24.75
Set, hinged 30.00

Globe, Dove and St. Stephen's Cathedral — A34

**1952, Dec. 8 Photo. *Perf. 13***

**118** A34 24pf brt carmine 1.50 *1.60*
**119** A34 35pf deep blue 1.50 *3.00*

Issued to publicize the Congress of Nations for Peace, Vienna, Dec. 12-19, 1952.

Pres. Wilhelm Pieck — A35

**1953 *Perf. 13x13½***

**120** A35 1m olive 14.00 .50
  *a.* 1m dark olive 22.50 2.50
**121** A35 2m red brown 10.00 .50

See Nos. 339-340, 532.

### Portrait Types of Russian Occupation, 1948

Designs as before.

*Perf. 13x12½*

**1953** **Typo.** **Wmk. 297**

**122** OS2 2pf gray 2.75 *3.25*
**123** OS2 6pf purple 2.75 2.00
**124** OS2 8pf red brown 2.00 2.00
**125** OS2 10pf blue grn 5.00 3.25
**126** OS2 15pf brown 12.50 12.50
**127** OS2 16pf turquoise 4.75 3.25
**128** OS2 20pf maroon 8.00 2.00
**129** OS2 25pf olive grn 180.00 *225.00*
**130** OS2 30pf red 20.00 8.00
**131** OS2 40pf red violet 4.00 4.00
**132** OS2 50pf dk ultra 24.00 17.50
**133** OS2 60pf dull green 4.75 3.25
**134** OS2 80pf dark blue 6.50 2.00
*a.* Varnish coating, dark ultramarine 11.00 7.50
**135** OS2 80pf crimson 12.00 8.00
**136** OS2 84pf brown lake 65.00 *80.00*
*Nos. 122-136 (15)* 354.00 376.00
Set, hinged 110.00

"Industry" and Red Flag — A36

Karl Marx Speaking — A38

Marx and Engels — A37

Karl Marx Medallion — A39

Designs: 12pf, Spasski tower and communist flag. 16pf, Marching workers. 24pf, Portrait of Karl Marx. 35pf, Marx addressing audience. 48pf, Karl Marx and Friedrich Engels. 60pf. Red banner above heads and shoulders of workers.

**1953** **Photo.** *Perf. 13*

**137** A36 6pf grnsh gray & red 1.25 .80
**138** A37 10pf grnsh gray & dk brn 3.50 .30
**139** A36 12pf grn, dp plum & dk grn .95 .30
**140** A37 16pf vio bl & dk car 2.50 1.75
**141** A38 20pf brown & buff 1.25 .75
**142** A38 24pf brown & red 2.50 .75
**143** A36 35pf dp pur & cr 2.50 2.50
**144** A36 48pf dk ol grn & red brn 1.90 .75
*a.* Souvenir sheet of 6 100.00 *175.00*
Hinged 35.00
**145** A37 60pf vio brn & red 3.25 2.50
**146** A39 84pf blue & brown 2.75 1.75
*a.* Souvenir sheet of 4 100.00 *175.00*
Hinged 35.00
*Nos. 137-146 (10)* 22.35 12.15

No. 144a contains one each of the denominations in types A36 and A38. Perf. and imperf.

No. 146a contains one each of the denominations in types A37 and A39. Perf. and imperf.

Maxim Gorky — A40

Bicycle Racers — A41

**1953, Mar. 28**
**147** A40 35pf brown .45 .45

**1953, May 2** **Wmk. 297** *Perf. 13*

24pf, 60pf, Different views of bicycle race.

**148** A41 24pf bluish green 2.00 2.00
**149** A41 35pf deep ultra 1.00 1.25
**150** A41 60pf chocolate 1.25 1.60
*Nos. 148-150 (3)* 4.25 4.85

6th International Bicycle Peace Race.

Heinrich von Kleist A42

Woman Mariner A43

20pf, Evangelical Marienkirche. 24pf, Sailboat on Oder River. 35pf, City Hall, Frankfurt-on-Oder.

**1953, July 6** **Litho.**

**151** A42 16pf chocolate 1.25 *2.00*
**152** A42 20pf blue green .80 *2.00*
**153** A42 24pf rose red 1.25 *2.00*
**154** A42 35pf violet blue 1.25 *2.50*
*Nos. 151-154 (4)* 4.55 8.50

700th anniversary of the founding of Frankfurt-on-Oder.

**1953** **Litho.** *Perf. 13x12½*

Designs: 1pf, Coal miner. 6pf, German and Soviet workers. 8pf, Mother teaching Marxist principles. 10pf, Machinists. 12pf, Worker, peasant and intellectual. 15pf, Teletype operator. 16pf, Steel worker. 20pf, Bad Elster. 24pf, Stalin Boulevard. 25pf, Locomotive building. 30pf, Dancing couple. 35pf, Sports Hall, Berlin. 40pf, Laboratory worker. 48pf, Zwinger Castle, Dresden. 60pf, Launching ship. 80pf, Agricultural workers. 84pf, Dove and East German family.

**155** A43 1pf black brown 1.25 .25
**156** A43 5pf emerald 1.60 .25
**157** A43 6pf violet 1.60 .25
**158** A43 8pf orange brn 2.25 .25
**159** A43 10pf blue green 1.60 .25
**160** A43 12pf blue 1.60 .25
**161** A43 15pf purple 2.60 .25
**162** A43 16pf dk violet 4.00 .25
**163** A43 20pf olive 3.75 .25
**163A** A43 24pf carmine 7.00 .25
**164** A43 25pf dk green 5.00 .25
**165** A43 30pf dp car 5.00 .25
**166** A43 35pf violet bl 15.00 .25
**167** A43 40pf rose red 12.50 .25
**168** A43 48pf rose red 12.50 .25
**169** A43 60pf deep blue 12.50 .25
**170** A43 80pf aqua 14.00 .25
**171** A43 84pf chocolate 12.50 .25
*Nos. 155-171 (18)* 116.25 4.50
Set, hinged 40.00

See Nos. 187-204, 227-230A, 330-338, 476-482. For surcharges see #216-223A.

Used values of Nos. 155-171 are for cto reprints with printed cancellations. The reprints differ slightly from originals in design and shade.

Power Shovel — A44

Design: 35pf, Road-building machine.

**1953, Aug. 29** **Photo.** *Perf. 13*

**172** A44 24pf red brown 1.75 2.00
**173** A44 35pf deep green 2.75 2.50

The 1953 Leipzig Fair.

G. W. von Knobelsdorff and Berlin State Opera House — A45

Design: 35pf, Balthasar Neumann and Wurzburg bishop's palace.

**1953, Sept. 16** *Perf. 13x12½*

**174** A45 24pf cerise 1.25 .90
**175** A45 35pf dk slate blue 2.00 1.50

200th anniv. of the deaths of G. W. von Knobelsdorff and Balthasar Neumann, architects.

Lucas Cranach — A46

**1953, Oct. 16** *Perf. 13x13½*

**176** A46 24pf brown 3.00 1.50

400th anniversary of the death of Lucas Cranach (1472-1553), painter.

Nurse Applying Bandage — A47

*Perf. 13½x13*

**1953, Oct. 23** **Wmk. 297**

**177** A47 24pf brown & red 2.10 1.50

Issued to honor the Red Cross.

Mail Delivery — A48

**1953, Oct. 25** **Photo.**

**178** A48 24pf blue gray 2.50 .70

Stamp Day, Oct. 24, 1953.

Lion and Lioness — A49

**1953, Nov. 2** *Perf. 13x13½*

**179** A49 24pf olive brown 2.10 .80

75th anniversary of Leipzig Zoo.

Thomas Muntzer and Attackers A50

16pf, H. F. K. vom Stein. 20pf, Ferdinand von Schill leading cavalry. 24pf, G. L. Blucher and battle scene. 35pf, Students fighting for National Unity. 48pf, Revolution of 1848.

**1953, Nov.** **Photo.** *Perf. 13x12½*

**180** A50 12pf brown 1.50 .65
**181** A50 16pf dp brown 1.50 .65
**182** A50 20pf dk car rose 1.50 .40
**183** A50 24pf deep blue 1.50 .40
**184** A50 35pf dk green 2.50 1.60
**185** A50 48pf dk brown 2.50 1.25
*Nos. 180-185 (6)* 11.00 4.95

Issued to honor German patriots.

Franz Schubert — A51

Gotthold E. Lessing — A52

**1953, Nov. 13** *Perf. 13½x13*

**186** A51 48pf brt orange brn 2.75 1.60

Death of Franz Schubert, 125th anniv.

### Types of 1953 Redrawn

Designs as before.

**1953-54** **Typo.** *Perf. 13x12½*

**187** A43 1pf black brn .80 .25
**188** A43 5pf emerald 3.00 .25
*a.* Bklt. pane, 3 #188 + 3 #227 24.00 28.00
*b.* Bklt. pane, 3 #188 + 3 #228 24.00 28.00
**189** A43 6pf purple 4.00 .25
**190** A43 8pf orange brn 5.00 .25
**191** A43 10pf blue grn 35.00 .25
**192** A43 12pf grnsh blue 5.50 .25
**193** A43 15pf brt vio ('54) 17.50 .25
**194** A43 16pf dk purple 4.00 .25
**195** A43 20pf olive ('54) 75.00 .25
**196** A43 24pf carmine 6.50 .25
**197** A43 25pf dk bl grn 4.00 .25
**198** A43 30pf dp carmine 8.00 .25
**199** A43 35pf dp vio bl 4.75 .25
**200** A43 40pf rose red ('54) 10.00 .25
**201** A43 48pf rose vio 10.00 .25
**202** A43 60pf blue 17.50 .25
**203** A43 80pf aqua 4.00 .25
**204** A43 84pf chocolate 16.00 .25
*Nos. 187-204 (18)* 230.55 4.50
Set, hinged 55.00

Nos. 155-171 were printed from screened halftones, and shading consists of dots. Shading in lines without screen on Nos. 187-204. Designers' and engravers' names added below design on all values except 6, 12, 16 and 35pf. There are many other minor differences.

See note on used values after No. 171.

**1954, Jan. 20** **Photo.** *Perf. 13*

**205** A52 20pf dark green 2.25 .95

225th anniversary of the birth of G. E. Lessing, dramatist.

Dove Over Conference Table — A53

Joseph V. Stalin — A54

**1954, Jan. 25** *Perf. 12½x13*

**206** A53 12pf blue 1.60 .90

Four Power Conference, Berlin, 1954.

**1954, Mar. 5** **Typo.** *Perf. 13x12½*

**207** A54 20pf gray, dk brn & red org 2.75 1.00

1st anniv. of the death of Joseph V. Stalin.

Cyclists A55

Design: 24pf, Cyclists passing farm.

**1954, Apr. 30** **Photo.**

**208** A55 12pf brown 1.20 .80
**209** A55 24pf dull green 2.00 1.20

7th International Bicycle Peace Race.

Dancers — A56

Fritz Reuter — A57

Design: 24pf, Boy, two girls and flag.

**1954, June 3** ***Perf. 13***

**210** A56 12pf emerald 1.10 .90
**211** A56 24pf rose brown 1.10 .90

Issued to publicize the 2nd German youth meeting for peace, unity and freedom.

**1954, July 12**

**212** A57 24pf sepia 1.50 1.10

Death of Fritz Reuter, writer, 80th anniv.

Ernst Thälmann — A58

**1954, Aug. 18** ***Perf. 13½x13***

**213** A58 24pf red org & indigo 1.00 .80

10th anniv. of the death of Ernst Thälmann (1886-1944), Communist leader.

Hall of Commerce, Leipzig Fair — A59

**1954, Sept. 4** ***Perf. 13x13½***

**214** A59 24pf dark red .75 .55
**215** A59 35pf gray blue .75 .70

Issued to publicize the 1954 Leipzig Fair.

**Redrawn Types of 1953-54 Surcharged with New Value and "X" in Black**

**1954** **Typo.** ***Perf. 13x12½***

**216** A43 5pf on 6pf purple 1.00 .25
**217** A43 5pf on 8pf org brn 1.40 .25
**218** A43 10pf on 12pf grnsh bl 1.00 .25
**219** A43 15pf on 16pf dk pur 1.00 .25
**220** A43 20pf on 24pf car 1.10 .25
**221** A43 40pf on 48pf rose vio 3.00 .25
**222** A43 50pf on 60pf blue 3.00 .25
**223** A43 70pf on 84pf choc 8.00 .25
*Nos. 216-223 (8)* 19.50 2.00

See note on used values after No. 171.

**No. 163A Surcharged with New Value and "X" in Black**

**1955** **Litho.**

**223A** A43 20pf on 24pf car .80 .45

Counterfeit surcharges exist on other values of the lithographed set (Nos. 155-171).

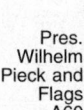

Pres. Wilhelm Pieck and Flags A60

**1954, Oct. 6** **Photo.**

**224** A60 20pf brown 2.25 1.10
**225** A60 35pf greenish blue 2.25 1.25

5th anniv. of the founding of the German Democratic Republic.

Cologne Cathedral, Leipzig Monument and Unissued Stamp Design — A61

**1954, Oct. 23** ***Perf. 13x13½***

**226** A61 20pf brt car rose 1.25 .80
*a.* Souvenir sheet, imperf. 40.00 40.00

Stamp Day. No. 226a has frame and inscription in blue. Size: 60x80mm.

**Redrawn Types of 1953-54**

Designs: 10pf, Worker, peasant and intellectual. 15pf, Steelworker. 20pf, Stalin Boulevard. 40pf, Zwinger Castle, Dresden. 50pf, Launching ship. 70pf, Dove and East German family.

**1955** **Typo.** ***Perf. 13x12½***

**227** A43 10pf blue 2.00 .25
*a.* Bklt. pane, 4 #227 + 2 #228 28.00 28.00
**227B** A43 15pf violet 2.40 .25
**228** A43 20pf carmine 1.75 .25
**229** A43 40pf rose violet 3.75 .25
**230** A43 50pf deep blue 6.25 .25
**230A** A43 70pf chocolate 8.50 .25
*Nos. 227-230A (6)* 24.65 1.50

See note on used values after No. 171.

Soviet Pavilion, Leipzig Spring Fair — A62

Design: 35pf, Chinese pavilion.

***Perf. 13x13½***

**1955, Feb. 21** **Photo.** **Wmk. 297**

**231** A62 20pf rose violet .90 .90
**232** A62 35pf violet blue 1.10 .90

Issued to publicize the Leipzig Spring Fair.

Women of Three Nations — A63

**1955, Mar. 1** ***Perf. 13x13½***

**233** A63 10pf green .90 .45
**234** A63 20pf red .90 .45

International Women's Day, 45th year.

Workers' Demonstration — A64

**1955, Mar. 15** ***Perf. 13x12½***

**235** A64 10pf black & red .90 .90

Intl. Trade Union Conference, Apr., 1955.

A65

A66

Monument to the Victims of Fascism.

**1955, Apr. 9** ***Perf. 13½x13***

**236** A65 10pf violet blue .70 .80
**237** A65 20pf cerise 1.00 1.25
*a.* Souv. sheet of 2, #236-237, imperf. 17.50 27.50

No. 237a sold for 50pf.

**1955, Apr. 15** ***Perf. 12½x13***

Russian War Memorial, Berlin.

**238** A66 20pf lilac rose 1.30 1.10

Nos. 236-238 issued for 10th anniv. of liberation, No. 237a for reconstruction of natl. memorial sites.

Cyclists — A67

**1955** **Wmk. 297** ***Perf. 13½x13***

**239** A67 10pf blue green .80 .60
**240** A67 20pf car rose .80 .75

8th International Bicycle Peace Race, Prague-Berlin-Warsaw.

Starting with the 1955 issues, commemorative stamps which are valued in italics were sold on a restricted basis.

Friedrich von Schiller — A68

Various Portraits of Schiller.

**1955, Apr. 20**

**241** A68 5pf dk gray grn *2.75* *2.40*
**242** A68 10pf brt blue .60 .25
**243** A68 20pf chocolate .60 .25
*a.* Souv. sheet, #241-243, imperf. *22.00* *24.00*
*Nos. 241-243 (3)* *3.95* *2.90*

150th anniv. of the death of Friedrich von Schiller, poet.

No. 243a sold for 50pf.

Karl Liebknecht — A69

Portraits: 10pf, August Bebel. 15pf, Franz Mehring. 20pf, Ernst Thalmann. 25pf, Clara Zetkin. 40pf, Wilhelm Liebknecht. 60pf, Rosa Luxemburg.

**1955, June 20** **Photo.** ***Perf. 13x12½***

**244** A69 5pf blue green .30 .30
**245** A69 10pf deep blue .40 .30
**246** A69 15pf violet *5.50* *3.25*
**247** A69 20pf red .40 .30
**248** A69 25pf slate .40 .30
**249** A69 40pf rose carmine 2.10 .30
**250** A69 60pf dk brown .40 .30
*Nos. 244-250 (7)* *9.50* *5.05*

Issued to honor German communists.

Optical Goods — A70

Design: 20pf, Pottery and china.

**1955, Aug. 29** **Photo.** ***Perf. 13x13½***

**253** A70 10pf dark blue .60 .45
**254** A70 20pf slate green .60 .45

Issued to publicize the 1955 Leipzig Fair.

Farmer Receiving Deed — A71

Harvesters A72

10pf, Construction of new farm community.

**1955, Sept. 3** ***Perf. 13½x13, 13x13½***

**255** A71 5pf dull green *5.25* *4.00*
**256** A71 10pf ultra .80 .35
**257** A72 20pf lake .80 .35
*Nos. 255-257 (3)* *6.85* *4.70*

10th anniv. of the Land-Reform Program.

Man Holding Badge of Peoples' Solidarity — A73

Engels at "First International," 1864 — A74

***Perf. 13½x13***

**1955, Oct. 10** **Wmk. 297**

**258** A73 10pf dark blue .60 .40

10th anniv. of the "Peoples' Solidarity."

**1955, Nov. 7** ***Perf. 13½x13***

Designs: 10pf, Marx and Engels writing the Communist Manifesto. 15pf, Engels as newspaper editor. 20pf, Friedrich Engels. 30pf, Friedrich Engels. 70pf, Engels on the barricades in 1848.

**259** A74 5pf Prus blue & olive .35 .25
**260** A74 10pf dk blue & yel .70 .25
**261** A74 15pf dk green & ol .70 .25
**262** A74 20pf brn vio & org 1.40 .25
**263** A74 30pf org brn & lt bl *8.00* *8.00*
**264** A74 70pf gray grn & rose car 4.00 .30
*a.* Souvenir sheet of 6, #259-264 *65.00* *140.00*
*Nos. 259-264 (6)* *15.15* *9.30*

Friedrich Engels, 135th birth anniv.

Cathedral at Magdeburg A75

Georgius Agricola A76

German Buildings: 10pf, German State Opera. 15pf, Old City Hall, Leipzig. 20pf, City Hall, Berlin. 30pf, Cathedral at Erfurt. 40pf, Zwinger at Dresden.

**1955, Nov. 14**

**265** A75 5pf black brown .75 .40
**266** A75 10pf gray green .75 .40
**267** A75 15pf purple .75 .40
**268** A75 20pf carmine .75 .80
**269** A75 30pf dk red brown *7.25* *10.50*
**270** A75 40pf indigo 1.50 .80
*Nos. 265-270 (6)* *11.75* *13.30*

For surcharges see Nos. B29-B30.

**1955, Nov. 21** **Wmk. 297**

**271** A76 10pf brown .60 .50

400th anniv. of the death of Georgius Agricola, mineralogist and scholar.

Paintings in Dresden Gallery — A77

Mozart — A78

Famous Paintings: 5pf, Portrait of a Young Man, by Dürer. 10pf, Chocolate Girl, by Liotard. 15pf, Portrait of a Boy, by Pinturicchio. 20pf, Self-portrait with Saskia, by Rembrandt. 40pf, Girl with Letter, by Vermeer. 70pf, Sistine Madonna, by Raphael.

**1955, Dec. 15** ***Perf. 13½x13***

**272** A77 5pf dk red brown .65 .25
**273** A77 10pf chestnut .65 .25
**274** A77 15pf pale purple *25.00 32.50*
**275** A77 20pf brown .65 .25
**276** A77 40pf olive green .65 .35
**277** A77 70pf deep blue 1.60 .75
*Nos. 272-277 (6) 29.20 34.35*

Issued to publicize the return of famous art works to the Dresden Art Gallery.
See Nos. 355-360, 439-443.

**1956, Jan. 27** **Photo.**

Designs: 20pf, Portrait facing left.

**278** A78 10pf gray green *11.00 8.00*
**279** A78 20pf copper brown 3.75 2.00

200th anniv. of the birth of Wolfgang Amadeus Mozart, composer.

Flag and Schoenefeld Airport, Berlin — A79

Lufthansa Plane A80

Designs: 15pf, Plane facing right. 20pf, Plane facing down and left.

**1956, Feb. 1** ***Perf. 13x12½***

**280** A79 5pf multicolored *12.00 8.50*
**281** A80 10pf gray green .70 .35
**282** A80 15pf dull blue .70 .35
**283** A80 20pf brown red .70 .35
*Nos. 280-283 (4) 14.10 9.55*

Issued to commemorate the opening of passenger service of the German Lufthansa.

Heinrich Heine — A81

Design: 20pf, Heine (different portrait.)

**1956, Feb. 17** ***Perf. 13½x13***

**284** A81 10pf Prus green *11.00 5.50*
**285** A81 20pf dark red *2.25* .60

Cent. of the death of Heinrich Heine, poet.

Railroad Cranes — A82

**1956, Feb. 26** ***Perf. 13x13½***

**286** A82 20pf brown red .60 .40
**287** A82 35pf violet blue .90 .75

Issued to publicize the Leipzig Spring Fair.

Ernst Thälmann A83

**1956, Apr. 16** **Litho.** ***Perf. 13x13½***

**288** A83 20pf black olive & red .75 .40
*a.* Souvenir sheet of 1, imperf *9.50 32.50*

Birth of Ernst Thälmann, 70th anniv.
No. 288a was sold at double face value. The proceeds were used for national memorials at former concentration camps.

Wheel, Hand and Olive Branch — A84

City Hall and Old Market — A85

Design: 20pf, Wheel and coats of arms of Warsaw, Berlin, Prague.

***Perf. 13½x13***

**1956, Apr. 30** **Wmk. 297**

**289** A84 10pf lt green .65 .30
**290** A84 20pf brt carmine .65 .30

9th International Bicycle Peace Race, Warsaw-Berlin-Prague, May 1-15, 1956.

**1956, June 1**

Designs: 20pf, Hofkirche and Elbe Bridge. 40pf, Technical College.

**291** A85 10pf green .40 .25
**292** A85 20pf carmine rose .40 .25
**293** A85 40pf brt purple *1.75 2.00*
*Nos. 291-293 (3) 2.55 2.50*

750th anniversary of Dresden.

Worker Holding Cogwheel Emblem — A86

**1956, June 30** ***Perf. 13½x13***

**294** A86 20pf rose red .45 .25

10th anniversary of nationalized industry.

Robert Schumann (Music by Schubert) A87

**1956, July 20** ***Perf. 13x13½***

**295** A87 10pf brt green *2.10 1.25*
**296** A87 20pf rose red 1.25 .25

Centenary of the death of Robert Schumann, composer. See Nos. 303-304.

Soccer Players — A88

Thomas Mann — A89

Designs: 10pf, Javelin Thrower. 15pf, Women Hurdlers. 20pf, Gymnast.

**1956, July 25** ***Perf. 13½x13***

**297** A88 5pf green .30 .25
**298** A88 10pf dk vio blue .30 .25
**299** A88 15pf red violet *2.10 1.40*
**300** A88 20pf rose red .30 .25
*Nos. 297-300 (4) 3.00 2.15*

Second Sports Festival, Leipzig, Aug. 2-5.

**1956, Aug. 13** **Wmk. 297**

**301** A89 20pf bluish black 1.00 .50

Death of Thomas Mann, novelist, 1st anniv.

Jakub Bart Cisinski — A90

**1956, Aug. 20** **Photo.**

**302** A90 50pf claret 1.00 .50

Birth centenary of Jakub Bart Cisinski, poet.

Robert Schumann (Music by Schumann) A91

**1956, Oct. 8** ***Perf. 13x13½***

**303** A91 10pf brt green *4.75 1.75*
**304** A91 20pf rose red 2.75 .40

See Nos. 295, 296.

Lace — A92

Olympic Rings, Laurel and Torch — A93

Design: 20pf, Sailboat.

**1956, Sept. 1** **Typo.** ***Perf. 13½x13***

**305** A92 10pf green & blk .30 .30
**306** A92 20pf rose red & blk .30 .30

Leipzig Fair, Sept. 2-9.

**1956, Sept. 28** **Litho.**

Design: 35pf, Classic javelin thrower.

**307** A93 20pf brown red .45 .35
**308** A93 35pf slate blue .65 .45

16th Olympic Games at Melbourne, Nov. 22-Dec. 8, 1956.

Post Runner of 1450 — A94

**1956, Oct. 27**

**309** A94 20pf red .50 .35

Issued to publicize the Day of the Stamp.

Greifswald University Seal — A95

**1956, Oct. 17** ***Perf. 13x13½***

**310** A95 20pf magenta .55 .35

500th anniv. of Greifswald University.

Ernst Abbe — A96

Zeiss Works, Jena A97

Portrait: 25pf, Carl Zeiss.

***Perf. 12½x13, 13x12½***

**1956, Nov. 9** **Photo.** **Wmk. 297**

**311** A96 10pf dark green .25 .25
**312** A97 20pf brown red .25 .25
**313** A96 25pf bluish black .35 .30
*Nos. 311-313 (3)* .85 .80

Carl Zeiss Optical Works, Jena, 110th anniv.

Chinese Girl with Flowers — A98

Designs: 10pf, Negro woman and child. 25pf, European man and dove.

**1956, Dec. 10** **Litho.** ***Perf. 13***

**314** A98 5pf ol, *pale lem* *1.25* .90
**315** A98 10pf brown, *pink* .25 .25
**316** A98 25pf vio bl, *pale vio bl* .25 .25
*Nos. 314-316 (3) 1.75 1.40*

Issued for Human Rights Day.

Elephants A99

**1956, Dec. 14** **Photo.** ***Perf. 13x12½***

**Design in Gray**

**317** A99 5pf shown .25 .25
**318** A99 10pf Flamingoes .25 .25
**319** A99 15pf White rhinoceros *4.50 3.00*
**320** A99 20pf Mouflon .25 .25
**321** A99 25pf Bison .25 .25
**322** A99 30pf Polar bear .25 .25
*Nos. 317-322 (6) 5.75 4.25*

Issued to publicize the Berlin Zoo.

Freighter A100

Design: 25pf, Electric Locomotive.

**1957, Mar. 1** **Litho.** **Wmk. 313**

**323** A100 20pf rose red .25 .25
**324** A100 25pf bright blue .25 .25

Leipzig Spring Fair.

Silver Thistle A101

10pf, Emerald lizard. 20pf, Lady's-slipper.

**1957, Apr. 12 Photo. Wmk. 313**

**325** A101 5pf chocolate .25 .25
**326** A101 10pf dk slate grn *2.40 2.25*
**327** A101 20pf red brown .25 .25
*Nos. 325-327 (3) 2.90 2.75*

Nature Conservation Week, Apr. 14-20.

Children at Play — A102

20pf, Friedrich Froebel and Children.

**1957, Apr. 18 Litho. *Perf. 13***

**328** A102 10pf dk slate grn & ol *1.20 .90*
**329** A102 20pf black & brown red .25 .25

175th anniv. of the birth of Friedrich Froebel, educator.

**Redrawn Types of 1953**

Designs: 5pf, Woman mariner. 10pf, Worker, peasant and intellectual. 15pf, Steel worker. 20pf, Stalin Boulevard. 25pf, Locomotive building. 30pf, Dancing couple. 40pf, Zwinger Castle, Dresden. 50pf, Launching ship. 70pf, Dove and East German family.

Imprint: "E. Gruner K. Wolf"
No imprint on 10pf, 15pf

***Perf. 13x12½, 14***

**1957-58 Typo. Wmk. 313**

**330** A43 5pf emerald .75 .25
a. Bklt. pane, 3 #330 + 3 #331b 27.50 27.50
b. Bklt. pane, 3 #330 + 3 #333 27.50 27.50
c. Booklet pane of 6 5.00 4.75
**331** A43 10pf blue ('58) .25 .25
a. Bklt. pane, 4 #331b + 2 #333 40.00 40.00
b. Perf. 13x12½ 5.50 .25
**332** A43 15pf violet ('58) .75 .25
a. Perf. 13x12½ .75 .25
**333** A43 20pf carmine .30 .25
a. Bklt. pane, 5 #333 + 1 #477 4.00 8.00
**334** A43 25pf bluish green .30 .25
**335** A43 30pf dull red .55 .25
**336** A43 40pf rose violet .95 .25
**337** A43 50pf bright blue 1.20 .25
**338** A43 70pf chocolate 2.40 .25

See Nos. 476-482.

**Pieck Type of 1953**

**Photo. *Perf. 13x13½***

**339** A35 1m dk olive grn ('58) 2.40 .40
**340** A35 2m red brown ('58) 4.75 .40
*Nos. 330-340 (11)* 14.60 3.05

No. 334 comes only perf 13x12½. Nos 330-333 and 335-338 come both perf 13x12½ and perf 14.

Bicycle Race Route — A103

***Perf. 13x13½***

**1957, Apr. 30 Litho. Wmk. 313**

**346** A103 5pf orange .35 .30

Issued to publicize the 10th International Bicycle Peace Race, Prague-Berlin-Warsaw.

Steam Shovel A104

Miner — A105

Design: 20pf, Coal conveyor.

***Perf. 13x12½, 13½x13 (25pf)***

**1957, May 3**

**347** A104 10pf green .25 .25
**348** A104 20pf redsh brown .25 .25
**349** A105 25pf blue violet *2.25 1.25*
*Nos. 347-349 (3) 2.75 1.75*

Issued in honor of the coal mining industry.

Henri Dunant and Globe A106

25pf, Henri Dunant facing right and globe.

**1957, May 7 Photo. *Perf. 13x12½***

**350** A106 10pf green, red & blk .25 .25
**351** A106 25pf brt blue, red & blk .25 .25

Tenth Red Cross world conference.

**Portrait Type of 1950, Redrawn**

Portraits: 5pf, Joachim Jungius. 10pf, Leonhard Euler. 20pf, Heinrich Hertz.

**1957, June 7 Litho.**

**352** A11 5pf brown *1.75 1.00*
**353** A11 10pf green .25 .25
**354** A11 20pf henna brown .25 .25
*Nos. 352-354 (3) 2.25 1.50*

Issued to honor famous German scientists.

**Painting Type of 1955.**

Famous Paintings: 5pf, Holy Family, by Mantegna. 10pf, The Dancer Campani, by Carriera. 15pf, Portrait of Morette, by Holbein. 20pf, The Tribute Money, by Titian. 25pf, Saskia with Red Flower, by Rembrandt. 40pf, Young Standard Bearer, by Piazetta.

***Perf. 13½x13***

**1957, June 26 Photo. Wmk. 313**

**355** A77 5pf dk brown .30 .25
**356** A77 10pf lt yellow grn .30 .25
**357** A77 15pf brown olive .30 .25
**358** A77 20pf rose brown .30 .25
**359** A77 25pf deep claret .30 .25
**360** A77 40pf dk blue gray *5.25 2.00*
*Nos. 355-360 (6) 6.75 3.25*

Clara Zetkin — A107

**1957, July 5 *Perf. 13x13½***

**361** A107 10pf dk green & red .60 .30

Centenary of the birth of Clara Zetkin, politician and founder of the socialist women's movement.

Bertolt Brecht — A108

**1957, Aug. 14 *Perf. 13½x13***

**362** A108 10pf dark green .30 .25
**363** A108 25pf deep blue .40 .25

Brecht (1898-1956), playwright and poet.

Congress Emblem — A109

Fair Emblem — A110

**1957, Aug. 23 Litho.**

**364** A109 20pf brt red & black .55 .30

4th Intl. Trade Union Congress, Leipzig, Oct. 4-15.

**1957, Aug. 30 Wmk. 313**

**365** A110 20pf crimson & ver .30 .25
**366** A110 25pf brt blue & lt blue .30 .25

Issued to publicize the 1957 Leipzig Fair.

Savings Book — A111

Postrider, 1563 — A112

**1957, Oct. 10 *Perf. 13½x13***

**367** A111 10pf grn & blk, *gray* *.80 .60*
**368** A111 20pf rose car & blk, *gray* .30 .30

Issued to publicize "Savings Weeks."

**1957, Oct. 25 Wmk. 313**

**369** A112 5pf black, *pale sepia* .50 .25

Issued for the Day of the Stamp.

Sputnik I A113

Storming of the Winter Palace A114

20pf, Stratospheric balloon above clouds. 25pf, Ship with plumb line exploring deep sea.

**1957-58 *Perf. 12½x13***

**370** A113 10pf blue black .40 .25
**371** A113 20pf car rose ('58) .55 .25
**372** A113 25pf brt blue ('58) *2.10 1.25*
*Nos. 370-372 (3) 3.05 1.75*

IGY. The 10pf also for the launching of the 1st artificial satellite.

**1957, Nov. 7 Photo.**

**373** A114 10pf yellow grn & red .25 .25
**374** A114 25pf brt blue & red .25 .25

40th anniv. of the Russian Revolution.

Guenther Ramin — A115

Portrait: 20pf, Hermann Abendroth.

***Perf. 13½x13***

**1957, Nov. 22 Litho. Wmk. 313**

**375** A115 10pf yellow grn & blk *1.00 .80*
**376** A115 20pf red orange & blk .25 .25

Ramin (1898-1956) and Abendroth (1883-1956), musicians, on the 1st anniv. of their death.

Dove and Globe — A116

**1958, Feb. 27 *Perf. 13x13½***

**377** A116 20pf rose red .30 .25
**378** A116 25pf blue .35 .25

Issued to publicize the 1958 Leipzig Fair.

Radio Tower, Morse Code and Post Horn A117

Design: 20pf, Radio tower and small post horn.

**1958, Mar. 6 *Perf. 13x12½***

**379** A117 5pf gray & blk *.80 .55*
**380** A117 20pf crim rose & dk red .40 .25

Conf. of Postal Ministers of Communist countries, Moscow, Dec. 3-17, 1957.

Sketch by Zille — A118

Symbolizing Quantum Theory — A119

Design: 20pf, Self-portrait of Zille.

**1958, Mar. 20 *Perf. 13½x13***

**381** A118 10pf green & gray *2.40 1.25*
**382** A118 20pf dp car & gray .55 .25

Centenary of the birth of Heinrich Zille, artist.

**1958, Apr. 23 Litho.**

Design: 20pf, Max Planck.

**383** A119 10pf gray green *1.20 1.00*
**384** A119 20pf magenta .40 .25

Centenary of the birth of Max Planck, physicist.

Prize Cow — A120

10pf, Mowing machine. 20pf, Beet harvester.

***Perf. 13x13½***

**1958, June 4 Wmk. 313**

**Size: 28x23mm**

**385** A120 5pf gray & blk *2.25 1.25*

**Size: 39x22mm**

***Perf. 13x12½***

**386** A120 10pf brt green .35 .25
**387** A120 20pf rose red .35 .25
*Nos. 385-387 (3) 2.95 1.75*

6th Agricultural Show, Markkleeberg.

Charles Darwin — A121

Portrait: 20pf, Carl von Linné.

**1958, June 19** *Perf. 13x13½*
**388** A121 10pf green & black *1.50 1.00*
**389** A121 20pf dk red & black .25 .25

Cent. of Darwin's theory of evolution and the bicent. of Linné's botanical system.

Seven Towers of Rostock and Ships — A122

Congress Emblem — A123

10pf, Ship at pier. 25pf, Ships in harbor.

**1958** *Perf. 13½x13*
**390** A122 10pf emerald .25 .25
**391** A122 20pf red orange .50 .25
**392** A122 25pf lt blue *1.10 1.10*
*Nos. 390-392 (3)* *1.85 1.60*

Establishment of Rostock as a seaport.
Issue dates: 20pf, July 5; 10pf and 25pf, Nov. 24.
For overprint see No. 500.

**1958, June 25** *Perf. 13x13½*
**393** A123 10pf rose red .35 .30

5th congress of the Socialist Party of the German Democratic Republic (SED).

Mare and Foal A124

Designs: 10pf, Trotter. 20pf, Horse race.

**1958, July 22 Photo.** *Perf. 13x12½*
**394** A124 5pf black brown *2.50 2.00*
**395** A124 10pf dark olive green .25 .25
**396** A124 20pf dark red brown .25 .25
*Nos. 394-396 (3)* *3.00 2.50*

Grand Prize of the DDR, 1958.

Jan Amos Komensky (Comenius) A125

Design: 20pf, Teacher and pupils, 17th cent.

**1958, Aug. 7 Litho.** *Perf. 13x13½*
**397** A125 10pf brt bl grn & blk *1.50 1.00*
**398** A125 20pf org brn & blk .25 .25

University Seal A126

Design: 20pf, Schiller University, Jena.

**1958, Aug. 19** *Perf. 13x12½*
**399** A126 5pf gray & black *1.50 1.00*
**400** A126 20pf dark red & gray .30 .25

Friedrich Schiller University in Jena, 400th anniv.

Soldier on Obstacle Course — A127

Design: 20pf, Spartacist emblem. 25pf, Marching athletes, map and flag.

*Perf. 13½x13*

**1958, Sept. 19 Litho. Wmk. 313**
**401** A127 10pf emerald & brn *1.50 .90*
**402** A127 20pf brown red & yel .30 .25
**403** A127 25pf lt blue & red .30 .25
*Nos. 401-403 (3)* *2.10 1.40*

1st Spartacist Sports Meet of Friendly Armies, Leipzig, Sept. 20-28.

Arms Breaking A-Bomb — A128

**1958, Sept. 19** *Perf. 13x13½*
**404** A128 20pf rose red .25 .25
**405** A128 25pf blue .40 .25

People's fight against atomic death.

Woman and Leipzig Railroad Station A129

Design: 25pf, Woman in Persian lamb coat and old City Hall, Leipzig.

**1958, Aug. 29** *Perf. 13x12½*
**406** A129 10pf green, brn & blk .25 .25
**407** A129 25pf blue & black .30 .25

Issued to publicize the 1958 Leipzig Fair.

Post Wagon, 17th Century A130

Design: 20pf, Mail train and plane.

**1958, Oct. 23 Wmk. 313**
**408** A130 10pf green *2.00 1.00*
**409** A130 20pf lake .40 .25

Issued for the Day of the Stamp.

Brandenburg Gate, Berlin — A131

**1958, Nov. 29** *Perf. 13x13½*
**410** A131 20pf rose red .40 .25
**411** A131 25pf dark blue *2.75 1.60*

Issued to commemorate 10 years of democratic city administration of Berlin.

Head from Greek Tomb — A132

20pf, Giant's head from Pergamum frieze.

**1958, Dec. 2** *Perf. 13½x13*
**412** A132 10pf blue grn & blk *1.40 .90*
**413** A132 20pf dp rose & black .25 .25

Return of art treasures from Russia. See #484-486.

Negro and Caucasian Men — A133

Design: 25pf, Chinese and Caucasian girls.

**1958, Dec. 10** *Perf. 13x12½*
**414** A133 10pf brt blue grn & blk .25 .25
**415** A133 25pf blue & black *1.75 1.00*

10th anniv. of the signing of the Universal Declaration of Human Rights.

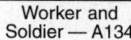

Worker and Soldier — A134

Otto Nuschke — A135

**1958, Nov. 7** *Perf. 12½x13*
**416** A134 20pf blk, ver & dl pur *9.00 15.00*

40th anniv. of the Revolution of Nov. 7. (Stamp inscribed Nov. 9.) Withdrawn from sale on day of issue.

*Perf. 13½x13*

**1958, Dec. 27 Wmk. 313**
**417** A135 20pf red .30 .30

First anniversary of the death of Otto Nuschke, vice president of the republic.

Communist Newspaper, "The Red Flag" — A136

**1958, Dec. 30** *Perf. 13x12½*
**418** A136 20pf red .45 .30

German Communist Party, 40th anniv.

Rosa Luxemburg Addressing Crowd — A137

20pf, Karl Liebknecht addressing crowd.

*Perf. 13x13½*

**1959, Jan. 15 Wmk. 313**
**419** A137 10pf blue green *2.00 1.10*
**420** A137 20pf henna brn & blk .25 .25

40th anniversary of the death of Rosa Luxemburg and Karl Liebknecht.

Gewandhaus, Leipzig — A138

Design: 25pf, Opening theme of Mendelssohn's A Major symphony.

**1959, Feb. 28 Engr.** *Perf. 14*
**421** A138 10pf green, *grnsh* .35 .30
**422** A138 25pf blue, *bluish* *1.50 2.50*

150th anniversary of the birth of Felix Mendelssohn-Bartholdy, composer.

President Wilhelm Pieck — A139

**1959, Jan. 3 Photo.** *Perf. 13½x13*
**423** A139 20pf henna brown .40 .25

83rd birthday of President Wilhelm Pieck. See No. 511.

"Black Pump" Plant A140

Design: 25pf, Photographic equipment.

**1959, Feb. 28 Litho.** *Perf. 13x12½*
**424** A140 20pf carmine rose .25 .25
**425** A140 25pf lt ultra .35 .25

1959 Leipzig Spring Fair.

Boy and Girl — A141

Statue of Handel, Halle — A142

**1959, Apr. 2** *Perf. 13½x13*
**426** A141 10pf blk, *lt grn* *1.50 .90*
**427** A141 20pf blk, *salmon* .25 .25

5 years of the Youth Consecration ceremony.

**1959, Apr. 27 Wmk. 313**

20pf, Handel by Thomas Hudson, 1749.

**428** A142 10pf bluish grn & blk *1.60 1.00*
**429** A142 20pf rose & blk .25 .25

Bicentenary of the death of George Frederick Handel, composer.

Alexander von Humboldt and Central American View — A143

Post Horn — A144

Design: 20pf, Portrait and Siberian view.

**1959, May 6**
**430** A143 10pf bluish grn *1.40 .90*
**431** A143 20pf rose .30 .25

Centenary of the death of Alexander von Humboldt, naturalist and geographer.

**1959, May 30** *Perf. 13½x13*
**432** A144 20pf scar, yel & blk .30 .25
**433** A144 25pf lt bl, yel & blk *.80 .80*

Conference of socialist postal ministers.

Gray Heron A145

10pf, Bittern. 20pf, Lily of the valley & butterfly. 25pf, Beaver. 40pf, Pussy willows and bee.

**1959, June 26** *Perf. 13x12½*

**434** A145 5pf lt bl, blk & lil .25 .25
**435** A145 10pf grnsh bl, dk brn & org .25 .25
**436** A145 20pf org red, grn & vio .25 .25
**437** A145 25pf lilac, yel & blk .35 .25
**438** A145 40pf gray bl, yel & blk *5.50 3.00*
*Nos. 434-438 (5)* *6.60 4.00*

Issued to publicize wildlife protection.

**Painting Type of 1955.**

Famous Paintings: 5pf, Portrait, by Angelica Kauffmann. 10pf, The Lady Lace Maker, by Gabriel Metsu. 20pf, Mademoiselle Lavergne, by Liotard. 25pf, Old Woman with Brazier, by Rubens. 40pf, Young Man in Black Coat, by Hals.

**1959, June 29 Photo.** *Perf. 13½x13*

**439** A77 5pf olive .25 .25
**440** A77 10pf green .25 .25
**441** A77 20pf dp org .25 .25
**442** A77 25pf chestnut .40 .25
**443** A77 40pf dp magenta *6.50 2.25*
*Nos. 439-443 (5)* *7.65 3.25*

Great Cormorant — A146

Youths of Three Races — A147

Birds: 10pf, Black Stork. 15pf, Eagle owl. 20pf, Black grouse. 25pf, Hoopoe. 40pf, Peregrine falcon.

*Perf. 13x13½*

**1959, July 2 Litho. Wmk. 313**

**Designs in Black**

**444** A146 5pf yellow .25 .25
**445** A146 10pf lt green .25 .25
**446** A146 15pf pale violet *5.25 2.50*
**447** A146 20pf deep pink .25 .25
**448** A146 25pf blue .25 .25
**449** A146 40pf vermilion .25 .25
*Nos. 444-449 (6)* *6.50 3.75*

Protection of native birds.

**1959, July 25** *Perf. 12½x13, 13x12½*

25pf, Swedish girl kissing African girl, horiz.

**450** A147 20pf crimson .30 .25
**451** A147 25pf bright blue *.75 .60*

7th World Youth Festival, Vienna, 7/26-8/14.

Glass Tea Service A148

Design: 25pf, Distilling apparatus, vert.

**1959, Sept. 1** *Perf. 13x12½, 12½x13*

**452** A148 10pf bluish green .25 .25
**453** A148 25pf bright blue *1.75 1.10*

75 years of Jena glassware.

Lunik 2 Hitting Moon — A149

**1959, Sept. 21** *Perf. 13½x13*

**454** A149 20pf rose red .60 .40

Landing of the Soviet rocket Lunik 2 on the moon, Sept. 13, 1959.

New Buildings, Leipzig, Globe and Fair Emblem A150

**1959, Aug. 17** *Perf. 13x12½*

**455** A150 20pf gray & rose .35 .30

1959 Leipzig Fall Fair.

Flag and Harvester — A151

10pf, Fritz Heckert rest home. 15pf, Zwinger, Dresden. 20pf, Steelworker. 25pf, Chemist. 40pf, Central Stadium, Leipzig. 50pf, Woman tractor driver. 60pf, Airplane. 70pf, Merchant ship. 1m, 1st atomic reactor of the DDR.

**1959, Oct. 6** *Perf. 13½x13*

**Flag in Black, Red & Orange Yellow Inscription and Design in Black & Red**

**456** A151 5pf yellow .25 .25
**457** A151 10pf gray .25 .25
**458** A151 15pf citron .25 .25
**459** A151 20pf gray .25 .25
**460** A151 25pf lt gray olive .25 .25
**461** A151 40pf citron .25 .25
**462** A151 50pf salmon .25 .25
**463** A151 60pf pale bluish grn .25 .25
**464** A151 70pf pale grnsh yel .25 .25
**465** A151 1m bister brn .40 .50
*Nos. 456-465 (10)* 2.65 2.75

German Democratic Republic, 10th anniv.

Johannes R. Becher — A152

**1959, Oct. 28 Litho.** *Perf. 13x13½*

**466** A152 20pf red & slate 1.30 .25

1st anniversary of the death of Johannes R. Becher, writer.

Printed with alternating yellow labels. The label carries in blue a verse from the national anthem and Becher's signature.

Schiller's Home, Weimar — A153

Design: 20pf, Friedrich von Schiller.

**1959, Nov. 10 Engr.** *Perf. 14*

**467** A153 10pf dull green, *grnsh* 1.50 1.00
**468** A153 20pf lake, *pink* .55 .25

Birth of Friedrich von Schiller, 200th anniv.

Post Rider and Mile Stone, 18th Century — A154

Design: 20pf, Motorized mailman.

**1959, Nov. 17 Litho.** *Perf. 13½x13*

**469** A154 10pf green *1.40 .90*
**470** A154 20pf dk car rose .25 .25

Issued for the Day of the Stamp.

Red Squirrels A155

**1959, Nov. 27** *Perf. 13x12½*

**471** A155 5pf shown .35 .25
**472** A155 10pf Hares .45 .25
**473** A155 20pf Roe deer .45 .25
**474** A155 25pf Red deer .50 .25
**475** A155 40pf Lynx *9.50 3.00*
*Nos. 471-475 (5)* *11.25 4.00*

**Redrawn Types of 1953 Without Imprint**

***Perf. 14, 13x12½ (#477)***

**1959-60 Wmk. 313 Typo.**

**476** A43 5pf emerald .25 .25
**477** A43 10pf lt bl grn *(Machinists)* .25 .25
*a.* Perf. 14 1.00 .40
*b.* Bklt. pane of 6 #477a 6.00 4.75
**478** A43 20pf carmine .25 .25
*a.* Se-tenant with DEBRIA label .95 .25
**479** A43 30pf dull red .25 .25
**480** A43 40pf rose violet .25 .25
**481** A43 50pf brt blue .25 .25
**482** A43 70pf choc ('60) .25 .25
*Nos. 476-482 (7)* 1.75 1.75

No. 478a was issued Sept. 3, 1959, to commemorate the 2nd German Stamp Exhibition, Berlin. Sheet contains 60 stamps, 40 labels.

Two other stamps without imprint are Nos. 331-332.

**Type of 1958 and**

Pergamum Altar of Zeus — A156

Designs: 5pf, Head of an Attic goddess, 580 B.C. 10pf, Head of a princess from Tell el Amarna, 1360 B.C. 20pf, Bronze figure from Toprak-Kale (Armenia), 7th century B.C.

**1959, Dec. 29 Litho.** *Perf. 13½x13*

**484** A132 5pf yellow & black .30 .25
**485** A132 10pf bluish grn & blk .30 .25
**486** A132 20pf rose & black .30 .25
**487** A156 25pf lt blue & blk *.80 .80*
*Nos. 484-487 (4)* *1.70 1.55*

Boxing — A157

10pf, Sprinters. 20pf, Ski jump. 25pf, Sailboat.

*Perf. 13x13½*

**1960, Jan. 27 Wmk. 313**

**488** A157 5pf brown & ocher *4.50 2.25*
**489** A157 10pf green & ocher .25 .25
**490** A157 20pf car & ocher .25 .25
**491** A157 25pf ultra & ocher .25 .25
*Nos. 488-491 (4)* *5.25 3.00*

1960 Winter and Summer Olympic Games.

Technical Fair, North Entrance A158

Design: 25pf, "Ring" Fair building.

**1960, Feb. 17** *Perf. 13x12½*

**492** A158 20pf red & gray .25 .25
**493** A158 25pf lt blue & gray .25 .25

1960 Leipzig Spring Fair.

Purple Foxglove A159

Lenin A160

Medicinal Plants: 10pf, Camomile. 15pf, Peppermint. 20pf, Poppy. 40pf, Dog rose.

**1960, Apr. 7** *Perf. 12½x13*

**494** A159 5pf grn, gray & car rose .25 .25
**495** A159 10pf citron, gray & grn .25 .25
**496** A159 15pf fawn, gray & grn .25 .25
**497** A159 20pf grnsh bl, gray & vio .25 .25
**498** A159 40pf brn, gray, grn & red *4.00 2.10*
*Nos. 494-498 (5)* *5.00 3.10*

**1960, Apr. 22 Engr.** *Perf. 14*

**499** A160 20pf lake .40 .25

90th anniversary of the birth of Lenin.

**No. 390 Overprinted: "Inbetriebnahme des Hochseehafens 1.Mai 1960"**

**1960, Apr. 28 Litho.** *Perf. 13½x13*

**500** A122 10pf emerald .50 .40

Inauguration of the seaport Rostock.

Russian Soldier and Liberated Prisoner — A161

**1960, May 5 Litho.** *Perf. 13x13½*

**501** A161 20pf rose red .40 .30

15th anniv. of Germany's liberation from fascism.

Model of Vacation Ship — A162

Designs: 25pf, Ship before Leningrad.

*Perf. 13½x13*

**1960, June 23 Wmk. 313**

**502** A162 5pf slate, cit & blk .25 .25
**503** A162 25pf blk, yel & ultra *4.25 4.75*
*Nos. 502-503,B58-B59 (4)* 5.00 5.50

Launching of the trade union (FDGB) vacation ship, June 25, 1960.

Masked Dancer in Porcelain A163 — Lenin Monument, Eisleben A164

Meissen porcelain: 10pf, Plate with Meissen mark and date. 15pf, Otter. 20pf, Potter. 25pf, Coffee pot.

**1960, July 28** *Perf. 12½x13*

**504** A163 5pf blue & orange .25 .25
**505** A163 10pf blue & emerald .25 .25
**506** A163 15pf blue & purple *3.50 3.50*
**507** A163 20pf blue & orange red .25 .25
**508** A163 25pf blue & apple grn .25 .25
*Nos. 504-508 (5)* *4.50 4.50*

Meissen porcelain works, 250th anniv.

*Perf. 13x13½*

**1960, July 2** **Wmk. 313**

Design: 20pf, Thälmann monument, gift for Pushkin, USSR.

**509** A164 10pf dark green .25 .25
**510** A164 20pf bright red .25 .25

### Pieck Type of 1959

**1960, Sept. 10 Litho.** *Perf. 13½x13*

**511** A139 20pf black .45 .30
*a.* Souv. sheet of 1, imperf. 1.60 2.25

Pres. Wilhelm Pieck (1876-1960).

Modern Postal Trucks A165

Design: 25pf, Railroad mail car, 19th cent.

**1960, Oct. 6** *Perf. 13x12½*

**512** A165 20pf car rose, blk & yel .25 .25
**513** A165 25pf blue, gray & blk *2.50 1.50*

Issued for the Day of the Stamp, 1960.

New Opera House, Leipzig A166

Design: 25pf, Car, sailboat, tent, campers.

**1960, Aug. 29** **Wmk. 313**

**514** A166 20pf rose brn & gray .25 .25
**515** A166 25pf blue & grysh brn .30 .30

1960 Leipzig Fall Fair.

Hans Burkmair Medal, 1518 A167 — Neidhardt von Gneisenau A168

25pf, Dancing Peasants by Albrecht Dürer.

**1960, Oct. 20 Litho.** *Perf. 12½x13*

**516** A167 20pf buff, grn & ocher .25 .25
**517** A167 25pf lt blue & blk *1.60 1.75*

400th anniv. of the Dresden Art Gallery.

**1960, Oct. 27** *Perf. 13x12½, 12½x13*

20pf, Neidhardt von Gneisenau, horiz.

**518** A168 20pf dk car & blk .25 .25
**519** A168 25pf ultra *1.30 1.30*

200th anniversary of the birth of Count August Neidhardt von Gneisenau, Prussian Field Marshal.

Rudolf Virchow A169

Humboldt University, Berlin — A170

10pf, Robert Koch. 25pf, Wilheim & Alexander von Humboldt medal. 40pf, Wilheim Griesinger.

**1960, Nov. 4 Litho.** *Perf. 13x12½*

**520** A169 5pf ocher & blk .25 .25
**521** A169 10pf green & blk .25 .25
**522** A170 20pf cop red, gray & blk .25 .25
**523** A170 25pf brt blue & blk .25 .25
**524** A169 40pf car rose & blk *2.25 1.40*
*Nos. 520-524 (5)* *3.25 2.40*

Nos. 520, 521, 524 for the 250th anniv. of the Charité (hospital), Berlin; Nos. 522-523 the 150th anniv. of Humboldt University, Berlin.

Nos. 520 and 523, and Nos. 521 and 522 are printed se-tenant.

Scientist and Chemical Formula — A171

Designs: 10pf, Chemistry worker (fertilizer). 20pf, Woman worker (automobile). 25pf, Laboratory assistant (synthetic fabrics).

*Perf. 13x13½*

**1960, Nov. 10** **Wmk. 313**

**525** A171 5pf dk red & gray .25 .25
**526** A171 10pf orange & brt grn .25 .25
**527** A171 20pf blue & red .25 .25
**528** A171 25pf yellow & ultra *1.75 2.25*
*Nos. 525-528 (4)* *2.50 3.00*

Day of the Chemistry Worker.

"Young Socialists' Express" A172

20pf, Sassnitz Harbor station & ferry. 25pf, Diesel locomotive & 1835 "Adler."

*Perf. 13x13½; 13x12½ (20pf)*

**1960, Dec. 5**

**Sizes: 10pf, 25pf, 28x23mm; 20pf, 38½x22mm**

**529** A172 10pf emerald & blk .25 .25
**530** A172 20pf red & blk .25 .25
**531** A172 25pf blue & blk *4.50 3.50*
*Nos. 529-531 (3)* *5.00 4.00*

125th anniv. of German railroads. No. 530 exists imperf. Value $3.50.

### Pieck Type of 1953 with Dates Added

**1961, Jan. 3 Photo.** *Perf. 13x13½*

**532** A35 20pf henna brn & blk .40 .30

Issued on the 85th anniversary of the birth of Pres. Wilhelm Pieck (1876-1960).

380 Kilovolt Switch A173 — Lilienstein A174

Design: 25pf, Leipzig Press Center.

**1961, Mar. 3 Litho.** *Perf. 13½x13*

**533** A173 10pf brt grn & dk gray .30 .25
**534** A173 25pf vio blue & dk gray .30 .25

Leipzig Spring Fair of 1961.

**1961 Typo.** *Perf. 14*

Designs: 5pf, Rudelsburg on Saale. 10pf, Wartburg. No. 538, City Hall, Wernigerode. 25pf, Brocken, Harz Mts., horiz.

**535** A174 5pf gray .25 .25
**536** A174 10pf blue green .25 .25
**537** A174 20pf red brown .25 .25
**538** A174 20pf dull red .25 .25
**539** A174 25pf dark blue .25 .25
*Nos. 535-539 (5)* 1.25 1.25

Issued: #538, 25pf, 3/14; 5pf, 10pf, #537, 6/22.

Trawler — A176

Designs: 20pf, Fishermen. 25pf, S.S. Robert Koch. 40pf, Cannery worker.

**1961, Apr. 4 Engr.** **Wmk. 313**

**545** A176 10pf gray green .25 .25
**546** A176 20pf claret .25 .25
**547** A176 25pf slate .25 .25
**548** A176 40pf dull violet *2.00 1.50*
*Nos. 545-548 (4)* *2.75 2.25*

Deep-sea fishing industry.

Vostok 1 Leaving Earth A177

Designs: 20pf, Cosmonaut in capsule. 25pf, Parachute landing of capsule.

**1961, Apr. Litho.** *Perf. 13x12½*

**549** A177 10pf lt blue grn & red 1.25 .80
**550** A177 20pf red 1.25 .80
**551** A177 25pf lt blue *4.75 4.75*
*Nos. 549-551 (3)* *7.25 6.35*

1st man in space, Yuri A. Gagarin, 4/12/61.

Issue dates: 10pf, Apr. 18; others, Apr. 20.

Zebra A178

Dresden Zoo cent.: 20pf, Black-and-white colobus monkeys.

**1961, May 9**

**552** A178 10pf green & blk *5.00 5.00*
**553** A178 20pf lilac rose & blk .80 .40

Engels, Marx, Lenin and Crowd — A179

**1961, Apr. 20 Litho.** *Perf. 13½x13*

**554** A179 20pf red .45 .30

15th anniversary of Socialist Unity Party of Germany (SED).

Stag Leap — A180

Designs: 20pf, Arabesque. 25pf, Exercise on parallel bars, horiz.

**1961, June 3** *Perf. 13½x13, 13x13½*

**555** A180 10pf blue green .25 .25
**556** A180 20pf rose pink .25 .25
**557** A180 25pf brt blue *5.00 4.25*
*Nos. 555-557 (3)* *5.50 4.75*

3rd Europa Cup for Women's Gymnastics.

Salt Miners and Castle Giebichenstein — A181

20pf, Chemist and "Five Towers" of Halle.

**1961, June 22** *Perf. 13x12½*

**558** A181 10pf blk, grn & yel *2.40 1.25*
**559** A181 20pf blk, dk red & yel .25 .25

1000th anniv. of the founding of Halle.

Kayak Slalom A182

10pf, Canoe. 20pf, Two seater canoe.

**1961, July 6 Litho.** **Wmk. 313**

**560** A182 5pf gray & Prus bl *2.75 2.25*
**561** A182 10pf gray & slate grn .25 .25
**562** A182 20pf gray & dk car rose .25 .25
*Nos. 560-562 (3)* *3.25 2.75*

Canoe Slalom and Rapids World Championships.

Target Line Casting A183

Design: 20pf, River fishing.

**1961, July 21**

**563** A183 10pf green & blue *1.25 1.00*
**564** A183 20pf dk red brn & blue 1.25 1.00

World Fishing Championships, Dresden.

Tulip — A184

"Alte Waage," Historical Building, Leipzig — A185

**1961, Sept. 13 Photo. *Perf. 14***

**565** A184 10pf shown .40 .25
**566** A184 20pf Dahlia .40 .25
**567** A184 40pf Rose *8.25 8.25*
*Nos. 565-567 (3) 9.05 8.75*

Intl. Horticulture Exhibition, Erfurt.

***Perf. 13½x13***
**1961, Aug. 23 Litho. Wmk. 313**

Design: 25pf, Old Exchange Building.

**568** A185 10pf citron & bl grn .25 .25
**569** A185 25pf lt blue & ultra 1.00 .30

1961 Leipzig Fall Fair. See Nos. 595-597.

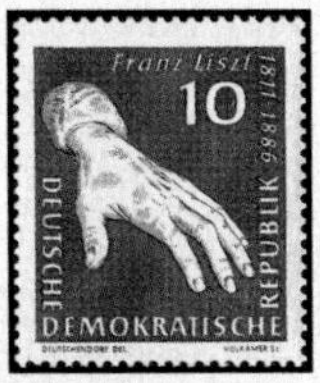


Liszt's Hand, French Sculpture — A186

Designs: 5pf, Liszt and Hector Berlioz. 20pf, Franz Liszt, medallion by Ernst Rietschel, 1852. 25pf, Liszt and Frederic Chopin.

**1961, Oct.-Nov. Engr. *Perf. 14***

**570** A186 5pf gray .25 .25
**571** A186 10pf blue green *2.00 2.00*
**572** A186 20pf dull red .25 .25
**573** A186 25pf chalky blue *2.50 2.50*
*Nos. 570-573 (4) 5.00 5.00*

150th anniversary of the birth of Franz Liszt, composer.

Television Camera and Screen — A187

Design: 20pf, Microphone and radio dial.

**1961, Oct. 25 *Perf. 13x13½***

**574** A187 10pf brt green & blk *1.60 1.60*
**575** A187 20pf brick red & blk .25 .25

Issued for Stamp Day, 1961.

Maj. Gherman Titov and Young Pioneers — A188

10pf, Titov in Leipzig, vert. 15pf, Titov in spaceship. 20pf, Titov & Walter Ulbricht. 25pf, Spaceship Vostok 2. 40pf, Titov & Ulbricht in Berlin.

**1961, Dec. 11 Litho. *Perf. 13½***

**576** A188 5pf carmine & vio .25 .25
**577** A188 10pf olive grn & car .25 .25
**578** A188 15pf blue & lilac *8.50 8.50*
**579** A188 20pf blue & car rose .25 .25
**580** A188 25pf carmine & blue .25 .25
**581** A188 40pf car & dk blue 1.50 .45
*Nos. 576-581 (6) 11.00 9.95*

Visit of Russian Maj. Gherman Titov to the German Democratic Republic.

Chairman Walter Ulbricht — A189

**1961-67 Wmk. 313 Typo. *Perf. 14***
**Size: 17x21mm**

**582** A189 5pf slate .25 .25
*a.* Booklet pane of 8 24.00 32.50
**583** A189 10pf brt green .25 .25
*a.* Booklet pane of 8 10.50 16.00
**584** A189 15pf red lilac .25 .25
**585** A189 20pf dark red .30 .25
**586** A189 25pf dull bl ('63) .30 .25
**587** A189 30pf car rose ('63) .25 .25
**588** A189 40pf brt vio ('63) .25 .25
**589** A189 50pf ultra ('63) .25 .25
**589A** A189 60pf dp yel grn ('64) .30 .25
**590** A189 70pf red brn ('63) .30 .25
**590A** A189 80pf brt blue ('67) .40 .40

**Engr.**
**Size: 24x28½mm**

**590B** A189 1dm dull grn ('63) .75 .35
**590C** A189 2dm brown ('63) 1.50 .50
*Nos. 582-590C (13) 5.35 3.75*

See #751-752, 1112A-1114A, 1483. Currency abbreviation is "DM" on #590B-590C, "MDN" on #751-752, "M" on #1113-1114A.

Red Ants A190

**1962, Feb. 16 Photo.**

**591** A190 5pf shown *3.75 5.25*
**592** A190 10pf Weasels .25 .25
**593** A190 20pf Shrews .25 .25
**594** A190 40pf Bat .50 .40
*Nos. 591-594 (4) 4.75 6.15*

See Nos. 663-667.

**Type of 1961**

Buildings: 10pf, "Coffee Tree House." 20pf, Gohlis Castle. 25pf, Romanus House.

**1962, Feb. 22 Litho. *Perf. 13x13½***

**595** A185 10pf olive grn & brn .25 .25
**596** A185 20pf orange red & blk .30 .25
**597** A185 25pf brt blue & brn .75 .75
*Nos. 595-597 (3) 1.30 1.25*

Leipzig Spring Fair of 1962.

Air Defense A191

Designs: 10pf, Motorized infantry. 20pf, Soldier and worker as protectors. 25pf, Sailor and destroyer escort. 40pf, Tank and tankman.

**1962, Mar. 1 *Perf. 13x12½***

**598** A191 5pf light blue .25 .25
**599** A191 10pf bright green .25 .25
**600** A191 20pf red .25 .25
**601** A191 25pf ultra .25 .25
**602** A191 40pf brown *1.60 1.25*
*Nos. 598-602 (5) 2.60 2.25*

National People's Army, 6th anniv.

Cyclists and Hradcany, Prague — A192

25pf, Cyclist, East Berlin City Hall and dove.

**1962, Apr. 26 Litho. Wmk. 313**

**603** A192 10pf multicolored .25 .25
**604** A192 25pf multicolored *1.25 1.25*
*Nos. 603-604,B89 (3) 1.75 1.75*

15th International Bicycle Peace Race, Berlin-Warsaw-Prague.

Johann Gottlieb Fichte — A193

10pf, Fichte's birthplace in Rammenau.

**1962, May 17 *Perf. 13x13½***

**605** A193 10pf brt green & blk *1.40 1.40*
**606** A193 20pf vermilion & blk .25 .25

Bicentenary of the birth of Johann Gottlieb Fichte, philosopher.

Cross, Crown of Thorns and Rose — A194

George Dimitrov at Reichstag Trial, Leipzig — A195

**1962, June 7 *Perf. 12½x13***

**607** A194 20pf red & black .25 .25
**608** A194 25pf brt blue & blk *1.10 1.10*

20th anniversary of the destruction of Lidice in Czechoslovakia by the Nazis.

**1962, June 18 Photo. *Perf. 14***

20pf, Dimitrov as Premier of Bulgaria.

**609** A195 5pf blue grn & blk *.55 .40*
**610** A195 20pf car rose & blk .25 .25
*a.* Pair, #609-610, + label 5.50 *40.00*

George Dimitrov, (1882-1949), communist leader and premier of the Bulgarian Peoples' Republic.

Nos. 609-610 also printed se-tenant, divided by a label inscribed with a Dimitrov quotation.

Corn Planter A196

20pf, Milking machine. 40pf, Combine harvester.

**1962, June 26 Litho. *Perf. 13x12½***

**611** A196 10pf multicolored .25 .25
**612** A196 20pf multicolored .25 .25
**613** A196 40pf yel, grn & dk red *1.60 1.40*
*Nos. 611-613 (3) 2.10 1.90*

10th Agricultural Exhibition, Markkleeberg.

Map of Baltic Sea and Emblem — A197

Designs: 20pf, Hotel, Rostock, vert. 25pf, Cargo ship "Frieden" in Rostock harbor.

***Perf. 13x13½, 13½x13 (20pf)***
**1962, July 2 Wmk. 313**

**614** A197 10pf bluish grn & ultra .25 .25
**615** A197 20pf dk red & yellow .25 .25
**616** A197 25pf blue & bister *2.25 2.25*
*Nos. 614-616 (3) 2.75 2.75*

5th Baltic Sea Week, Rostock, July 7-15.

Brandenburg Gate, Berlin — A198

#618 Heads of youths of three races. #619, Peace dove. #620, National Theater, Helsinki.

**1962, July 17 *Perf. 13½x13***

**617** A198 5pf multicolored *2.25 2.25*
**618** A198 5pf multicolored *2.25 2.25*
**619** A198 20pf multicolored *2.25 2.25*
**620** A198 20pf multicolored *2.25 2.25*
*a.* Block of 4, #617-620 *13.00 13.00*
*Nos. 617-620 (4) 9.00 9.00*

8th Youth Festival for Peace and Friendship, Helsinki, July 28-Aug. 6, 1962.

No. 620a forms the festival flower emblem.

Free Style Swimming A199

Designs: 10pf, Back stroke. 25pf, Butterfly stroke. 40pf, Breast stroke. 70pf, Water polo.

**1962, Aug. 7 Litho. *Perf. 13x13½***
**Design in Greenish Blue**

**621** A199 5pf orange .25 .25
**622** A199 10pf grnsh blue .25 .25
**623** A199 25pf ultra .25 .25
**624** A199 40pf brt violet *1.10 1.10*
**625** A199 70pf red brown .25 .25
*a.* Block of 6, #621-625, B92 *2.25 2.25*
*Nos. 621-625,B92 (6) 2.35 2.35*

10th European Swimming Championships. Leipzig, Aug. 18-25.

Nos. 621-625, B92 each printed in sheets of 50, No. 625a in sheet of 60.

Municipal Store, Leipzig — A200

Buildings: 20pf, Mädler Passage. 25pf, Leipzig Air Terminal and plane.

**Engr. & Photo.**
**1962, Aug. 28 Wmk. 313 *Perf. 14***

**626** A200 10pf black & emerald .25 .25
**627** A200 20pf black & red .30 .25
**628** A200 25pf black & blue .80 .80
*Nos. 626-628 (3) 1.35 1.30*

Leipzig Fall Fair of 1962.

"Transportation and Communication" — A201

**1962, Oct. 3 Litho. *Perf. 13½x13***

**629** A201 5pf light blue & black .30 .25

10th anniv. of the Friedrich List Transportation College.

### Souvenir Sheet

Pavel R. Popovich, Andrian G. Nikolayev and Space Capsules — A202

**1962, Sept. 13 Wmk. 313 *Imperf.***

| | | | |
|---|---|---|---|
| 630 | A202 70pf dk blue, lt grn & yel | *2.75* | *5.00* |

1st Russian group space flight of Vostoks III and IV, Aug. 11-13, 1962.

DDR Television Signal A203

Young Collectors and World Map — A204

**1962, Oct. 25 *Perf. 13½x13***

| | | | |
|---|---|---|---|
| 631 | A203 20pf green & gray | .25 | .25 |
| 632 | A204 40pf brt pink & blk | *1.75* | *1.75* |

No. 631 for the 10th anniv. of television in the German Democratic Republic; No. 632 is for Stamp Day.

Gerhart Hauptmann A205

**1962, Nov. 15 *Perf. 13x13½***

| | | | |
|---|---|---|---|
| 633 | A205 20pf red & black | .40 | .25 |

Centenary of the birth of Gerhart Hauptmann, playwright.

### Souvenir Sheet

Russian Space Flights and Astronauts — A206

**1962, Dec. 28 Litho. *Perf. 12½x13***

| | | | |
|---|---|---|---|
| 634 | A206 Sheet of 8 | 32.50 | 32.50 |
| *a.* | 5pf yellow | *1.60* | *1.60* |
| *b.* | 10pf emerald | *1.60* | *1.60* |
| *c.* | 15pf magenta | *3.25* | *3.25* |
| *d.* | 20pf red | *3.25* | *3.25* |
| *e.* | 25pf greenish blue | *3.25* | *3.25* |
| *f.* | 30pf red brown | *3.25* | *3.25* |
| *g.* | 40pf crimson | *1.60* | *1.60* |
| *h.* | 50pf ultramarine | *1.60* | *1.60* |

Issued to show the development of Russian space flights from Sputnik 1 to Vostoks 3 and 4, and to honor the Russian astronauts Gagarin, Titov, Nikolayev and Popovich.

Pierre de Coubertin — A207

Design: 25pf, Stadium and Olympic rings.

**1963, Jan. 2 *Perf. 13½x13***

| | | | |
|---|---|---|---|
| 635 | A207 20pf carmine & gray | .25 | .25 |
| 636 | A207 25pf blue & bister | *1.60* | *1.60* |

Baron Pierre de Coubertin, organizer of the modern Olympic Games, birth cent.

Congress Emblem, Flag with Marx, Engels and Lenin — A208

**1963, Jan. 15 *Perf. 13x13½***

| | | | |
|---|---|---|---|
| 637 | A208 10pf yel, org, red & blk | .30 | .25 |

6th congress of Socialist Unity Party of Germany (SED).

World Map and Exterminator — A209

Designs: 25pf, Map, cross and staff of Aesculapius. 50pf, Map, cross, mosquito.

**1963, Feb. 6 *Perf. 13x12½***

| | | | |
|---|---|---|---|
| 638 | A209 20pf dp org, dk red & blk | .25 | .25 |
| 639 | A209 25pf multicolored | .25 | .25 |
| 640 | A209 50pf multicolored | *1.10* | *1.10* |
| | *Nos. 638-640 (3)* | *1.60* | *1.60* |

WHO drive to eradicate malaria.

Silver Fox A210

Design: 25pf, Karakul.

**1963, Feb. 14 Photo. *Perf. 14***

| | | | |
|---|---|---|---|
| 641 | A210 20pf rose & black | .25 | .25 |
| 642 | A210 25pf blue & black | *1.50* | *1.50* |

Intl. Fur Auctions, Leipzig, 2/14-15, 4/21-24.

Barthels House, Leipzig — A211

Designs: 20pf, New Leipzig City Hall. 25pf, Belltower Building.

**Engr. & Photo.**

**1963, Feb. 26 Wmk. 313 *Perf. 14***

| | | | |
|---|---|---|---|
| 643 | A211 10pf black & citron | .25 | .25 |
| 644 | A211 20pf black & red org | .30 | .25 |
| 645 | A211 25pf black & blue | 1.00 | 1.00 |
| | *Nos. 643-645 (3)* | 1.55 | 1.50 |

1963 Leipzig Spring Fair.

### Souvenir Sheet

On March 12, 1963, a souvenir sheet publicizing "Chemistry for Peace and Socialism" was issued. It contains two imperforate stamps, 50pf and 70pf, printed on ungummed synthetic tissue. Size: 105x74mm. Value $4.50.

Richard Wagner and "The Flying Dutchman" — A213

Portrait & Scene from Play: 5pf, Johann Gottfried Seume (1763-1810). 10pf, Friedrich Hebbel (1813-63). 20pf, Georg Büchner (1813-37).

**1963, Apr. 9 Litho. *Perf. 13x12½***

| | | | |
|---|---|---|---|
| 647 | A213 5pf brt citron & blk | .25 | .25 |
| 648 | A213 10pf brt green & blk | .25 | .25 |
| 649 | A213 20pf orange & blk | .25 | .25 |
| 650 | A213 25pf dull blue & blk | *1.50* | *1.50* |
| | *Nos. 647-650 (4)* | *2.25* | *2.25* |

Anniversaries of German dramatists and the 150th anniv. of the birth of Richard Wagner, composer.

First Aid Station A214

Design: 20pf, Ambulance and hospital.

**1963, May 14 Wmk. 313**

| | | | |
|---|---|---|---|
| 651 | A214 10pf multicolored | *1.10* | *1.10* |
| 652 | A214 20pf red, blk & gray | .25 | .25 |

Centenary of International Red Cross.

Eugene Pottier, Writer — A215

25pf, Pierre-Chretien Degeyter, composer.

**1963, June 18 *Perf. 13x13½***

| | | | |
|---|---|---|---|
| 653 | A215 20pf vermilion & blk | .25 | .25 |
| 654 | A215 25pf vio blue & blk | *1.10* | *1.10* |

75th anniv. of the communist song "The International."

A216

No. 655, Valentina Tereshkova, Vostok 6. No. 656, Valeri Bykovski, Vostok 5.

**1963, July 18 Photo. *Perf. 13½***

| | | | |
|---|---|---|---|
| 655 | 20pf blue, blk & gray bl | .85 | .25 |
| 656 | 20pf blue, blk & gray bl | .85 | .25 |
| *a.* | A216 Pair, #655-656 | 1.75 | .50 |

Space flights of Valeri Bykovski, June 14-19, and Valentina Tereshkova, 1st woman cosmonaut, June 16-19, 1963.

Motorcyclist in "Motocross" at Apolda — A217

20pf, Motorcyclist at Sachsenring, horiz. 25pf, 2 motorcyclists at Sachsenring, horiz.

**Engr. & Photo.**

**1963, July 30 *Perf. 14***

**Size: 23x28mm**

| | | | |
|---|---|---|---|
| 657 | A217 10pf lt grn & dk grn | *3.50* | *3.50* |

**Size: 48½x21mm**

| | | | |
|---|---|---|---|
| 658 | A217 20pf rose & dk red | .25 | .25 |
| 659 | A217 25pf lt blue & dk blue | .25 | .25 |
| | *Nos. 657-659 (3)* | *4.00* | *4.00* |

Motorcycle World Championships.

Monument at Treblinka A218

***Perf. 13x13½***

**1963, Aug. 20 Litho. Wmk. 313**

| | | | |
|---|---|---|---|
| 660 | A218 20pf brick red & dk blue | .50 | .25 |

Erection of a memorial at Treblinka (Poland) concentration camp.

Globe, Car and Train — A219

Design: No. 662, Globe, plane and bus.

**1963, Aug. 27 *Perf. 13½x13***

| | | | |
|---|---|---|---|
| 661 | A219 10pf multicolored | .70 | .25 |
| 662 | A219 10pf multicolored | .70 | .25 |
| *a.* | Pair, #661-662 | 2.25 | .40 |

Issued to publicize the 1963 Leipzig Fall Fair.

### Fauna Type of 1962

10pf, Stag beetle. 20pf, Fire salamander. 30pf, Pond turtle. 50pf, Green toad. 70pf, Hedgehogs.

**1963, Sept. 10 Photo. *Perf. 14***

| | | | |
|---|---|---|---|
| 663 | A190 10pf emer, brn & blk | .25 | .25 |
| 664 | A190 20pf crimson, blk & yel | .25 | .25 |
| 665 | A190 30pf multicolored | .25 | .25 |
| 666 | A190 50pf multicolored | *3.50* | *3.50* |
| 667 | A190 70pf claret brn, brn & bis | .55 | .55 |
| | *Nos. 663-667 (5)* | *4.80* | *4.80* |

Neidhardt von Gneisenau and Gebhard Leberecht von Blücher — A220

Designs: 10pf, Cossacks and home guard, Berlin. 20pf, Ernst Moritz Arndt and Baron Heinrich vom Stein. 25pf, Lützow's volunteers before battle. 40pf, Gerhard von Scharnhorst and Prince Mikhail I. Kutuzov.

**1963, Oct. 10 Litho.** ***Perf. 13½x13***

**Center in Tan and Black**

| | | | | | |
|---|---|---|---|---|---|
| **668** | A220 | 5pf brt yellow | | .25 | .25 |
| **669** | A220 | 10pf emerald | | .25 | .25 |
| **670** | A220 | 20pf dp orange | | .25 | .25 |
| **671** | A220 | 25pf dp ultra | | .25 | .25 |
| **672** | A220 | 40pf dark red | | *2.00* | *1.10* |
| | | *Nos. 668-672 (5)* | | *3.00* | *2.10* |

150th anniversary of War of Liberation.

Valentina Tereshkova and Space Craft — A221

Burning Synagogue and Star of David in Chains — A222

#674, Tereshkova and map of DDR, vert. #675, Yuri A. Gagarin and map of DDR, vert. 25pf, Tereshkova in space capsule.

**1963** ***Perf. 13½x13, 13x13½***

**Size: 28x28mm (10pf, 25pf); 28x37mm (20pf)**

| | | | | |
|---|---|---|---|---|
| **673** | A221 | 10pf ultra & green | .25 | .25 |
| **674** | A221 | 20pf red, blk & ocher | .25 | .25 |
| **675** | A221 | 20pf red, grn & ocher | .25 | .25 |
| **676** | A221 | 25pf orange & blue | *3.75* | *2.25* |
| | | *Nos. 673-676 (4)* | *4.50* | *3.00* |

Visit of astronauts Valentina Tereshkova & Yuri A. Gagarin to the German Democratic Republic.

***Perf. 13½x13***

**1963, Nov. 8** **Wmk. 313**

| | | | | |
|---|---|---|---|---|
| **677** | A222 | 10pf multicolored | .50 | .25 |

25th anniv. of the "Crystal Night," the start of the systematic persecution of the Jews in Germany. Inscribed: "Never again Crystal Night."

Letter Sorting Machine A223

Design: 20pf, Mechanized mail loading.

**1963, Nov. 25** ***Perf. 13x12½***

| | | | | |
|---|---|---|---|---|
| **678** | A223 | 10pf multicolored | *1.60* | *1.60* |
| **679** | A223 | 20pf multicolored | .25 | .25 |

Issued for Stamp Day.

Ski Jump and Olympic Rings A224

**1963, Dec. 16 Litho.** ***Perf. 13½x13***

| | | | | |
|---|---|---|---|---|
| **680** | A224 | 5pf shown | .25 | .25 |
| **681** | A224 | 10pf Start | .25 | .25 |
| **682** | A224 | 25pf Landing | *2.00* | *2.00* |
| | | *Nos. 680-682,B111 (4)* | *2.75* | *2.75* |

9th Winter Olympic Games, Innsbruck, Jan. 29-Feb. 9, 1964.

Admiral — A225

Butterflies: 15pf, Alpine Apollo. 20pf, Swallowtail. 25pf, Postilion. 40pf, Great fox.

**Wmk. 313**

**1964, Jan. 15 Photo.** ***Perf. 14***

**Butterflies in Natural Colors**

| | | | | |
|---|---|---|---|---|
| **683** | A225 | 10pf citron & blk | .50 | .25 |
| **684** | A225 | 15pf pale violet & blk | .50 | .25 |
| **685** | A225 | 20pf lt brick red & blk | .50 | .25 |
| **686** | A225 | 25pf lt blue & dk brn | .50 | .25 |
| **687** | A225 | 40pf lt ultra & blk | *7.00* | *2.25* |
| | | *Nos. 683-687 (5)* | *9.00* | *3.25* |

William Shakespeare — A226

20pf, Quadriga, Brandenburg Gate, Berlin. 25pf, Keystone, History Museum (Zeughaus), Berlin.

**1964, Feb. 6 Litho.** ***Perf. 13x12½***

| | | | | |
|---|---|---|---|---|
| **688** | A226 | 20pf rose & dk blue | .25 | .25 |
| **689** | A226 | 25pf lt blue & mag | .25 | .25 |
| **690** | A226 | 40pf lt vio & dk bl grn | *1.30* | *1.00* |
| | | *Nos. 688-690 (3)* | *1.80* | *1.50* |

200th anniv. of the birth of the sculptor Johann Gottfried Schadow (20pf); 300th anniv. of the birth of the sculptor Andreas Schlüter (25pf); 400th anniv. of the birth of William Shakespeare, dramatist (40pf).

Electrical Engineering Exhibit — A227

20pf, Bräunigkes Court, exhibition hall, 1700.

***Perf. 13x13½***

**1964, Feb. 26** **Wmk. 313**

| | | | | |
|---|---|---|---|---|
| **691** | A227 | 10pf brt green & blk | 2.25 | .25 |
| **692** | A227 | 20pf red & black | 2.25 | .25 |
| *a.* | | Block, 1 each #691-692 + 2 labels | 16.00 | 1.50 |

Leipzig Spring Fair, Mar. 1-10, 1964.

Khrushchev and Inventors — A228

40pf, Khrushchev, Tereshkova & Gagarin.

**1964, May 15** ***Perf. 13x13½***

| | | | | |
|---|---|---|---|---|
| **693** | A228 | 25pf blue | .25 | .25 |
| **694** | A228 | 40pf lilac & grnsh blk | *2.60* | *1.75* |

Issued in honor of Premier Nikita S. Khrushchev of the Soviet Union.

Youth Training for Leadership A229

Designs: 20pf, Young athletes. 25pf, Accordion player and girl with flowers.

**1964, May 13** **Litho.**

**Center in Black**

| | | | | |
|---|---|---|---|---|
| **695** | A229 | 10pf ultra, mag & emer | .25 | .25 |
| **696** | A229 | 20pf emer, ultra & mag | .25 | .25 |
| **697** | A229 | 25pf magenta, emer & ultra | *1.50* | *.80* |
| | | *Nos. 695-697 (3)* | *2.00* | *1.30* |

German Youth Meeting, Berlin.

Television Antenna and Puppets — A230

Children's Day: Various characters from children's television programs.

**1964, June 1** ***Perf. 13x13½***

| | | | | |
|---|---|---|---|---|
| **698** | A230 | 5pf multicolored | .25 | .25 |
| **699** | A230 | 10pf multicolored | .25 | .25 |
| **700** | A230 | 15pf multicolored | .25 | .25 |
| **701** | A230 | 20pf multicolored | .25 | .25 |
| **702** | A230 | 40pf multicolored | *1.40* | *1.40* |
| | | *Nos. 698-702 (5)* | *2.40* | *2.40* |

Woman as Educator and Portrait of Jenny Marx — A231

Designs: 25pf, Women in industry and transistor diagram. 70pf, Women in agriculture.

***Perf. 13½x13***

**1964, June 26 Litho.** **Wmk. 313**

| | | | | |
|---|---|---|---|---|
| **703** | A231 | 20pf crimson, gray & yel | .30 | .25 |
| **704** | A231 | 25pf lt blue, gray & red | *.95* | *.80* |
| **705** | A231 | 70pf emerald, gray & yel | .50 | .25 |
| | | *Nos. 703-705 (3)* | *1.75* | *1.30* |

Congress of Women of the German Democratic Republic, June 25-27.

Bicycling A232

Diving — A233

**Litho. & Engr.**

**1964, July 15** ***Perf. 14***

| | | | | |
|---|---|---|---|---|
| **706** | A232 | 5pf shown | .25 | .25 |
| **707** | A232 | 10pf Volleyball | .25 | .25 |
| **708** | A232 | 20pf Judo | .25 | .25 |
| **709** | A232 | 25pf Woman diver | .25 | .25 |
| **710** | A232 | 70pf Equestrian | *1.60* | *1.60* |
| | | *Nos. 706-710,B118 (6)* | *2.90* | *2.85* |

**Litho.**

***Perf. 13x13½***

| | | | | |
|---|---|---|---|---|
| **711** | A233 | 10pf shown | 2.25 | 2.25 |
| **712** | A233 | 10pf Volleyball | 2.25 | 2.25 |
| **713** | A233 | 10pf Bicycling | 2.25 | 2.25 |
| **714** | A233 | 10pf Judo | 2.25 | 2.25 |
| *a.* | | Block of 6, #711-714, B119-B120 | 20.00 | 20.00 |

18th Olympic Games, Tokyo, Oct. 10-25, 1964. See Nos. B118-B120. No. 714a printed in 2 horiz. rows: (1st: #711, #B119, #712. 2nd: #713, #B120, #714). The Olympic rings extend over the 6 stamps.

Monument, Leningrad A234

**1964, Aug. 8 Litho.** ***Perf. 13x13½***

| | | | | |
|---|---|---|---|---|
| **715** | A234 | 25pf brt blue, blk & yel | .75 | .25 |

Issued to honor the victims of the siege of Leningrad, Sept. 1941-Jan. 1943.

Bertha von Suttner — A235

Designs: 20pf, Frederic Joliot Curie. 50pf, Carl von Ossietzky.

**1964, Sept. 1** ***Perf. 14***

| | | | | |
|---|---|---|---|---|
| **716** | A235 | 20pf red & black | .25 | .25 |
| **717** | A235 | 25pf ultra & black | .25 | .25 |
| **718** | A235 | 50pf lilac & black | *1.00* | *.80* |
| | | *Nos. 716-718 (3)* | *1.50* | *1.30* |

Issued to promote World Peace.

Medieval Glazier and Goblet — A236

15pf, Jena glass for chemical industry.

**1964, Sept. 3** ***Perf. 14***

| | | | | |
|---|---|---|---|---|
| **719** | A236 | 10pf lt ultra & multi | .70 | .25 |
| **720** | A236 | 15pf red & multi | .70 | .25 |
| *a.* | | Pair, #719-720 + label | 2.75 | .70 |

Issued for the Leipzig Fall Fair, 1964.

Handstamp of First Socialist International, 1864 — A237

**1964, Sept. 16 Photo.** **Wmk. 313**

| | | | | |
|---|---|---|---|---|
| **721** | A237 | 20pf orange red & blk | .25 | .25 |
| **722** | A237 | 25pf dull blue & blk | *.60* | *.60* |

Centenary of First Socialist International.

Stamp of 1955 (Dürer's Portrait of Young Man) — A238

**1964, Sept. 23 Litho.** ***Perf. 13x13½***

| | | | | |
|---|---|---|---|---|
| **723** | A238 | 50pf gray & dk red brn | *1.75* | *1.25* |
| | | *Nos. 723,B124-B125 (3)* | *2.30* | *1.75* |

Natl. Stamp Exhibition, Berlin, Oct. 3-18.

Coal Transport
A239

#724, Navigation. #725, Flag & new Berlin buildings. #727, Chemist. #728, Soldier. #729, Farm woman & cows. #730, Steel worker. #731, Woman scientist & lecture hall. #732, Heavy industry. #733, Optical industry. #734, Consumer goods (woman examining cloth). #735, Foreign trade, Leipzig fair emblem. #736, Buildings industry. #737, Sculptor. #738, Woman skier.

*Perf. 13½x13*

**1964, Oct. 6 Litho. Wmk. 313**

| | | | | | |
|---|---|---|---|---|---|
| **724** | A239 | 10pf blue & multi | | .30 | .30 |
| **725** | A239 | 10pf blue & multi | | .30 | .30 |
| **726** | A239 | 10pf gray & multi | | .30 | .30 |
| **727** | A239 | 10pf red & multi | | .30 | .30 |
| **728** | A239 | 10pf red & multi | | .30 | .30 |
| **729** | A239 | 10pf yel grn & multi | | .30 | .30 |
| **730** | A239 | 10pf red & multi | | .30 | .30 |
| **731** | A239 | 10pf red & multi | | .30 | .30 |
| **732** | A239 | 10pf gray & multi | | .30 | .30 |
| **733** | A239 | 10pf gray & multi | | .30 | .30 |
| **734** | A239 | 10pf blue & multi | | .30 | .30 |
| **735** | A239 | 10pf blue & multi | | .30 | .30 |
| **736** | A239 | 10pf yel grn & multi | | .30 | .30 |
| **737** | A239 | 10pf yel grn & multi | | .30 | .30 |
| **738** | A239 | 10pf blue & multi | | .30 | .30 |
| | | *Nos. 724-738 (15)* | | *4.50* | *4.50* |

German Democratic Republic, 15th anniv.

A souvenir sheet contains 15 imperf. stamps similar to #724-738. Size: 210x287mm. Values: $40 unused, $75 used.

For surcharge see No. B134.

Man from Mönchgut, Rügen — A240

Regional Costumes: No. 740, Woman from Mönchgut, Rügen. No. 741, Man from Spreewald. No. 742, Woman from Spreewald. No. 743, Man from Thuringia. No. 744, Woman from Thuringia.

**1964, Nov. 25 Photo. *Perf. 14***

| | | | | |
|---|---|---|---|---|
| **739** | A240 | 5pf multicolored | *7.00* | *4.25* |
| **740** | A240 | 5pf multicolored | *7.00* | *4.25* |
| *a.* | | Pair, #739-740 | *25.00* | *10.00* |
| **741** | A240 | 10pf multicolored | 1.75 | .90 |
| **742** | A240 | 10pf multicolored | 1.75 | .90 |
| *a.* | | Pair, #741-742 | 7.50 | 3.00 |
| **743** | A240 | 20pf multicolored | 1.75 | .90 |
| **744** | A240 | 20pf multicolored | 1.75 | .90 |
| *a.* | | Pair, #739-740 | 7.50 | 3.00 |
| | | *Nos. 739-744 (6)* | *21.00* | *12.10* |

Printed in checkerboard arrangement.

See Nos. 859-864.

Souvenir Sheets

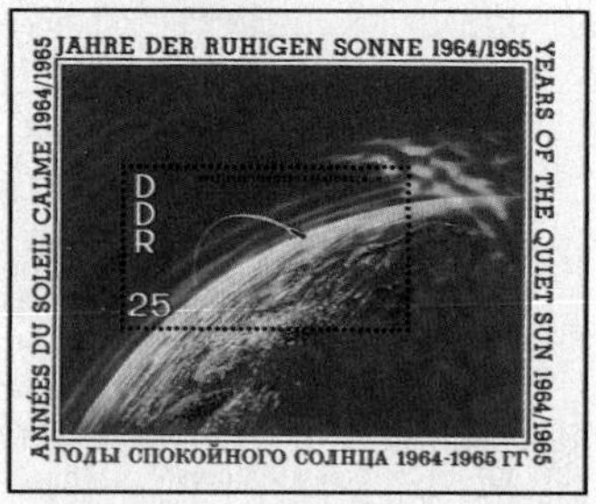


Exploration of Ionosphere — A241

Designs: 40pf, Exploration of sun activities. 70pf, Exploration of radiation belt.

**1964, Dec. 29 Litho. *Perf. 13½x13***

| | | | | |
|---|---|---|---|---|
| **745** | A241 | 25pf vio bl & yel | *5.50* | *8.00* |
| **746** | A241 | 40pf vio bl, yel & red | *2.75* | *4.00* |
| **747** | A241 | 70pf dp grn, vio bl & yel | *2.75* | *4.00* |
| | | *Nos. 745-747 (3)* | *11.00* | *16.00* |

Intl. Quiet Sun Year, 1964-65.

Albert Schweitzer as Physician
A242

Designs (Schweitzer): 20pf, As fighter against war and atom bomb. 25pf, At the organ with score of Organ Prelude by Bach.

**Wmk. 313**

**1965, Jan. 14 Photo. *Perf. 14***

| | | | | |
|---|---|---|---|---|
| **748** | A242 | 10pf emerald, blk & bis | .35 | .25 |
| **749** | A242 | 20pf crimson, blk & bis | .35 | .25 |
| **750** | A242 | 25pf blue, blk & bis | *3.00* | *1.75* |
| | | *Nos. 748-750 (3)* | *3.70* | *2.25* |

90th birthday of Dr. Albert Schweitzer, medical missionary.

**Ulbricht Type of 1961-63**

Currency in "Mark of the Deutsche Notenbank" (MDN)

**1965, Feb. 10 Engr.**

**Size: 24x28½mm**

| | | | | |
|---|---|---|---|---|
| **751** | A189 | 1mdn dull green | .60 | .60 |
| **752** | A189 | 2mdn brown | .70 | .70 |

See note below Nos. 590B-590C.

August Bebel — A243

10pf, Wilhelm Conrad Roentgen. #753A, Adolph von Menzel. 25pf, Wilhelm Külz. 40pf, Erich Weinert. 50pf, Dante Alighieri.

**1965 Photo. *Perf. 14***

| | | | | |
|---|---|---|---|---|
| **753** | A243 | 10pf dk brn, yel & emer | .40 | .25 |
| **753A** | A243 | 10pf dk brn, yel & org | .65 | .25 |
| **754** | A243 | 20pf ol brn, red & buff | .40 | .25 |
| **754A** | A243 | 25pf ol brn, yel & bl | .90 | .25 |
| **754B** | A243 | 40pf ol brn, buff & car rose | .50 | .25 |
| **755** | A243 | 50pf dk brn, yel & org | 1.90 | .25 |
| | | *Nos. 753-755 (6)* | 4.75 | 1.50 |

Roentgen (1845-1923), physicist, discoverer of X-rays. Sesquicentennial of the birth of Adolph von Menzel, painter and graphic artist. Bebel, labor leader (1840-1913). 90th anniv. of the birth of Wilhelm Külz, politician. 75th anniv. of the birth of Erich Weinert, poet. Alighieri (1265-1321), Italian poet.

Issued: #753, 3/24; #753A, 12/8; 20pf, 2/22; 25pf, 7/5; 40pf, 7/28; 50pf, 4/15.

A244

A245

Designs: 10pf, Gold Medal, Leipzig Fair. 15pf, Obverse of medal, arms of German Democratic Republic. 25pf, Chemical plant.

**1965, Feb. 25 Wmk. 313**

| | | | | |
|---|---|---|---|---|
| **756** | A244 | 10pf lilac rose & gold | .25 | .25 |
| **757** | A244 | 15pf lilac rose & gold | .25 | .25 |
| **758** | A244 | 25pf brt blue, yel & gold | .50 | .25 |
| | | *Nos. 756-758 (3)* | 1.00 | .75 |

1965 Leipzig Spring Fair; 800th anniv. of the Fair.

**1965, Mar. 24**

Designs: 10pf, Giraffe. 25pf, Common iguana, horiz. 30pf, White-tailed gnu.

| | | | | |
|---|---|---|---|---|
| **759** | A245 | 10pf green & gray | .25 | .25 |
| **760** | A245 | 25pf dk vio bl & gray | .25 | .25 |
| **761** | A245 | 30pf brown & gray | *2.10* | *1.25* |
| | | *Nos. 759-761 (3)* | *2.60* | *1.75* |

10th anniversary of Berlin Zoo.

Col. Pavel Belyayev and Lt. Col. Alexei Leonov
A246

25pf, Lt. Col. Leonov floating in space.

*Perf. 13½x13*

**1965, Apr. 15 Litho. Wmk. 313**

| | | | | |
|---|---|---|---|---|
| **762** | A246 | 10pf red | .30 | .25 |
| **763** | A246 | 25pf dk ultra | *2.25* | *1.50* |

Space flight of Voskhod 2 and the first man walking in space, Lt. Col. Alexei Leonov.

Boxing Glove and Laurel Wreath — A247

**1965, Apr. 27 Photo. *Perf. 14***

| | | | | |
|---|---|---|---|---|
| **764** | A247 | 20pf blk, red & gold | *.80* | *.80* |

16th European Boxing Championship, Berlin, May, 1965. See No. B126.

Walter Ulbricht and Erich Weinert Distributing "Free Germany" Leaflets on the Eastern Front — A248

50pf, Liberation of concentration camps. 60pf, Russian soldiers raising flag on Reichstag, Berlin. 70pf, Political demonstration.

**1965, May 5 Photo. *Perf. 14***

**Flags in Red, Black & Yellow**

| | | | | |
|---|---|---|---|---|
| **765** | A248 | 40pf blue grn & red | .25 | .25 |
| **766** | A248 | 50pf dull blue & red | .25 | .25 |
| **767** | A248 | 60pf brown & red | *4.00* | *4.00* |
| **768** | A248 | 70pf vio blue & red | .25 | .25 |
| | | *Nos. 765-768,B127-B131 (9)* | *6.00* | *6.00* |

20th anniv. of liberation from fascism.

Radio Tower and Globe
A249

ITU Emblem and Frequency Diagram
A250

40pf, Workers & broadcasting equipment.

**1965, May 12 Litho. *Perf. 12½x13***

| | | | | |
|---|---|---|---|---|
| **769** | A249 | 20pf dk car rose & blk | .30 | .25 |
| **770** | A249 | 40pf vio bl & blk | *1.10* | *.60* |

20th anniv. of the German Democratic broadcasting system.

**1965, May 17**

25pf, ITU emblem & telephone diagram.

| | | | | |
|---|---|---|---|---|
| **771** | A250 | 20pf olive, yel & blk | .40 | .25 |
| **772** | A250 | 25pf vio, pale vio & blk | *2.25* | *.45* |

Cent. of the ITU.

Emblem of Free German Trade Union — A251

Hemispheres with Crowd of Workers — A252

**1965, June 10 Photo. *Perf. 14***

| | | | | |
|---|---|---|---|---|
| **773** | A251 | 20pf red & gold | .35 | .25 |
| **774** | A252 | 25pf gold, blue & blk | *1.10* | *.45* |

20th anniv. of the Free German Trade Union (FDGB) and of the World Organization of Trade Unions.

Symbols of Industry — A253

Marx and Lenin — A254

Designs: 20pf, Red Tower. 25pf, City Hall.

**1965, June 16**

| | | | | |
|---|---|---|---|---|
| **775** | A253 | 10pf gold & emerald | .25 | .25 |
| **776** | A253 | 20pf gold & crimson | .25 | .25 |
| **777** | A253 | 25pf gold & brt blue | *.75* | *.45* |
| | | *Nos. 775-777 (3)* | *1.25* | *.95* |

800th anniv. of Chemnitz (Karl Marx City).

**1965, June 21 Litho. *Perf. 13½x13***

| | | | | |
|---|---|---|---|---|
| **778** | A254 | 20pf red, black & buff | .45 | .25 |

6th Conference of Postal Ministers of Communist Countries, Peking, June 21-July 15.

"Alte Waage" and New Building, Leipzig — A255

25pf, Old City Hall. 40pf, Opera House & General Post Office. 70pf, Hotel "Stadt Leipzig."

**Unwmk.**

**1965, Aug. 25 Photo. *Perf. 14***

| | | | | |
|---|---|---|---|---|
| **781** | A255 | 10pf gold, cl brn & ultra | .25 | .25 |
| *a.* | | Souv. sheet of 2, #781, 784 | *3.00* | *4.75* |
| **782** | A255 | 25pf gold, brn, & ocher | .25 | .25 |
| *a.* | | Souv. sheet of 2, #782-783 | *2.00* | *4.00* |

**783** A255 40pf gold, brn, ocher & yel grn .25 .25
**784** A255 70pf gold & ultra *1.60* *.70*
*Nos. 781-784 (4)* *2.35* *1.45*

800th anniv. of the City of Leipzig. No. 781a sold for 90pf; No. 782a for 80pf. The souvenir sheets were issued Sept. 4, 1965.

Cameras
A256

Equestrian
A257

Leipzig Fall Fair: 15pf, Electric guitar and organ. 25pf, Microscope.

**1965, Sept. 9** ***Perf. 14***

**785** A256 10pf green, blk & gold .25 .25
**786** A256 15pf multicolored .25 .25
**787** A256 25pf multicolored .70 .25
*Nos. 785-787 (3)* 1.20 .75

***Perf. 13½x13***

**1965, Sept. 15** **Litho.** **Unwmk.**

**789** A257 10pf shown .25 .25
**790** A257 10pf Swimmer .25 .25
**791** A257 10pf Runner *2.25* *2.25*
*Nos. 789-791,B135-B136 (5)* *3.25* *3.25*

Intl. Modern Pentathlon Championships, Leipzig.

Alexei Leonov and Brandenburg Gate — A258

Designs: No. 793, Pavel Belyayev and Berlin City Hall. 25pf, Leonov floating in space and space ship.

**Wmk. 313**

**1965, Nov. 1** **Litho.** ***Perf. 14***

**Size: 23½x28½mm**

**792** A258 20pf blue, sil & red *.45* *.55*
**793** A258 20pf blue, sil & red *.45* *.55*

**Size: 51x28½mm**

**794** A258 25pf blue, sil & red *.45* *.55*
*a.* Strip of 3, #792-794 *3.25* *4.25*

Visit of the Russian astronauts to the German Democratic Republic.

Memorial Monument, Putten — A259

**1965, Nov. 19** ***Perf. 13x13½***

**795** A259 25pf brt bl, pale yel & blk .85 .25

Issued in memory of the victims of a Nazi attack on Putten, Netherlands, Sept. 30, 1944.

Furnace
A260

After old woodcuts: 15pf, Ore miners. 20pf, Proustite crystals. 25pf, Sulphur crystals.

***Perf. 13x12½***

**1965, Nov. 11** **Litho.** **Unwmk.**

**796** A260 10pf black & multi .25 .25
**797** A260 15pf black & multi *.70* *.70*
**798** A260 20pf black & multi .25 .25
**799** A260 25pf black & multi .25 .25
*Nos. 796-799 (4)* *1.45* *1.45*

Mining Academy in Freiberg, bicent.

Red Kite
A261

Otto Grotewohl
A262

Birds: 10pf, Lammergeier. 20pf, Buzzard. 25pf, Kestrel. 40pf, Northern goshawk. 70pf, Golden eagle.

**1965, Dec. 8** **Photo.** ***Perf. 14***

**Gold Frame**

**800** A261 5pf orange & blk .25 .25
**801** A261 10pf emer, brn & blk .25 .25
**802** A261 20pf car, red brn & blk .30 .25
**803** A261 25pf blue, red brn & blk .30 .25
**804** A261 40pf lilac, blk & dk red .40 .25
**805** A261 70pf brn, blk & yel *3.75* *2.10*
*Nos. 800-805 (6)* *5.25* *3.35*

**1965, Dec. 14** **Photo.** **Wmk. 313**

**806** A262 20pf black .55 .25

Issued in memory of Otto Grotewohl (1894-1964), prime minister (1949-1964).

Souvenir Sheet

Spartacus Letter, Karl Liebknecht and Rosa Luxemburg — A263

**1966, Jan. 3** **Unwmk.**

**807** A263 Sheet of 2 1.90 *5.00*
*a.* 20pf red & black .35 .60
*b.* 50pf red & black .35 .60

50th anniv. of the natl. conf. of the Spartacus organization.

Tobogganing, Women's Singles
A264

20pf, Men's doubles. 25pf, Men's singles.

***Perf. 13½x13***

**1966, Jan. 25** **Litho.** **Unwmk.**

**808** A264 10pf citron & dp grn .25 .25
**809** A264 20pf car rose & dk vio bl .25 .25
**810** A264 25pf blue & dk blue *1.20* *.75*
*Nos. 808-810 (3)* *1.70* *1.25*

10th Intl. Tobogganing Championships, Friedrichroda, Feb. 8-13.

Electronic Computer
A265

Design: 15pf, Drill and milling machine.

**1966, Feb. 24** ***Perf. 13x12½***

**811** A265 10pf multicolored .25 .25
**812** A265 15pf multicolored .70 .25

Leipzig Spring Fair, 1966.

Jan Arnost Smoler and Linden Leaf — A266

25pf, House of the Sorbs, Bautzen, Saxony.

**1966, Mar. 1** ***Perf. 13x13½***

**813** A266 20pf brt bl, blk & brt red .25 .25
**814** A266 25pf brt red, blk & brt bl *.55* *.45*

Smoler (1816-84), philologist of the Sorbian language. The Sorbs are a small group of slavic people in Saxony.

Soldier and National Gallery, Berlin — A267

Designs (Soldier and): 10pf, Brandenburg Gate. 20pf, Factory. 25pf, Combine.

**Wmk. 313**

**1966, Mar. 1** **Photo.** ***Perf. 14***

**815** A267 5pf ol gray, blk & yel .25 .25
**816** A267 10pf ol gray, blk & yel .25 .25
**817** A267 20pf ol gray, blk & yel .25 .25
**818** A267 25pf ol gray, blk & yel *1.00* *.80*
*Nos. 815-818 (4)* *1.75* *1.55*

National People's Army, 10th anniversary.

Luna 9 on Moon — A268

**1966, Mar. 7** **Unwmk.**

**819** A268 20pf multicolored 1.75 .40

1st soft landing on the moon by Luna 9, 2/3/66.

Medal for Scholarship — A269

**1966, Mar. 7** **Litho.** ***Perf. 13½x13***

**820** A269 20pf multicolored .55 .25

20th anniv. of the State Youth Organization.

Traffic Signs — A270

Traffic safety: 15pf, Automobile and child with scooter. 25pf, Bicyclist and signaling hand. 50pf, Motorcyclist, ambulance and glass of beer.

**1966, Mar. 28** **Litho.** ***Perf. 13***

**821** A270 10pf dk & lt bl, red & blk .25 .25
**822** A270 15pf brt grn, citron & blk .25 .25
**823** A270 25pf ol bis, brt bl & blk .25 .25
**824** A270 50pf car, yel, gray & blk *.80* *.55*
*Nos. 821-824 (4)* *1.55* *1.30*

Marx, Lenin and Crowd — A271

Designs: 5pf, Party emblem and crowd, vert. 15pf, Marx, Engels and title page of Communist Manifesto, vert. 20pf, Otto Grotewohl and Wilhelm Pieck shaking hands, and Party emblem, vert. 25pf, Chairman Walter Ulbricht receiving flowers.

**1966, Mar. 31** **Photo.** ***Perf. 14***

**825** A271 5pf multicolored .25 .25
**826** A271 10pf multicolored .25 .25
**827** A271 15pf green & blk .25 .25
**828** A271 20pf dk carmine & blk .25 .25
**829** A271 25pf multicolored *1.50* *1.00*
*Nos. 825-829 (5)* *2.50* *2.00*

20th anniversary of Socialist Unity Party of Germany (SED).

WHO Headquarters, Geneva — A272

***Perf. 13x12½***

**1966, Apr. 26** **Litho.** **Unwmk.**

**830** A272 20pf multicolored .40 .30

Inauguration of WHO Headquarters, Geneva.

Rügen Island, Königsstuhl — A273

National Parks: 10pf, Spree River woodland. 20pf, Saxon Switzerland. 25pf, Dunes at Westdarss. 30pf, Thale in Harz, Devil's Wall. 50pf, Feldberg Lakes, Mecklenburg.

***Perf. 13x12½***

**1966, May 17** **Litho.** **Unwmk.**

**831** A273 10pf multicolored .25 .25
**832** A273 15pf multicolored .25 .25
**833** A273 20pf multicolored .25 .25
**834** A273 25pf multicolored .25 .25
**835** A273 30pf multicolored *1.60* *1.00*
**836** A273 50pf multicolored .25 *.25*
*Nos. 831-836 (6)* *2.85* *2.25*

Plauen Lace — A274

Various Lace Designs.

**1966, May 26** ***Perf. 13x13½***

**837** A274 10pf green & lt green .25 .25
**838** A274 20pf dk blue & lt blue .25 .25
**839** A274 25pf brown red & ver .25 .25
**840** A274 50pf dk vio & bluish lil *2.10* *1.00*
*Nos. 837-840 (4)* *2.85* *1.75*

Rhododendron
A275

Flowers: 20pf, Lilies of the Valley. 40pf, Dahlias. 50pf, Cyclamen.

**Photo. & Engr.**

**1966 Unwmk. *Perf. 14x13½***

**841** A275 20pf multicolored .25 .25
**842** A275 25pf multicolored .25 .25
**843** A275 40pf multicolored .30 .25
**844** A275 50pf multicolored 4.00 4.00
*Nos. 841-844 (4)* 4.80 4.75

Intl. Flower Show, Erfurt.
Issued: 20pf, Aug. 16; others, June 28.

Parachutist Landing on Target — A276

15pf, Group parachute jump. 20pf, Free fall.

**1966, July 12 Litho. *Perf. 12½x13***

**845** A276 10pf blue, blk & ol .25 .25
**846** A276 15pf multicolored .60 .60
**847** A276 20pf sky blue, blk & ol .25 .25
*Nos. 845-847 (3)* 1.10 1.10

8th Intl. Parachute Championships, Leipzig.

Hans Kahle, Song of German Fighters and Medal of Spanish Republic — A277

15pf, Hans Beimler and street fighting in Madrid.

**1966, July 15 Photo. *Perf. 14***

**848** A277 5pf multicolored .25 .25
**849** A277 15pf multicolored .25 .25
*Nos. 848-849,B137-B140 (6)* 2.75 2.45

German fighters in the Spanish Civil War.

Television Set
A278

Design: 15pf, Electric typewriter.

***Perf. 13x12½***

**1966, Aug. 29 Litho. Unwmk.**

**850** A278 10pf brt grn, blk & gray .60 .25
**851** A278 15pf red, blk & gray 1.40 .25

1966 Leipzig Fall Fair.

Women's Doubles Kayak Race — A279

**1966, Aug. 16**

**852** A279 15pf brt blue & multi 1.10 .85

7th Canoe World Championships, Berlin. See No. B141.

Oradour sur Glane Memorial and French Flag
A280

Emblem of the Committee for Health Education
A281

***Perf. 13x13½***

**1966, Sept. 9 Wmk. 313**

**853** A280 25pf ultra, blk & red .60 .25

Issued in memory of the victims of the Nazi attack on Oradour, France, June 10, 1944.

**1966, Sept. 13 *Perf. 14***

5pf, Symbolic blood donor & recipient, horiz.

**854** A281 5pf brt green & red .25 .25
**855** A281 40pf brt blue & red 1.75 .55
*Nos. 854-855,B142 (3)* 2.40 1.05

Blood donations and health education.

Weight Lifter — A282

***Perf. 13½x13***

**1966, Sept. 22 Litho. Unwmk.**

**856** A282 15pf lt brown & blk 1.75 1.40

Intl. and European Weight Lifting Championships, Berlin. See No. B143.

Congress Hall — A283

Emblem — A284

**1966, Oct. 10 *Perf. 13***

**857** A283 10pf multicolored .45 .40
**858** A284 20pf dk blue & yellow .25 .25

6th Cong. of the Intl. Organ. of Journalists, Berlin.

**Costume Type of 1964**

Regional Costumes: 5pf, Woman from Altenburg. No. 860, Man from Altenburg. No. 861, Woman from Mecklenburg. 15pf, Man from Mecklenburg. 20pf, Woman from Magdeburg area. 30pf, Man from Magdeburg area.

**1966, Oct. 25 Photo. *Perf. 14***

**859** A240 5pf multicolored .40 .25
**860** A240 10pf multicolored .40 .25
*a.* Pair, #859-860 1.25 .80
**861** A240 10pf lt green & multi .40 .25
**862** A240 15pf lt green & multi .40 .25
*a.* Pair, #861-862 1.25 .80
**863** A240 20pf yellow & multi 2.00 1.25
**864** A240 30pf yellow & multi 2.00 1.25
*a.* Pair, #863-864 4.50 3.25
*Nos. 859-864 (6)* 5.60 3.50

Printed in checkerboard arrangement.

Megalamphodus Megalopterus — A285

Various Tropical Fish in Natural Colors.

**1966, Nov. 8 Litho. *Perf. 13x12½***

**865** A285 5pf lt blue & gray .25 .25
**866** A285 10pf blue & indigo .25 .25
**867** A285 15pf citron & blk 2.40 1.75
**868** A285 20pf green & blk .25 .25
**869** A285 25pf ultra & blk .25 .25
**870** A285 40pf emerald & blk .30 .25
*Nos. 865-870 (6)* 3.70 3.00

Map of Oil Pipeline and Oil Field — A286

Design: 25pf, Map of oil pipelines and "Walter Ulbricht" Leuna chemical factory.

**1966, Nov. 8 *Perf. 13½x13***

**871** A286 20pf red & black .25 .25
**872** A286 25pf blue & black .65 .40

Chemical industry.

Detail from Ishtar Gate, Babylon, 580 B.C. — A287

Designs from Babylon c. 580 B.C.: 20pf, Mythological animal from Ishtar Gate. 25pf, Lion facing right and ornaments, vert. 50pf, Lion facing left and ornaments, vert.

***Perf. 13½x14, 14x13½***

**1966, Nov. 23 Photo.**

**873** A287 10pf multicolored .25 .25
**874** A287 20pf multicolored .25 .25
**875** A287 25pf multicolored .25 .25
**876** A287 50pf multicolored .55 1.00
*Nos. 873-876 (4)* 1.30 1.75

Near East Museum, Berlin.

Wartburg, Thuringia — A288

Gentian — A289

Design: 25pf, Wartburg, Palace.

**1966, Nov. 23 Litho. *Perf. 13x13½***

**877** A288 20pf olive .25 .25
**878** A288 25pf violet brown .55 .30
*Nos. 877-878,B145 (3)* 1.10 .80

900th anniv. (in 1967) of the Wartburg (castle) near Eisenach, Thuringia.

**1966, Dec. 8 Litho. *Perf. 12½x13***

Protected Flowers: 20pf, Cephalanthera rubra (orchid). 25pf, Mountain arnica.

**Black Background**

**879** A289 10pf yel, grn & bl .25 .25
**880** A289 20pf yel, grn & red .25 .25
**881** A289 25pf red, yel & grn 1.25 .80
*Nos. 879-881 (3)* 1.75 1.30

Son Leaving Home — A290

Various Scenes from Fairy Tale "The Table, the Ass and the Stick."

**1966, Dec. 8 *Perf. 13½x13***

**882** A290 5pf multicolored .25 .30
**883** A290 10pf multicolored .25 .30
**884** A290 20pf multicolored .65 .70
**885** A290 25pf multicolored .65 .70
**886** A290 30pf multicolored .25 .30
**887** A290 50pf multicolored .25 .30
*a.* Sheet of 6, #882-887 3.25 4.25

See Nos. 968-973, 1063-1068, 1087-1092, 1176-1181, 1339-1344.

City Hall, Stralsund — A291

Buildings: 5pf, Wörlitz Castle, horiz. 15pf, Chorin Convent. 20pf, Ribbeck House, Berlin, horiz. 25pf, Moritzburg, Zeitz. 40pf, Old City Hall, Potsdam.

***Perf. 14x13½, 13½x14***

**1967, Jan. 24 Photo.**

**888** A291 5pf multicolored .25 .25
**889** A291 10pf multicolored .25 .25
**890** A291 15pf multicolored .25 .25
**891** A291 20pf multicolored .25 .25
**892** A291 25pf multicolored .25 .25
**893** A291 40pf multicolored 1.00 .80
*Nos. 888-893 (6)* 2.25 2.05

See Nos. 1018, 1020, 1071-1076.

Rifle Shooting, Prone — A292

Designs: 20pf, Shooting on skis. 25pf, Relay race with rifles on skis.

**1967, Feb. 15 Litho. *Perf. 13x12½***

**894** A292 10pf Prus bl gray & brt pink .25 .25
**895** A292 20pf sl grn, brt bl & grn .25 .25
**896** A292 25pf ol grn, ol & grnsh bl .70 .45
*Nos. 894-896 (3)* 1.20 .95

World Biathlon Championships (skiing and shooting), Altenberg, Feb. 15-19.

Circular Knitting Machine — A293

Design: 15pf, Zeiss telescope and galaxy.

**1967, Mar. 2** *Perf. 13½x13*

| | | | | |
|---|---|---|---|---|
| **897** A293 | 10pf dull mag & brt grn | .25 | .25 |
| **898** A293 | 15pf ultra & gray | .65 | .25 |

Leipzig Spring Fair of 1967.

Mother and Child — A294

Design: 25pf, Working women.

**1967, Mar. 7** *Perf. 13x13½*

| | | | |
|---|---|---|---|
| **899** A294 | 20pf rose brn, red & gray | .25 | .25 |
| **900** A294 | 25pf dk bl, brt bl & brn | *.70* | *.60* |

20th anniv. of the Democratic Women's Federation of Germany.

Marx, Engels, Lenin and Electronic Control Center — A295

Designs (Portraits and): 5pf, Farmer driving combine. No. 903, Students and teacher. 15pf, Family. No. 905, Soldier, sailor and aviator. No. 906, Ulbricht among workers. 25pf, Soldier, sailor, aviator and factories. 40pf, Farmers with modern equipment. Nos. 901, 903-905 are vertical.

**1967** **Photo.** *Perf. 14*

| | | | |
|---|---|---|---|
| **901** A295 | 5pf multicolored | .25 | .25 |
| **902** A295 | 10pf multicolored | .25 | .25 |
| **903** A295 | 10pf multicolored | .25 | .25 |
| **904** A295 | 15pf multicolored | *.40* | *.40* |
| **905** A295 | 20pf multicolored | .25 | .25 |
| **906** A295 | 20pf multicolored | .25 | .25 |
| **907** A295 | 25pf multicolored | .25 | .25 |
| **908** A295 | 40pf multicolored | *.40* | *.70* |
| | *Nos. 901-908 (8)* | *2.30* | *2.60* |

7th congress of Socialist Unity Party of Germany (SED), Apr. 17.

Issued: #902, 906-908 3/22; #901, 903-905, 4/6.

Tahitian Women, by Paul Gauguin — A296

Paintings from Dresden Gallery: 20pf, Young Woman, by Ferdinand Hodler. 25pf, Peter in the Zoo, by H. Hakenbeck. 30pf, Venetian Episode (woman feeding pigeons), by R. Bergander. 50pf, Grandmother and Granddaughter, by J. Scholtz. 70pf, Cairn in the Snow, by Caspar David Friedrich.

**1967, Mar. 29**

| | | | |
|---|---|---|---|
| **909** A296 | 20pf multi, vert. | .25 | .25 |
| **910** A296 | 25pf multi, vert. | .25 | .25 |
| **911** A296 | 30pf multi, vert. | .25 | .25 |
| **912** A296 | 40pf multi | .25 | .25 |
| **913** A296 | 50pf multi, vert. | *1.60* | *1.25* |
| **914** A296 | 70pf multi | .30 | .25 |
| | *Nos. 909-914 (6)* | *2.90* | *2.50* |

Barn Owl — A297

Protected Birds: 10pf, Eurasian crane. 20pf, Peregrine falcon. 25pf, Bullfinches. 30pf, European kingfisher. 40pf, European roller.

**1967, Apr. 27** **Photo.** *Perf. 14*

**Birds in Natural Colors**

| | | | |
|---|---|---|---|
| **915** A297 | 5pf gray blue | .25 | .25 |
| **916** A297 | 10pf gray blue | .25 | .25 |
| **917** A297 | 20pf gray blue | .25 | .25 |
| **918** A297 | 25pf gray blue | .25 | .25 |
| **919** A297 | 30pf gray blue | *3.50* | *2.00* |
| **920** A297 | 40pf gray blue | .30 | .25 |
| | *Nos. 915-920 (6)* | *4.80* | *3.25* |

Arms of Warsaw, Berlin and Prague A298

Design: 25pf, Bicyclists and doves.

*Perf. 13x12½*

**1967, May 10** **Litho.** **Wmk. 313**

| | | | |
|---|---|---|---|
| **921** A298 | 10pf org, blk & lil | .25 | .25 |
| **922** A298 | 25pf lt bl & dk car | *.40* | *.35* |

20th Intl. Bicycle Peace Race, Berlin-Warsaw-Prague.

Cat A299

Children's Drawings: 10pf, Snow White and the Seven Dwarfs. 15pf, Fire truck. 20pf, Cock. 25pf, Flowers in vase. 30pf, Children playing ball.

**1967, June 1** **Unwmk.**

| | | | |
|---|---|---|---|
| **923** A299 | 5pf multicolored | .25 | .25 |
| **924** A299 | 10pf black & multi | .25 | .25 |
| **925** A299 | 15pf dk blue & multi | .25 | .25 |
| **926** A299 | 20pf orange & multi | .25 | .25 |
| **927** A299 | 25pf multicolored | .25 | .25 |
| **928** A299 | 30pf multicolored | *1.00* | *.70* |
| | *Nos. 923-928 (6)* | *2.25* | *1.95* |

Issued for International Children's Day.

Girl with Straw Hat, by Salomon Bray — A300

Exhibition Emblem and Map of DDR — A301

Paintings: 5pf, Three Horsemen, by Rubens, horiz. 10pf, Girl Gathering Grapes, by Gerard Dou. 20pf, Spring Idyl, by Hans Thoma, horiz. 25pf, Wilhelmine Schroder-Devrient, by Karl Begas. 50pf, The Four Evangelists, by Jacob Jordaens.

**1967, June 7** **Photo.** *Perf. 14*

| | | | |
|---|---|---|---|
| **929** A300 | 5pf lt & dk blue | .25 | .25 |
| **930** A300 | 10pf lt red brn & red brn | .25 | .25 |
| **931** A300 | 20pf lt & dp yel grn | .25 | .25 |
| **932** A300 | 25pf pale rose & rose lil | .25 | .25 |
| **933** A300 | 40pf pale grn & ol grn | .25 | .25 |
| **934** A300 | 50pf tan & sepia | *1.50* | *.95* |
| | *Nos. 929-934 (6)* | *2.75* | *2.20* |

Issued to publicize paintings missing from museums since World War II.

*Perf. 12½x13*

**1967, June 14** **Litho.** **Unwmk.**

| | | | |
|---|---|---|---|
| **935** A301 | 20pf dk grn, ocher & red | .35 | .25 |

15th Agricultural Exhib., Markkleeberg.

Marie Curie — A302

Portraits: 5pf, Georg Herwegh, poet. 20pf, Käthe Kollwitz. 25pf, Johann J. Winckelmann, archaeologist. 40pf, Theodor Storm, writer.

**1967** **Engr.** *Perf. 14*

| | | | |
|---|---|---|---|
| **936** A302 | 5pf brown | .25 | .25 |
| **937** A302 | 10pf dark blue | .25 | .25 |
| **938** A302 | 20pf dull red | .25 | .25 |
| **939** A302 | 25pf gray | .25 | .25 |
| **940** A302 | 40pf slate green | *.65* | *.55* |
| | *Nos. 936-940 (5)* | *1.65* | *1.55* |

150th anniv. of the birth of Herwegh, Winckelmann and Storm, and the birth centenaries of Curie and Kollwitz.

German Playing Cards — A303

Designs: Various German playing cards.

**1967, July 18** **Photo.**

| | | | |
|---|---|---|---|
| **941** A303 | 5pf red & multi | .25 | .25 |
| **942** A303 | 10pf green & multi | .25 | .25 |
| **943** A303 | 20pf multicolored | .25 | .25 |
| **944** A303 | 25pf multicolored | *4.00* | *2.75* |
| | *Nos. 941-944 (4)* | *4.75* | *3.50* |

Mare and Foal A304

Horses: 10pf, Stallion. 20pf, Horse race finish. 50pf, Colts, vert.

*Perf. 13½x13, 13x13½*

**1967, Aug. 15** **Litho.** **Unwmk.**

| | | | |
|---|---|---|---|
| **945** A304 | 5pf multicolored | .25 | .25 |
| **946** A304 | 10pf org, blk & dk brn | .25 | .25 |
| **947** A304 | 20pf blue & multi | .25 | .25 |
| **948** A304 | 50pf multicolored | *3.00* | *2.00* |
| | *Nos. 945-948 (4)* | *3.75* | *2.75* |

Thoroughbred Horse Show of Socialist Countries, Hoppegarten, Berlin.

Small Electrical Appliances A305

Leipzig Fall Fair: 15pf, Woman's fur coat and furrier's trademark.

*Perf. 14x13½*

**1967, Aug. 8** **Photo.** **Unwmk.**

| | | | |
|---|---|---|---|
| **949** A305 | 10pf brt bl, blk & yel | .35 | .25 |
| **950** A305 | 15pf yellow, brn & blk | .70 | .40 |

Max Reichpietsch and Warship — A306

15pf, Albin Köbis, warship. 20pf, Sailors marching with red flag, warship.

**1967, Sept. 5** **Litho.** *Perf. 13½x13*

**Bluish Paper**

| | | | |
|---|---|---|---|
| **951** A306 | 10pf dk blue, gray & red | .25 | .25 |
| **952** A306 | 15pf dk blue, gray & red | *.90* | *.50* |
| **953** A306 | 20pf dk blue, gray & red | .35 | .25 |
| | *Nos. 951-953 (3)* | *1.50* | *1.00* |

50th anniv. of the sailors' uprising at Kiel.

Monument at Kragujevac A307

**1967, Sept. 20** *Perf. 13x13½*

| | | | |
|---|---|---|---|
| **954** A307 | 25pf dk red, yel & blk | .75 | .30 |

Issued in memory of the victims of the Nazis at Kragujevac, Yugoslavia, Oct. 21, 1941.

Worker and Symbols of Electrification — A308

Communist Emblem and: 5pf, Worker, Communist newspaper masthead. 15pf, Russian War Memorial, Berlin-Treptow. 20pf, Russian and German soldiers, coat of arms. 40pf, Lenin, cruiser Aurora.

**1967, Oct. 6** **Photo.** *Perf. 14x14½*

| | | | |
|---|---|---|---|
| **955** A308 | 5pf multicolored | .25 | .25 |
| **956** A308 | 10pf multicolored | .25 | .25 |
| **957** A308 | 15pf multicolored | .25 | .25 |
| **958** A308 | 20pf multicolored | .30 | .25 |
| **959** A308 | 40pf multicolored | *2.25* | *1.75* |
| *a.* | Souvenir sheet of 2 | 1.40 | 3.25 |
| | *Nos. 955-959 (5)* | *3.30* | *2.75* |

50th anniv. of the Russian October Revolution. No. 959a contains 2 imperf. stamps similar to Nos. 958-959 with simulated perforations. It commemorates the Red October Jubilee Stamp Exhibition, Karl-Marx-Stadt, Oct. 6-15. Sold for 85pf.

Martin Luther, by Lucas Cranach — A309

Young Inventors and Fair Emblem — A310

Designs: 25pf, Luther's House, Wittenberg, horiz. 40pf, Castle Church, Wittenberg.

**Engraved and Photogravure**

**1967, Oct. 17** ***Perf. 14***

**960** A309 20pf black & rose lilac .25 .25
**961** A309 25pf black & blue .25 .25
**962** A309 40pf black & lemon *1.75* .80
*Nos. 960-962 (3)* *2.25* *1.30*

450th anniversary of the Reformation.

**1967, Nov. 15 Unwmk.** ***Perf. 14***

Designs: No. 964, Boy's and girl's heads and emblem of the Free German Youth Organization. 25pf, Young workers receiving awards, and medal.

**Size: 23x28½mm**

**963** A310 20pf multicolored .50 .40
**964** A310 20pf multicolored .50 .40

**Size: 51x28½mm**

**965** A310 25pf multicolored .50 .40
*a.* Strip of 3, #963-965 4.00 4.00

Issued to publicize the 10th Masters of Tomorrow Fair, Leipzig, Nov. 15-26.

Goethe House, Weimar A311

Design: 25pf, Schiller House, Weimar.

**1967, Nov. 27 Litho.** ***Perf. 13x12½***

**966** A311 20pf gray, blk & brn .25 .25
**967** A311 25pf citron, dk grn & brn *1.25* .45

Honoring German classical humanism.

**Fairy Tale Type of 1966**

Various Scenes from King Drosselbart.

**1967, Nov. 27** ***Perf. 13½x13***

**968** A290 5pf multicolored .25 .25
**969** A290 10pf multicolored .25 .25
**970** A290 15pf multicolored .80 .90
**971** A290 20pf multicolored .80 .90
**972** A290 25pf multicolored .25 .25
**973** A290 30pf multicolored .25 .25
*a.* Sheet of 6, #968-973 5.00 5.00

Farmers, Stables and Silos — A312

***Perf. 13x12½***

**1967, Dec. 6 Litho. Unwmk.**

**974** A312 10pf multicolored .35 .25

1st agricultural co-operatives, 15th anniv.

Nutcracker and Figurines — A313

Speed Skating — A314

20pf, Candle holders: angel and miner.

**1967, Dec. 6 Photo.** ***Perf. 13½x14***

**975** A313 10pf green & multi *.65* .40
**976** A313 20pf red & multi .25 .25

Issued to publicize local handicrafts of the Erzgebirge in Saxony (Ore Mountains).

***Perf. 13½x13***

**1968, Jan. 17 Litho. Unwmk.**

Sport and Olympic Rings: 15pf, Slalom. 20pf, Ice hockey. 25pf, Figure skating, pair. 30pf, Long-distance skiing.

**977** A314 5pf blue, dk bl & red .25 .25
**978** A314 15pf multicolored .25 .25
**979** A314 20pf grnsh bl, dk bl & red .25 .25
**980** A314 25pf multicolored .25 .25
**981** A314 30pf grnsh bl, vio bl & red *2.50* *1.10*
*Nos. 977-981,B146 (6)* *3.75* *2.35*

10th Winter Olympic Games, Grenoble, France, Feb. 6-18.

Actinometer, Sun and Potsdam Meteorological Observatory A315

Designs: 20pf, Antenna, Cloud Formation and Map of Europe. 25pf, Weather influence on farming (fields by day and night, produce).

**1968, Jan. 24** ***Perf. 13½x13***

**Size: 23x28mm**

**982** A315 10pf brt mag, org & blk .40 .30

**Size: 50x28mm**

**983** A315 20pf multicolored .40 .30

**Size: 23x28mm**

**984** A315 25pf olive, blk & yel .40 .30
*a.* Strip of 3, #982-984 4.50 4.50

75th anniversary of the Meteorological Observatory in Potsdam.

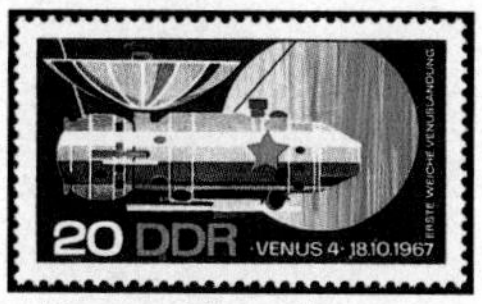

Venera 4 Interplanetary Station — A316

Design: 25pf, Earth satellites Kosmos 186 and 188 orbiting earth.

**1968, Jan. 24 Photo.** ***Perf. 14***

**985** A316 20pf multicolored .25 .25
**986** A316 25pf multicolored *.80* .50

Russian space explorations.

Fighters of The Underground A317

20pf, "The Liberation." 25pf, "The Partisans."

**1968, Feb. 21 Photo.** ***Perf. 14x13½***

**987** A317 10pf black & multi .25 .25
**988** A317 20pf black & multi .25 .25
**989** A317 25pf black & multi *.50* .25
*Nos. 987-989 (3)* *1.00* *.75*

The designs are from the stained glass window triptych by Walter Womacka in the Sachsenhausen Memorial Museum.

Diesel Locomotive — A318

Design: 15pf, Refrigerator fishing ship.

**1968, Feb. 29** ***Perf. 14***

**990** A318 10pf multicolored .30 .25
**991** A318 15pf multicolored .75 .40

The 1968 Leipzig Spring Fair.

Woman from Hoyerswerda A319

Maxim Gorky and View of Gorky A320

Sorbian Regional Costumes: 20pf, Woman from Schleife. 40pf, Woman from Crostwitz. 50pf, Woman from Spreewald.

**1968, Mar. 14**

**992** A319 10pf citron & multi .25 .25
**993** A319 20pf fawn & multi .25 .25
**994** A319 40pf blue grn & multi .25 .25
**995** A319 50pf green & multi *2.00* .85
*Nos. 992-995 (4)* *2.75* *1.60*

**1968, Mar. 14** **Engr.**

25pf, Stormy petrel and toppling towers.

**996** A320 20pf brown & rose car .25 .25
**997** A320 25pf brown & rose car *.55* .30

Maxim Gorky (1868-1936), Russian writer.

Ring-necked Pheasants A321

15pf, Gray partridges. 20pf, Mallards. 25pf, Graylag geese. 30pf, Wood pigeons. 40pf, Hares.

**1968, Mar. 26 Litho.** ***Perf. 13½x13***

**998** A321 10pf gray & multi .25 .25
**999** A321 15pf gray & multi .25 .25
**1000** A321 20pf gray & multi .25 .25
**1001** A321 25pf gray & multi .25 .25
**1002** A321 30pf gray & multi .30 .25
**1003** A321 40pf gray & multi *2.75* *4.75*
*Nos. 998-1003 (6)* *4.05* *6.00*

Karl Marx — A322

Fritz Heckert — A323

Designs: 10pf, Title page of the "Communist Manifesto." 25pf, Title page of "Das Kapital."

**1968, Apr. 25 Photo.** ***Perf. 14***

**1004** A322 10pf yel grn & blk .25 .25
**1005** A322 20pf mag, yel & blk .25 .25
**1006** A322 25pf lem, blk & red brn .25 .25
*a.* Strip of three 1.60 4.00
*b.* Souvenir sheet of 3 1.30 4.00

Karl Marx (1818-83). Nos. 1004-1006 are printed se-tenant. No. 1006a contains 3 imperf. stamps similar to Nos. 1004-1006 with simulated perforations.

**1968, Apr. 25**

Design: 20pf, Young workers, new apartment buildings and Congress emblem.

**1007** A323 10pf multicolored .25 .25
**1008** A323 20pf multicolored .25 .25

7th Congress of the Free German Trade Unions.

"Right to Work" — A324

Designs: 10pf, "Right to Live," tree and globe. 25pf, "Right for Peace," dove and sun.

**1968, May 8 Litho.** ***Perf. 13½x13***

**1009** A324 5pf maroon & pink .25 .25
**1010** A324 10pf brn ol & ol bister .25 .25
**1011** A324 25pf Prus bl & lt bl *.65* .40
*Nos. 1009-1011 (3)* *1.15* *.90*

International Human Rights Year.

Angler A325

Designs: No. 1013, Rowing (woman). No. 1014, High jump (woman).

**Unwmk.**

**1968, June 6 Photo.** ***Perf. 14***

**1012** A325 20pf ol grn, sl bl & dk red .75 .65
**1013** A325 20pf Prus bl, dk bl & ol .25 .25
**1014** A325 20pf cop red, dp cl & bl *.25* *.25*
*Nos. 1012-1014 (3)* *1.25* *1.15*

World angling championships, Gustrow (#1012); European women's rowing championships, Berlin (#1013); 2nd European youth athletic competition, Leipzig (#1014).

Brandenburg Gate, Torch — A326

Youth Festival Emblem — A327

Design: 25pf, Stadium and torch.

**1968, June 20 Litho.** ***Perf. 13½x13***

**1015** A326 10pf multicolored .25 .25
**1016** A326 25pf multicolored *.85* .50

2nd Children's and Youths' Spartakiad, Berlin.

**1968, June 20**

**1017** A327 25pf multicolored *.70* .40

9th Youth Festival for Peace & Friendship, Sofia.
See No. B148.

**Type of 1967 and**

Moritzburg Castle, Dresden — A328

Buildings: 10pf, City Hall, Wernigerode. 25pf, City Hall, Greifswald. 30pf, Sanssouci Palace, Potsdam.

**1968, June 25 Photo.** ***Perf. 13½x14***

**1018** A291 10pf multicolored .25 .25
**1019** A328 20pf multicolored .25 .25
**1020** A291 25pf multicolored .25 .25
**1021** A328 30pf multicolored *.60* .70
*Nos. 1018-1021 (4)* *1.35* *1.45*

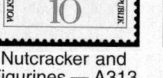

Walter Ulbricht and Arms of Republic A329

**Photo. & Engr.**

**1968, June 27** *Perf. 14*
**1022** A329 20pf org, dp car & blk .50 .25

75th birthday of Walter Ulbricht, chairman of the Council of State, Communist party secretary and deputy prime minister.

Old Rostock and Arms A330

Design: 25pf, Historic and modern buildings, 1968, and arms of Rostock.

**1968, July 9** **Photo.**
**1023** A330 20pf multicolored .25 .25
**1024** A330 25pf multicolored *.50 .40*

750th anniv. of Rostock and to publicize the 11th Baltic Sea Week.

Karl Landsteiner, M.D. (1868-1943) A331

Portraits: 15pf, Emanuel Lasker (1868-1941), chess champion and writer. 20pf, Hanns Eisler (1898-1962), composer. 25pf, Ignaz Semmelweis, M.D. (1818-1865). 40pf, Max von Pettenkofer (1818-1901), hygienist.

**1968, July 17** **Engr.** *Perf. 14*
**1025** A331 10pf gray green .25 .25
**1026** A331 15pf black .25 .25
**1027** A331 20pf brown .25 .25
**1028** A331 25pf gray blue .25 .25
**1029** A331 40pf rose lake *.70 .50*
*Nos. 1025-1029 (5)* *1.70 1.50*

"Trener" Stunt Plane — A332

25pf, 2 "Trener" stunt planes in parallel flight.

**1968, Aug. 13** **Litho.** *Perf. 12½x13*
**1030** A332 10pf multicolored .25 .25
**1031** A332 25pf blue & multi *.50 .40*

Peasant Woman, by Wilhelm Leibl — A333

Paintings from Dresden Gallery: 10pf, "On the Beach," by Walter Womacka, horiz. 15pf, Mountain Farmers Mowing, by Albin Egger-Lienz, horiz. 40pf, The Artist's daughter, by Venturelli. 50pf, High School Girl, by Michaelis. 70pf, Girl with Guitar, by Castelli.

***Perf. 14x13½, 13½x14***

**1968, Aug. 20** **Photo.**
**1032** A333 10pf multicolored .25 .25
**1033** A333 15pf multicolored .25 .25
**1034** A333 20pf multicolored .25 .25
**1035** A333 40pf multicolored .35 .25
**1036** A333 50pf multicolored .35 .25
**1037** A333 70pf multicolored *1.90 1.00*
*Nos. 1032-1037 (6)* *3.35 2.25*

Model Trains — A334

**1968, Aug. 29** *Perf. 14x13½*
**1038** A334 10pf lt ultra, red & blk .35 .25

The 1968 Leipzig Fall Fair.

Spremberg Dam — A335

Designs: 10pf, Pöhl Dam, vert. 15pf, Ohra Dam, vert. 20pf, Rappbode Dam.

***Perf. 13x12½, 12½x13***

**1968, Sept. 11** **Litho.**
**1039** A335 5pf multicolored .25 .25
**1040** A335 10pf multicolored .25 .25
**1041** A335 15pf multicolored *.40 .40*
**1042** A335 20pf multicolored .25 .25
*Nos. 1039-1042 (4)* *1.15 1.15*

Issued to publicize dams built since 1945.

Runner A336

Designs: 25pf, Woman gymnast, vert. 40pf, Water polo, vert. 70pf, Sculling.

**1968, Sept. 18** **Photo.** *Perf. 14*
**1043** A336 5pf multicolored .25 .25
**1044** A336 25pf multicolored .25 .25
**1045** A336 40pf multicolored .25 .25
**1046** A336 70pf blue & multi *1.40 1.10*
*Nos. 1043-1046,B149-B150 (6)* *2.65 2.35*

19th Olympic Games, Mexico City, 10/12-27.

Monument, Fort Breendonk, Belgium — A337

**1968, Oct. 10** **Litho.** *Perf. 13x13½*
**1047** A337 25pf multicolored .65 .25

Issued in memory of the victims of the Nazis at the Fort Breendonk Concentration Camp.

Tiger Beetle — A338

Insects: 15pf, Ground beetle (Cychrus caraboides). 20pf, Ladybug. 25pf, Ground beetle (Carabus arcensis hrbst.). 30pf, Hister beetle. 40pf, Checkered beetle.

**1968, Oct. 16** *Perf. 13½x13*
**1048** A338 10pf yellow & multi .25 .25
**1049** A338 15pf bluish lil & blk .25 .25
**1050** A338 20pf multicolored .25 .25
**1051** A338 25pf lt lilac & blk *2.10 1.75*
**1052** A338 30pf lt green, blk & red .25 .25
**1053** A338 40pf pink & black .25 .25
*Nos. 1048-1053 (6)* *3.35 3.00*

Lenin and Letter to Spartacists — A339

Designs: 20pf, Workers, soldiers and sailors with masthead and slogans. 25pf, Karl Liebknecht and Rosa Luxemburg.

**1968, Oct. 29** **Litho.** *Perf. 13x12½*
**1054** A339 10pf lemon, red & blk .25 .25
**1055** A339 20pf lemon, red & blk .25 .25
**1056** A339 25pf lemon, red & blk *.45 .45*
*Nos. 1054-1056 (3)* *.95 .95*

November Revolution in Germany, 50th anniv.

Cattleya — A340

Orchids: 10pf, Paphiopedilum albertianum. 15pf, Cattleya fabia. 20pf, Cattleya aclandiae. 40pf, Sobralia macrantha. 50pf, Dendrobium alpha.

**1968, Nov. 12** **Photo.** *Perf. 13*

**Flowers in Natural Colors**

**1057** A340 5pf bluish lilac .25 .25
**1058** A340 10pf green .25 .25
**1059** A340 15pf bister .25 .25
**1060** A340 20pf green .25 .25
**1061** A340 40pf light brown .25 .25
**1062** A340 50pf gray *2.00 1.25*
*Nos. 1057-1062 (6)* *3.25 2.50*

**Fairy Tale Type of 1966**

Various Scenes from Puss in Boots.

**1968, Nov. 27** **Litho.** *Perf. 13½x13*
**1063** A290 5pf multicolored .25 .25
**1064** A290 10pf multicolored .25 .25
**1065** A290 15pf multicolored .90 .90
**1066** A290 20pf multicolored .90 .90
**1067** A290 25pf multicolored .25 .25
**1068** A290 30pf multicolored .25 .25
*a.* Sheet of 6, #1063-1068 5.00 9.00

Young Pioneers A341

Design: 15pf, Five Young Pioneers.

**1968, Dec. 3** *Perf. 13x13½*
**1069** A341 10pf blue & multi .25 .25
**1070** A341 15pf multicolored *.50 .30*

20th anniv. of the founding of the Ernst Thalmann Young Pioneers' organization.

**Buildings Type of 1967**

Buildings: 5pf, City Hall, Tangermunde. 10pf, German State Opera, Berlin. 20pf, Wall Pavilion, Dresden. 25pf, Burgher's House, Luckau. 30pf, Rococo Palace, Dornburg. 40pf, "Stockfish" House, Erfurt.

**1969, Jan. 1** **Photo.** *Perf. 14*
**1071** A291 5pf multi .25 .25
**1072** A291 10pf multi, horiz. .25 .25
**1073** A291 20pf multi .25 .25
**1074** A291 25pf multi *.80 .55*
**1075** A291 30pf multi, horiz. .25 .25
**1076** A291 40pf multi .25 .25
*Nos. 1071-1076 (6)* *2.05 1.80*

Martin Andersen Nexö, Danish Writer — A342

Portraits: 20pf, Otto Nagel (1894-1967), painter. 25pf, Alexander von Humboldt (1769-1859), naturalist, traveler, statesman. 40pf, Theodor Fontane (1819-1898), writer.

**1969, Feb. 5** **Engr.** *Perf. 14*
**1077** A342 10pf grnsh black .25 .25
**1078** A342 20pf deep brown .25 .25
**1079** A342 25pf violet blue *.75 .40*
**1080** A342 40pf brown .25 .25
*Nos. 1077-1080 (4)* *1.50 1.15*

Issued to honor famous men.

Be Attentive and Considerate! A343

10pf, Watch ahead! (car, truck & traffic signal). 20pf, Watch railroad crossings! (train & car at crossing). 25pf, If in doubt don't pass! (cars & truck).

**1969, Feb. 18** **Litho.** *Perf. 13x13½*
**1081** A343 5pf lt blue & multi .25 .25
**1082** A343 10pf yellow & multi .25 .25
**1083** A343 20pf pink & multi .25 .25
**1084** A343 25pf multicolored *.45 .35*
*Nos. 1081-1084 (4)* *1.20 1.10*

Traffic safety campaign.

Combine A344

Leipzig Spring Fair: 15pf, Planeta-Variant offset printing press.

**1969, Feb. 26** **Photo.** *Perf. 14*
**1085** A344 10pf multicolored .25 .25
**1086** A344 15pf crimson, blk & bl .25 .25

Jorinde and Joringel A345

Various Scenes from Fairy Tale "Jorinde and Joringel."

**1969, Mar. 18** **Litho.** *Perf. 13½x13*
**1087** A345 5pf black & multi .25 .25
**1088** A345 10pf black & multi .25 .25
**1089** A345 15pf black & multi .45 .55
**1090** A345 20pf black & multi .45 .55
**1091** A345 25pf black & multi .25 .25
**1092** A345 30pf black & multi .25 .25
*a.* Sheet of 6, #1087-1092 2.25 2.75

See Nos. 1176-1181.

Spring Snowflake A346

Red Cross, Crescent, Lion and Sun Emblems A347

Protected Plants: 10pf, Adonis. 15pf, Globe-flowers. 20pf, Garden Turk's-cap. 25pf, Button snakeroot. 30pf, Dactylorchis latifolia.

**1969, Apr. 4 Photo. *Perf. 14***

**1093** A346 5pf green & multi .25 .25
**1094** A346 10pf green & multi .25 .25
**1095** A346 15pf green & multi .25 .25
**1096** A346 20pf green & multi .25 .25
**1097** A346 25pf green & multi *2.40 1.50*
**1098** A346 30pf green & multi .30 .25
*Nos. 1093-1098 (6)* *3.70 2.75*

**1969, Apr. 23 Litho. *Perf. 12½x13***

Design: 15pf, Large Red Cross, Red Crescent and Lion and Sun Emblems.

**1099** A347 10pf gray, red & yel .25 .25
**1100** A347 15pf multicolored *.90 .45*

League of Red Cross Societies, 50th anniv.

Conifer Nursery A348

Erythrite from Schneeberg A349

10pf, Forests as natural resources (timber & resin). 20pf, Forests as regulators of climate. 25pf, Forests as recreation areas (tents along lake).

**1969, Apr. 23**

**1101** A348 5pf multicolored .25 .25
**1102** A348 10pf multicolored .25 .25
**1103** A348 20pf multicolored .25 .25
**1104** A348 25pf multicolored *1.90 .85*
*Nos. 1101-1104 (4)* *2.65 1.60*

Prevention of forest fires.

**1969, May 21 Photo. *Perf. 13½x14***

Minerals: 10pf, Fluorite from Halsbrücke. 15pf, Galena from Neudorf. 20pf, Smoky quartz from Lichtenberg. 25pf, Calcite from Niederrabenstein. 50pf, Silver from Freiberg.

**1105** A349 5pf tan & multi .25 .25
**1106** A349 10pf multicolored .25 .25
**1107** A349 15pf gray & multi .25 .25
**1108** A349 20pf lemon & multi .25 .25
**1109** A349 25pf multicolored *.75 .55*
**1110** A349 50pf lt blue & multi .25 .25
*Nos. 1105-1110 (6)* *2.00 1.80*

Women and Symbols of Agriculture, Science and Industry — A350

Design: 25pf, Woman's head and symbols.

**1969, May 28 Engr. *Perf. 14***

**1111** A350 20pf dk red & blue .25 .25
**1112** A350 25pf blue & dk red *.70 .40*

2nd Women's Congress of the German Democratic Republic.

**Ulbricht Type of 1961-67**

**1969-71 Wmk. 313 Typo. *Perf. 14***

**Size: 17x21mm**

**1112A** A189 35pf Prus blue ('71) .45 .45

**Unwmk.**

**Engr.**

**Size: 24x28½mm**

**1113** A189 1m dull green .40 1.00
**1114** A189 2m brown .45 1.10
*Nos. 1112A-1114 (3)* 1.30 2.55

See note below Nos. 590B-590C.

**Coil Stamp**

**1970, Jan. 20 Typo. Wmk. 313**

**Size: 17x21mm**

**1114A** A189 1m olive .65 4.00

Emblem of DDR Philatelic Society — A351

**1969, June 4 Photo. Unwmk.**

**1115** A351 10pf red, gold & ultra .35 .25

National Philatelic Exhibition "20 Years DDR," Magdeburg, Oct. 31-Nov. 9.

Worker Protecting Children — A352

25pf, Workers of various races. 20pf+5pf, Berlin buildings: Brandenburg Gate, Council of State, Soviet Cenotaph, Town Hall Tower, Television Tower, Teachers' Building & Hall.

**Size: 23x28mm**

**1969, June 4 Litho. *Perf. 13***

**1116** A352 10pf lemon & multi .55 .70

**Size: 50x28mm**

**1117** A352 20pf + 5pf multi .55 .70

**Size: 23x28mm**

**1118** A352 25pf lemon & multi .55 .70
*a.* Strip of 3, #1116-1118 4.00 4.00

Intl. Peace Meeting, Berlin. The surtax on No. 1117 was for the Peace Council of the German Democratic Republic.

Opening Ceremony before Battle of Leipzig Monument — A353

15pf, Parading athletes & stadium. 25pf, Running, hurdling, javelin & flag waving. 30pf, Presentation of colors before old Leipzig Town Hall.

**Photo. & Engr.**

**1969, June 18 *Perf. 14***

**1119** A353 5pf multi & black .25 .25
**1120** A353 15pf multi & black .25 .25
**1121** A353 25pf multi & black *1.00 .40*
**1122** A353 30pf multi & black .25 .25
*Nos. 1119-1122,B152-B153 (6)* *2.25 1.65*

5th German Gymnastic and Sports Festival, Leipzig.

Pierre de Coubertin, by Wieland Forster — A354

Design: 25pf, Coubertin column, Memorial Grove, Olympia.

**1969, June 6 *Perf. 14x13½***

**1123** A354 10pf black & lt blue .25 .25
**1124** A354 25pf black & sal pink *.70 .55*

Revival of the Olympic Games, 75th anniv.

Knight — A355

#1126, Bicycle wheel. #1127, Volleyball.

**1969, July 29 Photo. *Perf. 14***

**1125** A355 20pf red, gold & dk brn .25 .25
**1126** A355 20pf green, gold & red .25 .25
**1127** A355 20pf multicolored .25 .25
*Nos. 1125-1127 (3)* .75 .75

16th Students' Chess World Championships, Dresden (No. 1125); Indoor Bicycle World Championships, Erfurt (No. 1126); 2nd Volleyball World Cup (No. 1127).

Merchandise A356

**1969, Aug. 27 Litho. *Perf. 12½x13***

**1128** A356 10pf multicolored .30 .25

Leipzig Fall Fair, Aug. 31-Sept. 7, 1969.

Arms of Republic and View of Rostock A357

1m, DDR Arms, Town Hall, Marienkirche and Television Tower, Berlin, vert.

**1969, Sept. 23 Photo. *Perf. 14***

**1129** A357 10pf Rostock .25 .25
**1130** A357 10pf Neubrandenburg .25 .25
**1131** A357 10pf Potsdam .25 .25
**1132** A357 10pf Eisenhüttenstadt .25 .25
**1133** A357 10pf Hoyerswerda .25 .25
**1134** A357 10pf Magdeburg .25 .25
**1135** A357 10pf Halle-Neustadt .25 .25
**1136** A357 10pf Suhl .25 .25
**1137** A357 10pf Dresden .25 .25
**1138** A357 10pf Leipzig .25 .25
**1139** A357 10pf Karl-Marx-Stadt .25 .25
**1140** A357 10pf Berlin .25 .25
*Nos. 1129-1140 (12)* 3.00 3.00

**Souvenir Sheet**

**1141** A357 1m multicolored 1.75 4.50

#1129-1141, 1142-1145 for 20th anniv. of the German Democratic Republic.
No. 1141 contains one 29x52mm stamp.

Television Tower, Berlin — A358

People and Flags — A359

Designs: 20pf, Sphere of Television Tower and TV test picture. No. 1144, Television Tower and TV test picture.

**1969, Oct. 6 *Perf. 14***

**1142** A358 10pf multicolored .25 .25
**1143** A358 20pf multicolored .25 .25

**Souvenir Sheets**

**1144** A358 1m dk blue & multi 1.40 3.50

***Perf. 13x12½***

**1145** A359 1m red & multi 1.60 3.50

No. 1144 contains one 21½x60mm stamp.

Cathedral, Otto von Guericke Monument and Hotel International, Magdeburg — A360

**1969, Oct. 28 Litho. *Perf. 13x12½***

**1146** A360 20pf multicolored .30 .25

Natl. Postage Stamp Exhibition in honor of the 20th anniv. of the German Democratic Republic, Magdeburg, Oct. 31-Nov. 9. See No. B154.

UFI Emblem — A361

**1969, Oct. 28 *Perf. 13x13½***

**1147** A361 10pf multicolored .25 .25
**1148** A361 15pf multicolored *1.10 .35*

36th UFI Congress (Union des Foires Internationales), Leipzig, Oct. 28-30.

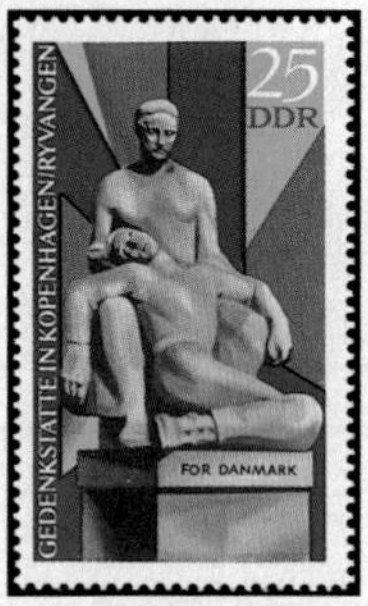


Memorial Monument, Copenhagen-Ryvangen — A362

**1969, Oct. 28** ***Perf. 13***

| | | | | |
|---|---|---|---|---|
| **1149** | A362 | 25pf multicolored | .75 | .25 |

Issued in memory of the victims of the Nazis in Denmark.

Rostock University Seal and Building — A363

Design: 15pf, Steam turbine, curve and Rostock University emblem.

**1969, Nov. 12** ***Perf. 12½x13***

| | | | | |
|---|---|---|---|---|
| **1150** | A363 | 10pf brt blue & multi | .25 | .25 |
| **1151** | A363 | 15pf violet & multi | *.80* | *.25* |

550th anniversary of Rostock University.

ILO Emblem — A364

Mold for Christmas Cookies — A365

**1969, Nov. 12** ***Perf. 13½x14***

| | | | | |
|---|---|---|---|---|
| **1152** | A364 | 20pf dp green & silver | .25 | .25 |
| **1153** | A364 | 25pf lil rose & silver | *1.10* | *.30* |

50th anniv. of the ILO.

**1969, Nov. 25** **Litho.** ***Perf. 13½x13***

50pf, Negro couple, shaped spice cookie.

| | | | | |
|---|---|---|---|---|
| **1154** | A365 | 10pf dull org, bl & red brn | .95 | .95 |
| **1155** | A365 | 50pf lt blue & multi | 1.60 | 1.60 |
| *a.* | | Pair, #1154-1155 | 6.00 | 4.75 |
| | | *Nos. 1154-1155,B155 (3)* | 2.85 | 2.85 |

Folk art of Lusatia.

Antonov An-24 A366

Planes: 25pf, Ilyushin Il-18. 30pf, Tupolev Tu-134. 50pf, Mi-8 helicopter.

**1969, Dec. 2** ***Perf. 13x12½***

| | | | | |
|---|---|---|---|---|
| **1156** | A366 | 20pf blue, red & blk | .25 | .25 |
| **1157** | A366 | 25pf vio, red & blk | *1.00* | *.90* |
| **1158** | A366 | 30pf ultra, red & blk | .25 | .25 |
| **1159** | A366 | 50pf olive, red & blk | .25 | .25 |
| | | *Nos. 1156-1159 (4)* | *1.75* | *1.65* |

Siberian Teacher, by D. K. Sveshnikov A367

Russian Paintings from Dresden Gallery of Modern Masters: 10pf, Steelworker, by V. A. Serov. 20pf, Still Life, by E. A. Aslamasjan. 25pf, Hot Day (boats on river), by J. D. Romas. 40pf, Spring is Coming (young woman and snow-covered street), by L. V. Kabatchek. 50pf, Man on River Bank, by V. J. Makovskij.

**1969, Dec. 10** **Photo.** ***Perf. 13***

| | | | | |
|---|---|---|---|---|
| **1160** | A367 | 5pf gray & multi | .25 | .25 |
| **1161** | A367 | 10pf gray & multi | .25 | .25 |
| **1162** | A367 | 20pf gray & multi | .25 | .25 |
| **1163** | A367 | 25pf gray & multi | *.80* | *.80* |
| **1164** | A367 | 40pf gray & multi | .25 | .25 |
| **1165** | A367 | 50pf gray & multi | .25 | .25 |
| | | *Nos. 1160-1165 (6)* | *2.05* | *2.05* |

Ernst Barlach (1870-1938), Sculptor and Writer — A368

Portraits: 10pf, Johann Gutenberg (1400-68). 15pf, Kurt Tucholsky (1890-1935), writer. 20pf, Ludwig van Beethoven. 25pf, Friedrich Hölderlin (1770-1843), poet. 40pf, Georg Wilhelm Friedrich Hegel (1770-1831), philosopher.

**1970, Jan. 20** **Engr.** ***Perf. 14***

| | | | | |
|---|---|---|---|---|
| **1166** | A368 | 5pf blue violet | .25 | .25 |
| **1167** | A368 | 10pf gray brown | .25 | .25 |
| **1168** | A368 | 15pf violet blue | .25 | .25 |
| **1169** | A368 | 20pf rose lilac | .30 | .25 |
| **1170** | A368 | 25pf blue green | *1.90* | *.60* |
| **1171** | A368 | 40pf rose claret | .30 | .25 |
| | | *Nos. 1166-1171 (6)* | *3.25* | *1.85* |

Rabbit — A369

**1970, Feb. 5** **Photo.** ***Perf. 13½x14***

| | | | | |
|---|---|---|---|---|
| **1172** | A369 | 10pf shown | .25 | .25 |
| **1173** | A369 | 20pf Red fox | .25 | .25 |
| **1174** | A369 | 25pf Mink | *2.40* | *2.10* |
| **1175** | A369 | 40pf Hamster | .30 | .25 |
| | | *Nos. 1172-1175 (4)* | *3.20* | *2.85* |

525th International Fur Auctions, Leipzig.

**Fairy Tale Type of 1969**

Various Scenes from Fairy Tale "Little Brother and Sister."

**1970, Feb. 17** **Litho.** ***Perf. 13½x13***

| | | | | |
|---|---|---|---|---|
| **1176** | A345 | 5pf lilac & multi | .25 | .25 |
| **1177** | A345 | 10pf lilac & multi | .25 | .25 |
| **1178** | A345 | 15pf lilac & multi | .55 | .55 |
| **1179** | A345 | 20pf lilac & multi | .55 | .55 |
| **1180** | A345 | 25pf lilac & multi | .25 | .25 |
| **1181** | A345 | 30pf lilac & multi | .25 | .25 |
| *a.* | | Sheet of 6, #1176-1181 | 5.50 | 3.75 |

Telephone Coordinating Station — A370

15pf, High voltage testing transformer, vert.

**1970, Feb. 24** ***Perf. 13x12½, 12½x13***

| | | | | |
|---|---|---|---|---|
| **1182** | A370 | 10pf multicolored | .25 | .25 |
| **1183** | A370 | 15pf multicolored | .40 | .25 |

Leipzig Spring Fair, Mar. 1-10, 1970.

Horseman's Tombstone (700 A.D.) — A371

Treasures from the Halle Museum: 20pf, Helmet (500 A.D.). 25pf, Bronze basin (1000 B.C.). 40pf, Clay drum (2500 B.C.).

**1970, Mar. 3** **Photo.** ***Perf. 13***

| | | | | |
|---|---|---|---|---|
| **1184** | A371 | 10pf dp grn, gray & dk brn | .25 | .25 |
| **1185** | A371 | 20pf multicolored | .25 | .25 |
| **1186** | A371 | 25pf yellow & multi | *.60* | *1.00* |
| **1187** | A371 | 40pf multicolored | .25 | .25 |
| | | *Nos. 1184-1187 (4)* | *1.35* | *1.75* |

Lenin and Clara Zetkin — A372

Designs: 10pf, Lenin, "ISKRA" (newspaper's name), composing frame and printing press. 25pf, Lenin and title page of German edition of "State and Revolution." 40pf, Lenin statue, Eisleben. 70pf, Lenin monument and Lenin Square, Berlin. 1m, Lenin portrait, vert.

**Photogravure and Engraved**

**1970, Apr. 16** ***Perf. 14***

| | | | | |
|---|---|---|---|---|
| **1188** | A372 | 10pf multicolored | .25 | .25 |
| **1189** | A372 | 20pf multicolored | .25 | .25 |
| **1190** | A372 | 25pf multicolored | *1.25* | *1.00* |
| **1191** | A372 | 40pf multicolored | .25 | .25 |
| **1192** | A372 | 70pf multicolored | .30 | .25 |
| | | *Nos. 1188-1192 (5)* | *2.30* | *2.00* |

**Souvenir Sheet**

| | | | | |
|---|---|---|---|---|
| **1193** | A372 | 1m dk carmine & multi | 1.60 | 8.00 |

Sea Kale — A373

Protected Plants: 20pf, European pasqueflower. 25pf, Fringed gentian. 30pf, Galeate orchis. 40pf, Marsh tea. 70pf, Round-leaved wintergreen.

**1970, Apr. 28** **Photo.**

| | | | | |
|---|---|---|---|---|
| **1194** | A373 | 10pf multicolored | .25 | .25 |
| **1195** | A373 | 20pf violet & multi | .25 | .25 |
| **1196** | A373 | 25pf multicolored | *1.60* | *1.60* |
| **1197** | A373 | 30pf multicolored | .25 | .25 |
| **1198** | A373 | 40pf multicolored | .25 | .25 |
| **1199** | A373 | 70pf multicolored | .30 | .25 |
| | | *Nos. 1194-1199 (6)* | *2.90* | *2.85* |

Red Army Soldier Raising Flag over Berlin Reichstag A374

20pf, Spasski Tower, Kremlin; State Council Building, Berlin; coats of arms of USSR and DDR, newspaper clipping about friendship treaty with USSR. 25pf, Mutual Economic Aid Building, Moscow, flags of member countries. 70pf, Memorial monument, Buchenwald.

**1970, May 5** **Litho.** ***Perf. 13x13½***

| | | | | |
|---|---|---|---|---|
| **1200** | A374 | 10pf multi | .25 | .25 |
| **1201** | A374 | 20pf multi | .25 | .25 |
| **1202** | A374 | 25pf multi | *.90* | *.60* |
| | | *Nos. 1200-1202 (3)* | *1.40* | *1.10* |

**Souvenir Sheet**

| | | | | |
|---|---|---|---|---|
| **1203** | A374 | 70pf multi, horiz. | 2.40 | 5.00 |

25th anniv. of liberation from Fascism.

Shortwave Antenna, RBI Emblem and Globe — A375

Grain and Globe — A376

15pf, Berlin Radio Station, emblems of Radio Berlin Intl. (RBI), Radio DDR & Radio Germany.

**1970, May 13** **Litho.** ***Perf. 13½x13***

**Size: 23x28mm**

| | | | | |
|---|---|---|---|---|
| **1204** | A375 | 10pf ap grn, vio bl & bl | .50 | .50 |

**Size: 50x28mm**

| | | | | |
|---|---|---|---|---|
| **1205** | A375 | 15pf vio bl, dp rose & ap grn | .75 | .75 |
| *a.* | | Pair, #1204-1205 | 3.25 | 2.40 |

DDR broadcasting system, 25th anniv.

**1970, May 19**

25pf, House of Culture, Dresden, and grain.

| | | | | |
|---|---|---|---|---|
| **1206** | A376 | 20pf vio bl, yel & bl | .70 | .70 |
| **1207** | A376 | 25pf vio bl, yel & bl | .70 | .70 |
| *a.* | | Strip of 2, #1206-1207 + label | 4.00 | 4.00 |

Issued to publicize the 5th World Cereal and Bread Congress, Dresden, May 24-29.

Fritz Heckert Medal A377

Design: 25pf, Globes and "FSM."

**1970, June 9** ***Perf. 13x12½***

| | | | | |
|---|---|---|---|---|
| **1208** | A377 | 20pf red, yel & brn | .25 | .25 |
| **1209** | A377 | 25pf red, bl & yel | *.55* | *.40* |

25th anniv. of the Free German Trade Union and of the World Organization of Trade Unions.

Traffic Policeman — A378

Designs: 10pf, Young Pioneers congratulating police woman. 15pf, Volga police car. 20pf, Railroad policeman with radio-telephone. 25pf, River police in Volga wing-type boat.

**1970, June 23** **Litho.** ***Perf. 13x12½***

| | | | | |
|---|---|---|---|---|
| **1210** | A378 | 5pf ocher & multi | .25 | .25 |
| **1211** | A378 | 10pf green & multi | .25 | .25 |
| **1212** | A378 | 15pf ultra & multi | .25 | .25 |
| **1213** | A378 | 20pf multicolored | .25 | .25 |
| **1214** | A378 | 25pf multicolored | *2.40* | *.30* |
| | | *Nos. 1210-1214 (5)* | *3.40* | *1.30* |

25th anniversary of the People's Police.

Gods Amon, Shu and Tefnut — A379

Designs from Lion Temple in Musawwarat: 15pf, Head of King Arnekhamani. 20pf, Cow from cattle frieze. 25pf, Head of Prince Arka. 30pf, Head of God Arensnuphis, vert. 40pf, Elephants and prisoners of war. 50pf, Lion God Apedemak.

***Perf. 13½x14, 14x13½***

**1970, June 23** **Photo.**

**1215** A379 10pf multicolored .35 .25
**1216** A379 15pf multicolored .35 .25
**1217** A379 20pf multicolored .35 .25
**1218** A379 25pf multicolored *.90 .70*
**1219** A379 30pf multicolored .35 .25
**1220** A379 40pf multicolored .35 .25
**1221** A379 50pf multicolored .35 .25
*Nos. 1215-1221 (7) 3.00 2.20*

Archaeological work in the Sudan by the Humboldt University, Berlin.

Arms and Flags of DDR and Poland — A380

**1970, July 1** **Litho.** ***Perf. 13x12½***

**1222** A380 20pf multicolored .35 .25

20th anniversary of the Görlitz Agreement concerning the Oder-Neisse border.

Culture Association Emblem — A381

Design: 25pf, Johannes R. Becher medal.

**1970, July 1** **Photo.** ***Perf. 14***

**1223** A381 10pf ultra, sil & brn 1.75 1.75
**1224** A381 25pf ultra, gold & brn 1.75 1.75
*a.* Strip of 2, #1223-1224 + label 8.75 10.00

25th anniv. of the German Kulturbund.

Athlete on Pommel Horse — A382

**1970, July 1** ***Perf. 14x13½***

**1225** A382 10pf blk, yel & brn red .30 .25

Issued to publicize the 3rd Children's and Youths' Spartakiad. See No. B156.

Meeting of the American, British and Russian Delegations — A383

10pf, Cecilienhof Castle. 20pf, "Potsdam Agreement" in German, English, French & Russian.

**1970, July 28** **Litho.** ***Perf. 13***

**Size: 23x28mm**

**1226** A383 10pf blk, cit & red .25 .25
**1227** A383 20pf blk, cit & red .25 .25

**Size: 77x28mm**

**1228** A383 25pf red & blk .25 .25
*a.* Strip of 3, #1226-1228 1.40 2.75

25th anniv. of the Potsdam Agreement among the Allies concerning Germany at the end of WWII.

Men's Pocket and Wrist Watches — A384

**1970, Aug. 25** **Photo.** ***Perf. 13½x14***

**1229** A384 10pf ultra, blk & gold .30 .25

Leipzig Fall Fair, 1970.

Theodor Neubauer and Magnus Poser — A385

"Homeland" from Soviet Cenotaph, Berlin-Treptow A386

**1970, Sept. 2** ***Perf. 13x12½, 12½x13***

**1230** A385 20pf dk bl, car & pale grn .25 .25
**1231** A386 25pf dp car, pale bl .25 .25

Issued in memory of fighters against "fascism and imperialistic wars."

Competition Map and Compass — A387

Design: 25pf, Competition map and runner at 3 different stations.

**1970, Sept. 15** **Litho.** ***Perf. 13x12½***

**1232** A387 10pf yellow & multi .25 .25
**1233** A387 25pf yellow & multi *1.10 .30*

World Orienting Championships.

Mother and Child, by Käthe Kollwitz — A388

Works of Art: 10pf, Forest Worker Scharf's Birthday, by Otto Nagel. 20pf, Portrait of a Girl, by Otto Nagel. 25pf, No More War, (Woman with raised arm) by Käthe Kollwitz. 40pf, Head from Gustrow Memorial, by Ernst Barlach. 50pf, The Flutist, by Ernst Barlach.

**Photo.; Litho. (25pf, 30pf)**

**1970, Sept. 22** ***Perf. 14x13½***

**1234** A388 10pf multicolored .25 .25
**1235** A388 20pf multicolored .25 .25
**1236** A388 25pf pink & dk brn *.75 .95*
**1237** A388 30pf sal & blk .25 .25
**1238** A388 40pf yel & blk .25 .25
**1239** A388 50pf yel & blk .25 .25
*Nos. 1234-1239 (6) 2.00 2.20*

Issued in memory of the artists Otto Nagel, Käthe Kollwitz and Ernst Barlach.

The Little Trumpeter A389

**1970, Oct. 1** **Photo.**

**1240** A389 10pf dp ultra, brn & org .25 .30

2nd Natl. Youth Stamp Exhib., Karl-Marx-Stadt, Oct. 4-11. The design shows the memorial in Halle for Fritz Weineck, trumpeter for the Red War Veterans' Organization. See No. B160.

Emblem with Flags of East Block Nations — A390

**1970, Oct. 1** **Litho.** ***Perf. 13x12½***

**1241** A390 10pf carmine & multi .25 .25
**1242** A390 20pf multicolored .25 .25

Issued to publicize the Brothers in Arms maneuvers of the East Bloc countries in the territory of the German Democratic Republic.

Musk Ox — A391

Berlin Zoo: 15pf, Shoebill. 20pf, Addax. 25pf, Malayan sun bear.

**1970, Oct. 6** **Photo.** ***Perf. 14***

**1243** A391 10pf blue & multi .30 .25
**1244** A391 15pf green & multi .30 .25
**1245** A391 20pf org & multi .55 .30
**1246** A391 25pf multicolored *5.00 5.00*
*Nos. 1243-1246 (4) 6.15 5.80*

UN Headquarters and Emblem — A392

**1970, Oct. 20** **Photo.** ***Perf. 13***

**1247** A392 20pf ultra & multi .55 .25

25th anniversary of the United Nations.

Friedrich Engels A393

Epiphyllum A394

20pf, Friedrich Engels and Karl Marx. 25pf, Engels and title page of his polemic against Dühring.

**Photogravure and Engraved**

**1970, Nov. 24** ***Perf. 14***

**1248** A393 10pf ver, gray & blk .25 .25
**1249** A393 20pf ver, dk grn & blk .25 .25
**1250** A393 25pf ver, dk car rose & blk *.80 .65*
*Nos. 1248-1250 (3) 1.30 1.15*

Friedrich Engels (1820-1895), socialist, collaborator with Karl Marx.

**1970, Dec. 2** **Photo.** ***Perf. 14***

Flowering Cactus Plants: 10pf, Astrophytum myriostigma. 15pf, Echinocereus salm-dyckianus. 20pf, Selenicereus grandiflorus. 25pf, Hamatocactus setispinus. 30pf, Mamillaria boolii.

**1251** A394 5pf multicolored .25 .25
**1252** A394 10pf dk blue & multi .25 .25
**1253** A394 15pf multicolored .25 .25
**1254** A394 20pf multicolored .25 .25
**1255** A394 25pf dk blue & multi *1.60 1.60*
**1256** A394 30pf purple & multi .25 .25
*Nos. 1251-1256 (6) 2.85 2.85*

Souvenir Sheet

Ludwig van Beethoven — A395

**1970, Dec. 10** **Engr.** ***Perf. 14***

**1257** A395 1m gray 1.60 3.25

Bicentenary of the birth of Ludwig van Beethoven (1770-1827), composer.

Dancer's Mask, South Seas A396

Works from Ethnological Museum, Leipzig: 20pf, Bronze head, Africa. 25pf, Tea pot, Asia. 40pf, Clay figure (jaguar), Mexico.

**1971, Jan. 12** **Photo.** ***Perf. 13***

**1258** A396 10pf multicolored .25 .25
**1259** A396 20pf multicolored .25 .25
**1260** A396 25pf multicolored *.60 .60*
**1261** A396 40pf multicolored .25 .25
*Nos. 1258-1261 (4) 1.35 1.35*

Venus 5, Soft-landing on Moon — A397

#1263, Model of space station. #1264, Luna 16 and Luna 10 satellites. #1265, Group flight of Sojuz 6, 7 and 8. #1266, Proton 1, radiation measuring satellite. #1267, Communications satellite Molniya 1. #1268, Yuri A. Gagarin, first flight of Vostok 1. #1269, Alexei Leonov walking in space, Voskhod 2.

**1971, Feb. 11 Litho. *Perf. 13x12½***

**1262** A397 20pf dk blue & multi .25 .25
**1263** A397 20pf dk blue & multi .25 .25
**1264** A397 20pf dk blue & multi .45 .45
**1265** A397 20pf dk blue & multi .45 .45
**1266** A397 20pf dk blue & multi .45 .45
**1267** A397 20pf dk blue & multi .45 .45
**1268** A397 20pf dk blue & multi .25 .25
**1269** A397 20pf dk blue & multi .25 .25
*a.* Sheet of 8, #1262-1269 4.25 4.25

Soviet space research.

Johannes R. Becher A398 Karl Liebknecht A399

Portraits: 10pf, Heinrich Mann. 15pf, John Heartfield. 20pf, Willi Bredel. 25pf, Franz Mehring. 40pf, Rudolf Virchow. 50pf, Johannes Kepler.

**1971 Engr. *Perf. 14***

**1270** A398 5pf brown .25 .25
**1271** A398 10pf vio blue .25 .25
**1272** A398 15pf black .25 .25
**1273** A398 20pf rose lake .25 .25
**1274** A398 25pf green *.45 .40*
**1274A** A398 40pf pale purple .40 .25
**1275** A398 50pf dp black .25 .25
*Nos. 1270-1275 (7) 2.10 1.90*

Honoring prominent Germans. See Nos. 1349-1353.

**1971, Feb. 23 Photo.**

Design: 25pf, Rosa Luxemburg.

**1276** A399 20pf gold, mag & blk .40 .40
**1277** A399 25pf gold, mag & blk .40 .40
*a.* Pair, #1276-1277 1.10 1.10

Karl Liebknecht (1871-1919) and Rosa Luxemburg (1871-1919), leaders of Spartacist Movement.

Soldier and Army Emblem — A400

**1971, Mar. 1 *Perf. 13½x14***

**1278** A400 20pf gray & multi .35 .25

15th anniv. of the National People's Army.

Crushing and Conveyor Plant, Magdeburg — A401

Leipzig Spring Fair: 15pf, Dredger for low temperature work.

**1971, Mar. 9 Litho. *Perf. 13x12½***

**1279** A401 10pf green & multi .25 .25
**1280** A401 15pf multicolored .25 .25

Proclamation of the Commune, Town Hall, Paris — A402

Designs: 20pf, Barricade at Place Blanche, defended by women. 25pf, Illustration by Theophile A. Steinlen for the International. 30pf, Title page for "The Civil War in France," by Karl Marx.

**1971, Mar. 9 *Perf. 13***

**1281** A402 10pf red, bis & blk .25 .25
**1282** A402 20pf red, bis & blk .25 .25
**1283** A402 25pf red, buff & blk *.45 .40*
**1284** A402 30pf red, gray & blk .25 .25
*Nos. 1281-1284 (4) 1.20 1.15*

Centenary of the Paris Commune.

Lunokhod 1 on Moon — A403

**1971, Mar. 30 Photo. *Perf. 14***

**1285** A403 20pf multicolored .55 .30

Luna 17 unmanned, automated moon mission, Nov. 10-17, and the 24th Communist Party Congress of the Soviet Union.

Discobolus — A404

**1971, Apr. 6 Litho. *Perf. 13½x13***

**1286** A404 20pf dull bl, lt bl & buff .55 .25

20th anniversary of the Olympic Committee of German Democratic Republic.

Köpenick Castle — A405

Berlin Buildings: 10pf, St. Mary's Church, vert. 20pf, Old Library. 25pf, Ermeler House, vert. 50pf, New Guard Memorial. 70pf, Natl. Gallery of Art.

***Perf. 13½x14, 14x13½***

**1971, Apr. 6 Photo.**

**1287** A405 10pf multicolored .25 .25
**1288** A405 15pf multicolored .25 .25
**1289** A405 20pf multicolored .25 .25
**1290** A405 25pf multicolored *2.40 2.25*
**1291** A405 50pf multicolored .25 .25
**1292** A405 70pf multicolored .30 .25
*Nos. 1287-1292 (6) 3.70 3.50*

Clasped Hands — A406

**Lithographed and Embossed**

**1971, Apr. 20 *Perf. 13x13½***

**1293** A406 20pf red, blk & gold .35 .25

25th anniversary of Socialist Unity Party of Germany (SED).

Dance Costume, Schleife — A407 Self-Portrait, by Dürer — A408

Sorbian Dance Costumes from: 20pf, Hoyerswerda. 25pf, Cottbus. 40pf, Kamenz.

**1971, May 4 Litho. *Perf. 13½x13***
**Size: 33x42mm**

**1294** A407 10pf multicolored .25 .25
**1295** A407 20pf green & multi .25 .25
**1296** A407 25pf blue & multi *.55 .75*
**1297** A407 40pf multicolored .25 .25
*Nos. 1294-1297 (4) 1.30 1.50*

**1971, Nov. 23 *Perf. 13½x13***
**Booklet Stamps**
**Size: 23x28mm**

**1297A** A407 10pf multicolored .25 .25
*c.* Booklet pane of 4 1.40 1.10
*d.* Booklet pane, 2 #1297A, 2 #1297B 3.25 2.50
**1297B** A407 20pf multicolored .55 .40

**1971, May 18 *Perf. 12½x13***

Art Works by Dürer: 40pf, Three Peasants. 70pf, Portrait of Philipp Melanchthon.

**1298** A408 10pf multicolored .25 .25
**1299** A408 40pf brown & multi .25 .25
**1300** A408 70pf gray & multi *1.50 .80*
*Nos. 1298-1300 (3) 2.00 1.30*

500th anniversary of the birth of Albrecht Dürer (1471-1528), painter and engraver.

Building Industry — A409 Congress Emblem — A410

Designs: 10pf, Science and technology. No. 1303, Farming. 25pf, Civilian defense.

**1971, June 9 Photo. *Perf. 14***

**1301** A409 5pf cream, red & blk .25 .25
**1302** A409 10pf cream, red & blk .25 .25
**1303** A409 20pf cream, red, bl & blk .25 .25
**1304** A410 20pf gold, dp car & red .25 .25
**1305** A409 25pf cream, red & blk *.30 .35*
*Nos. 1301-1305 (5) 1.30 1.35*

8th Congress of Socialist Unity Party of Germany (SED).

Golden Fleece, 1730 A411

Treasures from the Green Vault, Dresden: 5pf, Cherry stone with 180 heads carved on it, 1590. 15pf, Tankard, Nuremberg, 1530. 20pf, Moor with drums on horseback, 1720. 25pf, Decorated writing box, 1562. 30pf, St. George pendant, 1570.

**1971, June 22 *Perf. 13***

**1306** A411 5pf dp car & multi .25 .25
**1307** A411 10pf green & multi .25 .25
**1308** A411 15pf violet & multi .25 .25
**1309** A411 20pf multicolored .25 .25
**1310** A411 25pf multicolored *.55 .55*
**1311** A411 30pf multicolored .25 .25
*Nos. 1306-1311 (6) 1.80 1.80*

Prisoners, by Fritz Cremer A412

Design: 25pf, Brutality in Buchenwald Concentration Camp, by Fritz Cremer.

**1971, June 22 Litho. *Perf. 13***

**1312** A412 20pf bister & blk .45 .55
**1313** A412 25pf lt blue & blk .45 .55
*a.* Pair, #1312-1313 with label between 1.60 2.00

Intl. Federation of Resistance Fighters (FIR), 20th anniv.

Coat of Arms of Mongolia — A413

**1971, July 6 Litho. *Perf. 13***

**1314** A413 20pf dk red, yel & blk .35 .25

50th anniv. of the Mongolian People's Revolution.

Child's Head, UNICEF Emblem A414

**1971, July 13 Photo.**

**1315** A414 20pf multicolored .35 .25

25th anniv. of UNICEF.

Militiaman, Soldier and Brandenburg Gate — A415

Design: 35pf, Brandenburg Gate and new buildings in East Berlin.

**1971, Aug. 12**

**1316** A415 20pf red & multi .65 .25
**1317** A415 35pf yel & multi 1.75 .90

10 years of Berlin Wall.

Passenger Ship Iwan Franko — A416

Ships: 15pf, Freighter, type 17. 20pf, Freighter Rostock, type XD. 25pf, Fish processing ship "Junge Welt." 40pf, Container cargo ship. 50pf, Explorer ship Akademik Kurtschatow.

**1971, Aug. 24** **Engr.**

**1318** A416 10pf pale purple .25 .25
**1319** A416 15pf pale brn & ind .25 .25
**1320** A416 20pf gray green .25 .25
**1321** A416 25pf slate *1.00* *.90*
**1322** A416 40pf maroon .25 .25
**1323** A416 50pf grysh blue .25 .25
*Nos. 1318-1323 (6)* *2.25* *2.15*

Shipbuilding industry.

Butadiene Plant — A417

Leipzig Fall Fair: 25pf, Refinery.

**1971, Sept. 2** **Photo.** ***Perf. 13***

**1324** A417 10pf olive, vio & mag .25 .25
**1325** A417 25pf blue, vio & ol .25 .25

Raised Fists, Photo Montage by John Heartfield, 1937 A418

**1971, Sept. 23**

**1326** A418 35pf grnsh bl, blk & sil .35 .25

Intl. Year Against Racial Discrimination.

Karl Marx Monument A419

**1971, Oct. 5** **Photo.** ***Perf. 14x13½***

**1327** A419 35pf vio brn, pink & buff .40 .25

Unveiling of Karl Marx memorial at Karl-Marx-Stadt (Chemnitz).

Wiltz Memorial, Flag of Luxembourg A420

**1971, Oct. 5**

**1328** A420 25pf multicolored .50 .25

Memorial for Nazi victims, Wiltz, Luxembourg.

Postal Milestones, Saxony, and Zürner's Surveyor Carriage — A421

### Photo. & Engr.

**1971, Oct. 5** ***Perf. 14***

**1329** A421 25pf blue, olive & lilac .45 .45

Philatelists' Day 1971. See No. B162.

Darbuka, North Africa — A422

Musical Instruments: 15pf, Two morin chuur, Mongolia. 20pf, Violin, Germany. 25pf, Mandolin, Italy. 40pf, Bagpipes, Bohemia. 50pf, Kasso, Sudan.

**1971, Oct. 26** **Photo.** ***Perf. 14x13½***

**1330** A422 10pf multicolored .25 .25
**1331** A422 15pf multicolored .25 .25
**1332** A422 20pf ocher & multi .25 .25
**1333** A422 25pf blue & multi .25 .25
**1334** A422 40pf gray & multi .25 .25
**1335** A422 50pf multicolored *.85* *.85*
*Nos. 1330-1335 (6)* *2.10* *2.10*

Instruments from the Music Museum in Markneukirchen.

Geodetic Apparatus — A423

20pf, Ergaval microscope. 25pf, Planetarium.

**1971, Nov. 9** **Photo.** ***Perf. 13½x14***

**Size: 23½x28½mm**

**1336** A423 10pf blue, blk & red .40 .40
**1337** A423 20pf blue, blk & red .40 .40

**Size: 50½x28½mm**

**1338** A423 25pf blue, vio bl & yel .40 .40
*a.* Strip of 3, #1336-1338 3.25 3.25

Carl Zeiss optical works in Jena, 125th anniv.

### Fairy Tale Type of 1966

Designs: Various Scenes from Fairy Tale "The Bremen Town Musicians."

**1971, Nov. 23** **Litho.** ***Perf. 13½x13***

**1339** A290 5pf multicolored .25 .25
**1340** A290 10pf ocher & multi .25 .25
**1341** A290 15pf gray & multi .55 .80
**1342** A290 20pf ver & multi .55 .80
**1343** A290 25pf violet & multi .25 .25
**1344** A290 30pf yellow & multi .25 .25
*a.* Sheet of 6, #1339-1344 3.75 9.00

Olympic Rings and Sledding — A424

Olympic Rings and: 20pf, Long-distance skiing. 25pf, Biathlon. 70pf, Ski jump.

**1971, Dec. 7** **Photo.** ***Perf. 13½x14***

**1345** A424 5pf green, car & blk .25 .25
**1346** A424 20pf car rose, vio & blk .25 .25
**1347** A424 25pf vio, car & blk *1.40* *1.10*
**1348** A424 70pf vio bl, vio & blk .25 .25
*Nos. 1345-1348,B163-B164 (6)* *2.65* *2.35*

11th Winter Olympic Games, Sapporo, Japan, Feb. 3-13, 1972.

### Portrait Type of 1971

Portraits: 10pf, Johannes Tralow (1882-1968), playwright. 20pf, Leonhard Frank (1882-1961), writer. 25pf, K. A. Kocor (1822-1904), composer. 35pf, Heinrich Schliemann (1822-1890), archaeologist. 50pf, F. Caroline Neuber (1697-1760), actress.

**1972, Jan. 25** **Engr.** ***Perf. 14***

**1349** A398 10pf green .25 .25
**1350** A398 20pf rose claret .25 .25
**1351** A398 25pf dk blue .25 .25
**1352** A398 35pf brown .25 .25
**1353** A398 50pf rose violet *.80* *1.20*
*Nos. 1349-1353 (5)* *1.80* *2.20*

Honoring famous personalities.

Gypsum, Eisleben A425

Minerals found in East Germany: 10pf, Zinnwaldite, Zinnwald. 20pf, Malachite, Ullersreuth. 25pf, Amethyst, Wiesenbad. 35pf, Halite, Merkers. 50pf, Proustite, Schneeberg.

**1972, Feb. 22** **Photo.** ***Perf. 13***

**1354** A425 5pf grnsh bl & brn blk .25 .25
**1355** A425 10pf citron, brn & blk .25 .25
**1356** A425 20pf multicolored .25 .25
**1357** A425 25pf multicolored .25 .25
**1358** A425 35pf lt green, ind & blk .25 .25
**1359** A425 50pf gray & multi *.90* *1.00*
*Nos. 1354-1359 (6)* *2.15* *2.25*

Russian Pavilion and Fair Emblem A426

Design: 25pf, Flags of East Germany and Russia, and Fair emblem.

**1972, Mar. 3** **Photo.** ***Perf. 14***

**1360** A426 10pf vio blue & multi .25 .25
**1361** A426 25pf claret & multi .25 .25

50 years of Russian participation in the Leipzig Fair.

Miniature Sheets

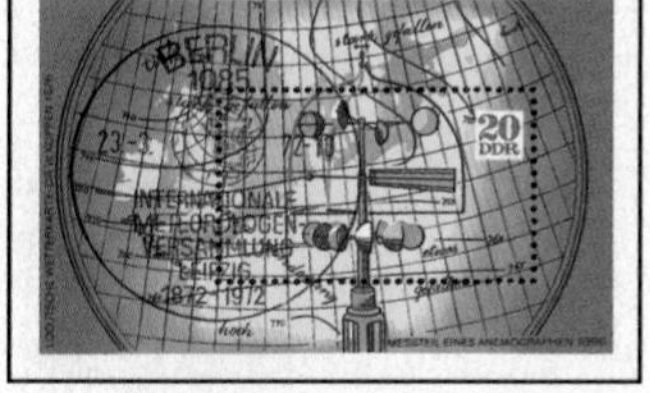


Anemometer, 1896, and Meteorological Chart, 1876 — A427

Designs: 35pf, Dipole and cloud photograph taken by satellite. 70pf, Meteor weather satellite and weather map.

**1972, Mar. 23** **Litho.** ***Perf. 13x12½***

**1362** A427 20pf multicolored .70 1.75
**1363** A427 35pf multicolored .70 1.75
**1364** A427 70pf green & multi .70 1.75
*Nos. 1362-1364 (3)* 2.10 5.25

Intl. Meteorologists' Cent. Meeting, Leipzig.

World Health Organization Emblem — A428

**1972, Apr. 4** **Photo.** ***Perf. 13***

**1365** A428 35pf lt bl, vio bl & sil .45 .25

World Health Day.

Kamov Helicopter A429

Aircraft: 10pf, Agricultural spray plane. 35pf, Ilyushin jet. 1m, Jet and tail with Interflug emblem.

**1972, Apr. 25** ***Perf. 14***

**1366** A429 5pf blue & multi .25 .25
**1367** A429 10pf multicolored .25 .25
**1368** A429 35pf blue grn & multi .25 .25
**1369** A429 1m multicolored *1.20* *1.50*
*Nos. 1366-1369 (4)* *1.95* *2.25*

Wrestling and Olympic Rings — A430

Sport and Olympic Rings: 20pf, Pole vault. 35pf, Volleyball. 70pf, Women's gymnastics.

**1972, May 16** **Photo.** ***Perf. 13½x14***

**1370** A430 5pf blue, gold & blk .25 .25
**1371** A430 20pf mag, gold & blk .25 .25
**1372** A430 35pf ol bis, gold & blk .25 .25
**1373** A430 70pf yel grn, gold & blk *2.50* *1.75*
*Nos. 1370-1373,B166-B167 (6)* *3.75* *3.00*

20th Olympic Games, Munich, 8/26-9/11.

Flags of USSR and German Democratic Republic — A431

20pf, Flags, Leonid Brezhnev & Erich Honecker.

**1972, May 24** **Engr. & Photo.**

**1374** A431 10pf red, yel & blk .85 .80
**1375** A431 20pf red, yel & blk .85 .80

Soc. for German-Soviet Friendship, 25th anniv.

Workers — A432

Design: 35pf, Students.

**1972, May 24 Litho. *Perf. 13***

**1376** A432 10pf dull yel, org & mag .25 .25
**1377** A432 35pf dull yel & ultra .25 .25
*a.* Strip of 2, #1376-1377 + label 1.00 1.00

8th Congress of Free German Trade Unions, Berlin.

Karneol Rose A433

**1972, June 13 Photo. *Perf. 13***
**Size: 36x36mm**

**1378** A433 5pf shown .25 .25
**1379** A433 10pf Berger's Erfurt Rose .25 .25
**1380** A433 15pf Charme *1.40 1.40*
**1381** A433 20pf Izetka Spree-Athens .25 .25
**1382** A433 25pf Kopenick summer .25 .25
**1383** A433 35pf Prof. Knoll .30 .25
*Nos. 1378-1383 (6) 2.70 2.65*

International Rose Exhibition.

**Redrawn**

**1972, Aug. 22 *Perf. 13½x13***
**Booklet Stamps**
**Size: 23x28mm**

**1383A** A433 10pf multicolored .25 .25
*d.* Booklet pane of 4 1.25 .80
**1383B** A433 25pf multicolored 1.10 .40
*e.* Booklet pane of 4 (2 #1383B, 2 #1383C) 5.25 3.75
**1383C** A433 35pf multicolored 1.10 .40
*Nos. 1383A-1383C (3) 2.45 1.05*

Young Mother and Child, by Cranach A434

Paintings by Lucas Cranach: 5pf, Young man. 35pf, Margarete Luther (Martin's mother). 70pf, Reclining nymph, horiz.

**1972, July 4 *Perf. 14x13½, 13½x14***

**1384** A434 5pf gold & multi .25 .25
**1385** A434 20pf gold & multi .25 .25
**1386** A434 35pf gold & multi .25 .25
**1387** A434 70pf gold & multi *1.80 2.50*
*Nos. 1384-1387 (4) 2.55 3.25*

Lucas Cranach (1472-1553), painter.

Compass and Motorcyclist — A435

Designs: 10pf, Parachute and light plane. 20pf, Target and military obstacle race. 25pf, Amateur radio transmitter, Morse key and tape. 35pf, Propeller and sailing ship.

**1972, Aug. 8 Photo. *Perf. 14***

**1388** A435 5pf multicolored .25 .25
**1389** A435 10pf multicolored .25 .25
**1390** A435 20pf multicolored .25 .25
**1391** A435 25pf multicolored *.55 .65*
**1392** A435 35pf multicolored .25 .25
*Nos. 1388-1392 (5) 1.55 1.65*

Society for Sport and Technology.

Young Worker Reading, by Jutta Damme — A436

**1972, Aug. 22 Photo. *Perf. 13½x14***

**1393** A436 50pf multicolored .55 .30

International Book Year 1972.

Polylux Writing Projector — A437

25pf, Pentacon-audiovision projector, horiz.

***Perf. 12½x13, 13x12½***

**1972, Aug. 29 Litho.**

**1394** A437 10pf crimson & blk .25 .25
**1395** A437 25pf brt green & blk .25 .25

Leipzig Fall Fair, 1972.

George Dimitrov — A438

**1972, Sept. 19 *Perf. 13x13½***

**1396** A438 20pf rose red & blk .35 .25

George Dimitrov (1882-1949), Bulgarian Communist party leader.

Bird Catchers, Egypt, c. 2400 B.C. — A439

Design: 20pf, Tapestry with animal design, Anatolia, c. 1400 A.D.

**1972, Sept. 19 Photo. *Perf. 14***

**1397** A439 10pf multicolored .25 .25
**1398** A439 20pf multicolored .25 .25
*Nos. 1397-1398,B168-B169 (4) 1.55 1.40*

Interartes Philatelic Exhib., Berlin, Oct. 4-Nov. 11.

Red Cross Trainees and Red Cross — A440

Designs: 15pf, Red Cross rescue launch in the Baltic. 35pf, Red Cross with world map, ship, plane and vehicles.

**1972, Oct. 3 Litho. *Perf. 13***
**Size: 23x28mm**

**1399** A440 10pf grnsh bl, dk bl & red .30 .25
**1400** A440 15pf grnsh bl, dk bl & red .30 .25

**Size: 50x28mm**

**1401** A440 35pf grnsh bl, dk bl & red .30 .25
*a.* Strip of 3, #1399-1401 1.50 1.75

Red Cross at work in the DDR.

Arab Celestial Globe, 1279 — A441

10pf, Globe, by Joachim R. Praetorius, 1568. 15pf, Globe clock, by Reinhold & Roll, 1586. 20pf, Globe clock, by J. Bürgi, c. 1590. 25pf, Armillary sphere, by J. Moeller, 1687. 35pf, Heraldic celestial globe, 1690.

**1972, Oct. 17 Photo. *Perf. 14x13½***

**1402** A441 5pf gray & multi .25 .25
**1403** A441 10pf gray & multi .25 .25
**1404** A441 15pf gray & multi *2.10 2.50*
**1405** A441 20pf gray & multi .25 .25
**1406** A441 25pf gray & multi .25 .25
**1407** A441 35pf gray & multi .25 .25
*Nos. 1402-1407 (6) 3.35 3.75*

Celestial and terrestrial globes from the National Mathematical and Physics Collection, Dresden.

Anti-Fascists Monument — A442

**1972, Oct. 24 Litho. *Perf. 12½x13***

**1408** A442 25pf multicolored .40 .25

Monument for Polish soldiers and German anti-Fascists, unveiled in Berlin, May 14, 1972.

Young Workers Receiving Technical Education — A443

25pf, Workers with modern welding machine.

**1972, Nov. 2 Photo. *Perf. 13½x14***

**1409** A443 10pf blue & multi .25 .25
**1410** A443 25pf blue & multi .25 .25
*a.* Strip of 2, #1409-1410 + label .90 1.25

15th Central Fair of Masters of Tomorrow.

Mauz and Hoppel A444

Designs: Children's television characters.

**1972, Nov. 28 Litho. *Perf. 13½x13***

**1411** A444 5pf shown .25 .25
**1412** A444 10pf Fox and magpie .25 .25
**1413** A444 15pf Mr. Owl .70 .70
**1414** A444 20pf Mrs. Hedgehog and Borstel .70 .70
**1415** A444 25pf Schnuffel and Peips .25 .25
**1416** A444 35pf Paul from the Library .25 .25
*a.* Sheet of 6, #1411-1416 3.00 3.00

Grandmother, Children, Magic Mirror — A445

Scenes from Hans Christian Andersen's "Snow Queen": 10pf, Kay and Snow Queen. 15pf, Gerda in magic garden. 20pf, Gerda and crows at palace. 25pf, Gerda and reindeer in Lapland. 35pf, Gerda and Kay at Snow Queen's palace.

**1972, Nov. 28 *Perf. 13x13½***

**1417** A445 5pf multicolored .25 .25
**1418** A445 10pf multicolored .55 .75
**1419** A445 15pf multicolored .25 .25
**1420** A445 20pf multicolored .25 .25
**1421** A445 25pf multicolored .55 .75
**1422** A445 35pf multicolored .25 .25
*a.* Sheet of 6, #1417-1422 4.00 9.00

See designs A469, A490.

Souvenir Sheet

Heinrich Heine — A446

**1972, Dec. 5 *Perf. 12½x13***

**1423** A446 1m brn ol, blk & red 1.60 3.00

150th anniversary of the birth of Heinrich Heine (1797-1856), poet.

Coat of Arms of USSR — A447

**1972, Dec. 5 Photo. *Perf. 13½x14***

**1424** A447 20pf red & multi .40 .25

50th anniversary of the Soviet Union.

Michelangelo da Caravaggio — A448

**1973 Litho. *Perf. 13½x13***

**1425** A448 5pf brown *.50 .60*
**1426** A448 10pf dull green .25 .25
**1427** A448 20pf rose lilac .25 .25
**1428** A448 25pf blue .25 .25

| | | | | | |
|---|---|---|---|---|---|
| **1429** | A448 | 35pf | brown red | .25 | .25 |
| **1429A** | A448 | 40pf | rose claret | .25 | .25 |
| | | | *Nos. 1425-1429A (6)* | *1.75* | *1.85* |

Michelangelo da Caravaggio (1565(?)-1609), Italian painter (5pf). Friedrich Wolf (1888-1953), writer (10pf). Max Reger (1873-1916), composer (20pf). Max Reinhardt (1873-1943), Austrian theatrical director (25pf). Johannes Dieckmann (1893-1969), member and president of People's Chamber (35pf). Hermann Matern (1893-1971), vice-president of DDR (40pf).

Lenin Square, Berlin — A449

Coat of Arms of DDR — A449a

Designs: 5pf, Pelican, Berlin Zoo. 10pf, Neptune Fountain, City Hall Street. 15pf, Fisherman's Island, Berlin. 25pf, World clock, Alexander Square, Berlin. 30pf, Workers' Memorial, Halle. 35pf, Marx monument, Karl-Marx-Stadt. 40pf, Brandenburg Gate, Berlin. 50pf, New Guardhouse, Berlin. 60pf, Zwinger, Dresden. 70pf, Old Town Hall, Office Building, Leipzig. 80pf, Old and new buildings, Rostock-Warnemunde. 1m, Soviet War Memorial, Treptow.

**1973-74 Engr. *Perf. 14x13¾***

**Size: 29x23½mm**

| | | | | | |
|---|---|---|---|---|---|
| **1430** | A449 | 5pf | blue green | .25 | .25 |
| **1431** | A449 | 10pf | emerald | .45 | .25 |
| **1432** | A449 | 15pf | rose lilac | .40 | .25 |
| **1433** | A449 | 20pf | rose magenta | .80 | .25 |
| **1434** | A449 | 25pf | grnsh blue | .95 | .25 |
| **1435** | A449 | 30pf | orange | .40 | .25 |
| **1436** | A449 | 35pf | grnsh blue | .80 | .30 |
| **1437** | A449 | 40pf | dull violet | .45 | .25 |
| **1438** | A449 | 50pf | blue, *bluish* | .55 | .25 |
| **1439** | A449 | 60pf | lilac ('74) | .80 | .30 |
| **1440** | A449 | 70pf | redsh brown | .70 | .35 |
| **1441** | A449 | 80pf | vio blue ('74) | .95 | .30 |
| **1442** | A449 | 1m | olive | 1.20 | .25 |
| **1443** | A449a | 2m | lake | 1.80 | .25 |
| **1443A** | A449a | 3m | rose lilac ('74) | 3.25 | 1.00 |
| | | | *Nos. 1430-1443A (15)* | 13.75 | 4.75 |

See Nos. 1610-1617, 2071-2085.

Lebachia Speciosa (Oldest Conifer) A450

Fossils from Natural History Museum, Berlin: 15pf, Sphenopteris hollandica (carbon fern). 20pf, Pterodactylus kochi (flying reptile). 25pf, Botryopteris (permian fern). 35pf, Archaeopteryx lithographica (primitive reptile-like bird). 70pf, Odontopieura ovata (trilobite).

**1973, Feb. 6 Photo. *Perf. 13***

| | | | | | |
|---|---|---|---|---|---|
| **1444** | A450 | 10pf | multicolored | .25 | .25 |
| **1445** | A450 | 15pf | ultra, gray & blk | .25 | .25 |
| **1446** | A450 | 20pf | yellow & multi | .25 | .25 |
| **1447** | A450 | 25pf | emerald, blk & brn | .25 | .25 |
| **1448** | A450 | 35pf | ocher & multi | .25 | .25 |
| **1449** | A450 | 70pf | ind, blk & yel | *1.40* | *1.40* |
| | | | *Nos. 1444-1449 (6)* | *2.65* | *2.65* |

Bobsled Track, Oberhof — A451

**1973, Feb. 13 Litho. *Perf. 12½x13***

| | | | | | |
|---|---|---|---|---|---|
| **1450** | A451 | 35pf | dk bl, bl & org | .40 | .30 |

15th Bobsledding Championships, Oberhof.

Combines A452

Leipzig Spring Fair: 25pf, Computerized threshing and silage producing machine.

**1973, Mar. 6 Litho. *Perf. 13x12½***

| | | | | | |
|---|---|---|---|---|---|
| **1451** | A452 | 10pf | olive & multi | .25 | .25 |
| **1452** | A452 | 25pf | blue & multi | .30 | .30 |

Firecrests A453

Songbirds: 10pf, White-winged crossbill. 15pf, Waxwing. 20pf, White-spotted and red-spotted bluethroats. 25pf, Goldfinch. 35pf, Golden oriole. 40pf, Gray wagtail. 50pf, Wall creeper.

**1973, Mar. 20 Photo. *Perf. 14x13½***

| | | | | | |
|---|---|---|---|---|---|
| **1453** | A453 | 5pf | multicolored | .25 | .25 |
| **1454** | A453 | 10pf | multicolored | .25 | .25 |
| **1455** | A453 | 15pf | multicolored | .25 | .25 |
| **1456** | A453 | 20pf | multicolored | .25 | .25 |
| **1457** | A453 | 25pf | multicolored | .25 | .25 |
| **1458** | A453 | 35pf | multicolored | .25 | .25 |
| **1459** | A453 | 40pf | multicolored | .25 | .25 |
| **1460** | A453 | 50pf | ocher & multi | *2.25* | *2.25* |
| | | | *Nos. 1453-1460 (8)* | *4.00* | *4.00* |

Copernicus and Title Page — A454

**1973, Feb. 13 Litho. *Perf. 13½x13***

| | | | | | |
|---|---|---|---|---|---|
| **1461** | A454 | 70pf | multicolored | .80 | .40 |

500th anniversary of the birth of Nicolaus Copernicus (1473-1543), astronomer.

Electric Locomotive — A455

Railroad Cars Manufactured in DDR: 10pf, Refrigerator car. 20pf, Long-distance coach. 25pf, Multiple tank car with pneumatic filling device. 35pf, Two-story coach. 85pf, International coaches.

**1973, May 22 Litho. *Perf. 13x12½***

| | | | | | |
|---|---|---|---|---|---|
| **1462** | A455 | 5pf | gray & multi | .25 | .25 |
| **1463** | A455 | 10pf | brt blue & multi | .25 | .25 |
| **1464** | A455 | 20pf | dk blue & multi | .25 | .25 |
| **1465** | A455 | 25pf | gray & multi | .25 | .25 |
| **1466** | A455 | 35pf | multicolored | .25 | .25 |
| **1467** | A455 | 85pf | green & multi | *2.00* | *2.00* |
| | | | *Nos. 1462-1467 (6)* | *3.25* | *3.25* |

King Lear, Staged by Wolfgang Langhoff A456

Great Theatrical Productions: 25pf, Midsummer Marriage, staged by Walter Felsenstein. 35pf, Mother Courage, staged by Bertolt Brecht.

**1973, May 29 Photo. *Perf. 13***

| | | | | | |
|---|---|---|---|---|---|
| **1468** | A456 | 10pf | maroon, rose & yel | .25 | .25 |
| **1469** | A456 | 25pf | vio bl, lt bl & rose | .25 | .25 |
| **1470** | A456 | 35pf | dk gray, bis & bl | *.70* | *.65* |
| | | | *Nos. 1468-1470 (3)* | *1.20* | *1.15* |

Goethe and his Home in Weimar — A457

Designs (Portraits and Houses): 15pf, Christoph Martin Wieland. 20pf, Friedrich von Schiller. 25pf, Johann Gottfried Herder. 35pf, Lucas Cranach, the Elder. 50pf, Franz Liszt.

**1973, June 26 Litho. *Perf. 12½x13***

| | | | | | |
|---|---|---|---|---|---|
| **1471** | A457 | 10pf | blue & multi | .25 | .25 |
| **1472** | A457 | 15pf | multicolored | .25 | .25 |
| **1473** | A457 | 20pf | multicolored | .25 | .25 |
| **1474** | A457 | 25pf | multicolored | .25 | .25 |
| **1475** | A457 | 35pf | green & multi | .25 | .25 |
| **1476** | A457 | 50pf | multicolored | *1.75* | *.95* |
| | | | *Nos. 1471-1476 (6)* | *3.00* | *2.20* |

Famous men and their homes in Weimar.

Fireworks, TV Tower, World Clock — A458

Designs (Festival Emblem and): 15pf, Vietnamese and European men, book and girder. 20pf, Construction workers and valve. 30pf, Negro and European students, dam and retort. 35pf, Emblems of World Federation of Democratic Youth and International Students Union. 50pf, Brandenburg Gate.

**1973**

| | | | | | |
|---|---|---|---|---|---|
| **1477** | A458 | 5pf | vio blue & multi | .25 | .25 |
| *a.* | | | Booklet pane of 4 | 1.60 | 1.25 |
| **1478** | A458 | 15pf | olive & multi | .25 | .25 |
| **1479** | A458 | 20pf | multicolored | .25 | .25 |
| *a.* | | | Booklet pane of 4 | 1.60 | 1.25 |
| **1480** | A458 | 30pf | blue & multi | *.80* | *.40* |
| **1481** | A458 | 35pf | green & multi | .25 | .25 |
| | | | *Nos. 1477-1481 (5)* | *1.80* | *1.40* |

**Souvenir Sheet**

| | | | | | |
|---|---|---|---|---|---|
| **1482** | A458 | 50pf | aqua & multi | 1.00 | 1.50 |

10th Festival of Youths and Students, Berlin, July 1973.

Issued: #1477-1481, July 3; #1482, July 26.

**Ulbricht Type of 1961-67**

**1973, Aug. 8 Engr. *Perf. 14***

**Size: 24x28½mm**

| | | | | | |
|---|---|---|---|---|---|
| **1483** | A189 | 20pf | black | .45 | .30 |

In memory of Walter Ulbricht (1893-1973), chairman of Council of State.

Pylon, Map of Electric Power System — A459

**1973, Aug. 14 Photo. *Perf. 14***

| | | | | | |
|---|---|---|---|---|---|
| **1484** | A459 | 35pf | magenta, org & lt bl | .40 | .30 |

10th anniversary of the united East European electric power system "Peace."

Sports Equipment — A460

Design: 25pf, Sailboat, guitar, electric drill.

**1973, Aug. 28 Photo. *Perf. 14***

| | | | | | |
|---|---|---|---|---|---|
| **1485** | A460 | 10pf | multicolored | .25 | .25 |
| **1486** | A460 | 25pf | multicolored | .30 | .25 |

Leipzig Fall Fair and EXPOVITA exhibition for leisure time equipment.

Militiaman and Emblem A461

Designs: 20pf, Militia guarding border at Brandenburg Gate. 50pf, Representatives of Red Veterans' League, International Brigade in Spain and Workers' Militia in DDR, vert.

**1973, Sept. 11 Litho. *Perf. 13x12½***

| | | | | | |
|---|---|---|---|---|---|
| **1487** | A461 | 10pf | multicolored | .25 | .25 |
| **1488** | A461 | 20pf | tan, red & blk | .30 | .25 |

**Souvenir Sheet**

***Perf. 12½x13***

| | | | | | |
|---|---|---|---|---|---|
| **1489** | A461 | 50pf | multicolored | .85 | 1.50 |

20th anniversary of Workers' Militia of the German Democratic Republic.

Globe and Red Flag Emblem A462

**1973, Sept. 11 Photo. *Perf. 13½x14***

| | | | | | |
|---|---|---|---|---|---|
| **1490** | A462 | 20pf | gold & red | .40 | .25 |

15th anniversary of the review "Problems of Peace and Socialism," published in Prague in 28 languages.

Memorial, Langenstein-Zwieberge — A463

**1973, Sept. 18 *Perf. 14x13½***

| | | | | | |
|---|---|---|---|---|---|
| **1491** | A463 | 25pf | multicolored | .45 | .25 |

In memory of the workers who perished in the subterranean munitions works at Langenstein-Zwieberge.

UN Headquarters, NY, UN and DDR Emblems — A464

**1973, Sept. 21** *Perf. 13*

| | | | | |
|---|---|---|---|---|
| **1492** | A464 | 35pf multicolored | .50 | .25 |

Admission of the DDR to the UN.

Union Emblem A465

**1973, Oct. 11** **Photo.** *Perf. 14x13½*

| | | | | |
|---|---|---|---|---|
| **1493** | A465 | 35pf silver & multi | .40 | .30 |

8th Congress of the World Federation of Trade Unions, Varna, Bulgaria.

Rocket Launching — A466

20pf, Emblem with map of Russia & hammer & sickle, horiz. 25pf, Oil refinery, Ryazan.

**1973, Oct. 23** *Perf. 14*

| | | | | |
|---|---|---|---|---|
| **1494** | A466 | 10pf violet bl & multi | .25 | .25 |
| **1495** | A466 | 20pf vio bl, red & sil | .25 | .25 |
| **1496** | A466 | 25pf multicolored | *.75* | *.65* |
| | | *Nos. 1494-1496 (3)* | *1.25* | *1.15* |

Soviet Science & Technology Days in DDR.

Madonna with the Rose, by Parmigianino A467

Paintings: 10pf Child with Doll, by Christian L. Vogel. 20pf, Woman with Plaited Blond Hair, by Rubens. 25pf, Lady in White, by Titian. 35pf, Archimedes, by Domenico Fetti. 70pf, Bouquet with Blue Iris, by Jan D. de Heem.

**1973, Nov. 13** **Photo.** *Perf. 14*

| | | | | |
|---|---|---|---|---|
| **1497** | A467 | 10pf gold & multi | .25 | .25 |
| **1498** | A467 | 15pf gold & multi | .25 | .25 |
| **1499** | A467 | 20pf gold & multi | .25 | .25 |
| **1500** | A467 | 25pf gold & multi | .25 | .25 |
| **1501** | A467 | 35pf gold & multi | .25 | .25 |
| **1502** | A467 | 70pf gold & multi | *2.25* | *1.60* |
| | | *Nos. 1497-1502 (6)* | *3.50* | *2.85* |

Human Rights Flame A468

**1973, Nov. 20** *Perf. 13*

| | | | | |
|---|---|---|---|---|
| **1503** | A468 | 35pf dp rose, dk car & sil | .50 | .30 |

25th anniv. of the Universal Declaration of Human Rights.

Boy Holding Pike — A469

Designs: Various scenes from Russian Folktale "At the Bidding of the Pike."

**1973, Dec. 4** **Litho.** *Perf. 13x13½*

| | | | | |
|---|---|---|---|---|
| **1504** | A469 | 5pf multicolored | .25 | .25 |
| **1505** | A469 | 10pf multicolored | .80 | 1.20 |
| **1506** | A469 | 15pf multicolored | .25 | .25 |
| **1507** | A469 | 20pf multicolored | .25 | .25 |
| **1508** | A469 | 25pf multicolored | .80 | 1.20 |
| **1509** | A469 | 35pf multicolored | .25 | .25 |
| *a.* | | Sheet of 6, #1504-1509 | 3.50 | 7.00 |

Edwin Hoernle — A470

#1511, Etkar Andre. #1512, Paul Merker. #1513, Hermann Duncker. #1514, Fritz Heckert. #1515, Otto Grotewohl. #1516, Wilhelm Florin. #1517, Georg Handke. #1518, Rudolf Breitscheid. #1519, Kurt Bürger. #1519A Carl Moltmann.

**1974** **Litho.** *Perf. 13½x13*

| | | | | |
|---|---|---|---|---|
| **1510** | A470 | 10pf gray green | .25 | .25 |
| **1511** | A470 | 10pf rose violet | .25 | .25 |
| **1512** | A470 | 10pf dark blue | .25 | .25 |
| **1513** | A470 | 10pf brown | .25 | .25 |
| **1514** | A470 | 10pf dull green | .25 | .25 |
| **1515** | A470 | 10pf red brown | .25 | .25 |
| **1516** | A470 | 10pf vio blue | .25 | .25 |
| **1517** | A470 | 10pf olive brown | .25 | .25 |
| **1518** | A470 | 10pf slate green | .25 | .25 |
| **1519** | A470 | 10pf dull violet | .25 | .25 |
| **1519A** | A470 | 10pf brown | .25 | .25 |
| | | *Nos. 1510-1519A (11)* | 2.75 | 2.75 |

Leaders of German labor movement. Issued: #1510-1517, Jan. 8; others July 9.

Flags of Comecon Members A471

**1974, Jan. 22** **Photo.** *Perf. 13*

| | | | | |
|---|---|---|---|---|
| **1520** | A471 | 20pf red & multi | .45 | .25 |

25th anniversary of the Council of Mutual Economic Assistance (Comecon).

Pablo Neruda and Chilean Flag A472

**1974, Jan. 22** *Perf. 14*

| | | | | |
|---|---|---|---|---|
| **1521** | A472 | 20pf multicolored | .45 | .25 |

Pablo Neruda (Neftali Ricardo Reyes, 1904-1973), Chilean poet.

Echinopsis Multiplex A473

Fieldball A474

Various Flowering Cacti: 10pf, Lobivia haageana. 15pf, Parodia sanguiniflora. 20pf, Gymnocal. monvillei. 25pf, Neoporteria rapifera. 35pf, Notocactus concinnus.

**1974, Feb. 12** **Photo.** *Perf. 14*

| | | | | |
|---|---|---|---|---|
| **1522** | A473 | 5pf multicolored | .25 | .25 |
| **1523** | A473 | 10pf tan & multi | .25 | .25 |
| **1524** | A473 | 15pf green & multi | *2.10* | *2.10* |
| **1525** | A473 | 20pf multicolored | .25 | .25 |
| **1526** | A473 | 25pf violet & multi | .25 | .25 |
| **1527** | A473 | 35pf multicolored | .25 | .25 |
| | | *Nos. 1522-1527 (6)* | *3.35* | *3.35* |

**1974, Feb. 26** **Litho.** *Perf. 13*

Design: Various fieldball scenes.

| | | | | |
|---|---|---|---|---|
| **1528** | A474 | 5pf green & multi | .30 | .30 |
| **1529** | A474 | 10pf green & multi | .30 | .30 |
| **1530** | A474 | 35pf green & multi | *.95* | *.95* |
| *a.* | | Strip of 3, #1528-1530 | *1.90* | *1.90* |

8th World Fieldball Championships for Men.

Power Testing Station — A475

Leipzig Spring Fair: 25pf, Robotron EC 2040 data processer, horiz.

**1974, Mar. 5** **Photo.** *Perf. 14*

| | | | | |
|---|---|---|---|---|
| **1531** | A475 | 10pf multicolored | .25 | .25 |
| **1532** | A475 | 25pf multicolored | .30 | .25 |

Poisonous European Mushrooms A476

Designs: 5pf, Rhodophyllus Sinuatus. 10pf, Boletus satanas. 15pf, Amanita pantherina. 20pf, Amanita muscaria. 25pf, Gyromitra esculenta. 30pf, Inocybe patouillardii. 35pf, Amanita phalloides. 40pf, Clitocybe dealbata.

**1974, Mar. 19** **Litho.** *Perf. 13x13½*

| | | | | |
|---|---|---|---|---|
| **1533** | A476 | 5pf buff & multi | .25 | .25 |
| **1534** | A476 | 10pf buff & multi | .25 | .25 |
| **1535** | A476 | 15pf buff & multi | .25 | .25 |
| **1536** | A476 | 20pf buff & multi | .25 | .25 |
| **1537** | A476 | 25pf buff & multi | .25 | .25 |
| **1538** | A476 | 30pf buff & multi | .25 | .25 |
| **1539** | A476 | 35pf buff & multi | .25 | .25 |
| **1540** | A476 | 40pf buff & multi | *1.40* | *1.00* |
| | | *Nos. 1533-1540 (8)* | *3.15* | *2.75* |

Gustav Robert Kirchhoff — A477

Portraits: 10pf, Immanuel Kant. 20pf, Ehm Welk. 25pf, Johann Gottfried Herder. 35pf, Lion Feuchtwanger.

**1974, Mar. 26** **Litho.** *Perf. 13½x13*

| | | | | |
|---|---|---|---|---|
| **1541** | A477 | 5pf black & gray | .25 | .25 |
| **1542** | A477 | 10pf vio bl & dull bl | .25 | .25 |
| **1543** | A477 | 20pf maroon & rose | .25 | .25 |
| **1544** | A477 | 25pf slate grn & grn | .25 | .25 |
| **1545** | A477 | 35pf brn & lt brn | *.50* | *.40* |
| | | *Nos. 1541-1545 (5)* | *1.50* | *1.40* |

"Peace" A477a

**1974, Apr. 16** *Perf. 13*

| | | | | |
|---|---|---|---|---|
| **1548** | A477a | 35pf silver & multi | .45 | .30 |

1st World Peace Congress, 25th anniv.

Oil Pipeline Operator and Arms of DDR A477b

**1974, Apr. 30** **Photo.** *Perf. 13*

| | | | | |
|---|---|---|---|---|
| **1549** | A477b | 10pf shown | .25 | .25 |
| **1550** | A477b | 20pf Students | .25 | .25 |
| **1551** | A477b | 25pf Woman worker | .25 | .25 |
| **1552** | A477b | 35pf Family | *.75* | *.75* |
| | | *Nos. 1549-1552 (4)* | *1.50* | *1.50* |

25th anniv. of the DDR.

Buk Lighthouse, 1878, and Map — A478

Lighthouses, Maps and Nautical Charts: 15pf, Warnemünde, 1898. 20pf, Darsser Ort, 1848. 35pf, Arkona, 1827 and 1902. 40pf, Greifswalder Oie, 1855.

**1974, May 7** **Litho.** *Perf. 14*

| | | | | |
|---|---|---|---|---|
| **1553** | A478 | 10pf multicolored | .25 | .25 |
| **1554** | A478 | 15pf multicolored | .25 | .25 |
| **1555** | A478 | 20pf multicolored | .25 | .25 |
| **1556** | A478 | 35pf multicolored | .25 | .25 |
| **1557** | A478 | 40pf multicolored | *1.25* | *.90* |
| | | *Nos. 1553-1557 (5)* | *2.25* | *1.90* |

Hydrographic Service of German Democratic Republic. See Nos. 1645-1649.

The Ages of Man, by C. D. Friedrich — A479

C. D. Friedrich, Self-portrait — A480

Paintings by Friedrich: 10pf, Two Men Observing Moon. 25pf, The Heath near Dresden. 35pf, View of Elbe Valley.

**1974, May 21 Photo. *Perf. 13½***

**1558** A479 10pf gold & multi .25 .25
**1559** A479 20pf gold & multi .25 .25
**1560** A479 25pf gold & multi *1.60 1.60*
**1561** A479 35pf gold & multi .25 .25
*Nos. 1558-1561 (4)* *2.35 2.35*

**Souvenir Sheet**

**Engr.**

***Perf. 14x13½***

**1562** A480 70pf sepia *1.50 2.00*

Caspar David Friedrich (1774-1840), German Romantic painter.

Plauen Lace — A481

Designs: Various Plauen lace patterns.

**1974, June 11 Litho. *Perf. 13***

**1563** A481 10pf violet, lil & blk .25 .25
**1564** A481 20pf brown ol & blk .25 .25
**1565** A481 25pf bl, lt bl & blk *1.10 1.10*
**1566** A481 35pf lil rose, rose & blk .25 .25
*Nos. 1563-1566 (4)* *1.85 1.85*

Trotter — A482

Designs: 10pf, Thoroughbred hurdling, vert. 25pf, Haflinger breed horses. 35pf, British thoroughbred race horse.

***Perf. 14x13½, 13½x14***

**1974, Aug. 13 Photo.**

**1570** A482 10pf olive & multi .25 .25
**1571** A482 20pf multicolored .25 .25
**1572** A482 25pf lt blue & multi *1.40 1.60*
**1573** A482 35pf ocher & multi .25 .25
*Nos. 1570-1573 (4)* *2.15 2.35*

International Horse Breeders' of Socialist Countries Congress, Berlin.

Crane Lifting Diesel Locomotive — A483

Leipzig Fall Fair: 25pf, Sugar beet harvester, type KS6.

**1974, Aug. 27 Litho. *Perf. 13x12½***

**1574** A483 10pf multicolored .25 .25
**1575** A483 25pf orange & multi .40 .25

Miniature China and Mirror Exhibits — A484

Designs: Scenes from 18th century Thuringia, Dolls' Village, Arnstadt Castle Museum.

**1974, Sept. 10 Photo. *Perf. 14x13½***

**1576** A484 5pf shown .25 .25
**1577** A484 10pf Harlequin barker at Fair .25 .25
**1578** A484 15pf Wine tasters .25 .25
**1579** A484 20pf Cooper and apprentice .25 .25
**1580** A484 25pf Bagpiper *1.25 1.25*
**1581** A484 35pf Butcher and beggar, women .25 .25
*Nos. 1576-1581 (6)* *2.50 2.50*

Bound Guerrillas, Ardeatine Caves, Rome — A485

Design: No. 1583, Resistance Fighters, monument near Chateaubriant, France.

**1974, Sept. 24 *Perf. 13½x14***

**1582** A485 35pf green, blk & red .50 .30
**1583** A485 35pf blue, blk & red .50 .30

International war memorials.

**Souvenir Sheet**

Family and Flag — A486

**1974, Oct. 3 Photo. *Perf. 13***

**1584** A486 1m multicolored 1.50 3.00

25th anniv. of the DDR.

Freighter and Paddle Steamer — A487

Cent. of the UPU: 20pf, Old steam locomotive and modern Diesel. 25pf, Bi-plane and jet. 35pf, Mail coach and truck.

**1974, Oct. 9 *Perf. 14***

**1585** A487 10pf green & multi .25 .25
**1586** A487 20pf multicolored .25 .25
**1587** A487 25pf blue & multi .25 .25
**1588** A487 35pf multicolored *.90 .80*
*Nos. 1585-1588 (4)* *1.65 1.55*

"In Praise of Dialectics" A488

Designs: 10pf+5pf, "Praise to the Revolutionaries." 25pf, "Praise to the Party." Designs are from bas-reliefs by Rossdeutscher, Jastram and Wetzel, illustrating poems by Bertholt Brecht.

**1974, Oct. 24 Litho. *Perf. 13x13½***

**1589** A488 10pf + 5pf multi *.25 .25*
**1590** A488 20pf multicolored *.25 .25*
**1591** A488 25pf multicolored *.25 .25*
*a.* Strip of 3, #1589-1591 *1.25 1.10*

DDR '74 Natl. Stamp Exhib., Karl-Marx-Stadt.

Souvenir Sheet

Drawings by Young Pioneers — A489

**1974, Nov. 26 Litho. *Perf. 14***

**1592** A489 Sheet of 4 *1.60 2.00*
*a.* 20pf Sun shines on everybody *.30 .30*
*b.* 20pf My Friend Sascha *.30 .30*
*c.* 20pf Carsten, the Best Swimmer *.30 .30*
*d.* 20pf Me at the Blackboard *.30 .30*

Young Pioneers' drawings (7-10 years old).

Man Cutting Tree, and Bird — A490

Designs: Various scenes from Russian folktale "Twittering To and Fro."

**1974, Dec. 3 *Perf. 13x13½***

**1593** A490 10pf multicolored *.25 .25*
**1594** A490 15pf multicolored *.90 .90*
**1595** A490 20pf multicolored *.25 .25*
**1596** A490 30pf multicolored *.25 .25*
**1597** A490 35pf multicolored *.90 .90*
**1598** A490 40pf multicolored *.25 .25*
*a.* Sheet of 6, #1593-1598 *3.50 4.25*

Meditating Girl, by Wilhelm Lachnit — A491

Paintings: 10pf, Still Life, by Ronald Paris, horiz. 20pf, Fisherman's House, Vitte, by Harald Hakenbeck. 35pf, Girl in Red, by Rudolf Bergander, horiz. 70pf, The Artist's Parents, by Willi Sitte.

**1974, Dec. 10 *Perf. 13½x14, 14x13½***

**1599** A491 10pf multicolored .25 .25
**1600** A491 15pf multicolored .25 .25
**1601** A491 20pf multicolored .25 .25
**1602** A491 35pf multicolored .25 .25
**1603** A491 70pf multicolored *1.75 1.50*
*Nos. 1599-1603 (5)* *2.75 2.50*

Paintings in Berlin Museums.

Banded Jasper — A492

Minerals from the collection of the Mining Academy in Freiberg: 15pf, Smoky quartz. 20pf, Topaz. 25pf, Amethyst. 35pf, Aquamarine. 70pf, Agate.

**1974, Dec. 17 Photo. *Perf. 14***

**1604** A492 10pf lt yellow & multi .25 .25
**1605** A492 15pf lt yellow & multi .25 .25
**1606** A492 20pf lt yellow & multi .25 .25
**1607** A492 25pf lt yellow & multi .25 .25
**1608** A492 35pf lt yellow & multi .25 .25
**1609** A492 70pf lt yellow & multi *1.60 1.50*
*Nos. 1604-1609 (6)* *2.85 2.75*

**Type of 1973**

Coil Stamps

**1974-75 Photo. *Perf. 14***

**Size: 21x17½mm**

**1610** A449 5pf blue grn ('74) .25 .25
**1611** A449 10pf emerald .35 .35
**1612** A449 20pf rose magenta .35 .35
**1613** A449 25pf green ('75) .35 .25
**1615** A449 50pf blue ('74) .70 .50
**1617** A449 1m olive ('74) 1.00 1.00
*Nos. 1610-1617 (6)* 3.00 2.70

Black control number on back of every fifth stamp.

The 20pf was issued in sheets of 100 in 1975.

Martha Arendsee (1885-1953), Communist Politician — A493

**1975, Jan. 14 Litho. *Perf. 13½x13***

**1618** A493 10pf dull red .40 .25

Souvenir Sheet

Peasants' War, Contemporary Woodcuts — A494

**1975, Feb. 11 *Perf. 12½x13***

**1619** A494 Sheet of 6 + label *3.25 3.00*
*a.* 5pf Forced labor *.30 .30*
*b.* 10pf Peasant paying tithe *.30 .30*
*c.* 20pf Thomas Munzer *.30 .30*
*d.* 25pf Armed peasants *.55 .55*
*e.* 35pf Peasant, "Liberty" flag *.55 .55*
*f.* 50pf Peasant on trial *.30 .30*

Peasants' War, 450th anniversary.

Black Women — A495

Designs: 20pf, Caucasian women. 25pf, Indian woman and child.

**1975, Feb. 25 Litho. *Perf. 13***

**1620** A495 10pf red & multi *.25 .25*
**1621** A495 20pf red & multi *.25 .25*
**1622** A495 25pf red & multi *.25 .25*
*a.* Strip of 3, Nos. 1620-1622 *1.10 1.00*

International Women's Year 1975.

Microfilm Pentakta Camera A496

Leipzig Spring Fair: 25pf, Sket cement plant.

**1975, Mar. 4 Photo. *Perf. 14***

| | | | | |
|---|---|---|---|---|
| **1623** | A496 | 10pf ultra & multi | .25 | .25 |
| **1624** | A496 | 25pf orange & multi | .25 | .25 |

A497

Portraits: 5pf, Hans Otto (1900-33), actor. 10pf, Thomas Mann (1875-1955), writer. 20pf, Albert Schweitzer (1875-1965), medical missionary. 25pf, Michelangelo (1475-1564), painter and sculptor. 35pf, André Marie Ampère (1775-1836), scientist.

**1975, Mar. 18 Litho. *Perf. 13½x13***

| | | | | |
|---|---|---|---|---|
| **1625** | A497 | 5pf dk blue | .25 | .25 |
| **1626** | A497 | 10pf dk car rose | .25 | .25 |
| **1627** | A497 | 20pf dk green | .25 | .25 |
| **1628** | A497 | 25pf sepia | .25 | .25 |
| **1629** | A497 | 35pf vio blue | *.80* | *.55* |
| | | *Nos. 1625-1629 (5)* | *1.80* | *1.55* |

Famous men, birth anniversaries.

A498

German Zoological Gardens: 5pf, Blue and yellow macaws, Magdeburg Zoo. 10pf, Orangutan family, Dresden. 15pf, Siberian chamois, Halle. 20pf, Rhinoceros, Berlin. 25pf, Dwarf hippopotamus, Erfurt. 30pf, Baltic seal and pup, Rostock. 35pf, Siberian tiger, Leipzig. 50pf, Boehm's zebra, Cottbus. 20pf, 25pf, 30pf, 35pf are horiz.

**1975, Mar. 25 *Perf. 13½x13, 13x13½***

| | | | | |
|---|---|---|---|---|
| **1630** | A498 | 5pf multicolored | .25 | .25 |
| **1631** | A498 | 10pf multicolored | .25 | .25 |
| **1632** | A498 | 15pf multicolored | .25 | .25 |
| **1633** | A498 | 20pf multicolored | .25 | .25 |
| **1634** | A498 | 25pf multicolored | .25 | .25 |
| **1635** | A498 | 30pf multicolored | .25 | .25 |
| **1636** | A498 | 35pf multicolored | .25 | .25 |
| **1637** | A498 | 50pf multicolored | *1.40* | *1.40* |
| | | *Nos. 1630-1637 (8)* | *3.15* | *3.15* |

Soldiers, Industry and Agriculture — A499

**1975, May 6 Photo. *Perf. 13½x14***

| | | | | |
|---|---|---|---|---|
| **1638** | A499 | 20pf multicolored | .90 | .30 |

20th anniv. of the signing of the Warsaw Treaty (Bulgaria, Czechoslovakia, DDR, Hungary, Poland, Romania, USSR).

Soviet War Memorial, Berlin-Treptow A500

Designs (Arms of German Democratic Rep. and): 20pf, Buchenwald Memorial (detail). 25pf, Woman reconstruction worker. 35pf, Skyscraper and statue at Orenburg (economic integration). 50pf, Soldier raising Red Flag on Reichstag Building, Berlin.

**1975, May 6 *Perf. 14x13½***

| | | | | |
|---|---|---|---|---|
| **1639** | A500 | 10pf red & multi | .25 | .25 |
| **1640** | A500 | 20pf red & multi | .25 | .25 |
| **1641** | A500 | 25pf red & multi | .25 | .25 |
| **1642** | A500 | 35pf red & multi | *.80* | *.60* |
| | | *Nos. 1639-1642 (4)* | *1.55* | *1.35* |

**Souvenir Sheet**

***Imperf***

| | | | | |
|---|---|---|---|---|
| **1643** | A500 | 50pf red & multi | 1.00 | 1.75 |

30th anniversary of liberation from fascism.

Ribbons, Youth Organization Emblems of DDR and USSR — A501

**1975, May 13 *Perf. 14***

| | | | | |
|---|---|---|---|---|
| **1644** | A501 | 10pf multicolored | .45 | .25 |

Third Friendship Festival of Russian and German Youths, Halle, 1975.

**Lighthouse Type of 1974**

Lighthouses, Maps and Nautical Charts: 5pf, Timmendorf, 1872. 10pf, Gellen, 1905. 20pf, Sassnitz, 1904. 25pf, Dornbush, 1888. 35pf, Peenemünde, 1954.

**1975, May 13 Litho. *Perf. 14***

| | | | | |
|---|---|---|---|---|
| **1645** | A478 | 5pf multicolored | .25 | .25 |
| **1646** | A478 | 10pf multicolored | .25 | .25 |
| **1647** | A478 | 20pf multicolored | .25 | .25 |
| **1648** | A478 | 25pf multicolored | .25 | .25 |
| **1649** | A478 | 35pf multicolored | *1.00* | *.75* |
| | | *Nos. 1645-1649 (5)* | *2.00* | *1.75* |

Hydrographic Service of the DDR.

Wilhelm Liebknecht, August Bebel — A502

20pf, Tivoli House & front page of Protocol of Gotha. 25pf, Karl Marx & Friedrich Engels.

**1975, May 21 Photo.**

| | | | | |
|---|---|---|---|---|
| **1650** | A502 | 10pf buff, brn & red | *.25* | *.25* |
| **1651** | A502 | 20pf salmon, brn & red | *.25* | *.25* |
| **1652** | A502 | 25pf buff, brn & red | *.25* | *.25* |
| *a.* | | Strip of 3, #1650-1652 | *1.00* | *1.00* |

Centenary of the Congress of Gotha, the beginning of German Socialist Workers' Party.

Construction Workers, Union Emblem — A503

**1975, June 10 Photo. *Perf. 14***

| | | | | |
|---|---|---|---|---|
| **1653** | A503 | 20pf red & multi | .40 | .25 |

Free German Association of Trade Unions (FDGB), 30th anniversary.

"Socialist Scientific Cooperation" Mosaic by Walter Womacka A504

**1975, June 10 Litho. *Perf. 13***

| | | | | |
|---|---|---|---|---|
| **1654** | A504 | 20pf multicolored | .40 | .25 |

Eisenhüttenstadt, first socialist city of DDR, 25th anniversary.

Automatic Clock by Paulus Schuster, 1585 — A505

Clocks, Dresden Museums: 10pf, Astronomical table clock, Augsburg, c. 1560. 15pf, Automatic clock, Hans Schlottheim, c. 1600. 20pf, Table clock, Johann Heinrich Köhler, c. 1720. 25pf, Table clock, Köhler, c. 1700. 35pf, Astronomical clock, Johannes Klein, 1738.

**1975, June 24 Photo. *Perf. 14***

| | | | | |
|---|---|---|---|---|
| **1655** | A505 | 5pf multicolored | .25 | .25 |
| **1656** | A505 | 10pf ultra & multi | .25 | .25 |
| **1657** | A505 | 15pf red & multi | *1.25* | *1.25* |
| **1658** | A505 | 20pf olive & multi | .25 | .25 |
| **1659** | A505 | 25pf multicolored | .25 | .25 |
| **1660** | A505 | 35pf ocher & multi | .25 | .25 |
| | | *Nos. 1655-1660 (6)* | *2.50* | *2.50* |

Dictionary, Compiled by Jacob and Wilhelm Grimm — A506

20pf, Karl-Schwarzschild Observatory, Tautenburg near Jena. 25pf, Electron microscope & chemical plant (scientific & practical cooperation). 35pf, Intercosmos 10 satellite.

**1975, July 2 Litho. *Perf. 13½x13***

| | | | | |
|---|---|---|---|---|
| **1661** | A506 | 10pf plum, ol & blk | .25 | .25 |
| **1662** | A506 | 20pf vio bl & blk | .25 | .25 |
| **1663** | A506 | 25pf green, yel & blk | .25 | .25 |
| **1664** | A506 | 35pf blue & multi | *.90* | *.75* |
| | | *Nos. 1661-1664 (4)* | *1.65* | *1.50* |

German Academy of Sciences, 275th anniv.

Torch Bearer — A507

**1975, July 15 *Perf. 13½x13***

| | | | | |
|---|---|---|---|---|
| **1665** | A507 | 10pf shown | .25 | .25 |
| **1666** | A507 | 20pf Hurdling | .25 | .25 |
| **1667** | A507 | 25pf Diving | .25 | .25 |
| **1668** | A507 | 35pf Gymnast on bar | *.90* | *.75* |
| | | *Nos. 1665-1668 (4)* | *1.65* | *1.50* |

5th Children and Youths Spartakiad.

Map of Europe A508

**1975, July 30 Photo. *Perf. 13***

| | | | | |
|---|---|---|---|---|
| **1669** | A508 | 20pf multicolored | .50 | .25 |

European Security and Cooperation Conference, Helsinki, July 30-Aug. 1.

China Aster — A509

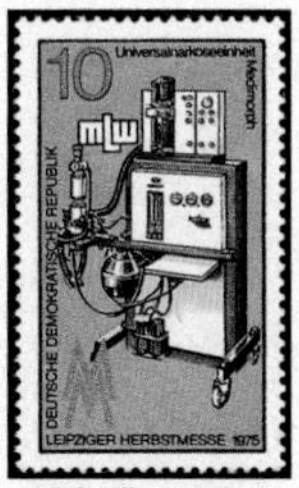


Medimorph Anesthesia Unit — A510

**1975, Aug. 19 Photo. *Perf. 13½x14***

| | | | | |
|---|---|---|---|---|
| **1670** | A509 | 5pf shown | .25 | .25 |
| **1671** | A509 | 10pf Geranium | .25 | .25 |
| **1672** | A509 | 20pf Transvaal daisies | .25 | .25 |
| **1673** | A509 | 25pf Carnation | .25 | .25 |
| **1674** | A509 | 35pf Chrysanthemum | .25 | .25 |
| **1675** | A509 | 70pf Pansies | *2.10* | *1.90* |
| | | *Nos. 1670-1675 (6)* | *3.35* | *3.15* |

**1975, Aug. 28 *Perf. 14***

Leipzig Fall Fair: 25pf, Motorcycle, type MZ TS 250, horiz.

| | | | | |
|---|---|---|---|---|
| **1676** | A510 | 10pf multicolored | .25 | .25 |
| **1677** | A510 | 25pf yellow & multi | .40 | .25 |

Children and Child Crossing Guard A511

Designs: 15pf, Traffic policewoman. 20pf, Policeman helping, motorist. 25pf, Motor vehicle inspection. 35pf, Volunteer instructor.

**1975, Sept. 9 Litho. *Perf. 13x12½***

| | | | | |
|---|---|---|---|---|
| **1678** | A511 | 10pf multicolored | .25 | .25 |
| **1679** | A511 | 15pf green & multi | *1.25* | *.70* |
| **1680** | A511 | 20pf brown & multi | .25 | .25 |
| **1681** | A511 | 25pf violet & multi | .25 | .25 |
| **1682** | A511 | 35pf multicolored | .25 | .25 |
| | | *Nos. 1678-1682 (5)* | *2.25* | *1.70* |

Traffic police serving and instructing the public.

Soyuz Take-off — A512

Designs: 20pf, Soyuz and Apollo in space. 70pf, Spacecraft after link-up, horiz., 79x28mm.

***Perf. 14x13½, 13½x14***

**1975, Sept. 15 Photo.**

**1683** A512 10pf multicolored .25 .25
**1684** A512 20pf multicolored .25 .25
**1685** A512 70pf multicolored 1.60 1.40
*Nos. 1683-1685 (3)* *2.10 1.90*

Apollo Soyuz space test project (Russo-American space cooperation), launching July 15; link-up, July 17.

Weimar, 1630, after Merian — A513

Designs: 20pf, Buchenwald Liberation Monument, vert. 35pf, Composite view of old and new buildings in Weimar.

**1975, Sept. 23 Litho. *Perf. 13½x13***

**1686** A513 10pf green, gray & blk .25 .25
**1687** A513 20pf red & multi .25 .25
**1688** A513 35pf ultra & multi *.45 .45*
*Nos. 1686-1688 (3)* *.95 .95*

Millennium of Weimar.

Monument, Vienna — A514

**1975, Oct. 14 Photo. *Perf. 14x13½***

**1689** A514 35pf red & multi .60 .25

Memorial for the victims of the struggle for a free Austria, 1934-1945.

Louis Braille and Dots — A515

Designs: 35pf, Hands reading Braille. 50pf, Eyeball and protective glasses.

**1975, Oct. 14**

**1690** A515 20pf gray & multi .25 .25
**1691** A515 35pf multicolored .25 .25
**1692** A515 50pf multicolored *1.50 1.20*
*Nos. 1690-1692 (3)* *2.00 1.70*

World Braille Year 1975. Sesquicentennial of the invention of Braille system of writing for the blind, by Louis Braille (1809-1852).

Post Office Bärenfels A516

**1975, Oct. 21 Photo. *Perf. 14***

**1693** A516 20pf multicolored .35 .25

Philatelists' Day 1975. See No. B177.

Emperor Ordering Clothes — A517

Designs: Scenes from "The Emperor's New Clothes," by Hans Christian Andersen and Andersen portrait.

**1975, Nov. 18 Litho. *Perf. 14x13***

**1694** A517 20pf ocher & multi *.40 .40*
**1695** A517 35pf ocher & multi *.65 .65*
**1696** A517 50pf ocher & multi *.40 .40*
*a.* Sheet of 3, #1694-1696 *2.25 2.25*

Tobogganing and Olympic Rings — A518

Olympic Rings and: 20pf, Speed-skating Rink, Berlin. 35pf, Figure-skating Hall, Karl-Marx Stadt. 70pf, Mass skiing at Schmiedefeld. 1m, Innsbruck & surrounding mountains.

**1975, Dec. 2 Photo. *Perf. 14***

**1697** A518 5pf multicolored .25 .25
**1698** A518 20pf olive & multi .25 .25
**1699** A518 35pf multicolored .25 .25
**1700** A518 70pf multicolored *1.60 1.50*
*Nos. 1697-1700,B178-B179 (6)* *2.85 2.75*

**Souvenir Sheet**

**1701** A518 1m ultra & multi *2.10 3.00*

12th Winter Olympic Games, Innsbruck, Austria, Feb. 4-15, 1976.

No. 1701 contains one 32x27mm stamp.

Pres. Wilhelm Pieck (1876-1960) A519

**1975, Dec. 30 Litho. *Perf. 13½x13***

**1702** A519 10pf lt ultra & blk .35 .25

Ernst Thälmann (1886-1944) A520

Labor Leaders: No. 1704, Georg Schumann (1886-1945). No. 1705, Wilhelm Koenen (1886-1963). No. 1706, John Schehr (1896-1934).

**1976, Jan. 13 *Perf. 13½x13***

**1703** A520 10pf rose & blk .25 .25
**1704** A520 10pf emerald & blk .25 .25
**1705** A520 10pf ocher & blk .25 .25
**1706** A520 10pf violet & blk .25 .25
*Nos. 1703-1706 (4)* *1.00 1.00*

See Nos. 1852-1854.

Silbermann Organ, Rötha — A521

Silbermann Organs: 20pf, Freiberg. 35pf, Fraureuth. 50pf, Dresden.

**1976, Jan. 27 Photo. *Perf. 14***

**1707** A521 10pf green & multi .25 .25
**1708** A521 20pf red & multi .25 .25
**1709** A521 35pf multicolored .25 .25
**1710** A521 50pf brown & multi *1.25 .80*
*Nos. 1707-1710 (4)* *2.00 1.55*

Organs built by Gottfried Silbermann (1683-1753).

Souvenir Sheet

Richard Sorge — A522

**1976, Feb. 3 Litho. *Imperf.***

**1711** A522 1m multicolored *2.00 3.50*

Dr. Richard Sorge (1895-1944), Soviet intelligence agent. No. 1711 contains one stamp with simulated perforations.

Military Flag, Sailor, Soldier, Aviator — A523

20pf, Military flag, ships, tanks, missile & planes.

**1976, Feb. 24 Litho. *Perf. 13½x14***

**1712** A523 10pf multicolored .25 .25
**1713** A523 20pf multicolored .30 .25

National People's Army, 20th anniversary.

Telephone A524

Apartment House, Leipzig A525

**1976, Mar. 2 *Perf. 13***

**1714** A524 20pf light blue .40 .25

Centenary of first telephone call by Alexander Graham Bell, March 10, 1876.

**1976, Mar. 9 Photo. *Perf. 14***

Design: 25pf, Ocean super trawler, horiz.

**1715** A525 10pf green & multi .25 .25
**1716** A525 25pf vio blue, blk & grn .35 .25

Leipzig Spring Fair.

Palace of the Republic — A526

**1976, Apr. 22 Photo. *Perf. 14***

**1717** A526 10pf vio blue & multi .70 .25

Inauguration of Palace of the Republic, Berlin. See No. 1721.

Post Office Radar Station — A527

**1976, Apr. 27 Photo. *Perf. 13½x14***

**1718** A527 20pf multicolored .40 .25

Intersputnik 1976.

Marx, Engels, Lenin and Party Flag — A528

20pf, New factories & apartment houses, party flag, horiz. 1m, Palace of the Republic.

**1976, May 11 *Perf. 14x13½, 13½x14***

**1719** A528 10pf dp mag, gold & red .25 .25
**1720** A528 20pf multicolored .25 .25

**Souvenir Sheet**

***Perf. 14***

**1721** A526 1m multicolored *1.50 2.50*

9th Congress of Unity Party (SED).

Peace Bicycle Race and Olympic Rings — A529

Designs: 20pf, Town and sport halls, Suhl. 25pf, Regatta course, Brandenburg. 70pf, 1500-meter race. 1m, Central Stadium, Leipzig.

**1976, May 18 Photo. *Perf. 13½x14***

**1722** A529 5pf green & multi .25 .25
**1723** A529 20pf blue & multi .25 .25
**1724** A529 25pf multicolored .25 .25
**1725** A529 70pf ultra & multi *2.00 1.75*
*Nos. 1722-1725,B180-B181 (6)* *3.25 3.00*

**Souvenir Sheet**

***Perf. 14***

**1726** A529 1m multicolored *1.60 2.50*

21st Olympic Games, Montreal, Canada, July 17-Aug. 1. No. 1726 contains one stamp (32x27mm).

Ribbons and Emblem A530

Design: 20pf, Young man and woman, industrial installations.

**1976, May 25 *Perf. 14***

**1727** A530 10pf blue & multi .25 .25
**1728** A530 20pf multicolored .25 .25

10th Parliamentary Meeting of the Free German Youth Organization.

Himantoglossum Hircinum — A531

Designs: European orchids.

**1976, June 15 Litho. *Perf. 12½x13***

| | | | | |
|---|---|---|---|---|
| **1729** | A531 | 10pf shown | .25 | .25 |
| **1730** | A531 | 20pf Dactylorhiza incarnata | .25 | .25 |
| **1731** | A531 | 25pf Anacamptis pyramidalis | .25 | .25 |
| **1732** | A531 | 35pf Dactylorhiza sambucina | .30 | .25 |
| **1733** | A531 | 40pf Orchis coriophora | .30 | .25 |
| **1734** | A531 | 50pf Cypripedium calceolus | 2.50 | 1.75 |
| | | *Nos. 1729-1734 (6)* | *3.85* | *3.00* |

Dancer at Rest, by Walter Arnold — A532

Small Sculptures: 10pf, Shetland Pony, by Heinrich Drake, horiz. 25pf, "At the Beach," by Ludwig Engelhardt. 35pf, Hermann Duncker, by Walter Howard. 50pf, "The Conversation," by Gustav Weidanz.

**1976, June 22 Photo. *Perf. 14***

| | | | | |
|---|---|---|---|---|
| **1735** | A532 | 10pf blk & bl grn | .25 | .25 |
| **1736** | A532 | 20pf ocher & blk | .25 | .25 |
| **1737** | A532 | 25pf ocher & blk | .25 | .25 |
| **1738** | A532 | 35pf yel grn & blk | .25 | .25 |
| **1739** | A532 | 50pf brick red & blk | 1.75 | 1.50 |
| | | *Nos. 1735-1739 (5)* | *2.75* | *2.50* |

Marx, Engels, Lenin, Red Flags, Berlin Buildings A533

**1976, June 29 Photo. *Perf. 14***

| | | | | |
|---|---|---|---|---|
| **1740** | A533 | 20pf blue, red & dk red | .40 | .25 |

European Communist Workers' Congress, Berlin.

Coronation Coach, 1790 — A534

Historic Coaches: 20pf, Open carriage, Russia, 1800. 25pf, Court landau, Saxony, 1840. 35pf, State carriage, Saxony, 1860. 40pf, Mail coach, 1850. 50pf, Town carriage, Saxony, 1889.

**1976, July 27**

| | | | | |
|---|---|---|---|---|
| **1741** | A534 | 10pf multicolored | .25 | .25 |
| **1742** | A534 | 20pf multicolored | .25 | .25 |
| **1743** | A534 | 25pf multicolored | .25 | .25 |
| **1744** | A534 | 35pf multicolored | .25 | .25 |
| **1745** | A534 | 40pf multicolored | .25 | .25 |
| **1746** | A534 | 50pf multicolored | 2.50 | 2.25 |
| | | *Nos. 1741-1746 (6)* | *3.75* | *3.50* |

View of Gera A535

Design: 10pf+5pf, View of Gera, c. 1652.

**1976, Aug. 5 Litho. *Perf. 13***

| | | | | |
|---|---|---|---|---|
| **1747** | A535 | 10pf + 5pf multi | .25 | .25 |
| **1748** | A535 | 20pf multicolored | .25 | .25 |
| *a.* | | Pair, #1747-1748 + label | 1.00 | .80 |

4th German Youth Philatelic Exhib., Gera.

Boxer — A536

Dogs: 10pf, Airedale terrier. 20pf, German shepherd. 25pf, Collie. 35pf, Giant schnauzer. 70pf, Great Dane.

**1976, Aug. 17 *Perf. 14***

| | | | | |
|---|---|---|---|---|
| **1749** | A536 | 5pf multicolored | .25 | .25 |
| **1750** | A536 | 10pf multicolored | .25 | .25 |
| **1751** | A536 | 20pf multicolored | .25 | .25 |
| **1752** | A536 | 25pf multicolored | .25 | .25 |
| **1753** | A536 | 35pf multicolored | .25 | .25 |
| **1754** | A536 | 70pf multicolored | 2.40 | 2.40 |
| | | *Nos. 1749-1754 (6)* | *3.65* | *3.65* |

Oil Distillery A537

Design: 25pf, German Library, Leipzig.

**1976, Sept. 1 *Perf. 13x12½***

| | | | | |
|---|---|---|---|---|
| **1755** | A537 | 10pf multicolored | .25 | .25 |
| **1756** | A537 | 25pf multicolored | .35 | .25 |

Leipzig Fall Fair.

Templin Lake Bridge — A538

Designs: 15pf, Overpass, Berlin-Adlergestell. 20pf, Elbe River Bridge, Rosslau. 25pf, Göltzschtal Viaduct. 35pf, Elbe River Bridge, Magdeburg. 50pf, Grosser Dreesch Overpass, Schwerin.

**1976, Sept. 21 Photo. *Perf. 14***

| | | | | |
|---|---|---|---|---|
| **1757** | A538 | 10pf multicolored | .25 | .25 |
| **1758** | A538 | 15pf multicolored | .25 | .25 |
| **1759** | A538 | 20pf multicolored | .25 | .25 |
| **1760** | A538 | 25pf multicolored | .25 | .25 |
| **1761** | A538 | 35pf multicolored | .25 | .25 |
| **1762** | A538 | 50pf multicolored | 1.60 | 1.60 |
| | | *Nos. 1757-1762 (6)* | *2.85* | *2.85* |

Memorial Monument (detail), Budapest — A539

**1976, Oct. 5 Photo. *Perf. 14***

| | | | | |
|---|---|---|---|---|
| **1763** | A539 | 35pf tan & multi | .60 | .30 |

Memorial to World War II victims.

Brass Jug, c. 1500 — A540

Artistic Handicraft Works: 20pf, Faience vase with lid, c. 1710. 25pf, Porcelain centerpiece (woman carrying bowl), c. 1768. 35pf, Porter, gilded silver, c. 1700. 70pf, Art Nouveau glass vase, c. 1900.

**1976, Oct. 19**

| | | | | |
|---|---|---|---|---|
| **1764** | A540 | 10pf dk car & multi | .25 | .25 |
| **1765** | A540 | 20pf ultra & multi | .25 | .25 |
| **1766** | A540 | 25pf green & multi | .25 | .25 |
| **1767** | A540 | 35pf vio blue & multi | .25 | .25 |
| **1768** | A540 | 70pf red brn & multi | 1.75 | 1.75 |
| | | *Nos. 1764-1768 (5)* | *2.75* | *2.75* |

Guppy A541

Designs: Various guppies.

**1976, Nov. 9 Litho. *Perf. 13½x13***

| | | | | |
|---|---|---|---|---|
| **1769** | A541 | 10pf multicolored | .25 | .25 |
| **1770** | A541 | 15pf multicolored | .25 | .25 |
| **1771** | A541 | 20pf multicolored | .25 | .25 |
| **1772** | A541 | 25pf multicolored | .25 | .25 |
| **1773** | A541 | 35pf multicolored | .25 | .25 |
| **1774** | A541 | 70pf multicolored | 1.80 | 1.60 |
| | | *Nos. 1769-1774 (6)* | *3.05* | *2.85* |

Vessels, c. 3000 B.C. — A542

20pf, Cult cart, c. 1300 B.C. 25pf, Roman gold coin, 270-273 A.D. 35pf, Gold pendant, 950 A.D. 70pf, Glass cup, 3rd cent. A.D.

**1976, Nov. 23 Photo. *Perf. 13***

| | | | | |
|---|---|---|---|---|
| **1775** | A542 | 10pf multicolored | .25 | .25 |
| **1776** | A542 | 20pf multicolored | .25 | .25 |
| **1777** | A542 | 25pf multicolored | .25 | .25 |
| **1778** | A542 | 35pf multicolored | .25 | .25 |
| **1779** | A542 | 70pf multicolored | 1.75 | 1.75 |
| | | *Nos. 1775-1779 (5)* | *2.75* | *2.75* |

Archaeological finds in DDR.

"Air," by Rosalba Carriera — A543

Paintings, Dresden Museum: 15pf, Virgin and Child, by Murillo. 20pf, Woman Viola da Gamba Player, by Bernardo Strozzi. 25pf, Ariadne Forsaken, by Angelica Kauffmann. 35pf, Old Man with Black Cap, by Bartolomeo Nazzari. 70pf, Officer Reading a Letter, by Gerard Terborch.

**1976, Dec. 14 Photo. *Perf. 13½x14***

| | | | | |
|---|---|---|---|---|
| **1780** | A543 | 10pf multicolored | .25 | .25 |
| **1781** | A543 | 15pf multicolored | .25 | .25 |
| **1782** | A543 | 20pf multicolored | .25 | .25 |
| **1783** | A543 | 25pf multicolored | .25 | .25 |
| **1784** | A543 | 35pf multicolored | .25 | .25 |
| **1785** | A543 | 70pf multicolored | 1.90 | 1.50 |
| | | *Nos. 1780-1785 (6)* | *3.15* | *2.75* |

Rumpelstiltskin and King — A544

Scenes from fairy tale "Rumpel-stiltskin."

**1976, Dec. 14 Litho. *Perf. 13***

| | | | | |
|---|---|---|---|---|
| **1786** | A544 | 5pf multicolored | .25 | .25 |
| **1787** | A544 | 10pf multicolored | .55 | .55 |
| **1788** | A544 | 15pf multicolored | .25 | .25 |
| **1789** | A544 | 20pf multicolored | .25 | .25 |
| **1790** | A544 | 25pf multicolored | .55 | .55 |
| **1791** | A544 | 30pf multicolored | .25 | .25 |
| *a.* | | Sheet of 6, #1786-1791 | 2.60 | 2.60 |

Arnold Zweig and Quotation A545

Designs: 20pf, Otto von Guericke and Magdeburg hemispheres. 35pf, Albrecht D. Thaer, wheat, plow and sheep. 40pf, Gustav Hertz and diagram of separation of isotopes.

**1977, Feb. 8 Litho. *Perf. 13x12½***

| | | | | |
|---|---|---|---|---|
| **1792** | A545 | 10pf rose & blk | .25 | .25 |
| **1793** | A545 | 20pf gray & blk | .25 | .25 |
| **1794** | A545 | 35pf lt green & blk | .25 | .25 |
| **1795** | A545 | 40pf blue & blk | .80 | .80 |
| | | *Nos. 1792-1795 (4)* | *1.55* | *1.55* |

Zweig (1887-1968), novelist; von Guericke (1602-86), physicist; Thaer (1752-1828), agronomist & physician; Hertz (1887-1975), physicist.

Spring near Plaue — A546

Natural Monuments: 20pf, Small Organ, Johnsdorf. 25pf, Ivenacker Oaks, Reuterstadt. 35pf, Stone Rose, Saalburg. 50pf, Rauenscher Stein (boulder), Furstenwalde.

**1977, Feb. 24 Litho. *Perf. 12½x13***

| | | | | |
|---|---|---|---|---|
| **1796** | A546 | 10pf multicolored | .25 | .25 |
| **1797** | A546 | 20pf multicolored | .25 | .25 |
| **1798** | A546 | 25pf multicolored | .25 | .25 |
| **1799** | A546 | 35pf multicolored | .25 | .25 |
| **1800** | A546 | 50pf multicolored | 1.20 | 1.20 |
| | | *Nos. 1796-1800 (5)* | *2.20* | *2.20* |

Fair Building, Book Fair A547

Leipzig Spring Fair: 25pf, Wide aluminum roll casting machine, Nachterstedt factory.

**1977, Mar. 8 Photo. *Perf. 14***

| | | | | |
|---|---|---|---|---|
| **1801** | A547 | 10pf multicolored | .25 | .25 |
| **1802** | A547 | 25pf multicolored | .25 | .25 |

Costume Senftenberg A548

Start after Wheel Change A549

Sorbian Costumes from: 20pf, Bautzen. 25pf, Klitten. 35pf, Nochten. 70pf, Muskau.

**1977, Mar. 22**

| | | | | |
|---|---|---|---|---|
| **1803** | A548 | 10pf multicolored | .25 | .25 |
| **1804** | A548 | 20pf multicolored | .25 | .25 |
| **1805** | A548 | 25pf multicolored | .25 | .25 |
| **1806** | A548 | 35pf multicolored | .25 | .25 |
| **1807** | A548 | 70pf multicolored | 2.00 | 1.60 |
| | | *Nos. 1803-1807 (5)* | 3.00 | 2.60 |

**1977, Apr. 19 Photo. *Perf. 14***

Designs: 20pf, Sprint. 35pf, At finish line.

| | | | | |
|---|---|---|---|---|
| **1808** | A549 | 10pf multicolored | .25 | .25 |
| **1809** | A549 | 20pf multicolored | .25 | .25 |
| **1810** | A549 | 35pf multicolored | .25 | .25 |
| *a.* | | Strip of 3, #1808-1810 | 1.30 | 1.30 |

30th International Peace Bicycling Race.

Carl Friedrich Gauss A550

**1977, Apr. 19 Litho. *Perf. 13x12½***

| | | | | |
|---|---|---|---|---|
| **1811** | A550 | 20pf lt ultra & blk | .65 | .25 |

Carl Friedrich Gauss (1777-1855), mathematician, 200th birth anniversary.

Flags and Handshake A551

**1977, May 3 Photo. *Perf. 13***

| | | | | |
|---|---|---|---|---|
| **1812** | A551 | 20pf vio bl & multi | .40 | .25 |

9th German Trade Union Congress, Berlin.

VKM Channel Converter, Filter and ITU Emblem — A552

**1977, May 17 Litho. *Perf. 14***

| | | | | |
|---|---|---|---|---|
| **1813** | A552 | 20pf multicolored | .45 | .25 |

International Telecommunications Day.

Pistol Shooting A553

Designs: 20pf, Deep-sea diver. 35pf, Radio controlled model boat.

**1977, May 17 Photo.**

| | | | | |
|---|---|---|---|---|
| **1814** | A553 | 10pf lt green & multi | .25 | .25 |
| **1815** | A553 | 20pf lt blue & multi | .25 | .25 |
| **1816** | A553 | 35pf salmon & multi | .70 | .70 |
| | | *Nos. 1814-1816 (3)* | 1.20 | 1.20 |

Organization for Physical and Technical Training.

Accordion, c. 1900 — A554

Designs: 20pf, Treble viola da gamba, 1747. 25pf, Oboe, 1785, Clarinet, 1830 and flute, 1817. 35pf, Concert zither, 1891. 70pf, Trumpet, 1860.

**1977, June 14**

| | | | | |
|---|---|---|---|---|
| **1817** | A554 | 10pf multicolored | .25 | .25 |
| **1818** | A554 | 20pf multicolored | .25 | .25 |
| **1819** | A554 | 25pf multicolored | .25 | .25 |
| **1820** | A554 | 35pf multicolored | .25 | .25 |
| **1821** | A554 | 70pf multicolored | 2.00 | 2.00 |
| | | *Nos. 1817-1821 (5)* | 3.00 | 3.00 |

Vogtland musical instruments from Markneukirchen Museum.

Mercury and Argus, by Rubens — A555

Rubens Paintings in Dresden Gallery: 10pf, Bath of Bathsheba, vert. 20pf, The Drunk Hercules, vert. 25pf, Diana Returning from the Hunt. 35pf, Old Woman with Brazier, vert. 50pf, Leda and the Swan.

**1977, June 28 Photo. *Perf. 14***

| | | | | |
|---|---|---|---|---|
| **1822** | A555 | 10pf multicolored | .25 | .25 |
| **1823** | A555 | 15pf multicolored | .25 | .25 |
| **1824** | A555 | 20pf multicolored | .25 | .25 |
| **1825** | A555 | 25pf multicolored | .25 | .25 |
| **1826** | A555 | 35pf multicolored | .25 | .25 |
| **1827** | A555 | 50pf multicolored | 3.25 | 2.25 |
| | | *Nos. 1822-1827 (6)* | 4.50 | 3.50 |

Peter Paul Rubens (1577-1640), Flemish painter, 400th birth anniversary.

Souvenir Sheet

Wreath, Flags of USSR and DDR — A556

**1977, June 28**

| | | | | |
|---|---|---|---|---|
| **1828** | A556 | 50pf multicolored | 1.25 | 2.00 |

Soc. for German-Soviet Friendship, 30th anniv.

Tractor with Plow — A557

Designs: 20pf, Fertilizer-spreader. 25pf, Potato digger and loader. 35pf, High-pressure harvester. 50pf, Rotating milking machine.

**1977, July 12 Litho. *Perf. 13x12½***

| | | | | |
|---|---|---|---|---|
| **1829** | A557 | 10pf multicolored | .25 | .25 |
| **1830** | A557 | 20pf multicolored | .25 | .25 |
| **1831** | A557 | 25pf multicolored | .25 | .25 |
| **1832** | A557 | 35pf multicolored | .25 | .25 |
| **1833** | A557 | 50pf multicolored | 1.75 | 1.60 |
| | | *Nos. 1829-1833 (5)* | 2.75 | 2.60 |

Motorized modern agriculture.

High Jump A558

Designs: 20pf, Hurdles, girls. 35pf, Dancing. 40pf, Torch bearer and flags.

**1977, July 19**

| | | | | |
|---|---|---|---|---|
| **1834** | A558 | 5pf red & multi | .25 | .25 |
| **1835** | A558 | 20pf lt green & multi | .25 | .25 |
| **1836** | A558 | 35pf green & multi | .25 | .25 |
| **1837** | A558 | 40pf blue & multi | 1.60 | 1.60 |
| | | *Nos. 1834-1837,B183-B184 (4)* | 2.35 | 2.35 |

6th Gymnastics and Sports Festival and 6th Children's and Youth Spartacist Games.

"Bread for all" by Wolfram Schubert A559

Konsument Department Store, Leipzig A560

Design: 25pf, "When Communists Dream," by Walter Womacka (detail) and Sozphilex emblem.

**1977, Aug. 16 Photo. *Perf. 14***

| | | | | |
|---|---|---|---|---|
| **1838** | A559 | 10pf multicolored | .25 | .25 |
| *a.* | | Souvenir sheet of 4 | 1.10 | .95 |
| **1839** | A559 | 25pf multicolored | .45 | .35 |
| *a.* | | Souvenir sheet of 4 | 2.10 | 2.00 |

SOZPHILEX '77 Philatelic Exhibition, Berlin, Aug. 19-28. See No. B185.

**1977, Aug. 30**

Design: 25pf, Glasses and wooden plate.

| | | | | |
|---|---|---|---|---|
| **1840** | A560 | 10pf blue & multi | .30 | .25 |
| **1841** | A560 | 25pf multicolored | .30 | .25 |

Leipzig Fall Fair.

Souvenir Sheet

Dzerzhinski and Quotation from Mayakovsky — A561

**1977, Sept. 6 Litho. *Perf. 12½x13***

| | | | | |
|---|---|---|---|---|
| **1842** | A561 | Sheet of 2 | 1.50 | 3.00 |
| *a.* | | 20pf multicolored | .45 | .70 |
| *b.* | | 35pf multicolored | .45 | 1.00 |

Feliks E. Dzerzhinski (1877-1926), organizer and head of Russian Secret Police (Cheka), birth centenary.

Muldenthal Locomotive, 1861 — A562

Designs: 10pf, Trolley car, Dresden, 1896. 20pf, First successful German plane, 1909. 25pf, 3-wheel car "Phäno-mobile," 1924. 35pf, Passenger steamship on the Elbe, 1837.

**1977, Sept. 13 Photo. *Perf. 14***

| | | | | |
|---|---|---|---|---|
| **1843** | A562 | 5pf green & multi | .25 | .25 |
| **1844** | A562 | 10pf green & multi | .25 | .25 |
| **1845** | A562 | 20pf green & multi | .25 | .25 |
| **1846** | A562 | 25pf green & multi | .25 | .25 |
| **1847** | A562 | 35pf green & multi | 2.25 | 1.75 |
| | | *Nos. 1843-1847 (5)* | 3.25 | 2.75 |

Transportation Museum, Dresden.

Cruiser "Aurora" A563

Designs: 25pf, Storming of the Winter Palace. 1m, Lenin, vert.

**1977, Sept. 20**

| | | | | |
|---|---|---|---|---|
| **1848** | A563 | 10pf multicolored | .30 | .25 |
| **1849** | A563 | 25pf multicolored | .50 | .40 |

**Souvenir Sheet**

***Perf. 12½x13***

| | | | | |
|---|---|---|---|---|
| **1850** | A563 | 1m carmine & blk | 2.25 | 3.00 |

60th anniversary of the Russian Revolution.

Mother Russia and Obelisk — A564

**1977, Sept. 20 Litho. *Perf. 14***

| | | | | |
|---|---|---|---|---|
| **1851** | A564 | 35pf multicolored | .45 | .25 |

Soviet soldiers' memorial, Berlin-Schönholz.

**Labor Leaders Type of 1976**

Portraits: No. 1852, Ernst Meyer (1887-1930). No. 1853, August Fröhlich (1877-1966). No. 1854, Gerhart Eisler (1897-1968).

**1977, Oct. 18 Litho. *Perf. 14***

| | | | | |
|---|---|---|---|---|
| **1852** | A520 | 10pf olive & brown | .25 | .25 |
| **1853** | A520 | 10pf rose & brown | .25 | .25 |
| **1854** | A520 | 10pf lt blue & blk brn | .25 | .25 |
| | | *Nos. 1852-1854 (3)* | .75 | .75 |

Souvenir Sheet

Heinrich von Kleist, by Peter Friedl, 1801 — A565

**1977, Oct. 18**

| | | | | |
|---|---|---|---|---|
| **1855** | A565 | 1m multicolored | 2.60 | 3.00 |

Heinrich von Kleist (1777-1811), poet and playwright, birth bicentenary.

Rocket A566

Design: 20pf, as 10pf, design reversed.

**1977, Nov. 8 Photo. *Perf. 14***

| | | | | |
|---|---|---|---|---|
| **1856** | A566 | 10pf red, blk & sil | *.25* | *.25* |
| **1857** | A566 | 20pf ultra, blk & gold | *.25* | *.25* |
| *a.* | | Pair, #1856-1857 + label | *.90* | *.90* |

20th Central Young Craftsmen's Exhibition (Masters of Tomorrow).

A567

A568

Hunting in East Germany: 10pf, Mouflons. 15pf, Red deer. 20pf, Retriever with pheasant, hunter. 25pf, Red fox, wild duck. 35pf, Tractor driver saving fawn. 70pf, Wild boars.

**1977, Nov. 15**

| | | | | |
|---|---|---|---|---|
| **1858** | A567 | 10pf multicolored | .25 | .25 |
| **1859** | A567 | 15pf multicolored | 2.00 | 2.00 |
| **1860** | A567 | 20pf multicolored | .25 | .25 |
| **1861** | A567 | 25pf multicolored | .25 | .25 |
| **1862** | A567 | 35pf multicolored | .25 | .25 |
| **1863** | A567 | 70pf multicolored | .30 | .25 |
| | | *Nos. 1858-1863 (6)* | *3.30* | *3.25* |

**1977, Nov. 22 Litho. *Perf. 14***

Firemen's Activities: 10pf, Firemen racing with ladders. 20pf, Children Visiting Firehouse. 25pf, Fire engines fighting forest and brush fires. 35pf, Artificial respiration. 50pf, Fireboat alongside freighter.

| | | | | |
|---|---|---|---|---|
| **1864** | A568 | 10pf multi, horiz. | .25 | .25 |
| **1865** | A568 | 20pf multi | .25 | .25 |
| **1866** | A568 | 25pf multi, horiz. | .25 | .25 |
| **1867** | A568 | 35pf multi | .25 | .25 |
| **1868** | A568 | 50pf multi, horiz. | 2.00 | 2.00 |
| | | *Nos. 1864-1868 (5)* | *3.00* | *3.00* |

Knight and King — A569

Designs: Various scenes from fairytale: "Six Men Around the World."

**1977, Nov. 22 *Perf. 13x13½***

| | | | | |
|---|---|---|---|---|
| **1869** | A569 | 5pf black & multi | .25 | .25 |
| **1870** | A569 | 10pf black & multi | .70 | .70 |
| **1871** | A569 | 20pf black & multi | .25 | .25 |
| **1872** | A569 | 25pf black & multi | .25 | .25 |
| **1873** | A569 | 35pf black & multi | .70 | .70 |
| **1874** | A569 | 60pf black & multi | .25 | .25 |
| *a.* | | Sheet of 6, #1869-1874 | 5.00 | 3.25 |

Hips and Dog Rose A570

Medicinal Plants: 15pf, Birch. 20pf, Chamomile. 25pf, Coltsfoot. 35pf, Linden. 50pf, Elder.

**1978, Jan. 10 Photo. *Perf. 14***

| | | | | |
|---|---|---|---|---|
| **1875** | A570 | 10pf multicolored | .25 | .25 |
| **1876** | A570 | 15pf multicolored | .25 | .25 |
| **1877** | A570 | 20pf multicolored | .25 | .25 |
| **1878** | A570 | 25pf multicolored | .25 | .25 |
| **1879** | A570 | 35pf multicolored | .25 | .25 |
| **1880** | A570 | 50pf multicolored | 2.00 | 2.00 |
| | | *Nos. 1875-1880 (6)* | *3.25* | *3.25* |

Amilcar Cabral — A571

**1978, Jan. 17 Litho. *Perf. 14***

| | | | | |
|---|---|---|---|---|
| **1881** | A571 | 20pf multicolored | .35 | .30 |

Amilcar Cabral (1924-1973), freedom movement leader from Guinea-Bissau.

Town Hall, Suhl-Heinrichs A572

Half-timbered Buildings, 17th-18th Centuries: 20pf, Farmhouse, Niederoderwitz. 25pf, Farmhouse, Strassen. 35pf, Townhouse, Quedlinburg. 40pf, Townhouse, Eisenach.

**1978, Jan. 24 Photo. *Perf. 14***

| | | | | |
|---|---|---|---|---|
| **1882** | A572 | 10pf multicolored | .25 | .25 |
| **1883** | A572 | 20pf multicolored | .25 | .25 |
| **1884** | A572 | 25pf multicolored | .25 | .25 |
| **1885** | A572 | 35pf multicolored | .25 | .25 |
| **1886** | A572 | 40pf multicolored | 1.80 | 1.80 |
| | | *Nos. 1882-1886 (5)* | *2.80* | *2.80* |

Mail Truck, 1921 A573

Past and Present Mail Transport: 20pf, Mail truck, 1978. 25pf, Railroad mail car, 1896. 35pf, Railroad mail car, 1978.

**1978, Feb. 9 Litho. *Perf. 13x12½***

| | | | | |
|---|---|---|---|---|
| **1887** | A573 | 10pf brown & multi | .25 | .25 |
| **1888** | A573 | 20pf brown & multi | .40 | .40 |
| **1889** | A573 | 25pf brown & multi | .45 | .45 |
| **1890** | A573 | 35pf brown & multi | .65 | .65 |
| *a.* | | Block of 4, #1887-1890 | 2.40 | 2.40 |

Earring, 11th Century — A574

Archaeological Artifacts: 20pf, Earring, 10th century. 25pf, Bronze sheath, 10th century. 35pf, Bronze horse, 12th century. 70pf, Arabian coin, 8th century.

**1978, Feb. 21 Photo. *Perf. 14***

| | | | | |
|---|---|---|---|---|
| **1891** | A574 | 10pf multicolored | .25 | .25 |
| **1892** | A574 | 20pf multicolored | .25 | .25 |
| **1893** | A574 | 25pf multicolored | .25 | .25 |
| **1894** | A574 | 35pf multicolored | .25 | .25 |
| **1895** | A574 | 70pf multicolored | 1.50 | 1.50 |
| | | *Nos. 1891-1895 (5)* | *2.50* | *2.50* |

Treasures found on Slavic sites.

Royal House, Leipzig — A575

Leipzig Spring Fair: 25pf, Universal measuring instrument by Carl Zeiss.

**1978, Mar. 7**

| | | | | |
|---|---|---|---|---|
| **1896** | A575 | 10pf multicolored | .25 | .25 |
| **1897** | A575 | 25pf multicolored | .35 | .30 |

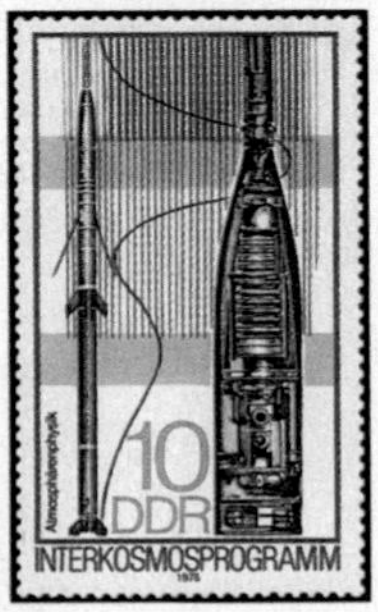

M-100 Meteorological Rocket — A576

Designs: 20pf, Intercosmos I satellite. 35pf, Meteor satellite with spectometric complex. 1m, MFK-6 multi-spectral camera over city.

**1978, Mar. 21 Photo. *Perf. 14x13½***

| | | | | |
|---|---|---|---|---|
| **1898** | A576 | 10pf multicolored | .25 | .25 |
| **1899** | A576 | 20pf multicolored | .25 | .25 |
| **1900** | A576 | 35pf multicolored | .90 | .90 |
| | | *Nos. 1898-1900 (3)* | *1.40* | *1.40* |

**Souvenir Sheet**

| | | | | |
|---|---|---|---|---|
| **1901** | A576 | 1m multicolored | *2.40* | *3.25* |

Achievements in atmospheric and space research.

Samuel Heinicke, Leipzig, c. 1800 A577

25pf, Deaf child learning sign language.

**1978, Apr. 4 Litho. *Perf. 13x12½***

| | | | | |
|---|---|---|---|---|
| **1902** | A577 | 20pf multicolored | .25 | .25 |
| **1903** | A577 | 25pf multicolored | *.65* | *.65* |

National Institute for the Education of the Deaf, established by Samuel Heinicke, 200th anniversary.

Radio Tower, Dequede, TV Truck — A578

Design: 20pf, TV equipment and tower, vert.

**1978, Apr. 25 *Perf. 13½x14, 14x13½***

| | | | | |
|---|---|---|---|---|
| **1904** | A578 | 10pf multicolored | .25 | .25 |
| **1905** | A578 | 20pf multicolored | *.25* | *.25* |

World Telecommunications Day.

Saxon Miner, 19th Century — A579

Dress Uniforms, 19th Century: 20pf, Foundry worker, Freiberg. 25pf, Mining Academy student. 35pf, Chief Inspector of Mines.

**1978, May 9 *Perf. 12½x13***

| | | | | |
|---|---|---|---|---|
| **1906** | A579 | 10pf silver & multi | .25 | .25 |
| **1907** | A579 | 20pf silver & multi | .25 | .25 |
| **1908** | A579 | 25pf silver & multi | .25 | .25 |
| **1909** | A579 | 35pf silver & multi | *1.10* | *.90* |
| | | *Nos. 1906-1909 (4)* | *1.85* | *1.65* |

Lion Cub — A580

Young Animals: 20pf, Leopard. 35pf, Tiger. 50pf, Snow leopard.

**1978, May 23 Photo. *Perf. 14***

| | | | | |
|---|---|---|---|---|
| **1910** | A580 | 10pf multicolored | .25 | .25 |
| **1911** | A580 | 20pf multicolored | .25 | .25 |
| **1912** | A580 | 35pf multicolored | .25 | .25 |
| **1913** | A580 | 50pf multicolored | *1.25* | *1.25* |
| | | *Nos. 1910-1913 (4)* | *2.00* | *2.00* |

Centenary of Leipzig Zoo.

Loading Container — A581

Designs: 20pf, Loading container on flatbed truck. 35pf, Container trains in terminal. 70pf, Loading container on ship.

**1978, June 13 Litho. *Perf. 12½x13***

| | | | | |
|---|---|---|---|---|
| **1914** | A581 | 10pf multicolored | .25 | .25 |
| **1915** | A581 | 20pf multicolored | .25 | .25 |
| **1916** | A581 | 35pf multicolored | .25 | .25 |
| **1917** | A581 | 70pf multicolored | *1.60* | *1.50* |
| | | *Nos. 1914-1917 (4)* | *2.35* | *2.25* |

Ceramic Bull — A582

Designs: 10pf, Woman's head, ceramic. 20pf, Gold armband, horiz. 25pf, Animal head, gold ring. 35pf, Seated family from signet ring. 40pf, Necklace, horiz.

***Perf. 14x13½, 13½x14***

**1978, June 20 Photo.**

| | | | | |
|---|---|---|---|---|
| **1918** | A582 | 5pf multicolored | .25 | .25 |
| **1919** | A582 | 10pf multicolored | .25 | .25 |
| **1920** | A582 | 20pf multicolored | .25 | .25 |
| **1921** | A582 | 25pf multicolored | .25 | .25 |
| **1922** | A582 | 35pf multicolored | .25 | .25 |
| **1923** | A582 | 40pf multicolored | *1.10* | *1.10* |
| | | *Nos. 1918-1923 (6)* | *2.35* | *2.35* |

African art from 1st and 2nd centuries in Berlin and Leipzig Egyptian museums.

Old and New Buildings, Cottbus — A583

Design: 10pf + 5pf, View of Cottbus, 1730.

**1978, July 18 Litho. *Perf. 13x12½***

| | | | |
|---|---|---|---|
| **1924** | 10pf + 5pf multi | *.25* | *.25* |
| **1925** | 20pf multicolored | *.25* | *.25* |
| *a.* | A583 Pair, #1924-1925 + label | *.65* | *.65* |

5th Youth Philatelic Exhibition, Cottbus.

Justus von Liebig, Wheat and Retort A584

Famous Germans: 10pf, Joseph Dietzgen (1828-1888) and title page. 15pf, Alfred Döblin (1878-1957) and title page. 20pf, Hans Loch (1898-1960) and signature, president of Liberal Democratic Party. 25pf, Dr. Theodor Brugsch (1878-1963), and blood circulation. 35pf, Friedrich Ludwig Jahn (1778-1852) and gymnast. 70pf, Dr. Albrecht von Graefe (1828-1870) and ophthalmological instruments.

Memorial Monument, Nordhausen A621

**1979, Aug. 28 Photo. *Perf. 14***
**2037** A621 35pf dull vio & blk .40 .30

Memorial to World War II victims.

Teddy Bear — A622

Leipzig Autumn Fair: 25pf, Grosser Blumenberg (building), Leipzig, horiz.

**1979, Aug. 28**
**2038** A622 10pf multicolored .25 .25
**2039** A622 25pf multicolored *.25 .25*

Philipp Dengel (1888-1948) A623

Working-Class Movement Leaders: No. 2041, Heinrich Rau (1899-1961). No. 2042, Otto Buchwitz (1879-1964). No. 2043, Bernard Koenen (1889-1964).

**1979, Sept. 11 Litho.**
**2040** A623 10pf multicolored .25 .25
**2041** A623 10pf multicolored .25 .25
**2042** A623 10pf multicolored .25 .25
**2043** A623 10pf multicolored .25 .25
*Nos. 2040-2043 (4)* 1.00 1.00

See Nos. 2166-2169, 2249-2253, 2314-2318, 2390-2392, 2452-2454.

DDR Arms and Flag, Worker A624

DDR Arms, Flag and: 10pf, Young man and woman. 15pf, Soldiers. 20pf, Workers.

**1979, Oct. 2 Photo. *Perf. 13***
**2044** A624 5pf multicolored .25 .25
**2045** A624 10pf multicolored .25 .25
**2046** A624 15pf multicolored *.35 .35*
**2047** A624 20pf multicolored .25 .25
*Nos. 2044-2047 (4)* *1.10 1.10*

**Souvenir Sheet**

**2048** A624 1m multicolored *1.60 2.10*

DDR, 30th anniv. No. 2048 contains one stamp (33x55mm).

Woman Applying Make-Up, 1967 — A625

Meissen Porcelain and Hallmark, 18th-20th Centuries: 10pf, Altozier coffee pot. 15pf, "Grosser Ausschnitt" coffee pot, 1974. 20pf, Covered vase. 25pf, Parrot. 35pf, Harlequin drinking. 50pf, Woman selling flowers. 70pf, Sake bottle.

**1979, Nov. 6 Photo. *Perf. 14***
**2049** A625 5pf multicolored *.25 .25*
**2050** A625 10pf multicolored *.25 .25*
**2051** A625 15pf multicolored *.25 .25*
**2052** A625 20pf multicolored *.30 .30*
*a.* Block of 4, #2049-2052 *3.00 2.25*
**2053** A625 25pf multicolored *.35 .35*
**2054** A625 35pf multicolored *.60 .60*
**2055** A625 50pf multicolored *.85 .85*
**2056** A625 70pf multicolored *1.10 1.10*
*a.* Block of 4, #2053-2056 *6.00 5.50*

Rag Doll, 1800 — A626

Historic Dolls: 15pf, Ceramic, 1960. 20pf, Wooden, 1780. 35pf, Straw, 1900. 50pf, Jointed, 1800. 70pf, Tumbler, 1820.

**1979, Nov. 20 Litho.**
**2057** A626 10pf multicolored *.25 .25*
**2058** A626 15pf multicolored *.95 .95*
**2059** A626 20pf multicolored *.25 .25*
**2060** A626 35pf multicolored *.25 .25*
**2061** A626 50pf multicolored *.95 .95*
**2062** A626 70pf multicolored *.25 .25*
*a.* Sheet of 6, #2057-2062 *4.00 4.00*

Bobsledding, by Gunter Rechn, Olympic Rings — A627

Olympic Rings and: 20pf, Figure Skating, by Johanna Stake, vert. 35pf, Speed Skating, by Axel Wunsch, vert. 1m, Cross-country Skiing, by Lothar Zitzmann.

**1980, Jan. 15 Photo. *Perf. 14***
**2063** A627 10pf multicolored .25 .25
**2064** A627 20pf multicolored .25 .25
**2065** A627 35pf multicolored *1.10 1.00*
*Nos. 2063-2065,B189 (4)* *1.85 1.75*

**Souvenir Sheet**

**2066** A627 1m multicolored *3.00 3.50*

13th Winter Olympic Games, Lake Placid, NY, Feb. 12-24. No. 2066 contains one 29x23½mm stamp. See Nos. 2098-2099, 2119-2121, B189-B190, B192.

"Quiet Music," Grossedlitz — A628

Baroque Gardens: 20pf, Orange grove, Belvedere, Weimar. 50pf, Flower garden, Dornburg Castle. 70pf, Park, Rheinsberg Castle.

**1980, Jan. 29**
**2067** A628 10pf multicolored .25 .25
**2068** A628 20pf multicolored .25 .25
**2069** A628 50pf multicolored .25 .25
**2070** A628 70pf multicolored *1.50 1.50*
*Nos. 2067-2070 (4)* *2.25 2.25*

**Type of 1973**

Designs as before and: 10pf, Palace of the Republic, Berlin.

**1980-81 Engr. *Perf. 14***
**Size: 22x17mm**

**2071** A449 5pf blue green .25 .25
**2072** A449 10pf emerald .25 .25
**2073** A449 15pf rose lilac .35 .30
**2074** A449 20pf rose mag .45 .25
**2075** A449 25pf grnsh bl .35 .30
**2076** A449 30pf org ('81) .45 .30
**2077** A449 35pf blue .45 .30
**2078** A449 40pf dull vio .90 .50
**2079** A449 50pf blue .55 .30
**2080** A449 60pf lilac ('81) .55 .30
**2081** A449 70pf redsh brn ('81) .70 .60
**2082** A449 80pf vio bl ('81) .85 .50
**2083** A449 1m olive .90 .80
**2084** A449a 2m red 1.60 1.10
**2085** A449a 3m rose lil ('81) 2.60 1.40
*Nos. 2071-2085 (15)* 11.20 7.45

Cable-Laying Vehicle, Dish Antenna — A629

20pf, Radio tower, television screen.

**1980, Feb. 5 Photo.**
**2086** A629 10pf multicolored .25 .25
**2087** A629 20pf multicolored .25 .25

**Famous Germans Type of 1979**

Designs: 5pf, Johann Wolfgang Dobereiner (1780-1849), chemist. 10pf, Frederic Joliot-Curie (1900-1958), French physicist. 20pf, Johann Friedrich Naumann (1780-1857), ornithologist. 25pf, Alfred Wegener (1880-1930), geophysicist and meteorologist. 35pf, Carl von Clausewitz (1780-1831), Prussian major general. 70pf, Helene Weigel (1900-1971), actress.

**1980, Feb. 26 Litho. *Perf. 13x12½***
**2088** A604 5pf pale yel & blk .25 .25
**2089** A604 10pf multicolored .25 .25
**2090** A604 20pf lt yel grn & blk .25 .25
**2091** A604 25pf multicolored .25 .25
**2092** A604 35pf lt blue & blk .25 .25
**2093** A604 70pf lt red brn & blk *1.30 1.10*
*Nos. 2088-2093 (6)* *2.55 2.35*

Type ZT-303 Tractor A630

1980 Leipzig Spring Fair: 10pf, Karl Marx University, Leipzig, vert.

**1980, Mar. 4 Photo. *Perf. 14***
**2094** A630 10pf multicolored .25 .25
**2095** A630 25pf multicolored .30 .25

Werner Eggerath (1900-1977), Labor Leader — A631

**1980, Mar. 18 Litho.**
**2096** A631 10pf brick red & blk .40 .30

Souvenir Sheet

Cosmonauts, Salyut 6 and Soyuz — A632

**1980, Apr. 11 Litho. *Perf. 14***
**2097** A632 1m multicolored *2.00 3.00*

Intercosmos cooperative space program.

**Olympic Type of 1980**

Designs: 10pf, On the Bars, by Erich Wurzer. 50pf, Scull's Crew, by Wilfried Falkenthal.

**1980, Apr. 22 Photo. *Perf. 14***
**2098** A627 10pf multicolored .25 .25
**2099** A627 50pf multicolored *1.20 1.00*
*Nos. 2098-2099,B190 (3)* *1.70 1.50*

22nd Summer Olympic Games, Moscow, July 19-Aug. 3. See No. B190.

Flags of Member Countries A633

Bauhaus Cooperative Society Building, 1928, Gropius A634

**1980, May 13 Photo.**
**2100** A633 20pf multicolored .40 .25

Signing of Warsaw Pact (Bulgaria, Czechoslovakia, DDR, Hungary, Poland, Romania, USSR), 25th anniv.

**1980, May 27**

Bauhaus Architecture: 10pf, Socialists' Memorial, 1926, by Mies van der Rohe, horiz. 15pf, Monument, 1922, by William Gropius. 20pf, Steel building, 1926, by Muche and Paulick, horiz. 50pf, Trade-Union School, 1928, by Meyer. 70pf, Bauhaus Building, 1926, by Gropius, horiz.

**2101** A634 5pf multicolored .25 .25
**2102** A634 10pf multicolored .25 .25
**2103** A634 15pf multicolored .25 .25
**2104** A634 20pf multicolored .25 .25
**2105** A634 50pf multicolored .30 .25
**2106** A634 70pf multicolored *1.80 1.60*
*Nos. 2101-2106 (6)* *3.10 2.85*

Rostock View A635

**1980, June 10 Photo. *Perf. 14***
**2107** A635 10pf shown .25 .25
**2108** A635 20pf Dancers .30 .25

18th Workers' Festival, Rostock, June 27-29.

Dish Antenna, Interflug Airlines A636

**1980, June 10 Litho. *Perf. 13x12½***

| | | | | | |
|---|---|---|---|---|---|
| **2109** | A636 | 20pf shown | .30 | .30 |
| **2110** | A636 | 25pf Jet | .30 | .30 |
| **2111** | A636 | 35pf Agricultural plane | .45 | .45 |
| **2112** | A636 | 70pf Aerial photography | .90 | .90 |
| *a.* | | Block of 4, #2109-2112 | 3.00 | 3.00 |

Interflug Airlines. See No. B191

Okapi — A637

**1980, June 24 *Perf. 14***

| | | | | |
|---|---|---|---|---|
| **2113** | A637 5pf shown | .25 | .25 |
| **2114** | A637 10pf Red pandas | .25 | .25 |
| **2115** | A637 15pf Prairie wolf | .25 | .25 |
| **2116** | A637 20pf Arabian oryx | .25 | .25 |
| **2117** | A637 25pf White-eared pheasant | .25 | .25 |
| **2118** | A637 35pf Musk oxen | 1.60 | 1.60 |
| | *Nos. 2113-2118 (6)* | 2.85 | 2.85 |

### Olympic Type of 1980

Designs: 10pf, Judo, by Erhard Schmidt. 50pf, Final Spurt, by Siegfried Schreiber. 1m, Spinnaker Yachts, by Karl Raetsch.

**1980, July 8 Photo. *Perf. 14***

| | | | |
|---|---|---|---|
| **2119** | A627 10pf multicolored | .25 | .25 |
| **2120** | A627 50pf multicolored | 1.40 | 1.00 |
| | *Nos. 2119-2120,B192 (3)* | 1.90 | 1.50 |

**Souvenir Sheet**

| | | | |
|---|---|---|---|
| **2121** | A627 1m multicolored | 2.50 | 3.25 |

22nd Summer Olympic Games, Moscow, 7/19-8/3. #2121 contains one 29x24mm stamp.

Old and New Buildings, Suhl A638

Design: 10pf + 5pf, View of Suhl, 1700.

**1980, July 22 Litho. *Perf. 13x12½***

| | | | |
|---|---|---|---|
| **2122** | A638 10pf + 5pf multi | .30 | .30 |
| **2123** | A638 20pf multicolored | .30 | .30 |
| *a.* | Pair, #2122-2123 + label | 1.10 | 1.10 |

6th National Youth Philatelic Exhibition, Suhl. Surtax for East German Association of Philatelists.

Huntley Microscope, London, 1740 — A639

Optical Museum, Karl Zeiss Foundation, Jena: 25pf, Magny microscope, Paris, 1751. 35pf, Amici microscope, Modena, 1845. 70pf, Zeiss microscope, Jena, 1873.

**1980, Aug. 12 Photo. *Perf. 14***

| | | | |
|---|---|---|---|
| **2124** | A639 20pf multicolored | .30 | .30 |
| **2125** | A639 25pf multicolored | .30 | .30 |
| **2126** | A639 35pf multicolored | .55 | .55 |
| **2127** | A639 70pf multicolored | .75 | .75 |
| *a.* | Block of 4, #2124-2127 | 3.00 | 3.00 |

Maidenek Memorial — A640

**1980, Aug. 26**

| | | | |
|---|---|---|---|
| **2128** | A640 35pf multicolored | .65 | .30 |

Leipzig 1980 Autumn Fair, Information Center — A641

**1980, Aug. 26**

| | | | |
|---|---|---|---|
| **2129** | A641 10pf shown | .25 | .25 |
| **2130** | A641 25pf Carpet loom | .40 | .25 |

67th Interparliamentary Conference, Berlin — A642

**1980, Sept. 9 Photo. *Perf. 14***

| | | | |
|---|---|---|---|
| **2131** | A642 20pf Republic Palace, Berlin | .70 | .25 |

Paintings by Frans Hals (1580-1666) A643

**1980, Sept. 23**

| | | | |
|---|---|---|---|
| **2132** | A643 10pf *Laughing Boy with Flute* | .25 | .25 |
| **2133** | A643 20pf *Man in Gray Coat* | .25 | .25 |
| **2134** | A643 25pf *The Mulatto* | .25 | .25 |
| **2135** | A643 35pf *Man in Black Coat* | .90 | .90 |
| | *Nos. 2132-2135 (4)* | 1.65 | 1.65 |

**Souvenir Sheet**

| | | | |
|---|---|---|---|
| **2136** | A643 1m *Self-portrait, horiz.* | 2.00 | 3.25 |

A644

Edible Mushrooms: 5pf, Leccinum Testaceo Scabrum. 10pf, Boletus erythropus. 15pf, Agaricus campester. 20pf, Xerocomus badius. 35pf, Boletus edulis. 70pf, Cantharellus cibarius.

**1980, Oct. 28 Litho. *Perf. 13x13½***

| | | | |
|---|---|---|---|
| **2137** | A644 5pf multicolored | .25 | .25 |
| **2138** | A644 10pf multicolored | .25 | .25 |
| **2139** | A644 15pf multicolored | .25 | .25 |
| **2140** | A644 20pf multicolored | .25 | .25 |
| **2141** | A644 35pf multicolored | .25 | .25 |
| **2142** | A644 70pf multicolored | 1.75 | 1.60 |
| | *Nos. 2137-2142 (6)* | 3.00 | 2.85 |

Exploration of Lignite Deposits (Gravimetry) — A645

Geophysical Exploration: 25pf, Bore-hole measuring (water). 35pf, Seismic geology. (mineral oil, natural gas). 50pf, Seismology.

**1980, Nov. 11 Litho. *Perf. 13***

| | | | |
|---|---|---|---|
| **2143** | A645 20pf multicolored | .30 | .25 |
| **2144** | A645 25pf multicolored | .35 | .30 |
| **2145** | A645 35pf multicolored | .45 | .45 |
| **2146** | A645 50pf multicolored | .75 | .75 |
| *a.* | Block of 4, #2143-2146 | 3.00 | 2.40 |

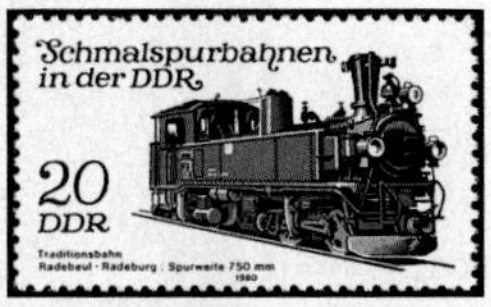


Radebeul-Radeburg Railroad Locomotive — A646

**1980, Nov. 25 *Perf. 13x12½***

| | | | |
|---|---|---|---|
| **2147** | Strip of 2 + label | 1.60 | 1.60 |
| *a.* | A646 20pf shown | .30 | .30 |
| *b.* | A646 25pf Passenger car | .30 | .30 |
| **2148** | Strip of 2 + label | 1.60 | 1.60 |
| *a.* | A646 20pf Bad Doberan-Osteebad Kuhlungsborn Locomotive | .30 | .30 |
| *b.* | A646 35pf Passenger car | .30 | .30 |

Labels show maps of routes and Moritzburg Castle (No. 2147), Bad Doberan Street (No. 2148).

See Nos. 2205-2206.

Toy Locomotive, 1850 — A647

**1980, Dec. 9 *Perf. 14***

| | | | |
|---|---|---|---|
| **2149** | Sheet of 6 | 3.75 | 3.75 |
| *a.* | A647 10pf shown | .30 | .30 |
| *b.* | A647 20pf Airplane, 1914 | .95 | .95 |
| *c.* | A647 25pf Steam roller, 1920 | .30 | .30 |
| *d.* | A647 35pf Ship, 1825 | .30 | .30 |
| *e.* | A647 40pf Car, 1900 | .95 | .95 |
| *f.* | A647 50pf Balloon, 1920 | .30 | .30 |

**Souvenir Sheet**

Wolfgang Amadeus Mozart, 225th Birth Anniv. — A648

**1981, Jan. 13 Litho.**

| | | | |
|---|---|---|---|
| **2150** | A648 1m multicolored | 2.40 | 3.00 |

St. John's Apple — A649

**1981, Jan. 13 Photo.**

| | | | |
|---|---|---|---|
| **2151** | A649 5pf shown | .25 | .25 |
| **2152** | A649 10pf Snow drop, horiz. | .25 | .25 |
| **2153** | A649 20pf Bladder bush | .25 | .25 |
| **2154** | A649 25pf Paulownia tomentose | .25 | .25 |
| **2155** | A649 35pf German honeysuckle, horiz. | .25 | .25 |
| **2156** | A649 50pf Genuine spice bush | 2.00 | 1.75 |
| | *Nos. 2151-2156 (6)* | 3.25 | 3.00 |

Heinrich von Stephan (1831-97), Founder of UPU — A650

**1981, Jan. 20 Litho. *Perf. 13x13½***

| | | | |
|---|---|---|---|
| **2157** | A650 10pf lt lemon & blk | .70 | .25 |

Dedication of National Commemorative Plaza, Sachsenhausen — A651

**1981, Jan. 27 Photo. *Perf. 14***

| | | | |
|---|---|---|---|
| **2158** | A651 10pf shown | .30 | .25 |
| **2159** | A651 20pf Changing of guard | .40 | .25 |

National People's Forces, 25th anniversary.

Socialist Union Party, 10th Congress — A652

**1981, Feb. 10**

| | | | |
|---|---|---|---|
| **2160** | A652 10pf multicolored | .40 | .25 |

Postal and Newspaper Apprentice Training — A653

**1981, Feb. 10 Litho.**

| | | | |
|---|---|---|---|
| **2161** | A653 5pf shown | .25 | .25 |
| **2162** | A653 10pf Telephone and telex service | .25 | .25 |
| **2163** | A653 15pf Radio communications | .25 | .25 |
| **2164** | A653 20pf School of Engineering, Leipzig | .25 | .25 |
| **2165** | A653 25pf Communications Academy, Dresden | 1.00 | .90 |
| | *Nos. 2161-2165 (5)* | 2.00 | 1.90 |

### Working-class Leader Type of 1979

Designs: No. 2166, Erich Baron (1881-1933). No. 2167, Conrad Blenkle (1901-1943). No. 2168, Arthur Ewert (1890-1959). No. 2169, Walter Stoecker (1891-1939).

**1981, Feb. 24 Litho. *Perf. 14***

| | | | |
|---|---|---|---|
| **2166** | A623 10pf gray grn & blk | .25 | .25 |
| **2167** | A623 10pf lemon & blk | .25 | .25 |
| **2168** | A623 10pf bl vio & blk | .25 | .25 |
| **2169** | A623 10pf lt red brn & blk | .25 | .25 |
| | *Nos. 2166-2169 (4)* | 1.00 | 1.00 |

Merkur Hotel, Leipzig — A654

1981 Leipzig Spring Fair: 25pf, Takraf mining conveyor system, horiz.

**1981, Mar. 10 Photo. *Perf. 14***

| | | | | | |
|---|---|---|---|---|---|
| **2170** | A654 | 10pf | multicolored | .25 | .25 |
| **2171** | A654 | 25pf | multicolored | .35 | .25 |

Ernst Thälmann, by Willi Sitte — A655

10th Communist Party Congress (Paintings): 20pf, Worker, by Bernhard Heising, 25pf, Festivities, by Rudolf Bergander. 35pf, Brotherhood in Arms, by Paul Michaelis. 1m, When Communists Dream, by Walter Womacka.

**1981, Mar. 24**

| | | | | | |
|---|---|---|---|---|---|
| **2172** | A655 | 10pf | multicolored | .25 | .25 |
| **2173** | A655 | 20pf | multicolored | .25 | .25 |
| **2174** | A655 | 25pf | multicolored | *.80* | *.65* |
| **2175** | A655 | 35pf | multicolored | .25 | .25 |
| | | | *Nos. 2172-2175 (4)* | *1.55* | *1.40* |

**Souvenir Sheet**

| | | | | | |
|---|---|---|---|---|---|
| **2176** | A655 | 1m | multicolored | *1.60* | *2.00* |

Souvenir Sheet

Opening of Sport and Recreation Center, Berlin — A656

**1981, Mar. 24 Litho.**

| | | | | | |
|---|---|---|---|---|---|
| **2177** | A656 | 1m | multicolored | *2.25* | *3.50* |

Energy Conservation A657

**1981, Apr. 21 Litho. *Perf. 12½x13***

| | | | | | |
|---|---|---|---|---|---|
| **2178** | A657 | 10pf | orange & blk | .25 | .25 |

Heinrich Barkhausen (1881-1956), Physicist — A658

Famous Men: 20pf, Johannes R. Becher (1891-1958), poet. 25pf, Richard Dedekind (1831-1916), mathematician. 35pf, Georg Philipp Telemann (1681-1767), composer. 50pf, Adelbert V. Chamisso (1781-1838), botanist. 70pf, Wilhelm Raabe (1831-1910), writer.

**1981, May 5 *Perf. 13x12½***

| | | | | | |
|---|---|---|---|---|---|
| **2179** | A658 | 10pf | dull bl & blk | .25 | .25 |
| **2180** | A658 | 20pf | brick red & blk | .25 | .25 |
| **2181** | A658 | 25pf | dull brn & blk | *2.10* | *1.60* |
| **2182** | A658 | 35pf | lt vio & blk | .25 | .25 |
| **2183** | A658 | 50pf | yel grn & blk | .30 | .25 |
| **2184** | A658 | 70pf | ol bis & blk | .45 | .25 |
| | | | *Nos. 2179-2184 (6)* | *3.60* | *2.85* |

Free German Youth Members A659

**1981, May 19**

| | | | | | |
|---|---|---|---|---|---|
| **2185** | A659 | 10pf | shown | *.25* | *.25* |
| **2186** | A659 | 20pf | Youths, diff. | *.25* | *.25* |
| *a.* | | | Pair, #2185-2186 + label | *.85* | *.80* |

Free German Youth, 11th Parliament, Berlin.

View and Map of Worlitz Park — A660

**1981, June 9 Litho. *Perf. 12½x13***

| | | | | | |
|---|---|---|---|---|---|
| **2187** | A660 | 5pf | shown | .25 | .25 |
| **2188** | A660 | 10pf | Tiefurt | .25 | .25 |
| **2189** | A660 | 15pf | Marxwalde | .25 | .25 |
| **2190** | A660 | 20pf | Branitz | .25 | .25 |
| **2191** | A660 | 25pf | Treptow | *1.50* | *1.20* |
| **2192** | A660 | 35pf | Wiesenburg | .25 | .25 |
| | | | *Nos. 2187-2192 (6)* | *2.75* | *2.45* |

Artistic Gymnastics — A661

8th Children's and Youth Spartacist Games: No. 2193, children and youths.

**1981, June 23 Photo. *Perf. 14***

| | | | | | |
|---|---|---|---|---|---|
| **2193** | A661 | 10pf + 5pf | multi | *.55* | *.35* |
| **2194** | A661 | 20pf | multicolored | .25 | .25 |

Javelin Throwers A662

**1981, June 23 Litho. *Perf. 13x12½***

| | | | | | |
|---|---|---|---|---|---|
| **2195** | A662 | 5pf | shown | .25 | .25 |
| **2196** | A662 | 15pf | Men at museum | .25 | .25 |
| *a.* | | | Pair, #2195-2196 + label | .60 | .55 |

Intl. Year of the Disabled.

Schinkel's Berlin Playhouse — A663

Karl Friedrich Schinkel, (1781-1841), Architect: 25pf, Old Museum, Berlin.

**1981, June 23 Litho. & Engr.**

| | | | | | |
|---|---|---|---|---|---|
| **2197** | A663 | 10pf | tan & blk | .85 | .25 |
| **2198** | A663 | 25pf | tan & blk | *1.90* | *.85* |

Sugar Loaf House, Gross Zicker — A664

Frame Houses: 10pf, Zaulsdorf, 19th cent., vert. 25pf, Farmhouse, stable, Weckersdorf, vert. 35pf, Restaurant (former farmhouse), Pillgram. 50pf, Eschenbach, vert. 70pf, Farmhouse, Lüdersdorf.

**1981, July 7 Photo.**

| | | | | | |
|---|---|---|---|---|---|
| **2199** | A664 | 10pf | multicolored | .25 | .25 |
| **2200** | A664 | 20pf | multicolored | .25 | .25 |
| **2201** | A664 | 25pf | multicolored | .25 | .25 |
| **2202** | A664 | 35pf | multicolored | .25 | .25 |
| **2203** | A664 | 50pf | multicolored | .30 | .25 |
| **2204** | A664 | 70pf | multicolored | *2.75* | *2.10* |
| | | | *Nos. 2199-2204 (6)* | *4.05* | *3.35* |

**Railroad Type of 1980**

**1981, July 21 Litho. *Perf. 13x12½***

| | | | |
|---|---|---|---|
| **2205** | Strip of 2 + label | *.85* | *.80* |
| *a.* | A646 5pf Locomotive, Freital-Kurort-Kipsdorf line | .25 | .25 |
| *b.* | A646 15pf Luggage car | .25 | .25 |
| **2206** | Strip of 2 + label | *.85* | *.80* |
| *a.* | A646 5pf Locomotive, Putbus-Gohren line | .25 | .25 |
| *b.* | A646 20pf Passenger car | .25 | .25 |

Labels show maps of train routes.

Ebers Papyrus (Egyptian Medical Text, 1600 B.C.), Leipzig — A665

Chemical Plant — A666

Literary Treasures in DDR Libraries: 35pf, Maya manuscript, 12th cent., Dresden. 50pf, Petrarch sonnet illustration, 16th century French manuscript, Berlin.

**1981, Aug. 18 Photo. *Perf. 14***

| | | | | | |
|---|---|---|---|---|---|
| **2207** | A665 | 20pf | multicolored | .25 | .25 |
| **2208** | A665 | 35pf | multicolored | .25 | .25 |
| **2209** | A665 | 50pf | multicolored | *1.40* | *1.40* |
| | | | *Nos. 2207-2209 (3)* | *1.90* | *1.90* |

**1981, Aug. 18**

Leipzig 1981 Autumn Fair: 25pf, Concert Hall, Leipzig, horiz.

| | | | | | |
|---|---|---|---|---|---|
| **2210** | A666 | 10pf | multicolored | .25 | .25 |
| **2211** | A666 | 25pf | multicolored | .35 | .30 |

Anti-Fascist Resistance Monument, Sassnitz A667

**1981, Sept. 8 Photo. *Perf. 14***

| | | | | | |
|---|---|---|---|---|---|
| **2212** | A667 | 35pf | multicolored | .45 | .30 |

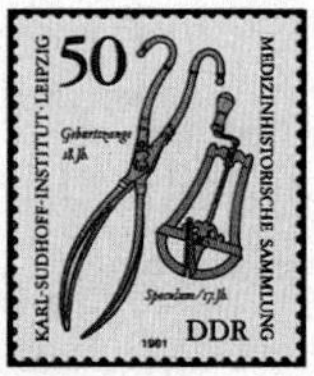

Forceps, 18th Cent., Speculum, 17th Cent. — A668

Historic Medical Instruments, Karl Sudhoff Institute, Leipzig: 10pf, Henbana, censer, 16th cent. 20pf, Pelican, dental elevator and extractors, 17th cent. 25pf, Seton forceps, 17th cent. 35pf, Lithotomy knife, 18th cent., hernia scissors, 17th cent. 85pf, Elevators, 17th cent. 10pf, 20pf, 25pf, 35pf horiz.

**1981, Sept. 22**

| | | | | | |
|---|---|---|---|---|---|
| **2213** | A668 | 10pf | multicolored | .25 | .25 |
| **2214** | A668 | 20pf | multicolored | .25 | .25 |
| **2215** | A668 | 25pf | multicolored | .25 | .25 |
| **2216** | A668 | 35pf | multicolored | .25 | .25 |
| **2217** | A668 | 50pf | multicolored | *2.25* | *2.25* |
| **2218** | A668 | 85pf | multicolored | .45 | .30 |
| | | | *Nos. 2213-2218 (6)* | *3.70* | *3.55* |

Philatelists' Day — A669

**1981, Oct. 6 Photo. *Perf. 14***

| | | | | | |
|---|---|---|---|---|---|
| **2219** | A669 | 10pf + 5pf | Letter by Engels, 1840 | *.75* | *.50* |
| **2220** | A669 | 20pf | Postcard by Marx, 1878 | .25 | .25 |

River Boat A670

**1981, Oct. 20**

| | | | | | |
|---|---|---|---|---|---|
| **2221** | A670 | 10pf | Tugboat | .25 | .25 |
| **2222** | A670 | 20pf | Tugboat, diff. | .25 | .25 |
| **2223** | A670 | 25pf | Diesel paddle liner | .25 | .25 |
| **2224** | A670 | 35pf | Ice breaker | .25 | .25 |
| **2225** | A670 | 50pf | Motor freighter | .30 | .25 |
| **2226** | A670 | 85pf | Bucket dredger | *2.40* | *2.40* |
| | | | *Nos. 2221-2226 (6)* | *3.70* | *3.65* |

Windmill, Dabel — A671

**1981, Nov. 10 Photo. *Perf. 14***

| | | | | | |
|---|---|---|---|---|---|
| **2227** | A671 | 10pf | shown | .25 | .25 |
| **2228** | A671 | 20pf | Pahrenz | .25 | .25 |
| **2229** | A671 | 25pf | Dresden-Gohlis | .25 | .25 |
| **2230** | A671 | 70pf | Ballstadt | *1.75* | *1.50* |
| | | | *Nos. 2227-2230 (4)* | *2.50* | *2.25* |

Toys — A672

**1981, Nov. 24 Litho. *Perf. 13½***

| | | | |
|---|---|---|---|
| **2231** | Sheet of 6 | *4.00* | *4.00* |
| *a.* | A672 10pf Jointed snake, 1850 | *.30* | *.30* |
| *b.* | A672 20pf Teddy bear, 1910 | *.30* | *.30* |
| *c.* | A672 25pf Fish, 1935 | *.95* | *.95* |
| *d.* | A672 35pf Hobby horse, 1850 | *.95* | *.95* |
| *e.* | A672 40pf Cuckoo, 1800 | *.30* | *.30* |
| *f.* | A672 70pf Frog, 1930 | *.30* | *.30* |

Meissen Porcelain Teapot, 1715 — A673

**1982, Jan. 26 Photo. *Perf. 14***

| | | | | | |
|---|---|---|---|---|---|
| **2232** | A673 | 10pf | shown | .25 | .25 |
| **2233** | A673 | 20pf | Vase, 1715 | .30 | .30 |
| **2234** | A673 | 25pf | Oberon figurine, 1969 | .45 | .45 |
| **2235** | A673 | 35pf | Day and Night vase, 1979 | .65 | .65 |
| *a.* | | | Block of 4, #2232-2235 | 2.25 | 1.90 |

**Souvenir Sheet**

| | | | |
|---|---|---|---|
| **2236** | Sheet of 2 | *2.60* | *3.25* |
| *a.* | A673 50pf Portrait | *.80* | *1.25* |
| *b.* | A673 50pf Emblem | *.80* | *1.25* |

Johann Friedrich Bottger (1682-1719), inventor of Dresden china. No. 2236 contains two 24x29mm stamps.

Post Offices — A674

**1982, Feb. 9**

| | | | | |
|---|---|---|---|---|
| **2237** | A674 | 20pf Liebenstein | .25 | .25 |
| **2238** | A674 | 25pf Berlin | .25 | .25 |
| **2239** | A674 | 35pf Erfurt | .25 | .25 |
| **2240** | A674 | 50pf Dresden | *1.50* | *1.50* |
| | | *Nos. 2237-2240 (4)* | *2.25* | *2.25* |

Intl. Fur Auction, Leipzig A675

**1982, Feb. 23 Photo. *Perf. 14***

| | | | | |
|---|---|---|---|---|
| **2241** | A675 | 10pf Marmot, vert. | .25 | .25 |
| **2242** | A675 | 20pf Polecat | .25 | .25 |
| **2243** | A675 | 25pf Mink | .25 | .25 |
| **2244** | A675 | 35pf Stone marten | *1.10* | *1.00* |
| | | *Nos. 2241-2244 (4)* | *1.85* | *1.75* |

Souvenir Sheet

Goethe-Schiller Awards, 1980-1984 — A676

**1982, Mar. 9 Litho.**

| | | | | |
|---|---|---|---|---|
| **2245** | A676 | Sheet of 2 | *2.60* | *3.50* |
| *a.* | | 50pf Goethe | *1.00* | *1.60* |
| *b.* | | 50pf Schiller | *1.00* | *1.60* |

1982 Leipzig Spring Fair A677

**1982, Mar. 9 *Perf. 13x12½***

| | | | | |
|---|---|---|---|---|
| **2246** | A677 | 10pf Entrance | .25 | .25 |
| **2247** | A677 | 25pf Exhibit | .30 | .25 |

Souvenir Sheet

TB Bacillus Centenary — A678

**1982, Mar. 23 *Perf. 14***

| | | | | |
|---|---|---|---|---|
| **2248** | A678 | 1m multi | *2.00* | *3.25* |

**Working-class Leader Type of 1979**

#2249, Max Fechner (1892-1973). #2250, Ottomar Greschke (1882-1957). #2251, Helmut Lehmann (1882-1959). #2252, Herbert Warnke (1902-75). #2253, Otto Winzer (1902-75).

**1982, Mar. 23 Engr.**

| | | | | |
|---|---|---|---|---|
| **2249** | A623 | 10pf dk red brn | .25 | .25 |
| **2250** | A623 | 10pf green | .25 | .25 |
| **2251** | A623 | 10pf violet | .25 | .25 |
| **2252** | A623 | 10pf dull blue | .25 | .25 |
| **2253** | A623 | 10pf gray olive | .25 | .25 |
| | | *Nos. 2249-2253 (5)* | 1.25 | 1.25 |

Poisonous Plants — A679

**1982, Apr. 6 Litho. *Perf. 14***

| | | | | |
|---|---|---|---|---|
| **2254** | A679 | 10pf Meadow saffron | .25 | .25 |
| **2255** | A679 | 15pf Water arum | .25 | .25 |
| **2256** | A679 | 20pf Marsh tea | .25 | .25 |
| **2257** | A679 | 25pf White bryony | .25 | .25 |
| **2258** | A679 | 35pf Common monks-hood | .25 | .25 |
| **2259** | A679 | 50pf Henbane | *1.60* | *1.40* |
| | | *Nos. 2254-2259 (6)* | *2.85* | *2.65* |

Free Federation of German Trade Unions, 10th Congress A680

Paintings: 10pf, Mother and Child, by Walter Womacka. 20pf, Discussion at the Innovator Collective, by Willi Neubert, horiz. 25pf, Young Couple, by Karl-Heinz Jacob.

**1982, Apr. 20 Photo.**

| | | | | |
|---|---|---|---|---|
| **2260** | A680 | 10pf multi | .25 | .25 |
| **2261** | A680 | 20pf multi | .25 | .25 |
| **2262** | A680 | 25pf multi | *.55* | *.55* |
| | | *Nos. 2260-2262 (3)* | *1.05* | *1.05* |

Intl. Book Art Exhibition, Leipzig — A681

**1982, Apr. 20**

| | | | | |
|---|---|---|---|---|
| **2263** | A681 | 15pf "I" | *.40* | *.40* |
| **2264** | A681 | 35pf Emblem | *.40* | *.40* |
| *a.* | | Pair, #2263-2264 + label | *1.50* | *1.20* |

A682

Protected species. 10pf, 25pf, 35pf vert.

***Perf. 13½x14, 14x13½***

**1982, May 18 Photo.**

| | | | | |
|---|---|---|---|---|
| **2265** | A682 | 10pf Fish hawk | .30 | .25 |
| **2266** | A682 | 20pf Sea eagle | .30 | .25 |
| **2267** | A682 | 25pf Tawny eagle | .30 | .25 |
| **2268** | A682 | 35pf Eagle owl | *2.10* | *1.50* |
| | | *Nos. 2265-2268 (4)* | *3.00* | *2.25* |

19th Workers' Festival, Neubrandenburg — A683

**1982, June 8 Photo. *Perf. 14***

| | | | | |
|---|---|---|---|---|
| **2269** | A683 | 10pf View of Neubrandenburg | .25 | .25 |
| **2270** | A683 | 20pf Traditional costumes | .40 | .30 |

Souvenir Sheet

Dimitrov Memorial Medal — A684

**1982, June 8**

| | | | | |
|---|---|---|---|---|
| **2271** | A684 | 1m multi | *2.60* | *3.25* |

George Dimitrov (1882-1947), first prime minister of Bulgaria.

Cargo Ship Frieden — A685

**1982, June 22**

| | | | | |
|---|---|---|---|---|
| **2272** | A685 | 5pf shown | .25 | .25 |
| **2273** | A685 | 10pf Fichtelberg | .25 | .25 |
| **2274** | A685 | 15pf Brocken | .25 | .25 |
| **2275** | A685 | 20pf Weimar | .25 | .25 |
| **2276** | A685 | 25pf Vorwarts | .25 | .25 |
| **2277** | A685 | 35pf Berlin | *1.20* | *1.20* |
| | | *Nos. 2272-2277 (6)* | *2.45* | *2.45* |

Society for Sport & Technology — A686

**1982, June 22 Litho. *Perf. 13x12½***

| | | | | |
|---|---|---|---|---|
| **2278** | A686 | 20pf multi | .55 | .25 |

Bird Wedding — A687

Sorbian Folklore: 20pf, Zampern masqueraders. 25pf, Easter egg game. 35pf, Painting Easter eggs. 40pf, St. John's Day parade. 50pf, Christmas celebration.

**1982, July 6 Litho. *Perf. 13x12½***

| | | | | |
|---|---|---|---|---|
| **2279** | A687 | Block of 6 | *4.00* | *4.00* |
| *a.* | | 10pf multi | *.25* | *.25* |
| *b.* | | 20pf multi | *.25* | *.25* |
| *c.* | | 25pf multi | *.30* | *.30* |
| *d.* | | 35pf multi | *.55* | *.55* |
| *e.* | | 40pf multi | *.65* | *.65* |
| *f.* | | 50pf multi | *.80* | *.80* |

View of Schwerin A688

7th Youth Stamp Exhibition, Schwerin: 10pf + 5pf, View, 1640.

**1982, July 6**

| | | | | |
|---|---|---|---|---|
| **2280** | A688 | 10pf + 5pf multi | *.30* | *.30* |
| **2281** | A688 | 20pf multi | *.30* | *.30* |
| *a.* | | Pair, #2280-2281 + label | *1.40* | *1.20* |

7th Pioneer Meeting, Dresden A689

**1982, July 20 Photo. *Perf. 14x13½***

| | | | | |
|---|---|---|---|---|
| **2282** | A689 | 10pf + 5pf Pioneers, banner | *.45* | *.45* |
| **2283** | A689 | 20pf Bugle, pennant | .25 | .25 |

Seascape, by Ludolf Backhuysen (1631-1708) — A690

17th Cent. Paintings in Natl. Museum, Schwerin: 10pf, Music Making at Home, by Frans van Mieris (1635-1681), vert. 20pf, The Gate Guard, by Carel Fabritius (1622-1654), vert. 25pf, Farmers Company, by Adriaen Brouwer (1606-1638). 35pf, Breakfast Table with Ham, by Willem Claesz Heda (1593-1680). 70pf, River Landscape, by Jan van Goyen (1596-1656).

**1982, Aug. 10 *Perf. 14***

| | | | | |
|---|---|---|---|---|
| **2284** | A690 | 5pf multi | .25 | .25 |
| **2285** | A690 | 10pf multi | .25 | .25 |
| **2286** | A690 | 20pf multi | .25 | .25 |
| **2287** | A690 | 25pf multi | .25 | .25 |
| **2288** | A690 | 35pf multi | .25 | .25 |
| **2289** | A690 | 70pf multi | *1.80* | *1.50* |
| | | *Nos. 2284-2289 (6)* | *3.05* | *2.75* |

1982 Leipzig Autumn Fair A691

**1982, Aug. 24 Litho. *Perf. 13x12½***

| | | | | |
|---|---|---|---|---|
| **2290** | A691 | 10pf Exhibition Hall | .25 | .25 |
| **2291** | A691 | 25pf Decorative box, ring | .25 | .25 |

Karl-Marx-Stadt Buildings and Monument — A692

**1982, Aug. 24 Photo. *Perf. 14***

| | | | | |
|---|---|---|---|---|
| **2292** | A692 | 10pf multi + label | .30 | .25 |

Org. for the Cooperation of Socialist Countries and Posts and Telecommunications Dept., 13th Conference, Karl-Marx-Stadt, Sept. 6-11.

Intl. Federation of Resistance Fighters, 9th Congress, Berlin — A693

**1982, Sept. 7 Litho. *Perf. 14***

| | | | | |
|---|---|---|---|---|
| **2293** | A693 | 10pf Emblem | .65 | .25 |

Auschwitz-Birkenau Intl. Memorial A694

**1982, Sept. 7 Photo.**

| | | | | |
|---|---|---|---|---|
| **2294** | A694 | 35pf multi | .65 | .30 |

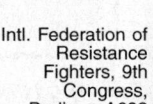

Autumn Flowers — A695

**1982, Sept. 21**

**2295** A695 5pf Autumn anemones .25 .25
**2296** A695 10pf Student flowers .25 .25
**2297** A695 15pf Hybrid gazanias .25 .25
**2298** A695 20pf Sunflowers .25 .25
**2299** A695 25pf Chrysanthemums .25 .25
**2300** A695 35pf Cosmos bipinnatus *1.80 1.50*
*Nos. 2295-2300 (6)* *3.05 2.75*

Ambulance — A696

**1982, Oct. 5 Litho.** ***Perf. 13x12½***

**2301** A696 5pf shown .25 .25
**2302** A696 10pf Street cleaner .25 .25
**2303** A696 20pf Bus .25 .25
**2304** A696 25pf Platform truck .25 .25
**2305** A696 35pf Platform truck, diff. .25 .25
**2306** A696 85pf Milk truck *2.25 1.75*
*Nos. 2301-2306 (6)* *3.50 3.00*

25th Masters of Tomorrow Central Fair — A697

**1982, Oct. 19** ***Perf. 14***

**2307** A697 20pf multicolored .35 .25

Martin Luther (1483-1546) A698

Designs: 10pf, Seal of Eisleben (town of birth and death). 20pf, Portrait, Eisenach, 1521. 35pf, Wittenberg seal, 1500. 85pf, Portrait, after Cranach, 1528.

**1982, Nov. 23 Photo.** ***Perf. 14x13½***

**2308** A698 10pf multi .25 .25
**2309** A698 20pf multi .25 .25
*a.* Miniature sheet of 10 6.50 6.50
**2310** A698 35pf multi .35 .25
**2311** A698 85pf multi *3.00 1.90*
*Nos. 2308-2311 (4)* *3.85 2.65*

Toy Carpenter, 1830 — A699

**1982, Nov. 23 Litho.** ***Perf. 14***

**2312** Sheet of 6 *3.75 3.75*
*a.* A699 10pf shown .25 .25
*b.* A699 20pf Cobbler 1.10 1.10
*c.* A699 25pf Baker .25 .25
*d.* A699 35pf Cooper .25 .25
*e.* A699 40pf Tanner 1.10 1.10
*f.* A699 70pf Carter .25 .25

Souvenir Sheet

Johannes Brahms (1833-1897), Composer — A700

**1983, Jan. 11 Litho.** ***Perf. 14***

**2313** A700 1.15m multi *3.25 4.25*

### Working-class Leader Type of 1979

#2314, Franz Dahlem (1892-1981). #2315, Karl Maron (1903-75). #2316, Josef Miller (1883-1964). #2317, Fred Oelssner (1903-77). #2318, Siegfried Radel (1893-1943).

**1983, Jan. 25 Photo.**

**2314** A623 10pf dark brown .25 .25
**2315** A623 10pf dark green .25 .25
**2316** A623 10pf dark olive grn .25 .25
**2317** A623 10pf deep plum .25 .25
**2318** A623 10pf dark blue .25 .25
*Nos. 2314-2318 (5)* 1.25 1.25

World Communications Year — A701

**1983, Feb. 8 Photo.** ***Perf. 14***

**2319** A701 5pf Telephone receiver, buttons .25 .25
**2320** A701 10pf Rugen radio .25 .25
**2321** A701 20pf Surface and air mail .25 .25
**2322** A701 35pf Optical conductors *1.10 1.10*
*Nos. 2319-2322 (4)* *1.85 1.85*

Otto Nuschke (1883-1957), Statesman A702

**1983, Feb. 8**

**2323** A702 20pf red brn, bl & blk .40 .25

Town Hall, Gera, 1576 — A703

**1983, Feb. 22 Photo.** ***Perf. 14***

**2324** A703 10pf Stolberg, 1482, horiz. .25 .25
**2325** A703 20pf shown .25 .25
**2326** A703 25pf Possneck, 1486 .25 .25
**2327** A703 35pf Berlin, 1869, horiz. *1.20 1.00*
*Nos. 2324-2327 (4)* *1.95 1.75*

1983 Leipzig Spring Fair — A704

**1983, Mar. 8**

**2328** A704 10pf Fair building .25 .25
**2329** A704 25pf Robotron microcomputer .40 .25

Paul Robeson (1898-1976), Singer — A705

**1983, Mar. 22 Litho.** ***Perf. 13x12½***

**2330** A705 20pf multicolored .55 .25

Souvenir Sheet

Schulze-Boysen/Harnack Resistance Org. — A706

Arvid Harnack (1901-42), Harro Schulze-Boysen (1909-42), John Sieg (1903-42).

**1983, Mar. 22**

**2331** A706 85pf multicolored 1.40 2.25

Karl Marx (1818-1883), and Newspaper Mastheads — A707

Portraits and: 20pf, Lyons silk weavers' revolt, 1831, French-German Yearbook. 35pf, Engels, Communist Manifesto. 50pf, Das Kapital titlepage. 70pf, Program of German Workers' Movement text. 85pf, Engels, Lenin, globe. 1.15m Portrait (24x29mm).

**1983, Apr. 11 Photo.** ***Perf. 13x12½***

**2332** A707 10pf multicolored .25 .25
**2333** A707 20pf multicolored .25 .25
**2334** A707 35pf multicolored .25 .25
**2335** A707 50pf multicolored .25 .25
**2336** A707 70pf multicolored .40 .25
**2337** A707 85pf multicolored *2.60 2.60*
*Nos. 2332-2337 (6)* *4.00 3.85*

### Souvenir Sheet

**Litho.** ***Perf. 14***

**2338** A707 1.15m multi *2.40 3.50*

Works of Art from Berlin State Museums — A708

**1983, Apr. 19 Photo.** ***Perf. 14***

**2339** A708 10pf Athena .25 .25
**2340** A708 20pf Amazon, bronze, 430 BC .35 .25

Narrow-Gauge Railroads — A709

**1983, May 17 Litho.** ***Perf. 13x12½***

**2341** Pair, Wernigerode-Nordhausen line *1.60 1.20*
*a.* A709 15pf Locomotive .40 .40
*b.* A709 20pf Passenger car .40 .40
**2342** Pair, Zittau-Oybin/Johnsdorf line *1.60 1.20*
*a.* A709 20pf Locomotive .40 .40
*b.* A709 50pf Freight car .40 .40

Nos. 2341 and 2342 se-tenant with labels showing maps. See Nos. 2405-2406.

Sand Glasses and Sundials A710

Cacti A711

**1983, June 7 Photo.** ***Perf. 14***

**2343** A710 5pf Sand glass, 1674 .25 .25
**2344** A710 10pf Sand glass, 1700 .25 .25
**2345** A710 20pf Sundial, 1611 .25 .25
*a.* Sheet of 8 3.00 3.00
**2346** A710 30pf Sundial, 1750 .25 .25
**2347** A710 50pf Sundial, 1760 .40 .25
**2348** A710 85pf Sundial, 1800 *2.40 2.40*
*Nos. 2343-2348 (6)* *3.80 3.65*

**1983, June 21**

**2349** A711 5pf Coryphantha elephantidens .25 .25
**2350** A711 10pf Thelocactus schwarzii .25 .25
**2351** A711 20pf Leuchtenbergia principis .25 .25
**2352** A711 25pf Submatucana madisoniorum .25 .25
**2353** A711 35pf Oroya peruviana .25 .25
**2354** A711 50pf Copiapoa cinerea *1.50 1.50*
*Nos. 2349-2354 (6)* *2.75 2.75*

Naumberg Cathedral Statues, 15th Cent. A712

**1983, July 5 Photo.** ***Perf. 13***

**2355** A712 20pf Thimo and Wilhelm .40 .40
**2356** A712 25pf Gepa and Gerburg .50 .50
**2357** A712 35pf Hermann and Reglindis .55 .55
**2358** A712 85pf Eckehard and Uta 1.30 1.30
*a.* Block of 4, #2355-2358 3.50 3.00

Technical Training, by Harald Metzkes (b. 1929) A713

SOZPHILEX '83 Junior Stamp Exhibition, Berlin: 10pf+5pf, Glasewaldt and Zinna Defending the Barricade-18th March, 1848, by Theodor Hosemann, vert. Surtax was for exhibition.

**1983, July 5 Litho.** ***Perf. 13x12½***

**2359** A713 10pf + 5pf multi *.65 .55*
**2360** A713 20pf multi .25 .25

Volleyball A714

**1983, July 19 Photo. *Perf. 14***

**2361** A714 10pf + 5pf Passing beach balls .50 .40
**2362** A714 20pf shown .25 .25

7th Gymnastic and Sports Meeting; 9th Children's and Youth Spartikiade, Leipzig.

Simon Bolivar (1783-1830) — A715

**1983, July 19**

**2363** A715 35pf Bolivar, Alexander von Humboldt .55 .30

A715A

A716

City Arms

**1983, Aug. 9**

**2364** A715A 50pf Berlin .80 .65
**2365** A716 50pf Cottbus .80 .65
**2366** A716 50pf Dresden .80 .65
**2367** A716 50pf Erfurt .80 .65
**2368** A716 50pf Frankfurt .80 .65
*Nos. 2364-2368 (5)* 4.00 3.25

See Nos. 2398-2402, 2464-2468.

1983 Leipzig Autumn Fair — A717

**1983, Aug. 30**

**2369** A717 10pf Central Palace .25 .25
**2370** A717 25pf Microelectronic pattern .45 .25

Leonhard Euler (1707-1783), Mathematician — A718

**1983, Sept. 6**

**2371** A718 20pf multi .45 .25

Souvenir Sheet

30th Anniv. of Working-Class Brigade Groups — A719

**1983, Sept. 6 Litho. *Perf. 12½x13***

**2372** A719 1m multicolored 2.10 2.50

Governmental Palaces, Potsdam Gardens — A720

**1983, Sept. 20 *Perf. 13x12½***

**2373** A720 10pf Sanssouci Palace .25 .25
**2374** A720 20pf Chinese teahouse .25 .25
**2375** A720 40pf Charlottenhof Palace .40 .25
**2376** A720 50pf Royal Stables, Film Museum 2.40 2.40
*Nos. 2373-2376 (4)* 3.30 3.15

Monument, Mamajew-Kurgan Hill — A721

**1983, Oct. 4 *Perf. 14***

**2377** A721 35pf Mother Home .50 .25

Souvenir Sheet

Martin Luther — A722

**1983, Oct. 18 Litho. *Perf. 14***

**2378** A722 1m multi 3.00 4.25

Margin shows title page from Luther Bible, 1541.

Thuringian Glass — A723

**1983, Nov. 8 Photo. *Perf. 13½x14***

**2379** A723 10pf Cock .25 .25
**2380** A723 20pf Cup .25 .25
**2381** A723 25pf Vase .25 .25
**2382** A723 70pf Ornamental Glass 1.60 1.50
*Nos. 2379-2382 (4)* 2.35 2.25

Souvenir Sheet

New Year 1984 — A724

**1983, Nov. 22 Litho. *Perf. 14***

**2383** Sheet of 4 2.00 3.25
*a.* A724 10pf multi .25 .25
*b.* A724 20pf multi .25 .40
*c.* A724 25pf multi .40 .70
*d.* A724 35pf multi .55 .80

Winter Olympics 1984, Sarajevo A725

**1983, Nov. 22 Photo. *Perf. 14***

**2384** A725 10pf + 5pf 2-man luge .25 .25
**2385** A725 20pf + 10pf Ski jump .25 .25
**2386** A725 25pf Skiing .25 .25
**2387** A725 35pf Biathlon 1.50 1.00
*Nos. 2384-2387 (4)* 2.25 1.75

**Souvenir Sheet**

**2388** A725 85pf Olympic Center 1.75 3.00

Jena Glass Centenary — A726

**1984, Jan. 10 Litho. *Perf. 12½x13***

**2389** A726 20pf Otto Schott .40 .25

**Working-class Leader Type of 1979**

Designs: No. 2390, Friedrich Ebert (1894-1979). No. 2391, Fritz Grosse (1904-1957). No. 2392, Albert Norden (1904-1982).

**1984, Jan. 24 Engr. *Perf. 14***

**2390** A623 10pf black .25 .25
**2391** A623 10pf dark green .25 .25
**2392** A623 10pf dark blue .25 .25
*Nos. 2390-2392 (3)* .75 .75

Souvenir Sheet

Felix Mendelssohn (1809-1847), Composer — A727

**1984, Jan. 24 Litho.**

**2393** A727 85pf multi 1.00 1.75

Margin shows Song Without Words score.

Postal Milestones — A728

Designs: 10pf, Muhlau, 1725; Oederan, 1722. 20pf, Johanngeorgenstadt, 1723; Schonbrunn, 1724. 35pf, Freiberg, 1723. 85pf, Pegau, 1723.

**1984, Feb. 7 Photo. *Perf. 14***

**2394** A728 10pf multi .25 .25
**2395** A728 20pf multi .30 .25
**2396** A728 35pf multi .40 .30
**2397** A728 85pf multi .80 .80
*Nos. 2394-2397 (4)* 1.75 1.60

**City Arms Type of 1983**

**1984, Feb. 21**

**2398** A716 50pf Gera .50 .40
**2399** A716 50pf Halle .50 .40
**2400** A716 50pf Karl-Marx-Stadt .50 .40
**2401** A716 50pf Leipzig .50 .40
**2402** A716 50pf Magdeburg .50 .40
*Nos. 2398-2402 (5)* 2.50 2.00

1984 Leipzig Spring Fair A729

**1984, Mar. 6 *Perf. 14***

**2403** A729 10pf Old Town Hall .25 .25
**2404** A729 25pf Factory .30 .25

**Railroad Type of 1983**

**1984, Mar. 20 Litho. *Perf. 13x12½***

**2405** Pair, Cranzahl Oberwiesenthal line 1.60 1.25
*a.* A709 30pf Locomotive .25 .25
*b.* A709 80pf Passenger car .65 .65
**2406** Pair, Selke Valley line 1.60 1.10
*a.* A709 40pf Locomotive .30 .30
*b.* A709 60pf Passenger car .40 .40

Labels show maps of routes.

Stone Door, Rostock — A730

Council Building — A731

Intl. Society of Monument Preservation 7th General Meeting: 10pf, Town Hall, Rostock. 15pf, Albrecht Castle, Meissen. 85pf, Stable Courtyard, Dresden. 10pf, 15pf, 85pf horiz.

**1984, Apr. 24 Photo. *Perf. 14***

**2407** A730 10pf multi .25 .25
**2408** A730 15pf multi .25 .25
**2409** A730 40pf multi .45 .35
**2410** A730 85pf multi 1.10 1.00
*Nos. 2407-2410 (4)* 2.05 1.85

**1984, May 8**

**2411** A731 70pf multi .70 .30

Standing Commission of Posts and Telecommunications of Council of Mutual Economic Aid, 25th meeting.

Cast-iron Bowl, 19th Cent. A732

Marionette A733

Cast-Iron, Lauchhammer: 85pf, Ascending Man, by Fritz Cremer, 1967.

**1984, May 22**

**2412** A732 20pf multi .25 .25
**2413** A732 85pf multi .90 .90

**1984, June 5**

**2414** A733 50pf shown .55 .55
**2415** A733 80pf Puppet .90 .90

Natl. Youth Festival A734

**1984, June 5 Litho. *Perf. 13x12½***

**2416** A734 10pf + 5pf Demonstration .25 .25
**2417** A734 20pf Construction workers .25 .25
*a.* Pair, #2416-2417 + label 1.20 .65

20th Workers' Festival A735

**1984, June 19**

**2418** A735 10pf View of Gera .25 .25
**2419** A735 20pf Traditional costumes .25 .25
*a.* Pair, #2418-2419 + label .85 .65

Natl. Stamp Exhib., Halle — A736

**1984, July 3 *Perf. 13½x14***

**2420** A736 10pf + 5pf Salt carrier .25 .25
**2421** A736 20pf Wedding couple .30 .25

Historic Seals, 1442 — A737

**1984, Aug. 7 Litho. *Perf. 14***

**2422** A737 5pf Baker, Berlin *.30* .25
**2423** A737 10pf Wool weaver, Berlin *.55* .30
**2424** A737 20pf Wool weaver, Cologne *1.00* .40
**2425** A737 35pf Shoemaker, Cologne *1.75* 1.60
*a.* Block of 4, #2422-2425 *4.50* 2.50

Building Renovation and Construction A738

Ironwork Collective Combine East — A739

**Litho., Photo. (#2427, 2429, 25pf)**

**1984 *Perf. 14x13½***

**2426** A738 10pf shown .25 .25
**2427** A739 10pf shown .25 .25
**2428** A738 20pf Surface mining .30 .30
**2429** A739 20pf Armed forces .25 .25
**2430** A739 25pf Petro-chemical Collective Combine, Schwedt .30 .30
*Nos. 2426-2430 (5)* 1.35 1.35

**Souvenir Sheets**

**2431** A738 1m Privy Council Building 1.10 2.10
**2432** A739 1m Family 1.10 2.10

DDR, 35th anniv. Issued: A738, 8/21; A739, 9/11.

1984 Leipzig Autumn Fair — A740

**1984, Aug. 28 Photo. *Perf. 14***

**2433** A740 10pf Frege House, Katharine St. .25 .25
**2434** A740 25pf Crystal bowl, Olbernhau .30 .25

Members of the Resistance, Sculpture by Arno Wittig — A741

**1984, Sept. 18 Photo. *Perf. 14***

**2435** A741 35pf multi .75 .30

View of Magdeburg — A742

**1984, Oct. 4 Litho. *Perf. 13x12½***

**2436** A742 10pf + 5pf shown .25 .25
**2437** A742 20pf Old & modern buildings .25 .25
*a.* Pair, #2436-2437 + label 1.00 .75

8th Youth Stamp Exhibition, Magdeburg.

35th Anniv. of Republic — A743

**1984, Oct. 4 Photo. *Perf. 14***

**2438** A743 10pf Construction .25 .25
**2439** A743 20pf Military .25 .25
**2440** A743 25pf Heavy industry .30 .30
**2441** A743 35pf Agriculture .35 .35
*Nos. 2438-2441 (4)* 1.15 1.15

**Souvenir Sheet**

**2442** A743 1m Arms, dove, vert. 1.10 2.10

Figurines, Green Vault of Dresden — A744

**1984, Oct. 23**

**2443** A744 10pf Spring .25 .25
**2444** A744 20pf Summer .25 .25
*a.* Miniature sheet of 8, litho., perf. 12½x13 2.75 2.75
**2445** A744 35pf Autumn .30 .30
**2446** A744 70pf Winter .75 .75
*Nos. 2443-2446 (4)* 1.55 1.55

Falkenstein Castle — A745

**1984, Nov. 6 Litho. *Perf. 14***

**2447** A745 10pf shown .25 .25
**2448** A745 20pf Kriebstein .25 .25
**2449** A745 35pf Ranis .55 .45
**2450** A745 80pf Neuenburg .85 .80
*Nos. 2447-2450 (4)* 1.90 1.75

See Nos. 2504-2507.

Dead Tsar's Daughter and the Seven Warriors A746

Various scenes from the fairytale.

**1984, Nov. 27 Litho. *Perf. 13***

**2451** Sheet of 6 *12.00* 4.75
*a.* A746 5pf multi *.40* .25
*b.* A746 10pf multi *.40* .25
*c.* A746 15pf multi *2.75* 1.60
*d.* A746 20pf multi *2.75* 1.60
*e.* A746 35pf multi *.40* .25
*f.* A746 50pf multi *.40* .25

**Working-class Leader Type of 1979**

Designs: No. 2452, Anton Ackermann (1905-1973). No. 2453, Alfred Kurella (1895-1975). No. 2454, Otto Schon (1905-1968).

**1985, Jan. 8 Engr. *Perf. 14***

**2452** A623 10pf blk brn .25 .25
**2453** A623 10pf red brn .25 .25
**2454** A623 10pf gray vio .25 .25
*Nos. 2452-2454 (3)* .75 .75

24th World Luge Championship — A747

**1985, Jan. 22 Photo.**

**2455** A747 10pf Single seat luge .30 .25

Antique Mailboxes — A748

**1985, Feb. 5 Litho. *Perf. 14***

**2456** A748 10pf 1850 .25 .25
**2457** A748 20pf 1860 .25 .25
**2458** A748 35pf 1900 .30 .30
**2459** A748 50pf 1920 .45 .45
*a.* Block of 4, Nos. 2456-2459 1.50 2.00

**Souvenir Sheet**

Dresden Opera House Reopening — A749

**Litho. & Engr.**

**1985, Feb. 12 *Perf. 13***

**2460** A749 85pf multicolored 1.00 1.50

1985 Leipzig Spring Fair — A750

**1985, Mar. 5 Photo. *Perf. 14***

**2461** A750 10pf Statue of Bach, Leipzig .25 .25
**2462** A750 25pf Porcelain pot, Meissen .30 .25

Souvenir Sheet

Bach, Handel and Schutz Tribute — A751

**1985, Mar. 19** **Litho.**

**2463** Sheet of 3 2.00 3.00
*a.* A751 10pf Bach .50 .70
*b.* A751 20pf Handel .50 .70
*c.* A751 85pf Heinrich Schutz (1585-1672) .70 1.30

### City Arms Type of 1983

**1985, Apr. 9** **Photo.** ***Perf. 14***

**2464** A716 50pf Neubrandenburg .50 .40
**2465** A716 50pf Potsdam .50 .40
**2466** A716 50pf Rostock .50 .40
**2467** A716 50pf Schwerin .50 .40
**2468** A716 50pf Suhl .80 .80
*Nos. 2464-2468 (5)* 2.80 2.40

Seelow Heights Memorial — A752

**1985, Apr. 16** **Photo.** ***Perf. 14***

**2469** A752 35pf multi .60 .30

Egon Erwin Kisch, Journalist (1885-1948) — A753

**1985, Apr. 23** **Photo.** ***Perf. 14***

**2470** A753 35pf multi .30 .25

No. 2470 was printed se-tenant with label showing the house where Kisch was born. Value, single with attached label: unused 50c; used 40c.

Liberation from Fascism, 40th Anniv. — A754

Designs: 10pf, German and Soviet astronauts. 20pf, Coal miner Adolf Hennecke, symbols of industry and energy. 25pf, farm workers, symbols of socialist agriculture. 50pf, Technicians manufacturing microchips, science and technology.

**1985, May 7** **Photo.** ***Perf. 14x13½***

**2471** A754 10pf multi .25 .25
**2472** A754 20pf multi .30 .30
**2473** A754 25pf multi .30 .30
**2474** A754 50pf multi .60 .60
*Nos. 2471-2474 (4)* 1.45 1.45

### Souvenir Sheet

***Perf. 12½x13***

**2475** A754 1m Berlin-Treptow Soviet Heroes Monument 1.40 2.00

Warsaw Treaty, 30th Anniv. — A755

**1985, May 14** **Litho.** ***Perf. 13x12½***

**2476** A755 20pf Flags of pact nations .45 .25

Historical and Modern Buildings A756

12th Youth Parliament, Berlin: 20pf, Ernst Thalmann, flags.

**1985, May 21** **Litho.**

**2477** A756 10pf + 5pf multi .25 .25
**2478** A756 20pf multi .25 .25
*a.* Pair, #2477-2478 + label .70 .70

Intl. Olympic Committee 90th Meeting — A757

**1985, May 28** **Litho.** ***Perf. 14***

**2479** A757 35pf Flag .50 .25

No. 2479 was printed setenant with label depicting Olympic Torches. Value of single with attached label: unused 90c; used 65c.

Free German Trade Unions, 40th Anniv. — A758

**1985, June 11** **Photo.**

**2480** A758 20pf Red flags .40 .25

Wildlife Preservation A759

**1985, June 25** **Photo.**

**2481** A759 5pf Harpy eagle, vert. .25 .25
**2482** A759 10pf Red-necked goose .25 .25
**2483** A759 20pf Spectacled bear .25 .25
**2484** A759 50pf Banteng (Javanese) buffalo .50 .45
**2485** A759 85pf Sunda Straits crocodile .95 .95
*Nos. 2481-2485 (5)* 2.20 2.15

19th Century Steam Engines A760

**1985, July 9** **Photo.**

**2486** A760 10pf Bock engine, vert. .25 .25
**2487** A760 85pf Beam engine 1.00 .80

12th World Youth and Student Festival, Moscow A761

**1985, July 23** **Litho.** ***Perf. 13x12½***

**2488** A761 20pf + 5pf Students reading .25 .25
**2489** A761 50pf Student demonstration .40 .40
*a.* Pair, #2488-2489 + label 1.05 .95

2nd World Orienteering and Deep-sea Diving Championship — A762

**1985, Aug. 13** **Photo.** ***Perf. 14***

**2490** A762 10pf Diver at turning buoy .25 .25
**2491** A762 70pf Long-distance divers .80 .80

Bose House Fair Building, St. Thomas Churchyard — A763

**1985, Apr. 27** **Photo.**

**2492** A763 10pf shown .25 .25
**2493** A763 25pf Bach trumpet .50 .25

Leipzig Autumn Fair.

A764

SOZPHILEX '85: 19th century coach and team, 1878, bas-relief by Hermann Steinemann, in the court of the former Berlin Post Office.

**1985, Sept. 10** **Litho.** ***Perf. 13x12½***

**2494** 5pf multi .25 .25
**2495** 20pf + 5pf multi .25 .25
*a.* Miniature sheet of 4 #2495b .75 .75
*b.* A764 Pair, #2494-2495 .45 .45

No. 2495b has a continuous design.

German Railways 150th Anniv. — A765

Socialist Railway Org.: 20pf, GS II signal box, track diagram. 25pf, 1838 Saxonia, first German locomotive, designer Johann Andreas Schubert (1808-1870), Model 250 electric locomotive. 50pf, Helicopter lifting cable drum, section electrification. 85pf, Leipzig Central Station.

**Litho.**

***Perf. 12½x13***

**1985, Sept. 24**

**2496** A765 20pf multi .30 .25
**2497** A765 25pf multi .40 .25
**2498** A765 50pf multi .75 .55
**2499** A765 85pf multi 1.20 1.20
*Nos. 2496-2499 (4)* 2.65 2.25

Bridges in East Berlin A766

**Photo.; Litho. (#2501a)**

**1985, Oct. 8** ***Perf. 14***

**2500** A766 10pf Gertrauden .25 .25
**2501** A766 20pf Jungfern .25 .25
*a.* Min. sheet of 8, perf. 13x12½ 3.25 3.25
**2502** A766 35pf Weidendammer .40 .40
**2503** A766 70pf Marx-Engels .65 .65
*Nos. 2500-2503 (4)* 1.55 1.55

### Castles Type of 1984

**1985, Oct. 15** **Litho.**

**2504** A745 10pf Hohnstein .25 .25
**2505** A745 20pf Rochsburg .25 .25
**2506** A745 35pf Schwarzenberg .40 .40
**2507** A745 80pf Stein 1.10 1.10
*Nos. 2504-2507 (4)* 2.00 2.00

Humboldt University, 175th Anniv. — A767

85pf, Charity Hospital, Berlin, 275th anniv.

**1985, Oct. 22** ***Perf. 14***

**2508** A767 20pf Administration bldg. .30 .25
**2509** A767 85pf Buildings, 1897, 1982 1.25 1.25

Castle Cacilienhof, UN Emblem A768

**1985, Oct. 22** **Photo.** ***Perf. 13***

**2510** A768 85pf multi .95 .45

UN, 40th Anniv.

Circus Art — A769

**1985, Nov. 12** ***Perf. 14***

**2511** A769 10pf Elephant training .30 .30
**2512** A769 20pf Trapeze artist .45 .45
**2513** A769 35pf Acrobats on unicycles .95 .95
**2514** A769 50pf Tiger training 1.40 1.40
*a.* Block of 4, #2511-2514 5.75 13.00

Souvenir Sheet

Brothers Grimm, Fabulists & Philologists — A770

Fairy tales compiled by Wilhelm (1786-1859) and Jacob (1785-1863) Grimm.

**1985, Nov. 26 Litho. *Perf. 13½x13***

**2515** Sheet of 6 3.25 7.25
*a.* A770 5pf Wilhelm & Jacob Grimm .25 .25
*b.* A770 10pf Valiant Tailor .25 .25
*c.* A770 20pf Lucky John .55 1.40
*d.* A770 25pf Puss-in-Boots .55 1.40
*e.* A770 35pf Seven Ravens .25 .25
*f.* A770 85pf Sweet Porridge .25 .25

Monuments to Water Power — A772

Designs: 10pf, Cast iron hand pump, c. 1900. 35pf, Berlin-Altglienicke water tower, c. 1900. 50pf, Berlin-Friedrichshagen waterworks, 1893. 70pf, Rapphoden Hydro-electric Dam, 1959.

**Engr., Photo. & Engr. (35pf)**

**1986, Jan. 21 *Perf. 14***

**2516** A772 10pf dk grn & lake .25 .25
**2517** A772 35pf buff, blk & dk grn .30 .30
**2518** A772 50pf dk red brn & lt ol grn .60 .60
**2519** A772 70pf dk bl & brn .75 .75
*Nos. 2516-2519 (4)* 1.90 1.90

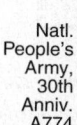

Postal Uniforms, c. 1850 — A773

**1986, Feb. 4 Photo. *Perf. 14½x14***

**2520** A773 10pf Saxon postillion .25 .25
*a.* Litho., perf. 12½x13 .25 .25
**2521** A773 20pf Prussian postman .35 .30
*a.* Litho., perf. 12½x13 .35 .30
**2522** A773 85pf Prussian P.O. clerk 1.10 1.05
*a.* Litho., perf. 12½x13 1.10 1.05
**2523** A773 1m Mecklenburg clerk 1.60 1.60
*a.* Litho., perf. 12½x13 1.60 1.60

Natl. People's Army, 30th Anniv. A774

**1986, Feb. 18 *Perf. 14***

**2524** A774 20pf multi .55 .30

No. 2524 printed se-tenant with gold and red inscribed label. Value of single with attached label: unused 80c; used 45c.

Free German Youth Org., 40th Anniv. — A775

**1986, Feb. 18**

**2525** A775 20pf multi .45 .30

Leipzig Spring Fair A776

**1986, Mar. 11 Litho. *Perf. 13x12½***

**2526** A776 35pf Fair grounds entrance, 1946 .35 .25
**2527** A776 50pf Trawler Atlantik 488 .50 .40

Manned Space Flight, 25th Anniv. — A777

Designs: 40pf, Yuri Gagarin, Soviet cosomonaut, Vostok rocket, 1961. 50pf, Cosmonauts V. Bykowski, USSR, and S. Jahn, DDR, Vega probe, 1986, Intercosmos emblem. 70pf, Venera probe, Venus, spectrometer. 85pf, MKF-6 multi-spectral reconnaissance camera.

**1986, Mar. 25 *Perf. 14***

**2528** A777 40pf multi .30 .40
**2529** A777 50pf multi .40 .40
**2530** A777 70pf multi .55 .60
**2531** A777 85pf multi .70 .75
*a.* Block of 4, #2528-2531 3.50 4.00

Socialist Unity 11th Party Day — A778

10pf, Marx, Engels & Lenin. 20pf, Ernst Thalmann. 50pf, Wilhelm Pieck & Otto Grotewohl, Uniting Party Day, 1946. 85pf,Family, motto. 1m, Construction worker, key to economic progress.

**1986, Apr. 8 *Perf. 13½x13***

**2532** A778 10pf multi .25 .25
**2533** A778 20pf multi .25 .25
**2534** A778 50pf multi .45 .45
**2535** A778 85pf multi .95 .95
*Nos. 2532-2535 (4)* 1.90 1.90

**Souvenir Sheet**

***Perf. 13x14***

**2536** A778 1m multi 1.25 2.10

Ernst Thalmann Park Opening, Berlin — A779

**1986, Apr. 15 Photo. *Perf. 14***

**2537** A779 20pf Memorial statue .60 .30

Trams and Streetcars — A780

Designs: 10pf, Dresden horse-drawn tram, 1886. 20pf, Leipzig streetcar, 1896. 40pf, Berlin streetcar, 1919. 70pf, Halle streetcar, 1928.

**1986, May 20 Photo. *Perf. 14***

**2538** A780 10pf multicolored .25 .25
**2539** A780 20pf multicolored .25 .25
**2540** A780 40pf multicolored .55 .65
**2541** A780 70pf multicolored .80 .80
*Nos. 2538-2541 (4)* 1.85 1.95

Dresden Zoo, 125th Anniv. — A781

Berlin, 750th Anniv. — A782

**1986, May 27 Litho. *Perf. 14***

**2542** A781 10pf Orangutan .25 .25
**2543** A781 20pf Colobus monkey .40 .30
**2544** A781 50pf Mandrill .85 .85
**2545** A781 70pf Lemur 1.05 1.05
*Nos. 2542-2545 (4)* 2.55 2.45

**Litho. & Engr., Engr. (70pf, 1m)**

**1986, June 3 *Perf. 12½x13, 13x12½***

20pf, 50pf are horiz.

**2546** A782 10pf City seal, 1253 .25 .25
**2547** A782 20pf Map, 1648 .45 .25
**2548** A782 50pf City arms, 1253 1.00 .65
**2549** A782 70pf Nicholas Church, 1832 1.75 1.00
*Nos. 2546-2549 (4)* 3.45 2.15

**Souvenir Sheet**

**2550** A782 1m Royal Palace, 1986 1.60 2.00

21st Workers' Games, Magdeburg — A783

20pf, Couple in folk dress, house construction. 50pf, Magdeburg Port, River Elbe.

**1986, June 17 Litho. *Perf. 13x12½***

**2551** A783 20pf multi .25 .25
**2552** A783 50pf multi .30 .30
*a.* Pair, #2551-2552 + label 1.00 1.00

9th Youth Stamp Exhibition, Berlin — A784

**1986, July 22 Litho. *Perf. 13x12½***

**2553** A784 10pf + 5pf Berlin, c. 1652 .25 .25
**2554** A784 20pf Art, architecture, 1986 .25 .25
*a.* Pair, #2553-2554 + label .50 .70

Castles A785

**1986, July 29 *Perf. 13x12½***

**2555** A785 10pf Schwerin .25 .25
*a.* Miniature sheet of 4 .80 .80
**2556** A785 20pf Gustrow .25 .25
*a.* Miniature sheet of 4 1.10 1.10
**2557** A785 85pf Rheinsberg .85 .85
**2558** A785 1m Ludwigslust 1.10 1.10
*Nos. 2555-2558 (4)* 2.45 2.45

Intl. Peace Year A786

**1986, Aug. 5 Photo. *Perf. 13***

**2559** A786 35pf multi .50 .40

Berlin Wall, 25th Anniv. — A787

**1986, Aug. 5 Litho. *Perf. 14***

**2560** A787 20pf Soldiers, Brandenburg Gate .55 .40

Souvenir Sheet

Leipzig Autumn Fair — A788

**1986, Aug. 19**

**2561** A788 Sheet of 2 1.40 2.10
*a.* 25pf Fair building .25 .40
*b.* 85pf Cloth merchants, 15th cent. .80 1.25

City Coins A789

**1986, Sept. 2 Photo. *Perf. 13***

**2562** A789 10pf Rostock, 1637 .25 .25
**2563** A789 35pf Nordhausen, 1660 .30 .30
**2564** A789 50pf Erfurt, 1633 .45 .40
**2565** A789 85pf Magdeburg, 1638 .80 .80
**2566** A789 1m Stralsund, 1622 1.25 1.25
*Nos. 2562-2566 (5)* 3.05 3.00

44th World Sports Shooting Championships, Suhl — A790

**1986, Sept. 2 *Perf. 14***

**2567** A790 20pf Rifle shooting .25 .25
**2568** A790 70pf Woman firing handgun .80 .70
**2569** A790 85pf Skeet-shooting .95 .85
*Nos. 2567-2569 (3)* 2.00 1.80

11th World Trade Unions Congress, Berlin — A791

**1986, Sept. 9**
**2570** A791 70pf multi+label .95 .80

Border Guards, 40th Anniv. — A792

**1986, Sept. 9**
**2571** A792 20pf multi .40 .30

Intl. Brigades in Spain, 50th Anniv. — A793

**1986, Sept. 11**
**2572** A793 20pf Memorial, Friedrichshain .35 .25

Natl. Memorial for Concentration Camp Victims, Sachsenhausem, 25th Anniv. — A794

**1986, Sept. 23**
**2573** A794 35pf multi .60 .30

Mukran-Klaipeda Train-Ferry, Inauguration — A795

**1986, Sept. 23**
**2574** A795 50pf Pier, Mukran .40 .40
**2575** A795 50pf Ferry .40 .40
*a.* Pair, #2574-2575 1.35 1.35

Souvenir Sheet

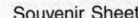

Carl Maria von Weber (1786-1826), Composer — A796

**1986, Nov. 4 Litho. *Perf. 14***
**2576** A796 85pf multi 1.20 2.00

Indira Gandhi (1917-1984), Prime Minister of India — A797

**1986, Nov. 18 Photo.**
**2577** A797 10pf multi .30 .25

Miniature Sheet

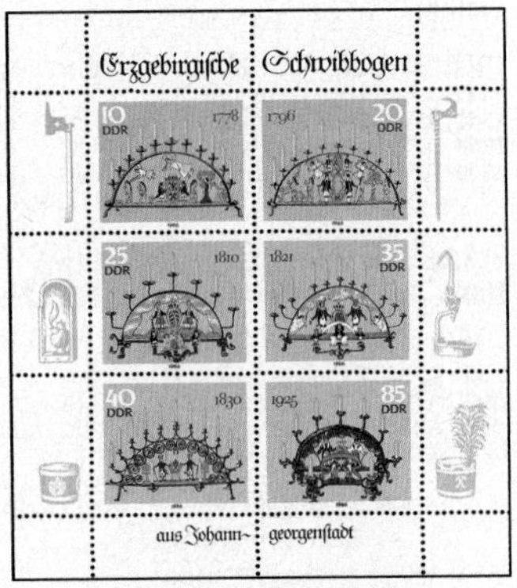


Chandeliers from the Ore Mountains — A798

Wrought iron candle-carrying chandeliers presented to Johann Georgenstadt miners annually by the mine blacksmith.

**1986, Nov. 18 Photo. *Perf. 14***
**2578** Sheet of 6 2.40 2.75
*a.* A798 10pf 1778 .25 .25
*b.* A798 20pf 1796 .25 .25
*c.* A798 25pf 1810 .55 .55
*d.* A798 35pf 1821 .55 .55
*e.* A798 40pf 1830 .25 .25
*f.* A798 85pf 1925 .25 .25

Statues of Roland, Medieval Hero — A799

**1987, Jan. 20 Photo. *Perf. 14½x14***
**2579** A799 10pf Stendal, 1525 .25 .25
**2580** A799 20pf Halle, 1719 .25 .25
**2581** A799 35pf Brandenburg, 1474 .30 .30
**2582** A799 50pf Quedlinburg, 1460 .55 .55
*Nos. 2579-2582 (4)* 1.35 1.35

See Nos. 2782-2785.

Historic Post Offices A800

**1987, Feb. 3 Photo. *Perf. 14x14½***
**2583** A800 10pf Freiberg, 1889 .25 .25
**2584** A800 20pf Perleberg, 1897 .25 .25
**2585** A800 70pf Weimar, 1889 .55 .55
**2586** A800 1.20m Kirschau, 1926 1.10 1.10
*a.* Block of 4, #2583-2586 2.60 2.60

Nos. 2583-2586 printed in sheets of fifty and se-tenant in sheets of 40.

Berlin, 750th Anniv. A801

Architecture: 20pf, Reconstructed Palais Ephraim, Nikolai Quarter, demolished 1936, reopened 1987, vert. 35pf, Old Marzahn Village, modern housing. 70pf, Marx-Engels Forum, Central Berlin. 85pf, Reconstructed Friedrichstadt Palace Theater, reopened 1984.

***Perf. 12½x13, 13x12½***
**1987, Feb. 17 Engr.**
**2587** A801 20pf vio brn & bluish grn .25 .25
**2588** A801 35pf sage grn & dk rose brn .40 .25
**2589** A801 70pf org & dk bl .80 .70
**2590** A801 85pf dk ol grn & yel grn 1.20 1.00
*Nos. 2587-2590 (4)* 2.65 2.20

See Nos. 2628-2631.

Democratic Women's Federation, 40th Anniv. — A802

**1987, Mar. 3 Litho. *Perf. 13½***
**2591** A802 10pf sil, dk bl & brt red .30 .25

Leipzig Spring Fair A803

**1987, Mar. 10 *Perf. 13x12½***
**2592** A803 35pf New Fair Hall No. 20 .30 .25
**2593** A803 50pf Traders at market, c. 1804 .65 .65

Leaders of the German Workers' Movement — A804

#2594, Fritz Gabler (1897-1974). #2595, Robert Siewert (1887-1973). #2596, Walter Vesper (1897-1978). #2597, Clara Zetkin (1857-1933).

**1987, Mar. 24 Engr. *Perf. 14***
**2594** A804 10pf dark gray .25 .25
**2595** A804 10pf dark green .25 .25
**2596** A804 10pf black .25 .25
**2597** A804 10pf vio black .25 .25
*Nos. 2594-2597 (4)* 1.00 1.00

See Nos. 2721-2724.

K.A. Lingner (1861-1916), Museum A805

**1987, Apr. 7 Photo. *Perf. 14***
**2598** A805 85pf multi .95 .80

German Hygiene Museum, Dresden, 75th anniv.

Free German Trade Unions 11th Congress A806

**1987, Apr. 7 Litho. *Perf. 13x12½***
**2599** A806 20pf Construction .25 .25
**2600** A806 50pf Computer, ship .45 .45
*a.* Pair, #2599-2600 + label .95 1.25

German Red Cross 10th Congress A807

**1987, Apr. 7 Photo. *Perf. 14***
**2601** A807 35pf multi .45 .25

Agricultural Cooperative, 35th Anniv. — A808

**1987, Apr. 21 Litho. *Perf. 13x12½***
**2602** A808 20pf multi .35 .30

Famous Men A809

Designs: 10pf, Ludwig Uhland (1787-1862), poet, philologist. 20pf, Arnold Zweig (1887-1968), novelist. 35pf, Gerhart Hauptmann (1862-1946), 1912 Nobel laureate for literature, and scene from The Weavers. 50pf, Gustav Hertz (1887-1975), physicist, and atomic energy transmission diagram.

**1987, May 5**
**2603** A809 10pf multi .25 .25
**2604** A809 20pf multi .25 .25
**2605** A809 35pf multi .35 .35
**2606** A809 50pf multi .60 .60
*Nos. 2603-2606 (4)* 1.45 1.45

Freshwater Fish — A810

**1987, May 19 Litho. *Perf. 13x12½***
**2607** A810 5pf Abramis brama .25 .25
**2608** A810 10pf Salmo trutta fario .25 .25
**2609** A810 20pf Silurus glanis .25 .25
**2610** A810 35pf Thymallus thymallus .40 .40
**2611** A810 50pf Barbus barbus .55 .40
**2612** A810 70pf Esox lucius .80 .80
*Nos. 2607-2612 (6)* 2.50 2.35

Nos. 2608-2609 exist in sheets of 4.

Fire Engines A811

**1987, June 16**

**2613** A811 10pf Hand-operated, 1756 .25 .25
**2614** A811 25pf Steam, 1903 .25 .25
**2615** A811 40pf LF 15, 1919 .45 .45
**2616** A811 70pf LF 16-TS 8, 1971 .80 .80
*a.* Block of 4, Nos. 2613-2616 2.25 2.25

Souvenir Sheet

Esperanto Movement, Cent. — A812

**1987, July 7** **Litho.** ***Perf. 14***

**2617** A812 85pf L.L. Zamenhof, globe 1.25 2.00

World Wildlife Fund A813

**1987, July 7** **Photo.**

**2618** A813 10pf Two otters .25 .25
**2619** A813 25pf Otter swimming .60 .25
**2620** A813 35pf Otter 1.25 .35
**2621** A813 60pf Close-up of head 2.50 1.00
*Nos. 2618-2621 (4)* 4.60 1.85

8th Sports Festival and 11th Youth Sports Championships, Leipzig — A814

**1987, July 21**

**2622** A814 5pf Tug-of-war .25 .25
**2623** A814 10pf Handball .25 .25
**2624** A814 20pf + 5pf Girls' long jump .25 .25
**2625** A814 35pf Table tennis .30 .30
**2626** A814 40pf Bowling .45 .45
**2627** A814 70pf Running .70 .70
*Nos. 2622-2627 (6)* 2.20 2.20

**Berlin Anniversary Type of 1987**

***Perf. 12½x13, 13x12½***

**1987, Feb. 17** **Engr.**

**2628** A801 10pf like No. 2587 .25 .25
*a.* Miniature sheet of 4 1.00 1.10
**2629** A801 10pf like No. 2588 .25 .25
*a.* Miniature sheet of 4 1.00 1.10
**2630** A801 20pf like No. 2589 .25 .25
*a.* Miniature sheet of 4 1.10 1.40
**2631** A801 20pf like No. 2590 .25 .25
*a.* Miniature sheet of 4 1.00 1.40
*Nos. 2628-2631 (4)* 1.00 1.00

Assoc. of Sports and Science, 35th Anniv. A815

**1987, Aug. 4** **Litho.** ***Perf. 13x12½***

**2632** A815 10pf multi .30 .25

Stamp Day A816

Designs: 10pf+5pf, Court Post Office, Berlin, 1760. 20pf, Wartenberg Palace, former Prussian General Post Office, 1770.

**1987, Aug. 11** **Photo.** ***Perf. 14***

**2633** A816 10pf +5pf multi .25 .25
**2634** A816 20pf multi .25 .25
*a.* Pair, #2633-2634 + label .60 1.10

Souvenir Sheet

Leipzig Autumn Fair — A817

**1987, Aug. 25** **Litho.** ***Perf. 13½***

**2635** A817 Sheet of 2 1.40 2.00
*a.* 40pf multi .40 .50
*b.* 50pf multi .60 .75

Intl. War Victims' Memorial, Budapest A818

**1987, Sept. 8** **Photo.** ***Perf. 14***

**2636** A818 35pf Statue by Jozsef Somogyi .60 .25

Souvenir Sheet

Thalmann Memorial — A819

**Litho. & Engr.**

**1987, Sept. 8** ***Perf. 14***

**2637** A819 1.35m buff, ver & blk 2.10 2.50

City of Berlin, 750th anniv.

10th Natl. Art Exhibition, Berlin — A820

Designs: 10pf, Weidendamm Bridge, Berlin, 1986, by Arno Mohr. 50pf, They Only Wanted to Learn How to Read and Write, Nicaragua, 1985-86, by Willi Sitte. 70pf, Large Figure of a Man in Mourning, 1983, scupture by Wieland Forster. 1m, Ceramic bowl, 1986, by Gerd Lucke. Nos. 2638-2640, vert.

**1987, Sept. 28** **Litho.**

**2638** A820 10pf multi .25 .25
**2639** A820 50pf multi .45 .45
**2640** A820 70pf multi .65 .70
**2641** A820 1m multi .95 1.10
*Nos. 2638-2641 (4)* 2.30 2.50

Lenin, Flag, Smolny Institute, Cruiser Aurora A821

**1987, Oct. 27** **Photo.** ***Perf. 14***

**2642** A821 10pf shown .25 .25
**2643** A821 20pf Spasski Tower .25 .25

October Revolution, Russia, 70th anniv.

Robot ZIM 10-S Welding A822

**1987, Nov. 3** **Litho.** ***Perf. 13x12½***

**2644** A822 10pf Personal computer .30 .25
**2645** A822 20pf shown .30 .25

30th MMM Science Fair and 10th Central Industrial Fair for Students and Youth Scientists, Leipzig.

Miniature Sheet

Christmas Candle Carousels from the Ore Mountains — A823

Designs: 10pf, Annaberg, c. 1810. 20pf, Freiberg, c. 1830. 25pf, Neustadtel, c. 1870. 35pf, Schneeberg, c. 1870. 40pf, Lossnitz, c. 1880. 85pf, Seiffen, c. 1910.

**1987, Nov. 3** **Litho.** ***Perf. 12½x13***

**2646** Sheet of 6 2.60 3.00
*a.* A823 10pf multi .25 .25
*b.* A823 20pf multi .55 .65
*c.* A823 25pf multi .25 .25
*d.* A823 35pf multi .25 .25
*e.* A823 40pf multi .55 .65
*f.* A823 85pf multi .25 .25

1988 Winter Olympics, Calgary — A824

**1988, Jan. 19** **Photo.** ***Perf. 14½x14***

**2647** A824 5pf Ski jumping .25 .25
**2648** A824 10pf Speed skating .25 .25
**2649** A824 20pf +10pf 4-Man bobsled .35 .30
**2650** A824 35pf Biathlon .45 .40
*Nos. 2647-2650 (4)* 1.30 1.20

**Souvenir Sheet**

***Perf. 13x12½***

**2651** A824 1.20m Single and double luge 1.60 2.00

No. 2649 surtaxed for the Olympic Promotion Society.

Postal Buildings, East Berlin A825

**1988, Feb. 2** ***Perf. 14***

**2652** A825 15pf Berlin-Buch post office .25 .25
**2653** A825 20pf Natl. Postal Museum .40 .25
**2654** A825 50pf General post office, Berlin-Marzahn .90 .65
*Nos. 2652-2654 (3)* 1.55 1.15

Souvenir Sheet

Bertolt Brecht (1898-1956), Playwright — A826

**1988, Feb. 2** **Litho.** ***Perf. 13x12½***

**2655** A826 70pf multi 1.00 1.75

Flowering Plants — A827

Leipzig Spring Fair — A828

**1988, Feb. 16** **Photo.** ***Perf. 14***

**2656** A827 10pf Tillandsia macrochlamys .25 .25
**2657** A827 25pf Tillandsia bulbosa .25 .25
**2658** A827 40pf Tillandsia kalmbacheri .45 .45
**2659** A827 70pf Guzmania blassii .75 .75
*Nos. 2656-2659 (4)* 1.70 1.70

**1988, Mar. 8 Litho. *Perf. 12½x13***

20pf, Entrance #8. 70pf, Faust & Mephistopheles, bronze statue by Matthieu Molitor.

| | | | | |
|---|---|---|---|---|
| **2660** | A828 | 20pf multi | .25 | .25 |
| **2661** | A828 | 70pf multi | .85 | .65 |

Madler Passage (arcade), 75th anniv.

Souvenir Sheet

A829

**1988, Mar. 8 *Perf. 14***

| | | | | |
|---|---|---|---|---|
| **2662** | A829 | 70pf multi | 1.25 | 2.00 |

Joseph von Eichendorff (1788-1857), poet.

Seals — A830

**1988, Mar. 22 Photo. *Perf. 14***

| | | | | |
|---|---|---|---|---|
| **2663** | A830 | 10pf Muhlhausen saddler, 1565 | .25 | .25 |
| **2664** | A830 | 25pf Dresden butcher, 1564 | .25 | .25 |
| **2665** | A830 | 35pf Nauen smith, 16th cent. | .30 | .30 |
| **2666** | A830 | 50pf Frankfurt-Oder clothier, 16th cent. | .40 | .40 |
| *a.* | | Block of 4, #2663-2666 | 1.75 | 1.75 |

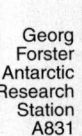

Georg Forster Antarctic Research Station A831

**1988, Mar. 22 Litho. *Perf. 13x12½***

| | | | | |
|---|---|---|---|---|
| **2667** | A831 | 35pf multi | .70 | .30 |

District Capitals A832

**1988, Apr. 5 Photo. *Perf. 14***

| | | | | |
|---|---|---|---|---|
| **2668** | A832 | 5pf Wismar | .25 | .25 |
| **2669** | A832 | 10pf Anklam | .25 | .25 |
| **2670** | A832 | 25pf Ribnitz-Damgarten | .25 | .25 |
| **2671** | A832 | 60pf Stralsund | .55 | .55 |
| **2672** | A832 | 90pf Bergen | .85 | .85 |
| **2673** | A832 | 1.20m Greifswald | 1.10 | 1.10 |
| | | *Nos. 2668-2673 (6)* | 3.25 | 3.25 |

Souvenir Sheet

Ulrich von Hutten (1488-1523), Promulgator of the Lutheran Movement — A833

**1988, Apr. 5 Litho. *Perf. 12½x13***

| | | | | |
|---|---|---|---|---|
| **2674** | A833 | 70pf multi | 1.10 | 1.40 |

USSR-DDR Manned Space Flight, 10th Anniv. — A834

Designs: 5pf, Cosmonauts S. Jahn and Valery Bykowski, Soyuz-29 landing, Sept. 3, 1978. 10pf, MKS-M multi-channel spectrometer. 20pf, MIR space station.

**1988, June 21 Litho. *Perf. 14***

| | | | | |
|---|---|---|---|---|
| **2675** | A834 | 5pf multi | .25 | .25 |
| **2676** | A834 | 10pf multi | .25 | .25 |
| **2677** | A834 | 20pf multi | .25 | .25 |
| | | *Nos. 2675-2677 (3)* | .75 | .75 |

See Nos. 2698-2700.

10th Youth Stamp Exhibitions in Erfurt and Karl-Marx-Stadt — A835

Designs: 10pf+5pf, Erfurt. c. 1520. 20+5pf, Chemnitz, c. 1620. 25pf, Historic and modern buildings of Erfurt. 50pf, Historic and modern buildings of Karl-Marx-Stadt.

**1988, June 21 Photo.**

| | | | | |
|---|---|---|---|---|
| **2678** | A835 | 10pf +5pf multi | .25 | .25 |
| **2679** | A835 | 20pf +5pf multi | .25 | .25 |
| **2680** | A835 | 25pf multi | .25 | .25 |
| *a.* | | Pair, #2678, 2680 + label | .60 | 1.00 |
| **2681** | A835 | 50pf multi | .55 | .55 |
| *a.* | | Pair, #2679, 2681 + label | .90 | 1.75 |

Nos. 2678-2679 surtaxed to benefit the Philatelists' League of the DDR Cultural Union.

22nd Workers' Games, Frankfurt-on-Oder — A836

**1988, June 7 Litho. *Perf. 13x12½***

| | | | | |
|---|---|---|---|---|
| **2682** | | 20pf multi | .25 | .25 |
| **2683** | | 50pf multi, diff. | .45 | .45 |
| *a.* | A836 | Pair, #2682-2683 + label | 1.00 | 1.00 |

Workers' Militia, 35th Anniv. — A837

**1988, July 5 Photo. *Perf. 14***

| | | | | |
|---|---|---|---|---|
| **2684** | A837 | 5pf Oath | .25 | .25 |
| **2685** | A837 | 10pf Ernst Thalmann tribute | .25 | .25 |
| **2686** | A837 | 15pf Roll call | .25 | .25 |
| **2687** | A837 | 20pf Weapons exchange | .25 | .25 |
| | | *Nos. 2684-2687 (4)* | 1.00 | 1.00 |

8th Young Pioneers' Congress, Karl-Marx-Stadt — A838

**1988, July 19 Litho. *Perf. 13x12½***

| | | | | |
|---|---|---|---|---|
| **2688** | A838 | 10pf shown | .25 | .25 |
| **2689** | A838 | 10pf +5pf Youths playing musical instruments | .25 | .25 |
| *a.* | | Pair, #2688-2689 + label | 1.10 | 1.10 |

Surtax financed the congress.

1988 Summer Olympics, Seoul A839

**1988, Aug. 9 Photo. *Perf. 14***

| | | | | |
|---|---|---|---|---|
| **2690** | A839 | 5pf Swimming | .25 | .25 |
| **2691** | A839 | 10pf Handball | .25 | .25 |
| **2692** | A839 | 20pf +10pf Hurdles | .35 | .35 |
| **2693** | A839 | 25pf Rowing | .35 | .35 |
| **2694** | A839 | 35pf Boxing | .35 | .35 |
| **2695** | A839 | 50pf +20pf Cycling | .70 | .70 |
| | | *Nos. 2690-2695 (6)* | 2.25 | 2.25 |

**Souvenir Sheet**

**Litho.**

***Perf. 13x12½***

| | | | | |
|---|---|---|---|---|
| **2696** | A839 | 85pf Relay race | 1.80 | 3.00 |

Souvenir Sheet

Leipzig Autumn Fair — A840

**1988, Aug. 30 Litho. *Perf. 14***

| | | | | |
|---|---|---|---|---|
| **2697** | A840 | Sheet of 3 | 1.60 | 2.25 |
| *a.* | | 5pf Fair, c. 1810 | .25 | .40 |
| *b.* | | 15pf Battle of Leipzig Memorial | .25 | .40 |
| *c.* | | 1m Fair, c. 1820 | .80 | 1.25 |

**DDR-USSR Manned Space Flight Type**

**1988, Aug. 30 Litho. *Perf. 14***

| | | | | |
|---|---|---|---|---|
| **2698** | A834 | 10pf like No. 2675 | .25 | .25 |
| *a.* | | Sheet of 4 | 1.00 | 1.00 |
| **2699** | A834 | 20pf like No. 2676 | .30 | .30 |
| *a.* | | Sheet of 4 | 1.30 | 1.30 |
| **2700** | A834 | 35pf like No. 2677 | .55 | .55 |
| *a.* | | Sheet of 4 | 2.10 | 2.10 |
| | | *Nos. 2698-2700 (3)* | 1.10 | 1.10 |

Fascism Resistance Memorial, Como, Italy — A841

**1988, Sept. 13 Photo.**

| | | | | |
|---|---|---|---|---|
| **2701** | A841 | 35pf multi | .40 | .30 |

Memorial at Buchenwald, 30th Anniv. — A842

**1988, Sept. 13 *Perf. 14***

| | | | | |
|---|---|---|---|---|
| **2702** | A842 | 10pf multi | .60 | .25 |

Mariner's Soc., Stralsund, 500th Anniv. — A843

Paintings: 5pf, *Adolph Friedrich* at Stralsund, by C. Leplow. 10pf, *Die Gartenlaube* (built in 1872) at Stralsund, by J.F. Kruger. 70pf, Brigantine *Auguste Mathilde* (built in 1830) at Stralsund, by I.C. Grunwaldt. 1.20m, Brig *Hoffnung* at Cologne, by G.A. Luther.

**1988, Sept. 20 Litho. *Perf. 13½x13***

| | | | | |
|---|---|---|---|---|
| **2703** | A843 | 5pf multi | .30 | .25 |
| **2704** | A843 | 10pf multi | .30 | .25 |
| **2705** | A843 | 70pf multi | .75 | .70 |
| **2706** | A843 | 1.20m multi | 1.10 | 1.10 |
| | | *Nos. 2703-2706 (4)* | 2.45 | 2.30 |

Ship Lifts and Bridges A844

**1988, Oct. 18 Photo. *Perf. 14x14½***

| | | | | |
|---|---|---|---|---|
| **2707** | A844 | 5pf Magdeburg | .25 | .25 |
| **2708** | A844 | 10pf Magdeburg-Rothensee | .25 | .25 |
| **2709** | A844 | 35pf Niederfinow | .30 | .25 |
| **2710** | A844 | 70pf Altfriesack | .65 | .65 |
| **2711** | A844 | 90pf Rugendamm | .80 | .80 |
| | | *Nos. 2707-2711 (5)* | 2.25 | 2.20 |

1st Nazi Pogrom (Kristallnacht), Nov. 9, 1938 — A845

**1988, Nov. 8 *Perf. 14***

| | | | | |
|---|---|---|---|---|
| **2712** | A845 | 35pf Menorah | .50 | .30 |

Paintings by Max Lingner (1888-1959) A846

**1988, Nov. 8**

2713 A846 5pf *In the Boat, 1931* .25 .25
2714 A846 10pf *Yvonne*, 1939 .25 .25
2715 A846 20pf *Free, Strong and Happy*, 1944 .30 .25
2716 A846 85pf *New Harvest*, 1951 .80 .80
*Nos. 2713-2716 (4)* 1.60 1.55

Souvenir Sheet

Friedrich Wolf (1888-1953), Playwright — A847

**1988, Nov. 22** **Litho.**

2717 A847 1.10m multi 1.30 3.00

WHO, 40th Anniv. — A848

**1988, Nov. 22** **Photo.**

2718 A848 85pf multi .95 .45

Miniature Sheet

Bone Lace from Erzgebirge — A849

Various lace designs.

**1988, Nov. 22 Litho.** ***Perf. 12½x13***

| | | | |
|---|---|---|---|
| 2719 | Sheet of 6 | 2.60 | 2.60 |
| *a.* | A849 20pf multi | .25 | .25 |
| *b.* | A849 25pf multi | .55 | .55 |
| *c.* | A849 35pf multi | .25 | .25 |
| *d.* | A849 40pf multi | .25 | .25 |
| *e.* | A849 50pf multi | .55 | .55 |
| *f.* | A849 85pf multi | .25 | .25 |

Council for Mutual Economic Aid, 40th Anniv. A850

**1989, Jan. 10 Photo.** ***Perf. 13***

2720 A850 20pf multi .35 .25

**Labor Leaders Type of 1987**

Portraits: No. 2721, Edith Baumann (1909-1973). No. 2722, Otto Meier (1889-1962). No. 2723, Fritz Selbmann (1899-1975). No. 2724, Alfred Oelssner (1879-1962).

**1989, Jan. 24 Engr.** ***Perf. 14***

2721 A804 10pf dark vio brn .25 .25
2722 A804 10pf dark grn .25 .25
2723 A804 10pf dark blue .25 .25
2724 A804 10pf brn blk .25 .25
*Nos. 2721-2724 (4)* 1.00 1.00

Telephones A851

Designs: 10pf, Philipp Reis, 1861. 20pf, Siemens & Halske wall model, 1882. 50pf, Wall model OB 03, 1903. 85pf, Table model OB 05, 1905.

**1989, Feb. 7** **Litho.**

2725 A851 10pf shown .25 .25
2726 A851 20pf multi .25 .25
2727 A851 50pf multi .45 .45
2728 A851 85pf multi .75 .75
*a.* Block of 4, #2725-2728 2.00 2.25

Famous Men A852

**1989, Feb. 28** **Photo.**

2729 A852 10pf Ludwig Renn (1889-1979) .25 .25
2730 A852 10pf Carl von Ossietzky (1889-1938) .25 .25
2731 A852 10pf Adam Scharrer (1889-1948) .25 .25
2732 A852 10pf Rudolf Mauersberger (1889-1971) .25 .25
2733 A852 10pf Johann Beckmann (1739-1811) .25 .25
*Nos. 2729-2733 (5)* 1.25 1.25

Leipzig Spring Fair — A853

**1989, Mar. 7** **Litho.**

2734 A853 70pf shown .75 .65
2735 A853 85pf Buildings, 1690 .90 .90

Handelshof, 80th anniv. (70pf).

Souvenir Sheet

Thomas Muntzer (c. 1468-1525), Religious Reformer — A854

**1989, Mar. 21** ***Perf. 13x12½***

2736 A854 1.10m multi 1.25 2.10

1st Long-distance German Railway, Leipzig-Dresden, Sesquicentennial — A855

15pf, Georg Friedrich List (1789-1846), industrialist, economist. 20pf, Dresden Station in Leipzig, 1839. 50pf, Leipzig Station in Dresden, 1839.

**1989, Apr. 4** ***Perf. 14***

2737 A855 15pf multi .30 .25
2738 A855 20pf multi .30 .25
2739 A855 50pf multi .55 .55
*Nos. 2737-2739 (3)* 1.15 1.05

A856

A857

Designs: Meissen Onion-pattern Porcelain, 250th anniv., and sword emblem.

**1989, Apr. 18 Litho.** ***Perf. 12½x13***

2740 A856 10pf Tea caddy .25 .25
2741 A856 20pf Vase .25 .30
2742 A856 35pf Breadboard .40 .50
2743 A856 70pf Teapot .80 .90
*Nos. 2740-2743 (4)* 1.70 1.95

**Size: 33x56mm**

***Perf. 14***

| | | | |
|---|---|---|---|
| 2744 | Block of 4 | 2.25 | 2.25 |
| *a.* | A856 10pf like No. 2740 | .30 | .30 |
| *b.* | A856 20pf like No. 2741 | .25 | .25 |
| *c.* | A856 35pf like No. 2742 | .35 | .35 |
| *d.* | A856 70pf like No. 2743 | .75 | .75 |

**1989, May 2 Photo.** ***Perf. 14½x14***

2745 A857 20pf "I" .25 .25
2746 A857 50pf "B" .45 .40
2747 A857 1.35m "A" 1.40 1.40
*Nos. 2745-2747 (3)* 2.10 2.05

Intl. Book Fair (IBA), Leipzig.

Student Government — A858

**1989, May 9 Litho.** ***Perf. 13½x12½***

2748 A858 20pf 8th World Youth Festival, Pyongyang .30 .40
2749 A858 20pf +5pf Whitsun meeting of Free German Youth .30 .40
*a.* Pair, #2748-2749 + label .60 .90

Princess Luise — A859

Carl Zeiss Foundation, Jena, Cent. — A860

Sculptures by Johann Gottfried Schadow (1764-1850), Prussian Court Sculptor.

**1989, May 16 Photo.** ***Perf. 14½x14***

2750 A859 50pf shown .60 .45
2751 A859 85pf Princess Friederike 1.10 .95

**1989, May 16**

Modern medical technology: 50pf, Interference microscope Jenaval. 85pf, Bicoordinate measuring instrument ZKM 01-250C.

2752 A860 50pf multi .40 .40
2753 A860 85pf multi .80 .80
*a.* Pair, #2752-2753 + label 1.60 1.60

Label pictures founder Ernst Abbe (1840-1905).

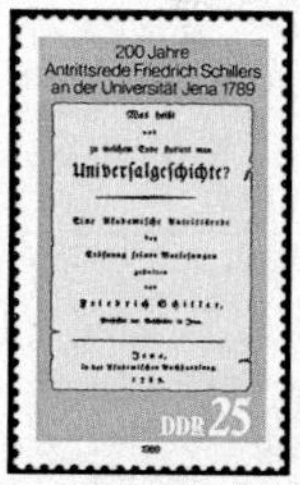


Jena University Inaugural Address, Bicent. — A861

**1989, May 23 Photo.** ***Perf. 14***

2754 A861 25pf Frontispiece .25 .25
2755 A861 85pf Excerpt .70 .70
*a.* Pair, #2754-2755 + label 1.10 1.10

Label pictures bust of Friedrich Schiller, author of the address.

Souvenir Sheet

Zoologists — A862

**1989, June 13** **Litho.**

| | | | |
|---|---|---|---|
| 2756 A862 | Sheet of 2 | 1.75 | 11.00 |
| *a.* | 50pf Alfred Brehm (1829-1884) | .50 | 3.50 |
| *b.* | 85pf Christian Brehm (1787-1864) | .95 | 5.75 |

French Revolution, Bicent. A863

5pf, Storming of the Bastille, July 14, 1789. 20pf, Revolutionaries, flag bearer. 90pf, Storming Tuileries Palace, Aug. 10, 1792.

**1989, July 4 Photo.** ***Perf. 13***

2757 A863 5pf multi .25 .25
2758 A863 20pf multi .25 .25
2759 A863 90pf multi .80 1.10
*Nos. 2757-2759 (3)* 1.30 1.60

Intl. Congress of Horse Breeders from Socialist States — A864

**1989, July 18 Litho. *Perf. 13½***

**2760** A864 10pf Haflinger .25 .25
**2761** A864 20pf English thoroughbred .25 .25
**2762** A864 70pf Cold blood .70 .70
**2763** A864 110pf Noble warm blood 1.10 1.10
*Nos. 2760-2763 (4)* 2.30 2.30

Natl. Stamp Exhibition, Magdeburg — A865

**1989, Aug. 8 Litho. *Perf. 13x12½***

**2764** A865 20pf Owlglass Fountain .25 .25
**2765** A865 70pf +5pf Demons Fountain .80 .70

No. 2765 surtaxed for the philatelic unit of the Kulturbund.

Souvenir Sheet

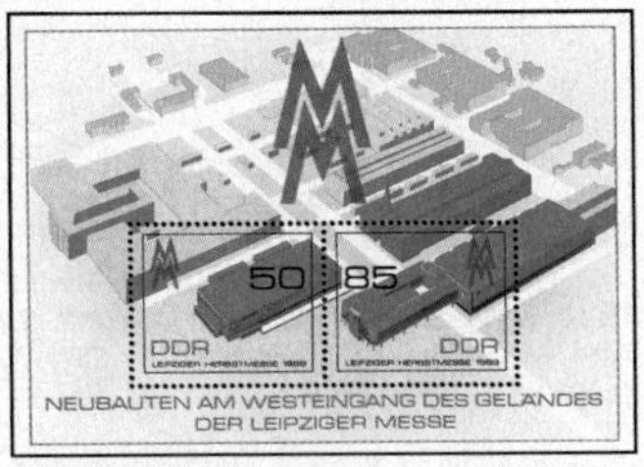


Leipzig Autumn Fair — A866

**1989, Aug. 22 *Perf. 14***

**2766** A866 Sheet of 2 1.50 2.50
*a.* 50pf Fairground .45 .80
*b.* 85pf Fairground, diff. .75 1.30

Thomas Muntzer (1489-1525), Religious Reformer A867

Various details of the painting *Early Bourgeois Revolution in Germany in 1525*, by W. Tubke.

**1989, Aug. 22**

**2767** A867 5pf Globe .25 .25
**2768** A867 10pf Fountain .25 .25
**2769** A867 20pf Battle scene .25 .25
*a.* Souvenir sheet of 4 2.00 2.00
**2770** A867 50pf Ark .45 .45
**2771** A867 85pf Rainbow, battle 1.10 1.10
*Nos. 2767-2771 (5)* 2.30 2.30

*Muttergruppe*, 1965, Bronze Statue in the Natl. Memorial, Ravensbruck A868

**1989, Sept. 5 Photo. *Perf. 14***

**2772** A868 35pf multi .55 .40

Natl. Memorial, Ravensbruck, 30th anniv.

Flowering Cacti (*Epiphyllum*) A869

**1989, Sept. 19 Litho. *Perf. 13***

**2773** A869 10m Adriana .25 .25
**2774** A869 35m Feuerzauber .40 .30
**2775** A869 50m Franzisko .65 .65
*Nos. 2773-2775 (3)* 1.30 1.20

DDR, 40th Anniv. — A870

**1989, Oct. 3 *Perf. 14***

**2776** A870 5pf Education .25 .25
**2777** A870 10pf Agriculture .25 .25
**2778** A870 20pf Construction .30 .25
**2779** A870 25pf Machinist, computer user .30 .30
*Nos. 2776-2779 (4)* 1.10 1.05

**Souvenir Sheet**

**2780** A870 135pf Two workers 4.50 4.50

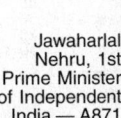

Jawaharlal Nehru, 1st Prime Minister of Independent India — A871

**1989, Nov. 7 Photo. *Perf. 14***

**2781** A871 35pf multicolored .45 .45

**Statues of Roland Type of 1987**

**1989, Nov. 7 *Perf. 14½x14***

**2782** A799 5pf Zerbst, 1445 .25 .25
**2783** A799 10pf Halberstadt, 1433 .25 .25
**2784** A799 20pf Buch-Altmark, 1611 .25 .25
**2785** A799 50pf Perleberg, 1546 .45 .45
*Nos. 2782-2785 (4)* 1.20 1.20

Miniature Sheet

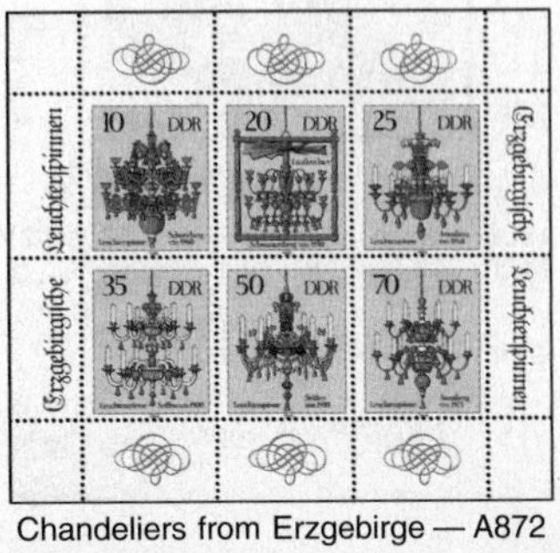


Chandeliers from Erzgebirge — A872

Designs: a, Schneeburg, circa 1860. b, Schwarzenberg, circa 1850. c, Annaberg, circa 1880. d, Seiffen, circa 1900. e, Seiffen, circa 1930. f, Annaberg, circa 1925.

**Litho. & Engr.**

**1989, Nov. 28 *Perf. 14***

**2786** Sheet of 6 2.50 2.50
*a.* A872 10pf multicolored .25 .25
*b.* A872 20pf multicolored .55 .55
*c.* A872 25pf multicolored .25 .25
*d.* A872 35pf multicolored .25 .25
*e.* A872 50pf multicolored .55 .55
*f.* A872 70pf multicolored .25 .25

Bees Collecting Nectar — A873

**1990, Jan. 9 Litho.**

**2787** A873 5pf Apple blossom .25 .25
**2788** A873 10pf Blooming heather .25 .25
**2789** A873 20pf Rape blossom .30 .30
**2790** A873 50pf Red clover .70 .70
*Nos. 2787-2790 (4)* 1.50 1.50

*The Young Post Rider*, an Engraving by Albrecht Durer — A874

**1990, Jan. 12 Litho. *Perf. 13***

**2791** A874 35pf multi .45 .55

Postal communications in Europe, 500th anniv.

See Austria No. 1486, Belgium No. 1332, Germany No. 1592 and Berlin No. 9N584.

Labor Leaders — A875

Portraits: #2792, Bruno Leuschner (1910-65). #2793, Erich Weinert (1890-1953).

**1990, Jan. 16 *Perf. 14***

**2792** A875 10pf gray brown .25 .25
**2793** A875 10pf deep blue .25 .25

Coats of Arms — A876

Early postal agency insignia: 10pf, Schwarzburg-Rudolstadt and Thurn & Taxis. 20pf, Royal Saxon letter collection. 50pf, Imperial Postal Agency. 1.10pf, Auxiliary post office.

**1990, Feb. 6 Photo. *Perf. 14***

**2794** A876 10pf multicolored .30 .25
**2795** A876 20pf multicolored .30 .25
**2796** A876 50pf multicolored .80 .65
**2797** A876 110pf multicolored 1.60 1.40
*Nos. 2794-2797 (4)* 3.00 2.55

**Size: 32x42mm**

***Perf. 13½***

**Litho.**

**2798** Block of 4 3.25 3.25
*a.* A876 10pf like No. 2794 .40 .25
*b.* A876 20pf like No. 2795 .40 .25
*c.* A876 50pf like No. 2796 .80 .65
*d.* A876 110pf like No. 2797 1.60 1.40

Posts & Telecommunications Workers' Day.

August Bebel (1840-1913), Co-founder of the Social Democratic Party — A877

**1990, Feb. 20 Photo.**

**2799** A877 20pf multicolored .40 .40

Flying Machine Designed by Leonardo da Vinci — A878

**1990, Feb. 20 Litho. *Perf. 13½x13***

**2800** A878 20pf shown .30 .25
**2801** A878 35pf +5pf Melchior Bauer .50 .50
**2802** A878 50pf Albrecht Berblinger .65 .55
**2803** A878 90pf Otto Lilienthal 1.25 1.25
*Nos. 2800-2803 (4)* 2.70 2.55

LILIENTHAL '91 airmail exhibition. No. 2801 surtaxed for philatelic promotion.

Leipzig Spring Fair Seals — A879

Dying Warriors — A880

**1990, Mar. 6 *Perf. 12½x13***

**2804** A879 70pf Seal, 1268 1.40 .70
**2805** A879 85pf Seal, 1497 1.40 .85

City of Leipzig and the Leipzig Spring Fair, 825th annivs.

**1990, Mar. 6 Photo. *Perf. 13½x14***

Sculptures by Andreas Schluter.

**2806** A880 40pf shown .60 .70
**2807** A880 70pf multi, diff. .80 .90

Museum of German History in the Zeughaus of Berlin.

Famous Men A881

Portraits: No. 2808, Friedrich Diesterweg (1790-1866), educator. No. 2809, Kurt Tucholsky (1890-1935), novelist, journalist.

**1990, Mar. 20 Photo. *Perf. 14***

**2808** A881 10pf multicolored .30 .30
**2809** A881 10pf multicolored .30 .30

Labor Day, Cent. — A882

**1990, Apr. 3**

**2810** A882 10pf shown .30 .30
**2811** A882 20pf Flower, "1890/1990" .70 .70

Dicraeosaurus — A883

***Perf. 13x12½, 12½x13***

**1990, Apr. 17 Litho.**

| | | | |
|---|---|---|---|
| **2812** | A883 10pf shown | .25 | .25 |
| **2813** | A883 25pf Kentrurosaurus | .25 | .25 |
| *a.* | Miniature sheet of 4 | 1.75 | 1.75 |
| **2814** | A883 35pf Dysalotosaurus | .30 | .30 |
| **2815** | A883 50pf Brachiosaurus | .50 | .50 |
| **2816** | A883 85pf Brachiosaurus skull | 1.10 | 1.10 |
| | *Nos. 2812-2816 (5)* | 2.40 | 2.40 |

Natural History Museum of Berlin, cent. Nos. 2815-2816 vert.

Penny Black, 150th Anniv. — A884

**1990, May 8** ***Perf. 14***

| | | | |
|---|---|---|---|
| **2817** | A884 20pf shown | .40 | .40 |
| **2818** | A884 35pf +15pf Saxony #1 | .80 | .80 |
| **2819** | A884 110pf No. 48 | 2.25 | 2.25 |
| | *Nos. 2817-2819 (3)* | 3.45 | 3.45 |

A885

Intl. Telecommunications Union, 125th Anniv.: 10pf, David Edward Hughes (1831-1900), type-printing telegraph, 1855. 20pf, Distribution linkage, Berlin-Kopenick post office. 25pf, TV and microwave tower. 50pf, Molniya news satellite, globe. 70pf, Philipp Reis (1834-1874), physicist, designed sound transmission equipment.

**1990, May 15**

| | | | |
|---|---|---|---|
| **2820** | A885 10pf multicolored | .30 | .30 |
| **2821** | A885 20pf multicolored | .30 | .30 |
| **2822** | A885 25pf multicolored | .30 | .30 |
| **2823** | A885 50pf multicolored | .80 | .80 |
| | *Nos. 2820-2823 (4)* | 1.70 | 1.70 |

**Souvenir Sheet**

| | | | |
|---|---|---|---|
| **2824** | A885 70pf multicolored | 2.50 | 3.00 |

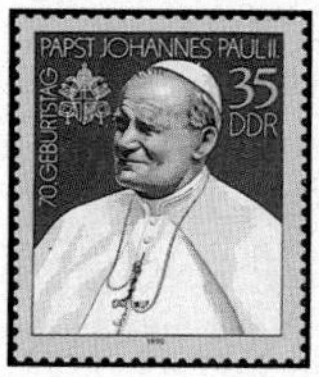


Pope John Paul II, 70th Birthday — A886

**1990, May 15**

| | | | |
|---|---|---|---|
| **2825** | A886 35pf multicolored | .80 | 1.00 |

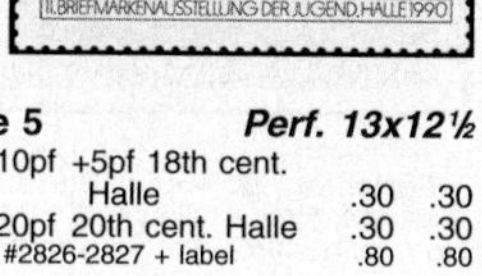

11th Youth Stamp Exhibition, Halle A887

**1990, June 5** ***Perf. 13x12½***

| | | | |
|---|---|---|---|
| **2826** | A887 10pf +5pf 18th cent. Halle | .30 | .30 |
| **2827** | A887 20pf 20th cent. Halle | .30 | .30 |
| *a.* | Pair, #2826-2827 + label | .80 | .80 |

Treasures in the German State Library, Berlin A888

Designs: 20pf, Rules of an order, 1264. 25pf, Rudimentum novitiorum, 1475. 50pf, Chosrou wa Schirin, 18th cent. 110pf, Book-cover of Amalienbibliothek, 18th cent.

**1990, June 19**

| | | | |
|---|---|---|---|
| **2828** | A888 20pf multicolored | .35 | .25 |
| **2829** | A888 25pf multicolored | .35 | .25 |
| **2830** | A888 50pf multicolored | 1.10 | .70 |
| **2831** | A888 110pf multicolored | 2.10 | 1.75 |
| | *Nos. 2828-2831 (4)* | 3.90 | 2.95 |

Castle Albrechtsburg and Cathedral, Meissen — A889

30pf, Goethe-Schiller Monument, Weimar. 50pf, Brandenburg Gate, Berlin. 60pf, Kyffhauser Monument. 70pf, Semper Opera, Dresden. 80pf, Castle Sanssouci, Potsdam. 100pf, Wartburg, Eisenach. 200pf, Magdeburg Cathedral. 500pf, Schwerin Castle.

**1990, July 2 Photo.** ***Perf. 14***

| | | | |
|---|---|---|---|
| **2832** | A889 10pf ultramarine | .40 | .30 |
| **2833** | A889 30pf olive green | .80 | .30 |
| **2834** | A889 50pf bluish green | .80 | .55 |
| **2835** | A889 60pf violet brown | .80 | .80 |
| **2836** | A889 70pf dark brown | .80 | .80 |
| **2837** | A889 80pf red brown | .80 | 1.00 |
| **2838** | A889 100pf dark carmine | 1.25 | .80 |
| **2839** | A889 200pf dark violet | 2.75 | 2.00 |
| **2840** | A889 500pf green | 5.25 | 5.25 |
| | *Nos. 2832-2840 (9)* | 13.65 | 11.80 |

Nos. 2832-2852 have face values based on the Federal Republic's Deutsche mark and were valid for postage in both countries.

Postal System, 500th Anniv. A890

30pf, 15th cent. postman. 50pf, 16th cent. postrider. 70pf, Post carriages c. 1595, 1750. 100pf, Railway mail carriages 1842, 1900.

**1990, Aug. 28 Litho.** ***Perf. 13x13½***

| | | | |
|---|---|---|---|
| **2841** | A890 30pf multicolored | .40 | .40 |
| **2842** | A890 50pf multicolored | .60 | .60 |
| **2843** | A890 70pf multicolored | .70 | 1.00 |
| **2844** | A890 100pf multicolored | 1.25 | 1.25 |
| | *Nos. 2841-2844 (4)* | 2.95 | 3.25 |

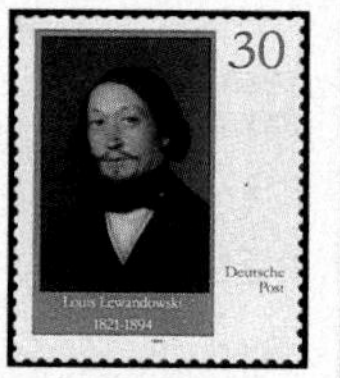


Louis Lewandowski (1821-94), Composer — A891

50pf+15pf, New Synagogue, Berlin.

**1990, Sept. 18** ***Perf. 14***

| | | | |
|---|---|---|---|
| **2845** | A891 30pf multicolored | .30 | .30 |
| **2846** | A891 50pf +15pf multi | .65 | .65 |

Heinrich Schliemann (1822-1890), Archaeologist A892

Design: 30pf, shown. 50pf, Schliemann, double pot c. 2600-1900 B.C., horiz.

**1990, Oct. 2 Photo.**

| | | | |
|---|---|---|---|
| **2847** | A892 30pf multicolored | .45 | .45 |
| **2848** | A892 50pf multicolored | .85 | .85 |

Intl. Astronautics Federation, 41st Congress, Dresden A893

**1990, Oct. 2**

| | | | |
|---|---|---|---|
| **2849** | A893 30pf Dresden skyline | .30 | .30 |
| **2850** | A893 50pf Globe | .50 | .50 |
| **2851** | A893 70pf Moon | .80 | 1.00 |
| **2852** | A893 100pf Mars | 1.25 | 1.25 |
| | *Nos. 2849-2852 (4)* | 2.85 | 3.05 |

Stamps of the German Democratic Republic were replaced starting Oct. 3, 1990 by those of the Federal Republic of Germany. #2832-2852 remained valid until Dec. 31, 1991.

---

## FOR USE IN ALL PROVINCES IN THE RUSSIAN ZONES

### SEMI-POSTALS

**Leipzig Fair Issue**

Type of German Semi-Postal Stamps

16pf+9pf, 1st New Year's Fair, 1459. 50pf+25pf, Arrival of clothmakers from abroad, 1469.

**Wmk. 292**

**1948, Aug. 29 Litho.** ***Perf. 13½***

| | | | |
|---|---|---|---|
| **10NB1** | SP252 16 + 9pf dk vio brn | .25 | .65 |
| **10NB2** | SP252 50 + 25pf dl vio bl | .25 | .65 |
| | Set, never hinged | 1.40 | |

The 1948 Leipzig Autumn Fair.

Emblem of Philatelic Institute — OSP1

Goethe — OSP2

**1948, Oct. 23** ***Perf. 13x13½***

| | | | |
|---|---|---|---|
| **10NB3** | OSP1 12 + 3pf red | .25 | 1.00 |
| | Never hinged | .80 | |

Stamp Day, Oct. 24, 1948.

**Type of German Semi-Postal Stamps of 1947**

30pf+15pf, First fair in newly built Town Hall, 1556. 50pf+25pf, Italians at the Fair, 1536.

**1949, Mar. 6 Litho.** ***Perf. 13½***

| | | | |
|---|---|---|---|
| **10NB4** | SP252 30 + 15pf red | 1.20 | 4.00 |
| **10NB5** | SP252 50 + 25pf blue | 1.60 | 4.50 |
| | Set, never hinged | 8.00 | |

1949 Leipzig Spring Fair.

**1949, July 20 Wmk. 292** ***Perf. 13***

Designs: Different Goethe portraits.

| | | | |
|---|---|---|---|
| **10NB6** | OSP2 6 + 4pf dl vio | .95 | 2.75 |
| **10NB7** | OSP2 12 + 8pf dl brn | .95 | 2.75 |
| **10NB8** | OSP2 24 + 16pf red brn | .80 | 2.40 |
| **10NB9** | OSP2 50 + 25pf dk bl | .80 | 2.40 |
| **10NB10** | OSP2 84 + 36pf ol gray | 1.20 | 4.75 |
| | *Nos. 10NB6-10NB10 (5)* | 4.70 | 15.05 |
| | Set, never hinged | 12.00 | |

Johann Wolfgang von Goethe, birth bicent.

Souvenir Sheet

Profile of Goethe — OSP3

**1949, Aug. 22 Engr.** ***Perf. 14***

| | | | |
|---|---|---|---|
| **10NB11** | OSP3 50pf + 4.50m blue | 120.00 | 475.00 |
| | Never hinged | 180.00 | |

The sheet measures 106x105mm. The surtax was for the reconstruction of Weimar.

**Type of German Semi-Postal Stamps**

12pf+8pf, Russian merchants at the Fair, 1650. 24pf+16pf, Young Goethe at the Fair, 1765.

**1949, Aug. 30 Litho.** ***Perf. 13½***

| | | | |
|---|---|---|---|
| **10NB12** | SP252 12 + 8pf gray | 2.00 | 8.00 |
| **10NB13** | SP252 24 + 16pf lake brn | 2.40 | 9.50 |
| | Set, never hinged | 10.50 | |

1949 Leipzig Autumn Fair.

---

## GERMAN DEMOCRATIC REPUBLIC SEMI-POSTAL STAMPS

**Catalogue values for unused stamps in this section, from this point to the end of the section, are for Never Hinged items.**

Canceled to Order

Used values are for CTO's from No. B14 to No. B203.

Some se-tenants include a semi-postal stamp. To avoid splitting the se-tenant piece the semi-postal is listed with the regular issue.

Bavaria No. 1 and Magnifier — SP4

**Wmk. 292**

**1949, Oct. 30 Litho.** ***Perf. 14***

| | | | |
|---|---|---|---|
| **B14** | SP4 12pf + 3pf gray blk | 5.75 | 5.75 |

Stamp Day, 1949. See No. B21a.

**Leipzig Fair Issue.**

German Type of 1947

Inscribed: "Deutsche Demokratische Republik"

Leipzig Spring Fair: 24pf+12pf, First porcelain at Fair, 1710. 30pf+14pf, First Fair at Municipal Store, 1894.

**1950, Mar. 5** ***Perf. 13***

| | | | |
|---|---|---|---|
| **B15** | SP252 24 + 12pf red vio | 8.00 | 9.50 |
| **B16** | SP252 30 + 14pf rose car | 8.75 | *11.00* |

Shepherd Boy with Double Flute — SP5

"Bach Year": 24pf+6pf, Girl with hand organ. 30pf+8pf, Johann Sebastian Bach. 50pf+16pf, Chorus.

**1950, June 14** *Perf. 14*

**B17** SP5 12pf + 4pf bl grn 5.00 4.75
**B18** SP5 24pf + 6pf olive 5.00 4.75
**B19** SP5 30pf + 8pf dk red 8.00 8.00
**B20** SP5 50pf + 16pf blue 15.00 14.00
*Nos. B17-B20 (4)* 33.00 31.50

Saxony No. 1, Globe and Dove — SP6

**1950, July 1** **Photo.** **Wmk. 292**

**B21** SP6 84 + 41pf brn red 37.50 9.00
*a.* Souv. sheet of 2, #B14, B21, imperf. *120.00 140.00*
No. B21a hinged 42.50

German Stamp Exhib. (DEBRIA) held at Leipzig for the cent. of Saxony's 1st postage stamp.

Clearing Land — SP7

Reconstruction program: 24pf+6pf, Bricklaying. 30pf+10pf, Carpentry. 50pf+10pf, Inspecting plans.

**1952, May 1** **Litho.**

**B22** SP7 12pf + 3pf brt vio 1.60 .80
**B23** SP7 24pf + 6pf henna brn 1.50 .80
**B24** SP7 30pf + 10pf dp grn 1.75 .80
**B25** SP7 50pf + 10pf vio bl 2.25 1.60
*Nos. B22-B25 (4)* 7.10 4.00

Dam — SP8

**1954, Aug. 16** **Unwmk.**

**B26** SP8 24pf + 6pf green .60 .80

The surtax was for flood victims.

Surcharged with New Value and "X"

**1955, Feb. 25**

**B27** SP8 20 +5pf on 24+6pf .75 .55

The surtax was for flood victims.

Buchenwald Memorial — SP9

*Perf. 13½x13*

**1956, Sept. 8** **Wmk. 297**

**B28** SP9 20pf + 80pf rose red *1.10 4.00*

The surtax was for the erection of national memorials at the concentration camps of Buchenwald, Ravensbruck and Sachsenhausen. See No. B43.

**Type of 1955 Surcharged "HELFT AGYPTEN +10" (#B29) or "HELFT DEM SOZIALISTISCHEN UNGARN +10" (#B30)**

*Perf. 13½x13*

**1956, Dec. 20** **Wmk. 313**

**B29** A75 20pf + 10pf carmine .55 .40
**B30** A75 20pf + 10pf carmine .55 .40

Monument to Ravensbrück SP10

Memorial Park and Lake — SP11

*Perf. 13x13½, 13½x13*

**1957, Apr. 25** **Litho.**

**B31** SP10 5pf + 5pf grn *.25 .25*
**B32** SP11 20pf + 10pf rose red *.30 .40*

Intl. Day of Liberation. See Nos. B54, B70.

Ernst Thälmann SP12

Bugler, Flag and Camp SP13

Portraits: 25pf+15pf, Rudolf Breitscheid. 40pf+20pf, Rev. Paul Schneider.

**1957, Dec. 3** **Photo.** *Perf. 13*

**Portraits in Gray**

**B33** SP12 20pf + 10pf dp plum .25 .25
**B34** SP12 25pf + 15pf dk blue .25 .25
**B35** SP12 40pf + 20pf violet .30 .35
*a.* Souv. sheet of 3, #B33-B35, imperf. 42.50 125.00
*Nos. B33-B35 (3)* .80 .85

No. B35a issued Sept. 15, 1958.

**1958, July 11** **Wmk. 313** *Perf. 13*

Portraits: 5pf+5pf, Albert Kuntz. 10pf+5pf, Rudi Arndt. 15pf+10pf, Kurt Adams. 20pf+10pf, Rudolf Renner. 25pf+15pf, Walter Stoecker.

**Portraits in Gray**

**B36** SP12 5pf + 5pf brn blk .25 .80
**B37** SP12 10pf + 5pf dk sl grn .25 .80
**B38** SP12 15pf + 10pf dp vio .25 3.25
**B39** SP12 20pf + 10pf dk red brn .25 .80
**B40** SP12 25pf + 15pf bl blk *.55 12.00*
*Nos. B36-B40 (5)* *1.55 17.65*

Issued to honor the murdered victims of the Nazis at Buchenwald. The surtax was for the erection of national memorials.

See Nos. B49-B53, B55-B57, B60-B64, B71-B75, B79-B81.

**1958, Aug. 7** **Litho.** *Perf. 12½*

Design: 20pf+10pf, Pioneers and flag.

**B41** SP13 10pf + 5pf green .25 .25
**B42** SP13 20pf + 10pf red .35 .25

Pioneer organization, 10th anniversary.

**Type of 1956 Overprinted in Black "14. September 1958"**

*Perf. 13½x13*

**1958, Sept. 15** **Unwmk.**

**B43** SP9 20pf + 20pf rose red *.60 .55*

Dedication of the memorial at Buchenwald concentration camp, Sept. 14, 1958.

Exercises with Hoops — SP14

Designs: 10pf+5pf, High jump. 20pf+10pf Vaulting. 25pf+10pf, Girl gymnasts. 40pf+20pf, Leipzig stadium and fireworks.

*Perf. 13x13½*

**1959, Aug. 10** **Litho.** **Wmk. 313**

**B44** SP14 5pf + 5pf org .25 .25
**B45** SP14 10pf + 5pf grn .25 .25
**B46** SP14 20pf + 10pf brt car .25 .25
**B47** SP14 25pf + 10pf brt bl .25 .25
**B48** SP14 40pf + 20pf red vio *1.75 .70*
*Nos. B44-B48 (5)* *2.75 1.70*

3rd German Sports Festival, Leipzig.

**Portrait Type of 1957-58**

Portraits: 5pf+5pf, Tilde Klose. 10pf+5pf, Kathe Niederkirchner. 15pf+10pf, Charlotte Eisenblatter. 20pf+10pf, Olga Benario-Prestes. 25pf+15pf, Maria Grollmuss.

**1959, Sept. 3** **Photo.** *Perf. 13*

**Portraits in Gray**

**B49** SP12 5pf + 5pf sep .25 .25
**B50** SP12 10pf + 5pf dp grn .25 .25
**B51** SP12 15pf + 10pf dp vio .25 .25
**B52** SP12 20pf + 10pf mag .25 .25
**B53** SP12 25pf + 15pf dk bl *.35 .95*
*Nos. B49-B53 (5)* *1.35 1.95*

Issued to honor women murdered by the Nazis at Buchenwald.

**Ravensbrück Type of 1957 Dated: "12. September 1959"**

*Perf. 13½x13*

**1959, Sept. 11** **Litho.** **Wmk. 313**

**B54** SP11 20pf + 10pf dp car & blk .50 .30

**Portrait Type of 1957-58**

5pf+5pf, Lothar Erdmann. 10pf+5pf, Ernst Schneller. 20pf+10pf, Lambert Horn.

**1960, Feb. 25** **Photo.** *Perf. 13½x13*

**Portraits in Gray**

**B55** SP12 5pf + 5pf ol bis .25 .25
**B56** SP12 10pf + 5pf dk grn .25 .25
**B57** SP12 20pf + 10pf dl mag .25 .25
*Nos. B55-B57 (3)* .75 .75

Issued to honor murdered victims of the Nazis at Sachsenhausen.

**Type of Regular Issue, 1960**

Designs: 10pf+5pf, Vacation ship under construction, Wismar. 20pf+10pf, Ship before Stubbenkammer and sailboat.

**Wmk. 313**

**1960, June 23** **Litho.** *Perf. 13*

**B58** A162 10pf + 5pf blk, yel & red .25 .25
**B59** A162 20pf + 10pf blk, red & bl .25 .25

**Portrait Type of 1957-58**

Portraits: 10pf+5pf, Max Lademann. 15pf+5pf, Lorenz Breunig. 20pf+10pf, Mathias Thesen. 25pf+10pf, Gustl Sandtner. 40pf+20pf, Hans Rothbarth.

**1960** **Wmk. 313** *Perf. 13½x13*

**Portraits in Gray**

**B60** SP12 10pf + 5pf grn .25 .25
**B61** SP12 15pf + 5pf dp vio *.80 .55*
**B62** SP12 20pf + 10pf maroon .25 .25
**B63** SP12 25pf + 10pf dk bl .25 .25
**B64** SP12 40pf + 20pf lt red brn *1.75 2.25*
*Nos. B60-B64 (5)* *3.30 3.55*

Issued to honor the murdered victims of the Nazis at Sachsenhausen.

Bicyclist — SP15

25pf+10pf, Bicyclists and spectators.

**1960, Aug. 3** *Perf. 13x13½, 13x12½*

**Size: 28x23mm**

**B65** SP15 20pf + 10pf multi .25 .25

**Size: 38½x21mm**

**B66** SP15 25pf + 10pf bl, gray & brn *1.50 2.75*

Bicycling World Championships, Aug. 3-14.

Rook and Congress Emblem SP16

20pf+10pf, Knight. 25pf+10pf, Bishop.

*Perf. 14x13½*

**1960, Sept. 19** **Engr.** **Wmk. 313**

**B67** SP16 10pf + 5pf blue green .25 .25
**B68** SP16 20pf + 10pf rose claret .25 .25
**B69** SP16 25pf + 10pf blue *1.00 3.00*
*Nos. B67-B69 (3)* *1.50 3.50*

14th Chess Championships, Leipzig.

**Type of 1957**

Design: Monument and memorial wall of Sachsenhausen National Memorial.

**1960, Sept. 8** **Litho.** *Perf. 13x13½*

**B70** SP10 20pf + 10pf dp car .35 .30

No. B70 was re-issued Apr. 20, 1961, with gray label adjoining each stamp in sheet, to commemorate the dedication of Sachsenhausen National Memorial. Value, $1.10.

**Type of 1957**

Portraits: 5pf+5pf, Werner Kube. 10pf+5pf, Hanno Gunther. 15pf+5pf, Elvira Eisenschneider. 20pf+10pf, Hertha Lindner. 25pf+10pf, Herbert Tschäpe.

**1961, Feb. 6** *Perf. 13½x13*

**Portraits in Black**

**B71** SP12 5pf + 5pf brt grn .25 .25
**B72** SP12 10pf + 5pf bl grn .25 .25
**B73** SP12 15pf + 5pf brt lilac *1.00 2.25*
**B74** SP12 20pf + 10pf dp rose .25 .25
**B75** SP12 25pf + 10pf brt bl .25 .25
*Nos. B71-B75 (5)* *2.00 3.25*

Surtax for the erection of natl. memorials.

Pioneers Playing Volleyball SP17

Designs: 20pf+10pf, Folk dancing. 25pf+10pf, Building model airplanes.

**1961, May 25** *Perf. 13x12½*

**B76** SP17 10pf + 5pf multi .25 .25
**B77** SP17 20pf + 10pf multi .25 .25
**B78** SP17 25pf + 10pf multi *2.75 2.40*
*Nos. B76-B78 (3)* *3.25 2.90*

Young Pioneers' meeting, Erfurt.

**Type of 1957 and**

Sophie and Hans Scholl SP18

Portraits: 5pf+5pf, Carlo Schönhaar. 10pf+5pf, Herbert Baum. 20pf+10pf, Liselotte Herrmann. 40pf+20pf, Hilde and Hans Coppi.

*Perf. 13½x13, 13x13½*

**1961, Sept. 7** **Litho.** **Wmk. 313**

**Portraits in Black**

**B79** SP12 5pf + 5pf green .25 .25
**B80** SP12 10pf + 5pf bl grn .25 .25
**B81** SP12 20pf + 10pf rose car .25 .25

**B82** SP18 25pf + 10pf blue .25 .25
**B83** SP18 40pf + 20pf rose brn *1.90 5.25*
*Nos. B79-B83 (5)* *2.90 6.25*

Surtax was the support of natl. memorials at Buchenwald, Ravensbrück & Sachsenhausen.

Danielle Casanova of France — SP19

Portraits: 10pf+5pf, Julius Fucik, Czechoslovakia. 20pf+10pf, Johanna Jannetje Schaft, Netherlands. 25pf+10pf, Pawel Finder, Poland. 40pf+20pf, Soya Anatolyevna Kosmodemyanskaya, Russia.

**1962, Mar. 22 Engr. *Perf. 13½***
**B84** SP19 5pf + 5pf gray .25 .25
**B85** SP19 10pf + 5pf green .25 .25
**B86** SP19 20pf + 10pf maroon .25 .25
**B87** SP19 25pf + 10pf deep blue .25 .25
**B88** SP19 40pf + 20pf sepia *1.60 2.10*
*Nos. B84-B88 (5)* *2.60 3.10*

Issued in memory of foreign victims of the Nazis.

### Type of Regular Issue, 1962

Design: 20pf+10pf, Three cyclists and Warsaw Palace of Culture and Science.

***Perf. 13x12½***
**1962, Apr. 26 Litho. Wmk. 313**
**B89** A192 20pf + 10pf ver, bl, blk & yel .25 .25

Folk Dance — SP20

15pf+5pf, Youths of three nations parading.

**1962, July 17 Wmk. 313 *Perf. 14***
**B90** SP20 10pf + 5pf multi .30 .25
**B91** SP20 15pf + 5pf multi .30 .25
*a.* Pair, #B90-B91 1.20 1.10

Issued to publicize the 8th Youth Festival for Peace and Friendship, Helsinki, July 28-Aug. 6, 1962.

No. B91a forms the festival emblem.

### Type of Regular Issue, 1962

Design: 20pf+10pf, Springboard diving.

**1962, Aug. 7 Wmk. 313 *Perf. 13***
**B92** A199 20pf + 10pf lil rose & grnsh bl .25 .25

René Blieck of Belgium — SP21

Seven Cervi Brothers of Italy SP22

Portraits: 10pf+5pf, Dr. Alfred Klahr, Austria. 15pf+5pf, José Diaz, Spain. 20pf+10pf, Julius Alpari, Hungary.

**1962, Oct. 4 Engr. *Perf. 14***
**B93** SP21 5pf + 5pf dk bl gray .25 .25
**B94** SP21 10pf + 5pf green .25 .25
**B95** SP21 15pf + 5pf brt vio .25 .25
**B96** SP21 20pf + 10pf dl red brn .25 .25
**B97** SP22 70pf + 30pf sepia *1.75 2.50*
*Nos. B93-B97 (5)* *2.75 3.50*

Issued to commemorate foreign victims of the Nazis.

Walter Bohne, Runner SP23

Gymnasts SP24

Portraits: 10pf+5pf, Werner Seelenbinder, wrestler. 15pf+5pf, Albert Richter, bicyclist. 20pf+10pf, Heinz Steyer, soccer player. 25pf+10pf, Kurt Schlosser, mountaineer.

### Engr. & Photo.

**1963, May 27 Wmk. 313 *Perf. 14***
**B98** SP23 5pf + 5pf yel & blk .25 .25
**B99** SP23 10pf + 5pf pale yel grn & blk .25 .25
**B100** SP23 15pf + 5pf rose lil & blk .25 .25
**B101** SP23 20pf + 10pf pink & blk .25 .25
**B102** SP23 25pf + 10pf pale bl & blk *1.75 4.75*
*Nos. B98-B102 (5)* *2.75 5.75*

Issued to commemorate sportsmen victims of the Nazis. Each stamp printed with alternating label showing sporting events connected with each person honored. The surtax went for the maintenance of national memorials. See Nos. B106-B110.

**1963, June 13 Litho. *Perf. 12½x13***

Designs: 20pf+10pf, Women gymnasts. 25pf+10pf, Relay race.

**B103** SP24 10pf + 5pf blk, yel grn & lem .25 .25
**B104** SP24 20pf + 10pf blk, red & vio .25 .25
**B105** SP24 25pf + 10pf blk, bl, & gray *3.25 2.75*
*Nos. B103-B105 (3)* *3.75 3.25*

4th German Gymnastic and Sports Festival, Leipzig. The surtax went to the festival committee.

### Type of 1963

Portraits: 5pf+5pf, Hermann Tops, gymnastics instructor. 10pf+5pf, Käte Tucholla, field hockey players. 15pf+5pf, Rudolph Seiffert, long-distance swimmers. 20pf+10pf, Ernst Grube, sportsmen demonstrating for peace. 40pf+20pf, Kurt Biedermann, kayak in rapids.

### Engraved and Photogravure

**1963, Sept. 24 Wmk. 313 *Perf. 14***
**B106** SP23 5pf + 5pf yel & blk .25 .25
**B107** SP23 10pf + 5pf grn & blk .25 .25
**B108** SP23 15pf + 5pf lil & blk .25 .25
**B109** SP23 20pf + 10pf pale pink & blk .25 .25
**B110** SP23 40pf + 20pf lt bl & blk *2.50 3.00*
*Nos. B106-B110 (5)* *3.50 4.00*

See note after No. B102.

### Type of Regular Issue, 1963

Design: 20pf+10pf, Ski jumper in mid-air.

***Perf. 13½x13***
**1963, Dec. 16 Litho. Wmk. 313**
**B111** A224 20pf + 10pf multi .25 .25

Surtax for the Natl. Olympic Committee.

Anton Saefkow SP25

Designs: 10pf+5pf, Franz Jacob. 15pf+5pf, Bernhard Bästlein. 20pf+5pf, Harro Schulze-Boysen. 25pf+10pf, Adam Kuckhoff. 40pf+10pf, Mildred and Arvid Harnack. Nos. B112-B114 show group posting anti-Hitler and pacifist posters. Nos. B115-B117 show production of anti-fascist pamphlets.

**1964, Mar. 24 Wmk. 313 *Perf. 13***
**Size: 41x32mm**
**B112** SP25 5pf + 5pf .25 .25
**B113** SP25 10pf + 5pf .25 .25
**B114** SP25 15pf + 5pf .25 .25
**B115** SP25 20pf + 5pf .25 .25
**B116** SP25 25pf + 10pf .35 .25
**Size: 48½x28mm**
**B117** SP25 40pf + 10pf *1.25 1.60*
*Nos. B112-B117 (6)* *2.60 2.85*

The surtax was for the support of national memorials for victims of the Nazis.

### Olympic Types of Regular Issues

Designs: 40pf+20pf, Two runners. #B119, Equestrian. #B120, Three runners.

### Lithographed and Engraved

**1964, July 15 Wmk. 313 *Perf. 14***
**B118** A232 40pf + 20pf multi .30 .25

**Litho.**
***Perf. 13***
**B119** A233 10pf + 5pf multi 2.40 2.75
**B120** A233 10pf + 5pf multi 2.40 2.75
*Nos. B118-B120 (3)* 5.10 5.75

See note after No. 714.

Pioneers Studying — SP26

Designs: 20pf+10pf, Pioneers planting tree. 25pf+10pf, Pioneers playing.

**1964, July 29**
**B121** SP26 10pf + 5pf multi 1.60 .40
**B122** SP26 20pf + 10pf multi 1.60 .40
**B123** SP26 25pf + 10pf multi *3.00 4.00*
*Nos. B121-B123 (3)* *6.20 4.80*

Fifth Young Pioneers Meeting, Karl-Marx-Stadt.

### Stamp Exhibition Type of 1964

Designs: 10pf+5pf, Stamp of 1958 (No. 390). 20pf+10pf, Stamp of 1950 (No. 73).

***Perf. 13x13½***
**1964, Sept. 23 Litho. Wmk. 313**
**B124** A238 10pf + 5pf org & emer .25 .25
**B125** A238 20pf + 10pf brt pink & bl .30 .25

### Boxing Type of Regular Issue

10pf+5pf, Two boxing gloves and laurel.

***Perf. 13½x14***
**1965, Apr. 27 Photo. Wmk. 313**
**B126** A247 10pf + 5pf blk, gold, red & blue .25 .25

The surtax went to the German Turner and Sport Organization.

### Type of Regular Issue, 1965

5pf+5pf, George Dimitrov at Leipzig trial & communist newspaper. 10pf+5pf, Anti-fascists clandestinely distributing leaflets. 15pf+5pf, Fighting in Spanish Civil War. 20pf+10pf, Ernst Thalman behind bars & demonstration for his release. 25pf+10pf, Founding of Natl. Committee for Free Germany & signatures.

**Wmk. 313**
**1965, May 5 Photo. *Perf. 14***
**Flags in Red, Black and Yellow**
**B127** A248 5pf + 5pf blk, org & red .25 .25
**B128** A248 10pf + 5pf grn & red .25 .25
**B129** A248 15pf + 5pf lil, red & yel .25 .25
**B130** A248 20pf + 10pf blk & red .25 .25
**B131** A248 25pf + 10pf ol grn, yel & blk .25 .25
*Nos. B127-B131 (5)* 1.25 1.00

The surtax went for the maintenance of national memorials.

Doves, Globe and Finnish Flag — SP27

**1965, July 5 Litho. *Perf. 13x13½***
**B132** SP27 10pf + 5pf vio bl & emer .25 .25
**B133** SP27 20pf + 5pf red & vio bl *.45 .30*

World Peace Congress, Helsinki, July 10-17. The surtax went to the peace council of the DDR.

No. 725 Surcharged

***Perf. 13½x13***
**1965, Aug. 23 Wmk. 313**
**B134** A239 10pf + 10pf multi .35 .25

Surtax was for North Viet Nam.

### Sports Type of Regular Issue

***Perf. 13½x13***
**1965, Sept. 15 Litho. Unwmk.**
**B135** A257 10pf + 5pf Fencer .25 .25
**B136** A257 10pf + 5pf Pistol shooter .25 .25

International Modern Pentathlon Championships, Leipzig.

### Type of Regular Issue

Designs: 10pf+5pf, Willi Bredel and instruction of International Brigade. 20pf+10pf, Heinrich Rau and parade after battle of Brunete. 25pf+10pf, Hans Marchwitza, international fighters and globe. 40pf+10pf, Artur Becker and battle on the Ebro.

**1966, July 15 Photo. *Perf. 14***
**B137** A277 10pf + 5pf multi .25 .25
**B138** A277 20pf + 10pf multi .25 .25
**B139** A277 25pf + 10pf multi .25 .25
**B140** A277 40pf + 10pf multi *1.50 1.20*
*Nos. B137-B140 (4)* *1.85 1.50*

The surtax was for the maintenance of national memorials.

### Canoe Type of Regular Issue

Design: 10pf+5pf, Men's single canoe race.

***Perf. 13x12½***
**1966, Aug. 16 Litho. Unwmk.**
**B141** A279 10pf + 5pf multi .25 .25

### Red Cross Type of Regular Issue

Design: ICY Red Crescent, Red Cross, and Red Lion and Sun emblems, horiz.

**1966, Sept. 13 Wmk. 313 *Perf. 14***
**B142** A281 20pf + 10pf vio & red .40 .25

International health cooperation. Surtax for German Red Cross.

### Sports Type of Regular Issue

Design: 20pf+5pf, Weight lifter.

***Perf. 13½x13***
**1966, Sept. 22 Litho. Unwmk.**
**B143** A282 20pf + 5pf ultra & blk .40 .25

Armed Woman Planting Flower — SP28

**1966, Oct. 25 *Perf. 13½x13***
**B144** SP28 20pf + 5pf blk & pink .45 .25

Surtax was for North Viet Nam.

### Wartburg Type of Regular Issue

Design: Wartburg, view from the East.

**1966, Nov. 23** ***Perf. 13x13½***
**B145** A288 10pf + 5pf slate .30 .25

See note after No. 878.

### Olympic Type of Regular Issue

Design: 10pf+5pf, Tobogganing.

**1968, Jan. 17 Litho.** ***Perf. 13½x13***
**B146** A314 10pf + 5pf grnsh bl, vio bl & red .25 .25

The surtax was for the Olympic Committee of the German Democratic Republic.

Armed Mother and Child — SP29

**1968, May 8** ***Perf. 13½x13***
**B147** SP29 10pf + 5pf yel & multi .25 .25

Surtax was for North Viet Nam.

### Festival Type of Regular Issue

**1968, June 20 Litho.** ***Perf. 13½x13***
**B148** A327 20pf + 5pf multi .30 .25

### Olympic Games Type of Regular Issue, 1968

Designs: 10pf+5pf, Pole vault, vert. 20pf+10pf, Soccer, vert.

**1968, Sept. 18 Photo.** ***Perf. 14***
**B149** A336 10pf + 5pf multi .25 .25
**B150** A336 20pf + 10pf multi .25 .25

The surtax was for the Olympic Committee.

Armed Vietnamese Couple — SP30

**1969, June 4**
**B151** SP30 10pf + 5pf multi .30 .25

Surtax was for North Viet Nam.

### Sports Type of Regular Issue, 1969

Designs: 10pf+5pf, Gymnastics. 20pf+5pf, Art Exhibition with sports motifs.

**Photo. & Engr.**

**1969, June 18** ***Perf. 14***
**B152** A353 10pf + 5pf multi .25 .25
**B153** A353 20pf + 5pf multi .25 .25

The surtax was for the German Gymnastic and Sports League.

Otto von Guericke's Vacuum Test with Magdeburg Hemispheres — SP31

**1969, Oct. 28 Litho.** ***Perf. 13x12½***
**B154** SP31 40pf + 10pf multi *1.00 .60*

See note after No. 1146.

### Folk Art Type of Regular Issue

Design: 20pf+5pf, Decorative plate.

**1969, Nov. 25 Litho.** ***Perf. 13½x13***
**B155** A365 20pf + 5pf yel blk & ultra .30 .30

### Sports Type of Regular Issue

Design: 20pf+5pf, Children hurdling.

**1970, July 1 Photo.** ***Perf. 14x13½***
**B156** A382 20pf + 5pf multi .40 .25

Pioneer Waving Kerchief, and Pioneer Activities — SP32

Design: 25pf+5pf, Girl Pioneer holding kerchief, and Pioneer activities.

**1970, July 28 Litho.** ***Perf. 13x12½***
**B157** SP32 10pf + 5pf multi .25 .25
**B158** SP32 25pf + 5pf multi .25 .25
*a.* Pair, #B157-B158 1.10 *2.40*

6th Youth Pioneer Meeting, Cottbus. No. B158a has continuous design.

Ho Chi Minh — SP33

**1970, Sept. 2** ***Perf. 13x13½***
**B159** SP33 20pf + 5pf rose, blk & red .40 .25

Surtax was for North Viet Nam.

German Democratic Republic No. 460 — SP34

**1970, Oct. 1 Photo.** ***Perf. 14x13½***
**B160** SP34 15pf + 5pf multi .25 *.30*

2nd National Youth Philatelic Exhibition, Karl-Marx-Stadt, Oct. 4-11.

Mother and Child — SP35

**Photo. & Engr.**

**1971, Sept. 2** ***Perf. 14***
**B161** SP35 10pf + 5pf multi .30 .25

Surtax was for North Viet Nam.

### Type of Regular Issue

10pf+5pf, Loading & unloading mail at airport.

**Photo. & Engr.**

**1971, Oct. 5** ***Perf. 14***
**B162** A421 10pf + 5pf multi .25 .25

### Olympic Games Type of Regular Issue

Olympic Rings and: 10pf+5pf, Figure skating, pairs. 15pf+5pf, Speed skating.

**1971, Dec. 7 Photo.** ***Perf. 13½x14***
**B163** A424 10pf + 5pf bl, car & blk .25 .25
**B164** A424 15pf + 5pf grn, blk & bl .25 .25

Vietnamese Farm Woman — SP36

**1972, Feb. 22 Litho.** ***Perf. 13½x13***
**B165** SP36 10pf + 5pf multi .30 .25

Surtax was for North Viet Nam.

### Olympic Games Type of Regular Issue

Sport and Olympic Rings: 10pf+5pf, Diving. 25pf+10pf, Rowing.

**1972, May 16 Photo.** ***Perf. 13½x14***
**B166** A430 10pf + 5pf grnsh bl, gold & blk .25 .25
**B167** A430 25pf + 10pf multi .25 .25

### Interartes Type of Regular Issue

Designs: 15pf+5pf, Spear carrier, Persia, 500 B.C. 35pf+5pf, Grape Sellers, by Max Lingner, 1949, horiz.

**1972, Sept. 19 Photo.** ***Perf. 14***
**B168** A439 15pf + 5pf multi *.80* *.65*
**B169** A439 35pf + 5pf multi .25 .25

Flags and World Time Clock SP37

Young Couple, by Günter Glombitza SP38

25pf+5pf, Youth group with guitar and dove.

**1973, Feb. 13 Litho.** ***Perf. 12½x13***
**B170** SP37 10pf + 5pf multi .25 .25
**B171** SP37 25pf + 5pf multi .30 .25

10th World Youth Festival, Berlin.

**1973, Oct. 4 Photo.** ***Perf. 13½x14***
**B172** SP38 20pf + 5pf multi .30 .25

Philatelists' Day and for the 3rd National Youth Philatelic Exhibition, Halle.

Child, Symbols of Reconstruction SP39

**1973, Oct. 11** ***Perf. 14x13½***
**B173** SP39 10pf + 5pf multi .30 .25

Surtax was for North Viet Nam.

Luis Corvalan, Red Flag — SP40

25pf+5pf, Salvador Allende, Chilean flag.

**1973, Nov. 5** ***Perf. 13½x14***
**B174** SP40 10pf + 5pf multi *.25 .25*
**B175** SP40 25pf + 5pf multi *.45 .45*

Solidarity with the people of Chile.

Raised Fist and Star — SP41

**1975, Sept. 23 Litho.** ***Perf. 13x13½***
**B176** SP41 10pf + 5pf multi .30 .25

Surtax was for the Solidarity Committee of the German Democratic Republic.

Restored Post Gate, Wurzen, 1734 — SP42

**1975, Oct. 21 Photo.** ***Perf. 14***
**B177** SP42 10pf + 5pf multi *.40 .40*

Philatelists' Day 1975.

### Olympic Games Type of 1975

Designs: 10pf+5pf, Luge run, Oberhof. 25pf+5pf, Ski jump, Rennsteig at Oberhof.

**1975, Dec. 2 Photo.** ***Perf. 14***
**B178** A518 10pf + 5pf multi .25 .25
**B179** A518 25pf + 5pf multi .25 .25

### Olympic Games Type of 1976

Designs: 10pf+5pf, Swimming pool, High School for Physical Education, Leipzig. 35pf+10pf, Rifle range, Suhl.

**1976, May 18 Photo.** ***Perf. 13½x14***
**B180** A529 10pf + 5pf multi .25 .25
**B181** A529 35pf + 10pf multi .25 .25

TV Tower, Berlin, and Perforations SP43

**1976, Oct. 19 Litho.** ***Perf. 13***
**B182** SP43 10pf + 5pf org & bl .30 .25

Surtax was for Sozphilex 77, Philatelic Exhibition of Socialist Countries, in connection with 60th anniversary of October Revolution.

### Sports Type of 1977

10pf+5pf, Young milers. 25pf+5pf, Girls artistic gymnastic performance.

**1977, July 19 Litho.** ***Perf. 13x12½***
**B183** A558 10pf + 5pf multi .25 .25
**B184** A558 25pf + 5pf multi .25 .25

### Sozphilex Type of 1977

Souvenir Sheet

Design: 50pf+20pf, World Youth Song, by Lothar Zitzmann, horiz.

**1977, Aug. 16 Photo.** ***Perf. 13***
**B185** A559 50pf + 20pf multi *1.50 3.00*

Hand Holding Torch — SP44

**1977, Oct. 18 Litho.** ***Perf. 14***
**B186** SP44 10pf + 5pf multi .30 .25

Surtax was for East German Solidarity Committee.

### Fountain Type of 1979

Design: 10pf+5pf, Goose Boy Fountain.

**1979, Aug. 7 Photo. *Perf. 14***

| | | | | |
|---|---|---|---|---|
| **B187** | A617 | 10pf + 5pf multi | *.50* | *.40* |

Vietnamese Soldier, Mother and Child — SP45

**1979, Nov. 6 Litho. *Perf. 14***

| | | | | |
|---|---|---|---|---|
| **B188** | SP45 | 10pf + 5pf red org & blk | .40 | .25 |

Surtax was for Vietnam.

### Olympic Type of 1980

Ski Jump, sculpture by Gunther Schutz.

**1980, Jan. 15 Photo.**

| | | | | |
|---|---|---|---|---|
| **B189** | A627 | 25pf + 10pf multi | .25 | .25 |

**1980, Apr. 22 Photo. *Perf. 14***

Design: 20pf+5pf, Runners at the Finish, by Lothar Zitzmann.

| | | | | |
|---|---|---|---|---|
| **B190** | A627 | 20 + 5pf multi | .25 | .25 |

### Interflug Type of 1980
Souvenir Sheet

**1980, June 10 Litho. *Perf. 13x12½***

| | | | | |
|---|---|---|---|---|
| **B191** | A636 | 1m + 10pf Jet, globe | *2.50* | *4.00* |

AEROSOZPHILEX 1980 International Airpost Exhibition, Berlin, Aug. 1-10.

### Olympic Type of 1980

Design: Swimmer, by Willi Sitte, vert.

**1980, July 8 Photo. *Perf. 14***

| | | | | |
|---|---|---|---|---|
| **B192** | A627 | 20pf + 10pf multi | .25 | .25 |

22nd Summer Olympic Games, Moscow, July 19-Aug. 3.

International Solidarity
SP46 SP47

**1980, Oct. 14 Photo. *Perf. 14***

| | | | | |
|---|---|---|---|---|
| **B193** | SP46 | 10pf + 5pf multi | .40 | .25 |

**1981, Oct. 6 Photo. *Perf. 14***

| | | | | |
|---|---|---|---|---|
| **B194** | SP47 | 10pf + 5pf multi | .35 | .25 |

Palestinian Solidarity — SP48

Palestinian family, Tree of Life.

**1982, Sept. 21 Litho. *Perf. 14***

| | | | | |
|---|---|---|---|---|
| **B195** | SP48 | 10pf + 5pf multi | .35 | .25 |

Nicaraguan Solidarity SP49

Literacy, home defense.

**1983, Nov. 8 Litho. *Perf. 14x13½***

| | | | | |
|---|---|---|---|---|
| **B196** | SP49 | 10pf + 5pf multi | .30 | .25 |

Solidarity — SP50

**1984, Oct. 23 Photo. *Perf. 14***

| | | | | |
|---|---|---|---|---|
| **B197** | SP50 | 10pf + 5pf Knot | .40 | .25 |

Solidarity SP51

**1985, May 28 Photo.**

| | | | | |
|---|---|---|---|---|
| **B198** | SP51 | 10pf + 5pf Globe, peace dove | .30 | .25 |

Surtax for the Solidarity Committee.

Technical Assistance to Developing Nations — SP52

**1986, Nov. 4 Photo.**

| | | | | |
|---|---|---|---|---|
| **B199** | SP52 | 10pf + 5pf multi | .30 | .25 |

Surtax for the Solidarity Committee.

Solidarity with South Africans Opposing Apartheid SP53

**1987, June 16 Litho. *Perf. 14***

| | | | | |
|---|---|---|---|---|
| **B200** | SP53 | 10pf +5pf multi | .30 | .25 |

Solidarity SP54

**1988, Oct. 4 Photo. *Perf. 14***

| | | | | |
|---|---|---|---|---|
| **B201** | SP54 | 10pf +5pf multi | .50 | .50 |

Surtax for the Solidarity Committee. No. B201 printed se-tenant with label containing a Wilhelm Pieck quote.

UNICEF Emblem and Children of Africa — SP55

**1989, Sept. 5 Photo. *Perf. 14½x14***

| | | | | |
|---|---|---|---|---|
| **B202** | SP55 | 10pf +5pf multi | .30 | .25 |

Surtax for the Solidarity Committee.

Leipzig Church, Municipal Arms SP56

**1990, Feb. 28 Photo. *Perf. 13***

| | | | | |
|---|---|---|---|---|
| **B203** | SP56 | 35pf +15pf multi | .75 | .50 |

We are the People.

Intl. Literacy Year — SP57

**1990, July 24 Photo. *Perf. 14***

| | | | | |
|---|---|---|---|---|
| **B204** | SP57 | 30pf+5pf on 10pf+5pf | 1.50 | 1.10 |

Not issued without surcharge.

---

## AIR POST STAMPS

**Catalogue values for unused stamps in this section, from this point to the end of the section, are for Never Hinged items.**

---

Canceled to Order
Used values are for CTO's.

---

Stylized Plane
AP1 AP2

***Perf. 13x12½, 13x13½ (AP2)***

**1957, Dec. 13 Litho. Wmk. 313**

| | | | | |
|---|---|---|---|---|
| **C1** | AP1 | 5pf gray & blk | 3.50 | .25 |
| **C2** | AP1 | 20pf brt car & blk | .25 | .25 |
| **C3** | AP1 | 35pf violet & blk | .25 | .25 |
| **C4** | AP1 | 50pf maroon & blk | .30 | .25 |
| **C5** | AP2 | 1m olive & yel | 1.00 | .25 |
| **C6** | AP2 | 3m choc & yel | 1.60 | .45 |
| **C7** | AP2 | 5m dk bl & yel | 3.75 | .70 |
| | | *Nos. C1-C7 (7)* | 10.65 | 2.40 |

Plane and Envelope — AP3

**1982-87 Photo. *Perf. 14***

| | | | | |
|---|---|---|---|---|
| **C8** | AP3 | 5pf lt bl & blk | .25 | .25 |
| **C9** | AP3 | 15pf brt rose lil & blk | .25 | .30 |
| **C10** | AP3 | 20pf ocher & blk | .25 | .25 |
| **C11** | AP3 | 25pf ol bis & blk | .35 | .35 |
| **C12** | AP3 | 30pf brt grn & blk | .25 | .25 |
| **C13** | AP3 | 40pf ol grn & blk | .35 | .25 |
| **C14** | AP3 | 1m blue & blk | 1.00 | .45 |
| **C15** | AP3 | 3m brown & blk | 3.00 | 1.75 |
| **C16** | AP3 | 5m dk red & blk | 4.50 | 1.50 |
| | | *Nos. C8-C16 (9)* | 10.20 | 5.35 |

Issued: 30, 40pf, 1m, 10/26; 5, 20pf, 10/4/83; 3m, 4/10/84; 5m, 9/10/85; 15, 25pf, 10/6/87.

---

## OFFICIAL STAMPS

While valid, these Official stamps were not sold to the public unused. After their period of use, some sets were sold abroad by the government stamp sales agency. Used values of Official stamps are for canceled-to-order examples. Reprints of type O1 stamps have printed cancellations.

**Catalogue values for unused stamps in this section, from this point to the end of the section, are for Never Hinged items.**

Arms of Republic — O1

***Perf. 13x12½***

**1954 Wmk. 297 Litho.**

| | | | | |
|---|---|---|---|---|
| **O1** | O1 | 5pf emerald | 13.50 | .25 |
| **O2** | O1 | 6pf violet | 7.50 | .25 |
| **O3** | O1 | 8pf org brown | 13.50 | .25 |
| **O4** | O1 | 10pf lt bl grn | 13.50 | .25 |
| **O5** | O1 | 12pf blue | 45.00 | .25 |
| **O6** | O1 | 15pf dark violet | 13.50 | .25 |
| **O7** | O1 | 16pf dark violet | 7.50 | .25 |
| **O8** | O1 | 20pf olive | 9.00 | .25 |
| **O9** | O1 | 24pf brown red | 9.00 | .25 |
| **O10** | O1 | 25pf sage green | 9.00 | .25 |
| **O11** | O1 | 30pf brown red | 6.00 | .25 |
| **O12** | O1 | 40pf red | 9.75 | .25 |
| **O13** | O1 | 48pf rose lilac | 5.25 | 1.20 |
| **O14** | O1 | 50pf rose lilac | 4.50 | .25 |
| **O15** | O1 | 60pf bright blue | 4.50 | .25 |
| **O16** | O1 | 70pf brown | 4.50 | .25 |
| **O17** | O1 | 84pf brown | 7.50 | 3.00 |
| | | *Nos. O1-O17 (17)* | 183.00 | 7.95 |

### Type of 1954 Redrawn

Arc of compass projects at right except on No. O22.

**1954-56 Typo.**

| | | | | |
|---|---|---|---|---|
| **O18** | O1 | 5pf emer ('54) | 3.75 | .25 |
| **O19** | O1 | 10pf bl grn | 2.25 | .25 |
| **O20** | O1 | 12pf dk bl ('54) | 2.25 | .25 |
| **O21** | O1 | 15pf dk vio | 2.75 | .25 |
| **O22** | O1 | 20pf ol, arc at left ('55) | *52.50* | .25 |
| *a.* | | Arc of compass projects at right ('56) | 550.00 | .25 |
| **O23** | O1 | 25pf dark green | 2.25 | .25 |
| **O24** | O1 | 30pf brown red | 4.50 | .25 |
| **O25** | O1 | 40pf red | 4.50 | .25 |
| **O26** | O1 | 50pf rose lilac | 2.25 | .25 |
| **O27** | O1 | 70pf brown | 2.25 | .25 |
| | | *Nos. O18-O27 (10)* | 79.25 | 2.50 |

Shaded background of emblem consists of vertical lines; on Nos. O1-O17 it consists of dots.

Granite paper was used for a 1956 printing of the 5pf, 10pf, 15pf, 20pf and 40pf. Value for set unused $1,800, used $5.50.

See Nos. O37-O43.

O2

**1956 Wmk. 297 *Perf. 13x12½***

| | | | | |
|---|---|---|---|---|
| **O28** | O2 | 5pf black | .30 | .25 |
| **O29** | O2 | 10pf black | .30 | .25 |
| **O30** | O2 | 20pf black | .40 | .25 |
| **O31** | O2 | 40pf black | .50 | .25 |
| **O32** | O2 | 70pf black | .60 | .45 |
| | | *Nos. O28-O32 (5)* | 2.10 | 1.45 |

O3

**1956 Litho. Wmk. 297**

| | | | | |
|---|---|---|---|---|
| **O33** | O3 | 10pf lilac & black | .90 | .75 |
| **O34** | O3 | 20pf lilac & black | *140.00* | 1.10 |
| **O35** | O3 | 40pf lilac & black | 1.50 | .75 |
| **O36** | O3 | 70pf lilac & black | 2.25 | 2.50 |
| | | *Nos. O33-O36 (4)* | *144.65* | 5.10 |

Nos. O33-O36 exist also with black or violet overprint of 4-digit control number.

See Nos. O44-O45.

*No. O34 was reprinted with watermark sideways ("DDR" vertical). Value $4.*

**Redrawn Type of 1954-56**
*Perf. 13x12½, 14*
**1957-60 Typo. Wmk. 313**
**Granite Paper**

**O37** O1 5pf emerald .25 .25
**O38** O1 10pf blue green .25 .25
**O39** O1 15pf dark vio .35 .25
**O40** O1 20pf olive .35 .25
**O41** O1 30pf dark red ('58) .75 .25
**O42** O1 40pf red .55 .25
**O42A** O1 50pf rose lilac ('60) 1.60 .40
**O43** O1 70pf brown ('58) 1.60 .40
*Nos. O37-O43 (8)* 5.70 2.30

Nos. O37-O43 were all issued in perf. 13x12½. Nos. O37-O40 were also issued perf. 14. Values are the same.

**Type of 1956**
**1957 Litho. *Perf. 13x12½***

**O44** O3 10pf lilac & black .80 .35
**O45** O3 20pf lilac & black .80 .35

Nos. O44-O45 have black or violet overprint of four-digit control number.

Stamps similar to type O3 were issued later, with denomination expressed in dashes: one for 10pf, two for 20pf.

## ISSUED UNDER RUSSIAN OCCUPATION

### BERLIN-BRANDENBURG

Berlin Bear — OS1

**1945 Litho. *Perf. 14***

**11N1** OS1 5pf shown .25 .55
**11N2** OS1 6pf Bear holding spade .25 .40
**11N3** OS1 8pf Bear on shield .25 .40
**11N4** OS1 10pf Bear holding brick .25 .55
**11N5** OS1 12pf Bear carrying board .25 .40
**11N6** OS1 20pf Bear on small shield .25 .55
**11N7** OS1 30pf Oak sapling, ruins .25 .80
*Nos. 11N1-11N7 (7)* 3.65
Set, never hinged 2.00

Issued: 5pf, 8pf, 6/9; 12pf, 7/5; others, 7/18.

**1945, Dec. 6 *Serrate Roulette 13½***

*11N1a* OS1 5pf .25 .55
*11N2a* OS1 6pf 3.75 90.00
*11N3a* OS1 8pf 2.25 90.00
*11N4a* OS1 10pf 3.75 90.00
*11N5a* OS1 12pf 4.50 125.00
*11N6a* OS1 20pf 3.00 97.50
*11N7a* OS1 30pf 4.50 125.00
*Nos. 11N1a-11N7a (7)* 22.00 618.05
Set, never hinged 110.00

No. 11N1a comes with two different roulettes. The roulette that matches Nos. 11N2a-11N7a is valued at $2. No. 11N5a in the second roulette is rare.

### MECKLENBURG-VORPOMMERN

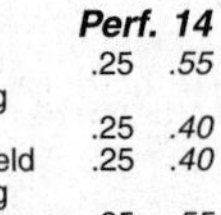
OS1

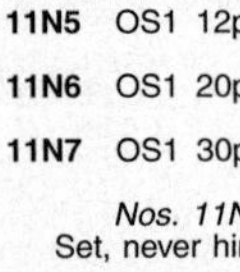
Plowman — OS2

Design: 12pf, Wheat.

**1945-46 Typo. *Perf. 10½***

**12N1** OS1 6pf black, *green* .25 1.90
**12N2** OS1 6pf purple 1.10 3.00
**12N3** OS1 6pf purple, *green* 1.10 3.00
**12N4** OS2 8pf red, *rose* .30 2.25
*a.* 8pf red lilac, *rose* .75 19.00
**12N5** OS2 8pf black, *rose* 1.90 9.75
**12N6** OS2 8pf red lilac, *green* .55 4.50
**12N7** OS2 8pf black, *green* 3.00 12.00
**12N8** OS2 8pf brown .45 4.50
**12N9** OS2 12pf black, *rose* .25 1.60
**12N10** OS2 12pf brown lilac .30 1.90
**12N11** OS2 12pf red 1.90 12.00
**12N12** OS2 12pf red, *rose* .30 2.40
*Nos. 12N1-12N12 (12)* 11.40 58.80
Set, never hinged 32.00

Many shades.

Issued: #12N1, 12N9, 8/28; #12N4, 10/6; #12N5, 10/19; #12N7, 11/2; #12N6, 11/3; #12N10, 11/9; #12N2, 11/16; #12N11, 12/20; #12N8, 1/7/46; #12N3, 1/11/46; #12N12, 1/30/46.

Buildings — OS3

Designs: 4pf, Deer. 5pf, Fishing boats. 6pf, Harvesting grain. 8pf, Windmill. 10pf, Two-horse plow. 12pf, Bricklayer on scaffolding. 15pf, Tractor plowing field. 20pf, Ship, warehouse. 30pf, Factory. 40pf, Woman spinning.

**1946 Typo. *Imperf.***

**12N13** OS3 3pf brown 1.10 35.00
**12N14** OS3 4pf blue 13.50 52.50
**12N15** OS3 4pf red brown 1.10 45.00
**12N16** OS3 5pf green 1.10 35.00
**12N17** OS3 8pf orange 1.10 35.00
**12N18** OS3 10pf brown .90 35.00

*Perf. 10½*

**12N19** OS3 6pf purple .75 6.00
**12N20** OS3 6pf blue 3.75 18.00
**12N21** OS3 12pf red .60 3.25
**12N22** OS3 15pf brown .60 5.75
**12N23** OS3 20pf blue .90 9.75
**12N24** OS3 30pf blue green .75 7.50
**12N25** OS3 40pf red violet .75 8.25
*Nos. 12N13-12N25 (13)* 26.90 296.00
Set, never hinged 52.50

Issued: 3pf, #12N14, 5pf, 6pf, 8pf, 1/17; 10pf, 12pf, 40pf, 1/22; 15pf, 1/24; 30pf, 1/26; 20pf, 1/29; #12N15, 2/25.

Nos. 12N13-12N21 exist on both white and toned paper.

### MECKLENBURG-VORPOMMERN SEMI-POSTAL STAMPS

Rudolf Breitscheid (1874-1944), Politician OSP1

Designs: 8pf+22pf, Dr. Erich Klausener (1885-1934), theologian. 12pf+28pf, Ernst Thalmann (1886-1944), politician.

**1945, Oct. 21 Typo. *Perf. 10½x11***

**12NB1** OSP1 6 +14pf green 10.50 60.00
**12NB2** OSP1 8 +22pf purple 10.50 60.00
**12NB3** OSP1 12 +28pf red 10.50 60.00
*Nos. 12NB1-12NB3 (3)* 31.50 180.00
Set, never hinged 90.00

Sower OSP2

Child Welfare OSP3

6pf+14pf, Horsedrawn Plow. 12pf+28pf, Reaper.

**1945**

**12NB4** OSP2 6 +14pf bl grn 2.40 40.00
**12NB5** OSP2 6 +14pf grn 2.75 40.00
**12NB6** OSP2 8 +22pf brn 2.40 40.00
**12NB7** OSP2 8 +22pf yel brn 2.40 40.00
**12NB8** OSP2 12 +28pf red 2.40 40.00
**12NB9** OSP2 12 +28pf org 2.40 40.00
*Nos. 12NB4-12NB9 (6)* 14.75 240.00
Set, never hinged 42.50

Issued: #12NB4, 12NB6, 12NB8, Dec. 8; others Dec. 31.

**1945, Dec. 31 *Perf. 11***

**12NB10** OSP3 6 +14pf Child in hand 2.75 47.50
**12NB11** OSP3 8 +22pf Girl in winter .95 47.50
**12NB12** OSP3 12 +28pf Boy .95 47.50
*Nos. 12NB10-12NB12 (3)* 4.65 142.50
Set, never hinged 12.00

### SAXONY PROVINCE

Coat of Arms — OS1

Land Reform — OS2

*Perf. 13x12½*
**1945-46 Typo. Wmk. 48**

**13N1** OS1 1pf slate .25 2.00
*a.* Imperf. .25 4.75
Never hinged .65
**13N2** OS1 3pf yellow brown .25 2.40
*a.* Imperf. .25 3.25
Never hinged .65
**13N3** OS1 5pf green .25 2.10
*a.* Imperf. .55 12.00
Never hinged 1.60
**13N4** OS1 6pf purple .25 2.40
*a.* Imperf. .35 2.00
Never hinged 1.10
**13N5** OS1 8pf orange .25 2.75
*a.* Imperf. .25 3.25
Never hinged .65
**13N6** OS1 10pf brown .25 2.75
*a.* Imperf. 2.75 120.00
Never hinged 7.25
**13N7** OS1 12pf red .25 2.00
*a.* Imperf. .25 2.00
Never hinged .65
**13N8** OS1 15pf red brown .25 20.00
**13N9** OS1 20pf blue .25 3.25
**13N10** OS1 24pf orange brown .25 3.25
**13N11** OS1 30pf olive green .25 3.25
**13N12** OS1 40pf lake .65 6.75
*Nos. 13N1-13N12 (12)* 3.40 52.90
Set, never hinged 6.00

Issued: #13N1-13N12, 12/1945; #13N1a-13N5a, 13N7a, 10/10/45; #13N6a, 1/1946.

**1945-46 Unwmk. *Imperf.***

**13N13** OS2 6pf green .25 1.90
**13N14** OS2 12pf red .25 1.90

**On Thin Transparent Paper**
**Wmk. 397**
*Perf. 13x13½*

**13N15** OS2 6pf green .25 6.00
**13N16** OS2 12pf red .25 6.00
*Nos. 13N13-13N16 (4)* 15.80
Set, never hinged 1.20

Issued: #13N13-13N14, 12/17/45; others 2/21/46.

### SAXONY PROVINCE SEMI-POSTAL STAMPS

Reconstruction OSP1

Designs: 6+4pf, Housing construction. 12+8pf, Bridge repair. 42+28pf, Locomotives.

**1946, Jan. 19 Typo. *Perf. 13***

**13NB1** OSP1 6pf +4pf green .25 1.90
*a.* Imperf. .25 16.00
**13NB2** OSP1 12pf +8pf red .25 1.90
*a.* Imperf. .25 20.00
**13NB3** OSP1 42pf +28pf violet .25 1.90
*a.* Imperf. .25 20.00
*Nos. 13NB1-13NB3 (3)* 5.70
Set, never hinged 1.00
Set, 13NB1a-13NB3a, never hinged 1.90

Nos. 13NB1a-13NB3a issued Feb. 21.

### WEST SAXONY

OS1

Leipzig Fair — OS2

**1945 Typo. Wmk. 48 *Perf. 13x12½***

**14N1** OS1 3pf brown .25 2.00
**14N2** OS1 4pf slate .25 3.75
**14N3** OS1 5pf green .25 2.00
*a.* Imperf. .25 2.00
Never hinged .25
**14N4** OS1 6pf violet .25 2.00
*a.* Imperf. .25 2.00
Never hinged .25
**14N5** OS1 8pf orange .25 4.75
*a.* Imperf. .25 2.00
Never hinged .25
**14N6** OS1 10pf gray .25 4.50
**14N7** OS1 12pf red .25 2.00
*a.* Imperf. .25 2.00
Never hinged .25
**14N8** OS1 15pf red brown .30 4.50
**14N9** OS1 20pf blue .25 4.00
**14N10** OS1 30pf olive green .30 2.40
**14N11** OS1 40pf red lilac .30 4.75
**14N12** OS1 60pf maroon .30 20.00
*Nos. 14N1-14N12 (12)* 3.20 56.65
Set, never hinged 8.00

Issued: 3-4, 20-30pf, 11/9; 5-8, 12pf, 11/12; 10, 15, 40-60pf, 11/15; imperfs., 9/28.

**1945, Oct. 18**

**14N13** OS2 6pf green .30 3.00
**14N14** OS2 12pf red .30 3.00
Set, never hinged 1.90

Leipzig Arms — OS3

Designs: 5pf, 6pf, St. Nicholas Church. 8pf, 12pf, Leipzig Town Hall.

**1946, Feb. 12**

**14N15** OS3 3pf brown .25 6.50
*a.* Unwatermarked .25 9.50
**14N16** OS3 4pf slate .25 6.50
*a.* Unwatermarked .25 9.50
**14N17** OS3 5pf green .25 6.50
*a.* Unwatermarked .25 9.50
**14N18** OS3 6pf violet .25 6.50
*a.* Unwatermarked .25 9.50
**14N19** OS3 8pf orange .25 6.50
*a.* Unwatermarked .25 9.50
**14N20** OS3 12pf red .25 6.50
*a.* Unwatermarked .25 9.50
*Nos. 14N15-14N20 (6)* 39.00
Set, never hinged 2.40
Set, 14NB15a-14NB20a, never hinged 2.40

Nos. 14N15a-14N20a issued Mar. 15.

### WEST SAXONY SEMI-POSTAL STAMPS

OSP1

Market, Old Town Hall — OSP2

**1946 Typo. Wmk. 48 *Perf. 13x12½***

**14NB1** OSP1 3 +2pf yel brn .25 3.25
**14NB2** OSP1 4 +3pf slate .25 3.25
**14NB3** OSP1 5 +3pf green .25 3.25
**14NB4** OSP1 6 +4pf violet .25 3.25

| | | | | |
|---|---|---|---|---|
| **14NB5** | OSP1 | 8 +4pf orange | .25 | *3.25* |
| **14NB6** | OSP1 | 10 +5pf gray | .25 | *3.25* |
| **14NB7** | OSP1 | 12 +6pf red | .25 | *3.25* |
| **14NB8** | OSP1 | 15 +10pf red brn | .25 | *3.25* |
| **14NB9** | OSP1 | 20 +10pf blue | .25 | *3.25* |
| **14NB10** | OSP1 | 30 +20pf olive grn | .25 | *4.00* |
| **14NB11** | OSP1 | 40 +30pf red lilac | .25 | *3.25* |
| **14NB12** | OSP1 | 60 +40pf lake | .25 | *4.75* |
| | | *Nos. 14NB1-14NB12 (12)* | 3.00 | *41.25* |
| | | Set, never hinged | 6.75 | |

Issue dates: Nos. 14NB1, 14NB4, 14NB7, 14NB11, Jan. 7; others, Jan. 28.

**1946, May 8** ***Perf. 13***

| | | | | |
|---|---|---|---|---|
| **14NB13** | OSP2 | 6 +14pf violet | .25 | *2.75* |
| *a.* | | Imperf. | .35 | *13.50* |
| *b.* | | Unwatermarked | .35 | 3.75 |
| **14NB14** | OSP2 | 12 +18pf bl gray | .25 | *4.75* |
| *a.* | | Imperf. | .35 | *13.50* |
| *b.* | | Unwatermarked | .25 | 6.50 |
| **14NB15** | OSP2 | 24 +26pf org brn | .25 | *2.75* |
| *a.* | | Imperf. | .35 | *13.50* |
| *b.* | | Unwatermarked | .25 | 2.40 |
| **14NB16** | OSP2 | 84 +66pf green | .25 | *6.50* |
| *a.* | | Imperf. | .35 | *27.50* |
| *c.* | | Sheet of 4, #14NB13a-14NB16a | *80.00* | *250.00* |
| | | *Nos. 14NB13-14NB16 (4)* | 1.00 | *16.75* |
| | | Set, never hinged | 2.00 | |
| | | Set, 14NB13a-14NB16a, never hinged | 4.00 | |
| | | Set, 14NB13b-14NB16b, never hinged | 3.00 | |

Issue date: Imperf., May 20.

## EAST SAXONY

OS1

OS2

**1945, June 23** **Photo.** ***Imperf.***

| | | | | |
|---|---|---|---|---|
| **15N1** | OS1 | 12pf red | *210.00* | *650.00* |
| | | Never hinged | 475.00 | |

Withdrawn on day of issue.

**Litho. (3pf, #15N9), Photo.**

**1945-46**

| | | | | |
|---|---|---|---|---|
| **15N2** | OS2 | 3pf sepia | .30 | *2.75* |
| **15N3** | OS2 | 4pf blue gray | .25 | *2.00* |
| *a.* | | 4pf gray | .25 | *.95* |
| **15N4** | OS2 | 5pf brown | .30 | *2.10* |
| **15N5** | OS2 | 6pf green | 2.50 | *9.00* |
| **15N6** | OS2 | 6pf violet | .25 | *.95* |
| **15N7** | OS2 | 8pf dark violet | .35 | *2.10* |
| **15N8** | OS2 | 10pf dark brown | .45 | *4.50* |
| **15N9** | OS2 | 10pf gray | .30 | *2.75* |
| **15N10** | OS2 | 12pf red | .30 | *2.10* |
| **15N11** | OS2 | 15pf lemon | .45 | *2.75* |
| **15N12** | OS2 | 20pf blue | .25 | *1.90* |
| *a.* | | 20pf gray blue | .65 | *2.75* |
| | | Never hinged | 1.25 | |
| **15N13** | OS2 | 25pf blue | .45 | *2.75* |
| **15N14** | OS2 | 30pf yellow | .25 | *2.00* |
| **15N15** | OS2 | 40pf lilac | .45 | *2.75* |

**Typo.**

***Perf. 13x12½***

| | | | | |
|---|---|---|---|---|
| **15N16** | OS2 | 3pf brown | .25 | *2.00* |
| **15N17** | OS2 | 5pf green | .25 | *2.00* |
| **15N18** | OS2 | 6pf violet | .25 | *2.00* |
| **15N19** | OS2 | 8pf orange | .25 | *2.00* |
| **15N20** | OS2 | 12pf vermilion | .25 | *2.00* |
| | | *Nos. 15N2-15N20 (19)* | 8.10 | *50.40* |
| | | Set, never hinged | 20.00 | |

Issued: 12pf, 6/28; #15N5, 6/30; 8pf, #15N8, 7/3; 25pf, 7/5; 5pf, 6/6; 40pf, 7/7; 15pf, 7/10; #15N12a, 7/26; #15N9, 15N12, 15N17-15N20, 11/3; #15N3, 30pf, 11/5; 3pf, 12/5; #15N15, 12/21; #15N6, 1/22/46.

## EAST SAXONY SEMI-POSTAL STAMPS

Zwinger, Dresden — OSP1

Design: 12pf+88pf, Rathaus, Dresden.

**1946, Feb. 6** **Photo.** ***Perf. 11***

| | | | | |
|---|---|---|---|---|
| **15NB1** | OSP1 | 6pf +44pf green | .25 | *6.00* |
| **15NB2** | OSP1 | 12pf +88pf red | .25 | *6.00* |
| | | Set, never hinged | 1.75 | |

## THURINGIA

Fir Trees — OS1

Designs: 6pf, 8pf, Posthorn. 12pf, Schiller. 20pf, 30pf, Goethe.

**1945-46** **Typo.** ***Perf. 11***

| | | | | |
|---|---|---|---|---|
| **16N1** | OS1 | 3pf brown | .25 | *3.25* |
| **16N2** | OS1 | 4pf black | .25 | *3.25* |
| **16N3** | OS1 | 5pf green | .25 | *4.00* |
| *a.* | | Souvenir sheet of 3, #16N1-16N3 | *160.00* | *875.00* |
| | | Never hinged | 325.00 | |
| **16N4** | OS1 | 6pf dark green | .25 | *2.40* |
| **16N5** | OS1 | 8pf orange | .25 | *2.75* |
| **16N6** | OS1 | 12pf red | .25 | *2.50* |
| **16N7** | OS1 | 20pf blue | .25 | *2.40* |
| *a.* | | Imperf. | .25 | *3.50* |
| | | Never hinged | .40 | |
| *b.* | | Souv. sheet of 4, #16N2, 16N4, 16N6-16N7, rouletted x imperf. btwn. | *600.00* | 2,500. |
| | | Never hinged | 1,350. | |
| **16N8** | OS1 | 30pf gray | .55 | *3.50* |
| *a.* | | Imperf. | 2.40 | *30.00* |
| | | Never hinged | 8.00 | |
| | | *Nos. 16N1-16N8 (8)* | 2.30 | 24.05 |
| | | Set, never hinged | 4.50 | |

#16N3a sold for 2m, #16N7b for 10m.

Issued: 6pf, 10/1; 12pf, 10/19; 5pf, 10/20; 8pf, 11/3; 20pf, 11/24; #16N3a, 16N7b, 12/18; 30pf, 12/22; 3pf, 4pf, 1/4/46.

Souvenir Sheet

Rebuilding of German Natl. Theater, Weimar — OS2

a, 6pf, Schiller. b, 10pf, Goethe. c, 12pf, Liszt. d, 16pf, Wieland. e, 40pf, Natl. Theater.

**1946, Mar. 27** **Wmk. 48** ***Imperf.***

| | | | | |
|---|---|---|---|---|
| **16N9** | OS2 | Sheet of 5, #a.-e. | 16.00 | *65.00* |
| *f.* | | Sheet, unwatermarked, roulettted | 28.00 | *175.00* |
| | | Never hinged | 55.00 | |

No. 16N9 was issued without gum. Sold for 7.50 marks.

## THURINGIA SEMI-POSTAL STAMPS

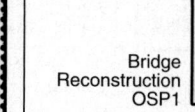

Bridge Reconstruction OSP1

Designs: 10pf+60pf, Saalburg Bridge. 12pf+68pf, Camsdorf Bridge, Jena. 16pf+74pf, Goschwitz Bridge. 24pf+76pf, Ilm Bridge, Mellingen.

**1946, Mar. 30** **Typo.** ***Imperf.***

| | | | | |
|---|---|---|---|---|
| **16NB1** | OSP1 | 10 +60pf red brn | .25 | *9.50* |
| **16NB2** | OSP1 | 12 +68pf red | .25 | *9.50* |
| **16NB3** | OSP1 | 16 +74pf dark grn | .25 | *9.50* |
| **16NB4** | OSP1 | 24 +76pf brown | .25 | *9.50* |
| *a.* | | Souv. sheet of 4, #16NB1-16NB4 | *160.00* | *1,350.* |
| | | Never hinged | 325.00 | |
| | | *Nos. 16NB1-16NB4 (4)* | | *38.00* |
| | | Set, never hinged | 2.75 | |

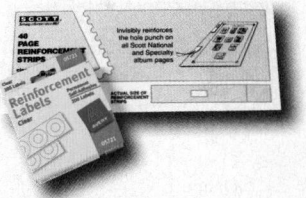

## GHANA

'gä-nə

LOCATION — West Africa between Benin and Ivory Coast
GOVT. — Republic
AREA — 92,010 sq. mi.
POP. — 18,101,000 (1997 est.)
CAPITAL — Accra

Ghana is the former British colony of Gold Coast, which achieved independence March 6, 1957. It includes the former trusteeship territory of British Togoland.

12 Pence = 1 Shilling
20 Shillings = 1 Pound
100 Pesewas = 1 Cedi (1965, 1972)
100 New Pesewas = 1 New Cedi (1967)

Used Values in Italics

In 1961 the government canceled all remainder stocks, using cancellations which closely resemble genuine postmarks. Catalogue values in italics for these stamps (Nos. 1-13, 61-65, 67-77) are for canceled-to-order stamps. Postally used stamps are worth more.

**Catalogue values for all unused stamps in this country are for Never Hinged items.**

**Watermark**

Wmk. 325 — Stars and G Multiple

Kwame Nkrumah, Map and Palm-nut Vulture — A1

***Perf. 14x14½***

**1957, Mar. 6 Wmk. 4 Photo.**

| | | | | | |
|---|---|---|---|---|---|
| **1** | A1 | 2p rose red | .25 | *.25* |
| **2** | A1 | 2½p green | .25 | *.25* |
| **3** | A1 | 4p brown | .25 | *.25* |
| **4** | A1 | 1sh3p dark blue | .25 | *.25* |
| | | *Nos. 1-4 (4)* | 1.00 | *1.00* |

Independence, Mar. 6, 1957.
For overprints see Nos. 28-31.

Stamps of Gold Coast, 1952-54, Overprinted in Black or Red

***Perf. 11½x12, 12x11½***

**1957, Mar. 6 Engr.**

| | | | | |
|---|---|---|---|---|
| **5** | A14 | ½p yel brown & car | .60 | *.25* |
| **6** | A14 | 1p deep blue (R) | .60 | *.25* |
| **7** | A14 | 1½p green | .60 | *.25* |
| **8** | A14 | 3p rose | 1.00 | *.25* |
| **9** | A15 | 6p org & black (R) | .60 | *.25* |
| **10** | A14 | 1sh red org & black | .60 | *.25* |
| **11** | A14 | 2sh rose car & ol brn | 1.50 | *.25* |
| **12** | A14 | 5sh gray & red vio | 2.40 | *.25* |
| **13** | A15 | 10sh olive grn & black | 2.75 | *.50* |
| | | *Nos. 5-13 (9)* | 10.65 | *2.50* |

Nos. 5-6 exist in vertical coils.
See Nos. 25-27.

Viking Ship and Angelfish A2

1sh3p, Medieval galleon and swordfish. 5sh, Modern cargo ship and flyingfish.

***Perf. 12x11½***

**1957, Dec. 27 Engr. Unwmk.**

| | | | | |
|---|---|---|---|---|
| **14** | A2 | 2½p emerald | .25 | .25 |
| **15** | A2 | 1sh3p dark blue | .30 | *1.25* |
| **16** | A2 | 5sh red lilac | 1.10 | *3.00* |
| | | *Nos. 14-16 (3)* | 1.65 | 4.50 |

Black Star Line inauguration.

Ambassador Hotel — A3

Coat of Arms — A4

Design: 2½p, Opening of Parliament. 1sh3p, National monument.

***Perf. 14x14½, 14½x14***

**1958, Mar. 6 Photo. Wmk. 4**

**Flags in Original Colors**

| | | | | |
|---|---|---|---|---|
| **17** | A3 | ½p car rose & black | .25 | *.40* |
| **18** | A3 | 2½p org yel, red & blk | .25 | .25 |
| **19** | A3 | 1sh3p blue & black | .25 | .25 |
| **20** | A4 | 2sh multicolored | .25 | *.50* |
| | | *Nos. 17-20 (4)* | 1.00 | 1.40 |

First anniversary of Independence.

Map of Africa — A5

Map and Torch — A6

**1958, Apr. 15** ***Perf. 13½x14½***

| | | | | |
|---|---|---|---|---|
| **21** | A5 | 2½p multicolored | .25 | .25 |
| **22** | A5 | 3p multicolored | .25 | .25 |
| **23** | A6 | 1sh multicolored | .25 | .25 |
| **24** | A6 | 2sh6p multicolored | .25 | *.65* |
| | | *Nos. 21-24 (4)* | 1.00 | 1.40 |

1st conf. of Independent African States, Accra, Apr. 15-22.

**Gold Coast Nos. 151-152 and 154 Overprinted Like Nos. 5-13**

***Perf. 11½x12, 12x11½***

**1958, May 26 Engr. Wmk. 4**

| | | | | |
|---|---|---|---|---|
| **25** | A15 | 2p chocolate | .75 | .35 |
| **26** | A15 | 2½p red | 2.10 | *1.40* |
| **27** | A14 | 4p deep blue | 8.25 | *8.50* |
| | | *Nos. 25-27 (3)* | 11.10 | 10.25 |

Nos. 25-27 were prepared in 1957 and some were sold without authorization. The set was officially released in 1958.

**Nos. 1-4 Overprinted: "Prime Minister's Visit U. S. A. and Canada"**

**1958, July 18 Photo. *Perf. 14x14½***

| | | | | |
|---|---|---|---|---|
| **28** | A1 | 2p rose red | .25 | *.40* |
| **29** | A1 | 2½p green | .25 | *.30* |
| **30** | A1 | 4p brown | .25 | *.50* |
| **31** | A1 | 1sh3p dark blue | .25 | *.25* |
| | | *Nos. 28-31 (4)* | 1.00 | *1.45* |

Prime Minister Kwame Nkrumah's visit to the US and Canada, July, 1958.

Palm-nut Vulture over Globe — A7

"Britannia" Plane — A8

Designs: 2sh, Stratocruiser and albatross. 2sh6p, Palm-nut vulture and jet plane, horiz.

**1958, July 15** ***Perf. 14x14½, 14½x14***

| | | | | |
|---|---|---|---|---|
| **32** | A7 | 2½p multicolored | .25 | .25 |
| **33** | A8 | 1sh3p multicolored | .35 | .25 |
| **34** | A8 | 2sh multicolored | .45 | .45 |
| **35** | A7 | 2sh6p olive bister & blk | .70 | .85 |
| | | *Nos. 32-35 (4)* | 1.75 | 1.80 |

Inauguration of Ghana Airways.

A9

***Perf. 14x14½***

**1958, Oct. 24 Wmk. 4 Litho.**

| | | | | |
|---|---|---|---|---|
| **36** | A9 | 2½p multicolored | .25 | .25 |
| **37** | A9 | 1sh3p multicolored | .25 | .25 |
| **38** | A9 | 2sh6p multicolored | .25 | .30 |
| | | *Nos. 36-38 (3)* | .75 | .80 |

United Nations Day, Oct. 24.

A10

Lincoln Memorial and Kwame Nkrumah.

***Perf. 14x14½***

**1959, Feb. 12 Photo. Wmk. 325**

| | | | | |
|---|---|---|---|---|
| **39** | A10 | 2½p dp plum & brt pink | .25 | .25 |
| **40** | A10 | 1sh3p dp blue & lt bl | .25 | .25 |
| **41** | A10 | 2sh6p ol gray & org yel | .25 | .30 |
| *a.* | | Souv. sheet of 3, #39-41, imperf. | .80 | 1.50 |
| | | *Nos. 39-41 (3)* | .75 | .80 |

Lincoln's birth sesquicentennial.

Kente Cloth with Traditional Symbols A11

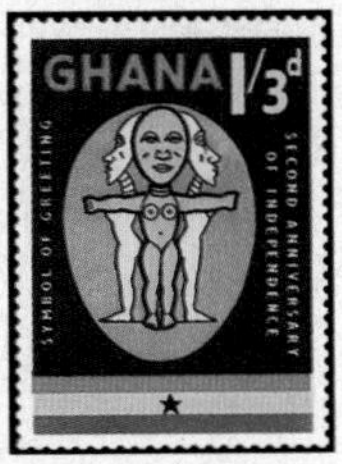


Symbol of Greeting — A12

2½p, Talking drums and elephant hornblower. 2sh, Map of Africa, flag and palm tree.

***Perf. 14½x14, 14x14½***

**1959, Mar. 6 Photo. Wmk. 325**

| | | | | |
|---|---|---|---|---|
| **42** | A11 | ½p multicolored | .25 | .25 |
| **43** | A11 | 2½p multicolored | .25 | .25 |
| **44** | A12 | 1sh3p multicolored | .25 | .25 |
| **45** | A11 | 2sh multicolored | .25 | 1.00 |
| | | *Nos. 42-45 (4)* | 1.00 | 1.75 |

Independence, 2nd anniversary.

Flags of Independent States of Africa and Globe — A13

**1959, Apr. 15** ***Perf. 14½x14***

| | | | | |
|---|---|---|---|---|
| **46** | A13 | 2½p multicolored | .25 | .25 |
| **47** | A13 | 8½p multicolored | .25 | .25 |

Africa Freedom Day, Apr. 15.

Kente Cloth and "God's Omnipotence" Symbol — A13a

Nkrumah Statue, Accra — A14

Shell Ginger — A15

Cacao A16

"God's Omnipotence" Symbol — A16a

Blackwinged Red Bishop — A17

1½p, Ghana timber. 2p, Volta river. 4p, Diamond and mine. 11p, Golden spider lily. 2sh6p, Great blue turaco. 5sh, Tiger orchid. 10sh, Jewelfish (tropical African cichlid).

***Perf. 11½x12, 12x11½, 14x14½, 14½x14***

**1959, Oct. 5 Photo. Wmk. 325**

**Size: 30½x21mm, 21x30½mm**

| | | | | | |
|---|---|---|---|---|---|
| 48 | A13a | ½p | multi *(God's Omnipotence)* | .45 | .25 |
| 49 | A14 | 1p | multicolored | .45 | .25 |

**Size: 26½x37mm, 37x26½mm**

| | | | | | |
|---|---|---|---|---|---|
| 50 | A15 | 1½p | multicolored | .45 | .25 |
| 51 | A16 | 2p | multicolored | .45 | .25 |
| 52 | A16 | 2½p | multicolored | .45 | .25 |
| 53 | A16a | 3p | multi *(God's Omnipotence)* | .45 | .25 |
| 54 | A16 | 4p | multicolored | .45 | .25 |
| 55 | A17 | 6p | multicolored | .45 | .25 |
| *a.* | | | Booklet pane of 4 | 2.00 | |
| 56 | A15 | 11p | multicolored | .70 | .25 |
| 57 | A15 | 1sh | multicolored | .50 | .25 |
| 58 | A17 | 2sh6p | multicolored | 1.25 | .40 |
| 59 | A15 | 5sh | multicolored | 2.75 | .70 |

**Size: 45x26mm**

| | | | | | |
|---|---|---|---|---|---|
| 60 | A16 | 10sh | multicolored | 5.00 | 2.25 |
| | | | *Nos. 48-60,C1-C2 (15)* | 15.70 | 6.70 |

Nos. 48 and 53 inscribed "God's Omnipotence." Nos. 95-96 inscribed "Gye Nyame."

For surcharges see Nos. 216-217, 219-225, 277-283.

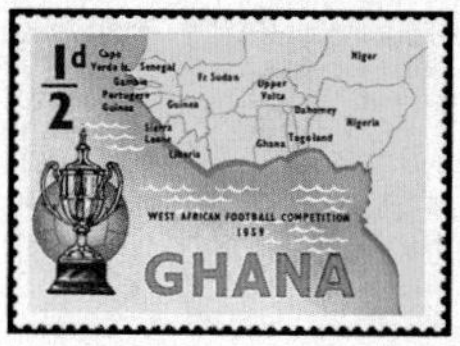

Map and Gold Cup — A18

1p, Soccer players, vert. 3p, Flags and goalkeeper in stadium. 8p, Soccer player at goal. 2sh6p, Kwame Nkrumah Gold Cup, vert.

**1959, Oct. 15 *Perf. 14½x14, 14x14½***

| | | | | | |
|---|---|---|---|---|---|
| 61 | A18 | ½p | multicolored | .25 | *.25* |
| 62 | A18 | 1p | multicolored | .25 | *.25* |
| 63 | A18 | 3p | multicolored | .25 | *.25* |
| 64 | A18 | 8p | multicolored | .25 | *.25* |
| 65 | A18 | 2sh6p | multicolored | .25 | *.30* |
| | | | *Nos. 61-65 (5)* | 1.25 | *1.30* |

West African Soccer Competitions.

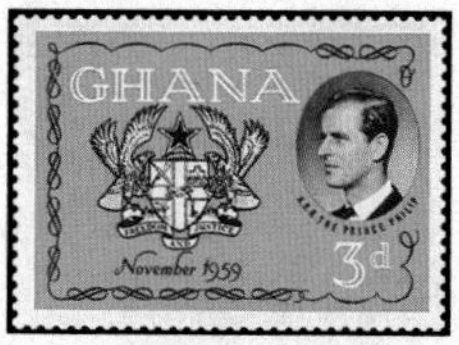

Prince Philip A19

***Perf. 14½x14***

**1959, Nov. 24 Photo. Wmk. 325**

| | | | | | |
|---|---|---|---|---|---|
| 66 | A19 | 3p | brt pink & black | .30 | .25 |

Visit of Prince Philip.

Talking Drums A20

Designs: 6p, 1sh3p, Ghana flag and UN emblem, vert. 2sh6p, Pile of Ceremonial Stools and "UNTC," vert.

**1959, Dec. 10 *Perf. 14½x14, 14x14½***

**Flag in Original Colors**

| | | | | | |
|---|---|---|---|---|---|
| 67 | A20 | 3p | violet & org yel | .25 | *.25* |
| 68 | A20 | 6p | Prus green & blk | .25 | *.25* |
| 69 | A20 | 1sh3p | grnsh bl, blk & vio | .25 | *.25* |
| 70 | A20 | 2sh6p | dark blue & black | .25 | *.25* |
| | | | *Nos. 67-70 (4)* | 1.00 | *1.00* |

United Nations Trusteeship Council.

Three Flying Eagles — A21

Designs: 3p, Three clusters of fireworks. 1sh3p, Ghana flag forming "3" and dove. 2sh, Ghana flag forming triple sail of symbolic ship.

***Perf. 13½x14½***

**1960, Mar. 6 Wmk. 325**

| | | | | | |
|---|---|---|---|---|---|
| 71 | A21 | ½p | multicolored | .25 | *.25* |
| 72 | A21 | 3p | multicolored | .25 | *.25* |
| 73 | A21 | 1sh3p | multicolored | .25 | *.25* |
| 74 | A21 | 2sh | multicolored | .25 | *.25* |
| | | | *Nos. 71-74 (4)* | 1.00 | *1.00* |

Independence, 3rd anniversary.

Flags Forming "A" and Map A22

Designs: 6p, Letter "F." 1sh, "D."

**1960, Apr. 15 Photo. Wmk. 325**

**Flags in Original Colors**

| | | | | | |
|---|---|---|---|---|---|
| 75 | A22 | 3p | green, red & black | .25 | *.25* |
| 76 | A22 | 6p | rose & black | .25 | *.25* |
| 77 | A22 | 1sh | blue, black & red | .25 | *.25* |
| | | | *Nos. 75-77 (3)* | .75 | *.75* |

Africa Freedom Day, Apr. 15.

President Kwame Nkrumah — A23

Designs: 1sh3p, Flag and star. 2sh, Hand holding torch. 10sh, Coat of Arms and flag of Ghana, horiz.

***Perf. 14x14½, 14½x14***

**1960, July 1 Litho.**

| | | | | | |
|---|---|---|---|---|---|
| 78 | A23 | 3p | multicolored | .25 | .25 |
| 79 | A23 | 1sh3p | multicolored | .25 | .25 |
| 80 | A23 | 2sh | multicolored | .30 | .30 |
| 81 | A23 | 10sh | multicolored | .70 | .70 |
| *a.* | | | Souv. sheet of 4, #78-81, imperf. | .50 | 1.00 |
| | | | *Nos. 78-81 (4)* | 1.50 | 1.50 |

Declaration of the Republic, July 1, 1960.

Olympic Rings and Hand Holding Torch — A24

Design: 1sh3p, 2sh6p, Runner, Map of Africa and Olympic Rings, horiz.

**1960, Aug. 15 Photo. Wmk. 325**

| | | | | | |
|---|---|---|---|---|---|
| 82 | A24 | 3p | multicolored | .25 | .25 |
| 83 | A24 | 6p | multicolored | .25 | .25 |
| 84 | A24 | 1sh3p | multicolored | .25 | .25 |
| 85 | A24 | 2sh6p | multicolored | .35 | .25 |
| | | | *Nos. 82-85 (4)* | 1.10 | 1.00 |

17th Olympic Games, Rome, Aug. 25-Sept. 11.

Map and Arch — A25

Designs: 3p, Flag and Kwame Nkrumah, horiz. 6p, Star and Nkrumah.

**1960, Sept. 21 Photo.**

| | | | | | |
|---|---|---|---|---|---|
| 86 | A25 | 3p | multicolored | .25 | .25 |
| 87 | A25 | 6p | multicolored | .25 | .25 |
| 88 | A25 | 1sh3p | multicolored | .25 | .30 |
| | | | *Nos. 86-88 (3)* | .75 | .80 |

Founder's Day, Sept. 21, birthday of Dr. Kwame Nkrumah.

UN Emblem and Ghana Flag — A26

6p, Flame & emblem. 1sh3p, UN Emblem.

**1960, Dec. 10 *Perf. 14x14½***

| | | | | | |
|---|---|---|---|---|---|
| 89 | A26 | 3p | multicolored | .25 | .25 |
| 90 | A26 | 6p | multicolored | .25 | .25 |
| 91 | A26 | 1sh3p | multicolored | .25 | .45 |
| | | | *Nos. 89-91 (3)* | .75 | .95 |

Human Rights Day, Dec. 10, 1960.

Talking Drums and Map — A27

Designs: 6p, Map of Africa showing 25 independent states. 2sh, Map of Africa and flags of independent nations in 1958, horiz.

***Perf. 14x14½, 14½x14***

**1961, Apr. 15 Wmk. 325**

| | | | | | |
|---|---|---|---|---|---|
| 92 | A27 | 3p | multicolored | .25 | .25 |
| 93 | A27 | 6p | multicolored | .25 | .25 |
| 94 | A27 | 2sh | multicolored | .25 | .35 |
| | | | *Nos. 92-94 (3)* | .75 | .85 |

Africa Freedom Day, Apr. 15, 1961.

**Types of 1959 Redrawn and**

Red-fronted Gazelle — A28

***Perf. 11½x12, 14½x14***

**1961, Apr. 29 Photo. Wmk. 325**

| | | | | | |
|---|---|---|---|---|---|
| 95 | A13a | ½p | "Gye Nyame" | .25 | .25 |
| 96 | A16a | 3p | "Gye Nyame" | .25 | .25 |
| *a.* | | | Booklet pane of 4 | 1.00 | |

***Perf. 14x14½***

| | | | | | |
|---|---|---|---|---|---|
| 97 | A28 | £1 | multicolored | 6.00 | 6.00 |
| | | | *Nos. 95-97 (3)* | 6.50 | 6.50 |

Nos. 95-96 are the same sizes as Nos. 48 and 53 which are inscribed "God's Omnipotence."

For surcharges see Nos. 218, 226, 284.

Column, Eagle and Star — A29

Designs: 1sh3p, Symbolic flower and star. 2sh, Star and 3 Ghana flags.

**1961, July 1 *Perf. 14x14½***

| | | | | | |
|---|---|---|---|---|---|
| 98 | A29 | 3p | multicolored | .25 | .25 |
| 99 | A29 | 1sh3p | multicolored | .25 | .25 |
| 100 | A29 | 2sh | multicolored | .25 | *1.00* |
| | | | *Nos. 98-100 (3)* | .75 | 1.50 |

First anniversary of the Republic.

Dove with Olive Branch — A30

World Map, Chain and Olive Branch A31

Design: 5sh, Rostrum and olive branch.

**1961, Sept. 1 *Perf. 14x14½, 14½x14***

| | | | | | |
|---|---|---|---|---|---|
| 101 | A30 | 3p | green | .25 | .25 |
| 102 | A31 | 1sh3p | dark blue | .25 | .25 |
| 103 | A31 | 5sh | rose carmine | .25 | *.90* |
| | | | *Nos. 101-103 (3)* | .75 | 1.40 |

Conference of Non-aligned Nations, Belgrade, Sept. 1961.

Kwame Nkrumah and Globe A32

Designs: 1sh3p, Kente cloth and Nkrumah, vert. 5sh, Kwame Nkrumah, vert.

***Perf. 14½x14, 14x14½***

**1961, Sept. 21 Wmk. 325**

| | | | | | |
|---|---|---|---|---|---|
| 104 | A32 | 3p | multicolored | .25 | .25 |
| *a.* | | | Souvenir sheet of 4, imperf. | 1.00 | *1.75* |
| 105 | A32 | 1sh3p | multicolored | .25 | .25 |
| *a.* | | | Souvenir sheet of 4, imperf. | 1.25 | *2.50* |
| 106 | A32 | 5sh | multicolored | .40 | *2.00* |
| *a.* | | | Souvenir sheet of 4, imperf. | 3.50 | *6.00* |
| | | | *Nos. 104-106 (3)* | .90 | 2.50 |

Founder's Day.

The souvenir sheets contain four imperf. stamps each with simulated perforations.

Elizabeth II and Map of Africa A33

**1961, Nov. 10 *Perf. 14½x14***

**Gold Inscriptions: Design in Black, Red, Yellow & Green**

| | | | | | |
|---|---|---|---|---|---|
| 107 | A33 | 3p | claret | .25 | .25 |
| 108 | A33 | 1sh3p | Prussian blue | .25 | .25 |
| 109 | A33 | 5sh | violet blue | 1.10 | .90 |
| *a.* | | | Souvenir sheet of 4 | 4.00 | *7.00* |
| | | | *Nos. 107-109 (3)* | 1.60 | 1.40 |

Visit of Queen Elizabeth II to Ghana, Nov. 10-22.

No. 109a contains four imperf. examples of No. 109 with simulated perforations.

Map of Tema Harbor and Ships
A34

***Perf. 14x13***

**1962, Feb. 10 Litho. Unwmk.**

**110** A34 3p multicolored .25 .25
*Nos. 110,C3-C4 (3)* 1.45 1.45

Opening of Tema Harbor, as part of Volta River Project.

Dove Flying over Map of Africa — A35

**1962, Mar. 6** ***Perf. 13x14***

**111** A35 3p multicolored .25 .25
*Nos. 111,C5-C6 (3)* 1.15 1.15

Conference of African heads of state at Casablanca, 1st anniv.

"Freedom" Illuminating Africa — A36

***Perf. 14x14½***

**1962, Apr. 15 Photo. Wmk. 325**

**112** A36 3p multicolored .25 .25
**113** A36 6p multicolored .25 .25
**114** A36 1sh3p multicolored .25 .25
*Nos. 112-114 (3)* .75 .75

Africa Freedom Day, Apr. 15.

"Five Continents at Peace" — A37

Designs: 6p, Atom bomb blast in shape of skull. 1sh3p, Peace dove and globe.

**1962, June 21 Wmk. 325**

**115** A37 3p deep rose & black .25 .25
**116** A37 6p black & dk red .25 *.30*
**117** A37 1sh3p greenish blue .30 *.50*
*Nos. 115-117 (3)* .80 1.05

Accra Assembly of Africans for a "World Without Bomb," June 21-28.

Patrice Lumumba
A38

**1962, June 30** ***Perf. 14½x14***

**118** A38 3p black & orange .25 .25
**119** A38 6p mar, grn & blk .25 *.30*
**120** A38 1sh3p dk grn, pink & blk .25 *.35*
*Nos. 118-120 (3)* .75 .90

1st anniv. (on Feb. 12) of the death of Patrice Lumumba, premier of Congo.

Arch and Star — A39

Designs: 6p, Torch in flag colors and globe. 1sh3p, Palm-nut vulture trailing flag, horiz.

***Perf. 13x13½, 13½x13***

**1962, July 1 Unwmk.**

**121** A39 3p multicolored .25 .25
**122** A39 6p multicolored .25 .25
**123** A39 1sh3p multicolored .25 .35
*Nos. 121-123 (3)* .75 .85

Second anniversary of the republic.

Kwame Nkrumah — A40

3p, Nkrumah medal. 1sh3p, Nkrumah's head & stars. 2sh, Hands with trowel & building block.

**1962, Sept. 21 Litho.** ***Perf. 13x14***

**124** A40 1p multicolored .25 .25
**125** A40 3p multicolored .25 .25
**126** A40 1sh3p ultra & black .25 .25
**127** A40 2sh multicolored .25 *1.00*
*Nos. 124-127 (4)* 1.00 1.75

Founder's Day, Nkrumah's 53rd birthday.

Malaria Eradication Emblem — A41

***Perf. 14x14½***

**1962, Dec. 1 Photo. Wmk. 325**

**128** A41 1p carmine rose .25 .25
**129** A41 4p yellow green .25 *1.00*
**130** A41 6p olive bister .25 *.30*
**131** A41 1sh3p violet .25 *.80*
*a.* Souvenir sheet of 4, imperf. 1.25 *1.50*
*Nos. 128-131 (4)* 1.00 *2.35*

WHO drive to eradicate malaria.

No. 131a contains one each of Nos. 128-131, with simulated perforation.

Wheat Emblem and Globe — A42

Designs: 4p, Hands holding Wheat Emblem, horiz. 1sh3p, Globe, horiz.

***Perf. 14x14½, 14½x14***

**1963, Mar. 21 Wmk. 325**

**132** A42 1p multicolored .30 .25
**133** A42 4p multicolored .45 *1.00*
**134** A42 1sh3p multicolored 1.75 1.50
*Nos. 132-134 (3)* 2.50 2.75

FAO "Freedom from Hunger" campaign.

Map of Africa in Sun — A43

Designs: 4p, Symbolic wood carving, horiz. 1sh3p, Map of Africa and ceremonial fire. 2sh6p, Gazelle and flag.

**1963, Apr. 15 Photo.**

**135** A43 1p crimson & gold .25 .25
**136** A43 4p orange, blk & red .25 .25
**137** A43 1sh3p multicolored .25 .25
**138** A43 2sh6p multicolored .25 *1.00*
*Nos. 135-138 (4)* 1.00 1.75

Africa Freedom Day, Apr. 15.

Cross, Flag and Centenary Emblem — A44

1½p, Centenary emblem, horiz. 4p, Family & emblem, horiz. 1sh3p, Emblem & globe.

***Perf. 14x14½, 14½x14***

**1963, May 28 Wmk. 325**

**139** A44 1p multicolored .45 .25
**140** A44 1½p multicolored .75 *1.75*
**141** A44 4p multicolored 1.00 .25
**142** A44 1sh3p multicolored 2.00 2.00
*a.* Souvenir sheet of 4, imperf. 4.25 *10.00*
*Nos. 139-142 (4)* 4.20 4.25

Cent. of the founding of the Intl. Red Cross.

No. 142a contains one each of Nos. 139-142, with simulated perforation.

A45

Designs: 4p, Three flags. 1sh3p, Map of Africa with Ghana, vert. 2sh6p, Torch, vert.

***Perf. 14½x14, 14x14½***

**1963, July 1 Photo.**

**143** A45 1p multicolored .25 .25
**144** A45 4p multicolored .25 .25
**145** A45 1sh3p multicolored .25 .25
**146** A45 2sh6p multicolored .25 *1.75*
*Nos. 143-146 (4)* 1.00 2.50

The 3rd anniversary of the republic.

Dancers, Fireworks and Nkrumah
A46

1p, Nkrumah & streamer. 4p, Nkrumah & flag. 5sh, Wisdom symbol.

***Perf. 14x14½, 14½x14***

**1963, Sept. 21**

**147** A46 1p multi, vert. .25 .25
**148** A46 4p multi, vert. .25 .25
**149** A46 1sh3p multi .25 .25
**150** A46 5sh multi .25 *.40*
*Nos. 147-150 (4)* 1.00 1.15

Founder's Day, Nkrumah's 54th birthday.

Ramses II at Abu Simbel — A47

Designs: 1½p, Rock painting, bird and fish, horiz. 2p, Queen Nefertari, horiz. 4p, Sphinx of Wadi es-Sebua. 1sh3p, Statues of Ramses II at Abu Simbel, horiz.

**1963, Nov. 1 Unwmk.** ***Perf. 11½x11***

**151** A47 1p multicolored .25 .25
**152** A47 1½p multicolored .25 *.50*
**153** A47 2p multicolored .25 .25
**154** A47 4p multicolored .50 .25
**155** A47 1sh3p multicolored 1.50 1.00
*Nos. 151-155 (5)* 2.75 2.25

UNESCO world campaign to save historic monuments in Nubia.

Steam and Diesel Engines
A48

***Perf. 14½x14***

**1963, Nov. 1 Wmk. 325**

**156** A48 1p multicolored .25 .25
**157** A48 6p multicolored .75 .25
**158** A48 1sh3p multicolored 1.20 .50
**159** A48 2sh6p multicolored 1.60 1.60
*Nos. 156-159 (4)* 3.80 2.60

The 60th anniversary of Ghana's railroads.

Eleanor Roosevelt and Flame — A49

6p, Mrs. Roosevelt & flag. 1sh3p, Mrs. Roosevelt, flag, flame & Ghanaian symbols, horiz.

***Perf. 11½x11, 11x11½***

**1963, Dec. 10 Unwmk.**

**160** A49 1p multicolored .25 .25
**161** A49 4p multicolored .25 .30
**162** A49 6p multicolored .25 .25
**163** A49 1sh3p multicolored .25 .25
*Nos. 160-163 (4)* 1.00 1.05

Eleanor Roosevelt; 15th anniv. of the Universal Declaration of Human Rights.

**Imperforates**
**Starting in 1964, certain sets of Ghana exist imperf.**

IQSY Emblem and Satellites — A50

**1964, June 1 Photo. *Perf. 14***

164 A50 3p multicolored .25 .25
165 A50 6p multicolored .25 .25
166 A50 1sh3p multicolored .25 .25
*a.* Souvenir sheet of 4 .90 *2.00*
*Nos. 164-166 (3)* .75 .75

Intl. Quiet Sun Year, 1964-65. No. 166a contains 4 imperf. stamps similar to No. 166 with simulated perforations.

See Nos. 186-188.

Harvest on State Farm A51

Designs: 6p, Oil refinery, Tema. 1sh3p, Communal labor. 5sh, Ghana flag and people.

**1964, July 1 *Perf. 13x14***

167 A51 3p multicolored .25 .25
168 A51 6p multicolored .25 .25
169 A51 1sh3p multicolored .25 .25
170 A51 5sh multicolored .25 .90
*a.* Souvenir sheet of 4 .80 *1.50*
*Nos. 167-170 (4)* 1.00 1.65

4th anniv. of the Republic. No. 170a contains four stamps similar to Nos. 167-170 with simulated perforations.

Dove, Globe, Olive Branch and Flag — A52

Designs: 6p, Map of Africa and quill pen, vert. 1sh3p, Knotted rope and map of Africa. 5sh, Hands planting symbolic tree, vert.

**1964, July 6 *Perf. 14***

171 A52 3p multicolored .25 .25
172 A52 6p black & red .25 .25
173 A52 1sh3p blue & multi .25 .25
174 A52 5sh yel & multi .25 .60
*Nos. 171-174 (4)* 1.00 1.35

Signing of the African Unity Charter, 1st anniv.

Nkrumah and Hibiscus — A53

***Perf. 14x14½***

**1964, Sept. 21 Photo. Wmk. 325**

**Design in Brown, Green and Rose Red**

175 A53 3p light blue .25 .25
176 A53 6p yellow .25 .25
177 A53 1sh3p gray .25 .25
178 A53 2sh6p emerald .25 *.90*
*a.* Souvenir sheet of 4 1.10 *2.00*
*Nos. 175-178 (4)* 1.00 1.65

Founder's Day, Nkrumah's 55th birthday.

No. 178a contains four of No. 178 with simulated perforation.

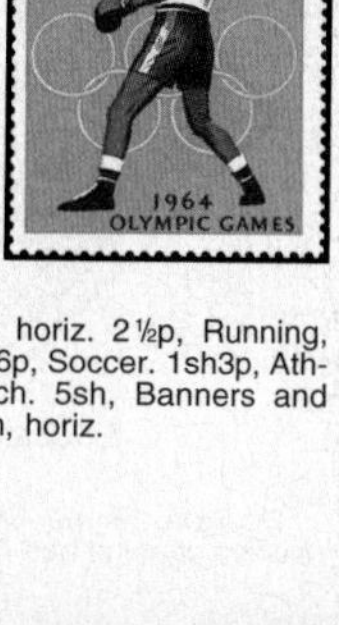

Boxing — A54

Sport: 1p, Hurdling, horiz. 2½p, Running, horiz. 4p, Broad jump. 6p, Soccer. 1sh3p, Athlete with Olympic torch. 5sh, Banners and Tokyo Olympic emblem, horiz.

**1964, Oct. 25 *Perf. 14½x14***

179 A54 1p yellow & multi .25 .25
180 A54 2½p multicolored .25 1.00
181 A54 3p red & multi .25 .25
182 A54 4p blue & multi .25 .25
183 A54 6p multicolored .25 .25
184 A54 1sh3p blue & multi .25 .25
185 A54 5sh gray & multi .25 *2.50*
*a.* Souvenir sheet of 3 1.30 *2.25*
*Nos. 179-185 (7)* 1.75 4.75

18th Olympic Games, Tokyo, Oct. 10-25.

No. 185a contains stamps similar to Nos. 183-185 with simulated perforation.

**Quiet Sun Year Type of 1964**

**Unwmk.**

**1964, Oct. Photo. *Perf. 14***

186 A50 3p gray, bl, grn, yel & red 1.25 1.25
187 A50 6p pink, bl, grn, yel & red 2.50 2.50
188 A50 1sh3p tan, bl, grn, yel, & red 3.75 3.75
*Nos. 186-188 (3)* 7.50 7.50

Each issued in sheets of 12, with star-strewn blue border inscribed "Ghana International Quiet Sun Year." Stamps arranged in square surrounding vignette of New York World's Fair Unisphere in blue.

G. W. Carver and Sweet Potato A55

Design: 1sh3p, Albert Einstein, theory of relativity formula and atom symbol.

**1964, Dec. 7 Wmk. 325 *Perf. 14½***

189 A55 6p grn & dk blue .30 .30
190 A55 1sh3p Prus bl & claret .45 .40
191 A55 5sh org ver & brn blk 1.50 *3.00*
*a.* Souvenir sheet of 3 3.00 2.00
*Nos. 189-191 (3)* 2.25 3.70

Human Rights Day; Albert Einstein (1878-1955) and George Washington Carver (1864-1943), scientists.

No. 191a commemorates UNESCO Week and contains one each of Nos. 189-191 with simulated perforations.

Secretary Bird — A56

Designs: 1p, Elephant, vert. 2½p, Purple wreath, vert. 3p, Gray parrot, vert. 4p, Blue-naped mousebird. 6p, African tulip tree flowers. 1sh3p, Amethyst starling. 2sh6p, Hippopotamuses.

***Perf. 11½x11, 11x11½***

**1964, Dec. 14 Photo. Unwmk.**

192 A56 1p blue & multi .50 .50
193 A56 1½p org & multi .80 1.40
194 A56 2½p lt green & multi .55 .90
*a.* Souv. sheet of 3, #192-194, imperf. 3.75 3.75
195 A56 3p lt green & multi 1.40 .50
196 A56 4p multicolored 1.40 .70
197 A56 6p multicolored .55 .30
198 A56 1sh3p multicolored 1.60 1.00
199 A56 2sh6p multicolored 1.60 3.50
*a.* Souv. sheet of 5, #195-199, imperf. 6.25 *10.00*
*Nos. 192-199 (8)* 8.40 8.80

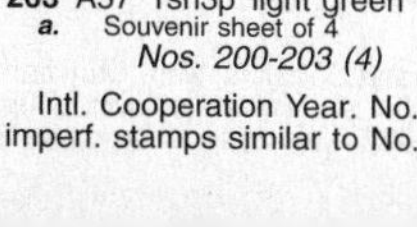

ICY Emblem A57

**1965, Feb. 15 Litho. *Perf. 14x13***

**Design in Black, Red and Green**

200 A57 1p gray .35 .60
201 A57 4p bister 1.25 1.50
202 A57 6p tan 1.25 .45
203 A57 1sh3p light green 1.60 2.25
*a.* Souvenir sheet of 4 4.75 4.75
*Nos. 200-203 (4)* 4.45 4.80

Intl. Cooperation Year. No. 203a contains 4 imperf. stamps similar to No. 203.

ITU Emblem, Old and New Communication Equipment — A58

**1965, Apr. 12 *Perf. 13½***

204 A58 1p multicolored .25 .25
205 A58 6p multicolored .25 .25
206 A58 1sh3p multicolored .75 .25
207 A58 5sh multicolored 2.00 2.00
*a.* Souvenir sheet of 4 10.00 10.00
*Nos. 204-207 (4)* 3.25 2.75

Cent. of the ITU. No. 207a contains 4 imperf. stamps similar to Nos. 204-207 with simulated perforations.

Lincoln's Home, Springfield, Ill. — A59

1sh3p, Inaugural Address and Lincoln. 2sh, Lincoln and his signature. 5sh, Adaptation of 1869 US Lincoln stamp (No. 122).

**Wmk. 325**

**1965, Apr. Photo. *Perf. 12½***

208 A59 6p multicolored .25 .25
209 A59 1sh3p multicolored .25 .25
210 A59 2sh multicolored .25 .35
211 A59 5sh red & black .50 1.25
*a.* Souvenir sheet of 4 1.60 2.50
*Nos. 208-211 (4)* 1.25 2.10

Centenary of death of Abraham Lincoln.

No. 211a contains one each of Nos. 208-211 with simulated perforation.

5-Pesewa Coin, Nkrumah's Head — A60

Coins: 10pa, 10 pesewas. 25pa, 25 pesewas. 50pa, 50 pesewas.

***Perf. 11x13***

**1965, July 19 Unwmk. Litho.**

**Coin in Silver and Black**

**Size: 45x32mm**

212 A60 5pa red, grn & lt grn .25 .25
213 A60 10pa red, grn, & pink .25 .25

**Size: 62x39mm**

214 A60 25pa red, grn, & pink .75 1.00

**Size: 71x43½mm**

215 A60 50pa red, grn & lt grn 1.75 2.25
*Nos. 212-215 (4)* 3.00 3.75

Introduction of decimal currency.

**Regular Issue of 1959-61 Surcharged in Red, Blue, Brown, Black or White with New Value and: "Ghana New Currency / 19th July, 1965"**

***Perf. 12x11½, 14½x14, 14x14½***

**1965, July 19 Photo. Wmk. 325**

216 A14 1pa on 1p (R) .25 .25
217 A16 2pa on 2p (Bl) .25 .25
218 A16a 3pa on 3p (#96, Br) 1.00 *3.50*
219 A16 4pa on 4p (Bl) 4.00 .50
220 A17 6pa on 6p (Bk) .50 .25
221 A15 11pa on 11p (W) .25 .25
222 A15 12pa on 1sh (Bl) .25 .25
223 A17 30pa on 2sh6p (Bl) 3.00 *6.00*
224 A15 60pa on 5sh (Bl) 4.00 .70
225 A16 1.20c on 10s (Bl) .75 *1.75*
226 A28 2.40c on £1 (Bl) 1.00 *6.25*
*Nos. 216-226,C7-C8 (13)* 19.25 21.00

The two lines of the overprint are diagonal on the 1pa, 11pa, 12pa, 60pa, 1.20c and 2.40c.

The surcharge exists double or inverted on six or more denominations.

Summit Conference, Accra — A61

Map of Africa and Flags A62

Designs: 2pa, "OAU" and three heads (triangle pointing up). 5pa, Symbol of African Unity. 15pa, Sunburst and map of Africa. 24pa, Map of Africa.

***Perf. 14, 14½x14***

**1965, Oct. 21 Photo.**

**Ghana Flag in Red, Black & Green**

227 A61 1pa multicolored .25 .25
228 A61 2pa multicolored .25 .25
229 A61 5pa multicolored .25 .25
230 A62 6pa orange & black .25 .25
231 A62 15pa light blue & blk .25 .30
232 A62 24pa lt ultra & green .25 .50
*Nos. 227-232 (6)* 1.50 1.80

Summit Conference of the Organization for African Unity, Accra, Oct. 1965.

Soccer Goalkeeper — A63

Designs: 15pa, Soccer player and cup, vert. 24pa, Two soccer players and cup.

***Perf. 14x13, 13x14***

**1965, Nov. 15 Unwmk.**

233 A63 6pa ocher & multi .25 .25
234 A63 15pa multicolored .40 .30
235 A63 24pa lt blue & multi .45 .60
*Nos. 233-235 (3)* 1.10 1.15

African Soccer Cup competition.

For overprints see Nos. 244-246.

John F. Kennedy and Eternal Flame — A64

Various Kennedy portraits.

**1965, Dec. 15 Wmk. 325 *Perf. 12½***

236 A64 6pa blk, yel, gold & grn .25 .25
237 A64 15pa vio, crim & brt grn .25 .30
238 A64 24pa dp pur & blk .25 .50
239 A64 30pa vio brn & blk .35 .80
*a.* Souvenir sheet of 4 ('66) 3.50 5.50
*Nos. 236-239 (4)* 1.10 1.85

President John F. Kennedy (1917-1963).

No. 239a contains four imperf. stamps similar to Nos. 236-239.

Generators, Volta River Project A65

Designs: 15pa, Dam and Lake Volta. 24pa, "Ghana" forming dam. 30pa, Grain.

***Perf. 11x11½***

**1966, Jan. 22** **Unwmk.**

| | | | | |
|---|---|---|---|---|
| **240** | A65 | 6pa sepia & multi | .25 | .25 |
| **241** | A65 | 15pa multicolored | .25 | .25 |
| **242** | A65 | 24pa multicolored | .25 | .25 |
| **243** | A65 | 30pa brt blue & blk | .35 | .50 |
| | | *Nos. 240-243 (4)* | 1.10 | 1.25 |

Opening of the Volta River dam and electric power station at Akosombo.

**Nos. 233-235 Overprinted Diagonally: "Black Stars Retain Africa Cup / 21st Nov. 1965"**

**1966, Feb. 7** ***Perf. 14x13, 13x14***

| | | | | |
|---|---|---|---|---|
| **244** | A63 | 6pa ocher & multi | .25 | .25 |
| **245** | A63 | 15pa multicolored | .30 | .30 |
| **246** | A63 | 24pa lt bl & multi | .55 | .65 |
| | | *Nos. 244-246 (3)* | 1.10 | 1.20 |

Ghana's soccer victory, Nov. 21, 1965.

Inauguration of WHO Headquarters, Geneva — A66

Designs: 24pa, 30pa, WHO Headquarters from the west and WHO emblem.

***Perf. 14x14½***

**1966, July 1** **Photo.** **Wmk. 325**

| | | | | |
|---|---|---|---|---|
| **247** | A66 | 6pa multicolored | .55 | .25 |
| **248** | A66 | 15pa multicolored | 1.10 | .50 |
| **249** | A66 | 24pa multicolored | 1.40 | 1.60 |
| **250** | A66 | 30pa multicolored | 1.60 | 3.00 |
| *a.* | | Souvenir sheet of 4 | 28.00 | 28.00 |
| | | *Nos. 247-250 (4)* | 4.65 | 5.35 |

No. 250a contains 4 imperf. stamps similar to Nos. 247-250 with simulated perforations.

Herring, Fishermen and Flag A67

Designs: 15pa, Flatfish and canoes. 24pa, Spadefish and schooner. 30pa, Red snapper and fishing trawler "Shama." 60pa, Mackerel and steamer.

**1966, Aug. 10** **Unwmk.** ***Perf. 14x13***

| | | | | |
|---|---|---|---|---|
| **251** | A67 | 6pa ocher & multi | .25 | .25 |
| **252** | A67 | 15pa yel grn & multi | .40 | .25 |
| **253** | A67 | 24pa ver & multi | .70 | .30 |
| **254** | A67 | 30pa blue & multi | 1.00 | 1.10 |
| *a.* | | Souvenir sheet of 4 | 12.00 | 12.00 |
| **255** | A67 | 60pa green & multi | 1.40 | 3.00 |
| | | *Nos. 251-255 (5)* | 3.75 | 4.90 |

1966 Freedom from Hunger campaign "Young World Against Hunger."

No. 254a contains 4 imperf. stamps similar to No. 254.

Flags of African Unity Charter Signers, Map and Diamond A68

Designs: 6p, Ghana flag and links enclosing map of Africa, vert. 24p, Ship's wheel enclosing map of Africa, and cacao pod.

**1966, Sept.** **Unwmk.** ***Perf. 13x13½***

| | | | | |
|---|---|---|---|---|
| **256** | A68 | 6pa brt blue & multi | .25 | .25 |
| **257** | A68 | 15pa blue & multi | .25 | .45 |
| **258** | A68 | 24pa dp green & multi | .25 | .50 |
| | | *Nos. 256-258 (3)* | .75 | 1.20 |

Signing of the African Unity Charter, 3rd anniv.

Soccer Player and Rimet Cup — A69

Various Soccer Scenes.

***Perf. 14½x14***

**1966, Nov. 14** **Photo.** **Wmk. 325**

| | | | | |
|---|---|---|---|---|
| **259** | A69 | 5pa brown & multi | .25 | .25 |
| **260** | A69 | 15pa blue & multi | .70 | .30 |
| **261** | A69 | 24pa green & multi | 1.00 | .50 |
| **262** | A69 | 30pa brt rose & multi | 1.20 | 1.20 |
| **263** | A69 | 60pa lilac & multi | 1.60 | 4.00 |
| *a.* | | Souvenir sheet of 4 | 28.00 | 28.00 |
| | | *Nos. 259-263 (5)* | 4.75 | 6.25 |

World Cup Soccer Championship, Wembley, England, July 11-30.

No. 263a contains 4 imperf. stamps similar to No. 263 with simulated perforations.

UNESCO Emblem A70

**1966, Dec. 23** **Wmk. 325** ***Perf. 14½***

| | | | | |
|---|---|---|---|---|
| **264** | A70 | 5pa multicolored | .25 | .25 |
| **265** | A70 | 15pa multicolored | .75 | .50 |
| **266** | A70 | 24pa multicolored | 1.00 | 1.00 |
| **267** | A70 | 30pa multicolored | 1.50 | 1.25 |
| **268** | A70 | 60pa multicolored | 2.25 | 5.00 |
| *a.* | | Souvenir sheet of 5 | 29.00 | 29.00 |
| | | *Nos. 264-268 (5)* | 5.75 | 8.00 |

UNESCO, 20th anniv. No. 268a contains 5 imperf. stamps similar to Nos. 264-268 with simulated perforations.

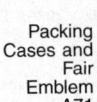

Packing Cases and Fair Emblem A71

Fair Emblem and: 15pa, World map and trade routes to Accra. 24pa, Freighters and loading crane, vert. 36pa, Hand holding cargo net.

**1967, Feb. 1** ***Perf. 14½x14, 14x14½***

| | | | | |
|---|---|---|---|---|
| **269** | A71 | 5pa multicolored | .25 | .25 |
| **270** | A71 | 15pa multicolored | .25 | .25 |
| **271** | A71 | 24pa multicolored | .25 | .30 |
| **272** | A71 | 36pa multicolored | .35 | 1.50 |
| | | *Nos. 269-272 (4)* | 1.10 | 2.30 |

International Trade Fair, Accra, Feb. 1-19.

Eagle and Flag — A72

**1967, Feb. 24** **Photo.** ***Perf. 14x14½***

**Flag in Red, Yellow, Black and Green**

| | | | | |
|---|---|---|---|---|
| **273** | A72 | 1np gray bl & dk brn | .25 | .75 |
| **274** | A72 | 4np ocher & dk brn | .25 | .25 |
| **275** | A72 | 12½np ol grn & dk brn | .35 | .50 |
| **276** | A72 | 25np dl cl & dk brn | .65 | 2.25 |
| *a.* | | Souvenir sheet of 4, #273-276 | 6.75 | 8.00 |
| | | *Nos. 273-276 (4)* | 1.50 | 3.75 |

1st anniv. of the revolution which overthrew the regime of Kwame Nkrumah.

No. 276a has dull claret marginal inscriptions. An imperf. sheet similar to No. 276a has solid margins of dull claret, colorless inscriptions. Value $10.

**Nos. 51, 54-58, 60 and 97 Surcharged in Black, Red or White**

**1967, Feb. 27** ***Perf. 14½x14, 14x14½***

**Size: 30½x21mm, 21x30½mm**

| | | | | |
|---|---|---|---|---|
| **277** | A16 | 1½np on 2p (B) | 3.50 | 7.00 |
| **278** | A16 | 3½np on 4p (R) | 6.00 | 3.00 |
| **279** | A17 | 5np on 6p (R) | 2.00 | 1.75 |
| **280** | A15 | 9np on 11p (W) | .30 | .50 |
| **281** | A15 | 10np on 1sh (W) | .35 | 1.00 |
| **282** | A17 | 25np on 2sh6p (R) | 3.50 | 7.50 |

**Size: 45x26mm**

| | | | | |
|---|---|---|---|---|
| **283** | A16 | 1nc on 10sh (R) | 3.00 | 20.00 |
| **284** | A28 | 2nc on £1 (R) | 6.00 | 30.00 |
| | | *Nos. 277-284,C9-C10 (10)* | 33.65 | 77.75 |

Corn — A73

Forest Kingfisher — A74

African Lungfish A75

Designs: 2np, Ghana Mace (golden staff). 2½np, Commelina flower. 4np, Rufous-crowned roller, vert. 6np, Akosombo Dam, Volta River. 8np, Adomi Bridge, Volta River. 9np, Chameleon. 10np, Quay No. 2, Tema Harbor. 20np, Cape hare. 50np, Black-winged stilt. 1nc, Chief's ceremonial stool. 2nc, Frangipani. 2.50nc, State Chair.

***Perf. 11½x12, 12x11½ (A73), 14x14½, 14½x14 (A74-A75)***

**1967** **Photo.** **Wmk. 325**

| | | | | |
|---|---|---|---|---|
| **286** | A73 | 1np multicolored | .25 | .25 |
| **287** | A74 | 1½np multicolored | 1.10 | 2.75 |
| **288** | A74 | 2np multicolored | .25 | .25 |
| **289** | A74 | 2½np multicolored | .40 | .25 |
| **290** | A75 | 3np multicolored | .25 | .45 |
| **291** | A73 | 4np multicolored | 1.90 | .25 |
| **292** | A75 | 6np multicolored | .25 | 1.75 |
| **293** | A73 | 8np multicolored | .25 | .75 |
| **294** | A75 | 9np multicolored | .90 | .25 |
| **295** | A75 | 10np multicolored | .25 | .25 |
| **296** | A74 | 20np blue | .25 | .25 |
| **297** | A74 | 50np multicolored | 6.50 | 2.75 |
| **298** | A74 | 1nc multicolored | 3.00 | 1.00 |
| **299** | A74 | 2nc multicolored | 2.50 | 4.00 |
| **300** | A74 | 2.50nc multicolored | 3.50 | 10.00 |
| | | *Nos. 286-300 (15)* | 21.55 | 25.20 |

For overprints & surcharges see #356-370, 858, 1091, 1092A-1092C, 1092E-1093, 1095, 1096B.

Kumasi Fort, 1896 A76

Castles on Ghana Coast: 12½np, Christiansborg Castle, 1659, and British galleon. 20np, Elmina Castle, 1482, and Portuguese galleon. 25np, Cape Coast Castle, 1664, and Spanish galleon.

**1967, June 12** ***Perf. 14½***

| | | | | |
|---|---|---|---|---|
| **301** | A76 | 4np grnsh bl & multi | .25 | .25 |
| **302** | A76 | 12½np red org & multi | .90 | 1.00 |
| **303** | A76 | 20np brt grn & multi | 1.90 | 2.25 |
| **304** | A76 | 25np lt red brn & multi | 2.40 | 3.00 |
| | | *Nos. 301-304 (4)* | 5.45 | 6.50 |

Orbiter 1 Landing on Moon — A77

Designs: 4np, Luna 10 on the moon, and globe. 12½np, Astronaut walking in space.

**1967, Aug. 16** **Unwmk.** ***Perf. 13½***

| | | | | |
|---|---|---|---|---|
| **305** | A77 | 4np multicolored | .25 | .25 |
| **306** | A77 | 10np multicolored | .25 | .30 |
| **307** | A77 | 12½np multicolored | .25 | .60 |
| *a.* | | Souvenir sheet of 3 | 2.25 | 4.00 |
| | | *Nos. 305-307 (3)* | .75 | 1.15 |

Achievements in space. Issued in Ghana in sheets of 30. Sheets of 12 with ornamented, inscribed border also exist; these were sold in Ghana in 1968.

No. 307a contains 3 imperf. stamps similar to Nos. 305-307.

Boy Scouts at Campfire A78

Designs: 10np, Hiking Boy Scout. 12½np, Lord Baden-Powell.

**1967, Sept. 18** **Photo.** ***Perf. 14x13½***

| | | | | |
|---|---|---|---|---|
| **308** | A78 | 4np multicolored | .25 | .25 |
| **309** | A78 | 10np multicolored | .40 | .40 |
| **310** | A78 | 12½np multicolored | .50 | .70 |
| *a.* | | Souvenir sheet of 3 | 7.25 | 10.00 |
| | | *Nos. 308-310 (3)* | 1.15 | 1.35 |

50th anniv. of the Ghana (Gold Coast) Boy Scouts. Issued in Ghana in sheets of 30. Sheets of 12 with ornamented, inscribed border also exist; these were sold in Ghana in 1968.

No. 310a contains 3 imperf. stamps similar to Nos. 308-310 with simulated perforations.

UN Secretariat Building — A79

Design: 50np, 2.50nc, UN Headquarters.

**1967, Oct. 24** **Litho.** ***Perf. 13½x13***

| | | | | |
|---|---|---|---|---|
| **311** | A79 | 4np multicolored | .25 | .25 |
| **312** | A79 | 10np multicolored | .25 | .25 |
| **313** | A79 | 50np multicolored | .30 | .60 |
| **314** | A79 | 2.50nc multicolored | 1.00 | 1.00 |
| *a.* | | Souvenir sheet | 5.75 | 9.00 |
| | | *Nos. 311-314 (4)* | 1.80 | 2.10 |

United Nations Day. No. 314a contains one imperf. stamp similar to No. 314 with simulated perforations.

Leopard — A80

Designs: 12½np, Christmas butterfly. 20np, Nubian carmine bee-eaters. 50np, Waterbuck.

**Wmk. 325**

**1967, Dec. 28 Photo. *Perf. 12½***

| | | | | |
|---|---|---|---|---|
| **315** | A80 | 4np multicolored | 1.75 | .25 |
| **316** | A80 | 12½np multicolored | 3.50 | 1.75 |
| **317** | A80 | 20np multicolored | 4.25 | 3.75 |
| **318** | A80 | 50np multicolored | 7.50 | 7.50 |
| *a.* | | Souvenir sheet of 3 | 22.00 | 25.00 |
| | | *Nos. 315-318 (4)* | 17.00 | 13.25 |

Intl. Tourist Year. No. 318a contains 3 imperf. stamps similar to Nos. 316-318 with simulated perforations.

Convoy Entering Accra A81

12½np, Victory parade. 20np, Waving crowd. 40np, Singing and dancing crowd.

**Unwmk.**

**1968, Feb. 24 Litho. *Perf. 14***

| | | | | |
|---|---|---|---|---|
| **319** | A81 | 4np sal & multi | .25 | .25 |
| **320** | A81 | 12½np multicolored | .25 | .25 |
| **321** | A81 | 20np multicolored | .30 | .30 |
| **322** | A81 | 25np yel & multi | .65 | *1.75* |
| | | *Nos. 319-322 (4)* | 1.45 | 2.55 |

2nd anniversary of Feb. 24th Revolution.

Cacao Beans and Microscope A82

4np, 25np, Cacao tree & beans, microscope.

***Perf. 14½x14***

**1968, Mar. 18 Photo. Wmk. 325**

| | | | | |
|---|---|---|---|---|
| **323** | A82 | 2½np grn & multi | .25 | *1.90* |
| **324** | A82 | 4np gray & multi | .25 | .25 |
| **325** | A82 | 10np scar & multi | .25 | .25 |
| **326** | A82 | 25np multicolored | .60 | *1.00* |
| *a.* | | Souvenir sheet of 4 | 3.50 | 3.50 |
| | | *Nos. 323-326 (4)* | 1.35 | 3.40 |

Issued to publicize Ghana's cocoa production. Sheets of 30.

No. 326a contains four imperf. stamps similar to Nos. 323-326 with simulated perforations.

Nos. 323-326 also exist in sheets of 12 believed not to have been on sale in Ghana.

Lt. Gen. E. K. Kotoka A83

Various portraits of Lt. Gen. Kotoka. 40np vert.

**1968, Apr. 17 Unwmk. *Perf. 14***

| | | | | |
|---|---|---|---|---|
| **327** | A83 | 4np pur & multi | .25 | .25 |
| **328** | A83 | 12½np grn & multi | .25 | .25 |
| **329** | A83 | 20np multicolored | .45 | *.60* |
| **330** | A83 | 40np gray & multi | .75 | *1.75* |
| | | *Nos. 327-330 (4)* | 1.70 | 2.85 |

Lt. Gen. Emmanuel Kwasi Kotoka (1926-67), leader of the Revolution of 1966 against Nkrumah.

Tobacco — A84

Designs: 5np, Crested porcupine. 12½np, Tapped rubber tree. 20np, Cymothoe sangaris butterfly. 40np, Charaxes ameliae butterfly.

**1968, Aug. Photo. *Perf. 14x14½***

| | | | | |
|---|---|---|---|---|
| **331** | A84 | 4np multicolored | .25 | .25 |
| **332** | A84 | 5np multicolored | .25 | *1.00* |
| **333** | A84 | 12½np multicolored | .75 | .75 |
| **334** | A84 | 20np multicolored | 2.50 | 2.75 |
| **335** | A84 | 40np multicolored | 2.75 | *5.00* |
| *a.* | | Souvenir sheet of 4 | 7.50 | 8.00 |
| | | *Nos. 331-335 (5)* | 6.50 | 9.75 |

No. 335a contains 4 stamps similar to Nos. 331, 332-335 with simulated perforations.

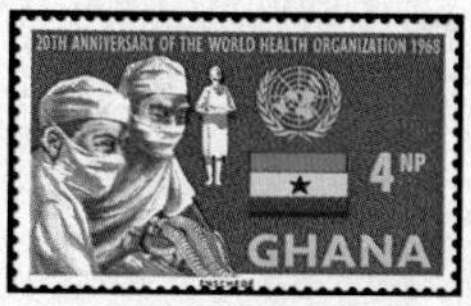


Surgical Team A85

**1968, Nov. 11 *Perf. 14x13***

| | | | | |
|---|---|---|---|---|
| **336** | A85 | 4np grn & multi | .25 | .25 |
| **337** | A85 | 12½np multicolored | .60 | .30 |
| **338** | A85 | 20np pur & multi | 1.00 | 1.00 |
| **339** | A85 | 40np bl & multi | 1.75 | *2.50* |
| *a.* | | Souvenir sheet of 4 | 4.75 | *7.00* |
| | | *Nos. 336-339 (4)* | 3.60 | 4.05 |

WHO, 20th anniv. No. 339a contains 4 imperf. stamps similar to Nos. 336-339.

Hurdling — A86

12½np, Boxing. 20np, Torch bearer, flags & Olympic rings. 40np, Soccer.

**1968, Dec. Unwmk. *Perf. 14x14½***

| | | | | |
|---|---|---|---|---|
| **340** | A86 | 4np gray & multi | .25 | .25 |
| **341** | A86 | 12½np gray & multi | .25 | .25 |
| **342** | A86 | 20np ultra & multi | .40 | *.70* |
| **343** | A86 | 40np gray & multi | .60 | *2.50* |
| *a.* | | Souvenir sheet of 4 | 4.75 | *7.00* |
| | | *Nos. 340-343 (4)* | 1.50 | 3.70 |

19th Olympic Games, Mexico City, Oct. 12-27, 1968. No. 343a contains 4 imperf. stamps with simulated perforations similar to Nos. 340-343.

UN Headquarters and Flags — A87

UN Day, 1968: 12np, UN emblem and Ghanaian staff and stool. 20np, UN Headquarters, New York, UN emblem and Ghana flag. 40np, UN emblem surrounded by flags.

**1969, Feb. 1 Litho. *Perf. 13x13½***

| | | | | |
|---|---|---|---|---|
| **344** | A87 | 4np multicolored | .25 | .25 |
| **345** | A87 | 12½np pink & multi | .25 | .25 |
| **346** | A87 | 20np blk & multi | .25 | *.35* |
| **347** | A87 | 40np lt bl & multi | .35 | *1.75* |
| *a.* | | Souvenir sheet of 4 | 1.25 | *3.25* |
| | | *Nos. 344-347 (4)* | 1.10 | 2.60 |

No. 347a contains 4 imperf. stamps with simulated perforations similar to #344-347.

Joseph Boakye Danquah A88

12½np, 20np, Dr. Martin Luther King, Jr., Human Rights flame & flag of Ghana.

**1969, Mar. 7 Photo. *Perf. 14½x14***

| | | | | |
|---|---|---|---|---|
| **348** | A88 | 4np gray & multi | .25 | .25 |
| **349** | A88 | 12½np multicolored | .25 | *.30* |
| **350** | A88 | 20np blue & multi | .55 | *.75* |
| **351** | A88 | 40np grn & multi | .70 | *2.00* |
| *a.* | | Souvenir sheet of 4 | 1.50 | *3.50* |
| | | *Nos. 348-351 (4)* | 1.75 | *3.30* |

Intl. Human Rights Year, Rev. Martin Luther King, Jr. (1929-1968), American civil rights leader, and Joseph Boakye Danquah (1895-1965), lawyer, writer and Ghanaian political leader.

No. 351a contains 4 imperf. stamps with simulated perforations similar to #348-351.

Parliament A89

Design: 12½np, 40np, Coat of Arms.

***Perf. 14½x14***

**1969, Sept. Wmk. 325**

| | | | | |
|---|---|---|---|---|
| **352** | A89 | 4np multicolored | .25 | .25 |
| **353** | A89 | 12½p multicolored | .25 | .25 |
| **354** | A89 | 20np multicolored | .25 | .25 |
| **355** | A89 | 40np multicolored | .25 | *.60* |
| *a.* | | Souvenir sheet of 4 | 1.10 | *2.50* |
| | | *Nos. 352-355 (4)* | 1.00 | 1.35 |

3rd anniv. of the revolution. No. 355a contains 4 imperf. stamps with simulated perforations similar to Nos. 352-355.

Nos. 286-300 Overprinted in Black, Yellow or Red

***Perf. 11½x12, 12x11½ (A73), 14x14½, 14½x14 (A74-A75)***

**1969, Oct. 1 Photo. Wmk. 325**

| | | | | |
|---|---|---|---|---|
| **356** | A73 | 1np multicolored | .25 | *2.25* |
| **357** | A74 | 1½np multicolored | 1.75 | *4.50* |
| **358** | A73 | 2np multicolored | .25 | *3.50* |
| **359** | A73 | 2½np multicolored | .25 | *2.25* |
| **360** | A75 | 3np multicolored | .70 | *2.50* |
| **361** | A73 | 4np multi (Y) | 2.25 | .75 |
| **362** | A75 | 6np multicolored | .25 | *2.75* |
| **363** | A73 | 8np multicolored | .25 | *3.00* |
| **364** | A75 | 9np multicolored | .25 | *3.00* |
| **365** | A75 | 10np multicolored | .25 | *3.00* |
| **366** | A74 | 20np blue | .65 | *2.25* |
| **367** | A74 | 50np multicolored | 5.00 | *8.50* |
| **368** | A74 | 1nc multicolored | 2.00 | *11.00* |
| **369** | A74 | 2nc multi (R) | 2.50 | *12.00* |
| **370** | A74 | 2.50nc multicolored | 2.50 | *13.00* |
| | | *Nos. 356-370 (15)* | 19.10 | 74.25 |

Overprint vertical on vertical stamps.

The 4np also exists with overprint in black and in red.

Map of Africa, Two Ghana Flags Rising from Ghana — A90

Designs: 12½np, "2" with laurel and star. 20np, Three hands and egg (symbol of rebirth) and Kente cloth. 40np, like 4np.

**Unwmk.**

**1969, Dec. 4 Litho. *Perf. 14***

| | | | | |
|---|---|---|---|---|
| **371** | A90 | 4np multicolored | .25 | .25 |
| **372** | A90 | 12½np bl & multi | .35 | .35 |
| **373** | A90 | 20np multicolored | .45 | .45 |
| **374** | A90 | 40np bl & multi | .95 | .95 |
| | | *Nos. 371-374 (4)* | 2.00 | 2.00 |

Inauguration of the 2nd Republic, Oct. 1969.

Cogwheels and ILO Emblem A91

***Perf. 14½x14***

**1970, Jan. 5 Photo. Wmk. 325**

| | | | | |
|---|---|---|---|---|
| **375** | A91 | 4np rose red & multi | .25 | .25 |
| **376** | A91 | 12½np multicolored | .25 | *.45* |
| **377** | A91 | 20np multicolored | .30 | *.90* |
| *a.* | | Souvenir sheet of 3 | 1.50 | *2.50* |
| | | *Nos. 375-377 (3)* | .80 | *1.60* |

ILO, 50th anniv. No. 377a contains 3 imperf. stamps similar to Nos. 375-377 with simulated perforations.

Nos. 375-377 printed in sheets of 12.

Red Cross Helping Wounded A92

4np, Red Cross & globe, vert. 12½np, Henri Dunant, Red Cross, Red Crescent, Lion & Sun emblems. 40np, Red Cross and first aid.

**1970, Feb. 2 *Perf. 14x14½, 14½x14***

| | | | | |
|---|---|---|---|---|
| **378** | A92 | 4np gold & multi | .50 | .50 |
| **379** | A92 | 12½np gold & multi | .60 | .60 |
| **380** | A92 | 20np blue & multi | .70 | *.85* |
| **381** | A92 | 40np multicolored | 1.00 | *2.50* |
| *a.* | | Souvenir sheet of 4 | 4.25 | *6.00* |
| | | *Nos. 378-381 (4)* | 2.80 | 4.45 |

League of Red Cross Societies, 50th anniv. No. 381a contains 4 imperf. stamps similar to Nos. 378-381 with simulated perforations.

Kotoka Airport, Gen. Kotoka and VC10 — A93

12½np, Control tower & tail section of VC10. 20np, Bird's eye view of airport and runway. 40np, Flags in front of Kotoka Airport.

***Perf. 13x14***

**1970, Apr. Unwmk. Litho.**

| | | | | |
|---|---|---|---|---|
| **382** | A93 | 4np multicolored | .25 | .25 |
| **383** | A93 | 12½np multicolored | .25 | .25 |
| **384** | A93 | 20np multicolored | .45 | .45 |
| **385** | A93 | 40np multicolored | .90 | .90 |
| | | *Nos. 382-385 (4)* | 1.85 | 1.85 |

Inauguration of Kotoka Airport.

Lunar Landing Module and Spacecraft — A94

Designs: 12½np, Neil A. Armstrong stepping onto the moon. 20np, Scientific experiments on the moon, horiz. 40np, Neil A. Armstrong, Michael Collins and Edwin E. Aldrin, Jr., after return to earth, horiz.

**1970, June 15 Litho. *Perf. 12½***

| | | | | |
|---|---|---|---|---|
| **386** | A94 | 4np multicolored | .25 | .25 |
| **387** | A94 | 12½np multicolored | .90 | .90 |
| **388** | A94 | 20np multicolored | 1.20 | 1.20 |
| **389** | A94 | 40np multicolored | 3.50 | 3.50 |
| *a.* | | Souvenir sheet of 4 | 7.00 | 10.00 |
| | | *Nos. 386-389 (4)* | 5.85 | 5.85 |

See note after US No. C76. No. 389a contains 4 imperf. stamps similar to Nos. 386-389. Exists with and without simulated perfs.

Nos. 386-389 and 389a were overprinted "PHILYMPIA/LONDON 1970" in black or silver in Sept. 1970. They are believed not to have been regularly issued.

Adult Education A95

Education Year Emblem and: 12½np, Children of various races studying together. 20np, "Ntesie" symbol of wisdom and knowledge. 40np, Nursery school children.

**1970, Aug. 10 Litho. *Perf. 13x12½***

| | | | | | |
|---|---|---|---|---|---|
| **390** | A95 | 4np | blue & multi | .25 | .25 |
| **391** | A95 | 12½np | blue & multi | .25 | .25 |
| **392** | A95 | 20np | blue & multi | .35 | .35 |
| **393** | A95 | 40np | blue & multi | .55 | .55 |
| | | | *Nos. 390-393 (4)* | 1.40 | 1.40 |

Issued for International Education Year.

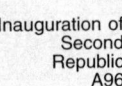

Inauguration of Second Republic A96

Designs: 12½np, Mace and words of proclamation by K. A. Busia. 20np, Mace and globe with doves. 40np, Opening of Parliament of Second Republic.

**1970, Oct. 1 Litho. *Perf. 13***

| | | | | | |
|---|---|---|---|---|---|
| **398** | A96 | 4np | multicolored | .25 | .25 |
| **399** | A96 | 12½np | multicolored | .30 | .30 |
| **400** | A96 | 20np | multicolored | .45 | .45 |
| **401** | A96 | 40np | lt bl & multi | .50 | .50 |
| | | | *Nos. 398-401 (4)* | 1.50 | 1.50 |

First anniversary of the Second Republic.

Amaryllis A97

***Perf. 14½x14***

**1970 Photo. Wmk. 325**

| | | | | | |
|---|---|---|---|---|---|
| **402** | A97 | 4np | shown | 2.50 | .25 |
| **403** | A97 | 12½np | Lioness | 2.50 | 1.25 |
| **404** | A97 | 20np | African orchid | 2.75 | 2.00 |
| **405** | A97 | 40np | Elephant | 8.00 | 8.50 |
| | | | *Nos. 402-405 (4)* | 15.75 | 12.00 |

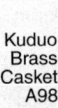

Kuduo Brass Casket A98

Designs: 12½np, Akan traditional house, Danmum. 20np, Larabanga Mosque. 40np, Akan funerary clay head.

**1970, Dec. 7 Litho. *Perf. 14½x14***

| | | | | | |
|---|---|---|---|---|---|
| **406** | A98 | 4np | gray & multi | .25 | .25 |
| **407** | A98 | 12½np | blue & multi | .40 | .30 |
| **408** | A98 | 20np | multicolored | .65 | .55 |
| *a.* | | | Souvenir sheet of 4 | 7.00 | *9.50* |
| **409** | A98 | 40np | blue & multi | 1.50 | 1.60 |
| | | | *Nos. 406-409 (4)* | 2.80 | 2.70 |

No. 408a contains stamps similar to Nos. 406 and 408, a 12½np (Pompeii Basilica) and a 40np (Pompeii scene). Simulated perforation.

Fair Building and Emblem A99

Fair Emblem and: 12½np, Drugstore merchandise. 20np, Automotives and tools. 40np, Cranes and trucks. 50np, Cargo, ship and plane, vert.

***Perf. 14½x14, 14x14½***

**1971, Feb. 5 Photo. Wmk. 325**

| | | | | | |
|---|---|---|---|---|---|
| **410** | A99 | 4np | multicolored | .25 | .25 |
| **411** | A99 | 12½np | lilac & multi | .40 | .40 |
| **412** | A99 | 20np | blue & multi | .70 | .70 |
| **413** | A99 | 40np | multicolored | 1.40 | 1.40 |
| **414** | A99 | 50np | multicolored | 1.75 | 1.75 |
| | | | *Nos. 410-414 (5)* | 4.50 | 4.50 |

2nd Ghana International Trade Fair, Accra, Feb. 1-14, 1971.

Crucifixion A100

Easter: 12½np, Jesus and disciples. 20np, Resurrection.

***Perf. 13½***

**1971, May 19 Litho. Unwmk.**

| | | | | | |
|---|---|---|---|---|---|
| **415** | A100 | 4np | multicolored | .25 | .25 |
| **416** | A100 | 12½np | multicolored | .45 | .45 |
| **417** | A100 | 20np | multicolored | .80 | .80 |
| | | | *Nos. 415-417 (3)* | 1.50 | 1.50 |

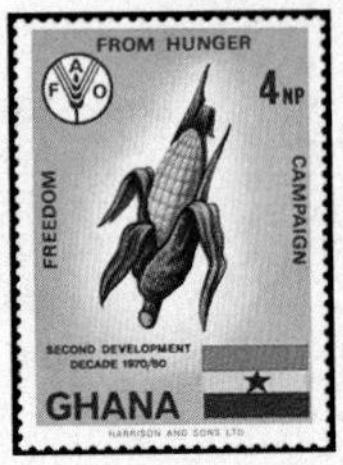


Corn and FAO Emblem — A101

***Perf. 14x14½***

**1971, June Wmk. 325 Photo.**

| | | | | | |
|---|---|---|---|---|---|
| **418** | A101 | 4np | lilac & multi | .25 | .25 |
| **419** | A101 | 12½np | lt bl & multi | .35 | .35 |
| **420** | A101 | 20np | multicolored | .60 | *1.25* |
| | | | *Nos. 418-420 (3)* | 1.20 | 1.85 |

Freedom from Hunger, second development decade, 1970-1980.

The overprint "In Memoriam / Lord Boyd ORR / 1880-1971" was applied to Nos. 418-420 in October, 1971. The 4np was also surcharged "60NP."

Girl Guide Emblem on Flag of Ghana A102

12½np, Mrs. Elsie Ofuatey-Kodjoe, national founder. 20np, Girl Guides at play. 40np, Campfire and tent. 50np, Girl Guides signalling.

**Unwmk.**

**1971, July 22 Litho. *Perf. 14***

| | | | | | |
|---|---|---|---|---|---|
| **421** | A102 | 4np | multicolored | .25 | .25 |
| **422** | A102 | 12½np | yel & multi | .75 | .70 |
| **423** | A102 | 20np | sal & multi | 1.40 | 1.40 |
| **424** | A102 | 40np | multicolored | 2.50 | 2.25 |
| **425** | A102 | 50np | lilac & multi | 2.75 | 2.50 |
| *a.* | | | Souvenir sheet of 5 | 13.00 | 13.00 |
| | | | *Nos. 421-425 (5)* | 7.65 | 7.10 |

50th anniversary of the Girl Guides of Ghana. No. 425a contains 5 imperf. stamps similar to Nos. 421-425.

Child Care Center — A103

YWCA Emblem and: 12½np, World Council Meeting and map of Ghana. 20np, Typing class. 40np, Building fund day.

**1971, Aug. 5 *Perf. 13***

| | | | | | |
|---|---|---|---|---|---|
| **426** | A103 | 4np | multicolored | .30 | .25 |
| **427** | A103 | 12½np | ultra & multi | .30 | .25 |
| **428** | A103 | 20np | blue & multi | .30 | .25 |
| **429** | A103 | 40np | yel & multi | .45 | *.80* |
| *a.* | | | Souvenir sheet of 4 | 1.25 | 1.25 |
| | | | *Nos. 426-429 (4)* | 1.35 | 1.55 |

World Council Meeting of Young Women's Christian Association, Accra, Aug. 5. No. 429a contains 4 stamps similar to Nos. 426-429 with simulated perforations.

African Nativity Scene A104

Christmas: 1np, Fireworks, vert. 6np, Flight into Egypt.

***Perf. 14x14½, 14½x14***

**1971, Nov. Photo. Wmk. 325**

| | | | | | |
|---|---|---|---|---|---|
| **433** | A104 | 1np | multicolored | .30 | *.70* |
| **434** | A104 | 3np | orange & multi | .30 | *.70* |
| **435** | A104 | 6np | blue & multi | .30 | *.70* |
| | | | *Nos. 433-435 (3)* | .90 | *2.10* |

UNICEF Emblem, and Child A105

UNICEF Emblem and: 5np, Infant weighed in net scale, vert. 30np, Student midwife, vert. 50np, Boy in day care center.

***Perf. 13½x13, 13x13½***

**1971, Dec. 20 Litho. Unwmk.**

| | | | | | |
|---|---|---|---|---|---|
| **436** | A105 | 5np | grn & multi | .25 | .25 |
| **437** | A105 | 15np | yel & multi | .25 | *.30* |
| **438** | A105 | 30np | pink & multi | .40 | *.70* |
| **439** | A105 | 50np | blue & multi | .60 | *1.75* |
| *a.* | | | Souvenir sheet of 4 | 4.75 | 6.50 |
| | | | *Nos. 436-439 (4)* | 1.50 | 3.00 |

25th anniv. of UNICEF. No. 439a contains 4 stamps with simulated perforations similar to Nos. 436-439.

Fair Emblem, Map of Africa, Symbol of Unity A106

Fair Emblem and: 15np, Horn of Plenty. 30np, Fireworks over Africa. 60np, 1nc, Names of participating nations over map of Africa.

**1972, Feb. 23 Litho. *Perf. 14***

| | | | | | |
|---|---|---|---|---|---|
| **440** | A106 | 5np | lt brn & multi | .25 | .25 |
| **441** | A106 | 15np | lt bl & multi | .25 | *.30* |
| **442** | A106 | 30np | green & multi | .25 | *.60* |
| **443** | A106 | 60np | yel & multi | .30 | *1.25* |
| **444** | A106 | 1nc | lt bl & multi | .45 | *1.75* |
| | | | *Nos. 440-444 (5)* | 1.50 | *4.15* |

First All-Africa Trade Fair, Nairobi, Kenya, Feb. 23-Mar. 5.

Nos. 440-444 were overprinted "BELGICA 72" in red for release June 24, 1972. The regularity of this issue has been questioned. Value $8.

Books for the Blind A107

Book and Flame of Knowledge A108

Book Year Emblem and: 15p, Books for Children ("Anansi and Snake the Postman"). 30p, Books for Recreation (Accra Central Library). 50p, Books for Students (2 students).

**1972, Apr. 21 *Perf. 13½***

| | | | | | |
|---|---|---|---|---|---|
| **445** | A107 | 5p | blue & multi | .25 | .25 |
| **446** | A107 | 15p | yel & multi | .60 | .50 |
| **447** | A107 | 30p | lilac & multi | .95 | 1.00 |
| **448** | A107 | 50p | green & multi | 1.75 | *2.25* |
| **449** | A108 | 1ce | blue & multi | 2.50 | *4.25* |
| *a.* | | | Souvenir sheet of 5 | 10.00 | *12.00* |
| | | | *Nos. 445-449 (5)* | 6.05 | *8.25* |

Intl. Book Year. No. 449a contains one each of Nos. 445-449 with simulated perforations.

Star Grass A109

**1972, July 3 Litho. *Perf. 13½***

| | | | | | |
|---|---|---|---|---|---|
| **450** | A109 | 5p | shown | .25 | .25 |
| **451** | A109 | 15p | Mona monkey | .75 | .75 |
| **452** | A109 | 30p | Amaryllis | 4.75 | 4.75 |
| **453** | A109 | 1ce | Side-striped squirrel | 5.25 | 5.25 |
| | | | *Nos. 450-453 (4)* | 11.00 | 11.00 |

Olympic Emblems, Soccer A110

**1972, Sept. 5 Litho. *Perf. 13½x13***

| | | | | | |
|---|---|---|---|---|---|
| **454** | A110 | 5p | shown | .25 | .25 |
| **455** | A110 | 15p | Running | .25 | .25 |
| **456** | A110 | 30p | Boxing | .45 | .45 |
| **457** | A110 | 50p | Long jump | .80 | *1.75* |
| **458** | A110 | 1ce | High jump | 1.75 | *3.00* |
| | | | *Nos. 454-458 (5)* | 3.50 | 5.70 |

**Souvenir Sheet**

| | | | | | |
|---|---|---|---|---|---|
| **459** | | | Sheet of 2 | 3.75 | *6.00* |
| *a.* | A110 | 40p | like 30p | 1.40 | *2.25* |
| *b.* | A110 | 60p | like 5p | 1.90 | *3.00* |

20th Olympic Games, Munich, 8/26-9/11.

Senior and Cub Scouts, Badge A111

Designs: 15p, Scout in front of tent. 30p, 40p, Sea Scouts in canoe. 50p, Cub Scouts with den mother. 60p, 1ce, Scouts studying.

**1972, Oct. Litho. *Perf. 14***

| | | | | | |
|---|---|---|---|---|---|
| **460** | A111 | 5p | blue grn & multi | .25 | .25 |
| **461** | A111 | 15p | ocher & multi | .50 | .45 |
| **462** | A111 | 30p | lilac & multi | .95 | .95 |
| **463** | A111 | 50p | multicolored | 1.75 | 1.75 |
| **464** | A111 | 1ce | blue & multi | 3.50 | 3.50 |
| | | | *Nos. 460-464 (5)* | 6.95 | 6.90 |

**Souvenir Sheet**

***Perf. 13½***

| | | | | | |
|---|---|---|---|---|---|
| **465** | | | Sheet of 2 | 4.50 | 4.50 |
| *a.* | A111 | 40p | brown & multi | 1.50 | 1.50 |
| *b.* | A111 | 60p | green & multi | 2.50 | 2.50 |

Boy Scout Movement, 65th anniversary. For overprints see Nos. 484-489.

Virgin and Child, by Holbein the Younger — A112

Paintings: 1p, Holy Night, by Correggio. 15p, Virgin and Child, by Andrea Rico. 30p, Melchior. 60p, Virgin and Child with Caspar. 1ce, Balthasar. 30p, 60p, 1ce, are from early 16th century stained glass windows.

**1972, Dec. 2** ***Perf. 14x13½***

**466** A112 1p black & multi .25 .25
**467** A112 3p black & multi .25 .25
**468** A112 15p black & multi .35 .35
**469** A112 30p black & multi .70 .70
**470** A112 60p black & multi 1.60 1.60
**471** A112 1ce black & multi 2.25 2.25
*a.* Souvenir sheet of 3 8.00 8.00
*Nos. 466-471 (6)* 5.40 5.40

Christmas. No. 471a contains one each of Nos. 469-471 with simulated perforations.

Market A113

Designs: 1p, Unity Declaration at Kumasi Durbar. 5p, Woman with child selling bananas, vert. 15p, Farmer at rest and produce, vert. 30p, Market. 40p, 1ce, Farmer cutting palm nuts with cutlass. 60p, Miners.

***Perf. 14x13½, 13½x14***

**1973, Apr.** **Litho.**

**472** A113 1p multicolored .25 .25
**473** A113 3p multicolored .25 .25
**474** A113 5p multicolored .25 .25
**475** A113 15p multicolored .25 .25
**476** A113 30p multicolored .25 *.40*
**477** A113 1ce multicolored .50 *1.25*
*Nos. 472-477 (6)* 1.75 2.65

**Souvenir Sheet**

**478** Sheet of 2 2.25 2.25
*a.* A113 40p multicolored .80 .80
*b.* A113 60p multicolored 1.20 1.20

Operation "Feed Yourself" and for 1st anniv. of the Oct. 13 Revolution.

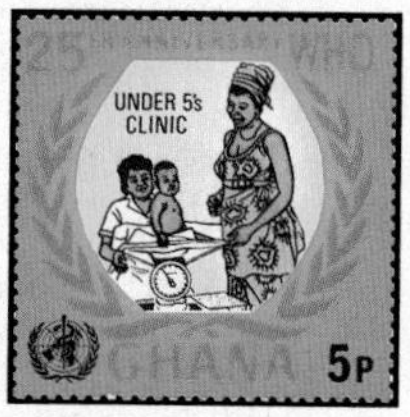

Children's Clinic — A114

WHO Emblem and: 15p, Radiology. 30p, Immunization. 50p, Fight against malnutrition (starving child). 1ce, WHO Headquarters, Geneva.

**1973, July** ***Perf. 14x13½***

**479** A114 5p rose red & multi .25 .25
**480** A114 15p blue & multi .25 .25
**481** A114 30p bister & multi .35 *.40*
**482** A114 50p green & multi .60 *.75*
**483** A114 1ce multicolored 1.05 *1.75*
*Nos. 479-483 (5)* 2.50 3.40

WHO, 25th anniversary.

**Nos. 460-465 Overprinted: "1st WORLD SCOUTING CONFERENCE IN AFRICA"**

**1973, July** **Litho.** ***Perf. 14***

**484** A111 5p green & multi .25 .25
**485** A111 15p ocher & multi .30 *.50*
**486** A111 30p lilac & multi .60 *1.25*
**487** A111 50p multicolored .95 *2.00*
**488** A111 1ce blue & multi 1.90 *3.00*
*Nos. 484-488 (5)* 4.00 *7.00*

**Souvenir Sheet**

***Perf. 13½***

**489** Sheet of 2 4.00 *10.00*
*a.* A111 40p brown & multi 1.40 *3.00*
*b.* A111 60p green & multi 2.10 *6.00*

24th Boy Scout World Conference (1st in Africa), Nairobi, Kenya, July 16-21.

Poultry Farming A115

FAO/UN Emblem and: 15p, 40p, Tractor. 50p, Cacao harvest. 60p, 1ce, FAO Headquarters, Rome.

**1973** **Litho.** ***Perf. 14½x14***

**490** A115 5p blue & multi .25 .25
**491** A115 15p blue & multi .25 .25
**492** A115 50p blue & multi .30 *.80*
**493** A115 1ce blue & multi .45 *1.60*
*Nos. 490-493 (4)* 1.25 2.90

**Souvenir Sheet**

**494** Sheet of 2 1.00 *2.25*
*a.* A115 40p blue & multi .30 *.80*
*b.* A115 60p blue & multi .45 *1.10*

World Food Program, 10th anniversary.

INTERPOL Emblem, Observer A116

INTERPOL Emblem and: 30p, Judge's wig, poison bottle, handcuffs. 50p, photograph and fingerprint. 1ce, Corpse and question mark.

**1973** ***Perf. 13x13½***

**495** A116 5p emerald & multi .25 .25
**496** A116 30p rose red & multi .80 .80
**497** A116 50p ultra & multi 1.90 1.90
**498** A116 1ce gray & multi 3.00 3.00
*Nos. 495-498 (4)* 5.95 5.95

50th anniv. the Intl. Criminal Police Org. (INTERPOL).

Handclasp and "OAU" A117

"OAU" and: 30p, Africa Hall, Addis Ababa. 50p, OAU emblem (map of Africa). 1ce, "X" in Ghana flag colors.

**1973, Oct. 22** **Litho.** ***Perf. 14x14½***

**499** A117 5p lt bl, blk & brn .25 .25
**500** A117 30p bluish grn, blk & brn .25 *.30*
**501** A117 50p pink, black & ol .25 *.75*
**502** A117 1ce multicolored .35 *1.10*
*Nos. 499-502 (4)* 1.10 *2.40*

Org. for African Unity, 10th anniv.

Weather Balloon, WMO Emblem A118

WMO Emblem and: 15p, 40p, Tiros weather satellite. 30p, 60p, Computer weather map. 1ce, Radar cloud scanner.

**1973, Nov. 16**

**503** A118 5p multicolored .25 .25
**504** A118 15p multicolored .25 .25
**505** A118 30p multicolored .35 *.60*
**506** A118 1ce multicolored .65 *1.75*
*Nos. 503-506 (4)* 1.50 2.85

**Souvenir Sheet**

**507** Sheet of 2 1.60 *3.25*
*a.* A118 40p multicolored .45 *.90*
*b.* A118 60p multicolored .85 *1.60*

Intl. meteorological cooperation, cent. No. 507 exists imperf.

Adoration of the Kings — A119

Christmas: 3p, 40p, Madonna and Child (contemporary). Nos. 510, 511d, Madonna and Child, by Murillo. No. 511, 60p, Adoration of the Kings, by Tiepolo. No. 511b as 1p.

**1973, Dec. 10** ***Perf. 14***

**508** A119 1p black & multi .25 .25
**509** A119 3p gray & multi .25 .25
**510** A119 30p multicolored .40 .40
**511** A119 50p multicolored .85 .85
*Nos. 508-511 (4)* 1.75 1.75

**Souvenir Sheet**

***Imperf***

**511A** Sheet of 4 2.00 2.00
*b.* A119 30p black & multi .30 .30
*c.* A119 40p gray & multi .40 .40
*d.* A119 50p multicolored .50 .50
*e.* A119 60p multicolored .60 .60

No. 511A has simulated perforations.

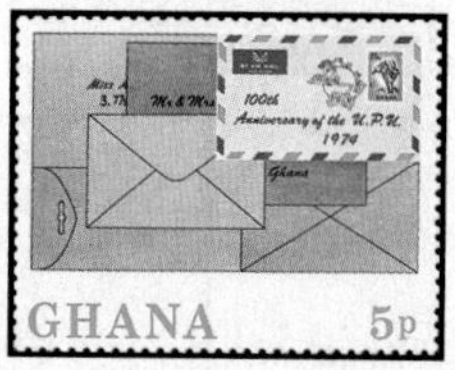

Various Envelopes A120

UPU Emblem and: 9p, 30p, UPU Headquarters, Bern. 40p, 50p, Airmail envelope with Ghana No. 296. 60p, 1ce, Ghana No. 296.

**1974, May** **Litho.** ***Perf. 14½***

**512** A120 5p blue, blk & org .25 .25
**513** A120 9p blue, blk & org .25 .25
**514** A120 50p blue, blk & org .25 *.80*
**515** A120 1ce blue, blk & org .50 *1.50*
*Nos. 512-515 (4)* 1.25 2.80

**Souvenir Sheet**

**515A** Sheet of 4 .90 *1.40*
*b.* A120 20p blue, blk & org .25 *.35*
*c.* A120 30p blue, blk & org .25 *.35*
*d.* A120 40p blue, blk & org .25 *.35*
*e.* A120 50p blue, blk & org .25 *.35*

Centenary of Universal Postal Union. No. 515A exists imperf. Value $20.

For overprints see Nos. 521-524A.

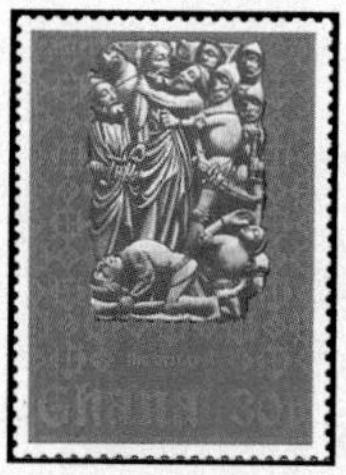
The Betrayal — A121

Designs: 5p, 15p, Jesus Carrying Cross, painting by Thomas de Coloswar, 1427. 20p, 30p, The Betrayal. 25p, 50p, The Deposition. 40p, 1ce, Risen Christ and Mary Magdalene. The designs (except 5p, 15p) are from 15th century English ivory carvings.

**1974, Apr.** **Litho.** ***Perf. 14***

**516** A121 5p black & multi .25 .25
**517** A121 30p sil, ultra & brn .25 *.30*
**518** A121 50p sil, red & brn .25 *.50*
**519** A121 1ce silver, ol & brn .35 *.90*
*Nos. 516-519 (4)* 1.10 *1.95*

**Souvenir Sheet**

***Imperf***

**520** Sheet of 4 1.00 *1.60*
*a.* A121 15p black & multi .25 *.40*
*b.* A121 20p silver, ultra & brn .25 *.40*
*c.* A121 25p silver, red & brn .25 *.40*
*d.* A121 40p silver, olive & brn .25 *.40*

Easter. No. 520 contains 4 stamps with simulated perforations.

**Nos. 512-515A Overprinted "INTERNABA 1974"**

**1974, June 7** ***Perf. 14½***

**521** A120 5p blue, blk & org .25 .25
**522** A120 9p blue, blk & org .25 .25
**523** A120 50p blue, blk & org .30 *.80*
**524** A120 1ce blue, blk & org .45 *1.25*
*Nos. 521-524 (4)* 1.25 2.55

**Souvenir Sheet**

**524A** Sheet of 4 2.00 *3.50*
*b.* A120 20p blue, blk & org .25 *.35*
*c.* A120 30p blue, blk & org .25 *.35*
*d.* A120 40p blue, blk & org .30 *.50*
*e.* A120 60p blue, blk & org .35 *.60*

INTERNABA 1974 International Philatelic Exhibition, Basel, June 7-16.

Overprint is applied to individual stamps of No. 524A.

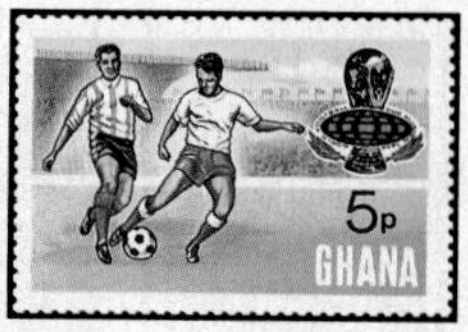

Soccer and World Cup Emblem A122

Designs: Various soccer scenes and world cup emblem.

**1974, June 17** **Litho.** ***Perf. 14½, 13***

**525** A122 5p multicolored .25 .25
**526** A122 30p multicolored .25 *.50*
**527** A122 50p multicolored .25 *.75*
**528** A122 1ce multicolored .25 *1.00*
*Nos. 525-528 (4)* 1.00 2.50

**Souvenir Sheet**

***Perf. 14½***

**529** Sheet of 4 1.75 *3.00*
*a.* A122 25p multicolored .25 *.30*
*b.* A122 40p multicolored .25 *.40*
*c.* A122 55p multicolored .25 *.45*
*d.* A122 60p multicolored .30 *.50*

World Cup Soccer Championship, June 13-July 7.

Nos. 525-528 were issued in sheets of 30, perf. 14½, and in sheets of 5 plus label, perf. 13.

For overprints, see Nos. 535-539, 549-553.

Traffic Diagram at Traffic Circle A123

Designs: 15p, Traffic sign "Two-way traffic." 30p, "Change to right hand drive!," vert. 50p, Warning hands sign, vert. 1ce, 2 hands and car symbolizing traffic change, vert.

**1974, July 16** ***Perf. 13½***

**Size: 35x28½mm**

**530** A123 5p yel grn, red & blk .25 .25
**531** A123 15p lilac, red & blk .25 *.30*

**Size: 28½x41mm**

***Perf. 14½***

**532** A123 30p multicolored .30 .30
**533** A123 50p multicolored .70 .70
**534** A123 1ce red, green & blk 1.40 1.40
*Nos. 530-534 (5)* 2.90 2.95

Publicity for change to right-hand driving, Aug. 4, 1974.

**Nos. 525-529 Overprinted: "WEST GERMANY WINNERS"**

**1974, Aug. 30** **Litho.** ***Perf. 14½, 13***

**535** A122 5p multicolored .25 .25
**536** A122 30p multicolored .40 .40
**537** A122 50p multicolored .60 .60
**538** A122 1ce multicolored 1.00 1.00
*Nos. 535-538 (4)* 2.25 2.25

**Souvenir Sheet**

**539** Sheet of 4 2.00 2.00
*a.* A122 25p multicolored .25 .25
*b.* A122 40p multicolored .40 .40
*c.* A122 55p multicolored .45 .45
*d.* A122 60p multicolored .50 .50

World Cup Soccer Championship, 1974, victory of German Federal Republic. Overprint is applied to individual stamps of No. 539.

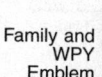

Family and WPY Emblem A124

**1974, Sept. 27** ***Perf. 12½***

**540** A124 5p shown .25 .25
**541** A124 30p Clinic .25 .30
**542** A124 50p Immunization of children .25 *.50*
**543** A124 1ce Census .50 *1.25*
*Nos. 540-543 (4)* 1.25 2.30

World Population Year.

Angel — A125

Nativity — A127

Three Kings, Candles — A126

Design: 60p, 1ce, Annunciation.

**Perf. 13½, 14 (7p)**

**1974, Dec. 19** — **Litho.**

| | | | |
|---|---|---|---|
| **544** A125 | 5p red & multi | .25 | .25 |
| **545** A126 | 7p blue & multi | .25 | .25 |
| **546** A127 | 9p orange & multi | .25 | .25 |
| **547** A127 | 1ce orange & multi | .50 | *1.25* |
| | *Nos. 544-547 (4)* | 1.25 | 2.00 |

### Souvenir Sheet
***Imperf***

| | | | |
|---|---|---|---|
| **548** | Sheet of 4 | 1.25 | *2.00* |
| *a.* | A125 15p red & multi | .25 | *.50* |
| *b.* | A126 30p blue & multi | .25 | *.50* |
| *c.* | A127 45p orange & multi | .25 | *.50* |
| *d.* | A127 60p orange & multi | .25 | *.50* |

Christmas. No. 548 contains 4 stamps with simulated perforations.

### Nos. 525-529 Overprinted "APOLLO / SOYUZ / JULY 15, 1975"

**1975, Aug. 15** — **Litho.** — ***Perf. 14½, 13***

| | | | |
|---|---|---|---|
| **549** A122 | 5p multicolored | .25 | .25 |
| **550** A122 | 30p multicolored | .25 | .25 |
| **551** A122 | 50p multicolored | .45 | .45 |
| **552** A122 | 1ce multicolored | .80 | .80 |
| | *Nos. 549-552 (4)* | 1.75 | 1.75 |

### Souvenir Sheet
***Perf. 14½***

| | | | |
|---|---|---|---|
| **553** | Sheet of 4 | 2.50 | 2.50 |
| *a.* | A122 25p multicolored | .25 | .25 |
| *b.* | A122 40p multicolored | .35 | .35 |
| *c.* | A122 55p multicolored | .55 | .55 |
| *d.* | A122 60p multicolored | .60 | .60 |

Apollo Soyuz space test project (Russo-American cooperation), launching July 15, link-up, July 17.

Overprint is applied to individual stamps of No. 553.

Nos. 549-552 with perf. 13 are from the sheets of 5 plus label.

IWY Emblem, Woman Tractor Driver — A128

Intl. Women's Year Emblem and: 15p, like 7p. 30p, 40p, Automobile mechanic. 60p, 65p, Factory workers. 80p, 1ce, Cocoa research.

**1975, Sept. 3** — **Litho.** — ***Perf. 14***

| | | | |
|---|---|---|---|
| **554** A128 | 7p multicolored | .25 | .25 |
| **555** A128 | 30p lt violet & multi | .50 | .50 |
| **556** A128 | 60p multicolored | 1.25 | 1.25 |
| **557** A128 | 1ce lilac & multi | 2.00 | 2.00 |
| | *Nos. 554-557 (4)* | 4.00 | 4.00 |

### Souvenir Sheet
***Imperf***

| | | | |
|---|---|---|---|
| **558** | Sheet of 4 | 3.50 | *5.00* |
| *a.* | A128 15p Prus green & multi | .25 | *.40* |
| *b.* | A128 40p light violet & multi | .65 | *.90* |
| *c.* | A128 65p dull green & multi | .90 | *1.25* |
| *d.* | A128 80p lilac & multi | 1.10 | *1.50* |

Intl. Women's Year. No. 558 contains 4 stamps with simulated perforations.

Angel over Child in Crib A129

Angel with Harp A130

Designs: 7p, 40p, Angels with lute and bell. 30p, 65p, Angel with viol. 1ce, 80p, Angels with trumpets. 15p, like 5p.

**1975, Dec. 31** — **Litho.** — ***Perf. 14x13½***

| | | | |
|---|---|---|---|
| **559** A129 | 2p org & multi | .25 | .25 |
| **560** A130 | 5p yel, brown & grn | .25 | .25 |
| **561** A130 | 7p yel, brown & grn | .25 | .25 |
| **562** A130 | 30p yel, brown & grn | .35 | .25 |
| **563** A130 | 1ce yel, brown & grn | .50 | .75 |
| | *Nos. 559-563 (5)* | 1.60 | 1.75 |

### Souvenir Sheet
***Imperf***

| | | | |
|---|---|---|---|
| **564** | Sheet of 4 | 1.60 | *2.50* |
| *a.* | A130 15p yellow, green & brown | .25 | *.25* |
| *b.* | A130 40p yellow, green & brown | .25 | *.25* |
| *c.* | A130 65p yellow, green & brown | .40 | *.65* |
| *d.* | A130 80p yellow, green & brown | .50 | *.75* |

Christmas. No. 564 has simulated perforations.

Boy Scouts Reading Map — A131

30p, 40p, Sailing. 60p, 65p, Hiking. 80p, 1ce, Life saving (swimmers). 15p, like 7p.

**1976, Jan. 5** — ***Perf. 13½x14***

| | | | |
|---|---|---|---|
| **565** A131 | 7p ocher & multi | .25 | .25 |
| **566** A131 | 30p blue & multi | .75 | .75 |
| **567** A131 | 60p green & multi | 1.60 | 1.60 |
| **568** A131 | 1ce multicolored | 2.40 | 2.40 |
| | *Nos. 565-568 (4)* | 5.00 | 5.00 |

### Souvenir Sheet

| | | | |
|---|---|---|---|
| **569** | Sheet of 4 | 4.50 | *6.00* |
| *a.* | A131 15p ocher & multi | .35 | *.50* |
| *b.* | A131 40p blue & multi | .80 | *1.10* |
| *c.* | A131 65p green & multi | 1.10 | *1.50* |
| *d.* | A131 80p rose claret & multi | 1.40 | *1.75* |

Nordjamb 75, 14th World Boy Scout Jamboree, Lillehammer, Norway, July 29-Aug. 7.

For overprints, see Nos. 578-582.

1¾ Pints Equal 1 Liter A132

Map of Ghana and: 30p, "2¼ lbs of jam a little more than a kilogram." 60p, "A meter of cloth will be a little more than 3 foot 3." 1ce, Thermometer, ice and boiling tea kettle.

**1976, Jan. 5** — **Litho.** — ***Perf. 14x13½***

| | | | |
|---|---|---|---|
| **570** A132 | 7p bluish gray & blk | .25 | .25 |
| **571** A132 | 30p vio blue & multi | .40 | .40 |
| **572** A132 | 60p ocher & multi | .80 | .80 |
| **573** A132 | 1ce multicolored | 1.40 | 1.40 |
| | *Nos. 570-573 (4)* | 2.85 | 2.85 |

Introduction of metric system, Sept. 1975.

Fair Grounds — A133

Designs: Various exhibition halls.

**1976, Apr. 6** — **Litho.** — ***Perf. 14***

| | | | |
|---|---|---|---|
| **574** A133 | 7p multicolored | .25 | .25 |
| **575** A133 | 30p yellow & multi | .25 | .25 |
| **576** A133 | 60p multicolored | .25 | *.60* |
| **577** A133 | 1ce salmon & multi | .40 | *1.00* |
| | *Nos. 574-577 (4)* | 1.15 | 2.10 |

International Trade Fair, Accra, Feb. 1-15.

### Nos. 565-569 Overprinted in Violet Blue

**1976, May 29** — **Litho.** — ***Perf. 13½x14***

| | | | |
|---|---|---|---|
| **578** A131 | 7p ocher & multi | .25 | .25 |
| **579** A131 | 30p blue & multi | .50 | .50 |
| **580** A131 | 60p green & multi | 1.00 | .75 |
| **581** A131 | 1ce multicolored | 1.40 | 1.25 |
| | *Nos. 578-581 (4)* | 3.15 | 2.75 |

### Souvenir Sheet

| | | | |
|---|---|---|---|
| **582** | Sheet of 4 | 2.00 | 2.00 |
| *a.* | A131 15p ocher & multi | .25 | .25 |
| *b.* | A131 40p blue & multi | .35 | .35 |
| *c.* | A131 65p green & multi | .45 | .45 |
| *d.* | A131 80p rose claret & multi | .45 | .45 |

Interphil 76 International Philatelic Exhibition, Philadelphia, Pa., May 29-June 6. Overprint applied to individual stamps of No. 582.

Shot Put — A134

Olympic Rings, Map of Ghana and: 15p, like 7p. 30p, 40p, Soccer. 60p, 65p, Women's 1500 meters. 80p, 1ce, Boxing.

**1976, Aug. 9** — **Litho.** — ***Perf. 14x13½***

| | | | |
|---|---|---|---|
| **583** A134 | 7p lt blue & multi | .25 | .25 |
| **584** A134 | 30p yellow & multi | .25 | .25 |
| **585** A134 | 60p multicolored | .60 | .60 |
| **586** A134 | 1ce yellow & multi | .90 | .90 |
| | *Nos. 583-586 (4)* | 2.00 | 2.00 |

### Souvenir Sheet

| | | | |
|---|---|---|---|
| **587** | Sheet of 4 | 1.60 | 1.60 |
| *a.* | A134 15p light blue & multi | .25 | .25 |
| *b.* | A134 40p yellow & multi | .25 | .25 |
| *c.* | A134 65p emerald & multi | .25 | .25 |
| *d.* | A134 80p yellow & multi | .35 | .35 |

21st Olympic Games, Montreal, Canada, July 17-Aug. 1.

For overprints see Nos. 606-610.

Supreme Court, Accra A135

Designs: Various views of Supreme Court Building, Scales of Justice, law book.

**1976, Sept. 7** — **Litho.** — ***Perf. 14***

| | | | |
|---|---|---|---|
| **588** A135 | 8p lilac & multi | .25 | .25 |
| **589** A135 | 30p blue & multi | .25 | .25 |
| **590** A135 | 60p ver & multi | .35 | *.50* |
| **591** A135 | 1ce multicolored | .65 | *1.00* |
| | *Nos. 588-591 (4)* | 1.50 | 2.00 |

Ghana Supreme Court, centenary.

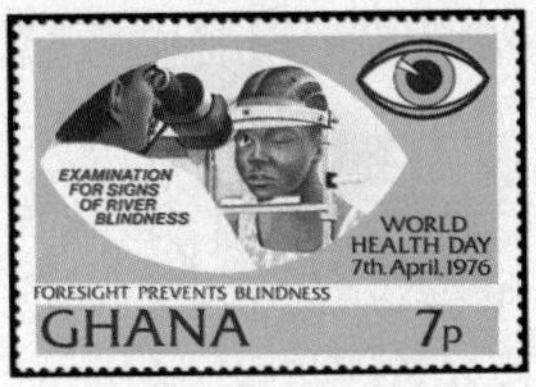


Examination for River Blindness — A136

Designs: 30p, Ghanaian entomologist with microscope. 60p, Flowers. 1ce, Boatmen checking effectiveness of black fly larvae insecticide.

**1976, Oct. 28** — **Litho.** — ***Perf. 14½x14***

| | | | |
|---|---|---|---|
| **592** A136 | 7p multicolored | .80 | .25 |
| **593** A136 | 30p multicolored | 2.10 | 1.75 |
| **594** A136 | 60p multicolored | 3.25 | 3.25 |
| **595** A136 | 1ce multicolored | 5.50 | 5.50 |
| | *Nos. 592-595 (4)* | 11.65 | 10.75 |

World Health Day. Prevention of blindness.

Children with Gifts and Christmas Tree — A137

Designs: 6p, 15p, Children with firecrackers. 30p, 65p, Family at Christmas dinner. 40p, 80p, 1ce, like 8p.

**1976, Dec. 15** — **Litho.** — ***Perf. 13½***

| | | | |
|---|---|---|---|
| **596** A137 | 6p multicolored | .25 | .25 |
| **597** A137 | 8p multicolored | .25 | .25 |
| **598** A137 | 30p multicolored | .60 | .60 |
| **599** A137 | 1ce multicolored | 1.40 | 1.40 |
| | *Nos. 596-599 (4)* | 2.50 | 2.50 |

### Souvenir Sheet
***Imperf***

| | | | |
|---|---|---|---|
| **600** | Sheet of 4 | 2.75 | 2.75 |
| *a.* | A137 15p multicolored | .25 | .25 |
| *b.* | A137 40p multicolored | .45 | .45 |
| *c.* | A137 65p multicolored | .75 | .75 |
| *d.* | A137 80p multicolored | 1.10 | 1.10 |

Christmas. No. 600 has simulated perfs.

1876 Gallows Frame Telephone and A. G. Bell — A138

A. G. Bell and: 15p, like 8p. 30p, 40p, 1895 telephone. 60p, 65p, 1929 telephone. 80p, 1ce, 1976 telephone.

**1976, Dec. 17** — ***Perf. 14½***

| | | | |
|---|---|---|---|
| **601** A138 | 8p multicolored | .25 | .25 |
| **602** A138 | 30p multicolored | .45 | .45 |
| **603** A138 | 60p multicolored | 1.30 | 1.30 |
| **604** A138 | 1ce multicolored | 1.50 | 1.50 |
| | *Nos. 601-604 (4)* | 3.50 | 3.50 |

### Souvenir Sheet
***Perf. 13***

| | | | |
|---|---|---|---|
| **605** | Sheet of 4 | 2.60 | 2.60 |
| *a.* | A138 15p multicolored | .25 | .25 |
| *b.* | A138 40p multicolored | .45 | .45 |
| *c.* | A138 65p multicolored | .75 | .75 |
| *d.* | A138 80p multicolored | .85 | .85 |

Centenary of first telephone call by Alexander Graham Bell, Mar. 10, 1876.

For overprints, see Nos. 616-620.

### Nos. 583-587 Overprinted

a. EAST GERMANY / WINNERS
b. U.S.S.R. WINNERS
c. U.S.A. WINNERS

**1977, Feb. 22 Litho. *Perf. 14x13½***
**606** A134(a) 7p multicolored .25 .25
**607** A134(a) 30p multicolored .30 .25
**608** A134(b) 60p multicolored .65 .65
**609** A134(c) 1ce multicolored 1.30 1.30
*Nos. 606-609 (4)* 2.50 2.45

**Souvenir Sheet**

**610** Sheet of 4 3.25 3.25
*a.* A134(a) 15p multicolored .25 .25
*b.* A134(a) 40p multicolored .65 .65
*c.* A134(b) 65p multicolored .95 .95
*d.* A134(c) 80p multicolored 1.00 1.00

1976 Montreal Olympic Games' winners.

Klama Dance, Dipo Tribe — A139

Festival Emblem and: 15p, like 8p. 30p, 40p, African artifacts. 60p, 65p, Acon dance. 80p, 1ce, Mud, straw and wooden huts.

**1977, Mar. 24 Litho. *Perf. 14x13½***
**611** A139 8p multicolored .25 .25
**612** A139 30p multicolored .45 *.60*
**613** A139 60p multicolored .70 *1.10*
**614** A139 1ce multicolored 1.10 *1.75*
*Nos. 611-614 (4)* 2.50 3.70

**Souvenir Sheet**

**615** Sheet of 4 3.00 3.00
*a.* A139 15p multicolored .30 .30
*b.* A139 40p multicolored .65 .65
*c.* A139 65p multicolored .85 .85
*d.* A139 80p multicolored 1.05 1.05

2nd World Black and African Festival of Arts and Culture, Lagos, Nigeria, Jan. 15-Feb. 12.

**Nos. 601-605 Overprinted: "PRINCE CHARLES / VISITS GHANA / 17th TO 25th / MARCH, 1977"**

**1977, June 2 Litho. *Perf. 14½***
**616** A138 8p multicolored .65 .65
**617** A138 30p multicolored 1.60 1.60
**618** A138 60p multicolored 2.50 2.50
**619** A138 1ce multicolored 3.25 3.25
*Nos. 616-619 (4)* 8.00 8.00

**Souvenir Sheet**
***Perf. 13***

**620** Sheet of 4 11.00 11.00
*a.* A138 15p multicolored 1.20 1.05
*b.* A138 40p multicolored 2.10 1.75
*c.* A138 65p multicolored 3.00 2.50
*d.* A138 80p multicolored 3.50 3.00

Visit of Prince Charles, Mar. 17-25. Overprint applied to individual stamps of No. 620.

Olive Colobus — A140

Wildlife Fund Emblem and: 15p, like 8p. 20p, 40p, Ebien palm squirrel. 30p, 65p, African wild dog. 60p, 80p, West African manatee.

**1977, June 22 Litho. *Perf. 13½x14***
**621** A140 8p multicolored *4.00* *1.50*
**622** A140 20p multicolored *9.00* *2.00*
**623** A140 30p multicolored *12.00* *5.00*
**624** A140 60p multicolored *16.00* *7.00*
*Nos. 621-624 (4)* *41.00* *15.50*

**Souvenir Sheet**

**625** Sheet of 4 20.00 20.00
*a.* A140 15p multicolored 2.50 2.50
*b.* A140 40p multicolored 4.50 4.50
*c.* A140 65p multicolored 5.50 5.50
*d.* A140 80p multicolored 6.50 6.50

Wildlife protection.

Suzanne Fourment in Velvet Hat, by Rubens — A141

Paintings: 15p, like 8p. 30p, 40p, Isabella of Portugal, by Titian. 60p, 65p, Duke and Duchess of Cumberland, by Gainsborough. 80p, 1ce, Rubens and his wife Isabella, by Rubens.

**1977, Sept. Litho. *Perf. 14x13½***
**626** A141 8p lt blue & multi .25 .25
**627** A141 30p lt blue & multi .50 .50
**628** A141 60p lt blue & multi 1.10 1.10
**629** A141 1ce lt blue & multi 2.00 2.00
*Nos. 626-629 (4)* 3.85 3.85

**Souvenir Sheet**

**630** Sheet of 4 3.50 3.50
*a.* A141 15p light blue & multi .25 .25
*b.* A141 40p light blue & multi .70 .70
*c.* A141 65p light blue & multi 1.10 1.10
*d.* A141 80p light blue & multi 1.25 1.25

Painters, birth annivs.: Peter Paul Rubens (1577-1640); Titian (1477-1576); Thomas Gainsborough (1727-1788).

Adoration of the Kings — A142

Guild of the Good Shepherd, Abossey Okai — A143

Designs: 6p, 40p, Methodist Church, Wesley, Accra. 8p, Virgin and Child, and Star. 15p, like 2p. 30p, 65p, Holy Spirit Cathedral, Accra. 80p, 1ce, Ebenezer Presbyterian Church, Osu, Accra. Type A143 designs include score of "Hark the Herald Angels Sing."

***Perf. 14x14½, 14***

**1977, Dec. 30 Litho.**
**631** A142 1p multicolored .25 .25
**632** A143 2p multicolored .25 .25
**633** A143 6p multicolored .25 .25
**634** A142 8p multicolored .25 .25
**635** A143 30p multicolored .50 .50
**636** A143 1ce multicolored 1.50 1.50
*Nos. 631-636 (6)* 3.00 3.00

**Souvenir Sheet**
***Imperf***

**637** Sheet of 4 4.00 4.00
*a.* A143 15p multicolored .25 .25
*b.* A143 40p multicolored .65 .65
*c.* A143 65p multicolored 1.05 1.05
*d.* A143 80p multicolored 1.25 1.25

Christmas. No. 637 has simulated perfs.

**No. 631-637 Overprinted: "REFERENDUM 1978 VOTE EARLY"**

***Perf. 14x14½, 14***

**1978, Mar. 28 Litho.**
**638** A142 1p multicolored .25 .25
**639** A143 2p multicolored .25 .25
**640** A143 6p multicolored .25 .25
**641** A142 8p multicolored .25 .25
**642** A143 30p multicolored .50 .50
**643** A143 1ce multicolored 1.75 1.75
*Nos. 638-643 (6)* 3.25 3.25

**Souvenir Sheet**
***Imperf***

**644** Sheet of 4 *35.00* *20.00*
*a.* A143 15p multicolored *2.60* *1.50*
*b.* A143 40p multicolored *6.50* *3.75*
*c.* A143 65p multicolored *11.00* *6.50*
*d.* A143 80p multicolored *13.00* *7.50*

Banana Harvest — A144

Designs: 8p, Vegetable garden. 30p, Produce market. 60p, Fishing. 1ce, Tractor.

**1978, May 15 *Perf. 14***
**645** A144 2p multicolored .25 .25
**646** A144 8p multicolored .25 .25
**647** A144 30p multicolored .40 .40
**648** A144 60p multicolored .95 .95
**649** A144 1ce multicolored 1.60 1.60
*Nos. 645-649 (5)* 3.45 3.45

Operation feed yourself.

Wright Biplane and Crowd — A145

Planes and Crowd: 15p, like 8p. 30p, 40p, Heracles, 1st practical airliner. 60p, 65p, D. H. Comet, 1st jet airliner. 80p, 1ce, Concorde, 1st supersonic airliner.

**1978, June 6 Litho. *Perf. 14x13½***
**650** A145 8p multicolored .25 .25
**651** A145 30p multicolored .65 .55
**652** A145 60p multicolored 1.25 1.10
**653** A145 1ce multicolored 2.00 1.40
*Nos. 650-653 (4)* 4.15 3.30

**Souvenir Sheet**

**654** Sheet of 4 6.00 3.25
*a.* A145 15p multicolored .35 .25
*b.* A145 40p multicolored 1.10 .60
*c.* A145 65p multicolored 1.90 1.00
*d.* A145 80p multicolored 2.10 1.10

75th anniversary of first powered flight. The cheering crowd forms a continuing design on Nos. 650-654.

**Nos. 650-653, 654a-654d Overprinted: "CAPEX 78 / JUNE 9-18 1978"**

**1978, June 9**
**655** A145 8p multicolored .25 .25
**656** A145 30p multicolored .40 .25
**657** A145 60p multicolored .65 .50
**658** A145 1ce multicolored 1.75 .80
*Nos. 655-658 (4)* 3.05 1.80

**Souvenir Sheet**

**659** Sheet of 4 2.50 2.25
*a.* A145 15p multicolored .25 .25
*b.* A145 40p multicolored .45 .40
*c.* A145 65p multicolored .70 .65
*d.* A145 80p multicolored .90 .80

CAPEX, Canadian International Philatelic Exhibition, Toronto, Ont., June 9-18.

Soccer, Africa Cup Emblem and Ghana Flag — A146

15p, like 8p. 30p, 40p, Three soccer players, Africa Cup emblem, Ghana flag. 60p, 65p, Two soccer players. Argentina '78 emblem, Argentine flag. 80p, 1ce, Goalkeeper, Argentina '78 emblem and Argentine flag.

**1978, July 1 Litho. *Perf. 13½x14***
**660** A146 8p multicolored .25 .25
**661** A146 30p multicolored .30 .30
**662** A146 60p multicolored .70 .70
**663** A146 1ce multicolored 1.30 1.30
*Nos. 660-663 (4)* 2.55 2.55

**Souvenir Sheet**

**664** Sheet of 4 1.75 1.75
*a.* A146 15p multicolored .25 .25
*b.* A146 40p multicolored .35 .35
*c.* A146 65p multicolored .55 .55
*d.* A146 80p multicolored .60 .60

11th African Cup of Nations, Ghana, Mar. 5-19, and 11th World Cup Soccer Championship, Argentina, June 1-25.

**Nos. 660-661, 664a-664b Overprinted: "GHANA WINNERS"**
**Nos. 662-663, 664c-664d Overprinted: "ARGENTINA WINS"**

**1978, Aug. 21 Litho. *Perf. 13½x14***
**665** A146 8p multicolored .25 .25
**666** A146 30p multicolored .40 .40
**667** A146 60p multicolored .80 .80
**668** A146 1ce multicolored 1.40 1.40
*Nos. 665-668 (4)* 2.85 2.85

**Souvenir Sheet**

**669** Sheet of 4 1.60 1.60
*a.* A146 15p multicolored .25 .25
*b.* A146 40p multicolored .25 .25
*c.* A146 65p multicolored .40 .40
*d.* A146 80p multicolored .60 .60

Winners, 11th African Cup and 11th World Cup Soccer Championships.
Overprint on 60p and 65p is in two lines.

The Betrayal, by Dürer — A147

Etchings by Albrecht Dürer: 39p, The Crucifixion. 60p, The Deposition. 1ce, The Resurrection.

**1978, Sept. 1 Litho. *Perf. 14x13½***
**670** A147 11p lilac & black .25 .25
**671** A147 39p salmon & black .30 .30
**672** A147 60p orange & black .45 .45
**673** A147 1ce yel green & black .75 .75
*Nos. 670-673 (4)* 1.75 1.75

Easter.

Bauhinia Purpurea A148

Flowers: 39p, Cassia fistula. 60p, Frangipani. 1ce, Jacaranda mimosifolia.

**1978, Nov. 20 Litho. *Perf. 14x13½***
**674** A148 11p multicolored .25 .25
**675** A148 39p multicolored .25 .25
**676** A148 60p multicolored .45 .45
**677** A148 1ce multicolored .65 .65
*Nos. 674-677 (4)* 1.60 1.60

Mail Railroad Car — A149

Ghana railroad, 75th Anniv.: 39p, Pay and bank car. 60p, Locomotive, 1922. 1ce, Diesel locomotive, 1960.

**1978, Dec. 4 Litho. *Perf. 13½***
**678** A149 11p multicolored .25 .25
**679** A149 39p multicolored .45 *.65*
**680** A149 60p multicolored .75 *1.00*
**681** A149 1ce multicolored 1.10 *1.50*
*Nos. 678-681 (4)* 2.55 *3.40*

Orbiter Spacecraft — A150

15p, like 11p. 39p, 40p, Multiprobe spacecraft. 60p, 65p, Orbiter and Multiprobe circling Venus. 2ce, 3ce, Radar chart of Venus.

**1979, July 5 Litho. *Perf. 14x13½***

**682** A150 11p multicolored .25 .25
**683** A150 39p multicolored .25 .25
**684** A150 60p multicolored .35 .35
**685** A150 3ce multicolored .55 *1.10*
*Nos. 682-685 (4)* 1.40 1.95

**Souvenir Sheet**

***Imperf***

**686** Sheet of 4 1.90 1.90
*a.* A150 15p multicolored .25 .25
*b.* A150 40p multicolored .25 .25
*c.* A150 65p multicolored .40 .40
*d.* A150 2ce multicolored .90 .90

Pioneer Venus Space Project.

O Come All Ye Faithful A152

Christmas Carols: 10p, O Little Town of Bethlehem. 15p, 65p, We Three Kings of Orient Are. 20p, I Saw Three Ships Come Sailing By. 25p, like 8p. No. 696, 1ce, Away in a Manger. 4ce, No. 698d, Ding Dong Merrily on High.

**1979, Dec. 20 *Perf. 14½***

**692** A152 8p multicolored .25 .25
**693** A152 10p multicolored .25 .25
**694** A152 15p multicolored .25 .25
**695** A152 20p multicolored .25 .25
**696** A152 2ce multicolored .25 *.60*
**697** A152 4ce multicolored .30 *1.10*
*Nos. 692-697 (6)* 1.55 2.70

**Souvenir Sheet**

**698** Sheet of 4 1.10 1.10
*a.* A152 25p multicolored .25 .25
*b.* A152 65p multicolored .25 .25
*c.* A152 1ce multicolored .25 .25
*d.* A152 2ce multicolored .50 .50

Christmas.

J.B. Danquah (1895-1965) A153

National Leaders: 65p, John Mensah Sarbah (1864-1910). 80p, J.E.K. Aggrey (1875-1925). 2ce, Kwame Nkrumah (1909-1972). 4ce, G.E. Grant (1878-1956).

**1980, Jan. 21 Litho. *Perf. 13½x14***

**699** A153 20p multicolored .25 .25
**700** A153 65p multicolored .25 .25
**701** A153 80p multicolored .25 .25
**702** A153 2ce multicolored .40 .40
**703** A153 4ce multicolored .75 .75
*Nos. 699-703 (5)* 1.90 1.90

Man with Clack Bells, Hill A154

Hill and: 25p, Man with clack bells. 50p, 65p, Chief, elephant staff. 1ce, 2ce, Drummer. 4ce, 5ce, Chief, ivory staff.

**1980, Mar. 12 Litho. *Perf. 14½***

**704** A154 20p multicolored .25 .25
**705** A154 65p multicolored .25 .25
**706** A154 2ce multicolored .45 .45
**707** A154 4ce multicolored .85 .85
*Nos. 704-707 (4)* 1.80 1.80

**Souvenir Sheet**

**708** Sheet of 4 1.75 1.75
*a.* A154 25p multicolored .25 .25
*b.* A154 50p multicolored .25 .25
*c.* A154 1ce multicolored .30 .30
*d.* A154 5ce multicolored .85 .85

Sir Rowland Hill (1795-1879), originator of penny postage.

Nos. 708a-708d also exist perf 13½, issued in small individual sheetlets. Values slightly more than perf 14½.

For overprints see Nos. 714-718.

Students, IYC Emblem — A155

IYC Emblem and: 25p like 20p. 50p, 65p, Boys playing soccer. 1ce, 2ce, Boys in canoe. 3ce, 4ce, Mother and child.

**1980, Apr. 2 Litho. *Perf. 15***

**709** A155 20p multicolored .25 .25
**710** A155 65p multicolored .25 *.30*
**711** A155 2ce multicolored .55 *.80*
**712** A155 4ce multicolored 1.10 *1.60*
*Nos. 709-712 (4)* 2.15 *2.95*

**Souvenir Sheet**

**713** Sheet of 4 2.25 2.25
*a.* A155 25p multicolored .25 .25
*b.* A155 50p multicolored .25 .25
*c.* A155 1ce multicolored .30 .30
*d.* A155 3ce multicolored .75 .75

Intl. Year of the Child (in 1979).

For overprints see Nos. 719-723.

**Nos. 704-708 Overprinted: "LONDON 1980" / 6th-14th May 1980**

**1980, May 6 Litho. *Perf. 14½***

**714** A154 20p multicolored .25 .25
**715** A154 65p multicolored .30 .30
**716** A154 2ce multicolored .80 .80
**717** A154 4ce multicolored 1.30 1.30
*Nos. 714-717 (4)* 2.65 2.65

**Souvenir Sheet**

**718** Sheet of 4 3.00 3.00
*a.* A154 25p multicolored .25 .25
*b.* A154 50p multicolored .25 .25
*c.* A154 1ce multicolored .45 .45
*d.* A154 5ce multicolored 1.90 1.90

London 1980 Intl. Stamp Exhib., May 6-14. #718a-718d also exist perf 13½, issued in small individual sheetlets. Value, unused or used, $15.

**Nos. 709-713 Overprinted: "PAPAL VISIT" / 8th-9th May / 1980**

**1980, May 8 *Perf. 15***

**719** A155 20p multicolored .75 .25
**720** A155 65p multicolored 1.40 .70
**721** A155 2ce multicolored 2.25 1.40
**722** A155 4ce multicolored 3.50 2.25
*Nos. 719-722 (4)* 7.90 4.60

**Souvenir Sheet**

**723** Sheet of 4 15.00 15.00
*a.* A155 25p multicolored 1.00 1.00
*b.* A155 50p multicolored 2.10 2.10
*c.* A155 1ce multicolored 3.25 3.25
*d.* A155 3ce multicolored 7.75 7.75

Visit of Pope John Paul II to Ghana, May 8-9.

Nos. 719-722 exist imperf. Value, set $25.

Parliament House A156

**1980, Aug. 4 Litho. *Perf. 14***

**724** A156 20p shown .25 .25
**725** A156 65p Supreme Court .25 .25
**726** A156 2ce The Castle .25 *.60*
*Nos. 724-726 (3)* .75 1.10

**Souvenir Sheet**

**727** Sheet of 3 .70 *1.00*
*a.* A156 25p like #724 .25 .25
*b.* A156 1ce like #725 .25 .25
*c.* A156 3ce like #726 .30 .30

Third Republic.

Map of West African Member Countries, Flag of Ghana, Jet — A157

**1980, Nov. 5 Litho. *Perf. 14½***

**728** A157 20p shown .25 .25
**729** A157 65p Dish antenna .25 .25
**730** A157 80p Cogwheels .25 .25
**731** A157 2ce Corn .25 .25
*Nos. 728-731 (4)* 1.00 1.00

5th Anniversary of ECOWAS (Economic Community of West African States).

A158

**1980, Nov. 26**

**732** A158 20p "OAU" .25 .25
**733** A158 65p OAU Banner, Maps .25 .25
**734** A158 80p Waves on map of Africa .25 .25
**735** A158 2ce Flag, banner, map .25 .25
*Nos. 732-735 (4)* 1.00 1.00

Org. for African Unity summit conference, Lagos, Nigeria, Apr. 28-29.

A159

Christmas (Fra Angelico Paintings): 15p, 25p, Adoration of the Magi. 20p, 50p, Virgin and Child Enthroned with Four Angels. 1ce, 2ce, Virgin and Child Enthroned with Eight Angels. 3ce, 4ce, Annunciation.

**1980, Dec. 10 *Perf. 14***

**736** A159 15p multicolored .25 .25
**737** A159 20p multicolored .25 .25
**738** A159 2ce multicolored .35 *.60*
**739** A159 4ce multicolored .75 *1.25*
*Nos. 736-739 (4)* 1.60 2.35

**Souvenir Sheet**

**740** Sheet of 4 1.00 1.00
*a.* A159 25p multicolored .25 .25
*b.* A159 50p multicolored .25 .25
*c.* A159 1ce multicolored .25 .25
*d.* A159 3ce multicolored .30 .30

Nurse Weighing Newborn, Rotary Emblem A160

**1980, Dec. 18**

**741** A160 20p shown .25 .25
**742** A160 65p Map of Ghana and world .25 .25
**743** A160 2ce Helping hands, world map .45 *.75*
**744** A160 4ce Food distribution .95 *1.40*
*Nos. 741-744 (4)* 1.90 2.65

**Souvenir Sheet**

**745** Sheet of 4 2.00 2.00
*a.* A160 25p like #741 .25 .25
*b.* A160 50p like #742 .25 .25
*c.* A160 1ce like #743 .25 .25
*d.* A160 3ce like #744 .80 .80

Rotary International, 75th anniv.

Narina Trogon — A161

**1981, Jan. 12 Litho. *Perf. 14***

**746** A161 20p shown 1.75 .25
**747** A161 65p White-crowned robin-chat 2.75 .60
**748** A161 2ce Swallow-tailed bee-eater 3.50 1.75
**749** A161 4ce Long-tailed parakeet 5.00 3.25
*Nos. 746-749 (4)* 13.00 5.85

**Souvenir Sheet**

**750** Sheet of 4 10.50 10.50
*a.* A161 25p like #746 .40 .30
*b.* A161 50p like #747 1.00 .45
*c.* A161 1ce like #748 1.75 .80
*d.* A161 3ce like #749 5.50 2.40

Pope John Paul II, Pres. Limann, Archbishop of Canterbury — A162

**1981, Mar. 3 Litho. *Perf. 14***

**751** A162 20p multicolored .25 .25
**752** A162 65p multicolored .55 .55
**753** A162 80p multicolored .70 .70
**754** A162 2ce multicolored 2.25 2.25
*Nos. 751-754 (4)* 3.75 3.75

Visit of Pope John Paul II, May 8-10, 1980.

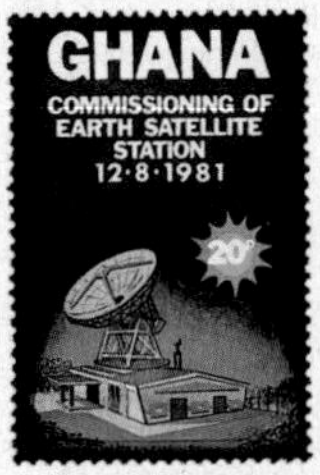


Earth Satellite Station — A163

**1981, Sept. 28 Litho. *Perf. 14***

**755** A163 20p shown .25 .25
**756** A163 65p Satellites orbiting earth .25 .25
**757** A163 80p Satellite .25 .25
**758** A163 4ce Satellite, earth 1.10 1.10
*Nos. 755-758 (4)* 1.85 1.85

**Souvenir Sheet**

**758A** Sheet of 4 1.40 1.40
*b.* A163 25p like #755 .25 .25
*c.* A163 50p like #756 .25 .25
*d.* A163 1ce like #757 .25 .25
*e.* A163 3ce like #758 .60 .60

Earth Satellite Station commission.

Common Design Types pictured following the introduction.

**Royal Wedding Issue**

Common Design Type

**1981 Litho. *Perf. 14***

**759** CD331a 20p Couple .25 .25
**759A** CD331a 65p like 20p .25 .25
**760** CD331a 80p Charles .25 .25
**760A** CD331a 1ce like 80p .25 .25
**760B** CD331a 3ce like 4ce .40 .40
**761** CD331a 4ce Royal yacht Britannia .50 .50
*Nos. 759-761 (6)* 1.90 1.90

**Souvenir Sheet**

**762** CD331 7ce St. Paul's Cathedral .80 .80

Nos. 759-761 each printed se-tenant with label showing heraldic design.

Issued: 20p, 80p, 4ce, 7ce, 7/8; 65p, 1ce, 3ce, 9/16.

For surcharges see Nos. 859, 866, 871, 880, 1168-1169, 1195-1197.

**1981, Sept. 16 Litho. *Perf. 14***

**763** CD331 2ce like 4ce .70 .70
**764** CD331 5ce like 20p 1.60 1.60
*a.* Bklt. pane, 2 each #763-764 4.75 4.75

Nos. 763-764 issued only in booklets.

World Food Day
A164

**1981, Oct. 16 Litho. *Perf. 14***

**765** A164 20p Women pounding fufu .25 .25
**766** A164 65p Plucking cocoa .25 .25
**767** A164 80p Preparing banku .40 .40
**768** A164 2ce Processing garri .75 .75
*Nos. 765-768 (4)* 1.65 1.65

**Souvenir Sheet**

**769** Sheet of 4 1.50 1.50
*a.* A164 25p like #765 .25 .25
*b.* A164 50p like #766 .25 .25
*c.* A164 1ce like #767 .30 .30
*d.* A164 3ce like #768 .85 .85

Angelic Musicians Play for Mary and Child, by Aachener Altares (1480-1520)
A165

Christmas (Paintings): 15p, The Betrothal of St. Catherine of Alexandria, by Lucas Cranach (1472-1553). 65p, Child Jesus Embracing His Mother, by Gabriel Metsu (1629-1667). 80p, Virgin and Child, by Fra Filippo Lippi (1406-1469). $2, The Virgin with Infant Jesus, by Barnaba da Modena (1361-1383). $4, The Immaculate Conception, by Bartolome Murillo (1618-1682). $6, Virgin and Child, by Hans Memling (1430-1494).

**1981, Nov. 26 *Perf. 14***

**770** A165 15p multicolored .25 .25
**771** A165 20p multicolored .25 .25
**772** A165 65p multicolored .25 .25
**773** A165 80p multicolored .25 .25
**774** A165 $2 multicolored .55 .55
**775** A165 $4 multicolored .75 .75
*Nos. 770-775 (6)* 2.30 2.30

**Souvenir Sheet**

**776** A165 $6 multicolored 1.40 1.40

Intl. Year of the Disabled
A166

**1982, Feb. 8 Litho. *Perf. 14***

**777** A166 20p Blind man .25 .25
**778** A166 65p Woman, crutch .30 .30
**779** A166 80p Girl reading Braille .40 .40
**780** A166 4ce Couple 1.50 1.50
*Nos. 777-780 (4)* 2.45 2.45

**Souvenir Sheet**

**781** A166 6ce Group 2.25 2.25

Clawless Otter — A167

**1982, Feb. 22**

**782** A167 20p shown .25 .25
**783** A167 65p Bushbuck .50 .50
**784** A167 80p Aardvark .60 .60
**785** A167 1ce Scarlet bell tree .80 .80
**786** A167 2ce Glory lilies 1.50 1.50
**787** A167 4ce Blue peas 3.25 3.25
*Nos. 782-787 (6)* 6.90 6.90

**Souvenir Sheet**

**788** A167 5ce Chimpanzees 3.25 3.25

Blue-spot Commodore
A168

**1982, Apr. 27 Litho. *Perf. 14***

**789** A168 20p shown .85 .85
**790** A168 65p Emperor swallowtail 1.40 1.40
**791** A168 2ce Orange admiral 2.50 2.50
**792** A168 4ce Giant charaxes 4.25 4.25
*Nos. 789-792 (4)* 9.00 9.00

**Souvenir Sheet**

***Perf. 14½***

**793** Sheet of 4 9.50 9.50
*a.* A168 25p like #789 .70 .70
*b.* A168 50p like #790 1.20 1.20
*c.* A168 1ce like #791 1.90 1.90
*d.* A168 3ce like #792 4.75 4.75

Scouting Year
A169

**1982, June 1 Litho. *Perf. 15***

**794** A169 20p Tree planting .25 .25
**795** A169 65p Camping .75 .75
**796** A169 80p Sailing .95 .95
**797** A169 3ce Watching elephant 2.50 2.50
*Nos. 794-797 (4)* 4.45 4.45

**Souvenir Sheet**

**798** A169 5ce Baden-Powell, vert. 4.25 4.25

For surcharges see Nos. 867, 870, 875, 877.

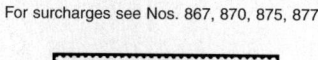

Kpong Hydroelectric Dam Opening — A170

**1982, June 28 Litho. *Perf. 14***

**799** A170 20p Cranes, lifts .50 .25
**800** A170 65p Construction 1.00 .55
**801** A170 80p Turbines 1.40 1.40
**802** A170 2ce Aerial view 3.00 3.00
*Nos. 799-802 (4)* 5.90 5.20

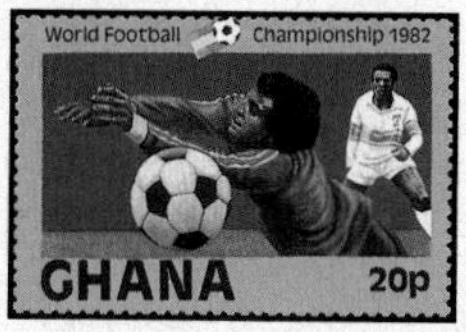


1982 World Cup
A171

***Perf. 15, 14½x15 (30p, No. 807, 1ce, 3ce)***

**1982, July 19 Litho.**

**803** A171 20p multi .25 .25
**804** A171 30p multi, like 20p .25 .25
**805** A171 65p multi .80 .80
**806** A171 80p multi, like 65p 1.00 1.00
**807** A171 80p multi, diff. .55 .55
**808** A171 1ce multi, like #807 .70 .70
**809** A171 3ce multi 1.60 1.60
**810** A171 4ce multi, like 3ce 2.50 2.50
*Nos. 803-810 (8)* 7.65 7.65

**Souvenir Sheet**

**811** A171 6ce multi 2.10 2.10

Nos. 804, 806, 808-809 in sheets of 5 plus label.

For overprints & surcharges see #826-834, 861-862, 864-865, 868-869, 872-873, 878-879, 912-917.

TB Bacillus Centenary
A172

**1982, Aug. 9 *Perf. 14***

**812** A172 20p Child immunization .50 .50
**813** A172 65p Koch, Berlin 1.40 1.40
**814** A172 80p Koch, Africa 1.75 1.75
**815** A172 1ce Looking through microscope 2.10 2.10
**816** A172 2ce Koch, 1905 Nobel medal 3.50 3.50
*Nos. 812-816 (5)* 9.25 9.25

Christmas — A173

**1982, Dec. Litho. *Perf. 15***

**817** A173 15p Nativity .25 .25
**818** A173 20p Holy Family .25 .25
**819** A173 65p Three Kings .30 .30
**820** A173 4ce Angel with banner 1.10 1.10
*Nos. 817-820 (4)* 1.90 1.90

**Souvenir Sheet**

**821** A173 6ce Nativity, diff. 2.00 2.00

A173a

**1983, Mar. 10 Litho. *Perf. 15***

**822** A173a 20p Flags .25 .25
**823** A173a 55p Aerial view .45 .45
**824** A173a 80p Minerals 1.10 1.10
**825** A173a 3ce Eagle 1.75 1.75
*Nos. 822-825 (4)* 3.55 3.55

Commonwealth Day. For surcharges see Nos. 860, 863, 874, 876.

**Nos. 803-811 Overprinted in Gold: "WINNER ITALY / 3-1"**

**1983, June Litho.**

**826** A171 20p multicolored .25 .25
**827** A171 30p multicolored .25 .25
**828** A171 65p multicolored .40 .40
**829** A171 80p multi, on #806 .40 .40
**830** A171 80p multi, on #807 1.25 1.25
**831** A171 1ce multicolored 1.40 1.40
**832** A171 3ce multicolored 2.75 2.75
**833** A171 4ce multicolored 2.50 2.50
*Nos. 826-833 (8)* 9.20 9.20

**Souvenir Sheet**

**834** A171 6ce multicolored 3.50 3.50

Italy's victory in 1982 World Cup.

For surcharges see Nos. 862, 865, 869, 873, 879, 913, 915, 917.

World Communications Year — A173b

**1983, Dec. 13 Litho. *Perf. 14***

**835** A173b 1ce shown .25 .25
**836** A173b 1.40ce Dish antenna .25 .25
**837** A173b 2.30ce Cable ship .55 .55
**838** A173b 3ce Switchboard .75 .75
**839** A173b 5ce Control tower 1.10 1.10
*Nos. 835-839 (5)* 2.90 2.90

**Souvenir Sheet**

**840** A173b 6ce Satellite .80 .80

For surcharges see Nos. 1107-1111.

Coastal Marine Mammals
A173c

**1983, Nov. 15 Litho. *Perf. 15***

**841** A173c 1ce Short fin pilot whale 2.25 2.25
**842** A173c 1.40ce Gray dolphin 2.40 2.40
**843** A173c 2.30ce False killer whale 2.75 2.75
**844** A173c 3ce Spinner dolphin 3.50 3.50
**845** A173c 5ce Atlantic humpback dolphin 4.25 4.25
*Nos. 841-845 (5)* 15.15 15.15

**Souvenir Sheet**

**846** A173c 6ce White Alantic humpback dolphin 6.50 6.50

For surcharges see Nos. 918-920.

A174

Christmas
A175

**1983, Dec. 28 *Perf. 14x13½, 14½x14***

**852** A174 70p Children receiving gifts .25 .25
**853** A175 1ce Nativity .25 .25
**854** A175 1.40ce Children playing .40 .40
**855** A175 2.30ce Family praying .50 .50
**856** A174 3ce Bongo drums, festivities .55 .55
*Nos. 852-856 (5)* 1.95 1.95

**Souvenir Sheet**

**857** A175 6ce like #855 .50 .50

For surcharge see No. 2676.

---

Surcharges

Many inverts, doubles, etc., exist on the surcharged stamps that follow.

---

**Previous Issues Surcharged**

**1984, Feb. 8**

**858** A74 1ce on 20np #296 .40 .25
**859** CD331 1ce on 20p #759 5.00 4.25

860 A173a 1ce on 20p #822 .40 .25
861 A171 1ce on 20p #803 .60 .40
862 A171 1ce on 20p #826 .40 .25
863 A173a 9ce on 55p #823 .90 .65
864 A171 9ce on 65p #805 1.60 1.00
865 A171 9ce on 65p #828 .90 .65
866 CD331 9ce on 80p #760 6.25 5.50
867 A169 10ce on 20p #794 .90 .65
868 A171 10ce on 80p #806 1.60 1.00
869 A171 10ce on 80p #830 .90 .65
870 A169 19ce on 65p #795 1.75 1.25
871 CD331 20ce on 4ce #761 8.00 *8.75*
872 A171 20ce on 4ce #810 3.50 2.40
873 A171 20ce on 4ce #833 1.75 1.25
874 A173a 30ce on 80p #824 3.50 2.40
875 A169 30ce on 3ce #797 3.50 2.40
876 A173a 50ce on 3ce #825 6.00 4.00
*Nos. 858-876 (19)* 47.85 37.95

### Souvenir Sheets

877 A169 60ce on 5ce #798 2.50 *4.75*
878 A171 60ce on 6ce #811 2.50 *3.25*
879 A171 60ce on 6ce #834 2.50 *4.75*
880 CD331 60ce on 7ce #762 2.50 *2.50*

For surcharges on this issue see #1092A-1092C.

Namibia Day A176

Scorpion Weight A177

**1984, Jan. 26** *Perf. 14*

881 A176 50p Soldiers raising rifles .25 .25
882 A176 1ce Soldiers, tank .25 .25
883 A176 1.40ce Machete cutting chains .25 .25
884 A176 2.30ce Namibian woman .25 .25
885 A176 3ce Soldiers in combat .25 .25
*Nos. 881-885 (5)* 1.25 1.25

**1983, Dec. 12** **Litho.** *Perf. 14*

886 A177 5p Hemichramis fasciatus, horiz. .35 .25
887 A177 10p Hemichramis fasciatus, map, horiz. .60 .25
888 A177 20p Haemanthus rupestris .70 .25
889 A177 50p Mounted warrior (gold statuette) .70 .30
890 A177 1ce shown .80 .25
891 A177 2ce Jet, horiz. .80 .30
892 A177 3ce Cercocebus torquatus 2.50 .30
893 A177 4ce Galagoides demidovii .70 .40
894 A177 5ce Kaempheria nigerica .80 .45
895 A177 10ce Camaroptera brevicaudata 1.00 1.00
*Nos. 886-895 (10)* 8.95 3.75

For surcharges see Nos. 1089A-1090, 1092, 1092D, 1093A-1094A, 1096-1096A.

Easter — A178

Local Flowers — A179

**1984, Apr.** **Litho.** *Perf. 14½*

906 A178 1ce Cross, crown of thorns .25 .25
907 A178 1.40ce Jesus praying .25 .25
908 A178 2.30ce Jesus going to Jerusalem .25 .25
909 A178 3ce Jesus entering Jerusalem .25 .25
910 A178 50ce Jesus with Disciples .90 *2.50*
*Nos. 906-910 (5)* 1.90 3.50

### Souvenir Sheet

911 A178 60ce Cross, crown of thorns 3.25 3.25

### Nos. 804, 806, 809, 827, 829, 832 Surcharged

**1984, Feb. 8** **Litho.**

912 A171 9ce on 3ce #809 .85 .85
913 A171 9ce on 3ce #832 .55 .55
914 A171 10ce on 30p #804 .85 .85
915 A171 10ce on 30p #827 .55 .55
916 A171 20ce on 80p #806 2.00 2.00
917 A171 20ce on 80p #829 1.00 1.00
*Nos. 912-917 (6)* 5.80 5.80

### Nos. 844-846 Surcharged and Overprinted in Red with UPU Emblem and:"19th U.P.U. CONGRESS-HAMBURG"

**1984** **Litho.** *Perf. 14½*

918 A173c 10ce on 3ce multi .50 .50
919 A173c 50ce on 5ce multi 2.50 2.50

### Souvenir Sheet

920 A173c 60ce on 6ce multi 3.00 3.00

**1984, July** **Litho.** *Perf. 14*

921 A179 1ce Amorphophallus johnsonii .25 .25
922 A179 1.40ce Pancratium trianthum .25 .25
923 A179 2.30ce Eulophia cucullata .25 .25
924 A179 3ce Amorphophallus abyssinicus .25 .25
925 A179 50ce Chlorophytum togoense 2.75 *2.75*
*Nos. 921-925 (5)* 3.75 3.75

### Souvenir Sheet

926 A179 60ce like 1ce 2.75 2.75

Endangered Species — A180

**1984, Aug.** *Perf. 14*

927 A180 1ce Bongo .60 .60
928 A180 2.30ce Males locking horns 1.25 1.25
929 A180 3ce Family 1.50 1.50
930 A180 20ce Herd 4.25 4.25
*Nos. 927-930 (4)* 7.60 7.60

### Souvenir Sheets

931 A180 70ce Kob 6.50 6.50
932 A180 70ce Bushbuck 6.50 6.50

Nos. 927-930 exist imperf. Value: set, $21.

1984 Summer Olympics — A181

Native Dancers — A182

**1984, Aug.** *Perf. 15*

933 A181 1ce Running .25 .25
934 A181 1.40ce Boxing .25 .25
935 A181 2.30ce Field hockey .25 .25
936 A181 3ce Hurdles .25 .25
937 A181 50ce Rhythmic gymnastics 3.00 *4.00*
*Nos. 933-937 (5)* 4.00 5.00

### Souvenir Sheet

938 A181 70ce Soccer 2.50 2.50

For surcharges see #945-950, 1112-1116.

**1984, Sept.** *Perf. 14*

939 A182 1ce Dipo .30 .25
940 A182 1.40ce Adowa .30 .25
941 A182 2.30ce Agbadza .30 .25
942 A182 3ce Damba .30 .25
943 A182 50ce Dipo, diff. 2.00 *3.00*
*Nos. 939-943 (5)* 3.20 4.00

### Souvenir Sheet

944 A182 70ce Mandolin player 4.00 4.00

### Nos. 933-938 Ovptd. in Gold with Winner and Country

**1984, Dec. 3** **Litho.** *Perf. 15*

945 A181 1ce Valerie Brisco-Hooks, US .25 .25
946 A181 1.40ce US winners .25 .25
947 A181 2.30ce Pakistan, (field hockey) .25 .25
948 A181 3ce Edwin Moses, US .25 .25
949 A181 50ce Lauri Fung, Canada 1.75 1.75
*Nos. 945-949 (5)* 2.75 2.75

### Souvenir Sheet

950 A181 70ce France 2.50 2.50

Christmas A183

Queen Mother, 85th Birthday A184

**1984, Nov. 19** *Perf. 12x12½*

951 A183 70p Adoration of the Magi .25 .25
952 A183 1ce Chorus of angels .25 .25
953 A183 1.40ce Adoration of the shepherds .25 .25
954 A183 2.30ce Flight into Egypt .25 .25
955 A183 3ce King holding Christ .25 .25
956 A183 50ce Adoration of the angels 1.50 1.50
*Nos. 951-956 (6)* 2.75 2.75

### Souvenir Sheet

957 A183 70ce like 70p 2.75 2.75

**1985** *Perf. 14*

Portraits.

958 A184 5ce multicolored .25 .25
959 A184 8ce like 5ce .25 .25
960 A184 12ce multicolored .25 .25
961 A184 20ce like 12ce .25 .25
962 A184 70ce multicolored .90 .90
963 A184 100ce like 70ce 1.10 1.10
*Nos. 958-963 (6)* 3.00 3.00

### Souvenir Sheet

964 A184 110ce multicolored 3.00 3.00

Issue dates: 5ce, 12ce, 100ce, 110ce, July 29. 8ce, 20ce, 70ce, Dec.

Nos. 959, 961-962 issued in sheets of 5 + label.

For surcharges see Nos. 1117-1119A, 1198-1200, 1311-1317.

Id-El-Fitr Islamic Festival — A185

**1985, Aug. 1**

965 A185 5ce Entering mosque .25 .25
966 A185 8ce Prayer rug .35 .35
967 A185 12ce Mosque .55 .55
968 A185 18ce Public Koran reading .95 .95
969 A185 50ce Map, Banda Nkwanta Mosque 2.40 2.40
*Nos. 965-969 (5)* 4.50 4.50

Intl. Youth Year — A186

**1985, Aug. 9**

970 A186 5ce Street clean-up .25 .25
971 A186 8ce Tree planting .25 .25
972 A186 12ce Food production .30 .30
973 A186 100ce Education 1.25 *2.50*
*Nos. 970-973 (4)* 2.05 3.30

### Souvenir Sheet

974 A186 110ce like 8ce 2.00 2.00

Motorcycle Centenary — A187

**1985, Sept. 9**

975 A187 5ce 1984 Honda Interceptor .50 .30
976 A187 8ce 1938 DKW .70 .40
977 A187 12ce 1923 BMW R 32 1.10 .85
978 A187 100ce 1900 NSU 6.00 6.00
*Nos. 975-978 (4)* 8.30 7.55

### Souvenir Sheet

979 A187 110ce 1973 Zundapp 5.25 5.25

Audubon Birth Bicent. — A188

**1985, Oct. 16**

980 A188 5ce York-tailed flycatcher 1.40 1.40
981 A188 8ce Barred owl 2.25 2.25
982 A188 12ce Black-throated mango 2.25 2.25
983 A188 100ce White-crowned pigeon 5.50 5.50
*Nos. 980-983 (4)* 11.40 11.40

### Souvenir Sheet

984 A188 110ce Downy woodpecker 7.50 7.50

For surcharges see Nos. 1124-1127.

UN, 40th Anniv. A189

**1985, Oct. 24** *Perf. 14½x14*

985 A189 5ce UN building .25 .25
986 A189 8ce UN building, diff. .25 .25
987 A189 12ce Dove .25 *.30*
988 A189 18ce General Assembly .25 *.40*
989 A189 100ce Flags 1.75 *2.25*
*Nos. 985-989 (5)* 2.75 3.45

### Souvenir Sheet

990 A189 110ce UN No. 36 1.75 1.75

UNCTAD, 20th Anniv. A190

**1985, Nov. 4** *Perf. 14*

**991** A190 5ce Coffee .25 .25
**992** A190 8ce Cocoa .25 .25
**993** A190 12ce Lumber .30 .30
**994** A190 18ce Bauxite mining 1.10 1.10
**995** A190 100ce Gold mining 6.50 6.50
*Nos. 991-995 (5)* 8.40 8.40

**Souvenir Sheet**

***Perf. 15x14***

**996** A190 110ce Produce 2.60 2.60

UN Child Survival Campaign A191

**1985, Dec. 16** *Perf. 14*

**997** A191 5ce Weighing .25 .25
**998** A191 8ce Oral rehydration therapy .25 .25
**999** A191 12ce Breast-feeding .50 .50
**1000** A191 100ce Immunization 4.00 4.00
*Nos. 997-1000 (4)* 5.00 5.00

**Souvenir Sheet**

***Perf. 15x14***

**1001** A191 110ce Emblem, pinwheel 2.10 2.10

AMERIPEX '86 — A192

***Perf. 14½x14, 14x14½***

**1986, Oct. 27** **Litho.**

**1002** A192 5ce Young collectors .30 .30
**1003** A192 25ce Earth, jet .85 .85
**1004** A192 100ce Stewardess, vert. 2.60 2.60
*Nos. 1002-1004 (3)* 3.75 3.75

**Souvenir Sheet**

**1005** A192 150ce Young collectors, diff. 3.50 3.50

INTER-TOURISM '86, Nov. 8-17 — A193

Designs: 5ce, Kejetia Roundabout, Kumasi. 15ce, Fort St. Jago, Elmina. 25ce, Warriors. 100ce, Chief, retinue. 150ce, Elephants.

**1986, Nov. 10** *Perf. 14*

**1006** A193 5ce multi .25 .25
**1007** A193 15ce multi .50 .50
**1008** A193 25ce multi .75 .75
**1009** A193 100ce multi 2.75 2.75
*Nos. 1006-1009 (4)* 4.25 4.25

**Souvenir Sheet**

***Perf. 15x14***

**1010** A193 150ce multi 5.00 5.00

1986 World Cup Soccer Championships, Mexico — A194

Fertility Dolls — A195

Various soccer plays.

**1987, Jan. 16** **Litho.** *Perf. 14x14½*

**1011** A194 5ce multi .30 .30
**1012** A194 15ce multi .35 .35
**1013** A194 25ce multi .55 .55
**1014** A194 100ce multi 2.00 2.00
*Nos. 1011-1014 (4)* 3.20 3.20

**Souvenir Sheet**

**1015** A194 150ce multi 2.40 2.40

For surcharges see Nos. 1120-1123D.

**1987, Jan. 22**

Various dolls.

**1016** A195 5ce multi .30 .30
**1017** A195 15ce multi .30 .30
**1018** A195 25ce multi .50 .50
**1019** A195 100ce multi 2.00 2.00
*Nos. 1016-1019 (4)* 3.10 3.10

**Souvenir Sheet**

**1020** A195 150ce like #1016 2.10 2.10

Intl. Peace Year A196

***Perf. 14½x14, 14x14½***

**1987, Mar. 2** **Litho.**

**1021** A196 5ce Children playing .30 .30
**1022** A196 25ce Plow .85 .85
**1023** A196 100ce Earth, doves, vert. 3.00 3.00
*Nos. 1021-1023 (3)* 4.15 4.15

**Souvenir Sheet**

**1024** A196 150ce Dove, plow, vert. 2.50 2.50

GIFEX '87 A197

**1987, Mar. 10** *Perf. 14*

**1025** A197 5ce Lumber, house construction .25 .25
**1026** A197 15ce Furniture .25 .25
**1027** A197 25ce Tree stumps .40 .40
**1028** A197 200ce Logs, art objects 2.25 2.25
*Nos. 1025-1028 (4)* 3.15 3.15

Ghana Intl. Forestry Exposition, Accra.

A198

Halley's Comet — A199

Designs: 5ce, Mikhail Vasilyevich Lomonosov (1711-1765), Russian scientist, and the Chamber of Curiosities. 25ce, Landing of the US probe Surveyor on the Moon's surface, 1966. 200ce, Wedgwood memorial to Sir Isaac Newton, the appearance of Halley's Comet in 1790 and US astronauts Armstrong and Aldrin landing Eagle on the Moon in 1969. 250ce, Comet over Fishermen near Christianborg Castle,

**1987, Apr. 8** *Perf. 14½x14*

**1029** A198 5ce multi .30 .25
**1030** A198 25ce multi .90 .90
**1031** A198 200ce multi 4.25 4.25
*Nos. 1029-1031 (3)* 5.45 5.40

**Souvenir Sheet**

**1032** A199 250ce multi 5.25 5.25

For surcharges see Nos. 1128-1131,

Solidarity with South Africans for Abolition of Apartheid — A200

**1987, May 18** *Perf. 14x14½*

**1033** A200 5ce Liberated prisoner .25 .25
**1034** A200 15ce Miner, gold ingots .30 .30
**1035** A200 25ce Zulu warrior .30 .30
**1036** A200 100ce Nelson Mandela, shackles 1.60 1.60
*Nos. 1033-1036 (4)* 2.45 2.45

**Souvenir Sheet**

**1037** A200 150ce Mandela, map, star 2.50 2.50

Traditional Musical Instruments — A201

**1987, July 13** *Perf. 14½x14*

**1038** A201 5ce Horns .25 .25
**1039** A201 15ce Xylophone .30 .30
**1040** A201 25ce String instruments .45 .45
**1041** A201 100ce Drums 1.30 1.30
*Nos. 1038-1041 (4)* 2.30 2.30

**Souvenir Sheet**

**1042** A201 200ce Percussion instruments 2.75 2.75

Intl. Year of Shelter for the Homeless A202

**1987, Sept. 21** **Litho.** *Perf. 14*

**1043** A202 5ce Public well .25 .25
**1044** A202 15ce Home construction .25 .25
**1045** A202 25ce Village, bridge, car .40 .40
**1046** A202 100ce Village, electric power lines 1.40 1.40
*Nos. 1043-1046 (4)* 2.30 2.30

Festivals — A203

Designs: Preparation of Kpokpoi, Homowo Festival. 15ce, Hunters with catch, Aboakyir Festival. 25ce, Chief dancing, Odwira Festival. 100ce, Chief held aloft in a palanquin, Yam Festival.

**1988, Jan. 6** **Litho.** *Perf. 15*

**1047** A203 5ce multi .25 .25
**1048** A203 15ce multi .25 .25
**1049** A203 25ce multi .35 .35
**1050** A203 100ce multi 1.25 1.25
*Nos. 1047-1050 (4)* 2.10 2.10

December 31, 1981 Revolution — A203a

**1988, Jan. 26** **Litho.** *Perf. 13*

**1050A** A203a 5ce Ports 1.50 .50
**1050B** A203a 15ce Railways 13.50 3.00
**1050C** A203a 25ce Cocoa industry 2.75 .75
**1050D** A203a 100ce Mining industry 16.00 16.00
*Nos. 1050A-1050D (4)* 33.75 20.25

UN Universal Immunization Campaign — A204

Child Survival Campaign emblem and: 5ce, Nurse immunizing woman. 15ce, Child receiving intramuscular vaccine. 25ce, Youth crippled by polio. 100ce, Nurse handing infant to mother.

**1988, Feb. 1** *Perf. 15*

**1051** A204 5ce multi .25 .25
**1052** A204 15ce multi .25 .25
**1053** A204 25ce multi .40 .40
**1054** A204 100ce multi 1.00 1.00
*Nos. 1051-1054 (4)* 1.90 1.90

Intl. Fund for Agricultural Development — A204a

**1988, Apr. 14** *Perf. 13*

**1054A** A204a 5ce Fishing 2.75 2.75
**1054B** A204a 15ce Harvesting 4.50 4.50
**1054C** A204a 25ce Cattle 7.75 7.75
**1054D** A204a 100ce Granary 17.00 17.00
*Nos. 1054A-1054D (4)* 32.00 32.00

Tribal Costumes — A205

**1988, May 9** **Litho.** *Perf. 14*

**1055** A205 5ce Akwadjan .25 .25
**1056** A205 25ce Banaa .55 .55
**1057** A205 250ce Agwasen 2.40 2.40
*Nos. 1055-1057 (3)* 3.20 3.20

For surcharges, see Nos. 2677, 2682.

1988 Summer Olympics, Seoul A206

**1988, Oct. 10**

**1058** A206 20ce Boxing .25 .25
**1059** A206 60ce Running .60 .60
**1060** A206 80ce Discus .80 .80

**1061** A206 100ce Javelin 1.00 1.00
**1062** A206 350ce Weight lifting 3.50 3.50
*Nos. 1058-1062 (5)* 6.15 6.15

### Souvenir Sheet

**1063** A206 500ce like 80ce 5.50 5.50

For overprints see Nos. 1084-1089.

Intl. Red Cross, 125th Anniv. — A207

**1988, Dec. 14 Litho. *Perf. 14***

**1064** A207 20ce Nutrition .60 .60
**1065** A207 50ce Voluntary service 1.25 1.25
**1066** A207 60ce Disaster relief (flood) 1.40 1.40
**1067** A207 200ce Medical assistance 3.50 3.50
*Nos. 1064-1067 (4)* 6.75 6.75

Christmas Symbolism — A208

**1988, Dec. 19 Litho. *Perf. 14***

**1068** A208 20ce shown .25 .25
**1069** A208 60ce Mother and child, vert. .50 .50
**1070** A208 80ce Mother, child, tree, vert. .55 .55
**1071** A208 100ce Magi follow star .75 .75
**1072** A208 350ce Abstract, diff., vert. 3.00 3.00
*Nos. 1068-1072 (5)* 5.05 5.05

### Souvenir Sheet

**1073** A208 500ce Mother and child, diff., vert. 3.75 3.75

For surcharges see Nos. 2678, 2680-2681.

Organization of African Unity, 25th Anniv. — A209

Titian, 500th Birth Anniv. (in 1988) — A210

**1989, Jan. 3**

**1074** A209 20ce Solidarity .25 .25
**1075** A209 50ce OAU, Addis Ababa .25 .25
**1076** A209 60ce Haile Selassie, Ethiopia .40 .40
**1077** A209 200ce Kwame Nkrumah, Ghana .60 .60
*Nos. 1074-1077 (4)* 1.50 1.50

"Selassie" is spelled incorrectly on No. 1076. Nos. 1076-1077 horiz.

**1989, Jan. 16**

**1078** A210 20ce Amor, 1515 .45 .25
**1079** A210 60ce The Appeal .80 .80
**1080** A210 80ce Bacchus and Ariadne, c. 1523 1.10 1.10
**1081** A210 100ce Portrait of a Musician, c. 1518 1.25 1.25
**1082** A210 350ce Philip II Seated 3.50 3.50
*Nos. 1078-1082 (5)* 7.10 6.90

### Souvenir Sheet

**1083** A210 500ce Portrait of a Gentleman, c. 1550 3.75 3.75

### Nos. 1058-1063 Ovptd. with Winners' Names

**1989, Jan. 23**

**1084** A206 20ce "A. ZUELOW / DDR / 60 KG" .40 .40
**1085** A206 60ce "G. BORDIN / ITALY / MARATHON" .50 .50
**1086** A206 80ce "J. SCHULT / DDR" .60 .60
**1087** A206 100ce "T. KORJUS / FINLAND" .70 .70
**1088** A206 350ce "B. GUIDIKOV / BULGARIA / 75 KG" 1.75 1.75
*Nos. 1084-1088 (5)* 3.95 3.95

### Souvenir Sheet

**1089** A206 500ce multi 4.00 4.00

1988 Summer Olympics, Seoul. Margin of No. 1089 ovptd. "GOLD / J. SCHULT DDR / SILVER / R. OUBARTAS USSR / BRONZE / R. DANNEBERG W. GERMANY."

### Stamps of 1967-1984 Surcharged

**1988-91**

**1089A** A177 20ce on 50p #889 .35 .30
**1090** A177 20ce on 1ce #890 .35 .30
**1091** A75 50ce on 10np #295 2.00 2.00
**1092** A177 50ce on 10p #887 1.00 2.00
*f.* 50ce' on 10p Denomination below obliterator — —
**1092A** A74 50ce on 1ce #858 6.00 5.00
**1092B** A74 50ce on 1ce #858 10.00 10.00
**1092C** A74 50ce on 1ce #858 10.00 10.00
**1092D** A177 50ce on 1ce #890 6.00 .50
**1092E** A73 60ce on 1np #286 6.00 .50
**1093** A73 60ce on 4np #291 6.00 .50
**1093A** A177 60ce on 3ce #892 1.00 .45
**1094** A177 80ce on 5p #886 1.00 .45
**1094A** A177 80ce on 5ce #894 10.00 10.00
**1095** A74 100ce on 20np #296 10.00 10.00
**1096** A177 100ce on 20p #888 1.00 1.00
**1096A** A177 100ce on 3ce #892 2.00 2.00
**1096B** A75 200ce on 6np #292 8.00 8.00

An additional 100ce surcharge exists in this set. The editors would like to examine it.

Surcharge has no decimal on No. 1092A, is vertical on No. 1092B and horizontal on No. 1092C.

No. 1090 also exists with 5mm spacing between block and $20.00.

Surcharge on No. 1093A has decimal point.

Unauthorized surchages exist.

Issued: Nos. 1089A, 1096B, 7/1/88; Nos. 1092A, 1092B, 1092D, 1092E, 1094A, 1096A, 1990; No. 1092C, 1991; others, 1989.

Minamoto-no-Yoritomo, by Fujiwara-no-Takanobu (1142-1205) — A211

Paintings: 50ce, Takami Senseki, by Watanabe Kazan (1793-1841). 60ce, Ikkyu Sojum, by Bokusai, Muromachi period. 75ce, Nakamura Kuranosuke, by Ogata Korin (1658-1716). 125ce, Portrait of a Lady, Kyoto branch of Kano school, Momoyama period. 150ce, Portrait of Zemmui, anonymous, 12th cent. 200ce, Ono no Komachi, the Poetess, by Hokusai. No. 1104, Kobo Daisi as a Child, anonymous, Kamakura period. No. 1105, Portrait of Kodai-no-Kimi, attributed to Fujiwara-no-Nobuzane, 12th cent. No. 1106, Portrait of Emperor Hanazono, by Fujiwara-no-Goshin, 14th cent.

**1989, Aug. 21 Litho. *Perf. 13½x14***

**1097** A211 20ce shown .25 .25
**1098** A211 50ce multi .40 .40
**1099** A211 60ce multi .45 .45
**1100** A211 75ce multi .65 .65
**1101** A211 125ce multi 1.00 1.00
**1102** A211 150ce multi 1.40 1.40
**1103** A211 200ce multi 1.75 1.75
**1104** A211 500ce multi 2.50 2.50
*Nos. 1097-1104 (8)* 8.40 8.40

### Souvenir Sheets

**1105** A211 500ce multi 6.25 6.25
**1106** A211 500ce multi 6.25 6.25

Hirohito (1901-1989) and enthronement of Akihito as emperor of Japan.

### Nos. 835-838 and 840 Surcharged

**1989, July 3 Litho. *Perf. 14***

**1107** A173b 60ce on 1ce 1.00 .60
**1108** A173b 80ce on 1.40ce 1.25 .75
**1109** A173b 200ce on 2.30ce 3.00 3.00
**1110** A173b 300ce on 3ce 3.75 3.75
*Nos. 1107-1110 (4)* 9.00 8.10

### Souvenir Sheet

**1111** A173b 500ce on 6ce 7.00 7.00

### Nos. 933-936 and 938 Surcharged

**1989, July 3 *Perf. 15***

**1112** A181 60ce on 1ce .40 .40
**1113** A181 80ce on 1.40ce .60 .60
**1114** A181 200ce on 2.30ce 1.50 1.50
**1115** A181 300ce on 3ce 2.00 2.00
*Nos. 1112-1115 (4)* 4.50 4.50

### Souvenir Sheet

**1116** A181 600ce on 70ce 4.00 4.00

### Nos. 958, 960 and 963-964 Surcharged

**1989, Nov. 20 Litho. *Perf. 14***

**1117** A184 80ce on 5ce #958 .60 .60
**1118** A184 250ce on 12ce #960 1.90 1.90
**1119** A184 300ce on 100ce #963 2.25 2.25
*Nos. 1117-1119 (3)* 4.75 4.75

### Souvenir Sheet

**1119A** A184 500ce on 110ce #964 5.00 5.00

### Nos. 1011-1013 and 1015 Surcharged

**1989 Litho. *Perf. 14x14½***

**1120** A194 60ce on 5ce #1011 .60 .60
**1121** A194 200ce on 15ce #1012 1.90 1.90
**1122** A194 300ce on 25ce #1013 2.50 2.50
*Nos. 1120-1122 (3)* 5.00 5.00

### Souvenir Sheet

**1123** A194 600ce on 150ce #1015 7.00 7.00

Nos. 1120-1123 Surcharged

**1989 Litho. *Perf. 14x14½***

**1123A** A194 60ce on 5ce .90 .90
**1123B** A194 200ce on 15ce 3.00 3.00
**1123C** A194 300ce on 25ce 4.75 4.75
*Nos. 1123A-1123C (3)* 8.65 8.65

### Souvenir Sheet

**1123D** A194 600ce on 150ce 10.00 10.00

### Nos. 980-982 and 984 Surcharged

**1989, Nov. 20 Litho. *Perf. 14***

**1124** A188 80ce on 5ce #980 1.90 1.90
**1125** A188 100ce on 8ce #981 3.25 3.25
**1126** A188 300ce on 12ce #982 3.75 3.75
*Nos. 1124-1126 (3)* 8.90 8.90

### Souvenir Sheet

**1127** A188 500ce on 110ce #984 10.00 10.00

### Nos. 1029-1032 Surcharged

**1989, Nov. 20 *Perf. 14½x14***

**1128** A198 60ce on 5ce #1029 1.00 1.00
*a.* With comet logo 1.00 1.00
**1129** A198 80ce on 25ce #1030 1.25 1.25
*a.* With comet logo 1.25 1.25
**1130** A198 500ce on 200ce #1031 4.25 4.25
*a.* With comet logo 4.25 4.25
*Nos. 1128-1130 (3)* 6.50 6.50
*Nos. 1128a-1130a (3)* 6.50 6.50

### Souvenir Sheet

**1131** A199 750ce on 250ce #1032 6.00 6.00
*a.* With comet logo 6.00 6.00

PHILEXFRANCE '89, French Revolution Bicent. — A212

Emblems, French arms and flags: 20ce, Tube-mounted field carriage, flag of 1643 to 1790. 60ce, Infantryman, flag of 1789. 80ce, Handgun, flag of 1789, diff. 350ce, Musket, flag of 1794 to 1814 and 1848 to present. 600ce, Map of Paris.

**1989, Sept. 22 Litho. *Perf. 14***

**1132** A212 20ce shown .75 .75
**1133** A212 60ce multi 1.40 1.40
**1134** A212 80ce multi 1.75 1.75
**1135** A212 350ce multi 4.00 4.00
*Nos. 1132-1135 (4)* 7.90 7.90

### Souvenir Sheet

**1136** A212 600ce multi 4.50 4.50

Mushrooms

A213 A214

**1989, Oct. 2 Litho. *Perf. 14***

**1137** A213 20ce Collybia .25 .25
**1138** A213 50ce Lawyer's wig .35 .35
**1139** A214 60ce *Xerocomus subtomentosus* .40 .40
**1140** A213 80ce Wood belwits .60 .60
**1141** A214 150ce *Suillus placidus* 1.20 1.20
**1142** A214 200ce *Lepista nuda* 1.50 1.50
**1143** A213 300ce Fairy rings 2.10 2.10
**1144** A213 500ce Field mushroom 3.50 3.50
*Nos. 1137-1144 (8)* 9.90 9.90

### Souvenir Sheets

**1145** A213 600ce Three *Amanita* species 4.50 4.50
**1146** A214 600ce Three *Boletus* species 4.50 4.50

Souvenir Sheet

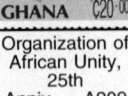

*A Midsummer Night's Dream*, by Shakespeare — A215

Designs: a, "The course of true love never did run smooth." b, "Love looks not with the eye but with the mind." c, "Nature here shows art." d, "Things growing are not ripe till their season." e, "He is defiled that draws a sword on thee." f, "It is not enough to speak but to speak true." g, "Thou art wise as thou art beautiful." h, Leopard behind trees. i, Theseus. j, Boy holding flower, trees. k, Oberon and Titania among trees. l, Bottom wearing head of a jackass. m, Bottom's leg, leopard behind trees. n, Hippolyta. o, Leopard, tree trunk. p, Tree trunk, foliage, lower portion of Theseus's robe. q, Wisps of fragrance, clouds, hills, foliage. r, Wisps of fragrance, flowering plants. s, Flowering plants. t, Lion, foliage. u, Lion's mane, foliage.

**1989, Oct. 9** ***Perf. 13½x13***

**1147** A215 Sheet of 21 18.00 18.00
*a.-u.* 40ce any single .80 .80

425th Birth anniv. of William Shakespeare, playwright.

Birds A216

**1989, Oct. 16** ***Perf. 14***

**1148** A216 20ce *Spermestes cuculatus* .40 .25
**1149** A216 50ce *Motacilla aguimp* .60 .35
**1150** A216 60ce *Halcyon malimbicus* 1.75 1.75
**1151** A216 80ce *Ispidina picta* 2.75 2.75
**1152** A216 150ce Striped kingfisher 2.25 2.25
**1153** A216 200ce Shikra 2.00 2.00
**1154** A216 300ce Gray parrot 2.75 2.75
**1155** A216 500ce Black kite 4.00 4.00
*Nos. 1148-1155 (8)* 16.50 16.10

**Souvenir Sheets**

**1156** A216 600ce Four birds 8.25 8.25
**1157** A216 600ce Three birds 8.25 8.25

Nos. 1152-1156 vert.

1st Moon Landing, 20th Anniv. A217

Highlights of the Apollo 11 mission.

**1989, Nov. 6** ***Perf. 14***

**1158** A217 20ce *Columbia* .25 .25
**1159** A217 80ce Footprint .75 .75
**1160** A217 200ce Aldrin on Moon 1.50 1.50
**1161** A217 300ce Splashdown 2.25 2.25
*Nos. 1158-1161 (4)* 4.75 4.75

**Souvenir Sheets**

**1162** A217 500ce Liftoff, vert. 4.25 4.25
**1163** A217 500ce Earth, vert. 4.25 4.25

World Environment Day — A218

**1989, Nov. 20** **Litho.** ***Perf. 14***

**1164** A218 20ce Desertification .25 .25
**1165** A218 60ce Bush fires .65 .65
**1166** A218 400ce Industrial pollution 3.75 3.75
**1167** A218 500ce Soil erosion 5.00 5.00
*Nos. 1164-1167 (4)* 9.65 9.65

Nos. 760 and 761 Surcharged

**1989, Nov. 20** **Litho.** ***Perf. 14***

**1168** CD331 100ce on 80p 1.00 1.00
**1169** CD331 500ce on 4ce 5.00 5.00

French Revolution, Bicent. — A219

Designs: 20ce, Storming of the Bastille, vert. 60ce, Declaration of Human Rights and Citizenship, vert. 80ce, Storming of the Bastille, diff. 200ce, *Departure of the Volunteers in 1792,* high relief on the Arc de Triomphe, 1833-35, by Francis Rude. 350ce, Planting the Liberty Tree.

***Perf. 14x13½, 13½x14***

**1989, Sept. 22**

**1170** A219 20ce multicolored .55 .55
**1171** A219 60ce multicolored 1.25 1.25
**1172** A219 80ce multicolored 1.50 1.50
**1173** A219 200ce multicolored 2.75 2.75
**1174** A219 350ce multicolored 3.50 3.50
*Nos. 1170-1174 (5)* 9.55 9.55

Butterflies A220

**1990, Feb. 15** **Litho.** ***Perf. 14***

**1175** A220 20ce *Bebearia arcadius* .50 .50
**1176** A220 60ce *Charaxes laodice* .65 .65
**1177** A220 80ce *Euryphura porphyrion* .85 .85
**1178** A220 100ce *Neptis nicomedes* .95 .95
**1179** A220 150ce *Citrinophila erastus* 1.10 1.10
**1180** A220 200ce *Epitola honorius* 1.60 1.60
**1181** A220 300ce *Precis westermanni* 2.10 2.10
**1182** A220 500ce *Cymothoe hypatha* 2.75 2.75
*Nos. 1175-1182 (8)* 10.50 10.50

**Souvenir Sheets**

**1183** A220 600ce *Telipna bimacula* 5.75 5.75
**1184** A220 600ce *Pentila phidia* 5.75 5.75

Seashells — A221

**1990, Feb. 20** ***Perf. 14x14½***

**1185** A221 20ce *Cymbium glans* .65 .65
**1186** A221 60ce *Cardium costatum* 1.10 1.10
**1187** A221 80ce *Conus genuanus* 1.40 1.40
**1188** A221 200ce *Ancilla tankervillei* 2.75 2.75
**1189** A221 350ce *Tectarius coronatus* 4.00 4.00
*Nos. 1185-1189 (5)* 9.90 9.90

Jawaharlal Nehru, 1st Prime Minister of Independent India — A222

Designs: 20ce, Greeting Pres. Kwame Nkrumah of Ghana. 60ce, Addressing Afro-Asian conference. 80ce, Return from tour of China, vert. 200ce, Releasing dove during a children's celebration in New Delhi, vert. 350ce, Portrait, vert.

***Perf. 14½x14, 14x14½***

**1990, Mar. 27** **Litho.**

**1190** A222 20ce shown .75 .75
**1191** A222 60ce multicolored .90 .90
**1192** A222 80ce multicolored 1.10 1.10
**1193** A222 200ce multicolored 1.60 1.60
**1194** A222 350ce multicolored 2.25 2.25
*Nos. 1190-1194 (5)* 6.60 6.60

**Nos. 759A and 760A-760B Surcharged**

**1990** ***Perf. 14***

**1195** CD331 80ce on 65p 1.00 1.00
**1196** CD331 100ce on 1ce 1.40 1.40
**1197** CD331 300ce on 3ce 4.25 4.25
*Nos. 1195-1197 (3)* 6.65 6.65

**Nos. 961, 959 and 962 Surcharged**

**1990**

**1198** A184 80ce on 20ce .75 .75
**1199** A184 200ce on 8ce 1.90 1.90
**1200** A184 250ce on 70ce 2.40 2.40
*Nos. 1198-1200 (3)* 5.05 5.05

Penny Black, 150th Anniv. A223

Great Britain No. 1 and: 20ce, City Medal containing portrait of Victoria by William Wyon adapted for use on the Penny Black. 60ce, No. 1208, Bath mail coach. 80ce, Leeds Mail coach. 200ce, Heath's engraving, based on the Wyon portrait. 350ce, Penny Black master die. 400ce, London mail coach. No. 1207, Printers and flat-bed presses of Perkins, Bacon & Petch, 1840.

**1990, May 3** ***Perf. 13½x14***

**1201** A223 20ce shown .35 .35
**1202** A223 60ce multicolored .65 .65
**1203** A223 80ce multicolored .90 .90
**1204** A223 200ce multicolored 1.75 1.75
**1205** A223 350ce multicolored 2.40 2.40
**1206** A223 400ce multicolored 2.40 2.40
*Nos. 1201-1206 (6)* 8.45 8.45

**Souvenir Sheets**

**1207** A223 600ce multicolored 4.75 4.75
**1208** A223 600ce multicolored 4.75 4.75

June 4, Revolution, 10th Anniv. (in 1989) — A224

**1990, June 5** **Litho.** ***Perf. 14½x14***

**1209** A224 20ce shown .25 .25
**1210** A224 60ce Pineapple, lobsters .50 .50
**1211** A224 80ce Corn, cacao beans .65 .65
**1212** A224 200ce Mining 1.60 1.60
**1213** A224 350ce Scales, sword 2.50 2.50
*Nos. 1209-1213 (5)* 5.50 5.50

Intelsat, 25th Anniv. A225

Satellites over: 60ce, Pacific Ocean. 80ce, Pacific, diff. 200ce, South Atlantic. 350ce, Pacific, Indian Oceans.

**1990, July 12** ***Perf. 14x14½***

**1214** A225 20ce multicolored .25 .25
**1215** A225 60ce multicolored .50 .50
**1216** A225 80ce multicolored .60 .60
**1217** A225 200ce multicolored 1.40 1.40
**1218** A225 350ce multicolored 2.00 2.00
*Nos. 1214-1218 (5)* 4.75 4.75

Introduction of Intl. Direct Dialing Service (in 1988) — A226

**1990, July 16**

**1219** A226 20ce shown .25 .25
**1220** A226 60ce Man using telephone .50 .50
**1221** A226 80ce Man using pay telephone .60 .60
**1222** A226 200ce Telephone booths 1.40 1.40
**1223** A226 350ce Satellite dish 2.00 2.00
*Nos. 1219-1223 (5)* 4.75 4.75

Miniature Sheet

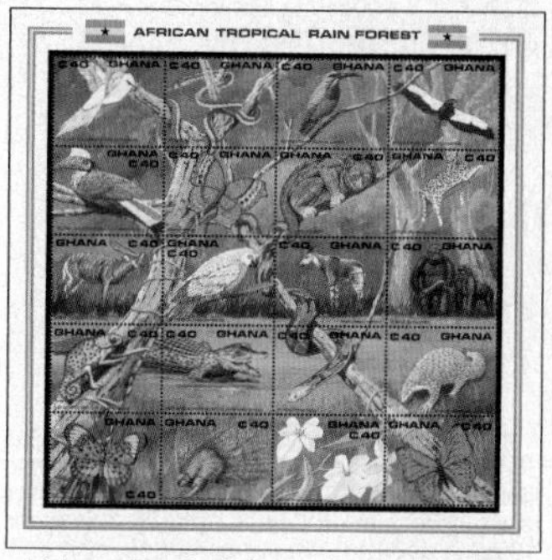


African Tropical Rain Forest — A227

Designs: No. 1224a, Blue fairy flycatcher. b, Boomslang. c, Superb sunbird. d, Bateleur eagle. e, Yellow-casqued hornbill. f, Salamis temora. g, Potto. h, Leopard. i, Bongo. j, Gray parrot. k, Okapi. l, Gorilla. m, Flap-necked chameleon. n, West African dwarf crocodile. o, Python. p, Giant pangolin. q, Pseudacraea boisduvali. r, African crested porcupine. s, Rosy-columned aerangis. t, Cymothoe sangaris.

No. 1225, Leopard, vert.

**1990, Oct. 25** **Litho.** ***Perf. 14x14½***

**1224** Sheet of 20 17.00 17.00
*a.-t.* A227 40ce any single .70 .70

**Souvenir Sheet**

**1225** A227 600ce multicolored 7.50 7.50

Miniature Sheet

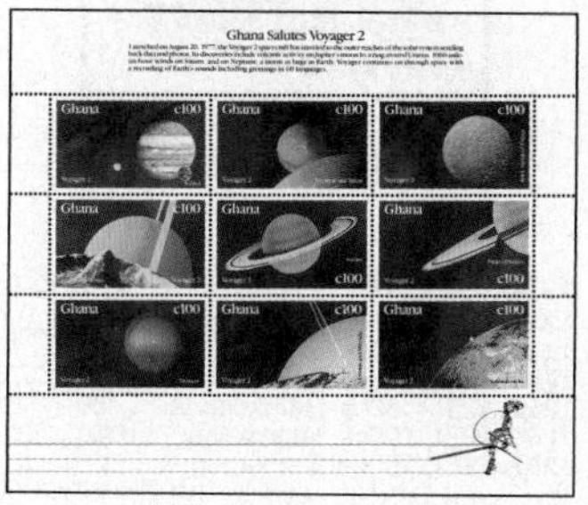

Voyager 2 — A228

Photographs from Voyager 2: No. 1226a, Jupiter. b, Neptune, Triton. c, Ariel, moon of Uranus. d, Saturn, Mimas. e, Saturn. f, Rings of Saturn. g, Neptune. h, Uranus, Miranda. i, Volcano on Io.

**1990, Dec. 13** **Litho.** ***Perf. 14***

**1226** A228 100ce Sheet of 9, #1226a-1226i 8.75 8.75

**Souvenir Sheets**

**1227** A228 600ce Voyager 2 liftoff, vert. 3.75 3.75
**1228** A228 600ce Voyager 2, vert. 3.75 3.75

Orchids — A229

Designs: 20ce, Eulophia guineensis. 40ce, Eurychone rothschildiana. 60ce, Bulbophyllum barbigerum. 80ce, Polystachya galeata. 200ce, Diaphananthe kamerunensis. 300ce, Podangis dactyloceras. 400ce, Ancistrochilus rothschildianus. 500ce, Rangaeris muscicola. No. 1237, Bolusiella imbricata. No. 1238, Diaphananthe rutila.

**1990, Dec. 17**

**1229** A229 20ce multicolored .25 .25
**1230** A229 40ce multicolored .30 .30
**1231** A229 60ce multicolored .55 .55
**1232** A229 80ce multicolored .70 .70
**1233** A229 200ce multicolored 1.75 1.75
**1234** A229 300ce multicolored 2.75 2.75
**1235** A229 400ce multicolored 3.75 3.75
**1236** A229 500ce multicolored 4.50 4.50
*Nos. 1229-1236 (8)* 14.55 14.55

### Souvenir Sheets

**1237** A229 600ce multicolored 7.25 7.25
**1238** A229 600ce multicolored 7.25 7.25

Mushrooms — A230

Designs: 20ce, Coprinus atramentarius. 50ce, Marasmius oreades. 60ce, Oudamansiella radicata. 80ce, Cep. 150ce, Hebeloma crustuliniforme. 200ce, Coprinus micaceus. 300ce, Lepiota procera. 500ce, Amanita phalloides.

**1990, Dec. 18**

**1239** A230 20ce multicolored .85 .55
**1240** A230 50ce multicolored 1.10 .85
**1241** A230 60ce multicolored 1.40 .85
**1242** A230 80ce multicolored 1.75 1.25
**1243** A230 150ce multicolored 2.25 1.75
**1244** A230 200ce multicolored 3.25 2.50
**1245** A230 300ce multicolored 3.25 3.25
*a.* Min. sheet of 4, #1240, 1243-1245 6.75 6.75
**1246** A230 500ce multicolored 4.25 4.25
*a.* Min. sheet of 4, #1239, 1241-1242, 1246 6.75 6.75
*Nos. 1239-1246 (8)* 18.10 15.25

World Cup Soccer Championships, Italy — A231

Players from participating countries.

**1990, Dec. 18 Litho. *Perf. 14***

**1247** A231 20ce Italy .50 .50
**1248** A231 50ce Egypt .65 .65
**1249** A231 60ce Cameroun .70 .70
**1250** A231 80ce Romania .85 .85
**1251** A231 100ce Yugoslavia 1.00 1.00
**1252** A231 150ce Cameroun, vert. 1.60 1.60
**1253** A231 400ce South Korea 2.60 2.60
**1254** A231 600ce West Germany 3.00 3.00
*Nos. 1247-1254 (8)* 10.90 10.90

### Souvenir Sheets

**1255** A231 800ce UAE 5.00 5.00
**1256** A231 800ce Colombia 5.00 5.00

Peter Paul Rubens (1577-1640), Painter A232

Portraits by Rubens: 20ce, Duke of Mantua. 50ce, Jan Brant. 60ce, Young man. 80ce, Michel Ophovius. 100ce, Caspar Gevaerts. 200ce, Head of a warrior (detail). 300ce, Bearded man. 400ce, Paracelsus. No. 1265, Archduke Ferdinand. No. 1266, Warrior with Two Pages.

**1990, Dec. 24 Litho. *Perf. 14***

**1257** A232 20ce multicolored .25 .25
**1258** A232 50ce multicolored .40 .40
**1259** A232 60ce multicolored .50 .50
**1260** A232 80ce multicolored .60 .60
**1261** A232 100ce multicolored .75 .75
**1262** A232 200ce multicolored 1.75 1.25
**1263** A232 300ce multicolored 2.25 2.25
**1264** A232 400ce multicolored 3.25 3.25
*Nos. 1257-1264 (8)* 9.75 9.25

### Souvenir Sheets

**1265** A232 600ce multicolored 4.75 4.75
**1266** A232 600ce multicolored 4.75 4.75

Minerals — A233

**1991, May 2 Litho. *Perf. 14½x14***

**1267** A233 20ce Manganese ore .55 .55
**1268** A233 60ce Iron ore .70 .70
**1269** A233 80ce Bauxite ore 1.25 1.25
**1270** A233 200ce Gold ore 3.00 3.00
**1271** A233 350ce Diamond 4.00 4.00
*Nos. 1267-1271 (5)* 9.50 9.50

### Souvenir Sheet

**1272** A233 600ce Diamonds 9.00 9.00

Tribal Drums — A234

**1991, May 9**

**1273** A234 20ce Damba .45 .25
**1274** A234 60ce Atumpan .85 .55
**1275** A234 80ce Kroboto 1.10 .70
**1276** A234 200ce Asafo 1.60 1.60
**1277** A234 350ce Obonu 2.50 2.50
*Nos. 1273-1277 (5)* 6.50 5.60

### Souvenir Sheet

**1278** A234 600ce Single drum 6.50 6.50

Flowers — A235 A236

**1991, May 15**

**1279** A235 20ce Amorphophallus dracontioides .75 .35
**1280** A235 60ce Anchomanes difformis 1.10 .55
**1281** A235 80ce Kaemferia nigerica 1.40 .70
**1282** A235 200ce Aframomum sceptrum 2.25 2.25
**1283** A235 350ce Amorphophallus flavovirens 2.50 2.50
*Nos. 1279-1283 (5)* 8.00 6.35

### Souvenir Sheet

**1284** A235 600ce White flowers 6.00 6.00

**1991, May 17 Litho. *Perf. 14½x14***

**1285** A235 20ce Urginea indica .55 .35
**1286** A235 60ce Hymenocallis littoralis 1.00 .55
**1287** A235 80ce Crinum jagus 1.40 .80
**1288** A235 200ce Dipcadi tacazzeanum 1.75 1.75
**1289** A235 350ce Haemanthus rupestris 2.25 2.25
*Nos. 1285-1289 (5)* 6.95 5.70

### Souvenir Sheet

**1290** A235 600ce Red flowers 6.00 6.00

**1991, June 21 Litho. *Perf. 13½x14***

Designs: 20ce, Satellite transmissions, airplane. 60ce, Scientific research, honey bee. 80ce, Literacy instruction. 200ce, Agricultural development. 350ce, Industry.

**1291** A236 20ce multicolored .25 .25
**1292** A236 60ce multicolored .85 .55
**1293** A236 80ce multicolored .90 .70
**1294** A236 200ce multicolored 1.50 1.50
**1295** A236 350ce multicolored 2.50 2.50
*Nos. 1291-1295 (5)* 6.00 5.50

UN Development Program, 40th anniv.

Lord Robert Baden-Powell (1857-1941), Founder of Boy Scouts — A237

Designs: 20ce, Sketch by Baden-Powell used in first scouting handbook, vert. 50ce, Portrait, vert. 80ce, Scout handbook illustration by Norman Rockwell. 100ce, Native runner, Cape of Good Hope #178. 200ce, Scouts aiding victims after V-1 attack, London, 1944. 500ce, Scout praying, vert. 600ce, Emblem, Cape of Good Hope No. 178 used. No. 1304, Cover with Cape of Good Hope No. 178 from Mafeking, 1900. No. 1305, Campsites, 17th World Scout Jamboree, Korea, 1991.

**1991, July 16 Litho. *Perf. 14***

**1296** A237 20ce buff & black .60 .25
**1297** A237 50ce multicolored .75 .40
**1298** A237 60ce multicolored .75 .50
**1299** A237 80ce black & buff 1.25 .65
**1300** A237 100ce multicolored 1.50 1.00
**1301** A237 200ce multicolored 1.90 1.90
**1302** A237 500ce multicolored 4.00 4.00
**1303** A237 600ce multicolored 4.50 4.50
*Nos. 1296-1303 (8)* 15.25 13.20

### Souvenir Sheets

**1304** A237 800ce multicolored 4.75 4.75
**1305** A237 800ce multicolored 4.75 4.75

For overprints see Nos. 1567-1572.

Chorkor Smoker A238

Designs: 20ce, Placing fish on racks. 60ce, Preparing smokers. 80ce, Preparing fish. 200ce, Preparing racks for smoker. 350ce, Placing racks in smoker.

**1991, July 22 Litho. *Perf. 14x14½***

**1306** A238 20ce multicolored .40 .25
**1307** A238 60ce multicolored .70 .45
**1308** A238 80ce multicolored .80 .65
**1309** A238 200ce multicolored 1.75 1.75
**1310** A238 350ce multicolored 2.25 2.25
*Nos. 1306-1310 (5)* 5.90 5.35

### Nos. 958-964 Overprinted "90th Birthday / 4th August 1990" and Surcharged

***Perf. 14, 12½x12 (#1312-1313, 1315)***

**1991, July 22**

**1311** A184 20ce on 5ce #958 .50 .50
**1312** A184 20ce on 8ce #959 .50 .50
**1313** A184 40ce on 20ce #961 .80 .80
**1314** A184 60ce on 12ce #960 1.50 1.50
**1315** A184 80ce on 70ce #962 1.75 1.75
**1316** A184 150ce on 100ce #963 3.50 3.50
*Nos. 1311-1316 (6)* 8.55 8.55

### Souvenir Sheet

**1317** A184 200ce on 110ce #964 5.00 5.00

Nos. 1312-1313, 1315 issued in sheets of 5 + label. Overprint is vertical on stamp in No. 1317, horizontal on sheet margin.

The status of this issue is uncertain.

Fish A239

**1991, July 29 Litho. *Perf. 14***

**1318** A239 20ce Cephalopholis taeniops .25 .25
**1319** A239 50ce Synodontis sorex .35 .35
**1320** A239 80ce Balistes forcipatus .35 .35
**1321** A239 100ce Petrocephalus bane .45 .45
**1322** A239 200ce Syngnathus rastellatus .85 .85
**1323** A239 300ce Gymnarchus niloticus 2.25 2.25
**1324** A239 400ce Hemichromis bimaculatus 3.00 3.00
**1325** A239 500ce Sphyrna zygaena 2.50 2.50
*Nos. 1318-1325 (8)* 10.00 10.00

### Souvenir Sheets

**1326** A239 800ce Bagrus bayad 5.25 5.25
**1327** A239 800ce Dactyloptena orientalis 3.75 3.75

While Nos. 1320-1322, 1325, 1327 have the same issue date as Nos. 1318-1319, 1323-1324, 1326, the value of Nos. 1320-1322, 1325, 1327 was lower when they were released.

For overprints see Nos. 1573-1578.

Paintings by Vincent Van Gogh A240

Designs: 20ce, Reaper with Sickle. 50ce, The Thresher. 60ce, The Sheaf Binder. 80ce, The Sheep Shearers. 100ce, Peasant Woman Cutting Straw. 200ce, The Sower. 500ce, The Plow and the Harrow, horiz. 600ce, The Woodcutter. No. 1336, Evening: The Watch. No. 1337, Evening: The End of the Day.

***Perf. 13x13½, 13½x13***

**1991, Aug. 12 Litho.**

**1328** A240 20ce multicolored .25 .25
**1329** A240 50ce multicolored .40 .40
**1330** A240 60ce multicolored .50 .50
**1331** A240 80ce multicolored .65 .65
**1332** A240 100ce multicolored .80 .80
**1333** A240 200ce multicolored 1.60 1.60
**1334** A240 500ce multicolored 3.50 3.50
**1335** A240 600ce multicolored 4.25 4.25
*Nos. 1328-1335 (8)* 11.95 11.95

**Size: 106x80mm**

***Imperf***

**1336** A240 800ce multicolored 6.00 6.00
**1337** A240 800ce multicolored 6.00 6.00

10th Non-aligned Ministers Conference, Accra — A241

Natl. Leaders: 20ce, Nasser, Egypt (1952-1970). 60ce, Tito, Yugoslavia (1945-1980). 80ce, Nehru, India (1947-1964). 200ce, Nkrumah, Ghana (1957-1966). 350ce, Sukarno, Indonesia (1945-1967).

**1991, Sept. 2 *Perf. 13½x14***

**1338** A241 20ce multicolored .45 .35
**1339** A241 60ce multicolored .55 .50
**1340** A241 80ce multicolored 3.50 1.50
**1341** A241 200ce multicolored 2.00 2.00
**1342** A241 350ce multicolored 2.50 2.50
*Nos. 1338-1342 (5)* 9.00 6.85

Birds of Ghana — A242

Designs: No. 1343a, Melba finch. b, Orange-cheeked waxbill. c, Paradise flycatcher. d, Blue plantain-eater, e, Red bishop.

f, Splendid glossy starling. g, Red-headed lovebird. h, Palm swift. i, Narina trogon. j, Tawny eagle. k, Bateleur eagle. l, Hoopoe. m, Secretary bird. n, White-backed vulture. o, Bare-headed rockfowl. p, Ground hornbill.

No. 1344a, Openbilled stork. b, African spoonbill. c, Pink-backed pelican. d, Little bittern. e, King reed-hen. f, Saddlebill stork. g, Glossy ibis. h, White-faced tree duck. i, Black-headed heron. j, Hammerkop. k, African darter. l, Woolly-necked stork. m, Yellow-billed stork. n, Black-winged stilt. o, Goliath heron. p, Lily trotter.

No. 1345a, Shikra. b, Abyssinian roller (c, g). c, Carmine bee-eater (g). d, Pintailed whydah (h). e, Purple glossy starling. f, Yellow-backed whydah (j). g, Pel's fishing owl. h, Verreaux's touraco (l). i, Red-cheeked cordon-bleu. j, Olive-bellied sunbird. k, Red-billed hornbill. l, Red-billed quelea. m, Crowned crane (i). n, Blue quail. o, Egyptian vulture (p). p, Helmeted guineafowl.

No. 1346, Marabou stork. No. 1347, Saddlebill stork, diff. No. 1348, African river eagle.

**1991, Oct. 14 Litho. *Perf. 14½x14***

**Sheets of 16**

**1343** A242 80ce #a.-p. 7.50 7.50
**1344** A242 100ce #a.-p. 11.50 11.50
**1345** A242 100ce #a.-p. 13.50 13.50
*Nos. 1343-1345 (3)* 32.50 32.50

**Souvenir Sheets**

**1346** A242 800ce multicolored 5.50 5.50
**1347** A242 800ce multicolored 5.50 5.50
**1348** A242 800ce multicolored 5.50 5.50

While No. 1344 has the same issue date as No. 1345, the value of No. 1344 was lower when it was released.

Insects
A243

**1991, Oct. 25 *Perf. 14x13½***

**1349** A243 20ce Nularda .75 .25
**1350** A243 50ce Zonocrus .90 .40
**1351** A243 60ce Gryllotalpa africana 1.25 .50
**1352** A243 80ce Weevil 1.75 1.25
**1353** A243 100ce Coenagrion 2.25 2.00
**1354** A243 150ce Sahlbergella 2.50 2.25
**1355** A243 200ce Anthia 3.00 3.00
**1356** A243 350ce Megacephala 4.00 3.00
*Nos. 1349-1356 (8)* 16.40 12.65

**Souvenir Sheet**

***Perf. 13x12***

**1357** A243 600ce Lacetus 13.50 13.50

Landmarks — A243a

Leucodon Cowrie — A243b

Achatina Achatina — A243c

Designs: 50ce, Boti Falls, vert. 60ce, Larabanga Mosque. 80ce, Fort Sebastian, Shama. 100ce, Cape Coast Castle.

100ce exists in four types:
Type I, "G" has angled curve, bars in "A"s slope down to left, "c" has straight line, bottom inscription 10mm.
Type II, "G" is rounded, bars in "A"s slope down to right, "c" has slanted line, bottom inscription 13mm.
Type III, "G" is rounded, bars in "A"s slope down to right, "c" has straight line, bottom inscription 10mm.
Type IV, "G" rounded, but cut off at top, bars in "A"s slope to right, "C" with slanted line, bottom inscription 10mm.

200ce, 400ce
Nos. 1357E, 1357Ej, 1357F, Type I: "G" has angled curve, bar in "A's" slope down to left.
Nos. 1357Ek, 1357Fl, Type II: "G" is rounded, bars in "A's" slope down to right.

***Perf. 13¾x13½, 13½x13¾***

**1991 Litho.**

**1357A** A243a 50ce multi — —
*o.* Perf. 13¾x14¼
**1357B** A243a 60ce multi — —
*p.* Perf. 14¼x13¾ — —
**1357C** A243a 80ce multi — —
**1357D** A243a 100ce multi (I) — —
*g.* Type II
*h.* Type I, perf 14¼x13¾
*i.* Type III, perf 14¼x13¾
*m.* Type IV — —
**1357E** A243b 200ce multi (I) — —
*j.* Type I, perf. 14¼x13¾ — —
*k.* Type II, perf. 14¼x13¾ — —
**1357F** A243c 400ce multi (I) — —
*l.* Type II, perf. 14¼x13¾ — —
*n.* Type I, perf. 11½ —

This set was printed locally. Shades exist.
Issue dates: 50ce, Nov. 21; others, Dec. 12. No. 1357Dm, 2004(?).

Adoration of the Magi by Hieronymus Bosch
A244

Details or entire paintings: 50ce, The Annunciation by Robert Campin. 60ce, Virgin and Child by Dirk Bouts. 80ce, Presentation in the Temple by Hans Memling. 100ce, The Virgin and Child Enthroned with an Angel and a Donor by Memling. 200ce, The Virgin and Child with Saints and a Donor by Jan van Eyck. 400ce, St. Luke Painting the Virgin by Rogier van der Weyden. 700ce, Virgin and Child by Bouts, diff. No. 1366, The Annunciation by Memling. No. 1367, The Virgin and Child Standing in a Niche by van der Weyden.

**1991, Dec. 23 *Perf. 12***

**1358** A244 20ce multicolored .25 .25
**1359** A244 50ce multicolored .40 .40
**1360** A244 60ce multicolored .50 .50
**1361** A244 80ce multicolored .60 .60
**1362** A244 100ce multicolored .80 .80
**1363** A244 200ce multicolored 1.50 1.50
**1364** A244 400ce multicolored 3.00 3.00
**1365** A244 700ce multicolored 5.25 5.25
*Nos. 1358-1365 (8)* 12.30 12.30

**Souvenir Sheets**

***Perf. 14½***

**1366** A244 800ce multicolored 5.50 5.50
**1367** A244 800ce multicolored 5.50 5.50

Christmas.

Reunification of Germany — A245

Designs: 20ce, Opening of German border, Nov. 9, 1989. 60ce, Signing of Two Plus Four Treaty, Sept. 12, 1990. 80ce, Opening of Brandenburg Gate, Dec. 22, 1989. 800ce, German leaders, Unity Day, Oct. 3, 1990. 1000ce, Currency union, July 1, 1990.

No. 1371Ab, USSR Pres. Mikhail Gorbachev, vert. c, Chancellor Helmut Kohl, vert. d, Map of West Germany, vert. e, Map of East Germany, vert.

No. 1371g, Doves. h, German Chancellor Helmut Kohl, Foreign Minister Hans-Dietrich Genscher.

**1992, Feb. 17 Litho. *Perf. 14***

**1368** A245 20ce multi .30 .25
**1369** A245 60ce multi .50 .50
**1370** A245 80ce multi .70 .70
**1371** A245 1000ce multi 8.00 8.00
*Nos. 1368-1371 (4)* 9.50 9.45

**Souvenir Sheets**

**1371A** A245 300ce Sheet of 4, #b.-e. 6.75 6.75
**1371F** A245 400ce Sheet of 2, #g.-h. 2.00 2.00
**1372** A245 800ce multicolored 4.75 4.75

While No. 1371F has the same issue date as No. 1371A, the dollar value of No. 1371F was lower when it was released.

1992 Summer Olympics, Barcelona
A246

Map and: 20ce, Eddie Blay, boxing, Ghana, 1964. 60ce, Mike Ahey, track, Ghana, 1964-1972. 80ce, T. Wilson, ski jumping, US, 1988. 100ce, East German 4-Man bobsled, 1988. 200ce, Greg Louganis, diving, US, 1984. 300ce, L. Visser, speed skating, Netherlands, 1988. 350ce, J. Passler, biathlon, Italy, 1988. 400ce, Mary Lou Retton, gymnastics, US, 1984. 500ce, Jurgen Hingsen, decathlon, Germany, 1984. 600ce, R. Neubert, heptathlon, West Germany, 1984. No. 1380, Jai alai player, vert. No. 1381, Windmill.

**1992, Mar. 3 Litho. *Perf. 14***

**1373** A246 20ce multi .40 .25
**1373A** A246 60ce multi .50 .45
**1374** A246 80ce multi .70 .55
**1375** A246 100ce multi 1.00 .90
**1376** A246 200ce multi 1.75 1.60
**1377** A246 300ce multi 1.75 2.10
**1378** A246 350ce multi 1.75 2.10
**1378A** A246 400ce multi 2.40 2.75
**1378B** A246 500ce multi 2.40 2.75
**1379** A246 600ce multi 2.40 2.75
*Nos. 1373-1379 (10)* 15.05 16.20

**Souvenir Sheets**

**1380** A246 800ce multi 6.00 6.00
**1381** A246 800ce multi 6.00 6.00

While Nos. 1373A, 1378A-1378B have the same issue date as rest of the set the dollar value of Nos. 1373A, 1378A-1378B were lower when they were released.

Phila Nippon '91
A247

**1992, Feb. 16 Litho. *Perf. 14***

**1382** A247 20ce shown .25 .25
**1383** A247 60ce Torii of Itsukushima Jingu shrine .35 .35
**1384** A247 80ce Geisha .45 .45
**1385** A247 100ce Samurai residence .60 .60
**1386** A247 200ce Bonsai tree 1.40 1.40
**1387** A247 400ce Olympic sports hall 2.75 2.75
**1388** A247 500ce Great Buddha 3.25 3.25
**1389** A247 600ce Nagoya castle 4.25 4.25
*Nos. 1382-1389 (8)* 13.30 13.30

**Souvenir Sheets**

**1390** A247 800ce Takamatsu castle 6.00 6.00
**1391** A247 800ce Heian shrine 6.00 6.00

Ghana Natl. Railways
A248

Designs: 20c, Engine, 1903, Gold Coast Railway. 50c, Diesel passenger locomotive, Ghana Railways Corp. 60ce, First class coach, 1931 Gold Coast Railway. 80ce, Official inspection coach, Gold Coast Railway. 100ce, Engine No. 401 on turntable. 200ce, Twin-bogie cocoa wagon, 1921, Gold Coast Railway. 500ce, Engine No. 223, "Prince of Wales." 600ce, Twin-bogie cattle wagon, Gold Coast Railway. No. 1400, German-made locomotive, Gold Coast Railway. No. 1401, Beyer-Garratt #301, 1943, Gold Coast Railway.

**1992, Mar. 2**

**1392** A248 20ce multicolored .25 .25
**1393** A248 50ce multicolored .25 .25
**1394** A248 60ce multicolored .35 .35
**1395** A248 80ce multicolored .45 .45
**1396** A248 100ce multicolored .55 .55
**1397** A248 200ce multicolored 1.20 1.20
**1398** A248 500ce multicolored 3.00 3.00
**1399** A248 600ce multicolored 4.00 4.00
*Nos. 1392-1399 (8)* 10.05 10.05

**Souvenir Sheets**

**1400** A248 800ce multicolored 5.00 5.00
**1401** A248 800ce multicolored 5.00 5.00

Decade of Revolutionary Progress
A249

**1992, Feb. 2 Litho. *Perf. 14x13½***

**1402** A249 20ce Bore hole water .25 .25
**1403** A249 50ce Mining industry .30 .30
**1404** A249 60ce Small scale industry .40 .40
**1405** A249 80ce Timber industry .45 .45
**1406** A249 200ce Cocoa rehabilitation .80 .80
**1407** A249 350ce Rural electrification 1.00 1.00
*Nos. 1402-1407 (6)* 3.20 3.20

Reptiles
A251

**1992, Mar. 30 Litho. *Perf. 14***

**1414** A251 20ce Angides lugubris .25 .25
**1415** A251 50ce Kinixys erosa .35 .35
**1416** A251 60ce Agama agama .35 .35
**1417** A251 80ce Chameleo gracilis .45 .45
**1418** A251 100ce Naja melanleuca .60 .60
**1419** A251 200ce Crocodylus niloticus 1.00 1.00
**1420** A251 400ce Chelonia mydas 2.00 2.00
**1421** A251 500ce Varanus exanthematicus 2.50 2.50
*Nos. 1414-1421 (8)* 7.50 7.50

**Souvenir Sheet**

**1422** A251 600ce Snake & tortoise 4.25 4.25

Numbers have been reserved for additional values in this set.

Easter
A252

Details from paintings: 20ce, The Four Apostles: Sts. John, Peter, Paul & Mark, by Durer. 50ce, The Last Judgment, by Rubens. 60ce, The Four Apostles: Sts. John, Peter, Paul and Mark, diff. by Durer. 80ce, The Last Judgment, diff. by Rubens. 100ce, Crucifixion, by Rubens. 200ce, The Last Judgment, diff. by Rubens. 500ce, Christum Videre, by Rubens. 600ce, The Last Judgment, diff. by Rubens. No. 1432, Last Communion of St. Francis of Assisi, by Rubens. No. 1432A, Scourging the Money Changers from the Temple, by El Greco, horiz.

**1992, Mar. 13 *Perf. 13½x14***

**1424** A252 20ce multi .25 .25
**1425** A252 50ce multi .35 .35
**1426** A252 60ce multi .45 .45
**1427** A252 80ce multi .55 .55
**1428** A252 100ce multi .65 .65
**1429** A252 200ce multi 1.00 1.00
**1430** A252 500ce multi 2.50 2.50
**1431** A252 600ce multi 2.75 2.75
*Nos. 1424-1431 (8)* 8.50 8.50

**Souvenir Sheets**

**1432** A252 800ce multi 5.25 5.25

***Perf. 14x13½***

**1432A** A252 800ce multi 5.25 5.25

Spanish Art — A253

Paintings by Velazquez: 20ce, Two Men at Table. 60ce, Christ in the House of Mary and Martha (detail). 80ce, The Supper at Emmaus. 100ce, Three Muscians. 200ce, Old Woman Cooking Eggs, vert. 400ce, Old Woman Cooking Eggs (detail), vert. 500ce, The Surrender of Breda (detail) diff., vert. 700ce, The Surrender of Breda (detail), vert.

No. 1441, They Still Say that Fish is Expensive, by Joaquin Sorolla y Bastida. No. 1442, The Waterseller of Seville.

**1992, May 4** *Perf. 13½*

| | | | | |
|---|---|---|---|---|
| **1433** | A253 | 20ce multicolored | .25 | .25 |
| **1434** | A253 | 60ce multicolored | .30 | .30 |
| **1435** | A253 | 80ce multicolored | .35 | .35 |
| **1436** | A253 | 100ce multicolored | .50 | .50 |
| **1437** | A253 | 200ce multicolored | 1.10 | 1.10 |
| **1438** | A253 | 400ce multicolored | 1.75 | 1.75 |
| **1439** | A253 | 500ce multicolored | 2.25 | 2.25 |
| **1440** | A253 | 700ce multicolored | 3.50 | 3.50 |

**Size: 120x95mm**

***Imperf***

| | | | | |
|---|---|---|---|---|
| **1441** | A253 | 900ce multicolored | 5.25 | 5.25 |
| **1442** | A253 | 900ce multicolored | 4.75 | 4.75 |
| | | *Nos. 1433-1442 (10)* | 20.00 | 20.00 |

Granada '92. While Nos. 1434-1435, 1438-1439, 1442 have the same issue date as Nos. 1433, 1436-1437, 1440-1441, the value in relation to the dollar of Nos. 1434-1435, 1438-1439, 1442 was lower when they were released.

Butterflies — A254 Dinosaurs — A255

**1992, May 25** **Litho.** *Perf. 14*

| | | | | |
|---|---|---|---|---|
| **1443** | A254 | 20ce African monarch | .25 | .25 |
| **1444** | A254 | 60ce Mocker swallowtail | .40 | .40 |
| **1445** | A254 | 80ce Painted lady | .55 | .55 |
| **1446** | A254 | 100ce Mountain beauty | .65 | .65 |
| **1447** | A254 | 200ce Blue temora | 1.50 | 1.50 |
| **1448** | A254 | 400ce Foxy charaxes | 3.00 | 3.00 |
| **1449** | A254 | 500ce Blue pansy | 3.50 | 3.50 |
| **1450** | A254 | 700ce Golden pansy | 4.75 | 4.75 |
| | | *Nos. 1443-1450 (8)* | 14.60 | 14.60 |

**Souvenir Sheets**

| | | | | |
|---|---|---|---|---|
| **1451** | A254 | 900ce Gaudy commodore | 5.50 | 5.50 |
| **1452** | A254 | 900ce Christmas butterfly | 5.50 | 5.50 |

Genoa '92. For overprints see Nos. 1471-1480.

**1992, June 1** **Litho.** *Perf. 14*

| | | | | |
|---|---|---|---|---|
| **1453** | A255 | 20ce Iguanodon | .45 | .35 |
| **1454** | A255 | 50ce Anchisaurus | .65 | .45 |
| **1455** | A255 | 60ce Heterodontosaurus | .70 | .45 |
| **1456** | A255 | 80ce Ouranosaurus | .75 | .55 |
| **1457** | A255 | 100ce Anatosaurus | 1.00 | .65 |
| **1458** | A255 | 200ce Elaphrosaurus | 1.60 | 1.60 |
| **1459** | A255 | 500ce Coelophysis | 2.75 | 2.75 |
| **1460** | A255 | 600ce Rhamphorynchus | 3.25 | 3.25 |
| | | *Nos. 1453-1460 (8)* | 11.15 | 10.05 |

**Souvenir Sheets**

| | | | | |
|---|---|---|---|---|
| **1461** | A255 | 1500ce like #1459 | 6.75 | 6.75 |
| **1462** | A255 | 1500ce like #1458 | 6.75 | 6.75 |

While Nos. 1453, 1456, 1458-1459 and 1462 have the same issue date as Nos. 1454-1455, 1457, 1460-1461, their value in relation to the dollar was lower when they were released.

Discovery of America, 500th Anniv. — A256

No. 1463: a, Capt. Martin Alonzo Pinzon, Pinta. b, Capt. Vicente Yanez Pinzon, Nina. c, Columbus, Fr. Marchena in La Rabida, 1485. d, Columbus in cabin. e, Land sighted, Oct. 12, 1492. f, Columbus lands on Samana Cay. g, Shipwreck of Santa Maria. h, Columbus returns to Spanish Court, 1493.

No. 1464, Columbus, ship.

**1992, July** **Litho.** *Perf. 14*

| | | | | |
|---|---|---|---|---|
| **1463** | A256 | 200ce Sheet of 8, #a.-h. | 9.50 | 9.50 |

**Souvenir Sheet**

| | | | | |
|---|---|---|---|---|
| **1464** | A256 | 500ce multicolored | 3.75 | 3.75 |

World Columbian Stamp Expo '92, Chicago.

Shells — A257

**1992, Oct. 5** **Litho.** *Perf. 14*

| | | | | |
|---|---|---|---|---|
| **1465** | A257 | 20ce Olivancillaria hiatula | .25 | .25 |
| **1465A** | A257 | 20ce Tympanotonus fuscatus | .25 | .25 |
| **1466** | A257 | 60ce Donax rugosus | .35 | .35 |
| **1466A** | A257 | 60ce Murex cornutus | .35 | .35 |
| **1467** | A257 | 80ce Sigaretus concavus | .45 | .45 |
| **1467A** | A257 | 80ce Tivela tripla | .45 | .45 |
| **1468** | A257 | 200ce Pila africana | 1.10 | 1.10 |
| **1468A** | A257 | 200ce Cypraea stercoraria | 1.10 | 1.10 |
| **1469** | A257 | 350ce Thais hiatula | 1.75 | 1.75 |
| **1469A** | A257 | 350ce Cassis tesselata | 1.75 | 1.75 |
| | | *Nos. 1465-1469A (10)* | 7.80 | 7.80 |

**Souvenir Sheet**

| | | | | |
|---|---|---|---|---|
| **1470** | A257 | 600ce Natica favel | 4.50 | 4.50 |
| **1470A** | A257 | 600ce Semifusos morio | 4.50 | 4.50 |

**Nos. 1443-1452 Ovptd. "40th / Anniversary / of the / Accession / of / HM Queen / Elizabeth II / 1952-1992" in Silver**

**1992, Aug. 10** **Litho.** *Perf. 14*

| | | | | |
|---|---|---|---|---|
| **1471** | A254 | 20ce on #1443 | .25 | .25 |
| **1472** | A254 | 60ce on #1444 | .30 | .30 |
| **1473** | A254 | 80ce on #1445 | .40 | .40 |
| **1474** | A254 | 100ce on #1446 | .50 | .50 |
| **1475** | A254 | 200ce on #1447 | 1.00 | 1.00 |
| **1476** | A254 | 400ce on #1448 | 1.75 | 1.75 |
| **1477** | A254 | 500ce on #1449 | 2.50 | 2.50 |
| **1478** | A254 | 700ce on #1450 | 3.25 | 3.25 |
| | | *Nos. 1471-1478 (8)* | 9.95 | 9.95 |

**Souvenir Sheets**

| | | | | |
|---|---|---|---|---|
| **1479** | A254 | 900ce on #1451 | 5.00 | 5.00 |
| **1480** | A254 | 900ce on #1452 | 5.00 | 5.00 |

Christmas A259

Details or entire paintings: 20ce, Presentation in the Temple, by Master of Brunswick. 50ce, Presentation in the Temple, by Master of St. Severin. 60ce, The Visitation, by Sebastiano del Piombo. 80ce, The Visitation, by Giotto. 100ce, The Circumcision, by Studio of Giovanni Bellini. 200ce, The Circumcision, by Workshop of Benvenuto Garofalo. 500ce, The Visitation, by Workshop of Rogier van der Weyden. 800ce, The Visitation, by Workshop of Rogier Van der Weyden. No. 1491, The Visitation, by Giotto. No. 1492, The Presentation in the Temple, by Bartolo di Fredi.

**1992** **Litho.** *Perf. 13½x14*

| | | | | |
|---|---|---|---|---|
| **1483** | A259 | 20ce multicolored | .25 | .25 |
| **1484** | A259 | 50ce multicolored | .30 | .30 |
| **1485** | A259 | 60ce multicolored | .35 | .35 |
| **1486** | A259 | 80ce multicolored | .40 | .40 |
| **1487** | A259 | 100ce multicolored | .50 | .50 |
| **1488** | A259 | 200ce multicolored | 1.00 | 1.00 |
| **1489** | A259 | 500ce multicolored | 2.75 | 2.75 |
| **1490** | A259 | 800ce multicolored | 4.25 | 4.25 |
| | | *Nos. 1483-1490 (8)* | 9.80 | 9.80 |

**Souvenir Sheet**

| | | | | |
|---|---|---|---|---|
| **1491** | A259 | 900ce multicolored | 4.50 | 4.50 |
| **1492** | A259 | 900ce multicolored | 4.50 | 4.50 |

No. 1492 exists imperf.

Anniversaries and Events
A260 A261

Designs: 20ce, LZ3, floating hangar at Lake Constance, horiz. 100ce, Lift-off of Ariane 4 rocket, horiz. 200ce, Leopard in tree, horiz. 300ce, Roman Colosseum, fruits and vegetables, horiz. 400ce, Wolfgang Amadeus Mozart. 600ce, Lift-off of H-1 rocket, Japan. 800ce, LZ10, Schwaben, horiz. No. 1501, Scene from "The Marriage of Figaro." No. 1502, Space shuttle, US. No. 1503, Count Ferdinand von Zeppelin. No. 1504, Bongo, horiz.

**1992, Dec.** **Litho.** *Perf. 14*

| | | | | |
|---|---|---|---|---|
| **1493** | A260 | 20ce multicolored | .25 | .25 |
| **1494** | A260 | 100ce multicolored | .50 | .50 |
| **1495** | A260 | 200ce multicolored | 1.00 | 1.00 |
| **1496** | A260 | 300ce multicolored | 1.60 | 1.60 |
| **1497** | A261 | 400ce multicolored | 2.25 | 2.25 |
| **1499** | A260 | 600ce multicolored | 3.50 | 3.50 |
| **1500** | A260 | 800ce multicolored | 4.50 | 4.50 |
| | | *Nos. 1493-1500 (7)* | 13.60 | 13.60 |

**Souvenir Sheets**

| | | | | |
|---|---|---|---|---|
| **1501** | A261 | 900ce multicolored | 4.75 | 4.75 |
| **1502** | A260 | 900ce multicolored | 4.75 | 4.75 |
| **1503** | A260 | 900ce multicolored | 4.75 | 4.75 |
| **1504** | A260 | 900ce multicolored | 4.75 | 4.75 |

Count Ferdinand von Zeppelin, 75th anniv. of death (#1493, 1500, 1503). Intl. Space Year (#1494, 1499, 1502). UN Earth Summit, Rio de Janeiro (#1495, 1504). WHO, Intl. Conference on Nutrition, Rome (1496). Mozart, bicent. of death (in 1991) (#1497, 1501).

Flowers — A262

Designs: Nos. 1505, 1514d (100ce), Lagerstroemia flos-reginae. No. 1506, Clerodendrum thomsoniae. Nos. 1507, 1514c (50ce), Spathodea campanulata. No. 1508, Cassia fistula. Nos. 1509, 1514e (150ce), Mellitea ferrugenea. Nos. 1510, 1514j (300ce), Hildegardia barteri. Nos. 1511, 1514i (150ce), Ipomoea asarifolia. No. 1512, Petrea volubilis. Nos. 1513, 1514f (300ce), Ritchiea reflexa. Nos. 1514, 1514h (100ce), Bryphyllum pinnatum.

**1993, Mar. 1** **Litho.** *Perf. 14*

| | | | | |
|---|---|---|---|---|
| **1505** | A262 | 20ce multicolored | .25 | .25 |
| **1506** | A262 | 20ce multicolored | .25 | .25 |
| **1507** | A262 | 60ce multicolored | .30 | .30 |
| **1508** | A262 | 60ce multicolored | .30 | .30 |
| **1509** | A262 | 80ce multicolored | .40 | .40 |
| **1510** | A262 | 80ce multicolored | .40 | .40 |
| **1511** | A262 | 200ce multicolored | .90 | .90 |
| **1512** | A262 | 200ce multicolored | .90 | .90 |
| **1513** | A262 | 350ce multicolored | 1.40 | 1.40 |
| **1514** | A262 | 350ce multicolored | 1.40 | 1.40 |
| | | *Nos. 1505-1514 (10)* | 6.50 | 6.50 |

**Souvenir Sheets**

| | | | | |
|---|---|---|---|---|
| **1514A** | A262 | Sheet of 4, #c.-f. | 3.50 | 3.50 |
| **1514B** | A262 | Sheet of 4, #g.-j. | 3.50 | 3.50 |

Intl. Conference on Nutrition, Rome — A263

**1993, Jan.** **Litho.** *Perf. 14*

| | | | | |
|---|---|---|---|---|
| **1515** | A263 | 20ce Energy foods | .25 | .25 |
| **1516** | A263 | 60ce Body-building foods | .30 | .30 |
| **1517** | A263 | 80ce Protective foods | .40 | .40 |
| **1518** | A263 | 200ce Disease prevention | 1.00 | 1.00 |
| **1519** | A263 | 400ce Food quality control, preservation | 1.75 | 1.75 |
| | | *Nos. 1515-1519 (5)* | 3.70 | 3.70 |

Crabs A264

Designs: 20ce, Clappa rubroguttata. 60ce, Cardisoma amatum. 80ce, Maia squinado. 400ce, Ocypoda cursor. 800ce, Grapus grapus.

**1993, Feb.** *Perf. 14x13½*

| | | | | |
|---|---|---|---|---|
| **1520** | A264 | 20ce multicolored | .25 | .25 |
| **1521** | A264 | 60ce multicolored | .35 | .35 |
| **1522** | A264 | 80ce multicolored | .45 | .45 |
| **1523** | A264 | 400ce multicolored | 2.10 | 2.10 |
| *a.* | | Souv. sheet of 4, #1520-1523 | 7.50 | 7.50 |
| **1524** | A264 | 800ce multicolored | 4.25 | 4.25 |
| | | *Nos. 1520-1524 (5)* | 7.40 | 7.40 |

Miniature Sheet of 8

Louvre Museum, Bicent. — A265

No. 1525 — Details or entire paintings, by Giovanni Domenico Tiepolo (1727-1804) (a-e) and Giovanni Battista Tiepolo (1696-1770) (f-h): a-c, Carnival Scene, (left, center, right). d-e, Tooth Puller, (left, right). f, Rebecca at the Well. g-h, Presenting Christ to the People, (left, right).

700ce, Chancellor Seguier, by Le Brun, horiz.

**1993, Mar. 1** **Litho.** *Perf. 12*

| | | | | |
|---|---|---|---|---|
| **1525** | A265 | 200ce Sheet of 8, #a.-h. + label | 9.00 | 9.00 |

**Souvenir Sheet**

***Perf. 14½***

| | | | | |
|---|---|---|---|---|
| **1526** | A265 | 700ce multicolored | 4.00 | 4.00 |

No. 1526 contains one 55x88mm stamp.

Oil Palm Fruit — A265a

**1993, Apr. Litho. *Perf. 13½***

**1526A** A265a 20ce multi — —

Faberge Eggs — A266

Easter: 50ce, Resurrection Egg. 80ce, Imperial Red Cross Egg with Resurrection Triptych. 100ce, Imperial Uspensky Cathedral Egg. 150ce, Imperial Red Cross Egg with portraits. 200ce, Orange Tree Egg. 250ce, Rabbit Egg. 400ce, Imperial Coronation Egg. 900ce, Silver-gilt enamel Easter Egg. No. 1535, Spring Flower Egg. No. 1536, Egg charms, horiz.

**1993, Apr. 26 *Perf. 14***

**1527** A266 50ce multi .30 .30
**1528** A266 80ce multi .50 .50
**1529** A266 100ce multi .60 .60
**1530** A266 150ce multi .90 .90
**1531** A266 200ce multi 1.25 1.25
**1532** A266 250ce multi 1.75 1.75
**1533** A266 400ce multi 3.50 3.50
**1534** A266 900ce multi 7.50 7.50
*Nos. 1527-1534 (8)* 16.30 16.30

**Souvenir Sheets**

**1535** A266 1000ce multi 6.50 6.50
**1536** A266 1000ce multi 6.50 6.50

Wild Animals — A267

**1993, May 24 Litho. *Perf. 14***

**1537** A267 20ce African buffalo .25 .25
**1538** A267 50ce Giant forest hog .50 .50
**1539** A267 60ce Potto .60 .60
**1540** A267 80ce Bay duiker .80 .80
**1541** A267 100ce Royal antelope 1.00 1.00
**1542** A267 200ce Serval 2.00 2.00
**1543** A267 500ce Golden cat 5.00 5.00
**1544** A267 800ce Megaloglossus woermanni 8.00 8.00
*Nos. 1537-1544 (8)* 18.15 18.15

**Souvenir Sheets**

**1545** A267 900ce Dormouse 6.50 6.50
**1546** A267 900ce White collared mangabey 6.50 6.50

4th Republic — A268

50ce, Kwame Nkrumah Mausoleum, horiz. 100ce, Kwame Nkrumah Conference Center, horiz. 200ce, Constitution book. 350ce, Independence Square. 400ce, Christiansborg Castle.

**1993, May Litho. *Perf. 14***

**1547** A268 50ce multicolored .25 .25
**1548** A268 100ce multicolored .50 .50
**1549** A268 200ce multicolored 1.05 1.05
**1550** A268 350ce multicolored 1.90 1.90
**1551** A268 400ce multicolored 2.25 2.25
*Nos. 1547-1551 (5)* 5.95 5.95

A269

Aviation and Automotive Anniversaries — A270

Designs: 50ce, Graf Zeppelin over Alps, vert. No. 1552, Mercedes Benz 300 SLR in 1955 Mille Miglia. No. 1553, LZ7 Deutschland. No. 1554, Vulcan bomber. No. 1555, Ford Trimotor. No. 1556, 1920 Ford Depot Wagon. No. 1557, Nieuport 27, vert. No. 1558, Graf Zeppelin taking aboard letters, vert. No. 1559, 1970 Ford Mach 1 Mustang.

No. 1560, LZ10 Schwaben. No. 1561, Mercedes wins 1937 Monaco Grand Prix. No. 1562, Graf Zeppelin over Rome. No. 1563, 1955 Mercedes Benz Type 196. No. 1564, Early US air mail flight. No. 1565, S.E.5A, 1918. No. 1566, 1910 Ford Super T, 999.

**1993 Litho. *Perf. 14***

**1551A** A269 50ce multi .35 .35
**1552** A270 150ce multi .90 .90
**1553** A269 150ce multi .90 .90
**1554** A269 400ce multi 2.75 2.75
**1555** A269 400ce multi 2.75 2.75
**1556** A270 400ce multi 2.75 2.75
**1557** A269 600ce multi 4.00 4.00
**1558** A269 600ce multi 4.00 4.00
**1559** A270 600ce multi 4.00 4.00
**1560** A269 800ce multi 5.00 5.00
**1561** A270 800ce multi 5.00 5.00
*Nos. 1551A-1561 (11)* 32.40 32.40

**Souvenir Sheets**

**1562** A269 1000ce multi 4.75 4.75
**1563** A270 1000ce multi 4.75 4.75
**1564** A269 1000ce multi 4.75 4.75
**1565** A269 1000ce multi 4.75 4.75
**1566** A270 1000ce multi 4.75 4.75

Capt. Hugo Eckener, 125th birth anniv. (Nos. 1551A, 1553-1554, 1562). Benz's first four-wheeled vehicle, cent. (Nos. 1552, 1561, 1563). Royal Air Force, 75th anniv. (Nos. 1554, 1557, 1564). Henry Ford's first gasoline powered engine, cent. (Nos. 1556, 1559, 1566).

No. 1564 contains one 57x42mm stamp. Nos. 1563, 1566 contains one 85x28mm stamp.

Issued: Nos. 1555-1556, 1558-1559, 1565-1566, May. Nos. 1551A-1554, 1557, 1560-1564, June.

**Nos. 1300-1305 Ovptd.**

**1993 Litho. *Perf. 14***

**1567** A237 100ce multicolored .65 .65
**1568** A237 200ce multicolored 1.60 1.60
**1569** A237 500ce multicolored 3.25 3.25
**1570** A237 600ce multicolored 4.50 4.50
*Nos. 1567-1570 (4)* 10.00 10.00

**Souvenir Sheet**

**1571** A237 800ce on #1304 5.50 5.50
**1572** A237 800ce on #1305 5.50 5.50

**Nos. 1321, 1323-1327 Ovptd.**

(a)

(b)

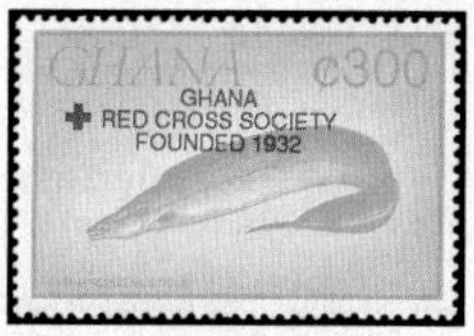


**1993**

**1573** A239(a) 100ce multi .75 .75
**1574** A239(b) 300ce multi 1.75 1.75
**1575** A239(b) 400ce multi 2.75 2.75
**1576** A239(a) 500ce multi 3.25 3.25
*Nos. 1573-1576 (4)* 8.50 8.50

**Souvenir Sheets**

**1577** A239(a) 800ce on #1326 5.25 5.25
**1578** A239(b) 800ce on #1327 5.25 5.25

A271

Mushrooms A272

Designs: 20ce, Cantharellus cibarius. 50ce, Russula cyanoxantha. 60ce, Clitocybe rivulosa. No. 1581, Boletus chrysenteron. No. 1582, Cortinarius elatior. No. 1583, Mycena galericulata. No. 1584, Boletus edulis. No. 1585, Tricholoma gambosum. No. 1586, Lepista saeva. 250ce, Gyroporus castaneus. No. 1589, Nolanea sericea. No. 1590, Hygrophorus puiceus. 500ce, Gomphidius glutinosus. No. 1592, Russula olivacea. 1000ce, Russula aurata.

No. 1594a, 100ce, Cantharellus cibarius. b, 150ce, Cortinarius elatior. c, 300ce, Tricholoma gambosum. d, 600ce, Hygrophorus puiceus.

No. 1595: a, 50ce, like #1581. b, 100ce, like #1583. c, 150ce, like #1584. d, 1000ce, like #1589.

**1993, July 30 Litho. *Perf. 14***

**1579** A271 20ce multi .25 .25
**1580** A271 50ce multi .25 .25
**1581** A271 60ce multi .25 .25
**1582** A271 80ce multi .35 .35
**1583** A271 80ce multi .35 .35
**1584** A271 200ce multi .85 .85
**1585** A271 200ce multi .85 .85
**1586** A272 200ce multi .85 .85
**1587** A272 250ce multi 1.05 1.05
**1588** A271 300ce multi 1.25 1.25
**1589** A271 350ce multi 1.60 1.60
**1590** A271 350ce multi 1.60 1.60
**1591** A272 500ce multi 2.50 2.50
**1592** A272 600ce multi 3.00 3.00
**1593** A272 1000ce multi 5.00 5.00
*Nos. 1579-1593 (15)* 20.00 20.00

**Souvenir Sheets**

**1594** A271 Sheet of 4, #a.-d. 7.25 7.25
**1595** A271 Sheet of 4, #a.-d. 7.25 7.25

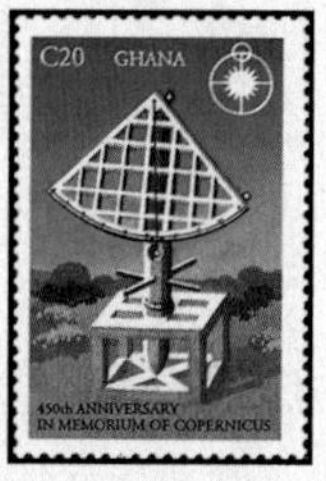


Copernicus (1473-1543) A273

Designs: 20ce, Early astronomical instrument. 200ce, Telescope. No. 1598, Copernicus, long hair. No. 1599, Copernicus, shorter hair.

**1993, Oct. 19 Litho. *Perf. 13½x14***

**1596** A273 20ce multicolored .50 .50
**1597** A273 200ce multicolored 3.00 3.00

**Souvenir Sheets**

***Perf. 12x13***

**1598** A273 1000ce multicolored 6.00 6.00
**1599** A273 1000ce multicolored 6.00 6.00

Picasso (1881-1973) A274

Paintings: 20ce, The Actor, 1905. 80ce, Portrait of Allen Stein, 1906. 800ce, Seated Male Nude, 1908-09.

**1993, Oct. 19 *Perf. 14***

**1600-1602** A274 Set of 3 5.50 5.50

**Souvenir Sheet**

**1603** A274 900ce Man with a Javelin, 1958 5.50 5.50

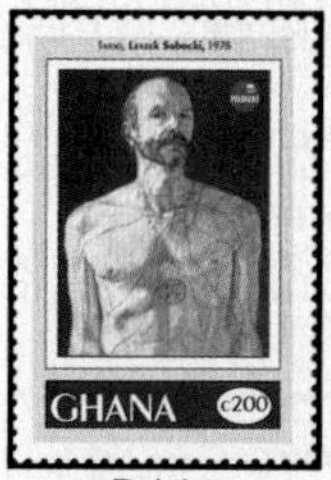


Polska '93 — A275

1994 World Cup Soccer, US — A276

Paintings: 200ce, Tattoo, by Sobocki, 1978. 600ce, Prison, by Blonder, 1934. 1000ce, Fable of the Fortunate Man, by Michalak, 1925, horiz.

**1993, Oct. 19**

**1604-1605** A275 Set of 2 5.00 5.00

**Souvenir Sheet**

**1606** A275 1000ce multicolored 5.00 5.00

**1993, Dec. 1 *Perf. 13½x14***

Designs: 50ce, Abedi Pele, Ghana. 80ce, Pedro Troglio, Argentina. 100ce, Fernando Alvez, Uruguay. 200ce, Franco Baresi, Italy. 250ce, Gomez, Colombia; Katanec, Yugoslavia. 600ce, Diego Maradona, Argentina. 800ce, Hasek, Czech Republic; Wynalda, US. 1000ce, Lothar Matthaeus, Germany.

No. 1615, Giuseppe Giannini, Italy. No. 1616, Rabie Yassein, Egypt; Ruud Gullit, Holland.

**1607** A276 50ce multi .25 .25
**1608** A276 80ce multi .45 .45
**1609** A276 100ce multi .55 .55
**1610** A276 200ce multi 1.10 1.10
**1611** A276 250ce multi 1.50 1.50
**1612** A276 600ce multi 3.25 3.25
**1613** A276 800ce multi 4.25 4.25
**1614** A276 1000ce multi 5.00 5.00
*Nos. 1607-1614 (8)* 16.35 16.35

**Souvenir Sheets**

***Perf. 13***

**1615** A276 1200ce multi 6.50 6.50
**1616** A276 1200ce multi 6.50 6.50

Domestic Animals A277

Designs: 50ce, Meleagris gallopvo. 100ce, Capra hircus. 150ce, Carina moschata. 200ce, Eguus asinus. 250ce, Male gallus gallus. 300ce, Sus vittatus. 400ce, Numida meleagris. 600ce, Canis domesticus. 800ce, Female gallus gallus. 1000ce, Ovis aries.

No. 1627: a, 100ce, Like #1618. b, 250ce, Like #1624. c, 350ce, Like #1622. d, 500ce, Like #1626.

No. 1628: a, 100ce, Like #1623. b, 250ce, Like #1621. c, 350ce, Like #1625. d, 500ce, Like #1617.

**1993, Dec. 8** ***Perf. 14***
**1617-1626** A277 Set of 10 18.00 18.00

**Souvenir Sheets**

**1627** A277 Sheet of 4, #a-d 7.00 7.00
**1628** A277 Sheet of 4, #a-d 7.00 7.00

Arts and Crafts — A278

Designs: No. 1629, 50ce, Doll. No. 1630, 50ce, Pot and lid. No. 1631, 200ce, Beads. No. 1632, 200ce, Snake charmers. No. 1633, 250ce, Hoe. No. 1634, 250ce, Scabbard. No. 1635, 600ce, Pipe. No. 1636, 600ce, Deer. No. 1637, 1000ce, Mask. No. 1638, 1000ce, Doll with baby.

No. 1639: a, 100ce, Like #1629. b, 250ce, Like #1631. c, 350ce, Like #1633. d, 500ce, Like #1635.

No. 1640: a, 100ce, Like #1630. b, 250ce, Like #1632. c, 350ce, Like #1634. d, 500ce, Like #1636.

**1994, Jan. 24** **Litho.** ***Perf. 14***
**1629-1638** A278 Set of 10 13.50 13.50

**Souvenir Sheets**

**1639** A278 Sheet of 4, #a-d 4.00 4.00
**1640** A278 Sheet of 4, #a-d 4.00 4.00

Christmas A279

Paintings and Woodcuts: 50ce, Adoration of the Magi. 100ce, The Virgin and Child with Saint John and an Angel, by Botticelli. 150ce, Mary as Queen of Heaven. 200ce, Saint Anne. 250ce, The Madonna of the Magnificat, by Botticelli. 400ce, The Madonna of the Goldfinch, by Tiepolo. 600ce, The Virgin and the Child with the Young St. John the Baptist, by Correggio. 1000ce, Adoration of the Shepherds.

No. 1649, Mystic Nativity (detail), by Botticelli, horiz. No. 1650, Madonna in a Circle, by Durer.

Woodcuts (50ce, 150ce, 200ce, 1000ce) are from Nuremberg Prayer Books, by Durer.

***Perf. 13½x14, 14x13½***

**1993, Dec. 20** **Litho.**
**1641-1648** A279 Set of 8 13.50 13.50

**Souvenir Sheets**

**1649** A279 1000ce multicolored 6.00 6.00
**1650** A279 1000ce multicolored 6.00 6.00

A280

Hong Kong '94 — A281

Stamps, tram from Kennedy Town to Shau Kei: No. 1651, Hong Kong #470, back of tram. No. 1652, Front of tram, #1392.

No. 1653 — Imperial Palace clocks: a, Windmill. b, Horse. c, Balloon. d, Zodiac. e, Shar-Pei dog. f, Cat.

**1994, Feb. 18** **Litho.** ***Perf. 14***
**1651** A280 200ce multicolored .90 .90
**1652** A280 200ce multicolored .90 .90
*a.* Pair, #1651-1652 1.80 1.80

**Miniature Sheet**

**1653** A281 100ce Sheet of 6, #a.-f. 6.50 6.50

Nos. 1651-1652 issued in sheets of 5 pairs. No. 1652a is a continuous design.

New Year 1994 (Year of the Dog) (#1653e).

Mickey Mouse, 65th Birthday A282

Mickey's films: 50ce, Steamboat Willie, 1928. 100ce, The Band Concert, 1937. 150ce, Moose Hunters, 1937. 200ce, Brave Little Taylor, 1938. 250ce, Fantasia, 1940. 400ce, The Nifty Nineties, 1941. 600ce, Canne Caddy, 1944. 1000ce, Mickey's Christmas Carol, 1983.

No. 1662, 1200ce, Mickey's Elephant, 1936. No. 1663, 1200ce, Mickey's Amateurs, 1937.

**1994, Mar. 1** **Litho.** ***Perf. 13½x14***
**1654-1661** A282 Set of 8 12.50 12.50

**Souvenir Sheets**

**1662-1663** A282 Set of 2 10.00 10.00

A283

Hummel Figurines: 50ce, Boy with backpack, walking stick. 100ce, Girl holding basket behind back. 150ce, Boy with rabbits. 200ce, Boy carrying chicks in basket. 250ce, Girl with chicks. 400ce, Girl petting lamb. 600ce, Lamb, girl waving handkerchief. 1000ce, Girl with basket, flowers.

No. 1672: a, 500ce, Like #1665; b, 150ce, Like #1671; c, 1200ce, Like #1667.

No. 1673: a, 300ce, Like #1668; b, 200ce, Like #1669; c, 500ce, Like #1670; d, 1000ce, Like #1666.

**1994, Apr. 6** ***Perf. 14***
**1664-1671** A283 Set of 8 9.50 9.50

**Souvenir Sheets**

**1672** A283 Sheet of 4, #a.-c., #1664 5.00 5.00
**1673** A283 Sheet of 4, #a.-d. 5.00 5.00

World Wildlife Fund — A284

Diana Monkeys: 50ce, Adult, young. 200ce, Sitting in tree. 500ce, Holding food. 800ce, Close-up of face.

**1994, May 16** **Litho.** ***Perf. 14***
**1674-1677** A284 Set of 4 7.50 7.50
*1677a* Sheet, 3 each #1674-1677 25.00 25.00

For surcharges see Nos. 2530-2533.

Wild Animals A285

Designs: 100ce, Bushbuck. 150ce, Spotted hyena. 1000ce, Aardvark. No. 1681, 2000ce, Leopard, vert. No. 1682, 2000ce, Waterbuck, vert.

**1994, May 16**
**1678-1680** A285 Set of 3 6.50 6.50

**Souvenir Sheets**

**1681-1682** A285 Set of 2 13.00 13.00

Cats A286

No. 1683, 200ce: a, Sorrel Abyssinian. b, Silver classic tabby. c, Chocolate-point Siamese. d, Brown tortie Burmese. e, Exotic shorthair. f, Havana brown. g, Devon rex. h, Black manx. i, British blue shorthair. j, Calico American wirehair. k, Spotted oriental Siamese. l, Red classic tabby.

No. 1684, 200ce: a, Norwegian forest cat. b, Blue longhair. c, Red self longhair. d, Black longhair. e, Chinchilla. f, Dilut calico longhair. g, Blue tabby-&-white longhair. h, Ruby somali. i, Blue smoke longhair. j, Calico longhair. k, Brown tabby longhair. l, Balinese.

No. 1685, 2000ce, Brown mackeral tabby Scottish fold. No. 1686, 2000ce, Seal-point colorpoint.

**1994, June 6** **Litho.** ***Perf. 14***

**Sheets of 12, #a-l**

**1683-1684** A286 Set of 2 16.00 16.00

**Souvenir Sheets**

**1685-1686** A286 Set of 2 11.00 11.00

Birds A287

No. 1687, 200ce: a, Red-bellied paradise flycatcher (b, e). b, Many-colored bush-shrike. c, Broad-tailed paradise whydah (b, e). d, White-crowned robin-chat. e, Violet plantain-eater. f, Village weaver. g, Fire-crowned bishop. h, Shoveler. i, Spur-winged goose (l). j, African crake. k, King reed-hen. l, Tiger bittern.

No. 1688, 200ce: a, Moho. b, Superb sunbird. c, Blue-breasted kingfisher. d, Blue cuckoo-shrike. e, Blue plantain-eater (d, g). f, Greater flamingo (i). g, Lily-trotter (j). h, Night heron. i, Black-winged stilt (l). j, White-spotted pigmy rail. k, Pigmy goose. k, Angola pitta.

No. 1689, 2000ce, Goliath heron. No. 1690, 2000ce, African spoonbill.

**1994, June 13**

**Sheets of 12, #a-l**

**1687-1688** A287 Set of 2 19.00 19.00

**Souvenir Sheets**

**1689-1690** A287 Set of 2 12.50 12.50

4th Republic, 1st Anniv. A288

Designs: 50ce, Rural water projects. 100ce, Honoring farmers. 200ce, Rural electrification. 600ce, Rural bridge construction. 800ce, Natl. Theater. 1000ce, Lighting Perpetual Flame.

**1994, July 11** **Litho.** ***Perf. 14***
**1691-1696** A288 Set of 6 6.50 6.50

D-Day, 50th Anniv. A289

Designs: 60ce, 15-inch Monitor HMS Roberts fires on Houlgate Battery. 100ce, HMS Warspite hits Villerville. 200ce, Flagship USS Augusta.

1500ce, USS Nevada bombards Utah Beach.

**1994, July 4** **Litho.** ***Perf. 14***
**1697-1699** A289 Set of 3 3.75 3.75

**Souvenir Sheet**

**1700** A289 1500ce multicolored 7.00 7.00

First Manned Moon Landing, 25th Anniv. A290

No. 1701 — German, Japanese, scientist-astronauts: a, Sigmund Jahn. b, Ulf Merbold. c, Hans Wilhelm Schlegal. d, Ulrich Walter. e, Reinhard Furrer. f, Ernst Messerschmid. g, Mamoru Mohri. h, Klaus-Dietrich Flade. i, Chaiki Naito-Mukai.

2000ce, "Frau im Mond."

**1994, July 4**
**1701** A290 300ce Sheet of 9, #a.-i. 8.75 8.75

**Souvenir Sheet**

**1702** A290 2000ce multicolored 8.00 8.00

Duiker Antelopes A291

Designs: 50ce, Crowned. 100ce, Red-flanked. 200ce, Yellow-backed. 400ce, Ogilby's. 600ce, Bay. 800ce, Jentink's.

No. 1709, 2000ce, Cephalophus natalensis. No. 1710, 2000ce, Cephalophus niger.

**1994, May 16** **Litho.** ***Perf. 14***
**1703-1708** A291 Set of 6 7.00 7.00

**Souvenir Sheets**

**1709-1710** A291 Set of 2 10.00 10.00

For surcharges see Nos. 2539-2544.

A292

Intl. Olympic Committee, Cent. — A293

Designs: 300ce, Dieter Modenburg, Germany, high jump, 1984. 400ce, Ruth Fuchs, German Democratic Republic, javelin, 1972, 1976.

1500ce, Jans Weissflog, Germany, large hill ski jump, 1994.

**1994, July 4 Litho. *Perf. 14***

| | | | |
|---|---|---|---|
| **1711** A292 | 300ce multicolored | 1.10 | 1.10 |
| **1712** A292 | 400ce multicolored | 1.40 | 1.40 |

**Souvenir Sheet**

| | | | |
|---|---|---|---|
| **1713** A293 | 1500ce multicolored | 5.00 | 5.00 |

A294

PHILAKOREA '94 — A295

Designs: 20ce, Ch'unghak-dong village elder in traditional clothes. 150ce, Stone pagoda, Punhwangsa, Korea. 300ce, Traditional country house, Andong region.

No. 1717 — Letter pictures, eight-panel screen, Choson Dynasty, 20th cent: a, Shown. b, f, Birds. c, Rooster. d, Animal with antennae. e, g, Flowers. h, Fish.

1500ce, Temple judges determine final afterlife judgments, horiz.

**1994, July 4 *Perf. 14, 13 (#1717)***

| | | | |
|---|---|---|---|
| **1714-1716** A294 | Set of 3 | 2.00 | 2.00 |
| **1717** A295 | 250ce Sheet of 8, #a.-h. | 7.25 | 7.25 |

**Souvenir Sheet**

| | | | |
|---|---|---|---|
| **1718** A294 | 1500ce multicolored | 6.00 | 6.00 |

Miniature Sheet of 6

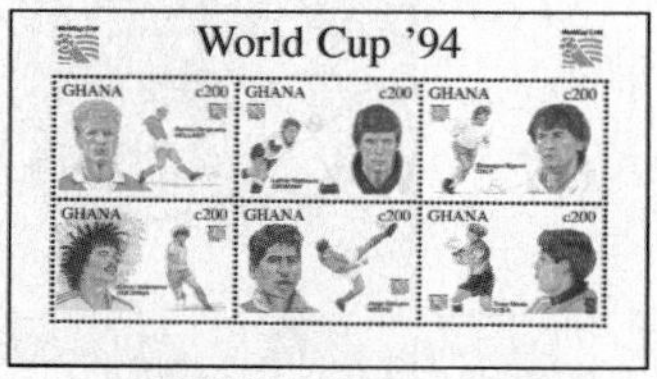


1994 World Cup Soccer Championships, US — A296

No. 1719: a, Dennis Bergkamp, Netherlands. b, Lothar Matthaus, Germany. c, Giuseppe Signori, Italy. d, Carlos Valderrama, Colombia. e, Jorge Campos, Mexico. f, Tony Meola, US.

No. 1720, 1200ce, Citrus Bowl, Orlando, FL, vert. No. 1721, 1200ce, Giants Stadium, Meadowlands, NJ, vert.

**1994, July 25 *Perf. 14***

| | | | |
|---|---|---|---|
| **1719** A296 | 200ce Sheet of 6, #a.-f. | 4.00 | 4.00 |

**Souvenir Sheets**

| | | | |
|---|---|---|---|
| **1720-1721** A296 | Set of 2 | 7.00 | 7.00 |

Christmas A297

Italian art: 100ce, Madonna of the Annunciation, by Simone Martini. 200ce, Madonna and Child, by Niccolo di Pietro Gerini. 250ce, Virgin and Child on the Throne with Angels and Saints, by Raffaello Botticelli. 300ce, Madonna and Child with Saints, by Antonio Fiorentino. 400ce, Adoration of the Magi, by Bartolo di Fredi. 500ce, The Annunciation, by Cima da Congeliano. 600ce, Virgin and Child with the Young St. John the Baptist, by Workshop of Botticelli. 1000ce, The Holy Family, by Giorgione.

Details from Adoration of the Kings, by Giorgione: No. 1730, 2000ce, Presenting gifts. No. 1731, 20000ce, Madonna & Child.

**1994, Dec. 5 Litho. *Perf. 13½x14***

| | | | |
|---|---|---|---|
| **1722-1729** A297 | Set of 8 | 10.00 | 10.00 |

**Souvenir Sheets**

| | | | |
|---|---|---|---|
| **1730-1731** A297 | Set of 2 | 10.00 | 10.00 |

Intl. Year of the Family — A298

Designs: 50ce, Family. 100ce, Technical training. 200ce, Child care. 400ce, Care for the aged. 600ce, Vocational training. 1000ce, Adult education.

**1994, Dec. 20 *Perf. 14***

| | | | |
|---|---|---|---|
| **1732-1737** A298 | Set of 6 | 6.00 | 6.00 |

Ghana Civil Aviation Authority, 50th Anniv. A299

Designs: 100ce, Control tower. 400ce, Insignia, marker light. 1000ce, Airplane leaving runway.

**1994, Dec. 20**

| | | | |
|---|---|---|---|
| **1738-1740** A299 | Set of 3 | 4.50 | 4.50 |

See Nos. 1766-1768. For surcharges see Nos. 2548-2550.

Red Cross & Red Crescent Societies in Ghana, 75th Anniv. A300

Designs: 50ce, Transporting victim. 200ce, Aiding mother, children. 600ce, Erecting tents.

**1994, Dec. 20 Litho. *Perf. 14***

| | | | |
|---|---|---|---|
| **1741-1743** A300 | Set of 3 | 4.25 | 4.25 |

**Souvenir Sheet**

| | | | |
|---|---|---|---|
| **1744** | Sheet of 3, #1741-1742, 1744a | 6.50 | 6.50 |
| *a.* A300 1000ce like #1743 | | 6.50 | 6.50 |

For surcharges see Nos. 2545-2547.

Fertility Dolls — A301

Various carvingswith background colors of: 50ce, Green. 100ce, Yellow (red frame). 150ce, Blue (black doll). 200ce, Rose. 400ce, Dull orange. 600ce, Yellow green. 800ce, Yellow (green frame). 1000ce, Blue (white doll).

**1994, Dec. 20**

| | | | |
|---|---|---|---|
| **1745-1752** A301 | Set of 8 | 9.25 | 9.25 |

**Souvenir Sheet**

| | | | |
|---|---|---|---|
| **1753** | Sheet of 4, #1745, 1748-1749, 1753a | 6.75 | 6.75 |
| *a.* A301 250ce like #1752 | | 1.60 | 1.60 |

For surcharges see Nos. 2551-2558.

Donald Duck, 60th Birthday (in 1994) — A302

Designs: 40ce, Pluto, Donald, Chip 'n Dale. 50ce, Mickey, pup. 60ce, Daisy. 100ce, Goofy. 150ce, Goofy, diff. 250ce, Donald, Goofy. 400ce, Ludwig Von Drake, Pluto. 500ce, Gramdma Duck, pups. 1000ce, Mickey, Minnie. 1500ce, Pluto.

No. 1764, 2000ce, Daisy, Donald, cake, Mickey, vert. No. 1765, 2000ce, Donald holding fork, spoon, vert.

**1995, Feb. 2 Litho. *Perf. 14x13½***

| | | | |
|---|---|---|---|
| **1754-1763** A302 | Set of 10 | 10.00 | 10.00 |

**Souvenir Sheets**

***Perf. 13½x14***

| | | | |
|---|---|---|---|
| **1764-1765** A302 | Set of 2 | 10.50 | 10.50 |

**Civil Aviation Authority Type of 1994 with ICAO Emblem and New Inscription**

Designs: 100ce, Like #1738. 400ce, Like #1739. 1000ce, Like #1740.

**1994, Dec. 20 Litho. *Perf. 14***

| | | | |
|---|---|---|---|
| **1766-1768** A299 | Set of 3 | 9.00 | 9.00 |

Nos. 1766-1768 are inscribed "50th Anniversary of The International Civil Aviation Organization (ICAO)."

For surcharges see Nos. 2559-2561.

Panafest '94 — A303

Designs: 50ce, Northern region dancer. 100ce, Relics with landmark. 200ce, Chief sitting in state. 400ce, Royalist ceremonial dress. 600ce, Cape Coast Castle. 800ce, Clay figurines of West Africa.

**1994, Dec. 9 Litho. *Perf. 13½***

| | | | |
|---|---|---|---|
| **1769-1774** A303 | Set of 6 | 9.00 | 9.00 |

Pan African Historical Theatre Festival, Dec. 1994.

Forts A304

Castles A305

Forts: 50ce, Apolonia, Beyin. 200ce, Patience, Apam. 250ce, Amsterdam, Kormantin. 300ce, St. Jago, Elmina. 400ce, William, Anomabo. 600ce, Kumasi.

Castles: 150ce, Cochem, Germany. 600ce, Hohenzollern, Germany. 800ce, Uwajima, Japan. 100ce, Hohenschwangau, Germany.

Castles: No. 1785a, Windsor, England. b, Osaka, Japan. c, Vaj Dahunyad, Hungary. d, Karlstejn, Czech Republic. e, Kronborg, Denmark. f, Alcazar of Segovia, Spain. g, Chambourd, France. h, Linderhof, Bavaria. i, Red Fort, India.

No. 1786, 800ce, Elmira Castle. No. 1787, 1000ce, Fort St. Antonio, Axim. No. 1788, 2500ce, Himeji Castle, Japan. No. 1789, 2500ce, Neuschwanstein Castle, Germany.

**1995, Apr. 3 *Perf. 14***

| | | | |
|---|---|---|---|
| **1775-1780** A304 | Set of 6 | 5.50 | 5.50 |
| **1781-1784** A305 | Set of 4 | 8.00 | 8.00 |
| **1785** A305 | 500ce Sheet of 9, #a.-i. | 11.00 | 11.00 |

**Souvenir Sheets**

| | | | |
|---|---|---|---|
| **1786-1787** A304 | Set of 2 | 4.50 | 4.50 |
| **1788-1789** A305 | Set of 2 | 8.50 | 8.50 |

Water Birds A306

Designs: 200ce, Eurasian pochard. 500ce, Maccoa duck. 800ce, Cape shoveler. 1000ce, Red-crested pochard.

No. 1794: a, African pygmy goose. b, Southern pochard. c, Cape teal. d, Ruddy shelduck. e, Fulvous whistling duck. f, White-faced whistling geese. g, Ferruginous white-eye. h, Hottentot teal. i, African black duck. j, Yellow-billed duck. k, White-checked pintail duck. l, Hartlaub's duck.

No. 1795, 2500ce, Roseate tern. No. 1796, 2500ce, Northern shoveler.

**1995, Apr. 28**

| | | | |
|---|---|---|---|
| **1790-1793** A306 | Set of 4 | 7.00 | 7.00 |
| **1794** A306 | 400ce Sheet of 12, #a.-l. | 10.50 | 10.50 |

**Souvenir Sheets**

| | | | |
|---|---|---|---|
| **1795-1796** A306 | Set of 2 | 11.00 | 11.00 |

Nos. 1794-1796 have a continuous design. Nos. 1790-1793 have a white border.

1996 Summer Olympics, Atlanta
A307 A308

Athletes: 500ce, Carl Lewis. 800ce, Eric Liddell. 900ce, Runner. 1000ce, Jim Thorpe.

No. 1801: a, Cycling. b, Archery. c, Diving. d, Swimming. e, Gymnastics-Floor Exercise. f, Fencing. g, Boxing. h, Gymnastics-Rings. i, Javelin. j, Tennis. k, Soccer. l, Equestrian.

No. 1802, 1200ce, John Akii Bua. No. 1803, 1200ce, Pierre de Cobertin.

**1995, May 2**

| | | | |
|---|---|---|---|
| **1797-1800** A307 | Set of 4 | 6.50 | 6.50 |

**1801** A308 300ce Sheet of 12, #a.-l. 7.50 7.50

**Souvenir Sheets**

**1802-1803** A308 Set of 2 5.00 5.00

UN, 50th Anniv. — A309

No. 1804 — Secretaries General: a, 200ce, Trygve Lie, Norway, 1946-52. b, 300ce, Dag Hammarskjold, Sweden, 1953-61. c, 400ce, U Thant, Burma, 1961-71. d, 500ce, Kurt Waldheim, Austria, 1972-81. e, 600ce, Javier Perez de Cuellar, Peru, 1982-91. f, 800ce, Boutros Boutros-Ghali, Egypt, 1992-.
No. 1805, UN flag, horiz.

**1995, July 6 Litho. *Perf. 14***

**1804** A309 Sheet of 6, #a.-f. 6.00 6.00

**Souvenir Sheet**

**1805** A309 1200ce multicolored 3.00 3.00

Miniature Sheets

A310

End of World War II, 50th Anniv. — A311

No. 1806 — Military decorations: a, US Navy Cross, US Purple Heart. b, UK Air Force Cross, UK Distinguished Flying Cross. c, US Navy and Marine Corps Medal, US Distinguished Service Cross. d, UK Distinguished Service Medal, UK Distinguished Conduct Medal. e, UK Military Medal, UK Military Cross. f, UK Distinguished Service Cross, UK Distinguished Service Order.
No. 1807: a, Churchill. b, Eisenhower. c, Air Chief Marshall Sir Arthur Tedder. d, Montgomery. e, Bradley. f, de Gaulle. g, French Resistance Organization. h, Patton.
No. 1808, 1200ce, U.S. Medal of Honor. No. 1809, 1200ce, Fuhrer's promise.

**1995, July 6 Litho. *Perf. 14***

**1806** A310 500ce Sheet of 6, #a.-f. + label 7.50 7.50
**1807** A311 400ce Sheet of 8, #a.-h. + label 7.50 7.50

**Souvenir Sheets**

**1808-1809** A310 Set of 2 6.50 6.50

No. 1809 contains one 42x56mm stamp.

FAO, 50th Anniv. A312

Designs: 200ce, Fish preservation. 300ce, Fishing. 400ce, Ox-drawn plow. 600ce, Harvesting. 800ce, Aforestation.
2000ce, Boat, shoreline, oxen, fruit.

**1995, July 6 Litho. *Perf. 14***

**1810-1814** A312 Set of 5 4.75 4.75

**Souvenir Sheet**

**1815** A312 2000ce multicolored 4.00 4.00

For surcharges see Nos. 2534-2538.

Rotary Intl., 90th Anniv. A313

Designs: 600ce, Natl. flag, Rotary emblem. 1200ce, Rotary emblem on banner, vert.

**1995, July 6**

**1816** A313 600ce multicolored 1.75 1.75

**Souvenir Sheet**

**1817** A313 1200ce multicolored 3.00 3.00

1995 Boy Scout Jamboree, Holland — A314

No. 1818: a, 400ce, Two boys. 800ce, Two boys, one wearing glasses. c, 1000ce, Two boys facing left.
1200ce, Boy with bamboo poles.

**1995, July 6**

**1818** A314 Strip of 3, #a.-c. 4.50 4.50

**Souvenir Sheet**

**1819** A314 1200ce multicolored 4.00 4.00

No. 1818 is a continuous design.

Queen Mother, 95th Birthday A315

No. 1820: a, Drawing. b, Bright green blue hat. c, Formal portrait. d, Coral outfit.
2500ce, Pale blue outfit.

**1995, July 6 *Perf. 13½x14***

**1820** A315 600ce Strip or block of 4, #a.-d. 5.00 5.00

**Souvenir Sheet**

**1821** A315 2500ce multicolored 4.50 4.50

No. 1820 was issued in sheets of 8 stamps.
For surcharges see Nos. 2333-2334.

Singapore '95 — A316

No. 1822, 400ce: a, Seismosaurus (d-f). b, Supersaurus (a, d). c, Ultrasaurus (f). d, Saurolophus (e). e, Lambeosaurus (d, g-h). f, Parasaurolophus (e, i). g, Triceratops (h). h, Styracosaurus (e, g i). i, Pachyrhinosaurus (h).

No. 1823, 400ce: a, Peteinosaurus (b, d-e). b, Quetzalcoatlus (a, c, e). c, Eudimorphodon (b). d, Allosaurus (e-f, h-i). e, Daspletosaurus (f). f, Tarbosaurus (i). g, Velociraptor (h-i). h, Herrerasaurus (i). i, Coelophysis.
No. 1824, 2500ce, Albertosaur. No. 1825, 2500ce, Tyrannosaurus rex.

**1995, Aug. 8 Litho. *Perf. 14***

**Sheets of 9, #a-i**

**1822-1823** A316 Set of 2 15.00 15.00

**Souvenir Sheets**

**1824-1825** A316 Set of 2 10.00 10.00

Nobel Prize Recipients — A317

No. 1826: a, Nelson Mandela, peace, 1993. b, Albert Schweitzer, peace, 1952. c, Wole Soyinka, literature, 1986. d, Emil Fischer, chemistry, 1902. e, Rudolf Mossbauer, physics, 1961. f, Archbishop Desmond Tutu, peace, 1984. g, Max Born, physics, 1954. h, Max Planck, physics, 1918. i, Hermann Hesse, literature, 1946.
1200ce, Paul Ehrlich, medicine, 1908.

**1995, Oct. 2 Litho. *Perf. 14***

**1826** A317 400ce Sheet of 9, #a.-i. 9.00 9.00

**Souvenir Sheet**

**1827** A317 1200ce multicolored 3.50 3.50

Asantehene, 25th Anniv. — A318

Designs: 50ce, Emblem. 100ce, Silver casket. 200ce, Golden stool. 400ce, Busummuru sword bearer. 600ce, 800ce, Diff. portraits of Otumfuo Opoku Ware II. 1000ce, Mponponsuo sword bearer.

**1995 *Perf. 13½x13***

**1828-1834** A318 Set of 7 6.25 6.25

A319

Fauna — A319a

Designs: 400ce, Cymothoe beckeri. 500ce, Graphium policene. 1000ce, Urotriorchis macrourus, vert. 2000ce, Xiphias gladius. 3000ce, Monodoctylus sabee. 5000ce, Ardea purpurea, vert.
400ce exists in two types:
Type I — Large flower bud under second "A" in "Ghana," the top of which is above cross line of "A" (shown in illustration).
Type II — Small flower bud under second "A" in "Ghana," the top of which is below cross line of "A."

***Perf. 14¼x13¾, 13¾x14¼***

**1995, June 19 Litho.**

| | | | | | |
|---|---|---|---|---|---|
| **1835** | A319 | 400ce multi | | .80 | .80 |
| **1835A** | A319 | 400ce multi, type II | | | — |
| **1836** | A319 | 500ce multi | | 1.00 | 1.00 |
| **1837** | A319 | 1000ce multi | | 2.00 | 2.00 |
| *a.* | | Perf. 11½ | | | |
| **1838** | A319a | 2000ce multi | | 4.25 | 4.25 |
| **1839** | A319 | 3000ce multi | | 6.00 | 6.00 |
| **1840** | A319 | 5000ce multi | | 10.00 | 10.00 |
| | | *Nos. 1835-1840 (7)* | | 24.05 | 24.05 |

No. 1838 has denomination at left. Compare with type A503. No. 1840 has green frame and "A's" of "Ghana" with cross lines sloping down to right.

Christmas A320

Details or entire paintings: 50ce, The Infant Jesus and the Young St. John, by Murillo. 80ce, Rest on Flight to Egypt, by Memling. 300ce, Sacred Family, by Van Dyck. 600ce, The Virgin and the Infant, by Uccello. 800ce, The Virgin and the Infant, by Van Eyck. 1000ce, Head of Christ, by Rembrandt.
No. 1847, 2500ce, Madonna, by Montagna. No. 1848, 2500ce, The Holy Family, by Pulzone.

**1995, Dec. 1 Litho. *Perf. 13½x14***

**1841-1846** A320 Set of 6 6.00 6.00

**Souvenir Sheets**

**1847-1848** A320 Set of 2 17.00 17.00

Motion Pictures, Cent. A321

No. 1849: a, 1903 H. Ernmann camera. b, Charles Chaplin. c, Rudolph Valentino. d, Will Rogers. e, Greta Garbo. f, Jackie Cooper. g, Bette Davis. h, John Barrymore. i, Shirley Temple.
No. 1850, Laurel and Hardy.

**1995, Dec. 8**

**1849** A321 400ce Sheet of 9, #a.-i. 10.50 10.50

**Souvenir Sheet**

**1850** A321 2500ce multi 7.00 7.00

A322

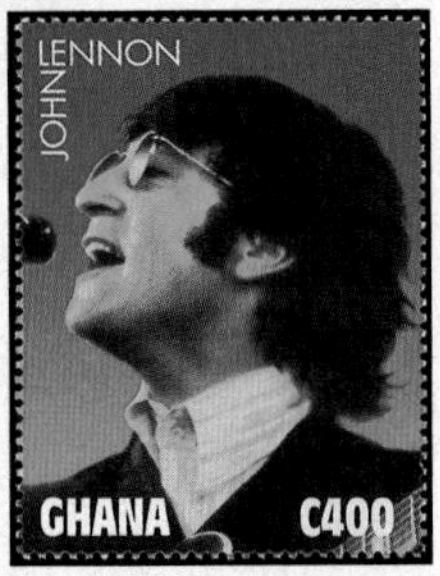


John Lennon (1940-80) A323

No. 1852: a-g, i, Various portraits. h, Like No. 1851.
2000ce, Lennon playing guitar, water in background.

**1995, Dec. 8 *Perf. 14***

**1851** A322 400ce shown 3.50 3.50

**Miniature Sheet**

***Perf. 13½x14***

**1852** A323 400ce Sheet of 9, #a.-i. 12.00 12.00

**Souvenir Sheet**

**1853** A323 2000ce multi 9.00 9.00

No. 1851 was issued in sheets of 16.

Louis Pasteur (1822-95) — A324

No. 1854: a, In laboratory. b, Discovery of rabies virus and vaccine. c, Pneumococcus discovery, 1880. d, Development of first vaccine with birds. e, Perfection of brewer's yeast culture.

**1995, Dec. 13** ***Perf. 14***

**1854** A324 600ce Sheet of 5, #a.-e. 7.25 7.25

Paintings from the Metropolitan Museum of Art — A325

No. 1855, 400ce: a, Portrait of a Man, by Van Der Goes. b, Paradise, by Giovanni di Paolo. c, Portrait of a Young Man, by Antonello da Messina. d, Tommaso Portinari, by Memling. e, Wife Maria Portinari, by Memling. f, Portrait of a Lady, by Ghirlandaio. g, St. Christopher & Infant Christ, by Ghirlandaio. h, Francesco D'Este, by van der Weyden.

No. 1856, 400ce: a, The Interrupted Sleep, by Boucher. b, Diana and Cupid, by Batoni. c, Boy Blowing Bubbles, by Chardin. d, Ancient Rome, by Pannini. e, Modern Rome, by Pannini. f, The Calmady Children, by Lawrence. g, The Triumph of Marius, by G.B. Tiepolo. h, Garden at Vaucresson, by E. Vuillard.

No. 1857, 2500ce, The Epiphany, by Giotto. No. 1858, 2500ce, The Calling of Matthew, by Hemessen.

**1996, Feb. 12 Litho.** ***Perf. 13½x14***

**Sheets of 8, #a-h, + Label**

**1855-1856** A325 Set of 2 14.00 14.00

**Souvenir Sheets**

***Perf. 14***

**1857-1858** A325 Set of 2 14.00 14.00

Nos. 1857-1858 each contain one 85x57mm stamp.

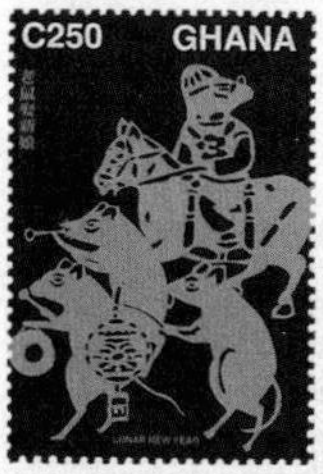


New Year 1996 (Year of the Rat) — A326

Nos. 1859-1860 — Stylized rats: a, With musical instruments, on horseback. b, Holding banners. c, Carrying rat in palanquin. d, Carrying box, holding fish.

1000ce, Four rats transporting rat in palanquin, horiz.

**1996, Jan. 28 Litho.** ***Perf. 14***

**Country Name in White**

**1859** A326 250ce Strip of 4, #a.-d. 4.50 4.50

**Country Name in Red**

**1860** A325 250ce Sheet of 4, #a.-d. 4.50 4.50

**Souvenir Sheet**

**1861** A325 1000ce red, pink & yellow 4.50 4.50

No. 1859 was issued in sheets of 12 stamps.

Fauna of the Rainforest — A327

No. 1862, 400ce: a, Ramphastos toco. b, Choloepus didactylus. c, Pongo pygmaeus. d, Spiaetus cirrhatus. e, Panthera tigris. f, Ibis leucocephallus. g, Ara chloroptera. h, Saimiri sciureus. i, Macaca fascicularis. j, Cithaerias menander, ithomiidae. k, Coryptophanes cristatus, gekkonidae. l, Boa caninus.

No. 1863, 400ce: a, Opisthoccomus hoazin. b, Tarsius bancanus. c, Leontopithecus rosalia. d, Pteropus gouldii. e, Rupicola rupicola. f, Pharomachrus mocino. g, Hyla boans, dendrobates leucomeles. h, Lemur catta. i, Iguana iguana. j, Heliconius burneyi. k, Mellisuga minima. l, Propithecus verreauxi.

No. 1864, 3000ce, Sarcoramphus papa. No. 1865, 3000ce, Pteridophora alberti.

**1996, Apr. 15**

**Sheets of 12, #a-l**

**1862-1863** A327 Set of 2 20.00 20.00

**Souvenir Sheets**

**1864-1865** A327 Set of 2 14.00 14.00

China '96 — A328

No. 1866: a, Kaiyuan Si Temple, Fujian. b, Kaiyuan Si Temple, Hebei. c, Fogong Si Temple, Shanxi. d, Xiangshan, Beijing.

No. 1867, Baima Si Temple, Henan.

**1996, May 13 Litho.** ***Perf. 14***

**1866** A328 400ce Strip of 4, #a.-d. 7.00 7.00

**Souvenir Sheet**

**1867** A328 1000ce multicolored 5.50 5.50

No. 1866 was issued in sheets of 8 stamps. See No. 1913.

Queen Elizabeth II, 70th Birthday A329

No. 1868: a, Portrait. b, Wearing blue hat, coat. c, Wearing printed dress, wide-brim hat.

2500ce, Riding in horse-drawn carriage, horiz.

**1996, June 10 Litho.** ***Perf. 13½x14***

**1868** A329 1000ce Strip of 3, #a.-c. 7.00 7.00

**Souvenir Sheet**

***Perf. 14x13½***

**1869** A329 2500ce multicolored 6.50 6.50

No. 1868 was issued in sheets of 9 stamps.

1996 Summer Olympics, Atlanta A330

Designs: 300ce, Two wrestlers, javelin thrower, Bas Relief, 500BC. 500ce, Wilma Rudolph, gold medalist in track and field, Rome, 1960, Olympic torch. 600ce, The Forum, St. Peter's Basilica, Colosseum, Olympic Stadium, Rome, 1960. 800ce, Soviet flag, ladies' kayak pairs gold medal winners, Rome, 1960.

No. 1874, 400ce — Medalists in swimming, diving: a, Aileen Riggin, springboard, 1920. b, Pat McCormick, platform, 1952. c, Dawn Fraser, 100m freestyle, 1956. d, Chris Von Saltza, 400m freestyle, 1960. e, Anita Lonsbrough, 200m breaststroke, 1960. f, Debbie Meyer, 400m freestyle, 1968. g, Shane Gould, 400m freestyle, 1972. h, Petra Thuemer, 800m freestyle, 1976. i, Marjorie Gestring, springboard, 1936.

No. 1875, 400ce, vert. — Soccer players: a, Abedi Pele, Ghana. b, Quico Navarez, Spain. c, Heino Hanson, Denmark. d, Mostafa Ismail, Egypt. e, Anthony Yeboah, Ghana. f, Jurgen Klinsmann, Germany. g, Cobi Jones, US. h, Franco Baresi, Italy. i, Igor Dobrovolski, Russia.

No. 1876, 2000ce, Kornella Ender, 200m freestyle gold medalist, 1976. No. 1877, 2000ce, Tracy Caulkins, 200m individual medlay gold medalist, 1984.

**1996, June 27** ***Perf. 14***

**1870-1873** A330 Set of 4 4.50 4.50

**Sheets of 9, #a-i**

**1874-1875** A330 Set of 2 17.00 17.00

**Souvenir Sheets**

**1876-1877** A330 Set of 2 11.00 11.00

Intl. Amateur Boxing Assoc., 50th Anniv. — A331

Boxers: 300ce, Serafim Todorow, Bulgaria. 400ce, Oscar de La Hoya, US. 800ce, Ariel Hernandez, Cuba. 1500ce, Arnaldo Mesa, Cuba.

3000ce, Tadahiro Sasaki, Japan.

**1996, July 31**

**1878-1881** A331 Set of 4 6.50 6.50

**Souvenir Sheet**

**1882** A331 3000ce multicolored 6.50 6.50

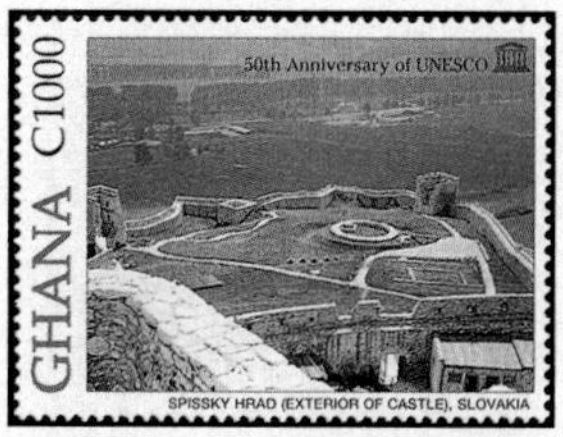


UNESCO, 50th Anniv. — A332

Designs: 400ce, The Citadel, Haiti, vert. 800ce, Ait-Ben-Haddou (Fortified Village), Morocco, vert. 1000ce, Spissky Hrad (exterior of castle), Slovakia.

2000ce, Cape Coast, Ghana.

**1996, July 31 Litho.** ***Perf. 14***

**1883-1885** A332 Set of 3 6.50 6.50

**Souvenir Sheet**

**1886** A332 2000ce multicolored 6.00 6.00

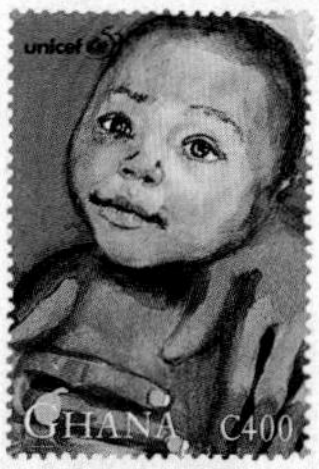


UNICEF, 50th Anniv. — A333

Designs: 400ce, Baby. 500ce, Mother, baby. 600ce, Mother, child drinking from glass.

1000ce, Child, diff.

**1996, July 31**

**1887-1889** A333 Set of 3 3.00 3.00

**Souvenir Sheet**

**1890** A333 1000ce multicolored 2.50 2.50

Jerusalem, 3000th Anniv. — A334

Landmark, flower: 400ce, St. Stephen's (Lion) Gate, Jasminum mesnyi. 600ce, Citadel and Tower of David, nerium oleander. 800ce, Chapel of the Ascension, romulea bulbocodium.

2000ce, Russian Church of St. Mary Magdalene.

**1996, July 31**

**1891-1893** A334 Set of 3 4.50 4.50

**Souvenir Sheet**

**1894** A334 2000ce multicolored 6.00 6.00

For overprints see Nos. 2032-2035.

Musical Instruments A335

No. 1895: a, Fiddles. b, Proverbial drum. c, Double clapless bell & castanet. d, Gourd rattle. e, Horns.

**1996, Aug. 5**

**1895** A335 500ce Sheet of 5, #a.-e. 5.00 5.00

Disney's Best Friends — A336

No. 1896, 60ce, Ariel, Flounder, Sebastian. No. 1897, 60ce, Pinocchio, Jiminy Cricket. No. 1898, 60ce, Cogsworth, Lumiere. No. 1899, 60ce, Copper, Tod. No. 1900, 60ce, Pocahontas, Meeko, Flit. No. 1901, 60ce, Bambi, Flower, Thumper.

No. 1902: a, 450ce, Pocahontas, Meeko, Flit. b, 150ce, Pinocchio, Jiminy Cricket. c, 200ce, Copper, Tod. d, 600ce, Aladdin, Abu. e, 700ce, Penny, Rufus. f, 350ce, Cogsworth, Lumiere. g, 800ce, Mowgli, Baloo. h, 200ce, Ariel, Flounder, Sebastian, i, 300ce, Bambi, Flower, Thumper.

No. 1903, Winnie the Pooh, vert. No. 1904, Simba, Pumbaa.

***Perf. 14x13½, 13½x14***

**1996, Aug. 25**

**1896-1901** A336 Set of 6 2.75 2.75

**1902** A336 Sheet of 9, #a.-i. 8.50 8.50

**Souvenir Sheets**

**1903** A336 3000ce multicolored 4.75 4.75
**1904** A336 3000ce multicolored 4.75 4.75

Stampshow '96 (No. 1902).

E.W. Agyare (1937-72), Ghana Broadcasting Corp. Technician — A337

**1996, July 31** ***Perf. 14***
**1905** A337 100ce multicolored .50 .50

Radio, Cent. A338

Entertainers: 500ce, Frank Sinatra. No. 1907, 600ce, Judy Garland. No. 1908, 600ce, Bing Crosby. 800ce, Dean Martin, Jerry Lewis. 2000ce, Edgar Bergen, Charlie McCarthy.

**1996, July 31** ***Perf. 13½x14***
**1906-1909** A338 Set of 4 3.25 3.25

**Souvenir Sheet**

**1910** A338 2000ce multicolored 3.25 3.25

Sylvester Stallone in Movie, "Rocky II" — A339

**1996, Nov. 21** **Litho.** ***Perf. 14***
**1911** A339 2000ce multi 2.40 2.40

Issued in sheets of 3.

New Year 1997 (Year of the Ox) — A340

Various scenes from Chinese story, "Herd Boy and Girl Weaver."

**1997, Jan. 22** **Litho.** ***Perf. 14***
**1912** A340 500ce Sheet of 9, #a.-i. 7.00 7.00

Souvenir Sheet

China '96 — A341

Statue of the Devil.

**1996, May 13** **Litho.** ***Perf. 14***
**1913** A341 1000ce multicolored 3.25 3.25

No. 1913 was not available until March 1997.

African Hair Styles — A342

No. 1914, 1000ce: a, Dipo. b, Oduku. c, Dansinkran. d, Mbobom. e, Oduku 2.

No. 1915, 1000ce: a, African corn row. b, Chinese raster. c, Chinese raster 2. d, Corn row. e, Mbakaa.

**1997, Mar. 3**

**Sheets of 5, #a-e**

**1914-1915** A342 Set of 2 9.00 9.00

Dr. Hideyo Noguchi (1876-1928), Pathologist A343

No. 1916: a, Tomb. b, Portrait. c, Birth place. d, Noguchi Institute, Legon. e, Noguchi Gardens, Accra.

No. 1917, 3000ce, Dr. Noguchi in laboratory. No. 1918, 3000ce, Statue.

**1997, Mar. 3**
**1916** A343 1000ce Sheet of 5, #a.-e. 7.00 7.00

**Souvenir Sheets**

**1917-1918** A343 Set of 2 7.00 7.00

Independence, 40th Anniv. — A344

Designs: 200ce, Emblem. 550ce, Dr. Kwame Nkrumah, first president of Ghana, vert. 800ce, Achievement in education. 1100ce, Akosombo Dam.

2000ce, Declaration of independence, Old Polo Grounds, vert. 3000ce, Kofi Annan, UN Secretary General, vert.

**1997, Mar. 6** **Litho.** ***Perf. 14***
**1919-1922** A344 Set of 4 7.25 7.25

**Souvenir Sheets**

**1923** A344 2000ce multicolored 2.75 2.75
**1924** A344 3000ce multicolored 4.50 4.50

Deng Xiaoping (1904-97), Chinese Leader — A345

No. 1925: a, 300ce, Smiling. b, 600ce, Wearing glasses. c, 800ce, Like #1925b. d, 1000ce, Like #1925a.

No. 1926: a, 500ce, Lips pursed. b, 600ce, Teeth showing. c, 800ce, Like #1926b. d, 1000ce, Like #1926a.

No. 1927, Reading. No. 1928, Hand in air.

**1997, Apr. 28** ***Perf. 14x13½***
**1925** A345 Sheet of 4, #a.-d. 3.50 3.50
**1926** A345 Sheet of 4, #a.-d. 3.50 3.50

**Souvenir Sheets**

***Perf. 13½***

**1927** A345 3000ce multicolored 3.50 3.50
**1928** A345 4000ce multicolored 4.00 4.00

Nos. 1927-1928 each contain one 51x38mm stamp.

Paintings by Hiroshige (1797-1858) A346

No. 1929: a, Nihonbashi Bridge and Edobashi Bridge. b, View of Nihonbashi Tori 1-chome. c, Open Garden at Fukagawa Hachiman Shrine. d, Inari Bridge and Minato Shrine, Teppozu. e, Bamboo Yards, Kyobashi Bridge. f, Hall of Thirty-Three Bays, Fukagawa.

No. 1930, 3000ce, Teppozu and Tsukiji Honganji Temple. No. 1931, 3000ce, Sumiyoshi Festival, Tsukudajima.

**1997, May 29** **Litho.** ***Perf. 13½x14***
**1929** A346 600ce Sheet of 6, #a.-f. 5.00 5.00

**Souvenir Sheets**

**1930-1931** A346 Set of 2 7.00 7.00

Queen Elizabeth II, Prince Philip, 50th Wedding Anniv. A347

No. 1932: a, Queen. b, Royal Arms. c, Queen, Prince waving. d, Queen, Prince. e, Royal carriage. f, Portrait of Prince Philip.

3000ce, Portrait of Queen Elizabeth II.

**1997, May 29** ***Perf. 14***
**1932** A347 800ce Sheet of 6, #a.-f. 5.50 5.50

**Souvenir Sheet**

**1933** A347 3000ce multicolored 2.00 2.00

Heinrich von Stephan (1831-97), Founder of UPU A348

No. 1934 — Portrait of Von Stephan and: a, Automobile used for postal delivery. b, UPU emblem. c, First airmail flight, Pierre Blanchard, 1784.

3000ce, African messenger with cleft stick.

**1997, May 29** **Litho.** ***Perf. 14***
**1934** A348 1000ce Sheet of 3, #a.-c. 3.50 3.50

**Souvenir Sheet**

**1935** A348 3000ce multicolored 3.50 3.50

PACIFIC 97.

Paul P. Harris (1868-1947), Founder of Rotary Intl. — A349

Portrait of Harris, Rotary emblem and: 2000ce, PolioPlus oral vaccine administration, Egypt. 3000ce, Emblem for PolioPlus vaccine, "A world free of disease."

**1997, May 29**
**1936** A349 2000ce multicolored 3.25 3.25

**Souvenir Sheet**

**1937** A349 3000ce multicolored 3.25 3.25

Chernobyl, 10th Anniv. A350

Designs: 800ce, UNESCO. 1000ce, Chabad's Children of Chernobyl.

**1997, May 29** ***Perf. 13½x14***
**1938** A350 800ce multicolored 2.25 2.25
**1939** A350 1000ce multicolored 2.50 2.50

Ajumpan Drums — A350a

Cyrestes Camillus — A350b

Kente Cloth — A350c

***Perf. 13½x14¼, 14¼x13½***

**1997** **Litho.**
**1939A** A350a 550ce multi — —
**1939B** A350b 800ce multi — —
**1939C** A350c 1100ce multi — —

Issued: 550ce, 5/30; 800ce, 6/4. 1100ce, 6/7.

For surcharges see Nos. 2360, 2360A, 2675.

A351

Entertainers — A352

No. 1940: a, Jackie Gleason. b, Danny Kaye. c, John Cleese. d, Lucille Ball. e, Jerry Lewis. f, Sidney James. g, Louis de Fuenes. h, Mae West. i, Bob Hope.

No. 1941: a, Professor Ajax Bukana with fingers making "V." b, Bukana with arms spread.

3000ce, Groucho Marx.

**1997, July 1** ***Perf. 13½x14***

**1940** A351 600ce Sheet of 9, #a.-i. 7.00 7.00

**Souvenir Sheets**

***Perf. 14***

**1941** A352 2000ce Sheet of 2, #a-b 3.25 3.25

***Perf. 13½x14***

**1942** A351 3000ce multicolored 2.25 2.25

Mushrooms A353

Designs: 200ce, Galerina calyptrata. 300ce, Lepiota ignivolvata. 400ce, Omphalotus olearius. 550ce, Amanita phalloides. 600ce, Entoloma conferendum. 800ce, Entoloma nitidum.

No. 1949: a, Coprinus picaceus. b, Stropharia aurantiaca. c, Cortinarius splendens. d, Gomphidius roseus. e, Russula sardonia. f, Geastrum schmidelia.

No. 1950, 3000ce, Mycena crocata. No. 1951, 3000ce, Craterellus cornucopioides.

**1997, July 9** ***Perf. 14***

**1943-1948** A353 Set of 6 3.50 3.50

**1949** A353 800ce Sheet of 6, #a.-f. 5.50 5.50

**Souvenir Sheets**

**1950-1951** A353 Set of 2 6.50 6.50

Fish A354

Seabirds, Marine Life A355

Designs: 400ce, African pygmy angelfish. 600ce, Angelfish. 800ce, Broomtail wrasse. 1000ce, Indian butterfly fish.

No. 1956: a, Violet crested turaco. b, Pied avocet. c, Bottle-nosed dolphin. d, Bottle-nosed dolphin, long-toed lapwing. e, Longfined spadefish (i). f, Imperial angelfish, manta ray. g, Raccoon butterfly fish, African pompano (h, k). h, Silvertip shark (g, l). i, Longfin banner fish (e, j). j, Longfin banner fish, manta ray (f, i). k, Rusty parrot fish (j). l, Coral trout.

No. 1957, 3000ce, Crown butterfly fish. No. 1958, 3000ce, King angelfish.

**1997, July 15**

**1952-1955** A354 Set of 4 3.50 3.50

**1956** A355 500ce Sheet of 12, #a.-l. 7.00 7.00

**Souvenir Sheets**

**1957-1958** A355 Set of 2 8.00 8.00

Flowers A356

Designs: 200ce, Eurychone rothschildiana. 550ce, Bulbophyllum lepidum. No. 1961, 800ce, Ansellia africana. 1100ce, Combretum grandiflorum.

No. 1963, vert: a, Strophanthus preusii. b, Ancistrochilus rothchildianus. c, Mussaendra arcuata. d, Microcoelia guyoniana. e, Gloriosa simplex. f, Brachycorythis kalbreyeri. g, Aframomum sceptrum. h, Thunbergia alata. i, Clerodendrum thomsoniae.

No. 1964, 3000ce, Kigelia africana. No. 1965, 3000ce, Spathodea campanulata.

**1997, Aug. 1** **Litho.** ***Perf. 14½***

**1959-1962** A356 Set of 4 3.75 3.75

**1963** A356 800ce Sheet of 9, #a.-i. 9.50 9.50

**Souvenir Sheets**

**1964-1965** A356 Set of 2 7.50 7.50

1998 World Cup Soccer Championships, France — A357

Stadiums: 200ce, Azteca, Mexico, 1970, 1986. 300ce, Rose Bowl, US, 1994. 400ce, Giuseppe Meazza, Italy, 1990. 500ce, Olympic, Germany, 1974. 1000ce, Maracana, Brazil, 1950. 2000ce, Bernabeu, Spain, 1982.

No. 1972 — Soccer players: a, Patrick Kluivert, Holland. b, Roy Deane, Ireland. c, Abedi Pele Ayew, Ghana. d, Peter Schmeichel, Denmark. e, Roberto di Matteo, Italy. f, Bebeto, Brazil. g, Steve McManaman, England. h, George Appong Weah, Liberia.

No. 1973, 3000ce, Juninho, Brazil. No. 1974, 3000ce, Seaman, England.

**1997, July 12** ***Perf. 14x13½***

**1966-1971** A357 Set of 6 4.50 4.50

**1972** A357 600ce Sheet of 8, #a.-h. + label 4.50 4.50

**Souvenir Sheets**

**1973-1974** A357 Set of 2 7.00 7.00

Nos. 1966-1971 were issued in sheets of 10 each.

Birds — A358

Designs: 200ce, Eurasian goldfinch. 300ce, Cape batis. 400ce, Bearded barbet. 500ce, White-necked raven. 600ce, Purple grenadier. 1000ce, Zebra waxbill.

No. 1981: a, Black bustard. b, Northern lapwing. c, Sandgrouse. d, Red-crested turaco. e, White-browed coucal. f, Lilac-breasted roller. g, Golden pipet. h, Crimson-breasted gonolek. i, Blackcap.

No. 1982, 3000ce, Nectarina famosa. No. 1983, 3000ce, Vidua regia.

**1997, Oct. 20** **Litho.** ***Perf. 14***

**1975-1980** A358 Set of 6 3.50 3.50

**1981** A358 800ce Sheet of 9, #a.-i. 8.00 8.00

**Souvenir Sheets**

**1982-1983** A358 Set of 2 7.50 7.50

Cats and Dogs A359

Cats, #1984-1989: 20ce, Havana. 50ce, Singapura. 100ce, Sphinx. 150ce, British white. 300ce, Snowshoe. 600ce, Persian.

Dogs, #1989A-1989F: 80ce, Papillon. 200ce, Bulldog. 400ce, Shetland sheepdog. 500ce, Schnauzer. 800ce, Shih tzu. 2000ce, Chow chow.

No. 1990, 1000ce — Dogs and cats: a, Russian wolfhound. b, Birman. c, Basset hound. d, Silver tabby. e, Afghan. f, Burmilla.

No. 1991, 1000ce: a, Abyssinian. b, Border terrier. c, Scottish fold. d, Boston terrier. e, Oriental. f, Keeshond.

No. 1992, 3000ce, Ragdoll. No. 1992A, 3000ce, Alaskan malamute.

**1997, Oct. 20**

**1984-1989** A359 Set of 6 2.75 2.75

**1989A-1989F** A359 Set of 6 8.00 8.00

**Sheets of 6, #a-f**

**1990-1991** A359 Set of 2 17.50 17.50

**Souvenir Sheets**

**1992-1992A** A359 Set of 2 8.00 8.00

Return of Hong Kong to China — A360

No. 1993: a, Lin Tsi-Hsu (1785-1850). b, Gwan Tian-Pei.

**1997, Nov. 10**

**1993** A360 1000ce Sheet of 4, 2 each #a.-b. 7.00 7.00

Huang Binhong (1865-1955) — A361

No. 1994 — Various details of "Color Landscape": a, 200ce. b, 300ce. c, 400ce. d, 500ce. e, 600ce. f, 800ce. g, 1000ce. h, 2000ce.

No. 1995: a, Detail with Chinese inscription. b, Detail without inscription.

**1997, Nov. 10**

**1994** A361 Sheet of 8, #a.-h. 7.00 7.00

**Souvenir Sheet**

**1995** A361 2000ce Sheet of 2, #a.-b. 5.50 5.50

Nos. 1994a-1994h are each 28x90mm.

Christmas A362

Entire paintings or details: 200ce, Cupid by Botticelli. 550ce, Zephyr and Chloris, by Botticelli. 800ce, Trumphant Cupid, by Caravaggio. 1100ce, The Seven Works of Mercy, by Caravaggio. 1500ce, The Toilet of Venus, by Diego Velazquez. 2000ce, Freeing of Saint Peter, by Raphael.

Sculptures: No. 2002, 5000ce, The Cavalcant Annunciation, by Donatello. No. 2003, 5000ce, Isis and Nepthys Protecting the Cartouches of Tutankhamen with their Wings.

**1997, Dec. 8** **Litho.** ***Perf. 14***

**1996-2001** A362 Set of 6 6.25 6.25

**Souvenir Sheets**

**2002-2003** A362 Set of 2 9.00 9.00

Diana, Princess of Wales (1961-97) — A363

Various portraits, background color of sheet margin: No. 2004, 1200ce, Pink. No. 2005, 1200ce, Blue.

Portraits with (in margin): No. 2006, 3000ce, Elizabeth Taylor. No. 2007, 3000ce, Henry Kissinger.

**1997, Dec. 22**

**Sheets of 6, #a-f**

**2004-2005** A363 Set of 2 11.00 11.00

**Souvenir Sheets**

**2006-2007** A363 Set of 2 7.00 7.00

Mickey and Friends A364

No. 2008, 1000ce — Characters, month: a, Mortie and Ferdie, Jan. b, Minnie, Feb. c, Goofy, Mar. d, Mickey, Minnie, & Pluto, Apr. e, Minnie, May. f, Daisy, June.

No. 2009, 1000ce: a, Donald, July. b, Donald and Daisy, Aug. c, Morty and Ferdie, Sept. d, Huey, Dewey, & Louie, Oct. e, Mickey, Nov. f, Mickey & Minnie, Dec.

Characters, season: No. 2010, 5000ce, Daisy, nephews, winter, horiz. No. 2011, 5000ce, Goofy, fall. No. 2012, 5000ce, Mickey, spring, horiz. No. 2013, 5000ce, Minnie, summer.

***Perf. 13½x14, 14x13½***

**1998, Jan. 29** **Litho.**

**Sheets of 6, #a-f**

**2008-2009** A364 Set of 2 16.00 16.00

**Sheets of 6 With Added Marginal Inscription**

*2008g-2009g* Set of 2 27.50 27.50

**Souvenir Sheets**

**2010-2013** A364 Set of 4 28.00 28.00

### Souvenir Sheets With Added Marginal Inscriptions

*2012a-2013a* Set of 2 57.50 57.50

Nos. 2008g, 2009g, 2012a, 2013a have added inscription in sheet margin showing "Happy Birthday," Mickey Mouse, and "1998" in emblem.

Issued: Nos. 2008g, 2009g, 2012a, 2013a, 8/4/98.

Trains A365

Designs: 300ce, Union Pacific SD60M, US. 500ce, ETR 450, Italy. No. 2018, 800ce, X200 Sweden. 1000ce, TGV Duplex, France. 2000ce, El Class Co-Co, Australia. 3000ce, Eurostar, Britain.

No. 2020, 800ce: a, SPS 4-4-0, Pakistan. b, Class WP 4-6-2, India. c, Class QI 2-10-2, China. d, Class 12 4-4-2, Belgium. e, Class P8 4-6-0, Germany. f, Castle Class 4-6-0, Britain. g, Tank engine 2-6-0, Austria. h, Class P36 4-8-4, Russia. i, William Mason 4-4-0, US.

No. 2021, 800ce: a, AVE, Spain. b, Class 1600, Luxembourg. c, Bullet train, Japan. d, GM F7 Warbonnet, US. e, Class E1500, Morocco. f, Deltic, Great Britain. g, XPT, Australia. h, Le Shuttle, France/Britain. i, Class 201, Ireland.

No. 2022, 5500ce, Duchess Class 4-6-2, Britain. No. 2023, 5500ce, TGV, France.

**1998, Feb. 26 Litho. *Perf. 14***

**2014-2019** A365 Set of 6 7.50 7.50

**Sheets of 9, #a-i**

**2020-2021** A365 Set of 2 13.50 13.50

**Souvenir Sheets**

**2022-2023** A365 Set of 2 10.00 10.00

Nos. 2022-2023 each contain one 57x42mm stamp.

Lunar New Year — A366

No. 2025 — Signs of Chinese zodiac: a, Horse. b, Monkey. c, Ram. d, Rooster. e, Dog. f, Ox. g, Rabbit. h, Boar. i, Snake. j, Dragon. k, Tiger. l, Rat.

**1998 Litho. *Perf. 13½***

**2025** A366 400ce Sheet of 12, #a.-l. 6.00 6.00

Numbers have been reserved for additional values in this set.

Great Black Writers of the 20th Century — A368

No. 2027: a, Maya Angelou. b, Alex Haley. c, Charles Johnson. d, Richard Wright. e, Toni Cade Bambara. f, Henry Louis Gates, Jr.

**1998, Mar. 25 Litho. *Perf. 14***

**2027** A368 350ce Sheet of 6, #a.-f. 5.00 5.00

Aircraft A369

No. 2028, 800ce: a, Messerschmitt Bf 109 E-7. b, Lockheed PV-2 Harpoon. c, Airspeed Oxford MK1. d, Junkers Ju87D-1. e, Yakovlev Yak-9D. f, North American P-51D Mustang. g, Douglas A-20 Havoc. h, Supermarine Attacker F1. i, Mikoyan-Gurevich MIG-15.

No. 2029, 800ce: a, Breguet 14 B2. b, Curtiss BF2C-1 Goshawk. c, Supermarine Spitfire MK IX. d, Fiat G.50. e, Douglas B-18A. f, Boeing FB-5. g, Bristol F.2B. h, Hawker Fury 1. i, Fiat CR42.

No. 2030, 3000ce, Mitsubishi AGM8 Reisen. No. 2031, 3000ce, Supermarine Spitfire MK XIV, Supermarine Spitfire MK 1.

**1998, May 5 Sheets of 9, #a-i**

**2028-2029** A369 Set of 2 14.00 14.00

**Souvenir Sheets**

**2030-2031** A369 Set of 2 6.00 6.00

#2030-2031 each contain one 57x42mm stamp.

Nos. 1891-1894 Overprinted

**1998, May 13**

**2032** A334 400ce multi .90 .90
**2033** A334 600ce multi 1.10 1.10
**2034** A334 800ce multi 1.50 1.50

**Souvenir Sheet**

**2035** A334 2000ce multi 4.50 4.50

No. 2035 contains additional inscription in sheet margin: "ISRAEL 98 — WORLD STAMP EXHIBITION / TEL-AVIV 13-21 MAY 1998." No. 2034 exists with an inverted surcharge.

Ships A370

No. 2036, 800ce — Ocean liners: a, Empress of Ireland. b, Transylvania. c, Mauritania. d, Reliance. e, Aquitania. f, Lapland. g, Cap Polonio. h, France. i, Imperator.

No. 2037, 800ce — Warships: a, HMS Rodney. b, USS Alabama. c, HMS Nelson. d, SS Ormonde. e, USS Radford. f, SS Empress of Russia. g, Type XIV, Germany. h, Type A Midget, Japan. i, Brin, Italy.

No. 2038, 5500ce, Titanic. No. 2039, 5500ce, Amistad.

**1998, May 5 Litho. *Perf. 14***

**Sheets of 9, #a-i**

**2036-2037** A370 Set of 2 14.00 14.00

**Souvenir Sheets**

**2038-2039** A370 Set of 2 9.75 9.75

#2038-2039 each contain one 42x56mm stamp.

Orchids — A371

No. 2040, 800ce: a, Renanthera imschootiana. b, Arachnis flosaeris. c, Restrepia lansbergi. d, Paphiopedilum tonsum. e, Phalaenopsis ebauche. f, Pleione limprichti.

No. 2041, 800ce: a, Phragmipedium schroderae. b, Zygopetalum clayii. c, Vanda coerulea. d, Odontonia boussole. e, Disa uniflora. f, Dendrobium bigibbum.

No. 2042, 5500ce, Cypripedium calceolus. No. 2043, 5500ce, Sobralia candida.

**1998, June 2 Sheets of 6, #a-f**

**2040-2041** A371 Set of 2 11.00 11.00

**Souvenir Sheets**

**2042-2043** A371 Set of 2 12.00 12.00

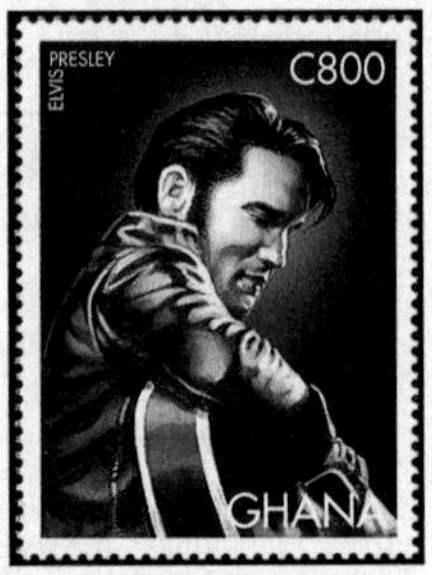


Elvis Presley (1935-77), Television Comeback Special, 30th Anniv. A372

Various portraits during performance.

**1998, June 16 Litho. *Perf. 13½***

**2044** A372 800ce Sheet of 6, #a.-f. 5.25 5.25

Japanese Flowers — A373

No. 2045, 2000ce — Predominant color of flowers, location of denomination : a, Green (bamboo), UR. b, Red, LR. c, Yellow, LR. d, Pale green & pink, UR.

No. 2046, 2000ce: a, Pale green, yellow & pink, LR. b, Red, UR. c, Pink, LR. d, White, LR.

No. 2047, 5500ce, Small pink & yellow, LR. No. 2048, 5500ce, Pink, UL.

**1998, June 2 Litho. *Perf. 14***

**Sheets of 4, #a-d**

**2045-2046** A373 Set of 2 13.50 13.50

**Souvenir Sheets**

**2047-2048** A373 Set of 2 11.00 11.00

Ghana Cocoa Board, 50th Anniv. A374

Designs: 200ce, Tetteh Quarshie, pioneer of Ghana Cocoa industry. 550ce, Ripe hybrid cocoa pods. 800ce, Opening of cocoa pods. 1100ce, Fermenting cocoa beans. 1500ce, Shipment of cocoa.

**1998, July 8 *Perf. 13x13½***

**2049-2053** A374 Set of 5 5.00 5.00

Metropolitan Assembly, Cent. — A375

Designs: 200ce, AMA Centennial emblem. 550ce, King Tackie Tawiah I (1862-1902). 800ce, Achimota School, Accra. 1100ce, Korle Bu Hospital, Accra. 1500ce, Christianborg Castle, Accra.

**1998, July 8**

**2054-2058** A375 Set of 5 4.50 4.50

Intl. Year of the Ocean A376

No. 2059: a, Dolphins. b, Dolphin (f). c, Seagull. d, Least tern, seagulls. e, Emperor angelfish (i). f, White ear. g, Blue shark, diver (k). h, Parrotfish. i, Dottyback. j, Blue-spotted stingray (m, n). k, Masked butterfly fish. l, Jack knife fish (h). m, Octopus (i). n, Turkeyfish (lionfish) (j, k, o). o, Seadragon. p, Rock cod.

No. 2060, 3000ce, Devil ray. No. 2061, 3000ce, Great white shark.

**1998, Aug. 18 *Perf. 14***

**2059** A376 500ce Sheet of 16, #a.-p. 17.50 17.50

**Souvenir Sheets**

**2060-2061** A376 Set of 2 14.50 14.50

Inventors and Inventions — A377

No. 2062, 1000ce: a, Edison, light bulb. b, Peephole kinetoscope, Edison. c, Tesla coil, Tesla. d, Nikola Tesla (1856-1943). e, Gottlieb Wilhelm Daimler (1834-1900). f, Motorcycle, Daimler. g, Transmitter circuit for telescope, Marconi. h, Guglielmo Marconi.

#2063, 1000ce: a, Orville & Wright. b, 1st Flyer, Wright Brothers. c, Neon lighting and signs, Claude. d, Georges Claude (1870-1960). e, Alexander Graham Bell. f, The telephone, transmitter, Bell. g, Various uses of lasers, Townes. h, Charles Townes (b. 1915).

No. 2064, 5500ce, Robert Goddard (1882-1945), physicist. No. 2065, 5500ce, Paul Ehrlich (1854-1915), chemist, bacteriologist.

**1998, Sept. 1 *Perf. 14***

**Sheets of 8, #a-h**

**2062-2063** A377 Set of 2 15.00 15.00

**Souenir Sheets**

**2064-2065** A377 Set of 2 10.00 10.00

Nos. 2062b-2062c, 2062f-2062g, 2063b-2063c, 2063f-2063g are each 53x38mm.

Christmas — A378

Cats and dogs in Christmas scenes: 500ce, British colorpoint. 600ce, American shorthair-Dilute calico. 800ce, Peke-faced Persian. 1000ce, Small German spitz. 2000ce, British shorthair blue. 3000ce, Persian Dilute calico.

No. 2072, 5500ce, English pointer. No. 2073, 5500ce, Rumpy max.

**1998, Dec. 1 Litho. *Perf. 14***

**2066-2071** A378 Set of 6 10.00 10.00

**Souvenir Sheets**

**2072-2073** A378 Set of 2 13.00 13.00

Ferrari Automobiles — A378a

No. 2073A: c, Lampredi. d, 250 GT Cabriolet. e, 121 LM.
3000ce, 365 GTS/4 Spyder.

**1998, Dec. 24 Litho. *Perf. 14***

| | | | | | |
|---|---|---|---|---|---|
| **2073A** | A378a | 2000ce Sheet of 3, #c-e | | 5.00 | 5.00 |

**Souvenir Sheet**

***Perf. 13¾x14¼***

| | | | | |
|---|---|---|---|---|
| **2073B** | A378a | 3000ce multi | 4.00 | 4.00 |

No. 2073A contains three 39x25mm stamps.

Diana, Princess of Wales (1961-97) — A379

**1998, Dec. 24 Litho. *Perf. 14½***

| | | | | |
|---|---|---|---|---|
| **2074** | A379 | 1000ce multicolored | 1.75 | 1.75 |

No. 2074 was issued in sheets of 6.

Gandhi — A380

No. 2075: a, After 8 month prison term in Poona, 1931. b, On Salt March, 1930. c, Picking up natural salt at end of Salt March, 1930. d, After graduating from high school in Rajkot, 1887.
5500ce, At age 61, 1931.

**1998, Dec. 24**

| | | | | |
|---|---|---|---|---|
| **2075** | A380 | 2000ce Sheet of 4, #a.-d. | 10.00 | 10.00 |

**Souvenir Sheet**

| | | | | |
|---|---|---|---|---|
| **2076** | A380 | 5500ce multi | 9.00 | 9.00 |

Nos. 2075b-2075c are each 53x38mm.

Pablo Picasso A381

Designs: No. 2077, 1000ce, Collage, Composition with Butterfly, 1932. No. 2078, 1000ce, Sculpture, Mandolin and Clarinet, 1913, vert. 2000ce, Painting, Ballplayers on the Beach, 1931.
5500ce, Tomato Plant, 1944, vert.

**1998, Dec. 24 *Perf. 14x14½***

| | | | | |
|---|---|---|---|---|
| **2077-2079** | A381 | Set of 3 | 3.75 | 3.75 |

**Souenir Sheet**

| | | | | |
|---|---|---|---|---|
| **2080** | A381 | 5500ce multicolored | 5.25 | 5.25 |

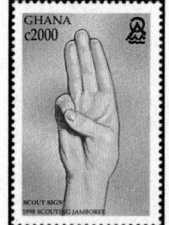


19th World Scouting Jamboree, Chile — A382

No. 2081: a, Scout sign. b, Camping. c, Tying a bowline.
5000ce, Robert Baden-Powell.

**1998, Dec. 24 *Perf. 14***

| | | | | |
|---|---|---|---|---|
| **2081** | A382 | 2000ce Sheet of 3, #a.-c. | 5.50 | 5.50 |

**Souvenir Sheet**

| | | | | |
|---|---|---|---|---|
| **2082** | A382 | 5000ce multicolored | 4.75 | 4.75 |

Royal Air Force, 80th Anniv. A383

No. 2083: a, C130 Hercules. b, Chinook HC2. c, C130 Hercules W2. d, Panavia Tornado F3ADV.
No. 2084, 5500ce, Eurofighter 2000, Chipmunk. No. 2085, 5500ce, Hawk's head, biplane.

**1998, Dec. 24**

| | | | | |
|---|---|---|---|---|
| **2083** | A383 | 2000ce Sheet of 4, #a.-d. | 7.25 | 7.25 |

**Souvenir Sheets**

| | | | | |
|---|---|---|---|---|
| **2084-2085** | A383 | Set of 2 | 10.00 | 10.00 |

New Year 1999 (Year of the Rabbit) A384

No. 2086 — Scenes showing farmer from "Farmer and Rabbit," by Han Fei Tzu: a, Working in field. b, Watching rabbit run into tree. c, Holding rabbit. d, Dreaming of rabbit.

**1999, Jan. 4**

| | | | | |
|---|---|---|---|---|
| **2086** | A384 | 1400ce Sheet of 4, #a.-d. | 5.50 | 5.50 |

Dinosaurs A385

Designs: 400ce, Corythosaurus. 600ce, Struthiomimus. 1000ce, Lambeosaurus. No. 2089A, 2000ce, Hesperosuchus.
No. 2090, 800ce: a, Ankylosaurus. b, Anatosaurus. c, Diplodocus. d, Monoclonius. e, Tyrannosaurus. f, Camptosaurus. g, Ornitholestes. h, Archaeopteryx. i, Allosaurus.
No. 2091, 800ce: a, Pterodactylus. b, Scelidosaurus. c, Pteranodon. d, Plateosaurus. e, Ornithosuchus. f, Kentrosaurus. g, Hypsognathus. h, Erythrosuchus. i, Stegoceros.
No. 2092, 5000ce, Dimorphodon, vert. No. 2093, 5000ce, Apatosaurus.

**1999, Mar. 1 Litho. *Perf. 13½***

| | | | | |
|---|---|---|---|---|
| **2087-2089A** | A385 | Set of 4 | 4.00 | 4.00 |

**Sheets of 9, #a-i**

| | | | | |
|---|---|---|---|---|
| **2090-2091** | A385 | 800ce Set of 2 | 14.00 | 14.00 |

**Souvenir Sheets**

| | | | | |
|---|---|---|---|---|
| **2092-2093** | A385 | 5000ce Set of 2 | 9.00 | 9.00 |

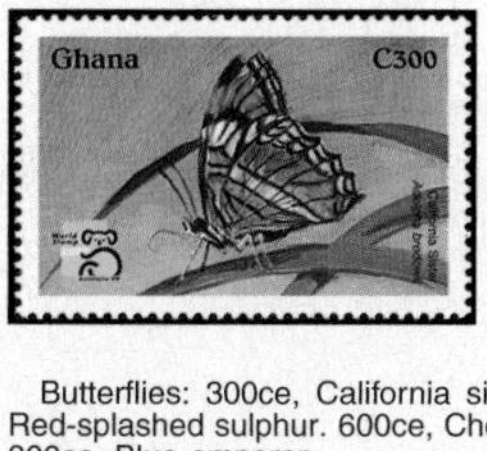


Australia '99, World Stamp Expo A386

Butterflies: 300ce, California sister. 500ce, Red-splashed sulphur. 600ce, Checked white. 800ce, Blue emperor.
No. 2098, 1000ce, vert: a, Red admiral. b, Buckeye. c, Desert checkered skipper. d, Orange sulphur. e, Tiger swallowtail. f, Orange-bordered blue. g, Agraulis vanillae. h, Monarch.
No. 2099, 1000ce, vert: a, Small tortoiseshell. b, Brimstone. c, Camberwell beauty. d, Marbled white. e, Purple emperor. f, Clouded yellow. g, Ladoga camilla. h, Marsh fritillary.
No. 2100, 5000ce, Papilio homerus, vert. No. 2101, 5000ce, Blue copper.

**1999, Apr. 26 Litho. *Perf. 14***

| | | | | |
|---|---|---|---|---|
| **2094-2097** | A386 | Set of 4 | 3.50 | 3.50 |

**Sheets of 8, #a-h**

| | | | | |
|---|---|---|---|---|
| **2098-2099** | A386 | Set of 2 | 16.00 | 16.00 |

**Souvenir Sheets**

| | | | | |
|---|---|---|---|---|
| **2100-2101** | A386 | Set of 2 | 10.00 | 10.00 |

Shirley Temple as "Curly Top" — A387

No. 2102, vert.: a, Saying prayers. b, Actor John Boles looking at portrait. c, Taking Boles' hand. d, Dressed as old woman.
No. 2103: a, Hugging older sister. b, Dressed as a man. c, Looking at stuffed animals. d, Pulling Boles' tie. e, With family. f, Looking at sister and Boles together.
5000ce, In pink dress, vert.

***Perf. 13½x14, 14x13½***

**1999, Mar. 1 Litho.**

| | | | | |
|---|---|---|---|---|
| **2102** | A387 | 1000ce Sheet of 4, #a.-d. | 3.50 | 3.50 |
| **2103** | A387 | 1000ce Sheet of 6, #a.-f. | 5.50 | 5.50 |

**Souvenir Sheet**

| | | | | |
|---|---|---|---|---|
| **2104** | A387 | 5000ce multicolored | 5.50 | 5.50 |

Amorphophallus Flavovirens — A387a

**1999, May 6 Litho. *Perf. 14x14¼***

| | | | | |
|---|---|---|---|---|
| **2104A** | A387a | 200ce multi | — | |

Trains A388

Designs: 400ce, ICE 2, Germany, 1966. 500ce, M41, Hungary, 1982. 600ce, DVR, Finland, 1963. 1000ce, AVE 100 class, Spain, 1982.
No. 2109, 1300ce: a, EMD GP7 Illinois Terminal RR, 1949-54. b, EMD SD 38-2, 1972-79. c, EMD SD 60M Soo Line, 1989-96. d, GE U25C, 1963-65. e, EMD GP 28, 1961-63. f, EMD SD 9, 1954-59.
No. 2110, 1300ce: a, Conrail EMD SD80, 1993-99. b, Columbus & Greenville RR EMD SDP35, 1964-66. c, Providence & Worcester RR, MLW M420 Loc. Works, 1973-77. d, Missouri Pacific C36-7, 1978-85. e, Alco C-420 Virginia & Maryland RR, 1963-68. f, Reading RR EMD GP30, 1961-63.
No. 2111, 5000ce, Swiss Federal RR Class RE 6/6 Co-Co, 1972. No. 2112, 5000ce, AGP44, ABB Traction, Inc. 1990-91.

**1999, May 10 *Perf. 14***

| | | | | |
|---|---|---|---|---|
| **2105-2108** | A388 | Set of 4 | 2.50 | 2.50 |

**Sheets of 6, #a-f**

| | | | | |
|---|---|---|---|---|
| **2109-2110** | A388 | Set of 2 | 13.00 | 13.00 |

**Souvenir Sheets**

| | | | | |
|---|---|---|---|---|
| **2111-2112** | A388 | Set of 2 | 9.00 | 9.00 |

Paintings by Hokusai (1760-1849) — A389

No. 2113: a, Girl Picking Plum Blossoms. b, Surveying a Region. c, Sumo Wrestlers (rear view). d, Sumo Wrestlers (front view). e, Landscape with Seaside Village. f, Courtiers Crossing a Bridge.
No. 2114: a, Climbing the Mountain. b, Nakahara in Sagami Province. c, Sumo Wrestlers (2 fighting). d, An Oiran and Maid by a Fence. e. Fujiwara Yoshitaka.
No. 2115, 5000ce, Palanquin Bearers on a Steep Hill, vert. No. 2116, 5000ce, Three Ladies by a Well, vert.

**1999, Aug. 3 Litho. *Perf. 13¾***

| | | | | |
|---|---|---|---|---|
| **2113** | A389 | 1300ce Sheet of 6, #a.-f. | 6.25 | 6.25 |
| **2114** | A389 | 1300ce Sheet of 6, #a.-e., 2113c | 6.25 | 6.25 |

**Souvenir Sheets**

| | | | | |
|---|---|---|---|---|
| **2115-2116** | A389 | Set of 2 | 8.00 | 8.00 |

IBRA '99, World Philatelic Exhibition, Nuremberg — A390

Exhibition emblem, sailing ship Schomberg and: No. 2117, 500ce, Hanover #1. No. 2119, 1000ce, Lubeck #1.
Emblem, Class P8 4-6-0 locomotive and: No. 2118, 800ce, Hamburg #1. No. 2120, 2000ce, Heligoland #1A.
5000ce, Germany #66 tied to airmail label on cover, vert.

**1999, Aug. 3 *Perf. 14x14½***

| | | | | |
|---|---|---|---|---|
| **2117-2120** | A390 | Set of 4 | 4.00 | 4.00 |

**Souvenir Sheet**

***Perf. 14½x14***

| | | | | |
|---|---|---|---|---|
| **2121** | A390 | 5000ce multicolored | 4.00 | 4.00 |

First Manned Moon Landing, 30th Anniv. — A391

No. 2122: a, Command Module. b, Lunar Module ascension. c, Giant moon rock. d, Lunar module signals home. e, Neil Armstrong. f, One small step.
5000ce, Earth rise, horiz.

**1999, Aug. 3 *Perf. 14***

| | | | | |
|---|---|---|---|---|
| **2122** | A391 | 1300ce Sheet of 6, #a.-f. | 8.00 | 8.00 |

**Souvenir Sheet**

| | | | | |
|---|---|---|---|---|
| **2123** | A391 | 5000ce multicolored | 4.75 | 4.75 |

Queen Mother, 100th Birthday (in 2000) — A392

Queen Mother, 100th Birthday (in 2000) — No. 2124: a, Lady Elizabeth Bowles-Lyon with brother David, 1904. b, Queen Elizabeth, 1957. c, Queen Mother, 1970. d, Queen Mother, 1992.
5000ce, Queen Mother, 1970, diff.

**1999, Aug. 4** **Gold Frames**

**2124** A392 2000ce Sheet of 4, #a.-d. + label 7.25 7.25

**Souvenir Sheet**

**2125** A392 5000ce multicolored 6.00 6.00

No. 2125 contains one 38x50mm stamp. Margins of sheets are embossed.
See Nos. 2273-2274.

Fauna A393

Designs: 200ce, Meles meles. 800ce, Vulpes vulpes.
No. 2128: a, Martes martes. b, Strix aluco. c, Sus scrofa. d, Accipiter gentilis. e, Eliomys quercinus. f, Lucanus cervus.
No. 2129: a, Merops apiaster. b, Upupa epops. c, Cervus elaphus. d, Circaetus gallicus. e, Lacerta ocellata. f, Lynx pardellus.
5000ce, Canis lupus, vert.

**1999, Mar. 29** **Litho.** ***Perf. 14***

**2126-2127** A393 Set of 2 2.00 2.00
**2128** A393 1000ce Sheet of 6, #a.-f. 5.00 5.00
**2129** A393 1000ce Sheet of 6, #a.-f. 5.00 5.00

**Souvenir Sheet**

**2130** A393 5000ce multicolored 5.00 5.00

**1999**

Birds: 400ce, Cyanopica cyana. 600ce, Ciconia ciconia. 2000ce, Aegypius monachus, vert. 3000ce, Garrulus glandarius, vert.
5000ce, Aquila heliaca adalberti.

**2131-2134** A393 Set of 4 5.50 5.50

**Souvenir Sheet**

**2135** A393 5000ce multicolored 4.50 4.50

Rights of the Child — A394

No. 2136: a, Child, UN building. b, Dove, earth. c, Mother, child.
5000ce, Child.

**1999, Aug. 3** **Litho.** ***Perf. 14***

**2136** A394 3000ce Sheet of 3, #a.-c. 7.50 7.50

**Souvenir Sheet**

**2137** A394 5000ce multicolored 5.00 5.00

Souvenir Sheets

PhilexFrance 99 — A395

Locomotives: No. 2138, 5000ce, 232-U1 Four cylinder compound 4-6-4. No. 2139, 5000ce, 0-6-0 Suburban tank engine.

**1999, Aug. 3** ***Perf. 14x13¾***

**2138-2139** A395 Set of 2 15.00 15.00

Johann Wolfgang von Goethe (1749-1832), German Poet — A396

No. 2140: a, Wagner entreats Faust in his study. b, Goethe and Friedrich von Schiller. c, Mephistopheles disguised as the fool.
5000ce, Faust attended by spirits.

**1999, Aug. 3** **Litho.** ***Perf. 14***

**2140** A396 2000ce Sheet of 3, #a.-c. 5.75 5.75

**Souvenir Sheet**

**2141** A396 5000ce multicolored 5.00 5.00

Return of Macao to People's Republic of China — A397

**1999, Aug. 20** **Litho.** ***Perf. 14x13¾***

**2142** A397 1000ce multicolored 3.00 3.00

Issued in sheets of 4.

Save the Ozone Layer — A398

Designs: 200ce, Fish. 550ce, Earth surrounded by ozone layer, man. 800ce, Crying Earth. 1100ce, People holding up shield against sunlight. 1500ce, Objects with ozone-depleting and non-harmful chemicals.

**1999** **Litho.** ***Perf. 13½x13***

**2143-2147** A398 Set of 5 8.50 8.50

SOS Children's Villages, 50th Anniv. A399

Designs: 200ce, Grandma Alice. 550ce, Kindergarten. 800ce, SOS Children's Village founder Herrmann Gmeiner (1919-86), Asikawa SOS building. 1100ce, Food preparation.

**1999** ***Perf. 13x13½***

**2148-2151** A399 Set of 4 3.00 3.00

Dr. Ephraim Apu, Musician, Birth Cent. — A400

Designs: 200ce, Apu, clef, note. 800ce, Apu playing Odurugya flute. 1100ce, Apu, indigenous flutes.

**1999** ***Perf. 13½x13***

**2152-2154** A400 Set of 3 2.00 2.00

Millennium — A401

Designs: 300ce, Millennium emblem, vert. 700ce, Emblem, Kwame Nkrumah. 1200ce, Emblem, University of Ghana, vert.

**1999, Dec. 28** **Litho.** ***Perf. 13¼***

**2155-2157** A401 Set of 3 6.00 6.00

New Year 2000 — A402

Various scenes from Chinese story, "Daughter of the Dragon King." Stamps from the two sheets are numbered 1-12 in Chinese numeral characters. The numerals are at the bottom of the top group of Chinese characters. See Chinese numerals in Illustrated Identifier.

**2000, Feb. 5** ***Perf. 14½x14¼***

**2158** A402 1600ce Sheet of 6, #a.-f. 5.00 5.00
**2159** A402 1700ce Sheet of 6, #a.-f. 5.50 5.50

Wildlife A403

Designs: 300ce, Black-faced impala. 500ce, Cheetah. 1000ce, Wildebeest. 3000ce, Hippopotamus.
No. 2164, vert.: a, Chimpanzee. b, Boomslang. c, Vulture. d, Leopard. e, Rhinoceros. f, Zebra. g, Crowned crane. h, Lesser kudu.
No. 2165, vert.: a, Purple roller. b, Pelicans. c, Egrets. d, Orange-breasted waxbill. e, Giraffe, f, African buffalo. g, African elephant. h, African lion.
No. 2166, 7000ce, Waterbuck. No. 2167, 7000ce, Ostrich.

**2000, Feb. 28** **Litho.** ***Perf. 14***

**2160-2163** A403 Set of 4 3.00 3.00
**2164** A403 1100ce Sheet of 8, #a.-h. 6.25 6.25
**2165** A403 1200ce Sheet of 8, #a.-h. 6.50 6.50

**Souvenir Sheets**

**2166-2167** A403 each 8.00 8.00

Tourism A404

No. 2168: a, 300ce, Building, palm trees. b, 300ce, Mud building, natives. c, 300ce, Elephants. d, 1100ce, Natives. e, 1200ce, Natives carrying animal. f, 1800ce, Natives, diff.

**2000** **Litho.** ***Perf. 13x13¼***

**2168** A404 Booklet pane of 6, #a.-h. 5.00 5.00
Complete booklet, 4 #2168 20.00

There are 2 types of No. 2168, which differ only by the arrangement of the stamps on the pane. The booklet contains 2 of each type.

Wildlife A405

Designs: 500ce, Zebra duiker. 600ce, Leopard. 2000ce, Bush buck. 3000ce, African wood owl.
No. 2173, 1600ce: a, Blotted genet. b, Tree pangolin. c, Bongo. d, Elephant. e, Flap-necked chameleon. f, West African dwarf crocodile.
No. 2174, 1600ce: a, Lowe's monkey. b, Diana monkey. c, Potto. d, Moustached monkey. e, Thomas's galago. f, Chimpanzee.
No. 2175, 1600ce: a, Gray parrot. b, Hoopoe. c, European roller. d, European bee-eater. e, Blue-breasted kingfisher. f, White-throated bee-eater.
No. 2176, 6000ce, Hippopotamus, vert. No. 2177, 6000ce, Great blue turaco, vert.

**2000, May 1** **Litho.** ***Perf. 14***

**2169-2172** A405 Set of 4 3.50 3.50

**Sheets of 6, #a.-f.**

**2173-2175** A405 Set of 3 13.00 13.00

**Souvenir Sheets**

**2176-2177** A405 Set of 2 7.50 7.50

Mushrooms — A406

No. 2178, horiz.: a, Slippery jack. b, Violet deceiver. c, Fairy stool. d, Honey fungus. e, Shaggy parasol. f, Russula sp.
No. 2179, horiz.: a, Grisette. b, Common puffball. c, Fan. d, Gray chanterelle. e, Fairies' bonnets. f, Russula sp., diff.
5000ce, Great orange elf-cup. 8000ce, Bitter boletus.

**2000, May 15**

**2178** A406 1500ce Sheet of 6, #a.-f. 6.00 6.00
**2179** A406 2000ce Sheet of 6, #a.-f. 8.00 8.00

**Souvenir Sheets**

**2180** A406 5000ce multi 3.00 3.00
**2181** A406 8000ce multi 4.00 4.00

The Stamp Show 2000, London.

Eurasian Goldfinch — A406a

**2000, June 1** **Litho.** ***Perf. 13¾x13¼***

**2181A** A406a 300ce multi — —

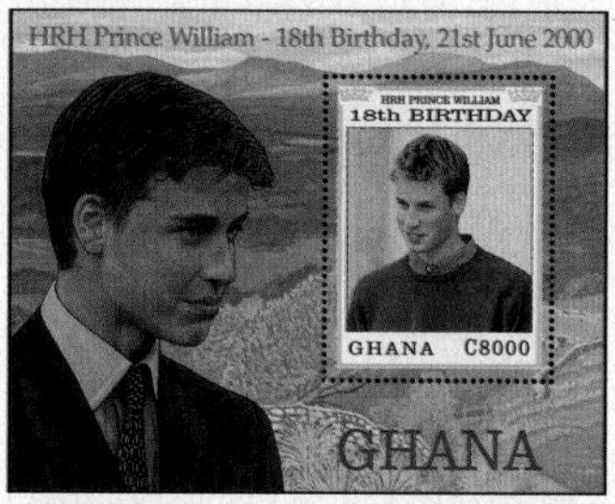


Prince William, 18th Birthday — A407

No. 2182: a, In ski gear. b, With ribbons wrapped around fingers. c, With jacket, no tie. d, Close-up.
8000ce, In sweater.

**2000, June 26 Litho. *Perf. 14***

**2182** A407 2000ce Sheet of 4, #a-d 5.50 5.50

**Souvenir Sheet**

***Perf. 13¾***

**2183** A407 8000ce multi 5.50 5.50

No. 2182 contains four 28x42mm stamps.

First Zeppelin Flight, Cent. — A408

No. 2184: a, LZ-129. b, LZ-9. c, LZ-4.
5000ce, LZ-11.

**2000, June 26 *Perf. 13¾***

**2184** A408 1600ce Sheet of 3, #a-c 3.50 3.50

**Souvenir Sheet**

**2185** A408 5000ce multi 4.25 4.25

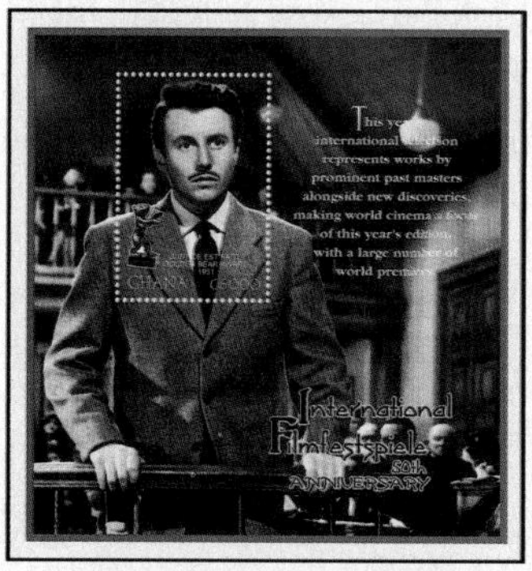


Berlin Film Festival, 50th Anniv. — A409

No. 2186: a, Wetherby. b, Die Frau und der Fremde. c, Hong Gao Liang (Red Sorghum). d, Skřivánci na Niti. e, Music Box. f, Tema.
6000ce, Justice Est Faite.

**2000, June 26 *Perf. 14***

**2186** A409 2000ce Sheet of 6, #a-f 7.50 7.50

**Souvenir Sheet**

**2187** A409 6000ce multi 4.00 4.00

Apollo-Soyuz Mission, 25th Anniv. — A410

No. 2188: a, Apollo 18. b, Docked spacecraft. c, Soyuz 19.
8000ce, Soyuz, Earth.

**2000, June 26**

**2188** A410 4000ce Sheet of 3, #a-c 6.50 6.50

**Souvenir Sheet**

**2189** A410 8000ce multi 5.00 5.00

Souvenir Sheets

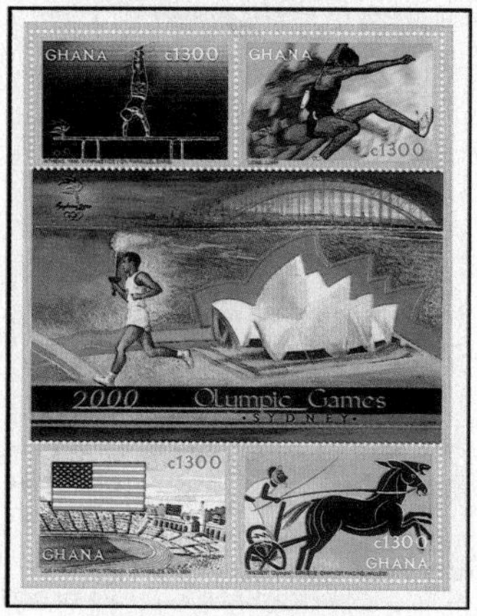


2000 Summer Olympics, Sydney — A411

No. 2190: a, Gymnastics. b, Long jump. c, Los Angeles Coliseum, and US flag. d, Ancient Greek chariot racer.

**2000, June 26**

**2190** A411 1300ce Sheet of 4, #a-d 4.50 4.50

Public Railways, 175th Anniv. — A412

No. 2191: a, Marc Seguin. b, Blenkinsop locomotive. c, Pumping station, Dawlish.

**2000, June 26**

**2191** A412 4000ce Sheet of 3, #a-c 7.00 7.00

Albert Einstein (1879-1955) — A413

**2000, June 26 *Perf. 13¾***

**2192** A413 8000ce multi 10.00 10.00

Ghana Home Economics Assoc. — A414

Designs: 300ce, Women, cooking pots. 700ce, Woman with home economics textbook, vert. 1200ce, Emblem, Alberta Ollennu, Patience A. Adow. 1800ce, Emblems, vert.

**2000 *Perf. 13x13¼, 13¼x13***

**2193-2196** A414 Set of 4 3.75 3.75

Space — A415

No. 2197, horiz.: a, Mercury. b, Gemini. c, Apollo. d, Vostok. e, Voskhod 2. f, Soyuz.

**2000, June 26 Litho. *Perf. 14***

**2197** A415 2000ce Sheet of 6, #a-f 7.75 7.75

**Souvenir Sheet**

**2198** A415 2000ce Challenger 51-L patch 6.00 6.00

World Stamp Expo 2000, Anaheim.

Cats and Dogs — A416

Designs: 1100ce, African shorthair. 1200ce, Russian Blue. 1800ce, Basenji. 2000ce, Basset hound.

No. 2203, horiz. a, 1600ce, Weimaraner. b, 1800ce, Keeshond. c, 1800ce, Fox terrier. d, 1800ce, Saluki. e, 1800ce, Dalmatian. f, 1800ce, English setter.

No. 2204, 1800ce, horiz.: a, Silver Persian. b, Creampoint Himalayan. c, British tortoise-shell shorthair. d, American shorthair tabby. e, Black Persian. f, Turkish Van.

No. 2205, 8000ce, Cocker spaniels. No. 2206, 8000ce, Lilac Persian.

**2000, Aug. 21**

**2199-2202** A416 Set of 4 3.25 3.25

**Sheets of 6, #a-f**

**2203-2204** A416 Set of 2 10.00 10.00

**Souvenir Sheets**

**2205-2206** A416 Set of 2 8.00 8.00

Scenes from Tale of the White Snake — A417

No. 2207, 2500ce: a, Xu Xian offers umbrella to White Lady and maid. b, White Lady (with basket) helps husband Xu Xian with business. c, Monk Fa Hai (with necklace) talks to Xu Xian. d, Xu Xian gives wine to wife. e, White Lady becomes snake, Xu Xian has heart attack. f, White Lady (with swords) trying to get medicinal herbs.

No. 2208, 2500ce: a, White Lady and maid at Fa Hai's temple. b, Maid threatens to kill Xu Xian. c, Fa Hai captures White Lady in bowl. d, Maid, Xu Xian at pagoda. e, Maid with sword attacks Fa Hai. f, Maid turns Fa Hai into crab.

Illustration reduced.

**2001, Jan. 2 Litho. *Perf. 14***

**Sheets of 6, #a-f**

**2207-2208** A417 Set of 2 8.50 8.50

New Year 2001 (Year of the snake).

Edward G. Robinson — A418

Color of photograph: a, Gray green. b, Lilac. c, Red violet (with hat). d, Brown (with cigar). e, Orange brown (with pipe). f, Blue green.

**2001, Apr. 16 Litho. *Perf. 14***

**2209** A418 4000ce Sheet of 6, #a-f 6.25 6.25

James Cagney — A419

Color of photograph: a, Olive green. b, Emerald. c, Blue. d, Brown. e, Red violet. f, Orange.

**2001, Apr. 16**

**2210** A419 4000ce Sheet of 6, #a-f 6.50 6.50

Millennium — A420

No. 2211, 2500ce — Architects: a, Walter Gropius. b, Aldo Rossi. c, Le Corbusier. d, Antonio Gaudi. e, Paolo Soleri. f, Ludwig Mies van de Rohe.

No. 2212, 2500ce — Artists: a, Wassily Kandinsky. b, Henry Moore. c, Marc Chagall. d, Norman Rockwell. e, Antonio López García. f, Frida Kahlo.

No. 2213, 14,000ce, Frank Lloyd Wright. No. 2214, 14,000ce, Pablo Picasso. No. 2215, 14,000ce, Human Genome Project.

**2001, Apr. 16 Sheets of 6, #a-f**

**2211-2212** A420 Set of 2 8.00 8.00

**Souvenir Sheets**

**2213-2215** A420 Set of 3 11.00 11.00

Jazz Musicians — A421

No. 2216, 4000ce: a, Scott Joplin. b, Clarence Williams. c, Sidney Bechet. d, Willie "The Lion" Smith. e, Ferdinand "Jelly Roll" Morton. f, Coleman "Bean" Hawkins.

No. 2217, 4000ce: a, Kid Ory. b, Earl "Fatha" Hines. c, Lil Hardin Armstrong. d, John Philip Sousa. e, James P. Johnson. f, Johnny St. Cyr.

No. 2218, 14,000ce, Joe "King" Oliver. No. 2219, 14,000ce, Louis "Satchmo" Armstrong.

**2001, Apr. 16** **Sheets of 6, #a-f**

**2216-2217** A421 Set of 2 12.50 12.50

**Souvenir Sheets**

**2218-2219** A421 Set of 2 7.50 7.50

Oriental Art A422

Designs: 500ce, Cranes, by Kano Eisenin Michinobu. 800ce, Flowers and Trees in Chen Chun's Style, by Tsubaki Chinzan. 1200ce, A Poetry Contest of 42 Matches, by unknown artist. 2000ce, Cranes, by Kano, diff. 5000ce, A Poetry Contest of 42 Matches, diff. 12,000ce, Plum Trees, by Tani Buncho.

No. 2226, 3000ce, vert. — The Tales of Ise, by Sumiyoshi Jokei: a, Chapter 1. b, Chapter 4. c, Chapter 6. d, Chapter 9 (Eastboud Trip, Mt. Utsu). e, Chapter 9, (Eastbound Trip, Mt. Fuji). f, Chapter 9, (Eastbound Trip, Black-headed Gulls). g, Chapter 23, (Crossing Kawachi). h, Chapter 23, (By the Well Wall).

No. 2227, 4000ce, vert. — The Story of Sakyamuni, by unknown artist: a, Siddhartha's Excursion Through the South Gate. b, Siddhartha's Excursion Through the East Gate. c, Siddhartha's Excursion Through the North Gate. d, Siddhartha's Excursion Through the West Gate. e, Sakyamuni Entering Nirvana. f, Untitled.

No. 2228, 14,000ce, Cranes, by Kano (red denomination), diff. No. 2229, 14,000ce, Cranes, by Kano (yellow denomination), diff. No. 2230, 14,000ce, Chapter 1, by Sumiyoshi. No. 2231, Chapter 12, by Sumiyoshi.

**2001, Apr. 30**

**2220-2225** A422 Set of 6 5.75 5.75

**2226** A422 3000ce Sheet of 8, #a-h 6.50 6.50

**2227** A422 4000ce Sheet of 6, #a-f 6.50 6.50

**Souvenir Sheets**

**2228-2231** A422 Set of 4 14.00 14.00

Phila Nippon '01, Japan.

Automobiles — A423

Designs: 2000ce, 1950 Bentley S Series convertible. 3000ce, 1948 Chrysler Town and Country. 5000ce, 1957 Lotus Elite. 6000ce, 1966 Chevrolet Corvette Sting Ray.

No. 2236, 4000ce: a, 1956-59 BMW 507. b, 1934 Bentley English Tourer. c, 1948 Morris Minor MM. d, 1954 Daimler SP-250 Dart. e, 1950 DeSoto custom convertible. f, 1955-60, Ford Thunderbird.

No. 2237, 4000ce: a,1959-63 Porshe 356B. b, 1962 Rolls-Royce Silver Cloud. c, 1958 Austin Healey Sprite MK-1. d, 1954-57 Mercedes 300SL. e, 1949 Citroen 2CV. f, 1949 Cadillac Series 62.

No. 2238, 14,000ce: a, 1933 Mercedes-Benz. No. 2239, 1953-55 Triumph TR-2.

**2001, June 18**

**2232-2235** A423 Set of 4 4.50 4.50

**Sheets of 6, #a-f**

**2236-2237** A423 Set of 2 12.50 12.50

**Souvenir Sheets**

**2238-2239** A423 Set of 2 7.50 7.50

Belgica 2001 Intl. Stamp Exhibition, Brussels. No. 2238-2239 each contain one 85x28mm stamp.

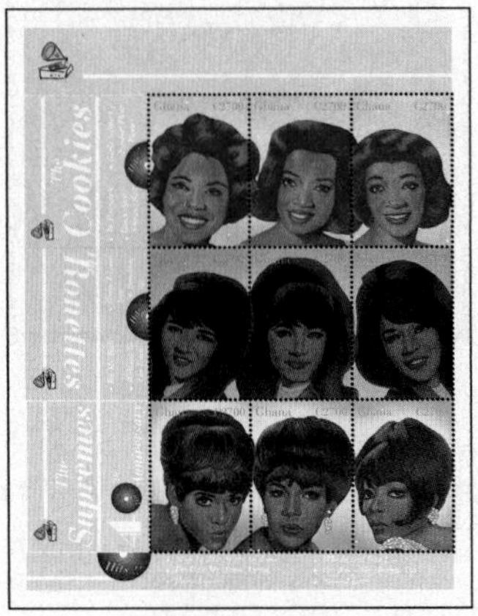


Female Recording Groups of the 1960s — A424

No. 2240 — Various members of: a-c, The Cookies. d-f, The Ronettes. g-i, The Supremes.

**2001, Apr. 16** **Litho.** ***Perf. 14***

**2240** A424 2700ce Sheet of 9, #a-i 6.50 6.50

Mao Zedong (1893-1976) — A425

No. 2241: a, With arm raised, orange and light orange background. b, Portrait. c, With arm raised, tan gray and blue background.

12,000ce, With flag.

**2001, Aug. 27**

**2241** A425 7000ce Sheet of 3, #a-c 6.00 6.00

**Souvenir Sheet**

**2242** A425 12,000ce multi 3.50 3.50

Giuseppe Verdi (1813-1901), Opera Composer — A426

No. 2243: a, Verdi. b, Scores for Aida and Rigoletto. c, Verdi's birthplace. d, Map of Italy.

13,000ce, Verdi and score.

**2001, Aug. 27**

**2243** A426 5000ce Sheet of 4, #a-d 5.50 5.50

**Souvenir Sheet**

**2244** A426 13,000ce multi 3.50 3.50

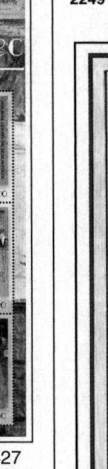

Toulouse-Lautrec Paintings — A427

No. 2245: a, Jane Avril Leaving the Moulin Rouge. b, Jane Avril Dancing. c, Jane Avril Entering the Moulin Rouge.

**2001, Aug. 27** ***Perf. 13¾***

**2245** A427 6700ce Sheet of 3, #a-c 5.50 5.50

Monet Paintings — A428

No. 2246, horiz.: a, Zaandam. b, On the Seine at Bennecourt. c, The Studio Boat. d, Houses on the Waterfront, Zaandam.

15,000ce, Madame Gaudibert.

**2001, Aug. 27**

**2246** A428 5000ce Sheet of 4, #a-d 5.50 5.50

**Souvenir Sheet**

**2247** A428 15,000ce multi 4.00 4.00

Queen Victoria (1819-1901) — A429

No. 2248: a, Victoria. b, Prince Albert. c, Albert and Victoria. d, Victoria and Albert on wedding day.

12,000ce, Victoria with green and white headpiece.

**2001, Aug. 27** ***Perf. 14***

**2248** A429 5000ce Sheet of 4, #a-d 5.50 5.50

**Souvenir Sheet**

**2249** A429 12,000ce multi 3.25 3.25

Queen Elizabeth II, 75th Birthday — A430

No. 2250, vert.: a, Bright pink hat. b, White hat. c, Peach hat. d, Crown. e, Blue and pink hat. f, In uniform.

15,000ce, with Prince Philip.

**2001, Aug. 27**

**2250** A430 4000ce Sheet of 6, #a-f 6.50 6.50

**Souvenir Sheet**

**2251** A430 15,000ce multi 4.00 4.00

Whales A431

Designs: 1000ce, Killer whale. 3000ce, Narwhal. 5000ce, Beluga. 6000ce, Bowhead whale.

No. 2256, 4000ce: a, Blue whale. b, Killer whale, diff. c, Northern bottlenose whale. d, Sperm whale. e, Southern right whale. f, Pygmy right whale.

No. 2257, 4000ce: a, Humpback whale. b, Fin whale. c, Bowhead whale, diff. d, Gray whale. e, Narwhal, diff. f, Beluga, diff.

No. 2258, 14,000ce, Sperm whale. No. 2259, 14,000ce, Blue whales.

**2001, Oct. 1**
**2252-2255** A431 Set of 4 7.00 7.00

**Sheets of 6, #a-f**
**2256-2257** A431 Set of 2 19.00 19.00

**Souvenir Sheets**
**2258-2259** A431 Set of 2 13.00 13.00

Rotary Intl. In Ghana, 40th Anniv. (in 1998) A432

Rotary Intl. emblem and: 300ce, Polio victim. 1100ce, Clean water. 1200ce, Founder Paul Harris. 1800ce, Blood donation.

**2001 ?** ***Perf. 13¼***
**2260-2263** A432 Set of 4 2.25 2.25

Orchids — A433

Designs: 1100ce, Paphiopedilum hennisianum. 1200ce, Vuylstekeara cambria Plush. 1800ce, Cymbidium ormoulu. 2000ce, Phalaenopsis Barbara Moler.

No. 2268, 4500ce: a, Cattleya capra. b, Odontoglossum rossii. c, Epidendrum pseudepidendrum. d, Encyclia cochleata. e, Cymbidium baldoyle Melbury. f, Phalaenopsis asean.

No. 2269, 4500ce: a, Odontocidium Tigersun. b, Miltonia Emotion. c, Odontonia sappho Excul. d, Cymbidium Bulbarrow. e, Dendrobium nobile. f, Paphiopedilum insigne.

No. 2270, 15,000ce, Calanthe vestita. No. 2271, 15,000ce, Angraecum eburneum.

**2001, Oct. 30 Litho.** ***Perf. 14***
**2264-2267** A433 Set of 4 2.75 2.75

**Sheets of 6, #a-f**
**2268-2269** A433 Set of 2 16.00 16.00

**Souvenir Sheets**
**2270-2271** A433 Set of 2 9.00 9.00

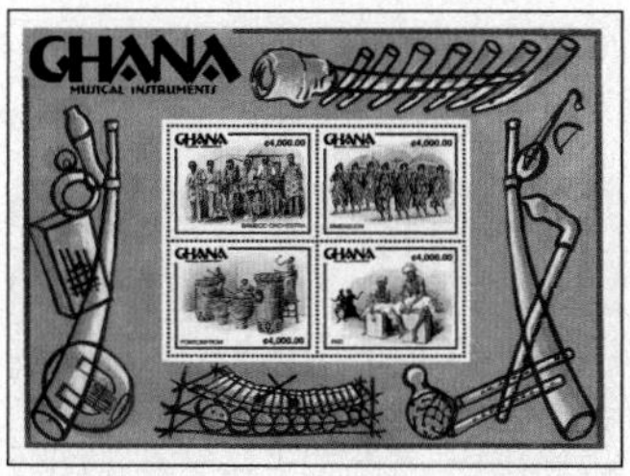


Musical Instruments — A434

No. 2272: a, Bamboo orchestra. b, Mmensuon. c, Fontomfrom. d, Pati.

**2001, Dec. 3** ***Perf. 14¼***
**2272** A434 4000ce Sheet of 4, #a-d 4.50 4.50

**Queen Mother Type of 1999 Redrawn**

No. 2273: a, Lady Elizabeth Bowles-Lyon with brother David, 1904. b, In Rhodesia, 1957. c, In 1970. d, In 1992.
5000ce, In 1970, diff.

**2001, Dec.** ***Perf. 14***
**Yellow Orange Frames**
**2273** A392 2000ce Sheet of 4, #a-d, + label 4.50 4.50

**Souvenir Sheet**
***Perf. 13¾***
**2274** A392 5000ce multi 3.00 3.00

Queen Mother's 101st birthday. No. 2274 contains one 38x50mm stamp with a darker background than on No. 2125. Sheet margins of Nos. 2273-2274 lack embossing and gold arms and frames found on Nos. 2124-2125.

Kwame Nkrumah University of Science and Technology, Kumasi, 50th Anniv. A435

Designs: 300ce, Emblem. No. 2276, 700ce, No. 2280a, 4000ce, Main gate. No. 2277, 1100ce, No. 2280b, 4000ce, Dairy production. No. 2278, 1200ce, No. 2280c, 4000ce, Pharmacy Department. No. 2279, 1800ce, No. 2280d, 4000ce, Residence hall.

**2001** ***Perf. 13x13¼***
**2275-2279** A435 Set of 5 2.00 2.00

**Souvenir Sheet**
**2280** A435 4000ce Sheet of 4, #a-d 4.25 4.25

For surcharge, see No. 2683.

Nobel Prizes, Cent. (In 2001) — A436

No. 2281, 4000ce — Chemistry laureates: a, George A. Olah, 1994. b, Kary Mullis, 1993. c, Sir Harold W. Kroto, 1996. d, Richard R. Ernst, 1991. e, Ahmed H. Zewail, 1999. f, Paul Crutzen, 1995.

No. 2282, 4000ce — Chemistry laureates: a, John E. Walker, 1997. b, Jens C. Skou, 1997. c, Alan G. MacDiarmid, 2000. d, Thomas Robert Cech, 1989. e, John Pole, 1998. f, Rudolph A. Marcus, 1992.

No. 2283, 4000ce — Chemistry laureates: a, Walter Kohn, 1998. b, F. Sherwood Rowland, 1995. c, Mario Molina, 1995. d, Hideki Shirakawa, 2000. e, Paul D. Boyer, 1997. f, Richard Smalley, 1996.

No. 2284, 15,000ce, Svante Arrhenius, Chemistry, 1903. No. 2285, 15,000ce, Alfred Werner, Chemistry, 1913. No. 2286, 15,000ce, Peter Debye, Chemistry, 1936. No. 2287, 15,000ce, Wole Soyinka, Literature, 1986. No. 2288, 15,000ce, Nelson Mandela, Peace, 1993.

**2002, Jan. 9** ***Perf. 14***
**Sheets of 6, #a-f**
**2281-2283** A436 Set of 3 19.00 19.00

**Souvenir Sheets**
**2284-2288** A436 Set of 5 20.00 20.00

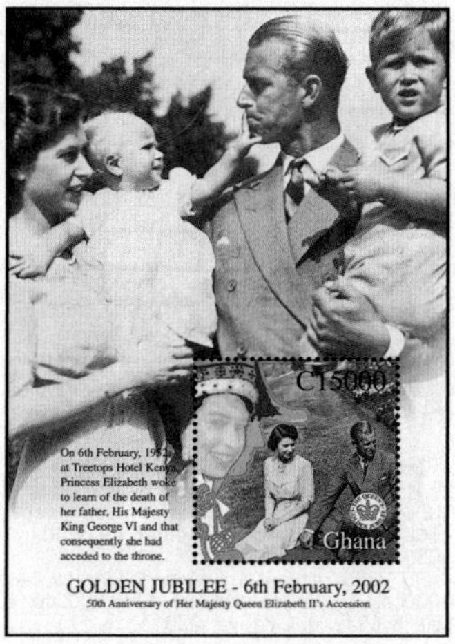


Reign of Queen Elizabeth II, 50th Anniv. — A437

No. 2289: a, Wearing pink dress. b, Sitting on horse. c. Looking at horses. d, In carriage with Prince Philip.

15,000ce, Sitting with Prince Philip (black and white photograph).

**2002, Feb. 6 Litho.** ***Perf. 14¼***
**2289** A437 6500ce Sheet of 4, #a-d 7.00 7.00

**Souvenir Sheet**
**2290** A437 15,000ce multi 4.25 4.25

Intl. Copyright Conference, Accra — A438

Designs: 300ce, Conference emblem, vert. 700ce, Person reading. 1100ce, Spider, web, map of Ghana. 1200ce, Map of Ghana, Kente cloth. 1800ce, Drummer.

**2002, Feb. 20** ***Perf. 14¼x14, 14x14¼***
**2291-2295** A438 Set of 5 1.75 1.75

2002 World Cup Soccer Championships, Japan and Korea — A439

World Cup trophy and: 100ce, Jay Jay Okacha, flag of Nigeria. 150ce, South African player and flag. 300ce, Pele, flag of Brazil. 400ce, Roger Milla, flag of Cameroun. 500ce, Bobby Charlton, flag of England. 800ce, Michel Platini, flag of France. 1000ce, Franz Beckenbauer, flag of West Germany. 1500ce, Ulsan Munsu Stadium, Korea, horiz. 2000ce, German player and flag. 3000ce, Brazilian player and flag. 4000ce, Korean player and flag. 5000ce, Yokohama Intl. Sports Stadium, Japan, horiz. 6000ce, Italian player and flag. 11,000ce, 1950 World Cup poster. 12,000ce, 1934 World Cup poster.

No. 2311, 15,000ce, Geoff Hurst's hat trick for England, 1966. No. 2312, 15,000ce, Gordon Banks making save on Pele, 1970.

**2002, Mar. 4** ***Perf. 14***
**2296-2310** A439 Set of 15 12.50 12.50

**Souvenir Sheets**
**2311-2312** A439 Set of 2 8.50 8.50

Souvenir Sheet

New Year 2002 (Year of the Horse) — A440

No. 2313: a, Brown panel at L, country name at LR. b, Brown panel at R, country name at UR. c, Brown panel at L, country name at LL. d, Brown panel at R, country name at LR.

**2002, Mar. 4** ***Perf. 13¾***
**2313** A440 4000ce Sheet of 4, #a-d 4.75 4.75

Visit of Netherlands Prince Willem-Alexander and Princess Máxima to Ghana — A441

Couple: a, With Prince wearing sash. b, Holding hands, Prince wearing hat. c, With windmills and flags. d, At wedding ceremony, with another man. e, In crowd. f, Kissing.

**2002** ***Perf. 14***
**2314** A441 6000ce Sheet of 6, #a-f 8.50 8.50

Amphilex 2002 Intl. Stamp Show, Amsterdam.

Paintings of Shunsho Katsukawa — A442

No. 2315, 9000ce — Activities of Women in the Twelve Months: a, Trying to retrieve a ball caught in a tree (March). b, Listening to a cuckoo in the bedroom (April). c, Holding a cage filled with fireflies for a woman to read a book (May).

No. 2316, 9000ce — Activities of Women in the Twelve Months: a, Mother and child taking a tub bath while woman holds a revolving lantern (June). b, Strips of paper with wishes and poems are tied on bamboo (July). c, Women enjoying the cool air on a boat (August).

No. 2317, 9000ce — Activities of Women in the Twelve Months: a, Celebrating Feast of the Chrysanthemum (September). b, Looking out for colored leaves (October). c, Mother reading picture book while sitting at a foot warmer (November).

No. 2318, 15,000ce, Three women decorating a gate (woman in blue kimono), from Activities of Women in the Twelve Months. No. 2319, 15,000ce, Part 1 (woman in red kimono) from Snow, Moonlight and Flowers. No. 2320, 15,000ce, Part 2 (woman in black kimono) from Snow, Moonlight and Flowers. No. 2321, 15,000ce, Part 3 (woman in gray kimono) from Snow, Moonlight and Flowers.

**2002, July 29 Litho.** ***Perf. 14¼***
**Sheets of 3, #a-c**
**2315-2317** A442 Set of 3 19.00 19.00

**Souvenir Sheets**
**2318-2321** A442 Set of 4 14.00 14.00

United We Stand — A443

**2002, Aug. 15** *Perf. 14*

**2322** A443 7000ce multi 3.25 3.25

Printed in sheets of 4.

2002 Winter Olympics, Salt Lake City — A444

Designs: No. 2323, 7000ce, Figure skaters. No. 2324, 7000ce, Freestyle skier.

**2002, Aug. 15**

**2323-2324** A444 Set of 2 3.50 3.50

*2324a* Souvenir sheet, #2323-2324 3.75 3.75

Intl. Year of Mountains — A445

No. 2325: a, Tateyama, Japan. b, Mt. Shivling, India. c, Wong Leng, Hong Kong. d, Mt. Blanc, France.

15,000ce, Mt. Fuji, Japan.

**2002, Aug. 15**

**2325** A445 6000ce Sheet of 4, #a-d 6.00 6.00

**Souvenir Sheet**

**2326** A445 15,000ce multi 3.75 3.75

20th World Scout Jamboree, Thailand — A446

No. 2327, horiz.: a, Scout with walking stick. b, Scout with backpack. c, Tent and campfire. d, Tent and scout tying knots.

15,000ce, Scout with red neckerchief.

**2002, Aug. 15**

**2327** A446 6500ce Sheet of 4, #a-d 6.00 6.00

**Souvenir Sheet**

**2328** A446 15,000ce multi 4.25 4.25

First Solo Transatlantic Flight, 75th Anniv. — A447

No. 2329, 8500ce, horiz.: a, Charles Lindbergh and Spirit of St. Louis. b, Charles and Anne Morrow Lindbergh in airplane.

15,000ce, Lindbergh wearing flying gear.

**2002, Aug. 15**

**2329** A447 8500ce Sheet of 2, #a-b 4.00 4.00

**Souvenir Sheet**

**2330** A447 15,000ce multi 3.75 3.75

Intl. Year of Ecotourism — A448

No. 2331: a, Nectarinia venusta. b, Panthera pardus. c, Kobus kob. d, Syncerus caffer. e, Pan troglodytes. f, Galago.

12,000ce, Loxodonta africana.

**2002, Aug. 15**

**2331** A448 4000ce Sheet of 6, #a-f 9.50 9.50

**Souvenir Sheet**

**2332** A448 12,000ce multi 5.00 5.00

Nos. 1820-1821 Surcharged

**2002, Aug. 15** *Perf. 13½x14*

**2333** Strip or block of 4 3.00 3.00

*a.* A315 3000ce on 600ce #1820a .75 .75

*b.* A315 3000ce on 600ce #1820b .75 .75

*c.* A315 3000ce on 600ce #1820c .75 .75

*d.* A315 3000ce on 600ce #1820d .75 .75

**Souvenir Sheet**

**2334** A315 20,000ce on 2500ce #1821 5.00 5.00

No. 2334 and sheets of No. 2333 are additionally overprinted in margin with black border and inscription "In Memoriam / 1900-2002."

Butterflies, Moths, Insects and Birds — A449

No. 2335, 4500ce — Butterflies: a, Iolaus menas. b, Neptis melicerta. c, Cymothoe lucasi. d, Euphaedra francina. e, Lilac nymph. f, Mocker swallowtail.

No. 2336, 4500ce — Moths: a, Phiala cunina. b, Mazuca strigicincta. c, Steindachner's emperor. d, Amphicallia pactolicus. e, Verdant sphinx. f, Oleander hawkmoth.

No. 2337, 4500ce — Insects: a, Bush hopper. b, Ant lion. c, Digger bee. d, Stag beetle. e, Mantis. f, Longhorn beetle.

No. 2338, 4500ce — Birds: a, Malachite kingfisher. b, Brown harrier eagle. c, Heuglin's masked weaver. d, Egyptian plover. e, Swallow-tailed bee-eater. f, Black-faced fire finch.

No. 2339, 15,000ce, Giant blue swallowtail butterfly. No. 2340, 15,000ce, African moon moth. No. 2341, 15,000ce, Mantis nymph. No. 2342, 15,000ce, Rufous fishing owl.

**2002, Aug. 26** *Perf. 14*

**Sheets of 6, #a-f**

**2335-2338** A449 Set of 4 25.00 25.00

**Souvenir Sheets**

**2339-2342** A449 Set of 4 14.00 14.00

Edina Bakatue Festival A450

Designs: No. 2343, 1000ce, No. 2349e, 4000ce, Casting of net. No. 2344, 2000ce, No. 2349b, 4000ce, Chief in palanquin. No. 2345, 2500ce, No. 2349c, 4000ce, Regatta. No. 2346, 3000ce, No. 2349d, 4000ce, Festival boat. No. 2347, 4000ce, Opening ritual. No. 2348, 5000ce, No. 2349a, 4000ce, Priestesses.

**2002, Oct. 21** *Perf. 14x13½*

**2343-2348** A450 Set of 6 4.00 4.00

**2349** A450 Sheet of 6, #2347, 2349a-e 5.50 5.50

Japan Overseas Cooperation Volunteers, 25th Anniv. in Ghana — A451

Designs: No. 2350, 1000ce, Health. No. 2351, 1000ce, Education (Home economics). 2000ce, Education (Science and math). 2500ce, Education (Computer technology). 3000ce, Sports.

No. 2355 (without white inscriptions): a, Like 2000ce. b, Like No. 2350. c, Like 3000ce. d, Like 2500ce. e, Like No. 2351.

**2002, Oct. 23** *Perf. 14*

**2350-2354** A451 Set of 5 2.40 2.40

**2355** A451 4000ce Sheet of 5, #a-e 5.00 5.00

Awarding of Nobel Peace Prize to UN Secretary General Kofi Annan — A452

Designs: 1000ce, With Ghana Pres. J. A. Kufuor at award ceremony. 2000ce, With Nobel medal and citation. 2500ce, Portrait. 3000ce, In academic procession at Kwame Nkrumah University.

**2002, Oct. 28**

**2356-2359** A452 Set of 4 3.50 3.50

Nos. 1939C, 1939B Surcharged

**Methods and Perfs As Before**

**2002, Mar. 7**

**2360** A350c 1000ce on 1100ce multi #1939C, 10½x6mm obliterator — —

**2360A** A350c 2500ce on 800ce multi #1939B — —

*b.* Obliterator 10½x4mm —

Obliterator on No. 2360 is 10½x6mm.

Charlie Chaplin (1889-1977) — A453

No. 2361: a, In suit and tie. b, As "Little Tramp," wearing hat. c, Wearing overalls. d, Holding Academy Award.

**2003, Jan. 14** **Litho.** *Perf. 14*

**2361** A453 6500ce Sheet of 4, #a-d 6.00 6.00

Marlene Dietrich (1901-92) — A454

No. 2362 — Background colors: a, Violet black (hair parted in middle, name at left). b, Gray (wearing scarf, name at right). c, Brown (name at left). d, Dark brown (wearing hat). e, Blue gray (name at left). f, Brown black (name at right).

15,000ce, Holding cigarette.

**2003, Jan. 14**
**2362** A454 4500ce Sheet of 6, #a-f 6.50 6.50

**Souvenir Sheet**

**2363** A454 15,000ce multi 3.50 3.50

Popeye in Amsterdam — A455

No. 2364: a, Along the canal. b, Anne Frank House. c, Restaurant Row. d, Downtown. e, Central Station. f, Windmills.

**2003, Jan. 14** ***Perf. 13¾***
**2364** A455 4500ce Sheet of 6, #a-f 6.50 6.50

**Souvenir Sheet**

**2365** A455 15,000ce shown 3.50 3.50

No. 2364 contains six 38x51mm stamps.

New Year 2003 (Year of the Ram) — A456

**2003, Feb. 24** ***Perf. 14***
**2366** A456 5000ce multi 3.00 3.00

Issued in sheets of 4.

Famous Women — A457

Designs: 1000ce, Nana Yaa Asantewaa (1822-1923), Asante warrior. 2000ce, Justice Annie Jiagge (1918-96). 2500ce, Dr. Esther Ocloo (1919-2002), industrialist. 3000ce, Dr. Efua T. Sutherland (1924-96), playwright. 5000ce, Rebecca Dedei Aryeetey (1924-60), activist.

**2003, Apr. 23** ***Perf. 13½x14***
**2367-2371** A457 Set of 5 3.00 3.00

British Council, 60th Anniv. — A458

Designs: 1000ce, Tomorrow's leaders. 2000ce, Women reading Africawoman Newspaper. 2500ce, Partners in culture. 3000ce, Window on the world. 5000ce, Leadership through sport.

**2003, June 12**
**2372-2376** A458 Set of 5 3.00 3.00

General Motors Automobiles — A459

No. 2377, 7000ce — Cadillacs: a, 1941 Sixty Special. b, 1953 Eldorado. c, 1957 Eldorado Brougham. d, 1959 Eldorado Convertible.
No. 2378, 7000ce — Corvettes: a, 1962. b, 1963 Sting Ray. c, 1964 Sting Ray. d, 1968.
No. 2379, 20,000ce, Cadillac. No. 2380, 20,000ce, 1966 Corvette Sting Ray.

**2003, July 2** ***Perf. 13¾***

**Sheets of 4, #a-d**

**2377-2378** A459 Set of 2 13.50 13.50

**Souvenir Sheets**

**2379-2380** A459 Set of 2 8.50 8.50

Coronation of Queen Elizabeth II, 50th Anniv. — A460

No. 2381: a, Wearing tiara. b, Wearing blue hat. c, Wearing black hat.
20,000ce, Wearing black hat, diff.

**2003, July 2** ***Perf. 14***
**2381** A460 10,000ce Sheet of 3, #a-c 7.00 7.00

**Souvenir Sheet**

**2382** A460 20,000ce multi 4.50 4.50

Tour de France Bicycle Race, Cent. — A461

No. 2383: a, Romain Maes, 1935. b, Sylvére Maes, 1936. c, Roger Lapebie, 1937. d, Gino Bartali, 1938.
20,000ce, Henri Pelissier, 1923.

**2003, July 2** ***Perf. 13½x13¼***
**2383** A461 7000ce Sheet of 4, #a-d 6.50 6.50

**Souvenir Sheet**

**2384** A461 20,000ce multi 4.50 4.50

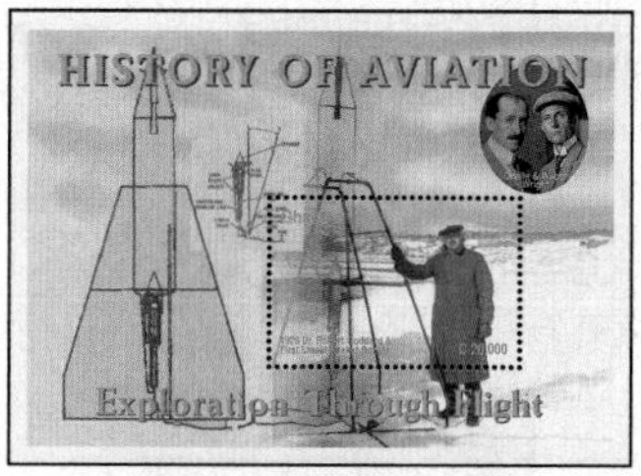

History of Aviation — A462

No. 2385: a, Charles Lindbergh makes first non-stop solo Atlantic crossing, 1927. b, Wiley Post makes first round-the-world solo flight, 1933. c, Heinkel He178, first turbojet powered aircraft, 1939. d, Chuck Yeager flies Bell X-1 to break sound barrier, 1947.
20,000ce, Dr. Robert Goddard and first liquid-fueled rocket, 1926.

**2003, July 2** ***Perf. 14***
**2385** A462 7000ce Sheet of 4, #a-d 6.50 6.50

**Souvenir Sheet**

**2386** A462 20,000ce multi 4.50 4.50

Christmas A463

Children's art: 2000ce, Preparation for Christmas, by Kwame Owusu Aduomi. 4000ce, Typical Christmas Present, by Thomas Kyerematteng, vert. 4500ce, Making Merry at Christmas, by Samuel Baffoe Maison. 5000ce, Christmas is Here, by Patrick Annan-Noonoo.

***Perf. 14x13¼, 13¼x14***

**2003, Dec. 1** **Litho.**
**2387-2390** A463 Set of 4 3.75 3.75

Boletus Edulis — A463a

**2003** **Litho.** ***Perf. 14x13½***
**2390A** A463a 1000ce multi — —

New Year 2004 (Year of the Monkey) — A464

No. 2391: a, Dark gray monkey. b, Light gray monkey. c, Buff monkey.

**2004, Jan. 29** **Litho.** ***Perf. 14***
**2391** A464 5000ce Sheet of 3, #a-c 5.00 5.00

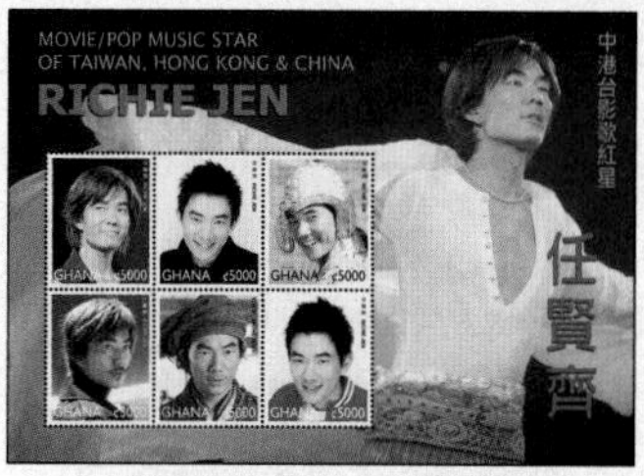

Chinese Actors — A465

No. 2392, 5000ce — Richie Jen: a, With hair below ears, wearing black shirt. b, With hair above ears, wearing black shirt. c, Wearing helmet. d, With mustache. e, Wearing head covering. f, Wearing red jacket.
No. 2393, 5000ce — Ray Lui: a, Wearing suit and tie. b, With shaved head. c, Wearing black hood. d, Wearing polka dot shirt. e, Wearing costume. f, Wearing costume with red headpiece. g, Wearing costume with wound on forehead.
No. 2394, 5000ce — Jiang Wen: a, Wearing glasses, fingers showing at LR. b, Wearing costume with headpiece. c, Sepia photograph, wearing glasses. d, Wearing suit and tie. e, Sepia photograph, without glasses. f, Wearing striped shirt.

**2004, Feb. 1** ***Perf. 13¾***

**Sheets of 6, #a-f**

**2392-2394** A465 Set of 3 21.00 21.00

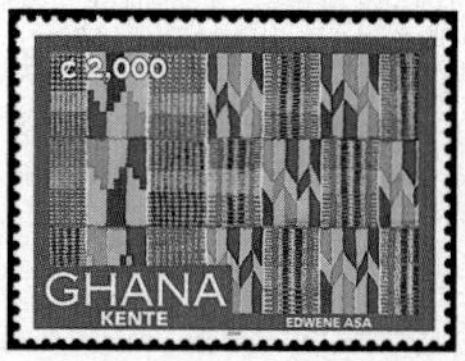

Kente Cloth Patterns A466

Designs: 2000ce, Edwene Asa. 4000ce, Fatia Fata Nkruma. 4500ce, Asam Takra. 5000ce, Toku Akra Ntoma. 6000ce, Sika Futuro.

**2004, Feb. 27** ***Perf. 14x13¼***
**2395-2399** A466 Set of 5 5.00 5.00

Hogbetsotso Festival — A467

Designs: 2000ce, Exodus from Notsie. 4000ce, Misego Dance. 4500ce, Royal stools. 5000ce, Pouring libation. 6000ce, King aloft.
No. 2405: a, Pouring libation, diff. b, Togbe Adeladza II, Awomefia of Anlo. c, Display of traditional symbols of wealth. d, Exodus from Notsie, diff. e, Procession of the royalty. f, Royalty at Durbar. g, Ewe cultural dance. h, Bountiful harvest. i, Royal stools, diff.

**2004, Mar. 1**
**2400-2404** A467 Set of 5 5.00 5.00
**2405** A467 3000ce Sheet of 9, #a-i 6.00 6.00

Paintings of Scouts by Norman Rockwell (1894-1978) — A468

No. 2406 — Paintings from 1974 Boy Scout Calendar: a, Female scout leader. b, Webelo

(plaid neckerchief). c, Boy scout (green cap). d, Cub scout (blue and yellow neckerchief).
20,000ce, Good Friends.

**2004, Mar. 18** ***Perf. 14***
**2406** A468 7000ce Sheet of 4, #a-d 6.50 6.50

**Souvenir Sheet**

**2407** A468 20,000ce multi 4.50 4.50

Paintings by Pablo Picasso (1881-1973) — A469

No. 2408: a, Jacqueline in a Black Scarf. b, Portrait of Olga. c, Woman in White (Sara Murphy). d, Portrait of Dora Maar.
16,000ce, Portrait of the Artist's Sister, Lola.

**2004, Mar. 18** ***Perf. 14¼***
**2408** A469 6500ce Sheet of 4, #a-d 7.50 7.50

***Imperf***

**2409** A469 16,000ce multi 4.50 4.50

No. 22408 contains four 37x50mm stamps.

Paintings of James Abbott McNeill Whistler (1834-1903) A470

Designs: 2000ce, Head of a Peasant Woman. 4000ce, The Master Smith of Lyme Regis. 5000ce, The Little Rose of Lyme Regis. 6000ce, Arrangement in Gray: Portrait of a Painter (self-portrait).
No. 2414: a, Rose and Siver: La Princesse du Pays de la Porcelaine. b, Variations in Flesh Color and Green: The Balcony. c, Caprice in Purple and Gold: The Golden Screen. d, Purple and Rose: The Lange Lijzen of the Six Marks.
20,000ce, Harmony in Green and Rose: The Music Room, horiz.

**2004, Mar. 18** ***Perf. 14¼***
**2410-2413** A470 Set of 4 4.00 4.00
**2414** A470 7500ce Sheet of 4, #a-d 6.75 6.75

**Souvenir Sheet**

**2415** A470 20,000ce multi 4.50 4.50

Paintings in the Hermitage, St. Petersburg, Russia A471

Designs: 2000ce, Portrait of Anne of Austria as Minerva, by Simon Vouet. 3000ce, Lasciviousness, by Pompeo Giroloamo Batoni. 10,000ce, Allegory of Faith, by Moretto da Brescia.
No. 2419: a, Allegory of the Arts, by Bernardo Strozzi. b, Vulcan's Forge, by Luca Giordano. c, Daedalus and Icarus, by Charles Lebrun. d, The Infant Hercules Strangling Serpents in His Cradle, by Sir Joshua Reynolds.
No. 2420, Cupid Undoing Venus's Belt, by Reynolds. No. 2421, Perseus Liberating Andromeda, by Peter Paul Rubens, horiz.

**2004, Mar. 18** ***Perf. 14¼***
**2416-2418** A471 Set of 3 3.50 3.50
**2419** A471 6500ce Sheet of 4, #a-d 6.00 6.00

***Imperf***

**Size: 55x78mm**

**2420** A471 20,000ce multi 4.50 4.50

**Size: 78x55mm**

**2421** A471 20,000ce multi 4.50 4.50

Rotary International, Cent. (in 2005) — A471a

Rotary International emblem and: 2000ce, Polio Plus emblem. 4000ce, Anopheles mosquito, flag of Ghana, vert. 4500ce, Paul P. Harris, flag of Ghana, vert. 5000ce, 2003-04 Rotary International President Jonathan B. Majiyagbe, flag of Ghana, vert. 6000ce, "100 Years," flag of Ghana, vert.
No. 2421F, vert.: g, Women filling water containers. h, Men building shelters. i, Women planting tree.

***Perf. 13x13¼, 13¼x13***

**2004, Sept. 14** **Litho.**
**2421A-2421E** A471a Set of 5 4.75 4.75

**Souvenir Sheet**

**2421F** A471a 10,000ce Sheet of 3, #g-i 6.75 6.75

No. 2421F contains three 28x42mm stamps.

Souvenir Sheet

Deng Xiaoping (1904-97), Chinese Leader — A472

**2004, Nov. 29** **Litho.** ***Perf. 14***
**2422** A472 20,000ce multi 4.50 4.50

Souvenir Sheet

World Peace — A473

No. 2423 — Dr. Martin Luther King, Jr. with: a, Country name at UL. b, Microphone. c, Hands at tie.

**2004, Nov. 29**
**2423** A473 10,000ce Sheet of 3, #a-c 9.25 9.25

Miniature Sheet

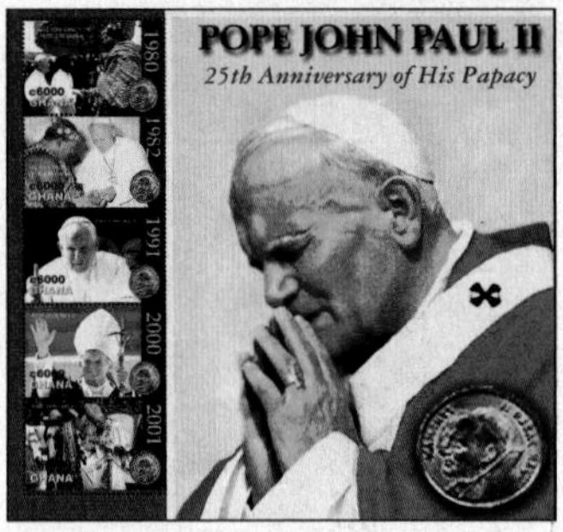


Election of Pope John Paul II, 25th Anniv. (in 2003) — A474

No. 2424 — Photos from: a, 1980. b, 1982. c, 1991. d, 2000. e, 2001.

**2004, Nov. 29**
**2424** A474 6000ce Sheet of 5, #a-e 6.75 6.75

2004 Summer Olympics, Athens A475

Designs: 500ce, Intl. Olympic Committee President Jacques Rogge. 800ce, Soccer player Abedi Ayew Pele. 7000ce, Athlete Margaret Simpson. 10,000ce, Art depicting athletes of ancient Greece, horiz.

**2004, Nov. 29** ***Perf. 14¼***
**2425-2428** A475 Set of 4 4.00 4.00

D-Day, 60th Anniv. — A476

No. 2429, vert.: a, Fleet Admiral Ernest J. King. b, Gen. William C. Lee. c, Lt. Commander John D. Bulkeley. d, Admiral Sir Bertram H. Ramsey.
20,000ce, Rear Admiral Alan G. Kirk.

**2004, Nov. 29**
**2429** A476 8000ce Sheet of 4, #a-d 7.25 7.25

**Souvenir Sheet**

**2430** A476 20,000ce multi 4.50 4.50

European Soccer Championships, Portugal — A477

No. 2431, vert.: a, Gerd Müller. b, Presentation of European Cup. c, Franz Beckenbauer. d, Heysel Stadium, Brussels.
20,000ce, 1972 German team.

**2004, Nov. 29** ***Perf. 14***
**2431** A477 7500ce Sheet of 4, #a-d 6.75 6.75

**Souvenir Sheet**

***Perf. 14¼***

**2432** A477 20,000ce multi 4.50 4.50

No. 2431 contains four 28x42mm stamps.

Worldwide Fund for Nature (WWF) — A478

No. 2433 — African lions: a, Three cubs. b, Lions in water. c, Male lion. d, Female and cubs.

**2004, Dec. 27** ***Perf. 14***
**2433** A478 5000ce Block or strip of 4, #a-d 4.50 4.50
*e.* Miniature sheet, 2 each #2433a-2433d 9.00 9.00

Mushrooms — A479

Designs: 500ce, Boletus badius. 3000ce, Clitocybe nebularis. 5000ce, Amanita muscaria. 8000ce, Russula vesca.
No. 2438, vert.: a, Boletus parasiticus. b, Cortinarius armillatus. c, Gymnopilus spectabilis. d, Cortinarius flexipes.
20,000ce, Chlorosplenium aeruginosum, vert.

**2004, Dec. 27**
**2434-2437** A479 Set of 4 5.00 5.00
**2438** A479 7500ce Sheet of 4, #a-d 8.00 8.00

**Souvenir Sheet**

**2439** A479 20,000ce multi 5.00 5.00

Orchids A480

Designs: 800ce, Oncidium desertorum. 3500ce, Oncidium variegatum. 4000ce, Anguloa uniflora, vert. 10,000ce, Oncidium gardneri, vert.
No. 2444: a, Vanda rothschildiana. b, Laelia cattleya. c, Laelia anceps. d, Odontioda dalmar.
20,000ce, Renanthera bella, vert.

**2004, Dec. 27**
**2440-2443** A480 Set of 4 6.00 6.00
**2444** A480 7500ce Sheet of 4, #a-d 7.50 7.50

**Souvenir Sheet**

**2445** A480 20,000ce multi 5.00 5.00

Mammals — A481

Designs: 1000ce, Serval. 1200ce, Sable antelope. 2000ce, Cheetah. 3000ce, Bohor reedbuck.

No. 2450, horiz.: a, White rhinoceros. b, Leopard. c, Burchell's zebra. d, Red river hog.

20,000ce, Hippopotamus, horiz.

**2004, Dec. 27**

**2446-2449** A481 Set of 4 2.50 2.50
**2450** A481 7500ce Sheet of 4, #a-d 7.50 7.50

**Souvenir Sheet**

**2451** A481 20,000ce multi 5.00 5.00

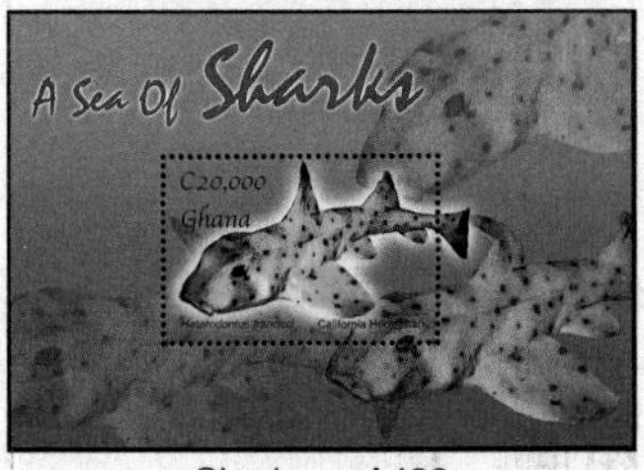


Sharks — A482

No. 2452: a, Zebra bullhead shark. b, Swell-shark. c, Port Jackson shark. d, Leopard shark.

20,000ce, California horn shark.

**2004, Dec. 27**

**2452** A482 7500ce Sheet of 4, #a-d 7.50 7.50

**Souvenir Sheet**

**2453** A482 20,000ce multi 5.00 5.00

New Juaben Akwantukese Afahye Festival — A483

Designs: 2000ce, State emblem Yiadom and Hwedie. No. 2455, 4000ce, Migrating to freedom. 4500ce, Crossing Suhyien River. 5000ce, Chief at State Durbar. 6000ce, Sacrificing at the cave.

No. 2459: a, Like 4500ce. b, Palace guards. c, Like 2000ce. d, Like 5000ce. e, Libation pouring. f, Parading the royal treasury.

**2005, Mar. 1** ***Perf. 13¼x13***

**2454-2458** A483 Set of 5 4.75 4.75
**2459** A483 4000ce Sheet of 6, #a-f 5.50 5.50

FIFA (Fédération Internationale de Football Association), Cent. — A484

No. 2460: a, Roberto Di Matteo. b, Marcel Desailly. c, Osei Kufuor. d, Eusebio.

20,000ce, Johan Cruyff.

**2005, Mar. 14** ***Perf. 13¼***

**2460** A484 7500ce Sheet of 4, #a-d 7.25 7.25

**Souvenir Sheet**

**2461** A484 20,000ce multi 4.75 4.75

Ipomoea Asarifolia — A485

**2005 ?** **Litho.** ***Perf. 13¾x13½***

**2462** A485 2000ce multi — —

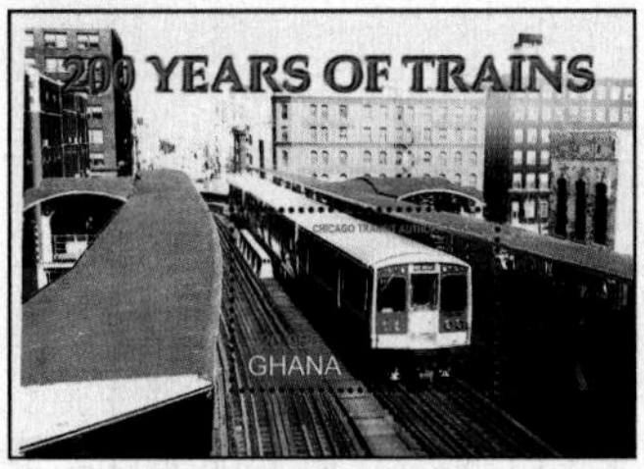


Trains — A486

No. 2463, 5000ce: a, Stanier Class 5-4-6-0. b, Central Pacific Jupiter. c, Robe River RSC3 Class 9401. d, Bangkok BTS train. e, Streamlined tank locomotive. f, ETR450.

No. 2464, 5000ce: a, Talgo train, Spain. b, VIA Turbotrain, Canada. c, Southern Pacific 4-8-4 #4449. d, Union Pacific "City of Portland." e, Shinkansen, Japan (white denomination). f, Deltic Diesel-electric engine, Great Britain.

No. 2465, 5000ce: a, Mogul 2-6-0. b, Milwaukee Railroad 4-6-2. c, Shinkansen (red denomination). d, Former Reading #2101 4-8-4. e, HST Inter-city 125. f, Daylight train.

No. 2466: a, Baldwin 4-6-0 steam train. b, Atchison, Topeka & Santa Fe 4-4-0 "American" steam train. c, Baldwin 4-6-0 Engine #44. d, Baldwin 2-6-0 #3 Three-spot.

No. 2467, 20,000ce, Chicago Transit Authority train. No. 2468, 20,000ce, Santa Fe train. No. 2469, 20,000ce, Empire Builder. No. 2470, 20,000ce, LMS 5305 steam train.

**2005, June 1** **Litho.** ***Perf. 12¾***

**Sheets of 6, #a-f**

**2463-2465** A486 Set of 3 20.00 20.00
**2466** A486 8000ce Sheet of 4, #a-d 7.00 7.00

**Souvenir Sheets**

**2467-2470** A486 Set of 4 18.00 18.00

Motor Vehicles A487

Designs: 2000ce, Setra State Transport bus. 4000ce, Albium double-decker bus. 4500ce, Bedford Mummy truck and trailer. 5000ce, 1925 Mail carrier. 6000ce, Morris truck.

**2005, June 21** **Litho.** ***Perf. 13x13¼***

**2471-2475** A487 Set of 5 5.00 5.00

Friedrich von Schiller (1759-1805), Writer — A488

No. 2476: a, Schiller, with hand touching head. b, Schiller and birthplace. c, Brahms with beard.

20,000ce, Portraits of Schiller and Johannes Brahms.

**2005** **Litho.** ***Perf. 13¼***

**2476** A488 11,000ce Sheet of 3, #a-c 7.25 7.25

***Imperf***

**2477** A488 20,000ce shown 4.75 4.75

No. 2476 contains three 42x28mm stamps.

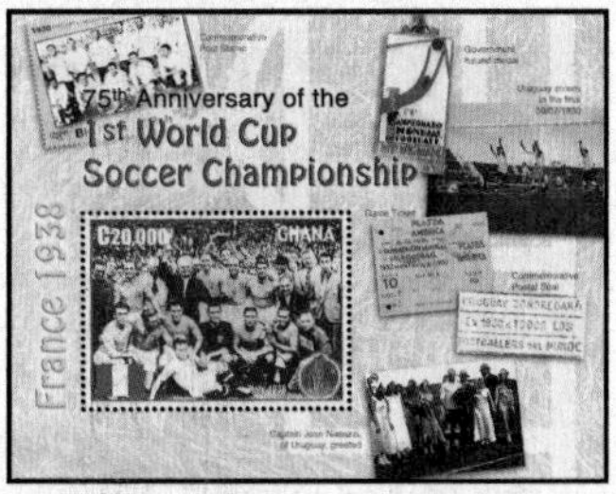


World Cup Soccer Championships, 75th Anniv. — A489

No. 2478: a, 1938 Italian team. b, Scene from 1938 Italy vs. Hungary match. c, Olympic Stadium. d, Silvio Piola.

20,000ce, Italian team with World Cup.

**2005** ***Perf. 13¼***

**2478** A489 8000ce Sheet of 4, #a-d 7.25 7.25

**Souvenir Sheet**

**2479** A489 20,000ce multi 4.75 4.75

Panafest 05 — A489a

Inscriptions: No. 2479A, Biribi wo soro (a symbol of hope). No. 2479B, A royal entry, horiz. No. 2479C, 4000ce, Let's hold hands together, horiz. No. 2479D, 4500ce, Clarion call for Black Unity, horiz. No. 2479E, Sankofa (back to your roots). No. 2479F, Bi-nnka-bi (bite not one another), horiz. No. 2479G, 6000ce, Nkyinkyim (changing oneself; playing many roles).

***Perf. 13½x13¼, 13¼x13½***

**2005 ?** **Litho.**

**2479A** A489a 2000ce multi —
**2479B** A489a 2000ce multi —
**2479C** A489a 4000ce multi —
**2479D** A489a 4500ce multi —
**2479E** A489a 5000ce multi —
**2479F** A489a 5000ce multi —
**2479G** A489a 6000ce multi —

The editors would like to examine any examples of any additional stamps that might exist in this set.

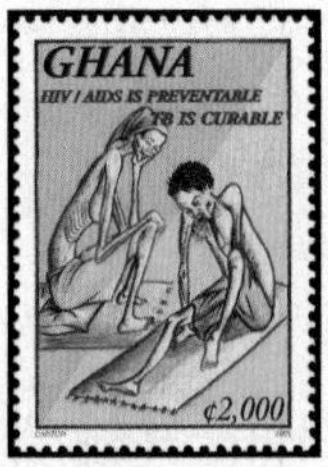


Disease Treatment and Prevention A490

Designs: No. 2480, 2000ce, Emaciated people on rugs. No. 2481, 2000ce, Map of Ghana, symbols of medicine, red ribbon. No. 2482, 2000ce, People holding signs, horiz. 3000ce, Red ribbon, head. 4000ce, Maps of Africa and Ghana, arms, stylized people. No. 2485, 4500ce, Diseases on ladder destroying human body of bricks. No. 2486, 4500ce, Hand holding egg depicting health care workers. No. 2487, 5000ce, Emaciated man carrying bags of diseases. No. 2488, 5000ce, Heart, man lifting stylized globe. 6000ce, Whistle, hands holding cards with slogans.

**2006, Jan. 26** ***Perf. 13¼x13, 13x13¼***

**2480-2489** A490 Set of 10 8.50 8.50

National Basketball Association Players and Team Emblems — A491

No. 2490, 3500ce: a, Carlos Boozer. b, Utah Jazz emblem

No. 2491, 3500ce: a, Carlos Arroyo. b, Detroit Pistons emblem.

No. 2492, 3500ce: a, Corey Magette. b, Los Angeles Clippers emblem.

No. 2493, 3500ce: a, David Wesley. b, Houston Rockets emblem.

No. 2494, 3500ce: a, Manu Ginobili. b, San Antonio Spurs emblem.

No. 2495, 3500ce: a, Al Harrington. b, Atlanta Hawks emblem.

**2006, Mar. 15** ***Perf. 13¼***

**Sheets of 12, 10 each #a, 2 each #b**

**2490-2495** A491 Set of 6 55.00 55.00

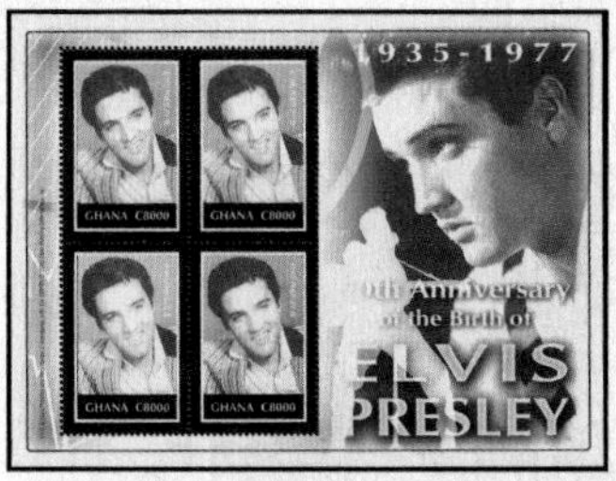


A492

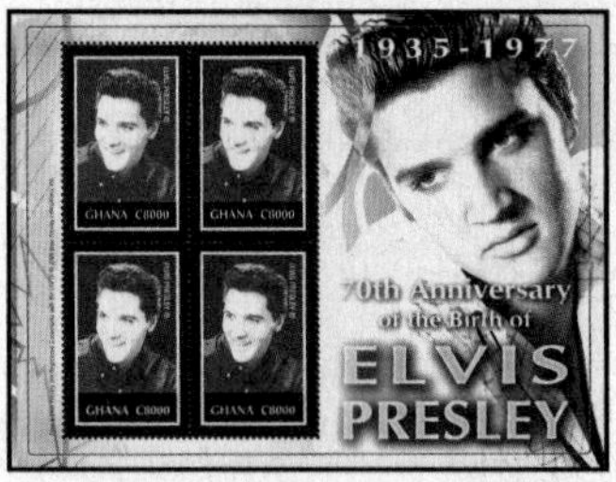


A493

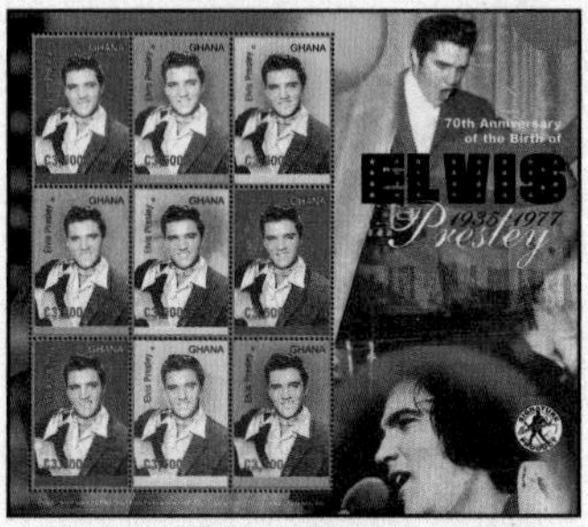


Elvis Presley (1935-77) — A494

No. 2496 — Background color: a, Lilac. b, Green. c, Yellow green. d, Blue.

No. 2497 — Face color: a, Lilac. b, Green. c, Yellow green. d, Blue.

No. 2498: a, Blue background. b, Green background with dark red halo, ghost image at right. c, Yellow background with orange halo. d, Green background with orange red halo, ghost image above head. e, Yellow background, ghost image showing teeth at left. f, Yellow background, gray area at right. g, Green background, blue halo.

**2006, Mar. 15** *Perf. 14*

**2496** A492 8000ce Sheet of 4, #a-d 7.00 7.00
**2497** A493 8000ce Sheet of 4, #a-d 7.00 7.00
**2498** A494 3500ce Sheet of 9, #a-f, 3 #g 7.00 7.00

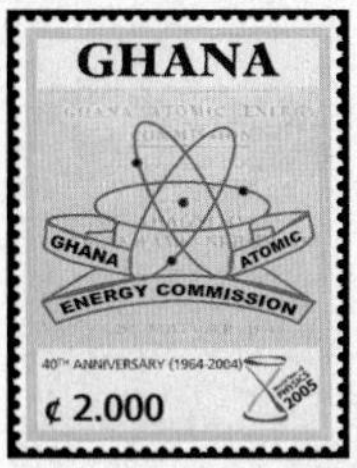

Intl. Year of Physics (in 2005) — A495

Designs: 2000ce, Emblem of Ghana Atomic Energy Commission. 4000ce, Ghana research reactor. 4500ce, Albert Einstein. 5000ce, Prof. Francis K. Allotey, physicist. 6000ce, Electricity experiment in physics laboratory.

**2006. Mar. 29** *Perf. 13¼x14*

**2499-2503** A495 Set of 5 7.25 7.25

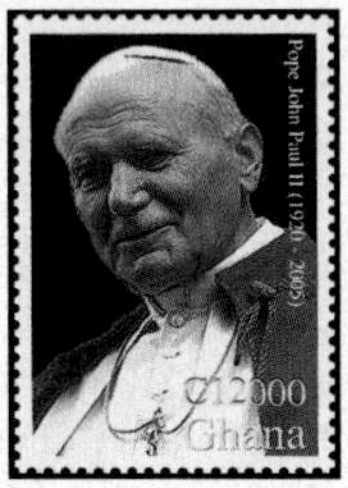

Pope John Paul II (1920-2005) A496

**2006, Apr. 7** *Perf. 13¼*

**2504** A496 12,000ce multi 2.75 2.75

Printed in sheets of 4.

Battle of Trafalgar, Bicent. (in 2005) A497

Designs: 2000ce, Sir John Jervis. 3000ce, Chase and Race. 5000ce, Goliath fires at Guerrier, horiz. 10,000ce, Death of Adm. Horatio Nelson, horiz.

20,000ce, Napoleon's flagships, Agamemnon. Vanguard, Elephant and Captain, horiz.

**2006, Apr. 7** *Perf. 13x13¼, 13¼x13*

**2505-2508** A497 Set of 4 4.50 4.50

**Souvenir Sheet**

*Perf. 12*

**2509** A497 20,000ce multi 4.50 4.50

Jules Verne (1828-1905), Writer — A498

No. 2510: a, Verne. b, Original book illustrations of balloons in flight. c, Montgolfier hot air balloon. d, Modern hot air balloon.

20,000ce, The Hindenburg.

**2006, Apr. 7** *Perf. 12¾*

**2510** A498 8000ce Sheet of 4, #a-d 7.50 7.50

**Souvenir Sheet**

**2511** A498 20,000ce multi 5.00 5.00

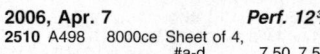

2006 World Cup Soccer Championships, Germany — A499

Designs: No. 2512, 2000ce, Line of Ghana Black Stars players. No. 2513, 2000ce, Captain Stephen Appiah and opposing player, vert. No. 2514, 4000ce, Exchange of pennants. No. 2515, 4000ce, Joy of success. No. 2516, 4500ce, Michael Essien. No. 2517, 4500ce, Franz Beckenbauer, FIFA World Cup Stadium, Hanover. No. 2518, 5000ce, Scene from Ghana vs. Burkina Faso match. No. 2519, 5000ce, Black Stars team photo. No. 2520, 6000ce, Scene from Ghana vs. South Africa match. No. 2521, 6000ce, Fans celebrating Black Stars victory.

No. 2522, 4000ce: a, Appiah. b, Issah Ahmed. c, John Paintsil. d, Laryea Kingston. e, Essien, diff. f, Sule Ali Muntari. g, Joe Tex Frimpong. h, Coach Ratomir Dujkovic.

No. 2523, 4000ce: a, Asamoah Gyan. b, Sammy Adjei. c, Matthew Amoah. d, John Mensah. e, Emmanuel Pappoe. f, Mark Caniel Edusei. g, Abubakari Yakubu. h, Godwin Attram.

**2006, May 18** *Perf. 13½*

**2512-2521** A499 Set of 10 9.50 9.50

**Sheets of 8, #a-h**

*Perf. 13¼*

**2522-2523** A499 Set of 2 14.00 14.00

Nos. 2522-2523 each contain eight 42x28mm stamps.

Tympanotonus Fuscatus — A500

Synodontis Ocellifer — A500a

Musa Sapientum — A501

Gomphidius Glutinosus — A501a

Bebearia Arcadius — A502

Polemaetus Bellicosus — A502a

Xaphia Gladius (Denomination at Center) — A503

Euphaedra Francina — A504

Falco Tinnunculus — A504a

Lagerstroemia Flos-reginae — A504b

Ardea Purpurea (With Brown Frame and "A's" of "Ghana" With Horizontal Cross Lines — A504c

Spathodea Campanulata — A505

**2003-07** **Litho.** *Perf. 13½*

| | | | | | |
|---|---|---|---|---|---|
| **2524** | A500 | 500ce | multi | | — |
| **2524A** | A500a | 500ce | multi | | — |
| **2525** | A501 | 800ce | multi | — | — |
| **2525A** | A501a | 1000ce | multi | | — |
| **2526** | A502 | 1500ce | multi | | — |
| **2526A** | A502a | 1500ce | multi | — | — |
| **2527** | A503 | 2000ce | multi | | — |
| **2528** | A504 | 2000ce | multi | — | — |
| **2528A** | A504a | 2500ce | multi | — | — |
| **2528B** | A504b | 4000ce | multi | | — |
| **2528C** | A504c | 5000ce | multi | | — |
| **2529** | A505 | 6000ce | multi | — | — |

Issued: No. 2524, July 2003; Nos. 2524A, 2528B, Oct. 2005. No. 2525A, 2529, 2006; Nos. 2526A, 2528A, 2528C, 2007; No. 2527, 2005.

For surcharge see No. 2679.

Nos. 1674-1677 Surcharged

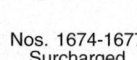

**2006, Aug. 28** **Litho.** *Perf. 14*

**2530** A284 2000ce on 50ce #1674 *29.00 10.00*
**2531** A284 2000ce on 200ce #1675 *29.00 10.00*
**2532** A284 2000ce on 500ce #1676 *29.00 10.00*
**2533** A284 2000ce on 800ce #1677 *29.00 10.00*
*Nos. 2530-2533 (4)* *116.00 40.00*

**Nos. 1810-1814 Surcharged**

**2006, Aug. 28** **Litho.** *Perf. 14*

**2534** A312 2000ce on 200ce #1810 .45 .45
**2535** A312 2000ce on 300ce #1811 .45 .45
**2536** A312 2000ce on 400ce #1812 .45 .45
**2537** A312 2000ce on 600ce #1813 .45 .45
**2538** A312 2000ce on 800ce #1814 .45 .45
*Nos. 2534-2538 (5)* 2.25 2.25

**Nos. 1703-1708 Surcharged**

**2006, Aug. 28** **Litho.** *Perf. 14*

**2539** A291 3000ce on 50ce #1703 .65 .65
**2540** A291 3000ce on 100ce #1704 .65 .65
**2541** A291 3000ce on 200ce #1705 .65 .65
**2542** A291 3000ce on 400ce #1706 .65 .65
**2543** A291 3000ce on 600ce #1707 .65 .65
**2544** A291 3000ce on 800ce #1708 .65 .65
*Nos. 2539-2544 (6)* 3.90 3.90

**Nos. 1741-1743 Surcharged**

**2006, Aug. 28** **Litho.** *Perf. 14*

**2545** A300 4000ce on 50ce #1741 .90 .90
**2546** A300 4000ce on 200ce #1742 .90 .90
**2547** A300 4000ce on 600ce #1743 .90 .90
*Nos. 2545-2547 (3)* 2.70 2.70

**Nos. 1738-1740 Surcharged**

**2006, Aug. 28** **Litho.** *Perf. 14*

**2548** A299 4500ce on 100ce #1738 1.00 1.00
**2549** A299 4500ce on 400ce #1739 1.00 1.00
**2550** A299 4500ce on 1000ce #1740 1.00 1.00
*Nos. 2548-2550 (3)* 3.00 3.00

Nos. 1745-1752 Surcharged

**2006, Aug. 28** **Litho.** *Perf. 14*

**2551** A301 5000ce on 50ce #1745 1.10 1.10
**2552** A301 5000ce on 100ce #1746 1.10 1.10
**2553** A301 5000ce on 150ce #1747 1.10 1.10
**2554** A301 5000ce on 200ce #1748 1.10 1.10
**2555** A301 5000ce on 400ce #1749 1.10 1.10
**2556** A301 5000ce on 600ce #1750 1.10 1.10
**2557** A301 5000ce on 800ce #1751 1.10 1.10
**2558** A301 5000ce on 1000ce #1752 1.10 1.10
*Nos. 2551-2558 (8)* 8.80 8.80

**Nos. 1766-1768 Surcharged**

**2006, Aug. 28 Litho. *Perf. 14***

**2559** A299 6000ce on 100ce #1766 1.25 1.25
**2560** A299 6000ce on 400ce #1767 1.25 1.25
**2561** A299 6000ce on 1000ce #1768 1.25 1.25
*Nos. 2559-2561 (3)* 3.75 3.75

Miniature Sheets

Ghana Soccer Players — A506

No. 2562, 4000ce: a, Asamoah Gyan. b, Sammy Adjei. c, Matthew Amoah. d, John Mensah. e, Emmanuel Pappoe. f, Mark Daniel Edusei. g, Abubakari Yakubu. h, Godwin Attram.

No. 2563, 4000ce: a, Stephen Appiah. b, Issah Ahmed. c, John Paintsil. d, Laryea Kingston. e, Michael Essien. f, Sule Ali Muntari. g, Joe Tex Frimpong. h, Ghana Team Coach Ratomir Dujkovic.

**2007, Jan. 22 Litho. *Perf. 13½***

**Sheets of 8, #a-h**

**2562-2563** A506 Set of 2 14.00 14.00

Queen Elizabeth II, 80th Birthday — A507

No. 2564: a, Holding flowers. b, Wearing purple hat. c, Wearing light green hat, denomination in purple. d, Wearing light green hat, denomination in white.

25,000ce, Wearing tiara.

**2007, Jan. 22**

**2564** A507 6000ce Sheet of 4, #a-d 5.25 5.25

**Souvenir Sheet**

**2565** A507 25,000ce multi 5.50 5.50

Marilyn Monroe (1926-62), Actress — A508

No. 2566: a, Wearing glasses. b, Wearing bathrobe. c, Looking left. d, Wearing red dress and earrings.

20,000ce, With eyes closed.

**2007, Jan. 22**

**2566** A508 9000ce Sheet of 4, #a-d 8.00 8.00

**Souvenir Sheet**

**2567** A508 20,000ce multi 4.50 4.50

Space Achievements — A509

No. 2568, horiz. — Luna 9: a, Distant view of spacecraft and moon, denomination in black. b, Spacecraft, denomination in white. c, Close-up view of spacecraft and moon, denomination in black. d, Spacecraft in frame, denomination in white.

No. 2569, 6500ce, horiz. — Apollo-Soyuz Test Project: a, Apollo and Soyuz spacecraft docked. b, Mission emblem. c, Astronaut Tom Stafford. d, Cosmonaut Aleksei Leonov. e, Astronaut Deke Slayton. f, Astronaut Vance Brand and Cosmonaut Valeri Kubasov.

No. 2570, 6500ce — Giotto Comet Probe: a, Probe in space, black background. b, Comet, probe in space, red text at bottom. c, Top of probe, white background. d, Comet, probe in space, purple background. e, Probe and schematic diagram. f, Bottom of probe.

No. 2571, 20,000ce, Astronaut Buzz Aldrin. No. 2572, 20,000ce, Apollo-Soyuz crew members shaking hands in space, horiz. No. 2573, 20,000ce, Viking 1, horiz.

**2007, Jan. 22**

**2568** A509 10,000ce Sheet of 4, #a-d 8.75 8.75

**Sheets of 6, #a-f**

**2569-2570** A509 Set of 2 17.00 17.00

**Souvenir Sheets**

**2571-2573** A509 Set of 3 13.00 13.00

Scouting, Cent. — A510

No. 2574, vert. — Dove, Scout emblem and Scout: a, Giving Scout sign. b, Blowing bugle. c, Carrying injured boy.

20,000ce, Scout emblem, Scout giving Scout sign.

**2007 *Perf. 13¼***

**2574** A510 12,000ce Sheet of 3, #a-c 8.00 8.00

**Souvenir Sheet**

**2575** A510 20,000ce multi 4.50 4.50

Independence, 50th Anniv. — A511

**2007, Sept. 15 Litho. *Perf. 13¼***

**2576** A511 4000ce multi .90 .90

Kente Cloth Designs — A512

Designs: 4000ce, Sika ne Barima. 7300ce, Edwene Si So. 7500ce, Dakoro Yesere. No. 2580, 9000ce, Agyenegyne Nsu. No. 2581, 9000ce, Nkatoa Sa. 10,000ce, Edwene Asa.

**2007, Sept. 15 *Perf. 13½x13¼***

**2577-2582** A512 Set of 6 10.00 10.00

Aburi Botanical Gardens — A513

Designs: 4000ce, Bamboo groves. 7300ce, School of Horticulture. 7500ce, Silk cotton tree, vert. 9000ce, Royal Palm Walkway. 10,000ce, Famous ficus tree, vert.

No. 2588: a, Like 9000ce. b, Like 7300ce. c, Silk cotton tree. d, Famous ficus tree. e, Like 4000ce. f, Sanatorium.

***Perf. 13¼x13½, 13½x13¼***

**2007, Sept. 15**

**2583-2587** A513 Set of 5 8.25 8.25
**2588** A513 6000ce Sheet of 6, #a-f 7.75 7.75

Cocoa — A514

Designs: 4000ce, Cocoa beverages and spread. 7300ce, Cocoa Pebbles. 7500ce, Assorted chocolates. 9000ce, Man at cocoa processing plant. 10,000ce, Finished cocoa products.

No. 2594: a, Like 10,000ce. b, Cacao pods. c, Like 7500ce. d, Like 9000ce. e, Like 7300ce. f, Workers packaging cocoa products.

**2007, Sept. 15 *Perf. 13¼x13½***

**2589-2593** A514 Set of 5 8.25 8.25
**2594** A514 6000ce Sheet of 6, #a-f 7.75 7.75

Cats and Dogs — A515

Designs: 6000ce, Chartreux cat. 7000ce, Blue-mitted ragdoll cat. 8000ce, Blue lynx point Birman cat, horiz. 9000ce, Norwegian Forest cat.

No. 2599, horiz.: a, American bulldog. b, Old English sheepdog. c, Shar-pei. d, Boston terrier.

No. 2600, 20,000ce, Cinnamon point Siamese cat. No. 2601, 20,000ce, Greyhound.

**2007, Sept. 15 *Perf. 14***

**2595-2598** A515 Set of 4 6.50 6.50
**2599** A515 7500ce Sheet of 4, #a-d 6.50 6.50

**Souvenir Sheets**

**2600-2601** A515 Set of 2 8.75 8.75

Orchids — A516

No. 2602: a, Epipactis atrorubens. b, Galeandra bicarinata. c, Platanthera tipuloides. d, Platanthera ciliaris.

20,000ce, Spathoglottis plicata.

**2007, Sept. 15**

**2602** A516 7500ce Sheet of 4, #a-d 6.50 6.50

**Souvenir Sheet**

**2603** A516 20,000ce multi 4.50 4.50

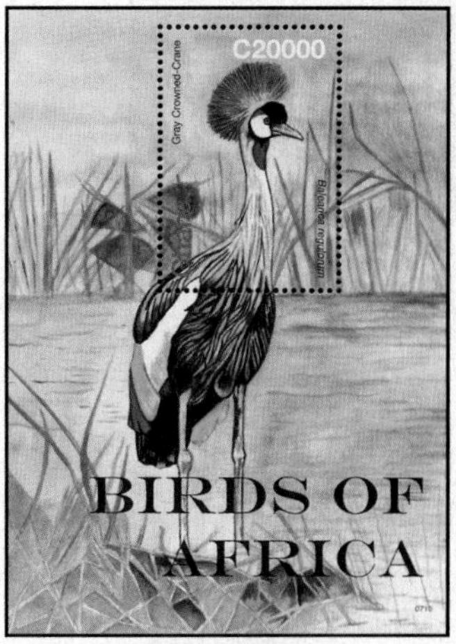


Birds — A517

No. 2604, horiz.: a, Red-billed hornbill. b, Bearded barbet. c, Hoopoe. d, Pygmy kingfisher.

20,000ce, Gray-crowned crane.

**2007, Sept. 15**

**2604** A517 7500ce Sheet of 4, #a-d 6.50 6.50

**Souvenir Sheet**

**2605** A517 20,000ce multi 4.50 4.50

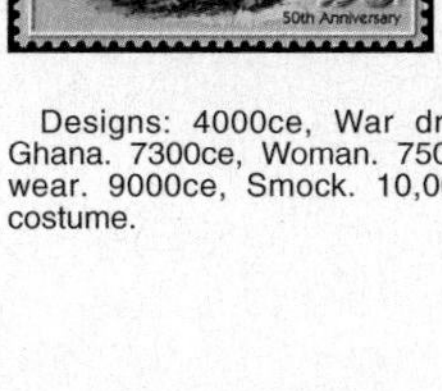


Traditional Costumes A518

Designs: 4000ce, War dress, Northern Ghana. 7300ce, Woman. 7500ce, Mourning wear. 9000ce, Smock. 10,000ce, Wulomo costume.

*Perf. 13½x13¼*

**2007, Sept. 15** **Litho.**
**2606-2610** A518 Set of 5 8.25 8.25

Famous People — A519

Designs: No. 2611, 4000ce, Sir Arko Korsah, first Chief Justice. No. 2612, 4000ce, Amon Kotei, designer of national coat of arms. No. 2613, 4000ce, Philip Gbeho, composer of national anthem. 4500ce, F. K. Buah, historian. 6000ce, Prof. Albert Adu Boahene, historian and politician. 7300ce, Leticia Obeng, aquatic biologist. 7500ce, Peter Cardinal Appiah Turkson, first Ghanaian cardinal. 9000ce, Susanna Alhassan, first femal government minister.

**2007, Sept. 15** *Perf. 13¼*
**2611-2618** A519 Set of 8 10.00 10.00

On July 3, 2007, Ghana's currency was revalued at a rate of 10,000 old cedis to 1 new cedi. Old cedis continued to be valid until Dec. 31, 2007. Nos. 2576-2618 and 2641-2646 were issued after July 3, but have denominations expressed in old cedis.

Antrak Air A520

Airplane: 40p, On ground. 73p, In flight.

**2007, Sept. 15** *Perf. 13¼*
**2619-2620** A520 Set of 2 2.25 2.25

Accra Tourist Attractions — A521

Designs: 20p, Independence Arch. 40p, Independence Square. 73p, Supreme Court. 75p, National Theater. 90p, Intl. Conference Center.

**2007, Sept. 15**
**2621-2625** A521 Set of 5 6.50 6.50

Agricultural Development Bank — A522

Designs: 40p, Emblem. 75p, Home Link Account, vert. 90p, Young Farmers Program, vert. 1ce, Gold Drive Motor Loan, vert.

**2007, Sept. 15**
**2626-2629** A522 Set of 4 6.75 6.75

Ghana Commercial Bank — A523

Designs: 40p, Emblem. 73p, Eagle, world map. 75p, Ghana Commercial Bank Tower, vert. 90p, Xpress Money Transfer, vert.

**2007, Sept. 15**
**2630-2633** A523 Set of 4 6.00 6.00

State Insurance Company A524

Designs: 40p, Emblem. 73p, Executives. 75p, New office building. 90p, Child pointing. 1ce, Three CIMG Awards, vert.

**2007, Sept. 15**
**2634-2638** A524 Set of 5 8.25 8.25

Ghanaian Heads of State — A525

Dr. Kwame Nkrumah and Pres. J. A. Kufuor With State Sword — A526

No. 2639: a, Dr. Kwame Nkrumah. b, Lieutenant General J. A. Ankrah. c, General A. A. Afrifa. d, Dr. Kofi Abrefa Busia. e, General I. K. Acheampong. f, Lieutenant General W. A. Akuffo. g, Dr. Hilla Limann. h, Flight Lieutenant J. J. Rawlings. i, Pres. J. A. Kufuor.

**2007, Sept. 15** *Perf. 13½x13¼*
**2639** A525 60p Sheet of 9, #a-i 11.00 11.00

**Souvenir Sheet**

**2640** A526 1ce multi 1.10 1.10

Pope Benedict XVI — A527

**2007, Nov. 15** *Perf. 13¼*
**2641** A527 4000ce multi .90 .90

Printed in sheets of 8.

Gold A528

Designs: 4000ce, Gold ore. 7300ce, Melting gold ore. 7500ce, Woman holding gold bar. 9000ce, Entrance of Obuasi Gold Mines, horiz. 10,000ce, Gold-plated chair.

**2007** *Perf. 13½x13¼, 13¼x13½*
**2642-2646** A528 Set of 5 8.25 8.25

24th UPU Congress, Nairobi A529

Designs: 40p, Dancers. 73p, Flags of Ghana and Kenya, warrior with shield, vert. 75p, UPU emblem in opened box. 90p, UPU emblem on map of Africa, vert.

No. 2651: a, Part of UPU emblem, folded map of world, denomination at LL. b, Part of UPU emblem, folded map of world, denomination at UR. c, Folded map of world, map and flag of Kenya.

**2007, Dec. 3** *Perf. 12½*
**2647-2650** A529 Set of 4 6.00 6.00

**Souvenir Sheet**

**2651** A529 1ce Sheet of 3, #a-c 6.50 6.50

**Miniature Sheet**

Wedding of Queen Elizabeth II and Prince Philip, 60th Anniv. (in 2007) — A530

No. 2652: a, Queen, denomination in green. b, Couple, denomination in green. c, Couple, denomination in orange. d, Queen, denomination in orange. e, Queen, denomination in blue. f, Couple, denomination in blue.

**2008, Jan. 31** **Litho.** *Perf. 13¼x13½*
**2652** A530 60p Sheet of 6, #a-f 7.75 7.75

Paintings by Qi Baishi (1864-1957) — A531

No. 2653: a, Top half of Lotus and Mandarin Ducks (lotus). b, Top half of River Landscape with Boats (boats). c, Bottom half of Lotus and Mandarin Ducks (ducks). d, Bottom half of River Landscape with Boats (trees).
3ce, Peony in a Dragon Vase.

**2008, Jan. 31** *Perf. 12x11½*
**2653** A531 90p Sheet of 4, #a-d 7.75 7.75

**Souvenir Sheet**

*Perf. 11½*

**2654** A531 3ce multi 6.50 6.50

No. 2653 contains four 30x40mm stamps.

**Miniature Sheet**

2008 Summer Olympics, Beijing — A532

No. 2655: a, Boxing. b, Relay race. c, Long jump. d, Soccer.

**2008, May 8** *Perf. 12¾*
**2655** A532 40p Sheet of 4, #a-d 3.25 3.25

**Souvenir Sheet**

Visit of US Pres. George W. Bush to Ghana — A533

No. 2656: a, US Pres. George W. Bush. b, Ghana Pres. John Agyekum Kufuor.

**2008, Sept. 17** ***Perf. 13½***
**2656** A533 1.25ce Sheet of 2, #a-b 4.50 4.50

Khilafat Ahmadiyya, Cent. — A533a

Designs: 40p, Flag, minaret, world map. 73p, T. I. Ahmadiyya Senior High School, Kumasi. 90p, Wheat. 1ce, Ahmadiuua Muslim Hospital, Daboase.

**2008** **Litho.** ***Perf. 14½***
**2656C-2656F** A533a Set of 4 *9.50 9.50*

Coat of Arms — A534

**2009, Mar. 31** **Litho.** ***Perf. 14x15***
**2657** A534 1ce gray + label 1.40 1.40

Vegetables A535

Designs: 1ce, Tomatoes. 1.20ce, Tomatoes and white eggplants. 1.30ce, White eggplants.

**2009, Mar. 31** **Litho.** ***Perf. 14¾x14***
**2658-2660** A535 Set of 3 5.00 5.00

Korle Bu Teaching Hospital A536

Designs: 1ce, Medical block. No. 2662, 1.10ce, Cardiothoracic Center. No. 2663, 1.10ce, New administration block. 1.20ce, Prof. Frimpong Boateng, heart surgeon, vert.

**2009, Mar. 31** ***Perf. 14¾x14, 14x14¾***
**2661-2664** A536 Set of 4 6.25 6.25

Tweneboa Kodua High School A537

Designs: 1ce, Administration block. 1.10ce, Girls domitory. 1.20ce, Students at ICT Center. 1.30ce, Students playing volleyball.

**2009, Mar. 31** ***Perf. 14¾x14***
**2665-2668** A537 Set of 4 6.50 6.50

Soccer Players — A538

Designs: No. 2669, 1ce, Edward Acquah. No. 2670, 1ce, Aggrey Fynn. No. 2671, 1ce, Nana Gyamfi II. No. 2672, 1ce, Robert Mensah. No. 2673, 1ce, Baba Yara.

**2009, Mar. 31** ***Perf. 14x14¾***
**2669-2673** A538 Set of 5 7.25 7.25

Peony A539

**2009, Apr. 10** ***Perf. 13¼***
**2674** A539 1ce multi 1.40 1.40

Printed in sheets of 8.

Pres. Kwame Nkrumah (1909-72) — A539a

Pres. Nkrumah: 1ce, At Afro-Asian Solidarity Conference.

**2009, Dec. 8** **Litho.** ***Perf. 13¼x13***
**2674A** A539a 1ce multi —

Two additional items were issued in this set. The editors would like to examine any examples. Numbers may change.

**Nos. 852, 1055, 1068, 1939B, and 2525 Surcharged**

No. 2675

No. 2676

No. 2677

No. 2678

No. 2679

**Methods and Perfs. As Before**

**2009 ?**

| | | | | |
|---|---|---|---|---|
| **2675** | A350a | 20p on 800ce #1939B | — | — |
| **2676** | A174 | 1ce on 70p #852 | — | — |
| **2677** | A205 | 1ce on 5ce #1055 | — | — |
| **2678** | A208 | 1ce on 20ce #1068 | — | — |
| **2679** | A501 | 1.20ce on 800ce #2525 | — | — |

The editors suspect more stamps may have been surcharged and would like to examine any examples.

**No. 1057 Surcharged Like No. 2677, Nos. 1069-1070 Surcharged Like No. 2678 and**

**Methods and Perfs As Before**

**2009 ?**

| | | | |
|---|---|---|---|
| **2680** | A208 | 1ce on 60ce #1069 | — |
| **2681** | A208 | 1ce on 80ce #1070 | — |
| **2682** | A205 | 1ce on 250ce #1057 | — |
| **2683** | A435 | 1.20ce on 1100ce #2277 | — |

The editors suspect more stamps may have been issued in this set and would like to examine any examples.

No. 2683 Volta River Authority — A539b

Designs: No. 2689A, 1ce, Kwame Nkrumah switching on Akosombo Generating Station. No. 2689C, 1.20ce, Kwame Nkrumah signing Akosombo Dam Agreement.

**2010, Mar. 2** **Litho.** ***Perf. 13x13¼***
**2689A** A539b 1ce multi —
**2689C** A539b 1.20ce multi —

Three additonal items were issued in this set. The editors would like to examine any examples. Numbers may change.

A540

Wedding of Prince William and Catherine Middleton — A541

Designs: Nos. 2690, 2692, Couple.
No. 2691: a, Prince William. b, Catherine Middleton.
No. 2693, Couple, diff.

**2011, June 15** **Litho.** ***Perf. 12***
**2690** A540 3.50ce multi 4.75 4.75
**2691** A541 3.50ce Horiz. pair, #a-b 9.25 9.25

**Souvenir Sheets**

**2692** A540 12ce multi 16.00 16.00
**2693** A541 12ce multi 16.00 16.00

No. 2690 was printed in sheets of 4. No. 2691 was printed in sheets containing 2 pairs.

Drafting of the Emancipation Proclamation by Abraham Lincoln, 150th Anniv. — A542

No. 2694: a, 1863 *Harper's Weekly* illustration, by Thomas Nast. b, 1863 photograph of Lincoln, by Thomas Le Mere. c, Watercolor by Henry L. Stephens. d, First Reading of the Emancipation Proclamation of President Lincoln, painting by Francis B. Carpenter.

No. 2695, horiz.: a, 1861 photograph of Lincoln, by Alexander Gardner. b, Text of Emancipation Proclamation from the *National Republican.*

**2012, July 9** ***Perf. 14***
**2694** A542 2ce Sheet of 4, #a-d 8.25 8.25

**Souvenir Sheet**

**2695** A542 3ce Sheet of 2, #a-b 6.25 6.25

Sinking of the Titanic, Cent. — A543

No. 2696: a, Dollar bill recovered from the Titanic wreckage. b, Captain Edward J. Smith. c, Titanic at sea. d, Spoons recovered from the Titanic wreckage.
5ce, Titanic at sea, horiz.

**2012, July 9** ***Perf. 12***
**2696** A543 2ce Sheet of 4, #a-d 8.25 8.25

**Souvenir Sheet**

**2697** A543 5ce multi 5.25 5.25

Burning of the Hindenburg, 75th Anniv. — A544

Hindenburg and: 2ce, Map of Europe. 5ce, Spotlights, vert.

**2012, July 9** ***Perf. 12***
**2698** A544 2ce multi 2.10 2.10

**Souvenir Sheet**

**2699** A544 5ce multi 5.25 5.25

No. 2699 contains one 30x50mm rectangular stamp.

Butterflies — A545

No. 2700: a, Acraea hypoleuca. b, Desmolycaena mazoensis. c, Aphnaeus erikssoni. d, Lycaena gigantea. e, Mimacraea marshalli. f, Iolaus alienus.

No. 2701: a, Female Durbania pallida. b, Male Durbania pallida.

**2012, July 9** ***Perf. 13 Syncopated***
**2700** A545 2ce Sheet of 6, #a-f 12.50 12.50

**Souvenir Sheet**

**2701** A545 3ce Sheet of 2, #a-b 6.25 6.25

Birds — A546

No. 2702: a, Hoopoe. b, Long-tailed glossy starling. c, Northern carmine bee-eater. d, Double-collared sunbird.
5ce, Ostrich.

**2012, July 9** ***Perf. 12***

**2702** A546 2ce Sheet of 4, #a-d 8.25 8.25

**Souvenir Sheet**

***Perf. 12¾***

**2703** A546 5ce multi 5.25 5.25

No. 2703 contains one 38x51mm stamp.

Parrots — A547

No. 2704: a, Cape parrot. b, Red-bellied parrot. c, Meyer's parrot. d, Ruppell's parrot. e, African gray parrot. f, Brown-headed parrot.
5ce, Senegal parrot.

**2012, July 9** ***Perf. 14***

**2704** A547 2ce Sheet of 6, #a-f 12.50 12.50

**Souvenir Sheet**

***Perf. 12***

**2705** A547 5ce multi 5.25 5.25

Worldwide Fund for Nature (WWF) — A548

No. 2706 — Bohor reedbuck: a, Three animals. b, Two animals butting heads. c, Two animals running. d, One animal in water.

**2012, Aug. 21** ***Perf. 14***

**2706** A548 1.50ce Block of 4, #a-d 6.50 6.50

*e.* Souvenir sheet of 8, 2 each #a-d 13.00 13.00

Souvenir Sheets

2012 Summer Olympics, London — A549

Designs: No. 2707, 1.50ce, Basketball. No. 2708, 1.50ce, Table tennis. No. 2709, 1.50ce, Synchronized swimming. No. 2710, 1.50ce, Cycling.

**2012, Aug. 21** ***Perf. 14***

**2707-2710** A549 Set of 4 6.50 6.50

Miniature Sheet

Primates — A550

No. 2711: a, Mandrills. b, Chimpanzees. c, Gorillas. d, Orangutans. e, Vervet monkeys.

**2012, Sept. 13** **Litho.**

**2711** A550 2ce Sheet of 5, #a-e 10.50 10.50

Souvenir Sheet

2009 Visit of President Barack Obama to Ghana — A551

No. 2712: a, U.S. flag and President Barack Obama. b, Ghana flag and Pres. John Atta Mills.

**2012, Oct. 1** ***Perf. 12¾***

**2712** A551 3ce Sheet of 2, #a-b 6.50 6.50

Souvenir Sheets

Mushrooms — A552

No. 2713, 3ce — Toxic mushrooms: a, Jack o'lantern mushrooms. b, Fly agaric. c, Death cap.
No. 2714, 3ce — Edible mushrooms: a, Oyster mushrooms. b, Almond mushrooms. c, Saffron milk caps.

**2012, Dec. 12** ***Perf. 12***

**Sheets of 3, #a-c**

**2713-2714** A552 Set of 2 19.00 19.00

Aircraft Carriers — A553

No. 2715: a, Arromanches. b, Béarn. c, Commandant Teste. d, HMS Hermes.
6ce, HMS Ark Royal.

**2012, Dec. 12** ***Perf. 12***

**2715** A553 2ce Sheet of 4, #a-d 8.50 8.50

**Souvenir Sheet**

***Perf. 12¾***

**2716** A553 6ce multi 6.25 6.25

No. 2715 contains four 47x27mm stamps.

Completion of the Painting of the Sistine Chapel, 500th Anniv. — A554

No. 2717: a, Libyan Sibyl. b, Cumaean Sibyl. c, Delphic Sibyl.
7ce, First Day of Creation.

**2012, Dec. 12** ***Perf. 13 Syncopated***

**2717** A554 2.75ce Sheet of 3, #a-c 8.75 8.75

**Souvenir Sheet**

**2718** A554 7ce multi 7.50 7.50

## SEMI-POSTAL STAMPS

Starlets, 1995 Under-17 World Soccer Champions — SP1

200ce+50ce, Holding gold cup won at Ecuador, vert. 550ce+50ce, Starlets '95 team photo. 800ce+50ce, Abu Idorisu, vert. 1100ce+50ce, Emmanuel Bentil, vert. 1500ce+50ce, Bashiru Gambo, vert.

***Perf. 13½x13, 13x13½***

**1997, Aug. 12** **Litho.**

**B1-B5** SP1 Set of 5 6.25 6.25

## AIR POST STAMPS

**Type of Regular Issue**

Designs: 1sh3p, Pennant-winged nightjar. 2sh, Crowned cranes, vert.

***Perf. 14½x14, 14x14½***

**1959, Oct. 5** **Photo.** **Wmk. 325**

**C1** A17 1sh3p multicolored .80 .25

*a.* Booklet pane of 4 4.50

**C2** A17 2sh multicolored 1.10 .60

For surcharges see Nos. C7-C10.

Ships, Tema Harbor and Jet — AP1

***Perf. 14x13***

**1962, Feb. 10** **Litho.** **Unwmk.**

**C3** AP1 1sh3p multicolored .35 .35

**C4** AP1 2sh6p multicolored .85 .85

*Nos. C3-C4,110 (3)* 1.60 1.60

Opening of Tema Harbor, as part of the Volta River Project.

**Type of Regular Issue, 1962**

**1962, Mar. 6** ***Perf. 13x14***

**C5** A35 1sh3p multicolored .30 .30

**C6** A35 2sh6p multicolored .60 .60

**Nos. C1-C2 Surcharged in White or Green with New Value and: "Ghana New Currency / 19th July, 1965"**

***Perf. 14½x14, 14x14½***

**1965, July 19** **Photo.** **Wmk. 325**

**C7** A17 15pa on 1sh3p multi (W) 2.00 .70

**C8** A17 24pa on 2sh multi (G) 2.00 .35

The two lines of the overprint are diagonal on No. C8.

**Nos. C1, C8 Surcharged in White or Red**

**1967, Feb. 27** **Photo.** **Wmk. 325**

**C9** A17 12½np on 1sh3p (W) 4.00 3.00

**C10** A17 20np on 24pa on 2sh 5.00 4.00

## POSTAGE DUE STAMPS

**Gold Coast Nos. J2-J6 Overprinted "GHANA" and Bar in Red**

***Perf. 14***

**1958, June 25** **Wmk. 4** **Typo.**

**J1** D1 1p black .25 *.45*

**J2** D1 2p black .25 *.45*

**J3** D1 3p black .25 *.45*

J4 D1 6p black .25 1.00
J5 D1 1sh black .25 2.00
*Nos. J1-J5 (5)* 1.25 4.35

### Type of Gold Coast Inscribed "Ghana"

**1958, Dec. 1** *Perf. 14*
J6 D1 1p carmine rose .25 .45
J7 D1 2p green .25 .45
J8 D1 3p orange .25 .45
J9 D1 6p ultramarine .25 1.00
J10 D1 1sh purple .25 2.00
*Nos. J6-J10 (5)* 1.25 4.35

### Nos. J6-J10 Surcharged in Black, Blue or Red with New Value and "Ghana New Currency / 19th July, 1965."

**1965, July 19**
J11 D1 1pa on 1p car rose .25 .75
J12 D1 2pa on 2p grn (Bl) .25 1.40
J13 D1 3pa on 3p org (Bl) .25 1.40
J14 D1 6pa on 6p ultra (R) .35 2.50
J15 D1 12pa on 1sh pur (Bl) .60 2.75
*Nos. J11-J15 (5)* 1.70 8.80

Surcharge diagonal on Nos. J11 and J15.

No. J12 with additional surcharge, "1 ½Np" in red, was reported to have been used at one branch post office (Burma Camp) despite official intention. Four similar added surcharges were prepared: 1np on 1pa, 2 ½np on 3pa, 5np on 6pa, and 10np on 12pa.

D2

**1970** **Unwmk.** **Litho.** *Perf. 14½x14*
J16 D2 1np carmine rose 1.30 5.00
J17 D2 1 ½np green 1.50 6.00
J18 D2 2 ½np orange 1.90 8.00
J19 D2 5np ultramarine 2.40 8.50
J20 D2 10np dull purple 3.50 9.50
*Nos. J16-J20 (5)* 10.60 37.00

**1981** **Litho.** *Perf. 14½x14*
J21 D2 2p red orange 1.50 5.25
J22 D2 3p brown 1.50 5.25

## GIBRALTAR

jə-ˈbrol-tər

LOCATION — A fortified promontory, including the Rock, extending from Spain's southeast coast at the entrance to the Mediterranean Sea
GOVT. — British Crown Colony
AREA — 2.5 sq. mi.
POP. — 29,165 (1999 est.)
CAPITAL — Gibraltar

12 Pence = 1 Shilling
20 Shillings = 1 Pound
100 Centimos = 1 Peseta (1889-95)
100 Pence = 1 Pound (1971)

**Catalogue values for unused stamps in this country are for Never Hinged items, beginning with Scott 119 in the regular postage section and Scott J1 in the postage due section.**

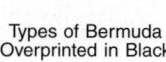

Types of Bermuda Overprinted in Black

**1886, Jan. 1** **Wmk. 2** *Perf. 14*
1 A6 ½p green 18.00 9.50
2 A1 1p rose 80.00 5.50
3 A2 2p violet brown 140.00 92.50
4 A8 2 ½p ultra 180.00 4.25
5 A7 4p orange brn 180.00 100.00
6 A4 6p violet 300.00 225.00
7 A5 1sh bister brn 500.00 400.00
*Nos. 1-7 (7)* 1,398. 836.75

Forged overprints of No. 7 are plentiful.

Victoria
A6 A7

A8 A9

**1886-98** **Typo.**
8 A6 ½p dull green ('87) 14.00 4.50
9 A6 ½p gray grn ('98) 11.00 2.00
10 A7 1p rose ('87) 50.00 5.00
11 A7 1p car rose ('98) 11.00 .55
12 A8 2p brn violet 35.00 27.00
13 A8 2p brn vio & ultra ('98) 27.50 2.00
14 A9 2 ½p brt ultra ('98) 36.00 .80
a. 2 ½p ultramarine 95.00 3.25
16 A8 4p orange brn 90.00 90.00
17 A8 4p org brn & grn ('98) 21.00 7.50
18 A8 6p violet 140.00 130.00
19 A8 6p vio & car rose ('98) 47.50 25.00
20 A8 1sh bister 275.00 225.00
21 A8 1sh bis & car rose ('98) 47.50 18.00
*Nos. 8-14,16-21 (13)* 805.50 537.35

Stamps of 1886 Issue Surcharged in Black

**1889, July**
22 A6 5c on ½p green 8.75 29.00
23 A7 10c on 1p rose 14.50 16.00
24 A8 25c on 2p brn vio 6.00 11.00
a. Small "I" in "CENTIMOS" 140.00 190.00
b. Broken "N" 140.00 190.00
25 A9 25c on 2 ½p ultra 25.00 2.75
a. Small "I" in "CENTIMOS" 400.00 125.00
b. Broken "N" 400.00 125.00
26 A8 40c on 4p org brn 62.50 87.50
27 A8 50c on 6p violet 67.50 87.50
28 A8 75c on 1sh bister 67.50 82.50
*Nos. 22-28 (7)* 251.75 316.25
Set, ovptd. "SPECIMEN" 375.00

There are two varieties of the figure "5" in the 5c, 25c, 50c and 75c.

A11

**1889-95**
29 A11 5c green 5.50 1.00
30 A11 10c rose 5.50 .60
a. Value omitted 6,500.
31 A11 20c ol green ('95) 15.00 100.00
31A A11 20c ol grn & brn ('95) 50.00 23.00
32 A11 25c ultra 23.00 .90
33 A11 40c orange brn 4.75 4.00
34 A11 50c violet 4.25 2.50
35 A11 75c olive green 42.50 42.50
36 A11 1p bister 92.50 25.00
36A A11 1p bis & bl ('95) 6.00 8.00
37 A11 2p blk & car rose ('95) 13.00 37.50
38 A11 5p steel blue 52.50 125.00
*Nos. 29-38 (12)* 314.50 370.00

A12 A13

King Edward VII

**1903, May 1**
39 A12 ½p grn & bl grn 12.00 11.00
40 A12 1p violet, *red* 37.50 .70
41 A12 2p grn & car rose 24.00 32.00
42 A12 2 ½p vio & blk, *bl* 7.50 .70
43 A12 6p violet & pur 30.00 26.00
44 A12 1sh blk & car rose 32.50 42.50
45 A13 2sh green & ultra 175.00 275.00
46 A13 4sh vio & green 120.00 200.00
47 A13 8sh vio & blk, *bl* 160.00 180.00
48 A13 £1 vio & blk, *red* 600.00 700.00
*Nos. 39-48 (10)* 1,198. 1,467.

**1904-12** **Wmk. 3**

**Ordinary or Chalky Paper**
49 A12 ½p blue grn ('07) 10.00 2.00
49A A12 ½p dull grn & br grn 16.00 3.00
50b A12 1p vio, *red* ('05) 8.00 1.00
a. Bisected, used as ½p on card 1,800.
51 A12 1p car ('07) 6.50 .70
52a A12 2p grn & car rose ('07) 10.00 11.00
53 A12 2p gray ('10) 10.00 13.00
54 A12 2 ½p vio & blk, *bl* ('07) 45.00 110.00
55 A12 2 ½p ultra ('07) 6.25 1.90
56b A12 6p vio & pur ('08) 35.00 18.00
a. 6p vio & red violet ('12) 160.00 450.00
57 A12 1sh blk & car rose ('05) 65.00 20.00
58 A12 1sh blk, *grn* ('10) 27.50 25.00
59a A13 2sh grn & ultra ('07) 97.50 120.00
60 A13 2sh vio & bl, *bl* ('10) 60.00 57.50
61 A13 4sh vio & grn 325.00 400.00
62 A13 4sh blk & red ('10) 150.00 175.00
63 A13 8sh vio & grn ('11) 225.00 250.00
64 A12 £1 vio & blk, *red* 600.00 650.00
*Nos. 49-64 (5)* 1,360. 1,532.

Nos. 51, 53, 55 are on ordinary paper. Nos. 54, 58, 60-64 are on chalky paper. Others come on both papers. The least expensive varieties are listed above. For detailed listings, see the *Scott Specialized Catalogue of Stamps and Covers.*

No. 56a, used, must have a 1912 cancellation. Stamps used later sell for about the same as unused.

A14 King George V — A15

**1912, July 17** **Ordinary Paper**
66 A14 ½p green 4.00 .80
67 A14 1p carmine 4.00 .90
a. 1p scarlet ('16) 5.00 1.60
68 A14 2p gray 15.00 1.75
69 A14 2 ½p ultra 10.00 2.50

**Chalky Paper**
70 A14 6p dl vio & red vio 11.00 19.00
71 A14 1sh black, *green* 12.00 4.25
a. 1sh black, *emerald* ('24) 24.00 110.00
b. 1sh blk, *bl grn*, ol back ('19) 21.00 30.00
c. 1sh blk, *emer*, ol back ('23) 30.00 82.50
72 A15 2sh vio & ultra, *bl* 30.00 4.00
73 A15 4sh black & scar 37.50 65.00
74 A15 8sh vio & green 90.00 120.00
75 A15 £1 vio & blk, *red* 160.00 230.00
*Nos. 66-75 (10)* 373.50 448.20

**1921-32** **Ordinary Paper** **Wmk. 4**
76 A14 ½p green ('26) 1.60 1.90
77 A14 1p rose red 2.25 1.40
78a A14 1 ½p pale red brown ('22) 2.25 .40
79 A14 2p gray 1.60 1.60
80 A14 2 ½p ultra 22.50 55.00
81 A14 3p ultra 2.75 1.75

**Chalky Paper**
82 A14 6p dl vio & red vio ('26) 1.75 4.00
a. 6p gray lilac & red violet ('23) 7.00 5.00
83 A14 1sh black, *emer* 12.00 23.00
84 A14 1sh ol grn & blk 17.50 27.50
a. 1sh brn olive & black ('32) 17.50 18.00
85a A15 2sh red vio & ultra, *blue* ('25) 8.25 47.50
86 A15 2sh red brn & black 11.00 37.50
87 A15 2sh6p green & blk 11.00 25.00
88 A15 4sh black & scar 75.00 130.00
89 A15 5sh car & black 17.50 75.00
90 A15 8sh vio & green 275.00 475.00
91 A15 10sh ultra & black 37.50 80.00
92 A15 £1 org & black 180.00 275.00
93 A15 £5 dl vio & blk 1,750. 5,500.
*Nos. 76-92 (15)* 668.95 1,213.

Years issued: Nos. 83, 85, 4sh, 8sh, 1924. 2sh6p, 5sh, 10sh, £5, 1925. £1, 1927. Nos. 84, 86, 1929.

### Type of 1912 Issue Inscribed: "THREE PENCE"

**1930, Apr. 12** **Ordinary Paper**
94 A14 3p ultramarine 9.50 2.25

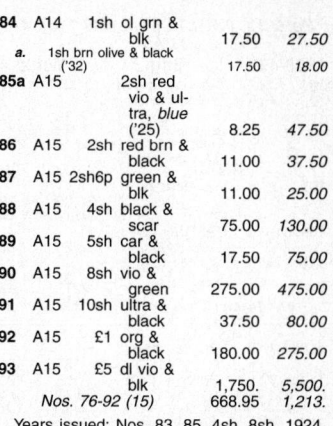

Rock of Gibraltar A16

**1931-33** **Engr.** *Perf. 14*
96 A16 1p red 2.50 3.50
a. Perf. 13½x14 17.50 7.00
97 A16 1 ½p red brown 2.75 3.25
a. Perf. 13½x14 14.50 5.00
98 A16 2p gray ('32) 8.75 2.25
a. Perf. 13½x14 18.00 3.75
99 A16 3p dk blue ('33) 7.75 4.25
a. Perf. 13½x14 30.00 40.00
*Nos. 96-99 (4)* 21.75 13.25
Set, never hinged 45.00
*Nos. 96a-99a (4)* 80.00 55.75
Set, never hinged 150.00

Common Design Types pictured following the introduction.

### Silver Jubilee Issue
Common Design Type

**1935, May 6** *Perf. 11x12*
100 CD301 2p black & ultra 1.40 2.50
101 CD301 3p ultra & brown 3.50 4.00
102 CD301 6p indigo & green 12.00 18.50
103 CD301 1sh brown vio & ind 12.00 16.00
*Nos. 100-103 (4)* 28.90 41.00
Set, never hinged 57.50

### Coronation Issue
Common Design Type

**1937, May 12** *Perf. 11x11½*
104 CD302 ½p deep green .25 .45
105 CD302 2p gray black .85 3.00
106 CD302 3p deep ultra 1.50 3.00
*Nos. 104-106 (3)* 2.60 6.45
Set, never hinged 5.00

George VI — A17

Rock of Gibraltar A18

Designs: 2p, Rock from north side. 3p, 5p, Europa Point. 6p, Moorish Castle. 1sh, Southport Gate. 2sh, Eliott Memorial. 5sh, Government House. 10sh, Catalan Bay.

***Perf. 13, 13½x14 (½p, No. 118), 14 (1½p)***

**1938-49 Engr. Wmk. 4**

**107** A17 ½p gray green .25 *.40*
**108** A18 1p red brn ('42) .35 *.55*
*a.* 1p chestnut, perf. 14 *27.50* 2.75
*b.* 1p chestnut, perf. 13½ 27.50 2.50
*c.* Perf. 13½, wmk. sideways ('41) *6.75* *8.25*
**109** A18 1½p carmine rose 30.00 .90
*b.* Perf. 13½ 275.00 45.00
**109A** A18 1½p gray vio ('43) .25 *1.60*
**110** A18 2p dk gray ('42) .35 1.40
*a.* Perf. 14 27.50 .55
*c.* Perf. 13½ 1.75 .45
*d.* Perf. 13½, wmk. sideways ('41) 650.00 52.50
**110B** A18 2p car rose ('44) .30 .55
**111** A18 3p blue ('42) .35 .35
*a.* Perf. 14 140.00 6.00
*b.* Perf. 13½ 22.50 1.10
**112** A18 5p red org ('47) 1.00 1.25
**113** A18 6p dl vio & car rose 3.75 1.90
*a.* Perf. 14 125.00 1.60
*b.* Perf. 13½ 50.00 4.00
**114** A18 1sh grn & blk ('42) 3.00 *4.50*
*a.* Perf. 14 45.00 27.50
*b.* Perf. 13½ 70.00 8.25
**115** A18 2sh org brn & blk ('42) 4.00 6.50
*a.* Perf. 14 70.00 30.00
*b.* Perf. 13½ 140.00 42.50
**116** A18 5sh dk car & blk ('44) 12.50 *21.00*
*a.* Perf 14 ('38) 100.00 *175.00*
*b.* Perf. 13½ 40.00 22.50
**117** A18 10sh bl & blk ('43) 27.50 27.50
*a.* Perf. 14 70.00 *150.00*
**118** A17 £1 orange 37.50 *47.50*
*Nos. 107-118 (14)* 121.10 115.90
Set, never hinged 190.00

Nos. 108c and 110d were issued in coils.

No. 108 (1p, perf. 13) exists with watermark both normal and sideways. Nos. 110 and 110B (both 2p, perf. 13) have watermark sideways.

For overprints see Nos. 127-130.

**Catalogue values for unused stamps in this section, from this point to the end of the section, are for Never Hinged items.**

### Peace Issue

Common Design Type

**1946, Oct. 12** ***Perf. 13½x14***

**119** CD303 ½p bright green .30 *.50*
**120** CD303 3p bright ultra .45 *.50*

### Silver Wedding Issue

Common Design Types

**1948, Dec. 1 Photo.** ***Perf. 14x14½***

**121** CD304 ½p dark green 1.00 *3.00*

**Engr.; Name Typo.**

***Perf. 11½x11***

**122** CD305 £1 brown orange 70.00 *87.50*
Set, hinged 55.00

### UPU Issue

Common Design Types

**Engr.; Name Typo. on 3p, 6p**

***Perf. 13½, 11x11½***

**1949, Oct. 10 Wmk. 4**

**123** CD306 2p rose carmine 1.00 1.25
**124** CD307 3p indigo 2.50 1.50
**125** CD308 6p rose violet 2.00 2.50
**126** CD309 1sh blue green 1.25 4.25
*Nos. 123-126 (4)* 6.75 9.50

### Nos. 110B, 111, 113-114 overprinted in Black or Carmine

**1950, Aug. 1** ***Perf. 13x12½***

**127** A18 2p carmine rose .40 *1.50*
**128** A18 3p blue 1.00 *1.25*
**129** A18 6p dl vio & car rose 1.25 *2.00*
*a.* Double overprint 1,000. *1,300.*
**130** A18 1sh grn & blk (C) 1.25 *2.00*
*Nos. 127-130 (4)* 3.90 *6.75*

Adoption of Constitution of 1950.

### Coronation Issue

Common Design Type

**1953, June 2 Engr.** ***Perf. 13½x13***

**131** CD312 ½p olive green & black .50 .50

Wharves A26

Moorish Castle — A27

Designs: 1p, South view. 1½p, Tunny fishing industry. 2p, Southport Gate. 2½p, Sailing in the bay. 3p, Ocean liner. 4p, Coaling wharf. 5p, Airport. 6p, Europa Point. 1sh, Strait from Buena Vista. 2sh, Rosia Bay. 5sh, Government House. £1, Arms of Gibraltar.

**1953, Oct. 19** ***Perf. 12½***

**132** A26 ½p dk grn & ind .25 .25
**133** A26 1p blue green 1.60 .60
**134** A26 1½p dark gray 1.00 *1.50*
**135** A26 2p sepia 1.75 1.25
**136** A26 2½p car lake 2.75 1.00
**137** A26 3p grnsh blue 4.25 1.25
**138** A26 4p ultra 6.00 3.50
**139** A26 5p deep plum 1.50 1.00
**140** A26 6p blue & black 3.50 1.75
**141** A26 1sh red brn & bl .60 *1.25*
**142** A26 2sh vio & org 29.00 6.00
**143** A26 5sh dark brown 37.50 15.00
**144** A27 10sh ultra & brn 47.50 40.00
**145** A27 £1 yellow & red 57.50 47.50
*Nos. 132-145 (14)* 194.70 121.85
Set, hinged 100.00

### Inscribed: "ROYAL VISIT 1954"

**1954, May 10**

**146** A26 3p greenish blue .50 .35

Candytuft — A28

Rock and Badge of Gibraltar Regiment — A30

Moorish Castle A29

Designs: 2p, St. George's Hall and cannons. 2½p, The keys. 3p, Rock by moonlight. 4p, Catalan Bay. 6p, Map. 7p, Air terminal. 9p, American war memorial. 1sh, Barbary ape. 2sh, Barbary partridge. 5sh, Blue rock thrush. 10sh, Narcissus.

**Wmk. 314**

**1960, Oct. 29 Photo.** ***Perf. 12½***

**147** A28 ½p brt green & lil .25 *.50*
**148** A29 1p black & yel grn .25 .25
**149** A29 2p org brn & sl 1.00 .25
**150** A28 2½p blue & black 1.00 .70
**151** A29 3p dk blue & ver .30 .25
**152** A29 4p choc & grnsh bl 3.00 .90
*a.* Wmkd. sideways ('66) .25 *1.00*
**153** A28 6p brown & emer 1.00 .70
**154** A28 7p gray & car 2.50 1.75
**155** A28 9p grnsh blue & bluish gray 1.00 .95
**156** A29 1sh brown & green 1.50 .70
**157** A29 2sh dark red brn & ultra 17.50 3.00
**158** A29 5sh ol & Prus grn 9.00 7.00
**159** A28 10sh blue, yel & grn 22.50 17.50

***Perf. 14***

**Engr.**

**160** A30 £1 org red & slate 19.00 17.50
*Nos. 147-160 (14)* 79.80 51.95

For overprints see Nos. 165-166.

### Freedom from Hunger Issue

Common Design Type

**1963, June 4** ***Perf. 14x14½***

**161** CD314 9p sepia 4.00 2.25

### Red Cross Centenary Issue

Common Design Type

**1963, Sept. 2 Litho.** ***Perf. 13***

**162** CD315 1p black & red .55 *1.40*
**163** CD315 9p ultra & red 6.50 4.00

### Shakespeare Issue

Common Design Type

**1964, Apr. 23 Photo.** ***Perf. 14x14½***

**164** CD316 7p brown .65 .55

Nos. 151 and 153 Overprinted

**1964, Oct. 16** ***Perf. 12½***

**165** A29 3p dk blue & ver .25 .25
**166** A28 6p brown & emer .35 *.50*
*a.* No period in overprint 17.00 *27.50*

### ITU Issue

Common Design Type

***Perf. 11x11½***

**1965, May 17 Litho. Wmk. 314**

**167** CD317 4p emerald & yel 2.75 .45
**168** CD317 2sh ap grn & dk bl 8.50 5.50

### Intl. Cooperation Year Issue

Common Design Type

**1965, Oct. 25** ***Perf. 14½***

**169** CD318 ½p lt violet & grn .25 *2.25*
**170** CD318 4p blue green & cl 1.10 .75

### Churchill Memorial Issue

Common Design Type

**1966, Jan. 24 Photo.** ***Perf. 14***

**Design in Black, Gold and Carmine Rose**

**171** CD319 ½p bright blue .25 *2.25*
**172** CD319 1p green .35 .25
**173** CD319 4p brown 1.10 .45
**174** CD319 9p violet 2.10 *2.50*
*Nos. 171-174 (4)* 3.80 5.45

### World Cup Soccer Issue

Common Design Type

**1966, July 1 Litho.** ***Perf. 14***

**175** CD321 2½p multicolored .75 *1.00*
**176** CD321 6p multicolored 1.25 .80

Sea Bream A30a

7p, Orange scorpionfish. 1sh, Stone bass, vert.

***Perf. 14x13½, 13½x14***

**1966, Aug. 27 Photo. Wmk. 314**

**177** A30a 4p ultra, rose red & black .30 .25
**178** A30a 7p ol, rose red & blk .35 *.70*
*a.* Value omitted *1,600.*
**179** A30a 1sh brt grn, brn & blk .55 .35
*Nos. 177-179 (3)* 1.20 1.30

European Sea Angling Championships, Gibraltar, Aug. 28-Sept. 3.

### WHO Headquarters Issue

Common Design Type

**1966, Sept. 20 Litho.** ***Perf. 14***

**180** CD322 6p multicolored 3.00 1.75
**181** CD322 9p multicolored 4.50 3.00

"Our Lady of Europa" A31

***Perf. 14x14½***

**1966, Nov. 15 Photo. Wmk. 314**

**182** A31 2sh ultra & black .60 *1.00*

Enthronement of the recovered statue of the Madonna in its new shrine, cent.

### UNESCO Anniversary Issue

Common Design Type

**1966, Dec. 1 Litho.** ***Perf. 14***

**183** CD323 2p "Education" .50 .25
**184** CD323 7p "Science" 2.00 .25
**185** CD323 5sh "Culture" 5.00 3.25
*Nos. 183-185 (3)* 7.50 3.75

Cable Ship Mirror — A32

Ships and Arms of Gibraltar: ½p Victory, Nelson's flagship. 1p, S.S. Arab. 2p, H.M.S. Carmania. 2½p, M.V. Mons Calpe. 3p, S.S. Canberra. 4p, H.M.S. Hood. 6p, Xebec, Moorish vessel. 7p, Amerigo Vespucci, Italian training ship (sails). 9p, Raffaello, Italian liner. 1sh, H.M.S. Royal Katherine, 17th century British warship. 2sh, H.M.S. Ark Royal, aircraft carrier. 5sh, H.M.S. Dreadnought, atomic submarine. 10sh, S.S. Neuralia, troopship. £1, Mary Celeste, 19th century mystery ship (sails).

***Perf. 14x14½***

**1967-69 Photo. Wmk. 314**

**Design in Black, Red and Gold; Background as Indicated**

**186** A32 ½p deep rose .25 .25
**187** A32 1p yellow .25 .25
**188** A32 2p ultra .25 .25
**189** A32 2½p orange .40 .30
**190** A32 3p violet .25 .25
**191** A32 4p rose .35 .25
**191A** A32 5p brn & multi ('69) 3.50 .65
**192** A32 6p gray .35 .60
**193** A32 7p yellow grn .35 .50
**194** A32 9p green .35 .95
**195** A32 1sh rose brown .35 .35
**196** A32 2sh brt yellow 4.00 2.50
**197** A32 5sh brick red 4.00 *6.75*
**198** A32 10sh emerald 14.00 *22.50*
**199** A32 £1 lt ultra 17.00 *22.50*
*Nos. 186-199 (15)* 45.65 *58.85*

Cable Car and ITY Emblem — A33

ITY emblem and: 9p, Bull shark, horiz. 1sh, Skin diver, horiz.

***Perf. 14½x14, 14x14½***

**1967, June 15 Photo. Wmk. 314**

**200** A33 7p red brn, red & blk .25 .25
**201** A33 9p brt blue, blk & slate .25 .25
**202** A33 1sh emer, blk & org brn .30 .25
*Nos. 200-202 (3)* .80 .75

International Tourist Year.

Holy Family A34

Christmas: 6p, Church window, vert.

**1967, Nov. 1** *Perf. 14½*

**203** A34 2p dark red & multi .25 .25
**204** A34 6p dark green & multi .25 .25

General Eliott and Map of Europe and Great Britain A35

Designs: 9p, Eliott Memorial and tower. 1sh, Gen. Eliott and map of Gibraltar, vert. 2sh, Gen. Eliott directing rescue operations for enemy sailors during Great Siege 1779-83.

*Perf. 14½x14, 14x14½*

**1967, Dec. 11 Photo. Wmk. 314**

**Size: 37x21mm, 21x37mm**

**205** A35 4p multicolored .25 .25
**206** A35 9p multicolored .25 .25
**207** A35 1sh multicolored .25 .25

**Size: 58x21½mm**

**208** A35 2sh multicolored .35 .25
*Nos. 205-208 (4)* 1.10 1.00

250th anniv. of the birth of General George Augustus Eliott (1717-1790), Governor of Gibraltar during Great Siege.

Lord Baden-Powell — A36

Designs: 7p, Scout flag, Rock of Gibraltar and globe with map of Europe. 9p, Symbolic tents, heads and Scout salute. 1sh, Three Scout badges.

*Perf. 14x14½*

**1968, Mar. 27 Photo. Wmk. 314**

**209** A36 4p dull yellow & pur .25 .25
**210** A36 7p brown org, brn & grn .25 .25
**211** A36 9p ultra, black & org .25 *.30*
**212** A36 1sh yellow & emerald .25 *.30*
*Nos. 209-212 (4)* 1.00 1.10

60th anniv. of the Gibraltar Scout Assoc.

Nurse and WHO Emblem A37

20th anniv. of WHO: 4p, Physician with microscope and WHO emblem.

**1968, July 1 Photo. Wmk. 314**

**213** A37 2p yellow, ultra & blk .25 .25
**214** A37 4p pink, black & slate .25 .25

King John Signing Magna Carta — A38

Shepherd, Lamb and Star — A39

Design: 2sh, Rock of Gibraltar, "Freedom" and Human Rights flame.

**1968, Aug. 26** *Perf. 13½x14½*

**215** A38 1sh org, gold & dk brn .25 .25
**216** A38 2sh brt green & gold .45 .45

International Human Rights Year.

**1968, Nov. 1** *Perf. 14x13½*

Christmas: 9p, Mary, Jesus and lamb.

**217** A39 4p lt brown & multi .25 .25
**218** A39 9p rose & multi .25 .25

Government House, Gibraltar — A40

9p, Rock of Gibraltar, Commonwealth Parliamentary Association emblem. 2sh, Big Ben, London, arms of Gibraltar.

*Perf. 14½x14, 14x14½*

**1969, May 26 Photo. Wmk. 314**

**219** A40 4p green & gold .25 .25
**220** A40 9p brt violet & gold .25 .25
**221** A40 2sh lt ultra, gold & red .25 .25
*Nos. 219-221 (3)* .75 .75

Meeting of the Executive Committee of the General Council of the Commonwealth Parliamentary Assoc., Gibraltar, May 1969.

Rock of Gibraltar A41

**1969, July 30** *Perf. 14½x13½*

**222** A41 ½p orange & gold .25 .25
**223** A41 5p emerald & silver .25 .25
**224** A41 7p brt rose lil & silver .25 .25
**225** A41 5sh ultra & gold 1.40 1.25
*Nos. 222-225 (4)* 2.15 2.00

Gibraltar's new constitution.

Nos. 222-225 are valued with surrounding selvage.

Royal Artillery Officer, 1758 — A42

Madonna della Seggiola, by Raphael — A43

Uniforms: 6p, Contemporary soldier of the Royal Anglian Regiment. 9p, Soldier, Royal Engineers, 1786. 2sh, Private of Fox's Marines, 1704.

**1969, Nov. 6 Photo.** *Perf. 14*

**226** A42 1p gold & multi .25 .25
**227** A42 6p silver, gold & multi .35 .30
**228** A42 9p silver, gold & multi .55 .40
**229** A42 2sh gold & multi 1.25 1.00
*Nos. 226-229 (4)* 2.40 1.95

Descriptions are printed on back on top of gum.

See Nos. 234-237, 276-279, 286-289, 299-302, 310-313, 318-321, 330-333.

**1969, Dec. 1** *Perf. 13½x Roulette 9*

Christmas (Paintings): 7p, Madonna and Child, by Luis Morales. 1sh, Virgin of the Rocks, by Leonardo da Vinci.

**230** A43 5p gold & multi .25 .25
**231** A43 7p gold & multi .35 .35
**232** A43 1sh gold & multi .55 .55
*a.* Triptych, Nos. 230, 232, 231 1.25 1.25

**Europa Issue**

Europa Point — A44

**1970, June 8** *Perf. 13½*

**233** A44 2sh multicolored .45 .40

**Uniform Type of 1969**

Uniforms: 2p, Royal Scots officer, 1839. 5p, Private of South Wales Borderers. 7p, Private of Queen's Royal Regiment, 1742. 2sh, Piper of Royal Irish Rangers, 1969.

**1970, Aug. 28 Photo.** *Perf. 14*

**234** A42 2p gold & multi .40 .25
**235** A42 5p gold & multi .60 .45
**236** A42 7p gold & multi .60 .55
**237** A42 2sh gold & multi 1.50 1.00
*Nos. 234-237 (4)* 3.10 2.25

Descriptions are printed on back on top of gum.

No. 178a and Rock of Gibraltar A45

Design: 2sh, No. 30a and Moorish Castle.

**1970, Sept. 18** *Perf. 13*

**238** A45 1sh red & olive .25 .25
**239** A45 2sh ultra & rose .40 .55

Philympia, London Phil. Exhib., Sept. 18-26.

Virgin Mary by Gabriel Loire A46

**1970, Dec. 1 Photo.** *Perf. 13x14*

**240** A46 2sh multicolored .35 .35

Christmas. The design is after a stained glass window in the Church of Our Lady of Perpetual Succour, Glasgow.

**Decimal Currency Issue**

Prince George of Cambridge Quarters, and Trinity Church — A47

Designs show for each denomination a 19th century print and a contemporary photograph of the same view: ½p Battery Rosia. 1½p, Wellington Monument, Alameda Gardens. 2p, View from North Bastion. 2½p, Catalan Bay. 3p, Convent, seen from garden. 4p, The Exchange and Spanish Chapel. 5p, Commercial Square, Library and Main Guard. 7p, South Barracks and Rosia Magazine. 8p, Moorish Mosque and Castle. 9p, Europa Pass. 10p, South Barracks, from Rosia Bay. 12½p, Southport Gates. 25p, Guards on Alameda. 50p, Europa Pass Gorge, vert. £1 Prince Edward Gate, vert.

In the listing the 1st number is for the 19th cent. design, the 2nd for the 20th cent. design.

**Wmk. 314 Sideways**

**1971, Feb. 15 Litho.** *Perf. 14*

**Multicolored and:**

**241** ½p brown red .25 .25
**242** ½p brown red .25 .25
*a.* A47 Pair, Nos. 241-242 .35 *.40*
**243** 1p light blue .85 .25
**244** 1p light blue .85 .25
*b.* A47 Pair, Nos. 243-244 1.75 .60
**245** 1½p emerald .25 *.30*
**246** 1½p emerald .25 *.30*
*a.* A47 Pair, Nos. 245-246 .50 *.90*
**247** 2p dark brown 1.50 *2.50*
**248** 2p dark brown 1.50 *2.50*
*b.* A47 Pair, Nos. 247-248 3.00 *5.75*
**249** 2½p vermilion .25 *.35*
**250** 2½p vermilion .25 *.35*
*a.* A47 Pair, Nos. 249-250 .35 *.75*
**251** 3p pale green .25 .25
**252** 3p pale green .25 .25
*a.* A47 Pair, Nos. 251-252 .35 .40
**253** 4p gray 2.00 *2.50*
**254** 4p gray 2.00 *2.50*
*b.* A47 Pair, Nos. 253-254 4.00 *6.50*
**255** 5p dark green .35 .35
**256** 5p dark green .35 .35
*a.* A47 Pair, Nos. 255-256 .75 .90
**257** 7p orange .70 .65
**258** 7p orange .70 .65
*a.* A47 Pair, Nos. 257-258 1.40 1.50
**259** 8p dark blue .75 .70
**260** 8p dark blue .75 .70
*a.* A47 Pair, Nos. 259-260 1.50 2.00
**261** 9p brick red .75 .70
**262** 9p brick red .75 .70
*a.* A47 Pair, Nos. 261-262 1.50 2.00
**263** 10p black .85 .80
**264** 10p black .85 .80
*a.* A47 Pair, Nos. 263-264 1.75 2.00
**265** 12½p bister 1.10 *1.75*
**266** 12½p bister 1.10 *1.75*
*a.* A47 Pair, Nos. 265-266 2.25 *5.00*
**267** 25p deep purple 1.10 *1.75*
**268** 25p deep purple 1.10 *1.75*
*a.* A47 Pair, Nos. 267-268 2.25 *5.00*
**269** 50p blue 1.40 *2.75*
**270** 50p blue 1.40 *2.75*
*a.* A47 Pair, Nos. 269-270 3.25 *7.25*
**271** £1 sepia 2.25 *4.25*
**272** £1 sepia 2.25 *4.25*
*a.* A47 Pair, Nos. 271-272 5.00 *10.50*
*Nos. 241-272 (32)* 29.20 *40.20*

Se-tenant both horizontally and vertically.

**1973, Sept. 12 Wmk. 314 Upright**

*247a* A47 2p dark brown & multi 1.80 *2.75*
*248a* A47 2p dark brown & multi 1.80 *2.75*
*c.* Pair, Nos. 247a-248a 4.00 *7.00*
*253a* A47 4p gray & multi 2.30 *2.50*
*254a* A47 4p gray & multi 2.30 *2.50*
*c.* Pair, Nos. 253a-254a 5.00 *7.00*
*Nos. 247a-254a (4)* 8.20 *10.50*

**1975, July 9 Wmk. 373**

*243a* A47 1p blue & multi 3.00 *3.25*
*244a* A47 1p blue & multi 3.00 *3.25*
*c.* Pair, Nos. 243a-244a 6.50 *8.00*

Elizabeth II — A48

Regimental Coat of Arms — A49

**Coil Stamps**

*Perf. 14½x14*

**1971, Feb. 15 Photo. Wmk. 314**

**273** A48 ½p red orange .25 *.25*
**274** A48 1p bright blue .35 *.25*
**275** A48 2p lt yellow green .55 *.80*
*a.* Strip of 5 (½p, ½p, 1p, 1p, 2p) 1.60 *26.00*
*Nos. 273-275 (3)* 1.15 *1.30*

**Uniform Type of 1969**

Uniforms: 1p, Soldier, Black Watch, 1845. 2p, Drum Major with antelope mascot, Royal Fusiliers, 1971. 4p, Soldier, Kings Own Royal Border Regiment, 1704. 10p, Soldier, Devonshire and Dorset Regiment, 1801.

**1971, Sept. 6 Litho. *Perf. 14***

| | | |
|---|---|---|
| **276** A42 1p silver & multi | .40 | .30 |
| **277** A42 2p gold & multi | .70 | .30 |
| **278** A42 4p gold & multi | 1.00 | .50 |
| **279** A42 10p sil, gold & multi | 3.25 | 2.75 |
| *Nos. 276-279 (4)* | 5.35 | 3.85 |

Descriptions are printed on back on top of gum.

**1971, Sept. 25 *Perf. 13x12***

| | | |
|---|---|---|
| **280** A49 3p red, bister & black | .50 | .40 |

Presentation of colors to Gibraltar Regiment, Sept. 25, 1971.

Nativity — A50

Christmas: 5p, Journey to Bethlehem.

**1971, Dec. 1 Photo. *Perf. 13x13½***

| | | |
|---|---|---|
| **281** A50 3p silver & multi | .50 | .50 |
| **282** A50 5p gold & multi | .70 | .70 |

Artificer, 1773 — A51

3p, Tunneler with drill, 1969. 5p, Royal Engineers, 1772 and 1972, and regimental crest, horiz.

**1972, Mar. 6 *Perf. 14x13½, 13½x14***

| | | |
|---|---|---|
| **283** A51 1p dk blue & multi | .55 | *.60* |
| **284** A51 3p red & multi | .65 | *.80* |
| **285** A51 5p green & multi | .75 | *1.00* |
| *Nos. 283-285 (3)* | 1.95 | 2.40 |

Bicent. of the Royal Engineers in Gibraltar.

**Uniform Type of 1969**

Uniforms: 1p, Soldier, Duke of Cornwall's Light Infantry, 1704. 3p, Officer, King's Royal Rifle Corps, 1830. 7p, Officer, 37th North Hampshire Regiment, 1825. 10p, Sailor, Royal Navy, 1972.

**1972, July 19 Litho. *Perf. 14***

| | | |
|---|---|---|
| **286** A42 1p silver & multi | .65 | .25 |
| **287** A42 3p slate & multi | 1.50 | .40 |
| **288** A42 7p silver & multi | 2.25 | .80 |
| **289** A42 10p gold & multi | 2.75 | 1.60 |
| *Nos. 286-289 (4)* | 7.15 | 3.05 |

Design descriptions printed on back on top of gum.

"Our Lady of Europa" — A52

**1972, Oct. 1 *Perf. 14½x14***

| | | |
|---|---|---|
| **290** A52 3p brown & multi | .25 | .25 |
| **291** A52 5p green & multi | .25 | .40 |

Christmas. Design description printed on back.

**Silver Wedding Issue, 1972**
Common Design Type

Design: Queen Elizabeth II, Prince Philip, keys of Gibraltar and white narcissus.

**1972, Nov. 20 Photo. *Perf. 14x14½***

| | | |
|---|---|---|
| **292** CD324 5p car rose & multi | .25 | .25 |
| **293** CD324 7p slate green & multi | .25 | .25 |

Flags of EEC Members and EEC Emblem — A53

***Perf. 14½x14***

**1973, Feb. 22 Litho. Unwmk.**

| | | |
|---|---|---|
| **294** A53 5p red & multi | .55 | .40 |
| **295** A53 10p ultra & multi | .85 | .85 |

Entry into European Economic Community.

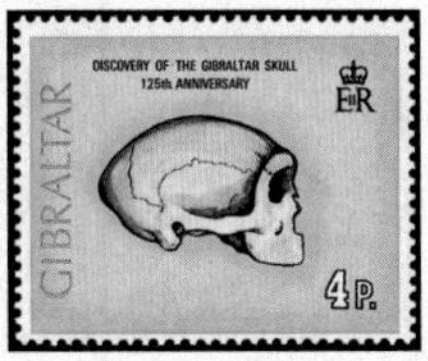


Gibraltar Skull — A54

Designs: 6p, Head of Neanderthal man. 10p, Neanderthal family.

**1973, May 22 Wmk. 314 *Perf. 13½***

| | | |
|---|---|---|
| **296** A54 4p lilac rose & multi | 1.50 | .60 |
| **297** A54 6p lt ultra & multi | 1.60 | 1.25 |
| **298** A54 10p yel green & multi | 2.25 | 2.25 |
| *Nos. 296-298 (3)* | 5.35 | 4.10 |

125th anniv. of the discovery of the Gibraltar skull.

**Uniform Type of 1969**

Uniforms: 1p, Fifer, King's Own Scottish Borderers, 1770. 4p, Officer, Royal Welsh Fusiliers, 1800. 6p, Soldier, Royal Northumberland Fusiliers, 1736. 10p, Private, Grenadier Guards, 1898.

**1973, Aug. 22 Litho. *Perf. 14***

| | | |
|---|---|---|
| **299** A42 1p multicolored | .50 | .30 |
| **300** A42 4p multicolored | 1.50 | .55 |
| **301** A42 6p multicolored | 2.25 | .95 |
| **302** A42 10p multicolored | 3.00 | *2.00* |
| *Nos. 299-302 (4)* | 7.25 | *3.80* |

Descriptions printed on back on top of gum.

Nativity, by Justus Danckerts — A55

**1973, Oct. 17 Litho. *Perf. 12½x12***

| | | |
|---|---|---|
| **303** A55 4p brown org & blue | .45 | .25 |
| **304** A55 6p green & claret | .50 | *.80* |

Christmas.

**Princess Anne's Wedding Issue**
Common Design Type

**1973, Nov. 14 *Perf. 14***

| | | |
|---|---|---|
| **305** CD325 6p bl grn & multi | .25 | .25 |
| **306** CD325 14p brt grn & multi | .45 | .45 |

Wedding of Princess Anne and Capt. Mark Phillips, Nov. 14, 1973.

V.R. (Queen Victoria) Pillar Box — A56

Pillar Boxes: 6p, G.R. (King George). 14p, E.R. (Queen Elizabeth).

**1974, May 2 Litho. *Perf. 14***

| | | |
|---|---|---|
| **307** A56 2p yel green & multi | .25 | *.25* |
| **308** A56 6p gray & multi | .35 | .35 |
| **309** A56 14p dull yel & multi | .50 | .50 |
| *a.* Souvenir booklet | 11.00 | |
| *Nos. 307-309 (3)* | 1.10 | 1.10 |

UPU, cent.

No. 309a contains 2 self-adhesive panes printed on peelable paper backing with multicolored advertising on back. One pane of 6 contains 3 each similar to Nos. 307-308; the other pane of 3 contains one each similar to Nos. 307-309. Stamps are imperf. x roulette.

**Uniform Type of 1969**

Uniforms: 4p, Officer, East Lancashire Regiment, 1742. 6p, Sergeant, Somerset Light Infantry, 1833. 10p, Company man, Royal Sussex Regiment, 1790. 16p, Officer, Royal Air Force, 1974.

**1974, Aug. 21 *Perf. 14***

| | | |
|---|---|---|
| **310** A42 4p silver & multi | .60 | .50 |
| **311** A42 6p silver & multi | 1.00 | .85 |
| **312** A42 10p silver & multi | 1.50 | *1.60* |
| **313** A42 16p silver & multi | 3.25 | *3.75* |
| *Nos. 310-313 (4)* | 6.35 | *6.70* |

Descriptions are printed on back on top of gum.

Virgin with Green Cushion, Andrea Solario — A57

Christmas (Painting): 6p, Madonna of the Meadow, by Giovanni Bellini.

**1974, Nov. 5 Litho.**

| | | |
|---|---|---|
| **314** A57 4p gold & multi | .45 | .35 |
| **315** A57 6p gold & multi | .75 | *1.00* |

Churchill, Parliament and Big Ben A58

20p, Churchill & George V-class battleship.

**1974, Nov. 30 *Perf. 14x14½***

| | | |
|---|---|---|
| **316** A58 6p violet & multi | .25 | .25 |
| **317** A58 20p multicolored | .55 | .60 |
| *a.* Souvenir sheet of 2, #316-317 | 5.25 | *6.00* |

Sir Winston Churchill (1874-1965).

**Uniform Type of 1969**

Uniforms: 4p, Officer, East Surrey Regiment, 1846. 6p, Private, Highland Light Infantry, 1777. 10p, Officer, Coldstream Guards, 1704. 20p, Sergeant, Gibraltar Regiment, 1974.

**1975, Mar. 14 Wmk. 373 *Perf. 14***

| | | |
|---|---|---|
| **318** A42 4p multicolored | .40 | .25 |
| **319** A42 6p multicolored | .60 | *.50* |
| **320** A42 10p multicolored | 1.10 | *.90* |
| **321** A42 20p multicolored | 1.60 | *2.25* |
| *Nos. 318-321 (4)* | 3.70 | *3.90* |

Descriptions are printed on back on top of gum.

Girl Guides Emblem A59

**1975, Oct. 10 *Perf. 13½x13***

| | | |
|---|---|---|
| **322** A59 5p violet, gold & blue | .35 | *.45* |
| **323** A59 7p red brn, gold & blk | .50 | *.50* |
| **324** A59 15p ocher, silver & blk | .80 | *1.00* |
| *Nos. 322-324 (3)* | 1.65 | 1.95 |

Girl Guides, 50th anniversary.

Child and Bird — A60

b, Angel playing lute. c, Singing boy. d, Mother & children. e, Praying child. f, Child & lamb.

**1975, Nov. 25 *Perf. 14x14½***

| | | |
|---|---|---|
| **325** Block of 6 | 2.75 | *3.25* |
| *a.-f.* A60 6p any single | .45 | *.55* |

Christmas. No. 325 printed in sheets of 60 containing 10 blocks of 6 (3x2) stamps with horizontal and vertical gutters between blocks.

Bruges Madonna, by Michelangelo A61

Sculptures by Michelangelo: 9p, Traddei Madonna. 15p, Pietà.

**1975, Dec. 17 Litho. *Perf. 14x13½***

| | | |
|---|---|---|
| **326** A61 6p violet blk & multi | .25 | .25 |
| **327** A61 9p black brn & multi | .35 | *.45* |
| **328** A61 15p dk purple & multi | .40 | *.95* |
| *a.* Souvenir booklet | 6.00 | |
| *Nos. 326-328 (3)* | 1.00 | *1.65* |

500th birth anniv. of Michelangelo Buonarroti (1475-1564), Italian sculptor, painter and architect.

No. 328a contains 2 self-adhesive panes printed on peelable paper backing with stamp dealer's advertisements on back. One pane of 6 contains 2 each similar to Nos. 326-328; the other pane of 3 contains one each similar to Nos. 326-328. Stamps are imperf. x roulette.

American Bicentennial Emblem, Arms of Gibraltar — A62

**1976, May 28 *Perf. 14x14½***

| | | |
|---|---|---|
| **329** A62 25p multicolored | .80 | .70 |
| *a.* Souvenir sheet of 4 | 5.00 | *7.00* |

American Bicentennial. No. 329a is rouletted all around.

**Uniform Type of 1969**

Uniforms: 1p, Suffolk Regiment, 1795. 6p, Northamptonshire Regiment, 1779. 12p, Lancashire Fusiliers, 1793. 25p, Royal Army Ordinance Corps. 1896.

**1976, July 21 *Perf. 14***

| | | |
|---|---|---|
| **330** A42 1p multicolored | .25 | .25 |
| **331** A42 6p multicolored | .40 | .25 |
| **332** A42 12p multicolored | .65 | .50 |
| **333** A42 25p multicolored | .90 | *1.25* |
| *Nos. 330-333 (4)* | 2.20 | 2.25 |

Descriptions printed on back on top of gum.

Holy Family — A63

Stained Glass Windows: 9p, St. Bernard of Clairvaux. 12p, St. John the Evangelist. 20p, Archangel Michael.

**1976, Nov. 3 Litho. Wmk. 373**

**334** A63 6p ultra & multi .25 .25
**335** A63 9p brt green & multi .35 .25
**336** A63 12p orange & multi .50 *.60*
**337** A63 20p dk carmine & multi .95 *1.25*
*Nos. 334-337 (4)* 2.05 2.35

Christmas.

Elizabeth II and Royal Crest — A64

**1977, Feb. 7 Litho. *Perf. 14x13½***

**338** A64 6p multicolored .25 .25
**339** A64 £1 multicolored 1.50 *1.75*
*a.* Souv. sheet of 2, #338-339, perf. 13 2.00 *2.50*

25th anniv. of the reign of Queen Elizabeth II. Nos. 338-339 issued in sheets of 9.

Red Mullet A65

Designs: ½p, 3p, 9p, 15p, 25p, Flowers. 1p, 4p, 10p, 50p, Fish. 2p, 5p, 12p, £1, Butterflies. 2½p, 6p, 20p, £2, Birds. ½p, 2½p, 3p, 6p, 9p, 15p, 20p, 25p, £2, £5, vertical.

**1977-80 *Perf. 14½x14, 14x14½***

**Inscribed "1977," except as noted**

**340** A65 ½p Toothed orchid .50 *2.00*
*a.* Chalky paper, inscribed "1982" 5.00 4.00
**341** A65 1p shown .25 *.45*
**342** A65 2p Large blue .25 *1.00*
**343** A65 2½p Sardinian warbler 1.25 *1.50*
**344** A65 3p Giant squill .25 .25
**345** A65 4p Gray wrasse .25 .25
**346** A65 5p Red admiral .40 *.80*
**347** A65 6p Black kite 2.00 .45
**348** A65 9p Scorpion vetch .55 .55
*a.* Inscribed "1978" .60 .60
**349** A65 10p John Dory .35 .25
**350** A65 12p Clouded yellow .90 .35
**350A** A65 15p Winged asparagus pea (inscr. "1980") 1.50 .45
**351** A65 20p Andouin's gull 1.75 *2.75*
**352** A65 25p Barbary nut 1.20 *1.75*
**353** A65 50p Swordfish 1.60 .80
**354** A65 £1 Swallowtail 4.00 *5.00*
**355** A65 £2 Hoopoe 8.75 *11.00*
**355A** A65 £5 Coat of Arms (inscr. "1979") 9.00 *12.00*
*Nos. 340-355A (18)* 34.75 *41.60*

Issued: No. 348a, 2/1/78; £ 5, 5/16/79; 15p, 11/12/80; No. 340a, 2/22/82; others, 4/1/77.

**Inscribed "1981"**

**1981, Apr. 21 Chalky Paper**

*345a* A65 4p multicolored .50 *.70*
*349a* A65 10p multicolored 1.00 *1.50*
*350a* A65 12p multicolored 4.00 4.00
*352a* A65 25p multicolored 5.00 *5.50*
*353a* A65 50p multicolored 6.50 6.50
*Nos. 345a-353a (5)* 17.00 *18.20*

Gibraltar No. 182 — A66

12p, Gibraltar #233. 25p, Gibraltar #294.

**1977, May 27 Litho. *Perf. 14***

**356** A66 6p multi .25 .25
**357** A66 12p multi, vert. .30 *.45*
**358** A66 25p multi, vert. .30 *.55*
*Nos. 356-358 (3)* .85 1.25

Amphilex 77 Intl. Phil. Exhib., Amsterdam, May 26-June 5. Issued in sheets of 6.

Annunciation, by Rubens — A67

Rubens Paintings: 9p, Nativity. 12p, Adoration of the Kings. 15p, Holy Family under Apple Tree.

***Perf. 14x13½, 13½x14***

**1977, Nov. 2 Litho.**

**359** A67 3p multi .25 .25
**360** A67 9p multi .25 .25
**361** A67 12p multi, horiz. .35 .35
**362** A67 15p multi .35 .35
*a.* Souvenir sheet of 4, #359-362 4.00 *4.00*
*Nos. 359-362 (4)* 1.20 1.20

Christmas and 400th birth anniv. of Peter Paul Rubens.

Gibraltar from Space A68

Design: 25p, Strait of Gibraltar, aerial view.

**1978, May 3 Litho. *Perf. 13½***

**363** A68 12p multicolored .35 *.50*

**Souvenir Sheet**

**364** A68 25p multicolored .90 .90

No. 363 issued in sheets of 10. No. 364 contains one stamp.

Holyroodhouse — A69

Royal Houses: 9p, St. James Palace. 12p, Sandringham House. 18p, Balmoral.

**1978, June 12 Litho. *Perf. 13½***

**365** A69 6p multicolored .25 .25
**366** A69 9p multicolored .25 .25
**367** A69 12p multicolored .40 .35
**368** A69 18p multicolored .50 .50
*a.* Souvenir booklet 3.75
*Nos. 365-368 (4)* 1.40 1.35

25th anniv. of coronation of Queen Elizabeth II. No. 368a contains 2 panes printed on peelable paper backing with pictures of castles. One pane contains 6 rouletted stamps, 3 each similar to Nos. 367-368; the other pane contains one 25p (Windsor Castle) rouletted stamp.

Sunderland Seaplane Landing — A70

Gibraltar and: 9p, Two-tiered Caudron taking off, 1918. 12p, Shackleton, 1953-1966. 16p, Hunter warplane, 1954-1966. 18p, Nimrod, 1969-1978.

**1978, Sept. 6 Litho. *Perf. 14***

**369** A70 3p multicolored .25 .25
**370** A70 9p multicolored .25 *.35*
**371** A70 12p multicolored .40 *.45*
**372** A70 16p multicolored .55 *.80*
**373** A70 18p multicolored .75 *1.00*
*Nos. 369-373 (5)* 2.20 *2.85*

Royal Air Force, 60th anniversary.

Madonna with Goldfinch, by Dürer — A71

Christmas (Paintings by Albrecht Dürer): 5p, Madonna with Animals. 9p, Nativity. 15p, Adoration of the Kings.

**1978, Nov. 1 Litho. *Perf. 14***

**374** A71 5p multicolored .25 .25
**375** A71 9p multicolored .25 .25
**376** A71 12p multicolored .35 *.40*
**377** A71 15p multicolored .40 *.75*
*Nos. 374-377 (4)* 1.25 1.65

Rowland Hill and Gibraltar No. 10 — A72

Sir Rowland Hill (1795-1879), originator of penny postage and: 9p, Gibraltar No. 274. 12p, Parchment scroll with early postal regulations. 25p, "Barred G" cancellation used on British stamps in Gibraltar.

**1979, Feb. 7 Litho. *Perf. 13½***

**378** A72 3p multicolored .25 .25
**379** A72 9p multicolored .25 .25
**380** A72 12p yellow grn & black .25 .25
**381** A72 25p yellow & black .35 *.55*
*Nos. 378-381 (4)* 1.10 1.30

Satellite Earth Station, Post Horn, Telephone — A73

**1979, May 16 *Perf. 13½x14***

**382** A73 3p lt green & green .25 .25
**383** A73 9p lt brown & brown .25 *.65*
**384** A73 12p gray & ultra .40 *1.10*
*Nos. 382-384 (3)* .90 *2.00*

European telecommunications system.

Children, IYC Emblem, Nativity — A74

a, African girl. b, Chinese girl. c, Pacific islands girl. d, American Indian girl. e, Shown. f, Scandinavian boy.

**Litho.; Silver Embossed**

**1979, Nov. 14 *Perf. 14***

**385** Block of 6 1.75 1.75
*a.-f.* A74 12p any single .25 .25

Christmas; IYC. No. 385 printed in sheets of 12 containing 2 No. 385 with vertical rouletted gutter between.

Officers, Exchange and Commercial Library, 1830 — A75

Gibraltar Police Force, 150th anniv.: 6p, Early and modern uniforms, Rock of Gibraltar. 12p, Traffic Officer, ambulance. 37p, Policeman and woman, Police Station, Irish Town.

***Perf. 14x14½***

**1980, Feb. 5 Litho. Wmk. 373**

**386** A75 3p multicolored .25 .25
**387** A75 6p multicolored .25 .25
**388** A75 12p multicolored .35 .35
**389** A75 37p multicolored .55 *.95*
*Nos. 386-389 (4)* 1.40 1.80

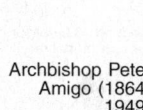

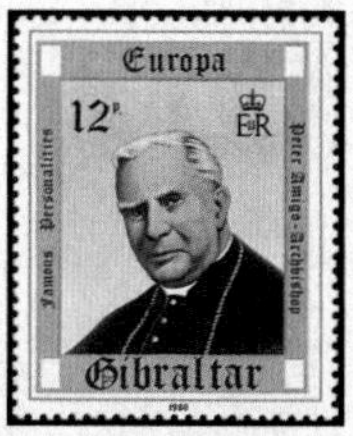


Archbishop Peter Amigo (1864-1949) A76

Europa: No. 391, Gustavo Charles Bacarisas (1872-1971), artist. No. 392, John Mackintosh (1865-1940), philanthropist.

**1980, May 6 Wmk. 373 *Perf. 14½***

**390** A76 12p multicolored .25 *.30*
**391** A76 12p multicolored .25 *.30*
**392** A76 12p multicolored .25 *.30*
*Nos. 390-392 (3)* .75 .90

**Queen Mother Elizabeth Birthday Issue**

Common Design Type

**1980, Aug. 4 Litho. *Perf. 14***

**393** CD330 15p multicolored .35 .35

"Victory" and Rock of Gibraltar, by Monamy Swaine A77

Paintings: 3p, Lord Nelson, by John Francis Rigaud, 1781, vert. 15p, Lord Nelson, by William Beechey, vert. 40p, Victory Towed into Gibraltar by Clarkson Stanfield.

**1980, Aug. 20 Litho. *Perf. 14***

**394** A77 3p multicolored .25 .25
**395** A77 9p multicolored .25 .25
**396** A77 15p multicolored .35 .35
*a.* Souvenir sheet 1.00 *1.40*
**397** A77 40p multicolored .80 *1.00*
*Nos. 394-397 (4)* 1.65 1.85

Horatio Nelson (1758-1805).

Holy Family A78

**1980, Nov. 12**

**398** A78 15p shown .30 *.40*
**399** A78 15p Three kings .30 *.40*
*a.* Pair, #398-399 .80 *.80*

Christmas. No. 399a has continuous design.

Hercules Separating Africa and Europe — A79

Europa: 15p, Hercules standing on Rock of Gibraltar and Morocco.

***Perf. 14x13½***

**1981, Feb. 24** **Wmk. 373**

**400** A79 9p multicolored .25 .25
**401** A79 15p multicolored .35 *.40*

Dining Room, The Convent — A80

**1981, May 22 Litho.** ***Perf. 14½x14***

**402** A80 4p shown .25 .25
**403** A80 14p King's Chapel .25 .25
**404** A80 15p Aerial view .40 .25
**405** A80 55p Cloister .80 .80
*Nos. 402-405 (4)* 1.70 1.55

450th anniv. of The Convent (Governor's residence, originally Franciscan monastery).

Prince Charles and Lady Diana A81

**1981, July 27** **Litho.** ***Perf. 14½***

**406** A81 £1 multicolored 2.00 2.00

Royal wedding. Se-tenant with decorative label.

Queen Elizabeth II — A82

**1981, Sept. 29** ***Perf. 14½***

**Booklet Stamps**

**407** A82 1p black .45 .45
*a.* Bklt. pane of 10 + 2 labels (2 #407, 2 #408, 6 #409) 4.50
*b.* Bklt. pane of 5 + label (#407, #408, 3 #409) 2.25
**408** A82 4p dark blue .45 .45
**409** A82 15p green .45 .45
*Nos. 407-409 (3)* 1.35 1.35

Airmail Service, 50th Anniv. A83

**1981, Sept. 29** ***Perf. 14½***

**410** A83 14p Paper plane .35 .35
**411** A83 15p Envelopes, aerogram .35 .35
**412** A83 55p Airplane circling globe 1.00 1.00
*Nos. 410-412 (3)* 1.70 1.70

Intl. Year of the Disabled A84

**1981, Nov. 19** **Litho.** **Wmk. 373**

**413** A84 14p multicolored .35 .35

Christmas A85

**1981, Nov. 19** ***Perf. 14***

**414** A85 15p Children singing carols .35 .25
**415** A85 55p Decorated mailbox, vert. 1.25 .80

Douglas DC-3 — A86

**1982, Feb. 10** **Litho.** ***Perf. 14***

**416** A86 1p shown .25 *1.00*
**417** A86 2p Vickers Viking .25 *1.00*
*a.* Wmk. 384, dated 1986 ('87) 3.25 4.00
**418** A86 3p Airspeed Ambassador .25 *.50*
**419** A86 4p Vickers Viscount .40 .25
**420** A86 5p Boeing 727 .50 .30
*a.* Wmk. 384, dated 1986 ('87) 3.25 4.00
**421** A86 10p Vickers Vanguard .90 .55
**422** A86 14p Short Solent 1.00 *1.75*
**423** A86 15p Fokker F-27 Friendship 1.75 *2.00*
**424** A86 17p Boeing 737 .85 .90
**425** A86 20p BAC One-eleven 1.00 .65
*a.* Inscribed "1985" 1.60 1.60
**426** A86 25p Lockheed Constellation 3.75 *4.00*
**427** A86 50p De Havilland Comet 4B 4.00 2.25
**428** A86 £1 Saro Windhover 5.50 2.25
**429** A86 £2 Hawker Siddeley Trident 2 7.00 7.00
**430** A86 £5 DH-89A Dragon Rapide 10.00 *15.00*
*Nos. 416-430 (15)* 37.40 39.40

Royal Navy Ship Crests — A87

**1982, Apr. 14** **Litho.** ***Perf. 14***

**431** A87 ½p Opossum .25 .25
**432** A87 15½p Norfolk .50 .50
**433** A87 17p Fearless .65 .65
**434** A87 60p Rooke 1.25 *2.75*
*Nos. 431-434 (4)* 2.65 *4.15*

See Nos. 449-452, 465-468, 474-477, 492-495, 501-504, 528-531, 552-555, 574-577, 587-590.

Europa A88

**1982, June 11** **Litho.** ***Perf. 14***

**435** A88 14p Planes preparing for takeoff .25 *.70*
**436** A88 17p Generals Eisenhower and Giraud .40 *.80*

Operation Torch, 1943.

Chamber of Commerce Centenary — A89

Anniversaries: 15½p, British Forces Postal Service centenary. 60p, Scouting year.

**1982, Sept. 22**

**437** A89 ½p multicolored .25 .25
**438** A89 15½p multicolored .45 .45
**439** A89 60p multicolored 1.40 *1.75*
*Nos. 437-439 (3)* 2.10 2.45

Intl. Direct Telephone Dialing System Inauguration — A90

**1982, Oct. 1** ***Perf. 14½***

**440** A90 17p Map .45 .45

Christmas A91

***Perf. 14x14½***

**1982, Nov. 18** **Litho.** **Wmk. 373**

**441** A91 14p Holly .30 .30
**442** A91 17p Mistletoe .40 .40

A92

**1983, Mar. 14** **Litho.** ***Perf. 14***

**443** A92 4p Local street .25 .25
**444** A92 14p Scouts on parade .35 .35
**445** A92 17p Flag, vert. .45 .45
**446** A92 60p Queen Elizabeth II, vert. 1.10 *1.40*
*Nos. 443-446 (4)* 2.15 *2.45*

Commonwealth Day.

Europa A93

**1983, May 21** ***Perf. 14x13½***

**447** A93 16p St. George's Hall .35 .35
**448** A93 19p Water catchments .45 .45

**Royal Navy Crest Type of 1982**

**1983, July 1** **Litho.** ***Perf. 14***

**449** A87 4p Faulknor .25 .25
**450** A87 14p Renown 1.10 .40
**451** A87 17p Ark Royal 1.25 .50
**452** A87 60p Sheffield 1.90 1.75
*Nos. 449-452 (4)* 4.50 2.90

Fortresses — A94

**1983, Sept. 13** ***Perf. 13½x14***

**453** A94 4p Landport Gate, 1729 .25 .25
**454** A94 17p Koehler gun, 1782 .45 .45
**455** A94 77p King's Bastion, 1799 1.50 1.50
*a.* Souvenir sheet of 3, #453-455 3.00 3.00
*Nos. 453-455 (3)* 2.20 2.20

Christmas A95

Raphael Paintings.

**1983, Nov. 17** **Litho.** ***Perf. 14***

**456** A95 4p Adoration of the Magi .30 .25
**457** A95 17p Madonna of Foligno, vert. .80 .35
**458** A95 60p Sistine Madonna, vert. 2.10 1.50
*Nos. 456-458 (3)* 3.20 2.10

Europa (1959-1984) A96

Intl. Postal and Telecommunication Links.

**1984, Mar. 6** **Litho.** ***Perf. 14½***

**459** A96 17p No. 98 .40 *.50*
**460** A96 23p Communications circuit .50 *.90*

Field Hockey A97

**1984, May 25** **Litho.** ***Perf. 14***

**461** A97 20p shown .75 *.80*
**462** A97 21p Basketball .75 *.80*
**463** A97 26p Rowing .75 *1.10*
**464** A97 29p Soccer .85 *1.40*
*Nos. 461-464 (4)* 3.10 *4.10*

**Royal Navy Crest Type of 1982**

**1984, Sept. 21** **Litho.** ***Perf. 13½x13***

**465** A87 20p Active 1.90 *1.75*
**466** A87 21p Foxhound 1.90 *2.10*
**467** A87 26p Valiant 2.10 *2.10*
**468** A87 29p Hood 2.25 *2.50*
*Nos. 465-468 (4)* 8.15 *8.45*

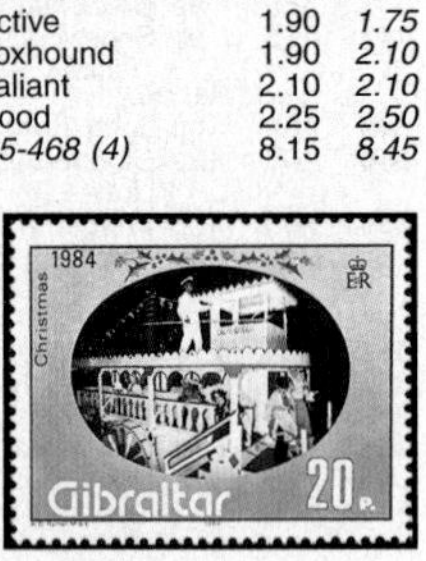


Christmas A98

***Perf. 14x14½***

**1984, Nov. 7** **Litho.** **Wmk. 373**

**469** A98 20p Parade float .55 .55
**470** A98 80p Float, diff. 2.25 2.25

**Europa Issue**

Musical Symbols — A99

**1985, Feb. 26 Photo. *Perf. 12½***
**Granite Paper**

| | | | |
|---|---|---|---|
| **471** A99 20p multi, diff. | .45 | .40 |
| **472** A99 29p shown | .65 | *1.60* |

Save the Children Fund A100

Globe and legend in various positions.

**1985, May 3 Litho. *Perf. 13x13½***

| | | |
|---|---|---|
| **473** Strip of 4 | 5.00 | *5.00* |
| ***a.-d.*** A100 26p any single | 1.10 | *1.10* |

**Royal Navy Crest Type of 1982**

**1985, July 3 Litho. *Perf. 14***

| | | |
|---|---|---|
| **474** A87 4p Duncan | 1.00 | .50 |
| **475** A87 9p Fury | 1.40 | 1.40 |
| **476** A87 21p Firedrake | 2.75 | *2.75* |
| **477** A87 80p Malaya | 4.50 | *5.00* |
| *Nos. 474-477 (4)* | 9.65 | *9.65* |

Intl. Youth Year — A101

**1985, Sept. 6 *Perf. 14½***

| | | |
|---|---|---|
| **478** A101 4p Emblem | .55 | .25 |
| **479** A101 20p Hands, diamond | 1.90 | 1.50 |
| **480** A101 80p Girl Guides anniv. emblem | 4.25 | *4.00* |
| *Nos. 478-480 (3)* | 6.70 | *5.75* |

St. Joseph's Parish Church, Cent. — A102

Creche, Detail — A103

***Perf. 13½xRoulette 7 Between, 13½***

**1985, Oct. 25 Wmk. 373 Litho.**

| | | |
|---|---|---|
| **481** A102 Pair | 1.75 | *1.40* |
| ***a.*** 4p Centenary seal | .85 | .60 |
| ***b.*** 4p Church | .85 | .60 |
| ***c.*** No. 481a, perf. 13½ on 4 sides | .80 | .60 |
| **482** A103 80p multicolored | 5.75 | *4.75* |

Christmas. Nos. 481a-481b rouletted between. Printed in sheets of 10 pairs with the bottom row containing 5 No. 481c. Strips of 3, Nos. 481a-481c exist.

Europa A104

**1986, Feb. 10 Litho. *Perf. 13x13½***

| | | |
|---|---|---|
| **483** A104 22p Butterfly, house | *.80* | *.55* |
| **484** A104 29p Seagull, hotel | *1.40* | *3.25* |

Postage Stamp Cent. — A105

Elizabeth II, 60th Birthday — A106

**1986, Mar. 25 *Perf. 13½x13***

| | | |
|---|---|---|
| **485** A105 4p No. 18 | .35 | .25 |
| **486** A105 22p No. 42 | 1.40 | 1.25 |
| **487** A105 32p No. 67 | 2.25 | *2.40* |
| **488** A105 36p No. 118 | 2.25 | *2.75* |

**Size: 32x48mm**

***Perf. 14***

| | | |
|---|---|---|
| **489** A105 44p No. 131 | 3.25 | *3.75* |
| *Nos. 485-489 (5)* | 9.50 | *10.40* |

**Souvenir Sheet**

| | | |
|---|---|---|
| **490** A105 29p No. 2 | 4.00 | 4.00 |

**1986, May 22 Litho. *Perf. 14***

| | | |
|---|---|---|
| **491** A106 £1 multicolored | 2.50 | *3.25* |

**Royal Navy Crest Type of 1982**

**1986, Aug. 28 Litho. *Perf. 14***

| | | |
|---|---|---|
| **492** A87 22p Lightning | 2.50 | 1.00 |
| **493** A87 29p Hermione | 2.75 | 1.75 |
| **494** A87 32p Laforey | 3.00 | *3.25* |
| **495** A87 44p Nelson | 3.50 | *4.50* |
| *Nos. 492-495 (4)* | 11.75 | *10.50* |

Christmas, Intl. Peace Year — A107

**1986, Oct. 14 Litho. *Perf. 14½x14***

| | | |
|---|---|---|
| **496** A107 18p St. Mary the Crowned Cathedral | 1.25 | .50 |
| **497** A107 32p St. Andrew's Church | 1.75 | *2.75* |

Souvenir Sheet

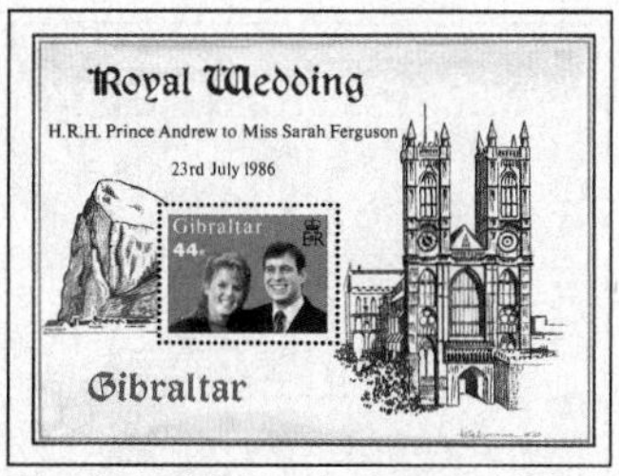
Wedding of Prince Andrew and Sarah Ferguson — A108

**1986, Aug. 28 Litho. *Perf. 15***

| | | |
|---|---|---|
| **498** A108 44p multicolored | 1.50 | *2.00* |

Europa — A109

**1987, Feb. 17 Wmk. 384 *Perf. 15***

| | | |
|---|---|---|
| **499** A109 22p Neptune House | *1.50* | *.50* |
| **500** A109 29p Ocean Heights | *2.00* | *3.75* |

**Royal Navy Crest Type of 1982**

**1987, Apr. 2 *Perf. 13½x13***

| | | |
|---|---|---|
| **501** A87 18p Wishart | 1.90 | .70 |
| **502** A87 22p Charybdis | 2.10 | 1.10 |
| **503** A87 32p Antelope | 3.00 | *3.00* |
| **504** A87 44p Eagle | 3.50 | *3.75* |
| *Nos. 501-504 (4)* | 10.50 | *8.55* |

Warrant Granted to the Royal Engineers, 200th Anniv. — A110

**1987, Apr. 25 Wmk. 373 *Perf. 14½***

| | | |
|---|---|---|
| **505** A110 18p Victoria Stadium | 1.60 | .55 |
| **506** A110 32p Casket, Freedom Scroll | 2.40 | *3.25* |
| **507** A110 44p Monogram | 3.25 | *4.25* |
| *Nos. 505-507 (3)* | 7.25 | *8.05* |

Guns and Artillery A111

Designs: 1p, 13-inch mortar, 1783. 2p, 6-inch Coast, 1909. 3p, 8-inch Howitzer, 1783. 4p, Bofors L40/70, 1951. 5p, 100-ton RML, 1882. 10p, 5.25 HAA, 1953. 18p, 25-pounder Gun-howitzer, 1943. 19p, 64-pounder RML, 1873. 22p, 12-pounder, 1758. 50p, 10-inch RML, 1870. £1, Russian 24-pounder, 1854. £3, 9.2-inch Coast Mk. 10, 1935. £5, 24-pounder, 1779.

**1987, June 1 Wmk. 373 *Perf. 12½***

| | | |
|---|---|---|
| **508** A111 1p multicolored | .25 | *.60* |
| **509** A111 2p multicolored | *.35* | *.50* |
| **510** A111 3p multicolored | .35 | *.40* |
| **511** A111 4p multicolored | .45 | .25 |
| **512** A111 5p multicolored | .45 | .50 |
| **513** A111 10p multicolored | .45 | .50 |
| **514** A111 18p multicolored | .70 | *.95* |
| **515** A111 19p multicolored | .70 | *1.50* |
| **516** A111 22p multicolored | .70 | .40 |
| **517** A111 50p multicolored | 1.40 | *2.75* |
| **518** A111 £1 multicolored | 3.00 | 3.50 |
| **519** A111 £3 multicolored | 6.00 | 4.50 |
| **520** A111 £5 multicolored | 10.00 | 18.00 |
| *Nos. 508-520 (13)* | 24.80 | *34.35* |

For surcharge see No. 595.

Christmas — A112

**1987, Nov. 12 Wmk. 384 *Perf. 14½***

| | | |
|---|---|---|
| **521** A112 4p Three Wise Men | .25 | .25 |
| **522** A112 22p Holy Family | 1.40 | .95 |
| **523** A112 44p Shepherds | 2.40 | *3.00* |
| *Nos. 521-523 (3)* | 4.05 | *4.20* |

Europa — A113

Transport and communication: No. 524, Rock of Gibraltar, Cruise Ship. No. 525, Passenger jet, yacht, dish aerial. No. 526, Bus, buggy. No. 527, Rock of Gibraltar, automobile, telephone.

***Perf. 14½x14 on 3 Sides; Rouletted Between***

**1988, Feb. 16 Litho. Wmk. 373**

| | | |
|---|---|---|
| **524** 22p multicolored | *1.50* | *1.60* |
| **525** 22p multicolored | *1.50* | *1.60* |
| ***a.*** A113 Pair, #524-525 | *3.25* | *3.25* |
| **526** 32p multicolored | *2.10* | *2.25* |
| **527** 32p multicolored | *2.10* | *2.25* |
| ***a.*** A113 Pair, #526-527 | *4.75* | *4.75* |
| *Nos. 524-527 (4)* | *7.20* | *7.70* |

Nos. 525a, 527a have continuous design.

**Royal Navy Crest Type of 1982**

***Perf. 13½x13***

**1988, Apr. 7 Wmk. 384**

| | | |
|---|---|---|
| **528** A87 18p Clyde | 2.10 | .65 |
| **529** A87 22p Foresight | 2.25 | 1.25 |
| **530** A87 32p Severn | 3.00 | *3.25* |
| **531** A87 44p Rodney | 3.75 | *4.75* |
| *Nos. 528-531 (4)* | 11.10 | *9.90* |

Birds A114

**1988, June 15 Wmk. 373 *Perf. 14***

| | | |
|---|---|---|
| **532** A114 4p Bee eater | .75 | .25 |
| **533** A114 22p Common puffin | 2.25 | 1.00 |
| **534** A114 32p Honey buzzard | 3.25 | *3.25* |
| **535** A114 44p Blue rock thrush | 4.00 | *4.25* |
| *Nos. 532-535 (4)* | 10.25 | *8.75* |

Operation Raleigh, 1984-88 A115

Designs: 19p, Square-rigger. 22p, Sir Walter Raleigh and expedition emblem. 32p, Maps and modern transport ship Sir Walter Raleigh. 44p, Ship Sir Walter Raleigh.

***Perf. 13x13½***

**1988, Sept. 14 Litho. Wmk. 373**

| | | |
|---|---|---|
| **536** A115 19p multicolored | .85 | .85 |
| **537** A115 22p multicolored | 1.00 | 1.00 |
| **538** A115 32p multicolored | 1.40 | 1.40 |
| *Nos. 536-538 (3)* | 3.25 | 3.25 |

**Souvenir Sheet**

| | | |
|---|---|---|
| **539** Sheet of 2, #537, 539a | 5.75 | 5.75 |
| ***a.*** A115 44p multicolored | 2.25 | 2.25 |

400th anniv. of Sir Walter Raleigh's voyage to the New World to establish the 1st English-speaking colony, in what is now North Carolina.

Christmas
A116

Children's drawings: 4p, Snowman, by Rebecca Falero. 22p, Nativity, by Dennis Penalver. 44p, Santa Claus, by Gavin Key.

**1988, Nov. 2** **Wmk. 384** ***Perf. 14***

**540** A116 4p multicolored .25 .25
**541** A116 22p multicolored .60 .75

**Size: 25x33mm**

**542** A116 44p multicolored 1.40 *1.90*
*Nos. 540-542 (3)* 2.25 *2.90*

Europa
A117

Toys: 32p, Doll, doll house, puppy, ball, boat.

***Perf. 13x13½***

**1989, Feb. 15** **Wmk. 384**

**543** A117 25p shown *1.25* *.80*
**544** A117 32p multicolored *1.75* *2.50*

Gibraltar Regiment, 50th Anniv. — A118

***Perf. 13½x13***

**1989, Apr. 28** **Wmk. 373**

**545** A118 4p The Port Sergeant .50 .25
**546** A118 22p Regimental colors, Queen's colors 1.75 1.00
**547** A118 32p Drum Major 2.50 *3.00*
*Nos. 545-547 (3)* 4.75 4.25

**Souvenir Sheet**

**548** Sheet of 2, Nos. 546, 548a 5.00 *5.50*
*a.* A118 44p Regimental arms 2.25 2.25

Intl. Red Cross, 125th Anniv. — A119

***Perf. 15x14½***

**1989, July 7** **Wmk. 384**

**549** A119 25p Mother and child 1.10 .60
**550** A119 32p Malnourished children 1.50 *1.50*
**551** A119 44p Accident victims 2.10 *2.50*
*Nos. 549-551 (3)* 4.70 *4.60*

**Royal Navy Crest Type of 1982**

**1989, Sept. 7** **Litho.** ***Perf. 14***

**552** A87 22p Blankney 2.00 .70
**553** A87 25p Deptford 2.00 1.50
**554** A87 32p Exmoor 2.75 2.50
**555** A87 44p Stork 3.75 *4.25*
*Nos. 552-555 (4)* 10.50 8.95

Souvenir Sheets

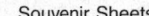

Coins — A120

No. 556: a, 1p Barbary Partridge. b, 2p Lighthouse at Europa Point. c, 10p Tower of Homage. d, 5p Barbary Ape.

No. 557: a, 50p Gibraltar Candytuft. b, £5 Pillars of Hercules. c, £2 Cannon from the Great Siege Period, 1779-1783. d, £1 Natl. coat of arms. e, Common obverse side of coins picturing Maklouf head of Queen Elizabeth II. f, 20p Our Lady of Europa.

**1989, Oct. 10** ***Perf. 14½x15***

**556** Sheet of 4 2.25 2.25
*a.-d.* A120 4p any single .55 .55
**557** Sheet of 6 7.75 7.75
*a.-f.* A120 22p any single 1.25 1.25

Christmas
A121

**Wmk. 384**

**1989, Oct. 11** **Litho.** ***Perf. 14½***

**558** A121 4p Santa's sleigh .25 .25
**559** A121 22p Shepherds see star 1.40 .85
**560** A121 32p Holy family 2.10 *2.10*
**561** A121 44p Adoration of the Magi 3.25 *3.50*
*Nos. 558-561 (4)* 7.00 *6.70*

Europa 1990 — A122

Post offices: No. 562, G.P.O. exterior. No. 563, Carved crown and "VR" from p.o. archway and G.P.O. interior. No. 564, South District P.O. interior. No. 565, South District P.O. exterior.

***Perf. 14½, Rouletted 9½ Between***

**1990, Mar. 6** **Litho.** **Unwmk.**

**562** 22p multicolored *1.25* *1.25*
**563** 22p multicolored *1.25* *1.25*
*a.* A122 Pair, #562-563 *3.00* *3.00*
**564** 32p multicolored *1.75* *1.75*
**565** 32p multicolored *1.75* *1.75*
*a.* A122 Pair, #564-565 *4.00* *4.00*
*Nos. 562-565 (4)* 6.00 *6.00*

Pairs are rouletted between.

Early Fire Truck
A123

**1990, Apr. 2** ***Perf. 14½x14***

**566** A123 4p Early firemen, hose, vert. 1.50 .25
**567** A123 20p shown 3.00 1.00
**568** A123 42p Modern truck 3.25 3.25
**569** A123 44p Modern fireman, vert. 3.50 3.50
*Nos. 566-569 (4)* 11.25 8.00

Fire Service, 125th anniv.

Penny Black, 150th Anniv. — A124

19p, Henry Corbould, Great Britain No. 1. 22p, 1st Royal Mail coach, Bristol-London. 32p, Sir Rowland Hill, Great Britain No. 1. 44p, Great Britain No. 1, Maltese Cross cancel.

**1990, May 3** ***Perf. 13½x14***

**570** A124 19p multicolored 1.25 .90
**571** A124 22p multicolored 1.50 .95
**572** A124 32p multicolored 3.00 3.00
*Nos. 570-572 (3)* 5.75 4.85

**Souvenir Sheet**

**573** A124 44p multicolored 6.25 6.25

**Royal Navy Crest Type of 1982**

**1990, July 10** **Litho.** ***Perf. 14***

**574** A87 22p Calpe 2.00 .80
**575** A87 25p Gallant 2.25 1.90
**576** A87 32p Wrestler 2.75 *3.00*
**577** A87 44p Greyhound 3.50 *4.00*
*Nos. 574-577 (4)* 10.50 9.70

Europort Model
A125

**1990, Oct. 10** **Litho.** ***Perf. 14½***

**578** A125 22p shown 1.00 .95
**579** A125 23p Building components 1.00 *1.40*
**580** A125 25p Land reclamation 1.10 *1.40*
*Nos. 578-580 (3)* 3.10 *3.75*

Christmas — A126

**1990, Oct. 10** ***Perf. 13½***

**581** A126 4p shown .25 .25
**582** A126 22p Santa Claus .90 .55
**583** A126 42p Christmas tree 2.25 *2.50*
**584** A126 44p Creche 2.25 *2.50*
*Nos. 581-584 (4)* 5.65 *5.80*

Europa
A127

**1991, Feb. 26** **Litho.** ***Perf. 13½***

**585** A127 25p Spaceplane, satellite *.90* *.75*
**586** A127 32p ERS-1 satellite *1.25* *1.75*

**Royal Navy Crest Type of 1982**

**1991, Apr. 9** **Litho.** ***Perf. 13½x13***

**587** A87 4p Hesperus .60 .25
**588** A87 21p Forester 2.10 1.50
**589** A87 22p Furious 2.10 1.50
**590** A87 62p Scylla 5.00 *6.00*
*Nos. 587-590 (4)* 9.80 *9.25*

Birds
A128

**1991, May 30** **Litho.** ***Perf. 13½***

**591** A128 13p Black stork 1.60 1.25
**592** A128 13p Egyptian vulture 1.60 1.25
**593** A128 13p Barbary partridge 1.60 1.25
**594** A128 13p Shag 1.60 1.25
*a.* Block of 4, #591-594 7.00 *7.50*

World Wildlife Fund.

No. 519 Surcharged

**Wmk. 373**

**1991, May 30** **Litho.** ***Perf. 12½***

**595** A111 £1.05 on £3 multi 6.50 3.25

Views of Gibraltar
A129

Paintings: 22p, North View of Gibraltar, by Gustavo Bacarisas (1873-1971). 26p, Parson's Lodge, by Elena Mifsud (1906-1989). 32p, Governor's Parade, by Jacobo Azabury, OBE (1890-1980). 42p, Waterport Wharf, by Rudesindo Mannia (1899-1982), vert.

**1991, Sept. 10** **Litho.** ***Perf. 15x14***

**596** A129 22p multicolored 1.25 .50
**597** A129 26p multicolored 1.40 .90
**598** A129 32p multicolored 2.10 *2.25*

***Perf. 14x15***

**599** A129 42p multicolored 3.00 *3.50*
*Nos. 596-599 (4)* 7.75 *7.15*

Christmas
A130

Christmas carols: 4p, Once in Royal David's City. 24p, Silent Night. 25p, Angels We Have Heard on High. 49p, O Come All Ye Faithful.

**1991, Oct. 15** **Litho.** ***Perf. 14½***

**600** A130 4p multicolored .25 .25
**601** A130 24p multicolored 2.00 .75
**602** A130 25p multicolored 2.00 1.50
**603** A130 49p multicolored 3.50 *4.50*
*Nos. 600-603 (4)* 7.75 *7.00*

Souvenir Sheet

Phila Nippon '91 — A131

**1991, Nov. 15**

**604** A131 £1.05 Plain tiger 5.25 5.25

**Queen Elizabeth II's Accession to the Throne, 40th Anniv.**

Common Design Type

**Wmk. 373**

**1992, Feb. 6 Litho. *Perf. 14***

**605** CD349 4p multicolored .25 .25
**606** CD349 20p multicolored .80 .80
**607** CD349 24p multicolored 1.00 *1.10*
**608** CD349 44p multicolored 2.00 *2.10*
**609** CD349 54p multicolored 2.50 *2.75*
*Nos. 605-609 (5)* 6.55 *7.00*

Discovery of America, 500th Anniv. — A132

**1992, Feb. 6 Unwmk. *Perf. 14½***

**610** A132 24p Columbus, Santa Maria 2.10 1.75
**611** A132 24p Map, Nina 2.10 1.75
*a.* Pair, #610-611 4.25 3.50
**612** A132 34p Map, Pinta 2.30 1.90
**613** A132 34p Map, sailor 2.30 1.90
*a.* Pair, #612-613 4.75 3.75
*Nos. 610-613 (4)* 8.80 *7.30*

Europa. Printed in sheets containing 4 pairs.

Around the World Yacht Rally, 1991-92 A133

Compass rose, sail and maps of routes through: 21p, Atlantic Ocean, vert. 24p, Malay Archipelago. 25p, Indian Ocean. 49p, Mediterranean and Red Seas, vert.

**1992, Apr. 15 Litho. *Perf. 13½***

**614** A133 21p multicolored 1.10 .90
**615** A133 24p multicolored 1.40 *1.50*
**616** A133 25p multicolored 1.40 *1.60*
*Nos. 614-616 (3)* 3.90 *4.00*

**Souvenir Sheet**

**617** A133 Sheet of 2, #614 & 617a 3.00 3.00
*a.* A133 49p multicolored 2.00 2.00

Anglican Diocese of Gibraltar, 150th Anniv. A134

4p, Holy Trinity Cathedral, vert. 24p, Crest and map. 44p, Construction work on Cathedral during 1800's. 54p, Bishop Tomlinson, first Bishop of Diocese (1842-1863), vert.

**1992, Aug. 21 Litho. *Perf. 14***

**618** A134 4p multicolored .40 .25
**619** A134 24p multicolored 1.25 .60
**620** A134 44p multicolored 2.25 *2.50*
**621** A134 54p multicolored 2.50 *3.25*
*Nos. 618-621 (4)* 6.40 *6.60*

Christmas A135

Designs: 4p, Church of the Sacred Heart of Jesus. 24p, Cathedral of St. Mary the Crowned. 34p, St. Andrew's Church. 49p, St. Joseph's Church.

**1992, Nov. 10 Litho. *Perf. 14***

**622** A135 4p multicolored .25 .25
**623** A135 24p multicolored 1.60 .50
**624** A135 34p multicolored 2.75 2.25
**625** A135 49p multicolored 3.25 *4.50*
*Nos. 622-625 (4)* 7.85 7.50

Contemporary Art — A136

Europa: No. 626, Masks of Comedy and Tragedy, record. No. 627, Painting, dancer, pottery. No. 628, Architecture, sculpture. No. 629, Video camera, 35mm film.

**1993, Mar. 2 Litho. *Perf. 14½***

**626** A136 24p multicolored 1.75 1.50
**627** A136 24p multicolored 1.75 1.50
*a.* Pair, #626-627 3.50 *4.25*
**628** A136 34p multicolored 2.25 2.25
**629** A136 34p multicolored 2.25 2.25
*a.* Pair, #628-629 4.50 *5.25*
*Nos. 626-629 (4)* 8.00 7.50

Souvenir Sheet

World War II Warships — A137

Designs: a, HMS Hood. b, HMS Ark Royal c, HMAS Waterhen. d, USS Gleaves.

**1993, Apr. 27 Litho. *Perf. 14***

**630** A137 24p Sheet of 4, #a.-d. 12.00 12.00

See Nos. 660, 684, 714, 732.

Architectural Heritage A138

**1993-94 Litho. *Perf. 13***

**631** A138 1p Landport Gate .25 *.75*
**632** A138 2p St. Mary the Crowned .30 *.75*
**633** A138 3p Parsons Lodge Battery .30 .25
**634** A138 4p Moorish Castle .30 .25
**635** A138 5p General Post Office .40 .25
**636** A138 10p South Barracks .40 .25
**637** A138 21p American War Memorial 1.00 .85
**638** A138 24p Garrison Library 1.10 .95
**639** A138 25p Southport Gates 1.10 .95
**640** A138 26p Casemates Gate 1.25 1.00
**641** A138 50p Central Police Station 2.00 1.75
**642** A138 £1 Prince Edward's Gate 3.00 3.00
**643** A138 £3 Lighthouse 9.00 *10.00*
**644** A138 £5 Coat of arms, keys to fortress, vert. 15.00 15.00
*Nos. 631-644 (14)* 35.40 36.00

Nos. 631, 635, 637, 639, 642-643 are vert.

Portions of the design on No. 644 were applied by a thermographic process producing a shiny, raised effect.

Issued: £5, 6/6/94; others, 6/28/93.

See Nos. 686-693.

Anniversaries — A139

**1993, Sept. 21 Litho. *Perf. 13***

**645** A139 21p Coins 1.25 .75
**646** A139 24p Jet, biplane fighters 2.00 1.00
**647** A139 34p Garrison Library 2.00 2.25
**648** A139 49p Churchill, searchlights 4.00 4.00
*Nos. 645-648 (4)* 9.25 8.00

First decimal coins, 25th anniv. Royal Air Force, 75th anniv. Garrison Library, bicent. Churchill's visit to Gibraltar, 50th anniv.

Christmas A140

Mice and: 5p, Christmas tree. 24p, Christmas cracker. 44p, Singing carols. 49p, Snowman.

**1993, Nov. 16 Litho. *Perf. 13½***

**649** A140 5p multicolored .25 .25
**650** A140 24p multicolored 1.25 .70
**651** A140 44p multicolored 2.50 2.50
**652** A140 49p multicolored 3.25 3.25
*Nos. 649-652 (4)* 7.25 6.70

European Discoveries — A141

Europa: No. 653, Atoms exploding, Lord Penney (1909-91). No. 654, Chemistry flasks, polonium, radium, Marie Curie. No. 655, Diesel engine, Rudolf Diesel. No. 656, Telescope, Galileo.

**1994, Mar. 1 Litho. *Perf. 13½***

**653** A141 24p multicolored 1.25 1.25
**654** A141 24p multicolored 1.25 1.25
*a.* Pair, #653-654 3.00 3.00
**655** A141 34p multicolored 1.50 1.50
**656** A141 34p multicolored 1.50 1.50
*a.* Pair, #655-656 3.75 3.50
*Nos. 653-656 (4)* 5.50 5.50

1994 World Cup Soccer Championships, US — A142

26p, FIFA cup, US map, flag. 39p, Players, US map as playing field. 49p, Leg action.

**1994, Apr. 19 Litho. *Perf. 13½***

**657** A142 26p multi 1.25 .65
**658** A142 39p multi 1.75 2.00
**659** A142 49p multi, vert. 2.25 2.75
*Nos. 657-659 (3)* 5.25 5.40

**World War II Warships Type of 1993**

Souvenir Sheet

Designs: a, 5p, HMS Penelope. b, 25p, HMS Warspite. c, 44p, USS McLanahan. d, 49p, HNLMS Isaac Sweers.

**1994, June 6 Litho. *Perf. 13½x13***

**660** A137 Sheet of 4, #a.-d. 11.50 11.50

Souvenir Sheet

PHILAKOREA '94 — A143

**1994, Aug. 16 Litho. *Perf. 13***

**661** A143 £1.05 multicolored 4.75 4.75

Marine Life — A144

**1994, Sept. 27 Litho. *Perf. 14***

**662** A144 21p Golden star coral 1.00 1.00
**663** A144 24p Star fish 1.25 1.25
**664** A144 34p Gorgonian sea fan 2.00 2.25
**665** A144 49p Turkish wrasse 2.75 3.00
*Nos. 662-665 (4)* 7.00 7.50

Intl. Olympic Committee, Cent. — A145

**1994, Nov. 22 Litho. *Perf. 14***

**666** A145 49p Discus 2.75 2.25
**667** A145 54p Javelin 2.75 2.50

Christmas Songbirds A146

**1994, Nov. 22 *Perf. 13½***

**668** A146 5p Great tit, vert. .60 .25
**669** A146 24p Robin 2.75 1.00
**670** A146 34p Blue tit 3.00 1.75
**671** A146 54p Goldfinch, vert. 3.75 *4.25*
*Nos. 668-671 (4)* 10.10 7.25

New Members in European Union A147

Flags: 24p, Austria. 26p, Finland. 34p, Sweden. 49p, Sweden, Finland, Austria, emblem of European Union.

**1995, Jan. 3 Litho. *Perf. 14***

**672** A147 24p multicolored .90 .90
**673** A147 26p multicolored 1.00 1.00
**674** A147 34p multicolored 1.25 1.50
**675** A147 49p multicolored 1.90 2.50
*Nos. 672-675 (4)* 5.05 5.90

Peace & Freedom — A148

Europa: No. 676, Cross, barbed wire, text. No. 677, Rainbow, dove, hands. No. 678, Shackles, text. No. 679, Doves, hands.

**1995, Feb. 28 Litho. *Perf. 13½***

**676** 24p multicolored 1.50 1.25
**677** 24p multicolored 1.50 1.25
*a.* A148 Pair, #676-677 3.25 3.00
**678** 34p multicolored 1.75 1.75
**679** 34p multicolored 1.75 1.75
*a.* A148 Pair, #678-679 4.25 4.25
*Nos. 676-679 (4)* 6.50 *6.00*

Island Games — A149

**1995, May 8 Litho. *Perf. 14x13½***

**680** A149 24p Sailing 1.00 .90
**681** A149 44p Running 2.00 2.00
**682** A149 49p Swimming 2.00 2.00
*Nos. 680-682 (3)* 5.00 4.90

*680a* Booklet pane of 3 4.00
*681a* Booklet pane of 3 7.00
*682a* Booklet pane of 3 8.50
*682b* Bklt. pane, 1 ea. #680-682 6.50
Commemorative booklet, 1 each #680a-682b 27.00

Souvenir Sheet

VE Day, 50th Anniv. — A150

**1995, May 8**

**683** A150 £1.05 multicolored 6.00 6.00

### World War II Warships Type of 1993

Designs: a, 5p, HMS Calpe. b, 24p, HMS Victorious. c, 44p, USS Weehawken. d, 49p, FFS Savorgnan de Brazza.

**Souvenir Sheet**

**1995, June 6 Litho. *Perf. 13½x14***

**684** A137 Sheet of 4, #a.-d. 11.50 11.50

Singapore '95 — A151

Orchids: a, 22p, Bee. b, 23p, Brown bee. c, 24p, Pyramidal. d, 25p, Mirror. e, 26p, Sawfly.

**1995, Sept. 1 Litho. *Perf. 14x14½***

**685** A151 Strip of 5, #a.-e. 9.00 6.25

### Architectural Heritage Type of 1993

**1995, Sept. 1 Litho. *Perf. 13***

**686** A138 6p House of Assembly .70 .40
**687** A138 7p Bleak House .70 .40
**688** A138 8p Bust of Gen. Eliott .90 .40
**689** A138 9p Supreme Court Bldg. 1.10 .65
**690** A138 20p Convent 1.25 .70
**691** A138 30p St. Bernard's Hospital 1.40 1.50
**692** A138 40p City Hall 1.60 2.00
**693** A138 £2 Church of Sacred Heart of Jesus 6.00 7.50
*Nos. 686-693 (8)* 13.65 13.55

Nos. 686, 688, 691, 693 are vert.

UN, 50th Anniv. A152

**1995, Oct. 24 Litho. *Perf. 13½***

**694** A152 34p shown 2.00 2.00
**695** A152 49p Peace dove 2.25 2.25

Miniature Sheets of 4 + 4 Labels

Motion Pictures, Cent. — A153

Designs: No. 696: a, Ingrid Bergman. b, Vittorio De Sica. c, Marlene Dietrich. d, Laurence Olivier.

No. 697: a, 38p, Audrey Hepburn. b, 25p, Romy Schneider. c, 28p, Yves Montand. d, 5p, Marilyn Monroe.

**1995, Nov. 13 Litho. *Perf. 14½x14***

**696** A153 24p #a.-d. 4.00 4.00
**697** A153 #a.-d. 4.00 4.00

Christmas A154

Designs: 5p, Santa Claus. 24p, Sack of toys. 34p, Reindeer. 54p, Santa with sleigh, reindeer flying over rooftops.

**1995, Nov. 27 *Perf. 14***

**698** A154 5p multicolored .40 .25
**699** A154 24p multicolored 1.50 .75
**700** A154 34p multicolored 2.00 2.00
**701** A154 54p multicolored 3.25 3.75
*Nos. 698-701 (4)* 7.15 6.75

Miniature Sheet

Puppies — A155

#702: a, 5p, Shih tzu. b, 21p, Dalmatian. c, Cocker spaniel. d, 25p, West Highland white terrier. e, 34p, Labrador. f, 35p, Boxer.

**1996, Jan. 24 Litho. *Perf. 14***

**702** A155 Sheet of 6, #a.-f. 6.50 6.50

No. 702 is a continuous design.

Women of the British Royal Family A156

**1996, Feb. 9 Litho. *Perf. 13½***

**703** A156 24p Princess Anne 1.50 1.50
**704** A156 24p Princess Diana 1.50 1.50
**705** A156 34p Queen Mother 1.75 1.75
**706** A156 34p Queen Elizabeth II 1.75 1.75
*Nos. 703-706 (4)* 6.50 6.50

Europa.

European Soccer — A157

Team members in action scenes: 21p, West Germany, 1980. 24p, France, 1964. 34p, Holland, 1988. £1.20, Denmark, 1992.

**1996, Apr. 2 Litho. *Perf. 13***

**707** A157 21p multicolored .70 .70
**708** A157 24p multicolored .90 .90
**709** A157 34p multicolored 1.40 1.40
**710** A157 £1.20 multicolored 3.50 3.50
*a.* Souvenir sheet, Nos. 707-710 10.00 10.00
*Nos. 707-710 (4)* 6.50 6.50

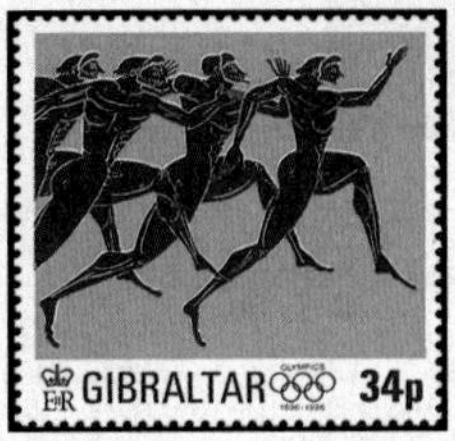


Modern Olympic Games, Cent. A158

**1996, May 2 Litho. *Perf. 13½***

**711** A158 34p Ancient athletes 1.25 1.25
**712** A158 49p Athletes, 1896 1.75 1.75
**713** A158 £1.05 Athletes, 1990s 3.50 3.50
*Nos. 711-713 (3)* 6.50 6.50

### World War II Warships Type of 1993

Souvenir Sheet

a, 5p, HMS Starling. b, 25p, HMS Royalist. c, 49p, USS Philadelphia. d, 54p, HMCS Prescott.

**1996, June 8 Litho. *Perf. 13½x14***

**714** A137 Sheet of 4, #a.-d. 8.00 8.00

UNICEF, 50th Anniv. A159

a, 21p, Girl, boy. b, 24p, Three children. c, 49p, Three children, diff. d, 54p, Girl, boy, diff.

**1996, June 8 *Perf. 13½x13***

**715** A159 Strip of 4, #a.-d. 5.75 5.75

World Wildlife Fund A160

Red kite: a, In flight. b, One adult. c, One on rock, one in flight. d, Adults, young in nest.

**1996, July 12 Litho. *Perf. 14½***

**716** A160 34p Block or strip of 4, #a.-d. 7.75 7.75

Christmas Images Formed with "Lego" Blocks — A161

**1996, Nov. 27 Litho. *Perf. 14***

**717** A161 5p Pudding .25 .25
**718** A161 21p Snowman .85 .85
**719** A161 24p Present 1.00 1.00
**720** A161 34p Santa Claus 1.25 1.25
**721** A161 54p Candle 1.75 1.75
*Nos. 717-721 (5)* 5.10 5.10

Sailing Ship "Mary Celeste" — A162

Europa: No. 722, "Mary Celeste" in rough seas. No. 723, Men on board ship. No. 724, Boat approaching "Mary Celeste." No. 725, In full sail.

**1997, Feb. 12 Litho. *Perf. 14***

**722** A162 28p multicolored 1.10 1.10
**723** A162 28p multicolored 1.10 1.10
**724** A162 30p multicolored 1.25 1.25
**725** A162 30p multicolored 1.25 1.25
*Nos. 722-725 (4)* 4.70 4.70

Kittens A163

Designs: a, 5p, Silver tabby American shorthair. b, 24p, "Rumpy" Manx red tabby. c, 26p, Blue point Birmans. d, 28p, Red self longhair. e, 30p, British shorthair, tortoiseshell & white. f, 35p, British bicolor shorthairs.

**1997, Feb. 12**

**726** A163 Sheet of 6, #a.-f. 8.00 8.00
*g.* Bklt. pane of 3, #726a, 726c, 726e 3.00 3.00
*h.* Bklt. pane of 3, #726b, 726c, 726d 4.25
*i.* Bklt. pane of 4, #726a, 726b, 726e, 726f 5.00
*j.* Bklt. pane of 4, #726c, 726d, 726e, 726f 6.00
*k.* Booklet pane, #726 8.25
Complete booklet, #726g-726k 26.00

Hong Kong '97. No. 726k is rouletted at left and does not have Hong Kong '97 emblem and inscription in bottom slevage.

Butterflies — A164

Designs: 23p, Anthocharis belia euphenoides. 26p, Charaxes jasius. 30p, Vanessa cardui. £1.20, Iphiclides podalirius.

**1997, Apr. 7 Litho. *Perf. 14x13½***

**728** A164 23p multicolored .95 .95
**729** A164 26p multicolored 1.10 1.10
**730** A164 30p multicolored 1.50 1.50
**731** A164 £1.20 multicolored 4.00 4.00
*a.* Souvenir sheet of 4, #728-731 8.75 8.75
*Nos. 728-731 (4)* 7.55 7.55

### World War II Warships Type of 1993

Souvenir Sheet

a, 24p, HMS Enterprise. b, 26p, HMS Cleopatra. c, 38p, USS Iowa. d, 50p, Polish Warship Orkan.

**1997, June 9 Litho. *Perf. 13½***

**732** A137 Sheet of 4, #a.-d. 6.25 6.25

Queen Elizabeth II and Prince Philip, 50th Wedding Anniv. — A165

Designs: £1.20, Prince Philip driving a four-in-hand, Queen beside him. £1.40, Queen, Prince Philip at Royal Ascot, Queen "Trooping the Color."

**1997, July 10 Litho. *Perf. 14x13½***

**733** A165 £1.20 multicolored 5.00 5.00
**734** A165 £1.40 multicolored 6.00 6.00
*a.* Pair, #733-734 11.00 11.00

1997 Dior Fashion Designs, by John Galliano — A166

30p, Long black dress, hat. 35p, Mini skirt, lace top. 50p, Formal gown. 62p, Suit, hat. £1.20, Formal gown, diff.

**1997, Sept. 9 Litho.** ***Perf. 13½x13***

**735** A166 30p multicolored 1.00 1.00
**736** A166 35p multicolored 1.25 1.25
**737** A166 50p multicolored 1.40 1.40
*a.* Pair, #735, 737 3.25 3.25
**738** A166 62p multicolored 2.00 2.00
*a.* Pair, #736, 738 4.25 4.25
*Nos. 735-738 (4)* 5.65 5.65

**Souvenir Sheet**

**739** A166 £1.20 multicolored 4.50 4.50

Christmas A167

Stained glass windows: 5p, Our Lady and St. Bernard. 26p, The Epiphany of the Lord. 38p, St. Joseph holding Jesus. 50p, The Holy Family. 62p, The Miraculous Medal Madonna.

**1997, Nov. 18 Litho.** ***Perf. 13½***

**740** A167 5p multicolored .25 .25
**741** A167 26p multicolored 1.10 1.10
**742** A167 38p multicolored 1.40 1.40
**743** A167 50p multicolored 2.00 2.00
**744** A167 62p multicolored 2.25 *3.25*
*Nos. 740-744 (5)* 7.00 8.00

A168

**1997, Dec. 15 Litho.** ***Perf. 13***

**745** A168 26p multicolored 1.20 1.20

Sir Joshua Hassan (1915-97), government leader.

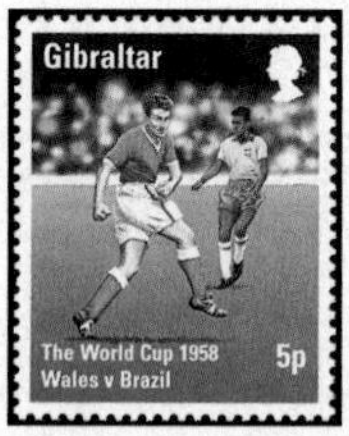


A169

Scenes from previous World Cup Championships: 5p, Wales v. Brazil, 1958. 26p, N. Ireland v. France, 1958. 38p, Scotland v. Holland, 1978. £1.20, England v. W. Germany, 1966.

**1998, Jan. 23**

**746** A169 5p multicolored .35 .35
**747** A169 26p multicolored 1.20 1.20
**748** A169 38p multicolored 1.50 1.50
**749** A169 £1.20 multicolored 4.00 4.00
*a.* Souvenir sheet, #746-749 8.00 8.00
*Nos. 746-749 (4)* 7.05 7.05

1998 World Cup Soccer Championships, France.

**Diana, Princess of Wales (1961-97)**

Common Design Type

Various portraits: a, 26p, Wearing black & white outfit. b, 26p, Wearing pink & white outfit. c, 38p, In black dress. d, 38p, In blue & gold jacket.

**1998, Mar. 31 Litho.** ***Perf. 14½x14***

**754** CD355 Sheet of 4, #a.-d. 5.50 5.50

The 20p surtax from international sales was donated to the Princess Diana Memorial Fund and the surtax from national sales was donated to a designated local charity.

**Royal Air Force, 80th Anniv.**

Common Design Type of 1993 Re-inscribed

Designs: 24p, Saro London. 26p, Fairey Fox. 38p, Handley Page Halifax GR.VI. 50p, Hawker Siddeley Buccaneer S.2B.

No. 759: a, 24p, Sopwith 1½ Strutter. b, 26p, Bristol M.1B. c, 38p, Supermarine Spitfire XII. d, 50p, Avro York.

**1998, Apr. 1** ***Perf. 14***

**755** CD350 24p multicolored 1.00 1.00
**756** CD350 26p multicolored 1.10 1.10
**757** CD350 38p multicolored 1.75 1.75
**758** CD350 50p multicolored 2.10 2.10
*Nos. 755-758 (4)* 5.95 5.95

**Souvenir Sheet of 4**

**759** CD350 #a.-d. 6.25 6.25

Europa — A170

Costumes worn by Miss Gibraltar for National Day: No. 760, Military style. No. 761, Long skirt, long-sleeved top. No. 762, Short skirt, long cape. No. 763, Black lace scarf, ruffled petticoat.

**1998, May 22 Litho.** ***Perf. 13***

**760** A170 26p multicolored .95 .95
**761** A170 26p multicolored .95 .95
**762** A170 38p multicolored 1.40 1.40
**763** A170 38p multicolored 1.40 1.40
*Nos. 760-763 (4)* 4.70 4.70

UNESCO 1998 Intl. Year of the Ocean A171

Marine life: a, 5p, Striped dolphin. b, 26p, Killer whale, vert. c, £1.20, Blue whale. d, 5p, Common dolphin, vert.

**1998, May 22** ***Perf. 14***

**764** A171 Sheet of 4, #a.-d. 7.75 7.75

Italia '98 and Portugal '98.

Battle of the Nile — A172

**1998, Aug. 1 Litho.** ***Perf. 13½***

**765** A172 12p Nileus .65 .65
**766** A172 26p Lord Nelson 1.25 1.25
*a.* Booklet pane of 1 1.60
**767** A172 28p Frances Nisbet 1.40 1.40
*a.* Bklt. pane, #765-767 3.75
**768** A172 35p HMS Vanguard 1.60 1.60

**Size: 45x27mm**

**769** A172 50p Battle of the Nile 2.50 2.50
*a.* Bklt. pane, #768-769, 2 #766 7.50
*b.* Bklt. pane, #766, 768-769 6.00
*c.* Bklt. pane, #765-769 8.50
Complete booklet, #766a, 767a, 769a-769c 27.50
*Nos. 765-769 (5)* 7.40 7.40

Quotations From Famous People A173

#770, "Love comforts like sunshine after rain," Shakespeare. #771, "The price of greatness is responsibility," Churchill. #772, "Hate the sin, love the sinner," Gandhi. #773, "Imagination is more important than knowledge," Einstein.

**1998, Oct. 6 Litho.** ***Perf. 14½***

**770** A173 26p multicolored 1.00 1.00
**771** A173 26p multicolored 1.00 1.00
**772** A173 38p multicolored 1.75 1.75
**773** A173 38p multicolored 1.75 1.75
*Nos. 770-773 (4)* 5.50 5.50

Nos. 770-773 were each printed in sheets of 6 with se-tenant labels.

A174

A175

**1998, Nov. 10 Litho.** ***Perf. 13***

**774** A174 5p Nativity .45 .45
**775** A174 26p Star over manger 1.10 1.10
**776** A174 30p Balthasar 1.25 1.25
**777** A174 35p Melchoir 1.40 1.40
**778** A174 50p Caspar 1.75 1.75
*Nos. 774-778 (5)* 5.95 5.95

Christmas.

**1999, Mar. 4 Litho.** ***Perf. 13½***

**779** A175 1p claret .25 .25
**780** A175 2p brown .25 .25
**781** A175 4p blue .25 .25
**782** A175 5p green .25 .25
**783** A175 10p brown orange .40 .40
**784** A175 12p red .45 .45
**785** A175 20p blue green .75 .75
**786** A175 28p lilac rose 1.00 1.00
**787** A175 30p vermilion 1.10 1.10
**788** A175 40p gray olive 1.50 1.50
**789** A175 42p slate 1.60 1.60

**Size: 22½x28mm**

***Perf. 14½***

**790** A175 50p olive bister 1.90 1.90
**791** A175 £1 black 4.00 4.00
**792** A175 £3 ultramarine 10.00 10.00

**Self-Adhesive**

***Die Cut Perf. 9x9½***

**793** A175 1st vermilion 1.50 1.50
*Nos. 779-793 (15)* 25.20 25.20

No. 793 was valued at 26p on day of issue.
See Nos. 885-886.

Nature Reserves — A176

**1999, Mar. 4** ***Perf. 13½x13***

**794** A176 30p Barbary macaque 1.60 1.60
**795** A176 30p Dartford warbler 1.60 1.60
**796** A176 42p Kingfisher 2.00 2.00
**797** A176 42p Dusky perch 2.00 2.00
*Nos. 794-797 (4)* 7.20 7.20

Europa.

Maritime Heritage — A177

Designs: 5p, Roman Anchorage. 30p, Medieval galley house. 42p, British relief ships. £1.20, HMS Berwick.

**1999, Mar. 19** ***Perf. 12½***

**798** A177 5p multicolored .25 .25
**799** A177 30p multicolored 1.50 1.50
**800** A177 42p multicolored 2.25 2.25
**801** A177 £1.20 multicolored 5.75 5.75
*a.* Souvenir sheet, #798-801 10.00 10.00
*Nos. 798-801 (4)* 9.75 9.75

John Lennon (1940-80) A178

Portraits: 20p, With flower over one eye. 30p, Black and white photo. 40p, Wearing glasses.

No. 805, Holding marriage license in front of Rock of Gibraltar. No. 806, Standing in front of airplane.

**1999, Mar. 20** ***Perf. 13***

**802** A178 20p multicolored 1.00 1.00
**803** A178 30p multicolored 1.50 1.50
**804** A178 40p multicolored 1.75 1.75
*Nos. 802-804 (3)* 4.25 4.25

**Souvenir Sheets**

**805** A178 £1 multicolored 7.00 7.00
**806** A178 £1 multicolored 7.00 7.00

UPU, 125th Anniv. — A179

**1999, June 7 Litho.** ***Perf. 12½***

**807** A179 5p Postal van .25 .25
**808** A179 30p Space station 1.50 1.50

Fighter Planes and Raptors A180

Designs: No. 809, RAF Eurofighter 2000 Typhoon. No. 810, RAF F3 Tornado. No. 811, RAF GR7 Harrier II. No. 812, Lesser kestrel. No. 813, Peregrine falcon. No. 814, Kestrel.

**1999, June 7** ***Perf. 13x13¼***

**809** A180 30p multicolored 1.10 1.10
**810** A180 30p multicolored 1.10 1.10
**811** A180 30p multicolored 1.10 1.10
*a.* Sheet of 3, #809-811 3.50 3.50
**812** A180 42p multicolored 1.25 1.25
*a.* Pair, #809, 812 3.25 3.25
**813** A180 42p multicolored 1.25 1.25
*a.* Pair, #810, 813 3.25 3.25
**814** A180 42p multicolored 1.25 1.25
*a.* Pair, #811, 814 3.25 3.25
*b.* Sheet of 3, #812-814 6.50 6.50

See Nos. 851-853, 887-889.

Wedding of Prince Edward and Sophie Rhys-Jones A181

***Perf. 13x13¼, 13¼x13***

**1999, June 19** **Litho.**

**815** A181 30p shown 1.50 1.50
**816** A181 42p Couple, vert. 1.75 1.75

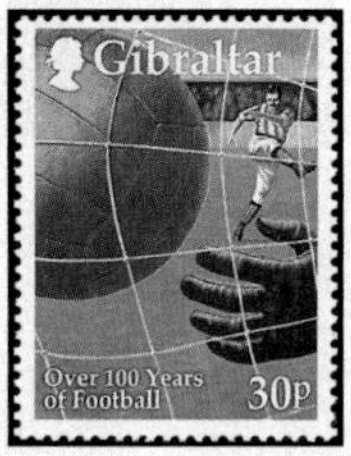


Sports in Gibraltar, Cent. — A182

**1999, July 2** ***Perf. 13***

**817** A182 30p Soccer 1.25 1.25
**818** A182 42p Rowing 1.75 1.75
**819** A182 £1.20 Cricket 3.75 3.75
*Nos. 817-819 (3)* 6.75 6.75

Wedding of Prince Edward to Sophie Rhys-Jones A183

***Perf. 13x13¼, 13¼x13***

**1999, Oct. 11** **Litho.**

**820** A183 54p shown 2.00 2.00
**821** A183 66p Couple standing, vert. 2.25 2.25

Christmas and New Year's Greetings A184

Designs: No. 822, "Happy Christmas," Santa, sleigh. No. 823, "Season's Greetings." No. 824, "Happy Millennium." No. 825, "Happy Christmas," Santa, reindeer. 42p, "Yo ho ho." 54p, Santa, tree, fireplace.

**1999, Nov. 11** **Litho.** ***Perf. 14***

**822** A184 5p multicolored .25 .25
**823** A184 5p multicolored .25 .25
**824** A184 30p multicolored 1.10 1.10
**825** A184 30p multicolored 1.10 1.10
**826** A184 42p multicolored 1.75 1.75
**827** A184 54p multicolored 2.00 2.00
*Nos. 822-827 (6)* 6.45 6.45

Stampin' the Future Children's Stamp Design Contest Winners A185

Artwork by: 30p, Colin Grech. 42p, Kim Barea. 54p, Stephan Williamson-Fa. 66p, Michael Podesta.

**2000. Jan. 28** **Litho.** ***Perf. 14½x14***

**828** A185 30p multi 1.50 1.50
**829** A185 42p multi 1.50 1.50
**830** A185 54p multi 1.50 1.50
**831** A185 66p multi 1.50 1.50
*a.* Block or strip of 4, #828-831 8.00 8.00

European Soccer — A186

**2000, Apr. 17** **Litho.** ***Perf. 12½***

**832** A186 30p France 1.00 1.00
**833** A186 30p Holland 1.00 1.00
**834** A186 42p Denmark 1.25 1.25
**835** A186 42p Germany 1.25 1.25
*a.* Souvenir sheet, #832-835 6.00 6.00
**836** A186 54p England 1.50 1.50
*a.* Souvenir sheet of 4 7.50 7.50
*Nos. 832-836 (5)* 6.00 6.00

The Stamp Show 2000, London (#836a).

Europa — A187

**2000, Apr. 17** ***Perf. 13¼x13***

**837** A187 30p Fountain 1.25 1.25
**838** A187 40p Hands 1.50 1.50
**839** A187 42p Airplane 1.50 1.50
**840** A187 54p Rainbow 2.00 2.00
*Nos. 837-840 (4)* 6.25 6.25

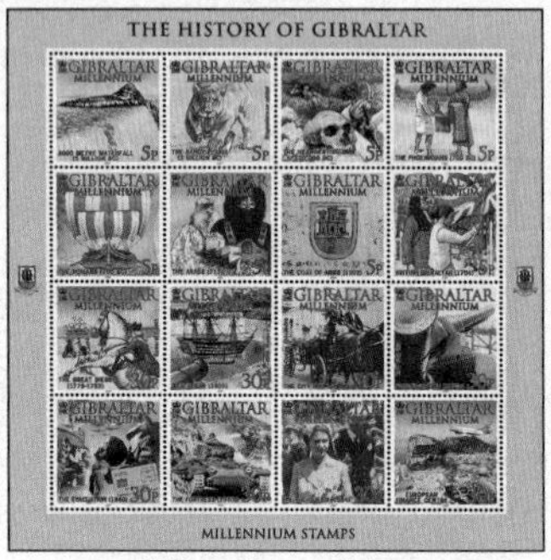


Millennium — A188

History of Gibraltar: a, 3000-meter waterfall. b, The sandy plains. c, The Neanderthals. d, The Phoenicians. e, The Romans. f, The Arabs. g, Coat of arms, 1502. h, British Gibraltar. i, The great siege. j, Trafalgar. k, The city. l, Fortifications. m, The evacuation. n, The fortress. o, Queen Elizabeth II. p, European finance center.

**2000, May 9** ***Perf. 14***

**841** A188 Sheet of 16 14.00 14.00
*a.-h.* 5p Any single .30 .30
*i.-p.* 30p Any single 1.40 1.40
*q.* Souvenir booklet 30.00

No. 841q contains a pane of 2 of each of Nos. 841a-841j and a pane of 3 of each of Nos. 841k-841p.

Prince William, 18th Birthday — A189

Designs: 30p, With Princess Diana. 42p, As child. 54p, With Prince Charles. 66p, In suit.

**2000, June 21** **Litho.** ***Perf. 12½***

**842** A189 30p multi 1.00 1.00
**843** A189 42p multi 1.50 1.40
**844** A189 54p multi 1.75 1.75
**845** A189 66p multi 2.00 2.00
*a.* Souvenir sheet, #842-845 8.00 8.00
*Nos. 842-845 (4)* 6.25 6.15

Queen Mother, 100th Birthday — A190

Designs: 30p, As young woman. 42p, With King George VI. 54p, With blue hat. 66p, With orange hat.

**2000, Aug. 4**

**846** A190 30p multi 1.00 1.00
**847** A190 42p multi 1.50 1.50
**848** A190 54p multi 1.75 1.75
**849** A190 66p multi 2.00 2.00
*a.* Souvenir sheet, #846-849 7.50 7.50
*Nos. 846-849 (4)* 6.25 6.25

Moorish Castle A191

**Photo. & Engr.**

**2000, Sept. 15** ***Perf. 11½x11¾***

**850** A191 £5 multi 17.50 17.50

**Fighter Planes and Raptors Type**

No. 851: a, RAF "Gibraltar" Supermarine Spitfire. b, Male merlin.
No. 852: a, RAF "City of Lincoln" Avro Lancaster B1-3. b, Bonelli's eagle.
No. 853: a, RAF Hawker Hurricane MK IIC. b, Female merlin.

**2000, Sept. 15** **Litho.** ***Perf. 14½x14***

**851** Pair 4.50 4.50
*a.* A180 30p multi 1.75 1.75
*b.* A180 42p multi 2.25 2.25
**852** Pair 4.50 4.50
*a.* A180 30p multi 1.75 1.75
*b.* A180 42p multi 2.25 2.25
**853** Pair 4.50 4.50
*a.* A180 30p multi 1.75 1.75
*b.* A180 42p multi 2.25 2.25
*c.* Souvenir sheet, #851a, 852a, 853a 5.50 5.50
*d.* Souvenir sheet, #851b, 852b, 853b 8.00 8.00
*Nos. 851-853 (3)* 13.50 13.50

Christmas A192

5p, Baby Jesus. No. 855, 30p, Joseph, Mary, donkey. No. 856, 30p, Mary, Jesus. 40p, Joseph, Mary, innkeeper. 42p, Holy Family, donkey. 54p, Holy Family, Magi.

**2000, Nov. 13** ***Perf. 14***

**854-859** A192 Set of 6 7.50 7.50

Queen Victoria (1819-1901) A193

Designs: 30p, On wedding day. 42p, Portrait. 54p, In carriage. 66p, Jubilee portrait.

**2001, Jan. 22** ***Perf. 12¾***

**860-863** A193 Set of 4 8.00 8.00

New Year 2001 (Year of the Snake) — A194

Snakes: No. 864, 5p, Grass. No. 865, 5p, Ladder. No. 866, 5p, Montpelier. No. 867, 30p, Viperine. No. 868, 30p, Southern smooth. No. 869, 30p, False smooth. 66p, Horseshoe whip.

**2001, Feb. 1** **Litho.** ***Perf. 13¾***

**864-870** A194 Set of 7 7.00 7.00
*870a* Souvenir sheet, #864-870 10.00 10.00

Size of No. 870: 31x62mm. Hong Kong 2001 Stamp Exhibition (No. 870a).

Europa — A195

Designs: 30p, Long-snouted seahorse. 40p, Snapdragon. 42p, Yellow-legged gull. 54p, Goldfish.

**2001, Feb. 1** ***Perf. 13¼x13***

**871-874** A195 Set of 4 10.00 10.00

Queen Elizabeth II, 75th Birthday A196

Designs: No. 875, 30p, As child. No. 876, 30p, As young woman. No. 877, 42p, In wedding dress. No. 878, 42p, At coronation. 54p, Wearing hat.
£2, In blue dress.

**2001, Apr. 21** **Litho.** ***Perf. 14***

**875-879** A196 Set of 5 8.00 8.00

**Souvenir Sheet**

***Perf. 13¾***

**880** A196 £2 multi 7.50 7.50

No. 880 contains one 35x48mm stamp.

Gibraltar Chronicle, Bicent. — A197

Designs: 30p, Battle of Trafalgar. 42p, Invention of the telephone. 54p, The end of World War II. 66p, First man on the Moon.

**2001, May 21** ***Perf. 14x14½***

**881-884** A197 Set of 4 9.00 9.00

**Queen Type of 1999**

**2001, June 1** **Litho.** ***Perf. 14x14¼***

**Size: 22x28mm**

**885** A175 £1.20 carmine 5.00 5.00
**886** A175 £1.40 blue 5.50 5.50

**Fighter Planes and Raptors Type of 1999**

No. 887: a, 40p, RAF Jaguar GR1B. b, 40p, Hobby.
No. 888: a, 40p, Royal Navy Sea Harrier FA MK 2. b, 40p, Marsh harrier.
No. 889: a, 40p, RAF Hawk T MK 1. b, 40p, Sparrowhawk.

**2001, Sept. 3** **Litho.** ***Perf. 14½x14***

**Pairs, #a-b**

**887-889** A180 Set of 3 10.00 10.00
*889c* Souvenir sheet, #887a, 888a, 889a 5.00 5.00
*889d* Souvenir sheet, #887b, 888b, 889b 5.00 5.00

Christmas A198

Snoopy, from Peanuts comic strip: 5p, In Santa Claus suit ringing bell, Woodstock. 30p, Charlie Brown, Christmas tree. 40p, Wreath. 42p, In Santa Claus suit carrying cookies, Woodstock. 54p, On dog house.

**2001, Nov. 12** ***Perf. 14***

**890-894** A198 Set of 5 7.00 7.00
*894a* Souvenir sheet, #890-894 8.00 8.00

Souvenir Sheet

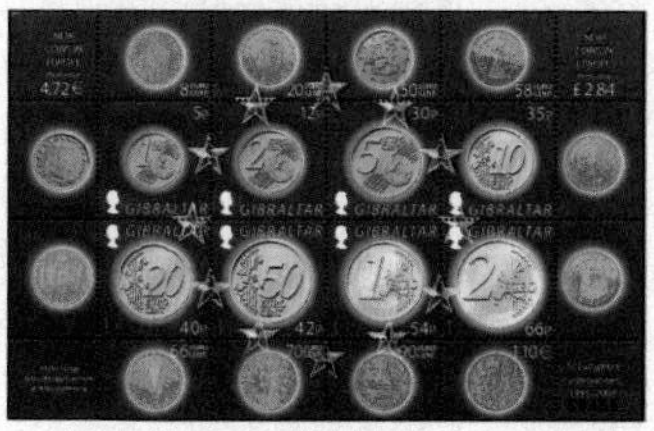


Introduction of Euro Coinage to Europe — A199

Coins in denominations of: a, 5p, 1 cent. b, 12p, 2 cents. c, 30p, 5 cents. d, 35p, 10 cents. e, 40p, 20 cents. f, 42p, 50 cents. g, 54p, 1 euro. h, 66p, 2 euro.

**2002, Jan. 1 Litho. *Perf. 13¼x13***
**895** A199 Sheet of 8, #a-h 11.00 11.00

A clear varnish was applied by a thermographic process producing a shiny, raised effect.

**Reign Of Queen Elizabeth II, 50th Anniv. Issue**

Common Design Type

Designs: No. 896, 30p, Princess Elizabeth in field, 1942. No. 897, 30p, Wearing tiara, 1961. No. 898, 30p, With Princess Margaret, microphones. No. 899, 30p, Wearing hat, 1993. 75p, 1955 portrait by Annigoni (38x50mm).

***Perf. 14¼x14½, 13¾ (75p)***

**2002, Feb. 6 Litho. Wmk. 373**
**896-900** CD360 Set of 5 8.00 8.00
*900a* Souvenir sheet, #896-900 10.00 10.00

Europa — A200

Famous clowns: 30p, Joseph Grimaldi (1778-1831). 40p, Karl Adrien Wettach (1880-1959). 42p, Nicholai Polakovs (1900-74). 54p, Hubert Jean Charles Cairoli (1910-80).

***Perf. 13¼x13***

**2002, Mar. 4 Litho. Unwmk.**
**901-904** A200 Set of 4 6.25 6.25

Bobby Moore, English Soccer Player — A201

Moore in 1966: 30p, Holding up World Cup. 42p, Kissing World Cup. 54p, With Queen Elizabeth II. 66p, In action.

***Perf. 13¼x13***

**2002, May 1 Litho. Unwmk.**
**905-908** A201 Set of 4 8.00 8.00
*908a* Souvenir sheet, #905-908 8.00 8.00

Wildlife A202

Designs: No. 909, 30p, Red fox. No. 910, 30p, Barbary macaque, vert. 40p, White tooth shrew. £1, Rabbit, vert.

***Perf. 14¼x14, 14x14¼***

**2002, June 6 Litho. Unwmk.**
**909-912** A202 Set of 4 8.50 8.50
*912a* Souvenir sheet, #909-912 9.00 9.00

Prince Harry, 18th Birthday — A203

Designs: 30p, As child in Princess Diana's arms. 42p, Waving. 54p, Wearing baseball cap. 66p, In suit and tie.

**2002, Sept. 15 Litho. *Perf. 12½***
**913-916** A203 Set of 4 8.25 8.25
*916a* Souvenir sheet, #913-916 9.50 9.50

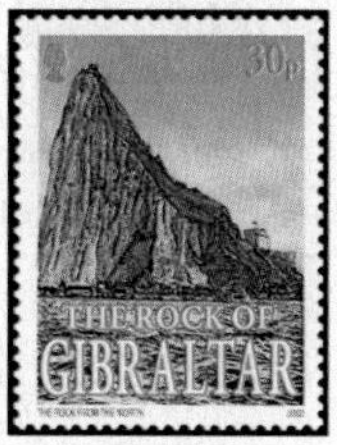


Rock of Gibraltar — A204

View of Rock from: a, North. b, South. c, East (46x38mm). d, West (46x38mm).

**2002, Sept. 15 Litho. *Perf. 13¼x13***
**917** Horiz. strip of 4 11.00 11.00
*a.-b.* A204 30p Either single 1.10 1.10
*c.-d.* A204 £1 Either single 3.50 3.50

Particles of the Rock of Gibraltar were applied to portions of the designs by a thermographic process.

Christmas — A205

Creche scenes from: 5p, Cathedral of St. Mary the Crowned. 30p, St. Joseph's Parish Church. 40p, St. Theresa's Parish Church. 42p, Our Lady of Sorrows Church, Catalan Bay. 52p, St. Bernard's Church. 54p, Cathedral of the Holy Trinity.

**2002, Nov. 13 *Perf. 13***
**918-923** A205 Set of 6 9.50 9.50

Coronation of Queen Elizabeth II, 50th Anniv. — A206

Designs: No. 924, 30p, Queen receiving crown. No. 925, 30p, Queen on throne. 40p, Queen holding orb. £1, Queen in profile.

***Perf. 12½***

**2003, Feb. 20 Litho. Unwmk.**
**924-927** A206 Set of 4 8.00 8.00
*927a* Souvenir sheet, #924-927 8.50 8.50

Europa — A207

Poster art for: 30p, Drama Festival. 40p, Spring Festival. 42p, Art Festival. 54p, Dance Festival.

**2003, Mar. 3 *Perf. 14x14½***
**928-931** A207 Set of 4 6.50 6.50

Powered Flight, Cent. A208

Designs: 30p, Wright Flyer, 1903. No. 933, 40p, Charles Lindbergh and Spirit of St. Louis, 1927. No. 934, 40p, Boeing 314 Yankee Clipper, 1939. 42p, Saunders Roe SARO-21 Windhover Amphibian, 1931 (77x27mm). 44p, Concorde, 1976 (77x27mm). 66p, Space Shuttle Columbia, 1981, vert. (37x57mm).

**2003, Mar. 31 Litho. *Perf. 13x13¼***
**932-937** A208 Set of 6 13.00 13.00
*937a* Souvenir sheet, #932-937, perf. 12½ 14.00 14.00

Martyrdom of St. George, 1700th Anniv. — A209

Designs: 30p, Cross of St. George. 40p, Constantinian Order of St. George. £1.20, Stained glass window depiction of St. George, vert. (31x63mm).

**2003, Apr. 23 *Perf. 13¾***
**938-940** A209 Set of 3 7.50 7.50
*940a* Souvenir sheet, #938-940 8.00 8.00

Big Ben, Swift and Rock of Gibraltar A210

**Photo. & Engr.**

**2003, June 21 *Perf. 11½***
**941** A210 (£3) multi 12.00 12.00

Prince William, 21st Birthday — A211

Prince William: No. 942, 30p, As a child, with Princess Diana. No. 943, 30p, With hands in pockets. 40p, Close-up, wearing suit. £1, Wearing sweatshirt.

**2003, June 21 Litho. *Perf. 12½***
**942-945** A211 Set of 4 12.00 12.00
*945a* Souvenir sheet, #942-945 12.00 12.00

Enlargement of European Union — A212

National flowers of newly-added countries: 30p, Daisy (Latvia), Cornflower (Estonia), Rue (Lithuania). 40p, Rose (Cyprus), Maltese centaury (Malta). 42p, Tulip (Hungary), Carnation (Slovenia), Dog rose (Slovakia). 54p, Corn poppy (Poland), Scented thyme (Czech Republic).

**2003, Sept. 15 Litho. *Perf. 13¾***
**946-949** A212 Set of 4 7.00 7.00

Mushrooms A213

Designs: No. 950, 30p, Lepista nuda. No. 951, 30p, Clitocybe odora. No. 952, 30p, Hypholoma fasciculare. £1.20, Agaricus campestris.

**2003, Sept. 15 *Perf. 14¼***
**950-953** A213 Set of 4 10.00 10.00
*953a* Souvenir sheet, #950-953 10.50 10.50

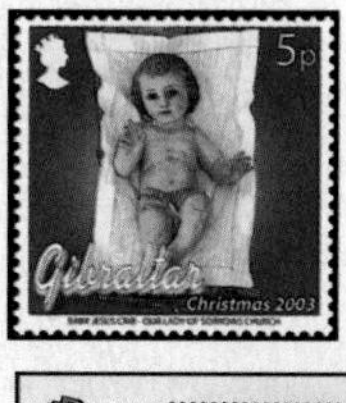


A214

Christmas — A215

Designs: 5p, Baby Jesus crib, Our Lady of Sorrows Church. 30p, Building a traditional creche at home. 40p, Three Kings Cavalcade on January 5. 42p, Children's provisions for Santa and reindeer on Christmas Eve. 54p, Christmas Eve midnight mass at the Cathedral of St. Mary the Crowned.

**2003, Nov. 17 Litho. *Perf. 14***
**954-958** A214 Set of 5 6.50 6.50

**Souvenir Sheet**

***Perf. 12¼x12***

**959** A215 £1 multi 5.50 5.50

Europa — A216

Designs: No. 960, 40p, Outdoor cafe. No. 961, 40p, St. Michael's Cave. No. 962, 54p, Seaside cafe. No. 963, 54p, Dolphin.

**2004, Feb. 20 Litho. *Perf. 14x14½***
**960-963** A216 Set of 4 7.50 7.50

British Gibraltar, 300th Anniv. A217

Designs: 8p, British flag, Gibraltar coat of arms.

No. 965: a, Ship with large flag. b, Ship, rowboat, cannons. c, Soldiers. d, Military uniform. e, Telephone booth, police hat. f, Mail box. g, Neckties, university documents, graduates in caps and gowns. h, Crowd waving flags. i. British flag.

**2004 Litho. *Perf. 13x13¼***

**964** A217 8p multi .75 .75
**965** Sheet of 9 16.00 16.00
*a.-h.* A217 30p Any single 1.10 1.10
*i.* A217 £1.20 multi 4.50 4.50
*j.* Souvenir sheet, #965i 5.25 5.25

Issued: Nos. 964-965i, 4/26. No. 965j, 9/10.

Sir Elton John's Tercentenary Concert (No. 965j).

A perforated "black print" sheet of No. 965 exists with cancels.

Visit of Queen Elizabeth II to Gibraltar, 50th Anniv. — A218

Queen: 38p, Holding flowers. 40p, With arm extended. 47p, In limousine. £1, With children and soldiers.

£1.50, Standing in limousine with Prince Philip.

**2004, May 4 *Perf. 12½***

**966-969** A218 Set of 4 9.00 9.00

**Souvenir Sheet**

**970** A218 £1.50 multi 7.00 7.00

European Soccer — A219

Designs: 30p, Goalie defending shot. No. 972, 40p, Players near side of goal. No. 973, 40p, Player making scissor kick. £1, Goalie playing ball near goal post.

£1.50, Player with arms extended, horiz.

**2004, June 6**

**971-974** A219 Set of 4 8.25 8.25
*974a* Souvenir sheet, #971-974 8.25 8.25

**Souvenir Sheet**

**975** A219 £1.50 multi 6.00 6.00

No. 975 contains one 48x37mm stamp.

D-Day, 60th Anniv. A220

Designs: 38p, Soldiers leaving landing craft. 40p, Tank approaching beach. 47p, Airplane. £1, Ships.

**2004, June 6 *Perf. 13x13¼***

**976-979** A220 Set of 4 9.75 9.75
*979a* Souvenir sheet, #976-979 9.75 9.75

Flowers — A221

Designs: 1p, Mallow-leaved bindweed. 2p, Gibraltar sea lavender. 5p, Gibraltar chickweed. G, Romulea. 10p, Common centaury. G1, Pyramidal orchid. S, Friar's cowl. UK, Corn poppy. E, Giant Tangier fennel. U, Snapdragon. 50p, Common gladiolus. £1, Yellow horned poppy. £3, Gibraltar candytuft.

**2004, Sept. 10 Litho. *Perf. 13¼***

**980** A221 1p multi .25 .25
*a.* Booklet pane of 1 .25 —
**981** A221 2p multi .25 .25
*a.* Booklet pane of 1 .25 —
**982** A221 5p multi .25 .25
*a.* Booklet pane of 1 .25 —
**983** A221 G multi .25 .25
*a.* Booklet pane of 1 .25 —
**984** A221 10p multi .40 .40
*a.* Booklet pane of 1 .40 —
**985** A221 G1 multi .55 .55
*a.* Booklet pane of 1 .55 —
**986** A221 S multi 1.20 1.20
*a.* Booklet pane of 1 1.20 —
**987** A221 UK multi 1.75 1.75
*a.* Booklet pane of 1 1.75 —
**988** A221 E multi 1.90 1.90
*a.* Booklet pane of 1 1.90 —
**989** A221 U multi 2.10 2.10
*a.* Booklet pane of 1 2.10 —
**990** A221 50p multi 2.25 2.25
*a.* Booklet pane of 1 2.25 —
**991** A221 £1 multi 4.25 4.25
*a.* Booklet pane of 1 4.25 —
**992** A221 £3 multi 13.00 13.00
*a.* Booklet pane of 1 13.00 —
Complete booklet, #980a-992a 28.00
*Nos. 980-992 (13)* 28.40 28.40

Nos. 983, 985, 986, 987, 988 and 989 sold for 7p, 12p, 28p, 38p, 40p and 47p respectively on day of issue.

See Nos. 1033B-1036.

Ferrari Race Cars A222

Designs: No. 993, 5p, F2003GA. No. 994, 5p, F2004. No. 995, 30p, F2001. No. 996, 30p, F2002. No. 997, 75p, F399. No. 998, 75p, F1-2000.

**2004, Nov. 12 *Perf. 14¾x14¼***

**993-998** A222 Set of 6 10.00 10.00
*998a* Souvenir sheet, #993-998 10.00 10.00

Christmas A223

Christmas tree ornaments: 7p, Santa Claus. 28p, Angel. 38p, Red star. 40p, Gold bell. 47p, Red ball. 53p, White star.

**2004, Nov. 12 *Perf. 12½***

**999-1004** A223 Set of 6 10.00 10.00

Battle of Trafalgar, Bicent. — A224

Designs: 38p, Soldier guarding wine cask containing Admiral Horatio Nelson's body. 40p, HMS Entrepenante. 47p, Admiral Nelson, vert. £1.60, HMS Victory.

£2, HMS Vctory being towed to Gibraltar.

**2005, Jan. 29 Litho. *Perf. 13¼***

**1005-1008** A224 Set of 4 14.50 14.50

**Souvenir Sheet**

***Perf. 13¾***

**1009** A224 £2 multi 12.00 12.00

No. 1008 has particles of wood from the HMS Victory embedded in the areas covered by a thermographic process that produces a raised, shiny effect. No. 1009 contains one 44x44mm stamp.

See Nos. 1027-1028.

Europa — A225

Designs: No. 1010, 47p, Sherry trifle. No. 1011, 47p, Spinach pie. No. 1012, 47p, Veal birds. No. 1013, 47p, Grilled sea bass.

***Perf. 14¼x14¾***

**2005, Mar. 31 Litho.**

**1010-1013** A225 Set of 4 9.00 9.00

V-E Day, 60th Anniv. — A226

Designs: 38p, Winston Churchill. 40p, Woman, children, British flags. 47p, Servicewomen in car waving flags. £1, People at dock.

**2005, May 8**

**1014-1017** A226 Set of 4 9.50 9.50
*1017a* Souvenir sheet, #1014-1017 9.50 9.50

Anniversaries — A227

Designs: 38p, Royal Gibraltar Police, 175th anniv. 47p, Gibraltar Museum, 75th anniv. £1, Grant of Charter of Justice, 175th anniv.

**2005, June 17 *Perf. 14¾x14¼***

**1018-1020** A227 Set of 3 9.00 9.00

Cruise Ships A228

Designs: 38p, Circassia. 40p, Nevassa. 47p, Black Prince. £1, Arcadia.

**2005, June 17 *Perf. 13x13¼***

**1021-1024** A228 Set of 4 9.75 9.75
*1024a* Souvenir sheet, #1021-1024 9.75 9.75

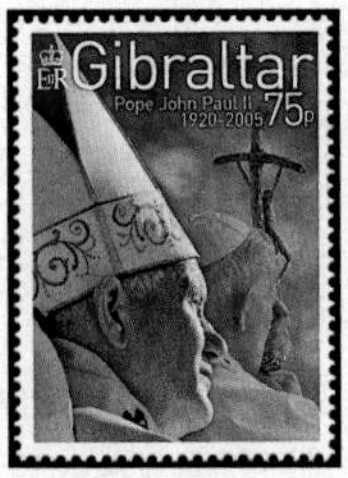


Pope John Paul II (1920-2005) A229

**2005, July 15 *Perf. 14¼x14¾***

**1025** A229 75p multi 3.75 3.75

Printed in sheets of 6.

Europa Stamps, 50th Anniv. (in 2006) — A230

**Litho. With Foil Application**

**2005, Sept. 30 *Perf. 14¼***

**1026** A230 £5 multi 18.50 18.50

**Battle of Trafalgar Type of 2005**

**Souvenir Sheets**

Designs: Nos. 1027, 1028a, Admiral Nelson mortally wounded.

**2005, Oct. 21 Litho. *Perf. 13¼***

**1027** A224 £1 multi 4.25 4.25
**1028** Sheet, #1028a, Isle of Man #1127a 8.75 8.75
*a.* A224 £1 multi, 47x30mm 4.25 4.25

No. 1028 has a Gibraltar Post emblem in sheet margin. See Isle of Man No. 1127.

Christmas A231

Various angels: 7p, 28p, 40p, 47p, 53p.

**2005, Oct. 21 *Perf. 13¼x13***

**1029-1033** A231 Set of 5 8.50 8.50
*1033a* Souvenir sheet, #1029-1033 8.75 8.75

**Flowers Type of 2004**

Designs: 3p, Gibraltar restharrow. 15p, Paper-white narcissus. 53p, Gibraltar campion. £1.60, Sea daffodil.

**2006, Jan. 31 Litho. *Perf. 13¼***

**1033B** A221 3p multi .25 .25
**1034** A221 15p multi .65 .65
**1035** A221 53p multi 2.10 2.10
**1036** A221 £1.60 multi 6.25 6.25
*Nos. 1033B-1036 (4)* 9.25 9.25

Worldwide Fund for Nature (WWF) A232

Various depictions of Giant devil ray.

**2006, Feb. 20 *Perf. 13x13¼***

**1037** Strip of 4 10.50 10.50
*a.* A232 38p multi 1.50 1.50
*b.* A232 40p multi 1.75 1.75
*c.* A232 47p multi 2.00 2.00
*d.* A232 £1 multi 4.00 4.00

Queen Elizabeth II, 80th Birthday A233

Various photographs.

**2006, Mar. 31 *Perf. 14¾x14***

**1038** Block of 4 10.50 10.50
*a.* A233 38p multi 1.50 1.50
*b.* A233 40p multi 1.75 1.75
*c.* A233 47p multi 2.00 2.00
*d.* A233 £1 multi 4.00 4.00
*e.* Souvenir sheet, #1038b, 1038c 3.25 3.25
*f.* Souvenir sheet, #1038a, 1038d 4.75 4.75

Miniature Sheet

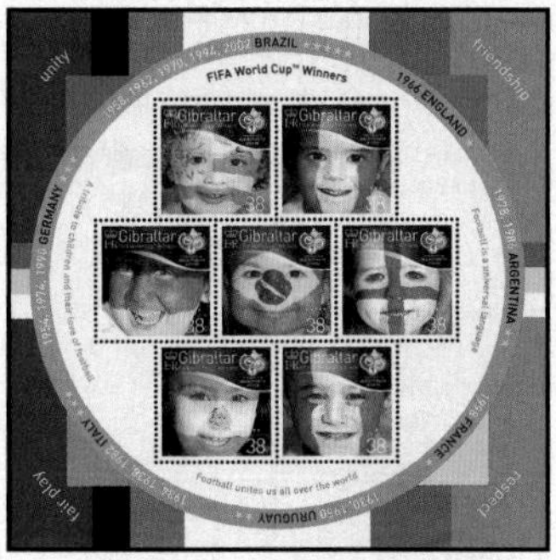


2006 World Cup Soccer Championships, Germany — A234

No. 1039 — Children with faces painted as flags of World Cup champions: a, Uruguay. b, Italy. c, Germany. d, Brazil. e, England. f, Argentina. g, France.

**2006, May 4** ***Perf. 15***

**1039** A234 Sheet of 7 12.00 12.00
*a.-g.* 38p Any single 1.60 1.60

Europa A235

Children: No. 1040, 47p, Holding books and notebook paper. No. 1041, 47p, Playing musical instruments. No. 1042, 47p, Building birdhouse. No. 1043, 47p, Playing soccer.

**2006, June 30** ***Perf. 13x13¼***

**1040-1043** A235 Set of 4 8.00 8.00

Gibraltar Packet Agency, Bicent. A236

Ships: 8p, Cornwallis. 40p, Meteor. 42p, Carteret. 68p, Prince Regent.

***Perf. 14¾x14¼***

**2006, Sept. 15** **Litho.**

**1044-1047** A236 Set of 4 8.00 8.00

Airmail Service, 75th Anniv. A237

Airplanes: 8p, Saro A21 Windhover. 40p, Vickers Vanguard. 49p, Vickers Viscount. £1.60, Boeing 737.

**2006, Sept. 15**

**1048-1051** A237 Set of 4 13.00 13.00

Cruise Ships A238

Designs: 40p, Coral. 42p, Legend of the Seas. 66p, Saga Ruby. 78p, Costa Concordia.

**2006, Sept. 15** ***Perf. 13***

**1052-1055** A238 Set of 4 10.50 10.50
*1055a* Souvenir sheet, #1052-1055 12.50 12.50

See Nos. 1076-1079, 1153-1156.

Christopher Columbus (1451-1506), Explorer — A239

Designs: 40p, Navigational equipment. 42p, Columbus on ship. 66p, Santa Maria. 78p, Columbus and Indian.
£1.60, Nina, Pinta and Santa Maria

**2006, Nov. 1** **Litho.** ***Perf. 13x13¼***

**1056-1059** A239 Set of 4 11.00 11.00

**Souvenir Sheet**

***Perf. 13¼***

**1060** A239 £1.60 multi 8.00 8.00

No. 1060 contains one 48x48mm stamp.

Christmas A240

Various depictions of Santa Claus with panel colors of: 8p, Red brown. 40p, Prussian blue. 42p, Olive bister. 49p, Green. 55p, Gray blue.

**2006, Nov. 1** ***Perf. 13¼x13***

**1061-1065** A240 Set of 5 9.50 9.50
*1065a* Souvenir sheet, #1061-1065, perf. 13¼x12½ 9.50 9.50

Miniature Sheet

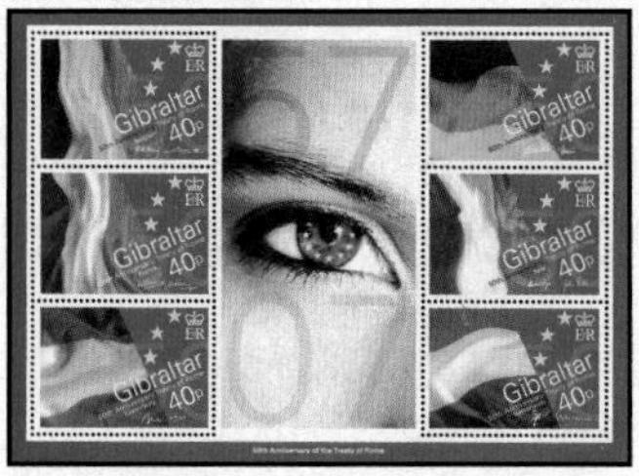


Treaty of Rome, 50th Anniv. — A241

No. 1066 — European Union flag and flag of: a, Belgium. b, Germany. c, France. d, Italy. e, Luxembourg. f, Netherlands.

***Perf. 14½x14¼***

**2007, Feb. 28** **Litho.**

**1066** A241 40p Sheet of 6, #a-f 10.50 10.50

Wedding of Queen Elizabeth II and Prince Philip, 60th Anniv. — A242

Designs: 40p, Royal engagement, 1947. 42p, Royal wedding, 1947. 66p, Silver anniversary, 1972. 78p, Ruby anniversary, 1987.
£1.60, Wedding party.

**2007, Feb. 28** ***Perf. 13½***

**1067-1070** A242 Set of 4 10.50 10.50

**Souvenir Sheet**

***Perf. 13½x13***

**1071** A242 £1.60 multi 8.50 8.50

No. 1071 contains one 85x85mm diamond-shaped stamp.

Princess Diana (1961-97) A243

Various photographs: 8p, 40p, 42p, £1.60.

**2007, Mar. 31** ***Perf. 13½***

**1072-1075** A243 Set of 4 11.00 11.00
*1075a* Souvenir sheet, #1072-1075 11.00 11.00

**Cruise Ships Type of 2006**

Designs: 40p, Oriana. 42p, Oceana. 66p, Queen Elizabeth 2.78p, Queen Mary 2.

**2007, May 15** **Litho.** ***Perf. 14¾x14***

**1076-1079** A238 Set of 4 10.50 10.50
*1079a* Souvenir sheet, #1076-1079 10.50 10.50

Europa — A244

Designs: 8p, Scout from 1908. 40p, Scout from 1950s, 42p, Sea Scout from 1980s. £1, Scout from 2007.

**2007, June 30** **Litho.** ***Perf. 13***

**1080-1083** A244 Set of 4 10.00 10.00

Gibraltar Postal Anniversaries — A245

Designs: 8p, Last-day-of-validity postcard from Fez, Morocco (cessation of Gibraltar's responsibility for the British postal service in Morocco in 1907). 40p, Stampless cover with last Gibraltar datestamp of the Packet Agency (creation of Gibraltar Post Office in 1857). 42p, Cover franked with stamps of Great Britain (sale of British stamps in Gibraltar in 1857). £1, Cover to London from Morocco via Gibraltar (placement of British postal service in Morocco under control of Gibraltar in 1857).

**2007, Sept. 26** ***Perf. 14¾x14***

**1084-1087** A245 Set of 4 11.00 11.00

Stork Carrying Baby, Baby Bottle, Pacifier, Rubber Duck — A246

Diamond Ring and Heart — A247

Sheep, Lion, Dog at Party — A248

Lamb, Dolphins, Rock of Gibraltar — A249

Shell, Crab and Heart — A250

**2007, Sept. 26** ***Perf. 12½x13***

**1088** A246 G multi + label .40 .40
**1089** A247 G multi + label .40 .40
**1090** A248 G multi + label .40 .40
**1091** A249 G multi + label .40 .40
**1092** A250 G multi + label .40 .40
**1093** A246 E multi + label 2.00 2.00
**1094** A247 E multi + label 2.00 2.00
**1095** A248 E multi + label 2.00 2.00
**1096** A249 E multi + label 2.00 2.00
**1097** A250 E multi + label 2.00 2.00
*Nos. 1088-1097 (10)* 12.00 12.00

On day of issue Nos. 1088-1092 each sold for 8p, and Nos. 1093-1097 each sold for 42p. Labels shown with each stamp are the generic labels for that stamp type. Labels could be personalized for an additional fee.

Prehistoric Wildlife of Gibraltar A251

Designs: 8p, Bears and dolphins. 40p, Eagle owl. 42p, Great auk and eagle. 55p, Red deer and bear. 78p, Wolf and vulture eating horse.
£2, Ibex.

**2007, Sept. 26** ***Perf. 13***

**1098-1102** A251 Set of 5 9.50 9.50
*1098a* Booklet pane of 1 .40 —
*1099a* Booklet pane of 1 1.75 —
*1100a* Booklet pane of 1 2.00 —
*1101a* Booklet pane of 1 2.50 —
*1102a* Booklet pane of 1 3.50 —
Complete booklet, #1098a-1103a, 1103b 20.00

**Souvenir Sheet**

**1103** A251 £2 multi 9.50 9.50
*a.* Booklet pane of 1 9.50 —
*b.* Booklet pane of 6, #1098-1102 10.50 —

No. 1103a has text in margin not found on the margin of No. 1103.

Views of Gibraltar — A252

Trinity Lighthouse — A253

Various views: 40p, 42p, 55p, 78p.

**2007, Nov. 2 Litho. *Perf. 13¼***
**1104-1107** A252 Set of 4 10.00 10.00

**Souvenir Sheet**

***Perf. 13¼x13***

**1108** A253 £1.70 multi 8.00 8.00

Christmas A254

Porcelain Nativity figurines: No. 1109, 8p, Joseph. No. 1110, 8p, Baby Jesus. 40p, Mary. 42p, King Melchior. 49p, King Balthasar. 55p, King Gaspar.

**2007, Nov. 2 *Perf. 13¼x13***
**1109-1114** A254 Set of 6 9.00 9.00
*1114a* Miniature sheet, #1109-1114 9.00 9.00

***Perf. 12½x13***

**Size: 32x32mm**

**1114B** A254 8p multi + label .35 .35
**1114C** A254 40p multi + label 1.75 1.75

Nos. 1114B and 1114C were available with generic labels. Labels could be personalized for an additional fee.

Birds — A255

Designs: 1p, Woodchat shrike. 2p, Balearic shearwater. 5p, Eagle owl. G, European bee-eater. 10p, Razorbill. S, Egyptian vulture. UK, Blue rock thrush. E, Hoopoe. U, Bonelli's eagle. 50p, Greater flamingo. 55p, Mediterranean shag. £1, Honey buzzard. £5, Lesser kestrel.

**2008, Feb. 15 Litho. *Perf. 13x12½***
**1115** A255 1p multi .25 .25
**1116** A255 2p multi .25 .25
**1117** A255 5p multi .25 .25
**1118** A255 G multi .35 .35
**1119** A255 10p multi .40 .40
**1120** A255 S multi 1.25 1.25
**1121** A255 UK multi 1.60 1.60
**1122** A255 E multi 1.75 1.75
**1123** A255 U multi 1.90 1.90
**1124** A255 50p multi 2.00 2.00
**1125** A255 55p multi 2.25 2.25

**Size: 32x45mm**

***Perf. 13x13¼***

**1126** A255 £1 multi 4.00 4.00
**1127** A255 £5 multi 18.00 18.00
*Nos. 1115-1127 (13)* 34.25 34.25

On day of issue Nos. 1118, 1120, 1121, 1122 and 1123 sold for 8p, 30p, 40p, 42p and 49p, respectively. See Nos. 1202-1204, 1244-1246.

Admiral Horatio Nelson (1758-1805) A256

Designs: No. 1128, 40p, HMS Agamemnon. No. 1129, 40p, HMS La Minerve. No. 1130, 42p, HMS Captain. No. 1131, 42p, HMS Vanguard. No. 1132, 49p, HMS Amphion. No. 1133, 49p, HMS Victory.
£2, Nelson's Birthplace, Burnham Thorpe, England, horiz.

***Perf. 14¼x14¾***

**2008, Mar. 15 Litho.**
**1128-1133** A256 Set of 6 10.50 10.50

**Souvenir Sheet**

***Perf. 14¾x14¼***

**1134** A256 £2 multi 8.00 8.00

Royal Air Force, 90th Anniv. — A257

Rock of Gibraltar and airplanes: No. 1135, 40p, Short 184, Saro London. No. 1136, 40p, Spitfire IV, Hurricane IIc. No. 1137, 42p, Beaufighter II, Lancaster TS III. No. 1138, 42p, Hunter Mk. 6, Shackleton MR2. No. 1139, 49p, Vulcan, Mosquito. No. 1140, 49p, Tornado GR4, Jaguar GR3.
£2, Felixstowe F3.

**2008, Mar. 15 *Perf. 14¼x14¾***
**1135-1140** A257 Set of 6 10.50 10.50

**Souvenir Sheet**

**1141** A257 £2 multi 8.00 8.00

Europa — A258

Famous letter writers: 10p, Sir Winston Churchill. 42p, Admiral Horatio Nelson. 44p, Pres. John F. Kennedy. £1, Mohandas K. Gandhi.

**2008, June 1 Litho. *Perf. 14x14¾***
**1142-1145** A258 Set of 4 7.75 7.75

New Seven Wonders of the World — A259

Designs: No. 1146, 8p, Roman Colosseum. No. 1147, 8p, Christ the Redeemer Statue, Rio de Janeiro. No. 1148, 38p, Great Wall of China. No. 1149, 38p, Petra, Jordan. No. 1150, 40p, Chichen Itza Pyramid, Mexico. No. 1151, 40p, Machu Picchu, Peru. 66p, Taj Mahal, India.

**2008, June 1**
**1146-1152** A259 Set of 7 9.50 9.50

**Cruise Ships Type of 2006**

Designs: 40p, Century. 42p, Grand Princess. 66p, Queen Victoria. 78p, Costa Mediterranea.

**2008, Sept. 15 Litho. *Perf. 13x13¼***
**1153-1156** A238 Set of 4 8.00 8.00
*1156a* Souvenir sheet, #1153-1156 8.00 8.00

**Miniature Sheet**

National Aeronautics and Space Administration, 50th Anniv. — A260

No. 1157: a, Liftoff of Apollo 11. b, Earthrise from Moon. c, Lunar Module leaving Moon. d, US flag on Moon.

**2008, Sept. 15 *Perf. 13¼***
**1157** A260 Sheet of 4 9.75 9.75
*a.* 10p multi .35 .35
*b.* 17p multi .60 .60
*c.* 42p multi 1.50 1.50
*d.* £2 multi 7.25 7.25

Royal Gibraltar Regiment — A261

Designs: No. 1158, 10p, Gibraltar Volunteer Corps in World War I. No. 1159, 10p, Gibraltar Defense Force in World War II. No. 1160, 10p, National Service recruits at Buena Vista Barracks. No. 1161, 42p, Soldiers and large guns, Thomson's Battery of Gibraltar Regiment, 1958-91. No. 1162, 42p, Soldier from Infantry Company of Gibraltar Regiment, 1958-99. No. 1163, 44p, Soldier from Air Defense Troop of Gibraltar Regiment, 1958-91. No. 1164, 44p, Royal Gibraltar Regiment soldier guarding the rock. No. 1165, 51p, Royal Gibraltar Regiment soldier training African Peacekeepers. No. 1166, 51p, Royal Gibraltar Regiment soldier serving in operations in Iraq. £2, Royal Gibraltar Regiment soldier serving in operations in Afghanistan.

**2008, Nov. 11 Litho. *Perf. 15x14***
**1158-1167** A261 Set of 10 15.00 15.00

Christmas A262

Songs: 10p, When Santa Got Stuck in a Chimney. 42p, Rudolph, the Red-nosed Reindeer. 44p, Oh, Christmas Tree. 51p, Away in a Manger. 59p, Jingle Bells.

**2008, Nov. 11 *Perf. 12½***
**1168-1172** A262 Set of 5 6.25 6.25

King Henry VIII, 500th Anniv. of Accession to the Throne — A263

Designs: No. 1173, 10p, Catherine of Aragon (first wife). No. 1174, 10p, Anne Boleyn (second wife). No. 1175, 42p, Jane Seymour (third wife). No. 1176, 42p, Anne of Cleves (fourth wife). No. 1177, 44p, Catherine Howard (fifth wife). No. 1178, 44p, Catherine Parr (sixth wife). No. 1179, 51p, Henry VIII. No. 1180, 51p, The Mary Rose.
£2, King Henry VIII at Hampton Court.

**2009, Jan. 10 Litho. *Perf. 12½***
**1173-1180** A263 Set of 8 8.25 8.25

**Souvenir Sheet**

**1181** A263 £2 multi 5.50 5.50

Gibraltar Shrine to Our Lady of Europe, 700th Anniv. — A264

**2009, Feb. 10 *Perf. 14x14¾***
**1182** A264 61p multi 1.75 1.75

Printed in sheets of 4. See Vatican City No. 1402.

Naval Aviation, Cent. — A265

Designs: No. 1183, 42p, Short 184. No. 1184, 42p, Short S27. No. 1185, 42p, SS Type non-rigid airship. No. 1186, 42p, Caudron G-III. No. 1187, 42p, Avro 504. No. 1188, 42p, Morane-Saulnier L and Zeppelin LZ-37.
£2, Short 184 and ships.

**2009, Mar. 15**
**1183-1188** A265 Set of 6 7.50 7.50

**Souvenir Sheet**

**1189** A265 £2 multi 6.00 6.00

Grandchildren of Queen Elizabeth II — A266

Designs: No. 1190, 42p, Prince William of Wales. No. 1191, 42p, Prince Henry of Wales. No. 1192, 42p, Princess Beatrice of York. No. 1193, 42p, Princess Eugenie of York. No. 1194, 42p, Viscount Severn. No. 1195, 42p, Lady Louise Windsor. No. 1196, 42p, Peter Phillips. No. 1197, 42p, Zara Phillips.

**2009, May 1 *Perf. 12½***
**1190-1197** A266 Set of 8 10.00 10.00

Europa — A267

Designs: 10p, Aristotle (384-322 B.C), philosopher. 42p, Galileo Galilei (1564-1642), astronomer and physicist. 44p, Nicolaus Copernicus (1473-1543), astronomer. £1.50, Sir Isaac Newton (1642-1727), physicist and mathematician.

**2009, June 1 *Perf. 13x12½***
**1198-1201** A267 Set of 4 8.00 8.00

Intl. Year of Astronomy.

### Birds Type of 2008

Designs: 10p, Black stork. £2, Northern gannet. £3, Osprey.

**2009, Sept. 16 Litho. *Perf. 13***
**1202** A255 10p multi .35 .35

**Size: 32x45mm**
***Perf. 13x13¼***

**1203** A255 £2 multi 6.50 6.50
**1204** A255 £3 multi 9.50 9.50
*Nos. 1202-1204 (3)* 16.35 16.35

Old Views of Gibraltar — A268

Designs: No. 1205, 10p, Road to the frontier. No. 1206, 42p, Catalan Bay village. No. 1207, 44p, Rock of Gibraltar. 51p, Moorish Castle. 59p, South Barracks.

No. 1210: a, 10p, Garrison Library. b, 42p, Piazza. c, 44p, Piazza Casemates. d, £1, Main Street.

**2009, Sept. 16 *Perf. 14x14¾***
**1205-1209** A268 Set of 5 6.75 6.75

**Souvenir Sheet**

**1210** A268 Sheet of 4, #a-d 6.25 6.25

Charles Darwin (1809-82), Naturalist — A269

Darwin and: 10p, HMS Beagle, bird and books. 42p, Books and pages with scientific drawings. 44p, Books and pages with drawings of horse and bone. £2, Book, page with drawing of bird, notebook.

£2.42, Darwin, book and house.

**2009, Nov. 12 *Perf. 14x14¾***
**1211-1214** A269 Set of 4 10.00 10.00

**Souvenir Sheet**

**1215** A269 £2.42 multi 8.00 8.00

Christmas A270

Christmas tree ornaments: 10p, Santa Claus. 42p, Angel. 44p, Teddy bear. 51p, Christmas tree. £2, Bells.

**2009, Nov. 12 *Perf. 13½x13***
**1216-1220** A270 Set of 5 11.50 11.50

Miniature Sheet

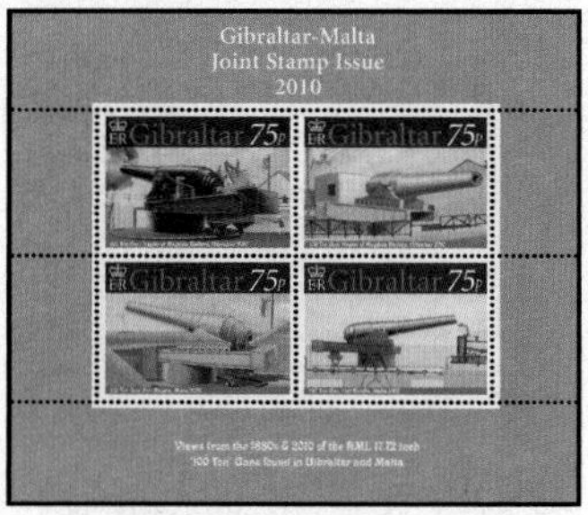


100-Ton Guns of Gibraltar and Malta — A271

No. 1221 — 100-ton gun from: a, Napier of Magdala Battery, Gibraltar, 1880. b, Napier of Magdala Battery, 2010. c, Fort Rinella, Malta, 2010. d, Fort Rinella, 1882.

**2010, Feb. 19 Litho. *Perf. 13¾***
**1221** A271 75p Sheet of 4, #a-d 9.25 9.25

See Malta No. 1400.

Battle of Britain, 70th Anniv. A272

Airplanes: No. 1222, 50p, Boulton Paul Defiant. No. 1223, 50p, Bristol Blenheim. No. 1224, 50p, Gloster Gladiator. No. 1225, 50p, Hawker Hurricane. No. 1226, 50p, Miles Master. No. 1227, 50p, Supermarine Spitfire. £2, Douglas Bader, British ace pilot, vert.

**2010, Feb. 21 *Perf. 14***
**1222-1227** A272 Set of 6 9.25 9.25

**Souvenir Sheet**

**1228** A272 £2 multi 6.25 6.25

Accession to Throne of King George V, Cent. A273

King George V: 10p, As child, with family. 42p, Examining stamp collection. 44p, On horse, reviewing troops. £2, On deck of gunship.

**2010, Mar. 26 *Perf. 13***
**1229-1232** A273 Set of 4 9.00 9.00

Europa A274

Scenes from children's stories by Roald Dahl: 10p, Charlie and the Chocolate Factory. 42p, Matilda. 44p, The Twits. £1.50, The BFG.

**2010, May 4 Litho. *Perf. 13***
**1233-1236** A274 Set of 4 7.50 7.50

Miniature Sheet

Sites in San Marino and Gibraltar — A275

No. 1237: a, Second Tower, San Marino. b, Moorish Castle, Gibraltar. c, Mt. Titano, San Marino. d, Rock of Gibraltar.

**2010, June 30 *Perf. 14¾x14***
**1237** A275 75p Sheet of 4, #a-d 9.25 9.25

See San Marino No. 1822.

Souvenir Sheet

Emblem of Miss World Pageant and Name of 2009 Winner — A276

**Litho. With Foil Application**

**2010, June 30 *Perf. 14x14¾***
**1238** A276 £2 gold & black 6.25 6.25

Aviation Centenaries — A277

Designs: No. 1239, 10p, Airplane of Baroness Raymonde de Laroche, first woman to obtain pilot's license. No. 1240, 42p, LZ-7, first Zeppelin flight with fare-paying customers. No. 1241, 49p, Antoinette VII, airplane of Hubert Latham, setting altitude record of 4,541 feet. No. 1242, £2, Clément-Bayard No. 2, first airship to cross the English Channel.

No. 1243 — Seaplanes: a, 10p, Le Canard, seaplane of Henri Fabre, first seaplane to take off from water. b, 42p, Supermarine S.6B, first aircraft to surpass 400 miles per hour in speed. c, 49p, Short Sunderland of 204th Squadron. d, £2, Saunders-ROE Princess.

**2010, Aug. 20 Litho. *Perf. 14¾x14***
**1239-1242** A277 Set of 4 9.50 9.50

**Souvenir Sheet**

**1243** A277 Sheet of 4, #a-d 9.50 9.50

### Birds Type of 2008

Designs: 59p, Barbary partridge. 76p, Ortolan bunting. £2, Pallid swift.

**2010, Oct. 20 Litho. *Perf. 13***
**1244** A255 59p multi 1.90 1.90
**1245** A255 76p multi 2.50 2.50
**1246** A255 £2 multi 6.50 6.50
*Nos. 1244-1246 (3)* 10.90 10.90

Girl Guides, Cent. A278

Uniform of: 10p, Rainbow. 42p, Brownie. 44p, Guide. £2, Senior.

**2010, Oct. 20 *Perf. 13½***
**1247-1250** A278 Set of 4 9.75 9.75

Souvenir Sheet

2010 Commonwealth Games, Delhi — A279

**2010, Oct. 20 *Perf. 14¼x14¾***
**1251** A279 £2 multi 6.50 6.50

Souvenir Sheet

Dicoese of Gibraltar, Cent. — A280

**2010, Nov. 16 Litho. *Perf. 15x14***
**1252** A280 £2 multi 6.50 6.50

Christmas A281

Designs: 10p, Christmas crackers, gifts, ornaments, stocking, candle, bell and candy cane. 42p, Stockings hung on mantle. 44p, Santa Claus and reindeer in flight. 51p, Three snowmen.

**2010, Nov. 26 *Perf. 13x13¼***
**1253-1256** A281 Set of 4 4.75 4.75

Royal British Legion A282

British troops in action in: No. 1257, 50p, World War I. No. 1258, 50p, World War II. No. 1259, 50p, Northern Ireland. No. 1260, 50p, The Falkland Islands. No. 1261, 50p, The Gulf War. No. 1262, 50p, The Balkans. No. 1263, 50p, Afghanistan. No. 1264, 50p, Iraq.

£2, Statue, poppies, words from poem, "In Flanders Fields."

**2011, Jan. 14 Litho. *Perf. 13***
**1257-1264** A282 Set of 8 13.00 13.00

**Souvenir Sheet**
***Perf. 13x13½***

**1265** A282 £2 multi 6.50 6.50

Nos. 1257-1264 each were printed in sheets of 6.

Souvenir Sheet

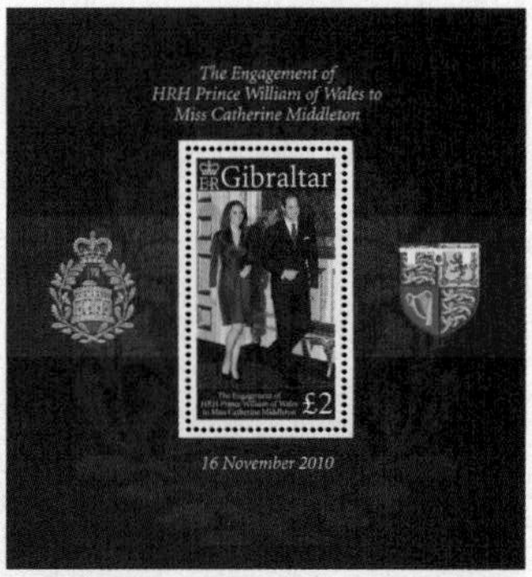


Engagement of Prince William and Catherine Middleton — A283

**2011, Jan. 14 *Perf. 14¾x14¼***
**1266** A283 £2 multi 6.50 6.50

Service of Queen Elizabeth II and Prince Philip — A284

Designs: 10p, Queen Elizabeth II. 42p, Queen and Prince Philip. 44p, Queen and Prince Philip, diff. 51p, Queen and Prince Philip, diff. 55p, Queen and Prince Philip, diff. £2, Prince Philip.

£3, Queen and Prince Philip at wedding, diff.

*Perf. 13¼*

**2011, Feb. 6 Litho. Unwmk.**

**1267-1272** A284 Set of 6 13.00 13.00

*1272a* Sheet of 6, #1267-1272, + 3 labels 13.00 13.00

**Souvenir Sheet**

**1273** A284 £3 multi 9.75 9.75

Europa — A285

Designs: 10p, Alpine forest, Swiss National Forest, Switzerland. 42p, Amazon rainforest, Brazil. 44p, Forest and waterfall, Yosemite National Park, US. £1.50, Forest and waterfall, Plitvice Lakes National Park, Croatia.

**2011, Apr. 4** *Perf. 12½*

**1274-1277** A285 Set of 4 8.25 8.25

Intl. Year of Forests.

Gibraltar Postage Stamps, 125th Anniv. — A286

Details from Gibraltar stamps: 10p, #7. 42p, #48. 44p, #93. 55p, #118. £1.50, #131.

**2011, Apr. 15** *Perf. 13¼*

**1278-1282** A286 Set of 5 10.00 10.00

Souvenir Sheet

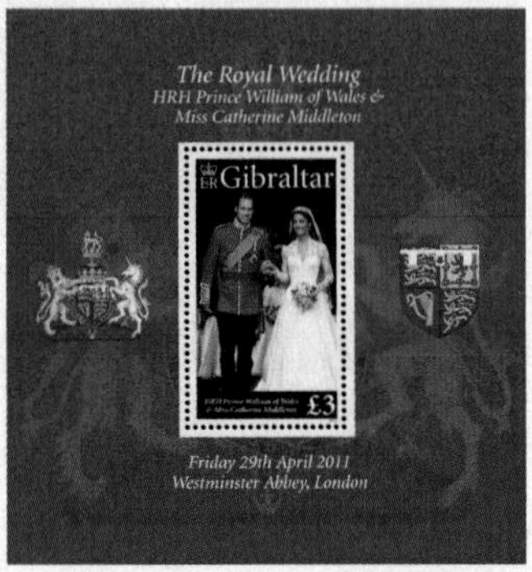


Wedding of Prince William and Catherine Middleton — A287

**2011, July 15 Litho.** ***Perf. 14¾x14¼***

**1283** A287 £3 multi 10.00 10.00

Endangered Animals — A288

Designs: No. 1284, 42p, Asian elephant. No. 1285, 42p, Bengal tiger. No. 1286, 42p, Black rhinoceros. No. 1287, 42p, Giant panda. No. 1288, 42p, Polar bear. No. 1289, 42p, Sumatran orangutan.

**2011, July 31** ***Perf. 14x14¾***

**1284-1289** A288 Set of 6 8.00 8.00

*1289a* Souvenir sheet of 6, #1284-1289 8.00 8.00

See Nos. 1353-1358.

Barbary Macaques — A289

Design: 10p, Macaque on tourist binoculars. 42p, Macaque on rock. 44p, Macaque on branch. 51p, Macaque on wall. 59p, Macaque on rock, diff. £1.50, Two macaques on rock.

**2011, Sept. 28** ***Perf. 15x14***

**1290-1295** A289 Set of 6 11.50 11.50

Supermarine Spitfire Airplanes, 75th Anniv. — A290

Designs: 10p, Spitfire K5054 modified to Mk 1 standard, in flight. 42p, Pilot in Spitfire on ground for first flight, Mar. 5, 1936. 49p, Ground crew testing Spitfire before first flight. No. 1299, £2, Spitfire prototype K5054 under construction.

No. 1300, £2, Pilot in Royal Air Force 92nd Squadron Spitfire Mk 1B.

**2011, Sept. 28** ***Perf. 14¾x14***

**1296-1299** A290 Set of 4 9.50 9.50

**Souvenir Sheet**

**1300** A290 £2 multi 6.25 6.25

Tariq Ibn Ziyad, 8th Century Muslim General A291

Scenes from Tariq Ibn Ziyad's invasion of Gibraltar in 711: 42p, Soldiers rowing boat. 44p, Boats on shore. 66p, Soldiers on horses. £2, Battle scene.

**2011, Nov. 7** ***Perf. 13¼***

**1301-1304** A291 Set of 4 11.50 11.50

Christmas A292

Nativity paintings by: 10p, Charles Le Brun. 42p, Lorenzo Lotto, 44p, Il Bronzino. 51p, Gerard van Honthorst. £2, Giorgione da Castelfranco.

**2011, Nov. 7** ***Perf. 14¼***

**1305-1309** A292 Set of 5 11.50 11.50

Gibraltar Intl. Chess Festival, 10th Anniv. — A293

Chessboard positions in matches between: 2p, Viktor Bologan and Pia Cramling. 30p, Michael Adams and Natalia Zhukova. 75p, Fabiano Caruana and Viktor Korchnoi. £2, Vassily Ivanchuk and Nigel Short.

**2012, Jan. 23** ***Perf. 13x13¼***

**1310-1313** A293 Set of 4 9.75 9.75

Sinking of the Titanic, Cent. A294

Milestones in history of the Titanic: 10p, Fitting of Titanic completed Mar. 31, 1912. 42p, Titanic sets sail on maiden voyage, April 10, 1912. 44p, Iceberg strikes starboard bow, April 14, 1912. 54p, First lifeboats lowered to the sea, April 15, 1912. 66p, Stern rises and starts sinking, April 15, 1912.

**2012, Jan. 30** ***Perf. 13¼***

**1314-1318** A294 Set of 5 7.00 7.00

Reign of Queen Elizabeth II, 60th Anniv. — A295

Queen Elizabeth II wearing: 10p, Light green hat. 42p, Tiara. 44p, Flowered hat. 51p, Large pendant earrings. 55p, Pearl necklace. £2, Red Cross hat.

£3, Queen Elizabeth II wearing sash and crown.

**2012, Feb. 27**

**1319-1324** A295 Set of 6 13.00 13.00

*1324a* Souvenir sheet of 6, #1319-1324, + 3 labels 13.00 13.00

**Souvenir Sheet**

**1325** A295 £3 multi 9.50 9.50

**Birds Type of 2008**

Designs: S, Red-necked nightjar. UK, Little owl. £3.44, Spotted flycatcher.

**2012, Apr. 16** ***Perf. 13x13¼***

**1326** A255 S multi 1.00 1.00

**1327** A255 UK multi 1.40 1.40

**1328** A255 £3.44 multi 11.00 11.00

*Nos. 1326-1328 (3)* 13.40 13.40

On day of issue, No. 1326 sold for 31p and No. 1327 sold for 41p.

Royal Air Force Squadron Emblems and Aircraft A296

Royal Air Force Squadron Emblems — A297

Designs: No. 1329, 10p, Westland WS-61 Sea King helicopter, emblem of 22nd Squadron. No. 1330, 42p, Gloster Javelin FAW.7 Mk IV airplane, emblem of 89th Squadron. No. 1331, 76p, Panavia tornado airplane, emblem of 111th Squadron. No. 1332, £2, Bristol Type 156 Beaufighter airplane, emblem of 248th Squadron.

No. 1333 — Emblem of: a, 22nd Squadron. b, 89th Squadron. c, 111th Squadron. d, 248th Squadron.

**2012, Apr. 16** ***Perf. 13¼***

**1329-1332** A296 Set of 4 11.00 11.00

**1333** A297 Sheet of 4 11.00 11.00

*a.* 10p multi .35 .35

*b.* 42p multi 1.40 1.40

*c.* 76p multi 2.50 2.50

*d.* £2 multi 6.50 6.50

Tourism — A298

Designs: 10p, Aerial view of harbor, city and Rock of Gibraltar. 42p, Tower of Homage, Moorish Castle. 44p, Aerial view of city and Rock of Gibraltar. 51p, St. Michael's Cave. 54p, Trinity Lighthouse. 66p, Eliott's Column, Alameda Botanical Gardens.

**2012, June 15 Litho.** ***Perf. 13¼***

**1334-1339** A298 Set of 6 8.25 8.25

Europa (42p, 44p).

Gibraltar Intl. Jazz Festival A299

**2012, June 19** ***Perf. 13x13¼***

**1340** A299 75p multi 2.40 2.40

Old Views of Gibraltar — A300

Designs: No. 1341, 10p, Moorish Castle. 30p, Grand Casemates. 61p, Landing Pier. 78p, Waterport. £1.75, Alameda Gardens.

No. 1346: a, 10p, Marching band on Sand Hill Road. b, 42p, South Port Gates. c, 50p, Victoria Monument. d, £1, Hargraves Barracks.

**2012, Sept. 14** ***Perf. 13¼***

**1341-1345** A300 Set of 5 11.50 11.50

**Souvenir Sheet**

**1346** A300 Sheet of 4, #a-d 6.50 6.50

Charles Dickens (1812-70), Writer — A301

Photograph of Dickens and: 10p, Cover and illustration from *David Copperfield.* 42p, First page and illustration from *Oliver Twist.* 44p, Cover and first page from *A Tale of Two Cities.* No. 1350, £2, Cover and illustration from *A Christmas Carol.*

No. 1351, £2, Photograph of Dickens over book cover.

**2012, Sept. 14** ***Perf. 14¼x15***

**1347-1350** A301 Set of 4 9.50 9.50

**Souvenir Sheet**

**1351** A301 £2 multi 6.50 6.50

Souvenir Sheet

Visit to Gibraltar of Earl and Countess of Wessex — A302

**2012, Sept. 14** ***Perf. 13¼***

**1352** A302 £1 Sheet of 3, #a-c 9.75 9.75

**Endangered Animals Type of 2011**

Designs: No. 1353, 42p, Arabian oryx. No. 1354, 42p, Asian one-horned rhinoceros. No. 1355, 42p, European wolf. No. 1356, 42p, Iberian lynx. No. 1357, 42p, Snow leopard. No. 1358, 42p, Western lowland gorilla.

**2012, Nov. 2** ***Perf. 13¼x13***

**1353-1358** A288 Set of 6 8.25 8.25

*1358a* Souvenir sheet of 6, #1353-1358 8.25 8.25

Christmas A303

Designs: 10p, Santa Claus, gifts and "Merry Christmas." 42p, Santa Claus with sack of gifts and lantern. 44p, Snowman, Christmas tree, gifts, flying sleigh and reindeer. 51p, Santa Claus in flying sleigh. £2, Reindeer, elf, Santa Claus holding bell.

**2012, Nov. 2** ***Perf. 13x13¼***

**1359-1363** A303 Set of 5 11.50 11.50

New Year 2013 (Year of the Snake) — A304

No. 1364: a, Head of snake. b, Entire snake.

**Litho. & Embossed With Foil Application**

**2013, Jan. 30** ***Perf. 12¾***

**1364** A304 Horiz. pair 4.75 4.75

*a.* 42p multi 1.40 1.40

*b.* £1 multi 3.25 3.25

Coronation of Queen Elizabeth II, 60th Anniv. — A305

Various black-and-white photographs of Queen Elizabeth II on day of coronation: 10p, 42p, 44p, £1.50.

£3, Color photograph of Queen Elizabeth II.

**2013, Jan. 30** **Litho.** ***Perf. 13¼***

**1365-1368** A305 Set of 4 7.75 7.75

**Souvenir Sheet**

**1369** A305 £3 multi 9.50 9.50

**POSTAGE DUE STAMPS**

**Catalogue values for unused stamps in this section are for Never Hinged items.**

D1

***Perf. 14***

**1956, Dec. 1** **Wmk. 4** **Typo.**

**Chalky Paper**

| | | | | |
|---|---|---|---|---|
| **J1** | D1 | 1p green | 1.75 | *2.00* |
| **J2** | D1 | 2p brown | 2.60 | *3.25* |
| **J3** | D1 | 4p ultramarine | 3.25 | *3.75* |
| | | *Nos. J1-J3 (3)* | 7.60 | *9.00* |

**"p" instead of "d"**

***Perf. 17½x18***

**1971, Feb. 15** **Typo.** **Wmk. 314**

**Chalky Paper**

| | | | | |
|---|---|---|---|---|
| **J4** | D1 | ½p green | .50 | *.60* |
| **J5** | D1 | 1p dark brown | .50 | *.55* |
| **J6** | D1 | 2p dark blue | .60 | *.60* |
| | | *Nos. J4-J6 (3)* | 1.60 | *1.75* |

D2

***Perf. 14x13½***

**1976, Oct. 13** **Litho.** **Wmk. 373**

| | | | | |
|---|---|---|---|---|
| **J7** | D2 | 1p orange | .25 | .35 |
| **J8** | D2 | 3p bright ultra | .25 | .35 |
| **J9** | D2 | 5p vermilion | .25 | *.50* |
| **J10** | D2 | 7p bright red lilac | .25 | *.60* |
| **J11** | D2 | 10p gray | .45 | *1.10* |
| **J12** | D2 | 20p green | .80 | *1.50* |
| | | *Nos. J7-J12 (6)* | 2.25 | *4.40* |

D3

**1984, July 2** ***Perf. 14½x14***

| | | | | |
|---|---|---|---|---|
| **J13** | D3 | 1p black | .25 | .25 |
| **J14** | D3 | 3p red | .25 | .25 |
| **J15** | D3 | 5p blue | .25 | .25 |
| **J16** | D3 | 10p sky blue | .40 | .40 |
| **J17** | D3 | 25p lilac | 1.25 | 1.25 |
| **J18** | D3 | 50p orange | 2.25 | 2.25 |
| **J19** | D3 | £1 green | 4.50 | 4.50 |
| | | *Nos. J13-J19 (7)* | 9.15 | 9.15 |

D4

Landmarks: 1p, Water Port Gates. 10p, HM Dockyard. 25p, Military Hospital. 50p, Governor's Cottage. £1, Laguna. £2, Catalan Bay.

**1996, Sept. 30** **Litho.** ***Perf. 14½x14***

| | | | | |
|---|---|---|---|---|
| **J20** | D4 | 1p multicolored | .25 | .25 |
| **J21** | D4 | 10p multicolored | .35 | .35 |
| **J22** | D4 | 25p multicolored | .80 | .80 |
| **J23** | D4 | 50p multicolored | 1.60 | 1.60 |
| **J24** | D4 | £1 multicolored | 3.25 | 3.25 |
| **J25** | D4 | £2 multicolored | 7.00 | 7.00 |
| | | *Nos. J20-J25 (6)* | 13.25 | 13.25 |

Finches — D5

Designs: 5p, Greenfinch. 10p, Serin. 20p, Siskin. 50p, Linnet. £1, Chaffinch. £2, Goldfinch.

***Perf. 13x13¼***

**2002, June 6** **Litho.** **Unwmk.**

**J26-J31** D5 Set of 6 15.00 15.00

**WAR TAX STAMP**

No. 66 Overprinted

**1918, Apr.** **Wmk. 3** ***Perf. 14***

**MR1** A14 ½p green 1.75 *2.40*

*a.* Double overprint 900.00

## GILBERT & ELLICE ISLANDS

ˈgil-bərt ənˌdˌ ˈe-ləs ˈī-lənds

LOCATION — Groups of islands in the Pacific Ocean northeast of Australia
GOVT. — British Crown Colony
AREA — 375 sq. mi.
POP. — 57,816 (est. 1973)
CAPITAL — Tarawa

The Gilbert group of which Butaritari, Tarawa and Tamana are the more important, is on the Equator. Ellice Islands, Phoenix Islands, Line Islands (Fanning, Washington and Christmas), and Ocean Island are included in the Colony. The islands were annexed by Great Britain in 1892 and formed into the Gilbert and Ellice Islands Colony in 1915 on request of the native governments.

The colony divided into the Gilbert Islands and Tuvalu, Jan. 1, 1976.

12 Pence = 1 Shilling
20 Shillings = 1 Pound
100 Cents = 1 Dollar (1966)

**Catalogue values for unused stamps in this country are for Never Hinged items, beginning with Scott 52.**

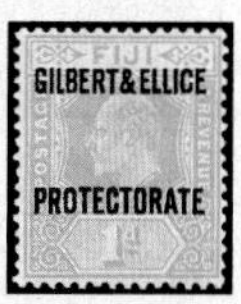

Stamps and Type of Fiji Overprinted in Black or Red

**1911, Jan. 1** **Wmk. 3** ***Perf. 14***

**Ordinary Paper**

| | | | | |
|---|---|---|---|---|
| **1** | A22 | ½p green | 7.50 | *50.00* |
| **2** | A22 | 1p carmine | 50.00 | 30.00 |
| *a.* | | Pair, one without overprint | | |
| **3** | A22 | 2p gray | 15.00 | *17.50* |
| **4** | A22 | 2½p ultramarine | 16.00 | *45.00* |

**Chalky Paper**

| | | | | |
|---|---|---|---|---|
| **5** | A22 | 5p violet & ol grn | 65.00 | *95.00* |
| **6** | A22 | 6p violet | 25.00 | *50.00* |
| **7** | A22 | 1sh black, *green* | 25.00 | *70.00* |
| | | *Nos. 1-7 (7)* | 203.50 | *357.50* |

Nos. 1-7 are known with a forged Ocean Island postmark dated "JY 15 11."

Pandanus — A2

**1911, Mar.** **Engr.** **Ordinary Paper**

| | | | | |
|---|---|---|---|---|
| **8** | A2 | ½p green | 5.00 | *20.00* |
| **9** | A2 | 1p carmine | 2.75 | *8.50* |
| **10** | A2 | 2p gray | 1.50 | *7.50* |
| **11** | A2 | 2½p ultramarine | 6.50 | *12.50* |
| | | *Nos. 8-11 (4)* | 15.75 | *48.50* |

King George V — A3

For description of Dies I and II, see front section of the Catalogue.

**1912-24** **Die I** **Typo.**

| | | | | |
|---|---|---|---|---|
| **14** | A3 | ½p deep green | .60 | *6.00* |
| **15** | A3 | 1p carmine | 2.50 | *9.00* |
| *a.* | | 1p scarlet ('15) | 4.25 | *15.00* |
| **16** | A3 | 2p gray ('16) | 16.00 | *26.00* |
| **17** | A3 | 2½p ultra ('16) | 2.00 | *11.00* |

**Chalky Paper**

| | | | | |
|---|---|---|---|---|
| **18** | A3 | 3p vio, *yel* ('19) | 2.75 | *9.00* |
| **19** | A3 | 4p blk & red, *yel* | .90 | *6.50* |
| **20** | A3 | 5p vio & ol grn | 2.00 | *6.25* |
| **21** | A3 | 6p vio & red vio | 1.50 | *6.75* |
| **22** | A3 | 1sh black, *green* | 1.50 | *5.25* |
| **23** | A3 | 2sh vio & ultra, *bl* | 15.00 | *30.00* |
| **24** | A3 | 2sh6p blk & red, *bl* | 18.00 | *25.00* |
| **25** | A3 | 5sh grn & red, *yel* | 37.50 | *65.00* |

**Die II**

| | | | | |
|---|---|---|---|---|
| **26** | A3 | £1 vio & blk, *red* ('24) | 600.00 | *1,500.* |
| | | *Nos. 14-26 (13)* | 700.25 | *1,705.* |

**Die II**

**1921-27** **Wmk. 4** **Ordinary Paper**

| | | | | |
|---|---|---|---|---|
| **27** | A3 | ½p green | 3.25 | *3.25* |
| **28** | A3 | 1p deep vio ('27) | 5.00 | *6.00* |
| **29** | A3 | 1½p scarlet ('24) | 5.00 | *2.50* |
| **30** | A3 | 2p gray | 8.00 | *35.00* |

**Chalky Paper**

| | | | | |
|---|---|---|---|---|
| **31** | A3 | 10sh green & red, *emer* ('24) | 160.00 | *375.00* |
| | | *Nos. 27-31 (5)* | 181.25 | *421.75* |

Common Design Types pictured following the introduction.

**Silver Jubilee Issue**

Common Design Type

**1935, May 6** **Engr.** ***Perf. 11x12***

| | | | | |
|---|---|---|---|---|
| **33** | CD301 | 1p black & ultra | 2.25 | *12.00* |
| **34** | CD301 | 1½p car & blue | 1.75 | *4.00* |
| **35** | CD301 | 3p ultra & brn | 5.50 | *17.50* |
| **36** | CD301 | 1sh brn vio & indigo | 30.00 | *20.00* |
| | | *Nos. 33-36 (4)* | 39.50 | *53.50* |
| | | Set, never hinged | 65.00 | |

**Coronation Issue**

Common Design Type

**1937, May 12** ***Perf. 13½x14***

| | | | | |
|---|---|---|---|---|
| **37** | CD302 | 1p dark purple | .25 | .65 |
| **38** | CD302 | 1½p carmine | .25 | .65 |
| **39** | CD302 | 3p bright ultra | .45 | .70 |
| | | *Nos. 37-39 (3)* | .95 | 2.00 |
| | | Set, never hinged | 1.25 | |

Great Frigate Bird — A4

Pandanus — A5

Designs: 1½p, Canoe crossing reef. 2p, Canoe and boat house. 2½p, Islander's house. 3p, Seascape. 5p, Ellice Islands canoe. 6p, Coconut trees. 1sh, Phosphate loading jetty, Ocean Island. 2sh, Cutter "Nimanoa." 2sh6p, Gilbert Islands canoe. 5sh, Coat of arms of colony.

***Perf. 11½x11 (Nos. 40, 43, 50), 12½ (Type A5), 13½ (Nos. 42, 44, 45, 48)***

**1939, Jan. 14 Engr. Wmk. 4**

| | | | | |
|---|---|---|---|---|
| **40** | A4 | ½p dk grn & sl bl | .40 | *.90* |
| **41** | A5 | 1p dk vio & brt bl green | .25 | *1.25* |
| **42** | A4 | 1½p car & black | .25 | *.90* |
| **43** | A4 | 2p black & brn | .40 | *.95* |
| **44** | A4 | 2½p dp olive & blk | .30 | *.70* |
| **45** | A4 | 3p ultra & black | .30 | *.90* |
| *a.* | | Perf. 12 ('55) | .40 | *2.25* |
| **46** | A5 | 5p dk brn & dp ultra | 3.25 | 1.50 |
| **47** | A5 | 6p dl vio & olive | .45 | *.60* |
| **48** | A4 | 1sh gray bl & blk | 5.50 | 3.75 |
| *b.* | | Perf. 12 ('51) | 2.00 | *16.00* |
| **49** | A5 | 2sh red org & ultra | 7.00 | 10.00 |
| **50** | A4 | 2sh6p brt bl grn & bl | 7.00 | *11.00* |
| **51** | A5 | 5sh dp blue & red | 8.50 | *14.00* |
| | | *Nos. 40-51 (12)* | 33.60 | *46.45* |
| | | Set, never hinged | 70.00 | |

**Catalogue values for unused stamps in this section, from this point to the end of the section, are for Never Hinged items.**

### Peace Issue
Common Design Type

**1946, Dec. 16** ***Perf. 13½x14***

| | | | | |
|---|---|---|---|---|
| **52** | CD303 | 1p deep magenta | .25 | .25 |
| **53** | CD303 | 3p deep blue | .25 | .25 |

### Silver Wedding Issue
Common Design Types

**1949, Aug. 29 Photo.** ***Perf. 14x14½***

| | | | | |
|---|---|---|---|---|
| **54** | CD304 | 1p violet | .25 | .25 |

**Engraved; Name Typographed**

***Perf. 11½x11***

| | | | | |
|---|---|---|---|---|
| **55** | CD305 | £1 red | 15.00 | *24.00* |

### UPU Issue
Common Design Types

**Engr.; Name Typo. on 2p, 3p**

**1949, Oct. 1** ***Perf. 13½, 11x11½***

| | | | | |
|---|---|---|---|---|
| **56** | CD306 | 1p rose violet | .75 | *1.25* |
| **57** | CD307 | 2p gray black | 2.50 | *2.75* |
| **58** | CD308 | 3p indigo | .80 | *2.75* |
| **59** | CD309 | 1sh blue | .80 | *2.00* |
| | | *Nos. 56-59 (4)* | 4.85 | *8.75* |

### Coronation Issue
Common Design Type

**1953, June 2 Engr.** ***Perf. 13½x13***

| | | | | |
|---|---|---|---|---|
| **60** | CD312 | 2p gray & black | .65 | 2.25 |

### Types of 1939-42 with Portrait of Queen Elizabeth II, and

Canoe Crossing Reef — A6

***Perf. 11½x11 (Nos. 61, 63, 70), 12½ (Type A5), 12 (Nos. 64-65, 68, 72)***

**1956, Aug. 1**

| | | | | |
|---|---|---|---|---|
| **61** | A4 | ½p brt ultra & blk | .65 | *1.40* |
| **62** | A5 | 1p violet & olive | .60 | *1.40* |
| **63** | A4 | 2p dull pur & brt green | .90 | *2.75* |
| **64** | A4 | 2½p green & black | .50 | *.65* |
| **65** | A4 | 3p dk car & black | .50 | .65 |
| **66** | A5 | 5p red orange & brt ultra | 8.00 | 2.75 |
| **67** | A5 | 6p dk gray & red brown | .85 | *3.00* |
| **68** | A4 | 1sh ol green & blk | 2.75 | .65 |
| **69** | A5 | 2sh dk brown & brt ultra | 5.50 | 4.25 |
| **70** | A4 | 2sh6p dp ultra & rose red | 8.50 | 4.75 |
| **71** | A5 | 5sh green & blue | 9.50 | 6.50 |
| **72** | A6 | 10sh turq blue & blk | 24.00 | 13.00 |
| | | *Nos. 61-72 (12)* | 62.25 | *41.75* |

See Nos. 84-85.

Loading Phosphate on Freighter A7

2½p, Original lump of phosphate. 1sh, Loading phosphate on truck, Ocean Island.

**Wmk. 314**

**1960, May 1 Photo.** ***Perf. 12***

| | | | | |
|---|---|---|---|---|
| **73** | A7 | 2p rose lilac & green | .80 | *.85* |
| **74** | A7 | 2½p olive & black | .80 | *.85* |
| **75** | A7 | 1sh grnsh blue & blk | .80 | *.85* |
| | | *Nos. 73-75 (3)* | 2.40 | 2.55 |

60th anniversary of the discovery of phosphate deposits at Ocean Island.

### Freedom from Hunger Issue
Common Design Type

**1963, June 4** ***Perf. 14x14½***

| | | | | |
|---|---|---|---|---|
| **76** | CD314 | 10p ultramarine | 1.40 | .40 |

### Red Cross Centenary Issue
Common Design Type

**1963, Sept. 2 Litho.** ***Perf. 13***

| | | | | |
|---|---|---|---|---|
| **77** | CD315 | 2p black & red | .75 | .75 |
| **78** | CD315 | 10p ultra & red | 1.50 | *2.50* |

Plane and Fiji-Ellice-Gilbert Route — A8

Designs: 1sh, Eastern reef heron in flight, horiz. 3sh7p, Plane and Tarawa sailboat.

**1964, July 20** ***Perf. 11½x11, 11x11½***

| | | | | |
|---|---|---|---|---|
| **79** | A8 | 3p lt blue, bl & blk | .75 | .35 |
| **80** | A8 | 1sh dk blue, bl & blk | .90 | .35 |
| **81** | A8 | 3sh7p lt green, grn & blk | 1.50 | 1.50 |
| | | *Nos. 79-81 (3)* | 3.15 | 2.20 |

Inauguration of air service between Fiji and Gilbert and Ellice Islands.

### Queen Types of 1956

***Perf. 11½x11, 12½***

**1964-65 Engr. Wmk. 314**

| | | | | |
|---|---|---|---|---|
| **84** | A4 | 2p dull pur & brt green | 1.10 | 1.60 |
| **85** | A5 | 6p dk gray & red brown | 1.75 | 1.75 |

Issue dates: 2p, Oct. 30. 6p, Apr. 1965.

### ITU Issue
Common Design Type

**1965, June 4 Litho.** ***Perf. 11x11½***

| | | | | |
|---|---|---|---|---|
| **87** | CD317 | 3p dp org & turq blue | .25 | .25 |
| **88** | CD317 | 2sh6p grnsh bl & red lilac | .70 | .50 |

Village Elder Blowing Conch and Meeting House (Maneaba) — A9

Designs: 1p, Ellice Islanders torch fishing. 2p, Gilbertese girl weaving frangipani garland. 3p, Gilbertese woman dancing The Ruoia. 4p, Gilbertese man dancing. 5p, Gilbertese woman drawing water. 6p, Ellice kosu dance. 7p, Fatele taua dance, Ellice men. 1sh, Gilbertese woman harvesting taro roots (babai). 1sh6p, Ellice man and woman dancing fatele toka. 2sh, Ellice Islanders pounding taro roots. 3sh7p, Gilbertese sitting dance, ruoia, horiz. 5sh, Gilbertese boys playing stick game, horiz. 10sh, Ellice men beating box-drum, horiz. £1, Coat of arms, horiz.

***Perf. 12x11, 11x12***

**1965, Aug. 16 Litho. Wmk. 314**

| | | | | |
|---|---|---|---|---|
| **89** | A9 | ½p blue grn & multi | .25 | .25 |
| **90** | A9 | 1p vio bl & multi | .25 | .25 |
| **91** | A9 | 2p lt olive & multi | .25 | .25 |
| **92** | A9 | 3p red & multi | .25 | .25 |
| **93** | A9 | 4p purple & multi | .25 | .25 |
| **94** | A9 | 5p car rose & multi | .25 | .25 |
| **95** | A9 | 6p multicolored | .25 | .25 |
| **96** | A9 | 7p brown & multi | .40 | .25 |
| **97** | A9 | 1sh bl vio & multi | .70 | .25 |
| **98** | A9 | 1sh6p yel & multi | 1.40 | 1.00 |
| **99** | A9 | 2sh multicolored | 1.40 | 1.25 |
| **100** | A9 | 3sh7p ultra & multi | 2.50 | .70 |
| **101** | A9 | 5sh multicolored | 2.50 | .90 |
| **102** | A9 | 10sh green & multi | 3.25 | 1.40 |
| **103** | A9 | £1 blue & multi | 4.00 | 2.00 |
| | | *Nos. 89-103 (15)* | 17.90 | 9.50 |

See #135-149. For surcharges see #110-124.

### Intl. Cooperation Year Issue
Common Design Type

**1965, Oct. 25 Litho.** ***Perf. 14½***

| | | | | |
|---|---|---|---|---|
| **104** | CD318 | ½p blue grn & cl | .25 | .25 |
| **105** | CD318 | 3sh7p lt violet & grn | .70 | .35 |

### Churchill Memorial Issue
Common Design Type

**1966, Jan. 24 Photo.** ***Perf. 14***

**Design in Black, Gold and Carmine Rose**

| | | | | |
|---|---|---|---|---|
| **106** | CD319 | ½p brt blue | .25 | .25 |
| **107** | CD319 | 3p green | .35 | .25 |
| **108** | CD319 | 3sh brown | .55 | .40 |
| **109** | CD319 | 3sh7p violet | .60 | .40 |
| | | *Nos. 106-109 (4)* | 1.75 | 1.30 |

Nos. 89-103 Surcharged

***Perf. 12x11, 11x12***

**1966, Feb. 14 Litho.**

| | | | | |
|---|---|---|---|---|
| **110** | A9 | 1c on 1p multi | .25 | .25 |
| **111** | A9 | 2c on 2p multi | .25 | .25 |
| **112** | A9 | 3c on 3p multi | .25 | .25 |
| **113** | A9 | 4c on ½p multi | .25 | .25 |
| **114** | A9 | 5c on 6p multi | .25 | .25 |
| **115** | A9 | 6c on 4p multi | .25 | .25 |
| **116** | A9 | 8c on 5p multi | .25 | .25 |
| **117** | A9 | 10c on 1sh multi | .25 | .25 |
| **118** | A9 | 15c on 7p multi | .80 | .60 |
| **119** | A9 | 20c on 1sh6p multi | .60 | .40 |
| **120** | A9 | 25c on 2sh multi | .60 | .35 |
| **121** | A9 | 35c on 3sh7p multi | 1.25 | .25 |
| **122** | A9 | 50c on 5sh multi | .75 | .45 |
| **123** | A9 | $1 on 10sh multi | .75 | .50 |
| **124** | A9 | $2 on £1 multi | 1.75 | *3.00* |
| | | *Nos. 110-124 (15)* | 8.50 | 7.55 |

### World Cup Soccer Issue
Common Design Type

**1966, July 1 Litho.** ***Perf. 14***

| | | | | |
|---|---|---|---|---|
| **125** | CD321 | 3c multicolored | .25 | .25 |
| **126** | CD321 | 35c multicolored | .55 | .35 |

### WHO Headquarters Issue
Common Design Type

**1966, Sept. 20 Litho.** ***Perf. 14***

| | | | | |
|---|---|---|---|---|
| **127** | CD322 | 3c multicolored | .25 | .25 |
| **128** | CD322 | 12c multicolored | .55 | .45 |

### UNESCO Anniversary Issue
Common Design Type

**1966, Dec. 1 Litho.** ***Perf. 14***

| | | | | |
|---|---|---|---|---|
| **129** | CD323 | 5c "Education" | .50 | *.50* |
| **130** | CD323 | 10c "Science" | .75 | .25 |
| **131** | CD323 | 20c "Culture" | 1.25 | .90 |
| | | *Nos. 129-131 (3)* | 2.50 | 1.65 |

H.M.S. Royalist, 1892, and Union Jack A10

10c, Cutter & canoe at trading post. 35c, Family.

***Perf. 14½x14***

**1967, Sept. 1 Photo. Wmk. 314**

| | | | | |
|---|---|---|---|---|
| **132** | A10 | 3c green, blue & red | .25 | .35 |
| **133** | A10 | 10c multicolored | .25 | .25 |
| **134** | A10 | 35c multicolored | .30 | .45 |
| | | *Nos. 132-134 (3)* | .80 | 1.05 |

75th anniv. as a British Protectorate.

### Type of 1965

***Perf. 12x11, 11x12***

**1968, Jan. 1 Litho. Wmk. 314**

| | | | | |
|---|---|---|---|---|
| **135** | A9 | 1c like 1p | .25 | .25 |
| **136** | A9 | 2c like 2p | .25 | .25 |
| **137** | A9 | 3c like 3p | .25 | .25 |
| **138** | A9 | 4c like ½p | .25 | .25 |
| **139** | A9 | 5c like 6p | .25 | .25 |
| **140** | A9 | 6c like 4p | .25 | .25 |
| **141** | A9 | 8c like 5p | .25 | .25 |
| **142** | A9 | 10c like 1sh | .25 | .25 |
| **143** | A9 | 15c like 7p | .50 | .25 |
| **144** | A9 | 20c like 1sh6p | .70 | .25 |
| **145** | A9 | 25c like 2sh | 1.25 | .25 |
| **146** | A9 | 35c like 3sh7p | 1.50 | .25 |
| **147** | A9 | 50c like 5sh | 1.50 | 2.50 |
| **148** | A9 | $1 like 10sh | 1.75 | 3.50 |
| **149** | A9 | $2 like £1 | 4.50 | 3.75 |
| | | *Nos. 135-149 (15)* | 13.70 | 12.75 |

Map of Tarawa Atoll — A11

Designs: 10c, US Marines wading ashore at Betio. 15c, Battle scene on Betio. 35c, Raising US and British flags on Betio.

**1968, Nov. 21 Photo.** ***Perf. 14***

| | | | | |
|---|---|---|---|---|
| **150** | A11 | 3c multicolored | .25 | .25 |
| **151** | A11 | 10c multicolored | .25 | .25 |
| **152** | A11 | 15c multicolored | .25 | .25 |
| **153** | A11 | 35c multicolored | .30 | .30 |
| | | *Nos. 150-153 (4)* | 1.05 | 1.05 |

Battle of Tarawa against Japan, 25th anniv.

School Boy and Map of Abemama Atoll A12

Designs: 10c, Secondary school boy and girl on map of Tarawa, with rest of Gilbert and Ellice Islands. 35c, Student in cap and gown on main Fiji island (Viti Levu) and map of South Pacific Islands.

**1969, June 2 Litho.** ***Perf. 12½***

| | | | | |
|---|---|---|---|---|
| **154** | A12 | 3c dull org & multi | .25 | .25 |
| **155** | A12 | 10c black & multi | .25 | .25 |
| **156** | A12 | 35c dull grn & multi | .25 | .35 |
| | | *Nos. 154-156 (3)* | .75 | .85 |

1st anniv. of the University of the South Pacific in Fiji, and to show the progress of education in the area it serves.

Polynesian Madonna — A13

**1969, Oct. 20** — *Perf. 11½*

| | | | | | |
|---|---|---|---|---|---|
| **157** | A13 | 2c | multicolored | .25 | .25 |
| **158** | A13 | 10c | multicolored | .25 | .25 |

Christmas.

---

Canceled to Order

The Philatelic Bureau of Gilbert and Ellice Islands began in 1970 to sell canceled sets of new issues. Values in the second ("used") column are for these canceled-to-order stamps.

---

Mouth-to-Mouth Resuscitation — A14

**1970, Mar. 9** — **Litho.** — *Perf. 14½*

| | | | | | |
|---|---|---|---|---|---|
| **159** | A14 | 10c | multi | .25 | .25 |
| **160** | A14 | 15c | multi, diff. | .35 | *.40* |
| **161** | A14 | 35c | multi, diff. | .50 | *.85* |
| | | | *Nos. 159-161 (3)* | 1.10 | 1.50 |

Centenary of the British Red Cross.

Mother and Child Care — A15

Designs: 10c, Woman physician and laboratory equipment. 15c, Chest X-ray and technician. 35c, Map of Gilbert and Ellice Islands and UN emblem.

*Perf. 12½x13*

**1970, June 26** — **Litho.** — **Wmk. 314**

| | | | | | |
|---|---|---|---|---|---|
| **162** | A15 | 5c | lilac & multi | .25 | .25 |
| **163** | A15 | 10c | black, gray & red | .25 | .25 |
| **164** | A15 | 15c | yellow & multi | .25 | .25 |
| **165** | A15 | 35c | blue grn, bl & blk | .35 | .35 |
| | | | *Nos. 162-165 (4)* | 1.10 | 1.10 |

25th anniv. of the United Nations.

Map of Onotoa, Beru, Tamana and Arorae Islands — A16

Designs: 10c, Sailing ship "John Williams III," vert. 25c, Rev. Samuel James Whitmee, vert. 35c, Map of Islands and steamship "John Williams VII."

*Perf. 14x14½, 14½x14*

**1970, Sept. 1** — **Litho.** — **Wmk. 314**

| | | | | | |
|---|---|---|---|---|---|
| **166** | A16 | 2c | blue & multi | .25 | .25 |
| **167** | A16 | 10c | brt green & black | .35 | .25 |
| **168** | A16 | 25c | lt ultra & red brn | .25 | .25 |
| **169** | A16 | 35c | ver, blk & lt gray | .65 | .65 |
| | | | *Nos. 166-169 (4)* | 1.50 | 1.40 |

Centenary of the landing in the Southern Gilbert Islands by the first missionaries of the London Missionary Society.

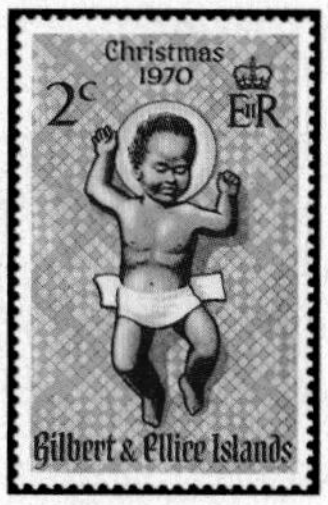


Island Child with Halo on Pandanus Mat — A17

Christmas: 10c, Sanctuary of New Tarawa Cathedral. 35c, Three Gilbertese sailing canoes within Star of Bethlehem.

**1970, Oct. 3** — *Perf. 14½*

| | | | | | |
|---|---|---|---|---|---|
| **170** | A17 | 2c | ocher & multi | .25 | .25 |
| **171** | A17 | 10c | ocher & multi | .25 | .25 |
| **172** | A17 | 35c | pink & multi | .25 | .25 |
| | | | *Nos. 170-172 (3)* | .75 | .75 |

Harvesting Copra — A18

Lagoon Fishing A19

3c, Women cleaning pandanus leaves. 4c, Fishermen casting nets. 5c, Gilbertese canoes. 6c, Dehusking coconuts. 8c, Woman weaving pandanus fronds. 10c, Basket weaving. 15c, Tiger shark. 20c, Beating rolled pandanus leaf. 25c, Loading copra. 35c, Night fishing. 50c, Local handicraft. $1, Woman weaving coconut screen. $2, Coat of arms.

**Wmk. 314 Upright (A18), Sideways (A19)**

**1971, May 31** — **Litho.** — *Perf. 14*

| | | | | | |
|---|---|---|---|---|---|
| **173** | A18 | 1c | multicolored | .25 | .25 |
| **174** | A19 | 2c | multicolored | .25 | .25 |
| **175** | A19 | 3c | multicolored | .25 | .25 |
| **176** | A19 | 4c | multicolored | .30 | .25 |
| **177** | A19 | 5c | multicolored | .60 | .25 |
| **178** | A18 | 6c | multicolored | .40 | .35 |
| **179** | A18 | 8c | multicolored | .55 | .35 |
| **180** | A18 | 10c | multicolored | .50 | .45 |
| **181** | A18 | 15c | multicolored | 3.25 | .90 |
| **182** | A19 | 20c | multicolored | 2.00 | 1.75 |
| **183** | A19 | 25c | multicolored | 2.50 | 1.40 |
| **184** | A19 | 35c | multicolored | 3.00 | 1.00 |
| **185** | A18 | 50c | multicolored | 1.60 | 2.40 |
| **186** | A18 | $1 | multicolored | 2.25 | 4.75 |
| **187** | A18 | $2 | multicolored | 6.50 | 9.25 |
| | | | *Nos. 173-187 (15)* | 24.20 | 23.85 |

**Wmk. 314 Upright (A19), Sideways (A18)**

**1972-73**

| | | | | | |
|---|---|---|---|---|---|
| *174a* | A19 | 2c | multicolored | 11.00 | *15.50* |
| *177a* | A19 | 5c | multicolored | 4.25 | 7.25 |
| *178a* | A18 | 6c | multicolored | 11.00 | *16.50* |
| *181a* | A18 | 15c | multicolored | 4.50 | 7.50 |
| *182a* | A19 | 20c | multicolored | 4.75 | 8.00 |
| | | | *Nos. 174a-182a (5)* | 35.50 | 54.75 |

Issue dates: Sept. 7, 1972, June 13, 1973.

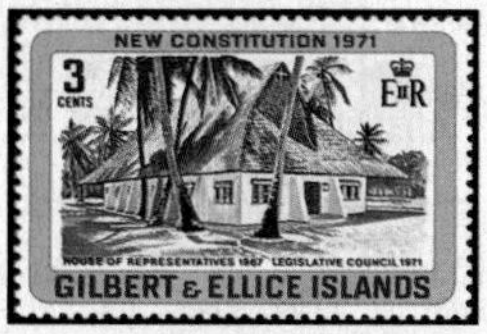


Legislative Council, 1971 (former House of Representatives) — A20

New Constitution: 10c, Meeting House.

**1971, Aug. 1** — **Wmk. 314** — *Perf. 14*

| | | | | | |
|---|---|---|---|---|---|
| **188** | A20 | 3c | orange & multi | .25 | .25 |
| **189** | A20 | 10c | green & multi | .25 | .25 |

Nativity Scene — A21

Christmas: 10c, Star of Bethlehem and palm fronds. 35c, Fishermen in outrigger canoe looking at Star.

**1971, Oct. 1**

| | | | | | |
|---|---|---|---|---|---|
| **190** | A21 | 3c | vio blue, blk & yel | .25 | .55 |
| **191** | A21 | 10c | grnsh bl, blk & gold | .25 | .25 |
| **192** | A21 | 35c | car rose, blk & rose | .25 | .25 |
| | | | *Nos. 190-192 (3)* | .75 | 1.05 |

Children and UNICEF Emblem A22

25th Anniv. of UNICEF: 10c, Seated child. 35c, Child's head.

**1971, Dec. 11**

| | | | | | |
|---|---|---|---|---|---|
| **193** | A22 | 3c | brt pink & multi | .25 | .45 |
| **194** | A22 | 10c | black & multi | .25 | .25 |
| **195** | A22 | 35c | blue & multi | .65 | .80 |
| | | | *Nos. 193-195 (3)* | 1.15 | 1.50 |

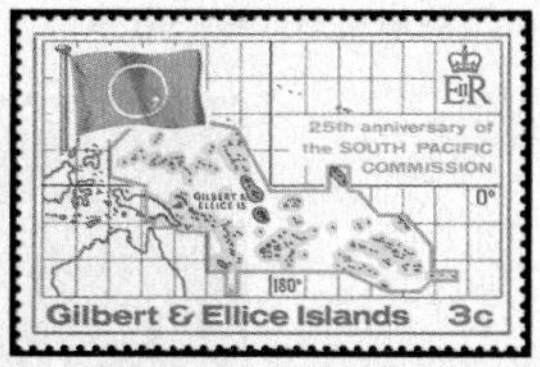


Commission Flag, Map of South Pacific — A23

South Pacific Commission, 25th Anniv.: 10c, Island boats. 35c, Flags of 8 member nations plus Tonga, a non-member.

**1972, Feb. 21** — *Perf. 13½x14*

| | | | | | |
|---|---|---|---|---|---|
| **196** | A23 | 3c | gray & multi | .25 | .55 |
| **197** | A23 | 10c | tan, ultra & brown | .25 | .25 |
| **198** | A23 | 35c | ultra & multi | .25 | .80 |
| | | | *Nos. 196-198 (3)* | .75 | 1.60 |

Corals A24

**1972, May 26** — *Perf. 14x14½*

| | | | | | |
|---|---|---|---|---|---|
| **199** | A24 | 3c | Alveopora | .25 | .35 |
| **200** | A24 | 10c | Euphyllia | .50 | .25 |
| **201** | A24 | 15c | Melithea | .65 | .35 |
| **202** | A24 | 35c | Spongodes | 1.90 | 1.10 |
| | | | *Nos. 199-202 (4)* | 3.30 | 2.05 |

"Peace" on Star of Bethlehem A25

Christmas: 10c, Holy Family, made of shells. 35c, Christ child sleeping in giant clam and covered with dawn cowrie, horiz.

**1972, Sept. 15** — *Perf. 13½*

| | | | | | |
|---|---|---|---|---|---|
| **203** | A25 | 3c | gold & multi | .25 | .25 |
| **204** | A25 | 10c | gold & multi | .25 | .25 |
| **205** | A25 | 35c | gold & multi | .30 | .30 |
| | | | *Nos. 203-205 (3)* | .80 | .80 |

**Silver Wedding Issue, 1972**

Common Design Type

Design: Queen Elizabeth II, Prince Philip and kaue floral headdress.

**1972, Nov. 20** — **Photo.** — *Perf. 14x14½*

| | | | | | |
|---|---|---|---|---|---|
| **206** | CD324 | 3c | olive & multi | .25 | .25 |
| **207** | CD324 | 35c | rose brown & multi | .25 | .25 |

Funafuti, Land of Bananas A26

Designs: 10c, Butaritari, the smell of the sea. 25c, Tarawa, the center of the world. 35c, Abemama, the land of the moon.

**1973, Mar. 5** — **Litho.** — *Perf. 14½x14*

| | | | | | |
|---|---|---|---|---|---|
| **208** | A26 | 3c | yellow & multi | .25 | *.45* |
| **209** | A26 | 10c | brt green & multi | .30 | .35 |
| **210** | A26 | 25c | dull blue & multi | .45 | .65 |
| **211** | A26 | 35c | orange & multi | .50 | .75 |
| | | | *Nos. 208-211 (4)* | 1.50 | 2.20 |

Legends of island names.

Ellice Dancer — A27

Christmas (Within Outline of Nautilus Shell): 10c, Outrigger canoe in lagoon. 35c, Evening on the lagoon. 50c, Map of Christmas Island, Pacific Ocean.

**1973, Sept. 24** — *Perf. 14*

| | | | | | |
|---|---|---|---|---|---|
| **212** | A27 | 3c | vio blue & multi | .25 | .25 |
| **213** | A27 | 10c | multicolored | .25 | .25 |
| **214** | A27 | 35c | multicolored | .25 | .25 |
| **215** | A27 | 50c | vio blue & multi | .35 | *1.00* |
| | | | *Nos. 212-215 (4)* | 1.10 | 1.75 |

**Princess Anne's Wedding Issue**

Common Design Type

**1973, Nov. 14** — *Perf. 14*

| | | | | | |
|---|---|---|---|---|---|
| **216** | CD325 | 3c | brt green & multi | .25 | .25 |
| **217** | CD325 | 35c | slate & multi | .25 | .25 |

Meteorological Observation — A28

WMO Emblem and: 10c, Island observation station. 35c, Wind finding radar. 50c, Map of Gilbert and Ellice Islands world weather watch stations.

**1973, Nov. 26** — **Litho.** — *Perf. 14½*

| | | | | | |
|---|---|---|---|---|---|
| **218** | A28 | 3c | orange & multi | .90 | .55 |
| **219** | A28 | 10c | dp bister & multi | .95 | .40 |
| **220** | A28 | 35c | gray & multi | 1.25 | .55 |
| **221** | A28 | 50c | dk blue & multi | 1.90 | 2.25 |
| | | | *Nos. 218-221 (4)* | 5.00 | 3.75 |

Cent. of intl. meteorological cooperation.

Te-Mataaua Crest and Canoe — A29

Designs: Various family crests and canoes.

**1974, Mar. 4 Litho. *Perf. 13½***

| | | | | |
|---|---|---|---|---|
| **222** | A29 | 3c tan & multi | .25 | .25 |
| **223** | A29 | 10c lt blue & multi | .25 | .25 |
| **224** | A29 | 35c yellow & multi | .25 | .25 |
| **225** | A29 | 50c pink & multi | .30 | .65 |
| *a.* | | Souvenir sheet of 4, #222-225 | 7.00 | *8.50* |
| | | *Nos. 222-225 (4)* | 1.05 | 1.40 |

UPU Emblem, "Te Koroba" and No. 26 — A30

UPU cent.: 10c, Sailing ship "Kiakia" and No. 51. 25c, BAC 111 jet and No. 187. 35c, UPU emblem.

**1974, June 10 *Perf. 14***

| | | | | |
|---|---|---|---|---|
| **226** | A30 | 4c blue green & multi | .25 | .25 |
| **227** | A30 | 10c orange & multi | .25 | .25 |
| **228** | A30 | 25c dp blue & multi | .30 | .25 |
| **229** | A30 | 35c red orange & black | .40 | .30 |
| | | *Nos. 226-229 (4)* | 1.20 | 1.05 |

Toy Canoe, Star and Boat A31

Star of Bethlehem and: 10c, Pinwheel and boat. 25c, Coconut ball (crate) and boat. 35c, Three boats (Wise Men) and stars.

**1974, Sept. 23**

| | | | | |
|---|---|---|---|---|
| **230** | A31 | 4c yel green & multi | .25 | .25 |
| **231** | A31 | 10c red brown & multi | .25 | .25 |
| **232** | A31 | 25c multicolored | .25 | .45 |
| **233** | A31 | 35c red brown & multi | .30 | .50 |
| | | *Nos. 230-233 (4)* | 1.05 | 1.45 |

Christmas.

Blenheim Palace, Entrance — A32 Churchill Painting — A33

Design: 35c, Churchill Statue, London.

**1974, Nov. 30 Litho. *Perf. 14***

| | | | | |
|---|---|---|---|---|
| **234** | A32 | 4c multicolored | .25 | .25 |
| **235** | A33 | 10c ultra & black | .25 | .25 |
| **236** | A33 | 35c blue, ocher & blk | .25 | .25 |
| | | *Nos. 234-236 (3)* | .75 | .75 |

Sir Winston Churchill (1874-1965).

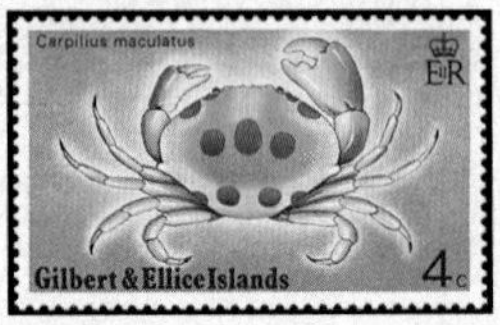


Carpilius Maculatus — A34

Crabs: 10c, Ranina ranina. 25c, Portunus pelagicus. 35c, Ocypode ceratophthalma.

**1975, Jan. 27 Litho. *Perf. 14***

| | | | | |
|---|---|---|---|---|
| **237** | A34 | 4c violet & multi | .25 | .25 |
| **238** | A34 | 10c green & multi | .50 | .50 |
| **239** | A34 | 25c buff & multi | 1.25 | 1.25 |
| **240** | A34 | 35c lt blue & multi | 1.75 | 1.75 |
| | | *Nos. 237-240 (4)* | 3.75 | 3.75 |

Living Cowries and Empty Shells — A35

**1975, May 26 Wmk. 314 *Perf. 14***

| | | | | |
|---|---|---|---|---|
| **241** | A35 | 4c Cypraea argus | .60 | .60 |
| **242** | A35 | 10c Cypraea cribraria | .85 | .85 |
| **243** | A35 | 25c Cypraea talpa | 1.60 | 1.60 |
| **244** | A35 | 35c Cypraea mappa | 2.50 | 2.50 |
| *a.* | | Souvenir sheet of 4, #241-244 | 17.50 | 17.50 |
| | | *Nos. 241-244 (4)* | 5.55 | 5.55 |

Map of Beru (The Bud) A36

Designs: 10c, Map of Onotoa (Six Giants). 25c, Map of Abaiang (Land to the North). 35c, Map of Marakei (Floating fish trap).

**Wmk. 314**

**1975, Aug. 1 Litho. *Perf. 14***

| | | | | |
|---|---|---|---|---|
| **245** | A36 | 4c brt green & multi | .25 | .25 |
| **246** | A36 | 10c brown & multi | .25 | .25 |
| **247** | A36 | 25c vio blue & multi | .30 | .30 |
| **248** | A36 | 35c org red & multi | .45 | .45 |
| | | *Nos. 245-248 (4)* | 1.25 | 1.25 |

Legends of island names.

Christ Child Within Coconut — A37

Christmas: 10c, Sadd Memorial Chapel (Protestant), Tarawa. 25c, R.C. Church, Ocean Island. 35c, Fishermen in outrigger canoes seeing star.

**1975, Sept. 22 *Perf. 14***

| | | | | |
|---|---|---|---|---|
| **249** | A37 | 4c brown & multi | .25 | *.40* |
| **250** | A37 | 10c brt blue & multi | .25 | .25 |
| **251** | A37 | 25c violet & multi | .40 | *.55* |
| **252** | A37 | 35c green & multi | .50 | *.80* |
| | | *Nos. 249-252 (4)* | 1.40 | *2.00* |

## POSTAGE DUE STAMPS

D1

**1940, Aug. Typo. Wmk. 4 *Perf. 12***

| | | | | |
|---|---|---|---|---|
| **J1** | D1 | 1p emerald | 5.50 | *24.00* |
| **J2** | D1 | 2p dark red | 6.00 | *24.00* |
| **J3** | D1 | 3p chocolate | 8.25 | *25.00* |
| **J4** | D1 | 4p deep blue | 10.00 | *35.00* |
| **J5** | D1 | 5p deep green | 13.00 | *35.00* |
| **J6** | D1 | 6p brt red vio | 13.00 | *35.00* |
| **J7** | D1 | 1sh dull violet | 22.50 | *50.00* |
| **J8** | D1 | 1sh6p turq green | 32.50 | *90.00* |
| | | *Nos. J1-J8 (8)* | 110.75 | *318.00* |
| | | Set, never hinged | 175.00 | |

## WAR TAX STAMP

No. 15a Overprinted

**1918 Wmk. 3 *Perf. 14***

| | | | | |
|---|---|---|---|---|
| **MR1** | A3 | 1p scarlet | .70 | *6.50* |

# GILBERT ISLANDS

'gil-bərt 'ī-ləndz

LOCATION — A group of islands in the Pacific Ocean northeast of Australia.
GOVT. — British Crown Colony
AREA — 270 sq. mi.
POP. — 52,000 (1973)
CAPITAL — Tarawa

The Gilbert Islands Colony consists of the Gilbert Islands, Phoenix, Ocean and Line Islands. They were part of the Gilbert and Ellice Islands colony until 1976. See Tuvalu.

**Catalogue values for all unused stamps in this country are for Never Hinged items.**

Stamps and Types of Gilbert and Ellice Islands 1971 Overprinted in Red, Black or Gold

**Wmk. 373; 314 (2c, 4c)**

**1976, Jan. 2 Litho. *Perf. 14***

| | | | | |
|---|---|---|---|---|
| **253** | A18 | 1c multi (R) | .25 | *.70* |
| *a.* | | Watermark 314 | .25 | *.30* |
| **254** | A19 | 2c multi (R) | .40 | *.25* |
| *a.* | | Watermark upright | .50 | 2.25 |
| **255** | A19 | 3c multi (R) | .40 | *1.60* |
| *a.* | | Watermark 314 | 19.00 | 15.00 |
| **256** | A19 | 4c multi (R) | .30 | *.90* |
| **257** | A19 | 5c multi (R) | .50 | *.90* |
| **258** | A18 | 6c multi (B) | .50 | *.90* |
| **259** | A18 | 8c multi (R) | .50 | *.90* |
| **260** | A18 | 10c multi (B) | .50 | *.90* |
| **261** | A18 | 15c multi (B) | 2.50 | 1.10 |
| **262** | A19 | 20c multi (R) | 1.10 | 1.75 |
| *a.* | | Watermark 314 sideways | 6.00 | 3.25 |
| *b.* | | Watermark 314 upright | | *125.00* |
| **263** | A19 | 25c multi (B) | 1.75 | 1.10 |
| *a.* | | Watermark 314 | 30.00 | 47.50 |
| **264** | A19 | 35c multi (G) | 2.25 | 1.50 |
| *a.* | | Watermark 314 | 950.00 | 1,000. |
| **265** | A18 | 50c multi (B) | 2.25 | 1.90 |
| *a.* | | Watermark 314 | *950.00* | *1,000.* |
| **266** | A18 | $1 multi (R) | 5.50 | 8.25 |
| | | *Nos. 253-266 (14)* | 18.70 | 22.65 |

Location of overprint varies.

Maps of Tarawa and Funafuti A38

4c, Charts of Gilbert and Tuvalu Islands.

**1976, Jan. 2 Wmk. 373**

| | | | | |
|---|---|---|---|---|
| **267** | A38 | 4c multicolored | .45 | *1.00* |
| **268** | A38 | 35c multicolored | .80 | 1.60 |

Separation of the Gilbert and Ellice Islands.

M.V. Teraaka A39

3c, M.V. Tautunu. 4c, Moorish idol. 5c, Hibiscus. 6c, Reef egret. 7c, Roman Catholic Cathedral, Tarawa. 8c, Frangipani. 10c, Maneaba meeting house. 12c, Betio Harbor. 15c, Sunset. 20c, Marakei Atoll. 35c, Chapel, Tangintebu. 40c, Flamboyant tree. 50c, Hypolimnas bolina elliciana (butterfly). $1, Landing craft, Tabakea. $2, Gilbert Islands flag.

**1976, July 1 Litho. *Perf. 14***

| | | | | |
|---|---|---|---|---|
| **269** | A39 | 1c multicolored | .45 | *.60* |
| **270** | A39 | 3c multicolored | .60 | *.70* |
| **271** | A39 | 4c multicolored | .35 | *.60* |
| **272** | A39 | 5c multicolored | .40 | .25 |
| **273** | A39 | 6c multicolored | 1.50 | .90 |
| **274** | A39 | 7c multicolored | .25 | *.25* |
| **275** | A39 | 8c multicolored | .25 | *.25* |
| **276** | A39 | 10c multicolored | .25 | *.25* |
| **277** | A39 | 12c multicolored | .45 | .45 |
| **278** | A39 | 15c multicolored | .50 | .45 |
| **279** | A39 | 20c multicolored | .50 | .35 |
| **280** | A39 | 35c multicolored | .50 | .35 |
| **281** | A39 | 40c multicolored | .50 | .50 |
| **282** | A39 | 50c multicolored | 1.50 | *1.75* |
| **283** | A39 | $1 multicolored | 1.00 | *2.75* |
| **284** | A39 | $2 multicolored | 1.00 | *2.75* |
| | | *Nos. 269-284 (16)* | 10.00 | 13.15 |

Church A40

Children's Drawings: 15c, Feasting (vegetables, fish, pig, chicken), vert. 20c, Communal meeting house, vert. 35c, Children watching dancer.

**1976, Sept. 15 Litho. *Perf. 14***

| | | | | |
|---|---|---|---|---|
| **285** | A40 | 5c blue & multi | .25 | .25 |
| **286** | A40 | 15c green & multi | .60 | .25 |
| **287** | A40 | 20c rose & multi | .60 | .60 |
| **288** | A40 | 35c salmon & multi | .60 | .60 |
| | | *Nos. 285-288 (4)* | 2.05 | 1.70 |

Christmas.

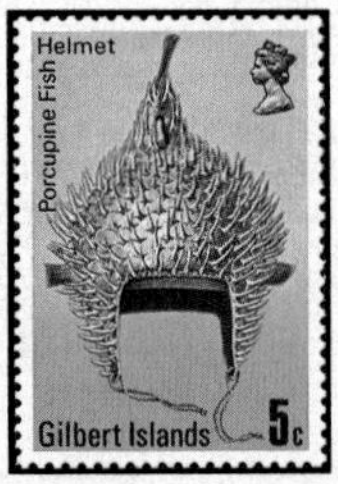


Porcupine Fish Helmet — A41

Artifacts: 15c, Shark's teeth dagger. 20c, Fighting gauntlet. 35c, Coconut body armor.

**1976, Dec. 6 Litho. *Perf. 13½x13***

| | | | | |
|---|---|---|---|---|
| **289** | A41 | 5c multicolored | .25 | .25 |
| **290** | A41 | 15c multicolored | .35 | .35 |
| **291** | A41 | 20c multicolored | .35 | .45 |
| **292** | A41 | 35c multicolored | .80 | .90 |
| *a.* | | Souvenir sheet of 4, #289-292 | 9.00 | 9.00 |
| | | *Nos. 289-292 (4)* | 1.75 | 1.95 |

Prince Charles, 1970 Visit — A42

Designs: 20c, Prince Philip, 1959 visit. 40c, Queen in coronation robes.

**1977, Feb. 7** *Perf. 14*

**293** A42 8c multicolored .25 .25
**294** A42 20c multicolored .25 .25
**295** A42 40c multicolored .40 .40
*Nos. 293-295 (3)* .90 .90

Reign of Queen Elizabeth II, 25th anniv.

John Byron and Dolphin, 1765
A43

Explorers: 15c, Edmund Fanning, 1798, and "Betsey." 20c, Fabian Gottlieb von Bellingshausen, 1820, and "Vostok." 35c, Charles Wilkes, 1838-42, and "Vincennes."

**1977, June 1** **Wmk. 373** *Perf. 14*

**296** A43 5c multicolored .65 *1.40*
**297** A43 15c multicolored .85 2.75
**298** A43 20c multicolored .85 *2.75*
**299** A43 35c multicolored 1.00 *4.25*
*Nos. 296-299 (4)* 3.35 *11.15*

Resolution and Discovery off Christmas Island — A44

15c, Capt. Cook's logbook entry, 1777. 20c, Capt. Cook on board ship. 40c, Capt. Cook landing on Christmas Island.

**1977, Sept. 12** **Litho.** *Perf. 14*

**300** A44 8c multi .50 .25
**301** A44 15c multi, horiz .50 .25
**302** A44 20c multi .75 .45
**303** A44 40c multi, horiz. .75 .80
*a.* Souvenir sheet of 4, #300-303 9.00 7.50
*Nos. 300-303 (4)* 2.50 1.75

Christmas; bicentenary of Capt. Cook's discovery of Christmas Island.

Scout Emblem, Beach Scene — A45

15c, Patrol meeting. 20c, Scout weaving mat. 40c, Canoeing.

**1977, Dec. 5** **Litho.** *Perf. 13*

**304** A45 8c gold & multi .35 .25
**305** A45 15c gold & multi, horiz. .40 .25
**306** A45 20c gold & multi, horiz. .40 .45
**307** A45 40c gold & multi .85 .90
*Nos. 304-307 (4)* 2.00 1.85

50th anniversary of Gilbert Islands Scouting.

Taurus with Aldebaran — A46

Night Sky over Gilbert Islands: 20c, Canis Major with Sirius. 25c, Scorpio with Antares. 45c, Orion with Betelgeuse and Rigel.

**1978, Feb. 20** **Litho.** *Perf. 14*

**308** A46 10c blue & black .45 .35
**309** A46 20c dp rose & black .50 .25
**310** A46 25c olive grn & black .50 .55
**311** A46 45c orange & black .75 1.00
*Nos. 308-311 (4)* 2.20 2.15

Common Design Types pictured following the introduction.

### Elizabeth II Coronation Anniversary

Common Design Types
Souvenir Sheet

**1978, Apr. 21** **Unwmk.**

**312** Sheet of 6 1.40 1.40
*a.* CD326 45c Unicorn of Scotland .25 .25
*b.* CD327 45c Elizabeth II .25 .25
*c.* CD328 45c Great frigate bird .25 .25

Arrows, Tarawa and Abemama Islands, School Insignia
A47

10c, Birds inscribed Bikenibeu, Abemama, Bairiki (school locations). 25c, Children greeting each other from maps of Islands. 45c, Abemama & Tarawa school buildings.

*Perf. 14x13½*

**1978, June 5** **Wmk. 373**

**313** A47 10c multicolored .25 .25
**314** A47 20c multicolored .25 .25
**315** A47 25c multicolored .25 .25
**316** A47 45c multicolored .25 .25
*Nos. 313-316 (4)* 1.00 1.00

King George V School, 25th anniversary of return from Abemama to Tarawa.

Garland
A48

Christmas: Various garlands.

**1978, Sept. 4** **Litho.** *Perf. 14*

**317** A48 10c multicolored .25 .25
**318** A48 20c multicolored .25 .25
**319** A48 25c multicolored .25 .25
**320** A48 45c multicolored .50 .35
*a.* Souvenir sheet of 4, #317-320, perf. 13x13½ 2.25 *3.50*
*Nos. 317-320 (4)* 1.25 1.10

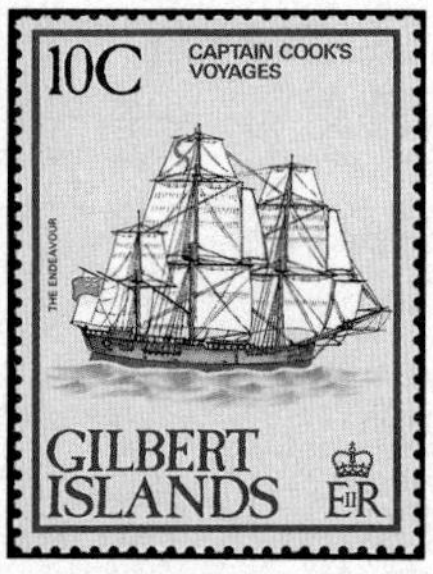


Endeavour
A49

Designs: 20c, Green turtle. 25c, Quadrant. 45c, Capt. Cook after Flaxman/Wedgwood medallion.

**1979, Jan. 15** **Litho.** *Perf. 11*

**321** A49 10c multicolored .30 .35
**322** A49 20c multicolored .40 .40
**323** A49 25c multicolored .40 .40

**Litho.; Embossed**

**324** A49 45c multicolored .40 .80
*Nos. 321-324 (4)* 1.50 1.95

Capt. Cook's voyages.

Gilbert Islands stamps were replaced in 1979 by those of Kiribati.

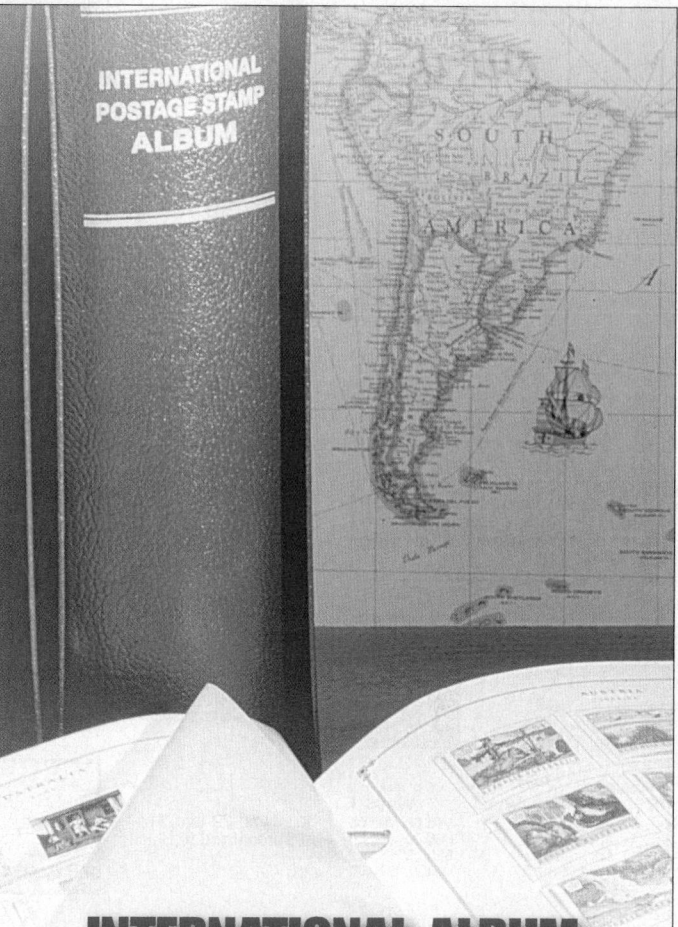

# GOLD COAST

'gōld 'kōst

LOCATION — West Africa between Dahomey and Ivory Coast
GOVT. — Former British Crown Colony
AREA — 91,843 sq. mi.
POP. — 3,089,000 (1952)
CAPITAL — Accra

Attached to the colony were Ashanti and Northern Territories (protectorate). Togoland, under British mandate, was also included for administrative purposes.
Gold Coast became the independent state of Ghana in 1957.
See Ghana.

12 Pence = 1 Shilling
20 Shillings = 1 Pound

**Catalogue values for unused stamps in this country are for Never Hinged items, beginning with Scott 128.**

Queen Victoria — A1

***Perf. 12½***

**1875, July Typo. Wmk. 1**
**1** A1 1p blue 550.00 95.00
**2** A1 4p red violet 525.00 140.00
**3** A1 6p orange 825.00 75.00
*Nos. 1-3 (3)* 1,900. 310.00

**1876-79 *Perf. 14***
**4** A1 ½p bister ('79) 90.00 32.50
**5** A1 1p blue 30.00 8.00
*a.* Half used as ½p on cover *4,500.*
**6** A1 2p green ('79) 110.00 11.50
*a.* Half used as 1p on cover *4,250.*
*b.* Quarter used as ½p on cover *7,500.*
**7** A1 4p red violet 250.00 7.25
*a.* Quarter used as 1p on cover *10,000.*
*b.* Half used as 2p on cover *7,750.*
**8** A1 6p orange 250.00 23.00
*a.* One sixth used as 1p on cover *13,000.*
*b.* Half used as 3p on cover *10,000.*
*Nos. 4-8 (5)* 730.00 82.25

**Handstamp Surcharged "1D" in Black**

**1883, May**
**9** A1 1p on 4p red violet

Some experts question the status of No. 9. One canceled example is in the British Museum. Another example is supposed to exist (Ferrari).

**1883-91 Wmk. 2**
**10** A1 ½p bister ('83) 210.00 75.00
**11** A1 ½p green ('84) 4.25 1.50
**12** A1 1p blue ('83) 1,000. 85.00
**13** A1 1p rose ('84) 4.75 .60
*a.* Half used as ½p on cover *5,000.*
**14** A1 2p gray ('84) 25.00 5.00
*b.* Half used as 1p on cover *5,000.*
**15** A1 2½p bl & org ('91) 9.00 .85
**16** A1 3p ol green ('89) 18.00 9.00
*a.* 3p olive bister 18.00 8.00
**17** A1 4p dull vio ('84) 18.00 3.25
*a.* 4p claret 23.00 5.50
*b.* Half used as 2p on cover —
**18** A1 6p orange ('89) 18.00 6.00
*a.* One sixth used as 1p on cover —
**19** A1 1sh purple ('88) 10.00 2.00
*a.* 1sh violet 37.50 15.00
**20** A1 2sh brown ('84) 60.00 17.50
*a.* 2sh yellow brown ('88) 95.00 42.50

No. 18 Surcharged in Black

**1889, Mar.**
**21** A1 1p on 6p orange 140.00 60.00
*a.* Double surcharge *4,500.*

The surcharge exists in two spacings between "PENNY" and bar: 7mm (normal) and 8mm.
No. 21a does not exist unused.

Queen Victoria — A3

**1889**
**22** A3 5sh lilac & ultra 75.00 21.00
**23** A3 10sh lilac & red 95.00 17.50
**24** A3 20sh green & red 3,250.

**1894**
**25** A3 20sh vio & blk, *red* 190.00 40.00

**1898-1902**
**26** A3 ½p lilac & green 4.75 1.25
**27** A3 1p lil & car rose 5.50 .60
**28** A3 2p lil & red ('02) 60.00 *175.00*
**29** A3 2½p lilac & ultra 8.50 8.50
**30** A3 3p lilac & yel 8.50 3.25
**31** A3 6p lilac & purple 9.00 3.00
**32** A3 1sh gray grn & blk 15.00 *28.00*
**33** A3 2sh gray grn & car rose 26.00 *29.00*
**34** A3 5sh grn & lil ('00) 75.00 45.00
**35** A3 10sh grn & brn ('00) 175.00 65.00
*Nos. 26-35 (10)* 387.25 *358.60*

Numerals of 2p, 3p and 6p of type A3 are in color on colorless tablet.

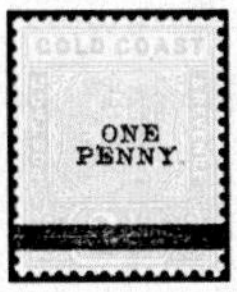


Nos. 29 and 31 Surcharged in Black

**1901, Oct. 6**
**36** A3 1p on 2½p lil & ultra 6.50 5.00
*a.* "ONE" omitted 1,200.
**37** A3 1p on 6p lilac & pur 6.50 4.25
*a.* "ONE" omitted 325.00 *650.00*

Beware of copies offered as No. 37a that have part of "ONE" showing.

King Edward VII — A5

**1902 Wmk. 2**
**38** A5 ½p violet & green 1.75 .50
**39** A5 1p vio & car rose 1.75 .25
**40** A5 2p vio & red org 29.00 8.50
**41** A5 2½p vio & ultra 5.50 *11.00*
**42** A5 3p vio & orange 4.50 2.00
**43** A5 6p violet & pur 5.00 2.25
**44** A5 1sh green & blk 17.00 4.00
**45** A5 2sh grn & car rose 18.00 28.00
**46** A5 5sh green & violet 60.00 *110.00*
**47** A5 10sh green & brn 75.00 *150.00*
**48** A5 20sh vio & blk, *red* 170.00 *210.00*
*Nos. 38-48 (11)* 387.50 *526.50*

Numerals of 2p, 3p, 6p and 2sh6p of type A5 are in color on colorless tablet.

**1904-07 Wmk. 3 Ordinary Paper**
**49** A5 ½p vio & grn ('07) 3.00 *8.50*
**50** A5 1p vio & car rose 15.00 .40
**51** A5 2p vio & red org 9.00 1.25
**52** A5 2½p vio & ultra ('06) 60.00 *65.00*
*53a* A5 3p vio & org ('06) 22.00 .60
**54** A5 6p vio & pur ('06) 80.00 4.50
**55** A5 2sh6p grn & yel ('06) 32.50 *130.00*
*Nos. 49-55 (7)* 221.50 *210.25*

Nos. 50, 51 and 54 exist on both ordinary and chalky paper. No. 55 is on chalky paper only. No. 53a, is the chalky-paper variety of the more expensive No. 53. For detailed listings, see the *Scott Classic Specialized Catalogue of Stamps and Covers.*

**1907-13 Ordinary Paper**
**56** A5 ½p green 9.00 .40
**57** A5 1p carmine 14.50 .50
**58** A5 2p gray ('09) 2.75 .55
**59** A5 2½p ultramarine 15.00 4.00

**Chalky Paper**
**60** A5 3p violet, *yel* ('09) 9.50 .65
**61** A5 6p dull violet ('08) 27.50 1.00
*a.* 6p dull violet & red violet 5.00 4.50
**62** A5 1sh blk, *grn* ('09) 20.00 .65
*63a* A5 2sh Ordinary paper 9.50 19.00
**64** A5 2sh6p blk & red, *blue* ('11) 37.50 *105.00*
**65** A5 5sh grn & red, *yel* ('13) 65.00 *225.00*
*Nos. 56-65 (9)* 200.75 *337.75*

No. 63 is on both ordinary and chalky paper.

King Edward VII — A6

**1908, Nov. Ordinary Paper**
**66** A6 1p carmine 6.00 .25

King George V
A7 A8

For description of Dies I and II, see front section of the Catalogue.

**Die I**

**1913-21 Ordinary Paper**
**69** A7 ½p green 3.00 1.75
**70** A8 1p carmine 1.50 .25
*a.* 1p scarlet 2.75 .60
**71** A7 2p gray 8.00 3.00
**72** A7 2½p ultramarine 11.00 1.50

**Chalky Paper**
**73** A7 3p vio, *yel* ('15) 3.25 1.00
*a.* Die II ('19) 60.00 6.00
**74** A7 6p dull vio & red vio 7.50 2.75
**75** A7 1sh black, *green* 4.50 1.75
*a.* 1sh black, *emerald* 2.50 2.50
*b.* 1sh black, *bl grn,* ol back 11.00 .95
*c.* Die II ('21) 1.75 .60
**76** A7 2sh vio & bl, *bl* 10.50 4.00
*a.* Die II ('21) 190.00 77.50
**77** A7 2sh6p blk & red, *bl* 10.00 *16.00*
*a.* Die II ('21) 27.50 *50.00*
**78** A7 5sh grn & red, *yel* 22.50 *65.00*
*a.* Die II ('21) 37.50 *160.00*
**79** A7 10sh grn & red, *grn* ('16) 60.00 *110.00*
*a.* 10sh grn & red, *emer* 40.00 *180.00*
*b.* 10sh grn & red, *bl grn,* ol back 28.00 *85.00*
**80** A7 20sh vio & blk, *red* ('16) 150.00 100.00

**Surface-colored Paper**
**81** A7 3p violet, *yel* 2.10 1.00
**82** A7 5sh grn & red, *yel* 22.00 *72.50*
*Nos. 69-82 (14)* 315.85 *380.50*

Numerals of 2p, 3p, 6p and 2sh6p of type A7 are in color on plain tablet.

**Die II**

**1921-25 Ordinary Paper Wmk. 4**
**83** A7 ½p green ('22) 1.00 .60
**84** A8 1p brown ('22) .90 .25
**85** A7 1½p carmine ('22) 2.10 .25
**86** A7 2p gray 2.10 .40
**87** A7 2½p orange ('23) 1.75 *11.00*
**88** A7 3p ultra ('22) 2.10 1.00

**Chalky Paper**
**89** A7 6p dl vio & red vio ('22) 3.25 *3.50*
**90** A7 1sh blk, *emer* ('25) 5.50 4.00
**91** A7 2sh vio & bl, *bl* ('24) 4.00 *4.00*
**92** A7 2sh6p blk & red, *bl* ('25) 8.50 *35.00*
**93** A7 5sh grn & red, *yel* ('25) 18.00 *77.50*

**Die I**
**94** A7 15sh dl vio & grn ('21) 180.00 *475.00*
*a.* Die II ('25) 140.00 *475.00*
**95** A7 £2 grn & org 500.00 *1,300.*
*Nos. 83-95 (13)* 729.20 *1,912.*

Christiansborg Castle — A9

**1928, Aug. 1 Photo. *Perf. 13½x14½***
**98** A9 ½p green 1.20 .50
**99** A9 1p red brown 1.00 .25
**100** A9 1½p scarlet 3.00 1.75
**101** A9 2p slate 3.00 .25
**102** A9 2½p yellow 3.25 *4.25*
**103** A9 3p ultramarine 3.00 .50
**104** A9 6p dull vio & blk 3.50 .50
**105** A9 1sh red org & blk 4.50 1.00
**106** A9 2sh purple & black 30.00 6.00
**107** A9 5sh ol green & car 72.50 52.50
*Nos. 98-107 (10)* 124.95 67.50

Common Design Types pictured following the introduction.

**Silver Jubilee Issue**
Common Design Type

**1935, May 6 Engr. *Perf. 11x12***
**108** CD301 1p black & ultra 1.00 .60
**109** CD301 3p ultra & brown 3.25 *7.25*
**110** CD301 6p indigo & green 17.00 *22.50*
**111** CD301 1sh brn vio & indigo 5.50 *32.50*
*Nos. 108-111 (4)* 26.75 *62.85*
Set, never hinged 40.00

**Coronation Issue**
Common Design Type

**1937, May 12 *Perf. 11x11½***
**112** CD302 1p brown .85 *2.50*
**113** CD302 2p dark gray 1.00 *4.75*
**114** CD302 3p deep ultra 1.25 *2.75*
*Nos. 112-114 (3)* 3.10 *10.00*
Set, never hinged 6.00

A10

George VI and Christiansborg Castle — A11

**1938-41 Wmk. 4 *Perf. 12***
**115** A10 ½p green .35 *.50*
**116** A10 1p red brown .35 .25
**117** A10 1½p rose red .35 *.50*
**118** A10 2p gray black .35 .25
**119** A10 3p ultramarine .35 .35
**120** A10 4p rose lilac .70 *1.25*
**121** A10 6p rose violet .70 .25
**122** A10 9p red orange 1.10 .55
**123** A11 1sh gray grn & blk 1.40 .65
**124** A11 1sh3p turq grn & red brown 1.75 .50
**125** A11 2sh dk vio & dp bl 4.75 *19.00*
**126** A11 5sh rose car & ol green 9.25 *22.00*
**127** A11 10sh purple & black 6.50 *29.00*
*Nos. 115-127 (13)* 27.90 *75.05*
Set, never hinged 40.00

Issued: 10sh, July, 1940; 1sh3p, Apr. 12, 1941; others, Apr. 1.

**Catalogue values for unused stamps in this section, from this point to the end of the section, are for Never Hinged items.**

**Peace Issue**
Common Design Type

**1946, Oct. 14 *Perf. 13½***
**128** CD303 2p purple .25 .25
*a.* Perf. 13½x14 19.00 3.00
**129** CD303 4p deep red violet 1.60 *3.50*
*a.* Perf. 13½x14 3.50 3.75

A12

A13

½p, Mounted Constable. 1p, Christiansborg Castle. 1½p, Emblem of Joint Provincial Council. 2p, Talking Drums. 2½p, Map. 3p, Manganese mine. 4p, Lake Bosumtwi. 6p, Cacao farmer. 1sh, Breaking cacao pods. 2sh, Trooping the colors. 5sh, Surfboats. 10sh, Forest.

**1948, July 1 Engr. *Perf. 12***

| | | | | | |
|---|---|---|---|---|---|
| **130** | A12 | ½p | emerald | .25 | *.40* |
| **131** | A13 | 1p | deep blue | .25 | .25 |
| **132** | A13 | 1½p | red | 1.50 | 1.00 |
| **133** | A12 | 2p | chocolate | .65 | .25 |
| **134** | A13 | 2½p | lt brown & red | 2.50 | *4.50* |
| **135** | A13 | 3p | blue | 5.00 | 1.00 |
| **136** | A13 | 4p | dk car rose | 4.25 | 4.00 |
| **137** | A12 | 6p | org & black | .40 | .40 |
| **138** | A13 | 1sh | red org & blk | 2.25 | .40 |
| **139** | A13 | 2sh | rose car & ol brn | 6.50 | 4.00 |
| **140** | A13 | 5sh | gray & red vio | 35.00 | 11.00 |
| **141** | A12 | 10sh | ol grn & black | 16.00 | 11.00 |
| | | | *Nos. 130-141 (12)* | 74.55 | 38.20 |

### Silver Wedding Issue

Common Design Types

**1948, Dec. 20 Photo. *Perf. 14x14½***

| | | | | | |
|---|---|---|---|---|---|
| **142** | CD304 | 1½p | scarlet | .25 | .25 |

**Engraved; Name Typographed**

***Perf. 11½x11***

| | | | | | |
|---|---|---|---|---|---|
| **143** | CD305 | 10sh | dk brn olive | 29.00 | 29.00 |

### UPU Issue

Common Design Types

**Engr.; Name Typo. on 2½p and 3p**

**1949, Oct. 10 *Perf. 13½, 11x11½***

| | | | | | |
|---|---|---|---|---|---|
| **144** | CD306 | 2p | red brown | .25 | .25 |
| **145** | CD307 | 2½p | deep orange | 1.90 | *4.50* |
| **146** | CD308 | 3p | indigo | .45 | *1.75* |
| **147** | CD309 | 1sh | blue green | .45 | .45 |
| | | | *Nos. 144-147 (4)* | 3.05 | *6.95* |

Map of West Africa — A14

Mounted Constable — A15

Designs: 1p, Christiansborg Castle. 1½p, Emblem of Joint Provincial Council. 2p, Talking drums. 3p, Manganese mine. 4p, Lake Bosumtwi. 6p, Cacao farmer. 1sh, Breaking cacao pods. 2sh, Trooping the colors. 5sh, Surfboats. 10sh, Forest.

***Perf. 11½x12, 12x11½***

**1952-54 Engr.**

| | | | | | |
|---|---|---|---|---|---|
| **148** | A14 | ½p | yel brn & car | .25 | .25 |
| **149** | A14 | 1p | deep blue | .40 | .25 |
| **150** | A14 | 1½p | green | .40 | *1.50* |
| **151** | A15 | 2p | chocolate | .40 | .25 |
| **152** | A15 | 2½p | red | .45 | *1.00* |
| **153** | A14 | 3p | rose | .95 | .25 |
| **154** | A14 | 4p | deep blue | .45 | *.45* |
| **155** | A15 | 6p | orange & black | .50 | .25 |
| **156** | A14 | 1sh | red org & black | 1.50 | .25 |
| **157** | A14 | 2sh | rose car & ol brn | 13.00 | 1.00 |
| **158** | A14 | 5sh | gray & red vio | 23.00 | 6.00 |
| **159** | A15 | 10sh | olive grn & blk | 22.50 | 15.00 |
| | | | *Nos. 148-159 (12)* | 63.80 | 26.45 |

Nos. 148-149 exist in vertical coils.

Issued: 2½p, 12/19/52; ½p, 1½p, 3p, 4p, 4/1/53; 1p, 2p, 6p, 1sh-10sh, 3/1/54.

For overprints see Ghana #5-13, 25-27.

### Coronation Issue

Common Design Type

**1953, June 2 *Perf. 13½x13***

| | | | | | |
|---|---|---|---|---|---|
| **160** | CD312 | 2p | dk brown & black | .95 | .25 |

### POSTAGE DUE STAMPS

D1

**1923 Typo. Wmk. 4 *Perf. 14***

**Yellowish Toned Paper**

| | | | | | |
|---|---|---|---|---|---|
| **J1** | D1 | ½p | black | 19.00 | *125.00* |
| **J2** | D1 | 1p | black | .95 | *1.50* |
| **J3** | D1 | 2p | black | 13.00 | *3.50* |
| **J4** | D1 | 3p | black | 22.50 | *3.00* |
| | | | *Nos. J1-J4 (4)* | 55.45 | *133.00* |

**1951-52 Typo. Wmk. 4 *Perf. 14***

**Chalk-Surfaced Paper**

| | | | | | |
|---|---|---|---|---|---|
| **J5** | D1 | 2p | black | 3.75 | *27.50* |
| *a.* | | | Wmk. 4a (error) | 600.00 | |
| *b.* | | | Wmk. 4, crown missing (error) | 1,100. | |
| **J6** | D1 | 3p | black | 3.25 | *26.00* |
| *a.* | | | Wmk. 4a (error) | 550.00 | |
| *b.* | | | Wmk. 4, crown missing (error) | 1,100. | |
| **J7** | D1 | 6p | black ('52) | 2.10 | *13.00* |
| *a.* | | | Wmk. 4a (error) | 1,000. | |
| *b.* | | | Wmk. 4, crown missing (error) | 1,600. | |
| **J8** | D1 | 1sh | black ('52) | 2.10 | *80.00* |
| *a.* | | | Wmk. 4a (error) | 1,200. | |
| | | | *Nos. J5-J8 (4)* | 11.20 | *146.50* |

Issued: #J7-J8, 10/1.

### WAR TAX STAMP

Regular Issue of 1913 Surcharged

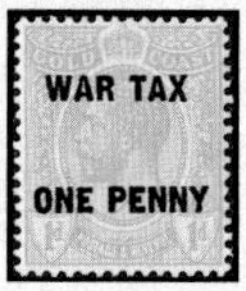


**1918, June Wmk. 3 *Perf. 14***

| | | | | | |
|---|---|---|---|---|---|
| **MR1** | A8 | 1p on 1p scarlet | 3.25 | 1.00 |

## GRAND COMORO

'grand 'kä-mə-ˌrō

LOCATION — One of the Comoro Islands in the Mozambique Channel between Madagascar and Mozambique.

GOVT. — French Colony

AREA — 385 sq. mi. (approx.)

POP. — 50,000 (approx.)

CAPITAL — Moroni

100 Centimes = 1 Franc

See Comoro Islands.

Navigation and Commerce — A1

***Perf. 14x13½***

**1897-1907 Typo. Unwmk.**

**Name of Colony in Blue or Carmine**

| | | | | | |
|---|---|---|---|---|---|
| **1** | A1 | 1c | blk, *lil bl* | 1.25 | 1.25 |
| **2** | A1 | 2c | brn, *buff* | 2.00 | 2.00 |
| **3** | A1 | 4c | claret, *lav* | 2.50 | 2.50 |
| **4** | A1 | 5c | grn, *grnsh* | 4.50 | 4.50 |
| **5** | A1 | 10c | blk, *lavender* | 10.00 | 6.50 |
| **6** | A1 | 10c | red ('00) | 11.00 | 11.00 |
| **7** | A1 | 15c | blue, quadrille paper | 20.00 | 14.50 |
| **8** | A1 | 15c | gray, *lt gray* ('00) | 11.00 | 11.00 |
| **9** | A1 | 20c | red, *grn* | 12.50 | 12.50 |
| **10** | A1 | 25c | blk, *rose* | 18.50 | 17.00 |
| **11** | A1 | 25c | blue ('00) | 21.50 | 21.50 |
| **12** | A1 | 30c | brn, *bister* | 22.50 | 20.00 |
| **13** | A1 | 35c | blk, *yel* ('06) | 21.00 | 20.00 |
| **14** | A1 | 40c | red, *straw* | 22.50 | 20.00 |
| **15** | A1 | 45c | blk, *gray grn* ('07) | 80.00 | 67.50 |
| **16** | A1 | 50c | car, *rose* | 45.00 | 24.00 |
| **17** | A1 | 50c | brn, *bluish* ('00) | 47.50 | 45.00 |
| **18** | A1 | 75c | dp vio, *org* | 60.00 | 40.00 |
| **19** | A1 | 1fr | brnz grn, *straw* | 42.50 | 36.00 |
| | | | *Nos. 1-19 (19)* | 455.75 | 376.75 |

Perf. 13½x14 stamps are counterfeits.

**Issues of 1897-1907 Surcharged in Black or Carmine**

**1912**

| | | | | |
|---|---|---|---|---|
| **20** | A1 | 5c on 2c brn, *buff* | 1.50 | 1.50 |
| *a.* | | Inverted surcharge | 240.00 | |
| **21** | A1 | 5c on 4c cl, *lav* (C) | 1.60 | 1.60 |
| **22** | A1 | 5c on 15c blue (C) | 1.50 | 1.50 |
| **23** | A1 | 5c on 20c red, *grn* | 1.75 | 1.75 |
| **24** | A1 | 5c on 25c blk, *rose* (C) | 1.60 | 1.60 |
| **25** | A1 | 5c on 30c brn, *bis* (C) | 1.75 | 1.75 |
| **26** | A1 | 10c on 40c red, *straw* | 2.00 | 2.00 |
| **27** | A1 | 10c on 45c blk, *gray grn* (C) | 2.75 | 2.75 |
| **28** | A1 | 10c on 50c car, *rose* | 2.50 | 2.50 |
| **29** | A1 | 10c on 75c dp vio, *org* | 3.00 | 3.00 |
| | | *Nos. 20-29 (10)* | 19.95 | 19.95 |

Two spacings between the surcharged numerals are found on Nos. 20-29. For detailed listings, see the *Scott Classic Specialized Catalogue of Stamps and Covers.*

Nos. 20-29 were available for use in Madagascar and the entire Comoro archipelago.

Stamps of Grand Comoro were superseded by those of Madagascar, and in 1950 by those of Comoro Islands.

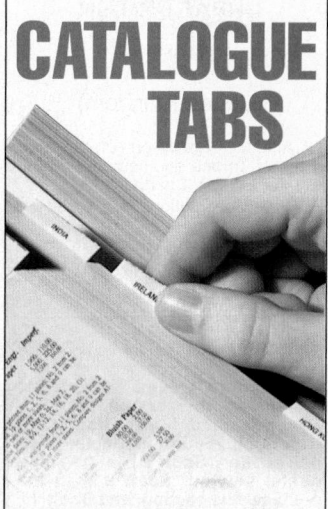

## GREAT BRITAIN

'grāt 'bri-tən

(United Kingdom)

LOCATION — Northwest of the continent of Europe and separated from it by the English Channel
GOVT. — Constitutional monarchy
AREA — 94,511 sq. mi.
POP. — 59,128,000 (1998 est.)
CAPITAL — London

12 Pence = 1 Shilling
20 Shillings = 1 Pound
100 Pence = 1 Pound (1970)

**Catalogue values for unused stamps in this country are for Never Hinged items, beginning with Scott 264 in the regular postage section, Scott B1 in the semi-postal section. Scott J34 in the postage due section, and Scott 93, Scott 246 and Scott 521 in British Offices in Morocco. All of the listings in British Offices — Middle East Forces, for Use in Eritrea, for Use in Somalia and for Use in Tripolitania are valued as never-hinged.**

The letters in the corners of the early postage issues indicate position in the horizontal and vertical rows in which that particular specimen was placed.

In the case of illustration A1, this stamp came from the 15th horizontal row (O) and was the second stamp (B) from the left in that row. The left corner refers to the horizontal row and the right corner to the vertical row. Thus no two stamps on the plate bore the same combination of letters.

When four corner letters are used (starting in 1858), the lower ones indicate the stamp's position in the sheet and the top ones are the same letters reversed.

### Watermarks

Wmk. 18 — Small Crown

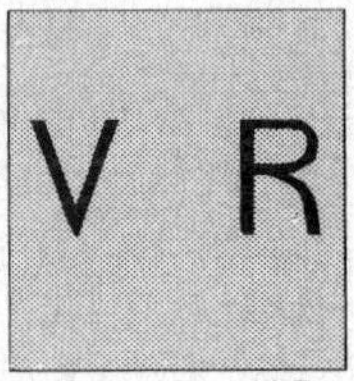
Wmk. 19 — V R

Wmk. 20 — Large Crown

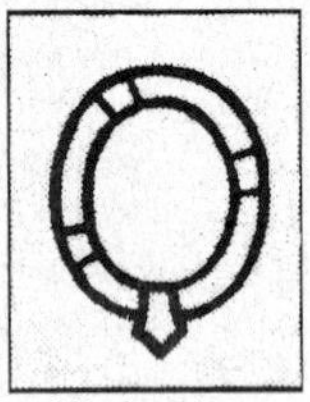
Wmk. 21 — Small Garter

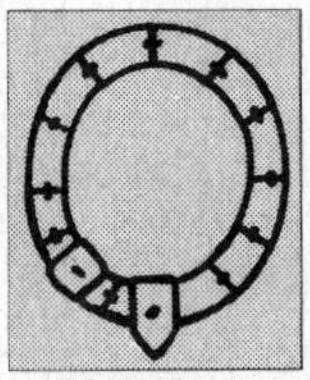
Wmk. 22 — Medium Garter

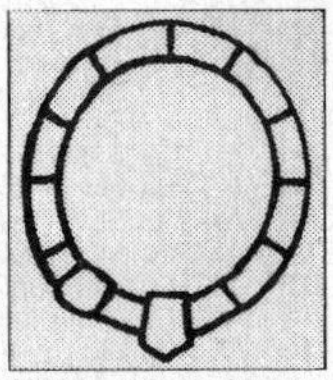
Wmk. 23 — Large Garter

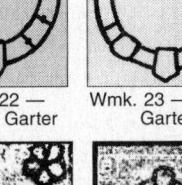

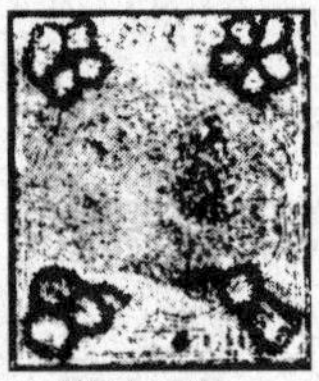
Wmk. 24 — Heraldic Emblems

Wmk. 25 — Spray of Rose

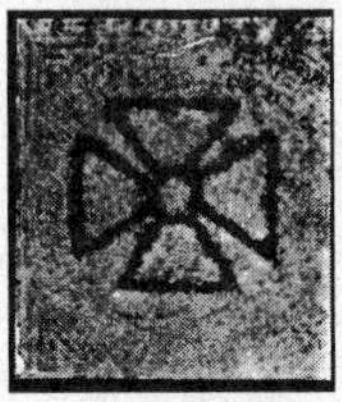
Wmk. 26 — Maltese Cross

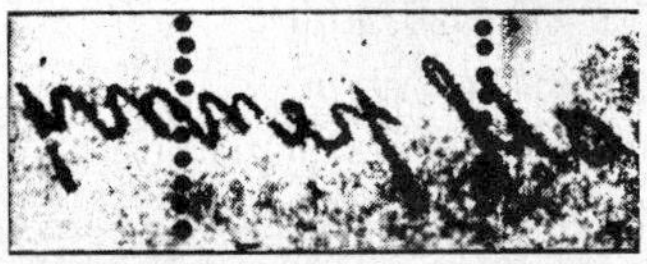
Wmk. 27 — "Half Penny" in Script

Wmk. 28 — Anchor

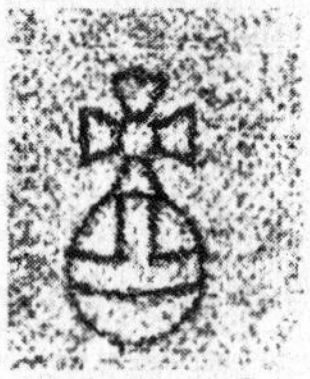
Wmk. 29 — Orb

Wmk. 30 — Imperial Crown

Wmk. 31 — Anchor

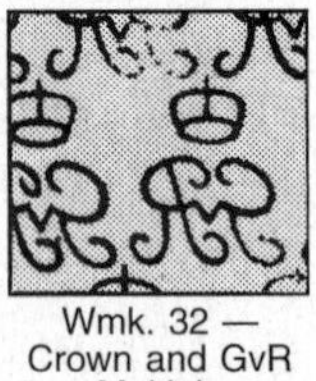
Wmk. 32 — Crown and GvR Multiple

Wmk. 33 — Crown and GvR

Wmk. 33 — In the normal watermark (sometimes termed the "repeated" watermark) the letters "GvR" are extended. The royal cyphers are placed one above the other and usually two appear on each stamp. In the multiple watermark the letters "GvR" are condensed, the cyphers are smaller and are so placed that those in each succeeding row are below the spaces between the cyphers in the row above.

Wmk. 34 — Large Crown and GvR

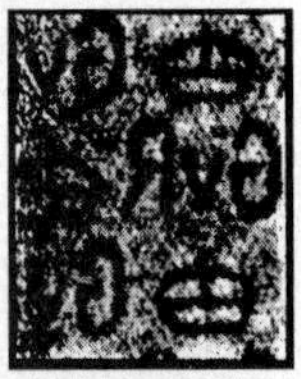
Wmk. 35 — Crown and Block GvR Multiple

Wmk. 219 — Large Crown and GvR

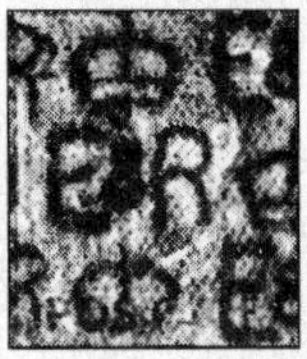
Wmk. 250 — Crown and E8R Multiple

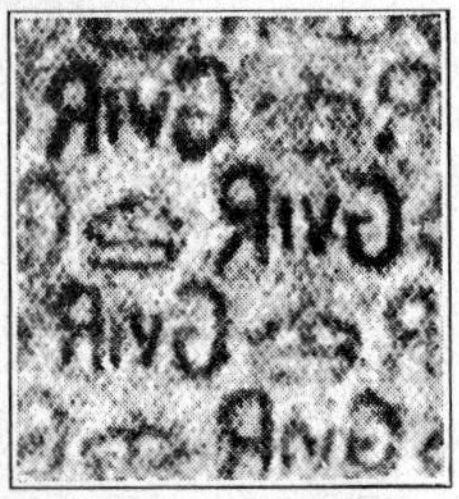
Wmk. 251 — Crown and GviR Multiple

Wmk. 259 — Crown and Large G VI R

Wmk. 298 — Tudor Crown and E 2 R Multiple

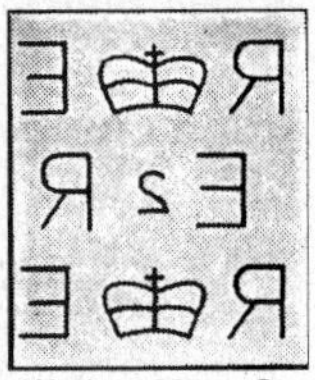
Wmk. 308 — St. Edward's Crown and E 2 R Multiple

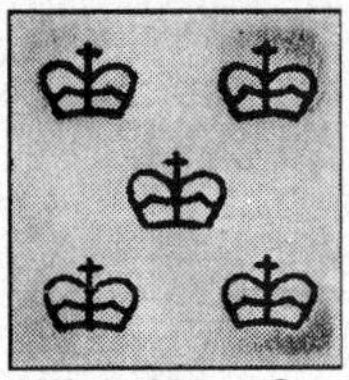
Wmk. 322 — St. Edward's Crown Multiple

Wmk. 401

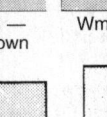

Values for unused stamps are for examples with original gum as defined in the catalogue introduction. Very fine stamps will be sound and have fresh color, but expect Nos. 8-56, 58-73, 78-89, 94-95, and the Official overprints on these designs, to have perforations touching the design on at least one side due to the narrow spacing of the stamps on the plates. Stamps with perfs clear of the design on all four sides range from scarce to very rare and command substantially higher prices.

Cancellations on stamps from the 1847 issue to the 1884 issues, and in many cases beyond, are usually heavy. Values quoted are for stamps with better than average cancellations. Stamps with circular date stamps (especially those with a steel cds) range from scarce to very rare and command much higher prices.

Queen Victoria — A1

**1840, May Wmk. 18 Engr. *Imperf.***
**White Paper**

| | | | | |
|---|---|---|---|---|
| 1 | A1 | 1p black | 10,000. | 300.00 |
| 2 | A1 | 2p blue | 32,000. | 700.00 |

No. 1 was printed from 11 plates; No. 2 from 2 plates. The 1p plates 1, 2, 5, 6, 8 and 9 can be found in two or more states. Stamp values are for the most common plates.

Issue dates: 1p, May 6; 2p, May 7.

See Nos. 3, 8-9, 11-12, 14, 16, 18, 20, O1.

Compare designs A1-A2 with A8, A10.

A1a

A2

**1841 Bluish Paper**

3 A1a 1p red brown 550.00 24.00
c. Rouletted 12 *25,000.*
d. "A" missing in lower right corner (position BA, P77) — *24,000.*
4 A2 2p blue 4,500. 85.00
c. 2p violet blue *20,000.* 1,400.

No. 3 exists on silk thread paper, but was not regularly issued.
No. 4 was printed from two plates.
See Nos. 10, 13, 15, 17, 19, 21.
For shades, see the *Scott Classic Specialized Catalogue of Stamps and Covers.*

During the reigns of Victoria and Edward VII, many color trials were produced on perfed, gummed and watermarked papers.

Nos. 5-7 were printed one stamp at a time on the sheet. Space between the stamps usually is very small. Impressions that touch, or even overlap, are numerous.

Stamps with margins ½mm beyond the outer frame are considered as having full margins.

Values for Nos. 5-6 are for examples with complete frames and clear white margins on all four sides. Values for No. 7 are for examples with complete design but not necessarily clear margins around the design.

A3

A3a

**With Vertical Silk Threads**

**1847 Embossed Unwmk.**

5 A3 1sh pale green 17,500. 850.00
a. 1sh green 17,500. 900.00
Cut to shape 25.00

Die numbers (on base of bust): 1 and 2.

**1848**

6 A3a 10p red brown 8,000. 1,200.
Cut to shape *500.00* 35.00

Die numbers (on base of bust): 1, 2, 3, 4; also without die number.

A4

**1854 Wmk. 19**

7 A4 6p red violet 15,000. 900.00
a. 6p dull violet 15,000. 900.00
b. 6p deep violet *20,000.* 3,250.
Cut to shape 20.00

**1854-55 Wmk. 18 Engr. *Perf. 16***
**Bluish Paper**

8 A1 1p red brown 325.00 25.00
a. 1p yellow brown 375.00 45.00
9 A1 1p red brown, re-engraved ('55) 400.00 60.00
a. Imperf. —
10 A2 2p blue 4,000. 90.00
a. 2p pale blue 4,500. 100.00

In the re-engraved 1p stamps, the lines of the features are deeper and stronger, the fillet behind the ear more distinct, the shading about the eye heavier, the line of the nostril is turned downward at right and an indentation of color appears between lower lip and chin.

***Perf. 14***

11 A1 1p red brown ('55) 625.00 80.00
a. Imperf. —
12 A1 1p red brown, re-engraved ('55) 600.00 67.50
a. 1p org brn, re-engraved 1,700. 150.00
13 A2 2p blue ('55) 9,000. 200.00
a. Imperf. (P5) *7,000.*

Wmk. 20 exists in two types. The first includes two vertical prongs, rising from the top of the crown's headband and extending into each of the two balancing midsections. The second type (illustrated), introduced in 1861, omits these prongs.

**1855 Wmk. 20 *Perf. 16***
**Bluish Paper**

14 A1 1p red brown, re-engraved 2,000. 110.00
15 A2 2p blue 14,000. 400.00
a. Imperf. (P5) *7,500.*

Some specialists regard No. 15a as a proof.

**1855 Bluish Paper *Perf. 14***

16 A1 1p red brown, re-engraved 225.00 21.00
a. 1p orange brn, re-engraved 650.00 62.50
b. 1p brown rose, re-engraved 300.00 50.00
c. Imperf. 4,250. 3,500.
17 A2 2p blue 2,250. 60.00

**1856-58 White Paper *Perf. 16***

18 A1 1p rose red, re-engraved ('57) 2,400. 72.50
19 A2 2p blue, thin lines ('58) 12,000. 375.00

***Perf. 14***

20 A1 1p rose red, re-engraved ('57) 60.00 11.50
a. Imperf. 4,500. 3,250.
b. 1p red brown, re-engraved 1,500. 340.00
21 A2 2p blue, thin lines ('57) 2,850. 67.50
a. Imperf. — *8,000.*
b. Vertical pair, imperf horiz. —

Queen Victoria — A5

**1855 Typo. Wmk. 21**

22 A5 4p rose, *bluish* 7,250. 375.00
23 A5 4p rose, *white* — 850.00

Compare design A5 with A11, A16, A31.

**1856 Wmk. 22**

24 A5 4p rose, *bluish* *9,000.* 450.
25 A5 4p rose, *white* 8,250. 375.

**1857 Wmk. 23**

26 A5 4p rose, *white* 1,300. 110.00

A6

A7

**1856 Wmk. 24**

27 A6 6p lilac 1,100. 100.00
a. 6p deep lilac 1,500. 130.00
b. Wmk. 3 roses and shamrock
28 A7 1sh green 2,500. 275.00
a. 1sh pale green 2,500. 260.00
b. 1sh deep green 4,750. 425.00
e. Imperf —

Compare design A6 with A13, A18, A22. Compare A7 with A15, A21, A29.

A8

A9

**1858-69 Engr. Wmk. 20 *Perf. 14***

29 A8 2p deep blue (P9) 325.00 22.50
Plate 7 1,400. 52.50
Plate 8 1,300. 37.50
Plate 12 2,200. 125.00
b. Imperf. (P9) *8,500.*

Plate numbers are contained in the scroll work at the sides of the stamp.

**Lines Above and Below Head Thinner**

30 A8 2p blue ('69) (P13) 325.00 32.50
Plate 14 425.00 32.50
Plate 15 400.00 32.50
a. Imperf. (P13) *8,500.*

**1860-70**

31 A9 1½p lilac rose, *bluish* (P1) ('60) 7,000.
32 A9 1½p dull rose ('70) (P3) 400.00 60.00
a. 1½p lake red 500.00 60.00
Plate 1 600.00 80.00
c. Imperf (P1, 3) *8,500.*

The 1½p stamps from Plate 1 carry no plate number. The Plate 3 number is in the border at each side above the lower corner letters.
No. 31 was prepared but not issued.

Queen Victoria — A10

**1864**

33 A10 1p rose red 19.00 2.50
a. 1p brick red 19.00 2.50
b. 1p lake red 19.00 2.50
c. Imperf. (P116, see footnote) *1,800.* *1,000.*

Plate numbers are contained in the scroll work at the sides of the stamp.
No. 33 was printed from 1864 to 1879.
Thirty-nine plate numbers besides Plate 116 (No. 33c) are also known imperforate and used. Values for used examples start at $450.
Stamps from plate 177 have been altered and offered as plate 77.

**Plate Numbers**

| | | |
|---|---|---|
| Plate 71 | 42.50 | 3.75 |
| Plate 72 | 47.50 | 4.75 |
| Plate 73 | 47.50 | 3.75 |
| Plate 74 | 47.50 | 2.50 |
| Plate 76 | 42.50 | 2.50 |
| Plate 77 | — | *175,000.* |
| Plate 78 | 110.00 | 2.50 |
| Plate 79 | 37.50 | 2.50 |
| Plate 80 | 52.50 | 2.50 |
| Plate 81 | 52.50 | 3.00 |
| Plate 82 | 110.00 | 4.75 |
| Plate 83 | 140.00 | 8.50 |
| Plate 84 | 70.00 | 3.00 |
| Plate 85 | 47.50 | 4.00 |
| Plate 86 | 60.00 | 4.75 |
| Plate 87 | 37.50 | 2.50 |
| Plate 88 | 170.00 | 9.00 |
| Plate 89 | 50.00 | 2.50 |
| Plate 90 | 50.00 | 2.50 |
| Plate 91 | 65.00 | 7.00 |
| Plate 92 | 42.50 | 2.50 |
| Plate 93 | 60.00 | 2.50 |
| Plate 94 | 52.50 | 6.00 |
| Plate 95 | 47.50 | 2.50 |
| Plate 96 | 52.50 | 2.50 |
| Plate 97 | 47.50 | 4.25 |
| Plate 98 | 60.00 | 7.00 |
| Plate 99 | 65.00 | 6.00 |
| Plate 100 | 70.00 | 3.00 |
| Plate 101 | 70.00 | 10.50 |
| Plate 102 | 52.50 | 2.50 |
| Plate 103 | 60.00 | 4.25 |
| Plate 104 | 85.00 | 6.00 |
| Plate 105 | 105.00 | 8.50 |
| Plate 106 | 65.00 | 2.50 |
| Plate 107 | 70.00 | 8.50 |
| Plate 108 | 90.00 | 3.00 |
| Plate 109 | 95.00 | 4.25 |
| Plate 110 | 70.00 | 10.75 |
| Plate 111 | 60.00 | 3.00 |
| Plate 112 | 80.00 | 3.00 |
| Plate 113 | 60.00 | 15.00 |
| Plate 114 | 300.00 | 15.00 |
| Plate 115 | 110.00 | 3.00 |
| Plate 116 | 85.00 | 10.75 |
| Plate 117 | 52.50 | 2.50 |
| Plate 118 | 60.00 | 2.50 |
| Plate 119 | 52.50 | 2.50 |
| Plate 120 | 29.00 | 2.50 |
| Plate 121 | 47.50 | 10.75 |
| Plate 122 | 19.00 | 2.50 |
| Plate 123 | 47.50 | 2.50 |
| Plate 124 | 35.00 | 2.50 |
| Plate 125 | 47.50 | 2.50 |
| Plate 127 | 65.00 | 3.00 |
| Plate 129 | 47.50 | 9.50 |
| Plate 130 | 65.00 | 3.00 |
| Plate 131 | 75.00 | 20.00 |
| Plate 132 | 160.00 | 27.50 |
| Plate 133 | 135.00 | 10.75 |
| Plate 134 | 19.00 | 2.25 |
| Plate 135 | 105.00 | 30.00 |
| Plate 136 | 105.00 | 24.00 |
| Plate 137 | 35.00 | 3.00 |
| Plate 138 | 24.00 | 2.50 |
| Plate 139 | 70.00 | 20.00 |
| Plate 140 | 24.00 | 2.50 |
| Plate 141 | 135.00 | 10.75 |
| Plate 142 | 80.00 | 30.00 |
| Plate 143 | 70.00 | 17.00 |
| Plate 144 | 105.00 | 24.00 |
| Plate 145 | 37.50 | 2.50 |
| Plate 146 | 47.50 | 7.00 |
| Plate 147 | 60.00 | 3.75 |
| Plate 148 | 47.50 | 3.75 |
| Plate 149 | 47.50 | 7.00 |
| Plate 150 | 19.00 | 2.50 |
| Plate 151 | 70.00 | 10.75 |
| Plate 152 | 70.00 | 6.50 |
| Plate 153 | 115.00 | 10.75 |
| Plate 154 | 60.00 | 2.50 |
| Plate 155 | 60.00 | 2.50 |
| Plate 156 | 52.50 | 2.50 |
| Plate 157 | 60.00 | 2.50 |
| Plate 158 | 37.50 | 2.50 |
| Plate 159 | 37.50 | 2.50 |
| Plate 160 | 37.50 | 2.50 |
| Plate 161 | 70.00 | 8.50 |
| Plate 162 | 60.00 | 8.50 |
| Plate 163 | 60.00 | 3.75 |
| Plate 164 | 60.00 | 3.75 |
| Plate 165 | 52.50 | 2.50 |
| Plate 166 | 52.50 | 7.00 |
| Plate 167 | 52.50 | 2.50 |
| Plate 168 | 60.00 | 9.50 |
| Plate 169 | 70.00 | 8.50 |
| Plate 170 | 42.50 | 2.50 |
| Plate 171 | 19.00 | 2.50 |
| Plate 172 | 37.50 | 2.50 |
| Plate 173 | 80.00 | 10.75 |
| Plate 174 | 37.50 | 2.50 |
| Plate 175 | 70.00 | 4.25 |
| Plate 176 | 70.00 | 3.00 |
| Plate 177 | 47.50 | 2.50 |
| Plate 178 | 70.00 | 4.25 |
| Plate 179 | 60.00 | 2.50 |
| Plate 180 | 70.00 | 6.00 |
| Plate 181 | 52.50 | 2.50 |
| Plate 182 | 105.00 | 6.00 |
| Plate 183 | 65.00 | 3.75 |
| Plate 184 | 37.50 | 2.50 |
| Plate 185 | 60.00 | 3.75 |
| Plate 186 | 75.00 | 3.00 |
| Plate 187 | 60.00 | 2.50 |
| Plate 188 | 80.00 | 12.00 |
| Plate 189 | 80.00 | 8.00 |
| Plate 190 | 60.00 | 7.00 |
| Plate 191 | 37.50 | 8.50 |
| Plate 192 | 60.00 | 2.50 |
| Plate 193 | 37.50 | 2.50 |
| Plates 194-195 | 60.00 | 9.50 |
| Plate 196 | 60.00 | 6.00 |
| Plate 197 | 65.00 | 10.75 |
| Plate 198 | 47.50 | 7.00 |
| Plate 199 | 65.00 | 7.00 |
| Plate 200 | 70.00 | 2.50 |

| | | |
|---|---|---|
| Plate 201 | 37.50 | 6.00 |
| Plate 202 | 70.00 | 9.50 |
| Plate 203 | 37.50 | 20.00 |
| Plate 204 | 65.00 | 2.50 |
| Plate 205 | 65.00 | 3.75 |
| Plate 206 | 65.00 | 8.25 |
| Plate 207 | 70.00 | 10.75 |
| Plate 208 | 65.00 | 20.00 |
| Plate 209 | 60.00 | 10.75 |
| Plate 210 | 75.00 | 14.00 |
| Plate 211 | 80.00 | 24.00 |
| Plate 212 | 70.00 | 13.00 |
| Plate 213 | 70.00 | 13.00 |
| Plate 214 | 75.00 | 21.50 |
| Plate 215 | 75.00 | 21.50 |
| Plate 216 | 80.00 | 21.50 |
| Plate 217 | 80.00 | 8.50 |
| Plate 218 | 75.00 | 9.50 |
| Plate 219 | 105.00 | 80.00 |
| Plate 220 | 47.50 | 8.50 |
| Plate 221 | 80.00 | 20.00 |
| Plate 222 | 90.00 | 47.50 |
| Plate 223 | 120.00 | 70.00 |
| Plate 224 | 150.00 | 60.00 |
| Plate 225 | 3,000. | 750.00 |

A11

**1862 Typo. Wmk. 23**

| | | |
|---|---|---|
| **34** A11 4p vermilion | 1,500. | 95.00 |
| *b.* Hair lines (P4) | 2,000. | 120.00 |
| *d.* Imperf. (P4) | 3,500. | |

Hair lines on No. 34b are fine colorless lines drawn diagonally across the corners of the stamp. For more detail, see *Scott Classic Specialized Catalogue of Stamps & Covers 1840-1940.*

A12

A13

A14

A15

**1862 Wmk. 24**

| | | |
|---|---|---|
| **37** A12 3p pale rose | 2,000. | 260.00 |
| *a.* 3p deep rose | 4,000. | 375.00 |
| *b.* With white dots under side ornaments | 40,000. | 11,000. |
| **39** A13 6p lilac (P3) | 1,700. | 95.00 |
| *c.* 6p lilac, wmk. 3 roses & thistle | — | 8,000. |
| *d.* 6p lilac, hair lines (P4) ('64) | 2,400. | 190.00 |
| *e.* As "d," imperf. | 4,000. | |
| *h.* 6p deep lilac (P3) | 2,100. | 115.00 |
| **40** A14 9p straw (p2) | 3,500. | 375.00 |
| *c.* 9p straw, wmk. 3 roses & thistle | | — |
| *d.* 9p bister (P2) | 4,750. | 500.00 |
| *e.* 9p bister, hair lines (P3) | 27,500. | 10,000. |
| **42** A15 1sh green | 2,500. | 225.00 |
| *a.* 1sh deep green (P1) | 3,800. | 375.00 |
| *b.* As "c," imperf. | 5,500. | |
| *c.* 1sh deep green, with hair lines (P2) | 32,000. | |

Hair lines on Nos. 39d, 39e, 39f, 39g, 40e and 42c are fine colorless lines drawn diagonally across the corners of the stamp. For details, see *Scott Classic Specialized Catalogue of Stamps & Covers 1840-1940.*

Compare design A14 with A19.

Forgeries exist of Nos. 39a and 40a.

A16

**1865 Wmk. 23**

| | | |
|---|---|---|
| **43** A16 4p vermilion (P12) | 475.00 | 60.00 |
| Plate 9 | 525.00 | 65.00 |
| Plate 10 | 700.00 | 140.00 |
| Plate 11 | 525.00 | 65.00 |
| Plate 13 | 550.00 | 60.00 |
| Plate 14 | 600.00 | 90.00 |
| *a.* 4p dull vermilion (P8) | 550.00 | 90.00 |
| Plate 7 | 600.00 | 100.00 |
| Plates 9, 13 | 525.00 | 65.00 |
| *b.* Imperf. (P11,12) | 5,000. | |

A17

(Hyphen after SIX) — A18

A19

A20

A21

**1865 Wmk. 24**

| | | |
|---|---|---|
| **44** A17 3p rose (P4) | 1,800. | 190.00 |
| *a.* Wmk. 3 roses & shamrock | 4,250. | 950.00 |
| **45** A18 6p lilac (P5) | 875.00 | 85.00 |
| *a.* 6p deep lilac | 1,500. | 135.00 |
| Plate 6 | 2,700. | 160.00 |
| *b.* Double impression (P6) | | 13,000. |
| *c.* Wmk. 3 roses & shamrock (P5) | | 1,400. |
| As "c," Plate 6 | | 1,600. |
| **46** A19 9p straw (P4) | 4,250. | 550.00 |
| Plate 5 | 20,000. | |
| *a.* Wmk. 3 roses & shamrock (P4) | — | 2,250. |
| **47** A20 10p red brn (P1) | | 45,000. |
| **48** A21 1sh green (P4) | 2,250. | 210.00 |
| *b.* Wmk. 3 roses & shamrock | | 1,500. |
| *c.* Vert. pair, imperf. btwn. | | 15,000. |

No. 46, plate 5 is from a proof sheet.

See Nos.49-50, 52-54. Compare design A17 with A27.

(No hyphen after SIX) — A22

A23

**1867-80 Wmk. 25**

| | | |
|---|---|---|
| **49** A17 3p rose (P5) | 450.00 | 60.00 |
| *a.* 3p deep rose | 800.00 | 90.00 |
| Plate 4 | 1,500. | 250.00 |
| Plate 6 | 475.00 | 60.00 |
| Plate 7 | 600.00 | 65.00 |
| Plate 8 | 575.00 | 60.00 |
| Plate 9 | 575.00 | 65.00 |
| Plate 10 | 775.00 | 120.00 |
| *b.* Imperf. (P5,6,8,9) | 5,000. | |
| **50** A18 6p dull violet (P6) | 1,500. | 85.00 |
| *a.* 6p bright violet (P6) | 1,500. | 95.00 |
| *b.* Imperf. (P6) | | 5,000. |
| **51** A22 6p red violet ('69) (P9) | 550.00 | 85.00 |
| *a.* 6p violet (P9) | 600.00 | 85.00 |
| Plate 8 | 600.00 | 115.00 |
| Plate 10 | | 30,000. |
| *b.* Imperf. (P8, 9) | 10,000. | 4,500. |
| **52** A19 9p bister (P4) ('67) | 2,000. | 300.00 |
| *a.* Imperf. (P4) | 10,000. | |
| **53** A20 10p red brown (P1) | 2,800. | 325.00 |
| Plate 2 | 45,000. | 14,000. |
| *a.* 10p deep red brown | 4,000. | 525.00 |
| *b.* Imperf. (P1) | 10,000. | |
| **54** A21 1sh green (P4) | 1,200. | 60.00 |
| Plate 5 | 650.00 | 37.50 |
| Plate 6 | 1,000. | 37.50 |
| Plate 7 | 1,200. | 70.00 |
| *a.* 1sh deep green | 775.00 | 45.00 |
| *b.* Imperf. (P4) | 8,000. | 5,000. |
| **55** A23 2sh blue (P1) | 3,000. | 180.00 |
| *a.* 2sh pale blue | 3,750. | 210.00 |
| Plate 3 | | 12,000. |
| *b.* Imperf. (P1) | 15,000. | |
| **56** A23 2sh pale brn (P1) ('80) | 22,000. | 3,500. |
| *a.* Imperf. | 25,000. | |

No. 51, plate 10 and No. 53, plate 2, are from proof sheets.

A24

**1867 Wmk. 26 *Perf. 15½x15***

| | | |
|---|---|---|
| **57** A24 5sh rose (P1) | 8,000. | 600.00 |
| Plate 2 | 12,000. | 600.00 |
| *a.* 5sh pale rose | 8,000. | 650.00 |
| Plate 2 | 12,000. | 1,200. |
| *b.* Imperf. (P1) | 15,000. | |

See No. 90. Compare design A24 with A51.

A25

**1870 Engr. Wmk. 27 *Perf. 14***

| | | |
|---|---|---|
| **58** A25 ½p rose (P5) | 95.00 | 19.00 |
| Plate 1 | 275.00 | 80.00 |
| Plate 3 | 200.00 | 42.50 |
| Plate 4 | 140.00 | 32.50 |
| Plate 6 | 105.00 | 19.00 |
| Plate 8 | 500.00 | 100.00 |
| Plate 9 | 5,500. | 750.00 |
| Plate 10 | 115.00 | 19.00 |
| Plate 11-14 | 105.00 | 19.00 |
| Plate 15 | 160.00 | 42.50 |
| Plate 19 | 180.00 | 60.00 |
| Plate 20 | 275.00 | 80.00 |
| *a.* Imperf (see footnote) | — | — |

Plates 1, 4-6, 8, and 14 are known imperf. Values: from $3,750 unused, $2,500 used.

A26

A27

A28

A29

Type A28 has a lined background.

**1872-73 Wmk. 25 Typo.**

| | | |
|---|---|---|
| **59** A26 6p brown (P11) | 700.00 | 52.50 |
| Plate 12 | | 3,500. |
| *a.* 6p deep brown (P11) | 1,100. | 95.00 |
| Plate 12 | | 3,250. |
| *b.* 6p pale buff (P11) | 725.00 | 90.00 |
| Plate 12 | 3,000. | 265.00 |
| **60** A26 6p gray (P12) ('73) | 1,600. | 240.00 |
| *a.* Imperf. | 10,000. | |

**1873-80**

| | | |
|---|---|---|
| **61** A27 3p rose (shades) (P11) | 400.00 | 47.50 |
| Plates 12 | 400.00 | 47.50 |
| Plate 14 | 450.00 | 47.50 |
| Plates 15-16 | 350.00 | 45.00 |
| Plates 17-18 | 400.00 | 47.50 |
| Plate 19 | 350.00 | 45.00 |
| Plate 20 | 650.00 | 100.00 |
| **62** A28 6p gray (P13-16) | 400.00 | 65.00 |
| Plate 17 | 750.00 | 150.00 |
| **63** A28 6p buff (P13) | | 21,000. |
| **64** A29 1sh pale green (P12, 13) | 525.00 | 105.00 |
| Plate 10 | 600.00 | 150.00 |
| Plate 11 | 600.00 | 130.00 |
| Plate 14 | | 35,000. |
| *a.* 1sh deep green (P8, 9) | 625.00 | 130.00 |
| **65** A29 1sh sal (P13) ('80) | 4,000. | 600.00 |

No. 63, plate 13, and No. 64, plate 14, are from proof sheets.

See Nos. 83, 86-87. For surcharges see Nos. 94-95. For overprints see Nos. O6, O30.

A30

**1875 Wmk. 28**

| | | |
|---|---|---|
| **66** A30 2½p claret (P1, 2) | 525.00 | 85.00 |
| Plate 3 | 850.00 | 130.00 |
| *a.* Bluish paper (P1) | 750.00 | 130.00 |
| Plate 2 | 7,500. | 1,450. |
| Plate 3 | | 5,000. |
| *b.* Lettered "LH-FL" | 22,000. | 2,250. |

Forgeries exist of 66a.

**1876-80 Wmk. 29**

| | | |
|---|---|---|
| **67** A30 2½p claret (P4-9, 11-16) | 425.00 | 52.50 |
| Plate 3 | 1,100. | 115.00 |
| Plate 10 | 500.00 | 70.00 |
| Plate 17 | 1,400. | 275.00 |
| **68** A30 2½p ultra ('80) (P19, 20) | 500.00 | 42.50 |
| Plate 17 | 475.00 | 50.00 |
| Plate 18 | 475.00 | 40.00 |

A31

A32

**1876-80 Wmk. 23**

| | | |
|---|---|---|
| **69** A31 4p vermilion (P15) | 2,400. | 450.00 |
| Plate 16 | | 30,000. |
| **70** A31 4p pale ol grn ('77) (P16) | 1,000. | 275.00 |
| Plate 15 | 1,000. | 300.00 |
| Plate 17 | | 17,500. |
| *a.* Imperf (P15) | 1,300. | |
| **71** A31 4p gray brn (P17) ('80) | 2,400. | 475.00 |
| **72** A32 8p brn lilac (P1) ('76) | 11,750. | |
| **73** A32 8p org (P1) ('76) | 1,500. | 325.00 |

Some specialists consider No. 70a a proof.

No. 72 was never placed in use.

No. 69, plate 16, is from proof sheets.

A33

A34

**1878 Wmk. 26 *Perf. 15½x15***

| | | |
|---|---|---|
| **74** A33 10sh slate (P1) | 50,000. | 2,900. |
| **75** A34 £1 brn lilac (P1) | 80,000. | 4,000. |

See Nos. 91-92. Compare design A34 with A52.

A35

A36

A37

A38

A39

A40

**1880-81 Wmk. 30 *Perf. 14***

| | | |
|---|---|---|
| **78** A35 ½p deep green | 47.50 | 12.00 |
| *a.* Imperf. | 4,000. | |
| *b.* No watermark | 7,500. | |
| **79** A36 1p red brown | 24.00 | 12.00 |
| *a.* Imperf. | 4,000. | |
| *b.* Wmk. 29, error | | |
| **80** A37 1½p red brown | 200.00 | 47.50 |
| **81** A38 2p lilac rose | 275.00 | 90.00 |
| **82** A30 2½p ultra ('81) (P23) | 350.00 | 30.00 |
| Plate 21 | 400.00 | 40.00 |
| Plate 22 | 350.00 | 40.00 |
| *a.* Imperf. (P23) | 600.00 | |

**83** A27 3p rose ('81) (P21) 425.00 85.00
Plate 20 750.00 150.00
**84** A31 4p gray brown (P17, 18) 375.00 65.00
**85** A39 5p dp indigo ('81) 675.00 110.00
*a.* Imperf. *6,500.* *4,000.*
**86** A28 6p gray (P18) 375.00 40.00
Plate 17 400.00 40.00
**87** A29 1sh salmon (P14) ('81) 550.00 150.00
Plate 13 700.00 150.00
*Nos. 78-87 (10)* 3,296. 641.50

Some specialists consider No. 82a a proof.
The 1sh in purple was not issued. Value, unused, $8,750.
See No. 98. For overprints, see Nos. O2-O3.
Compare design A35 with A54.

**1881**
**88** A40 1p lilac (14 dots in each angle) 200.00 32.50
**89** A40 1p lilac (16 dots in each angle) 2.75 2.00
*a.* Printed on both sides 800.
*b.* Imperf., pair 7,000.
*c.* Unwmkd. 7,500.
*d.* Bluish paper 4,500.
*e.* Printed on the gummed side 800.

For overprints, see Nos. O4, O37, O45 and O55.

**1882-83** **Wmk. 31**
**90** A24 5sh rose, *bluish* (P4) 32,000. 4,000.
*a.* White paper 27,000. 3,250.
**91** A33 10sh slate, *bluish* (P1) 125,000. 5,250.
*a.* White paper 140,000. 4,000.
**92** A34 £1 brown lilac, *bluish* (P1) 140,000. 9,250.
*a.* White paper 170,000. 7,750.

A41

**1882** **Wmk. Two Anchors (31)**
**93** A41 £5 brt orange (P1) 12,750. 4,500.
*a.* £5 pale dull orange, *bluish* *57,000.* *13,000.*
*b.* £5 bright orange, *bluish* *60,000.* *13,000.*

The paper of No. 93b is less bluish than that of No. 93a, and it is a later printing.

Types of 1873-80 Surcharged in Carmine

**1883** **Wmk. 30**
**94** A27 3p on 3p violet 500.00 140.00
**95** A28 6p on 6p violet 550.00 140.00
*a.* Double surcharge 10,000.

A44

**1883** **Wmk. 31**
**96** A44 2sh6p lilac 500.00 140.00
*a.* Bluish paper *8,000.* *3,500.*

**See British Offices Abroad for overprints on types A44-A133.**
**These overprints include "M.E.F.," "B.A.," "B.M.A.," "E.A.F.," "CHINA," "Morocco Agencies," "TANGIER," "LEVANT," "PARAS," and "PIASTRE(S)."**

A45

A46

A47

A48

A49

A50

**1883-84** **Wmk. 30**
**98** A35 ½p slate blue ('84) 27.50 8.50
**99** A45 1½p lilac ('84) 110.00 40.00
**100** A46 2p lilac ('84) 185.00 75.00
**101** A47 2½p lilac ('84) 80.00 16.00
**102** A48 3p lilac ('84) 225.00 95.00
**103** A49 4p green ('84) 450.00 200.00
**104** A45 5p green ('84) 450.00 200.00
**105** A46 6p green ('84) 475.00 225.00
**106** A50 9p green 950.00 425.00
**107** A48 1sh green ('84) 1,100. 250.00
*Nos. 98-107 (10)* 4,052. 1,534.

Nos. 99-107 were printed by De La Rue in a newly invented doubly fugitive ink that was only available in lilac and green. The stamps were unpopular with the public and postal clerks because they were unattractive and the different denominations were difficult to distinguish from one another.
Values are for stamps of good color. Faded stamps sell for much less. Soaking stamps will cause the color to run.
No. 104 with line instead of period under "d" was not regularly issued. Value, $27,500.
Nos. 98-105 and 107 exist imperf. Values from $3,500 to $5,000 each for Nos. 98-105, $7,500 for No. 107.
For overprints see Nos. O5, O7, O27-O29.

A51

A52

**1884** **Wmk. 31**
**108** A51 5sh carmine rose 950.00 220.00
*a.* Bluish paper 15,000. 3,750.
**109** A52 10sh ultra 2,000. 500.00
*a.* 10sh cobalt *35,000.* 7,500.
*b.* Bluish paper *37,500.* *8,000.*
*c.* As "a," bluish paper *60,000.* *14,000.*

Nos. 99-107 were printed by De La Rue in a newly invented doubly fugitive ink that was only available in lilac and green. The stamps were unpopular with the public and postal clerks because they were unattractive and the different denominations were difficult to distinguish from one another. For overprints see Nos. O8-O9.

A53

**1884** **Wmk. 30**
**110** A53 £1 brown violet 30,000. 3,250.

See Nos. 123-124. For overprints see Nos. O10, O13, O15.

**Queen Victoria Jubilee Issue**

A54

A55

A56

A57

A58

A59

A60

A61

A62

A63

A64

A65

Two types of 5p:
I — Squarish dots beside "d."
II — Tiny vertical dashes beside "d."

**1887-92** **Wmk. 30**
**111** A54 ½p vermilion 1.60 1.00
*a.* Printed on both sides
*b.* Double impression 25,000.
**112** A55 1½p violet & grn 15.00 7.50
**113** A56 2p grn & car rose 30.00 13.00
*a.* 2p green & vermilion 400.00 240.00
**114** A57 2½p violet, *blue* 24.00 3.50
**115** A58 3p violet, *yellow* 24.00 3.50
*a.* 3p violet, *orange* 750.00 175.00
**116** A59 4p brown & grn 32.50 14.00
**117** A60 4½p car rose & grn ('92) 10.00 42.50
**118** A61 5p lilac & bl, II 37.50 11.50
*a.* Type I 600.00 100.00
**119** A62 6p violet, *rose* 32.50 11.00
**120** A63 9p blue & lilac 65.00 42.50
**121** A64 10p car rose & lilac ('90) 45.00 40.00
**122** A65 1sh green 220.00 60.00
*Nos. 111-122 (12)* 537.10 250.00

The unpopular green and lilac issue (Nos. 98-107) were replaced by these stamps in colored inks and papers that made it easier to distinguish the different denominations.
Soaking these stamps will cause the color to run.
See Nos. 125-126. For overprints see Nos. O11-O12, O14, O16-O18, O31-O36, O38, O44, O46-O48, O54, O56-O58, O65-O66.

**1888** **Wmk. Three Orbs (29)**
**123** A53 £1 brown violet 65,000. 4,250.

**1891** **Wmk. 30**
**124** A53 £1 green 3,750. 750.00

**1900** **Wmk. 30**
**125** A54 ½p blue green 1.90 *2.10*
*a.* Imperf *6,500.*
**126** A65 1sh car rose & green 60.00 *135.00*

No. 125 in bright blue is a color changeling.

King Edward VII
A66 A67

A68

A69

A70

A71

A72

A73

A74

A75

A76

A77

A78

**1902-11 Wmk. 30 *Perf. 14***

**Ordinary Paper**

**127** A66 ½p gray green 2.25 1.75
**128** A66 1p scarlet 2.25 1.60
*c.* 1p aniline rose ('11) 225.00 125.00
*e.* Booklet pane of 6 110.00
*f.* No watermark ('11) 45.00 45.00
*g.* Imperf., pair *27,500.*
**129** A67 1½p vio & green 45.00 22.50
**130** A68 2p yel grn & car 52.50 22.50
*b.* 2p deep grn & red ('11) 20.00 10.00
**131** A66 2½p ultra 22.50 11.50
**132** A69 3p dull pur, *org yel* 45.00 19.00
**133** A70 4p gray brn & grn 57.50 35.00
**134** A71 5p dull pur & ultra 67.50 22.50
**135** A66 6p pale dull vio 45.00 22.50
*a.* 6p slate purple 45.00 22.50
*b.* 6p red violet 45.00 22.50
*c.* 6p dark violet 45.00 30.00
**136** A72 9p ultra & dull vio 100.00 70.00
**137** A73 10p car & dull pur 100.00 70.00
*a.* 10p scarlet & dull pur 92.50 85.00
**138** A74 1sh car & dull grn 92.50 40.00
*a.* 1sh scar & dark green ('11) 115.00 70.00

**Wmk. 31**

**139** A75 2sh6p lilac 260.00 150.00
*a.* 2sh6p dark violet ('11) 260.00 175.00
**140** A76 5sh car rose 400.00 225.00
*b.* 5sh carmine 400.00 225.00
**141** A77 10sh ultra 775.00 525.00

**Wmk. Three Imperial Crowns (30)**

**142** A78 £1 blue green 2,000. 750.00
*Nos. 127-138 (12)* 632.00 338.85

Nos. 129, 130 and 132 to 139 inclusive exist on both ordinary and chalky paper.

See Nos. 143, 144, 146-150. For overprints see Nos. O19-O26, O39-O43, O49-O53, O59-O64, O67-O83.

**See British Offices Abroad for overprints on types A44-A133. These overprints include "M.E.F.," "B.A.," "B.M.A.," "E.A.F.," "CHINA," "Morocco Agencies," "TANGIER," "LEVANT," "PARAS," and "PIASTRE(S)."**

**1904 Wmk. 30**

**143** A66 ½p pale yel grn 2.25 1.75
*b.* Booklet pane of 5 + label 500.00
*c.* Booklet pane of 6 175.00
*d.* Double impression *29,000.*
*e.* Imperf., pair *27,500.*

Edward VII — A79

**1909-10**

**144** A70 4p pale orange ('10) 20.00 15.00
**145** A79 7p gray ('10) 13.50 *22.50*

**1911 *Perf. 15x14***

**146** A66 ½p dull yel green 45.00 *50.00*
**147** A66 1p carmine rose 17.50 17.50
**148** A66 2½p brt ultra 25.00 17.50
**149** A69 3p violet, *yellow* 52.50 17.50
*a.* 3p gray, *lemon* *3,250.*
**150** A70 4p orange 35.00 17.50
*Nos. 146-150 (5)* 175.00 120.00

King George V
A80 A81

***Perf. 15x14***

**1911, June 22 Wmk. 30**

**151** A80 ½p yellow green 5.75 4.50
*a.* Booklet pane of 6 175.00
*b.* Perf. 14 (error) *18,000.* 1,000.
**152** A81 1p carmine 5.25 3.00
*a.* Booklet pane of 6 175.00
*b.* Perf. 14 (error) — —
*c.* 1p pale carmine 16.00 3.50
*d.* As "c," booklet pane of 6 *125.00*

**1912, Jan. 1 Re-engraved**

**153** A80 ½p yellow green 10.00 4.50
**154** A81 1p scarlet 7.50 3.50
*b.* 1p aniline scarlet 175.00 100.00

In the re-engraved stamps the lines of the hair and beard are clearer. The re-engraved ½p has 3 lines of shading instead of 4 between the point of neck and frame; in the 1p the body of the lion is nearly covered by lines of shading.

**1912, Aug. Wmk. 33 *Perf. 15x14***

**Die I (Before Re-engraving)**

**155** A80 ½p yellow green 45.00 45.00
*a.* Booklet pane of 6 270.00
**156** A81 1p scarlet 30.00 30.00
*a.* Booklet pane of 6 210.00

**Die II (Re-engraved)**

**157** A80 ½p yellow green 8.00 3.50
**158** A81 1p scarlet 9.25 3.50

**1912-21 Wmk. 32**

**158A** A80 ½p yellow green 14.00 9.25
*e.* Imperf., pair 300.00
**158B** A81 1p scarlet 20.00 11.50
*e.* Imperf., pair 300.00

A82

A83

A84

A85

A86

A87

A88

A89

King George V — A90

TWO PENCE:

Die I — Four horizontal lines above the head. Heavy colored lines above and below the bottom tablet. The inner frame line is closer to the central design than it is to the outer frame line.

Die II — Three lines above the head. Thinner lines above and below the bottom tablet. The inner frame line is midway between the central design and the outer frame line.

**1912-13 Wmk. 33 *Perf. 15x14***

**159** A82 ½p green ('13) 1.10 1.10
*a.* Double impression *25,000.*
*b.* Booklet pane of 6 90.00
**160** A83 1p scarlet 1.10 1.10
*a.* Booklet pane of 6 100.00
*b.* Tete beche pair *67,500.*
**161** A84 1½p red brown 4.50 1.75
*a.* "PENCF" 350.00 250.00
*b.* 1½p orange brown 12.00 15.00
*e.* 1½p chocolate brown 10.00 2.25
*f.* As "e," Unwmkd. 200.00 140.00
*g.* Booklet pane of 6 125.00
*h.* Booklet pane of 4 + 2 labels 675.00
**162** A85 2p deep org (I) 5.00 3.50
*a.* 2p deep orange (II) ('21) 5.75 4.25
*b.* Booklet pane of 6 (I) 200.00
*c.* Booklet pane of 6 (II) 350.00
**163** A86 2½p ultramarine 14.00 4.50
**164** A87 3p bluish violet ('13) 8.00 2.25
**165** A88 4p slate green 17.50 2.25
**166** A89 5p yellow brown 17.50 5.75
*a.* Unwmkd. 1,100.
**167** A89 6p rose lilac 17.50 8.00
*a.* 6p dull violet ('13) 30.00 11.50
*b.* Perf. 14 90.00 *100.00*
**168** A89 7p ol grn ('13) 22.50 10.00
**169** A89 8p black, *yellow* ('13) 37.50 12.50
**170** A90 9p black brown ('13) 22.50 6.75
**171** A90 10p light blue ('13) 25.00 22.50
**172** A90 1sh bister ('13) 24.00 4.50
*Nos. 159-172 (14)* 217.70 86.45

No. 167 is on chalky paper.

Nos. 159-172 were printed in a variety of shades.

See #177-178, 183, 187-200, 210, 212-220. Compare design A82 with A97.

**See British Offices Abroad for overprints on types A44-A133. These overprints include "M.E.F.," "B.A.," "B.M.A.," "E.A.F.," "CHINA," "Morocco Agencies," "TANGIER," "LEVANT," "PARAS," and "PIASTRE(S)."**

**Waterlow Brothers & Layton Printing (1913)**

"Britannia Rule the Waves" A91

Measure 22mm vertically. Perforation holes are larger and evenly spaced.

**1913 Engr. Wmk. 34 *Perf. 11x12***

**173** A91 2sh6p dark brown 275.00 180.00
**174** A91 5sh rose car 500.00 375.00
**175** A91 10sh indigo blue 950.00 475.00
**176** A91 £1 green 3,250. 1,550.
*Nos. 173-176 (4)* 4,975. 2,580.

**De La Rue & Co. Printing (1915)**

Measure 22mm vertically. Gum tends to be yellowish and patchy. The top right and top left perf teeth are wider than the others. Perforation holes are smaller.

**1915 Engr. Wmk. 34 *Perf. 11x12***

**173a** A91 2sh6p lt brn (worn plate) 250.00 225.00
**174a** A91 5sh br carmine 475.00 375.00
**175a** A91 10sh light blue 2,500. 800.00

See Nos. 179-181, 222-224.

**1913 Wmk. 32 Typo. *Perf. 15x14***

**Coil Stamps**

**177** A82 ½p green 175.00 *210.00*
**178** A83 1p scarlet 260.00 *260.00*

**Bradbury, Wilkinson & Co. Printing (1918-19)**

**Seahorses Types of 1913-15 Retouched**

**1919 Engr. Wmk. 34 *Perf. 11x12***

**179** A91 2sh6p olive brown 125.00 75.00
**180** A91 5sh car rose 300.00 125.00
**181** A91 10sh blue 425.00 160.00
*Nos. 179-181 (3)* 850.00 360.00

The retouched stamps usually have a dot above the middle of the top frame. They are 22¾mm high, whereas Nos. 173-176 are 22mm high.

**Type of 1912-13**

**1922 Typo. Wmk. 33 *Perf. 15x14***

**183** A90 9p olive green 120.00 35.00

**British Empire Exhibition Issue**

British Lion and George V
A92

**Wmk. 35**

**1924, Apr. 23 Engr. *Perf. 14***

**185** A92 1p vermilion 9.00 9.00
Never hinged 15.00
**186** A92 1½p dark brown 14.00 14.00
Never hinged 22.50

See Nos. 203-204.

**Types of 1912-13 Issue**

**1924 Typo. *Perf. 15x14***

**187** A82 ½p green .75 .90
Never hinged 1.25
*a.* Wmk. sideways 9.00 4.00
Never hinged 16.00
*b.* Booklet pane of 6 90.00
Never hinged 140.00
*c.* Double impression *11,000.*
**188** A83 1p scarlet .75 .90
Never hinged 1.25
*a.* Wmk. sideways 20.00 20.00
Never hinged 35.00
*b.* Booklet pane of 6 90.00
Never hinged 140.00
**189** A84 1½p red brown .75 .90
Never hinged 1.25
*a.* Tête bêche pair 550.00 *875.00*
Never hinged 800.00
*b.* Wmk. sideways 10.00 6.00
Never hinged 20.00
*c.* Booklet pane of 6 50.00
Never hinged 75.00
*d.* Bklt. pane of 4 + 2 labels 200.00
Never hinged 325.00
*e.* Double impression *18,000.*
**190** A85 2p dp orange (II) 1.75 2.50
Never hinged 3.50
*a.* Wmk. sideways 90.00 *90.00*
Never hinged 225.00
*b.* Unwatermarked 950.00
Never hinged 1,450.
**191** A86 2½p ultra 4.75 4.00
Never hinged 12.00
*a.* Unwatermarked 2,000.
Never hinged 2,750.
**192** A87 3p violet 11.50 3.25
Never hinged 22.50
**193** A88 4p slate green 15.00 3.25
Never hinged 29.00
**194** A89 5p yel brown 24.00 4.00
Never hinged 55.00
**195** A89 6p dull violet 4.00 1.75
Never hinged 6.50
**198** A90 9p olive green 13.50 4.00
Never hinged 30.00
**199** A90 10p dull blue 47.50 42.50
Never hinged 110.00
**200** A90 1sh bister 22.50 3.75
Never hinged 60.00
*Nos. 187-200 (12)* 146.75 71.70

Nos. 187a, 188a, 189b, 190a issued in coils.

Inverted watermarks on the three lowest values are usually from booklet panes.

Nos. 188-189 were issued also on experimental paper with variety of Wmk. 35: closer spacing; letters shorter, rounder.

**British Empire Exhibition Issue**

Type of 1924, Dated "1925"

**1925, May 9 Engr. *Perf. 14***

**203** A92 1p vermilion 12.00 *20.00*
Never hinged 21.00
**204** A92 1½p brown 35.00 *60.00*
Never hinged 57.50

A93

A94

A95

St. George Slaying the Dragon A96

**1929, May 10 Typo. *Perf. 15x14***

205 A93 ½p green 2.00 2.00
Never hinged 3.75
a. Wmk. sideways 45.00 35.00
Never hinged 120.00
b. Booklet pane of 6 150.00
206 A94 1p scarlet 2.00 2.00
Never hinged 3.75
a. Wmk. sideways 82.50 67.50
Never hinged 120.00
b. Booklet pane of 6 150.00
207 A94 1½p dark brown 2.00 1.75
Never hinged 4.00
a. Wmk. sideways 45.00 35.00
Never hinged 90.00
b. Booklet pane of 6 60.00
c. Booklet pane of 4 + 2 labels 350.00
208 A95 2½p deep blue 9.50 9.50
Never hinged 24.00
*Nos. 205-208 (4)* 15.50 15.25

Inverted watermarks on the three lowest values are usually from booklet panes.

Nos. 205a, 206a and 207a were issued in coils.

**Wmk. 219**

**Engr. *Perf. 12***

209 A96 £1 black 800.00 800.00
Never hinged 1,400.

Universal Postal Union, 9th Congress.

A97

Type A97 designs are re-engraved versions of the types of the 1912-13 issue, with the most obvious difference being the solid appearance of the central field. The backgrounds appear to be solid, although the photoengraving screen can be seen under magnification.

***Perf. 14½x14***

**1934-36 Photo. Wmk. 35**

210 A97 ½p dark green .45 .45
Never hinged .90
a. Wmk. sideways 8.00 3.25
Never hinged 17.50
b. Booklet pane of 6 85.00
211 A97 1p carmine .45 .45
Never hinged .90
a. Wmk. sideways 15.00 15.00
Never hinged 40.00
b. Booklet pane of 6 85.00
c. Imperf., pair 5,000.
d. Pair, imperf. btwn. 7,000.
212 A97 1½p red brown .45 .45
Never hinged .90
a. Imperf., pair 1,100.
b. Wmk. sideways 6.00 2.00
Never hinged 18.00
c. Booklet pane of 6 30.00
d. Booklet pane of 4 + 2 labels 160.00
213 A97 2p red org ('35) .55 .55
Never hinged 1.60
a. Imperf., pair 5,000.
b. Wmk. sideways 90.00 70.00
Never hinged 275.00
214 A97 2½p ultra ('35) .90 .75
Never hinged 3.00
215 A97 3p dk violet ('35) .90 1.00
Never hinged 3.00
216 A97 4p dk sl grn ('35) 1.75 1.00
Never hinged 4.00
217 A97 5p yel brown ('36) 6.00 1.50
Never hinged 19.00
218 A97 9p dk ol grn ('35) 9.00 2.75
Never hinged 19.00
219 A97 10p Prus blue ('36) 15.00 11.00
Never hinged 32.50
220 A97 1sh bister brn ('36) 15.00 1.25
Never hinged 40.00
*Nos. 210-220 (11)* 50.45 21.15

The designs in this set are slightly smaller than the 1912-13 issue.

Inverted watermarks on the three lowest values are usually from booklet panes.

Nos. 210a, 211a, 212b and 213b were issued in coils.

**Britannia Type of 1913-19 Reengraved**

**1934 Engr. Wmk. 34 *Perf. 11x12***

222 A91 2sh6p brown 80.00 25.00
Never hinged 150.00
223 A91 5sh carmine 175.00 60.00
Never hinged 375.00
224 A91 10sh dark blue 375.00 65.00
Never hinged 750.00
*Nos. 222-224 (3)* 630.00 150.00

Printed by Waterlow & Sons. Can be distinguished by the crossed lines in background of portrait. Previous issues have horizontal lines only.

**Silver Jubilee Issue**

A98

***Perf. 14½x14***

**1935, May 7 Photo. Wmk. 35**

226 A98 ½p dark green 1.00 .60
Never hinged 1.40
a. Booklet pane of 4 40.00
227 A98 1p carmine 1.25 *1.75*
Never hinged 2.00
a. Booklet pane of 4 40.00
228 A98 1½p red brown 1.00 .60
Never hinged 1.40
a. Booklet pane of 4 17.50
229 A98 2½p ultra 4.00 *4.50*
Never hinged 6.50
a. 2½p Prussian blue *9,500.* *11,000.*
Never hinged *11,000.*
*Nos. 226-229 (4)* 7.25 *7.45*

25th anniv. of the reign of George V. Device at right differs on 1½p and 2½p.

Inverted watermarks on the three lowest values are usually from booklet panes.

Edward VIII — A99

**1936 Wmk. 250**

230 A99 ½p dark green .25 .25
Never hinged .40
a. Booklet pane of 6 2.00
Never hinged 2.75
231 A99 1p crimson .50 .50
Never hinged .70
a. Booklet pane of 6 17.50
Never hinged 25.00
232 A99 1½p red brown .25 *.35*
Never hinged .40
a. Booklet pane of 6 11.00
Never hinged 15.00
b. Booklet pane of 4 + 2 labels 62.50
Never hinged 85.00
c. Booklet pane of 2 20.00
Never hinged 30.00
233 A99 2½p bright ultra .25 *1.00*
Never hinged .40
*Nos. 230-233 (4)* 1.25 *2.10*

Inverted watermarks on the three lowest values are usually from booklet panes.

King George VI and Queen Elizabeth A100

***Perf. 14½x14***

**1937, May 13 Wmk. 251**

234 A100 1½p purple brown .25 .25
Never hinged .35

Coronation of George VI and Elizabeth.

**See British Offices Abroad for overprints on types A44-A133. These overprints include "M.E.F.," "B.A.," "B.M.A.," "E.A.F.," "CHINA," "Morocco Agencies," "TANGIER," "LEVANT," "PARAS," and "PIASTRE(S)."**

A101

A102

King George VI — A103

Nos. 235-240 show face and neck highlighted, background solid.

**1937-39**

235 A101 ½p deep green .25 .25
Never hinged .30
a. Wmk. sideways .40 .45
Never hinged .55
b. Booklet pane of 6 32.50
Never hinged 45.00
c. Booklet pane of 4 60.00 32.50
Never hinged 85.00
d. Booklet pane of 2 70.00
Never hinged 100.00
236 A101 1p scarlet .25 .25
Never hinged .30
a. Wmk. sideways 8.50 7.50
Never hinged 22.50
b. Booklet pane of 6 40.00
Never hinged 55.00
c. Booklet pane of 4 100.00 *100.00*
Never hinged 150.00
d. Booklet pane of 2 70.00
Never hinged 100.00
237 A101 1½p red brown .25 .25
Never hinged .40
a. Wmk. sideways .65 *1.25*
Never hinged 1.40
b. Booklet pane of 6 35.00
Never hinged 50.00
c. Booklet pane of 4 + 2 labels 85.00
Never hinged 120.00
d. Booklet pane of 2 20.00
Never hinged 30.00
238 A101 2p orange ('38) .60 .50
Never hinged 1.00
a. Wmk. sideways 30.00 32.50
Never hinged 80.00
b. Booklet pane of 6 100.00
Never hinged 150.00
239 A101 2½p bright ultra .25 .25
Never hinged .35
a. Wmk. sideways 45.00 32.50
Never hinged 90.00
b. Booklet pane of 6 85.00
Never hinged 120.00
c. Tête bêche pair *22,000.*
240 A101 3p dk purple ('38) 3.00 .95
Never hinged 5.00
241 A102 4p gray green ('38) .45 .75
Never hinged .70
a. Imperf., pair *7,000.*
Never hinged *8,500.*
b. Horiz. pair, imperf. on 3 sides *7,500.*
Never hinged *9,000.*
242 A102 5p lt brown ('38) 1.10 .80
Never hinged 3.00
a. Imperf., pair *6,500.*
Never hinged *8,000.*
b. Horiz. pair, imperf. on 3 sides *7,000.*
Never hinged *8,500.*
243 A102 6p rose lilac ('39) .80 .60
Never hinged 1.50
244 A103 7p emerald ('39) 2.00 .60
Never hinged 6.00
a. Horiz. pair, imperf. on 3 sides *6,500.*
Never hinged *8,500.*
245 A103 8p brt rose ('39) 3.25 .80
Never hinged 7.00
246 A103 9p dp ol green ('39) 3.25 .80
Never hinged 6.50
247 A103 10p royal bl ('39) 3.25 .80
Never hinged 6.50
a. Imperf., pair 5,700.
Never hinged 7,000.
248 A103 1sh brown ('39) 3.25 1.00
Never hinged 9.00
*Nos. 235-248 (14)* 21.95 8.60
Set, never hinged 47.00

Nos. 235a, 236a, 237a, 238a and 239a were issued in coils.

Nos. 235c and 236c are watermarked sideways.

The 1½p, 1p, 1½p, 2p and 2½p with watermark inverted are from booklet panes.

No. 238 bisects were used in Guernsey from 12/27/40 to 2/24/41. Value, on cover $32.50.

See Nos. 258-263, 266, 280-285.

**Oman Surcharges**

**Various definitive and commemorative stamps between Nos. 243 and 372 were surcharged in annas (a), new paisa (np) and rupees (r) for use in Oman. The surcharges do not indicate where the stamps were used.**

King George VI and Royal Arms — A104

King George VI — A105

**1939-42 Engr. Wmk. 259 *Perf. 14***

249 A104 2sh6p chestnut 42.50 6.00
Never hinged 110.00
249A A104 2sh6p yel green ('42) 8.00 1.50
Never hinged 16.00
250 A104 5sh dull red 10.00 2.00
Never hinged 25.00
251 A105 10sh indigo 150.00 24.00
Never hinged 325.00
251A A105 10sh ultra ('42) 17.50 5.00
Never hinged 45.00
*Nos. 249-251A (5)* 228.00 38.50

See No. 275.

Victoria and George VI A106

***Perf. 14½x14***

**1940, May 6 Photo. Wmk. 251**

252 A106 ½p deep green .25 .25
Never hinged .30
253 A106 1p scarlet 1.00 .40
Never hinged 1.10
254 A106 1½p red brown .25 *.75*
Never hinged .55
255 A106 2p orange .50 .75
Never hinged 1.00
256 A106 2½p brt ultra 1.00 .55
Never hinged 2.25
257 A106 3p dark purple 1.75 *3.50*
Never hinged 3.00
*Nos. 252-257 (6)* 4.75 6.20

Centenary of the postage stamp.

No. 255 bisects were used in Guernsey from 12/27/40 to 2/24/41. Value, on cover, $40.

**Type of 1937-39, with Background Lightened**

**1941-42**

258 A101 ½p green .25 .25
Never hinged .30
a. Booklet pane of 6 14.00
Never hinged 20.00
b. Booklet pane of 2 7.00
Never hinged 10.00
c. Imperf., pair *6,500.*
Never hinged *8,500.*
d. Tete beche pair *8,000.*
Never hinged *17,500.*
e. Booklet pane of 4
259 A101 1p vermilion .25 .25
Never hinged .30
a. Wmk. sideways ('42) 3.00 5.75
Never hinged 5.00
b. Booklet pane of 2 35.00
Never hinged 50.00
c. Imperf., pair *6,000.*
Never hinged *8,000.*
d. Booklet pane of 4
e. Horiz. pair, imperf on 3 sides *6,000.*
Never hinged *8,500.*
260 A101 1½p lt red brn ('42) .30 .85
Never hinged .60
a. Booklet pane of 2 7.00
Never hinged 10.00
b. Booklet pane of 4
261 A101 2p light orange .25 .50
Never hinged .50
a. Wmk. sideways ('42) 16.50 *21.00*
Never hinged 32.50
b. Booklet pane of 6 17.50
Never hinged 25.00
c. Imperf., pair *5,500.*
Never hinged *7,500.*
d. Tete beche pair *11,500.*
Never hinged *17,500.*
262 A101 2½p ultra .25 .40
Never hinged .35
a. Wmk. sideways ('42) 9.00 *11.00*
Never hinged 17.50
b. Booklet pane of 6 11.00
Never hinged 15.00
c. Imperf., pair *3,350.*
Never hinged *4,750.*
d. Tete beche pair *11,500.*
Never hinged *17,500.*

**263** A101 3p violet 1.40 1.10
Never hinged 5.00
*Nos. 258-263 (6)* 2.70 3.35

The ½p, 2p and 2½p with inverted watermarks are from booklets.

Nos. 259a, 261a and 262a were issued in coils.

Nos. 258b, 258e, 259b, 259d, 260a-260b are made from sheets.

**Catalogue values for unused stamps in this section, from this point to the end of the section, are for Never Hinged items.**

### Peace Issue

A107

King George VI and Symbols of Peace and Industry
A108

*Perf. 14½x14*

**1946, June 11 Photo. Wmk. 251**
**264** A107 2½p bright ultra .25 .25
**265** A108 3p violet .25 .45

Return to peace at the close of WW II.

### George VI Type of 1939

**1947, Dec. 29**
**266** A103 11p violet brown 2.50 2.00

A109

King George VI and Queen Elizabeth
A110

**1948, Apr. 26** *Perf. 14½x14, 14x14½*
**267** A109 2½p brt ultra .40 .25
**268** A110 £1 dp chalky blue 40.00 40.00

25th anniv. of the marriage of King George VI and Queen Elizabeth.

A111

Vraicking (Gathering Seaweed)
A112

**1948, May 10** *Perf. 14½x14*
**269** A111 1p red .25 .25
**270** A112 2½p bright ultra .25 .25

3rd anniversary of the liberation of the Channel Islands from German occupation.

Sold at post offices in the Channel Islands and at major philatelic windows in the United Kingdom, and valid for postage throughout Great Britain.

A113

A114

A115

A116

**1948, July 29**
**271** A113 2½p bright ultra .40 .25
**272** A114 3p deep violet .65 .50
**273** A115 6p red violet 2.75 .75
**274** A116 1sh dark brown 4.25 1.75
*Nos. 271-274 (4)* 8.05 3.25

1948 Olympic Games held at Wembley during July and August.

### George VI Type of 1939
### Wmk. 259

**1948, Oct. 1 Engr.** *Perf. 14*
**275** A105 £1 red brown 25.00 20.00

A117

A118

A119

A120

*Perf. 14½x14*

**1949, Oct. 10 Photo. Wmk. 251**
**276** A117 2½p bright ultra .25 .25
**277** A118 3p brt violet .25 .50
**278** A119 6p red violet .45 .55
**279** A120 1sh brown .90 *1.10*
*Nos. 276-279 (4)* 1.85 2.40

UPU, 75th anniversary.

### Types of 1937

**1950-51 Wmk. 251** *Perf. 14½x14*
**280** A101 ½p light orange .25 .25
*a.* Booklet pane of 2 10.00
*b.* Booklet pane of 4 15.00
*c.* Booklet pane of 6 10.00
*d.* Imperf., pair *6,000.*
*e.* Tete beche pair *18,000.*
**281** A101 1p ultramarine .25 .25
*a.* Wmk. sideways .50 .90
*b.* Booklet pane of 2 10.00
*c.* Booklet pane of 4 20.00
*d.* Booklet pane of 6 35.00
*e.* Booklet pane of 3 + 3 labels 20.00
*f.* Imperf., pair *5,000.*
*g.* Horiz. pair, imperf on 3 sides *6,500.*
**282** A101 1½p green .50 .50
*a.* Wmk. sideways 2.00 *3.00*
*b.* Booklet pane of 2 10.00
*c.* Booklet pane of 4 15.00
*d.* Booklet pane of 6 25.00
**283** A101 2p lt red brown .60 .45
*a.* Wmk. sideways 1.50 *1.25*
*b.* Booklet pane of 6 25.00
*c.* Tete beche pair *18,000.*
*d.* Horiz. pair, imperf on 3 sides *8,000.*
**284** A101 2½p vermilion .50 .45
*a.* Wmk. sideways 1.00 1.00
*b.* Booklet pane of 6 8.00
*c.* Tete beche pair
**285** A102 4p ultra ('50) 1.50 1.50
*a.* Double impression *8,250.*
*Nos. 280-285 (6)* 3.60 3.40

Inverted watermarks on Nos. 280-284 are usually from booklets.

Nos. 281a, 282a, 283a and 284a were issued in coils.

H.M.S. Victory
A121

St. George Slaying the Dragon
A122

Royal Arms
A123

Design: 5sh, White Cliffs, Dover.

*Perf. 11x12*

**1951, May 3 Engr. Wmk. 259**
**286** A121 2sh6p green 9.00 1.10
**287** A121 5sh dull red 30.00 1.75
**288** A122 10sh ultra 32.50 9.75
**289** A123 £1 lt red brown 35.00 18.00
*Nos. 286-289 (4)* 106.50 30.60

Britannia, Symbols of Commerce and Prosperity, King George VI — A124

Festival Symbol
A125

*Perf. 14½x14*

**1951, May 3 Photo. Wmk. 251**
**290** A124 2½p scarlet .25 .25
**291** A125 4p bright ultra .35 .75

Festival of Britain, 1951.

Queen Elizabeth
A126 A127

A128

A129

A130

A131

A132

The 2½d exists in two types: Type I, in the front cross of the diadem, the top line extends half the width of the cross; Type II, the top line extends across the full width of the top of the cross.

*Perf. 14½x14*

**1952-54 Photo. Wmk. 298**
**292** A126 ½p red orange ('53) .25 .25
*a.* Booklet pane of 2 .70
*b.* Booklet pane of 4 1.25
*c.* Booklet pane of 6 1.50
**293** A126 1p ultra ('53) .25 .25
*a.* Booklet pane of 2 .90
*b.* Booklet pane of 4 1.75
*c.* Booklet pane of 6 2.25
*d.* Booklet pane 3 + 3 labels 35.00
**294** A126 1½p green ('52) .25 .25
*a.* Booklet pane of 2 .70
*b.* Booklet pane of 4 1.25
*c.* Booklet pane of 6 ('53) 1.50
*d.* Wmk. sideways .55 *.80*
*e.* As "c," imperf. (error) *750.00*
**295** A126 2p red brn ('53) .25 .25
*a.* Booklet pane of 6 25.00
*b.* Wmk. sideways 1.25 *2.25*
**296** A127 2½p scarlet, Type I ('52) .25 .25
*a.* Booklet pane of 6, Type II ('53) 7.00
*b.* Wmk. sideways, Type I ('54) 8.00 *9.25*
*c.* Type II 1.40 1.40
**297** A127 3p dk purple .85 .65
**298** A128 4p ultra ('53) 3.25 1.10
**299** A129 5p lt brn ('53) .75 *1.50*
**300** A129 6p lilac rose 4.00 .90
**301** A129 7p emerald 8.50 4.00
**302** A130 8p brt rose ('53) .75 .75
**303** A130 9p dp ol grn 21.00 4.25
**304** A130 10p royal blue 16.50 4.00
**305** A130 11p vio brown 30.00 11.50
**306** A131 1sh brown ('53) .75 .55
**307** A132 1sh3p dk grn ('53) 4.50 2.50
**308** A131 1sh6p dk bl ('53) 15.00 3.50
*Nos. 292-308 (17)* 107.10 36.45

Nos. 294d, 295b, 296b issued in coils.

Nos. 292-296 with watermark inverted are from booklets.

Type II stamps of No. 296 come only from booklet panes.

See Nos. 317-333, 353-369, 1801-1803, 2022-2023, 2086, 2125.

Compare design A128 with A139.

See regional issues, Guernsey, Jersey and Isle of Man for other stamps showing this portrait of the Queen, which have different frames or devices added to the design.

**See British Offices Abroad for overprints on types A44-A133. These overprints include "M.E.F.," "B.A.," "B.M.A.," "E.A.F.," "CHINA," "Morocco Agencies," "TANGIER," "LEVANT," "PARAS," and "PIASTRE(S)."**

Windsor, England
A133

Castles: 2sh6p, Carrickfergus, Ireland. 5sh, Caernarfon Castle, Wales. 10sh, Edinburgh, Scotland.

**1955 Engr. Wmk. 308** *Perf. 11x12*
**309** A133 2sh6p dark brown 12.50 1.50
**310** A133 5sh crimson 32.50 3.50
**311** A133 10sh brt ultra 75.00 12.50
**312** A133 £1 intense blk 120.00 35.00
*Nos. 309-312 (4)* 240.00 52.50

See Nos. 371-374, 525-528, 2278.

A134

A135

A136

A137

*Perf. 14½x14*

**1953, June 3 Photo. Wmk. 298**

| | | | | |
|---|---|---|---|---|
| **313** | A134 | 2½p scarlet | .30 | .25 |
| **314** | A135 | 4p ultra | 1.00 | *1.75* |
| **315** | A136 | 1sh3p dark green | 4.50 | 2.50 |
| **316** | A137 | 1sh6p dark blue | 9.50 | 4.25 |
| | | *Nos. 313-316 (4)* | 15.30 | 8.75 |

See Nos. 1942, 2126.

### Types of 1952-54

**1955-57 Wmk. 308 *Perf. 14½x14***

| | | | | |
|---|---|---|---|---|
| **317** | A126 | ½p red orange ('56) | .25 | .25 |
| *a.* | | Booklet pane of 6 | 1.75 | |
| *b.* | | Booklet pane of 4 | 1.50 | |
| *d.* | | Booklet pane of 2 | .70 | |
| **318** | A126 | 1p ultra ('56) | .25 | .25 |
| *a.* | | Bklt. pane of 3 + 3 labels | 16.00 | |
| *b.* | | Booklet pane of 6 | 2.00 | |
| *c.* | | Booklet pane of 4 | 1.50 | |
| *e.* | | Tete Beche pair | — | |
| *f.* | | Booklet pane of 2 | .80 | |
| **319** | A126 | 1½p green ('56) | .25 | .25 |
| *a.* | | Booklet pane of 6 | 8.50 | |
| *b.* | | Booklet pane of 4 | 6.50 | |
| *c.* | | Wmk. sideways ('56) | .35 | *.65* |
| *e.* | | Tete beche pair | *3,000.* | |
| *f.* | | Booklet pane of 2 | 1.50 | |
| **320** | A126 | 2p red brown | .25 | .25 |
| *a.* | | Wmk. sideways | .50 | *.65* |
| *b.* | | Booklet pane of 6 | 3.00 | |
| *d.* | | Tete beche pair | *2,000.* | |
| *e.* | | Vert. pair, imperf. between | *4,500.* | |
| *f.* | | As "a," horiz. pair, imperf. between | *4,500.* | |
| *h.* | | Imperf., pair | *350.00* | |
| **321** | A127 | 2½p scar, Type I ('56) | .25 | *.25* |
| *a.* | | Booklet pane of 6, Type II | 4.50 | |
| *b.* | | Wmk. sideways, Type I ('56) | 1.40 | 1.40 |
| *d.* | | Type II | .40 | .40 |
| *e.* | | Tete beche pair | *3,000.* | |
| *f.* | | Imperf., pair | *300.00* | |
| **322** | A127 | 3p dk purple ('56) | .25 | *.25* |
| *a.* | | Booklet pane of 6 | 4.50 | |
| *b.* | | Booklet pane of 4 | 6.00 | |
| *c.* | | Wmk. sideways | 16.00 | 12.00 |
| *e.* | | Tete beche pair | *3,000.* | |
| **323** | A128 | 4p ultra | 1.40 | .50 |
| **324** | A129 | 5p lt brn ('56) | 5.00 | 4.50 |
| **325** | A129 | 6p lilac rose ('56) | 4.25 | 1.25 |
| **326** | A129 | 7p emerald | 47.50 | 10.00 |
| **327** | A130 | 8p brt rose ('56) | 6.50 | 1.10 |
| **328** | A130 | 9p dp ol grn ('56) | 21.00 | 2.75 |
| **329** | A130 | 10p royal bl ('56) | 20.00 | 2.50 |
| **330** | A130 | 11p vio brown | .50 | *.80* |
| **331** | A131 | 1sh brown | 20.00 | .60 |
| **332** | A132 | 1sh3p dk grn ('56) | 26.00 | 1.50 |
| **333** | A131 | 1sh6p dark blue | 27.50 | 1.50 |
| | | *Nos. 317-333 (17)* | 181.15 | 28.50 |

Nos. 319c, 320a, 321b, 322c issued in coils.

Nos. 317-322 with watermark inverted are from booklets. See Nos. 353-369.

### Black Graphite Lines on Back

**1957-59 Wmk. 308**

| | | | | |
|---|---|---|---|---|
| *317c* | A126 | ½p red orange | .25 | .25 |
| *p.* | | Phosphor. ('59) | 4.00 | 4.00 |
| *318d* | A126 | 1p ultra | .40 | .25 |
| *p.* | | Phosphor. ('59) | 14.00 | 8.00 |
| *319d* | A126 | 1½p green | 1.10 | *1.60* |
| *p.* | | Phosphor. ('59) | 3.75 | 3.75 |
| *320c* | A126 | 2p red brown | 1.50 | *1.75* |
| *p.* | | Phosphor. ('59) | 160.00 | 125.00 |
| *321c* | A127 | 2½p scarlet (II) | 6.50 | 5.50 |
| *322d* | A127 | 3p dark purple | .70 | .45 |
| | | *Nos. 317c-322d (6)* | 10.45 | 9.80 |

The vertical black graphite lines were applied to facilitate mail sorting by an electronic machine. The 2p has one line (at right, seen from back), the others two.

---

Phosphorescent bands were overprinted vertically in Nov. 1959 on the face of the preceding ½p, 1p, 1½p and 2p graphite-lined stamps, plus the 2p, 2½p, 3p, 4p and 4½p graphite-lined stamps with Wmk. 322, in a letter-sorting experiment. These faint bands can be seen best with an ultraviolet lamp; without it they can be seen best on unused stamps.

---

Scout Emblem and Rolling Hitch Knot A138

4p, Swallows. 1sh3p, Globe encircled by compass.

*Perf. 14½x14*

**1957, Aug. 1 Wmk. 308**

| | | | | |
|---|---|---|---|---|
| **334** | A138 | 2½p scarlet | .45 | .35 |
| **335** | A138 | 4p ultra | .75 | *1.10* |
| **336** | A138 | 1sh3p dk green | 4.50 | 4.00 |
| | | *Nos. 334-336 (3)* | 5.70 | 5.45 |

50th anniv. of the Boy Scout movement and the World Scout Jubilee Jamboree, Sutton Coldfield, Aug. 1-12.

A139

**1957, Sept. 12 Photo.**

| | | | | |
|---|---|---|---|---|
| **337** | A139 | 4p ultra | .85 | *.85* |

46th Conf. of the Inter-Parliamentary Union, London, Sept. 12-19.

Welsh Dragon A140

Designs: 6p, Flag with British Empire and Commonwealth Games Emblem. 1sh3p, Welsh dragon holding laurel.

**1958, July 18 *Perf. 14½x14***

| | | | | |
|---|---|---|---|---|
| **338** | A140 | 3p dk purple | .25 | .25 |
| **339** | A140 | 6p red lilac | .40 | .40 |
| **340** | A140 | 1sh3p green | 1.75 | 1.75 |
| | | *Nos. 338-340 (3)* | 2.40 | 2.40 |

6th British Empire and Commonwealth Games, Cardiff, July 18-26.

---

Regional Issues of Great Britain for Guernsey, Jersey, Isle of Man, Northern Ireland, Scotland and Wales-Monmouthshire are listed in separate sections following Great Britain Envelopes.

---

### Types of 1952-55

*Perf. 14½x14*

**1958-65 Photo. Wmk. 322**

| | | | | |
|---|---|---|---|---|
| **353** | A126 | ½p red orange | .25 | .25 |
| *a.* | | Booklet pane of 6 | .70 | |
| *b.* | | Booklet pane of 4 | 4.00 | |
| *e.* | | Booklet pane of 4 (3 No. 353 + No. 357) ('63) | 10.50 | 10.50 |
| *f.* | | Tete beche pair | *2,250.* | |
| *g.* | | Booklet pane of 4 (2 Nos. 353 + 2 No. 357) ('64) | 2.50 | 2.50 |
| *h.* | | Wmk. sideways | .30 | .35 |
| **354** | A126 | 1p ultra ('59) | .25 | .25 |
| *a.* | | Booklet pane of 6 ('59) | 1.50 | |
| *b.* | | Booklet pane of 4 | 5.25 | |
| *e.* | | Imperf., pair | — | |
| *f.* | | Bklt. pane, #2 #354, 2 #358 ('65) | 11.50 | 11.50 |
| *g.* | | Tete-beche pair | | |
| *h.* | | Wmk. sideways | 1.00 | .75 |
| **355** | A126 | 1½p green | .25 | .25 |
| *a.* | | Booklet pane of 6 | 1.50 | |
| *b.* | | Booklet pane of 4 | 40.00 | |
| *e.* | | Tete-beche pair | | |
| *f.* | | Wmk. sideways | 8.00 | 6.50 |
| **356** | A126 | 2p red brown | .25 | .25 |
| *a.* | | Wmk. sideways | .60 | *.80* |
| *b.* | | Booklet pane of 6 | 6.00 | |
| **357** | A127 | 2½p scarlet, type II ('59) | .25 | .25 |
| *a.* | | Type I ('61) | .65 | .65 |
| *b.* | | Wmk. sideways, type I | .65 | .40 |
| *c.* | | Booklet pane of 6, Type II ('59) | 1.50 | |
| *f.* | | Tete beche pair, type II | *5,000.* | |
| *g.* | | Booklet pane of 4, type II ('64) | 2.50 | |
| *h.* | | Imperf., pair | — | |
| *i.* | | Wmk. sideways, type II ('59) | .75 | .75 |
| **358** | A127 | 3p dark purple | .25 | .25 |
| *a.* | | Booklet pane of 6 | 1.75 | |
| *b.* | | Booklet pane of 4 | 3.75 | |
| *e.* | | Imperf., pair | 250.00 | |
| *g.* | | Wmk. sideways | .30 | .35 |
| **359** | A128 | 4p ultra | .40 | .35 |
| *b.* | | Booklet pane of 6 ('65) | 6.00 | |
| *c.* | | Booklet pane of 4 ('65) | 3.75 | |
| *d.* | | Wmk. sideways | .90 | .55 |
| **360** | A128 | 4½p henna brn | .25 | .25 |
| **361** | A129 | 5p light brown | .30 | .40 |
| **362** | A129 | 6p lil rose ('59) | .30 | .25 |
| **363** | A129 | 7p emerald | .45 | .45 |
| **364** | A130 | 8p brt rose ('60) | .55 | .40 |
| **365** | A130 | 9p dp ol grn ('59) | .55 | .40 |
| **366** | A130 | 10p royal blue | 1.00 | .65 |
| **367** | A131 | 1sh brown | .50 | .35 |
| **368** | A132 | 1sh3p dk grn ('59) | .50 | .35 |
| **369** | A131 | 1sh6p dark blue | 5.00 | .60 |
| | | *Nos. 353-369 (17)* | 11.30 | 5.95 |

Nos. 356a and 357b were issued in coils. The 3p and 4p watermarked sideways may be from a coil or booklet pane of 4.

Booklet panes of this issue have watermarks normal, inverted or sideways.

Part perf. booklet panes exist of No. 353a and No. 354a.

### Black Graphite Lines on Back

**1958-59 Wmk. 322**

| | | | | |
|---|---|---|---|---|
| *353c* | A126 | ½p red orange ('59) | 8.50 | 8.50 |
| *d.* | | Booklet pane of 6 | 52.50 | |
| *354c* | A126 | 1p ultra | 2.00 | 1.10 |
| *d.* | | Booklet pane of 6 | 17.50 | |
| *355c* | A126 | 1½p green ('59) | 80.00 | 65.00 |
| *d.* | | Booklet pane of 6 | 600.00 | |
| *356c* | A126 | 2p red brown | 6.75 | 2.75 |
| *cp.* | | Phosphor. ('59) | 5.00 | 4.75 |
| *357d* | A127 | 2½p scarlet (II) ('59) | 9.00 | 7.50 |
| *dp.* | | Phosphor. ('59) | 17.50 | 15.00 |
| *e.* | | Booklet pane of 6 | 100.00 | |
| *358c* | A127 | 3p dark purple | .55 | .55 |
| *cp.* | | Phosphor. ('59) | 8.00 | 7.75 |
| *d.* | | Booklet pane of 6 | 5.50 | |
| *359a* | A128 | 4p ultra ('59) | 3.75 | 3.75 |
| *ap.* | | Phosphor. ('59) | 17.00 | 14.00 |
| *360a* | A128 | 4½p henna brn ('59) | 5.00 | 4.50 |
| *ap.* | | Phosphor. ('59) | 27.50 | 19.00 |
| | | *Nos. 353c-360a (8)* | 115.55 | 93.65 |

The vertical black graphite lines were applied to facilitate mail sorting by an electronic machine. The 2p has one line; the others two. Missing or misplaced lines occur on 1p, 3p and 4p.

Nos. 353c and 354c were issued only in booklets or coils; No. 355c only in booklets.

### Phosphorescent Stamps of 1958-65

**1960-67 Wmk. 322**

| | | | | |
|---|---|---|---|---|
| *353p* | A126 | ½p red orange | .25 | .25 |
| *ap.* | | Booklet pane of 6 | 4.00 | |
| *bp.* | | Booklet pane of 4 | 50.00 | |
| *hp.* | | Wmk. sideways ('61) | 8.50 | 8.00 |
| *354p* | A126 | 1p ultra | .25 | .25 |
| *ap.* | | Booklet pane of 6 | 5.00 | |
| *bp.* | | Booklet pane of 4 | 12.00 | |
| *fp.* | | Booklet pane of 2 each #354p, 358p | 40.00 | |
| *hp.* | | Wmk. sideways ('61) | .50 | .50 |
| *355p* | A126 | 1½p green | .25 | .25 |
| *ap.* | | Booklet pane of 6 | 5.00 | |
| *bp.* | | Booklet pane of 4 | 50.00 | |
| *fp.* | | Wmk. sideways ('61) | 8.50 | 7.50 |
| *356p* | A126 | 2p red brown | .25 | .25 |
| *ap.* | | Watermark sideways | .30 | *.35* |
| *357p* | A127 | 2½p scarlet (II) | .25 | *.30* |
| *ap.* | | Type I ('61) | 35.00 | 25.00 |
| *cp.* | | Booklet pane of 6 | 60.00 | |
| *358p* | A127 | 3p dark purple | .45 | *.50* |
| *ap.* | | Booklet pane of 6 | 7.50 | |
| *bp.* | | Booklet pane of 4 | 12.50 | |
| *gp.* | | Watermark sideways | 1.00 | .55 |
| *359p* | A128 | 4p ultramarine | .25 | .25 |
| *bp.* | | Booklet pane of 6 | 6.25 | |
| *cp.* | | Booklet pane of 4 | 5.00 | |
| *dp.* | | Watermark sideways | .30 | *.50* |
| *360p* | A128 | 4½p henna brown ('61) | .25 | .25 |
| *361p* | A129 | 5p lt brown ('67) | .25 | .25 |
| *362p* | A129 | 6p lilac rose | .35 | .30 |
| *363p* | A129 | 7p emerald ('67) | .65 | .60 |
| *364p* | A130 | 8p brt rose ('67) | .45 | .45 |
| *365p* | A130 | 9p dp ol grn ('67) | .60 | .55 |
| *366p* | A130 | 10p royal blue ('67) | .60 | .60 |
| *367p* | A131 | 1sh brown ('67) | .45 | .40 |
| *368p* | A132 | 1sh3p dark green | 1.60 | *2.25* |
| *369p* | A131 | 1sh6p dark blue ('66) | 2.00 | 1.50 |
| | | *Nos. 353p-369p (17)* | 9.15 | 9.20 |

The 2p, 2½p (II) and 3p were issued with both one and two phosphorescent bands. The less expensive is valued here.

Watermarked sideways, the 2p is from a coil; the 3p and 4p from booklet pane or coil; the ½p, 1p and 1½p from booklet panes (hence unlisted in this state).

Booklet panes of 4 with phosphorescent bands; ½p, 1p, 1½p, 3p (2 bands), 4p, and 1p se-tenant with 3p (1 or 2 bands). Booklet panes of 6 with phosphorescent bands: ½p, 1p, 1½p, 2½p (II) (1 or 2 bands), 3p (1 or 2 bands), 4p.

*Perf. 11x12*

**1959-68 Engr. Wmk. 322**

| | | | | |
|---|---|---|---|---|
| **371** | A133 | 2sh6p dark brown | .35 | .35 |
| **372** | A133 | 5sh crimson | 1.00 | .50 |
| **373** | A133 | 10sh bright ultra | 14.00 | 4.00 |
| **374** | A133 | £1 intense blk | 11.50 | 6.00 |
| | | *Nos. 371-374 (4)* | 26.85 | 10.85 |

See Nos 525-528.

Postboy on Horseback A147

Queen Elizabeth II, Oak Leaves and 1660 Post Horn — A148

*Perf. 14½x14, 14x14½*

**1960, July 7 Photo. Wmk. 322**

| | | | | |
|---|---|---|---|---|
| **375** | A147 | 3p bright violet | .50 | .50 |
| **376** | A148 | 1sh3p dark green | 3.00 | *3.25* |

Tercentenary of the act establishing the General Letter Office (General Post Office).

Symbolic Wheel CD3

*Perf. 14½x14*

**1960, Sept. 19 Wmk. 322**

| | | | | |
|---|---|---|---|---|
| **377** | CD3 | 6p red lilac & grn | 1.50 | .50 |
| **378** | CD3 | 1sh6p dk bl & red brn | 8.25 | 4.50 |

1st anniv. of the establishment of CEPT.

Symbolic Thrift Plant — A150

Nut Tree, Nest, Squirrel, Owl A151

Thrift Plant A152

*Perf. 14x14½, 14½x14*

**1961, Aug. 28 Photo. Wmk. 322**

| | | | | |
|---|---|---|---|---|
| **379** | A150 | 2½p scar & blk | .25 | .25 |
| *a.* | | Black omitted | *27,500.* | |
| **380** | A151 | 3p pur & org | .25 | .25 |
| *a.* | | Orange omitted | 550.00 | *250.00* |
| **381** | A152 | 1sh6p dk bl & ver | 1.75 | 1.75 |
| | | *Nos. 379-381 (3)* | 2.25 | 2.25 |

Centenary of Post Office Savings Bank.

CEPT Emblem A153

Nineteen Doves Flying as One CD4

Design: 10p, Queen at right.

**1961, Sept. 18** *Perf. 14½x14*

**382** A153 2p red brn, yel & rose .25 .25
*a.* Orange omitted 18,000.
**383** CD4 4p ultra, pink & buff .25 .25
**384** CD4 10p dk bl, yel grn & Prus blue .25 *.40*
*a.* Yellow green omitted 24,000.
*b.* Dark blue omitted 7,500.
*Nos. 382-384 (3)* .75 .90

Hammer Beam Roof of Westminster Hall — A155

Parliament — A156

*Perf. 14½x14, 14x14½*

**1961, Sept. 25** **Wmk. 322**

**385** A155 6p red lil & gold .25 .25
*a.* Gold omitted 2,500.
**386** A156 1sh3p green & slate 1.75 1.75
*a.* Slate (Queen's head) omitted 40,000.

7th Commonwealth Parliamentary Conf.

National Productivity Symbol — A157

Designs: 3p, Two arrows and map of the British Isles. 1sh3p, Five arrows pointing up.

*Perf. 14½x14*

**1962, Nov. 14** **Photo.** **Wmk. 322**

**387** A157 2½p car rose & dk grn .25 .25
**388** A157 3p violet & blue .30 .25
*a.* Queen's head omitted 6,000.
**389** A157 1sh3p dk grn, car rose & bl 1.50 *1.50*
*a.* Queen's head omitted 16,000.
*Nos. 387-389 (3)* 2.05 2.00

**Phosphorescent**

*387p* A157 2½p car rose & dk grn .55 .50
*388p* A157 3p violet & blue 1.50 .80
*389p* A157 1sh3p dk grn, car rose & bl 25.00 17.50
*Nos. 387p-389p (3)* 27.05 18.80

National Productivity Year. The watermark on Nos. 387-388 is inverted.

Phosphorescent Commemorative stamps between Nos. 387-493 were issued both with and without phosphorescence on the front unless otherwise noted with the issue.

Starting with No. 514, commemorative stamps were issued only with phosphorescence on the front unless otherwise noted.

Phosphorescent Regulars: Starting in 1967, all small stamps (lower values) of the regular series were issued only with phosphorescence.

Wheat Emblem and People A158

1sh3p, Children of different races.

**1963, Mar. 21** **Wmk. 322**

**390** A158 2½p pink & dp car .25 .25
*p.* Phosphor. 2.50 1.00
**391** A158 1sh3p yellow & brn 1.75 1.75
*p.* Phosphor. 22.50 14.50

FAO "Freedom from Hunger" campaign.

Paris Postal Conference A159

**1963, May 7** **Wmk. 322**

**392** A159 6p purple & green .35 .35
*a.* Green omitted 6,000.
*p.* Phosphor. 6.25 6.00

Cent. of the 1st Intl. Postal Conf., Paris, 1863, and Paris Postal Conf., May 7-9, 1963.

Buttercups, Daisies and Bee A160

Design: 4½p, Badger, Fawn, woodpecker, lark, titmouse, butterfly, mouse and wild plants.

**1963, May 16** *Perf. 14½x14*

**393** A160 3p multicolored .25 .25
*p.* Phosphor. .50 .50
**394** A160 4½p multicolored .25 *.35*
*p.* Phosphor. 2.75 2.75

Natl. Nature Week, May 18-25, and the importance of wildlife conservation.

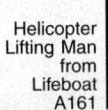

Helicopter Lifting Man from Lifeboat A161

Lifeboat Men A162

Design: 4p, 19th cent. lifeboat under sail.

**1963, May 31** **Photo.**

**395** A161 2½p multicolored .25 .25
**396** A161 4p multicolored .40 *.45*
**397** A162 1sh6p multicolored 2.25 *2.50*
*Nos. 395-397 (3)* 2.90 3.20

**Phosphorescent**

*395p* A161 2½p multicolored .50 *.60*
*396p* A161 4p multicolored .50 *.60*
*397p* A162 1sh6p multicolored 37.50 25.00
*Nos. 395p-397p (3)* 38.50 26.20

9th Intl. Life-Boat Conf., Edinburgh, 6/3-5.

Red Cross and Elizabeth II — A163

1sh3p, Cross at UL. 1sh6p, Cross in center.

**1963, Aug. 15** **Wmk. 322**

**Cross in Red**

**398** A163 3p purple .25 .25
*a.* Red cross omitted 18,000.
**399** A163 1sh3p gray & blue 2.00 2.00
**400** A163 1sh6p dl bl & ol bister 2.00 2.00
*Nos. 398-400 (3)* 4.25 4.25

**Phosphorescent**

*398p* A163 3p purple 1.10 1.00
*a.* Red cross omitted 45,000.
*399p* A163 1sh3p gray & blue 29.00 19.00
*400p* A163 1sh6p dull blue & ol bister 29.00 19.00
*Nos. 398p-400p (3)* 59.10 39.00

Red Cross Cent. Cong., Geneva, Sept. 2.

Cable Around World and Under Sea A164

**1963, Dec. 3** *Perf. 14½x14*

**401** A164 1sh6p blue & blk 2.00 *2.00*
*a.* Black omitted 8,000.
*p.* Phosphor. 13.50 11.50

Opening of the Commonwealth Pacific (telephone) cable service, COMPAC.

Puck and Bottom from "A Midsummer Night's Dream," Shakespeare — A165

Hamlet Holding Yorick's Skull A166

First Folio Portrait of Shakespeare and: 6p, Feste the Clown, from "Twelfth Night." 1sh3p, Romeo and Juliet. 1sh6p, Henry V praying at Agincourt.

*Perf. 14½x14*

**1964, Apr. 23** **Photo.** **Wmk. 322**

**402** A165 3p multicolored .25 .25
**403** A165 6p multicolored .30 .30
**404** A165 1sh3p multicolored .65 .65
**405** A165 1sh6p multicolored .85 .75

*Perf. 11x12*

**Engr.**

**406** A166 2sh6p dark gray 1.25 1.25
*Nos. 402-406 (5)* 3.30 3.20

**Phosphorescent**

*402p* A165 3p multicolored .30 *.30*
*403p* A165 6p multicolored .75 *1.00*
*404p* A165 1sh3p multicolored 3.50 *4.50*
*405p* A165 1sh6p multicolored 6.25 5.00
*Nos. 402p-405p (4)* 10.80 10.80

400th anniv. of the birth of William Shakespeare. No. 406 was not issued with phosphorescence.

Apartment Buildings, London A170

Designs: 4p, Shipyards, Belfast. 8p, Beddgelert Forest Park, Snowdonia. 1sh6p, Dounreay nuclear reactor and sheaves of wheat.

**1964, July 1** **Photo.** *Perf. 14½x14*

**410** A170 2½p multicolored .25 .25
**411** A170 4p multicolored .30 .30
*a.* Violet ("4d") omitted 300.00
*b.* Ocher omitted 475.00
*c.* Violet & ocher omitted 550.00
**412** A170 8p multicolored .65 .65
*a.* Green omitted 22,500.
**413** A170 1sh6p multicolored 2.60 2.60
*Nos. 410-413 (4)* 3.80 3.80

**Phosphorescent**

*410p* A170 2½p multicolored .40 .50
*411p* A170 4p multicolored 1.25 1.25
*412p* A170 8p multicolored 2.25 2.25
*413p* A170 1sh6p multicolored 20.00 18.00
*Nos. 410p-413p (4)* 23.90 22.00

20th Intl. Geographical Cong., London, July 20-28.

Spring Gentian A171

**1964, Aug. 5** **Wmk. 322**

**414** A171 3p shown .25 .25
*a.* Blue omitted 21,000.
*b.* Sage green omitted 24,000.
**415** A171 6p Dog rose .40 .40
**416** A171 9p Honeysuckle 1.25 1.25
*a.* Light green omitted 23,000.
**417** A171 1sh3p Fringed water lily 1.75 1.75
*a.* Yellow omitted 45,000.
*Nos. 414-417 (4)* 3.65 3.65

**Phosphorescent**

*414p* A171 3p shown .40 .40
*415p* A171 6p Dog rose 2.00 2.00
*416p* A171 9p Honeysuckle 3.50 3.00
*417p* A171 1sh3p Fringed water lily 19.00 16.00
*Nos. 414p-417p (4)* 24.90 21.40

10th Intl. Botanical Cong., Edinburgh, Aug. 3-12.

Forth Road Bridge A172

Design: 6p, Bridge and railroad bridge.

**1964, Sept. 4** *Perf. 14½x14*

**418** A172 3p blk, lil & blue .25 .25
*p.* Phosphor. .75 .75
**419** A172 6p vio blk, grnsh bl & car lake .35 .35
*a.* Greenish blue omitted 7,000. *1,500.*
*p.* Phosphor. 4.00 4.00

Opening of Forth Road Bridge, Scotland.

Winston Churchill A173

Design: 1sh3p, Large portrait.

**1965, July 8** **Photo.** **Wmk. 322**

**420** A173 4p dk brown & blk .25 .25
*p.* Phosphor. .30 .30
**421** A173 1sh3p gray & black .45 .45
*p.* Phosphor. 2.25 *2.75*

Sir Winston Spencer Churchill (1874-1965), statesman and WWII leader.

Seal of Simon de Montfort A174

St. Stephen's Hall, Westminster Hall and Abbey, Engraving by Wenceslaus Hollar, 1647 — A175

**1965, July 19** *Perf. 14½x14*

422 A174 6p dark olive .25 .25
*p.* Phosphor. .75 .90
423 A175 2sh6p brown black .75 1.00

700th anniv. of Parliament. No. 423 was not issued with phosphorescence; size: 58x21mm.

Salvation Army Band and "Blood and Fire" Flag A176

1sh6p, Salvation Army officers and flag.

**1965, Aug. 9**

424 A176 3p dk bl, yel & brt car .25 .25
*p.* Phosphor. .25 .40
425 A176 1sh6p red, yel & brt bl .85 1.00
*p.* Phosphor. 2.00 2.25

Centenary of the Salvation Army.

Lister's Carbolic Spray A177

1sh, Joseph Lister & carbolic acid formula.

**1965, Sept. 1**

426 A177 4p gray, bluish blk & red brn .25 .25
*a.* Red brown (tubing) omitted 600.00
*b.* Bluish black omitted 7,000.
*p.* Phosphor. .25 .25
427 A177 1sh blk, blue & pur .75 1.00
*p.* Phosphor. 2.00 2.25

Introduction of antiseptic surgery by Joseph Lister, cent.

Trinidad Folk Dancers, Shrove Monday Carnival A178

Design: 1sh6p, French Canadian folk dancers, Les Feux Follets.

*Perf. 14½x14*

**1965, Sept. 1 Photo. Wmk. 322**

428 A178 6p orange & blk .25 .25
*p.* Phosphor. .30 .45
429 A178 1sh6p brt vio & blk .80 1.00
*p.* Phosphor. 2.50 2.75

1st Commonwealth Arts Festival, 9/16-10/2.

Supermarine Spitfire Fighters — A179

Anti-Aircraft Gun Battery in Action A180

Designs: No. 431, Pilot in cockpit of Hawker Hurricane fighter. No. 432, Wing tips of Messerschmitt ME-109 and Spitfire. No. 433, Two Spitfires attacking Heinkel HE-111 bomber. No. 434, Spitfire attacking Junkers JU-187B Stuka dive bomber. No. 435, Hurricanes returning over wreckage of Dornier DO-17 Z bomber. 1sh3p, Vapor trails over St. Paul's Cathedral, London.

*Perf. 14½x14*

**1965, Sept. 13 Photo. Wmk. 322**

430 A179 4p slate & dk ol .40 .40
431 A179 4p slate & dk ol .40 .40
432 A179 4p sl, dk ol, brt bl & red .40 .40
433 A179 4p slate & dk ol .40 .40
434 A179 4p slate & dk ol .40 .40
435 A179 4p sl, dk ol & brt blue .40 .40
*a.* Bright blue omitted 6,500.
*b.* Block of 6, #430-435 4.50 5.00
436 A180 9p vio bl, org & vio black 1.75 1.75
437 A180 1sh3p brt bl, sl & grnsh gray 1.75 1.75
*Nos. 430-437 (8)* 5.90 5.90

**Phosphorescent**

*430p* A179 4p slate & dark ol .90 .90
*431p* A179 4p slate & dark ol .90 .90
*432p* A179 4p sl, dk ol, brt bl & red .90 .90
*433p* A179 4p slate & dark ol .90 .90
*434p* A179 4p slate & dark ol .90 .90
*435p* A179 4p sl, dk ol & brt bl .90 .90
*a.* Block of 6, #430p-435p 9.50 12.00
*436p* A180 9p vio bl, org & vio black 1.90 2.00
*437p* A180 1sh3p brt bl, slate & grnsh gray 1.90 2.00
*Nos. 430p-437p (8)* 9.20 9.40

25th anniv. of the Battle of Britain. Nos. 430-435 printed in blocks of 6 (3x2) in sheets of 120.

Post Office Tower and Georgian Buildings — A181

Design: 1sh3p, Post Office Tower and Nash Terrace, Regents Park, horiz.

**1965, Oct. 8** *Perf. 14x14½, 14½x14*

438 A181 3p brt bl, lem & ol green .25 .25
*a.* Lemon omitted 6,000. 2,250.
*p.* Phosphor. .25 .25
439 A181 1sh3p grn, ol grn & bl .30 .40
*p.* Phosphor. .30 .40

Opening of the Post Office Tower, London.

UN Emblem A182

ICY Emblem A183

**1965, Oct. 25** *Perf. 14½x14*

440 A182 3p multicolored .25 .25
*p.* Phosphor. .30 .30
441 A183 1sh6p multicolored .60 .60
*p.* Phosphor. 2.25 2.40

20th anniv. of the UN and Intl. Cooperation Year, 1965.

"World Telecommunication Stations" — A184

ITU Cent.: 1sh6p, "Radio waves & switchboard."

**1965, Nov. 15 Photo. Wmk. 322**

442 A184 9p multicolored .30 .30
*p.* Phosphor. 1.00 .85
443 A184 1sh6p bl, red, blk, ind & pink .85 .85
*a.* Pink omitted 4,200.
*p.* Phosphor. 4.25 5.25

Robert Burns and Saltier Cross of St. Andrew A185

Design: 1sh3p, Alexander Nasmyth portrait of Burns, his signature and symbols of his life. Portrait of Burns on 4p stamp is adaptation of Archibald Skirvings', chalk drawing, 1798.

**1966, Jan. 25** *Perf. 14½x14*

444 A185 4p blue, blk & dk sl .25 .25
*p.* Phosphor. .30 .35
445 A185 1sh3p org, blk & Prus blue .35 .55
*p.* Phosphor. 1.90 2.25

Robert Burns (1759-1796), Scottish national poet.

Westminster Abbey — A186

Fan Vaulting, Chapel of Henry VII A187

**1966, Feb. 28 Photo.** *Perf. 14½x14*

452 A186 3p blue, blk, & red brn .25 .25
*p.* Phosphor. .25 .25

*Perf. 11x12*

**Engr.**

453 A187 2sh6p black .50 .65

900th anniv. of Westminster Abbey. No. 453 issued only without phosphor.

Landscape near Hassock, Sussex A188

Views: 6p, Antrim, Northern Ireland. 1sh3p, Harlech Castle, Wales. 1sh6p, The Cairngorms (mountains), Scotland.

*Perf. 14½x14*

**1966, May 2 Photo. Wmk. 322**

454 A188 4p multicolored .25 .25
455 A188 6p multicolored .25 .25
456 A188 1sh3p multicolored .25 .30
457 A188 1sh6p multicolored .40 .35
*Nos. 454-457 (4)* 1.15 1.15

**Phosphorescent**

*454p* A188 4p multicolored .25 .25
*455p* A188 6p multicolored .25 .25
*456p* A188 1sh3p multicolored .25 .30
*457p* A188 1sh6p multicolored .40 .40
*Nos. 454p-457p (4)* 1.15 1.20

Soccer Players — A189

Players and Crowd A190

1sh3p, Goalkeeper and two players.

*Perf. 14x14½, 14½x14*

**1966, June 1 Photo. Wmk. 322**

458 A189 4p multicolored .25 .25
459 A190 6p multicolored .25 .25
*a.* Black omitted 200.00
*b.* Yellow green omitted 6,000.
*c.* Red omitted 12,000.
460 A190 1sh3p multicolored .40 .50
*a.* Blue omitted 350.00
*Nos. 458-460 (3)* .90 1.00

**Phosphorescent**

*458p* A189 4p multicolored .25 .25
*459p* A190 6p multicolored .25 .25
*d.* Black omitted 2,750.
*460p* A190 1sh3p multicolored .40 .50
*Nos. 458p-460p (3)* .90 1.00

Final games of the 1965-66 World Soccer Championship for the Jules Rimet Cup, Wembley, July 11-30.

See No. 465.

Blackheaded Gull — A191

*Perf. 14½x14*

**1966, Aug. 8 Photo. Wmk. 322**

**Birds in Natural Colors**

461 A191 4p shown .25 .25
*p.* Phosphor. .25 .25
462 A191 4p Blue tit .25 .25
*p.* Phosphor. .25 .25
463 A191 4p European robin .25 .25
*p.* Phosphor. .25 .25
464 A191 4p European blackbird .25 .25
*p.* Phosphor. .25 .25
*a.* Block of 4, #461-464 1.00 1.75
*b.* Block of 4, #461p-464p 1.25 1.75

Seven colors have been found omitted (singly or in combinations) on Nos. 461-464; green, red, ultramarine, brown, red brown, yellow and black. Values range from $125 to $20,000.

**No. 458 Inscribed: "ENGLAND WINNERS"**

**1966, Aug. 18** *Perf. 14x14½*

465 A189 4p multicolored .25 .25

England's victory in the World Soccer Cup Championship.

Jodrell Bank Radio Telescope A192

Designs: 6p, Automobiles (Jaguar and 3 Mini-Minors). 1sh3p, SR N6 Hovercraft. 1sh6p, Windscale atomic reactor.

**1966, Sept. 19** *Perf. 14½x14*

466 A192 4p yellow & blk .25 .25
467 A192 6p org, red & dk bl .25 .25
*a.* Red (Mini-Minors) omitted 20,000.
*b.* Dark blue (Jaguar & imprint) omitted 17,000.
468 A192 1sh3p sl, blk, org & bl .30 .30
469 A192 1sh6p multicolored .35 .30
*Nos. 466-469 (4)* 1.15 1.10

**Phosphorescent**

*466p* A192 4p yellow & black .25 .25
*467p* A192 6p org, red & dk bl .25 .25
*468p* A192 1sh3p slate, blk, org & bl .30 .35
*469p* A192 1sh6p multicolored .40 .50
*Nos. 466p-469p (4)* 1.20 1.35

British technology.

Battle of Hastings A193

Battle of Hastings from Bayeux Tapestry: No. 471, Two knights on horseback, one killed, one attacking. No. 472, Slain Harold on horseback and knight with shield. No. 473, Knight with shield and axe fighting horseman. No. 474, Knight on foot killing man, and horseman attacking with lance. No. 475, Four knights and two horses in battle scene. 6p, Norman ship. 1sh3p, King Harold's housecarls (body guard) battling Normans.

**Photo.; Gold Impressed on 6p, 1sh3p**
*Perf. 14½x14*

**1966, Oct. 14** **Wmk. 322**

**Size: 38½x22mm**

**470** A193 4p multicolored .25 .25
**471** A193 4p multicolored .25 .25
**472** A193 4p multicolored .25 .25
**473** A193 4p multicolored .25 .25
**474** A193 4p multicolored .25 .25
**475** A193 4p multicolored .25 .25
*a.* Strip of 6, #470-475 2.00 —
**476** A193 6p multi & gold .25 .25

**Size: 58x22mm**

**477** A193 1sh3p multi & gold .30 .55
*Nos. 470-477 (8)* 2.05 2.30

**Phosphorescent**

*470p* A193 4p multicolored .25 .25
*471p* A193 4p multicolored .25 .25
*472p* A193 4p multicolored .25 .25
*473p* A193 4p multicolored .25 .25
*474p* A193 4p multicolored .25 .25
*475p* A193 4p multicolored .25 .25
*b.* Strip of 6, #470p-475p 2.00 —
*476p* A193 6p multi & gold .25 .25
*477p* A193 1sh3p multi & gold .30 .55
*Nos. 470p-477p (8)* 2.05 2.30

900th anniv. of the Battle of Hastings.

Eight colors have been found omitted (singly or in pair) on Nos. 470-475 and 470p-477p: gray, orange, blue, dark blue, bright green, olive green, brown and magenta. Also violet on 1sh3p. Values for various color-omitted examples of Nos. 470-475 and 470p-475p, $65-$75. Values for color-omitted examples of No. 477, $5,000.; No. 477p, $1,250.

Gold Omitted

The variety "Gold (Queen's head) omitted" can be forged by chemically removing the gold.

Christmas — A194

**Photo.; Gold Impressed**

**1966, Dec. 1** *Perf. 14x14½*

**478** A194 3p King .25 .25
*b.* Green omitted —
*p.* Phosphor. .25 .25
**479** A194 1sh6p Snowman .30 .35
*b.* Pink omitted 4,500.
*p.* Phosphor. .30 .35

Loading Ship at Dock and Train A195

Design: 1sh6p, Loading plane from trucks and flags of EFTA members.

*Perf. 14½x14*

**1967, Feb. 20** **Photo.** **Wmk. 322**

**480** A195 9p blue & multi .25 .25
*p.* Phosphor. .25 .25
**481** A195 1sh6p violet & multi .35 .35
*p.* Phosphor. .25 .30

European Free Trade Assoc. Tariffs were abolished Dec. 31, 1966, among EFTA members (Austria, Denmark, Finland, Great Britain, Norway, Portugal, Sweden, Switzerland).

Colors omitted include: 9p — yellow, brown, light blue, light violet and green singly; black, brown, light blue and yellow simultaneously. 1sh6p — dark blue, bister, yellow, red, ultramarine and gray. 9p, value range for one-color omissions, $75 to $200. 1sh6p, value for red omitted $5,000 (used), dark blue omitted $500, value for other color-omitted errors $75 to $125 each.

Hawthorn and Wild Blackberry A196

Flowers: No. 489, Morning-glory and viper's bugloss. No. 490, Ox-eye daisy, coltsfoot and buttercup. No. 491, Bluebell, red campion and wood anemone. 9p, Dog violet. 1sh9p, Primrose.

*Perf. 14½x14*

**1967, Apr. 24** **Photo.** **Wmk. 322**

**488** A196 4p multicolored .25 .25
**489** A196 4p multicolored .25 .25
**490** A196 4p multicolored .25 .25
**491** A196 4p multicolored .25 .25
**492** A196 9p multicolored .25 .25
**493** A196 1sh9p multicolored .25 .35
*Nos. 488-493 (6)* 1.50 1.60

**Phosphorescent**

*488p* A196 4p multicolored .25 .25
*489p* A196 4p multicolored .25 .25
*490p* A196 4p multicolored .25 .25
*491p* A196 4p multicolored .25 .25
*492p* A196 9p multicolored .25 .25
*493p* A196 1sh9p multicolored .25 .30
*Nos. 488p-493p (6)* 1.50 1.55

Four colors have been found omitted on Nos. 488-491 and three on 488p-491p: dark brown, red, violet and dull purple. Values range from $500 to $5,000.

For QEII Machin definitives, see listings following Regional Issues and preceding Booklets.

Master Lambton, by Thomas Lawrence — A198

Mares and Foals, by George Stubbs A199

Design: 1sh6p, Children Coming out of School, by Laurence Stephen Lowry.

**Photo.; Gold Impressed on 4p, 1sh6p**
*Perf. 14x14½, 14½x14*

**1967, July 10** **Unwmk.**

**514** A198 4p multi .25 .25
*a.* Gold (Queen's head & value) omitted 350.00
*b.* Blue omitted 18,000.
**515** A199 9p multi .25 .25
*a.* Black (Queen's head & value) omitted 950.00
*b.* Black (Queen's head only) omitted 2,400.
**516** A199 1sh6p multi .25 .25
*a.* Blue omitted 300.00
*b.* Gray omitted 160.00
*c.* Gold (Queen's head) omitted 13,500.
*Nos. 514-516 (3)* .75 .75

See Nos. 568-571.

Gipsy Moth IV — A200

**1967, July 24** **Photo.** *Perf. 14½x14*

**517** A200 1sh9p multicolored .25 .25

Sir Francis Chichester's one-man voyage around the world, Aug. 27, 1966-May 28, 1967.

Radar Screen A201

British Discoveries: 1sh, Penicillin mold. 1sh6p, Vickers 10 twin jet engines. 1sh9p, Television camera, vert.

*Perf. 14½x14, 14x14½*

**1967, Sept. 19** **Photo.** **Wmk. 322**

**518** A201 4p multicolored .25 .25
**519** A201 1sh multicolored .25 .25
**520** A201 1sh6p multicolored .25 .25
**521** A201 1sh9p multicolored .25 .25
*a.* Gray omitted 4,500.
*Nos. 518-521 (4)* 1.00 1.00

Adoration of the Shepherds, Ascribed to School of Seville — A202

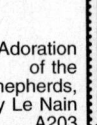

Adoration of the Shepherds, by Le Nain A203

Christmas 1967: 4p, Madonna and Child, by Murillo.

**Photo.; Gold Impressed**
*Perf. 14x14½, 14½x14*

**1967** **Unwmk.**

**522** A202 3p multi .25 .25
*a.* Gold (Queen's head & value) omitted 110.00
*b.* Pink omitted 3,750.
**523** A202 4p multi .25 .25
*a.* Gold (Queen's head & value) omitted 80.00
*b.* Gold ("4d" only) omitted 3,000.
*c.* Yellow omitted 7,500.
*d.* Greenish yellow & gold omitted 15,000.
**524** A203 1sh6p multi .25 .25
*a.* Gold (Queen's head & value) omitted 17,000.
*b.* Blue omitted 800.00
*c.* Yellow omitted 20,000.
*d.* Gold (Queen's head only) omitted 3,000.
*Nos. 522-524 (3)* .75 .75

Issue dates: 4p, Oct. 18; 3p, 1sh6p, Nov. 27.

**Castle Type of 1955**
*Perf. 11x12*

**1967-68** **Engr.** **Unwmk.**

**525** A133 2sh6p dk brown ('68) .35 .35
**526** A133 5sh crimson ('68) .70 .55
**527** A133 10sh brt ultra ('68) 5.25 3.25
**528** A133 £1 intense black 6.50 4.00
*Nos. 525-528 (4)* 12.80 8.15

Aberfeldy Bridge, Perthshire A204

Designs: 4p, Prehistoric Tarr Steps, Exmoor. 1sh6p, Menai Bridge, North Wales, 1826. 1sh9p, Viaduct, Highway M4.

*Perf. 14½x14*

**1968, Apr. 29** **Photo.** **Unwmk.**

**560** A204 4p gold & multi .25 .25
**561** A204 9p gold & multi .25 .25
*a.* Blue omitted 7,000.
*b.* Gold (Queen's head) omitted 225.00
**562** A204 1sh6p gold & multi .25 .30
*a.* Gold (Queen's head) omitted 400.00
*b.* Red omitted 400.00
**563** A204 1sh9p gold & multi .25 .35
*a.* Gold (Queen's head) omitted 400.00
*Nos. 560-563 (4)* 1.00 1.15

Emmeline Pankhurst Statue A205

Designs: 4p, Letters "TUC" and faces. 1sh, Sopwith Camel 1914-1918 fighter plane and formation of Lightning jets. 1sh9p, Capt. Cook's "Endeavour" and signature.

**1968, May 29**

**564** A205 4p brt grn, blk, ol & bl .25 .25
**565** A205 9p gray, violet & blk .25 .25
**566** A205 1sh gray, ol, red, bl & blk .25 .25
**567** A205 1sh9p blk & bister .30 .30
*Nos. 564-567 (4)* 1.05 1.05

Cent. of Trades Union Congress (4p); 50th anniv. of women's suffrage (9p); 50th anniv. of the Royal Air Force (1sh); bicent. of Captain Cook's first discovery voyage (1sh9p).

**Paintings Types of 1967**

Paintings: 4p, Elizabeth I, c. 1575, artist unknown. 1sh, Pinkie (Miss Sarah Moulton-Barrett) by Sir Thomas Lawrence. 1sh6p, St. Mary le Port, by John Piper. 1sh9p, The Hay Wain (landscape), by John Constable.

**Photo.; Gold Impressed**
*Perf. 14x14½, 14½x14*

**1968, Aug. 12**

**568** A198 4p multi .25 .25
*a.* Gold (Queen's head & value) omitted 350.00
*b.* Vermilion omitted 700.00
**569** A198 1sh multi .25 .25
*a.* Gold (Queen's head & value) omitted 7,000.
**570** A198 1sh6p multi .25 .25
*a.* Gold (Queen's head & value) omitted 300.00
**571** A199 1sh9p multi .25 .40
*a.* Gold (Queen's head & value) omitted 950.00
*b.* Red omitted 13,500.
*Nos. 568-571 (4)* 1.00 1.15

Sizes: 4p, 27x37½mm; 1sh, 25½x37½mm; 1sh6p, 31x37½mm; 1sh9p, 38x28mm.

Boy and Girl with Rocking Horse A206

Girl Playing with Dolls and Dollhouse — A207

Christmas: 1sh6p, Boy with toy train and building blocks.

*Perf. 14½x14, 14x14½*

**1968, Nov. 25** **Photo.**

**572** A206 4p gold & multi .25 .25
*a.* Gold omitted 9,000.
*b.* Vermilion omitted 600.00
*c.* Ultramarine omitted 500.00
**573** A207 9p gold & multi .25 .25
*a.* Yellow omitted 160.00
**574** A207 1sh6p gold & multi .25 .35
*a.* Turquoise-green omitted 20,000.
*Nos. 572-574 (3)* .75 .85

British Ships — A208

Designs: 5p, R.M.S. Queen Elizabeth 2. No. 576, Elizabethan Galleon. No. 577, East Indiaman. No. 578, Cutty Sark. No. 579, S.S. Great Britain. No. 580, R.M.S. Mauretania.

**1969, Jan. 15** *Perf. 14½x14*

**Size: 58x22mm**

**575** A208 5p multicolored .25 .25
*a.* Black omitted 3,250.
*b.* Gray omitted 250.00
*c.* Red omitted 275.00

**Size: 38½x22mm**

**576** A208 9p multicolored .25 .25
*a.* Red & blue omitted 3,500.
*b.* Blue omitted 3,500.
**577** A208 9p multicolored .25 .30
**578** A208 9p multicolored .25 .30
*a.* Strip of 3, #576-578 .50

**Size: 58x22mm**

**579** A208 1sh multicolored .35 .35
*a.* Greenish yellow omitted 4,500.

**580** A208 1sh multicolored .35 .35
 *a.* Pair, #579-580 1.00
 *b.* Carmine (hull overlay) omitted 40,000.
 *c.* Red (funnels) omitted 27,500.
 *d.* Carmine and red omitted 27,500.
 *Nos. 575-580 (6)* 1.70 1.80

British seamen and shipbuilders.

Concorde over Great Britain and France A209

Designs: 9p, Concorde seen from above and from side, flags of France and Great Britain. 1sh6p, Outlines of plane's nose and tail superimposed.

**1969, Mar. 3 Photo. *Perf. 14½x14***
**581** A209 4p multicolored .25 .25
 *a.* Violet omitted 700.00
 *b.* Orange omitted 700.00
**582** A209 9p multicolored .30 .30
**583** A209 1sh6p multicolored .35 .40
 *a.* Silver omitted 700.00
 *Nos. 581-583 (3)* .90 .95

First flight of the prototype Concorde plane at Toulouse, France, Mar. 1, 1969.

Alcock, Brown, Daily Mail and Vickers Vimy Plane A210

"EUROPA" and "CEPT" CD12

Hand Holding Wrench A212

Flags of NATO Nations Forming one Flag A213

Vickers-Vimy Plane and Globe — A214

**1969, Apr. 2**
**584** A210 5p multicolored .25 .25
**585** CD12 9p multicolored .25 .25
**586** A212 1sh multicolored .25 .25
**587** A213 1sh6p multicolored .25 .25
 *a.* Black omitted 120.00
 *b.* Green omitted 90.00
 *c.* Yellow omitted 4,500.
**588** A214 1sh9p multicolored .25 .35
 *Nos. 584-588 (5)* 1.25 1.35

50th anniv. of the 1st non-stop Atlantic flight from Newfoundland to Ireland of Capt. John Alcock and Lt. Arthur Whitten Brown; 10th anniv. of the Conference of European Postal and Telecommunications Administrations; 50th anniv. of the ILO (1sh); 20th anniv. of NATO; 50th anniv. of the first England to Australia flight (1sh9p).

Durham Cathedral A215

British Cathedrals: No. 590, York Minster. No. 591, St. Giles', Edinburgh. No. 592, Canterbury. 9p, St. Paul's. 1sh6p, Liverpool Metropolitan.

***Perf. 14½x14***
**1969, May 28 Photo. Unwmk.**
**589** A215 5p multicolored .25 .25
 *a.* Bluish violet omitted 20,000.
**590** A215 5p multicolored .25 .25
 *a.* Bluish violet omitted 20,000.
**591** A215 5p multicolored .25 .25
 *a.* Green omitted 100.00
**592** A215 5p multicolored .25 .25
 *a.* Block of 4, #589-592 1.10 1.10
**593** A215 9p multicolored .25 .25
 *a.* Black (denomination) omitted 275.00
**594** A215 1sh6p multicolored .25 .30
 *a.* Black (denomination) omitted 5,000.
 *Nos. 589-594 (6)* 1.50 1.55

King's Gate, Caernarvon Castle, Wales — A216

Celtic Cross, Margam Abbey, Glamorgan A217

Prince of Wales — A218

Designs: No. 596, Eagle Tower, Caernarvon Castle (2 flags). No. 597, Queen Eleanor's Gate, Caernarvon Castle.

***Perf. 14x14½***
**1969, July 1 Photo. Unwmk.**
**595** A216 5p silver & multi .25 .25
**596** A216 5p silver & multi .25 .25
**597** A216 5p silver & multi .25 .25
 *a.* Strip of 3, #595-597 .25 .25
**598** A217 9p gold, gray & black .25 .25
**599** A218 1sh black & gold .25 .25
 *Nos. 595-599 (5)* 1.25 1.25

Investiture of Prince Charles as Prince of Wales, July 1.

Mahatma Gandhi and Flag of India A219

**1969, Aug. 13 *Perf. 14½x14***
**600** A219 1sh6p orange, blk & grn .25 .25

Mohandas K. Gandhi (1869-1948), leader in India's fight for independence.

Emblem of Post Office Bank A220

International Subscriber Dialing — A221

Automatic Letter Sorting A222

Design: 1sh, Telecommunications (pulse code modulation graph).

***Perf. 13½x14***
**1969, Oct. 1 Litho. Unwmk.**
**601** A220 5p blue & multi .25 .25
**602** A221 9p ultra & multi .25 .25
**603** A221 1sh green & multi .25 .25
**604** A222 1sh6p multicolored .25 .30
 *Nos. 601-604 (4)* 1.00 1.05

Technological advancements of the British Post Office, transfer of responsibility from the government to the Post Office Corporation.

Angel A223

Christmas: 5p, Three shepherds. 1sh6p, The Three Kings.

**Photo.; Gold Embossed**
**1969, Nov. 26 *Perf. 14x15***
**605** A223 4p multicolored .25 .25
**606** A223 5p multicolored .25 .25
**607** A223 1sh6p multicolored .25 .25
 *Nos. 605-607 (3)* .75 .75

Fife Harling House, Scotland A224

British Rural Architecture: 9p, Cotswold limestone house, Gloucestershire, England. 1sh, Aberaeron town house, Wales. 1sh6p, Irish cottage with Ulster thatching.

***Perf. 14x15***
**1970, Feb. 11 Photo. Unwmk.**
**Size: 38½x22mm**
**608** A224 5p multicolored .25 .25
**609** A224 9p multicolored .25 .25
**Size: 38½x27mm**
**610** A224 1sh multicolored .25 .25
**611** A224 1sh6p multicolored .25 .25
 *Nos. 608-611 (4)* 1.00 1.00

Mayflower Leaving Plymouth, England A225

Designs: 5p, Signing of the Declaration of Arbroath. 9p, Florence Nightingale and soldiers in Scutari Hospital. 1sh, Earl Grey, Great Britain; Charles Robert, France; Victor Bohmert, Germany; De Keussler, Russia, and document in 4 languages. 1sh9p, Sir William Herschel, Francis Bailey, Sir John Herschel and telescope.

**Photo.; Gold Embossed**
**1970, Apr. 1 *Perf. 14x15***
**612** A225 5p red & multi .25 .25
**613** A225 9p blue & multi .25 .25
**614** A225 1sh lt blue & multi .25 .25
**615** A225 1sh6p olive & multi .25 .30
**616** A225 1sh9p brt pink & multi .25 .30
 *Nos. 612-616 (5)* 1.25 1.35

650th anniv. of the Declaration of Arbroath (5p); Florence Nightingale (1820-1910), nurse and hospital reformer (9p); Intl.Cooperative Alliance, 75th anniv. (1sh); 350th anniv. of Mayflower sailing (1sh6p); sesquicentennial of the Royal Astronomical Soc. (1sh9p).

Missing colors or embossing occur on each denomination.

"The Pickwick Papers," by Dickens A226

Wordsworth's Grasmere, Lake District A227

Designs: No. 618, Mr. and Mrs. Micawber ("David Copperfield"). No. 619, David Copperfield and Betsy Trotwood ("David Copperfield"). No. 620, "Oliver Twist."

***Perf. 14x14½***
**1970, June 3 Photo. Unwmk.**
**617** A226 5p orange & multi .25 .25
**618** A226 5p lil rose & multi .25 .25
**619** A226 5p grnsh blue & multi .25 .25
**620** A226 5p lemon & multi .25 .25
 *a.* Block of 4, #617-620 1.10 1.10
**621** A227 1sh6p citron & multi .25 .40
 *Nos. 617-621 (5)* 1.25 1.40

Charles Dickens (1812-70), novelist. William Wordsworth (1770-1850), poet, No. 621.

No. 620a exists imperf. Value $2,250.

Athletics A228

**1970, July 15 Litho. *Perf. 14x14½***
**639** A228 5p shown .25 .25
**640** A228 1sh6p Swimming .25 .25
**641** A228 1sh9p Bicycling .25 .25
 *Nos. 639-641 (3)* .75 .75

9th British Commonwealth Games, Edinburgh, July 16-25.

Philympia, London Phil. Exhib., Sept. 18-26 — A229

5p, Penny black. 9p, 1847 1-shilling stamp, #5. 1sh6p, 1855 4-pence stamp, #22.

**1970, Sept. 18 Photo. *Perf. 14x14½***
**642** A229 5p multicolored .25 .25
**643** A229 9p multicolored .25 .25
**644** A229 1sh6p multicolored .25 .35
 *Nos. 642-644 (3)* .75 .85

Christmas (Illuminations from 14th Century de Lisle Psalter) — A230

Designs: 4p, Angel and Shepherds. 5p, Nativity. 1sh6p, Adoration of the Kings.

**1970, Nov. 25 Photo. *Perf. 14x14½***
**645** A230 4p red & multi .25 .25
**646** A230 5p violet & multi .25 .25
 *a.* Imperf., pair 500.00
**647** A230 1sh6p olive & multi .25 .25
 *Nos. 645-647 (3)* .75 .75

### Decimal Currency Issue

Mountain Road, by T.P. Flanagan A231

Paintings from Northern Ireland: 7½p, Deer's Meadow, by Thomas Carr. 9p, Tollymore Forest Park, by Colin Middleton.

**"P" instead of "D"**

**1971, June 16 Photo. *Perf. 14½x14***

| | | | | |
|---|---|---|---|---|
| **648** | A231 | 3p multicolored | .25 | .25 |
| **649** | A231 | 7½p multicolored | .30 | .30 |
| **650** | A231 | 9p multicolored | .35 | *.40* |
| | | *Nos. 648-650 (3)* | .90 | .95 |

Ulster '71 Festival, Belfast, May-Oct.

John Keats (1795-1821) — A232

Writers and their signatures: 5p, Thomas Gray (1716-71). 7½p, Sir Walter Scott (1771-1832).

**1971, July 28 Photo. *Perf. 14½x14***

| | | | | |
|---|---|---|---|---|
| **651** | A232 | 3p dull bl, blk & gold | .25 | .25 |
| **652** | A232 | 5p olive, blk & gold | .30 | *.35* |
| **653** | A232 | 7½p yel brn, blk & gold | .35 | .35 |
| | | *Nos. 651-653 (3)* | .90 | .95 |

Soldier, Sailor, Airman, Nurse, 1921, and Poppy A233

Designs: 7½p, Roman centurion on horseback, York Castle and coat of arms. 9p, Rugby players 100 years ago, and rose.

**1971, Aug. 25**

| | | | | |
|---|---|---|---|---|
| **654** | A233 | 3p ultra & multi | .25 | .25 |
| **655** | A233 | 7½p ocher & multi | .30 | .30 |
| **656** | A233 | 9p olive & multi | .35 | *.40* |
| | | *Nos. 654-656 (3)* | .90 | .95 |

50th anniv. of the British Legion (3p); 1900th anniv. of the founding of York (7½p); cent. of the Rugby Football Union (9p).

Physical Sciences Building, University College of Wales, Aberystwyth — A234

Modern University Buildings: 5p, Faraday Building, Engineering Faculty, University of Southampton. 7½p, Engineering Building, University of Leicester. 9p, Hexagon Restaurant, University of Essex.

**1971, Sept. 22 Photo. *Perf. 14½x14***

| | | | | |
|---|---|---|---|---|
| **657** | A234 | 3p citron & multi | .25 | .25 |
| **658** | A234 | 5p rose vio & multi | .25 | .25 |
| **659** | A234 | 7½p dp brn & multi | .35 | .35 |
| **660** | A234 | 9p dk blue & multi | .50 | .50 |
| | | *Nos. 657-660 (4)* | 1.35 | 1.35 |

No. 658 exists with large "p" in "5p." These are from plate combination 1A1B1C1D and were not officially issued.

Dream of the Kings A235

Christmas (from Stained Glass Windows, Canterbury Cathedral): 3p, Adoration of the Kings. 7½p, Journey of the Kings.

**1971, Oct. 13**

| | | | | |
|---|---|---|---|---|
| **661** | A235 | 2½p scarlet & multi | .25 | .25 |
| **662** | A235 | 3p ultra & multi | .25 | .25 |
| **663** | A235 | 7½p green & multi | .30 | .35 |
| | | *Nos. 661-663 (3)* | .80 | .85 |

James Clark Ross (1800-1862) and Map of South Polar Sea — A236

British Polar Explorers: 5p, Martin Frobisher (1535-1594), and Desceliers map, 1550. 7½p, Henry Hudson (c. 1560-1611) and Petrus Plancius map, 1592. 9p, Robert Falcon Scott (1868-1912) and map of Antarctica.

**1972, Feb. 16** ***Perf. 14x14½***

| | | | | |
|---|---|---|---|---|
| **664** | A236 | 3p dp bister & multi | .25 | .25 |
| **665** | A236 | 5p brick red & multi | .25 | .25 |
| **666** | A236 | 7½p violet & multi | .35 | .35 |
| **667** | A236 | 9p blue & multi | .50 | *.55* |
| | | *Nos. 664-667 (4)* | 1.35 | 1.40 |

See Nos. 689-693.

Head of Tutankhamen as Fisherman — A237

Coast Guard A238

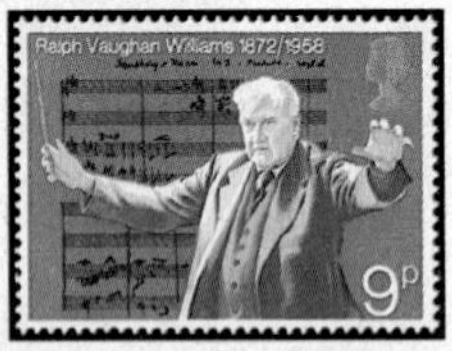


Ralph Vaughan Williams and "Sea Symphony" A239

**1972, Apr. 26 Photo. *Perf. 14½x14***

| | | | | |
|---|---|---|---|---|
| **668** | A237 | 3p gold & multi | .25 | .25 |

**Photo.; Queen's Head Gold Embossed**

| | | | | |
|---|---|---|---|---|
| **669** | A238 | 7½p blue & multi | .30 | .30 |
| **670** | A239 | 9p multicolored | .30 | .45 |
| | | *Nos. 668-670 (3)* | .85 | 1.00 |

50th anniv. of the discovery of the tomb of Tutankhamen by Howard Carter and Lord Carnarvon; sesquicentennial of the British Coast guard; Ralph Vaughan Williams (1872-1958), composer.

St. Andrew's, Greensted-Juxta-Ongar — A240

Old Village Churches: 4p, All Saints, Earls Barton. 5p, St. Andrew's, Letheringsett. 7½p, St. Andrew's, Helpringham. 9p, St. Mary the Virgin, Huish Episcopi.

**Photo.; Queen's Head Gold Embossed**

**1972, June 21** ***Perf. 14x14½***

| | | | | |
|---|---|---|---|---|
| **671** | A240 | 3p dull blue & multi | .25 | .25 |
| **672** | A240 | 4p olive & multi | .25 | .25 |
| **673** | A240 | 5p dp grn & multi | .25 | .25 |
| **674** | A240 | 7½p red & multi | .35 | *.40* |
| **675** | A240 | 9p blue & multi | .35 | *.50* |
| | | *Nos. 671-675 (5)* | 1.45 | 1.65 |

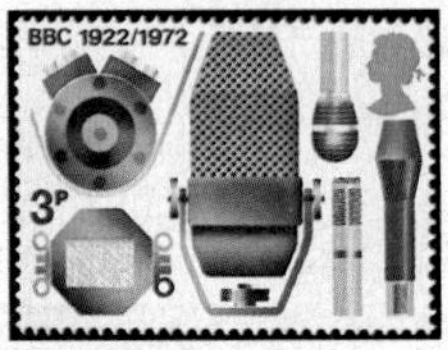


Various BBC Microphones — A241

Designs: 5p, Wooden horn loudspeaker 1925. 7½p, Color TV camera, 1972. 9p, Marconi's oscillator and spark transmitter, 1897.

**1972, Sept. 13 Photo. *Perf. 14½x14***

| | | | | |
|---|---|---|---|---|
| **676** | A241 | 3p black, brn & yel | .25 | .25 |
| **677** | A241 | 5p henna brn & blk | .25 | .25 |
| **678** | A241 | 7½p black & magenta | .35 | *.40* |
| **679** | A241 | 9p black & yel | .40 | .40 |
| | | *Nos. 676-679 (4)* | 1.25 | 1.30 |

Daily broadcasting in the United Kingdom, 50th anniv. (British Broadcasting Corp., Nos. 676-678), Marconi-Kemp experiments resulting in the 1st radio transmission across water, 75th anniv. (No. 679).

Angel with Trumpet — A242

**Photo.; Gold Embossed**

**1972, Oct. 18** ***Perf. 14x14½***

| | | | | |
|---|---|---|---|---|
| **680** | A242 | 2½p shown | .25 | .25 |
| **681** | A242 | 3p Angel with lute | .25 | .25 |
| **682** | A242 | 7½p Angel with harp | .30 | .30 |
| | | *Nos. 680-682 (3)* | .80 | .80 |

Christmas.

Queen Elizabeth II, Prince Philip — A243

**1972, Nov. 20 Photo. *Perf. 14x14½***

| | | | | |
|---|---|---|---|---|
| **683** | A243 | 3p dk bl, sep & sil | .25 | .25 |
| **684** | A243 | 20p dk pur, sepia & sil | .75 | .75 |

25th anniv. of the marriage of Queen Elizabeth II and Prince Philip. No. 684 is without phosphor.

Britain as Part of European Community A244

**1973, Jan. 3**

| | | | | |
|---|---|---|---|---|
| **685** | A244 | 3p brown org & multi | .25 | .25 |
| **686** | A244 | 5p blue & multi | .25 | .25 |
| **687** | A244 | 5p emerald & multi | .25 | .25 |
| *a.* | | Pair, #686-687 | .90 | *1.50* |
| | | *Nos. 685-687 (3)* | .75 | .75 |

Britain's entry into the European Community.

Oak A245

**1973, Feb. 28 Photo. *Perf. 14½x14***

| | | | | |
|---|---|---|---|---|
| **688** | A245 | 9p multicolored | .25 | .30 |

Tree Planting Year.

**Explorer Type of 1972**

British Explorers: No. 689, David Livingstone and map of Africa. No. 690, Henry Stanley and map of Africa. 5p, Sir Francis Drake and world map. 7½p, Sir Walter Raleigh and world map. 9p, Charles Sturt and map of Australia.

**1973, Apr. 8 Photo. *Perf. 14x14½***

| | | | | |
|---|---|---|---|---|
| **689** | A236 | 3p multicolored | .25 | .25 |
| **690** | A236 | 3p multicolored | .25 | .25 |
| *a.* | | Pair, #689-690 | .75 | *1.00* |
| **691** | A236 | 5p multicolored | .25 | .25 |
| **692** | A236 | 7½p multicolored | .30 | .30 |
| **693** | A236 | 9p multicolored | .45 | *.60* |
| | | *Nos. 689-693 (5)* | 1.50 | 1.65 |

William Gilbert Grace — A246

Designs: Caricatures of William Gilbert Grace, the Great Cricketer, by Harry Furniss.

**1973, May 16 Photo. *Perf. 14x14½***

| | | | | |
|---|---|---|---|---|
| **694** | A246 | 3p brown & black | .25 | .25 |
| **695** | A246 | 7½p green & black | .50 | .50 |
| **696** | A246 | 9p blue & black | .75 | .75 |
| | | *Nos. 694-696 (3)* | 1.50 | 1.50 |

Centenary of British County Cricket.

Sir Joshua Reynolds, Self-portrait A247

Paintings: 5p, Sir Henry Raeburn (1756-1823), self-portrait. 7½p, Nelly O'Brien, by Reynolds (1723-92). 9p, Rev. R. Walker (The Skater), by Raeburn.

**1973, July 4 Photo. *Perf. 14x14½***

| | | | | |
|---|---|---|---|---|
| **697** | A247 | 3p multicolored | .25 | .25 |
| **698** | A247 | 5p multicolored | .25 | .25 |
| **699** | A247 | 7½p multicolored | .25 | .25 |
| **700** | A247 | 9p gray & multi | .35 | .35 |
| | | *Nos. 697-700 (4)* | 1.10 | 1.10 |

Tuscan Portico, St. Paul's Church, Covent Garden
A248

Designs: No. 701, Costumes for Oberon and Titania. No. 703, Prince's Lodging, Newmarket. No. 704, Stage scenery for Oberon.

**Litho. and Typo.**

**1973, Aug. 15** ***Perf. 14½x14***

| | | | | |
|---|---|---|---|---|
| **701** | A248 | 3p black, pur & gold | .25 | .25 |
| **702** | A248 | 3p gold, brn & blk | .25 | .25 |
| *a.* | | Pair, #701-702 | .50 | .50 |
| **703** | A248 | 5p black, blue & gold | .30 | .40 |
| **704** | A248 | 5p gold, olive & blk | .30 | .40 |
| *a.* | | Pair, #703-704 | 1.10 | 1.10 |
| | | *Nos. 701-704 (4)* | 1.10 | 1.30 |

400th birth anniv. of Inigo Jones (1573-1652), architect and designer.

Parliament, from Millbank
A249

Design: 8p, Parliament, from Whitehall.

**1973, Sept. 12** **Engr. and Typo.**

| | | | | |
|---|---|---|---|---|
| **705** | A249 | 8p buff, gray & blk | .25 | .25 |
| **706** | A249 | 10p black & gold | .30 | .30 |

Opening by the Queen of the 19th Commonwealth Parliamentary Assoc. Conf., Westminster Hall.

Princess Anne and Mark Phillips
A250

**1973, Nov. 14** **Photo.** ***Perf. 14½x14***

| | | | | |
|---|---|---|---|---|
| **707** | A250 | 3½p violet & silver | .25 | .25 |
| **708** | A250 | 20p brown & silver | .50 | .50 |

Wedding of Princess Anne and Captain Mark Phillips, Nov. 14, 1973.

Good King Wenceslas
A251

Christmas: Illustrations for Christmas carol "Good King Wenceslas" showing king and page.

**1973, Nov. 28**

| | | | | |
|---|---|---|---|---|
| **709** | A251 | 3p shown | .30 | .30 |
| **710** | A251 | 3p Page looking out of window | .30 | .30 |
| **711** | A251 | 3p Page leaving castle | .30 | .30 |
| **712** | A251 | 3p Page in storm | .30 | .30 |
| **713** | A251 | 3p Page bringing gifts | .30 | .30 |
| *a.* | | Strip of 5, #709-713 | 2.10 | 2.10 |
| **714** | A251 | 3½p Page and peasant | .35 | .35 |
| | | *Nos. 709-714 (6)* | 1.85 | 1.85 |

Horse Chestnut
A252

**1974, Feb. 27** **Photo.** ***Perf. 14½x14***

| | | | | |
|---|---|---|---|---|
| **715** | A252 | 10p green & multi | .35 | .35 |

Fire Engine, 1766
A253

Designs: 3½p, First motorized fire engine, 1904. 5½p, Prize winning Sutherland fire engine, 1863. 8p, First steam engine, 1830.

**1974, Apr. 24**

| | | | | |
|---|---|---|---|---|
| **716** | A253 | 3½p multicolored | .25 | .25 |
| **717** | A253 | 5½p multicolored | .25 | .25 |
| **718** | A253 | 8p multicolored | .30 | .30 |
| **719** | A253 | 10p multicolored | .35 | .35 |
| | | *Nos. 716-719 (4)* | 1.15 | 1.15 |

Fire Prevention (Metropolis) Act, bicent.

Packet "Peninsular," 1888, and "Southampton Packet Letter" Postmark — A254

Development of Overseas Mail Transport: 5½p, Farnham Biplane and "Aerial Post" postmark. 8p, Truck and pillar box for airmail and "London F.S. Air Mail" postmark. 10p, Imperial Airways flying boat and "Southampton Airport" postmark.

**1974, June 12** ***Perf. 14½x14***

| | | | | |
|---|---|---|---|---|
| **720** | A254 | 3½p multicolored | .25 | .25 |
| **721** | A254 | 5½p multicolored | .25 | .25 |
| **722** | A254 | 8p multicolored | .25 | .25 |
| **723** | A254 | 10p multicolored | .25 | .25 |
| | | *Nos. 720-723 (4)* | 1.00 | 1.00 |

UPU, Cent.

Robert the Bruce
A255

"Great Britons" on caparisoned chargers.

**1974, July 10** ***Perf. 14½x14***

| | | | | |
|---|---|---|---|---|
| **724** | A255 | 4½p shown | .25 | .25 |
| **725** | A255 | 5½p Owain Glyndwr | .25 | .25 |
| **726** | A255 | 8p King Henry V | .25 | .25 |
| **727** | A255 | 10p Black Prince | .35 | .35 |
| | | *Nos. 724-727 (4)* | 1.10 | 1.10 |

Churchill, Lord Warden of the Cinque Ports, 1942 — A256

Designs (Churchill): 5½p, with bowler and cigar, 1940. 8p, with top hat, as Secretary of War and Air, 1919. 10p, in uniform of South African Light Horse Regiment, 1899.

**1974, Oct. 9** **Photo.** ***Perf. 14x14½***

| | | | | |
|---|---|---|---|---|
| **728** | A256 | 4½p silver & multi | .25 | .25 |
| **729** | A256 | 5½p silver & multi | .30 | .30 |
| **730** | A256 | 8p silver & multi | .35 | .35 |
| **731** | A256 | 10p silver & multi | .45 | .45 |
| | | *Nos. 728-731 (4)* | 1.35 | 1.35 |

Sir Winston Spencer Churchill (1874-1965).

Adoration of the Kings, York Minster, c. 1355
A257

Christmas (Roof Bosses): 4½p, Nativity, St. Helen's, Norwich, c. 1480. 8p, Virgin and Child, Church of Ottery St. Mary, Devonshire, c. 1350. 10p, Virgin and Child, Lady Chapel, Worcester Cathedral, c. 1224.

**1974, Nov. 27** ***Perf. 14½x14***

| | | | | |
|---|---|---|---|---|
| **732** | A257 | 3½p gold & multi | .25 | .25 |
| **733** | A257 | 4½p gold & multi | .25 | .25 |
| **734** | A257 | 8p gold & multi | .25 | .25 |
| **735** | A257 | 10p gold & multi | .30 | .30 |
| | | *Nos. 732-735 (4)* | 1.05 | 1.05 |

"Peace-Burial at Sea," by Turner — A258

Paintings: 5½p, "Snowstorm-Steamer off a Harbour's Mouth." 8p, "Arsenal, Venice." 10p, "View of St. Laurent."

**1975, Feb. 19** **Photo.** ***Perf. 14½x14***

| | | | | |
|---|---|---|---|---|
| **736** | A258 | 4½p multicolored | .25 | .25 |
| **737** | A258 | 5½p multicolored | .25 | .25 |
| **738** | A258 | 8p multicolored | .25 | .25 |
| **739** | A258 | 10p multicolored | .30 | .30 |
| | | *Nos. 736-739 (4)* | 1.05 | 1.05 |

Birth bicent. of Joseph Mallord William Turner (1775-1851), painter.

Charlotte Square, Edinburgh
A259

National Theater, London
A260

Designs: No. 740, The Rows, Chester (double-storied medieval shopping streets). 8p, Sir Christopher Wren's Flamsteed House, Royal Observatory, Greenwich. 10p, St. George's Chapel, Windsor.

**1975, Apr. 23** ***Perf. 14½x14***

| | | | | |
|---|---|---|---|---|
| **740** | A259 | 7p multicolored | .25 | .25 |
| **741** | A259 | 7p multicolored | .25 | .25 |
| *a.* | | Pair, #740-741 | .60 | .60 |
| **742** | A259 | 8p multicolored | .25 | .25 |
| **743** | A259 | 10p multicolored | .30 | .30 |
| **744** | A260 | 12p multicolored | .35 | .35 |
| | | *Nos. 740-744 (5)* | 1.40 | 1.40 |

European Architectural Heritage Year 1975. Nos. 740-741 printed se-tenant in sheets of 100. 300th anniv. of Royal Observatory, (No. 742) and 500th anniv. of St. George's Chapel (No. 743).

Dinghies
A261

**1975, June 11** **Photo. & Engr.**

| | | | | |
|---|---|---|---|---|
| **745** | A261 | 7p shown | .25 | .25 |
| **746** | A261 | 8p Racing keelboats | .25 | .25 |
| **747** | A261 | 10p Cruising yachts | .30 | .30 |
| **748** | A261 | 12p Multihulls | .40 | .40 |
| | | *Nos. 745-748 (4)* | 1.20 | 1.20 |

Royal Thames Yacht Club bicent. and other sailing club anniversaries.

Stephenson's Locomotion, 1825 — A262

Locomotives: 8p, Abbotsford, Waverley Class, 1876. 10p, Caerphilly Castle, 1923. 12p, High-speed train, 1975.

**1975, Aug. 13** **Photo.** ***Perf. 14½x14***

| | | | | |
|---|---|---|---|---|
| **749** | A262 | 7p multicolored | .25 | .25 |
| **750** | A262 | 8p multicolored | .25 | .25 |
| **751** | A262 | 10p multicolored | .30 | .30 |
| **752** | A262 | 12p multicolored | .40 | .40 |
| | | *Nos. 749-752 (4)* | 1.20 | 1.20 |

Sesquicentennial of public railroads in Great Britain.

Parliament
A263

**1975, Sept. 3**

| | | | | |
|---|---|---|---|---|
| **753** | A263 | 12p multicolored | .30 | .30 |

62nd Inter-Parliamentary Conference, London, Sept. 1975.

Emma and Mr. Woodhouse from "Emma" — A264

Designs (Illustrations by Barbara Brown of Characters from Jane Austen's Novels): 10p, Catherine Morland from "Northanger Abbey." 11p, Mr. Darcy from "Pride and Prejudice." 13p, Mary and Henry Crawford from "Mansfield Park."

**1975, Oct. 22** **Photo.** ***Perf. 14x14½***

| | | | | |
|---|---|---|---|---|
| **754** | A264 | 8½p multicolored | .25 | .25 |
| **755** | A264 | 10p multicolored | .30 | .30 |
| **756** | A264 | 11p multicolored | .30 | .30 |
| **757** | A264 | 13p multicolored | .35 | .35 |
| | | *Nos. 754-757 (4)* | 1.20 | 1.20 |

Jane Austen (1775-1817), novelist.

Angels with Lute and Harp
A265

Christmas: 8½p, Angel with mandolin. 11p, Angel with horn. 13p, Angel with trumpet.

**1975, Nov. 26** **Photo.** ***Perf. 14½x14***

| | | | | |
|---|---|---|---|---|
| **758** | A265 | 6½p violet & multi | .25 | .25 |
| **759** | A265 | 8½p multicolored | .25 | .25 |
| **760** | A265 | 11p multicolored | .30 | .30 |
| **761** | A265 | 13p ocher & multi | .30 | .30 |
| | | *Nos. 758-761 (4)* | 1.10 | 1.10 |

Woman Making Social Call
A266

Designs: 10p, Policeman making emergency call. 11p, District nurse making social welfare call. 13p, Refinery worker making field call.

**1976, Mar. 10 Photo. *Perf. 14½x14***

| | | | | | |
|---|---|---|---|---|---|
| **777** | A266 | 8½p | multicolored | .25 | .25 |
| **778** | A266 | 10p | multicolored | .30 | .30 |
| **779** | A266 | 11p | multicolored | .35 | .35 |
| **780** | A266 | 13p | multicolored | .40 | .40 |
| | | | *Nos. 777-780 (4)* | 1.30 | 1.30 |

1st telephone call by Alexander Graham Bell, Mar. 10, 1876.

Coal Miner's Hands (Thomas Hepburn)
A267

Designs: 10p, Child's hands, textile mill (Robert Owen). 11p, Boy's hand sweeping chimney (Lord Shaftesbury). 13p, Woman's hands holding prison bars (Elizabeth Frey).

**1976, Apr. 28 Photo. *Perf. 14½x14***

| | | | | | |
|---|---|---|---|---|---|
| **781** | A267 | 8½p | gray & black | .25 | .25 |
| **782** | A267 | 10p | multicolored | .30 | .30 |
| **783** | A267 | 11p | multicolored | .35 | .35 |
| **784** | A267 | 13p | multicolored | .40 | .40 |
| | | | *Nos. 781-784 (4)* | 1.30 | 1.30 |

19th cent. industrial & social reformers: Hepburn formed 1st miners' union in 1831; Owen, improved working conditions in his mill and established schools; Lord Shaftesbury, philanthropist and sponsor of reform work laws; Frey, pioneer of women's prison reforms.

Benjamin Franklin, by Jean-Jacques Caffieri — A268

**1976, June 2 *Perf. 14x14½***

| | | | | | |
|---|---|---|---|---|---|
| **785** | A268 | 11p | multicolored | .30 | .30 |

American Bicentennial.

Royal National Rose Society, Centenary
A269

Roses Painted by Kristin Rosenberg.

**1976, June 30 Photo. *Perf. 14x14½***

| | | | | | |
|---|---|---|---|---|---|
| **786** | A269 | 8½p | Elizabeth of Glamis Rose | .25 | .25 |
| **787** | A269 | 10p | Grandpa Dickson | .30 | .30 |
| **788** | A269 | 11p | Rosa Mundi | .35 | .35 |
| **789** | A269 | 13p | Sweet Briar | .40 | .40 |
| | | | *Nos. 786-789 (4)* | 1.30 | 1.30 |

Archdruid, Eisteddfod
A270

Morris Dancing — A271

British Cultural Traditions: 11p, Piper and dancers, Highland gathering. 13p, Woman playing Welsh harp (telyn), Eisteddfod.

**1976, Aug. 4 Photo. *Perf. 14x14½***

| | | | | | |
|---|---|---|---|---|---|
| **790** | A270 | 8½p | multicolored | .25 | .25 |
| **791** | A271 | 10p | multicolored | .30 | .30 |
| **792** | A271 | 11p | multicolored | .35 | .35 |
| **793** | A270 | 13p | multicolored | .40 | .40 |
| | | | *Nos. 790-793 (4)* | 1.30 | 1.30 |

Squire, from Canterbury Tales — A272

Designs: 10p, Page from Tretyse of Love, c. 1493, set in Caxton typeface. 11p, Philosopher, from The Game and Playe of Chesse, c. 1483. 13p, Printing press and printers, early 16th century woodcut.

**Photo.; Queen's Head Gold Embossed**

**1976, Sept. 29 *Perf. 14x14½***

| | | | | | |
|---|---|---|---|---|---|
| **794** | A272 | 8½p | blue & indigo | .25 | .25 |
| **795** | A272 | 10p | olive & dk grn | .30 | .30 |
| **796** | A272 | 11p | gray & black | .30 | .30 |
| **797** | A272 | 13p | ocher & red brn | .40 | .40 |
| | | | *Nos. 794-797 (4)* | 1.25 | 1.25 |

500 years of British printing, introduced by William Caxton (1422-1491).

Virgin and Child, Clare Chasuble
A273

Christmas (English medieval embroideries): 8½p, Angel with crown. 11p, Angel appearing to the shepherds. 13p, Three Kings bringing gifts, Butler-Bowden cope.

**1976, Nov. 24 Photo. *Perf. 14½x14***

| | | | | | |
|---|---|---|---|---|---|
| **798** | A273 | 6½p | multicolored | .25 | .25 |
| **799** | A273 | 8½p | multicolored | .30 | .30 |
| **800** | A273 | 11p | multicolored | .35 | .35 |
| **801** | A273 | 13p | multicolored | .40 | .40 |
| | | | *Nos. 798-801 (4)* | 1.30 | 1.30 |

Racket Sports
A274

**1977, Jan. 12 Photo. *Perf. 14½x14***

| | | | | | |
|---|---|---|---|---|---|
| **802** | A274 | 8½p | Tennis | .25 | .25 |
| **803** | A274 | 10p | Table tennis | .30 | .30 |
| **804** | A274 | 11p | Squash | .35 | .35 |
| **805** | A274 | 13p | Badminton | .40 | .40 |
| | | | *Nos. 802-805 (4)* | 1.30 | 1.30 |

Wimbledon Tennis Championships, cent. and 1977 World Table Tennis Championships, Birmingham.

Steroids Conformational Analysis — A275

Designs: 10p, Vitamin C synthesis (formula and orange). 11p, Starch chromatography. 13p, Salt crystallography.

**1977, Mar. 2 Photo. *Perf. 14½x14***

| | | | | | |
|---|---|---|---|---|---|
| **806** | A275 | 8½p | multicolored | .25 | .25 |
| **807** | A275 | 10p | multicolored | .30 | .30 |
| **808** | A275 | 11p | multicolored | .35 | .35 |
| **809** | A275 | 13p | multicolored | .40 | .40 |
| | | | *Nos. 806-809 (4)* | 1.30 | 1.30 |

British chemists who won Nobel prize. Derek Barton, 1969 (8½p); Walter Norman Haworth, 1937 (10p); Archer J. P. Martin and Richard L. M. Synge, 1952 (11p); William and Lawrence Bragg, 1915 (13p).

Queen Elizabeth II — A276

**1977 Photo. *Perf. 14½x14***

| | | | | | |
|---|---|---|---|---|---|
| **810** | A276 | 8½p | silver & multi | .25 | .25 |
| **811** | A276 | 9p | silver & multi | .25 | .25 |
| **812** | A276 | 10p | silver & multi | .30 | .30 |
| **813** | A276 | 11p | silver & multi | .35 | .35 |
| **814** | A276 | 13p | silver & multi | .40 | .40 |
| | | | *Nos. 810-814 (5)* | 1.55 | 1.55 |

25th anniv. of the reign of Elizabeth II.
Issue dates: 9p, June 15;.others, May 11.

Pentagons, Symbolic of Continents and Nations — A277

**1977, June 8 Photo. *Perf. 14x14½***

| | | | | | |
|---|---|---|---|---|---|
| **815** | A277 | 13p | multicolored | .40 | .40 |

Summit Conference of Commonwealth Heads of Government, London, June 1977.

Wildlife Protection — A278

**1977, Oct. 5 Photo. *Perf. 14x14½***

| | | | | | |
|---|---|---|---|---|---|
| **816** | A278 | 9p | Hedgehog | .25 | .25 |
| **817** | A278 | 9p | Brown hare | .25 | .25 |
| **818** | A278 | 9p | Red squirrel | .25 | .25 |
| **819** | A278 | 9p | Otter | .25 | .25 |
| **820** | A278 | 9p | Badger | .25 | .25 |
| *a.* | | | Strip of 5, #816-820 | 1.75 | |

"Two Turtle Doves, Three French Hens. . ." — A279

The Twelve Days of Christmas: No. 822, 4 colly birds, 5 gold rings, 6 geese a-laying. No. 823, 7 swans a-swimming, 8 maids a-milking. No. 824, 9 drummers drumming, 10 pipers piping. No. 825, 11 ladies dancing, 12 lords a-leaping. 9p, A partridge in a pear tree.

**1977, Nov. 23 Photo. *Perf. 14½x14***

| | | | | | |
|---|---|---|---|---|---|
| **821** | A279 | 7p | multicolored | .25 | .25 |
| **822** | A279 | 7p | multicolored | .25 | .25 |
| **823** | A279 | 7p | multicolored | .25 | .25 |
| **824** | A279 | 7p | multicolored | .25 | .25 |
| **825** | A279 | 7p | multicolored | .25 | .25 |
| *a.* | | | Strip of 5, #821-825 | 1.25 | |
| **826** | A279 | 9p | multicolored | .30 | .30 |
| | | | *Nos. 821-826 (6)* | 1.55 | 1.55 |

Oil Production Platform, North Sea — A280

Designs: 10½p, Coal, pithead. 11p, Natural gas, flame. 13p, Electricity-producing nuclear power plant and uranium atom diagram.

**1978, Jan. 25 Photo. *Perf. 14x14½***

| | | | | | |
|---|---|---|---|---|---|
| **827** | A280 | 9p | multicolored | .25 | .25 |
| **828** | A280 | 10½p | multicolored | .25 | .25 |
| **829** | A280 | 11p | multicolored | .35 | .25 |
| **830** | A280 | 13p | multicolored | .40 | .25 |
| | | | *Nos. 827-830 (4)* | 1.25 | 1.00 |

Great Britain's wealth of energy resources.

Tower of London
A281

British Architecture: 10½p, Abbey and Palace, Holyrood House, Edinburgh. 11p, Caernarvon Castle, Wales. 13p, Hampton Court Palace, London.

**1978, Mar. 1 Photo. *Perf. 14½x14***

| | | | | | |
|---|---|---|---|---|---|
| **831** | A281 | 9p | multicolored | .25 | .25 |
| **832** | A281 | 10½p | multicolored | .30 | .25 |
| **833** | A281 | 11p | multicolored | .30 | .25 |
| **834** | A281 | 13p | multicolored | .40 | .25 |
| *a.* | | | Souv. sheet of 4, #831-834 | 1.30 | 1.30 |
| | | | *Nos. 831-834 (4)* | 1.25 | 1.00 |

No. 834a issued to publicize London 1980 Intl. Stamp Exhib. and sold for 53½p. The surtax went to exhibition fund.

Gold State Coach — A282

Designs: 10½p, St. Edward's crown. 11p, Orb. 13p, Imperial State crown.

**1978, May 31 Photo. *Perf. 14x14½***

| | | | | | |
|---|---|---|---|---|---|
| **835** | A282 | 9p | vio blue & gold | .25 | .25 |
| **836** | A282 | 10½p | car lake & gold | .30 | .25 |
| **837** | A282 | 11p | dp green & gold | .35 | .30 |
| **838** | A282 | 13p | purple & gold | .40 | .35 |
| | | | *Nos. 835-838 (4)* | 1.30 | 1.15 |

25th anniv. of coronation of Elizabeth II.

Shire Horse A283

British Horses: 10½p, Shetland pony. 11p, Merlyn Cymreig Welsh pony. 13p, Thoroughbred.

**1978, July 5 Photo.** ***Perf. 14½x14***

| | | | | |
|---|---|---|---|---|
| **839** | A283 | 9p multicolored | .25 | .25 |
| **840** | A283 | 10½p multicolored | .30 | .25 |
| **841** | A283 | 11p multicolored | .35 | .25 |
| **842** | A283 | 13p multicolored | .40 | .35 |
| | | *Nos. 839-842 (4)* | 1.30 | 1.10 |

"Penny-farthing," 19th Century — A284

British bicycles: 10½p, 1920 touring bicycles. 11p, Modern small-wheel bicycles. 13p, Road racers.

**1978, Aug. 2 Photo.** ***Perf. 14½x14***

| | | | | |
|---|---|---|---|---|
| **843** | A284 | 9p multicolored | .25 | .25 |
| **844** | A284 | 10½p multicolored | .30 | .25 |
| **845** | A284 | 11p multicolored | .35 | .25 |
| **846** | A284 | 13p multicolored | .40 | .35 |
| | | *Nos. 843-846 (4)* | 1.30 | 1.10 |

Cent. of 1st natl. cycling organizations: British Cycling Fed. and Cyclists Touring Club.

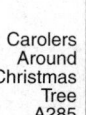

Carolers Around Christmas Tree A285

Christmas: 9p, Christmas waits (watchmen). 11p, 18th century carolers. 13p, Boar's head carol.

**1978, Nov. 22 Photo.** ***Perf. 14½x14***

| | | | | |
|---|---|---|---|---|
| **847** | A285 | 7p multicolored | .25 | .25 |
| **848** | A285 | 9p multicolored | .25 | .25 |
| **849** | A285 | 11p multicolored | .35 | .25 |
| **850** | A285 | 13p multicolored | .40 | .35 |
| | | *Nos. 847-850 (4)* | 1.25 | 1.10 |

Old English Sheepdog A286

British dogs: 10½p, Welsh springer spaniel. 11p, West Highland white terrier. 13p, Irish setter.

**1979, Feb. 7 Photo.** ***Perf. 14½x14***

| | | | | |
|---|---|---|---|---|
| **851** | A286 | 9p multicolored | .25 | .25 |
| **852** | A286 | 10½p multicolored | .30 | .25 |
| **853** | A286 | 11p multicolored | .35 | .25 |
| **854** | A286 | 13p multicolored | .40 | .35 |
| | | *Nos. 851-854 (4)* | 1.30 | 1.10 |

British Wild Flowers — A287

**1979, Mar. 21 Photo.** ***Perf. 14x14½***

| | | | | |
|---|---|---|---|---|
| **855** | A287 | 9p Primroses | .25 | .25 |
| **856** | A287 | 10½p Daffodils | .30 | .25 |
| **857** | A287 | 11p Bluebells | .35 | .25 |
| **858** | A287 | 13p Snowdrops | .40 | .35 |
| | | *Nos. 855-858 (4)* | 1.30 | 1.10 |

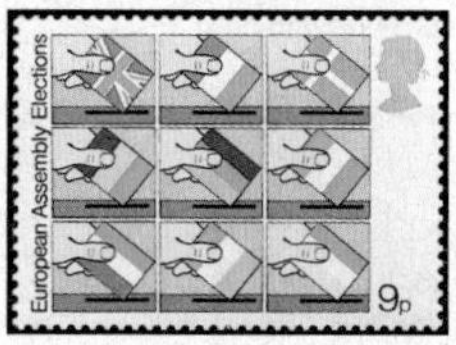

Flags of Member Nations as Ballots A288

Flags of European Community Members: United Kingdom, Italy, Denmark, Belgium, Fed. Rep. of Germany, France, Netherlands, Ireland, Luxembourg. Positions of hands and flags different on each denomination.

**1979, May 9 Photo.** ***Perf. 14½x14***

| | | | | |
|---|---|---|---|---|
| **859** | A288 | 9p multicolored | .25 | .25 |
| **860** | A288 | 10½p multicolored | .30 | .25 |
| **861** | A288 | 11p multicolored | .35 | .25 |
| **862** | A288 | 13p multicolored | .40 | .35 |
| | | *Nos. 859-862 (4)* | 1.30 | 1.10 |

European Parliament, 1st direct elections, 6/7-10.

Saddling of Mahmoud, 1936 Derby, by Alfred Munnings A289

200th Anniv. of the Derby: 10½p, Liverpool Great National Steeple Chase, 1839, aquatint by F. C. Turner. 11p, First Spring Meeting, Newmarket, 1793, by J. N. Sartorius. 13p, Charles II watching racing at Dorsett Ferry, Windsor, 1684, by Francis Barlow.

**1979, June 6 Photo.** ***Perf. 14½x14***

| | | | | |
|---|---|---|---|---|
| **863** | A289 | 9p multicolored | .25 | .25 |
| **864** | A289 | 10½p multicolored | .30 | .25 |
| **865** | A289 | 11p multicolored | .35 | .25 |
| **866** | A289 | 13p multicolored | .40 | .35 |
| | | *Nos. 863-866 (4)* | 1.30 | 1.10 |

Peter Rabbit — A290

Children's books: 10½p, The Wind in the Willows. 11p, Winnie the Pooh. 13p, Alice's Adventures in Wonderland.

**1979, July 11 Photo.** ***Perf. 14x14½***

| | | | | |
|---|---|---|---|---|
| **867** | A290 | 9p multicolored | .30 | .25 |
| **868** | A290 | 10½p multicolored | .35 | .25 |
| **869** | A290 | 11p multicolored | .35 | .25 |
| **870** | A290 | 13p multicolored | .45 | .25 |
| | | *Nos. 867-870 (4)* | 1.45 | 1.00 |

International Year of the Child.

Rowland Hill — A291

Designs: 11½p, Bellman, early 19th cent. 13p, London post office and mailman, early 19th cent. 15p, Victorian woman and child mailing letter.

**1979, Aug. 22 Photo.** ***Perf. 14x14½***

| | | | | |
|---|---|---|---|---|
| **871** | A291 | 10p multicolored | .25 | .25 |
| **872** | A291 | 11½p multicolored | .25 | .25 |
| **873** | A291 | 13p multicolored | .35 | .25 |
| **874** | A291 | 15p multicolored | .40 | .30 |
| *a.* | | Souvenir sheet of 4, #871-874 | 1.20 | 1.20 |
| | | *Nos. 871-874 (4)* | 1.25 | 1.05 |

Sir Rowland Hill (1795-1879), originator of penny postage.

No. 874a issued 10/24/79 to publicize London 1980 Intl. Stamp Exhib. and sold for 59½p. The surtax went to exhibition fund.

Police Constable and Children A292

Designs: 11½p, Police constable directing traffic. 13p, Police woman on horseback. 15p, River patrol boat.

**1979, Sept. 26 Photo.** ***Perf. 14½x14***

| | | | | |
|---|---|---|---|---|
| **875** | A292 | 10p multicolored | .25 | .25 |
| **876** | A292 | 11½p multicolored | .30 | .25 |
| **877** | A292 | 13p multicolored | .35 | .25 |
| **878** | A292 | 15p multicolored | .40 | .35 |
| | | *Nos. 875-878 (4)* | 1.30 | 1.10 |

London Metropolitan Police, 150th anniv.

Three Kings Following Star A293

Christmas: 10p, Angel appearing before the shepherds. 11½p, Nativity. 13p, Joseph and Mary traveling to Bethlehem. 15p, Annunciation.

**1979, Nov. 21 Photo.** ***Perf. 14½x14***

| | | | | |
|---|---|---|---|---|
| **879** | A293 | 8p multicolored | .25 | .25 |
| **880** | A293 | 10p multicolored | .25 | .25 |
| **881** | A293 | 11½p multicolored | .30 | .25 |
| **882** | A293 | 13p multicolored | .35 | .30 |
| **883** | A293 | 15p multicolored | .40 | .30 |
| | | *Nos. 879-883 (5)* | 1.55 | 1.35 |

Kingfisher — A294

**1980, Jan. 16 Photo.** ***Perf. 14x14½***

| | | | | |
|---|---|---|---|---|
| **884** | A294 | 10p shown | .25 | .25 |
| **885** | A294 | 11½p Dipper | .30 | .25 |
| **886** | A294 | 13p Moorhen | .35 | .25 |
| **887** | A294 | 15p Yellow wagtail | .40 | .35 |
| | | *Nos. 884-887 (4)* | 1.30 | 1.10 |

"Rocket" Locomotive A295

**1980, Mar. 12 Photo.** ***Perf. 14½x14***

| | | | | |
|---|---|---|---|---|
| **904** | A295 | 12p shown | .25 | .25 |
| **905** | A295 | 12p 1st, 2nd class cars | .25 | .25 |
| **906** | A295 | 12p 3rd class and sheep cars | .25 | .25 |
| **907** | A295 | 12p Flat cars | .25 | .25 |
| **908** | A295 | 12p Flat car, mail coach | .25 | .25 |
| *a.* | | Strip of 5, #904-908 | 1.75 | 1.75 |

Liverpool-Manchester Railroad, 150th anniv. No. 908a has a continuous design.

London View A296

**1980, Apr. 9 Engr.** ***Perf. 14½***

| | | | | |
|---|---|---|---|---|
| **909** | A296 | 50p multicolored | 1.40 | 1.25 |
| *a.* | | Souvenir sheet | 1.45 | 1.45 |

London 1980, Intl. Stamp Exhib., May 6-14. No. 909a, issued May 7, sold for 75p.

Buckingham Palace — A297

**1980, May 7 Photo.** ***Perf. 14x14½***

| | | | | |
|---|---|---|---|---|
| **910** | A297 | 10½p shown | .25 | .25 |
| **911** | A297 | 12p Albert Memorial | .35 | .25 |
| **912** | A297 | 13½p Royal Opera House | .35 | .25 |
| **913** | A297 | 15p Hampton Court | .40 | .25 |
| **914** | A297 | 17½p Kensington Palace | .45 | .35 |
| | | *Nos. 910-914 (5)* | 1.80 | 1.35 |

Emily Bronte and "Wuthering Heights" A298

Victorian novelists and scenes from their novels: 12p, Charlotte Bronte, "Jane Eyre." 13½p, George Eliot, "The Mill on the Floss." 17½p, Mrs. Gaskell, "North and South." 12p and 13½p show CEPT (Europa) emblem.

**1980, July 9 Photo.** ***Perf. 15x14***

| | | | | |
|---|---|---|---|---|
| **915** | A298 | 12p multicolored | .35 | .30 |
| **916** | A298 | 13½p multicolored | .40 | .35 |
| **917** | A298 | 15p multicolored | .45 | .40 |
| **918** | A298 | 17½p multicolored | .50 | .45 |
| | | *Nos. 915-918 (4)* | 1.70 | 1.50 |

Queen Mother Elizabeth, 80th Birthday — A299

**1980, Aug. 4 Photo.** ***Perf. 14x14½***

| | | | | |
|---|---|---|---|---|
| **919** | A299 | 12p multicolored | .40 | .25 |

English Conductors A300

Designs: 12p, Henry Wood (1869-1944). 13½p, Thomas Beecham (1879-1961). 15p,

Malcolm Sargent (1895-1967). 17½p, John Barbirolli (1899-1970).

**1980, Sept. 10**

| | | | | | |
|---|---|---|---|---|---|
| **920** | A300 | 12p | multicolored | .35 | .30 |
| **921** | A300 | 13½p | multicolored | .40 | .30 |
| **922** | A300 | 15p | multicolored | .45 | .40 |
| **923** | A300 | 17½p | multicolored | .50 | .45 |
| | | | *Nos. 920-923 (4)* | 1.70 | 1.45 |

Running — A301

**1980, Oct. 10 Litho. *Perf. 14x14½***

| | | | | | |
|---|---|---|---|---|---|
| **924** | A301 | 12p | shown | .35 | .30 |
| **925** | A301 | 13½p | Rugby | .40 | .30 |
| **926** | A301 | 15p | Boxing | .45 | .40 |
| **927** | A301 | 17½p | Cricket | .50 | .45 |
| | | | *Nos. 924-927 (4)* | 1.70 | 1.45 |

Centenaries: Amateur Athletics Assoc.; Welsh Rugby Union; Amateur Boxing Assoc.; 1st cricket test match against Australia.

Christmas Tree with Candles A302

Christmas (Traditional Decorations): 12p, Candles, ivy, ribbons. 13½p, Mistletoe, apples. 15p, Paper chain and bell. 17½p, Holly wreath.

**1980, Nov. 19 Photo. *Perf. 14½x14***

| | | | | | |
|---|---|---|---|---|---|
| **928** | A302 | 10p | multicolored | .25 | .25 |
| **929** | A302 | 12p | multicolored | .35 | .30 |
| **930** | A302 | 13½p | multicolored | .35 | .35 |
| **931** | A302 | 15p | multicolored | .40 | .40 |
| **932** | A302 | 17½ | multicolored | .45 | .45 |
| | | | *Nos. 928-932 (5)* | 1.80 | 1.75 |

Lovebirds, Angels and Heart (Valentine's Day) A303

Folklore: 18p, Morris Dancers, 16th century window, Shropshire. 22p, Wheat, fruit, farm couple dancing (Lammastide). 25p, Medieval mummers, 14th century manuscript illustration. 14p and 18p show CEPT (Europa) emblem.

**1981, Feb. 6 Photo. *Perf. 14½x14***

| | | | | | |
|---|---|---|---|---|---|
| **933** | A303 | 14p | multicolored | *.45* | .30 |
| **934** | A303 | 18p | multicolored | *.60* | *.60* |
| **935** | A303 | 22p | multicolored | .75 | .75 |
| **936** | A303 | 25p | multicolored | .80 | .80 |
| | | | *Nos. 933-936 (4)* | 2.60 | 2.45 |

Guide Dog Leading Blind Man A304

**1981, Mar. 25 Photo.**

| | | | | | |
|---|---|---|---|---|---|
| **937** | A304 | 14p | shown | .35 | .30 |
| **938** | A304 | 18p | Sign language | .45 | .40 |
| **939** | A304 | 22p | Man in wheelchair | .60 | .55 |
| **940** | A304 | 25p | Foot painting | .65 | .60 |
| | | | *Nos. 937-940 (4)* | 2.05 | 1.85 |

International Year of the Disabled.

Small Tortoiseshell A305

**1981, May 13 *Perf. 14x14½***

| | | | | | |
|---|---|---|---|---|---|
| **941** | A305 | 14p | shown | .40 | .30 |
| **942** | A305 | 18p | Large blue | .45 | .40 |
| **943** | A305 | 22p | Peacock | .60 | .55 |
| **944** | A305 | 25p | Checkered skipper | .65 | .60 |
| | | | *Nos. 941-944 (4)* | 2.10 | 1.85 |

Glenfinnan, Highlands, Scotland A306

50th anniv. of National Trust for Scotland: 18p, Derwentwater, Lake District, England. 20p, Stackpole Head, Dyfed, Wales. 22p, Giant's Causeway, County Antrim, Northern Ireland. 25p, St. Kilda, Scotland.

**1981, June 24 Photo. *Perf. 14½x14***

| | | | | | |
|---|---|---|---|---|---|
| **945** | A306 | 14p | multicolored | .35 | .25 |
| **946** | A306 | 18p | multicolored | .45 | .35 |
| **947** | A306 | 20p | multicolored | .50 | .30 |
| **948** | A306 | 22p | multicolored | .55 | .40 |
| **949** | A306 | 25p | multicolored | .60 | .45 |
| | | | *Nos. 945-949 (5)* | 2.45 | 1.75 |

Prince Charles and Lady Diana — A307

**1981, July 22 Photo. *Perf. 14x14½***

| | | | | | |
|---|---|---|---|---|---|
| **950** | A307 | 14p | multicolored | .55 | .25 |
| **951** | A307 | 25p | multicolored | 1.20 | 1.00 |

Wedding of Charles, Prince of Wales, and Lady Diana Spencer, St. Paul's Cathedral, July 29.

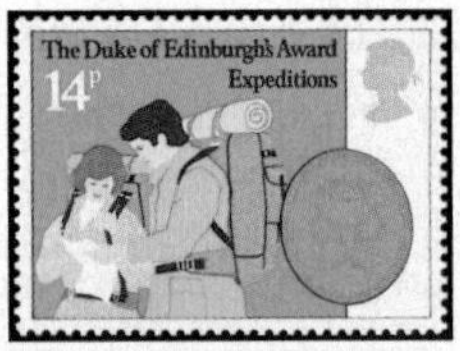

Hikers Reading Map A308

**1981, Aug. 12 Litho. *Perf. 14***

| | | | | | |
|---|---|---|---|---|---|
| **952** | A308 | 14p | shown | .35 | .25 |
| **953** | A308 | 18p | Girl at potter's wheel | .45 | .35 |
| **954** | A308 | 22p | Woman administering artificial respiration | .60 | .45 |
| **955** | A308 | 25p | Hurdler | .65 | .50 |
| | | | *Nos. 952-955 (4)* | 2.05 | 1.55 |

The Duke of Edinburgh's Awards (expeditions, skills, service, recreation), 25th anniv.

Cockle Dredging A309

**1981, Sept. 23 Photo. *Perf. 14½x14***

| | | | | | |
|---|---|---|---|---|---|
| **956** | A309 | 14p | shown | .35 | .25 |
| **957** | A309 | 18p | Hauling trawl net | .45 | .35 |
| **958** | A309 | 22p | Lobster potting | .60 | .40 |
| **959** | A309 | 25p | Hauling seine net | .65 | .50 |
| | | | *Nos. 956-959 (4)* | 2.05 | 1.50 |

Fishermen's Year and Royal Natl. Mission to Deep Sea Fishermen centenary.

Joseph and Mary Arriving at Bethlehem A310

Christmas: Children's Drawings.

**1981, Nov. 18 Photo.**

| | | | | | |
|---|---|---|---|---|---|
| **960** | A310 | 11½p | Santa Claus | .30 | .25 |
| **961** | A310 | 14p | Jesus | .35 | .30 |
| **962** | A310 | 18p | Angel | .45 | .40 |
| **963** | A310 | 22p | shown | .60 | .50 |
| **964** | A310 | 25p | Three Kings | .65 | .60 |
| | | | *Nos. 960-964 (5)* | 2.35 | 2.05 |

Death Centenary of Charles Darwin (1809-1882) — A311

**1982, Feb. 10 Photo.**

| | | | | | |
|---|---|---|---|---|---|
| **965** | A311 | 15½p | Giant tortoises | .40 | .35 |
| **966** | A311 | 19½p | Iguanas | .50 | .40 |
| **967** | A311 | 26p | Darwin's finches | .70 | .50 |
| **968** | A311 | 29p | Skulls | .75 | .60 |
| | | | *Nos. 965-968 (4)* | 2.35 | 1.85 |

Youth Organizations A312

**1982, Mar. 24 Photo. *Perf. 14x14½***

| | | | | | |
|---|---|---|---|---|---|
| **983** | A312 | 15½p | Boy's Brigade | .40 | .35 |
| **984** | A312 | 19½p | Girl's Brigade | .50 | .40 |
| **985** | A312 | 26p | Boy Scouts | .70 | .50 |
| **986** | A312 | 29p | Girl Guides | .75 | .60 |
| | | | *Nos. 983-986 (4)* | 2.35 | 1.85 |

75th anniv. of scouting and 125th birth anniv. of founder Robert Baden-Powell (26p).

Performing Arts — A313

**1982, Apr. 28 Photo. *Perf. 14x14½***

| | | | | | |
|---|---|---|---|---|---|
| **987** | A313 | 15½p | Ballet | *.50* | *.25* |
| **988** | A313 | 19½p | Pantomime | *.65* | *.50* |
| **989** | A313 | 26p | Shakespearean drama | *.85* | *.85* |
| **990** | A313 | 29p | Opera | *1.00* | *1.00* |
| | | | *Nos. 987-990 (4)* | *3.00* | *2.60* |

Nos. 987-990 show CEPT (Europa) emblem.

King Henry VIII and the Mary Rose A314

**1982, June 16 *Perf. 14½x14***

| | | | | | |
|---|---|---|---|---|---|
| **991** | A314 | 15½p | shown | .40 | .25 |
| **992** | A314 | 19½p | Admiral Blake, Triumph | .50 | .35 |
| **993** | A314 | 24p | Lord Nelson, Victory | .55 | .45 |
| **994** | A314 | 26p | Lord Fisher, Dreadnought | .75 | .55 |
| **995** | A314 | 29p | Viscount Cunningham, Warspite | .80 | .60 |
| | | | *Nos. 991-995 (5)* | 3.00 | 2.20 |

Textile Designs — A315

**1982, July 23 Photo. *Perf. 14x14½***

| | | | | | |
|---|---|---|---|---|---|
| **996** | A315 | 15½p | Strawberry Thief, 1883 | .40 | .25 |
| **997** | A315 | 19½p | Tulips, 1906 | .55 | .35 |
| **998** | A315 | 26p | Cherry Orchard, 1930 | .75 | .55 |
| **999** | A315 | 29p | Chevron, 1973 | .80 | .60 |
| | | | *Nos. 996-999 (4)* | 2.50 | 1.75 |

Information Technology — A316

15½p, Hieroglyphics, library, word processor. 26p, Viewdata set, satellite, laser pen.

**1982, Sept. 8 Photo.**

| | | | | | |
|---|---|---|---|---|---|
| **1000** | A316 | 15½p | multicolored | .35 | .25 |
| **1001** | A316 | 26p | multicolored | .65 | .45 |

Austin's Seven (1922) and Metro A317

Cars: 19½p, Ford Model T (1913) and Escort. 26p, Jaguar SS (1931) and XJ6 (1967). 29p, Rolls-Royce Silver Ghost (1907) and Silver Spirit (1982).

**1982, Oct. 13 Litho. *Perf. 14½x14***

| | | | | | |
|---|---|---|---|---|---|
| **1002** | A317 | 15½p | multicolored | .45 | .35 |
| **1003** | A317 | 19½p | multicolored | .60 | .45 |
| **1004** | A317 | 26p | multicolored | .80 | .55 |
| **1005** | A317 | 29p | multicolored | .85 | .60 |
| | | | *Nos. 1002-1005 (4)* | 2.70 | 1.95 |

Christmas 1982 A318

Designs: Christmas carols.

**1982, Nov. 17 Photo.**

| | | | | | |
|---|---|---|---|---|---|
| **1006** | A318 | 12½p | While Shepherds Watched | .35 | .25 |
| **1007** | A318 | 15½p | The Holly and the Ivy | .40 | .30 |
| **1008** | A318 | 19½p | I Saw Three Ships | .55 | .40 |
| **1009** | A318 | 26p | We Three Kings | .70 | .45 |
| **1010** | A318 | 29p | Good King Wenceslas | .75 | .55 |
| | | | *Nos. 1006-1010 (5)* | 2.75 | 1.95 |

River Fish
A319

**1983, Jan. 26 Photo. *Perf. 15x14***

| | | | | | |
|---|---|---|---|---|---|
| **1011** | A319 | 15½p | Salmon | .40 | .25 |
| **1012** | A319 | 19½p | Pike | .55 | .35 |
| **1013** | A319 | 26p | Trout | .70 | .40 |
| **1014** | A319 | 29p | Perch | .75 | .50 |
| | | | *Nos. 1011-1014 (4)* | 2.40 | 1.50 |

Commonwealth Day — A320

Landscapes by Donald Hamilton Fraser.

**1983, Mar. 9 Photo. *Perf. 14x14½***

| | | | | | |
|---|---|---|---|---|---|
| **1015** | A320 | 15½p | Tropical island | .40 | .30 |
| **1016** | A320 | 19½p | Desert | .50 | .35 |
| **1017** | A320 | 26p | Farmland | .70 | .40 |
| **1018** | A320 | 29p | Mountains | .75 | .50 |
| | | | *Nos. 1015-1018 (4)* | 2.35 | 1.55 |

Engineering Achievements (Europa) — A321

**1983, May 25 Photo. *Perf. 15x14***

| | | | | | |
|---|---|---|---|---|---|
| **1019** | A321 | 16p | Humber Bridge | *.55* | *.25* |
| **1020** | A321 | 20½p | Thames Flood Barrier | *.75* | *.75* |
| **1021** | A321 | 28p | Emergency oil rig support vessel Lolair | *1.00* | *1.00* |
| | | | *Nos. 1019-1021 (3)* | *2.30* | *2.00* |

A322

Designs: 16p, The Royal Scots (Royal Regiment). 20½p, Royal Welsh Fusiliers. 26p, Royal Green Jackets. 28p, Irish Guards. 31p, Parachute Regiment.

**1983, July 6 *Perf. 14x14½***

| | | | | | |
|---|---|---|---|---|---|
| **1022** | A322 | 16p | multicolored | .40 | .30 |
| **1023** | A322 | 20½p | multicolored | .50 | .35 |
| **1024** | A322 | 26p | multicolored | .70 | .40 |
| **1025** | A322 | 28p | multicolored | .75 | .45 |
| **1026** | A322 | 31p | multicolored | .80 | .50 |
| | | | *Nos. 1022-1026 (5)* | 3.15 | 2.00 |

A323

Designs: 16p, 20th cent. garden, Sissinghurst. 20½p, Biddulph Grange, 19th cent. 28p, Blenheim, 18th cent. 31p, Pitmeeden, 17th cent.

**1983, Aug. 24 Litho. *Perf. 14***

| | | | | | |
|---|---|---|---|---|---|
| **1027** | A323 | 16p | multicolored | .40 | .30 |
| **1028** | A323 | 20½p | multicolored | .50 | .35 |
| **1029** | A323 | 28p | multicolored | .75 | .45 |
| **1030** | A323 | 31p | multicolored | .80 | .50 |
| | | | *Nos. 1027-1030 (4)* | 2.45 | 1.60 |

British Fairs
A324

**1983, Oct. 5 Photo. *Perf. 14½x14***

| | | | | | |
|---|---|---|---|---|---|
| **1031** | A324 | 16p | Merry-go-round | .40 | .25 |
| **1032** | A324 | 20½p | Animals, rides | .50 | .35 |
| **1033** | A324 | 28p | Games | .75 | .45 |
| **1034** | A324 | 31p | Ancient market fair | .80 | .50 |
| | | | *Nos. 1031-1034 (4)* | 2.45 | 1.55 |

850th anniv. of St. Bartholomew's Fair.

Christmas
A325

**1983, Nov. 16 Photo.**

| | | | | | |
|---|---|---|---|---|---|
| **1035** | A325 | 12½p | Birds mailing cards | .35 | .25 |
| **1036** | A325 | 16p | Three Kings chimney pots | .40 | .25 |
| **1037** | A325 | 20½p | Birds under umbrella | .50 | .35 |
| **1038** | A325 | 28p | Birds under street lamp | .75 | .50 |
| **1039** | A325 | 31p | Topiary dove | .80 | .55 |
| | | | *Nos. 1035-1039 (5)* | 2.80 | 1.90 |

Heraldry
A326

Designs: 16p, Arms of The College of Arms. 20½p, Arms of Richard III, founder. 28p, Arms of The Earl Marshal. 31p, Arms of The City of London.

**1984, Jan. 17 Photo. *Perf. 14½***

| | | | | | |
|---|---|---|---|---|---|
| **1040** | A326 | 16p | multicolored | .40 | .25 |
| **1041** | A326 | 20½p | multicolored | .50 | .35 |
| **1042** | A326 | 28p | multicolored | .75 | .50 |
| **1043** | A326 | 31p | multicolored | .80 | .55 |
| | | | *Nos. 1040-1043 (4)* | 2.45 | 1.65 |

National Cattle Breeders' Association
A327

**1984, Mar. 6 Litho. *Perf. 15x14½***

| | | | | | |
|---|---|---|---|---|---|
| **1044** | A327 | 16p | Highland Cow | .40 | .25 |
| **1045** | A327 | 20½p | Chillingham Wild Bull | .50 | .35 |
| **1046** | A327 | 26p | Hereford Bull | .70 | .40 |
| **1047** | A327 | 28p | Welsh Black Bull | .75 | .45 |
| **1048** | A327 | 31p | Irish Moiled Cow | .80 | .50 |
| | | | *Nos. 1044-1048 (5)* | 3.15 | 1.95 |

Royal Institute of British Architects Sesquicentennial — A328

Urban renewal projects and plans.

**1984, Apr. 3 Photo.**

| | | | | | |
|---|---|---|---|---|---|
| **1049** | A328 | 16p | Liverpool | .40 | .25 |
| **1050** | A328 | 20½p | Durham | .50 | .35 |
| **1051** | A328 | 28p | Bristol | .75 | .45 |
| **1052** | A328 | 31p | Perth | .80 | .50 |
| | | | *Nos. 1049-1052 (4)* | 2.45 | 1.55 |

Europa (1959-1984) — A329

**1984, May 9 Photo. *Perf. 14½x14***

| | | | | | |
|---|---|---|---|---|---|
| **1053** | A329 | 16p | Bridge | *.50* | *.25* |
| **1054** | A329 | 16p | Abduction of Europa | *.50* | *.25* |
| *a.* | | | Pair, #1053-1054 | *1.25* | *.75* |
| **1055** | A329 | 20½p | like No. 1053 | *.70* | *.40* |
| **1056** | A329 | 20½p | like No. 1054 | *.70* | *.40* |
| *a.* | | | Pair, #1055-1056 | *2.25* | *2.25* |
| | | | *Nos. 1053-1056 (4)* | *2.40* | *1.30* |

Nos. 1054, 1056 also for 2nd Election of the European Parliament.

London Economic Summit, June 7-9 — A330

**1984, June 5 Photo. *Perf. 14x15***

| | | | | | |
|---|---|---|---|---|---|
| **1057** | A330 | 31p | Lancaster House | 1.00 | 1.00 |

Greenwich Meridian, Cent. — A331

**1984, June 26 Litho. *Perf. 14x14½***

| | | | | | |
|---|---|---|---|---|---|
| **1058** | A331 | 16p | View from Apollo 11 | .40 | .25 |
| **1059** | A331 | 20½p | English Channel map | .50 | .35 |
| **1060** | A331 | 28p | Greenwich Observatory | .70 | .45 |
| **1061** | A331 | 31p | Airy's transit telescope, 1850 | .80 | .50 |
| | | | *Nos. 1058-1061 (4)* | 2.40 | 1.55 |

Bath-Bristol-London Mail Coach Bicentenary — A332

18th century drawings by James Pollard.

**Photo. & Engr.**

**1984, July 31 *Perf. 14½x14***

| | | | | | |
|---|---|---|---|---|---|
| **1062** | A332 | 16p | Bath, 1784 | .40 | .35 |
| **1063** | A332 | 16p | Exeter, 1816 | .40 | .35 |
| **1064** | A332 | 16p | Norwich, 1827 | .40 | .35 |
| **1065** | A332 | 16p | Holyhead & Liverpool | .40 | .35 |
| **1066** | A332 | 16p | Edinburgh, 1831 | .40 | .35 |
| *a.* | | | Strip of 5, #1062-1066 | 2.75 | 2.50 |

50th Anniv. of British Council
A333

**1984, Sept. 25 Photo.**

| | | | | | |
|---|---|---|---|---|---|
| **1067** | A333 | 17p | Education for development | .40 | .25 |
| **1068** | A333 | 22p | Promoting the arts | .55 | .30 |
| **1069** | A333 | 31p | Technical training | .80 | .40 |
| **1070** | A333 | 34p | Language & libraries | .90 | .50 |
| | | | *Nos. 1067-1070 (4)* | 2.65 | 1.45 |

Christmas 1984
A334

Crayon Sketches by Yvonne Gilbert.

**1984, Nov. 20 Photo. *Perf. 15x14***

| | | | | | |
|---|---|---|---|---|---|
| **1088** | A334 | 13p | Holy Family | .35 | .30 |
| *a.* | | | Booklet pane of 20 (BK770) | 10.50 | |
| **1089** | A334 | 17p | Arrival in Bethlehem | .45 | .35 |
| **1090** | A334 | 22p | Shephard and Lamb | .60 | .35 |
| **1091** | A334 | 31p | Virgin and child | .80 | .50 |
| **1092** | A334 | 34p | Offering Frankincense | .90 | .60 |
| | | | *Nos. 1088-1092 (5)* | 3.10 | 2.10 |

Bklt. of 20 13p sold at 30p discount. Stamps have blue stars printed on the back.

Great Western Railway Sesquicentennial — A335

**1985, Jan. 22 Photo. *Perf. 15x14***

| | | | | | |
|---|---|---|---|---|---|
| **1093** | A335 | 17p | Flying Scotsman | .50 | .30 |
| **1094** | A335 | 22p | Golden Arrow | .65 | .55 |
| **1095** | A335 | 29p | Cheltenham Flyer | .85 | .75 |
| **1096** | A335 | 31p | Royal Scot | .90 | .90 |
| **1097** | A335 | 34p | Cornish Riviera | 1.00 | .90 |
| | | | *Nos. 1093-1097 (5)* | 3.90 | 3.40 |

Insects — A336

**1985, Mar. 12 Photo. *Perf. 15x14½***

| | | | | | |
|---|---|---|---|---|---|
| **1098** | A336 | 17p | Buff tailed bumble bee | .50 | .35 |
| **1099** | A336 | 22p | Seven spotted ladybird | .65 | .50 |
| **1100** | A336 | 29p | Wart-biter bushcricket | .85 | .65 |
| **1101** | A336 | 31p | Stag beetle | .90 | .70 |
| **1102** | A336 | 34p | Emperor dragonfly | .95 | .75 |
| | | | *Nos. 1098-1102 (5)* | 3.85 | 2.95 |

Music Year (Europa)
A337

British Composers: 17p, Water Music, by George Frideric Handel. 22p, The Planets

Suite, by Gustav Holst. 31p, The First Cockoo, by Frederick Delius. 34p, Sea Pictures, by Edward Elgar.

**1985, May 14 Perf. 14½**

**1103** A337 17p Reflections in pool .65 .25
**1104** A337 22p View of planets .90 .90
**1105** A337 31p Roosting cuckoo 1.20 1.10
**1106** A337 34p Waves, wing 1.30 1.25
*Nos. 1103-1106 (4) 4.05 3.50*

Safety at Sea A338

**1985, June 18 Litho. Perf. 14**

**1107** A338 17p Lifeboat .45 .25
**1108** A338 22p Beachy Head Lighthouse, chart .60 .55
**1109** A338 31p Marecs-A satellite .80 .75
**1110** A338 34p Signal buoy, yacht .90 .85
*Nos. 1107-1110 (4) 2.75 2.40*

Royal Mail Service, 350th Anniv. — A339

Designs: 17p, Royal Mail Datapost motorcyclist and plane. 22p, Postbus on country road. 31p, Parcel service delivery. 34p, Postman delivering mail.

**1985, July 30 Photo. Perf. 14x14½**

**1111** A339 17p multicolored .45 .25
**1112** A339 22p multicolored .60 .55
**1113** A339 31p multicolored .80 .75
**1114** A339 34p multicolored .90 .85
*Nos. 1111-1114 (4) 2.75 2.40*

Arthurian Legends A340

Designs: 17p, Arthur consulting with Merlin. 22p, The Lady of the Lake with the sword "Excalibur." 31p, Guinevere and Lancelot fleeing from Camelot. 34p, Sir Galahad praying during his quest for the Holy Grail.

**1985, Sept. 3 Photo. Perf. 15x14**

**1115** A340 17p multicolored .45 .25
**1116** A340 22p multicolored .60 .55
**1117** A340 31p multicolored .80 .75
**1118** A340 34p multicolored .90 .85
*Nos. 1115-1118 (4) 2.75 2.40*

500th anniv. of William Caxton's edition of Le Morte D'Arthur, by Sir Thomas Mallory.

20th Cent. Stars and Directors of Film — A341

Photographs: 17p, Peter Sellers (1925-80). 22p, David Niven (1910-83). 29p, Charlie Chaplin (1889-1977). 31p, Vivien Leigh (1913-67). 34p, Sir Alfred Hitchcock (1899-1980), director.

**1985, Oct. 8 Photo. Perf. 14½**

**1119** A341 17p multicolored .55 .25
**1120** A341 22p multicolored .75 .60
**1121** A341 29p multicolored .90 .80
**1122** A341 31p multicolored 1.00 .90
**1123** A341 34p multicolored 1.10 1.00
*Nos. 1119-1123 (5) 4.30 3.55*

Christmas Pantomime A342

**1985, Nov. 19 Photo. Perf. 15x14½**

**1124** A342 12p Principal boy .35 .30
*a.* Booklet pane of 20 (BK 780) 10.00
**1125** A342 17p Genie .45 .40
**1126** A342 22p Grande dame .60 .50
**1127** A342 31p Good fairy .85 .75
**1128** A342 34p Cat .90 .85
*Nos. 1124-1128 (5) 3.15 2.80*

No. 1124a has random star design printed on back.

Industry Year A343

**1986, Jan. 14 Litho. Perf. 15x14**

**1129** A343 17p North Sea oil rig, light bulb .45 .25
**1130** A343 22p Medical research lab, thermometer .60 .55
**1131** A343 31p Steel mill, garden hoe .85 .75
**1132** A343 34p Cornfield, bread .90 .85
*Nos. 1129-1132 (4) 2.80 2.40*

Halley's Comet A344

Designs: 17p, Caricature, Edmond Halley (1656-1742), astronomer. 22p, European Space Agency Giotto spacecraft pursuing comet. 31p, Comet and legend, Maybe Twice in a Lifetime. 34p, Comet orbiting sun.

**1986, Feb. 18 Photo.**

**1133** A344 17p multicolored .45 .25
**1134** A344 22p multicolored .60 .55
**1135** A344 31p multicolored .85 .75
**1136** A344 34p multicolored .90 .85
*Nos. 1133-1136 (4) 2.80 2.40*

A345

Queen Elizabeth II, 60th Birthday A346

**1986, Apr. 21 Photo.**

**1137** A345 17p multicolored .50 .25
**1138** A346 17p multicolored .50 .25
*a.* Pair, #1137-1138 1.25 1.25
**1139** A345 34p multicolored 1.00 .50
**1140** A346 34p multicolored 1.00 .50
*a.* Pair, #1139-1140 2.25 2.25

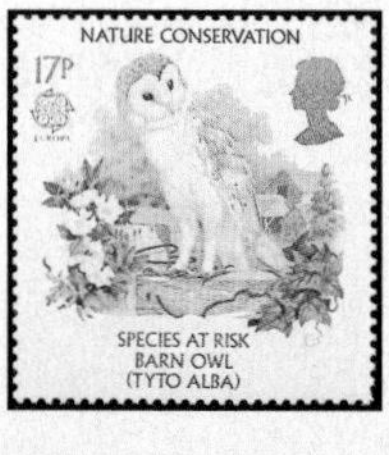


Europa A347

**1986, May 20 Photo. Perf. 14½**

**1141** A347 17p Barn owl .55 .25
**1142** A347 22p Pine marten .80 .85
**1143** A347 31p Wild cat 1.10 1.00
**1144** A347 34p Natterjack toad 1.20 1.20
*Nos. 1141-1144 (4) 3.65 3.30*

Domesday Book, 900th Anniv. A348

**1986, June 17 Photo.**

**1145** A348 17p Peasant .50 .25
**1146** A348 22p Freeman .60 .60
**1147** A348 31p Knight .90 1.25
**1148** A348 34p Lord 1.00 1.25
*Nos. 1145-1148 (4) 3.00 3.35*

Domesday Book, first nationwide survey in British history.

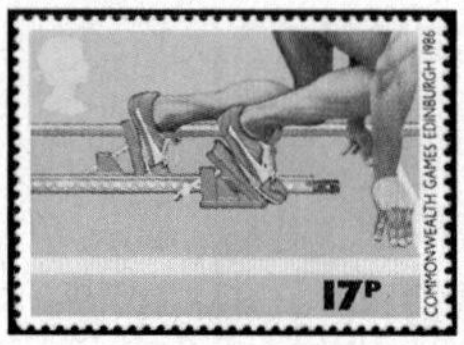

Sports A349

**1986, July 15 Photo. Perf. 15x14**

**1149** A349 17p Track and field .50 .25
**1150** A349 22p Rowing .60 .55
**1151** A349 29p Weight lifting .80 .80
**1152** A349 31p Shooting .85 .85
**1153** A349 34p Field hockey .90 .90
*Nos. 1149-1153 (5) 3.65 3.35*

1986 Commonwealth Games, Edinburgh. World Hockey Cup, London.

Wedding of Prince Andrew and Sarah Ferguson — A350

**1986, July 22 Perf. 14x15**

**1154** A350 12p multicolored .45 .30
**1155** A350 17p multicolored .75 .75

Commonwealth Parliamentary Assoc. Conf., London — A351

**1986, Aug. 19 Litho. Perf. 14x14½**

**1156** A351 34p multicolored 1.10 .85

Royal Air Force Commanders and Aircraft A352

Designs: 17p, Lord Dowding (1882-1970), Hurricane. 22p, Lord Tedder (1890-1967), Hawker Typhoon. 29p, Lord Trenchard (1873-1956), De Havilland 9A World War I bomber. 31p, Sir Arthur Harris (1892-1984), Avro Lancaster. 34p, Lord Portal (1893-1971), De Havilland Mosquito.

**1986, Sept. 16 Photo. Perf. 14½**

**1157** A352 17p multicolored .50 .25
**1158** A352 22p multicolored .65 .65
**1159** A352 29p multicolored .80 .75
**1160** A352 31p multicolored .90 .80
**1161** A352 34p multicolored .95 .90
*Nos. 1157-1161 (5) 3.80 3.35*

Christmas A353

Customs: 12p, 13p, Glastonbury Thorn. 18p, Tanad Valley Plygain. 22p, Hebrides Tribute. 31p, Dewsbury Church Knell. 34p, Hereford Boy Bishop.

**1986, Nov. 18 Photo. Perf. 15x14½**

**1162** A353 12p multicolored .40 .30
**1163** A353 13p multicolored .40 .25
*a.* Pane of 36 18.00
**1164** A353 18p multicolored .50 .25
**1165** A353 22p multicolored .60 .60
**1166** A353 31p multicolored .85 .85
**1167** A353 34p multicolored .90 .90
*Nos. 1162-1167 (6) 3.65 3.15*

No. 1163a printed in two panes of 18 with gutter between, stars on back; folded and sold in discount booklet for £4.30.

Flora — A354

Photographs by Alfred Lammer.

**1987, Jan. 20 Photo. Perf. 14½**

**1168** A354 18p Gaillardia .60 .25
**1169** A354 22p Echinops .80 .80
**1170** A354 31p Echeveria 1.10 1.10
**1171** A354 34p Colchicum 1.20 1.20
*Nos. 1168-1171 (4) 3.70 3.35*

Sir Isaac Newton (1642-1727), Physicist, Mathematician A355

Manuscripts and principles: 18p, Philosophiae Naturalis Principia Mathematica, 1687. 22p, Motion of bodies in ellipses. 31p, Opticks Treatise of the Refraction, Reflections and Colors of Light. 34p, The System of the World.

**1987, Mar. 24 Photo. Perf. 14**

**1172** A355 18p multicolored .50 .25
**1173** A355 22p multicolored .60 .60
**1174** A355 31p multicolored .90 .90
**1175** A355 34p multicolored .95 .95
*Nos. 1172-1175 (4) 2.95 2.70*

Europa A356

Modern architecture: 18p, Willis Faber & Dumas Building, Ipswich, designed by Norman Foster. 22p, Pompidou Centre, Paris, designed by Richard Rogers and Renzo Piano. 31p, Staatsgalerie, Stuttgart, designed by James Stirling and Michael Wilford. 34p, European Investment Bank, Luxembourg, designed by Sir Denys Lasdun.

**1987, May 12 Photo. Perf. 15x14**

**1176** A356 18p multicolored .60 .25
**1177** A356 22p multicolored .90 .80
**1178** A356 31p multicolored 1.10 1.10
**1179** A356 34p multicolored 1.40 1.25
*Nos. 1176-1179 (4) 4.00 3.40*

St. John Ambulance, Cent. — A357

First aid.

**1987, June 16 Litho. *Perf. 14x14½***

| | | | | | |
|---|---|---|---|---|---|
| **1180** | A357 | 18p | Ambulance, 1887 | .50 | .25 |
| **1181** | A357 | 22p | War victims, 1940 | .60 | .60 |
| **1182** | A357 | 31p | Public event, 1965 | .90 | .90 |
| **1183** | A357 | 34p | Transplant organ flight, 1987 | .95 | .95 |
| | | | *Nos. 1180-1183 (4)* | 2.95 | 2.70 |

Order of the Thistle, Scotland, 300th Anniv. of Revival A358

Coats of arms: 18p, Lord Lyon, King of Arms, 1687. 22p, Duke of Rothesay, bestowed on Prince Charles in 1974. 31p, Royal Scottish Academy of Painting, Sculpture & Architecture, 1826. 34p, The Royal Society of Edinburgh, 1783.

**1987, July 21 Photo. *Perf. 14½***

| | | | | | |
|---|---|---|---|---|---|
| **1184** | A358 | 18p | multicolored | .50 | .25 |
| **1185** | A358 | 22p | multicolored | .60 | .60 |
| **1186** | A358 | 31p | multicolored | .90 | .90 |
| **1187** | A358 | 34p | multicolored | .95 | .95 |
| | | | *Nos. 1184-1187 (4)* | 2.95 | 2.70 |

Accession of Queen Victoria, 150th Anniv. A359

Portraits of Victoria and: 18p, Great Exhibition (1851) at the Crystal Palace, Grace Darling's rescue (1838) of the Forfashire's survivors, and Monarch of the Glen, by Sir Edwin Henry Landseer. 22p, Launching of Brunel's ship Great Eastern, portrait of Prince Consort Albert, Mrs. Beeton's Book of Household Management (1889). 31p, The Albert Memorial, Prime Minister Disraeli and 1st ballot box. 34p, The Boer War, Guglielmo Marconi's wireless telegraph communications linking Paris and London (1898), and diamond jubilee emblem.

**Photo. & Engr.**

**1987, Sept. 8 *Perf. 15x14***

| | | | | | |
|---|---|---|---|---|---|
| **1188** | A359 | 18p | multicolored | .50 | .25 |
| **1189** | A359 | 22p | multicolored | .60 | .60 |
| **1190** | A359 | 31p | multicolored | .90 | .90 |
| **1191** | A359 | 34p | multicolored | .95 | .95 |
| | | | *Nos. 1188-1191 (4)* | 2.95 | 2.70 |

Studio Pottery A360

**1987, Oct. 13 Photo. *Perf. 14½***

| | | | | | |
|---|---|---|---|---|---|
| **1192** | A360 | 18p | Bernard Leach | .50 | .25 |
| **1193** | A360 | 26p | Elizabeth Fritsch | .75 | .75 |
| **1194** | A360 | 31p | Lucie Rie | .90 | .90 |
| **1195** | A360 | 34p | Hans Coper | .95 | .95 |
| | | | *Nos. 1192-1195 (4)* | 3.10 | 2.85 |

Christmas A361

Childhood memories: 13p, Decorating tree. 18p, Looking out window, Christmas eve. 26p, Sweet dreams. 31p, Reading new book to toys, Christmas morning. 34p, Playing horn, snowman.

**1987, Nov. 17 Photo. *Perf. 15x14***

| | | | | | |
|---|---|---|---|---|---|
| **1196** | A361 | 13p | multicolored | .40 | .25 |
| *a.* | | | Pane of 36 | 18.00 | |
| **1197** | A361 | 18p | multicolored | .50 | .25 |
| **1198** | A361 | 26p | multicolored | .75 | .75 |
| **1199** | A361 | 31p | multicolored | .90 | .90 |
| **1200** | A361 | 34p | multicolored | .95 | .95 |
| | | | *Nos. 1196-1200 (5)* | 3.50 | 3.10 |

No. 1196a printed in two panes of 18 with gutter between, stars on back; folded and sold in discount booklets for £4.30.

Linnean Society of London, 200th Anniv. A362

**1988, Jan. 19 *Perf. 15x14½***

| | | | | | |
|---|---|---|---|---|---|
| **1201** | A362 | 18p | Bull-rout fish | .50 | .25 |
| **1202** | A362 | 26p | Yellow waterlily | .75 | .75 |
| **1203** | A362 | 31p | Bewick's swan | .90 | .90 |
| **1204** | A362 | 34p | Morel | .95 | .95 |
| | | | *Nos. 1201-1204 (4)* | 3.10 | 2.85 |

Linnaeus (Carl von Linne, 1707-78), inventor of system of taxonomic nomenclature.

Welsh Bible, 400th Anniv. — A363

**1988, Mar. 1 Photo. *Perf. 14½***

| | | | | | |
|---|---|---|---|---|---|
| **1205** | A363 | 18p | William Morgan | .50 | .25 |
| **1206** | A363 | 26p | William Salesbury | .75 | .75 |
| **1207** | A363 | 31p | Richard Davies | .90 | .90 |
| **1208** | A363 | 34p | Richard Parry | .95 | .95 |
| | | | *Nos. 1205-1208 (4)* | 3.10 | 2.85 |

Sports — A364

**1988, Mar. 22 Photo. *Perf. 14½***

| | | | | | |
|---|---|---|---|---|---|
| **1209** | A364 | 18p | Balance beam | .50 | .25 |
| **1210** | A364 | 26p | Downhill skiing | .75 | .75 |
| **1211** | A364 | 31p | Tennis | .90 | .90 |
| **1212** | A364 | 34p | Soccer | .95 | .95 |
| | | | *Nos. 1209-1212 (4)* | 3.10 | 2.85 |

Ski Club of Great Britain and centenaries of the British Amateur Gymnastics Assoc., Lawn Tennis Assoc. and the Soccer League.

Europa 1988 A365

Transportation and communication, 1938.

**1988, May 10 *Perf. 15x14***

| | | | | | |
|---|---|---|---|---|---|
| **1213** | A365 | 18p | Mallard locomotive | *.60* | *.25* |
| **1214** | A365 | 26p | Queen Elizabeth ocean liner | *.90* | *.90* |
| **1215** | A365 | 31p | Tram No. 1173, Glasgow | *1.00* | *1.00* |
| **1216** | A365 | 34p | Handley Page aircraft, Croydon Airport | *1.10* | *1.10* |
| | | | *Nos. 1213-1216 (4)* | *3.60* | *3.25* |

Defeat of the Spanish Armada by the Royal Navy, 400th Anniv. A366

Designs: No. 1217, Armada approaching The Lizard, July 19, 1588. No. 1218, Royal Navy vessels sailing from Plymouth to engage Spaniards in battle, July 21. No. 1219, Battle scene off the Isle of Wight, July 25. No. 1220, Battle scene off Calais, France, July 28-29. No. 1221, Spanish ships foundering in the North Sea storms, July 30-Aug. 2. Printed in a continuous design.

**1988, July 19**

| | | | | | |
|---|---|---|---|---|---|
| **1217** | A366 | 18p | multicolored | .50 | .25 |
| **1218** | A366 | 18p | multicolored | .50 | .25 |
| **1219** | A366 | 18p | multicolored | .50 | .25 |
| **1220** | A366 | 18p | multicolored | .50 | .25 |
| **1221** | A366 | 18p | multicolored | .50 | .25 |
| *a.* | | | Strip of 5, Nos. 1217-1221 | 3.00 | 2.25 |

Australia Bicentennial A367

Designs: No. 1222, Colonist, First Fleet vessel. No. 1223, British and Australian parliaments, Queen Elizabeth II. No. 1224, Cricketer W.G. Grace. No. 1225, John Lennon (1940-1980), William Shakespeare (1564-1616) and Sydney Opera House. Flag of Australia appears on Nos. 1223a, 1225a.

**1988, June 21 Litho. *Perf. 14½***

| | | | | | |
|---|---|---|---|---|---|
| **1222** | A367 | 18p | multicolored | .45 | .25 |
| **1223** | A367 | 18p | multicolored | .45 | .25 |
| *a.* | | | Pair, #1222-1223 | 1.10 | 1.00 |
| **1224** | A367 | 34p | multicolored | .90 | .50 |
| **1225** | A367 | 34p | multicolored | .90 | .50 |
| *a.* | | | Pair, #1224-1225 | 2.25 | 2.00 |
| | | | *Nos. 1222-1225 (4)* | 2.70 | 1.50 |

See Australia Nos. 1082-1085.

Nonsensical Drawings by Edward Lear (1812-1888) — A368

Illustrations and text: 19p, *The Owl and the Pussycat*, 1867. 27p, Self-portrait as a bird, pen-and-ink sketch from a letter. 32p, "C" is for Cat, alphabet book character. 35p, Girl, birds and part of a limerick.

**1988, Sept. 6 Photo. *Perf. 15x14***

| | | | | | |
|---|---|---|---|---|---|
| **1226** | A368 | 19p | multicolored | .55 | .25 |
| **1227** | A368 | 27p | multicolored | .75 | .75 |
| **1228** | A368 | 32p | multicolored | .95 | .95 |
| **1229** | A368 | 35p | multicolored | 1.00 | 1.00 |
| *a.* | | | Souv. sheet of 4, #1226-1229 | 6.00 | 5.50 |
| | | | *Nos. 1226-1229 (4)* | 3.25 | 2.95 |

No. 1229a sold for £1.35. The surtax benefited Stamp World London '90.

Photographs of Castles by Prince Andrew — A369

**1988, Oct 18 Engr.**

| | | | | | |
|---|---|---|---|---|---|
| **1230** | A369 | £1 | Carrickfergus | 2.75 | .50 |
| **1231** | A369 | £1.50 | Caernarfon | 4.00 | 1.00 |
| **1232** | A369 | £2 | Edinburgh | 5.50 | 1.50 |
| **1233** | A369 | £5 | Windsor | 14.00 | 4.50 |
| | | | *Nos. 1230-1233 (4)* | 26.25 | 7.50 |

See Nos. 1445-1448.

Christmas Cards A370

**1988, Nov. 15 Photo. *Perf. 15x14½***

| | | | | | |
|---|---|---|---|---|---|
| **1234** | A370 | 14p | Journey to Bethlehem | .40 | .25 |
| **1235** | A370 | 19p | Shepherds see star | .55 | .25 |
| **1236** | A370 | 27p | Magi follow star | .75 | .75 |
| **1237** | A370 | 32p | Nativity | .95 | .95 |
| **1238** | A370 | 35p | The Annunciation | 1.00 | 1.00 |
| | | | *Nos. 1234-1238 (5)* | 3.65 | 3.20 |

Birds — A371

**1989, Jan. 17 *Perf. 14x15***

| | | | | | |
|---|---|---|---|---|---|
| **1239** | A371 | 19p | Puffin | .55 | .25 |
| **1240** | A371 | 27p | Avocet | .75 | .75 |
| **1241** | A371 | 32p | Oystercatcher | .95 | .95 |
| **1242** | A371 | 35p | Gannet | 1.00 | 1.00 |
| | | | *Nos. 1239-1242 (4)* | 3.25 | 2.95 |

Special Occasions A372

**1989, Jan. 31 Photo. *Perf. 15x14***

**Booklet Stamps**

| | | | | | |
|---|---|---|---|---|---|
| **1243** | A372 | 19p | Rose | 3.00 | 3.00 |
| **1244** | A372 | 19p | Cupid | 3.00 | 3.00 |
| **1245** | A372 | 19p | Ships | 3.00 | 3.00 |
| **1246** | A372 | 19p | Fruit bowl | 3.00 | 3.00 |
| **1247** | A372 | 19p | Teddy Bear | 3.00 | 3.00 |
| *a.* | | | Bklt. pane of 10 (2 each #1243-1247) +12 labels (BK733) | 55.00 | |
| | | | *Nos. 1243-1247 (5)* | 15.00 | 15.00 |

Labels inscribed "CONGRATULATIONS," "BEST WISHES," "HAPPY BIRTHDAY," "HAPPY ANNIVERSARY," "WITH LOVE," or "THANK YOU."

No. 1247a is valued with perfs guillotined. Full perfs sell for more.

Food and Farming Year — A373

Foods and tile mosaics in agricultural motifs.

**1989, Mar. 7 Photo. *Perf. 14½***

**1248** A373 19p Fruit and vegetables .55 .25
**1249** A373 27p Meat, fish, fruit .75 .75
**1250** A373 32p Dairy products .95 .95
**1251** A373 35p Breads, cake, cereal 1.00 1.00
*Nos. 1248-1251 (4)* 3.25 2.95

Fireworks — A374

**1989, Apr. 11 Photo. *Perf. 14x14½***

**1252** A374 19p Mortarboard .55 .25
**1253** A374 19p "X" on ballot .55 .25
*a.* Pair, #1252-1253 1.25 1.25
**1254** A374 35p Posthorn 1.00 .50
**1255** A374 35p Globe 1.00 .50
*a.* Pair, #1254-1255 2.25 2.25
*Nos. 1252-1255 (4)* 3.10 1.50

Public education in England and Wales, 150th anniv. (No. 1252); European Parliament 3rd elections (No. 1253); 26th world congress of Postal Telegraph and Telephone Intl., Brighton, Sept. 18-23 (No. 1254); Interparliamentary Union Cent. Conf., 82nd session, Sept. 4-9 (No. 1255).

Europa 1989 — A375

Children's toys.

**1989, May 16 *Perf. 14x15***

**1256** A375 19p Airplane, locomotive *.75 .25*
**1257** A375 27p Building-block tower *.90 .80*
**1258** A375 32p Checkerboard, die, ladder, chips *1.10 .90*
**1259** A375 35p Doll house, boat, robot *1.25 1.00*
*Nos. 1256-1259 (4) 4.00 2.95*

Industrial Archaeology A376

**1989, July 4 Photo. *Perf. 14x15***

**1280** A376 19p Ironbridge .55 .25
**1281** A376 27p Tin Mine .75 .75
**1282** A376 32p Mills .95 .95
**1283** A376 35p Pontcysyllte Aqueduct 1.00 1.00
*Nos. 1280-1283 (4)* 3.25 2.95

**1989, July 25 Souvenir Sheet**

**1284** Sheet of 4 4.00 *4.00*
*a.* A376 19p like #1280, horiz. .60 *.50*
*b.* A376 27p like #1281, horiz. .85 *.75*
*c.* A376 32p like #1282, horiz. 1.10 *.95*
*d.* A376 35p like #1283, horiz. 1.25 *1.00*

No. 1284 sold for £1.40.

Microscopy A377

Specimens under magnification: 19p, Snowflake, the soc. emblem. 27p, Blue fly. 32p, Blood cells. 35p, Microchip.

**1989, Sept. 5 Litho. *Perf. 14½x14***

**1285** A377 19p multicolored .55 .25
**1286** A377 27p multicolored .75 .75
**1287** A377 32p multicolored .95 .95
**1288** A377 35p multicolored 1.00 1.00
*Nos. 1285-1288 (4)* 3.25 2.95

Royal Microscopical Soc., 150th anniv.

The Lord Mayor's Show, London — A378

Procession of the Lord Mayor's coach from Guildhall to the Law Courts in the Strand: No. 1289, Royal mail coach and The Guildhall. No. 1290, Drummer, cavalrymen and Mansion House. No. 1291, Gold coach, 1757, and The Royal Exchange. No. 1292, Coachman and St. Paul's Cathedral. No. 1293, Drummer, cavalryman and the Law Courts.

**1989, Oct. 17 Litho. *Perf. 14x15***

**1289** A378 20p multicolored .45 .35
*a.* Perf. 14x14¼ 1.50 .30
*b.* Booklet pane of 4 #1289a (BK189) 6.00 —
**1290** A378 20p multicolored .45 .35
**1291** A378 20p multicolored .45 .35
**1292** A378 20p multicolored .45 .35
**1293** A378 20p multicolored .45 .35
*a.* Strip of 5, #1289-1293 2.75 2.50

Issued. Nos. 1289a, 1289b, 8/19/09.

Ely Cathedral, Cambridgeshire, 800th Anniv. — A379

**1989, Nov. 14 Photo. *Perf. 15x14***

**1294** A379 15p Gothic arches, 4 peasants .40 .25
*Nos. 1294,B2-B5 (5)* 3.20 3.00

Christmas.

Royal Soc. for the Prevention of Cruelty to Animals, 150th Anniv. — A381

**1990, Jan. 23 Litho. *Perf. 14x15***

**1300** A381 20p Kitten .65 .50
**1301** A381 29p Rabbit .95 .95
**1302** A381 34p Duckling 1.00 1.00
**1303** A381 37p Puppy 1.20 1.20
*Nos. 1300-1303 (4)* 3.80 3.65

A382

A382a

A382b

A382c

A382d

A382e

A382f

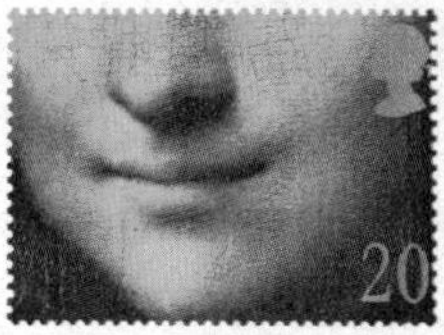

A382g

A382h

Famous Smiles — A382i

**1990, Feb. 6 Photo. *Perf. 15x14***

**1304** A382 20p Teddy bear 2.00 2.00
**1305** A382a 20p Dennis the Menace 2.00 2.00
**1306** A382b 20p Mr. Punch 2.00 2.00
**1307** A382c 20p Cheshire Cat 2.00 2.00
**1308** A382d 20p Man in the Moon 2.00 2.00
**1309** A382e 20p The Laughing Policeman 2.00 2.00
**1310** A382f 20p Clown 2.00 2.00
**1311** A382g 20p Mona Lisa 2.00 2.00
**1312** A382h 20p Queen of Hearts 2.00 2.00
**1313** A382i 20p Stan Laurel 2.00 2.00
*a.* Pane of 10, #1304-1313 27.50 27.50
*Nos. 1304-1313 (10)* 20.00 20.00

No. 1313a sold folded and unattached in booklet cover.

See Nos. 1364-1373.

A383

Europa 1990: No. 1314, Alexandra Palace. No. 1315, School of Art, Glasgow. 29p, British Philatelic Bureau, Edinburgh. 37p, Templeton Carpet Factory, Glasgow.

**1990, Mar. 6 Photo. *Perf. 14x15***

**1314** A383 20p multicolored .70 .25
*a.* Bklt. pane of 4 + printed margin 5.00
**1315** A383 20p multicolored .70 .25
**1316** A383 29p multicolored 1.00 1.00
**1317** A383 37p multicolored 1.10 1.10
*Nos. 1314-1317 (4)* 3.50 2.60

Stamp World '90, London (No. 1314); Glasgow, European City of Culture (Nos. 1315, 1317).

For Prestige booklet containing pane No. 1314a, see listings in the Booklets section.

Queen's Awards for Export and Technological Achievement, 25th Anniv. — A384

**1990, Apr. 10 Litho.**

**1318** A384 20p Export .60 .30
**1319** A384 20p Technology .60 .30
*a.* Pair, #1318-1319 1.40 1.40
**1320** A384 37p like No. 1318 1.00 .60
**1321** A384 37p like No. 1319 1.00 .60
*a.* Pair, #1320-1321 2.50 2.50
*Nos. 1318-1321 (4)* 3.20 1.80

Se-tenant pairs have continuous designs.

Kew Gardens, 150th Anniv. — A385

**1990, June 5 Photo.**

**1322** A385 20p Cycad .50 .25
**1323** A385 29p Stone pine .75 .75
**1324** A385 34p Willow tree .90 .90
**1325** A385 37p Cedar 1.00 1.00
*Nos. 1322-1325 (4)* 3.15 2.90

Thomas Hardy (1840-1928), Writer and Clyffe Clump, Dorset — A386

**1990, July 10 Photo. *Perf. 14x15***

**1326** A386 20p multicolored .55 .55

Queen Mother, 90th Birthday — A387

Designs: Portraits of Queen Elizabeth, The Queen Mother.

**1990, Aug. 2** *Perf. 14x15, 14½*

**1327** A387 20p Recent portrait .70 .35
**1328** A387 29p As Queen Consort, 1937 1.05 1.05
**1329** A387 34p As Duchess of York 1.45 1.45
**1330** A387 37p As Lady Elizabeth Bowes-Lyon 1.50 1.50
*Nos. 1327-1330 (4)* 4.70 4.35

Gallantry Awards — A388

Designs: No. 1331, Victoria Cross. No. 1332, George Cross. No. 1333, Military Cross, Military Medal. No. 1334, Distinguished Flying Cross, Distinguished Flying Medal. No. 1335, Distinguished Service Cross, Distinguished Service Medal. Nos. 1333-1335 horiz.

**1990, Sept. 11** *Perf. 14x15, 15x14*

**1331** A388 20p multicolored .55 .50
*a.* Litho., perf. 14x14¼, black denomination ('06) 7.00 2.00
*b.* Booklet pane of 4 #1331a (BK180) 28.00 —
**1332** A388 20p multicolored .55 .50
**1333** A388 20p multicolored .55 .50
**1334** A388 20p multicolored .55 .50
**1335** A388 20p multicolored .55 .50
*Nos. 1331-1335 (5)* 2.75 2.50

Denomination on No. 1331 is gray.
Nos. 1331a, 1331b issued 9/21/2006.

Astronomy A389

Designs: 22p, Armagh Observatory, Jodrell Bank and La Palma telescopes. 26p, Early telescope, celestial diagram. 31p, Greenwich Old Observatory, sextant, chronometer. 37p, Stonehenge, celestial navigation.

**1990, Oct. 16** *Perf. 14*

**1336** A389 22p multicolored .60 .25
**1337** A389 26p multicolored .75 .75
**1338** A389 31p multicolored .90 .90
**1339** A389 37p multicolored 1.00 1.00
*Nos. 1336-1339 (4)* 3.25 2.90

Christmas A390

**1990, Nov. 13** **Litho.** *Perf. 15x14*

**1340** A390 17p Building snowman .45 .25
*a.* Booklet pane of 20 10.00
**1341** A390 22p Carrying Christmas tree .60 .25
**1342** A390 26p Caroling .75 .75
**1343** A390 31p Sledding .90 .90
**1344** A390 37p Ice skating 1.00 1.00
*Nos. 1340-1344 (5)* 3.70 3.15

Dogs — A391

Paintings by George Stubbs: 22p, King Charles Spaniel. 26p, A Pointer. 31p, Two Hounds in a Landscape. 33p, A Rough Dog. 37p, Fino and Tiny.

**1991, Jan. 8** **Photo.** *Perf. 14x14½*

**1345** A391 22p multicolored .60 .25
**1346** A391 26p multicolored .75 .75
**1347** A391 31p multicolored .90 .90
**1348** A391 33p multicolored .95 .95
**1349** A391 37p multicolored 1.00 1.00
*Nos. 1345-1349 (5)* 4.20 3.85

Royal Veterinary College bicentennial, National Canine Defense League and Cruft's Dog Show, centennial.

Symbols of Good Luck A392

**1991, Feb. 5** **Photo.** *Perf. 15x14*

**Booklet Stamps**

**1350** A392 1st shown 1.25 .70
**1351** A392 1st Shooting star, rainbow 1.25 .70
**1352** A392 1st Bird, charm bracelet 1.25 .70
**1353** A392 1st Black cat 1.25 .70
**1354** A392 1st Bluebird, key 1.25 .70
**1355** A392 1st Duck, frog 1.25 .70
**1356** A392 1st Black boot, shamrocks 1.25 .70
**1357** A392 1st Rainbow, pot of gold 1.25 .70
**1358** A392 1st Peacock moths 1.25 .70
**1359** A392 1st Wishing well, sixpence 1.25 .70
*a.* Bklt. pane of 10, #1350-1359 (BK1160) 16.00

No. 1359a printed se-tenant with 12 greetings labels. No. 1359a sold for £2.20 at date of issue.

Scientists & Their Technology A393

Designs: No. 1360, Michael Faraday, electricity. No. 1361, Charles Babbage, computers. 31p, Radar, developed by Robert Watson-Watt. 37p, Jet engine developed by Frank Whittle.

**1991, Mar. 5** *Perf. 14x15*

**1360** A393 22p multicolored .60 .50
**1361** A393 22p multicolored .60 .50
**1362** A393 31p multicolored .90 .90
**1363** A393 37p multicolored 1.00 1.00
*Nos. 1360-1363 (4)* 3.10 2.90

**Famous Smiles Type of 1990**

**1991, Mar. 26** **Photo.** *Perf. 15x14*

**Booklet Stamps**

**1364** A382 1st Teddy bear 1.25 .75
*a.* Sheet of 20 + 20 labels, litho., perf. 14¼x14 37.50 —
**1365** A382a 1st Dennis the Menace 1.25 .75
*a.* Sheet, 10 each #1364-1365 + 20 labels 32.50
*b.* Sheet of 20 + 20 labels, litho., perf. 14¼x14 37.50 —
**1366** A382b 1st Mr. Punch 1.25 .75
**1367** A382c 1st Cheshire Cat 1.25 .75
**1368** A382d 1st Man in the Moon 1.25 .75
**1369** A382e 1st The Laughing Policeman 1.25 .75
**1370** A382f 1st Clown 1.25 .75
**1371** A382g 1st Mona Lisa 1.25 .75
**1372** A382h 1st Queen of Hearts 1.25 .75
**1373** A382i 1st Stan Laurel 1.25 .75
*a.* Booklet pane of 10 14.00 —
*b.* Sheet, #1364-1373 + 10 labels 22.00

No. 1373a sold for £2.20 at date of issue. No. 1373a was affixed to booklet cover and was printed se-tenant with 12 greetings labels.

No. 1373b issued 5/22/00. Labels depict ribbons and are inscribed "The Stamp Show / 2000". The sheet with ribbon labels sold for £2.95, while the sheet with personalized labels sold for £5.95.

A sheet similar to No. 1373b with labels inscribed "Collect British Stamps" was specially produced for stamp dealers. Value, $225.

No. 1365a issued 2002. It sold for £5.95 and had labels that could be personalized.

Nos. 1364a, 1365b issued 2002. Each sold for £14.95 and has labels that can be personalized.

A394

Europa — A395

**1991, Apr. 23** **Photo.** *Perf. 14x15*

**1374** A394 22p Planets .60 .40
**1375** A394 22p Stars .60 .40
*a.* Pair, #1374-1375 1.75 1.75
**1376** A395 37p shown 1.00 .60
**1377** A395 37p Crescent eye 1.00 .60
*a.* Pair, #1376-1377 3.75 3.75
*Nos. 1374-1377 (4)* 3.20 2.00

Sports — A396

**1991, June 11** **Photo.** *Perf. 14½x14*

**1378** A396 22p Fencing .60 .25
**1379** A396 26p Hurdling .75 .75
**1380** A396 31p Diving .90 .90
**1381** A396 37p Rugby 1.00 1.00
*Nos. 1378-1381 (4)* 3.25 2.90

World Student Games, Nos. 1378-1380. Rugby World Cup, No. 1381.

Roses — A397

**1991, July 16** **Litho.** *Perf. 14½x14*

**1382** A397 22p Silver Jubilee .60 .25
**1383** A397 26p Mme. Alfred Carriere .75 .75
**1384** A397 31p Rosa moyesii .90 .90
**1385** A397 33p Harvest Fayre .95 .95
**1386** A397 37p Mutabilis 1.00 1.00
*Nos. 1382-1386 (5)* 4.20 3.85

Dinosaurs A398

**1991, Aug. 20** **Photo.** *Perf. 14½x14*

**1387** A398 22p Iguanodon .75 .25
**1388** A398 26p Stegosaurus .90 .90
**1389** A398 31p Tyrannosaurus 1.00 1.00
**1390** A398 33p Protoceratops 1.10 1.10
**1391** A398 37p Triceratops 1.25 1.25
*Nos. 1387-1391 (5)* 5.00 4.50

First use of word "dinosaur" by Sir Richard Owen, 150th anniv.

Ordnance Survey Maps, Bicent. — A399

Maps of village of Hamstreet, Kent.

**1991, Sept. 17** **Litho. & Engr.**

**1392** A399 24p 1816 .70 .25

**Litho.**

**1393** A399 28p 1906 .75 .75
**1394** A399 33p 1959 .95 .95
**1395** A399 39p 1991 1.10 1.10
*Nos. 1392-1395 (4)* 3.50 3.05

Christmas A400

Illuminated letters from Venetian manuscript "Acts of Mary and Jesus": 18p, "P," Adoration of the Magi. 24p, "M," Mary placing Jesus in manger. 28p, "A," Angel warning Joseph. 33p, "Q," The Annunciation. 39p, "N," Flight into Egypt.

**1991, Nov. 12** **Photo.** *Perf. 15x14*

**1416** A400 18p multicolored .50 .25
*a.* Booklet pane of 20 10.00
**1417** A400 24p multicolored .70 .70
**1418** A400 28p multicolored .75 .75
**1419** A400 33p multicolored .95 .85
**1420** A400 39p multicolored 1.10 1.10
*Nos. 1416-1420 (5)* 4.00 3.65

Animals in Winter A401

**1992, Jan. 14** **Photo.** *Perf. 15x14*

**1421** A401 18p Fallow deer .50 .25
**1422** A401 24p Brown hare .70 .35
**1423** A401 28p Fox .75 .75
**1424** A401 33p Redwing .95 .90
**1425** A401 39p Welsh mountain sheep 1.10 1.10
*a.* Booklet pane of 4 4.50
*Nos. 1421-1425 (5)* 4.00 3.35

For Prestige booklet containing pane No. 1425a, see BK156.
Issue date: No. 1425a, Mar. 1.

Memories A402

**1992, Jan. 28** **Litho.** *Perf. 15x14*

**Booklet Stamps**

**1426** A402 1st Flowers 1.25 .85
**1427** A402 1st Locket 1.25 .85
**1428** A402 1st Key 1.25 .85
**1429** A402 1st Model car 1.25 .85
**1430** A402 1st Compass, 4-leaf clover 1.25 .85
**1431** A402 1st Pocket watch 1.25 .85
**1432** A402 1st Envelope, fountain pen 1.25 .85
**1433** A402 1st Buttons, pearls 1.25 .85
**1434** A402 1st Marbles 1.25 .85

| | | | | |
|---|---|---|---|---|
| 1435 | A402 | 1st Starfish, shovel and bucket | 1.25 | .85 |
| a. | | Bklt. pane of 10, #1426-1435 (BK1171) | 15.00 | — |

No. 1435a printed se-tenant with 12 greeting labels and sold for £2.40 at date of issue.

Queen Elizabeth II's Accession to the Throne, 40th Anniv. A403

Queen Elizabeth II: No. 1436, In coronation regalia. No. 1437, Facing right, wearing garter robes as head of Church of England. No. 1438, Holding infant Prince Andrew. No. 1439, Wearing military uniform at Trooping of the Color. No. 1440, Wearing purple hat.

**1992, Feb. 6 Litho. *Perf. 14½x14***

| | | | | |
|---|---|---|---|---|
| 1436 | A403 | 24p multicolored | .80 | .60 |
| 1437 | A403 | 24p multicolored | .80 | .60 |
| 1438 | A403 | 24p multicolored | .80 | .60 |
| 1439 | A403 | 24p multicolored | .80 | .60 |
| 1440 | A403 | 24p multicolored | .80 | .60 |
| a. | | Strip of 5, #1436-1440 | 5.25 | *5.25* |

Alfred, Lord Tennyson, Death Cent. — A404

Portraits and illustrations for poems: 24p, The Beguiling of Merlin by Sir Edward Burne-Jones. 28p, April Love by Arthur Hughes. 33p, The Lady of Shalott by John William Waterhouse. 39p, Mariana by Dante Gabriel Rossetti.

**1992, Mar. 10 Photo.**

| | | | | |
|---|---|---|---|---|
| 1441 | A404 | 24p multicolored | .70 | .25 |
| 1442 | A404 | 28p multicolored | .75 | .75 |
| 1443 | A404 | 33p multicolored | .95 | .90 |
| 1444 | A404 | 39p multicolored | 1.10 | 1.00 |
| | | *Nos. 1441-1444 (4)* | 3.50 | 2.90 |

### Castle Type of 1988

Nos. 1445-1448 have been re-engraved to show greater detail than on Nos. 1230-1233. The silhouette of the Queen's head on Nos. 1445-1448 is printed in a special ink that changes color from green to gold.

***Perf. 15x14 Syncopated***

**1992-95 Engr.**

| | | | | |
|---|---|---|---|---|
| 1445 | A369 | £1 like #1230 | 3.00 | 1.00 |
| 1446 | A369 | £1.50 like #1231 | 4.50 | 1.00 |
| 1447 | A369 | £2 like #1232 | 6.00 | 2.50 |
| 1447A | A369 | £3 like #1230 | 14.00 | 3.00 |
| 1448 | A369 | £5 like #1233 | 14.00 | 3.00 |
| | | *Nos. 1445-1448 (5)* | 41.50 | 10.50 |

Nos. 1445-1447, 1448 were re-issued 12/6/94 with lines strengthened. Castles appear darker than on original issue.
Issued: £3, 8/22/95; others, 3/24/92.

### Castle Type Re-engraved

**1997, July 29**

| | | | | |
|---|---|---|---|---|
| *1446a* | A369 | £1.50 Caernarfon | 10.00 | 2.50 |
| *1447b* | A369 | £2 Edinburgh | 12.00 | 1.50 |
| *1447Ac* | A369 | £3 Carrickfergus | 25.00 | 2.00 |
| *1448a* | A369 | £5 Windsor | 30.00 | 4.50 |

Queen's head is silkscreened and feels smooth on Nos. 1446a, 1447b, 1447Ac, 1448a. Letters "C" and "S" in Castle do not have serifs. Letters in castle names also differ from the 1992 and 1995 printings. The elliptical perforation begins one perf hole higher than on the earlier printings.

Discovery of America, 500th Anniv. A405

Design: 39p, Sailing ship, Operation Raleigh Grand Regatta.

**Litho. & Engr.**

**1992, Apr. 7 *Perf. 14½***

| | | | | |
|---|---|---|---|---|
| 1449 | A405 | 24p multicolored | *1.25* | *.40* |
| 1450 | A405 | 39p multicolored | *1.75* | *.90* |

Europa.

Events A406

Designs: No. 1451, British Olympic Assoc. flag. No. 1452, Flying torch flag of British Paralympic Assoc. No. 1453, British pavilion.

**1992, Apr. 7 Litho.**

| | | | | |
|---|---|---|---|---|
| 1451 | A406 | 24p multicolored | .50 | .40 |
| 1452 | A406 | 24p multicolored | .50 | .40 |
| a. | | Pair, #1451-1452 | 1.40 | 1.50 |
| 1453 | A406 | 39p multicolored | 1.25 | 1.00 |
| | | *Nos. 1451-1453 (3)* | 2.25 | 1.80 |

1992 Summer Olympics (No. 1451) and Paralympics (No. 1452), Barcelona. Expo '92, Seville (No. 1453).

English Civil War, 350th Anniv. — A407

**1992, June 16 Photo. *Perf. 14½***

| | | | | |
|---|---|---|---|---|
| 1454 | A407 | 24p Pikeman | .70 | .25 |
| 1455 | A407 | 28p Drummer | .75 | .75 |
| 1456 | A407 | 33p Musketeer | .95 | .95 |
| 1457 | A407 | 39p Standard bearer | 1.10 | 1.00 |
| | | *Nos. 1454-1457 (4)* | 3.50 | 2.95 |

Yeoman of the Guard, by Gilbert & Sullivan A408

Scenes from comic operas: 24p, The Gondoliers. 28p, The Mikado. 33p, The Pirates of Penzance. 39p, Iolanthe.

**1992, July 21 Photo. *Perf. 14½x14***

| | | | | |
|---|---|---|---|---|
| 1458 | A408 | 18p multicolored | .50 | .25 |
| 1459 | A408 | 24p multicolored | .70 | .25 |
| 1460 | A408 | 28p multicolored | .75 | .75 |
| 1461 | A408 | 33p multicolored | .95 | .95 |
| 1462 | A408 | 39p multicolored | 1.10 | 1.10 |
| | | *Nos. 1458-1462 (5)* | 4.00 | 3.30 |

Sir Arthur Sullivan, 150th anniv. of birth.

Protect the Environment A409

Children's drawings: 24p, Acid rain kills. 28p, Ozone layer. 33p, Greenhouse effect. 39p, Bird of hope.

**1992, Sept. 15 Photo. *Perf. 14½***

| | | | | |
|---|---|---|---|---|
| 1463 | A409 | 24p multicolored | .70 | .25 |
| 1464 | A409 | 28p multicolored | .80 | .80 |
| 1465 | A409 | 33p multicolored | .90 | .90 |
| 1466 | A409 | 39p multicolored | 1.10 | 1.10 |
| | | *Nos. 1463-1466 (4)* | 3.50 | 3.05 |

Single European Market A410

**1992, Oct. 13 Photo. *Perf. 15x14***

| | | | | |
|---|---|---|---|---|
| 1467 | A410 | 24p multicolored | .65 | .65 |

Christmas A411

Stained glass windows: 18p, Angel Gabriel. 24p, Madonna and Child. 28p, King offering gold crown. 33p, Shepherds. 39p, Kings offering frankincense and myrrh.

**1992, Nov. 10 Photo. *Perf. 15x14***

| | | | | |
|---|---|---|---|---|
| 1468 | A411 | 18p multicolored | .50 | .25 |
| a. | | Booklet pane of 20 | 10.00 | |
| 1469 | A411 | 24p multicolored | .70 | .25 |
| 1470 | A411 | 28p multicolored | .80 | .80 |
| 1471 | A411 | 33p multicolored | .90 | .90 |
| 1472 | A411 | 39p multicolored | 1.10 | 1.10 |
| | | *Nos. 1468-1472 (5)* | 4.00 | 3.30 |

Mute Swans — A412

Designs: 18p, Male, St. Catherine's Chapel, Abbotsbury. 24p, Cygnet, reed bed, Abbotsbury Swannery. 28p, Pair, cygnet. 33p, Eggs in nest, Tithe Barn. 39p, Head of young swan.

**1993, Jan. 19 Photo. *Perf. 14x15***

| | | | | |
|---|---|---|---|---|
| 1473 | A412 | 18p multicolored | 1.00 | .50 |
| 1474 | A412 | 24p multicolored | 1.00 | .50 |
| 1475 | A412 | 28p multicolored | 1.25 | 1.25 |
| 1476 | A412 | 33p multicolored | 1.60 | 1.60 |
| 1477 | A412 | 39p multicolored | 1.80 | 1.80 |
| | | *Nos. 1473-1477 (5)* | 6.65 | 5.65 |

Abbotsbury Swannery, 600th anniv.

Britannia — A413

**Litho., Typo. and Embossed**

***Perf. 14x14½ Syncopated***

**1993, Mar. 2 Granite Paper**

| | | | | |
|---|---|---|---|---|
| 1478 | A413 | £10 multicolored | 32.50 | 12.50 |
| a. | | Silver (Queen's head, security crosses) omitted | *1,750.* | |

Soaking may damage these stamps.

Greetings Stamps A414

Children's Characters: No. 1479, Long John Silver, parrot. No. 1480, Tweedledum, Tweedledee. No. 1481, Just William, Violet Elizabeth. No. 1482, Toad, Mole. No. 1483, Bash Street Kids, teacher. No. 1484, Peter Rabbit, Mrs. Rabbit. No. 1485, Father Christmas, Snowman. No. 1486, Big Friendly Giant, Sophie. No. 1487, Rupert Bear, Bill Badger. No. 1488, Aladdin, Genie.

***Perf. 15x14 Syncopated***

**1993, Feb. 2 Litho.**

| | | | | |
|---|---|---|---|---|
| 1479 | A414 | (1st) multicolored | 1.25 | .85 |
| 1480 | A414 | (1st) multicolored | 1.25 | .85 |
| 1481 | A414 | (1st) multicolored | 1.25 | .85 |
| 1482 | A414 | (1st) multicolored | 1.25 | .85 |
| 1483 | A414 | (1st) multicolored | 1.25 | .85 |
| 1484 | A414 | (1st) multicolored | 1.25 | .85 |
| a. | | Booklet pane of 4 (BK1172) | 5.50 | — |
| 1485 | A414 | (1st) multicolored | 1.25 | .85 |
| 1486 | A414 | (1st) multicolored | 1.25 | .85 |
| 1487 | A414 | (1st) multicolored | 1.25 | .85 |
| 1488 | A414 | (1st) multicolored | 1.25 | .85 |
| a. | | Bklt. pane of 10, #1479-1488 | 15.00 | |

No. 1479-1488 sold for 24p on day of issue. No. 1488a printed se-tenant with 20 greetings labels. See note above No. 1445.
Issue date: No. 1484a, Aug. 10.
For booklets containing panes of No. 1484a and No. 1488a, see BK158 and BK1172, respectively.

Marine Chronometer No. 4 — A415

Designs: 24p, Face. 28p, Escapement, remontoire and fusee. 33p, Balance spring, temperature compensator. 39p, Back of movement.

**1993, Feb. 16 Litho. *Perf. 14½***

| | | | | |
|---|---|---|---|---|
| 1489 | A415 | 24p multicolored | .70 | .25 |
| 1490 | A415 | 28p multicolored | .80 | .80 |
| 1491 | A415 | 33p multicolored | .90 | .90 |
| 1492 | A415 | 39p multicolored | 1.10 | 1.10 |
| | | *Nos. 1489-1492 (4)* | 3.50 | 3.05 |

John Harrison (1693-1776), inventor of marine chronometer.

Orchids A416

14th World Orchid Conf., Glasgow: 18p, Dendrobium hellwigianum. 24p, Paphiopedilum Maudiae "Magnificum." 28p, Cymbidium lowianum. 33p, Vanda Rothschildiana. 39p, Dendrobium vexillarius.

**1993, Mar. 16 Litho. *Perf. 15x14***

| | | | | |
|---|---|---|---|---|
| 1493 | A416 | 18p multicolored | .50 | .30 |
| 1494 | A416 | 24p multicolored | .70 | .30 |
| 1495 | A416 | 28p multicolored | .80 | .80 |
| 1496 | A416 | 33p multicolored | .90 | .90 |
| 1497 | A416 | 39p multicolored | 1.10 | 1.10 |
| | | *Nos. 1493-1497 (5)* | 4.00 | 3.40 |

Contemporary Art — A417

Europa: 24p, Sculpture, Family Group, by Henry Moore. 28p, Print, Kew Gardens, by Edward Bawden. 33p, Painting, St. Francis and the Birds, by Stanley Spencer. 39p, Painting, Still Life, Odyssey 1, by Ben Nicholson.

**1993, May 11 Photo. *Perf. 14x14½***

| | | | |
|---|---|---|---|
| **1498** | A417 24p multicolored | .75 | .25 |
| **1499** | A417 28p multicolored | .85 | .85 |
| **1500** | A417 33p multicolored | .95 | .95 |
| **1501** | A417 39p multicolored | 1.10 | 1.10 |
| | *Nos. 1498-1501 (4)* | 3.65 | 3.15 |

Roman Artifacts A418

24p, Gold aureus of Claudius. 28p, Bronze bust of Hadrian. 33p, Gemstone carved with head of Roma. 39p, Mosaic of Christ.

**1993, June 15 Photo. *Perf. 14½x14***

| | | | |
|---|---|---|---|
| **1502** | A418 24p multicolored | .70 | .25 |
| **1503** | A418 28p multicolored | .80 | .80 |
| **1504** | A418 33p multicolored | .90 | .90 |
| **1505** | A418 39p multicolored | 1.10 | 1.10 |
| | *Nos. 1502-1505 (4)* | 3.50 | 3.05 |

British Canals, Bicent. A419

Designs: 24p, Grand Junction Canal boats. 28p, Stainforth and Keadby Canal. 33p, Brecknock and Abergavenny Canal boats, horse. 39p, Crinan Canal, steamers and fishing boats.

**1993, July 20 Litho. *Perf. 14½x14***

| | | | |
|---|---|---|---|
| **1506** | A419 24p multicolored | .70 | .25 |
| **1507** | A419 28p multicolored | .80 | .80 |
| **1508** | A419 33p multicolored | .90 | .90 |
| **1509** | A419 39p multicolored | 1.10 | 1.10 |
| | *Nos. 1506-1509 (4)* | 3.50 | 3.05 |

Autumn Fruits A420

**1993, Sept. 14 Photo. *Perf. 15x14***

| | | | |
|---|---|---|---|
| **1510** | A420 18p Horse chestnut | .50 | .30 |
| **1511** | A420 24p Blackberries | .70 | .30 |
| **1512** | A420 28p Filbert | .80 | .80 |
| **1513** | A420 33p Rowanberries | .90 | .90 |
| **1514** | A420 39p Pears | 1.10 | 1.10 |
| | *Nos. 1510-1514 (5)* | 4.00 | 3.40 |

Sherlock Holmes — A421

Holmes and: No. 1515, Dr. Watson, The Reigate Squire. No. 1516, Sir Henry, The Hound of the Baskervilles. No. 1517, Lestrade, The Six Napoleons. No. 1518, Mycroft, The Greek Interpreter. No. 1519, Moriarty, The Final Problem.

**1993, Oct. 12 Litho. *Perf. 14x14½***

| | | | |
|---|---|---|---|
| **1515** | A421 24p multicolored | .65 | .40 |
| **1516** | A421 24p multicolored | .65 | .40 |
| **1517** | A421 24p multicolored | .65 | .40 |
| **1518** | A421 24p multicolored | .65 | .40 |
| **1519** | A421 24p multicolored | .65 | .40 |
| *a.* | Strip of 5, #1515-1519 | 4.00 | 4.00 |

"A Christmas Carol," by Charles Dickens, 150th Anniv. A423

Designs: 19p, Tiny Tim, Bob Cratchit. 25p, Mr. & Mrs. Fezziwig. 30p, Scrooge. 35p, Prize Turkey. 41p, Mr. Scrooge's Nephew.

**1993, Nov. 9 Photo. *Perf. 15x14***

| | | | |
|---|---|---|---|
| **1528** | A423 19p multicolored | .55 | .25 |
| *a.* | Booklet pane of 20 | 14.00 | |
| **1529** | A423 25p multicolored | .70 | .25 |
| **1530** | A423 30p multicolored | .85 | .85 |
| **1531** | A423 35p multicolored | .95 | .95 |
| **1532** | A423 41p multicolored | 1.20 | 1.20 |
| | *Nos. 1528-1532 (5)* | 4.25 | 3.50 |

For booklet containing No. 1528a, see BK857.

Age of Steam — A424

Designs: 19p, Tandem locomotives, West Highland Line, North British Railway. 25p, Locomotive No. 60149, Kings Cross Station, London. 30p, Locomotive No. 43000 on turntable, Blyth North engine shed. 35p, Locomotive entering station. 41p, Locomotive on bridge over Worcester & Birmingham Canal.

**1994, Jan. 18 Photo. *Perf. 14½***

| | | | |
|---|---|---|---|
| **1533** | A424 19p black & green | .65 | .35 |
| **1534** | A424 25p black & purple | .80 | .80 |
| **1535** | A424 30p black & red brn | .95 | .95 |
| **1536** | A424 35p black & red violet | 1.05 | 1.05 |
| **1537** | A424 41p black & dark blue | 1.30 | 1.30 |
| | *Nos. 1533-1537 (5)* | 4.75 | 4.45 |

Dan Dare A425

The Three Bears A426

Rupert the Bear A427

Alice in Wonderland — A428

Noggin the Nog A429

Peter Rabbit A430

Little Red Riding Hood A431

Orlando, the Marmalade Cat A432

Biggles A433

Paddington A434

***Perf. 15x14 Syncopated***

**1994, Feb. 1 Photo.**

**Booklet Stamps**

| | | | |
|---|---|---|---|
| **1538** | A425 (1st) multicolored | 1.25 | .95 |
| **1539** | A426 (1st) multicolored | 1.25 | .95 |
| **1540** | A427 (1st) multicolored | 1.25 | .95 |
| **1541** | A428 (1st) multicolored | 1.25 | .95 |
| **1542** | A429 (1st) multicolored | 1.25 | .95 |
| **1543** | A430 (1st) multicolored | 1.25 | .95 |
| **1544** | A431 (1st) multicolored | 1.25 | .95 |
| **1545** | A432 (1st) multicolored | 1.25 | .95 |
| **1546** | A433 (1st) multicolored | 1.25 | .95 |
| **1547** | A434 (1st) multicolored | 1.25 | .95 |
| *a.* | Bklt. pane of 10, #1538-1547 | 14.50 | |

Nos. 1538-1547 sold for 25p on day of issue. No. 1547a was printed se-tenant with 20 greetings labels.

For booklet containing No. 1547a, see BK1182.

Investiture of Prince of Wales, 25th Anniv. A435

Watercolor landscapes, by Prince Charles: 19p, Chirk Castle, Clwyd, Wales. 25p, Ben Arkle, Sutherland, Scotland. 30p, Mourne Mountains, County Down, Northern Ireland. 35p, Dersingham, Norfolk, England. 41p, Dolwyddelan, Gwynedd, Wales.

**1994, Mar. 1 Photo. *Perf. 15x14***

| | | | |
|---|---|---|---|
| **1548** | A435 19p multicolored | .60 | .35 |
| **1549** | A435 25p multicolored | .75 | .35 |
| **1550** | A435 30p multicolored | .90 | .90 |
| *a.* | Booklet pane of 4 | 3.75 | |
| **1551** | A435 35p multicolored | 1.00 | 1.00 |
| **1552** | A435 41p multicolored | 1.15 | 1.15 |
| | *Nos. 1548-1552 (5)* | 4.40 | 3.75 |

For booklet containing pane No. 1550a, see No. BK159.

British Picture Postcards, Cent. — A436

Seaside characters: 19p, "Bather at Blackpool." 25p, "Where's my Little Lad." 30p, "Wish You Were Here." 35p, "Punch and Judy Show." 41p, "The Tower Crane."

**1994, Apr. 12 Litho. *Perf. 14x14½***

| | | | |
|---|---|---|---|
| **1553** | A436 19p multicolored | .55 | .30 |
| **1554** | A436 25p multicolored | .70 | .30 |
| **1555** | A436 30p multicolored | .85 | .85 |
| **1556** | A436 35p multicolored | .95 | .95 |
| **1557** | A436 41p multicolored | 1.20 | 1.20 |
| | *Nos. 1553-1557 (5)* | 4.25 | 3.60 |

Blackpool Tower, cent. (No. 1553). Tower Bridge, cent. (No. 1557).

Opening of Channel Tunnel — A437

Nos. 1558, 1560, British lion, French rooster, meeting over Channel. Nos. 1559, 1561, Joined hands above speeding train.

**1994, May 3 Photo. *Perf. 14x14½***

| | | | |
|---|---|---|---|
| **1558** | A437 25p dk blue & multi | .65 | .45 |
| **1559** | A437 25p dk blue & multi | .65 | .45 |
| *a.* | Pair, #1558-1559 | 1.60 | 1.25 |
| **1560** | A437 41p lt blue & multi | 1.10 | .70 |
| **1561** | A437 41p multicolored | 1.10 | .70 |
| *a.* | Pair, #1560-1561 | 2.60 | 2.60 |
| | *Nos. 1558-1561 (4)* | 3.50 | 2.30 |

See France Nos. 2421-2424.

D-Day, 50th Anniv. — A438

Photographs from Imperial War Museum's archives: No. 1562, Ground crew reloading FAF Bostons. No. 1563, Coastal bombardment by HMS Warspite. No. 1564, Commandos landing on Gold Beach. No. 1565, Infantry regrouping on Sword Beach. No. 1566, Advancing inland from Ouistreham.

**1994, June 6 Litho. *Perf. 14***

| | | | |
|---|---|---|---|
| **1562** | A438 25p multicolored | .65 | .45 |
| **1563** | A438 25p multicolored | .65 | .45 |
| **1564** | A438 25p multicolored | .65 | .45 |
| **1565** | A438 25p multicolored | .65 | .45 |
| **1566** | A438 25p multicolored | .65 | .45 |
| *a.* | Strip of 5, #1562-1566 | 4.25 | 4.00 |

Honorable Company of Edinburgh Golfers, 250th Anniv. — A439

Golf courses: 19p, St. Andrews, old course. 25p, Muirfield, 18th hole. 30p, Carnoustie, 15th hole. 35p, Royal Troon, "postage stamp" 8th hole. 41p, Turnberry, 9th hole.

**1994, July 5 Photo. *Perf. 14***

| | | | |
|---|---|---|---|
| **1567** | A439 19p multicolored | .55 | .30 |
| **1568** | A439 25p multicolored | .70 | .30 |
| **1569** | A439 30p multicolored | .85 | .85 |

| | | | | |
|---|---|---|---|---|
| **1570** | A439 35p multicolored | 1.00 | 1.00 |
| **1571** | A439 41p multicolored | 1.25 | 1.25 |
| | *Nos. 1567-1571 (5)* | 4.35 | 3.70 |

Summertime Events — A440

Designs: 19p, Royal Welsh Agricultural Show, Llanelwedd. 25p, Wimbledon. 30p, Yachts on Solent during Cowes Week. 35p, Cricket at Lord's. 41p, Scottish Highland Games, Braemar.

**1994, Aug. 2** *Perf. 14½x14*

| | | | |
|---|---|---|---|
| **1572** | A440 19p multicolored | .55 | .25 |
| **1573** | A440 25p multicolored | .70 | .25 |
| **1574** | A440 30p multicolored | .85 | .85 |
| **1575** | A440 35p multicolored | .95 | .95 |
| **1576** | A440 41p multicolored | 1.20 | 1.20 |
| | *Nos. 1572-1576 (5)* | 4.25 | 3.50 |

Medical Discoveries — A441

Europa: 25p, Ultrasonic imaging. 30p, Scanning electron microscopy. 35p, Magnetic resonance imaging. 41p, Computed tomography.

**1994, Sept. 27 Photo.** *Perf. 14x14½*

| | | | |
|---|---|---|---|
| **1577** | A441 25p multicolored | .80 | .30 |
| **1578** | A441 30p multicolored | 1.00 | 1.00 |
| **1579** | A441 35p multicolored | 1.10 | 1.10 |
| **1580** | A441 41p multicolored | 1.35 | 1.35 |
| | *Nos. 1577-1580 (4)* | 4.25 | 3.75 |

Christmas A442

School children portraying: 19p, Mary, Joseph, with infant Jesus. 25p, Magi. 30p, Mary holding Jesus. 35p, Shepherds. 41p, Angels.

**1994, Nov. 1 Photo.** *Perf. 15x14*

| | | | |
|---|---|---|---|
| **1581** | A442 19p multicolored | .55 | .25 |
| *a.* | Booklet pane of 20 | 12.00 | |
| **1582** | A442 25p multicolored | .70 | .25 |
| **1583** | A442 30p multicolored | .85 | .85 |
| **1584** | A442 35p multicolored | .95 | .95 |
| **1585** | A442 41p multicolored | 1.20 | 1.20 |
| | *Nos. 1581-1585 (5)* | 4.25 | 3.50 |

For booklet containing No. 1581a, see No. BK858.

Cats A443

Designs: 19p, Black cat. 25p, Siamese, tabby cats. 30p, Yellow cat. 35p, Calico, Abyssinian cats. 41p, Black & white cat.

**1995, Jan. 17 Litho.** *Perf. 15x14*

| | | | |
|---|---|---|---|
| **1586** | A443 19p multicolored | .55 | .25 |
| **1587** | A443 25p multicolored | .75 | .35 |
| **1588** | A443 30p multicolored | .90 | .85 |
| **1589** | A443 35p multicolored | 1.00 | .95 |
| **1590** | A443 41p multicolored | 1.20 | 1.20 |
| | *Nos. 1586-1590 (5)* | 4.40 | 3.60 |

Springtime A444

Sculptures from natural materials, by Andy Goldsworthy: 19p, Dandelions. 25p, Chestnut leaves. 30p, Garlic leaves. 35p, Hazel leaves. 41p, Spring grass.

**1995, Mar. 14 Photo.** *Perf. 15x14*

| | | | |
|---|---|---|---|
| **1591** | A444 19p multicolored | .55 | .25 |
| **1592** | A444 25p multicolored | .70 | .25 |
| **1593** | A444 30p multicolored | .85 | .85 |
| **1594** | A444 35p multicolored | .95 | .95 |
| **1595** | A444 41p multicolored | 1.20 | 1.20 |
| | *Nos. 1591-1595 (5)* | 4.25 | 3.50 |

La Danse a la Campagne, by Renoir A445

Troilus and Criseyde, by Peter Brookes A446

The Kiss, by Rodin A447

Girls on the Town, by Beryl Cook A448

Jazz, by Andrew Mockett A449

Girls Performing aKathal Dance (Aurangzeb Period) A450

Alice Keppel with her Daughter, by Alice Hughes A451

Children Playing, by L.S. Lowry A452

Circus Clowns, by Emily Firmin and Justin Mitchell A453

Decoration from All the Love Poems of Shakespeare, by Eric Gill — A454

***Perf. 14 Syncopated***

**1995, Mar. 21 Litho.**

| | | | |
|---|---|---|---|
| **1596** | A445 1st multicolored | 1.25 | .70 |
| **1597** | A446 1st multicolored | 1.25 | .70 |
| **1598** | A447 1st multicolored | 1.25 | .70 |
| **1599** | A448 1st multicolored | 1.25 | .70 |
| **1600** | A449 1st multicolored | 1.25 | .70 |
| **1601** | A450 1st multicolored | 1.25 | .70 |
| **1602** | A451 1st multicolored | 1.25 | .70 |
| **1603** | A452 1st multicolored | 1.25 | .70 |
| **1604** | A453 1st multicolored | 1.25 | .70 |
| **1605** | A454 1st multicolored | 1.25 | .70 |
| *a.* | Bklt. pane of 10, #1596-1605 | 13.50 | |

Complete booklet sold for £2.50 on day of issue.

For booklet containing No. 1605a, see No. BK1183.

National Trust, Cent. — A455

Designs: 19p, Celebrating 100 years. 25p, Protecting land. 30p, Conserving art. 35p, Saving coast. 41p, Repairing buildings.

**1995, Apr. 11 Photo.** *Perf. 14x15*

| | | | |
|---|---|---|---|
| **1606** | A455 19p multicolored | .55 | .25 |
| **1607** | A455 25p multicolored | .70 | .25 |
| *a.* | Booklet pane of 6 | 4.25 | |
| **1608** | A455 30p multicolored | .85 | .85 |
| **1609** | A455 35p multicolored | .95 | .95 |
| **1610** | A455 41p multicolored | 1.20 | 1.20 |
| | *Nos. 1606-1610 (5)* | 4.25 | 3.50 |

For booklet containing panes No. 1607a, see No. BK160.

Issued: No. 1607a, 4/25/95.

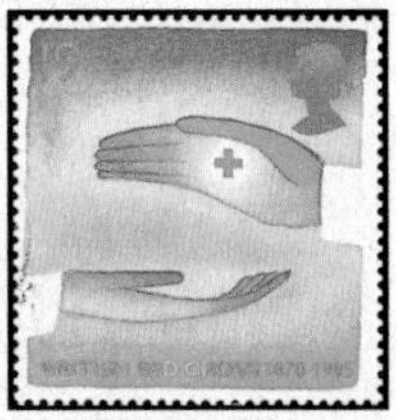

Peace & Freedom A456

Designs: No. 1611, Hands, British Red Cross 1870-1995. No. 1612, British troops, people celebrating liberation of Paris. No. 1613, Dove, outstretched hand, UN, 1945-95. No. 1614, St. Paul's Cathedral, floodlights forming Victory V. 30p, Hands above earth, UN 1945-95.

**1995, May 2 Photo.** *Perf. 14½x14*

| | | | |
|---|---|---|---|
| **1611** | A456 19p multicolored | .55 | .40 |
| **1612** | A456 19p multicolored | .55 | .40 |
| **1613** | A456 25p multicolored | .70 | .70 |
| **1614** | A456 25p multicolored | .70 | .70 |
| **1615** | A456 30p multicolored | .85 | .85 |
| | *Nos. 1611-1615 (5)* | 3.35 | 3.05 |

End of World War II, 50th anniv. (Nos. 1612, 1614), Europa (Nos. 1613, 1615).

See No. 2294a.

H. G. Wells (1866-1946), Science Fiction Writer — A457

Novels: 25p, The Time Machine. 30p, The First Men on the Moon. 35p, The War of the Worlds. 41p, The Shape of Things to Come.

**1995, June 6 Litho.** *Perf. 14½x14*

| | | | |
|---|---|---|---|
| **1616** | A457 25p multicolored | .70 | .30 |
| **1617** | A457 30p multicolored | .85 | .85 |
| **1618** | A457 35p multicolored | .95 | .95 |
| **1619** | A457 41p multicolored | 1.20 | 1.20 |
| | *Nos. 1616-1619 (4)* | 3.70 | 3.30 |

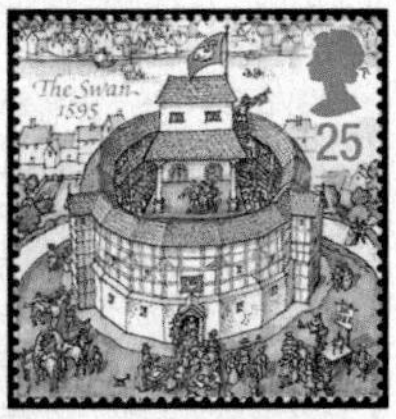


Opening of Shakespeare's New Globe Theatre A458

Bankside theatres: No. 1620, Swan, 1595. No. 1621, The Rose, 1595. No. 1622, The Globe, 1599. No. 1623, The Hope, 1613. No. 1624, The Globe, 1614.

**1995, Aug. 8 Litho.** *Perf. 14½x14*

| | | | |
|---|---|---|---|
| **1620** | A458 25p multicolored | .65 | .50 |
| **1621** | A458 25p multicolored | .65 | .50 |
| **1622** | A458 25p multicolored | .65 | .50 |
| **1623** | A458 25p multicolored | .65 | .50 |
| **1624** | A458 25p multicolored | .65 | .50 |
| *a.* | Strip of 5, #1620-1624 | 3.50 | 3.50 |

Pioneers of Communication — A459

Designs: 19p, Sir Rowland Hill, introduction of uniform penny postage. 25p, Hill as older man, design A1. 41p, Guglielmo Marconi, early wireless equipment. 60p, Marconi as older man using radiophone, sinking *Titanic.*

**Litho. & Engr.**

**1995, Sept. 5** *Perf. 14½*

| | | | |
|---|---|---|---|
| **1625** | A459 19p multicolored | .55 | .30 |
| **1626** | A459 25p multicolored | .70 | .50 |
| **1627** | A459 41p multicolored | 1.20 | 1.20 |
| **1628** | A459 60p multicolored | 1.75 | 1.75 |
| | *Nos. 1625-1628 (4)* | 4.20 | 3.75 |

Rugby League, Cent. — A460

**1995, Oct. 3 Photo.** *Perf. 14x14½*

| | | | |
|---|---|---|---|
| **1629** | A460 19p Harold Wagstaff | .55 | .30 |
| **1630** | A460 25p Gus Risman | .75 | .40 |
| **1631** | A460 30p Jim Sullivan | .85 | .85 |
| **1632** | A460 35p Billy Batten | .95 | .95 |
| **1633** | A460 41p Brian Bevan | 1.10 | 1.10 |
| | *Nos. 1629-1633 (5)* | 4.20 | 3.60 |

Christmas — A461

Designs showing robin in winter scene: 19p, In pillar box. 25p, On fence rail, holly bush. 30p, Standing on snow covered milk bottle. 41p, Sitting on snow covered road sign, blue fence. 60p, Sitting on door knob, Christmas decoration on door.

**1995, Oct. 30 Photo. *Perf. 14¾x14***

**1634** A461 19p multicolored .55 .25
*a.* Booklet pane of 20 11.00
*b.* Sheet of 20 + 20 labels 225.00
**1635** A461 25p multicolored .70 .25
**1636** A461 30p multicolored .85 .85
**1637** A461 41p multicolored 1.20 1.20
**1638** A461 60p multicolored 1.75 1.75
*a.* Booklet pane of 4 7.25
*Nos. 1634-1638 (5)* 5.05 4.30

No. 1634b was issued 10/3/00. It sold for £3.99 and has labels that read "Seasons Greetings" and "Glad Tidings." Sheets with personalized labels were made available only to select Royal Post customers via mail order purchases, and sold for more.

For booklets containing Nos. 1634a and 1638a, see Nos. BK859 and BK792, respectively.

Robert Burns (1759-1796), Poet — A462

Lines from poems: 19p, "Wee sleeket, cowran, tim'rous beastie." 25p, "O my luve's like a red, red rose." 41p, "Scots, wha hae wi Wallace bled." 60p, "Should auld acquaintance be forgot."

**1996, Jan. 25 Litho. *Perf. 14½***

**1639** A462 19p multicolored .55 .30
**1640** A462 25p multicolored .70 .40
**1641** A462 41p multicolored 1.20 1.20
**1642** A462 60p multicolored 1.75 1.75
*Nos. 1639-1642 (4)* 4.20 3.65

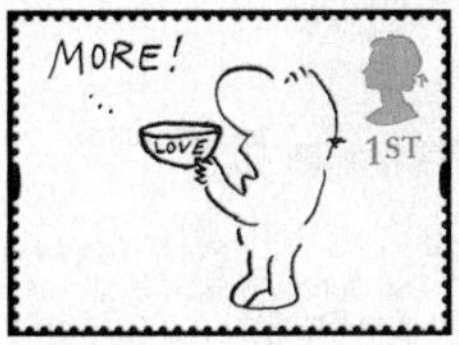


Greetings Cartoons A463

No. 1643, More Love. No. 1644, Sincerely. No. 1645, Human condition. No. 1646, Mental Floss. No. 1647, Don't ring. No. 1648, Dear lottery prize winner. No. 1649, I'm writing to you... No. 1650, Fetch this... No. 1651, My day starts... No. 1652, The check in the post.

***Perf. 14½ Syncopated***

**1996-2001 Litho.**

**1643** A463 1st black & lilac 1.25 .60
**1644** A463 1st black & green 1.25 .60
**1645** A463 1st black & blue 1.25 .60
**1646** A463 1st black & purple 1.25 .60
**1647** A463 1st black & red 1.25 .60
**1648** A463 1st black & blue 1.25 .60
**1649** A463 1st black & red 1.25 .60
**1650** A463 1st black & purple 1.25 .60
**1651** A463 1st black & green 1.25 .60
**1652** A463 1st black & lilac 1.25 .60
*a.* Booklet pane, #1643-1652+20 labels 12.50
*b.* Sheet of 10, #1643-1652, + 10 labels, perf. 14½x14 60.00 —
*c.* Sheet of 20, 2 each #1643-1652, + 20 labels, perf. 14¼ — —

Issued: No. 1652b, 12/18/01. 1652a, 2/26/96. 1652c, 7/29/03.

No. 1652b lacks perforation syncopation. Labels could be personalized for an additional amount.

Nos. 1643-1652 sold for 25p on day of issue.

No. 1652c sold for £6.15.

For booklet containing No. 1652a, see No. BK1184.

Wildfowl and Wetlands Trust, 50th Anniv. A464

Paintings by Charles Tunnicliffe RA (1901-79): 19p, Muscovy duck. 25p, Lapwing. 30p, White-fronted goose. 35p, Bittern. 41p, Whooper swan.

**1996, Mar. 12 Photo. *Perf. 14x14½***

**1653** A464 19p multicolored .55 .30
**1654** A464 25p multicolored .70 .35
**1655** A464 30p multicolored .85 .85
**1656** A464 35p multicolored 1.00 1.00
**1657** A464 41p multicolored 1.20 1.20
*Nos. 1653-1657 (5)* 4.30 3.70

Motion Pictures, Cent. — A465

Designs: 19p, Exterior of Odeon at Harrogate, 1930s theater. 25p, Laurance Olivier, Vivien Leigh in scene from "That Hamilton Woman." 30p, Cinema ticket from "The Picture House." 35p, Rooster emblem of Pathe News, motion picture newsreels. 41p, Theater marquee.

**1996, Apr. 16 Photo. *Perf. 14x14½***

**1658** A465 19p multicolored .55 .25
**1659** A465 25p multicolored .70 .25
**1660** A465 30p multicolored .85 .85
**1661** A465 35p multicolored 1.00 1.00
**1662** A465 41p multicolored 1.20 1.20
*Nos. 1658-1662 (5)* 4.30 3.55

1996 European Soccer Championships — A466

Lengendary players: 19p, Dixie Dean (1907-80). 25p, Bobby Moore (1941-93). 35p, Duncan Edwards (1936-58). 41p, Billy Wright (1924-94). 60p, Danny Blanchflower (1926-93).

**1996, May 14 Litho. *Perf. 15x14***

**1663** A466 19p gray, red & blk .55 .25
*a.* Bklt. pane of 4 + printed margin (BK161) 2.25
**1664** A466 25p gray, grn & blk .70 .25
*a.* Bklt. pane of 4 + printed margin (BK161) 3.00
**1665** A466 35p gray, yel & blk 1.00 1.00
**1666** A466 41p blk, blue & gray 1.20 1.20
**1667** A466 60p gray, org & blk 1.75 1.75
*a.* Bklt. pane, 2 ea #1665-1667 (BK161) 7.25
*Nos. 1663-1667 (5)* 5.20 4.45

1996 Summer Olympic, Paralympic Games, Atlanta A467

**1996, July 9 Litho. *Perf. 15x14***

**1688** A467 26p Sprinting .60 .45
**1689** A467 26p Javelin .60 .45
**1690** A467 26p Basketball .60 .45
**1691** A467 26p Swimming .60 .45
**1692** A467 26p Victorious athlete .60 .45
*a.* Strip of 5, #1688-1692 3.75 3.75

Compare with Type A588.

20th Century Women of Achievement A468

Designs: 20p, Dorothy Hodgkin (1910-94), chemist. 26p, Margot Fonteyn (1919-91), ballerina. 31p, Elisabeth Frink (1930-93), sculptor. 37p, Daphne du Maurier (1907-89), novelist. 43p, Marea Hartman (1920-94), sports administrator.

**1996, Aug. 6 Photo. *Perf. 14½***

**1693** A468 20p multicolored .60 .30
**1694** A468 26p multicolored .80 .30
**1695** A468 31p multicolored .90 .90
**1696** A468 37p multicolored 1.10 1.10
**1697** A468 43p multicolored 1.25 1.25
*Nos. 1693-1697 (5)* 4.65 3.85

Europa, Nos. 1694-1695.

British Television Programs for Children, 50th Anniv. A469

Designs: 20p, Annette Mills, "Muffin the Mule." 26p, Sooty. 31p, String puppets Troy Tempest and Lord Titan. 37p, The Clangers. 43p, Dangermouse.

**1996, Sept. 3 *Perf. 14½x14***

**1698** A469 20p multicolored .70 .25
*a.* Pane of 4 #1698b + printed margin 8.00
*b.* Perf. 15x14 1.75 1.50
**1699** A469 26p multicolored .90 .25
**1700** A469 31p multicolored 1.00 1.00
**1701** A469 37p multicolored 1.25 1.25
**1702** A469 43p multicolored 1.40 1.40
*Nos. 1698-1702 (5)* 5.25 4.15

For Prestige booklet containing pane No. 1698a, see BK162.

Issued: No. 1698a, 9/23/97.

Classic British Sports Cars — A470

Designs: 20p, 1955 Triumph TR3. 26p, MG TD. 37p, Austin-Healy 100. 43p, 1948 Jaguar XK 120. 63p, Morgan Plus Four.

**1996, Oct. 1 Photo. *Perf. 14½***

**1703** A470 20p multicolored .70 .30
**1704** A470 26p multicolored .90 .30
**1705** A470 37p multicolored 1.25 1.25
**1706** A470 43p multicolored 1.40 1.40
**1707** A470 63p multicolored 1.90 1.90
*Nos. 1703-1707 (5)* 6.15 5.15

Christmas A471

Designs: 2nd, Three kings, star. 1st, The Annunciation. 31p, Mary, Joseph on journey to Bethlehem. 43p, Madonna and Child. 63p, Angel telling shepherds of Christ's birth.

**1996, Oct. 28 Photo. *Perf. 14½x14***

**1708** A471 2nd multicolored .60 .25
*a.* Booklet pane of 20 14.00
**1709** A471 1st multicolored .80 .25
**1710** A471 31p multicolored 1.00 1.00
**1711** A471 43p multicolored 1.40 1.40
**1712** A471 63p multicolored 1.90 1.90
*Nos. 1708-1712 (5)* 5.70 4.80

Nos. 1708-1709 sold for 20p and 26p respectively on day of issue.

For booklet containing No. 1708a, see No. BK1220.

Gentiana Acaulis A472

Magnolia Altissima A473

Camellia Japonica A474

Tulip A475

Fuchsia "Princess of Wales" A476

Le Perroquet Rouge A477

Gazania Splendens A478

Iris Latifolia A479

Amaryllis Bresiliensis A480

Granadilla A481

***Perf. 14½x14 Syncopated***

**1997, Jan. 6 Litho.**

**Booklet Stamps**

**1713** A472 1st multicolored 1.25 .65
*a.* Perf 15x14 7.50 3.25
**1714** A473 1st multicolored 1.25 .65
**1715** A474 1st multicolored 1.25 .65
**1716** A475 1st multicolored 1.25 .65
*a.* Perf 15x14 4.75 2.00
**1717** A476 1st multicolored 1.25 .65
**1718** A477 1st multicolored 1.25 .65
**1719** A478 1st multicolored 1.25 .65
**1720** A479 1st multicolored 1.25 .65
*a.* Perf 15x14 7.50 3.25
*b.* Booklet pane, #1713a, 1720a, 2 #1716a (BK176) 25.00 —

| No. | Type | Description | Unused | Used |
|---|---|---|---|---|
| 1721 | A480 | 1st multicolored | 1.25 | .65 |
| 1722 | A481 | 1st multicolored | 1.25 | .65 |
| a. | | Bklt. pane of 10, #1713-1722 | 14.00 | |
| b. | | Sheet, 2 each #1713-1722, + 20 labels, perf. 14¼ | 37.50 | |

Nos. 1713-1722, 1722a issued 1/9/97. 1722a sold for £2.50 on day of issue, but stamps each had 26p of franking value.

No. 1722b issued 2003. It sold for £14.95 and had labels that could be personalized.

No. 1720a issued 5/25/04. 1720a sold for £1.12 on day of issue.

For booklet containing No. 1722a, see No. BK1195.

See Nos. 2671-2672.

King Henry VIII and His Six Wives A482

### 1997, Jan. 21 Photo. *Perf. 15*

| No. | Type | Description | Unused | Used |
|---|---|---|---|---|
| 1723 | A482 | 26p shown | .70 | .70 |

**Size: 27x38mm**

***Perf. 14x15***

| No. | Type | Description | Unused | Used |
|---|---|---|---|---|
| 1724 | A482 | 26p Catherine of Aragon | .70 | .70 |
| 1725 | A482 | 26p Anne Boleyn | .70 | .70 |
| 1726 | A482 | 26p Jane Seymour | .70 | .70 |
| 1727 | A482 | 26p Anne of Cleves | .70 | .70 |
| 1728 | A482 | 26p Catherine Howard | .70 | .70 |
| 1729 | A482 | 26p Catherine Parr | .70 | .70 |
| a. | | Strip of 6, #1724-1729 | 6.00 | 6.00 |
| | | *Nos. 1723-1729 (7)* | 4.90 | 4.90 |

St. Augustine of Canterbury & St. Columba of Iona — A483

Designs: 26p, St. Columba's journey across Irish Sea to Iona. 37p, St. Columba at work, Ionian Sea. 43p, St. Augustine baptizing King Ethelbert. 63p, St. Augustine outside Cathedral at Canterbury, Kent coastline.

### 1997, Mar. 11 Photo. *Perf. 14½x14*

| No. | Type | Description | Unused | Used |
|---|---|---|---|---|
| 1730 | A483 | 26p multicolored | .90 | .45 |
| 1731 | A483 | 37p multicolored | 1.25 | 1.25 |
| 1732 | A483 | 43p multicolored | 1.40 | 1.40 |
| 1733 | A483 | 63p multicolored | 1.90 | 1.90 |
| | | *Nos. 1730-1733 (4)* | 5.45 | 5.00 |

Stories and Legends — A484

Europa: 26p, Dracula. 31p, Frankenstein. 37p, Dr. Jekyll and Mr. Hyde. 43p, The Hound of the Baskervilles.

### 1997, May 13 Photo. *Perf. 14x15*

| No. | Type | Description | Unused | Used |
|---|---|---|---|---|
| 1754 | A484 | 26p multicolored | *.90* | *.45* |
| 1755 | A484 | 31p multicolored | *1.00* | *1.00* |
| 1756 | A484 | 37p multicolored | *1.25* | *1.25* |
| 1757 | A484 | 43p multicolored | *1.40* | *1.40* |
| | | *Nos. 1754-1757 (4)* | *4.55* | *4.10* |

Aircraft, Designers A485

20p, Supermarine Spitfire, R.J. Mitchell. 26p, Avro Lancaster, Roy Chadwick. 37p, DeHavilland Mosquito, R.E. Bishop. 43p, Gloster Meteor, George Carter. 63p, Hawker Hunter, Sidney Camm.

### 1997, June 10 Photo. *Perf. 15x14*

| No. | Type | Description | Unused | Used |
|---|---|---|---|---|
| 1758 | A485 | 20p multicolored | .60 | .50 |
| a. | | Litho., perf. 14¼x14 (#2587b) ('08) | .85 | .90 |
| 1759 | A485 | 26p multicolored | .90 | 1.10 |
| 1760 | A485 | 37p multicolored | 1.25 | 1.25 |
| 1761 | A485 | 43p multicolored | 1.40 | 1.60 |
| 1762 | A485 | 63p multicolored | 1.90 | 1.90 |
| | | *Nos. 1758-1762 (5)* | 6.05 | 6.35 |

Issued: No. 1758a, 9/18/08.

All the Queen's Horses A486

20p, 43p, Carriage horses from Royal Mews. 26p, 63p, Mount horses from Household Cavalry.

### 1997, July 9 Litho. *Perf. 14x14½*

| No. | Type | Description | Unused | Used |
|---|---|---|---|---|
| 1763 | A486 | 20p multicolored | .60 | .40 |
| 1764 | A486 | 26p multicolored | .90 | .90 |
| 1765 | A486 | 43p multicolored | 1.40 | 1.40 |
| 1766 | A486 | 63p multicolored | 1.90 | 1.90 |
| | | *Nos. 1763-1766 (4)* | 4.80 | 4.60 |

British Horse Society, 50th anniv.

Post Offices A487

Designs: 20p, Haroldswick, Shetland Islands, Scotland. 26p, Painswick, Gloucestershire, England. 43p, Beddgelert, Gwynedd, Wales. 63p, Ballyroney, County Down, Northern Ireland.

### 1997, Aug. 12 Litho. *Perf. 14½x14*

| No. | Type | Description | Unused | Used |
|---|---|---|---|---|
| 1767 | A487 | 20p multicolored | .55 | .35 |
| 1768 | A487 | 26p multicolored | .75 | .75 |
| 1769 | A487 | 43p multicolored | 1.20 | 1.20 |
| 1770 | A487 | 63p multicolored | 1.75 | 1.75 |
| | | *Nos. 1767-1770 (4)* | 4.25 | 4.05 |

Enid Blyton, Author of Children's Stories, Birth Cent. — A488

Characters from books: 20p, "Noddy." 26p, "Famous Five." 37p, "Secret Seven." 43p, "Faraway Tree." 63p, "Malory Towers."

### 1997, Sept. 9 Litho. *Perf. 14x14½*

| No. | Type | Description | Unused | Used |
|---|---|---|---|---|
| 1771 | A488 | 20p multicolored | .55 | .25 |
| 1772 | A488 | 26p multicolored | .75 | .75 |
| 1773 | A488 | 37p multicolored | 1.05 | 1.05 |
| 1774 | A488 | 43p multicolored | 1.20 | 1.20 |
| 1775 | A488 | 63p multicolored | 1.75 | 1.75 |
| | | *Nos. 1771-1775 (5)* | 5.30 | 5.00 |

Christmas Crackers A489

Designs: 2nd, Santa as Man in Moon sharing cracker with two children. 1st, Santa bursting through wrapping paper with cracker. 31p, Santa riding across sky on giant cracker. 43p, Santa on giant snowball holding cracker. 63p, Santa climbing into chimney with sack full of crackers.

### 1997, Oct. 27 Photo. *Perf. 15x14*

| No. | Type | Description | Unused | Used |
|---|---|---|---|---|
| 1776 | A489 | 2nd multicolored | .65 | .30 |
| a. | | Booklet pane of 20 | 13.00 | |
| 1777 | A489 | 1st multicolored | .90 | .35 |
| b. | | Sheet of 10 + 10 labels | *200.00* | |
| c. | | Sheet of 20 + 20 labels, litho., perf 14½x14 | 40.00 | |
| 1778 | A489 | 31p multicolored | .90 | .80 |
| 1779 | A489 | 43p multicolored | 1.10 | 1.10 |
| 1780 | A489 | 63p multicolored | 1.75 | 1.75 |
| | | *Nos. 1776-1780 (5)* | 5.30 | 4.30 |

Nos. 1776-1777 were sold for 20p and 26p, respectively, on day of issue.

No. 1777b issued 10/3/00. It sold for £2.95 and has labels that read "Seasons Greetings" and "Ho Ho Ho." Sheets with personalized labels were made available only to select Royal Post customers via mail order purchases, and sold for more.

No. 1777c issued 2003. It sold for £5.95 and had labels that could be personalized.

For booklet containing No. 1776a, see No. BK1221.

Queen Elizabeth II, Prince Philip, 50th Wedding Anniv. A490

Designs: 20p, 43p, Wedding portrait, 1947. 26p, 63p, Anniversary portrait, 1997.

### 1997, Nov. 13 Photo. *Perf. 15*

| No. | Type | Description | Unused | Used |
|---|---|---|---|---|
| 1781 | A490 | 20p multicolored | .55 | .30 |
| 1782 | A490 | 26p multicolored | .70 | .70 |
| 1783 | A490 | 43p multicolored | 1.10 | 1.10 |
| 1784 | A490 | 63p multicolored | 1.75 | 1.75 |
| | | *Nos. 1781-1784 (4)* | 4.10 | 3.85 |

Endangered Species — A491

Designs: 20p, Common dormouse. 26p, Lady's slipper orchid. 31p, Song thrush. 37p, Shining ram's horn snail. 43p, Mole cricket. 63p, Devil's bolete.

### 1998, Jan. 20 Litho. *Perf. 14x14½*

| No. | Type | Description | Unused | Used |
|---|---|---|---|---|
| 1785 | A491 | 20p multicolored | .55 | .40 |
| 1786 | A491 | 26p multicolored | .70 | .40 |
| 1787 | A491 | 31p multicolored | .90 | .80 |
| 1788 | A491 | 37p multicolored | 1.00 | 1.00 |
| 1789 | A491 | 43p multicolored | 1.15 | 1.15 |
| 1790 | A491 | 63p multicolored | 1.75 | 1.75 |
| | | *Nos. 1785-1790 (6)* | 6.05 | 5.50 |

Diana, Princess of Wales (1961-97) — A492

Portraits of Diana wearing: No. 1791, Choker. No. 1792, Blue dress. No. 1793, Tiara. No. 1794, Checked dress. No. 1795, Black dress.

### 1998, Feb. 3 Photo. *Perf. 14x15*

| No. | Type | Description | Unused | Used |
|---|---|---|---|---|
| 1791 | A492 | 26p multicolored | .60 | .45 |
| 1792 | A492 | 26p multicolored | .60 | .45 |
| 1793 | A492 | 26p multicolored | .60 | .45 |
| 1794 | A492 | 26p multicolored | .60 | .45 |
| 1795 | A492 | 26p multicolored | .60 | .45 |
| a. | | Strip of 5, #1791-1795 | 3.50 | 3.50 |
| b. | | As "a," imperf. | — | |

Order of the Garter, 650th Anniv. A493

Queen's Beasts (supporters of Royal Arms created for Queen Elizabeth II's coronation in 1953): No. 1796, Lion of England, Griffin of Edward III. No. 1797, Falcon of Plantagenet, Bull of Clarence. No. 1798, Lion of Mortimer, Yale of Beaufort. No. 1799, Greyhound of Richmond, Dragon of Wales. No. 1800, Unicorn of Scotland, Horse of Hanover.

**Litho. & Engr.**

### 1998, Feb. 24 *Perf. 15x14*

| No. | Type | Description | Unused | Used |
|---|---|---|---|---|
| 1796 | A493 | 26p multicolored | .60 | .50 |
| 1797 | A493 | 26p multicolored | .60 | .50 |
| 1798 | A493 | 26p multicolored | .60 | .50 |
| 1799 | A493 | 26p multicolored | .60 | .50 |
| 1800 | A493 | 26p multicolored | .60 | .50 |
| a. | | Strip of 5, #1796-1800 | 3.75 | 3.75 |

**Queen Type of 1952 with Face Values in Decimal Currency**

***Perf. 14 Syncopated***

### 1998, Mar. 10 Litho.

| No. | Type | Description | Unused | Used |
|---|---|---|---|---|
| 1801 | A129 | 20p dk grn & lt grn | .70 | .50 |
| a. | | Booklet pane of 6 + printed margin (BK163) | 4.75 | |
| 1802 | A129 | 26p dk brn & lt brn | .90 | .80 |
| a. | | Booklet pane of 9 + printed margin (BK163) | 10.50 | |
| 1803 | A129 | 37p dk red lil & lt lil | 2.50 | 2.00 |
| a. | | Booklet pane 3 each #1802-1803 + printed margin (BK163) | 11.00 | |
| b. | | Booklet pane, 4 #1801, 2 ea #1802-1803 + printed margin (BK163) | 11.00 | |

Lighthouses A494

### 1998, Mar. 24 *Perf. 14x14½*

| No. | Type | Description | Unused | Used |
|---|---|---|---|---|
| 1804 | A494 | 20p St. John's Point | .55 | .40 |
| 1805 | A494 | 26p The Smalls | .75 | .45 |
| 1806 | A494 | 37p Needles Rocks | 1.10 | 1.10 |
| 1807 | A494 | 43p Bell Rock | 1.20 | 1.20 |
| 1808 | A494 | 63p Eddystone | 1.75 | 1.75 |
| | | *Nos. 1804-1808 (5)* | 5.35 | 4.90 |

Comedians A495

20p, Tommy Cooper (1922-84). 26p, Eric Morecambe (1926-84). 37p, Joyce Grenfell (1910-79). 43p, Les Dawson (1933-93). 63p, Peter Cook (1937-95).

### 1998, Apr. 23 Litho. *Perf. 14½x14*

| No. | Type | Description | Unused | Used |
|---|---|---|---|---|
| 1809 | A495 | 20p multicolored | .55 | .45 |
| 1810 | A495 | 26p multicolored | .75 | .75 |
| 1811 | A495 | 37p multicolored | 1.10 | 1.10 |
| 1812 | A495 | 43p multicolored | 1.20 | 1.20 |
| 1813 | A495 | 63p multicolored | 1.75 | 1.75 |
| | | *Nos. 1809-1813 (5)* | 5.35 | 5.25 |

National Health Service, 50th Anniv. — A496

Designs: 20p, Hands forming heart, "10,000 donors give blood every day." 26p, Adult hand clasping child's, "1,700,000 prescriptions dispensed every day." 43p, Hands forming cradle, "2,000 babies delivered every day." 63p, Taking pulse, "130,000 hospital outpatients seen every day."

**1998, June 23 Litho.** ***Perf. 14x14½***

**1814** A496 20p multicolored .60 .50
**1815** A496 26p multicolored .75 .75
**1816** A496 43p multicolored 1.20 1.20
**1817** A496 63p multicolored 1.90 1.90
*Nos. 1814-1817 (4)* 4.45 4.35

Magical World of Children's Literature A496a

Stories depicted: 20p, "The Hobbit," by J.R.R. Tolkien. 26p, "The Lion, The Witch and the Wardrobe," by C.S. Lewis. 37p, "The Phoenix and the Carpet," by E. Nesbit. 43p, "The Borrowers," by Mary Norton. 63p, "Through the Looking Glass," by Lewis Carroll.

**1998, July 21 Photo.** ***Perf. 15x14***

**1820** A496a 20p multicolored .55 .40
**1821** A496a 26p multicolored .75 .55
**1822** A496a 37p multicolored 1.05 1.05
**1823** A496a 43p multicolored 1.20 1.20
**1824** A496a 63p multicolored 1.75 1.75
*Nos. 1820-1824 (5)* 5.30 4.95

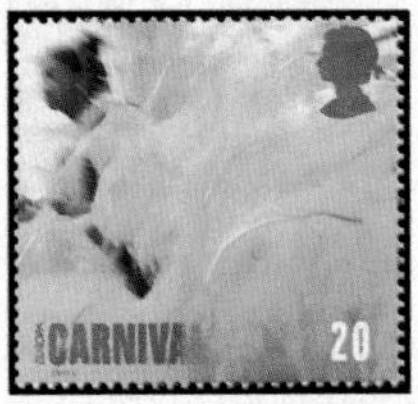

Notting Hill Carnival A497

Expressionist photographic images of dancers, color of costumes: 20p, Yellow. 26p, Blue. 43p, Gold and white. 63p, Green.

**1998, Aug. 25** ***Perf. 14x14½***

**1825** A497 20p multicolored *.60 .40*
**1826** A497 26p multicolored *.85 .55*
**1827** A497 43p multicolored 1.25 1.25
**1828** A497 63p multicolored 1.90 1.90
*Nos. 1825-1828 (4)* *4.60 4.10*

Europa (Nos. 1825-1826).

Land Speed Records A498

Car, driver, year, record speed: 20p, Bluebird, Sir Malcolm Campbell, 1925, 151 mph. 26p, Red Sunbeam, Sir Henry Segrave, 1926, 152 mph. 30p, Babs, John G. Parry Thomas, 1926, 171 mph. 43p, Railton Mobil Special, John R. Cobb, 1947, 394 mph. 63p, Bluebird CN7, Donald Campbell, 1964, 403 mph.

**1998, Sept. 29 Photo.** ***Perf. 15x14***

**1829** A498 20p multicolored .55 .35
*a.* Perf. 14½x13½ 2.50 1.25
*b.* As "a," booklet pane of 4 + printed margin (BK164) 12.00
**1830** A498 26p multicolored .75 .55
**1831** A498 30p multicolored .85 .85
**1832** A498 43p multicolored 1.20 1.20
**1833** A498 63p multicolored 1.75 1.75
*Nos. 1829-1833 (5)* 5.10 4.70

Christmas Angels A499

**1998, Nov. 2 Photo.** ***Perf. 15x14***

**1834** A499 20p shown .60 .45
*a.* Booklet pane of 20 13.00
**1835** A499 26p Praying .80 .45
**1836** A499 30p Playing flute .90 .90
**1837** A499 43p Playing lute 1.25 1.25
**1838** A499 63p Praying, diff. 1.90 1.90
*Nos. 1834-1838 (5)* 5.45 4.95

British Achievements During Past 1000 Years — A500

Inventions: 20p, Timekeeping, John Harrison's chronometer. 26p, Development of steam power. 43p, William Henry Fox Talbot's use of negatives to create photographs. 63p, Development of computers.

Transportation: 20p, Jet travel. 26p, Development of bicycle. 43p, Isambard Kingdom Brunel's Clifton Suspension Bridge, Great Western Railway. 63p, Capt. Cook's expeditions.

Health care: 20p, First smallpox vaccination, by Edward Jenner. 26p, Development of nursing care. 43p, Discovery of penicillin, by Alexander Fleming. 63p, First "test tube" baby (in vitro fertilization), pioneered by Patrick Steptoe and Robert Edwards.

Emigration: 20p, Migration to Scotland. 26p, Pilgrim fathers. 43p, Destination Australia. 63p, Migration to UK.

Workers: 19p, Weavers. 26p, Mill towns. 44p, Ship building. 64p, City finance.

Entertainment and sports: 19p, Freddie Mercury, lead singer of Queen. 26p, Bobby Moore, 1966 World Cup Soccer Champions. 44p, Dalek from "Dr. Who" television series. 64p, Charlie Chaplin.

Citizens' Rights: 19p, Equal rights. 26p, Right to health. 44p, Right to learn. 64p, First rights.

Scientists: 19p, Decoding DNA. 26p, Darwin's theory. 44p, Faraday's electricity. 64p, Newton, Hubble Telescope.

Farmers: 19p, Strip farming (Europa). 26p, Mechanical farming. 44p, Food from afar. 64p, Satellite agriculture.

Soldiers: 19p, Battle of Bannockburn. 26p, Civil War. 44p, World Wars, cemetery. 64p, Peace keeping.

Christians: 19p, John Wesley (1703-91), founder of Methodism, and "Hark, The Herald Angels Sing," hymn by brother Charles (1707-88). 26p, King James Bible. 44p, St. Andrews Pilgrimage. 64p, First Christmas.

Artists: 19p, World of the stage. 26p, World of music. 44p, World of literature. 64p, New worlds.

**1999 Photo.** ***Perf. 14¼x14½***

**Inventions**

**1839** A500 20p multi (48) .60 .60
**1840** A500 26p multi (47) .75 .80
**1841** A500 43p multi (46) 1.25 1.40
**1842** A500 63p multi (45) 1.75 1.75
*a.* Perf. 13¾ 3.50
*b.* Booklet pane, 4 #1842a (BK166) 17.00

**Transportation**

**1843** A500 20p multi (44) .60 .60
**1844** A500 26p multi (43) .75 .80
**1845** A500 43p multi (42) 1.25 1.40
**1846** A500 63p multi (41) 1.75 1.75

**Health Care**

***Perf. 13¾x14***

**1847** A500 20p multi (40) .60 .60
*a.* Booklet pane of 4 (BK166) 3.25
**1848** A500 26p multi (39) .75 .80
**1849** A500 43p multi (38) 1.25 1.40
**1850** A500 63p multi (37) 1.75 1.75

**Emigration**

***Perf. 14¼x14½***

**1851** A500 20p multi (36) .60 .60
**1852** A500 26p multi (35) .75 .80
**1853** A500 43p multi (34) 1.25 1.40
**1854** A500 63p multi (33) 1.75 1.75

**Workers**

***Perf. 14¼x14½***

**1855** A500 19p multi (32) .60 .60
**1856** A500 26p multi (31) .75 .80
*a.* Booklet pane #1852, 1856 (BK1141) 3.00
**1857** A500 44p multi (30) 1.25 1.40
**1858** A500 64p multi (29) 1.80 1.80

**Entertainment & Sports**

***Perf. 14¼x14½***

**1859** A500 19p multi (28) .60 .60
**1860** A500 26p multi (27) .75 .80
**1861** A500 44p multi (26) 1.25 1.40
**1862** A500 64p multi (25) 1.80 1.80

**Citizen's Rights**

***Perf. 14¼x14½***

**1863** A500 19p multi (24) .60 .60
**1864** A500 26p multi (23) .75 .80
**1865** A500 44p multi (22) 1.25 1.40
**1866** A500 64p multi (21) 1.80 1.80

**Scientists**

***Perf. 14¼ (#1868-1869), 13¾ (#1867, 1870)***

**1867** A500 19p multi (20) .60 .60
**1868** A500 26p multi (19) .75 .80
*a.* Perf. 14¼x14 2.50 2.50
*b.* Booklet pane, 4 #1868a (BK166) 15.00
**1869** A500 44p multi (18) 1.25 1.40
*a.* Perf. 14¼x14 3.50 3.50
*b.* Booklet pane, 4 #1869a (BK166) 16.00
**1870** A500 64p multi (17) 1.90 1.90
*a.* Perf. 14¼ 4.50 4.50
*b.* Souvenir sheet, 4 #1870a 22.50 22.50

**Farmers**

***Perf. 14¼x14½***

**1871** A500 19p multi (16) .60 .60
**1872** A500 26p multi (15) .75 .80
*a.* Booklet pane of 2 (BK1142) 1.50
**1873** A500 44p multi (14) 1.25 1.40
**1874** A500 64p multi (13) 1.80 1.80

Europa, No. 1871.

**Soldiers**

***Perf. 14¼x14½***

**1875** A500 19p multi (12) .60 .60
**1876** A500 26p multi (11) .75 .80
**1877** A500 44p multi (10) 1.25 1.40
**1878** A500 64p multi (9) 1.80 1.80

**Christians**

**1879** A500 19p multi (8) .60 .60
*a.* Booklet pane of 20 12.00
**1880** A500 26p multi (7) .75 .80
**1881** A500 44p multi (6) 1.25 1.40
**1882** A500 64p multi (5) 1.80 1.80

**Artists**

***Perf. 14¼x14½***

**1883** A500 19p multi (4) .60 .60
**1884** A500 26p multi (3) .75 .80
**1885** A500 44p multi (2) 1.25 1.40
**1886** A500 64p multi (1) 1.80 1.80
*Nos. 1839-1886 (48)* 52.70 55.10

Issued: Nos. 1839-1842, 1/12; Nos. 1843-1846, 2/2; Nos. 1847-1850, 3/2; Nos. 1851-1854, 4/6; Nos. 1855-1858, 5/4; Nos. 1859-1862, 6/1; Nos. 1863-1866, 7/6; Nos. 1867-1870, 8/3; Nos. 1871-1874, 9/7; Nos. 1870b, 8/11; Nos. 1875-1878, 10/5; Nos. 1879-1882, 11/2; Nos. 1883-1886, 12/7.

See Nos. 1889, 1890-1937, 1938.

Marriage of Prince Edward and Sophie Rhys-Jones — A501

**1999, June 15 Photo.** ***Perf. 15x14***

**1887** A501 26p shown .75 .75
**1888** A501 64p Profile portrait 1.75 1.75

Souvenir Sheet

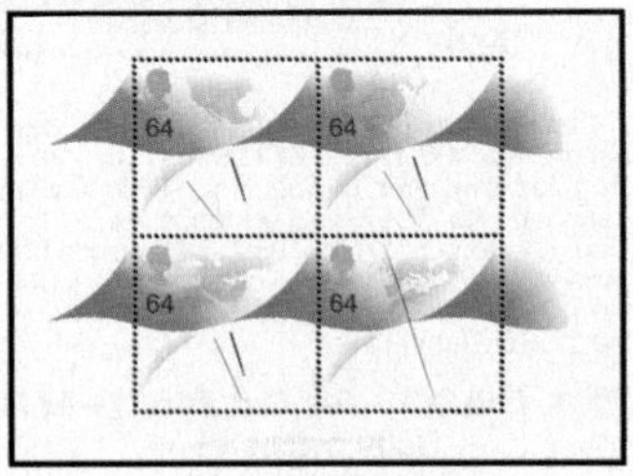

Millennium — A502

Clock and globe showing: a, North America. b, Southeast Asia. c, Middle East. d, Europe.

***Perf. 14¼x14½***

**1999, Dec. 14 Photo.**

**1889** Sheet of 4 22.50 22.50
*a.-d.* A502 64p any single 5.00 3.50

No. 1889 exists overprinted "EARLS COURT, LONDON...STAMP SHOW 2000." It was sold at a substantial premium as part of a premium entrance fee.

Millennium Projects A503

Above and Beyond: 19p, Barn owl's head, 3rd Millennium conservation projects, Muncaster. 26p, Night sky, National Space Center, Leicester. 44p, Buildings and waterfall, Torrs Walkway project, Derbyshire. 64p, Sea birds, Scottish Sea Bird Center.

Fire & Light: 19p, Beacon, Beacon Millennium project. 26p, Rheilffordd Eryri / Snowdonia, Welsh Highland Railway rebuilding project. 44p, Lightning bolt, Dynamic Earth project. 64p, Lights, Croydon Skyline project.

Water & Coast: 19p, Stones, Durham Coast restoration project. 26p, Frog, flowers, National Pondlife Center, conservation project. 44p, Parc Arfordirol project. 64p, Portsmouth Harbor project.

Life & Earth: 2nd, Wetlands, ECOS/Ballymena Project. 1st, Ants, Web of Life Exhibition at London Zoo. 44p, Solar cells, Earth Center, Doncaster. 64p, Plant leaves in water, Project SUZY, Teeside.

Art & Craft: 2nd, Ceramica project, Stoke-on-Trent. 1st, Tate Gallery of Modern Art, London. 45p, Cycle Network Artworks Project. 65p, The Lowry Arts Complex, Balford.

People & Place: 2nd, Millennium Greens project. 1st, Gateshead Millennium Bridge, Newcastle. 45p, Mile End Park, London. 65p, On the Line project.

Stone & Soil: 2nd, Raising of Strangford Stone, Killyleagh, Northern Ireland. 1st, Trans Pennine Trail project. 45p, Kingdom of Fife Cycle Ways project, Scotland. 65p, Changing Places project of Groundwork Foundation.

Tree & Leaf: 2nd, Yews for the Millennium project. 1st, Eden Project, St. Austell. 45p, Millennium Seed Bank project, Ardingly. 65p, Forest for Scotland project.

Mind & Matter: 2nd, Ant's head, Wildscreen at Bristol Project. 1st, People in rowboat, Norfolk and Norwich Project, Newport. 45p, X-ray image of hand and computer mouse, Millennium Point Project, Birmingham. 65p, Plaid globe, Scottish Cultural Resources Access Network.

Body & Bone: 2nd, Dancers, Millennium Dome project, Greenwich. 1st, Soccer players, Hampden Park project, Glasgow. 45p, Bath Spa project. 65p, Center for Life, Newcastle.

Spirit & Faith: 2nd, Stained glass window, St. Edmundsbury Cathedral project. 1st, Church floodlighting project. 45p, St. Patrick Center project, Downpatrick. 65p, York mystery plays.

Sound & Vision: 2nd, Bells, Ringing in the Millennium project. 1st, Eye, Year of the Artist. 45p, Harp, Camofym Millennium Center, Cardiff. 65p, TS2K Talent and Skills project.

**Above & Beyond**

**Photo., Litho. (#1892, 1900, 1911, 1913)**

***Perf. 13¾x14, 14¼x14½ (#1892)***

**2000**

**1890** A503 19p multi (1) .60 .60
**1891** A503 26p multi (2) .85 .85
**1892** A503 44p multi (3) 1.40 1.40
**1893** A503 64p multi (4) 2.10 2.10

***Perf. 14¼x14½***

**Fire & Light**

**1894** A503 19p multi (5) .60 .60
**1895** A503 26p multi (6) .85 .85
**1896** A503 44p multi (7) 1.40 1.40
**1897** A503 64p multi (8) 2.10 2.10

**Water & Coast**

**1898** A503 19p multi (9) .60 .60
**1899** A503 26p multi (10) .85 .85
**1900** A503 44p multi (11) 1.40 1.40
**1901** A503 64p multi (12) 2.10 2.10

**Life & Earth**

**1902** A503 2nd multi (13) .70 .70
**1903** A503 1st multi (14) .95 .95
**1904** A503 44p multi (15) 1.40 1.40
**1905** A503 64p multi (16) 2.10 2.10

**Art & Craft**

**1906** A503 2nd multi (17) .70 .70
**1907** A503 1st multi (18) .95 .95
**1908** A503 45p multi (19) 1.40 1.40
**1909** A503 65p multi (20) 2.10 2.10

**People & Place**

**1910** A503 2nd multi (21) .70 .70
**1911** A503 1st multi (22) .95 .95
**1912** A503 45p multi (23) 1.40 1.40
**1913** A503 65p multi (24) 2.10 2.10

**Stone & Soil**

**1914** A503 2nd multi (25) .70 .70
**1915** A503 1st multi (26) .95 .95
**1916** A503 45p multi (27) 1.40 1.40

**1917** A503 65p multi (28) 2.10 2.10
*a.* Booklet pane of 2 (BK169) 4.25

### Tree & Leaf

**1918** A503 2nd multi (29) .70 .70
*a.* Bklt. pane of 4 (BK169) 3.00
**1919** A503 1st multi (30) .95 .95
*a.* Bklt. pane, #1915, 1919 (BK1202) 2.25
**1920** A503 45p multi (31) 1.40 1.40
*a.* Bklt. pane of 4 (BK169) 5.75
**1921** A503 65p multi (32) 2.10 2.10
*a.* Bklt. pane of 2 (BK169) 4.25

### Mind & Matter

### Litho.

**1922** A503 2nd multi (33) .70 .70
**1923** A503 1st multi (34) .95 .95
**1924** A503 45p multi (35) 1.40 1.40
**1925** A503 65p multi (36) 2.10 2.10

### Body & Bone

**1926** A503 2nd multi (37) .70 .70

### Photo.

### *Perf. 13¾*

**1927** A503 1st multi (38) .95 .95
**1928** A503 45p multi (39) 1.40 1.40
**1929** A503 65p multi (40) 2.10 2.10

### *Perf. 14¼*

### Spirit & Faith

**1930** A503 2nd multi (41) .70 .70
*a.* Bklt. pane of 20 (BK1211) 15.00
**1931** A503 1st multi (42) .95 .95
**1932** A503 45p multi (43) 1.40 1.40
**1933** A503 65p multi (44) 2.10 2.10

### Sound & Vision

**1934** A503 2nd multi (45) .70 .70
**1935** A503 1st multi (46) .95 .95
**1936** A503 45p multi (47) 1.40 1.40
**1937** A503 65p multi (48) 2.10 2.10
*Nos. 1890-1937 (48)* 61.20 61.20

Nos. 1902, 1906, 1910, 1914, 1918, 1922, 1926, 1930, 1934 sold for 19p; No. 1903, sold for 26p; Nos. 1907, 1911, 1915, 1919, 1923, 1927, 1931, 1935 sold for 27p on day of issue.

Issued: Nos. 1890-1893, 1/18; Nos. 1894-1897, 2/1; Nos. 1898-1901, 3/7; Nos. 1902-1905, 4/4; Nos. 1906-1909, 5/2; Nos. 1910-1913, 6/6; Nos. 1914-1917, 7/4; Nos. 1918-1921, 8/1; Nos. 1917a-1921a, 9/18; Nos. 1922-1925, 9/5; Nos. 1926-1929, 10/3; Nos. 1930-1933, 11/7; Nos. 1934-1937, 12/5.

**2000-02 Photo. *Perf. 14¼x14½***
**1938** A503 (1st) Like #1891 6.75 4.75
*a.* Booklet pane, #1903, 1938 (BK1201) 8.00
*b.* Booklet pane of 4 (BK172) 30.00

Issued: No. 1938, 5/26. No. 1938b, 9/24/02.

Nos. 1938 sold for 27p on day of issue, and was issued only in booklets.

### Types of 1953 and 2000

Stamp Show 2000, London — A503a

Souvenir Sheet

**2000, May 23 Photo. *Perf. 14¾x14***
**1942** Sheet, #1942a, 4 #MH335 21.00 21.00
*a.* A136 £1 dark green 18.00 15.00

Souvenir Sheet

Queen Mother's 100th Birthday — A504

Designs: a, Queen Elizabeth II. b, Prince William. c, Queen Mother. d, Prince Charles.

**2000, Aug. 4 Photo. *Perf. 14½***
**1943** A504 Sheet of 4 9.50 9.50
*a.-d.* 27p Any single 1.75 .50
*e.* Booklet pane, #1943 with silver border (BK168) 12.00 12.00
*f.* Booklet pane, 4 #1943c (BK168) 5.00

Millennium 2001 A505

Painted faces of children: 2nd, Flower. 1st, Tiger. 45p, Owl. 65p, Butterfly.

### *Perf. 14¼x14½*

**2001, Jan. 16 Photo.**
**1944** A505 2nd multi .70 .70
**1945** A505 1st multi .95 .95
**1946** A505 45p multi 1.40 1.40
**1947** A505 65p multi 2.10 2.10
*Nos. 1944-1947 (4)* 5.15 5.15

Stamps inscribed "2nd" and "1st" sold for 19p and 27p respectively on day of issue.

Greetings A506

**2001, Feb. 6 Photo. *Perf. 14¼***
**1948** A506 1st shown 1.25 1.25
**1949** A506 1st Cheers 1.25 1.25
**1950** A506 1st Love 1.25 1.25
**1951** A506 1st Thanks 1.25 1.25
**1952** A506 1st Welcome 1.25 1.25
*a.* Sheet, 4 vert. strips #1948-1952 + 20 labels, litho. 200.00 25.00
*Nos. 1948-1952 (5)* 6.25 6.25

Nos. 1948-1952 each sold for 27p on day of issue.

No. 1952a issued 6/5/01. No. 1952a sold for £5.95.

A sheet containing 7 No. 1949 and 3 No. 1951 + 10 labels depicting Spiderman was specially produced for stamp dealers.

Dogs and Cats A507

Designs: No. 1953, Dog and man on park bench. No. 1954, Dog in bathtub. No. 1955, Dog looking over carrel. No. 1956, Cat in handbag. No. 1957, Cat on fence. No. 1958, Dog in automobile. No. 1959, Cat in curtained window. No. 1960, Dog looking over fence. No. 1961, Cat looking at bird through window. No. 1962, Cat in sink.

**2001, Feb. 13 *Die Cut Perf. 14½x14***

### Self- Adhesive

### Booklet Stamps

**1953** A507 1st blk & sil 1.25 1.25
**1954** A507 1st blk & sil 1.25 1.25
**1955** A507 1st blk & sil 1.25 1.25
**1956** A507 1st blk & sil 1.25 1.25
**1957** A507 1st blk & sil 1.25 1.25
**1958** A507 1st blk & sil 1.25 1.25
**1959** A507 1st blk & sil 1.25 1.25
**1960** A507 1st blk & sil 1.25 1.25
**1961** A507 1st blk & sil 1.25 1.25
**1962** A507 1st blk & sil 1.25 1.25
*a.* Booklet, #1953-1962 14.00
*b.* Booklet, #1953-1962, 2 #MH297 30.00
*Nos. 1953-1962 (10)* 12.50 12.50

Nos. 1953-1962 each sold for 27p on day of issue.

The Weather A508

Designs: 19p, Rain. 27p, Fair. 45p, Much rain, storms. 65p, Very dry, set fair.

### *Perf. 14¼x14½*

**2001, Mar. 13 Photo.**
**1963** A508 19p multi .70 .70
**1964** A508 27p multi .95 .95
**1965** A508 45p multi 1.40 1.40
**1966** A508 65p multi 2.25 2.25
*a.* Souvenir sheet, #1963-1966 18.00 18.00
*Nos. 1963-1966 (4)* 5.30 5.30

Purple cloud at bottom of No. 1964 is printed with thermochromic ink and changes color to blue when warmed.

Submarines — A509

Designs: 2nd, Vanguard Class, 1992. 1st, Swiftsure Class, 1973. 45p, Unity Class, 1939. 65p, Holland Class, 1901.

**2001 Photo. *Perf. 14¾x14***
**1967** A509 2nd multi .70 .70
*a.* Perf. 15¼x14¾ 5.00 5.00
**1968** A509 1st multi .95 .95
*a.* Perf. 15¼x14¾ 5.00 4.00
**1969** A509 45p multi 1.40 1.40
*a.* Perf. 15¼x14¾ 5.00 4.00
*b.* Booklet pane, 2 each #1967a, 1969a (BK170) 12.00
**1970** A509 65p multi 2.25 2.25
*a.* Perf. 15¼x14¾ 5.00 4.00
*b.* Booklet pane, 2 each #1968a, 1970a (BK170) 20.00
*Nos. 1967-1970 (4)* 5.30 5.30

### Self-Adhesive

### *Die Cut Perf. 15½x14¼*

**1971** A509 1st multi 57.50 45.00
*a.* Booklet, 2 #1971, 4 #MH298 125.00

Issued: Nos. 1967-1970, 4/10; No. 1971, 4/17; Nos. 1967a, 1968a, 1969a, 1970a, 10/22/01.

On day of issue No. 1967 sold for 19p and Nos. 1968 and 1971 sold for 27p.

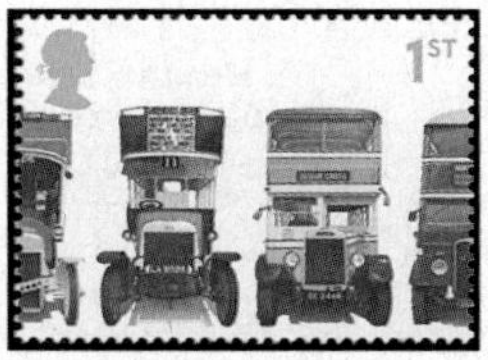

Buses A510

Designs: No. 1972, Blue and red Leyland X-type (half), London General (No. 11), yellow green and orange Leyland Titan, dark green and yellow AEC Regent I (half). No. 1973, AEC Regent I (half), Daimler COG5 (No. 8), Guy Arab Mk II (No. 51), green and yellow AEC Regent (half). No. 1974, AEC Regent (half), Bristol KSW 5G (No. 68), AEC Routemaster (No. 21), red and yellow Bristol Lodekka (half). No. 1975, Bristol Lodekka (half), Leyland Titan (No. 12B), Leyland Atlantean (No. 53X), red and yellow Daimler Fleetline (half). No. 1976, Daimler Fleetline (half), MCW Metrobus (No. 770), Leyland Olympian (No. 12), red and blue Dennis Trident (half).

**2001, May 15 Photo. *Perf. 14¼x14***
**1972** A510 1st multi 1.25 1.25
**1973** A510 1st multi 1.25 1.25
**1974** A510 1st multi 1.25 1.25
**1975** A510 1st multi 1.25 1.25
**1976** A510 1st multi 1.25 1.25
*a.* Horiz. strip, #1972-1976 5.75 5.75
*b.* Souvenir sheet, #1972-1976 10.00 10.00

Nos. 1972-1976 each sold for 27p on day of issue.

Women's Hats — A511

Hats designed by: 1st, Pip Hackett. E, Dai Rees. 45p, Stephen Jones. 65p, Philip Treacy.

### *Perf. 14½x14¼*

**2001, June 19 Litho.**
**1977** A511 1st multi 1.10 1.10
**1978** A511 E multi 1.50 1.50
**1979** A511 45p multi 1.40 1.40
**1980** A511 65p multi 2.10 2.10
*Nos. 1977-1980 (4)* 6.10 6.10

Nos. 1977 and 1978 sold for 27p and 36p respectively on day of issue.

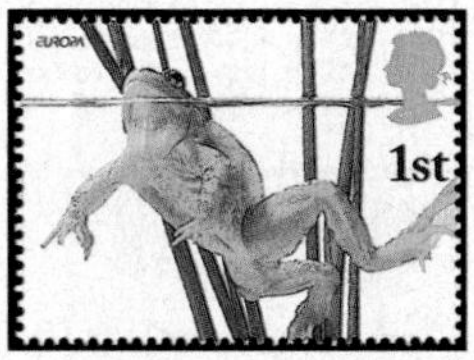

Europa A512

**2001, July 10 Photo. *Perf. 14¾x14***
**1981** A512 1st Frog .90 .90
**1982** A512 E Great diving beetle 1.75 1.75
**1983** A512 45p Stickleback 1.75 1.75
**1984** A512 65p Dragonfly 2.10 2.10
*Nos. 1981-1984 (4)* 6.50 6.50

Nos. 1981 and 1982 sold for 27p and 36p respectively on day of issue.

Puppets — A513

**2001, Sept. 4 Photo. *Perf. 14x15***
**1985** A513 1st Policeman .85 .55
**1986** A513 1st Clown .85 .55
**1987** A513 1st Punch .85 .55
**1988** A513 1st Judy .85 .55
**1989** A513 1st Beadle .85 .55
**1990** A513 1st Crocodile .85 .55
*a.* Horiz. strip of 6, #1985-1990 6.50 6.50
*Nos. 1985-1990 (6)* 5.10 3.30

### Booklet Stamps

### Self-Adhesive

### *Die Cut Perf. 14x15½*

**1991** A513 1st Punch 11.50 10.00
**1992** A513 1st Judy 11.50 10.00
*a.* Booklet, Nos. 1991-1992, 4 #MH298 30.00

Nos. 1985-1992 sold for 27p on day of issue.

Nobel Prizes, Cent. — A514

Items symbolic of prize categories: 2nd, Carbon 60 molecule (Chemistry). 1st, Globe (Economics). E, Dove (Peace). 40p, Crosses (Physiology or Medicine). 45p, The Addressing of Cats, by T.S. Eliot (Literature). 65p, Boron atom (Physics)

**2001, Oct. 2 Photo. *Perf. 14½x14¼***
**1993** A514 2nd multi .95 .65

### Photo. & Engr.

**1994** A514 1st multi 1.50 .90

**Photo. & Embossed**

**1995** A514 E multi 2.00 1.25

**Photo.**

**1996** A514 40p multi 2.00 1.50
**1997** A514 45p multi 3.00 2.00

**Photo. With Hologram Affixed**

**1998** A514 65p multi 5.00 2.50
*Nos. 1993-1998 (6)* 14.45 8.80

Nos. 1993-1995 each sold for 19p, 27p and 37p respectively on day of issue. Molecule on No. 1993 is covered with a thermochromic film that changes color when warmed. No. 1996 has a scrach and sniff coating with a eucalyptus odor. Soaking in water may affect holographic images.

Flags — A515

Designs: Nos. 1999a, 2001, White ensign. No. 1999b, Union flag. Nos. 1999c, 2000, Jolly Roger. No. 1999d, Flag of the Chief of the Defense Staff.

**2001, Oct. 22 Photo. *Perf. 14¾***

**Miniature Sheet**

**1999** A515 Sheet of 4 10.00 10.00
*a.-d.* 1st Any single 1.75 1.00
*e.* Booklet pane, #1999 + selvage at L (BK170) 12.00
*f.* Sheet of 20 #1999b + 20 labels, litho. 50.00 —
*g.* Sheet of 20 #1999a + 20 labels, litho. 27.50 —
*h.* Booklet pane of 3 #1999a, litho. (BK178) 4.75 —
*i.* Booklet pane of 4, 2 each #1999a, 1999b, litho. (BK184) 12.00 —
*j.* Booklet pane of 4, 2 each #1999a, 1999b, litho. (BK190) 5.00 —

**Booklet Stamps**

**Self-Adhesive**

***Die Cut Perf. 14¾***

**2000** A515 1st multi 12.50 9.00
**2001** A515 1st multi 12.50 9.00
*a.* Booklet, #2000-2001, 4 #MH298 32.50

Nos. 1999a-1999d, 2000-2001 each sold for 27p on day of issue. The left edge of No. 1999 is straight while rouletting separates the selvage from the sheet on No. 1999e.

No. 1999f issued 2004. It sold for £14.95 and has labels that can be personalized.

No. 1999h issued 10/18/2005. No. 1999i issued 1/8/2008. No. 1999j issued 9/17/2009.

Christmas A516

Robins and: 2nd, Snowman. 1st, Birdhouse. E, Birdbath. 45p, Suet ball. 65b, Nest.

***Die Cut Perf. 14¼x14½***

**2001, Nov. 6 Photo.**

**Self-Adhesive**

**2002** A516 2nd multi .75 .25
*a.* Booklet of 24 18.00
*b.* Sheet of 20 + 20 labels, litho. 27.50 —
**2003** A516 1st multi 1.10 .25
*a.* Booklet of 12 16.50
*b.* Sheet of 20 + 20 labels, litho. 27.50
*c.* Sheet, 10 each #2002-2003 +20 labels, litho. 22.50 —
**2004** A516 E multi 1.50 1.50
**2005** A516 45p multi 1.40 1.40
**2006** A516 65p multi 2.10 2.10
*Nos. 2002-2006 (5)* 6.85 5.50

Nos. 2002-2004 each sold for 19p, 27p, and 37p respectively on day of issue.

Issued: No. 2003b, 9/30/03. No. 2003b sold for £6.15 and had labels that could be personalized.

Issued: No. 2202b, 2203c, 2005. No. 2002b sold for £9.95 and had labels that could be personalized. No. 2003c sold for £5.60.

Just So Stories, by Rudyard Kipling, Cent. A517

Designs: No. 2007, How the Whale Got His Throat (whale in bed). No. 2008, How the Camel Got His Hump (genie, camel). No. 2009, How the Rhinoceros Got His Skin (man in palm tree, rhinoceros). No. 2010, How the Leopard Got His Spots (man putting spots on leopard). No. 2011, The Elephant's Child (crocodile, elephant, snake). No. 2012, The Sing-song of Old Man Kangaroo (dog chasing kangaroo). No. 2013, The Beginning of the Armadilloes (jaguar, armadillo). No. 2014, The Crab That Played With the Sea (people in boat, giant crab). No. 2015, The Cat That Walked by Himself (people, dog, cat and shadow in cave). No. 2016, The Butterfly That Stamped (castle, giant butterfly).

***Serpentine Die Cut 14½x14***

**2002, Jan. 15 Photo.**

**Booklet Stamps**

**Self-Adhesive**

**2007** A517 1st multi .85 .65
**2008** A517 1st multi .85 .65
**2009** A517 1st multi .85 .65
**2010** A517 1st multi .85 .65
**2011** A517 1st multi .85 .65
**2012** A517 1st multi .85 .65
**2013** A517 1st multi .85 .65
**2014** A517 1st multi .85 .65
**2015** A517 1st multi .85 .65
**2016** A517 1st multi .85 .65
*a.* Booklet, #2007-2016 12.00

Nos. 2007-2016 each sold for 27p on day of issue. Titles of stories are not on stamps, but in margin.

Reign of Queen Elizabeth II, 50th Anniv. — A518

Photographs of Queen by: 2nd, Dorothy Wilding, 1952. 1st, Cecil Beaton, 1968. E, Lord Snowdon, 1978, 45p, Yousef Karsh, 1984. 65p, Tim Graham, 1996.

***Perf. 14½x14¼***

**2002, Feb. 6 Photo. Wmk. 401**

**2017** A518 2nd blk & sil .75 .50
**2018** A518 1st blk & sil 1.10 .85
**2019** A518 E blk & sil 1.50 .90
**2020** A518 45p blk & sil 1.40 1.40
*a.* Booklet pane, #2017-2020 (BK171) 4.75 —
**2021** A518 65p blk & sil 2.10 1.75
*a.* Booklet pane, #2018-2021 (BK171) 6.25 —
*Nos. 2017-2021 (5)* 6.85 5.40

Nos. 2017-2019 each sold for 19p, 27p, and 37p respectively on day of issue.

**Queen Types of 1952**

**Tan Surface-colored Paper**

***Perf. 14¾x14 Syncopated***

**2002, Feb. 6 Photo. Wmk. 401**

**2022** A127 2nd red 1.50 1.00
**2023** A126 1st green 1.75 1.50
*a.* Booklet pane, 5 #2022, 4 #2023, + label (BK171) 14.50 —

Nos. 2022 and 2023 sold for 19p and 27p respectively on day of issue.

A New Baby A519

Hello A520

Moving A521

Best Wishes A522

Love A523

***Perf. 14¾x14***

**2002-3 Litho. Unwmk.**

**2024** A519 1st multi 1.15 .60
*a.* Perf. 14¼ + label 2.50 2.50
**2025** A520 1st multi 1.15 .60
*a.* Perf. 14¼ + label 2.50 2.50
**2026** A521 1st multi 1.15 .60
*a.* Perf. 14¼ + label 2.50 2.50
**2027** A522 1st multi 1.15 .60
*a.* Perf. 14¼ + label 2.50 2.50
**2028** A523 1st multi 1.15 .65
*a.* Perf. 14¼ + label 2.50 2.50
*c.* Sheet of 20, 4 each #2024-2028, + 20 labels, perf. 14¼ — —
*Nos. 2024-2028 (5)* 5.75 3.05

**Self-Adhesive**

**Booklet Stamp**

***Die Cut Perf. 14¾x14***

**2028A** A520 1st multi 6.00 .65
*b.* Booklet pane, 2 #2028A, 4 #MH300 14.00

Nos. 2024-2028A each sold for 27p on day of issue.

Nos. 2024a-2028a each sold for £14.95 and have labels that can be personalized. No. 2028c sold for £5.95.

Sheets of No. 2025a with a Washington 2006 World Philatelic Exhibition margin and labels sold for £6.95. Value $27.50. Sheets with other margins exist.

Issued, Nos. 2024-2028, 3/5/02; No. 2028c, 4/23/02; Nos. 2024a-2028a, 2002; No. 2028A, 3/4/03.

Aerial Photographs of Coastline A524

**2002, Mar. 19 *Perf. 14¼x14½***

**2029** A524 27p Studland Bay 1.10 .80
**2030** A524 27p Luskentyre 1.10 .80
**2031** A524 27p Dover 1.10 .80
**2032** A524 27p Padstow 1.10 .80
**2033** A524 27p Broadstairs 1.10 .80
**2034** A524 27p St. Abb's Head 1.10 .80
**2035** A524 27p Dunster Beach 1.10 .80
**2036** A524 27p Newquay 1.10 .80
**2037** A524 27p Portrush 1.10 .80
**2038** A524 27p Conwy 1.10 .80
*a.* Block of 10, #2029-2038 11.00 10.00

Circus — A525

Designs: 2nd, High wire performer. 1st, Lion tamer. E, Trick tricyclists. 45p, Krazy kar. 65p, Equestrienne.

**2002, Apr. 9 Photo. *Perf. 14¼x14½***

**2039** A525 2nd multi .95 .50
**2040** A525 1st multi 1.35 .80
**2041** A525 E multi 1.90 1.00
**2042** A525 45p multi 1.80 1.40
**2043** A525 65p multi 2.60 1.75
*Nos. 2039-2043 (5)* 8.60 5.45

Europa (Nos. 2040-2041). Nos. 2039-2041 sold for 19p, 27p and 37p respectively on day of issue.

First day covers of Nos. 2039-2043 bear an April 9, 2001, date, but the issue of the stamps was delayed until April 10 due to the funeral of the Queen Mother.

Queen Mother (1900-2002) A526

**2002, Apr. 25 *Perf. 14x14¾***

**2044** A526 1st 1990 photo 1.10 .80
**2045** A526 E 1948 photo 1.50 1.00
**2046** A526 45p 1930 photo 1.40 1.40
**2047** A526 65p 1907 photo 2.10 1.75
*Nos. 2044-2047 (4)* 6.10 4.95

Nos. 2044-2045 sold for 27p and 37p respectively on day of issue. Compare with Type A387.

Jet Aircraft — A527

Designs: 2nd, Airbus A340-600, 2002. 1st, Concorde, 1976. E, Trident, 1964. 45p, VC10, 1964. 65p, Comet, 1952.

**2002, May 2 *Perf. 14½***

**2048** A527 2nd multi .95 .50
**2049** A527 1st multi 1.35 .80
*a.* Litho. (#2619a) ('09) 8.00 .55
**2050** A527 E multi 1.90 1.00
**2051** A527 45p multi 1.80 1.40
**2052** A527 65p multi 2.60 1.75
*a.* Souvenir sheet, #2048-2052 13.00 9.50
*Nos. 2048-2052 (5)* 8.60 5.45

**Booklet Stamp**

**Self-Adhesive**

***Die Cut Perf. 14½***

**2053** A527 1st multi 5.00 5.00
*a.* Booklet, 2 #2053, 4 #MH297 16.00

Nos. 2048-2052 sold for 19p, 27p and 37p respectively on day of issue.

No. 2049a issued 1/13/09. No. 2049a sold for 36p on day of issue.

A528

2002 World Cup Soccer Championships, Japan and Korea — A529

Soccer ball and: Nos. 2056a, 2057, Upper left portion of English flag. Nos. 2056b, 2058, Upper right portion of English flag. No. 2056c, Lower left portion of English flag. Nos. 2055, 2056d, Lower right portion of English flag.

**Photo., Litho. (#2055)**

**2002, May 21** ***Perf. 14¼***

| | | | | | |
|---|---|---|---|---|---|
| **2054** | A528 | 1st multi | | 1.80 | 1.50 |
| **2055** | A529 | 1st dull blue & multi | | 1.80 | 1.50 |

**Souvenir Sheet**

| | | | |
|---|---|---|---|
| **2056** | Sheet, #2054, #2056a-2056d | 6.50 | 6.50 |
| *a.-d.* | A529 1st deep blue & multi, perf. 14¾x14, any single | 1.60 | 1.50 |

**Booklet Stamps**

***Die Cut Perf. 14¾x14***

**Self-Adhesive**

| | | | |
|---|---|---|---|
| **2057** | A529 1st deep blue & multi | 7.00 | 3.50 |
| **2058** | A529 1st deep blue & multi | 7.00 | 3.50 |
| *a.* | Booklet, #2057, 2058, 4 #MH298 | 17.50 | |

Nos. 2054, 2056a-2056d, 2057-2058 sold for 27p on day of sale. No. 2055 was issued only in sheets of 20 stamps + 16 labels that sold for £5.95, and which could have the labels personalized for an additional fee.

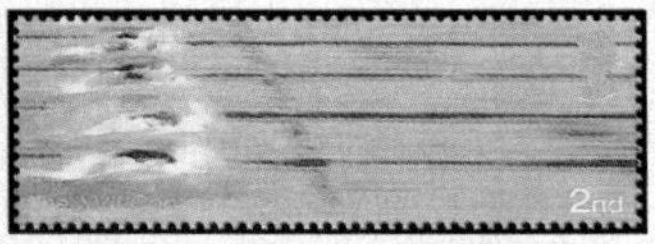

17th Commonwealth Games, Manchester — A530

Designs: 2nd, Swimming. 1st, Running. E, Cycling. 47p, Long jump. 68p, Wheelchair racing.

***Perf. 14¾x14¼***

**2002, July 16** **Photo.**

| | | | | |
|---|---|---|---|---|
| **2059** | A530 | 2nd multi | .75 | .35 |
| **2060** | A530 | 1st multi | 1.10 | .55 |
| **2061** | A530 | E multi | 1.50 | 1.00 |
| **2062** | A530 | 47p multi | 1.50 | 1.00 |
| **2063** | A530 | 68p multi | 2.10 | 1.40 |
| | | *Nos. 2059-2063 (5)* | 6.95 | 4.30 |

Nos. 2059-2061 each sold for 19p, 27p and 37p respectively on day of issue.

Peter Pan, by J. M. Barrie, 150th Anniv. A531

Designs: 2nd, Tinkerbell. 1st, Darling children. E, Crocodile and clock. 47p, Captain Hook. 68p, Peter Pan.

***Perf. 14¾x14¼***

**2002, Aug. 20** **Photo.**

| | | | | |
|---|---|---|---|---|
| **2064** | A531 | 2nd multi | .75 | .35 |
| **2065** | A531 | 1st multi | 1.10 | .55 |
| **2066** | A531 | E multi | 1.50 | 1.00 |
| **2067** | A531 | 47p multi | 1.50 | 1.00 |
| **2068** | A531 | 68p multi | 2.15 | 1.40 |
| | | *Nos. 2064-2068 (5)* | 7.00 | 4.30 |

Nos. 2064-2066 each sold for 19p, 27p and 37p respectively on day of issue.

Thames River Bridges in London A532

**2002, Sept. 10 Litho.** ***Perf. 14¾x14***

| | | | | |
|---|---|---|---|---|
| **2069** | A532 | 2nd Millennium | 1.05 | .35 |
| **2070** | A532 | 1st Tower | 1.25 | .55 |
| **2071** | A532 | E Westminster | 1.90 | 1.00 |
| **2072** | A532 | 47p Blackfriars | 1.90 | 1.00 |
| **2073** | A532 | 68p London | 2.50 | 1.40 |
| | | *Nos. 2069-2073 (5)* | 8.60 | 4.30 |

**Booklet Stamp**

***Serpentine Die Cut 14¾x14***

| | | | |
|---|---|---|---|
| **2074** | A532 1st Tower | 7.50 | *6.00* |
| *a.* | Booklet, 2 #2074, 4 #MH300 | 19.00 | |

Nos. 2070 and 2074 sold for 27p; Nos. 2069, 2071 sold for 19p and 37p respectively on day of sale.

Souvenir Sheet

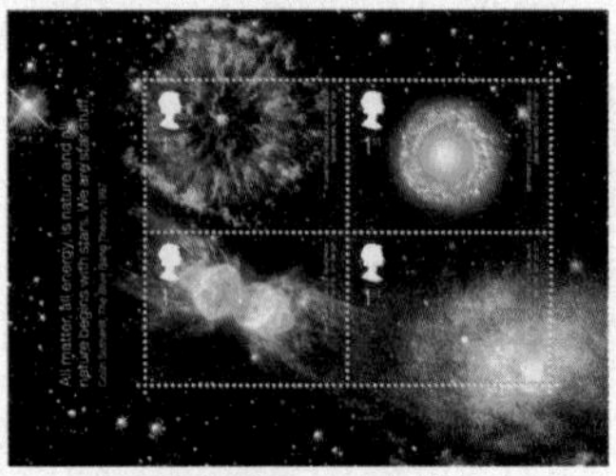

Astronomy — A533

No. 2075: a, Planetary nebula in Aquila. b, Seyfert 2 galaxy in Pegasus. c, Planetary nebula in Norma. d, Seyfert 2 galaxy in Circinus.

***Perf. 14¾x14¼***

**2002, Sept. 24** **Photo.**

| | | | |
|---|---|---|---|
| **2075** | A533 Sheet of 4 | 5.25 | 5.00 |
| *a.-d.* | (1st) Any single | 1.25 | .75 |
| *e.* | Booklet pane, #2075, rouletted at left (BK172) | 5.50 | |

Nos. 2075a-2075d each sold for 27p on day of issue.

Pillar Boxes, 150th Anniv. — A534

Designs: 2nd, Decorative box, 1857. 1st, Mainland box, 1874. E, Airmail box, 1934. 47p, Oval dual-aperture box, 1939. 68p, Modern box, 1980.

**Litho. & Engr.**

**2002, Oct. 8** ***Perf. 14x14¼***

| | | | | |
|---|---|---|---|---|
| **2076** | A534 | 2nd multi | .85 | .35 |
| **2077** | A534 | 1st multi | 1.20 | .55 |
| **2078** | A534 | E multi | 1.75 | 1.00 |
| **2079** | A534 | 47p multi | 1.75 | 1.00 |
| **2080** | A534 | 68p multi | 2.40 | 1.40 |
| | | *Nos. 2076-2080 (5)* | 7.95 | 4.30 |

Nos. 2076-2078 each sold for 19p, 27p and 37p on day of issue.

Christmas A535

***Die Cut Perf. 14½x14***

**2002, Nov. 5** **Photo.**

**Self-Adhesive**

| | | | |
|---|---|---|---|
| **2081** | A535 2nd Spruce branches | .75 | .25 |
| *a.* | Booklet pane of 24 | 18.00 | |
| **2082** | A535 1st Holly | 1.10 | .25 |
| *a.* | Booklet pane of 12 | 13.50 | |
| **2083** | A535 E Ivy | 7.50 | .80 |
| **2084** | A535 47p Mistletoe | 1.50 | .95 |
| **2085** | A535 68p Pine cone | 2.15 | 1.40 |
| | *Nos. 2081-2085 (5)* | 13.00 | 3.65 |

Nos. 2081-2085 each sold for 19p, 27p and 37p on day of issue.

**Types of 1952-54**

Souvenir Sheet

**Tan Surface-colored Paper**

***Perf. 14¾x14 Syncopated***

**2002, Dec. 5 Photo. Wmk. 401**

| | | | |
|---|---|---|---|
| **2086** | Sheet of 9, #2022-2023, 2086a-2086g + label | 10.00 | 8.50 |
| *a.* | A126 1p red orange | .30 | .25 |
| *b.* | A126 2p ultramarine | .30 | .25 |
| *c.* | A126 5p brown | .30 | .25 |
| *d* | A129 33p light brown | 1.60 | .90 |
| *e.* | A130 37p bright rose | 2.00 | 1.00 |
| *f.* | A131 47p brown | 2.40 | 1.10 |
| *g.* | A132 50p dark green | 2.75 | 1.25 |

Barn Owl in Flight — A536

Barn Owl in Flight — A537

Barn Owl in Flight — A538

Barn Owl in Flight — A539

Barn Owl in Flight — A540

Kestrel in Flight — A541

Kestrel in Flight — A542

Kestrel in Flight — A543

Kestrel in Flight — A544

Kestrel in Flight — A545

**2003, Jan. 14 Litho.** ***Perf. 14¼x14½***

| | | | | |
|---|---|---|---|---|
| **2087** | A536 | 1st multi | 1.10 | .80 |
| **2088** | A537 | 1st multi | 1.10 | .80 |
| **2089** | A538 | 1st multi | 1.10 | .80 |
| **2090** | A539 | 1st multi | 1.10 | .80 |
| **2091** | A540 | 1st multi | 1.10 | .80 |
| **2092** | A541 | 1st multi | 1.10 | .80 |
| **2093** | A542 | 1st multi | 1.10 | .80 |
| **2094** | A543 | 1st multi | 1.10 | .80 |
| **2095** | A544 | 1st multi | 1.10 | .80 |
| **2096** | A545 | 1st multi | 1.10 | .80 |
| *a.* | | Block of 10, #2087-2096 | 11.00 | 11.50 |

Nos. 2087-2096 each sold for 27p on day of issue.

Check-off Slogans A546

Designs: No. 2097, Gold star, See me, Playtime. No. 2098, I love you, XXXX, S.W.A.L.K. No. 2099, Angel, Poppet, Little terror. No. 2100, Yes, No, Maybe. No. 2101, Oops!, Sorry, Will try harder. No. 2102, I did it!, You did it!, We did it!

**2003, Feb. 4 Litho.** ***Perf. 14¼x14***

| | | | | |
|---|---|---|---|---|
| **2097** | A546 | 1st multi | 1.05 | .80 |
| **2098** | A546 | 1st multi | 1.05 | .80 |
| **2099** | A546 | 1st multi | 1.05 | .80 |
| **2100** | A546 | 1st multi | 1.05 | .80 |
| **2101** | A546 | 1st multi | 1.05 | .80 |
| **2102** | A546 | 1st multi | 1.05 | .80 |
| *a.* | | Block of 6, #2097-2102 | 6.50 | 6.25 |
| *b.* | | Sheet, 3 each #2097, 2099, 2101-2102, 4 each #2098, 2100 + 20 labels | 35.00 | |

No. 2102b sold for £5.95 and had labels that could be personalized.

Genetics A548

Designs: 2nd, Scientists with jigsaw puzzle. 1st, Chimpanzee and scientist. E, Scientist, DNA double helix, snake. 47p, Scientists with animals. 68p, Scientist with doctor's satchel, crystal ball.

***Perf. 14¼x14½***

**2003, Feb. 25** **Litho.**

| | | | | |
|---|---|---|---|---|
| **2103** | A548 | 2nd multi | .70 | .35 |
| **2104** | A548 | 1st multi | 1.00 | .45 |
| *a.* | | Booklet pane, 2 each #2103-2104 (BK173) | 3.50 | |
| **2105** | A548 | E multi | 1.40 | .90 |
| *a.* | | Booklet pane of 4 (BK173) | 5.75 | |
| **2106** | A548 | 47p multi | 1.40 | .90 |
| **2107** | A548 | 68p multi | 2.00 | 1.40 |
| | | *Nos. 2103-2107 (5)* | 6.50 | 4.00 |

Nos. 2103-2105 sold for 19p, 27p and 37p respectively on day of issue.

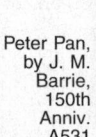

Fruit and Vegetables A549

*Die Cut Perf. 14¼x14*

**2003, Mar. 25 Photo.**

**Self-Adhesive**

**Booklet Stamps**

| | | | | |
|---|---|---|---|---|
| **2108** | A549 | 1st Strawberry | 1.10 | .75 |
| **2109** | A549 | 1st Potato | 1.10 | .75 |
| **2110** | A549 | 1st Apple | 1.10 | .75 |
| **2111** | A549 | 1st Pepper | 1.10 | .75 |
| **2112** | A549 | 1st Pear | 1.10 | .75 |
| **2113** | A549 | 1st Orange | 1.10 | .75 |
| **2114** | A549 | 1st Tomato | 1.10 | .75 |
| **2115** | A549 | 1st Lemon | 1.10 | .75 |
| **2116** | A549 | 1st Brussels sprout | 1.10 | .75 |
| **2117** | A549 | 1st Eggplant | 1.10 | .75 |
| *a.* | | Pane, #2108-2117 + 76 stickers | 11.00 | |
| *b.* | | Sheet, 2 each #2108-2117, litho., + 20 labels +93 stickers ('06) | 35.00 | |

Nos. 2108-2117 each sold for 27p on day of issue.

No. 2117b issued 3/7/06. No. 2117b sold for £6.55.

Adventurers — A550

Designs: 2nd, Amy Johnson (1903-41), first woman to fly to Australia. 1st, British Mount Everest expedition of 1953. E, Freya Stark (1893-1993), Middle East traveler and writer. 42p, Ernest Shackleton (1874-1922), Antarctic explorer. 47p, Francis Chichester (1901-72), sailor. 68p, Robert Falcon Scott (1868-1912), Antarctic explorer.

*Perf. 14¾x14¼*

**2003, Apr. 29 Photo. Unwmk.**

| | | | | |
|---|---|---|---|---|
| **2118** | A550 | 2nd multi | .80 | .35 |
| **2119** | A550 | 1st multi | 1.15 | .50 |
| **2120** | A550 | E multi | 1.60 | .85 |
| **2121** | A550 | 42p multi | 1.40 | .85 |
| **2122** | A550 | 47p multi | 1.60 | 1.00 |
| **2123** | A550 | 68p multi | 2.25 | 1.40 |
| | | *Nos. 2118-2123 (6)* | 8.80 | 4.95 |

**Booklet Stamp**

**Self-Adhesive**

*Die Cut Perf. 14¾x14¼*

| | | | | |
|---|---|---|---|---|
| **2124** | A550 | 1st multi | 6.75 | 1.25 |
| *a.* | | Booklet pane, 2 #2124, 4 #MH300 | 14.00 | |

Nos. 2118-2120 each sold for 19p, 27p and 38p respectively on day of issue.

**Types of 1952-54**

A550a

*Perf. 14¾x14 Syncopated*

**2003, May 20 Photo. Wmk. 401**

**Tan Surface-colored Paper**

**Souvenir Sheet**

| | | | | |
|---|---|---|---|---|
| **2125** | | Sheet of 9 + label | 9.50 | 11.00 |
| *a.* | A127 | 4p purple | .25 | .25 |
| *b.* | A128 | 8p ultramarine | .30 | .25 |
| *c.* | A129 | 10p lilac rose | .35 | .25 |
| *d.* | A129 | 20p emerald | .65 | .40 |
| *e.* | A130 | 28p deep olive green | .90 | .50 |
| *f.* | A130 | 34p violet brown | 1.10 | .65 |
| *g.* | A128 | E henna brown | 1.50 | .80 |
| *h.* | A130 | 42p royal blue | 1.45 | .75 |
| *i.* | A131 | 68p dark blue | 2.50 | 1.25 |

**Booklet Stamp**

*Perf. 14¾x14*

| | | | | |
|---|---|---|---|---|
| **2126** | A136 | £1 dark green | 65.00 | 55.00 |
| *a.* | | Booklet pane, #2126, 2 each #2086f, 2125i (BK174) | 72.50 | |

No. 2125g sold for 38p on day of issue.

Coronation of Queen Elizabeth II, 50th Anniv. — A551

Designs: No. 2127, Aerial view of parade entering circle. No. 2128, Children reading coronation party sign. No. 2129, Queen at coronation. No. 2130, Children at wall of pictures. No. 2131, Queen holding orb and scepter. No. 2132, Children running in street. No. 2133, Royal carriage under arch. No. 2134, Children standing in front of house. No. 2135, Royal carriage. No. 2136, Children at party.

*Perf. 14½x14¼*

**2003, June 2 Photo. Wmk. 401**

| | | | | |
|---|---|---|---|---|
| **2127** | A551 | 1st multi | 1.05 | .80 |
| **2128** | A551 | 1st multi | 1.05 | .80 |
| **2129** | A551 | 1st multi | 1.05 | .80 |
| **2130** | A551 | 1st multi | 1.05 | .80 |
| **2131** | A551 | 1st multi | 1.05 | .80 |
| **2132** | A551 | 1st multi | 1.05 | .80 |
| **2133** | A551 | 1st multi | 1.05 | .80 |
| **2134** | A551 | 1st multi | 1.05 | .80 |
| *a.* | | Booklet pane, #2127, 2129, 2132, 2134 (BK174) | 5.50 | |
| **2135** | A551 | 1st multi | 1.05 | .80 |
| **2136** | A551 | 1st multi | 1.05 | .80 |
| *a.* | | Block of 10, #2127-2136 | 11.00 | 10.00 |
| *b.* | | Booklet pane, #2128, 2131, 2133, 2136 (BK174) | 5.50 | |

Nos. 2127-2136 each sold for 28p on day of issue.

Prince William, 21st Birthday A552

Various portraits.

**2003, June 17 Photo. *Perf. 14¼***

**Background Color**

| | | | | |
|---|---|---|---|---|
| **2137** | A552 | 28p silver | 1.00 | .55 |
| **2138** | A552 | E brown | 2.00 | 1.10 |
| **2139** | A552 | 47p green | 2.25 | 1.60 |
| **2140** | A552 | 68p olive green | 3.50 | 2.75 |
| | | *Nos. 2137-2140 (4)* | 8.75 | 6.00 |

No. 2138 sold for 38p on day of issue. Background colors are printed with Iriodin ink, giving the stamp a three dimensional appearance.

Scottish Scenery A553

Designs: 2nd: Loch Assynt, Sutherland. 1st, Ben More, Isle of Mull. E, Rothiemurchus, Cairngorms. 42p, Dalveen Pass, Lowther Hills. 47p, Glenfinnan Viaduct, Lochaber. 68p, Papa Little, Shetland Islands.

**2003, July 15 Photo. *Perf. 14½***

| | | | | |
|---|---|---|---|---|
| **2141** | A553 | 2nd multi | .75 | .45 |
| **2142** | A553 | 1st multi | 1.10 | .60 |
| **2143** | A553 | E multi | 1.50 | .90 |
| **2144** | A553 | 42p multi | 1.35 | 1.10 |
| **2145** | A553 | 47p multi | 1.50 | 1.25 |
| **2146** | A553 | 68p multi | 2.10 | 1.75 |
| | | *Nos. 2141-2146 (6)* | 8.30 | 6.05 |

**Booklet Stamp**

**Self-Adhesive**

*Die Cut Perf. 14½*

| | | | | |
|---|---|---|---|---|
| **2147** | A553 | 1st multi | 6.00 | 2.00 |
| *a.* | | Booklet pane, 2 #2147, 4 #MH300 | 16.00 | |

Nos. 2141 and 2143 each sold for 20p and 38p respectively on day of issue, while Nos. 2142 and 2147 sold for 28p on day of issue.

Pub Signs — A554

Designs: 1st, The Station, Thurnscoe. E, Black Swan, Lincoln. 42p, The Cross Keys, London. 47p, The Mayflower, Southsea. 68p, The Barley Sheaf, Bodmin.

**2003, Aug. 12 Photo. *Perf. 14x14¼***

| | | | | |
|---|---|---|---|---|
| **2148** | A554 | 1st multi | 1.15 | .55 |
| *a.* | | Booklet pane of 4 (BK175) | 4.75 | — |
| **2149** | A554 | E multi | 1.00 | .85 |
| **2150** | A554 | 42p multi | 1.45 | 1.00 |
| **2151** | A554 | 47p multi | 1.60 | 1.10 |
| **2152** | A554 | 68p multi | 2.25 | 1.60 |
| | | *Nos. 2148-2152 (5)* | 7.45 | 5.10 |

Europa (Nos. 2148-2149).

Nos. 2148 and 2149 each sold for 28p and 38p, respectively, on day of issue.

Toys A555

Designs: 1st, Meccano Constructor Biplane, c. 1931. E, Wells-Brimtoy Clockwork Double-decker Omnibus, c. 1938. 42p, Hornby M1 Clockwork Locomotive and Tender, c. 1948. 47p, Dinky Toys Ford Zephyr, c. 1956. 68p, Mettoy Friction drive Space Ship Eagle c. 1960.

**2003, Sept. 18 Photo. *Perf. 14¼x14***

| | | | | |
|---|---|---|---|---|
| **2153** | A555 | 1st multi | 1.15 | .55 |
| **2154** | A555 | E multi | 1.60 | .85 |
| **2155** | A555 | 42p multi | 1.45 | 1.00 |
| **2156** | A555 | 47p multi | 1.60 | 1.10 |
| **2157** | A555 | 68p multi | 2.25 | 1.60 |
| *a.* | | Souvenir sheet, #2153-2157 | 10.00 | 10.00 |
| | | *Nos. 2153-2157 (5)* | 8.05 | 5.10 |

**Booklet Stamp**

**Self-Adhesive**

*Die Cut Perf. 14¼x14*

| | | | | |
|---|---|---|---|---|
| **2158** | A555 | 1st multi | 6.00 | 2.00 |
| *a.* | | Booklet, 2 #2158, 4 #MH300 | 16.00 | |

Nos. 2153 and 2158 each sold for 28p on day of issue. No. 2154 sold for 38p on day of issue.

British Museum, 250th Anniv. — A556

Museum Exhibits: 2nd, Coffin of Denytenamun, c. 900 B.C. 1st, Bust of Alexander the Great, c. 200 B.C. E, Sutton Hoo Helmet, c. 600. 42p, Sculpture of Indian Goddess Parvati, c. 1500. 47p, Mask of Xiuhtecuhtli, c. 1500. 68p, Hoa Hakananai'a Easter Island moai, c. 1000.

**2003, Oct. 7 *Perf. 14x14¼***

| | | | | |
|---|---|---|---|---|
| **2159** | A556 | 2nd multi | .80 | .45 |
| **2160** | A556 | 1st multi | 1.15 | .55 |
| **2161** | A556 | E multi | 1.60 | .85 |
| **2162** | A556 | 42p multi | 1.45 | 1.00 |
| **2163** | A556 | 47p multi | 1.60 | 1.10 |
| **2164** | A556 | 68p multi | 2.25 | 1.60 |
| | | *Nos. 2159-2164 (6)* | 8.85 | 5.55 |

Nos. 2159-2161 each sold for 20p, 28p and 38p respectively on day of issue.

Christmas A557

Ice and snow sculptures by Andy Goldsworthy: 2nd, Ice Spiral. 1st, Icicle Star. E, Wall of Frozen Snow. 53p, Ice Ball. 68p, Ice Hole. £1.12, Snow Pyramids.

*Die Cut Perf. 14¼x14*

**2003, Nov. 4 Photo.**

**Self-Adhesive**

| | | | | |
|---|---|---|---|---|
| **2165** | A557 | 2nd multi | .75 | .25 |
| *a.* | | Booklet pane of 24 | 18.50 | |
| *b.* | | Sheet of 20 + 20 labels, litho. | 25.00 | |
| **2166** | A557 | 1st multi | 1.10 | .25 |
| *a.* | | Booklet pane of 12 | 14.00 | |
| *b.* | | Sheet of 20 + 20 labels, litho. | 37.50 | |
| **2167** | A557 | E multi | 1.50 | 1.00 |
| **2168** | A557 | 53p multi | 1.75 | 1.20 |
| **2169** | A557 | 68p multi | 2.25 | 1.60 |
| **2170** | A557 | £1.12 multi | 3.75 | 2.40 |
| | | *Nos. 2165-2170 (6)* | 11.10 | 6.70 |

Nos. 2165-2167 sold for 20p, 28p and 38p respectively on day of issue.

Nos. 2165b and 2166b sold for £4.20 and £6.15 respectively and had labels that could be personalized.

Souvenir Sheet

England, Winners of 2003 Rugby World Cup Championships — A558

No. 2171: a, English flags. b, Players with red shirts in huddle. c, World Cup. d, Players in white jerseys, celebrating.

**2003, Dec. 19 Litho. *Perf. 13¾x14***

| | | | | |
|---|---|---|---|---|
| **2171** | A558 | Sheet of 4 | 14.00 | 14.00 |
| *a.-b.* | | 1st Either single | 2.00 | .75 |
| *c.-d.* | | 68p Either single | 4.00 | 1.75 |

Nos. 2171a-2171b sold for 28p on day of issue.

Locomotives — A559

Designs: 20p, Dolgoch 0-4-0T. 28p, CR 439 0-4-4T. E, GCR 8K 2-8-0. 42p, GWR Manor 4-6-0. 47p, SR West Country 4-6-2. 68p, BR Standard 4 2-6-4T.

**2004, Jan. 13 Litho. *Perf. 14¾x14¼***

| | | | | |
|---|---|---|---|---|
| **2172** | A559 | 20p multi | .70 | .40 |
| **2173** | A559 | 28p multi | 1.00 | .60 |
| **2174** | A559 | E multi | 1.75 | .90 |
| **2175** | A559 | 42p multi | 1.60 | 1.00 |
| *a.* | | Booklet pane, #2173-2175 (BK175) | 4.50 | — |
| **2176** | A559 | 47p multi | 1.75 | 1.10 |
| **2177** | A559 | 68p multi | 2.50 | 1.60 |
| *a.* | | Souvenir sheet, #2172-2177 | 45.00 | 45.00 |
| | | *Nos. 2172-2177 (6)* | 9.30 | 5.60 |

First steam locomotive, bicent. No. 2174 sold for 38p on day of issue.

Special Occasions A560

**2004, Feb. 3 Litho. *Perf. 14¼x14***

| | | | | |
|---|---|---|---|---|
| **2178** | A560 | 1st Postman | 1.35 | .55 |
| **2179** | A560 | 1st Face | 1.35 | .55 |
| **2180** | A560 | 1st Duck | 1.35 | .55 |
| **2181** | A560 | 1st Baby | 1.35 | .55 |

| | | | | |
|---|---|---|---|---|
| **2182** | A560 1st Airplane | | 1.35 | .55 |
| *a.* | Horiz. strip of 5, #2178-2182 | | 6.75 | 3.25 |
| *c.* | Sheet, 4 each #2178-2182, + 20 labels | | 27.50 | — |

Nos. 2178-2182 each sold for 28p on day of issue. No. 2182c sold for £6.15 and had labels that could not be personalized.

Map — A561

Forest of Lothlórien A562

The Fellowship of the Ring — A563

Rivendell A564

Hall at Bag-End A565

Orthanc A566

Doors of Durin — A567

Barad-Dur A568

Minas Tirith — A569

Fangorn Forest A570

**2004, Feb. 26** ***Perf. 14½x14¼***

| | | | | |
|---|---|---|---|---|
| **2183** | A561 1st multi | | 1.10 | .65 |
| **2184** | A562 1st multi | | 1.10 | .65 |
| **2185** | A563 1st multi | | 1.10 | .65 |
| **2186** | A564 1st multi | | 1.10 | .65 |
| **2187** | A565 1st multi | | 1.10 | .65 |
| **2188** | A566 1st multi | | 1.10 | .65 |
| **2189** | A567 1st multi | | 1.10 | .65 |
| **2190** | A568 1st multi | | 1.10 | .65 |
| **2191** | A569 1st multi | | 1.10 | .65 |
| **2192** | A570 1st multi | | 1.10 | .65 |
| *a.* | Block of 10, #2183-2192 | | 11.00 | 6.50 |

Publication of *The Lord of the Rings,* by J.R.R. Tolkein, 50th anniv. Nos. 2183-2192 each sold for 28p on day of issue.

Northern Ireland Scenery A571

Designs: 2nd, Ely, Island, Lower Lough Erne. 1st, Giant's Causeway, Antrim Coast. E, Slemish, Antrim Mountains. 42p, Banns Road, Mourne Mountain. 47p, Glenelly Valley, Sperrins. 68p, Islandmore, Strangford Lough.

**2004, Mar. 16** **Photo.** ***Perf. 14½***

| | | | | |
|---|---|---|---|---|
| **2193** | A571 2nd multi | | .75 | .40 |
| **2194** | A571 1st multi | | 1.10 | .55 |
| **2195** | A571 E multi | | 1.50 | .75 |
| **2196** | A571 42p multi | | 1.35 | .85 |
| **2197** | A571 47p multi | | 1.50 | .95 |
| **2198** | A571 68p multi | | 2.10 | 1.40 |
| | *Nos. 2193-2198 (6)* | | 8.30 | 4.90 |

**Booklet Stamp**
**Self-Adhesive**
***Die Cut Perf. 14½***

| | | | | |
|---|---|---|---|---|
| **2199** | A571 1st multi | | 6.50 | 2.00 |
| *a.* | Booklet, 2 #2199, 4 #MH300 | | 15.00 | |

Nos. 2193-2195 each sold for 20p, 28p and 38p respectively on day of issue.

Entente Cordiale, Cent. — A572

Designs: 28p, Lace 1 (trial proof) 1968, by Sir Terry Frost. 57p, Coccinelle, by Sonia Delaunay.

**2004, Apr. 6** **Photo.** ***Perf. 14x14¼***

| | | | | |
|---|---|---|---|---|
| **2200** | A572 28p multi | | .90 | .50 |
| **2201** | A572 57p multi | | 1.80 | 1.10 |

See France Nos. 3009-3010.

Ocean Liners A573

Designs: 1st, RMS Queen Mary 2, 2004. E, SS Canberra, 1961. 42p, RMS Queen Mary, 1936. 47p, RMS Mauretania, 1907. 57p, SS City of New York, 1888. 68p, PS Great Western, 1838.

**2004, Apr. 13** ***Perf. 14¼x14***

| | | | | |
|---|---|---|---|---|
| **2202** | A573 1st multi | | 1.10 | .50 |
| **2203** | A573 E multi | | 1.50 | .80 |
| **2204** | A573 42p multi | | 1.40 | .85 |
| **2205** | A573 47p multi | | 1.50 | .90 |
| **2206** | A573 57p multi | | 1.80 | 1.40 |
| **2207** | A573 68p multi | | 2.10 | 1.40 |
| *a.* | Souvenir sheet, #2202-2207 | | 17.50 | 10.00 |
| *b.* | Litho. (from #2356a) | | 2.70 | 1.40 |
| | *Nos. 2202-2207 (6)* | | 9.40 | 5.85 |

**Booklet Stamp**
**Self-Adhesive**
***Serpentine Die Cut 14¼x14***

| | | | | |
|---|---|---|---|---|
| **2208** | A573 1st multi | | 6.00 | 2.00 |
| *a.* | Booklet pane, 2 #2208, 4 #MH300 | | 16.00 | |

Nos. 2202 and 2203 sold for 28p and 40p respectively on day of issue.

No. 2207b is contained in the booklet pane No. 2356a, issued 2/23/06.

Royal Horticultural Society, Bicent. A574

Designs: 2nd, Dianthus Allwoodii Group. 1st, Dahlia "Garden Princess." E, Clematis "Arabella." 42p, Miltonia "French Lake." 47p, Lilium "Lemon Pixie." 68p, Delphinium "Clifford Sky."

**2004, May 25** **Photo.** ***Perf. 14½***

| | | | | |
|---|---|---|---|---|
| **2209** | A574 2nd multi | | .75 | .35 |
| **2210** | A574 1st multi | | 1.10 | .50 |
| *a.* | Perf. 14¼ + label, litho. | | 2.25 | 1.10 |
| **2211** | A574 E multi | | 1.50 | .85 |
| **2212** | A574 42p multi | | 1.40 | .85 |
| **2213** | A574 47p multi | | 1.50 | 1.00 |
| *a.* | Booklet pane, 2 each #2210, 2213 (BK176) | | 6.50 | — |
| **2214** | A574 68p multi | | 2.10 | 1.40 |
| *a.* | Souvenir sheet, #2209-2214 | | 15.00 | 10.00 |
| *b.* | Booklet pane, #2209, 2211, 2212, 2214 (BK176) | | 7.25 | — |
| | *Nos. 2209-2214 (6)* | | 8.35 | 4.95 |

Nos. 2209-2211 each sold for 21p, 28p and 40p respectively on day of issue.

No. 2210a was printed in sheets of 20 stamps + 20 labels that sold for £6.15.

Wales Scenery A575

Designs: 2nd, Barmouth Bridge. 1st, Hyddgen, Plynlimon. 40p, Brecon Beacons National Park. 43p, Pen-pych, Rhondda Valley. 47p, Rhewl, Dee Valley. 68p, Marloes Sands.

**2004, June 15** **Photo.** ***Perf. 14½***

| | | | | |
|---|---|---|---|---|
| **2215** | A575 2nd multi | | .75 | .45 |
| **2216** | A575 1st multi | | 1.10 | .55 |
| **2217** | A575 40p multi | | 1.30 | .90 |
| **2218** | A575 43p multi | | 1.40 | 1.00 |
| **2219** | A575 47p multi | | 1.50 | 1.10 |
| **2220** | A575 68p multi | | 2.10 | 1.60 |
| | *Nos. 2215-2220 (6)* | | 8.15 | 5.60 |

**Booklet Stamp**
**Self-Adhesive**
***Die Cut Perf. 14½***

| | | | | |
|---|---|---|---|---|
| **2221** | A575 1st multi | | 7.50 | 2.00 |
| *a.* | Booklet pane, 2 #2221, 4 #MH300 | | 19.00 | |

Europa (Nos. 2216, 2217, 2221). Nos. 2215-2216 each sold for 21p and 28p respectively on day of issue.

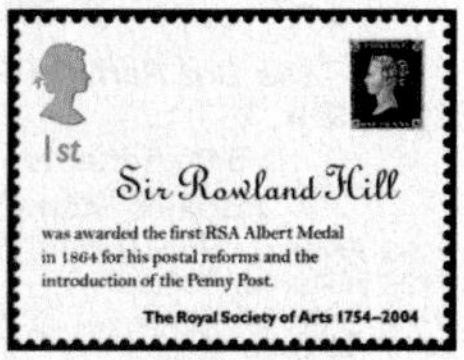

Royal Society of Arts, 250th Anniv. A576

Designs: 1st, Great Britain #1. 40p, William Shipley, Society founder. 43p, Stylized typewriter keys, shorthand. 47p, Apparatus for sweeping chimneys invented by George Smart. 57p, Typeface designed by Eric Gill. 68p, Zero waste.

***Perf. 13¾x14¼***

**2004, Aug. 10** **Litho.**

| | | | | |
|---|---|---|---|---|
| **2222** | A576 1st multi | | 1.10 | .55 |
| **2223** | A576 40p multi | | 1.40 | .90 |
| **2224** | A576 43p multi | | 1.50 | 1.00 |
| **2225** | A576 47p multi | | 1.60 | 1.10 |
| **2226** | A576 57p multi | | 2.00 | 1.40 |
| **2227** | A576 68p multi | | 2.25 | 1.60 |
| | *Nos. 2222-2227 (6)* | | 9.85 | 6.55 |

No. 2222 sold for 28p on day of issue.

Mammals A577

***Perf. 14½x14¼***

**2004, Sept. 16** **Photo.**

| | | | | |
|---|---|---|---|---|
| **2228** | A577 1st Pine marten | | 1.10 | .50 |
| **2229** | A577 1st Roe deer | | 1.10 | .50 |
| **2230** | A577 1st Badger | | 1.10 | .50 |
| **2231** | A577 1st Yellow-necked mouse | | 1.10 | .50 |
| **2232** | A577 1st Wild cat | | 1.10 | .50 |
| **2233** | A577 1st Red squirrel | | 1.10 | .50 |
| **2234** | A577 1st Stoat | | 1.10 | .50 |
| **2235** | A577 1st Natterer's bat | | 1.10 | .50 |
| **2236** | A577 1st Mole | | 1.10 | .50 |
| **2237** | A577 1st Fox | | 1.10 | .50 |
| *a.* | Block of 10, #2228-2237 | | 11.00 | 8.00 |

Nos. 2228-2237 each sold for 28p on day of issue.

Crimean War, 150th Anniv. — A578

Photographs of Crimean War heroes: 2nd, Private Michael MacNamara. 1st, Piper David Muir. 40p, Sergeant Major Edward Edwards. 57p, Sergeant William Powell. 68p, Sergeant Major John Poole. £1.12, Sergeant Robert Glasgow.

**2004, Oct. 12** **Litho.** ***Perf. 14x13¾***

| | | | | |
|---|---|---|---|---|
| **2238** | A578 2nd multi | | .75 | .45 |
| **2239** | A578 1st multi | | 1.10 | .55 |
| **2240** | A578 40p multi | | 1.30 | .95 |
| **2241** | A578 57p multi | | 1.80 | 1.40 |
| **2242** | A578 68p multi | | 2.10 | 1.60 |
| **2243** | A578 £1.12 multi | | 3.75 | 2.25 |
| | *Nos. 2238-2243 (6)* | | 10.80 | 7.20 |

Nos. 2238-2239 each sold for 21p and 28p respectively on day of issue.

Christmas
A579

Santa Claus: Nos. 2244a, 2245, Walking toward chimney in snow. Nos. 2244b, 2246, Looking at rising sun. Nos. 2244c, 2247, In wind. Nos. 2244d, 2248, With umbrella in rain storm. Nos. 2244e, 2249, With flashlight in fog. Nos. 2244f, 2250, Taking protection from hail storm.

**2004, Nov. 2 Photo. *Perf. 14½x14***

**2244** Sheet of 6 11.00 7.75
*a.* A579 (2nd) multi .75 .45
*b.* A579 (1st) multi 1.10 .60
*c.* A579 40p multi 1.30 .95
*d.* A579 57p multi 1.80 1.40
*e.* A579 68p multi 2.10 1.60
*f.* A579 £1.12 multi 3.75 2.25

**Self-Adhesive**

***Die Cut Perf. 14½x14***

**2245** A579 (2nd) multi .95 .25
*a.* Booklet pane of 24 23.00
*b.* Sheet of 20 + 20 personalized labels, litho. 40.00
**2246** A579 (1st) multi 1.35 .55
*a.* Booklet pane of 12 16.00 .25
*b.* Sheet, 10 each #2245-2246, + 20 labels, litho. 27.50
*c.* Sheet of 20 + 20 personalized labels, litho. 57.50
**2247** A579 40p multi 1.60 .85
**2248** A579 57p multi 2.30 1.25
**2249** A579 68p multi 2.70 1.40
**2250** A579 £1.12 multi 4.50 2.10
*Nos. 2245-2250 (6)* 13.40 6.40

Nos. 2244a and 2245 each sold for 21p and Nos. 2244b and 2246 each sold for 28p on day of issue.

No. 2245b sold for £9.95; No. 2246b sold for £5.40; No. 2246c sold for £14.95.

Farm Animals
A580

Designs: No. 2251, British Saddleback pigs. No. 2252, Two Khaki Campbell ducks. No. 2253, Clydesdale horses. No. 2254, Shorthorn cattle. No. 2255, Border collie. No. 2256, Chicks. No. 2257, Suffolk sheep. No. 2258, Bagot goat. No. 2259, Norfolk Black turkeys. No. 2260, Three Embden geese.

**2005, Jan. 11 Photo. *Perf. 14½***

**2251** A580 1st multi 1.10 .60
**2252** A580 1st multi 1.10 .60
**2253** A580 1st multi 1.10 .60
**2254** A580 1st multi 1.10 .60
**2255** A580 1st multi 1.10 .60
**2256** A580 1st multi 1.10 .60
**2257** A580 1st multi 1.10 .60
**2258** A580 1st multi 1.10 .60
**2259** A580 1st multi 1.10 .60
**2260** A580 1st multi 1.10 .60
*a.* Block of 10, #2251-2260 11.00 8.00
*b.* Sheet, 2 each #2251-2260 + 20 labels, litho. 34.00 —

Nos. 2251-2260 each sold for 28p on day of issue. No. 2260b sold for £6.15.

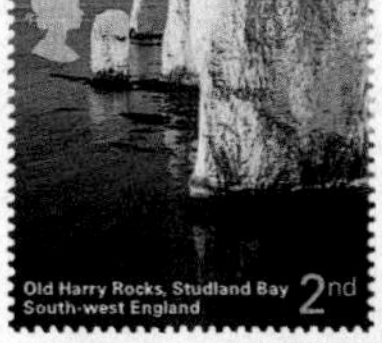


Southwestern England Scenery
A581

Designs: 2nd, Old Harry Rocks, Studland Bay. 1st, Wheal Coates mine, St. Agnes. 40p, Start Point and Start Bay. 43p, Norton Down, Wiltshire. 57p, Chiselcombe, Exmoor. 68p, St. James Stone, Lundy.

**2005, Feb. 8 Photo. *Perf. 14½***

**2261** A581 2nd multi .75 .45
**2262** A581 1st multi 1.10 .55
**2263** A581 40p multi 1.30 .90
**2264** A581 43p multi 1.40 1.00
**2265** A581 57p multi 1.80 1.40
**2266** A581 68p multi 2.10 1.60
*Nos. 2261-2266 (6)* 8.45 5.90

Nos. 2261 and 2262 sold for 21p and 28p respectively on day of issue.

Jane Eyre, by Charlotte Bronte (1816-55) — A582

Various characters.

**2005, Feb. 24 Litho. *Perf. 14¼***

**2267** A582 2nd multi .75 .45
**2268** A582 1st multi 1.10 .55
*a.* Booklet pane, 2 each #2267-2268 (BK177) 5.50 —
**2269** A582 40p multi 1.30 .95
**2270** A582 57p multi 1.80 1.40
**2271** A582 68p multi 2.10 1.60
**2272** A582 £1.12 multi 3.75 2.40
*a.* Souvenir sheet, #2267-2272 10.50 8.50
*b.* Booklet pane, #2269-2272 (BK177) 11.00 —
*Nos. 2267-2272 (6)* 10.80 7.35

Nos. 2267 and 2268 sold for 21p and 28p respectively on day of issue.

Magic Tricks
A583

Designs: 1st, Magician, "heads or tails" coin. 40p, Rabbit and hat. 47p, Popper. 68p, Ace of Hearts. £1.12, Pyramids and fezzes.

**2005, Mar. 15 Photo. *Perf. 14¼x14***

**2273** A583 1st multi, unscratched coin 1.10 .60
*a.* Scratched coin, heads 1.10 .60
*b.* Scratched coin, tails 1.10 .60
*c.* Vert. pair, unscratched 2.25 1.25
*d.* Sheet of 20 + 20 labels, unscratched, litho. 27.00 —
**2274** A583 40p multi 1.30 .90
**2275** A583 47p multi 1.50 1.05
**2276** A583 68p multi 2.10 1.60
**2277** A583 £1.12 multi 3.75 2.40
*Nos. 2273-2277 (5)* 9.75 6.55

No. 2273 sold for 28p on day of issue. No. 2273 has a chalky covering over the coin that can be scratched away with a coin or other metal object to reveal a "heads" picture, showing a face composed of a planet, star and a crescent, or a "tails" picture, showing a shooting star. The chalky covering may, like earlier British chalky paper stamps, dissolve in any fluid.

No. 2273c will have both versions of the stamp. Vertical or horizontal pairs from No. 2273d will have both versions of the stamp. No. 2273d sold for £6.15.

Portions of the designs of Nos. 2275 and 2277 are printed with a thermochromic ink that changes color when warmed.

**Castles Type of 1955**

Miniature Sheet

**Litho. & Engr.**

**2005, Mar. 22 *Perf. 11x11¾***

**On Cream-Colored Paper**

**2278** Sheet of 4 10.00 10.00
*a.* A133 50p Carrickfergus (brown) 1.60 1.00
*b.* A133 50p Windsor (black) 1.60 1.00
*c.* A133 £1 Caernarfon (red) 3.25 2.00
*d.* A133 £1 Edinburgh (blue) 3.25 2.00
*e.* Booklet pane of 4 #2278b (BK197) 7.00 —

Issued: No. 2278e, 9/9/11. Stamps from No. 2278e have a pale yellow background.

Miniature Sheet

Wedding of Prince Charles and Camilla Parker Bowles — A584

No. 2279 — Couple: a, 30p, Prince wearing blue, red and green tie. b, 68p, Prince wearing vest.

**2005, Apr. 8 Litho. *Perf. 13½x14***

**2279** A584 Sheet, 2 each #a-b 8.50 8.50
*a.* 30p multi 1.75 .60
*b.* 68p multi 2.75 1.40

The marginal inscription states that the wedding took place on Apr. 8, but it was delayed until Apr. 9, due to Prince Charles's attendance at the Apr. 8 funeral of Pope John Paul II. Post offices were requested not to sell the stamps until Apr. 9, but first day covers have Apr. 8 cancels.

UNESCO World Heritage Sites in Great Britain and Australia
A585

Designs: No. 2280, Hadrian's Wall, England. No. 2281, Ayers Rock, Uluru-Kata Tjuta National Park, Australia. No. 2282, Stonehenge, England No. 2283, Wet Tropics of Queensland, Australia. No. 2284, Blenheim Palace, England. No. 2285, Greater Blue Mountains Area, Australia. No. 2286, Heart of Neolithic Orkney, Scotland. No. 2287, Purnululu National Park, Australia.

**2005, Apr. 21 *Perf. 14½***

**2280** A585 2nd multi .75 .45
**2281** A585 2nd multi .75 .45
*a.* Horiz. pair, #2280-2281 1.50 1.00
**2282** A585 1st multi 1.10 .60
**2283** A585 1st multi 1.10 .60
*a.* Horiz. pair, #2282-2283 2.25 1.50
**2284** A585 47p multi 1.50 1.10
**2285** A585 47p multi 1.50 1.10
*a.* Horiz. pair, #2284-2285 3.25 2.50
**2286** A585 68p multi 2.10 1.60
**2287** A585 68p multi 2.10 1.60
*a.* Horiz. pair, #2286-2287 4.25 3.25
*Nos. 2280-2287 (8)* 10.90 7.50

Nos. 2280 and 2281 each sold for 21p, and Nos. 2282 and 2283 each sold for 30p on day of issue.

See Australia Nos. 2369-2376.

Trooping the Color Ceremony
A586

Designs: 2nd, Soldier holding regimental flag. 1st, Queen Elizabeth II saluting. 42p, Bugler on horseback. 60p, Soldier holding scabbard. 68p, Queen on horseback. £1.12, Queen and soldier in phaeton.

**2005, June 7 Litho. *Perf. 14½***

**2288** A586 2nd multi .75 .45
**2289** A586 1st multi 1.10 .60
**2290** A586 42p multi 1.40 .95
**2291** A586 60p multi 1.90 1.40
**2292** A586 68p multi 2.10 1.40
**2293** A586 £1.12 multi 3.75 2.25
*a.* Souvenir sheet, #2288-2293 11.50 11.50
*Nos. 2288-2293 (6)* 11.00 7.05

Nos. 2288 and 2289 sold for 21p and 30p respectively on day of issue.

**St. Paul's Cathedral Type of 1995**

Souvenir Sheet

**2005, July 5 Photo. *Perf. 14½***

**2294** Sheet of 6, #2294a, 5 #MH287 5.75 5.75
*a.* A456 (1st) deep blue & silver 1.35 .50

No. 2294a issued 6/21/2005 and sold for 30p on day of issue. End of World War II, 60th anniv.

Motorcycles — A587

Designs: 1st, 1991 Norton F.1. 40p, 1969 BSA Rocket 3. 42p, 1949 Vincent Black Shadow. 47p, 1938 Triumph Speed Twin. 60p, 1930 Brough Superior. 68p, 1914 Royal Enfield.

**2005, July 19 Litho. *Perf. 13¾x14***

**2295** A587 1st multi 1.10 .60
**2296** A587 40p multi 1.30 .90
**2297** A587 42p multi 1.40 .95
**2298** A587 47p multi 1.50 1.10
**2299** A587 60p multi 1.90 1.40
**2300** A587 68p multi 2.10 1.60
*Nos. 2295-2300 (6)* 9.30 6.55

No. 2295 sold for 30p on day of issue.

Miniature Sheet

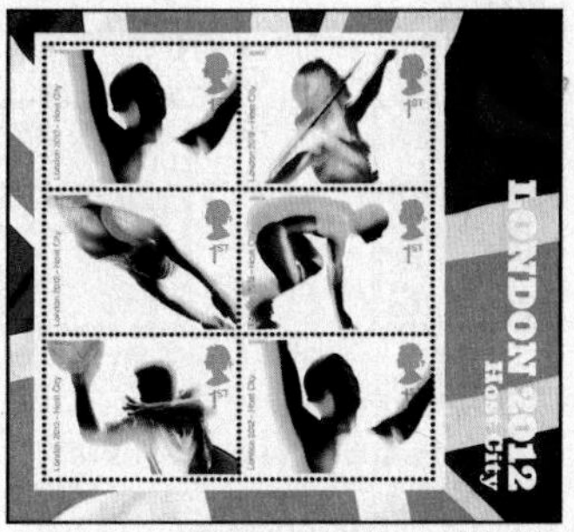


Selection of London as Host of 2012 Summer Olympics — A588

No. 2301: a, Javelin. b, Swimming. c, Sprinting. d, Basketball. e, Victorious athlete.

**2005, Aug. 5 *Perf. 14¼***

**2301** A588 Sheet of 6, #a-d, 2 #e 6.50 6.50
*a.-e.* 1st Any single 1.05 .55

Nos. 2301a-2301e each sold for 30p on day of issue. Compare with Type A467.

Changing Tastes in Britain — A589

Designs: 2nd, Woman with rice bowl and chopsticks. 1st, Woman with mug of tea. 42p, Man eating sushi. 47p, Woman with pasta bowl and wine glass. 60p, Woman with bag of French fries. 68p, Man with bowl of fruit.

**2005, Aug. 23 Photo. *Perf. 14½***

**2302** A589 2nd multi .75 .45
**2303** A589 1st multi 1.10 .60
**2304** A589 42p multi 1.40 1.00
**2305** A589 47p multi 1.50 1.10
**2306** A589 60p multi 1.90 1.40
**2307** A589 68p multi 2.10 1.60
*Nos. 2302-2307 (6)* 8.75 6.15

Europa (Nos. 2303, 2304). Nos. 2302 and 2303 sold for 21p and 30p respectively on day of issue.

Television Shows A590

Designs: 2nd, Inspector Morse. 1st, Emmerdale. 42p, Rising Damp. 47p, The Avengers. 60p, The South Bank Show. 68p, Who Wants To Be a Millionaire?

**2005, Sept. 15 Litho. *Perf. 14¼x14***

| | | | | |
|---|---|---|---|---|
| **2308** | A590 | 2nd multi | .75 | .45 |
| **2309** | A590 | 1st multi | 1.10 | .60 |
| *a.* | | Sheet of 20 + 20 labels | 27.00 | — |
| **2310** | A590 | 42p multi | 1.40 | .95 |
| **2311** | A590 | 47p multi | 1.50 | 1.10 |
| **2312** | A590 | 60p multi | 1.90 | 1.40 |
| **2313** | A590 | 68p multi | 2.10 | 1.60 |
| | | *Nos. 2308-2313 (6)* | 8.75 | 6.10 |

Independent Television, 50th anniv. Nos. 2308 and 2309 sold for 21p and 30p respectively on day of issue. No. 2309a sold for £6.65.

Labels on No. 2309a could be personalized for a fee.

Flower A591

Hello A592

Love — A593

Flag — A594

Teddy Bear — A595

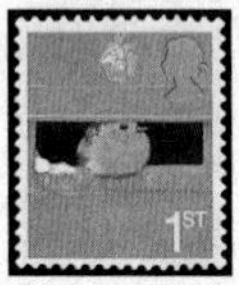


Bird — A596

***Serpentine Die Cut 14¾x14***

**2005, Oct. 4 Photo.**

**Self-Adhesive**

**Booklet Stamps**

| | | | | |
|---|---|---|---|---|
| **2314** | A591 | 1st multi | 2.00 | .75 |
| *a.* | | Sheet of 20 + 20 labels, litho. | 52.50 | — |
| **2315** | A592 | 1st multi | 2.00 | .75 |
| *a.* | | Sheet of 20 + 20 labels, litho. | 52.50 | — |
| **2316** | A593 | 1st multi | 2.00 | .75 |
| *a.* | | Sheet of 20 + 20 labels, litho. | 52.50 | — |
| **2317** | A594 | 1st multi | 2.00 | .75 |
| *a.* | | Sheet of 20 + 20 labels, litho. | 52.50 | — |
| **2318** | A595 | 1st multi | 2.00 | .75 |
| *a.* | | Sheet of 20 + 20 labels, litho. | 52.50 | — |
| **2319** | A596 | 1st multi | 2.00 | .75 |
| *a.* | | Booklet pane, #2314-2319 | 13.00 | |
| *b.* | | Sheet of 20 + 20 labels, litho. | 52.50 | — |
| *c.* | | Sheet, 4 each #2315-2316, 3 each #2314, 2317-2319, + 20 labels, litho. ('06) | 42.50 | |

Each stamp sold for 30p on day of issue.

Nos. 2314a-2318a, 2319b each sold for £14.95 and had labels that could be personalized.

No. 2319 issued 7/4/06. No. 2319c sold for £6.95.

See Nos. 2427, 2537-2538a, 2545, 2793.

Souvenir Sheet

Great Britain's Victory Over Australia in Ashes Cricket Test Match Series — A597

No. 2320: a, Players celebrating with trophy. b, Players celebrating. c, Batsman. d, Players in action.

**2005, Oct. 6 Litho. *Perf. 14¼x14***

| | | | | |
|---|---|---|---|---|
| **2320** | A597 | Sheet of 4 | 7.00 | 7.00 |
| *a.-b.* | | 1st Either single | 1.35 | .55 |
| *c.-d.* | | 68p Either single | 2.70 | 1.40 |

Nos. 2320a and 2320b each sold for 30p on day of issue.

Battle of Trafalgar, Bicent. — A598

Designs: No. 2321, Ships in battle. No. 2322, Wounded Admiral Horatio Nelson on deck of HMS Victory. No. 2323, Ship on fire. No. 2324, Ships in battle, diff. No. 2325, Columns of British ships. No. 2326, French and Spanish ships.

**2005, Oct. 18 Litho. *Perf. 14¾x14¼***

| | | | | |
|---|---|---|---|---|
| **2321** | A598 | 1st multi | 1.10 | .60 |
| **2322** | A598 | 1st multi | 1.10 | .60 |
| *a.* | | Horiz. pair, #2321-2322 | 2.25 | 1.40 |
| **2323** | A598 | 42p multi | 1.30 | .95 |
| **2324** | A598 | 42p multi | 1.30 | .95 |
| *a.* | | Horiz. pair, #2323-2324 | 2.75 | 2.00 |
| **2325** | A598 | 68p multi | 2.10 | 1.60 |
| *a.* | | Booklet pane, #2321, 2323, 2325 (BK178) | 5.25 | — |
| **2326** | A598 | 68p multi | 2.10 | 1.60 |
| *a.* | | Horiz. pair, #2325-2326 | 4.25 | 3.50 |
| *b.* | | Booklet pane, #2322, 2324, 2326 (BK178) | 5.75 | — |
| *c.* | | Souvenir sheet, #2321-2326 | 10.00 | 10.00 |
| | | *Nos. 2321-2326 (6)* | 9.00 | 6.30 |

Nos. 2321-2322 each sold for 30p on day of issue.

Christmas A599

Madonna and Child in artistic style of: 2nd, Haiti. 1st, Europe. 42p, Europe. 60p, Native Americans. 68p, India. £1.12, Australian Aborigines.

**2005, Nov. 1 Photo. *Perf. 14½x14***

| | | | | |
|---|---|---|---|---|
| **2327** | | Sheet of 6 | 10.50 | 10.50 |
| *a.* | | A599 2nd multi | .70 | .40 |
| *b.* | | A599 1st multi | 1.00 | .55 |
| *c.* | | A599 42p multi | 1.20 | .90 |
| *d.* | | A599 60p multi | 1.60 | 1.25 |
| *e.* | | A599 68p multi | 1.90 | 1.40 |
| *f.* | | A599 £1.12 multi | 3.25 | 2.00 |

**Self-Adhesive**

***Die Cut Perf. 14½x14***

| | | | | |
|---|---|---|---|---|
| **2328** | A599 | 2nd multi | .70 | .25 |
| *a.* | | Booklet pane of 24 | 17.00 | |
| **2329** | A599 | 1st multi | 1.00 | .25 |
| *a.* | | Booklet pane of 12 | 12.50 | |
| **2330** | A599 | 42p multi | 1.20 | 1.00 |
| **2331** | A599 | 60p multi | 1.60 | 1.40 |
| **2332** | A599 | 68p multi | 1.90 | 1.60 |
| **2333** | A599 | £1.12 multi | 3.25 | 2.25 |
| | | *Nos. 2328-2333 (6)* | 9.65 | 6.75 |

Nos. 2327a and 2328 each sold for 21p and Nos. 2327b and 2329 each sold for 30p on day of issue.

Animals From Children's Books — A600

Designs: No. 2334, Jeremy Fisher, from *The Tale of Mr. Jeremy Fisher,* by Beatrix Potter. No. 2335, Kipper, from *Kipper,* by Mick Inkpen. No. 2336, The Enormous Crocodile, from *The Enormous Crocodile,* by Roald Dahl. No. 2337, Paddington Bear, from *More About Paddington,* by Michael Bond. No. 2338, Boots, from *The Comic Adventures of Boots,* by Satoshi Kitamura. No. 2339, White Rabbit, from *Alice's Adventures in Wonderland,* by Lewis Carroll. No. 2340, The Very Hungry Caterpillar, from *The Very Hungry Caterpillar,* by Eric Carle. No. 2341, Maisy, from *Maisy's ABC,* by Lucy Cousins.

No. 2342, Like #2337.

**2006, Jan. 10 Litho. *Perf. 14½***

| | | | | |
|---|---|---|---|---|
| **2334** | A600 | 2nd multi | .80 | .45 |
| **2335** | A600 | 2nd multi | .80 | .45 |
| *a.* | | Horiz. pair, #2334-2335 | 1.60 | .95 |
| **2336** | A600 | 1st multi | 1.10 | .60 |
| **2337** | A600 | 1st multi | 1.10 | .60 |
| *a.* | | Horiz. pair, #2336-2337 | 2.25 | 1.40 |
| **2338** | A600 | 42p multi | 1.45 | .85 |
| **2339** | A600 | 42p multi | 1.45 | .85 |
| *a.* | | Horiz. pair, #2338-2339 | 3.00 | 1.75 |
| **2340** | A600 | 68p multi | 2.25 | 1.60 |
| **2341** | A600 | 68p multi | 2.25 | 1.60 |
| *a.* | | Horiz. pair, #2340-2341 | 4.50 | 3.25 |
| | | *Nos. 2334-2341 (8)* | 11.20 | 7.00 |

**Self-Adhesive**

***Serpentine Die Cut 14½***

| | | | | |
|---|---|---|---|---|
| **2342** | A600 | 1st multi + label | 2.25 | .75 |

Nos. 2334-2335 each sold for 21p, and Nos. 2336-2337 each sold for 30p on day of issue. No. 2340 has two die cut holes repesenting holes eaten by the caterpillar.

See United States Nos. 3987, 3990.

No. 2342 had a franking value of 30p on the day of issue, and was issued in sheets of 20 stamps + 20 different labels that sold for £6.55.

English Scenery A601

Designs: No. 2343, Carding Mill Valley, Shropshire. No. 2344, Beachy Head, Sussex coast. No. 2345, St. Paul's Cathedral, London. No. 2346, Brancastle, Norfolk coast. No. 2347, Derwent Edge, Peak District. No. 2348, Robin Hood's Bay, Yorkshire coast. No. 2349, Buttermere, Lake District. No. 2350, Chipping Campden, Cotswolds. No. 2351, St. Boniface Down, Isle of Wight. No. 2352, Chamberlain Square, Birmingham.

**2006, Feb. 7 Photo. *Perf. 14½***

| | | | | |
|---|---|---|---|---|
| **2343** | A601 | 1st multi | 1.10 | .60 |
| **2344** | A601 | 1st multi | 1.10 | .60 |
| **2345** | A601 | 1st multi | 1.10 | .60 |
| **2346** | A601 | 1st multi | 1.10 | .60 |
| **2347** | A601 | 1st multi | 1.10 | .60 |
| **2348** | A601 | 1st multi | 1.10 | .60 |
| **2349** | A601 | 1st multi | 1.10 | .60 |
| **2350** | A601 | 1st multi | 1.10 | .60 |
| **2351** | A601 | 1st multi | 1.10 | .60 |
| **2352** | A601 | 1st multi | 1.10 | .60 |
| *a.* | | Block of 10, #2343-2352 | 11.00 | 8.50 |
| | | *Nos. 2343-2352 (10)* | 11.00 | 6.00 |

Nos. 2343-2352 each sold for 30p on day of issue.

Isambard Kingdom Brunel (1806-1859), Engineer — A602

Engineering projects of Brunel: 1st, Royal Albert Bridge. 40p, Box Tunnel. 42p, Paddington Station. 47p, PSS Great Eastern. 60p, Clifton Suspension Bridge design. 68p, Maidenhead Bridge.

**2006, Feb. 23 Litho. *Perf. 14x13¼***

| | | | | |
|---|---|---|---|---|
| **2353** | A602 | 1st multi | 1.35 | .55 |
| **2354** | A602 | 40p multi | 1.60 | .80 |
| **2355** | A602 | 42p multi | 1.70 | .90 |
| **2356** | A602 | 47p multi | 1.90 | 1.00 |
| *a.* | | Booklet pane, #2356, 2 #2207b (BK179) | 7.25 | — |
| **2357** | A602 | 60p multi | 2.40 | 1.25 |
| *a.* | | Booklet pane, #2354, 2356, 2357 (BK179) | 6.00 | — |
| **2358** | A602 | 68p multi | 2.70 | 1.40 |
| *a.* | | Souvenir sheet, #2353-2358 | 12.00 | 7.50 |
| *b.* | | Booklet pane, #2353, 2355, 2358 (BK179) | 5.75 | — |
| | | *Nos. 2353-2358 (6)* | 11.65 | 5.90 |

No. 2353 sold for 30p on day of issue.

Ice Age Animals A603

Designs: 1st, Saber-tooth cat. 42p, Giant deer. 47p, Woolly rhinoceros. 68p, Woolly mammoth. £1.12, Cave bear.

***Perf. 14¼x14½***

**2006, Mar. 21 Litho.**

| | | | | |
|---|---|---|---|---|
| **2359** | A603 | 1st gray & blk | 1.35 | .55 |
| **2360** | A603 | 42p gray & blk | 1.70 | .90 |
| **2361** | A603 | 47p gray & blk | 1.90 | 1.00 |
| **2362** | A603 | 68p gray & blk | 2.70 | 1.40 |
| **2363** | A603 | £1.12 gray & blk | 4.50 | 2.00 |
| | | *Nos. 2359-2363 (5)* | 12.15 | 5.85 |

No. 2359 sold for 30p on day of issue.

Queen Elizabeth II, 80th Birthday A604

Queen: No. 2364, Wearing sunglasses, 1972. No. 2365, With horse, 1985. No. 2366, Wearing hat, 2001. No. 2367, As child, with mother, 1931. No. 2368, Wearing tiara, 1951. No. 2369, Wearing hat, 1960. No. 2370, As teenager, 1940. No. 2371, With Prince Philip, 1950.

**2006, Apr. 18 Photo. *Perf. 14¼x14***

| | | | | |
|---|---|---|---|---|
| **2364** | A604 | 2nd gray & blk | .80 | .45 |
| **2365** | A604 | 2nd gray & blk | .80 | .45 |
| *a.* | | Horiz. pair, #2364-2365 | 1.60 | 1.00 |
| **2366** | A604 | 1st gray & blk | 1.10 | .60 |
| **2367** | A604 | 1st gray & blk | 1.10 | .60 |
| *a.* | | Horiz. pair, #2366-2367 | 2.25 | 1.50 |
| **2368** | A604 | 44p gray & blk | 1.50 | 1.00 |
| **2369** | A604 | 44p gray & blk | 1.50 | 1.00 |
| *a.* | | Horiz. pair, #2368-2369 | 3.25 | 2.25 |
| **2370** | A604 | 72p gray & blk | 2.50 | 1.60 |
| **2371** | A604 | 72p gray & blk | 2.50 | 1.60 |
| *a.* | | Horiz. pair, #2370-2371 | 5.25 | 3.25 |
| | | *Nos. 2364-2371 (8)* | 11.80 | 7.30 |

On day of issue, Nos. 2364-2365 each sold of 23p; Nos. 2366-2367 each sold for 32p.

2006 World Cup Soccer Championships, Germany — A605

Globe, soccer player and flag from: 1st, England. 42p, Italy. 44p, Argentina. 50p, Germany. 64p, France. 72p, Brazil.

**2006, June 6 Litho. *Perf. 14½***

| | | | | |
|---|---|---|---|---|
| **2372** | A605 | 1st multi | 1.20 | .60 |
| *a.* | | Sheet of 20 + 20 labels | 27.00 | — |
| **2373** | A605 | 42p multi | 1.50 | .85 |
| **2374** | A605 | 44p multi | 1.60 | .90 |
| **2375** | A605 | 50p multi | 1.80 | 1.00 |
| **2376** | A605 | 64p multi | 2.25 | 1.25 |
| **2377** | A605 | 72p multi | 2.60 | 1.40 |
| | | *Nos. 2372-2377 (6)* | 10.95 | 6.00 |

No. 2372 sold for 32p on day of issue. No.2372a sold for £6.95.

Modern Architecture A606

Designs: 1st, 30 St. Mary Axe, London, designed by Sir Norman Foster. 42p, Maggie's Center, Dundee, designed by Frank Gehry. 44p, Selfridges, Birmingham, designed by

Future Systems. 50p, Downland Gridshell, Chichester, by Edward Cullinan. 64p, An Turas, Isle of Tiree, by Sutherland Hussey Architects. 72p, The Deep Hull, by Terry Farrell and Partners.

**2006, June 20** **Photo.**

| | | | | |
|---|---|---|---|---|
| **2378** | A606 | 1st multi | 1.35 | .60 |
| **2379** | A606 | 42p multi | 1.70 | .85 |
| **2380** | A606 | 44p multi | 1.75 | .90 |
| **2381** | A606 | 50p multi | 2.00 | 1.00 |
| **2382** | A606 | 64p multi | 2.50 | 1.40 |
| **2383** | A606 | 72p multi | 2.90 | 1.50 |
| | | *Nos. 2378-2383 (6)* | 12.20 | 6.25 |

No. 2378 sold for 32p on day of issue.

National Portrait Gallery, 150th Anniv. — A607

Famous Britons in art from National Portrait Gallery: No. 2384, Sir Winston Churchill, by Walter Sickert. No. 2385, Self-portrait of Sir Joshua Reynolds. No. 2386, T. S. Eliot, by Patrick Heron. No. 2387, Emmeline Pankhurst, by Georgina Brakenbury. No. 2388, Virginia Woolf, photograph by George Beresford. No. 2389, Sir Walter Scott, bust by Sir Francis Chantry. No. 2390, Mary Seacole, by Albert Challen. No. 2391, William Shakespeare, by John Taylor. No. 2392, Dame Cicely Saunders, by Catherine Goodman. No. 2393, Charles Darwin, by John Collier.

**2006, July 18** ***Perf. 14¼***

| | | | | |
|---|---|---|---|---|
| **2384** | A607 | 1st multi | 1.10 | .65 |
| **2385** | A607 | 1st multi | 1.10 | .65 |
| **2386** | A607 | 1st multi | 1.10 | .65 |
| **2387** | A607 | 1st multi | 1.10 | .65 |
| **2388** | A607 | 1st multi | 1.10 | .65 |
| **2389** | A607 | 1st multi | 1.10 | .65 |
| **2390** | A607 | 1st multi | 1.10 | .65 |
| **2391** | A607 | 1st multi | 1.10 | .65 |
| **2392** | A607 | 1st multi | 1.10 | .65 |
| **2393** | A607 | 1st multi | 1.10 | .65 |
| *a.* | | Block of 10, #2384-2393 | 11.00 | 7.50 |
| | | *Nos. 2384-2393 (10)* | 11.00 | 6.50 |

Nos. 2384-2393 each sold for 32p on day of issue.

Recipients of Victoria Cross A608

Designs: No. 2394, Corporal Agansing Rai. No. 2395, Boy Seaman First Class Jack Cornwell. No. 2396, Midshipman Charles Lucas. No. 2397, Captain Noel Chavasse. No. 2398, Captain Albert Ball. No. 2399, Captain Charles Upham.

**2006, Sept. 21** **Litho.** ***Perf. 14¼x14***

| | | | | |
|---|---|---|---|---|
| **2394** | A608 | 1st multi | 1.35 | .60 |
| **2395** | A608 | 1st multi | 1.35 | .60 |
| *a.* | | Horiz. pair, #2394-2395 | 2.70 | 1.50 |
| **2396** | A608 | 64p multi | 2.50 | 1.40 |
| **2397** | A608 | 64p multi | 2.50 | 1.40 |
| *a.* | | Horiz. pair, #2396-2397 | 5.00 | 3.25 |
| **2398** | A608 | 72p multi | 2.90 | 1.00 |
| *a.* | | Booklet pane, #2394, 2396, 2398 (BK180) | 6.75 | — |
| **2399** | A608 | 72p multi | 2.90 | 1.50 |
| *a.* | | Horiz. pair, #2398-2399 | 5.75 | 3.75 |
| *b.* | | Booklet pane #2395, 2397, 2399 (BK180) | 6.75 | — |
| *c.* | | Souvenir sheet, #1331a, 2394-2399 | 20.00 | 8.00 |
| | | *Nos. 2394-2399 (6)* | 13.50 | 6.50 |

Nos. 2394-2395 each sold for 32p on day of issue.

Musicians and Dancers A609

Designs: 1st, Sitar player and dancer. 42p, Guitarist and drummer. 50p, Violinist and harpist. 72p, Saxophone player and guitarist. £1.19, Maracas player and dancers.

**2006, Oct. 3** ***Perf. 14¼x14½***

| | | | | |
|---|---|---|---|---|
| **2400** | A609 | 1st multi | 1.35 | .60 |
| **2401** | A609 | 42p multi | 1.70 | .90 |
| **2402** | A609 | 50p multi | 2.00 | 1.05 |
| **2403** | A609 | 72p multi | 2.90 | 1.50 |
| **2404** | A609 | £1.19 multi | 4.75 | 2.25 |
| | | *Nos. 2400-2404 (5)* | 12.70 | 6.30 |

Europa (No. 2402).

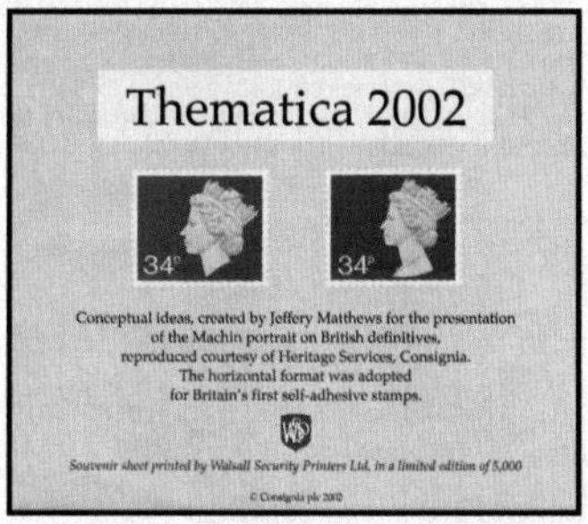


The gummed souvenir sheets shown above, created for the 2002 and 2006 Thematica stamp shows, contain invalid imperforate stamps with simulated perforations that were never issued by Royal Mail. The stamps on these sheets have no obliterators.

The gummed 2005 Thematica sheet reproduces reduced versions of Nos. 440, 441, 683, 1040 and 1796. These reproduced images lack obliterators, and are also invalid for postage.

Gummed Thematica sheets for other years exist, each showing reproductions of other stamps with obliterations to invalidate the images.

"New Baby" A610

"Best Wishes" A611

"Thank You" A612

Balloons A613

Fireworks A614

Flowers, Butterflies and Champagne Bottle A615

***Die Cut Perf. 14¾x14¼***

**2006, Oct. 17** **Photo.**

**Self-Adhesive**

| | | | | |
|---|---|---|---|---|
| **2405** | A610 | 1st multi | 1.50 | .80 |
| **2406** | A611 | 1st multi | 1.50 | .80 |
| **2407** | A612 | 1st multi | 1.50 | .80 |
| **2408** | A613 | 1st multi | 1.50 | .80 |
| **2409** | A614 | 1st multi | 1.50 | .80 |
| **2410** | A615 | 1st multi | 1.50 | .80 |
| *a.* | | Booklet pane, #2405-2410 | 10.00 | |
| *b.* | | Sheet, 3 each #2406-2409, 4 each #2405, 2410 + 20 labels, litho. | 32.50 | |
| | | *Nos. 2405-2410 (6)* | 9.00 | 4.80 |

Nos. 2405-2410 each sold for 32p on day of issue. No. 2410b sold for £6.95.

See Nos. 2546-2548, 2794.

Christmas

A616 A617

Designs: Nos. 2411a, 2411c, 2412, 2414, Snowman. Nos. 2411b, 2411d, 2413, 2415, Santa Claus. Nos. 2411e, 2416, Reindeer. Nos. 2411f, 2417, Christmas tree.

**2006, Nov. 7** **Photo.** ***Perf. 14¾x14***

| | | | | |
|---|---|---|---|---|
| **2411** | | Sheet of 6 | 13.00 | 6.50 |
| *a.* | A616 | 2nd multi | .95 | .45 |
| *b.* | A616 | 1st multi | 1.35 | .60 |
| *c.* | A617 | 2nd Large multi | 1.50 | .80 |
| *d.* | A617 | 1st Large multi | 1.75 | .90 |
| *e.* | A616 | 72p multi | 2.90 | 1.50 |
| *f.* | A616 | £1.19 multi | 4.75 | 2.40 |

**Self-Adhesive**

***Die Cut Perf. 14¾x14***

| | | | | |
|---|---|---|---|---|
| **2412** | A616 | 2nd multi | .95 | .25 |
| *a.* | | Booklet pane of 12 | 11.50 | |
| **2413** | A616 | 1st multi | 1.35 | .25 |
| *a.* | | Booklet pane of 12 | 16.00 | |
| *b.* | | Sheet, 10 each #2412-2413, + 20 labels, litho. | 24.00 | — |
| **2414** | A617 | 2nd Large multi | 1.50 | .80 |
| **2415** | A617 | 1st Large multi | 1.75 | .90 |
| **2416** | A616 | 72p multi | 2.90 | 1.50 |
| **2417** | A616 | £1.19 multi | 4.75 | 2.40 |
| | | *Nos. 2412-2417 (6)* | 13.20 | 6.10 |

On day of issue, Nos. 2411a and 2412 each sold for 23p, Nos. 2411b and 2413 each sold for 32p, Nos. 2411c and 2414 each sold for 37p, and Nos. 2411d and 2415 each sold for 44p. No. 2413b sold for £6.

Souvenir Sheet

Battle of the Somme, 90th Anniv. — A618

***Perf. 14½x14¼ (#2418a), 14¾x14 Syncopated***

**2006, Nov. 9** **Photo.**

| | | | | |
|---|---|---|---|---|
| **2418** | A618 | Sheet of 5 | 13.00 | 6.50 |
| *a.* | | 1st Poppies | 1.35 | .60 |
| *b.* | | Sheet of 20 #2418a + 20 labels, litho. | 27.50 | — |
| *c.* | | Single stamp, litho. (#2614b) ('08) | 1.10 | .55 |

No. 2418 contains #2418a, England #13, Northern Ireland #24, Scotland #27 and Wales & Monmouthshire #27. No. 2418a sold for 32p on day of issue. No. 2418b sold for £6.95.

No. 2418c issued 11/6/08. It sold for 36p on day of issue.

Souvenir Sheet

Heritage of Scotland — A619

No. 2419: a, National flag (Scotland type A5). b, St. Andrew (58x22mm). c, Edinburgh Castle (58x22mm).

***Perf. 14¾x14 Syncopated, 14¾x14 (#2419b, 2419c)***

**2006, Nov. 30** **Photo.**

| | | | | |
|---|---|---|---|---|
| **2419** | A619 | Sheet of 4, #2419a-2419c, Scotland #21 | 9.50 | 6.50 |
| *a.* | | 1st multi | 1.50 | .75 |
| *b.-c.* | | 72p Either single | 3.25 | 1.75 |

No. 2419a sold for 32p on day of issue.

Beatles Memorabilia — A620

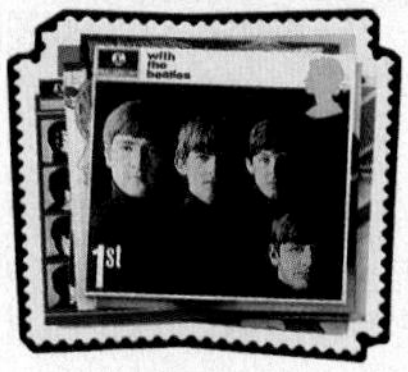


Beatles Album Covers A621

No. 2420: a, Toy guitar, button. b, Lunch box, buttons. c, 45RPM record of "Love Me Do." d, Tray picturing the Beatles, buttons.

No. 2421, "With The Beatles." No. 2422, "Sgt. Pepper's Lonely Hearts Club Band." No. 2423, "Help!" No. 2424, "Abbey Road." No. 2425, "Let It Be." No. 2426, "Revolver."

**2007, Jan. 9** **Litho.** ***Perf. 14***

| | | | | |
|---|---|---|---|---|
| **2420** | A620 | Sheet of 4 | 5.00 | 3.00 |
| *a.-d.* | | 1st Any single | 1.25 | .60 |

**Self-Adhesive**

**Photo.**

***Die Cut Perf. 13x13¾***

| | | | | |
|---|---|---|---|---|
| **2421** | A621 | 1st multi | 1.20 | .65 |
| **2422** | A621 | 1st multi | 1.20 | .65 |
| **2423** | A621 | 64p multi | 2.25 | 1.40 |
| **2424** | A621 | 64p multi | 2.25 | 1.40 |
| **2425** | A621 | 72p multi | 2.75 | 1.75 |
| **2426** | A621 | 72p multi | 2.75 | 1.75 |
| | | *Nos. 2421-2426 (6)* | 12.40 | 7.60 |

Nos. 2420a-2420d, 2421-2422 each sold for 32p on day of issue.

**Love Type of 2005**

***Serpentine Die Cut 14¾x14 Syncopated***

**2007-08** **Photo.**

**Self-Adhesive**

**Booklet Stamp**

| | | | | |
|---|---|---|---|---|
| **2427** | A593 | 1st multi | 10.00 | .65 |
| *a.* | | Booklet pane, #2427, 5 #MH380 | 15.00 | |
| *b.* | | Booklet pane, 2 #2427, 4 #MH300 + 3 labels | 8.25 | |
| *c.* | | As #2427, litho. (from 2538a) | 1.50 | 1.50 |

No. 2427 sold for 32p on day of issue. Compare with No. 2316 which is not syncopated.

Issued: Nos. 2427, 2427a, 1/16/07. Nos. 2427b, 2427c, 1/15/08.

No. 2427c had a franking value of 34p on day of issue.

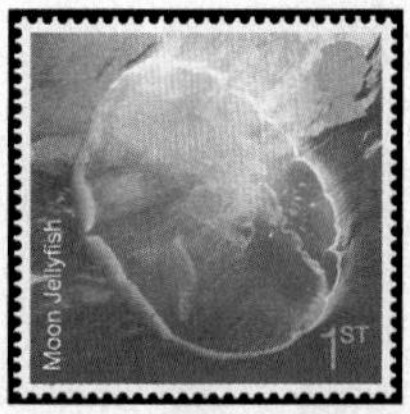


Marine Life — A622

Designs: No. 2428, Moon jellyfish. No. 2429, Common starfish. No. 2430, Beadlet anemone. No. 2431, Bass. No. 2432, Thornback ray. No. 2433, Lesser octopus. No. 2434, Common mussels. No. 2435, Gray seal. No. 2436, Shore crab. No. 2437, Common sun star.

**2007, Feb. 1** **Litho.** ***Perf. 14½***

| | | | | |
|---|---|---|---|---|
| **2428** | A622 | 1st multi | 1.10 | .65 |
| **2429** | A622 | 1st multi | 1.10 | .65 |
| **2430** | A622 | 1st multi | 1.10 | .65 |
| **2431** | A622 | 1st multi | 1.10 | .65 |

**2432** A622 1st multi 1.10 .65
**2433** A622 1st multi 1.10 .65
**2434** A622 1st multi 1.10 .65
**2435** A622 1st multi 1.10 .65
**2436** A622 1st multi 1.10 .65
**2437** A622 1st multi 1.10 .65
*a.* Block of 10, #2428-2437 11.00 6.50

Nos. 2428-2437 each sold for 32p on day of issue.

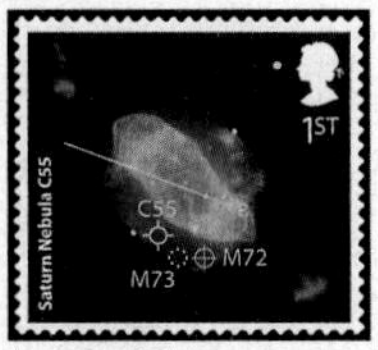

Astronomical Objects — A623

Designs: No. 2438, Saturn Nebula (C55). No. 2439, Eskimo Nebula (C39). No. 2440, Cat's Eye Nebula (C6). No. 2441, Helix Nebula (C63). No. 2442, Flaming Star Nebula (C31). No. 2443, Spindle Galaxy (C53).

***Serpentine Die Cut 14¼x14***

**2007, Feb. 13 Photo.**
**2438** A623 1st multi 1.20 .70
**2439** A623 1st multi 1.20 .70
**2440** A623 50p multi 1.80 1.10
**2441** A623 50p multi 1.80 1.10
**2442** A623 72p multi 2.75 1.60
**2443** A623 72p multi 2.75 1.60
*Nos. 2438-2443 (6)* 11.50 6.80

Nos. 2438-2439 each sold for 32p on day of issue.

World of Invention A624

Designs: Nos. 2444, 2450, Man thinking about bridge. Nos. 2445, 2451, Locomotive and tracks. Nos. 2446, 2452, People using telephones, maps of Great Britain, Ireland and Australia. Nos. 2447, 2453, Television camera, man with microphone, man watching television. Nos. 2448, 2454, Man at computer with cord in large ball. Nos. 2449, 2455, Man and woman travelers on cratered planet.

**2007, Mar. 1 Photo. *Perf. 14½x14***
**2444** A624 1st multi 1.75 .65
**2445** A624 1st multi 1.75 .65
**2446** A624 64p multi 3.00 1.40
**2447** A624 64p multi 3.00 1.40
*a.* Booklet pane, #2444-2447 (BK181) 9.75 —
**2448** A624 72p multi 5.00 2.00
**2449** A624 72p multi 5.00 2.00
*a.* Souvenir sheet, #2444-2449 19.50 10.00
*b.* Booklet pane, #2444-2445, 2448-2449 11.00 —
*Nos. 2444-2449 (6)* 19.50 8.10

**Self-Adhesive**

***Die Cut Perf. 14½x14***
**2450** A624 1st multi 1.35 .60
**2451** A624 1st multi 1.35 .60
**2452** A624 64p multi 2.50 1.25
**2453** A624 64p multi 2.50 1.25
**2454** A624 72p multi 3.00 1.50
**2455** A624 72p multi 3.00 1.50
*Nos. 2450-2455 (6)* 13.70 6.70

Nos. 2444-2445, 2450-2451 each sold for 32p on day of issue.

Abolition of the Slave Trade, Bicent. — A625

Designs: No. 2456, William Wilberforce (1759-1833), abolitionist leader in Parliament, and poster. No. 2457, Olaudah Equiano (c. 1750-97), freed slave and abolitionist writer, and map. No. 2458, Granville Sharp (1735-1813), abolitionist, and ship. No. 2459, Thomas Clarkson (1760-1846), abolitionist and diagram of slaves in slave ship. No. 2460, Hannah More (1745-1833), religious writer, and illustration from Cheap Repository Tracts. No. 2461, Ignatius Sancho (c. 1729-80), abolitionist and actor, poster for performance by Sancho.

**2007, Mar. 22 Litho. *Perf. 14¼***
**2456** A625 1st multi 1.25 .60
**2457** A625 1st multi 1.25 .60
*a.* Horiz. pair, #2456-2457 2.50 1.20
**2458** A625 50p multi 2.00 1.00
**2459** A625 50p multi 2.00 1.00
*a.* Horiz. pair, #2458-2459 4.00 2.00
**2460** A625 72p multi 3.00 1.50
**2461** A625 72p multi 3.00 1.50
*a.* Horiz. pair, #2460-2461 6.00 3.00
*Nos. 2456-2461 (6)* 12.50 6.20

Nos. 2456-2457 each sold for 32p on day of issue.

Souvenir Sheet

Heritage of England — A626

No. 2462: a, English flag (18x22mm). b, St. George slaying dragon (59x22mm). c, Parliament (59x22mm).

***Perf. 14 Syncopated, 14¾x14 (#2462b, 2642c)***

**2007, Apr. 23 Photo.**
**2462** A626 Sheet of 4, #2462a-2462c, England #7 9.00 4.50
*a.* 1st multi 1.40 .70
*b.-c.* 78p Either single 3.00 1.50

On day of issue, No. 2462a and England No. 7 sold for 34p.

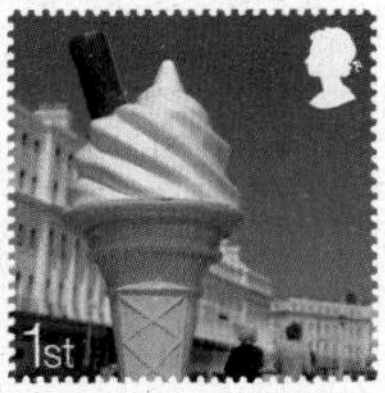

Seaside Resort Scenes A627

Designs: 1st, Giant ice cream cone. 46p, Sand castle. 48p, Carousel horses. 54p, Beach cabins. 69p, Beach chairs. 78p, Hitched donkeys.

**2007, May 15 Photo. *Perf. 14½***
**2463** A627 1st multi 1.40 .70
**2464** A627 46p multi 1.90 .95
**2465** A627 48p multi 2.00 1.00
**2466** A627 54p multi 2.10 1.10
**2467** A627 69p multi 2.75 1.40
**2468** A627 78p multi 3.25 1.60
*Nos. 2463-2468 (6)* 13.40 6.75

No. 2463 sold for 34p on day of issue.
See No. 2573.

Crowned Lion of England — A628

**2007, May 17 Litho. *Perf. 14½x14¼***
**2469** A628 1st gray bl & dk red + label 2.25 2.25

**Souvenir Sheet**

**Photo.**
**2470** Sheet, #2470a, 2 each England #6, 15 + label 9.50 9.50
*a.* A628 1st bl grn & brt red 1.40 .70

No. 2469 was issued in sheets of 20 stamps + 20 labels that sold for £7.35. No. 2470 sold for £2.38 on day of issue. Nos. 2469 and 2470 each had a franking value of 34p on day of issue.

Souvenir Sheet

Definitive Stamps Designed by Arnold Machin, 40th Anniv. — A629

Design: No. 2472, Arnold Machin.

***Perf. 14½x14¼ (#2471a-2471b, 2472)***
**Photo. & Embossed (#2471a-2471b)**

**2007, June 5**
**2471** A629 Sheet, #2471a, 2471b, MH237, MH373 11.50 11.50
*a.* 1st Arnold Machin 1.40 .70
*b.* 1st #MH6 1.40 .70
*c.* Booklet pane, 2 each #2471a, 2471b (BK182) 5.75 —

**Photo.**
**2472** A629 1stnulti + label 1.50 .75

Nos. 2471a and 2471b each sold for 34p on day of issue and were only issued in the souvenir sheet and the booklet pane.

No. 2472, having a franking value of 34p on day of issue, was issued only in sheets of 20 stamps + 20 labels. The sheets sold for £7.35.

Grand Prix Race Cars and Drivers A630

Designs: No. 2473, 1957 Vanwall 2.5-liter, Stirling Moss. No. 2474, 1962 BRM P57, Graham Hill. No. 2475, 1963 Lotus 25 Climax, Jim Clark. No. 2476, 1973 Tyrrell 006/2, Jackie Stewart. No. 2477, 1976 McLaren M23, James Hunt. No. 2478, 1986 Williams FW11, Nigel Mansell.

**2007, July 3 Litho. *Perf. 14¼x14***
**2473** A630 1st multi 1.25 .75
**2474** A630 1st multi 1.25 .75
**2475** A630 54p multi 2.00 1.25
**2476** A630 54p multi 2.00 1.25
**2477** A630 78p multi 3.00 1.75
**2478** A630 78p multi 3.00 1.75
*Nos. 2473-2478 (6)* 12.50 7.50

Nos. 2473 and 2474 each sold for 34p on day of issue.

Publication of Last Harry Potter Novel by J. K. Rowling A631

Coats of Arms From Harry Potter Novels A632

Novels: No. 2479, Harry Potter and the Philosopher's Stone. No. 2480, Harry Potter and the Chamber of Secrets. No. 2481, Harry Potter and the Prisoner of Azkaban. No. 2482, Harry Potter and the Goblet of Fire. No. 2483, Harry Potter and the Order of the Phoenix. No. 2484, Harry Potter and the Half-Blood Prince. No. 2485, Harry Potter and the Deathly Hallows.

Arms of: Nos. 2486a, 2487, Gryffindor. Nos. 2486b, 2488, Hufflepuff. Nos. 2486c, 2489, Hogwarts. Nos. 2486d, 2490, Ravenclaw. Nos. 2486e, 2491, Slytherin.

**2007, July 17 *Perf. 14x14¼***
**2479** A631 1st multi 1.40 .70
**2480** A631 1st multi 1.40 .70
**2481** A631 1st multi 1.40 .70
**2482** A631 1st multi 1.40 .70
**2483** A631 1st multi 1.40 .70
**2484** A631 1st multi 1.40 .70
**2485** A631 1st multi 1.40 .70
*a.* Horiz. strip of 7, #2479-2485 9.80 4.90

**Souvenir Sheet**

***Perf. 14¾x14***
**2486** Sheet of 5 7.00 7.00
*a.-e.* A632 1st Any single 1.40 .70

**Self-Adhesive**

***Die Cut Perf. 14¾x14***
**2487** A632 1st multi + label 2.00 2.00
**2488** A632 1st multi + label 2.00 2.00
**2489** A632 1st multi + label 2.00 2.00
**2490** A632 1st multi + label 2.00 2.00
**2491** A632 1st multi + label 2.00 2.00
*a.* Vert. strip of 5, #2487-2491, + 5 labels 11.00
*Nos. 2487-2491 (5)* 10.00 10.00

Nos. 2479-2485, 2486a-2486e, each sold for 34p on day of issue. Nos. 2487-2491, having a franking value of 34p on day of issue, were sold in a sheet of 20 stamps + 20 labels that sold for £7.35. Labels could be personalized for an extra fee.

Scouting, Cent. A633

Designs: 1st, Scouts around campfire, Scout looking at sky. 46p, Scouts climbing rocks. 48p, Scout planting tree. 54p, Scout learning archery from volunteer. 69p, Scouts and glider. 78p, Nine Scouts.

**2007, July 26 *Perf. 14¼x14***
**2492** A633 1st multi 1.25 .75
**2493** A633 46p multi 1.75 1.05
**2494** A633 48p multi 1.80 1.10
**2495** A633 54p multi 2.00 1.25
**2496** A633 69p multi 2.50 1.50
**2497** A633 78p multi 3.00 1.75
*Nos. 2492-2497 (6)* 12.30 7.40

Europa (Nos. 2492, 2494). No. 2492 sold for 34p on day of issue.

Endangered Birds — A634

**2007, Sept. 4 Litho. *Perf. 14½***
**2498** A634 1st White-tailed eagle 1.25 .80
**2499** A634 1st Bearded tit 1.25 .80
**2500** A634 1st Red kite 1.25 .80
**2501** A634 1st Cirl bunting 1.25 .80
**2502** A634 1st Marsh harrier 1.25 .80
**2503** A634 1st Avocet 1.25 .80
**2504** A634 1st Bittern 1.25 .80
**2505** A634 1st Dartford warbler 1.25 .80
**2506** A634 1st Corncrake 1.25 .80
**2507** A634 1st Peregrine falcon 1.25 .80
*a.* Block of 10, #2498-2507 12.50 8.75

Nos. 2498-2507 each sold for 34p on day of issue.

British Army Uniforms — A635

Designs: No. 2508, Non-commissioned officer, Royal Military Police, 1999. No. 2509, Tank commander, 5th Royal Tank Regiment, 1944. No. 2510, Observer, Royal Field Artillery, 1917. No. 2511, Rifleman, 95th Rifles, 1813. No. 2512, Grenadier, Royal Regiment of Foot of Ireland, 1704. No. 2513, Trooper, Earl of Oxford's Horse, 1661.

**2007, Sept. 20 Litho. *Perf. 14¼***
**2508** A635 1st multi 1.40 .70
**2509** A635 1st multi 1.40 .70
**2510** A635 1st multi 1.40 .70
*a.* Horiz. strip of 3, #2508-2510 4.20 2.10
*b.* Booklet pane of 3, #2508-2510 (BK183) 4.20 —
**2511** A635 78p multi 3.25 1.60
**2512** A635 78p multi 3.25 1.60

**2513** A635 78p multi 3.25 1.60
*a.* Horiz. strip of 3, #2511-2513 9.75 4.80
*b.* Booklet pane of 3, #2511-2513 (BK183) 9.75 —
*Nos. 2508-2513 (6)* 13.95 6.90

Nos. 2508-2510 each sold for 34p on day of sale.

Wedding of Queen Elizabeth II and Prince Philip, 60th Anniv. A636

Royal Family — A637

Various photographs of couple from: No. 2514, 2006. No. 2515, 1997. No. 2516, 1980. No. 2517, 1969. No. 2518, 1961. No. 2519, 1947.

No. 2520: a, Royal family, log and flowers (35x35mm). b, Queen Elizabeth II and Prince Philip (40x30mm). c, Royal family, baby carriage (41x30mm). d, Queen Elizabeth II, Prince Philip, Princess Anne and Prince Charles (27x38mm).

**2007, Oct. 26 Litho.** ***Perf. 14¼x14***

**2514** A636 1st black 1.40 .70
**2515** A636 1st black 1.40 .70
*a.* Horiz. pair, #2514-2515 2.80 1.40
**2516** A636 54p black 2.25 1.10
**2517** A636 54p black 2.25 1.10
*a.* Horiz. pair, #2516-2517 4.50 2.10
**2518** A636 78p black 3.25 1.60
**2519** A636 78p black 3.25 1.60
*a.* Horiz. pair, #2518-2519 6.50 3.20
*Nos. 2514-2519 (6)* 13.80 6.80

**Souvenir Sheet**

**Self-Adhesive**

**2520** A637 Sheet of 4 9.00
*a.* 1st multi, die cut perf. 14½ 1.40 .70
*b.* 1st multi, die cut perf. 14½x14¼ 1.40 .70
*c.* 69p multi, die cut perf. 14¼x14 2.75 1.40
*d.* 78p multi, die cut perf. 14¼ 3.25 1.60

Nos. 2514-2515, 2520a and 2520b each sold for 34p on day of sale.

Madonna and Child, by William Dyce A638

Madonna of Humility, by Lippo di Dalmasio A639

***Die Cut Perf. 14¾x14 Syncopated***

**2007, Nov. 6 Photo.**

**Self-Adhesive**

**2521** A638 2nd multi 1.00 .50
**2522** A639 1st multi 1.50 .75

On day of issue, No. 2521 sold for 24p; No. 2522 for 34p.

Christmas

A640 A641

Angels with banners inscribed: Nos. 2523a, 2523c, 2524, 2526, Peace. Nos. 2523b, 2523d, 2525, 2527, Goodwill. Nos. 2523e, 2528, Joy. Nos. 2523f, 2529, Glory.

**2007, Nov. 6 Photo.** ***Perf. 14¾x14***

**2523** Sheet of 6 15.00 15.00
*a.* A640 2nd multi 1.00 .50
*b.* A640 1st multi 1.50 .75
*c.* A641 2nd Large multi 1.75 .85
*d.* A641 1st Large multi 2.00 1.00
*e.* A640 78p multi 3.25 1.60
*f.* A640 £1.24 multi 5.25 2.60

**Self-Adhesive**

***Die Cut Perf. 14¾x14***

**2524** A640 2nd multi 1.00 .50
*a.* Booklet pane of 12 12.00
*b.* Sheet of 20 + 20 labels, litho. 35.00
**2525** A640 1st multi 1.50 .75
*a.* Booklet pane of 12 18.00
*b.* Sheet of 20 + 20 labels, litho. 57.50
**2526** A641 2nd Large multi 1.75 .85
**2527** A641 1st Large multi 2.00 1.00
**2528** A640 78p multi 3.25 1.60
*a.* Sheet, 8 each #2524-2525, 4 #2528, + 20 labels, litho. 35.00
*b.* Sheet of 10 + 10 labels, litho. 57.50
**2529** A640 £1.24 multi 5.25 2.60
*Nos. 2524-2529 (6)* 14.75 7.30

On day of issue, Nos. 2523a and 2524 sold for 24p, Nos. 2523b and 2425 sold for 34p, Nos. 2523c and 2426 sold for 40p, and Nos. 2523d and 2427 sold for 48p. No. 2528a sold for £8.30. No. 2524b sold for £8.50, Nos. 2525b and 2528b each sold for £13.50. Labels on Nos. 2524b, 2525b, and 2528b were personalizable.

Poppy and Soldiers A642

**2007, Nov. 8 Litho.** ***Perf. 14½x14¼***

**2530** A642 1st multi 2.25 .90
*a.* Souvenir sheet of 5 14.50 14.50

Battle of Passchendaele, 90th anniv. No. 2530a contains #2530, England #15, Northern Ireland #26, Scotland #29, and Wales & Monmouthshire #30. No. 2530 was also printed in a sheet of 20 + 5 labels that sold for £7.35, and a limited-quantity privately-contracted sheet of 10 + 10 labels, that sold for £28.50.

Book Covers of James Bond Novels by Ian Fleming — A643

Designs: No. 2531, Casino Royale. No. 2532, Doctor No. No. 2533, Goldfinger. No. 2534, Diamonds Are Forever. No. 2535, For Your Eyes Only. No. 2536, From Russia, with Love.

**2008, Jan. 8 Litho.** ***Perf. 14¾x14¼***

**2531** A643 1st multi 1.25 .80
**2532** A643 1st multi 1.25 .80
**2533** A643 54p multi 2.00 1.25
**2534** A643 54p multi 2.00 1.25
**2535** A643 78p multi 3.00 1.75
*a.* Booklet pane of 3, #2531, 2533, 2535 (BK184) 6.75 —
**2536** A643 78p multi 3.00 1.75
*a.* Miniature sheet of 6, #2531-2536 13.50 13.50
*b.* Booklet pane of 3, #2532, 2534, 2536 (BK184) 6.75 —
*Nos. 2531-2536 (6)* 12.50 7.60

On day of issue, Nos. 2531-2532 each sold for 34p.

**Hello and Flag Types of 2005**

***Die Cut Perf 14¾x14 Syncopated***

**2008, Jan. 15 Litho.**

**Self-Adhesive**

**2537** A592 1st Hello 1.50 1.50
*a.* Sheet of 20 + 20 labels 25.00

Issued: No. 2537a, 5/8/10. No. 2537a sold for £8.50. Labels could not be personalized.

**2538** A594 1st Flag 1.50 1.50
*a.* Sheet, 8 #2427c, 6 each #2537-2538, + 20 labels 30.00

No. 2538a sold for £7.35. Nos. 2537-2538 each had a franking value of 34p on day of issue.

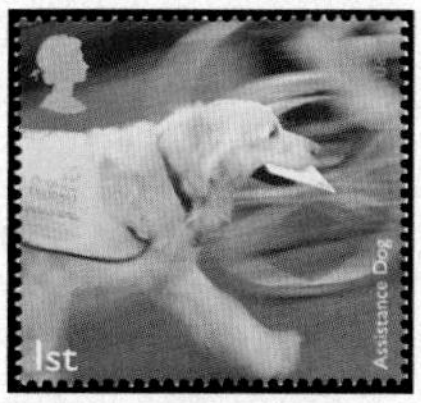


Working Dogs — A644

Designs: 1st, Assistance dog. 46p, Mountain rescue dog. 48p, Police dog. 54p, Customs dog. 69p, Sheepdog. 78p, Guide dog.

**2008, Feb. 5 Litho.** ***Perf. 14¼x14½***

**2539** A644 1st multi 1.25 .80
**2540** A644 46p multi 1.60 1.00
**2541** A644 48p multi 1.75 1.05
**2542** A644 54p multi 1.90 1.25
**2543** A644 69p multi 2.50 1.50
**2544** A644 78p multi 3.00 1.75
*Nos. 2539-2544 (6)* 12.00 7.35

No. 2539 sold for 34p on day of issue. Europa (No. 2539).

**Types of 2005-06**

***Die Cut Perf. 14¾x14 Syncopated***

**2008, Feb. 28 Litho.**

**Booklet Stamps**

**Self-Adhesive**

**2545** A591 1st multi 1.40 .70
**2546** A613 1st multi 1.40 .70
**2547** A614 1st multi 1.40 .70
*a.* Sheet of 20 + 20 labels 37.50
**2548** A615 1st multi 1.40 .70
*a.* Booklet pane of 6, #2537-2538, 2545-2548 8.50

On day of issue, Nos. 2545-2548 each sold for 34p.

Issued: No. 2547a, 1/20/12. No. 2547a sold for £11.47. Labels could not be personalized.

British Royalty and History — A645

Designs: No. 2549, King Henry IV. No. 2550, King Henry V. No. 2551, King Henry VI. No. 2552, King Edward IV. No. 2553, King Edward V. No. 2554, King Richard III.

No. 2555: a, Owen Glendower (Owain Glyn Dwr), Welsh rebel. b, Battle of Agincourt. c, Battle of Tewkesbury. d, William Caxton, first English printer.

**2008, Feb. 28 Litho.** ***Perf. 14¼***

**2549** A645 1st multi 1.25 .80
**2550** A645 1st multi 1.25 .80
**2551** A645 54p multi 2.00 1.25
**2552** A645 54p multi 2.00 1.25
**2553** A645 69p multi 2.50 1.50
**2554** A645 69p multi 2.50 1.50
*Nos. 2549-2554 (6)* 11.50 7.10

**Souvenir Sheet**

**2555** Sheet of 4 6.50 6.50
*a.-b.* A645 1st Either single 1.40 .70
*c.-d.* A645 78p Either single 3.25 1.60

On day of issue, Nos. 2549, 2550, 2555a and 2555b each sold for 34p.

See Nos. 2653-2659, 2767-2774, 2807-2814, 2940-2946, 2990-2995.

Souvenir Sheet

Heritage of Northern Ireland — A646

No. 2556: a, Carrickfergus Castle (18x21mm). b, Giant's Causeway, ocean and sky (18x21mm). c, St. Patrick (57x21mm). d, Queen's Bridge and Friendship Beacon, Belfast (57x21mm).

***Perf. 14¾x14¼ Syncopated, 14¾x14¼ (78p)***

**2008, Mar. 11 Litho.**

**2556** A646 Sheet of 4 8.00 8.00
*a.-b.* 1st Either single 1.40 .70
*c.-d.* 78p Either single 3.25 1.60

On day of issue Nos. 2556a-2556b each sold for 34p.

Rescue at Sea A647

Sea rescuers in action near: 1st, Barra. 46p, Appledore. 48p, Portland. 54p, St. Ives. 69p, Lee-on-Solent. 78p, Tenby.

***Perf. 14¼x14 Syncopated***

**2008, Mar. 13**

**2557** A647 1st multi 1.20 .80
**2558** A647 46p multi 1.60 1.05
**2559** A647 48p multi 1.75 1.10
**2560** A647 54p multi 1.90 1.20
**2561** A647 69p multi 2.40 1.50
**2562** A647 78p multi 2.75 1.75
*Nos. 2557-2562 (6)* 11.60 7.40

No. 2557 sold for 34p on day of issue.

Endangered Insects A648

Designs: No. 2563, Adonis blue butterfly. No. 2564, Southern damselfly. No. 2565, Red-barbed ant. No. 2566, Barberry carpet moth. No. 2567, Stag beetle. No. 2568, Hazel pot beetle. No. 2569, Field cricket. No. 2570, Silver-spotted skipper. No. 2571, Purbeck mason wasp. No. 2572, Noble chafer.

**2008, Apr. 15 Litho.** ***Perf. 14½***

**2563** A648 1st multi 1.25 .80
**2564** A648 1st multi 1.25 .80
**2565** A648 1st multi 1.25 .80
**2566** A648 1st multi 1.25 .80
**2567** A648 1st multi 1.25 .80
**2568** A648 1st multi 1.25 .80
**2569** A648 1st multi 1.25 .80
**2570** A648 1st multi 1.25 .80
**2571** A648 1st multi 1.25 .80
**2572** A648 1st multi 1.25 .80
*a.* Block of 10, #2563-2572 12.50 10.00

Nos. 2563-2572 each sold for 36p on day of issue.

**Seaside Resorts Type of 2007**

***Die Cut Perf. 14½***

**2008, May 13 Photo.**

**Booklet Stamp**

**Self-Adhesive**

**2573** A627 1st Like #2463 3.50 2.00
*a.* Booklet pane, 2 #2573, 4 #MH300 12.00

No. 2573 sold for 36p on day of issue.

A649

Cathedrals — A650

Designs: No. 2574, Lichfield Cathedral. 48p, Belfast Cathedral. 50p, Gloucester Cathedral. 56p, St. David's Cathedral, Wales. 72p, Westminster Cathedral. 81p, St. Magnus Cathedral, Orkney.

No. 2580 — St. Paul's Cathedral: a, Ceiling, denomination at UL. b, Ceiling, denomination at UR. c, Floor, denomination at UL. d, Floor, denomination at UR.

**2008, May 13 Litho. *Perf. 14¼***

| | | | | |
|---|---|---|---|---|
| **2574** | A649 | 1st black | 1.20 | .80 |
| **2575** | A649 | 48p black | 1.60 | 1.05 |
| **2576** | A649 | 50p black | 1.75 | 1.10 |
| **2577** | A649 | 56p black | 1.90 | 1.20 |
| **2578** | A649 | 72p black | 2.50 | 1.60 |
| **2579** | A649 | 81p black | 2.75 | 1.75 |
| | | *Nos. 2574-2579 (6)* | 11.70 | 7.50 |

**Souvenir Sheet**

| | | | | |
|---|---|---|---|---|
| **2580** | A650 | Sheet of 4 | 8.00 | 8.00 |
| *a.-b.* | | 1st Either single | 1.20 | .70 |
| *c.-d.* | | 81p Either single | 2.75 | 1.60 |

Nos. 2574, 2580a-2580b each sold for 36p on day of issue.

Posters of British Comedy and Horror Films A651

Poster for: 1st, Carry On Sergeant. 48p, Dracula. 50p, Carry On Cleo. 56p, The Curse of Frankenstein. 72p, Carry On Screaming. 81p, The Mummy.

**2008, June 10 Litho. *Perf. 13¾x14***

| | | | | |
|---|---|---|---|---|
| **2581** | A651 | 1st multi | 1.20 | .80 |
| **2582** | A651 | 48p multi | 1.60 | 1.05 |
| **2583** | A651 | 50p multi | 1.75 | 1.10 |
| **2584** | A651 | 56p multi | 1.90 | 1.20 |
| **2585** | A651 | 72p multi | 2.50 | 1.60 |
| **2586** | A651 | 81p multi | 2.75 | 1.75 |
| | | *Nos. 2581-2586 (6)* | 11.70 | 7.50 |

No. 2581 sold for 36p on day of issue.

First Powered Flight in Great Britain, Cent. A652

Air displays: 1st, Red Arrow aerobatic team. 48p, Royal Air Force Falcons parachuting squad. 50p, Boy watching airplanes in formation. 56p, Avro Vulcans and Avro 707s in flight. 72p, Parachutist Robert Wyndham on wing of Avro 504 biplane. 81p, Blériot airplane and air race tower.

**2008, July 17 Photo. *Perf. 14¼x14***

| | | | | |
|---|---|---|---|---|
| **2587** | A652 | 1st multi | 1.30 | .80 |
| *a.* | | Sheet of 20 + 17 labels, litho. | 27.50 | — |
| *b.* | | Litho. | 1.25 | .65 |
| *c.* | | Booklet pane of 4, 2 each #1758a, 2587b (BK185) | 4.00 | — |
| **2588** | A652 | 48p multi | 1.60 | 1.05 |
| **2589** | A652 | 50p multi | 1.75 | 1.10 |
| **2590** | A652 | 56p multi | 1.90 | 1.20 |
| **2591** | A652 | 72p multi | 2.50 | 1.60 |
| **2592** | A652 | 81p multi | 2.75 | 1.75 |
| | | *Nos. 2587-2592 (6)* | 11.80 | 7.50 |

No. 2587 sold for 36p on day of issue. No. 2587a sold for £7.75. Labels could not be personalized.

No. 2587c issued 9/18.

Souvenir Sheet

2008 Olympic Games, Beijing and 2012 Olympic Games, London — A653

No. 2593: a, National Stadium, Beijing. b, London Eye. c, Tower of London. d, Corner Tower, Forbidden City, Beijing.

**Litho. & Silk Screened**

**2008, Aug. 22 *Perf. 14½***

| | | | | |
|---|---|---|---|---|
| **2593** | A653 | Sheet of 4 | 7.00 | 5.75 |
| *a.-d.* | | 1st Any single | 1.40 | .70 |

On day of issue Nos. 2593a-2593d each sold for 36p.

Royal Air Force Uniforms — A654

Designs: No. 2594, Drum major, Royal Air Force Central Band, 2007. No. 2595, Helicopter rescue winchman, 1984. No. 2596, Hawker Hunter pilot, 1951. No. 2597, Lancaster air gunner, 1944. No. 2598, Plotter, Women's Army Air Force, 1940. No. 2599, Pilot, 1918.

**2008, Sept. 18 Litho. *Perf. 14¼***

| | | | | |
|---|---|---|---|---|
| **2594** | A654 | 1st multi | 1.05 | .75 |
| **2595** | A654 | 1st multi | 1.05 | .75 |
| **2596** | A654 | 1st multi | 1.05 | .75 |
| *a.* | | Horiz. strip of 3, #2594-2596 | 3.75 | 2.00 |
| *b.* | | Booklet pane of 3, #2594-2596 (BK185) | 3.75 | — |
| **2597** | A654 | 81p multi | 2.50 | 1.75 |
| **2598** | A654 | 81p multi | 2.50 | 1.75 |
| **2599** | A654 | 81p multi | 2.50 | 1.75 |
| *a.* | | Horiz. strip of 3, #2597-2599 | 9.00 | 4.50 |
| *b.* | | Booklet pane of 3, #2597-2599 (BK185) | 9.00 | — |
| | | *Nos. 2594-2599 (6)* | 10.65 | 7.50 |

Nos. 2594-2596 each sold for 36p on day of issue.

Miniature Sheet

Country Definitive Stamps, 50th Anniv. — A655

***Perf. 14¾x14 Syncopated***

**2008, Sept. 29 Photo.**

**Buff Paper**

| | | | | |
|---|---|---|---|---|
| **2600** | A655 | Sheet of 9 + label | 10.50 | 6.00 |
| *a.* | | 1st Wales & Monmouthshire Type A1 | 1.25 | .65 |
| *b.* | | 1st Scotland Type A1 | 1.25 | .65 |
| *c.* | | 1st Wales & Monmouthshire Type A3 | 1.25 | .65 |
| *d.* | | 1st Scotland Type A3 | 1.25 | .65 |
| *e.* | | 1st Northern Ireland Type A1 | 1.25 | .65 |
| *f.* | | 1st Wales & Monmouthshire Type A2 | 1.25 | .65 |
| *g.* | | 1st Scotland Type A2 | 1.25 | .65 |
| *h.* | | 1st Northern Ireland Type A2 | 1.25 | .65 |
| *i.* | | 1st Northern Ireland Type A3 | 1.25 | .65 |
| *j.* | | As #2600e, litho., white paper | 1.25 | .65 |
| *k.* | | As #2600i, litho., white paper | 1.25 | .65 |
| *l.* | | As #2600h, litho., white paper | 1.25 | .65 |
| *m.* | | As #2600a, litho., white paper | 1.25 | .65 |
| *n.* | | As #2600c, litho., white paper | 1.25 | .65 |
| *o.* | | As #2600f, litho., white paper | 1.25 | .65 |
| *p.* | | As #2600b, litho., white paper | 1.25 | .65 |
| *q.* | | As #2600d, litho., white paper | 1.25 | .65 |
| *r.* | | As #2600g, litho., white paper | 1.25 | .65 |
| *s.* | | Booklet pane of 9, #2600j-2600r (BK186) | 11.50 | |
| *t.* | | Booklet pane of 6, #2600p-2600r, 3 Scotland #21a (BK186) | 7.50 | |
| *u.* | | Booklet pane of 6, #2600j-2600l, 3 Northern Ireland #18a (BK186) | 7.50 | |
| *v.* | | Booklet pane of 6, #2600m-2600o, 3 Wales & Monmouthshire #21b (BK186) | 7.50 | |

Nos. 2600a-2600r each sold for 36p on day of issue.

Famous Women A656

Designs: 1st, Millicent Garrett Fawcett (1847-1929), suffragist. 48p, Elizabeth Garrett Anderson (1836-1917), first female physician in Britain. 50p, Marie Stopes (1880-1958), birth control advocate. 56p, Eleanor Rathbone (1872-1946), politician and advocate for family allowance. 72p, Claudia Jones (1915-64), civil rights activist. 81p, Barbara Castle (1910-2002), politician and advocate for equal pay for women.

***Perf. 14¼x14½***

**2008, Oct. 14 Photo.**

| | | | | |
|---|---|---|---|---|
| **2601** | A656 | 1st multi | 1.05 | .65 |
| **2602** | A656 | 48p multi | 1.40 | .90 |
| **2603** | A656 | 50p multi | 1.40 | .90 |
| **2604** | A656 | 56p multi | 1.60 | 1.05 |
| **2605** | A656 | 72p multi | 2.00 | 1.40 |
| **2606** | A656 | 81p multi | 2.25 | 1.50 |
| | | *Nos. 2601-2606 (6)* | 9.70 | 6.40 |

On day of issue, No. 2601 sold for 36p.

Christmas
A657 A658

Pantomime actors: Nos. 2607a, 2607c, 2608, 2610, Ugly sisters from Cinderella. Nos. 2607b, 2607e, 2609, 2612, Genie from Aladdin. 50p, Captain Hook from Peter Pan. 81p, Wicked queen from Snow White.

**2008, Nov. 4 Photo. *Perf. 14¾x14***

| | | | | |
|---|---|---|---|---|
| **2607** | | Sheet of 6 | 8.00 | 8.00 |
| *a.* | | A657 2nd multi | .70 | .40 |
| *b.* | | A657 1st multi | .95 | .55 |
| *c.* | | A658 2nd Large multi | 1.20 | .70 |
| *d.* | | A657 50p multi | 1.40 | .80 |
| *e.* | | A658 1st Large multi | 1.40 | .80 |
| *f.* | | A657 81p multi | 2.25 | 1.40 |

**Self-Adhesive**

***Die Cut Perf. 14¾x14 Syncopated***

| | | | | |
|---|---|---|---|---|
| **2608** | A657 | 2nd multi | .70 | .40 |
| *a.* | | Booklet pane of 12 | 9.00 | |
| *b.* | | Litho. + label | .80 | .90 |
| **2609** | A657 | 1st multi | .95 | .55 |
| *a.* | | Booklet pane of 12 | 12.00 | |
| *b.* | | Litho. + label | 1.00 | 1.25 |
| **2610** | A658 | 2nd Large multi | 1.20 | .70 |
| **2611** | A657 | 50p multi | 1.40 | .80 |
| **2612** | A658 | 1st Large multi | 1.40 | .80 |
| **2613** | A657 | 81p multi | 2.25 | 1.40 |
| *a.* | | Litho. + label | 2.40 | 2.75 |
| *b.* | | Sheet of 20, 8 each #2608b, 2609b, 4 #2613a + 20 labels | 25.00 | — |
| | | *Nos. 2608-2613 (6)* | 7.90 | 4.65 |

On day of issue, the franking value of Nos. 2607a, 2608, and 2608b was 27p, and that of Nos. 2607b, 2609 and 2609b was 36p. On day of issue, Nos. 2607c and 2610 sold for 42p, and Nos. 2607e and 2612 sold for 52p. No. 2613b sold for £8.85. Labels could not be personalized.

No. 2608 was also printed in sheets of 20 stamps + 20 labels that could be personalized. No. 2609b was also printed in sheets of 10 stamps + 10 labels and 20 stamps + 20 labels that could be personalized. No. 2613a was also available in a sheet of 10 stamps + 10 labels that could be personalized.

Poppy With Soldier's Face — A659

**2008, Nov. 6 Litho. *Perf. 14½x14¼***

| | | | | |
|---|---|---|---|---|
| **2614** | A659 | 1st multi | 2.25 | .75 |
| *a.* | | Souvenir sheet of 5 | 10.00 | 10.00 |
| *b.* | | Horiz. strip, #2418c, 2530, 2614 | 3.00 | 2.50 |

End of World War I, 90th anniv. On day of issue, No. 2614 sold for 36p. No. 2614a contains #2614, England #18, Northern Ireland #29, Scotland #32, and Wales and Monmouthshire #32. No. 2614 also was printed in a sheet of 20 + 5 labels that sold for £7.75, and in a series of limited-quantity privately contracted sheets of 10 + 10 labels that sold for various prices.

British Design A660

Designs: No. 2615, Supermarine Spitfire, designed by R. J. Mitchell. No. 2616, Miniskirt, designed by Mary Quant. No. 2617, Mini Cooper, designed by Sir Alec Issigonis. No. 2618, Anglepoise lamp, designed by George Carwardine. No. 2619, Concorde, designed by Aérospatiale-BAC. No. 2620, K2 telephone kiosk, designed by Sir Giles Gilbert Scott. No. 2621, Polypropylene chair, designed by Robin Day. No. 2622, Penguin books, designed by Edward Young. No. 2623, London Underground map, designed by Harry Beck. No. 2624, Routemaster Bus, designed by AAM Durrant.

**2009, Jan. 13 Litho. *Perf. 14½***

| | | | | |
|---|---|---|---|---|
| **2615** | A660 | 1st multi | 1.10 | .55 |
| *a.* | | Sheet of 20 + 20 labels | 26.00 | — |
| **2616** | A660 | 1st multi | 1.10 | .55 |
| **2617** | A660 | 1st multi | 1.10 | .55 |
| *a.* | | Sheet of 20 + 20 labels | 24.00 | — |
| **2618** | A660 | 1st multi | 1.10 | .55 |
| **2619** | A660 | 1st multi | 1.10 | .55 |
| *a.* | | Booklet pane of 4, 2 each #2049a, 2619 (BK187) | 16.00 | — |
| *b.* | | Sheet of 20 + 20 labels | 25.00 | — |
| **2620** | A660 | 1st multi | 1.10 | .55 |
| **2621** | A660 | 1st multi | 1.10 | .55 |
| **2622** | A660 | 1st multi | 1.10 | .55 |
| **2623** | A660 | 1st multi | 1.10 | .55 |
| *a.* | | Booklet pane of 6, #2616, 2618, 2620-2623 (BK187) | 6.75 | — |
| **2624** | A660 | 1st multi | 1.10 | .55 |
| *a.* | | Block of 10, #2615-2624 | 11.00 | 5.50 |
| *b.* | | Booklet pane of 4, #2615, 2617, 2 #2624 (BK187) | 4.50 | — |

On day of issue, Nos. 2615-2624 each sold for 36p. Nos. 2617a, 2619b sold for £7.74. Labels on No. 2617a, No. 2619b could not be personalized.

Issued: No. 2619b, 3/2/09. No. 2615a, 9/15/10. No. 2615a sold for £8.50 and labels could not be personalized.

See Nos. 2640-2644, 2833.

Miniature Sheet

Robert Burns (1759-96), Poet — A661

No. 2625: a, Man with plow, text, "A Man's a Man for a' that". b, Portrait of Burns by Alexander Naysmith.

***Perf. 14½ (#2625a, 2625b), 14¾x14 Syncopated***

**2009, Jan. 22 Photo.**

| | | | | |
|---|---|---|---|---|
| **2625** | A661 | Sheet of 6, #2625a, 2625b, Scotland #20, 21, 31, 32 | 9.00 | 5.00 |
| *a.-b.* | | 1st Either single | 1.25 | .60 |

On day of issue, Nos. 2625a and 2625b each sold for 36p.

Miniature Sheet

Wildlife and HMS Beagle Map of Galapagos Islands — A662

No. 2626: a, Flightless cormorant. b, Giant tortoise, cactus finch. c, Marine iguana. d, Floreana mockingbird.

**2009, Feb. 12** *Perf. 14¼*
**2626** A662 Sheet of 4 7.00 3.50
*a.-b.* 1st Either single 1.10 .55
*c.-d.* 81p Either single 2.40 1.25
*e.* Booklet pane, #2626, litho. (BK188) 7.00 —

On day of issue, Nos. 2626a and 2626b each sold for 36p. No. 2626e has a rouletted label to the left of the sheet.

Charles Darwin (1809-82), Naturalist A663

Designs: Nos. 2627, 2633, Photograph of Darwin. Nos. 2628, 2634, Head of marine iguana (zoology). Nos. 2629, 2635, Heads of finches (ornithology). Nos. 2630, 2636, Island (geology). Nos. 2631, 2637, Bee orchid (botany). Nos. 2632, 2638, Orangutan (anthropology).

**2009, Feb. 12** *Perf. 14 Syncopated*
**Booklet Stamps (#2627-2632)**
**2627** A663 1st multi (2632a) 2.05 1.50
**2628** A663 48p multi (2630a) 2.05 1.80
**2629** A663 50p multi (2630a) 4.50 2.00
**2630** A663 56p multi (2630a) 5.25 2.50
*a.* Booklet pane of 3, #2628-2630 (BK188) 15.00 —
**2631** A663 72p multi (2632a) 5.75 2.50
**2632** A663 81p multi (2632a) 7.00 5.00
*a.* Booklet pane of 3, #2627, 2631, 2632 (BK188) 15.00 —
*Nos. 2627-2632 (6)* 26.60 15.30

**Self-Adhesive**
***Die Cut Perf. 14 Syncopated***
**2633** A663 1st multi 1.10 .55
**2634** A663 48p multi 1.40 .70
**2635** A663 50p multi 1.50 .75
**2636** A663 56p multi 1.60 .80
**2637** A663 72p multi 2.10 1.10
**2638** A663 81p multi 2.40 1.25
*Nos. 2633-2638 (6)* 10.10 5.15

On day of issue, Nos. 2627 and 2633 each sold for 36p.

Miniature Sheet

Heritage of Wales — A664

No. 2639: a, Flag of Wales (18x22mm). b, Red dragon (18x21mm). c, St. David (58x22mm). d, Welsh Assembly, Cardiff (58x22mm).

***Perf. 14¾x14 Syncopated (#2639a), 14¾x14 (#2639b, 2639c)***
**2009, Feb. 26** **Litho.**
**2639** A664 Sheet of 4 8.75 5.00
*a.-b.* 1st Either single 1.25 .60
*c.-d.* 81p Either single 2.50 1.40

On day of issue, Nos. 2639a and 2639b each sold for 36p.

**British Design Types of 2009**

Designs: No. 2640, K2 telephone kiosk. No. 2641, Routemaster Bus. No. 2642, Mini Cooper automobile. No. 2643, Concorde. No. 2644, Miniskirt.

**2009** **Photo.** ***Die Cut Perf. 14½***
**Booklet Stamps**
**Self-Adhesive**
**2640** A660 1st multi 2.50 1.00
**2641** A660 1st multi 2.50 1.00
*a.* Booklet pane, #2640-2641, 4 #MH384a 9.50
**2642** A660 1st multi 2.75 1.25
*a.* Booklet pane, 2 #2642, 4 #MH384a 11.00
**2643** A660 1st multi 2.75 1.25
*a.* Booklet pane of 6, 2 #2643, 4 #MH384a 11.00
**2644** A660 1st multi 2.75 1.25
*a.* Booklet pane of 6, 2 #2644, 4 #MH384a 11.00

Issued: Nos. 2640, 2641, 2641a, 3/10; Nos. 2642, 2642a, 4/21; Nos. 2643, 2643a, 8/18; Nos. 2644, 2644a, 9/17. On day of issue, Nos. 2640-2641 each sold for 36p; Nos. 2642, 2643, 2644 sold for 39p.

Pioneers of the Industrial Revolution A665

Designs: No. 2645, Matthew Boulton (1728-1809), steam engine manufacturer. No. 2646, James Watt (1736-1819), steam engine pioneer and inventor. No. 2647, Richard Arkwright (1732-92), inventor of textile machines. No. 2648, Josiah Wedgwood (1730-95), manufacturer of decorative ceramics. No. 2649, George Stephenson (1781-1848), steam locomotive inventor. No. 2650, Henry Maudslay (1771-1831), engineer and machine tool inventor. No. 2651, James Brindley (1716-72), canal engineer. No. 2652, John McAdam (1756-1836), engineer, road builder.

***Perf. 14¼x14½***
**2009, Mar. 10** **Litho.**
**2645** A665 1st multi 1.10 .60
**2646** A665 1st multi 1.10 .60
*a.* Horiz. pair, #2645-2646 2.25 1.25
**2647** A665 50p multi 1.50 .85
**2648** A665 50p multi 1.50 .85
*a.* Horiz. pair, #2647-2648 3.00 1.75
**2649** A665 56p multi 1.75 .95
**2650** A665 56p multi 1.75 .95
*a.* Horiz. pair, #2649-2650 3.50 1.90
**2651** A665 72p multi 2.25 1.20
**2652** A665 72p multi 2.25 1.20
*a.* Horiz. pair, #2651-2652 4.50 2.50
*Nos. 2645-2652 (8)* 13.20 7.20

On day of issue, Nos. 2645-2646 each sold for 36p.

**British Royalty and History Type of 2008**

Designs: No. 2653, King Henry VII. No. 2654, King Henry VIII. No. 2655, King Edward VI. No. 2656, Lady Jane Grey. No. 2657, Queen Mary I. No. 2658, Queen Elizabeth I.

No. 2659: a, Warship Mary Rose. b, Field of Cloth of Gold Royal Conference. c, Royal Exchange. d, Sir Francis Drake, first English circumnavigator.

**2009, Apr. 21** *Perf. 14¼*
**2653** A645 1st multi 1.25 .65
**2654** A645 1st multi 1.25 .65
**2655** A645 62p multi 1.90 1.05
**2656** A645 62p multi 1.90 1.05
**2657** A645 81p multi 2.40 1.40
**2658** A645 81p multi 2.40 1.40
*Nos. 2653-2658 (6)* 11.10 6.20

**Souvenir Sheet**
**2659** Sheet of 4 7.75 4.00
*a.-b.* A645 1st Either single 1.25 .60
*c.-d.* A645 90p Either single 2.60 1.25

On day of issue, Nos. 2653, 2654, 2659a and 2659b sold for 39p.

Endangered Plants A666

Designs: No. 2660, Round-headed leek. No. 2661, Floating water plantain. No. 2662, Lady's slipper orchid. No. 2663, Dwarf milkwort. No. 2664, Marsh saxifrage. No. 2665, Downy woundwort. No. 2666, Upright spurge. No. 2667, Plymouth pear. No. 2668, Sea knotgrass. No. 2669, Deptford pink.

**2009, May 19** *Perf. 14½*
**2660** A666 1st multi 1.25 .75
**2661** A666 1st multi 1.25 .75
**2662** A666 1st multi 1.25 .75
**2663** A666 1st multi 1.25 .75
**2664** A666 1st multi 1.25 .75
**2665** A666 1st multi 1.25 .75
**2666** A666 1st multi 1.25 .75
**2667** A666 1st multi 1.25 .75
**2668** A666 1st multi 1.25 .75
**2669** A666 1st multi 1.25 .75
*a.* Block of 10, #2660-2669 12.50 7.50

On day of issue, Nos. 2660-2669 each sold for 39p.

Miniature Sheet

Royal Botanic Gardens, Kew — A667

No. 2670: a, Palm House. b, Millennium Seed Bank, Wakehurst Place. c, Pagoda. d, Sackler Crossing.

**2009, May 19** *Perf. 14¼x14½*
**2670** A667 Sheet of 4 8.00 4.00
*a.-b.* 1st Either single 1.25 .60
*c.-d.* 90p Either single 2.75 1.40

On day of issue, Nos. 2670a and 2670b each sold for 39p.

**Flowers Type of 1997**
***Die Cut Perf. 14½x14 Syncopated***
**2009, May 21** **Photo.**
**Booklet Stamps**
**Self-Adhesive**
**2671** A475 1st multi 3.00 .85
**2672** A479 1st multi 3.00 .85
*a.* Booklet pane, #2671-2672, 4 #MH384a 11.00

On day of issue Nos. 2671-2672 each sold for 39p.

Mythical Creatures A668

**2009, June 16** **Photo.** *Perf. 14½*
**2673** A668 1st Dragon 1.40 .70
**2674** A668 1st Unicorn 1.40 .70
**2675** A668 62p Giant 2.10 1.10
**2676** A668 62p Pixie 2.10 1.10
**2677** A668 90p Mermaid 3.00 1.50
**2678** A668 90p Fairy 3.00 1.50
*Nos. 2673-2678 (6)* 13.00 6.60

On day of issue, Nos. 2673-2674 each sold for 39p.

Miniature Sheet

Post Boxes — A669

No. 2679: a, George V type B wall box. b, Edward VII Ludlow box. c, Victorian lamp box. d, Elizabeth II type A wall box.

**2009, Aug. 18** **Litho.** *Perf. 14¼*
**2679** A669 Sheet of 4 9.00 9.00
*a.* 1st multi 1.25 .65
*b.* 56p multi 1.90 .95
*c.* 81p multi 2.75 1.40
*d.* 90p multi 3.00 1.50
*e.* Booklet pane of 4, #2679a-2679d (BK189) 9.00 —
*f.* Sheet of 20 #2679a + 20 labels 27.50 —

No. 2679 sold for 39p on day of issue. No. 2679f sold for £8.35 on day of issue and its labels could not be personalized.

Fire and Rescue Service A670

Designs: 1st, Firefighting. 54p, Chemical fire. 56p, Emergency rescue. 62p, Flood rescue. 81p, Search and rescue. 90p, Fire safety.

***Perf. 14¼x14½***
**2009, Sept. 1** **Photo.**
**2680** A670 1st multi 1.25 .70
**2681** A670 54p multi 1.75 1.00
**2682** A670 56p multi 1.90 1.05
**2683** A670 62p multi 2.10 1.20
**2684** A670 81p multi 2.75 1.50
**2685** A670 90p multi 3.00 1.60
*Nos. 2680-2685 (6)* 12.75 7.05

No. 2680 sold for 39p on day of issue.

Royal Navy Uniforms — A671

Designs: No. 2686, Flight deck officer, 2009. No. 2687, Captain, 1941. No. 2688, Second officer WRNS, 1918. No. 2689, Able seaman, 1880. No. 2690, Royal Marine, 1805. No. 2691, Admiral, 1795.

**2009, Sept. 17** **Litho.** *Perf. 14¼*
**2686** A671 1st multi 1.25 .70
**2687** A671 1st multi 1.25 .70
**2688** A671 1st multi 1.25 .70
*a.* Horiz. strip of 3, #2686-2688 3.75 2.25
*b.* Booklet pane of 3, #2686-2688 (BK190) 3.75 —
**2689** A671 90p multi 3.00 1.75
**2690** A671 90p multi 3.00 1.75
**2691** A671 90p multi 3.00 1.75
*a.* Horiz. strip of 3, #2689-2691 9.00 5.50
*b.* Booklet pane of 3, #2689-2691 (BK190) 9.00 —
*Nos. 2686-2691 (6)* 12.75 7.35

Nos. 2686-2688 each sold for 39p on day of issue.

Famous People A672

Designs: No. 2692, Fred Perry (1909-95), tennis player. No. 2693, Henry Purcell (1659-95), composer and musician. No. 2694, Sir Matt Busby (1909-94), soccer player and manager. No. 2695, William Gladstone (1809-98), prime minister. No. 2696, Mary Wollstonecraft (1759-97), writer on feminist themes. No. 2697, Sir Arthur Conan Doyle (1859-1930), writer and creator of Sherlock Holmes stories. No. 2698, Donald Campbell (1921-67), breaker of land and water speed records. No. 2699, Judy Fryd (1909-2000), founder of Royal Society for Mentally Handicapped Children. No. 2700, Samuel Johnson (1709-84), lexicographer, critic and poet. No. 2701, Sir Martin Ryle (1918-84), radio astronomer.

**2009, Oct. 8** **Litho.** *Perf. 14½*
**2692** A672 1st multi 1.25 .70
**2693** A672 1st multi 1.25 .70
**2694** A672 1st multi 1.25 .70
**2695** A672 1st multi 1.25 .70
**2696** A672 1st multi 1.25 .70
*a.* Horiz. strip of 5, #2692-2696 6.25 3.50
**2697** A672 1st multi 1.25 .70
**2698** A672 1st multi 1.25 .70
**2699** A672 1st multi 1.25 .70
**2700** A672 1st multi 1.25 .70
**2701** A672 1st multi 1.25 .70
*a.* Horiz. strip of 5, #2697-2701 6.25 3.50
*Nos. 2692-2701 (10)* 12.50 7.00

On day of issue, Nos. 2692-2701 each sold for 39p. Europa (No. 2701).

Sports of the 2012 Summer Olympics and Paralympics, London A673

Olympics or Paralympics emblem and: No. 2702, Canoe slalom. Nos. 2703, 2713, Archery (Paralympics). Nos. 2704, 2714, Track. No. 2705, Aquatics. No. 2706, Boccie (Paralympics). Nos. 2707, 2712, Judo. No. 2708, Equestrian (Paralympics). No. 2709, Badminton. No. 2710, Weight lifting. Nos. 2711, 2715, Basketball.

**2009-10 Litho. *Perf. 14½***

| | | | | |
|---|---|---|---|---|
| **2702** | A673 | 1st multi | 1.40 | .70 |
| **2703** | A673 | 1st multi | 1.40 | .70 |
| **2704** | A673 | 1st multi | 1.40 | .70 |
| **2705** | A673 | 1st multi | 1.40 | .70 |
| **2706** | A673 | 1st multi | 1.40 | .70 |
| *a.* | | Horiz. strip of 5, #2702-2706 | 7.00 | 3.50 |
| **2707** | A673 | 1st multi | 1.40 | .70 |
| **2708** | A673 | 1st multi | 1.40 | .70 |
| *a.* | | Booklet pane of 2, #2703, 2708 (BK200) | 4.00 | — |
| **2709** | A673 | 1st multi | 1.40 | .70 |
| **2710** | A673 | 1st multi | 1.40 | .70 |
| **2711** | A673 | 1st multi | 1.40 | .70 |
| *a.* | | Horiz. strip of 5, #2707-2711 | 7.00 | 3.50 |
| | | *Nos. 2702-2711 (10)* | 14.00 | 7.00 |

**Booklet Stamps**

**Self-Adhesive**

**Photo.**

***Die Cut Perf. 14½***

| | | | | |
|---|---|---|---|---|
| **2712** | A673 | 1st multi (2713a) | 2.75 | .90 |
| **2713** | A673 | 1st multi (2713a) | 2.75 | .90 |
| *a.* | | Booklet pane of 6, #2712, 2713, 4 #MH384a | 11.50 | |
| **2714** | A673 | 1st multi | 2.75 | .85 |
| **2715** | A673 | 1st multi | 2.75 | .85 |
| *a.* | | Booklet pane of 6, #2714-2715, 4 #MH384a | 11.50 | |

On day of issue, Nos. 2702-2715 each sold for 39p. Issued: Nos. 2702-2711, 10/22; Nos. 2712-2713, 1/7/10; Nos. 2714-2715, 2/25/10. No. 2708a, 7/27/12.

See Nos. 2815-2826, 2840-2841, 2916-2927.

Christmas

A674 A675

Stained-glass windows: Nos. 2716a, 2716c, 2717, 2719, Angel, Church of St. James, Staveley. Nos. 2716b, 2716e, 2718, 2721, Madonna and Child, Church of Ormesby St. Michael, Great Yarmouth. 56p, Joseph, Church of St. Michael, Minehead. 90p, Wise Man, Church of St. Mary the Virgin, Rye. £1.35, Shepherd, Church of St. Mary's, Upavon.

***Perf. 14¾x14 Syncopated***

**2009, Nov. 3 Photo.**

| | | | | |
|---|---|---|---|---|
| **2716** | | Sheet of 7 | 15.50 | 7.75 |
| *a.* | A674 | 2nd multi | 1.00 | .50 |
| *b.* | A674 | 1st multi | 1.40 | .70 |
| *c.* | A675 | 2nd Large multi | 1.50 | .75 |
| *d.* | A674 | 56p multi | 1.90 | .95 |
| *e.* | A675 | 1st Large multi | 2.00 | 1.00 |
| *f.* | A674 | 90p multi | 3.00 | 1.50 |
| *g.* | A674 | £1.35 multi | 4.50 | 2.25 |
| *h.* | | Litho. (2716i) | 1.50 | 1.50 |
| *i.* | | Booklet pane of 4 #2716h + label (BK196) | 6.25 | — |

**Self-Adhesive**

***Die Cut Perf. 14¾x14 Syncopated***

| | | | | |
|---|---|---|---|---|
| **2717** | A674 | 2nd multi | 1.00 | .50 |
| *a.* | | Booklet pane of 12 | 12.00 | |
| *b.* | | Litho., serpentine die cut 14¾x14 + label | 1.10 | 1.10 |
| **2718** | A674 | 1st multi | 1.40 | .70 |
| *a.* | | Booklet pane of 12 | 17.00 | |
| *b.* | | Litho., serpentine die cut 14¾x14 + label | 1.50 | 1.50 |
| **2719** | A675 | 2nd Large multi | 1.50 | .75 |
| **2720** | A674 | 56p multi | 1.90 | .95 |
| *a.* | | Litho., serpentine die cut 14¾x14 + label | 2.00 | 2.00 |
| **2721** | A675 | 1st Large multi | 2.00 | 1.00 |
| **2722** | A674 | 90p multi | 3.00 | 1.50 |
| *a.* | | Litho., serpentine die cut 14¾x14 + label | 3.25 | 3.25 |
| *b.* | | Sheet of 20, 8 each #2717b, 2718b, 2 each #2720a, 2722a, + 20 labels | 32.00 | |
| **2723** | A674 | £1.35 multi | 4.50 | 2.25 |
| | | *Nos. 2717-2723 (7)* | 15.30 | 7.65 |

On day of issue, Nos. 2716a and 2717 each sold for 30p; Nos. 2716b and 2718, 39p; Nos. 2716c and 2719, 47p; Nos. 2716e and 2721, 61p. No. 2722b sold for £9, and contains 20 labels that could not be personalized. No. 2717b was additionally sold in a sheet of 20 + 20 labels that could be personalized that sold for £9.50. No. 2718b was additionally sold in a sheet of 20 + 20 labels that could be personalized that sold for £13.50. No. 2720a was additionally sold in a sheet of 10 + 10 labels that could be personalized that sold for £9.50. No. 2722b was additionally sold in a sheet of 10 + 10 labels that could be personalized that sold for £13.50.

Issued: Nos. 2716h, 2716i, 5/5/11.

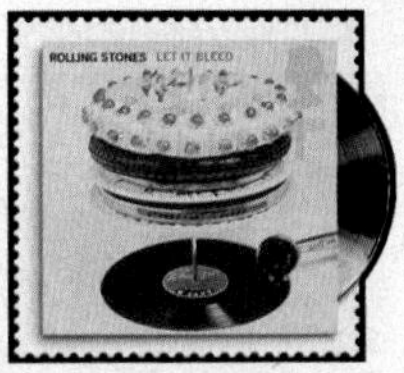

Let It Bleed, by The Rolling Stones A676

Led Zeppelin IV, by Led Zeppelin A677

The Rise and Fall of Ziggy Stardust and the Spiders from Mars, by David Bowie A678

Power, Corruption and Lies, by New Order — A679

Screamadelica, by Primal Scream — A680

The Division Bell, by Pink Floyd — A681

Tubular Bells, by Mike Oldfield A682

London Calling, by The Clash — A683

Parklife, by Blur — A684

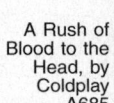

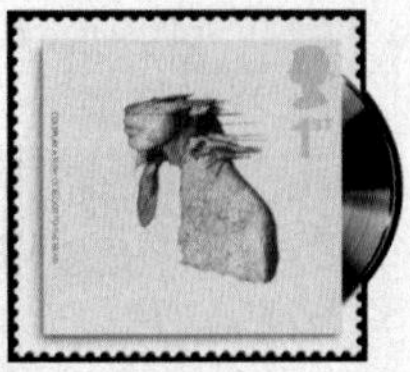

A Rush of Blood to the Head, by Coldplay A685

***Perf. 14¾ Syncopated***

**2010, Jan. 7 Litho.**

| | | | | |
|---|---|---|---|---|
| **2724** | A676 | 1st multi | 2.75 | .70 |
| **2725** | A677 | 1st multi | 2.75 | .70 |
| **2726** | A678 | 1st multi | 2.75 | .70 |
| **2727** | A679 | 1st multi | 2.75 | .70 |
| **2728** | A680 | 1st multi | 2.75 | .70 |
| **2729** | A681 | 1st multi | 2.75 | .70 |
| *a.* | | Booklet pane of 6, #2724-2729 (BK191) | 14.00 | — |
| **2730** | A682 | 1st multi | 2.75 | .70 |
| **2731** | A683 | 1st multi | 2.75 | .70 |
| **2732** | A684 | 1st multi | 2.75 | .70 |
| **2733** | A685 | 1st multi | 2.75 | .70 |
| *a.* | | Booklet pane of 4, #2730-2733 (BK191) | 10.00 | — |
| *b.* | | Souvenir sheet, #2724-2733 | 28.00 | 14.00 |

No. 2733b has simulated creases and toning at the sides and corners of the album cover sheet margin.

**Self-Adhesive**

**Photo.**

***Die Cut Perf. 14¾***

| | | | | |
|---|---|---|---|---|
| **2734** | A681 | 1st multi | 1.40 | .70 |
| **2735** | A685 | 1st multi | 1.40 | .70 |
| **2736** | A684 | 1st multi | 1.40 | .70 |
| **2737** | A679 | 1st multi | 1.40 | .70 |
| **2738** | A676 | 1st multi | 1.40 | .70 |
| *a.* | | Horiz. strip of 5, #2734-2738 | 7.00 | |
| **2739** | A683 | 1st multi | 1.40 | .70 |
| **2740** | A682 | 1st multi | 1.40 | .70 |
| **2741** | A677 | 1st multi | 1.40 | .70 |
| **2742** | A680 | 1st multi | 1.40 | .70 |
| **2743** | A678 | 1st multi | 1.40 | .70 |
| *a.* | | Horiz. strip of 5, #2739-2743 | 7.00 | |

On day of issue, Nos. 2724-2743 each sold for 39p.

Miniature Sheet

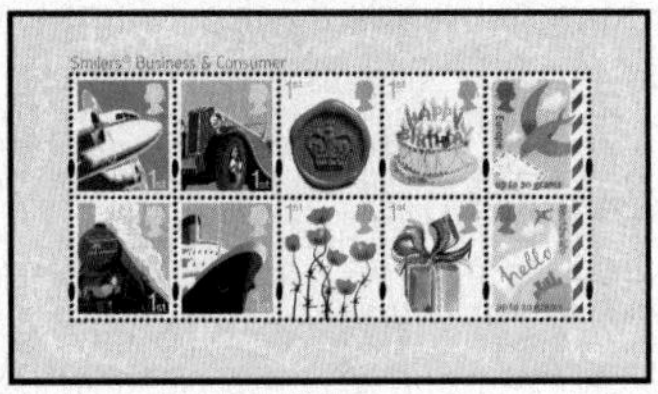

A686

Nos. 2744 and 2745: a, Airplane with propellers. b, Automobile. c, Sealing wax with crown impression. d, Birthday cake. e, Steam locomotive. f, Ocean liner. g, Poppies. h, Gift box. i, Bird carrying airmail letter. j, "Hello" in airplane's contrail.

***Perf. 14¾x14 Syncopated***

**2010, Jan. 26 Litho.**

| | | | | |
|---|---|---|---|---|
| **2744** | A686 | Sheet of 10 | 15.00 | 15.00 |
| *a.-h.* | | 1st Any single | 1.25 | .60 |
| *i.* | | (56p) multi | 1.90 | .95 |
| *j.* | | (90p) multi | 3.00 | 1.50 |

**Self-Adhesive**

***Die Cut Perf. 14¾x14 Syncopated***

| | | | | |
|---|---|---|---|---|
| **2745** | A686 | Sheet of 20, 2 each #a-j, + 20 labels | 33.00 | |
| *a.-h.* | | 1st Any single + label | 1.40 | 1.40 |
| *i.* | | (56p) multi + label | 2.00 | 2.00 |
| *j.* | | (90p) multi + label | 3.25 | 3.25 |
| *k.* | | Sheet of 20 #2745d + 20 labels | 44.00 | |
| *l.* | | Sheet of 20 #2745g + 20 labels | 44.00 | |
| *m.* | | Sheet of 10 #2745h + 10 labels | 31.00 | |
| *n.* | | Sheet of 10 #2745i + 10 labels | 44.00 | |
| *o.* | | Sheet of 20 #2745c + 20 labels | 30.00 | |

On day of issue, Nos. 2744a-2744h sold for 39p. No. 2745 sold for £9.70, and Nos. 2745a-2745h had a franking value of 39p. Labels could not be personalized.

Nos. 2745k and 2745l each sold for £13.63; No. 2745m for £9.58; and No. 2745n for £13.60. Labels could be personalized on Nos. 2745k-2745n.

Issued: No. 2745o, 9/15/11. No. 2745o sold for £9.50. Labels could not be personalized. No. 2745g was printed in sheets of 50 in 2012.

Miniature Sheet

Girl Guides, Cent. — A687

No. 2746 — Girl Guides and: a, Kite, handprint, drawing of flower. b, Cupcake, magnifying glass, leaves, colored pencils. c, Archery target, climber's rope. d, Photographs, swimming goggles, map of Manchester.

**2010, Feb. 2 *Perf. 14¼x14½***

| | | | | |
|---|---|---|---|---|
| **2746** | A687 | Sheet of 4 | 8.75 | 8.75 |
| *a.* | | 1st multi | 1.25 | .60 |
| *b.* | | 56p multi | 1.75 | .85 |
| *c.* | | 81p multi | 2.60 | 1.25 |
| *d.* | | 90p multi | 3.00 | 1.50 |

No. 2746a sold for 39p on day of issue.

Royal Society, 350th Anniv. A688

Scientists: No. 2747, Robert Boyle (1627-91), air pump. No. 2748, Sir Isaac Newton (1642-1727), color spectrum and optics diagram. No. 2749, Benjamin Franklin (1706-90), lightning. No. 2750, Edward Jenner (1749-1823), smallpox virus. No. 2751, Charles Babbage (1792-1871), gear diagram. No. 2752, Alfred Russel Wallace (1823-1913), oak tree. No. 2753, Sir Joseph Lister (1827-1912), spray. No. 2754, Ernest Rutherford (1871-1937), atom. No. 2755, Dorothy Hodgkin (1910-94), crystal diagram. No. 2756, Sir Nicholas Shackleton (1937-2006), microfossils.

**2010, Feb. 25 Litho. *Perf. 14½***

| | | | | |
|---|---|---|---|---|
| **2747** | A688 | 1st multi | 1.25 | .60 |
| **2748** | A688 | 1st multi | 1.25 | .60 |
| **2749** | A688 | 1st multi | 1.25 | .60 |
| **2750** | A688 | 1st multi | 1.25 | .60 |
| **2751** | A688 | 1st multi | 1.25 | .60 |
| **2752** | A688 | 1st multi | 1.25 | .60 |
| **2753** | A688 | 1st multi | 1.25 | .60 |
| **2754** | A688 | 1st multi | 1.25 | .60 |
| *a.* | | Booklet pane of 4, #2748, 2749, 2 #2754 (BK192) | 5.00 | — |
| **2755** | A688 | 1st multi | 1.25 | .60 |
| *a.* | | Booklet pane of 4, #2753, 2755, 2 #2750 (BK192) | 5.00 | — |
| **2756** | A688 | 1st multi | 1.25 | .60 |
| *a.* | | Block of 10, #2747-2756 | 12.50 | 6.00 |
| *b.* | | Booklet pane of 4, #2747, 2751, 2752, 2756 (BK192) | 5.00 | — |
| | | *Nos. 2747-2756 (10)* | 12.50 | 6.00 |

On day of issue, Nos. 2747-2756 each sold for 39p.

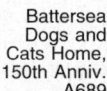

Battersea Dogs and Cats Home, 150th Anniv. A689

Designs: No. 2757, Pixie (dog). No. 2758, Button (cat). No. 2759, Herbie (dog). No. 2760, Mr. Tumnus (cat). No. 2761, Tafka (dog). No. 2762, Boris (dog). No. 2763, Casey (dog). No. 2764, Tigger (cat). No. 2765, Leonard (dog). No. 2766, Tia (dog).

**2010, Mar. 11 *Perf. 14½***

| | | | | |
|---|---|---|---|---|
| **2757** | A689 | 1st multi | 1.25 | .60 |
| **2758** | A689 | 1st multi | 1.25 | .60 |
| **2759** | A689 | 1st multi | 1.25 | .60 |
| **2760** | A689 | 1st multi | 1.25 | .60 |
| **2761** | A689 | 1st multi | 1.25 | .60 |
| **2762** | A689 | 1st multi | 1.25 | .60 |
| **2763** | A689 | 1st multi | 1.25 | .60 |
| **2764** | A689 | 1st multi | 1.25 | .60 |
| **2765** | A689 | 1st multi | 1.25 | .60 |
| **2766** | A689 | 1st multi | 1.25 | .60 |
| *a.* | | Block of 10, #2757-2766 | 12.50 | 6.00 |
| | | *Nos. 2757-2766 (10)* | 12.50 | 6.00 |

On day of issue, Nos. 2757-2766 each sold for 39p.

**British Royalty and History Type of 2008**

Designs: No. 2767, King James I of Scotland (1406-37). No. 2768, King James II of Scotland (1437-60). No. 2769, King James III. No. 2770, King James IV. No. 2771, King James V. No. 2772, Mary, Queen of Scots. No. 2773, King James VI.

No. 2774: a, Founding of St. Andrew's University, 1413. b, College of Surgeons, Edinburgh, 1505. c, Court of Session, 1532. d, John Knox, religious reformer.

**2010, Mar. 23** *Perf. 14¼*

| | | | | |
|---|---|---|---|---|
| **2767** | A645 | 1st multi | 1.25 | .60 |
| **2768** | A645 | 1st multi | 1.25 | .60 |
| **2769** | A645 | 1st multi | 1.25 | .60 |
| **2770** | A645 | 62p multi | 1.90 | .95 |
| **2771** | A645 | 62p multi | 1.90 | .95 |
| **2772** | A645 | 81p multi | 2.50 | 1.25 |
| **2773** | A645 | 81p multi | 2.50 | 1.25 |
| | | *Nos. 2767-2773 (7)* | 12.55 | 6.20 |

**Souvenir Sheet**

| | | | |
|---|---|---|---|
| **2774** | Sheet of 4 | 7.50 | 7.50 |
| *a.-b.* | A645 1st Either single | 1.25 | .60 |
| *c.-d.* | A645 81p Either single | 2.50 | 1.25 |

On day of issue, Nos. 2767-2769, 2774a-2774b each sold for 39p.

Land and Sea Mammals A690

Designs: No. 2775, Humpback whale. No. 2776, Wildcat. No. 2777, Brown long-eared bat. No. 2778, Polecat. No. 2779, Sperm whale. No. 2780, Water vole. No. 2781, Greater horseshoe bat. Nos. 2782, 2785, Otter. No. 2783, Dormouse. Nos. 2784, 2786, Hedgehog.

**2010** *Perf. 14½*

| | | | | |
|---|---|---|---|---|
| **2775** | A690 | 1st multi | 1.25 | .65 |
| **2776** | A690 | 1st multi | 1.25 | .65 |
| **2777** | A690 | 1st multi | 1.25 | .65 |
| **2778** | A690 | 1st multi | 1.25 | .65 |
| **2779** | A690 | 1st multi | 1.25 | .65 |
| **2780** | A690 | 1st multi | 1.25 | .65 |
| **2781** | A690 | 1st multi | 1.25 | .65 |
| **2782** | A690 | 1st multi | 1.25 | .65 |
| **2783** | A690 | 1st multi | 1.25 | .65 |
| **2784** | A690 | 1st multi | 1.25 | .65 |
| *a.* | | Block of 10, #2775-2784 | 12.50 | 6.50 |
| | | *Nos. 2775-2784 (10)* | 12.50 | 6.50 |

**Photo.**

**Booklet Stamps**

**Self-Adhesive**

***Die Cut Perf. 14½***

| | | | | |
|---|---|---|---|---|
| **2785** | A690 | 1st multi | 2.50 | .65 |
| **2786** | A690 | 1st multi | 2.50 | .65 |
| *a.* | | Booklet pane of 6, #2785-2786, 4 #MH384a | 11.00 | |

Issued: Nos. 2775-2784, 4/13; Nos. 2785-2786, 6/15. On day of issue, Nos. 2775-2786 each sold for 41p.

King George V and Queen Elizabeth II — A691

British Empire Exhibition Stamps of 1924 — A692

"Britannia Rules the Waves" Stamps of 1913 — A693

Heads of King George V and Lion From Types A81 and A82 — A694

Designs: No. 2788, Great Britain #185. No. 2789, Great Britain #186. No. 2790, Great Britain #176. No. 2791, Great Britain #175.

***Perf. 14½x14 (#2787, 2792), 14¾x14¼***

**Litho. (#2787, 2792), Litho. & Engr.**

**2010**

| | | | | |
|---|---|---|---|---|
| **2787** | A691 | 1st red | 1.25 | .60 |
| **2788** | A692 | 1st multi | 1.25 | .60 |
| **2789** | A692 | 1st multi | 1.25 | .60 |
| *a.* | | Booklet pane of 4, 2 each #2788-2789 (BK193) | 5.00 | — |
| **2790** | A693 | £1 multi | 3.00 | 1.50 |
| **2791** | A693 | £1 multi | 3.00 | 1.50 |
| *a.* | | Souvenir sheet of 4, #2788-2791 | 8.50 | 4.25 |
| *b.* | | Booklet pane of 2, #2790-2791 (BK193) | 6.00 | — |
| **2792** | A694 | £1 brown & silver | 3.00 | 1.50 |
| *a.* | | Souvenir sheet of 2, #2787, 2792 | 4.25 | 2.10 |
| *b.* | | Booklet pane of 6, 3 each #2787, 2792 (BK193) | 13.00 | — |
| | | *Nos. 2787-2792 (6)* | 12.75 | 6.30 |

Issued: No. 2787, 5/6; others, 5/8. London 2010 Festival of Stamps. Nos. 2787-2789 each sold for 41p on day of issue.

**Bird and Thank You Types of 2005-06**

***Die Cut Perf. 14¾x14 Syncopated***

**2010, May 8** **Litho.**

**Self-Adhesive**

| | | | | |
|---|---|---|---|---|
| **2793** | A596 | 1st multi + label (2794a) | 17.50 | 5.00 |
| **2794** | A612 | 1st multi + label (2794a) | 17.50 | 5.00 |
| *a.* | | Sheet of 20, #2427, 2546, 2547, 2793, 2794, 2 each #2745i, 2745j, 3 #2538, 4 each #2745d, 2745g + 20 labels | 40.00 | |

No. 2794a sold for £10. Labels could not be personalized. Nos. 2793 and 2794 each had a franking value of 41p on day of issue.

Britain in World War II — A695

Designs: No. 2795, Prime Minister Winston Churchill reviewing troops. No. 2796, Girl on tractor. No. 2797, Home Guard. No. 2798, Evacuees. No. 2799, Air raid warden. No. 2800, Woman in factory. No. 2801, Firemen at fire. No. 2802, Royal broadcast.

No. 2803, Soldiers in water. No. 2804, Flotilla of small boats. No. 2805, Soldiers in boat. No. 2806, Soldiers on two boats.

**2010, May 13** *Perf. 14½*

| | | | | |
|---|---|---|---|---|
| **2795** | A695 | 1st multi | 1.25 | .60 |
| **2796** | A695 | 1st multi | 1.25 | .60 |
| **2797** | A695 | 60p multi | 1.75 | .85 |
| **2798** | A695 | 60p multi | 1.75 | .85 |
| **2799** | A695 | 67p multi | 2.00 | 1.00 |
| **2800** | A695 | 67p multi | 2.00 | 1.00 |
| **2801** | A695 | 97p multi | 3.00 | 1.50 |
| *a.* | | Booklet pane of 4, #2797-2799, 2801 (BK194) | 8.50 | — |
| **2802** | A695 | 97p multi | 3.00 | 1.50 |
| *a.* | | Booklet pane of 4, #2795-2796, 2800, 2802 (BK194) | 7.50 | — |

**Inscribed "Dunkirk"**

| | | | | |
|---|---|---|---|---|
| **2803** | A695 | 1st multi | 1.25 | .60 |
| **2804** | A695 | 60p multi | 1.75 | .85 |
| **2805** | A695 | 88p multi | 2.60 | 1.25 |
| **2806** | A695 | 97p multi | 3.00 | 1.50 |
| *a.* | | Souvenir sheet of 4, #2803-2806 | 8.75 | 8.75 |
| *b.* | | Booklet pane of 4, #2803-2806 (BK194) | 8.75 | — |
| | | *Nos. 2795-2806 (12)* | 24.60 | 12.10 |

Nos. 2795, 2796 and 2803 each sold for 41p on day of issue.

**British Royalty and History Type of 2008**

Designs: No. 2807, King James I of Great Britain (1603-25). No. 2808, King Charles I. No. 2809, King Charles II. No. 2810, King James II of Great Britain (1685-88). No. 2811, King William III. No. 2812, Queen Mary II. No. 2813, Queen Anne.

No. 2814: a, William Harvey, discoverer of blood circulation, 1628. b, Civil War Battle of Naseby, 1645. c, John Milton, author of Paradise Lost, 1667. d, Castle Howard, designed by John Vanbrugh.

**2010, June 15** *Perf. 14¼*

| | | | | |
|---|---|---|---|---|
| **2807** | A645 | 1st multi | 1.25 | .60 |
| **2808** | A645 | 1st multi | 1.25 | .60 |
| **2809** | A645 | 60p multi | 1.90 | .95 |
| **2810** | A645 | 60p multi | 1.90 | .95 |
| **2811** | A645 | 67p multi | 2.10 | 1.10 |
| **2812** | A645 | 67p multi | 2.10 | 1.10 |
| **2813** | A645 | 88p multi | 2.75 | 1.40 |
| | | *Nos. 2807-2813 (7)* | 13.25 | 6.70 |

**Souvenir Sheet**

| | | | |
|---|---|---|---|
| **2814** | Sheet of 4 | 9.00 | 9.00 |
| *a.* | A645 1st multi | 1.25 | .60 |
| *b.* | A645 60p multi | 1.90 | .95 |
| *c.* | A645 88p multi | 2.75 | 1.40 |
| *d.* | A645 97p multi | 3.00 | 1.50 |

On day of issue, Nos. 2807, 2808 and 2814a each sold for 41p.

**Sports of the 2012 Olympics and Paralympics Type of 2009-10**

Olympics or Paralympics emblem and: Nos. 2815, 2825, Rowing (Paralympics). No. 2816, Shooting. Nos. 2817, Modern pentathlon. No. 2818, Taekwondo. No. 2819, Cycling. Nos. 2820, 2826, Table tennis (Paralympics). No. 2821, Field hockey. No. 2822, Soccer. No. 2823, Goalball (Paralympics). No. 2824, Boxing.

**2010, July 27** **Litho.** *Perf. 14½*

| | | | | |
|---|---|---|---|---|
| **2815** | A673 | 1st multi | 1.40 | .70 |
| **2816** | A673 | 1st multi | 1.40 | .70 |
| **2817** | A673 | 1st multi | 1.40 | .70 |
| **2818** | A673 | 1st multi | 1.40 | .70 |
| **2819** | A673 | 1st multi | 1.40 | .70 |
| *a.* | | Horiz. strip of 5, #2815-2819 | 7.00 | 3.50 |
| **2820** | A673 | 1st multi | 1.40 | .70 |
| **2821** | A673 | 1st multi | 1.40 | .70 |
| **2822** | A673 | 1st multi | 1.40 | .70 |
| *a.* | | Booklet pane of 2, #2704, 2822 (BK200) | 4.00 | — |
| **2823** | A673 | 1st multi | 1.40 | .70 |
| **2824** | A673 | 1st multi | 1.40 | .70 |
| *a.* | | Horiz. strip of 5, #2820-2824 | 7.00 | 3.50 |
| | | *Nos. 2815-2824 (10)* | 14.00 | 7.00 |

**Booklet Stamps**

**Self-Adhesive**

**Photo.**

***Die Cut Perf. 14½***

| | | | | |
|---|---|---|---|---|
| **2825** | A673 | 1st multi (2826a) | 1.40 | .70 |
| **2826** | A673 | 1st multi (2826a) | 1.40 | .70 |
| *a.* | | Booklet pane of 6, #2825, 2826, 4 #MH384a | 8.50 | |

Nos. 2815-2826 each sold for 41p on day of issue. See Nos. 2840-2841.

Issued: No. 2822a, 7/27/12.

Locomotives — A696

Designs: No. 2827, London Midland and Scottish Railway Coronation Class. No. 2828, British Rail Class 9F. No. 2829, Great Western Railway King Class. No. 2830, London North Eastern Railway Class A1. No. 2831, London Midland and Scottish Railway Northern Counties Committee Class WT. No. 2832, Southern Railway King Arthur Class.

**2010, Aug. 19** **Photo.** *Perf. 14¼x14*

| | | | | |
|---|---|---|---|---|
| **2827** | A696 | 1st multi | 1.40 | .70 |
| **2828** | A696 | 1st multi | 1.40 | .70 |
| **2829** | A696 | 67p multi | 2.10 | 1.10 |
| **2830** | A696 | 67p multi | 2.10 | 1.10 |
| **2831** | A696 | 97p multi | 3.25 | 1.60 |
| **2832** | A696 | 97p multi | 3.25 | 1.60 |
| | | *Nos. 2827-2832 (6)* | 13.50 | 6.80 |

Nos. 2827-2828 each sold for 41p on day of issue.

**British Design Type of 2009**

Design: Supermarine Spitfire.

***Die Cut Perf. 14½***

**2010, Sept. 15** **Photo.**

**Booklet Stamp**

**Self-Adhesive**

| | | | | |
|---|---|---|---|---|
| **2833** | A660 | 1st multi | 3.00 | .65 |
| *a.* | | Booklet pane of 6, 2 #2833, 4 #MH384a | 12.00 | |

No. 2833 sold for 41p on day of issue.

Medical Breakthroughs — A697

Designs: 1st, Heart-regulating beta blockers synthesized by Sir James Black, 1962. 58p, Antibiotic properties of penicillin discovered by Sir Alexander Fleming, 1928. 60p, Total hip replacement operation pioneered by Sir John Charnley, 1962. 67p, Artificial lens implant surgery pioneered by Sir Harold Ridley, 1949. 88p, Malaria parasite transmitted by mosquitoes proved by Sir Ronald Ross, 1897. 97p, Computed tomography scanner invented by Sir Godfrey Hounsfield, 1971.

***Perf. 14¼x14½***

**2010, Sept. 16** **Litho.**

| | | | | |
|---|---|---|---|---|
| **2834** | A697 | 1st multi | 1.25 | .65 |
| **2835** | A697 | 58p multi | 1.75 | .90 |
| **2836** | A697 | 60p multi | 1.90 | .95 |
| **2837** | A697 | 67p multi | 2.10 | 1.10 |
| **2838** | A697 | 88p multi | 2.75 | 1.40 |
| **2839** | A697 | 97p multi | 3.00 | 1.50 |
| | | *Nos. 2834-2839 (6)* | 12.75 | 6.50 |

No. 2834 sold for 41p on day of issue. See No. 2866.

**Sports of the 2012 Olympics and Paralympics Type of 2009-10**

Designs: No. 2840, Soccer. No. 2841, Cycling.

***Die Cut Perf. 14½***

**2010, Oct. 12** **Photo.**

**Booklet Stamps**

**Self-Adhesive**

| | | | | |
|---|---|---|---|---|
| **2840** | A673 | 1st multi (2841a) | 3.00 | .70 |
| **2841** | A673 | 1st multi (2841a) | 3.00 | .70 |
| *a.* | | Booklet pane of 6, #2840, 2841, 4 #MH384a | 12.00 | |

Nos. 2840-2841 each sold for 41p on day of issue.

Characters From Winnie-the-Pooh Stories by A. A. Milne — A698

Winnie-the-Pooh and: No. 2842, Christopher Robin. 58p, Piglet. No. 2844, Rabbit. 67p, Eeyore. No. 2846, Friends. No. 2847, Tigger.

No. 2848 — Winnie-the-Pooh and Christopher Robin with inscriptions: a, Wherever I am, there's always Pooh. b, There's always Pooh and Me, Whatever I do, he wants to do. c, "Where are you going to-day?" says Pooh: "Well, that's very odd 'cos I was too." d, "Let's go together," says Pooh, says he. "Let's go together," says Pooh.

**2010, Oct. 12** **Litho.** *Perf. 14¼x14½*

| | | | | |
|---|---|---|---|---|
| **2842** | A698 | 1st multi | 1.40 | .70 |
| **2843** | A698 | 58p multi | 1.90 | .95 |
| **2844** | A698 | 60p multi | 1.90 | .95 |
| **2845** | A698 | 67p multi | 2.10 | 1.10 |

**2846** A698 88p multi 2.75 1.40
**2847** A698 97p multi 3.25 1.60
*Nos. 2842-2847 (6)* 13.30 6.70

### Souvenir Sheet
***Perf. 14½***

**2848** Sheet of 4 9.50 9.50
*a.* A698 1st multi 1.40 .70
*b.* A698 60p multi 1.90 .95
*c.* A698 88p multi 2.75 1.40
*d.* A698 97p multi 3.25 1.60

Europa (Nos. 2842, 2848a). Nos. 2842 and 2848a each sold for 41p on day of issue.

Christmas
A699 A700

Designs: 2nd, Wallace and Gromit singing Christmas carols. 1st, Gromit mailing Christmas cards. 2nd Large, Wallace and Gromit singing Christmas carols, Christmas tree at left. 60p, Wallace and Gromit decorating Christmas tree. 1st Large, Gromit mailing Christmas cards, Feathers McGraw at left. 97p, Gromit carrying Christmas pudding. £1.46, Gromit wearing large sweater.

***Perf. 14¾x14 Syncopated***

**2010, Nov. 2** **Photo.**
**2849** Sheet of 7 16.50 8.25
*a.* A699 2nd multi 1.10 .55
*b.* A699 1st multi 1.40 .70
*c.* A700 2nd Large multi 1.75 .85
*d.* A699 60p multi 2.00 1.00
*e.* A700 1st Large multi 2.10 1.10
*f.* A699 97p multi 3.25 1.60
*g.* A699 £1.46 multi 4.75 2.40

### Self-Adhesive
***Die Cut Perf. 14¾x14 Syncopated***

**2850** A699 2nd multi 1.10 .55
*a.* Booklet pane of 12 13.50
*b.* Litho., serpentine die cut 14¾x14 syncopated, + label (2855b) 1.10 1.10
*c.* Sheet of 20 #2850b 32.50 —
**2851** A699 1st multi 1.40 .70
*a.* Booklet pane of 12 17.00
*b.* Litho., serpentine die cut 14¾x14 syncopated, + label (2855b) 1.40 1.40
*c.* Sheet of 20 #2851b 45.00 —
**2852** A700 2nd Large multi 1.75 .85
**2853** A699 60p multi 2.00 1.00
*a.* Litho., serpentine die cut 14¾x14 syncopated, + label (2855b) 2.00 2.00
*b.* Sheet of 10 #2853a 32.50 —
**2854** A700 1st Large multi 2.10 1.10
**2855** A699 97p multi 3.25 1.60
*a.* Litho., serpentine die cut 14¾x14 syncopated, + label (2855b) 3.25 3.25
*b.* Sheet of 20, 8 each #2850b, 2851b, 2 each #2853a, 2855a, + 20 labels 31.00
*c.* Sheet of 10 #2855a 47.50 —
**2856** A699 £1.46 multi 4.75 2.40
*Nos. 2850-2856 (7)* 16.35 8.20

On day of issue, Nos. 2849a and 2850 each sold for 32p, Nos. 2849b and 2851 each sold for 41p, Nos. 2849c and 2852 each sold for 51p, and Nos. 2849e and 2854 each sold for 66p. No. 2855b sold for £9.30 and contained 20 labels that could not be personalized.

Nos. 2850c, 2851c, 2853b and 2855c had labels that could be personalized. Nos. 2850a and 2853b each sold for £9.95; No. 2851c sold for £13.95; No. 2855c sold for £14.50. Sheets of 10 No. 2850b were also sold but these were halves of No. 2850c torn along the sheet's central row of rouletting. Nos. 2853b and 2855c have rouletting along the left or right side of the sheet, but these stamps were not sold in sheets of 20.

Television Shows Created By Gerry Anderson
A701

Designs: No. 2857, Joe 90. No. 2858, Captain Scarlet. Nos. 2859, 2864, Thunderbirds. No. 2860, Stingray. No. 2861, Fireball XL5. No. 2862, Supercar.

No. 2863 — Opening sequence of show depicting Thunderbird: a, "4." b, "3." c, "2." d, "1."

**2011, Jan. 11** **Litho.** ***Perf. 14¼***
**2857** A701 1st multi 1.40 .70
**2858** A701 1st multi 1.40 .70
**2859** A701 1st multi 1.40 .70
*a.* Horiz. strip of 3, #2857-2859 4.20 2.10
**2860** A701 97p multi 3.25 1.60
**2861** A701 97p multi 3.25 1.60
**2862** A701 97p multi 3.25 1.60
*a.* Horiz. strip of 3, #2860-2862 9.75 4.80
*Nos. 2857-2862 (6)* 13.95 6.90

### Souvenir Sheet
### Litho. With Three-Dimensional Plastic Affixed

**2863** Sheet of 4 9.50 9.50
*a.* A701 41p multi 1.40 1.40
*b.* A701 60p multi 1.90 1.90
*c.* A701 88p multi 2.75 2.75
*d.* A701 97p multi 3.25 3.25

### Booklet Stamp
### Self-Adhesive
***Die Cut Perf. 14¼x14***

**2864** A701 1st multi 3.00 .70
*a.* Booklet pane of 6, 2 #2864, 4 #MH384a 12.00

On day of issue, Nos. 2857-2859, 2864 each sold for 41p.

Miniature Sheet

Locomotives — A702

No. 2865: a, British Railways Dean Goods No. 2532. b, Peckett R2 Thor. c, Lancashire & Yorkshire Railway 1093 No. 1100. d, British Railways WD No. 90662.

**2011, Feb. 1** **Litho.** ***Perf. 14¼***
**2865** A702 Sheet of 4 9.75 9.75
*a.* 1st multi 1.40 .70
*b.* 60p multi 2.00 1.00
*c.* 88p multi 3.00 1.50
*d.* 97p multi 3.25 1.60

No. 2865a sold for 41p on day of issue. See No. 2930.

### Medical Breakthroughs Type of 2010

Design: Heart-regulating beta blockers, synthesized by Sir James Black, 1962.

***Die Cut Perf. 14¼x14½***
**2011, Feb. 24** **Photo.**

### Booklet Stamp
### Self-Adhesive

**2866** A697 1st multi 3.00 .70
*a.* Booklet pane of 6, 2 #2866, 4 #MH384a 12.00

No. 2866 sold for 41p on day of issue.

Musicals — A703

Designs: No. 2867, Oliver! No. 2868, Blood Brothers. No. 2869, We Will Rock You. No. 2870, Monty Python's Spamalot. No. 2871, Rocky Horror Show. No. 2872, Me and My Girl. No. 2873, Return to the Forbidden Planet. No. 2874, Billy Elliot.

**2011, Feb. 24** **Litho.** ***Perf. 14¼***
**2867** A703 1st multi 1.40 .70
**2868** A703 1st multi 1.40 .70
**2869** A703 1st multi 1.40 .70
**2870** A703 1st multi 1.40 .70
**2871** A703 97p multi 3.25 1.60
**2872** A703 97p multi 3.25 1.60
**2873** A703 97p multi 3.25 1.60
**2874** A703 97p multi 3.25 1.60
*Nos. 2867-2874 (8)* 18.60 9.20

On day of issue, Nos. 2867-2870 each sold for 41p.

Fictional Wizards and Magicians
A704

Designs: No. 2875, Rincewind, from Discworld, by Terry Pratchett. No. 2876, Nanny Ogg, from Discworld. No. 2877, Dumbledore, from Harry Potter stories, by J.K. Rowling. No. 2878, Lord Voldemort, from Harry Potter stories. No. 2879, Merlin, from Arthurian legend. No. 2880, Morgan Le Fay, from Arthurian legend. No. 2881, Aslan, from Narnia, by C. S. Lewis. No. 2882, The White Witch, from Narnia.

**2011, Mar. 8** **Photo.** ***Perf. 14½***
**2875** A704 1st multi 1.40 .70
**2876** A704 1st multi 1.40 .70
*a.* Vert. pair, #2875-2876 2.80 1.40
**2877** A704 1st multi 1.40 .70
**2878** A704 1st multi 1.40 .70
*a.* Vert. pair, #2877-2878 2.80 1.40
**2879** A704 60p multi 2.00 1.00
**2880** A704 60p multi 2.00 1.00
*a.* Vert. pair, #2879-2880 4.00 2.00
**2881** A704 97p multi 3.25 1.60
**2882** A704 97p multi 3.25 1.60
*a.* Vert. pair, #2881-2882 6.50 3.25
*Nos. 2875-2882 (8)* 16.10 8.00

On day of issue, Nos. 2875-2878 each sold for 41p.

A705

Worldwide Fund for Nature (WWF), 50th Anniv. — A706

Designs: No. 2883, African elephant. No. 2884, Mountain gorilla. No. 2885, Siberian tiger. No. 2886, Polar bear. No. 2887, Amur leopard. No. 2888, Iberian lynx. No. 2889, Red panda. No. 2890. Black rhinoceros. No. 2891, African wild dog. No. 2892, Golden lion tamarin.

No. 2893, a, Spider monkey. b, Hyacinth macaw. c, Poison dart frog. d, Jaguar.

**2011, Mar. 22** **Litho.** ***Perf. 14½***
**2883** A705 1st multi 1.40 .70
**2884** A705 1st multi 1.40 .70
**2885** A705 1st multi 1.40 .70
**2886** A705 1st multi 1.40 .70
**2887** A705 1st multi 1.40 .70
*a.* Horiz. strip of 5, #2883-2887 7.00 3.50
**2888** A705 1st multi 1.40 .70
**2889** A705 1st multi 1.40 .70
**2890** A705 1st multi 1.40 .70
*a.* Booklet pane of 6, #2885-2890 (BK195) 8.50 —
**2891** A705 1st multi 1.40 .70
**2892** A705 1st multi 1.40 .70
*a.* Horiz. strip of 5, #2888-2892 7.00 3.50
*b.* Booklet pane of 4, #2883-2884, 2891-2892 (BK195) 5.25 —
*Nos. 2883-2892 (10)* 14.00 7.00

***Perf. 14¼***

**2893** A706 Sheet of 4 9.75 9.75
*a.* 1st multi 1.40 .70
*b.* 60p multi 2.00 1.00
*c.* 88p multi 3.00 1.50
*d.* 97p multi 3.25 1.60
*e.* Booklet pane of 4, #2893a-2893d (BK195) 9.75 —

Europa (nos. 2893a, 2893e). On day of issue, Nos. 2883-2892 and 2893a each sold for 41p. No. 2893e is 150x96mm, and has additional printing in booklet pane margin beyond that shown in illustration A706.

A707

Royal Shakespeare Company, Stratford-on-Avon, 50th Anniv. — A708

Line from play by William Shakespeare and: No. 2894, David Tennant in *Hamlet*. 66p, Anthony Sher in *The Tempest*. No. 2896, Chuk Iwuji in *Henry VI*. No. 2897, Paul Schofield in *King Lear*. No. 2898, Sarah Kestelman in *A Midsummer Night's Dream*. £1.10, Ian McKellen and Francesca Annis in *Romeo and Juliet*.

No. 2900: a, Janet Suzman in *Hamlet* at Royal Shakespeare Theater. b, Patrick Stewart in *Antony and Cleopatra* at Swan Theater. c, Geoffrey Streatfeild in *Henry V* at the Courtyard Theater. d, Dame Judi Dench in *Macbeth*at the Other Place.

**2011, Apr. 12** **Photo.** ***Perf. 14½***
**2894** A707 1st red & black 1.50 .75
**2895** A707 66p black & red 2.25 1.10
**2896** A707 68p red & black 2.25 1.10
**2897** A707 76p black & red 2.50 1.25
**2898** A707 £1 red & black 3.25 1.60
**2899** A707 £1.10 black & red 3.75 1.90
*Nos. 2894-2899 (6)* 15.50 7.70

### Litho.
***Perf. 14¼***

**2900** A708 Sheet of 4 9.50 9.50
*a.* 1st multi 1.50 .75
*b.* 68p multi 2.25 1.10
*c.* 76p multi 2.50 1.25
*d.* £1 multi 3.25 1.60

On day of issue, Nos. 2894 and 2900 sold for 46p.

Souvenir Sheet

Wedding of Prince William and Catherine Middleton — A709

***Perf. 14½x14¼***
**2011, Apr. 21** **Photo.**
**2901** A709 Sheet of 4, 2 each #a-b 10.50 10.50
*a.* 1st Couple 1.50 .75
*b.* £1.10 Couple, diff. 3.75 1.90

No. 2901a sold for 46p on day of issue.

William Morris & Company, 150th Anniv.
A710

Designs: No. 2902, Floral fabric design, by William Morris, 1884. No. 2903, Cherry tree wall panel design, by Philip Webb, 1867. No. 2904, Floral wallpaper design, by John Henry Dearle, 1901. No. 2905, Floral ceramic tile design, by Kate Faulkner. No. 2906, Floral glazed tile design, by Morris and William De Morgan, 1876. No. 2907, The Merchant's Daughter, stained-glass by Edward Burne-Jones, c. 1864.

**2011, May 5** **Litho.** ***Perf. 14¼***
**2902** A710 1st multi 1.50 .75
**2903** A710 1st multi 1.50 .75
**2904** A710 76p multi 2.50 1.25
**2905** A710 76p multi 2.50 1.25
**2906** A710 £1.10 multi 3.75 1.90
*a.* Booklet pane of 4, #2902, 2904, 2905, 2906 (BK196) 11.00 —

**2907** A710 £1.10 multi 3.75 1.90
*a.* Booklet pane of 4, 2 each #2903, 2907 (BK196) 11.00 —
*Nos. 2902-2907 (6)* 15.50 7.80

No. 2902 sold for 46p on day of issue.

A711

Thomas the Tank Engine Children's Book Characters, by Rev. Wilbert Awdry (1911-97) — A712

Designs: No. 2908, Thomas. 66p, James. No. 2910, Percy. No. 2911, Daisy. No. 2912, Toby. £1.10, Gordon.

No. 2914 — Inscriptions: a, "Goodbye, Bertie," called Thomas. b, James was more dirty than hurt. c, "Yes, Sir," Percy shivered miserably. d, They told Henry, "We shall leave you there for always."

No. 2915, Like No. 2914a.

**2011, June 14** *Perf. 14¾x14¼*

**2908** A711 1st multi 1.50 .75
**2909** A711 66p multi 2.10 1.10
**2910** A711 68p multi 2.25 1.10
**2911** A711 76p multi 2.50 1.25
**2912** A711 £1 multi 3.25 1.60
**2913** A711 £1.10 multi 3.50 1.75
*Nos. 2908-2913 (6)* 15.10 7.55

*Perf. 14¼*

**2914** A712 Sheet of 4 9.50 9.50
*a.* 1st multi 1.50 .75
*b.* 68p multi 2.25 1.10
*c.* 76p multi 2.50 1.25
*d.* £1 multi 3.25 1.60

**Booklet Stamp**
**Self-Adhesive**
**Photo.**
*Die Cut Perf. 14¼*

**2915** A712 1st multi 1.50 .75
*a.* Booklet pane of 6, 2 #2915, 4 #MH384a 9.00

On day of issue, Nos. 2908, 2914a and 2915 each sold for 46p.

## Sports of the 2012 Summer Olympics and Paralympics Type of 2009-10

Olympics or Paralympics emblem and: Nos. 2916, 2927, Sailing (Paralympics). No. 2917, High jump. No. 2918, Volleyball. Nos. 2919, 2926, Wheelchair rugby (Paralympics). No. 2920, Wrestling. No. 2921, Wheelchair tennis (Paralympics). Nos. 2922, 2929, Fencing. Nos. 2923, 2928, Gymnastics. No. 2924, Triathlon. No. 2925, Handball.

**2011** **Litho.** *Perf. 14½*

**2916** A673 1st multi 1.50 .75
**2917** A673 1st multi 1.50 .75
*a.* Booklet pane of 2, #2705, 2917 (BK200) 4.00 —
**2918** A673 1st multi 1.50 .75
**2919** A673 1st multi 1.50 .75
**2920** A673 1st multi 1.50 .75
*a.* Horiz. strip of 5, #2916-2920 7.50 3.75
**2921** A673 1st multi 1.50 .75
**2922** A673 1st multi 1.50 .75
**2923** A673 1st multi 1.50 .75
**2924** A673 1st multi 1.50 .75
**2925** A673 1st multi 1.50 .75
*a.* Horiz. strip of 5, #2921-2925 7.50 3.75
*b.* Sheet of 30, #2702-2711, 2815-2824, 2916-2925 47.50 47.50
*Nos. 2916-2925 (10)* 15.00 7.50

**Booklet Stamps**
**Self-Adhesive**
**Photo.**
*Die Cut Perf. 14½*

**2926** A673 1st multi 1.50 .75
**2927** A673 1st multi 1.50 .75
*a.* Booklet pane of 6, #2926-2927, 4 #MH384a 9.00
**2928** A673 1st multi 1.50 .75
**2929** A673 1st multi 1.50 .75
*a.* Booklet pane of 6, #2928-2929, + 4 #MH384a 9.00

Issued: Nos. 2916-2927, 7/27. Nos. 2928-2929, 9/15. No. 2917a, 7/27/12. No. 2925b, 7/27. Nos. 2916-2929 each sold for 46p on day of issue. No. 2925b sold for £13.80.

## Locomotives Type of 2011

Design: British Railways Dean Goods No. 2532.

*Die Cut Perf. 14¼*

**2011, Aug. 23** **Photo.**

**Booklet Stamp**
**Self-Adhesive**

**2930** A702 1st multi 1.50 .75
*a.* Booklet pane of 6, 2 #2930, 4 #MH384a 9.00

No. 2930 sold for 46p on day of issue.

British Crown Jewels A713

Designs: No. 2931, Sovereign's scepter with cross. No. 2932, St. Edward's crown. No. 2933, Rod and scepter with doves. No. 2934, Queen Mary's crown. No. 2935, Sovereign's orb. No. 2936, Jeweled sword of offering. No. 2937, Imperial state crown. No. 2938, Coronation spoon.

*Perf. 14¼x14½*

**2011, Aug. 23** **Litho.**

**2931** A713 1st multi 1.50 .75
**2932** A713 1st multi 1.50 .75
**2933** A713 68p multi 2.25 1.10
**2934** A713 68p multi 2.25 1.10
**2935** A713 76p multi 2.40 1.25
**2936** A713 76p multi 2.40 1.25
**2937** A713 £1.10 multi 3.50 1.75
**2938** A713 £1.10 multi 3.50 1.75
*Nos. 2931-2938 (8)* 19.30 9.70

On day of issue Nos. 2931-2932 each sold for 46p.

Miniature Sheet

First Air Mail Flight in Great Britain, Cent. — A714

No. 2939: a, Pilot Gustav Hamel receives first mail bag. b, Hamel in plane ready to leave Hendon Aerodrome. c, Clement Greswell near his Blériot airplane at Windsor Castle. d, Air mail delivered at Windsor Castle.

**2011, Sept. 9** **Litho.** *Perf. 14¼x14*

**2939** A714 Sheet of 4 10.50 10.50
*a.* 1st multi 1.50 .75
*b.* 68p multi 2.25 1.10
*c.* £1 multi 3.25 1.60
*d.* £1.10 multi 3.50 1.75
*e.* Booklet pane of 3, #2939c, 2 #2939b (BK197) 8.25 —
*f.* Booklet pane of 3, #2939d, 2 #2939a (BK197) 7.25 —

No. 2939a sold for 46p on day of issue.

## British Royalty and History Type of 2008

Designs: No. 2940, King George I. No. 2941, King George II. No. 2942, King George III. No. 2943, King George IV. No. 2944, King William IV. No. 2945, Queen Victoria.

No. 2946: a, Robert Walpole, first Prime Minister. b, Interior of Kedleston Hall, designed by architect Robert Adam. c, Great Britain #1. d, Queen Victoria in 1897.

**2011, Sept. 15** *Perf. 14¼*

**2940** A645 1st multi 1.50 .75
**2941** A645 1st multi 1.50 .75
**2942** A645 76p multi 2.40 1.25
**2943** A645 76p multi 2.40 1.25
**2944** A645 £1.10 multi 3.50 1.75
**2945** A645 £1.10 multi 3.50 1.75
*Nos. 2940-2945 (6)* 14.80 7.50
**2946** Sheet of 4 9.50 9.50
*a.* A645 1st multi 1.50 .75
*b.* A645 68p multi 2.25 1.10
*c.* A645 76p multi 2.40 1.25
*d.* A645 £1 multi 3.25 1.60

On day of issue, Nos. 2940, 2941 and 2946a each sold for 46p.

Great Britain Landmarks in Alphabetical Order — A715

Designs: No. 2947, Angel of the North sculpture, Gateshead. No. 2948, Blackpool Tower. No. 2949, Carrick-a-Rede rope bridge, near Ballintoy, Northern Ireland. No. 2950, 10 Downing Street (Prime Minister's residence, London). No. 2951, Edinburgh Castle. No. 2952, Forth Railway Bridge. No. 2953, Glastonbury Tor. No. 2954, Harlech Castle. No. 2955, Ironbridge. No. 2956, Jodrell Bank radio telescope. No. 2957, Kursaal, Southend. No. 2958, Lindisfarne Priory, Lindisfarne Island. No. 2959, Manchester Town Hall. No. 2960, Narrow Water Castle, near Warrenpoint, Northern Ireland. No. 2961, Old Bailey Courthouse, London. No. 2962, Portmeirion, Wales. No. 2963, Queen's College, Oxford University. No. 2964, Roman Baths, Bath. No. 2965, Stirling Castle, Stirling, Scotland. No. 2966, Tyne Bridge, Newcastle. No. 2967, Urquhart Castle, near Drumnadrochit, Scotland. No. 2968, Victoria and Albert Museum, London. No. 2969, White Cliffs of Dover. No. 2970, Station X, Bletchley Park. No. 2971, York Minster. No. 2972, ZSL London Zoo.

**2011** *Perf. 14½*

**2947** A715 1st multi 1.50 .75
**2948** A715 1st multi 1.50 .75
**2949** A715 1st multi 1.50 .75
**2950** A715 1st multi 1.50 .75
**2951** A715 1st multi 1.50 .75
**2952** A715 1st multi 1.50 .75
*a.* Horiz. strip of 6, #2947-2952 9.00 4.50
**2953** A715 1st multi 1.50 .75
**2954** A715 1st multi 1.50 .75
**2955** A715 1st multi 1.50 .75
**2956** A715 1st multi 1.50 .75
**2957** A715 1st multi 1.50 .75
**2958** A715 1st multi 1.50 .75
*a.* Horiz. strip of 6, #2953-2958 9.00 4.50
*Nos. 2947-2958 (12)* 18.00 9.00
**2959** A715 1st multi 1.50 .75
**2960** A715 1st multi 1.50 .75
**2961** A715 1st multi 1.50 .75
**2962** A715 1st multi 1.50 .75
**2963** A715 1st multi 1.50 .75
**2964** A715 1st multi 1.50 .75
*a.* Horiz. strip of 6, #2959-2964 9.00 4.50
**2965** A715 1st multi 1.50 .75
**2966** A715 1st multi 1.50 .75
**2967** A715 1st multi 1.50 .75
**2968** A715 1st multi 1.50 .75
**2969** A715 1st multi 1.50 .75
**2970** A715 1st multi 1.50 .75
*a.* Horiz. strip of 6, #2965-2970 9.00 4.50
**2971** A715 1st multi 1.50 .75
**2972** A715 1st multi 1.50 .75
*a.* Horiz. pair, #2971-2972 3.00 1.50
*b.* Sheet of 26, #2947-2972, + 4 labels 39.00 39.00
*Nos. 2959-2972 (14)* 21.00 10.50
*Nos. 2947-2972 (26)* 39.00 19.50

Europa (No. 2968).

Issued: Nos. 2947-2958, 10/13. Nos. 2959-2972, 4/10/12. On day of issue, Nos. 2947-2972 each sold for 46p.

A716

A717

Designs: Nos. 2973a, 2973c, 2974, 2976, Angel visiting Joseph. Nos. 2973b, 2975, Madonna and Child, Nos. 2973e, 2978, Madonna and Child, livestock, dove. 68p, Baby Jesus in manger, livestock. £1.10, Angel visiting shepherds. £1.65, Magi and Star of Bethlehem.

*Perf. 14¾x14 Syncopated*

**2011, Nov. 8** **Photo.**

**2973** Sheet of 7 18.50 9.00
*a.* A716 2nd multi 1.25 .60
*b.* A716 1st multi 1.50 .75
*c.* A717 2nd Large multi 1.90 .95
*d.* A716 68p multi 2.25 1.10
*e.* A717 1st Large multi 2.40 1.25
*f.* A716 £1.10 multi 3.50 1.75
*g.* A716 £1.65 multi 5.25 2.60

**Self-Adhesive**
*Die Cut Perf. 14¾x14 Syncopated*

**2974** A716 2nd multi 1.25 .60
*a.* Booklet pane of 12 15.00
*b.* Sheet of 20 #2974 + 20 labels, litho. 35.00
**2975** A716 1st multi 1.50 .75
*a.* Booklet pane of 12 18.00
*b.* Sheet of 10 #2975 + 10 labels, litho. 26.00
**2976** A717 2nd Large multi 1.90 .95
**2977** A716 68p multi 2.25 1.10
*a.* Sheet of 10 #2977 + 10 labels, litho. 34.00
**2978** A717 1st Large multi 2.40 1.25
**2979** A716 £1.10 multi 3.50 1.75
*a.* Sheet of 20, 8 each #2974-2975, 2 each #2977, 2979, + 20 labels, litho. 33.00
*b.* Sheet of 10 #2979 + 10 labels, litho. 50.00
**2980** A716 £1.65 multi 5.25 2.60
*Nos. 2974-2980 (7)* 18.05 9.00

On day of issue, Nos. 2973a and 2974 each sold for 36p; Nos. 2973b and 2975 for 46p; Nos. 2973c and 2976 for 58p; Nos. 2973e and 2978 for 75p. No. 2979a sold for £10.45. Labels on No. 2979a could not be personalized.

Nos. 2974b, 2975b, 2977a and 2979b had labels that could be personalized. No. 2974b sold for £10.95; No. 2975b, for £8.30; No. 2977a, for £10.75; and No. 2979b, for £15.80. No. 2975b was half of a larger sheet of 20 stamps and 20 labels that sold for £14.95, which was torn along central row of rouletting. Nos. 2977a and 2979b have rouletting along the left or right side of the sheet, but these stamps were not sold in sheets of 20.

Emblem of 2012 Summer Olympics A718

Emblem of 2012 Paralympics A719

*Die Cut Perf. 14¾x14 Syncopated*

**2012, Jan. 5** **Photo.**

**Self-Adhesive**

**2981** A718 1st gray, org & blk 1.50 .75
**2982** A719 1st gray, org & blk 1.50 .75
*a.* Booklet pane of 6, 3 each #2981-2982, #2981 at UL 9.00
*b.* As "a," #2982 at UL 9.00 9.00

See Nos. 3044-3045, C6-C9.

Illustratrions From Children's Books by Roald Dahl (1916-90) — A720

Designs: 1st, Charlie and the Chocolate Factory. 66p, Fantastic Mr. Fox. 68p, James and the Giant Peach. 76p, Matilda. £1, The Twits. £1.10, The Witches.

No. 2989 — Scenes from The BFG (Big Friendly Giant): a, Giant holding Sophie in hand. b, Big Friendly Giant and Sophie awakening other Giants. c, Sophie on Queen's window sill. d, Giant and Sophie at desk.

**2012, Jan. 10** **Litho.** *Perf. 14¼*

**2983** A720 1st multi 1.50 .75
**2984** A720 66p multi 2.10 1.10
**2985** A720 68p multi 2.25 1.10
**2986** A720 76p multi 2.40 1.25
*a.* Booklet pane of 3, #2983, 2985, 2986 (BK198) 6.50 —
**2987** A720 £1 multi 3.25 1.60
**2988** A720 £1.10 multi 3.50 1.75
*a.* Booklet pane of 3, #2984, 2987, 2988 (BK198) 9.50 —
*Nos. 2983-2988 (6)* 15.00 7.55

**Souvenir Sheet**
*Perf. 14¼x14½*

**2989** Sheet of 4 9.50 9.50
*a.* A720 1st multi 1.50 .75
*b.* A720 68p multi 2.25 1.10
*c.* A720 76p multi 2.40 1.25

| | | | |
|---|---|---|---|
| *d.* | A720 £1 multi | 3.25 | 1.60 |
| *e.* | Booklet pane of 4, #2989a-2989d (BK198) | 10.00 | — |

On day of issue, Nos. 2983 and 2989a sold for 46p. No. 2989 contains four 36x35mm stamps.

### British Royalty and History Type of 2008

Designs: No. 2990, King Edward VII. No. 2991, King George V. No. 2992, King Edward VIII. No. 2993, King George VI. £1.10, Queen Elizabeth II.

No. 2995: a, 1912 Scott Expedition to the South Pole. b, King Georg VI and Queen Mary talking with man amidst World War II damage. c, Victory of 1966 English World Cup soccer team. d, Opening of Channel Tunnel, 1994.

**2012, Feb. 2 Litho. *Perf. 14¼***

| | | | | |
|---|---|---|---|---|
| **2990** | A645 | 1st multi | 1.50 | .75 |
| **2991** | A645 | 68p multi | 2.25 | 1.10 |
| **2992** | A645 | 76p multi | 2.40 | 1.25 |
| **2993** | A645 | £1 multi | 3.25 | 1.60 |
| **2994** | A645 | £1.10 multi | 3.50 | 1.75 |
| | | *Nos. 2990-2994 (5)* | 12.90 | 6.45 |

**Souvenir Sheet**

| | | | |
|---|---|---|---|
| **2995** | Sheet of 4 | 9.50 | 9.50 |
| *a.* | A645 1st multi | 1.50 | .75 |
| *b.* | A645 68p multi | 2.25 | 1.10 |
| *c.* | A645 76p multi | 2.40 | 1.25 |
| *d.* | A645 £1 multi | 3.25 | 1.60 |

On day of issue, Nos. 2990 and 2995a each sold for 46p.

Miniature Sheet

Reign of Queen Elizabeth II, 60th Anniv. — A721

No. 2996 — Image of Queen Elizabeth II: a, Great Britain Type A131 redrawn. b, From 1960 one-pound banknote ("ND" at upper left). c, From 1971 five-pound banknote. d, From coin, without tiara. e, From coin, with tiara. f, Great Britain Type MH2 with iridescent overprint of "Diamond Jubilee" in wavy lines.

***Perf. 14¾x14 Syncopated***

**2012, Feb. 6 Photo.**

| | | | | |
|---|---|---|---|---|
| **2996** | A721 | Sheet of 6 | 9.00 | 4.50 |
| *a.-f.* | | 1st Any single | 1.50 | .75 |
| **2996G** | A721 | 1st As #2996a, litho. (2996Gh) | 2.00 | 2.00 |
| *h.* | | Booklet pane of 8, 4 each #2996G, MH419, + central label (BK199) | 16.00 | — |

Nos. 2996a-2996f each sold for 46p on day of issue.

Issued: No. 2996G, 2996Gh, 5/31. No. 2996G sold for 60p on day of issue.

Britons of Distinction A722

Designs: No. 2997, New Coventry Cathedral, designed by Sir Basil Spence (1907-76). No. 2998, Frederick Delius (1862-1934), composer. No. 2999, Orange Tree embroidery by Mary "May" Morris (1862-1938), designer and textile artist. No. 3000, Odette Hallowes (1912-95), Special Operations Executive agent in World War II. No. 3001, Atmospheric steam engine invented by Thomas Newcomen (1664-1729). No. 3002, Kathleen Ferrier (1912-53), opera singer. No. 3003, Interior of Palace of Westminster, designed by Augustus Pugin (1812-53). No. 3004, Montague Rhodes James (1862-1936), medieval scholar and writer of ghost stories. No. 3005, Bombe codebreaking machine designed by Alan Turing (1912-54), mathematician and cryptanalyst. No. 3006, Joan Mary Fry (1862-1955), relief worker and social reformer.

**2012, Feb. 23 Litho. *Perf. 14½***

| | | | | |
|---|---|---|---|---|
| **2997** | A722 | 1st multi | 1.50 | .75 |
| **2998** | A722 | 1st multi | 1.50 | .75 |
| **2999** | A722 | 1st multi | 1.50 | .75 |
| **3000** | A722 | 1st multi | 1.50 | .75 |
| **3001** | A722 | 1st multi | 1.50 | .75 |
| *a.* | | Horiz. strip of 5, #2997-3001 | 7.50 | 3.75 |
| **3002** | A722 | 1st multi | 1.50 | .75 |
| **3003** | A722 | 1st multi | 1.50 | .75 |
| **3004** | A722 | 1st multi | 1.50 | .75 |
| **3005** | A722 | 1st multi | 1.50 | .75 |
| **3006** | A722 | 1st multi | 1.50 | .75 |
| *a.* | | Horiz. strip of 5, #3002-3006 | 7.50 | 3.75 |
| | | *Nos. 2997-3006 (10)* | 15.00 | 7.50 |

Nos. 2997-3006 each sold for 46p on day of issue.

Miniature Sheet

Scottish Locomotives — A723

No. 3007: a, British Railways D34 Nos. 62471 and 62496. b, British Railways D40 No. 62276. c, Andrew Barclay No. 807. d, British Railways 4P No. 54767.

**2012, Mar. 8 *Perf. 14¼***

| | | | | |
|---|---|---|---|---|
| **3007** | A723 | Sheet of 4 | 10.50 | 5.25 |
| *a.* | | 1st multi | 1.50 | .75 |
| *b.* | | 68p multi | 2.25 | 1.10 |
| *c.* | | £1 multi | 3.25 | 1.60 |
| *d.* | | £1.10 multi | 3.50 | 1.75 |

No. 3007a sold for 46p on day of issue. See No. 3111.

Comic Book Covers and Characters A724

Designs: No. 3008, The Dandy. No. 3009, The Beano. No. 3010, Eagle. No. 3011, The Topper. No. 3012, Tiger. No. 3013, Bunty. No. 3014, Buster. No. 3015, Valiant. No. 3016, Twinkle. No. 3017, 2000 A.D.

**2012, Mar. 20 *Perf. 14½***

| | | | | |
|---|---|---|---|---|
| **3008** | A724 | 1st multi | 1.50 | .75 |
| **3009** | A724 | 1st multi | 1.50 | .75 |
| **3010** | A724 | 1st multi | 1.50 | .75 |
| **3011** | A724 | 1st multi | 1.50 | .75 |
| **3012** | A724 | 1st multi | 1.50 | .75 |
| *a.* | | Horiz. strip of 5, #3008-3012 | 7.50 | 3.75 |
| **3013** | A724 | 1st multi | 1.50 | .75 |
| **3014** | A724 | 1st multi | 1.50 | .75 |
| **3015** | A724 | 1st multi | 1.50 | .75 |
| **3016** | A724 | 1st multi | 1.50 | .75 |
| **3017** | A724 | 1st multi | 1.50 | .75 |
| *a.* | | Horiz. strip of 5, #3013-3017 | 7.50 | 3.75 |
| | | *Nos. 3008-3017 (10)* | 15.00 | 7.50 |

Nos. 3008-3017 each sold for 46p on day of issue.

Fashion A725

Clothing designed by: No. 3018, Hardy Amies. No. 3019, Norman Hartnell. No. 3020, Granny Takes a Trip. No. 3021, Ossie Clark. No. 3022, Tommy Nutter. No. 3023, Jean Muir. No. 3024, Zandra Rhodes. No. 3025, Vivienne Westwood. No. 3025, Paul Smith. No. 3026, Alexander McQueen.

**2012, May 15 Litho. *Perf. 14½***

| | | | | |
|---|---|---|---|---|
| **3018** | A725 | 1st multi | 1.90 | .95 |
| **3019** | A725 | 1st multi | 1.90 | .95 |
| **3020** | A725 | 1st multi | 1.90 | .95 |
| **3021** | A725 | 1st multi | 1.90 | .95 |
| **3022** | A725 | 1st multi | 1.90 | .95 |
| *a.* | | Horiz. strip of 5, #3018-3022 | 9.50 | 4.75 |
| **3023** | A725 | 1st multi | 1.90 | .95 |
| **3024** | A725 | 1st multi | 1.90 | .95 |
| **3025** | A725 | 1st multi | 1.90 | .95 |
| **3026** | A725 | 1st multi | 1.90 | .95 |
| **3027** | A725 | 1st multi | 1.90 | .95 |
| *a.* | | Horiz. strip of 5, #3023-3027 | 9.50 | 4.75 |
| | | *Nos. 3018-3027 (10)* | 19.00 | 9.50 |

Nos. 3018-3027 each sold for 60p on day of issue.

Reign of Queen Elizabeth II, 60th Anniv. A726

Photographs of Queen Elizabeth II at: Nos. 3028, 3036, Golden Jubilee, 2002. No. 3029, Trooping the Color, 1967. No. 3030, The Royal Welsh, 2007. No. 3031, First Christmas TV Broadcast, 1957. No. 3032, Silver Jubilee Walkabout, 1977. No. 3033, Garter Ceremony, 1997. No. 3034, United Nations Address, 1957. No. 3035, Commonwealth Games, 1982.

***Perf. 14¼x14½***

**2012, May 31 Photo.**

| | | | | |
|---|---|---|---|---|
| **3028** | A726 | 1st multi | 2.00 | 1.00 |
| *a.* | | Litho. (3034b) | 2.10 | 2.10 |
| **3029** | A726 | 1st black | 2.00 | 1.00 |
| *a.* | | Litho. (3030b) | 2.10 | 2.10 |
| *b.* | | Horiz. pair, #3028-3029 | 4.00 | 2.00 |
| **3030** | A726 | 77p multi | 2.50 | 1.25 |
| *a.* | | Litho. (3030b) | 2.60 | 2.60 |
| *b.* | | Booklet pane of 2, #3029a, 3030a (BK199) | 4.75 | — |
| **3031** | A726 | 77p black | 2.50 | 1.25 |
| *a.* | | Litho. (3035c) | 2.60 | 2.60 |
| *b.* | | Horiz. pair, #3030-3031 | 4.00 | 2.00 |
| **3032** | A726 | 87p black | 3.00 | 1.50 |
| *a.* | | Litho. (3034b) | 2.60 | 2.60 |
| **3033** | A726 | 87p multi | 3.00 | 1.50 |
| *a.* | | Litho. (3034b) | 2.60 | 2.60 |
| *b.* | | Horiz. pair, #3032-3033 | 6.00 | 3.00 |
| **3034** | A726 | £1.28 black | 4.25 | 2.10 |
| *a.* | | Litho. (3034b) | 4.50 | 4.50 |
| *b.* | | Booklet pane of 4, #3028a, 3032a, 3033a, 3034a (BK199) | 12.00 | — |
| **3035** | A726 | £1.28 multi | 4.25 | 2.10 |
| *a.* | | Litho. (3035c) | 4.50 | 4.50 |
| *b.* | | Horiz. pair, #3034-3035 | 8.50 | 4.25 |
| *c.* | | Booklet pane of 2, #3031a, 3035a (BK199) | 7.25 | — |
| | | *Nos. 3028-3035 (8)* | 23.50 | 11.70 |

**Booklet Stamp Self-Adhesive**

***Die Cut Perf. 14¾x14½***

| | | | | |
|---|---|---|---|---|
| **3036** | A726 | 1st multi | 2.00 | 1.00 |
| *a.* | | Booklet pane of 6, 2 #3036, 4 #MH414 | 12.00 | |

On day of issue, Nos. 3028, 3029 and 3036 each sold for 60p.

A727

Characters and Scenes From Novels by Charles Dickens (1812-70) — A728

Designs: 2nd, Mr. Bumble from *Oliver Twist.* No. 3038, Mr. Pickwick from *The Pickwick Papers.* 77p, The Marchioness from *The Old Curiosity Shop.* 87p, Mrs. Gamp from *Martin Chuzzlewit.* £1.28, Captain Cuttle from *Dombey and Son.* £1.90, Mr. Micawber from *David Copperfield.*

No. 3043 — Scenes from: a, *Nicholas Nickleby.* b, *Bleak House.* c, *Little Dorrit.* d, *A Tale of Two Cities.*

**2012, June 19 Litho. *Perf. 14¼***

| | | | | |
|---|---|---|---|---|
| **3037** | A727 | 2nd multi | 1.60 | .80 |
| **3038** | A727 | 1st multi | 1.90 | .95 |
| **3039** | A727 | 77p multi | 2.40 | 1.25 |
| **3040** | A727 | 87p multi | 2.75 | 1.40 |
| **3041** | A727 | £1.28 multi | 4.00 | 2.00 |
| **3042** | A727 | £1.90 multi | 6.00 | 3.00 |
| | | *Nos. 3037-3042 (6)* | 18.65 | 9.40 |

**Miniature Sheet**

| | | | |
|---|---|---|---|
| **3043** | Sheet of 4 | 7.75 | 7.75 |
| *a.-d.* | A728 1st Any single | 1.90 | .95 |

On day of issue No. 3037 sold for 50p, and Nos. 3038, 3043a-3043d each sold for 60p.

### Olympics and Paralympics Emblems Type of 2012

***Perf. 14¾x14 Syncopated***

**2012, July 27 Litho.**

**Booklet Stamps**

| | | | | |
|---|---|---|---|---|
| **3044** | A718 | 1st gray, org & blk (C9a) | 2.10 | 2.10 |
| **3045** | A719 | 1st gray, org & blk (C9a) | 2.10 | 2.10 |

On day of issue Nos. 3044-3045 each sold for 60p.

Miniature Sheet

Welcome to the Summer Olympics — A729

No. 3046: a, Fencing, Tower Bridge. b, Runners, Olympic Stadium. c, Diver, Tate Modern Museum. d, Cyclist at left, London Eye.

**2012, July 27 Litho. *Perf. 14¾***

| | | | | |
|---|---|---|---|---|
| **3046** | A729 | Sheet of 4 | 12.00 | 12.00 |
| *a.-b.* | | 1st Either single | 1.90 | .95 |
| *c.-d.* | | £1.28 Either single | 4.00 | 2.00 |

On day of issue Nos. 3046a-3046b each sold for 60p.

Britsh Gold Medalists at 2012 Summer Olympics — A730

Photographs of gold medalists and inscription: No. 3047, Team GB, Rowing, Women's Pairs. No. 3048, Bradley Wiggins, Cycling: Road, Men's Time Trial. No. 3049, Team GB, Canoe Slalom: Men's, Canoe Double (C2). No. 3050, Peter Wilson, Shooting: Shotgun, Men's Double Trap. No. 3051, Team GB, Cycling: Track, Men's Team Sprint. No. 3052, Team GB, Rowing, Women's Double Sculls. No. 3053, Team GB, Cycling: Track, Men's Team Pursuit. No. 3054, Victoria Pendleton, Cycling: Track, Women's Keirin. No. 3055, Team GB, Rowing, Men's Fours. No. 3056, Team GB, Rowing: Lightweight Women's Double Sculls. No. 3057, Team GB, Cycling: Track Women's Team Pursuit. No. 3058, Jessica Ennis, Athletics: Combined Women's Heptathlon. No. 3059, Greg Rutherford, Athletics: Field, Men's Long Jump. No. 3060, Mo Farah, Athletics: Track, Men's 10,000m. No. 3061, Ben Ainslie, Sailing: Finn, Men's Heavyweight Dinghy. No. 3062, Andy Murray, Tennis, Men's Singles. No. 3063, Team GB, Equestrian: Jumping, Team. No. 3064, Jason Kenny, Cycling: Track, Men's Sprint. No. 3065, Alistair Brownlee, Triathlon, Men's. No. 3066, Team GB, Equestrian: Dressage, Team. No. 3067, Laura Trott, Cycling: Track, Women's Omnium. No. 3068, Chris Hoy, Cycling: Track, Men's Keirin. No. 3069, Charlotte Dujardin, Equestrian: Dressage, Individual. No. 3070, Nicola Adams, Boxing, Women's Flyweight. No. 3071, Jade Jones, Taekwondo, Women's Under 57kg. No. 3072, Ed McKeever, Canoe Sprint: Men's, Kayak Single (K1) 200m. No. 3073, Mo Farah, Athletics: Track, Men's 5000m. No. 3074, Luke Campbell, Boxing, Men's Bantamweight. No. 3075, Anthony Joshua, boxing, Men's Super Heavyweight.

**Litho. With Digital Printing**

**2012 *Die Cut Perf. 14¾x14½***

**Self-Adhesive**

| | | | | |
|---|---|---|---|---|
| **3047** | A730 | 1st multi | 1.90 | .95 |
| **3048** | A730 | 1st multi | 1.90 | .95 |
| **3049** | A730 | 1st multi | 1.90 | .95 |
| **3050** | A730 | 1st multi | 1.90 | .95 |
| **3051** | A730 | 1st multi | 1.90 | .95 |
| **3052** | A730 | 1st multi | 1.90 | .95 |
| **3053** | A730 | 1st multi | 1.90 | .95 |
| **3054** | A730 | 1st multi | 1.90 | .95 |
| **3055** | A730 | 1st multi | 1.90 | .95 |
| **3056** | A730 | 1st multi | 1.90 | .95 |
| **3057** | A730 | 1st multi | 1.90 | .95 |
| **3058** | A730 | 1st multi | 1.90 | .95 |
| **3059** | A730 | 1st multi | 1.90 | .95 |
| **3060** | A730 | 1st multi | 1.90 | .95 |
| **3061** | A730 | 1st multi | 1.90 | .95 |
| **3062** | A730 | 1st multi | 1.90 | .95 |
| **3063** | A730 | 1st multi | 1.90 | .95 |
| **3064** | A730 | 1st multi | 1.90 | .95 |
| **3065** | A730 | 1st multi | 1.90 | .95 |
| **3066** | A730 | 1st multi | 1.90 | .95 |

| | | | | |
|---|---|---|---|---|
| **3067** | A730 | 1st multi | 1.90 | .95 |
| **3068** | A730 | 1st multi | 1.90 | .95 |
| **3069** | A730 | 1st multi | 1.90 | .95 |
| **3070** | A730 | 1st multi | 1.90 | .95 |
| **3071** | A730 | 1st multi | 1.90 | .95 |
| **3072** | A730 | 1st multi | 1.90 | .95 |
| **3073** | A730 | 1st multi | 1.90 | .95 |
| **3074** | A730 | 1st multi | 1.90 | .95 |
| **3075** | A730 | 1st multi | 1.90 | .95 |
| | | *Nos. 3047-3075 (29)* | 55.10 | 27.55 |

Issued: Nos. 3047-3048, 8/2; Nos. 3049-3051, 8/3; Nos. 3052-3055, 8/4; Nos. 3056-3060, 8/5; Nos. 3061-3062, 8/6; Nos. 3063-3064, 8/7; Nos. 3065-3068, 8/8; Nos. 3069-3071, 8/10; Nos. 3072-3075, 8/12.

Nos. 3047-3075 were each issued in sheets of six. Each stamp sold for 60p on day of issue

Miniature Sheet

Welcome to the Paralympics — A731

No. 3076: a, Runner with artificial leg, Olympic Stadium. b, Wheelchair basketball player, Palace of Westminster. c, Weight lifter, St. Paul's Cathedral and Millennium Bridge. d, London Eye, cyclist on right.

**2012, Aug. 29 Litho. *Perf. 14¾***

| | | | | |
|---|---|---|---|---|
| **3076** | A731 | Sheet of 4 | 12.50 | 12.50 |
| *a.-b.* | | 1st Either single | 2.00 | 1.00 |
| *c.-d.* | | £1.28 Either single | 4.25 | 2.10 |

On day of issue Nos. 3076a-3076b each sold for 60p.

British Gold Medalists at 2012 Summer Paralympics — A732

Photograph of gold medalist and inscription: No. 3077, Sarah Storey, Cycling: Track, Women's C5 Pursuit. No. 3078, Jonathan Fox, Swimming: Men's, 100m Backstroke, S7. No. 3079, Mark Colbourne, Cycling: Track, Men's C1 Pursuit. No. 3080, Hannah Cockroft, Athletics: Track, Women's 100m, T34. No. 3081, Paralympics GB, Cycling: Track, Men's B 1km Time Trial. No. 3082, Richard Whitehead, Athletics: Track, Men's 200m, T42. No. 3083, Natasha Baker, Equestrian: Individual, Championship Test, Grade II. No. 3084, Sarah Storey, Cycling: Track, Women's C4-5 500m Time Trial. No. 3085, Ellie Simmonds, Swimming: Women's, 400m Freestyle, S6. No. 3086, Paralympics GB, Rowing: Mixed, Coxed Four, LTA Mix 4+. No. 3087, Aled Davies, Athletics: Field, Men's Discus, F42. No. 3088, Paralympics GB, Cycling: Track, Men's B Sprint. No. 3089, Jessica-Jane Applegate, Swimming: Women's, 200m Freestyle, S14. No. 3090, Sophie Christiansen, Equestrian: Individual, Championship Test, Grade Ia. No. 3091, David Weir, Athletics: Track, Men's 5000m, T54. No. 3092, Natasha Baker, Equestrian: Individual, Freestyle Test, Grade II. No. 3093, Ellie Simmonds, Swimming: Women's, 200m Individual Medley, SM6. No. 3094, Mickey Bushell, Atheltics: Track, Men's 100m, T53. No. 3095, Danielle Brown, Archery: Women's, Individual Compound, Open. No. 3096, Heather Frederiksen, Swimming: Women's, 100m Backstroke, S8. No. 3097, Sophie Christiansen, Equestrian: Individual, Freestyle Test, Grade Ia. No. 3098, David Weir, Athletics: Track, Men's 1500m, T54. No. 3099, Sarah Storey, Cycling: Road, Women's C5 Time Trial. No. 3100, Ollie Hynd, Swimming: Men's, 200m Individual Medley, SM8. No. 3101, Paralympics GB, Equestrian, Team, Open. No. 3102, Helena Lucas, Sailing: Single-person, Keelboat 2.4mR. No. 3103, Sarah Storey, Cycling: Road, Women's C4-5 Road Race. No. 3104, Josef Craig, Swimming: Men's, 400m Freestyle, S7. No. 3105, Hannah Cockroft, Athletics: Track, Women's 200m, T34. No. 3106, David Weir, Atheltics: Track, Men's 800m, T54. No. 3107, Jonnie Peacock, Athletics: Track, Men's 100m, T44. No. 3108, Josie Pearson, Athletics: Field, Women's Discus, F51/52/53. No. 3109, David Stone, Cycling: Road, Mixed T1-2 Road Race. No. 3110, David Weir, Athletics: Road, Men's Marathon, T54.

**Litho. With Digital Printing**

**2012 *Die Cut Perf. 14¾x14½***

**Self-Adhesive**

| | | | | |
|---|---|---|---|---|
| **3077** | A732 | 1st multi | 2.00 | 1.00 |
| **3078** | A732 | 1st multi | 2.00 | 1.00 |
| **3079** | A732 | 1st multi | 2.00 | 1.00 |
| **3080** | A732 | 1st multi | 2.00 | 1.00 |
| **3081** | A732 | 1st multi | 2.00 | 1.00 |
| **3082** | A732 | 1st multi | 2.00 | 1.00 |
| **3083** | A732 | 1st multi | 2.00 | 1.00 |
| **3084** | A732 | 1st multi | 2.00 | 1.00 |
| **3085** | A732 | 1st multi | 2.00 | 1.00 |
| **3086** | A732 | 1st multi | 2.00 | 1.00 |
| **3087** | A732 | 1st multi | 2.00 | 1.00 |
| **3088** | A732 | 1st multi | 2.00 | 1.00 |
| **3089** | A732 | 1st multi | 2.00 | 1.00 |
| **3090** | A732 | 1st multi | 2.00 | 1.00 |
| **3091** | A732 | 1st multi | 2.00 | 1.00 |
| **3092** | A732 | 1st multi | 2.00 | 1.00 |
| **3093** | A732 | 1st multi | 2.00 | 1.00 |
| **3094** | A732 | 1st multi | 2.00 | 1.00 |
| **3095** | A732 | 1st multi | 2.00 | 1.00 |
| **3096** | A732 | 1st multi | 2.00 | 1.00 |
| **3097** | A732 | 1st multi | 2.00 | 1.00 |
| **3098** | A732 | 1st multi | 2.00 | 1.00 |
| **3099** | A732 | 1st multi | 2.00 | 1.00 |
| **3100** | A732 | 1st multi | 2.00 | 1.00 |
| **3101** | A732 | 1st multi | 2.00 | 1.00 |
| **3102** | A732 | 1st multi | 2.00 | 1.00 |
| **3103** | A732 | 1st multi | 2.00 | 1.00 |
| **3104** | A732 | 1st multi | 2.00 | 1.00 |
| **3105** | A732 | 1st multi | 2.00 | 1.00 |
| **3106** | A732 | 1st multi | 2.00 | 1.00 |
| **3107** | A732 | 1st multi | 2.00 | 1.00 |
| **3108** | A732 | 1st multi | 2.00 | 1.00 |
| **3109** | A732 | 1st multi | 2.00 | 1.00 |
| **3110** | A732 | 1st multi | 2.00 | 1.00 |
| | | *Nos. 3077-3110 (34)* | 68.00 | 34.00 |

Issued: No. 3077, 8/31; No. 3078, 9/1; Nos. 3079-3085, 9/3; Nos. 3086-3093, 9/4; Nos. 3094-3097, 9/5; Nos. 3098-3101, 9/7. Nos. 3102-3105, 9/8; Nos. 3106-3110, 9/10.

Nos. 3077-3110 were each issued in sheets of two. Each stamp sold for 60p on day of issue

**Scottish Locomotives Type of 2012**

Design: British Railways D34 Nos. 62471 and 62496.

***Die Cut Perf. 14¼***

**2012, Sept. 27 Photo.**

**Booklet Stamp**

**Self-Adhesive**

| | | | | |
|---|---|---|---|---|
| **3111** | A723 | 1st multi | 2.00 | 1.00 |
| *a.* | | Booklet pane of 6, 2 #3111, 4 #MH414 | 12.00 | |

No. 3111 sold for 60p on day of issue.

Miniature Sheet

Scenes From 2012 Summer Olympics and Paralympics — A733

No. 3112: a, British Paralympics Team in procession. b, Athletes walking near stadium. c, Paralympic Games Opening Ceremonies. d, Olympic Closing Ceremony.

**2012, Sept. 27 Litho. *Perf. 14¾***

| | | | | |
|---|---|---|---|---|
| **3112** | A733 | Sheet of 4 | 12.50 | 12.50 |
| *a.-b.* | | 1st Either single | 2.00 | 1.00 |
| *c.-d.* | | £1.28 Either single | 4.25 | 2.10 |

On day of issue Nos. 3112a-3112b each sold for 60p.

Astronomical Bodies — A734

Designs: No. 3113, Sun. No. 3114, Venus. No. 3115, Mars. No. 3116, Asteroid Lutetia. No. 3117, Saturn. No. 3118, Titan, moon of Saturn.

**2012, Oct. 10 *Perf. 14¼x14***

| | | | | |
|---|---|---|---|---|
| **3113** | A734 | 1st multi | 1.90 | .95 |
| **3114** | A734 | 1st multi | 1.90 | .95 |
| **3115** | A734 | 77p multi | 2.50 | 1.25 |
| **3116** | A734 | 77p multi | 2.50 | 1.25 |
| **3117** | A734 | £1.28 multi | 4.25 | 2.10 |
| **3118** | A734 | £1.28 multi | 4.25 | 2.10 |
| | | *Nos. 3113-3118 (6)* | 17.30 | 8.60 |

First British satellite, 50th anniv. On day of issue, Nos. 3113-3114 each sold for 60p.

Christmas

A735 A736

Designs: 2nd, Reindeer with Christmas ornaments on antlers. 1st, Bird on hand of Santa Claus. 2nd Large, Reindeer with Christmas ornaments on antlers, trees. 87p, Penguin and snowman. 1st Large, Bird on hand of Santa Claus, tree. £1.28, Bird carrying star Christmas ornament on holly branch. £1.90, Cat, mouse and Christmas tree.

***Perf. 14¾x14 Syncopated***

**2012, Nov. 6 Photo.**

| | | | | |
|---|---|---|---|---|
| **3119** | | Sheet of 7 | 22.00 | 22.00 |
| *a.* | | A735 2nd multi | 1.60 | .80 |
| *b.* | | A735 1st multi | 1.90 | .95 |
| *c.* | | A736 2nd Large multi | 2.25 | 1.10 |
| *d.* | | A735 87p multi | 2.75 | 1.40 |
| *e.* | | A736 1st Large multi | 3.00 | 1.50 |
| *f.* | | A735 £1.28 multi | 4.25 | 2.10 |
| *g.* | | A735 £1.90 multi | 6.25 | 3.25 |

**Self-Adhesive**

***Die Cut Perf. 14¾x14 Syncopated***

| | | | | |
|---|---|---|---|---|
| **3120** | A735 | 2nd multi | 1.60 | .80 |
| *a.* | | Booklet pane of 12 | 19.50 | |
| *b.* | | Litho., + label (3125b) | 1.75 | 1.75 |
| **3121** | A735 | 1st multi | 1.90 | .95 |
| *a.* | | Booklet pane of 12 | 23.00 | |
| *b.* | | Litho., + label (3125b) | 2.00 | 2.00 |
| **3122** | A736 | 2nd Large multi | 2.25 | 1.10 |
| **3123** | A735 | 87p multi | 2.75 | 1.40 |
| *a.* | | Litho., + label (3125b) | 3.00 | 3.00 |
| **3124** | A736 | 1st Large multi | 3.00 | 1.50 |
| **3125** | A735 | £1.28 multi | 4.25 | 2.10 |
| *a.* | | Litho., + label (3125b) | 4.50 | 4.50 |
| *b.* | | Sheet of 20, 8 each #3120b, 3121b, 2 each #3123a, 3125a, + 20 labels | 45.00 | |
| **3126** | A735 | £1.90 multi | 6.25 | 3.25 |
| | | *Nos. 3120-3126 (7)* | 22.00 | 11.10 |

On day of issue, Nos. 3119a and 3120 each sold for 50p, Nos. 3119b and 3121 each sold for 60p, Nos. 3119c and 3122 each sold for 69p, and Nos. 3119e and 3124 each sold for 90p. No. 3125b sold for £13.60. Labels could not be personalized.

London Underground, 150th Anniv. — A737

Advertisements in London Underground — A738

Designs: No. 3127, Train and cars in tunnel, 1863. No. 3128, Workers tunneling under London streets, 1898. No. 3129, Suburban commuters in train car, 1911. Nos. 3130, 3134, Boston Manor Art Deco station exterior, 1934. No. 3131, Train cars, 1938. No. 3132, Escalators at Canary Wharf Jubilee Line Station, 1999.

No. 3133 — Underground emblem and various advertising posters promoting travel on the Underground.

**2013, Jan. 9 Litho. *Perf. 14¼***

| | | | | |
|---|---|---|---|---|
| **3127** | A737 | 2nd multi | 1.75 | .85 |
| **3128** | A737 | 2nd multi | 1.75 | .85 |
| **3129** | A737 | 1st multi | 2.00 | 1.00 |
| **3130** | A737 | 1st multi | 2.00 | 1.00 |
| **3131** | A737 | £1.28 multi | 4.25 | 2.10 |
| **3132** | A737 | £1.28 multi | 4.25 | 2.10 |
| | | *Nos. 3127-3132 (6)* | 16.00 | 7.90 |

**Miniature Sheet**

***Perf. 14¾***

| | | | | |
|---|---|---|---|---|
| **3133** | A738 | Sheet of 4 | 12.00 | 12.00 |
| *a.* | | 1st multi | 2.00 | 1.00 |
| *b.* | | 77p multi | 2.50 | 1.25 |
| *c.* | | 87p multi | 3.00 | 1.50 |
| *d.* | | £1.28 multi | 4.25 | 2.10 |

**Booklet Stamp**

**Self-Adhesive**

***Die Cut Perf. 14¼***

| | | | | |
|---|---|---|---|---|
| **3134** | A737 | 1st multi | 2.00 | 1.00 |
| *a.* | | Booklet pane of 6, 2 #3134, 4 #MH426 | 12.00 | |

On day of issue, Nos.3127-3128 each sold for 50p, and Nos, 3129-3130, 3133a and 3134 each sold for 60p.

Scenes From Novels by Jane Austen — A739

Scene from: No. 3135, Sense and Sensibility. No. 3136, Pride and Prejudice. No. 3137, Mansfield Park. No. 3138, Emma. No. 3139, Northanger Abbey. No. 3140, Persuasion.

**2013, Feb. 21 *Perf. 14¼***

| | | | | |
|---|---|---|---|---|
| **3135** | A739 | 1st multi | 1.90 | .95 |
| **3136** | A739 | 1st multi | 1.90 | .95 |
| **3137** | A739 | 77p multi | 2.40 | 1.25 |
| **3138** | A739 | 77p multi | 2.40 | 1.25 |
| **3139** | A739 | £1.28 multi | 4.00 | 2.00 |
| **3140** | A739 | £1.28 multi | 4.00 | 2.00 |
| | | *Nos. 3135-3140 (6)* | 16.60 | 8.40 |

On day of issue, Nos. 3135-3136 each sold for 60p.

## SEMI-POSTAL STAMPS

**Catalogue values for unused stamps in this section are for Never Hinged items.**

Handicapped Person — SP1

***Perf. 14½x14***

**1975, Jan. 22 Photo. Unwmk.**

| | | | | |
|---|---|---|---|---|
| **B1** | SP1 | 4½p +1½p blue & lt blue | .25 | .25 |

For the benefit of health and handicap charities. No. B1 is phosphorescent.

**Christmas Type of 1989**

Ely Cathedral, Cambridgeshire: No. B2, Romanesque arches, west front. No. B3, Central tower. No. B4, Interlocking arches, Romanesque arcades, west transept. No. B5, Peasant, stained-glass window in triple arch, west front.

**1989, Nov. 14 Photo. *Perf. 15x14***

| | | | | |
|---|---|---|---|---|
| **B2** | A379 | 15p +1p multicolored | .40 | .40 |
| **B3** | A379 | 20p +1p multicolored | .50 | .55 |
| **B4** | A379 | 34p +1p multicolored | .90 | .85 |
| **B5** | A379 | 37p +1p multicolored | 1.00 | .95 |
| | | *Nos. B2-B5 (4)* | 4.25 | 2.75 |

## AIR POST STAMPS

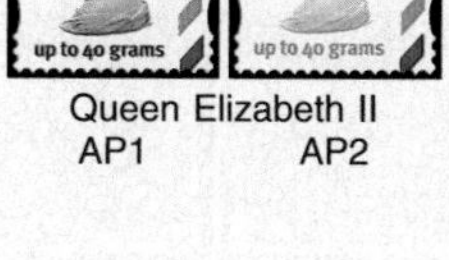

Queen Elizabeth II

AP1 AP2

***Serpentine Die Cut 14¾x14 Syncopated***
**2003, Mar. 27** **Photo.**
**Self-Adhesive**
**Booklet Stamps**
**C1** AP1 (52p) blue & red 2.75 .85
*a.* Booklet pane of 4 11.00
**C2** AP2 (£1.12) red & blue 4.50 1.90
*a.* Booklet pane of 4 18.00

Queen Elizabeth II — AP3

***Die Cut Perf. 14¾x14 Syncopated***
**2004, Apr. 1** **Photo.**
**Self-Adhesive**
**C3** AP3 (43p) blk, red & blue 2.00 .80
*a.* Booklet of 4 + 4 etiquettes 8.00

Nos. C1-C3 were sold for 52p, £1.12 and 43p, respectively, when issued.

Queen Elizabeth II
AP4 AP5

***Die Cut Perf. 14¾x14 Syncopated***
**2010, Mar. 30** **Photo.**
**Booklet Stamps**
**Self-Adhesive**
**C4** AP4 (60p) grn, red & blue 1.90 .95
*a.* Booklet pane of 4 7.75
**C5** AP5 (97p) pur, red & blue 3.00 1.50
*a.* Booklet pane of 4 12.00

Emblem of 2012 Olympics
AP6

Emblem of 2012 Paralympics
AP7

***Die Cut Perf. 14¾x14 Syncopated***
**2012, Jan. 5** **Photo.**
**Self-Adhesive**
**C6** AP6 (£1.10) multi 3.50 1.75
**C7** AP7 (£1.10) multi 3.50 1.75
*a.* Sheet of 20, 8 each #2981-2982, 2 each #C6-C7, + 20 labels, litho. 47.50

Issued: No. C7a, 7/27/12. No. C7a sold for £15.22. Labels on No. C7a could not be personalized.

**Olympic and Paralympic Emblems Type of 2012**
***Perf. 14¾x14 Syncopated***
**2012, July 27** **Litho.**
**Booklet Stamps**
**C8** AP6 (£1.28) multi 4.25 4.25
**C9** AP7 (£1.28) multi 4.25 4.25
*a.* Booklet pane of 8, #C8, C9, 3 each #3044-3045 (BK200) 21.50 —

On day of issue Nos. C8-C9 each had a franking value of £1.28.

## SPECIAL DELIVERY STAMPS

Queen Elizabeth II
SD1 SD2

***Die Cut Perf. 14¾x14 Syncopated***
**2010, Oct. 26** **Photo.**
**Self-Adhesive**
**E1** SD1 (£5.05) dk bl & gray 16.50 8.25
**E2** SD2 (£5.50) gray & dk bl 18.00 9.00

## POSTAGE DUE STAMPS

D1

D2

***Perf. 14x14½***
**1914-24** **Typo.** **Wmk. 33**
**J1** D1 ½p emerald .50 .30
Never hinged 2.00
**J2** D1 1p rose .50 .30
Never hinged 2.00
**J3** D1 1½p red brown ('22) 47.50 20.00
Never hinged 160.00
**J4** D1 2p brown black .50 .30
Never hinged 2.00
**J5** D1 3p violet ('18) 6.50 .85
Never hinged 30.00
**J6** D1 4p gray green ('21) 47.50 5.75
Never hinged 150.00
**J7** D1 5p org brown 8.00 4.00
Never hinged 22.50
**J8** D1 1sh blue ('15) 45.00 5.50
Never hinged 170.00
*Nos. J1-J8 (8)* 156.00 37.00

**1924-30** **Wmk. 35**
**J9** D1 ½p emerald 1.10 .85
Never hinged 3.00
**J10** D1 1p car rose .65 .30
Never hinged 3.00
**J11** D1 1½p red brown 52.50 22.50
Never hinged 175.00
**J12** D1 2p black brown 1.60 .30
Never hinged 10.50
**J13** D1 3p violet 2.25 .30
Never hinged 11.50
*a.* Experimental wmk. 75.00 55.00
Never hinged 110.00
*b.* Printed on the gummed side 125.00
Never hinged 160.00
**J14** D1 4p deep green 17.50 4.00
Never hinged 67.50
**J15** D1 5p org brown ('30) 65.00 45.00
Never hinged 165.00
**J16** D1 1sh blue 11.50 1.10
Never hinged 45.00
**J17** D2 2sh6p brown, *yellow* 85.00 2.25
Never hinged 250.00
*Nos. J9-J17 (9)* 237.10 76.60

The experimental watermark of No. J13a resembles Wmk. 35 but is spaced more closely, with letters short and rounded, crown with flat arch and sides high, lines thicker.

**1936-37** **Wmk. 250**
**J18** D1 ½p emerald ('37) 7.50 *10.00*
Never hinged 13.50
**J19** D1 1p car rose ('37) 1.50 *1.75*
Never hinged 2.50
**J20** D1 2p blk brown ('37) 10.00 *12.50*
Never hinged 17.50
**J21** D1 3p violet ('37) 1.50 *2.00*
Never hinged 2.25
**J22** D1 4p slate green 24.00 *32.50*
Never hinged 50.00
**J23** D1 5p bister ('37) 20.00 *26.00*
Never hinged 30.00
*a.* 5p orange brown 35.00 *30.00*
Never hinged 75.00
**J24** D1 1sh blue ('36) 7.50 *8.50*
Never hinged 16.00
**J25** D2 2sh6p brn, *yel* ('37) 140.00 12.50
Never hinged 350.00
*Nos. J18-J25 (8)* 212.00 *105.75*

**1938-39** **Wmk. 251**
**J26** D1 ½p emerald 8.50 5.75
Never hinged 13.00
**J27** D1 1p carmine rose 1.40 .85
Never hinged 3.50
**J28** D1 2p black brown 1.50 .85
Never hinged 3.00
**J29** D1 3p violet 7.00 1.10
Never hinged 14.00
**J30** D1 4p slate green 40.00 10.00
Never hinged 110.00
**J31** D1 5p bister ('39) 6.75 .85
Never hinged 16.00
**J32** D1 1sh blue 25.00 2.25
Never hinged 80.00
**J33** D2 2sh6p brown, *yel* ('39) 40.00 3.00
Never hinged 95.00
*Nos. J26-J33 (8)* 130.15 24.65

**Catalogue values for unused stamps in this section, from this point to the end of the section, are for Never Hinged items.**

**1951-52**
**J34** D1 ½p orange 3.50 3.50
**J35** D1 1p violet blue 1.50 .75
**J36** D1 1½p green ('52) 2.00 *2.50*
**J37** D1 4p bright blue 50.00 24.00
**J38** D1 1sh olive bister 32.50 10.00
*Nos. J34-J38 (5)* 89.50 40.75

**1954-55** **Wmk. 298**
**J39** D1 ½p orange ('55) 9.00 9.25
**J40** D1 2p brn black ('55) 35.00 27.50
**J41** D1 3p purple ('55) 70.00 60.00
**J42** D1 4p brt blue ('55) 35.00 32.50
*a.* Imperf., pair 250.00
**J43** D1 5p bister brn ('55) 22.50 19.00
**J44** D2 2sh6p dk pur brn, *yel* 150.00 9.00
*Nos. J39-J44 (6)* 321.50 157.25

**1955-57** **Wmk. 308** ***Perf. 14x14½***
**J45** D1 ½p orange ('56) 5.50 3.25
**J46** D1 1p ultra ('56) 9.75 1.50
**J47** D1 1½p green ('56) 12.50 7.00
**J48** D1 2p brown blk ('56) 52.50 4.50
**J49** D1 3p purple ('56) 6.00 2.25
**J50** D1 4p brt blue ('56) 30.00 6.00
**J51** D1 5p bister brn ('56) 27.50 17.50
**J52** D1 1sh dp olive bister 70.00 2.75
**J53** D2 2sh6p dk red brn, *yel* ('57) 200.00 8.25
**J54** D2 5sh red, *yellow* 140.00 27.50
*Nos. J45-J54 (10)* 553.75 80.50

**1959-63** **Wmk. 322** ***Perf. 14x14½***
**J55** D1 ½p orange ('61) .25 1.10
**J56** D1 1p ultra ('60) .25 .50
**J57** D1 1½p green ('60) 2.60 *2.25*
**J58** D1 2p brown black 1.25 .60
**J59** D1 3p purple .40 .35
**J60** D1 4p brt blue ('60) .40 .35
**J61** D1 5p bister brn ('62) .50 .70
**J62** D1 6p dp mag ('62) .60 .35
**J63** D1 1sh dp ol bis ('60) 1.00 .35
**J64** D2 2sh6p dark red brown, *yellow* ('61) 4.00 .85
**J65** D2 5sh red, *yellow* ('61) 8.25 1.10
**J66** D2 10sh ultra, *yel* ('63) 13.00 5.00
**J67** D2 £1 blk, *yellow* ('63) 47.50 7.50
*Nos. J55-J67 (13)* 80.00 21.00

Nos. J1-J67 are watermarked sideways.

***Perf. 14x14½***
**1968-69** **Unwmk.** **Typo.**
**J68** D1 2p greenish black .50 1.00
**J69** D1 3p purple 1.00 .85
**J70** D1 4p bright blue 1.00 .75
**J71** D1 5p brown org ('69) 5.00 6.00
**J72** D1 6p deep magenta 2.25 1.50
**J73** D1 1sh bister ('69) 4.00 2.00
*Nos. J68-J73 (6)* 13.75 12.10

**1968-69** **Photo.**
**J74** D1 4p bright blue ('69) 7.00 6.00
**J75** D1 8p bright red .75 1.00

D3

D4

***Perf. 14x14½***
**1970-75** **Photo.** **Unwmk.**
**J79** D3 ½p grnsh blue ('71) .25 .60
**J80** D3 1p magenta ('71) .25 .25
**J81** D3 2p green ('71) .25 .25
**J82** D3 3p ultra ('71) .25 .25
**J83** D3 4p olive bister ('71) .25 .25
**J84** D3 5p bluish lilac ('71) .25 .25
**J85** D3 7p brown red ('74) .40 .90
**J86** D4 10p carmine rose .40 .25
**J87** D4 11p slate ('75) .60 1.10
**J88** D4 20p olive .75 .50
**J89** D4 50p ultramarine 3.00 1.00
**J90** D4 £1 black 5.00 2.25
**J91** D4 £5 org & black ('73) 30.00 3.50
*Nos. J79-J91 (13)* 41.65 11.35

D5

**1982, June 9** **Photo.** ***Perf. 14x14½***
**J92** D5 1p rose carmine .25 .35
**J93** D5 2p ultramarine .35 .35
**J94** D5 3p deep rose lilac .25 .35
**J95** D5 4p dark blue .25 .30
**J96** D5 5p sepia .25 .30
**J97** D5 10p brown .35 .45
**J98** D5 20p dark ol green .60 .70
**J99** D5 25p slate blue .90 1.00
**J100** D5 50p black 1.75 1.25
**J101** D5 £1 vermilion 3.50 1.40
**J102** D5 £2 greenish blue 7.00 2.75
**J103** D5 £5 yellow bister 12.50 2.25
*Nos. J92-J103 (12)* 27.95 11.45

D6

***Perf. 15x14 Syncopated, Type C (2 Sides)***
**1994, Feb. 15** **Photo. & Embossed**
**J104** D6 1p vermilion & org .25 .60
**J105** D6 2p red lilac & red .25 .60
**J106** D6 5p yel & brn .25 .40
**J107** D6 10p yel & grn .50 .50
**J108** D6 20p green & blue 1.00 .80
**J109** D6 25p red 1.50 .85
**J110** D6 £1 vio & red lilac 7.50 3.00
**J111** D6 £1.20 blue & green 10.00 4.00
**J112** D6 £5 green & black 27.50 20.00
*Nos. J104-J112 (9)* 48.75 30.75

## OFFICIAL STAMPS

**Type of Regular Issue of 1840 "V R" in Upper Corners**

O1

**1840** **Wmk. 18** ***Imperf.***
**O1** O1 1p black *35,000. 27,500.*

No. O1 was never placed in use but examples are known used and on covers that passed through the mails by oversight. The stamp also was used experimentally to test cancellations.

Postage stamps perforated with a crown and initials "H.M.O.W.," "O.W.," "B.T." or "S.O.," or with only the initials "H.M.S.O." or "D.S.I.R.," were used for official purposes.

Counterfeits exist of Nos. O2-O83.

**Inland Revenue**
Regular Issues Overprinted in Black

a

b

Type "a" is overprinted on the stamps of ½ penny to 1 shilling inclusive, type "b" on the higher values.

**1882-85** **Wmk. 30** ***Perf. 14***
**O2** A35 ½p pale green 75.00 30.00
**O3** A35 ½p slate bl ('85) 70.00 26.00
**O4** A40 1p lilac 6.00 4.00
*a.* "OFFICIAL" omitted *8,500.*
*b.* Ovpt. lines transposed
**O5** A47 2½p lilac ('85) 400.00 120.00
**O6** A28 6p gray 450.00 150.00
**O7** A48 1sh green ('85) *5,500.* 1,400.
**Wmk. 31**
**O8** A51 5sh car rose ('85) 7,000. 2,000.
*a.* Bluish paper ('85) *12,000.* 4,500.
**O9** A52 10sh ultra *10,000.* 3,750.
*a.* 10sh cobalt *20,000.* 6,500.
*b.* Bluish paper *22,000.* 6,500.
**Wmk. Three Imperial Crowns (30)**
**O10** A53 £1 brown vio *60,000. 22,500.*

**1888-89** **Wmk. 30**

**O11** A54 ½p vermilion 9.50 3.50
*a.* "I.R." omitted *5,500.*
**O12** A65 1sh green ('89) 650.00 220.00

**1890** **Wmk. Three Orbs (29)**

**O13** A53 £1 brown vio *70,000. 30,000.*

**1891** **Wmk. 30**

**O14** A57 2½p violet, *blue* 130.00 16.00

**Wmk. Three Imperial Crowns (30)**

**1892**

**O15** A53 £1 green *10,000.* 2,250.
*a.* No period after "R" — *3,500.*

**1901** **Wmk. 30**

**O16** A54 ½p blue green 16.00 10.00
**O17** A62 6p violet, *rose* 350.00 100.00
**O18** A65 1sh car rose & green 4,500. 1,250.

**1902-04**

**O19** A66 ½p gray green 30.00 3.25
**O20** A66 1p carmine 20.00 2.25
**O21** A66 2½p ultra 900.00 250.00
**O22** A66 6p dull vio ('04) *375,000. 170,000.*
**O23** A74 1sh car rose & green 3,500. 450.00

**Wmk. 31**

**O24** A76 5sh car rose *30,000. 9,000.*
**O25** A77 10sh ultra *120,000. 45,000.*

**Wmk. Three Imperial Crowns (30)**

**O26** A78 £1 green *60,000. 24,000.*

Nos. O4, O8, O9 and O13 also exist with overprint in blue black.

**Government Parcels**

Overprinted 

**1883-86** **Wmk. 30**

**O27** A45 1½p lilac ('86) 350.00 70.00
**O28** A46 6p green ('86) 2,100. 875.00
**O29** A50 9p green 1,750. 700.00
**O30** A29 1sh salmon (P13) 1,050. 250.00
Plate 14 2,500. 350.00
*Nos. O27-O30 (4)* 5,250. 1,895.

**1887-92**

**O31** A55 1½p violet & green 175.00 24.00
**O32** A56 2p green & car rose ('91) 125.00 19.00
**O33** A60 4½p car rose & grn ('92) 300.00 220.00
**O34** A62 6p violet, *rose* 250.00 50.00
**O35** A63 9p blue & lil ('88) 300.00 75.00
**O36** A65 1sh green 550.00 225.00
*Nos. O31-O36 (6)* 1,700. 613.00

**1897**

**O37** A40 1p lilac 82.50 17.50
*a.* Inverted overprint 6,500. 2,800.

**1900**

**O38** A65 1sh car rose & grn 525.00 200.00
*a.* Inverted overprint *13,000.*

**1902**

**O39** A66 1p carmine 40.00 14.00
**O40** A68 2p green & car 160.00 35.00
**O41** A66 6p dull violet 275.00 35.00
**O42** A72 9p ultra & violet 600.00 175.00
**O43** A74 1sh car rose & grn 1,300. 275.00
*Nos. O39-O43 (5)* 2,375. 534.00

**Office of Works**

Overprinted 

**1896**

**O44** A54 ½p vermilion 250.00 120.00
**O45** A40 1p lilac 400.00 120.00

**1901-02**

**O46** A54 ½p blue green 350.00 175.00
**O47** A61 5p lilac & ultra 3,000. 1,000.
**O48** A64 10p car rose & lil 5,000. 1,500.

**1902**

**O49** A66 ½p gray green 600.00 160.00
**O50** A66 1p carmine 600.00 160.00
**O51** A68 2p green & car 1,900. 400.00
**O52** A66 2½p ultramarine 3,250. 600.00
**O53** A73 10p car rose & vio *35,000.* 6,750.

**Army**

Overprinted

a

b

**1896**

**O54** A54(a) ½p vermilion 5.25 2.75
*a.* "OFFICIAI" 240.00 110.00
**O55** A40(a) 1p lilac 5.00 10.00
*a.* "OFFICIAI" 175.00 110.00
**O56** A57(b) 2½p violet, *blue* 35.00 24.00
*Nos. O54-O56 (3)* 45.25 36.75

**1900**

**O57** A54(a) ½p blue green 5.00 *10.00*

**1901**

**O58** A62(b) 6p violet, *rose* 87.50 47.50

**1902**

**O59** A66(a) ½p gray green 6.00 2.40
**O60** A66(a) 1p carmine 6.00 2.40
*a.* "ARMY" omitted —
**O61** A66(a) 6p dull violet 175.00 80.00
*Nos. O59-O61 (3)* 187.00 84.80

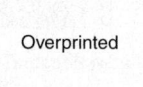

Overprinted 

**1903**

**O62** A66 6p dull violet 3,000. 1,200.

**Royal Household**

Overprinted 

**1902**

**O63** A66 ½p gray green 400.00 220.00
**O64** A66 1p carmine 350.00 175.00

**Board of Education**

Overprinted 

**1902**

**O65** A61 5p lilac & ultra 3,700. 850.00
**O66** A65 1sh car rose & grn 9,500. 4,500.

**1902-04**

**O67** A66 ½p gray green 175.00 37.50
**O68** A66 1p carmine 175.00 37.50
**O69** A66 2½p ultramarine 4,500. 400.00
**O70** A71 5p lilac & ultra ('04) 27,500. 9,000.
**O71** A74 1sh car rose & grn *140,000.* —

**Admiralty**

Overprinted 

**1903**

**O72** A66 ½p gray green 30.00 14.00
**O73** A66 1p carmine 17.50 7.00
**O74** A67 1½p vio & green 325.00 140.00
**O75** A68 2p green & car 325.00 150.00
**O76** A66 2½p ultra 450.00 140.00
**O77** A69 3p violet, *yel* 400.00 150.00
*Nos. O72-O77 (6)* 1,547. 601.00

Overprinted 

**1903**

**O78** A66 ½p gray green 60.00 24.00
**O79** A66 1p carmine 60.00 24.00
**O80** A67 1½p vio & green 1,100. 600.00
**O81** A68 2p green & car 2,600. 800.00
**O82** A66 2½p ultramarine 2,750. 850.00
**O83** A69 3p violet, *yel* 2,400. 350.00

The two types of the "Admiralty Official" overprint differ principally in the shape of the letter "M."

**ENVELOPES**

Britannia Sending Letters to World (William Mulready, Designer) — E1

**1840**

**U1** E1 1p black 375.00 *500.00*
**U2** E1 2p blue 450.00 *2,000.*

**LETTER SHEETS**

**U3** E1 1p black 375.00 *500.00*
**U4** E1 2p blue 425.00 *2,000.*

**REGIONAL ISSUES**

Sold only at post offices within the respective regions, but valid for postage throughout Great Britain. Issues for Guernsey, Jersey and Isle of Man are listed with the Bailiwick issues that follow.

Starting in 1967, all Regional stamps were issued only with phosphorescence.

**Catalogue values for unused stamps in this section are for Never Hinged items.**

## ENGLAND

Three Lions — A1 

***Perf. 15x14 Syncopated***

**2001-02** **Photo.**

**1** A1 2nd shown .95 .40
**2** A1 1st Crowned Lion 1.35 .55
**3** A1 E Oak tree 1.90 1.00
**4** A1 65p Tudor rose 2.60 2.00
**5** A1 68p Tudor rose 2.90 1.50
*Nos. 1-5 (5)* 9.70 5.45

Issued: Nos. 1-4, 4/23/01. No. 5, 7/4/02.

Nos. 1-3 sold for 19p, 27p and 36p respectively on day of issue.

Three Lions — A2

Crowned Lion — A3

Oak Tree — A4

Tudor Rose — A5

***Perf. 14¾x14 Syncopated***

**2003, Oct. 14**

**6** A2 2nd multi .95 .40
**7** A3 1st multi 1.35 .60
*a.* Litho. (Wales #21a) 1.35 .60
**8** A4 E multi 1.90 1.00
**9** A5 68p multi 2.90 1.50
*Nos. 6-9 (4)* 7.10 3.50

Nos. 6-8 each sold for 20p, 28p and 38p respectively on day of issue.

**2004, May 11**

**10** A4 40p multi 1.60 .80
*a.* Booklet pane, 2 each #6, 10 + label (BK177) 5.00 —

No. 10a issued 2/24/05.

**2005, Apr. 5**

**11** A4 42p multi 1.70 .85

**2006, Mar. 28**

**12** A4 44p multi 1.75 .90
**13** A5 72p multi 2.90 1.50

**2007**

**14** A4 48p multi 1.90 .95
**15** A5 78p multi 3.25 1.60

**Litho.**

**Self-Adhesive**

***Die Cut Perf. 14¾x14***

**Stamp + Label**

**16** A3 1st multi 1.50 1.50

Issued: Nos. 14, 15, 3/27; No. 16, 4/23. No. 16 was issued in sheets of 20 stamps + 20 labels that sold for £7.35 and had a franking value of 34p on day of issue.

***Perf. 14¾x14 Syncopated***

**2008, Apr. 1** **Photo.**

**17** A4 50p multi 2.00 1.00
**18** A5 81p multi 3.25 1.60

**2009, Mar. 31**

**19** A4 56p multi 1.75 .85
**20** A5 90p multi 2.75 1.40

**Heritage of England Type of 2007**

Design: English flag (like #2462a).

**Self-Adhesive**

*Die Cut Perf. 14¾x14*

**2009, Apr. 21** **Litho.**
**21** A626 1st multi + label 2.50 1.25

No. 21 was issued in a sheet of 20 stamps + 20 labels that sold for £8.35, and had a franking value of 39p on day of issue.

**Types of 2003**

*Perf. 14¾x14 Syncopated*

**2010, Mar. 30** **Photo.**
**22** A4 60p multi 1.90 .95
**23** A5 97p multi 3.00 1.50

**2011, Mar. 29** **Litho.**
**24** A4 68p multi 2.25 1.10
**25** A5 £1.10 multi 3.75 1.90

**2012, Apr. 25**
**26** A4 87p multi 3.00 1.50
**27** A5 £1.28 multi 4.25 2.10

## NORTHERN IRELAND

A1

A2

Flax and Red Hand of Ulster — A3

*Perf. 15x14*

**1958-67** **Photo.** **Wmk. 322**
**1** A1 3p dark purple .25 .25
*p.* Phosphor. ('67) .25 .25
**2** A1 4p ultra ('66) .25 .25
*p.* Phosphor. ('67) .25 .25
**3** A2 6p rose lilac .30 .25
**4** A2 9p dk green ('67) .35 .80
**5** A3 1sh3p dark green .35 .80
**6** A3 1sh6p dark blue ('67) .35 .80
*Nos. 1-6 (6)* 1.85 3.15

Nos. 4, 6 and following are phosphorescent. For stamps with denomination of "1st" see No. 2600.

**1968-69** **Unwmk.**

Design: 1sh6p, Flax plant, Red Right Hand of Ulster and Ulster field gate.

**7** A1 4p ultramarine .25 .25
**8** A1 4p olive brown .25 .25
**9** A1 4p bright red ('69) .30 .25
**10** A1 5p dark blue .25 .25
**11** A3 1sh6p dark blue ('69) 3.00 3.00
*Nos. 7-11 (5)* 4.05 4.00

Giants Causeway — A4

*Perf. 14¾x14 Syncopated*

**2001-02** **Litho.**
**12** A4 2nd shown .95 .25
**13** A4 1st Farm fields 1.35 .60
*a.* Booklet pane, 5 #12, 4 #13 (BK173) 10.00
**14** A4 E Linen 1.90 .90
**15** A4 65p Parian China 2.60 1.35
**16** A4 68p Parian China 2.70 1.40
*Nos. 12-16 (5)* 9.50 4.50

Issued: Nos. 12-15, 3/6/01; No. 16, 7/4/02; No. 13a, 2/25/03.

Nos. 12-14 sold for 19p, 27p and 36p respectively on day of issue.

Giants Causeway A5

Farm Fields A6

Linen — A7

Parian China — A8

**2003, Oct. 14**
**17** A5 2nd multi .95 .40
*a.* Photo. .95 .40
**18** A6 1st multi 1.35 .50
*a.* Photo. ('07) 1.25 .65
**19** A7 E multi 1.90 .90
**20** A8 68p multi 2.70 1.40
*Nos. 17-20 (4)* 6.90 3.20

Nos. 17-19 each sold for 20p, 28p and 38p respectively on day of issue.

No. 21a issued 9/28/08.

**2004, May 11**
**21** A7 40p multi 1.60 .80

**2005, Apr. 5**
**22** A7 42p multi 1.70 .90

**2006, Mar. 28**
**23** A7 44p multi 1.75 .90
**24** A8 72p multi 2.90 1.50

**2007, Mar. 27** **Photo.**
**25** A7 48p multi 1.90 .95
**26** A8 78p multi 3.25 1.60

**Self-Adhesive**
**Stamp + Label**
*Die Cut Perf. 14¾x14*

**2008, Mar. 11** **Litho.**
**27** A6 1st multi 3.00 1.50

No. 27 was issued in sheets of 20 stamps + 20 labels that sold for £7.35, and had a franking value of 34p on day of issue.

*Perf. 14¾x14 Syncopated*

**2008, Apr. 1** **Photo.**
**28** A7 50p multi 2.00 1.00
**29** A8 81p multi 3.25 1.60

**2009**
**30** A7 56p multi 1.75 .85
**31** A8 90p multi 2.75 1.40

**Litho.**
**Self-Adhesive**
**Stamp + Label**
*Die Cut Perf. 14¾x14 Syncopated*

**32** A6 1st multi 1.25 1.25
*Nos. 30-32 (3)* 5.75 3.50

Issued: Nos. 30-31, 3/31; No. 32, 4/21. No. 32 was issued in a sheet of 20 stamps + 20 labels that sold for £8.35, and had a franking value of 39p on day of issue.

*Perf. 14¾x14 Syncopated*

**2010, Mar. 30** **Photo.**
**33** A7 60p multi 1.90 .95
**34** A8 97p multi 3.00 1.50

**2011, Mar. 29** **Litho.**
**35** A7 68p multi 2.25 1.10
**36** A8 £1.10 multi 3.75 1.90

**2012, Apr. 25**
**37** A7 87p multi 3.00 1.50
**38** A8 £1.28 multi 4.25 2.10

## SCOTLAND

St. Andrew's Cross and Thistle — A1

A2

A3

*Perf. 15x14*

**1958-67** **Photo.** **Wmk. 322**
**1** A1 3p dark purple .25 .25
*p.* Phosphor. .25 .25
**2** A1 4p ultra ('66) .25 .25
*p.* Phosphor. ('67) .25 .25
**3** A2 6p rose lilac .25 .25
*p.* Phosphor. ('63) .25 .25
**4** A2 9p dark green ('67) .40 .45
**5** A3 1sh3p dark green .45 .45
*p.* Phosphor. ('63) .45 .45
**6** A3 1sh6p dark blue ('67) .50 .55
*Nos. 1-6 (6)* 2.10 2.20

The 3p with two phosphorescent bands was issued in 1963; with one side band in 1965, and one center band in 1967. The value of No. 1p is for one center band. Nos. 4, 6 and following are phosphorescent. For stamps with denomination of "1st" see No. 2600.

**1967-70** **Unwmk.**
**7** A1 3p purple ('68) .25 .25
**8** A1 4p ultramarine .25 .25
**9** A1 4p olive brown ('68) .25 .25
**10** A1 4p brt red ('69) .25 .25
**11** A1 5p dark blue ('68) .25 .25
**12** A2 9p dark green ('70) 6.50 5.75
**13** A3 1sh6p dark blue ('68) 1.60 1.60
*Nos. 7-13 (7)* 9.35 8.60

Natl. Flag (St. Andrew's Cross) — A4

*Perf. 14¾x14 Syncopated*

**1999-2002** **Photo.**
**14** A4 (2nd) shown .95 .30
**15** A4 (1st) Lion Rampant 1.35 .45
*a.* Booklet pane, #15, 4 England #1, 4 England #2 (BK172) 10.50
**16** A4 (E) Thistle 1.10 .50
*a.* Booklet pane, 4 each #15-16, + label (BK170) 8.25
**17** A4 64p Tartan 10.00 2.50
**18** A4 65p As #17 2.40 1.25
*a.* Booklet pane, 6 #14, 2 #18 + label (BK168) 9.00
**19** A4 68p Tartan 2.50 1.40
*Nos. 14-19 (6)* 18.30 6.40

#14-16 sold for 19p, 26p, & 30p, respectively, on day of issue.

Issued: #14-17, 6/8; #18, 4/25/00; #18a, 8/4/00; #16a, 10/22/01. #19, 7/4/02. #15a, 9/24/02.

Natl. Flag (St. Andrew's Cross) A5

Lion Rampant A6

Thistle — A7

Tartan — A8

**2003, Oct. 14**
**20** A5 2nd multi .95 .40
*a.* Booklet pane, 3 each England #9, Scotland #20 (BK175) 11.50 —
**21** A6 1st multi 1.35 .50
*21a* Litho. (Wales #21a, GB 2600t) 1.25 .65
**22** A7 E multi 1.90 .90
**23** A8 68p multi 2.70 1.30
*Nos. 20-23 (5)* 8.15 3.75

Nos. 20-22 each sold for 20p, 28p and 38p respectively on day of issue.

No. 20a issued 3/16/04. No. 21a issued 9/28/08.

See Great Britain No. 2419a for National Flag stamp inscribed "1st."

**2004, May 11**
**24** A7 40p multi 1.60 .80
*a.* Souvenir sheet, #20, 2 each #21, 24 6.75 4.50

No. 24a issued 10/5/04.

**2005, Apr. 5**
**25** A7 42p multi 1.70 .85

**2006, Mar. 28**
**26** A7 44p multi 1.75 .90
**27** A8 72p multi 2.90 1.50

**2007, Mar. 27**
**28** A7 48p multi 1.90 .95
**29** A8 78p multi 3.25 1.60

**Self-Adhesive**
**Stamp + Label**
*Die Cut Perf. 14¾x14*

**2007, Nov. 30** **Litho.**
**30** A6 1st multi 3.50 1.75

No. 30 was issued in sheets of 20 stamps + 20 labels that sold for £8.50, and had a franking value of 34p on day of issue.

*Perf. 14¾x14 Syncopated*

**2008, Apr. 1** **Photo.**
**31** A7 50p multi 2.00 1.00
**32** A8 81p multi 3.25 1.60

**2009, Mar. 31**
**33** A7 56p multi 1.75 .85
**34** A8 90p multi 2.75 1.40

Flag of Scotland — A9

**35** A9 1st multi + label 1.40 1.40

No. 35 was printed in a sheet of 20 + 20 labels that could not be personalizd that sold for £8.35. See No. 2419a for similar stamp with water-activated gum.

**Types of 2003**

**2010, Mar. 30**
**36** A7 60p multi 1.90 .95
**37** A8 97p multi 3.00 1.50

**2011, Mar. 29** **Litho.**
**38** A7 68p multi 2.25 1.10
**39** A8 £1.10 multi 3.75 1.90

**2012, Apr. 25**
**40** A7 87p multi 3.00 1.50
**41** A8 £1.28 multi 4.25 2.10

## WALES & MONMOUTHSHIRE

A1

A2

Welsh Dragon — A3

Designs: 6p, 9p, Dragon in rectangular panel at bottom. 1sh3p, 1sh6p, Dragon and leek.

*Perf. 15x14*

**1958-67 Photo. Wmk. 322**

| | | | | |
|---|---|---|---|---|
| 1 | A1 | 3p dark purple | .25 | .25 |
| *p.* | | Phosphor. band ('67) | .25 | .25 |
| 2 | A1 | 4p ultra ('66) | .25 | .25 |
| *p.* | | Phosphor. bands ('67) | .25 | .25 |
| 3 | A2 | 6p rose lilac | .40 | .35 |
| 4 | A2 | 9p dark green ('67) | .45 | .40 |
| 5 | A3 | 1sh3p dark green | .45 | .45 |
| 6 | A3 | 1sh6p dark blue ('67) | .45 | .45 |
| | | *Nos. 1-6 (6)* | 2.25 | 2.15 |

Nos. 4, 6 and following are phosphorescent. For stamps with denomination of "1st" see No. 2600.

**1967-69 Unwmk.**

| | | | | |
|---|---|---|---|---|
| 7 | A1 | 3p dark purple | .25 | .25 |
| 8 | A1 | 4p ultra ('68) | .25 | .25 |
| 9 | A1 | 4p olive brown ('68) | .25 | .25 |
| 10 | A1 | 4p brt red ('69) | .25 | .25 |
| 11 | A1 | 5p dark blue ('68) | .25 | .25 |
| 12 | A3 | 1sh6p dark blue ('69) | 4.00 | 4.00 |
| | | *Nos. 7-12 (6)* | 5.25 | 5.25 |

Leek — A4

*Perf. 15x14 Syncopated*

**1999-2002 Photo.**

| | | | | |
|---|---|---|---|---|
| 13 | A4 | 2nd shown | .95 | .30 |
| 14 | A4 | 1st Dragon | 1.35 | .45 |
| 15 | A4 | E Daffodil | 1.90 | .75 |
| 16 | A4 | 64p Prince of Wales feathers | 10.00 | 3.50 |
| 17 | A4 | 65p Prince of Wales feathers | 2.60 | 1.30 |
| | | *Nos. 13-17 (5)* | 16.80 | 6.30 |
| 18 | A2 | 2nd Leek, perf 13¾x14¼ | 5.50 | .30 |
| *a.* | | Booklet pane, 4 each #18, MH336 + label (BK169) | 27.50 | |
| 19 | A4 | 68p Prince of Wales Feathers | 3.00 | 1.50 |

#13, 18 sold for 19p; #14, 26p; & #15, 30p, on day of issue.

Issued: #13-16, 6/8; #17, 4/25/00. #19, 7/4/02.

No. 18 is a booklet stamp.

Leek — A5

Dragon — A6

Daffodil A7

Prince of Wales Feathers A8

*Perf. 14¾x14 Syncopated*

**2003, Oct. 14**

| | | | | |
|---|---|---|---|---|
| 20 | A5 | 2nd multi | .95 | .40 |
| 21 | A6 | 1st multi | 1.35 | .50 |
| *a.* | | Booklet pane, litho., England #7a, Northern Ireland #18, Scotland, #21a, Wales & Monmouthshire #21b, + 5 labels (BK183) ('07) | 5.75 | |
| *b.* | | Litho. (#21a, GB #2600v) ('07) | 1.25 | .65 |
| 22 | A7 | E multi | 1.90 | .70 |
| 23 | A8 | 68p multi | 2.70 | 1.40 |
| *a.* | | Souvenir sheet, #20, 2 each #21, 23 ('06) | 9.00 | 5.00 |
| | | *Nos. 20-23 (4)* | 6.90 | 3.00 |

Nos. 20-22 each sold for 20p, 28p and 38p respectively on day of issue.

No. 23a issued 3/1/06. No. 21b issued 9/28/08

**2004, May 11**

| | | | | |
|---|---|---|---|---|
| 24 | A7 | 40p multi | 1.60 | .80 |

**2005, Apr. 5**

| | | | | |
|---|---|---|---|---|
| 25 | A7 | 42p multi | 1.70 | .85 |

**2006-07**

| | | | | |
|---|---|---|---|---|
| 26 | A7 | 44p multi | 1.75 | .90 |
| *a.* | | Booklet pane, 3 each Scotland #20, Wales & Monmouthshire #26 (BK181) ('07) | 8.00 | — |
| 27 | A8 | 72p multi | 2.90 | 1.50 |

**Self-Adhesive**

**Litho.**

**Stamp + Label**

***Die Cut Perf. 14¾x14***

| | | | | |
|---|---|---|---|---|
| 28 | A6 | 1st multi | 3.00 | 1.40 |
| *a.* | | Sheet, 5 each #28, England #16, Northern Ireland #27, Scotland #30, + 20 labels, die cut perf. 14¾x14 syncopated ('08) | 27.50 | — |

No. 28 was issued in a sheet of 20 stamps + 20 different se-tenant labels that sold for £6.95. The franking value of No. 28 was 32p on day of issue.

No. 28a issued 9/29/08. No. 28a sold for £7.74. Labels could not be personalized.

Issued: Nos. 26, 27, 3/28; Nos. 26a, 28 issued 3/1/07.

*Perf. 14¾x14 Syncopated*

**2007, Mar. 27 Photo.**

| | | | | |
|---|---|---|---|---|
| 29 | A7 | 48p multi | 1.90 | .95 |
| 30 | A8 | 78p multi | 3.25 | 1.60 |

**2008, Apr. 1**

| | | | | |
|---|---|---|---|---|
| 31 | A7 | 50p multi | 2.00 | 1.00 |
| 32 | A8 | 81p multi | 3.25 | 1.60 |

**2009, Mar. 31**

| | | | | |
|---|---|---|---|---|
| 33 | A7 | 56p multi | 1.75 | .85 |
| 34 | A8 | 90p multi | 2.75 | 1.40 |

Flag of Wales — A9

***Die Cut Perf. 14¾x14 Syncopated***

**2010, Mar. 1 Self-Adhesive Litho.**

| | | | | |
|---|---|---|---|---|
| 35 | A9 | 1st multi + label | 1.25 | 1.25 |

No. 35 was printed in a sheet of 20 + 20 labels that could not be personalizd that sold for £8.35. See No. 2639a for similar stamp with water-activated gum.

**Types of 2003**

***Perf. 14¾x14 Syncopated***

**2010, Mar. 30 Photo.**

| | | | | |
|---|---|---|---|---|
| 36 | A7 | 60p multi | 1.90 | .95 |
| 37 | A8 | 97p multi | 3.00 | 1.50 |

**2011, Mar. 29 Litho.**

| | | | | |
|---|---|---|---|---|
| 38 | A7 | 68p multi | 2.25 | 1.10 |
| 39 | A8 | £1.10 multi | 3.75 | 1.90 |

**2012, Apr. 25**

| | | | | |
|---|---|---|---|---|
| 40 | A7 | 87p multi | 3.00 | 1.50 |
| 41 | A8 | £1.28 multi | 4.25 | 2.10 |

## MACHINS

### MACHIN DEFINITIVE STAMPS

**Sterling Currency Issue**

MA1

Type I Type II

Two types of 2p:

Type I — Head off-center to right. Foot of "2" 1mm from left margin.

Type II — Head centered. Foot of "2" ½mm from left margin.

MH21 MH168

Two types of "£" symbol:

No. MH21 has a loop at the bottom and the numeral is a figure "1."

No. MH168 has no loop and numeral is like a capital "I."

*Perf. 15x14*

**1967-69 Photo. Unwmk.**

**Size: 17½x21½mm**

| | | | |
|---|---|---|---|
| MH1 | ½ brown orange | .25 | .25 |
| MH2 | 1p olive | .25 | .25 |
| *a.* | Booklet pane of 6 (BK101-BK104, BK121) | 1.00 | |
| MH3 | 2p maroon (I) | .25 | .25 |
| MH4 | 2p maroon (II) | .35 | .25 |
| MH5 | 3p dark violet | .25 | .25 |
| *a.* | Booklet pane of 6 (BK121) | 12.00 | |
| *b.* | Booklet pane, 2 ea #MH2, MH5 (BK83) | 3.50 | |
| *c.* | imperf, pair | *850.00* | |
| MH6 | 4p brown black | .25 | .25 |
| *a.* | Bklt. pane of 2 + 2 labels (BK84) | 1.10 | |
| *b.* | Bklt. pane of 4 (BK83-BK84) | 1.10 | |
| *c.* | Booklet pane of 6 (BK101-BK102, BK114-BK115, BK121-BK122) | 1.50 | |
| *d.* | Booklet pane, 4 #MH2, 2 #MH6 (BK122) | 4.50 | |
| MH7 | 4p bright red | .25 | .25 |
| *a.* | Bklt. pane of 2 + 2 labels (BK85) | 1.10 | |
| *b.* | Booklet pane of 4 (BK85) | 1.10 | |
| *c.* | Booklet pane of 6 (BK103-BK104, BK116-BK117, BK123-BK124) | 1.10 | |
| *d.* | Booklet pane of 15 + recipe (BK125-BK126) | 5.00 | |
| *e.* | Booklet pane, 4 #MH2, 2 #MH7 (BK123-BK124) | 4.00 | |
| *f.* | Coil strip of 5, #MH2, #MH5, #MH7, 2 #MH4 | 3.00 | |
| MH8 | 5p dark blue | .25 | .25 |
| *a.* | Booklet pane of 6 (BK110-BK112, BK122-BK124) | 1.50 | |
| *b.* | Booklet pane, 6 each #MH2, #MH7, 3 #MH8 + recipe (BK125-BK126) | 16.00 | |
| *c.* | Booklet pane of 15 + recipe (BK125-BK126) | 6.00 | |
| MH9 | 6p magenta | .30 | .30 |
| MH10 | 7p bright green | .45 | .40 |
| MH11 | 8p scarlet | .25 | .50 |
| MH12 | 8p lt greenish blue | .60 | .70 |
| MH13 | 9p dark green | .45 | .30 |
| MH14 | 10p gray | .65 | .65 |
| MH15 | 1sh light violet | .50 | .30 |
| MH16 | 1sh6p indigo & greenish bl | .60 | .60 |
| *a.* | Greenish blue omitted | 150.00 | |
| MH17 | 1sh9p black & orange | .60 | .50 |

*Perf. 12*

**Engr.**

**Size: 27x31mm**

| | | | |
|---|---|---|---|
| MH18 | 2sh6p brown | .55 | .25 |
| MH19 | 5sh dark carmine | 2.25 | .70 |
| MH20 | 10sh ultramarine | 7.00 | 7.00 |
| MH21 | £1 bluish black | 4.00 | 1.75 |
| | *Nos. MH1-MH21 (21)* | 20.30 | 15.95 |

Nos. MH10-MH13 have denomination at right. Many of Nos. MH1-MH17 exist with phosphor bands omitted in error.

Issued: ½p, 1p, #MH3, 6p, 2/5/68; #MH4, 8/27/69; 3p, 4/6/68; #MH6, 1sh, 1sh9p, 6/5/67; #MH7, #MH12, 1/6/69; 5p, 7p, #MH11, 10p, 7/1/68; 9p, 1sh6p, 8/8/67; #MH18-MH21, 3/5/69.

**Decimal Currency Issues**

(P Instead of D)

MA2

Nos. MH22-MH189, MH199-MH243 are Type MA2. Specialized illustrations are shown for identification purposes.

Two types of 1p: Type I: Thick numeral and "p," which are 2½mm from bottom of design. Type II: Thinner numeral and "p," which are 3mm from bottom of design.

*Perf. 15x14*

**1970-95 Photo. Unwmk.**

**Size: 17½x21½mm**

| | | | |
|---|---|---|---|
| MH22 | ½p greenish blue | .25 | .25 |
| *a.* | Booklet pane of 5 + label (BK129-BK130, BK132, BK138, BK143) | 4.50 | |
| MH23 | 1p magenta, Type I | .25 | .25 |
| MH23A | 1p magenta, Type II | .60 | .60 |
| MH24 | 1½p black | .25 | .25 |
| *a.* | Booklet pane, 2 each #MH23-MH24 (BK127-BK128) | 2.00 | |

Issued: ½p, #MH23, 1½p, 2/15/71. #MH23A, 8/4/80.

a b c

Three types of 2p:

a, Wide "2," thick at bottom of curve.

b, Wide "2," thin at bottom of curve.

c, Narrow "2."

| | | | |
|---|---|---|---|
| MH25 | 2p light green (a) | .25 | .25 |
| *a.* | Coil strip, 2 ea #MH22-MH23, 1 #MH25 | .60 | |
| MH26 | 2p light green (b) | .55 | .25 |
| *a.* | Booklet pane, 2 each #MH22, MH26(BK127-BK128) | 4.00 | |
| *b.* | Booklet pane of 6 + printed margin (BK145) | .60 | |
| MH27 | 2p dark green (c) | .35 | .25 |
| MH28 | 2p light green (c) | 6.25 | 3.00 |

**Litho.**

| | | | |
|---|---|---|---|
| MH29 | 2p dk grn, perf 14 (a) | .40 | .25 |
| MH30 | 2p dark green (a) | .55 | .25 |
| MH31 | 2p dark green (c) | 1.00 | .80 |
| MH31A | 2p dk grn, perf 14 (c) | 2.00 | .25 |

Nos. MH24a, MH26a exist with with stamps se-tenant vertically or horizontally.

Issued: #MH25, 12/12/79; #MH26, 2/15/71; #MH27, 9/5/88; #MH28, 7/26/88; #MH29, 5/21/80; #MH30, 7/10/84; #MH31, 2/23/88; MH31A, 2/9/93.

No. MH31A comes from #MH128a (BK420) only.

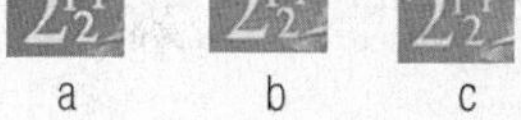

a b c

Three types of 2½p:

a, Thick numerals & "P," end of curve of small "2" is thick.

b, Thinner numerals & "P," end of curve of small "2" is thin.

c, Very thin numerals & "P," end of curve of small "2" is pointy.

| | | | |
|---|---|---|---|
| MH32 | 2½p pink (a) | .25 | .25 |
| *a.* | Booklet pane of 4 + 2 labels (BK129-BK130, BK132) | 5.75 | |
| *b.* | Booklet pane of 5 + label (BK129-BK130, BK132, BK138, BK143) | 5.50 | |
| MH33 | 2½p pink (b) | .30 | .60 |
| MH34 | 2½p pink (c) | 2.00 | *3.00* |
| *a.* | Booklet pane, 3 #MH22, 9 #MH34 + printed margin (BK144) | 25.00 | |
| *b.* | Booklet pane, 4 #MH22, 2 #MH34 + printed margin (BK144) | 75.00 | |

#MH34a, MH34b valued in F-VF condition.

| | | | |
|---|---|---|---|
| MH35 | 2½p vermilion (b) | .45 | .70 |

Issued: #MH32 2/15/71; MH33, 5/21/75; #MH34, 5/24/72; MH35, 1/14/81.

#MH34 issued only in booklets.

a b

Two types of 3p:

a, Thick numeral with top serif.

b, Thin numeral without serif.

| | | | |
|---|---|---|---|
| MH36 | 3p ultramarine (a) | .25 | .25 |
| *a.* | Booklet pane, 2 #MH32, 4 #MH36 (BK138, BK143) | 8.00 | |
| *b.* | Booklet pane, 5 + label (BK131, BK133-BK136, BK139) | 5.00 | |
| *c.* | Bklt. pane of 6 (BK138, BK143) | 5.00 | |

*d.* Booklet pane of 12, 6 each #MH34, #MH36 + printed margin (BK144) 18.00
*e.* Booklet pane of 12 + printed margin (BK144) 10.00

**MH37** 3p deep lilac rose (a) .25 .25
*a.* Coil strip, #MH35, 3 #MH37 .75 .35
**MH38** 3p deep lilac rose (b) 1.75 .75

Issued: #MH36, 9/10/73; #MH37, 10/22/80; #MH38, 1/21/92.

a b

Two types of 3½p:
a, Numerals in fraction aligned diagonally.
b, Numerals in fraction aligned vertically.

**MH39** 3½p gray green (a) .40 .40
*a.* Booklet pane of 5 + label (BK137, BK139-BK141) 6.00
**MH40** 3½p violet brown (b) 1.25 1.40

Issued: #MH39, 6/24/74; #MH40, 3/30/83.

a b c

Three types of 4p:
a, Wide "4" with large serif and thick crossbar.
b, Wide "4" with small serif and thin crossbar.
c, Narrow "4."

**MH41** 4p olive bister (a) .30 .25
*a.* Imperf., pair
**MH42** 4p greenish blue (a) .75 *.75*
*a.* Coil strip, #MH22, 3 MH42 1.75 *2.50*
**MH43** 4p brt greenish bl (a) .25 .25
*a.* Coil strip, #MH23, 3 MH43 3.25
*b.* Coil strip, #MH28, 3 MH43 4.25
**MH44** 4p greenish blue (b) 2.25 2.25
**MH45** 4p brt greenish bl (c) 1.90 2.25
**MH46** 4p bright blue (c) 1.25 .25
*a.* Coil strip, #MH38, 3 MH46 5.25
**MH47** 4p Prussian blue, litho., perf 13½x14 (b) .40 .40
**MH48** 4p Prus blue, litho. (c) 1.10 .85
**MH49** 4½p grayish blue .50 .25
*a.* Booklet pane of 5 + label (BK140, BK142) 6.00

Issued: #MH41, 2/15/71; #MH42-MH42a, 12/30/81; #MH43-MH43a, 8/14/84; #MH43b, 9/5/88. #MH44, 8/26/81; #MH45, 9/3/84; #MH46, 7/26/88; #MH46a, 9/19/89. #MH47, 1/30/80; #MH48, 5/13/86; 4 1/2p, 10/24/73.
#MH43 issued only in strips.

a b

Two types of 5p:
a, 5p is 3.25mm wide.
b, 5p is 2.75mm wide.

**MH50** 5p bluish lilac (a) .30 .25
**MH51** 5p lilac, litho., perf 13½x14 (a) .45 .45
**MH52** 5p red brown, litho., perf 13½x14 (a) .75 .60
**MH53** 5p red brown, litho. (a) .90 .25
**MH54** 5p red brown (b) 2.50 1.25
**MH55** 5p brown (b) .45 .35
*a.* Coil strip, #MH55, 3 #MH46 4.00
*b.* Coil strip, 2 ea #MH46, MH55 2.75
*c.* Coil strip, #MH46, 3 MH55 1.75
**MH56** 5½p dark violet .35 .35

Issued: #MH50, 2/15/71; #MH51, 5/21/80; #MH52, 1/27/82; #MH53, 2/21/84; #MH54, 10/20/86; #MH55, 7/26/88; #MH55a, 11/27/90; #MH55b, 10/1/91. #MH55c, 1/31/95. 5 1/2p, 10/24/73.

a b c

Three types of 6p:
a, Thick numeral and "P."
b, Thinner numeral and "P," numeral is pointed at top and very thin where loop joins.
c, Narrow numeral.

**MH57** 6p light emerald (a) .35 .25
**MH58** 6p light emerald (b) .85 .25
*a.* Booklet pane, #MH58, 2 MH22, 3 MH23 (BK225) 1.50
*b.* Coil strip, #MH23, MH26, MH58, 2 #MH22 1.10
**MH59** 6p brt olive green (c) .40 .25
**MH60** 6½p Prussian blue .35 .40

Issued: #MH57, 2/15/71; #MH58, 6/9/76; #MH58b, 12/3/75. #MH59, 9/10/91; 6 1/2p, 9/4/74.
#MH58 issued only in booklets and strips.

a b

Two types of 7p:
a, Wide numeral.
b, Narrow numeral.

**MH61** 7p dark red brown (a) .35 .40
*a.* Coil strip, #MH61, 2 ea MH22-MH23 .60
*b.* Booklet pane, #MH61, 2 ea MH22-MH23 + label (BK226) .75
**MH62** 7p henna brown (b) 1.25 *1.50*
**MH63** 7½p lt red brown .40 .40
**MH64** 8p red .35 .25
*a.* Coil strip, #MH64, 2 MH23 + 2 labels .60
*b.* Booklet pane, #MH64, 2 MH23 + label (BK227) .75
**MH65** 8½p yellow green .35 .25
*a.* Bklt. pane, 2 ea #MH22-MH23, MH60, 4 MH65 (BK228) 5.25

No. MH65a exists with the four 8 1/2p stamps se-tenant on either the left or right side of the pane.

**MH66** 9p black & ocher .65 .25
**MH67** 9p violet blue .45 .25
*a.* Booklet pane, 2 #MH23, 3 ea MH61, MH67 (BK229-BK230) 3.50
*b.* Booklet pane, 10 ea #MH61, MH67 (BK672) 6.50

No. MH67a exists with the three 9p stamps se-tenant on either the left or right side of the pane.

**MH68** 9½p bright lilac .40 .50

Issued: #MH61, 1/15/75; #MH61a, 12/14/77. #MH62, 10/29/85; 7 1/2p, 2/15/71; 8p, 10/24/73; #MH64a, 1/16/80. 8½p, 9/24/75; #MH66, 2/15/71; #MH67, 9 1/2p, 2/25/76.

a b c

Three types of 10p:
a, Round "0."
b, Thin part of "0" at upper left, lower right.
c, Thin part of "0" at top, bottom.

**MH69** 10p org brn & lt org (a) .65 .35
**MH70** 10p light org brn (b) .45 .30
*a.* Bklt. pane of 9 + printed margin (BK145) 2.50
*b.* Booklet pane, 2 ea #MH26, MH64, 3 #MH70 + label (BK231-BK232) 2.50
*c.* Booklet pane, 10 ea #MH64, MH70 (BK709) 6.25
**MH70D** 10p light org brn (c) 35.00 20.00

No. MH70b exists with the three 10p stamps se-tenant on either the left or right side of the pane.

**MH71** 10p brn orange (c) .60 .50
**MH72** 10½p yellow .50 .50
**MH73** 10½p steel blue .80 .60
**MH74** 11p pink .50 .25

Issued: #MH69, 8/11/71; #MH70, MH72, 11p, 2/25/76; #MH71, 9/4/90; #MH73, 4/26/78; #MH70D, 9/4/84.

a b

Two types of 11½p:
a, Thin numerals in fraction.
b, Thick numerals in fraction.

**MH75** 11½p olive bister (a) .65 .65
**MH76** 11½p gray brown (a) .50 .40
*a.* Booklet pane, 2 #MH42, 3 each MH35, MH76 (BK236) 4.50
**MH77** 11½p gray brown (b) 1.00 .25

#MH77 comes from #MH86c (BK826), only.
Issued: #MH75, 8/15/79; #MH76, 1/14/81; #MH77, 11/11/81;

a b

Two types of 12p:
a, Wide numerals.
b, Narrow, thin numerals.

**MH78** 12p yellow green (a) .55 .50
*a.* Booklet pane of 9 + printed margin (BK145) 3.00
*b.* Booklet pane of 9 (#MH26, 4 each #MH70, MH78) + printed margin (BK145) 13.50
*c.* Booklet pane of 10 each #MH70, MH78 (BK759) 9.00
*d.* Booklet pane, 3 #MH26, 2 each MH70, MH78 + label (BK233) 2.25
**MH79** 12p bright green (b) .60 .35
*a.* Booklet pane of 9 + printed margin (BK140) 6.00
*b.* Booklet pane, 2 #MH23, 4 MH79 (BK245) 8.00

Issued: #MH78, 1/30/80; #MH79, 10/29/85.

a b

Two types of 12½p:
a, Thin, narrow numerals.
b, Thick, wider numerals.

**MH80** 12½p light emerald (a) .50 .25
*a.* Booklet pane of 6 + printed margin (BK146-BK147) 5.00
*b.* Booklet pane of 9, #MH25, MH37, 7 MH80 + printed margin (BK146) 6.00
*c.* Booklet pane, #MH22, 4 MH37, 3 MH80 (BK237-BK238) 3.00
*d.* Booklet pane, 2 #MH23, 3 each MH40, MH80 (BK239) 7.50
*e.* Booklet pane of 20 (BK760) 8.00

No. MH80c exists with the three 12½p stamps se-tenant on either the left or right side of the pane. Booklets with 20 #MH80 were sold at a discount. Stamps in these booklets had 5-point double-lined stars printed on the reverse.

**MH81** 12½p green (b) .80 .25

No. MH81 comes from #MH93d (BK572).
Issued: #MH80, 1/27/82; #MH81, 2/1/82.

a b

Two types of 13p:
a, "3" with serif.
b, "3" without serif.

**MH82** 13p gray green (a) .60 .55
**MH83** 13p lt red brown (b) .50 .25
*a.* Booklet pane of 6 + printed margin (BK148, BK151) 3.50
*b.* Booklet pane of 9 + printed margin (BK149, BK151) 5.00
*c.* Booklet pane, 2 #MH45, 3 each MH23, MH83 (BK240) 4.75
*d.* Booklet pane, #MH23, 2 MH54, 3 MH83 (BK244, BK248) 5.00
*e.* Booklet pane of 4, margins all around (BK285) 3.00
*f.* Booklet pane of 10, margins all around (BK534) 6.00
*g.* As "d," imperf edges (BK248A, BK250-BK251) 5.00

Panes of #MH83 with stars printed on the reverse were sold at a discount.

**MH84** 13p lt red brn, litho. (b) 1.00 .85
*a.* Booklet pane of 6 + printed margin (BK152) 6.00
**MH85** 13½p brown purple .70 .70

Issued: #MH82, 8/15/79; #MH83, 8/28/84; #MH84, 2/9/88; 13½p, 1/30/80.

a b

Two types of 14p:
a, Wide "4."
b, Narrow "4."

**MH86** 14p gray blue (a) .70 .60
*a.* Bklt. pane, #MH22-MH23, MH86, 3 MH76 (BK234-BK235) 2.25
*b.* Booklet pane, 4 #MH76, 6 MH86 (BK524) 5.25
*c.* Booklet pane, 10 each #MH77, MH86 (BK826) 12.50
**MH87** 14p dark blue (b) .60 .40
*a.* Booklet pane of 4, margins all around (BK295) *5.00*
*b.* Booklet pane of 4, imperf on T, B (BK296) *5.00*
*c.* Booklet pane of 4, imperf on T, B, R (BK297) *19.00*
*d.* Boolet pane of 10, margins all around (BK558) 5.50
*e.* Booklet pane of 10, imperf on T, B (BK560) 8.00
**MH88** 14p dark blue, litho. (b) 2.50 2.00
**MH89** 14p dark blue, litho., perf 14 (b) 6.25 1.00

No. MH89 comes from #MH108a (BK412), only.

**MH90** 15p deep ultramarine .70 .70
**MH91** 15p bright blue .75 .25

Issued: #MH86, 1/14/81; #MH87, 9/5/88; #MH88, 10/11/88; #MH89, 4/25/89; #MH90, 8/15/79; #MH91, 9/26/89.

a b

Two types of 15½p:
a, Thin numerals in fraction, top bar of "5" thin.
b, Thick numerals in fraction, top bar of "5" thick.

**MH92** 15½p light violet (a) .70 .60
*a.* Booklet pane of 6 + printed margin (BK146) 4.25
*b.* Booklet pane of 9 + printed margin (BK146) 6.50
**MH93** 15½p light violet (b) .80 .35
*c.* Booklet pane, 4 #MH80, 6 MH93 (BK573-BK574) 6.75
*d.* Booklet pane, 4 #MH81, 6 MH93 (BK572) 8.25
*e.* Booklet pane, 10 each #MH80, MH93 (BK802) 11.00

No. MH93e was printed with 10-point single-line blue stars on the reverse over the gum.

**MH94** 16p brownish gray .65 .65
*a.* Booklet pane, #MH37, 2 MH40 6 MH94 + printed margin (BK147) 4.50
*b.* Booklet pane of 9 + printed margin (BK147) 5.50
*c.* Booklet pane, 4 #MH80, 6 MH94 (BK594) 12.00

Panes of #MH94 with double-line D printed on reverse were sold at a discount in BK584.

**MH95** 16½p fawn 1.00 .85

Issued: #MH92, 1/14/81; #MH93, 2/1/82; 16p, 3/30/83; 16½p, 1/27/82.
#MH93 issued only in booklets.

a b

Two types of 17p:
a, Wide "7."
b, Narrow "7."

**MH96** 17p light green (a) .85 .70
**MH97** 17p blue gray (b) .70 .70
*a.* Booklet pane of 3 + label (star printed on reverse-BK241-BK242) 2.50
*b.* Booklet pane of 9 + printed margin (BK149-BK150) 7.00
*c.* Booklet pane of 6 + printed margin (BK148-BK150) 4.00
*d.* Booklet pane, #MH70D, MH83, 7 MH97 + printed margin (BK148) 45.00
*e.* Booklet pane, 4 #MH79, 6 MH97 (BK616-BK618) 7.00
*f.* Booklet pane, 4 #MH83, 6 MH97 (BK641) 6.00
*g.* Booklet pane of 10 (double-lined "D" printed on reverse-BK652) 6.00
**MH98** 17p dark blue (b) 1.25 .35
*a.* Bklt. pane of 3 + label (BK256) 3.00
**MH99** 17p dk bl, litho. (b) 1.20 .35
*a.* Booklet pane of 6 + printed margin (BK155) 7.50
**MH100** 17½p lt red brown .90 .85
**MH101** 18p violet blue .80 .80
**MH102** 18p olive green .85 .70
*a.* Booklet pane of 9 + printed margin (BK151) 7.00
*b.* Booklet pane, #MH23, MH83, 2 MH102 (BK246-BK247, BK249) 3.00
*c.* Booklet pane of 4, margins all around (BK328) 4.00
*d.* Booklet pane, #MH83, 5 MH102 (BK406-BK407) 6.00
*e.* Booklet pane of 10, margins all around (BK714) 8.75
*f.* As "d," imperf edges (BK408-BK410) 6.00
**MH103** 18p ol grn, litho. 1.00 1.10
*a.* Booklet pane of 6 + printed margin (BK152) 5.75
*b.* Booklet pane of 9 + printed margin (BK152) 7.75
**MH104** 18p brt yel grn .90 .40
**MH105** 18p brt yel grn, litho. 1.40 1.60
*a.* Booklet pane of 6 + printed margin (BK157) 7.75

**MH106** 19p brt orange 1.25 .35
*a.* Bklt. pane, #MH87, 2 #MH106 + label (BK252-BK253) 3.75
*b.* Booklet pane, 2 #MH87, 4 MH106 (BK411, BK413) 8.00
*c.* Booklet pane of 4, margins all around (BK348) *8.00*
*d.* Booklet pane of 4, imperf on T, B (BK349) *9.75*
*e.* Booklet pane of 4, imperf on T, B, R (BK350) *19.00*
*f.* Booklet pane of 10, margins all around (BK729) 14.00
*g.* Booklet pane of 10, imperf on T, B (BK730) *10.00*
**MH107** 19p red org, litho. 2.25 2.25
**MH108** 19p red org, litho., perf 14 3.50 1.25
*a.* Booklet pane, 2#MH89, 4 #MH108 (BK412) 22.50
**MH110** 19½p olive gray 2.25 1.50

Issued: #MH96, 1/30/80; #MH97, 3/30/80; #MH98, 9/4/90; #MH99, 3/19/91; 17½p, 1/30/80; #MH101, 1/14/81; #MH102, 8/28/84; #MH103, 2/9/88; #MH104, 9/10/91; #MH105, 10/27/92; #MH106, 8/3/88; #MH107, 10/11/88; #MH108, 4/25/89; 19½p, 1/27/82.

#MH99, MH103, MH105, MH108 issued only in booklets.

a b

Two types of 20p:
a, Thin part of "0" at upper left, lower right.
b, Thin part of "0" at top, bottom.

**MH111** 20p dp pur brn (a) 1.25 .25
**MH112** 20p dp pur brn, litho., perf 13¾x14 (a) 1.75 1.10
**MH113** 20p dp pur brn, litho., perf 15x14 (b) 2.00 1.25
**MH114** 20p greenish bl (b) 1.00 .80
**MH115** 20p brown black (b) 1.10 1.10
*a.* Booklet pane, 2 #MH91, MH115 + label (BK254) 5.00
*b.* Booklet pane of 5 + label (BK414) 8.00
**MH116** 20½p ultramarine 1.50 1.10
**MH117** 22p dark blue 1.00 .85
**MH118** 22p yellow green 1.00 .90
**MH119** 22p yel grn, litho. (MH150a) 14.00 3.00
**MH120** 22p orange red 1.20 .90
*a.* Booklet pane, 2 #MH98, 3 MH120 + 3 labels (BK417) 4.00
**MH121** 22p org red, litho. 1.40 1.00
*a.* Booklet pane of 9 + printed margin (BK155) 10.00
**MH122** 23p rose pink 1.50 .50
**MH123** 23p brt yel grn 1.40 1.00
**MH124** 24p violet 1.75 1.75
**MH125** 24p brown red 2.25 1.90
**MH126** 24p brown 1.00 .90
*a.* Booklet pane, 2 each #MH23, MH126 (BK257-BK259) 1.75
*b.* Booklet pane, 2 #MH27, 4 MH126 + 2 labels (BK418-BK419) 3.50
**MH127** 24p brown, litho. 1.25 1.25
*a.* Booklet pane of 6 + printed margin (BK157) 8.00
**MH128** 24p brn, litho. perf 14 1.50 .35
*a.* Booklet pane, 2 #MH31A, 4 MH128 + 2 labels (BK420) 9.50
**MH129** 25p lilac 1.00 1.10
**MH129A** 25p salmon 15.00 14.00

Issued: #MH111, 2/25/76; #MH112, 5/21/80; #MH113, 5/13/86; #MH114, 8/23/88; #MH115, 9/26/89; 20½p, 3/30/83; #MH117, 10/22/80; #MH118, 8/28/84; #MH119, 2/9/88; #MH120, 9/4/90; #MH121, 3/19/91; #MH122, 3/30/83; #MH123, 8/3/88; #MH124, 8/28/84; MH125, 9/26/89; #MH126, 9/10/91; #MH127, 10/27/92; #MH128, 2/9/93; 25p, 1/14/81.

#MH119, MH121, MH127 issued only in booklets.

No. MH129A was issued 2/6/96 only in coils.

a b

Two types of 26p:
a, Wide numerals.
b, Narrow numerals.

**MH130** 26p red (a) 1.25 .70
*a.* Booklet pane, #MH23, MH130, 2 MH83, 5 MH102 + printed margin (BK151) 20.00
**MH131** 26p red (b) 6.00 6.00
*a.* Booklet pane of 4, margins all around (BK446) 24.00
**MH132** 26p olive gray (b) 1.75 1.40
**MH133** 27p brown 1.50 1.50
*a.* Booklet pane of 4, margins all around (BK456) 14.50
*b.* Booklet pane of 4, horiz. edges imperf (BK457) 35.00
**MH134** 27p violet 1.75 1.40
**MH135** 28p deep violet blue 1.40 1.40
**MH136** 28p dk olive bister 1.60 1.40
**MH137** 28p dull blue green 1.60 1.40

Issued: #MH130, 1/27/82; #MH131, 8/4/87; #MH132, 9/4/90; #MH133, 8/3/88; #MH134, 9/4/90; #MH135, 3/30/83; #MH136, 8/23/88; #MH137, 9/10/91.

#MH131 issued only in booklets.

a b

Two types of 29p:
a, Wide numerals.
b, Narrow numerals.

**MH138** 29p brown olive (a) 2.25 2.00
**MH139** 29p dp rose lilac (b) 2.50 2.00
**MH140** 29p dp rose lilac, litho., perf 14 (b) 4.75 3.00
*a.* Booklet pane of 4, imperf edges (BK150) 20.00
**MH141** 30p dk olive green 1.75 1.40
**MH142** 31p brt rose lilac 1.40 1.40
*a.* Bklt. pane, #MH142, 6 MH79, 2 MH97 + printed margin (BK150) 17.00
**MH143** 31p ultramarine 1.90 1.75
**MH144** 31p ultra, litho., perf 14 2.75 1.60
*a.* Booklet pane of 4, imperf on T, B (BK503) 11.00
**MH145** 32p Prussian blue 2.25 2.00
**MH146** 33p emerald 2.00 1.90
**MH147** 33p emerald, litho. 3.00 3.00
*a.* Bklt. pane, 6 #MH121, 2 MH147 + label, printed margin (BK155) 15.00
**MH148** 33p emer, litho. perf 14 2.75 .45
*a.* Booklet pane of 4, margins all around (BK544) 11.00
**MH149** 34p dark brown 2.00 2.00
*a.* Bklt. pane, #MN149, 2 MH45, 4 MH83, 2 MH97 + printed margin (BK149) 17.00
**MH150** 34p dark brn, litho. 11.00 2.00
*a.* Bklt. pane, 6 #MH84, 1 ea MH103, MH119, MH150 + printed margin (BK152) 27.50
**MH151** 34p dull blue green 2.25 2.10
**MH152** 34p brt rose lilac 2.00 2.00
**MH153** 35p dark brown 2.25 1.90
**MH154** 35p orange yellow 2.00 1.90
**MH155** 37p scarlet 2.25 2.00
**MH156** 39p brt rose lilac 2.25 1.75
**MH157** 39p brt rose lil, litho. perf 14 3.00 .80
*a.* Booklet pane of 4, imperf on T, B (BK662) 12.00
**MH158** 39p brt rose lil, litho. (MH178a, MH187b) 2.50 .80

Issued: #MH138, 1/27/82; #MH139, 9/26/89; #MH140, 10/2/89; #MH141, 9/26/89; #MH142, 3/30/83; #MH143, 9/4/90; #MH144, 9/17/90; #MH145, 8/23/88; #MH146, 9/4/90; #MH147, 3/19/91; #MN148, 9/16/91; #MH149, 8/28/84; #MH150, 2/9/88; #MH151, 9/26/89; #MH152, 9/10/91; #MH153, 8/23/88; #MH154, 9/10/91; #MH155, 9/26/89; #MH156, 9/10/91; #MH157, 9/16/91; #MH158, 10/27/92.

#MH144, MH147-MH148, MH150 issued only in booklets.

a b

Two types of 50p:
a, Wide numerals.
b, Narrow numerals.

**MH159** 50p bister brown (a) 2.75 .35
**MH160** 50p ocher (b) 2.50 .80

Issued: #MH159, 2/2/77; #MH160, 5/21/80.

a b

Two types of 75p:
a, Wide numerals.
b, Narrow numerals.

**MH161** 75p black, litho., perf 13½x14 (a) 4.00 1.50
**MH162** 75p black, litho. (a) 4.00 1.50
**MH163** 75p black, litho. (b) 12.00 9.75
**MH164** 75p black (b) 4.00 2.00

Issued: #MH161, 3/1/80; #MH162, 2/21/84; #MH163, 2/23/88; #MH164, 7/26/88.

### Engr.
### *Perf. 12*
### Size: 27x31mm

**MH165** 10p carmine rose .90 *1.00*
**MH166** 20p olive 1.00 .25
**MH167** 50p ultramarine 2.00 .60
*p.* Phosphor 2.50 .60
**MH168** £1 bluish black 4.75 1.25

For illustration of £1, see above #MH1.

No. MH168, imperf, are from printers' waste.

Issued: #MH165-MH167, 6/17/70; £1, 12/6/72.

### Photo.
### *Perf. 14x15*
### Size: 27x38mm

**MH169** £1 olive grn & yel 4.00 .60
**MH170** £1.30 slate bl & buff 6.25 *7.00*
**MH171** £1.33 black & pale rose lilac 8.75 8.00
**MH172** £1.41 indigo & buff 11.00 9.75
**MH173** £1.50 blk & lt pink 7.50 5.75
**MH174** £1.60 indigo & buff 7.50 8.00
**MH175** £2 mar & lt grn 14.00 1.50
**MH176** £5 dk bl & pink 32.50 4.00

Issued: £1, 2/2/77; £1.30, 8/3/83; £1.33, 8/28/84; £1.41, 9/17/85; £1.50, 9/2/86; £1.60, 9/15/87; £2, £5, 2/2/77.

## 2nd or 1st Class (Non-Denominated)

2nd and 1st class stamps sell for the current rates and remain valid indefinitely for the indicated service

### *Perf. 15x14*

**MH177** 2nd bright blue 1.50 1.10
*a.* Booklet pane of 4, imperf on T, B, R (BK961) 25.00
*b.* Booklet pane of 10, imperf on T, B (BK1028, BK1078) 15.00
**MH178** 2nd bright blue, litho. 1.25 1.00
*a.* Booklet pane, 2 each #MH105, MH147, MH158, MH178 + label, printed margin (BK158) 15.00
**MH179** 2nd bright blue, litho., perf 14 1.25 1.10
*a.* Booklet pane of 4, imperf on T, B, R (BK960) 5.00
*b.* Booklet pane of 4, imperf on T, B (BK963-BK964) 5.00
*c.* Booklet pane of 10, imperf on T, B (BK1034-BK1035) 12.50

Nos. MH177-MH179 each sold for 14p on day of issue.

**MH180** 2nd dark blue 1.75 .30
*a.* Booklet pane of 10, imperf on T, B (BK1030) 17.50
**MH181** 2nd dark blue, litho. 2.50 .30
**MH182** 2nd dark blue, litho., perf 14 .95 .30
*a.* Booklet pane of 4, imperf on T, B (BK962) 3.75
*b.* Booklet pane of 10, imperf on T, B (BK1032) 9.50

Nos. MH180-MH182 each sold for 15p on day of issue.

**MH183** 1st brown black 2.00 .65
*a.* Booklet pane of 4, imperf on T, B, R (BK995) 25.00
*b.* Booklet pane of 10, imperf on T, B (BK1041) 20.00
**MH184** 1st brown black, litho., perf 14 3.00 .75
*a.* Booklet pane of 4, imperf on T, B, R (BK994) 12.00
**MH185** 1st brown black, litho. 2.50 .65

Nos. MH183-MH185 each sold for 19p on day of issue.

**MH186** 1st orange red 1.35 .40
*a.* Booklet pane of 10, imperf on T, B (BK1068, BK1091) 13.50
**MH187** 1st orange red, litho. 1.35 .40
*a.* Booklet pane, 3 each #MH178, MH187 + printed margin (BK158) 7.75
*b.* Booklet pane, #MH178, MH187, 2 ea MH105, MH127, MH158 + label, printed margin (BK157) *15.00*
*c.* Booklet pane of 8+ label, printed margin (BK156) 10.50
*d.* Booklet pane of 10, imperf on T, B (BK1092-BK1093) 13.50

No. MH187c contains #MH178, MH187, 2 each MH147, WMMH34, WMMH45.

**MH188** 1st orange red, litho., perf 14 1.35 .40
*a.* Booklet pane of 4, imperf on T, B (BK996-BK997) 5.50
*b.* Booklet pane of 10, imperf on T, B (BK1070) 13.50
**MH189** 1st orange red, litho., perf 13x13½ 4.25 1.50

Nos. MH186-MH189 each sold for 20p on day of issue.

Distance of denomination to the margin and bust may vary on different printings of the same stamp.

Issued: #MH177, 8/22/89; #MH178, 9/18/89; #MH179, 8/22/89; #MH180-MH182, 8/7/90; #MH183-MH184, 8/22/89; #MH185, 9/19/89; #MH186-MH188, 8/7/90; #MH189, 10/90.

#MH177-MH189 issued only in booklets.

Victoria and Elizabeth II — MA3

**1990-2000 Photo. *Perf. 15x14***

**MH190** 15p bright blue .90 .90
*a.* Booklet pane of 10, imperf on T, B (BK619) 11.50
**MH191** 15p brt bl, litho., perf 14 1.75 2.00
*a.* Booklet pane of 4 with imperf on T, B, R (BK307) 8.00
*b.* Booklet pane of 10 with imperf on T, B, R (BK620) 14.00
**MH192** 15p bright blue, litho. 2.50 2.50
*a.* Booklet pane of 10 (BK621) 22.50
**MH193** 20p black & brown black .90 .90
*a.* Booklet pane, #MH193, 2 MH190 + label (BK255) 3.00
*b.* Booklet pane of 4 with imperf on T, B, R (BK371) 6.00
*c.* Bklt. pane of 5 + label (BK415) 4.00
*d.* Booklet pane of 6 + printed margin (BK154) 4.00
*e.* Booklet pane of 10 with imperf on T, B (BK743) 12.00
*f.* Souvenir sheet of 1 7.00 7.00
**MH194** 20p black & brn blk, litho., perf 14 2.25 2.00
*a.* Booklet pane of 4 with imperf on T, B, R (BK372) 11.50
*b.* Bklt. pane of 5 + label (BK416) 12.00
*c.* Booklet pane of 10 with imperf on T, B, R (BK744) 22.50
**MH195** 20p black & brn blk, litho. 2.75 2.75
*a.* Booklet pane of 10 (BK745) 27.50
**MH196** 29p deep rose lilac 2.00 2.00
*a.* Booklet pane, #MH91, MH115, MH160, MH177, MH183, MH190, MH193, MH196 + label, printed margin (BK154) 22.50
**MH197** 34p dull blue green 2.25 2.25
**MH198** 37p scarlet 2.50 2.50

### *Perf. 13¾x14¼ Syncopated*

**MH198A** 1st blk & yel 2.50 1.60
*b.* Booklet pane of 6 (BK167) 15.00

Nos. MH191-MH192, MH194-MH195, MH198A were issued only in booklets.

No. MH198A sold for 26p on day of issue.

Issued: #MH190, MH193, MH196-MH198, 1/10; #MH191, MH194, 1/30; #MH192, MH195, 4/17; #MH198A, 2/15/00.

### *Syncopated Perf. 15x14*

**1993-97 Type MA2**

**MH199** 1p magenta .25 .25
**MH200** 1p mag, litho. (MH216b) .90 .45
**MH201** 2p dark green .25 .25
**MH202** 4p Prussian blue .45 .25
**MH203** 5p rose brown .35 .25
**MH204** 6p bright olive green .55 .35
**MH205** 6p bright olive green, litho. (MH214a) 15.00 15.00
**MH206** 10p brown orange .50 .35
**MH207** 10p brown orange, litho. (MH231a) 7.25 5.50
**MH208** 19p olive green .75 .70
**MH209** 19p ol grn, litho. (MH214a, MH231a) 2.25 2.00
*a.* Booklet pane of 6 + printed margin (BK160) 13.50
**MH210** 20p greenish blue 1.20 1.00
**MH211** 20p bright yel grn 1.40 .80
**MH212** 20p brt yel grn, litho. (MH216a-MH216b) 3.75 2.50
**MH213** 25p salmon 1.00 .40
*a.* Booklet pane of 2 + 2 labels (BK260-BK262) 2.00

**MH214** 25p sal, litho. (MH231a) 1.25 1.25
*a.* Bklt. pane, #MH205, MH209, 4 MH214 + printed margin (BK159) 22.50
*b.* Booklet pane of 8 + label, printed margin (see footnote) (BK161) 11.00

No. MH214b contains 2 each #MH214, NIMH59, SMH65, WMMH60.

**MH215** 26p brown 1.75 1.25
**MH216** 26p brown, litho. 1.10 1.10
*a.* Bklt. pane, #MH212, 7 MH216 (BK749) 10.00
*b.* Bklt. pane, #MH212, 2 MH200, 3 MH216 + 2 labels (BK426) 4.00
**MH218** 29p gray 1.50 1.40
**MH219** 30p olive green 1.50 1.25
**MH220** 30p olive green, litho. (MH231a) 8.00 4.75
**MH221** 31p deep rose lilac 1.75 1.25
**MH222** 35p orange yellow 2.00 1.75
**MH223** 35p org yel, litho. 2.00 2.00
*a.* Booklet pane of 4 (BK562-BK563) 10.00
**MH224** 36p blue 1.75 1.75
**MH225** 37p bright rose lilac 2.10 2.10
**MH226** 37p brt rose lilac, litho. 4.25 3.00
*a.* Booklet pane of 4 (BK605) 18.00
**MH227** 38p red 2.00 2.00
**MH228** 39p bright pink 2.10 2.10
**MH230** 41p drab 2.50 1.60
**MH231** 41p drab, litho. 3.50 2.00
*a.* Booklet pane, #MH207, MH220, MH223, MH231, 2 each MH209, MH214 + label, printed margin (BK160) 17.50
*b.* Booklet pane of 4 (BK685-BK686) 15.00
**MH232** 43p dark brown 2.75 2.75
**MH233** 50p ocher 2.75 1.10
**MH234** 60p slate blue, litho. 2.75 2.75
*a.* Booklet pane of 4 (BK790-BK791) 11.00
**MH235** 63p bright green 3.25 2.25
**MH236** 63p brt grn, litho. 5.00 3.50
*a.* Bklt. pane of 4 (BK815) 18.00
**MH237** £1 violet 4.50 3.25

No. MH237 is printed with Iriodin ink, giving stamp design a three dimensional appearance.

**MH238** 2nd bright blue 1.00 1.00
**MH239** 2nd bright blue, litho. 1.00 1.00
**MH240** 1st orange red 1.75 1.40
**MH241** 1st orange red, litho. 1.35 1.00
*a.* Miniature sheet of 1 6.50 6.50
*b.* Booklet pane of 4 + label (BK1000, BK1002, BK1004) 6.50
*c.* Booklet pane of 9 + printed margin (BK165) 12.00

No. MH241a was sold for £1 on day of issue in pre-packaged greeting cards at Boots pharmacy. Unfolded examples were later sold by British Philatelic Bureau. Value indicated is for unfolded example.

MH243

MH309

## Size: 21½x17½mm
## Self-Adhesive
### *Die Cut 14x15 Syncopated*
### Litho.

**MH243** 1st orange red 1.60 1.25
*a.* Booklet pane of 20 32.50

Nos. MH238-MH239 each sold for 18p on day of issue; Nos. MH240-MH241, MH243 each for 24p.

Issued: No. MH201, 4/11/95; No. MH204, 4/27/93; No. MH219, 7/27/93; No. MH222, 8/17/93; No. MH234, 8/9/94; No. MH237, 8/22/95; No. MH238, 9/7/93; No. MH241, 9/6/93. No. MH241c, 2/16/99.
Nos. MH239, MH240, 4/6/93.
Nos. MH199, MH203, MH212, MH206, 6/8/93.
No. MH243, 10/19/93.
Nos. MH208, MH213, MH218, MH224, MH227, MH230, 10/26/93.
Nos. MH214, MH223, MH223, 11/1/93.
Nos. MH202, MH210, MH233, 12/14/93.
Nos. MH205, MH209, 7/26/94.
Nos. MH207, MH220, 4/25/95.
Nos. MH215, MH221, MH225, MH228, MH232, MH235, 6/25/96.
Nos. MH200, MH216, MH226, MH236, 7/8/96.
Nos. MH200, MH205, MH207, MH209, MH212, MH216, MH219, MH226, MH231, MH236 issued only in booklets.
No. MH243a is a complete booklet.

## Queen Type of 1970 with Redrawn Portrait

Type MA2: Upper lip not defined by sharp line, nostril is incomplete, hairlines not sharply defined, upper corners of cross formeé are widely separated.

Redrawn portrait: Upper lip sharply outlined, nostril is complete and defined by two lines, hairlines are sharply defined, upper corners of cross formeé are close together so they nearly complete a square.

5p Type c — The top line of the 5 has a curved top edge.

### *Perf. 15x14 Syncopated, 13¾x14¼ Syncopated (#MH251, MH254A, MH264B, MH269, MH285, MH289)*

**1996-2010 Photo.**

**MH245** 1p magenta .25 .25
*a.* Litho. (MH372c) 3.50 .75
**MH246** 2p dark green .25 .25
*a.* Litho. (MH401b) .25 .25
**MH247** 4p Prussian blue .70 .30
**MH248** 5p rose brown (b) .25 .25
*a.* Litho. (b) (MH363c) 2.50 .30
**MH248B** 5p red brown, litho. (c) (MH350Ad) 5.25 .30
**MH249** 6p bright olive green 1.00 .30
**MH249A** 7p gray 5.00 1.00
**MH249B** 8p dk olive bister .90 .90
**MH250** 10p brown orange .40 .25
*a.* Litho. (MH363c) 1.75 .35
**MH251** 10p brn org, perf 13¾x14¼ 4.00 .30
**MH254** 19p bister 1.75 .40
**MH254A** 19p bister (MH264c), perf 13¾x14¼ 2.25 2.25
**MH255** 20p bright yellow green 1.60 1.60
*a.* Litho. (MH368c) 2.50 .30
**MH256** 26p gold 1.75 1.10
**MH257** 26p brown 1.50 .40
*a.* Booklet pane, 3 each #MH255, MH257 + printed margin (BK162) 9.50
*b.* Bklt. pane, #MH255, 2 MH245, 3 MH257 + 2 labels (BK427) 16.50
*c.* Booklet pane, #MH255, 7 MH257 (BK751) 22.00
*d.* Booklet pane, #MH245-MH246, MH254, 3 #MH257 + 2 labels (BK428) 9.00
*e.* Booklet pane, #MH254, 7 #MH257 (BK752) 13.00
*f.* Booklet pane, 4 #MH245, 3 #MH254, 1 #MH257 + label 4.50
**MH259** 30p olive green 2.00 .50
**MH260** 31p deep rose lil 2.00 .55
**MH261** 33p dk blue green 1.75 1.25
**MH261A** 34p olive green 7.50 1.40
**MH262** 37p brt rose lilac 2.50 1.75
**MH263** 37p black 1.90 1.25
**MH264** 38p dark blue 2.25 1.75
**MH264B** 38p dk blue, perf 13¾x14¼ 7.50 1.00
*c.* Booklet pane, 4 #MH254A, 2 #MH264B (BK167) 20.00
**MH265** 39p brt pink 2.50 .30
**MH266** 40p chalky blue 2.00 1.40
*a.* Booklet pane of 4 (BK676) 8.00
**MH267** 41p carmine rose 2.00 1.40
**MH267A** 42p olive 2.00 1.40
**MH268** 43p dark brown 3.00 .70
**MH269** 43p dk brn, perf 13¾x14¼ 2.25 2.25
*a.* Booklet pane, #NIMH70, SMH76, WMMH71, 3 MH269 + printed margin (BK164) 12.00
**MH270** 44p brown 6.75 2.50
**MH270A** 45p brt rose lilac 2.10 1.50
**MH270B** 47p blue green 2.25 1.75
**MH271** 50p ocher 2.00 1.10
**MH275** 63p bright green 4.00 1.25
**MH276** 64p greenish blue 3.50 2.50
**MH277** 65p Prussian blue 3.50 2.10
*a.* Booklet pane of 4 (BK830) 14.00
**MH278** 68p drab 3.25 2.10
**MH279** £1 violet 4.50 3.00
*a.* Souv. sheet, see footnote 32.50 12.00

No. MH279 is printed with Iriodin ink, giving stamp design a three dimensional appearance.

No. MH279a contains #MH247-MH249, MH250, MH260, MH265, MH276, MH279 + 2 labels.

Issued: No. MH246a, 5/8/10.

**MH280** £1.50 red, engr. 6.00 2.25
**MH281** £2 slate blue, engr. 8.00 3.25
**MH282** £3 purple, engr. 12.00 4.75
**MH283** £5 brown, engr. 20.00 8.00

**MH284** 2nd bright blue .95 .30
*a.* Litho. (#MH287h) ('08) 4.00 .75
**MH285** 2nd bright blue, perf 13¾x14¼ 1.75 .30
*a.* Booklet pane, #NIMH74, SMH80, WMMH75, 3 MH285 + printed margin (BK164) 11.00
*b.* Booklet pane, 2 #MH251, 3 each MH269, MH285 + label, printed margin (BK164) 16.50
**MH287** 1st gold 1.35 .30
*a.* Bklt. pane, 4 ea #MH256, MH287 + label, printed margin (BK162) 10.50
*b.* Booklet pane, 4 each #MH284, MH287 + label (BK174) 9.25
*c.* Booklet pane, 4 each #MH263, MH287 + label 11.50 —
*d.* Booklet pane, 2 each #MH267A, MH270B, 4 #MH287, + label (BK176) 11.00
*e.* Booklet pane, 2 each #MH271, MH278, 4 #MH287 + label (BK178) 15.00 —
*f.* Booklet pane of 8 + central label , litho. (BK184) 11.00 —
*g.* Litho. (#MH287f) ('08) 2.00 .75
*h.* Booklet pane of 8, 4 each #MH284a, MH287g + label (BK185) ('08) 24.00 —
**MH288** 1st orange red (BK1005, BK1140) 1.35 .30
*a.* Booklet pane of 8, label + printed margin (BK165) 11.00
*b.* Booklet pane of 8 (BK1141-BK1142) 11.00
*c.* Booklet pane of 4 + label (BK1006) 5.50
*d.* Booklet pane, #MH284, 3 #MH288 + 4 labels (BK429) 6.25
*e.* Bklt. pane, 2 #MH284, 4 #MH288 (BK753) 7.25
**MH289** 1st org red, perf 13¾x14¼ 3.25 .50
*a.* Booklet pane of 10 (BK1139A) 20.00
**MH290** E dark blue 2.10 .50
*a.* Booklet pane of 4 (BK1010) 8.50
*b.* Booklet pane, 4 each #MH284, MH290, + label (BK171) 13.00 —
*c.* Booklet pane, 4 #MH287, 4 #MH290 + label (BK172, BK173) 14.50

#MH284-MH285 sold for 20p on day of issue; #MH287-MH289 for 26p; #MH290 for 30p. #MH284-MH285 were later sold for 19p. Selling prices for booklets containing these stamps will be considered to have 20p stamps.

## Queen Type of 1970 with Redrawn Portrait

MH292

MH294

MH297

MH299

MH300

MH301

On Nos. MH292 and MH297, the numeral and letters are thinner, and perf tips are flat with distinct corners, while on MH294 and MH299, numeral and letters are thicker and bolder, and perf tips have a slight arc and are rounded at the corners.

On No. MH300 the numeral and letters are thick and bold and perf tips have a slight arc and are rounded at the corners, while on No. MH301, the numeral and letters are thin and perf tips are distinctly serpentine with little flatness on the peaks or valleys.

### *Die Cut Perf. 14¾x14 Sync., Die Cut Perf. 15x14¼ Sync. (MH 293, MH298)*
### Self-Adhesive
### Booklet Stamps (MH293, MH298)

**MH292** 2nd bright blue 1.75 .35
*a.* Booklet pane of 6 10.50
*b.* Booklet pane of 12 20.00
**MH293** 2nd bright blue 1.50 .30
*a.* Booklet pane of 10 15.00
*b.* Booklet pane of 12 18.00
**MH294** 2nd bright blue 1.75 .30
*a.* Booklet of 12 21.00
**MH297** 1st vermilion 1.75 .45
*a.* Booklet pane of 6 10.50
*b.* Booklet pane of 12 21.00
**MH298** 1st vermilion 1.75 .40
*a.* Booklet pane of 10 17.50
*b.* Booklet pane of 12 21.00
**MH299** 1st vermilion 2.50 .40
*a.* Booklet of 6 15.00
**MH300** 1st gold 1.35 .40
*a.* Booklet of 6 8.00
**MH301** 1st gold 1.35 .40
*a.* Booklet of 6 8.00
*b.* Booklet of 12 16.00
**MH302** E dark blue 3.75 .75
*a.* Booklet of 6 22.00
**MH304** 42p olive 7.00 1.25
*a.* Booklet of 6 42.50
**MH306** 68p drab 7.00 1.25
*a.* Booklet of 6 42.50

Nos. MH292, MH297 and MH301 were also issued as coils, which have no selvage surrounding stamps.

No. MH293 & single stamps from No. MH292a sold for 19p on day of issue; #MH292, 20p; #MH297, 26p; #MH298 & single stamps from #MH297a, MH297b, 27p.

Nos. MH292a, MH293a, MH293b, MH297a, MH297b, MH298a, and MH298b are complete booklets.

No. MH297a exists with self-adhesive label depicting Queen Victoria.

### *Die Cut Perf. 14x15 Syncopated*
### Self-Adhesive Coil Stamps
### Size: 21x17mm

**MH308** 2nd bright blue 7.00 3.00
**MH309** 1st orange red 3.50 3.50

### Size: 30x40mm
### *Perf. 14x14½*

**MH310** 1st black, engr. 4.00 3.00
*a.* Booklet pane of 4 + printed margin (BK165) 16.00
**MH311** 1st black, typo. 3.50 2.50
*a.* Booklet pane of 4 + printed margin (BK165) 14.00

### Self-Adhesive
### *Die Cut Perf. 14x14½*

**MH312** 1st gray, litho. & embossed 3.75 .50
*a.* Booklet pane of 4 + printed margin (BK165) 15.00

No. MH312 is valued in used condition on piece. Soaking and pressing No. MH312 removes the embossed image of the Queen.

No. MH300 sold for 20p on day of issue. Nos. MH305, MH310-MH312 sold for 26p on day of issue.

Issued: No. MH268, 7/8/96. Nos. MH245, MH249, MH268, MH271, MH279, 4/1/97; Nos. MH256, MH287, 4/21/97. Nos. MH255, MH284, MH308, MH309, 4/29/97; Nos. MH246-MH248, MH250, MH259, MH265, 5/27/97; Nos. MH260, MH262, MH275, MH288, 8/26/97; No. MH257, 11/18/97; Nos. MH292, MH297, 4/6/98; Nos. MH251, MH269, MH285, 10/13/98; No. MH289, 12/1/98; No. MH290, 1/12/99; No. MH288c, 5/12/99; Nos. MH280-MH283, 3/9/99; Nos. MH310-MH312, 2/16/99; Nos. MH249A, MH254, MH264, MH270, MH276, 4/20/99; Nos. MH254A, MH264B, 2/15/00; Nos. MH249B, MH261, MH266, MH267, MH270A, MH277, MH288d, MH288e, 4/25/00; No. MH279a, 5/22/00; Nos. MH292a, MH293, MH293c, MH297a, MH297b, MH298, MH298c, 1/29/01; Nos. MH300-MH301, 6/5/02; Nos. MH263, MH267A, MH278, MH270B, MH294, MH299, MH302, MH304, MH306, 7/4/02; No. MH290c, 9/24/02; No. MH261A, 5/6/03; No. MH287b, 6/2/03. Nos. MH284a, MH287h, 9/18/08; No. MH287g, 1/8/08. Nos. MH248a, MH250a, 2/12/09. Nos. MH249B, MH255a, 1/7/10.

Nos. MH251, MH254A, MH264B, MH269, MH285 (BK164), MH289 (BK1139A), MH290 (BK1010) issued only in booklets.

No. MH290b issued 2/6/02. E stamps from MH 290b sold for 37p on day of issue. No. MH294 sold for 19p, Nos. MH299, MH300 and MH301 sold for 27p, and No. MH302 sold for 37p on day of issue.

This is an expanding set. Nos. MH245-MH312 may change.

## Queen Type of 1970 With Redrawn Portraits
### Printed in Iriodin Ink
### *Perf. 14¾x14 Syncopated*

**2003, July 1 Photo.**

**MH321** £1.50 rose 6.00 5.00
**MH322** £2 greenish blue 8.00 7.00
*a.* Pound symbol missing in denomination *200.00* —
**MH323** £3 violet 12.00 11.00
*a.* Souvenir sheet of 1 ('06) 12.00 11.00
**MH324** £5 light blue 20.00 17.50
*Nos. MH321-MH324 (4)* 46.00 40.50

Issued: £1.50, £2, £3, £5, 7/1. No. MH323a, 8/31/06.

No. MH323a has margin depicting invalid imperforate examples of Nos. 211, 231, and 236.

Queen Elizabeth II (No Frame, Perforations Touch Vignette) — MA4

***Perf. 14¾x14 Syncopated***

**2000 Photo. Design MA4**

**MH335** 1st olive green 1.35 .45
*a.* Bklt. pane of 8 (BK1201) 11.00
*b.* Bklt. pane of 9 (BK168) 12.25
*c.* Bklt. pane of 4 + label (BK1007) 5.50

***Perf. 13¾x14¼ Syncopated***

**MH336** 1st olive green 1.75 .50
*a.* Booklet pane of 10 (BK1144) 17.50
*b.* Booklet pane of 8 + label (BK167) 14.00

Issued: #MH335, MH336, 1/6; #MH336b, 2/15; #MH335a, 5/26; #MH335b, 8/4.

No. MH335c comes in two versions (as does No. BK1007): with Postman Pat on label and with Botanical Garden of Wales on label.

No. MH336 issued only in booklets. Perforations are Syncopated.

No. MH335 and MH336 sold for 26p on day of issue.

### Queen Type of 1970 With Redrawn Portraits

54p Type a — "5" has thick straight top line, "4" has thick cross line.

Type b — "5" has thinner, slightly curved top line, "4" has thin cross line.

***Perf. 14¾x14 Syncopated***

**2004-10 Type MA2 Photo.**

**MH344** 7p bright pink .75 .25
**MH346** 9p brt orange .35 .25
*a.* Litho. (MH401b) .50 .25
**MH347** 12p blue green .75 .25
**MH348** 14p vermilion .70 .25
**MH348A** 15p brt pink .75 .30
**MH349** 16p lilac rose .75 .30
*a.* Litho. (MH365b) ('09) 4.25 .35
**MH350** 17p olive green .55 .25
*b.* Litho. (MH368b) 1.00 .30
**MH350A** 22p brown .65 .30
*c.* Litho. (MH368b) 3.50 .40
*d.* Booklet pane of 9, 5 #MH250a, 2 each #MH248B, MH350Ac (BK191) 26.00 —
**MH351** 35p brown 1.75 .65
**MH352** 35p olive green 1.75 .75
**MH353** 37p olive green 1.75 .75
**MH354** 39p gray 2.00 .75
*a.* Booklet pane, 4 #MH284, 2 each #MH267A, MH354 + label (BK177) 11.00 —
**MH355** 40p Prussian blue 2.00 .75
*a.* Booklet pane, 4 #MH287, 2 each #MH352, MH355 + central label (BK179) 12.50 —
**MH358** 43p emerald 2.50 .80
**MH359** 44p bright blue 2.00 .80
**MH361** 46p dk ol bister 2.00 .85
**MH363** 48p brt rose lil 2.00 .95
*a.* Booklet pane, 4 #MH246, 2 each #MH361, MH363, + label (BK182) 7.75 —
*b.* Litho. (MH363c) 4.75 .80
*c.* Booklet pane, 2 each #MH248a, MH250a, MH287g, MH363b + label (BK188) 21.00 —
**MH364** 49p brown 2.25 .85
**MH365** 50p gray 2.25 1.00
*a.* Litho. (MH365b) ('09) 5.50 .75
*b.* Booklet pane, 4 each #MH349a, MH365a, + central label (BK187) ('09) 26.00 —
**MH366** 54p brown (a) 2.25 1.10
*a.* Booklet pane, 2 each #MH245, MH366, 4 #MH361, + label (BK183) 12.50
**MH366B** 54p brown, litho. (b) (MH368c) 4.75 .85
*c.* Booklet pane of 8, 4#MH350Ac, 4 #MH366B, + label (BK192) 33.00 —
**MH367** 56p lt olive grn 2.25 1.10
**MH368** 62p carmine 1.90 .95
*a.* Litho. (MH368b) 4.00 1.25
*b.* Booklet pane of 8, 4 #MH350b, 2 each #MH350Ac, MH368a + central label (BK189) 19.00 —
*c.* Booklet pane of 8, 4 #MH255a, 2 each #MH366B, MH368a + label (BK191) 27.50 —
**MH370** 72p carmine rose 3.00 1.25
**MH371** 78p emerald 3.25 1.60
**MH372** 81p greenish blue 3.25 1.60
**MH372A** 90p dark blue 2.75 1.40
*b.* Litho. (MH372c) 6.25 1.75
*c.* Booklet pane of 8, 4 #MH350b, 2 each #MH245a, MH372Ab + central label (BK190) 23.50 —
**MH373** £1 cerise 4.25 2.00
*a.* Booklet pane of 2 + label (BK182) 8.50 —
*Nos. MH344-MH373 (28)* 55.15 22.90

Issued: 7p, 35p, 39p, 40p, 43p, 4/1. MH354a, 2/24/05. 9p, No. MH352, 46p, 4/5/05. No. MH355a, 2/23/06. 37p, 44p, 49p, 72p, 3/28/06. 12p, 14p, 8/1/06. 16p, 48p, 50p, 54p, 78p, 3/27/07. Nos. MH363a, MH373, 6/5/07. MH366a, 9/20/07. 15p, 56p, 81p, 4/1/08. Nos. MH349a, MH365a, MH365b, 1/13/09. Nos. MH363b, MH363c, 2/17/09. Nos. MH350, MH350A, MH368, MH372A, 3/31/09. Nos. MH350b, MH350Ac, MH368a, MH368b, 8/18/09. Nos. MH350Ad, MH366Bb, MH368c, 1/7/10. No. MH366Bc, 2/25/10. MH356a, 5/8/10.

Queen Elizabeth II
MA5 MA6

***Perf. 14¾x14 Syncopated***

**2006 Photo.**

**MH375** MA5 2nd bright blue 1.25 .45
**MH376** MA5 1st gold 1.60 .60
*a.* Booklet pane, 4 each #MH271, MH376 + central label (BK180) 24.00 —
*b.* Booklet pane, 4 each #MH248, MH376, + central label (BK181) 8.50 —

**Inscribed "Large"**

**MH377** MA6 2nd bright blue 2.00 .70
**MH378** MA6 1st gold 2.25 .85
*a.* Booklet pane, #MH375, MH376, 2 each #MH377-MH378, + label (BK182) 11.00 —
*Nos. MH375-MH378 (4)* 7.10 2.60

**Booklet Stamps**

**Self-Adhesive**

***Serpentine Die Cut 14¾x14 Syncopated***

**MH379** MA5 2nd bright blue 1.50 .45
*a.* Booklet pane of 12 18.00
**MH380** MA5 1st gold 1.60 .60
*a.* Booklet pane of 6 9.75
*b.* Booklet pane of 12 19.50

**Inscribed "Large"**

**MH381** MA6 2nd bright blue 2.25 .70
*a.* Booklet pane of 4 9.00
**MH382** MA6 1st gold 2.60 .85
*a.* Booklet pane of 4 11.00
*Nos. MH379-MH382 (4)* 7.95 2.60

Issued: Nos. MH375-MH378, 8/1; Nos. MH379-MH380, 9/12; Nos. MH381-MH382, 8/15. No. MH376a, 9/21. No. MH376b, 3/1/07. No. MH378a, 6/5/07.

On day of issue, Nos. MH375 and MH379 each sold for 23p, Nos. MH376 and MH380 each sold for 32p, Nos. MH377 and MH381 each sold for 37p, and Nos. MH378 and MH382 each sold for 44p.

Beginning with No. MH383, an iridescent "ROYAL MAIL" overprint was added to the design of many Machin-head stamps. These are identified in the listings below as having an "Iridescent Overprint of Royal Mail in Wavy Lines". Subsequent to the initial release of stamps with the overprint, both source and date codes were worked into the overprint as shown in the illustration.

The source codes currently in use are: MAIL (no code letter)—from counter sheets; ROYBL—from business sheets; MCIL—from "custom" booklets, including special stamps; MFIL—from booklets of four; MPIL—from prestige booklets; MRIL—from coil rolls; MSIL—from booklets of six; MTIL—from booklets of twelve.

Date codes were first used in 2010 and have a variety of forms: MA10—for 2010; MA11 or MIIL—for 2011; M12L—for 2012.

Diamond Jubilee definitives have an iridescent "DIAMOND JUBILEE" wavy line overprint. On these stamps the source code replaces a letter at the end of "DIAMOND": DIAMBND—from business sheets; DIAMTND—from booklets of 12; DIAMMND—from miniature sheet.

New codes, when they appear, will be included in the above list.

### Queen Type of 1970 With Redrawn Portraits and Type of 2006 With Two Die Cut Slits on Stamp and Iridescent Overprint of "Royal Mail" in Wavy Lines

**Self-Adhesive**

***Die Cut Perf. 14¾x14 Syncopated***

**2009 Type MA2 Photo.**

**MH383** 2nd bright blue 1.25 .40
*b.* Booklet pane of 12 #MH383 15.00
**MH384** 1st gold 1.50 .55
*b.* Booklet pane of 6 #MH384 9.00
*c.* Booklet pane of 12 #MH384 18.00
**MH385** 50p gray 1.50 .75
*a.* Booklet pane of 8, 4 #MH384, 2 each #MH383, MH385, + central label (BK193) 12.00
**MH386** £1 cerise 3.00 1.50
**MH387** £1.50 brown red 4.25 2.10
**MH388** £2 greenish blue 5.75 2.75
**MH389** £3 violet 8.75 4.25
**MH390** £5 light blue 14.50 7.25

**Type MA6**

**MH391** 2nd Large bright blue 1.75 .60
*b.* Booklet pane of 4 #MH391 7.00
**MH392** 1st Large gold 2.25 .75
*b.* Booklet pane of 4 #MH392 9.00
*Nos. MH383-MH392 (10)* 44.50 20.90

Issued: Nos. MH383-MH392, 2/17; Nos. MH383b, MH384b, MH384c, MH391b, MH392b, 3/31. MH385a, 5/8/10. On day of issue, No. MH383 sold for 27p; No. MH384, 36p; No. MH391, 42p; No. MH392, 52p.

No. MH383 was also issued in coils in 2012.

### Victoria and Elizabeth II Type of 1990

**Booklet Stamps**

***Perf. 14¾x14 Syncopated***

**2009 Type MA3 Litho.**

**MH393** 20p black (MH394a) 2.00 .35
**MH394** 1st black (MH394a) 2.75 .45
*a.* Booklet pane of 8, 4 each #MH393-MH394 + central label (BK189) 19.00 —

No. MH394 sold for 39p on day of issue.

MA7

MA8

**With Two Die Cut Slits**

**Self-Adhesive**

***Die Cut Perf. 14¾x14 Syncopated***

**2009, Nov. 17 Photo.**

**MH395** MA7 1st yel & org 3.75 1.90

***Die Cut Perf. 14½x14***

**MH396** MA8 1st Large yel & org 4.50 2.25

On day of issue, No. MH395 sold for £1.14; No. MH396, £1.36.

### Queen Type of 1970 With Redrawn Portraits

***Perf. 14¾x14 Syncopated***

**2010, Mar. 30 Type MA2 Photo.**

**MH397** 60p emerald 1.90 .95
*a.* Litho. (MH397b) 4.00 .85
*b.* Booklet pane of 8, 4 #MH248a, 2 each #MH250a, MH397a, + central label (BK194) 19.00 —
**MH398** 67p red violet 2.10 1.10
*a.* Litho. (MH401b) 2.00 1.00
**MH399** 88p cerise 2.75 1.40
*a.* Litho. (MH401b) 2.60 1.40
**MH400** 97p violet 3.00 1.50
*a.* Litho. (MH401b) 8.25 1.50
*b.* Booklet pane of 8, #MH398a, MH400a, 3 each # MH248a, MH250a + label (BK195) 12.50 —
**MH401** £1.46 Prussian blue 4.50 2.25
*a.* Litho. (MH401b) 4.25 2.10
*b.* Sheet of 11 + label (see contents below) 16.00 16.00
*Nos. MH397-MH401 (5)* 14.25 7.20

Issued: Nos. MH397a, MH397b, 5/13/10.

London 2010 Festival of Stamps (No. MH401b). Issued: Nos. MH398a, MH399a, MH400a, MH401a, MH401b, 5/8/10; No. MH400b, 3/22/11. No. MH401b contains Nos. MH245a, MH246a, MH248a, MH250a, MH255a, MH346a, MH397a, MH398a, MH399a, MH400a, MH401a + label.

### Queen Type of 1970 With Redrawn Portrait With Iridescent Overprint of "Royal Mail" in Wavy Lines

**Coil Stamps**

***Perf. 14¾x14 Syncopated***

**2010, May 13 Type MA2 Photo.**

**MH401C** 2nd bright blue .95 .45
**MH401D** 1st gold 1.25 .60

On day of issue, No. MH401C sold for 32p, and No. MH401D sold for 41p.

### Queen Type of 1970 With Redrawn Portrait and 2 Die Cut Slits With Die Cut Slits

**Self-Adhesive**

***Die Cut Perf. 14¾x14 Syncopated***

**2011 Type MA2 Photo.**

**MH402** 1p magenta .25 .25
**MH403** 2p dark green .25 .25
**MH404** 5p red brown .25 .25
**MH405** 10p brn orange .35 .25
*a.* Booklet pane of 8, 2 each #MH385, MH405, 4 #MH404 + label (BK196) 5.25
**MH406** 20p brt yel grn .65 .30

**With Iridescent Overprint of "Royal Mail" in Wavy Lines**

**MH407** 68p greenish blue 2.25 1.10
**MH408** 76p pink 2.50 1.25
**MH409** £1.10 olive green 3.75 1.90
**MH410** £1.65 dk olive green 5.50 2.25
*Nos. MH402-MH410 (9)* 15.75 7.80

Issued: Nos. MH402, MH403, MH404, MH405, MH406, 3/8; Nos. MH407-MH410, 3/29; Nos. MH404a, MH405a, MH405b, 5/5.

See Nos. MH420-MH424 for stamps with iridescent overprint that are similar to Nos. MH402-MH406.

**Queen Type of 1970 with Redrawn Portrait and Iridescent Overprint of "Royal Mail" in Wavy Lines**

*Perf. 14¾x14 Syncopated*

**2011, Sept. 9 Type MA2 Litho.**

**MH411** 1st gold (MH412a) 4.00 .75
*a.* Miniature sheet of 10 15.00 7.50
**MH412** 76p pink (MH412a) 4.75 1.25
*a.* Booklet pane of 8, 4 #MH248a, 2 each #MH411, MH412 (BK197) 17.00 —

Isseud: No. MH411a, 9/14. No. MH411 sold for 46p on day of issue.

**Queen Type of 1970 with Redrawn Portrait and Iridescent Overprint of "Royal Mail" in Wavy Lines**

*Perf. 14¾x14 Syncopated*

**2012, Jan. 5 Type MA2 Litho.**

**MH413** 68p greenish blue (MH413a) 2.25 1.10
*a.* Booklet pane of 8, 4 #MH413, 2 each #MH246a, MH250a + central label (BK198) 10.00 —

**Queen Type of 1970 With Redrawn Portrait and Iridescent Overprint of "Diamond Jubilee" in Wavy Lines Booklet Stamp Self-Adhesive With Two Oval Slits**

*Die Cut Perf. 14¾x14 Syncopated*

**2012, Feb. 6 Type MA2 Photo.**

**MH414** 1st gray blue 1.50 .75
*a.* Booklet pane of 12 18.00
*b.* Booklet pane of 6 9.00

No. MH414 sold for 46p on day of issue. See No. 2996f for photogravure stamp with water-activated gum.

Issued: No. MH414b, 10/1.

**Queen Type of 2006 With Redrawn Portrait and Iridescent Overprint of "Diamond Jubilee" in Wavy Lines Self-Adhesive With Two Oval Slits**

*Die Cut Perf. 14¾x14 Syncopated*

**2012, Apr. 25 Type MA6 Photo.**

**MH415** 1st Large gray blue 2.50 1.25
*a.* Booklet pane of 4 10.00

No. MH415 sold for 75p on day of issue.

**Queen Type of 1970 With Redrawn Portrait and Iridescent Overprint of "Royal Mail" in Wavy Lines Self-Adhesive With Two Oval Slits**

*Die Cut Perf. 14¾x14 Syncopated*

**2012, Apr. 25 Type MA2 Photo.**

**MH416** 87p orange 3.00 1.50
**MH417** £1.28 green 4.25 2.10
**MH418** £1.90 red violet 6.25 3.00
*Nos. MH416-MH418 (3)* 13.50 6.60

**Queen Type of 1970 With Redrawn Portrait and Iridescent Overprint of "Diamond Jubilee" in Wavy Lines Booklet Stamp**

*Perf. 14¾x14 Syncopated*

**2012, May 31 Type MA2 Litho.**

**MH419** 1st gray blue (2996Gh) 2.00 2.00

No. MH419 sold for 60p on day of issue. See No. 2996f for photogravure stamp with water-activated gum.

**Queen Type of 1970 With Redrawn Portrait and Type of 2006 With Iridescent Overprint of "Royal Mail" in Wavy Lines Self-Adhesive With Two Oval Slits**

*Die Cut Perf. 14¾x14 Syncopated*

**2013, Jan. 3 Type MA2 Photo.**

**MH420** 1p magenta .25 .25
**MH421** 2p dark green .25 .25
**MH422** 5p red brown .25 .25
**MH423** 10p brn orange .35 .25
**MH424** 20p brt yel grn .65 .35
**MH425** 50p dark gray 1.75 .85
**MH426** 1st bright red 2.00 1.00
*a.* Booklet pane of 6 12.00
*b.* Booklet pane of 12 24.00
**MH427** £1 brown 3.25 1.60

**Type MA6**

**MH428** 1st Large brt red 3.00 1.50
*a.* Booklet pane of 4 12.00
*Nos. MH420-MH428 (9)* 11.75 6.30

On day of issue, No. MH426 sold for 60p, and No. MH428 sold for 90p. For stamps similar to Nos. MH420-MH424 but without the iridescent overprint, see Nos. MH402-MH406.

## MACHINS REGIONAL ISSUES

## NORTHERN IRELAND

All stamps are Design MA2 unless noted.

Type I

Type II

Two types of crown:

Type I: All pearls individually drawn, screened background.

Type II: Large pearls with strong white line below them.

First three pearls at left joined together. Solid background.

**1971-93 Photo. *Perf. 15x14***

**NIMH1** 2 ½p bright pink .75 .50
**NIMH2** 3p ultramarine .40 .30
**NIMH3** 3 ½p slate .30 .30
**NIMH4** 4 ½p dark blue .30 .30
**NIMH5** 5p bright violet 1.40 1.40
**NIMH6** 5 ½p dark violet .30 .25
**NIMH7** 6 ½p Prussian blue .30 .25
**NIMH8** 7p dark red brn .40 .30
**NIMH9** 7 ½p chestnut 2.25 2.00
**NIMH10** 8p red .40 .40
**NIMH11** 8 ½p yellow green .40 .45
**NIMH12** 9p violet blue .45 .45
**NIMH13** 10p orange brown .45 .55
**NIMH14** 10 ½p steel blue .55 .55
**NIMH15** 11p red .55 .55
**NIMH16** 11 ½p gray brn, litho,, perf 13 ½x14 1.00 1.00
**NIMH17** 12p yellow green .70 .60
**NIMH18** 12p brt grn, litho. .95 .90
**NIMH19** 12 ½p lt emer, litho., perf 13 ½x14 .70 .70
**NIMH20** 12 ½p lt emer, litho. 6.00 4.50
**NIMH21** 13p lt red brown, litho., type II 2.00 .55
*a.* Type I 1.25 .50
**NIMH22** 13 ½p brown purple .80 .80
**NIMH23** 14p gray bl, litho., perf 13 ½x14 .90 .85
**NIMH24** 14p dark bl, litho. 1.00 .70
**NIMH25** 15p deep ultra 1.00 .70

**Litho.**

**NIMH26** 15p bright blue 1.00 .70
**NIMH27** 15 ½p light violet, perf 13 ½x14 .90 .90
**NIMH28** 16p brownish gray, perf 13 ½x14 1.10 1.25
**NIMH29** 16p brownish gray 9.50 6.00
**NIMH30** 17p blue gray, type I .95 1.10
*a.* Type II 250.00
**NIMH31** 17p dark blue 1.10 .90
**NIMH32** 18p violet blue, perf 13 ½x14 1.10 1.10
**NIMH33** 18p olive green 1.10 1.00
**NIMH34** 18p bright yel grn 1.10 1.00
**NIMH35** 18p bright yel grn, perf 13 ½x14 7.00 1.90
**NIMH36** 19p red orange 1.10 1.10
**NIMH37** 19 ½p olive gray, perf 13 ½x14 2.25 2.50
**NIMH38** 20p brown black 1.10 .90
**NIMH39** 20 ½p ultramarine, perf 13 ½x14 4.75 4.00
**NIMH40** 22p dark blue, perf 13 ½x14 1.25 1.25
**NIMH41** 22p yellow green 1.25 1.25
**NIMH42** 22p red orange 1.40 1.00
**NIMH43** 23p bright yel grn 1.40 1.25
**NIMH44** 24p brown red 1.75 1.10
**NIMH45** 24p brown 1.25 1.00
*a.* Bklt. pane, see footnote (BK158) 4.25

#NIMH45a contains NIMH34, NIMH45, SMH35, SMH47, WMMH34, WMMH45.

**NIMH46** 26p red, perf 13 ½x14, type I 1.40 1.40
**NIMH47** 26p red, type II 4.50 4.00
**NIMH48** 26p olive gray 1.75 1.50
**NIMH49** 28p deep viol bl, perf 13 ½x14, type I 1.60 1.40
**NIMH50** 28p deep viol bl, type II 2.25 1.40
**NIMH51** 28p dull blue green 1.90 1.60
**NIMH52** 31p brt rose lil, type I 1.75 1.75
*a.* Type II 3.75 2.00
**NIMH53** 32p Prussian blue 2.00 2.00
**NIMH54** 34p dull blue green 2.25 2.25
**NIMH55** 37p scarlet 2.50 2.50
**NIMH56** 39p brt rose lilac 2.50 2.50

Issued: #NIMH1, 3p, 5p, NIMH9, 7/7/71; #NIMH3, NIMH6, 8p, 1/23/74; #NIMH4, 11/6/74;

#NIMH7, NIMH11, 1/14/76; 10p, 11p, 10/20/76; 7p, 9p, NIMH14, 1/18/78.

#NIMH17, NIMH22, #NIMH25, 7/23/80; #NIMH16, #NIMH23, NIMH32, NIMH40, 4/8/81; #NIMH19, 1/24/82; #NIMH27, #NIMH28, NIMH37, NIMH46, 2/24/82; NIMH39, #NIMH49, 4/27/83;

#NIMH20, #NIMH29, 2/28/84; 13p, #NIMH30, NIMH41, 31p, 10/23/84; #NIMH18, 1/7/86; #NIMH33, 1/6/87; #NIMH50, 1/27/87; #NIMH24, 19p, 23p, 32p, 11/8/88; #NIMH26, 30p, NIMH44, 34p, 11/28/89; #NIMH31, NIMH42, NIMH48, 37p, 12/4/90; #NIMH34, NIMH45, NIMH51, 39p, 12/3/91; #NIMH35, NIMH45a, 8/10/93; #NIMH47, 12/7/93.

*Perf. 15x14 Syncopated*

**1993-96 Litho.**

**NIMH57** 19p olive green 1.00 .90
**NIMH58** 20p brt yel green 1.75 1.40
**NIMH59** 25p salmon 1.00 .90
*a.* Bklt. pane, see footnote (BK160) 5.00

No. NIMH59a contains #NIMH57, NIMH59, SMH63, SMH65, WMMH58, WMMH60 + label, printed margin.

**NIMH60** 26p brown 2.25 1.60
**NIMH61** 30p olive green 1.75 1.60
**NIMH62** 37p bright rose lilac 3.25 2.50
**NIMH63** 41p drab 2.00 1.75
*a.* Bklt. pane, #NIMH61, NIMH63, 2 #NIMH57, 4 #NIMH59 + label, printed margin (BK159) 6.25
*b.* Bklt. pane, #NIMH57, NIMH59, NIMH61, NIMH63 + printed margin (BK159) 3.50
**NIMH64** 63p bright green 5.50 4.00

Issued: 19p, 25p, 30p, 41p, 12/7/93; #NIMH59a, 4/25/95; 20p, 26, 37p, 63p, 7/23/96.

**Queen Design of 1970 with Redrawn Portrait**

*Perf. 15x14 Syncopated*

**1997-2000 Photo.**

**NIMH68** 19p olive green 4.50 .80
**NIMH69** 20p brt yel grn 1.75 .80
**NIMH70** 20p brt yel grn, perf 14 5.50 2.10
**NIMH73** 26p brown 2.50 1.10
**NIMH74** 26p brown, perf 14 5.50 2.00
**NIMH81** 37p bright rose lilac 3.25 1.40
*a.* Bklt. pane, see footnote (BK162) 7.50

No. NIMH81a contains #NIMH73, NIMH81, SMH79, SMH87, WMMH74, WMMH82 + printed margin.

**NIMH82** 38p dark blue 10.00 7.50
**NIMH83** 40p chalky blue 5.00 2.50
**NIMH91** 63p bright green 6.50 5.00
**NIMH92** 64p greenish blue 11.00 8.00
**NIMH93** 65p Prussian blue 4.00 3.00

Issued: #NIMH69, NIMH73, 37p, 63p, 7/1/97; #NIMH81a, 9/24/97; #NIMH70, NIMH74, 10/13/98; #NIMH68, NIMH82, NIMH92, 6/8/99; 40p, 65p, 4/25/00.

Nos. NIMH70, NIMH74 issued only in booklets (BK164).

*Perf. 13¾x14¼ Syncopated*

**2000 Photo.**

**NIMH96** 1st orange red (WM-MH96a) 3.50 2.75

*Perf. 15x14 Syncopated*

**NIMH99** 1st org red 11.00 7.50

#NIMH96, NIMH99 sold for 26p on day of issue. #NIMH96 issued only in booklets.

Issued: #NIMH96, 2/15/00; #NIMH99, 4/25/00.

## SCOTLAND

All stamps are Design MA2 unless noted.

Type I

Type II

Two types of lion:

Type I: Thin tongue, no line across bridge of nose, three "feathers" on left of tail are widely separated.

Type II: Thick tongue where it enters mouth, eye connected to background by solid line, three "feathers" on left of tail are close together.

**1971-93 Photo. *Perf. 15x14***

**SMH1** 2 ½p bright pink .30 .25
**SMH2** 3p ultramarine .40 .25
**SMH3** 3 ½p slate .30 .25
**SMH4** 4 ½p dark blue .35 .30
**SMH5** 5p brt violet 1.50 1.25
**SMH6** 5 ½p dark violet .30 .25
**SMH7** 6 ½p Prussian blue .30 .25
**SMH8** 7p dark red brn .35 .35
**SMH9** 7 ½p chestnut 1.50 1.50
**SMH10** 8p red .50 .40
**SMH11** 8 ½p yellow green .50 .45
**SMH12** 9p violet blue .50 .45
**SMH13** 10p orange brown .50 .60
**SMH14** 10 ½p steel blue .50 .55
**SMH15** 11p red .55 .55
**SMH16** 11 ½p gray brn, litho., perf 13 ½x14 1.00 .90
**SMH17** 12p yellow green .55 .55
**SMH18** 12p brt green, litho., perf 13 ½x14 2.25 1.90
**SMH19** 12p green, litho. 2.10 2.10
**SMH20** 12 ½p lt emer, litho., perf 13 ½x14 .70 .80
**SMH21** 13p lt red brown, litho., perf 13 ½x14, type I 1.10 1.10
*a.* Type II 11.00 5.00
**SMH22** 13p lt red brn, litho. 1.25 .85
**SMH23** 13 ½p brown purple .80 .90
**SMH24** 14p gray blue, litho., perf 13 ½x14 .85 .85
**SMH25** 14p dk bl, litho. .75 .35
*a.* Booklet pane of 6 + printed margin (BK153) 3.50
**SMH26** 15p deep ultra .70 .80

**Litho.**

**SMH27** 15p bright blue .80 .80

*Perf. 13½x14*

**SMH28** 15 ½p light violet .90 .90
**SMH29** 16p brownish gray .90 .95
**SMH30** 17p blue gray, type II 2.50 1.10
*a.* Type I 4.50 2.50

*Perf. 15x14*

**SMH31** 17p blue gray 4.50 4.50
**SMH32** 17p dark blue 1.10 1.25
**SMH33** 18p violet blue, perf 13 ½x14 1.00 .75
**SMH34** 18p olive green 1.25 1.00
**SMH35** 18p bright yel grn 1.00 .30
**SMH36** 18p brt yel grn, perf 13 ½x14 2.50 1.00
**SMH37** 19p red orange .80 .80
*a.* Booklet pane of 6 + printed margin (BK153) 5.25
*b.* Booklet pane of 9 + printed margin (BK153) 6.50
**SMH38** 19 ½p olive gray, perf 13 ½x14 2.00 2.00
**SMH39** 20p brown black 1.10 1.10

*Perf. 13½x14*

**SMH40** 20 ½p ultra 4.75 .75
**SMH41** 22p dk blue 1.25 1.00
**SMH42** 22p yel grn, type I 4.50 2.00
*a.* Type II 50.00 40.00

*Perf. 15x14*

**SMH43** 22p yellow green 2.00 1.75
**SMH44** 22p red orange 1.40 1.00
**SMH45** 23p bright yel grn 1.50 1.25
*a.* Booklet pane #SMH45, 2 #SMH37, 5 #SMH25 + printed margin (BK153) 5.25

**SMH46** 24p brown red 1.75 1.10
**SMH47** 24p brown 1.60 1.40
**SMH48** 24p chestnut, perf 13½x14 9.25 3.25
**SMH49** 26p red, perf 13½x14, type I 4.50 .90
**SMH50** 26p red 3.75 3.50
**SMH51** 26p olive gray 1.40 1.40
**SMH52** 28p dp vio bl, perf 13½x14 1.40 1.40
**SMH53** 28p deep violet blue 1.75 .90
**SMH54** 28p dull bl grn 1.75 1.60
**SMH55** 28p dull bl grn, perf 13½x14 10.00 4.00
**SMH56** 31p brt rose lilac, perf 13½x14 3.00 2.10
*a.* Type II 190.00 90.00
**SMH57** 31p brt rose lilac 2.50 .90
**SMH58** 32p Prussian blue 2.00 1.75
**SMH59** 34p dull bl grn 2.25 2.25
**SMH60** 37p scarlet 2.25 2.25
**SMH61** 39p brt rose lilac 2.25 2.25
**SMH62** 39p brt rose lilac, perf 13½x14 16.00 2.75

Issued: #SMH1, 3p, 5p, #SMH9, 7/7/71; #SMH3, SMH6, 8p, 1/23/74; #SMH4, 11/6/74; #SMH7, SMH11, 1/14/76; 10p, 11p, 10/20/76; 7p, 9p, #SMH14, 1/18/78; #SMH17, SMH23, #SMH26, 7/23/80.

#SMH16, #SMH24, SMH33, SMH41, 4/8/81; #SMH20, SMH28, SMH38, #SMH49, 2/24/82;

16p, #SMH40, #SMH52, 4/27/83; #SMH21, SMH30, SMH42, SMH56, 10/23/84; #SMH18, 1/7/86; #SMH19, 1/24/86; #SMH31, SMH57, 4/29/86; #SMH22, 11/4/86; #SMH34, 1/6/87.

#SMH43, SMH50, SMH53, 1/27/87; #SMH25, 19p, 23p, 32p, 11/8/88; #SMH27, 20p, SMH46, 34p, 1/28/89; #SMH32, SMH44, SMH51, 37p, 12/4/90;

#SMH35, SMH47, SMH54, SMH61, 12/3/91; #SMH36, 9/26/92; #SMH48, 10/92; #SMH62, 11/92; #SMH55, 2/18/93.

### *Perf. 15x14 Syncopated*

**1993-96 Litho.**

**SMH63** 19p olive green 1.00 .80
**SMH64** 20p brt yel green 1.75 1.10
**SMH65** 25p salmon 1.25 1.10
**SMH66** 26p brown 2.25 1.75
**SMH67** 30p olive green 2.00 1.40
**SMH68** 37p bright rose lilac 3.25 2.50
**SMH69** 41p drab 2.25 2.25
**SMH70** 63p bright green 4.75 3.75

Issued: 19p, 20p, 30p, 41p, 12/7/93; 20p, 26p, 37p, 63p, 7/23/96.

### Queen Design of 1970 with Redrawn Portrait

### *Perf. 15x14 Syncopated*

**1997-98 Photo.**

**SMH75** 20p brt yel green 1.50 .70
**SMH76** 20p brt yel grn, perf 14 5.75 2.50
**SMH79** 26p brown 2.25 1.25
**SMH80** 26p brown, perf 14 5.75 3.00
**SMH87** 37p bright rose lilac 3.50 1.50
**SMH97** 63p bright green 6.00 3.75

Issued: #SMH75, SMH79, 37p, 63p, 7/1/97; #SMH76, SMH80, 10/13/98.

Nos. SMH76, SMH80 issued only in booklets (BK164).

This is an expanding set, numbers may change.

### *Perf. 13¾x14¼ Syncopated*

**2000 Photo.**

**SMH101** 1st org red (WMMH96a) 3.50 3.00

Issued: No. SMH96, 2/15/00. No. SMH96 sold for 26p on day of issue and was issued only in booklets.

## WALES & MONMOUTHSHIRE

All stamps are Design MA2 unless noted.

Type I

Type II

Two types of dragon:

Type I: Eye is complete with white dot in center. Wing tips, tail and tongue are thin.

Type II: Eye is joined to nose by solid line. Wing tips, tail and tongue are thick.

**1971-93 Photo. *Perf. 15x14***

**WMMH1** 2½p bright pink .30 .25
**WMMH2** 3p ultra .30 .25
**WMMH3** 3½p slate .30 .35
**WMMH4** 4½p dark blue .35 .35
**WMMH5** 5p brt violet 1.25 1.25
**WMMH6** 5½p dark violet .30 .35
**WMMH7** 6½p Prussian blue .30 .25
**WMMH8** 7p dark red brn .30 .25
**WMMH9** 7½p chestnut 1.75 *2.00*
**WMMH10** 8p red .40 .40
**WMMH11** 8½p yel grn .40 .40
**WMMH12** 9p violet blue .45 .45
**WMMH13** 10p orange brn .45 .45
**WMMH14** 10½p steel blue .55 .50
**WMMH15** 11p red .55 .50
**WMMH16** 11½p gray brn, litho., perf 13½x14 1.00 .90
**WMMH17** 12p yel grn .60 .55

**Litho.**

**WMMH18** 12p brt grn 1.75 1.40
**WMMH19** 12½p lt emer, perf 13½x14 .80 .80
**WMMH20** 12½p lt emer 6.00 5.75
**WMMH21** 13p lt red brn, type I .70 .70
*a.* Type II 3.50

**Photo.**

**WMMH22** 13½p brown pur .85 .75
**WMMH23** 14p gray blue, litho., perf 13½x14 .85 .85
**WMMH24** 14p dark blue .85 .85
**WMMH25** 15p deep ultra .70 .80

**Litho.**

**WMMH26** 15p bright blue .90 .85
**WMMH27** 15½p light violet 1.10 .85
**WMMH28** 16p brownish gray, perf 13½x14 1.75 1.90
**WMMH29** 16p brownish gray 2.00 2.25
**WMMH30** 17p blue gray, type I .95 .90
*a.* Type II 72.50 25.00
**WMMH31** 17p dark blue 1.00 .90
**WMMH32** 18p vio bl, perf 13½x14 1.10 1.10
**WMMH33** 18p olive green 1.10 1.00
**WMMH34** 18p brt yel grn .85 .85
*a.* Booklet pane of 6 + printed margin (BK156) 3.90
**WMMH35** 18p brt yel grn, perf 13½x14 13.00 4.00
**WMMH36** 19p red orange 1.10 .90
**WMMH37** 19½p ol gray, perf 13½x14 2.00 2.00
**WMMH38** 20p brown black 1.00 1.00
**WMMH39** 20½p ultra 3.75 3.75
**WMMH40** 22p dk bl, perf 13½x14 1.25 1.25
**WMMH41** 22p yel grn 1.10 1.25
**WMMH42** 22p orange red 1.10 1.25
**WMMH43** 23p brt yel grn 1.40 1.25
**WMMH44** 24p brown red 1.50 1.25
**WMMH45** 24p brown .95 .85
*a.* Booklet pane of 6 + printed margin (BK156) 5.75
**WMMH46** 24p brown, perf 13½x14 12.50 3.25
**WMMH47** 26p red, type I, perf 13½x14 1.25 1.25
**WMMH48** 26p red, type II 6.25 5.75
**WMMH49** 26p olive gray 1.60 1.60
**WMMH50** 28p dp vio bl, type I, perf 13½x14 1.40 1.40
**WMMH51** 28p dp vio bl, type II 2.00 2.00
**WMMH52** 28p dull bl grn 1.75 1.60
**WMMH53** 31p brt rose lil 1.60 1.60
**WMMH54** 32p Prus blue 1.75 1.75
**WMMH55** 34p dull bl grn 1.75 1.75
**WMMH56** 37p scarlet 2.25 2.25
**WMMH57** 39p brt rose lil 2.50 2.50

Issued: #WMMH1, 3p, 5p, WMMH9, 7/7/71; #WMMH3, WMMH6, 8p, 1/23/74; #WMMH4, 11/6/74; #WMMH7, WMMH11, 1/14/76; 10p, 11p, 10/20/76.

7p, 9p, #WMMH14, 1/18/78; #WMMH17, WMMH22, WMMH25, 7/23/80; #WMMH16, #WMMH23, WMMH32, WMMH40, 4/8/81;

#WMMH19, WMMH27, WMMH37, WMMH47, 2/24/82; #WMMH28, WMMH39, WMMH50, 4/27/83; #WMMH20, WMMH29, 1/10/84.

#WMMH30, WMMH41, 31p, 10/23/84; #WMMH18, 1/7/86; #WMMH33, 1/6/87; #WMMH48, WMMH51, 1/27/87; #WMMH24, 19p, 23p, 32p, 8/11/88; #WMMH26, 20p, WMMH44, 34p, 11/28/89.

#WMMH31, WMMH42, WMMH49, 37p, 12/4/90; #WMMH34, WMMH45, WMMH52, 39p, 12/3/91; #WMMH46, 9/14/92; #WMMH35, 1/12/93.

### *Perf. 15x14 Syncopated*

**1993-96 Litho.**

**WMMH58** 19p olive green 1.10 1.00
**WMMH59** 20p brt yel grn 2.00 1.75
**WMMH60** 25p salmon 1.40 1.10
**WMMH61** 26p brown 2.25 2.00
**WMMH62** 30p olive green 2.00 1.50
**WMMH63** 37p bright rose lilac 3.25 2.75
**WMMH64** 41p drab 2.25 2.25
**WMMH65** 63p bright green 5.00 4.50

Issued: 19p, 25p, 30p, 41p, 12/7/93. 20p, 26p, 37p, 63p, 7/23/96.

### Queen Design of 1970 with Redrawn Portrait

"P" Removed

### *Perf. 15x14 Syncopated*

**1997-98 Photo.**

**WMMH70** 20p brt yel grn 1.75 .90
**WMMH71** 20p brt yel grn, perf 14 5.50 2.25
**WMMH74** 26p brown 2.00 1.10
**WMMH75** 26p brown, perf 14 5.50 2.25
**WMMH82** 37p bright rose lilac 6.00 2.50
**WMMH92** 63p brt yel grn 5.00 4.00

Issued: #WMMH70, WMMH74, 37p, 63p, 7/1/97; #WMMH71, WMMH75, 10/13/98.

Nos. WMMH71, WMMH75 issued only in booklets (BK164).

This is an expanding set, numbers may change.

### *Perf. 13¾x14¼ Syncopated*

**2000 Photo.**

**WMMH96** 1st orange red 3.50 2.50
*a.* Bklt. pane, 3 ea #NIMH96, SMH101, WMMH96 (BK167) 30.00

Issued: No. WMMH96, 2/15/00. No. WMMH96 sold for 26p on day of issue and was issued only in booklets.

See Isle of Man #8-11 for additional Machin Head definitives.

## BOOKLETS

Booklets are listed in denomination sequence by reign. Numbers in parenthesis following each listing reflect the number of cover varieties or edition numbers that apply to each cover style.

Values shown for complete booklets are for examples containing most panes having full perforations on two edges of the pane only. Booklets containing most or all panes with very fine, full perforations on all sides are scarce and will sell for more. Also, in booklets where most of the value is contained in only one pane of several, it is assumed that this pane has full perforations on two sides only. If this pane is very fine, the booklet will be worth a considerable premium over the value given.

This section does not contain complete booklets consisting solely of self-adhesive stamps. These are catalogued as minors under stamp listings.

### Sterling Currency

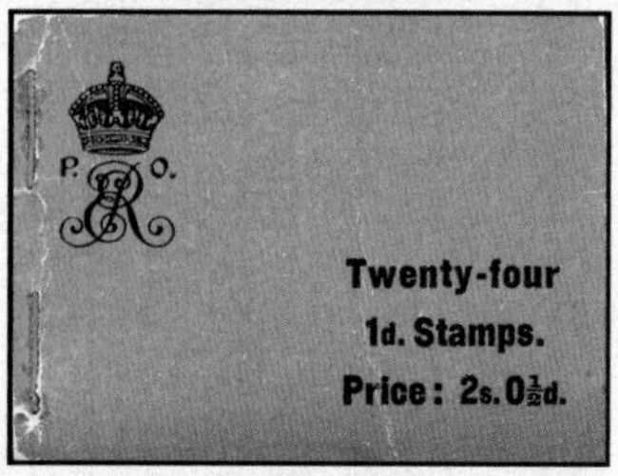


BC1

**1904**

**BK1** BC1 2sh½p *red,* 4 #128e 350.00

**1906-11**

**BK2** BC1 2sh *red,* 2 #128e, 3 #143c, #143b 950.00
**BK3** BC1 2sh *red,* 3 #128e, 1 each #143b-143c (4) 1,150.

Cover inscription on Nos. BK2-BK3 revised to reflect changed contents.

**1911**

**BK4** BC1 2sh *red,* 2#151a, 3 #152a 750.00

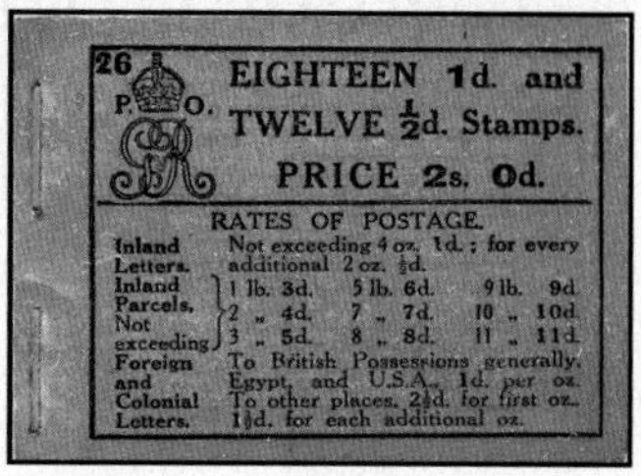


BC2

**1912-13**

**BK5** BC2 2sh *red,* 2 #151a, 3 #152a 1,050.
**BK6** BC2 2sh *red,* 2 #155a, 3 #156a (4) 1,000.

Cover inscription on Nos. BK5-BK6 shows only Inland Postage Rates.

**1913**

**BK7** BC2 2sh *red,* 2 #159b, 3 #160a (35) 500.00
**BK8** BC2 2sh *org,* 2 #159b,3 #160a (20) 525.00

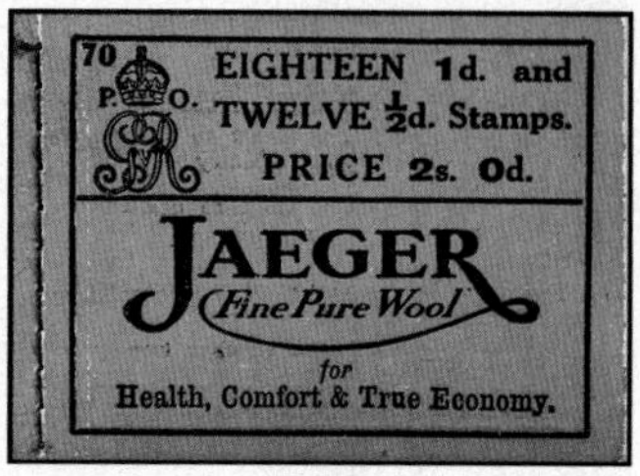


BC3

**1917**

**BK9** BC3 2sh *org,* 2 #159b, 3 #160a (17) 500.00

BC4

**1924-34**

**BK10** BC4 2sh *blue,* #159b, 160a, 161d-161e (2) 1,250.
**BK11** BC4 2sh *blue,* #187b, 188b, 189c-189d (277) 475.00

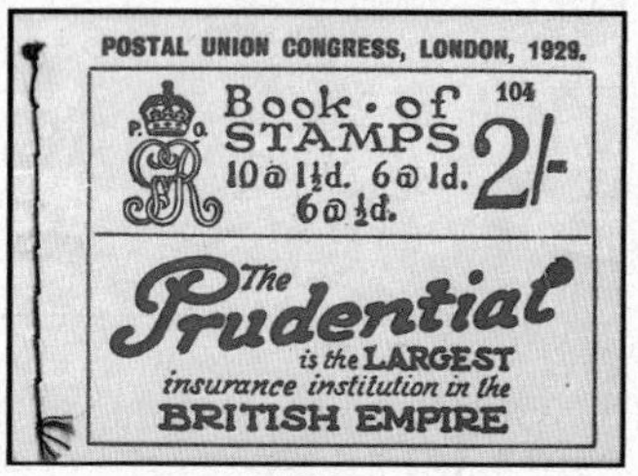


BC5

**1929**

**BK12** BC5 2sh blue, *buff,* #205b-207b, 207c 550.00

**1935**

**BK13** BC4 2sh *blue,* #210b-211b, 212c-212d (58) 550.00

BC6

**1935**

**BK14** BC6 2sh blue, *buff,* #226a-227a, 3 #228a — 100.00

**1918-19**

**BK15** BC4 3sh *org,* 2 each #159b, 160a, 161d (11) — 650.00
**BK16** BC4 3sh *org,* #159b, 160a, 3 #161d (15) — 650.00

Cover used for Nos. BK15-BK16 does not have inscription above top line.

**1921**

**BK17** BC4 3sh *blue,* 3 #162b (3) — 850.00
**BK18** BC4 3sh *blue,* 3 #162c (3) — 900.00

**1922**

**BK19** BC4 3sh *scar,* #159b, 160a, 3 #161d (33) — 850.00
**BK20** BC4 3sh *blue,* 4 #161d (2) — 900.00

**1924-34**

**BK21** BC4 3sh *scar,* #187b-188b, 3 #189c (237) — 375.00

**1929**

**BK22** BC5 3sh blue, *buff,* #205b-206b, 3 #207b (5) — 450.00

**1935**

**BK23** BC4 3sh *scar,* #210b-211b, 3 #212c (27) — 375.00
**BK24** BC6 3sh red, *buff,* #226a-227a, 5 #228a (4) — 100.00

**1920**

**BK25** BC4 3sh6p *org,* #160a, 3 #162b (6) — 850.00

Cover used for No. BK25 does not have inscription above top line.

**1921**

**BK26** BC4 3sh6p *org red,* #159b, 160a, 161d, 2 #162b (7) — 900.00
**BK27** BC4 3sh6p *org red,* #159b, 160a, 161d, 2 #162c (13) — 900.00

**1931-35**

**BK28** BC4 5sh *grn,* #187b-188b, 189d, 5 #189c — 4,000.
**BK29** BC4 5sh *buff,* #187b-188b, 189d, 5 #189c (7) — 1,250.
**BK30** BC4 5sh *buff,* #210b-211b, 212d, 5 #212c (7) — 450.00

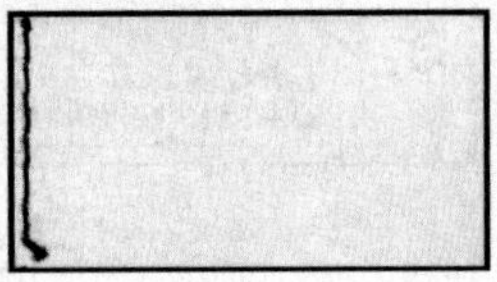

BC7

**1936**

**BK31** BC7 6p *buff,* 2 #232c — 70.00

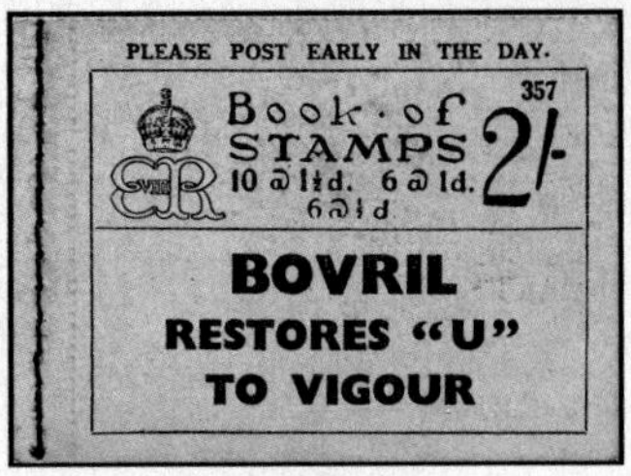


BC8

**BK32** BC8 2sh *blue,* #230a-231a, #232a-232b (31) — 140.00
**BK33** BC8 3sh *scar,* #230a-231a, 3 #232a (12) — 110.00
**BK34** BC8 5sh *buff,* #230a-231a, 6 #232a (2) — 250.00

**1938-40**

**BK35** BC7 6p *buff,* 2 #237d — 70.00
**BK36** BC7 6p *pink,* #235d-237d — 325.00
**BK37** BC7 6p *pale grn,* #235c-236c — 150.00

No. BK37 is 53x41mm.

**1947-51**

**BK38** BC7 1sh *buff,* 2 each #258b-259b, 260a — 27.50
**BK39** BC7 1sh *buff,* 2 each #280a, 281b-282b — 27.50
**BK40** BC7 1sh *buff,* #258e, 259d, 260b — 6,000.
**BK41** BC7 1sh *buff,* #280b-282b — 32.50

Nos. BK40-BK41 are 53x41mm.

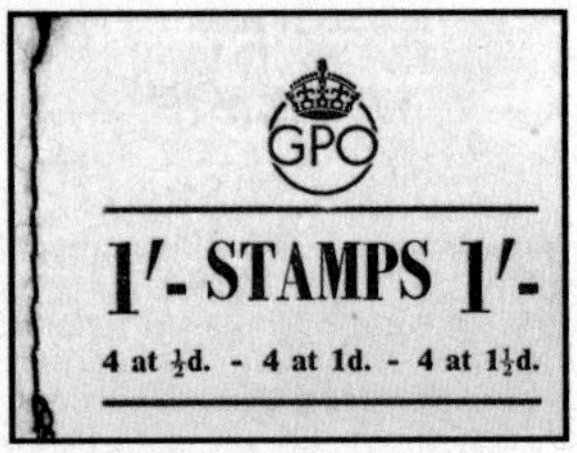


Round GPO Emblem — BC9

**1952-53**

**BK42** BC9 1sh *buff,* #280b, 281c-282c — 22.50
*a.* Inland postage rate corrected in ink on inside booklet cover — 25.00

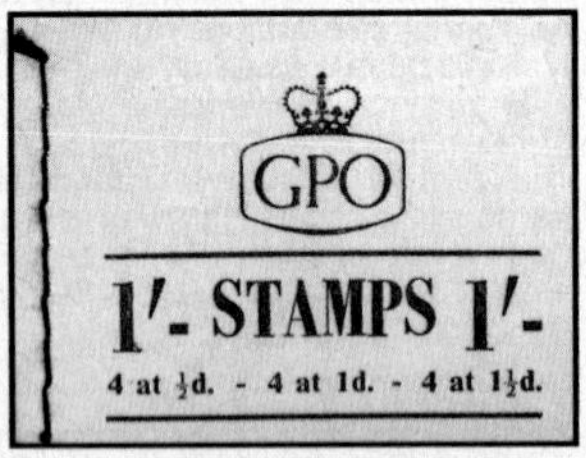


Oval GPO Emblem — BC10

**1954**

**BK43** BC10 1sh *buff,* #280b, 281c-282c — 32.50

**1937**

**BK44** BC8 2sh *blue,* #235b-236b, #237b-237c (26) — 450.00

BC11

**1938**

**BK45** BC11 2sh *blue,* #235b-236b, #237b-237c (95) — 450.00

**1940-42** **2sh6p Booklets**

**BK46** BC11 *scar,* #235b, #238b-239b (7) — 1,050.
**BK47** BC11 *blue,* #235b, #238b-239b (6) — 1,050.

Denomination part of cover of Nos. BK46-BK47 is printed in white on black background.

**BK48** BC11 *grn,* #235b, #238b-239b (80) — 550.00
**BK49** BC11 *grn,* #258a, #261b-262b (120) — 550.00

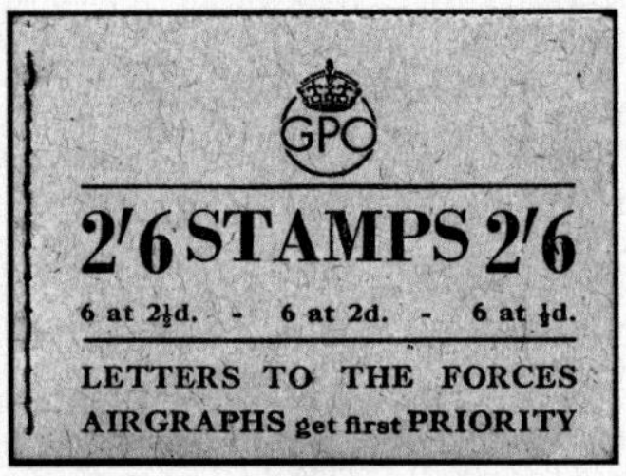


BC12

**1943**

**BK50** BC12 *grn,* #258a, #261b-262b (90) — 65.00

With booklets issued in August and September 1943, commercial advertising on British booklets was discontinued. Covers and interleaving were used for Post Office slogans. Booklets were no longer numbered, but carried the month and year of issue.

**1951-52**

**BK51** BC12 *grn,* #280c, #283b-284b (10) — 42.50
**BK52** BC12 *grn,* #280c, 281e, #282d, 284b (15) — 40.00

**1937-38** **3sh Booklets**

**BK53** BC8 *scar,* #235a-236a, 3 #237b (10) — 850.00
**BK54** BC11 *scar,* #235a-236a, 3 #237b (34) — 850.00

**1937-43** **5sh Booklets**

**BK55** BC8 *buff,* #235b-236b, 237c, 5 #237b (3) — 1,000.
**BK56** BC11 *buff,* #235b-236b, 237c, 5 #237b (9) — 950.00
**BK57** BC11 *buff,* #235b, 238b, 3 #239b (16) — 975.00
**BK58** BC11 *buff,* #258a, 261b, 3 #262b (20) — 950.00

**1943-53**

**BK59** BC12 *tan,* #258a, 261b, 3 #262b (49) — 110.00
**BK60** BC12 *tan,* #258a, 261b, 3 #262b (20) — 1,250.

Cover on No. BK60 has thick horizontal lines separating the GPO emblem and the various inscriptions.

**BK61** BC12 *tan,* #280a, 283b, 3 #284b (5) — 62.50
**BK62** BC12 *tan,* #280c, 281e, 282d, 3 #284b (5) — 62.50
**BK63** BC12 *tan,* #280c, 281d-282d, 283b, 2 #284b (2) — 62.50

BC13

**1953-54** **2sh6p Booklets**

**BK64** BC12 *grn,* #280c, 281e, 294c, #296a (6) — 29.00
**BK65** BC13 *grn,* #280c, 281e, 294c, 296a (7) — 32.50
**BK66** BC13 *grn,* #281e, 292c, 294c, 296a — 500.00

**5sh Booklets**

**BK67** BC12 *brn,* #280c, 281d, 283b, 294c, 2 #296a (3) — 40.00
**BK68** BC13 *brn,* #280c, 281d, 283b, 294c, 2 #296a (2) — 45.00
**BK69** BC13 *brn,* #281d, 283b, 292c, 294c, 2 #296a — 300.00
**BK70** BC13 *brn,* #283b, 292c-294c, 2 #296a — 160.00

**1953-57**

**1sh Booklets**

**BK71** BC7 *buff,* 2 each #292a-294a — 8.50
**BK72** BC7 *buff,* 2 each #317d, 318f, 319f — 25.00

**1954-59**

**BK73** BC10 *buff,* #292b-294b (2) — 8.00
**BK74** BC10 *buff,* #317b, 318c, 319b (3) — 8.00
**BK75** BC10 *buff,* #353b-355b (2) — 10.00

**1959**

**2sh Booklets**

**BK76** BC10 *salmon,* #317b, 318c, 319b, 322b — 6.50

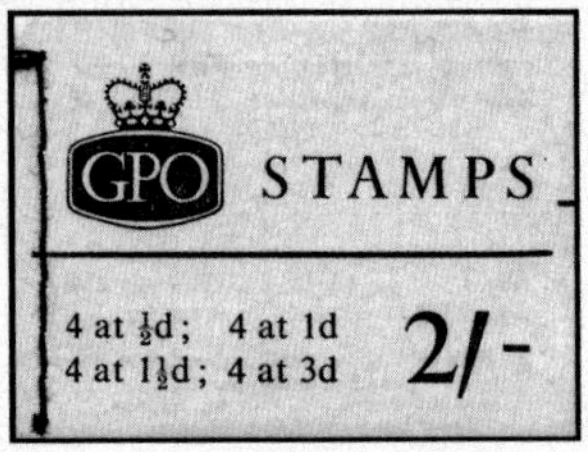


BC14

**1960-65** **2sh Booklets**

**BK77** BC14 *sal,* #353b-355b, 358b — 40.00
**BK77A** BC14 *pale yel,* 353b-355b, 358b — 40.00
**BK78** BC14 red, *pale yel,* #353e, 2 #357g — 4.00
*a.* White stiching — 4.00
**BK79** BC14 *pale yel,* #353b-355b, 358b (17) — 40.00
*a.* #353bp-355bp, 358bp (13) — 100.00
**BK80** BC14 red, *pale yel,* 4 #353g — 5.00
**BK81** BC14 *org yel,* #354f, 359c (7) — 3.50
*a.* #354fp, 359cp (12) — 17.50
**BK82** BC14 red, *org yel,* 2 #358b — 8.00

**1968-69**

**BK83** BC14 *org yel,* #MH5b, MH6b (3) — 1.40
**BK84** BC14 *gray,* #MH6a-MH6b (5) — 1.00
**BK85** BC14 *gray,* #MH7a-MH7b (12) — 1.25

**1954, Mar.** **2sh6p Booklets**

**BK86** BC13 *grn,* #292c, 293d, 294c, 296a (19) — 37.50

No. BK86 inscribed Apr. 1954 through Aug. 1955 are valued. Booklet inscribed Mar. 1954 is valued at $325.

No. BK86 inscribed Aug. 1955 through Nov. 1955, may contain one or more panes watermarked 308 substituted for those listed. Value $50.

**1955, Dec.**

**BK87** BC13 *grn,* #317a, 318b, 319a, 321a (16) — 40.00

No. BK87 inscribed Dec. 1955 through June 1956 may contain one or more panes watermarked 298 substituted for those listed. Value $15.

**1957**

**BK88** BC13 *grn,* #317a, 320b, 321a (9) — 40.00

**1958, Jan.** **3sh Booklets**

**BK89** BC13 *red,* #317a, 318b, 319a, 322a (9) — 25.00

No. BK89 inscribed Nov. 1958, may contain one or more panes watermarked 322 substituted for those listed. Value $13.

**1958, Dec.-59**

**BK90** BC13 *red,* #353a-355a, 358a (5) 29.00
*a.* #353d, 354d, 355d, 358d (2) 300.00

No. BK90 dated Dec. 1958, may contain one or more panes watermarked 308 substituted for those listed. Value $14.

**BK91** BC13 *brick red,* #353a-355a, 358a (14) 32.50
*a.* #353d, 354d, 355d, 358d (4) 325.00
*b.* #353ap, 354ap, 355ap, 358ap (2) 65.00

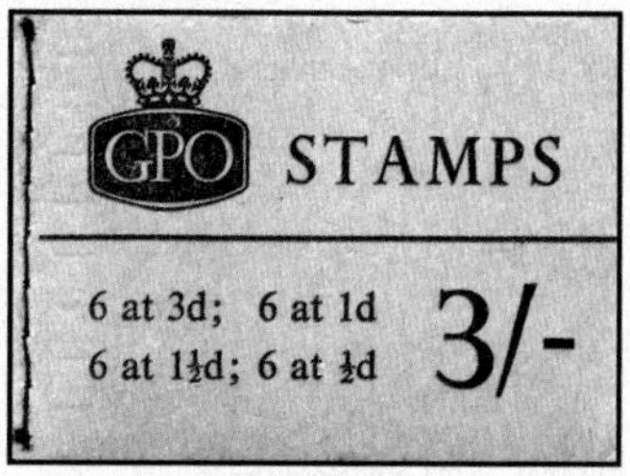


BC15

**1960**

**BK92** BC15 *brick red,* #353a-355a, 358a (46) 32.50
*a.* #353ap-355ap, 358ap (35) 75.00

**1953, Nov. 3sh9p Booklets**

**BK93** BC13 *red,* 3 #296a (10) 35.00

No. BK93 inscribed Oct. or Dec. 1955 may contain one or more panes watermarked 308 substituted for those listed. Value $16.

**1956, Feb.**

**BK94** BC13 *red,* 3 #321a (10) 25.00

**4sh6p Booklets**

**1957, Oct.-Dec. 1960**

**BK95** BC13 *dull mauve,* 3 #322a (7) 25.00
**BK96** BC13 *dull mauve,* 3 #358a 90.00
**BK97** BC14 *dull mauve,* 3 #358a (4) 26.00
*a.* 3 #358d 37.50
**BK98** BC14 *pale reddish lil,* 3 #358a (9) 37.50
*a.* 3 #358d (4) 25.00
*b.* 3 #358ap 30.00
**BK99** BC15 *pale reddish lil,* 3 #358a (36) 45.00
*a.* 3 #358ap (31) 35.00

**1965**

**BK100** BC15 *slate bl,* #354a, 2 #359b (7) 25.00
*a.* #354ap, 2 #359bp (13) 32.50

**1968**

**BK101** BC15 *slate bl,* #MH2a, 2 #MH6c 7.50

Ship with GPO Emblem — BC16

**1968-70 4sh6p Booklets**

**BK102** BC16 *blue,* #MH2a, 2 #MH6c (3) 2.00
**BK103** BC16 *blue,* #MH2a, 2 #MH7c (9) 3.75

**Ship Type with St. Edward's Crown instead of GPO emblem**

**BK104** BC16 *blue,* #MH2a, 2 #MH7c (2) 4.50

**1954, Mar. 5sh Booklets**

**BK105** BC13 *brn,* #292c-294c, 295a-296a (10) 45.00

No. BK105 inscribed Sept. 1955 may contain one or more panes watermarked 308 substituted for those listed. Value $16.

**1955, Nov.**

**BK106** BC13 *brn,* #317a, 318b, 319a, 320b, 321a (14) 40.00

No. BK106 inscribed Nov. 1955, Jan. 1956 or May 1956 may contain one or more panes watermarked 298 substituted for those listed. Value $17.

**1958**

**BK107** BC13 *brn,* #317a, 318b, 321a, 2 #322a (5) 40.00

No. BK107 inscribed July or Nov. 1958 may contain one or more panes watermarked 322 substituted for those listed. Value $15.

**1959, Jan.**

**BK108** BC14 *bl,* #353a-354a, 357c, 2 #358a (11) 32.50
*a.* #353d-354d, 357e, 2 #358d (3) 150.00
*b.* #353ap-354ap, 357cp, 2 #358ap 125.00

No. BK108 inscribed Jan. 1959 may contain one or more panes watermarked 308 substituted for those listed. Value $15.

**1961, Jan.**

**BK109** BC15 *bl,* #353a-354a, 357c, 2 #358a (27) 50.00
*a.* #353ap-354ap, 357cp, 2 #358ap (24) 150.00

House with GPO Emblem — BC17

**1968-70**

**BK110** BC17 *org brn,* 2 #MH8a (5) 3.00

**House Type with St. Edward's Crown instead of GPO Emblem**

**BK111** BC17 5sh *org brn,* 2 #MH8a (7) 3.25

BC18

**1970**

**BK112** BC18 *org brn,* 2 #MH8a 3.50

**1965 6sh Booklets**

**BK113** BC15 *claret,* 3 #359b (23) 30.00
*a.* 3 #359bp (27) 37.50

**1967**

**BK114** BC15 *claret,* 3 #MH6c (10) 50.00

Bird with GPO Emblem — BC19

**1968-70**

**BK115** BC19 *org,* 3 #MH6c (8) 2.25
**BK116** BC19 *org,* 3 #MH7c (5) 2.25

**Bird Type with St. Edward's Crown instead of GPO Emblem**

**BK117** BC19 *org,* 3 #MH7c (5) 4.25

**1961-67 10sh Booklets**

**BK118** BC15 *grn,* #353a-355a, 356b, 5 #358a (2) 140.00
**BK119** BC15 *gray grn,* #354a-355a, 357c, 5 #358a (7) 115.00
**BK120** BC15 *tan,* #354a, 358a, 4 #359b (5) 30.00
*a.* #354ap, 358ap, 4 #359bp (3) 9.25

Explorers with GPO Emblem — BC20

**1968-70**

**BK121** BC20 *pur,* #MH2a, MH5a, 4 #MH6c (2) 6.75

**Explorer Type with clear GPO Emblem**

**BK122** BC20 *yel grn,* #MH6d, 2 ea #MH6c, #MH8a 6.75
**BK123** BC20 *yel grn,* #MH7c, MH7e, MH8a (4) 4.00

**Explorer Type with St. Edward's Crown instead of GPO Emblem**

**BK124** BC20 *yel grn,* #MH7e, 2 ea #MH7c, MH8a (2) 8.00

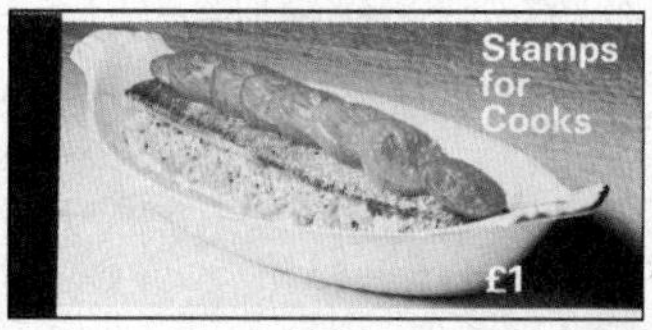


BC21

**1969 £1 Booklets**

**BK125** BC21 multi, 2 #MH7d, MH8b-MH8c 17.50
**BK126** BC21 2 #MH7d, MH8b-MH8c, stapled 400.00

**Decimal Currency Booklets (Stitched)**

BC22

**1971-74**

**BK127** BC22 10p *org yel,* #MH24a, MH26a (21) 2.50

BC23

**1974-76**

**BK128** BC23 10p *org yel,* #MH24a, MH26a (9) 2.75

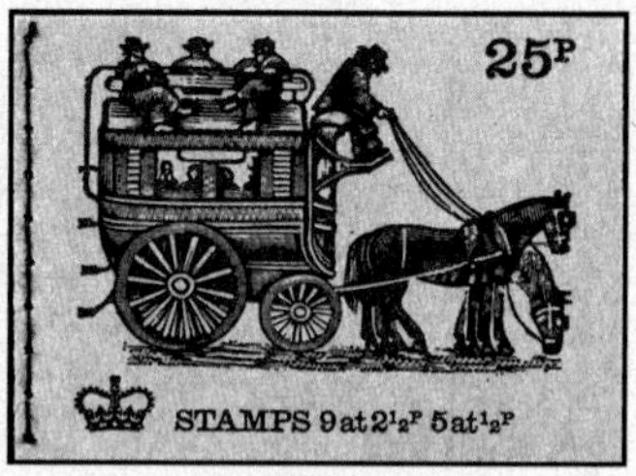


BC24

**1971-73**

**BK129** BC24 25p *dull purple* (12) 5.00

Contents: #MH22a, MH32a-MH32b.

BC25

**1971**

**BK130** BC25 25p *dull purple* 8.25

Contents: #MH22a, MH32a-MH32b.

**BK131** BC25 30p *bright pur,* #MH36b 5.75

BC26

**1973-74**

**BK132** BC26 25p *dull mauve* 10.50

Contents: #MH22a, MH32a-MH32b.

**BK133** BC26 30p *vermilion,* 2 #MH36b 6.50

**Bird Type with St. Edward's Crown instead of GPO Emblem**

**1971-73**

**BK134** BC19 30p *pur,* 2 #MH36b (16) 5.50
**BK135** BC19 30p *buff,* 2 #MH36b 8.25

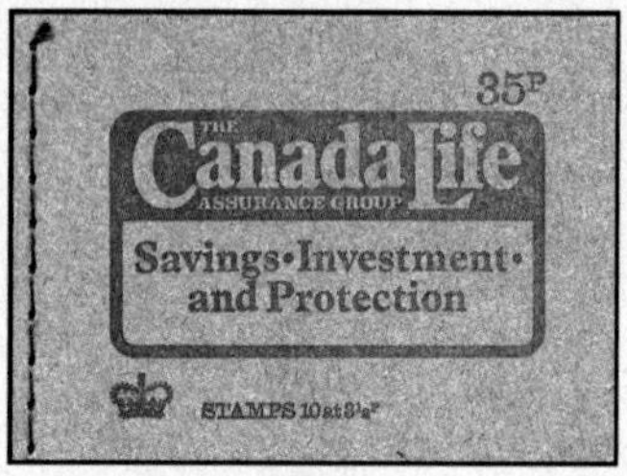


BC27

**1973-74**

**BK136** BC27 30p *red,* 2 #MH36b 6.00
**BK137** BC27 35p *blue,* 2 #MH39a 4.00
**BK138** BC27 50p *pale bluish grn* 12.00

Contents: #MH22a, MH32b, MH36a, MH36c (4).

**BK139** BC27 50p *pale grn, MH36b, 2 #MH39a (2)* 10.50
**BK140** BC27 85p *purple, #MH39a, 3 #MH49a* 10.50

BC28

**1973-74**
**BK141** BC28 35p *bl,* 2 #MH39a (3) 4.25
**BK142** BC28 45p *yel brn,* 2 #MH49a (3) 7.00

BC29

**1971-72**
**BK143** BC29 50p *pale bluish green* 11.50

Contents: #MH22a, MH32b, MH36a, MH36c (8).

---

**Prestige Booklets**

BC30

**1972, May 24**
**BK144** BC30 £1 *Wedgwood* 150.00

Contents: #MH34a-MH34b, #MH36d-MH36e. Valued with a F-VF 1/2p stamp.

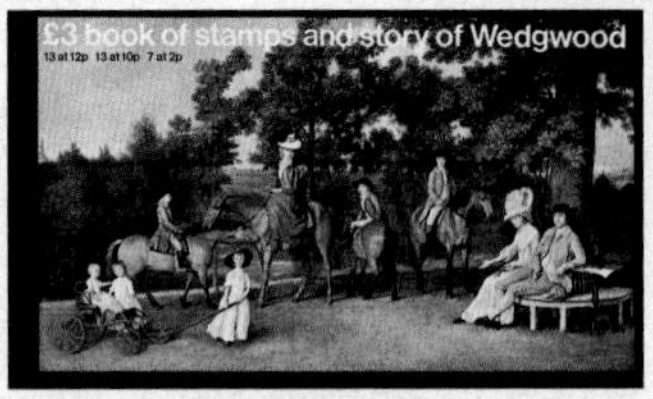


BC31

**1980, Apr. 16**
**BK145** BC31 £3 *Wedgwood* 20.00

Contents: #MH26b, MH70a, MH78a-MH78b.

**1982, May 19**
**BK146** £4 *Stanley Gibbons* 20.00

Contents: #MH80a-MH80b, MH92a-MH92b.

**1983, Sept. 14**
**BK147** £4 *Royal Mint* 19.00

Contents: #MH94a-MH94b, 2 #MH80a.

**1984, Sept. 4**
**BK148** £4 *Christian Heritage* 55.00

Contents: #MH97c-MH97d, 2 #MH83a.

**1985, Jan. 8**
**BK149** £5 *The Times* 50.00

Contents: #MH83b, MH97b-MH97c, MH149a.

**1986, Mar. 18**
**BK150** £5 *British Rail* 50.00

Contents: #MH79a, MH97b-MH97c, MH142a.

**1987, Mar. 3**
**BK151** £5 *P & O* 32.50

Contents: #MH83a-MH83b, MH102a, MH130a.

**1988, Feb. 9**
**BK152** £5 *The Financial Times* 47.50

Contents: #MH84a, MH103a-MH103b, MH150a.

**1989, Mar. 21**
**BK153** £5 *Scots Connection* 30.00

Contents: #SMH25a,SMH37a-SMH37b, SMH45a.

**1990, Mar. 20**
**BK154** £5 *London Life* 37.50

Contents: #1314a, MH196a, 2 #MH193d.

**1991, Mar. 19**
**BK155** £6 *Agatha Christie* 37.50

Contents: #MH121a, MH147a, 2 #MH99a.

**1992, Feb. 25**
**BK156** £6 *Cymru-Wales* 30.00

Contents: #1425a, MH187c, WMMH34a, WMMH45a.

**1992, Oct. 27**
**BK157** £6 *J.R.R. Tolkien* 32.50

Contents: #MH105a, MH187b, 2 #MH127a.

**1993, Aug. 10**
**BK158** £5.64 *Beatrix Potter* 30.00

Although inscribed £6 on the cover, No. BK158 was sold for £5.64, the face value of its contents, which were #1484a, MH178a, MH187a, NIMH45a.

**1994, July 26**
**BK159** £6.04 *N. Ireland* 45.00

Contents: #1550a, MH214a, NIMH63a-NIMH63b, 2 postal cards.

**1995, Apr. 25**
**BK160** £6 *National Trust* 40.00

Contents: #1607a, MH209a, MH231a, NIMH59a.

**1996, May 14**
**BK161** £6.48 *European Soccer Championships* 25.00

Contents: #1663a, 1664a, 1667a, MH214b.

**1997, Sept. 23**
**BK162** £6.15 *75th Anniv. of BBC* 30.00

Contents: #1698a, MH287a, MH257a, NIMH81a.

**1998, Mar. 10**
**BK163** £7.49 *Definitive Portrait* 35.00

Contents: #1801a, 1802a, 1803a-1803b.

**1998, Oct. 13**
**BK164** £6.16 *Breaking Barriers* 45.00

Contents: #1829b, MH269a, MH285a-MH285b.

**1999, Feb. 16**
**BK165** (£7.54) *Profile on Print* 50.00

Contents: #MH241c, MH288a, MH310a-MH312a.

**1999, Sept. 21**
**BK166** (£6.99) *World Changers* 55.00

Contents: #1842b, 1847a, 1868b, 1869b, MH257f.

**2000, Feb. 15**
**BK167** (£7.50) *Special by Design* 60.00

Contents: #MH198Ab, MH264Bc, MH336b, WMMH96a.

**2000, Aug. 4**
**BK168** (£7.03) *The Life of the Century* 35.00

Contents: #1943e, 1943f, Scotland 18a, MH335b.

**2000, Sept. 18**
**BK169** (£7) *A Treasury of Trees* 45.00

Contents: #1917a, 1918a, 1920a, 1921a, Wales and Monmouthshire 18a.

**2001, Oct. 22**
**BK170** (£6.76) *Unseen and Unheard* 50.00

Contents: #1969b, 1970b, 1999e, Scotland 16a.

**2002, Feb. 6**
**BK171** (£7.23) *A Gracious Accession* 45.00

Contents: #2020a, 2021a, 2023a, MH290b.

**2002, Sept. 24**
**BK172** (£6.83) *Across the Universe* 45.00

Contents: 1938b, 2075e, Scotland 15a, MH290c.

**2003, Feb. 25**
**BK173** (£6.99) *Microcosmos* 35.00

Contents: #2104a, 2105a, Northern Ireland 13a, MH290c.

**2003, June 2**
**BK174** (£7.46) *A Perfect Coronation* 90.00

Contents: #2126a, 2134a, 2136b, MH287b.

**2004, Mar. 16**
**BK175** (£7.44) *Letters by Night* 30.00

Contents: #2148a, 2175a, Scotland 20a, MH287c.

**2004, May 25**
**BK176** (£7.23) *The Glory of the Garden* 45.00

Contents: #1720b, 2213a, 2214b, MH287d.

**2005, Feb. 24**
**BK177** (£7.43) *The Bronte Sisters* 30.00

Contents: #2268a, 2272b, England 10a, MH354a.

**2005, Oct. 18**
**BK178** (£7.26) *Battle of Trafalgar* 30.00

Contents: #1999h, 2325a, 2326b, MH287e.

**2006, Feb. 23**
**BK179** (£7.40) *Isambard Kingdom Brunel* 30.00

Contents: #2356a, 2357a, 2358b, MH355a.

**2006, Sept. 21**
**BK180** (£7.44) *Victoria Cross* 50.00

Contents: #1331b, 2398a, 2399b, MH376a.

**2007, Mar. 1**
**BK181** (£7.49) *World of Invention* 37.50

Contents: #2447a, 2449b, Wales & Monmouthshire 26a, MH376b.

**2007, June 5**
**BK182** (£7.66) *The Machin* 31.00

Contents: #2471c, MH363a, MH373a, MH378a.

**2007, Sept. 20**
**BK183** (£7.66) *British Army Uniforms* 32.00

Contents: #2510b, 2513b, MH366a, Wales & Monmouthshire #21a.

**2008, Jan. 8**
**BK184** (£7.40) *Ian Fleming's James Bond* 30.00

Contents: #1999i, 2535a, 2536b, MH287f.

**2008, Sept. 18**
**BK185** (£7.15) *RAF Uniforms* 30.00

Contents: #2587c, 2596b, 2599b, MH287h.

**2008, Sept. 29**
**BK186** (£9.72) *The Regional Definitives: Heraldry and Symbol* 35.00

Contents: #2600s, 2600t, 2600u, 2600v.

**2009, Jan. 13**
**BK187** (£7.68) *British Design Classics* 50.00

Contents: #2619a, 2623a, 2624b, MH365b.

**2009, Feb. 12**
**BK188** (£7.75) *Charles Darwin* 55.00

Contents: #2626e, 2630a, 2632a, MH363c.

**2009, Aug. 18**
**BK189** (£8.18) *Treasures of the Archive* 28.00

Contents: #1289b, 2679e, MH368b, MH394a.

**2009, Sept. 17**
**BK190** (£7.93) *Royal Navy Uniforms* 30.00

Contents: #1999j, 2688b, 2691b, MH372Ac.

**2010, Jan. 7**
**BK191** (£8.06) *Classic Album Covers* 55.00

Contents: #2729a, 2733a, MH350Ad, MH368c.

**2010, Feb. 25**

**BK192** (£7.72) *The Royal Society* 35.00

Contents: #2754a, 2755a, 2756b, MH366Bc.

**2010, May 8**

**BK193** (£11.15) *King George V* 33.00

Contents: #2792b, 2791b, 2789a, MH385a.

**2010, May 13**

**BK194** (£9.76) *Britain Alone* 30.00

Contents: #MH397b, 2802a, 2801a, 2806b.

**2011, Mar. 11**

**BK195** (£9.05) *WWF For a Living Planet* 31.00

Contents: #2890a, 2892b, 2893e, MH400b.

**2011, May 5**

**BK196** (£9.44) *Morris & Co.* 34.00

No. BK196 sold for £9.99. Contents: #2716i, 2906a, 2907a, MH405a.

**2011, Sept. 9**

**BK197** (£9.02) *First United Kingdom Aerial Post* 32.00

No. BK197 sold for £9.97. Contents: Nos, 2278e, 2939e, 2939f, MH412a.

**2012, Jan. 10**

**BK198** (£10.52) *Roald Dahl: Master Stroyteller* 36.00

No. BK198 sold for £11.47. contents: Nos. 2986a, 2988a, 2989e, MH413a.

**2012, May 31**

**BK199** (£11.84) *The Diamond Jubilee* 40.00

No. BK199 sold for £12.77. contents: Nos. 2996Gh, 3030b, 3034b, 3035c.

**2012, July 27**

**BK200** (£9.76) *Keeping the Flame Alive* 33.50

No. BK200 sold for £10.71. contents: Nos. 2708a, 2822a, 2917a, C9a.

Numbers have been reserved for future prestige booklets.

---

**Decimal Currency Booklets (Folded)**

Booklets are listed in denomination sequence in chronological order in this section.

BC32

**1976-77**

**BK225** BC32 10p red, *gray*, #MH58a (3) 1.25

BC33

**1978**

**BK226** BC33 10p brn, *bl*, #MH61b (6) 1.25

**1979-80**

**BK227** BC33 10p *London '80*, #MH64b (2) .75

BC34

**1977**

**BK228** BC34 50p #MH65a 5.25
**BK229** BC34 50p #MH67a 3.50

**Nos. BK228-BK229, BK230-BK231, BK237-BK238 exist with either version of #MH65a, MH67a, MH70b, MH80c. See the notes following the listings for these panes.**

---

Commercial Vehicles — BC35

**50p Booklets, Cover BC35**

**1978-95**

**BK230** *Commercial Vehicles*, #MH67a (6) 5.75
**BK231** *Commercial Vehicles*, #MH70b 3.75
**BK232** *Veteran Cars*, #MH70b 3.00
**BK233** *Veteran Cars*, #MH78d (3) 3.00
**BK234** *Veteran Cars*, #MH86a (2) 3.00
**BK235** *Follies*, #MH86a 3.00
**BK236** *Follies*, #MH76a (2) 8.25
**BK237** *Follies*, #MH80c (4) 3.50
**BK238** *Rare Farm Animals*, #MH80c 3.75
**BK239** *Rare Farm Animals*, #MH80d (4) 7.50
**BK240** *Orchids*, #MH83c (4) 4.75
**BK241** *Pillar Box*, #MH97a 5.50
**BK242** *Pond Life*, #MH97a (2) 3.50

Nos. BK241-BK242 sold for a 1p discount. Some panes have stars on reverse.

**BK244** *Pond Life*, #MH83d (2) 5.00
**BK245** *Roman Britain*, #MH79b 11.50
**BK246** *Roman Britain*, #MH102b (2) 5.25
**BK247** *Marylebone Cricket Club*, #MH102b (4) 3.50
**BK248** *Botanical Gardens*, #MH83d (2) 6.00
**BK248A** *Botanical Gardens*, #MH83g (2) 5.75
**BK249** *London Zoo*, #MH102b (2) 4.00
**BK250** *London Zoo*, #MH83g 5.00
**BK251** *Marine Life*, #MH83g 5.00
**BK252** *Marine Life*, #MH106a 4.00
**BK253** *Gilbert & Sullivan Operas*, #MH106a (3) 6.00
**BK254** *Aircraft*, #MH115a 14.00
**BK255** *Aircraft*, #MH193a 10.50
**BK256** *Aircraft*, #MH98a (2) 6.25
**BK257** *Archaeology*, #MH126a (4) 3.50
**BK258** *Sheriff's Millennium*, #MH126a 2.50
**BK259** *Postal History*, #MH126a (3) 3.00
**BK260** *Postal History*, #MH213a 3.00
**BK261** *Coaching Inns*, #MH213a (4) 3.00
**BK262** *Sea Charts*, #MH213a (4) 3.00

With Window — BC36

Without Window — BC37

**1987**

**BK285** BC36 52p #MH83e 4.50

**1988-89**

**BK295** BC36 56p #MH87a (2) 7.00
**BK296** BC37 56p #MH87b 11.00
**BK297** BC37 56p #MH87c 45.00

**1990**

**BK307** BC37 60p #MH191a 7.50

**1976-77**

**BK317** BC34 65p 10 #MH60 10.50
**BK325** BC34 70p 10 #MH61 7.00

**Nos. BK317, BK325-BK327, BK370, BK394, BK404-BK405, BK467-BK468, BK488-BK492, BK513-BK514, BK524-BK533, BK554-BK557, BK573-BK574, BK584, BK594, BK616-BK618, BK631, BK641, BK651-BK652, BK673-BK675, BK696-BK699, BK709-BK713, BK715-BK718, BK728, BK732-BK733 exist with stamps affixed to cover by selvage at either right or left edges of block or pane of stamps.**

---

BC38

**1978-79** **70p Booklets**

**BK326** BC38 *Country Crafts*, 10 #MH61 (6) 5.75
**BK327** BC38 *Derby Mechanized Letter Office*, 10 #MH61 10.50

**1987**

**BK338** BC36 72p red, yel & blk, #MH102c 4.50

**1988-89**

**BK348** BC36 76p #MH106c (2) 9.00
**BK349** BC37 76p #MH106d 9.00
**BK350** BC37 76p #MH106e 45.00

BC39

**1992**

**BK360** BC39 78p 2 #MH157 4.00

Cover of #BK360 does not show the numeral four. Contents of #BK360 is 1/2 of #MH157a, the right hand vertical pair of stamps being removed.

**1979**

**BK370** BC38 80p *Military Aircraft*, 10 #MH64 3.00

**1990**

**BK371** BC37 80p red, yel & blk, #MH193b 10.00
**BK372** BC37 80p red, yel & blk, #MH194a 7.50

**1976-79**

**BK382** BC34 85p gray & ol grn, 10 #MH65 10.50
**BK392** BC34 90p lt & dk bl, 10 #MH67 7.00
**BK393** BC38 90p *British Canals*, 10 #MH67 (6) 8.00
**BK394** BC38 90p *Derby Letter Office*, 10 #MH67 12.50

**1979-95** **£1 Booklets**

**BK403** BC38 *Industrial Archaeology*, 10 #MH70 5.25
**BK404** BC38 *Military Aircraft*, 10 #MH70 (3) 5.25
**BK405** BC35 *Violin*, 6 #MH97 5.75
**BK406** BC35 *Musical Instruments*, #MH102d (2) 6.00
**BK407** BC35 *Sherlock Holmes*, #MH102d (2) 6.00
**BK408** BC35 *Sherlock Holmes*, #MH102f (2) 6.00
**BK409** BC35 *London Zoo*, #MH102f 6.00
**BK410** BC35 *Oliver Twist*, #MH102f 8.00
**BK411** BC35 *Nicholas Nickleby*, #MH106b (2) 8.00
**BK412** BC35 *Great Expectations*, #MH108a 15.00
**BK413** BC35 *Marine Life*, #MH106b 8.00
**BK414** BC35 *Wicken Fen*, #MH115b 11.00
**BK415** BC35 *Click Mill*, #MH193c 8.50
**BK416** BC35 *Wicken Fen*, #MH194b 8.00
**BK417** BC35 *Jack & Jill Mills*, #MH120a (2) 5.00
**BK418** BC35 *Punch Magazine*, #MH126b (4) 4.00
**BK419** BC35 *Sheriff's Millennium*, #MH126b 4.25
**BK420** BC35 *Educational Institutions*, #MH128a (3) 8.25
**BK421** BC35 *Educational Institutions*, 4 #MH214 8.25
**BK422** BC35 *Prime Ministers*, 4 #MH214 3.75
**BK423** BC35 *Prime Ministers*, 4 #MH213 (3) 4.00
**BK424** BC35 *End of World War II*, 4 #MH213 (4) 4.00

BC40

**1996-2000**

**BK425** BC40 £1 multi, 4 #MH214 8.00
**BK426** BC40 £1 multi, #MH216b 8.00
**BK427** BC40 £1 multi, #MH257b 12.50
**BK428** BC40 £1 multi, #MH257d 7.00
**BK429** BC40 £1 #MH288d 6.00

**1987-88 £1.04 Booklet**

**BK446** BC36 #MH131a 24.00

**£1.08 Booklets**

**BK456** BC36 #MH133a 16.00
**BK457** BC37 #MH133b 40.00

**1981 £1.15 Booklets**

**BK467** BC38 *Military Aircraft,* 10 #MH76 (2) 5.75
**BK468** BC38 *Museums,* 10 #MH76 (2) 5.75

**1989 £1.16 Booklet**

**BK478** BC37 multi, #MH140a 25.00

**1980-86 £1.20 Booklets**

**BK488** BC38 *Industrial Archaeology,* 10 #MH78 (3) 5.75
**BK489** BC38 *Pillar Box,* 10 #MH79 8.00
**BK490** BC38 *National Gallery,* 10 #MH79 7.50
**BK491** BC38 *Handwriting,* 10 #MH79 7.50
**BK492** BC38 *Christmas,* 10 #MH83 10.00

No. BK492 was sold at a discount. Each stamp has a blue double-line star printed on reverse.

BC41

**1998 £1.20 Booklet**

**BK493** BC41 multi, 4 #MH259 4.75

**1990 £1.24 Booklet**

**BK503** BC39 multi, #MH144a 8.00

**1982-83 £1.25 Booklets**

**BK513** BC38 *Museums,* 10 #MH81 (4) 6.25
**BK514** BC38 *Railway Engines,* 10 #MH81 (5) 8.00

**1981-88 £1.30 Booklets**

**BK524** BC38 *Postal History,* #MH86b (2) 8.00
**BK525** BC38 *Trams,* 10 #MH83 (4) 6.25
**BK526** BC38 *Books for Children,* 10 #MH83 6.25
**BK527** BC38 *Keep in Touch,* 10 #MH83 6.25
**BK528** BC38 *Ideas for your Garden,* 10 #MH83 6.25
**BK529** BC38 *Brighter Writer,* 10 #MH83 6.25
**BK530** BC38 *Jolly Postman,* 10 #MH83 6.50
**BK531** BC38 *Linnean Society,* 10 #MH83 7.75
**BK532** BC38 *Recipe Cards,* 10 #MH83 6.25
**BK533** BC38 *Party Pack,* 10 #MH83 6.25
**BK534** BC36 red, yel & blk, #MH83f 7.00

**1991 £1.32 Booklet**

**BK544** BC39 multi, #MH148a 11.00

**1981-89 £1.40 Booklets**

**BK554** BC38 *Industrial Archaeology,* 10 #MH86 (2) 6.25
**BK555** BC38 *Women's Costumes,* 10 #MH86 (2) 6.25
**BK556** BC38 *Pocket Planner,* 10 #MH87 6.25
**BK557** BC38 *William Henry Fox Talbot,* 10 #MH87 6.50

**1988-95 £1.40 Booklets**

**BK558** BC36 #MH87d 9.50
**BK559** BC36 10 #MH88 20.00
**BK560** BC37 #MH87e 11.50
**BK561** BC37 10 #MH88 20.00
**BK562** BC39 4 #MH223 8.00
**BK563** BC41 4 #MH223 (2) 8.00

**1982 £1.43 Booklets**

**BK572** BC38 *James Chalmers,* #MH93d 7.00
**BK573** BC38 *Postal History,* #MH93c (4) 7.00
**BK574** BC38 *Holiday Postcard Stamp Book,* #MH93c 7.00

**1983 £1.45 Booklet**

**BK584** BC38 *Britain's Countryside,* 10 #MH94 5.50

Stamps in #BK584 have double-lined D printed on reverse.

**1983 £1.46 Booklet**

**BK594** BC38 *Postal History,* #MH94c (4) 12.50

BC42

**1996-97 £1.48 Booklets**

**BK605** BC41 #MH226a (2) 11.50
**BK606** BC42 4 #MH262 11.50

**1986-90 £1.50 Booklets**

**BK616** BC38 *Pillar Box,* #MH97e 8.00
**BK617** BC38 *National Gallery,* #MH97e 8.00
**BK618** BC38 *Handwriting,* #MH97e 8.00
**BK619** BC37 #MH190a 7.50
**BK620** BC37 #MH191b 12.00
**BK621** BC37 #MH192a 11.00

**1999 £1.52 Booklet**

**BK630** BC41 4 #MH264 8.00

**1985 £1.53 Booklet**

**BK631** BC38 *Royal Mail, 350th Anniv.,* 10 #1111 7.00

**1984 £1.54 Booklet**

**BK641** BC38 *Postal History,* #MH97f (4) 7.00

**1982-85 £1.55 Booklets**

**BK651** BC38 *Women's Costumes,* 10 #MH93 (4) 6.50
**BK652** BC38 *Social Letter Writing,* 10 #MH97 6.50

No. BK652 sold for a 15p discount. Panes have double-lined "D" printed on reverse.

**1991 £1.56 Booklet**

**BK662** BC39 #MH157a 12.50

**1978-2000 £1.60 Booklets**

**BK672** BC38 *Christmas,* #MH67b 8.00
**BK673** BC38 *Birthday Box,* 10 #MH97 (2) 8.00
**BK674** BC38 *Britain's Countryside,* 10 #MH94 7.00
**BK675** BC38 *Write It,* 10 #MH97 8.00
**BK676** BC41 #MH266a 8.75

**1993-96 £1.64 Booklets**

**BK685** BC39 #MH231b 10.00
**BK686** BC41 #MH231b (2) 10.00

**1984-86 £1.70 Booklets**

**BK696** BC38 *Love Letters,* 10 #MH97 (2) 8.00
**BK697** BC38 *Pillar Box,* 10 #MH97 (2) 8.00
**BK698** BC38 *National Gallery,* 10 #MH97 8.00
**BK699** BC38 *Handwriting,* 10 #MH97 8.00

**1979-88 £1.80 Booklets**

**BK709** BC38 *Christmas,* #MH70c 10.50
**BK710** BC38 *Books for Children,* 10 #MH102 8.00
**BK711** BC38 *Keep in Touch,* 10 #MH102 8.00
**BK712** BC38 *Ideas for your Garden,* 10 #MH102 8.00
**BK713** BC38 *Brighter Writer,* 10 #MH102 8.00
**BK714** BC36 red, yel & blk, #MH102e 10.50
**BK715** BC38 *Jolly Postman,* 10 #MH102 8.00
**BK716** BC38 *Linnean Society,* 10 #MH102 8.00
**BK717** BC38 *Recipe Cards,* 10 #MH102 8.00
**BK718** BC38 *Party Pack,* 10 #MH102 8.00

**1988-89 £1.90 Booklets**

**BK728** BC38 *Pocket Planner,* 10 #MH106 10.00
**BK729** BC36 red, yel & blk, #MH106f 14.00
**BK730** BC37 #MH106g 14.00
**BK731** BC37 10 #MH107 27.50
**BK732** BC38 *William Henry Fox Talbot,* 10 #MH106 10.00

BC43

**1989 £1.90 Booklet**

**BK733** BC43 *Greetings,* #1247a 65.00

Artwork for #BC43 spanned six booklet covers. Only portions of the design appear on each cover.

Value is for pane with perfs guillotined. Value for booklet with pane having full perfs is approximately 60% more.

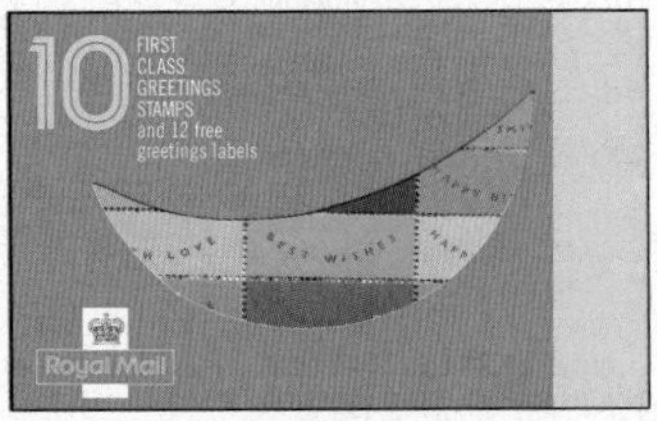


BC44

**1990 £2 Booklets**

**BK742** BC44 #1313a 40.00
**BK743** BC37 #MH193e 12.00
**BK744** BC37 #MH194c 12.00
**BK745** BC37 #MH195a 20.00
**BK746** BC35 *Postal Vehicles,* 8 #MH213 (3) 8.50
**BK747** BC35 *Rowland Hill,* 8 #MH213 (4) 8.50
**BK748** BC40 8 #MH214 8.00
**BK749** BC40 #MH216a 9.00

**1998-2000**

**BK751** BC40 #MH257c 15.00
**BK752** BC40 #MH257e 8.50
**BK753** BC40 #MH288e 8.00

**1980-93 £2.20 Booklets**

**BK759** BC38 *Christmas,* #MH78c 9.00
**BK760** BC38 *Christmas,* 20 #MH80 8.00

**£2.30 Booklet**

**BK770** BC38 *Christmas,* 20 #1088 11.00

**£2.40 Booklet**

**BK780** BC38 *Christmas,* 20 #1124 10.50

Stamps in #BK760, BK770, BK780 have double-line star printed on reverse over gum.

BC45

**1994-95 £2.40 Booklets**

**BK790** BC39 #MH234a (2) 9.25
**BK791** BC41 #MH234a (2) 9.25
**BK792** BC45 #1638a 7.25

**1981-94 £2.50 Booklets**

**BK802** BC38 *Christmas,* #MH93e 10.50

No. BK802 was sold for a 30p discount. Stamps in #BK802 have a 10-point single-line blue star printed on reverse over gum.

**BK803** BC45 *Santa, Reindeer,* 10 #1529 11.50
**BK804** BC45 *Christmas Play Props,* 10 #1582 9.00
**BK805** BC45 *Christmas Robin,* 10 #1635 9.00

**1996-97 £2.52 Booklet**

**BK815** BC41 #MH236a (3) 15.00

**1981 £2.55 Booklet**

**BK826** BC38 *Christmas,* #MH86c 11.00

**1999 £2.56 Booklet**

**BK827** BC41 4 #MH276 10.50

**2000 £2.60 Booklet**

**BK830** BC41 #MH277a 11.50

**1990-95 £3.40 Booklet**

**BK836** BC45 *Snowman,* #1340a 10.00

**£3.60 Booklets**

**BK846** BC45 *Holly,* #1416a 10.00
**BK847** BC45 *Santa, Reindeer,* #1468a 10.00

**£3.80 Booklets**

**BK857** BC45 *Santa, Reindeer,* #1528a 11.00
**BK858** BC45 *Christmas Play Props,* #1581a 11.00
**BK859** BC45 *Christmas Robin,* #1634a 11.00

**No-Value Indicated Booklets**

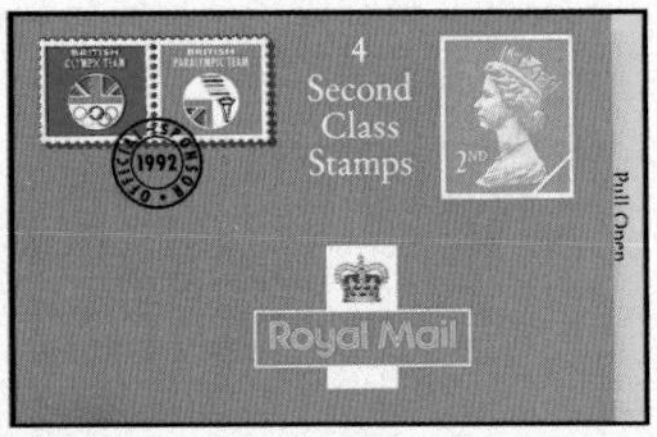


BC46

**1989-2000**

**BK960** BC37 (56p) #MH179a 10.00
**BK961** BC37 (60p) #MH177a 30.00
**BK962** BC39 (60p) #MH182a 4.50
**BK963** BC39 (68p) #MH179b 5.00
**BK964** BC46 (72p) #MH179b 8.00
**BK965** BC39 (72p) 4 #MH238 4.50
**BK966** BC39 (72p) 4 #MH239 4.50
**BK967** BC41 (76p) 4 #MH238 4.50
**BK968** BC41 (76p) 4 #MH239 (2) 4.50
**BK969** BC41 (80p) 4 #MH284 (2) 5.00
**BK994** BC37 (76p) #MH184a 10.00
**BK995** BC37 (80p) #MH183a 40.00
**BK996** BC39 (80p) #MH188a (2) 4.50
**BK997** BC46 (96p) #MH188a 4.00
**BK998** BC39 (96p) 4 #MH240 4.50
**BK999** BC39 (96p) 4 #MH241 5.00
**BK1000** BC39 (£1) #MH241b 11.00
**BK1001** BC41 (£1) 4 #MH241 (4) 5.00
**BK1002** BC41 (£1) #MH241b (4) 7.00

**(£1.04) Booklets**

**BK1003** BC41 4 #MH288 5.75
**BK1004** BC41 #MH241b 7.00
**BK1005** BC41 4 #MH288 8.50

**BK1006** BC41 4 #MH288+label 9.75

### (£1.20) Booklet

**BK1007** BC41 #MH335c 5.50
**BK1010** BC41 #MH290a 6.50

### (£1.40) Booklets

**BK1028** BC37 #MH177b 15.00
**BK1029** BC37 10 #MH178 12.50

### (£1.50) Booklets

**BK1030** BC39 #MH180a 8.50
**BK1031** BC39 10 #MH181 20.00
**BK1032** BC39 #MH182b 9.50

### (£1.70) Booklets

**BK1033** BC39 10 #MH178 12.50
**BK1034** BC39 #MH179c 12.50

### (£1.80) Booklets

**BK1035** BC46 #MH179c 12.50
**BK1036** BC46 10 #MH178 12.50
**BK1037** BC39 #MH177b 15.00
**BK1038** BC39 10 #MH239 (3) 10.00

### (£1.90) Booklets

**BK1039** BC41 10 #MH239 (5) 10.00
**BK1040** BC41 10 #MH238 (4) 10.00
**BK1041** BC37 #MH183b 20.00

### (£2) Booklets

**BK1068** BC39 #MH186a (2) 13.50
**BK1069** BC39 10 #MH187 (3) 13.50
**BK1070** BC39 #MH188b (3) 13.50
**BK1071** BC41 10 #MH284 9.50
**BK1072** BC41 10 #MH285 9.50

### (£2.40) Booklets

**BK1091** BC46 #MH186a 13.50
**BK1092** BC46 #MH187d 13.50
**BK1093** BC39 #MH187d 13.50
**BK1094** BC39 10 #MH240 14.00
**BK1095** BC39 10 #MH241 (11) 14.00

### (£2.50) Booklets

**BK1116** BC41 10 #MH240 (11) 12.50
**BK1117** BC41 10 #MH241 (12) 11.00

### (£2.60) Booklets

**BK1137** BC41 10 #MH287 12.50
**BK1139** BC41 10 #MH288 12.50
**BK1139A** BC41 #MH289a 20.00
**BK1140** BC41 10 #MH288 12.50
**BK1141** BC41 #1856a, MH288b 11.00
**BK1142** BC41 #1872a, MH288b 11.00
**BK1143** BC41 10 #MH335 12.50
**BK1144** BC41 #MH336a 12.50

BC47

### 1991-2000 (£2.20) Booklets

**BK1160** BC47 #1359a 11.50
**BK1161** BC47 *Laughing Pillar Box,* #1373a 12.00

### (£2.40) Booklets

**BK1171** BC47 *Memories,* #1435a 11.00
**BK1172** BC47 *Rupert Bear,* #1488a (3) 11.00

### (£2.50) Booklets

**BK1182** BC47 *Rupert Bear, Paddington Bear,* #1547a 11.00
**BK1183** BC47 *Clown,* #1605a 11.00
**BK1184** BC47 *More Love,* #1652a 11.00

### (£2.60) Booklets

**BK1194** BC47 *Christmas,* 10 #1709 15.00
**BK1195** BC47 *Flower,* #1722a (4) 11.00
**BK1196** BC47 *Chocolates,* #1722a 14.00
**BK1197** BC47 *Memorable Post,* #1722a 14.00
**BK1198** BC47 *Santa Claus,* 10 #1777 11.50
**BK1199** BC47 *Christmas,* 10 #1835 10.50
**BK1200** BC47 10 #1880 10.50

### (£2.70) Booklets

**BK1201** BC41 #1938a, MH335a 11.00
**BK1202** BC47 #1919a, MH335a 11.00
**BK1203** BC47 10 #1931 13.50

### (£3.80) Booklet

**BK1210** BC47 #1879a 11.00
**BK1211** BC47 #1930a 15.00

### (£4) Booklets

**BK1220** BC47 *Magi,* #1708a 19.00
**BK1221** BC47 *Santa Claus, Children,* #1776a 13.00
**BK1222** BC47 *Christmas,* #1834a 13.00

# BRITISH OFFICES ABROAD

## OFFICES IN AFRICA

**Catalogue values for unused stamps in this section are for Never Hinged stamps.**

### MIDDLE EAST FORCES

For use in Ethiopia, Cyrenaica, Eritrea, the Dodecanese and Somalia

Stamps of Great Britain, 1937-42 Overprinted in Black or Blue Black

**London Printing — ovpt. 14mm long, square dots**

**1942-43 Wmk. 251** ***Perf. 14½x14***

**1** A101 1p scarlet 2.00 *3.00*
**2** A101 2p orange 1.50 *4.00*
**3** A101 2½p bright ultra 1.10 *1.40*
**4** A101 3p dark purple .90 .35
*a.* Double overprint *4,000.*
**5** A102 5p lt brn (Blk) .80 .35
*a.* Blue black overprint ('43) 4.25 .25
**6** A102 6p rose lilac ('43) .45 .25
**7** A103 9p dp olive grn ('43) 1.00 .25
**8** A103 1sh brown ('43) .55 .25

**Wmk. 259**

***Perf. 14***

**9** A104 2sh6p yel green ('43) 8.00 1.10
*Nos. 1-9 (9)* 16.30 10.95

**Same Overprint in Blue Black on Nos. 259, 261, 262 and 263**

**1943, Jan. 1 Wmk. 251**

**10** A101 1p vermilion 1.75 .25
**11** A101 2p light orange 1.75 1.40
**12** A101 2½p ultramarine .55 .25
**13** A101 3p violet 1.75 .25
*Nos. 10-13 (4)* 5.80 2.15

There were two printings of Nos. 1-5, both issued Mar. 2, 1942, and both black. Nos. 5a and 6-13 compose a third printing, also made in London. On these stamps, issued Jan. 1, 1943, the overprint is 13½mm wide. The 2sh6p overprint is black, the others blue black.

**Same Ovpt. in Black on #250, 251A**

**1947 Wmk. 259** ***Perf. 14***

**14** A104 5sh dull red 15.00 *20.00*
**15** A105 10sh ultramarine 17.50 11.50

In 1950 Nos. 1-15 were declared valid for use in Great Britain. Used values are for stamps postmarked in territory of issue. Others sell for about 25 percent less.

### POSTAGE DUE STAMPS

**Catalogue values for unused stamps in this section are for Never Hinged items.**

Postage Due Stamps of Great Britain Overprinted in Blue

**1942 Wmk. 251** ***Perf. 14x14½***

**J1** D1 ½p emerald .35 *14.00*
**J2** D1 1p carmine rose .35 *2.00*
**J3** D1 2p black brown 1.40 1.40
**J4** D1 3p violet .55 *4.75*
**J5** D1 1sh blue 4.25 *14.00*
*Nos. J1-J5 (5)* 6.90 *36.15*

No. J1-J5 were used in Eritrea.

### FOR USE IN ERITREA

**Catalogue values for unused stamps in this section are for Never Hinged items.**

100 Cents = 1 Shilling

Stamps of Great Britain 1937-42 Surcharged — a

***Perf. 14½x14***

**1948, June -49 Wmk. 251**

**1** A101 5c on ½p green (II) 1.60 .75
**2** A101 10c on 1p vermilion (II) 1.60 *2.75*
**3** A101 20c on 2p light org (II) 1.10 *2.50*
**4** A101 25c on 2½p ultra (II) 1.40 .70
**5** A101 30c on 3p violet (II) 1.60 *5.00*
**6** A101 40c on 5p light brown 1.10 *4.75*
**7** A101 50c on 6p rose lilac .70 *1.10*
**8** A103 75c on 9p deep ol grn 1.40 *.85*
**9** A103 1sh on 1sh brown 1.40 .55

Great Britain Nos. 249A, 250 and 251A Surcharged

**Wmk. 259**

***Perf. 14***

**10** A104 2sh50c on 2sh6p yel grn 9.25 *11.50*
**11** A104 5sh on 5sh dl red 9.25 *18.00*
**12** A105 10sh on 10sh ultra 25.00 25.00

**Great Britain No. 245 Surcharged Type "a"**

**Wmk. 251**

***Perf. 14½x14***

**13** A103 65c on 8p brt rose ('49) 8.00 2.25
*Nos. 1-13 (13)* 63.40 *75.70*

"B. M. A." stands for British Military Administration.

Stamps of Great Britain 1937-42 Surcharged — c

**1950, Feb. 6**

**14** A101 5c on ½p green (II) 1.60 *9.25*
**15** A101 10c on 1p ver (II) .45 *3.50*
**16** A101 20c on 2p lt orange (II) .55 *.90*
**17** A101 25c on 2½p ultra (II) .55 *.70*
**18** A101 30c on 3p violet (II) .45 *2.50*
**19** A102 40c on 5p light brown .80 *2.00*
**20** A102 50c on 6p rose lilac .45 .25
**21** A103 65c on 8p bright rose 3.25 1.75
**22** A103 75c on 9p dp ol grn .65 .30
**23** A103 1sh on 1sh brown .45 .25

Great Britain Nos. 249A, 250, 251A Surcharged

**Wmk. 259** ***Perf. 14***

**24** A104 2sh50c on 2sh6p yel grn 8.00 5.50
**25** A104 5sh on 5sh dl red 8.00 *14.00*
**26** A105 10sh on 10sh ultra 70.00 62.50
*Nos. 14-26 (13)* *95.20* *103.40*

**Great Britain Nos. 280, 281, 283 and 284 Surcharged Type "c"**

***Perf. 14½x14***

**1951, May 3 Wmk. 251**

**27** A101 5c on ½p lt orange .55 *.95*
**28** A101 10c on 1p ultra .55 *.85*
**29** A101 20c on 2p lt red brown .55 .35
**30** A101 25c on 2½p vermilion .55 .35

**Great Britain Nos. 286-288 Surcharged**

***Perf. 11x12***

**1951, May 31 Wmk. 259**

**31** A121 2sh50c on 2sh6p grn 11.50 *26.00*
**32** A121 5sh on 5sh dl red 24.00 *26.00*
**33** A122 10sh on 10sh ultra 25.00 *26.00*
*Nos. 27-33 (7)* 62.70 *80.50*

Surcharge arranged to fit the design on #33.

### POSTAGE DUE STAMPS

**Catalogue values for unused stamps in this section are for Never Hinged items.**

Great Britain Nos. J26-J29, J32 Surcharged

**1948 Wmk. 251** ***Perf. 14x14½***

**J1** D1 5c on ½p emer 11.00 *25.00*
**J2** D1 10c on 1p car rose 11.00 *27.50*
**J3** D1 20c on 2p blk brn 12.00 *18.00*
**J4** D1 30c on 3p violet 11.00 *18.00*
**J5** D1 1sh on 1sh blue 20.00 *35.00*
*Nos. J1-J5 (5)* 65.00 *123.50*

Great Britain Nos. J26 to J29 and J32 Surcharged

**1950, Feb. 6**

**J6** D1 5c on ½p emer 13.00 *55.00*
**J7** D1 10c on 1p car rose 13.00 *18.50*
*a.* "C" of CENTS omitted *2,750.*
Lightly hinged *1,850.*
**J8** D1 20c on 2p blk brn 13.00 *20.00*
**J9** D1 30c on 3p violet 17.50 *28.00*
**J10** D1 1sh on 1sh blue 17.50 *28.00*
*Nos. J6-J10 (5)* 74.00 *149.50*

## EAST AFRICAN FORCES

### FOR USE IN SOMALIA (ITALIAN SOMALILAND)

**Catalogue values for unused stamps in this section are for Never Hinged items.**

12 Pence = 1 Shilling
100 Cents = 1 Shilling

Stamps of Great Britain 1938-42 Overprinted in Blue

***Perf. 14½x14***

**1943, Jan. 15 Wmk. 251**

**1** A101 1p vermilion .80 .65
**2** A101 2p light orange 1.75 1.40
**3** A101 2½p ultramarine .80 *3.75*
**4** A101 3p violet 1.10 .25
**5** A101 5p light brown 1.90 .45
**6** A101 6p rose lilac 1.10 *1.40*
**7** A103 9p dp olive green 1.60 *2.40*
**8** A103 1sh brown 3.00 .25

**On Great Britain No. 249A**

**1946 Wmk. 259** ***Perf. 14***

**9** A104 2sh6p yellow green 16.00 8.00
*Nos. 1-9 (9)* 28.05 *18.55*

Stamps of Great Britain, 1937-42 Surcharged

***Perf. 14½x14***

**1948, May 27 Wmk. 251**

**10** A101 5c on ½p grn (II) 1.40 *2.10*
**11** A101 15c on 1½p lt red brn (II) 2.00 *17.50*
**12** A101 20c on 2p lt org (II) 3.50 *5.00*
**13** A101 25c on 2½p ultra (II) 2.50 *5.00*
**14** A101 30c on 3p vio (II) 2.50 *10.50*
**15** A102 40c on 5p lt brown 1.40 .25
**16** A102 50c on 6p rose lilac .55 *2.25*
**17** A103 75c on 9p dp ol grn 2.25 *21.00*
**18** A103 1sh on 1sh brown 1.40 .25

Great Britain Nos. 249A and 250 Surcharged

**Wmk. 259** ***Perf. 14***

**19** A104 2sh50c on 2sh6p yel grn 5.00 *29.00*
**20** A104 5sh on 5sh dl red 11.00 *45.00*
*Nos. 10-20 (11)* 33.50 *137.85*

Stamps of Great Britain 1937-42 Surcharged

***Perf. 14½x14***

**1950, Jan. 2 Wmk. 251**

**21** A101 5c on ½p grn (II) .25 *3.50*
**22** A101 15c on 1½p lt red brn (II) .85 *19.00*
**23** A101 20c on 2p lt org (II) .85 *8.50*
**24** A101 25c on 2½p ultra (II) .55 *8.50*
**25** A101 30c on 3p violet (II) 1.40 *5.00*
**26** A102 40c on 5p light brn .65 *1.10*
**27** A102 50c on 6p rose lilac .55 *1.10*
**28** A103 75c on 9p deep ol grn 2.25 *8.00*
**29** A103 1sh on 1sh brown .70 *1.75*

Great Britain Nos. 249A and 250 Surcharged

**Wmk. 259** ***Perf. 14***

**30** A104 2sh50c on 2sh 6p yel grn 4.50 *27.50*
**31** A104 5sh on 5sh dull red 12.50 *35.00*
*Nos. 21-31 (11)* 25.05 *118.95*

### FOR USE IN TRIPOLITANIA

**Catalogue values for unused stamps in this section are for Never Hinged items.**

Stamps of Great Britain, 1937-42, Surcharged

**M.A.L.=Military Authority Lire**

*Perf. 14½x14*

**1948, July 1 Wmk. 251**

| | | | | |
|---|---|---|---|---|
| 1 | A101 | 1 l on ½p green (II) | 1.00 | *1.75* |
| 2 | A101 | 2 l on 1p ver (II) | .35 | .25 |
| 3 | A101 | 3 l on 1½p lt red brn (II) | .35 | *.55* |
| 4 | A101 | 4 l on 2p lt org (II) | .35 | *.80* |
| 5 | A101 | 5 l on 2½p ultra (II) | .35 | .25 |
| 6 | A101 | 6 l on 3p violet (II) | .35 | *.45* |
| 7 | A102 | 10 l on 5p lt brown | .35 | .25 |
| 8 | A102 | 12 l on 6p rose lilac | .35 | .25 |
| 9 | A103 | 18 l on 9p dp ol grn | .90 | *.75* |
| 10 | A103 | 24 l on 1sh brown | .80 | *1.75* |

Great Britain Nos. 249A, 250 and 251A Surcharged

**Wmk. 259** ***Perf. 14***

| | | | | |
|---|---|---|---|---|
| 11 | A104 | 60 l on 2sh6p yel grn | 4.00 | *9.75* |
| 12 | A104 | 120 l on 5sh dl red | 17.50 | *21.00* |
| 13 | A105 | 240 l on 10sh ultra | 25.00 | *110.00* |
| | | *Nos. 1-13 (13)* | 51.65 | *147.80* |

Stamps of Great Britain 1937-42 Surcharged

*Perf. 14½x14*

**1950, Feb. 6 Wmk. 251**

| | | | | |
|---|---|---|---|---|
| 14 | A101 | 1 l on ½p green (II) | 3.00 | *14.00* |
| 15 | A101 | 2 l on 1p ver (II) | 2.75 | *.45* |
| 16 | A101 | 3 l on 1½p lt red brn (II) | 1.10 | *14.00* |
| 17 | A101 | 4 l on 2p lt org (II) | 1.10 | *5.00* |
| 18 | A101 | 5 l on 2½p ultra (II) | .80 | *.80* |
| 19 | A101 | 6 l on 3p violet (II) | 2.00 | *3.75* |
| 20 | A102 | 10 l on 5p lt brown | .55 | *4.50* |
| 21 | A102 | 12 l on 6p rose lilac | 2.25 | .55 |
| 22 | A103 | 18 l on 9p dp ol grn | 2.50 | *2.75* |
| 23 | A103 | 24 l on 1sh brown | 2.75 | *4.25* |

Great Britain Nos. 249A, 250 and 251A Surcharged

**Wmk. 259** ***Perf. 14***

| | | | | |
|---|---|---|---|---|
| 24 | A104 | 60 l on 2sh6p yel grn | 7.50 | *14.00* |
| 25 | A104 | 120 l on 5sh dl red | 22.50 | *25.00* |
| 26 | A105 | 240 l on 10sh ultra | 42.50 | *57.50* |
| | | *Nos. 14-26 (13)* | 91.30 | *146.55* |

**Great Britain Nos. 280-284 Surcharged like Nos. 14-23**

*Perf. 14½x14*

**1951, May 3 Wmk. 251**

| | | | | |
|---|---|---|---|---|
| 27 | A101 | 1 l on ½p lt org | .25 | *7.00* |
| 28 | A101 | 2 l on 1p ultra | .25 | *1.10* |
| 29 | A101 | 3 l on 1½p green | .35 | *9.25* |
| 30 | A101 | 4 l on 2p lt red brown | .25 | *1.40* |
| 31 | A101 | 5 l on 2½p ver | .30 | *8.50* |

**Great Britain Nos. 286-288 Surcharged**

**1951, May 3 Wmk. 259** ***Perf. 11x12***

| | | | | |
|---|---|---|---|---|
| 32 | A121 | 60 l on 2sh6p grn | 6.25 | *25.00* |
| 33 | A121 | 120 l on 5sh dl red | 10.00 | *30.00* |
| 34 | A122 | 240 l on 10sh ultra | 42.50 | *57.50* |
| | | *Nos. 27-34 (8)* | 60.15 | *139.75* |

Surcharge arranged to fit the design on #34.

## POSTAGE DUE STAMPS

**Catalogue values for unused stamps in this section are for Never Hinged items.**

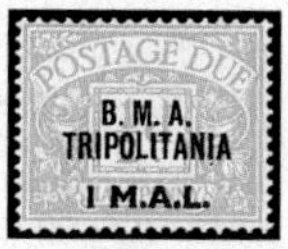


Great Britain Nos. J26-J29, J32 Surcharged

**1948 Wmk. 251** ***Perf. 14x14½***

| | | | | |
|---|---|---|---|---|
| J1 | D1 | 1 l on ½p emer | 6.25 | *57.50* |
| J2 | D1 | 2 l on 1p car rose | 2.75 | *30.00* |
| J3 | D1 | 4 l on 2p blk brn | 8.50 | *37.50* |
| J4 | D1 | 6 l on 3p violet | 8.50 | *24.00* |
| J5 | D1 | 24 l on 1sh blue | 32.50 | *110.00* |
| | | *Nos. J1-J5 (5)* | 58.50 | *259.00* |

Great Britain Nos. J26-J29, J32 Surcharged

**1950, Feb. 6**

| | | | | |
|---|---|---|---|---|
| J6 | D1 | 1 l on ½p emer | 14.00 | *92.50* |
| J7 | D1 | 2 l on 1p car rose | 3.00 | *30.00* |
| J8 | D1 | 4 l on 2p blk brn | 4.50 | *40.00* |
| J9 | D1 | 6 l on 3p violet | 21.00 | *70.00* |
| J10 | D1 | 24 l on 1sh blue | 55.00 | *160.00* |
| | | *Nos. J6-J10 (5)* | 97.50 | *392.50* |

# CHINA

100 Cents = 1 Dollar

Stamps of Hong Kong, 1912-14, Overprinted

**1917 Wmk. 3** ***Perf. 14***

**Ordinary Paper**

| | | | | |
|---|---|---|---|---|
| 1 | A11 | 1c brown | 4.50 | 3.00 |
| 2 | A11 | 2c deep green | 8.00 | .35 |
| 3 | A12 | 4c scarlet | 6.25 | .35 |
| 4 | A13 | 6c orange | 6.25 | .70 |
| 5 | A12 | 8c gray | 14.00 | 1.40 |
| 6 | A11 | 10c ultramarine | 14.00 | .35 |

**Chalky Paper**

| | | | | |
|---|---|---|---|---|
| 7 | A14 | 12c violet, *yel* | 12.50 | 5.00 |
| 8 | A14 | 20c olive grn & vio | 14.00 | .70 |
| 9 | A15 | 25c red vio & dl vio (on #117) | 9.25 | *17.50* |
| 10 | A13 | 30c orange & violet | 40.00 | 6.25 |
| 11 | A14 | 50c black, *emerald* | 40.00 | 6.50 |
| *a.* | | 50c blk, *blue green*, ol back | 75.00 | 1.75 |
| *b.* | | 50c blk, *emerald*, ol back | 50.00 | 9.75 |
| 12 | A11 | $1 blue & vio, *bl* | 80.00 | 2.90 |
| 13 | A14 | $2 black & red | 260.00 | 62.50 |
| 14 | A13 | $3 violet & grn | 625.00 | 210.00 |
| 15 | A14 | $5 red & grn, *bl grn*, ol back | 400.00 | 290.00 |
| 16 | A13 | $10 blk & vio, *red* | 1,000. | 550.00 |
| | | *Nos. 1-16 (16)* | 2,533. | 1,157. |

Stamps of Hong Kong, 1921-26, Overprinted

**1922-27 Wmk. 4**

**Ordinary Paper**

| | | | | |
|---|---|---|---|---|
| 17 | A11 | 1c brown | 2.60 | *4.25* |
| 18 | A11 | 2c green | 4.00 | 2.60 |
| 19 | A12 | 4c scarlet | 7.00 | 2.60 |
| 20 | A13 | 6c orange | 5.00 | 4.75 |
| 21 | A12 | 8c gray | 9.25 | *17.50* |
| 22 | A11 | 10c ultramarine | 10.00 | 4.00 |

**Chalky Paper**

| | | | | |
|---|---|---|---|---|
| 23 | A14 | 20c ol grn & vio | 16.00 | 5.75 |
| 24 | A15 | 25c red violet & dull vio | 26.00 | *80.00* |
| 25 | A14 | 50c blk, *emerald* ('27) | 70.00 | *210.00* |
| 26 | A11 | $1 ultra & vio, *bl* | 85.00 | *70.00* |
| 27 | A14 | $2 black & red | 225.00 | *290.00* |
| | | *Nos. 17-27 (11)* | 459.85 | *691.45* |

# MOROCCO

100 Centimos = 1 Peseta
12 Pence = 1 Shilling
20 Shillings = 1 Pound
100 Centimes = 1 Franc

These stamps were issued for various purposes:

a — For general use at the British Post Offices throughout Morocco.

b — For use in the Spanish Zone of Northern Morocco.

c — For use in the French Zone of Southern Morocco.

d — For use in the International Zone of Tangier.

For convenience these stamps are listed in four groups according to the coinage expressed or surcharged on the stamps, namely:

#1-108: Value expressed in Spanish currency.
#201-280: Value in British currency.
#401-440: Value in French currency.
#501-611: Stamps overprinted "Tangier."

## Spanish Currency

Gibraltar Stamps of 1889-95 Overprinted

**1898 Wmk. 2** ***Perf. 14***

**Black Overprint**

| | | | | |
|---|---|---|---|---|
| 1 | A11 | 5c green | 3.00 | *3.00* |
| 2 | A11 | 10c carmine rose | 5.00 | .85 |
| *b.* | | Double overprint | 625.00 | |
| 3 | A11 | 20c olive green | 11.00 | 6.25 |
| 4 | A11 | 25c ultramarine | 4.50 | .70 |
| 5 | A11 | 40c orange brown | 7.00 | 3.75 |
| 6 | A11 | 50c violet | 20.00 | *26.00* |
| 7 | A11 | 1pe bister & blue | 20.00 | *30.00* |
| 8 | A11 | 2pe blk & car rose | 25.00 | *30.00* |
| | | *Nos. 1-8 (8)* | 95.50 | *100.55* |

**Dark Blue Overprint**

| | | | | |
|---|---|---|---|---|
| 9 | A11 | 40c orange brown | *50.00* | *35.00* |
| 10 | A11 | 50c violet | 14.00 | 14.00 |
| 11 | A11 | 1pe bister & blue | *175.00* | *210.00* |

**Inverted "V" for "A"**

| | | | | |
|---|---|---|---|---|
| *1a* | A11 | 5c | 40.00 | *50.00* |
| *2a* | A11 | 10c | 260.00 | 310.00 |
| *3a* | A11 | 20c | 85.00 | *95.00* |
| *4a* | A11 | 25c | 140.00 | *150.00* |
| *5a* | A11 | 40c | 190.00 | 210.00 |
| *6a* | A11 | 50c | 290.00 | *375.00* |
| *7a* | A11 | 1pe | 275.00 | *400.00* |
| *8a* | A11 | 2pe | 350.00 | *400.00* |

**Overprinted in Black**

(Narrower "M," ear of "g" horiz.)

**1899**

| | | | | |
|---|---|---|---|---|
| 12 | A11 | 5c green | .55 | *1.10* |
| 13 | A11 | 10c carmine rose | 2.90 | .35 |
| 14 | A11 | 20c olive green | 8.00 | .80 |
| 15 | A11 | 25c ultramarine | 12.50 | 1.00 |
| 16 | A11 | 40c orange brown | 47.50 | 35.00 |
| 17 | A11 | 50c violet | 11.00 | 4.00 |
| 18 | A11 | 1pe bister & blue | 32.50 | *50.00* |
| 19 | A11 | 2pe blk & car rose | 62.50 | *55.00* |
| | | *Nos. 12-19 (8)* | 177.45 | *147.25* |

**"M" with long serif**

| | | | | |
|---|---|---|---|---|
| *12a* | A11 | 5c | 10.00 | *15.00* |
| *13a* | A11 | 10c | 11.50 | *13.50* |
| *14a* | A11 | 20c | 40.00 | *42.50* |
| *15a* | A11 | 25c | 50.00 | *55.00* |
| *16a* | A11 | 40c | 260.00 | *290.00* |
| *17a* | A11 | 50c | 125.00 | *140.00* |
| *18a* | A11 | 1pe | *175.00* | *290.00* |
| *19a* | A11 | 2pe | 375.00 | *400.00* |

**Type of Gibraltar, 1903, with Value in Spanish Currency, Overprinted**

**1903-05**

| | | | | |
|---|---|---|---|---|
| 20 | A12 | 5c gray grn & bl grn | 11.00 | 4.00 |
| 21 | A12 | 10c violet, *red* | 9.75 | .45 |
| 22 | A12 | 20c gray grn & car rose ('04) | 20.00 | *52.50* |
| 23 | A12 | 25c vio & blk, *bl* | 9.25 | .35 |
| 24 | A12 | 50c violet | 100.00 | *190.00* |
| 25 | A12 | 1pe blk & car rose | 47.50 | *175.00* |
| 26 | A12 | 2pe black & ultra | 57.50 | *140.00* |
| | | *Nos. 20-26 (7)* | 255.00 | *562.30* |

**"M" with long serif**

| | | | | |
|---|---|---|---|---|
| *20a* | A12 | 5c | 57.50 | *62.50* |
| *21a* | A12 | 10c | 50.00 | 45.00 |
| *22a* | A12 | 20c | 110.00 | *210.00* |
| *23a* | A12 | 25c | 57.50 | 50.00 |
| *24a* | A12 | 50c | 400.00 | *700.00* |
| *25a* | A12 | 1pe | 260.00 | *575.00* |
| *26a* | A12 | 2pe | 300.00 | *550.00* |

**1905-06 Wmk. 3 Chalky Paper**

| | | | | |
|---|---|---|---|---|
| 27 | A12 | 5c gray grn & bl grn | 11.00 | *3.50* |
| 28 | A12 | 10c violet, *red* | 12.50 | 2.25 |
| 29 | A12 | 20c gray grn & car rose ('06) | 6.25 | *35.00* |
| 30 | A12 | 25c violet & blk, *bl* ('06) | 45.00 | 9.75 |
| 31 | A12 | 50c violet | 8.50 | *50.00* |
| 32 | A12 | 1pe blk & car rose | 32.50 | *92.50* |
| 33 | A12 | 2pe black & ultra | 18.00 | *40.00* |
| | | *Nos. 27-33 (7)* | 133.75 | *233.00* |

No. 29 is on ordinary paper. Nos. 27 and 28 are on both ordinary and chalky paper.

**"M" with long serif**

| | | | | |
|---|---|---|---|---|
| *27a* | A12 | 5c | 62.50 | 50.00 |
| *28a* | A12 | 10c | 62.50 | 42.50 |
| *29a* | A12 | 20c | 57.50 | *175.00* |
| *30a* | A12 | 25c | 350.00 | 175.00 |
| *31a* | A12 | 50c | 175.00 | *290.00* |
| *32a* | A12 | 1pe | 225.00 | *375.00* |
| *33a* | A12 | 2pe | 210.00 | *290.00* |

Numerous other minor overprint varieties exist of Nos. 1-33.

**British Stamps of 1902-10 Surcharged in Spanish Currency**

#34-42, 46-48

#43-45

**1907-10 Wmk. 30**

| | | | | |
|---|---|---|---|---|
| 34 | A66 | 5c on ½p pale grn | 9.25 | .25 |
| 35 | A66 | 10c on 1p car | 13.50 | .25 |
| 36 | A67 | 15c on 1½p vio & grn | 3.50 | .25 |
| *a.* | | "1" of "15" omitted | 5,400. | |
| 37 | A68 | 20c on 2p grn & car | 3.00 | .25 |
| 38 | A66 | 25c on 2½p ultra | 2.00 | .25 |
| 39 | A70 | 40c on 4p brn & grn | 1.40 | *3.50* |
| 40 | A70 | 40c on 4p org ('10) | 1.10 | .70 |
| 41 | A71 | 50c on 5p lil & ultra | 2.25 | *3.75* |
| 42 | A73 | 1pe on 10p car rose & vio | 25.00 | *14.00* |

**Wmk. 31**

| | | | | |
|---|---|---|---|---|
| 43 | A75 | 3pe on 2sh6p vio | 24.00 | *29.00* |
| 44 | A76 | 6pe on 5sh car rose | 40.00 | *52.50* |
| 45 | A77 | 12pe on 10sh ultra | 85.00 | 85.00 |
| | | *Nos. 34-45 (12)* | 210.00 | *189.70* |

Nos. 36-37, 39-43 are on chalky paper.

**Great Britain Nos. 153, 154 and 148 Surcharged**

**1912 Wmk. 30** ***Perf. 15x14***

| | | | | |
|---|---|---|---|---|
| 46 | A80 | 5c on ½p yel grn | 3.50 | .25 |
| 47 | A81 | 10c on 1p scarlet | 1.10 | .25 |
| 48 | A66 | 25c on 2½p ultra | 42.50 | 30.00 |
| | | *Nos. 46-48 (3)* | 47.10 | 30.50 |

**British Stamps of 1912-18 Surcharged in Black or Carmine**

c

d

e

**1914-18** **Wmk. 33**

49 A82(a) 5c on ½p grn .85 .25
50 A83(d) 10c on 1p scar 1.75 .25
51 A84(c) 15c on 1 ½p red brn('15) 1.10 .25
52 A85(d) 20c on 2p org (I) 1.10 .25
53 A86(d) 25c on 2 ½p ultra 2.00 .25
54 A90(d) 1pe on 10p lt bl 4.00 *8.00*

**Wmk. 34**

***Perf. 11x12***

55 A91(e) 3pe on 2sh6p lt brn 35.00 *160.00*
*a.* 3pe on 2sh6p dark brown 45.00 *125.00*
56 A91(e) 6pe on 5sh car 32.50 *55.00*
*a.* 6pe on 5sh light carmine 150.00 *210.00*
57 A91(e) 12pe on 10sh dk bl(C) 110.00 *190.00*
*a.* 12pe on 10sh blue 100.00 *190.00*
*Nos. 49-57 (9)* 188.30 *414.25*

**Great Britain Nos. 159, 165 Surcharged in Spanish Currency**

f

g

**1917-23** **Wmk. 33** ***Perf. 15x14***

58 A82(f) 3c on ½p green 1.40 *5.00*
59 A88(g) 40c on 4p sl green 3.50 *4.50*

**Great Britain Nos. 189, 191, 179 Surcharged in Spanish Currency**

**1926** **Wmk. 35**

60 A84(c) 15c on 1 ½p red brn 8.50 *26.00*
61 A86(d) 25c on 2 ½p ultra 2.90 *2.90*

**Wmk. 34**

***Perf. 11x12***

62 A91(e) 3pe on 2sh6p brn 26.00 *85.00*
*Nos. 60-62 (3)* 37.40 *113.90*

**British Stamps of 1924 Surcharged in Spanish Currency**

**1929-31** **Wmk. 35** ***Perf. 15x14***

63 A82(a) 5c on ½p grn('31) 3.00 *17.50*
64 A83(d) 10c on 1p scar 21.00 *30.00*
65 A85(d) 20c on 2p org (II) ('31) 3.50 *10.00*
66 A88(g) 40c on 4p sl grn ('30) 2.90 2.90
*Nos. 63-66 (4)* 30.40 *60.40*

**Silver Jubilee Issue**

Great Britain Nos. 226-229 Srchd. in Blue or Red

**1935, May 8** ***Perf. 14½x14***

67 A98 5c on ½p dk grn 1.10 1.10
68 A98 10c on 1p car 3.00 2.50
*a.* Pair, one reading "CEN-TIMES" 1,600. 1,800.
69 A98 15c on 1 ½p red brn 6.25 *20.00*
70 A98 25c on 2 ½p ultra (R) 4.00 2.50
*Nos. 67-70 (4)* 14.35 *26.10*

25th anniv. of the reign of King George V.

**Catalogue values for unused stamps in this section, from this point to the end of the section, are for Never Hinged items.**

**Great Britain Nos. 210-214, 216, 219 Surcharged in Spanish Currency**

**1935-37** **Photo.**

71 A97(a) 5c on ½p dk grn('36) 1.25 *21.00*
72 A97(d) 10c on 1p car 3.25 *11.00*
73 A97(c) 15c on 1 ½p red brn 7.00 3.75
74 A97(d) 20c on 2p red org ('36) .75 .30
75 A97(d) 25c on 2 ½p ultra('36) 1.75 *5.00*
76 A97(d) 40c on 4p dk sl grn ('37) .75 *3.50*
77 A97(d) 1pe on 10p Prus bl ('37) 7.00 .35
*Nos. 71-77 (7)* 21.75 *44.90*

Great Britain Nos. 230-233 Surcharged

**"MOROCCO" 14mm**

**1936** **Wmk. 250**

78 A99 5c on ½p dk green .25 .25
79 A99 10c on 1p crimson .55 *2.25*
*a.* "Morocco" 15mm long 4.00 *16.00*
80 A99 15c on 1 ½p red brown .25 .25
81 A99 25c on 2 ½p brt ultra .25 .25
*Nos. 78-81 (4)* 1.30 *3.00*

**Great Britain #234 Surcharged in Blue**

***Perf. 14½x14***

**1937, May 13** **Wmk. 251**

82 A100 15c on 1 ½p purple brn .80 .80

Coronation of George VI and Elizabeth.

**Great Britain Nos. 235-237, 239, 241, 244 Surcharged in Blue or Black**

h

**1937-40**

83 A101 5c on ½p dp grn (Bl) 1.40 .35
84 A101 10c on 1p scarlet 1.10 .25
85 A101 15c on 1 ½p red brown (Bl) 1.40 .30
86 A101 25c on 2 ½p brt ultra 2.25 1.40
87 A102 40c on 4p gray green ('40) 35.00 15.00
88 A103 70c on 7p emer ('40) 2.00 *16.00*
*Nos. 83-88 (6)* 43.15 *33.30*

Great Britain Nos. 252-254, 256 Surcharged in Blue or Black

**1940, May 6**

89 A106 5c on ½p deep grn (Bl) .35 *3.00*
90 A106 10c on 1p scarlet 4.25 *2.90*
91 A106 15c on 1 ½p red brn (Bl) .80 *2.90*
92 A106 25c on 2 ½p brt ultra .90 *1.10*
*Nos. 89-92 (4)* 6.30 *9.90*

Centenary of the postage stamp.

**Great Britain Nos. 267 and 268 Surcharged in Black**

i

j

***Perf. 14½x14, 14x14½***

**1948, Apr. 26** **Wmk. 251**

93 A109(i) 25c on 2 ½p 1.10 .35
94 A110(j) 45pe on £1 19.00 *25.00*

25th anniv. of the marriage of King George VI and Queen Elizabeth.

**Great Britain Nos. 271-274 Surcharged "MOROCCO AGENCIES" and New Value**

**1948, July 29** ***Perf. 14½x14***

95 A113 25c on 2 ½p brt ultra .55 *1.40*
96 A114 30c on 3p dp vio .55 *1.40*
97 A115 60c on 6p red vio .55 *1.40*
98 A116 1.20pe on 1sh dk brn .70 *1.40*
*a.* Double surcharge 925.00
*Nos. 95-98 (4)* 2.35 *5.60*

1948 Olympic Games, Wembley, July-Aug.

A square of dots obliterates the original denomination on No. 98.

**Great Britain Nos. 280-282, 284-285, 247 Surcharged Type "h"**

**1951-52** **Wmk. 251** ***Perf. 14½x14***

99 A101 5c on ½p lt orange 2.25 *5.00*
100 A101 10c on 1p ultra 3.75 *8.50*
101 A101 15c on 1 ½p green 2.00 *19.00*
102 A101 25c on 2 ½p ver 2.00 *11.00*
103 A102 40c on 4p ultra ('52) .70 *11.50*
104 A103 1pe on 10p ryl bl ('52) 2.50 *4.00*
*Nos. 99-104 (6)* 13.20 *59.00*

**Great Britain Nos. 292-293 Surcharged Type "h"**

**1954-55** **Wmk. 298**

105 A126 5c on ½c red org .25 *2.00*
106 A126 10c on 1p ultra ('55) .50 *3.00*

**Great Britain Nos. 317 and 323 Surcharged type "h"**

**1956** **Wmk. 308** ***Perf. 14x14½***

107 A126 5c on ½p red org .25 *2.00*
108 A128 40c on 4p ultra 1.10 *3.00*

**BRITISH CURRENCY**

Stamps of Morocco Agencies were accepted for postage in Great Britain, starting in mid-1950. Examples with contemporaneous Morocco cancellations sell for more.

**British Stamps of 1902-11 Overprinted**

a

b

**Overprint "a" 14½mm long**

**1907-12** **Wmk. 30** ***Perf. 14***

**Ordinary Paper**

201 A66 ½p pale yel grn 2.50 *9.75*
202 A66 1p carmine 11.00 6.25

**Chalky Paper**

203 A68 2p green & car 11.50 6.25
204 A70 4p brown & grn 4.25 *4.50*
205 A70 4p orange ('12) 11.50 *12.50*
*a.* Perf. 15x14 25.00 *27.50*
206 A66 6p dull vio 17.00 *21.00*
207 A74 1sh car rose & grn 30.00 *19.00*

**Overprinted Type "b"**

**Wmk. 31**

208 A75 2sh6p violet 92.50 *140.00*
*Nos. 201-208 (8)* 180.25 *219.25*

**British Stamps of 1912-18 Overprinted Type "a"**

***Perf. 14½x14, 15x14***

**1914-21** **Wmk. 33**

209 A82 ½p green ('18) 4.00 .55
210 A83 1p scarlet ('17) 1.00 .25
211 A84 1 ½p red brn ('21) 3.75 *14.00*
212 A85 2p orange ('18) 4.50 .70
213 A87 3p violet ('21) 1.40 .40
214 A88 4p slate grn ('21) 3.75 1.40
215 A89 6p dull vio ('21) 5.50 *17.50*
216 A90 1sh bister ('17) 6.25 1.40

c

**Wmk. 34** ***Perf. 11x12***

217 A91 2sh6p lt brown 42.50 *57.50*
*a.* 2sh6p brown 55.00 35.00
*b.* 2sh6p black brown 52.50 *62.50*
*c.* Double overprint 1,900. 1,350.
*Nos. 209-217 (9)* 72.65 *93.70*

**Same Overprint on Great Britain Nos. 179-180**

**1925-31**

218 A91 2sh6p gray brown 42.50 29.00
219 A91 5sh car rose ('31) 62.50 *100.00*

**British Stamps of 1924 Overprinted Type "a" (14½mm long)**

**1925-31** **Wmk. 35** ***Perf. 15x14***

220 A82 ½p green 2.25 .55
221 A84 1 ½p red brn ('31) 13.50 *15.00*
222 A85 2p dp org (Die II) 2.50 1.10
223 A86 2 ½p ultra 2.50 *5.75*
224 A89 6p red vio ('31) 2.25 *9.50*
225 A90 1sh bister 19.00 5.75
*Nos. 220-225 (6)* 42.00 *37.65*

**Silver Jubilee Issue**
**Great Britain Nos. 226-229 Overprinted in Blue or Red**

**1935, May 8** ***Perf. 14½x14***

226 A98 ½p dark green (Bl) 1.40 *7.50*
227 A98 1p carmine (Bl) 1.40 *7.50*
228 A98 1 ½p red brown (Bl) 2.50 *11.00*
229 A98 2 ½p ultramarine (R) 2.90 2.90
*Nos. 226-229 (4)* 8.20 *28.90*

25th anniversary of the reign of King George V.

**British Stamps of 1924 Overprinted Type "a" (15½mm long)**

**1935-36**

230 A82 ½p green 9.50 *45.00*
231 A86 2 ½p ultra *110.00* 35.00
232 A88 4p slate green 8.00 *40.00*
233 A89 6p red violet 1.10 .70
234 A90 1sh bister 62.50 57.50
*Nos. 230-234 (5)* 191.10 *178.20*

**British Stamps of 1934-36 Overprinted "MOROCCO AGENCIES"**

**1935-36**

235 A97 1p carmine 3.50 *16.00*
236 A97 1 ½p red brn ('36) 3.50 *19.00*
237 A97 2p red org ('36) 1.40 *9.00*
238 A97 2 ½p ultra ('36) 2.00 *4.75*
239 A97 3p dk violet ('36) .55 .35
240 A97 4p dk slate grn ('36) .55 .35
241 A97 1sh bis brn ('36) .90 *4.00*

### Overprinted Type "c"

**Wmk. 34**

***Perf. 11x12***

| | | | | |
|---|---|---|---|---|
| 242 | A91 | 2sh6p brown | 45.00 | 70.00 |
| 243 | A91 | 5sh carmine ('37) | 27.50 | 110.00 |
| | | *Nos. 235-243 (9)* | 84.90 | 233.45 |

**Catalogue values for unused stamps in this section, from this point to the end of the section, are for Never Hinged items.**

Great Britain Nos. 231, 233 Overprinted

### "MOROCCO" 14mm

**1936 Wmk. 250 *Perf. 14½x14***

| | | | | |
|---|---|---|---|---|
| 244 | A99 | 1p crimson | .25 | .25 |
| a. | | "Morocco" 15mm long | 7.00 | 19.00 |
| 245 | A99 | 2½p bright ultra | .25 | .25 |
| a. | | "Morocco" 15mm long | 1.10 | 4.75 |

### Great Britain Nos. 258-263, 241-248, 266, 249A-250 Overprinted "MOROCCO AGENCIES" (14½mm long)

**1949, Aug. 16 Wmk. 251**

| | | | | |
|---|---|---|---|---|
| 246 | A101 | ½p green | 2.00 | 8.00 |
| 247 | A101 | 1p vermilion | 3.00 | 10.00 |
| 248 | A101 | 1½p lt red brown | 3.00 | 9.50 |
| 249 | A101 | 2p lt orange | 3.50 | 10.00 |
| 250 | A101 | 2½p ultra | 3.75 | 11.50 |
| 251 | A101 | 3p violet | 1.75 | 2.00 |
| 252 | A102 | 4p gray green | .55 | 1.40 |
| 253 | A102 | 5p lt brown | 3.50 | 17.00 |
| 254 | A102 | 6p rose lilac | 1.75 | 1.75 |
| 255 | A103 | 7p emerald | .55 | 18.00 |
| 256 | A103 | 8p brt rose | 3.50 | 7.50 |
| 257 | A103 | 9p dp olive grn | .55 | 12.50 |
| 258 | A103 | 10p royal blue | .55 | 7.50 |
| 259 | A103 | 11p violet brn | .80 | 8.50 |
| 260 | A103 | 1sh brown | 3.00 | 7.00 |

### "MOROCCO AGENCIES"

**17½mm long**

**Wmk. 259**

***Perf. 14***

| | | | | |
|---|---|---|---|---|
| 261 | A104 | 2sh6p yellow grn | 18.00 | 40.00 |
| 262 | A104 | 5sh dull red | 32.50 | 70.00 |
| | | *Nos. 246-262 (17)* | 82.25 | 242.15 |

### Great Britain Nos. 280-284, 286-287 Overprinted "MOROCCO AGENCIES" (14½mm long)

***Perf. 14½x14***

**1951, May 3 Wmk. 251**

| | | | | |
|---|---|---|---|---|
| 263 | A101 | ½p lt orange | 2.25 | 1.10 |
| 264 | A101 | 1p ultra | 2.25 | 1.60 |
| 265 | A101 | 1½p green | 2.25 | 3.00 |
| 266 | A101 | 2p lt red brown | 2.50 | 4.50 |
| 267 | A101 | 2½p vermilion | 2.25 | 4.75 |

### "MOROCCO AGENCIES"

**17½mm long**

**Wmk. 259**

***Perf. 11x12***

| | | | | |
|---|---|---|---|---|
| 268 | A121 | 2sh6p green | 15.00 | 24.00 |
| 269 | A121 | 5sh dull red | 15.00 | 26.00 |
| | | *Nos. 263-269 (7)* | 41.50 | 64.95 |

### Great Britain Nos. 292-296, 298-300, 302 and 306 Overprinted "MOROCCO AGENCIES" (14½mm long)

**1952-55 Wmk. 298 *Perf. 14½x14***

| | | | | |
|---|---|---|---|---|
| 270 | A126 | ½p red orange | .25 | .25 |
| 271 | A126 | 1p ultramarine | .25 | 2.00 |
| 272 | A126 | 1½p green ('52) | .25 | .25 |
| 273 | A126 | 2p red brown | .30 | 2.25 |
| 274 | A127 | 2½p scarlet ('52) | .25 | 1.40 |
| 275 | A128 | 4p ultra ('55) | 1.75 | 4.00 |
| 276 | A129 | 5p light brown | .75 | .70 |
| 277 | A129 | 6p lilac rose ('55) | 1.00 | 4.00 |
| 278 | A130 | 8p bright rose | .80 | .80 |
| 279 | A131 | 1sh brown | .80 | .70 |
| | | *Nos. 270-279 (10)* | 6.40 | 16.35 |

### Same Ovpt. on Great Britain No. 321

**1956 Wmk. 308**

| | | | | |
|---|---|---|---|---|
| 280 | A127 | 2½p scarlet | 1.00 | 3.75 |

### French Currency

### British Stamps of 1912-22 Surcharged in French Currency in Red or Black

h

i

***Perf. 14½x14, 15x14***

**1917-24 Wmk. 33**

| | | | | |
|---|---|---|---|---|
| 401 | A82(h) | 3c on ½p green (R) | 1.10 | 2.90 |
| 402 | A82(h) | 5c on ½p green | .45 | 1.75 |
| 403 | A83(h) | 10c on 1p scarlet | 3.75 | .45 |
| 404 | A84(h) | 15c on 1½p red brn | 2.90 | .25 |
| 405 | A86(h) | 25c on 2½p ultra | 2.25 | .25 |
| 406 | A88(h) | 40c on 4p slate grn | 2.90 | 1.75 |
| 407 | A89(h) | 50c on 5p yel brn ('23) | .90 | 3.00 |
| 408 | A90(h) | 75c on 9p ol grn ('24) | 1.10 | .85 |
| 409 | A90(i) | 1fr on 10p lt blue | 8.00 | 3.50 |
| | | *Nos. 401-409 (9)* | 23.35 | 14.70 |

### Great Britain No. 179 Surcharged

k

**1924 Wmk. 34 *Perf. 11x12***

| | | | | |
|---|---|---|---|---|
| 410 | A91(k) | 3fr on 2sh6p brn | 8.50 | 1.75 |

### British Stamps of 1924 Surcharged in French Currency as in 1917-24

**1925-26 Wmk. 35 *Perf. 15x14***

| | | | | |
|---|---|---|---|---|
| 411 | A82(h) | 5c on ½p green | .35 | 7.50 |
| 412 | A83(h) | 10c on 1p scarlet | .35 | 2.25 |
| 413 | A84(h) | 15c on 1½p red brn | 1.10 | 2.00 |
| 414 | A86(h) | 25c on 2½p ultra | 1.75 | .55 |
| 415 | A88(h) | 40c on 4p sl green | .70 | .90 |
| 416 | A89(h) | 50c on 5p yel brown | 1.75 | .25 |
| 417 | A90(h) | 75c on 9p ol green | 4.00 | .25 |
| 418 | A90(i) | 1fr on 10p dl blue | 1.40 | .25 |
| | | *Nos. 411-418 (8)* | 11.40 | 13.95 |

### Great Britain Nos. 180, 198 and 200 Surcharged type "k"

**1932 Wmk. 34 *Perf. 11x12***

| | | | | |
|---|---|---|---|---|
| 419 | A91 | 6fr on 5sh car rose | 42.50 | 47.50 |

**1934 Wmk. 35 *Perf. 14½x14***

| | | | | |
|---|---|---|---|---|
| 420 | A90 | 90c on 9p ol green | 18.00 | 8.50 |
| 421 | A90 | 1.50fr on 1sh bister | 11.50 | 2.50 |

### Silver Jubilee Issue

### Great Britain Nos. 226-229 Surcharged in Blue or Red

**1935, May 8 *Perf. 14½x14***

| | | | | |
|---|---|---|---|---|
| 422 | A98 | 5c on ½p dk green | .25 | .25 |
| 423 | A98 | 10c on 1p carmine | 3.00 | .85 |
| 424 | A98 | 15c on 1½p red brn | .40 | .55 |
| 425 | A98 | 25c on 2½p ultra (R) | .25 | .35 |
| | | *Nos. 422-425 (4)* | 3.90 | 2.00 |

25th anniv. of the reign of King George V.

### British Stamps of 1934-36 Surcharged Types "h" or "k"

***Perf. 14½x14***

**1935-37 Photo. Wmk. 35**

| | | | | |
|---|---|---|---|---|
| 426 | A97(h) | 5c on ½p dk grn | .55 | 5.75 |
| 427 | A97(h) | 10c on 1p car ('36) | .40 | .35 |
| 428 | A97(h) | 15c on 1½p red brn | 5.50 | 6.25 |
| 429 | A97(h) | 25c on 2½p ultra | .35 | .25 |
| 430 | A97(h) | 40c on 4p dk sl grn | .35 | .25 |
| 431 | A97(h) | 50c on 5p yel brn | .35 | .25 |
| 432 | A97(h) | 90c on 9p dk ol grn | .40 | 2.00 |
| 433 | A97(k) | 1fr on 10p Prus bl | .35 | .35 |
| 434 | A97(h) | 1.50fr on 1sh bister brn ('37) | .85 | 3.75 |

### Waterlow Printing

**Wmk. 34 *Perf. 11x12***

| | | | | |
|---|---|---|---|---|
| 435 | A91(k) | 3fr on 2sh6p brn | 5.50 | 14.00 |
| 436 | A91(k) | 6fr on 5sh car ('36) | 7.00 | 24.00 |
| | | *Nos. 426-436 (11)* | 21.60 | 57.20 |

Great Britain Nos. 230, 232 Surcharged

**1936 Wmk. 250 *Perf. 14½x14***

| | | | | |
|---|---|---|---|---|
| 437 | A99 | 5c on ½p dark green | .25 | .25 |
| 438 | A99 | 15c on 1½p red brown | .25 | .25 |

### Great Britain No. 234 Surcharged in Blue

**1937, May 13 Wmk. 251**

| | | | | |
|---|---|---|---|---|
| 439 | A100 | 15c on 1½p purple brn | .35 | .25 |

Coronation of George VI and Elizabeth.

Great Britain No. 235 Surcharged in Blue

**1937**

| | | | | |
|---|---|---|---|---|
| 440 | A101 | 5c on ½p deep green | 2.50 | 2.90 |

### For Use in the International Zone of Tangier

Great Britain Nos. 187-190 Overprinted in Black — a

**1927 Wmk. 35 *Perf. 15x14***

| | | | | |
|---|---|---|---|---|
| 501 | A82 | ½p green | 3.50 | .25 |
| 502 | A83 | 1p scarlet | 3.50 | .30 |
| 503 | A84 | 1½p red brown | 7.00 | 4.25 |
| 504 | A85 | 2p orange (II) | 3.75 | .25 |
| | | *Nos. 501-504 (4)* | 17.75 | 5.05 |

### Same Overprint on Great Britain Nos. 210-212

**1934-35 Photo. *Perf. 14½x14***

| | | | | |
|---|---|---|---|---|
| 505 | A97 | ½p dark green | 1.40 | 1.75 |
| 506 | A97 | 1p carmine | 4.75 | 2.75 |
| 507 | A97 | 1½p red brown | .55 | .25 |
| | | *Nos. 505-507 (3)* | 6.70 | 4.75 |

### Silver Jubilee Issue

### Great Britain Nos. 226-228 Overprinted in Blue

b

**1935, May 8**

| | | | | |
|---|---|---|---|---|
| 508 | A98 | ½p dark green | 1.40 | 5.75 |
| 509 | A98 | 1p carmine | 16.00 | 17.00 |
| 510 | A98 | 1½p red brown | 1.40 | 1.10 |
| | | *Nos. 508-510 (3)* | 18.80 | 23.85 |

25th anniv. of the reign of King George V.

### Great Britain Nos. 230-232 Overprinted Type "a"

**1936 Wmk. 250**

| | | | | |
|---|---|---|---|---|
| 511 | A99 | ½p dark green | .25 | .25 |
| 512 | A99 | 1p crimson | .25 | .25 |
| 513 | A99 | 1½p red brown | .25 | .25 |
| | | *Nos. 511-513 (3)* | .75 | .75 |

### Great Britain No. 234 Overprinted Type "b" in Blue

**1937, May 13 Wmk. 251**

| | | | | |
|---|---|---|---|---|
| 514 | A100 | 1½p purple brown | .55 | .55 |

Coronation of George VI and Elizabeth.

Great Britain Nos. 235-237 Overprinted in Blue or Black — c

**1937 *Perf. 14½x14***

| | | | | |
|---|---|---|---|---|
| 515 | A101 | ½p deep green (Bl) | 2.75 | 1.75 |
| 516 | A101 | 1p scarlet (Bk) | 8.00 | 1.75 |
| 517 | A101 | 1½p red brown (Bl) | 2.75 | .30 |
| | | *Nos. 515-517 (3)* | 13.50 | 3.80 |

### Great Britain Nos. 252-254 Ovptd. Type "a" in Blue or Black

**1940, May 6**

| | | | | |
|---|---|---|---|---|
| 518 | A106 | ½p deep green (Bl) | .35 | 5.50 |
| 519 | A106 | 1p scarlet (Bk) | .50 | .60 |
| 520 | A106 | 1½p red brown (Bl) | 2.25 | 5.75 |
| | | *Nos. 518-520 (3)* | 3.10 | 11.85 |

Centenary of the postage stamp.

### Great Britain Nos. 258 and 259 Overprinted Type "c" in Blue or Black

**1944-45**

| | | | | |
|---|---|---|---|---|
| 521 | A101 | ½p green (Bl) | 12.50 | 5.00 |
| 522 | A101 | 1p ver (Bk) ('45) | 12.50 | 3.50 |

**Catalogue values for unused stamps in this section, from this point to the end of the section, are for Never Hinged items.**

### Great Britain Nos. 264-265 Overprinted

d

e

**1946, June 11**

| | | | | |
|---|---|---|---|---|
| 523 | A107(d) | 2½p bright ultra | .75 | .75 |
| 524 | A108(e) | 3p violet | .75 | 2.25 |

Return to peace at close of World War II.

### Great Britain Nos. 267 and 268 Overprinted Type "a"

**1948, Apr. 26 *Perf. 14½x14, 14x14½***

| | | | | |
|---|---|---|---|---|
| 525 | A109 | 2½p bright ultra | .60 | .25 |
| a. | | Pair, one without overprint | 5,400. | |
| 526 | A110 | £1 dp chalky bl | 22.50 | 29.00 |

25th anniv. of the marriage of King George VI and Queen Elizabeth.

### Great Britain Nos. 271 to 274 Overprinted Type "a"

**1948, July 29 *Perf. 14½x14***

| | | | | |
|---|---|---|---|---|
| 527 | A113 | 2½p bright ultra | 1.10 | 2.25 |
| 528 | A114 | 3p deep violet | 1.10 | 2.25 |
| 529 | A115 | 6p red violet | 1.10 | 2.25 |
| 530 | A116 | 1sh dark brown | 1.10 | 1.40 |
| | | *Nos. 527-530 (4)* | 4.40 | 8.15 |

1948 Olympic Games, Wembley, July-Aug.

### Stamps of Great Britain, 1937-47, and Nos. 249A, 250 and 251A Overprinted Type "c"

**1949, Jan. 1**

| | | | | |
|---|---|---|---|---|
| 531 | A101 | 2p lt org (II) | 5.75 | 7.00 |
| 532 | A101 | 2½p ultra (II) | 2.00 | 7.00 |
| 533 | A101 | 3p violet (II) | .80 | 1.40 |
| 534 | A102 | 4p gray green | 12.50 | 11.50 |
| 535 | A102 | 5p light brown | 4.25 | 22.50 |
| 536 | A102 | 6p rose lilac | .80 | .35 |
| 537 | A103 | 7p emerald | 1.40 | 15.00 |
| 538 | A103 | 8p bright rose | 4.25 | 12.50 |
| 539 | A103 | 9p deep ol grn | 1.40 | 13.50 |
| 540 | A103 | 10p royal blue | 1.40 | 15.00 |

541 A103 11p violet brn 1.75 *12.50*
542 A103 1sh brown 1.40 *3.00*

**Wmk. 259**

***Perf. 14***

543 A104 2sh6p yellow grn 5.00 *13.50*
544 A104 5sh dull red 15.00 *42.50*
545 A105 10sh ultra 50.00 *110.00*
*Nos. 531-545 (15)* 107.70 *287.25*

### Great Britain Nos. 276 to 279 Overprinted Type "a"

***Perf. 14½x14***

**1949, Oct. 10** **Wmk. 251**

546 A117 2½p bright ultra .80 *3.00*
547 A118 3p bright violet .80 *2.00*
548 A119 6p red violet .80 *1.40*
549 A120 1sh brown .80 *3.75*
*Nos. 546-549 (4)* 3.20 *10.15*

### Great Britain Nos. 280-288 Overprinted Type "c" or "a" (Shilling Values)

**1950-51**

550 A101 ½p lt orange 1.00 *1.75*
551 A101 1p ultra 1.10 *3.50*
552 A101 1½p green 1.10 *16.00*
553 A101 2p lt red brn 1.10 *2.90*
554 A101 2½p vermilion 1.10 *5.75*
555 A102 4p ultra ('50) 3.50 3.50

**Wmk. 259**

***Perf. 11x12***

556 A121 2sh6p green 11.00 5.75
557 A121 5sh dull red 17.50 *19.00*
558 A122 10sh ultra 22.50 19.00
*Nos. 550-558 (9)* 59.90 *77.15*

### Great Britain Nos. 292-308 Overprinted Type c

**1952-54** **Wmk. 298** ***Perf. 14½x14***

559 A126 ½p red org ('53) .25 *.35*
560 A126 1p ultra ('53) .25 *.45*
561 A126 1½p green ('52) .25 *.35*
562 A126 2p red brn ('53) .25 *.90*
563 A127 2½p scarlet ('52) .25 *1.10*
564 A127 3p dk pur (Dk Bl) .25 *1.40*
565 A128 4p ultra ('53) .70 *2.25*
566 A129 5p lt brown ('53) .70 *2.25*
567 A129 6p lilac rose .50 .25
568 A129 7p emerald .90 *3.00*
569 A130 8p brt rose ('53) .70 *1.75*
570 A130 9p dp olive grn 1.60 .85
571 A130 10p royal blue 1.60 *3.00*
572 A130 11p violet brn 1.60 *3.75*
573 A131 1sh brown ('53) .55 .80
574 A132 1sh3p dk grn ('53) .75 *4.75*
575 A131 1sh6p dk blue ('53) 1.10 *2.00*
*Nos. 559-575 (17)* 12.20 *29.20*

### Stamp and Type of Great Britain 1955 Overprinted Type a

***Perf. 11x12***

**1955, Sept. 23** **Engr.** **Wmk. 308**

576 A133 2sh6p dark brown 4.00 *10.00*
577 A133 5sh crimson 5.00 *18.00*
578 A133 10sh brt ultra 18.00 *24.00*
*Nos. 576-578 (3)* 27.00 *52.00*

### Coronation Issue Great Britain Nos. 313-316 Overprinted Type a

**1953, June 3** **Photo.** **Wmk. 298**

579 A134 2½p scarlet .50 .40
580 A135 4p brt ultra .90 .65
581 A136 1sh3p dark green 2.75 1.90
582 A137 1sh6p dark blue 3.25 2.25
*Nos. 579-582 (4)* 7.40 5.20

### Great Britain Nos. 317-323, 325 and 332 Overprinted Type c

**1956** **Wmk. 308** ***Perf. 14½x14***

583 A126 ½p red orange .25 *.55*
584 A126 1p ultramarine .35 *.55*
585 A126 1½p green .65 *1.40*
586 A126 2p red brown 1.10 .55
587 A127 2½p scarlet .75 .55
588 A127 3p dark purple .85 *1.00*
589 A128 4p ultra 1.75 *4.00*
590 A129 6p lilac rose 1.10 1.00
591 A132 1sh3p dark green 1.25 *15.00*
*Nos. 583-591 (9)* 8.05 *24.60*

### Great Britain Nos. 317-333 and 309-311 Overprinted 1857-1957 TANGIER

**1957, Apr. 1** **Photo.** **Wmk. 308**

592 A126 ½p red orange .25 .25
593 A126 1p ultramarine .25 .25
594 A126 1½p green .25 .25
595 A126 2p red brown .25 .25
596 A127 2½p scarlet .25 *1.40*
597 A127 3p dark purple .25 *.45*
598 A128 4p ultramarine .35 .25
599 A129 5p lt brown .35 *.40*
600 A129 6p lilac rose .35 *.40*
601 A129 7p emerald .35 *.40*
602 A130 8p brt rose .35 *1.10*
603 A130 9p dp olive grn .35 .35
*a.* "TANGIER" omitted *5,500.*
604 A130 10p royal blue .35 .35
605 A130 11p violet brown .35 .35
606 A131 1sh brown .35 .35
607 A132 1sh3p dark green .50 *5.50*
608 A131 1sh6p dark blue .55 *1.75*

**Engr.**

***Perf. 11x12***

609 A133 2sh6p dark brown 2.25 *4.25*
610 A133 5sh crimson 3.00 *7.00*
611 A133 10sh ultramarine 4.25 *8.50*
*Nos. 592-611 (20)* 15.20 *33.80*

Centenary of British P.O. in Tangier.

Nos. 609-611 are found with hyphen omitted (one stamp in sheet of 40).

British stamps overprinted "Tangier" were discontinued Apr. 30, 1957.

## TURKISH EMPIRE

40 Paras = 1 Piaster
12 Pence = 1 Shilling (1905)

a

b

c

d

### Surcharged on Great Britain Nos. 101, 104, 96

**1885, Apr. 1** **Wmk. 30** ***Perf. 14***

1 A47(a) 40pa on 2½p lil 110.00 1.50
2 A45(b) 80pa on 5p grn 210.00 12.50

**Wmk. 31**

3 A44(c) 12pi on 2sh6p lilac 52.50 27.50
*a.* Bluish paper 400.00 260.00
*Nos. 1-3 (3)* 372.50 41.50

### Great Britain Nos. 114, 118 Surcharged

**1887** **Wmk. 30**

4 A57(a) 40pa on 2½p vio, *bl* 4.75 .25
*a.* Double surcharge *2,250.* *2,900.*
5 A61(b) 80pa on 5p lil & bl 17.50 .35
*a.* Small "0" in "80" 225.00 100.00

### Great Britain No. 111 Handstamp Surcharged

**1893, Feb. 25**

6 A54(d) 40pa on ½p ver *500.00* *125.00*

No. 6 was a provisional, made and used at Constantinople for five days. Excellent forgeries are known.

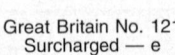

Great Britain No. 121 Surcharged — e

**1896**

7 A64(e) 4pi on 10p car rose & lil 47.50 9.25

### British Stamps of 1902 Surcharged

**1902-05** **Wmk. 30**

8 A66(a) 40pa on 2½p ultra 17.50 .25
9 A71(b) 80pa on 5p lil & bl 9.00 2.90
*a.* Small "0" in "80" 250.00 210.00
10 A73(e) 4pi on 10p car rose & vio 13.50 4.50

**Wmk. 31**

11 A75(c) 12pi on 2sh6p vio ('03) 40.00 40.00
12 A76(c) 24pi on 5sh car rose ('05) 35.00 47.50
*Nos. 8-12 (5)* 115.00 *95.15*

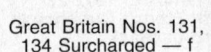

Great Britain Nos. 131, 134 Surcharged — f

**1906** **Wmk. 30**

13 A66(f) 1pi on 2½p ultra 17.50 .25
14 A71(f) 2pi on 5p lil & ultra 32.50 2.75

Nos. 10, 11, 14 are on both ordinary and chalky paper.

Great Britain Nos. 127-135, 138 Overprinted — g

**1905**

15 A66 ½p pale green 10.00 .25
16 A66 1p carmine 9.50 .25
17 A67 1½p violet & grn 6.25 2.00
18 A68 2p green & car 3.50 *8.00*
19 A66 2½p ultra 10.00 *22.50*
20 A69 3p violet, *yel* 7.25 *13.50*
21 A70 4p brown & grn 10.00 *50.00*
22 A71 5p lilac & ultra 19.00 *32.50*
23 A66 6p dull violet 15.00 *29.00*
24 A74 1sh car rose & grn 42.50 *57.50*
*Nos. 15-24 (10)* 133.00 *215.50*

Nos. 17, 18 and 24 are on both ordinary and chalky paper.

No. 18 Surcharged

**1906, July 2**

25 A68 1pi on 2p grn & car 1,500. 700.00

### British Stamps of 1902-09 Surcharged

j

k

**1909**

26 A67 30pa on 1½p vio & grn 11.50 1.40
27 A69 1pi10pa on 3p vio, *yel* 13.50 *40.00*
28 A70 1pi30pa on 4p brn & grn 5.75 *19.00*
29 A70 1pi30pa on 4p org 20.00 *70.00*
30 A66 2pi20pa on 6p dl violet 22.50 *70.00*
31 A74 5pi on 1sh car rose & grn 5.00 *11.00*
*Nos. 26-31 (6)* 78.25 *211.40*

No. 29 is on ordinary paper, the others are on chalky paper.

### Great Britain Nos. 132, 144, 135 Surcharged

m

n

**1910**

32 A69(m) 1¼pi on 3p vio, *yel* .60 *1.25*
33 A70(m) 1¾pi on 4p orange .60 *.75*
34 A66(n) 2½pi on 6p dl vio 1.60 .80
*Nos. 32-34 (3)* 2.80 2.80

There are three different varieties of "4" in the fraction of the 1¾ piastre.

### Great Britain Nos. 151-154 Overprinted Type g

**1911-12** ***Perf. 15x14***

35 A80 ½p yellow green 2.25 1.75
36 A81 1p carmine .55 *7.00*

### Re-engraved

37 A80 ½p yel grn ('12) .90 .25
38 A81 1p scarlet ('12) .90 *1.75*

Great Britain No. 148 Surcharged — o

39 A66(o) 1pi on 2½p ultra 15.00 3.00
*Nos. 35-39 (5)* 19.60 13.75

The surcharge on No. 39 exists in two types with the letters 2½ and 3mm high respectively. The stamp also differs from No. 13 in the perforation.

### British Stamps of 1912-13 Surcharged with New Values

**1913-14** **Wmk. 33**

40 A84(j) 30pa on 1½p red brown 4.00 *16.00*
41 A86(o) 1pi on 2½p ultra 8.50 .25
42 A87(m) 1¼pi on 3p vio 5.50 4.75
43 A88(m) 1¾pi on 4p sl grn 3.50 *7.00*
44 A90(o) 4pi on 10p lt bl 9.00 *22.50*
45 A90(o) 5pi on 1sh bis 45.00 *70.00*
*Nos. 40-45 (6)* *75.50* 120.50

### British Stamps of 1912-19 Overprinted Type "g"

**1913-21**

46 A82 ½p green .45 *1.40*
47 A83 1p scarlet .35 *5.75*
48 A85 2p orange ('21) 1.40 *32.50*
49 A87 3p violet ('21) 8.50 *11.50*
50 A88 4p sl grn ('21) 5.75 *16.00*
51 A89 5p yel brn ('21) 13.50 *32.50*
52 A89 6p dl vio ('21) 30.00 *10.00*
53 A90 1sh bister ('21) 15.00 *10.00*

**Wmk. 34**

***Perf. 11x12***

54 A91 2sh6p brn ('21) 42.50 *100.00*
*Nos. 46-54 (9)* 117.45 *219.65*

### British Stamps of 1912-19 Surcharged as in 1909-10 and

p

q

**1921** **Wmk. 33** ***Perf. 14½x14***

55 A82(j) 30pa on ½p grn .90 *13.50*
*a.* Inverted surcharge 100.00
56 A83(p) 1½pi on 1p scar 1.75 1.40
57 A86(p) 3¾pi on 2½p ultra 1.50 .35
58 A87(p) 4½pi on 3p vio 2.25 *4.25*
59 A89(p) 7½pi on 5p yel brn .60 .25
60 A90(p) 15pi on 10p lt bl .85 .25
61 A90(p) 18¾pi on 1sh bis 5.00 *5.00*

**Wmk. 34**

***Perf. 11x12***

62 A91(q) 45pi on 2sh6p brown 22.50 *52.50*
63 A91(q) 90pi on 5sh car rose 30.00 *35.00*
64 A91(q) 180pi on 10sh blue 52.50 45.00
*Nos. 55-64 (10)* 117.85 *157.50*

# GUERNSEY

'gərn-zē

LOCATION — A group of islands in the English Channel
GOVT. — Dependent territory (bailiwick) of the British Crown
AREA — 30 sq. mi.
POP. — 58,681 (1996)
CAPITAL — St. Peter Port

The bailiwick includes the islands of Guernsey, Alderney, Sark, Herm, Jethou and Lithou.

Following the establishment of the British General Post Office as a public corporation on October 1, 1969, the post office of the Bailiwick of Guernsey became a separate entity and British postage stamps ceased to be valid.

**Catalogue values for unused stamps in this country are for Never Hinged items.**

### Watermark

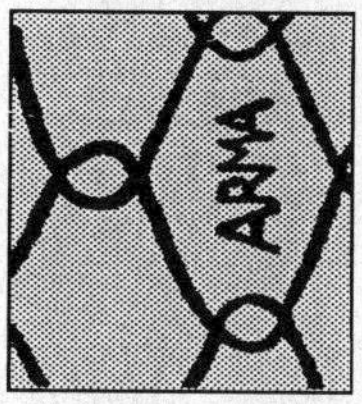

Wmk. 396 — Link Fence

### British Regional Issue

Guernsey Lily and Crown of William the Conqueror
A1 A2

*Perf. 15x14*

**1958-69 Photo. Wmk. 322**

1 A1 2½p rose red ('64) .35 .35
2 A2 3p light purple .30 .25
p. Phoshor. ('67) .25 .25
3 A2 4p ultra ('66) .30 .25
p. Phosphor. ('67) .25 .25

**Unwmk.**

4 A2 4p ultra ('68) .25 .25
5 A2 4p olive brown ('68) .25 .25
6 A2 4p bright red ('69) .25 .25
7 A2 5p dark blue ('68) .25 .25
*Nos. 1-7 (7)* 1.95 1.85

Nos. 4-7 are phosphorescent.

Sold to the general public only at post offices within Guernsey, but valid for postage throughout Great Britain.

See also Great Britain Nos. 269-270, which were sold only in the Channel Islands and at a few philatelic windows in Great Britain, and may be considered to be precursors to the regional issues.

### Bailiwick Issues

William the Conqueror, Queen Elizabeth II and Map of Bailiwick — A3

Creux Harbor, Sark — A4

Designs (Queen Elizabeth II and): ½p, Castle Cornet and Edward the Confessor. 1½p, Martello Tower and Henry II. 2p, Arms of Sark and King John. 3p, Arms of Alderney and Edward III. 4p, Guernsey lily and Henry V. 5p, Arms of Guernsey and Queen Elizabeth I. 6p, Arms of Alderney and Charles II. 9p, Arms of Sark and George III. 1sh, Arms of Guernsey and Queen Victoria. 1sh6p, Map of Bailiwick and William I. 1sh9p, Guernsey lily and Queen Elizabeth I. 2sh6p, Martello Tower and King John. 10sh, Braye Harbor, Alderney. £1, St. Peter Port, Guernsey.

*Perf. 14½x14*

**1969-70 Photo. Unwmk.**

8 A3 ½p magenta & blk .25 .25
9 A3 1p ultra & black .25 .25
10 A3 1½p bister & blk .25 .25
11 A3 2p dk blue & multi .25 .25
12 A3 3p deep org & multi .30 .25
13 A3 4p yel green & multi .40 .40
a. Booklet pane of 1 1.00 1.00
14 A3 5p vio blue & multi .35 .25
a. Booklet pane of 1 1.50 1.50
15 A3 6p ol green & multi .40 *.50*
16 A3 9p plum & multi .50 *.60*
17 A3 1sh dk olive & multi .40 *.50*
18 A3 1sh6p blue grn & blk .40 *.50*
19 A3 1sh9p magenta & multi 1.50 1.40
20 A3 2sh6p purple & blk 7.00 6.00

*Perf. 12½*

21 A4 5sh multicolored 4.00 3.00
22 A4 10sh multicolored 27.50 25.00
a. Perf. 13½x13 57.50 50.00

*Perf. 13½x13*

23 A4 £1 multicolored 3.75 3.50
a. Perf. 12½ 4.50 4.50
*Nos. 8-23 (16)* 47.50 42.90

Issued: #22a, 23, 3/4/70; others, 10/1/69.
Nos. 9 and 18 are inscribed "40o 30' N."
See Nos. 28-29, 41-55, 749.

Col. Isaac Brock — A5

Designs: 5p, Sir Isaac Brock as major general. 1sh9p, as ensign, flags of 1789 and 1969. 2sh6p, Regimental coat of arms and flags, horiz.

*Perf. 14x13½, 13½x14*

**1969, Dec. 1 Litho. Unwmk.**

24 A5 4p multicolored .25 .25
25 A5 5p black & multi .25 .25
26 A5 1sh9p dp blue & multi 1.25 1.10
27 A5 2sh6p purple & multi 1.25 1.10
*Nos. 24-27 (4)* 3.00 2.70

Sir Isaac Brock (1769-1812), born on Guernsey, commander of Quebec garrison.

### Map Type of 1969 Redrawn

**1969-70 Photo. *Perf. 14½x14***

28 A3 1p "49o 30'N" .25 .25
a. Booklet pane of 1 .45 .45
Complete booklet, 3 #13a, 2 #14a, 2 #28a 3.50
Complete booklet, 6 #13a, 4 #14a, 4 #28a 5.50
Complete booklet, 9 #13a, 6 #14a, 6 #28a 8.00
29 A3 1sh6p "49o 30'N" 3.00 2.00

Issued: No. 28a, 12/12/69; Nos. 28-29, 2/4/70.
Nos. 9 and 18 are inscribed "40o 30' N."

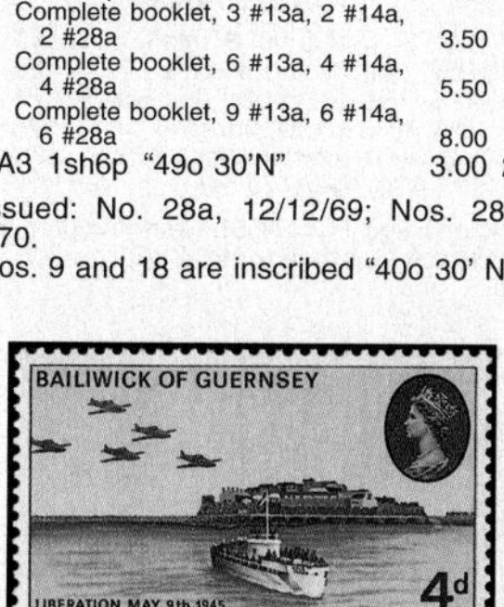


Destroyer "Bulldog" near Castle Cornet — A6

Designs: 5p, Liberation fleet in roadsteads between Guernsey, Herm and Jethou. 1sh6p, Brigadier A. E. Snow reading proclamation of King George VI on steps of Elizabeth College in Guernsey, vert.

**1970, May 9 Photo. *Perf. 11½***

30 A6 4p vio blue & lt blue .25 .25
31 A6 5p dp plum & gray .25 .25
32 A6 1sh6p dk brown & bis 1.75 1.75
*Nos. 30-32 (3)* 2.25 2.25

25th anniv. of Guernsey's liberation from the Germans.

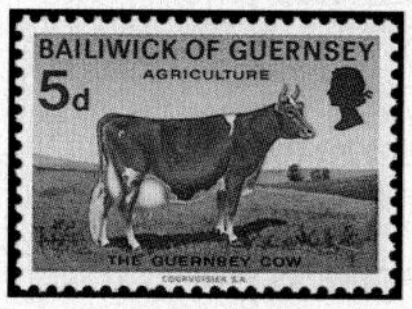


Guernsey Cow — A7

**1970, Aug. 12 Photo. *Perf. 11½***

33 A7 4p Tomatoes 1.10 .45
34 A7 5p shown 1.10 .45
35 A7 9p Guernsey bull 5.50 2.25
36 A7 1sh6p Freesias 6.00 4.50
*Nos. 33-36 (4)* 13.70 7.65

For similar design see No. 68.

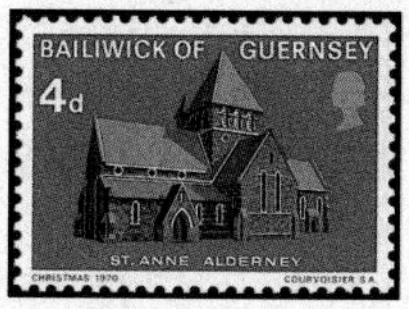


St. Anne, Alderney A8

Christmas (Churches): 5p, St. Peter, Town Church, Guernsey. 9p, St. Peter, Sark, vert. 1sh6p, St. Tugual Chapel, Herm, vert.

**1970, Nov. 11 Photo. *Perf. 11½***

37 A8 4p blue, gold & brn .30 .25
38 A8 5p brt grn, gold & brn .40 .25
39 A8 9p rose red, gold & brown 1.10 1.00
40 A8 1sh6p brt purple, gold & brown 2.10 1.60
*Nos. 37-40 (4)* 3.90 3.10

### Decimal Currency Issue Types of 1969 "p" instead of "d"

Designs: ½p, Castle Cornet and Edward the Confessor. 1p, 5p, Map of Bailiwick and William the Conqueror. 1½p, Martello Tower and Henry II. 2p, Guernsey lily and Henry V. 2½p, Arms of Guernsey and Elizabeth I. 3p, Arms of Alderney and Edward III. 3½p, Guernsey lily and Elizabeth I. 4p, Arms of Sark and King John. 6p, Arms of Alderney and Charles II. 7½p, Arms of Guernsey and Queen Victoria. 9p, Arms of Sark and George III. 10p, Martello Tower and King John. 20p, Creux Harbor. 50p, Braye Harbor.

**1971 Photo. *Perf. 14½x14***

41 A3 ½p magenta & blk .25 .25
a. Booklet pane of 1 .20
42 A3 1p ultra & black .25 .25
43 A3 1½p bister & blk .25 .25
44 A3 2p yel green & multi .25 .25
a. Booklet pane of 1 .35
45 A3 2½p vio blue & multi .25 .25
a. Booklet pane of 1 .35
Complete booklet, 2 each #41a, 44a, 45a .60
Complete booklet, 4 each #41a, 44a, 45a 1.20
Complete booklet, 6 each #41a, 44a, 45a 1.80
46 A3 3p dp orange & multi .30 .30
47 A3 3½p magenta & multi .30 .30
48 A3 4p dk blue & multi .30 .30
49 A3 5p brt green & multi .30 .30
50 A3 6p dk green & multi .30 .30
51 A3 7½p brn olive & multi .40 .40
52 A3 9p plum & multi .80 .80
53 A3 10p purple & black 1.60 1.60

*Perf. 13*

54 A4 20p dk red & multi 1.00 1.00
55 A4 50p multicolored 2.40 2.40
*Nos. 41-55 (15)* 8.95 8.95

Issue dates: #53-55, Jan. 6; others Feb. 15.

Thomas de la Rue, Hong Kong No. 1 — A9

Thomas de la Rue and: 2½p, GB No. 22. 4p, Italy No. 26. 7½p, US Confederate States No. 6.

**1971, June 2 Engr. *Perf. 14x13½***

56 A9 2p brown .60 .25
57 A9 2½p carmine .60 .25
58 A9 4p dark green 1.90 1.60
59 A9 7½p violet blue 2.25 1.60
*Nos. 56-59 (4)* 5.35 3.70

Thomas de la Rue (1793-1866), founder of Thomas de la Rue & Co., Ltd., security printers.

Ebenezer Methodist Church — A10

Historic Churches of Guernsey: 2½p, St. Pierre du Bois. 5p, St. Joseph's, vert. 7½p, St. Philippe de Torteval, vert.

**1971, Oct. 27 Photo. *Perf. 11½***

60 A10 2p green, sil & blk .35 .35
61 A10 2½p blue, sil & blk .40 .35
62 A10 5p pur, silver & blk 1.75 1.40
63 A10 7½p red, silver & blk 2.50 2.25
*Nos. 60-63 (4)* 5.00 4.35

Christmas 1971.

Mail Boat, Earl of Chesterfield, 1794 — A11

**1972, Feb. 10 Photo. *Perf. 11½***

64 A11 2p shown .25 .25
65 A11 2½p *Dasher, 1827* .25 .25
66 A11 7½p *Ibex, 1891* .35 .35
67 A11 9p *Alberta, 1900* .55 .55
*Nos. 64-67 (4)* 1.40 1.40

See Nos. 77-80.

Guernsey Bull — A12

**1972, May 22 Photo. *Perf. 11½***

68 A12 5p brown & multi .65 .55

Guernsey Breeders, 2nd World Conf. For similar designs see Nos. 33-36.

Wild Flowers A13

**1972, May 24**

69 A13 2p Sorrel .25 .25
70 A13 2½p Orchis maculata, vert. .25 .25
71 A13 7½p Carpobrotus edulis .40 .40
72 A13 9p Pimpernel, vert. .50 .50
*Nos. 69-72 (4)* 1.40 1.40

Angels, St. Martin's Church — A14

Stained Glass Windows from Guernsey Churches: 2½p, Virgin and Child, St. André's.

7½p, Virgin Mary, St. Sampson's. 9p, Christ Victorious, St. Pierre's.

**1972, Nov. 20 Photo. *Perf. 11½***

**73** A14 2p brick red & multi .25 .25
**74** A14 2½p lt violet & multi .25 .25
**75** A14 7½p yellow & multi .30 .30
**76** A14 9p lt green & multi .30 .30
*Nos. 73-76 (4)* 1.10 1.10

Christmas 1972 and for the 25th anniv. of the marriage of Queen Elizabeth II and Prince Philip.

**Mail Boat Type of 1972**

**1973, Mar. 9 Photo. *Perf. 11½***

**77** A11 2½p *St. Julien, 1925* .25 .25
**78** A11 3p *Isle of Sark, 1932* .25 .25
**79** A11 7½p *St. Patrick, 1947* .40 .40
**80** A11 9p *Sarnia, 1961* .40 .40
*Nos. 77-80 (4)* 1.30 1.30

No. 78 is incorrectly inscribed "Isle of Guernsey 1930."

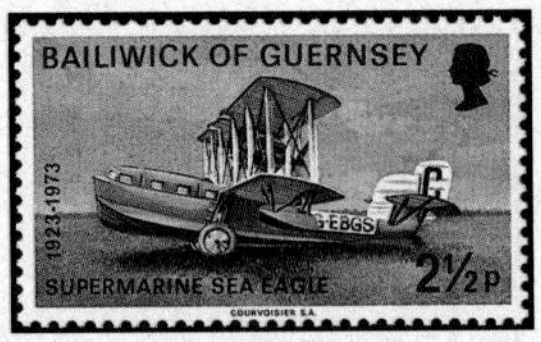


Supermarine Sea Eagle — A15

Airplanes: 3p, Westland Wessex. 5p, De Havilland Rapide. 7½p, Douglas Dakota. 9p, Vickers Viscount.

**1973, July 4 Photo. *Perf. 11½***

**81** A15 2½p multicolored .25 .25
**82** A15 3p multicolored .25 .25
**83** A15 5p multicolored .25 .25
**84** A15 7½p multicolored .40 .40
**85** A15 9p multicolored .50 .50
*Nos. 81-85 (5)* 1.65 1.65

50th anniversary of air service to Guernsey.

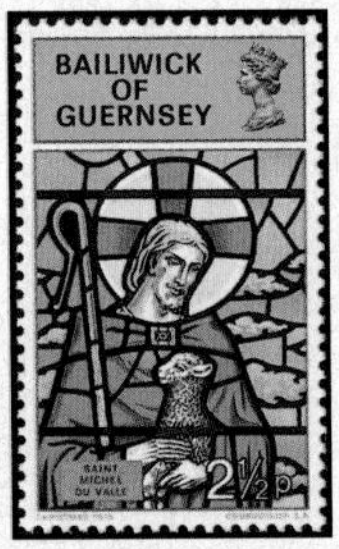


The Good Shepherd, St. Michel du Valle — A16

Stained-glass Windows from Guernsey Churches: 3p, Jesus preaching, St. Marie du Castel. 7½p, St. Dominic, Notre Dame du Rosaire. 20p, Virgin and Child, St. Sauveur.

**1973, Oct. 24 Photo. *Perf. 11½***

**86** A16 2½p salmon & multi .25 .25
**87** A16 3p blue & multi .25 .25
**88** A16 7½p yellow & multi .25 .25
**89** A16 20p multicolored .50 .50
*Nos. 86-89 (4)* 1.25 1.25

Christmas 1973.

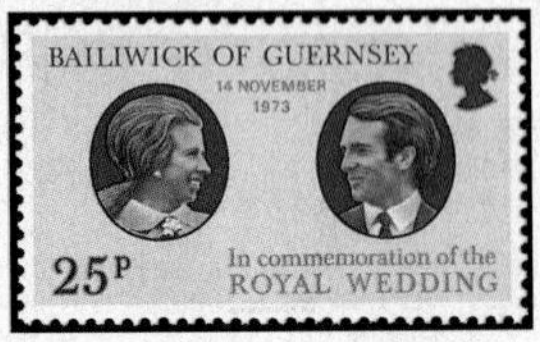


Princess Anne and Mark Phillips — A17

**1973, Nov. 14**

**90** A17 25p blue & multi .70 .70

Wedding of Princess Anne and Capt. Mark Phillips, Nov. 14, 1973.

"John Lockett," 1875 — A18

Guernsey Lifeboats: 3p, "Arthur Lionel," 1875. 8p, "Euphrosyne Kendal," 1954. 10p, "Arun," 1972.

**1974, Jan. 15 Photo. *Perf. 11½***
**Granite Paper**

**91** A18 2½p multicolored .25 .25
**92** A18 3p multicolored .25 .25
**93** A18 8p multicolored .25 .25
**94** A18 10p multicolored .25 .25
*Nos. 91-94 (4)* 1.00 1.00

Sesqui. of Royal Natl. Lifeboat Institution.

A19

Militia — A20

**1974-78 Photo. *Perf. 11½***
**Granite Paper (Nos. 95-107)**

**95** A19 ½p 1815 .25 .25
**96** A19 1p 1825 .25 .25
**97** A19 1½p 1787 .25 .25
**98** A19 2p 1815 .25 .25
**99** A19 2½p Royal, 1868 .25 .25
Complete booklet, pane of 8 (5 #95, 3 #99) .35
**100** A19 3p Royal, 1895 .25 .25
Complete booklet, pane of 16 (4 #95, 6 #99 and 6 #100) 1.10
**101** A19 3½p Royal, 1867 .25 .25
**102** A19 4p 1822 .25 .25
**102A** A19 5p Royal, 1895 .25 .25
Complete booklet, pane of 8 (4 #96, #100, 2 #102, #102A) ('77) .85
Complete booklet, pane of 4 (#96, 2 #98, #102A) ('78) .55
**103** A19 5½p Royal. 1833 .25 .25
**104** A19 6p Royal. 1832 .25 .25
**104A** A19 7p 1822 .35 .35
**105** A19 8p Royal, 1868 .25 .25
**106** A19 9p 1785 .25 .25
**107** A19 10p 1824 .25 .25

***Perf. 13x13½, 13½x13***

**108** A20 20p Royal, 1848, vert. .70 .50
**109** A20 50p Royal, 1868, vert. 1.50 1.40
**110** A20 £1 1814 3.00 2.50
*Nos. 95-110 (18)* 9.05 8.25

Issued: Nos. 95-107, 4/2/74; Nos. 108-110, 4/1/75; No. 102A, 104A, 5/29/76; No. 96a, 2/8/77; No. 96b, 2/7/78.

Stamps in booklet panes are from special sheets of 80 (two 8x5 panes) which were sold separately.

Bailiwick Seal and UPU Emblem — A21

UPU Cent.: 3p, Map of Guernsey. 8p, UPU Headquarters, Bern, flag of Guernsey. 10p, Legislative Chamber, Parliament.

**1974, June 11 Photo. *Perf. 11½***
**Granite Paper**

**111** A21 2½p multicolored .25 .25
**112** A21 3p ultra & multi .25 .25
**113** A21 8p multicolored .25 .25
**114** A21 10p multicolored .25 .25
*Nos. 111-114 (4)* 1.00 1.00

Cradle Rock, by Renoir A22

Paintings by Renoir: 5½p, Moulin-Huet Bay. 8p, Woman at the Shore, vert. 10p, Self-portrait, vert.

**1974, Sept. 21 Photo. *Perf. 13¼***

**115** A22 3p multicolored .25 .25
**116** A22 5½p multicolored .25 .25
**117** A22 8p multicolored .25 .25
**118** A22 10p multicolored .25 .25
*Nos. 115-118 (4)* 1.00 1.00

Pierre Auguste Renoir (1841-1919), who painted pictures shown on Nos. 115-117 while visiting Guernsey.

Guernsey Spleenwort — A23

Designs: Guernsey ferns.

**1975, Jan. 7 Photo. *Perf. 11½***

**119** A23 3½p shown .25 .25
**120** A23 4p Sand quillwort .25 .25
**121** A23 8p Guernsey fern .25 .25
**122** A23 10p Least adder's tongue .25 .25
*Nos. 119-122 (4)* 1.00 1.00

Hauteville, Hugo's House A24

Victor Hugo Statue, Candie Gardens — A25

Designs: 8p, United Europe Oak, Hauteville (planted by Hugo). 10p, Departure for the Hunt, Aubusson tapestry, Hauteville.

**1975, June 6 Photo. *Perf. 11½***
**Granite Paper**

**123** A24 3½p dull yel & multi .25 .25
**124** A25 4p lt blue & multi .25 .25
**125** A25 8p yel green & multi .25 .25
**126** A24 10p multicolored .25 .25
*a.* Souvenir sheet of 4, #123-126 .80 .80
*Nos. 123-126 (4)* 1.00 1.00

Victor Hugo (1802-85), French writer, political exile in Guernsey (1855-70).

Arms and Map of Guernsey — A26

Designs (Globe with Map of Bailiwick): 6p, Flag of Guernsey. 10p, Flag of Guernsey and arms of Alderney, horiz. 12p, Flag of Guernsey and arms of Sark, horiz.

**1975, Oct. 7 Photo. *Perf. 13½***

**127** A26 4p olive green & multi .25 .25
**128** A26 6p rose lilac & multi .25 .25
**129** A26 10p brt green & multi .25 .25
**130** A26 12p orange & multi .25 .25
*Nos. 127-130 (4)* 1.00 1.00

Christmas 1975.

Lighthouses — A27

**1976, Feb. 10 Photo. *Perf. 11½***
**Granite Paper**

**131** A27 4p Les Hanois .25 .25
**132** A27 6p Les Casquets .25 .25
**133** A27 11p Quesnard, Alderney .25 .25
**134** A27 13p Point Robert, Sark .30 .30
*Nos. 131-134 (4)* 1.05 1.05

Guernsey Milk Can — A28

Europa: 25p, Silver christening cup.

**1976, May 29 Photo. *Perf. 11½***
**Granite Paper**

**135** A28 10p multicolored *.35* *.30*
**136** A28 25p multicolored *.70* *.50*

Sheets of 9.

Pine Forest, Guernsey — A29

Guernsey Views: 7p, Herm Harbor and Jethou. 11p, Grande Grave Bay, Sark Cliffs, vert. 13p, Trois Vaux Bay, Alderney Cliffs, vert.

**1976, Aug. 3 Photo. *Perf. 11½***
**Granite Paper**

**137** A29 5p multicolored .25 .25
**138** A29 7p multicolored .25 .25
**139** A29 11p multicolored .25 .25
**140** A29 13p multicolored .25 .25
*Nos. 137-140 (4)* 1.00 1.00

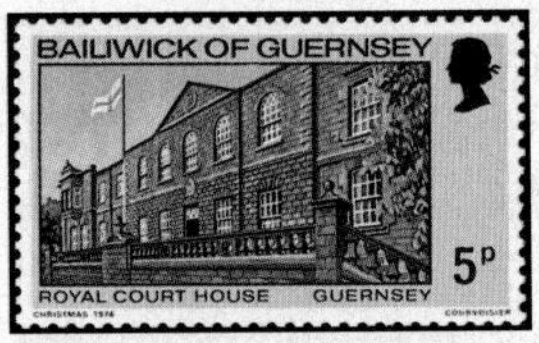


Royal Court House, Guernsey — A30

Christmas (Buildings in the Bailiwick): 7p, Elizabeth College, Guernsey. 11p, La Seigneurie, Sark. 13p, Island Hall, Alderney.

**1976, Oct. 14 Photo. *Perf. 11½***
**Granite Paper**

**141** A30 5p multicolored .25 .25
**142** A30 7p multicolored .25 .25
**143** A30 11p multicolored .25 .25
**144** A30 13p multicolored .25 .25
*Nos. 141-144 (4)* 1.00 1.00

Elizabeth II with Order of the Garter — A31

Design: 7p, Queen Elizabeth II.

**1977, Feb. 8 Photo. *Perf. 12x11½***

**145** A31 7p blue & multi .25 .25
**146** A31 35p purple & multi .70 .70

25th anniv. of the reign of Elizabeth II.

Talbots Valley — A32

Europa: 25p, Fields and hedges, Talbots Valley.

**1977, May 17 Photo. *Perf. 11½***
**Granite Paper**

**147** A32 7p multicolored .25 .25
**148** A32 25p multicolored *.70 .70*

Megalithic Tomb, Le Catioroc — A33

Prehistoric monuments: 5p, Menhir (statue), Castel, vert. 11p, Roc à l'Épine Tourgis. 13p, Gràn mère du Chim' quière, vert.

**1977, Aug. 2 Photo. *Perf. 11½***

**149** A33 5p multicolored .25 .25
**150** A33 7p multicolored .25 .25
**151** A33 11p multicolored .30 .30
**152** A33 13p multicolored .30 .30
*Nos. 149-152 (4)* 1.10 1.10

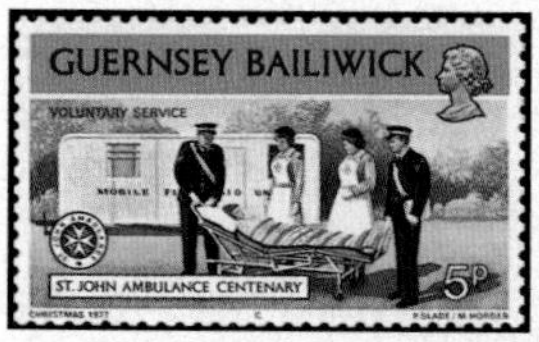


Mobile First Aid Unit A34

7p, Mobile radar & rescue coordination unit, for ships in distress. 11p, Marine ambulance "Flying Christine II," vert. 13p, Cliff rescue, vert.

**1977, Oct. 25 Photo. *Perf. 11½***

**153** A34 5p multicolored .25 .25
**154** A34 7p multicolored .25 .25
**155** A34 11p multicolored .30 .30
**156** A34 13p multicolored .30 .30
*Nos. 153-156 (4)* 1.10 1.10

St. John Ambulance Assoc. cent. (in GB).

View from Clifton, c. 1830 A35

19th Century Prints, Guernsey: 7p, Market Square, c. 1838. 11p, Petit-Bo Bay, c. 1839. 13p, The Quay, c. 1830.

**1978, Feb. 7 Litho. *Perf. 14x13½***

**157** A35 5p pale green & black .25 .25
**158** A35 7p buff & black .25 .25
**159** A35 11p pink & black .30 .30
**160** A35 13p lt violet & black .30 .30
*Nos. 157-160 (4)* 1.10 1.10

See Nos. 236-239.

Memorial to Seamen of Ship Prosperity; Sank 1974 — A36

Europa: 7p, Victoria monument, vert.

**1978, May 2 Litho. *Perf. 14½***

**161** A36 5p multicolored .25 .25
**162** A36 7p multicolored *.25 .25*

Elizabeth II — A37

**1978, May 2 Photo. *Perf. 11½***

**163** A37 20p ultra & black .70 .70

25th anniv. of coronation of Elizabeth II.

Inscribed: "VISIT OF/H.M. THE QUEEN AND/H.R.H. THE DUKE OF EDINBURGH/JUNE 28-29, 1978"

**1978, June 28**

**164** A37 7p emerald & black .30 .30

Gannet A38

Birds: 7p, Firecrest. 11p, Dartford warbler. 13p, Spotted redshank.

**1978, Aug. 29 Photo. *Perf. 11½***

**165** A38 5p multicolored .25 .25
**166** A38 7p multicolored .25 .25
**167** A38 11p multicolored .30 .30
**168** A38 13p multicolored .40 .40
*Nos. 165-168 (4)* 1.20 1.20

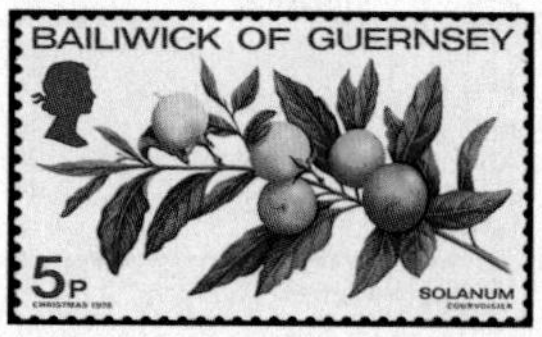


Solanum — A39

Christmas: 7p, Christmas rose. 11p, Holly, vert. 13p, Mistletoe, vert.

**1978, Oct. 31 Photo. *Perf. 11½***

**169** A39 5p multicolored .25 .25
**170** A39 7p multicolored .25 .25
**171** A39 11p multicolored .30 .30
**172** A39 13p multicolored .30 .30
*Nos. 169-172 (4)* 1.10 1.10

1 Double, 1930 — A40

**1979, Feb. 13 Granite Paper**

**173** A40 ½p 1 double, 1930 .25 .25
**174** A40 1p 2 doubles, 1899 .25 .25
**175** A40 2p 4 doubles, 1902 .25 .25
**176** A40 4p 8 doubles, 1959 .25 .25
**177** A40 5p 3 pence, 1956 .25 .25
**178** A40 6p 5 new pence, 1968 .25 .25
*a.* Horiz. strip of 4, #175, 178, 2 #174 1.00
**179** A40 7p 50 new pence, 1969 .25 .25
**180** A40 8p 10 new pence, 1970 .25 .25
*a.* Horiz. strip of 5, #175, 2 each #178, 180 1.25
Complete booklet of 10, 5 each #176, 180 2.25
**181** A40 9p ½ new penny, 1971 .25 .25
**182** A40 10p 1 new penny, 1971 .30 .25
**183** A40 11p 2 new pence, 1971 .30 .25
**184** A40 12p 1 penny, 1977 .30 .25
Complete booklet of 15, 5 each #176, 180, 184 3.50
**185** A40 13p 2 pence, 1977 .30 .25
Complete booklet of 10, 2 #176, 3 #181, 5 #185 2.25
Complete booklet of 15, 5 each #176, 181, 185 3.50
**186** A40 14p 5 pence, 1977 .35 .25
**187** A40 15p 10 pence, 1977 .35 .25
**188** A40 20p 25 pence, 1977 .45 .25
*Nos. 173-188 (16)* 4.60 4.00

No. 177 is dark brown, No. 182, green & bronze. See Nos. 198B-203A.

Booklets were produced from sheets of 40, 30 and 20. These sheets were sold both as complete sheets and as strips, folded and affixed by the sheet selvage or inserted unattached into booklet covers.

Oldest Pillar Box, 1853 Cancel, Truck — A41

Europa: 8p, Telephone, 1897, telex machine.

**1979, May 8 Photo. *Perf. 11½***

**189** A41 6p multicolored .25 .25
**190** A41 8p multicolored .25 .25

Steam Tram, 1879 A42

Public Transportation: 8p, Electric tram, 1896. 11p, Autobus, 1911. 13p, Autobus, 1979.

**1979, Aug. 7 Photo. *Perf. 11½***

**191** A42 6p multicolored .25 .25
**192** A42 8p multicolored .25 .25
**193** A42 11p multicolored .30 .30
**194** A42 13p multicolored .30 .30
*Nos. 191-194 (4)* 1.10 1.10

Centenary of public transportation.

Postal Bureau and Headquarters — A43

Designs: 8p, Mail and telegram deliverymen. 13p, Parcel trucks. 15p, Post Office philatelic room.

**1979, Oct. 1 Photo. *Perf. 11½***

**195** A43 6p multicolored .25 .25
**196** A43 8p multicolored .25 .25
**197** A43 13p multicolored .30 .30
**198** A43 15p multicolored .40 .40
*a.* Souvenir sheet of 4, Nos. 195-198 1.25 1.25
*Nos. 195-198 (4)* 1.20 1.20

Guernsey PO, 10th anniv.; Christmas 1979.

**Coin Type of 1979**

Designs: 10p, like No. 182. 11½p, ½ pence, 1979. 50p, Battle of Hastings coin, 1966. £1, Queen Elizabeth II 25th anniv., 1977, horiz. £2, Queen Elizabeth II 25th wedding anniv., 1972, horiz. £5, Official seal.

**1980-81 Photo. *Perf. 11½***

**198B** A40 5p orange brown & multi .45 .45
Complete booklet of 15, 5 each #180, 185, 198B 2.00
Complete booklet of 10, #185, 4 #180, 5 #198B 3.50
**199** A40 10p orange & bronze .25 .25
Complete booklet of 10, #177, 179, 199, 2 each #173, 175, 3 each #174 2.00
Complete booklet of 10, #174, 2 each #173, 175, 179, 3 #199 2.50
**200** A40 11½p red & bronze .30 .25

**Size: 26x45, 45x26mm**

**201** A40 50p red org & sil 1.60 1.25
**202** A40 £1 green & sil 3.25 2.25
**203** A40 £2 blue & silver 6.50 3.50
**203A** A40 £5 multi ('81) 16.00 12.00
*Nos. 198B-203A (7)* 28.35 19.95

No. 177 is dark brown.
For booklets, see note following No. 188.
Issue dates: £5, May 22, others, Feb. 5.

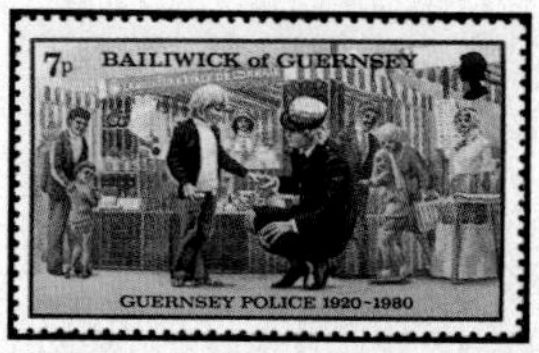


Policewoman Helping Child — A44

Guernsey Police Force, 60th Anniv.: 15p, Policeman on motorcycle. 17½p, Police dog and officer.

**1980, May 6 Litho. *Perf. 14***

**204** A44 7p multicolored .25 .25
**205** A44 15p multicolored .40 .40
**206** A44 17½p multicolored .45 .45
*Nos. 204-206 (3)* 1.10 1.10

Major Gen. John Gaspard Le Marchant — A45

Europa: 13½p, Admiral James Lord de Saumarez (1757-1836).

**1980, May 6 Photo. *Perf. 11½***
**Granite Paper**

**207** A45 10p multicolored *.25 .25*
**208** A45 13½p multicolored *.40 .40*

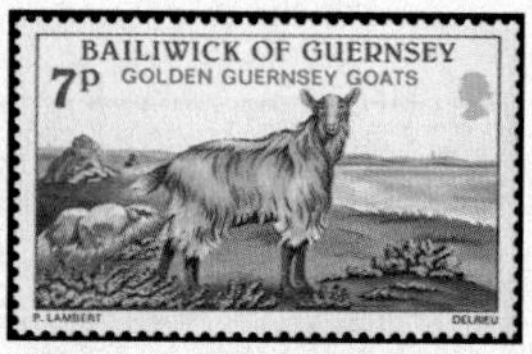


Guernsey Golden Goat — A46

Designs: Various Guernsey golden goats.

**1980, Aug. 5 Photo. *Perf. 13***

**209** A46 7p multicolored .25 .25
**210** A46 10p multicolored .25 .25
**211** A46 15p multicolored .40 .40
**212** A46 17½p multicolored .50 .50
*Nos. 209-212 (4)* 1.40 1.40

Sark Cottage, by Peter Le Lievre, 1847 — A47

Christmas 1980 (Le Lievre Paintings): 10p, Moulin Huet, 1850. 13½p, Boats at Sea, 1850. 15p, Cow Lane, 1852, vert. 17½p, Portrait, by Le Lievre's sister, vert.

**1980, Nov. 15 Photo. *Perf. 12***

**Granite Paper**

| | | | | |
|---|---|---|---|---|
| **213** | A47 | 7p multicolored | .25 | .25 |
| **214** | A47 | 10p multicolored | .25 | .25 |
| **215** | A47 | 13½p multicolored | .40 | .40 |
| **216** | A47 | 15p multicolored | .45 | .45 |
| **217** | A47 | 17½p multicolored | .50 | .50 |
| | | *Nos. 213-217 (5)* | 1.85 | 1.85 |

Common Blue A48

**1981, Feb. 24 Photo. *Perf. 14½***

| | | | | |
|---|---|---|---|---|
| **218** | A48 | 8p shown | .25 | .25 |
| **219** | A48 | 12p Red Admiral | .25 | .25 |
| **220** | A48 | 22p Small Tortoiseshell | .60 | .60 |
| **221** | A48 | 25p Wall Brown | .70 | .70 |
| | | *Nos. 218-221 (4)* | 1.80 | 1.80 |

Le Petit Bonhomme Andriou (Head-shaped Rock) — A49

**1981, May 22 Litho. *Perf. 14½***

| | | | | |
|---|---|---|---|---|
| **222** | A49 | 12p shown | *.35* | *.35* |
| **223** | A49 | 18p Guernsey lily | *.55* | *.55* |

Europa.

Prince Charles and Lady Diana — A50

Royal Wedding: a, Charles. c, Diana.

**1981, July 29 Litho. *Perf. 14½x15***

| | | | | |
|---|---|---|---|---|
| **224** | | Strip of 3 | .90 | .90 |
| *a.-c.* | | A50 8p any single | .30 | .30 |
| **225** | | Strip of 3 | 1.25 | 1.25 |
| *a.-c.* | | A50 12p any single | .40 | .40 |

**Size: 49x32mm**

| | | | | |
|---|---|---|---|---|
| **226** | A50 | 25p Royal family | .90 | .90 |
| *a.* | | Souv. sheet, #224-226, perf. 14x14½ | 3.25 | 3.25 |
| | | *Nos. 224-226 (3)* | 3.05 | 3.05 |

Sark Launch — A51

Designs: Interisland transportation.

**1981, Aug. 25 Photo. *Perf. 11½***

**Granite Paper**

| | | | | |
|---|---|---|---|---|
| **227** | A51 | 8p shown | .25 | .25 |
| **228** | A51 | 12p Trislander plane | .35 | .35 |
| **229** | A51 | 18p Hydrofoil | .55 | .55 |
| **230** | A51 | 22p Herm catamaran | .75 | .75 |
| **231** | A51 | 25p Alderney coaster | .80 | .80 |
| | | *Nos. 227-231 (5)* | 2.70 | 2.70 |

Rifle-shooting Competition A52

**1981, Nov. 17 Litho. *Perf. 14¾***

| | | | | |
|---|---|---|---|---|
| **232** | A52 | 8p shown | .25 | .25 |
| **233** | A52 | 12p Riding | .35 | .35 |
| **234** | A52 | 22p Swimming | .70 | .70 |
| **235** | A52 | 25p Electronics workers | .80 | .80 |
| | | *Nos. 232-235 (4)* | 2.10 | 2.10 |

Intl. Year of the Disabled.

**Print Type of 1978**

**1982, Feb. 2 Litho. & Engr.**

| | | | | |
|---|---|---|---|---|
| **236** | A35 | 8p Jethou | .25 | .25 |
| **237** | A35 | 12p Fermain Bay | .35 | .35 |
| **238** | A35 | 22p The Terres | .70 | .70 |
| **239** | A35 | 25p St. Pierre Port | .80 | .80 |
| | | *Nos. 236-239 (4)* | 2.10 | 2.10 |

La Societe Guernesiaise Centenary A53

Society Emblem and Activities: 8p, Sir Edgar MacCulloch, founding president. 13p, William the Conqueror's fleet, Battle at Hastings (history). 20p, Sir James Saumarez's Crescent rescued from French fleet (history). 24p, Dragonfly (entomology). 26p, Vale Parish Church bird sanctuary (ornithology). 29p, Samian bowl, King's Road excavation (archaeology). 13p and 20p show CEPT (Europa) emblem.

**1982, Apr. 28 Photo. *Perf. 11½***

**Granite Paper**

| | | | | |
|---|---|---|---|---|
| **240** | A53 | 8p multicolored | .30 | .30 |
| **241** | A53 | 13p multicolored | .40 | .40 |
| **242** | A53 | 20p multicolored | .65 | .65 |
| **243** | A53 | 24p multicolored | .80 | .80 |
| **244** | A53 | 26p multicolored | .80 | .80 |
| **245** | A53 | 29p multicolored | .85 | .85 |
| | | *Nos. 240-245 (6)* | 3.80 | 3.80 |

Scouting Year — A54

**1982, July 13 Litho. *Perf. 14½***

| | | | | |
|---|---|---|---|---|
| **246** | A54 | 8p Sea scouts, Castle Cornet, St. Peter Port | .25 | .25 |
| **247** | A54 | 13p Boy scouts building bridge | .35 | .35 |
| **248** | A54 | 26p Cub scouts parading | .80 | .80 |
| **249** | A54 | 29p Air scouts reading chart | .85 | .85 |
| | | *Nos. 246-249 (4)* | 2.25 | 2.25 |

Christmas 1982 — A55

**1982, Oct. 12 Photo. *Perf. 14½***

| | | | | |
|---|---|---|---|---|
| **250** | A55 | 8p Midnight mass, St. Peter Port Church | .25 | .25 |
| **251** | A55 | 13p Exchanging presents | .35 | .35 |
| **252** | A55 | 24p Dinner | .70 | .70 |
| **253** | A55 | 26p Exchanging cards | .75 | .75 |
| **254** | A55 | 29p Watching Queen's TV greeting | .90 | .90 |
| | | *Nos. 250-254 (5)* | 2.95 | 2.95 |

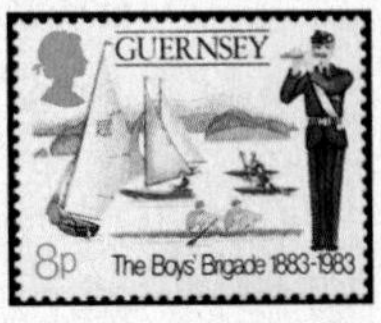

Centenary of Boys' Brigade — A56

Designs: Various brigade activities.

**1983, Jan. 18 *Perf. 14***

| | | | | |
|---|---|---|---|---|
| **255** | A56 | 8p multicolored | .25 | .25 |
| **256** | A56 | 13p multicolored | .40 | .40 |
| **257** | A56 | 24p multicolored | .75 | .75 |
| **258** | A56 | 26p multicolored | .90 | .90 |
| **259** | A56 | 29p multicolored | 1.10 | 1.10 |
| | | *Nos. 255-259 (5)* | 3.40 | 3.40 |

Europa 1983 — A57

Views of the development of St. Peter Port Harbor.

**1983, Mar. 14 Photo. *Perf. 11½***

**Granite Paper**

| | | | | |
|---|---|---|---|---|
| **260** | A57 | 13p multicolored | *.40* | *.40* |
| **261** | A57 | 13p multicolored | *.40* | *.40* |
| *a.* | | Pair, #260-261 | *.90* | *.90* |
| **262** | A57 | 20p multicolored | *.65* | *.65* |
| **263** | A57 | 20p multicolored | *.65* | *.65* |
| *a.* | | Pair, #262-263 | *1.40* | *1.40* |

View at Guernsey, by Renoir — A58

Centenary of Renoir's Visit: 13p, Children at the Seashore (26x39mm). 26p, Marine Guernsey. 28p, Moulin Huet Bay through the Trees. 31p, Fog in Guernsey.

***Perf. 12, 11½x12 (13p)***

**1983, Sept. 6 Photo.**

**Granite Paper**

| | | | | |
|---|---|---|---|---|
| **264** | A58 | 9p multicolored | .30 | .30 |
| **265** | A58 | 13p multicolored | .40 | .40 |
| **266** | A58 | 26p multicolored | .85 | .85 |
| **267** | A58 | 28p multicolored | .90 | .90 |
| **268** | A58 | 31p multicolored | 1.00 | 1.00 |
| | | *Nos. 264-268 (5)* | 3.45 | 3.45 |

Star of the West, 1869 Merchant Ship, Capt. J.G. Lenfestey — A59

**1983, Nov. 15 Photo. *Perf. 14½***

| | | | | |
|---|---|---|---|---|
| **269** | A59 | 9p Launching | .30 | .30 |
| **270** | A59 | 13p Leaving St. Peter Port | .40 | .40 |
| **271** | A59 | 26p Rio Grande Bar | .85 | .85 |
| **272** | A59 | 28p St. Lucia | .90 | .90 |
| **273** | A59 | 31p Voyage Map | 1.00 | 1.00 |
| | | *Nos. 269-273 (5)* | 3.45 | 3.45 |

Dame of Sark (Sibyl Hathaway, 1884-1974) — A60

Biographical Scenes: 9p, Portrait, La Seigneurie (residence). 13p, German occupation, 1940-45. 26p, Royal visit, 1957. 28p, Chief Pleas (parliament). 31p, Dame of Sark rose.

**1984, Feb. 7 Litho. *Perf. 14½***

| | | | | |
|---|---|---|---|---|
| **274** | A60 | 9p multicolored | .30 | .30 |
| **275** | A60 | 13p multicolored | .40 | .40 |
| **276** | A60 | 26p multicolored | .85 | .85 |
| **277** | A60 | 28p multicolored | 1.00 | 1.00 |
| **278** | A60 | 31p multicolored | 1.10 | 1.10 |
| | | *Nos. 274-278 (5)* | 3.65 | 3.65 |

Links with the Commonwealth — A61

Designs: 9p, Flag of Guernsey, Royal Court. 31p, Union Jack, Castle Cornet.

**1984, Apr. 10 Litho. *Perf. 14½***

| | | | | |
|---|---|---|---|---|
| **279** | A61 | 9p multicolored | .30 | .30 |
| **280** | A61 | 31p multicolored | 1.25 | 1.25 |

Europa (1959-84) — A62

**1984, Apr. 10 *Perf. 15***

| | | | | |
|---|---|---|---|---|
| **281** | A62 | 13p multicolored | *.50* | *.50* |
| **282** | A62 | 20½p multicolored | *.75* | *.75* |

Petit Port — A63

***Perf. 15x14½, 14½x15***

**1984-85 Litho.**

| | | | | |
|---|---|---|---|---|
| **283** | A63 | 1p Little Chapel, vert. ('85) | .25 | .25 |
| **284** | A63 | 2p Ft. Grey ('85) | .25 | .25 |
| **285** | A63 | 3p St. Apolline Chapel, vert. | .25 | .25 |
| **286** | A63 | 4p shown | .25 | .25 |
| **287** | A63 | 5p Little Russel ('85) | .25 | .25 |
| **288** | A63 | 6p The Harbour, Herm ('85) | .25 | .25 |
| **289** | A63 | 7p Saints ('85) | .25 | .25 |
| **290** | A63 | 8p St. Saviour, vert. ('85) | .25 | .25 |
| **291** | A63 | 9p Cambridge Berth | .25 | .25 |
| **292** | A63 | 10p Belvoir, Herm | .35 | .25 |
| *a.* | | Min. sheet, 2 2p, 4 4p, 2 5p, 2 10p | 2.50 | |
| **293** | A63 | 11p La Seigneurie, Sark ('85) | .25 | .25 |
| **294** | A63 | 13p St. Saviour's Reservoir | .35 | .35 |
| *a.* | | Min. sheet, 2 4p, 3 9p, 5 13p | 3.00 | |
| *b.* | | Min. sheet, 5 each 4p, 9p, 13p | 5.00 | |
| **295** | A63 | 14p St. Peter Port, vert. | .25 | .25 |
| *a.* | | Min. sheet, 4 9p, 6 14p | 4.50 | |
| *b.* | | Min. sheet, 2 9p, 8 14p | 4.75 | |
| *c.* | | Min. sheet, 5 10p, 5 14p | 4.50 | |
| **296** | A63 | 15p Havelet, vert. ('85) | .35 | .25 |
| *a.* | | Min. sheet, 3p, 2 4p, 4 11p, 3 15p | 3.75 | |
| *b.* | | Min. sheet, 5 each 11p, 15p | 4.50 | |
| **297** | A63 | 20p La Coupee, Sark | .60 | .25 |
| *a.* | | Booklet pane, 4 6p, 4 14p, 2 20p | 3.00 | |
| *b.* | | Booklet pane, 5 14p, 5 20p | 3.50 | |
| **298** | A63 | 30p Grandes Rocques ('85) | 1.00 | 1.00 |
| **299** | A63 | 40p St. Torteval Church, vert. | 1.25 | 1.25 |
| **300** | A63 | 50p Bordeaux | 1.60 | 1.60 |
| **301** | A63 | £1 Albecq | 3.50 | 3.50 |
| **302** | A63 | £2 L'Ancresse ('85) | 7.00 | 7.00 |
| | | *Nos. 283-302 (20)* | 18.75 | 18.20 |

Issued: 1p, 2p, 5p, 6p, 7p, 8p, 11p, 15p, 30p, £2, 7/23/84; 3p, 4p, 9p, 10p, 13p, 14p, 20p, 40p, 50p, £1, 9/18/84; #292a, 12/2/85; #294a-294b, 9/18/84; #295a-295b, 3/19/85; #295c, 4/1/86; #296a-296b, 3/30/87; #297a-297b, 12/27/89.

Miniature sheets have surrounding selvage and were sold folded and unattached in booklet covers. Nos. 297a, 297b with straight edges around stamps and attached to booklet covers by tabs.

See Nos. 372-378, 453-454.

Lieutenant-General John Doyle (1756-1834) — A64

Designs: 13p, Portrait by James Ramsey, 1817. 29p, American War of Independence battle. 31p, Land fill, Grand Havre Bay. 34p, Ship approaching Casquets Reef, 1811. 29p, 31p, 34p horiz.

**1984, Nov. 20 Photo. *Perf. 11½***

**303** A64 13p multicolored .40 .40
**304** A64 29p multicolored .95 .95
**305** A64 31p multicolored 1.00 1.00
**306** A64 34p multicolored 1.10 1.00
*Nos. 303-306 (4)* 3.45 3.35

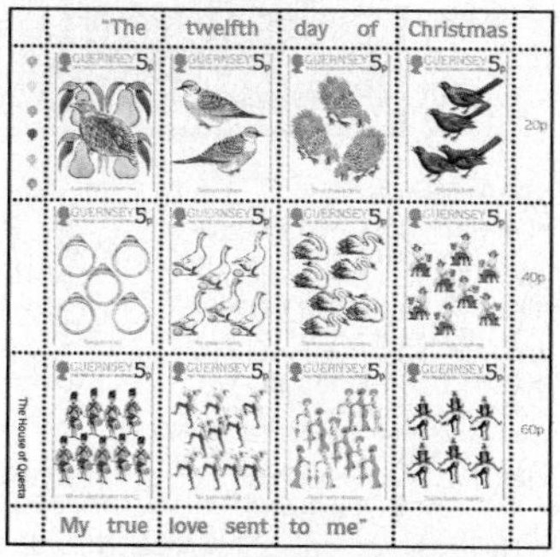


Christmas 1984 — A65

Twelve Days of Christmas: a, Partridge in a Pear Tree. b, 2 Turtle Doves. c, 3 French Hens. d, 4 Colly Birds. e, 5 Golden Rings. f, 6 Geese-a-Laying. g, 7 Swans a-Swimming. h, 8 Maids a-Milking. i, 9 Drummers Drumming. j, 10 Pipers Piping. k, 11 Ladies Dancing. l, 12 Lords a-Leaping.

**1984, Nov. 20 Litho. *Perf. 14½***

**307** A65 Sheet of 12 2.50 2.50
*a.-l.* 5p any single .25 .25

Indigenous Fish — A66

**1985, Jan. 22 Photo. *Perf. 12***

**308** A66 9p Cockoo Wrasse .40 .40
**309** A66 13p Red Gurnard .65 .65
**310** A66 29p Red Mullet 1.25 1.25
**311** A66 31p Mackerel 1.60 1.60
**312** A66 34p Sunfish 1.75 1.75
*Nos. 308-312 (5)* 5.65 5.65

Liberation from German Forces, 40th Anniv. A67

**1985, May 9 Litho. *Perf. 14x14½***

**313** A67 22p Peace dove 1.00 1.00

Celebrating the end of the war in Europe (VE-Day).

Europa 1985 — A68

Designs: 14p, Musical staff, flags of Great Britain, Netherlands, Germany, Italy, Cross of St. George. 22p, Music, cello, French horn.

**1985, May 14 Litho. *Perf. 14½***

**314** A68 14p multicolored .55 .55
**315** A68 22p multicolored .90 .90

Intl. Youth Year — A69

**1985, May 14 Litho. *Perf. 14***

**316** A69 9p IYY emblem, circle of children .35 .35
**317** A69 31p Girl Guides in camp 1.25 1.25

Children's drawings.

Girl Guides, 75th Anniv. — A70

**1985, May 14 Litho. *Perf. 14***

**318** A70 34p Leader, guide and brownie 1.40 1.40

Child's drawing.

Christmas 1985 — A71

Religious and folk figures: a, Santa Claus. b, Lussibruden. c, Balthasar. d, St. Nicholas. e, La Befana. f, Julenisse. g, Christkind. h, King Wenceslas. i, Shepherd of Les Baux. j, Caspar. k, Baboushka. l, Melchior.

**1985, Nov. 19 Litho. *Perf. 12½***
**Granite Paper**

**319** A71 Sheet of 12 *5.00 5.00*
*a.-l.* 5p any single .40 .40

Watercolors by Paul Jacob Naftel — A72

**1985, Nov. 19 *Perf. 15x14½***

**320** A72 9p Vraicing .35 .35
**321** A72 14p Castle Cornet .55 .55
**322** A72 22p Rocquaine Bay .90 .90
**323** A72 31p Little Russel 1.25 1.25
**324** A72 34p Seaweed Gatherers 1.40 1.40
*Nos. 320-324 (5)* 4.45 4.45

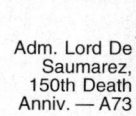

Adm. Lord De Saumarez, 150th Death Anniv. — A73

Designs: 9p, Squadron off Nargue Is., 1809. 14p, Battle of the Nile, 1798. 29p, Battle of St. Vincent, 1797. 31p, HMS Crescent off Cherbourg, 1793. 34p, Battle of the Saints, 1782.

**1986, Feb. 4 Litho. *Perf. 12x11½***
**Granite Paper**

**325** A73 9p multicolored .35 .35
**326** A73 14p multicolored .55 .55
**327** A73 29p multicolored 1.10 1.10
**328** A73 31p multicolored 1.40 1.40
**329** A73 34p multicolored 1.50 1.50
*Nos. 325-329 (5)* 4.90 4.90

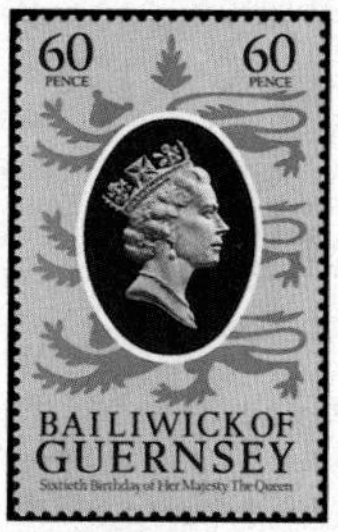


Queen Elizabeth II, 60th Birthday — A74

**1986, Apr. 21 *Perf. 14***

**330** A74 60p multicolored 2.50 2.50

Europa 1986 — A75

**1986, May 22 *Perf. 11½***
**Granite Paper**

**331** A75 10p Operation Gannet *.40 .40*
**332** A75 14p Whitsun orchid *.55 .55*
**333** A75 22p Guernsey elm *.90 .90*
*Nos. 331-333 (3)* 1.85 1.85

Wedding of Prince Andrew and Sarah Ferguson — A76

**1986, July 23 Litho. *Perf. 14***

**334** A76 14p Couple .60 .60

**Size: 48x32mm**

**335** A76 34p Couple, diff. 1.50 1.50

Sports A77

**1986, July 24 *Perf. 14½***

**336** A77 10p Lawn bowling, vert. .40 .40
**337** A77 14p Cricket, vert. .55 .55
**338** A77 22p Badminton, vert. .90 .90
**339** A77 29p Field hockey, vert. 1.10 1.10
**340** A77 31p Swimming 1.25 1.25
**341** A77 34p Rifle shooting 1.40 1.40
*Nos. 336-341 (6)* 5.60 5.60

Museums A78

**1986, Nov. 18 Litho. *Perf. 14½***

**342** A78 14p Guernsey Museum and Art Gallery .55 .55
**343** A78 29p Ft. Grey Maritime Museum 1.10 1.10
**344** A78 31p Castle Cornet 1.25 1.25
**345** A78 34p Natl. Trust of Guernsey Folk Museum 1.40 1.40
*Nos. 342-345 (4)* 4.30 4.30

Miniature Sheet

Christmas — A79

Carols: a, "While Shepherds Watched Their Flocks by Night." b, "In the Bleak Mid-Winter." c, "O Little Town of Bethlehem." d, "The Holly and the Ivy." e, "O Little Christmas Tree." f, "Away in a Manger." g, "Good King Wenceslas." h, "We Three Kings of Orient Are." i, "Hark the Herald Angels Sing." j, "I Saw Three Ships." k, "Little Donkey." l, "Jingle Bells."

**1986, Nov. 18 *Perf. 12½***

**346** A79 Sheet of 12 2.75 2.75
*a.-l.* 6p any single .25 .25

Souvenir Sheet

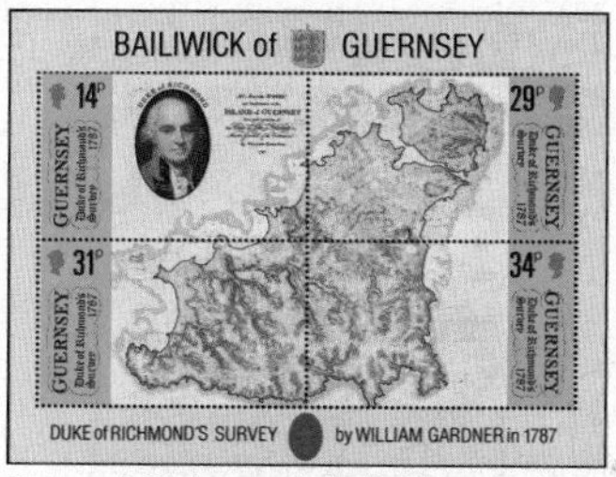


Duke of Richmond, 18th Century Map Detail — A80

14p, Duke of Richmond, part of map in bottom right corner. 29p, North. 31p, Southwest. 34p, Southeast.

**1987, Feb. 10 Litho. *Perf. 14½***

**347** Sheet of 4 4.50 4.50
*a.* A80 14p multicolored .55 .55
*b.* A80 29p multicolored 1.10 1.10
*c.* A80 31p multicolored 1.25 1.25
*d.* A80 34p multicolored 1.40 1.40

Duke of Richmond's survey of Guernsey, bicent.

Europa 1987 — A81

Modern architecture.

**1987, May 5 Litho. *Perf. 13x13½***

**348** A81 15p Postal headquarters *.60 .60*
**349** A81 15p Headquarters, schematic view *.60 .60*
*a.* Pair, #348-349 *1.25 1.25*
**350** A81 22p Grammar school entrance *.90 .90*
**351** A81 22p School, schematic view *.90 .90*
*a.* Pair, #350-351 *1.90 1.90*

Andros and La Plaiderie Court House, Guernsey A82

Andros and: 29p, Governor's Palace, Virginia. 31p, "Governor Andros and the Boston People," print from Harper's New Monthly Magazine. 34p, Map of New Amsterdam (New York City).

**1987, July 7 Granite Paper** ***Perf. 12***

**352** A82 15p multicolored .60 .60
**353** A82 29p multicolored 1.10 1.10
**354** A82 31p multicolored 1.25 1.25
**355** A82 34p multicolored 1.40 1.40
*Nos. 352-355 (4)* 4.35 4.35

Sir Edmund Andros (1637-1714), lieutenant-governor of Guernsey (1704-1706) and statesman of Colonial America (1672-1710).

William the Conqueror (c. 1028-1087), King of England (1066-1087) — A83

11p, Jester warning young William of a plot to murder him. #357, Battle of Hastings. #358, King William, his banner at the Battle of Hastings. #359, William the Conqueror. #360, Abbey at Caen & Queen Matilda of Flanders (d. 1083). 34p, Halley's Comet & regalia of William I.

**1987, Sept. 9** ***Perf. 13½x14***

**356** A83 11p multicolored .45 .50
**357** A83 15p multicolored .60 .65
**358** A83 15p multicolored .60 .65
*a.* Pair, #357-358 1.25 1.40
**359** A83 22p multicolored .90 .95
**360** A83 22p multicolored .90 .95
*a.* Pair, #359-360 1.90 2.00
**361** A83 34p multicolored 1.40 1.50
*Nos. 356-361 (6)* 4.85 5.20

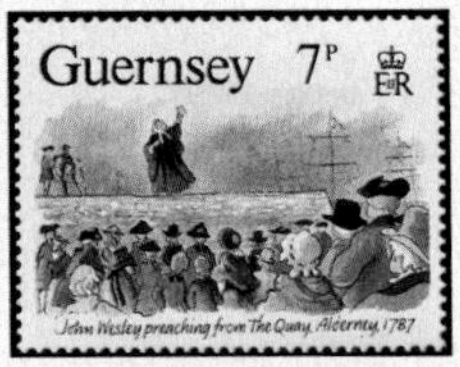


Visit of John Wesley (1703-1791), Religious Reformer, Bicent. — A84

Designs: 7p, Preaching at the quay, Alderney. 15p, Preaching at Mon Plaisir. 29p, Preaching at Assembly Rooms, St. Peter Port. 31p, Wesley and La Ville Baudu, an early Methodist meeting place, Vale Parish. 34p, Wesley and Ebenezer Methodist Church, first Methodist chapel, Union Street, 1816.

**1987, Nov. 17 Litho.** ***Perf. 14½***

**362** A84 7p multicolored .30 .30
**363** A84 15p multicolored .60 .60
**364** A84 29p multicolored 1.10 1.10
**365** A84 31p multicolored 1.25 1.25
**366** A84 34p multicolored 1.40 1.40
*Nos. 362-366 (5)* 4.65 4.65

Voyage of the Golden Spur, Apr. 12, 1872-Jan. 4, 1874 — A85

Designs: 11p, Off St. Sampson's Harbor. 15p, Entering Hong Kong Harbor. 29p, Anchored off Macao. 31p, In China Tea Race. 34p, Golden Spur, map of voyage.

**1988, Feb. 9 Litho.** ***Perf. 13½x14***

**367** A85 11p multicolored .45 .45
**368** A85 15p multicolored .60 .60
**369** A85 29p multicolored 1.10 1.10
**370** A85 31p multicolored 1.25 1.25
**371** A85 34p multicolored 1.40 1.40
*Nos. 367-371 (5)* 4.80 4.80

Guernsey's Golden Age of Shipping: largest vessel built on Guernsey, the Golden Spur, launched Oct. 15, 1864, wrecked at Haiphong on Feb. 27, 1879.

**Landscape Type of 1984**

***Perf. 14½x15, 15x14½***

**1988-89** **Litho.**

**372** A63 12p Petit Bot beach, vert. .50 .50
**373** A63 16p St. John's Hostel for the Aged .65 .65
*a.* Min. sheet, 5 each 12p, 16p 6.50
*b.* Min. sheet, 4 4p, 3 12p, 3 16p 5.00
**374** A63 18p Le Variouf, vert. .70 .70
*a.* Booklet pane, 4p, 6p, 3 12p, 3 18p 4.00
*b.* Booklet pane, 4 12p, 4 18p 3.50
*Nos. 372-374 (3)* 1.85 1.85

Nos. 373a-373b have surrounding selvage and were sold unattached in booklet covers. Nos. 374a, 374b with straight edges around stamps and attached to booklet covers by tabs.

Issued: Nos. 372-373b, 3/28/88; Nos. 374-374b, 2/28/89.

**Coil Stamps**

**Sizes: 21½x17½mm, 17½x21½mm**

***Perf. 14x14½, 14½x14***

**375** A63 11p La Seigneurie, Sark .45 .45
**376** A63 12p Petit Bot beach .50 .50
**377** A63 15p Havelet, vert. .60 .60
**378** A63 16p St. John's Hostel for the Aged .65 .65
*Nos. 375-378 (4)* 2.20 2.20

Issued: 11p, 15p, 5/15/87; 12p, 16p, 3/28/88.

Waves, Map — A85a

***Perf. 14½x14***

**1989, Apr. 3 Photo. Coil Stamp**

**380** A85a (18p) green 1.00 1.00

Inscribed "MINIMUM FIRST CLASS POSTAGE TO UK PAID." See No. 431.

Europa 1988 A86

Communication and transportation: No. 381, Bedford Rascal postal van, Lihou Is. rowboat. No. 382, Rowboat, Viscount plane. No. 383, Horse and buggy, front wheel of bicycle. No. 384, Back wheel of bicycle, No. 4 coach.

**1988, May 10 Litho.** ***Perf. 14½***

**381** A86 16p multicolored .65 .65
**382** A86 16p multicolored .65 .65
*a.* Pair, #381-382 1.40 1.40
**383** A86 22p multicolored .90 .90
**384** A86 22p multicolored .90 .90
*a.* Pair, #383-384 1.90 1.90
*Nos. 381-384 (4)* 3.10 3.10

#382a, 384a have continuous designs.

Frederick Corbin Lukis (1788-1871), Archaeologist A87

Designs: 12p, Entrance to Lukis House, St. Peter Port, and portrait. 16p, Bound manuscript containing illustrations painted by Lukis's daughter Mary Anne (born 1822). 29p, Lukis supervising excavation of Le Creux es Faies dolmen at L'Eree, Guernsey. 31p, Rear of Lukis House and garden. 34p, Artifacts recovered by Lukis and preserved as part of the museum collection.

**1988, July 12 Photo.** ***Perf. 12½***

**Granite Paper**

**385** A87 12p multicolored .50 .50
**386** A87 16p multicolored .65 .65
**387** A87 29p multicolored 1.10 1.10
**388** A87 31p multicolored 1.25 1.25
**389** A87 34p multicolored 1.40 1.40
*Nos. 385-389 (5)* 4.90 4.90

1988 World Offshore Powerboat Championships — A88

Designs: 16p, Racing boats, Royal Navy helicopter. 30p, Boats racing through Gouliot Passage (separating Sark from Brecqhou). 32p, Boats, helicopter, St. John's Ambulance rescue ship, vert. 35p, Race course marked in red on Admiralty Chart, vert.

**1988, Sept. 6** ***Perf. 12***

**Granite Paper**

**390** A88 16p multicolored .65 .65
**391** A88 30p multicolored 1.25 1.25
**392** A88 32p multicolored 1.25 1.25
**393** A88 35p multicolored 1.40 1.40
*Nos. 390-393 (4)* 4.55 4.55

Publication of *Flora Sarniensis,* Bicent. — A89

Designs: 12p, Joshua Gosselin (1739-1813), botanist, and herbarium made by Rollo Sherwill in 1976. No. 395, *Lagurus ovatus* (pressed specimen). No. 396, *Lagurus ovatus,* diff. No. 397, *Silene gallica quinquevulnera* (pressed specimen). No. 398, *Silene gallica quinquevulnera,* diff. 35p, *Limonium binervosum sarniense serquense.*

**1988, Nov. 15 Litho.** ***Perf. 14***

**394** A89 12p shown .50 .50
**395** A89 16p multicolored .65 .65
**396** A89 16p multicolored .65 .65
*a.* Pair, #395-396 1.40 1.40
**397** A89 23p multicolored .90 .90
**398** A89 23p multicolored .90 .90
*a.* Pair, #397-398 1.90 1.90
**399** A89 35p multicolored 1.40 1.40
*Nos. 394-399 (6)* 5.00 5.00

Miniature Sheet

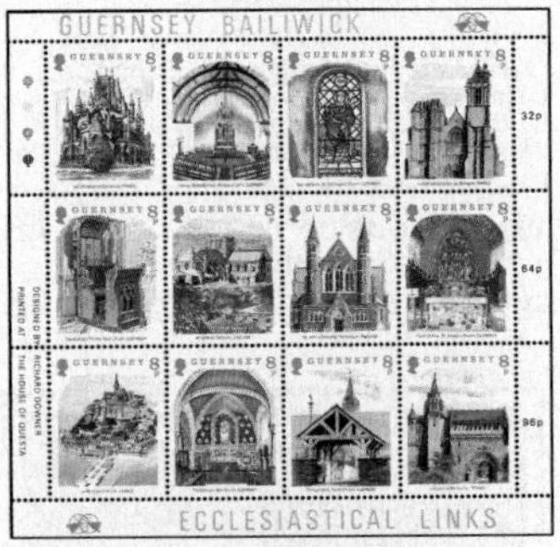


Ecclesiastical Links to France and Great Britain — A90

Church interiors, exteriors and artifacts: a, Coutances Cathedral, France. b, Notre Dame du Rosaire Church interior, Guernsey. c, Stained-glass window, St. Sampson's Church, Guernsey. d, Dol-de-Bretagne Cathedral, France. e, Bishop's Throne, Town Church, Guernsey. f, Winchester Cathedral, England. g, St. John's Cathedral, Portsmouth, England. h, High Altar, St. Joseph's Church, Guernsey. i, Mont Saint-Michel, France. j, Chancel, Vale Church, Guernsey. k, The Lychgate, Forest Church, Guernsey. l, Marmoutier Abbey, France.

**1988, Nov. 15** ***Perf. 14½x15***

**400** A90 Sheet of 12 4.00 4.00
*a.-l.* 8p any single .30 .30

Christmas 1988.

Europa 1989 — A91

Traditional children's toys and games.

**1989, Feb. 28 Litho.** ***Perf. 13½***

**401** A91 12p Tip cat (Le Cat) .50 .50
**402** A91 16p Girl, Cobo Alice doll .65 .65
**403** A91 23p Hopscotch (Le Colimachaon) .90 .90
*Nos. 401-403 (3)* 2.05 2.05

Aircraft A92

**1989, May 5**

**404** A92 12p DH86 Express .50 .50
*a.* Booklet pane of 6 3.25
**405** A92 12p Southampton .50 .50
**406** A92 18p DH89 Rapide .70 .70
*a.* Booklet pane of 6 4.75
**407** A92 18p Sunderland .70 .70
**408** A92 35p BAe 146 1.40 1.40
*a.* Booklet pane of 6 9.50
Complete booklet, #404a, 406a, 408a 17.50
**409** A92 35p Shackleton 1.40 1.40
*Nos. 404-409 (6)* 5.20 5.20

Guernsey Airport, 50th anniv. (Nos. 404, 406, 408); others, 201st Squadron Affiliation, 50th anniv.

Visit of Queen Elizabeth II, May 23-24 — A93

**1989, May 23** ***Perf. 15x14***

**410** A93 30p Portrait by June Mendoza 1.25 1.25

Great Western Railway Steamer Service Between Weymouth and the Channel Isls., Cent. — A94

**1989, Sept. 5 Litho.** ***Perf. 13½***

**411** A94 12p S.S. *Ibex,* 1891 .50 .50
**412** A94 18p P.S. *Great Western,* 1872 .70 .70
**413** A94 29p S.S. *St. Julien,* 1925 1.10 1.10
**414** A94 34p S.S. *Roebuck,* 1925 1.40 1.40
**415** A94 37p S.S. *Antelope,* 1889 1.50 1.50
*a.* Souvenir sheet of 5, #411-415 5.50 5.50
*Nos. 411-415 (5)* 5.20 5.20

Zoological Trust of Guernsey — A95

**1989, Nov. 17 Litho. *Perf. 14x13½***

**416** A95 18p Two-toed sloth .70 .70
**417** A95 29p Capuchin monkey 1.10 1.10
**418** A95 32p White-lipped tamarin 1.25 1.25
**419** A95 34p Squirrel monkey 1.40 1.40
**420** A95 37p Lar gibbon 1.50 1.50
*a.* Strip of 5, #416-420 6.00 6.00

Animals of the rainforest.

Miniature Sheet

Christmas — A96

Ornaments on tree: a, Star. b, Angel. c, Candles. d, Robin red breast. e, Presents on sled. f, Caroler. g, Santa Claus pictured on Christmas cracker. h, Herald and stars pictured on glass ball. i, Presents in stocking. j, Bell. k, Reindeer. l, Chapel.

**1989, Nov. 17 *Perf. 13***

**421** A96 Sheet of 12 5.00 5.00
*a.-l.* 10p any single .40 .40

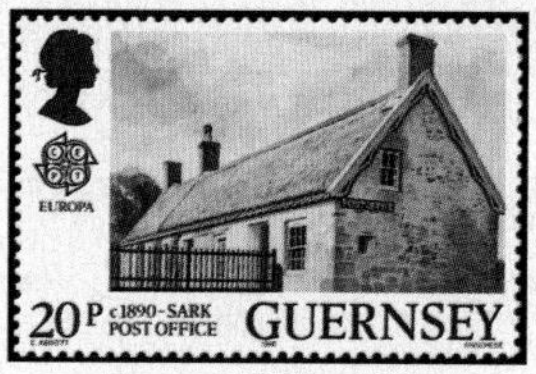


Europa 1990 — A97

Post offices.

**1990, Feb. 27 Litho. *Perf. 13½x14***

**422** A97 20p Sark, c. 1890 *.80 .80*
**423** A97 20p Sark, 1990 *.80 .80*
**424** A97 24p Arcade, c. 1840 *.95 .95*
**425** A97 24p Arcade, 1990 *.95 .95*
*Nos. 422-425 (4)* 3.50 3.50

Penny Black, 150th Anniv. A98

Designs: 14p, Great Britain No. 1, Maltese Cross cancellation in red, mail steamer in St. Peter Port Harbor. 20p, Great Britain No. 3, Maltese Cross cancellation in black, pedestrians, mailbox at Elm Grove and Union Street in 1852. 32p, Great Britain No. 255 bisected, 1940, and military band. 34p, Guernsey No. 2, crown of William the Conqueror, Guernsey lily. 37p, Guernsey No. 10, crowd in line outside Guernsey P.O.

**1990, May 3 *Perf. 14***

**426** A98 14p multicolored .55 .55
**427** A98 20p multicolored .80 .80
**428** A98 32p multicolored 1.25 1.25
**429** A98 34p multicolored 1.40 1.40
**430** A98 37p multicolored 1.50 1.50
*a.* Souvenir sheet of 5, #426-430 6.00 6.00
*b.* No. 430a ovptd. "NZ 1990" emblem, "FROM LONDON 90 TO NEW ZEALAND 90" 16.00 16.00
*Nos. 426-430 (5)* 5.50 5.50

**Map and Waves Type of 1989**

**1989, Dec. 27 Photo. *Perf. 14½x14***

**Coil Stamp**

**431** A85a (14p) ultra & lt ultra .85 .85

Inscribed "MINIMUM BAILIWICK POSTAGE PAID."

Lord Anson's Circumnavigation of the World, 250th Anniv. — A99

Designs: 14p, Philip Saumarez writing ship's log. 20p, *Centurion, Gloucester, Severn, Pearle, Wager* and *Tryal* departing from Portsmouth. 29p, Landfall at St. Catherine's Is. off Brazil, 1740. 34p, *Tryal* rounding Cape Horn, 1741. 37p, Camp at Juan Fernandez, 1741.

**1990, July 24 Litho. *Perf. 13½x14***

**436** A99 14p multicolored .55 .55
**437** A99 20p multicolored .80 .80
**438** A99 29p multicolored 1.10 1.10
**439** A99 34p multicolored 1.40 1.40
**440** A99 37p multicolored 1.50 1.50
*Nos. 436-440 (5)* 5.35 5.35

Gray Seal A100

**1990, Oct. 16 Litho. *Perf. 14½***

**441** A100 20p shown *1.25* .75
**442** A100 26p Bottlenose dolphin *2.25* 1.10
**443** A100 31p Basking shark *2.50* 1.40
**444** A100 37p Harbor porpoise *2.75* 1.60
*Nos. 441-444 (4)* *8.75* 4.85

World Wildlife Fund.

Miniature Sheet

Christmas — A101

Winter birds: a, Blue and Great Tits. b, Snow Bunting. c, Kestrel. d, Starling. e, Greenfinch. f, Robin. g, Wren. h, Barn owl. i, Mistle Thrush. j, Heron. k, Chaffinch. l, Kingfisher.

**1990, Oct. 16 *Perf. 13½***

**445** A101 Sheet of 12 5.00 5.00
*a.-l.* 10p any single .40 .40

Occupation Stamp No. N1, 50th Anniv. — A102

**1991, Feb. 18 Litho. *Perf. 13½***

**446** A102 37p shown 1.50 1.50
**447** A102 53p No. N2 2.10 2.10
**448** A102 57p No. N3 2.25 2.25
*a.* Booklet pane of 3, #446-448 6.00
Complete booklet, 3 #448a 18.00
*Nos. 446-448 (3)* 5.85 5.85

No. 448a printed in three formats with Nos. 446-448 in different order.

Europa — A103

Designs: No. 449, Royal Visit to Guernsey, discovery of Neptune, 1846. No. 450, Royal Visit to Sark, launch of Sputnik, 1957. No. 451, Maiden voyage of ferry Sarnia, first manned space flight, 1961. No. 452, Independence of Guernsey Post Office, first man on moon, 1969.

**1991, Apr. 1 Litho. *Perf. 13½x14***

**449** A103 21p multicolored *.85 .85*
**450** A103 21p multicolored *.85 .85*
**451** A103 26p multicolored *1.00 1.00*
**452** A103 26p multicolored *1.00 1.00*
*Nos. 449-452 (4)* 3.70 3.70

**Landscape Type of 1984**

**1991 Litho. *Perf. 15x14½, 14½x15***

**453** A63 21p King's Mills, St. Saviours .85 .85
*a.* Booklet pane, 3 each #453, #296, 2 each #287, #288) 3.50
*b.* Booklet pane, 5 each #453, #296) 6.00
**454** A63 26p Town Church, St. Peter Port, vert. 1.00 1.00

Issued: 21p, 26p, 4/1; #453a, 453b, 4/2.

#453a, 453b with straight edges around stamps and attached to booklet covers by tabs.

Guernsey Yacht Club, Cent. — A104

**1991, July 2 Litho. *Perf. 14***

**459** A104 15p Guernsey Sailing Trust .60 .60
**460** A104 21p Guernsey Regatta .80 .80
**461** A104 26p Channel Islands Challenge 1.00 1.00
**462** A104 31p Rolex Swan Regatta 1.25 1.25
**463** A104 37p Old Gaffers Assoc. 1.50 1.50
*a.* Souvenir sheet of 5, #459-463 5.50 5.50
*Nos. 459-463 (5)* 5.15 5.15

"Guernsey" and denomination in white on sheet stamps, yellow on souvenir sheet stamps.

Miniature Sheet

Christmas — A105

Children's Paintings: a, Reindeer by Melanie Sharpe. b, Christmas pudding by James Quinn. c, Snowman by Lisa Marie Guille. d, Snowman by Jessica Ede-Golightly. e, Birds by Sharon Le Page. f, Shepherds, sheep, angels by Anna Coquelin. g, Manger scene by Claudine Lihou. h, Three kings by Jonathan Le Noury. i, Children, angels, Star of Bethlehem by Marcia Mahy. j, Christmas tree, presents by Laurel Garfield. k, Santa Claus by Rebecca Driscoll. l, Snowman by Ian Lowe.

**1991, Oct. 15 Litho. *Perf. 13***

**464** A105 Sheet of 12 5.75 5.75
*a.-l.* 12p any single .45 .45

Nature Conservation A106

Birds and plants: No. 465: a, Two oyster catchers. b, Three turnstones. c, Two dunlins, two turnstones. d, Curlew, two turnstones. e, Ringed plover, chicks.

No. 466: a, Violet and white flowers. b, Yellow flowers. c, Small yellow flowers. d, Violet, yellow and white flowers. e, Long-stemmed yellow flowers.

**1991, Oct. 15 *Perf. 14½***

**465** Strip of 5 3.00 3.00
*a.-e.* A106 15p any single .60 .60
**466** Strip of 5 4.25 4.25
*a.-e.* A106 21p any single .85 .85

Discovery of America, 500th Anniv. — A107

**1992, Feb. 6 Litho. *Perf. 13½x14***

**467** A107 23p Columbus *.90 .90*
**468** A107 23p Columbus' signatures *.90 .90*
**469** A107 28p Map of 1st voyage *1.10 1.10*
**470** A107 28p Santa Maria *1.10 1.10*
*a.* Souvenir sheet, #467-470 *7.00 7.00*
*b.* No. 470a overprinted in brown in sheet margin *8.00 8.00*
*Nos. 467-470 (4)* 4.00 4.00

Europa. No. 470b overprint shows emblem of World Columbian Stamp Expo '92.

Issue date: No. 470b, May 22.

Queen Elizabeth II's Accession to Throne, 40th Anniv. — A108

Various portraits of Queen Elizabeth II from 1952, 1977, 1986 and 1992.

**1992, Feb. 6 Litho. *Perf. 14***

**471** A108 23p multicolored .90 .90
**472** A108 28p multicolored 1.10 1.10
**473** A108 33p multicolored 1.25 1.25
**474** A108 39p multicolored 1.60 1.60
*Nos. 471-474 (4)* 4.85 4.85

Souvenir Sheet

Guernsey Cows — A109

**1992, May 22 Litho. *Perf. 14***

**475** A109 75p multicolored 3.00 3.00

Royal Guernsey Agricultural and Horticultural Society, 150th anniv.

Flowers — A110

**1992-96** *Perf. 13*

**476** A110 1p Stephanotis floribunda .25 .25
**477** A110 2p Potted hydrangea .25 .25
**478** A110 3p Stock .25 .25
**479** A110 4p Anemones .25 .25
**480** A110 5p Gladiolus .25 .25
**481** A110 6p Gypsophila paniculata, asparagus plumosus .25 .25
**482** A110 7p Guernsey lily .25 .25
**483** A110 8p Enchantment lily .30 .30
**484** A110 9p Clematis freckles .35 .35
**485** A110 10p Alstroemeria .40 .40
**486** A110 16p Standard carnation, horiz. .65 .55
*a.* Perf. 14 on 3 sides, inscribed "1993" .65 .55
*b.* Booklet pane of 8 #486a 5.00
Complete booklet, 1 #486b 5.00
*c.* Inscribed "1992" .65 .55
**487** A110 20p Spray rose .80 .75
**488** A110 23p Mixed freesia, horiz. .90 .85
*a.* Perf. 14 on 3 sides .90 .85
*b.* Bklt. pane of 5 #486c, 3 #488a 6.50 6.50
Complete booklet, 1 #488b 6.50
*c.* Booklet pane of 8, #488a 8.00 8.00
Complete booklet, 1 #488c 8.00
**489** A110 24p Standard rose, horiz. .95 .80
*a.* Perf. 14 on 3 sides 1.00 .80
*b.* Booklet pane of 8 #489a 8.00
Complete booklet, 1 #489b 8.00
**490** A110 25p Iris ideal 1.00 .80
*a.* Perf. 14½ on 3 sides 1.10 .80
*b.* As "a," booklet pane of 4 4.50
Complete booklet, 1 #490b 4.50
**491** A110 28p Lisianthus, horiz. 1.10 .75
*a.* Perf. 14 on 3 sides 1.25 .80
*b.* Booklet pane of 4 #491a 5.00
Complete booklet, 1 #491b 5.00
**492** A110 30p Spray chrysanthemum, horiz. 1.25 1.10
**493** A110 40p Spray carnation 1.60 1.25
**494** A110 50p Single freesia, horiz. 2.00 1.50

**Size: 39x30mm**

*Perf. 13¾*

**495** A110 £1 Bouquet, horiz., inscribed "1992" 4.00 3.00
*a.* Souv. sheet of 1 + label, perf. 13, inscribed "1994" 4.50 4.50
*b.* Souv. sheet of 1 + label, perf. 13, inscribed "1995" 4.50 4.50
**496** A110 £2 Chelsea flower show, horiz. 8.00 8.00

**Size: 39x31mm**

*Perf. 13¼*

**497** A110 £3 Floral fantasia, horiz. 12.00 10.00
*Nos. 476-497 (22)* 37.05 32.15

PHILAKOREA '94 (#495a). Singapore '95 (#495b).

Issued: 3p, 4p, 5p, 10p, 16p, 20p, 23p, 40p, 50p, £1, 5/22/92; 1p, 2p, 6p, 7p, 8p, 9p, 24p, 28p, 30p, £2, #486a, 3/2/93; #486b, 489b, 491b, 3/3/93: #488a, 488b, 5/22/92; 25p, 2/18/94; #490b, 2/18/94; #495a, 8/94; #495b, 9/1/95; £3, 1/24/96.

Perf 14 or 14½ stamps issued only in booklets.

See Nos. 584-585.

Operation Asterix A111

**1992, Sept. 18** **Litho.** *Perf. 13*

**498** A111 16p Ship construction .65 .65
**499** A111 23p Loading cargo .90 .90
**500** A111 28p Ship at sea 1.10 1.10
**501** A111 33p Ship on fire 1.25 1.25
**502** A111 39p Ship sinking 1.50 1.50
*a.* Bklt. pane of #498-502 + label 5.50
Complete booklet, 4 #502a 22.50
*Nos. 498-502 (5)* 5.40 5.40

No. 502a exists with four different labels: Great Britain, France, Italy, Germany. Booklet contains one of each type.

Historic Trams A112

Designs: 16p, Tram No. 10 decorated for Battle of Flowers. 23p, No. 10 passing Hougue a la Perre. 28p, Tram No. 1 at St. Sampsons. 33p, First steam tram, St. Peter Port, 1879. 39p, Last electric tram, 1934.

**1992, Nov. 17** **Litho.** *Perf. 13½x14*

**503** A112 16p multicolored .65 .65
**504** A112 23p multicolored .90 .90
**505** A112 28p multicolored 1.10 1.10
**506** A112 33p multicolored 1.25 1.25
**507** A112 39p multicolored 1.50 1.50
*Nos. 503-507 (5)* 5.40 5.40

Christmas — A113

a, Father dressed as Santa. b, Girl pulling end of cracker. c, Mother. d, Champagne, mince pies. e, Turkey. f, Plum pudding. g, Cake. h, Cookies. i, Wine, blue cheese. j, Nuts. k, Ham. l, Cake roll.

**1992, Nov. 17** *Perf. 13½*

**508** A113 Sheet of 12 6.25 6.25
*a.-l.* 13p any single .50 .50

A114

Rupert Bear and friends, created by Mary Tourtel: No. 509: Rupert Bear, Bingo, and dog. No. 510a, 24p, Bill Badger, Willie Mouse, Reggie Rabbit, and Podgy Pig with snowman. No. 510b, 16p, Airplane above castle tower. No. 510c, 24p, Balloonist leaping away from Gregory on sled. No. 510d, 16p, Professor's servant and Autumn Elf. No. 510e, 16p, Algy Pug. No. 510f, 16p, Baby Badger on sled. No. 510g, 24p, Tiger Lily and Edward Trunk.

**1993, Feb. 2** **Litho.** *Perf. 13½x13*

**509** A114 24p multicolored .95 .95
**510** A114 Sheet of 8, #a.-g. & #509 7.00 7.00

No. 510 printed in continuous design. Nos. 510b, 510d-510f are 25x26mm.

Contemporary Art — A115

Europa: No. 511, Tapestry, by Kelly Fletcher. No. 512, The Fish Market, by Sally Reed. No. 513, Dress Shop, King's Road, by Damon Bell. No. 514, Red Abstract, by Molly Harris.

**1993, May 7** **Litho.** *Perf. 13½x14*

**Size: 45x30mm (#512, 513)**

**511** A115 24p multicolored *.95 .95*
**512** A115 24p multicolored *.95 .95*
**513** A115 28p multicolored *1.10 1.10*
**514** A115 28p multicolored *1.10 1.10*
*Nos. 511-514 (4)* 4.10 4.10

Siege of Castle Cornet, 1643-51 — A116

16p, Shipboard arrest of Parliamentarian officials. 24p, Parliamentarian warships firing on castle. 28p, Captured officials fleeing from castle. 33p, Cannon firing from castle into St. Peter Port. 39p, Surrender of castle.

**1993, May 7** *Perf. 15x14*

**515** A116 16p multicolored .65 .65
**516** A116 24p multicolored .95 .95
**517** A116 28p multicolored 1.10 1.10
**518** A116 33p multicolored 1.25 1.25
**519** A116 39p multicolored 1.50 1.50
*a.* Souvenir sheet of 5, #515-519 5.50 5.50
*Nos. 515-519 (5)* 5.45 5.45

Thomas de la Rue, Printer, Birth Bicent. — A117

Designs: 16p, Playing card king, queen and jack. 24p, Swift reservoir fountain pens. 28p, Envelope folding machine. 33p, Great Britain type A5. 39p, £1 Mauritius bank note, portrait of de la Rue.

**1993, July 27** **Litho.** *Perf. 13½*

**520** A117 16p multicolored .65 .65
**521** A117 24p multicolored .95 .95
**522** A117 28p multicolored 1.10 1.10

**Engr.**

**523** A117 33p rose carmine 1.25 1.25
**524** A117 39p green 1.50 1.50
*Nos. 520-524 (5)* 5.45 5.45

*520a* Booklet pane of 4 3.00
*521a* Booklet pane of 4 4.25
*522a* Booklet pane of 4 4.75
*523a* Booklet pane of 4 5.50
*524a* Booklet pane of 4 6.50
Complete booklet, #520a-524a 24.00

Miniature Sheet

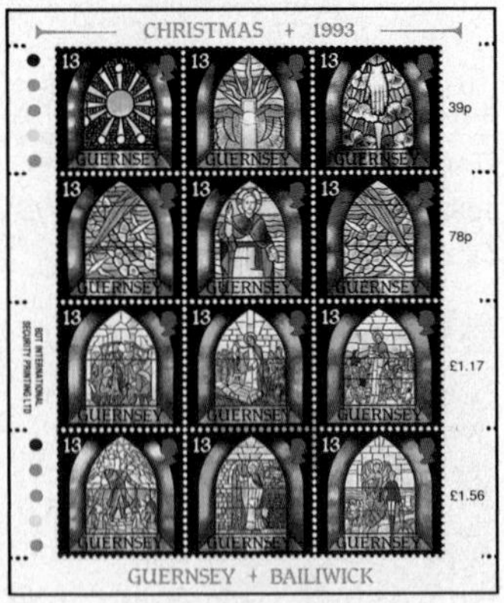


Christmas — A118

Stained glass windows, Chapel of Christ the Healer: a, Sunburst. b, Light from sun. c, Hand of God. d, Doves descending left. e, Christ raising hand. f, Doves descending right. g, Christ Child sitting in temple. h, Christ raising daughter of Jairus from dead. i, "Suffer little children to come unto me." j, Scene from Pilgrim's Progress. k, The Light of the World. l, Archangel of Healing.

**1993, Nov. 2** **Litho.** *Perf. 13x13½*

**525** A118 Sheet of 12 6.25 6.25
*a.-l.* 13p any single .50 .45

Archaeological Discoveries — A119

Europa: No. 526, Warrior on horseback. No. 527, Burial site, Les Fouaillages. No. 528, Sword, scabbard, spear. No. 529, Cerny-style pots, arrowheads, axe.

**1994, Feb. 18** **Litho.** *Perf. 13½*

**526** A119 24p multicolored .95 .95
*a.* Sheet of 10 with added inscription 12.00 12.00
**527** A119 24p multicolored .95 .95
**528** A119 30p multicolored 1.25 1.25
**529** A119 30p multicolored 1.25 1.25
*Nos. 526-529 (4)* 4.40 4.40

No. 526a inscribed in sheet margin with Hong Kong '94 emblem and "PHILATELIC EXHIBITION / 18-21 FEBRUARY 1994" in English and Chinese.

Souvenir Sheet

D-Day, 50th Anniv. — A120

£2, Canadian Wing Spitfires flying over Normandy coastline.

**1994, June 6** **Litho.** *Perf. 14*

**530** A120 £2 multicolored 8.00 5.00

Classic Cars A121

Designs: 16p, 1894 Peugeot Type 3. 24p, 1903 Mercedes Simplex. 35p, 1906 Humber 14.4hp. 41p, 1936 Bentley 4¼ L. 60p, 1948 MG TC.

**1994, July 19** **Litho.** *Perf. 15x14*

**531** A121 16p multicolored .65 .65
**532** A121 24p multicolored .95 .95
**533** A121 35p multicolored 1.40 1.40
**534** A121 41p multicolored 1.60 1.60
**535** A121 60p multicolored 2.40 2.40
*Nos. 531-535 (5)* 7.00 7.00

*531a* Booklet pane of 4 3.00
*532a* Booklet pane of 4 4.25
*533a* Booklet pane of 4 6.00
*534a* Booklet pane of 4 6.50
*535a* Booklet pane or 4 9.75
Complete booklet, #531a-535a 29.50

Guernsey Post Office, 25th Anniv. A122

Designs: 16p, Trident ferry. 24p, Handley Page Super Dart Herald of Channel Express. 35p, Aurigny Air Services' JOEY. 41p, Bon Marin de Serk ferry. 60p, Map of Guernsey, Herm, Alderney, Sark.

**1994, Oct. 1** **Litho.** *Perf. 14*

**536** A122 16p multicolored .65 .65
**537** A122 24p multicolored .95 .95
**538** A122 35p multicolored 1.40 1.40
**539** A122 41p multicolored 1.60 1.60

**540** A122 60p multicolored 2.40 2.40
*a.* Souvenir sheet, #536-540 7.50 7.50
*Nos. 536-540 (5)* 7.00 7.00

See Jersey Nos. 685-689a.

### Miniature Sheets

Christmas — A123

Antique toys — #541: a, Doll house. b, Doll. c, Small teddy bear in carriage. d, Cards, post boxes with candy. e, Top. f, Picture puzzle blocks.

#542: a, Rocking horse. b, Large teddy bear. c, Tricycle. d, Wooden pull duck. e, Tin plate locomotive. f, Ludo game.

**1994, Oct. 1** ***Perf. 13***
**541** A123 Sheet of 6 3.25 3.25
*a.-f.* 13p any single .50 .50
**542** A123 Sheet of 6 5.75 5.75
*a.-f.* 24p any single .90 .90

Greetings — A124

Faces formed by: No. 543, Shrimp, oyster, lobster, fish. No. 544, Sand buckets, shovel, sand. No. 545, Flowers. No. 546, Lettuce, tomatoes, mushroom, squash. No. 547, Seaweed, shells. No. 548, Anchor, life preservers. No. 549, Wine, cork, knife, fork. No. 550, Butterflies, caterpillars.

**1995, Feb. 2 Litho.** ***Perf. 14***
**543** A124 24p multicolored .95 .95
**544** A124 24p multicolored .95 .95
**545** A124 24p multicolored .95 .95
**546** A124 24p multicolored .95 .95
**547** A124 24p multicolored .95 .95
**548** A124 24p multicolored .95 .95
**549** A124 24p multicolored .95 .95
**550** A124 24p multicolored .95 .95
*a.* Miniature sheet of 8, #543-550 8.00 7.25
Complete booklet, #550a 8.00
*Nos. 543-550 (8)* 7.60 7.60

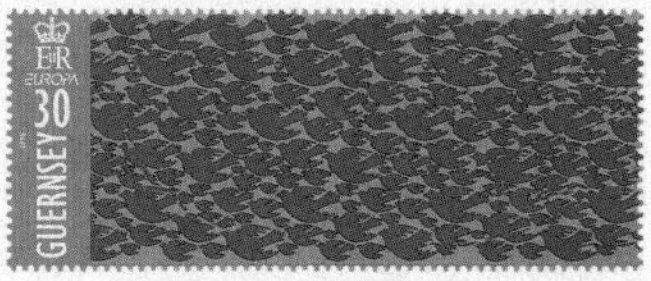


Doves — A125

Europa: 25p, Doves standing. 30p, Doves in flight.

**1995, May 9 Litho.** ***Perf. 14***
**551** A125 25p green *1.00 1.00*
**552** A125 30p blue *1.25 1.25*

Nos. 551-552 contain a three-dimensional image hidden in the patterns composed of doves.

Liberation of Guernsey, 50th Anniv. — A126

Designs: 16p, Churchill making broadcast, crowd. 24p, St. Peter Port harbor. 35p, Military band. 41p, Red Cross ship Vega. 60p, Soldier kissing civilian woman.

**1995, May 9** ***Perf. 13½x14***
**553** A126 16p multicolored .65 .65
**554** A126 24p multicolored .95 .95
**555** A126 35p multicolored 1.40 1.40
**556** A126 41p multicolored 1.60 1.60
**557** A126 60p multicolored 2.40 2.40
*a.* Souvenir sheet of 5, #553-557 7.50 7.50
*Nos. 553-557 (5)* 7.00 7.00

Visit by Prince of Wales A127

**1995, May 9** ***Perf. 14***
**558** A127 £1.50 multicolored 6.00 6.00

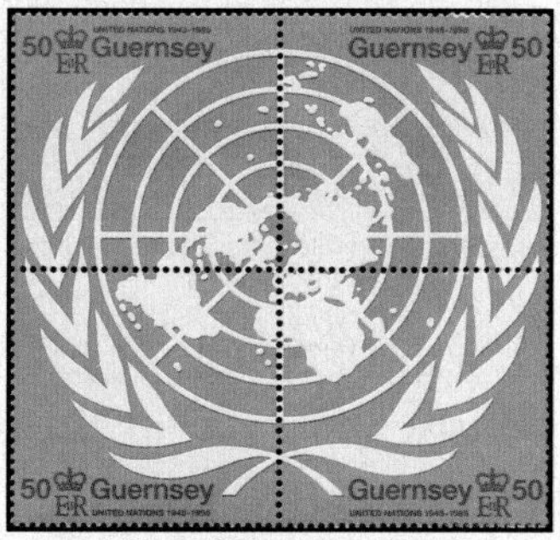


UN, 50th Anniv. — A128

Portion of UN emblem, denomination: a, UL. b, UR. c, LL. d, LR.

### Litho. & Embossed

**1995, Oct. 24** ***Perf. 14x13½***
**559** A128 Block of 4 8.00 8.00
*a.-d.* 50p any single 2.00 2.00

Christmas — A129

Designs, with denomination at:
Shops in the city, children playing in snow — #560: a, LL. b, LR.
Homes in winter, children playing in snow — #561: a, LL. b, LR.
Children playing instruments, singing — #562: a, LL. b, LR.
Children of many nations — #563: a, LL. b, LR.

**1995, Nov. 16 Litho.** ***Perf. 13½x13***
**560** A129 Pair 1.00 1.00
*a.-b.* 13p any single .50 .50
**561** A129 Pair 1.00 1.00
*a.-b.* 13p +1p, any single .50 .50
**562** A129 Pair 1.90 1.90
*a.-b.* 24p any single .95 .95
**563** A129 Pair 1.90 1.90
*a.-b.* 24p +2p, any single .95 .95
*Nos. 560-563 (4)* 5.80 5.80

Nos. 560-563 are each continuous designs. UNICEF, 50th anniv.

Women of Achievement — A130

Europa: 25p, Princess Anne, children of different nations. 30p, Queen Elizabeth II, people of different nations.

**1996, Apr. 21 Litho.** ***Perf. 14***
**564** A130 25p multicolored *1.00 1.00*
**565** A130 30p multicolored *1.25 1.25*

Queen Elizabeth II, 70th birthday (#565). See Isle of Man Nos. 679-680.

1996 European Soccer Championships — A131

Various flags from participating countries and: No. 566a, USSR player kicking ball. No. 566b, English players in white shirts, 1968. No. 567a, Italian player in blue shirt with ball. No. 567b, Belgium player in red, Italian players, 1972. No. 568a, Irish player in green kicking. No. 568b, Dutch player in blue, 1988. No. 569a, German player in white with ball. No. 569b, Danish player in red, 1992.

**1996, Apr. 25** ***Perf. 14x13½***
**566** A131 Pair 1.25 1.25
*a.-b.* 16p any single .60 .60
**567** A131 Pair 1.90 1.90
*a.-b.* 24p any single .95 .95
**568** A131 Pair 3.00 3.00
*a.-b.* 35p any single 1.40 1.40
**569** A131 Pair 3.25 3.25
*a.-b.* 41p any single 1.60 1.60
*Nos. 566-569 (4)* 9.40 9.40

### Souvenir Sheet

Sir Isaac Brock (1769-1812), British Commander in Upper Canada — A132

Designs: a, 24p, Brock shaking hands with Tecumseh. b, £1, Brock on horse.

**1996, June 8 Litho.** ***Perf. 14x13½***
**570** A132 Sheet of 2, #a.-b. 5.00 5.00

CAPEX '96.

Modern Olympic Games, Cent. — A133

The original pentathlon.

**1996, July 19 Litho.** ***Perf. 14***
**571** A133 16p Running .65 .65
**572** A133 24p Javelin .95 .95
**573** A133 41p Discus 1.60 1.60
**574** A133 55p Wrestling 2.25 2.25
**575** A133 60p Jumping 2.40 2.40
*a.* Souvenir sheet, #571-575 8.00 8.00
*Nos. 571-575 (5)* 7.85 7.85

No. 574 is 53x31mm. Olymphilex'96 (#574).

Motion Pictures, Cent. A134

Classic Movie Detectives: 16p, Humphrey Bogart as Philip Marlowe. 24p, Peter Sellers as Inspector Clouseau. 35p, Basil Rathbone as Sherlock Holmes. 41p, Margaret Rutherford as Miss Marple. 60p, Warner Oland as Charlie Chan.

**1996, Nov. 6 Litho.** ***Perf. 15x14***
**576** A134 16p multicolored .65 .65
**577** A134 24p multicolored .95 .95
**578** A134 35p multicolored 1.40 1.40
**579** A134 41p multicolored 1.60 1.60
**580** A134 60p multicolored 2.40 2.40
*Nos. 576-580 (5)* 7.00 7.00

*576a* Booklet pane of 3 2.00
*577a* Booklet pane of 3 3.00
*578a* Booklet pane of 3 4.25
*579a* Booklet pane of 3 5.00
*580a* Booklet pane of 3 7.25
*580b* Bklt. pane of 5, #576-580 7.50
Complete booklet, #576a-580b 30.00

Christmas A135

Scenes depicting the Christmas story: 24p, Madonna and Child. 25p, Nativity.

No. 583, vert: a, Annuniciation by Angel Gabriel. b, Mary, Joseph on way to Bethlehem. c, Inn keeper turning them away. d, Angel appearing before shepherds. e, Holy Family in stable. f, Adoration of the shepherds. g, Magi following star. h, Magi presenting gifts. i, Prophet's warning to Mary, Joseph. j, Madonna and Child. k, Angel appearing in Joseph's dream. l, Flight into Egypt.

**1996, Nov. 6** ***Perf. 13***
**581** A135 24p multicolored .95 .95
**582** A135 25p multicolored 1.00 1.00

### Miniature Sheet

**583** Sheet of 12 6.25 6.25
*a.-l.* A135 13p Any single .50 .50

### Flower Type of 1992

**1997 Litho.** ***Perf. 13***
**584** A110 18p Standard rose .70 .60
*a.* Perf. 14 on 3 Sides .75 .65
*b.* As "a," booklet pane of 8 7.50
Complete booklet, #584b 7.50
**585** A110 26p Freesia pink glow, horiz. 1.00 .80
*a.* Perf. 14 on 3 Sides 1.10 .80
*b.* As "a," booklet pane of 4 5.25
Complete booklet, #585b 5.25

Butterflies and Moths A136

Designs: 18p, Holly blue. 25p, Hummingbird hawk-moth. 26p, Emperor moth. 37p, Brimstone.
£1, Painted lady.

**1997, Feb. 12 Litho.** ***Perf. 14***
**586** A136 18p multicolored 1.10 1.10
**587** A136 25p multicolored 1.40 1.40
**588** A136 26p multicolored 1.60 1.60
**589** A136 37p multicolored 2.25 2.25
*Nos. 586-589 (4)* 6.35 6.35

### Souvenir Sheet

***Perf. 13½***

**590** A136 £1 multicolored 4.00 4.00

World Wildlife Fund (#586-589), Hong Kong '97 (#590).

Stories and Legends — A137

The Toilers of the Sea, by Victor Hugo: 26p, Man fighting sea monster, face in sea, ship. 31p, Ship, man seated on rock visualizing woman.

**1997, Apr. 24 Litho.** ***Perf. 13½***
**591** A137 26p multicolored 1.00 1.00
**592** A137 31p multicolored 1.25 1.25

Nos. 591-592 each issued in sheets of 10. Europa.

Island Scenes — A138

18p, Shell Beach, Herm. 25p, La Seigneurie, Sark, vert. 26p, Castle Comet, Guernsey.

***Die Cut Perf. 9½x9, 9x9½***

**1997, Apr. 24**

**Self-Adhesive**

| | | | | |
|---|---|---|---|---|
| **593** | A138 | 18p multicolored | .70 | .70 |
| *a.* | | Booklet pane of 8 | 6.50 | |
| | | Complete booklet, #593a | 6.50 | |
| **594** | A138 | 25p multicolored | 1.00 | 1.00 |
| *a.* | | Booklet pane of 8 | 9.00 | |
| | | Complete booklet, #594a | 9.00 | |
| **595** | A138 | 26p multicolored | 1.00 | 1.00 |
| *a.* | | Booklet pane of 4 | 4.50 | |
| | | Complete booklet, #595a | 4.50 | |
| | | *Nos. 593-595 (3)* | 2.70 | 2.70 |

See Nos. 625-628.

Souvenir Sheet

PACIFIC 97 — A139

a, 30p, St. Peter Port, 1868. b, £1, Sailing ships.

**1997, May 29 Litho. *Perf. 14***

| | | | | |
|---|---|---|---|---|
| **596** | A139 | Sheet of 2, #a.-b. | 5.25 | 5.25 |

Communications — A140

**1997, Aug. 21 Litho. *Perf. 13½x13***

| | | | | |
|---|---|---|---|---|
| **597** | A140 | 18p Radio | .70 | .70 |
| **598** | A140 | 25p Television | 1.00 | 1.00 |
| **599** | A140 | 26p Telephone | 1.00 | 1.00 |
| **600** | A140 | 37p Newspaper | 1.50 | 1.50 |
| **601** | A140 | 43p Post system | 1.60 | 1.60 |
| **602** | A140 | 63p Computer network | 2.50 | 2.50 |
| | | *Nos. 597-602 (6)* | 8.30 | 8.30 |

Queen Elizabeth II and Prince Philip, 50th Wedding Anniv. — A141

Designs: 18p, At St. George's Hall, Guernsey, 1957. 25p, Queen being saluted by guardsman, 1953. 26p, Queen, family on horseback, 1957. 37p, Prince, Queen in casual attire, 1972. 43p, Queen saluting, at Trooping of the Color, 1987. 63p, Portrait, 1997.

**1997, Nov. 20 Litho. *Perf. 14***

| | | | | |
|---|---|---|---|---|
| **603** | A141 | 18p multicolored | .70 | .70 |
| **604** | A141 | 25p multicolored | 1.00 | 1.00 |
| *a.* | | Bklt. pane, 3 each #603-604 | 5.75 | |
| **605** | A141 | 26p multicolored | 1.00 | 1.00 |
| **606** | A141 | 37p multicolored | 1.50 | 1.50 |
| *a.* | | Bklt. pane, 3 each #605-606 | 8.50 | |
| **607** | A141 | 43p multicolored | 1.60 | 1.60 |
| **608** | A141 | 63p multicolored | 2.50 | 2.50 |
| *a.* | | Bklt. pane, 3 each #607-608 | 13.50 | |
| *b.* | | Booklet pane, #603-608 | 9.00 | |
| | | Complete booklet, #604a, 606a, 608a, 608b | 37.50 | |
| | | *Nos. 603-608 (6)* | 8.30 | 8.30 |

A142

Teddy Bears celebrating Christmas: 15p, Baking in kitchen. 25p, Beside Christmas tree. 26p, Seated in chair reading story. 37p, As Santa Claus. 43p, With presents. 63p, Seated at Christmas dinner.

**1997, Nov. 6**

| | | | | |
|---|---|---|---|---|
| **609** | A142 | 15p multicolored | .60 | .60 |
| **610** | A142 | 25p multicolored | 1.00 | 1.00 |
| **611** | A142 | 26p multicolored | 1.00 | 1.00 |
| **612** | A142 | 37p multicolored | 1.50 | 1.50 |
| **613** | A142 | 43p multicolored | 1.60 | 1.60 |
| **614** | A142 | 63p multicolored | 2.50 | 2.50 |
| *a.* | | Souvenir sheet, #609-614 | 8.25 | 7.50 |
| | | *Nos. 609-614 (6)* | 8.20 | 8.20 |

A143

Millennium Tapestries: Embroidered panels showing images of Guernsey during last ten centuries, Guernsey-French inscriptions.

**1998, Feb. 10 Litho. *Perf. 14½***

| | | | | |
|---|---|---|---|---|
| **615** | A143 | 25p 11th century | 1.00 | 1.00 |
| **616** | A143 | 25p 12th century | 1.00 | 1.00 |
| **617** | A143 | 25p 13th century | 1.00 | 1.00 |
| **618** | A143 | 25p 14th century | 1.00 | 1.00 |
| *a.* | | Bklt. pane, 2 each #615-616, 1 each #617-618 | 6.50 | |
| **619** | A143 | 25p 15th century | 1.00 | 1.00 |
| **620** | A143 | 25p 16th century | 1.00 | 1.00 |
| *a.* | | Bklt. pane, 2 each #617-618, 1 each #619-620 | 6.50 | |
| **621** | A143 | 25p 17th century | 1.00 | 1.00 |
| **622** | A143 | 25p 18th century | 1.00 | 1.00 |
| *a.* | | Bklt. pane, 2 each #619-620, 1 each #621-622 | 6.50 | |
| **623** | A143 | 25p 19th century | 1.00 | 1.00 |
| **624** | A143 | 25p 20th century | 1.00 | 1.00 |
| *a.* | | Bklt. pane, 2 each #621-622, 1 each #623-624 | 6.50 | |
| *b.* | | Bklt. pane, 2 each #623-624, 1 each #615-616 | 6.50 | |
| | | Complete booklet, #618a, 620a, 622a, 624a-624b | 35.00 | |
| *c.* | | Strip of 10, #615-624 | 10.00 | 10.00 |

**Island Scenes Type of 1997**

***Die Cut Perf. 9½x9***

**1998, Mar. 25 Litho.**

**Self-Adhesive**

| | | | | |
|---|---|---|---|---|
| **625** | A138 | (20p) Fort Grey | .80 | .80 |
| **626** | A138 | (20p) Grand Havre | .80 | .80 |
| *a.* | | Booklet pane, 4 each #625-626 | 7.50 | |
| | | Complete booklet, #626a | 7.50 | |
| **627** | A138 | (25p) Little Chapel | 1.00 | 1.00 |
| **628** | A138 | (25p) Guernsey cow | 1.00 | 1.00 |
| *a.* | | Booklet pane, 4 each #627-628 | 8.75 | |
| | | Complete booklet, #628a | 8.75 | |
| | | *Nos. 625-628 (4)* | 3.60 | 3.60 |

Nos. 625-626 are inscribed "Bailwick Minimum Postage Paid" and were valued at 20p on day of issue. Nos. 627-628 are inscribed "UK Minimum Postage Paid" and were valued at 25p on day of issue.

Aircraft A144

Designs: 20p, Fairey IIIC, Balloon, Sopwith Camel, Avro 504. 25p, Fairey Swordfish, Tiger Moth, Supermarine Walrus, Gloster Gladiator. 30p, Hawker Hurricane, Supermarine Spitfire, Vickers Wellington, Short Sunderland, Westland Lysander, Bristol Blenheim. 37p, De Havilland Mosquito, Avro Lancaster, Auster III, Gloster Meteor, Horsa glider. 43p, Canberra, Hawker Sea Fury, Bristol Sycamore, Hawker Hunter, Handley Page Victor, BAe Lightning. 63p, Pavania Tornado GRI, BAe Hawk, BAe Sea Harrier, Westland Lynx, Hawker Siddeley Nimrod.

**1998, May 7 *Perf. 13½x13***

| | | | | |
|---|---|---|---|---|
| **629** | A144 | 20p multicolored | .80 | .80 |
| **630** | A144 | 25p multicolored | 1.00 | 1.00 |
| **631** | A144 | 30p multicolored | 1.25 | 1.25 |
| **632** | A144 | 37p multicolored | 1.50 | 1.50 |
| **633** | A144 | 43p multicolored | 1.60 | 1.60 |
| **634** | A144 | 63p multicolored | 2.50 | 2.50 |
| | | *Nos. 629-634 (6)* | 8.65 | 8.65 |

Royal Air Force, 80th anniv.

Souvenir Sheet

Cambridge Rules for Soccer, 150th Anniv. — A145

a, 30p, Jules Rimet, first president of FIFA. b, £1.75, Bobby Moore, Queen Elizabeth II.

**1998, May 7 *Perf. 13½x14***

| | | | | |
|---|---|---|---|---|
| **635** | A145 | Sheet of 2, #a.-b. | 8.25 | 8.25 |

Natl. Holidays and Festivals — A146

Europa: 20p, People in traditional costumes watching animals, West Show. 25p, Band in parade, Battle of Flowers, North Show. 30p, Prince Charles, Liberation Monument under Guernsey flag, tank, Liberation Day. 37p, Goat, equestrian event, flowers, South Show.

**1998, Aug. 11 Litho. *Perf. 13½***

| | | | | |
|---|---|---|---|---|
| **636** | A146 | 20p multicolored | *.80* | *.80* |
| **637** | A146 | 25p multicolored | *1.00* | *1.00* |
| **638** | A146 | 30p multicolored | *1.25* | *1.25* |
| **639** | A146 | 37p multicolored | *1.50* | *1.50* |
| | | *Nos. 636-639 (4)* | 4.55 | 4.55 |

A147

Royal Yacht Britannia — A148

Designs: 1p, Small fishing boat. 2p, St. John Ambulance Inshore Rescue inflatable dinghy. 3p, Pilot boat. 4p, St. John Ambulance boat, Flying Christine III. 5p, Crab boat. 6p, Herm Island Ferry. 7p, St. Peter Port Harbor Authority launch, Sarnia. 8p, Fisheries Protecton vessel, Leopardess. 9p, Trawler. 10p, Powerboat. 20p, Dart 18 racing catamaran. 30p, Bermudan rigged sloop. 40p, Motor cruiser. 50p, Ocean-going yacht. 75p, Motor cruiser anchored. £1, Ocean liner, Queen Elizabeth II. £3, Cruise ship Oriana

**1998-2000 Litho. *Perf. 14***

| | | | | |
|---|---|---|---|---|
| **640** | A147 | 1p multicolored | .25 | .25 |
| **641** | A147 | 2p multicolored | .25 | .25 |
| **642** | A147 | 3p multicolored | .25 | .25 |
| **643** | A147 | 4p multicolored | .25 | .25 |
| **644** | A147 | 5p multicolored | .25 | .25 |
| **645** | A147 | 6p multicolored | .25 | .25 |
| **646** | A147 | 7p multicolored | .25 | .25 |
| **647** | A147 | 8p multicolored | .30 | .30 |
| **648** | A147 | 9p multicolored | .35 | .35 |

**Size: 27x27mm**

***Perf. 14½x14¼***

| | | | | |
|---|---|---|---|---|
| **649** | A147 | 10p multicolored | .40 | .40 |
| **650** | A147 | 20p multicolored | .80 | .80 |
| **651** | A147 | 30p multicolored | 1.25 | 1.25 |
| **652** | A147 | 40p multicolored | 1.60 | 1.60 |
| **654** | A147 | 50p multicolored | 2.00 | 2.00 |
| **656** | A147 | 75p multicolored | 3.00 | 3.00 |

**Size: 34x26mm**

**Litho. & Embossed**

***Perf. 14¼x14½***

| | | | | |
|---|---|---|---|---|
| **658** | A148 | £1 multicolored | 4.00 | 4.00 |
| **660** | A148 | £3 multicolored | 12.00 | 12.00 |

**Size: 48x36mm**

***Perf. 14¾x14½***

| | | | | |
|---|---|---|---|---|
| **663** | A148 | £5 gold & multi | 20.00 | 20.00 |
| | | *Nos. 640-663 (18)* | 47.45 | 47.45 |

Issued: £5, 8/11; 1p, 2p, 3p, 4p, 5p, 6p, 7p, 8p, 10p, 40p, 50p, 75p, £1, 7/27/99; 20p, 30p, £3, 8/4/00.

See also No. 867.

Introduction of Christmas Tree to Britain, 150th Anniv. — A149

Christmas tree and toys from past 150 years: 17p, Teletubby "Po," video game machine, 1998. 25p, Doll, double decker bus, c. 1968. 30p, Stuffed panda, toy army tank, c. 1938. 37p, Model of Bluebird race car, doll, c. 1928. 43p, Teddy bear, train pull toy, c. 1908. 63p, Spinning top, wooden doll, c. 1850.

**1998, Nov. 10 Litho. *Perf. 13½***

| | | | | |
|---|---|---|---|---|
| **664** | A149 | 17p multicolored | .65 | .65 |
| **665** | A149 | 25p multicolored | 1.00 | 1.00 |
| **666** | A149 | 30p multicolored | 1.25 | 1.25 |
| **667** | A149 | 37p multicolored | 1.50 | 1.50 |
| **668** | A149 | 43p multicolored | 1.60 | 1.60 |
| **669** | A149 | 63p multicolored | 2.50 | 2.50 |
| *a.* | | Souvenir sheet, #664-669 | 8.50 | 8.50 |
| | | *Nos. 664-669 (6)* | 8.50 | 8.50 |

Queen Elizabeth, the Queen Mother — A150

Three strings of pearls and photographs: No. 670, As a child, 1907. No. 671, At wedding, 1923. No. 672, Holding newly-born Princess Elizabeth, 1926. No. 673, Wearing crown at coronation of King George VI, 1937. No. 674, In green hat, 1940. No. 675, Holding fishing pole, 1966. No. 676, Wearing tiara, 1963. No. 677, Holding flowers, 1992. No. 678, Presenting trophy, 1989. No. 679, In blue hat, 1990.

**1999, Feb. 4 Litho. *Perf. 13***

**Color of LL Corner**

| | | | | |
|---|---|---|---|---|
| **670** | A150 | 25p pink | 1.00 | 1.00 |
| **671** | A150 | 25p blue | 1.00 | 1.00 |
| **672** | A150 | 25p red brown | 1.00 | 1.00 |
| **673** | A150 | 25p purple | 1.00 | 1.00 |
| *a.* | | Bklt. pane, 2 each #670-671, 1 each #672-673 | 6.50 | |
| **674** | A150 | 25p green | 1.00 | 1.00 |
| **675** | A150 | 25p green | 1.00 | 1.00 |
| *a.* | | Bklt. pane, 2 each #672-673, 1 each #673-674 | 6.50 | |
| **676** | A150 | 25p purple | 1.00 | 1.00 |
| **677** | A150 | 25p red brown | 1.00 | 1.00 |
| **678** | A150 | 25p blue | 1.00 | 1.00 |
| *a.* | | Bklt. pane, 2 each #674-675, 1 each #676-677 | 6.50 | |
| **679** | A150 | 25p pink | 1.00 | 1.00 |
| *a.* | | Bklt. pane, 2 each #676-677, 1 each #678-679 | 6.50 | |
| *b.* | | Bklt. pane, 2 each #678-679, 1 each #670-671 | 6.50 | |
| | | Complete booklet, #673a, 675a, 678a, 679a, 679b | 35.00 | |
| *c.* | | Strip of 10, #670-679 | 10.00 | 10.00 |

Herm Island — A151

Local Carriage Labels and: 20p, Burnet roses, Shell Beach. 25p, Puffins, Belvoir Bay. 30p, Small Heath butterfly. 38p, Various shells, Shell Beach.

**1999, Apr. 27 Litho. *Perf. 13½x13***

| | | | | |
|---|---|---|---|---|
| **680** | A151 20p multicolored | | *.80* | *.80* |
| **681** | A151 25p multicolored | | *1.00* | *1.00* |
| **682** | A151 30p multicolored | | *1.25* | *1.25* |
| **683** | A151 38p multicolored | | *1.50* | *1.50* |
| | *Nos. 680-683 (4)* | | 4.55 | 4.55 |

Europa.

Royal Lifeboat Assoc., 175th Anniv. A152

20p, Spirit of Guernsey, 1995. 25p, Sir William Arnold, 1973. 30p, Euphrosyne Kendal, 1954. 38p, Queen Victoria, 1929. 44p, Arthur Lionel, 1912. 64p, Vincent Kirk Ella, 1888.

**1999, Apr. 27**

| | | | |
|---|---|---|---|
| **684** | A152 20p multicolored | .80 | .80 |
| **685** | A152 25p multicolored | 1.00 | 1.00 |
| **686** | A152 30p multicolored | 1.25 | 1.25 |
| **687** | A152 38p multicolored | 1.50 | 1.50 |
| **688** | A152 44p multicolored | 1.75 | 1.75 |
| **689** | A152 64p multicolored | 2.50 | 2.50 |
| | *Nos. 684-689 (6)* | 8.80 | 8.80 |

Souvenir Sheet

Wedding of Prince Edward and Sophie Rhys-Jones — A153

**1999, June 19 Litho. *Perf. 13½***

| | | | |
|---|---|---|---|
| **690** | A153 £1 multicolored | 4.00 | 4.00 |

Royal Military Academy, Sandhurst, Bicent. — A154

20p, Major General Le Marchant, founder, 1799. 25p, Duke of York, sponsor, 1802. 30p, Field Marshal Earl Haig, 1884-85. 38p, Field Marshal Montgomery, 1907-08. 44p, Major David Niven, actor, 1928-30. 64p, Sir Winston Churchill, 1893-95.

**1999, July 27 Litho. *Perf. 14***

| | | | |
|---|---|---|---|
| **691** | A154 20p multicolored | .80 | .80 |
| **692** | A154 25p multicolored | 1.00 | 1.00 |
| **693** | A154 30p multicolored | 1.25 | 1.25 |
| **694** | A154 38p multicolored | 1.50 | 1.50 |
| **695** | A154 44p multicolored | 1.75 | 1.75 |
| **696** | A154 64p multicolored | 2.50 | 2.50 |
| | *Nos. 691-696 (6)* | 8.80 | 8.80 |

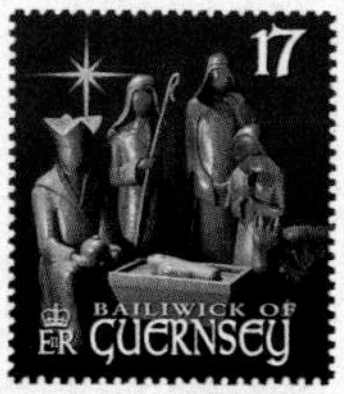


Christmas A155

Creche figures around manger: 17p, Magus, shepherd, Mary, Joseph, donkey. 25p, Mary. 30p, Joseph, Mary. 38p, Donkey, Mary, cow. 44p, Mary, two shepherds. 64p, Three Magi.

**1999, Oct. 19 Litho. *Perf. 13¾x14¼***

| | | | |
|---|---|---|---|
| **697** | A155 17p multicolored | .65 | .65 |
| **698** | A155 25p multicolored | 1.00 | 1.00 |
| **699** | A155 30p multicolored | 1.25 | 1.25 |
| **700** | A155 38p multicolored | 1.50 | 1.50 |
| **701** | A155 44p multicolored | 1.75 | 1.75 |
| **702** | A155 64p multicolored | 2.50 | 2.50 |
| *a.* | Souvenir sheet, #697-702 | 11.00 | 11.00 |
| | *Nos. 697-702 (6)* | 8.65 | 8.65 |

Millennium A156

Children's drawings by: 20p, Fallon Ephgrave. 25p, Abigail Downing. 30p, Laura Martin. 38p, Sarah Haddow. 44p, Sophie Medland. 64p, Danielle McIver.

**2000, Jan. 1 Litho. *Perf. 14¼x14½***

| | | | |
|---|---|---|---|
| **703** | A156 20p multi | .80 | .80 |
| **704** | A156 25p multi | 1.00 | 1.00 |
| **705** | A156 30p multi | 1.25 | 1.25 |
| **706** | A156 38p multi | 1.50 | 1.50 |
| **707** | A156 44p multi | 1.75 | 1.75 |
| **708** | A156 64p multi | 2.50 | 2.50 |
| | *Nos. 703-708 (6)* | 8.80 | 8.80 |

Nos. 703-708 depict the winning designs in the Future Children's Stamp Design Contest.

**Europa, 2000**

Common Design Type and

A157

Designs: 21p, Kite. 26p, Yacht sails. 65p, Rainbow and doves.

**2000, May 9 Litho. *Perf. 13¼***

| | | | |
|---|---|---|---|
| **709** | A157 21p multi | *.85* | *.85* |
| **710** | A157 26p multi | *1.00* | *1.00* |
| **711** | CD17 36p multi | *1.40* | *1.40* |
| **712** | A157 65p multi | *2.50* | *2.50* |
| | *Nos. 709-712 (4)* | 5.75 | 5.75 |

Battle of Britain, 60th Anniv. A158

Designs: 21p, Bristol Blenheim. 26p, Hawker Hurricane. 36p, Boulton Paul Defiant II. 40p, Gloster Gladiator. 45p, Bristol Beaufighter IF. 65p, Supermarine Spitfire IIc.

**2000, April 28 Litho. *Perf. 13¼x13***

| | | | |
|---|---|---|---|
| **713** | A158 21p multi | .85 | .85 |
| **714** | A158 26p multi | 1.00 | 1.00 |
| **715** | A158 36p multi | 1.40 | 1.40 |
| **716** | A158 40p multi | 1.60 | 1.60 |
| **717** | A158 45p multi | 1.75 | 1.75 |
| *a.* | Booklet pane, #713-715, 717 | 5.75 | |
| *b.* | Booklet pane, #713, 715-717 | 6.25 | |
| *c.* | Booklet pane, #714-717 | 6.25 | |
| **718** | A158 65p multi | 2.50 | 2.50 |
| *a.* | Booklet pane of 2 | 5.75 | |
| *b.* | Bklt. pane, #713-714, 716, 718 | 6.50 | |
| | Complete booklet, #717a-717c, 718a-718b | 32.50 | |
| | *Nos. 713-718 (6)* | 9.10 | 9.10 |

The Stamp Show 2000, London (Nos. 717a-717c, 718a-718b).

Flowers in Candie Gardens — A159

No. 719: a, Long styled iris. b, Watsonia. c, Arum lily. d, Hoop petticoat daffodil. e, Triteleia laxa. f, Peacock flower. g, African blue lily. h, Corn lily. i, Sea lily. j, Guernsey lily.

**2000, Aug. 4 Litho. *Perf. 13½x13***

| | | | |
|---|---|---|---|
| **719** | Horiz. strip of 10 | 10.50 | 10.50 |
| *a.-j.* | A159 26p Any single | 1.00 | 1.00 |

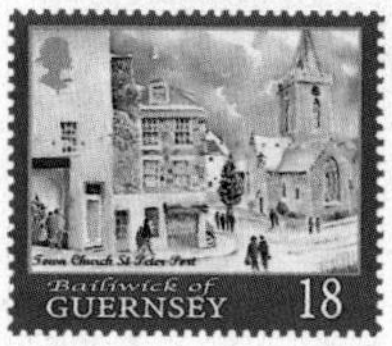


Christmas A160

Snow-covered churches: 18p, Town Church, St. Peter's Port. 26p, St. Sampson's Church. 36p, Vale Church. 40p, St. Pierre du Bois Church. 45p, St. Martin's Church. 65p, St. John's Church, St. Peter's Port.

**2000, Oct. 19 Litho. *Perf. 14¼x13¾***

| | | | |
|---|---|---|---|
| **720** | A160 18p multi | .70 | .70 |
| **721** | A160 26p multi | 1.00 | 1.00 |
| **722** | A160 36p multi | 1.40 | 1.40 |
| **723** | A160 40p multi | 1.60 | 1.60 |
| **724** | A160 45p multi | 1.75 | 1.75 |
| **725** | A160 65p multi | 2.50 | 2.50 |
| *a.* | Souvenir sheet, #720-725 | 9.25 | 9.25 |
| | *Nos. 720-725 (6)* | 8.95 | 8.95 |

Queen Victoria (1819-1901) — A161

Various portraits and: 21p, Statue of Victoria. 26p, Document. 36p, Statues of Victoria and Prince Albert. 40p, Commemoration stone, St. Peter's Port. 45p, Statue of Prince Albert. 65p, Victoria Tower.

**2001, Jan. 22 *Perf. 14¾***

| | | | |
|---|---|---|---|
| **726** | A161 21p multi | .85 | .85 |
| **727** | A161 26p multi | 1.00 | 1.00 |
| **728** | A161 36p multi | 1.40 | 1.40 |
| **729** | A161 40p multi | 1.60 | 1.60 |
| **730** | A161 45p multi | 1.75 | 1.75 |
| **731** | A161 65p multi | 2.50 | 2.50 |
| *a.* | Souvenir sheet, #726-731 | 9.25 | 9.25 |
| | *Nos. 726-731 (6)* | 9.10 | 9.10 |

Hong Kong 2001 Stamp Exhibition (No. 731a).

Birds A162

**2001, Feb. 1 Litho. *Perf. 14x14¾***

| | | | |
|---|---|---|---|
| **732** | A162 21p Kingfisher | .85 | .85 |
| **733** | A162 26p Garganey | 1.00 | 1.00 |
| **734** | A162 36p Little egret | 1.40 | 1.40 |
| **735** | A162 65p Little ringed plover | 2.50 | 2.50 |
| | *Nos. 732-735 (4)* | 5.75 | 5.75 |

Europa (26p, 36p).

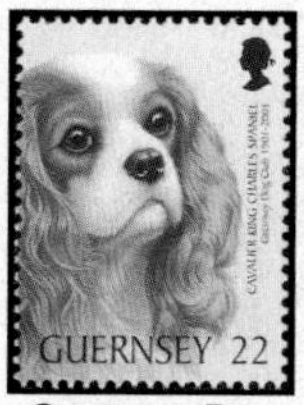


Guernsey Dog Club, Cent. — A163

Island Views — A164

Designs: 22p, Cavalier King Charles spaniel. 27p, Miniature schnauzer. 36p, German shepherd. 40p, Cocker spaniel. 45p, West Highland terrier. 65p, Dachshund.

**2001, Apr. 26 Litho. *Perf. 13x13¼***

| | | | |
|---|---|---|---|
| **736** | A163 22p multi | .85 | .85 |
| **737** | A163 27p multi | 1.00 | 1.00 |
| **738** | A163 36p multi | 1.40 | 1.40 |
| **739** | A163 40p multi | 1.60 | 1.60 |
| **740** | A163 45p multi | 1.75 | 1.75 |
| **741** | A163 65p multi | 2.50 | 2.50 |
| | *Nos. 736-741 (6)* | 9.10 | 9.10 |

***Serpentine Die Cut 14¼x14***

**2001, Apr. 26 Litho.**

No. 742: a, La Corbière sunset. b, Rue des Hougues. c, St. Saviour's Reservoir. d, Shell Beach, Herm. e, Telegraph Bay, Alderney. f, Alderney Railway. g, Vazon Bay. h, La Coupée, Sark. i, Les Hanois. j, Albecq,

**Self-Adhesive**

| | | | |
|---|---|---|---|
| **742** | Sheet of 10 | 9.50 | |
| *a.-e.* | A164 GY Any single | .85 | .85 |
| *f.-j.* | A164 UK Any single | 1.00 | 1.00 |
| *k.* | Booklet, 2 each #742a-742e | 9.50 | |
| *l.* | Booklet, 2 each #742f-742j | 11.00 | |
| *m.-q.* | As "a-e," photo., any single | .85 | .85 |
| *r.* | Strip, #742m-742q | 4.25 | |
| *s.-w.* | As "f-j," photo., any single | 1.00 | 1.00 |
| *x.* | Strip, #742s-742w | 5.00 | |

The photogravure stamps have a fuzzier appearance overall than the lithographed stamps. This is most noticeable in the crown where under magnification the bumps on the crown's outline are clearly distinct and well-defined as semicircles on the lithographed stamps, while ragged and ill-defined with a pointy appearance, on the photogravure stamps.

Nos. 742a-742e each sold for 22p, and Nos. 742f-742j each sold for 27p on day of issue.

No. 742 itself was available only from the Philatelic Bureau.

**Type of 1969 and**

Change of Guernsey Post Office to Guernsey Post Ltd., Oct. 1, 2001 — A165

Designs: 22p, Vision (water droplet on leaf). 27p, Understanding (hummingbird and flower). 36p, Individuality (butterfly's wing). 40p, Strength (nautilus shell cross-section). 45p, Community (honeycomb). 65p, Maturity (Dandelion gone to seed). £1, Like No. 23.

**2001, Aug. 1 Litho. *Perf. 13¼x13***

| | | | |
|---|---|---|---|
| **743** | A165 22p multi | .85 | .85 |
| *a.* | Booklet pane of 3 | 3.00 | — |
| **744** | A165 27p multi | 1.00 | 1.00 |
| *a.* | Booklet pane of 3 | 3.25 | — |
| **745** | A165 36p multi | 1.40 | 1.40 |
| *a.* | Booklet pane of 3 | 4.50 | — |
| **746** | A165 40p multi | 1.60 | 1.60 |
| *a.* | Booklet pane of 3 | 5.50 | — |
| **747** | A165 45p multi | 1.75 | 1.75 |
| *a.* | Booklet pane of 3 | 6.00 | — |
| **748** | A165 65p multi | 2.50 | 2.50 |
| *a.* | Booklet pane of 3 | 8.25 | — |

***Perf. 14x14¼***

| | | | |
|---|---|---|---|
| **749** | A4 £1 Booklet pane of 1 | 8.50 | 8.50 |
| | Booklet, #743a, 744a, 745a, 746a, 747a, 748a, 749 | 40.00 | |
| | *Nos. 743-749 (7)* | 17.60 | 17.60 |

Panels on the at top and bottom of No. 749 are dark blue and clouds in silver margin are distinct. Never-bound examples (without stitching holes) of No. 749 with Prussian blue panels and less distinct clouds in the silver margin were given to standing order subscribers at no charge.

Christmas
A166

Decorations: 19p, Tree of Joy, St. Peter Port. 27p, Cross, Les Cotils Christian Center. 36p, Les Ruettes Cottage, St. Saviour's. 40p, 17th cent. farmhouse. 45p, Sark Post Office. 65p, High Street, St. Peter Port.

**2001, Oct. 16** ***Perf. 14¼x14½***

| | | | | |
|---|---|---|---|---|
| **750** | A166 | 19p multi | .75 | .75 |
| **751** | A166 | 27p multi | 1.00 | 1.00 |
| **752** | A166 | 36p multi | 1.40 | 1.40 |
| **753** | A166 | 40p multi | 1.60 | 1.60 |
| **754** | A166 | 45p multi | 1.75 | 1.75 |
| **755** | A166 | 65p multi | 2.50 | 2.50 |
| *a.* | | Souvenir sheet, #750-755 | 9.00 | 9.00 |
| | | *Nos. 750-755 (6)* | 9.00 | 9.00 |

Hafnia 01 Philatelic Exhibition, Copenhagen (#755a).

Circus — A167

Designs: 22p, Juggler. 27p, Clowns. 36p, Trapeze artists. 40p, Knife thrower. 45p, Acrobat. 65p, High-wire cyclist.

**2002, Feb. 6 Litho.** ***Perf. 14¾x14½***

| | | | | |
|---|---|---|---|---|
| **756** | A167 | 22p multi | .85 | .85 |
| **757** | A167 | 27p multi | *1.00* | *1.00* |
| **758** | A167 | 36p multi | *1.40* | *1.40* |
| **759** | A167 | 40p multi | 1.60 | 1.60 |
| **760** | A167 | 45p multi | 1.75 | 1.75 |
| **761** | A167 | 65p multi | 2.50 | 2.50 |
| | | *Nos. 756-761 (6)* | 9.10 | 9.10 |

Europa (27p, 36p).

Victor Hugo (1802-85), Writer — A168

Designs: 22p, Hugo and St. Peter Port. 27p, Cosette from Les Misérables. 36p, Valjean from Les Misérables. 40p, Javert from Les Misérables. 45p, Cosette and Marius from Les Misérables. 65p, Les Misérables, score from play based on book.

**2002, Feb. 6** ***Perf. 13¼x13***

| | | | | |
|---|---|---|---|---|
| **762** | A168 | 22p multi | .85 | .85 |
| **763** | A168 | 27p multi | 1.00 | 1.00 |
| **764** | A168 | 36p multi | 1.40 | 1.40 |
| **765** | A168 | 40p multi | 1.60 | 1.60 |
| **766** | A168 | 45p multi | 1.75 | 1.75 |
| **767** | A168 | 65p multi | 2.50 | 2.50 |
| *a.* | | Souvenir sheet of 6, #762-767 | 9.25 | 9.25 |
| | | *Nos. 762-767 (6)* | 9.10 | 9.10 |

Souvenir Sheet

Pillar Boxes, 150th Anniv. — A169

**2002, Apr. 30** ***Perf. 14½x14¼***

| | | | | |
|---|---|---|---|---|
| **768** | A169 | £1.75 multi | 5.25 | 5.25 |

Reign of Queen Elizabeth II, 50th Anniv. — A170

Various views of Queen.

**2002, Apr. 30** ***Perf. 13½***

| | | | | |
|---|---|---|---|---|
| **769** | A170 | 22p multi | .85 | .85 |
| **770** | A170 | 27p multi | 1.00 | 1.00 |
| **771** | A170 | 36p multi | 1.40 | 1.40 |
| **772** | A170 | 40p multi | 1.60 | 1.60 |
| **773** | A170 | 45p multi | 1.75 | 1.75 |
| *a.* | | Booklet pane, #770-773 | 6.00 | |
| **774** | A170 | 65p multi | 2.50 | 2.50 |
| *a.* | | Booklet pane, #769, 772-774 | 6.50 | |
| *b.* | | Booklet pane, #769-771, 774 | 5.75 | |
| *c.* | | Booklet pane, #769-774 | 9.00 | |
| | | *Nos. 769-774 (6)* | 9.10 | 9.10 |

For complete booklet, see Alderney No. 184a.

Vacations in Sark — A171

No. 775: a, Family on dock, boat near dock. b, Family disembarking tractor-pulled transport. c, Family at campground. d, Family with bicycles at La Coupée. e, Swimming at Venus Pool. f, Family at La Seigneurie Gardens. g, Family at village pillar box. h, Family in horse-drawn cart. i, Family dining outdoors. j, Family at beach.

**2002, July 30** ***Perf. 13¼***

| | | | | |
|---|---|---|---|---|
| **775** | | Block of 10 | 10.00 | 10.00 |
| *a.-j.* | | A171 27p Any single | 1.00 | 1.00 |

Awarding of Victoria Cross to Major Herbert Wallace Le Patourel, 60th Anniv.
A172

Designs: 22p, Parade of Elizabeth College Combined Cadet Corps, 1934. 27p, In battle, Tunisia, 1942. 36p, As repatriated prisoner of war, 1943. 40p, Presentation of Victoria Cross ribbon, 1943. 45p, Return to Guernsey, 1948. 65p, Carrying King's Colors, 1968.

**2002, July 30** ***Perf. 13¼x13***

| | | | | |
|---|---|---|---|---|
| **777** | A172 | 22p multi | .85 | .85 |
| **778** | A172 | 27p multi | 1.00 | 1.00 |
| **779** | A172 | 36p multi | 1.40 | 1.40 |
| **780** | A172 | 40p multi | 1.60 | 1.60 |
| **781** | A172 | 45p multi | 1.75 | 1.75 |
| **782** | A172 | 65p multi | 2.50 | 2.50 |
| | | *Nos. 777-782 (6)* | 9.10 | 9.10 |

Souvenir Sheet

Queen Mother Elizabeth (1900-2002) — A173

**Litho. With Foil Application**

**2002, Aug. 4** ***Perf. 13¼***

| | | | | |
|---|---|---|---|---|
| **783** | A173 | £2 multi | 8.00 | 8.00 |

Christmas
A174

Designs: 22p, Madonna and Child. 27p, Holy Family. 36p, Angel announcing birth to shepherds. 40p, Adoration of the shepherds. 45p, Three Kings. 65p, Star of Bethlehem.

**2002, Oct. 17 Litho.** ***Perf. 13¼x13***

| | | | | |
|---|---|---|---|---|
| **784** | A174 | 22p multi | .85 | .85 |
| **785** | A174 | 27p multi | 1.00 | 1.00 |
| **786** | A174 | 36p multi | 1.40 | 1.40 |
| **787** | A174 | 40p multi | 1.60 | 1.60 |
| **788** | A174 | 45p multi | 1.75 | 1.75 |
| **789** | A174 | 65p multi | 2.50 | 2.50 |
| *a.* | | Souvenir sheet, #784-789 | 9.25 | 9.25 |
| | | *Nos. 784-789 (6)* | 9.10 | 9.10 |

World War II — A175

Designs: 22p, Pilots and airplanes. 27p, Airplanes over shoreline. 36p, Airplanes and searchlights. 40p, Airplanes dropping bombs. £1.50, HMS Charybdis and HMS Limbourne.

**2003, Jan. 30** ***Perf. 14***

| | | | | |
|---|---|---|---|---|
| **790** | A175 | 22p multi | .85 | .85 |
| **791** | A175 | 27p multi | 1.00 | 1.00 |
| **792** | A175 | 36p multi | 1.40 | 1.40 |
| **793** | A175 | 40p multi | 1.60 | 1.60 |

**Size: 40x31mm**

***Perf. 14¼x14½***

| | | | | |
|---|---|---|---|---|
| **794** | A175 | £1.50 multi | 6.00 | 6.00 |
| | | *Nos. 790-794 (5)* | 10.85 | 10.85 |

Dambusters Raid (#790-793), Operation Tunnel (#794), 60th anniv. See Nos. 827-831, 855-859.

Island Games — A176

Designs: 22c, Hurdles. 27p, Cycling. 36p, Gymnastics. 40p, Windsurfing. 45p, Golf. 65p, Triathlon.

**2003, Jan. 30** ***Perf. 12½***

| | | | | |
|---|---|---|---|---|
| **795** | A176 | 22p multi | .85 | .85 |
| **796** | A176 | 27p multi | 1.00 | 1.00 |
| **797** | A176 | 36p multi | 1.40 | 1.40 |
| **798** | A176 | 40p multi | 1.60 | 1.60 |
| **799** | A176 | 45p multi | 1.75 | 1.75 |
| **800** | A176 | 65p multi | 2.50 | 2.50 |
| *a.* | | Souvenir sheet, #795-800 | 9.25 | 9.25 |
| | | *Nos. 795-800 (6)* | 9.10 | 9.10 |

Poster Art — A177

Poster art from: 22p, 2003. 27p, 1995. 36p, 1988. 40p, 1978. 45p, 1968. 65p, 1956.

**2003, Apr. 10** ***Perf. 14¾x14½***

| | | | | |
|---|---|---|---|---|
| **801** | A177 | 22p multi | .85 | .85 |
| **802** | A177 | 27p multi | *1.00* | *1.00* |
| **803** | A177 | 36p multi | *1.40* | *1.40* |
| **804** | A177 | 40p multi | 1.60 | 1.60 |
| **805** | A177 | 45p multi | 1.75 | 1.75 |
| **806** | A177 | 65p multi | 2.50 | 2.50 |
| | | *Nos. 801-806 (6)* | 9.10 | 9.10 |

Europa (#802, 803).

Souvenir Sheet

Decommissioning of HMS Guernsey — A178

**2003, Apr. 10** ***Perf. 13¾x14¼***

| | | | | |
|---|---|---|---|---|
| **807** | A178 | £1.50 multi | 6.00 | 6.00 |

Prince William, 21st Birthday — A179

No. 808: a, With Princess Diana, 1983. b, With Princes Charles and Harry, 1985. c, At play in military uniform, 1986. d, In school uniform, with Prince Harry, 1989. e, Holding hand of Prince Charles, 1990. f, In ski jacket, with Princess Diana, 1991. g, In suit, 1995. h, With Princes Charles and Harry, 1997. i, Wearing helmet, 2000. j, Playing polo, 2002.

**2003, June 21** ***Perf. 13½x13***

| | | | |
|---|---|---|---|
| **808** | Horiz. strip of 10 | 10.00 | 10.00 |
| *a.-j.* | A179 27p Any single | 1.00 | 1.00 |
| *k.* | As #808a, perf. 13½x14 | 1.00 | 1.00 |
| *l.* | As #808b, perf. 13½x14 | 1.00 | 1.00 |
| *m.* | As #808c, perf. 13½x14 | 1.00 | 1.00 |
| *n.* | As #808d, perf. 13½x14 | 1.00 | 1.00 |
| *o.* | As #808e, perf. 13½x14 | 1.00 | 1.00 |
| *p.* | As #808f, perf. 13½x14 | 1.00 | 1.00 |
| *q.* | As #808g, perf. 13½x14 | 1.00 | 1.00 |
| *r.* | As #808h, perf. 13½x14 | 1.00 | 1.00 |
| *s.* | As #808i, perf. 13½x14 | 1.00 | 1.00 |
| *t.* | As #808j, perf. 13½x14 | 1.00 | 1.00 |
| *u.* | Booklet pane, #808k, 808m, 808p, 808q, 808s, 808t | 6.00 | — |
| *v.* | Booklet pane, #808l, 808m, 808np, 808o, 808r, 808s | 6.00 | — |
| *w.* | Booklet pane, #808k, 808n, 808p, 808q, 808r, 808t | 6.00 | — |
| *x.* | Booklet pane, #808k, 808l, 808m, 808o, 808r, 808t | 6.00 | — |
| *y.* | Booklet pane, #808l, 808n, 808o, 808p, 808q, 808s | 6.00 | — |
| | Complete booklet, #808u-808y | 30.00 | |

Nos. 808k-808t come only from Nos. 808u-808y.

Letters
A180

**Litho. With Foil Application**

**2003, July 3** *Perf. 13¼*

**809** A180 £5 multi 20.00 20.00

No. 809 is printed with thermochromatic ink that changes color when warmed.

Christmas A181

Scenes from *'Twas the Night Before Christmas*: 10p, Boy in bed, Christmas tree. 27p, Arrival of St. Nicholas. 36p, St. Nicholas near chimney. 40p, St. Nicholas carrying gifts. 45p, St. Nicholas placing gifts near tree. 65p, Departure of St. Nicholas.

**2003, Oct. 16 Litho.** *Perf. 14¼*

**810** A181 10p multi .40 .40
**811** A181 27p multi 1.00 1.00
**812** A181 36p multi 1.40 1.40
**813** A181 40p multi 1.60 1.60
**814** A181 45p multi 1.75 1.75
**815** A181 65p multi 2.50 2.50
*a.* Souvenir sheet, #810-815 8.75 8.75
*Nos. 810-815 (6)* 8.65 8.65

Souvenir Sheet

Golden Snub-nosed Monkey — A182

**2004, Jan. 29 Litho.** *Perf. 13¾x14¼*

**816** A182 £2 multi 8.25 8.25

Clematis Flower Varieties — A183

***Serpentine Die Cut 12½***

**2004, Jan. 29 Litho.**

**Self-Adhesive**

**Inscribed "GY"**

**817** A183 (22p) Rosemoor .85 .85
**818** A183 (22p) Arctic Queen .85 .85
**819** A183 (22p) Harlow Carr .85 .85
**820** A183 (22p) Guernsey Cream .85 .85
**821** A183 (22p) Josephine .85 .85
*a.* Booklet pane, 2 each #817-821 8.50
Complete booklet, No. 821a 8.50
*b.* Booklet pane, 2 each #817-821 (see note) 8.50
Complete booklet, 10 No. 821b 85.00

**Inscribed "UK"**

**822** A183 (27p) Blue Moon 1.10 1.10
**823** A183 (27p) Wisley 1.10 1.10
**824** A183 (27p) Liberation 1.10 1.10
**825** A183 (27p) Royal Velvet 1.10 1.10
**826** A183 (27p) Hyde Hall 1.10 1.10
*a.* Sheetlet, #817-826 10.00
*b.* Booklet pane, 2 each #822-826 11.00
Complete booklet, #826b 11.00
*c.* Booklet pane, 2 each #822-826 (see note) 11.00
Complete booklet, 10 #826c 110.00
*Nos. 817-826 (10)* 9.75 9.75

Booklet panes Nos. 821a and 826b have blocks of 6 and 4 separated by a space with text. Nos. 821b and 826c do not have a space between stamps.

**World War II Type of 2003**

Scenes of D-Day: 26p, Royal Air Force Spitfire. 32p, Arrival of landing craft. 36p, Soldiers approaching Gold Beach, open door of landing craft. 40p, Soldiers seeking shelter behind obstacles. £1.50, SS Vega.

**2004, May 12** *Perf. 14¼*

**827** A175 26p multi 1.00 1.00
**828** A175 32p multi 1.25 1.25
**829** A175 36p multi 1.40 1.40
**830** A175 40p multi 1.60 1.60

***Perf. 14¾x14¼***

**Size: 40x30mm**

**831** A175 £1.50 multi 6.00 6.00
*Nos. 827-831 (5)* 11.25 11.25

Vacations — A184

Inscriptions: 26p, Sand, Beaches, Sunshine. 32p, Views, Walking, Cliff top trails. 36p, Marina, Yachts, Cruisers. 40p, Dining, Seafood, A la carte. 45p, Churches, History, Monuments. 65p, Fauna, Flora, Colors.

**2004, May 12** *Perf. 13½*

**832** A184 26p multi 1.00 1.00
**833** A184 32p multi *1.25 1.25*
**834** A184 36p multi *1.40 1.40*
**835** A184 40p multi 1.60 1.60
**836** A184 45p multi 1.75 1.75
**837** A184 65p multi 2.50 2.50
*Nos. 832-837 (6)* 9.50 9.50

Europa (32p, 36p).

Loyalty to the British Crown, 800th Anniv. — A185

**2004, June 24** *Perf. 13¼x14*

**838** A185 26p Loyalty 1.00 1.00
**839** A185 32p Trade 1.25 1.25
**840** A185 36p Unity 1.40 1.40
**841** A185 40p Protection 1.60 1.60
**842** A185 45p Justice 1.75 1.75
**843** A185 65p Industry 2.50 2.50
*a.* Souvenir sheet, #838-843, perf. 14x13¼ 10.00 10.00
*Nos. 838-843 (6)* 9.50 9.50

2004 Summer Olympics, Athens — A186

**2004, July 29** *Perf. 13½*

**844** A186 32p Discus 1.25 1.25
**845** A186 36p Javelin 1.40 1.40
**846** A186 45p Runners 1.75 1.75
*a.* Booklet pane, #845, 846, 2 #844 5.75 —
**847** A186 65p Wrestlers 2.50 2.50
*a.* Booklet pane, #846, 847, 2 #845 7.25 —
*b.* Booklet pane, #844, 847, 2 #846 7.25 —
*c.* Booklet pane, #844, 845, 2 #847 7.75 —
*d.* Booklet pane, #844-847 7.00 —
*Nos. 844-847 (4)* 6.90 6.90

Nos. 846a, 847a-847d are perf 14¾x14.

**Souvenir Sheet**

***Perf. 14¾x14***

**848** A186 £1 Athletes, horiz. 4.00 4.00
*a.* Booklet pane, #848 4.00 —
Complete booklet, Nos. 846a, 847a-847d, 848a 40.00

No. 848 contains one 40x30mm stamp. No. 848a has binding stub at left.

Christmas A187

Designs: No. 849a, Little Donkey. No. 849b, While Shepherds Watched. No. 849c, Away in a Manger. No. 849d, Unto Us a Child is Born. No. 849e, We Three Kings.

32p, Angel wings. 36p, Christmas tree ornament. 40p, Holly leaf and berries. 45p, Snowman's scarf and buttons. 65p, Christmas tree star.

**2004, Oct. 28 Litho.** *Perf. 13*

**849** Horiz. strip of 5 4.00 4.00
*a.-e.* A187 20p Any single .80 .80
**850** A187 32p multi 1.25 1.25
**851** A187 36p multi 1.40 1.40
**852** A187 40p multi 1.60 1.60
**853** A187 45p multi 1.75 1.75
**854** A187 65p multi 2.50 2.50
*Nos. 849-854 (6)* 12.50 12.50

**World War II Type of 2003**

Designs: 26p, Soldiers on Army Landrover greet Guernsey residents. 32p, Woman celebrating liberation from German rule. 36p, Parents reunite with children. 40p, Soldiers return home. £1.50, Winston Churchill.

**2005, Feb. 3 Litho.** *Perf. 14¼*

**855** A175 26p multi 1.00 1.00
**856** A175 32p multi 1.25 1.25
**857** A175 36p multi 1.40 1.40
**858** A175 40p multi 1.60 1.60

**Size: 40x30mm**

***Perf. 14¾x14¼***

**859** A175 £1.50 multi 6.00 6.00
*Nos. 855-859 (5)* 11.25 11.25

Paintings of Flowers by William John Caparne — A188

Designs: 26p, Iris "Dorothea" and "Royal." 32p, Nerine fothergilli "Major." 36p, Iris "Garnet." 40p, Narcissus "Sir Watkin." 45p, Narcissus "Rip Van Winkle." 65p, Narcissus "Sulphur Phoenix."

**2005, Feb. 3** *Perf. 13¼*

**860** A188 26p multi 1.00 1.00
**861** A188 32p multi 1.25 1.25
**862** A188 36p multi 1.40 1.40
**863** A188 40p multi 1.60 1.60
**864** A188 45p multi 1.75 1.75
**865** A188 65p multi 2.50 2.50
*a.* Souvenir sheet, #860-865 10.00 10.00
*Nos. 860-865 (6)* 9.50 9.50

Liberation of Guernsey, 60th Anniv. A189

No. 866: a, King George VI. b, Queen Elizabeth II.

**Litho. With Foil Application**

**2005, May 9** *Perf. 14¾x14*

**866** Horiz. pair 8.50 8.50
*a.-b.* A189 £1 Either single 4.00 4.00

Queen Mary 2 Ocean Liner — A190

**Litho. & Embossed With Foil Application**

**2005, May 9** *Perf. 13¼*

**867** A190 £4 multi 16.00 16.00

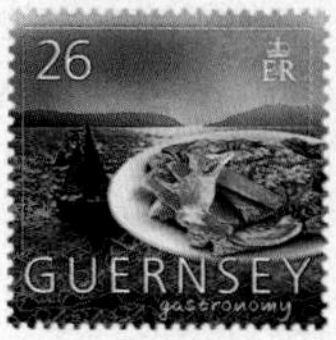

Gastronomy A191

Dishes: 26p, Spider crab. 32p, Red mullet and crab cake. 36p, Lobster salad. 40p, Brill on spinach with mussels. 45p, Prawn salad. 65p, Salmon wrapped in spinach with mussels.

**2005, May 9 Litho.** *Perf. 14x13¼*

**868** A191 26p multi 1.00 1.00
**869** A191 32p multi 1.25 1.25
**870** A191 36p multi 1.40 1.40
**871** A191 40p multi 1.60 1.60
**872** A191 45p multi 1.75 1.75
**873** A191 65p multi 2.50 2.50
*Nos. 868-873 (6)* 9.50 9.50

Europa (32p, 36p).

Souvenir Sheet

Basking Shark — A192

**2005, July 21** *Perf. 13¼*

**874** A192 £2 multi 8.50 8.50

SeaGuernsey 2005 — A193

Designs: 26p, Fishing boat and gulls. 32p, Sailboat. 36p, Windsurfer. 40p, Fisherman. 65p, Horse and rider on beach.

**2005, July 21** *Perf. 13¼x13¾*

**875** A193 26p multi 1.00 1.00
**876** A193 32p multi 1.25 1.25
*a.* Booklet pane, 2 each #875-876 4.75 —
**877** A193 36p multi 1.40 1.40
*a.* Booklet pane, 2 each #876-877 5.50 —
**878** A193 40p multi 1.60 1.60
*a.* Booklet pane, 2 each #877-878 6.25 —
**879** A193 65p multi 2.50 2.50
*a.* Booklet pane, 2 each #878-879 8.50 —
*b.* Booklet pane, 2 each #875, 879 7.50 —
*c.* Booklet pane, #876-879 7.00 —
Complete booklet, #876a, 877a, 878a, 879a, 879b, 879c 40.00
*Nos. 875-879 (5)* 7.75 7.75

Christmas — A194

No. 880 — Stained glass windows from: a, St. Pierre du Bois Church. b, St. Saviour's Church. c, St. Martin's Church. d, Torteval Church. e, St. Sampson's Church.

32p, Vale Church. 36p, Castel Church. 40p, St. Anne's Church, Alderney. 45p, St. Andrew's Church. 65p, Forest Church.

**2005, Oct. 27** *Perf. 14x14¼*

**880** Horiz. strip of 5 4.00 4.00
*a.-e.* A194 20p Any single .80 .80
**881** A194 32p multi 1.25 1.25
**882** A194 36p multi 1.40 1.40
**883** A194 40p multi 1.60 1.60
**884** A194 45p multi 1.75 1.75
**885** A194 65p multi 2.50 2.50
*Nos. 880-885 (6)* 12.50 12.50

Victoria Cross, 150th Anniv. A195

Battle scenes and medals from: 29p, Iraq Conflict, 2004. 34p, Falklands Conflict, 1982. 38p, Battle of El Alamein, World War II, 1942. 42p, Battle of Gallipoli, World War I, 1915. 47p, Battle of Rorke's Drift, Zulu War, 1879. 68p, Charge of the Light Brigade, Crimean War, 1854.

*Perf. 13¾x13½*

**2006, Feb. 16** **Litho.**

**886** A195 29p multi 1.10 1.10
**887** A195 34p multi 1.40 1.40
**888** A195 38p multi 1.50 1.50
**889** A195 42p multi 1.60 1.60
**890** A195 47p multi 1.90 1.90
**891** A195 68p multi 2.75 2.75
*Nos. 886-891 (6)* 10.25 10.25

Souvenir Sheet

Endangered Species of the Florida Everglades — A196

No. 892: a, £1, Leatherback turtle. b, £1.50, Wood stork.

**2006, Feb. 16** *Perf. 14x14¾*

**892** A196 Sheet of 2, #a-b 10.00 10.00

International Tourist Attractions — A197

Designs: 29p, Eiffel Tower, Paris. 34p, Sphinx, Egypt. 42p, Great Wall of China. 45p, Uluru (Ayers Rock), Australia. 47p, Statue of Liberty, New York. 68p, Taj Mahal, India.

**2006, May 20** *Perf. 13¼x13½*

**893** A197 29p multi 1.10 1.10
**894** A197 34p multi 1.40 1.40
**895** A197 42p multi 1.60 1.60
**896** A197 45p multi 1.75 1.75
**897** A197 47p multi 1.90 1.90
**898** A197 68p multi 2.75 2.75
*Nos. 893-898 (6)* 10.50 10.50

Europa (34p, 42p).

Isambard Kingdom Brunel (1806-59) — A198

Designs: 29p, Brunel, mailbags for Guernsey at Paddington Station, London. 34p, Mail train leaving Paddington Station. 42p, Train on Wharncliffe Viaduct. 45p, Mail train and ship at harbor, Weymouth. 47p, Mailboat Ibex in English Channel. 68p, Ibex at St. Peter Port.

**2006, May 20** *Perf. 13¼x13*

**899** A198 29p multi 1.10 1.10
**900** A198 34p multi 1.40 1.40
**901** A198 42p multi 1.60 1.60
**902** A198 45p multi 1.75 1.75
*a.* Booklet pane, #899-902 6.00 —
**903** A198 47p multi 1.90 1.90
*a.* Booklet pane, #900-903 6.75 —
**904** A198 68p multi 2.75 2.75
*a.* Booklet pane, #901-904 8.00 —
*b.* Booklet pane, #899, 902-904 7.50 —
*c.* Booklet pane, #899-900, 903-904 7.00 —
*d.* Booklet pane, #899-901, 904 7.00 —
Complete booklet, #902a, 903a, 904a-904d 42.50
*Nos. 899-904 (6)* 10.50 10.50

Andy Priaulx, Race Car Driver A199

Priaulx, car and events: 29p, British Speed Hill Climb Championship, 1995. 34p, Renault Spider Cup, 1999. 42p, British Formula 3, 2001. 45p, FIA European Touring Car Championship, 2004. 47p, Nürburgring, Germany, 2005. 68p, FIA World Touring Car Championship, 2005.

**2006, May 20** *Perf. 13½*

**905** A199 29p multi 1.10 1.10
**906** A199 34p multi 1.40 1.40
**907** A199 42p multi 1.60 1.60
**908** A199 45p multi 1.75 1.75
**909** A199 47p multi 1.90 1.90
**910** A199 68p multi 2.75 2.75
*a.* Souvenir sheet, #905-910 11.00 11.00
*Nos. 905-910 (6)* 10.50 10.50

Queen Elizabeth II, 80th Birthday A200

**Litho. & Embossed with Foil Application**

**2006, June 17** *Perf. 14¾x14¼*

**911** A200 £10 multi 40.00 40.00

L'Erée Wetlands A201

Designs: 29p, Gray seal. 34p, Ormer. 42p, Common blenny. 45p, Le Creux ès Faies. 47p, Yellow-horned poppy. 68p, Oyster catchers.

**2006, July 27** **Litho.** *Perf. 14x13¼*

**912** A201 29p multi 1.10 1.10
**913** A201 34p multi 1.40 1.40
**914** A201 42p multi 1.60 1.60
**915** A201 45p multi 1.75 1.75
**916** A201 47p multi 1.90 1.90
**917** A201 68p multi 2.75 2.75
*a.* Souvenir sheet, #912-917 11.00 11.00
*Nos. 912-917 (6)* 10.50 10.50

Addition of L'Erée Wetlands to Ramsar Convention Protected Wetlands List. See Nos. 972-977.

The Twelve Days of Christmas — A202

No. 918: a, A partridge in a pear tree. b, Two turtle doves. c, Three French hens. d, Four calling birds. e, Five gold rings. f, Six geese a-laying.

29p, Seven swans a-swimming. 34p, Eight maids a-milking. 42p, Nine ladies dancing. 45p, Ten lords a-leaping. 47p, Eleven pipers piping. 68p, Twelve drummers drumming.

**2006, Nov. 2** **Litho.** *Perf. 14¾x15*

**918** Horiz. strip of 6 5.00 5.00
*a.-f.* A202 22p Any single .80 .80
**919** A202 29p multi 1.10 1.10
**920** A202 34p multi 1.40 1.40
**921** A202 42p multi 1.60 1.60
**922** A202 45p multi 1.75 1.75
**923** A202 47p multi 1.90 1.90
**924** A202 68p multi 2.60 2.60
*Nos. 918-924 (7)* 15.35 15.35

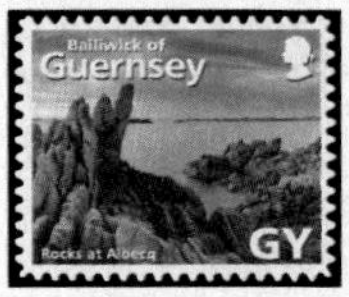


La Société Guernesiaise, 125th Anniv. — A203

No. 925: a, Rocks, Albecq. b, Ivy bee. c, Vale Church. d, Common frog. e, Parasol mushroom. f, Southern marsh orchid. g, Shore crab. h, Alderney blonde hedgehog. i, Barn owl. j, Le Trépied dolmen.

***Serpentine Die Cut 12½***

**2007, Mar. 8** **Self-Adhesive**

**925** Sheet of 10 13.50
*a.-e.* A203 (32p) Any single 1.25 1.25
*f.-j.* A203 (37p) Any single 1.40 1.40
*k.* Booklet pane of 10, 2 each #925a-925e 12.50
Complete booklet, 1 #925k 12.50
*l.* Booklet pane of 10, 2 each #925f-925j 14.00
Complete booklet, 1 #925l 14.00
*m.* Booklet pane of 10, 2 each #925a-925e (see note) 12.50
Complete booklet, 10 #925m 125.00
*n.* Booklet pane of 10, 2 each #925f-925j (see note) 14.00
Complete booklet, 10 #925n 140.00

Nos. 925a-925e are inscribed "GY"; Nos. 925f-925j, "UK."

Booklet panes Nos. 925k and 925l have blocks of 6 and 4 separated by a space between stamps. Booklet panes Nos. 925m and 925n do not have a space between stamps.

See No. 997.

Falkland Islands War, 25th Anniv. A204

Designs: 32p, Troops leaving for war. 37p, Landing at San Carlos Bay. 45p, Harriers flying over SS Canberra. 48p, Lieutenant Colonel H. Jones firing gun. 50p, Helicopter evacuating men from ship. 71p, Troops marching toward Port Stanley.

**2007, Mar. 8** *Perf. 13½*

**926** A204 32p multi 1.25 1.25
**927** A204 37p multi 1.40 1.40
**928** A204 45p multi 1.75 1.75
**929** A204 48p multi 1.90 1.90
**930** A204 50p multi 1.90 1.90
**931** A204 71p multi 2.75 2.75
*a.* Souvenir sheet, #926-931 11.00 11.00

Scouting, Cent. — A205

Designs: 32p, 1907 Scout camping. 37p, 1924 Scout sailing. 45p, 1947 Scouts fishing. 48p, 1968 Scouts making model airplanes. 50p, 1990 Scouts exploring cave. 71p, 2007 Scouts on rollerblades.

**2007, May 24** **Litho.** *Perf. 13¼x13*

**932** A205 32p multi 1.25 1.25
**933** A205 37p multi 1.50 1.50
**934** A205 45p multi 1.75 1.75
**935** A205 48p multi 1.90 1.90
**936** A205 50p multi 2.00 2.00
**937** A205 71p multi 3.00 3.00
*Nos. 932-937 (6)* 11.40 11.40

Europa (37p, 45p).

British Formula 1 World Championship Cars and Drivers — A206

Driver and championship year: No. 938, Mike Hawthorn, 1958. No. 939, Jackie Stewart, 1971. No. 940, Graham Hill, 1962. No. 941, James Hunt, 1976. 45p, Jim Clark, 1963. 48p, Nigel Mansell, 1992. 50p, John Surtees, 1964. 71p, Damon Hill, 1996.

**2007, May 24** *Perf. 14x13¾*

**938** A206 32p multi 1.25 1.25
**939** A206 32p multi 1.25 1.25
**940** A206 37p multi 1.50 1.50
**941** A206 37p multi 1.50 1.50
**942** A206 45p multi 1.75 1.75
**943** A206 48p multi 1.90 1.90
**944** A206 50p multi 2.00 2.00
**945** A206 71p multi 3.00 3.00
*Nos. 938-945 (8)* 14.15 14.15

See Nos. 1142-1145.

Wedding of Queen Elizabeth II and Prince Philip, 60th Anniv. — A207

Designs: 32p, Princess Elizabeth and Prince Philip, c. 1947. 37p, With baby Princess Anne. 45p, Off duty, wearing casual clothes. 48p, On tour, Queen in jacket and hat. 50p, With grandchildren Princes William and Henry. 71p, Recent photo.

**2007, Aug. 2** *Perf. 13¼x13¾*

**Background Color**

**946** A207 32p red brown 1.40 1.40
**947** A207 37p tan 1.50 1.50
*a.* Booklet pane, 2 each #946-947 6.00 —
**948** A207 45p light blue 1.90 1.90
*a.* Booklet pane, 2 each #947-948 7.00 —
**949** A207 48p light green 2.00 2.00
*a.* Booklet pane, 2 each #948-949 8.00 —
**950** A207 50p orange 2.10 2.10
*a.* Booklet pane, 2 each #949-950 8.25 —
**951** A207 71p lilac 3.00 3.00
*a.* Booklet pane, 2 each #950-951 10.50 —
*b.* Booklet pane, 2 each #946, 951 9.00 —
Complete booklet, #947a, 948a, 949a, 950a, 951a, 951b 49.00
*Nos. 946-951 (6)* 11.90 11.90

Souvenir Sheet

Mountain Gorilla — A208

**2007, Aug. 2** *Perf. 14*

**952** A208 £2.50 multi 10.50 10.50

Seaside Views A209

Designs: 32p, St. Peter Port Harbor. 37p, Fort Grey, Rocquaine. 45p, Point Robert Lighthouse, Sark. 48p, Brecqhou Island as seen from Sark. 50p, Vazon Bay. 71p, Fontenelle Bay.

**2007, Oct. 1** **Litho.** *Perf. 13¾x13½*

**953** A209 32p multi 1.40 1.40
**954** A209 37p multi 1.50 1.50
**955** A209 45p multi 1.90 1.90
**956** A209 48p multi 2.00 2.00
**957** A209 50p multi 2.10 2.10
**958** A209 71p multi 3.00 3.00
*Nos. 953-958 (6)* 11.90 11.90

See Nos. 1057-1062, 1098, 1136-1141.

Christmas — A210

Decorations: No. 959, Crystal snowflake in snow. No. 960, Crystal snowflake pendant. No. 961, Angel candle accent. No. 962, Crystal angel pendant. No. 963, Pine cone in snow. No. 964, Spherical ornament with leaf pattern. 32p, Spherical ornament with spiral pattern. 37p, Candles. 45p, Bell. 48p, Ribbon bow. 50p, Christmas tree star. 71p, Porcelain angel.

**2007, Oct. 25** *Perf. 14½x15*

| | | | | |
|---|---|---|---|---|
| **959** | A210 | 27p multi | 1.10 | 1.10 |
| **960** | A210 | 27p multi | 1.10 | 1.10 |
| **961** | A210 | 27p multi | 1.10 | 1.10 |
| **962** | A210 | 27p multi | 1.10 | 1.10 |
| **963** | A210 | 27p multi | 1.10 | 1.10 |
| **964** | A210 | 27p multi | 1.10 | 1.10 |
| **965** | A210 | 32p multi | 1.40 | 1.40 |
| **966** | A210 | 37p multi | 1.50 | 1.50 |
| **967** | A210 | 45p multi | 1.90 | 1.90 |
| **968** | A210 | 48p multi | 2.00 | 2.00 |
| **969** | A210 | 50p multi | 2.10 | 2.10 |
| **970** | A210 | 71p multi | 3.00 | 3.00 |
| | | *Nos. 959-970 (12)* | 18.50 | 18.50 |

Souvenir Sheet

Race Cars Used by World Touring Car Champion Andy Priaulx — A211

Race cars used by Priaulx in: a, 2005 (40x30mm). b, 2006 (40x30mm). c, 2007 (60x48mm).

**2008, Jan. 18 Litho.** *Perf. 13¾x14¼*

| | | | | |
|---|---|---|---|---|
| **971** | A211 | Sheet of 3 | 12.00 | 12.00 |
| *a.-c.* | | £1 Any single | 4.00 | 4.00 |

**Wetlands Type of 2006**

Designs: 34p, Beadlet anemones. 40p, Sand crocus. 48p, Fulmars. 51p, Sheep's bit. 53p, Thick-lipped gray mullets. 74p, Light bulb sea squirts.

**2008, Feb. 28** *Perf. 13x13¼*

| | | | | |
|---|---|---|---|---|
| **972** | A201 | 34p multi | 1.40 | 1.40 |
| **973** | A201 | 40p multi | 1.60 | 1.60 |
| **974** | A201 | 48p multi | 1.90 | 1.90 |
| **975** | A201 | 51p multi | 2.00 | 2.00 |
| **976** | A201 | 53p multi | 2.10 | 2.10 |
| **977** | A201 | 74p multi | 3.00 | 3.00 |
| *a.* | | Miniature sheet, #972-977 | 12.00 | 12.00 |
| | | *Nos. 972-977 (6)* | 12.00 | 12.00 |

Addition of Gouliot Headland and Caves, Sark to Ramsar Convention Protected Wetlands List.

Flowers — A212

Designs: 10p, Red campion. 20p, Great bindweed. 30p, Spear thistle. 40p, Greater bird's foot trefoil. 50p, Sheep's bit. £1, Marguerite, vert. £2, Sea campion, vert.

**2008, Feb. 28 Litho.** *Perf. 14*

| | | | | |
|---|---|---|---|---|
| **978** | A212 | 10p multi | .40 | .40 |
| **979** | A212 | 20p multi | .80 | .80 |
| **980** | A212 | 30p multi | 1.25 | 1.25 |
| **981** | A212 | 40p multi | 1.60 | 1.60 |
| **982** | A212 | 50p multi | 2.00 | 2.00 |

**Litho. & Embossed**

| | | | | |
|---|---|---|---|---|
| **983** | A212 | £1 multi | 4.00 | 4.00 |
| **984** | A212 | £2 multi | 8.00 | 8.00 |
| | | *Nos. 978-984 (7)* | 18.05 | 18.05 |

See Nos. 1029-1038.

Mr. Men and Little Miss Children's Book Characters A213

Designs: 34p, Mr. Happy. 40p, Mr. Bump. 48p, Little Miss Naughty. 51p, Mr. Greedy. 53p, Mr. Strong. 74p, Mr. Tickle.

**2008, May 15 Litho.** *Perf. 14x13½*

| | | | | |
|---|---|---|---|---|
| **985** | A213 | 34p multi | 1.40 | 1.40 |
| **986** | A213 | 40p multi | 1.60 | 1.60 |
| **987** | A213 | 48p multi | 1.90 | 1.90 |
| **988** | A213 | 51p multi | 2.00 | 2.00 |
| **989** | A213 | 53p multi | 2.10 | 2.10 |
| **990** | A213 | 74p multi | 3.00 | 3.00 |
| | | *Nos. 985-990 (6)* | 12.00 | 12.00 |

Guernesiais Phrases — A214

Guernesias phrases for: 34p, Till the next time. 40p, Hello. 48p, Oh! There you are. 51p, Good gracious. 53p, Cor blimey. 74p, How are things?

**2008, May 15** *Perf. 13¼x13*

| | | | | |
|---|---|---|---|---|
| **991** | A214 | 34p multi | 1.40 | 1.40 |
| **992** | A214 | 40p multi | 1.60 | 1.60 |
| **993** | A214 | 48p multi | 1.90 | 1.90 |
| **994** | A214 | 51p multi | 2.00 | 2.00 |
| **995** | A214 | 53p multi | 2.10 | 2.10 |
| **996** | A214 | 74p multi | 3.00 | 3.00 |
| | | *Nos. 991-996 (6)* | 12.00 | 12.00 |

Europa (40p, 48p).

**La Société Guernsiaise Type of 2007**

No. 997 — Photographs of Guernsey: a, Pleimont Point. b, Saint's Harbor. c, Rocks at Albecq. d, Groins at Vazon Bay. e, La Bette Bay. f, Bordeaux Harbor. g, St. Saviour's Reservoir. h, Vazon Bay. i, St. Peter Port Lighthouse. j, Petit Port.

***Serpentine Die Cut 12½***

**2008, June 9** **Litho.**

**Self-Adhesive**

| | | | | |
|---|---|---|---|---|
| **997** | | Sheet of 10 | 15.00 | |
| *a.-e.* | | A203 (34p) Any single | 1.40 | 1.40 |
| *f.-j.* | | A203 (40p) Any single | 1.60 | 1.60 |
| *k.* | | Booklet pane of 10, 2 each #997a-997e | 14.00 | |
| *l.* | | Booklet pane of 10, 2 each #997f-997j | 16.00 | |

Nos. 997a-997e are inscribed "GY"; Nos. 997f-997j, "UK."

Ford Model T, Cent. A215

Model T: 34p, And house. 40p, Converted to truck. 48p, Converted to pickup truck. 51p, On tree-lined street. 53p, Converted to World War I army ambulance. 74p, Red 1912 Roadster.

**2008, July 31** *Perf. 13¼*

| | | | | |
|---|---|---|---|---|
| **998** | A215 | 34p multi | 1.40 | 1.40 |
| **999** | A215 | 40p multi | 1.60 | 1.60 |
| **1000** | A215 | 48p multi | 1.90 | 1.90 |
| **1001** | A215 | 51p multi | 2.00 | 2.00 |
| *a.* | | Booklet pane of 4, #998-1001 | 7.00 | — |
| **1002** | A215 | 53p multi | 2.10 | 2.10 |
| *a.* | | Booklet pane of 4, #998-999, 1001-1002 | 7.25 | — |
| **1003** | A215 | 74p multi | 3.00 | 3.00 |
| *a.* | | Booklet pane of 4, #1000-1003 | 9.00 | — |
| *b.* | | Booklet pane of 4, #998-999, 1002-1003 | 8.25 | — |
| *c.* | | Booklet pane of 4, #999-1000, 1002-1003 | 8.75 | — |
| *d.* | | Booklet pane of 4, #998, 1000-1001, 1003 | 8.50 | — |
| | | Complete booklet, #1001a, 1002a, 1003a, 1003b, 1003c, 1003d | 49.00 | |
| | | *Nos. 998-1003 (6)* | 12.00 | 12.00 |

St. Paul's Cathedral, London, 300th Anniv. — A216

Blocks of granite from Guernsey and various depictions of cathedral.

**2008, Oct. 30** *Perf. 13¼*

| | | | | |
|---|---|---|---|---|
| **1004** | A216 | 34p multi | 1.10 | 1.10 |
| **1005** | A216 | 40p multi | 1.40 | 1.40 |
| **1006** | A216 | 48p multi | 1.60 | 1.60 |
| **1007** | A216 | 51p multi | 1.75 | 1.75 |
| **1008** | A216 | 53p multi | 1.75 | 1.75 |
| **1009** | A216 | 74p multi | 2.40 | 2.40 |
| | | *Nos. 1004-1009 (6)* | 10.00 | 10.00 |

Particles of granite were applied to parts of the designs by a thermographic process.

Christmas — A217

**2008, Oct. 30** *Perf. 13¾x13¼*

| | | | | |
|---|---|---|---|---|
| **1010** | A217 | 29p Spruce | .95 | .95 |
| **1011** | A217 | 29p Butchers broom | .95 | .95 |
| **1012** | A217 | 29p Mistletoe | .95 | .95 |
| **1013** | A217 | 29p Ivy | .95 | .95 |
| **1014** | A217 | 29p Christmas cactus | .95 | .95 |
| **1015** | A217 | 29p Cyclamen | .95 | .95 |
| **1016** | A217 | 34p Holly | 1.10 | 1.10 |
| **1017** | A217 | 40p Poinsettia | 1.40 | 1.40 |
| **1018** | A217 | 48p Bracken | 1.60 | 1.60 |
| **1019** | A217 | 51p Hawthorn | 1.75 | 1.75 |
| **1020** | A217 | 53p Clematis peppermint | 1.75 | 1.75 |
| **1021** | A217 | 74p Pyracantha | 2.40 | 2.40 |
| | | *Nos. 1010-1021 (12)* | 15.70 | 15.70 |

Animals Encountered on Charles Darwin's Scientific Expeditions A218

Designs: 36p, Land iguana. 43p, Wallaby. 51p, Giant tortoise. 54p, Marine iguana. 56p, Guanaco. 77p, Komodo dragon.

**2009, Feb. 26 Litho.** *Perf. 14*

| | | | | |
|---|---|---|---|---|
| **1022** | A218 | 36p multi | 1.10 | 1.10 |
| **1023** | A218 | 43p multi | 1.25 | 1.25 |
| **1024** | A218 | 51p multi | 1.50 | 1.50 |
| **1025** | A218 | 54p multi | 1.60 | 1.60 |
| **1026** | A218 | 56p multi | 1.60 | 1.60 |
| **1027** | A218 | 77p multi | 2.25 | 2.25 |
| *a.* | | Miniature sheet of 6, #1022-1027 | 9.50 | 9.50 |
| | | *Nos. 1022-1027 (6)* | 9.30 | 9.30 |

Souvenir Sheet

Amur Leopard — A219

**2009, Feb. 26** *Perf. 13¼x14*

| | | | | |
|---|---|---|---|---|
| **1028** | A219 | £3 multi | 8.75 | 8.75 |

**Flowers Type of 2008**

Designs: 1p, Stinking onion. 2p, Common mallow. 3p, Primrose. 4p, Loose-flowered orchid. 5p, Common centaury. 6p, Yellow horned poppy. 7p, Sea kale. 8p, Bluebell. 9p, Sea bindweed. £3, Common poppy, vert.

**2009, May 28 Litho.** *Perf. 13¼*

| | | | | |
|---|---|---|---|---|
| **1029** | A212 | 1p multi | .25 | .25 |
| **1030** | A212 | 2p multi | .25 | .25 |
| **1031** | A212 | 3p multi | .25 | .25 |
| **1032** | A212 | 4p multi | .25 | .25 |
| **1033** | A212 | 5p multi | .25 | .25 |
| **1034** | A212 | 6p multi | .25 | .25 |
| **1035** | A212 | 7p multi | .25 | .25 |
| **1036** | A212 | 8p multi | .25 | .25 |
| **1037** | A212 | 9p multi | .30 | .30 |

**Litho. & Embossed**

| | | | | |
|---|---|---|---|---|
| **1038** | A212 | £3 multi | 9.75 | 9.75 |
| | | *Nos. 1029-1038 (10)* | 12.05 | 12.05 |

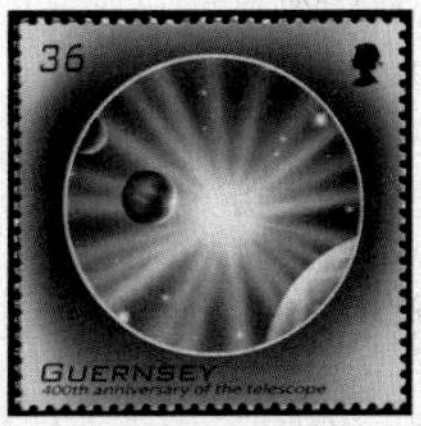


Invention of Telescope, 400th Anniv. A220

Designs: 36p, Quasar. 43p, Asteroid. 51p, Sun and Earth. 54p, Sun and Jupiter. 56p, Total solar eclipse. 77p, Solar eruption.

**2009, May 28 Litho.** *Perf. 13¼*

| | | | | |
|---|---|---|---|---|
| **1039** | A220 | 36p multi | 1.25 | 1.25 |
| **1040** | A220 | 43p multi | 1.40 | 1.40 |
| **1041** | A220 | 51p multi | 1.60 | 1.60 |
| **1042** | A220 | 54p multi | 1.75 | 1.75 |
| **1043** | A220 | 56p multi | 1.75 | 1.90 |
| **1044** | A220 | 77p multi | 2.50 | 2.50 |
| | | *Nos. 1039-1044 (6)* | 10.40 | 10.40 |

Europa (43p, 51p).

Coronation of King Henry VIII, 500th Anniv. A221

King Henry VIII: 36p, With hawk. 43p, On throne beside Catherine of Aragon. 51p, Meeting Francis I of France. 54p, With Cardinal Wolsey. 56p, With Anne Boleyn. 77p, And ships.

**2009, July 30 Litho.** *Perf. 13½*

| | | | | |
|---|---|---|---|---|
| **1045** | A221 | 36p multi | 1.25 | 1.25 |
| *a.* | | Booklet pane of 4 | 5.00 | 5.00 |
| **1046** | A221 | 43p multi | 1.50 | 1.50 |
| *a.* | | Booklet pane of 4 | 6.00 | 6.00 |
| **1047** | A221 | 51p multi | 1.75 | 1.75 |
| *a.* | | Booklet pane of 4 | 7.00 | 7.00 |
| **1048** | A221 | 54p multi | 2.00 | 2.00 |
| *a.* | | Booklet pane of 4 | 8.00 | 8.00 |
| **1049** | A221 | 56p multi | 2.00 | 2.00 |
| *a.* | | Booklet pane of 4 | 8.00 | 8.00 |
| **1050** | A221 | 77p multi | 2.60 | 2.60 |
| *a.* | | Booklet pane of 4 | 10.50 | 10.50 |
| | | Complete booklet, #1045a-1050a | 44.50 | |
| | | *Nos. 1045-1050 (6)* | 11.10 | 11.10 |

Postal Independence, 40th Anniv. — A222

"1969" and "2009" with inscription: 36p, The Psychedelic 60's. 43p, God Save the 70's. 51p, The POPular 80's. 54p, The Urban 90's. 56p, The Seductive 00's. 77p, Looking to the Future.

**2009, July 30 Litho. *Perf. 14x13¾***

| | | | | |
|---|---|---|---|---|
| **1051** | A222 | 36p multi | 1.25 | 1.25 |
| **1052** | A222 | 43p multi | 1.50 | 1.50 |
| **1053** | A222 | 51p multi | 1.75 | 1.75 |
| **1054** | A222 | 54p multi | 1.90 | 1.90 |
| **1055** | A222 | 56p multi | 1.90 | 1.90 |
| **1056** | A222 | 77p multi | 2.60 | 2.60 |
| | | *Nos. 1051-1056 (6)* | 10.90 | 10.90 |

### Seaside Views Type of 2007

Designs: 36p, Jerbourg Point. 43p, Vazon Bay. 51p, Saints Bay Moorings. 54p, Le Jaonnet Bay. 56p, Rocquaine Bay. 77p, Bordeaux Harbor.

**2009, Sept. 16 Litho. *Perf. 13½***

| | | | | |
|---|---|---|---|---|
| **1057** | A209 | 36p multi | 1.25 | 1.25 |
| **1058** | A209 | 43p multi | 1.40 | 1.40 |
| **1059** | A209 | 51p multi | 1.60 | 1.60 |
| **1060** | A209 | 54p multi | 1.75 | 1.75 |
| **1061** | A209 | 56p multi | 1.75 | 1.75 |
| **1062** | A209 | 77p multi | 2.50 | 2.50 |
| | | *Nos. 1057-1062 (6)* | 10.25 | 10.25 |

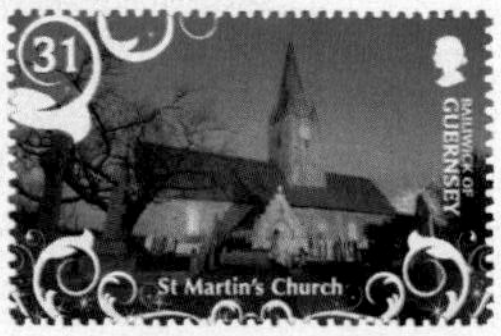


Christmas — A223

Designs: No. 1063, St. Martin's Church. No. 1064, Castel Church. No. 1065, Torteval Church. No. 1066, St. John's Church. No. 1067, St. Peter Port Church. No. 1068, St. Sampson's Church. 36p, St. Matthew's Church. 43p, St. Saviour's Church. 51p, Forest Church. 54p, St. Andrew's Church. 56p, Vale Church. 77p, St. Peter's Church.

**2009, Oct. 29**

| | | | | |
|---|---|---|---|---|
| **1063** | A223 | 31p multi | 1.10 | 1.10 |
| **1064** | A223 | 31p multi | 1.10 | 1.10 |
| **1065** | A223 | 31p multi | 1.10 | 1.10 |
| **1066** | A223 | 31p multi | 1.10 | 1.10 |
| **1067** | A223 | 31p multi | 1.10 | 1.10 |
| **1068** | A223 | 31p multi | 1.10 | 1.10 |
| **1069** | A223 | 36p multi | 1.25 | 1.25 |
| **1070** | A223 | 43p multi | 1.40 | 1.40 |
| **1071** | A223 | 51p multi | 1.75 | 1.75 |
| **1072** | A223 | 54p multi | 1.75 | 1.75 |
| **1073** | A223 | 56p multi | 1.90 | 1.90 |
| **1074** | A223 | 77p multi | 2.60 | 2.60 |
| | | *Nos. 1063-1074 (12)* | 17.25 | 17.25 |

### Souvenir Sheet

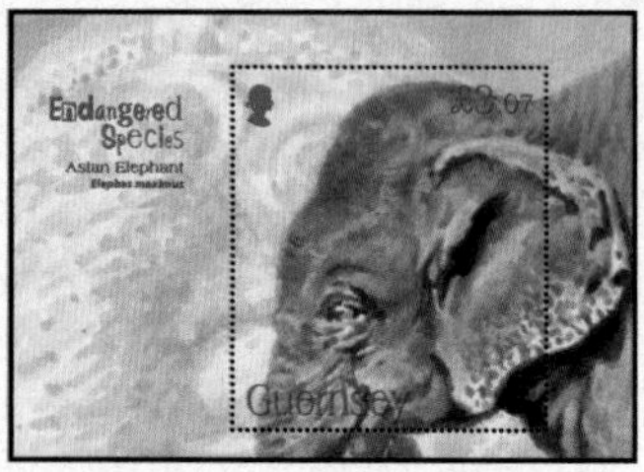


Asian Elephant — A224

**2010, Feb. 25 Litho. *Perf. 14***

| | | | | |
|---|---|---|---|---|
| **1075** | A224 | £3.07 multi | 9.50 | 9.50 |

Views of Guernsey A225

Designs: Nos. 1076, 1082a, Port à la Jument, Sark. Nos. 1077, 1082b, Dog and Lion Rocks. Nos. 1078, 1082c, Fort Grey. Nos. 1079, 1082d, West coast of Guernsey. Nos. 1080, 1082e, Slipway, Havelet Bay. Nos. 1081, 1082f, Castle Cornet.

**2010, Mar. 18 *Perf. 13¼***

| | | | | |
|---|---|---|---|---|
| **1076** | A225 | (48p) multi | 1.50 | 1.50 |
| **1077** | A225 | (48p) multi | 1.50 | 1.50 |
| *a.* | | Vert. pair, #1076-1077 | 3.00 | 3.00 |
| **1078** | A225 | (50p) multi | 1.60 | 1.60 |
| **1079** | A225 | (58p) multi | 1.75 | 1.75 |
| **1080** | A225 | (58p) multi | 1.75 | 1.75 |
| *a.* | | Vert. pair, #1079-1080 | 3.50 | 3.50 |
| **1081** | A225 | (80p) multi | 2.50 | 2.50 |
| | | *Nos. 1076-1081 (6)* | 10.60 | 10.60 |

### Self-Adhesive

***Serpentine Die Cut 12½***

| | | | | |
|---|---|---|---|---|
| **1082** | | Sheet of 6 | 11.00 | |
| *a.-b.* | | A225 (48p) Either single | 1.50 | 1.50 |
| *c.* | | A225 (50p) multi | 1.60 | 1.60 |
| *d.-e.* | | A225 (58p) Either single | 1.75 | 1.75 |
| *f.* | | A225 (80p) multi | 2.50 | 2.50 |
| *g.* | | Booklet pane of 4, 2 each #1082a-1082b | 6.00 | |
| *h.* | | Booklet pane of 4, 2 each #1082d-1082e | 7.00 | |

Nos. 1076-1077, 1082a-1082b are inscribed "GY LARGE"; Nos. 1078, 1082c, "EUR"; Nos. 1079-1080, 1082d-1082e, "UK LARGE"; Nos. 1081, 1082f, "ROW."

The Adventures of Penny the Postie A226

Children on treasure chest with sail and: 45p, Volcano. 50p, Map. £2, Pirate and ship.

**2010, May 4 Litho. *Perf. 13¼***

| | | | | |
|---|---|---|---|---|
| **1083** | A226 | 45p multi | 1.40 | 1.40 |

### Size: 38x51mm

***Perf. 14¼***

| | | | | |
|---|---|---|---|---|
| **1084** | A226 | 50p multi | 1.50 | 1.50 |
| **1085** | A226 | £2 multi | 6.00 | 6.00 |
| *a.* | | Souvenir sheet, #1083-1085 | 9.00 | 9.00 |
| | | *Nos. 1083-1085 (3)* | 8.90 | 8.90 |

Europa (Nos. 1083-1084).

Girl Guides, Cent. — A227

Designs: 36p, Outdoor activities. 45p, Help during World Wars I and II. 48p, Crystal Palace Maze. 50p, Agnes Baden-Powell. 58p, Mount Everest. 80p, Queen's Guide award.

**2010, May 27 Litho. *Perf. 13¼***

| | | | | |
|---|---|---|---|---|
| **1086** | A227 | 36p multi | 1.10 | 1.10 |
| **1087** | A227 | 45p multi | 1.40 | 1.40 |
| **1088** | A227 | 48p multi | 1.40 | 1.40 |
| **1089** | A227 | 50p multi | 1.50 | 1.50 |
| **1090** | A227 | 58p multi | 1.75 | 1.75 |
| **1091** | A227 | 80p multi | 2.40 | 2.40 |
| | | *Nos. 1086-1091 (6)* | 9.55 | 9.55 |

National Trust of Guernsey, 50th Anniv. — A228

Designs: 36p, Victorian Shop, 26 Cornet Street, St. Peter Port. 45p, Field, Jerbourg. 48p, Martello Tower, Fermain Bay. 50p, Ivy Gates. 58p, Pleinmont Headland. 80p, Moulin de Quanteraine.

**2010, July 5 Litho. *Perf. 13½***

| | | | | |
|---|---|---|---|---|
| **1092** | A228 | 36p multi | 1.10 | 1.10 |
| **1093** | A228 | 45p multi | 1.40 | 1.40 |
| **1094** | A228 | 48p multi | 1.50 | 1.50 |
| **1095** | A228 | 50p multi | 1.50 | 1.50 |
| **1096** | A228 | 58p multi | 1.75 | 1.75 |
| **1097** | A228 | 80p multi | 2.40 | 2.40 |
| | | *Nos. 1092-1097 (6)* | 9.65 | 9.65 |

### Seaside Views Type of 2007

Design: Point Robert Lighthouse, Sark.

**2010, July 29 *Perf. 13¾x13½***

| | | | | |
|---|---|---|---|---|
| **1098** | A209 | 55p multi | 1.75 | 1.75 |

Evacuation of Guernsey, 70th Anniv. A229

Designs: 36p, Gas masks being loaded onto a truck, 1939. 45p, Guernsey children waiting to leave, 1940. 48p, German soldiers leaving Guernsey, 1945. 50p, Evacuees arriving back in Guernsey, 1945. 58p, Royal visit to Guernsey, June 1945. 80p, Liberation Day, 1946.

**2010, July 29 *Perf. 13¾***

| | | | | |
|---|---|---|---|---|
| **1099** | A229 | 36p multi | 1.10 | 1.10 |
| **1100** | A229 | 45p multi | 1.40 | 1.40 |
| **1101** | A229 | 48p multi | 1.50 | 1.50 |
| **1102** | A229 | 50p multi | 1.60 | 1.60 |
| **1103** | A229 | 58p multi | 1.90 | 1.90 |
| **1104** | A229 | 80p multi | 2.50 | 2.50 |
| | | *Nos. 1099-1104 (6)* | 10.00 | 10.00 |

2010 Commonwealth Games, Delhi — A230

Designs: 36p, Tennis. 45p, Lawn bowling. 48p, Shooting. 50p, Swimming. 58p, Track. 80p, Cycling.

**2010, Sept. 23 *Perf. 13½***

| | | | | |
|---|---|---|---|---|
| **1105** | A230 | 36p multi | 1.25 | 1.25 |
| *a.* | | Booklet pane of 4 | 5.00 | — |
| **1106** | A230 | 45p multi | 1.50 | 1.50 |
| *a.* | | Booklet pane of 4 | 6.00 | — |
| **1107** | A230 | 48p multi | 1.60 | 1.60 |
| *a.* | | Booklet pane of 4 | 6.50 | — |
| **1108** | A230 | 50p multi | 1.60 | 1.60 |
| *a.* | | Booklet pane of 4 | 6.50 | — |
| **1109** | A230 | 58p multi | 1.90 | 1.90 |
| *a.* | | Booklet pane of 4 | 7.75 | — |
| **1110** | A230 | 80p multi | 2.60 | 2.60 |
| *a.* | | Booklet pane of 4 | 10.50 | — |
| | | Complete booklet, #1005a, 1106a, 1107a, 1108a, 1109a, 1110a | 42.50 | |
| | | *Nos. 1105-1110 (6)* | 10.45 | 10.45 |

Christmas Carols A231

Designs: 31p, The Holly and the Ivy. 36p, Little Donkey. 45p, Silent Night. 48p, I Saw Three Ships. 50p, Joy to the World. 58p, Ding Dong Merrily on High. 80p, We Three Kings.

**2010, Nov. 4 Litho. *Perf. 13¼x14***

| | | | | |
|---|---|---|---|---|
| **1111** | A231 | 31p multi | 1.00 | 1.00 |
| **1112** | A231 | 36p multi | 1.25 | 1.25 |
| **1113** | A231 | 45p multi | 1.50 | 1.50 |
| **1114** | A231 | 48p multi | 1.60 | 1.60 |
| **1115** | A231 | 50p multi | 1.60 | 1.60 |
| **1116** | A231 | 58p multi | 1.90 | 1.90 |
| **1117** | A231 | 80p multi | 2.60 | 2.60 |
| | | *Nos. 1111-1117 (7)* | 11.45 | 11.45 |

Royal British Legion, 90th Anniv. — A232

Emblem, soldiers or veterans and word: 36p, Hope. 45p, Reflection. 52p, Comradeship. 58p, Selflessness. 65p, Service. 70p, Dedication.

**2011, Feb. 23 Litho. *Perf. 13¼x13***

| | | | | |
|---|---|---|---|---|
| **1118** | A232 | 36p multi | 1.25 | 1.25 |
| **1119** | A232 | 45p multi | 1.50 | 1.50 |
| **1120** | A232 | 52p multi | 1.75 | 1.75 |
| **1121** | A232 | 58p multi | 1.90 | 1.90 |
| **1122** | A232 | 65p multi | 2.10 | 2.10 |
| **1123** | A232 | 70p multi | 2.25 | 2.25 |
| *a.* | | Souvenir sheet of 6, #1118-1123 | 11.00 | 11.00 |
| | | *Nos. 1118-1123 (6)* | 10.75 | 10.75 |

### Souvenir Sheet

Blue Whale — A233

**2011, Feb. 23 *Perf. 13¼***

| | | | | |
|---|---|---|---|---|
| **1124** | A233 | £3 multi | 9.75 | 9.75 |

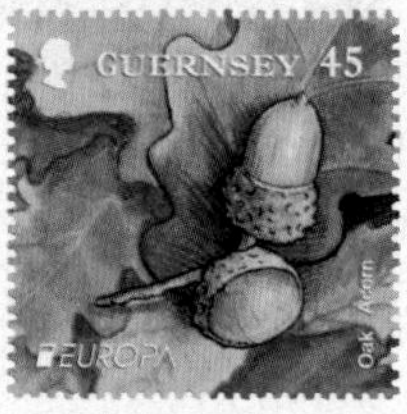


Intl. Year of Forests A234

Designs: 45p, Oak leaves, acorn. 52p, Hazel leaves, hazel nut. £2, Horse chestnut leaves and horse chestnut.

**2011, May 4 *Perf. 13¾***

| | | | | |
|---|---|---|---|---|
| **1125** | A234 | 45p multi | 1.50 | 1.50 |
| **1126** | A234 | 52p multi | 1.75 | 1.75 |
| **1127** | A234 | £2 multi | 6.75 | 6.75 |
| *a.* | | Souvenir sheet of 3, #1125-1127 | 10.00 | 10.00 |
| | | *Nos. 1125-1127 (3)* | 10.00 | 10.00 |

Europa (#1125-1126).

### Souvenir Sheets

Wedding of Prince William and Catherine Middleton — A235

Designs: No. 1128, Engagement photo. No. 1129, Bride and groom on wedding day.

**2011, June 2 *Perf. 14***

| | | | | |
|---|---|---|---|---|
| **1128** | A235 | £2 multi | 6.50 | 6.50 |
| **1129** | A235 | £2 multi | 6.50 | 6.50 |

The Guernsey Literary and Potato Peel Pie Society, Book by Mary Ann Shaffer and Annie Barrows
A236

Depictions of scenes from book: 36p, How to roast your pig. 47p, The books enjoyed by the Guernsey Literary and Potato Peel Pie Society. 48p, Juliet arrives at St. Peter Port weaing her red cloak. 52p, The view through Elizabeth's cottage window. 61p, Juliet and Dawsey's pivotal moment on the cliffs. 65p, Isola's legendary parrot, Zenobia.

**2011, July 28** ***Perf. 13¼***

**1130** A236 36p multi 1.25 1.25
**1131** A236 47p multi 1.50 1.50
**1132** A236 48p multi 1.60 1.60
**1133** A236 52p multi 1.75 1.75
**1134** A236 61p multi 2.00 2.00
**1135** A236 65p multi 2.10 2.10
*Nos. 1130-1135 (6)* 10.20 10.20

### Seaside Views Type of 2007

Designs: 36p, Victoria Marina, St. Peter Port. 45p, L'Ancresse Bay. 52p, Bordeaux Harbor Slipway. 58p, South Coast sunset. 65p, Salerie Harbor. 70p, Petit Port.

**2011, Sept. 28** **Litho.** ***Perf. 14¼***

**1136** A209 36p multi 1.25 1.25
**1137** A209 45p multi 1.40 1.40
**1138** A209 52p multi 1.60 1.60
**1139** A209 58p multi 1.90 1.90
**1140** A209 65p multi 2.10 2.10
**1141** A209 70p multi 2.25 2.25
*Nos. 1136-1141 (6)* 10.50 10.50

### British Formula 1 World Championship Cars and Drivers Type of 2007

Driver and championship year: 36p, Lewis Hamilton, 2008 (red background). 47p, Jenson Button, 2009 (purple background). 61p, Hamilton, 2008 (blue background). 65p, Button, 2009 (orange background).

**2011, Oct. 27** ***Perf. 13¼x13***

**1142** A206 36p multi 1.25 1.25
**1143** A206 47p multi 1.50 1.50
**1144** A206 61p multi 2.00 2.00
**1145** A206 65p multi 2.10 2.10
*a.* Souvenir sheet of 4, #1142-1145 7.00 7.00
*Nos. 1142-1145 (4)* 6.85 6.85

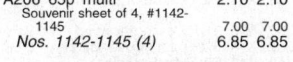

Guernsey in Winter
A237

Winning entries in "Guernsey in Winter" photography contest: 31p, Forest Church, by John Shakerley. 36p, L'Ancresse Common, by Nigel Byrom. 47p, Guernsey Cows, by Sarah Plumley. 48p, St. Peter Port, by Karen Millard. 52p, La Coupée, by Sue Daly. 61p, St. Peter's Church, by Jason Bishop. 65p, Cobo Bay, by Eric Ferbrache.

**2011, Oct. 27** ***Perf. 13½x13¼***

**1146** A237 31p multi 1.00 1.00
**1147** A237 36p multi 1.25 1.25
**1148** A237 47p multi 1.50 1.50
**1149** A237 48p multi 1.60 1.60
**1150** A237 52p multi 1.75 1.75
**1151** A237 61p multi 2.00 2.00
**1152** A237 65p multi 2.10 2.10
*Nos. 1146-1152 (7)* 11.20 11.20

Souvenir Sheet

Bengal Tiger — A238

**2012, Feb. 22** ***Perf. 13¾***

**1153** A238 £3 multi 9.50 9.50

Reign of Queen Elizabeth II, 60th Anniv. — A239

Gem and: 36p, Queen at coronation, birth of Prince Andrew. 47p, Queen receiving Jules Rimet trophy, ocean liner Queen Elizabeth 2. 48p, Queen, Sydney Opera House, emblem of 1976 Montreal Summer Olympics. 52p, Queen riding horse, Princes William and Harry in school uniforms, 1989. 61p, Queen, Queen Mother, Nelson Mandela. 65p, Queen at Guernsey Liberation Day, Queen with Pres. Barack Obama.

**2012, Feb. 22** ***Perf. 12½***

**1154** A239 36p multi 1.25 1.25
**1155** A239 47p multi 1.50 1.50
**1156** A239 48p multi 1.60 1.60
**1157** A239 52p multi 1.75 1.75
**1158** A239 61p multi 2.00 2.00
**1159** A239 65p multi 2.10 2.10
*a.* Souvenir sheet of 6, #1154-1159 10.50 10.50
*Nos. 1154-1159 (6)* 10.20 10.20

Tourist Attractions
A240

Designs: (39p), Surfer, Vazon Bay. (52p), Shell Beach, Herm. (53p), Grande Greve Beach, Sark. (59p), Bluestone Bay, Alderney. (69p), Sailboat off the coast of Herm. (74p), La Coupée, Sark.

**2012, May 1** ***Perf. 13x13¼***

**1160** A240 (39p) multi 1.25 1.25
**1161** A240 (52p) multi 1.75 1.75
**1162** A240 (53p) multi 1.75 1.75
**1163** A240 (59p) multi 1.90 1.90
**1164** A240 (69p) multi 2.25 2.25
**1165** A240 (74p) multi 2.40 2.40
*a.* Souvenir sheet of 6, #1160-1165 11.50 11.50
*Nos. 1160-1165 (6)* 11.30 11.30

Europa (53p, 59p). Inscriptions on: No. 1160, "GY Letter"; No. 1161, "GY Large"; No. 1162, "UK Letter"; No. 1163, "INT Letter 20G"; No. 1164, "UK Large"; No. 1165, "INT Letter 40G."

Duke of Cambridge, 30th Birthday — A241

Prince William: 36p, Carrying log, Chile, 2006. 47p, At St. Andrews University graduation ceremonies, 2005. 48p, Playing soccer, 2006. 52p, Climbing mountain, 2007. 67p, Riding motorcycle at Endura Africa Charity Motorcycle Ride, 2008. 65p, As rescue pilot, 2010.

**2012, May 8** ***Perf. 13½***

**1166** A241 36p multi 1.10 1.10
*a.* Booklet pane of 4 4.50 —
**1167** A241 47p multi 1.50 1.50
*a.* Booklet pane of 4 6.00 —
**1168** A241 48p multi 1.50 1.50
*a.* Booklet pane of 4 6.00 —
**1169** A241 52p multi 1.60 1.60
*a.* Booklet pane of 4 6.50 —
**1170** A241 61p multi 1.90 1.90
*a.* Booklet pane of 4 7.75 —
**1171** A241 65p multi 2.00 2.00
*a.* Booklet pane of 4 8.00 —
Complete booklet, #1166a, 1167a, 1168a, 1169a, 1170a, 1171a 39.00
*Nos. 1166-1171 (6)* 9.60 9.60

War of 1812 — A242

No. 1172: a, Sir Isaac Brock (1769-1812), British Major General. b, Tecumseh (1768-1813), leader of Indian confederacy.

**2012, June 15** ***Perf. 13¼x12½***

**1172** A242 Horiz. pair 6.50 6.50
*a.-b.* £1 Either single 3.25 3.25

See Canada Nos. 2554-2555.

Royal Channel Islands Yacht Club, 150th Anniv. — A243

Various sailors on yachts.

**2012, July 25** ***Perf. 13¼x13½***

**Denomination Color**

**1173** A243 39p purple 1.25 1.25
**1174** A243 52p blue gray 1.60 1.60
**1175** A243 53p blue 1.75 1.75
**1176** A243 59p blue 1.90 1.90
**1177** A243 69p olive green 2.25 2.25
**1178** A243 74p orange brown 2.40 2.40
*Nos. 1173-1178 (6)* 11.15 11.15

A244

Floral Guernsey, 20th Anniv. — A245

Designs: 39p, Flowers in wheelbarrow. 52p, Flowers and building. 53p, Flower display and rope. 59p, Flowers and lake. 69p, Potted flowers in and near shelf. 74p, Flowers and building, diff.

£3, Floral Guernsey daffodil.

**2012, Sept. 27** ***Perf. 13½***

**1179** A244 39p multi 1.25 1.25
**1180** A244 52p multi 1.75 1.75
**1181** A244 53p multi 1.75 1.75
**1182** A244 59p multi 1.90 1.90
**1183** A244 69p multi 2.25 2.25
**1184** A244 74p multi 2.40 2.40
*Nos. 1179-1184 (6)* 11.30 11.30

**Souvenir Sheet**

***Perf. 14***

**1185** A245 £3 multi 9.75 9.75

Christmas
A246

Designs: 34p, Annunciation. 39p, Innkeeper shows Mary and Joseph to the stable. 52p, Jesus is born in a stable. 53p, Angels come down amongst the shepherds. 59p, The Three Kings. 69p, Mary and baby Jesus with Angels. 74p, Flight to Egypt.

**2012, Oct. 31** ***Perf. 13¼x13***

**1186** A246 34p multi 1.10 1.10
**1187** A246 39p multi 1.25 1.25
**1188** A246 52p multi 1.75 1.75
**1189** A246 53p multi 1.75 1.75
**1190** A246 59p multi 1.90 1.90
**1191** A246 69p multi 2.25 2.25
**1192** A246 74p multi 2.40 2.40
*Nos. 1186-1192 (7)* 12.40 12.40

Souvenir Sheet

Giant Panda — A247

**2013, Feb. 20** ***Perf. 14x14¼***

**1193** A247 £3 multi 9.25 9.25

Fish — A248

Designs: 39p, Tompot blenny. 52p, Leopard-spotted goby. 53p, Red gurnard. 59p, Female cuckoo wrasse. 69p, Male cuckoo wrasse. 74p, John Dory.

£5, Black-face blenny.

**2013, Feb. 20** ***Perf. 12½***

**1194** A248 39p multi 1.25 1.25
**1195** A248 52p multi 1.60 1.60
**1196** A248 53p multi 1.60 1.60
**1197** A248 59p multi 1.75 1.75
**1198** A248 69p multi 2.10 2.10
**1199** A248 74p multi 2.25 2.25
*Nos. 1194-1199 (6)* 10.55 10.55

**Souvenir Sheet**

***Perf. 13¼x13½***

**1200** A248 £5 multi 15.50 15.50

No. 1200 contains one 48x66mm stamp.

---

## POSTAGE DUE STAMPS

Castle Cornet and St. Peter Port — D1

***Perf. 12½x12***

**1969, Oct. 1** **Photo.** **Unwmk.**

**Black Numeral**

**J1** D1 1p deep magenta 1.75 1.00
**J2** D1 2p yellow green 2.25 1.75
**J3** D1 3p red 3.00 3.00

| | | | | |
|---|---|---|---|---|
| **J4** | D1 | 4p ultra | 4.00 | 4.00 |
| **J5** | D1 | 5p yellow bister | 7.00 | 4.00 |
| **J6** | D1 | 6p greenish blue | 8.00 | 4.50 |
| **J7** | D1 | 1sh red brown | 21.00 | 13.00 |
| | | *Nos. J1-J7 (7)* | 47.00 | 31.25 |

**Type of 1969**
**"p" instead of "d"**

**1971-76**

**Black Numeral**

| | | | | |
|---|---|---|---|---|
| **J8** | D1 | ½p deep magenta | .25 | .25 |
| **J9** | D1 | 1p yellow green | .25 | .25 |
| **J10** | D1 | 2p red | .25 | .25 |
| **J11** | D1 | 3p ultra | .25 | .25 |
| **J12** | D1 | 4p yellow bister | .25 | .25 |
| **J13** | D1 | 5p greenish blue | .25 | .25 |
| **J14** | D1 | 6p purple ('76) | .25 | .25 |
| **J15** | D1 | 8p orange ('75) | .25 | .25 |
| **J16** | D1 | 10p red brown | .50 | .50 |
| **J17** | D1 | 15p gray ('76) | .50 | .50 |
| | | *Nos. J8-J17 (10)* | 3.00 | 3.00 |

Town Church, St. Peter Port — D2

**1977-80 Photo. *Perf. 13½x13***
**Arms and Denomination in Black**

| | | | | |
|---|---|---|---|---|
| **J18** | D2 | ½p red brown | .25 | .25 |
| **J19** | D2 | 1p lilac rose | .25 | .25 |
| **J20** | D2 | 2p orange | .25 | .25 |
| **J21** | D2 | 3p red | .25 | .25 |
| **J22** | D2 | 4p greenish blue | .25 | .25 |
| **J23** | D2 | 5p olive green | .25 | .25 |
| **J24** | D2 | 6p greenish blue | .25 | .25 |
| **J25** | D2 | 8p ocher | .25 | .25 |
| **J26** | D2 | 10p dark blue | .30 | .30 |
| **J27** | D2 | 14p green ('80) | .40 | .40 |
| **J28** | D2 | 15p purple | .40 | .40 |
| **J29** | D2 | 16p salmon rose ('80) | .50 | .50 |
| | | *Nos. J18-J29 (12)* | 3.60 | 3.60 |

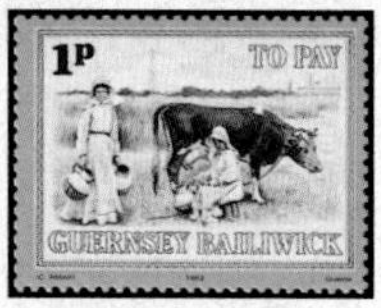

Woman Milking Cow — D3

**1982, July 13 Litho. *Perf. 14½***

| | | | | |
|---|---|---|---|---|
| **J30** | D3 | 1p shown | .25 | .25 |
| **J31** | D3 | 2p Vale Mill | .25 | .25 |
| **J32** | D3 | 3p Sark cottage | .25 | .25 |
| **J33** | D3 | 4p St. Peter Port | .25 | .25 |
| **J34** | D3 | 5p Well, Moulin Huet | .25 | .25 |
| **J35** | D3 | 16p Seaweed gathering | .40 | .40 |
| **J36** | D3 | 18p Upper Walk, White Rock | .45 | .45 |
| **J37** | D3 | 20p Cobo Bay | .50 | .50 |
| **J38** | D3 | 25p Saints' Bay | .55 | .55 |
| **J39** | D3 | 30p La Coupee, Sark | .75 | .75 |
| **J40** | D3 | 50p Old Harbor, St. Peter Port | 1.10 | 1.10 |
| **J41** | D3 | £1 Greenhouses, Victoria Tower | 2.50 | 2.50 |
| | | *Nos. J30-J41 (12)* | 7.50 | 7.50 |

---

**OCCUPATION STAMPS**

**Issued Under German Occupation**

Bisects of Great Britain Nos. 238 and 255 were used in Guernsey from 12/27/40 to 2./24/41. Values, on cover or postcard: No. 238, $45; No. 255, $40.

OS1

***Rouletted 14x7***

**1941-44 Typo. Unwmk.**

| | | | | |
|---|---|---|---|---|
| **N1** | OS1 | ½p light green | 3.50 | 3.50 |
| **N2** | OS1 | 1p red | 3.00 | 2.00 |
| **N3** | OS1 | 2½p ultramarine | 8.00 | 12.00 |
| | | *Nos. N1-N3 (3)* | 14.50 | 17.50 |

Issued: #N1b, 4/7/41; #N1c, 6/41; #N1d, 11/41; #N1e, 2/42; #N1a, 9/42; #N1f, 2/43; #N1, from 7/43; #N2, 2/18/41; #N2a, 7/43; #N2b, 1943; #N3, 4/12/44; #N3a, 7/44.

Additional shades and papers exist. The rouletting is very crude and may not be measurable. This is not a defect.

**Bluish French Bank Note Paper**

**Wmk. 396 Chain Link Fence**

**1942 *Rouletted 14x7***

| | | | | |
|---|---|---|---|---|
| **N4** | OS1 | ½p green | 27.50 | 27.50 |
| **N5** | OS1 | 1p red | 14.50 | *21.00* |

Issue dates: ½p, Mar. 11; 1p, Apr. 9.
Nos. N1-N5 remained valid until 4/13/46.

---

## ALDERNEY

'ol-dər-nē

LOCATION — Northernmost of the Channel Islands in the Guernsey Bailiwick
GOVT. — Dependent territory under Bailiwick of Guernsey.
AREA — 3 sq. mi.
POP. — 2,373 (1994 est.)
CAPITAL — St. Anne's

Part of the Bailiwick of Guernsey, this island began issuing its own stamps.

**Catalogue values for unused stamps in this section are for Never Hinged items.**

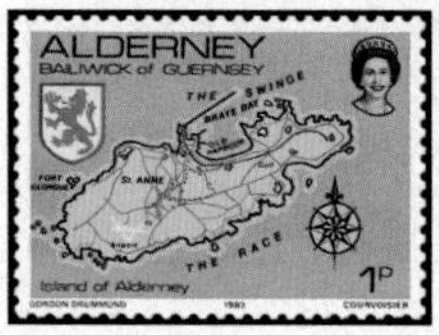

Map of Alderney, Arms — A1

**1983, June 14 Litho. *Perf. 12***

| | | | | |
|---|---|---|---|---|
| **1** | A1 | 1p shown | .40 | .40 |
| **2** | A1 | 4p Hanging Rock | .40 | .40 |
| **3** | A1 | 9p States Building | .45 | .45 |
| **4** | A1 | 10p St. Anne's Church | .45 | .45 |
| **5** | A1 | 11p Yachts, Braye Bay | .50 | .50 |
| **6** | A1 | 12p Victoria St., St. Anne | .50 | .50 |
| **7** | A1 | 13p Map, arms | .50 | .50 |
| **8** | A1 | 14p Ft. Clonque | .55 | .55 |
| **9** | A1 | 15p Corblets Bay Port | .55 | .55 |
| **10** | A1 | 16p Old Tower, St. Anne | .65 | .65 |
| **11** | A1 | 17p Essex Castle Golf Course | .70 | .70 |
| **12** | A1 | 18p Ships in Old Harbor | .70 | .70 |
| | | *Nos. 1-12 (12)* | 6.35 | 6.35 |

See Nos. 42-46, which is considered to be the higher-denomination continuation of this definitive set.

Oystercatcher, Telegraph Bay — A2

**1984, June 12 *Perf. 14½***

| | | | | |
|---|---|---|---|---|
| **13** | A2 | 9p shown | *1.50* | *1.10* |
| **14** | A2 | 13p Turnstone, Corblets Bay | *1.50* | *1.00* |
| **15** | A2 | 26p Ringed plover, Corblets Bay | *4.00* | *3.00* |
| **16** | A2 | 28p Dunlin, Arch Bay | *4.00* | *3.25* |
| **17** | A2 | 31p Curlew, Old Harbor | *4.00* | *3.25* |
| | | *Nos. 13-17 (5)* | *15.00* | *11.60* |

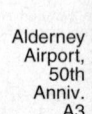

Alderney Airport, 50th Anniv. A3

Aircraft: 9p, Wessex helicopter of the Queen's Flight, 1984. 13p, Aurigny Air Joey Britten-Norman Trislander, 1981. 29p, Morton Air Services DeHavilland Heron, 1946. 31p, DeHavilland Dragon Rapide, c. 1930. 34p, Saunders-Roe Saro Windhover, 1935.

**1985, Mar. 19 *Perf. 12x11½***

| | | | | |
|---|---|---|---|---|
| **18** | A3 | 9p multicolored | *1.75* | *1.50* |
| **19** | A3 | 13p multicolored | *2.50* | *1.50* |
| **20** | A3 | 29p multicolored | *4.25* | *3.50* |
| **21** | A3 | 31p multicolored | *5.25* | *3.75* |
| **22** | A3 | 34p multicolored | *5.25* | *3.75* |
| | | *Nos. 18-22 (5)* | *19.00* | *14.00* |

Regimental Uniforms, Alderney Garrison — A4

**1985, Sept. 24 *Perf. 14½***

| | | | | |
|---|---|---|---|---|
| **23** | A4 | 9p Royal Engineers, 1890 | *.30* | *.30* |
| **24** | A4 | 14p Duke of Albany's Own Highlanders, 1856 | *1.10* | *.55* |
| **25** | A4 | 29p Royal Artillery, 1855 | *1.10* | *1.10* |
| **26** | A4 | 31p South Hampshire Regiment, 1810 | *1.50* | *1.25* |
| **27** | A4 | 34p Royal Irish Regiment, 1782 | *1.75* | *1.40* |
| | | *Nos. 23-27 (5)* | *5.75* | *4.60* |

Forts — A5

**1986, Sept. 23 Litho. *Perf. 13x13½***

| | | | | |
|---|---|---|---|---|
| **28** | A5 | 10p Grosnez | 1.25 | 1.25 |
| **29** | A5 | 14p Tourgis | 1.50 | 1.50 |
| **30** | A5 | 31p Clonque | 3.50 | 3.50 |
| **31** | A5 | 34p Albert | 3.75 | 3.75 |
| | | *Nos. 28-31 (4)* | 10.00 | 10.00 |

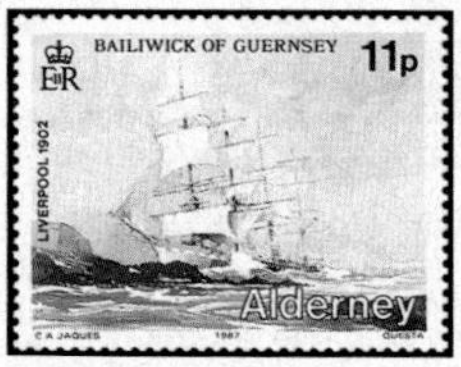

Shipwrecks A6

**1987, May 5 Litho. *Perf. 14½***

| | | | | |
|---|---|---|---|---|
| **32** | A6 | 11p Liverpool, 1902 | *2.00* | *.80* |
| **33** | A6 | 15p Petit Raymond, 1906 | *2.50* | *.80* |
| **34** | A6 | 29p Maina, 1910 | *5.00* | *5.00* |
| **35** | A6 | 31p Burton, 1911 | *5.25* | *5.00* |
| **36** | A6 | 34p Point Law, 1975 | *5.25* | *5.25* |
| | | *Nos. 32-36 (5)* | *20.00* | *16.85* |

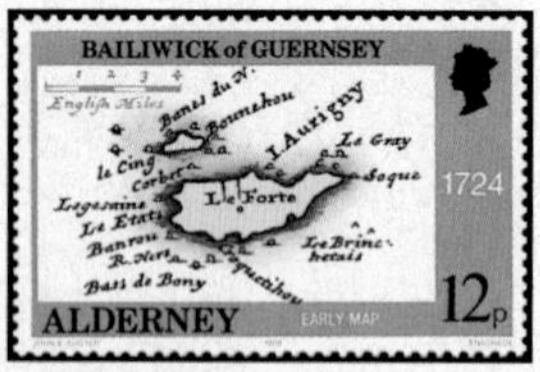

18th-20th Cent. Maps — A7

Designs: 12p, Herman Moll map, 1724. 18p, Survey by J.H. Bastide, 1739. 27p, Land survey by M.P. Goodwin, 1830. 32p, Wartime occupation map, 1943. 35p, Ordnance survey, 1988.

**1989, July 7 Litho. *Perf. 13½x14***

| | | | | |
|---|---|---|---|---|
| **37** | A7 | 12p multicolored | .50 | .50 |
| **38** | A7 | 18p multicolored | .75 | .75 |
| **39** | A7 | 27p multicolored | 1.10 | 1.10 |
| **40** | A7 | 32p multicolored | 1.25 | 1.25 |
| **41** | A7 | 35p multicolored | 1.40 | 1.40 |
| | | *Nos. 37-41 (5)* | 5.00 | 5.00 |

Quesnard Lighthouse A8

Designs: 21p, Inner Harbor, Braye. 23p, The Island Hall, Alderney. 24p, Alderney Railway locomotive, J. T. Daly. 28p, Lifeboat, Louis Marchesi of Round Table.

**1989-93 Litho. *Perf. 15x14***

| | | | | |
|---|---|---|---|---|
| **42** | A8 | 20p multicolored | 1.25 | 1.00 |
| **43** | A8 | 21p multicolored | 1.25 | 1.00 |
| **44** | A8 | 23p multicolored | .85 | .75 |
| **45** | A8 | 24p multicolored | 2.25 | 2.00 |
| **46** | A8 | 28p multicolored | 2.40 | 2.00 |
| | | *Nos. 42-46 (5)* | 8.00 | 6.75 |

Issued: 20p, 12/27; 21p, 4/2/91; 23p, 2/6/92; 24p, 28p, 3/3/93.

Ships Called HMS *Alderney* A9

**1990, May 3 Litho. *Perf. 13½***

| | | | | |
|---|---|---|---|---|
| **55** | A9 | 14p Bomb ketch, 1738 | .55 | .55 |
| **56** | A9 | 20p Sixth-rate, 1742 | .70 | .70 |
| **57** | A9 | 29p Sloop, 1755 | 1.00 | 1.00 |
| **58** | A9 | 34p A-Class submarine, 1945 | 1.25 | 1.25 |
| **59** | A9 | 37p Fishery protection vessel, 1979 | 1.50 | 1.50 |
| | | *Nos. 55-59 (5)* | 5.00 | 5.00 |

Automation of Casquets Lighthouse — A10

**1991, Apr. 20 Litho. *Perf. 14x13½***

| | | | | |
|---|---|---|---|---|
| **60** | A10 | 21p Wreck of HMS Victory, 1744 | *1.90* | *1.90* |
| **61** | A10 | 26p Returning by rowboat | *2.10* | *2.10* |
| **62** | A10 | 31p Helicopter relief | *2.50* | *2.50* |
| **63** | A10 | 37p Lighthouse, birds | *3.00* | *3.00* |
| **64** | A10 | 50p MV Patricia | *4.00* | *4.00* |
| | | *Nos. 60-64 (5)* | *13.50* | *13.50* |

Battle of La Hogue, 300th Anniv. — A11

23p, 28p, and 33p, Various details from painting by unknown artist. 50p, Entire painting.

**1992, Sept. 18 Litho. *Perf. 13½***

| | | | | |
|---|---|---|---|---|
| **65** | A11 | 23p multicolored | *2.00* | *2.00* |
| **66** | A11 | 28p multicolored | *2.50* | *2.50* |
| **67** | A11 | 33p multicolored | *3.00* | *3.00* |

**Size: 45x30mm**

***Perf. 14x14½***

| | | | | |
|---|---|---|---|---|
| **68** | A11 | 50p multicolored | *3.75* | *3.75* |
| | | *Nos. 65-68 (4)* | *11.25* | *11.25* |

Marine Life — A12

Designs: a, 24p, Palinurus elephas. b, 28p, Metridium senile. c, 33p, Luidia ciliaris. d, 39p, Psammechinus miliaris.

**1993, Nov. 2 Litho. *Perf. 15x14½***
**69** A12 Strip of 4, #a.-d. *9.50 9.50*

Flora and Fauna — A13

Designs: 1p, Ischnura elegans, ranunculus trichophyllus, sparganium erectum. 2p, Crocidura russula, hypericum linarifolium. 3p, Fulmarus glacialis, carpobrotus edulis. 4p, Colias croceus, trifolium pratense. 5p, Bombus lucorum, orobanche rapum-genistae, cytisus scoparius. 6p, Sylvia undata, cuscuta epithymum, ulex europaeus. 7p, Inachis io, cirsium acaule. 8p, Talpa europaea, endymion non-scripta. 9p, Tettigonia viridissima, ulex europaeus. 10p, Zygaena filipendulae, echium vulgare. 16p, Polyommatus icarus, anacamptis pyramidalis. 20p, Oryctolagus cuniculus, rannunculus repens, pteridium aquilinum. 24p, Larus marinus, romulea columnae. 30p, Fratercula arctica, sedum anglicum. 40p, Saturnia pavonia, rubus fruticosus. 50p, Erinaceus europaeus, oxalis articulata. £1, Sterna hirundo, cynodon dactylon, horiz. £2, Morus bassanus, fucus vesiculosus.

**1994-95 Litho. *Perf. 14***
**70** A13 1p multicolored .25 .25
**71** A13 2p multicolored .25 .25
**72** A13 3p multicolored .25 .25
**73** A13 4p multicolored .25 .25
**74** A13 5p multicolored .25 .25
**75** A13 6p multicolored .25 .25
**76** A13 7p multicolored .25 .25
**77** A13 8p multicolored .30 .30
**78** A13 9p multicolored .35 .35
**79** A13 10p multicolored .40 .40
**80** A13 16p multicolored .60 .60
*a.* Perf. 14x15 on three sides .65 .65
*b.* As "a," booklet pane of 8 5.75
Complete booklet, #80b 5.75
**81** A13 20p multicolored .80 .80
*a.* Perf. 14x15 on three sides .85 .85
*b.* As "a," booklet pane of 8 7.25
Complete booklet, #81b 7.25
**82** A13 24p multicolored .95 .95
*a.* Perf. 14x15 on three sides 1.00 1.00
*b.* As "a," booklet pane of 8 9.00
Complete booklet, #82b 9.00
**83** A13 30p multicolored 1.10 1.10
**84** A13 40p multicolored 1.60 1.60
**85** A13 50p multicolored 2.00 2.00
**86** A13 £1 multicolored 4.00 4.00

***Perf. 14x15***
**87** A13 £2 multicolored 8.00 8.00
*Nos. 70-87 (18)* 21.85 21.85

No. 81 is dated "1994." Nos. 81a-81b are dated "1998."
Issued: £2, 2/28/95; others, 5/5/94.
See Nos. 98-100.

Career of Flt. Lt. Tommy Rose DFC (1895-1968) — A14

No. 88: a, 1917-18 Royal Flying Corps. b, 1939-45 Chief Test Pilot. c, Phillips & Powis (Miles) Aircraft.
No. 89: a, Winner, 1935 King's Cup Air Race. b, Winner, 1947 Manx Air Derby. c, UK-Cape-UK Speed Record, 1936.

**1995, Sept. 1 Litho. *Perf. 14x15***
**88** A14 35p Strip of 3, #a.-c. 4.25 4.25
**89** A14 41p Strip of 3, #a.-c. 5.00 5.00

Nos. 88-89 printed in sheets of 12 stamps + 3 labels.

Souvenir Sheet

Return of Islanders, 50th Anniv. — A15

**1995, Nov. 16 Litho. *Perf. 13½***
**90** A15 £1.65 multicolored 6.50 6.50

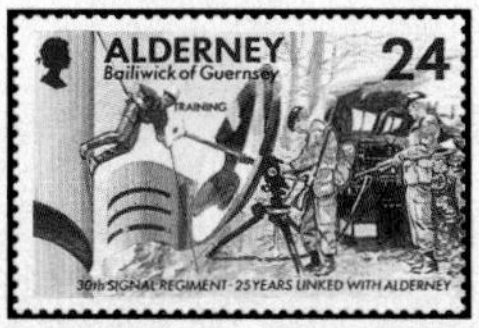


30th Signal Regiment Activities in Alderney, 25th Anniv. A16

a, 24p, Training. b, 41p, Natl. contingencies overseas. c, 60p, Strategic communications. d, 75p, UN operations.

**1996, Jan. 24 Litho. *Perf. 14***
**91** A16 Strip of 4, #a.-d. 8.00 8.00

Domestic Cats — A17

16p, Butterfly, brown & white cat. 24p, Gray cat on table. 25p, Two cats on chair. 35p, Cat pulling on table cloth. 41p, Calico cat in toy cart, white cat. 60p, Siamese cat with yarn.

**1996, July 19 Litho. *Perf. 13½***
**92** A17 16p multicolored .60 .60
**93** A17 24p multicolored .95 .95
**94** A17 25p multicolored 1.00 1.00
**95** A17 35p multicolored 1.40 1.40
**96** A17 41p multicolored 1.60 1.60
**97** A17 60p multicolored 2.40 2.40
*a.* Souvenir sheet, #92-97 8.00 8.00
*Nos. 92-97 (6)* 7.95 7.95

No. 97a is a continuous design.

### Fauna and Flora Type of 1994

Designs: 18p, Aglais urticae, Buddleja davidii. 25p, Anthus petrosus, matthiola incana. 26p, Ammophila sabulosa, calystegia soldanella, horiz.

**1997, Jan. 2 Litho. *Perf. 14½***
**98** A13 18p multicolored .70 .70
*a.* Perf. 14x15 on 3 sides 1.00
*b.* As "a," booklet pane of 8 8.75
Complete booklet, #98b 8.75
**99** A13 25p multicolored 1.00 1.00
*a.* Perf. 14x15 on 3 sides 1.00
*b.* As "a," booklet pane of 8 8.75
Complete booklet, #99b 8.75
**100** A13 26p multicolored 1.00 1.00
*Nos. 98-100 (3)* 2.70 2.70

Alderney Cricket Club, 150th Anniv. — A18

**1997, Aug. 21 Litho. *Perf. 13½***
**101** A18 18p Harold Larwood .70 .70
**102** A18 25p John Arlott 1.00 1.00
**103** A18 37p Pelham J. Warner 1.40 1.40
**104** A18 43p W.G. Grace 1.60 1.60
**105** A18 63p John Wisden 2.50 2.50
*a.* Souvenir sheet, #101-105 + label 8.00 8.00
*Nos. 101-105 (5)* 7.20 7.20

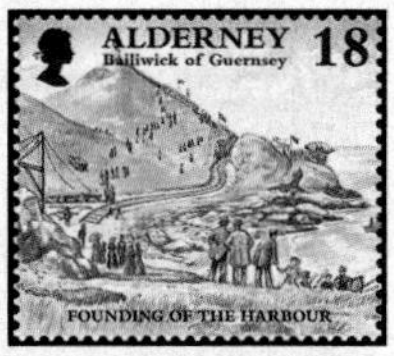


Garrison Island — A19

#106, Founding of the harbor. #107, Ariadne at anchor. #108, Quarrying at Mannez. #109, Earliest train ferrying stone. #110, Queen Victoria arrives ashore. #111, Royal yacht at anchor. #112, Railway and quarry workers greet the Queen. #113, Queen Victoria tours the island.

**1997, Nov. 20 Litho. *Perf. 14½x14***
**106** A19 18p multicolored .70 .70
**107** A19 18p multicolored .70 .70
*a.* Pair, #106-107 1.40 1.40
**108** A19 25p multicolored 1.00 1.00
**109** A19 25p multicolored 1.00 1.00
*a.* Pair, #108-109 2.00 2.00
*b.* Booklet pane, #107a, 109a ('98) 3.75
**110** A19 26p multicolored 1.00 1.00
**111** A19 26p multicolored 1.00 1.00
*a.* Pair, #110-111 2.00 2.00
*b.* Booklet pane, #107a, 111a ('98) 3.75
**112** A19 31p multicolored 1.25 1.25
**113** A19 31p multicolored 1.25 1.25
*a.* Pair, #112-113 2.50 2.50
*b.* Booklet pane, #111a, 113a ('98) 4.75
*c.* Booklet pane, #109a, 113a ('98) 4.75
*Nos. 106-113 (8)* 7.90 7.90

Nos. 109b, 111b, 113b, 113c issued 11/10/98.
See Nos. 119-126, 134-141, 155-162, 176-183.

Alderney Diving Club, 21st Anniv. — A20

20p, Modern superlite helmet. 30p, Cousteau-Gagnan demand valve, 1943. 37p, Heinke closed helmet, 1845. 43p, Siebe closed helmet, 1840. 63p, Deane open helmet, 1829.

**1998, Feb. 10 Litho. *Perf. 13***
**114** A20 20p multicolored .80 .80
**115** A20 30p multicolored 1.10 1.10
**116** A20 37p multicolored 1.40 1.40
**117** A20 43p multicolored 1.60 1.60
**118** A20 63p multicolored 2.50 2.50
*a.* Souvenir sheet, #114-118 + label 7.50 7.50
*Nos. 114-118 (5)* 7.40 7.40

### Garrison Island Type of 1997

#119, Alderney Post Office. #120, Traders in Victoria Street. #121, Court House. #122, Police Station and Fire Service. #123, St. Anne's Church. #124, Wedding Party at The Albert Gate. #125, SS Courier unloading. #126, Fishermen at quay.

**1998, Nov. 10 Litho. *Perf. 14½x14***
**119** A19 20p multicolored .80 .80
**120** A19 20p multicolored .80 .80
*a.* Pair, #119-120 1.60 1.60
**121** A19 25p multicolored 1.00 1.00
**122** A19 25p multicolored 1.00 1.00
*a.* Pair, #121-122 2.00 2.00
*b.* Booklet pane, #120a, 122a 3.75
**123** A19 30p multicolored 1.25 1.25
**124** A19 30p multicolored 1.25 1.25
*a.* Pair, #123-124 2.50 2.50
*b.* Booklet pane, #120a, 124a 4.25
**125** A19 37p multicolored 1.60 1.60
**126** A19 37p multicolored 1.60 1.60
*a.* Pair, #125-126 3.25 3.25
*b.* Booklet pane, #124a, 126a 6.00
*c.* Booklet pane, #122a, 126a 5.75
Complete booklet, #109b, 111b, 113b, 113c, 122b, 124b, 126b, 126c 37.50
*Nos. 119-126 (8)* 9.30 9.30

Souvenir Sheet

The Wreck of the SS Stella, Cent. — A21

a, 25p, Stained glass window, Anglican Cathedral, Liverpool, dedicated to Mary Rogers, chief stewardess. b, £1.75, Ship leaving Southampton.

**1999, Feb. 4 Litho. *Perf. 14***
**127** A21 Sheet of 2, #a.-b. 8.00 8.00

Total Solar Eclipse — A22

Stages of eclipse on 8/11/99: 20p, 10:15. 25p, 10:51. 30p, 11:14. 38p, 11:16. 44p, 11:17. 64p, 11:36.

**1999, Apr. 27 Litho. *Perf. 13½x13***
**128** A22 20p multicolored .80 .80
**129** A22 25p multicolored 1.00 1.00
**130** A22 30p multicolored 1.25 1.25
**131** A22 38p multicolored 1.50 1.50
**132** A22 44p multicolored 1.75 1.75
**133** A22 64p multicolored 2.50 2.50
*a.* Souvenir sheet, #128-133 + label 8.75 8.75
*Nos. 128-133 (6)* 8.80 8.80

### Garrison Island Type of 1997

Designs: No. 134, Fort Grosnez, c. 1855. No. 135, Ninth Battalion, Royal Garrison Artillery. No. 136, Arsenal, Fort Albert. No. 137, Royal Engineer Unit. No. 138, Fort Tourgis, c. 1865. No. 139, Second Battalion, Royal Scots Regiment. No. 140, Fort Houmet Herbé, c. 1870. No. 141, Royal Alderney Artillery Militia.

**1999, Oct. 19 Litho. *Perf. 14¼x13¾***
**134** A19 20p multicolored .80 .80
**135** A19 20p multicolored .80 .80
*a.* Pair, #134-135 1.60 1.60
**136** A19 25p multicolored 1.00 1.00
**137** A19 25p multicolored 1.00 1.00
*a.* Pair, #136-137 2.00 2.00
*b.* Booklet pane, #135a, 137a 3.75
**138** A19 30p multicolored 1.25 1.25
**139** A19 30p multicolored 1.25 1.25
*a.* Pair, #138-139 2.50 2.50
*b.* Booklet pane, #135a, 139a 4.50
*c.* Booklet pane, #137a, 139a 4.75
**140** A19 38p multicolored 1.50 1.50
**141** A19 38p multicolored 1.50 1.50
*a.* Pair, #140-141 3.25 3.25
*b.* Booklet pane, #135a, 141a 5.25
*c.* Booklet pane, #137a, 141a 5.50
*d.* Booklet pane, #139a, 141a 6.00
Complete booklet, #137b, 139b, 139c, 141b, 141c, 141d 32.50
*Nos. 134-141 (8)* 9.10 9.10

Peregrine Falcon — A23

Falcons: 21p, Attacking turnstone near lighthouse. 26p, With prey. 34p, With eggs. 38p, With chicks. 44p, With young near Fort Clonque. 64p, Preparing to fly.

**2000, Feb. 4 Litho. *Perf. 14½x14***
**142** A23 21p multi 1.10 1.10
*a.* Booklet pane of 10 11.00
Complete booklet 11.00
**143** A23 26p multi 1.25 1.25
*a.* Booklet pane of 10 12.00
Complete booklet 12.00
**144** A23 34p multi 1.50 1.50
**145** A23 38p multi 1.60 1.60

**146** A23 44p multi 2.00 2.00
**147** A23 64p multi 2.75 2.75
*Nos. 142-147 (6)* 10.20 10.20

Worldwide Fund for Nature, Nos. 144-147.

The Wombles on Vacation A24

Wombles: 21p, With map. 26p, On beach. 36p, At lighthouse. 40p, Picnicking. 45p, On golf course. 65p, At airport.

**2000, Apr. 28 Litho.** ***Perf. 14¼x13¾***
**148** A24 21p multi .85 .85
**149** A24 26p multi 1.00 1.00
**150** A24 36p multi 1.40 1.40
**151** A24 40p multi 1.60 1.60
**152** A24 45p multi 1.75 1.75
**153** A24 65p multi 2.50 2.50
*a.* Souvenir sheet, #148-153 9.25 9.25
*Nos. 148-153 (6)* 9.10 9.10

The Stamp Show 2000, London (No. 153a).

Souvenir Sheet

Queen Mother, 100th Birthday — A25

### Litho. with Foil Application

**2000, Aug. 4** ***Perf. 13¼***
**154** A25 £1.50 multi 6.00 6.00

### Garrison Island Type of 1997

#155, Regimental boxing tournament. #156, Sports Day of Alderney Gala Week, 1924. #157, Regimental Band of 15th entertains. #158, Garrison Ball, 1873, Fort Albert mess room. #159, Garrison assembly for Queen's birthday celebrations, 1859. #160, Demonstration of field guns on the Butes. #161, Inspection of honor guard, 1863. #162, Arrival of Lt. Gov. Major Gen. Marcus Slade.

**2000, Oct. 19 Litho.** ***Perf. 13¼x13***
**155** A19 21p multi .85 .85
**156** A19 21p multi .85 .85
*a.* Pair, #155-156 1.75 1.75
**157** A19 26p multi 1.00 1.00
**158** A19 26p multi 1.00 1.00
*a.* Pair, #157-158 2.00 2.00
*b.* Booklet pane, #156a, 158a 4.00
**159** A19 36p multi 1.40 1.40
**160** A19 36p multi 1.40 1.40
*a.* Pair, #159-160 3.00 3.00
*b.* Booklet pane, #158a, 160a 5.50
**161** A19 40p multi 1.60 1.60
**162** A19 40p multi 1.60 1.60
*a.* Pair, #161-162 3.25 3.25
*b.* Booklet pane, #156a, 162a 5.00
*c.* Booklet pane, #160a, 162a 6.25
Booklet, #158b, 162c, 2 each #160b, 162b 30.00
*Nos. 155-162 (8)* 9.70 9.70

Each of the two panes of Nos. 160b and 162b in the booklet have different selvages.

Souvenir Sheet

Queen Elizabeth, 75th Birthday — A26

**2001, Feb. 1 Litho.** ***Perf. 14¼***
**163** A26 £1.75 multi 7.00 7.00

Community Health Services A27

Health care workers and: 22p, Hospital x-ray department. 27p, Mignot Memorial Hospital in 1980s. 36p, Princess Anne visiting hospital, 1972. 40p, Nurse with infant, 1960s. 45p, Queen Elizabeth II laying hospital cornerstone, 1957. 65p, Opening of original hospital, 1920s.

**2001-02 Litho.** ***Perf. 14¼x14½***
**164** A27 22p multi .85 .85
*a.* Perf. 13¼x13 .90 .90
**165** A27 27p multi 1.00 1.00
*a.* Perf. 13¼x13 2.50 2.50
**166** A27 36p multi 1.40 1.40
*a.* Perf. 13¼x13 1.40 1.40
**167** A27 40p multi 1.60 1.60
*a.* Perf. 13¼x13 1.60 1.60
*b.* Booklet pane, #164a, 165a, 166a, 167a 5.50 —
**168** A27 45p multi 1.75 1.75
*a.* Perf. 13¼x13 1.75 1.75
**169** A27 65p multi 2.50 2.50
*a.* Perf. 13¼x13 2.40 2.40
*b.* Booklet pane, #166a, 167a, 168a, 169a 7.25 —
*c.* Booklet pane, #164a, 165a, 168a, 169a 6.50 —
*Nos. 164-169 (6)* 9.10 9.10

Issued: Nos. 164-169, 4/26/01; Nos. 164a-169a, 10/17/02.

See Nos. 196-201, 215-220, 239-244.

Alderney Golf Club — A28

Designs: 22p, Golf ball with core of feathers, 1901. 27p, Golfing fashions, 1920s. 36p, Player and ball on Alderney Golf Club green, 1970s. 40p, Modern putter. 45p, Golf accessories. 65p, Modern lofted wood.

**2001, Aug. 1 Litho.** ***Perf. 14¾***
**170** A28 22p multi .85 .85
**171** A28 27p multi 1.00 1.00
**172** A28 36p multi 1.40 1.40
**173** A28 40p multi 1.60 1.60
**174** A28 45p multi 1.75 1.75
**175** A28 65p multi 2.50 2.50
*a.* Souvenir sheet, #170-175 9.25 9.25
*Nos. 170-175 (6)* 9.10 9.10

Phila Nippon '01 (#175a).

### Garrison Island Type of 1997

Designs: No. 176, Work continues at the breakwater. No. 177, Officials observe work in progress. No. 178, Steam frigate Emerald grounded. No. 179, Soldiers disembarking Emerald. No. 180, Torpedo boats moored at breakwater. No. 181, Railway provides mobile artillery. No. 182, HMS Majestic at anchor, 1901. No. 183, Torpedo boats maneuver at speed.

**2001, Oct. 16 Litho.** ***Perf. 13¼x13***
**176** A19 22p multi .85 .85
**177** A19 22p multi .85 .85
*a.* Pair, #176-177 1.75 1.75
**178** A19 27p multi 1.00 1.00
**179** A19 27p multi 1.00 1.00
*a.* Pair, #178-179 2.00 2.00
*b.* Booklet pane, #177a, 179a 4.00 —
**180** A19 36p multi 1.40 1.40
**181** A19 36p multi 1.40 1.40
*a.* Pair, #180-181 3.00 3.00
*b.* Booklet pane, #179a, 181a 5.25 —
**182** A19 40p multi 1.60 1.60
**183** A19 40p multi 1.60 1.60
*a.* Pair, #182-183 3.25 3.25
*b.* Booklet pane, #177a, 183a 4.75 —
*c.* Booklet pane, #179a, 183a 5.25 —
*d.* Booklet pane, #181a, 183a 5.25 —
Booklet, #179b, 181b, 183c, 183d, 2 #183b 32.50
*Nos. 176-183 (8)* 9.70 9.70

Booklet sold for £7.50. Each of the two panes of No. 183b in the booklet have different selvages.

Souvenir Sheet

Reign of Queen Elizabeth II, 50th Anniv. — A29

**2002, Feb. 6 Litho.** ***Perf. 13¾x13½***
**184** A29 £2 multi 8.00 8.00
*a.* Booklet pane of 1 8.00
Complete booklet, #184a, Guernsey #773a, 774a, 774b, 774c 37.50

No. 184a is sewn into booklets, but is otherwise identical to No. 184.

Issued: #184: 2/6; #184a, 4/30.

Birds — A30

**2002, Apr. 30** ***Perf. 13¾***
**185** A30 22p Hobby .85 .85
**186** A30 27p Black kite 1.00 1.00
**187** A30 36p Merlin 1.40 1.40
**188** A30 40p Honey buzzard 1.60 1.60
**189** A30 45p Osprey 1.75 1.75
**190** A30 65p Marsh harrier 2.50 2.50
*a.* Souvenir sheet, #185-190 9.25 9.25
*Nos. 185-190 (6)* 9.10 9.10

See Nos. 209-214, 233-238, 256-261.

Lighting at Les Casquets Lighthouse — A31

Designs: 22p, Coal fire, 1725. 27p, Oil lantern, 1779. 36p, Argand lamp, 1790. 45p, Revolving apparatus, 1818. 65p, Electrification, 1952.

**2002, July 30** ***Perf. 12¾x13¼***
**191** A31 22p multi .85 .85
**192** A31 27p multi 1.00 1.00
**193** A31 36p multi 1.40 1.40
**194** A31 45p multi 1.75 1.75
**195** A31 65p multi 2.50 2.50
*Nos. 191-195 (5)* 7.50 7.50

Emergency Medical Services A32

Designs: 22p, Ambulance technician, crew running to ambulance. 27p, Emergency medical technician on radio, ambulance on road. 36p, Doctor, transfer of patient to airplane. 40p, Pilot, Aurigny Trislander airplane. 45p, Emergency dispatch operator, transfer of patient to lifeboat. 65p, Lifeboat crewman, speeding lifeboat.

**2002, Oct. 17 Litho.** ***Perf. 14x14½***
**196** A32 22p multi .85 .85
*a.* Perf. 13¼x13 .85 .85
**197** A32 27p multi 1.00 1.00
*a.* Perf. 13¼x13 1.00 1.00
**198** A32 36p multi 1.40 1.40
*a.* Perf. 13¼x13 1.40 1.40
**199** A32 40p multi 1.60 1.60
*a.* Perf. 13¼x13 1.60 1.60
*b.* Booklet pane, #196a, 197a, 198a, 199a 5.00 —
**200** A32 45p multi 1.75 1.75
*a.* Perf. 13¼x13 1.75 1.75
**201** A32 65p multi 2.50 2.50
*a.* Perf. 13¼x13 2.50 2.50
*b.* Booklet pane, #198a, 199a, 200a, 201a 6.25 —
*c.* Booklet pane, #196a, 197a, 200a, 201a 5.50 —
Complete booklet, #167b, 169b, 169c, 199b, 201b, 201c 35.00
*Nos. 196-201 (6)* 9.10 9.10

Souvenir Sheet

Coronation of Queen Elizabeth II, 50th Anniv. — A33

### Litho. & Embossed

**2003, Jan. 30** ***Perf. 13½***
**202** A33 £2 multi 8.00 8.00

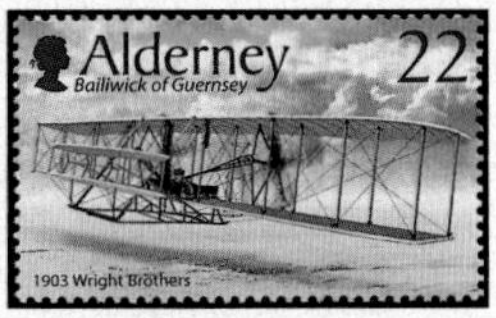


Powered Flight, Cent. A34

Designs: 22p, Wright Flyer, 1903. 27p, Vickers Vimy, 1919. 36p, Douglas DC-3, 1936. 40p, Comet, 1946. 45p, Concorde, 1969. 65p, Airbus A380.

**2003, Apr. 10** **Litho.**
**203** A34 22p multi .85 .85
**204** A34 27p multi 1.00 1.00
**205** A34 36p multi 1.40 1.40
**206** A34 40p multi 1.60 1.60
**207** A34 45p multi 1.75 1.75
**208** A34 65p multi 2.50 2.50
*Nos. 203-208 (6)* 9.10 9.10

### Bird Type of 2002

**2003, July 3** ***Perf. 13¾***
**209** A30 22p Arctic tern .85 .85
**210** A30 27p Great skua 1.00 1.00
**211** A30 36p Sandwich tern 1.40 1.40
**212** A30 40p Sooty shearwater 1.60 1.60
**213** A30 45p Arctic skua 1.75 1.75
**214** A30 65p Manx shearwater 2.50 2.50
*a.* Souvenir sheet, #209-214 9.25 9.25
*Nos. 209-214 (6)* 9.10 9.10

Island Police — A35

Police officer and: 22p, Policemen patrolling streets. 27p, Police vehicle. 36p, Member of forensics team. 40p, Policeman assisting child on bicycle. 45p, Police at car accident. 65p, Policeman working with customs officer.

**2003, Oct. 16 Litho.** ***Perf. 13¼x13***
**215** A35 22p multi .85 .85
**216** A35 27p multi 1.00 1.00
**217** A35 36p multi 1.40 1.40
**218** A35 40p multi 1.60 1.60
*a.* Booklet pane, #215-218 5.00 —
**219** A35 45p multi 1.75 1.75
*a.* Booklet pane, #215-217, 219 5.25 —
**220** A35 65p multi 2.50 2.50
*a.* Booklet pane, #215-216, 219-220 6.25 —
*b.* Booklet pane, #217-220 7.25 —

| | | | | |
|---|---|---|---|---|
| *c.* | | Booklet pane, #215-216, 218, 220 | 6.00 | — |
| | | Complete booklet, #218a, 219a, 220a, 220c, 2 #220b | 37.50 | |
| | | *Nos. 215-220 (6)* | 9.10 | 9.10 |

The two examples of No. 220b in the booklet have different margins.

Fungi — A36

Designs: 22p, Sulphur tuft. 27p, Orange peel fungus. 36p, Shining ink-cap. 40p, Giant puffball. 45p, Parasol. 65p, Candle snuff fungus.

**2004, Jan. 29 Litho. *Perf. 13¼***

| | | | | |
|---|---|---|---|---|
| **221** | A36 | 22p multi | .85 | .85 |
| **222** | A36 | 27p multi | 1.00 | 1.00 |
| **223** | A36 | 36p multi | 1.40 | 1.40 |
| **224** | A36 | 40p multi | 1.60 | 1.60 |
| **225** | A36 | 45p multi | 1.75 | 1.75 |
| **226** | A36 | 65p multi | 2.50 | 2.50 |
| | | *Nos. 221-226 (6)* | 9.10 | 9.10 |

FIFA (Fédération Internationale de Football Association), Cent. — A37

Designs: 26p, Challenge on Tourgis Close. 32p, Soccer on the beach. 36p, Playground school soccer. 40p, Friendly kickabout. 45p, Turning the defender. 65p, Tackling Dad at Arch Bay.

**2004, May 12 Litho. *Perf. 13¼***

| | | | | |
|---|---|---|---|---|
| **227** | A37 | 26p multi | 1.00 | 1.00 |
| **228** | A37 | 32p multi | 1.25 | 1.25 |
| **229** | A37 | 36p multi | 1.40 | 1.40 |
| **230** | A37 | 40p multi | 1.60 | 1.60 |
| **231** | A37 | 45p multi | 1.75 | 1.75 |
| **232** | A37 | 65p multi | 2.50 | 2.50 |
| | | *Nos. 227-232 (6)* | 9.50 | 9.50 |

Values are for stamps with surrounding selvage.

### Birds Type of 2002

**2004, July 29 Litho. *Perf. 13¼***

| | | | | |
|---|---|---|---|---|
| **233** | A30 | 26p Wheatear | 1.00 | 1.00 |
| **234** | A30 | 32p Redstart | 1.25 | 1.25 |
| **235** | A30 | 36p Yellow wagtail | 1.40 | 1.40 |
| **236** | A30 | 40p Hoopoe | 1.60 | 1.60 |
| **237** | A30 | 45p Ring ouzel | 1.75 | 1.75 |
| **238** | A30 | 65p Sand martin | 2.50 | 2.50 |
| *a.* | | Souvenir sheet, #233-238 | 9.50 | 9.50 |
| | | *Nos. 233-238 (6)* | 9.50 | 9.50 |

Fire Services A38

Designs: 26p, Fireman and fire truck. 32p, Firemen and fire truck. 36p, Fireman and airport fire truck. 40p, Fire chief, fire truck at station. 45p, Training grounds at airport. 65p, Road accicent training exercise.

**2004, Oct. 28 Litho. *Perf. 13¼x13***

| | | | | |
|---|---|---|---|---|
| **239** | A38 | 26p multi | 1.00 | 1.00 |
| **240** | A38 | 32p multi | 1.25 | 1.25 |
| **241** | A38 | 36p multi | 1.40 | 1.40 |
| **242** | A38 | 40p multi | 1.60 | 1.60 |
| *a.* | | Booklet pane, #239-242 | 5.50 | — |
| **243** | A38 | 45p multi | 1.75 | 1.75 |
| *a.* | | Booklet pane, #239-241, 243 | 5.75 | — |
| **244** | A38 | 65p multi | 2.50 | 2.50 |
| *a.* | | Booklet pane, #239-240, 243-244 | 6.75 | — |
| *b.* | | Booklet pane, #241-244 | 7.50 | — |
| *c.* | | Booklet pane, #239-240, 242, 244 | 6.50 | — |
| | | Complete booklet, #242a, 243a, 244a, 244c, 2 #244b | 42.50 | |
| | | *Nos. 239-244 (6)* | 9.50 | 9.50 |

The two examples of No. 244b in the complete booklet have different margins.

Hans Christian Andersen (1805-75), Author — A39

Scenes from "The Little Mermaid": 26p, Mermaid, fish, castle. 32p, Mermaid rescues prince. 36p, Mermaid and sea witch. 40p, Mermaid and prince on land. 65p, Dead mermaid and angels.

**2005, Feb. 3 Litho. *Perf. 13½***

| | | | | |
|---|---|---|---|---|
| **245** | A39 | 26p multi | 1.00 | 1.00 |
| **246** | A39 | 32p multi | 1.25 | 1.25 |
| **247** | A39 | 36p multi | 1.40 | 1.40 |
| **248** | A39 | 40p multi | 1.60 | 1.60 |
| **249** | A39 | 65p multi | 2.50 | 2.50 |
| | | *Nos. 245-249 (5)* | 7.75 | 7.75 |

Battle of Trafalgar, Bicent. — A40

Designs: 26p, Admiral Horatio Nelson. 32p, HMS Victory. 36p, Enemy in sight. 40p, Fall of Nelson. 45p, Breaking the line. 65p, Admiral James de Saumarez.

**2005, May 9 Litho. *Perf. 14x13¼***

| | | | | |
|---|---|---|---|---|
| **250** | A40 | 26p multi | 1.00 | 1.00 |
| **251** | A40 | 32p multi | 1.25 | 1.25 |
| **252** | A40 | 36p multi | 1.40 | 1.40 |
| **253** | A40 | 40p multi | 1.60 | 1.60 |
| *a.* | | Booklet pane, #250-253 | 5.50 | — |
| **254** | A40 | 45p multi | 1.75 | 1.75 |
| **255** | A40 | 65p multi | 2.50 | 2.50 |
| *a.* | | Booklet pane, #250-251, 254-255 | 6.50 | — |
| *b.* | | Booklet pane, #252-255 | 7.25 | |
| *c.* | | Booklet pane, #251-252, 254-255 | 7.00 | |
| *d.* | | Booklet pane, #250, 253-255 | 6.75 | |
| | | Complete booklet, #255a, 255b, 255c, 255d, 2 #253a | 42.50 | |
| | | *Nos. 250-255 (6)* | 9.50 | 9.50 |

The two examples of No. 253a in the complete booklet have different pane margins.

### Bird Type of 2002

**2005, July 21 *Perf. 13¼***

| | | | | |
|---|---|---|---|---|
| **256** | A30 | 26p Little stint | 1.00 | 1.00 |
| **257** | A30 | 32p Greenshank | 1.25 | 1.25 |
| **258** | A30 | 36p Golden plover | 1.40 | 1.40 |
| **259** | A30 | 40p Bar-tailed godwit | 1.60 | 1.60 |
| **260** | A30 | 45p Green sandpiper | 1.75 | 1.75 |
| **261** | A30 | 65p Sanderling | 2.50 | 2.50 |
| *a.* | | Souvenir sheet, #256-261 | 11.00 | 11.00 |
| | | *Nos. 256-261 (6)* | 9.50 | 9.50 |

### Souvenir Sheet

Homecoming of World War II Evacuees, 60th Anniv. — A41

**2005, Oct. 27 *Perf. 13¾***

| | | | | |
|---|---|---|---|---|
| **262** | A41 | £2 multi | 8.00 | 8.00 |

T.H. White, Author of *The Once and Future King*, Birth Centenary — A42

Authorian legends: 29p, King Arthur. 34p, Merlyn. 38p, Morgause. 42p, Queen Guenever. 47p, Lancelot. 68p, Mordred.

**2006, Feb. 16 Litho. *Perf. 13½x14***

| | | | | |
|---|---|---|---|---|
| **263** | A42 | 29p multi | 1.10 | 1.10 |
| **264** | A42 | 34p multi | 1.40 | 1.40 |
| **265** | A42 | 38p multi | 1.50 | 1.50 |
| **266** | A42 | 42p multi | 1.60 | 1.60 |
| **267** | A42 | 47p multi | 1.90 | 1.90 |
| **268** | A42 | 68p multi | 2.75 | 2.75 |
| *a.* | | Souvenir sheet, #263-268 | 10.50 | 10.50 |
| | | *Nos. 263-268 (6)* | 10.25 | 10.25 |

Queen Elizabeth II, 80th Birthday — A43

Various photographs of Queen with predominant background colors of:
No. 269: a, Blue violet. b, Red violet.
No. 270: a, Green. b, Orange brown.
No. 271: a, Yellow brown. b, Bright red.
No. 272: a, Red. b, Violet.

**2006, Apr. 21 *Perf. 13¾***

| | | | | |
|---|---|---|---|---|
| **269** | A43 | Horiz. pair | 2.25 | 2.25 |
| *a.-b.* | | 29p Either single | 1.10 | 1.10 |
| **270** | A43 | Horiz. pair | 3.00 | 3.00 |
| *a.-b.* | | 34p Either single | 1.50 | 1.50 |
| **271** | A43 | Horiz. pair | 3.25 | 3.25 |
| *a.-b.* | | 42p Either single | 1.60 | 1.60 |
| **272** | A43 | Horiz. pair | 3.50 | 3.50 |
| *a.-b.* | | 45p Either single | 1.75 | 1.75 |
| | | *Nos. 269-272 (4)* | 12.00 | 12.00 |

Birds — A44

Designs: 29p, Fulmar. 34p, Gannet. 42p, Lesser black-backed gull. 45p, Storm petrel. 47p, Kittiwake. 68p, Puffin.

**2006, July 27 Litho. *Perf. 13¾***

| | | | | |
|---|---|---|---|---|
| **273** | A44 | 29p multi | 1.10 | 1.10 |
| *a.* | | Booklet pane of 4 | 4.50 | — |
| **274** | A44 | 34p multi | 1.50 | 1.50 |
| *a.* | | Booklet pane of 4 | 6.00 | — |
| **275** | A44 | 42p multi | 1.60 | 1.60 |
| *a.* | | Booklet pane of 4 | 6.50 | — |
| **276** | A44 | 45p multi | 1.75 | 1.75 |
| *a.* | | Booklet pane of 4 | 7.00 | — |
| **277** | A44 | 47p multi | 2.00 | 2.00 |
| *a.* | | Booklet pane of 4 | 8.00 | — |
| **278** | A44 | 68p multi | 2.75 | 2.75 |
| *a.* | | Booklet pane of 4 | 11.00 | — |
| | | Complete booklet, #273a, 274a, 275a, 276a, 277a, 278a | 45.00 | |
| | | *Nos. 273-278 (6)* | 10.70 | 10.70 |

See Nos. 297-302, 319-324, 344-349.

Corals and Anemones — A45

Designs: 1p, Burrowing anemone. 2p, Colonial anemone. 3p, Jewel anemone. 4p, Sagartia elegans. 5p, Red fingers. 6p, Plumose anemone. 7p, Fan coral. 8p, Jewel anemone, diff. 9p, Actinothoe sphyrodeta. 10p, Snakelocks anemone. £1, Beadlet anemone. £2, Sunset cup coral.

**2006, Nov. 2 Litho. *Perf. 13x13½***

| | | | | |
|---|---|---|---|---|
| **279** | A45 | 1p multi | .25 | .25 |
| **280** | A45 | 2p multi | .25 | .25 |
| **281** | A45 | 3p multi | .25 | .25 |
| **282** | A45 | 4p multi | .25 | .25 |
| **283** | A45 | 5p multi | .25 | .25 |
| **284** | A45 | 6p multi | .25 | .25 |
| **285** | A45 | 7p multi | .25 | .25 |
| **286** | A45 | 8p multi | .30 | .30 |
| **287** | A45 | 9p multi | .35 | .35 |
| **288** | A45 | 10p multi | .40 | .40 |

**Litho. & Embossed**
**Size: 22x27mm**
***Perf. 12¾x13¼***

| | | | | |
|---|---|---|---|---|
| **289** | A45 | £1 multi | 3.75 | 3.75 |
| **290** | A45 | £2 multi | 7.75 | 7.75 |
| | | *Nos. 279-290 (12)* | 14.30 | 14.30 |

See Nos. 303-306.

Alderney Wetlands A46

Designs: 32p, Cushion starfish. 37p, Gannet. 45p, Spiny squat lobster. 48p, Gray seal. 50p, Golden samphire. 71p, Little egret.

**2007, Mar. 8 Litho. *Perf. 13¼***

| | | | | |
|---|---|---|---|---|
| **291** | A46 | 32p multi | 1.25 | 1.25 |
| **292** | A46 | 37p multi | 1.50 | 1.50 |
| **293** | A46 | 45p multi | 1.75 | 1.75 |
| **294** | A46 | 48p multi | 1.90 | 1.90 |
| **295** | A46 | 50p multi | 2.00 | 2.00 |
| **296** | A46 | 71p multi | 2.75 | 2.75 |
| *a.* | | Souvenir sheet, #291-296 | 11.50 | 11.50 |
| | | *Nos. 291-296 (6)* | 11.15 | 11.15 |

Addition of Alderney Wetlands and Burhou Islands to Ramsar Convention Protected Wetlands List.

### Birds Type of 2006

Designs: 32p, Blackbird. 37p, Dartford warbler. 45p, Blue tit. 48p, Wren. 50p, House sparrow. 71p, Jackdaw.

**2007, May 24 Litho. *Perf. 13¾***

| | | | | |
|---|---|---|---|---|
| **297** | A44 | 32p multi | 1.25 | 1.25 |
| *a.* | | Booklet pane of 4 | 5.00 | — |
| **298** | A44 | 37p multi | 1.50 | 1.50 |
| *a.* | | Booklet pane of 4 | 6.00 | — |
| **299** | A44 | 45p multi | 1.75 | 1.75 |
| *a.* | | Booklet pane of 4 | 7.00 | — |
| **300** | A44 | 48p multi | 1.90 | 1.90 |
| *a.* | | Booklet pane of 4 | 7.75 | — |
| **301** | A44 | 50p multi | 2.00 | 2.00 |
| *a.* | | Booklet pane of 4 | 8.00 | — |
| **302** | A44 | 71p multi | 3.00 | 3.00 |
| *a.* | | Booklet pane of 4 | 12.00 | — |
| | | Complete booklet, #297a-302a | 46.00 | |
| | | *Nos. 297-302 (6)* | 11.40 | 11.40 |

### Corals and Anemones Type of 2006

Designs: 20p. Devonshire cup coral. 40p, Fried egg anemone. 50p, Parasitic anemone. £4, Strawberry anemone.

**2007, Aug. 2 Litho. *Perf. 14***
**Size: 27x23mm**

| | | | | |
|---|---|---|---|---|
| **303** | A45 | 20p multi | .80 | .80 |
| **304** | A45 | 40p multi | 1.60 | 1.60 |
| **305** | A45 | 50p multi | 2.10 | 2.10 |

**Litho. & Embossed**
**Size: 27x28mm**

| | | | | |
|---|---|---|---|---|
| **306** | A45 | £4 multi | 16.00 | 16.00 |
| | | *Nos. 303-306 (4)* | 20.50 | 20.50 |

Just So Stories, by Rudyard Kipling — A47

Designs: 32p, How the Camel Got His Hump. 37p, How the Whale Got His Throat. 45p, The Elephant's Child. 48p, How the Leopard Got His Spots. 50p, The Cat That Walked by Himself. 71p, How the Rhinoceros Got His Skin.

**2007, Oct. 25 Litho. *Perf. 13x13¼***

| | | | | |
|---|---|---|---|---|
| **307** | A47 | 32p multi | 1.40 | 1.40 |
| **308** | A47 | 37p multi | 1.50 | 1.50 |
| **309** | A47 | 45p multi | 1.90 | 1.90 |
| **310** | A47 | 48p multi | 2.00 | 2.00 |
| **311** | A47 | 50p multi | 2.10 | 2.10 |
| **312** | A47 | 71p multi | 3.00 | 3.00 |
| *a.* | | Miniature sheet, #307-312 | 12.00 | 12.00 |
| | | *Nos. 307-312 (6)* | 11.90 | 11.90 |

Butterflies A48

Butterflies: 34p, Painted lady. 40p, Grayling. 48p, Green hairstreak. 51p, Speckled wood. 53c, Common blue. 74p, Glanville fritillary.

**2008, Feb. 28 Litho. *Perf. 13¾***

**313** A48 34p multi 1.40 1.40
**314** A48 40p multi 1.60 1.60
**315** A48 48p multi 1.90 1.90
**316** A48 51p multi 2.00 2.00
**317** A48 53p multi 2.10 2.10
**318** A48 74p multi 3.00 3.00
*a.* Miniature sheet, #313-318 12.00 12.00
*Nos. 313-318 (6)* 12.00 12.00

**Birds Type of 2006**

Designs: 34p, Common buzzard. 40p, Peregrine falcon. 48p, Kestrel. 51p, Barn owl. 53p, Long-eared owl. 74p, Sparrowhawk.

**2008, May 15 Litho. *Perf. 13¾***

**319** A44 34p multi 1.40 1.40
*a.* Booklet pane of 4 5.75 —
**320** A44 40p multi 1.60 1.60
*a.* Booklet pane of 4 6.50 —
**321** A44 48p multi 1.90 1.90
*a.* Booklet pane of 4 7.75 —
**322** A44 51p multi 2.00 2.00
*a.* Booklet pane of 4 8.00 —
**323** A44 53p multi 2.10 2.10
*a.* Booklet pane of 4 8.50 —
**324** A44 74p multi 3.00 3.00
*a.* Booklet pane of 4 12.00 —
Complete booklet, #319a-324a 49.00
*Nos. 319-324 (6)* 12.00 12.00

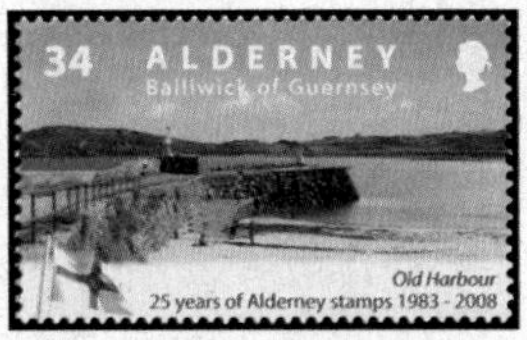


Alderney Postage Stamps, 25th Anniv. — A49

Flag and tourist sites: 34p, Old Harbor. 40p, Breakwater. 48p, Fort Clonque Causeway. 51p, Golf course. 53p, Hanging Rock. 74p, Fort Clonque.

**2008, June 14 Litho. *Perf. 14x13¾***

**325** A49 34p multi 1.40 1.40
**326** A49 40p multi 1.60 1.60
**327** A49 48p multi 1.90 1.90
**328** A49 51p multi 2.00 2.00
**329** A49 53p multi 2.10 2.10
**330** A49 74p multi 3.00 3.00
*Nos. 325-330 (6)* 12.00 12.00

See No. 376.

Heraldic Lion — A50

**Litho. & Embossed With Foil Application**

**2008, June 14 *Perf. 14¼x13½***

**331** A50 £5 multi 20.00 20.00

Aurigny Air Services, 40th Anniv. — A51

Airplanes: 34p, Britten-Norman Islander. 40p, Britten-Norman Trislander. 48p, DHC-6 Twin Otter. 51p, Short 360. 53p, Saab 340. 74p, ATR 72.

**2008, Oct. 30 Litho. *Perf. 13½***

**332** A51 34p multi 1.10 1.10
**333** A51 40p multi 1.25 1.25
**334** A51 48p multi 1.60 1.60
**335** A51 51p multi 1.75 1.75
**336** A51 53p multi 1.75 1.75
**337** A51 74p multi 2.40 2.40
*a.* Souvenir sheet, #332-337 10.00 10.00
*Nos. 332-337 (6)* 9.85 9.85

Bees — A52

Flowers and: 36p, Tawny mining bee. 43p, Early bumblebee. 51p, Bug mining bee. 54p, Cuckoo bee. 56p, Solitary bee. 77p, Honey bee.

**2009, Feb. 26 Litho. *Perf. 13¾***

**338** A52 36p multi 1.10 1.10
**339** A52 43p multi 1.25 1.25
**340** A52 51p multi 1.50 1.50
**341** A52 54p multi 1.60 1.60
**342** A52 56p multi 1.60 1.60
**343** A52 77p multi 2.25 2.25
*a.* Miniature sheet of 6, #338-343 9.50 9.50
*Nos. 338-343 (6)* 9.30 9.30

**Birds Type of 2006**

Designs: 36p, Turnstone. 43p, Curlew. 51p, Oystercatcher. 54p, Snipe. 56p, Dunlin. 77p, Ringed plover.

**2009, May 28 Litho. *Perf. 13¾***

**344** A44 36p multi 1.25 1.25
*a.* Booklet pane of 4 5.00 —
**345** A44 43p multi 1.40 1.40
*a.* Booklet pane of 4 5.75 —
**346** A44 51p multi 1.60 1.60
*a.* Booklet pane of 4 6.50 —
**347** A44 54p multi 1.75 1.75
*a.* Booklet pane of 4 7.00 —
**348** A44 56p multi 1.90 1.90
*a.* Booklet pane of 4 7.75 —
**349** A44 77p multi 2.50 2.50
*a.* Booklet pane of 4 10.00 —
Complete booklet, #344a-349a 42.00
*Nos. 344-349 (6)* 10.40 10.40

Naval Aviation, Cent. — A53

Designs: 36p, Flying Boat over Castle Cornet. 43p, Fairey Swordfish attacking U-boat. 51p, Skuas divebombing Scharnhorst. 54p, Sea Fury over Alderney. 56p, Sea Hawk and Sea Fury. 77p, Merlin helicopter landing on HMS Daring.

**2009, July 30 *Perf. 14¼x13¾***

**350** A53 36p multi 1.25 1.25
**351** A53 43p multi 1.50 1.50
**352** A53 51p multi 1.75 1.75
**353** A53 54p multi 1.90 1.90
**354** A53 56p multi 1.90 1.90
**355** A53 77p multi 2.60 2.60
*Nos. 350-355 (6)* 10.90 10.90

Scenes From Sherlock Holmes and the Curious Case of the Alderney Bull, by Sir Arthur Conan Doyle (1859-1930) — A54

Designs: 36p, Alice West reporting theft to Holmes. 43p, Holmes and policeman studying message, arrest of suspect. 51p, Holmes looking for clues with magnifying glass. 54p, Holmes with two men outside building. 56p, Holmes pointing to partially-built lighthouse. 77p, Holmes pointing to thief.

**2009, Oct. 29 Litho. *Perf. 13¼x13***

**356** A54 36p multi 1.25 1.25
**357** A54 43p multi 1.50 1.50
**358** A54 51p multi 1.75 1.75
**359** A54 54p multi 1.90 1.90
**360** A54 56p multi 1.90 1.90
**361** A54 77p multi 2.60 2.60
*Nos. 356-361 (6)* 10.90 10.90

A miniature sheet of six containing one of each stamp was sold together with a special lens and a DVD for £9.99. The sheet was not available separately.

Dragonflies A55

Designs: 36p, Common darter. 45p, Emperor dragonfly. 56p, Blue-tailed damselfly. 66p, Brown hawker. 75p, Black-tailed skimmer. 83p, Red-veined darter.

**2010, Feb. 25 Litho. *Perf. 13¾***

**362** A55 36p multi 1.10 1.10
**363** A55 45p multi 1.40 1.40
**364** A55 56p multi 1.75 1.75
**365** A55 66p multi 2.00 2.00
**366** A55 75p multi 2.40 2.40
**367** A55 83p multi 2.60 2.60
*a.* Souvenir sheet, #362-367 11.50 11.50
*Nos. 362-367 (6)* 11.25 11.25

Battle of Britain, 70th Anniv. A56

Designs: 36p, Pilot Keith Gilman. 45p, Hawker Hurricanes in flight. 48p, Pilots scrambling to planes. 50p, Spitfire sortie. 58p, Air raid warden. 80p, Evacuees.
£2, Sir Douglas Bader, vert.

**2010, May 4 *Perf. 14***

**369** A56 36p blk & gray 1.10 1.10
**370** A56 45p blk & gray 1.40 1.40
**371** A56 48p blk & gray 1.50 1.50
**372** A56 50p blk & gray 1.50 1.50
**373** A56 58p blk & gray 1.75 1.75
**374** A56 80p blk & gray 2.40 2.40
*Nos. 369-374 (6)* 9.65 9.65

**Souvenir Sheet**

**375** A56 £2 blk & gray 6.00 6.00

**Alderney Postage Stamps, 25th Anniv. Type of 2008**

Design: Hanging Rock.

**2010, July 29 *Perf. 14x13¾***

**376** A49 55p multi 1.75 1.75

Florence Nightingale (1820-1910), Nurse — A57

Various quotes of Nightingale and: 36p, Hand carrying lantern. 45p, Hand reaching out. 48p, Hand holding bucket. 50p, Hands unwrapping gauze bandage. 58p, Hand writing. 80p, Hands in prayer.

**2010, July 29 *Perf. 14½x14***

**377** A57 36p multi 1.10 1.10
**378** A57 45p multi 1.40 1.40
**379** A57 48p multi 1.50 1.50
**380** A57 50p multi 1.60 1.60
**381** A57 58p multi 1.90 1.90
**382** A57 80p multi 2.50 2.50
*Nos. 377-382 (6)* 10.00 10.00

Peter Pan, by Sir James M. Barrie (1860-1937) — A58

Designs: 36p, Children flying above London. 45p, Captain Hook and crocodile. 48p, Peter Pan visits Captain Hook's ship. 50p, Peter Pan waving a rainbow. 58p, Children on Neverpeak. 80p, Bonfire.
£3, Peter Pan, vert.

**2010, Nov. 4 Litho. *Perf. 13¼x13½***

**383** A58 36p multi 1.25 1.25
**384** A58 45p multi 1.50 1.50
**385** A58 48p multi 1.60 1.60
**386** A58 50p multi 1.60 1.60
**387** A58 58p multi 1.90 1.90
**388** A58 80p multi 2.60 2.60
*Nos. 383-388 (6)* 10.45 10.45

**Souvenir Sheet**

***Perf. 13½x13¼***

**389** A58 £3 multi 10.00 10.00

Christmas Carols A59

Designs: 31p, O Christmas Tree. 36p, Away in a Manger. 45p, While Shepherds Watched Their Flocks By Night. 48p, Hark the Herald Angels Sing. 50p, O Holy Night. 58p, O Little Town of Bethlehem. 80p, Good King Wenceslas.

**2010, Nov. 4 Litho. *Perf. 13¼x14***

**390** A59 31p multi 1.00 1.00
**391** A59 36p multi 1.25 1.25
**392** A59 45p multi 1.50 1.50
**393** A59 48p multi 1.60 1.60
**394** A59 50p multi 1.60 1.60
**395** A59 58p multi 1.90 1.90
**396** A59 80p multi 2.60 2.60
*Nos. 390-396 (7)* 11.45 11.45

Moths A60

Designs: 36p, Elephant hawkmoth. 45p, Hummingbird hawkmoth. 52p, Convolvulus hawkmoth. 58p, Poplar hawkmoth. 65p, Striped hawkmoth. 70p, Privet hawkmoth.

**2011, Feb. 23 Litho. *Perf. 13¾***

**397** A60 36p multi 1.25 1.25
**398** A60 45p multi 1.50 1.50
**399** A60 52p multi 1.75 1.75
**400** A60 58p multi 1.90 1.90
**401** A60 65p multi 2.10 2.10
**402** A60 70p multi 2.25 2.25
*a.* Souvenir sheet of 6, #397-402 11.00 11.00
*Nos. 397-402 (6)* 10.75 10.75

See Nos. 440-445.

Birds — A61

Designs: 36p, Mediterranean gull. 45p, Shelduck. 48p, Firecrest. 52p, Balearic shearwater. 58p, Woodcock, 65p, Little grebe.

**2011, May 4**

| | | | |
|---|---|---|---|
| **403** | A61 36p multi | 1.25 | 1.25 |
| **404** | A61 45p multi | 1.50 | 1.50 |
| **405** | A61 48p multi | 1.60 | 1.60 |
| **406** | A61 52p multi | 1.75 | 1.75 |
| **407** | A61 58p multi | 1.90 | 1.90 |
| **408** | A61 65p multi | 2.10 | 2.10 |
| *a.* | Souvenir sheet of 6, #403-408 | 10.50 | 10.50 |
| | *Nos. 403-408 (6)* | 10.10 | 10.10 |

Queen Elizabeth II, 85th Birthday, Prince Philip, 90th Birthday — A62

Various photographs of Queen and Prince.

**2011, June 2** ***Perf. 13¾x13¼***

| | | | |
|---|---|---|---|
| **409** | A62 36p silver & sepia | 1.25 | 1.25 |
| *a.* | Booklet pane of 4 | 5.00 | — |
| **410** | A62 45p silver & sepia | 1.50 | 1.50 |
| *a.* | Booklet pane of 4 | 6.00 | — |
| **411** | A62 48p silver & sepia | 1.60 | 1.60 |
| *a.* | Booklet pane of 4 | 6.50 | — |
| **412** | A62 52p silver & sepia | 1.75 | 1.75 |
| *a.* | Booklet pane of 4 | 7.00 | — |
| **413** | A62 58p silver & sepia | 1.90 | 1.90 |
| *a.* | Booklet pane of 4 | 7.75 | — |
| **414** | A62 65p silver & sepia | 2.10 | 2.10 |
| *a.* | Booklet pane of 4 | 8.50 | — |
| | Complete booket, #409a, 410a, 411a, 412a, 413a, 414a | 41.00 | |
| | *Nos. 409-414 (6)* | 10.10 | 10.10 |

Red Cross Uniforms, Cent. — A63

Designs: 36p, Women's Voluntary Aid Detachment uniform, c. 1915. 47p, Men's Voluntary Aid Detachment uniform, 1915. 48p, Nurse's uniform, c. 1966-78. 52p, Women's uniform, 1981-2001. 61p, Man's uniform, c. 2001. 65p, Women's uniform, c. 2011.

**2011, July 28** ***Perf. 14¼x13¾***

| | | | |
|---|---|---|---|
| **415** | A63 36p multi | 1.25 | 1.25 |
| **416** | A63 47p multi | 1.50 | 1.50 |
| **417** | A63 48p multi | 1.60 | 1.60 |
| **418** | A63 52p multi | 1.75 | 1.75 |
| **419** | A63 61p multi | 2.00 | 2.00 |
| **420** | A63 65p multi | 2.10 | 2.10 |
| | *Nos. 415-420 (6)* | 10.20 | 10.20 |

Alderney in Winter A64

Designs: 31p, Victoria Street. 36p, St. Anne's Church. 47p, Les Estacs Gannet Colonies, reindeer in flight. 48p, Reindeer pulling Santa's sleigh, Mannez Lighthouse. 52p, Alderney train. 61p, Children playing in snow, snowman. 65p, Boat in harbor.

**2011, Oct. 27 Litho.** ***Perf. 13½x14¼***

| | | | |
|---|---|---|---|
| **421** | A64 31p multi | 1.00 | 1.00 |
| **422** | A64 36p multi | 1.25 | 1.25 |
| **423** | A64 47p multi | 1.50 | 1.50 |
| **424** | A64 48p multi | 1.60 | 1.60 |
| **425** | A64 52p multi | 1.75 | 1.75 |
| **426** | A64 61p multi | 2.00 | 2.00 |
| **427** | A64 65p multi | 2.10 | 2.10 |
| | *Nos. 421-427 (7)* | 11.20 | 11.20 |

Sinking of the Titanic, Cent. A65

Designs: 36p, Titanic leaving port. 47p, Rocket exploding over Titanic. 48p, Grand staricase. 52p, Musicians. 61p, Capt. Edward J. Smith. 65p, Lifeboat near sinking Titanic.

**2012, Feb. 22** ***Perf. 13¼x13¾***

| | | | |
|---|---|---|---|
| **428** | A65 36p multi | 1.25 | 1.25 |
| *a.* | Booklet pane of 4 | 5.00 | — |
| **429** | A65 47p multi | 1.50 | 1.50 |
| *a.* | Booklet pane of 4 | 6.00 | — |
| **430** | A65 48p multi | 1.60 | 1.60 |
| *a.* | Booklet pane of 4 | 6.50 | — |
| **431** | A65 52p multi | 1.75 | 1.75 |
| *a.* | Booklet pane of 4 | 7.00 | — |
| **432** | A65 61p multi | 2.00 | 2.00 |
| *a.* | Booklet pane of 4 | 8.00 | — |
| **433** | A65 65p multi | 2.10 | 2.10 |
| *a.* | Booklet pane of 4 | 8.50 | — |
| | Complete booklet, #428a, 429a, 430a, 431a, 432a, 433a | 41.00 | |
| | *Nos. 428-433 (6)* | 10.20 | 10.20 |

Charles Dickens (1812-70), Writer — A66

Various illustrations by George Cruikshank for original printing of Oliver Twist.

**2012, May 8** ***Perf. 14***

| | | | |
|---|---|---|---|
| **434** | A66 36p blk & ol brn | 1.10 | 1.10 |
| **435** | A66 47p blk & ol brn | 1.50 | 1.50 |
| **436** | A66 48p blk & ol brn | 1.50 | 1.50 |
| **437** | A66 52p blk & ol brn | 1.60 | 1.60 |
| **438** | A66 61p blk & ol brn | 1.90 | 1.90 |
| **439** | A66 65p blk & ol brn | 2.00 | 2.00 |
| | *Nos. 434-439 (6)* | 9.60 | 9.60 |

**Moths Type of 2011**

Designs: 39p, Garden tiger moth. 52p, Cream spot tiger moth. 53p, Buff ermine. 59p, Ruby tiger moth. 69p, Jersey tiger moth. 74p, Cinnabar.

**2012, July 25** ***Perf. 13¾***

| | | | |
|---|---|---|---|
| **440** | A60 39p multi | 1.25 | 1.25 |
| **441** | A60 52p multi | 1.60 | 1.60 |
| **442** | A60 53p multi | 1.75 | 1.75 |
| **443** | A60 59p multi | 1.90 | 1.90 |
| **444** | A60 69p multi | 2.25 | 2.25 |
| **445** | A60 74p multi | 2.40 | 2.40 |
| *a.* | Souvenir sheet of 6, #440-445 | 11.50 | 11.50 |
| | *Nos. 440-445 (6)* | 11.15 | 11.15 |

Alderney Harbor A67

Designs: 39p, Douglas Quay, Braye Harbor, c.1800. 52p, Breakwater completed, 1856. 53p, SS Courier, c. 1926. 59p, Little Crabby Harbor, 1985. 69p, RNLI Lifeboat Roy Baker I, c. 1995. 74p, Commercial Quay, 2011.

**2012, Oct. 31**

| | | | |
|---|---|---|---|
| **446** | A67 39p multi | 1.25 | 1.25 |
| **447** | A67 52p multi | 1.75 | 1.75 |
| **448** | A67 53p multi | 1.75 | 1.75 |
| **449** | A67 59p multi | 1.90 | 1.90 |
| **450** | A67 69p multi | 2.25 | 2.25 |
| **451** | A67 74p multi | 2.40 | 2.40 |
| *a.* | Souvenir sheet of 6, #446-451 | 11.50 | 11.50 |
| | *Nos. 446-451 (6)* | 11.30 | 11.30 |

Christmas A68

Designs: 34p, Annunciation. 39p, No room at the inn. 52p, Birth of Jesus. 53p, Whilst shepherds watch their flocks. 59p, The Three Kings. 69p, Children of Bethlehem visiting baby Jesus. 74p, Flight to Egypt.

**2012, Oct. 31** ***Perf. 13¼x12½***

| | | | |
|---|---|---|---|
| **452** | A68 34p multi | 1.10 | 1.10 |
| **453** | A68 39p multi | 1.25 | 1.25 |
| **454** | A68 52p multi | 1.75 | 1.75 |
| **455** | A68 53p multi | 1.75 | 1.75 |
| **456** | A68 59p multi | 1.90 | 1.90 |
| **457** | A68 69p multi | 2.25 | 2.25 |
| **458** | A68 74p multi | 2.40 | 2.40 |
| | *Nos. 452-458 (7)* | 12.40 | 12.40 |

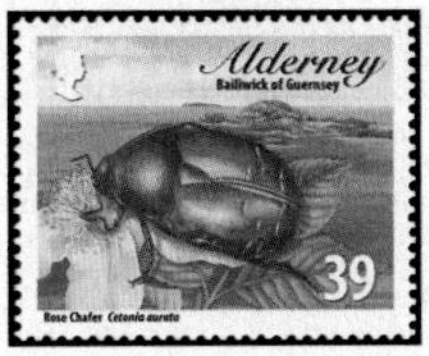


Beetles A69

Designs: 39p, Rose chafer. 52p, Burying beetle. 53p, Green tiger beetle. 59p, May bug. 69p, Netocia moria. 74p, Oil beetle.

**2013, Feb. 20** ***Perf. 13¾***

| | | | |
|---|---|---|---|
| **459** | A69 39p multi | 1.25 | 1.25 |
| **460** | A69 52p multi | 1.60 | 1.60 |
| **461** | A69 53p multi | 1.60 | 1.60 |
| **462** | A69 59p multi | 1.75 | 1.75 |
| **463** | A69 69p multi | 2.10 | 2.10 |
| **464** | A69 74p multi | 2.25 | 2.25 |
| *a.* | Souvenir sheet of 6, #459-464 | 11.00 | 11.00 |
| | *Nos. 459-464 (6)* | 10.55 | 10.55 |

## JERSEY

jər-zē

LOCATION — Island in the English Channel
GOVT. — Dependent territory (bailiwick) of the British Crown
AREA — 45 sq. mi.
POP. — 89,721 (1999 est.)
CAPITAL — St. Helier

Following the establishment of the British General Post Office as a public corporation on October 1, 1969, the post office of the Bailiwick of Jersey became a separate entity and British postage stamps ceased to be valid.

**Catalogue values for unused stamps in this country are for Never Hinged items.**

**British Regional Issue**

A1

Royal Mace and Arms of Jersey — A2

***Perf. 15x14***

**1958-69 Photo. Wmk. 322**

| | | | | |
|---|---|---|---|---|
| **1** | A1 | 2½p rose red ('64) | .35 | .25 |
| **2** | A2 | 3p light purple | .35 | .25 |
| *p.* | | Phosphor. ('67) | .25 | .25 |
| **3** | A2 | 4p ultra ('66) | .35 | .25 |
| *p.* | | Phosphor. ('67) | .25 | .25 |

**Unwmk.**

| | | | | |
|---|---|---|---|---|
| **4** | A2 | 4p olive brown ('68) | .25 | .25 |
| **5** | A2 | 4p brt red ('69) | .25 | .25 |
| **6** | A2 | 5p dark blue ('68) | .25 | .25 |
| | | *Nos. 1-6 (6)* | 1.80 | 1.50 |

Nos. 4-6 are phosphorescent.

Sold to the general public only at post offices within Jersey, but valid for postage throughout Great Britain.

See also Great Britain Nos. 269-270, which were sold only in the Channel Islands and at a few philatelic windows in Great Britain, and may be considered to be precursors to the regional issues.

**Bailiwick Issues**

Elizabeth Castle and Queen Elizabeth II — A3

Queen Elizabeth II — A4

Designs (Queen Elizabeth II and): 1p, La Hougue Bie (prehistoric tomb). 2p, Portelet Bay. 3p, La Corbière Lighthouse. 4p, Mont Orgueil by night. 5p, Arms of Jersey and Royal Mace. 6p, Jersey cow. 9p, 1sh6p, Map of English Channel with Jersey. 1sh, Mont Orgueil. 2sh6p, Airport. 5sh, Legislative Chamber. 10sh, Royal Court. £1, Queen Elizabeth II, photograph by Cecil Beaton.

***Perf. 14½***

**1969, Oct. 1 Photo. Unwmk.**

| | | | | |
|---|---|---|---|---|
| **7** | A3 | ½p ocher & multi | .25 | .25 |
| **8** | A3 | 1p brown & multi | .25 | .25 |
| *a.* | | Booklet pane of 1 | .35 | |
| *b.* | | Booklet pane of 2 | .90 | |
| **9** | A3 | 2p multicolored | .25 | .25 |
| **10** | A3 | 3p dp blue & multi | .25 | .25 |
| **11** | A3 | 4p multicolored | .25 | .25 |
| *a.* | | Booklet pane of 1 | .60 | |
| | | Complete booklet, 4 #8a, 5 #11a | 2.00 | |
| *b.* | | Booklet pane of 2 | 1.10 | |
| **12** | A3 | 5p multicolored | .25 | .25 |
| *a.* | | Booklet pane of 2 | 1.75 | |
| | | Complete booklet, 3 each #8b & 12a, 6 #11b | 17.50 | |
| | | Complete booklet, 2 #8b, 7 #11b, 6 #12a | 12.50 | |
| **13** | A3 | 6p multicolored | .40 | .25 |
| **14** | A3 | 9p multicolored | .60 | *.30* |
| **15** | A3 | 1sh lilac & multi | .80 | .70 |
| **16** | A3 | 1sh6p green & multi | 1.40 | 1.40 |
| **17** | A4 | 1sh9p multicolored | 2.00 | 2.00 |

***Perf. 12***

| | | | | |
|---|---|---|---|---|
| **18** | A3 | 2sh6p multicolored | 3.50 | 2.75 |
| **19** | A3 | 5sh multicolored | 12.00 | 10.00 |
| **20** | A3 | 10sh gray & multi | 27.50 | 20.00 |
| *a.* | | 10sh green & multi (error) | *4,000.* | |
| **21** | A4 | £1 tan & multi | 4.00 | 3.50 |
| | | *Nos. 7-21 (15)* | 53.70 | 42.40 |

A second post-1971 printing of No. 21 shows the background drapery less purple and more blue. Value, $3.

See Nos. 34-48, 107-109.

Jersey Post Office First Day Cover A5

**1969, Oct. 1** ***Perf. 14½***

| | | | | |
|---|---|---|---|---|
| **22** | A5 | 4p multicolored | .35 | .25 |
| **23** | A5 | 5p blue & multi | .40 | .25 |
| **24** | A5 | 1sh6p brown & multi | 1.10 | *1.25* |
| **25** | A5 | 1sh9p emerald & multi | 1.75 | *2.10* |
| | | *Nos. 22-25 (4)* | 3.60 | 3.85 |

Inauguration of independent postal service.

Jersey Woman Reaching for Royal Mace, Flags of USSR, US and Great Britain — A6

4p, Lord Coutanche, Bailiff of Jersey, by James Gunn, vert. 5p, Sir Winston Churchill, by D. Van Praag, vert. 1sh9p, Swedish Red Cross ship "Vega."

**1970, May 9 Photo.** ***Perf. 11½***

| | | | | |
|---|---|---|---|---|
| **26** | A6 | 4p gold & multi | .50 | .25 |
| **27** | A6 | 5p gold & multi | .50 | .25 |
| **28** | A6 | 1sh6p gold & multi | 2.00 | 2.00 |
| **29** | A6 | 1sh9p gold & multi | 2.00 | 2.00 |
| | | *Nos. 26-29 (4)* | 5.00 | 4.50 |

25th anniv. of Jersey's liberation from the Germans.

"Rags to Riches" Cinderella — A7

Designs (Parade Floats Made of Flowers): 4p, "A Tribute to Enid Blyton," author of children's books. 1sh6p, "Gourmet's Delight." 1sh9p, "We're the Greatest" (ostriches and trees).

**1970, July 28 Photo. *Perf. 11½***

**30** A7 4p gold & multi .60 .25
**31** A7 5p gold & multi .60 .60
**32** A7 1sh6p gold & multi 8.00 5.00
**33** A7 1sh9p gold & multi 8.00 6.50
*Nos. 30-33 (4)* 17.20 12.35

"Battle of Flowers" annual parade.

### Decimal Currency Issue
### Types of 1969
### "p" instead of "d"

Designs: ½p, Elizabeth Castle. 1p, La Corbiere Lighthouse. 1½p, Jersey cow. 2p, Mont Orgueil by night. 2½p, Arms of Jersey and Royal Mace. 3p, La Hougue Bie. 3½p, Portelet Bay. 4p, 7½p, Map of English Channel and Jersey. 5p, Mont Orgueil by day. 6p, Martello Tower at Archirondel. 9p, Queen Elizabeth II, by Cecil Beaton. 10p, Airport. 20p, Legislative Chamber. 50p, Royal Court.

**1970-75 Photo. *Perf. 14½***

**34** A3 ½p ocher & multi ('71) .25 .25
*a.* Booklet pane of 1 .25
**35** A3 1p multicolored ('71) .25 .25
*a.* Booklet pane of 2 ('75) .25
*b.* Booklet pane of 4 ('75) .35
**36** A3 1½p multicolored ('71) .25 .25
**37** A3 2p multicolored ('71) .25 .25
*a.* Booklet pane of 1 .25
*b.* Booklet pane of 2 .35
**38** A3 2½p multicolored ('71) .25 .25
*a.* Booklet pane of 1 .35
Complete booklet, 2 each #34a, 37a, 38a 1.25
*b.* Booklet pane of 2 .45
Complete booklet,5 #37b, 3 #38b 1.75
Complete booklet,5 #37b, 6 #38b 3.75
Complete booklet, 4 #38b 4.00
**39** A3 3p brn & multicolored ('71) .25 .25
*a.* Booklet pane of 1 ('72) .35
Complete booklet, 3 #34a, 1 #38a, 2 #39a 1.00
*b.* Booklet pane of 2 ('72) .45
Complete booklet, 5 #39b 40.00
Complete booklet, 4 #38b, 5 #59b 4.00
**40** A3 3½p multicolored ('71) .25 .25
*a.* Booklet pane of 1 ('74) .35
Complete booklet, #39a, 2 #40a 1.00
Complete booklet, #34a, #40a, 2 #39a .60
Complete booklet, 2 #39a, 4 #40a .90
*b.* Booklet pane of 2 ('74) .50
Complete booklet, 3 #39b, 6 #40b 3.00
**41** A3 4p multicolored ('71) .25 .25
*a.* Booklet pane of 2 ('75) .50
*b.* Booklet pane of 4 ('75) .75
**42** A3 5p lilac & multi ('71) .25 .25
*a.* Booklet pane of 2 ('75) .55
Complete booklet, 3 each #35a, #41a, 2 #42a 2.75
*b.* Booklet pane of 4 ('75) .95
Complete booklet, 4 each #35b, 41b, 6 #42b 5.00
**43** A3 6p green & multi ('71) .25 .25
**44** A3 7½p multicolored ('71) .25 .25
**45** A4 9p multicolored ('71) .35 .35

***Perf. 12***

**46** A3 10p multicolored .40 .40
**47** A3 20p multicolored .75 .75
**48** A3 50p multicolored 1.90 1.90
*Nos. 34-48 (15)* 6.15 6.15

See also Nos. 107-109.

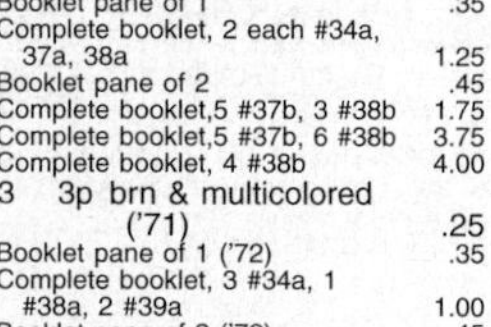

White-eared Pheasant — A8

2½p, Thick-billed parrots, vert. 7½p, Ursine colobus monkeys, vert. 9p, Ring-tailed lemurs.

**1971, Mar. 9 Photo. *Perf. 11½***

**49** A8 2p deep plum & multi .70 .25
**50** A8 2½p dark gray & multi .80 .25
**51** A8 7½p olive & multi 6.00 5.00
**52** A8 9p vio blue & multi 8.00 8.00
*Nos. 49-52 (4)* 15.50 13.50

Jersey Wildlife Preservation Trust.
See Nos. 65-68.

British Legion Emblem A9

2½p, Poppy field & poppy emblem. 7½p, Jack Counter (1899-1970) & Victoria Cross. 9p, Flags of France & Great Britain.

**1971, June 15 Litho. *Perf. 14½***

**53** A9 2p multicolored .35 .25
**54** A9 2½p multicolored .35 .25
**55** A9 7½p multicolored 2.25 2.00
**56** A9 9p multicolored 2.25 2.25
*Nos. 53-56 (4)* 5.20 4.75

50th anniversary of the British Legion.

English Fleet in Channel, by Peter Monamy A10

Paintings by Jersey Artists: 2p, Tante Elizabeth (women in farm kitchen), by Edmund Blampied, vert. 7½p, Boyhood of Raleigh (man and boys at seashore), by Sir John Millais. 9p, The Blind Beggar (old man and girl), by W. W. Ouless, vert.

**1971, Oct. 5 Photo. *Perf. 11½***

**57** A10 2p gold & multi .30 .25
**58** A10 2½p gold & multi .40 .25
**59** A10 7½p gold & multi 3.00 2.50
**60** A10 9p gold & multi 3.00 2.50
*Nos. 57-60 (4)* 6.70 5.50

Jersey Fern — A11

Jersey Wild Flowers: 5p, Thrift. 7½p, Orchid (laxiflora). 9p, Viper's bugloss.

**1972, Jan. 18**

### Flowers in Natural Colors

**61** A11 3p brown & blk .35 .25
**62** A11 5p lt blue & blk .75 .35
**63** A11 7½p lilac & blk 2.25 1.90
**64** A11 9p green & blk 2.25 2.00
*Nos. 61-64 (4)* 5.60 4.50

### Wildlife Type of 1971

2½p, Cheetahs. 3p, Rothschild's mynahs, vert. 7½p, Spectacled bear. 9p, Tuatara reptiles.

**1972, Mar. 17 Photo. *Perf. 11½***

### Queen's Head in Gold

**65** A8 2½p Prus blue & multi .85 .25
**66** A8 3p dk pur & multi .60 .25
**67** A8 7½p yel bis & multi 1.25 1.25
**68** A8 9p multicolored 1.75 1.75
*Nos. 65-68 (4)* 4.45 3.50

Jersey Wildlife Preservation Trust.

Jersey Royal Artillery Shako — A12

**1972, June 27**

**69** A12 2½p shown .25 .25
**70** A12 3p 2nd North Regiment .25 .25
**71** A12 7½p South West Regiment .60 .30
**72** A12 9p 3rd (South) Light Infantry .85 .65
*Nos. 69-72 (4)* 1.95 1.45

Royal Jersey Militia shakos of 19th century.

Princess Anne — A13

Designs: 3p, Queen Elizabeth II and Prince Philip, horiz. 7½p, Prince Charles. 20p, Queen Elizabeth II and family, horiz.

**1972, Nov. 1 Photo. *Perf. 11½***

**73** A13 2½p citron & multi .25 .25
**74** A13 3p rose & multi .25 .25
**75** A13 7½p blue & multi .25 .25
**76** A13 20p gray & multi .75 .50
*Nos. 73-76 (4)* 1.50 1.25

25th anniversary of the marriage of Queen Elizabeth II and Prince Philip.

Silver Wine and Christening Cups, 18th Century A14

Designs: 3p, Gold torque, Bronze Age, vert. 7½p, Seal of Charles II, 1659, vert. 9p, Armorican (Brittany) coins, c. 55 B.C.

**1973, Jan. 23 Photo. *Perf. 11½***

**77** A14 2½p ultra & multi .25 .25
**78** A14 3p dp car & multi .25 .25
**79** A14 7½p org & multi .25 .25
**80** A14 9p blue & multi .35 .25
*Nos. 77-80 (4)* 1.10 1.00

Cent. of the Jersey Soc. Designs are from exhibits in the Soc. museum in St. Helier.

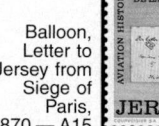

Balloon, Letter to Jersey from Siege of Paris, 1870 — A15

5p, Astra seaplane, 1912. 7½p, Supermarine Sea Eagle, 1923. 9p, De Havilland DH86, 1933.

**1973, May 16 Photo. *Perf. 11½***

**81** A15 3p brt blue & multi .25 .25
**82** A15 5p blue grn & multi .25 .25
**83** A15 7½p ultra & multi .35 .35
**84** A15 9p vio blue & multi .45 .45
*Nos. 81-84 (4)* 1.30 1.30

Aviation history connected with Jersey before 1939.

19th Century Locomotives A16

**1973, Aug. 6 Photo. *Perf. 11½***

**85** A16 2½p North Western .25 .25
**86** A16 3p Calvados .25 .25
**87** A16 7½p Carteret .35 .30
**88** A16 9p Caesarea .45 .35
*Nos. 85-88 (4)* 1.30 1.15

Centenary of Jersey Eastern Railroad.

Princess Anne and Mark Phillips A17

**1973, Nov. 14 Photo. *Perf. 11½***

**89** A17 3p lt blue & multi .25 .25
**90** A17 20p pink & multi .60 *.80*

Wedding of Princess Anne and Capt. Mark Phillips, Nov. 14, 1973.

Spider Crab A18

**1973, Nov. 15 Photo. *Perf. 11½***

**91** A18 2½p shown .25 .25
**92** A18 3p Conger eel .25 .25
**93** A18 7½p Lobster .30 .25
**94** A18 20p Ormer .60 .30
*Nos. 91-94 (4)* 1.40 1.05

Jersey Spring Flowers — A19

**1974, Feb. 13 Photo. *Perf. 12x11½***

**95** A19 3p Freesias .25 .25
**96** A19 5½p Anemones .25 .25
**97** A19 8p Carnations & gladioli .25 .25
**98** A19 10p Daffodils & iris .35 .35
*Nos. 95-98 (4)* 1.10 1.10

First Letter Box, Letter with 1852 Cancel A20

UPU Cent.: 3p, Postmen, 1862 and 1969. 5½p, Contemporary pillar box and first day cover of No. 101. 20p, BAC 111 and paddle steamer "Aquila," 1874.

**1974, June 7 Photo. *Perf. 11½***

**99** A20 2½p multicolored .25 .25
**100** A20 3p ultra & multi .25 .25
**101** A20 5½p olive & multi .25 .25
**102** A20 20p gray & multi .75 .40
*Nos. 99-102 (4)* 1.50 1.15

John Wesley — A21

### Lithographed and Engraved

**1974, July 31 *Perf. 13½x14***

**103** A21 3p shown .25 .25
**104** A21 3½p Hillary .25 .25
**105** A21 8p Wace .25 .25
**106** A21 20p Churchill .75 .50
*Nos. 103-106 (4)* 1.50 1.25

Anniversaries: Methodism in Jersey, bicen.; John Wesley, theologian, founder of Methodism. Sesquicentennial of Royal Natl. Lifeboat Institution, Lt. Col. Sir William Hillary, founder. 800th death anniv. of Canon Wace, poet and chronicler. Sir Winston Churchill, birth centenary.

### Type of 1969

4½p, Arms of Jersey and Royal Mace. 5½p, Jersey cow. 8p, Mont Orgueil by night.

**1974, Oct. 31 Photo. *Perf. 14½***

| | | | | |
|---|---|---|---|---|
| **107** | A3 | 4½p olive & multi | .25 | .25 |
| **108** | A3 | 5½p magenta & multi | .25 | .25 |
| **109** | A3 | 8p yellow & multi | .30 | .30 |
| | | *Nos. 107-109 (3)* | .80 | .80 |

English Yacht, 1660, by Peter Monamy A22

Marine paintings by Peter Monamy (d. 1749): 5½p, French ship. 8p, Dutch ship, horiz. 25p, Naval battle, 1662.

**1974, Nov. 22 Photo. *Perf. 11½***

**Size: 31x38, 38x31mm**

| | | | | |
|---|---|---|---|---|
| **116** | A22 | 3½p gold & multi | .25 | .25 |
| **117** | A22 | 5½p gold & multi | .25 | .25 |
| **118** | A22 | 8p gold & multi | .25 | .25 |

**Size: 54x25mm**

| | | | | |
|---|---|---|---|---|
| **119** | A22 | 25p gold & multi | .65 | .65 |
| | | *Nos. 116-119 (4)* | 1.40 | 1.40 |

Potato Digger — A23

19th cent. farming tools: 3½p, Cider apple crusher. 8p, Six-horse plow. 10p, Hay cart.

**1975, Feb. 25 Photo. *Perf. 11½***

| | | | | |
|---|---|---|---|---|
| **120** | A23 | 3p multicolored | .25 | .25 |
| **121** | A23 | 3½p multicolored | .25 | .25 |
| **122** | A23 | 8p multicolored | .40 | .30 |
| **123** | A23 | 10p multicolored | .70 | .35 |
| | | *Nos. 120-123 (4)* | 1.60 | 1.15 |

Shell Design as Letter "J" — A24

Posters: 8p, Beach umbrella. 10p, Beach chair. 12p, Sand castle with Union Jacks & Jersey flag.

**1975, June 8 Photo. *Perf. 11½***

| | | | | |
|---|---|---|---|---|
| **124** | A24 | 5p multicolored | .25 | .25 |
| **125** | A24 | 8p multicolored | .25 | .25 |
| **126** | A24 | 10p multicolored | .30 | .30 |
| **127** | A24 | 12p multicolored | .40 | .40 |
| *a.* | | Souvenir sheet of 4 | 1.25 | 1.25 |
| | | *Nos. 124-127 (4)* | 1.20 | 1.20 |

Tourist publicity. No. 127a contains Nos. 124-127 in continuous design extending into margin.

Queen Mother Elizabeth A25

**1975, May 30 Photo. *Perf. 11½***

| | | | | |
|---|---|---|---|---|
| **128** | A25 | 20p multicolored | .75 | .50 |

Visit of Queen Mother Elizabeth to Jersey.

Common Tern — A26

**1975, July 28 Photo. *Perf. 11½***

| | | | | |
|---|---|---|---|---|
| **129** | A26 | 4p shown | .25 | .25 |
| **130** | A26 | 5p Storm petrel | .25 | .25 |
| **131** | A26 | 8p Brent geese | .40 | .25 |
| **132** | A26 | 25p Shag | .80 | .35 |
| | | *Nos. 129-132 (4)* | 1.70 | 1.10 |

Siskin 3A, 1925 — A27

R.A.F. Planes: 5p, Southampton 1, 1925. 10p, Spitfire 1, 1931. 25p, Gnat T.1, 1962.

**1975, Oct. 30 Photo. *Perf. 11½***

| | | | | |
|---|---|---|---|---|
| **133** | A27 | 4p blue & multi | .25 | .25 |
| **134** | A27 | 5p lt green & multi | .25 | .25 |
| **135** | A27 | 10p yellow & multi | .40 | .35 |
| **136** | A27 | 25p ultra & multi | .70 | .70 |
| | | *Nos. 133-136 (4)* | 1.60 | 1.55 |

Royal Air Force Assoc., Jersey Branch, 50th anniv.

Map of Jersey with 12 Parishes A28

Arms of Trinity and Zoo — A29

Queen Elizabeth II — A30

Arms and scene: 5p, Church of St. Mary. 6p, Grouville, Seymour Tower. 7p, St. Brelade, La Corbière Lighthouse. 8p, Church of St. Saviour. 9p, St. Helier, Elizabeth Castle. 10p, St. Martin, Gorey Harbor. 11p, St. Peter, Jersey Airport. 12p, St. Ouen, Grosnez Castle. 13p, St. John, Bonne Nuit Harbor. 14p, St. Clement and Le Hocq Tower. 15p, St. Lawrence, Morel Farm. 20p, 12 Parishes, view of harbor. 30p, Jersey flag, map of Island. 40p, Postal Administration emblem, PO Headquarters. 50p, Jersey, Parliament and Royal Court. £1, Flag of Lt.-Governor, Government House.

**1976-77 Litho. *Perf. 14½***

**Size: 33x23mm**

| | | | | |
|---|---|---|---|---|
| **137** | A28 | ½p lt blue & multi | .25 | .25 |
| **138** | A29 | 1p bister & multi | .25 | .25 |
| *a.* | | Bklt. pane of 2 + 2 labels | .80 | |
| *b.* | | Booklet pane of 4 | .80 | |
| **139** | A29 | 5p rose & multi | .25 | .25 |
| *a.* | | Booklet pane of 4 | .80 | |
| **140** | A29 | 6p vio blue & multi | .25 | .25 |
| *a.* | | Booklet pane of 4 ('78) | 1.00 | |
| | | Complete booklet, #138b, 4 #140a | 3.75 | |
| **141** | A29 | 7p fawn & multi | .25 | .25 |
| *a.* | | Booklet pane of 4 | 1.10 | |
| | | Complete booklet, #138a, 139a, 141a | 2.25 | |
| | | Complete booklet, #138b, 2 each #139a, 141a | 4.00 | |
| **142** | A29 | 8p yel grn & multi | .25 | .25 |
| *a.* | | Booklet pane of 4 ('78) | 1.10 | |
| | | Complete booklet, #138b, 3 #142a | 3.75 | |
| | | Complete booklet, 2 each #138b, 140a, 142a | 5.00 | |
| **143** | A29 | 9p lil rose & multi | .25 | .25 |
| *a.* | | Booklet pane of 4 ('80) | 1.25 | |
| | | Complete booklet, 3 #138b, 2 each #141a, 143a | 5.50 | |
| **144** | A29 | 10p ol bis & multi | .30 | .30 |
| **145** | A29 | 11p bl grn & multi | .35 | .35 |
| **146** | A29 | 12p org & multi | .35 | .35 |
| **147** | A29 | 13p blue & multi | .35 | .35 |
| **148** | A29 | 14p yel org & multi | .50 | .50 |
| **149** | A29 | 15p vio & multi | .50 | .50 |

**Photo.**

***Perf. 12***

**Size: 41x26mm, 26x41mm**

| | | | | |
|---|---|---|---|---|
| **150** | A29 | 20p gold & multi | .55 | .55 |
| **151** | A28 | 30p gold & multi | .70 | .70 |
| **152** | A29 | 40p gold & multi | 1.00 | 1.00 |
| **153** | A29 | 50p gold & multi | 1.25 | 1.25 |
| **154** | A29 | £1 gold & multi | 3.50 | 3.50 |
| **155** | A30 | £2 multicolored ('77) | 5.00 | 5.00 |
| | | *Nos. 137-155 (19)* | 16.10 | 16.10 |

Issue dates: Nos. 137-149, Jan. 29; Nos. 150-154, Aug. 20. No. 155, Nov. 16.

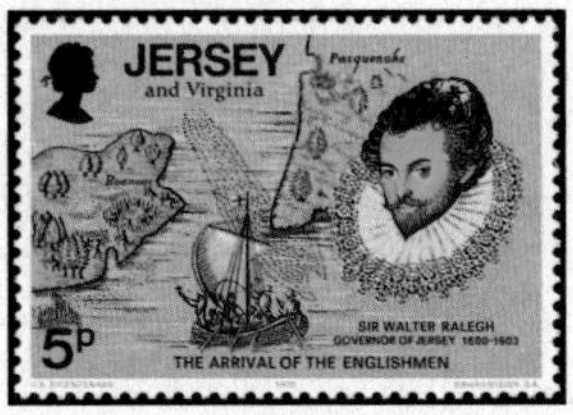

Sir Walter Raleigh and Old Map of Virginia — A31

US Bicentennial: 7p, Sir George Carteret and old map of New Jersey. 11p, Philippe Dauvergne and ships landing on Long Island. 13p, John Singleton Copley and his "Death of Major Pierson."

**1976, May 29 Photo. *Perf. 11½***

| | | | | |
|---|---|---|---|---|
| **160** | A31 | 5p multicolored | .25 | .25 |
| **161** | A31 | 7p multicolored | .25 | .25 |
| **162** | A31 | 11p multicolored | .35 | .35 |
| **163** | A31 | 13p multicolored | .45 | .45 |
| | | *Nos. 160-163 (4)* | 1.30 | 1.30 |

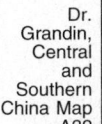

Dr. Grandin, Central and Southern China Map A32

7p, Yangtze River journey. 11p, On horseback to Chaotung. 13p, Dr. Grandin holding infant.

**1976, Nov. 25 Photo. *Perf. 11½***

| | | | | |
|---|---|---|---|---|
| **164** | A32 | 5p multicolored | .25 | .25 |
| **165** | A32 | 7p multicolored | .25 | .25 |
| **166** | A32 | 11p multicolored | .35 | .35 |
| **167** | A32 | 13p multicolored | .45 | .45 |
| | | *Nos. 164-167 (4)* | 1.30 | 1.30 |

Lilian Mary Grandin (1876-1924), Jersey-born missionary doctor in China.

Queen Wearing St. Edward's Crown — A33

7p, Queen with Jersey Bailiff Sir Alexander Coutanche, 1957. 25p, Portrait, 1976.

**1977, Feb. 7 Photo. *Perf. 11½***

| | | | | |
|---|---|---|---|---|
| **168** | A33 | 5p multicolored | .25 | .25 |
| **169** | A33 | 7p multicolored | .30 | .30 |
| **170** | A33 | 25p multicolored | .70 | .70 |
| | | *Nos. 168-170 (3)* | 1.25 | 1.25 |

25th anniv. of the reign of Elizabeth II.

1/13th sh, 1871 and 1/12th sh, 1877 A34

Coins: 7p, 1/12th sh, 1949. 11p, Silver crown, 1966. 13p, Silver £2, 1972.

**1977, Mar. 25 Litho. *Perf. 14***

| | | | | |
|---|---|---|---|---|
| **171** | A34 | 5p multicolored | .25 | .25 |
| **172** | A34 | 7p multicolored | .25 | .25 |
| **173** | A34 | 11p multicolored | .40 | .40 |
| **174** | A34 | 13p multicolored | .45 | .45 |
| | | *Nos. 171-174 (4)* | 1.35 | 1.35 |

Centenary of Jersey's currency reform.

Sir William Weston and Santa Anna, 1530 A35

Designs: 7p, Sir William Drogo and horse-drawn ambulance, 1877. 11p, Duke of Connaught and Jersey ambulance, 1917. 13p, Richard, Duke of Gloucester and ambulance team, 1977.

**1977, June 24 Litho. *Perf. 14x13½***

| | | | | |
|---|---|---|---|---|
| **175** | A35 | 5p multicolored | .25 | .25 |
| **176** | A35 | 7p multicolored | .25 | .25 |
| **177** | A35 | 11p multicolored | .35 | .35 |
| **178** | A35 | 13p multicolored | .45 | .45 |
| | | *Nos. 175-178 (4)* | 1.30 | 1.30 |

St. John Ambulance Assoc. cent. (in GB).

Victoria and Albert Arriving in Jersey, 1846 A36

Designs: 10½p, Victoria College, 1852. 11p, Statue of Sir Galahad near college gate, vert. 13p, College Hall, interior, vert.

**1977, Sept. 29 Litho. *Perf. 14½***

| | | | | |
|---|---|---|---|---|
| **179** | A36 | 7p multicolored | .25 | .25 |
| **180** | A36 | 10½p multicolored | .25 | .25 |
| **181** | A36 | 11p multicolored | .35 | .35 |
| **182** | A36 | 13p multicolored | .45 | .45 |
| | | *Nos. 179-182 (4)* | 1.30 | 1.30 |

Jersey Victoria College, 125th anniv.

Harry Vardon Statuette, Layout of Golf Course A37

Designs: 8p, Golf grip and swing perfected by Vardon. 11p, Vardon's putting grip and stance. 13p, Vardon's British and US Open Golf trophies, his book "The Complete Golfer" and biography.

**1978, Feb. 28 Litho. *Perf. 14***

| | | | | |
|---|---|---|---|---|
| **183** | A37 | 6p multicolored | .25 | .25 |
| **184** | A37 | 8p multicolored | .30 | .30 |
| **185** | A37 | 11p multicolored | .35 | .35 |
| **186** | A37 | 13p multicolored | .40 | .40 |
| | | *Nos. 183-186 (4)* | 1.30 | 1.30 |

Cent. of Royal Jersey Golf Club and to honor Vardon (1870-1937), Jersey-born golfer.

Mont Orgueil — A38

Europa: 8p, St. Aubin's Fort. 10½p, Elizabeth Castle.

**1978, May 1 Photo. *Perf. 11½***

| | | | | | |
|---|---|---|---|---|---|
| **187** | A38 | 6p | multicolored | .25 | .25 |
| **188** | A38 | 8p | multicolored | .25 | .25 |
| **189** | A38 | 10½p | multicolored | .35 | .35 |
| | | | *Nos. 187-189 (3)* | .85 | .85 |

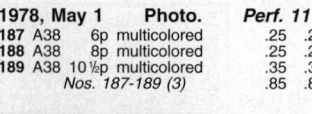

Gaspe Basin, by P. J. Ouless — A39

8p, Early map of Gaspe Peninsula, after Capt. Cook. 10½p, Sailing ship Century. 11p, Early map of Jersey. 13p, St. Aubin's Bay Town & Harbor.

**1978, June 9 Litho. *Perf. 14x15***

| | | | | | |
|---|---|---|---|---|---|
| **190** | A39 | 6p | multicolored | .25 | .25 |
| **191** | A39 | 8p | multicolored | .25 | .25 |
| **192** | A39 | 10½p | multicolored | .30 | .25 |
| **193** | A39 | 11p | multicolored | .35 | .25 |
| **194** | A39 | 13p | multicolored | .45 | .30 |
| | | | *Nos. 190-194 (5)* | 1.60 | 1.30 |

Jersey's links with Canada and for CAPEX, Canadian Intl. Phil. Exhib., Toronto, Ont., June 9-18.

Elizabeth II, Portraits 1953 and 1977 — A40

Design: 8p, Elizabeth II and Prince Philip.

**1978, June 27 Photo. *Perf. 11½***

| | | | | | |
|---|---|---|---|---|---|
| **195** | A40 | 8p | car, sil & black | .25 | .25 |
| **196** | A40 | 25p | blue, sil & black | .75 | .70 |

25th anniv. of coronation of Queen Elizabeth II and for Royal visit, June 27.

Mail Cutter — A41

Packets: 8p, Flamer, paddle vessel. 10½p, Diana, screw steamer. 11p, Ibex, steamer. 13p, Caesarea, mini-liner.

**1978, Oct. 18 Litho. *Perf. 14½x14***

| | | | | | |
|---|---|---|---|---|---|
| **197** | A41 | 6p | multicolored | .25 | .25 |
| **198** | A41 | 8p | multicolored | .25 | .25 |
| **199** | A41 | 10½p | multicolored | .30 | .25 |
| **200** | A41 | 11p | multicolored | .35 | .25 |
| **201** | A41 | 13p | multicolored | .45 | .30 |
| | | | *Nos. 197-201 (5)* | 1.60 | 1.30 |

First Government packet between Britain and Jersey, bicentenary.

Jersey Pillar Box, 1860 — A42

Europa: No. 203, Mailman emptying 1979 mailbox. No. 204, Telephone switchboard, c. 1900. No. 205, Technician working on contemporary telecommunications system.

***Perf. 14, 14½x15***

**1979, Mar. 1 Litho.**

| | | | | | |
|---|---|---|---|---|---|
| **202** | A42 | 8p | yellow & blk | .25 | .25 |
| **203** | A42 | 8p | carmine & blk | .25 | .25 |
| *a.* | | | Pair, #202-203 | .50 | .50 |
| **204** | A42 | 10½p | violet & blk | .45 | .45 |
| **205** | A42 | 10½p | blue & blk | .45 | .45 |
| *a.* | | | Pair, #204-205 | .90 | .90 |
| | | | *Nos. 202-205 (4)* | 1.40 | 1.40 |

Nos. 203a, 205a have continuous design. Both exist perf. 14 and 14½x15.

Soft-colored Jersey Heifer — A43

25p, Milk-laden Jersey cow with 1st Prize ribbon.

***Perf. 14 (#206), 13¾ (#207)***

**1979, Mar. 1**

| | | | | | |
|---|---|---|---|---|---|
| **206** | A43 | 6p | multicolored | .30 | .30 |

**Size: 48x31mm**

| | | | | | |
|---|---|---|---|---|---|
| **207** | A43 | 25p | multicolored | .95 | .95 |

30th anniv. of 1st Intl. Conf. of Jersey Breed Societies and 9th Conf. of the World Jersey Cattle Bureau.

Percival Mew Gull — A44

Planes: 8p, De Havilland Chipmunk. 10½p, Druine D-31 Turbulent. 11p, De Havilland Tiger Moth. 13p, North American Harvard Mk. 4.

**1979, Apr. 24 Photo. *Perf. 11½***

| | | | | | |
|---|---|---|---|---|---|
| **208** | A44 | 6p | multicolored | .25 | .25 |
| **209** | A44 | 8p | multicolored | .25 | .25 |
| **210** | A44 | 10½p | multicolored | .25 | .25 |
| **211** | A44 | 11p | multicolored | .40 | .40 |
| **212** | A44 | 13p | multicolored | .50 | .50 |
| | | | *Nos. 208-212 (5)* | 1.65 | 1.65 |

25th International Air Rally.

My First Sermon, by Millais — A45

Paintings by Millais: 10½p, Orphan. 11p, The Princes in the Tower. 25p, Jesus in the Home of His Parents, horiz.

**1979, Aug. 13 Photo. *Perf. 11½***

**Size: 25x35mm**

| | | | | | |
|---|---|---|---|---|---|
| **213** | A45 | 8p | multicolored | .30 | .30 |
| **214** | A45 | 10½p | multicolored | .35 | .35 |
| **215** | A45 | 11p | multicolored | .35 | .35 |

**Size: 49x30mm**

***Perf. 12x12½***

| | | | | | |
|---|---|---|---|---|---|
| **216** | A45 | 25p | multicolored | .75 | .75 |
| | | | *Nos. 213-216 (4)* | 1.75 | 1.75 |

IYC and for John Everett Millais (1829-96).

Waldrapp Ibis — A46

**1979, Nov. 8 Photo. *Perf. 11½***

| | | | | | |
|---|---|---|---|---|---|
| **217** | A46 | 6p | Pink pigeons | .25 | .25 |
| **218** | A46 | 8p | Orangutans | .25 | .25 |
| **219** | A46 | 11½p | shown | .25 | .25 |
| **220** | A46 | 13p | Lowland gorillas | .40 | .40 |
| **221** | A46 | 15p | Rodrigues fruit bats | .60 | .60 |
| | | | *Nos. 217-221 (5)* | 1.75 | 1.75 |

Nos. 217-218, 220-221 vertical.

Mont Orgueil Fortress A47

Fortresses, 300th Anniversary: 11½p, St. Aubin Tower. 13p, Elizabeth. 25p, Map of Jersey showing fortress locations.

**1980, Feb. 5 Litho. *Perf. 14½x13½***

| | | | | | |
|---|---|---|---|---|---|
| **222** | A47 | 8p | multicolored | .25 | .25 |
| **223** | A47 | 11½p | multicolored | .30 | .30 |
| **224** | A47 | 13p | multicolored | .35 | .35 |

***Perf. 13½x14***

**Size: 37½x26mm**

| | | | | | |
|---|---|---|---|---|---|
| **225** | A47 | 25p | multicolored | .70 | .70 |
| | | | *Nos. 222-225 (4)* | 1.60 | 1.60 |

Potato Harvest — A48

Royal Jersey Potato Cent.: 7p, Planting potatoes. 17½p, Loading dock, Weighbridge.

**1980, May 6 Litho. *Perf. 14***

| | | | | | |
|---|---|---|---|---|---|
| **226** | A48 | 7p | multicolored | .25 | .25 |
| **227** | A48 | 15p | multicolored | .40 | .40 |
| **228** | A48 | 17½p | multicolored | .55 | .55 |
| | | | *Nos. 226-228 (3)* | 1.20 | 1.20 |

A49

Europa (Wax Figures from Mont Orgueil and Elizabeth Castles): No. 229a, Sir Walter Raleigh; 229b, Paul Ivy. No. 230a, Charles II and Sir George Carteret; 230b, Lady Carteret. Pairs in continuous design.

**1980, May 6**

| | | | | | |
|---|---|---|---|---|---|
| **229** | A49 | | Pair | .60 | .60 |
| *a.-b.* | | | 9p any single | .30 | .30 |
| **230** | A49 | | Pair | .70 | .70 |
| *a.-b.* | | | 13½p any single | .35 | .35 |

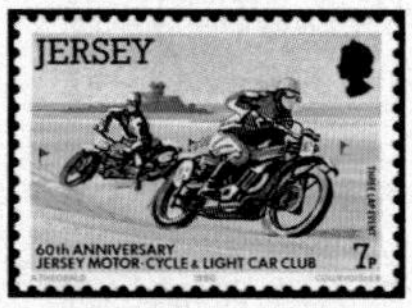

Three-lap Motorcycle Race — A51

**1980, July 24 Litho. *Perf. 12***

**Granite Paper**

| | | | | | |
|---|---|---|---|---|---|
| **231** | A51 | 7p | shown | .25 | .25 |
| **232** | A51 | 9p | Intl. road race | .25 | .25 |
| **233** | A51 | 13½p | Motorcycle scrambling | .45 | .45 |
| **234** | A51 | 15p | Sand racing, saloon cars | .50 | .50 |
| **235** | A51 | 17½p | Natl. Hill climb | .55 | .55 |
| | | | *Nos. 231-235 (5)* | 2.00 | 2.00 |

Jersey Motorcycle and Light Car Club, 60th anniv.

"Eye of the Wind" Leaving St. Helier — A52

Designs: 9p, Medical research, Cuna Indians, Panama. 13½p, Exploration, Papua New Guinea. 14p, Capt. Scott's ship, Antarctica. 15p, Conservation, Sulawesi. 17½p, Marine studies.

**1980, Oct. 1 Litho. *Perf. 14½***

| | | | | | |
|---|---|---|---|---|---|
| **236** | A52 | 7p | multicolored | .25 | .25 |
| **237** | A52 | 9p | multicolored | .25 | .25 |
| **238** | A52 | 13½ | multicolored | .30 | .30 |
| **239** | A52 | 14p | multicolored | .30 | .30 |
| **240** | A52 | 15p | multicolored | .45 | .45 |
| **241** | A52 | 17½p | multicolored | .55 | .55 |
| | | | *Nos. 236-241 (6)* | 2.10 | 2.10 |

Operation Drake, a two-year, round-the-world scientific expedition in tribute to Royal Geographic Society sesquicentennial.

Armed Soldiers and Wounded Drummer A53

Designs: Details from The Death of Major Peirson, by John Singleton Copley.

**1981, Jan. 6 Photo. *Perf. 12½***

**Granite Paper**

| | | | | | |
|---|---|---|---|---|---|
| **242** | A53 | 7p | multicolored | .25 | .25 |
| **243** | A53 | 10p | multicolored | .30 | .30 |
| **244** | A53 | 15p | multicolored | .45 | .45 |
| **245** | A53 | 17½p | multicolored | .60 | .60 |
| *a.* | | | Souvenir sheet of 4, #242-245 | 2.00 | 2.00 |
| | | | *Nos. 242-245 (4)* | 1.60 | 1.60 |

Battle of Jersey bicentenary. No. 245a has continuous design.

De Bagot Family Arms — A54

Jersey, Channel Map A54a

Queen Elizabeth II, by Norman Hepple — A54b

**1981-83 Litho. *Perf. 14***

| | | | | | |
|---|---|---|---|---|---|
| **246** | A54 | ½p | shown | .25 | .25 |
| **247** | A54 | 1p | De Carteret | .25 | .25 |
| *a.* | | | Booklet pane of 6 | .35 | |
| **248** | A54 | 2p | La Cloche | .25 | .25 |
| *a.* | | | Booklet pane of 6 | .55 | |
| **249** | A54 | 3p | Dumaresq | .25 | .25 |
| *a.* | | | Booklet pane of 6 | .65 | |
| **250** | A54 | 4p | Payn | .25 | .25 |
| **251** | A54 | 5p | Janvrin | .25 | .25 |
| **252** | A54 | 6p | Poingdestre | .25 | .25 |
| **253** | A54 | 7p | Pipon | .30 | .25 |
| *a.* | | | Booklet pane of 6 | 1.90 | |
| **254** | A54 | 8p | Marett | .35 | .30 |
| *a.* | | | Booklet pane of 6 ('83) | 2.40 | |
| **255** | A54 | 9p | Le Breton | .35 | .25 |
| **256** | A54 | 10p | Le Maistre | .40 | .25 |
| *a.* | | | Booklet pane of 6 | 2.75 | |
| | | | Complete booklet, 2 #247a, 1 each #249a, 253a, 256a | 6.00 | |
| | | | Complete booklet, #247a, 248a, 253a, 256a | 6.00 | |
| **257** | A54 | 11p | Bisson | .45 | .25 |
| *b.* | | | Booklet pane of 6 ('83) | 3.25 | |
| | | | Complete booklet, #247a, #248a, 254a, 257b | 6.00 | |
| **258** | A54 | 12p | Robin | .45 | .30 |
| **259** | A54 | 13p | Herault | .50 | .30 |
| **260** | A54 | 14p | Messervy | .55 | .30 |
| **261** | A54 | 15p | Fiott | .60 | .35 |
| **262** | A54 | 20p | Badier | .80 | .35 |
| **263** | A54 | 25p | L'Arbalestier | 1.00 | .35 |
| **264** | A54 | 30p | Journeaulx | 1.25 | .45 |
| **265** | A54 | 40p | Lempriere | 1.40 | .60 |
| **266** | A54 | 50p | D'Auvergne | 1.60 | .75 |
| **267** | A54a | £1 | shown | 3.00 | 1.50 |

**Photo.**

***Perf. 12½x12***

| | | | | |
|---|---|---|---|---|
| **268** | A54b | £5 multi | 15.00 | 10.00 |
| | | *Nos. 246-268 (23)* | 29.75 | 18.30 |

Issued: #246-256, 2/24; #248a, 12/1; #257-262, 7/28; #263-267, 2/23/82; #254a, 257a, 4/19/83; £5, 11/17/83.

**1984-88** ***Perf. 15x14***

| | | | | |
|---|---|---|---|---|
| *247b* | A54 | 1p ('88) | .35 | .25 |
| *248b* | A54 | 2p Bklt. pane of 6 ('86) | .65 | |
| *248c* | A54 | 2p ('84) | .25 | .25 |
| *249b* | A54 | 3p Bklt. pane of 6 ('84) | .75 | |
| *249c* | A54 | 3p ('84) | .30 | .25 |
| *250a* | A54 | 4p Bklt. pane of 6 ('87) | 1.25 | |
| *250b* | A54 | 4p ('86) | .30 | .25 |
| *251a* | A54 | 5p ('86) | .35 | .30 |
| *252a* | A54 | 6p ('86) | .30 | .25 |
| *255a* | A54 | 9p Bklt. pane of 6 ('84) | 1.75 | |
| *255b* | A54 | 9p ('84) | .60 | .50 |
| *256b* | A54 | 10p Bklt. pane of 6 ('86) | 2.50 | |
| *256c* | A54 | 10p ('86) | .50 | .35 |
| *257a* | A54 | 11p Bklt. pane of 6 ('87) | 3.00 | |
| *257c* | A54 | 11p ('87) | .55 | .45 |
| *258a* | A54 | 12p Bklt. pane of 6 ('84) | 3.00 | |
| | | Complete booklet, 2 each #249b, 255a, 1 #258a | 10.00 | |
| *258b* | A54 | 12p ('84) | .80 | .60 |
| *259a* | A54 | 13p ('84) | .50 | .25 |
| *260a* | A54 | 14p Bklt. pane of 6 ('86) | 3.25 | |
| | | Complete booklet, 2 each #248b, 256b, 1 #260a | 14.00 | |
| *260b* | A54 | 14p ('84) | .45 | .25 |
| *261a* | A54 | 15p ('87) | .60 | .45 |
| *261b* | A54 | 15p Bklt. pane of 6 ('87) | 3.50 | |
| | | Complete booklet, 2 each #250a, 257a, 1 #261b | 15.00 | |
| *262a* | A54 | 20p ('86) | .85 | .60 |
| *264a* | A54 | 30p ('86) | 1.50 | 1.25 |
| *265a* | A54 | 40p ('87) | 2.00 | 1.50 |
| *266a* | A54 | 50p ('87) | 2.75 | 2.25 |

Issued: #251a, 252a, 262a, 264a, Mar. 4.

No. 247a dated "February 1981," "December 1981" or "April 1983"; No. 248a dated "December 1981" or "April 1983"; Nos. 253a, 256a dated "February 1981" or "December 1981;" No. 250a dated "April 1987" or "May 1988." No. 258a dated "April 1984" or "May 1988."

See Nos. 381-388.

Knight of Hamby Killing the Dragon A55

Europa (Legends): 10p, La Hougue Bie. 18p, Easter Voyage of St. Brelade. No. 272, Servant killing Knight of Hamby. No. 273, Shipwreck of St. Brelade. No. 274, Fish, ships' departure.

**1981, Apr. 7** ***Perf. 14½***

| | | | | |
|---|---|---|---|---|
| **271** | A55 | 10p multicolored | .35 | .35 |
| **272** | A55 | 10p multicolored | .35 | .35 |
| *a.* | | Pair, #271-272 | .70 | .70 |
| **273** | A55 | 18p multicolored | .55 | .55 |
| **274** | A55 | 18p multicolored | .55 | .55 |
| *a.* | | Pair, #273-274 | 1.10 | 1.10 |
| | | *Nos. 271-274 (4)* | 1.80 | 1.80 |

Royal Square by Gaslight A56

**1981, May 22 Photo.** ***Perf. 12***

**Granite Paper**

| | | | | |
|---|---|---|---|---|
| **275** | A56 | 7p The Harbor | .25 | .25 |
| **276** | A56 | 10p The Quay | .30 | .30 |
| **277** | A56 | 18p shown | .45 | .45 |
| **278** | A56 | 22p Halkett Place | .55 | .55 |
| **279** | A56 | 25p Central Market | .65 | .65 |
| | | *Nos. 275-279 (5)* | 2.20 | 2.20 |

Gas light sesquicentennial.

Prince Charles and Lady Diana A57

**1981, July 28 Photo.** ***Perf. 12***

**Granite Paper**

| | | | | |
|---|---|---|---|---|
| **280** | A57 | 10p multicolored | .30 | .30 |
| **281** | A57 | 25p multicolored | 1.40 | 1.40 |

Royal Wedding.

Christmas Tree, Royal Square, St. Helier — A58

**1981, Sept. 29 Litho.** ***Perf. 14½***

| | | | | |
|---|---|---|---|---|
| **282** | A58 | 7p shown | .25 | .25 |
| **283** | A58 | 10p East window, St. Helier's Church, choir | .35 | .35 |
| **284** | A58 | 18p Boxing Day, Jersey Drag Hunt | .60 | .60 |
| | | *Nos. 282-284 (3)* | 1.20 | 1.20 |

Christmas 1981.

Europa 1982 — A59

Designs: Maps showing formation of Channel Islands resulting from rise in sea level.

**1982, Apr. 20 Litho.** ***Perf. 14½***

| | | | | |
|---|---|---|---|---|
| **285** | A59 | 11p 16,000 BC | .35 | .35 |
| **286** | A59 | 11p 10,000 BC, vert. | .35 | .35 |
| **287** | A59 | 19½p 7,000 BC, vert. | .55 | .55 |
| **288** | A59 | 19½p 4,000 BC | .55 | .55 |
| | | *Nos. 285-288 (4)* | 1.80 | 1.80 |

Rollon Duke of Normandy, William the Conqueror, Clameur de Haro (Plea of Injunction) — A60

Links with France: No. 290, Kings John and Philippe Auguste, Siege of Rouen. No. 291, Jean Martell (1694-1753), brandy merchant. No. 292, Victor Hugo. No. 293, Pierre Teilhard de Chardin (1881-1955), theologian. No. 294, Charles Rey (1897-1981), meteorologist.

**1982, June 11 Litho.** ***Perf. 14***

| | | | | |
|---|---|---|---|---|
| **289** | A60 | 8p multicolored | .25 | .25 |
| **290** | A60 | 8p multicolored | .25 | .25 |
| *a.* | | Bklt. pane of 4+label, 2 each #289-290 | 1.00 | 1.00 |
| *b.* | | Pair, #289-290 | .50 | .50 |
| **291** | A60 | 11p multicolored | .35 | .35 |
| **292** | A60 | 11p multicolored | .35 | .35 |
| *a.* | | Bklt. pane of 4+label, 2 each #291-292 | 1.50 | 1.50 |
| *b.* | | Pair, #291-292 | .70 | .70 |
| **293** | A60 | 19½p multicolored | .60 | .60 |
| **294** | A60 | 19½p multicolored | .60 | .60 |
| *a.* | | Bklt. pane of 4+label, 2 each #293-294 | 2.75 | 2.75 |
| *b.* | | Pair, #293-294 | 1.25 | 1.25 |
| | | Complete booklet, 2 each #290a, 292a, 294a | 11.00 | |
| | | *Nos. 289-294 (6)* | 2.40 | 2.40 |

Issue date: Nos. 290a-294a, Sept. 7. Two versions of Nos. 290a, 292a and 294a exist: the label is inscribed in English or French.

Scouting Year A61

Designs: 8p, Sir William Smith (Boys Brigade founder). 11p, Liberation parade, 1945, vert. 24p, Boys Brigade annual display, 1903. 26p, The Baden-Powells, 1924, vert. 29p, Scouts.

**1982, Nov. 18 Photo.** ***Perf. 12***

**Granite Paper**

| | | | | |
|---|---|---|---|---|
| **295** | A61 | 8p multicolored | .30 | .30 |
| **296** | A61 | 11p multicolored | .40 | .40 |
| **297** | A61 | 24p multicolored | .75 | .75 |
| **298** | A61 | 26p multicolored | .80 | .80 |
| **299** | A61 | 29p multicolored | .95 | .85 |
| | | *Nos. 295-299 (5)* | 3.20 | 3.10 |

Port Egmont A62

250th Birth Anniv. of Capt. Philippe de Carteret (1733-97): 18th cent. engravings.

**1983, Feb. 15 Litho.** ***Perf. 14¼***

| | | | | |
|---|---|---|---|---|
| **300** | A62 | 8p shown | .30 | .30 |
| **301** | A62 | 11p Dolphin, Swallow | .40 | .40 |
| **302** | A62 | 19½p Discovering Pitcairn Is. | .65 | .65 |
| **303** | A62 | 24p English Cove, New Ireland | .80 | .80 |
| **304** | A62 | 26p Sinking pirate ship | .85 | .85 |
| **305** | A62 | 29p Endymion | 1.00 | 1.00 |
| | | *Nos. 300-305 (6)* | 4.00 | 4.00 |

No. 19 — A63

Royal Mace — A64

**1983, Apr. 19** **Litho.**

| | | | | |
|---|---|---|---|---|
| **306** | A63 | 11p shown | .45 | .45 |
| **307** | A64 | 11p shown | .45 | .45 |
| *a.* | | Pair, #306-307 | .90 | .90 |
| **308** | A63 | 19½p No. 20a | .65 | .65 |
| **309** | A64 | 19½p Bailiff's seal | .65 | .65 |
| *a.* | | Pair, #308-309 | 1.40 | 1.40 |
| | | *Nos. 306-309 (4)* | 2.20 | 2.20 |

Europa.

World Communications Year — A65

1st Postmaster Charles William LeGeyt (1733-1827): 8p, Commanding Grenadier Co., 25th Foot, Battle of Minden, 1759. 11p, London-Weymouth mail coach. 24p, PO Mail Packet attacked by French privateer. 26p, Hue St. PO. 29p, St. Helier Harbor.

**1983, June 21 Litho.** ***Perf. 14***

| | | | | |
|---|---|---|---|---|
| **310** | A65 | 8p multicolored | .35 | .35 |
| **311** | A65 | 11p multicolored | .45 | .45 |
| **312** | A65 | 24p multicolored | .85 | .85 |
| **313** | A65 | 26p multicolored | .90 | .90 |
| **314** | A65 | 29p multicolored | 1.10 | 1.10 |
| | | *Nos. 310-314 (5)* | 3.65 | 3.65 |

Intl. Assoc. of French-Speaking Parliamentarians 1983 General Assembly — A66

**1983, June 21** ***Perf. 15***

| | | | | |
|---|---|---|---|---|
| **315** | A66 | 19½p multicolored | .80 | .80 |

Cardinal Newman, by Walter William Ouless (1848-1933) A67

**1983, Sept. 20 Photo.** ***Perf. 11½***

| | | | | |
|---|---|---|---|---|
| **316** | A67 | 8p shown | .35 | .35 |
| **317** | A67 | 11p M. De Cazotte and his Daughter | .55 | .55 |
| **318** | A67 | 20½p Thomas Hardy | .85 | .85 |

**Size: 41x34mm**

| | | | | |
|---|---|---|---|---|
| **319** | A67 | 31p David with the Head of Goliath | 1.25 | 1.25 |
| | | *Nos. 316-319 (4)* | 3.00 | 3.00 |

Jersey Wildlife Preservation Trust — A68

**1984, Jan. 17 Litho.** ***Perf. 14***

| | | | | |
|---|---|---|---|---|
| **320** | A68 | 9p Golden Lion Tamarin | .40 | .40 |
| **321** | A68 | 12p Snow Leopard | .45 | .45 |
| **322** | A68 | 20½p Jamaican Boa | .75 | .75 |
| **323** | A68 | 26p Round Island Gecko | 1.00 | 1.00 |
| **324** | A68 | 28p Coscoroba Swan | 1.00 | 1.00 |
| **325** | A68 | 31p St. Lucia Parrot | 1.10 | 1.10 |
| | | *Nos. 320-325 (6)* | 4.70 | 4.70 |

Europa 1984 (25th Anniv.) — A69

**1984, Mar. 12** ***Perf. 14½x15***

| | | | | |
|---|---|---|---|---|
| **326** | A69 | 9p multicolored | .35 | .35 |
| **327** | A69 | 12p multicolored | .40 | .40 |
| **328** | A69 | 20½p multicolored | .70 | .70 |
| | | *Nos. 326-328 (3)* | 1.45 | 1.45 |

Souvenir Sheet

Jersey Links with the Commonwealth — A70

**1984, Mar. 12** ***Perf. 15x14½***

| | | | | |
|---|---|---|---|---|
| **329** | A70 | 75p multicolored | 3.00 | 3.00 |

Commonwealth Postal Administrations Conf.

Royal Natl. Lifeboat Institution Centenary A71

Rescue Scenes (Lifeboats and Ships).

**1984, June 1 Litho.** ***Perf. 14½***

| | | | | |
|---|---|---|---|---|
| **330** | A71 | 9p Sarah Brooshoft, Demie de Pas Light | .35 | .35 |
| **331** | A71 | 9p Hearts of Oak, Maurice Georges | .35 | .35 |
| **332** | A71 | 12p Elizabeth Rippon, Hanna | .45 | .45 |

**333** A71 12p Elizabeth Rippon, Santa Maria .45 .45
**334** A71 20½p Elizabeth Rippon, Bacchus .75 .75
**335** A71 20½p Thomas James King, Cythara .75 .75
*Nos. 330-335 (6)* 3.10 3.10

40th Anniv. of Intl. Civil Aviation Org. A72

**1984, July 24 Litho. *Perf. 14***
**Granite Paper**

**336** A72 9p Bristol Type 170 .35 .35
**337** A72 12p Airspeed AS-57 Ambassador 2 .50 .50
**338** A72 26p De Havilland Heron 1B .90 .90
**339** A72 31p DH-89A Dragon Rapide 1.25 1.25
*Nos. 336-339 (4)* 3.00 3.00

Robinson Crusoe, by John Alexander Gilfillan (1793-1864) — A73

"Links with Australia" paintings by J.A. Gilfillan.

**1984, Sept. 21 Photo. *Perf. 11½***

**340** A73 9p shown .35 .35
**341** A73 12p Edinburgh Castle .45 .45
**342** A73 20½p Maori Village .70 .70
**343** A73 26p Australian Landscape .95 .95
**344** A73 28p Waterhouse's Corner, Adelaide 1.00 1.00
**345** A73 31p Capt. Cook at Botany Bay 1.10 1.10
*Nos. 340-345 (6)* 4.55 4.55

Christmas 1984 — A74

**1984, Nov. 15 Photo. *Perf. 12x11½***

**346** A74 9p St. Helier orchid .60 .60
**347** A74 12p Mt. Bingham orchid .80 .80

Ship Paintings by Philip John Ouless (1817-85) — A75

**1985, Feb. 26 Photo. *Perf. 14x14½***

**348** A75 9p Hebe, 1874 .30 .30
**349** A75 12p Gaspe .35 .35
**350** A75 22p London, 1856 .75 .75
**351** A75 31p Rambler 1.25 1.25
**352** A75 34p Elizabeth Castle 1.40 1.40
*Nos. 348-352 (5)* 4.05 4.05

Europa 1985 A76

Performing Arts: 10p, John Ireland, composer (1879-1962). 13p, Ivy St. Helier, actress (1886-1971). 22p, Claude Debussy, composer.

**1985, Apr. 23 Litho. *Perf. 14***

**353** A76 10p multicolored .35 .35
**354** A76 13p multicolored .45 .45
**355** A76 22p multicolored .80 .80
*Nos. 353-355 (3)* 1.60 1.60

Intl. Youth Year — A77

**1985, May 30 Litho. *Perf. 14½***

**356** A77 10p Girls' Brigade .35 .35
**357** A77 13p Girl Guides .45 .45
**358** A77 29p Jersey Youth Service .95 .95
**359** A77 31p Sea Cadet Corps 1.00 1.00
**360** A77 34p Air Training Corps 1.25 1.25
*Nos. 356-360 (5)* 4.00 4.00

Railway History A78

**1985, July 16 Photo. *Perf. 12x11½***

**361** A78 10p Duke of Normandy, Cheapside .45 .45
**362** A78 13p Saddletank, First Tower .50 .50
**363** A78 22p La Moye, Millbrook .90 .90
**364** A78 29p St. Helier's, St. Aubin 1.10 1.10
**365** A78 34p St. Aubyns, Corbiere 1.40 1.40
*Nos. 361-365 (5)* 4.35 4.35

Centenary of Jersey's first train from St. Helier to Corbiere.

Huguenot Heritage A79

300th anniv. of revocation of the Edict of Nantes (religious tolerance) by King Louis XIV of France: No. 366, James Hemery (1814-1849), Dean of Jersey, Rector of St. Helier. No. 367, Francis Henry Jeune, Baron St. Helier, law lord and junior counsel in the Tichbourne case. No. 368, Francois Voisin, merchant. No. 369, Pierre Amiraux, silversmith. No. 370, George Henry Ingouville, Victoria Cross recipient. No. 371, Robert Brohier, co-founder of Schweppes soft-drink company.

**1985, Sept. 10 Litho. *Perf. 14***

**366** A79 10p Memorial window, St. Helier Town Church .40 .40
*a.* Booklet pane of 4 1.60
**367** A79 10p Houses of Parliament, Westminster .40 .40
*a.* Booklet pane of 4 1.60
**368** A79 13p Great Fair, Nijni-Novgorod, Russia .45 .45
*a.* Booklet pane of 4 1.90
**369** A79 13p Silver coffee pot, pitcher .45 .45
*a.* Booklet pane of 4 1.90
**370** A79 22p Naval Battle of Viborg .70 .70
*a.* Booklet pane of 4 3.25
**371** A79 22p Glass bottles, carbonated water commercial patent .70 .70
*a.* Booklet pane of 4 3.25
Complete booklet, #366a-371a 14.00
*Nos. 366-371 (6)* 3.10 3.10

Thomas Benjamin Frederick Davis (1867-1942), Shipping Magnate, Philanthropist — A80

Portrait and endowments: 10p, Howard Davis Hall, Victoria College. 13p, Yacht, racing schooner Westward. 31p, Howard Davis Park, St. Helier. 34p, Howard Davis Agricultural Development Farm, Trinity.

**1985, Oct. 25 *Perf. 13½***

**372** A80 10p multicolored .40 .40
**373** A80 13p multicolored .45 .45
**374** A80 31p multicolored 1.10 1.10
**375** A80 34p multicolored 1.25 1.25
*Nos. 372-375 (4)* 3.20 3.20

50th anniv. of Howard Davis Hall, Victoria College, donated by Davis in memory of his son.

**Arms Type of 1981-82 and**

Elizabeth II, 60th Birthday — A80a

**1985-91 Litho. *Perf. 15x14***

**381** A54 16p Malet .55 .35
*a.* Booklet pane of 6 ('88) 3.50
Complete booklet, 2 each #248b, 258a, 381a 15.00
**382** A54 17p Mabon .55 .45
**383** A54 18p De St. Martin ('88) .80 .75
**384** A54 19p Hamptonne ('88) .95 .80
**386** A54 26p De Bagot ('88) .80 .65
**388** A54 75p Remon ('87) 2.40 1.75

***Perf. 11½x12***

**389** A80a £1 multicolored 3.50 3.25

**Photo.**
**Granite Paper**

**390** A80a £2 multicolored 6.50 4.00
*Nos. 381-390 (8)* 16.05 12.00

Issued: 16, 17p, 10/25; £1, 4/21/86; 75p, 4/23/87; 18, 19, 26p, 4/26/88; £2, 3/19/91.
No. 381a inscribed "May 1988."

Jersey Lily — A81

Lillie Langtry, by Sir John Millais — A82

**1986, Jan. 28 Litho. *Perf. 15x14½***

**391** A81 13p multicolored .60 .60
**392** A82 34p multicolored 1.40 1.40
*a.* Souvenir sheet of 5 (4 13p, 34p) 4.25 4.25

Intl. Flower Gala, June 10-14.

Halley's Comet Sightings A83

Comet and coinciding historic events: 10p, Conquest of England, Bayeux Tapestry, A.D. 912 and 1066 sightings. 22p, Lady Carteret signing New Jersey over to William Penn, Edmond Halley observing comet, comets of 1301 & 1682. 31p, Giotto spacecraft and technology developed in 1910, 1986. Caesarea maiden voyage.

**1986, Mar. 4 *Perf. 13½x13***

**393** A83 10p multicolored .35 .35
**394** A83 22p multicolored .90 .90
**395** A83 31p multicolored 1.25 1.25
*Nos. 393-395 (3)* 2.50 2.50

Europa 1986 — A84

**1986, Apr. 21 *Perf. 14½***

**396** A84 10p Dwarf pansy .35 .35
**397** A84 14p Sea stock .60 .60
**398** A84 22p Sand crocus .95 .95
*Nos. 396-398 (3)* 1.90 1.90

Environmental conservation.

Jersey Natl. Trust, 50th Anniv. A85

**1986, June 17 Litho. *Perf. 13½x13***

**399** A85 10p Le Rat cottage .40 .40
**400** A85 14p The Elms, headquarters .45 .45
**401** A85 22p Morel Farm entrance .70 .70
**402** A85 29p Quetivel Mill 1.10 1.10
**403** A85 31p La Vallette 1.25 1.25
*Nos. 399-403 (5)* 3.90 3.90

Wedding of Prince Andrew and Sarah Ferguson — A86

**1986, July 23 *Perf. 13½***

**404** A86 14p multicolored .55 .55
**405** A86 40p multicolored 1.90 1.90

Paintings by Edmund Blampied (1886-1966), Artist — A87

**1986, Aug. 28 Litho. *Perf. 14***

**406** A87 10p Gathering Vraic .40 .40
**407** A87 14p Driving Home in the Rain .55 .55
**408** A87 29p The Miller 1.10 1.10
**409** A87 31p The Joy Ride 1.25 1.25
**410** A87 34p Tante Elizabeth 1.40 1.40
*Nos. 406-410 (5)* 4.70 4.70

Christmas, Intl. Peace Year — A88

**1986, Nov. 4** *Perf. 14½*

**411** A88 10p Dove, map, flower .40 .40
**412** A88 14p Lovebirds .55 .55
**413** A88 34p Dove, noise-maker 1.40 1.40
*Nos. 411-413 (3)* 2.35 2.35

Racing Schooner Westward A89

**1987, Jan. 15** **Litho.** *Perf. 13½*

**414** A89 10p Under full sail .40 .40
**415** A89 14p T.B. Davis, owner .55 .55
**416** A89 31p Overhauling Britannia 1.25 1.25
**417** A89 34p Dry dock, St. Helier 1.50 1.50
*Nos. 414-417 (4)* 3.70 3.70

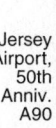

Jersey Airport, 50th Anniv. A90

**1987, Mar. 3** **Litho.** *Perf. 14*

**418** A90 10p DH86 Belcroute Bay .40 .40
**419** A90 14p Boeing 757, Douglas DC-9 .55 .55
**420** A90 22p Britten Norman Trislander, Islander .85 .85
**421** A90 29p Short SD330, Vickers Viscount 1.10 1.10
**422** A90 31p BAC1-11, HPR.7 Dart Herald 1.25 1.25
*Nos. 418-422 (5)* 4.15 4.15

Europa 1987 A91

Modern architecture.

**1987, Apr. 23** *Perf. 15x14*

**423** A91 11p St. Mary and St. Peter's Church .45 .45
**424** A91 15p Villa Devereux .60 .60

**Size: 61x31mm**

**425** A91 22p Fort Regent, St. Helier .85 .85
*Nos. 423-425 (3)* 1.90 1.90

Adm. Philippe D'Auvergne (1754-1816) — A92

Ships: 11p, Racehorse trapped in the Arctic. 15p, Alarm burned at Rhode Island. 29p, Arethusa wrecked off Ushant, France. 31p, Rattlesnake stranded on Trinidad. 34p, Mont Orgueil Castle.

**1987, July 9** *Perf. 14*

**426** A92 11p multicolored .40 .40
**427** A92 15p multicolored .50 .50
**428** A92 29p multicolored 1.00 1.00
**429** A92 31p multicolored 1.00 1.00
**430** A92 34p multicolored 1.10 1.10
*Nos. 426-430 (5)* 4.00 4.00

William the Conqueror (c. 1028-87), King of England (1066-87) — A93

Designs in the style of the Bayeux Tapestry: 11p, King Charles negotiating peace with the Vikings, 911, and cession of Jersey to Rollo's son William, 933. 15p, Duke Robert I and King Edward ashore Jersey after storm, 1030; Edward's succession to the throne of England, 1042. 22p, William the Conqueror's coronation, 1066, and succession of William II, 1087. 29p, Death of King William Rufus, and Henry defeating Duke Robert to unite England and Normandy, 1106. 31p, Death of Henry, battle for the throne and succession of King Stephen, 1135. 34p, Successions of Henry II, 1154, and John Lackland, 1189.

**1987** *Perf. 13½*

**431** A93 11p multicolored .45 .45
*a.* Booklet pane of 4 + label 2.00
**432** A93 15p multicolored .60 .60
*a.* Booklet pane of 4 + label 2.50
**433** A93 22p multicolored .85 .85
*a.* Booklet pane of 4 + label 3.75
**434** A93 29p multicolored 1.10 1.10
*a.* Booklet pane of 4 + label 4.75 4.75
**435** A93 31p multicolored 1.25 1.25
*a.* Booklet pane of 4 + label 5.50
**436** A93 34p multicolored 1.40 1.40
*a.* Booklet pane of 4 + label 6.50
Complete booklet, #431a-436a 26.00
*Nos. 431-436 (6)* 5.65 5.65

Paintings by John Le Capelain (1812-1848) — A94

**1987, Nov. 3** **Photo.** *Perf. 12x11½*

**437** A94 11p Grosnez Castle .45 .45
**438** A94 15p St. Aubin's Bay .60 .60
**439** A94 22p Mt. Orgueil Castle .85 .85
**440** A94 31p Town Fort and Harbor, St. Helier 1.25 1.25
**441** A94 34p The Hermitage 1.40 1.40
*Nos. 437-441 (5)* 4.55 4.55

Christmas.

Hybrids, Eric Young Orchid Foundation, Trinity — A95

Nos. 443, 445 are vertical.

**1988, Jan. 12** **Litho.** *Perf. 14*

**442** A95 11p Cymbidium pontac .45 .45
**443** A95 15p Odontioda Eric Young .60 .60
**444** A95 29p Lycaste auburn Seaford and Ditchling 1.10 1.10
**445** A95 31p Odontoglossum St. Brelade 1.25 1.25
**446** A95 34p Cymbidium mavourneen Jester 1.40 1.40
*Nos. 442-446 (5)* 4.80 4.80

Jersey Dog Club, Cent. A96

**1988, Mar. 2**

**447** A96 11p Labrador retriever .45 .45
**448** A96 15p Wire-haired dachshund .60 .60
**449** A96 22p Pekingese .85 .85
**450** A96 31p Cavalier King Charles spaniel 1.25 1.25
**451** A96 34p Dalmatian 1.40 1.40
*Nos. 447-451 (5)* 4.55 4.55

Europa 1988 A97

Nos. 453 and 455 vert.

***Perf. 14x13½, 13½x14***

**1988, Apr. 26** **Litho.**

**452** A97 16p Air transport .65 .65
**453** A97 16p Air communication .65 .65
**454** A97 22p Sea transport .85 .85
**455** A97 22p Sea communication .85 .85
*Nos. 452-455 (4)* 3.00 3.00

Wildlife Preservation Trust, 25th Anniv. — A98

**1988, July 6** **Litho.**

**456** A98 12p Rodrigues fody, vert. .45 .45
**457** A98 16p Volcano rabbit .65 .65
**458** A98 29p White-faced marmoset, vert. 1.10 1.10
**459** A98 31p Ploughshare tortoise 1.25 1.25
**460** A98 34p Mauritius kestrel, vert. 1.40 1.40
*Nos. 456-460 (5)* 4.85 4.85

Operation Raleigh A99

Activities: 12p, Rain Forest Leaf Frog, Costa Rica. 16p, Archaeological Survey, Peru. 22p, Glacier Climbing, Chile. 29p, Medical Assistance, Solomon Isls. 31p, Underwater Exploration, Australia. 34p, *Zebu* returns to St. Helier, Jersey.

**1988, Sept. 27** **Photo.** *Perf. 12*

**461** A99 12p multicolored .45 .45
**462** A99 16p multicolored .65 .65
**463** A99 22p multicolored .85 .85
**464** A99 29p multicolored 1.10 1.10
**465** A99 31p multicolored 1.25 1.25
**466** A99 34p multicolored 1.40 1.40
*Nos. 461-466 (6)* 5.70 5.70

Operation Raleigh: voyage of the *Zebu*, on which youths were trained with the aim of remotivating them and helping them to earn new self-respect.

WHO 40th anniv. (29p).

Parish Churches A100

**1988, Nov. 15** **Litho.** *Perf. 14*

**467** A100 12p St. Clement .45 .45
**468** A100 16p St. Ouen .55 .55
**469** A100 31p St. Brelade 1.10 1.10
**470** A100 34p St. Lawrence 1.25 1.25
*Nos. 467-470 (4)* 3.35 3.35

Christmas. See Nos. 549-552, 610-613.

Classic Cars A101

Designs: 12p, 1912 Talbot Tourer, seaweed harvest at Le Hocq. 16p, 1920 De Dion Bouton, Grosnez Castle ruins. 23p, 1926 Austin Chummy, brick kiln at Mont a l'Abbe. 30p, 1926 Ford Model T, harvest of the Jersey royal potato crop. 32p, 1930 Bentley 8-Litre, Guard House and Gate at Government House. 35p, 1931 Cadillac V16 Fleetwood Sports Phaeton, St. Ouen's Manor.

**1989, Jan. 31**

**471** A101 12p multicolored .45 .45
**472** A101 16p multicolored .60 .60
**473** A101 23p multicolored .80 .80
**474** A101 30p multicolored 1.00 1.00
**475** A101 32p multicolored 1.10 1.10
**476** A101 35p multicolored 1.25 1.25
*Nos. 471-476 (6)* 5.20 5.20

See Nos. 604-609, 903-908.

Scenic Views — A102

Coronation of Queen Elizabeth II, 40th Anniv. — A102a

Royal Arms A102b

**1989-95** **Litho.** *Perf. 13½*

**477** A102 1p Belcroute Bay .25 .25
**478** A102 2p High St., St. Aubin .25 .25
**480** A102 4p Royal Jersey Golf Course .25 .25
*a.* Booklet pane of 6 .80 .80
**481** A102 5p Portelet Bay .25 .25
*a.* Booklet pane of 6 1.40 1.40
**485** A102 10p Les Charrieres D'Anneport .30 .30
**486** A102 13p St. Helier Marina .45 .45
**487** A102 14p St. Ouen's Bay .45 .45
*a.* Booklet pane of 6 3.00 3.00
*b.* Booklet pane of 8 4.25 4.25
Complete booklet, #487b ('92) 4.25
**488** A102 15p Rozel Harbor .50 .50
*a.* Booklet pane of 6 3.25 3.25
**489** A102 16p St. Aubin's Harbor .55 .55
*a.* Booklet pane of 8 5.00 5.00
Complete booklet, #489a ('92) 5.00
**490** A102 17p Jersey Airport .55 .55
**491** A102 18p Corbiere Lighthouse .60 .60
*a.* Booklet pane of 6 4.25 4.25
Complete booklet, 2 each #480a, 487a, 491a ('90) 17.50
**492** A102 19p Val de la Mare .60 .60
**493** A102 20p Elizabeth Castle .50 .50
*a.* Booklet pane of 6 3.25 3.25
Complete booklet, 2 each #481a, 488a, 493a ('91) 20.00
**494** A102 21p Greve de Lecq .55 .55
**495** A102 22p Samares Manor .50 .50
*a.* Booklet pane of 8 4.50 4.50
Complete booklet, #495a ('92) 4.50
**496** A102 23p Bonne Nuit Harbor .85 .85
**497** A102 24p Grosnez Castle .70 .70
**498** A102 25p Augres Manor .80 .80
**499** A102 26p Central Market .90 .90
**500** A102 27p St. Brelade's Bay 1.00 1.00

**501** A102 30p St. Ouen's Manor 1.10 1.10
**502** A102 40p La Hougue Bie 1.40 1.40
**503** A102 50p Mont Orgueil Castle 1.60 1.60
**504** A102 75p Royal Square 2.50 2.50

*Perf. 14½*

**505** A102a £1 multicolored 3.50 3.50

*Perf. 15x14*

**506** A102b £4 multicolored 13.00 13.00
*Nos. 477-506 (26)* 33.90 33.90

Pane Nos. 480a, 487a and 491a issued for Stamp World London '90 and are inscribed "May 1990."

Issued: 1p-20p, 3/21/89; 21p-27p, 1/16/90; 30p-75p, 3/13/90; #481a, 488a, 493a, 2/12/91; £1, 6/2/93; £4, 1/2/95. Nos. 487b, 489a, 495a were released on May 22, but were not readily available until September 1992. Other booklet panes, 1990.

World Wildlife Fund — A103

**1989, Apr. 25 Litho. *Perf. 13x13¼***

**507** A103 13p Large checkered skipper *2.50 2.50*

*Perf. 13¼x13*

**508** A103 13p Agile frog, horiz. *2.50 2.50*
**509** A103 17p Green lizard, horiz. *2.50 2.50*

*Perf. 13½x13¾*

**510** A103 17p Barn owl *2.50 2.50*
*Nos. 507-510 (4)* *10.00 10.00*

Europa 1989 — A104

Children's games.

**1989, Apr. 25 *Perf. 14***

**511** A104 17p Playpen .65 .65
**512** A104 17p Playground .65 .65
**513** A104 23p Magician, games .90 .90
**514** A104 23p Cricket, rugby, tennis .90 .90
*Nos. 511-514 (4)* 3.10 3.10

Visit of Queen Elizabeth II — A105

**1989, May 24 Litho. *Perf. 14½***

**515** A105 £1 Ferry Terminal, St. Helier 4.00 4.00

French Revolution, Bicent. A106

Designs: 13p, D'Auvergne meets Louis XVI, 1786. 17p, Storming the Bastille, 1789. 23p, Marie de Bouillon at the Chateau de Navarre, 1790. 30p, Mission from Mont Orgueil, 1795. 32p, Support for the Chouans, 1796. 35p, The last Chouannerie, 1799.

**1989, July 7 *Perf. 13½***

**516** A106 13p multicolored .45 .45
*a.* Booklet pane of 4 1.90
**517** A106 17p multicolored .55 .55
*a.* Booklet pane of 4 2.50
**518** A106 23p multicolored .75 .75
*a.* Booklet pane of 4 3.50
**519** A106 30p multicolored 1.00 1.00
*a.* Booklet pane of 4 4.25
**520** A106 32p multicolored 1.10 1.10
*a.* Booklet pane of 4 5.50
**521** A106 35p multicolored 1.25 1.25
*a.* Booklet pane of 4 5.00
Complete booklet, #516a-521a 23.00
*Nos. 516-521 (6)* 5.10 5.10

Great Western Railway Steamer Service Between Weymouth and the Channel Isls., Cent. — A107

**1989, Sept. 5 Litho. *Perf. 13½x14***

**522** A107 13p *St. Helier,* 1925 .45 .45
**523** A107 17p *Caesarea II,* 1910 .55 .55
**524** A107 27p *Reindeer,* 1897 .95 .95
**525** A107 32p *Ibex* and *Frederica,* 1891 1.25 1.10
**526** A107 35p *Lynx,* 1889 1.40 1.40
*Nos. 522-526 (5)* 4.60 4.45

Paintings by Sarah Louisa Kilpack (1839-1909) — A108

**1989, Oct. 24 Litho. *Perf. 13x12½***

**527** A108 13p Gorey Harbour .50 .50
**528** A108 17p La Corbiere .65 .65
**529** A108 23p Greve de Lecq .90 .90
**530** A108 32p Bouley Bay 1.25 1.25
**531** A108 35p Mont Orgueil 1.40 1.40
*Nos. 527-531 (5)* 4.70 4.70

Europa 1990 A109

Post offices.

*Perf. 13½x14, 14x13½*

**1990, Mar. 13 Litho.**

**532** A109 18p Broad Street, 1969 .70 .70
**533** A109 18p Mont Millais, 1990 .70 .70
**534** A109 24p Hue Street, 1815 .95 .95
**535** A109 24p Halkett Place, 1890 .95 .95
*Nos. 532-535 (4)* 3.30 3.30

Nos. 532-533 vert.

Festival of Tourism — A110

**1990, May 3 Litho. *Perf. 14x13½***

**536** A110 18p Battle of Flowers .80 .80
**537** A110 24p Recreation 1.00 1.00
**538** A110 29p History 1.10 1.10
**539** A110 32p Salon Culinaire 1.25 1.25
*a.* Souvenir sheet of 4, #536-539 4.50 4.50
*Nos. 536-539 (4)* 4.15 4.15

News Media A111

**1990, June 26 Litho. *Perf. 13½***

**540** A111 14p Print (newspapers), 1784-1889 .55 .55
**541** A111 18p The Evening Post, 1890 .70 .70
**542** A111 34p BBC Radio Jersey, 1982 1.50 1.50
**543** A111 37p Channel Television, 1962 1.60 1.60
*Nos. 540-543 (4)* 4.35 4.35

UNESCO World Literacy Year.

Battle of Britain, 50th Anniv. A112

**1990, Sept. 4 *Perf. 14***

**544** A112 14p Hawk .65 .65
**545** A112 18p Spitfire .75 .75
**546** A112 24p Hurricane 1.00 1.00
**547** A112 34p Wellington 1.50 1.50
**548** A112 37p Lancaster 1.60 1.60
*Nos. 544-548 (5)* 5.50 5.50

**Parish Churches Type of 1988**

**1990, Nov. 13 Litho. *Perf. 13½x14***

**549** A100 14p St. Helier .55 .55
**550** A100 18p Grouville .70 .70
**551** A100 34p St. Saviour 1.50 1.50
**552** A100 37p St. John 1.60 1.60
*Nos. 549-552 (4)* 4.35 4.35

Christmas.

Prince's Tower, La Hougue Bie, 1801 A113

Philippe d'Auvergne: 20p, Arrested in Paris, 1802. 26p, Plotting against Napoleon, 1803. 31p, Execution of Cadoudal, 1804. 37p, H.M. Cutter Surly, 1809. 44p, Prince de Bouillon, 1816.

**1991, Jan. 22 Litho. *Perf. 13½***

**553** A113 15p multicolored .60 .60
**554** A113 20p multicolored .80 .80
**555** A113 26p multicolored 1.00 1.00
**556** A113 31p multicolored 1.25 1.25
**557** A113 37p multicolored 1.50 1.50
**558** A113 44p multicolored 1.75 1.75
*Nos. 553-558 (6)* 6.90 6.90

A114

Europa (Satellites and their functions): No. 559, ERS-1, oceanography. No. 560, Landsat, Earth resources. No. 561, Meteosat, meteorology. No. 562, Olympus, communications.

**1991, Mar. 19 Litho. *Perf. 14½x13***

**559** A114 20p multicolored .80 .80
**560** A114 20p multicolored .80 .80
**561** A114 26p multicolored 1.00 1.00
**562** A114 26p multicolored 1.00 1.00
*Nos. 559-562 (4)* 3.60 3.60

A115

15p, German Occupation Stamps for Jersey, 50th anniv. 20p, Eastern Railway extension to Gorey Pier, 100th anniv. 26p, Jersey Herd Book, 125th anniv. 31p, Victoria Harbor, 150th anniv. 53p, Hospital bequest of Marie Bartlett, 250th anniv.

**1991, May 16 Litho. *Perf. 13½***

**563** A115 15p multicolored .60 .60
**564** A115 20p multicolored .80 .80
**565** A115 26p multicolored 1.00 1.00
**566** A115 31p multicolored 1.25 1.25
**567** A115 53p multicolored 2.10 2.10
*Nos. 563-567 (5)* 5.75 5.75

Butterflies & Moths A116

**1991, July 9 Litho. *Perf. 13x12½***

**568** A116 15p Glanville fritillary .60 .60
**569** A116 20p Jersey tiger .80 .80
**570** A116 37p Small elephant hawk-moth 1.90 1.90
**571** A116 57p Peacock 2.40 2.40
*Nos. 568-571 (4)* 5.70 5.70

See Nos. 727-731.

Overseas Aid — A117

Designs: 15p, Water drilling rig, Ethiopia. 20p, Construction work, Rwanda. 26p, Technical school, Kenya. 31p, Leprosy and eye care, Tanzania. 37p, Agriculture and cultivation aid, Zambia. 44p, Health care and immunization, Lesotho.

**1991, Sept. 3 Litho. *Perf. 13½***

**572** A117 15p multicolored .60 .60
**573** A117 20p multicolored .80 .80
**574** A117 26p multicolored 1.00 1.00
**575** A117 31p multicolored 1.25 1.25
**576** A117 37p multicolored 1.50 1.50
**577** A117 44p multicolored 1.75 1.75
*Nos. 572-577 (6)* 6.90 6.90

Christmas — A118

Illustrations by Edmund Blampied from Peter Pan: 15p, This is the place for me. 20p, The Island Come True. 37p, The Never Bird. 53p, The Great White Father.

**1991, Nov. 5 Litho. *Perf. 14***

**578** A118 15p multicolored .60 .60
**579** A118 20p multicolored .80 .80
**580** A118 37p multicolored 1.50 1.50
**581** A118 53p multicolored 2.10 2.10
*Nos. 578-581 (4)* 5.00 5.00

Winter Birds — A119

**1992, Jan. 7 Litho. *Perf. 13½x14***

| | | | | |
|---|---|---|---|---|
| **582** | A119 16p Pied wagtail | .55 | .55 |
| **583** | A119 22p Firecrest | .75 | .75 |
| **584** | A119 28p Snipe | 1.00 | 1.00 |
| **585** | A119 39p Lapwing | 1.50 | 1.50 |
| **586** | A119 57p Fieldfare | 2.10 | 2.10 |
| | *Nos. 582-586 (5)* | 5.90 | 5.90 |

Shanghai Harbor, 1860 A120

William Mesny, 150th birth anniv: No. 588, Running the Taiping blockade, 1862. No. 589, General Mesny, River Gate, 1874. No. 590, Mesny accompanying Gill to Burma, 1877. No. 591, Mesny advises Governor Chang, 1882. No. 592, Mesny, Mandarin First Class, 1886.

**1992, Feb. 25 Litho. *Perf. 13½***

| | | | |
|---|---|---|---|
| **587** | A120 16p multicolored | .60 | .60 |
| **588** | A120 16p multicolored | .60 | .60 |
| **589** | A120 22p multicolored | .90 | .90 |
| **590** | A120 22p multicolored | .90 | .90 |
| **591** | A120 33p multicolored | 1.25 | 1.25 |
| **592** | A120 33p multicolored | 1.25 | 1.25 |
| | *Nos. 587-592 (6)* | 5.50 | 5.50 |
| *587a* | Booklet pane of 4 | 2.40 | 2.40 |
| *588a* | Booklet pane of 4 | 2.40 | 2.40 |
| *589a* | Booklet pane of 4 | 3.75 | 3.75 |
| *590a* | Booklet pane of 4 | 3.75 | 3.75 |
| *591a* | Booklet pane of 4 | 5.25 | 5.25 |
| *592a* | Booklet pane of 4 | 5.25 | 5.25 |
| | Complete booklet, #587a-592a | 23.00 | |

Discovery of America, 500th Anniv. A121

Columbus, ship and: 22p, John Bertram (1796-1882). 28p, Sir George Carteret (1610-1680). 39p, Sir Walter Raleigh (1554-1618).

**1992, Apr. 14 Litho. *Perf. 14½***

| | | | |
|---|---|---|---|
| **593** | A121 22p multicolored | .85 | .85 |
| **594** | A121 28p multicolored | 1.10 | 1.10 |
| **595** | A121 39p multicolored | 1.60 | 1.60 |
| | *Nos. 593-595 (3)* | 3.55 | 3.55 |

Europa.

Jersey-Built Sailing Ships — A122

**1992, Apr. 14 Litho. *Perf. 14***

| | | | |
|---|---|---|---|
| **596** | A122 16p Tickler | .55 | .55 |
| **597** | A122 22p Hebe | .75 | .75 |
| **598** | A122 50p Gemini | 1.75 | 1.75 |
| **599** | A122 57p Percy Douglas | 1.90 | 1.90 |
| *a.* | Souvenir sheet of 4, #596-599 | 5.25 | 5.25 |
| | *Nos. 596-599 (4)* | 4.95 | 4.95 |

Batik — A123

16p, Snow leopards. 22p, Three elements. 39p, Three men in a tub. 57p, Cockatoos.

**1992, June 23 Litho. *Perf. 14½***

| | | | |
|---|---|---|---|
| **600** | A123 16p multicolored | .65 | .65 |
| **601** | A123 22p multicolored | .90 | .90 |
| **602** | A123 39p multicolored | 1.50 | 1.50 |
| **603** | A123 57p multicolored | 2.10 | 2.10 |
| | *Nos. 600-603 (4)* | 5.15 | 5.15 |

### Classic Car Type of 1989

Designs: 16p, 1925 Morris Cowley "Bullnose." 22p, 1932 Rolls Royce 20/25. 28p, 1924 Chenard & Walcker T5. 33p, 1932 Packard 900 Series Light Eight. 39p, 1927 Lanchester 21. 50p, 1913 Buick 30 Roadster.

**1992, Sept. 8 Litho. *Perf. 13x12½***

| | | | |
|---|---|---|---|
| **604** | A101 16p multicolored | .50 | .50 |
| **605** | A101 22p multicolored | .70 | .70 |
| **606** | A101 28p multicolored | .90 | .90 |
| **607** | A101 33p multicolored | 1.10 | 1.10 |
| **608** | A101 39p multicolored | 1.25 | 1.25 |
| **609** | A101 50p multicolored | 1.60 | 1.60 |
| | *Nos. 604-609 (6)* | 6.05 | 6.05 |

### Parish Church Type of 1988

**1992, Nov. 3 Litho. *Perf. 13½x14***

| | | | |
|---|---|---|---|
| **610** | A100 16p Trinity | .50 | .50 |
| **611** | A100 22p St. Mary | .70 | .65 |
| **612** | A100 39p St. Martin | 1.25 | 1.25 |
| **613** | A100 57p St. Peter | 1.75 | 1.75 |
| | *Nos. 610-613 (4)* | 4.20 | 4.15 |

Christmas.

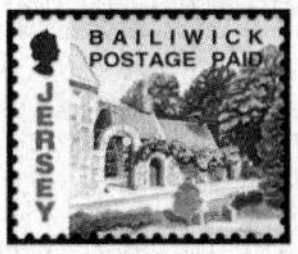

Non-Value Indicator Stamps — A124

Scenic views: No. 614, Building with arches. No. 615, Cemetery, Trinity Church. No. 616, Daffodils, cattle. No. 617, Cattle in pasture.

Beach scenes: No. 618, People lying on beach with umbrella. No. 619, Man with windsurfer. No. 620, Crab facing right. No. 621, Crab, facing left.

Parade floats: No. 622, Smiling face, rainbow. No. 623, Dragon head, Oriental theme. No. 624, Umbrellas, Asian theme. No. 625, Elephant's tusks, African theme.

**1993, Jan. 26 Litho. *Perf. 13½***

| | | | |
|---|---|---|---|
| **614** | A124 (17p) Bailiwick | .55 | .55 |
| **615** | A124 (17p) Bailiwick | .55 | .55 |
| **616** | A124 (17p) Bailiwick | .55 | .55 |
| **617** | A124 (17p) Bailiwick | .55 | .55 |
| *a.* | Block of 4, #614-617 | 2.25 | 2.25 |
| *b.* | Booklet pane of 8, 2 each #614-617 | 4.50 | |
| | Complete booklet, #617b | 5.00 | |
| **618** | A124 (23p) UK | .70 | .70 |
| **619** | A124 (23p) UK | .70 | .70 |
| **620** | A124 (23p) UK | .70 | .70 |
| **621** | A124 (23p) UK | .70 | .70 |
| *a.* | Block of 4, #618-621 | 3.00 | 3.00 |
| *b.* | Booklet pane of 8, 2 each #618-621 | 6.00 | |
| | Complete booklet, #621b | 6.75 | |
| **622** | A124 (28p) European | .85 | .85 |
| **623** | A124 (28p) European | .85 | .85 |
| **624** | A124 (28p) European | .85 | .85 |
| **625** | A124 (28p) European | .85 | .85 |
| *a.* | Block of 4, #622-625 | 3.25 | 3.25 |
| *b.* | Booklet pane of 8, 2 each #622-625 | 7.00 | 7.00 |
| | Complete booklet, #625b | 7.75 | |
| | *Nos. 614-625 (12)* | 8.40 | 8.40 |

The minimum postage rate is represented for each area where mail is delivered.

Orchids — A125

17p, Phragmipedium Eric Young "Jersey." 23p, Odontoglossum Augres "Trinity." 28p, Miltonia Saint Helier "Colomberie." 39p, Phragmipedium pearcei. 57p, Calanthe Grouville "Gorey."

**1993, Jan. 26 Litho. *Perf. 14½x13***

| | | | |
|---|---|---|---|
| **626** | A125 17p multicolored | .60 | .60 |
| **627** | A125 23p multicolored | .90 | .90 |
| **628** | A125 28p multicolored | 1.10 | 1.10 |
| **629** | A125 39p multicolored | 1.50 | 1.50 |
| **630** | A125 57p multicolored | 2.00 | 2.00 |
| | *Nos. 626-630 (5)* | 6.10 | 6.10 |

Europa — A126

Contemporary Art: 23p, Jersey Opera House, by Ian Rolls. 28p, The Ham and Tomato Bap, by Jonathan Hubbard. 39p, Vase of Flowers, by Neil MacKenzie.

**1993, Apr. 1 Litho. *Perf. 13½x14***

| | | | |
|---|---|---|---|
| **631** | A126 23p multicolored | .90 | .90 |
| **632** | A126 28p multicolored | 1.10 | 1.10 |
| **633** | A126 39p multicolored | 1.50 | 1.50 |
| | *Nos. 631-633 (3)* | 3.50 | 3.50 |

Royal Air Force, 75th Anniv. A127

Designs: 17p, Douglas Dakota. 23p, Wight Seaplane. 28p, Avro Shakleton AEW2. 33p, Gloster Meteor, DeHavilland Vampire. 39p, BAe Harrier GR1A. 57p, Panavia Tornado F3.

**1993, Apr. 1 *Perf. 14***

| | | | |
|---|---|---|---|
| **634** | A127 17p multicolored | .65 | .65 |
| **635** | A127 23p multicolored | .90 | .90 |
| **636** | A127 28p multicolored | 1.10 | 1.10 |
| **637** | A127 33p multicolored | 1.25 | 1.25 |
| **638** | A127 39p multicolored | 1.50 | 1.50 |
| **639** | A127 57p multicolored | 2.25 | 2.25 |
| *a.* | Souvenir sheet of 2, #635, 639 | 7.75 | 7.75 |
| | *Nos. 634-639 (6)* | 7.65 | 7.65 |

Stamps from No. 639a do not have white border.

German Occupation Stamps by Edmund Blampied, 50th Anniv. A128

**1993, June 2 Litho. *Perf. 13½***

| | | | |
|---|---|---|---|
| **640** | A128 17p No. N3 | .65 | .65 |
| **641** | A128 23p No. N4 | .90 | .90 |
| **642** | A128 28p No. N5 | 1.10 | 1.10 |
| **643** | A128 33p No. N6 | 1.25 | 1.25 |
| **644** | A128 39p No. N7 | 1.50 | 1.50 |
| **645** | A128 50p No. N8 | 2.00 | 2.00 |
| | *Nos. 640-645 (6)* | 7.40 | 7.40 |

Birds — A129

**1993, Sept. 7 Litho. *Perf. 13½x14***

| | | | |
|---|---|---|---|
| **646** | A129 17p Short-toed treecreeper | .65 | .65 |
| **647** | A129 23p Dartford warbler | .90 | .90 |
| **648** | A129 28p Wheatear | 1.10 | 1.10 |
| **649** | A129 39p Cirl bunting | 1.50 | 1.50 |
| **650** | A129 57p Jay | 2.25 | 2.25 |
| | *Nos. 646-650 (5)* | 6.40 | 6.40 |

Christmas — A130

Stained glass windows by Henry Bosdet, from St. Aubin on the Hill.

**1993, Nov. 2 Litho. *Perf. 14½x13***

| | | | |
|---|---|---|---|
| **651** | A130 17p multicolored | .65 | .65 |
| **652** | A130 23p multicolored | .90 | .90 |
| **653** | A130 39p multicolored | 1.50 | 1.50 |
| **654** | A130 57p multicolored | 2.25 | 2.25 |
| | *Nos. 651-654 (4)* | 5.30 | 5.30 |

Mushrooms A131

**1994, Jan. 11 Litho. *Perf. 14½***

| | | | |
|---|---|---|---|
| **655** | A131 18p Shaggy ink cap | .70 | .70 |
| **656** | A131 23p Fly agaric | .90 | .90 |
| **657** | A131 30p Chanterelle | 1.25 | 1.25 |
| **658** | A131 41p Parasol mushroom | 1.60 | 1.60 |
| **659** | A131 60p Latticed stinkhorn | 2.40 | 2.40 |
| | *Nos. 655-659 (5)* | 6.85 | 6.85 |

### Souvenir Sheet

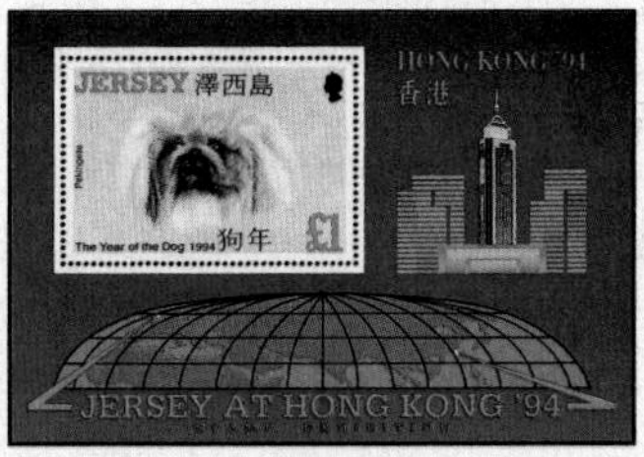

New Year 1994 (Year of the Dog) — A132

**1994, Feb. 18 Litho. *Perf. 15x14½***

| | | | |
|---|---|---|---|
| **660** | A132 £1 multicolored | 4.00 | 4.00 |

Hong Kong '94.

Cats — A133

**1994, Apr. 5 Litho. *Perf. 13½***

| | | | |
|---|---|---|---|
| **661** | A133 18p Maine coon, vert. | .70 | .70 |
| **662** | A133 23p British shorthair | .90 | .90 |
| **663** | A133 35p Persian, vert. | 1.40 | 1.40 |
| **664** | A133 41p Siamese | 1.60 | 1.60 |
| **665** | A133 60p Non-pedigree, vert. | 2.40 | 2.40 |
| | *Nos. 661-665 (5)* | 7.00 | 7.00 |

Jersey Cat Club, 21st anniv., and 4th Championship Show.

Europa A134

Designs: No. 666, Mammoths on cliff, c. 250,000 B.C. No. 667, Paleolithic hunters dragging mammoth by tusks. No. 668, Neolithic dolmen, "La Hougue Bie," c. 4,000 B.C. No. 669, Exterior of "La Hougue Bie," during construction.

**1994, Apr. 5 Litho. *Perf. 13½x14***

**666** A134 23p multicolored .90 .90
**667** A134 23p multicolored .90 .90
*a.* Pair, #666-667 1.90 1.90
**668** A134 30p multicolored 1.25 1.25
**669** A134 30p multicolored 1.25 1.25
*a.* Pair, #668-669 2.50 2.50
*Nos. 666-669 (4)* 4.30 4.30

D-Day, 50th Anniv. A135

#670, Airborne Forces enroute to drop zones. #671, Allied Fleet of Normandy Coast. #672, Coming ashore, Gold Beach. #673, Coming ashore, Sword Beach. #674, Spitfires on beachead patrol. #675, Normandy invasion map.

**1994, June 6 Litho. *Perf. 13½***

**670** A135 18p multicolored .70 .70
**671** A135 18p multicolored .70 .70
*a.* Bklt. pane, 3 each #670-671 4.50
**672** A135 23p multicolored .90 .90
**673** A135 23p multicolored .90 .90
*a.* Bklt. pane, 3 each #672-673 6.00
**674** A135 30p multicolored 1.25 1.25
**675** A135 30p multicolored 1.25 1.25
*a.* Bklt. pane, 3 each #674-675 8.00
*b.* Bklt. pane of 6, #670-675 6.50
Complete booklet, #671a, #673a, 675a, 675b 25.00
*Nos. 670-675 (6)* 5.70 5.70

No. 675b also sold by the Philatelic Bureau separate from the booklet. without stitching, as a souvenir sheet.

Intl. Olympic Committee, Cent. — A136

**1994, June 6 *Perf. 14***

**676** A136 18p Sailing .70 .70
**677** A136 23p Rifle shooting .90 .90
**678** A136 30p Hurdles 1.25 1.25
**679** A136 41p Swimming 1.60 1.60
**680** A136 60p Field hockey 2.40 2.40
*Nos. 676-680 (5)* 6.85 6.85

Marine Life A137

Designs: 18p, Strawberry anemone. 23p, Hermit crab, parasitic anemone. 41p, Velvet swimming crab. 60p, Common jellyfish.

**1994, Aug. 2 Litho. *Perf. 13½x13***

**681** A137 18p multicolored .70 .70
**682** A137 23p multicolored .90 .90
**683** A137 41p multicolored 1.60 1.60
**684** A137 60p multicolored 2.40 2.40
*Nos. 681-684 (4)* 5.60 5.60

Postal Independence, 25th Anniv. — A138

Designs: 18p, Condor 10 Wavepiercer. 23p, Map of Jersey, postbox. 35p, BEA "Vanguard" aircraft. 41p, Aurigny "Short 360" aircraft. 60p, Sealink vessel "Caesarea."

**1994, Oct. 1 Litho. *Perf. 14***

**685** A138 18p multicolored .70 .70
**686** A138 23p multicolored .90 .90
**687** A138 35p multicolored 1.40 1.40
**688** A138 41p multicolored 1.60 1.60
**689** A138 60p multicolored 2.40 2.40
*a.* Souvenir sheet, #685-689 + label 7.25 7.25
*Nos. 685-689 (5)* 7.00 7.00

See Guernsey Nos. 536-540a.

Christmas A139

Christmas carols: 18p, "Away in the manger..." 23p, "Hark! the herald angels sing..." 41p, "While shepherds watched..." 60p, "We three kings of Orient are..."

**1994, Nov. 8**

**690** A139 18p multicolored .70 .70
**691** A139 23p multicolored .90 .90
**692** A139 41p multicolored 1.60 1.60
**693** A139 60p multicolored 2.40 2.40
*Nos. 690-693 (4)* 5.60 5.60

Greetings Stamps — A140

Designs: No. 694, Dog, "Good Luck." No. 695, Rose, "With Love." No. 696, Chick, "Congratulations." No. 697, Bouquet of flowers, "Thank You."

No. 698, Dove, "With love." No. 699, Cat, "Good Luck." No. 700, Carnations, "Thank You." No. 701, Parrot, "Congratulations."

60p, Boar, "Happy New Year."

**1995, Jan. 24 Litho. *Perf. 13½x13***

**694** A140 18p multicolored .70 .70
**695** A140 18p multicolored .70 .70
**696** A140 18p multicolored .70 .70
**697** A140 18p multicolored .70 .70
*a.* Strip of 4, #694-697 3.00 3.00
**698** A140 23p multicolored .90 .90
**699** A140 23p multicolored .90 .90
**700** A140 23p multicolored .90 .90
**701** A140 23p multicolored .90 .90
*a.* Strip of 4, #698-701 3.75 3.75

**Size: 25x64mm**

**702** A140 60p multicolored 2.40 2.40
*a.* Booklet pane, #697a, #701a, #702 10.00
Complete booklet, #702a 10.00
*Nos. 694-702 (9)* 8.80 8.80

New Year 1995 (Year of the Boar) (#702).

Camellias A141

**1995, Mar. 21 Litho. *Perf. 14***

**703** A141 18p Captain Rawes .70 .70
**704** A141 23p Brigadoon .90 .90
**705** A141 30p Elsie Jury 1.25 1.25
**706** A141 35p Augusto L'Gouveia Pinto 1.40 1.40
**707** A141 41p Bella Romana 1.60 1.60
*Nos. 703-707 (5)* 5.85 5.85

International Camellia Society conference, Jersey, Mar. 30-Apr. 4, 1995.

Liberation, by Philip Jackson A142

**1995, May 9 Litho. *Perf. 13½***

**708** A142 23p gray & black .90 .90
**709** A142 30p pink & black 1.25 1.25

Europa.

Liberation, 50th Anniv. A143

#710, Bailiff, Crown Officers taken to HMS Beagle. #711, Red Cross ship SS Vega. #712, Germans surrender on board HMS Beagle. #713, First troops of task force 135, Ordinance Yard, St. Helier. #714, Royal visitors, June 1945. #715, Supplies come ashore from LSTs, Operation Nestegg.

£1, Princess Elizabeth, Queen Elizabeth, Winston Churchill, King George VI, Princess Margaret at Buckingham Palace, VE Day.

**1995, May 9 Litho. *Perf. 14½x14***

**710** A143 18p multicolored .70 .70
**711** A143 18p multicolored .70 .70
*a.* Bklt. pane, 3 each #710-711 4.75
**712** A143 23p multicolored .90 .90
**713** A143 23p multicolored .90 .90
*a.* Bklt. pane, 3 each #712-713 6.25
**714** A143 60p multicolored 2.40 2.40
**715** A143 60p multicolored 2.40 2.40
*a.* Bklt. pane, 3 each #714-715 16.00
*Nos. 710-715 (6)* 8.00 8.00

**Souvenir Sheet**

**716** A143 £1 multicolored 4.00 4.00
*a.* Booklet pane, #716 4.50
Complete booklet, #711a, #713a, #715a, #716a 32.50

No. 716 contains one 81x29mm stamp.

Wild Flowers — A144

**1995, July 4 Litho. *Perf. 13½***

**717** A144 19p Bell heather .75 .75
**718** A144 19p Sea campion .75 .75
**719** A144 19p Spotted rock-rose .75 .75
**720** A144 19p Thrift .75 .75
**721** A144 19p Sheep's-bit scabious .75 .75
*a.* Strip of 5, #717-721 3.75 3.75
**722** A144 23p Field bind-weed .90 .90
**723** A144 23p Common bird's-foot trefoil .90 .90
**724** A144 23p Sea holly .90 .90
**725** A144 23p Common centaury .90 .90
**726** A144 23p Dwarf pansy .90 .90
*a.* Strip of 5, #722-726 4.75 4.75
*Nos. 717-726 (10)* 8.25 8.25

**Butterfly & Moth Type of 1991**

**1995, Sept. 1 Litho. *Perf. 14***

**727** A116 19p Peacock pansy .75 .75
**728** A116 23p Green-barred swallowtail .90 .90
**729** A116 30p Orange emigrant 1.25 1.25
**730** A116 41p Scarlet mormon 1.60 1.60
**731** A116 60p Common birdwing 2.40 2.40
*a.* Souvenir sheet of 2, #730-731 4.00 4.00
*Nos. 727-731 (5)* 6.90 6.90

Singapore '95 (#731a).

Stamps from No. 731a do not have border around the designs or inscriptions at bottom.

Christmas Pantomimes — A145

Childrens' stories: 19p, Puss in Boots. 23p, Cinderella. 41p, Sleeping Beauty. 60p, Aladdin.

**1995, Oct. 24 Litho. *Perf. 13½***

**732** A145 19p multicolored .75 .75
**733** A145 23p multicolored .90 .90
**734** A145 41p multicolored 1.60 1.60
**735** A145 60p multicolored 2.40 2.40
*Nos. 732-735 (4)* 5.65 5.65

UN, 50th Anniv. A146

**1995, Oct. 24 Litho. *Perf. 13x14***

**736** A146 19p Doves, emblem .75 .75
**737** A146 23p Wheat ear, emblem .90 .90
**738** A146 41p As 23p 1.60 1.60
**739** A146 60p As 19p 2.40 2.40
*Nos. 736-739 (4)* 5.65 5.65

UNICEF, 50th Anniv. A147

Children, map areas of UNICEF activities: 19p, Africa. 23p, Globe. 30p, Europe, Balkans. 35p, South America, Caribbean. 41p, South Asia. 60p, Australasia, South Pacific.

**1996, Feb. 19 Litho. *Perf. 14½***

**740** A147 19p multicolored .75 .75
**741** A147 23p multicolored .90 .90
**742** A147 30p multicolored 1.25 1.25
**743** A147 35p multicolored 1.40 1.40
**744** A147 41p multicolored 1.60 1.60
**745** A147 60p multicolored 2.40 2.40
*Nos. 740-745 (6)* 8.30 8.30

**Souvenir Sheet**

New Year 1996 (Year of the Rat) — A148

**1996, Feb. 19 *Perf. 14***

**746** A148 £1 multicolored 4.00 4.00

Queen Elizabeth II, 70th Birthday — A149

**1996, Apr. 21 Litho. *Perf. 14x15***

**747** A149 £5 multicolored 20.00 20.00

Women of Achievement A150

Europa: 23p, Elizabeth Garrett, first British woman physician. 30p, Emmeline Pankhurst (1858-1928), suffragist.

**1996, Apr. 25 *Perf. 14***

**748** A150 23p multicolored .90 .90
**749** A150 30p multicolored 1.25 1.25

1996 European Soccer Chamionships — A151

Various soccer plays.

**1996, Apr. 25**

**750** A151 19p multicolored .75 .75
**751** A151 23p multicolored .90 .90
**752** A151 35p multicolored 1.40 1.40
**753** A151 41p multicolored 1.60 1.60
**754** A151 60p multicolored 2.40 2.40
*Nos. 750-754 (5)* 7.05 7.05

Modern Olympic Games, Cent. A152

**1996, June 8 Litho. *Perf. 14***

**755** A152 19p Rowing .75 .75
**756** A152 23p Judo .90 .90
**757** A152 35p Fencing 1.40 1.40
**758** A152 41p Boxing 1.60 1.60
**759** A152 60p Basketball 2.40 2.40
*Nos. 755-759 (5)* 7.05 7.05

**Souvenir Sheet**

**760** A152 £1 Olympic torch, flame 4.00 4.00

Intl. Amateur Boxing Assoc., 50th anniv. (#758). CAPEX '96 (#760). No. 760 contains one 50x38mm stamp.

Tourism A153

**1996, June 8 Litho. *Perf. 14***

**761** A153 19p North Coast .75 .75
**762** A153 23p Portelet Bay .90 .90
*a.* Bklt. pane, 3 each #761-762 5.75
**763** A153 30p Greve de Lecq Bay 1.25 1.25
**764** A153 35p Beauport Beach 1.25 1.25
*a.* Bklt. pane, 3 each #763-764 8.50
**765** A153 41p Plemont Bay 1.60 1.60
**766** A153 60p St. Brelade's Bay 2.40 2.40
*a.* Bklt. pane, 1 each #761-766 8.75
*b.* Bklt. pane, 3 each #765-766 13.00
Complete booklet, #762a, 764a, 766a, 766b 37.50
*Nos. 761-766 (6)* 8.15 8.15

Horses A154

**1996, Sept. 13 Litho. *Perf. 13½x14***

**767** A154 19p Drag hunt .75 .75
**768** A154 23p Horse driving .90 .90
**769** A154 30p Race training 1.25 1.25
**770** A154 35p Show jumping 1.40 1.40
**771** A154 41p Pony club 1.60 1.60
**772** A154 60p Shire horses 2.40 2.40
*Nos. 767-772 (6)* 8.30 8.30

Christmas A155

19p, Journey to Bethlehem. 23p, Archangel Gabriel visits shepherds. 30p, Nativity. 60p, Magi.

**1996, Nov. 12 *Perf. 13x13½***

**773** A155 19p multicolored .75 .75
**774** A155 23p multicolored .90 .90
**775** A155 30p multicolored 1.25 1.25
**776** A155 60p multicolored 2.40 2.40
*Nos. 773-776 (4)* 5.30 5.30

Souvenir Sheet

New Year 1997 (Year of the Ox) — A156

**1997, Feb. 7 Litho. *Perf. 13½***

**777** A156 £1 multicolored 4.00 4.00
*a.* With added inscription in sheet margin 4.00 4.00

No. 777a inscribed in sheet margin with "JERSEY AT HONG KONG '97" in red and Hong Kong '97 emblem in black.

Birds — A157

**1997, Feb. 12 *Perf. 14½***

**Inscribed "1997"**

**778** A157 1p Red-breasted merganser .25 .25
**779** A157 10p Common tern .40 .40
**780** A157 15p Black-headed gull .60 .60
**781** A157 20p Dunlin .80 .80
**782** A157 24p Puffin .95 .95
**783** A157 37p Oystercatcher 1.50 1.50
**784** A157 75p Redshank 3.00 3.00
**785** A157 £2 Shag 8.00 8.00
*a.* Souv. sheet of 8, #778-785 16.00 16.00
*b.* As "a," with added inscription in sheet margin 16.00 16.00

No. 785b contains PACIFIC '97 World Philatelic Exhibition emblem in sheet margin. Issued: 5/29.

See Nos. 825-832, 864-871, 909-916.

**1998, Apr. 4 Inscribed "1998"**

*781a* A157 20p Dunlin — —
*782a* A157 24p Puffin — —

Lillie the Cow — A158

Designs: No. 786, Building sand castle. No. 787, Taking photographs. No. 788, Lying on beach. No. 789, In restaurant.

**1997, Feb. 12 *Die Cut Perf 9½x9***

**Self-Adhesive**

**Inscribed "1997"**

**786** A158 (23p) multicolored .90 .90
**787** A158 (23p) multicolored .90 .90
**788** A158 (23p) multicolored .90 .90
**789** A158 (23p) multicolored .90 .90
*b.* Strip of 4, #786-789 3.75

Peelable backing is rouletted 9 between stamps.

**1999, Apr. 16 Inscribed "1999 ©"**

*786d* (25p) multi 7.00 7.00
*787d* (25p) multi 7.00 7.00
*788d* (25p) multi 7.00 7.00
*789d* (25p) multi 7.00 7.00
*789e* Strip of 4, #786d-789d 28.00

**2000, Dec. 9 Coil Stamps**

**Inscribed "2000 ©"**

*786f* (26p) Die cut perf. 8¾x9 6.00 6.00
*787f* (26p) Die cut perf. 8¾x9 6.00 6.00
*788f* (26p) Die cut perf. 8¾x9 6.00 6.00
*789f* (26p) Die cut perf. 8¾x9 6.00 6.00
*789g* Strip of 4, #786f-789f 25.00

Nos. 786-789 are inscribed "U.K. MINIMUM POSTAGE PAID."

Jersey Airport, 60th Anniv. A159

**1997, Mar. 10 Litho. *Perf. 13½x14***

**790** A159 20p DH95 Flamingo .80 .80
**791** A159 24p HPR1 Marathon .95 .95
**792** A159 31p DH114 Heron 1.25 1.25
**793** A159 37p Boeing 737-236 1.40 1.40
**794** A159 43p BN Trislander 1.75 1.75
**795** A159 63p BAe 146-200 2.50 2.50
*Nos. 790-795 (6)* 8.65 8.65

Stories and Legends A160

Europa: 20p, Bull of St. Clement. 24p, Black Horse of St. Ouen. 31p, Black Dog of Bouley Bay. 63p, Les Fontaines des Mittes.

**1997, Apr. 15 Litho. *Perf. 14½x14***

**796** A160 20p multicolored .75 .75
**797** A160 24p multicolored .85 .85
**798** A160 31p multicolored 1.10 1.10
**799** A160 63p multicolored 2.10 2.10
*Nos. 796-799 (4)* 4.80 4.80

1997 Jersey Island Games A161

**1997, June 28 Litho. *Perf. 13½x14***

**800** A161 20p Cycling .75 .75
**801** A161 24p Archery .85 .85
*a.* Booklet pane, 3 each #800-801 4.75 —
**802** A161 31p Windsurfing 1.10 1.10
**803** A161 37p Gymnastics 1.40 1.40
*a.* Booklet pane, 3 each #802-803 7.50 —
**804** A161 43p Volleyball 1.60 1.60
**805** A161 63p Running 2.50 2.50
*a.* Booklet pane, 3 each #804-805 12.00 —
*b.* Booklet pane, #800-805 8.25 —
Complete booklet, #801a, 803a, 805a-805b 32.50
*Nos. 800-805 (6)* 8.20 8.20

Jesey Wildlife Preservation Trust A162

Endangered species: 20p, Mallorcan midwife toad. 24p, Aye-aye. 31p, Echo parakeet. 37p, Pigmy hog. 43p, St. Lucia whip-tail. 63p, Madagascar teal.

**1997, Sept. 2 Litho. *Perf. 13***

**806** A162 20p multicolored .80 .80
**807** A162 24p multicolored .95 .95
**808** A162 31p multicolored 1.25 1.25
**809** A162 37p multicolored 1.50 1.50
**810** A162 43p multicolored 1.75 1.75
**811** A162 63p multicolored 2.50 2.50
*Nos. 806-811 (6)* 8.75 8.75

Trees — A163

**1997, Sept. 2 *Perf. 14½***

**812** A163 20p Ash .80 .80
**813** A163 24p Elder .95 .95
**814** A163 31p Beech 1.25 1.25
**815** A163 37p Sweet chestnut 1.50 1.50
**816** A163 43p Hawthorn 1.75 1.75
**817** A163 63p Common oak 2.50 2.50
*Nos. 812-817 (6)* 8.75 8.75

Christmas A164

Santa Claus at various Jersey landmarks: 20p, Jersey Airport. 24p, St. Aubin's Harbor. 31p, Mont Orgueil Castle. 63p, Royal Square, St. Helier.

**1997, Nov. 11 Litho. *Perf. 14***

**818** A164 20p multicolored .80 .80
**819** A164 24p multicolored .95 .95
**820** A164 31p multicolored 1.25 1.25
**821** A164 63p multicolored 2.50 2.50
*Nos. 818-821 (4)* 5.50 5.50

Queen Elizabeth II and Prince Philip, 50th Wedding Anniv. A165

Designs: No. 822, Wedding portrait. No. 823, Anniversary portrait.

£1.50, Full length wedding portrait, vert.

**1997, Nov. 20 Litho. *Perf. 14½***

**822** A165 50p multicolored 2.00 2.00
**823** A165 50p multicolored 2.00 2.00
*a.* Pair, #822-823 4.00 4.00

**Souvenir Sheet**

***Perf. 13½x14***

**824** A165 £1.50 multicolored 4.75 4.75

No. 824 contains one 38x51mm stamp.

**Bird Type of 1997**

**1998, Jan. 28 Litho. *Perf. 14½***

**825** A157 2p Sanderling .25 .25
**826** A157 5p Great crested grebe .25 .25
**827** A157 21p Sandwich tern .80 .80
**828** A157 25p Brent goose 1.00 1.00
**829** A157 30p Fulmar 1.25 1.25
**830** A157 40p Turnstone 1.60 1.60
**831** A157 60p Avocet 2.50 2.50
**832** A157 £1 Razorbill 4.00 4.00
*a.* Souvenir sheet of 8, #825-832 12.00 12.00
*Nos. 825-832 (8)* 11.65 11.65

Souvenir Sheet

New Year 1998 (Year of the Tiger) — A166

**1998, Jan. 28 *Perf. 14***

**833** A166 £1 multicolored 4.00 4.00

Buses A167

Designs: 20p, JMT Bristol 4 Tonner, 1923. 24p, SCS Regent Double Decker, 1934. 31p, Slade's Dennis Lancet, 1936. 37p, Tantivy Leyland PLSC Lion, 1947. 43p, JBS Morris Bus, 1958. 63p, JMT Leyland Titan TD4 Double Decker, 1961.

**1998, Apr. 2 Litho. *Perf. 14***

**834** A167 20p multicolored .80 .80
**835** A167 24p multicolored .95 .95
*a.* Bklt. pane, 3 each #834-835 5.75

**836** A167 31p multicolored 1.25 1.25
**837** A167 37p multicolored 1.50 1.50
*a.* Bklt. pane, 3 each #836-837 8.50
**838** A167 43p multicolored 1.75 1.75
**839** A167 63p multicolored 2.50 2.50
*a.* Bklt. pane, 3 each #838-839 13.50
*b.* Bklt. pane, 1 each, #834-839 9.00
Complete booklet, #835a, 837a, 839a, 839b 37.50
*Nos. 834-839 (6)* 8.75 8.75

National Festivals — A168

Europa: 20p, Creative Arts Festival. 24p, Jazz Festival. 31p, Good Food Festival. 63p, Floral Festival.

**1998, Apr. 2** *Perf. 14x13½*
**840** A168 20p multicolored .80 .80
**841** A168 24p multicolored .95 .95
**842** A168 31p multicolored 1.25 1.25
**843** A168 63p multicolored 2.50 2.50
*Nos. 840-843 (4)* 5.50 5.50

Yachting — A169

Nos. 844-848: Various Hobie Cats sailing in St. Aubin's Bay.
Nos. 849-853: Various yachts racing in annual "Lombard Challenge."

**1998, May 18** **Litho.** *Perf. 13*
**844** A169 20p multicolored .80 .80
**845** A169 20p multicolored .80 .80
**846** A169 20p multicolored .80 .80
**847** A169 20p multicolored .80 .80
**848** A169 20p multicolored .80 .80
*a.* Strip of 5, #844-848 4.25 4.25
**849** A169 24p multicolored .95 .95
**850** A169 24p multicolored .95 .95
**851** A169 24p multicolored .95 .95
**852** A169 24p multicolored .95 .95
**853** A169 24p multicolored .95 .95
*a.* Strip of 5, #849-853 5.00 5.00

"Days Gone By" — A170

Jersey lily and: No. 854, Cider making. No. 855, Potato barrels transported by horse and cart. No. 856, Gathering seaweed for fertilizer. No. 857, Milking Jersey cows by hand.

***Serpentine Die Cut Perf. 11¼***
**1998, Aug. 11** **Litho.**
**Self-Adhesive**
**Inscribed "1998"**
**854** A170 (20p) multicolored 1.10 1.10
**855** A170 (20p) multicolored 1.10 1.10
**856** A170 (20p) multicolored 1.10 1.10
**857** A170 (20p) multicolored 1.10 1.10
*a.* Strip of 4, #854-857 4.50

**Inscribed "1999"**
*854b* (20p) multi 7.50 7.50
*855b* (20p) multi 7.50 7.50
*856b* (20p) multi 7.50 7.50
*857b* (20p) multi 7.50 7.50
*857c* Strip of 4, #854b-857b 30.00

**Inscribed "2000"**
*854d* (20p) multi 6.50 6.50
*855d* (20p) multi 6.50 6.50
*856d* (20p) multi 6.50 6.50
*857d* (20p) multi 6.50 6.50
*857e* Strip of 4, #854d-857d 26.00

**Inscribed "2001"**
*854f* (20p) multi 3.75 3.75
*855f* (20p) multi 3.75 3.75
*856f* (20p) multi 3.75 3.75
*857f* (20p) multi 3.75 3.75
*857g* Strip of 4, #854f-857f 15.00

**Inscribed "2003"**
*854h* (20p) multi 3.75 3.75
*855h* (20p) multi 3.75 3.75
*856h* (20p) multi 3.75 3.75
*857h* (20p) multi 3.75 3.75
*857i* Strip of 4, #854h-857h 15.00

Nos. 854-857h are inscribed "Bailiwick / Minimum Postage Paid."

Marine Life A171

**1998, Aug. 11** **Litho.** *Perf. 15x14½*
**858** A171 20p Bass .80 .80
**859** A171 24p Red gurnard .95 .95
**860** A171 31p Skate 1.25 1.25
**861** A171 37p Mackerel 1.50 1.50
**862** A171 43p Tope 1.75 1.75
**863** A171 63p Cuckoo wrasse 2.50 2.50
*Nos. 858-863 (6)* 8.75 8.75

Intl. Year of the Ocean.

**Bird Type of 1997**

**1998, Aug. 11** *Perf. 14½*
**864** A157 4p Gannet .25 .25
**865** A157 22p Ringed plover .85 .85
**866** A157 26p Grey plover 1.00 1.00
**867** A157 31p Golden plover 1.25 1.25
**868** A157 32p Greenshank 1.25 1.25
**869** A157 35p Curlew 1.40 1.40
**870** A157 44p Herring gull 1.75 1.75
**871** A157 50p Great black-backed gull 2.00 2.00
*a.* Souvenir sheet of 8, #864-871 9.75 9.75
*Nos. 864-871 (8)* 9.75 9.75

Jersey Autumn Flowers A172

**1998, Oct. 23** **Litho.** *Perf. 14½*
**872** A172 20p Iris .80 .80
**873** A172 24p Carnations .95 .95
**874** A172 31p Chrysanthemums 1.25 1.25
**875** A172 37p Pinks 1.50 1.50
**876** A172 43p Roses 1.75 1.75
**877** A172 63p Lilies 2.50 2.50
*Nos. 872-877 (6)* 8.75 8.75

**Souvenir Sheet**
***Perf. 14***
**878** A172 £1.50 Lilium star gazer 6.00 6.00

No. 878 contains one 50x38mm stamp. Italia '98 (#878).

Christmas A173

Island manger (crib), service club sponsor: 20p, Central Market, Jersey Round Table. 24p, St. Thomas' Church, Soroptimist Intl. of Jersey. 31p, Trinity Parish Church, Rotary Club of Jersey. 63p, Royal Square, Lions Club of Jersey.

**1998, Nov. 10** *Perf. 13x13½*
**879** A173 20p multicolored .80 .80
**880** A173 24p multicolored .95 .95
**881** A173 31p multicolored 1.25 1.25
**882** A173 63p multicolored 2.50 2.50
*Nos. 879-882 (4)* 5.50 5.50

Souvenir Sheet

New Year 1999 (Year of the Rabbit) — A174

**1999, Feb. 16** **Litho.** *Perf. 13½*
**883** A174 £1 multicolored 4.00 4.00

UPU, 125th Anniv. A175

Jersey mail transport: 20p, Eastern Railway train. 24p, Mail steamer, "Brighton." 43p, DH 86A, first airmail arrival. 63p, Morris Minor P.O. van.

**1999, Feb. 16** *Perf. 14*
**884** A175 20p multicolored .80 .80
**885** A175 24p multicolored .95 .95
**886** A175 43p multicolored 1.75 1.75
**887** A175 63p multicolored 2.50 2.50
*Nos. 884-887 (4)* 6.00 6.00

Royal Natl. Lifeboat Institution, 175th Anniv. A176

**1999, Feb. 16** *Perf. 14½*
**888** A176 75p Jessica Eliza, St. Catherine 3.00 3.00
**889** A176 £1 Alexander Coutanche, St. Helier 4.00 4.00
*a.* Pair, #888-889 7.00 7.00

Orchids — A177

Designs: 21p, Cymbidium Maufant "Jersey." 25p, Miltonia Millbrook "Jersey." 31p, Paphiopedilum Transvaal. 37p, Paphiopedilum Elizabeth Castle. 43p, Calanthe Five Oaks. 63p, Cymbidium Icho Tower "Trinity."
£1.50, Miltonia Portelet.

***Perf. 14¼x13¼***
**1999, Mar. 19** **Litho.**
**890** A177 21p multicolored .80 .80
**891** A177 25p multicolored 1.00 1.00
**892** A177 31p multicolored 1.25 1.25
**893** A177 37p multicolored 1.50 1.50
**894** A177 43p multicolored 1.75 1.75
**895** A177 63p multicolored 2.50 2.50
*Nos. 890-895 (6)* 8.80 8.80

**Souvenir Sheet**
***Perf. 13½***
**896** A177 £1.50 multicolored 6.00 6.00

Australia '99 World Stamp Expo (#896).

IBRA'99 Intl. Philatelic Exhibition, Nuremberg A178

National Parks: 21p, Howard Davis Park. 25p, Sir Winston Churchill Memorial Park. 31p, Coronation Park. 63p, La Collette Gardens.

**1999, Apr. 27** *Perf. 13x13½*
**897** A178 21p multicolored .80 .80
**898** A178 25p multicolored 1.00 1.00
**899** A178 31p multicolored 1.25 1.25
**900** A178 63p multicolored 2.25 2.25
*Nos. 897-900 (4)* 5.30 5.30

Europa (#898-899).

Wedding of Prince Edward and Sophie Rhys-Jones — A179

**1999, June 19** **Litho.** *Perf. 14½*
**901** A179 35p yellow & multi 1.40 1.40
**902** A179 35p blue & multi 1.40 1.40
*a.* Pair, #901-902 3.00 3.00

**Classic Car Type of 1989**

Designs: 21p, 1899 Jersey-built Benz. 25p, 1910 Star Tourer. 31p, 1938 Citroen "Traction Avant." 37p, 1937 Talbot BG110 Tourer. 43p, 1934 Morris Cowley Six Special Coupé. 63p, 1946 Ford Anglia E04A Saloon.

**1999, July 2** **Litho.** *Perf. 14*
**903** A101 21p multicolored .80 .80
**904** A101 25p multicolored 1.00 1.00
*a.* Bklt. pane, 3 each #903-904 5.75
**905** A101 31p multicolored 1.25 1.25
**906** A101 37p multicolored 1.50 1.50
*a.* Bklt. pane, 3 each #905-906 8.75
**907** A101 43p multicolored 1.75 1.75
**908** A101 63p multicolored 2.50 2.50
*a.* Bklt. pane, 3 each #907-908 13.50
*b.* Booklet pane, #903-908 9.25
Complete booklet, #904a, 906a, 908a, 908b 40.00
*Nos. 903-908 (6)* 8.80 8.80

PhilexFrance '99 (#904a, 906a, 908a-908b).

**Bird Type of 1997**

**1999, Aug. 21** **Litho.** *Perf. 14¾*
**909** A157 23p Bar-tailed godwit .90 .90
**910** A157 27p Common scoter 1.10 1.10
**911** A157 28p Lesser black-backed gull 1.10 1.10
**912** A157 29p Little egret 1.10 1.10
**913** A157 33p Little grebe 1.25 1.25
**914** A157 34p Cormorant 1.25 1.25
**915** A157 45p Rock pipit 1.75 1.75
**916** A157 65p Gray heron 2.50 2.50
*a.* Souvenir sheet of 8, #909-916 11.00 11.00
*Nos. 909-916 (8)* 10.95 10.95

Small Mammals A180

Designs: 21p, Hedgehog. 25p, Red squirrel. 31p, Nathusius pipestrelle. 37p, Jersey bank vole. 43p, Lesser white-toothed shrew. 63p, Common mole.

**1999, Aug. 21** **Litho.** *Perf. 13¼x13*
**917** A180 21p multicolored .80 .80
**918** A180 25p multicolored 1.00 1.00
**919** A180 31p multicolored 1.25 1.25
**920** A180 37p multicolored 1.50 1.50
**921** A180 43p multicolored 1.75 1.75
**922** A180 63p multicolored 2.50 2.50
*Nos. 917-922 (6)* 8.80 8.80

Lighthouses A181

**1999, Oct. 5 Litho. *Perf. 14***

**923** A181 21p Gorey Pierhead .80 .80
**924** A181 25p La Corbiere 1.00 1.00
**925** A181 34p Noirmont Point 1.40 1.40
**926** A181 38p Demie de Pas 1.50 1.50
**927** A181 44p Greve d'Azette 1.75 1.75
**928** A181 64p Sorel Point 2.50 2.50
*Nos. 923-928 (6)* 8.95 8.95

Christmas A182

Poinsettias and: 21p, Mistletoe. 25p, Holly. 34p, Ivy. 64p, Christmas rose.

**1999, Nov. 9 Litho. *Perf. 13¾***

**929** A182 21p multi .80 .80
**930** A182 25p multi 1.00 1.00
**931** A182 34p multi 1.40 1.40
**932** A182 64p multi 2.50 2.50
*Nos. 929-932 (4)* 5.70 5.70

Coat of Arms A183

**Litho. & Embossed with Foil Application**

**2000, Jan. 1 *Perf. 13¼***

**933** A183 £10 gold & multi 40.00 40.00

Millennium.

Souvenir Sheet

New Year 2000 (Year of the Dragon) — A184

**2000, Feb. 5 Litho. *Perf. 13¾***

**934** A184 £1 multi 4.00 4.00

**Europa, 2000**

Common Design Type and

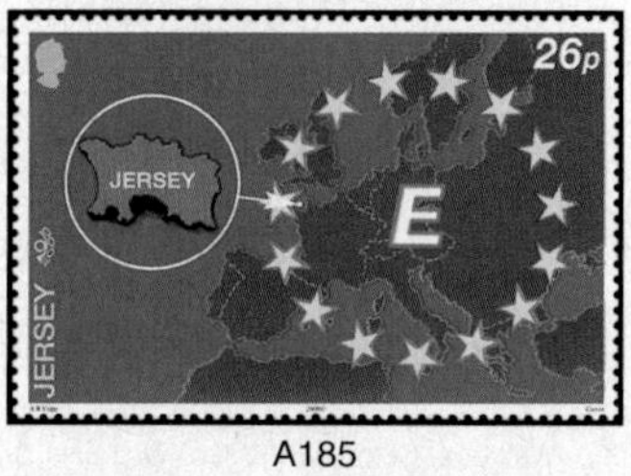


A185

**2000, May 9 *Perf. 13¼x13***

**935** A185 26p multi 1.00 1.00
**936** CD17 34p multi 1.40 1.40

Stampin' the Future — A186

Children's Stamp Design Contest Winners: No. 937, Ocean Adventure, by Gemma Carré. No. 938, Solar Power, by Chantal Varley-Best. No. 939, Floating City and Space Cars, by Nicola Singleton. No. 940, Conservation, by Carly Logan.

**2000, May 9 Litho. *Perf. 14***

**937** A186 22p multi .85 .85
**938** A186 22p multi .85 .85
**939** A186 22p multi .85 .85
**940** A186 22p multi .85 .85
*a.* Souvenir sheet, #937-940 3.50 3.50
*Nos. 937-940 (4)* 3.40 3.40

Ships — A187

#941, Roman merchant ship. #942, Viking long boat. #943, Warship, 13th cent. #944, Merchant ship, 14th-15th cent. #945, Tudor warship, 16th cent.

#946, Warship, 17th cent. #947, Navy cutter, 18th cent. #948, Barque, 19th cent. #949, Oyster cutter, 19th cent. #950, Ketch, 20th cent.

**2000, May 22 *Perf. 13¾***

**941** A187 22p multi .85 .85
**942** A187 22p multi .85 .85
**943** A187 22p multi .85 .85
**944** A187 22p multi .85 .85
**945** A187 22p multi .85 .85
*a.* Strip of 5, #941-945 4.25 4.25
**946** A187 26p multi 1.00 1.00
**947** A187 26p multi 1.00 1.00
**948** A187 26p multi 1.00 1.00
**949** A187 26p multi 1.00 1.00
*a.* Booklet pane, #941-944, 946-949 7.50 7.50
**950** A187 26p multi 1.00 1.00
*a.* Strip of 5, #946-950 5.00 5.00
*b.* Souvenir sheet, #941-950 9.25 9.25
*c.* Booklet pane, #941-942, 944-946, 948-950 7.50
*d.* Booklet pane, #941, 943-947, 949-950 7.50
*e.* Booklet pane, #941-943, 945-948, 950 7.50
*f.* Bklt. pane, #942-945, 947-950 7.50
Booklet, #949a, 950c-950f 37.50
*g.* As "b," with Stamp Show 2000 emblem added in sheet margin 9.25 9.25

Marine Mammals A188

Designs: 22p, Bottle-nosed dolphin. 26p, Long-finned pilot whale. 34p, Harbor porpoise. 38p, Atlantic gray seal. 44p, Risso's dolphin. 64p, White-beaked dolphin.

£1.50, Common dolphin.

**2000, June 5 *Perf. 14¾x14***

**951** A188 22p multi .85 .85
**952** A188 26p multi 1.00 1.00
**953** A188 34p multi 1.25 1.25
**954** A188 38p multi 1.50 1.50
**955** A188 44p multi 1.75 1.75
**956** A188 64p multi 2.50 2.50
*Nos. 951-956 (6)* 8.85 8.85

**Souvenir Sheet**

**957** A188 £1.50 multi 6.00 6.00
*a.* As #957, with World Stamp Expo 2000 emblem in margin 6.00 6.00

No. 957 contains one 81x29mm stamp. Issued: No. 957a, 7/7/00.

Prince William, 18th Birthday A189

William &: #958, Mountain. #959, Polo player. #960, Fireworks. #961, Beaumarais Castle.

**2000, June 21 *Perf. 14¼x14½***

**958** A189 75p multi 3.00 3.00
**959** A189 75p multi 3.00 3.00
**960** A189 75p multi 3.00 3.00
**961** A189 75p multi 3.00 3.00
*Nos. 958-961 (4)* 12.00 12.00

Queen Mother, 100th Birthday A190

**Litho. with Foil Application**

**2000, Aug. 4 *Perf. 14½x14¼***

**962** A190 50p Purple hat 2.00 2.00
**963** A190 50p Pink hat 2.00 2.00
*a.* Souvenir sheet, #962-963 4.00 4.00

Battle of Britain, 60th Anniv. A191

Designs: 22p, Supermarine Spitfire Mk. Ia. 26p, Hawker Hurricane Mk. I. 36p, Bristol Blenheim Mk. IV. 40p, Vickers Wellington Mk. Ic. 45p, Boulton Paul Defiant Mk. I. 65p, Short Sunderland Mk. I.

**2000, Sept. 15 Litho. *Perf. 14¼x14***

**964** A191 22p multi .85 .85
**965** A191 26p multi 1.00 1.00
**966** A191 36p multi 1.40 1.40
**967** A191 40p multi 1.60 1.60
**968** A191 45p multi 1.75 1.75
**969** A191 65p multi 2.50 2.50
*Nos. 964-969 (6)* 9.10 9.10

Christmas A192

**2000, Nov. 7 *Perf. 13***

**970** A192 22p Virgin Mary .85 .85
**971** A192 26p Shepherd 1.00 1.00
**972** A192 36p Angel 1.40 1.40
**973** A192 65p Magus 2.50 2.50
*Nos. 970-973 (4)* 5.75 5.75

Souvenir Sheet

New Year 2001 (Year of the Snake) — A193

**2001, Jan. 24 Litho. *Perf. 13¾***

**974** A193 £1 multi 4.25 4.25

Steamships on Jersey-France Route — A194

**2001, Jan. 24 *Perf. 13x13¼***

**975** A194 22p Rose .85 .85
**976** A194 26p Comete 1.00 1.00
**977** A194 36p Cygne 1.40 1.40
**978** A194 40p Victoria 1.60 1.60
**979** A194 45p Attala 1.75 1.75
**980** A194 65p Brittany 2.50 2.50
*Nos. 975-980 (6)* 9.10 9.10

Agricultural Products — A195

No. 981: a, Jersey cows. b, Royal potatoes. c, Tomatoes. d, Cauliflower and purple broccoli. e, Zucchini and peppers.

***Serpentine Die Cut 11¼***

**2001, Apr. 3 Self-Adhesive**

**Inscribed "2001"**

**981** Strip of 5 14.00
*a.-e.* A195 (26p) Any single 2.75 2.75
*f.* As No. 981, inscribed "2002" 14.00
*g.* As No. 981, inscribed "2003" 14.00
*h.* As No. 981, inscribed "2005" 14.00

Navy Ships Named Jersey A196

Ships in service from: 23p, 1654-91. 26p, 1694-98. 37p, 1698-1731. 41p, 1736-83. 46p, 1860-73. 66p, 1938-41.

**2001, Apr. 3 *Perf. 14***

**982** A196 23p multi .90 .90
**983** A196 26p multi 1.00 1.00
**984** A196 37p multi 1.50 1.50
**985** A196 41p multi 1.60 1.60
**986** A196 46p multi 1.75 1.75
**987** A196 66p multi 2.50 2.50
*Nos. 982-987 (6)* 9.25 9.25

Queen Elizabeth II, 75th Birthday — A197

**2001, Apr. 21 *Perf. 14x14¾***

**988** A197 £3 multi 12.00 12.00

Pond Life
A198

Designs: 23p, Agile frog. 26p, Trout. 37p, White water lily. 41p, Common blue damselfly. 46p, Palmate newt. 66p, Tufted duck.

**2001, May 22** ***Perf. 14¾x14***

| | | | | | |
|---|---|---|---|---|---|
| **989** | A198 | 23p multi | | .90 | .90 |
| **990** | A198 | 26p multi | | 1.00 | 1.00 |
| **991** | A198 | 37p multi | | 1.40 | 1.40 |
| **992** | A198 | 41p multi | | 1.50 | 1.50 |
| **993** | A198 | 46p multi | | 1.60 | 1.60 |
| **994** | A198 | 66p multi | | 2.40 | 2.40 |
| | | *Nos. 989-994 (6)* | | 8.80 | 8.80 |

**Souvenir Sheet**

***Perf. 14¼***

| | | | | |
|---|---|---|---|---|
| **995** | A198 £1.50 Kingfisher | | 6.00 | 6.00 |
| *a.* | As #995, with Belgica 2001 emblem in margin | | 6.50 | 6.50 |

Europa (#990-991). No. 995 contains one 38x50mm stamp.

Issued: No. 995a, 6/9/01.

Birds of Prey — A199

Designs: 23p, Long-eared owl. 26p, Peregrine falcon. 37p, Short-eared owl. 41p, Marsh harrier. 46p, Sparrowhawk. 66p, Tawny owl. £1.50, Barn owl.

**2001, July 3** **Litho.** ***Perf. 13½***

| | | | | |
|---|---|---|---|---|
| **996** | A199 23p multi | | .90 | .90 |
| **997** | A199 26p multi | | 1.00 | 1.00 |
| **998** | A199 37p multi | | 1.50 | 1.50 |
| **999** | A199 41p multi | | 1.60 | 1.60 |
| **1000** | A199 46p multi | | 1.75 | 1.75 |
| *a.* | Booklet pane, #997, 998, 2 each #996, 1000 | | 8.00 | — |
| **1001** | A199 66p multi | | 2.50 | 2.50 |
| *a.* | Booklet pane, #996-1001 | | 9.25 | — |
| *b.* | Booklet pane, 2 each #996, 998, 1001 | | 9.75 | — |
| *c.* | Booklet pane, #996-998, 1001, 2 #999 | | 8.75 | — |
| | *Nos. 996-1001 (6)* | | 9.25 | 9.25 |
| **1002** | A199 £1.50 Booklet pane of 1 | | 17.50 | 12.50 |
| | Booklet, #1000a, 1001a, 1001b, 1001c, 1002 | | 55.00 | |

**Souvenir Sheet**

| | | | | |
|---|---|---|---|---|
| **1003** | A199 £1.50 multi | | 6.00 | 6.00 |
| *a.* | Like #1003, with Hafnia 01 emblem | | 6.00 | 6.00 |

Issued: No. 1003a, 10/16/01.

On No. 1002, "Tyto" is 4mm from the owl's head (owl is in center of stamp), while on No. 1003, it is 9mm from the head (owl is at right of stamp). The size of No. 1002 is 154x100mm, while the size of No. 1003 is 110x75.

Souvenir Sheet

Racing Yacht Jersey Clipper — A200

**2001, Sept. 17** ***Perf. 13¾***

**1004** A200 £1.50 multi 6.00 6.00

Fire Engines
A201

Designs: 23p, Tilley 26 manual, c. 1845. 26p, Albion Merryweather, c. 1935. 37p, Dennis Ace, c. 1940. 41p, Dennis F8 pump escape, c. 1952. 46p, Land Rover Merryweather, c. 1968. 66p, Dennis Carmichael, c. 1989.

**2001, Sept. 25** ***Perf. 13x13¼***

| | | | | |
|---|---|---|---|---|
| **1005** | A201 23p multi | | 1.00 | 1.00 |
| **1006** | A201 26p multi | | 1.25 | 1.25 |
| **1007** | A201 37p multi | | 1.50 | 1.50 |
| **1008** | A201 41p multi | | 1.75 | 1.75 |
| **1009** | A201 46p multi | | 1.90 | 1.90 |
| **1010** | A201 66p multi | | 2.50 | 2.50 |
| | *Nos. 1005-1010 (6)* | | 9.90 | 9.90 |

Christmas
A202

No. 1011: a, Nativity. b, Street decorations. c, Carolers. d, Santa Claus. e, Bells and other ornaments on Christmas tree.

No. 1012: a, Adoration of the Shepherds. b, Carolers, Santa Claus, reindeer. c, Bell ornament, Christmas tree with candles. d, Church bells. e, Cracker with bells on wrapper.

***Serpentine Die Cut 11x11¼***

**2001, Nov. 6** **Self-Adhesive**

**Coil Stamps**

**Inscribed "2001"**

| | | | |
|---|---|---|---|
| **1011** | Horiz. strip of 5 | 4.75 | |
| *a.-e.* | A202 (23p) green & multi, any single | .90 | .90 |
| **1012** | Horiz. strip of 5 | 5.75 | — |
| *a.-e.* | A202 (29p) red & multi, any single | 1.10 | 1.10 |
| *f.* | Booklet pane of 16, 2 each #1011a, 1011c-1011e, 1012a-1012b, 1012d-1012e | 16.00 | |

On Nos. 1011-1012, the matrix was stripped from around the stamps; on the booklets, the matrix remains surrounding the stamps.

**2002, Nov. 23** **Inscribed "2002"**

| | | | |
|---|---|---|---|
| *1011f* | Horiz. strip of 5 | 4.75 | |
| *g.-k.* | A202 (23p) any single | .90 | .90 |
| *1012g* | Horiz. strip of 5 | 5.75 | |
| *h.-l.* | A202 (29p) any single | 1.10 | 1.10 |

**2003, Nov. 10** **Inscribed "2003"**

| | | | |
|---|---|---|---|
| *1011l* | Horiz. strip of 5 | 4.75 | |
| *m.-q.* | A202 (23p) any single | .90 | .90 |

Jersey State Vessels
A203

Designs: 23p, Launch "Duchess of Normandy." 29p, Tugboat "Duke of Normandy." 38p, Customs patrol boat "Challenger." 47p, Pilot boat "Le Fret." 68p, Sea fisheries protection boat "Norman Le Brocq."

**2002, Jan. 22** **Litho.** ***Perf. 13x13¼***

| | | | | |
|---|---|---|---|---|
| **1013** | A203 23p multi | | .90 | .90 |
| **1014** | A203 29p multi | | 1.10 | 1.10 |
| **1015** | A203 38p multi | | 1.50 | 1.50 |
| **1016** | A203 47p multi | | 1.75 | 1.75 |
| **1017** | A203 68p multi | | 2.75 | 2.75 |
| | *Nos. 1013-1017 (5)* | | 8.00 | 8.00 |

Reign of Queen Elizabeth II, 50th Anniv. — A204

**Litho. & Embossed With Foil Application**

**2002, Feb. 6** ***Perf. 13¼***

**1018** A204 £3 multi 12.00 12.00

Souvenir Sheet

New Year 2002 (Year of the Horse) — A205

**2002, Feb. 12** **Litho.** ***Perf. 13¾***

**1019** A205 £1 multi 4.75 4.75

Battle of Flowers Depictions of Circus Figures — A206

**2002, Mar. 12** **Litho.** ***Perf. 13¾***

| | | | | |
|---|---|---|---|---|
| **1020** | A206 23p Elephant, cats | | .90 | .90 |
| **1021** | A206 29p Clown | | 1.10 | 1.10 |
| **1022** | A206 38p Clown, diff. | | 1.50 | 1.50 |
| **1023** | A206 68p Seal | | 2.75 | 2.75 |
| | *Nos. 1020-1023 (4)* | | 6.25 | 6.25 |

Europa (#1021-1022).

La Moye Golf Club, Cent.
A207

Designs: 23p, Aubrey Boomer. 29p, Harry Vardon. 38p, Sir Henry Cotton. 47p, Golfer's swing. 68p, Golfer addressing ball.

**2002, Apr. 16** ***Perf. 14***

| | | | | |
|---|---|---|---|---|
| **1024** | A207 23p multi | | 1.00 | 1.00 |
| **1025** | A207 29p multi | | 1.25 | 1.25 |
| **1026** | A207 38p multi | | 1.50 | 1.50 |
| **1027** | A207 47p multi | | 2.00 | 2.00 |
| **1028** | A207 68p multi | | 3.00 | 3.00 |
| | *Nos. 1024-1028 (5)* | | 8.75 | 8.75 |

Police Vehicles
A208

Designs: 23p, Vauxhall 12, c. 1952. 29p, 1959-60 Jaguar 2.4 MkII. 38p, 1972-73 Austin 1800. 40p, Ford Cortina MkIV, c. 1978. 47p, 1995-2000 Honda motorcycle. 68p, 1998-2000 Vauxhall Vectra.

**2002, May 24** **Litho.** ***Perf. 13x13¼***

| | | | | |
|---|---|---|---|---|
| **1029** | A208 23p multi | | .90 | .90 |
| **1030** | A208 29p multi | | 1.10 | 1.10 |
| **1031** | A208 38p multi | | 1.50 | 1.50 |
| **1032** | A208 40p multi | | 1.60 | 1.60 |
| **1033** | A208 47p multi | | 1.75 | 1.75 |
| **1034** | A208 68p multi | | 2.75 | 2.75 |
| | *Nos. 1029-1034 (6)* | | 9.60 | 9.60 |

Insects
A209

Designs: 23p, Honeybee. 29p, Seven-spot ladybug. 38p, Great green bush cricket. 40p, Greater horntail. 47p, Emperor dragonfly. 68p, Hawthorn shield bug.

**2002, June 18** ***Perf. 14¾x14***

| | | | | |
|---|---|---|---|---|
| **1035** | A209 23p multi | | .90 | .90 |
| **1036** | A209 29p multi | | 1.10 | 1.10 |
| **1037** | A209 38p multi | | 1.50 | 1.50 |
| **1038** | A209 40p multi | | 1.60 | 1.60 |
| **1039** | A209 47p multi | | 1.75 | 1.75 |
| **1040** | A209 68p multi | | 2.75 | 2.75 |
| | *Nos. 1035-1040 (6)* | | 9.60 | 9.60 |

Queen Mother Elizabeth (1900-2002) — A210

**Litho. with Foil Application**

**2002, Aug. 4** ***Perf. 14x14¾***

**1041** A210 £2 multi 8.00 8.00

Battle of Flowers, Cent.
A211

Designs: 23p, Hydrangeas. 29p, Chrysanthemums. 38p, Hare's tails, pampas grass. 40p, Asters. 47p, Carnations. 68p, Gladioli. £2, Float "Zanzibar."

**2002, Aug. 8** **Litho.** ***Perf. 13x13¼***

| | | | | |
|---|---|---|---|---|
| **1042** | A211 23p multi | | .90 | .90 |
| **1043** | A211 29p multi | | 1.10 | 1.10 |
| **1044** | A211 38p multi | | 1.50 | 1.50 |
| **1045** | A211 40p multi | | 1.60 | 1.60 |
| **1046** | A211 47p multi | | 1.75 | 1.75 |
| **1047** | A211 68p multi | | 2.75 | 2.75 |
| *a.* | Booklet pane, #1042-1047 | | 9.75 | |
| | *Nos. 1042-1047 (6)* | | 9.60 | 9.60 |

**Souvenir Sheet**

***Perf. 13***

| | | | | |
|---|---|---|---|---|
| **1048** | A211 £2 multi | | 8.00 | 8.00 |
| *a.* | Booklet pane of 1 | | 8.00 | |
| | Booklet, #1048a, 3 #1047a | | 37.50 | |

No. 1047a has three different layouts of stamps on pane. No. 1048 contains one 76x39mm stamp. No. 1048a is larger than No. 1048, having extra selvage at left, with rouletting separating the selvage from the rest of the sheet.

Cats
A212

Designs: 23p, British dilute tortoiseshell. 29p, Cream Persian. 38p, Blue exotic shorthair. 40p, Black smoke Devon Rex. 47p, British silver tabby. 68p, Usual Abyssinian. £2, British cream and white bi-color, vert.

**2002, Oct. 12** ***Perf. 14¾x14¼***

| | | | | |
|---|---|---|---|---|
| **1049** | A212 23p multi | | .90 | .90 |
| **1050** | A212 29p multi | | 1.10 | 1.10 |
| **1051** | A212 38p multi | | 1.50 | 1.50 |
| **1052** | A212 40p multi | | 1.60 | 1.60 |
| **1053** | A212 47p multi | | 1.75 | 1.75 |
| **1054** | A212 68p multi | | 2.75 | 2.75 |
| | *Nos. 1049-1054 (6)* | | 9.60 | 9.60 |

**Souvenir Sheet**

***Perf. 14¼***

**1055** A212 £2 multi 8.00 8.00

No. 1055 contains one 38x50mm stamp.

Letter Boxes, 150th Anniv. — A213

Designs: 23p, Pillar box, Central Market. 29p, Wall box, Colomberie. 38p, Wall box, St.

Clement's Inner Road. 40p, Ship box. 47p, Pillar box, Parade, 1952. 68p, Pillar box, La Collette, 2000.
£2, First letter box, David Place, 1852.

**2002, Nov. 23** ***Perf. 14½x14¼***

**1056** A213 23p multi .90 .90
**1057** A213 29p multi 1.10 1.10
**1058** A213 38p multi 1.50 1.50
**1059** A213 40p multi 1.60 1.60
**1060** A213 47p multi 1.75 1.75
**1061** A213 68p multi 2.75 2.75
*Nos. 1056-1061 (6)* 9.60 9.60

**Souvenir Sheet**

***Perf. 14¾***

**1062** A213 £2 multi 8.50 8.50

No. 1062 contains one 39x76mm stamp.

Airplanes A214

Designs: 23p, Sanchez-Besa Hydroplane. 29p, Supermarine S.6B. 38p, De Havilland DH84 Dragon. 40p, De Havilland DH89a Rapide. 47p, Vickers 701 Viscount. 68p, BAC One-Eleven.
£2, 1906 Biplane of Jacob Christian Hansen Ellehammer.

**2003, Jan. 21 Litho.** ***Perf. 13x13¼***

**1063** A214 23p multi .90 .90
**1064** A214 29p multi 1.10 1.10
**1065** A214 38p multi 1.50 1.50
**1066** A214 40p multi 1.60 1.60
**1067** A214 47p multi 1.75 1.75
**1068** A214 68p multi 2.75 2.75
*a.* Booklet pane, #1063-1068 9.75 —
*Nos. 1063-1068 (6)* 9.60 9.60

**Souvenir Sheet**

***Perf. 13¼x13***

**1069** A214 £2 multi 8.00 8.00
*a.* Booklet pane, #1069 8.00 —
Complete booklet, #1069a, 3 #1068a 37.50

No. 1069 contains one 60x40mm stamp.
The booklet contains three examples of No. 1068a, each with different margins. No. 1069a has a larger margin than No. 1069, which contains additional text and illustrations. The £2 stamp from the booklet pane No. 1069a has the date under the second "e" of "Ellehammer," while the date on the stamp from the souvenir sheet No. 1069 has the date under the first "m" of "Ellehammer."

Souvenir Sheet

New Year 2003 (Year of the Ram) — A215

**2003, Feb. 1** ***Perf. 13¾***

**1070** A215 £1 multi 4.50 4.50

Poster Art A216

Designs: 23p, Portelet, c. 1935. 29p, Southern British Railways, c. 1952, vert. 38p, Chemins de Fer de l'Ouest, c. 1910, vert. 68p, Jersey, the Sunny Channel Island, c. 1947.

**2003, Mar. 11** ***Perf. 13½***

**1071** A216 23p multi .90 .90
**1072** A216 29p multi 1.10 1.10
**1073** A216 38p multi 1.50 1.50
**1074** A216 68p multi 2.75 2.75
*Nos. 1071-1074 (4)* 6.25 6.25

Europa (29p, 38p).

Lighthouses and Buoys — A217

No. 1075: a, St. Catherine's Breakwater Light. b, Violet Channel Buoy.
No. 1076: a, Mont Ubé Lighthouse. b, Frouquie Aubert Buoy.
No. 1077: a, Gronez Point Lighthouse. b, Banc des Ormes Buoy.

**2003, Apr. 15** ***Perf. 13¾***

**1075** A217 Horiz. pair 2.25 2.25
*a.-b.* 29p Either single 1.10 1.10
**1076** A217 Horiz. pair 2.50 2.50
*a.-b.* 30p Either single 1.25 1.25
**1077** A217 Horiz. pair 4.00 4.00
*a.-b.* 48p Either single 1.90 1.90
*Nos. 1075-1077 (3)* 8.75 8.75

Wild Orchids — A218

Designs: 29p, Southern-marsh orchid. 30p, Loose-flowered orchid. 39p, Spotted orchid. 50p, Autumn Ladies Tresses. 53p, Green-winged orchid. 69p, Pyramidal orchid.
£2, Loose-flowered orchid, diff.

**2003, May 13** ***Perf. 13¼x13***

**1078** A218 29p multi 1.10 1.10
**1079** A218 30p multi 1.25 1.25
**1080** A218 39p multi 1.60 1.60
**1081** A218 50p multi 2.00 2.00
**1082** A218 53p multi 2.25 2.25
**1083** A218 69p multi 2.75 2.75
*Nos. 1078-1083 (6)* 10.95 10.95

**Souvenir Sheet**

**1084** A218 £2 multi 8.00 8.00
*a.* As #1084, with added marginal inscription 8.25 8.25

No. 1084a has Bangkok 2003 Philatelic Exhibition emblem and text, "Jersey at Bangkok 2003," added in margin. Issued, 10/4.

Coronation of Queen Elizabeth II, 50th Anniv. A219

Designs: 29p, Sovereign's orb. 30p, St. Edward's Crown. 39p, Scepter with Cross. 50p, Ampulla and Spoon. 53p, Sovereign's Ring. 69p, Armills.

**Litho. With Foil Application**

**2003, June 2** ***Perf. 14¾x14***

**1085** A219 29p multi 1.10 1.10
**1086** A219 30p multi 1.25 1.25
**1087** A219 39p multi 1.60 1.60
**1088** A219 50p multi 2.00 2.00
**1089** A219 53p multi 2.10 2.10
**1090** A219 69p multi 2.75 2.75
*a.* Souvenir sheet, #1085-1090 11.00 11.00
*Nos. 1085-1090 (6)* 10.80 10.80

Souvenir Sheet

Prince William, Prince Charles and Queen Elizabeth II — A220

**2003, June 21 Litho.** ***Perf. 13¾***

**1091** A220 £2 multi 8.00 8.00

Prince William, 21st birthday.

Offshore Reefs and Flowers — A221

No. 1092: a, Les Ecrehous Reef, tree mallow. b, Les Minquiers Reef, smooth sow-thistle. c, Les Minquiers Reef, thrift. d, Paternosters Reef, rock samphire. e, Les Ecrehous Reef, bluebells.
No. 1092g, Like No. 1092a. No. 1092h, Like No. 1092b. No. 1092i, Like No. 1092c. No. 1092j, Like No. 1092d. No. 1092k, Like No. 1092e.

***Serpentine Die Cut 11***

**2003, Aug. 5 Photo. Coil Stamps**

**Self-Adhesive**

**1092** Horiz. strip of 5 5.50 5.50
*a.-e.* A221 (29p) Any single 1.10 1.10
*f.* Like #1092, serp. die cut 11¼, inscribed "2004" 7.00
*g.-k.* A221 (32p) Any single, serp. die cut 11¼ 1.40 1.40
*l.* Like #1092, serp. die cut 11¼, inscribed "2006" 7.00
*m.-q.* A221 (32p) Any single, serp. die cut 11¼, inscribed "2006" 1.40 1.40

Nos. 1092f-1092k issued 11/3/04. Nos. 1092l-1092q issued 11/16/06.

Pets — A222

Designs: 29p, Albino Rex rabbit. 30p, Labrador retriever. 38p, Canary and budgerigar. 53p, Hamster. 69p, Guinea pig.
£2, Border collie.

**2003, Sept. 9 Litho.** ***Perf. 13¾***

**1093** A222 29p multi 1.10 1.10
**1094** A222 30p multi 1.25 1.25
**1095** A222 38p multi 1.50 1.50
**1096** A222 53p multi 2.10 2.10
**1097** A222 69p multi 2.75 2.75
*Nos. 1093-1097 (5)* 8.70 8.70

**Souvenir Sheet**

***Perf. 13¼***

**1098** A222 £2 multi 8.00 8.00

No. 1098 contains one 39x51mm stamp.

Winter Flowers A223

Designs: 29p, Japanese quince. 30p, Winter jasmine. 39p, Snowdrop. 48p, Winter heath. 53p, Chinese witch hazel. 69p, Winter daphne.

**2003, Nov. 10** ***Perf. 14¼***

**1099** A223 29p multi 1.10 1.10
**1100** A223 30p multi 1.25 1.25
**1101** A223 39p multi 1.60 1.60
**1102** A223 48p multi 1.90 1.90
**1103** A223 53p multi 2.10 2.10
**1104** A223 69p multi 2.75 2.75
*Nos. 1099-1104 (6)* 10.70 10.70

Souvenir Sheet

New Year 2004 (Year of the Monkey) — A224

**2004, Jan. 22 Litho.** ***Perf. 13¾***

**1105** A224 £1 multi 4.75 4.75

British Chess Federation, Cent. — A225

**2004, Jan. 22**

**1106** A225 29p Rook 1.10 1.10
**1107** A225 30p Knight 1.25 1.25
**1108** A225 39p Bishop 1.75 1.75
**1109** A225 48p Pawn 2.00 2.00
**1110** A225 53p Queen 2.25 2.25
**1111** A225 69p King 2.75 2.75
*Nos. 1106-1111 (6)* 11.10 11.10

Tourist Attractions A226

Designs: 29p, St. Aubin's Harbor. 30p, Mont Orgueil Castle. 39p, Corbiere Lighthouse. 69p, Rozel Harbor.

**2004, Mar. 9** ***Perf. 13x13¼***

**1112** A226 29p multi 1.10 1.10
**1113** A226 30p multi 1.25 1.25
**1114** A226 39p multi 1.60 1.60
**1115** A226 69p multi 2.75 2.75
*Nos. 1112-1115 (4)* 6.70 6.70

Europa (#1113, 1114).

Waterfowl A227

Designs: 32p, Eurasian teal. 33p, Mute swan. 40p, Northern shoveler. 49p, Common pochard. 62p, Black swan. 70p, Eurasian wigeon.
£2, Mallard, vert.

**2004, Apr. 6** ***Perf. 14¾x14***

**1116** A227 32p multi 1.25 1.25
**1117** A227 33p multi 1.25 1.25
**1118** A227 40p multi 1.60 1.60
**1119** A227 49p multi 2.00 2.00
**1120** A227 62p multi 2.50 2.50
**1121** A227 70p multi 2.75 2.75
*Nos. 1116-1121 (6)* 11.35 11.35

**Souvenir Sheet**

***Perf. 14¼***

**1122** A227 £2 multi 8.00 8.00

No. 1122 contains one 38x50mm stamp.

Orchids A228

Designs: 32p, Cymbidium lowianum "Concolor." 33p, Phragmipedium besseae var. flavum. 40p, Peristeria elata. 54p, Cymbidium tracyanum. 62p, Paphiopedilum "Victoria Village Isle of Jersey." 70p, Paphiopedilum hirsutissimum.
£2, Phragmipedium "Jason Fischer."

**2004, May 25** *Perf. 13x13¼*

**1123** A228 32p multi 1.25 1.25
**1124** A228 33p multi 1.25 1.25
**1125** A228 40p multi 1.60 1.60
**1126** A228 54p multi 2.10 2.10
**1127** A228 62p multi 2.50 2.50
**1128** A228 70p multi 2.75 2.75
*a.* Booklet pane, #1123-1128 11.50 —
*Nos. 1123-1128 (6)* 11.45 11.45

**Souvenir Sheet**

**1129** A228 £2 multi 8.00 8.00
*a.* Booklet pane #1129 8.00 —
Complete booklet, #1129a, 3 #1128a 42.50
*b.* Like #1129, with added marginal inscription 8.25 8.25

The booklet contains three examples of No. 1128a each with different arrangements of the stamps. No. 1129a has a larger margin than No. 1129.

No. 1129b issued 6/26. It is inscribed "Jersey at / Le Salon du Timbre 2004" in margin.

Souvenir Sheet

D-Day, 60th Anniv. — A229

**2004, June 4** *Perf. 13*

**1130** A229 £2 multi 8.00 8.00

Mont Orgueil Castle and Monarchs — A230

No. 1131: a, Castle in 13th century (49x32mm). b, King John, vert. (29x32mm).

No. 1132: a, Castle in 17th century (49x32mm). b, King Charles II, vert. (29x32mm).

No. 1133: a, Castle in 21st century (49x32mm). b, Queen Elizabeth II, vert. (29x32mm).

**2004, June 25** *Perf. 14¾*

**1131** A230 Horiz. pair 2.50 2.50
*a.-b.* 32p Either single 1.25 1.25
**1132** A230 Horiz. pair 2.50 2.50
*a.-b.* 33p Either single 1.25 1.25
**1133** A230 Horiz. pair 3.25 3.25
*a.-b.* 40p Either single 1.60 1.60
*Nos. 1131-1133 (3)* 8.25 8.25

Worldwide Fund for Nature (WWF) A231

Designs: 32p, Wall lizard. 33p, Ant lion. 49p, Field cricket. 70p, Dartford warbler.

**2004, July 27** *Perf. 14¾x14*

**1134** A231 32p multi 1.25 1.25
**1135** A231 33p multi 1.25 1.25
**1136** A231 49p multi 2.00 2.00
**1137** A231 70p multi 2.75 2.75
*a.* Miniature sheet, 2 each #1134-1137 14.50 14.50
*Nos. 1134-1137 (4)* 7.25 7.25

Corals A232

Designs: 32p, Dead man's fingers. 33p, Devonshire cup. 40p, White sea fan. 54p, Pink sea fan. 62p, Sunset cup. 70p, Red fingers.

**2004, Sept. 28 Litho.** *Perf. 13x13¼*

**1138** A232 32p multi 1.25 1.25
**1139** A232 33p multi 1.25 1.25
**1140** A232 40p multi 1.60 1.60
**1141** A232 54p multi 2.10 2.10
**1142** A232 62p multi 2.50 2.50
**1143** A232 70p multi 2.75 2.75
*a.* Souvenir sheet, #1141-1143 7.50 7.50
*Nos. 1138-1143 (6)* 11.45 11.45

Christmas A233

No. 1144: a, Nativity. b, Street with Christmas decorations. c, Santa Claus, children, Christmas tree. d, Church interior. e, Candles and holly. Each inscribed "Jersey Minimum Postage Paid."

No. 1145: a, Madonna and Child, lilies. b, Christmas stocking on mantle. c, Candles and flowers. d, Angel and candle. e, Candles in window. Each inscribed "U.K. Minimum Postage Paid."

***Serpentine Die Cut 11¼x11½***

**2004, Nov. 2 Litho. Self-Adhesive**

**Coil Stamps**

**1144** Horiz. strip of 5 6.00
*a.-e.* A233 (32p) Any single 1.25 1.25
*f.* Like #1144, inscribed "2005" 6.00
*g.-k.* A233 (32p) Any single 1.25 1.25
*l.* Like #1144, inscribed "2006" 6.00
*m.-q.* A233 (32p) Any single 1.25 1.25
**1145** Horiz. strip of 5 6.25
*a.-e.* A233 (33p) Any single 1.25 1.25
*f.* Like #1145, inscribed "2005" 6.25
*g.-k.* A233 (33p) Any single 1.25 1.25
*l.* Like #1145, inscribed "2006" 6.25
*m.-q.* A233 (33p) Any single 1.25 1.25

Nos. 1144f-1144k, 1145f-1145k issued 10/21/05. Nos. 1144l-1144q, 1145l-1145q issued 10/31/06.

Rescue Craft A234

Designs: 32p, Channel Islands Air Search airplane. 33p, Burby helicopter. 40p, Beach Lifeguard Service Surf Rescue boat. 49p, Fire Rescue inflatable boat. 70p, Royal Air Force Sea King helicopter.

**2005, Jan. 18 Litho.** *Perf. 13x13¼*

**1146** A234 32p multi 1.25 1.25
**1147** A234 33p multi 1.25 1.25
**1148** A234 40p multi 1.60 1.60
**1149** A234 49p multi 2.00 2.00
**1150** A234 70p multi 2.75 2.75
*Nos. 1146-1150 (5)* 8.85 8.85

Souvenir Sheet

New Year 2005 (Year of the Rooster) — A235

**2005, Feb. 9** *Perf. 14¼*

**1151** A235 £1 multi 5.00 5.00

Gastronomy A236

Designs: 32p, Conger eel soup. 33p, Oysters. 40p, Bean crock. 70p, Bourdélots with black butter.

**2005, Mar. 8 Litho.** *Perf. 13¾*

**1152** A236 32p multi 1.25 1.25
**1153** A236 33p multi 1.50 1.50
**1154** A236 40p multi 1.75 1.75
**1155** A236 70p multi 2.75 2.75
*Nos. 1152-1155 (4)* 7.25 7.25

Europa (33p, 40p).

Fairy Tales A237

Designs: 33p, Little Red Riding Hood. 34p, The Little Mermaid. 41p, Beauty and the Beast. 50p, Rumpelstiltskin. 73p, The Goose That Laid the Golden Egg.
£2, The Ugly Duckling.

**2005, Apr. 2** *Perf. 13x13¼*

**1156** A237 33p multi 1.25 1.25
**1157** A237 34p multi 1.40 1.40
**1158** A237 41p multi 1.60 1.60
**1159** A237 50p multi 2.00 2.00
**1160** A237 73p multi 3.00 3.00
*Nos. 1156-1160 (5)* 9.25 9.25

**Souvenir Sheet**

***Perf. 13¼***

**1161** A237 £2 multi 8.00 8.00
*a.* As No. 1161, with Nordia 2005 emblem in sheet margin 7.75 7.75

No. 1161 contains one 49x35mm stamp, and has a hologram applied in the sheet margin. Hans Christian Andersen, birth bicentennial.

No. 1161a issued 5/26.

Souvenir Sheet

Jersey Soccer Association and Muratti Vase Soccer Competition, Cent. — A238

**2005, Apr. 27** *Perf.*

**1162** A238 £2 multi 8.00 8.00

Souvenir Sheet

End of World War II, 60th Anniv. — A239

**2005, May 9 Litho.** *Perf. 14¼*

**1163** A239 £2 multi 8.00 8.00

Jersey Motor Festival A240

Automobiles: 33p, MGB GT. 34p, Mini Cooper. 41p, Citroen DS. 50p, Jaguar E Type. 56p, Volkswagen Beetle. 73p, Aston Martin DB5.

**2005, June 6** *Perf. 13x13¼*

**1164** A240 33p multi 1.25 1.25
**1165** A240 34p multi 1.40 1.40
**1166** A240 41p multi 1.60 1.60
**1167** A240 50p multi 2.00 2.00
**1168** A240 56p multi 2.25 2.25
**1169** A240 73p multi 3.00 3.00
*a.* Booklet pane, #1164-1169 11.50 —
Complete booklet, 3 #1169a 35.00
*Nos. 1164-1169 (6)* 11.50 11.50

Complete booklet contains three examples of No. 1169a, each with a different margin and layout of the stamps.

Flowers — A241

Designs: 2p, Scarlet pimpernel. 4p, Common knapweed. 20p, Greater stitchwort. 30p, Common mallow. 40p, White campion. 50p, Common dog-violet. 65p, Herb Robert. £1, Three-cornered garlic.

**2005, July 19** *Perf. 13¼*

**1170** A241 2p multi .25 .25
**1171** A241 4p multi .25 .25
**1172** A241 20p multi .80 .80
**1173** A241 30p multi 1.25 1.25
**1174** A241 40p multi 1.60 1.60
**1175** A241 50p multi 2.00 2.00
**1176** A241 65p multi 2.50 2.50
**1177** A241 £1 multi 4.00 4.00
*a.* Souvenir sheet, #1170-1177 12.50 12.50
*Nos. 1170-1177 (8)* 12.65 12.65

See Nos. 1228-1235a, 1267-1274a.

Martello Towers — A242

**2005, Aug. 9** *Perf. 13¾*

**1178** A242 33p Le Hocq 1.25 1.25
**1179** A242 34p Seymour 1.40 1.40
**1180** A242 41p Archirondel 1.60 1.60
**1181** A242 56p Kempt 2.25 2.25
**1182** A242 73p Le Rocco 3.00 3.00
*Nos. 1178-1182 (5)* 9.50 9.50

Mushrooms A243

Designs: 33p, Pink waxcap. 34p, Boletus erythropus. 41p, Inocybe godeyi. 50p, Pepper-pot earthstar. 56p, White elfin saddle. 73p, Red waxy cap.

£2, Fairy ring mushrooms, horiz.

**2005, Sept. 13** ***Perf. 13¾***

| | | | | |
|---|---|---|---|---|
| **1183** | A243 33p multi | | 1.25 | 1.25 |
| **1184** | A243 34p multi | | 1.40 | 1.40 |
| **1185** | A243 41p multi | | 1.60 | 1.60 |
| **1186** | A243 50p multi | | 2.00 | 2.00 |
| **1187** | A243 56p multi | | 2.25 | 2.25 |
| **1188** | A243 73p multi | | 3.00 | 3.00 |
| | *Nos. 1183-1188 (6)* | | 11.50 | 11.50 |

**Souvenir Sheet**

***Perf. 14¼***

| | | | |
|---|---|---|---|
| **1189** | A243 £2 multi | 8.00 | 8.00 |

No. 1189 contains one 50x38mm stamp.

Battle of Trafalgar, Bicent. A244

Designs: 33p, HMS Belleisle. 34p, HMS Royal Sovereign. 41p, HMS Neptune. 50p, HMS Euryalus. 73p, HMS Mars.

£2, HMS Victory.

**2005, Oct. 21** ***Perf. 14***

| | | | |
|---|---|---|---|
| **1190** | A244 33p multi | 1.25 | 1.25 |
| **1191** | A244 34p multi | 1.40 | 1.40 |
| **1192** | A244 41p multi | 1.60 | 1.60 |
| **1193** | A244 50p multi | 2.00 | 2.00 |
| **1194** | A244 73p multi | 3.00 | 3.00 |
| | *Nos. 1190-1194 (5)* | 9.25 | 9.25 |

**Souvenir Sheet**

***Perf. 14¼***

| | | | |
|---|---|---|---|
| **1195** | A244 £2 multi | 8.00 | 8.00 |

No. 1195 contains one 50x38mm stamp.

Royal Jersey Militia Uniforms and Badges A245

Uniforms and badges from: 33p, Royal Jersey Regiment, ca. 1830. 34p, Royal Jersey Regiment, ca. 1844. 41p, Royal Jersey Artillery, ca. 1881. 50p, Royal Jersey Light Infantry ca. 1890. 73p, Royal Engineers, present day.

**2006, Jan. 6** **Litho.** ***Perf. 13¼***

| | | | |
|---|---|---|---|
| **1196** | A245 33p multi | 1.25 | 1.25 |
| **1197** | A245 34p multi | 1.40 | 1.40 |
| **1198** | A245 41p multi | 1.60 | 1.60 |
| **1199** | A245 50p multi | 2.00 | 2.00 |
| **1200** | A245 73p multi | 3.00 | 3.00 |
| | *Nos. 1196-1200 (5)* | 9.25 | 9.25 |

Souvenir Sheet

New Year 2006 (Year of the Dog) — A246

**2006, Jan. 29** **Litho.** ***Perf. 14¼***

| | | | |
|---|---|---|---|
| **1201** | A246 £1 multi | 5.00 | 5.00 |

Souvenir Sheet

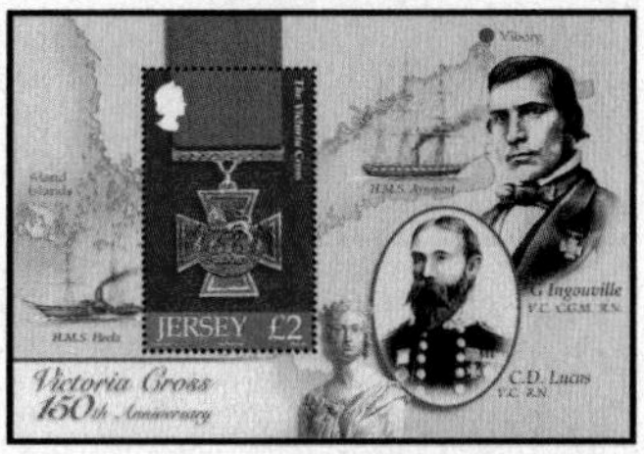


Victoria Cross, 150th Anniv. — A247

**2006, Jan. 29** ***Perf. 13¼x14***

| | | | |
|---|---|---|---|
| **1202** | A247 £2 multi | 9.00 | 9.00 |

Multiculturalism — A248

Designs: 33p, Chinese costumes. 34p, Portuguese Fado Music Festival. 41p, Polish Pisanki Easter egg tradition. 73p, Indian costumes.

**2006, Mar. 7** ***Perf. 14***

| | | | |
|---|---|---|---|
| **1203** | A248 33p multi | 1.25 | 1.25 |
| **1204** | A248 34p multi | 1.40 | 1.40 |
| **1205** | A248 41p multi | 1.60 | 1.60 |
| **1206** | A248 73p multi | 3.00 | 3.00 |
| | *Nos. 1203-1206 (4)* | 7.25 | 7.25 |

Europa (34p, 41p).

Shells A249

Designs: 34p, Flat periwinkle. 37p, Painted top shell. 42p, Dog cockle. 51p, Variegated scallop. 57p, Blue-rayed limpet. 74p, European cowrie.

£2, Ormer shell.

**2006, Apr. 4** **Litho.** ***Perf. 13x13¼***

| | | | |
|---|---|---|---|
| **1207** | A249 34p multi | 1.40 | 1.40 |
| **1208** | A249 37p multi | 1.50 | 1.50 |
| **1209** | A249 42p multi | 1.60 | 1.60 |
| **1210** | A249 51p multi | 2.00 | 2.00 |
| **1211** | A249 57p multi | 2.25 | 2.25 |
| **1212** | A249 74p multi | 3.00 | 3.00 |
| | *Nos. 1207-1212 (6)* | 11.75 | 11.75 |

**Souvenir Sheet**

**Litho. & Embossed With Hologram Affixed**

***Perf.***

| | | | |
|---|---|---|---|
| **1213** | A249 £2 multi | 8.00 | 8.00 |
| *a.* | Like #1213, with Belgica '06 emblem added in sheet margin | 9.00 | 9.00 |

Portions of the designs of Nos. 1207-1212 were applied by a thermographic process producing a shiny, raised effect. No. 1213 contains one 46x30 oval stamp.

Issued: No. 1213a, 11/16.

Wedding of Prince Charles and Camilla Parker-Bowles, 1st Anniv. — A250

**2006, Apr. 9** **Litho.** ***Perf. 13¼***

| | | | |
|---|---|---|---|
| **1214** | A250 £2 multi | 8.00 | 8.00 |

Queen Elizabeth II, 80th Birthday A251

**Litho. & Embossed With Foil Application**

**2006, Apr. 21** ***Perf. 13½***

| | | | |
|---|---|---|---|
| **1215** | A251 £5 dk bl & multi | 20.00 | 20.00 |
| *a.* | Prussian blue & multi | 20.00 | 20.00 |
| *b.* | Souvenir sheet, #1215a, New Zealand #2068a | 27.50 | 27.50 |

See New Zealand No. 2068. No. 1215b sold for £7.

Souvenir Sheet

2006 World Cup Soccer Championships, Germany — A252

**2006, June 9** **Litho.** ***Perf. 14¼***

| | | | |
|---|---|---|---|
| **1216** | A252 £2 multi | 9.00 | 9.00 |

Island Views — A253

***Serpentine Die Cut 11¼***

**2006, July 11** **Self-Adhesive**

**Coil Stamps**

**Inscribed "2006"**

| | | | |
|---|---|---|---|
| **1217** | A253 (37p) Greve de Lecq | 1.75 | 1.75 |
| *a.* | Inscribed "2009" | 1.75 | 1.75 |
| **1218** | A253 (37p) La Rocque | 1.75 | 1.75 |
| *a.* | Inscribed "2009" | 1.75 | 1.75 |
| **1219** | A253 (37p) Portelet | 1.75 | 1.75 |
| *a.* | Inscribed "2009" | 1.75 | 1.75 |
| **1220** | A253 (37p) St. Brelade's Bay | 1.75 | 1.75 |
| *a.* | Inscribed "2009" | 1.75 | 1.75 |
| *b.* | Horiz. strip of 4, #1217-1220 | 7.50 | |
| *c.* | Horiz. strip of 4, #1217a-1220a | 7.50 | |

Butterflies & Moths A254

Designs: 34p, Red underwing moth. 37p, Comma buttterfly. 42p, Black arches moth. 51p, Small copper butterfly. 57p, Holly blue butterfly. 74p, Orange-tip butterfly.

**2006, Aug. 1** ***Perf. 14¾x14***

**Stamps With White Margin**

| | | | |
|---|---|---|---|
| **1221** | A254 34p multi | 1.50 | 1.50 |
| **1222** | A254 37p multi | 1.60 | 1.60 |
| **1223** | A254 42p multi | 1.75 | 1.75 |
| **1224** | A254 51p multi | 2.25 | 2.25 |
| **1225** | A254 57p multi | 2.50 | 2.50 |
| **1226** | A254 74p multi | 3.25 | 3.25 |
| | *Nos. 1221-1226 (6)* | 12.85 | 12.85 |

**Souvenir Sheet**

**Stamps Without White Margin**

| | | | |
|---|---|---|---|
| **1227** | Sheet of 3 | 8.50 | 8.50 |
| *a.* | A254 51p multi | 2.25 | 2.25 |
| *b.* | A254 57p multi | 2.50 | 2.50 |
| *c.* | A254 74p multi | 3.25 | 3.00 |

**Flowers Type of 2005**

Designs: 1p, Yellow bartsia. 3p, Wild angelica. 5p, Marsh St. John's wort. 15p, Bog pimpernel. 70p, Ragged robin. 75p, Brooklime. 85p, Cuckoo flower. 90p, Yellow iris.

**2006, Sept. 26** **Litho.** ***Perf. 13¼***

| | | | |
|---|---|---|---|
| **1228** | A241 1p multi | .25 | .25 |
| **1229** | A241 3p multi | .25 | .25 |
| **1230** | A241 5p multi | .25 | .25 |
| **1231** | A241 15p multi | .75 | .75 |
| **1232** | A241 70p multi | 3.00 | 3.00 |
| **1233** | A241 75p multi | 3.25 | 3.25 |
| **1234** | A241 85p multi | 3.75 | 3.75 |
| **1235** | A241 90p multi | 4.00 | 4.00 |
| *a.* | Souvenir sheet, #1228-1235 | 15.00 | 15.00 |
| | *Nos. 1228-1235 (8)* | 15.50 | 15.50 |

Jersey Post Vehicles A255

Designs: 34p, 2004 LDV Luton Van. 37p, 1999-2004 Renault Kangaroo. 42p, 1994-2004 LDV Pilot. 51p, 1988-96 Ford Transit Luton Body. 57p, Morris Marina 440/575, c. 1978. 74p, Morris Minor, c. 1969.

**2006, Oct. 31** ***Perf. 13x13¼***

| | | | |
|---|---|---|---|
| **1236** | A255 34p multi | 1.40 | 1.40 |
| **1237** | A255 37p multi | 1.50 | 1.50 |
| **1238** | A255 42p multi | 1.60 | 1.60 |
| **1239** | A255 51p multi | 2.00 | 2.00 |
| **1240** | A255 57p multi | 2.25 | 2.25 |
| **1241** | A255 74p multi | 3.00 | 3.00 |
| *a.* | Booklet pane, #1236-1241 | 12.00 | — |
| *b.* | Booklet pane, #1239-1241 + binding stub | 7.50 | — |
| | Complete booklet, #1241b, 3 #1241a | 45.00 | |
| *c.* | Souvenir sheet, #1239-1241 | 7.50 | 7.50 |

No. 1241a has three different layouts of stamps on pane and three different margins. No. 1241c has a straight edge at left, while No. 1241b is separated from binding stub by a row of rouletting.

Minerals A256

Designs: 34p, Molybdenite. 37p, Muscovite in pegmatite vein, feldspar and quartz. 42p, Orthoclase and plagioclase. 51p, Quartz coated with manganese oxide. 74p, Smoky quartz.

**2007, Jan. 23** **Litho.** ***Perf. 13x13¼***

| | | | |
|---|---|---|---|
| **1242** | A256 34p multi | 1.50 | 1.50 |
| **1243** | A256 37p multi | 1.75 | 1.75 |
| **1244** | A256 42p multi | 1.75 | 1.75 |
| **1245** | A256 51p multi | 2.25 | 2.25 |
| **1246** | A256 74p multi | 3.25 | 3.25 |
| | *Nos. 1242-1246 (5)* | 10.50 | 10.50 |

Souvenir Sheet

New Year 2007 (Year of the Pig) — A257

**2007, Feb. 18** ***Perf. 14¼***

| | | | |
|---|---|---|---|
| **1247** | A257 £1 multi | 5.00 | 5.00 |

Scouting, Cent. A258

Lord Robert Baden-Powell and Scouts: 34p, With kayak, sailboard and kite-propelled vehicle. 37p, With musical instruments and flags. 42p, In go-carts and wagons, scouts climbing. 74p, With uniform patches.

**2007, Mar. 6** ***Perf. 14***

| | | | | |
|---|---|---|---|---|
| **1248** | A258 | 34p multi | 1.40 | 1.40 |
| **1249** | A258 | 37p multi | 1.50 | 1.50 |
| **1250** | A258 | 42p multi | 1.60 | 1.60 |
| **1251** | A258 | 74p multi | 3.00 | 3.00 |
| | | *Nos. 1248-1251 (4)* | 7.50 | 7.50 |

Europa (37p, 42p).

Mammals A259

Designs: 34p, Long-tailed field mouse. 37p, Rabbits. 42p, Polecat. 51p, Common shrew. 57p, Stoat. 74p, Brown rat.

**2007, Apr. 10** ***Perf. 14¾x14***

**Stamps With White Frames**

| | | | | |
|---|---|---|---|---|
| **1252** | A259 | 34p multi | 1.50 | 1.50 |
| **1253** | A259 | 37p multi | 1.75 | 1.75 |
| **1254** | A259 | 42p multi | 2.00 | 2.00 |
| **1255** | A259 | 51p multi | 2.25 | 2.25 |
| **1256** | A259 | 57p multi | 2.50 | 2.50 |
| **1257** | A259 | 74p multi | 3.25 | 3.25 |
| | | *Nos. 1252-1257 (6)* | 13.25 | 13.25 |

**Souvenir Sheet**

**Stamps Without White Frames**

| | | | |
|---|---|---|---|
| **1258** | Sheet of 3 | 8.00 | 8.00 |
| *a.* | A259 51p multi | 2.25 | 2.25 |
| *b.* | A259 57p multi | 2.50 | 2.50 |
| *c.* | A259 74p multi | 3.25 | 3.25 |

Birds A260

Designs: 34p, House sparrow. 37p, Chaffinch. 42p, Blue tit. 51p, Blackbird. 57p, Magpie. 74p, Great tit.

**2007, June 19 Litho.** ***Perf. 13x13½***

**Stamps With White Frames**

| | | | | |
|---|---|---|---|---|
| **1259** | A260 | 34p multi | 1.50 | 1.50 |
| **1260** | A260 | 37p multi | 1.75 | 1.75 |
| **1261** | A260 | 42p multi | 2.00 | 2.00 |
| **1262** | A260 | 51p multi | 2.25 | 2.25 |
| **1263** | A260 | 57p multi | 2.50 | 2.50 |
| **1264** | A260 | 74p multi | 3.25 | 3.25 |
| *a.* | | Miniature sheet, #1259-1264 | 13.00 | 13.00 |
| | | *Nos. 1259-1264 (6)* | 13.25 | 13.25 |

**Souvenir Sheet**

**Stamps Without White Frames**

| | | | |
|---|---|---|---|
| **1265** | Sheet of 3 | 8.00 | 8.00 |
| *a.* | A260 51p multi | 2.25 | 2.25 |
| *b.* | A260 57p multi | 2.50 | 2.50 |
| *c.* | A260 74p multi | 3.25 | 3.25 |

See Nos. 1342-1348, 1389-1395, 1429-1435.

Souvenir Sheet

Gorey Regatta — A261

**2007, June 22** ***Perf. 12¾x13½***

| | | | | |
|---|---|---|---|---|
| **1266** | A261 | £2 multi | 8.50 | 8.50 |

**Flowers Type of 2005**

Designs: 10p, Black bryony. 25p, Horseshoe vetch. 35p, English stonecrop. 45p, Tutsan. 55p, Ox-eye daisy. 60p, Rock sea-spurrey. 80p, Mouse-ear hawkweed. £1.50, Devil's-bit scabious.

**2007, July 25** ***Perf. 13¼***

| | | | | |
|---|---|---|---|---|
| **1267** | A241 | 10p multi | .40 | .40 |
| **1268** | A241 | 25p multi | 1.00 | 1.00 |
| **1269** | A241 | 35p multi | 1.40 | 1.40 |
| **1270** | A241 | 45p multi | 1.90 | 1.90 |
| *a.* | | Dated "2011" | 1.50 | 1.50 |
| **1271** | A241 | 55p multi | 2.25 | 2.25 |
| **1272** | A241 | 60p multi | 2.50 | 2.50 |
| **1273** | A241 | 80p multi | 3.25 | 3.25 |
| **1274** | A241 | £1.50 multi | 6.25 | 6.25 |
| *a.* | | Miniature sheet, #1267-1274 | 19.00 | 19.00 |
| | | *Nos. 1267-1274 (8)* | 18.95 | 18.95 |

Issued: No. 1270a, 6/16/11.

Summer Flowers A262

Designs: 34p, Clematis. 37p, Roses. 42p, Honeysuckles. 51p, Fuchsias. 57p, Sweet peas. 74p, Lilacs.

**2007, July 25** ***Perf. 13½***

| | | | | |
|---|---|---|---|---|
| **1275** | A262 | 34p multi | 1.50 | 1.50 |
| **1276** | A262 | 37p multi | 1.75 | 1.75 |
| **1277** | A262 | 42p multi | 2.00 | 2.00 |
| **1278** | A262 | 51p multi | 2.25 | 2.25 |
| **1279** | A262 | 57p multi | 2.50 | 2.50 |
| **1280** | A262 | 74p multi | 3.25 | 3.25 |
| | | *Nos. 1275-1280 (6)* | 13.25 | 13.25 |

Airplanes A263

Designs: 34p, Dornier Do 24 ATT. 37p, Avro Vulcan B-2. 42p, Junkers Ju-52. 51p, Sukhoi Su-27 Flanker. 57p, Boeing B-52 Stratofortress. 74p, Concorde.

£2.50, Red Arrows in formation.

**2007, Sept. 13** ***Perf. 13x13¼***

| | | | | |
|---|---|---|---|---|
| **1281** | A263 | 34p multi | 1.40 | 1.40 |
| **1282** | A263 | 37p multi | 1.50 | 1.50 |
| **1283** | A263 | 42p multi | 1.75 | 1.75 |
| **1284** | A263 | 51p multi | 2.10 | 2.10 |
| **1285** | A263 | 57p multi | 2.40 | 2.40 |
| **1286** | A263 | 74p multi | 3.00 | 3.00 |
| *a.* | | Booklet pane, #1281-1286 | 12.50 | — |
| | | Complete booklet, #1287a, 3 #1286a | 48.00 | |
| | | *Nos. 1281-1286 (6)* | 12.15 | 12.15 |

**Souvenir Sheet**

***Perf. 13¼x13***

| | | | | |
|---|---|---|---|---|
| **1287** | A263 | £2.50 multi | 10.50 | 10.50 |
| *a.* | | Booklet pane, #1287 | 10.50 | — |

No. 1287 contains one 60x40mm stamp. Size of No. 1287a: 150x100mm. The complete booklet contains three examples of No. 1286a, each of which has a different arrangement of the stamps.

Jersey Attractions — A264

Designs: 34p, Queen's Valley Reservoir. 37p, Mont Orgueil Castle. 42p, Bonne Nuit Harbor. 51, La Hogue Bie. 57p, Bouley Bay. 74p, Le Corbiere Lighthouse.

**2007, Oct. 1** ***Perf. 14x13½***

| | | | | |
|---|---|---|---|---|
| **1288** | A264 | 34p multi | 1.50 | 1.50 |
| **1289** | A264 | 37p multi | 1.75 | 1.75 |
| **1290** | A264 | 42p multi | 2.00 | 2.00 |
| **1291** | A264 | 51p multi | 2.25 | 2.25 |
| **1292** | A264 | 57p multi | 2.50 | 2.50 |
| **1293** | A264 | 74p multi | 3.25 | 3.25 |
| | | *Nos. 1288-1293 (6)* | 13.25 | 13.25 |

See Nos. 1396-1401, 1541-1546..

Christmas Songs A265

No. 1294: a, Minuit Chrétiens. b, While Shepherds Watched. c, O Come, All Ye Faithful. d, O Christmas Tree. e, Jingle Bells.

No. 1295: a, Hark! The Herald Angels Sing. b, We Three Kings. c, Ding Dong! Merrily On High. d, Holly and the Ivy. e, Good King Wenceslas.

***Serpentine Die Cut 11¼***

**2007, Nov. 7 Litho. Self-Adhesive**

**Coil Stamps**

**Inscribed "2007"**

| | | | |
|---|---|---|---|
| **1294** | Horiz. strip of 5 | 7.50 | |
| *a.-e.* | A265 (35p) Any single | 1.40 | 1.40 |
| *g.* | As #1294, inscribed "2008" | 5.50 | |
| *h.-l.* | A265 (35p) As #1294a-1294e, any single, inscribed "2008" | 1.10 | 1.10 |
| *m.* | As #1294, inscribed "2009" | 7.00 | |
| *n.-r.* | A265 (39p) As #1294a-1294e, any single, inscribed "2009" | 1.40 | 1.40 |
| **1295** | Horiz. strip of 5 | 8.50 | |
| *a.-e.* | A265 (39p) Any single | 1.60 | 1.60 |
| *g.* | As #1295, inscribed "2008" | 6.25 | |
| *h.-l.* | A265 (39p) As #1295a-1295e, any single, inscribed "2008" | 1.25 | 1.25 |
| *m.* | As #1295, inscribed "2009" | 7.00 | |
| *n.-r.* | A265 (42p) As #1295a-1295e, any single, inscribed "2009" | 1.40 | 1.40 |

Issued: Nos. 1294g, 1295g, 11/14/08; Nos. 1294m, 1295m, 11/10/09.

Wedding of Queen Elizabeth II and Prince Philip, 60th Anniv. — A266

**2007, Nov. 20** ***Perf. 13¼***

| | | | | |
|---|---|---|---|---|
| **1296** | A266 | £3 multi | 12.50 | 12.50 |

Jersey Signal Station, 300th Anniv. A267

Designs: 35p, Sun, sunshine recorder, clouds. 39p, Clouds, weather symbols for wind speed, weather vane. 43p, Clouds, raindrops, weather symbols and barometer. 58p, Sun, thermometer and weather station. 76p, Tide measuring device, French flag, Moon.

**2008, Jan. 15 Litho.** ***Perf. 14***

| | | | | |
|---|---|---|---|---|
| **1297** | A267 | 35p multi | 1.40 | 1.40 |
| **1298** | A267 | 39p multi | 1.60 | 1.60 |
| **1299** | A267 | 43p multi | 1.75 | 1.75 |
| **1300** | A267 | 58p multi | 2.40 | 2.40 |
| **1301** | A267 | 76p multi | 3.00 | 3.00 |
| | | *Nos. 1297-1301 (5)* | 10.15 | 10.15 |

Letters A268

Designs: 35p, Thank-you letter. 39p, Love letter. 43p, Letter to Santa Claus. 76p, Family letter.

**2008, Feb. 14** ***Perf. 13½x14***

| | | | | |
|---|---|---|---|---|
| **1302** | A268 | 35p multi | 1.40 | 1.40 |
| **1303** | A268 | 39p multi | 1.60 | 1.60 |
| **1304** | A268 | 43p multi | 1.75 | 1.75 |
| **1305** | A268 | 76p multi | 3.00 | 3.00 |
| | | *Nos. 1302-1305 (4)* | 7.75 | 7.75 |

Europa (39p, 43p).

Jersey Eisteddfod, Cent. A269

Designs: 35p, Arts and crafts. 39p, Dance and drama. 43p, Speech. 58p, Films and photography. 76p, Music.

**2008, Mar. 3** ***Perf. 14***

| | | | | |
|---|---|---|---|---|
| **1306** | A269 | 35p multi | 1.40 | 1.40 |
| **1307** | A269 | 39p multi | 1.60 | 1.60 |
| **1308** | A269 | 43p multi | 1.75 | 1.75 |
| **1309** | A269 | 58p multi | 2.40 | 2.40 |
| **1310** | A269 | 76p multi | 3.25 | 3.25 |
| | | *Nos. 1306-1310 (5)* | 10.40 | 10.40 |

Buses A270

Designs: 35p, Grey Bus Services Daimler CB bus. 39p, Safety Coach Service Ex LGOC K single decker bus. 43p, Jersey Motor Transport horse-drawn town bus. 52p, Jersey Motor Transport Leyland Lion Charcoal Burner bus. 58p, Jersey Bus Service Bedford WLB bus. 76p, Jersey Motor Transport Commer Commando bus.

£2.50, Jersey Motor Transport Ford Willowbrook bus.

**2008, Apr. 8** ***Perf. 14¼x14***

| | | | | |
|---|---|---|---|---|
| **1311** | A270 | 35p multi | 1.40 | 1.40 |
| **1312** | A270 | 39p multi | 1.60 | 1.60 |
| **1313** | A270 | 43p multi | 1.75 | 1.75 |
| **1314** | A270 | 52p multi | 2.10 | 2.10 |
| **1315** | A270 | 58p multi | 2.40 | 2.40 |
| **1316** | A270 | 76p multi | 3.00 | 3.00 |
| | | *Nos. 1311-1316 (6)* | 12.25 | 12.25 |

**Souvenir Sheet**

***Perf. 13½x13¾***

| | | | | |
|---|---|---|---|---|
| **1317** | A270 | £2.50 multi | 10.00 | 10.00 |
| *a.* | | As #1317, with WIPA 08 emblem in sheet margin | 9.00 | 9.00 |

No. 1317 contains one 75x30mm stamp.

No. 1317a issued 9/18.

Souvenir Sheet

World Jersey Cattle Bureau Conference — A271

**2008, May 18** ***Perf. 13***

| | | | | |
|---|---|---|---|---|
| **1318** | A271 | £2 multi | 8.00 | 8.00 |

Orchids A272

Designs: 35p, Cymbidium Avranches "Victoria Village." 39p, Miltonia "Tesson Mill." 43p, Anguloa Victoire "Trinity." 52p, Phragmipedium La Hougette. 58p, Phragmipedium Havre des Pas "Jersey." 76p, Paphiopedilum Rolfei "Trinity."

£2.50, Paphiopedilum Rocco Tower.

**2008, May 20** ***Perf. 13x13¼***

| | | | | |
|---|---|---|---|---|
| **1319** | A272 | 35p multi | 1.40 | 1.40 |
| **1320** | A272 | 39p multi | 1.60 | 1.60 |
| **1321** | A272 | 43p multi | 1.75 | 1.75 |
| **1322** | A272 | 52p multi | 2.10 | 2.10 |

| | | | | |
|---|---|---|---|---|
| **1323** | A272 | 58p multi | 2.40 | 2.40 |
| **1324** | A272 | 76p multi | 3.00 | 3.00 |
| | | *Nos. 1319-1324 (6)* | 12.25 | 12.25 |

**Souvenir Sheet**

| | | | | |
|---|---|---|---|---|
| **1325** | A272 | £2.50 multi | 10.00 | 10.00 |

Souvenir Sheet

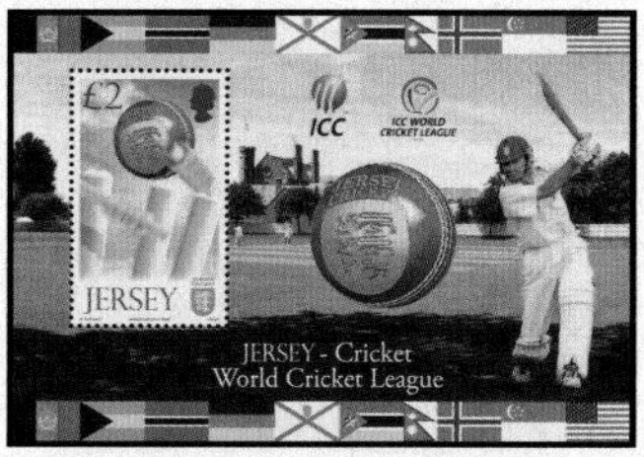


2008 World Cricket League Division 5 Tournament, Jersey — A273

**2008, May 23 Litho. *Perf. 12¾x13¼***

| | | | | |
|---|---|---|---|---|
| **1326** | A273 | £2 multi | 8.00 | 8.00 |

Royal Navy Vessels A274

Designs: 35p, HMS Roebuck. 39p, HMS Monmouth. 43p, HMS Edinburgh. 52p, HMS Express. 58p, HMS Severn. 76p, HMS Cottesmore.

£2.50, HMY Britannia.

**2008, June 24 Litho. *Perf. 13x13¼***

| | | | | |
|---|---|---|---|---|
| **1327** | A274 | 35p multi | 1.40 | 1.40 |
| **1328** | A274 | 39p multi | 1.60 | 1.60 |
| **1329** | A274 | 43p multi | 1.75 | 1.75 |
| **1330** | A274 | 52p multi | 2.10 | 2.10 |
| **1331** | A274 | 58p multi | 2.40 | 2.40 |
| **1332** | A274 | 76p multi | 3.00 | 3.00 |
| *a.* | | Booklet pane, #1327-1332 | 12.50 | 12.50 |
| | | *Nos. 1327-1332 (6)* | 12.25 | 12.25 |

**Souvenir Sheet**

***Perf. 13¼x13***

| | | | | |
|---|---|---|---|---|
| **1333** | A274 | £2.50 multi | 10.00 | 10.00 |
| *a.* | | Booklet pane of 1 #1333 | 10.00 | 10.00 |
| | | Complete booklet, #1333a, 3 #1332a | 47.50 | |

No. 1333 contains one 60x40mm stamp.

No. 1333a has a binding stub at left. Complete booklet contains 3 examples of No. 1332a, each with a different margin and different arrangement of the stamps.

Souvenir Sheet

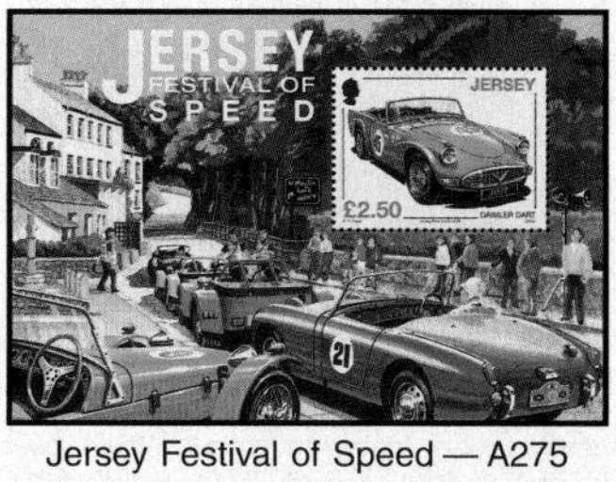


Jersey Festival of Speed — A275

**2008, Aug. 23 Litho. *Perf. 13x13¼***

| | | | | |
|---|---|---|---|---|
| **1334** | A275 | £2.50 multi | 9.25 | 9.25 |

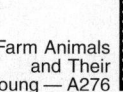

Farm Animals and Their Young — A276

No. 1335: a, Rooster, hen and chicks. b, Sheep and lambs. c, Sow and piglets. d, Ducks and ducklings. e, Cows and calf.

***Serpentine Die Cut 11¼***

**2008, Aug. 26**

**Coil Stamps**

**Self-Adhesive**

| | | | | |
|---|---|---|---|---|
| **1335** | | Horiz. strip of 5 | 6.50 | |
| *a.-e.* | A276 | (35p) Any single | 1.25 | 1.25 |
| *f.* | | Horiz. strip of 5, dated "2010" | 5.50 | |
| *g.-k.* | | (36p) As #1335a-1335e, dated "2011," any single | 1.10 | 1.10 |

Issued: No. 1335f, 4/2/10.

Insects A277

Designs: 35p, Carpenter bee. 39p, Buff-tailed bumblebee. 43p, Clown-faced bug. 52p, Large migrant hoverfly. 58p, Ruby-tailed wasp. 76p, 22-spot ladybug.

**2008, Sept. 8 *Perf. 13x13¼***

| | | | | |
|---|---|---|---|---|
| **1336** | A277 | 35p multi | 1.25 | 1.25 |
| **1337** | A277 | 39p multi | 1.40 | 1.40 |
| **1338** | A277 | 43p multi | 1.60 | 1.60 |
| **1339** | A277 | 52p multi | 1.90 | 1.90 |
| **1340** | A277 | 58p multi | 2.10 | 2.10 |
| **1341** | A277 | 76p multi | 2.75 | 2.75 |
| | | *Nos. 1336-1341 (6)* | 11.00 | 11.00 |

**Birds Type of 2007**

Designs: 35p, Northern wheatear. 39p, Whinchat. 43p, Pied flycatcher. 52p, Yellow wagtail. 58p, Ring ouzel. 76p, Common redstart.

**2008, Oct. 21 Litho.**

**Stamps With White Frames**

| | | | | |
|---|---|---|---|---|
| **1342** | A260 | 35p multi | 1.10 | 1.10 |
| **1343** | A260 | 39p multi | 1.25 | 1.25 |
| **1344** | A260 | 43p multi | 1.40 | 1.40 |
| **1345** | A260 | 52p multi | 1.75 | 1.75 |
| **1346** | A260 | 58p multi | 1.90 | 1.90 |
| **1347** | A260 | 76p multi | 2.50 | 2.50 |
| *a.* | | Souvenir sheet, #1342-1347 | 10.00 | 10.00 |
| | | *Nos. 1342-1347 (6)* | 9.90 | 9.90 |

**Souvenir Sheet**

**Stamps Without White Frames**

| | | | | |
|---|---|---|---|---|
| **1348** | | Sheet of 3 | 6.25 | 6.25 |
| *a.* | | A260 52p multi | 1.75 | 1.75 |
| *b.* | | A260 58p multi | 1.90 | 1.90 |
| *c.* | | A260 76p multi | 2.50 | 2.50 |

Prince Charles, 60th Birthday A278

**2008, Nov. 14 *Perf. 13¼***

| | | | | |
|---|---|---|---|---|
| **1349** | A278 | £4 multi | 12.00 | 12.00 |
| *a.* | | Souvenir sheet of 1 | 12.00 | 12.00 |

Airplanes A279

Designs: 35p, Douglas C-47 Dakota 3 Pionair. 39p, Vickers Viscount 833. 43p, Handley Page HPR7 Dart-Herald. 52p, Bristol Superfreighter 32. 58p, Fokker F-27 Friendship. 76p, Bombardier Q400 Dash 8.

£3, De Havilland D.H. 84 Dragon 2.

**2009, Jan. 13 Litho. *Perf. 14***

| | | | | |
|---|---|---|---|---|
| **1350** | A279 | 35p multi | 1.00 | 1.00 |
| **1351** | A279 | 39p multi | 1.10 | 1.10 |
| **1352** | A279 | 43p multi | 1.25 | 1.25 |
| **1353** | A279 | 52p multi | 1.50 | 1.50 |
| **1354** | A279 | 58p multi | 1.60 | 1.60 |
| **1355** | A279 | 76p multi | 2.10 | 2.10 |
| | | *Nos. 1350-1355 (6)* | 8.55 | 8.55 |

**Souvenir Sheet**

| | | | | |
|---|---|---|---|---|
| **1356** | A279 | £3 multi | 8.25 | 8.25 |

First flight from Jersey to Southampton, 75th anniv. (#1356).

Intl. Year of Astronomy A280

Galileo Galilei, one quarter of Jupiter and: 35p, Jupiter's moon Io, Ursa Major and Cassiopeia constellations. 39p, Jupiter's moon Europa, Boötes and Corona Borealis constellations. 43p, Jupiter's moon Ganymede, Cygnus and Pegasus constellations. 76p, Jupiter's moon Callisto, Perseus and Orion constellations.

**Litho. & Embossed With Foil Application**

**2009, Feb. 10 *Perf. 13x13¼***

| | | | | |
|---|---|---|---|---|
| **1357** | A280 | 35p multi | 1.00 | 1.00 |
| **1358** | A280 | 39p multi | 1.10 | 1.10 |
| **1359** | A280 | 43p multi | 1.25 | 1.25 |
| **1360** | A280 | 76p multi | 2.25 | 2.25 |
| | | *Nos. 1357-1360 (4)* | 5.60 | 5.60 |

Europa (39p, 43p).

Endangered Species — A281

Designs: 35p, Blue iguana. 39p, Madagascar giant jumping rat. 43p, Mountain chicken frog. 52p, Livingstone's fruit bat. 58p, Andean bear. 76p, Western lowland gorilla.

**2009, Mar. 10 Litho. *Perf. 14¾x14***

| | | | | |
|---|---|---|---|---|
| **1361** | A281 | 35p multi | 1.10 | 1.10 |
| **1362** | A281 | 39p multi | 1.25 | 1.25 |
| **1363** | A281 | 43p multi | 1.25 | 1.25 |
| **1364** | A281 | 52p multi | 1.60 | 1.60 |
| **1365** | A281 | 58p multi | 1.75 | 1.75 |
| **1366** | A281 | 76p multi | 2.25 | 2.25 |
| | | *Nos. 1361-1366 (6)* | 9.20 | 9.20 |

Durrell Wildlife Conservation Trust, 50th anniv.

Spring Flowers A282

Designs: 35p, Crocus and grape hyacinth. 39p, Daffodils. 43p, Anemones de Caen. 52p, Tulips. 58p, Hyacinths. 76p, Polyanthus and primulas.

**2009, Apr. 1 *Perf. 13¼***

| | | | | |
|---|---|---|---|---|
| **1367** | A282 | 35p multi | 1.10 | 1.10 |
| **1368** | A282 | 39p multi | 1.25 | 1.25 |
| **1369** | A282 | 43p multi | 1.25 | 1.25 |
| **1370** | A282 | 52p multi | 1.60 | 1.60 |
| **1371** | A282 | 58p multi | 1.75 | 1.75 |
| **1372** | A282 | 76p multi | 2.25 | 2.25 |
| | | *Nos. 1367-1372 (6)* | 9.20 | 9.20 |

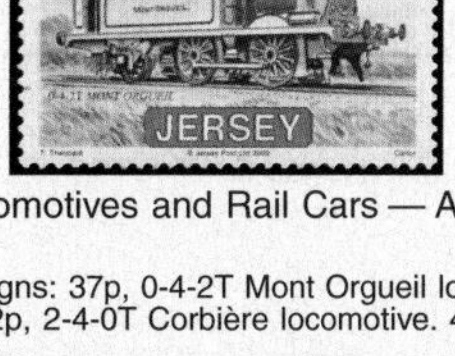

Locomotives and Rail Cars — A283

Designs: 37p, 0-4-2T Mont Orgueil locomotive. 42p, 2-4-0T Corbière locomotive. 45p, 0-4-2T Carteret locomotive. 55p, Pioneer rail car. 61p, 2-4-0T La Moye locomotive. 80p, 2-4-0T St. Brelades locomotive.

£3, 2-4-0T Corbière locomotive, diff.

**2009, May 6 *Perf. 13x13¼***

| | | | | |
|---|---|---|---|---|
| **1373** | A283 | 37p multi | 1.25 | 1.25 |
| **1374** | A283 | 42p multi | 1.40 | 1.40 |
| **1375** | A283 | 45p multi | 1.50 | 1.50 |
| **1376** | A283 | 55p multi | 1.75 | 1.75 |
| **1377** | A283 | 61p multi | 2.00 | 2.00 |
| **1378** | A283 | 80p multi | 2.60 | 2.60 |
| *a.* | | Booklet pane of 6, #1373-1378 | 10.50 | 10.50 |
| | | *Nos. 1373-1378 (6)* | 10.50 | 10.50 |

**Souvenir Sheet**

***Perf. 13¼x13***

| | | | | |
|---|---|---|---|---|
| **1379** | A283 | £3 multi | 9.75 | 9.75 |
| *a.* | | Booklet pane of 1 #1379 | 9.75 | 9.75 |
| | | Complete booklet, #1379a, 3 #1378a | 42.00 | |
| *b.* | | As #1379, with IBRA emblem in sheet margin | 9.75 | 9.75 |

No. 1379 contains one 60x40mm stamp.

No. 1379a has a binding stub at left.

Complete booklet contains three examples of No. 1378a, each with a different margin and different arrangement of the stamps.

Souvenir Sheet

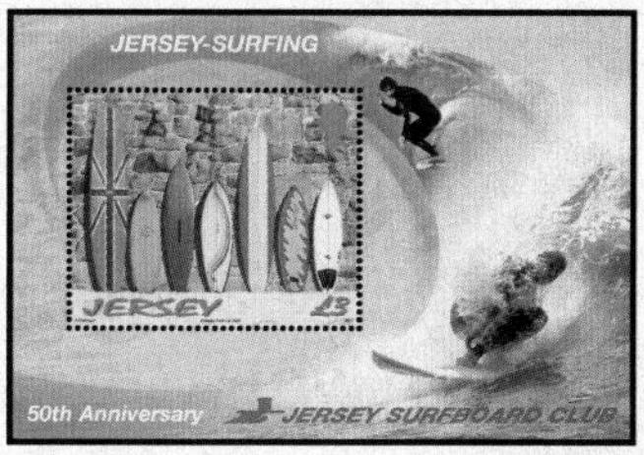


Surfing — A284

**2009, June 2 *Perf. 13¼***

| | | | | |
|---|---|---|---|---|
| **1380** | A284 | £3 multi | 9.75 | 9.75 |

Jersey Surfboard Club, 50th anniv.

Souvenir Sheet

St. Helier Broad Street Post Office, Cent. — A285

**2009, June 21 *Perf. 14***

| | | | | |
|---|---|---|---|---|
| **1381** | A285 | £3 multi | 9.75 | 9.75 |

Souvenir Sheet

Investiture of Prince Charles as Prince of Wales, 40th Anniv. — A286

**2009, July 1 *Perf. 13¼***

| | | | | |
|---|---|---|---|---|
| **1382** | A286 | £3 multi | 9.75 | 9.75 |

Seaweeds A287

Designs: 37p, Egg wrack. 42p, Gutweed. 45p, Red rags. 55p, Sea lettuce. 61p, Laminaria hyperborea. 80p, Velvet horn.

**2009, July 7** ***Perf. 13x13¼***

| | | | | |
|---|---|---|---|---|
| **1383** | A287 37p multi | 1.25 | 1.25 |
| **1384** | A287 42p multi | 1.40 | 1.40 |
| **1385** | A287 45p multi | 1.50 | 1.50 |
| **1386** | A287 55p multi | 1.90 | 1.90 |
| **1387** | A287 61p multi | 2.00 | 2.00 |
| **1388** | A287 80p multi | 2.60 | 2.60 |
| | *Nos. 1383-1388 (6)* | 10.65 | 10.65 |

**Birds Type of 2007**

Designs: 37p, Dunnock. 42p, Song thrush. 45p, Wren. 55p, Blackcap. 61p, Mistle thrush. 80p, Robin.

**2009, Aug. 4 Litho.** ***Perf. 13x13¼***

**Stamps With White Frames**

| | | | |
|---|---|---|---|
| **1389** | A260 37p multi | 1.25 | 1.25 |
| **1390** | A260 42p multi | 1.40 | 1.40 |
| **1391** | A260 45p multi | 1.50 | 1.50 |
| **1392** | A260 55p multi | 1.90 | 1.90 |
| **1393** | A260 61p multi | 2.10 | 2.10 |
| **1394** | A260 80p multi | 2.75 | 2.75 |
| *a.* | Souvenir sheet, #1389-1394 | 11.00 | 11.00 |
| | *Nos. 1389-1394 (6)* | 10.90 | 10.90 |

**Souvenir Sheet**

**Stamps Without White Frames**

| | | | |
|---|---|---|---|
| **1395** | Sheet of 3 | 6.75 | 6.75 |
| *a.* | A260 55p multi | 1.90 | 1.90 |
| *b.* | A260 61p multi | 2.10 | 2.10 |
| *c.* | A260 80p multi | 2.75 | 2.75 |

**Jersey Attractions Type of 2007**

Designs: 37p, Green Island. 42p, Gorey Castle. 45p, St. Aubin's Harbor. 55p, St. Peter's Valley. 61p, La Rocque Harbor. 80p, Greve de Lecq.

**2009, Sept. 16 Litho.** ***Perf. 14x13½***

| | | | |
|---|---|---|---|
| **1396** | A264 37p multi | 1.25 | 1.25 |
| **1397** | A264 42p multi | 1.40 | 1.40 |
| **1398** | A264 45p multi | 1.50 | 1.50 |
| **1399** | A264 55p multi | 1.75 | 1.75 |
| **1400** | A264 61p multi | 2.00 | 2.00 |
| **1401** | A264 80p multi | 2.60 | 2.60 |
| | *Nos. 1396-1401 (6)* | 10.50 | 10.50 |

Mushrooms A288

Designs: 37p, Parrot wax-cap. 42p, Russula sardonia. 45p, Velvet foot. 55p, Honey fungus. 61p, Orange peel fungus. 80p, Jewelled deathcap.

**2009, Oct. 15 Litho.** ***Perf. 13¼x13***

| | | | |
|---|---|---|---|
| **1402** | A288 37p multi | 1.25 | 1.25 |
| **1403** | A288 42p multi | 1.40 | 1.40 |
| **1404** | A288 45p multi | 1.50 | 1.50 |
| **1405** | A288 55p multi | 1.90 | 1.90 |
| **1406** | A288 61p multi | 2.10 | 2.10 |
| **1407** | A288 80p multi | 2.75 | 2.75 |
| | *Nos. 1402-1407 (6)* | 10.90 | 10.90 |

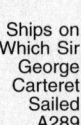

Ships on Which Sir George Carteret Sailed A289

Designs: 37p, HMS Garland. 42p, HMS Eighth Lion's Whelp. 45p, HMS Unicorn. 55p, HMS Mary Rose. 61p, HMS Antelope. 80p, HMS Rainbow.

**2009, Oct. 15 Litho.** ***Perf. 13¼x13***

| | | | |
|---|---|---|---|
| **1408** | A289 37p multi | 1.25 | 1.25 |
| **1409** | A289 42p multi | 1.40 | 1.40 |
| **1410** | A289 45p multi | 1.50 | 1.50 |
| **1411** | A289 55p multi | 1.90 | 1.90 |
| **1412** | A289 61p multi | 2.10 | 2.10 |
| **1413** | A289 80p multi | 2.75 | 2.75 |
| | *Nos. 1408-1413 (6)* | 10.90 | 10.90 |

Girl Guides, Cent. A290

Inscriptions: 37p, Healthy lifestyles. 42p, Global awareness. 45p, Skills & relationships. 61p, Celebrating diversity. 80p, Discovery.

**2010, Jan. 12 Litho.** ***Perf. 14***

| | | | |
|---|---|---|---|
| **1414** | A290 37p multi | 1.25 | 1.25 |
| **1415** | A290 42p multi | 1.40 | 1.40 |
| **1416** | A290 45p multi | 1.50 | 1.50 |
| **1417** | A290 61p multi | 2.00 | 2.00 |
| **1418** | A290 80p multi | 2.60 | 2.60 |
| | *Nos. 1414-1418 (5)* | 8.75 | 8.75 |

Maps of Jersey — A291

No. 1419 — Map: a, Circa 1685. b, Circa 1844. c, Circa 1980s. d, Circa 2000. e, Satellite view.

***Serpentine Die Cut 11¼***

**2010, Feb. 9 Self-Adhesive**

**Coil Stamps**

| | | | |
|---|---|---|---|
| **1419** | Horiz. strip of 5 | 6.50 | |
| *a.-e.* | A291 (42p) Any single | 1.25 | 1.25 |

Children's Book Characters A292

Designs: 37p, Pushmi-pullyu from *Dr. Doolittle,* by Hugh Lofting. 42p, Elephant from *How the Elephant Got His Trunk,* by Rudyard Kipling. 45p, Mad Hatter from *Alice in Wonderland,* by Lewis Carroll. 80p, *The Dong with a Luminous Nose,* by Edward Lear.

**2010, Feb. 9** ***Perf. 13x13¼***

| | | | |
|---|---|---|---|
| **1420** | A292 37p multi | 1.10 | 1.10 |
| **1421** | A292 42p multi | 1.25 | 1.25 |
| **1422** | A292 45p multi | 1.40 | 1.40 |
| **1423** | A292 80p multi | 2.50 | 2.50 |
| | *Nos. 1420-1423 (4)* | 6.25 | 6.25 |

Europa (42p, 45p).

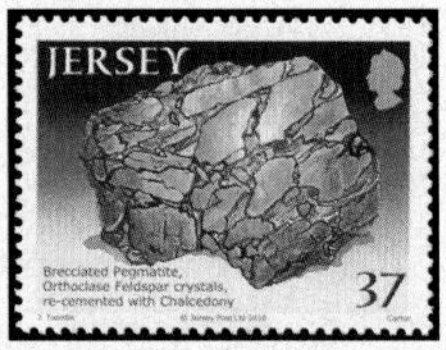


Rocks A293

Designs: 37p, Brecciated pegmatite, orthoclase feldspar crystals re-cemented with chalcedony. 42p, Diorite with incipient orbicular structure. 45p, Granite. 61p, Jasper in andesite. 80p, Pebbles of granite, andesite and shale in Rozel conglomerate.

**2010, Mar. 9** ***Perf. 13x13¼***

| | | | |
|---|---|---|---|
| **1424** | A293 37p multi | 1.10 | 1.10 |
| **1425** | A293 42p multi | 1.25 | 1.25 |
| **1426** | A293 45p multi | 1.40 | 1.40 |
| **1427** | A293 61p multi | 1.90 | 1.90 |
| **1428** | A293 80p multi | 2.50 | 2.50 |
| | *Nos. 1424-1428 (5)* | 8.15 | 8.15 |

**Birds Type of 2007**

Designs: 37p, Jay. 42p, Great spotted woodpecker. 45p, Short-toed treecreeper. 55p, Chiffchaff. 61p, Long-tailed tit. 80p, Turtle dove.

**2010, Apr. 1**

**Stamps With White Frames**

| | | | |
|---|---|---|---|
| **1429** | A260 37p multi | 1.10 | 1.10 |
| **1430** | A260 42p multi | 1.25 | 1.25 |
| **1431** | A260 45p multi | 1.40 | 1.40 |
| **1432** | A260 55p multi | 1.75 | 1.75 |
| **1433** | A260 61p multi | 1.90 | 1.90 |
| **1434** | A260 80p multi | 2.50 | 2.50 |
| *a.* | Souvenir sheet, #1429-1434 | 10.00 | 10.00 |
| | *Nos. 1429-1434 (6)* | 9.90 | 9.90 |

**Souvenir Sheet**

**Stamps Without White Frames**

| | | | |
|---|---|---|---|
| **1435** | Sheet of 3 | 6.25 | 6.25 |
| *a.* | A260 55p multi | 1.75 | 1.75 |
| *b.* | A260 61p multi | 1.90 | 1.90 |
| *c.* | A260 80p multi | 2.50 | 2.50 |

British Regional Stamps of 1958-69 A294

Designs: 36p, Jersey #2. 39p, Jersey #1. 45p, Jersey #3. 55p, Jersey #4. 60p, Jersey #6. 72p, Jersey #5.

**2010, May 8** ***Perf. 13x13¼***

| | | | |
|---|---|---|---|
| **1436** | A294 36p multi | 1.10 | 1.10 |
| **1437** | A294 39p multi | 1.10 | 1.10 |
| **1438** | A294 45p multi | 1.40 | 1.40 |
| **1439** | A294 55p multi | 1.60 | 1.60 |
| **1440** | A294 60p multi | 1.75 | 1.75 |
| **1441** | A294 72p multi | 2.10 | 2.10 |
| *a.* | Souvenir sheet, #1436-1441 | 9.25 | 9.25 |
| | *Nos. 1436-1441 (6)* | 9.05 | 9.05 |

Mail Ships A295

Designs: 39p, Royal Charlotte. 45p, Dispatch. 55p, Diana. 60p, Reindeer. 72p, Caesarea (II). 80p, St. Patrick (III).
£3, Watersprite.

**2010, May 8** ***Perf. 13x13¼***

| | | | |
|---|---|---|---|
| **1442** | A295 39p multi | 1.10 | 1.10 |
| **1443** | A295 45p multi | 1.40 | 1.40 |
| **1444** | A295 55p multi | 1.60 | 1.60 |
| **1445** | A295 60p multi | 1.75 | 1.75 |
| **1446** | A295 72p multi | 2.10 | 2.10 |
| **1447** | A295 80p multi | 2.40 | 2.40 |
| *a.* | Booklet pane, #1442-1447 | 10.50 | — |
| *b.* | Souvenir sheet, #1442-1447 | 10.50 | 10.50 |
| | *Nos. 1442-1447 (6)* | 10.35 | 10.35 |

**Souvenir Sheet**

***Perf. 13¼x13***

| | | | |
|---|---|---|---|
| **1448** | A295 £3 multi | 8.75 | 8.75 |
| *a.* | Booklet pane of 1 + binding stub | 8.75 | — |
| | Complete booklet, #1448a, 3 #1447a | 41.00 | |

No. 1448 contains one 60x40mm stamp.

Complete booklet contains three examples of No. 1447a, each with a different margin and different arrangement of the stamps.

Roses A296

Rose varieties: 36p, Nostalgia. 39p, Mountbatten. 45p, Royal William. 55p, Elina. 60p, New Dawn. 72p, Lovers Meeting.
£3, Pride of England.

**2010, June 8** ***Perf. 13x13¼***

| | | | |
|---|---|---|---|
| **1449** | A296 36p multi | 1.10 | 1.10 |
| **1450** | A296 39p multi | 1.10 | 1.10 |
| **1451** | A296 45p multi | 1.40 | 1.40 |
| **1452** | A296 55p multi | 1.60 | 1.60 |
| **1453** | A296 60p multi | 1.75 | 1.75 |
| **1454** | A296 72p multi | 2.10 | 2.10 |
| | *Nos. 1449-1454 (6)* | 9.05 | 9.05 |

**Souvenir Sheet**

| | | | |
|---|---|---|---|
| **1455** | A296 £3 multi | 8.75 | 8.75 |
| *a.* | As #1455, with Salon du Timbre emblem in sheet margin | 9.25 | 9.25 |

Issued: No. 1455a, 6/12.

Sea Anemones A297

Designs: 36p, Strawberry anemone. 39p, Snakelock anemone. 45p, Jewel anemone. 55p, Parasitic anemone. 60p, Tube anemone. 72p, Beadlet anemone.
£3, Dahlia anemone.

**2010, July 6** **Litho.**

| | | | |
|---|---|---|---|
| **1456** | A297 36p multi | 1.10 | 1.10 |
| **1457** | A297 39p multi | 1.25 | 1.25 |
| **1458** | A297 45p multi | 1.40 | 1.40 |
| **1459** | A297 55p multi | 1.75 | 1.75 |
| **1460** | A297 60p multi | 1.90 | 1.90 |
| **1461** | A297 72p multi | 2.25 | 2.25 |
| | *Nos. 1456-1461 (6)* | 9.65 | 9.65 |

**Souvenir Sheet**

| | | | |
|---|---|---|---|
| **1462** | A297 £3 multi | 9.00 | 9.00 |

Automobiles — A298

Designs: 39p, 1912 Rolls Royce Silver Ghost. 45p, 1926 Bugatti Type 37. 55p, 1933 Austin Seven. 60p, 1938 Citroen Light 15. 72p, 1946 Morris 10. 80p, 1949 Rover 75 Sports Saloon.

**2010, Aug. 3** ***Perf. 14¼x14***

| | | | |
|---|---|---|---|
| **1463** | A298 39p multi | 1.25 | 1.25 |
| **1464** | A298 45p multi | 1.50 | 1.50 |
| **1465** | A298 55p multi | 1.75 | 1.75 |
| **1466** | A298 60p multi | 1.90 | 1.90 |
| **1467** | A298 72p multi | 2.40 | 2.40 |
| **1468** | A298 80p multi | 2.60 | 2.60 |
| | *Nos. 1463-1468 (6)* | 11.40 | 11.40 |

Fish A299

Designs: 36p, Perch. 39p, Tench. 45p, Roach. 55p, Rudd. 60p, Mirror carp. 72p, Common bream.
£3, Brown trout.

**2010, Sept. 7 Litho.** ***Perf. 14¾x14***

| | | | |
|---|---|---|---|
| **1469** | A299 36p multi | 1.10 | 1.10 |
| **1470** | A299 39p multi | 1.25 | 1.25 |
| **1471** | A299 45p multi | 1.40 | 1.40 |
| **1472** | A299 55p multi | 1.75 | 1.75 |
| **1473** | A299 60p multi | 1.90 | 1.90 |
| **1474** | A299 72p multi | 2.25 | 2.25 |
| | *Nos. 1469-1474 (6)* | 9.65 | 9.65 |

**Souvenir Sheet**

| | | | |
|---|---|---|---|
| **1475** | A299 £3 multi | 9.25 | 9.25 |

La Cotte de St. Brelade Archaeological Site — A300

Designs: 39p, Human teeth, models of head of Neanderthal man. 45p, Skull of Woolly rhinoceros. 55p, Tooth and tusks of Woolly mammoth. 60p, Flint tools and timeline. 80p, Antler of Giant deer.

**2010, Oct. 12** ***Perf. 14***

| | | | |
|---|---|---|---|
| **1476** | A300 39p multi | 1.25 | 1.25 |
| **1477** | A300 45p multi | 1.50 | 1.50 |
| **1478** | A300 55p multi | 1.90 | 1.90 |
| **1479** | A300 60p multi | 2.00 | 2.00 |
| **1480** | A300 80p multi | 2.60 | 2.60 |
| | *Nos. 1476-1480 (5)* | 9.25 | 9.25 |

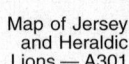

Map of Jersey and Heraldic Lions — A301

Inscriptions: (36p), Standard Letter. (39p), Priority Letter. (45p), UK Letter.

***Serpentine Die Cut 11½x11¼***

**2010, Nov. 1** **Self-Adhesive**

**Coil Stamps**

**Background Color**

| | | | | |
|---|---|---|---|---|
| **1481** | A301 | (36p) dark red | 1.25 | 1.25 |
| **1482** | A301 | (39p) blue | 1.25 | 1.25 |
| **1483** | A301 | (45p) green | 1.50 | 1.50 |
| | | *Nos. 1481-1483 (3)* | 4.00 | 4.00 |

Buses A302

Designs: 36p, Paragon C10 AEC B, c. 1926. 45p, Ramblers Tours Chevrolet, c. 1935. 55p, JMT Leyland Lioness, c. 1938. 60p, JMT Leyland PLSC1 Lion, c. 1939. 72p, Mascot Motors Morris C/F 13/5, c. 1948. 80p, Mascot Motors AEC Regal 4, c. 1961.

**2011, Jan. 11** **Litho.** ***Perf. 14***

| | | | | |
|---|---|---|---|---|
| **1484** | A302 | 36p multi | 1.25 | 1.25 |
| **1485** | A302 | 45p multi | 1.50 | 1.50 |
| **1486** | A302 | 55p multi | 1.75 | 1.75 |
| **1487** | A302 | 60p multi | 1.90 | 1.90 |
| **1488** | A302 | 72p multi | 2.40 | 2.40 |
| **1489** | A302 | 80p multi | 2.60 | 2.60 |
| | | *Nos. 1484-1489 (6)* | 11.40 | 11.40 |

Intl. Year of Forests A303

Tree branches: 39p, Silver birch. 45p, English oak. 55p, Beech. 80p, Lime.

**2011, Feb. 8** **Litho.** ***Perf. 133¼***

| | | | | |
|---|---|---|---|---|
| **1490** | A303 | 39p multi | 1.25 | 1.25 |
| **1491** | A303 | 45p multi | 1.50 | 1.50 |
| **1492** | A303 | 55p multi | 1.75 | 1.75 |
| **1493** | A303 | 80p multi | 2.60 | 2.60 |
| | | *Nos. 1490-1493 (4)* | 7.10 | 7.10 |

Europa (45p, 55p).

Famous Women A304

Designs: 36p, Dame Margot Fonteyn (1919-91), ballerina. 45p, Florence Nightingale (1820-1910), nurse. 60p, Marie Curie (1867-1934), chemist. 72p, Mother Teresa (1910-97), humanitarian.

**2011, Mar. 8**

| | | | | |
|---|---|---|---|---|
| **1494** | A304 | 36p multi | 1.25 | 1.25 |
| **1495** | A304 | 45p multi | 1.50 | 1.50 |
| **1496** | A304 | 60p multi | 2.00 | 2.00 |
| **1497** | A304 | 72p multi | 2.40 | 2.40 |
| | | *Nos. 1494-1497 (4)* | 7.15 | 7.15 |

Marine Life A305

Designs: (36p), Gooseberry sea squirt. (39p), Finger sponge. (45p), Purse sponge. 60p, Star squirt. 72p, Light bulb sea squirt. 80p, Red sea squirt.

**2011, Apr. 7** ***Perf. 14¾x14***

**Stamps With White Frames**

| | | | | |
|---|---|---|---|---|
| **1498** | A305 | (36p) multi | 1.25 | 1.25 |
| **1499** | A305 | (39p) multi | 1.25 | 1.25 |
| **1500** | A305 | (45p) multi | 1.50 | 1.50 |
| **1501** | A305 | 60p multi | 2.00 | 2.00 |
| **1502** | A305 | 72p multi | 2.40 | 2.40 |
| **1503** | A305 | 80p multi | 2.60 | 2.60 |
| | | *Nos. 1498-1503 (6)* | 11.00 | 11.00 |

**Souvenir Sheet**

**Stamps Without White Frames**

| | | | | |
|---|---|---|---|---|
| **1504** | | Sheet of 3 | 7.00 | 7.00 |
| *a.* | | A305 60p multi | 2.00 | 2.00 |
| *b.* | | A305 72p multi | 2.40 | 2.40 |
| *c.* | | A305 80p multi | 2.60 | 2.60 |

Queen Elizabeth II, 85th Birthday A306

**2011, Apr. 21** ***Perf. 13¼x13½***

| | | | | |
|---|---|---|---|---|
| **1505** | A306 | £3 multi | 10.00 | 10.00 |
| *a.* | | Souvenir sheet of 1 | 10.00 | 10.00 |

Wedding of Prince William and Catherine Middleton — A307

**2011, Apr. 29** ***Perf. 13½x13¼***

| | | | | |
|---|---|---|---|---|
| **1506** | A307 | £3.50 multi | 11.50 | 11.50 |

Printed in sheets of 4.

Orchids A308

Designs: (36p), Paphiopedilum La Garenne "Saint John." (39p), Odontioda Les Brayes "Pontac." (45p), Phragmipedium Don Wimber. 55p, Kriegerara Kemp Tower "Trinity." 60p, Angulocaste Noirmont "Isle of Jersey." 72p, Calanthe Beresford "Victoria Village."

£3, Miltonia Pointe des Pas "Jersey."

**2011, May 17** ***Perf. 13x13¼***

| | | | | |
|---|---|---|---|---|
| **1507** | A308 | (36p) multi | 1.25 | 1.25 |
| **1508** | A308 | (39p) multi | 1.25 | 1.25 |
| **1509** | A308 | (45p) multi | 1.50 | 1.50 |
| **1510** | A308 | 55p multi | 1.90 | 1.90 |
| **1511** | A308 | 60p multi | 2.00 | 2.00 |
| **1512** | A308 | 72p multi | 2.40 | 2.40 |
| | | *Nos. 1507-1512 (6)* | 10.30 | 10.30 |

**Souvenir Sheet**

| | | | | |
|---|---|---|---|---|
| **1513** | A308 | £3 multi | 10.00 | 10.00 |

**Birds Type of 2007**

Designs: 42p, Barn swallow. 50p, Spotted flycatcher. 59p, Cuckoo. 64, Whitethroat. 79p, Linnet. 86p, Swift.

**2011, June 16** **Litho.**

**Stamps With White Frames**

| | | | | |
|---|---|---|---|---|
| **1514** | A260 | 42p multi | 1.40 | 1.40 |
| **1515** | A260 | 50p multi | 1.60 | 1.60 |
| **1516** | A260 | 59p multi | 1.90 | 1.90 |
| **1517** | A260 | 64p multi | 2.10 | 2.10 |
| **1518** | A260 | 79p multi | 2.60 | 2.60 |
| **1519** | A260 | 86p multi | 2.75 | 2.75 |
| *a.* | | Souvenri sheet of 6, #1514-1519 | 12.50 | 12.50 |
| | | *Nos. 1514-1519 (6)* | 12.35 | 12.35 |

**Souvenir Sheet**

**Stamps Without White Frames**

| | | | | |
|---|---|---|---|---|
| **1520** | | Sheet of 3 | 7.50 | 7.50 |
| *a.* | | A260 64p multi | 2.10 | 2.10 |
| *b.* | | A260 79p multi | 2.60 | 2.60 |
| *c.* | | A260 86p multi | 2.75 | 2.75 |

Shipwrecks — A309

Designs: 37p, TSS Princess Ena, 1935. 49p, SS Caledonia, 1881. 59p, TSS Ibex, 1897. 64p, SS Schokland, 1943. 79p, PT509, 1944. 86p, PS Superb, 1950.

£3, TSS Roebuck, 1911

**2011, July 12** ***Perf. 13x13¼***

| | | | | |
|---|---|---|---|---|
| **1521** | A309 | 37p multi | 1.25 | 1.25 |
| **1522** | A309 | 49p multi | 1.60 | 1.60 |
| **1523** | A309 | 59p multi | 2.00 | 2.00 |
| **1524** | A309 | 64p multi | 2.10 | 2.10 |
| **1525** | A309 | 79p multi | 2.60 | 2.60 |
| **1526** | A309 | 86p multi | 2.75 | 2.75 |
| *a.* | | Booklet pane of 6, #1521-1526 | 12.50 | — |
| | | *Nos. 1521-1526 (6)* | 12.30 | 12.30 |

**Souvenir Sheet**

| | | | | |
|---|---|---|---|---|
| **1527** | A309 | £3 multi | 10.00 | 10.00 |
| *a.* | | Booklet pane of 1 | 10.00 | — |
| | | Complete booklet, #1527a, 3 #1526a | 47.50 | |

No. 1527 is 110x75mm; No. 1527a, 150x100mm. No. 1526ahas three different layouts of stamps on pane and three different margins.

National Trust for Jersey, 75th Anniv. A310

Designs: 42p, Marsh harrier, La Caumine à Marie Best, painted white. 50p, Swallowtail butterfly, Victoria Tower. 59p, Dartford warbler, La Cotte Battery. 64p, Red squirrel, Le Moulin de Quétivel. 75p, Marsh harrier, La Caumine à Marie Best, painted green. 79p, Puffins, North Coast sea cliffs.

**2011, Aug. 3** ***Perf. 14¾x14***

| | | | | |
|---|---|---|---|---|
| **1528** | A310 | 42p multi | 1.40 | 1.40 |
| **1529** | A310 | 50p multi | 1.60 | 1.60 |
| **1530** | A310 | 59p multi | 2.00 | 2.00 |
| **1531** | A310 | 64p multi | 2.10 | 2.10 |
| **1532** | A310 | 75p multi | 2.50 | 2.50 |
| **1533** | A310 | 79p multi | 2.60 | 2.60 |
| | | *Nos. 1528-1533 (6)* | 12.20 | 12.20 |

Ancient Celtic Coins Found Buried on Jersey A311

Obverse and reverse of: 37p, Billon stater of XN series. 49p, Durotriges base gold quarter stater. 59p, Baiocasses gold stater. 64p, Gold chute type stater. 79p, Southern British silver unit. 86p, Billon stater Coriosolite Tribe coin.

**2011, Aug. 30**

| | | | | |
|---|---|---|---|---|
| **1534** | A311 | 37p multi | 1.25 | 1.25 |
| **1535** | A311 | 49p multi | 1.60 | 1.60 |
| **1536** | A311 | 59p multi | 1.90 | 1.90 |
| **1537** | A311 | 64p multi | 2.10 | 2.10 |
| **1538** | A311 | 79p multi | 2.50 | 2.50 |
| **1539** | A311 | 86p multi | 2.75 | 2.75 |
| | | *Nos. 1534-1539 (6)* | 12.10 | 12.10 |

Souvenir Sheet

Jersey's Finance Industry, 50th Anniv. — A312

**Litho. & Embossed**

**2011, Sept. 12** ***Perf. 13x13¼***

| | | | | |
|---|---|---|---|---|
| **1540** | A312 | £3 multi | 9.50 | 9.50 |

**Jersey Attractions Type of 2007**

Designs: 42p, Beauport. 49p, St. Ouen's Bay. 50p, Ouaisné. 64p, St. Brelade's Bay. 79p, Mont Orgueil. 86p, Portelet Bay.

**2011, Sept. 28** **Litho.** ***Perf. 13½***

| | | | | |
|---|---|---|---|---|
| **1541** | A264 | 42p multi | 1.40 | 1.40 |
| **1542** | A264 | 49p multi | 1.60 | 1.60 |
| **1543** | A264 | 50p multi | 1.60 | 1.60 |
| **1544** | A264 | 64p multi | 2.00 | 2.00 |
| **1545** | A264 | 79p multi | 2.50 | 2.50 |
| **1546** | A264 | 86p multi | 2.75 | 2.75 |
| | | *Nos. 1541-1546 (6)* | 11.85 | 11.85 |

Mills A313

Designs: 37p, Rozel Windmill. 42p, Tesson Mill. 49p, St. Peter's Windmill. 50p, Ponterrin Mill. 59p, Quétivel Mill. 79p, Greve de Lecq Mill.

**2011, Oct. 11** ***Perf. 14***

| | | | | |
|---|---|---|---|---|
| **1547** | A313 | 37p multi | 1.25 | 1.25 |
| **1548** | A313 | 42p multi | 1.40 | 1.40 |
| **1549** | A313 | 49p multi | 1.60 | 1.60 |
| **1550** | A313 | 50p multi | 1.60 | 1.60 |
| **1551** | A313 | 59p multi | 1.90 | 1.90 |
| **1552** | A313 | 79p multi | 2.60 | 2.60 |
| | | *Nos. 1547-1552 (6)* | 10.35 | 10.35 |

Christmas A314

Various Christmas tree ornaments and decorations.

**2011, Nov. 8** ***Perf. 13x13¼***

| | | | | |
|---|---|---|---|---|
| **1553** | A314 | 37p multi | 1.25 | 1.25 |
| **1554** | A314 | 42p multi | 1.40 | 1.40 |
| **1555** | A314 | 49p multi | 1.60 | 1.60 |
| **1556** | A314 | 50p multi | 1.60 | 1.60 |
| **1557** | A314 | 79p multi | 2.50 | 2.50 |
| **1558** | A314 | 86p multi | 2.75 | 2.75 |
| | | *Nos. 1553-1558 (6)* | 11.10 | 11.10 |

Jersey Symphony Orchestra, 25th Anniv. — A315

Various musical scores and: 37p, Violin. 50p, Trumpets. 59p, Harp. 64p, Timpani. 79p, Bassoons. 86p, French horn.

**2011, Nov. 15** ***Perf. 14***

| | | | | |
|---|---|---|---|---|
| **1559** | A315 | 37p multi | 1.25 | 1.25 |
| **1560** | A315 | 50p multi | 1.60 | 1.60 |
| **1561** | A315 | 59p multi | 1.90 | 1.90 |
| **1562** | A315 | 64p multi | 2.00 | 2.00 |
| **1563** | A315 | 79p multi | 2.50 | 2.50 |
| **1564** | A315 | 86p multi | 2.75 | 2.75 |
| | | *Nos. 1559-1564 (6)* | 12.00 | 12.00 |

Tourism — A316

Designs: 42p, Food and wine bottle. 49p, Surfer, sailboats, land yachts. 59p, Cyclist, people on pathways. 86p, Military reenactment.

**2012, Jan. 10** *Perf. 13¼*

**1565** A316 42p multi 1.40 1.40
**1566** A316 49p multi 1.60 1.60
**1567** A316 59p multi 1.90 1.90
**1568** A316 86p multi 2.75 2.75
*Nos. 1565-1568 (4)* 7.65 7.65

Europa (49p, 59p).

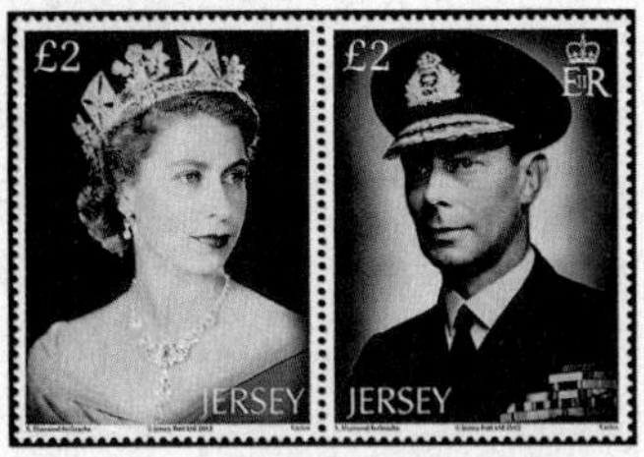


Reign of Queen Elizabeth II, 60th Anniv. — A317

Nos. 1569 and 1570: a, Queen Elizabeth II. b, King George VI.

**2012, Feb. 6** **Litho.** *Perf. 13½*

**Stamps With White Frames**

**1569** A317 Horiz. pair 13.00 13.00
*a.-b.* £2 Either single 6.50 6.50

**Souvenir Sheet**
**Stamps Without White Frames**

**1570** A317 Sheet of 2 13.00 13.00
*a.-b.* £2 Either single 6.50 6.50

A sheet similar to No. 1570 having a diamond attached to the crown in the sheet margin was produced in limited quantities and sold for £131.95.

Jersey Airport, 75th Anniv. A318

Aircraft at Jersey Airport: 37p, DeHavilland DH86. 49p, Bristol 170 Wayfarer. 50p, Airspeed Ambassador. 64p, Hawker Siddeley Trident. 79p, Britten-Norman Trislander. 86p, Vickers VC10.
£3, Fairchild Dornier 328-110.

**2012, Mar. 10** *Perf. 13x13¼*

**1571** A318 37p multi 1.25 1.25
**1572** A318 49p multi 1.60 1.60
**1573** A318 50p multi 1.60 1.60
**1574** A318 64p multi 2.10 2.10
**1575** A318 79p multi 2.50 2.50
**1576** A318 86p multi 2.75 2.75
*a.* Booklet pane of 6, #1571-1576 12.00 —
*Nos. 1571-1576 (6)* 11.80 11.80

**Souvenir Sheet**
*Perf. 13¼x13*

**1577** A318 £3 multi 9.50 9.50
*a.* Booklet pane of 1, 163x100mm 9.50 9.50
Complete booklet, #1577a, 3 #1576a 46.00

No. 1577 contains one 60x40mm stamp. Sheet size of No. 1577: 110x75mm. Complete booklet contains three examples of No. 1576a, each with different arrangements of the stamps.

Souvenir Sheet

Sinking of the Titanic, Cent. — A319

**2012, Apr. 14** *Perf. 14¼*

**1578** A319 £3 multi 9.75 9.75

Butterflies and Moths A320

Designs: (45p), Broad-bordered yellow underwing moth. (55p), Painted lady butterfly. (60p), Merveille du jour moth. (68p), Queen of Spain fritillary butterfly. (72p), Large emerald moth. (86p), Red admiral butterfly.

**2012, May 8** *Perf. 13x13¼*

**Stamps With White Frames**

**1579** A320 (45p) multi 1.40 1.40
**1580** A320 (55p) multi 1.75 1.75
**1581** A320 (60p) multi 1.90 1.90
**1582** A320 (68p) multi 2.10 2.10
**1583** A320 (72p) multi 2.25 2.25
**1584** A320 (86p) multi 2.75 2.75
*Nos. 1579-1584 (6)* 12.15 12.15

**Souvenir Sheet**
**Stamps Without White Frame**

**1585** Sheet of 3 7.25 7.25
*a.* A320 (68p) multi 2.10 2.10
*b.* A320 (72p) multi 2.25 2.25
*c.* A320 (86p) multi 2.75 2.75

Inscriptions: No. 1579, "Local Letter." No. 1580, "UK Letter." No. 1581, "Europe." Nos. 1582, 1585a, "Local Large." Nos. 1583, 1585b, "UK Large." Nos. 1584, 1585c, "International."

Reign of Queen Elizabeth II, 60th Anniv. A325

**Litho. with Hologram Affixed**

**2012, June 1** *Perf. 13¼*

**1590** A325 £10 black & silver 31.00 31.00

Duke of Cambridge, 30th Birthday A326

Prince William wearing various military uniforms. 68p, 70p, horiz.

**2012, June 21** **Litho.** *Perf. 14*

**1591** A326 45p multi 1.40 1.40
**1592** A326 68p multi 2.10 2.10
**1593** A326 70p multi 2.25 2.25
**1594** A326 88p multi 2.75 2.75
*Nos. 1591-1594 (4)* 8.50 8.50

Trees — A327

Designs: 45p, Magnolia. 55p, Swamp cypress. 60p, Flowering cherry. 68p, Maidenhair. 70p, Hill cherry. 88p, London plane.

**2012, July 3** *Perf. 13¼x14*

**1595** A327 45p multi 1.40 1.40
**1596** A327 55p multi 1.75 1.75
**1597** A327 60p multi 1.90 1.90
**1598** A327 68p multi 2.10 2.10
**1599** A327 70p multi 2.25 2.25
**1600** A327 88p multi 2.75 2.75
*Nos. 1595-1600 (6)* 12.15 12.15

Celebrations — A328

Designs: No. 1601, Champagne flutes. No. 1602, Flower. No. 1603, Curled ribbons. No. 1604, Teddy bear. No. 1605, Balloons. No. 1606, Birthday candles on cake. No. 1607, Ribbon bow. No. 1608, Ribbon in shape of heart.

***Serpentine Die Cut 12½x12***

**2012, Aug. 2** **Self-Adhesive**

**Inscribed "Local Letter"**

**1601** A328 (48p) multi 1.50 1.50
**1602** A328 (48p) multi 1.50 1.50
**1603** A328 (48p) multi 1.50 1.50
**1604** A328 (48p) multi 1.50 1.50

**Inscribed "UK Letter"**

**1605** A328 (55p) multi 1.75 1.75
**1606** A328 (55p) multi 1.75 1.75
**1607** A328 (55p) multi 1.75 1.75
**1608** A328 (55p) multi 1.75 1.75
*a.* Miniature sheet of 8, #1601-1608 13.00
*Nos. 1601-1608 (8)* 13.00 13.00

Nos. 1601-1608 were each available in sheets of 20 stamps + 20 labels that could be personalized.

**Birds Type of 2007**

Designs: 45p, Lesser spotted woodpecker. 55p, Stonechat. 60p, Yellowhammer. 68p, Serin. 70p, Bullfinch. 88p, Cirl bunting.

**Stamps With White Frames**

**2012, Aug. 14** *Perf. 13x13½*

**1609** A260 45p multi 1.50 1.50
**1610** A260 55p multi 1.75 1.75
**1611** A260 60p multi 2.00 2.00
**1612** A260 68p multi 2.25 2.25
**1613** A260 70p multi 2.25 2.25
**1614** A260 88p multi 3.00 3.00
*a.* Souvenir sheet of 6, #1609-1614 13.00 13.00
*Nos. 1609-1614 (6)* 12.75 12.75

**Souvenir Sheet**
**Stamps Without White Frames**

**1615** Sheet of 3 7.50 7.50
*a.* A260 68p multi 2.25 2.25
*b.* A260 70p multi 2.25 2.25
*c.* A260 88p multi 3.00 3.00

Jambo the Gorilla (1972-92), First Male Gorilla Born in Captivity A329

Jambo: 45p, With bushes in background. 60p, Amidst trees. 80p, With two other gorillas. 88p, Head.
£1, Jambo facing right, vert.

**2012, Sept. 15** **Litho.** *Perf. 14¾x14*

**1616** A329 45p multi 1.50 1.50
**1617** A329 60p multi 2.00 2.00
**1618** A329 80p multi 2.60 2.60
**1619** A329 88p multi 3.00 3.00
*Nos. 1616-1619 (4)* 9.10 9.10

**Souvenir Sheet**
*Perf. 14x14¾*

**1620** A329 £1 multi 3.25 3.25

Towers A330

Designs: 45p, Flicquet Tower. 55p, Portelet Tower. 60p, Ouaisné Tower. 68p, Lewis Tower. 70p, Noirmont Tower. 80p, St. Catherine's Tower.

**2012, Oct. 12** *Perf. 14*

**1621** A330 45p multi 1.50 1.50
**1622** A330 55p multi 1.75 1.75
**1623** A330 60p multi 1.90 1.90
**1624** A330 68p multi 2.25 2.25
**1625** A330 70p multi 2.25 2.25
**1626** A330 80p multi 2.60 2.60
*Nos. 1621-1626 (6)* 12.25 12.25

Christmas A332

Scenes from *A Christmas Carol,* by Charles Dickens, with inscriptions of: 40p, A Merry Christmas one and all! 45p, Bah Humbug! 50p, The End of It. 55p, Scrooge with Marley's ghost. 60p, The Ghost of Christmas Past. 68p, The Ghost of Christmas Present. 80p, The Ghost of Christmas Future. 88p, Bob Cratchit and Tiny Tim.

**2012, Nov. 15** **Litho.** *Perf. 13x13½*

**1632** A332 40p multi 1.25 1.25
**1633** A332 45p multi 1.50 1.50
**1634** A332 50p multi 1.60 1.60
**1635** A332 55p multi 1.75 1.75
**1636** A332 60p multi 2.00 2.00
**1637** A332 68p multi 2.25 2.25
**1638** A332 80p multi 2.60 2.60
**1639** A332 88p multi 3.00 3.00
*Nos. 1632-1639 (8)* 15.95 15.95

Flora A333

Designs: 45p, Camellia sasonqua "Paradise Belinda." 55p, Butcher's broom. 60p, Snowdrop. 68p, Mistletoe. 80p, Bramble. 88p, Hawthorn.

**2013, Jan. 8**

**1640** A333 45p multi 1.50 1.50
**1641** A333 55p multi 1.90 1.90
**1642** A333 60p multi 2.00 2.00
**1643** A333 68p multi 2.25 2.25
**1644** A333 80p multi 2.60 2.60
**1645** A333 88p multi 3.00 3.00
*Nos. 1640-1645 (6)* 13.25 13.25

## POSTAGE DUE STAMPS

Numeral — D1

Map of Jersey — D2

**Unwmk.**

**1969, Oct. 1** **Litho.** *Perf. 14*

**J1** D1 1p violet blue 2.75 2.50
**J2** D1 2p sepia 4.00 3.75
**J3** D1 3p brt carmine 5.50 5.25
**J4** D2 1sh emerald 15.00 14.50
**J5** D2 2sh6p gray green 25.00 *27.50*
**J6** D2 5sh red orange 42.50 42.50
*Nos. J1-J6 (6)* 94.75 96.00

**Type of 1969**
**Decimal Currency**

**1971-75** **Litho.** *Perf. 14*

**J7** D2 ½p black .25 .25
**J8** D2 1p pale violet .25 .25
**J9** D2 2p brown .25 .25
**J10** D2 3p bright pink .25 .25
**J11** D2 4p orange .25 .25
**J12** D2 5p emerald .25 .25
**J13** D2 6p orange ('74) .25 .25
**J14** D2 7p brt yellow ('74) .25 .25
**J15** D2 8p grnsh blue ('75) .30 .30
**J16** D2 10p gray .35 .35
**J17** D2 11p bister ('75) .40 .40
**J18** D2 14p lilac .50 .50
**J19** D2 25p dull green ('74) .90 .90
**J20** D2 50p plum ('75) 1.90 1.90
*Nos. J7-J20 (14)* 6.35 6.35

St. Clement Arms, Dovecote, Samares — D3

Arms and Scenes from Jersey Parishes: 2p, St. Lawrence and Handois Reservoir. 3p, St. John and Sorel Point. 4p, St. Ouen and Pinnacle Rock. 5p, St. Peter and Quetivel Mill. 10p, St. Martin and St. Catherine's Breakwater. 12p, St. Helier and St. Helier Harbor. 14p, St. Saviour and Highlands College. 15p, St. Brelade and Beauport Bay. 20p, Grouville and La Hougue Bie. 50p, St. Mary and Perry Farm. £1, Trinity and Bouley Bay.

**1978, Jan. 17 Litho. *Perf. 14***

| | | | | | |
|---|---|---|---|---|---|
| **J21** | D3 | 1p | brt green & blk | .25 | .25 |
| **J22** | D3 | 2p | orange & blk | .25 | .25 |
| **J23** | D3 | 3p | maroon & blk | .25 | .25 |
| **J24** | D3 | 4p | vermilion & blk | .25 | .25 |
| **J25** | D3 | 5p | dp ultra & blk | .25 | .25 |
| **J26** | D3 | 10p | olive & blk | .25 | .25 |
| **J27** | D3 | 12p | blue & blk | .30 | .30 |
| **J28** | D3 | 14p | red org & blk | .35 | .35 |
| **J29** | D3 | 15p | lilac rose & blk | .40 | .40 |
| **J30** | D3 | 20p | yel green & blk | .45 | .45 |
| **J31** | D3 | 50p | brown & blk | 1.10 | 1.10 |
| **J32** | D3 | £1 | violet & blk | 2.40 | 2.40 |
| | | | *Nos. J21-J32 (12)* | 6.50 | 6.50 |

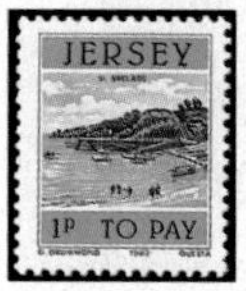


St. Brelade — D4

**1982, Sept. 4 Litho. *Perf. 13½x14***

| | | | | | |
|---|---|---|---|---|---|
| **J33** | D4 | 1p | shown | .25 | .25 |
| **J34** | D4 | 2p | St. Aubin | .25 | .25 |
| **J35** | D4 | 3p | Rozel | .25 | .25 |
| **J36** | D4 | 4p | Greve de Lecq | .25 | .25 |
| **J37** | D4 | 5p | Bouley Bay | .25 | .25 |
| **J38** | D4 | 6p | St. Catherine | .25 | .25 |
| **J39** | D4 | 7p | Gorey | .25 | .25 |
| **J40** | D4 | 8p | Bonne Nuit | .25 | .25 |
| **J41** | D4 | 9p | La Rocque | .30 | .30 |
| **J42** | D4 | 10p | St. Helier | .35 | .35 |
| **J43** | D4 | 20p | Ronez | .60 | .60 |
| **J44** | D4 | 30p | La Collette | 1.00 | 1.00 |
| **J45** | D4 | 40p | Elizabeth Castle | 1.25 | 1.25 |
| **J46** | D4 | £1 | Upper Harbor Marina | 2.75 | 2.75 |
| | | | *Nos. J33-J46 (14)* | 8.25 | 8.25 |

## OCCUPATION STAMPS

### Issued Under German Occupation

OS1

**1941-42 Typo. Unwmk. *Perf. 11***

| | | | | | |
|---|---|---|---|---|---|
| **N1** | OS1 | ½p | bright green | 5.00 | 6.00 |
| **N2** | OS1 | 1p | vermilion | 5.00 | 5.00 |

Issue dates: #N1, 1/29/42; #N1d, 1/43; #N2, 4/1/41; #N2e, 1/43.

Jersey Views — OS2

Designs: ½p, Old Jersey farm; 1p, Portelet Bay; 1½p, Corbiere Lighthouse; 2p, Elizabeth Castle; 2½p, Mont Orgueil Castle; 3p, Gathering seaweed.

**1943-44 *Perf. 13½***

| | | | | | |
|---|---|---|---|---|---|
| **N3** | OS2 | ½p | dark green | 7.25 | 12.00 |
| *a.* | | | On rough, gray paper | 9.00 | 14.00 |
| **N4** | OS2 | 1p | scarlet | 1.75 | .80 |
| *a.* | | | On newsprint | 2.10 | 1.50 |
| **N5** | OS2 | 1½p | brown | 7.25 | 5.75 |
| **N6** | OS2 | 2p | orange | 6.75 | 2.00 |
| **N7** | OS2 | 2½p | blue | 2.00 | 1.40 |
| *a.* | | | On newsprint | .90 | 1.75 |
| **N8** | OS2 | 3p | red violet | 2.00 | 2.75 |
| | | | *Nos. N3-N8 (6)* | 27.00 | 24.70 |

Issued: ½p, 1p, 6/1/43; 1½p, 2p, 6/8/43; 2½p, 3p, 6/29/43; #N4a, 2/28/44; #N7a, 2/25/44.

Nos. N1-N8 remained valid until 4/13/46.

# ISLE OF MAN

ˈī(ə)l əv ˈman

LOCATION — In the Irish Sea, off Northwest coast of England
GOVT. — Semi-autonomous within the British Commonwealth
AREA — 221 sq. mi.
POP. — 75,686 (1999 est.)
CAPITAL — Douglas

**Catalogue values for unused stamps in this section are for Never Hinged items, beginning with Scott 1 in the regular postage section and Scott J1 in the postage due section.**

### British Regional Issues

A1

A2

Manx Emblem — A3

**1958-69 Photo. Wmk. 322**
***Perf. 15x14***

| | | | | | |
|---|---|---|---|---|---|
| **1** | A1 | 2½p | rose red ('64) | .60 | .50 |
| **2** | A2 | 3p | purple | .25 | .25 |
| *p.* | | | Phosphor. ('68) | .25 | .25 |
| **3** | A2 | 4p | ultra ('66) | 1.50 | .25 |
| *p.* | | | Phosphor. ('67) | .25 | .25 |

**Unwmk.**

| | | | | | |
|---|---|---|---|---|---|
| **4** | A2 | 4p | ultra ('68) | .25 | .25 |
| **5** | A2 | 4p | olive brown ('68) | .25 | .25 |
| **6** | A2 | 4p | bright red ('69) | .65 | .30 |
| **7** | A2 | 5p | dark blue ('68) | .65 | .30 |
| | | | *Nos. 1-7 (7)* | 4.15 | 2.10 |

Nos. 4-7 are phosphorescent.
A 1963 printing of No. 2 is on chalky paper.

**1971, July 7 Photo. Unwmk.**

| | | | | | |
|---|---|---|---|---|---|
| **8** | A3 | 2½p | bright pink | .35 | .25 |
| **9** | A3 | 3p | ultramarine | .35 | .25 |
| **10** | A3 | 5p | bluish lilac | .65 | .60 |
| **11** | A3 | 7½p | light red brown | .65 | .70 |
| | | | *Nos. 8-11 (4)* | 2.00 | 1.80 |

Sold to the general public only at post offices within the Isle of Man, but valid for postage throughout Great Britain.

### Bailiwick Issues

Castletown and Manx Emblem A4

Manx Cat — A5

***Perf. 11½***
**1973, July 5 Photo. Unwmk.**

| | | | | | |
|---|---|---|---|---|---|
| **12** | A4 | ½p | shown | .25 | .25 |
| *a.* | | | Booklet pane of 2 | 2.75 | |
| *b.* | | | Booklet pane of 4 ('74) | .90 | |
| **13** | A4 | 1p | Port Erin | .25 | .25 |
| **14** | A4 | 1½p | Mt. Snaefell | .25 | .25 |
| **15** | A4 | 2p | Laxey Village | .25 | .25 |
| *a.* | | | Booklet pane of 2 | 2.75 | |
| **16** | A4 | 2½p | Tynwald Hill | .25 | .25 |
| *a.* | | | Booklet pane of 2 | .75 | |
| | | | Complete booklet, #12a, 15a, 16a | 12.00 | |
| | | | Complete booklet, 5 #16a | 4.00 | |
| **17** | A4 | 3p | Douglas Promenade | .25 | .25 |
| *a.* | | | Booklet pane of 2 | .70 | |
| | | | Complete booklet, 5 #17a | 22.50 | |
| | | | Complete booklet, 4 #16a, 5 #17a | 10.00 | |
| *b.* | | | Booklet pane of 4 ('74) | .90 | |
| **18** | A4 | 3½p | Port St. Mary | .25 | .25 |
| *a.* | | | Booklet pane of 4 ('74) | 5.00 | |
| | | | Complete booklet, 2 #12b, 1 each #17b, 18a | 5.00 | |
| | | | Complete booklet, 2 #17b, 1 each #12b, 18a | 5.00 | |
| | | | Complete booklet, 3 #17b, 1 #18a | 5.00 | |
| **19** | A4 | 4p | Fairy Bridge | .25 | .25 |
| **20** | A4 | 5p | Peel, Castle and shore | .25 | .25 |
| **21** | A4 | 6p | Cregneish Village | .35 | .35 |
| **22** | A4 | 7½p | Ramsey Bay | .35 | .35 |
| **23** | A4 | 9p | Douglas Bay | .35 | .35 |
| **24** | A5 | 10p | shown | .45 | .45 |
| **25** | A5 | 20p | Manx ram | .75 | .75 |
| **26** | A5 | 50p | Manx shearwaters | 2.00 | 2.00 |
| **27** | A5 | £1 | Viking longship | 4.00 | 4.00 |
| | | | *Nos. 12-27 (16)* | 10.50 | 10.50 |

See Nos. 52-59.

Vikings Landing on Man, 938 — A6

**1973, July 5 *Perf. 14***

| | | | | | |
|---|---|---|---|---|---|
| **28** | A6 | 15p | multicolored | .60 | .60 |

Inauguration of postal independence.
Compare with No. 251. Inscription under "Isle of Man" reads "Post Office Decennium" on No. 251.

Engine No. 1, Sutherland, 1873 — A7

**1973, Aug. 4 *Perf. 14½x14***

| | | | | | |
|---|---|---|---|---|---|
| **29** | A7 | 2½p | shown | .25 | .25 |
| **30** | A7 | 3p | Caledonia, 1885 | .25 | .25 |
| **31** | A7 | 7½p | Kissack, 1910 | .50 | .50 |
| **32** | A7 | 9p | Pender, 1873 | .60 | .60 |
| | | | *Nos. 29-32 (4)* | 1.60 | 1.60 |

Centenary of Manx steam railroad.

Leslie Randles, 1923 Winner A8

3½p, Alan Holmes, 1957 double winner.

**1973, Sept. 4 Litho. *Perf. 14***

| | | | | | |
|---|---|---|---|---|---|
| **33** | A8 | 3p | multicolored | .25 | .25 |
| **34** | A8 | 3½p | multicolored | .25 | .25 |

Manx Grand Prix Motorcycle Race, 50th anniversary.

Princess Anne and Mark Phillips — A9

**Litho. & Engr.**
**1973 Nov. 14 *Perf. 14x13½***

| | | | | | |
|---|---|---|---|---|---|
| **35** | A9 | 25p | lt blue & multi | .95 | .95 |

Wedding of Princess Anne and Capt. Mark Phillips, Nov. 14, 1973.

William Hillary, R.N.L.I. Badge A10

Wreck of "St. George" A11

Designs: 8p, Tower of Refuge and lifeboat "Manchester & Salford." 10p, "Osman Gabriel" at Port Erin. 3½p and 8p are from paintings.

**1974, Mar. 4 Photo. *Perf. 11½***

| | | | | | |
|---|---|---|---|---|---|
| **36** | A10 | 3p | black & multi | .25 | .25 |
| **37** | A11 | 3½ | black & multi | .25 | .25 |
| **38** | A11 | 8p | black & multi | .45 | .45 |
| **39** | A11 | 10p | black & multi | .55 | .55 |
| | | | *Nos. 36-39 (4)* | 1.50 | 1.50 |

Sesqui. of the founding of the Royal Natl. Lifeboat Institution by Sir William Hillary.

Stanley Woods on Moto Guzzi Motorcycle — A12

Designs: 3½p, Freddie Frith on Norton. 8p, Max Deubel on BMW with sidecar. 10p, Mike Hailwood on Honda.

**1974, May 29 Litho. *Perf. 13***

| | | | | | |
|---|---|---|---|---|---|
| **40** | A12 | 3p | yellow grn & multi | .25 | .25 |
| **41** | A12 | 3½p | crimson & multi | .25 | .25 |
| **42** | A12 | 8p | yellow & multi | .30 | .25 |
| **43** | A12 | 10p | ultra & multi | .40 | .35 |
| | | | *Nos. 40-43 (4)* | 1.20 | 1.10 |

Tourist Trophy Motorcycle Races on the Isle of Man.

Arms and Ruins of Rushen Abbey A13

Designs: 4½p, King Edgar of England visiting Chester in boat rowed by 8 kings including King Magnus Haraldson. 8p, Fleet under King Magnus' command and arms he gave to Isle of Man. 10p, Bridge at Avignon, Bishop's mitre and Three Legs of Man.

**1974, Sept. 18 Litho. *Perf. 14***

| | | | | | |
|---|---|---|---|---|---|
| **44** | A13 | 3½p | multicolored | .25 | .25 |
| **45** | A13 | 4½p | multicolored | .25 | .25 |
| **46** | A13 | 8p | multicolored | .30 | .30 |
| **47** | A13 | 10p | multicolored | .40 | .40 |
| | | | *Nos. 44-47 (4)* | 1.20 | 1.20 |

1,000th death anniv. of Magnus Haraldson, King of Many Islands (Nos. 45-46), and 600th death anniv. of William Russell, Bishop of Sodor and Mann (Nos. 44, 47).

Churchill and "Bugler Dunne at Colenso, 1899" — A14

Sir Winston Churchill: 4½p, Government Buildings, Douglas, and Warrant of Appointment. 8p, Manx A.A. Regiment in action. 20p, Freedom of Douglas Scroll, and scroll casket.

**1974, Nov. 22 Photo. *Perf. 11½***

| | | | | | |
|---|---|---|---|---|---|
| 48 | A14 | 3½p | multicolored | .25 | .25 |
| 49 | A14 | 4½p | multicolored | .25 | .25 |
| 50 | A14 | 8p | multicolored | .25 | .25 |
| 51 | A14 | 20p | multicolored | .65 | .65 |
| *a.* | | | Souvenir sheet of 4, #48-51 | 1.40 | 1.40 |
| | | | *Nos. 48-51 (4)* | 1.40 | 1.40 |

**Type of 1973**

**1975 Unwmk. *Perf. 11½***

| | | | | | |
|---|---|---|---|---|---|
| 52 | A4 | 4½p | Tynwald Hill | .25 | .25 |
| 53 | A4 | 5½p | Douglas Promenade | .25 | .25 |
| 54 | A4 | 7p | Laxey Village | .40 | .40 |
| 55 | A4 | 8p | Ramsey Bay | .40 | .40 |
| 58 | A4 | 11p | Monk's Bridge | .45 | .45 |
| 59 | A4 | 13p | Derbyhaven | .60 | .60 |
| | | | *Nos. 52-59 (6)* | 2.35 | 2.35 |

Issued: #52, 55, 1/8; #53-54, 5/28; #58-59, 10/29.

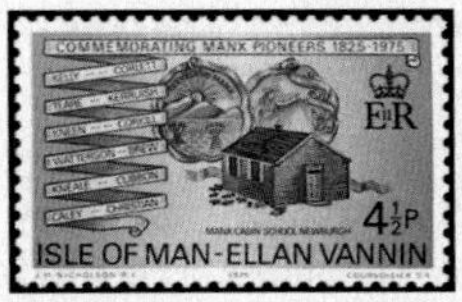


Log Cabin School, Cleveland Medal, Names of Settlers A15

Designs: 5½p, Terminal Tower Building, Cleveland, John Gill and Robert Carran. 8p, Clague House Museum, Margaret and Robert Clague. 10p, Thomas Quayle and S. S. William T. Graves.

**1975, Mar. 14 Photo. *Perf. 11½***

| | | | | | |
|---|---|---|---|---|---|
| 62 | A15 | 4½p | multicolored | .25 | .25 |
| 63 | A15 | 5½p | multicolored | .25 | .25 |
| 64 | A15 | 8p | multicolored | .30 | .30 |
| 65 | A15 | 10p | multicolored | .35 | .35 |
| | | | *Nos. 62-65 (4)* | 1.15 | 1.15 |

Sesquicentennial of arrival of Manx settlers in Cleveland, Ohio area.

Tom Sheard and "Douglas" — A16

Designs: 7p, Walter L. Handley and "Rex-Acme." 10p, Geoffrey Duke and "Gilera." 12p, Peter Williams and "Norton."

**1975, May 28 Litho. *Perf. 13½***

| | | | | | |
|---|---|---|---|---|---|
| 66 | A16 | 5½p | bister & multi | .25 | .25 |
| 67 | A16 | 7p | salmon & multi | .25 | .25 |
| 68 | A16 | 10p | lt green & multi | .35 | .35 |
| 69 | A16 | 12p | ultra & multi | .40 | .40 |
| | | | *Nos. 66-69 (4)* | 1.25 | 1.25 |

Tourist Trophy Motorcycle races on Isle of Man.

Sir George Goldie and his Birthplace A17

Designs (Sir George Goldie and): 7p, Map of Africa with Niger River basin, vert. 10p, Goldie as president of Royal Geographical Society and Society emblem, vert. 12p, River boats: trading hulk, native canoe, sternwheeler.

**1975, Sept. 9 Photo. *Perf. 11½***

| | | | | | |
|---|---|---|---|---|---|
| 70 | A17 | 5½p | multicolored | .25 | .25 |
| 71 | A17 | 7p | multicolored | .25 | .25 |
| 72 | A17 | 10p | multicolored | .35 | .35 |
| 73 | A17 | 12p | multicolored | .40 | .40 |
| | | | *Nos. 70-73 (4)* | 1.25 | 1.25 |

Sir George Dashwood Goldie-Taubman (1846-1925), founder of Royal Niger Company.

Manx Bible — A18

Bicentenary of Manx Bible and Christmas 1975: 7p, Rev. Philip Moore and Old Ballaugh Church. 11p, Bishop Mark Hildesley and Bishops Court. 13p, Shipwreck off Cumberland Coast with John Kelly holding manuscript above water.

**1975, Oct. 29 Litho. *Perf. 14***

| | | | | | |
|---|---|---|---|---|---|
| 74 | A18 | 5½p | multicolored | .25 | .25 |
| 75 | A18 | 7p | multicolored | .25 | .25 |
| 76 | A18 | 11p | multicolored | .35 | .35 |
| 77 | A18 | 13p | multicolored | .40 | .40 |
| | | | *Nos. 74-77 (4)* | 1.25 | 1.25 |

William Christian Listening to Patrick Henry — A19

Designs: 7p, Christian carrying Fincastle Resolutions to Williamsburg. 13p, Col. Patrick Henry and Lt. Col. William Christian of 1st Virginia Regiment. 20p, Christian as frontiersman and Indians.

**1976, Mar. 12 Litho. *Perf. 13½***

| | | | | | |
|---|---|---|---|---|---|
| 78 | A19 | 5½p | multicolored | .25 | .25 |
| 79 | A19 | 7p | multicolored | .25 | .25 |
| 80 | A19 | 13p | multicolored | .40 | .40 |
| 81 | A19 | 20p | multicolored | .45 | .45 |
| *a.* | | | Souv. sheet of 4, #78-81, perf. 14 | 1.75 | 1.75 |
| | | | *Nos. 78-81 (4)* | 1.35 | 1.35 |

American Bicentennial. William Christian (1743-1786), patriot, son of a Manx-man and Patrick Henry's brother-in-law.

First Double-decker Tram Car — A20

Designs: 7p, Toast-rack tram, 1890. 11p, Horse bus, 1895. 13p, Decorated tram with Queen Elizabeth II and Prince Philip.

**1976, May 26 Photo. *Perf. 11½***

| | | | | | |
|---|---|---|---|---|---|
| 82 | A20 | 5½p | multicolored | .25 | .25 |
| 83 | A20 | 7p | multicolored | .25 | .25 |
| 84 | A20 | 11p | multicolored | .40 | .40 |
| 85 | A20 | 13p | multicolored | .40 | .40 |
| | | | *Nos. 82-85 (4)* | 1.30 | 1.30 |

Douglas horse trams, centenary.

Barroose Beaker, Bronze Age — A21

Virgin and Child, on Sodor and Man Banner — A22

Europa (Manx Ceramic Art): No. 87, Souvenir teapot (3-legged man), 19th cent. No. 88, Laxey jug, 1854. No. 89, Cronk Aust food vessel, early Bronze Age. No. 90, Sansbury bowl, 1851. No. 91, Knox urn, 20th cent. Nos. 89-91, horiz.

**1976, July 28 Photo. *Perf. 11½***

| | | | | | |
|---|---|---|---|---|---|
| 86 | A21 | 5p | multicolored | .25 | .25 |
| 87 | A21 | 5p | multicolored | .25 | .25 |
| 88 | A21 | 5p | multicolored | .25 | .25 |
| *a.* | | | Strip of 3, #86-88 | .80 | .80 |
| 89 | A21 | 10p | multicolored | .25 | .25 |
| 90 | A21 | 10p | multicolored | .25 | .25 |
| 91 | A21 | 10p | multicolored | .25 | .25 |
| *a.* | | | Strip of 3, #89-91 | .80 | .80 |
| | | | *Nos. 86-91 (6)* | 1.50 | 1.50 |

Printed in sheets of 9 (3x3).

**1976, Oct. 14 Litho. *Perf. 14¾x14½***

Virgin and Child on Embroidered Church Banners: 7p, St. Peter's, Onchan, Mothers' Union. 11p, Castletown. 13p, St. Olav's, Ramsey.

| | | | | | |
|---|---|---|---|---|---|
| 92 | A22 | 6p | multicolored | .25 | .25 |
| 93 | A22 | 7p | multicolored | .25 | .25 |
| 94 | A22 | 11p | multicolored | .35 | .35 |
| 95 | A22 | 13p | multicolored | .45 | .45 |
| | | | *Nos. 92-95 (4)* | 1.30 | 1.30 |

Christmas 1976 & cent. of Mothers' Union.

Elizabeth II and Arms of Man A23

Designs: 7p, Queen Elizabeth II and Prince Philip, vert. 25p, Queen, 1976 portrait.

***Perf. 13½x14, 14x13½***

**1977, Mar. 1 Litho. & Engr.**

| | | | | | |
|---|---|---|---|---|---|
| 96 | A23 | 6p | multicolored | .25 | .25 |
| 97 | A23 | 7p | multicolored | .25 | .25 |
| 98 | A23 | 25p | multicolored | .75 | .75 |
| | | | *Nos. 96-98 (3)* | 1.25 | 1.25 |

25th anniv. of the reign of Elizabeth II.

Carrick Bay from Tom-the-Dipper's — A24

Europa: 10p, Looking south from Mooragh Park, Ramsey.

**1977, May 25 Litho. *Perf. 14***

| | | | | | |
|---|---|---|---|---|---|
| 99 | A24 | 6p | multicolored | .25 | .25 |
| 100 | A24 | 10p | multicolored | .35 | .35 |

"Pa" Applebee at Ballig Bridge, 1912 — A25

Designs: 7p, Hairpin curve at Governor's Bridge and ambulance attendants. 11p, Boy Scouts tending scoreboards. 13p, John Williams at Windy Corner on Snaefell Mountain, winner of 1976 Open Classic Race.

**1977, May 25 *Perf. 13½***

| | | | | | |
|---|---|---|---|---|---|
| 101 | A25 | 6p | multicolored | .25 | .25 |
| 102 | A25 | 7p | multicolored | .30 | .30 |
| 103 | A25 | 11p | multicolored | .40 | .40 |
| 104 | A25 | 13p | multicolored | .45 | .45 |
| | | | *Nos. 101-104 (4)* | 1.40 | 1.40 |

Tourist Trophy Motorcycle Races, and Boy Scouts, 70th anniv.; St. John Ambulance Assoc. cent. (in GB).

Meeting House, Mt. Morrison — A26

Designs: 7p, John Wesley preaching at Castletown, 1777. 11p, Wesley preaching outside Braddan Church. 13p, Methodist Church on Douglas Promenade, 1976.

**1977, Oct. 19 Photo. *Perf. 11½***

**Size: 30x24mm**

| | | | | | |
|---|---|---|---|---|---|
| 105 | A26 | 6p | multicolored | .25 | .25 |

**Size: 37½x24mm**

| | | | | | |
|---|---|---|---|---|---|
| 106 | A26 | 7p | multicolored | .30 | .30 |
| 107 | A26 | 11p | multicolored | .40 | .40 |

**Size: 30x24mm**

| | | | | | |
|---|---|---|---|---|---|
| 108 | A26 | 13p | multicolored | .45 | .45 |
| | | | *Nos. 105-108 (4)* | 1.40 | 1.40 |

Bicentenary of John Wesley's first visit to the Isle of Man.

Seaplane and Carrier Ben My Chree — A27

Royal Air Force, 60th Anniv.: 7p, Bristol Scout and carrier Vindex, 1915. 11p, Boulton Paul Defiant over Douglas Bay, 1941. 13p, RAF Jaguar over Ramsey, 1977.

**1978, Feb. 28 Litho. *Perf. 13½x14***

| | | | | | |
|---|---|---|---|---|---|
| 109 | A27 | 6p | multicolored | .25 | .25 |
| 110 | A27 | 7p | multicolored | .30 | .30 |
| 111 | A27 | 11p | multicolored | .40 | .40 |
| 112 | A27 | 13p | multicolored | .45 | .45 |
| | | | *Nos. 109-112 (4)* | 1.40 | 1.40 |

Watch Tower, Langness — A28

Jurby Church — A29

Fuchsia — A30

Landmarks: 6p, Government buildings. 7p, Tynwald Hill. 8p, Milner's Tower. 9p, Laxey Wheel. 10p, Castle Rushen. 11p, St. Ninian's Church. 12p, Tower of Refuge. 13p, St. German's Cathedral. 14p, Point of Ayre Lighthouse. 15p, Corrin's Tower. 16p, Douglas Head Lighthouse. 25p, Manx cat. 50p, Chough (crows). £1, Viking warrior.

**1978 Litho. *Perf. 14***

| | | | | | |
|---|---|---|---|---|---|
| 113 | A28 | ½p | multicolored | .25 | .25 |
| 114 | A29 | 1p | multicolored | .25 | .25 |
| 115 | A28 | 6p | multicolored | .25 | .25 |
| 116 | A29 | 7p | multicolored | .25 | .25 |
| 117 | A28 | 8p | multicolored | .25 | .25 |
| 118 | A28 | 9p | multicolored | .30 | .30 |
| 119 | A29 | 10p | multicolored | .45 | .45 |
| 120 | A28 | 11p | multicolored | .45 | .45 |
| 121 | A29 | 12p | multicolored | .50 | .50 |
| 122 | A29 | 13p | multicolored | .70 | .70 |
| 123 | A29 | 14p | multicolored | .70 | .70 |
| 124 | A29 | 15p | multicolored | .85 | .85 |
| 125 | A29 | 16p | multicolored | .60 | .60 |

**Photo.**

***Perf. 11½***

| | | | | | |
|---|---|---|---|---|---|
| **126** | A30 | 20p | multicolored | .60 | .60 |
| **127** | A30 | 25p | multicolored | .90 | .90 |
| **128** | A30 | 50p | multicolored | 1.60 | 1.60 |
| **129** | A30 | £1 | multicolored | 3.50 | 3.50 |
| | | *Nos. 113-129 (17)* | | 12.40 | 12.40 |

Issued: #113-125, 2/28; #126-129, 10/18.

***Perf. 14½***

| | | | | | |
|---|---|---|---|---|---|
| *113a* | A28 | ½p | multicolored | .25 | .25 |
| *114a* | A29 | 1p | multicolored | .25 | .25 |
| *116a* | A29 | 7p | multicolored | 9.00 | 7.00 |
| *117a* | A28 | 8p | multicolored | .40 | .40 |
| *118a* | A28 | 9p | multicolored | .30 | .30 |
| *119a* | A29 | 10p | multicolored | .40 | .40 |
| *120a* | A28 | 11p | multicolored | .45 | .45 |
| *121a* | A29 | 12p | multicolored | .60 | .60 |
| *122a* | A29 | 13p | multicolored | .35 | .35 |
| *123a* | A29 | 14p | multicolored | .35 | .35 |
| *124a* | A29 | 15p | multicolored | .35 | .35 |
| *125a* | A29 | 16p | multicolored | 30.00 | 25.00 |
| | | *Nos. 113a-125a (12)* | | 42.70 | 35.70 |

Elizabeth II — A31

**1978, May 24 Litho.** ***Perf. 14½x14¼***

| | | | | |
|---|---|---|---|---|
| **130** | A31 | 25p blue & multi | .80 | .80 |

25th anniv. of coronation of Elizabeth II.

Keeil Chiggyrt Stone — A32

Europa (Carved Gravestones): No. 132, Wheel-headed cross slab. No. 133, Celtic Wheel cross. No. 134, Thor cross. No. 135, Olaf Liotulfson cross. No. 136, Odd's and Thorleif's crosses.

**1978, May 24** ***Perf. 11½***

| | | | | | |
|---|---|---|---|---|---|
| **131** | A32 | 6p | multicolored | .25 | .25 |
| **132** | A32 | 6p | multicolored | .25 | .25 |
| **133** | A32 | 6p | multicolored | .25 | .25 |
| *a.* | | Strip of 3, #131-133 | | .50 | .50 |
| **134** | A32 | 11p | multicolored | .35 | .35 |
| **135** | A32 | 11p | multicolored | .35 | .35 |
| **136** | A32 | 11p | multicolored | .35 | .35 |
| *a.* | | Strip of 3, #134-136 | | 1.10 | 1.10 |
| | | *Nos. 131-136 (6)* | | 1.80 | 1.80 |

Printed se-tenant in sheets of 9 (3x3).

J. K. Ward, Ward Library, Peel — A33

13p, Lumber camp at Three Rivers & J. K. Ward.

**1978, June 10 Litho.** ***Perf. 13½***

| | | | | | |
|---|---|---|---|---|---|
| **137** | A33 | 6p | multicolored | .25 | .25 |
| **138** | A33 | 13p | multicolored | .35 | .35 |

James K. Ward (1819-1910), Manx pioneer in Canada.

Athletes, Games' Emblem and Manx Arms A34

Eagle, Manx Arms, Maple Leaf A35

**1978, June 10**

| | | | | | |
|---|---|---|---|---|---|
| **139** | A34 | 7p | multicolored | .25 | .25 |
| **140** | A35 | 11p | multicolored | .35 | .35 |

11th Commonwealth Games, Edmonton, Aug. 3-12 (7p); North American Manx Soc., 50th anniv. (11p).

"Hunt the Wren" — A36

**1978, Oct. 18 Litho.** ***Perf. 13***

| | | | | |
|---|---|---|---|---|
| **141** | A36 | 5p multicolored | .35 | .25 |

Christmas 1978.

Philip M. C. Kermode and Nassa Kermodei A37

7p, Peregrine falcons. 11p, Fulmars. 13p, Asilid fly.

**1979, Feb. 27 Litho.** ***Perf. 14***

| | | | | | |
|---|---|---|---|---|---|
| **142** | A37 | 6p | multicolored | .25 | .25 |
| **143** | A37 | 7p | multicolored | .30 | .30 |
| **144** | A37 | 11p | multicolored | .35 | .35 |
| **145** | A37 | 13p | multicolored | .45 | .45 |
| | | *Nos. 142-145 (4)* | | 1.35 | 1.35 |

Isle of Man Natural History and Antiquarian Society.

Viking Ship — A38

A39

Viking Raid at Garwick A40

Designs (Tynwald Emblem and): 7p, 10th century meeting at Tynwald. 11p, Tynwald Hill and St. John's Church. 13p, Contemporary Tynwald Day parade.

***Perf. 14½x14 (#146-147), 13¼ (#148-151)***

**1979, May 16** **Litho.**

| | | | | | |
|---|---|---|---|---|---|
| **146** | A38 | 3p | *Insularem* | .25 | .25 |
| *a.* | | Bklt. pane, 4 #146, 2 #147 | | .60 | |
| | | Complete booklet, #146a | | 1.00 | |
| | | Complete booklet, 2 #146a | | 1.50 | |
| | | Complete booklet, 3 #146a | | 2.00 | |
| *b.* | | *Insularum* (inscribed "1980") | | .25 | .25 |
| *c.* | | Bklt. pane, 4 #146b, 2 #147a | | 1.25 | |
| **147** | A39 | 4p | multicolored | .25 | .25 |
| *a.* | | Inscribed "1980" | | .25 | .25 |
| **148** | A40 | 6p | multicolored | .25 | .25 |
| **149** | A40 | 7p | multicolored | .25 | .25 |
| **150** | A40 | 11p | multicolored | .30 | .30 |
| **151** | A40 | 13p | multicolored | .35 | .35 |
| | | *Nos. 146-151 (6)* | | 1.65 | 1.65 |

Millennium of Tynwald, Legislative Council. #146-147 printed se-tenant in sheets of 80. No. 146a comes in two arrangements.

19th Century Mailman — A41

Europa: 11p, Contemporary mailman.

**1979, May 16** ***Perf. 14½***

| | | | | | |
|---|---|---|---|---|---|
| **152** | A41 | 6p | multicolored | .25 | .25 |
| **153** | A41 | 11p | multicolored | .40 | .40 |

Ceremony on Tynwald Hill — A42

Design: 13p, Procession from St. John's Church to Tynwald Hill.

**1979, July 5 Litho.** ***Perf. 14½***

| | | | | | |
|---|---|---|---|---|---|
| **154** | A42 | 7p | multicolored | .25 | .25 |
| **155** | A42 | 13p | multicolored | .45 | .45 |

Visit of Queen Elizabeth II for the celebration of millennium of Tynwald.

Girl Holding Teddy Bear — A43

Christmas and IYC: 7p, Children with Santa.

**1979, Oct. 19 Litho.** ***Perf. 13¼x13½***

| | | | | | |
|---|---|---|---|---|---|
| **156** | A43 | 5p | multicolored | .25 | .25 |
| **157** | A43 | 7p | multicolored | .30 | .30 |

Capt. John Quilliam and Spencer A44

Capt. Quilliam: 6p, Seized by press gang. 8p, Battle of Trafalgar. 15p, Castle Rushen.

**1979, Oct. 19** ***Perf. 14***

| | | | | | |
|---|---|---|---|---|---|
| **158** | A44 | 6p | multicolored | .25 | .25 |
| **159** | A44 | 8p | multicolored | .25 | .25 |
| **160** | A44 | 13p | multicolored | .35 | .35 |
| **161** | A44 | 15p | multicolored | .45 | .45 |
| | | *Nos. 158-161 (4)* | | 1.30 | 1.30 |

Capt. John Quilliam (1771-1829), British naval hero and member of House of Keys.

"Odin's Raven" A45

**1979, Oct. 19** ***Perf. 14x14½***

| | | | | |
|---|---|---|---|---|
| **162** | A45 | 15p multicolored | .65 | .65 |

Voyage of replica Viking longboat across North Sea (Trondheim to Peel), May 27-July 4. See No. 176a.

Conglomerate Arch, Langness, and Emblem — A46

Royal Geographical Society Emblem and: 8p, Braaid Circle. 12p, Cashtal yn Ard (Neolithic burial ground). 13p, Volcanic rocks, Scarlett. 15p, Sugar-loaf Rock.

**1980, Feb. 5 Litho.** ***Perf. 14½***

| | | | | | |
|---|---|---|---|---|---|
| **163** | A46 | 7p | multicolored | .25 | .25 |
| **164** | A46 | 8p | multicolored | .30 | .30 |
| **165** | A46 | 12p | multicolored | .40 | .40 |
| **166** | A46 | 13p | multicolored | .40 | .40 |
| **167** | A46 | 15p | multicolored | .40 | .40 |
| | | *Nos. 163-167 (5)* | | 1.75 | 1.75 |

Royal Geographical Society, 150th anniv.

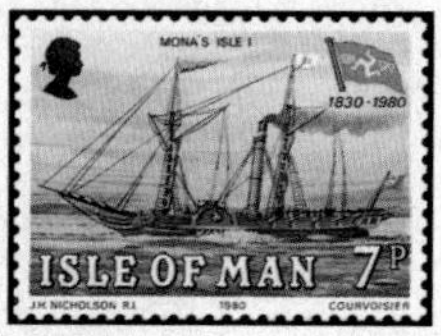

"Mona's Isle I" A47

**1980, May 6 Photo.** ***Perf. 11½***

**Granite Paper**

| | | | | | |
|---|---|---|---|---|---|
| **168** | A47 | 7p | *shown* | .25 | .25 |
| **169** | A47 | 8p | *Douglas I* | .25 | .25 |
| **170** | A47 | 11½p | *Mona's Queen II, sinking U-boat* | .30 | .30 |
| **171** | A47 | 12p | *King Orry III* | .35 | .35 |
| **172** | A47 | 13p | *Ben-My-Chree IV* | .40 | .40 |
| **173** | A47 | 15p | *Lady of Mann II* | .50 | .50 |
| *a.* | | Souvenir sheet of 6, #168-173 | | 2.25 | 2.25 |
| | | *Nos. 168-173 (6)* | | 2.05 | 2.05 |

Isle of Man Steam Packet Co. sesqui.; London 80 Intl. Stamp Exhib., May 6-14.

Thomas Edward Brown and Characters from his Poems — A48

Europa (Brown (1830-1897), Poet and Scholar): 13½p, Cricket game, Clifton College Bristol.

**1980, May 6**

| | | | | | |
|---|---|---|---|---|---|
| **174** | A48 | 7p | multicolored | .30 | .30 |
| **175** | A48 | 13½p | multicolored | .40 | .40 |

Visit of King Olav V of Norway A49

**1980, June 13 Litho.** ***Perf. 14½***

| | | | | |
|---|---|---|---|---|
| **176** | A49 | 12p multicolored | .75 | .75 |
| *a.* | | Souv. sheet of 2, #162, 176 | 1.25 | 1.25 |

Visit of King Olav V of Norway, Aug. 2-7, 1979, and NORWEX 80 stamp exhibition, Oslo, June 13-22.

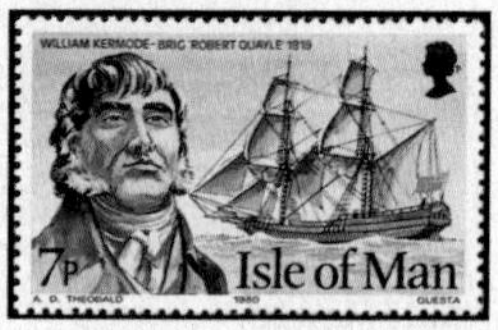

William Kermode and "Robert Quayle" A50

Kermode Family (First Manx Pioneers in Tasmania): 9p, First homestead, Mona Vale, Merino sheep, 1834. 13½p, Ross Bridge, W.

Kermode. 15p, Calendar House, 1868. 17½p, Parliament Buildings, Hobart, Robert Quayle Kermode.

**1980, Sept. 29 Litho.**

| | | | | |
|---|---|---|---|---|
| 177 | A50 | 7p multicolored | .25 | .25 |
| 178 | A50 | 9p multicolored | .30 | .30 |
| 179 | A50 | 13½p multicolored | .45 | .45 |
| 180 | A50 | 15p multicolored | .50 | .50 |
| 181 | A50 | 17½p multicolored | .55 | .55 |
| | | *Nos. 177-181 (5)* | 2.05 | 2.05 |

Wren A51

**1980, Sept. 29 Litho. *Perf. 13½x14***

| | | | | |
|---|---|---|---|---|
| 182 | A51 | 6p shown | .25 | .25 |
| 183 | A51 | 8p Robin | .25 | .25 |

Wildlife conservation and Christmas 1980.

Luggers, Red Pier, Douglas A52

**1981, Feb. 24 Litho. *Perf. 14***

| | | | | |
|---|---|---|---|---|
| 184 | A52 | 8p shown | .25 | .25 |
| 185 | A52 | 9p Wanderer saving Lusitania Survivors | .25 | .25 |
| 186 | A52 | 18p Nickey, Port St. Mary | .50 | .50 |
| 187 | A52 | 20p Nobby, Ramsey Harbor | .60 | .60 |
| 188 | A52 | 22p Sunbeam and Zebra, Port Erin | .65 | .65 |
| | | *Nos. 184-188 (5)* | 2.25 | 2.25 |

Royal National Mission to Deep Sea Fishermen centenary.

Peregrine Falcon — A53

**1980, Sept. 29 Litho. *Perf. 14½x14***

**Booklet Stamps**

| | | | | |
|---|---|---|---|---|
| 189 | A53 | 1p shown | .35 | .35 |
| 190 | A53 | 5p Loaghtyn ram | .35 | .35 |
| *a.* | | Bklt. pane, 2 each #147a, 189, 190 | 1.25 | |
| | | Complete booklet, #146c, 190a | 2.50 | |
| | | Complete booklet, 2 each #146c, 190a | 5.00 | |

Crosh Cuirn (Cross of Mountain Ash Twigs, Harvest Charm) — A54

Europa: 18p, Bollan fish cross-bone (fishermen's charm).

**1981, May 22 Litho. *Perf. 14½***

| | | | | |
|---|---|---|---|---|
| 191 | A54 | 8p multicolored | .25 | .25 |
| 192 | A54 | 18p multicolored | .65 | .65 |

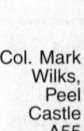

Col. Mark Wilks, Peel Castle A55

**1981, May 22 *Perf. 14***

| | | | | |
|---|---|---|---|---|
| 193 | A55 | 8p shown | .30 | .30 |
| 194 | A55 | 20p Wilks, Fort. St. George, Madras | .50 | .50 |
| 195 | A55 | 22p Wilks, Napoleon | .65 | .65 |
| 196 | A55 | 25p Wilks at Kirby estate | .75 | .75 |
| | | *Nos. 193-196 (4)* | 2.20 | 2.20 |

Wilks (d. 1831), governor of St. Helena.

Suffragettes Emmeline Goulden Pankhurst and Sophia Jane Goulden — A56

**1981, May 22 *Perf. 14***

| | | | | |
|---|---|---|---|---|
| 197 | A56 | 9p multicolored | .40 | .40 |

Centenary of women's suffrage and of House of Keys Election Act (granting widows and unmarried women voting rights).

Prince Charles and Lady Diana A57

**1981, July 29 Litho. *Perf. 14***

| | | | | |
|---|---|---|---|---|
| 198 | A57 | 9p multicolored | .25 | .25 |
| 199 | A57 | 25p multicolored | 1.00 | 1.00 |
| *a.* | | Souv. sheet, 2 each #198-199 | 2.75 | 2.75 |

Royal Wedding.

Queen Elizabeth II — A58

**1981, Sept. 29 Photo. *Perf. 11½***

**Granite paper**

| | | | | |
|---|---|---|---|---|
| 200 | A58 | £2 multicolored | 6.00 | 6.00 |

Douglas War Memorial, Poppies, Quote from Laurence Binyon's For the Fallen — A59

**1981, Sept. 29 Granite Paper**

| | | | | |
|---|---|---|---|---|
| 201 | A59 | 8p shown | .25 | .25 |
| 202 | A59 | 10p Maj. R.H. Cain, Battle of Arnhem, 1944 | .30 | .30 |
| 203 | A59 | 18p Festival of Remembrance | .60 | .60 |
| 204 | A59 | 20p Tynwald and Spitfire, Dunkirk, 1940 | .70 | .70 |
| | | *Nos. 201-204 (4)* | 1.85 | 1.85 |

Royal British Legion, 60th anniv.

Nativity Stained-glass Window, 1865, St. George's Church, Douglas — A60

9p: Christmas pageant, Glencrutchery Special School, Douglas.

**1981, Sept. 29 Litho. *Perf. 14½x14***

| | | | | |
|---|---|---|---|---|
| 205 | A60 | 7p multicolored | .25 | .25 |

**Size: 47x28mm**

| | | | | |
|---|---|---|---|---|
| 206 | A60 | 9p multicolored | .35 | .35 |

Christmas and St. George's Church bicen. (7p), IYD (9p).

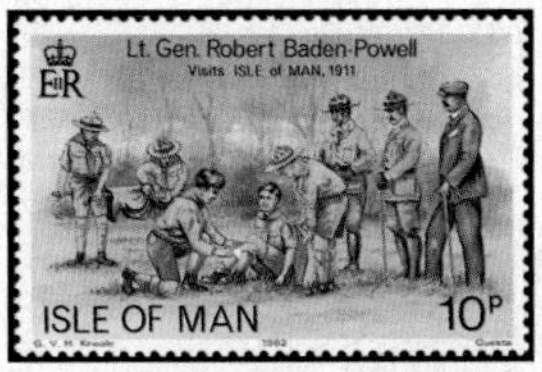


Scouting Year — A61

Designs: 9p, Cunningham House (Man Scout Headquarters). 10p, Baden-Powell's visit, 1911. 19½p, Portrait (32x41mm., Perf. 14½). 24p, Baden-Powell with scouts, message. 29p, Sign, handshake, globe, emblem.

**1982, Feb. 23 Litho. *Perf. 13½x14***

| | | | | |
|---|---|---|---|---|
| 207 | A61 | 9p multicolored | .25 | .25 |
| 208 | A61 | 10p multicolored | .25 | .25 |
| 209 | A61 | 19½p multicolored | .65 | .65 |
| 210 | A61 | 24p multicolored | .80 | .80 |
| 211 | A61 | 29p multicolored | 1.00 | 1.00 |
| | | *Nos. 207-211 (5)* | 2.95 | 2.95 |

Europa 1982 — A62

Designs: 9p, Bishop Thomas Wilson (1663-1755) and his "The Principles and Duties of Christianity," first book printed in Manx, 1707. 19½p, Visit of Thomas, 2nd Earl of Derby, 1507.

**1982, June 1 Photo. *Perf. 12½***

**Granite Paper**

| | | | | |
|---|---|---|---|---|
| 212 | A62 | 9p multicolored | .30 | .30 |
| 213 | A62 | 19½p multicolored | .60 | .60 |

75th Anniv. of Tourist Trophy Motorcycle Races — A63

Designs: Winners on their bikes.

**1982, June 1 Litho. *Perf. 14***

| | | | | |
|---|---|---|---|---|
| 214 | A63 | 9p Charlie Collier, 431 Matchless, 1907 | .25 | .25 |
| 215 | A63 | 10p Freddie Dixon, Douglas, 1923 | .25 | .25 |
| 216 | A63 | 24p Jimmie Simpson, Norton, 1932 | .90 | .90 |
| 217 | A63 | 26p Mike Hailwood, Norton, 1961 | .90 | .90 |
| 218 | A63 | 29p Jock Taylor, 700 Fowler Yamaha, '80 | .90 | .90 |
| | | *Nos. 214-218 (5)* | 3.20 | 3.20 |

Isle of Man Steam Packet Co. Mail Contract Sesquicentennial — A64

**1982, Oct. 5 Litho. *Perf. 13½x14***

| | | | | |
|---|---|---|---|---|
| 219 | A64 | 12p Mona I | .55 | .55 |
| 220 | A64 | 19½p Manx Maid II | .80 | .80 |

Christmas 1982 A65

***Perf. 13¼x13½, 13½x13¼***

**1982, Oct. 5**

| | | | | |
|---|---|---|---|---|
| 221 | A65 | 8p Three Kings | .30 | .30 |
| 222 | A65 | 11p Robin, Christmas tree, vert. | .55 | .55 |

Souvenir Sheet

Princess Diana and Prince William — A66

**1982, Oct. 12 *Perf. 14½x14¼***

| | | | | |
|---|---|---|---|---|
| 223 | A66 | 50p multicolored | 2.75 | 2.75 |

Birth of Prince William of Wales (June 21) and 21st birthday of Princess Diana (July 1).

Marine Birds A67

**1983, Feb. 15 Litho. *Perf. 14½***

| | | | | |
|---|---|---|---|---|
| 224 | A67 | 1p Puffins, Cranstal | .25 | .25 |
| 225 | A67 | 2p Gannets, Point of Ayre | .25 | .25 |
| 226 | A67 | 5p Lesser black-backed gulls, Santon | .25 | .25 |
| 227 | A67 | 8p Cormorants, Maughold Head | .35 | .35 |
| 228 | A67 | 10p Kittiwakes, White Strand | .45 | .45 |
| 229 | A67 | 11p Shags, Calf of Man | .50 | .50 |
| 230 | A67 | 12p Herons, Douglas Foreshore | .55 | .55 |
| 231 | A67 | 13p Herring gulls, Peel | .60 | .60 |
| 232 | A67 | 14p Razorbills, Calf of Man | .60 | .60 |
| 233 | A67 | 15p Great black-backed gulls, Calf of Man | .70 | .70 |
| 234 | A67 | 16p Shelducks, Poyll Vaaish | .75 | .75 |
| 235 | A67 | 18p Oystercatchers, Langness | .80 | .80 |

**1983, Sept. 14 *Perf. 14***

**Size: 39x25mm**

| | | | | |
|---|---|---|---|---|
| 236 | A67 | 20p Arctic terns, Blue Point | .90 | .90 |
| 237 | A67 | 25p Guillemots, Calf of Man | 1.10 | 1.10 |
| 238 | A67 | 50p Redshanks, Langness | 2.00 | 2.00 |
| 239 | A67 | £1 Mute swans, Port St. Mary Bay | 4.00 | 4.00 |
| | | *Nos. 224-239 (16)* | 14.05 | 14.05 |

Centenary of Salvation Army in Isle of Man — A68

Designs: 10p, Citadel opening ceremony, 1932, T.H. Cannell. 12p, Founder William Booth, early meeting place (former Unitarian Church, Douglas). 19½p, Band, Bandmaster Gordon Cowley, 1981. 26p, Lt.-Col. Thomas Bridson, treating lepers in Dutch East Indies.

**1983, Feb. 15 Photo. *Perf. 11½***
**Granite Paper**

**240** A68 10p multicolored .35 .35
**241** A68 12p multicolored .45 .45
**242** A68 19½ multicolored .75 .75
**243** A68 26p multicolored .95 .95
*Nos. 240-243 (4)* 2.50 2.50

Europa 1983 — A69

**1983, May 18 *Perf. 14***

**244** A69 10p Laxey Wheel .45 .45
**245** A69 20½p Designer Robert Casement .80 .80

King William's College Sesquicentennial — A70

Graduates: 10p, Nick Keig, Yachtsman. 12p, College, arms. 28p, William Bragg, 1915 Nobel Prize winner in physics, ionization spectrometer. 31p, Gen. George Stuart White, Defense of Ladysmith, Boer War.

**1983, May 18 Photo. *Perf. 11½***
**Granite Paper**

**246** A70 10p multicolored .30 .30
**247** A70 12p multicolored .40 .40
**248** A70 28p multicolored 1.10 1.10
**249** A70 31p multicolored 1.25 1.25
*Nos. 246-249 (4)* 3.05 3.05

World Communications Year and 10th Anniv. of Post Office — A71

**1983, July 5 Litho. *Perf. 15***

**250** A71 10p New P.O. Headquarters .45 .45
**251** A6 15p Viking landing, 938 .75 .75

Compare No. 251 with No. 28.

Christmas 1983 A72

**1983, Sept. 14 Litho. *Perf. 13x13½***

**252** A72 9p Shepherds .40 .40
**253** A72 12p Three Kings .50 .50

Karran Fleet A73

Links with Falkland Islands — A74

**1984, Feb. 14 Litho. *Perf. 14***

**254** A73 10p Manx King, 1884 .30 .30
**255** A73 13p Hope, 1858 .45 .45
**256** A73 20½p Rio Grande, 1868 .65 .65
**257** A73 28p Lady Elizabeth, 1879 1.10 1.10
**258** A73 31p Sumatra, 1858 1.25 1.25
*Nos. 254-258 (5)* 3.75 3.75

**1984, Feb. 14**

**259** Sheet of 2, #257, 259a 3.50 3.50
*a.* A74 31p multicolored 1.50 1.50

Europa (1959-1984) A75

**1984, Apr. 27 Photo. *Perf. 11½***

**260** A75 10p dk yel org, dk brn & buff .40 .40
**261** A75 20½p blue, dk bl & lt bl .75 .75

DH-48, Ronaldsway Airport — A76

**1984, Apr. 27 Litho. *Perf. 14***

**262** A76 11p shown .50 .50
**263** A76 13p DH-86, Calf of Man .55 .55
**264** A76 26p DC-3, Ronaldsway Airport 1.00 1.00
**265** A76 28p Vickers Viscount, Douglas 1.00 1.00
**266** A76 31p Islander, Ronaldsway Airport 1.00 1.00
*Nos. 262-266 (5)* 4.05 4.05

50th Anniv. of official airmail service and 40th anniv. of Intl. Civil Aviation Org.

William Cain as Mayor of Melbourne, 1886-87 — A77

**1984, Sept. 21 Litho. *Perf. 14½***

**267** A77 11p Ballasalla (birthplace) .45 .45
**268** A77 22p Voyage to Australia .80 .80
**269** A77 28p Railway, Victoria 1.00 1.00
**270** A77 30p shown 1.10 1.10
**271** A77 33p Royal Exhibition Buildings, Melbourne 1.10 1.10
*Nos. 267-271 (5)* 4.45 4.45

William Cain (1831-1914), building contractor and public servant in Australia.

Queen Elizabeth II, CPA Emblem A78

**1984, Sept. 21 *Perf. 14***

**272** A78 14p shown .50 .50
**273** A78 33p Arms, Elizabeth II 1.25 1.25

30th Conference of Commonwealth Parliamentary Assoc., Sept. 28-Oct. 5.

Christmas — A79

Stained-glass windows.

**1984, Sept. 21**

**274** A79 10p Birds, Glencrutchery House .50 .50
**275** A79 13p Arms, Lonan Old Church .60 .60

75th Anniv. of Girl Guides — A80

Designs: 11p, Cunningham House (headquarters), Mrs. W. and J. Cunningham (early Island Commissioners). 14p, Princess Margaret (president), color guard. 29p, Lady Olave Baden-Powell, headquarters opening. 31p, Uniforms, 1910-85. 34p, Sign, handclasp, trefoil.

**1985, Jan. 31 Photo. *Perf. 12***

**276** A80 11p multicolored .50 .50
**277** A80 14p multicolored .65 .65
**278** A80 29p multicolored 1.10 1.10
**279** A80 31p multicolored 1.25 1.25
**280** A80 34p multicolored 1.50 1.50
*Nos. 276-280 (5)* 5.00 5.00

Elizabeth II A81

**1985, Jan. 31 Litho. *Perf. 14***

**281** A81 £5 multicolored 15.00 15.00

Europa 1985 — A82

Manx composers and excerpts from their works: No. 282a, "O'Land of our Birth." No. 282b, William H. Gill (1839-1922). No. 283a, Hymn "Crofton;" No. 283b, Dr. John Clague (1842-1908).

**1985, Apr. 24 Photo. *Perf. 12***

**282** A82 Pair 1.25 1.25
*a.-b.* 12p any single .65 .65
**283** A82 Pair 1.50 1.50
*a.-b.* 22p any single .75 .75

Motoring — A83

Motor races and winning vehicles: No. 284a, 1906 Tourist Trophy Race. No. 284b, 1922 Tourist Trophy Race. No. 285a, 1950 British Empire Trophy Race. No. 285b, 1934 Manin Moar Race. No. 286a, 1984 Tourist Trophy Motorcycle Race (official car). No. 286b, 1981 Rothmans Manx Intl. Rally.

**1985, May 25 Litho. *Perf. 14***

**284** A83 Pair 1.00 1.00
*a.-b.* 12p any single .45 .45
**285** A83 Pair 1.25 1.25
*a.-b.* 14p any single .60 .60
**286** A83 Pair 2.50 2.50
*a.-b.* 31p any single 1.25 1.25
*Nos. 284-286 (3)* 4.75 4.75

H.R.H. Alexandra (1885-1925), Princess of Wales — A84

SSA presidents: 15p, Queen Mary (1925-1953). 29p, Earl Mountbatten of Burma (1953-1979). 34p, Prince Michael of Kent (1982- ).

**1985, Sept. 4 Litho. *Perf. 14***

**287** A84 12p multicolored .45 .45
**288** A84 15p multicolored .60 .60
**289** A84 29p multicolored 1.10 1.10
**290** A84 34p multicolored 1.40 1.40
*Nos. 287-290 (4)* 3.55 3.55

Soldier's, Sailors' & Airmen's Families Assoc., cent.

Lt.-Gen. Sir Mark Cubbon, K.C.B. (1785-1861), Commissioner of Mysore — A85

**1985, Oct. 2 Litho. *Perf. 14***

**291** A85 12p Kirk Maughold Parish Church, 14th century .50 .50
**292** A85 22p Portrait, vert. .90 .90
**293** A85 45p Equestrian monument, 1866 Bangalore, India, vert. 1.75 1.75
*Nos. 291-293 (3)* 3.15 3.15

Christmas 1985 A86

**1985, Oct. 2 Litho. *Perf. 13½***

**294** A86 11p Onchan Parish Church, 1833 .40 .40
**295** A86 14p St. John's Church .65 .65
**296** A86 31p Bride Parish Church, 1876 1.50 1.50
*Nos. 294-296 (3)* 2.55 2.55

1986 Commonwealth Games, Edinburgh — A87

**1986, Feb. 5 Litho. *Perf. 14***

**297** A87 12p Women's swimming .50 .50
**298** A87 15p Walking .65 .65
**299** A87 31p Rifle shooting 1.10 1.10
**300** A87 34p Bicycling 1.50 1.50
*Nos. 297-300 (4)* 3.75 3.75

Viking Necklace, Peel Castle
A88

Artifacts, architecture: 15p, Meayll Circle burial ground, Rushen. 22p, Prehistoric Cervus giganteus skeleton, Glose-y-Garey, vert. 26p, Norwegian viking longship, vert. 29p, Open-air Museum, Cregneash.

**1986, Feb. 5** *Perf. 14½x14, 14x14½*

**301** A88 12p multicolored .50 .50
**302** A88 15p multicolored .60 .60
**303** A88 22p multicolored .90 .90
**304** A88 26p multicolored 1.00 1.00
**305** A88 29p multicolored 1.25 1.25
*Nos. 301-305 (5)* 4.25 4.25

Centenaries of Manx Museum and Ancient Monuments Act.

Europa 1986, Manx National Trust — A89

Designs: No. 306a, Bride hills and the Ayres. No. 306b, Calf of Man. No. 307a, Eary Cushlin. No. 307b, St. Michael's Isle.

**1986, Apr. 10** **Litho.** *Perf. 12*

**306** A89 Pair 1.00 1.00
*a.-b.* 12p any single .50 .50
**307** A89 Pair 2.00 2.00
*a.-b.* 22p any single 1.00 1.00

Settling of Plymouth — A90

Designs: 12p, Ellanbane, Isle of Man, Myles Standish's home. 15p, The Mayflower. 31p, Pilgrims landing, 1620. 34p, Capt. Myles Standish (c. 1584-1656).

**1986, May 22** *Perf. 13½*

**308** A90 12p multicolored .50 .50
**309** A90 15p multicolored .60 .60
**310** A90 31p multicolored 1.25 1.25
**311** A90 34p multicolored 1.50 1.50
*a.* Souvenir sheet of 2, #310-311, perf. 13x12½ 3.00 3.00
*Nos. 308-311 (4)* 3.85 3.85

AMERIPEX '86, Chicago, May 22-June 1.

Heritage Year — A91

**1986, Apr. 10** **Litho.** *Perf. 15x14*

**Booklet Stamps**

**312** A91 2p Viking longship bow .25 .25
*a.* Bklt. pane of 6, 2 #312, 4 #313 4.50
**313** A91 10p Celtic cross .90 .90
*a.* Bklt. pane of 3 + 3 labels 2.75
Complete booklet, #190a, 313a 4.50
Complete booklet, #146c, 190a, 312a, 313a 10.00

Wedding of Prince Andrew and Sarah Ferguson
A92

**1986, July 23**

**314** A92 15p Wedding date .80 .80
**315** A92 40p Engagement date 1.75 1.75

Royal Birthdays — A93

No. 316: a, Prince Philip, 65. #b, Elizabeth II, 60. No. 317 is the same size as No. 316.

**1986, Aug. 28** *Perf. 11½*

**316** A93 Pair 1.40 1.40
*a.-b.* 15p any single .70 .70
**317** A93 34p Royal couple 1.40 1.40

STOCKHOLMIA '86, Swedish Post Office 350th anniv. Stamps issued in sheets of 6.

Intl. Peace Year — A94

**1986, Sept. 25** **Litho.** *Perf. 14*

**318** A94 11p Robins, globe, Braille .45 .45
**319** A94 14p Hands, dove .55 .55
**320** A94 31p Hand-holding, sign language 1.25 1.25
*Nos. 318-320 (3)* 2.25 2.25

Accession of Queen Victoria to the British Throne, 150th Anniv.
A95

Photographs of Victorian Douglas, by John Miller Nicholson.

**1987, Jan. 21** **Litho.** *Perf. 14½*

**321** A95 2p North Quay .25 .25
**322** A95 3p The Old Fish Market .25 .25
**323** A95 10p Breakwater .40 .40
*a.* Bklt. pane of 8 (2 2p, 2 3p, 4 10p) ('87) 2.10
Complete booklet, #323a 2.10
**324** A95 15p Jubilee Clock .60 .60
*a.* Bklt. pane of 8 (2 2p, 2 3p, 2 10p, 2 15p) ('87) 2.40
Complete booklet, #323a, #324a 4.50
**325** A95 31p Loch Promenade 1.40 1.40
**326** A95 34p Beach 1.50 1.50
*Nos. 321-326 (6)* 4.40 4.40

No. 323a comes in two arrangements.

19th Century Paintings by John Miller Nicholson (1840-1913) — A96

Harbor scenes: 12p, The Old Fish Market and Harbor, Douglas. 26p, Red Sails at Douglas. 29p, The Double Corner. 34p, Peel Harbor.

**1987, Feb. 18** *Perf. 13½*

**327** A96 12p multicolored .50 .50
**328** A96 26p multicolored 1.00 1.00
**329** A96 29p multicolored 1.10 1.10
**330** A96 34p multicolored 1.40 1.40
*Nos. 327-330 (4)* 4.00 4.00

Promenade, Douglas — A97

**1987, Apr. 29** **Litho.** *Perf. 13½*

**331** A97 12p Sea Terminal, 1965 .65 .65
**332** A97 12p Tower of Refuge, 1832 .65 .65
*a.* Pair, #331-332 1.25 1.25
**333** A97 22p Gaiety Theater, c. 1900 1.00 1.00
**334** A97 22p Villa Marina 1.00 1.00
*a.* Pair, #333-334 2.00 2.00
*Nos. 331-334 (4)* 3.30 3.30

Europa 1987.

Tourist Trophy Motorcycle Races, 80th Anniv. — A98

**1987, May 27** *Perf. 13½x13*

**335** A98 12p 1939 Supercharged BMW 500CC .45 .45
**336** A98 15p 1953 Manx "Kneeler" Norton 350CC .60 .60
**337** A98 29p 1956 MV Agusta 500CC 4 1.10 1.10
**338** A98 31p 1957 Guzzi 500CC V8 1.25 1.25
**339** A98 34p 1967 Honda 250CC 6 1.40 1.40
*a.* Souv. sheet of 5, #335-339 + 7 labels, perf 14x13½ 5.00 5.00
*Nos. 335-339 (5)* 4.80 4.80

Wildflowers — A99

**1987, Sept. 9** **Litho.** *Perf. 14½x13½*

**340** A99 16p Fuchsia, wild roses .60 .60
**341** A99 29p Field scabius, ragwort 1.10 1.10
**342** A99 31p Wood anemone, celandine 1.25 1.25
**343** A99 34p Violets, primroses 1.40 1.40
*Nos. 340-343 (4)* 4.35 4.35

Christmas — A100

Victorian family scenes based on drawings by Alfred Hunt for The Illustrated London News, c. 1870-1890.

**1987, Oct. 16** *Perf. 14*

**344** A100 12p Stirring the pudding .50 .50
**345** A100 15p Christmas tree selection .60 .60
**346** A100 31p Decorating tree 1.40 1.40
*Nos. 344-346 (3)* 2.50 2.50

Railways & Tramways
A101

Designs: 1p, Horse-drawn "Toast Rack" tram, Douglas Bay, 1884. 2p, No. 5 electric tram, Snaefell Mountain Railway, 1895. 3p, No. 3 open-top double-deck electric tram, Marine Drive-Port Soderick line, Douglas Southern Electric Tramway, 1896. 5p, Tower of Refuge and open tram, Douglas Head Incline Railway. 10p, Electric tram at Maughold Head, 1893, Douglas and Laxey Coast Electric Tramway. 13p, Douglas Cable Car No. 72, 1896. 14p, Manx Northern Railway No. 4 Caledonia, a Dubs 0-6-0T, 1885, at Gob-y-Deigan. 15p, Great Laxey Mine Railway Lewin steam engine Ant pulling coal cars. 16p, Henry B. Loch, first locomotive on the island, Port Erin Breakwater Railway, 1864. 17p, Locomotive No. 1, Ramsey Harbor Tramway. 18p, Engine No. 7 Tynwald, 1880, Foxdale Railway. 19p, Douglas Corp. engine, Baldwin Reservoir Railway. 20p, "Kissack" leaving St. John's for Peel. 25p, "Hutchinson" leaving Douglas Station. 50p, "Polar Bear" of Groudle Glen Railway. £1, The Royal Train.

**1988** **Litho.** *Perf. 13½*

**Inscribed 1988**

**347** A101 1p multicolored .25 .25
**348** A101 2p multicolored .25 .25
**349** A101 3p multicolored .25 .25
*a.* Inscribed "1989" .25 .25
**350** A101 5p multicolored .25 .25
**351** A101 10p multicolored .40 .40
**352** A101 13p multicolored .50 .50
**353** A101 14p multicolored .55 .55
*a.* Inscribed "1989" .55 .55
**354** A101 15p multicolored .60 .60
*a.* Inscribed "1990" .60 .60
**355** A101 16p multicolored .65 .65
*b.* Bklt. pane, 2 #349, #352, 2 #355 2.25
Complete booklet #355b 3.00
*c.* Bklt. pane, 4 #352, 6 #355 6.00
Complete booklet, #355b, 355c 11.50
**356** A101 17p multicolored .70 .70
*a.* Bklt. pane, 2 #349a, 2 #353a, #356c 2.25
Complete booklet, #356a 3.00
*b.* Booklet pane, 4 #353a, 6 #356c 6.50
Complete booklet, #356a, 356b 9.50
*c.* Inscribed "1989" .70 .70
*d.* Inscribed "1991" .70 .70
**357** A101 18p multicolored .70 .70
**358** A101 19p multicolored .75 .75
*e.* Inscribed "1990" .75 .75
*f.* Bklt. pane, 4 #354a, 6 #358e 7.00
Complete booklet, 4 #354a, 6 #358e 7.50
*g.* Bklt. pane, 1 #354a, 2 #358e 2.10
Complete booklet, #354a, 358e 2.50

*Perf. 15*

**358A** A101 20p multicolored .80 .80
**358B** A101 25p multicolored 1.00 1.00
**358C** A101 50p multicolored 2.00 2.00
*a.* Inscribed "1992" 4.00 4.00
**358D** A101 £1 multicolored 4.00 4.00
*a.* Inscribed "1992" 8.50 8.50
*Nos. 347-358D (16)* 13.65 13.65

Nos. 356a and 356b also exist in special booklet sheets of 50 stamps containing either 10 #356a or 5 #356b.

Issued: 1p-19p, 2/10; #355b-355c, 3/16; 20p-£1, 9/21; #356a, 356b, 10/16/89; #358f, 2/14/90.

See Nos. 448-459.

Car Racing — A102

Winning automobiles, drivers: 13p, Vauxhall Opel, Russell Brookes, 1985. 26p, Ford Escort, Ari Vatanen of Finland, 1976. 31p, Repco March 761, Terry Smith, 1980. 34p, Williams/Honda Nigel Mansell, 1986-87.

**1988, Feb. 10** *Perf. 13½x14½*

**359** A102 13p multicolored .60 .60
**360** A102 26p multicolored 1.25 1.25
**361** A102 31p multicolored 1.40 1.40
**362** A102 34p multicolored 1.50 1.50
*Nos. 359-362 (4)* 4.75 4.75

Europa 1988
A103

Telecommunications: No. 363, IOM-UK optical fiber cable-laying plow. No. 364, Cable-laying ship. No. 365, 1st IOM Earth station, Braddan, established by Manx Telecom. No. 366, Intelsat V satellite.

**1988, Apr. 14 Litho. *Perf. 14x13½***

**363** A103 13p multicolored .60 .60
**364** A103 13p multicolored .60 .60
*a.* Pair, #363-364 1.25 1.25
**365** A103 22p multicolored 1.00 1.00
**366** A103 22p multicolored 1.00 1.00
*a.* Pair, #365-366 2.00 2.00
*Nos. 363-366 (4)* 3.20 3.20

Submarine cable linking the Isle of Man and Silecroft in Cumbria, 1987 (13p). Nos. 364a, 366a have continuous designs.

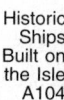

Historic Ships Built on the Isle — A104

Isle of Man flag, Australia bicen. emblem or US flag and: 16p, Euterpe, 1863, built in Ramsey. 29p, Vixen leaving Peel for Australia, 1853. 31p, Ramsey, an immigrant ship in Brisbane, 1870. 34p, Star of India (renamed in 1906, was the Euterpe), restored 1960-1976, Maritime Museum at San Diego.

**1988, May 11 Litho. *Perf. 14***

**367** A104 16p multicolored .60 .60
**368** A104 29p multicolored 1.10 1.10
**369** A104 31p multicolored 1.10 1.10
**370** A104 34p multicolored 1.25 1.25
*a.* Souvenir sheet of 2 (16p, 34p) 2.75 2.75
*Nos. 367-370 (4)* 4.05 4.05

Fuchsia Blossoms — A105

**1988, Sept. 21 Litho. *Perf. 13½x14***

**371** A105 13p Magellanica .45 .45
**372** A105 16p Pink cloud .55 .55
**373** A105 22p Leonora .80 .80
**374** A105 29p Satellite 1.10 1.10
**375** A105 31p Preston Guild 1.25 1.25
**376** A105 34p Thalia 1.40 1.40
*Nos. 371-376 (6)* 5.55 5.55

British Fuchsia Society, 50th anniv.

Christmas A106

**1988, Oct. 12 *Perf. 14***

**377** A106 12p Long-earred owl .75 .75
**378** A106 15p Robin .90 .90
**379** A106 31p Partridge 1.75 1.75
*Nos. 377-379 (3)* 3.40 3.40

Manx Cats A107

Designs: 16p, Ginger. 27p, Black and white. 30p, Tortoiseshell and white. 40p, Tortoiseshell.

**1989, Feb. 8**

**380** A107 16p multicolored .65 .65
**381** A107 27p multicolored 1.10 1.10
**382** A107 30p multicolored 1.40 1.40
**383** A107 40p multicolored 1.60 1.60
*Nos. 380-383 (4)* 4.75 4.75

Celtic Works of Art by Archibald Knox (1864-1933) — A108

Designs: 13p, Tudric pewter and enamel clock, 1903, vert. 16p, Cross, a watercolor, vert. 23p, Silver tankard, 1902, vert. 32p, Liberty silver and Cymric gold brooches. 35p, Silver jewel box with inlaid turquoise, mother-of-pearl and enamel, 1900.

**1989, Feb. 8 Litho. *Perf. 13***

**384** A108 13p multicolored .50 .50
**385** A108 16p multicolored .60 .60
**386** A108 23p multicolored .85 .85
**387** A108 32p multicolored 1.10 1.10
**388** A108 35p multicolored 1.40 1.40
*Nos. 384-388 (5)* 4.45 4.45

Mutiny on the *Bounty* A109

Designs: 13p, William Bligh, Old Onchan Church. 16p, Bligh and crewmen cast adrift. 30p, Peter Heywood on Tahiti, 1770. 32p, *Bounty* off Pitcairn. 35p, Fletcher Christian on Pitcairn.

**1989, Apr. 28 Litho. *Perf. 14***

**389** A109 13p multicolored .45 .45
**390** A109 16p multicolored .60 .60
**391** A109 30p multicolored 1.00 1.00
**392** A109 32p multicolored 1.10 1.10
**393** A109 35p multicolored 1.25 1.25
*Nos. 389-393 (5)* 4.40 4.40

**Souvenir Sheet**

**394** Sheet of 3 + label 4.50 4.50
*a.* A109 23p Pitcairn Isls. No. 321d .80 .80
*b.* A109 27p Norfolk Is. No. 453 .95 .95
*c.* Booklet pane, #394 4.50
*d.* Booklet pane, 1 each #389-393, 394a 5.50
*e.* Bklt. pane of 6, #389-393, #394b 5.50
*f.* Booklet pane, 3 each #394a, #394b 5.25
Complete booklet, #394c, 394d, 394e, 394f 22.00

See Norfolk Is. Nos. 452-456 and Pitcairn Isls. Nos. 320-322.
No. 394 contains Nos. 393, 394a-394b.
No. 394c is 145x101mm and is rouletted at left.

Europa 1989 A110

Children's games: No. 395, Jumping rope, hopscotch, London Bridge is falling down. No. 396, Running, wheelbarrow race, leap frog, piggyback ride. No. 397, Boy building fort, girl blowing soap bubbles, puzzle. No. 398, Doll house, blocks, girl playing with rag doll and puzzle.

**1989, May 17 *Perf. 13½***

**395** A110 13p multicolored .50 .50
**396** A110 13p multicolored .50 .50
*a.* Pair, #395-396 1.00 1.00
**397** A110 23p multicolored 1.00 1.00
**398** A110 23p multicolored 1.00 1.00
*a.* Pair, #397-398 2.00 2.00
*Nos. 395-398 (4)* 3.00 3.00

Nos. 396a, 398a have continuous designs.

World Wildlife Fund — A111

**1989, Sept. 20 Litho. *Perf. 14***

**399** A111 13p Puffin 1.50 1.50
**400** A111 13p Black guillemot 1.50 1.50
**401** A111 13p Cormorant 1.50 1.50
**402** A111 13p Kittiwake 1.50 1.50
*a.* Block or strip of 4, #399-402 7.50 7.50
*Nos. 399-402 (4)* 6.00 6.00

Exists as sheetlet of 16 with "World Stamp Expo '89" printed in selvage.

Intl. Red Cross, 125th Anniv. A112

**1989, Oct. 16 Litho. *Perf. 14***

**403** A112 14p Training youths .55 .55
**404** A112 17p Emblems .65 .65
**405** A112 23p Signing 1st Geneva convention, 1864 .90 .90
**406** A112 30p Ambulance services 1.25 1.25
**407** A112 35p Henri Dunant, founder 1.40 1.40
*Nos. 403-407 (5)* 4.75 4.75

Noble's Hospital, Douglas, cent.

Christmas — A113

**1989, Oct. 16 *Perf. 14½x15***

**408** A113 13p Maternity home .45 .45
**409** A113 16p Mother and child .55 .55
**410** A113 34p Madonna and child, scripture 1.25 1.25
**411** A113 37p Church, baptismal ceremony 1.40 1.40
*Nos. 408-411 (4)* 3.65 3.65

Jane Crookall Maternity Home 50th anniv. (13p) and 75th anniv. of the consecration of St. Ninian's Church (37p).

Queen Elizabeth II, Lord of Man, Trooping the Colors — A114

**1990, Feb. 14 Litho. *Perf. 14½***

**412** A114 £2 multicolored 6.50 6.50

Humorous Edwardian Postcards — A115

15p, The Isle of Man Express Going Up a Gradient. 19p, A Way We Have in the Isle of Man. 32p, Douglas — Waiting for the Male Boat. 34p, The Last Toast Rack Home Douglas Parade. 37p, The Last Isle of Man Boat.

**1990, Feb. 14 *Perf. 14***

**413** A115 15p multicolored .55 .55
**414** A115 19p multicolored .75 .75
**415** A115 32p multicolored 1.25 1.25
**416** A115 34p multicolored 1.50 1.50
**417** A115 37p multicolored 1.75 1.75
*Nos. 413-417 (5)* 5.80 5.80

Europa 1990 — A116

Mailmen and post offices.

**1990, Apr. 18 Litho. *Perf. 13½***
**Size of Nos. 419, 421: 42x28mm**

**418** A116 15p Mailman, 1990 .75 .75
**419** A116 15p Ramsey P.O., 1990 .75 .75
*a.* Pair, #418-419 1.50 1.50
**420** A116 24p Mailman, c. 1890 1.25 1.25
**421** A116 24p Douglas P.O., c. 1890 1.25 1.25
*a.* Pair, #420-421 2.50 2.50
*Nos. 418-421 (4)* 4.00 4.00

Great Britain No. 1 — A117

Designs: 19p, Wyon Medal. 32p, William Wyon's essay. 34p, Perkins Bacon engine-turned essay of 1839. 37p, Great Britain No. 2.

No. 423 (various Penny Blacks and text): a.-e. Positions AA-AE. f.-j. Positions BA-BE. k.-n. Positions CA-CE. p.-t. Positions DA-DE. u.-y. Positions EA-EE.

**Note** that A-A top of square on No. 423a, centered on No. 422a.

**1990, May 3 Litho. *Perf. 14x13½***

**422** Pane of 5 5.25 5.25
*a.* A117 1p shown .25 .25
*b.* A117 19p multicolored .75 .75
*c.* A117 32p multicolored 1.25 1.25
*d.* A117 34p multicolored 1.40 1.40
*e.* A117 37p multicolored 1.50 1.50
*g.* Bklt. pane, 2 each #422b-422e 10.00
*h.* No. 422 ovptd. "From STAMP WORLD LONDON '90 / To NEW ZEALAND '90" *16.00* *16.00*

**Miniature Sheet**

**423** Sheet of 25 2.50 2.50
*a.-y.* A117 1p like #422a, any single .25 .25
*z.* Pane of 8, #a.-d., f.-i. .55

**Souvenir Sheet**
**Litho. & Engr.**

**424** A117 £1 4 Great Britain #1 4.50 4.50
*a.* Booklet pane of 1 4.50 4.50
Complete booklet, #422g, 423z, 424a 15.00

Left margin of #422g, 423z and 424a rouletted.

Queen Mother, 90th Birthday — A118

**1990, Aug. 4 Litho. *Perf. 13x13½***

**425** A118 90p multicolored 3.75 3.75

Sheets of 10 alternating with 10 labels.

Battle of Britain, 50th Anniv. A119

**1990, Sept. 5 Litho. *Perf. 14***

**426** A119 15p Home defense .70 .70
**427** A119 15p Air sea rescue .70 .70
*a.* Pair, #426-427 1.40 1.40
**428** A119 24p Rearming fighters 1.00 1.00
**429** A119 24p Height of battle 1.00 1.00
*a.* Pair, #428-429 2.00 2.00
**430** A119 29p Civil defense 1.25 1.25
**431** A119 29p Anti-aircraft defense 1.25 1.25
*a.* Pair, #430-431 2.50 2.50
*Nos. 426-431 (6)* 5.90 5.90

Sir Winston Churchill (1874-1965) — A120

**1990, Sept. 5** *Perf. 13½*

**432** A120 19p multicolored .75 .75
**433** A120 32p multicolored 1.25 1.25
**434** A120 34p multicolored 1.40 1.40
**435** A120 37p multicolored 1.50 1.50
*Nos. 432-435 (4)* 4.90 4.90

Christmas — A121

**1990, Oct. 10** *Perf. 13x13½*

**436** A121 14p Mailing letters .55 .55
**437** A121 18p Sledding, skating .70 .70
**438** A121 34p Snowman 1.25 1.25
**439** A121 37p Throwing snowball 1.40 1.40
*a.* Souvenir sheet of 4, #436-439 4.25 4.25
*Nos. 436-439 (4)* 3.90 3.90

Denominations on stamps in No. 439a are black.

Manx Photographers A122

Designs: 17p, Henry Bloom Noble, by Marshall Wane. 21p, Douglas, by Frederic Frith & Co. 26p, Studio Portrait, by Hilda Newby. 31p, Cashtal yn Ard, by Christopher Killip. 40p, Peel, by Colleen Corlett.

**1991, Jan. 6** **Litho.** *Perf. 14x14½*

**440** A122 17p multicolored .60 .60
**441** A122 21p multicolored .70 .70
**442** A122 26p multicolored .90 .90
**443** A122 31p multicolored 1.25 1.25
**444** A122 40p multicolored 1.60 1.60
*Nos. 440-444 (5)* 5.05 5.05

**Railways and Tramways Type of 1988 with Queen's Head in White (#448, 458)**

Designs: 18p, TPO Special leaving Douglas Station, 1991. 23p, Double decker horse tram.

**1991-92** **Litho.** *Perf. 13½*

**448** A101 4p like No. 352 .25 .25
**456** A101 18p multicolored .70 .70
**458** A101 21p like No. 353 .85 .85
*a.* Souv. sheet, 2 each #448, #458 2.75 2.75
*b.* Bklt. pane, #458, 3 #448, 4 #356d 3.75
Complete booklet, #458b 4.00
*c.* Bklt. pane, 3 #448, 1 each #356d, #458 1.90
Complete booklet, #458c 2.00
**459** A101 23p multicolored .90 .90
*a.* Bklt. pane, 6 #456, 4 #459 9.00
Complete booklet, #459a 2.00
*b.* Bklt. pane, 3 #456, 2 #459 5.00
Complete booklet, #459b 2.00
*Nos. 448-459 (4)* 2.70 2.70

No. 458a for Ninth Conf. of Commonwealth Postal Administrations, Douglas, Isle of Man.

Issued: 4p, 21p, #458b, 458c, 1/9; #458a, 7/1; 18p, 23p, #459a, 1/8/92.

No. 458b exists in special booklet sheets containing 5 #458b and 5 each #448, #458.

No. 458b dated 1991.

Manx Lifeboats A123

**1991, Feb. 13** *Perf. 14*

**463** A123 17p Sir William Hillary .65 .65
**464** A123 21p Osman Gabriel .85 .85
**465** A123 26p James & Ann Ritchie 1.00 1.00
**466** A123 31p The Gough Ritchie 1.25 1.25
**467** A123 37p John Batstone 1.40 1.40
*Nos. 463-467 (5)* 5.15 5.15

Europa — A124

**1991, Apr. 24** **Litho.** *Perf. 14*

**468** A124 17p Satellites .80 .80
**469** A124 17p Boats, Ariane rocket .80 .80
*a.* Vert. pair, #468-469 1.60 1.60
**470** A124 26p Satellites, diff. 1.25 1.25
**471** A124 26p Space shuttle, jet 1.25 1.25
*a.* Vert. pair, #470-471 2.50 2.50
*Nos. 468-471 (4)* 4.10 4.10

Tourist Trophy Mountain Course, 80th Anniv. A125

Designs: 17p, Oliver Godfrey, Indian 500cc, Bray Hill, 1911. 21p, Freddie Dixon, Douglas banking sidecar, Ballacraine, 1923. 26p, Bill Ivy, Yamaha 125cc, Waterworks, 1968. 31p, Giacomo Agostini, MV Agusta 500cc, Cregny-Baa, 1972. 37p, Joey Dunlop, RVF Honda 750cc, Ballaugh Bridge, 1985.

**1991, May 30** **Litho.** *Perf. 14½x13*

**472** A125 17p multicolored .70 .70
**473** A125 21p multicolored .85 .85
**474** A125 26p multicolored 1.00 1.00
**475** A125 31p multicolored 1.25 1.25
**476** A125 37p multicolored 1.50 1.50
*a.* Souv. sheet of 5, #472-476 + 7 labels 5.50 5.50
*b.* As "a," ovptd. in black & red in sheet margin 15.00 15.00
*Nos. 472-476 (5)* 5.30 5.30

No. 476b overprint includes show emblem and "PHILA / NIPPON '91."

Issue date: No. 476b, Nov. 16.

Fire Engines A126

Designs: 17p, Laxey hand cart. 21p, Douglas horse drawn steamer. 30p, Merryweather Hatfield pump. 33p, Dennis F8 pumping appliance. 37p, Volvo turntable ladder.

**1991, Sept. 18** **Litho.** *Perf. 14½*

**477** A126 17p multicolored .60 .60
**478** A126 21p multicolored .80 .80
**479** A126 30p multicolored 1.10 1.10
**480** A126 33p multicolored 1.25 1.25
**481** A126 37p multicolored 1.40 1.40
*Nos. 477-481 (5)* 5.15 5.15

Swans A127

Designs: No. 482, Mute swans, Douglas Harbor. No. 483, Black swans, Curraghs Wildlife Park. No. 484, Whooper swans, Bishops Dub, Ballaugh. No. 485, Bewick's swans, Eairy Dam, Foxdale. No. 486, Coscaroba swans, Curraghs Wildlife Park. No. 487, Trumpeter swans, Corraghs Wildlife Park.

**1991, Sept. 18** *Perf. 13*

**482** A127 17p multicolored .75 .75
**483** A127 17p multicolored .75 .75
*a.* Pair, #482-483 1.50 1.50
**484** A127 26p multicolored 1.25 1.25
**485** A127 26p multicolored 1.25 1.25
*a.* Pair, #484-485 2.75 2.75
**486** A127 37p multicolored 1.60 1.60
**487** A127 37p multicolored 1.60 1.60
*a.* Pair, #486-487 3.50 3.50
*Nos. 482-487 (6)* 7.20 7.20

Pairs have continuous designs.

Christmas — A128

**1991, Oct. 14** *Perf. 14x14½*

**488** A128 16p Three kings .55 .55
**489** A128 20p Jesus in manger, Mary .70 .70
**490** A128 26p Shepherds .90 .90
**491** A128 37p Angels 1.25 1.25
*Nos. 488-491 (4)* 3.40 3.40

**Litho.**

***Die Cut***

**Self-Adhesive Booklet Stamps**

**492** A128 16p like #488 1.00 1.00
**493** A128 20p like #489 1.25 1.25
*a.* Bklt. pane, 8 #492, 4 #493 13.50 13.50
Complete booklet, 2 #493a 27.00

Queen Elizabeth II's Accession to the Throne, 40th Anniv. — A129

Various portraits of Queen Elizabeth II.

**1992, Feb. 6** **Litho.** *Perf. 14*

**494** A129 18p multicolored .60 .60
**495** A129 23p multicolored .80 .80
**496** A129 28p multicolored 1.00 1.00
**497** A129 33p multicolored 1.10 1.10
**498** A129 39p multicolored 1.50 1.50
*Nos. 494-498 (5)* 5.00 5.00

Parachute Regiment, 50th Anniv. A130

Designs: No. 499, North Africa & Italy, 1942-43. No. 500, Operation Overlord, Normandy, 1944. No. 501, Operation Market Garden, Arnhem, 1944. No. 502, Operation Varsity, Rhine, 1945. No. 503, Near, Middle and Far East, 1945-68. No. 504, Operation Corporate, Falkland Islands, 1982, and Utrinque Paratus, 1992.

**1992, Feb. 6** *Perf. 14*

**499** A130 23p multicolored .80 .80
**500** A130 23p multicolored .80 .80
*a.* Pair, #499-500 1.60 1.60
**501** A130 28p multicolored 1.00 1.00
**502** A130 28p multicolored 1.00 1.00
*a.* Pair, #501-502 2.00 2.00
**503** A130 39p multicolored 1.50 1.50
**504** A130 39p multicolored 1.50 1.50
*a.* Pair, #503-504 3.00 3.00
*Nos. 499-504 (6)* 6.60 6.60

Printed in sheets of 8.

Pilgrims' Voyage to America, 1620 — A131

Europa: No. 505, Pilgrims in longboats. No. 506, Speedwell, Delfshaven, Holland. No. 507, Mayflower. No. 508, Speedwell, Dartmouth, England.

**1992, Apr. 16** **Litho.** *Perf. 14x13½*

**505** A131 18p multicolored .80 .80
**506** A131 18p multicolored .80 .80
*a.* Pair, #505-506 1.60 1.60
**507** A131 28p multicolored 1.75 1.75
**508** A131 28p multicolored 1.75 1.75
*a.* Pair, #507-508 3.50 3.50
*Nos. 505-508 (4)* 5.10 5.10

Nos. 506a, 508a have continuous design.

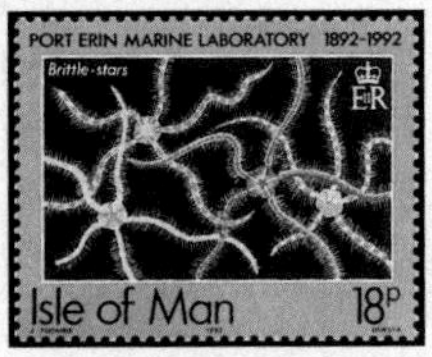


Port Erin Marine Laboratory, Cent. A132

**1992, Apr. 16** *Perf. 14½*

**509** A132 18p Brittle stars .65 .65
**510** A132 23p Phytoplankton .85 .85
**511** A132 28p Herring 1.00 1.00
**512** A132 33p Great scallop 1.10 1.10
**513** A132 39p Dahlia anemone, delesseria 1.40 1.40
*Nos. 509-513 (5)* 5.00 5.00

Union Pacific, First Transcontinental Railroad — A133

#514, "Jupiter," 1869. #515, "#119," 1869. #516, "#844," 1992. #517, "#3985," 1992. £1.50, Golden Spike Ceremony, Union Pacific and Central Pacific Railroads, 1869.

**1992, May 22** **Litho.** *Perf. 13½x14*

**514** A133 33p multicolored 1.10 1.10
**515** A133 33p multicolored 1.10 1.10
*a.* Pair, #514-515 + label 2.25 2.25
**516** A133 39p multicolored 1.40 1.40
**517** A133 39p multicolored 1.40 1.40
*a.* Pair, #516-517 + label 3.00 3.00
*b.* Bklt. pane, 1 ea #515a, 517a 5.25

**Souvenir Sheet**

**518** A133 £1.50 multicolored 6.00 6.00
*a.* Booklet pane, #518 6.00
*b.* Bklt. pane, #518a, 2 #517b 17.00
Complete booklet, #518b 17.00

World Columbian Stamp Expo '92. No. 518 contains one 60x50mm stamp.

Nos. 514-515 and 516-517 issued in sheets of 10.

Nos. 515a, 517a have 3 different labels. No. 517b exists with two different pairs of labels. No. 518a has a roulletted white border at left and right.

Manx Harbors — A134

#519, King Orry V, Douglas Harbor. 23p, Castletown Harbor. 37p, Port St. Mary Harbor. 40p, Ramsey Harbor. a, King Orry. b, St. Eloi.

**1992, Sept. 18** **Litho.** *Perf. 14½x14*

**519** A134 18p multicolored .60 .60
**520** A134 23p multicolored .75 .75
**521** A134 37p multicolored 1.40 1.40
**522** A134 40p multicolored 1.75 1.75
*Nos. 519-522 (4)* 4.50 4.50

**Souvenir Sheet**

**523** Sheet of 2 4.75 4.75
*a.* A134 18p multicolored .75 .75
*b.* A134 £1 multicolored 4.00 4.00

Genoa '92. #523 contains 30x24mm stamps.

Christmas — A135

Designs: 17p, Nativity window, St. German's Cathedral, Peel. 22p, Adoration of the Magi panel, St. Matthew's Church, Douglas. 28p, Nativity window, St. George's Church, Douglas. 37p, Reredos of The Annunciation, St. Mary of the Isle, Douglas. 40p, Good Shepherd window, Trinity Methodist Church, Douglas.

**1992, Oct. 13 Litho. *Perf. 14½***

**524** A135 17p multicolored .55 .55
**525** A135 22p multicolored .75 .75
**526** A135 28p multicolored 1.00 1.00
**527** A135 37p multicolored 1.25 1.25
**528** A135 40p multicolored 1.40 1.40
*Nos. 524-528 (5)* 4.95 4.95

Nigel Mansell, Formula I World Champion, 1992 A136

Williams Renault FW 14B at: 20p, British Grand Prix, 1992. 24p, French Grand Prix, 1992.

**1992, Nov. 8 *Perf. 13½***

**529** A136 20p multicolored .85 .85
**530** A136 24p multicolored 1.00 1.00

Ships A137

Royal Ensign of the Isle of Man — A137a

Queen Elizabeth II — A137b

**1993-96 Litho. *Perf. 13½***

**531** A137 1p HMS Amazon .25 .25
**532** A137 2p Fingal .25 .25
**533** A137 4p Sir Winston Churchill .25 .25
*a.* Inscribed "1997" .25 .25
**534** A137 5p Dar Mlodziezy .25 .25
**543** A137 20p Tynwald I .45 .45
*a.* Inscribed "1995" .45 .45
**544** A137 21p Ben Veg .55 .55
*a.* Inscribed "1997" .55 .55
**545** A137 22p Waverley .55 .55
**546** A137 23p HMY Britannia .60 .60
*a.* Souv. sheet of 1, Perf. 13 1.00 1.00
**547** A137 24p Francis Drake .55 .55
*a.* Bklt. pane, 4 #543, 6 #547 5.50
Complete booklet, #547a 5.50
*b.* Bklt. pane, 2 #543, 3 #547 2.75
Complete booklet, #547b 2.75
*c.* Inscribed "1995" .55 .55
**548** A137 25p Royal Viking Sky .65 .65
*a.* Booklet pane, 2 #533, 2 #544, 2 #548 4.25
Complete booklet, #548a 4.25
*b.* Inscribed "1997" .65 .65
**549** A137 26p Lord Nelson .70 .70
**550** A137 27p Europa .70 .70
**551** A137 30p Snaefell V .80 .80
**551A** A137 35p Sea Cat .95 .95
**552** A137 40p Lady of Mann I 1.10 1.10
**553** A137 50p Mona's Queen II 1.40 1.40
**553A** A137 £1 QE2, Mona's Queen V 3.50 3.50
*a.* Inscribed "1997" 3.50 3.50

***Perf. 14½***

**553B** A137a £2 multicolored 6.00 6.00
**553C** A137b £5 multicolored 17.00 17.00
*Nos. 531-553C (19)* 36.50 36.50

#546a, for return of Hong Kong to China, is wmk. 373.

No. 553C has a holographic image. Soaking in water may affect the hologram.

Issued: 1p-5p, 20p-27p, 1/4/93; 30p, 40p-£1, 9/15/93; £2, 1/24/94; £5, 7/5/94; 35p, 1/11/96; #546a, 7/1/97; #548a, 1997.

Nos. 533, 544, 546a, 548, 548a, 553A dated "1997."

See Nos. 683-697.

Manx Electric Railway, Cent. — A138

20p, #13 trailer, #1 motor car. 24p, #19 trailer, #9 tunnel car. 28p, #59 Royal trailer special saloon car, #19 motor car. 39p, #33 motor car, #45 trailer, #13 small van.

**1993, Feb. 3 *Perf. 14***

**554** A138 20p multicolored .75 .75
**555** A138 24p multicolored .85 .85
**556** A138 28p multicolored 1.10 1.10
**557** A138 39p multicolored 1.25 1.25
*a.* Booklet pane of #554-557 4.25 4.25
Complete booklet, 4 #557a 17.00
*Nos. 554-557 (4)* 3.95 3.95

No. 557a exists with four different marginal inscriptions and in four different arrangements.

Contemporary Art by Bryan Kneale — A139

Europa: No. 558, Statue of Sir Hall Caine. No. 559, Painting, The Brass Bedstead. No. 560, Abstract bronze. No. 561, Drawing of polar bear skeleton.

**1993, Apr. 14 Litho. *Perf. 14***

**558** A139 20p multicolored .80 .80
**559** A139 20p multicolored .80 .80
*a.* Pair, #558-559 1.60 1.60
**560** A139 28p multicolored 1.00 1.00
**561** A139 28p multicolored 1.00 1.00
*a.* Pair, #560-561 2.00 2.00
*Nos. 558-561 (4)* 3.60 3.60

Motorcycling Events — A140

Riders and events: 20p, Gold Medalists Graham Oates, Bill Marshall, Intl. Six-Day Trial, 1933, Ariel Square Four. 24p, Geoff Duke, Team Sergeant, Royal Signals Display Team, 1947, Triumph Twin. 28p, Denis Parkinson, winner of Senior Manx Grand Prix, 1953, Manx Norton. 33p, Richard Swallow, winner of Junior Classic Manx Grand Prix, 1991, Aermacchi. 39p, Steve Colley, winner of Scottish Six-Day Trial, 1992, Beta Zero.

**1993, June 3 Litho. *Perf. 13½x14***

**562** A140 20p multicolored .80 .80
**563** A140 24p multicolored .85 .85
**564** A140 28p multicolored 1.00 1.00
**565** A140 33p multicolored 1.25 1.25
**566** A140 39p multicolored 1.40 1.40
*a.* Souv. sheet of 5, #562-566 + 4 labels 5.50 5.50
*Nos. 562-566 (5)* 5.30 5.30

Butterflies A141

**1993, Sept. 15 Litho. *Perf. 14½***

**567** A141 24p Dark green fritillary .85 .85
**568** A141 24p Painted lady .85 .85
**569** A141 24p Holly blue .85 .85
**570** A141 24p Red admiral .85 .85
**571** A141 24p Peacock .85 .85
*a.* Strip of 5, #567-571 4.50 4.50

Christmas — A142

Designs: 19p, Children decorating Christmas tree. 23p, Snowman, girl. 28p, Boy unwrapping presents. 39p, Girl, teddy bear. 40p, Girl with holly basket, boy on sled.

**1993, Oct. 12 *Perf. 14***

**572** A142 19p multicolored .70 .70
Complete booklet, 10 #572 7.00
**573** A142 23p multicolored .80 .80
Complete booklet, 10 #573 8.00
**574** A142 28p multicolored 1.00 1.00
**575** A142 39p multicolored 1.40 1.40
**576** A142 40p multicolored 1.40 1.40
*Nos. 572-576 (5)* 5.30 5.30

Tourism A143

No. 577, Gaiety Theatre, Douglas. No. 578, Field hockey, golf, soccer (#577). No. 579, Yacht racing, artist's hand painting picture of castle (#580). No. 580, TT Motorcycle Races, Red Arrows demonstration squadron. (#581). No. 581, Musical instruments. No. 582, Laxey Wheel, Manx cat. No. 583, Tower of Refuge, beach, sand bucket (#584). No. 584, Cyclist. No. 585, Tynwald Day, classic racing car (#579, 580, 584, 586). No. 586, Santa Claus riding Mince Pie Train, Groudle Glen.

**1994, Feb, 18 Litho. *Perf. 13½***

**Booklet Stamps**

**577** A143 24p multicolored .80 .80
**578** A143 24p multicolored .80 .80
**579** A143 24p multicolored .80 .80
**580** A143 24p multicolored .80 .80
**581** A143 24p multicolored .80 .80
**582** A143 24p multicolored .80 .80
**583** A143 24p multicolored .80 .80
**584** A143 24p multicolored .80 .80
**585** A143 24p multicolored .80 .80
**586** A143 24p multicolored .80 .80
*a.* Booklet pane of 10, #577-586 8.25
Complete booklet, #586a 8.25

Birds A144

Magpie, Calf of Man Bird Observatory — A145

**1994, Feb. 18 *Perf. 14***

**587** A144 20p White-throated robin .80 .80
**588** A144 20p Black-eared wheatear .80 .80
*a.* Pair, #587-588 1.60 1.60
**589** A144 24p Goldcrest .95 .95
**590** A144 24p Northern oriole .95 .95
*a.* Pair, #589-590 1.90 1.90
**591** A144 30p Kingfisher 1.25 1.25
**592** A144 30p Hoopoe 1.25 1.25
*a.* Pair, #591-592 2.50 2.50
*Nos. 587-592 (6)* 6.00 6.00

**Souvenir Sheet**

***Perf. 13½x13***

**593** A145 £1 shown 4.00 4.00

Hong Kong '94 (#593).

Europa A146

Designs, Forbes and Discoveries: No. 594, Eubranchus tricolor. No. 595, Loligo forbesii. No. 596, Edward Forbes (1815-54), naturalist. No. 597, Solaster moretonis. No. 598, Adamsia carciniopados on hermit crab. No. 599, Solaster endeca.

**1994, May 5 Litho. *Perf. 13¼x14½***

**594** A146 20p multicolored .80 .80
**595** A146 20p multicolored .80 .80
**596** A146 20p multicolored .80 .80
*a.* Strip of 3, #594-596 2.40 2.40
**597** A146 30p multicolored 1.25 1.25
**598** A146 30p multicolored 1.25 1.25
**599** A146 30p multicolored 1.25 1.25
*a.* Strip of 3, #597-599 3.75 3.75

D-Day, 50th Anniv. A147

Designs: No. 600, Transport Ben-My-Chree IV, landing ships, US Maj. Gen. Walter Bedell Smith. No. 601, Transports Victoria, Lady of Mann I, Adm. Sir Bertram Ramsay, RN, Naval Commander. No. 602, Infantry, tanks on Gold, Juno, Sword Beaches, Gen. Montgomery, Commander, 21st Army Group. No. 603, Tanks, landing craft on Gold, Juno, Sword Beaches, Lt. Gen. Sir Miles C. Dempsey, Commander, British 2nd Army. No. 604, US 8th, 9th Air Forces, Air Chief Marshal Sir Trafford Leigh-Mallory, RAF, Air Force Commander. No. 605, Air Chief Marshall Sir Arthur Tedder, RAF, Deputy Supreme Allied Commander, RAF 2nd Tactical Air Force & Bomber Command. No. 606, Landing craft, Omaha, Utah Beaches, Lt. Gen. Omar N. Bradley, Commander, US 1st Army. No. 607, Infantry, tanks on Omaha, Utah Beaches, Gen. Eisenhower, Supreme Allied Commander.

**1994, June 6 Litho. *Perf. 14***

**600** A147 4p multicolored .25 .25
**601** A147 4p multicolored .25 .25
*a.* Pair, #600-601 .25 .25
**602** A147 20p multicolored .75 .75
**603** A147 20p multicolored .75 .75
*a.* Pair, #602-603 1.50 1.50
**604** A147 30p multicolored 1.10 1.10
**605** A147 30p multicolored 1.10 1.10
*a.* Pair, #604-605 2.25 2.25
**606** A147 41p multicolored 1.60 1.60
**607** A147 41p multicolored 1.60 1.60
*a.* Pair, #606-607 3.25 3.25
*Nos. 600-607 (8)* 7.40 7.40

Nos. 601a, 603a, 605a, 607a are continuous designs.

Postman Pat
A148

Postman Pat at: 1p, Sea Terminal, Douglas. 20p, Laxey Wheel. 24p, Cregneash. 30p, Manx Electric Railway. 36p, Peel Harbor. 41p, Tourist office, Douglas Promenade.
£1, Postman Pat.

**1994, Sept. 14 Litho. *Perf. 14½x14***

| | | | | | |
|---|---|---|---|---|---|
| 608 | A148 | 1p multicolored | .25 | .25 |
| a. | | Booklet pane of 2 | .20 | |
| 609 | A148 | 20p multicolored | .65 | .65 |
| a. | | Booklet pane of 2 | 1.40 | |
| 610 | A148 | 24p multicolored | .80 | .80 |
| a. | | Booklet pane of 2 | 1.60 | |
| 611 | A148 | 30p multicolored | 1.00 | 1.00 |
| a. | | Booklet pane of 2 | 2.10 | |
| 612 | A148 | 36p multicolored | 1.25 | 1.25 |
| a. | | Booklet pane of 2 | 2.50 | |
| 613 | A148 | 41p multicolored | 1.40 | 1.40 |
| a. | | Booklet pane of 2 | 3.00 | |
| | | *Nos. 608-613 (6)* | 5.35 | 5.35 |

**Souvenir Sheet**

| | | | | |
|---|---|---|---|---|
| 614 | A148 | £1 multicolored | 4.00 | 4.00 |
| a. | | Booklet pane of 1 | 4.00 | 4.00 |
| | | Complete booklet, #608a-614a | 16.00 | |

No. 614a is rouletted 9 at left.

Intl. Olympic Committee, Cent. — A149

**1994, Oct. 11 *Perf. 14***

| | | | | |
|---|---|---|---|---|
| 615 | A149 | 10p Cycling | .40 | .40 |
| 616 | A149 | 20p Alpine skiing | .75 | .75 |
| 617 | A149 | 24p Swimming | .90 | .90 |
| 618 | A149 | 35p Steeplechase | 1.40 | 1.40 |
| 619 | A149 | 48p Emblem | 1.60 | 1.60 |
| | | *Nos. 615-619 (5)* | 5.05 | 5.05 |

A150

Christmas: 19p, Santa, Mrs. Claus greeting children on Santa Train to Santon, horiz. 23p, Santa Claus on tractor, Postman Pat. 60p, Santa Claus arriving by boat, Port St. Mary, horiz.

**1994, Oct. 11**

| | | | | |
|---|---|---|---|---|
| 620 | A150 | 19p multicolored | .75 | .75 |
| 621 | A150 | 23p multicolored | 1.00 | 1.00 |
| 622 | A150 | 60p multicolored | 2.00 | 2.00 |
| | | *Nos. 620-622 (3)* | 3.75 | 3.75 |

Snaefell Mountain Electric Railway, Cent. — A151

Designs: 20p, Opening day, Car No. 2. 24p, Car 3 ascending Laxey Valley, Car 4 in green livery. 35p, Car 5, Car 6. 42p, Caledonia on construction duty, Goods Car 7.
£1, Bungalow Hotel & Station, Snaefell.

**1995, Feb. 8 Litho. *Perf. 14***

| | | | | |
|---|---|---|---|---|
| 623 | A151 | 20p multicolored | .75 | .75 |
| 624 | A151 | 24p multicolored | .95 | .95 |
| 625 | A151 | 35p multicolored | 1.40 | 1.40 |
| 626 | A151 | 42p multicolored | 1.60 | 1.60 |
| a. | | Bklt. pane, #623-626 | 4.75 | |
| | | *Nos. 623-626 (4)* | 4.70 | 4.70 |

**Souvenir Sheet**

***Perf. 14x13½***

| | | | | |
|---|---|---|---|---|
| 627 | A151 | £1 multicolored | 4.00 | 4.00 |
| a. | | Sheet from souvenir booklet | 4.00 | 4.00 |
| | | Complete booklet, 3 #626a, #627a | 18.50 | |

No. 627 contains one 61x38mm stamp.

No. 626a comes with three different arrangements of the stamps. Value the same for each.

No. 627a is rouletted in margin at left with additional vertical sheet margin inscriptions. At left is a description of the design. At right is "1895-Centenary Snaefell Mountain Railway-1995."

Steam-Powered Vehicles — A152

Designs: 20p, Foden Wagon, 5 ton. 24p, Clayton & Shuttleworth, 7hp, Fowler, 6hp. 30p, Wallis & Steevens, 6hp. 35p, Marshall, 6hp. 41p, Marshall Convertible, 5hp.

**1995, Feb. 8 *Perf. 13½***

| | | | | |
|---|---|---|---|---|
| 628 | A152 | 20p multicolored | .70 | .70 |
| 629 | A152 | 24p multicolored | .90 | .90 |
| 630 | A152 | 30p multicolored | 1.10 | 1.10 |
| 631 | A152 | 35p multicolored | 1.40 | 1.40 |
| 632 | A152 | 41p multicolored | 1.50 | 1.50 |
| | | *Nos. 628-632 (5)* | 5.60 | 5.60 |

Peace & Freedom — A153

Europa: 20p, Flight of doves forming tidal wave, Tower of Refuge, Douglas Bay. 30p, Dove with olive branch breaking barbed wire.

**1995, Apr. 28 Litho. *Perf. 13½***

| | | | | |
|---|---|---|---|---|
| 633 | A153 | 20p multicolored | .80 | .80 |
| 634 | A153 | 30p multicolored | 1.25 | 1.25 |

VE Day, 50th Anniv. A154

Designs: No. 635, Spitfire, tank, 1939-45 Star, African Star. No. 636, France and Germany Star, Italy Star, Hawker Typhoon, artillery. No. 637, Lancaster bomber, aircraft carrier, Air Crew Europe Star, Atlantic Star. No. 638, Pacific Star, Burma Star, Avenger torpedo bomber, soldiers. No. 639, Parliament, Manx flag. No. 640, British flag, crowd celebrating. No. 641, Children celebrating at street party, Manx flag. No. 642, British flag, visit of Queen Elizabeth, King George VI, 1945.

**1995, May 8 *Perf. 14***

| | | | | |
|---|---|---|---|---|
| 635 | A154 | 10p multicolored | .40 | .40 |
| 636 | A154 | 10p multicolored | .40 | .40 |
| a. | | Pair, #635-636 | .80 | .80 |
| 637 | A154 | 20p multicolored | .75 | .75 |
| 638 | A154 | 20p multicolored | .75 | .75 |
| a. | | Pair, #637-638 | 1.50 | 1.50 |
| 639 | A154 | 24p multicolored | .85 | .85 |
| 640 | A154 | 24p multicolored | .85 | .85 |
| a. | | Pair, #639-640 | 1.75 | 1.75 |
| 641 | A154 | 40p multicolored | 1.50 | 1.50 |
| 642 | A154 | 40p multicolored | 1.50 | 1.50 |
| a. | | Pair, #641-642 | 3.25 | 3.25 |
| | | *Nos. 635-642 (8)* | 7.00 | 7.00 |

British Motor Car Racing, 90th Anniv. A155

Tourist Trophy Race drivers, cars: 20p, R. Parnell, 1951 Maserati 4 CLT. 24p, S. Moss, 1951 Frazer Nash. 30p, R.J.B. Seaman, 1936 Delage. 36p, Prince Bira, 1937 ERA R2B Romulus. 41p, K. Lee Guinness, 1914 Sunbeam 1. 42p, F. Dixon, 1934 Riley.
£1, John S. Napier, 1905 Arrol Johnston.

**1995, May 8**

| | | | | |
|---|---|---|---|---|
| 643 | A155 | 20p multicolored | .75 | .75 |
| 644 | A155 | 24p multicolored | .90 | .90 |
| 645 | A155 | 30p multicolored | 1.10 | 1.10 |
| 646 | A155 | 36p multicolored | 1.40 | 1.40 |
| 647 | A155 | 41p multicolored | 1.50 | 1.50 |
| 648 | A155 | 42p multicolored | 1.60 | 1.60 |
| | | *Nos. 643-648 (6)* | 7.25 | 7.25 |

**Souvenir Sheet**

| | | | | |
|---|---|---|---|---|
| 649 | A155 | £1 multicolored | 4.00 | 4.00 |

No. 649 contains one 47x58mm stamp.

Mushrooms A156

Designs: 20p, Amanita muscaria. 24p, Boletus edulis. 30p, Coprinus disseminatus. 35p, Pleurotus ostreatus. 45p, Geastrum triplex.
£1, Shaggy ink cap, bee orchid.

**1995, Sept. 1 Litho. *Perf. 13½x14***

| | | | | |
|---|---|---|---|---|
| 650 | A156 | 20p multicolored | .80 | .80 |
| 651 | A156 | 24p multicolored | .95 | .95 |
| 652 | A156 | 30p multicolored | 1.25 | 1.25 |
| 653 | A156 | 35p multicolored | 1.40 | 1.40 |
| 654 | A156 | 45p multicolored | 1.75 | 1.75 |
| | | *Nos. 650-654 (5)* | 6.15 | 6.15 |

**Souvenir Sheet**

***Perf. 14x13½***

| | | | | |
|---|---|---|---|---|
| 655 | A156 | £1 multicolored | 4.00 | 4.00 |

No. 655 contains one 51x60mm stamp. Singapore '95 (#655).

Thomas the Tank Engine A157

Designs: 20p, Bertie arrives on the quayside. 24p, Mail train and Thomas. 30p, Bertie and trains at Ballasalla. 36p, Viking and Thomas at Port Erin. 41p, The mail gets through. 45p, Race at Laxey Wheel.

**1995, Sept. 1 *Perf. 14***

| | | | | |
|---|---|---|---|---|
| 656 | A157 | 20p multicolored | .75 | .75 |
| 657 | A157 | 24p multicolored | .85 | .85 |
| a. | | Booklet pane of 2, #656-657 | 1.60 | |
| 658 | A157 | 30p multicolored | 1.10 | 1.10 |
| a. | | Booklet pane of 2, #657-658 | 2.00 | |
| 659 | A157 | 36p multicolored | 1.40 | 1.40 |
| a. | | Booklet pane of 2, #658-659 | 2.50 | |
| 660 | A157 | 41p multicolored | 1.50 | 1.50 |
| a. | | Booklet pane of 2, #659-660 | 3.00 | |
| 661 | A157 | 45p multicolored | 1.60 | 1.60 |
| a. | | Booklet pane of 2, #656, 661 | 2.50 | |
| b. | | Booklet pane of 2, #660-661 | 3.25 | |
| | | Complete booklet, #657a, 658a, 659a, 660a, 661a-661b | 16.00 | |
| | | *Nos. 656-661 (6)* | 7.20 | 7.20 |

Christmas A158

Designs: 19p, Church, holly. 23p, Bird on holly branch. 42p, Snow crocuses, church. 50p, Antique farming equipment in snow.

**1995, Oct. 10 Litho. *Perf. 14x14½***

| | | | | |
|---|---|---|---|---|
| 662 | A158 | 19p multicolored | .70 | .70 |
| 663 | A158 | 23p multicolored | .80 | .80 |
| 664 | A158 | 42p multicolored | 1.50 | 1.50 |
| 665 | A158 | 50p multicolored | 1.75 | 1.75 |
| | | *Nos. 662-665 (4)* | 4.75 | 4.75 |

Lighthouses — A159

Location, year opened: 20p, Langness, 1880, vert. 24p, Point of Ayre, 1818. 30p, Chicken Rock, 1873, vert. 36p, Calf of Man, 1818. 41p, Douglas Head, 1832. vert. 42p, Maughold Head, 1914.

**1996, Feb. 27 Litho. *Perf. 14***

| | | | | |
|---|---|---|---|---|
| 666 | A159 | 20p multicolored | .70 | .70 |
| a. | | Booklet pane of 4 + 4 labels | 3.00 | |
| 667 | A159 | 24p multicolored | .80 | .80 |
| a. | | Booklet pane of 4 | 3.25 | |
| 668 | A159 | 30p multicolored | 1.10 | 1.10 |
| 669 | A159 | 36p multicolored | 1.25 | 1.25 |
| 670 | A159 | 41p multicolored | 1.50 | 1.50 |
| a. | | Booklet pane, 2 each #668, 670 + 4 labels | 5.25 | |
| 671 | A159 | 42p multicolored | 1.50 | 1.50 |
| a. | | Bklt. pane, 2 ea #669, 671 | 5.50 | |
| | | Complete booklet, #666a, 667a, 670a, 671a | 17.50 | |
| | | *Nos. 666-671 (6)* | 6.85 | 6.85 |

Manx Cats A160

Various cats and: 20p, Arms of Man. 24p, British Union Flag as of ball yarn. 36p, Brandenburg Gate. 42p, US flag, Statue of Liberty. 48p, Australian flag, map.
£1.50, Gray adult cat, gray and yellow kittens.

**1996, Mar. 14**

| | | | | |
|---|---|---|---|---|
| 672 | A160 | 20p multicolored | .70 | .70 |
| 673 | A160 | 24p multicolored | .80 | .80 |
| 674 | A160 | 36p multicolored | 1.25 | 1.25 |
| 675 | A160 | 42p multicolored | 1.50 | 1.50 |
| 676 | A160 | 48p multicolored | 1.75 | 1.75 |
| | | *Nos. 672-676 (5)* | 6.00 | 6.00 |

**Souvenir Sheet**

| | | | | |
|---|---|---|---|---|
| 677 | A160 | £1.50 multicolored | 6.00 | 6.00 |
| a. | | With additional inscription | 12.00 | 12.00 |

No. 677 contains one 51x60mm stamp. No. 677a contains CAPEX '96 exhibition emblem in sheet margin. Issued 6/8/96.

Douglas Borough, Cent. — A161

***Die Cut Perf. 9x9½***

**1996, Mar. 14 Litho.**

**Self-Adhesive**

| | | | | |
|---|---|---|---|---|
| 678 | A161 | (40p) multicolored | 1.50 | 1.50 |

The backing of No. 678 is rouletted 13.

Women of Achievement — A162

Europa: 24p, Princess Anne, children of different nations. 30p, Queen Elizabeth II, people of different nations.

**1996 *Perf. 14***

| | | | | |
|---|---|---|---|---|
| 679 | A162 | 24p multicolored | .90 | .90 |
| 680 | A162 | 30p multicolored | 1.25 | 1.25 |

Queen Elizabeth II, 70th birthday (#680).
See Guernsey Nos. 564-565.

### Ship Type of 1993

**1996** **Litho.** *Perf. 14*

**Size: 21x19mm**

**683** A137 4p like #533 .25 .25
**693** A137 20p like #543 .80 .80
**697** A137 24p like #547 .90 .90
*Nos. 683-697 (3)* 1.95 1.95
*a.* Bklt. pane, 2 ea 4p, 20p, 24p 4.00
Complete booklet, No. 697a 4.00

Irish Winners of Tourist Trophy Motorcycle Races — A163

20p, Alec Bennett. 24p, Stanley Woods. 45p, Artie Bell. 60p, Robert & Joey Dunlop.
£1, Demonstration squadron Hawks flying over motorcycles, vert.

**1996, May 30** **Litho.** *Perf. 14*

**701** A163 20p multicolored .75 .75
**702** A163 24p multicolored .85 .85
**703** A163 45p multicolored 1.60 1.60
**704** A163 60p multicolored 2.10 2.10
*Nos. 701-704 (4)* 5.30 5.30

**Souvenir Sheet**

**705** A163 £1 multicolored 3.75 3.75

See Ireland Nos. 1010-1014.

Royal British Legion, 75th Anniv. — A164

Poppies and: 20p, National poppy appeal trophy. 24p, Manx war memorial. 42p, Poppy appeal. 75p, Crest.

**1996, June 8**

**706** A164 20p multicolored .75 .75
**707** A164 24p multicolored .85 .85
**708** A164 42p multicolored 1.60 1.60
**709** A164 75p multicolored 2.75 2.75
*Nos. 706-709 (4)* 5.95 5.95

UNICEF, 50th Anniv. A165

Children receiving aid, map of country: #710, Mexico. #711, Sri Lanka. #712, Colombia. #713, Zambia. #714, Afghanistan. #715, Viet Nam.

**1996, Sept. 18** **Litho.** *Perf. 13½x14*

**710** A165 24p multicolored .85 .85
**711** A165 24p multicolored .85 .85
*a.* Pair, #710-711 1.75 1.75
**712** A165 30p multicolored 1.10 1.10
**713** A165 30p multicolored 1.10 1.10
*a.* Pair, #712-713 2.25 2.25
**714** A165 42p multicolored 1.60 1.60
**715** A165 42p multicolored 1.60 1.60
*a.* Pair, #714-715 3.25 3.25
*Nos. 710-715 (6)* 7.10 7.10

Dogs — A166

**1996, Sept. 18** *Perf. 14½*

**716** A166 20p Labrador .75 .75
*a.* Booklet pane of 4 3.00
**717** A166 24p Border collie .80 .80
*a.* Booklet pane of 4 3.25
**718** A166 31p Dalmatian 1.10 1.10
**719** A166 38p Mongrel 1.40 1.40
**720** A166 43p English setter 1.60 1.60
**721** A166 63p Alsatian 2.40 2.40
*a.* Booklet pane, 1 each #718-721 6.50
*Nos. 716-721 (6)* 8.05 8.05

**Souvenir Sheet**

*Perf. 13½x14*

**722** A166 £1.20 Border collie, labrador 4.75 4.75
*a.* Booklet pane of 1 4.75
Complete booklet, #716a, 717a, 721a, 722a 19.00

Nos. 716-721 are each printed with se-tenant label. No. 722 contains one 38x50mm stamp. No. 722a is rouletted around margin of sheet.

Christmas A167

Children's drawings: 19p, Snowman. 23p, Santa, "Happy Christmas" in Manx. 50p, Family, Christmas tree, presents. 75p, Santa in sleigh flying over rooftops.

**1996, Nov. 2** **Litho.** *Perf. 14x14½*

**723** A167 19p multicolored .70 .70
**724** A167 23p multicolored .80 .80
**725** A167 50p multicolored 1.60 1.60
**726** A167 75p multicolored 2.75 2.75
*Nos. 723-726 (4)* 5.85 5.85

Owls — A168

**1997, Feb. 12** **Litho.** *Perf. 14*

**727** A168 20p Barn owl .75 .75
*a.* Booklet pane of 4 3.00
**728** A168 24p Short-eared owl .85 .85
*a.* Booklet pane of 4 3.50
**729** A168 31p Long-eared owl 1.10 1.10
**730** A168 36p Little owl 1.25 1.25
**731** A168 43p Snowy owl 1.60 1.60
**732** A168 56p Tawny owl 2.00 2.00
*a.* Booklet pane of 4, #729-732 6.00
*Nos. 727-732 (6)* 7.55 7.55

**Souvenir Sheet**

*Perf. 13*

**733** A168 £1.20 Long-eared owl 4.00 4.00
*a.* Booklet pane of 1 4.00
Complete booklet, #727a, 728a, 732a, 733a 16.50

No. 733, 733a each contain one 56x60mm stamp. No. 733a is rouletted at left. Hong Kong '97 (#733, 733a).

Springtime A169

**1997, Feb. 12** *Perf. 14*

**734** A169 20p Spring flowers .70 .70
**735** A169 24p Sheep .80 .80
**736** A169 43p Waterfowl 1.60 1.60
**737** A169 63p Frog, ducks 2.40 2.40
*Nos. 734-737 (4)* 5.50 5.50

Stories and Legends A170

21p, Moddey Dhoo. 25p, The Trammen Tree. 31p, Fairy Bridge. 36p, Fin Macooil. 37p, The Buggane of St. Trinian's. 43p, Fynoderee.

**1997, Apr. 24** **Litho.** *Perf. 13½x14*

**738** A170 21p multicolored .70 .70
**739** A170 25p multicolored .85 .85
**740** A170 31p multicolored 1.10 1.10
**741** A170 36p multicolored 1.25 1.25
**742** A170 37p multicolored 1.25 1.25
**743** A170 43p multicolored 1.60 1.60
*Nos. 738-743 (6)* 6.75 6.75

Europa (#739-740).

Aircraft A171

Designs: No. 744, Sopwith Tabloid. No. 745, Grumman Tiger. No. 746, Manx Airlines BAe ATP. No. 747, Manx Airlines BAe 146-200. No. 748 Boeing 757-200. No. 749, Farman biplane. No. 750, Spitfire. No. 751, Hurricane.

**1997, Apr. 24** *Perf. 14*

**744** A171 21p multicolored .70 .70
**745** A171 21p multicolored .70 .70
*a.* Pair, #744-745 1.40 1.40
**746** A171 25p multicolored .85 .85
**747** A171 25p multicolored .85 .85
*a.* Pair, #746-747 1.75 1.75
**748** A171 31p multicolored 1.10 1.10
**749** A171 31p multicolored 1.10 1.10
*a.* Pair, #748-749 2.25 2.25
**750** A171 36p multicolored 1.25 1.25
**751** A171 36p multicolored 1.25 1.25
*a.* Pair, #750-751 2.50 2.50
*Nos. 744-751 (8)* 7.80 7.80

Golf Courses A172

1997 Ryder Cup, Valderrama, Spain — A173

21p, 14th Hole, Ramsey Golf Club. 25p, 15th Hole, King Edward Bay Golf and Country Club. 43p, 17th Hole, Rowany Golf Club. 50p, 8th Hole, Castletown Golf Links.

**1997, May 29** **Litho.** *Perf. 14*

**752** A172 21p multicolored .70 .70
*a.* Booklet pane of 3 2.10
**753** A172 25p multicolored .90 .90
*a.* Booklet pane of 3 2.75
**754** A172 43p multicolored 1.60 1.60
**755** A172 50p multicolored 1.75 1.75
*a.* Bklt. pane, 2 ea #754-755 6.75
*Nos. 752-755 (4)* 4.95 4.95

**Souvenir Sheet**

**756** A173 £1.30 multicolored 5.25 5.25
*a.* Booklet pane of 1 5.25
Complete booklet, #752a, 753a, 755a, 756a 17.00

PACIFIC 97 (#756). No. 756 contains one 40mm diameter stamp.

No. 756a has a large white border, is 155x96mm and is sewn into booklet.

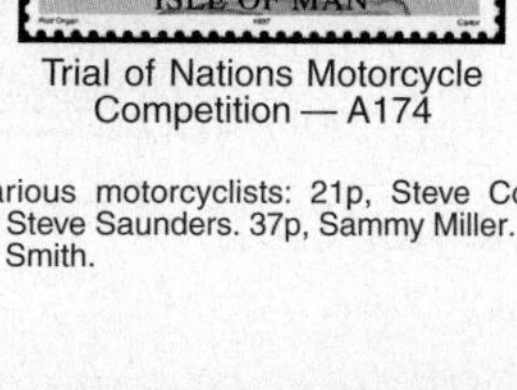

Trial of Nations Motorcycle Competition — A174

Various motorcyclists: 21p, Steve Colley. 25p, Steve Saunders. 37p, Sammy Miller. 44p, Don Smith.

**1997, Sept. 29** **Litho.** *Perf. 13½*

**757** A174 21p multicolored .70 .70
**758** A174 25p multi, vert. .85 .85
**759** A174 37p multi, vert. 1.40 1.40
**760** A174 44p multicolored 1.60 1.60
*Nos. 757-760 (4)* 4.55 4.55

Queen Elizabeth II and Prince Philip, 50th Wedding Anniv. — A175

Designs: a, Early drawing of couple. b, Wedding portrait. c, Drawing of Queen waving, Prince in top hat. d, Portrait, 1997.
£1, Queen, Prince touring Isle of Man, 1989.

**1997, Nov. 3** **Litho.** *Perf. 14x14½*

**761** A175 50p Strip of 4, #a.-d. 7.00 7.00

**Souvenir Sheet**

*Perf. 14*

**762** A175 £1 multicolored 3.75 3.75

No. 761 was issued in sheets of 16 stamps. No. 762 contains one 48x58mm stamp.

Christmas — A176

**1997, Nov. 3** *Perf. 14*

**763** A176 20p Angel, shepherd .75 .75
**764** A176 24p Wise man, angel .85 .85

**Size: 54x39mm**

**765** A176 63p Angel and one of the Three Kings 2.40 2.40
*Nos. 763-765 (3)* 4.00 4.00

Flowers — A177

**1998, Feb. 12** **Litho.** *Perf. 13x13½*

**766** A177 4p Shamrocks .25 .25
*a.* Inscribed "1999" .40 .40
**767** A177 21p Cushag .80 .80
**768** A177 25p Princess of Wales Rose 1.00 1.00
Complete booklet, 2 each #766-768 4.00
**769** A177 50p Daffodil 2.00 2.00
**770** A177 £1 Spear thistle 4.00 4.00
*Nos. 766-770 (5)* 8.05 8.05

Nos. 766-768 also exist in special booklet sheets containing 10 of each denomination. Booklet panes made from these sheets contain 2 each #766-768.

See Nos. 794-801.

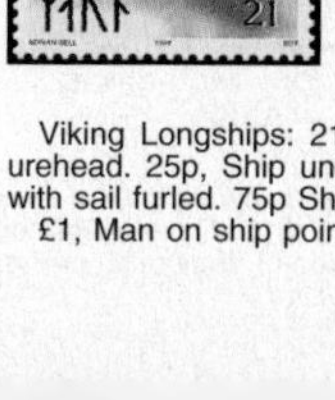


A178

Viking Longships: 21p, Dragon's head figurehead. 25p, Ship under full sail. 31p, Ship with sail furled. 75p Ship's stern.
£1, Man on ship pointing, fortress.

**1998, Feb. 14** *Perf. 14*

| | | | | |
|---|---|---|---|---|
| **771** | A178 | 21p multicolored | .80 | .80 |
| **772** | A178 | 25p multicolored | 1.00 | 1.00 |
| **773** | A178 | 31p multicolored | 1.25 | 1.25 |
| **774** | A178 | 75p multicolored | 3.00 | 3.00 |
| | | *Nos. 771-774 (4)* | 6.05 | 6.05 |

**Souvenir Sheet**

| | | | | |
|---|---|---|---|---|
| **775** | A178 | £1 multicolored | 4.00 | 4.00 |

Marine Life A179

Designs: 10p, Bottle-nosed dolphin. 21p, Basking shark swimming right. 25p, Basking shark swimming forward. 31p, Minke whale. 63p, Killer whale.

**1998, Mar. 14** **Litho.** *Perf. 14*

| | | | | |
|---|---|---|---|---|
| **776** | A179 | 10p multicolored | .40 | .40 |
| **777** | A179 | 21p multicolored | .80 | .80 |
| *a.* | | Booklet pane of 6, 3 each #776-777 + 3 labels | 3.75 | |
| **778** | A179 | 25p multicolored | 1.00 | 1.00 |
| **779** | A179 | 31p multicolored | 1.25 | 1.25 |
| **780** | A179 | 63p multicolored | 2.40 | 2.40 |
| *a.* | | Bklt. pane of 8, #776-777, 2 ea #778-780 + label | 11.00 | |
| | | Souvenir booklet, #777a, 780a | 15.00 | |
| | | *Nos. 776-780 (5)* | 5.85 | 5.85 |

Trains A180

Designs: 21p, Hutchinson 2-4-0. 25p, G.H. Wood 2-4-0. 31p, Maitland 2-4-0. 63p, Loch 2-4-0.

**1998, May 2** **Litho.** *Perf. 14½x14*

| | | | | |
|---|---|---|---|---|
| **781** | A180 | 21p multicolored | .80 | .80 |
| **782** | A180 | 25p multicolored | 1.00 | 1.00 |
| **783** | A180 | 31p multicolored | 1.25 | 1.25 |
| **784** | A180 | 63p multicolored | 2.40 | 2.40 |
| *a.* | | Bklt. pane of 4, #781-784 | 5.50 | 5.50 |
| | | *Nos. 781-784 (4)* | 5.45 | 5.45 |

**Souvenir Sheet**

| | | | | |
|---|---|---|---|---|
| **785** | A180 | Sheet of 2 | 5.50 | 5.50 |
| *a.* | | £1 Engine | 4.50 | 4.50 |
| *b.* | | 25p Passenger cars | 1.00 | 1.00 |
| *c.* | | Booklet pane of 1 | 5.50 | 5.50 |
| | | Complete bklt., #785c, 2 #784a | 17.00 | |
| *d.* | | As #785, inscribed in sheet margin | 5.50 | 5.50 |

No. 784a exists with two different backgrounds and stamps in different order. Complete booklets contain one of each pane.

No. 785d is inscribed in sheet margin with PhilexFrance '99, World Philatelic Exhibition emblem and was issued 7/2/99.

Europa A181

National Days celebration: 25p, People under tent, seated in stand, watching ceremony. 30p, Women dancing in traditional costumes.

**1998, July 2** *Perf. 13x13½*

| | | | | |
|---|---|---|---|---|
| **786** | A181 | 25p multicolored | 1.00 | 1.00 |
| **787** | A181 | 30p multicolored | 1.25 | 1.25 |

1998 Tourist Trophy Motorcycle Races — A182

Designs: 21p, Eight-man pyramid. 25p, Joey Dunlop rounding curve. 31p, Dave Molyneux with side car. 43p, Naomi Taniguchi racing. 63p, Mike Hailwood racing.

**1998, June 1** **Litho.** *Perf. 14*

| | | | | |
|---|---|---|---|---|
| **788** | A182 | 21p multicolored | .80 | .80 |
| **789** | A182 | 25p multicolored | 1.00 | 1.00 |
| **790** | A182 | 31p multicolored | 1.25 | 1.25 |
| **791** | A182 | 43p multicolored | 1.60 | 1.60 |
| **792** | A182 | 63p multicolored | 2.50 | 2.50 |
| | | *Nos. 788-792 (5)* | 7.15 | 7.15 |

A183

Diana, Princess of Wales (1961-97): a, In black evening dress. b, Accepting flowers. c, Holding hand to face. d, In protective clothing.

**1998, June 19** *Perf. 13*

| | | | | |
|---|---|---|---|---|
| **793** | A183 | 25p Strip of 4, #a.-d. | 4.00 | 4.00 |

**Flower Type**

***Perf. 13, 13x13½ (5p, 22p, 26p)***

**1998-99** **Litho.**

Flowers: 1p, Bearded iris. 2p, Daisy. 5p, Silver jubilee rose. 10p, Oriental poppy. 20p, Heath spotted orchid. 22p, Gorse. 26p, Dog rose. 30p, Fuchsia - lady thumb.

| | | | | |
|---|---|---|---|---|
| **794** | A177 | 1p multicolored | .25 | .25 |
| **795** | A177 | 2p multicolored | .25 | .25 |
| **796** | A177 | 5p multicolored | .25 | .25 |
| **797** | A177 | 10p multicolored | .40 | .40 |
| **798** | A177 | 20p multicolored | .80 | .80 |
| **799** | A177 | 22p multicolored | .85 | .85 |
| **800** | A177 | 26p multicolored | 1.00 | 1.00 |
| *a.* | | Bklt. pane, #800, 2 #766, 3 #799 | 4.00 | |
| | | Complete booklet, #800a | 4.00 | |
| **801** | A177 | 30p multicolored | 1.25 | 1.25 |
| | | *Nos. 794-801 (8)* | 5.05 | 5.05 |

Issued: 5p, 22p, 26p, 4/26/99; others, 7/2/98.

Queen Mother and Queen Elizabeth II A185

**1998, July 2** **Litho.** *Perf. 13*

| | | | | |
|---|---|---|---|---|
| **802** | A185 | £2.50 multicolored | 10.00 | 10.00 |

Christmas A186

Santa Claus: 20p, Loading sleigh at North Pole. 24p, With list, reindeer standing in clouds, Isle of Man below. 30p, Going over Spring Valley Sorting Office. 43p, Passing through Baldrine. 63p, Leaving presents, children inside house.

**1998, Sept. 25** **Litho.** *Perf. 14½x14*

| | | | | |
|---|---|---|---|---|
| **803** | A186 | 20p multicolored | .70 | .70 |
| **804** | A186 | 24p multicolored | .85 | .85 |
| **805** | A186 | 30p multicolored | 1.25 | 1.25 |
| **806** | A186 | 43p multicolored | 1.60 | 1.60 |
| **807** | A186 | 63p multicolored | 2.50 | 2.50 |
| | | *Nos. 803-807 (5)* | 6.90 | 6.90 |

Manx Nature Reserve and Parks (Europa) — A187

Designs: 25p, Cottage, Ballaglass Glen. 30p, Glen Maye Waterfall.

**1999, Mar. 4** **Litho.** *Perf. 14*

| | | | | |
|---|---|---|---|---|
| **808** | A187 | 25p multicolored | 1.00 | 1.00 |
| **809** | A187 | 30p multicolored | 1.25 | 1.25 |

Post Boxes — A188

10p, Oval box, Kirk Onchan Post Office. 20p, Wall box, Ballaterson, Ballaugh. 21p, Cylindrical box, Laxey Station. 25p, Wall box, Spaldrick, Port Erin. 44p, Oval box, Derby Road, Douglas. 63p, Wall box, Baldrine Station.

**1999, Mar. 4**

| | | | | |
|---|---|---|---|---|
| **810** | A188 | 10p multicolored | .40 | .40 |
| **811** | A188 | 20p multicolored | .80 | .80 |
| **812** | A188 | 21p multicolored | .80 | .80 |
| **813** | A188 | 25p multicolored | .95 | .95 |
| **814** | A188 | 44p multicolored | 1.60 | 1.60 |
| **815** | A188 | 63p multicolored | 2.40 | 2.40 |
| | | *Nos. 810-815 (6)* | 6.95 | 6.95 |

Royal Natl. Lifeboat Institution, 175th Anniv. — A189

**1999, Mar. 4**

| | | | | |
|---|---|---|---|---|
| **816** | A189 | 21p Ramsey lifeboat | .80 | .80 |
| **817** | A189 | 25p Douglas lifeboat | 1.00 | 1.00 |
| **818** | A189 | 37p Peel lifeboat | 1.50 | 1.50 |
| **819** | A189 | 43p Port Erin lifeboat | 1.60 | 1.60 |
| **820** | A189 | 56p Port St. Mary lifeboat | 2.25 | 2.25 |
| *a.* | | Bklt. pane, #816-820 + 4 labels | 7.25 | |
| | | *Nos. 816-820 (5)* | 7.15 | 7.15 |

**Booklet Stamps**

| | | | | |
|---|---|---|---|---|
| **821** | A189 | 43p #38 | 1.60 | 1.60 |
| **822** | A189 | 56p #464 | 2.25 | 2.25 |
| *a.* | | Booklet pane, #816-818, #821-822 + 4 labels | 7.25 | |

**Souvenir Sheet**

| | | | | |
|---|---|---|---|---|
| **823** | A189 | £1 William Hillary (1771-1847) | 4.00 | 4.00 |
| *a.* | | Booklet pane of 1 | 4.00 | |
| | | Complete booklet, #820a, #822a, #823a | 19.00 | |

IBRA '99 (#822a), Australia '99, World Stamp Expo. (#823). No. 823 contains one 38x50mm stamp.

Celtic Jewelry Depicting Seasons — A190

**1999, May 14** *Perf. 14½x14*

| | | | | |
|---|---|---|---|---|
| **824** | A190 | 22p Winter | .85 | .85 |
| **825** | A190 | 26p Spring | 1.00 | 1.00 |
| **826** | A190 | 50p Summer | 1.90 | 1.90 |
| **827** | A190 | 63p Autumn | 2.50 | 2.50 |
| | | *Nos. 824-827 (4)* | 6.25 | 6.25 |

20th Century British Monarchs A191

Monarch: a, Victoria. b, Edward VII. c, George V. d, Edward VIII. e, George VI. f, Elizabeth II.

**1999, June 2** **Litho.** *Perf. 14*

| | | | | |
|---|---|---|---|---|
| **828** | A191 | 26p Sheet of 6, #a.-f. | 6.00 | 6.00 |

Manx Buses A192

22p, 1922 Tilling Stevens 46 double-decker. 26p, 1928 Thornycroft BC 28-seat. 28p, 1927 ADC 416 28-seat. 37p, 1914 Staker Squire 25-seat. 38p, 1927 Thornycroft A2 20-seat. 40p, 1938 Leyland Lion LT9 34-seat.

**1999, June 18**

| | | | | |
|---|---|---|---|---|
| **829** | A192 | 22p multicolored | .85 | .85 |
| **830** | A192 | 26p multicolored | 1.00 | 1.00 |
| **831** | A192 | 28p multicolored | 1.10 | 1.10 |
| **832** | A192 | 37p multicolored | 1.50 | 1.50 |
| **833** | A192 | 38p multicolored | 1.50 | 1.50 |
| **834** | A192 | 40p multicolored | 1.60 | 1.60 |
| | | *Nos. 829-834 (6)* | 7.55 | 7.55 |
| *831a* | | Bklt. pane, #829-830, 2 #831 | 4.25 | |
| *832a* | | Bklt. pane, #829-830, 2 #832 | 5.00 | |
| *833a* | | Bklt. pane, #829-830, 2 #833 | 5.00 | |
| *834a* | | Bklt. pane, #829-830, 2 #834 | 5.25 | |
| | | Complete booklet, #831a-834a | 19.50 | |

Wedding of Prince Edward and Sophie Rhys-Jones — A193

**1999, June 19**

| | | | | |
|---|---|---|---|---|
| **835** | A193 | 22p Sophie, vert. | .85 | .85 |
| **836** | A193 | 39p Prince Edward, vert. | 1.40 | 1.40 |
| **837** | A193 | 44p Couple | 1.60 | 1.60 |
| | | *Nos. 835-837 (3)* | 3.85 | 3.85 |

Royal Wedding Photos — A193a

Designs: 26p, Couple standing. 53p, Couple seated in carriage, horiz.

**1999, Sept. 1** **Litho.** *Perf. 14¼*

| | | | | |
|---|---|---|---|---|
| **837A** | A193a | 26p multi | 1.00 | 1.00 |
| **837B** | A193a | 53p multi | 2.00 | 2.00 |

Churches — A194

***Perf. 13¼x13½***

**1999, Sept. 22** **Litho.**

| | | | | |
|---|---|---|---|---|
| **838** | A194 | 21p St. Luke, Baldwin | .80 | .80 |
| **839** | A194 | 25p St. Mark's, Malew | .95 | .95 |
| **840** | A194 | 30p St. Germain Parish Church and Cathedral, Peel | 1.10 | 1.10 |
| **841** | A194 | 64p Kirk Christ Church, Rushan | 2.50 | 2.50 |
| | | *Nos. 838-841 (4)* | 5.35 | 5.35 |

Bee Gees Songs
A195

Designs: 22p, "Massachusetts." 26p, "Words." 29p, "I've Gotta Get a Message to You." 37p, "Ellan Vannin." 38p, "You Win Again." 66p, "Night Fever."
60p, "Immortality." 90p, "Stayin' Alive."

**1999, Oct. 12 Litho. *Perf. 13¼x13½***

| | | | | |
|---|---|---|---|---|
| **842** | A195 | 22p multicolored | .85 | .85 |
| **843** | A195 | 26p multicolored | 1.00 | 1.00 |
| **844** | A195 | 29p multicolored | 1.10 | 1.10 |
| **845** | A195 | 37p multicolored | 1.40 | 1.40 |
| **846** | A195 | 38p multicolored | 1.40 | 1.40 |
| **847** | A195 | 66p multicolored | 2.50 | 2.50 |
| | | *Nos. 842-847 (6)* | 8.25 | 8.25 |

**Souvenir Sheets**

| | | | | |
|---|---|---|---|---|
| **848** | A195 | 60p multicolored | 4.00 | 4.00 |
| **849** | A195 | 90p multicolored | 6.00 | 6.00 |

Nos. 848-849 each contain one 40mm diameter stamp. Nos. 842-847 each issued in sheets of 9 stamps and 3 labels.

Souvenir Sheet

Millennium
A196

Objects in the night sky: a, 50p, Mars, stars Deneb, Altair, Vega. b, £2, Constellations Lynx, Draco, Ursa Minor, Ursa Major. c, 50p, Mercury, Venus, Deneb, Vega, Altair, orbit of International Space Station (ISS).

***Perf. 14¼x14½***

**1999, Dec. 31 Litho.**

| | | | | |
|---|---|---|---|---|
| **850** | A196 | Sheet of 3, #a.-c. | 13.00 | 13.00 |

History of Time — A197

Clock escapements of: 22p, 1735 by John Harrison. 26p, 2000 by George Daniels. 29p, 1767 by Harrison. 34p, 1769 by Thomas Mudge. 38p, 1779 by John Arnold. 44p, 1780 by Thomas Earnshaw.

**2000, Jan. 24 Litho. *Perf. 13x13½***

| | | | | |
|---|---|---|---|---|
| **851** | A197 | 22p multi | 1.00 | 1.00 |
| **852** | A197 | 26p multi | 1.10 | 1.10 |
| **853** | A197 | 29p multi | 1.25 | 1.25 |
| **854** | A197 | 34p multi | 1.50 | 1.50 |
| **855** | A197 | 38p multi | 1.75 | 1.75 |
| **856** | A197 | 44p multi | 2.00 | 2.00 |
| | | *Nos. 851-856 (6)* | 8.60 | 8.60 |

Queen Mother (b. 1900) — A198

Pictures of Queen Mother from — No. 857: a, 1923. b, 1940. c, 1944.
No. 858: a, 1954. b, 1985. c, 1988.
No. 859, 1984.
£1, Queen Mother on Isle of Man.

**2000, Feb. 29 Litho. *Perf. 14***

| | | | | |
|---|---|---|---|---|
| **857** | | Strip of 3 | 3.00 | 3.00 |
| *a.* | A198 | 22p multi | .80 | .80 |
| *b.* | A198 | 26p multi | 1.00 | 1.00 |
| *c.* | A198 | 30p multi | 1.10 | 1.10 |
| **858** | | Strip of 3 | 6.00 | 6.00 |
| *a.* | A198 | 44p multi | 1.60 | 1.60 |
| *b.* | A198 | 52p multi | 1.90 | 1.90 |
| *c.* | A198 | 64p multi | 2.40 | 2.40 |

**Souvenir Sheet**

***Perf. 14¼***

| | | | | |
|---|---|---|---|---|
| **859** | A198 | £1 multi | 3.75 | 3.75 |
| *a.* | | With emblem of The Stamp Show 2000 in margin | 7.00 | 7.00 |

Size of Nos. 857a-857c, 858a-858c, 42x28mm.
Issued: No. 859a, 5/22/00.

Song Birds — A199

**2000, May 5 *Perf. 14½x14¼***

| | | | | |
|---|---|---|---|---|
| **860** | | Strip of 4 | 8.50 | 8.50 |
| *a.* | A199 | 22p Swallow | 1.00 | 1.00 |
| *b.* | A199 | 26p Spotted flycatcher | 1.10 | 1.10 |
| *c.* | A199 | 64p Skylark | 2.75 | 2.75 |
| *d.* | A199 | 77p Yellowhammer | 3.25 | 3.25 |

World Wildlife Fund.

Military Leaders and Isle of Man Military Personnel
A200

Battle of Britain, 60th Anniv. — A201

#861: a, John Quilliam (1771-1829), Admiral Lord Nelson (1758-1805). b, Caesar Bacon (1791-1876), Duke of Wellington (1769-1852).
#862: a, Thomas Leigh Goldie (1807-54), Earl of Cardigan (1797-1868). b, John Dunne (1884-1950), Sir Robert Baden-Powell (1857-1941).
#863: a, George Kneale (1896-1917), Viscount Kitchener (1850-1916). b, Alan Watterson (1910-42), Sir Winston Churchill (1874-1965).
#864: a, Planes in air. b, Plane on ground.

**2000, May 22 Litho. *Perf. 13¼***

| | | | | |
|---|---|---|---|---|
| **861** | | Pair, #a-b, + central label | 1.90 | 1.90 |
| *a.* | A200 | 22p multi | .80 | .80 |
| *b.* | A200 | 26p multi | 1.00 | 1.00 |
| **862** | | Pair, #a-b, + central label | 3.25 | 3.25 |
| *a.* | A200 | 36p multi | 1.40 | 1.40 |
| *b.* | A200 | 48p multi | 1.75 | 1.75 |
| **863** | | Pair, #a-b, + central label | 4.75 | 4.75 |
| *a.* | A200 | 50p multi | 1.90 | 1.90 |
| *b.* | A200 | 77p multi | 2.75 | 2.75 |
| *c.* | | Booklet pane, #861a, 861b, 862a, 862b, 863a | 7.00 | |
| *d.* | | Booklet pane, #861a, 862b, 863a, 863b | 6.75 | |
| | | *Nos. 861-863 (3)* | 9.90 | 9.90 |

**Souvenir Sheet**

***Perf. 14¾x14¼***

| | | | | |
|---|---|---|---|---|
| **864** | A201 | 60p Sheet of 2, #a-b | 5.25 | 5.25 |
| *c.* | | Booklet pane, #864 | 5.25 | |
| | | Booklet, #863c, 863d, 864c | 21.00 | |

No. 864c has stitched margin at left.

Souvenir Sheet

Prince William, 18th Birthday — A202

**2000, June 21 Litho. *Perf. 14***

| | | | | |
|---|---|---|---|---|
| **865** | | Sheet of 5 | 6.50 | 6.50 |
| *a.* | A202 | 22p As toddler | .80 | .80 |
| *b.* | A202 | 26p With Queen Mother | 1.00 | 1.00 |
| *c.* | A202 | 45p In checked shirt | 1.75 | 1.75 |
| *d.* | A202 | 52p With Princes Charles, Harry | 1.90 | 1.90 |
| *e.* | A202 | 56p In ski gear | 2.00 | 2.00 |

Gaiety Theater, Cent.
A203

**2000, July 16**

| | | | | |
|---|---|---|---|---|
| **866** | A203 | 22p Ballet | .80 | .80 |
| **867** | A203 | 26p Comedy | 1.00 | 1.00 |
| **868** | A203 | 36p Drama | 1.40 | 1.40 |
| **869** | A203 | 45p Pantomime | 1.75 | 1.75 |
| **870** | A203 | 52p Opera | 1.90 | 1.90 |
| **871** | A203 | 65p Musicals | 2.40 | 2.40 |
| | | *Nos. 866-871 (6)* | 9.25 | 9.25 |

Global Challenge Yacht Race — A204

Sail from yacht "Isle of Man," and ports of call: 22p, Southampton. 26p, Sydney. 36p, Wellington. 40p, Buenos Aires. 44p, Boston. 65p, Cape Town.

***Perf. 13¼x13¾***

**2000, Sept. 10 Litho.**

| | | | | |
|---|---|---|---|---|
| **872** | A204 | 22p multi | .80 | .80 |
| **873** | A204 | 26p multi | 1.00 | 1.00 |
| **874** | A204 | 36p multi | 1.40 | 1.40 |
| **875** | A204 | 40p multi | 1.50 | 1.50 |
| **876** | A204 | 44p multi | 1.60 | 1.60 |
| **877** | A204 | 65p multi | 2.40 | 2.40 |
| | | *Nos. 872-877 (6)* | 8.70 | 8.70 |

Travel Poster Art of Isle of Man Steam Packet Co. — A205

Designs: 22p, Three legs of Man, ship. 26p, Cliffs and sailboats. 36p, Woman and Isle of Man. 45p, Woman, ship, flag. 65p, Ship.

**2000, Oct. 16 *Perf. 13½x13¼***

| | | | | |
|---|---|---|---|---|
| **878** | A205 | 22p multi | .80 | .80 |
| **879** | A205 | 26p multi | 1.00 | 1.00 |
| **880** | A205 | 36p multi | 1.40 | 1.40 |
| **881** | A205 | 45p multi | 1.75 | 1.75 |
| **882** | A205 | 65p multi | 2.40 | 2.40 |
| | | *Nos. 878-882 (5)* | 7.35 | 7.35 |

**Europa, 2000**

Common Design Type

**2000, Nov. 7 *Perf. 14***

| | | | | |
|---|---|---|---|---|
| **883** | CD17 | 36p multi | 1.50 | 1.50 |

Christmas
A206

**2000, Nov. 7**

| | | | | |
|---|---|---|---|---|
| **884** | A206 | 21p Peace | .80 | .80 |
| **885** | A206 | 25p Hope | .90 | .90 |
| **886** | A206 | 45p Love | 1.75 | 1.75 |
| **887** | A206 | 65p Faith | 2.40 | 2.40 |
| | | *Nos. 884-887 (4)* | 5.85 | 5.85 |

Souvenir Sheet

New Year 2001 (Year of the Snake) — A207

**Litho. with Foil Application**

**2001, Jan. 22 *Perf. 13¾***

| | | | | |
|---|---|---|---|---|
| **888** | A207 | £1 St. Patrick | 4.50 | 4.50 |

Hong Kong 2001 Stamp Exhibition.

Queen Victoria (1819-1901) — A208

Designs: 22p, Wyon medal, Queen Victoria, Great Britain Type A1. 26p, Great Exhibition medal, Albert Tower. 34p, Coin, Steamship Great Britain. 39p, Coin, scene from Oliver Twist, St. Thomas' Church, Douglas. 40p, Coin, first train to arrive in Vancouver, Canada and Jubilee streetlamp standard. 52p, Coin, Foxdale Clock Tower, family of diamond magnate Joe Mylchreest.

**2001, Jan. 22 Litho. *Perf. 13½***

| | | | | |
|---|---|---|---|---|
| **889** | A208 | 22p multi | .85 | .85 |
| **890** | A208 | 26p multi | 1.00 | 1.00 |
| **891** | A208 | 34p multi | 1.40 | 1.40 |
| **892** | A208 | 39p multi | 1.50 | 1.50 |
| **893** | A208 | 40p multi | 1.60 | 1.60 |
| **894** | A208 | 52p multi | 2.00 | 2.00 |
| | | *Nos. 889-894 (6)* | 8.35 | 8.35 |

Insects
A209

Designs: 22p, White-tailed bumblebee. 26p, Seven-spot ladybug. 29p, Lesser mottled grasshopper. 58p, Manx robber fly. 66p, Elephant hawkmoth.

**2001, Feb. 1 *Perf. 14½***

| | | | | |
|---|---|---|---|---|
| **895** | A209 | 22p multi | .85 | .85 |
| **896** | A209 | 26p multi | 1.00 | 1.00 |
| **897** | A209 | 29p multi | 1.10 | 1.10 |
| **898** | A209 | 58p multi | 2.25 | 2.25 |
| **899** | A209 | 66p multi | 2.50 | 2.50 |
| | | *Nos. 895-899 (5)* | 7.70 | 7.70 |

Souvenir Sheet

Queen Elizabeth II, 75th Birthday — A210

Stamps: 29p, Great Britain #MH1. 34p, Great Britain #300. 37p, Isle of Man #8. 50p, Isle of Man #3.

**2001, Apr. 18 Litho. *Perf. 14***

**900** A210 Sheet of 4, #a-d 6.00 6.00
*e.* As #900, with Hafnia 01 emblem added in sheet margin 7.50 7.50

No. 900e issued 10/29.

Manx Postmen and Cancels — A211

**2001, Apr. 18**

**901** A211 22p 1805 .85 .85
**902** A211 26p 1859 1.00 1.00
**903** A211 36p 1910 1.40 1.40
**904** A211 39p 1933 1.50 1.50
**905** A211 40p 1983 1.60 1.60
**906** A211 66p 2001 2.50 2.50
*Nos. 901-906 (6)* 8.85 8.85

William Joseph Dunlop (1952-2000), Motorcycle Racer — A212

Various photographs.

**2001, May 17**

**907** A212 22p multi .85 .85
**908** A212 26p multi 1.00 1.00
**909** A212 36p multi 1.40 1.40
**910** A212 45p multi 1.75 1.75
**911** A212 65p multi 2.50 2.50
**912** A212 77p multi 2.75 2.75
*Nos. 907-912 (6)* 10.25 10.25

Horse Racing A213

Designs: 22p, Manx Derby. 26p, Post Haste. 36p, Red Rum. 52p, Hyperion. 63p, Isle of Man.

**2001, May 18 *Perf. 13¼x13½***

**913** A213 22p multi .85 .85
**914** A213 26p multi 1.00 1.00
**915** A213 36p multi 1.40 1.40
**916** A213 52p multi 1.90 1.90
**917** A213 63p multi 2.40 2.40
*Nos. 913-917 (5)* 7.55 7.55

Gourmet Food — A214

**2001, Aug. 10 Litho. *Perf. 14¼***

**918** A214 22p Beef .80 .80
**919** A214 26p Queenies .90 .90
*a.* Sheet of 10 9.00 —
**920** A214 36p Seafood 1.25 1.25
*a.* Sheet of 10 12.50 —
**921** A214 45p Lamb 1.60 1.60
**922** A214 50p Kippers 1.90 1.90
**923** A214 66p Lemon tart 2.40 2.40
*Nos. 918-923 (6)* 8.85 8.85

Europa (#919, 920).

Architecture of Mackay Hugh Baillie Scott — A215

Designs: 22p, Castletown Police Station, 1901. 26p, Leafield/Braeside, 1897. 37p, Red House, 1893. 40p, Ivydene, 1893. 80p, Onchan Village Hall, 1898.

**2001, Sept. 3 *Perf. 13¼x13½***

**924** A215 22p multi .85 .85
**925** A215 26p multi 1.00 1.00
**926** A215 37p multi 1.40 1.40
**927** A215 40p multi 1.60 1.60
**928** A215 80p multi 3.00 3.00
*Nos. 924-928 (5)* 7.85 7.85

Reign of Queen Elizabeth II, 50th Anniv. (in 2002) — A216

Drawings of Queen: 22p, At dining table. 26p, With crowd, holding flower bouquet. 39p, With dogs. 40p, With men wearing hats. 45p, With correspondence. 65p, Alone, holding flower bouquet.

**Litho. With Foil Application**

**2001-02 *Perf. 14¼***

**929** A216 22p multi .85 .85
**930** A216 26p multi 1.00 1.00
**931** A216 39p multi 1.60 1.60
*a.* Booklet pane of 3, #929-931 3.50 —
**932** A216 40p multi 1.60 1.60
**933** A216 45p multi 1.75 1.75
**934** A216 65p multi 2.50 2.50
*a.* Booklet pane of 3, #932-934 6.00 —
*Nos. 929-934 (6)* 9.30 9.30

Issued: Nos. 929-934, 10/29/01. Nos. 931a, 934a, 2/6/02.

Christmas A217

Floral arrangements: 21p, Holly on Christmas tree-shaped frame. 25p, Wreath. 37p, Table decoration with candles. 45p, Topiary tree. 65p, Wreath, diff.

**2001, Nov. 5 Litho. *Perf. 14x14½***

**Stamp + Label**

**Background Color**

**935** A217 21p green .80 .80
**936** A217 25p red 1.00 1.00
**937** A217 37p gold 1.40 1.40
**938** A217 45p silver 1.75 1.75
**939** A217 65p violet 2.40 2.40
*Nos. 935-939 (5)* 7.35 7.35

Reign of Queen Elizabeth II, 50th Anniv. — A218

No. 940 — Paintings: a, The Coronation, by Terence Cuneo. b, Her Majesty the Queen as Colonel in Chief, Grenadier Guards on Imperial, by Cuneo (Queen on horse). c, Her Majesty in Evening Dress, by June Mendoza. d, Her Majesty the Queen, by Chen Yan Ning. e, The Royal Family, by John Wonnacott.

£1, Her Majesty Queen Elizabeth II Lord of Mann, sculpture by David Cregeen.

**Litho. with Foil Application**

**2002, Feb. 6 *Perf. 14***

**940** Vert. strip of 5 10.00 10.00
*a.-e.* A218 50p Any single 2.00 2.00
*f.* Booklet pane of 3, #940a-940c 6.25 —
*g.* Booklet pane of 2, #940d-940e 4.25 —

**Souvenir Sheet**

***Perf. 14½x14***

**941** A218 £1 multi 4.00 4.00
*a.* Booklet pane of 1 with larger margin 4.00 —
Booklet, #931a, 934a, 940f, 940g, 941a 24.00
*b.* As 941, inscribed in sheet margin in purple The Isle of Man Celebrates The Jubilee / 4th June 2002 6.00 6.00

No. 941 contains one 60x40mm stamp.

17th Commonwealth Games, Manchester, England — A219

Designs: 22p, Cycling. 26p, Running. 29p, Javelin, women's high jump. 34p, Swimming. 40p, Hurdles, pole vault. 45p, Wheelchair racing.

**2002, Mar. 11 Litho. *Perf. 14***

**942** A219 22p multi .80 .80
**943** A219 26p multi .90 .90
**944** A219 29p multi 1.10 1.10
**945** A219 34p multi 1.25 1.25
**946** A219 40p multi 1.50 1.50
**947** A219 45p multi 1.60 1.60
*Nos. 942-947 (6)* 7.15 7.15

Queen Mother Elizabeth (1900-2002) A220

**2002, Apr. 23 *Perf. 13x13¼***

**948** A220 £3 multi 12.00 12.00

Paintings by Toni Onley A221

Designs: 22p, Monks' Bridge, Ballasalla. 26p, Laxey. 37p, Langness Lighthouse. 45p, King William's College. 65p, The Mull Circle & Bradda Head.

**2002, May 1 *Perf. 13¼x13½***

**949** A221 22p multi .85 .85
**950** A221 26p multi 1.00 1.00
**951** A221 37p multi 1.50 1.50
**952** A221 45p multi 1.75 1.75
**953** A221 65p multi 2.50 2.50
*Nos. 949-953 (5)* 7.60 7.60

2002 World Cup Soccer Championships, Japan and Korea — A222

Various players.

**2002, May 1 *Perf. 13½***

**954** A222 22p multi .85 .85
**955** A222 26p multi 1.00 1.00
**956** A222 39p multi 1.60 1.60
**957** A222 40p multi 1.60 1.60
**958** A222 66p multi 2.50 2.50
**959** A222 68p multi 2.75 2.75
*Nos. 954-959 (6)* 10.30 10.30

Flower Sketches by Sir Paul McCartney A223

Various sketches.

**2002, July 1 Litho. *Perf. 13¼x12¾***

**960** A223 22p multi .85 .85
**961** A223 26p multi 1.00 1.00
**962** A223 29p multi 1.10 1.10
**963** A223 52p multi 2.00 2.00
**964** A223 63p multi 2.50 2.50
**965** A223 77p multi 3.00 3.00
*Nos. 960-965 (6)* 10.45 10.45

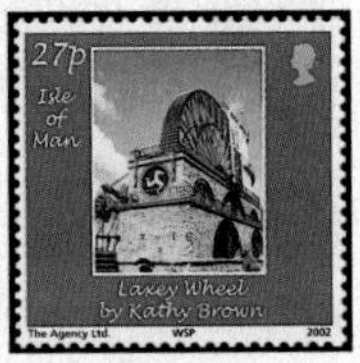

Photographs of Local Scenes — A224

Nos. 966-967: a, Laxey Wheel, by Kathy Brown. b, Sheep at Druidale, by John Hall. c, Carousel at Silverdale, by Colin Edwards. d, Grandma, by Stephanie Corkill. e, Manx Rock, by Ruth Nicholls. f, TT Riders at Signpost, by Neil Brew. g, Groudle Railway, by Albert Lowe. h, Royal Cascade, by Brian Speedie. i, St. Johns, by John Hall. j, Niarbyl Cottages with Poppies, by Cathy Galbraith.

**2002 Litho. *Perf. 14***

**966** Block of 10 11.00 11.00
*a.-j.* A224 27p Any single 1.10 1.10

**Self-Adhesive**

***Serpentine Die Cut 6¼***

**967** Booklet of 10 11.00
*a.-j.* A224 27p Any single 1.10 1.10

Designs: a, Manx Milestone, by Mrs. B. J. Trimble. b, Plow Horses, by Miss D. Flint. c, Manx Emblem, by Ruth Nicholls. d, Loaghtan Sheep, by Diana Buford. e, Fishing Fleet at Port St. Mary, by Phil Thomas. f, Peel, by Michael Thompson. g, Daffodils, by Michael Thompson. h, Millennium Sword, by Mr. F. K. Smith. i, Peel Castle, by Kathy Brown. j, Snaefell Railway, by Joan Burgess.

**Litho.**

***Perf. 14***

**968** Block of 10 9.00 9.00
*a.-j.* A224 23p Any single .90 .90

**Self-Adhesive**

***Serpentine Die Cut 6¼***

**969** Booklet of 10 9.00
*a.-j.* A224 23p Any single .90 .90

Issued: Nos. 966-967, 8/30; Nos. 968-969, 10/1.

Christmas and Europa — A225

Designs: 22p, Santa Claus. 26p, Madonna and Child. 37p, Clown. 47p, Cymbal player. 68p, Fairy.
£1.30, "Christmas."

**2002, Nov. 5** *Perf. 14x14½*

**970** A225 22p multi .80 .80
**971** A225 26p multi .95 .95
**972** A225 37p multi 1.50 1.50
*a.* Sheet of 10 + 10 labels 15.00 15.00
**973** A225 47p multi 1.75 1.75
**974** A225 68p multi 2.75 2.75
*Nos. 970-974 (5)* 7.75 7.75

**Miniature Sheet**

***Perf. 14¾***

**975** A225 £1.30 multi 5.25 5.25

Europa (#972). No. 975 contains one 99x38mm stamp.

Post Office Vehicles A226

Designs: 23p, Handcart. 27p, Morris Z van. 37p, Morris LD van. 42p, DI BSA Bantam motorcycle. 89p, Ford Escort 55 delivery van.

**2003, Feb. 14** *Perf. 14¼*

**976** A226 23p multi 1.00 1.00
**977** A226 27p multi 1.25 1.25
**978** A226 37p multi 1.50 1.50
**979** A226 42p multi 1.75 1.75
**980** A226 89p multi 3.50 3.50
*Nos. 976-980 (5)* 9.00 9.00

Space Exploration — A227

No. 981: a, Tromode Teleport. b, Satellite earth station.
No. 982: a, Pioneering the space frontier (denomination at left). b, Pioneering the space frontier (denomination at right).
No. 983: a, Sea Launch Odyssey launch platform. b, Sea Launch Commander.
No. 984: a, Loral Skynet Telstar 1. b, Loral Skynet Telstar 8.
No. 985: a, Space station, Phobos. b, Astronauts, Mars.

**2003, Feb. 14** *Perf. 13¼x13½*

**981** A227 Horiz. pair 1.90 1.90
*a.-b.* 23p Either single .90 .90
**982** A227 Horiz. pair 2.25 2.25
*a.-b.* 27p Either single 1.10 1.10
**983** A227 Horiz. pair 3.00 3.00
*a.-b.* 37p Either single 1.50 1.50
**984** A227 Horiz. pair 3.25 3.25
*a.-b.* 42p Either single 1.60 1.60
*Nos. 981-984 (4)* 10.40 10.40

**Souvenir Sheet**

***Perf. 13¼x13***

**985** A227 Horiz. pair 6.00 6.00
*a.-b.* 75p Either single 3.00 3.00

No. 985 contains two 29x38mm stamps.

Coronation of Queen Elizabeth II, 50th Anniv. — A228

No. 986: a, Queen wearing St. Edward's Crown (brown background, 29x59mm). b, Queen wearing Sovereign's ring and armills (29x29mm). c, Sovereign's orb (29x29mm). d, Scepter with Cross, Rod with Dove (29x29mm). e, Queen wearing Imperial State Crown (blue green background, 29x59mm) f, Queen in State Coach (89x29mm).

**Litho. With Foil Application**

**2003, Apr. 12** *Perf. 13¼*

**986** A228 Block of 6 12.00 12.00
*a.-f.* 50p Any single 2.00 2.00

Powered Flight, Cent. — A229

No. 987: a, DH 83 Fox Moth, Saro Cloud. b, DH 61 Giant Moth, DH Puss Moth. c, Avro Anson, B-17 Flying Fortress.
No. 988: a, Eurofighter Typhoon, Avro Vulcan. b, Handley Page Herald, Bristol Wayfarer. c, Concorde, A380 Airbus.

**2003, May 9** **Litho.** *Perf. 13¼*

**987** Strip of 3 3.50 3.50
*a.* A229 23p multi .90 .90
*b.* A229 27p multi 1.10 1.10
*c.* A229 37p multi 1.50 1.50
**988** Strip of 3 8.00 8.00
*a.* A229 40p multi 1.60 1.60
*b.* A229 67p multi 2.75 2.75
*c.* A229 89p multi 3.50 3.50

**Souvenir Sheet**

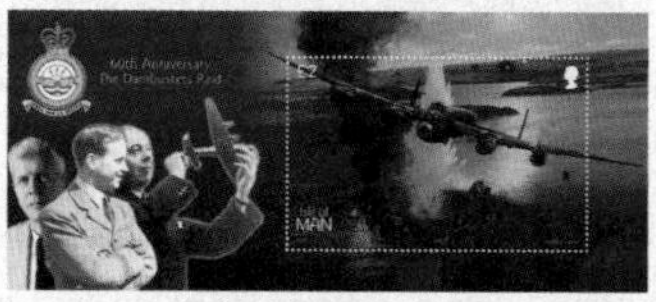

Dambuster's Raid, 60th Anniv. — A230

**2003**

**989** A230 £2 multi 8.00 8.00
*a.* With "Ticino 2003" emblem in margin 8.50 8.50

Issued: No. 989, 5/9; No. 989a, 6/18.

Prince William, 21st Birthday A231

Various photographs.

**2003, June 9** *Perf. 13¼x13½*

**990** A231 42p black 1.60 1.60
**991** A231 47p black 1.90 1.90
**992** A231 52p black 2.00 2.00
**993** A231 68p black 2.50 2.50
*Nos. 990-993 (4)* 8.00 8.00

Literature With Manx Connections — A232

Designs: 23p, Manx Gold, by Agatha Christie. 27p, Quartermass and the Pit, by Nigel Kneale. 30p, Flashman at the Charge, by George MacDonald Fraser. 38p, The Eternal City, by Hall Caine. 40p, Islanders, by Mona Douglas. 53p, Emma's Secret, by Barbara Taylor Bradford.

**2003, July 9** *Perf. 13¼*

**Stamp + Label**

**994** A232 23p multi .90 .90
**995** A232 27p multi 1.10 1.10
**996** A232 30p multi 1.25 1.25
**997** A232 38p multi 1.50 1.50
*a.* Sheet of 10 + 10 labels 15.00 15.00
**998** A232 40p multi 1.60 1.60
**999** A232 53p multi 2.00 2.00
*Nos. 994-999 (6)* 8.35 8.35

Europa (#997).

End of Tudor Reign, 400th Anniv. A233

Designs: 23p, Crowning of King Henry VII at Bosworth. 27p, King Henry VIII, Dissolution of the Monasteries. 38p, Queen Elizabeth I, Sir Francis Drake circumnavigates the globe. 40p, King Henry VIII, Hampton Court. 47p, Queen Mary I, Tudor rose. 67p, Queen Elizabeth I, Spanish Armada.

**2003, Sept. 15** *Perf. 14*

**1000** A233 23p multi .90 .90
**1001** A233 27p multi 1.10 1.10
**1002** A233 38p multi 1.50 1.50
**1003** A233 40p multi 1.60 1.60
**1004** A233 47p multi 1.90 1.90
**1005** A233 67p multi 2.50 2.50
*Nos. 1000-1005 (6)* 9.50 9.50

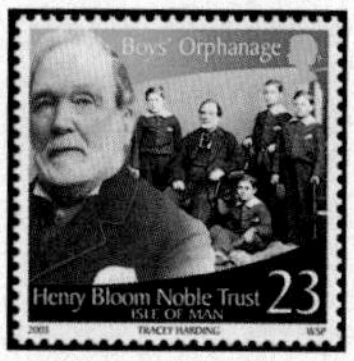


Henry Bloom Noble Trust, Cent. — A234

No. 1006: a, Boys' Orphanage. b, Ramsey Cottage Hospital. c, Children's Home. d, Noble's Baths. e, Scout Headquarters.
No. 1007: a, Noble's Hospital. b, Villa Marina. c, Noble's Park. d, St. Ninian's Church. e, Noble's Library.

**2003, Oct. 1**

**1006** Horiz. strip of 5 4.50 4.50
*a.-e.* A234 23p Any single .90 .90
**1007** Horiz. strip of 5 5.50 5.50
*a.-e.* A234 27p Any single 1.10 1.10

**Booklet Stamps**

**Self-Adhesive**

***Serpentine Die Cut 6¼***

**1007F** A234 23p Like #1006a .90 .90
**1007G** A234 23p Like #1006b .90 .90
**1007H** A234 23p Like #1006c .90 .90
**1007I** A234 23p Like #1006d .90 .90
**1007J** A234 23p Like #1006e .90 .90
*p.* Booklet pane, 2 each #1007F-1007J 9.00
**1007K** A234 27p Like #1007a 1.10 1.10
**1007L** A234 27p Like #1007b 1.10 1.10
**1007M** A234 27p Like #1007c 1.10 1.10
**1007N** A234 27p Like #1007d 1.10 1.10
**1007O** A234 27p Like #1007e 1.10 1.10
*q.* Booklet pane, 2 each #1007K-1007O 11.00
*Nos. 1007F-1007O (10)* 10.00 10.00

Nos. 1007Jp and 1007Oq are complete booklets, the backing serving as the booklet covers.

Christmas A235

Various snowmen, based on Raymond Briggs' children's story *The Snowman.*

**Litho. With Foil Application**

**2003, Nov. 5** *Perf. 14¼*

**Background Color**

**1008** A235 22p red .90 .90
**1009** A235 26p deep blue 1.00 1.00
**1010** A235 38p blue green 1.50 1.50
**1011** A235 47p orange 1.90 1.90
**1012** A235 68p yellow 2.50 2.50
*Nos. 1008-1012 (5)* 7.80 7.80

Debut of Movie *The Lord of the Rings: The Return of the King* — A236

Designs: 23p, Aragorn. 27p, Gimli. 30p, Gandalf the White. 38p, Legolas on horseback. 42p, Gollum. 47p, Frodo Baggins and Samwise Gamgee. 68p, Legolas with bow and arrow. 85p, Aragorn on horseback.
£2, Ring.

**2003, Dec. 17** **Litho.** *Perf. 13¼*

**1013** A236 23p multi .90 .90
**1014** A236 27p multi 1.10 1.10
**1015** A236 30p multi 1.25 1.25
**1016** A236 38p multi 1.50 1.50
**1017** A236 42p multi 1.60 1.60
**1018** A236 47p multi 1.90 1.90
**1019** A236 68p multi 2.75 2.75
**1020** A236 85p multi 3.50 3.50
*Nos. 1013-1020 (8)* 14.50 14.50

**Souvenir Sheet**

***Perf. 13½***

**1021** A236 £2 multi 8.50 8.50

No. 1021 contains one 44x39mm stamp. Nos. 1013-1020 were each printed in sheets of six.

Steam Locomotives — A237

Designs: 23p, Maitland. 27p, Evening Star. 40p, Penydarren Tramroad locomotive. 57p, Duchess of Hamilton. 61p, City of Truro. 90p, Mallard.

**2004, Feb. 21** **Litho.** *Perf. 13x13½*

**1022** A237 23p multi 1.00 1.00
**1023** A237 27p multi 1.25 1.25
**1024** A237 40p multi 1.75 1.75
**1025** A237 57p multi 2.25 2.25
**1026** A237 61p multi 2.50 2.50
**1027** A237 90p multi 3.50 3.50
*Nos. 1022-1027 (6)* 12.25 12.25

D-Day, 60th Anniv. — A238

No. 1028: a, Two soldiers near walkways, tanks on beach. b, Soldiers in water, tanks on beach.
No. 1029: a, Soldiers in water between two boats. b, Soldiers in water, landing craft with gangway open.
No. 1030: a, Lady of Mann, two blimps. b, Ben-my-Chree, three landing craft, five blimps.
No. 1031: a, Two US B-24 Liberators, RAF Horsa glider. b, Three RAF Horsa gliders.
No. 1032: a, Sir Winston Churchill. b, Soldiers near airplane propeller. c, Military vehicles on street in residential area. d, Soldiers reading book.
Illustration reduced.

**2004, Apr. 6** *Perf. 14*

**1028** A238 Horiz. pair 1.90 1.90
*a.-b.* 23p Either single .90 .90
**1029** A238 Horiz. pair 2.25 2.25
*a.-b.* 27p Either single 1.10 1.10
**1030** A238 Horiz. pair 4.00 4.00
*a.-b.* 47p Either single 1.90 1.90
**1031** A238 Horiz. pair 5.50 5.50
*a.-b.* 68p Either single 2.75 2.75
*Nos. 1028-1031 (4)* 13.65 13.65

**Souvenir Sheet**

***Perf. 13¼x13¾***

**1032** A238 Sheet of 4 8.00 8.00
*a.-d.* 50p Any single 2.00 2.00

Flowers A239

Designs: 25p, Lesser celandine. 28p, Red campion. 37p, Devil's bit scabious. 40p, Northern harebell. 68p, Wood anemone. 85p, Common spotted orchid.

**2004, May 3** *Perf. 13½*

| | | | |
|---|---|---|---|
| 1033 | A239 25p multi | 1.00 | 1.00 |
| 1034 | A239 28p multi | 1.10 | 1.10 |
| 1035 | A239 37p multi | 1.50 | 1.50 |
| 1036 | A239 40p multi | 1.60 | 1.60 |
| 1037 | A239 68p multi | 2.75 | 2.75 |
| 1038 | A239 85p multi | 3.50 | 3.50 |
| | *Nos. 1033-1038 (6)* | 11.45 | 11.45 |

George Formby (1904-61), Movie Actor — A240

Various scenes from film *No Limit* and text: 25p, No Limit. 28p, George. 40p, Speed Demon. 43p, Florence. 50p, Shuttleworth. 74p, Formby.

**2004, May 26** *Perf. 13¼*

| | | | |
|---|---|---|---|
| 1039 | A240 25p multi | 1.00 | 1.00 |
| 1040 | A240 28p multi | 1.10 | 1.10 |
| 1041 | A240 40p multi | 1.60 | 1.60 |
| 1042 | A240 43p multi | 1.75 | 1.75 |
| 1043 | A240 50p multi | 2.00 | 2.00 |
| 1044 | A240 74p multi | 3.00 | 3.00 |
| | *Nos. 1039-1044 (6)* | 10.45 | 10.45 |

2004 Summer Olympics, Athens — A241

Designs: 25p, Johnny Weismuller, Paris Olympics, 1924. 28p, Jesse Owens, runners, Berlin Olympics, 1936. 43p, John Mark, torch bearer, London Olympics, 1948. 55p, Fanny Blankers-Koen, runners, London Olympics, 1948. 91p, Sir Steve Redgrave, rowers, Sydney Olympics, 2000.

**2004, July 1** **Litho.** *Perf. 14*

| | | | |
|---|---|---|---|
| 1045 | A241 25p multi | 1.00 | 1.00 |
| 1046 | A241 28p multi | 1.25 | 1.25 |
| 1047 | A241 43p multi | 1.75 | 1.75 |
| 1048 | A241 55p multi | 2.25 | 2.25 |
| 1049 | A241 91p multi | 3.75 | 3.75 |
| | *Nos. 1045-1049 (5)* | 10.00 | 10.00 |

Manx History — A242

Designs: Nos. 1050a, 1052, Celtic islander and Viking invaders. Nos. 1050b, 1053, Ships and the sea. Nos. 1050c, 1054, Laxey miners. Nos. 1050d, 1055, Kings and Lords of Mann. Nos. 1050e, 1056, Farmers and crofters. Nos. 1051a, 1057, Calf of Man. Nos. 1051b, 1058, Peel Castle. Nos. 1051c, 1059, Laxey Wheel. Nos. 1051d, 1060, Castle Rushen. Nos. 1051e, 1061, Cregneash.

**2004, Aug. 3** *Perf. 14¼*

| | | | |
|---|---|---|---|
| 1050 | Horiz. strip of 5 | 5.00 | 5.00 |
| *a.-e.* | A242 (25p) Any single | 1.00 | 1.00 |
| 1051 | Horiz. strip of 5 | 5.50 | 5.50 |
| *a.-e.* | A242 (28p) Any single | 1.10 | 1.10 |

**Booklet Stamps**

**Self-Adhesive**

***Serpentine Die Cut 12½***

| | | | |
|---|---|---|---|
| 1052 | A242 (25p) multi | 1.00 | 1.00 |
| 1053 | A242 (25p) multi | 1.00 | 1.00 |
| 1054 | A242 (25p) multi | 1.00 | 1.00 |
| 1055 | A242 (25p) multi | 1.00 | 1.00 |
| 1056 | A242 (25p) multi | 1.00 | 1.00 |
| *a.* | Booklet pane, 2 each #1052-1056 | 10.00 | |
| 1057 | A242 (28p) multi | 1.10 | 1.10 |
| 1058 | A242 (28p) multi | 1.10 | 1.10 |
| 1059 | A242 (28p) multi | 1.10 | 1.10 |
| 1060 | A242 (28p) multi | 1.10 | 1.10 |
| 1061 | A242 (28p) multi | 1.10 | 1.10 |
| *a.* | Booklet pane, 2 each #1057-1061 | 11.00 | |
| | *Nos. 1050-1061 (12)* | 21.00 | 21.00 |

Nos. 1056a and 1061a are complete booklets, the backing serving as the booklet covers.

Souvenir Sheet

Laxey Wheel, 150th Anniv. — A243

**2004, Aug. 3** *Perf. 14¼*

| | | | |
|---|---|---|---|
| 1062 | A243 £2 multi | 8.00 | 8.00 |
| *a.* | With Sindelfingen 2004 emblem added in sheet margin | 10.00 | 10.00 |

No. 1062a issued 10/29.

Watercolors by Alfred Heaton Cooper (1864-1929) A244

Designs: 25p, Maughold Church. 28p, Port St. Mary. 40p, Ballaugh Old Church. 41p, Douglas Bay (A Midsummer's Night). 43p, Point of Ayre. 74p, Peel Harbor and Castle.

**2004, Oct. 21** **Litho.** *Perf. 13¼x12¾*

| | | | |
|---|---|---|---|
| 1063 | A244 25p multi | 1.00 | 1.00 |
| 1064 | A244 28p multi | 1.10 | 1.10 |
| *a.* | Sheet of 10 + 10 labels | 11.00 | 11.00 |
| 1065 | A244 40p multi | 1.60 | 1.60 |
| *a.* | Sheet of 10 + 10 labels | 16.00 | 16.00 |
| 1066 | A244 41p multi | 1.60 | 1.60 |
| 1067 | A244 43p multi | 1.75 | 1.75 |
| 1068 | A244 74p multi | 3.00 | 3.00 |
| | *Nos. 1063-1068 (6)* | 10.05 | 10.05 |

Europa (#1064-1065).

Robins A245

Robin on: 25p, Flowerpot. 28p, Rock. 40p, Branch. 47p, Window sill. 68p, Log.

**2004, Nov. 9** *Perf. 12½x13*

| | | | |
|---|---|---|---|
| 1069 | A245 25p multi | 1.00 | 1.00 |
| 1070 | A245 28p multi | 1.25 | 1.25 |
| 1071 | A245 40p multi | 1.75 | 1.75 |
| 1072 | A245 47p multi | 2.00 | 2.00 |
| 1073 | A245 68p multi | 2.75 | 2.75 |
| *a.* | Miniature sheet, 2 each #1069-1073 | 22.50 | 22.50 |
| | *Nos. 1069-1073 (5)* | 8.75 | 8.75 |

Scenes from *Harry Potter and the Prisoner of Azkaban* A246

Designs: 25p, Harry Potter, Ron Weasley and Hermione Granger. 28p, Owl Post. 39p, Harry and Petronus. 40p, Hogwarts Express. 49p, Hagrid. 55p, Knight Bus. 57p, Harry and Dementor. 68p, Harry and Buckbeak.

**2004, Dec. 7** *Perf. 13¼*

| | | | |
|---|---|---|---|
| 1074 | A246 25p multi | 1.00 | 1.00 |
| 1075 | A246 28p multi | 1.25 | 1.25 |
| 1076 | A246 39p multi | 1.75 | 1.75 |
| 1077 | A246 40p multi | 1.90 | 1.90 |
| 1078 | A246 49p multi | 2.00 | 2.00 |
| 1079 | A246 55p multi | 2.25 | 2.25 |
| 1080 | A246 57p multi | 2.50 | 2.50 |
| 1081 | A246 68p multi | 2.75 | 2.75 |
| | *Nos. 1074-1081 (8)* | 15.40 | 15.40 |

Each printed in sheets of 5.

Battle of Trafalgar, Bicent. — A247

No. 1082: a, Nile Campaign. b, Battle of Copenhagen.
No. 1083: a, Emma Horatia Nelson. b, Band of brothers.
No. 1084: a, Prepare for battle. b, Victory in sight.
No. 1085: a, Fall of Nelson. b, Death of Nelson.
No. 1086: a, #861a. b, #159.

**2005** *Perf. 12½x13*

| | | | |
|---|---|---|---|
| 1082 | A247 Horiz. pair | 2.00 | 2.00 |
| *a.-b.* | 25p Either single | 1.00 | 1.00 |
| 1083 | A247 Horiz. pair | 2.25 | 2.25 |
| *a.-b.* | 28p Either single | 1.10 | 1.10 |
| 1084 | A247 Horiz. pair | 4.00 | 4.00 |
| *a.-b.* | 50p Either single | 2.00 | 2.00 |
| 1085 | A247 Horiz. pair | 5.00 | 5.00 |
| *a.-b.* | 65p Either single | 2.50 | 2.50 |
| | *Nos. 1082-1085 (4)* | 13.25 | 13.25 |

**Souvenir Sheet**

| | | | |
|---|---|---|---|
| 1086 | A247 Sheet of 2 | 8.00 | 8.00 |
| *a.-b.* | £1 Either single | 4.00 | 4.00 |

Issued: Nos. 1082-1085, 1/9; No. 1086, 2/1.

Victory in World War II, 60th Anniv. — A248

No. 1087: a, Women and sailors. b, Soldiers and women marching together.
No. 1088: a, Soldier trying on hat. b, Servicewomen.
No. 1089: a, Winston Churchill and Royal family waving. b, Royal family in carriage.
No. 1090: a, Servicemen without shirts. b, Cemetery.
No. 1091: a, Manx Regiment. b, Royal visit, 1945.

**2005, Apr. 15** **Litho.** *Perf. 13¼x13¾*

| | | | |
|---|---|---|---|
| 1087 | A248 Horiz. pair | 2.25 | 2.25 |
| *a.-b.* | 26p Either single | 1.10 | 1.10 |
| 1088 | A248 Horiz. pair | 2.50 | 2.50 |
| *a.-b.* | 29p Either single | 1.25 | 1.25 |
| 1089 | A248 Horiz. pair | 5.00 | 5.00 |
| *a.-b.* | 60p Either single | 2.50 | 2.50 |
| 1090 | A248 Horiz. pair | 5.50 | 5.50 |
| *a.-b.* | 65p Either single | 2.75 | 2.75 |
| | *Nos. 1087-1090 (4)* | 15.25 | 15.25 |

**Souvenir Sheet**

| | | | |
|---|---|---|---|
| 1091 | A248 Sheet of 2 | 9.00 | 9.00 |
| *a.-b.* | £1 Either single | 4.50 | 4.50 |

Paintings of Isle of Man Steam Packet Company Ships — A249

No. 1092: a, Mona's Isle, by Samuel Walters. b, Viking, by Norman Wilkinson.
No. 1093: a, King Orry, by Robert Lloyd. b, Mona's Queen, by Arthur Burgess.
No. 1094: a, Ben-my-Chree, by John Nicholson. b, King Orry, by Robert Lloyd, diff.
No. 1095: a, Ben-my-Chree, by Robert Lloyd. b, Lady of Mann, by Robert Lloyd.

**2005, May 6** *Perf. 14*

| | | | |
|---|---|---|---|
| 1092 | A249 Horiz. pair | 2.25 | 2.25 |
| *a.-b.* | 26p Either single | 1.10 | 1.10 |
| 1093 | A249 Horiz. pair | 2.50 | 2.50 |
| *a.-b.* | 29p Either single | 1.25 | 1.25 |
| *c.* | Booklet pane, #1092, 1093 | 4.75 | — |
| 1094 | A249 Horiz. pair | 3.50 | 3.50 |
| *a.-b.* | 40p Either single | 1.75 | 1.75 |
| *c.* | Booklet pane, #1092, 1094 | 5.75 | — |
| 1095 | A249 Horiz. pair | 5.50 | 5.50 |
| *a.-b.* | 66p Either single | 2.75 | 2.75 |
| *c.* | Booklet pane, #1093, 1095 | 8.00 | — |
| *d.* | Booklet pane, #1094, 1095 | 9.00 | — |
| *e.* | Booklet pane, #1095 | 5.50 | — |
| | Complete booklet, #1093c, 1094c, 1095c, 1095d, 1095e | 35.00 | |
| | *Nos. 1092-1095 (4)* | 13.75 | 13.75 |

Complete booklet sold for £7.80.

Motorcycle Racers — A250

Designs: 26p, Bill Ivy, Phil Read. 29p, Joey Dunlop, Ray McCullough. 40p, Steve Hislop. 42p, Carl Fogarty. 68p, David Jefferies. 78p, John McGuinness.

**2005, May 17**

| | | | |
|---|---|---|---|
| 1096 | A250 26p multi | 1.00 | 1.00 |
| 1097 | A250 29p multi | 1.10 | 1.10 |
| 1098 | A250 40p multi | 1.60 | 1.60 |
| 1099 | A250 42p multi | 1.75 | 1.75 |
| 1100 | A250 68p multi | 2.75 | 2.75 |
| 1101 | A250 78p multi | 3.00 | 3.00 |
| *a.* | Miniature sheet, 2 each #1096-1101 | 22.50 | 22.50 |
| | *Nos. 1096-1101 (6)* | 11.20 | 11.20 |

Yamaha motorcycles, 50th anniv.

Rotary International, Cent. — A251

Rotary International emblem, various photos and inscription: 26p, Paul Harris, The Man Behind The Movement. 29p, Rotary's Dreams For The Future. 40p, Polioplus: Rotary's Finest Hour. 42p, Youth Programme: Junior Masterchef. 64p, A Day In The Life of Rotary International. 68p, Serving The World Community.

***Perf. 13¼x13½***

**2005, June 15** **Litho.**

| | | | |
|---|---|---|---|
| 1102 | A251 26p multi | 1.00 | 1.00 |
| 1103 | A251 29p multi | 1.10 | 1.10 |
| 1104 | A251 40p multi | 1.60 | 1.60 |
| 1105 | A251 42p multi | 1.75 | 1.75 |
| *a.* | Sheet of 10 + 10 labels | 17.50 | 17.50 |
| 1106 | A251 64p multi | 2.50 | 2.50 |
| 1107 | A251 68p multi | 2.75 | 2.75 |
| | *Nos. 1102-1107 (6)* | 10.70 | 10.70 |

No. 1105 is inscribed "Europa 2005."

Photographs of Everyday Life — A252

Inscriptions: Nos. 1108a, 1110, Guttin' Herrin'. Nos. 1108b, 1111, Pickin' Spuds. Nos. 1108c, 1112, Master Butcher. Nos. 1108d, 1113, Winckles: Foxdale. Nos. 1108e, 1114, Palace Ballroom. Nos. 1109a, 1115, Land Army. Nos. 1109b, 1116, Farmyard Glen Maye. Nos. 1109c, 1117, Summer Season Stars. Nos. 1109d, 1118, Donkey Rides. Nos. 1109e, 1119, Give us a go Mister!

**2005, Aug. 12** *Perf. 12½x13*

| | | | |
|---|---|---|---|
| 1108 | Horiz. strip of 5 | 5.00 | 5.00 |
| *a.-e.* | A252 26p Any single | 1.00 | 1.00 |
| 1109 | Horiz. strip of 5 | 5.50 | 5.50 |
| *a.-e.* | A252 29p Any single | 1.10 | 1.10 |

**Booklet Stamps**

**Self-Adhesive**

***Serpentine Die Cut 10½x10¼***

| | | | |
|---|---|---|---|
| 1110 | A252 26p multi | 1.00 | 1.00 |
| *a.* | Die cut perf 12½x13 | 1.00 | 1.00 |
| 1111 | A252 26p multi | 1.00 | 1.00 |
| *a.* | Die cut perf 12½x13 | 1.00 | 1.00 |
| 1112 | A252 26p multi | 1.00 | 1.00 |
| *a.* | Die cut perf 12½x13 | 1.00 | 1.00 |
| 1113 | A252 26p multi | 1.00 | 1.00 |
| *a.* | Die cut perf 12½x13 | 1.00 | 1.00 |
| 1114 | A252 26p multi | 1.00 | 1.00 |
| *a.* | Booklet pane, 2 each #1110-1114 | 10.00 | |
| | Complete booklet, #1114a | 10.00 | |
| *b.* | Die cut perf 12½x13 | 1.00 | 1.00 |
| *c.* | Strip of 5, #1110a-1113a, 1114b | 5.00 | |
| 1115 | A252 29p multi | 1.10 | 1.10 |
| *a.* | Die cut perf 12½x13 | 1.10 | 1.10 |
| 1116 | A252 29p multi | 1.10 | 1.10 |
| *a.* | Die cut perf 12½x13 | 1.10 | 1.10 |
| 1117 | A252 29p multi | 1.10 | 1.10 |
| *a.* | Die cut perf 12½x13 | 1.10 | 1.10 |

**1118** A252 29p multi 1.10 1.10
*a.* Die cut perf 12½x13 1.10 1.10
**1119** A252 29p multi 1.10 1.10
*a.* Booklet pane, 2 each #1115-1119 11.00
Complete booklet, #1119a 11.00
*b.* Die cut perf 12½x13 1.10 1.10
*c.* Strip of 5, #1115a-1118a, 1119b 5.50
*Nos. 1110-1119 (10)* 10.50 10.50

Nos. 1114a and 1119a are complete booklets, the backing serving as booklet covers. The die-cut 12½x13 stamps are from sheets of 50.

Souvenir Sheet

20th World Youth Day, Cologne, Germany — A253

***Perf. 14x14¾ on 3 Sides***

**2005, Aug. 15**

**1120** A253 Sheet of 2 + 2 labels 8.00 8.00
*a.* 42p Apostolic Palace 1.75 1.75
*b.* £1.50 St. Peter's Basilica 6.00 6.00

Scenes From *Harry Potter and the Goblet of Fire* — A254

Designs: 26p, Harry Potter. 29p, Harry, Ron Weasley, Hermione Granger, Goblet of Fire. 33p, Triwizard Cup. 64p, Hungarian Horntail. 68p, Hogwarts coat of arms. 75p, Murcus.

**2005, Oct. 21** ***Perf. 13¼***

**1121** A254 26p multi 1.00 1.00
**1122** A254 29p multi 1.10 1.10
**1123** A254 33p multi 1.40 1.40
**1124** A254 64p multi 2.50 2.50
**1125** A254 68p multi 2.75 2.75
**1126** A254 75p multi 3.00 3.00
*Nos. 1121-1126 (6)* 11.75 11.75

Souvenir Sheet

Battle of Trafalgar, Bicent. — A255

**2005, Oct. 21** **Litho.** ***Perf. 13¼***

**1127** A255 Sheet, #1127a, Gibraltar #1028a 8.00 8.00
*a.* £1 Funeral of Admiral Nelson 4.00 4.00

See Gibraltar No. 1028. No. 1127 has an Isle of Man Post emblem in the margin.

Christmas — A256

Stained glass windows: 26p, Madonna and Child, St. German's Cathedral, Peel. 29p, Angel with Crown of Glory, St. German's Cathedral. 42p, Adoration of the Shepherds, St. German's Cathedral. 60p, Nativity, Kirk Church, Rushen. 68p, Adoration of the Magi, Kirk Church.

**2005, Nov. 7** **Litho.** ***Perf. 13½x13***

**1128** A256 26p multi 1.00 1.00
**1129** A256 29p multi 1.10 1.10
**1130** A256 42p multi 1.75 1.75
**1131** A256 60p multi 2.40 2.40
**1132** A256 68p multi 2.75 2.75
*Nos. 1128-1132 (5)* 9.00 9.00

Queen Elizabeth II, 80th Birthday A257

No. 1133: a, At age 5 with family, 1931. b, In uniform, 1944. c, Wearing tiara, 1952. d, With husband and children, 1972.

No. 1134: a, With Prince Philip, 1972. b, Seated in Throne Room, 2001. c, With Prince William. d, With crowd, 2002.

**2006, Jan. 16** ***Perf. 13¾***

**1133** Horiz. strip of 4 3.25 3.25
*a.-d.* A257 20p Any single .80 .80
**1134** Horiz. strip of 4 13.00 13.00
*a.-d.* A257 80p Any single 3.25 3.25

Isle of Man Natural History and Antiquarian Society — A258

Designs: 26p, Jurby Church, chalice. 29p, Peel Castle, Viking pinhead. 64p, Meayll Hill, Neolithic potsherd. 68p, Cronk Sumark, Manx stoat. 78p, South Barrule Hill, hen harrier. 97p, Scarlett Point, ammonite fossil.

**2006, Feb. 15** **Litho.** ***Perf. 14***

**1135** A258 26p multi 1.00 1.00
**1136** A258 29p multi 1.10 1.10
**1137** A258 64p multi 2.50 2.50
**1138** A258 68p multi 2.75 2.75
**1139** A258 78p multi 3.00 3.00
**1140** A258 97p multi 3.75 3.75
*Nos. 1135-1140 (6)* 14.10 14.10

Birds — A259

No. 1141: a, Peregrine falcon. b, Puffin. c, Manx shearwater. d, Chough. e, Guillemot.

No. 1142: a, Whinchat. b, Hen harrier. c, Goldcrest. d, Gray wagtail. e, Wren.

No. 1142G: i, Peregrine falcon. j, Puffin. k, Manx shearwater. l, Chough. m, Guillemot.

No. 1142H: n, Whinchat. o, Hen harrier. p, Goldcrest. q, Gray wagtail. r, Wren.

**2006, Apr. 17** ***Perf. 12½***

**1141** Horiz. strip of 5 5.50 5.50
*a.-e.* A259 28p multi 1.10 1.10
**1142** Horiz. strip of 5 6.25 6.25
*a.-e.* A259 31p multi 1.25 1.25
*f.* Miniature sheet, #1141a-1141e, 1142a-1142e 12.00 12.00

**Self-Adhesive**

**1142G** Horiz. strip of 5 5.25 5.25
*i.-m.* A259 28p Any single 1.00 1.00
**1142H** Horiz. strip of 5 5.75 5.75
*n.-r.* A259 31p Any single 1.10 1.10

No. 1142f issued 10/11, for Belgica '06 Intl. Philatelic Exhibition.

Souvenir Sheet

Queen Elizabeth II, 80th Birthday — A260

No. 1143: a, Queen, swordbearer, Manx flag, 2003. b, Queen, crowd, cross, 1972.

**2006, Apr. 21** ***Perf. 14***

**1143** A260 Sheet of 2 8.00 8.00
*a.-b.* £1 Either single 4.00 4.00

Souvenir Sheet

Europa Stamps, 50th Anniv. — A261

No. 1144: a, #100. b, #419a.

**2006, May 2** ***Perf. 13¼x13¾***

**1144** A261 Sheet of 2 5.25 5.25
*a.* 42p multi 1.75 1.75
*b.* 83p multi 3.50 3.50

2006 World Cup Soccer Championships, Germany — A262

Various photographs of English team's 1966 World Cup championship match and celebrations.

**2006, May 2** ***Perf. 12½***

**1145** A262 28p multi 1.10 1.10
**1146** A262 31p multi 1.25 1.25
**1147** A262 44p multi 1.75 1.75
**1148** A262 72p multi 2.75 2.75
**1149** A262 83p multi 3.25 3.25
**1150** A262 94p multi 3.75 3.75
*Nos. 1145-1150 (6)* 13.85 13.85

Manx Ties to Washington, D.C. A263

Designs: 28p, Letitia Tyler, wife of Pres. John Tyler, White House. 31p, Speaker of the House Joseph G. Cannon, Cannon House Office Building. 45p, Matthew Quay, Medal of Honor recipient, battle scene. 50p, Mary Clemmer, journalist, inkwell and U.S. Constitution. 76p, Ewan Clague, economist, Castletown. 83p, Henry "Marse" Watterson, newspaper publisher, Pres. Theodore Roosevelt.

**2006, May 23** ***Perf. 13¾***

**1151** A263 28p multi 1.10 1.10
**1152** A263 31p multi 1.25 1.25
**1153** A263 45p multi 1.75 1.75
**1154** A263 50p multi 2.00 2.00
**1155** A263 76p multi 3.00 3.00
**1156** A263 83p multi 3.25 3.25
*Nos. 1151-1156 (6)* 12.35 12.35

Peel Cars — A264

Designs: 28p, Peel P50. 31p, Trident. 38p, Viking Sport. 41p, BMC GRP Mini. 54p, Manxcar. 94p, P1000.

**2006, July 23** ***Perf. 13¼***

**1157** A264 28p multi 1.10 1.10
**1158** A264 31p multi 1.25 1.25
**1159** A264 38p multi 1.50 1.50
**1160** A264 41p multi 1.60 1.60
**1161** A264 54p multi 2.10 2.10
**1162** A264 94p multi 3.75 3.75
*Nos. 1157-1162 (6)* 11.30 11.30

National Portrait Gallery, London, 150th Anniv. A265

Portraits: 28p, Ewan Christian, by unknown artist. 31p, Dame Agatha Christie, by John Gay. 38p, Sir Hall Caine, by Harry Furniss. 41p, William Bligh, by John Condé. 44p, Lady Maria Callcott, by Sir Thomas Lawrence. 54p, John Martin, by Henry Warren. 64p, Sir John Betjeman, by Stephen Hyde. 96p, Sir Edward Elgar, by Herbert Lambert.

**2006, Aug. 25** **Litho.** ***Perf. 13½***

**1163** A265 28p multi 1.10 1.10
**1164** A265 31p multi 1.25 1.25
**1165** A265 38p multi 1.50 1.50
**1166** A265 41p multi 1.60 1.60
**1167** A265 44p multi 1.75 1.75
**1168** A265 54p multi 2.10 2.10
**1169** A265 64p multi 2.50 2.50
**1170** A265 96p multi 3.75 3.75
*Nos. 1163-1170 (8)* 15.55 15.55

Souvenir Sheet

Tales of Beatrix Potter — A266

No. 1171: a, Benjamin Bunny. b, Jemima Puddle-duck, horiz. c, Peter Rabbit, horiz. d, Jeremy Fisher.

**2006, Oct. 11** ***Perf. 13***

**1171** A266 Sheet of 4 9.00 9.00
*a.* 28p multi 1.10 1.10
*b.* 50p multi 2.00 2.00
*c.* 72p multi 2.75 2.75
*d.* 75p multi 3.00 3.00

Christmas — A267

Various Christmas trees with panel colors of: 28p, Red. 31p, Dark violet. 41p, Green. 44p, Light blue. 72p, Purple. 94p, Orange.

**Litho. with Foil Application**

**2006, Oct. 11** ***Perf. 14¼***

**1172** A267 28p multi 1.10 1.10
**1173** A267 31p multi 1.25 1.25
*a.* Sheet of 10 12.50
**1174** A267 41p multi 1.60 1.60
**1175** A267 44p multi 1.75 1.75
*a.* Sheet of 10 17.50
**1176** A267 72p multi 2.75 2.75
**1177** A267 94p multi 3.75 3.75
*Nos. 1172-1177 (6)* 12.20 12.20

**Self-Adhesive**

**Booklet Stamps**

***Die Cut Perf. 9x9½***

**1178** A267 28p multi 1.10 1.10
*a.* Booklet pane of 10 11.00
**1179** A267 31p multi 1.25 1.25
*a.* Booklet pane of 10 12.50

Europa (31p, 44p).

Nos. 1178a and 1179a are complete booklets, the backing serving as the booklet covers.

TT Motorcycle Races, Cent. — A268

No. 1180 — Various racers with panel color of: a, Pink. b, Light blue. c, Purple. d, Indigo. e, Orange.

No. 1181: a, Red violet. b, Green. c, Gray blue. d, Red. e, Red brown.

**2007, Jan. 1 Litho. *Perf. 14¼***

| | | | |
|---|---|---|---|
| **1180** | Horiz. strip of 5 | 6.25 | 6.25 |
| *a.-e.* | A268 UK Any single | 1.25 | 1.25 |
| **1181** | Horiz. strip of 5 | 8.75 | 8.75 |
| *a.-e.* | A268 E Any single | 1.75 | 1.75 |
| *f.* | Sheet of 10, #1180a-1180e, 1181a-1181e, + 10 labels | 15.00 | 15.00 |

On day of issue Nos. 1180a-1180e each sold for 31p, Nos. 1181a-1181e each sold for 44p.

Issued: No. 1181f, 7/9.

A269

Scouting, Cent. — A270

Designs: 28p, Hiking expedition near South Barrule. 31p, Scout investiture on Douglas Beach. 44p, Backpacking below Cronk-ny-Arrey-Laa. 72p, Manx Scouts on parade at St. Johns. 83p, Sea kayaking off Laxey Beach. £1, Manx Scouts operating the TT scoreboard.

No. 1188: a, Scouts and table (43x29mm). b, Scouts, tent and campfire (43x57mm).

**2007, Feb. 22 Litho. *Perf. 14***

| | | | |
|---|---|---|---|
| **1182** | A269 28p multi | 1.10 | 1.10 |
| **1183** | A269 31p multi | 1.25 | 1.25 |
| *a.* | Sheet of 10 | 12.50 | |
| **1184** | A269 44p multi | 1.75 | 1.75 |
| *a.* | Booklet pane, #1182-1184 | 4.25 | — |
| *a.* | Sheet of 10 | 17.50 | |
| **1185** | A269 72p multi | 2.75 | 2.75 |
| **1186** | A269 83p multi | 3.25 | 3.25 |
| *a.* | Booklet pane, #1182, 1184, 1186 | 6.25 | — |
| **1187** | A269 £1 multi | 4.00 | 4.00 |
| *a.* | Booklet pane, #1185-1187 | 10.00 | — |
| *b.* | Booklet pane, #1183, 1185, 1187 | 8.00 | — |
| | *Nos. 1182-1187 (6)* | 14.10 | 14.10 |

**Souvenir Sheet**

| | | | |
|---|---|---|---|
| **1188** | A270 Sheet of 2 | 7.75 | 7.75 |
| *a.* | 50p multi | 2.00 | 2.00 |
| *b.* | £1.50 multi | 5.75 | 5.75 |
| *c.* | Booklet pane, #1188 (154x96mm) | 7.75 | — |
| | Complete booklet, #1184a, 1186a, 1187a, 1187b, 1188c | 36.50 | |
| *d.* | As No. 1188, with 2007 Intl. Scout Jamboree emblem in margin | 8.25 | 8.25 |

Europa (31p, 44p).

No. 1188d issued 7/26.

Wedding of Queen Elizabeth II and Prince Philip, 60th Anniv. — A271

Various photos of Queen and Prince with denomination colors of: a, Dark blue. b, Lilac. c, Rose pink. d, Light blue. e, Dark green. f, Yellow bister.

**2007, Feb. 22 *Perf. 14***

| | | | |
|---|---|---|---|
| **1189** | Horiz. strip of 6 | 14.00 | 14.00 |
| *a.-f.* | A271 60p Any single | 2.25 | 2.25 |

Paintings by Norman Sayle A272

Designs: Nos. 1190, 1198, Headland, Cornaa. Nos. 1191, 1199, Headland, Sound. Nos. 1192, 1200, St. Mark's Church. Nos. 1193, 1201, Castletown Harbour Moonlight. 42p, Bridge House, Castletown. 44p, Winter Sun. 65p, In Ancient Times. 75p, Bracken Mountain.

**2007, Apr. 12 *Perf. 12½x13***

| | | | |
|---|---|---|---|
| **1190** | A272 28p multi | 1.10 | 1.10 |
| **1191** | A272 28p multi | 1.10 | 1.10 |
| **1192** | A272 31p multi | 1.25 | 1.25 |
| **1193** | A272 31p multi | 1.25 | 1.25 |
| **1194** | A272 42p multi | 1.75 | 1.75 |
| **1195** | A272 44p multi | 1.75 | 1.75 |
| **1196** | A272 65p multi | 2.60 | 2.60 |
| **1197** | A272 75p multi | 3.00 | 3.00 |
| | *Nos. 1190-1197 (8)* | 13.80 | 13.80 |

**Booklet Stamps**

**Self-Adhesive**

***Serpentine Die Cut 10x9½***

| | | | |
|---|---|---|---|
| **1198** | A272 28p multi | 1.10 | 1.10 |
| **1199** | A272 28p multi | 1.10 | 1.10 |
| *a.* | Booklet pane, 5 each #1198-1199 | 11.00 | |
| **1200** | A272 31p multi | 1.25 | 1.25 |
| **1201** | A272 31p multi | 1.25 | 1.25 |
| *a.* | Booklet pane, 5 each #1200-1201 | 12.50 | |
| | *Nos. 1198-1201 (4)* | 4.70 | 4.70 |

Nos. 1199a and 1201a are complete booklets, the backing serving as the booklet covers.

Settlement of Jamestown, Virginia, 400th Anniv. — A273

Designs: 28p, Map. 31p, Capt. John Smith and ships. 44p, Aerial view of settlement. 54p, Indians and colonists. 78p, Settlement buildings. 90p, Indian village.

**2007, Apr. 26 *Perf. 13½***

| | | | |
|---|---|---|---|
| **1202** | A273 28p multi | 1.10 | 1.10 |
| **1203** | A273 31p multi | 1.25 | 1.25 |
| **1204** | A273 44p multi | 1.75 | 1.75 |
| **1205** | A273 54p multi | 2.25 | 2.25 |
| **1206** | A273 78p multi | 3.25 | 3.25 |
| **1207** | A273 90p multi | 3.75 | 3.75 |
| | *Nos. 1202-1207 (6)* | 13.35 | 13.35 |

Royal Charter of Liverpool, 800th Anniv. A274

Designs: 31p, King John and Royal Charter. 48p, The spiritual heart of Liverpool. 54p, Liverpool war heroes. 74p, Liverpool heritage. 80p, Port of Liverpool. £1, Wall of Fame.

No. 1214: a, James Brown, Manx election pioneer. b, Joseph Cunningham, philantropist. c, William Gill, ship captain. d, Dalrymple Maitland, industrialist.

**2007, Apr. 26 *Perf. 14***

| | | | |
|---|---|---|---|
| **1208** | A274 31p multi | 1.25 | 1.25 |
| **1209** | A274 48p multi | 1.90 | 1.90 |
| **1210** | A274 54p multi | 2.25 | 2.25 |
| **1211** | A274 74p multi | 3.00 | 3.00 |
| **1212** | A274 80p multi | 3.25 | 3.25 |
| **1213** | A274 £1 multi | 4.00 | 4.00 |
| | *Nos. 1208-1213 (6)* | 15.65 | 15.65 |

**2007, May 10 Souvenir Sheet**

| | | | |
|---|---|---|---|
| **1214** | Sheet of 4 | 9.00 | 9.00 |
| *a.* | A274 25p multi | 1.00 | 1.00 |
| *b.* | A274 40p multi | 1.50 | 1.50 |
| *c.-d.* | A274 80p Either single | 3.25 | 3.25 |

Historical Maps of Isle of Man A275

Designs: 28p, Map by John Speed, 1605. 31p, Map by Capt. Greenville Collins, 1693. 44p, Map by John Drinkwater, 1826. 48p, Ordnance Survey County Series map, 1870. 75p, Six-inch Series map, 1975. 88p, 1:100,000 map by Isle of Man Government Mapping Office, 2006.

**2007, Aug. 1 Litho. *Perf. 12½x13***

| | | | |
|---|---|---|---|
| **1215** | A275 28p multi | 1.10 | 1.10 |
| **1216** | A275 31p multi | 1.25 | 1.25 |
| **1217** | A275 44p multi | 1.75 | 1.75 |
| **1218** | A275 48p multi | 2.00 | 2.00 |
| **1219** | A275 75p multi | 3.00 | 3.00 |
| **1220** | A275 88p multi | 3.75 | 3.75 |
| | *Nos. 1215-1220 (6)* | 12.85 | 12.85 |

Intl. Polar Year A276

Designs: 28p, Capt. John Ross, ship Victory trapped in ice. 31p, Flares shot from Victory. 55p, Victory crewmen hunting with Inuit. 75p, Musk ox hunted by Victory crewmen. 90p, Victory crewmen pulling sled after abandoning ship. 117p, Whaler Isabella rescuing Victory crewmen.

**2007, Aug. 20**

| | | | |
|---|---|---|---|
| **1221** | A276 28p multi | 1.10 | 1.10 |
| **1222** | A276 31p multi | 1.25 | 1.25 |
| **1223** | A276 55p multi | 2.25 | 2.25 |
| **1224** | A276 75p multi | 3.00 | 3.00 |
| **1225** | A276 90p multi | 3.75 | 3.75 |
| **1226** | A276 117p multi | 4.75 | 4.75 |
| | *Nos. 1221-1226 (6)* | 16.10 | 16.10 |

**Souvenir Sheet**

Manx Connections With Northern Canada — A277

No. 1227: a, Ben-My-Chree Cabin, British Columbia. b, Graham "Jimmy" Oates, first man to reach Hudson Bay on rubber-tired vehicle, vert. c, Kermode bear, vert. d, Hudson Bay Post Office and dog team.

**2007, Aug. 20 *Perf. 13***

| | | | |
|---|---|---|---|
| **1227** | A277 Sheet of 4 | 10.00 | 10.00 |
| *a.-b.* | 50p Either single | 2.00 | 2.00 |
| *c.-d.* | 75p Either single | 3.00 | 3.00 |

Intl. Polar Year.

Europen Vintage Plowing Championships — A278

Designs: 28p, Manx-style plowing. 31p, Vintage plowing. 48p, Horse and digger plow. 71p, Swing plow. 90p, World-style plowing. £1.27, Jean Burns, first woman to compete in Manx plowing contest, on tractor.

**2007, Sept. 1 *Perf. 13¼***

| | | | |
|---|---|---|---|
| **1228** | A278 28p multi | 1.10 | 1.10 |
| **1229** | A278 31p multi | 1.25 | 1.25 |
| **1230** | A278 48p multi | 2.00 | 2.00 |
| **1231** | A278 71p multi | 3.00 | 3.00 |
| **1232** | A278 90p multi | 3.75 | 3.75 |
| **1233** | A278 £1.27 multi | 5.25 | 5.25 |
| | *Nos. 1228-1233 (6)* | 16.35 | 16.35 |

Christmas — A279

Various angels with panel color of: 28p, Blue. 31p, Pink. 69p, Orange. 78p, Green. £1.24, Dark blue.

***Serpentine Die Cut 13x13¼***

**2007, Oct. 19**

**Self-Adhesive**

| | | | |
|---|---|---|---|
| **1234** | A279 28p multi | 1.25 | 1.25 |
| **1235** | A279 31p multi | 1.40 | 1.40 |
| **1236** | A279 69p multi | 3.00 | 3.00 |
| **1237** | A279 78p multi | 3.25 | 3.25 |
| **1238** | A279 £1.24 multi | 5.25 | 5.25 |
| | *Nos. 1234-1238 (5)* | 14.15 | 14.15 |

**Souvenir Sheet**

Cunard Ocean Liners — A280

No. 1239: a, Queen Elizabeth 2. b, Queen Mary 2. c, Queen Victoria.

**2008, Jan. 13 Litho. *Perf. 14x13¼***

| | | | |
|---|---|---|---|
| **1239** | A280 Sheet of 3 | 12.00 | 12.00 |
| *a.-c.* | £1 Any single | 4.00 | 4.00 |
| *d.* | Sheet of 10 #1239a + 10 labels | 40.00 | — |
| *e.* | Sheet of 10 #1239b + 10 labels | 40.00 | — |
| *f.* | Sheet of 10 #1239c + 10 labels | 40.00 | — |

Royal Air Force, 90th Anniv. A281

Aircraft: No. 1240, H.P. 0/400, Bristol F2B fighter. No. 1241, Avro 504N, Westland Wapiti. No. 1242, Hawker Hurricane, Short Sunderland. No. 1243, Gloster Meteor, Westland Whirlwind. No. 1244, Hawker Hunter, E.E. Canberra. No. 1245, BAE Harrier, Lockheed Hercules.

**2008, Jan. 15 *Perf. 13¼***

| | | | |
|---|---|---|---|
| **1240** | A281 31p multi | 1.25 | 1.25 |
| **1241** | A281 31p multi | 1.25 | 1.25 |
| **1242** | A281 31p multi | 1.25 | 1.25 |
| *a.* | Horiz. strip, #1240-1242 | 3.75 | 3.75 |
| **1243** | A281 90p multi | 3.75 | 3.75 |
| *a.* | Booklet pane, #1240-1243 | 7.50 | — |
| **1244** | A281 90p multi | 3.75 | 3.75 |
| *a.* | Booklet pane, #1240-1241, 1243-1244 | 10.00 | — |
| **1245** | A281 90p multi | 3.75 | 3.75 |
| *a.* | Horiz. strip, #1243-1245 | 11.25 | 11.25 |
| *b.* | Booklet pane, #1242-1245 | 12.50 | — |
| *c.* | Booklet pane, #1240-1241, 1244-1245 | 10.00 | — |
| | Complete booklet, #1243a, 1244a, 1245b, 1245c | 40.00 | |
| | *Nos. 1240-1245 (6)* | 15.00 | 15.00 |

Vikings on Isle of Man — A282

Designs: 28p, Pagan Lady of Peel. 31p, Ship burial. 44p, Godred Crovan (King Orry). 54p, Gautr Bjornsson the Sculptor. 69p, Sigurd the Dragon Slayer. £1.24, Coming of Christianity.

**2008, Feb. 18 Litho. *Perf. 13¼***

| | | | | |
|---|---|---|---|---|
| **1246** | A282 | 28p multi | 1.10 | 1.10 |
| **1247** | A282 | 31p multi | 1.25 | 1.25 |
| **1248** | A282 | 44p multi | 1.75 | 1.75 |
| **1249** | A282 | 54p multi | 2.25 | 2.25 |
| **1250** | A282 | 69p multi | 2.75 | 2.750 |
| **1251** | A282 | £1.24 multi | 5.00 | 5.00 |
| | | *Nos. 1246-1251 (6)* | 14.10 | 14.10 |

Manx Bank Notes A283

Designs: 30p, 1956 Isle of Man Bank one-pound note. 31p, 1972 Isle of Man Government ten-pound note. 44p, 1882 Manx Bank one-pound note. 56p, 1969 Isle of Man Government fifty-pence note. 85p, 1983 Isle of Man Government fifty-pound note. 114p, 1918 Parr's Bank one-pound note.

**2008, Apr. 7 *Perf. 14***

| | | | | |
|---|---|---|---|---|
| **1252** | A283 | 30p multi | 1.25 | 1.25 |
| **1253** | A283 | 31p multi | 1.25 | 1.25 |
| **1254** | A283 | 44p multi | 1.75 | 1.75 |
| **1255** | A283 | 56p multi | 2.25 | 2.25 |
| **1256** | A283 | 85p multi | 3.50 | 3.50 |
| **1257** | A283 | 114p multi | 4.50 | 4.50 |
| | | *Nos. 1252-1257 (6)* | 14.50 | 14.50 |

**Booklet Stamp**

**Self-Adhesive**

***Die Cut Perf. 12x12¼***

| | | | | |
|---|---|---|---|---|
| **1258** | A283 | 30p multi | 1.25 | 1.25 |
| *a.* | | Booklet pane of 10 | 10.00 | |
| | | Complete booklet, #1258a | 12.50 | |

Miniature Sheet

2008 Summer Olympics, Beijing — A284

**2008, Apr. 21 *Perf. 13¼***

| | | | | |
|---|---|---|---|---|
| **1259** | A284 | Sheet of 4 | 4.00 | 4.00 |
| *a.* | | 1p Archery | .25 | .25 |
| *b.* | | 2p Equestrian | .25 | .25 |
| *c.* | | 3p Cycling | .25 | .25 |
| *d.* | | 94p Olympic torch | 3.75 | 3.75 |
| *e.* | | As No. 1259, with Olympex inscription in sheet margin | 4.00 | 4.00 |
| *f.* | | Souvenir sheet, #1259c, #1259d | 4.00 | 4.00 |

Issued: No. 1259e, 8/8; No. 1259f, 8/9.

Interceltic Music Festival, Lorient, France A285

Flags of regions with Celtic language heritage: 20p, Cornwall. 30p, Isle of Man. 31p, Scotland. 48p, Brittany. 50p, Ireland. 56p, Asturias. 72p, Wales. £1.13, Galicia.

**2008, May 12 *Perf. 13¼***

| | | | | |
|---|---|---|---|---|
| **1260** | A285 | 20p multi | .80 | .80 |
| **1261** | A285 | 30p multi | 1.25 | 1.25 |
| **1262** | A285 | 31p multi | 1.25 | 1.25 |
| *a.* | | Sheet of 10 | 12.50 | 12.50 |
| **1263** | A285 | 48p multi | 1.90 | 1.90 |
| **1264** | A285 | 50p multi | 2.00 | 2.00 |
| *a.* | | Sheet of 10 | 20.00 | 20.00 |
| **1265** | A285 | 56p multi | 2.25 | 2.25 |
| **1266** | A285 | 72p multi | 3.00 | 3.00 |
| **1267** | A285 | £1.13 multi | 4.50 | 4.50 |
| *a.* | | Sheet of 8, #1260-1267 (Aug. 1) | 17.00 | — |
| | | *Nos. 1260-1267 (8)* | 16.95 | 16.95 |

Europa (31p, 50p).

Famous Race Drivers and Their Cars A286

Designs: 20p, Reg Parnell. 30p, Mike Hawthorn. 70p, Tony Brooks. 81p, Roy Salvadori. 94p, Stirling Moss. £1.22, Jim Clark.

**2008, July 10 Litho. *Perf. 14***

| | | | | |
|---|---|---|---|---|
| **1268** | A286 | 20p multi | .80 | .80 |
| **1269** | A286 | 30p multi | 1.25 | 1.25 |
| **1270** | A286 | 70p multi | 2.75 | 2.75 |
| **1271** | A286 | 81p multi | 3.25 | 3.25 |
| **1272** | A286 | 94p multi | 3.75 | 3.75 |
| **1273** | A286 | £1.22 multi | 5.00 | 5.00 |
| | | *Nos. 1268-1273 (6)* | 16.80 | 16.80 |

Miniature Sheet

Race Cars — A287

No. 1274: a, 1961 Aston Martin DB4 GT Zagato. b, 1965 Ferrari 250 LM. c, 1962 Ferrari 250 GTO. d, 1965 Ford GT40. e, 1955 Mercedes-Benz 300 SLR. f, 1964 Shelby Cobra.

**2008, July 10 *Perf. 14¾x14***

| | | | | |
|---|---|---|---|---|
| **1274** | A287 | Sheet of 6 | 12.00 | 12.00 |
| *a.-f.* | | 50p Any single | 2.00 | 2.00 |

Famous People — A288

No. 1275: a, Mary Louisa Wood (1839-1925), founder of Isle of Man Fine Arts and Industrial Guild. b, Harry Kelly (1852-1935), last native Manx speaker. c, Sir Frank Gill (1866-1950), telephone and communications engineer. d, Ramsey Gelling Johnson (1889-1972), judge, president of Royal Manx Agricultural Society. e, John Nicholson (1911-88), stamp designer.

No. 1276: a, Dr. Dorothy Pantin (1896-1985), first female doctor. b, Richard Costain (1839-1902), construction business entrepreneur. c, Sir William Percy Cowley (1886-1958), judge. d, Rev. Fred Cubbon (1902-80), philanthropist. e, William Henry Gill (1839-1922), author, musician.

**2008, Aug. 1 *Perf. 13¼***

| | | | | |
|---|---|---|---|---|
| **1275** | | Horiz. strip of 5 | 6.25 | 6.25 |
| *a.-e.* | | A288 31p Any single | 1.25 | 1.25 |
| **1276** | | Horiz. strip of 5 | 10.00 | 10.00 |
| *a.-e.* | | A288 50p Any single | 2.00 | 2.00 |

End of World War I, 90th Anniv. — A289

Poppy and letter from soldier: 30p, Second Lieutenant Roy F. Corlett. 31p, Second Lieutenant John W. Lewis. 44p, Private Joseph Killey. 56p, Lieutenant Colonel W. A. W. Crellin. 81p, Lance Corporal Tom Quilliam. 94p, Private Robert Oates. £2, National War Memorial, St. John's.

**2008, Oct. 1 Litho. *Perf. 14***

| | | | | |
|---|---|---|---|---|
| **1277** | A289 | 30p multi | 1.10 | 1.10 |
| **1278** | A289 | 31p multi | 1.10 | 1.10 |
| **1279** | A289 | 44p multi | 1.60 | 1.60 |
| **1280** | A289 | 56p multi | 2.00 | 2.00 |
| **1281** | A289 | 81p multi | 3.00 | 3.00 |
| **1282** | A289 | 94p multi | 3.50 | 3.50 |
| | | *Nos. 1277-1282 (6)* | 12.30 | 12.30 |

**Souvenir Sheet**

| | | | | |
|---|---|---|---|---|
| **1283** | A289 | £2 multi | 7.25 | 7.25 |

Flora and Fauna of Ballaugh Curragh A290

Designs: 30p, Orange-tip butterfly. 31p, Curlew. 50p, Birch bracket fungus. 70p, Large red damselfly. 82p, Marsh cinquefoil. £1.38, Royal fern.

**2008, Oct. 1 *Perf. 13¼***

| | | | | |
|---|---|---|---|---|
| **1284** | A290 | 30p multi | 1.10 | 1.10 |
| **1285** | A290 | 31p multi | 1.10 | 1.10 |
| **1286** | A290 | 50p multi | 1.75 | 1.75 |
| **1287** | A290 | 70p multi | 2.50 | 2.50 |
| **1288** | A290 | 82p multi | 3.00 | 3.00 |
| **1289** | A290 | £1.38 multi | 5.00 | 5.00 |
| | | *Nos. 1284-1289 (6)* | 14.45 | 14.45 |

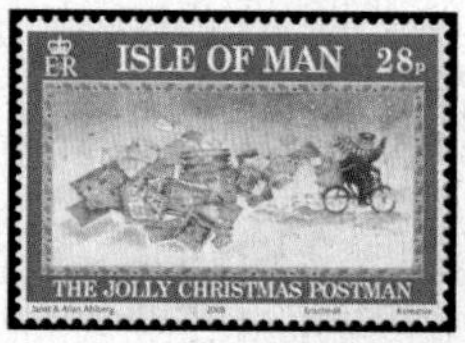

Christmas A291

Postman from *The Jolly Christmas Postman,* by Janet and Allen Ahlberg: 28p, On bicycle, letters. 31p, And mouse in cracker box. 48p, And bear family. 50p, And Toy Town. 56p, On bicycle, with truck and horsecart on winding road. £1.56, At home.

**2008, Oct. 20 *Perf. 14x14¼***

| | | | | |
|---|---|---|---|---|
| **1290** | A291 | 28p multi | .90 | .90 |
| **1291** | A291 | 31p multi | 1.00 | 1.00 |
| **1292** | A291 | 48p multi | 1.60 | 1.60 |
| **1293** | A291 | 50p multi | 1.60 | 1.60 |
| **1294** | A291 | 56p multi | 1.90 | 1.90 |
| **1295** | A291 | £1.56 multi | 5.00 | 5.00 |
| | | *Nos. 1290-1295 (6)* | 12.00 | 12.00 |

Lewis Hamilton, Formula 1 Race Car Driver A292

No. 1296: a, Hamilton driving race car. b, Hamilton celebrating victory with champagne spray.

No. 1297: a, Hamilton driving past finish line. b, Hamilton in race car cockpit.

No. 1298: a, Hamilton driving race car, diff. b, Hamilton in helmet with arms extended.

**2009, Jan. 15 Litho. *Perf. 14***

| | | | | |
|---|---|---|---|---|
| **1296** | | Horiz. pair | 1.75 | 1.75 |
| *a.* | | A292 30p multi | .85 | .85 |
| *b.* | | A292 31p multi | .90 | .90 |
| **1297** | | Horiz. pair | 4.00 | 4.00 |
| *a.* | | A292 56p multi | 1.60 | 1.60 |
| *b.* | | A292 85p multi | 2.40 | 2.40 |
| **1298** | | Horiz. pair | 6.75 | 6.75 |
| *a.* | | A292 98p multi | 2.75 | 2.75 |
| *b.* | | A292 £1.42 multi | 4.00 | 4.00 |
| | | *Nos. 1296-1298 (3)* | 12.50 | 12.50 |

Naval Aviation, Cent. A293

No. 1299: a, Fairey Barracuda II. b, Blackburn Buccaneer S.2. c, Fairey Flycatcher.

No. 1300: a, EH101 Merlin helicopter. b, BAe Sea Harrier FRS.1. c, Sea Scout SS.24 airship.

**2009, Jan. 15**

| | | | | |
|---|---|---|---|---|
| **1299** | | Horiz. strip of 3 | 3.75 | 3.75 |
| *a.* | | A293 30p multi | .85 | .85 |
| *b.* | | A293 31p multi | .90 | .90 |
| *c.* | | A293 72p multi | 2.00 | 2.00 |
| *d.* | | Booklet pane of 4, 2 each #1299a, 1299b | 3.50 | — |
| **1300** | | Horiz. strip of 3 | 9.00 | 9.00 |
| *a.* | | A293 85p multi | 2.40 | 2.40 |
| *b.* | | A293 98p multi | 2.75 | 2.75 |
| *c.* | | A293 £1.36 multi | 3.75 | 3.75 |
| *d.* | | Booklet pane of 4, #1299a, 1299b, 1299c, 1300a | 6.25 | — |
| *e.* | | Booklet pane of 4, #1299a, 1299b, 1300b, 1300c | 8.25 | — |
| *f.* | | Booklet pane of 4, #1299c, 1300a, 1300b, 1300c | 11.00 | — |
| | | Complete booklet, #1299d, 1300d, 1300e, 1300f | 29.00 | |

Accession to the Throne of Henry VIII, 500th Anniv. A294

No. 1301: a, King Henry VIII. b, Catherine of Aragon (first wife). c, Anne Boleyn (second wife). d, Jane Seymour (third wife).

No. 1302: a, Anne of Cleves (fourth wife). b, Catherine Howard (fifth wife). c, Catherine Parr (sixth wife). d, Hampton Court.

**2009, Feb. 18 *Perf. 13¼***

| | | | | |
|---|---|---|---|---|
| **1301** | | Horiz. strip of 4 | 5.75 | 5.75 |
| *a.-d.* | | A294 50p Any single | 1.40 | 1.40 |
| **1302** | | Horiz. strip of 4 | 5.75 | 5.75 |
| *a.-d.* | | A294 50p Any single | 1.40 | 1.40 |

Photographs of Mills and Millers by Chris Killip — A295

No. 1303: a, Ballakilley Farm. b, Grenaby Farm.

No. 1304: a, Mr. Cubbon. b, Glenmoar Mill.

No. 1305: a, Golden Meadow Mill. b, Bernie Mylcraine.

No. 1306: a, Golden Meadow Mill, diff. b, Loughtan Farm.

No. 1307, Like #1303a. No. 1308, Like #1303b. No. 1309, Like #1304b. No. 1310, Like #1304a.

**2009, Apr. 1 *Perf. 13¼***

| | | | | |
|---|---|---|---|---|
| **1303** | | Pair | 1.90 | 1.90 |
| *a.-b.* | | A295 32p Either single | .95 | .95 |
| **1304** | | Pair | 2.00 | 2.00 |
| *a.-b.* | | A295 33p Either single | 1.00 | 1.00 |
| **1305** | | Pair | 3.00 | 3.00 |
| *a.-b.* | | A295 50p Either single | 1.50 | 1.50 |
| **1306** | | Pair | 4.75 | 4.75 |
| *a.-b.* | | A295 78p Either single | 2.25 | 2.25 |
| | | *Nos. 1303-1306 (4)* | 11.65 | 11.65 |

**Booklet Stamps**

**Self-Adhesive**

***Serpentine Die Cut 12½***

| | | | | |
|---|---|---|---|---|
| **1307** | A295 | 32p black | .95 | .95 |
| **1308** | A295 | 32p black | .95 | .95 |
| *a.* | | Booklet pane of 10, 5 each #1307-1308 | 9.00 | |
| | | Complete booklet, #1308a | 9.00 | |
| **1309** | A295 | 33p black | 1.00 | 1.00 |
| **1310** | A295 | 33p black | 1.00 | 1.00 |
| *a.* | | Booklet pane of 10, 5 each #1309-1310 | 9.50 | |
| | | Complete booklet, #1310a | 10.00 | |
| | | *Nos. 1307-1310 (4)* | 3.90 | 3.90 |

Miniature Sheet

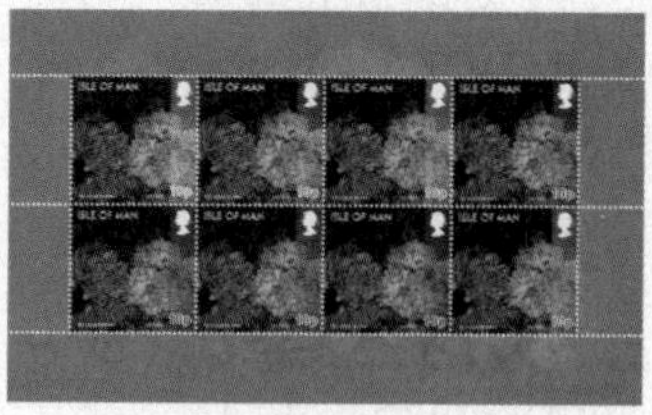

Peonies — A296

No. 1311 — Denomination color: a, Yellow. b, Light green. c, Pink. d, Blue. e, Violet. f, Red. g, Blue green. h, Olive green.

**2009, Apr. 10** ***Perf. 13¼***
**1311** A296 Sheet of 8 2.40 2.40
*a.-h.* 10p Any single .30 .30

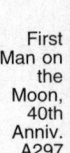

First Man on the Moon, 40th Anniv. A297

Paintings by Astronaut Alan Bean: 33p, First Boot Print, Sunrise Over Antares. 50p, Clan MacBean Arrives on the Moon, Documenting the Sample. 56p, Pete and Me. 81p, Headed for the Last Parking Lot. 105p, The Eagle is Headed Home, In the Beginning. 135p, Ceremony on the Plain at Hadley, The Hoer. £2.50, On the Rim, vert.

**2009, Apr. 12** ***Perf. 12½***
**1312** A297 33p multi 1.00 1.00
*a.* Sheet of 10 10.00 10.00
**1313** A297 50p multi 1.50 1.50
**1314** A297 56p multi 1.75 1.75
*a.* Sheet of 10 17.50 17.50
**1315** A297 81p multi 2.40 2.40
**1316** A297 105p multi 3.25 3.25
**1317** A297 135p multi 4.00 4.00
*Nos. 1312-1317 (6)* 13.90 13.90

**Souvenir Sheet**

**1318** A297 £2.50 multi 7.50 7.50
*1318a* As #1318, with 40th anniversary emblem in sheet margin, perf. 12 8.50 8.50

Europa (33p, 56p).
Issued: No. 1318a, 7/20.

Honda Racing Motorcycles — A298

Motorcycle from the: 32p, 1950s. 33p, 1960s. 56p, 1970s. 62p, 1980s. 90p, 1990s. £1.77, 2000s.

**2009, May 11** ***Perf. 14***
**1319** A298 32p multi 1.00 1.00
**1320** A298 33p multi 1.10 1.10
**1321** A298 56p multi 1.75 1.75
**1322** A298 62p multi 2.00 2.00
**1323** A298 90p multi 3.00 3.00
**1324** A298 £1.77 multi 5.75 5.75
*Nos. 1319-1324 (6)* 14.60 14.60

**Souvenir Sheet**

2009 England Vs. Australia The Ashes Cricket Test Match — A299

No. 1325: a, W. G. Grace at Lord's Cricket Ground (42x28mm). b, Marylebone Cricket Club Ashes trophy and urn (30x40mm). c, England vs. Australia, Lord's Cricket Ground, 2005 (42x28mm).

***Perf. 14 (#1325a, 1325c), 14x14¾***
**2009, June 20**
**1325** A299 Sheet of 3 9.75 9.75
*a.-c.* £1 Any single 3.25 3.25

The Bee Gees, 50th Anniv. — A300

No. 1326: a, Barry, Robin and Maurice Gibb as children. b, "Children of the World" album cover. c, "Spirits Having Flown" album cover. d, "Still Waters" album cover.

No. 1327: a, "One Night Only" album cover. b, "This Is Where I Came In" album cover. c, "Number Ones" album cover. d, "The Studio Albums 1967-1968" album cover.

**2009, July 1** ***Perf. 13x12½***
**1326** Horiz. strip of 4 + central label 5.50 5.50
*a.* A300 32p multi 1.00 1.00
*b.* A300 33p multi 1.10 1.10
*c.* A300 50p multi 1.60 1.60
*d.* A300 54p multi 1.75 1.75
**1327** Horiz. strip of 4 + central label 11.00 11.00
*a.* A300 56p multi 1.90 1.90
*b.* A300 62p multi 2.10 2.10
*c.* A300 78p multi 2.60 2.60
*d.* A300 £1.28 multi 4.25 4.25

Paintings of Wildlife by Jeremy Paul A301

Paintings: 32p, Brown Hare. 33p, Hedgehogs. 54p, Pheasants. 90p, Barn Owl. 92p, Cockerel. £1.58, On the Hill.

**2009, Sept. 1** **Litho.** ***Perf. 12½***
**1328** A301 32p multi 1.10 1.10
**1329** A301 33p multi 1.10 1.10
**1330** A301 54p multi 1.75 1.75
**1331** A301 90p multi 3.00 3.00
**1332** A301 92p multi 3.00 3.00
**1333** A301 £1.58 multi 5.25 5.25
*a.* Sheet of 6, #1328-1333 15.50 15.50
*Nos. 1328-1333 (6)* 15.20 15.20

Watercolors by Archibald Knox A302

Watercolors: 32p, Bridge Possibly at Laxey. 33p, Willows and Blue Mountain Possibly Greeba. 56p, Kew. 62p, Eairy Beg Glen Helen. 81p, Leaning Trees. 182p, Old Laxey.

**2009, Sept. 16** ***Perf. 12½***
**1334** A302 32p multi 1.00 1.00
**1335** A302 33p multi 1.10 1.10
**1336** A302 56p multi 1.75 1.75
**1337** A302 62p multi 2.00 2.00
**1338** A302 81p multi 2.60 2.60
**1339** A302 182p multi 5.75 5.75
*Nos. 1334-1339 (6)* 14.20 14.20

**Souvenir Sheet**

Sinking of the Ellan Vannin, Cent. — A303

No. 1340: a, Captain James Teare and Ellan Vannan at sea. b, Ellan Vannan in harbor.

**2009, Oct. 1** ***Perf. 14***
**1340** A303 Sheet of 2 9.50 9.50
*a.-b.* £1.50 Either single 4.75 4.75

Christmas — A304

Santa Claus: 30p, Filling stocking. 33p, Making a list. 56p, Holding bag of toys. 62p, Near chimney, holding gift. 81p, Holding staff and bag. 90p, Holding chalice.

**2009, Oct. 20** ***Perf. 14***
**1341** A304 30p multi 1.00 1.00
**1342** A304 33p multi 1.10 1.10
**1343** A304 56p multi 1.90 1.90
**1344** A304 62p multi 2.10 2.10
**1345** A304 81p multi 2.75 2.75
**1346** A304 90p multi 3.00 3.00
*Nos. 1341-1346 (6)* 11.85 11.85

**Size: 23x34mm**
**Self-Adhesive**
***Die Cut Perf. 13x13½***

**1347** A304 30p multi 1.00 1.00
**1348** A304 33p multi 1.10 1.10

A305

A306

A307

A308

A309

A310

A311

A312

A313

Island Life — A314

**2010, Jan. 12** ***Perf. 12½***
**1349** Horiz. strip of 4 4.25 4.25
*a.* A305 (32p) multi 1.00 1.00
*b.* A306 (32p) multi 1.00 1.00
*c.* A307 (32p) multi 1.00 1.00
*d.* A308 (32p) multi 1.00 1.00
**1350** Horiz. strip of 4 4.50 4.50
*a.* A309 (33p) multi 1.10 1.10
*b.* A310 (33p) multi 1.10 1.10
*c.* A311 (33p) multi 1.10 1.10
*d.* A312 (33p) multi 1.10 1.10
**1351** A313 56p multi 1.75 1.75
**1352** A314 90p multi 3.00 3.00
*Nos. 1349-1352 (4)* 13.50 13.50

**Booklet Stamps**
**Self-Adhesive**
***Serpentine Die Cut 13¾x13***

**1353** A305 (32p) multi 1.00 1.00
**1354** A306 (32p) multi 1.00 1.00
**1355** A307 (32p) multi 1.00 1.00
**1356** A308 (32p) multi 1.00 1.00
*a.* Booklet pane of 12, 3 each #1353-1356 12.00
**1357** A309 (33p) multi 1.10 1.10
**1358** A310 (33p) multi 1.10 1.10
**1359** A311 (33p) multi 1.10 1.10
**1360** A312 (33p) multi 1.10 1.10
*a.* Booklet pane of 12, 3 each #1357-1360 13.50
*Nos. 1353-1360 (8)* 8.40 8.40

Girl Guides, Cent. — A315

No. 1361 — Rainbows with denomination in: a, Red. b, Blue.
No. 1362 — Brownies with denomination in: a, Red. b, Blue.
No. 1363 — Girl Guides with denomination in: a, Red. b, Blue.
No. 1364 — Senior Section members with denomination in: a, Red. b, Blue.
No. 1365 — Adult volunteers with denomination in: a, Red. b, Blue.

**2010** ***Perf. 14***
**1361** A315 Horiz. pair 2.00 2.00
*a.-b.* 32p Either single 1.00 1.00
**1362** A315 Horiz. pair 2.00 2.00
*a.-b.* 33p Either single 1.00 1.00
*c.* Sheet of 10 #1362a 10.00 10.00
**1363** A315 Horiz. pair 3.50 3.50
*a.-b.* 56p Either single 1.75 1.75
*c.* Sheet of 10 #1363a 17.50 17.50
**1364** A315 Horiz. pair 6.00 6.00
*a.-b.* £1 Either single 3.00 3.00
*Nos. 1361-1364 (4)* 13.50 13.50

**Souvenir Sheet**

**1365** A315 Sheet of 2 9.00 9.00
*a.-b.* £1.50 Either single 4.50 4.50
*c.* As #1365, with Centenary Camp emblem added in sheet margin 9.75 9.75

Issued: Nos. 1361-1365, 2/18; No. 1365c, 7/31. Europa (Nos. 1362a, 1363a).

A316

Battle of Britain, 70th Anniv. — A317

No. 1366: a, Messerschmitt BF110 and Hurricane. b, Blenheim I and Junkers 88. c, Heinkel III and Spitfire.

No. 1367: a, Messerschmitt BF109 and Defiant. b, Spitfire and Messerschmitt BF109. c, Junkers JU-87 and Hurricane.

No. 1368: a, Ben My Chree arriving at Folkstone with troops evacuated from Dunkirk, Isle of Man #204. b, Airmen running to planes, Isle of Man #429a.

**2010, Apr. 20** ***Perf. 13¼***

| | | | | |
|---|---|---|---|---|
| **1366** | | Horiz. strip of 3 | 6.50 | 6.50 |
| *a.-c.* | A316 | 70p Any single | 2.10 | 2.10 |
| **1367** | | Horiz. strip of 3 | 6.50 | 6.50 |
| *a.-c.* | A316 | 70p Any single | 2.10 | 2.10 |

**Souvenir Sheet**

***Perf. 13¾***

| | | | | |
|---|---|---|---|---|
| **1368** | A317 | Sheet of 2 | 9.25 | 9.25 |
| *a.-b.* | | £1.50 Either single | 4.50 | 4.50 |

Accession to Throne of King George V, Cent. — A318

Photographs of 1920 royal visit to Isle of Man and items from Royal Philatelic Collection: 55p, Royal party at Bishops Court, Ballaugh, cast of proposed 1913 stamp depicting King George V. 60p, King George V and Queen Mary on Tynwald Hill, two used pairs of Cape of Good Hope 1p triangle stamps. 67p, Queen's Pier, Ramsey, unissued 2p plum stamp of Great Britain. 96p, Visit to war disabled at Ramsey Cottage Hospital, Niger Coast Protectorates #35. 97p, Tree planting at Bishops Court, Great Britain #151. £1.10, Royal party at Castletown, Mauritius #2.

**2010, May 6** ***Perf. 14***

| | | | | |
|---|---|---|---|---|
| **1369** | A318 | 55p multi | 1.60 | 1.60 |
| **1370** | A318 | 60p multi | 1.75 | 1.75 |
| **1371** | A318 | 67p multi | 2.00 | 2.00 |
| **1372** | A318 | 96p multi | 3.00 | 3.00 |
| **1373** | A318 | 97p multi | 3.00 | 3.00 |
| **1374** | A318 | £1.10 multi | 3.25 | 3.25 |
| | | *Nos. 1369-1374 (6)* | 14.60 | 14.60 |

Model T Fords — A319

Designs: 35p, 1915 Speedster. 36p, 1926 Coupe. 60p, 1923 Van. 74p, 1912 Town Car. 97p, 1922 Charabanc. 172p, 1912 Tourer.

**2010, May 7** ***Perf. 13¼***

| | | | | |
|---|---|---|---|---|
| **1375** | A319 | 35p multi | 1.10 | 1.10 |
| **1376** | A319 | 36p multi | 1.10 | 1.10 |
| **1377** | A319 | 60p multi | 1.75 | 1.75 |
| **1378** | A319 | 74p multi | 2.25 | 2.25 |
| **1379** | A319 | 97p multi | 3.00 | 3.00 |
| **1380** | A319 | 172p multi | 5.25 | 5.25 |
| | | *Nos. 1375-1380 (6)* | 14.45 | 14.45 |

Railways A320

Designs: 35p, Caledonia at summit of Snaefell Mountain. 36p, Isle of Man Railways steam locomotive No. 1 and Manx Electric Railway car No. 1 at Laxey. 55p, Caledonia at Bulgham. 88p, Isle of Man Railways Loch locomotive at Skinscoe Curve. £1.32, Manx Electric Railway car No. 33 approaching Keristal. £1.46, Loch and Maitland locomotives near White Hoe.

**2010, June 24** ***Perf. 14***

| | | | | |
|---|---|---|---|---|
| **1381** | A320 | 35p multi | 1.10 | 1.10 |
| **1382** | A320 | 36p multi | 1.10 | 1.10 |
| **1383** | A320 | 55p multi | 1.75 | 1.75 |
| **1384** | A320 | 88p multi | 2.75 | 2.75 |
| **1385** | A320 | £1.32 multi | 4.00 | 4.00 |
| **1386** | A320 | £1.46 multi | 4.50 | 4.50 |
| *a.* | | Sheet of 6, #1381-1386 + 3 labels | 15.50 | 15.50 |
| | | *Nos. 1381-1386 (6)* | 15.20 | 15.20 |

History of Manx Coinage A321

Designs: 35p, 1709 Lord Derby halfpenny, Castle Rushen. 36p, 1798 Cartwheel penny, Soho Mint, Birmingham. 55p, 1839 Queen Victoria Farthing, Douglas. 60p, 1965 gold coin, Castle Rushen. 67p, 1971 Decimal currency 5p coin, Tower of Refuge. £1.87, 2010 £5 Laxey Wheel coin, Laxey Wheel.

**2010, June 24** ***Perf. 12¾***

| | | | | |
|---|---|---|---|---|
| **1387** | A321 | 35p multi | 1.10 | 1.10 |
| **1388** | A321 | 36p multi | 1.10 | 1.10 |
| **1389** | A321 | 55p multi | 1.75 | 1.75 |
| **1390** | A321 | 60p multi | 1.90 | 1.90 |
| **1391** | A321 | 67p multi | 2.10 | 2.10 |
| **1392** | A321 | £1.87 multi | 5.75 | 5.75 |
| | | *Nos. 1387-1392 (6)* | 13.70 | 13.70 |

**Souvenir Sheet**

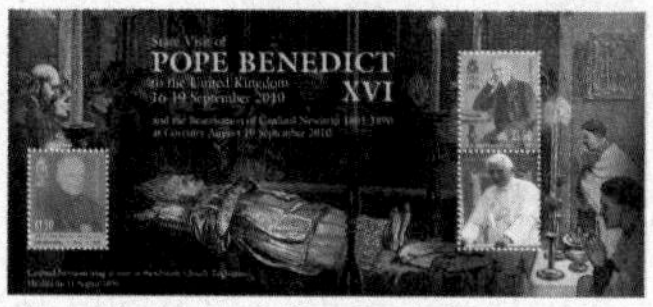


Beatification of Cardinal John Henry Newman (1801-90) — A322

No. 1393: a, Newman, table and book. b, Newman.

**2010, Aug. 11** ***Perf. 13¼***

| | | | | |
|---|---|---|---|---|
| **1393** | A322 | Sheet of 2 + label | 9.50 | 9.50 |
| *a.-b.* | | £1.50 Either single | 4.75 | 4.75 |

State visit of Pope Benedict XVI.

Artwork by Internees in Isle of Man World War II Internment Camps A323

Designs: 35p, Three-legged Postman, by Bertram. 36p, Peveril Camp, Peel, by Herbert Kaden. 55p, Life at Palace Camp, Douglas, by Imre Goth. 67p, Douglas, Isle of Man, by Hermann Fechenbach. 132p, Violinist at Onchan Camp, by Ernst Eisenmayer. 172p, Portrait of Klaus E. Hinrichsen, by Kurt Schwitters.

**2010, Sept. 24** **Litho.**

| | | | | |
|---|---|---|---|---|
| **1394** | A323 | 35p multi | 1.10 | 1.10 |
| **1395** | A323 | 36p multi | 1.10 | 1.10 |
| **1396** | A323 | 55p multi | 1.75 | 1.75 |
| **1397** | A323 | 67p multi | 2.10 | 2.10 |
| **1398** | A323 | 132p multi | 4.00 | 4.00 |
| **1399** | A323 | 172p multi | 5.25 | 5.25 |
| | | *Nos. 1394-1399 (6)* | 15.30 | 15.30 |

**Souvenir Sheet**

The Christmas Story — A324

No. 1400 — Characters from Friends and Heroes animated TV show depicting the Nativity: a, Jesus is born. b, Shepherds hear first. c, The Magi see a star.

**2010, Oct. 1** **Litho.** ***Perf. 13¼x13¾***

| | | | | |
|---|---|---|---|---|
| **1400** | A324 | Sheet of 3 | 9.75 | 9.75 |
| *a.-c.* | | £1 Any single | 3.25 | 3.25 |

Photographs of Snowfall of 2009-10 Winter — A325

Photographs of: 35p, Old Braddan Church, by Bill Dale. 36p, The Braaid, by Seamus Whelan. 60p, Dhoon Glen, by Simon Park. 88p, Dhoon Beach, by Park. 97p, Cronk ny Aree Laa, by Dale. £1.46, St. Patrick's Isle in Snow, by Victoria Harrop.

**2010, Oct. 20** ***Perf. 13x13¼***

| | | | | |
|---|---|---|---|---|
| **1401** | A325 | 35p multi | 1.25 | 1.25 |
| **1402** | A325 | 36p multi | 1.25 | 1.25 |
| **1403** | A325 | 60p multi | 2.00 | 2.00 |
| **1404** | A325 | 88p multi | 3.00 | 3.00 |
| **1405** | A325 | 97p multi | 3.25 | 3.25 |
| **1406** | A325 | £1.46 multi | 4.75 | 4.75 |
| | | *Nos. 1401-1406 (6)* | 15.50 | 15.50 |

**Souvenir Sheet**

Engagement of Prince William of Wales and Catherine Middleton — A326

No. 1407 — Prince William: a, Close-up, no shirt visible. b, Shirt visible.

**2010, Nov. 26** **Litho.** ***Perf. 14¾x14***

| | | | | |
|---|---|---|---|---|
| **1407** | A326 | Sheet of 2 | 9.50 | 9.50 |
| *a.-b.* | | £1.50 Either single | 4.75 | 4.75 |

Service of Queen Elizabeth II and Prince Philip — A327

Designs: 35p, Queen Elizabeth II, 1953 coronation photograph. 36p, Queen and Prince Philip, 2007. 55p, Queen and Prince Philip as newlyweds. 60p, Queen and Prince Philip in uniforms, 1971. £1.14, Queen and Prince Philip, 2002. £1.46, Prince Philip at 1953 coronation.

£3, Queen and Prince Philip, 1970s.

**2011, Feb. 6** ***Perf. 13¼***

| | | | | |
|---|---|---|---|---|
| **1408** | A327 | 35p multi | 1.10 | 1.10 |
| **1409** | A327 | 36p multi | 1.25 | 1.25 |
| **1410** | A327 | 55p multi | 1.75 | 1.75 |
| **1411** | A327 | 60p multi | 1.90 | 1.90 |
| **1412** | A327 | £1.14 multi | 3.75 | 3.75 |
| **1413** | A327 | £1.46 multi | 4.75 | 4.75 |
| *a.* | | Souvenir sheet of 6, #1408-1413, + 3 labels | 14.50 | 14.50 |
| | | *Nos. 1408-1413 (6)* | 14.50 | 14.50 |

**Souvenir Sheet**

| | | | | |
|---|---|---|---|---|
| **1414** | A327 | £3 multi | 9.75 | 9.75 |
| *a.* | | Sheet of 13, #1413, 1414, 3 #1411, 2 each #1408-1410, 1412, + 16 labels | 36.00 | 36.00 |

Issued: No. 1414a, 6/4/12.

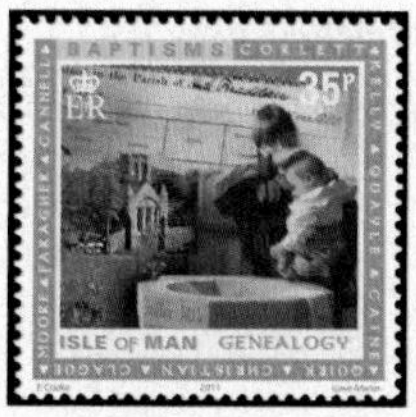


Genealogy A328

Inscription in frame at UL: No. 1415, Baptisms. No. 1416, School Days. No. 1417, Working Life. No. 1418, Weddings. No. 1419, Family Album. No. 1420, Emigration. No. 1421, Memorials. No. 1422, Family Tree.

**2011, Feb. 18** **Litho.** ***Perf. 13½***

**Frame Color**

| | | | | |
|---|---|---|---|---|
| **1415** | A328 | 35p org brown | 1.10 | 1.10 |
| **1416** | A328 | 35p deep claret | 1.10 | 1.10 |
| **1417** | A328 | 36p car rose | 1.25 | 1.25 |
| **1418** | A328 | 36p Prus blue | 1.25 | 1.25 |
| **1419** | A328 | 67p slate grn | 2.25 | 2.25 |
| **1420** | A328 | 67p emerald | 2.25 | 2.25 |
| **1421** | A328 | £1.10 ol green | 3.50 | 3.50 |
| **1422** | A328 | £1.10 brown | 3.50 | 3.50 |
| | | *Nos. 1415-1422 (8)* | 16.20 | 16.20 |

Greatest TT Motorcycle Races — A329

No. 1423: a, Stanley Woods v. Jimmy Guthrie, 1935 Senior race. b, Mike Hailwood v. Giacomo Agostini, 1967 Senior race. c, John Williams v. Tom Herron, 1976 Senior race. d, George O'Dell and Kenny Arthur v. Dick Greasley and Mick Skeels, 1977 Sidecar A race. e, Alex George v. Mike Hailwood, 1979 Classic race.

No. 1424: a, Steve Hislop v. Carl Fogarty, 1992 Senior race. b, Joey Dunlop v. David Jefferies, 2000 Formula 1 race. c, John McGuiness v. Cameron Donald, 2008 Senior race. d, Klaus Klaffenbock and Dan Sayle v. John Holden and Andy Winkle, 2010 Sidecar 2 race. e, Ian Hutchinson v. Ryan Farquhar, 2010 Superstock race.

£3, Hislop v. Fogarty, 1992 Senior race, horiz..

**2011, Apr. 1** **Litho.** ***Perf. 14¼***

| | | | | |
|---|---|---|---|---|
| **1423** | | Horiz. strip of 5 | 6.25 | 6.25 |
| *a.-e.* | A329 | 38p Any single | 1.25 | 1.25 |
| **1424** | | Horiz. strip of 5 | 11.50 | 11.50 |
| *a.-e.* | A329 | 68p Any single | 2.25 | 2.25 |

**Souvenir Sheet**

***Perf. 14¼x15***

| | | | | |
|---|---|---|---|---|
| **1425** | A329 | £3 multi | 10.00 | 10.00 |

No. 1425 contains one 45x30mm stamp.

Butterflies A330

Designs: No. 1426, Wall butterfly. No. 1427, Dark green fritillary. No. 1428, Comma butterfly. No. 1429, Red admiral. Nos. 1430, 1434, Small tortoiseshell butterfly. No. 1431, Common blue butterfly. No. 1432, Green-veined white butterfly. No. 1433, Speckled wood butterfly.

**2011, Apr. 1** ***Perf. 13¼***

**With WWF Emblem at Lower Left**

| | | | | |
|---|---|---|---|---|
| **1426** | A330 | 37p multi | 1.25 | 1.25 |
| **1427** | A330 | 38p multi | 1.25 | 1.25 |
| **1428** | A330 | 58p multi | 1.90 | 1.90 |
| **1429** | A330 | 115p multi | 3.75 | 3.75 |
| *a.* | | Sheet of 16, 4 each #1426-1429 | 33.00 | 33.00 |

**Without WWF Emblem**

| | | | | |
|---|---|---|---|---|
| **1430** | A330 | 37p multi | 1.25 | 1.25 |
| **1431** | A330 | 38p multi | 1.25 | 1.25 |
| **1432** | A330 | 58p multi | 1.90 | 1.90 |
| **1433** | A330 | 115p multi | 3.75 | 3.75 |
| | | *Nos. 1426-1433 (8)* | 16.30 | 16.30 |

**Booklet Stamp**
**Self-Adhesive**

***Serpentine Die Cut 13¼***

| | | | | |
|---|---|---|---|---|
| **1434** | A330 | 37p multi | 1.25 | 1.25 |
| *a.* | | Booklet pane of 12 | 15.00 | |

**Souvenir Sheet**

Wedding of Prince William and Catherine Middleton — A331

No. 1435: a, Middleton. b, Prince William.

**2011, Apr. 15** ***Perf. 14¾x14***

**1435** A331 Sheet of 2 6.50 6.50
*a.-b.* £1 Either single 3.25 3.25
*c.* Sheet of 10, 5 each #1435a-1435b, + 10 labels 32.50 32.50

Political Cartoons by Harold "Dusty" Miller (1898-1964) A332

Designs: 37p, The Southern Hundred. 38p, I'm Staking My Claim On the Sands at Douglas. 68p, Over the Water - I Must Get Me a Bigger Horse. 76p, Will Uncle Sam Provide the Third Leg? 110p, Bob a Job Week. 165p, Well, Councilor - Did You Vote For Evening Meetings?

**2011, May 10** ***Perf. 13¼***

**Color of Panel and Frame**

**1436** A332 37p red 1.25 1.25
**1437** A332 38p purple 1.25 1.25
**1438** A332 68p green 2.25 2.25
**1439** A332 76p red violet 2.50 2.50
**1440** A332 110p Prussian blue 3.75 3.75
**1441** A332 165p bister 5.50 5.50
*Nos. 1436-1441 (6)* 16.50 16.50

Picture Post Cards Depicting Manx Cats A333

Various post cards depicting cats and arms of Isle of Man.

**2011, June 23** ***Perf. 13¼x13½***

**Panel Color**

**1442** A333 37p dark blue 1.25 1.25
**1443** A333 38p bister 1.25 1.25
**1444** A333 58p light blue 1.90 1.90
**1445** A333 76p red violet 2.50 2.50
**1446** A333 115p red 3.75 3.75
**1447** A333 165p brown 5.25 5.25
*Nos. 1442-1447 (6)* 15.90 15.90

Postal History of Knockaloe Internment Camp — A334

No. 1448: a, Post card depicting troops marching, half of 1908 Camp Knockaloe cancel. b, Address side of post card, Great Britain #143 with 1908 Camp Knockaloe cancel.

No. 1449: Post card depicting camp, part of 1914 Peel cancel. b, Address side of post card, pair of Great Britain #159 with 1914 Peel cancel.

No. 1450: a, Easter post card from 1915-19, half of registry label. b, Half of registry label, registered mail envelope with camp cancel.

No. 1451: a, Post card depicting camp, Knockaloe cancel. b, Internee-produced local stamp, local stamp on cover.

No. 1452: a, Post card depicting camp huts, Camp Knockaloe censor marking. b, Great Britain #160 with 1915 Camp Knockaloe cancel, prisoner-of-war cover. c, 1917 Easter post card, 1915 Camp Knockaloe cancel. d, Great Britain envelope stamp with 1915 Camp Knockaloe cancel, registered mail envelope.

**2011, Aug. 8** ***Perf. 13¼x13½***

**1448** A334 Horiz. pair 2.50 2.50
*a.-b.* 37p Either single 1.25 1.25
**1449** A334 Horiz. pair 2.50 2.50
*a.-b.* 38p Either single 1.25 1.25
**1450** A334 Horiz. pair 3.80 3.80
*a.-b.* 58p Either single 1.90 1.90
**1451** A334 Horiz. pair 7.50 7.50
*a.-b.* £1.15 Either single 3.75 3.75
*Nos. 1448-1451 (4)* 16.30 16.30

**Souvenir Sheet**

**1452** A334 Sheet of 4 10.00 10.00
*a.-b.* 50p Either single 1.75 1.75
*c.-d.* £1 Either single 3.25 3.25

Miniature Sheet

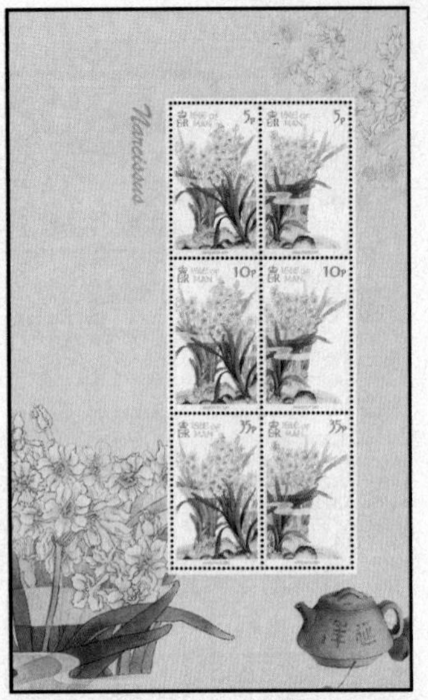

Narcissi — A335

No. 1453: a, c, and e, Flowers, flower to right of "Man." b, d, and f, Flowers, diff, leaf to right of "Man."

**2011, Sept. 1** **Litho.** ***Perf. 13¾x13½***

**1453** A335 Sheet of 6 3.25 3.25
*a.-b.* 5p Either single .20 .20
*c.-d.* 10p Either single .30 .30
*e.-f.* 35p Either single 1.10 1.10

Miniature Sheet

2011 Commonwealth Youth Games, Isle of Man — A336

No. 1454 — Mascot: a, Running (48x32mm). b, Playing badminton (24x26mm). c, Boxing (24x26mm). d, Playing rugby (24x26mm). e, Cycling (24x26mm). f, On gymnastics horse (24x26mm). g, Crossing finish line (24x26mm). h, Swimming (24x26mm).

***Perf. 14x14¾ on 3 or 4 Sides***

**2011, Sept. 1**

**1454** A336 Sheet of 8 10.00 10.00
*a.-h.* 38p Any single 1.25 1.25

Birds in Winter — A337

Designs: (37p), Robin. (38p), Redwing. 58p, Goldfinch. 68p, Siskin. 76p, Waxwing. £2, Long-tailed tit.

**2011, Sept. 28** ***Perf. 13¼x13***

**Panel Color**

**1455** A337 (37p) bright red 1.25 1.25
**1456** A337 (38p) olive brown 1.25 1.25
**1457** A337 58p bluish black 1.90 1.90
**1458** A337 68p dark green 2.25 2.25
*1458a* Perf. 12½x12 2.25 2.25
**1459** A337 76p maroon 2.40 2.40
**1460** A337 £2 gray blue 6.25 6.25
*Nos. 1455-1460 (6)* 15.30 15.30

**Self-Adhesive**

**Panel Color**

***Rouletted 14***

**1461** A337 (37p) bright red 1.25 1.25
**1462** A337 (38p) olive brown 1.25 1.25

Europa (#1458). No. 1458a was printed in sheets of 10.

Transportation Created on *Top Gear* Television Show — A338

Designs: 37p, Triumph Herald Sailboat. 38p, Citroen Grand Design. 58p, Polar Hilux. 68p, Hammerhead Eagle I-thrust. £1.10, Robin Reliant Space Shuttle. £1.82, Caravan Airship.

**2011, Nov. 5** **Litho.** ***Perf. 13***

**1463** A338 37p multi + label 1.25 1.25
**1464** A338 38p multi + label 1.25 1.25
**1465** A338 58p multi + label 1.90 1.90
**1466** A338 68p multi + label 2.25 2.25
**1467** A338 £1.10 multi + label 3.50 3.50
**1468** A338 £1.82 multi + label 6.00 6.00
*Nos. 1463-1468 (6)* 16.15 16.15

**Self-Adhesive**

***Die Cut***

**1469** A338 £1.10 multi + label 3.50 3.50
**1470** A338 £1.82 multi + label 6.00 6.00

Nos. 1469 and 1470 each were printed in sheets of 5.

2012 Summer Olympics, London A339

Designs: 37p, Sailing. 38p, Cycling. 58p, Swimming. 68p, Tennis. 76p, Rowing. £1, Track. £1.15, Archery.

£3, Cycling, diff.

**2012, Jan. 1** ***Perf. 13½***

**1471** A339 37p multi 1.25 1.25
**1472** A339 38p multi 1.25 1.25
**1473** A339 58p multi 1.90 1.90
**1474** A339 68p multi 2.10 2.10
**1475** A339 76p multi 2.40 2.40
**1476** A339 £1 multi 3.25 3.25
**1477** A339 £1.15 multi 3.75 3.75
*a.* Souvenir sheet of 14, 2 each #1471-1477 32.00 32.00
*Nos. 1471-1477 (7)* 15.90 15.90

**Souvenir Sheet**

***Perf. 13***

**1478** A339 £3 multi 9.50 9.50
*a.* Sheet of 6, 3 each #1472, 1478, + 6 labels 32.50 32.50

No. 1478 contains one 52x40mm stamp. No. 1478a sold for £10.

Reign of Queen Elizabeth II, 60th Anniv. — A340

Photographs of Queen Elizabeth II: 37p, Wearing tiara, 1990. 38p, Trooping the colors, 1979. 58p, Wearing tiara, 1955. 68p, Wearing blue hat, 1982. £1.10, Without hat, 1968. £1.82, Wearing red hat, 2008.

£3, Queen Elizabeth II wearing crown, 2005.

**2012** ***Perf. 13¼***

**1479** A340 37p multi 1.25 1.25
**1480** A340 38p multi 1.25 1.25
**1481** A340 58p multi 1.90 1.90
**1482** A340 68p multi 2.25 2.25
**1483** A340 £1.10 multi 3.50 3.50
**1484** A340 £1.82 multi 5.75 5.75
*a.* Souvenir sheet of 6, #1478-1484, + 3 labels 16.00 16.00
*Nos. 1479-1484 (6)* 15.90 15.90

**Souvenir Sheet**

**1485** A340 £3 multi 9.75 9.75
*a.* Sheet of 11, #1483-1485, 2 each #1479-1482, + 18 labels 32.50 32.50

Issued: Nos. 1479-1484, 2/6; No. 1485, 4/21; No. 1484a, 2/6; No. 1485a, 6/5.

Frost Arbory, by William Hoggatt (1879-1961) — A341

A Colby Mill, by Hoggatt A342

Landing the Catch, Port St. Mary, by Hoggatt A343

Early Spring, by Hoggatt A344

Port Erin Bay, by Hoggatt A345

**2012, Feb. 20** ***Perf. 14***

**1486** A341 38p multi 1.25 1.25
**1487** A342 38p multi 1.25 1.25
**1488** A343 38p multi 1.25 1.25
**1489** A344 38p multi 1.25 1.25
**1490** A345 38p multi 1.25 1.25
*a.* Horiz. strip of 5, #1486-1490 6.25 6.25
*Nos. 1486-1490 (5)* 6.25 6.25

Sinking of the Titanic, Cent. A346

No. 1491: a, Titanic at dock and at sea, breakfast menu. b, Male passenger, dining room. c, Capt. Edward J. Smith, White Star Line stationery, life preserver.

No. 1492: a, Titanic sinking, life preserver. b, Lifeboats, newspaper boy with newspaper announcing sinking. c, Newspaper, Titanic, passengers.

**2012, Apr. 2** **Litho.**

**1491** Horiz. strip of 3 4.75 4.75
*a.* A346 37p multi 1.25 1.25
*b.* A346 38p multi 1.25 1.25
*c.* A346 68p multi 2.25 2.25
**1492** Horiz. strip of 3 11.50 11.50
*a.* A346 76p multi 2.50 2.50
*b.* A346 £1.15 multi 3.75 3.75
*c.* A346 £1.65 multi 5.25 5.25

| | | | | |
|---|---|---|---|---|
| *d.* | Souvenir sheet of 9, #1491a-1491c, 2 each #1492a-1492c, + 9 labels | | 28.00 | 28.00 |

Lighthouses — A347

Designs: 1p, Castletown Harbor Lighthouse. 68p, Douglas Harbor Lighthouse. 75p, Peel Harbor Lighthouse. £1, Laxey Harbor Lighthouse. £1.30, Ramsey Harbor Lighthouse. £1.60, Port St. Mary Harbor Lighthouse.

**2012, Apr. 2** ***Perf. 13¾***

| | | | | |
|---|---|---|---|---|
| **1493** | A347 | 1p multi | .25 | .25 |
| **1494** | A347 | 68p multi | 2.25 | 2.25 |
| *a.* | | Sheet of 10 | 22.50 | 22.50 |
| **1495** | A347 | 75p multi | 2.40 | 2.40 |
| **1496** | A347 | £1 multi | 3.25 | 3.25 |
| **1497** | A347 | £1.30 multi | 4.25 | 4.25 |
| **1498** | A347 | £1.60 multi | 5.25 | 5.25 |
| | | *Nos. 1493-1498 (6)* | 17.65 | 17.65 |

Europa (#1494).

Manx Tourist Memorabilia — A348

Designs: (38p), Goss China Manx cottage. (41p), Crown Devon Manx race car. 58p, Royal Doulton Postman at Maughold spittoon. 68p, Willow Art China Manx dog. £1.10, Kettlespring Kilns commemorative plate depicting Ginger the Manx cat. £1.82, Archibald Knox Jewel.

**2012, May 8** ***Perf. 14¾x14¼***

| | | | | |
|---|---|---|---|---|
| **1499** | A348 | (38p) multi | 1.25 | 1.25 |
| **1500** | A348 | (41p) multi | 1.25 | 1.25 |
| **1501** | A348 | 58p multi | 1.90 | 1.90 |
| **1502** | A348 | 68p multi | 2.10 | 2.10 |
| **1503** | A348 | £1.10 multi | 3.50 | 3.50 |
| **1504** | A348 | £1.82 multi | 5.75 | 5.75 |
| | | *Nos. 1499-1504 (6)* | 15.75 | 15.75 |

Inscriptions: No. 1499, "IOM." No. 1500, "UK."

Miniature Sheet

Thames Diamond Jubilee Pageant — A349

No. 1505: a, Eighteen-oarsman barge Gloriana (42x28mm). b, Lady of Mann near London Eye (42x28mm). c, Viking longboat Vital Spark (42x28mm). d, Royal barge Spirit of Chartwell (85x28mm).

**2012, June 3** ***Perf. 14***

| | | | | |
|---|---|---|---|---|
| **1505** | A349 | Sheet of 4 | 9.75 | 9.75 |
| *a.-c.* | | 50p Any single | 1.60 | 1.60 |
| *d.* | | £1.50 multi | 4.75 | 4.75 |
| *e.* | | Souvenir sheet of 12, 3 each #1505a-1505d, + 9 labels | 30.00 | 30.00 |

Mark Cavendish, Cyclist A350

Cavendish: 38p, Holding Manx flag after winning 2006 Commonwealth Games Scratch race. 41p, Cycling in 2007 Scheldeprijs Vlaanderen. 65p, Cycling in 2009 Milan-San Remo Classic. 71p, Cycling in 2011 Tour de France. 80p, Celebrating victory in 2011 World Road Race Championships. 105p, Wearing rainbow jersey and medal. 116p, Cycling with rainbow jersey.

**2012, June 19** ***Perf. 13***

| | | | | |
|---|---|---|---|---|
| **1506** | A350 | 38p multi | 1.25 | 1.25 |
| **1507** | A350 | 41p multi | 1.25 | 1.25 |
| **1508** | A350 | 65p multi | 2.00 | 2.00 |
| **1509** | A350 | 71p multi | 2.25 | 2.25 |
| **1510** | A350 | 80p multi | 2.50 | 2.50 |
| **1511** | A350 | 105p multi | 3.25 | 3.25 |
| **1512** | A350 | 116p multi | 3.75 | 3.75 |
| *a.* | | Sheet of 13, #1510, 2 each #1506-1509, 1511-1512, + 7 labels | 30.00 | 30.00 |
| | | *Nos. 1506-1512 (7)* | 16.25 | 16.25 |

Bees — A351

Designs: 38p, Colletes succinctus. 41p, Epeolus variegatus. £1, Osmia rufa. £1.05, Halictus rubicundus. £1.30, Bombus monticola. £1.47, Apis mellifera.

**2012, Aug. 8** ***Perf. 13***

| | | | | |
|---|---|---|---|---|
| **1513** | A351 | 38p multi | 1.25 | 1.25 |
| **1514** | A351 | 41p multi | 1.25 | 1.25 |
| **1515** | A351 | £1 multi | 3.25 | 3.25 |
| **1516** | A351 | £1.05 multi | 3.25 | 3.25 |
| **1517** | A351 | £1.30 multi | 4.25 | 4.25 |
| **1518** | A351 | £1.47 multi | 4.75 | 4.75 |
| | | *Nos. 1513-1518 (6)* | 18.00 | 18.00 |

**Booklet Stamps**
**Self-Adhesive**

***Die Cut Perf. 13¼x12¾***

| | | | | |
|---|---|---|---|---|
| **1519** | A351 | 38p multi | 1.25 | 1.25 |
| *a.* | | Booklet pane of 10 | 12.50 | |
| **1520** | A351 | 41p multi | 1.25 | 1.25 |
| *a.* | | Booklet pane of 10 | 12.50 | |

Nos. 1513-1518 were impregnated with a honey scent.

Royal Flying Corps, Cent. A352

Military aircraft: 38p, AW FK.8 B5773, 1918. 41p, MS Type L 3253, 1915. 65p, DH.2 5964, 1916. 80p, Sopwith Camel B5648, 1918. £1.37, RAF BE.2C, 4359, 1917. £1.91, Short S.32 402, 1912.

**2012, Sept. 20** ***Perf. 13¼x13½***

| | | | | |
|---|---|---|---|---|
| **1521** | A352 | 38p multi | 1.25 | 1.25 |
| **1522** | A352 | 41p multi | 1.40 | 1.40 |
| **1523** | A352 | 65p multi | 2.10 | 2.10 |
| **1524** | A352 | 80p multi | 2.60 | 2.60 |
| **1525** | A352 | £1.37 multi | 4.50 | 4.50 |
| **1526** | A352 | £1.91 multi | 6.25 | 6.25 |
| | | *Nos. 1521-1526 (6)* | 18.10 | 18.10 |

Souvenir Sheet

Antarctic Expedition of Robert Falcon Scott, Cent. — A353

No. 1527: a, Expedition ship, Dicovery, and ice. b, Memorial cairn.

**2012, Oct. 2** ***Perf. 13¼x13***

| | | | | |
|---|---|---|---|---|
| **1527** | A353 | Sheet of 2 | 9.75 | 9.75 |
| *a.-b.* | | £1.50 Either single | 4.75 | 4.75 |

Christmas A354

Designs: 38p, Ramsey Christmas lights. 41p, Mail carrier delivering mail in Glen Auldyn. 71p, Castletown Police Station. £1.05, Sulby Glen. £1.16, Martin's Sweet Shop, Ramsey. £1.73, Lake Lane, Peel.

**2012, Oct. 20** ***Perf. 13***

| | | | | |
|---|---|---|---|---|
| **1528** | A354 | 38p multi | 1.25 | 1.25 |
| **1529** | A354 | 41p multi | 1.40 | 1.40 |
| **1530** | A354 | 71p multi | 2.25 | 2.25 |
| **1531** | A354 | £1.05 multi | 3.50 | 3.50 |
| **1532** | A354 | £1.16 multi | 3.75 | 3.75 |
| **1533** | A354 | £1.73 multi | 5.50 | 5.50 |
| | | *Nos. 1528-1533 (6)* | 17.65 | 17.65 |

**Self-Adhesive**

***Serpentine Die Cut 11¼***

| | | | | |
|---|---|---|---|---|
| **1534** | A354 | 38p multi | 1.25 | 1.25 |
| **1535** | A354 | 41p multi | 1.40 | 1.40 |

Chronicles of Man and Lewis Chessmen A355

Various chessmen and segments of text from Chronicles with panel color of: 38p, Gray. 41p, Red violet. 71p, Bister. 80p, Purple. 130p, Green. 191p, Brown.

**2013, Jan. 11** ***Perf. 13½***

| | | | | |
|---|---|---|---|---|
| **1536** | A355 | 38p multi | 1.25 | 1.25 |
| **1537** | A355 | 41p multi | 1.40 | 1.40 |
| **1538** | A355 | 71p multi | 2.40 | 2.40 |
| **1539** | A355 | 80p multi | 2.60 | 2.60 |
| **1540** | A355 | 130p multi | 4.25 | 4.25 |
| **1541** | A355 | 191p multi | 6.25 | 6.25 |
| | | *Nos. 1536-1541 (6)* | 18.15 | 18.15 |

Items Produced to Commemorate Coronations — A356

Items depicting: 38p, Queen Victoria. 41p, King Edward VII. 65p, King George V. £1.05, King George VI. £1.37, Queen Elizabeth II. £1.73, Queen Elizabeth II, diff.

**2013, Feb. 6** ***Perf. 14***

| | | | | |
|---|---|---|---|---|
| **1542** | A356 | 38p multi | 1.25 | 1.25 |
| **1543** | A356 | 41p multi | 1.40 | 1.40 |
| **1544** | A356 | 65p multi | 2.10 | 2.10 |
| **1545** | A356 | £1.05 multi | 3.50 | 3.50 |
| **1546** | A356 | £1.37 multi | 4.50 | 4.50 |
| **1547** | A356 | £1.73 multi | 5.50 | 5.50 |
| | | *Nos. 1542-1547 (6)* | 18.25 | 18.25 |

Miniature Sheet

New Year 2013 (Year of the Snake) — A357

No. 1548: a, Snake. b, Chinese character with fish, flowers and butterfly. c, Chinese character with cranes and peaches. d, Chinese character with deer. e, Chinese character with birds and flowers. f, Snake coiled in spiral.

**2013, Feb. 8** ***Perf. 12***

| | | | | |
|---|---|---|---|---|
| **1548** | A357 | Sheet of 6, #a-f | 9.25 | 9.25 |
| *a.* | | 5p multi | .25 | .25 |
| *b.-e.* | | 20p Any single | .60 | .60 |
| *f.* | | £2.15 multi | 6.50 | 6.50 |

Isle of Man Constabulary, 150th Anniv. — A358

Designs: 38p, Uniforms. 41p, Vehicles. 71p, Dogs. 80p, Communications. £1.47, Community. £1.82, Stations.

**2013, Feb. 20** ***Perf. 14***

| | | | | |
|---|---|---|---|---|
| **1549** | A358 | 38p multi | 1.25 | 1.25 |
| **1550** | A358 | 41p multi | 1.25 | 1.25 |
| **1551** | A358 | 71p multi | 2.25 | 2.25 |
| **1552** | A358 | 80p multi | 2.50 | 2.50 |
| **1553** | A358 | £1.47 multi | 4.50 | 4.50 |
| **1554** | A358 | £1.82 multi | 5.50 | 5.50 |
| | | *Nos. 1549-1554 (6)* | 17.25 | 17.25 |

Souvenir Sheet

Isle of Man Fire and Rescue Services — A359

**2013, Feb. 20** ***Perf. 13¾x14***

| | | | | |
|---|---|---|---|---|
| **1555** | A359 | £3 multi | 9.25 | 9.25 |

## POSTAGE DUE STAMPS

**Catalogue values for unused stamps in this section are for Never Hinged items.**

D1

D2

**Imprint: "1973 Questa"**

***Perf. 13½***

**1973, July 5** **Litho.** **Unwmk.**

**Inscriptions and Coat of Arms in Black and Red**

| | | | | |
|---|---|---|---|---|
| **J1** | D1 | ½p yellow | .25 | .25 |
| **J2** | D1 | 1p buff | .30 | .30 |
| **J3** | D1 | 2p lt yellow grn | 1.10 | 1.10 |
| **J4** | D1 | 3p gray | 2.00 | 2.00 |
| **J5** | D1 | 4p dull rose | 3.00 | 3.00 |
| **J6** | D1 | 5p light blue | 3.25 | 3.25 |
| **J7** | D1 | 10p light violet | 7.50 | 7.50 |
| **J8** | D1 | 20p lt grnsh blue | 18.00 | 18.00 |
| | | *Nos. J1-J8 (8)* | 35.40 | 35.40 |

**Inscribed: "1973 A Questa"**

**1973, Sept.**

| | | | | |
|---|---|---|---|---|
| *J1a* | D1 | ½p | 1.75 | 1.50 |
| *J2a* | D1 | 1p | .90 | .45 |
| *J3a* | D1 | 2p | .25 | .25 |
| *J4a* | D1 | 3p | .25 | .25 |
| *J5a* | D1 | 4p | .25 | .25 |
| *J6a* | D1 | 5p | .25 | .25 |
| *J7a* | D1 | 10p | .45 | .40 |
| *J8a* | D1 | 20p | .90 | .65 |
| | | *Nos. J1a-J8a (8)* | 5.00 | 4.00 |

**1975, Jan. 8** **Litho.** ***Perf. 14***

**Inscriptions and Coat of Arms in Black and Red**

| | | | | |
|---|---|---|---|---|
| **J9** | D2 | ½p yellow | .25 | .25 |
| **J10** | D2 | 1p buff | .25 | .25 |
| **J11** | D2 | 4p lilac rose | .25 | .25 |
| **J12** | D2 | 7p blue | .30 | .30 |
| **J13** | D2 | 9p sepia | .35 | .35 |
| **J14** | D2 | 10p lilac | .40 | .40 |
| **J15** | D2 | 50p orange | 1.25 | 1.25 |
| **J16** | D2 | £1 bright green | 2.50 | 2.50 |
| | | *Nos. J9-J16 (8)* | 5.55 | 5.55 |

D3

D4

**1982-92** **Litho.** ***Perf. 15x14***

| | | | | |
|---|---|---|---|---|
| **J17** | D3 | 1p light green | .25 | .25 |
| **J18** | D3 | 2p bright pink | .25 | .25 |
| **J19** | D3 | 5p grnsh blue | .25 | .25 |
| **J20** | D3 | 10p bright lilac | .40 | .40 |
| **J21** | D3 | 20p gray | .75 | .75 |

| | | | | |
|---|---|---|---|---|
| **J22** | D3 50p dull yellow | | 2.00 | 2.00 |
| **J23** | D3 £1 brick red | | 3.00 | 3.00 |
| **J24** | D3 £2 blue | | 6.00 | 6.00 |

**Litho.**

*Perf. 13x13½*

| | | | |
|---|---|---|---|
| **J25** | D4 £5 multicolored | 15.00 | 15.00 |
| | *Nos. J17-J25 (9)* | 27.90 | 27.90 |

Issued: £5, 9/16/92; others, 10/5/82.

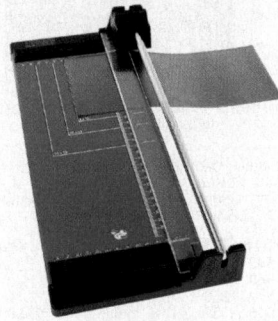

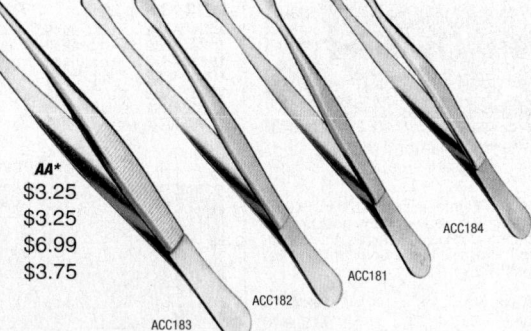

# GREECE

'grēs

## (Hellas)

LOCATION — Southern part of the Balkan Peninsula in southeastern Europe, bordering on the Ionian, Aegean and Mediterranean Seas
GOVT. — Republic
AREA — 50,949 sq. mi.
POP. — 10,511,000 (1997 est.)
CAPITAL — Athens

In 1923 the reigning king was forced to abdicate and the following year Greece was declared a republic. In 1935, the king was recalled by a "plebiscite" of the people. Greece became a republic in June 1973. The country today includes the Aegean Islands of Chios, Mytilene (Lesbos), Samos, Icaria (Nicaria) and Lemnos, the Ionian Islands (Corfu, etc.) Crete, Macedonia, Western Thrace and part of Eastern Thrace, the Mount Athos District, Epirus and the Dodecanese Islands.

100 Lepta = 1 Drachma
100 Cents = 1 Euro (2002)

**Catalogue values for unused stamps in this country are for Never Hinged items, beginning with Scott 472 in the regular postage section, Scott B1 in the semipostal section, Scott C48 in the airpost section, Scott CB1 in the airpost semi-postal section, Scott RA69 in the postal tax section, and Scott N239 in the occupation and annexation section.**

Values for unused stamps are for examples with original gum as defined in the catalogue introduction. Any exceptions will be noted.

Values for Large Hermes Head stamps with double control numbers on the back, Nos. 20e, 21c, 27a, et al, are for examples with two distinct and separate impressions, not for blurred or "slide doubles" caused by paper slippage on the press.

### Watermarks

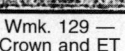

Wmk. 129 — Crown and ET

Wmk. 252 — Crowns

### Paris Print

Hermes (Mercury) — A1

Paris Print, Fine Impression

The enlarged illustrations show the head in various states of the plates. The differences are best seen in the shading lines on the cheek and neck.

**1861 Unwmk. Typo. *Imperf.***

**Without Figures on Back**

| | | | | |
|---|---|---|---|---|
| **1** | A1 | 1 l choc, *brnish* | 600.00 | 550.00 |
| *a.* | | 1 l red brown, *brnish* | 725.00 | 600.00 |
| *b.* | | 1 l brown | 575.00 | 475.00 |
| **2** | A1 | 2 l ol bis, *straw* | 67.50 | 87.50 |
| *a.* | | 2 l brown buff, *buff* | 55.00 | 75.00 |
| *b.* | | 2 l yellowish bister | 55.00 | 75.00 |
| **3** | A1 | 5 l yel grn, *grnsh* | 700.00 | 150.00 |
| *a.* | | 5 l emerald green | 875.00 | 175.00 |
| **4** | A1 | 20 l bl, *bluish* | 1,150. | 95.00 |
| *a.* | | 20 l deep blue, *bluish* | 1,100. | 340.00 |
| *b.* | | On pelure paper | 1,350. | *275.00* |
| **5** | A1 | 40 l vio, *bl* | 325.00 | 130.00 |
| **6** | A1 | 80 l rose, *pink* | 250.00 | 120.00 |
| *a.* | | 80 l carmine, *pink* | 250.00 | 120.00 |

**Large Figures, 8mm high, on Back**

| | | | | |
|---|---|---|---|---|
| **7** | A1 | 10 l red org, *bl* | 1,040. | 500.00 |
| *a.* | | "10" on back inverted | — | — |
| *c.* | | "0" of "10" invtd. on back | — | *1,850.* |
| *d.* | | "1" of "10" invtd. on back | — | *2,750.* |

No. 7 without "10" on back is a proof.

Trial impressions of Paris prints exist in many shades, some being close to those of the issued stamps. The gum used was thin and smooth instead of thick, brownish and crackly as on the issued stamps.

See #8-58. For surcharges see #130, 132-133, 137-139, 141-143, 147-149, 153-154, 157-158.

Faint quadrille, horizontal or vertical lines are visible in the background of some Athens print large Hermes head stamps.

Nos. 16, 16a, 16b are the only 1 l stamps that have these lines.

### Athens Prints

Athens Print, Typical Fine Impression

Athens Print, Typical Coarse Impression

**Figures on Back**

5 l:

#11 #18-45

**Fine Printing (F)**
**Fine Printing (F, '62) see footnote**
**Coarse Printing (C)**

**1861-62 Without Figures on Back**

| | | | | |
|---|---|---|---|---|
| **8** | A1 | 1 l choc, *brnish* (F, '62) | 490.00 | *490.00* |
| | | No gum | 350.00 | |
| *a.* | | 1 l dk chocolate, *brnish* (F) | 1,300. | 1,325. |
| | | No gum | 700.00 | |
| *b.* | | 1 l chocolate, *brnish* (F) | 590.00 | 590.00 |
| | | No gum | 460.00 | |
| **9** | A1 | 2 l bis brn, *bister* (F) | 75.00 | *110.00* |
| | | No gum | 40.00 | |
| *a.* | | 2 l dark brown, *straw,* (C) | *6,750.* | — |
| *b.* | | 2 l bister brown, *bister* (C) | 90.00 | *135.00* |
| *c.* | | 2 l bister brown, *bister* (F, '62) | 90.00 | *135.00* |
| **10** | A1 | 20 l dk bl, *bluish* (C) | | *15,000.* |

**With Figures on Back**

| | | | | |
|---|---|---|---|---|
| **11** | A1 | 5 l grn, *grnsh* (F) | 300.00 | 135.00 |
| | | No gum | 175.00 | |
| *a.* | | 5 l green, *greenish* (C) | 375.00 | 190.00 |
| *b.* | | As "a," double "5" on back (F, C) | | *2,850.* |
| *c.* | | 5 l green, *greenish,* bl grn figures on back (F, '62) | 350.00 | 135.00 |
| **12** | A1 | 10 l org, *grnsh* (F, '62) | 600.00 | 90.00 |
| | | No gum | 325.00 | |
| *a.* | | 10 l orange, *greenish* (C) | 1,950. | 300.00 |
| *c.* | | 10 l orange, *greenish* (F) | 600.00 | 135.00 |
| **13** | A1 | 20 l blue, *bluish* (F, '62) | *475.00* | 57.50 |
| *a.* | | 20 l dull blue, *bluish* (C) | *6,750.* | 245.00 |
| *b.* | | 20 l dark blue, *bluish,* (F) | *3,500.* | 110.00 |
| **14** | A1 | 40 l red vio, *pale bl* (F, '62) | *5,250.* | 475.00 |
| *a.* | | 40 l red violet, *blue* (C) | *10,000.* | 600.00 |
| *b.* | | 40 l red violet, *blue,* (F) | *5,250.* | 475.00 |
| **15** | A1 | 80 l carmine, *pink* (F, '62) | 1,200. | 165.00 |
| *a.* | | 80 l carmine, *pink* (F) | 1,200. | 165.00 |
| *b.* | | 80 l dl rose, *pink* (F) | 1,200. | 165.00 |

Nos. 8-15 are known as the "Athens Provisionals." The first printings were not very successful, producing the "coarse printings." Later printings used an altered printing method that gave better results (the "fine printings"). All these were issued in the normal manner by the Post Office.

Nos. 8, 9c, 11c, 12, 13, 14, 15 have uninterrupted and even shading lines that do not taper off at the ends. They were produced in May 1862 (F, '62). Other fine printing stamps were produced in Feb.-Apr. 1862 (F).

The numerals on the back are strongly shaded in the right lines with the corresponding left lines being quite thin. The colors of the numerals are generally strong and often show clumps of ink.

Nos. 15a and 15b have vermilion figures on the back, while those of all later printings are carmine.

Athens Print, Consecutive Print

**With Figures on Back**
**Except 1 l, 2 l**

**1862-67**

| | | | | |
|---|---|---|---|---|
| **16** | A1 | 1 l brn, *brnish* (poor print) | 60.00 | 60.00 |
| *a.* | | 1 l red brn, *brnish* (poor print) | 150.00 | 150.00 |
| *b.* | | 1 l choc, *brnish* | 67.50 | 67.50 |
| **17** | A1 | 2 l bister, *bister* | 55.00 | *60.00* |
| *a.* | | 2 l brnsh bis, *bister* | 13.00 | *24.00* |
| **18** | A1 | 5 l grn, *grnsh* | 250.00 | 24.00 |
| *a.* | | 5 l yellowish green, *grnsh* | 250.00 | 12.00 |
| **19** | A1 | 10 l org, *blue* ('64) | 400.00 | 47.50 |
| *a.* | | 10 l yel org, *bluish* | 650.00 | 60.00 |
| *b.* | | As "b," "10" inverted on front of stamp | | *23,500.* |
| *c.* | | 10 l red org, *bl* (Dec. '65) | *650.00* | 27.50 |
| *d.* | | "01" on back | *9,000.* | *175.00* |
| **20** | A1 | 20 l bl, *bluish* | 250.00 | 24.00 |
| *a.* | | 20 l lt bl, *bluish* (fine print) | 375.00 | 24.00 |
| *b.* | | 20 l dark blue, *bluish* | 2,000. | 67.50 |
| *c.* | | 20 l blue, *greenish* | *1,700.* | 37.50 |
| *d.* | | "80" on back | | *2,450.* |
| *e.* | | Double "20" on back | | *1,500.* |
| *f.* | | Without "20" on back | | *5,500.* |
| **21** | A1 | 40 l lilac, *bl* | 550.00 | 37.50 |
| *a.* | | 40 l grayish lilac, *blue* | 1,750. | 37.50 |
| *b.* | | 40 l lilac brown, *lil gray* | *1,500.* | 47.50 |
| *c.* | | Double "40" on back | | 1,600. |
| **22** | A1 | 80 l car, *pale rose* | 80.00 | 24.00 |
| *a.* | | 80 l rose, *pale rose* | 80.00 | 24.00 |
| *b.* | | "8" on back inverted | — | 550.00 |
| *c.* | | "80" on back inverted | | — |
| *d.* | | "8" only on back | | 700.00 |
| *e.* | | "0" only on back | | 700.00 |

Nos. 16-22 represent a series of printings for each value, from 1862 through 1867, until a major cleaning of the plates was done in 1868. Impressions range from very fine and clear to coarse and blotchy.

Some printings of Nos. 16, 16a, 16b show faint vertical, horizontal or quadrilled lines in the background. Later 1 l stamps do not show these lines.

Many stamps of this and succeeding issues which are normally imperforate are known privately rouletted, pin-perforated, percé en scie, etc.

### With Figures on Back, Except 1 l, 2 l

**1868 From Cleaned Plates**

23 A1 1 l gray brn, *brnish* 67.50 75.00
24 A1 2 l gray bis, *bister* 32.50 *47.50*
25 A1 5 l grn, *grnsh* *6,500.* 150.00
a. 5 l yellow green, *grnsh* 6,500. 50.00
26 A1 10 l pale org, *bluish* *1,650.* 40.00
a. "01" on back — —
27 A1 20 l pale bl, *bluish* *1,500.* 24.00
a. Double "20" on back — *1,450.*
28 A1 40 l rose vio, *bl* 325.00 37.50
a. "20" on back, corrected to "40" — *2,750.*
29 A1 80 l rose car, *pale rose* 190.00 250.00

The "0" on the back of No. 29 is printed more heavily than the "8."

### With Figures on Back, Except 1 l

**1870**

30 A1 1 l deep reddish brn, *brnish* 175.00 *200.00*
a. 1 l redsh brn, *brnish* 200.00 *240.00*
31 A1 20 l lt bl, *bluish* *1,900.* 24.00
a. 20 l blue, *bluish* *2,000.* 35.00
b. "02" on back 1,225.
c. "20" on back inverted 675.00

Nos. 30 and 30a have short lines of shading on cheek. The spandrels of No. 31 are very pale with the lines often broken or missing.

This was an Athens Printing made under supervision of German workmen.

### Medium to Thin Paper
### With Figures on Back, Except 1 l, 2 l

**1870 Without Mesh**

32 A1 1 l brn, *brnish* 325.00 325.00
a. 1 l purple brown, *brnish* 325.00 325.00
33 A1 2 l sal bis, *bister* 19.00 *45.00*
34 A1 5 l grn, *grnsh* *6,000.* 120.00
35 A1 10 l lt red org, *grnsh* — 240.00
a. "01" on back — —
b. "10" on back inverted — —
36 A1 20 l bl, *bluish* *1,400.* 24.00
a. "02" on back — 600.00
b. Double "20" on back — 1,375.
37 A1 40 l sal, *grnsh* 825.00 82.50
a. 40 l lilac, *greenish* *75,000.*

The stamps of this issue have rather coarse figures on back.

No. 37a is printed in the exact shade of the numerals on the back of No. 37.

### Thin Transparent Paper
### With Figures on Back, Except 1 l

**1872 Showing Mesh**

38 A1 1 l grayish brown, *straw* 55.00 *75.00*
a. 1 l red brn, *yelsh* 82.50 *115.00*
39 A1 5 l grn, *greenish* 675.00 30.00
a. 5 l dark green, *grnsh* 725.00 40.00
b. Double "5" on back 225.00
40 A1 10 l red org, *grnsh* *1,050.* 37.50
a. 10 l red orange, *pale lilac* *7,750.* 150.00
b. As #40, "10" on back inverted — 90.00
c. Double "10" on back — 1,125.
d. "0" on back — 525.00
e. "01" on back — *2,100.*
41 A1 20 l dp bl, *bluish* 1,375. 30.00
a. 20 l blue, *bluish* 1,375. 32.50
b. 20 l dark blue, *blue* 2,500. 55.00
42 A1 40 l brn, *bl* 45.00 *67.50*
a. 40 l olive brown, *blue* 45.00 *70.00*
b. 40 l red violet, *blue* 1,000. 95.00
c. 40 l gray violet, *blue* 825.00 75.00
d. Figures on back bister (#42b, 42c) 1,100. 95.00

The mesh is not apparent on Nos. 38, 38a.

### On Cream Paper Unless Otherwise Stated
### With Figures on Back, Except 1 l, 2 l

**1875**

43 A1 1 l gray brn 15.00 12.00
a. 1 l Deep red brown 35.00 20.00
b. 1 l black brown, *yellowish* 175.00 *160.00*
c. 1 l red brown 45.00 *60.00*
d. 1 l dark red brown 75.00 *87.50*
e. 1 l purple brown 75.00 *87.50*
44 A1 2 l bister 30.00 *32.50*
45 A1 5 l pale yellow green 200.00 30.00
a. 5 l dk yel grn 275.00 40.00
46 A1 10 l orange 425.00 45.00
a. 10 l orange, *yellow* 240.00 25.00
c. "00" on back 925.00 200.00
d. "1" on back — 260.00
e. "0" on back — 225.00
f. "01" on back — 535.00
g. Double "10" on back — 800.00
47 A1 20 l ultra 160.00 24.00
a. 20 l blue 290.00 24.00
b. 20 l deep Prussian blue 1,600. 60.00
c. "02" on back — 475.00
d. "20" on back inverted — *11,000.*
e. "2" instead of "20," inverted — *3,000.*
f. Double "20" on back — 1,350.
g. "20" inverted, on front of stamp 210,000.
48 A1 40 l salmon 30.00 *90.00*

The back figures are found in many varieties, including "1" and "0" inverted in "10."

Value for No. 47e is for example with "2" of "02" broken (deformed). Also known with unbroken "2"; value used about $600.

### Paris Print, Clear Impression

**1876 Without Figures on Back**

49 A1 30 l ol brn, *yelsh* 290.00 60.00
a. 30 l brown, *yellowish* 500.00 135.00
50 A1 60 l grn, *grnsh* 40.00 *115.00*

### Athens Print, Coarse Impression, Yellowish Paper

51 A1 30 l dark brown 75.00 13.50
a. 30 l black brown 75.00 13.50
52 A1 60 l green 625.00 67.50

### Without Figures on Back

**1880-82 Cream Paper**

53 A1 5 l green 30.00 9.50
54 A1 10 l orange 27.50 9.50
a. 10 l yellow 27.50 9.50
b. 10 l red orange *8,250.* 75.00
55 A1 20 l ultra 450.00 190.00
56 A1 20 l pale rose (aniline ink) ('82) 8.25 8.25
a. 20 l rose (aniline ink) ('82) 8.25 8.25
b. 20 l deep carmine *275.00* 17.50
57 A1 30 l ultra ('82) 225.00 17.50
a. 30 l slate blue 230.00 17.50
58 A1 40 l lilac 67.50 15.00
a. 40 l violet 67.50 24.00

Stamps of type A1 were not regularly issued with perf. 11½ but were freely used on mail.

Hermes — A2

Lepta denominations have white numeral tablets.

### Belgian Print, Clear Impression

**1886-88 *Imperf.***

64 A2 1 l brown ('88) 4.00 4.00
65 A2 2 l bister ('88) 9.50 *225.00*
66 A2 5 l yel grn ('88) 12.00 2.75
67 A2 10 l yellow ('88) 16.00 2.40
68 A2 20 l car rose ('88) 45.00 4.00
69 A2 25 l blue 160.00 2.75
70 A2 40 l violet ('88) 105.00 30.00
71 A2 50 l gray grn 8.25 2.75
72 A2 1d gray 120.00 4.00
*Nos. 64-72 (9)* 479.75 277.65

See Nos. 81-116. For surcharges see Nos. 129, 134, 140, 144, 150, 151-152, 155-156.

**1891 *Perf. 11½***

81 A2 1 l brown 8.25 3.50
82 A2 2 l bister 13.50 —
83 A2 5 l yel grn 27.50 13.00
84 A2 10 l yellow 40.00 13.00
85 A2 20 l car rose 55.00 18.00
86 A2 25 l blue 275.00 25.00
87 A2 40 l violet 190.00 190.00
88 A2 50 l gray grn 22.50 6.50
89 A2 1d gray 200.00 8.25
*Nos. 81-89 (9)* 831.75 277.25

The Belgian Printings perf. 13½ and most of the values perf. 11½ (Nos. 82-86) were perforated on request of philatelists at the main post office in Athens. While not regularly issued they were freely used for postage.

### Athens Print, Poor Impression
### Wmk. Greek Words in Some Sheets

**1889-95 *Imperf.***

90 A2 1 l black brn 6.75 2.75
a. 1 l brown 6.75 4.00
91 A2 2 l pale bister 1.75 1.60
a. 2 l buff 2.75 *2.75*
92 A2 5 l green 11.00 1.60
a. Double impression *200.00* —
b. 5 l deep green 40.00 9.50
93 A2 10 l yellow 125.00 5.50
a. 10 l orange 47.50 4.00
b. 10 l dull yellow 125.00 5.50
94 A2 20 l carmine 11.00 8.25
a. 20 l rose 75.00 40.00
95 A2 25 l dull blue 125.00 9.50
a. 25 l indigo 150.00 6.75
b. 25 l ultra 125.00 6.75
c. 25 l brt blue 135.00 9.50
96 A2 25 l lilac 13.50 2.75
a. 25 l red vio ('93) 20.00 4.00
97 A2 40 l red vio ('91) 125.00 27.50
98 A2 40 l blue ('93) 9.50 2.75
99 A2 1d gray ('95) 475.00 8.25

***Perf. 13½***

100 A2 1 l brown 80.00 —
101 A2 2 l buff 2.00 1.60
104 A2 20 l carmine 67.50 5.25
a. 20 l rose 80.00 6.25
105 A2 40 l red violet 130.00 47.50

Other denominations of type A2 were not officially issued with perf. 13½.

***Perf. 11½***

107 A2 1 l brown 3.00 1.60
a. 1 l black brown 7.25 5.75
108 A2 2 l pale bister 2.50 2.00
a. 2 l buff 2.75 2.75
109 A2 5 l pale green 13.50 2.00
a. 5 l deep green 55.00 3.00
110 A2 10 l yellow 95.00 1.25
a. 10 l dull yellow 165.00 2.50
b. 10 l orange 300.00 5.75
111 A2 20 l carmine 55.00 .75
a. 20 l rose 160.00 1.60
112 A2 25 l dull blue 110.00 3.75
a. 25 l indigo 300.00 21.00
b. 25 l ultra 110.00 52.50
c. 25 l bright blue 160.00 9.00
113 A2 25 l lilac 6.75 1.60
a. 25 l red violet 20.00 2.75
114 A2 40 l red violet 160.00 37.50
115 A2 40 l blue 16.50 2.75
116 A2 1d gray 600.00 10.00

Partly-perforated varieties sell for about twice as much as normal stamps.

The watermark on Nos. 90-116 consists of three Greek words meaning Paper for Public Service. It is in double-lined capitals, measures 270x35mm, and extends across three panes.

Boxers — A3

Discobolus by Myron — A4

Vase Depicting Pallas Athene (Minerva) — A5

Chariot Driving A6

Stadium and Acropolis A7

Statue of Hermes by Praxiteles — A8

Statue of Victory by Paeonius — A9

Acropolis and Parthenon A10

***Perf. 14x13½, 13½x14***

**1896 Unwmk.**

117 A3 1 l ocher 4.00 3.00
118 A3 2 l rose 3.00 3.00
a. Without engraver's name 30.00 21.00
119 A4 5 l lilac 12.50 5.25
120 A4 10 l slate gray 12.50 7.25
121 A5 20 l red brn 25.00 8.25
122 A6 25 l red 30.00 10.50
123 A5 40 l violet 14.50 9.50
124 A6 60 l black 42.50 21.00
125 A7 1d blue 115.00 26.00
126 A8 2d bister 325.00 105.00
a. Horiz. pair, imperf. btwn. — —
127 A9 5d green 575.00 500.00
128 A10 10d brown 625.00 550.00
*Nos. 117-128 (12)* 1,784. 1,248.

1st intl. Olympic Games of the modern era, held at Athens. Counterfeits of Nos. 123-124 and 126-128 exist.

For surcharges see Nos. 159-164.

Preceding Issues Surcharged

**1900 *Imperf.***

129 A2 20 l on 25 l dl bl, #95c 3.00 1.60
a. 20 l on 25 l indigo, #95a 67.50 47.50
b. 20 l on 25 l ultra, #95b 70.00 55.00
c. Double surcharge 57.50 57.50
d. Triple surcharge 85.00 85.00
e. Inverted surcharge 60.00 57.50
f. "20" above word 110.00 105.00
g. Pair, one without surcharge 250.00 250.00
h. "20" without word 165.00 165.00
130 A1 30 l on 40 l vio, *cr*, #58a 6.50 6.25
a. 30 l on 40 l lilac, #58 15.50 15.50
b. Broad "0" in "30" 10.50 8.25
c. First letter of word is "A" 135.00 135.00
d. Double surcharge *625.00* *625.00*
132 A1 40 l on 2 l bis, *cr*, #44 8.50 8.25
a. Broad "0" in "40" 12.50 12.50
b. First letter of word is "A" 165.00 165.00
133 A1 50 l on 40 l sal, *cr*, #48 6.25 6.25
a. Broad "0" in "50" 10.00 8.25
b. First letter of word is "A" 135.00 135.00
c. "50" without word 200.00 175.00
d. "50" above word 200.00 175.00
134 A2 1d on 40 l red vio (No. 97) 15.50 6.25
137 A1 3d on 10 l org, *cr*, #54 52.50 52.50
a. 3d on 10 l yellow, #54a 52.50 52.50
138 A1 5d on 40 l red vio, *bl*, #21 150.00 150.00
a. 5d on 40 l red vio, *bl*, #28 190.00 *190.00*
b. "20" on back corrected to "40" *1,400.*
139 A1 5d on 40 l red vio, *bl*, #42b 575.00

***Perf. 11½***

140 A2 20 l on 25 l dl bl, #112 3.25 3.25
a. 20 l on 25 l indigo, #112a 100.00 90.00
b. 20 l on 25 l ultra, #112b 80.00 77.50
c. Double surcharge 67.50 70.00
d. Triple surcharge 95.00 95.00
e. Inverted surcharge 67.50 67.50
f. "20" above word 150.00 150.00
141 A1 30 l on 40 l vio, *cr*, #58a 10.50 10.50
a. 30 l on 40 l lilac, #58 17.50 17.50
b. Broad "0" in "30" 12.50 12.50
c. First letter of word is "A" 150.00 150.00
d. Double surcharge
142 A1 40 l on 2 l bis, *cr*, #44 15.50 15.50
a. Broad "0" in "40" 15.50 15.50
b. First letter of word is "A" 165.00 165.00
143 A1 50 l on 40 l sal, *cr*, #48 10.50 10.50
a. Broad "0" in "50" 12.50 12.50
b. First letter of word is "A" 135.00 135.00
c. "50" without word 200.00 175.00
144 A2 1d on 40 l red vio, #114 145.00 160.00
147 A1 3d on 10 l yel, *cream*, #54a 57.50 57.50
a. 3d on 10 l org, *cr*, #54 60.00 *65.00*
148 A1 5d on 40 l red vio, *bl*, #21 150.00 175.00
a. 5d on 40 l red vio, *bl*, #28 175.00 *225.00*
149 A1 5d on 40 l red vio, *bl*, #42b 625.00

***Perf. 13½***

150 A2 2d on 40 l red vio, #105 12.00 12.50

The 1d on 40 l perf. 13½ and the 2d on 40 l, both imperf. and perf. 13½, were not officially issued.

### Surcharge Including "A M"

"A M" = "Axia Metalliki" or "Value in Metal (gold)."

**1900 *Imperf.***

151 A2 25 l on 40 l vio, #70 6.00 10.50
152 A2 50 l on 25 l bl, #69 26.50 24.00
153 A1 1d on 40 l brn, *bl*, #42b 125.00 *150.00*
154 A1 2d on 5 l grn, *cr*, #53 16.00 *21.00*

*Perf. 11½*

| | | | | |
|---|---|---|---|---|
| **155** | A2 | 25 l on 40 l vio, #87 | 12.00 | 15.50 |
| **156** | A2 | 50 l on 25 l bl, #86 | 52.50 | 62.50 |
| **157** | A1 | 1d on 40 l brn, *bl,* #42b | 160.00 | 160.00 |
| **158** | A1 | 2d on 5 l grn, *cr,* #53 | 20.00 | 26.00 |
| | | *Nos. 151-158 (8)* | 418.00 | 469.50 |

Partly-perforated varieties of Nos. 129-158 sell for about two to three times as much as normal stamps.

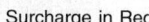

Surcharge in Red

**1900-01** *Perf. 14x13½*

| | | | | |
|---|---|---|---|---|
| **159** | A7 | 5 l on 1d blue | 15.00 | 9.50 |
| *a.* | | Wrong font "M" with serifs | 75.00 | *80.00* |
| *b.* | | Double surcharge | 225.00 | 200.00 |
| **160** | A5 | 25 l on 40 l vio | 70.00 | 67.50 |
| *a.* | | Double surcharge | 900.00 | |
| **161** | A8 | 50 l on 2d bister | 80.00 | 62.50 |
| *a.* | | Broad "0" in "50" | 80.00 | 62.50 |
| **162** | A9 | 1d on 5d grn ('01) | 250.00 | 200.00 |
| *a.* | | Greek "Λ" instead of "A" as 3rd letter | 650.00 | 700.00 |
| **163** | A10 | 2d on 10d brn ('01) | 70.00 | *100.00* |
| *a.* | | Greek "Λ" instead of "A" as 3rd letter | 275.00 | 250.00 |
| | | *Nos. 159-163 (5)* | 485.00 | 439.50 |

Black Surcharge on No. 160

| | | | | |
|---|---|---|---|---|
| **164** | A5 | 50 l on 25 l on 40 l vio (R + Bk) | 500.00 | 475.00 |
| *a.* | | Broad "0" in "50" | 475.00 | *575.00* |

Nos. 151-164 and 179-183, gold currency stamps, were generally used for parcel post and foreign money orders. They were also available for use on letters, but cost about 20 per cent more than the regular stamps of the same denomination.

Counterfeit surcharges exist of #159-164.

Giovanni da Bologna's Hermes
A11 A12

A13

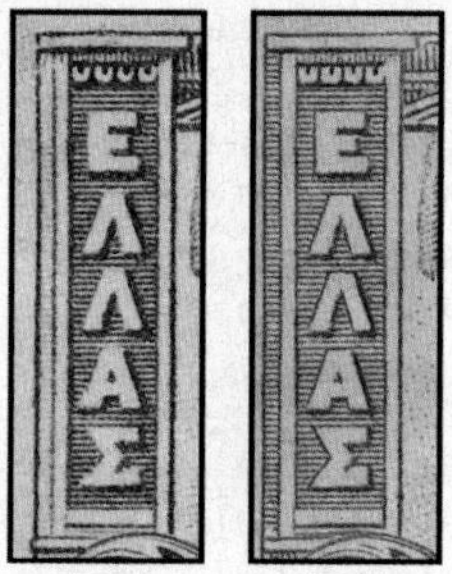

Type I Type II

FIVE LEPTA.

Type I — Letters of "ΕΛΛΑΣ" not outlined at top and left. Only a few faint horizontal lines between the outer vertical lines at sides.

Type II — Letters of "ΕΛΛΑΣ" fully outlined. Heavy horizontal lines between the vertical frame lines.

*Perf. 11½, 12½, 13½*

**1901** **Engr.** **Wmk. 129**

| | | | | |
|---|---|---|---|---|
| **165** | A11 | 1 l yellow brn | .40 | .25 |
| **166** | A11 | 2 l gray | .60 | .25 |
| **167** | A11 | 3 l orange | .65 | .30 |
| **168** | A12 | 5 l grn, type I | .80 | .25 |
| *a.* | | 5 l yellow green, type I | .60 | .25 |
| *b.* | | 5 l yellow green, type II | .60 | .25 |
| **169** | A12 | 10 l rose | 3.25 | .25 |
| **170** | A11 | 20 l red lilac | 6.50 | .25 |
| **171** | A12 | 25 l ultra | 6.50 | .25 |
| **172** | A11 | 30 l dl vio | 12.00 | 2.00 |
| **173** | A11 | 40 l dk brn | 25.00 | 3.00 |
| **174** | A11 | 50 l brn lake | 20.00 | 1.50 |

*Perf. 12½, 14 and Compound*

| | | | | |
|---|---|---|---|---|
| **175** | A13 | 1d black | 47.50 | 3.00 |
| *a.* | | Horiz. pair, imperf. btwn. | 325.00 | |
| *c.* | | Horiz. pair, imperf. vert. | 300.00 | |
| *d.* | | Vert. pair, imperf. horiz. | 300.00 | |

**Litho.**

*Perf. 12½*

| | | | | |
|---|---|---|---|---|
| **176** | A13 | 2d bronze | 11.00 | 8.00 |
| **177** | A13 | 3d silver | 11.00 | *12.00* |
| **178** | A13 | 5d gold | 13.00 | *15.00* |
| | | *Nos. 165-178 (14)* | 158.20 | 46.30 |
| | | Set, never hinged | 325.00 | |

All values 1 l through 1d issued on both thick and thin paper. Nos. 173-174 are values for thin paper — values for thick paper are higher.

For overprints and surcharges see Nos. RA3-RA13, N16, N109.

**Imperf., Pairs**

| | | | |
|---|---|---|---|
| *165a* | A11 | 1 l | 12.00 |
| *166a* | A11 | 2 l | 15.00 |
| *167a* | A11 | 3 l | 15.00 |
| *168c* | A12 | 5 l | 12.00 |
| *169a* | A12 | 10 l | 19.00 |
| *170a* | A11 | 20 l | 15.00 |
| *171a* | A12 | 25 l | 15.00 |
| *172a* | A11 | 30 l | 250.00 |
| *173a* | A11 | 40 l | 300.00 |
| *174a* | A11 | 50 l | 70.00 |
| *175b* | A13 | 1d | 250.00 |

Nos. 165a-175a were issued on both thick and thin paper. Values are for the less expensive thin paper.

Hermes — A14

**1902, Jan. 1** **Engr.** *Perf. 13½*

| | | | | |
|---|---|---|---|---|
| **179** | A14 | 5 l deep orange | 2.00 | 1.10 |
| *a.* | | Imperf., pair | 82.50 | |
| **180** | A14 | 25 l emerald | 30.00 | 3.00 |
| **181** | A14 | 50 l ultra | 30.00 | 3.75 |
| *a.* | | Imperf., pair | 550.00 | |
| **182** | A14 | 1d rose red | 30.00 | 8.25 |
| **183** | A14 | 2d orange brn | 52.50 | 50.00 |
| | | *Nos. 179-183 (5)* | 144.50 | 66.10 |
| | | Set, never hinged | 375.00 | |

See note after No. 164. In 1913 remainders of Nos. 179-183 were used as postage dues.

Apollo Throwing Discus A15

Jumper, with Jumping Weights A16

Victory — A17

Atlas and Hercules A18

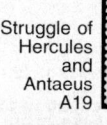

Struggle of Hercules and Antaeus A19

Wrestlers A20

Daemon of the Games A21

Foot Race A22

Nike, Priest and Athletes in Pre-Games Offering to Zeus A23

**Wmk. Crown and ET (129)**

**1906, Mar.** **Engr.** *Perf. 13½, 14*

| | | | | |
|---|---|---|---|---|
| **184** | A15 | 1 l brown | .55 | .40 |
| *a.* | | Imperf., pair | *300.00* | |
| **185** | A15 | 2 l gray | .55 | .40 |
| *a.* | | Imperf., pair | *300.00* | |
| **186** | A16 | 3 l orange | .55 | .40 |
| *a.* | | Imperf., pair | 300.00 | |
| **187** | A16 | 5 l green | 1.25 | .40 |
| *a.* | | Imperf., pair | 110.00 | |
| **188** | A17 | 10 l rose red | 3.00 | .60 |
| *a.* | | Imperf., pair | *300.00* | |
| **189** | A18 | 20 l magenta | 5.00 | .60 |
| *a.* | | Imperf., pair | *575.00* | |
| **190** | A19 | 25 l ultra | 6.00 | .85 |
| *a.* | | Imperf., pair | *575.00* | |
| **191** | A20 | 30 l dl pur | 5.00 | 2.75 |
| *a.* | | Double impression | *1,100.* | |
| **192** | A21 | 40 l dk brown | 5.00 | 2.75 |
| **193** | A18 | 50 l brn lake | 10.00 | 3.25 |
| **194** | A22 | 1d gray blk | 65.00 | 13.00 |
| *a.* | | Imperf., pair | *1,100.* | |
| **195** | A22 | 2d rose | 100.00 | 35.00 |
| **196** | A22 | 3d olive yel | 155.00 | 125.00 |
| **197** | A23 | 5d dull blue | 160.00 | 140.00 |
| | | *Nos. 184-197 (14)* | 516.90 | 325.40 |
| | | Set, never hinged | 1,500. | |

Greek Special Olympic Games of 1906 at Athens, celebrating the 10th anniv. of the modern Olympic Games.

Surcharged stamps of this issue are revenues.

A24

Iris Holding Caduceus A25

Hermes Donning Sandals A26

Hermes Carrying Infant Arcas — A27

Hermes, from Old Cretan Coin — A28

Designs A24 to A28 are from Cretan and Arcadian coins of the 4th Century, B.C.

*Serrate Roulette 13½*

**1911-21** **Engr.** **Unwmk.**

| | | | | |
|---|---|---|---|---|
| **198** | A24 | 1 l green | .65 | .30 |
| **199** | A25 | 2 l car rose | .65 | .30 |
| **200** | A24 | 3 l vermilion | .95 | .30 |
| **201** | A26 | 5 l green | 2.00 | .30 |
| **202** | A24 | 10 l car rose | 9.50 | .30 |
| **203** | A25 | 20 l gray lilac | 3.00 | .80 |
| **204** | A25 | 25 l ultra | 15.00 | .80 |
| *a.* | | Rouletted in black | 190.00 | 140.00 |
| **205** | A26 | 30 l car rose | 4.50 | 1.60 |
| **206** | A25 | 40 l deep blue | 10.00 | 4.00 |
| **207** | A26 | 50 l dl vio | 15.00 | 3.00 |
| **208** | A27 | 1d ultra | 20.00 | .80 |
| **209** | A27 | 2d vermilion | 27.50 | .95 |
| **210** | A27 | 3d car rose | 27.50 | 1.40 |
| *a.* | | Size 20¼x25½mm ('21) | 100.00 | 50.00 |
| **211** | A27 | 5d ultra | 35.00 | 4.00 |
| *a.* | | Size 20¼x25½mm ('21) | 200.00 | 25.00 |
| **212** | A27 | 10d dp bl ('21) | 140.00 | 70.00 |
| *a.* | | Size 20x26½mm ('11) | 300.00 | 125.00 |
| **213** | A28 | 25d deep blue | 87.50 | 55.00 |
| | | *Nos. 198-213 (16)* | 398.75 | 143.85 |
| | | Set, never hinged | 750.00 | |

The 1921 reissues of the 3d, 5d and 10d measure 20¼x25½mm instead of 20x26½mm.

See Nos. 214-231. For overprints see Nos. 233-248B, N1, N10-N15, N17-N52A, N110-N148, Thrace 22-30, N26-N75.

**Imperf., Pairs**

| | | | | | |
|---|---|---|---|---|---|
| *198a* | A24 | 1 l | | 90.00 | 90.00 |
| *200a* | A24 | 3 l | | 240.00 | 240.00 |
| *201a* | A26 | 5 l | | 30.00 | 30.00 |
| *202a* | A24 | 10 l | | 52.50 | 52.50 |
| *203a* | A25 | 20 l | | 225.00 | 225.00 |
| *204b* | A25 | 25 l | | 300.00 | 300.00 |
| *206a* | A25 | 40 l | | 350.00 | |
| *207a* | A26 | 50 l | | 350.00 | |
| *208a* | A27 | 1d | | 350.00 | |
| *209a* | A27 | 2d | | 350.00 | |
| *210b* | A27 | 3d | | 350.00 | |
| *211b* | A27 | 5d | | 240.00 | |
| *212b* | A27 | 10d | As "a" | *1,600.* | |
| *213a* | A28 | 25d | | *2,250.* | |

*Serrate Roulette 10½x13½, 13½*

**1913-23** **Litho.**

| | | | | |
|---|---|---|---|---|
| **214** | A24 | 1 l green | .25 | .25 |
| *a.* | | Without period after "ΕΛΛΑΣ" | 77.50 | — |
| **215** | A25 | 2 l rose | .25 | .25 |
| **216** | A24 | 3 l vermilion | .25 | .25 |
| **217** | A26 | 5 l green | .25 | .25 |
| **218** | A24 | 10 l carmine | .25 | .25 |
| **219** | A25 | 15 l dl bl ('18) | .35 | .25 |
| **220** | A25 | 20 l slate | .35 | .25 |
| **221** | A25 | 25 l ultra | 4.00 | .50 |
| *a.* | | 25 l blue | .20 | |
| *c.* | | Double impression | — | |
| **222** | A26 | 30 l rose ('14) | .95 | .40 |
| **223** | A25 | 40 l indigo ('14) | 2.10 | .70 |
| **224** | A26 | 50 l vio brn ('14) | 4.25 | .35 |
| **225** | A26 | 80 l vio brn ('23) | 5.25 | 1.40 |
| **226** | A27 | 1d ultra ('19) | 7.00 | .70 |
| **227** | A27 | 2d ver ('19) | 6.50 | .70 |
| **228** | A27 | 3d car rose ('20) | 8.50 | .80 |
| **229** | A27 | 5d ultra ('22) | 12.00 | 1.00 |

| | | | | |
|---|---|---|---|---|
| **230** | A27 | 10d dp bl ('22) | 12.00 | 1.25 |
| **231** | A28 | 25d indigo ('22) | 16.00 | 4.75 |
| | | *Nos. 214-231 (18)* | 80.50 | 14.30 |
| | | Set, never hinged | 225.00 | |

Nos. 221, 223 and 226 were re-issued in 1926, printed in Vienna from new plates. There are slight differences in minor details.

The 10 lepta brown, on thick paper, type A28, is not a postage stamp. It was issued in 1922 to replace coins of this denomination during a shortage of copper.

**Imperf., Pairs**

| | | | | |
|---|---|---|---|---|
| *214b* | A24 | 1 l | 65.00 | |
| *215a* | A25 | 2 l | 110.00 | |
| *216a* | A24 | 3 l | 175.00 | |
| *217a* | A26 | 5 l | 65.00 | |
| *218a* | A24 | 10 l | 82.50 | |
| *220a* | A25 | 20 l | 82.50 | |
| *221b* | A25 | 25 l | 175.00 | |
| *222a* | A26 | 30 l | 175.00 | |
| *223a* | A25 | 40 l | 175.00 | |
| *224a* | A26 | 50 l | 300.00 | |
| *225b* | A26 | 80 l | 92.50 | |
| *226a* | A27 | 1d | | 250.00 |
| *227a* | A27 | 2d | 100.00 | |
| *228b* | A27 | 3d | 300.00 | |
| *229a* | A27 | 5d | 360.00 | |

Raising Greek Flag at Suda Bay, Crete
A29

**1913, Dec. 1 Engr. *Perf. 14½***

| | | | | |
|---|---|---|---|---|
| **232** | A29 | 25 l blue & black | 8.00 | 5.00 |
| | | Never hinged | 16.00 | |
| *a.* | | Imperf., pair | *1,400.* | |

Union of Crete with Greece. Used only in Crete.

Stamps of 1911-14 Overprinted in Red or Black

***Serrate Roulette 13½***

**1916, Nov. 1 Litho.**

| | | | | |
|---|---|---|---|---|
| **233** | A24 | 1 l green (R) | .25 | .25 |
| **234** | A25 | 2 l rose | .25 | .25 |
| **235** | A24 | 3 l vermilion | .25 | .25 |
| **236** | A26 | 5 l green (R) | .50 | .40 |
| **237** | A24 | 10 l carmine | .75 | .40 |
| **238** | A25 | 20 l slate (R) | 1.50 | .40 |
| **239** | A25 | 25 l blue (R) | 1.50 | .40 |
| *a.* | | 25 l ultra | 140.00 | 26.00 |
| **240** | A26 | 30 l rose | 1.50 | .90 |
| *a.* | | Pair, one without ovpt. | | |
| **241** | A25 | 40 l indigo (R) | 11.00 | 3.00 |
| **242** | A26 | 50 l vio brn (R) | 37.50 | 2.50 |

**Engr.**

| | | | | |
|---|---|---|---|---|
| **243** | A24 | 3 l vermilion | .50 | .50 |
| **244** | A26 | 30 l car rose | 1.25 | 1.25 |
| **245** | A27 | 1d ultra (R) | 40.00 | .80 |
| *a.* | | Rouletted in black | 325.00 | 225.00 |
| **246** | A27 | 2d vermilion | 24.00 | 3.50 |
| **247** | A27 | 3d car rose | 14.00 | 3.50 |
| **248** | A27 | 5d ultra (R) | 95.00 | 15.00 |
| **248B** | A27 | 10d dp bl (R) | 24.00 | 22.50 |
| | | *Nos. 233-248B (17)* | 253.75 | 55.80 |
| | | Set, never hinged | 500.00 | |

Most of Nos. 233-248B exist with overprint double, inverted, etc. Minimum value of errors $18. Excellent counterfeits of the overprint varieties exist.

**Issued by the Venizelist Provisional Government**

Iris — A32

**1917, Feb. 5 Litho. *Perf. 14***

| | | | | |
|---|---|---|---|---|
| **249** | A32 | 1 l dp green | .40 | .25 |
| **250** | A32 | 5 l yel grn | .40 | .25 |
| **251** | A32 | 10 l rose | .80 | .35 |
| **252** | A32 | 25 l lt blue | 1.10 | .35 |
| **253** | A32 | 50 l gray vio | 9.00 | 2.50 |
| **254** | A32 | 1d ultra | 2.25 | .75 |
| **255** | A32 | 2d lt red | 4.50 | 1.50 |
| **256** | A32 | 3d claret | 25.00 | 7.75 |
| **257** | A32 | 5d gray bl | 5.75 | 3.00 |
| **258** | A32 | 10d dk blue | 70.00 | 20.00 |
| **259** | A32 | 25d slate | 125.00 | *160.00* |
| | | *Nos. 249-259 (11)* | 244.20 | 196.70 |
| | | Set, never hinged | 400.00 | |

The 4d was used only as a revenue stamp.

**Imperf., Pairs**

| | | | |
|---|---|---|---|
| *249a* | A32 | 1 l | 9.50 |
| *250a* | A32 | 5 l | 9.50 |
| *251a* | A32 | 10 l | 9.50 |
| *252a* | A32 | 25 l | 17.50 |
| *253a* | A32 | 50 l | 25.00 |
| *254a* | A32 | 1d | 22.50 |
| *255a* | A32 | 2d | 30.00 |
| *256a* | A32 | 3d | 65.00 |
| *257a* | A32 | 5d | 65.00 |
| *258a* | A32 | 10d | 110.00 |
| *259a* | A32 | 25d | 125.00 |

Stamps of 1917 Surcharged

**1923**

| | | | | |
|---|---|---|---|---|
| **260** | A32 | 5 l on 10 l rose | .25 | .25 |
| *a.* | | Inverted surcharge | 24.00 | *35.00* |
| **261** | A32 | 50 l on 50 l gray vio | .25 | .25 |
| **262** | A32 | 1d on 1d ultra | .25 | .25 |
| *a.* | | 1d on 1d gray | .25 | .25 |
| **263** | A32 | 2d on 2d lt red | .55 | .55 |
| **264** | A32 | 3d on 3d claret | 1.60 | 1.60 |
| **265** | A32 | 5d on 5d dk bl | 2.00 | 2.00 |
| **266** | A32 | 25d on 25d slate | 27.50 | 27.50 |
| | | *Nos. 260-266 (7)* | 32.40 | 32.40 |
| | | Set, never hinged | 125.00 | |

**Same Surcharge on Occupation of Turkey Stamps, 1913**

***Perf. 13½***

| | | | | |
|---|---|---|---|---|
| **267** | O2 | 5 l on 3 l org | .25 | .25 |
| *a.* | | Inverted surcharge | 19.00 | |
| **268** | O1 | 10 l on 20 l vio | 1.50 | 1.50 |
| *a.* | | Inverted surcharge | 82.50 | |
| **269** | O2 | 10 l on 25 l pale bl | .25 | .25 |
| *a.* | | Inverted surcharge | 60.00 | 35.00 |
| **270** | O1 | 10 l on 30 l gray grn | .25 | .25 |
| **271** | O2 | 10 l on 40 l ind | 1.25 | 1.25 |
| **272** | O1 | 50 l on 50 l dk bl | .25 | .25 |
| *a.* | | Inverted surcharge | 72.50 | 37.50 |
| **273** | O1 | 2d on 2d gray brn | 60.00 | 60.00 |
| **274** | O2 | 3d on 3d dl bl | 4.50 | *6.00* |
| *a.* | | Imperf., pair | 500.00 | |
| **275** | O1 | 5d on 5d gray | 4.00 | *7.00* |
| **276** | O2 | 10d on 1d vio brn | 15.00 | *22.50* |
| **276A** | O2 | 10d on 10d car | 800.00 | |
| | | *Nos. 267-276 (10)* | 87.25 | 99.25 |
| | | Set, never hinged | 150.00 | |

Dangerous counterfeits of No. 276A exist.

**Same Surcharge on Stamps of Crete**

***Perf. 14***

**On Crete #50, 52, 59**

| | | | | |
|---|---|---|---|---|
| **276B** | A6 | 5 l on 1 l red brn | 27.50 | 27.50 |
| **277** | A8 | 10 l on 10 l red | .25 | .25 |
| **277B** | A8 | 10 l on 25 l bl | 110.00 | 110.00 |

**On Crete #66-69, 71**

| | | | | |
|---|---|---|---|---|
| **278** | A8 | 10 l on 25 l blue | .25 | .25 |
| **279** | A6 | 50 l on 50 l lilac | .45 | *.70* |
| **279A** | A6 | 50 l on 50 l ultra | 8.50 | *14.00* |
| **280** | A9 | 50 l on 1d gray vio | 3.00 | *4.00* |
| **280A** | A11 | 50 l on 5d grn & blk | 27.50 | 27.50 |

**On Crete #77-82**

| | | | | |
|---|---|---|---|---|
| **281** | A15 | 10 l on 20 l bl grn | 125.00 | 125.00 |
| **282** | A16 | 10 l on 25 l ultra | .45 | .45 |
| *a.* | | Double surcharge | 50.00 | 50.00 |
| **283** | A17 | 50 l on 50 l yel brn | .25 | .35 |
| **284** | A18 | 50 l on 1d rose car & brn | 2.00 | 1.75 |
| *a.* | | Imperf., pair | 425.00 | |
| **285** | A19 | 3d on 3d org & blk | 14.00 | 14.00 |
| **286** | A20 | 5d on 5d ol grn & blk | 9.00 | 9.00 |

**On Crete #83-84**

| | | | | |
|---|---|---|---|---|
| **287** | A21 | 10 l on 25 l bl & blk | 3.25 | 1.75 |
| *a.* | | Imperf., pair | | |
| **287B** | A22 | 50 l on 1d grn & blk | 8.00 | 4.50 |

**On Crete #96**

| | | | | |
|---|---|---|---|---|
| **288** | A23 | 10 l on 10 l brn red | .25 | .25 |
| *a.* | | Inverted surcharge | 45.00 | 40.00 |

**On Crete #91**

| | | | | |
|---|---|---|---|---|
| **288B** | A17 | 50 l on 50 l yel brn | *800.00* | |

Dangerous counterfeits of the overprint on No. 288B are plentiful.

**On Crete #109**

| | | | | |
|---|---|---|---|---|
| **289** | A19 | 3d on 3d org & blk | 17.50 | 17.50 |

**On Crete #111, 113-120**

| | | | | |
|---|---|---|---|---|
| **290** | A6 | 5 l on 1 l vio brn | .25 | .25 |
| *a.* | | Inverted surcharge | 25.00 | |
| **291** | A13 | 5 l on 5 l grn | .25 | .25 |
| *a.* | | Inverted surcharge | 47.50 | |
| **292** | A23 | 10 l on 10 l brn red | .25 | .25 |
| *a.* | | Inverted surcharge | 47.50 | |
| **293** | A15 | 10 l on 20 l bl grn | .30 | .30 |
| *a.* | | Inverted surcharge | 47.50 | |
| **294** | A16 | 10 l on 25 l ultra | .35 | .35 |
| *a.* | | Inverted surcharge | 47.50 | |
| **295** | A17 | 50 l on 50 l yel brn | .40 | .40 |
| **296** | A18 | 50 l on 1d rose car & brn | 5.25 | 5.25 |
| *a.* | | Inverted surcharge | | |
| *b.* | | Double surcharge | 225.00 | |
| *c.* | | Double surch., one invtd. | | |
| *d.* | | Imperf., pair | | |
| **297** | A19 | 3d on 3d org & blk | 16.00 | 16.00 |
| **298** | A20 | 5d on 5d ol grn & blk | 200.00 | 200.00 |

Dangerous counterfeits of No. 298 exist.

**Crete #J2-J9**

| | | | | |
|---|---|---|---|---|
| **299** | D1 | 5 l on 5 l red | .25 | .25 |
| *a.* | | Inverted surcharge | 45.00 | 6.75 |
| **300** | D1 | 5 l on 10 l red | .30 | .30 |
| **301** | D1 | 10 l on 20 l red | 12.00 | 12.00 |
| *a.* | | Inverted surcharge | | |
| **302** | D1 | 10 l on 40 l red | .30 | .30 |
| **303** | D1 | 50 l on 50 l red | .30 | *.55* |
| **304** | D1 | 50 l on 1d red | .30 | .50 |
| *a.* | | Double surcharge | | |
| **305** | D1 | 50 l on 1d on 1d red | 9.50 | 9.50 |
| **306** | D1 | 2d on 2d red | 1.25 | 1.25 |

**On Crete #J11-J13**

| | | | | |
|---|---|---|---|---|
| **307** | D1 | 5 l on 5 l red | 6.00 | 6.00 |
| **308** | D1 | 5 l on 10 l red | 1.50 | 1.50 |
| *a.* | | "ΕΛΛΑΣ" inverted | 6.50 | |
| **309** | D1 | 10 l on 20 l red | 55.00 | 55.00 |

**On Crete #J20-J22, J24-J26**

| | | | | |
|---|---|---|---|---|
| **310** | D1 | 5 l on 5 l red | .25 | .25 |
| **311** | D1 | 5 l on 10 l red | .25 | .25 |
| *a.* | | Inverted surcharge | 12.00 | |
| **312** | D1 | 10 l on 20 l red | .25 | .25 |
| **313** | D1 | 50 l on 50 l red | .55 | .55 |
| **314** | D1 | 50 l on 1d red | 4.00 | 4.00 |
| **315** | D1 | 2d on 2d red | 7.00 | 7.00 |

These surcharged Postage Due stamps were intended for the payment of ordinary postage.

Nos. 260 to 315 were surcharged in commemoration of the revolution of 1922.

Nos. 59, 91, 109, 111, 113-120, J11-J13, J20-J22, J24-J26 are on stamps previously overprinted by Crete.

**Issues of the Republic**

Lord Byron — A33

Byron at Missolonghi — A34

**1924, Apr. 16 Engr. *Perf. 12***

| | | | | |
|---|---|---|---|---|
| **316** | A33 | 80 l dark blue | .55 | .25 |
| **317** | A34 | 2d dk vio & blk | 1.25 | .65 |
| | | Set, never hinged | 3.25 | |

Death of Lord Byron (1788-1824) at Missolonghi.

Tomb of Markos Botsaris — A35

***Serrate Roulette 13½***

**1926, Apr. 24 Litho.**

| | | | | |
|---|---|---|---|---|
| **318** | A35 | 25 l lilac | .85 | .50 |
| | | Never hinged | 1.75 | |

Centenary of the defense of Missolonghi against the Turks.

Corinth Canal
A36

Dodecanese Costume
A37

Macedonian Costume
A38

Monastery of Simon Peter on Mt. Athos
A39

White Tower of Salonika
A40

Temple of Hephaestus
A41

The Acropolis — A42

Cruiser "Georgios Averoff" — A43

Academy of Sciences, Athens — A44

Temple of Hephaestus
A45

Acropolis
A46

***Perf. 12½x13, 13, 13x12½, 13½, 13½x13***

**1927, Apr. 1 Engr.**

| | | | | |
|---|---|---|---|---|
| **321** | A36 | 5 l dark green | .25 | .25 |
| *a.* | | Vert. pair, imperf. horiz. | 140.00 | 92.50 |
| **322** | A37 | 10 l orange red | .30 | .25 |
| *a.* | | Horiz. pair, imperf. between | 140.00 | 92.50 |
| *c.* | | Double impression | 77.50 | |
| **323** | A38 | 20 l violet | .30 | .25 |
| **324** | A39 | 25 l slate blue | .50 | .25 |
| *a.* | | Imperf., pair | 140.00 | 140.00 |
| *b.* | | Vert. pair, imperf. between | 150.00 | 110.00 |
| **325** | A40 | 40 l slate blue | .50 | .25 |
| **326** | A36 | 50 l violet | 1.10 | .25 |
| **327** | A36 | 80 l dk bl & blk | .95 | .25 |
| *a.* | | Imperf., pair | 825.00 | |
| **328** | A41 | 1d dk bl & bis brn (I) | 1.10 | .25 |
| *a.* | | Imperf., pair | 150.00 | 125.00 |
| *b.* | | Center inverted | | *6,500.* |
| *c.* | | Double impression of center | 325.00 | 225.00 |
| *d.* | | Double impression of frame | 325.00 | 225.00 |
| **329** | A42 | 2d dk green & blk | 6.50 | .30 |
| *a.* | | Imperf., pair | 600.00 | *800.00* |
| **330** | A43 | 3d dp violet & blk | 6.00 | .30 |
| *a.* | | Double impression of center | 225.00 | *275.00* |
| *b.* | | Center inverted | | *8,000.* |

| | | | | |
|---|---|---|---|---|
| **331** | A44 | 5d yellow & blk | 15.00 | 2.00 |
| *a.* | | Imperf., pair | 925.00 | 925.00 |
| *b.* | | Center inverted | 10,000. | *4,500.* |
| *c.* | | 5d yellow & green | 110.00 | 37.50 |
| **332** | A45 | 10d brn car & blk | 45.00 | 11.00 |
| **333** | A44 | 15d brt yel grn & blk | 57.50 | 16.00 |
| **334** | A46 | 25d green & blk | 110.00 | 18.00 |
| *a.* | | Double impression of center | | — |
| | | *Nos. 321-334 (14)* | 245.00 | 49.60 |
| | | Set, never hinged | 700.00 | |

See Nos. 364-371 and notes preceding No. 364. For overprints see Nos. RA55, RA57, RA60, RA66, RA70-RA71.

This series as prepared, included a 1 lepton dark brown, type A37, but that value was never issued. Most stamps were burned. Value $300.

Gen. Charles N. Fabvier and Acropolis A47

**1927, Aug. 1** *Perf. 12*

| | | | | |
|---|---|---|---|---|
| **335** | A47 | 1d red | .30 | .25 |
| **336** | A47 | 3d dark blue | 2.00 | .60 |
| **337** | A47 | 6d green | 12.00 | 9.00 |
| | | *Nos. 335-337 (3)* | 14.30 | 9.85 |
| | | Set, never hinged | 42.50 | |

Cent. of the liberation of Athens from the Turks in 1826.

For surcharges see Nos. 376-377.

Bay of Navarino and Pylos A48

Battle of Navarino A49

"Edward" omitted — A50

"Edward" added — A51

Admiral de Rigny — A52

Admiral van der Heyden — A53

Designs: #340-341, Sir Edward Codrington.

***Perf. 13½x12½, 12½x13½, 13x12½, 12½x13***

**1927-28** **Litho.**

| | | | | |
|---|---|---|---|---|
| **338** | A48 | 1.50d gray green | 1.60 | .35 |
| *a.* | | Imperf., pair | 275.00 | |
| *b.* | | Horiz. pair, imperf. btwn. | 875.00 | |
| *c.* | | Horiz. pair, imperf. vert. | 250.00 | |
| **339** | A49 | 4d dk gray bl ('28) | 7.00 | 1.50 |
| **340** | A50 | 5d dk brn & gray | 5.50 | *4.75* |
| *a.* | | 5d blk brn & blk ('28) | 13.00 | 6.50 |
| **341** | A51 | 5d dk brn & blk ('28) | 35.00 | 12.00 |
| **342** | A52 | 5d vio bl & blk ('28) | 35.00 | 12.00 |
| **343** | A53 | 5d lake & blk ('28) | 20.00 | 9.50 |
| | | *Nos. 338-343 (6)* | 104.10 | 40.10 |
| | | Set, never hinged | 275.00 | |

Centenary of the naval battle of Navarino.

For surcharges see Nos. 372-375.

Admiral Lascarina Bouboulina A54

Athanasios Diakos A55

Map of Greece in 1830 and 1930 — A56

Sortie from Missolonghi A58

Patriots Declaring Independence — A57

Portraits: 10 l, Constantine Rhigas Ferreos. 20 l, Gregorios V. 40 l, Prince Alexandros Ypsilantis. No. 345, Bouboulina. No. 355, Diakos. No. 346, Theodoros Kolokotronis. No. 356, Konstantinos Kanaris. No.347, Georgios Karaiskakis. No. 357, Markos Botsaris. 2d, Andreas Miaoulis. 3d, Lazaros Koundouriotis. 5d, Count John Capo d'Istria (Capodistria), statesman and doctor. 10d, Petros Mavromichalis. 15d, Dionysios Solomos. 20d, Adamantios Korais.

### Various Frames

**1930, Apr. 1 Engr.** ***Perf. 13½, 14***

**Imprint of Perkins, Bacon & Co.**

| | | | | |
|---|---|---|---|---|
| **344** | A55 | 10 l brown | .25 | .25 |
| **345** | A54 | 50 l red | .25 | .25 |
| **346** | A54 | 1d car rose | .30 | .30 |
| **347** | A55 | 1.50d lt blue | .40 | .40 |
| **348** | A55 | 2d orange | .45 | .45 |
| **349** | A55 | 5d purple | 1.50 | 1.50 |
| **350** | A54 | 10d gray blk | 6.50 | 6.50 |
| **351** | A54 | 15d yellow grn | 12.00 | 12.00 |
| **352** | A55 | 20d blue blk | 17.50 | 17.50 |

**Imprint of Bradbury, Wilkinson & Co.**

***Perf. 12***

| | | | | |
|---|---|---|---|---|
| **353** | A55 | 20 l black | .25 | .25 |
| **354** | A55 | 40 l blue grn | .25 | .25 |
| **355** | A55 | 50 l brt blue | .25 | .25 |
| **356** | A55 | 1d brown org | .30 | .30 |
| **357** | A55 | 1.50d dk red | .40 | .40 |
| **358** | A55 | 3d dk brown | .65 | .65 |
| **359** | A56 | 4d dk blue | 3.00 | 3.00 |
| **360** | A57 | 25d black | 17.50 | 17.50 |
| **361** | A58 | 50d red brn | 45.00 | 45.00 |
| | | *Nos. 344-361 (18)* | 106.75 | 106.75 |
| | | Set, never hinged | 275.00 | |

Greek independence, cent. Some exist imperf.

Arcadi Monastery and Abbot Gabriel (Mt. Ida in Background) A60

**1930, Nov. 8** ***Perf. 12***

| | | | | |
|---|---|---|---|---|
| **363** | A60 | 8d deep violet | 13.00 | 1.10 |
| | | Never hinged | 55.00 | |

### Issue of 1927 Re-engraved

50 l, Design is clearer, especially "50" and the 10 letters.

Type I

Type II

1d. Type I — Greek letters "Λ," "Α," "Δ" have sharp pointed tops; numerals "1" are 1½mm wide at the foot, and have a straight slanting serif at top.

1d. Type II — Greek letters "Λ," "Α," "Δ" have flat tops; numerals "1" are 2mm wide at foot and the serif at top is slightly curved. Perf. 14.

There are many minor differences in the lines of the two designs.

1d. Type III — The "1" in lower left corner has no serif at left of foot. Lines of temple have been deepened, so details stand out more clearly.

2d. On 1927 stamp the Parthenon is indistinct and blurred. On 1933 stamp it is strongly outlined and clear. Between the two pillars at lower right are four blocks of marble. These blocks are clear and distinct on the 1933 stamp but run together on the 1927 issue.

3d. Design is clearer, especially vertical lines of shading in smoke stacks and reflections in the water. Two or more sides perf. 11½.

10d. Background and shading of entire stamp have been lightened. Detail of frame is clearer and more distinct.

15d. Many more lines of shading in sky and foreground. Engraving is sharp and clear, particularly in frame. Two or more sides perf. 11½.

25d. Background has been lightened and foreground reduced until base of larger upright column is removed and fallen column appears nearly submerged.

Sizes in millimeters:

50 l, 1927, 18x24¾. 1933, 18½x24½.

1d, 1927, 24¾x17¾. 1931, 24¾x17¼. 1933, 24½x18¼.

2d, 1927, 24½x17¾. 1933, 24½x18½.

***Perf. 11½, 11½x12½, 12½x10, 13, 13x12½, 14***

**1931-35**

| | | | | |
|---|---|---|---|---|
| **364** | A36 | 50 l dk vio ('33) | 4.00 | 1.00 |
| **365** | A41 | 1d dk bl & org brn, type II | 10.00 | 1.00 |
| **366** | A41 | 1d dk bl & org brn, type III ('33) | 5.75 | .25 |
| **367** | A42 | 2d dk grn & blk ('33) | 2.75 | .50 |
| **368** | A43 | 3d red vio & blk ('34) | 3.25 | .25 |
| *a.* | | Imperf., pair | | |
| **369** | A45 | 10d brn car & blk ('35) | 47.50 | 1.50 |
| **370** | A44 | 15d pale yel grn & blk ('34) | 82.50 | 17.50 |
| *a.* | | Imperf., pair | *1,100.* | |
| **371** | A46 | 25d dk grn & blk ('35) | 25.00 | 17.00 |
| | | *Nos. 364-371 (8)* | 180.75 | 39.00 |
| | | Set, never hinged | 600.00 | |

Nos. 336-337, 340-343 Surcharged in Red

**1932** ***Perf. 12½x13½, 12½x13***

| | | | | |
|---|---|---|---|---|
| **372** | A52 | 1.50d on 5d | 2.00 | .25 |
| **373** | A53 | 1.50d on 5d | 2.00 | .25 |
| *a.* | | Double surcharge | 110.00 | |
| **374** | A50 | 2d on 5d | 5.00 | .25 |
| **375** | A51 | 2d on 5d | 9.00 | .25 |

***Perf. 12***

| | | | | |
|---|---|---|---|---|
| **376** | A47 | 2d on 3d | 2.25 | .25 |
| *a.* | | Double surcharge | 125.00 | |
| **377** | A47 | 4d on 6d | 2.50 | 1.10 |
| | | *Nos. 372-377 (6)* | 22.75 | 2.35 |
| | | Set, never hinged | 50.00 | |

Adm. Pavlos Koundouriotis and Cruiser "Averoff" — A61

Pallas Athene — A62

Youth of Marathon — A63

**1933** ***Perf. 13½x13, 13x13½***

| | | | | |
|---|---|---|---|---|
| **378** | A61 | 50d black & ind | 50.00 | 1.60 |
| *a.* | | Imperf., pair | *2,250.* | |
| **379** | A62 | 75d blk & vio brn | 110.00 | *175.00* |
| *a.* | | Imperf., pair | 825.00 | |
| | | Never hinged | 1,700. | |
| **380** | A63 | 100d brn & dull grn | 625.00 | 29.00 |
| *a.* | | Imperf., pair | 2,750. | |
| | | *Nos. 378-380 (3)* | 785.00 | *205.60* |
| | | Set, never hinged | 1,800. | |

The imperf pairs are without gum.

For surcharges see Nos. 386-387.

Approach to Athens Stadium A64

***Perf. 11½, 11½x10, 13½x11½***

**1934, Dec. 10**

| | | | | |
|---|---|---|---|---|
| **381** | A64 | 8d blue | 65.00 | 2.25 |
| | | Never hinged | 200.00 | |

Perforations on No. 381 range from 10½ to 13, including compounds.

Church of Pantanassa, Mistra — A65

**1935, Nov. 1** ***Perf. 13x12½***

| | | | | |
|---|---|---|---|---|
| **382** | A65 | 4d brown | 17.00 | 1.60 |
| | | Never hinged | 47.50 | |
| *a.* | | Horiz. pair, imperf. between | 725.00 | |
| *b.* | | Imperf., pair | 725.00 | |

### Issues of the Monarchy

J71, J76, J82, 380, 379 Surcharged in Red or Blue

Nos. 383-385

Nos. 386-387

***Serrate Roulette 13½***

**1935, Nov. 24** **Litho.**

| | | | | |
|---|---|---|---|---|
| **383** | D3 | 50 l on 40 l indigo (R) | .25 | .25 |
| *a.* | | Double surcharge | | 27.50 |
| **384** | D3 | 3d on 3d car (Bl) | .55 | .40 |

***Perf. 13***

| | | | | |
|---|---|---|---|---|
| **385** | D3 | 3d on 3d rose red (Bl) | 2.75 | 2.00 |

***Perf. 13x13½***

| | | | | |
|---|---|---|---|---|
| **386** | A63 | 5d on 100d (R) | 2.25 | 2.00 |
| **387** | A62 | 15d on 75d (Bl) | 6.50 | 6.00 |
| | | *Nos. 383-387 (5)* | 12.30 | 10.65 |
| | | Set, never hinged | 30.00 | |

King Constantine — A66

**Center Engr., Frame Litho.**
***Perf. 12x13½***

**1936, Nov. 18** **Wmk. 252**

| | | | | |
|---|---|---|---|---|
| **389** | A66 | 3d black & brown | .55 | .40 |
| *a.* | | Pair, printer's name in Greek | 22.50 | |
| *b.* | | Pair, printer's name in English | 22.50 | |
| **390** | A66 | 8d black & blue | 1.10 | .90 |
| *a.* | | Pair, printer's name in Greek | 22.50 | |
| *b.* | | Pair, printer's name in English | 22.50 | |
| | | Set, never hinged | 3.25 | |

Re-burial of the remains of King Constantine and Queen Sophia.

Two printings exist, the first containing varieties "a" and "b" with gray border; second with black border.

King George II — A67

Pallas Athene — A68

**1937, Jan. 24** **Engr.** ***Perf. 12½x12***

| | | | | |
|---|---|---|---|---|
| **391** | A67 | 1d green | .25 | .25 |
| **392** | A67 | 3d red brown | .25 | .25 |
| **393** | A67 | 8d dp blue | .90 | .40 |
| **394** | A67 | 100d carmine lake | 12.00 | 12.00 |
| | | *Nos. 391-394 (4)* | 13.40 | 12.90 |
| | | Set, never hinged | 30.00 | |

For surcharges see Nos. 484-487, 498-500, RA86-RA87, N241-N242.

**1937, Apr. 17** **Unwmk.** ***Perf. 11½***

| | | | | |
|---|---|---|---|---|
| **395** | A68 | 3d yellow brown | .55 | .25 |
| | | Never hinged | 1.10 | |

Centenary of the University of Athens.

Contest with Bull — A69

Lady of Tiryns — A70

Zeus of Dodona — A71

Coin of Amphictyonic League A72

Diagoras of Rhodes, Victor at Olympics A73

Venus of Melos — A74

Battle of Salamis A75

Chariot of Panathenaic Festival A76

Alexander the Great at Battle of Issos — A77

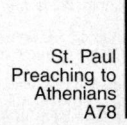

St. Paul Preaching to Athenians A78

St. Demetrius' Church at Salonika A79

Leo III Victory over Arabs — A80

Allegorical Figure of Glory — A81

***Perf. 13½x12, 12x13½***

**1937, Nov. 1** **Litho.** **Wmk. 252**

| | | | | |
|---|---|---|---|---|
| **396** | A69 | 5 l brn red & bl | .25 | .25 |
| *a.* | | Double impression of frame | 60.00 | |
| **397** | A70 | 10 l bl & brn red | .25 | .25 |
| *a.* | | Double impression of frame | 60.00 | |
| **398** | A71 | 20 l black & grn | .25 | .25 |
| **399** | A72 | 40 l green & blk | .25 | .25 |
| *a.* | | Green impression doubled | 60.00 | |
| **400** | A73 | 50 l brown & blk | .25 | .25 |
| **401** | A74 | 80 l ind & yel brn | .25 | .25 |
| | | **Engr.** | | |
| **402** | A75 | 2d ultra | .25 | .25 |
| **403** | A76 | 5d red | .25 | .25 |
| *a.* | | Printer's name omitted | 5.50 | |
| **404** | A77 | 6d olive brn | .25 | .25 |
| **405** | A78 | 7d dk brown | .55 | .50 |
| **406** | A79 | 10d red brown | .25 | .25 |
| **407** | A80 | 15d green | .25 | .25 |
| **408** | A81 | 25d dk blue | .25 | .25 |
| | | *Nos. 396-408 (13)* | 3.55 | 3.50 |
| | | Set, never hinged | 4.00 | |

See Nos. 413, 459-466. For overprints and surcharges see Nos. 455-458, 476-477, RA75-RA78, RA83-RA85, N202-N217, N246-N247.

Cerigo, Paxos, Lefkas

Greek stamps with Italian overprints for the islands of Cerigo (Kithyra), Paxos and Lefkas (Santa Maura) are fraudulent.

**Royal Wedding Issue**

Princess Frederika-Louise and Crown Prince Paul — A82

**1938** **Wmk. 252** ***Perf. 13½x12***

| | | | | |
|---|---|---|---|---|
| **409** | A82 | 1d green | .25 | .25 |
| **410** | A82 | 3d orange brn | .30 | .25 |
| **411** | A82 | 8d dark blue | .55 | .65 |
| | | *Nos. 409-411 (3)* | 1.10 | 1.15 |
| | | Set, never hinged | 2.75 | |

Arms of Greece, Romania, Yugoslavia and Turkey — A83

***Perf. 12x12½***

**1938, Feb. 8** **Litho.** **Unwmk.**

| | | | | |
|---|---|---|---|---|
| **412** | A83 | 6d blue | 5.50 | 1.75 |
| | | Never hinged | 14.00 | |

Balkan Entente.

**Tiryns Lady Type of 1937**
**Corrected Inscription**

**1938** **Wmk. 252** ***Perf. 12x13½***

| | | | | |
|---|---|---|---|---|
| **413** | A70 | 10 l blue & brn red | .50 | *.70* |
| | | Never hinged | .85 | |

The first four letters of the third word of the inscription read "TIPY" instead of "TYPI."

Statue of King Constantine — A84

***Perf. 12x13½***

**1938, Oct. 8** **Engr.** **Unwmk.**

| | | | | |
|---|---|---|---|---|
| **414** | A84 | 1.50d green | .45 | .25 |
| **415** | A84 | 30d orange brn | 2.25 | *3.25* |
| | | Set, never hinged | 5.50 | |

For overprint see No. N218.

Coats of Arms of Ionian Islands — A85

Fort at Corfu — A86

King George I of Greece and Queen Victoria of England A87

***Perf. 12½x12, 13½x12***

**1939, May 21** **Engr.** **Unwmk.**

| | | | | |
|---|---|---|---|---|
| **416** | A85 | 1d dk blue | .85 | .25 |
| **417** | A86 | 4d green | 2.90 | 1.00 |
| **418** | A87 | 20d yellow org | 17.00 | 17.00 |
| **419** | A87 | 20d dull blue | 17.00 | 17.00 |
| **420** | A87 | 20d car lake | 17.00 | 17.00 |
| | | *Nos. 416-420 (5)* | 54.75 | 52.25 |
| | | Set, never hinged | 125.00 | |

75th anniv. of the union of the Ionian Islands with Greece.

Runner with Shield — A88

10th Pan-Balkan Games: 3d, Javelin thrower. 6d, Discus thrower. 8d, Jumper.

***Perf. 12x13½***

**1939, Oct. 1** **Litho.** **Unwmk.**

| | | | | |
|---|---|---|---|---|
| **421** | A88 | 50 l slate grn & grn | .25 | .25 |
| **422** | A88 | 3d henna brn & dl rose | 1.25 | .55 |
| **423** | A88 | 6d cop brn & dl org | 3.00 | 2.25 |
| **424** | A88 | 8d ultra & gray | 3.00 | 2.50 |
| | | *Nos. 421-424 (4)* | 7.50 | 5.55 |
| | | Set, never hinged | 18.00 | |

Arms of Greece, Romania, Turkey and Yugoslavia — A92

***Perf. 13x12½***

**1940, May 27** **Wmk. 252**

| | | | | |
|---|---|---|---|---|
| **425** | A92 | 6d blue | 10.00 | 2.25 |
| **426** | A92 | 8d blue gray | 7.00 | 2.25 |
| | | Set, never hinged | 45.00 | |

Balkan Entente.

Emblem of Youth Organization A93

Boy Member — A94

Designs: 3d, 100d, Emblem of Greek Youth Organization. 10d, Girl member. 15d, Javelin Thrower. 20d, Column of members. 25d, Flag bearers and buglers. 30d, Three youths. 50d, Line formation. 75d, Coat of arms.

***Perf. 12½, 13½x12½***

**1940, Aug. 3** **Litho.** **Wmk. 252**

| | | | | |
|---|---|---|---|---|
| **427** | A93 | 3d sil, dp ultra & red | .85 | *1.25* |
| **428** | A94 | 5d dk bl & blk | 6.50 | *7.50* |
| **429** | A94 | 10d red org & blk | 7.50 | *10.00* |
| **430** | A94 | 15d dk grn & blk | 30.00 | *32.50* |
| **431** | A94 | 20d lake & blk | 25.00 | 25.00 |
| **432** | A94 | 25d dk bl & blk | 25.00 | 25.00 |
| **433** | A94 | 30d rose vio & blk | 25.00 | 25.00 |
| **434** | A94 | 50d lake & blk | 30.00 | 30.00 |
| **435** | A94 | 75d dk bl, brn & gold | 30.00 | 32.50 |
| **436** | A93 | 100d sil, dp ultra & red | 50.00 | *37.50* |
| | | *Nos. 427-436,C38-C47 (20)* | 555.70 | 529.00 |
| | | Set, never hinged | 1,000. | |

4th anniv. of the founding of the Greek Youth Organization. The stamps were good for postal duty Aug. 3-5, 1940, only. They remained on sale until Feb. 3, 1941.

For overprints see Nos. N219-N238.

Windmills on Mykonos
A103

Bourtzi Fort — A104

Aspropotamos River — A105

Candia Harbor, Crete — A106

Houses at Hydra — A107

Meteora Monasteries
A108

Edessa
A109

Pantokratoros Monastery and Port — A110

Bridge at Konitsa
A111

Ekatontapiliani Church, Paros — A112

Ponticonissi, Corfu (Mouse Island)
A113

***Perf. 12½, 13½x12½***

**1942-44 Litho. Wmk. 252**

**437** A103 2d red brown .25 .25
**438** A104 5d lt bl grn .25 .25
*a.* "ΝΑΥΟΛΙΟΝ" instead of "ΝΑΥΠΛΙΟΝ" 8.25 8.25
**439** A105 10d lt blue .25 .25
**440** A106 15d red vio .25 .25
**441** A107 25d org red .25 .25
**442** A108 50d sapphire .25 .25
**443** A109 75d dp rose .25 .25
**444** A110 100d black .25 .25
**445** A110 200d ultra .25 .25
*a.* Imprint omitted 3.90 3.90
**446** A111 500d dk olive .25 .25
**447** A112 1000d org brn .25 .25
**448** A113 2000d dp blue .25 .25
**449** A111 5000d rose red .25 .25
**450** A112 15,000d rose lil .25 .25
**451** A113 25,000d green .25 .25
**452** A105 500,000d blue .25 .25
**453** A103 2,000,000d turq grn .25 .25
**454** A104 5,000,000d rose brn .25 .30
*Nos. 437-454 (18)* 4.50 4.55
Set, never hinged 4.50

Double impressions exist of 10d, 25d, 50d, 100d, 200d, 1,000d and 2,000d. Value, each $30.

Issued: #439-442, 9/1; 200d, 12/1; #446-448, 3/15/44; #449-451, 7/1/44; #452-454, 9/15/44.

For surcharges and overprint see Nos. 472C, 473B-475, 478-481, 501-505, B1-B5, B11-B15, RA72-RA74, N239-N240, N243-N245, N248.

**Imperf., Pairs**

*439a* A105 10d 57.50
*440a* A106 15d 57.50
*441a* A107 25d 45.00
*442a* A108 50d 45.00
*446a* A111 500d 45.00
*447a* A112 1000d 45.00
*448a* A113 2000d 45.00
*449a* A111 5000d 45.00
*450a* A112 15,000d 45.00
*451a* A113 25,000d 45.00
*452a* A105 500,000d 45.00
*454a* A104 5,000,000d 45.00

Nos. 400, 402-404 Surcharged in Blue Black

**1944-45** ***Perf. 13½x12***

**455** A73 50 l brn & blk .25 .25
*a.* Double surcharge 40.00 40.00
**456** A75 2d ultra .25 .25
**457** A76 5d red .25 .25
*a.* Inverted surcharge 47.50
*b.* Double surcharge 47.50
*c.* Printer's name omitted (403a) 12.00 12.00
*d.* Pair, one without surcharge 20.00
**458** A77 6d olive brn ('45) .25 .25
*Nos. 455-458 (4)* 1.00
Set, never hinged .90

**Glory Type of 1937**

***Perf. 12½x13½***

**1945 Litho. Wmk. 252**

**459** A81 1d dull rose vio .40 .25
**460** A81 3d rose brown .40 .25
*a.* Imperf., pair 160.00
**461** A81 5d ultra .40 .25
*a.* Imperf., pair 160.00
**462** A81 10d dull brown .40 .25
**463** A81 20d dull violet .40 .25
**464** A81 50d olive black .40 .25
**465** A81 100d pale blue 6.00 6.00
*a.* Imperf., pair 190.00
**466** A81 200d slate 5.25 4.75
*Nos. 459-466 (8)* 13.65 12.25
Set, never hinged 27.50

Doric Column and Greek Flag
A114

Franklin D. Roosevelt
A115

**1945, Oct. 28 Unwmk.**

**467** A114 20d orange brown .25 .25
**468** A114 40d blue .25 .25
*a.* Double impression 30.00
Set, never hinged .75

Vote of Oct. 28, 1940, refusing Italy's ultimatum. "OXI" means "No."
Exist imperf.

**1945, Dec. 21 Unwmk.**

**469** A115 30d blk & red brn .30 .25
*a.* Center double 27.00
*c.* Inverted frame 72.50
*d.* Imperf., pair 45.00
**470** A115 60d blk & sl gray .30 .25
*a.* Center double 27.50
*b.* 60d black & blue gray 11.00 11.00
*c.* Imperf., pair 27.50
*d.* Inverted frame 65.00
**471** A115 200d blk & vio brn .30 .25
*a.* Center double 27.50 *77.50*
*b.* Imperf., pair 45.00
*Nos. 469-471 (3)* .90 .75
Set, never hinged 1.50

Death of Pres. Franklin D. Roosevelt.

**Catalogue values for unused stamps in this section, from this point to the end of the section, are for Never Hinged items.**

Nos. C61, C63, 447-451, 453, 398, 401, 454 and 452 Surcharged in Black or Carmine

***Perf. 12½, 12x13½, 13½x12½***

**1946 Wmk. 252**

**472** AP35 10d on 10d .40 .25
*a.* Inverted surcharge 100.00 —
*b.* Double surcharge 22.50
**472C** A113 10d on 2000d (C) .40 .25
**473** AP35 20d on 50d (C) .40 .25
*a.* Inverted surcharge 125.00
**473B** A112 20d on 1000d .40 .25
**474** A113 50d on 25,000d (C) .55 .25
**475** A103 100d on 2,000,000d (C) .95 .30
**476** A71 130d on 20 l (C) 1.00 .25
*b.* Double surcharge 27.50
**476A** A71 250d on 20 l (C) 1.25 .25
*c.* Double surcharge 92.50
**477** A74 300d on 80 l 1.00 .25
*a.* Purple brown surcharge 17.00 17.00
*b.* Double surcharge 90.00
**478** A104 500d on 5,000,000d 4.00 .80
*a.* Inverted surcharge 85.00
*b.* Double surcharge 85.00
**479** A105 1000d on 500,000d (C) 14.00 2.25
*a.* Double surcharge 45.00
**480** A111 2000d on 5000d 52.50 4.50
**481** A112 5000d on 15,000d 160.00 35.00
*a.* Blue surcharge 160.00 140.00
*Nos. 472-481 (13)* 236.85 44.85

The surcharge exists in various shades on most denominations. A 150d on 20 l is fraudulent.

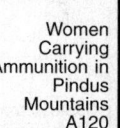

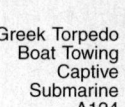

Eleutherios K. Venizelos — A116

***Perf. 12x13½***

**1946, Mar. 25 Litho. Wmk. 252**

**482** A116 130d brn ol & buff .40 .25
*a.* Double impression of brn olive 7.25
**483** A116 300d red brn & pale brn .40 .25
*a.* Double impression of red brown 14.00

Venizelos (1864-1936), statesman.

Nos. 391 to 394 Surcharged in Blue Black

**1946, Sept. 28** ***Perf. 12½x12***

**484** A67 50d on 1d .70 .25
**485** A67 250d on 3d 1.60 .25
*a.* Date omitted 32.50
*b.* Inverted surcharge 32.50 —
**486** A67 600d on 8d 11.00 1.25
*a.* Additional surcharge on back, inverted 72.50
*b.* Carmine surcharge 150.00
**487** A67 3000d on 100d 27.50 2.00
*Nos. 484-487 (4)* 40.80 3.75

Plebiscite of Sept. 1, 1946, which resulted in the return of King George II to Greece.

Panaghiotis Tsaldaris — A117

***Perf. 12½x13½***

**1946, Nov. 15 Litho. Unwmk.**

**488** A117 250d red brn & buff 4.00 1.25
**489** A117 600d dp bl & pale bl 4.00 1.25
*a.* Double impression 22.50

Naval Convoy
A118

Torpedoing of Cruiser Helle — A119

Women Carrying Ammunition in Pindus Mountains
A120

Troops in Albania
A121

Campaign of Greek Troops in Italy — A122

Allegory of Flight — A123

Greek Torpedo Boat Towing Captive Submarine
A124

Design: 5000d, Memorial Tomb, El Alamein.

**1946-47 Unwmk. Engr.** ***Perf. 13***

**490** A118 50d dk bl grn .25 .25
**491** A119 100d dp ultra .65 .25
**492** A120 250d yel grn ('46) .65 .25
**493** A121 500d yel brn 1.05 .25
**494** A122 600d dk brown 1.40 .85
**495** A123 1000d dull lil 7.25 .40
**496** A124 2000d dp ultra 30.00 2.50
**497** A119 5000d dk car 40.00 2.50
*a.* Imperf., pair 1,500.
*Nos. 490-497 (8)* 81.25 7.25

1947 stamps issued May 1.

**King George II Memorial Issue**

Nos. 391-393
Surcharged in Black

*Perf. 12½x12*

**1947, Apr. 15** **Wmk. 252**

| | | | | |
|---|---|---|---|---|
| **498** | A67 | 50d on 1d grn | .60 | .25 |
| *a.* | | Double surcharge | 72.50 | |
| **499** | A67 | 250d on 3d red brn | 1.25 | .25 |
| *a.* | | Double surcharge | 72.50 | |
| *b.* | | Pair, one without surcharge | 72.50 | |
| **500** | A67 | 600d on 8d dp bl | 10.00 | .55 |
| *a.* | | Double surcharge | 72.50 | |
| | | *Nos. 498-500 (3)* | 11.85 | 1.05 |

Nos. 446, 438, 442, 439 and 443
Surcharged in Carmine or Black

**1947** ***Perf. 12½***

| | | | | |
|---|---|---|---|---|
| **501** | A111 | 20d on 500d | .30 | .25 |
| *a.* | | Double surcharge | 27.50 | |
| **502** | A104 | 30d on 5d | .95 | .40 |
| **503** | A108 | 50d on 50d | .45 | .25 |
| **504** | A105 | 100d on 10d | 1.60 | .25 |
| **505** | A109 | 450d on 75d (Bk) | 2.50 | .25 |
| | | *Nos. 501-505 (5)* | 5.80 | 1.40 |

Castellorizo Castle
A126

Dodecanese Vase
A127

Dodecanese Costume
A128

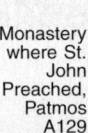

Monastery where St. John Preached, Patmos
A129

Emanuel Xanthos — A130

Sailing Vessel of 1824 — A131

Revolutionary Stamp of 1912 — A132

Statue of Hippocrates
A133

Colossus of Rhodes
A134

*Perf. 12½x13½, 13½x12½*

**1947-48** **Litho.** **Wmk. 252**

| | | | | |
|---|---|---|---|---|
| **506** | A126 | 20d ultra | .30 | .25 |
| **507** | A127 | 30d blk brn & buff | .30 | .25 |
| **508** | A128 | 50d chlky bl | .50 | .25 |
| **509** | A129 | 100d blk grn & pale grn | .50 | .25 |
| **510** | A130 | 250d gray grn & pale grn | 1.00 | .25 |
| **511** | A132 | 450d dp bl ('48) | 2.25 | .25 |
| **512** | A131 | 450d dp bl & pale bl ('48) | 1.75 | .25 |
| *a.* | | Imperf., pair | 275.00 | |
| **513** | A132 | 500d red | 1.40 | .25 |
| **514** | A133 | 600d vio brn & pale pink | 1.40 | .25 |
| **515** | A134 | 1000d brn & cream | 2.00 | .25 |
| *a.* | | Imperf., pair | 250.00 | |
| | | *Nos. 506-515 (10)* | 11.40 | 2.50 |

Return of the Dodecanese to Greece. See Nos. 520-522, 525-534.

Battle of Crete — A135

**1948, Sept. 15** **Engr.** ***Perf. 13x13½***

| | | | | |
|---|---|---|---|---|
| **516** | A135 | 1000d dark green | 6.50 | .50 |

Battle of Crete, 7th anniversary.

Abduction of Children
A136

Concentration Camp — A137

Protective Mother — A138

*Perf. 13½x12½, 12½x13½*

**1949, Feb. 1** **Litho.** **Wmk. 252**

| | | | | |
|---|---|---|---|---|
| **517** | A136 | 450d dk & lt violet | 3.75 | .65 |
| **518** | A137 | 1000d dk & lt brown | 13.50 | 4.00 |
| **519** | A138 | 1800d dk red & cream | 17.50 | .40 |
| | | *Nos. 517-519 (3)* | 34.75 | 5.05 |

**Types of 1947**

**1950, Apr. 5** ***Perf. 12½x13½***

| | | | | |
|---|---|---|---|---|
| **520** | A127 | 2000d org brn & sal | 50.00 | .55 |
| *a.* | | Imperf., pair | 140.00 | |
| **521** | A133 | 5000d rose vio | 55.00 | .55 |
| **522** | A134 | 10,000d ultra | 95.00 | 1.25 |
| | | *Nos. 520-522 (3)* | 200.00 | 2.35 |

Map of Crete and Flags
A139

*Perf. 13½x13*

**1950, Apr. 28** **Engr.** **Wmk. 252**

| | | | | |
|---|---|---|---|---|
| **523** | A139 | 1000d deep blue | 17.50 | .40 |
| *a.* | | Imperf., pair | *1,500.* | |

Battle of Crete, 9th anniversary.

Youth of Marathon — A140

**Engraved and Lithographed**

**1950, May 21** ***Perf. 13x13½***

| | | | | |
|---|---|---|---|---|
| **524** | A140 | 1000d cream & dp grn | 2.00 | .60 |
| *a.* | | Without dates | 450.00 | |
| *b.* | | "1949" only | 450.00 | |
| *c.* | | Dates inverted | 450.00 | |
| *d.* | | Dates doubled | 450.00 | |

75th anniv. (in 1949) of the UPU.
Exists imperf., used only.

**Types of 1947-48**

*Perf. 12½x13½, 13½x12½*

**1950** **Litho.** **Wmk. 252**

| | | | | |
|---|---|---|---|---|
| **525** | A130 | 200d orange | .70 | .25 |
| **526** | A128 | 300d orange | .95 | .25 |
| **527** | A129 | 400d blue | 1.75 | .25 |
| **528** | A133 | 700d lilac rose | 2.25 | .25 |
| **529** | A133 | 700d blue green | 27.50 | .25 |
| *a.* | | Imperf., pair | 290.00 | |
| **530** | A131 | 800d pur & pale grn | 2.75 | .25 |
| **531** | A132 | 1300d carmine | 12.00 | .25 |
| **532** | A126 | 1500d brn org | 82.50 | 1.10 |
| **533** | A127 | 1600d ultra & bl gray | 8.50 | .25 |
| **534** | A134 | 2600d emer & pale grn | 11.50 | .85 |
| | | *Nos. 525-534 (10)* | 150.40 | 3.95 |

Altar and Sword
A141

St. Paul — A142

St. Paul by El Greco — A143

Preaching to Athenians — A144

*Perf. 13½x12, 12x13½*

**1951, June 15** **Engr.** **Unwmk.**

| | | | | |
|---|---|---|---|---|
| **535** | A141 | 700d red vio | 3.50 | 1.00 |
| **536** | A142 | 1600d lt blue | 14.50 | 8.75 |
| **537** | A143 | 2600d dk ol bis | 25.00 | 9.00 |
| **538** | A144 | 10,000d red brn | 175.00 | 80.00 |
| | | *Nos. 535-538 (4)* | 218.00 | 98.75 |

1900th anniv. of St. Paul's visit to Athens.

Industrialization
A145

Designs: 800d, Fishing. 1300d, Rebuilding. 1600d, Farming. 2600d, Home Industries. 5000d, Electrification and map of Greece.

*Perf. 12½x13½*

**1951, Sept. 20** **Wmk. 252**

| | | | | |
|---|---|---|---|---|
| **539** | A145 | 700d red org | 5.00 | .30 |
| **540** | A145 | 800d aqua | 7.25 | .30 |
| **541** | A145 | 1300d grnsh bl | 10.00 | .30 |
| **542** | A145 | 1600d olive grn | 30.00 | .50 |
| **543** | A145 | 2600d vio gray | 75.00 | 2.25 |
| **544** | A145 | 5000d dp plum | 100.00 | .50 |
| | | *Nos. 539-544 (6)* | 227.25 | 4.15 |

Issued to publicize Greek recovery under the Marshall Plan.

King Paul I — A146

Allegorical Figure and Medal — A147

**1952, Dec. 14** **Engr.** ***Perf. 12½x12***

| | | | | |
|---|---|---|---|---|
| **545** | A146 | 200d deep green | 2.00 | .25 |
| **546** | A146 | 1000d red | 6.00 | .35 |
| **547** | A147 | 1400d blue | 20.00 | 2.25 |
| **548** | A146 | 10,000d dk red lil | 60.00 | 14.00 |
| | | *Nos. 545-548 (4)* | 88.00 | 16.85 |

50th birthday of King Paul I.

Oranges
A148

Tobacco — A149

National Products: 1000d, Olive oil, Pallas Athene. 1300d, Wine. 2000d, Figs. 2600d, Grapes and bread. 5000d, Bacchus holding grapes.

**1953, July 1** ***Perf. 13½x13, 13x13½***

| | | | | |
|---|---|---|---|---|
| **549** | A148 | 500d dp car & org | 1.90 | .25 |
| **550** | A149 | 700d dk brn & org yel | 1.90 | .25 |
| **551** | A148 | 1000d bl & lt ol grn | 4.00 | .25 |
| *a.* | | Imperf., pair | 450.00 | |
| **552** | A149 | 1300d dp plum & org brn | 5.50 | .25 |
| **553** | A149 | 2000d dk brn & lt grn | 13.50 | .40 |
| **554** | A149 | 2600d vio & ol bis | 37.50 | 1.75 |
| **555** | A149 | 5000d dk brn & yel grn | 37.50 | .90 |
| | | *Nos. 549-555 (7)* | 101.80 | 4.05 |

Pericles
A150

Homer
A151

Hunting Wild
Boar — A152

Shepherd
Carrying
Calf — A152a

Designs: 200d, Mycenaean oxhead vase. 500d, Zeus of Istiaea. 600d, Head of a youth. 1000d, Alexander the Great. 1200d, Charioteer of Delphi. 2000d, Vase of Dipylon. 4000d, Voyage of Dionysus. 20,000d, Pitcher bearers.

***Perf. 13½x13, 12½x12, 13x13½***

**1954, Jan. 15** **Litho.**

| | | | | | |
|---|---|---|---|---|---|
| **556** | A150 | 100d | red brn | .50 | .25 |
| **557** | A150 | 200d | black | .50 | .25 |
| **558** | A151 | 300d | blue vio | 1.25 | .25 |
| **559** | A151 | 500d | green | 2.00 | .25 |
| **560** | A151 | 600d | rose pink | 2.00 | .25 |
| **561** | A151 | 1000d | dl bl & blk | 2.50 | .25 |
| **562** | A150 | 1200d | ol grn | 2.50 | .25 |
| **563** | A150 | 2000d | red brn | 11.00 | .25 |
| **564** | A152 | 2400d | grnsh bl | 11.00 | .40 |
| *a.* | | | Double impression | 150.00 | |
| **565** | A152a | 2500d | dk bl grn | 11.00 | .25 |
| **566** | A151 | 4000d | dk car | 27.50 | .40 |
| **567** | A150 | 20,000d | rose lilac | 225.00 | 1.25 |
| | | | *Nos. 556-567 (12)* | 296.75 | 4.30 |

See Nos. 574-581, 632-638, and 689.

British
Parliamentary
Debate and Ink
Blot — A153

**1954, Sept.** ***Perf. 12½***

**Center in Black**

| | | | | | |
|---|---|---|---|---|---|
| **568** | A153 | 1.20d | cream | 4.00 | .45 |
| **569** | A153 | 2d | orange | 20.00 | 3.75 |
| **570** | A153 | 2d | lt bl | 20.00 | 9.25 |
| **571** | A153 | 2.40d | lilac | 20.00 | 2.50 |
| **572** | A153 | 2.50d | pink | 20.00 | 2.50 |
| **573** | A153 | 4d | citron | 60.00 | 3.75 |
| | | | *Nos. 568-573 (6)* | 144.00 | 22.20 |

Document in English on Nos. 569, 572, 573; in French on Nos. 570, 571 and in Greek on No. 568.

Issued to promote the proposed union between Cyprus and Greece.

**Types of 1954**

***Perf. 13½x13, 12½x12, 13x13½***

**1955** **Litho.** **Wmk. 252**

Designs: 20 l, Mycenaean oxhead vase. 30 l, Pericles. 50 l, Zeus of Istiaea. 1d, Head of a youth. 2d, Alexander the Great. 3d, Hunting wild boar. 3.50d, Homer. 4d, Voyage of Dionysus.

| | | | | | |
|---|---|---|---|---|---|
| **574** | A150 | 20 l | dk green | .40 | .25 |
| **575** | A150 | 30 l | yellow brn | .60 | .25 |
| **576** | A151 | 50 l | car lake | .90 | .25 |
| **577** | A151 | 1d | blue grn | 2.25 | .25 |
| **578** | A151 | 2d | brown & blk | 7.25 | .25 |
| **579** | A152 | 3d | red org | 11.00 | .25 |
| **580** | A151 | 3.50d | rose crim | 11.00 | .70 |
| **581** | A151 | 4d | violet bl | 82.50 | .45 |
| | | | *Nos. 574-581 (8)* | 115.90 | 2.65 |

Samos Coin
Picturing
Pythagoras
A154

Pythagorean
Theorem
A155

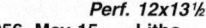

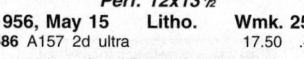

Samos
Mapped in
Antique
Style — A156

**1955, Aug. 20** ***Perf. 12x13½***

| | | | | | |
|---|---|---|---|---|---|
| **582** | A154 | 2d | green | 3.75 | .40 |
| **583** | A155 | 3.50d | intense blk | 13.50 | 3.00 |
| **584** | A154 | 5d | plum | 45.00 | 2.00 |
| **585** | A156 | 6d | blue | 57.50 | 32.50 |
| | | | *Nos. 582-585 (4)* | 119.75 | 37.90 |

2500th anniv. of the founding of the 1st School of Philosophy by Pythagoras on Samos.

Globe and Rotary
Emblem — A157

***Perf. 12x13½***

**1956, May 15** **Litho.** **Wmk. 252**

| | | | | | |
|---|---|---|---|---|---|
| **586** | A157 | 2d | ultra | 17.50 | .40 |

50th anniv. of Rotary Intl. (in 1955).

King
Alexander
A158

Crown Prince
Constantine — A159

Portraits: 30 l, George I. 50 l, Queen Olga. 70 l, King Otto. 1d, Queen Amalia. 1.50d, King Constantine. 2d, 7.50d, King Paul. 3d, George II. 3.50d, Queen Sophia. 4d, Queen Frederica. 5d, King Paul and Queen Frederica. 10d, King, Queen and Crown Prince.

***Perf. 13½x12, 12x13½***

**1956, May 21** **Engr.**

| | | | | | |
|---|---|---|---|---|---|
| **587** | A158 | 10 l | blue vio | .25 | .25 |
| **588** | A159 | 20 l | dull pur | .25 | .25 |
| **589** | A159 | 30 l | sepia | .25 | .25 |
| **590** | A159 | 50 l | red brn | .30 | .25 |
| **591** | A159 | 70 l | lt ultra | .50 | .25 |
| **592** | A159 | 1d | grnsh bl | .50 | .25 |
| **593** | A159 | 1.50d | gray bl | 3.50 | .25 |
| **594** | A159 | 2d | black | 4.75 | .25 |
| **595** | A159 | 3d | brown | 3.50 | .25 |
| **596** | A159 | 3.50d | copper brn | 11.50 | .25 |
| **597** | A159 | 4d | gray green | 11.50 | .25 |
| **598** | A158 | 5d | rose car | 11.50 | .25 |
| **599** | A159 | 7.50d | ultra | 11.50 | 2.00 |
| **600** | A158 | 10d | dk blue | 60.00 | 1.10 |
| | | | *Nos. 587-600 (14)* | 119.80 | 6.10 |

See Nos. 604-617.

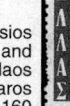

Dionysios
Solomos and
Nicolaos
Mantzaros
A160

Dionysios
Solomos — A161

5d, View on Zante and bust of Solomos.

***Perf. 13½x12, 12x13½***

**1957, Mar. 26** **Litho.** **Wmk. 252**

| | | | | | |
|---|---|---|---|---|---|
| **601** | A160 | 2d | red brn & ocher | 4.25 | .50 |
| **602** | A161 | 3.50d | bl & gray | 6.75 | 3.25 |
| **603** | A160 | 5d | dk grn & ol bis | 9.00 | 4.75 |
| | | | *Nos. 601-603 (3)* | 20.00 | 8.50 |

Centenary of the death of Dionysios Solomos (1798-1857), nationalist poet best known for the poem *Hymn to Liberty*, the first two stanzas of which were adopted as the lyrics of the Greek national anthem.

**Types of 1956**

Designs as before.

***Perf. 13½x12***

**1957** **Wmk. 252** **Engr.**

| | | | | | |
|---|---|---|---|---|---|
| **604** | A158 | 10 l | rose lake | .50 | .25 |
| **605** | A159 | 20 l | orange | .50 | .25 |
| **606** | A159 | 30 l | gray blk | .50 | .25 |
| **607** | A159 | 50 l | grnsh blk | .50 | .25 |
| **608** | A159 | 70 l | rose lil | 1.50 | .65 |
| **609** | A159 | 1d | rose red | 1.00 | .25 |
| **610** | A159 | 1.50d | lt ol grn | 1.75 | .25 |
| **611** | A159 | 2d | carmine | 3.25 | .25 |
| **612** | A159 | 3d | dk blue | 4.00 | .25 |
| **613** | A159 | 3.50d | blk vio | 10.00 | .25 |
| *a.* | | | Imperf., pair | | |
| **614** | A159 | 4d | red brn | 10.00 | .25 |
| **615** | A158 | 5d | gray blue | 10.00 | .25 |
| **616** | A159 | 7.50d | yel org | 3.00 | 1.25 |
| **617** | A158 | 10d | green | 75.00 | .80 |
| | | | *Nos. 604-617 (14)* | 121.50 | 5.45 |

Oil Tanker
A162

Ships: 1d, Ocean liner. 1.50d, Sailing ship, 1820. 2d, Byzantine vessel. 3.50d, Ship from 6th century B. C. 5d, "Argo."

**1958, Jan. 30** **Litho.** ***Perf. 13½x12***

| | | | | | |
|---|---|---|---|---|---|
| **618** | A162 | 50 l | multi | .50 | .25 |
| **619** | A162 | 1d | ultra, blk & bis | .50 | .25 |
| **620** | A162 | 1.50d | blk & car | 1.50 | .95 |
| *a.* | | | Double impression of blk | 160.00 | |
| **621** | A162 | 2d | vio bl, blk & red brn | .50 | .30 |
| **622** | A162 | 3.50d | lt bl, blk & red | 2.00 | 1.25 |
| *a.* | | | Double impression of blk | 160.00 | 125.00 |
| **623** | A162 | 5d | bl grn, blk & car | 13.50 | 10.00 |
| | | | *Nos. 618-623 (6)* | 18.50 | 13.00 |

Issued to honor the Greek merchant marine.

Narcissus — A163

Designs: 30 l, Daphne (laurel) and Apollo. 50 l, Adonis (hibiscus) and Aphrodite. 70 l, Pitys (pine) and Pan. 1d, Crocus. 2d, Iris. 3.50d, Tulips. 5d, Cyclamen.

**1958, Sept. 15** **Wmk. 252** ***Perf. 13***

**Size: 22½x38mm**

| | | | | | |
|---|---|---|---|---|---|
| **624** | A163 | 20 l | multi | .25 | .25 |
| **625** | A163 | 30 l | multi | .25 | .25 |
| **626** | A163 | 50 l | multi | .25 | .25 |
| **627** | A163 | 70 l | multi | .25 | .25 |

***Perf. 12½x12***

**Size: 21½x26mm**

| | | | | | |
|---|---|---|---|---|---|
| **628** | A163 | 1d | multi | .45 | .40 |

***Perf. 12x13½***

**Size: 22x32mm**

| | | | | | |
|---|---|---|---|---|---|
| **629** | A163 | 2d | multi | .25 | .25 |
| **630** | A163 | 3.50d | multi | 1.75 | 1.75 |
| *a.* | | | Imperf., pair | 325.00 | |
| **631** | A163 | 5d | multi | 5.00 | 5.00 |
| | | | *Nos. 624-631 (8)* | 8.45 | 8.40 |

International Congress for the Protection of Nature, held in Athens.

**Types of 1954**

Designs: 10 l, Pericles. 20 l, Mycenaean oxhead vase. 50 l, Zeus of Istiaea. 70 l, Charioteer of Delphi. 1d, Head of a youth. 1.50d, Pitcher bearers. 2.50d, Alexander the Great.

Two types of 2.50d:
I — 9 dots in upper half of right border.
II — 10 dots.

***Perf. 13½x13, 12½x12***

**1959** **Litho.** **Wmk. 252**

| | | | | | |
|---|---|---|---|---|---|
| **632** | A150 | 10 l | emerald | .50 | .25 |
| **633** | A150 | 20 l | magenta | .80 | .25 |
| **634** | A151 | 50 l | lt bl grn | 1.75 | .25 |
| **635** | A150 | 70 l | red org | .50 | .25 |
| **636** | A151 | 1d | reddish brn | 4.50 | .25 |
| **637** | A150 | 1.50d | brt bl | 25.00 | .25 |
| **638** | A151 | 2.50d | mag & blk (II) | 17.50 | .30 |
| *a.* | | | Type I | 60.00 | .55 |
| | | | *Nos. 632-638 (7)* | 50.55 | 1.80 |

Zeus-Eagle Coin — A164

Helios-Rose
Coin — A165

Ancient Greek Coins: 20 l, Athena & Owl. 50 l, Nymph Arethusa & Chariot. 70 l, Hercules & Zeus. 1.50d, Griffin & Square. 2.50d, Apollo & Lyre. 4.50d, Apollo & Labyrinth. 6d, Aphrodite & Apollo. 8.50d, Ram's Head & Incuse Squares.

**1959, Mar. 24** **Wmk. 252** ***Perf. 14***

**Coins in Various Shades of Gray**

| | | | | | |
|---|---|---|---|---|---|
| **639** | A164 | 10 l | red brn & blk | .45 | .25 |
| **640** | A164 | 20 l | dp bl & blk | .45 | .25 |
| **641** | A164 | 50 l | plum & blk | .60 | .25 |
| **642** | A164 | 70 l | ultra & blk | 1.10 | .30 |
| **643** | A165 | 1d | dk car rose & blk | 1.50 | .25 |
| **644** | A164 | 1.50d | ocher & blk | 1.75 | .25 |
| **645** | A164 | 2.50d | dp mag & blk | 2.50 | .25 |
| **646** | A165 | 4.50d | Prus grn & blk | 5.50 | .40 |
| **647** | A165 | 6d | ol grn & blk | 25.00 | .25 |
| **648** | A165 | 8.50d | dp car & blk | 10.00 | 1.75 |
| | | | *Nos. 639-648 (10)* | 48.85 | 4.20 |

See Nos. 750-758.

Audience, Vase 580
B. C. — A166

Theater, Delphi A167

Designs: 50 l, Clay tragedy mask, 3rd cent. B.C. 1d, Flute, drum and lyre. 2.50d, Clay statue of an actor, 3rd cent. B.C. 4.50d, Andromeda, vase, 4th cent. B.C. 6d, Actors, bowl 410 B.C.

*Perf. 13x13½, 13½x13*

**1959, June 20 Litho. Wmk. 252**

| | | | | |
|---|---|---|---|---|
| **649** | A166 | 20 l blk, fawn & gray | .30 | .25 |
| **650** | A166 | 50 l dk red brn & ol bis | .30 | .25 |
| **651** | A166 | 1d grn, brn & ocher | .30 | .25 |
| **652** | A166 | 2.50d brn & bl | .80 | .65 |
| **653** | A167 | 3.50d red brn, grn & sep | 15.00 | 10.50 |
| **654** | A167 | 4.50d blk & fawn | 1.50 | 1.25 |
| **655** | A166 | 6d blk, fawn & gray | 1.75 | 1.50 |
| | | *Nos. 649-655 (7)* | 19.95 | 14.65 |

Ancient Greek theater.

"Victory" and Soldiers — A168

*Perf. 13x13½*

**1959, Aug. 29 Wmk. 252**

| | | | | |
|---|---|---|---|---|
| **656** | A168 | 2.50d red brn, ultra & blk | 5.00 | .50 |

10th anniversary of civil war.

St. Basil — A169

The Good Samaritan A170

Designs: 20 l, Plane tree of Hippocrates. 50 l, Aesculapius. 2.50d, Achilles and Patroclus. 3d, Globe and Red Cross over people receiving help. 4.50d, Henri Dunant.

*Perf. 13½x12, 12x13½*

**1959, Sept. 21 Litho.**

| | | | | |
|---|---|---|---|---|
| **657** | A170 | 20 l multi | .25 | .25 |
| **658** | A169 | 50 l multi | .25 | .25 |
| **659** | A170 | 70 l multi | .25 | .25 |
| **660** | A169 | 2.50d multi | .60 | .50 |
| **661** | A169 | 3d multi | 10.00 | 10.00 |
| **662** | A169 | 4.50d multi | 1.60 | 1.60 |
| **663** | A170 | 6d multi | 1.50 | 1.50 |
| | | *Nos. 657-663 (7)* | 14.45 | 14.35 |

Cent. of the Red Cross idea. Sizes: Nos. 658-660, 662 24½x32mm, No. 661 32x47mm.

Imre Nagy — A171

Costis Palamas — A172

*Perf. 13x13½*

**1959, Dec. 8 Wmk. 252**

| | | | | |
|---|---|---|---|---|
| **664** | A171 | 4.50d org brn & dk brn | 1.75 | 1.75 |
| **665** | A171 | 6d brt bl, bl & blk | 1.75 | 1.75 |

3rd anniv. of the crushing of the 1956 Hungarian Revolution, and to honor Premier Imre Nagy, its leader.

**1960, Jan. 25** *Perf. 12x13½*

| | | | | |
|---|---|---|---|---|
| **666** | A172 | 2.50d multi | 7.00 | .75 |

Centenary of the birth of Costis Palamas (1859-1943), poet.

Ship Battling Storm A173

4.50d, Ship in calm sea and rainbow.

*Perf. 13½x13*

**1960, Apr. 7 Wmk. 252**

| | | | | |
|---|---|---|---|---|
| **667** | A173 | 2.50d multi | .50 | .40 |
| **668** | A173 | 4.50d multi | 2.00 | 1.40 |

Issued to publicize World Refugee Year, July 1, 1959-June 30, 1960.

Boy Scout on Horseback, St. George and Dragon — A174

Scouts Planting Tree A175

30 l, Scout taking oath & boy of ancient Athens. 40 l, Scouts helping in disaster. 70 l, Scouts reading map & tent. 1d, Boy Scout, Sea Scout & Air Scout. 2.50d, Crown Prince Constantine. 6d, Scout flag of Greece & Military Merit medal.

*Perf. 13x13½, 13½x13*

**1960, Apr. 23 Litho.**

| | | | | |
|---|---|---|---|---|
| **669** | A174 | 20 l multi | .25 | .25 |
| **670** | A174 | 30 l multi | .25 | .25 |
| **671** | A174 | 40 l multi | .25 | .25 |
| **672** | A175 | 50 l multi | .25 | .25 |
| **673** | A175 | 70 l multi | .25 | .25 |
| **674** | A175 | 1d multi | .80 | .40 |
| **675** | A174 | 2.50d multi | 2.00 | 1.25 |
| **676** | A175 | 6d multi | 2.50 | 1.50 |
| | | *Nos. 669-676 (8)* | 6.55 | 4.40 |

Greek Boy Scout Organization, 50th anniv.

Greek Holding Sacred Disk Proclaiming Armistice During Games — A176

Lighting Olympic Flame A177

Designs: 70 l, Youth taking oath. 80 l, Boy cutting olive branches for Olympic prizes. 1d, Judges entering stadium. 1.50d, Long jump. 2.50d, Discus thrower. 4.50d, Sprinters. 5d, Javelin thrower. 6d, Crowning the victors. 12.50d, Victor in chariot entering home town.

*Perf. 13x13½, 13½x13*

**1960, Aug. 12 Wmk. 252**

| | | | | |
|---|---|---|---|---|
| **677** | A176 | 20 l multi | .25 | .25 |
| **678** | A177 | 50 l multi | .25 | .25 |
| **679** | A176 | 70 l multi | .25 | .25 |
| **680** | A177 | 80 l multi | .25 | .25 |
| *a.* | | Imperf., pair | 450.00 | |
| **681** | A177 | 1d multi | .40 | .30 |
| **682** | A177 | 1.50d multi | .40 | .30 |
| **683** | A176 | 2.50d multi | .80 | .50 |
| **684** | A177 | 4.50d multi | .95 | .70 |
| *a.* | | Dbl. impression of black | 350.00 | 200.00 |
| **685** | A176 | 5d multi | 2.75 | 1.60 |
| **686** | A177 | 6d multi | 2.75 | 1.60 |
| **687** | A177 | 12.50d multi | 15.00 | 10.00 |
| | | *Nos. 677-687 (11)* | 24.05 | 16.00 |

17th Olympic Games, Rome, 8/25-9/11.

Common Design Types pictured following the introduction.

**Europa Issue, 1960**

Common Design Type

*Perf. 13½x12*

**1960, Sept. 19 Litho. Wmk. 252**

**Size: 33x23mm**

| | | | | |
|---|---|---|---|---|
| **688** | CD3 | 4.50d ultra | *5.00* | *2.00* |
| *a.* | | Double impression | *190.00* | |

**Shepherd Type of 1954**

**1960, Sept. 1 Wmk. 252** *Perf. 13*

| | | | | |
|---|---|---|---|---|
| **689** | A152a | 3d ultra | 2.25 | .40 |

Crown Prince Constantine and Yacht — A178

**1961, Jan. 18** *Perf. 13½x13*

| | | | | |
|---|---|---|---|---|
| **690** | A178 | 2.50d multi | 1.00 | .25 |

Victory of Crown Prince Constantine and his crew at the 17th Olympic Games, Rome (Gold medal, Yachting, Dragon class).

Castoria A179

Delphi — A180

Landscapes and Ancient Monuments: 20 l, Meteora. 50 l, Hydra harbor. 70 l, Acropolis, Athens. 80 l, Mykonos. 1d, St. Catherine's Church, Salonika. 1.50d, Olympia. 2.50d, Knossos. 3.50d, Rhodes. 4d, Epidauros amphitheater. 4.50d, Temple of Poseidon, Sounion. 5d, Temple of Zeus, Athens. 7.50d, Aslan's mosque, Ioannina. 8d, Mount Athos. 8.50d, Santorini. 12.50d, Marble lions, Delos.

*Perf. 13½x12½, 12½x13½*

**1961, Feb. 15 Engr. Wmk. 252**

| | | | | |
|---|---|---|---|---|
| **691** | A179 | 10 l dk gray bl | .25 | .25 |
| **692** | A179 | 20 l dk purple | .25 | .25 |
| **693** | A179 | 50 l blue | .25 | .25 |
| **694** | A179 | 70 l dk purple | .25 | .25 |
| **695** | A179 | 80 l brt ultra | .40 | .25 |
| **696** | A179 | 1d red brn | .70 | .25 |
| **697** | A179 | 1.50d brt grn | 1.00 | .25 |
| **698** | A179 | 2.50d carmine | 3.50 | .25 |
| **699** | A179 | 3.50d purple | 1.40 | .25 |
| **700** | A179 | 4d sl grn | 11.00 | .25 |
| **701** | A179 | 4.50d dk blue | 1.25 | .25 |
| **702** | A179 | 5d claret | 11.00 | .25 |
| **703** | A180 | 6d slate grn | 2.50 | .25 |
| **704** | A179 | 7.50d black | .70 | .25 |
| **705** | A180 | 8d dk vio bl | 4.50 | .25 |
| **706** | A180 | 8.50d org ver | 7.00 | .65 |
| **707** | A179 | 12.50d dk brn | 2.75 | 1.50 |
| | | *Nos. 691-707 (17)* | 48.70 | 5.90 |

Issued for tourist publicity.

Lily Vase — A181

Partridge and Fig Pecker A182

Minoan Art: 1d, Fruit dish. 1.50d, Rhyton bearer. 2.50d, Ladies of Knossos Palace. 4.50d, Sarcophagus of Hagia Trias. 6d, Dancer. 10d, Two vessels with spouts.

*Perf. 13x13½, 13½x13*

**1961, June 30 Litho.**

| | | | | |
|---|---|---|---|---|
| **708** | A181 | 20 l multi | .50 | .25 |
| **709** | A182 | 50 l multi | .50 | .25 |
| **710** | A182 | 1d multi | .50 | .25 |
| **711** | A181 | 1.50d multi | 1.00 | .25 |
| **712** | A182 | 2.50d multi | 7.00 | .25 |
| **713** | A181 | 4.50d multi | 3.00 | 2.00 |
| **714** | A182 | 6d multi | 13.50 | 1.60 |
| **715** | A182 | 10d multi | 15.00 | 8.00 |
| | | *Nos. 708-715 (8)* | 41.00 | 12.85 |

Democritus Nuclear Research Center — A183

Democritus — A184

**1961, July 31** *Perf. 13½x13*

| | | | | |
|---|---|---|---|---|
| **716** | A183 | 2.50d dp lil rose & rose lil | .50 | .25 |
| **717** | A184 | 4.50d vio bl & pale vio bl | 1.00 | .60 |

Inauguration of the Democritus Nuclear Research Center at Aghia Paraskevi.

**Europa Issue, 1961**

Common Design Type

**1961, Sept. 18** *Perf. 13½x12*

**Size: 32½x22mm**

| | | | | |
|---|---|---|---|---|
| **718** | CD4 | 2.50d ver & pink | *.40* | .25 |
| *a.* | | Pink omitted (inscriptions white) | *20.00* | *18.00* |
| **719** | CD4 | 4.50d ultra & lt ultra | *.40* | .25 |

Nicephoros Phocas — A185

**1961, Sept. 22** **Wmk. 252**

**720** A185 2.50d multi 1.00 .60

1000th anniv. of the liberation of Crete from the Saracens by the Byzantine general (later emperor) Phocas.

Hermes Head of 1861 — A186

Each denomination shows a different stamp of 1861 issue.

**1961, Dec. 20** **Litho.** ***Perf. 13x13½***

| | | | | | |
|---|---|---|---|---|---|
| **721** | A186 | 20 l | brn, red brn & cream | .25 | .25 |
| **722** | A186 | 50 l | brn, bis & straw | .25 | .25 |
| **723** | A186 | 1.50d | emer & gray | .25 | .25 |
| **724** | A186 | 2.50d | red org & ol bis | .25 | .25 |
| **725** | A186 | 4.50d | dk bl, bl & gray | .45 | .30 |
| **726** | A186 | 6d | rose lil, pale rose & bl | .75 | .50 |
| **727** | A186 | 10d | car, rose & cr | 1.50 | 1.50 |
| | | | *Nos. 721-727 (7)* | 3.70 | 3.30 |

Centenary of Greek postage stamps.

Tauropos Dam and Lake — A187

Ptolemais Power Station A188

Designs: 50 l, Ladhon river hydroelectric plant. 1.50d, Louros river dam. 2.50d, Aliverion power plant. 4.50d, Salonika hydroelectric sub-station. 6d, Agra river hydroelectric station, interior.

***Perf. 13x13½, 13½x13***

**1962, Apr. 14** **Wmk. 252**

| | | | | | |
|---|---|---|---|---|---|
| **728** | A187 | 20 l | multi | .25 | .25 |
| **729** | A187 | 50 l | multi | .25 | .25 |
| **730** | A188 | 1d | multi | .25 | .25 |
| **731** | A188 | 1.50d | multi | .25 | .25 |
| **732** | A188 | 2.50d | multi | 1.25 | .25 |
| **733** | A188 | 4.50d | multi | .95 | .70 |
| **734** | A188 | 6d | multi | 4.00 | 4.00 |
| | | | *Nos. 728-734 (7)* | 7.20 | 5.95 |

National electrification project.

Youth with Shield and Helmet from Ancient Vase — A189

Designs: 2.50d, Zappion hall, horiz. 4.50d, Kneeling soldier from Temple of Aphaea, Aegina. 6d, Standing soldier from stele of Ariston.

***Perf. 13¼x14, 12x13½***

**1962, May 3** **Litho.** **Wmk. 252**

**Sizes: 22x33mm, 33x22mm**

| | | | | | |
|---|---|---|---|---|---|
| **735** | A189 | 2.50d | grn, bl, red & brn | .25 | .25 |
| **736** | A189 | 3d | brn, buff & red brn | .25 | .25 |
| **737** | A189 | 4.50d | bl & gray | .40 | .40 |

**Size: 21x37mm**

| | | | | | |
|---|---|---|---|---|---|
| **738** | A189 | 6d | brn red & blk | .40 | .30 |
| | | | *Nos. 735-738 (4)* | 1.30 | 1.20 |

Ministerial congress of NATO countries, Athens, May 3-5.

**Europa Issue, 1962**

Common Design Type

**1962, Sept. 17** ***Perf. 13½x12***

**Size: 33x23mm**

| | | | | | |
|---|---|---|---|---|---|
| **739** | CD5 | 2.50d | ver & blk | *.75* | *.40* |
| **740** | CD5 | 4.50d | ultra & blk | *1.50* | *.75* |

Hands and Grain — A190

Demeter — A191

**1962, Oct. 30** ***Perf. 13x13½***

| | | | | | |
|---|---|---|---|---|---|
| **741** | A190 | 1.50d | dp car, blk & brn | *.50* | .25 |
| **742** | A190 | 2.50d | brt grn, blk & brn | *.75* | .25 |

Agricultural Insurance Program.

***Perf. 12x13½***

**1963, Apr. 25** **Wmk. 252**

Design: 4.50d, Wheat and globe.

| | | | | | |
|---|---|---|---|---|---|
| **743** | A191 | 2.50d | brn car, gray & blk | .40 | .25 |
| **744** | A191 | 4.50d | multicolored | .85 | .35 |

FAO "Freedom from Hunger" campaign.

George I, Constantine XII, Alexander I, George II and Paul I — A192

***Perf. 13½x12½***

**1963, June 29** **Engr.**

| | | | | | |
|---|---|---|---|---|---|
| **745** | A192 | 50 l | rose car | .25 | .25 |
| **746** | A192 | 1.50d | green | .45 | .25 |
| **747** | A192 | 2.50d | redsh brn | 1.00 | .25 |
| **748** | A192 | 4.50d | dk blue | 1.60 | 1.25 |
| **749** | A192 | 6d | violet | 3.50 | .60 |
| | | | *Nos. 745-749 (5)* | 6.80 | 2.60 |

Centenary of the Greek dynasty.

**Coin Types of 1959**

Ancient Greek Coins: 50 l, Nymph Arethusa & Chariot. 80 l, Hercules & Zeus. 1d, Helios & Rose. 1.50d, Griffin & Square. 3d, Zeus & Eagle. 3.50d, Athena & Owl. 4.50d, Apollo & Labyrinth. 6d, Aphrodite & Apollo. 8.50d, Ram's head & Incuse Squares.

***Perf. 13½x13, 13x13½***

**1963, July 5** **Litho.** **Wmk. 252**

**Coins in Various Shades of Gray**

| | | | | | |
|---|---|---|---|---|---|
| **750** | A164 | 50 l | violet bl | .25 | .25 |
| **751** | A164 | 80 l | dp magenta | .25 | .25 |
| **752** | A165 | 1d | emerald | .25 | .25 |
| **753** | A164 | 1.50d | lilac rose | .85 | .25 |
| **754** | A164 | 3d | olive | .60 | .25 |
| **755** | A164 | 3.50d | vermilion | .70 | .25 |
| **756** | A165 | 4.50d | redsh brn | .85 | .50 |
| **757** | A165 | 6d | blue grn | 1.10 | .25 |
| **758** | A165 | 8.50d | brt blue | 2.00 | .85 |
| | | | *Nos. 750-758 (9)* | 6.85 | 3.10 |

"Acropolis at Dawn" by Lord Baden-Powell — A193

Jamboree Badge (Boeotian Shield) — A194

Designs: 2.50d, Crown Prince Constantine, Chief Scout. 3d, Athanassios Lefkadites (founder of Greek Scouts) and Lord Baden-Powell. 4.50d, Scout bugling with conch shell.

**1963, Aug. 1**

| | | | | | |
|---|---|---|---|---|---|
| **759** | A193 | 1d | bl, sal & ol | .25 | .25 |
| **760** | A194 | 1.50d | dk bl, org brn & brn | .25 | .25 |
| **761** | A194 | 2.50d | multi | 1.25 | .25 |
| **762** | A193 | 3d | multi | .50 | .55 |
| **763** | A194 | 4.50d | multi | 1.25 | .55 |
| | | | *Nos. 759-763 (5)* | 3.50 | 1.85 |

11th Boy Scout Jamboree, Marathon, July 29-Aug. 16, 1963.

Athenian Treasury, Delphi — A195

2d, Centenary emblem. 2.50d, Queen Olga, founder of Greek Red Cross. 4.50d, Henri Dunant.

**1963, Sept. 16** ***Perf. 12x13½***

| | | | | | |
|---|---|---|---|---|---|
| **764** | A195 | 1d | multi | .50 | .25 |
| **765** | A195 | 2d | multi | .25 | .25 |
| **766** | A195 | 2.50d | multi | .30 | .25 |
| **767** | A195 | 4.50d | multi | .75 | .50 |
| | | | *Nos. 764-767 (4)* | 1.80 | 1.25 |

International Red Cross Centenary.

**Europa Issue, 1963**

Common Design Type

**1963, Sept. 16** ***Perf. 13½x12***

**Size: 33x23mm**

| | | | | | |
|---|---|---|---|---|---|
| **768** | CD6 | 2.50d | green | *2.25* | *.40* |
| **769** | CD6 | 4.50d | brt magenta | *3.00* | *1.50* |

Vatopethion Monastery A196

King Paul I (1901-1964) A197

Designs: 80 l, St. Denys' Monastery. 1d, "Protaton" (Founder's) Church, horiz. 2d, Stavronikita Monastery. 2.50d, Jeweled cover of Nicephoros Phocas Gospel. 3.50d, Fresco of St. Athanassios, founder of community. 4.50d, Presentation of Christ, 11th century manuscript. 6d, Great Lavra Church, horiz.

***Perf. 13x13½, 13½x13***

**1963, Dec. 5** **Litho.** **Wmk. 252**

| | | | | | |
|---|---|---|---|---|---|
| **770** | A196 | 30 l | multi | .25 | .25 |
| **771** | A196 | 80 l | multi | .25 | .25 |
| **772** | A196 | 1d | multi | .25 | .25 |
| **773** | A196 | 2d | multi | 1.00 | .25 |
| **774** | A196 | 2.50d | multi | 3.00 | .25 |
| **775** | A196 | 3.50d | multi | 1.00 | .85 |
| **776** | A196 | 4.50d | multi | 1.00 | .55 |
| **777** | A196 | 6d | multi | 1.10 | .55 |
| | | | *Nos. 770-777 (8)* | 7.85 | 3.20 |

Millennium of the founding of the monastic community on Mt. Athos.

**1964, May 6** ***Perf. 12x13½***

| | | | | | |
|---|---|---|---|---|---|
| **778** | A197 | 30 l | brown | .25 | .25 |
| **779** | A197 | 50 l | purple | .25 | .25 |
| **780** | A197 | 1d | green | .75 | .25 |
| **781** | A197 | 1.50d | orange | .40 | .25 |
| **782** | A197 | 2d | blue | .75 | .25 |
| **783** | A197 | 2.50d | chocolate | .75 | .25 |
| **784** | A197 | 3.50d | red brn | .75 | .25 |
| **785** | A197 | 4d | ultra | 2.00 | .25 |
| **786** | A197 | 4.50d | bluish blk | 2.00 | .80 |
| **787** | A197 | 6d | rose pink | 3.00 | 1.00 |
| | | | *Nos. 778-787 (10)* | 10.90 | 3.80 |

Archangel Michael — A198

Designs: 1d, Bulgaroctonus coin of Emperor Basil II. 1.50d, Two armed saints from ivory triptych by Harbaville, Louvre. 2.50d, Lady, fresco by Panselinos, Protaton Church, Mt. Athos. 4.50d, Angel, mosaic, Daphni Church, Athens.

**1964, June 10** ***Perf. 12x13½***

| | | | | | |
|---|---|---|---|---|---|
| **788** | A198 | 1d | multi | .25 | .25 |
| **789** | A198 | 1.50d | multi | .25 | .25 |
| **790** | A198 | 2d | multi | .25 | .25 |
| **791** | A198 | 2.50d | multi | .25 | .25 |
| **792** | A198 | 4.50d | multi | .80 | .50 |
| | | | *Nos. 788-792 (5)* | 1.80 | 1.50 |

Byzantine Art and for the Byzantine Art Exhibition, Athens, Apr.-June, 1964.

Exist imperf.

Birth of Aphrodite, Emblem of Kythera A199

Designs (emblems of islands): 20 l, Trident, Paxos. 1d, Head of Ulysses, Ithaca. 2d, St. George slaying dragon, Lefkas. 2.50d, Zakyntnos, Zante. 4.50d, Cephalus, dog and spear, Cephalonia. 6d, Trireme, Corfu.

***Perf. 13½x12***

**1964, July 20** **Litho.** **Wmk. 252**

| | | | | | |
|---|---|---|---|---|---|
| **793** | A199 | 20 l | multi | .25 | .25 |
| **794** | A199 | 30 l | multi | .25 | .25 |
| **795** | A199 | 1d | multi | .25 | .25 |
| **796** | A199 | 2d | multi | .25 | .25 |
| **797** | A199 | 2.50d | sl grn & dl grn | .50 | .25 |
| **798** | A199 | 4.50d | multi | 1.00 | .75 |
| **799** | A199 | 6d | multi | 1.00 | .40 |
| | | | *Nos. 793-799 (7)* | 3.50 | 2.40 |

Centenary of the union of the Ionian Islands with Greece.

Child and Sun — A200

**1964, Sept. 10** **Wmk. 252**
**800** A200 2.50d multi .80 .25

50th anniv. of the Natl. Institute of Social Welfare for the Protection of Children and Mothers (P.I.K.P.A.).

## Europa Issue, 1964

Common Design Type

**1964, Sept. 14 Litho.** ***Perf. 13x13½***

**Size: 23x39mm**

**801** CD7 2.50d lt grn & dk red *2.25 .40*
**802** CD7 4.50d gray & brn *2.75 1.50*

King Constantine II and Queen Anne-Marie A201

Peleus and Atalante Fighting, 6th Cent. B.C. Vase A202

**1964, Sept. 18 Engr.** ***Perf. 13½x14***
**803** A201 1.50d green .25 .25
**804** A201 2.50d rose car .25 .25
**805** A201 4.50d brt ultra .50 .25
*Nos. 803-805 (3)* 1.00 .75

Wedding of King Constantine II and Princess Anne-Marie of Denmark, Sept. 18, 1964.

***Perf. 12x13½, 13½x12***

**1964, Oct. 24 Litho. Wmk. 252**

Designs: 1d, Runners on amphora, horiz. 2d, Athlete on vase, horiz. 2.50d, Discus thrower and judge, pitcher. 4.50d, Charioteer, sculpture, horiz. 6d, Boxers, vase, horiz. 10d, Apollo, frieze from Zeus Temple at Olympia.

**806** A202 10 l multi .25 .25
**807** A202 1d multi .25 .25
**808** A202 2d multi .25 .25
**809** A202 2.50d multi .25 .25
**810** A202 4.50d multi .40 .30
**811** A202 6d multi .25 .25
**812** A202 10d multi .30 .25
*Nos. 806-812 (7)* 1.95 1.80

18th Olympic Games, Tokyo, Oct. 10-25.

Detail from "Christ Stripped of His Garments" by El Greco A203

Aesculapius Theatre, Epidauros A204

Paintings by El Greco: 1d, Concert of the Angels. 1.50d, El Greco's painted signature, horiz. 2.50d, Self-portrait. 4.50d, Storm-lashed Toledo.

***Perf. 12x13½, 13½x12***

**1965, Mar. 6 Litho. Wmk. 252**
**813** A203 50 l sepia & multi .25 .25
**814** A203 1d gray & multi .25 .25
*a.* Double impression of black *100.00*
**815** A203 1.50d multi .25 .25
**816** A203 2.50d slate & multi .25 .25
**817** A203 4.50d multi .30 .25
*Nos. 813-817 (5)* 1.30 1.25

350th anniv. of the death of Domenico Theotocopoulos, El Greco (1541-1614).

**1965, Apr. 30 Litho.** ***Perf. 12x13½***

Design: 4.50d, Herod Atticus Theatre, and Acropolis, Athens.

**818** A204 1.50d multi .25 .25
**819** A204 4.50d multi .30 .30

Epidauros and Athens theatrical festivals.

ITU Emblem, Old and New Telecommunication Equipment — A205

**1965, Apr. 30** ***Perf. 13½x12***
**820** A205 2.50d multi .40 .25

Cent. of the ITU.

Swearing-in Ceremony A206

Flag of Philiki Hetaeria, the Friends' Society A207

***Perf. 13½x12***

**1965, May 31 Litho. Wmk. 252**
**821** A206 1.50d multi .25 .25
**822** A207 4.50d gray & multi .25 .25

150th anniv. of the Friends' Society, a secret organization for the liberation of Greece from Turkey.

Emblem of A.H.E.P.A. A208

**1965, June 30**
**823** A208 6d lt bl, blk & ol .50 .25

Congress of the American Hellenic Educational Progressive Association, Athens.

Eleutherios Venizelos, Therissos, 1905 — A209

Designs: 2d, Venizelos signing Treaty of Sevres, 1920. 2.50d, Venizelos portrait.

**1965, June 30 Engr.** ***Perf. 12½x13***
**824** A209 1.50d green .25 .25
**825** A209 2d dark blue .40 .30
**826** A209 2.50d brown .25 .25
*Nos. 824-826 (3)* .90 .80

Cent. of the birth of Eleutherios Venizelos (1864-1936), statesman and prime minister.

Symbols of Planets — A210

Astronaut in Space — A211

Design: 6d, Two space ships over globe.

***Perf. 12½x13½***

**1965, Sept. 11 Litho. Wmk. 252**
**827** A210 50 l multi .25 .25
**828** A211 2.50d multi .25 .25
**829** A211 6d multi .25 .25
*Nos. 827-829 (3)* .75 .75

16th Astronautical Cong., Athens, 9/12-18.

Victory Medal — A212

Stadium, Phaleron A213

Design: 1d, Games' emblem and "JBA."

***Perf. 13½x13, 13x13½***

**1965, Sept. 11**
**830** A213 1d multicolored .25 .25
**831** A212 2d multicolored .25 .25
**832** A213 6d multicolored .25 .25
*Nos. 830-832 (3)* .75 .75

24th Balkan Games, Sept. 1-10.

## Europa Issue, 1965

Common Design Type

**1965, Oct. 21** ***Perf. 13½x12***

**Size: 33x23mm**

**833** CD8 2.50d bl gray, blk & dk bl *.75 .40*
**834** CD8 4.50d olive, blk & grn *1.50 .75*

Hipparchus and Astrolabe A214

**1965, Oct. 21 Litho. Wmk. 252**
**835** A214 2.50d bl grn, blk & dk red .40 .25

Opening of the Evghenides Planetarium, Athens.

St. Andrew's Church, Patras — A215

St. Andrew — A216

**1965, Nov. 30** ***Perf. 12x13½***
**836** A215 1d multicolored .25 .25
**837** A216 5d multicolored .25 .25

Return of the head of St. Andrew from St. Peter's, Rome to St. Andrew's, Patras. The design of the 5d is from an 11th cent. mosaic at St. Luke's Monastery, Boeotia.

Ants and Anthill — A217

Savings Bank and Book — A218

**1965, Nov. 30 Litho. Wmk. 252**
**838** A217 10 l grn, blk & bis .25 .25
**839** A218 2.50d multi .30 .25

50th anniv. of the Post Office Savings Bank.

Theodore Brysakes — A219

Greek Painters: 1d, Nikeforus Lytras. 2.50d, Constantin Volonakis. 4d, Nicolas Gyses. 5d, George Jacobides.

***Perf. 13x13½***

**1966, Feb. 28 Litho. Wmk. 252**
**840** A219 80 l multi .25 .25
**841** A219 1d multi .25 .25
**842** A219 2.50d multi .25 .25
**843** A219 4d multi .25 .25
**844** A219 5d multi .25 .25
*Nos. 840-844 (5)* 1.25 1.25

Jean Gabriel Eynard — A220

Banknote of 1867 — A221

2.50d, Georgios Stavros. 4d, Bank's 1st headquarters, etching by Yannis Kefallinos.

***Perf. 12x13½***

**1966, Mar. 30 Engr. Wmk. 252**
**845** A220 1.50d gray grn .25 .25
**846** A220 2.50d brown .25 .25
**847** A221 4d ultra .25 .25
**848** A221 6d black .25 .25
*Nos. 845-848 (4)* 1.00 1.00

National Bank of Greece, 125th anniv.

Symbolic Water Cycle — A222

UNESCO Emblem — A223

WHO Headquarters, Geneva — A224

*Perf. 12x13½, 13½x12*

**1966, Apr. 18** **Litho.**

**849** A222 1d multicolored .25 .25
**850** A223 3d multicolored .25 .25
**851** A224 5d multicolored .25 .25
*Nos. 849-851 (3)* .75 .75

Hydrological Decade (UNESCO), 1965-74, (1d); 20th anniv. of UNESCO (3d); inauguration of the WHO Headquarters, Geneva (5d).

Geannares Michael (Hatzes) — A225

Explosion at Arkadi Monastery A226

Map of Crete — A227

**1966, Apr. 18**

**852** A225 2d multi .25 .25
**853** A226 2.50d multi .25 .25
**854** A227 4.50d multi .25 .25
*Nos. 852-854 (3)* .75 .75

Cent. of the Cretan revolt against the Turks. Geannares Michael (Hatzes), the leader of the revolt, was a member of Cretan government and a writer.

Copper Mask, 4th Century, B.C. — A228

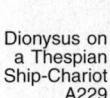

Dionysus on a Thespian Ship-Chariot A229

Designs: 2.50d, Old Theater of Dionysus, Athens, 6th Century B.C. 4.50d, Dancing Dionysus, from vase by Kleophrades, c. 500 B.C.

*Perf. 12x13½, 13½x12*

**1966, May 26** **Litho.** **Wmk. 252**

**855** A228 1d multi .25 .25
**856** A229 1.50d multi .25 .25
**857** A229 2.50d multi .25 .25
**858** A228 4.50d multi .25 .25
*Nos. 855-858 (4)* 1.00 1.00

2500th anniversary of Greek theater.

Boeing 707-320 over New York Buildings and Greek Column A230

**1966, May 26** ***Perf. 13x12½***

**859** A230 6d blue & dark blue .40 .25

Inauguration of transatlantic flights of Olympic Airways.

Tobacco Worker — A231

Design: 5d, Woman sorting tobacco leaves.

*Perf. 12½x13½*

**1966, Sept. 19** **Litho.** **Wmk. 252**

**860** A231 1d multicolored .25 .25
**861** A231 5d multicolored .45 .25

Greek tobacco industry, and 4th Intl. Scientific Tobacco Congress, Athens, Sept. 19-26.

**Europa Issue, 1966**
Common Design Type

**1966, Sept. 19** **Litho.** **Wmk. 252**
**Size: 23x33mm**

**862** CD9 1.50d olive *.75* *.35*
**863** CD9 4.50d lt red brown *1.50* *.70*

Carved Cases for Knitting Needles — A232

Bridegroom, Embroidery from Epirus A233

Designs (Popular Art): 50 l, Lyre, Crete. 1d, Massa (stringed instrument). 1.50d, Bas-relief (cross and angels). 2d, Icon (Sts. Constantine and Helena). 2.50d, Virgin (wood carving, Church of St. Nicholas, Galaxeidon). 3d, Embroidery (sailing ship from Skyros). 4d, Embroidery (wedding parade). 4.50d, Carved wooden distaff (Sts. George and Barbara). 5d, Silver and agate necklace and earrings. 20d, Handwoven cloth, Cyprus.

*Perf. 12x13½, 13½x12*

**1966, Nov. 21** **Litho.** **Wmk. 252**

**864** A232 10 l multi .25 .25
**865** A233 30 l multi .25 .25
**866** A232 50 l multi .25 .25
**867** A232 1d multi .25 .25
**868** A233 1.50d multi .25 .25
**869** A232 2d multi 1.60 .25
**870** A232 2.50d multi .25 .25
**871** A233 3d multi .25 .25
**872** A233 4d multi .65 .25
**873** A232 4.50d multi .30 .30
**874** A232 5d multi .70 .25
**875** A233 20d multi 1.50 .50
*Nos. 864-875 (12)* 6.50 3.30

King Constantine II, Queen Anne-Marie and Princess Alexia — A234

Designs: 2d, Princess Alexia. 3.50d, Queen Anne-Marie and Princess Alexia.

*Perf. 13½x14*

**1966, Dec. 19** **Engr.** **Wmk. 252**

**876** A234 2d green .30 .25
**877** A234 2.50d brown .30 .25
**878** A234 3.50d ultra .40 .25
*Nos. 876-878 (3)* 1.00 .75

Princess Alexia, successor to the throne of Greece.

"Night" by John Cossos (1830-73) — A235

Sculptures: 50 l, Penelope by Leonides Drosses (1836-1882). 80 l, Shepherd by George Fytales. 2d, Woman's torso by Constantine Demetriades (1881-1943). 2.50d, "Colocotrones" (equestrian statue) by Lazarus Sochos (1862-1911). 3d, Sleeping Young Lady by John Halepas (1851-1938), horiz. 10d, Woodcutter by George Filippotes (1839-1919), horiz.

*Perf. 12x13½, 13½x12*

**1967, Feb. 28** **Litho.** **Wmk. 252**

**879** A235 20 l Prus bl, gray & blk .25 .25
**880** A235 50 l brn, gray & blk .25 .25
**881** A235 80 l brn red, gray & blk .25 .25
**882** A235 2d vio bl, gray & blk .25 .25
**883** A235 2.50d ultra, blk & grn .25 .25
**884** A235 3d bl, lt bl, gray & blk .40 .25
**885** A235 10d bl & multi .30 .25
*Nos. 879-885 (7)* 1.95 1.75

Issued to honor modern Greek sculptors.

World Map and Olympic Rings A236

Discus Thrower by C. Demetriades A237

Designs: 1.50d, Runners on ancient clay vessel. 2.50d, Hurdler and map of Europe and Near East. 6d, Rising sun over Altis ruins at Olympia.

*Perf. 13½x12, 12x13½*

**1967, Apr. 6** **Litho.** **Wmk. 252**

**886** A236 1d multi .25 .25
**887** A236 1.50d multi .25 .25
**888** A236 2.50d multi .25 .25
**889** A237 5d multi .40 .30
**890** A236 6d multi .45 .25
*Nos. 886-890 (5)* 1.60 1.30

Olympic Games Day, Apr. 6 (1d); Classic Marathon Race, Apr. 6 (1.5d); athletic qualifying rounds for the Cup of Europe, June 24-25 (2.50d); 9th contest for the European Athletic Championships, 1969 (5d); founding of the Intl. Academy at Olympia and the 7th meeting of the Academy, July 29-Aug. 14, 1967 (6d).

**Europa Issue, 1967**
Common Design Type
*Perf. 12x13½*

**1967, May 2** **Litho.** **Wmk. 252**
**Size: 23x33½mm**

**891** CD10 2.50d buff, lt & dk brn *1.00* *.25*
**892** CD10 4.50d grn, lt & dk grn *2.75* *.75*

Chapel, Skopelos Island A238

Plaka District, Athens — A239

Intl. Tourist Year: 4.50d, Doric Temple of Epicurean Apollo, by Itkinus, c. 430 B.C.

*Perf. 13½x12, 12x13½*

**1967, June 26** **Litho.** **Wmk. 252**

**893** A238 2.50d multi .25 .25
**894** A238 4.50d multi .50 .30
*a.* Double impression of black
**895** A239 6d multi .50 .25
*Nos. 893-895 (3)* 1.25 .80

Destroyer and Sailor A240

Training Ship, Merchant Marine Academy — A241

Maritime Week: 2.50d, Merchant Marine Academy, Aspropyrgos, Attica, and rowing crew. 3d, Cruiser Georgios Averoff and Naval School, Poros. 6d, Merchant ship and bearded figurehead.

**1967, June 26**

**896** A240 20 l multi .25 .25
**897** A241 1d multi .25 .25
**898** A240 2.50d multi .25 .25
**899** A240 3d multi .30 .25
**900** A240 6d multi .40 .25
*Nos. 896-900 (5)* 1.45 1.25

Soldier and Rising Phoenix A242

Blast Furnaces A243

*Perf. 12x13½*

**1967, Aug. 30** **Litho.** **Wmk. 252**

**901** A242 2.50d blue & multi .25 .25
**902** A242 3d orange & multi .25 .25
**903** A242 4.50d multi .25 .25
*Nos. 901-903 (3)* .75 .75

Revolution of Apr. 21, 1967.

**1967, Nov. 29** ***Perf. 13x14***

**904** A243 4.50d brt bl & dk vio bl .40 .40

1st meeting of the UN Industrial Development Organization, Athens, Nov. 29-Dec. 20.

Sailboats A244

Children's Drawings: 1.50d, Steamship and island. 3.50d, Farmhouse. 6d, Church on hill.

**1967, Dec. 20** ***Perf. 13½x12½***

| | | | | |
|---|---|---|---|---|
| **905** | A244 | 20 l multi | .25 | .25 |
| **906** | A244 | 1.50d grn, dk bl & blk | .25 | .25 |
| **907** | A244 | 3.50d multi | .40 | .40 |
| **908** | A244 | 6d multi | .40 | .40 |
| | | *Nos. 905-908 (4)* | 1.30 | 1.30 |

Javelin A245

Apollo, Olympic Academy Seal A246

Discus Thrower by Demetriades A247

Designs: 1d, Jumping. 2.50d, Attic vase showing lighting of Olympic torch. 4d, Olympic rings and world map, horiz. 6d, Long-distance runners, vert.

**Wmk. 252**

**1968, Feb. 28** **Litho.** ***Perf. 12½***

| | | | | |
|---|---|---|---|---|
| **909** | A245 | 50 l ultra & bis | .25 | .25 |
| **910** | A245 | 1d grn, yel, blk & gray | .25 | .25 |
| **911** | A246 | 1.50d blk, bl & buff | .25 | .25 |
| **912** | A246 | 2.50d ol grn, blk & org brn | .25 | .25 |
| **913** | A246 | 4d gray & multi | .35 | .25 |
| **914** | A247 | 4.50d bl, grn, yel & blk | 1.25 | .35 |
| **915** | A245 | 6d brn, red & bl | .30 | .25 |
| | | *Nos. 909-915 (7)* | 2.90 | 1.85 |

50 l, 1d, 6d, 27th Balkan Games, Athens, Aug. 29-Sept. 1; 1.50d, Meeting of the Intl. Olympic Academy; 2.50d, Lighting of the Olympic torch for 19th Olympic Games, Mexico City; 4d, Olympic Day, Apr. 6; 4.50d, 9th European Athletic Championships, 1969.

## Europa Issue, 1968

Common Design Type

***Perf. 13½x12***

**1968, Mar. 29** **Litho.** **Wmk. 252**

**Size: 33x23mm**

| | | | | |
|---|---|---|---|---|
| **916** | CD11 | 2.50d cop red, bis & blk | *1.25* | *.40* |
| **917** | CD11 | 4.50d vio, bister & blk | *2.50* | *1.25* |

Emblems of Greek and International Automobile Clubs — A248

**1968, Mar. 29** ***Perf. 13x14***

| | | | | |
|---|---|---|---|---|
| **918** | A248 | 5d ultra & org brn | 1.00 | .40 |

General Assembly of the International Automobile Federation, Athens, Apr. 8-14.

Athena Defeating Alkyoneus, from Pergamos Altar, 180 B.C. — A249

Athena, 2nd Century, B.C. — A250

Winged Victory of Samothrace, c. 190 B.C. — A251

Designs: 50 l, Alexander the Great on horseback, from sarcophagus, c. 310 B.C. 1.50d, Emperors Constantine and Justinian bringing offerings to Virgin Mary, Byzantine mosaic. 2.50d, Emperor Constantine Paleologos, lithograph by D. Tsokos, 1859. 3d, Greece in Missolonghi, by Delacroix. 4.50d, Greek Soldier (evzone), by G. B. Scott.

***Perf. 13½x13, 13x13½, 13½x14 (A249)***

**1968, Apr. 27**

| | | | | |
|---|---|---|---|---|
| **919** | A249 | 10 l gray & multi | .25 | .25 |
| **920** | A250 | 20 l grn & multi | .25 | .25 |
| **921** | A250 | 50 l pur & multi | .25 | .25 |
| **922** | A249 | 1.50d gray & multi | .25 | .25 |
| **923** | A250 | 2.50d multi | .25 | .25 |
| **924** | A251 | 3d multi | .25 | .25 |
| **925** | A251 | 4.50d multi | .25 | .25 |
| **926** | A251 | 6d multi | .35 | .30 |
| | | *Nos. 919-926 (8)* | 2.10 | 2.05 |

"The Hellenic Fight for Civilization" exhibition

Monument to the Unknown Priest and Teacher, Rhodes A252

Map & Flag of Greece — A253

Cross and Globe — A254

***Perf. 14x13½, 13½x14***

**1968, July 11** **Litho.** **Wmk. 252**

| | | | | |
|---|---|---|---|---|
| **927** | A252 | 2d multicolored | .40 | .25 |
| **928** | A253 | 5d multicolored | .80 | .80 |

20th anniv. of the union of the Dodecanese Islands with Greece.

**1968, July 11** ***Perf. 13½x14***

| | | | | |
|---|---|---|---|---|
| **929** | A254 | 6d multicolored | .55 | .40 |

19th Biennial Congress of the Greek Orthodox Archdiocese of North and South America.

Antique Lamp (GAPA Emblem) A255

**1968, July 11** ***Perf. 14x13½***

| | | | | |
|---|---|---|---|---|
| **930** | A255 | 6d multicolored | .50 | .30 |

Regional Congress of the Greek-American Progressive Association, G.A.P.A.

Fragment of Bas-relief, Temple of Aesculapius, Athens — A256

***Perf. 13½x14***

**1968, Sept. 8** **Litho.** **Wmk. 252**

| | | | | |
|---|---|---|---|---|
| **931** | A256 | 4.50d multicolored | 1.50 | .90 |

Issued to publicize the 5th European Cardiology Congress, Athens, Sept. 8-14.

View of Olympia, Site of Ancient Games A257

Pindar and Olympic Ode — A258

Design: 2.50d, Panathenaic Stadium, site of 1896 Olympic Games.

***Perf. 14x13½, 13x13½***

**1968, Sept. 25** **Litho.** **Wmk. 252**

| | | | | |
|---|---|---|---|---|
| **932** | A257 | 2.50d multicolored | .30 | .25 |
| **933** | A257 | 5d green & multi | .60 | .25 |
| **934** | A258 | 10d bl, yel & brn | 1.50 | .80 |
| | | *Nos. 932-934 (3)* | 2.40 | 1.30 |

19th Olympic Games, Mexico City, 10/12-27.
On 10d, hyphen is omitted at end of 5th line of ode on 5 of 50 stamps in each sheet.

Hygeia and WHO Emblem — A259

**1968, Nov. 8** ***Perf. 13½x14***

| | | | | |
|---|---|---|---|---|
| **935** | A259 | 5d gray & multi | .70 | .40 |

20th anniv. of WHO.

Mediterranean, Breguet 19 and Flight Route, 1928 — A260

Farman, 1912, Plane and F-104G Jet — A261

St. Zeno, The Letter Bearer — A262

Design: 2.50d, Greek air force pilot ramming enemy plane over Langada.

**1968, Nov. 8** ***Perf. 14x13½, 13½x14***

| | | | | |
|---|---|---|---|---|
| **936** | A260 | 2.50d ultra, blk & yel | .25 | .25 |
| **937** | A260 | 3.50d multicolored | .25 | .25 |
| **938** | A261 | 8d multicolored | 1.25 | .90 |
| | | *Nos. 936-938 (3)* | 1.75 | 1.40 |

Exploits of Royal Hellenic Air Force.

***Perf. 13½x14***

**1969, Feb. 10** **Litho.** **Wmk. 252**

| | | | | |
|---|---|---|---|---|
| **939** | A262 | 2.50d multicolored | .50 | .25 |

Establishment of the feast day of St. Zeno as the day of Greek p.o. personnel.

Hephaestus and Cyclops, Bas-relief A263

Parade of Harvesters, Minoan Vase — A264

**1969, Feb. 10** ***Perf. 13½x12½***

| | | | | |
|---|---|---|---|---|
| **940** | A263 | 1.50d multicolored | .35 | .25 |
| **941** | A264 | 10d multicolored | .90 | .65 |

50th anniv. of the ILO.

Yachts in Vouliagmeni Harbor — A265

Athens Festival, Chorus of Elders — A266

View of Astypalaia — A267

***Perf. 13½x12½, 12½x13½***

**1969, Mar. 3**

| | | | | |
|---|---|---|---|---|
| **942** | A265 | 1d multicolored | .25 | .25 |
| **943** | A266 | 5d multicolored | .80 | .70 |
| **944** | A267 | 6d multicolored | .40 | .25 |
| | | *Nos. 942-944 (3)* | 1.45 | 1.20 |

Issued for tourist publicity.

Attic Shield and Helmet on Greek Coin, 461-450 B.C. — A268

Hoplites and Flutist, from Proto-Corinthian Pitcher, 640-630 B.C. — A269

***Perf. 12½x13½, 13½x12½***

**1969, Apr. 4 Litho. Wmk. 252**

**945** A268 2.50d rose red, blk & sl .35 .25
**946** A269 4.50d multi 1.00 .65

20th anniv. of NATO.

**Europa Issue, 1969**

Common Design Type

**1969, May 5** ***Perf. 13½x12½***

**Size: 33x23mm**

**947** CD12 2.50d multi *1.75* .25
**948** CD12 4.50d multi *3.25* *1.25*

Victory Medal A270

Pole Vault and Pentathlon (from Panathenaic Amphora) A271

5d, Relay race and runners from amphora, 525 B.C., horiz. 8d, Modern and ancient (Panathenaic amphora, c. 480 B.C.) discus throwers.

***Perf. 12½x13½, 13½x12½***

**1969, May 5**

**949** A270 20 l red & multi .25 .25
**950** A271 3d gray & multi .25 .25
**951** A271 5d multicolored .25 .25
**952** A271 8d multicolored 1.40 .75
*Nos. 949-952 (4)* 2.15 1.50

Issued to publicize the 9th European Athletic Championships, Athens, Sept. 16-21.

**Greece and the Sea Issue**

Oil Tanker A272

Merchant Vessels and Warships, 1821 — A273

Designs: 80 l, Brig and steamship, painting by Ioannis Poulakas, vert. 4.50d, Warships on maneuvers. 6d, Battle of Salamis, 480 B.C., painting by Constantine Volonakis.

***Perf. 12½x13½, 13½x12½, 13½x13***

**1969, June 28 Litho. Wmk. 252**

**953** A272 80 l multicolored .25 .25
**954** A272 2d blk, bl & gray .25 .25
**955** A273 2.50d dk bl & multi .25 .25
**956** A272 4.50d brn, gray & bl 1.00 .35
**957** A273 6d multicolored 1.50 .45
*Nos. 953-957 (5)* 3.25 1.55

Raising Greek Flag — A274

**1969, Aug. 31** ***Perf. 13x13½***

**958** A274 2.50d blue & multi .70 .25

20th anniv. of the Grammos-Vitsi victory.

Athena Promachos and Map of Greece A275

"National Resistance" A276

Greek Participation in World War II — A277

***Perf. 13x13½, 13½x14***

**1969, Oct. 12 Litho. Wmk. 252**

**959** A275 4d multicolored .25 .25
**960** A276 5d multicolored 1.50 .70
**961** A277 6d multicolored .65 .25
*Nos. 959-961 (3)* 2.40 1.20

25th anniv. of the liberation of Greece in WW II.

No. 960 exists imperf.

Demetrius Tsames Karatasios, by G. Demetriades A278

Pavlos Melas, by P. Mathiopoulos A279

2.50d, Emmanuel Pappas, statue by Nicholas Perantinos. 4.50d, Capetan Kotas.

***Perf. 12x13½***

**1969, Nov. 12 Litho. Wmk. 252**

**962** A278 1.50d multicolored .25 .25
**963** A278 2.50d blue & multi .25 .25
**964** A279 3.50d gray & multi .25 .25
**965** A279 4.50d multicolored .95 .55
*Nos. 962-965 (4)* 1.70 1.30

Issued to honor Greek heroes in Macedonia's struggle for liberation.

Angel of the Annunciation, Daphni Church, 11th Century — A280

Dolphins, Delos, 110 B.C. A281

Christ's Descent into Hell, Nea Moni Church, 11th Cent. A282

Greek Mosaics: 1.50d, The Holy Ghost (dove), Hosios Loukas Monastery, 11th cent. 2d, The Hunter, Pella, 4th cent. B.C. 5d, Bird, St. George's Church, Salonica, 5th cent.

***Perf. 12x13½, 13½x12 (1d), 13x13½ (6d)***

**1970, Jan. 16 Litho. Wmk. 252**

**966** A280 20 l multicolored .25 .25
**967** A281 1d multicolored .25 .25
**968** A280 1.50d blue & multi .25 .25
**969** A280 2d gray & multi .45 .25
**970** A280 5d bister & multi .55 .35
**971** A282 6d multicolored .75 .75
*Nos. 966-971 (6)* 2.50 2.10

Hercules and the Cretan Bull — A283

Hercules and the Erymanthian Boar — A284

Labors of Hercules: 30 l, Capture of Cerberus. 1d, Capture of the golden apples of the Hesperides. 1.50d, Lernean Hydra. 2d, Slaying of Geryon. 3d, Centaur Nessus. 4.50d, Fight with the river god Achelos. 5d, Nemean lion. 6d, Stymphalian birds. 20d, Giant Antaeus. Designs of 20 l and 1d are from Temple of Zeus, Olympia; others from various vessels; all from 7th-5th cent. B.C.

***Perf. 13½x12, 12x13½***

**1970, Mar. 16 Litho. Wmk. 252**

**972** A283 20 l gray, blk & yel .25 .25
**973** A283 30 l ocher & multi .25 .25
**974** A284 1d bl gray, blk & bl .25 .25
**975** A283 1.50d dk brn, bis & sl grn .30 .25
**976** A283 2d ocher & multi 2.25 .25
**977** A284 2.50d ocher, dk brn & dl red .30 .25
**978** A284 3d multicolored 2.25 .25
**979** A283 4.50d dk bl & multi .50 .25
**980** A283 5d multicolored .50 .25
**981** A283 6d multicolored .50 .25
**982** A283 20d black & multi 1.75 .85
*Nos. 972-982 (11)* 9.10 3.35

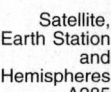

Satellite, Earth Station and Hemispheres A285

**1970, Apr. 21** ***Perf. 13½x12***

**983** A285 2.50d bl, gray & yel .50 .30
**984** A285 4.50d brn, ol & bl 1.25 1.10

Opening of the Earth Satellite Telecommunications Station "Thermopylae," Apr. 21, 1970.

**Europa Issue, 1970**

Common Design Type and

Owl (Post Horns and CEPT) — A287

**1970, Apr. 21** ***Perf. 13½x12, 12x13½***

**985** CD13 2.50d rose red & org *2.00* *.75*
**986** A287 3d brt bl, gray & vio bl *2.00* *.75*
**987** CD13 4.50d ultra & org *5.75* *1.25*
*Nos. 985-987 (3)* 9.75 2.75

St. Demetrius with Cyril and Methodius as Children A288

Emperor Michael III with Sts. Cyril and Methodius A290

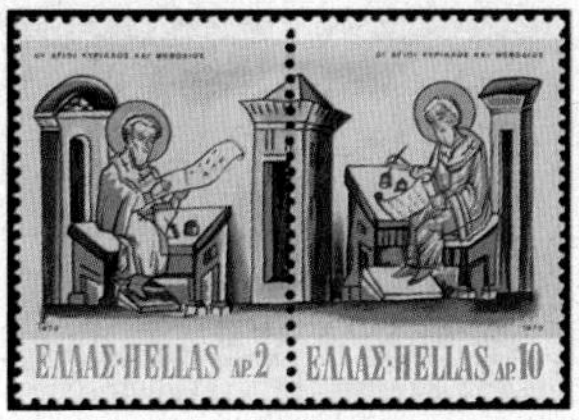

A289

***Perf. 13½x14 (50 l); 12x13½ (2d, 10d); 13x13½ (5d)***

**1970, Apr. 17 Litho. Wmk. 252**

**988** A288 50 l multi .25 .25
**989** A289 2d St. Cyril .60 .45
**990** A290 5d multi .50 .25
**991** A289 10d St. Methodius .70 .50
*a.* Pair, #989, 991 1.25 1.25
*Nos. 988-991 (4)* 2.05 1.45

Sts. Cyril and Methodius who translated the Bible into Slavonic.

Greek Fir A292

Jankaea Heldreichii A293

6d, Rock partridge, horiz. 8d, Wild goat.

***Perf. 13x14, 14x13, 12x13½ (2.50d)***

**1970, June 16 Litho. Wmk. 252**

| | | | | | |
|---|---|---|---|---|---|
| **992** | A292 | 80 l | multi | .35 | .35 |
| **993** | A293 | 2.50d | multi | 1.25 | .25 |
| **994** | A292 | 6d | multi | 2.40 | .55 |
| **995** | A292 | 8d | multi | 2.75 | 2.40 |
| | | | *Nos. 992-995 (4)* | 6.75 | 3.55 |

European Nature Conservation Year, 1970.

Map Showing Link Between AHEPA Members and Greece A294

**1970, Aug. 1** ***Perf. 13½x13***

| | | | | | |
|---|---|---|---|---|---|
| **996** | A294 | 6d | blue & multi | 1.00 | .40 |

48th annual AHEPA (American Hellenic Educational Progressive Assoc.) Cong., Athens, Aug. 1970.

UPU Headquarters, Bern — A295

Education Year Emblem — A296

Mahatma Gandhi — A297

United Nations Emblem — A298

Ludwig van Beethoven — A299

***Perf. 13½x12, 13x14, 12x13½***

**1970, Oct. 7 Litho. Wmk. 252**

| | | | | | |
|---|---|---|---|---|---|
| **997** | A295 | 50 l | bis & multi | .25 | .25 |
| **998** | A296 | 2.50d | bl & multi | .40 | .25 |
| **999** | A297 | 3.50d | multi | .25 | .25 |
| **1000** | A298 | 4d | bl & multi | .75 | .25 |
| **1001** | A299 | 4.50d | blk & multi | 1.50 | 1.10 |
| | | | *Nos. 997-1001 (5)* | 3.15 | 2.10 |

Inauguration of the UPU Headquarters, Bern (50 l); Intl. Education Year (2.50d); cent. of the birth of Mohandas K. Gandhi (1869-1948), leader in India's struggle for independence (3.50d); 25th anniv. of the UN (4d); Ludwig van Beethoven (1770-1827), composer (4.50d).

The Shepherds (Mosaic) — A300

Christmas (from Mosaic in the Monastery of Hosios Loukas, Boetia, 11th cent.): 4.50d, The Three Kings and Angel. 6d, Nativity, horiz.

**1970, Dec. 5** ***Perf. 13x14, 14x13***

| | | | | | |
|---|---|---|---|---|---|
| **1002** | A300 | 2d | bister & multi | .25 | .25 |
| **1003** | A300 | 4.50d | bister & multi | .40 | .30 |
| **1004** | A300 | 6d | bister & multi | .80 | .80 |
| | | | *Nos. 1002-1004 (3)* | 1.45 | 1.35 |

"Leonidas" A301

Priest Sworn in as Fighter, from Commemorative Medal — A302

Eugenius Voùlgaris (1716-1806) A303

Battle of Corinth A304

Kaltetsi Monastery, Seal of Peloponnesian Senate — A305

Death of Bishop Isaias, Battle of Alamana — A306

Designs: No. 1009, *Pericles.* No. 1010, Sacrifice of Kapsalis. 1.50d, *Terpsichore.* No. 1012, Patriarch Grigorius IV. No. 1013, Suliot women in battle, horiz. No. 1015, *Karteria.* No. 1016, Adamantios Korais, M.D. No. 1017, Memorial column, provincial administrative seal of Epidaurus. 3d, Naval battle, Samos, horiz. 5d, Battle of Athens. 6d, Naval battle, Yeronda. 6.50d, Battle of Maniaki. 9d, Battle of Karpenisi, death of Marcos Botsaris. 10d, Bishop Germanos blessing flag. 15d, *Secret School.* 20d, John Capodistrias' signature and seal.

**1971 Litho. Wmk. 252**

| | | | | | |
|---|---|---|---|---|---|
| **1005** | A301 | 20 l | multi | .25 | .25 |
| **1006** | A302 | 50 l | multi | .25 | .25 |
| **1007** | A303 | 50 l | multi | .25 | .25 |
| **1008** | A304 | 50 l | multi | .25 | .25 |
| **1009** | A301 | 1d | multi | .25 | .25 |
| **1010** | A304 | 1d | multi | .25 | .25 |
| **1011** | A301 | 1.50d | multi | .25 | .25 |
| **1012** | A302 | 2d | multi | .25 | .25 |
| **1013** | A304 | 2d | multi | .25 | .25 |
| **1014** | A305 | 2d | multi | .25 | .25 |
| **1015** | A301 | 2.50d | multi | .25 | .25 |
| **1016** | A303 | 2.50d | multi | .25 | .25 |
| **1017** | A305 | 2.50d | multi | .25 | .25 |
| **1018** | A304 | 3d | multi | .65 | .40 |
| **1019** | A306 | 4d | multi | .25 | .25 |
| **1020** | A304 | 5d | multi | .40 | .25 |
| **1021** | A301 | 6d | multi | 1.25 | .90 |
| **1022** | A301 | 6.50d | multi | .40 | .25 |
| **1023** | A301 | 9d | multi | 1.00 | .90 |
| **1024** | A306 | 10d | multi | 1.10 | .90 |
| **1025** | A306 | 15d | multi | 1.25 | 1.10 |
| **1026** | A305 | 20d | multi | 2.25 | 1.40 |
| | | | *Nos. 1005-1026 (22)* | 11.80 | 9.60 |

Sesquicentennial of Greece's uprising against the Turks. Emphasize role of Navy (#1005, 1009, 1011, 1015, 1018, 1021), issued 3/15; Church (#1006, 1012, 1019, 1024), 2/8; Instructors (#1007, 1016, 1025), 6/21; Land Forces (#1008, 1010, 1013, 1020, 1022-1023), 9/21; Provincial Administrations (#1014, 1017, 1026), 10/19.

Sizes: 37x24mm: #1005, 1009, 1011, 1015; 40x27½mm, #1021; 48x33mm, #1022, 1023.

Perfs.: 14x13, #1005, 1009, 1011, 1013, 1015, 1018; 13½x14, #1006, 1012; 12x13½, #1007, 1016, 1019, 1022-1025; 13x14, #1008, 1010, 1020; 13½x13, #1014, 1017, 1021, 1026.

Spyridon Louis, Winner of 1896 Marathon Race, Arriving at Stadium A307

Pierre de Coubertin and Memorial Column — A308

***Perf. 13½x13, 13x13½***

**1971, Apr. 10 Litho. Wmk. 252**

| | | | | | |
|---|---|---|---|---|---|
| **1027** | A307 | 3d | multi | .50 | .25 |
| **1028** | A308 | 8d | multi | 1.25 | .90 |

Olympic Games revival, 75th anniv.

**Europa Issue, 1971**

Common Design Type

**1971, May 18** ***Perf. 13½x12***

**Size: 33x22½mm**

| | | | | | |
|---|---|---|---|---|---|
| **1029** | CD14 | 2.50d | grn, yel & blk | *1.00* | *.30* |
| **1030** | CD14 | 5d | org, yel & blk | *3.00* | *1.50* |

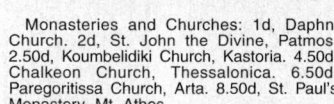

Hosios Lukas Monastery A309

Monasteries and Churches: 1d, Daphni Church. 2d, St. John the Divine, Patmos. 2.50d, Koumbelidiki Church, Kastoria. 4.50d, Chalkeon Church, Thessalonica. 6.50d, Paregoritissa Church, Arta. 8.50d, St. Paul's Monastery, Mt. Athos.

**1972, Jan. 17** ***Perf. 14x13***

| | | | | | |
|---|---|---|---|---|---|
| **1031** | A309 | 50 l | multi | .25 | .25 |
| **1032** | A309 | 1d | multi | .25 | .25 |
| **1033** | A309 | 2d | multi | .25 | .25 |
| **1034** | A309 | 2.50d | multi | .25 | .25 |
| **1035** | A309 | 4.50d | multi | .25 | .25 |
| **1036** | A309 | 6.50d | multi | .25 | .25 |
| **1037** | A309 | 8.50d | multi | 1.00 | 1.00 |
| | | | *Nos. 1031-1037 (7)* | 2.50 | 2.50 |

Cretan Costume — A310

Designs: Greek regional costumes.

**1972, Mar. 1** ***Perf. 12½x13½***

| | | | | | |
|---|---|---|---|---|---|
| **1038** | A310 | 50 l | shown | .25 | .25 |
| **1039** | A310 | 1d | Woman, Pindus | .25 | .25 |
| **1040** | A310 | 2d | Man, Missolonghi | .25 | .25 |
| **1041** | A310 | 2.50d | Woman, Sarakatsan, Attica | .25 | .25 |
| *a.* | | | "1972" omitted | 10.00 | 10.00 |
| **1042** | A310 | 3d | Woman, Island of Nisyros | .25 | .25 |
| **1043** | A310 | 4.50d | Woman, Megara | .25 | .25 |
| **1044** | A310 | 6.50d | Woman, Trikeri | .30 | .25 |
| **1045** | A310 | 10d | Woman, Pylaia, Macedonia | 3.00 | 1.00 |
| | | | *Nos. 1038-1045 (8)* | 4.80 | 2.75 |

See Nos. 1073-1089, 1121-1135.

Memorial Medal, Science and Industry A311

Flag and Map of Greece — A312

Honeycomb, Transportation and Industry — A313

***Perf. 13½x13, 13x13½***

**1972, Apr. 21 Wmk. 252**

| | | | | | |
|---|---|---|---|---|---|
| **1046** | A311 | 2.50d | blue & multi | .25 | .25 |
| **1047** | A312 | 4.50d | ocher & multi | .25 | .25 |
| **1048** | A313 | 5d | multi | .40 | .40 |
| | | | *Nos. 1046-1048 (3)* | .90 | .90 |

5th anniversary of the revolution.

**Europa Issue 1972**

Common Design Type

**1972, May 2** ***Perf. 12x13½***

**Size: 23x33mm**

| | | | | | |
|---|---|---|---|---|---|
| **1049** | CD15 | 3d | multi | *.50* | *.30* |
| **1050** | CD15 | 4.50d | blue & multi | *1.50* | *1.25* |

Acropolis and Car — A314

Route of Automobile Rally — A315

**1972, May 26** ***Perf. 13½x12***

| | | | | | |
|---|---|---|---|---|---|
| **1051** | A314 | 4.50d | multi | .60 | .60 |
| **1052** | A315 | 5d | bl & multi | .60 | .60 |

20th Acropolis Automobile Rally, May 26-29.

Gaia Handing Erecthonius to Athena, Cecrops A316

Designs: 2d, Uranus, from altar of Zeus at Pergamum. 2.50d, Gods defeating the Giants, Treasury of Siphnos. 5d, Zeus of Dodona.

**1972, June 26 Litho. *Perf. 14x13½***

**1053** A316 1.50d yel grn & blk .25 .25
**1054** A316 2d dk bl & blk .25 .25
**1055** A316 2.50d org brn & blk .25 .25
**1056** A316 5d dk brn & blk .50 .40
*a.* Strip of 4, #1053-1056 2.00 2.00

Greek mythology. No. 1056 issued only se-tenant with Nos. 1053-1055 in sheets of 40 (4x10). Nos. 1053-1055 issued also in sheets of 50 each.

Olympic Rings, Wrestlers A317

50 l, Young athlete, crowning himself, c. 480 B.C., vert. 3.50d, Spartan woman running, Archaic period, vert. 4.50d, Episkyros ball game, 6th century B.C. 10d, Running youths, from Panathenaic amphora.

***Perf. 13½x14, 14x13½***

**1972, July 28 Litho. Wmk. 252**

**1057** A317 50 l mar, blk & gray .25 .25
**1058** A317 1.50d brn, gray & blk .25 .25
**1059** A317 3.50d ocher & multi .50 .25
**1060** A317 4.50d grn, buff & blk .25 .25
**1061** A317 10d blk & fawn 1.00 .55
*Nos. 1057-1061 (5)* 2.25 1.55

20th Olympic Games, Munich, 8/26-9/11.

Young Stamp Collector — A318

**1972, Nov. 15 *Perf. 13x14***

**1062** A318 2.50d multi .25 .25

Stamp Day.

Three Kings and Angels — A319

**1972, Nov. 15**

**1063** A319 2.50d shown .25 .25
**1064** A319 4.50d Nativity .25 .25
*a.* Pair, #1063-1064 .40 .40

Christmas 1972.

Technical University, 1885, by Luigi Lanza — A320

**1973, Mar. 30 *Perf. 13½x13***

**1065** A320 2.50d multi .40 .25

Centenary of the Metsovion National Technical University.

"Spring," Fresco — A321

Breast-form Jug — A322

"Wooing and Twittering Swallows" Fresco — A323

Designs: 30 l, "Blue Apes" fresco. 1.50d, Jug decorated with birds. 5d, "Wild Goats" fresco. 6.50d, Wrestlers, fresco.

**1973, Mar. 30 *Perf. 13x13½, 13½x13***

**1066** A321 10 l multi .25 .25
**1067** A322 20 l multi .25 .25
**1068** A323 30 l multi .25 .25
**1069** A322 1.50d grn & multi .25 .25
**1070** A323 2.50d multi .25 .25
**1071** A323 5d multi .25 .25
**1072** A323 6.50d multi .80 .80
*Nos. 1066-1072 (7)* 2.30 2.30

Archaeological treasures from Santorini Island (Thera).

**Costume Type of 1972**

Women's costumes except 10 l, 20 l, 50 l, 5d, 15d.

**1973, Apr. 18 *Perf. 12½x13½***

**1073** A310 10 l Peloponnesus .25 .25
**1074** A310 20 l Central Greece .25 .25
**1075** A310 30 l Locris .25 .25
**1076** A310 50 l Skyros .25 .25
**1077** A310 1d Spetsai .25 .25
**1078** A310 1.50d Almyros .25 .25
**1079** A310 2.50d Macedonia .25 .25
**1080** A310 3.50d Salamis .25 .25
**1081** A310 4.50d Epirus .25 .25
**1082** A310 5d Lefkas .25 .25
**1083** A310 6.50d Skyros .25 .25
**1084** A310 8.50d Corinth .40 .25
**1085** A310 10d Corfu .40 .25
**1086** A310 15d Epirus .40 .25
**1087** A310 20d Thessaly 1.25 .25
**1088** A310 30d Macedonia 1.60 .35
**1089** A310 50d Thrace 3.25 1.60
*Nos. 1073-1089 (17)* 10.05 5.70

**Europa Issue 1973**

Common Design Type

**1973, May 2 *Perf. 13½x12½***

**Size: 35x22mm**

**1090** CD16 2.50d dp bl & lt bl *.30 .25*
**1091** CD16 3d dp car & dp org *.30 .30*
**1092** CD16 4.50d ol grn & yel *1.50 .85*
*Nos. 1090-1092 (3)* 2.10 1.40

Zeus Battling Typhoeus, from Amphora A324

1d, Mount Olympus, after photograph. 2.50d, Zeus battling Giants, from Pergamum Altar. 4.50d, Punishment of Atlas and Prometheus, from vase.

***Perf. 14x13½***

**1973, June 25 Wmk. 252**

**1093** A324 1d gray & blk .25 .25
**1094** A324 2d multi .25 .25
**1095** A324 2.50d gray, blk & buff .25 .25
**1096** A324 4.50d ocher & multi .45 .45
*a.* Strip of 4, #1093-1096 1.75 1.75

Greek mythology.

Dr. George Papanicolaou A325

***Perf. 13x13½***

**1973, Aug. 10 Litho. Wmk. 252**

**1097** A325 2.50d multi .25 .25
**1098** A325 6.50d multi .25 .25

Dr. George Papanicolaou (1883-1962), cytologist and cancer researcher.

Icon, The Annunciation A326

**1973, Aug. 10**

**1099** A326 2.50d multi .40 .25

Miraculous icon of Our Lady of the Annunciation found on Tinos, 1823.

A327

Triptolemus holding wheat on chariot.

***Perf. 13x14***

**1973, Oct. 22 Litho. Wmk. 252**

**1100** A327 4.50d buff, dk brn & red .30 .25

5th Symposium of the European Conf. of Transport Ministers, Athens, Oct. 22-25.

A328

National Benefactors: 1d, Georgios Averoff. 2d, Apostolos Arsakis. 2.50d, Constantine Zappas. 4d, Andrea Sygros. 6.50d, John Varvakis.

**1973, Nov. 15 Engr.**

**1101** A328 1.50d dk red brn .25 .25
**1102** A328 2d car rose .25 .25
**1103** A328 2.50d slate green .25 .25
**1104** A328 4d purple .25 .25
**1105** A328 6.50d black .25 .25
*Nos. 1101-1105 (5)* 1.25 1.25

Child Examining Stamp — A329

**1973, Nov. 15 Litho. *Perf. 14x13***

**1106** A329 2.50d multi .25 .25

Stamp Day.

Lord Byron in Souliot Costume — A330

Byron Taking Oath at Grave of Botsaris — A331

***Perf. 13x14***

**1974, Apr. 4 Wmk. 252 Litho.**

**1107** A330 2.50d multi .25 .25
**1108** A331 4.50d multi .25 .25

George Gordon, Lord Byron (1788-1824), English poet involved in Greek struggle for independence.

Harpist of Keros, c. 2800-2200 B.C. — A332

Europa: 4.50d, Statue of Young Women, c. 510 B.C. 6.50d, Charioteer of Delphi, c. 480-450 B.C.

**1974, May 10 *Perf. 13x14***

**1109** A332 3d dp bl & multi *.45 .25*
**1110** A332 4.50d dl red & multi *.65 .30*
**1111** A332 6.50d yel & multi *1.75 .80*
*Nos. 1109-1111 (3)* 2.85 1.35

Zeus and Hera Enthroned, and Iris — A333

Design from Mycenean Vase and UPU Emblem — A334

Greek mythology (from Vases, 5th Cent. B.C.): 2d, Birth of Athena, horiz. 2.50d, Artemis, Apollo, Leto, horiz. 10d, Hermes, the messenger.

**1974, June 24** ***Perf. 13x14, 14x13***

**1112** A333 1.50d ocher, blk & brn .25 .25
**1113** A333 2d blk, ocher & brn .25 .25
**1114** A333 2.50d blk, ocher & brn .25 .25
**1115** A333 10d blk, ocher & brn .25 .25
*Nos. 1112-1115 (4)* 1.00 1.00

**1974, Sept. 14** ***Perf. 12½x13½***

UPU cent.: 4.50d, Hermes on the Move, horiz. 6.50d, Woman reading letter.

**1116** A334 2d vio & blk .25 .25
**1117** A334 4.50d vio & blk .25 .25
**1118** A334 6.50d vio & blk .25 .30
*Nos. 1116-1118 (3)* .75 .80

Crete No. 80 A335

**1974, Nov. 15 Litho.** ***Perf. 13½x13***

**1119** A335 2.50d multi .25 .25

Stamp Day.

Flight into Egypt — A336

**1974, Nov. 15** ***Perf. 13½x14***

**1120** A336 Strip of 3 .80 .80
*a.* 2d ocher & multi .25 .25
*b.* 4.50d ocher & multi .25 .25
*c.* 8.50d ocher & multi .25 .25

Christmas 1974. Design is from 11th cent. Codex of Dionysos Monastery on Mount Athos.

### Costume Type of 1972

Designs: Women's costumes, except 1.50d.

**1974, Dec. 5** ***Perf. 12½x13½***

**1121** A310 20 l Megara .25 .25
**1122** A310 30 l Salamis .25 .25
**1123** A310 50 l Edipsos .25 .25
**1124** A310 1d Kyme .25 .25
**1125** A310 1.50d Sterea Hellas .25 .25
**1126** A310 2d Desfina .25 .25
**1127** A310 3d Epirus .25 .25
**1128** A310 3.50d Naousa .25 .25
**1129** A310 4d Hasia .25 .25
**1130** A310 4.50d Thasos .25 .25
**1131** A310 5d Skopelos .25 .25
**1132** A310 6.50d Epirus .25 .25
**1133** A310 10d Pelion .30 .25
**1134** A310 25d Kerkyra .70 .25
**1135** A310 30d Boeotia 2.25 .60
*Nos. 1121-1135 (15)* 6.25 4.10

Secret Vostitsa Assembly, 1821 — A337

Grigorios Dikeos-Papaflessas A338

Aghioi Apostoli Church, Kalamata A339

***Perf. 13½x12½, 12½x13½***

**1975, Mar. 24**

**1136** A337 4d multi .25 .25
**1137** A338 7d multi .25 .25
**1138** A339 11d multi .25 .25
*Nos. 1136-1138 (3)* .75 .75

Grigorios Dikeos-Papaflessas (1788-1825), priest and leader in Greece's uprising against the Turks, sesquicentennial of death.

Vase with Flowers — A340

Erotokritos and Aretussa — A341

Europa: 11d, Girl with Hat. All designs are after paintings by Theophilos Hatzimichael (d. 1934).

***Perf. 12½x13½***

**1975, May 10 Litho. Wmk. 252**

**1139** A340 4d multi *.50* .45
**1140** A341 7d multi *.70* .65
**1141** A340 11d multi *2.00* 1.25
*Nos. 1139-1141 (3)* *3.20* 2.35

House, Kastoria A342

Greek Houses, 18th Cent.: 40 l, Arnea, Halkidiki. 4d, Veria. 6d, Siatista. 11d, Ambelakia, Thessaly.

**1975, June 26** ***Perf. 13½x12½***

**1142** A342 10 l brt bl & blk .25 .25
**1143** A342 40 l red org & blk .25 .25
**1144** A342 4d bister & blk .25 .25
**1145** A342 6d ultra & multi .25 .25
**1146** A342 11d org & blk .25 .25
*Nos. 1142-1146 (5)* 1.25 1.25

IWY Emblem, Neolithic Goddess — A343

"Looking to the Future" — A344

8.50d, Confrontation between Antigone & Creon.

***Perf. 12½x13½***

**1975, Sept. 29 Litho. Wmk. 252**

**1147** A343 1.50d lilac & dk brn .25 .25
**1148** A343 8.50d bis, blk & brn .25 .25
**1149** A344 11d bl & blk .25 .25
*Nos. 1147-1149 (3)* .75 .75

International Women's Year 1975.

Papanastasiou and University Buildings — A345

First University Building A346

University City Plan A347

**1975, Sept. 29** ***Perf. 14x13½***

**1150** A345 1.50d tan & sepia .25 .25
**1151** A346 4d multi .25 .25
**1152** A347 11d multi .25 .25
*Nos. 1150-1152 (3)* .75 .75

Thessaloniki University, 50th anniversary. Alexandros Papanastasiou (1876-1936), founded University while Prime Minister.

Evangelos Zappas and Zappeion Building — A348

National Benefactors: 4d, Georgios Rizaris and Rizarios Ecclesiastical School. 6d, Michael Tositsas and Metsovion Technical University. 11d, Nicolaos Zosimas and Zosimea Academy.

***Perf. 14x13***

**1975, Nov. 15 Litho. Wmk. 252**

**1153** A348 1d blk & grn .25 .25
**1154** A348 4d blk & brn .25 .25
**1155** A348 6d blk & org .25 .25
**1156** A348 11d blk & brick red .25 .25
*Nos. 1153-1156 (4)* 1.00 1.00

Greece No. 380 — A349

**1975, Nov. 15** ***Perf. 13x14***

**1157** A349 11d dull grn & brn .40 .35

Stamp Day 1975.

Pontos Lyre — A350

Musicians, Byzantine Mural — A351

Designs: 1d, Cretan lyre. 1.50d, Tambourine. 4d, Guitarist, from amphora, horiz. 6d, Bagpipes. 7d, Lute. 10d, Barrel organ. 11d, Pipes and zournadas. 20d, Musicians and singers praising God, Byzantine mural, horiz. 25d, Drums. 30d, Kanonaki, horiz.

***Perf. 12½x13½, 13½x12½***

**1975, Dec. 15 Litho. Wmk. 252**

**1158** A350 10 l multi .25 .25
**1159** A351 20 l multi .25 .25
**1160** A350 1d ultra & multi .25 .25
**1161** A350 1.50d multi .25 .25
**1162** A351 4d multi .25 .25
**1163** A350 6d multi .25 .25
**1164** A350 7d multi .25 .25
**1165** A350 10d multi .25 .25
**1166** A350 11d red & multi .25 .25
**1167** A351 20d multi .25 .25
**1168** A350 25d multi .45 .25
**1169** A350 30d multi 1.00 1.00
*Nos. 1158-1169 (12)* 3.95 3.75

Popular musical instruments.

Early Telephone, Globe, Waves A352

11d, Globe, waves, telephone 1976.

***Perf. 13½x12½***

**1976, Mar. 23 Litho. Wmk. 252**

**1170** A352 7d blk & multi .25 .25
**1171** A352 11d blk & multi .25 .25
*a.* Pair, Nos. 1170-1171 .50 .50

1st telephone call by Alexander Graham Bell, Mar. 10, 1876.

Sortie of Missolonghi — A353

**1976, Mar. 23** ***Perf. 13½x13***

**1172** A353 4d multi .25 .25

Sortie of the garrison of Missolonghi, sesquicentennial.

Florina Jugn — A354

Avramidis Plate — A355

Europa: 11d, Egina pitcher with Greek flags.

***Perf. 13x14, 12½x12 (A355)***

**1976, May 10 Litho. Wmk. 252**

**1173** A354 7d buff & multi .40 .30
**1174** A355 8.50d blk & multi .50 .30
**1175** A354 11d gray & multi 1.50 .90
*Nos. 1173-1175 (3)* 2.40 1.50

Lion Attacking Bull — A356

Head of Silenus — A357

Designs: 4.50d, Flying aquatic birds. 7d, Wounded bull. 11d, Cow feeding calf, horiz. Designs from Creto-Mycenaean engraved seals, c. 1400 B.C.

***Perf. 13x12½, 13½x14, 14x13½***

**1976, May 10**

**1176** A356 2d bis & multi .25 .25
**1177** A356 4.50d multi .25 .25
**1178** A356 7d multi .25 .25
**1179** A357 8.50d pur & multi .25 .25
**1180** A357 11d brn & multi .25 .25
*Nos. 1176-1180 (5)* 1.25 1.25

Long Jump A358

Montreal and Athens Stadiums — A359

Designs (Classical and Modern Events): 2d, Basketball. 3.50d, Wrestling. 4d, Swimming. 25d, Lighting Olympic flame and Montreal Olympic Games torch.

***Perf. 14x13½, 12½x13½ (A359)***

**1976, June 25 Litho. Wmk. 252**

**1181** A358 50 l org & multi .25 .25
**1182** A358 2d org & multi .25 .25
**1183** A358 3.50d org & multi .25 .25
**1184** A358 4d bl & multi .25 .25
**1185** A359 11d multi .25 .25
**1186** A358 25d org & multi .75 .75
*Nos. 1181-1186 (6)* 2.00 2.00

21st Olympic Games, Montreal, Canada, July 17-Aug. 1.

Lesbos, View and Map A360

***Perf. 13½x14, 14x13½***

**1976, July 26 Litho. Wmk. 252**

**1187** A360 30d Lemnos, vert. .45 .25
**1188** A360 50d shown .75 .25
**1189** A360 75d Chios .90 .25
**1190** A360 100d Samos 2.10 1.75
*Nos. 1187-1190 (4)* 4.20 2.50

Greek Aegean Islands.

Three Kings Speaking to the Jews — A361

Christmas: 7d, Nativity. Designs from manuscripts in Esfigmenou Monastery, Mount Athos.

**1976, Dec. 8** ***Perf. 13½x14***

**1191** A361 4d yellow & multi .25 .25
**1192** A361 7d yellow & multi .25 .25

Greek Grammar of 1478 A362

**1976, Dec. 8** ***Perf. 14x13***

**1193** A362 4d multi .25 .25

500th anniversary of printing of first Greek book by Constantin Lascaris, Milan.

Heinrich Schliemann A363

Brooch with Figure of Goddess — A364

Designs: 4d, Gold bracelet, horiz. 7d, Gold diadem, horiz. 11d, Gold mask (Agamemnon). Treasures from Mycenaean tombs.

**1976, Dec. 8** ***Perf. 13x14, 14x13***

**1194** A363 2d multi .25 .25
**1195** A364 4d multi .25 .25
**1196** A364 5d grn & multi .25 .25
**1197** A364 7d multi .25 .25
**1198** A364 11d multi .50 .50
*Nos. 1194-1198 (5)* 1.50 1.50

Cent. of the discovery of the Mycenaean royal shaft graves by Heinrich Schliemann.

Aesculapius with Patients — A365

Patient in Clinic — A366

Designs: 1.50d, Aesculapius curing young man. 2d, Young Hercules with old nurse. 20d, Old man with votive offering of large leg.

***Perf. 12½x13½ (A365); 13x12 (A366)***

**1977, Mar. 15 Litho. Wmk. 252**

**1199** A365 50 l multi .25 .25
**1200** A366 1d multi .25 .25
**1201** A366 1.50d multi .25 .25
**1202** A366 2d multi .25 .25
**1203** A365 20d multi .25 .25
*Nos. 1199-1203 (5)* 1.25 1.25

International Rheumatism Year.

Winged Wheel, Modern Transportation — A367

**1977, May 16 Litho.** ***Perf. 14x13½***

**1204** A367 7d multi .25 .25

European Conference of Ministers of Transport (E.C.M.T.), Athens, June 1-3.

Mani Castle, Vathia A368

Europa: 7d, Santorini, vert. 15d, Windmills on Lasithi plateau.

***Perf. 14x13½, 13½x14***

**1977, May 16 Litho. Wmk. 252**

**1205** A368 5d multicolored .45 .25
**1206** A368 7d multicolored .45 .35
**1207** A368 15d multicolored 1.50 .50
*Nos. 1205-1207 (3)* 2.40 1.10

Alexandria Lighthouse, from Roman Coin — A369

Designs: 1d, Alexander places Homer's works into Achilles' tomb, fresco by Raphael. 1.50d, Alexander descends to the bottom of the sea, Flemish miniature. 3d, Alexander searching for water of life, Hindu plate. 7d, Alexander on horseback, Coptic carpet. 11d, Alexander hearing oracle that his days are numbered, Byzantine manuscript. 30d, Death of Alexander, Persian miniature. All designs include gold coin of Lysimachus with Alexander's head.

**1977, July 23** ***Perf. 14x13***

**1208** A369 50 l silver & multi .25 .25
**1209** A369 1d silver & multi .25 .25
**1210** A369 1.50d silver & multi .25 .25
**1211** A369 3d silver & multi .25 .25
**1212** A369 7d silver & multi .25 .25
**1213** A369 11d silver & multi .25 .25
**1214** A369 30d silver & multi .35 .35
*Nos. 1208-1214 (7)* 1.85 1.85

Cultural influence of Alexander the Great (356-323 B.C.), King of Macedonia.

"Greece Rising Again" A370

People in Front of University A371

Greek Flags, Laurel, University A372

***Perf. 13½x12½, 12x12½, 12½x12***

**1977, July 23 Unwmk.**

**1215** A370 4d multi .25 .25
**1216** A371 7d multi .25 .25
**1217** A372 20d multi .25 .25
*Nos. 1215-1217 (3)* .75 .75

Restoration of Democracy in Greece.

Archbishop Makarios, Map of Cyprus — A373

Design: 4d, Archbishop Makarios, vert.

***Perf. 13x13½, 13½x13***

**1977, Sept. 10 Litho. Unwmk.**

**1218** A373 4d sepia & blk .25 .25
**1219** A373 7d buff, brn & blk .25 .25

Archbishop Makarios (1913-1977), President of Cyprus.

Old Athens Post Office A374

Neo-Hellenic architecture: 1d, Institution for the Blind, Salonika. 1.50d, Townhall, Syros. 2d, National Bank of Greece, Piraeus. 5d, Byzantine Museum, Athens. 50d, Municipal Theater, Patras.

**1977, Sept. 22** ***Perf. 13½x13***

**1220** A374 50 l multi .25 .25
**1221** A374 1d multi .25 .25
**1222** A374 1.50d multi .25 .25
**1223** A374 2d multi .25 .25
**1224** A374 5d multi .25 .25
**1225** A374 50d multi .35 .35
*Nos. 1220-1225 (6)* 1.60 1.60

Battle of Navarino, Lithograph — A375

Adm. Van Heyden, Sir Edward Codrington, Count de Rigny — A376

**1977, Oct. 20** ***Perf. 13½x13***

**1226** A375 4d brn, buff & blk .25 .25
**1227** A376 7d multi .25 .25

150th anniversary of Battle of Navarino.

Parthenon and Refinery — A377

Caryatid and Factories — A379

Fish and Birds Suffering from Pollution A378

Design: 7d, Birds and trees in polluted air.

**1977, Oct. 20** ***Perf. 13½x14, 14x13½***

| | | | | |
|---|---|---|---|---|
| **1228** | A377 | 3d org & blk | .25 | .25 |
| **1229** | A378 | 4d multi | .25 | .25 |
| **1230** | A378 | 7d multi | .25 | .25 |
| **1231** | A379 | 30d blk, gray & slate | .40 | .40 |
| | | *Nos. 1228-1231 (4)* | 1.15 | 1.15 |

Protection of the environment.

Map of Greece and Ships — A380

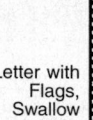

Globe and Swallows A381

Letter with Flags, Swallow A382

5d, Globe with Greek flag. 13d, World map showing dispersion of Greeks abroad.

**1977, Dec. 15** ***Perf. 13½x12½***

| | | | | |
|---|---|---|---|---|
| **1232** | A380 | 4d multi | .25 | .25 |
| **1233** | A380 | 5d multi | .25 | .25 |
| **1234** | A381 | 7d multi | .25 | .25 |
| **1235** | A382 | 11d multi | .25 | .25 |
| **1236** | A380 | 13d multi | .25 | .25 |
| | | *Nos. 1232-1236 (5)* | 1.25 | 1.25 |

Greeks living abroad.

Kalamata Harbor, by Constantine Parthenis — A383

Greek Paintings: 2.50d, Boats, Arsanas, by Spyros Papaloucas, vert. 4d, Santorini, by Constantine Maleas. 7d, The Engagement, by Nicolaus Gyzis. 11d, Woman with Straw Hat, by Nicolaus Lytras, vert. 15d, "Spring" (nude), by Georgio Iacovidis.

**1977, Dec. 15** ***Perf. 13½x13, 13x13½***

| | | | | |
|---|---|---|---|---|
| **1237** | A383 | 1.50d yel & multi | .25 | .25 |
| **1238** | A383 | 2.50d yel & multi | .25 | .25 |
| **1239** | A383 | 4d yel & multi | .25 | .25 |
| **1240** | A383 | 7d yel & multi | .25 | .25 |
| **1241** | A383 | 11d yel & multi | .25 | .25 |
| **1242** | A383 | 15d yel & multi | .25 | .25 |
| | | *Nos. 1237-1242 (6)* | 1.50 | 1.50 |

Ebenus Cretica — A384

Greek Flora: 2.50d, Dwarf lily. 3d, Campanula oreadum. 4d, Tiger lily. 7d, Viola delphinantha. 25d, Paeonia rhodia.

**1978, Mar. 30** **Litho.** ***Perf. 13x13½***

| | | | | |
|---|---|---|---|---|
| **1243** | A384 | 1.50d multi | .25 | .25 |
| **1244** | A384 | 2.50d multi | .25 | .25 |
| **1245** | A384 | 3d multi | .25 | .25 |
| **1246** | A384 | 4d multi | .25 | .25 |
| **1247** | A384 | 7d multi | .25 | .25 |
| **1248** | A384 | 25d multi | .30 | .25 |
| | | *Nos. 1243-1248 (6)* | 1.55 | 1.50 |

Postrider, Cancellation A385

5d, S.S. Maximilianos & Hermes Head. 7d, 19th cent. mail train & #122. 30d, Mailmen on motorcycles & #1062.

**1978, May 15** ***Perf. 13½x12½***

| | | | | |
|---|---|---|---|---|
| **1249** | A385 | 4d buff & multi | .25 | .25 |
| **1250** | A385 | 5d buff & multi | .25 | .25 |
| **1251** | A385 | 7d buff & multi | .25 | .25 |
| **1252** | A385 | 30d buff & multi | .25 | .25 |
| *a.* | | Souvenir sheet of 4 | 1.00 | 1.00 |
| | | *Nos. 1249-1252 (4)* | 1.00 | 1.00 |

150th anniv. of Greek postal service.

No. 1252a issued Sept. 25, contains Nos. 1249-1252 in slightly changed colors. Sold for 60d.

Lighting Olympic Flame, Olympia — A386

Start of 100-meter Race — A387

**1978, May 15** ***Perf. 13x14***

| | | | | |
|---|---|---|---|---|
| **1253** | A386 | 7d multi | .40 | .25 |
| **1254** | A387 | 13d multi | .85 | .40 |

80th session of International Olympic Committee, Athens, May 10-21.

**Europa Issue 1978**

St. Sophia, Salonica A388

Lysicrates Monument, Athens — A389

**1978, May 15** ***Perf. 13x14, 14x13***

| | | | | |
|---|---|---|---|---|
| **1255** | A388 | 4d multi | .75 | .30 |
| **1256** | A389 | 7d multi | 1.50 | .70 |

Aristotle, Roman Bust — A390

School of Athens, by Raphael — A391

Map of Chalcidice, Base of Statue from Attalus Arcade A392

Aristotle the Wise, Byzantine Fresco, St. George's Church, Ioannina A393

***Perf. 13x13½, 13½x14 (20d)***

**1978, July 10** **Litho.**

| | | | | |
|---|---|---|---|---|
| **1257** | A390 | 2d multi | .25 | .25 |
| **1258** | A391 | 4d multi | .25 | .25 |
| **1259** | A392 | 7d multi | .25 | .25 |
| **1260** | A393 | 20d multi | .25 | .25 |
| | | *Nos. 1257-1260 (4)* | 1.00 | 1.00 |

Aristotle (384-322 B.C.), systematic philosopher.

Rotary Emblem A394

Surgeons Operating — A395

Ugo Foscolo, View of Zante — A396

Hellenistic Bronze Head — A397

Charioteer's Hand, Delphi — A398

Wright Brothers' Plane, Daedalus and Icarus — A399

**1978, Sept. 21** **Litho.** ***Perf. 12½***

| | | | | |
|---|---|---|---|---|
| **1261** | A394 | 1d multi | .25 | .25 |
| **1262** | A395 | 1.50d multi | .25 | .25 |
| **1263** | A396 | 2.50d multi | .25 | .25 |
| **1264** | A397 | 5d multi | .25 | .25 |
| **1265** | A398 | 7d multi | .40 | .30 |
| **1266** | A399 | 13d multi | .40 | .40 |
| | | *Nos. 1261-1266 (6)* | 1.80 | 1.70 |

Rotary in Greece, 50th anniv. (1d); 11th Greek Surgery Cong., Salonica (1.50d); Ugo Foscolo (1778-1827), Italian writer (2.50d); European Convention on Human Rights, 25th anniv. (5d); 2nd Conf. of Ministers of Culture of the Council of Europe member countries, Athens, Oct. 23-27 (7d); 75th anniv. of 1st powered flight (13d).

Poor Woman and her 5 Children A400

Scenes from Fairy Tale "The 12 Months": 3d, The poor woman and the 12 months. 4d, The poor woman and the gold coins. 20d, Punishment of the greedy woman.

**1978, Nov. 6** **Litho.** ***Perf. 13½x13***

| | | | | |
|---|---|---|---|---|
| **1267** | A400 | 2d multi | .25 | .25 |
| **1268** | A400 | 3d multi | .25 | .25 |
| **1269** | A400 | 4d multi | .25 | .25 |
| **1270** | A400 | 20d multi | .25 | .25 |
| | | *Nos. 1267-1270 (4)* | 1.00 | 1.00 |

"Transplants" A401

The Miracle of St. Anarghiri A402

**1978, Nov. 6** ***Perf. 12½x13½***

| | | | | |
|---|---|---|---|---|
| **1271** | A401 | 4d multi | .25 | .25 |
| **1272** | A402 | 10d multi | .25 | .25 |

Advancements in organ transplants.

Cruiser A403

New and Old Greek Naval Ships: 1d, Torpedo boats. 2.50d, Submarine Papanicolis. 4d, Battleship Psara. 5d, Sailing ship "Madonna of Hydra." 7d, Byzantine corvette. 50d, Archaic trireme.

**1978, Dec. 15** **Litho.** ***Perf. 13½x12***

| | | | | |
|---|---|---|---|---|
| **1273** | A403 | 50 l multi | .25 | .25 |
| **1274** | A403 | 1d multi | .25 | .25 |
| **1275** | A403 | 2.50d multi | .25 | .25 |
| **1276** | A403 | 4d multi | .25 | .25 |
| **1277** | A403 | 5d multi | .25 | .25 |
| **1278** | A403 | 7d multi | .25 | .25 |
| **1279** | A403 | 50d multi | .45 | .45 |
| | | *Nos. 1273-1279 (7)* | 1.95 | 1.95 |

Cadet Officer, Military School, Nauplia
A404

Cadet Officers' School Emblem — A405

Design: 10d, Cadet Officers Military School, Athens, Cadet's uniform, 1978.

**1978, Dec. 15** ***Perf. 13½x12, 12x13½***

| | | | | |
|---|---|---|---|---|
| **1280** | A404 | 1.50d multi | .25 | .25 |
| **1281** | A405 | 2d multi | .25 | .25 |
| **1282** | A404 | 10d multi | .25 | .25 |
| | | *Nos. 1280-1282 (3)* | .75 | .75 |

Cadet Officers Military School, 150th anniv.

Virgin and Child — A406

Baptism of Christ — A407

Designs from 16th century icon stands in Stavronikita Monastery.

**1978, Dec. 15** ***Perf. 13x13½***

| | | | | |
|---|---|---|---|---|
| **1283** | A406 | 4d multi | .25 | .25 |
| **1284** | A407 | 7d multi | .25 | .25 |

Christmas 1978.

Map of Greece
A408

**1978, Dec. 28** ***Perf. 14x13***

| | | | | |
|---|---|---|---|---|
| **1285** | A408 | 7d multi | .25 | .25 |
| **1286** | A408 | 11d multi | .25 | .25 |
| **1287** | A408 | 13d multi | .25 | .25 |
| | | *Nos. 1285-1287 (3)* | .75 | .75 |

Kitsos Tzavellas — A409

Souli Castle
A410

10d, Fighting Souliots. 20d, Fight of Zalongo.

***Perf. 12½x13½, 13½x12½***

**1979, Mar. 12** **Litho.**

| | | | | |
|---|---|---|---|---|
| **1288** | A409 | 1.50d buff, blk & brn | .25 | .25 |
| **1289** | A410 | 3d multi | .25 | .25 |
| **1290** | A410 | 10d multi | .25 | .25 |
| **1291** | A409 | 20d buff, blk & brn | .25 | .25 |
| | | *Nos. 1288-1291 (4)* | 1.00 | 1.00 |

Struggle of the Souliots, 18th century fighters for freedom from Turkey.

Cycladic Figure from Amorgos — A411

**1979, Apr. 26** **Litho.** ***Perf. 12x13½***

| | | | | |
|---|---|---|---|---|
| **1292** | A411 | 20d multi | .35 | .35 |

Aegean art.

Mailmen from Crete — A412

Europa: 7d, Rural mailman on horseback, Crete.

**1979, May 11** ***Perf. 13½x14***

| | | | | |
|---|---|---|---|---|
| **1293** | A412 | 4d multi | *1.00* | .25 |
| **1294** | A412 | 7d multi | *1.00* | .55 |
| *a.* | | Pair, #1293-1294 | *2.25* | *2.25* |

Nicolas Scoufas
A413

Basketball
A415

Locomotives — A414

Mene Psarianosi Symeonidis Fossil
A416

Temple of Hephaestus and Byzantine Church
A417

Victory of Paeonius Statue, Flags of Balkan Countries
A418

**1979, May 12** ***Perf. 13x14, 14x13***

| | | | | |
|---|---|---|---|---|
| **1295** | A413 | 1.50d multi | .25 | .25 |
| **1296** | A414 | 2d multi | .25 | .25 |
| **1297** | A415 | 3d multi | .25 | .25 |
| **1298** | A416 | 4d multi | .25 | .25 |
| **1299** | A417 | 10d multi | .25 | .25 |
| **1300** | A418 | 20d multi | .35 | .35 |
| | | *Nos. 1295-1300 (6)* | 1.60 | 1.60 |

Nicolas Scoufas (1779-1818), founder of (patriotic) Friendly Society; Piraeus-Athens-to-the-frontier railroad, 75th anniv.; European Basketball Championship; 7th Intl. Cong. for the Study of the Neocene Period in the Mediterranean; Balkan Tourist Year 1979; 50 years of track and field competitions in Balkan countries.

Wheat with Members' Flags, Greek Coins — A419

European Parliament, Strasbourg — A420

***Perf. 13x14, 14x13***

**1979, May 28** **Litho.**

| | | | | |
|---|---|---|---|---|
| **1301** | A419 | 7d multi | .25 | .25 |
| **1302** | A420 | 30d multi | .35 | .35 |

Greece's entry into European Economic Community and Parliament.

Statue of a Girl, IYC Emblem — A421

Intl. Year of the Child: 8d, Girl & pigeons. 20d, Mother & Children, painting by Iacovides.

**1979, June 27** **Litho.** ***Perf. 13x14***

| | | | | |
|---|---|---|---|---|
| **1303** | A421 | 5d multi | .25 | .25 |
| **1304** | A421 | 8d multi | .25 | .25 |
| **1305** | A421 | 20d multi | .25 | .25 |
| | | *Nos. 1303-1305 (3)* | .75 | .75 |

Philip II, Bust — A422

Purple Heron — A423

Designs: 8d, Golden wreath. 10d, Copper vessel. 14d, Golden casket, horiz. 18d, Silver ewer. 20d, Golden quiver (detail). 30d, Gold and iron cuirass.

***Perf. 13½x14, 14x13½***

**1979, Sept. 15** **Litho.**

| | | | | |
|---|---|---|---|---|
| **1306** | A422 | 6d multi | .25 | .25 |
| **1307** | A422 | 8d multi | .25 | .25 |
| **1308** | A422 | 10d multi | .25 | .25 |
| **1309** | A422 | 14d multi | .25 | .25 |
| **1310** | A422 | 18d multi | .25 | .25 |
| **1311** | A422 | 20d multi | .25 | .25 |
| **1312** | A422 | 30d multi | .40 | .40 |
| | | *Nos. 1306-1312 (7)* | 1.90 | 1.90 |

Archaeological finds from Vergina, Macedonia.

**1979, Oct. 15**

Protected Birds: 8d, Gull. 10d, Falcon, horiz. 14d, Kingfisher, horiz. 20d, Pelican. 25d, White-tailed sea eagle.

| | | | | |
|---|---|---|---|---|
| **1313** | A423 | 6d multi | .25 | .25 |
| **1314** | A423 | 8d multi | .25 | .25 |
| **1315** | A423 | 10d multi | .25 | .25 |
| **1316** | A423 | 14d multi | .25 | .25 |
| **1317** | A423 | 20d multi | .25 | .25 |
| **1318** | A423 | 25d multi | .75 | .60 |
| | | *Nos. 1313-1318 (6)* | 2.00 | 1.85 |

Council of Europe wildlife and natural habitat protection campaign.

Agricultural Bank
A424

St. Cosmas — A425

Basil the Great — A426

Balkan Countries, Magnifier — A427

Aristotelis Valaoritis — A428

Golfer
A429

Hippocrates
A430

Parliament in Session
A431

***Perf. 14x13½, 13½x14***

**1979, Nov. 24** **Litho.**

| | | | | |
|---|---|---|---|---|
| **1319** | A424 | 3d multi | .25 | .25 |
| **1320** | A425 | 4d multi | .25 | .25 |
| **1321** | A426 | 6d multi | .25 | .25 |
| **1322** | A427 | 8d multi | .25 | .25 |
| **1323** | A427 | 10d multi, horiz. | .25 | .25 |
| **1324** | A428 | 12d multi | .25 | .25 |
| **1325** | A429 | 14d multi | .25 | .25 |
| **1326** | A430 | 18d multi | .30 | .30 |
| **1327** | A431 | 25d multi | .40 | .40 |
| | | *Nos. 1319-1327 (9)* | 2.45 | 2.45 |

Agricultural Bank of Greece, 50th anniv.; Cosmas the Aetolian (1714-79), Greek missionary and martyr; Basil the Great (330-379), Archbishop of Caesarea; Balkanfila, Balkan Stamp Exhibition, Athens, Nov. 24-Dec. 2; Aristotelis Valaoritis (1824-79), Greek poet; 27th World Golf Championship, Nov. 8-11; Intl. Hippocratic Foundation of Cos; Greek Parliament, 104th anniv.

Parnassus — A432

Tempe Valley A433

*Perf. 12½x13½, 13½x12½*

**1979, Dec. 15** **Litho.**

| | | | | | |
|---|---|---|---|---|---|
| **1328** | A432 | 50 l | shown | .25 | .25 |
| **1329** | A433 | 1d | shown | .25 | .25 |
| **1330** | A432 | 2d | Melos | .25 | .25 |
| **1331** | A432 | 4d | Vikos Gorge | .25 | .25 |
| **1332** | A433 | 5d | Missolonghi Salt Lake | .25 | .25 |
| **1333** | A432 | 6d | Louros Aqueduct | .25 | .25 |
| **1334** | A432 | 7d | Samothrace | .25 | .25 |
| **1335** | A433 | 8d | Sithonia-Halkidiki | .25 | .25 |
| **1336** | A433 | 10d | Samarias Gorge, vert | .25 | .25 |
| **1337** | A432 | 12d | Siphnos | .25 | .25 |
| **1338** | A433 | 14d | Kyme | .25 | .25 |
| **1339** | A432 | 18d | Ios | .25 | .25 |
| **1340** | A432 | 20d | Thasos | .25 | .25 |
| **1341** | A433 | 30d | Paros | .30 | .25 |
| **1342** | A432 | 50d | Cephalonia | .50 | .40 |
| | | | *Nos. 1328-1342 (15)* | 4.05 | 3.90 |

Byzantine Castle of Thessalonica A434

4d, Aegosthena Castle, vert. 8d, Cave of Perama Ioannina, vert. 10d, Cave of Dyros, Mani, vert. 14d, Arta Bridge. 20d, Kalogiros Bridge, Epirus.

*Perf. 12½x14, 14x12½*

**1980, Mar. 15** **Litho.**

| | | | | | |
|---|---|---|---|---|---|
| **1343** | A434 | 4d | multi | .25 | .25 |
| **1344** | A434 | 6d | multi | .25 | .25 |
| **1345** | A434 | 8d | multi | .25 | .25 |
| **1346** | A434 | 10d | multi | .25 | .25 |
| **1347** | A434 | 14d | multi | .25 | .25 |
| **1348** | A434 | 20d | multi | .25 | .25 |
| | | | *Nos. 1343-1348 (6)* | 1.50 | 1.50 |

Gate of Galerius A435

**1980, Mar. 15**

| | | | | | |
|---|---|---|---|---|---|
| **1349** | A435 | 8d | multi | .25 | .25 |

1st Hellenic Congress of Nephrology, Thessalonica, Mar. 20-22.

Solar System A436

Design: 10d, Temple of Hera, Aristarchus' theory and diagram.

**1980, May 5** **Litho.** ***Perf. 13½x12½***

| | | | | | |
|---|---|---|---|---|---|
| **1350** | A436 | 10d | multi | .25 | .25 |
| **1351** | A436 | 20d | multi | .40 | .35 |

Aristarchus of Samos, first astronomer to discover heliocentric theory of universe, 2300th birth anniv.; Intl. Scientific Congress on Aristarchus, Samos, June 17-19.

Maria Callas (1923-1977), Opera Singer A437

Europa: 8d, Georges Seferis (1900-1971), writer and diplomat.

**1980, May 5**

| | | | | | |
|---|---|---|---|---|---|
| **1352** | A437 | 8d | multi | *.40* | .40 |
| **1353** | A437 | 14d | multi | *1.60* | 1.20 |

Energy Conservation Manual A438

*Perf. 13½x12½, 12½x13½*

**1980, May 5**

| | | | | | |
|---|---|---|---|---|---|
| **1354** | A438 | 8d | shown | .25 | .25 |
| **1355** | A438 | 20d | Candle in bulb, vert. | .30 | .30 |

Firemen A439

St. Demetrius, Angel, Fresco — A440

Ancient Vase, Olives — A442

Soldiers Marching through Crete — A441

Federation Emblem, Newspaper A443

Constantinos Ikonomos A444

**1980, July 14** **Litho.** ***Perf. 12½***

| | | | | | |
|---|---|---|---|---|---|
| **1356** | A439 | 4d | multi | .25 | .25 |
| **1357** | A440 | 6d | multi | .25 | .25 |
| **1358** | A441 | 8d | multi | .25 | .25 |
| **1359** | A442 | 10d | multi | .25 | .25 |
| **1360** | A443 | 14d | multi | .25 | .25 |
| **1361** | A444 | 20d | multi | .40 | .40 |
| | | | *Nos. 1356-1361 (6)* | 1.65 | 1.65 |

Fire Brigade, 50th anniv.; St. Demetrius, 1700th birth anniv.; Therissos Revolution, 75th anniv.; 2nd Intl. Olive Oil Year; Intl. Federation of Journalists, 15th Cong., Athens, May 12-16; Constantinos Ikonomos (1780-1857), writer and revolutionary.

Olympic Stadium, Temple Coin, Olympia A445

Olympic Rings and: 14d, Stadium and coin of Delphi 18d, Epidaurus theater, coin of Olympia 20d, Rhodes Stadium, Cos coin. 50d, Panathenean Stadium; 1st Olympic Games medal.

**1980, Aug. 11** **Litho.** ***Perf. 13½x13***

| | | | | | |
|---|---|---|---|---|---|
| **1362** | A445 | 8d | multi | .25 | .25 |
| **1363** | A445 | 14d | multi | .35 | .30 |
| **1364** | A445 | 18d | multi | .25 | .25 |
| **1365** | A445 | 20d | multi | .30 | .25 |
| **1366** | A445 | 50d | multi | .65 | .55 |
| | | | *Nos. 1362-1366 (5)* | 1.80 | 1.60 |

22nd Summer Olympic Games, Moscow, July 19-Aug. 3.

Asbestos A446

*Perf. 13½x12½*

**1980, Sept. 22** **Litho.**

| | | | | | |
|---|---|---|---|---|---|
| **1367** | A446 | 6d | shown | .25 | .25 |
| **1368** | A446 | 8d | Gypsum, vert. | .25 | .25 |
| **1369** | A446 | 10d | Copper ore | .25 | .25 |
| **1370** | A446 | 14d | Barite, vert. | .35 | .35 |
| **1371** | A446 | 18d | Chromite | .25 | .25 |
| **1372** | A446 | 20d | Mixed sulphides, vert. | .25 | .25 |
| **1373** | A446 | 30d | Bauxite, vert. | .35 | .35 |
| | | | *Nos. 1367-1373 (7)* | 1.95 | 1.95 |

Tow Truck — A447

Air Force Jet — A448

Airplane and Hangar A449

Ships in Port A450

Students' Association Headquarters A451

**1980, Oct. 31** **Litho.** ***Perf. 12½***

| | | | | | |
|---|---|---|---|---|---|
| **1374** | A447 | 6d | multi | .25 | .25 |
| **1375** | A448 | 8d | multi | .25 | .25 |
| **1376** | A449 | 12d | multi | .25 | .25 |
| **1377** | A450 | 20d | multi | .35 | .30 |
| **1378** | A451 | 25d | multi | .40 | .40 |
| | | | *Nos. 1374-1378 (5)* | 1.50 | 1.45 |

Road Assistance Service of Automobile and Touring Club of Greece, 20th anniv.; Air Force, 50th anniv.; Flyers' Club of Thessaloniki, 50th anniv.; Piraeus Port Organization, 50th anniv.; Association for Macedon ian Studies, 40th anniv.

Madonna and Child, by Theodore Poulakis — A452

Christmas 1980: He is Happy Thanks to You, by Theodore Poulakis. No. 1381a has continuous design.

**1980, Dec. 10** ***Perf. 13½***

| | | | | | |
|---|---|---|---|---|---|
| **1379** | | 6d | multi | .25 | .25 |
| **1380** | | 14d | multi | .25 | .25 |
| **1381** | | 20d | multi | .30 | .30 |
| *a.* | A452 | | Strip of 3, #1379-1381 | .75 | .75 |

Vegetables for Export — A453

**1981, Mar. 16** **Litho.** ***Perf. 12½***

| | | | | | |
|---|---|---|---|---|---|
| **1382** | A453 | 9d | shown | .25 | .25 |
| **1383** | A453 | 17d | Fruits | .25 | .25 |
| **1384** | A453 | 20d | Cotton | .25 | .25 |
| **1385** | A453 | 25d | Marble | .40 | .40 |
| | | | *Nos. 1382-1385 (4)* | 1.15 | 1.15 |

**Europa Issue 1981**

Kira Maria Folk Dance, Alexandria — A454

**1981, May 4** **Litho.** ***Perf. 14x13***

| | | | | | |
|---|---|---|---|---|---|
| **1386** | A454 | 12d | shown | *.50* | .25 |
| **1387** | A454 | 17d | Cretan Sousta (dance) | *1.00* | .75 |

Runner, Olympic Stadium, Kalogreza A455

**1981, May 4**

| | | | | | |
|---|---|---|---|---|---|
| **1388** | A455 | 12d | shown | .25 | .25 |
| **1389** | A455 | 17d | Runners, Europe | .40 | .40 |

13th European Athletic Championship, Athens, 1982.

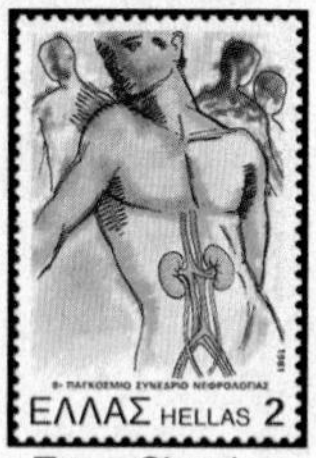
Torso Showing Kidneys A456

Sky Diver and Airplanes A457

Views of Thessaly and Epirus — A458

Oil Rig and Map of Thassos Island — A460

Vase with Painted Eyes A459

Globes and Ancient Coin A461

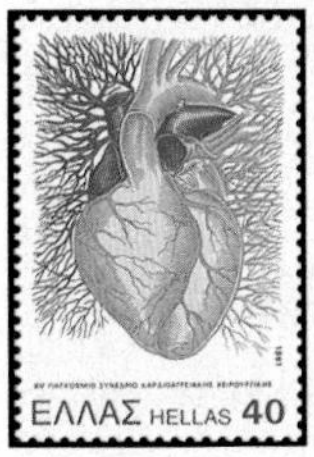


Heart and Vessels — A462

***Perf. 13½x14, 14x13½***

**1981, May 22** **Litho.**

| | | | | | |
|---|---|---|---|---|---|
| **1390** | A456 | 2d multi | .25 | .25 |
| **1391** | A457 | 3d multi | .25 | .25 |
| **1392** | A458 | 6d multi | .25 | .25 |
| **1393** | A459 | 9d multi | .25 | .25 |
| **1394** | A460 | 12d multi | .25 | .25 |
| **1395** | A461 | 21d multi | .50 | .45 |
| **1396** | A462 | 40d multi | .75 | .75 |
| | | *Nos. 1390-1396 (7)* | 2.50 | 2.45 |

8th Intl. Nephrology Conf., Athens, June 7-12; Greek National Air Club, 50th anniv.; Intl. Historical Symposium, Volos, Sept. 27-30; Greek Ophthalmological Society, 50th anniv.; inauguration of oil production at Thassos Island; World Assoc. for Intl. Relations, Athens, 2nd anniv.; 15th Intl. Cardiovascular Surgery Conference, Athens, Sept. 6-10.

Cockles A463

**1981, June 30** **Litho.** ***Perf. 14x13½***

| | | | | |
|---|---|---|---|---|
| **1397** | A463 | 4d shown | .25 | .25 |
| **1398** | A463 | 5d Parrot fish | .25 | .25 |
| **1399** | A463 | 12d Painted comber | .25 | .25 |
| **1400** | A463 | 15d Common dentex | .25 | .25 |
| **1401** | A463 | 17d Parnassius apollo | .50 | .30 |
| **1402** | A463 | 50d Colias hyale | 1.10 | .90 |
| | | *Nos. 1397-1402 (6)* | 2.60 | 2.20 |

Bell Tower, Epirus — A464

Altar Gate, St. Paraskevi's Church — A465

Bell Towers and Wood Altar Gates (Iconostases): 9d, Pelion, horiz. 12d, Church of Sts. Constantine and Helen, Epirus. 17d, St. Nicolas Church, Velvendos, horiz. 30d, St. Jacob icon, Church Museum, Alexandroupolis. 40d, St. Nicholas Church, Makrinitsa.

**1981, Sept. 30** **Litho.**

| | | | | |
|---|---|---|---|---|
| **1403** | A464 | 4d multi | .25 | .25 |
| **1404** | A465 | 6d multi | .25 | .25 |
| **1405** | A465 | 9d multi | .25 | .25 |
| **1406** | A464 | 12d multi | .25 | .25 |
| **1407** | A465 | 17d multi | .25 | .25 |
| **1408** | A465 | 30d multi | .35 | .35 |
| **1409** | A465 | 40d multi | .60 | .60 |
| | | *Nos. 1403-1409 (7)* | 2.20 | 2.20 |

European Urban Renaissance Year — A466

St. Simeon, Archbishop of Thessalonica A467

Promotion of Breastfeeding A468

Gina Bachauer, Pianist, 5th Death Anniv. A469

Constantine Broumidis, Artist, Death Centenary A470

Sesquicentennial of Greek Banknotes — A471

***Perf. 14x13½, 13½x14***

**1981, Nov. 20** **Litho.**

| | | | | |
|---|---|---|---|---|
| **1410** | A466 | 3d multi | .25 | .25 |
| **1411** | A467 | 9d multi | .25 | .25 |
| **1412** | A468 | 12d multi | .25 | .25 |
| **1413** | A469 | 17d multi | .40 | .25 |
| **1414** | A470 | 21d multi | .45 | .25 |
| **1415** | A471 | 50d multi | .75 | .60 |
| | | *Nos. 1410-1415 (6)* | 2.35 | 1.85 |

Old Parliament Building, Athens A472

Angelos Sikelianos (1884-1951), Poet A473

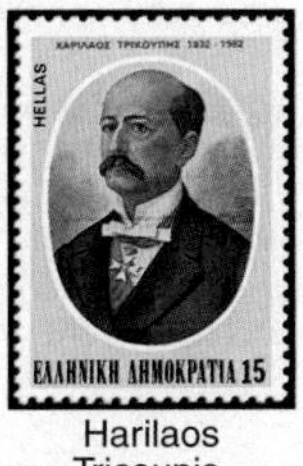


Harilaos Tricoupis, Politician, Birth Sesquicentennial A474

Aegean Islands Exhib., Rhodes, Athens — A475

Petralona Cave and Skull — A477

Olympic Airlines, 25th Anniv. A476

***Perf. 13½x12½, 12½x13½***

**1982, Mar. 15** **Litho.**

| | | | | |
|---|---|---|---|---|
| **1416** | A472 | 2d multi | .25 | .25 |
| **1417** | A473 | 9d multi | .25 | .25 |
| **1418** | A474 | 15d multi | .25 | .25 |
| **1419** | A475 | 21d multi | .40 | .40 |
| **1420** | A476 | 30d multi | .65 | .55 |
| **1421** | A477 | 50d multi | 1.10 | 1.00 |
| | | *Nos. 1416-1421 (6)* | 2.90 | 2.70 |

Historical and Ethnological Society centennial (2d); 3rd European Anthropology Congress, Halkidiki, Sept. (50d).

Europa 1982 — A478

**1982, May 10** **Litho.** ***Perf. 13½x14***

| | | | | |
|---|---|---|---|---|
| **1422** | A478 | 21d Battle of Marathon, 490 BC | *2.00* | 1.00 |
| **1423** | A478 | 30d 1826 Revolution | *4.00* | 2.00 |

13th European Athletic Championships, Athens — A479

**1982, May 10** ***Perf. 14x13½, 13½x14***

| | | | | |
|---|---|---|---|---|
| **1424** | A479 | 21d Pole vaulting, horiz. | .30 | .25 |
| **1425** | A479 | 25d Running | .40 | .25 |
| **1426** | A479 | 40d Sports, horiz. | .80 | .65 |
| | | *Nos. 1424-1426 (3)* | 1.50 | 1.15 |

Byzantine Book Illustrations A480

***Perf. 13½x12½, 12½x13½***

**1982, June 26** **Litho.**

| | | | | |
|---|---|---|---|---|
| **1427** | A480 | 4d Gospel book heading | .25 | .25 |
| **1428** | A480 | 6d Illuminated "E," vert. | .25 | .25 |
| **1429** | A480 | 12d Illuminated "T," vert. | .25 | .25 |
| **1430** | A480 | 15d Gospel reading canon table, vert. | .25 | .25 |
| **1431** | A480 | 80d Zoology book heading | 1.50 | 1.25 |
| | | *Nos. 1427-1431 (5)* | 2.50 | 2.25 |

Georgios Karaiskakis (1782-1827), Liberation Hero — A481

Amnesty Intl. — A482

Designs: 12d, Camp in Piraeus, by von Krazeisen. 50d, Meditating.

**1982, Sept. 20** **Litho.** ***Perf. 13x13½***

| | | | | |
|---|---|---|---|---|
| **1432** | A481 | 12d multi | .40 | .25 |
| **1433** | A481 | 50d multi | .80 | .50 |

**1982, Sept. 20** ***Perf. 13x14***

| | | | | |
|---|---|---|---|---|
| **1434** | A482 | 15d Vigil | .45 | .25 |
| **1435** | A482 | 75d Prisoners | 1.25 | 1.00 |

Natl. Resistance Movement, 1941-44 A483

Designs: 1d, Demonstration of Mar. 24, 1942. 2d, Sacrifice of Inhabitants of Kalavrita, by S. Vasiliou. 5d, Resistance Fighters in Thrace, by A. Tassos. 9d, The Start of Resistance in Crete, by P. Gravalos. 12d, Partisan Men and Women, by P. Gravalos. 21d, Blowing Up a Bridge, by A. Tassos. 30d, Fighters at a Barricade, by G. Sikeliotis. 50d, The Fight in Northern Greece, by B. Katraki, 5d, 9d, 12d, 21d vert.

**1982, Nov. 8** **Litho.** ***Perf. 12½***

| | | | | |
|---|---|---|---|---|
| **1436** | A483 | 1d multi | .25 | .25 |
| **1437** | A483 | 2d multi | .25 | .25 |
| **1438** | A483 | 5d multi | .25 | .25 |
| **1439** | A483 | 9d multi | .25 | .25 |
| **1440** | A483 | 12d multi | .25 | .25 |
| **1441** | A483 | 21d multi | .25 | .25 |
| *a.* | | Souv. sheet, 5d, 9d, 12d, 21d | 1.75 | 1.75 |
| **1442** | A483 | 30d multi | .50 | .35 |
| **1443** | A483 | 50d multi | 1.25 | .55 |
| *a.* | | Souv. sheet, 1d, 2d, 30d, 50d | 2.00 | 2.00 |
| | | *Nos. 1436-1443 (8)* | 3.25 | 2.40 |

Christmas 1982 — A484

Designs: Various Byzantine Nativity bas-reliefs, Byzantine Museum.

**1982, Dec. 6** **Litho.** ***Perf. 13½x12½***

| | | | | |
|---|---|---|---|---|
| **1444** | A484 | 9d multi | .25 | .25 |
| **1445** | A484 | 21d multi | .30 | .25 |
| *a.* | | Pair, #1444-1445 | .65 | .65 |

25th Anniv. of Intl. Maritime Org. A485

Ship Figureheads. 15d, 18d, 25d, 40d vert.

**1983, Mar. 14** ***Perf. 14x13½, 13½x14***

| | | | | |
|---|---|---|---|---|
| **1446** | A485 | 11d Ares, Tsamados | .25 | .30 |
| **1447** | A485 | 15d Ares, Miaoulis | .25 | .25 |
| **1448** | A485 | 18d Female figure | .25 | .25 |
| **1449** | A485 | 25d Spetses, Bouboulina | .40 | .25 |

**1450** A485 40d Epameinondas, K. Babas .60 .35
**1451** A485 50d Carteria 1.25 1.00
*Nos. 1446-1451 (6)* 3.00 2.40

Postal Code Inauguration A486

**1983, Mar. 14 Litho. *Perf. 12½***
**1452** A486 15d Cover, map .25 .25
**1453** A486 25d Hermes, post horn, vert. .45 .40

Rowing A487

**1983, Apr. 28 *Perf. 14x13, 13x14***
**1454** A487 15d shown .25 .25
**1455** A487 18d Water skiing, vert. .35 .25
**1456** A487 27d Wind surfing, vert. .65 .60
**1457** A487 50d Skiers on chair-lift, vert. .65 .60
**1458** A487 80d Skiing 2.00 1.75
*Nos. 1454-1458 (5)* 3.90 3.45

**Europa Issue 1983**

Acropolis — A488

Archimedes and His Hydrostatic Principle — A489

***Perf. 12½x13½, 13x13½***
**1983, Apr. 28 Litho.**
**1459** A488 25d multi *2.00* 1.00
**1460** A489 80d multi *4.00* 3.00

Marinos Antypas (1873-1907), Farmers' Movement Leader — A490

Designs: 9d, Nicholas Plastiras (1883-1953), prime minister. 15d, George Papandreou (1888-1968), statesman. 20d, Constantine Cavafy (1863-1933), poet. 27d, Nikos Kazantzakis (1883-1957), writer. 32d, Manolis Calomiris (1883-1962), composer. 40d, George Papanicolaou (1883-1962), medical researcher. 50d, Despina Achladioti (1890-1982), nationalist.

**1983, July 11 Litho. *Perf. 13½x14***
**1461** A490 6d multi .25 .25
**1462** A490 9d multi .25 .25
**1463** A490 15d multi .25 .25
**1464** A490 20d multi .30 .25
**1465** A490 27d multi .35 .25
**1466** A490 32d multi .60 .30
**1467** A490 40d multi .70 .30
**1468** A490 50d multi .85 .60
*Nos. 1461-1468 (8)* 3.55 2.45

A491

**1983, Sept. 26 Litho. *Perf. 13½x13***
**1469** A491 50d Portrait bust 1.00 .50

1st Intl. Conf. on the Works of Democritus (Philosopher, 460-370 BC), Xanthe, Oct.

A492

**1983, Nov. 17 Litho. *Perf. 13***
**1470** A492 15d Poster .25 .25
**1471** A492 30d Flight from school .45 .35

Polytechnic School Uprising, 1st anniv.

The Deification of Homer — A493

Homer Inspired Artworks: 3d, The Abduction of Helen by Paris, horiz. 4d, The Wooden Horse, horiz. 5d, Achilles Throwing Dice with Ajax, horiz. 6d, Achilles. 10d, Hector Receiving His Arms from His Parents. 14d, Single-handed Battle Between Ajax and Hector, horiz. 15d, Priam Requesting the Body of Hector, horiz. 20d, The Blinding of Polyphemus. 27d, Ulysses Escaping from Polyphemus' Cave, horiz. 30d, Ulysses Meeting with Nausica. 32d, Ulysses on the Island of the Sirens, horiz. 50d, Ulysses Slaying the Suitors, horiz. 75d, The Heroes of the Iliad, horiz. 100d, Homer.

**1983, Dec. 19 Litho. *Perf. 13***
**1472** A493 2d multi .25 .25
**1473** A493 3d multi .25 .25
**1474** A493 4d multi .25 .25
**1475** A493 5d multi .25 .25
**1476** A493 6d multi .25 .25
**1477** A493 10d multi .25 .25
**1478** A493 14d multi .25 .25
**1479** A493 15d multi .25 .25
**1480** A493 20d multi .25 .25
**1481** A493 27d multi .30 .25
**1482** A493 30d multi .40 .25
**1483** A493 32d multi .50 .25
**1484** A493 50d multi .60 .25
**1485** A493 75d multi 1.25 .60
**1486** A493 100d multi 1.90 .80
*Nos. 1472-1486 (15)* 7.20 4.65

Horse's Head from Chariot of Seline A494

Horsemen and Heroes A495

Nos. 1492a-1492b, Equestrian scene. Nos. 1492c-1492d, Athenian Elders.

**1984, Mar. 15 Litho. *Perf. 14½x14***
**1487** A494 14d shown .25 .25
**1488** A494 15d Dionysus .35 .25
**1489** A494 20d Hestia, Dione, Aphrodite .65 .30
**1490** A494 27d Ilissus .85 .30
**1491** A494 32d Lapith, centaur 1.50 .75
*Nos. 1487-1491 (5)* 3.60 1.85

**Souvenir Sheet**

***Perf. 13x13½***

**1492** Sheet of 4 4.50 4.50
*a.* A495 15d multi .75 .75
*b.* A495 21d multi .90 .90
*c.* A495 27d multi 1.00 1.00
*d.* A495 32d multi 1.25 1.25

Marble from the Parthenon. No. 1492 sold for 107d.

Nos. 1492a-1492b and 1492c-1492d have continuous designs.

Europa (1959-84) A496

**1984, Apr. 30 Litho. *Perf. 14x13½***
**1493** A496 15d multi *.75* *.40*
**1494** A496 27d multi *1.75* *1.00*
*a.* Pair, #1493-1494 *3.25* *3.25*

1984 Summer Olympics — A497

Designs: 14d, Ancient Olympic stadium crypt. 15d, Athletes training. 20d, Broad jump, discus thrower. 32d, Athletes, diff. 80d, Stadium, Demetrius Bikelos, poet, organizer of 1896 Athens games.

**1984, Apr. 30 *Perf. 13½x14***
**1495** A497 14d multi .30 .25
**1496** A497 15d multi .40 .35
**1497** A497 20d multi .50 .45
**1498** A497 32d multi .75 .65
**1499** A497 80d multi 1.75 1.40
*a.* Strip of 5, #1495-1499 4.50 4.50

Also issued in booklets.

Turkish Invasion of Cyprus, 10th Anniv. — A498

**1984, July 10 Litho. *Perf. 13***
**1500** A498 20d Tank, map, vert. .40 .25
**1501** A498 32d Map, barbed wire .60 .50

Also issued in booklets.

Greek Railway Centenary A499

***Perf. 13x13½, 13½x13***
**1984, July 20 Litho.**
**1502** A499 15d Pelion .65 .35
**1503** A499 20d Papadia Bridge, vert. 2.00 1.40
**1504** A499 30d Piraeus-Peloponnese .65 .35
**1505** A499 50d Cogwheel Calavryta, vert. 2.00 1.40
*Nos. 1502-1505 (4)* 5.30 3.50

Sesquicentenary of Athens as Capital City — A500

15d, 4d silver coin, 5th cent. BC, city plan, vert. 100d, Views of ancient & modern Athens.

***Perf. 13½x13, 13x13½***
**1984, Oct. 12 Litho.**
**1506** A500 15d multi .40 .25
**1507** A500 100d multi 1.60 1.00

10th Anniv. of Democratic Govt. — A501

**1984, Oct. 12 Litho. *Perf. 13x13½***
**1508** A501 95d "10" on flag 1.75 .75

Christmas 1984 — A502

Scenes from 18th cent. icon by Athanasios Tountas.

**1984, Dec. 6 Litho. *Perf. 13½x13***
**1509** A502 14d Annunciation .50 .30
**1510** A502 20d Nativity .50 .30
**1511** A502 25d Presentation in the Temple .50 .40
**1512** A502 32d Baptism of Christ .50 .50
*a.* Block of 4, #1509-1512 2.50 2.50

Also issued in booklets.

Runner A503

Palais des Sports A504

***Perf. 13, 13x13½ (#1515)***
**1985, Mar. 1 Litho.**
**1513** A503 12d shown .25 .25
**1514** A503 15d Shot put .35 .25
**1515** A504 20d shown .35 .25
**1516** A503 25d Hurdles .70 .25
**1517** A503 80d Women's high jump 1.40 .80
*Nos. 1513-1517 (5)* 3.05 1.80

European Indoor Athletics Championships, Palais des Sports, New Phaleron.

Europa 1985 — A505

CEPT emblem and: 27d, Musical contest between Marsyas and Apollo. 80d, Dimitris Mitropoulos (1896-1960) and Nikos Skalkottas (1904-1949), composers.

**1985, Apr. 29** *Perf. 14x14½*

**1518** A505 27d multi *.80* .50
**1519** A505 80d multi *1.50* 1.00

Exist se-tenant as strip of 3, 27d+80d+27d in booklets.

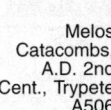

Melos Catacombs, A.D. 2nd Cent., Trypete — A506

**1985, Apr. 29** *Perf. 14½x14*

**1520** A506 15d Niche .25 .25
**1521** A506 20d Altar, Central Gallery .50 .25
**1522** A506 100d Catacombs 1.60 1.10
*Nos. 1520-1522 (3)* 2.35 1.60

Republic of Cyprus, 25th Anniv. — A507

**1985, June 24** *Perf. 13x13½*

**1523** A507 32d Map of Cyprus, urn 1.00 .50

Coin of King Cassander (315 B.C.), Personification of Salonika, Galerius Era Bas-relief — A508

Sts. Demetrius and Methodius, Mosaics — A509

Designs: 15d, Emperor sacrificing at Altar, Arch of Galerius, Roman era. 20d, Eastern walls of Salonika, Byzantine era. 32d, Houses in the Upper City. 50d, Liberation of Salonika by the Greek Army, 1912. 80d, German occupation, 1941-44, the Old Mosque. 95d, View of city, Trade Fair grounds, Aristotelian University tower.

***Perf. 14½x14 (A508), 14x14½ (A509)***

**1985, June 24**

**1524** A508 1d multi .25 .25
**1525** A509 5d multi .35 .25
**1526** A508 15d multi .40 .25
**1527** A508 20d multi .40 .25
**1528** A508 32d multi .45 .25
**1529** A508 50d multi .60 .25
**1530** A508 80d multi 1.25 .50
**1531** A509 95d multi 1.75 1.50
*Nos. 1524-1531 (8)* 5.45 3.50

Salonika City, 2300th anniv. Aristotelian University, Trade Fair, 60th annivs.

Athenian Cultural Heritage A510

Ancient art and architecture: 15d, Democracy Crowning the City, bas-relief from a column, Ancient Agora of Athens, vert. 20d, Mosaic pavement of tritons, nereids, dolphins, etc., Roman baths at Hieratus, Isthmia, A.D. 2nd cent. 32d, Angel, fresco, Grotto of Pentheli, A.D. 13th cent., vert. 80d, Capodistrian University, Athens.

**1985, Oct. 7** *Perf. 13½x13, 13x13½*

**1532** A510 15d multi .25 .25
**1533** A510 20d multi .25 .25
**1534** A510 32d multi .65 .30
**1535** A510 80d multi 1.40 1.10
*Nos. 1532-1535 (4)* 2.55 1.90

Intl. Youth Year — A511

UN 40th Anniv. — A512

#1540, Girl crowned with flowers, Stadium of Peace and Friendship, Athens.

**1985, Oct. 7** *Perf. 14x14½*

**1536** A511 15d Children, olive wreath .25 .25
**1537** A511 25d Children, doves .45 .25
**1538** A512 27d UN General Assembly, dove .55 .25
**1539** A512 100d UN building, emblem 1.60 1.50
*Nos. 1536-1539 (4)* 2.85 2.25

**Souvenir Sheet**

**1985, Nov. 22** *Perf. 14x13*

**1540** A511 100d multi 2.00 2.00

No. 1540 contains one 43x47mm stamp.

Pontic Hellenism Cultural Reformation A513

***Perf. 14x12½, 12½x14***

**1985, Dec. 9** **Litho.**

**1541** A513 12d Folk dance .25 .25
**1542** A513 15d Our Lady Soumela Monastery .25 .25
**1543** A513 27d Folk costumes, vert. .45 .30
**1544** A513 32d Trapezus High School .45 .30
**1545** A513 80d Sinope Castle 1.10 1.00
*Nos. 1541-1545 (5)* 2.50 2.10

Greek Gods — A514

**1986, Feb. 17** **Litho.** *Perf. 13*

**1546** A514 5d Hestia .25 .25
**1547** A514 18d Hermes .25 .25
**1548** A514 27d Aphrodite .30 .25
**1549** A514 32d Ares .45 .35
**1550** A514 35d Athena .60 .35
**1551** A514 40d Hephaestus .70 .25
**1552** A514 50d Artemis .95 .35
**1553** A514 110d Apollo 1.10 .35
**1554** A514 150d Demeter 1.75 .35
**1555** A514 200d Poseidon 2.50 .45
**1556** A514 300d Hera 4.25 .95
**1557** A514 500d Zeus 9.50 4.50
*Nos. 1546-1557 (12)* 22.60 8.65

Each denomination also sold in booklets containing 20 panes of 5 stamps, perf 13 horizontally only. Value for set of unused booklet stamps $25; used booklet stamps sell for approximately half the values shown for used sheet stamps.

Youth of Antikythera A515

Soccer Players A517

Diadoumenos, by Polycleitus A516

Wrestlers, Hellenic Era Statue — A518

Cyclists — A520

Volleyball Players A519

Commemorative Design for 1st Modern Olympic Games — A521

**1986, Mar. 3** *Perf. 12*

**1558** A515 18d multi .40 .25
**1559** A516 27d multi 1.40 .40
**1560** A517 32d multi 2.75 .90
**1561** A518 35d multi 1.40 1.25
**1562** A519 40d multi 1.40 .45
**1563** A520 50d multi 1.40 .45
**1564** A521 110d multi 4.50 1.60
*Nos. 1558-1564 (7)* 13.25 5.30

First World Junior Athletic Championships. Pan-European Junior Soccer Championships. Pan-European Free-style and Greco-Roman Wrestling Championships. Men's World Volleyball Championships. Sixth International Round-Europe Cycling Meet. Modern Olympic Games, 90th anniv.

European Traffic Safety Year — A522

**1986, Mar. 3** *Perf. 12½x14*

**1565** A522 18d Seat belts .25 .25
**1566** A522 27d Motorcycle .95 .95
**1567** A522 110d Speed limits 1.50 .50
*Nos. 1565-1567 (3)* 2.70 1.70

Prevention of Forest Fires A523

**1986, Apr. 23** **Litho.** *Perf. 14x13½*

**1568** A523 35d shown *3.00* 2.00
**1569** A523 110d Prespa Lakes wetlands *5.00* 4.00
*a.* Pair, 35d, 110d *9.00* 9.00
*b.* Bklt. pane, 2 each 35d, 110d *25.00*
*c.* As "b," pair, 35d, 110d 12.50 12.50

Europa.

No. 1569b is imperf horizontally.

New Postal Services — A524

May Day Strike, Chicago, Cent. — A525

**1986, Apr. 23** *Perf. 13½x14, 14x13½*

**1570** A524 18d Intelpost .40 .25
**1571** A524 110d Express mail, horiz. 1.60 .80

**1986, Apr. 23** *Perf. 12½*

**1572** A525 40d Strikers, monument .65 .50

Eleutherios K. Venizelos (1864-1936), Premier A526

18d, Venizelos, Ministers taking oath of office, 1917. 110d, Old Hania Harbor, Crete.

**1986, June 30** **Litho.** *Perf. 14x12½*

**1573** A526 18d multi .25 .25
**1574** A526 110d multi 1.75 .70

6th Intl. Cretological Conference, Crete.

Intl. Peace Year — A527

**1986, Oct. 6** **Litho.** *Perf. 12½*

**1575** A527 18d Dove, sun, vert. .25 .25
**1576** A527 35d Flags, dove, vert. .60 .40
**1577** A527 110d World cage, dove 1.50 .70
*Nos. 1575-1577 (3)* 2.35 1.35

Christmas A528

Aesop's Fables A529

Religious art in the Benaki Museum: 22d, Madonna and Child Enthroned, triptych center panel, 15th cent. 46d, Adoration of the Magi, 15th cent. 130d, Christ Enthroned with St. John the Evangelist, triptych panel.

**1986, Dec. 1** **Litho.** *Perf. 13½x14*

**1578** A528 22d multi .30 .25
**1579** A528 46d multi .65 .50
**1580** A528 130d multi 1.75 .40
*Nos. 1578-1580 (3)* 2.70 1.15

Size of No. 1579: 27x35mm.

**1987, Mar. 5** **Litho.** *Perf. 12½*

**1581** A529 2d Fox and the Grapes .25 .25
**1582** A529 5d North Wind and the Sun .25 .25
**1583** A529 10d Stag and the Lion .30 .30
**1584** A529 22d Zeus and the Snake .60 .25
**1585** A529 32d Crow and the Fox 1.10 .30
**1586** A529 40d Woodcutter and Hermes 1.25 .40
**1587** A529 46d Ass in a Lion's Skin 2.10 .65

**1588** A529 130d Tortoise and the Hare 4.50 1.60
*Nos. 1581-1588 (8)* 10.35 4.00

Each denomination also sold in booklets containing 20 panes of 5 stamps, perf 13½ horizontally only. Value for set of unused booklet stamps $32.50; used booklet stamps sell for approximately half the values shown for used sheet stamps.

Europa 1987 — A530

Modern art: 40d, Composition, by Achilleas Apergis. 130d, Delphic Light, by Gerassimos Sklavos.

**1987, May 4 Litho. *Perf. 12½***

**1589** A530 40d multi 3.00 2.00
**1590** A530 130d multi 4.00 3.00
*a.* Pair, #1589-1590 7.50 7.50
*b.* Bklt. pane, 2 each #1589-1590 21.00
*c.* As "b," pair, #1589-1590 10.00 10.00

Nos. 1590b and 1590c are imperf horizontally.

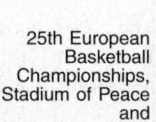

25th European Basketball Championships, Stadium of Peace and Friendship — A531

A532

**1987, May 4 *Perf. 13½x14, 12½***

**1591** A531 22d Jump shot, stadium, vert. .60 .60
**1592** A532 25d Emblem, spectators .40 .25
**1593** A531 130d Two players, vert. 1.90 1.10
*Nos. 1591-1593 (3)* 2.90 1.95

Higher Education Sesquicentenary — A533

***Perf. 14x13½, 13½x14***

**1987, May 4 Litho.**

**1594** A533 3d Students, tapestry .25 .25
**1595** A533 23d Owl, medallion .40 .25
**1596** A533 40d Institute, symbols of science .70 .40
**1597** A533 60d Institute, students 1.00 .75
*Nos. 1594-1597 (4)* 2.35 1.65

Capodistrias University of Athens (Nos. 1594-1595); The Natl. Metsovio Polytechnic Institute (Nos. 1596-1597). #1596-1597 vert.

Souvenir Sheet

25th European Men's Basketball Championships — A534

**1987, June 3 Litho. *Perf. 13x14***

**1598** Sheet of 3 6.00 6.00
*a.* A534 40d Jump ball .90 .90
*b.* A534 60d Layup 1.25 1.25
*c.* A534 100d Dunk shot 2.25 2.25

Architecture A535

Designs: 2d, Ionic and Corinthian capitals, Archaic Era. 26d, Doric capital, the Parthenon (detail). 40d, Ionic capital and the Erechteum. 60d, Corinthian capital and the Tholos in Epidaurus.

**1987, July 1 Litho. *Perf. 13½x12½***

**1599** A535 2d multi .25 .25
**1600** A535 26d multi .35 .25
**1601** A535 40d multi .55 .35
**1602** A535 60d multi 1.10 1.00
*Nos. 1599-1602 (4)* 2.25 1.85

Engraving by Yiannis Kephalinos — A536

Panteios School A537

***Perf. 12½x14, 14x12½***

**1987, Oct. 1 Litho.**

**1603** A536 26d multi .35 .25
**1604** A537 60d multi .85 .75

School of Fine Arts, 150th anniv. (26d), and Panteios School of Political Science, 60th anniv. (60d).

Greek Natl. Team, Winner, 25th European Men's Basketball Championship A538

**1987, Oct. 1 *Perf. 13x14***

**1605** A538 40d multi .90 .90

Traditional and Modern Greek Theater A539

Designs: 2d, Eleni Papadaki in Hecuba, by Euripides, and outdoor theater, Philippi. 4d, Christopher Nezer in The Wasps, by Aristophane, and outdoor theater, Dodona. 7d, Emilios Veakis in Oedipus Rex and theater, Delphi. 26d, Marika Cotopouli in The Shepherdess's Love, by Dimitris Koromilas. 40d, Katina Paxinou in Abraham's Sacrifice, by Vitzentzos Cornaros. 50d, Kyveli in Countess Valeraina's Secret, by Gregory Xenopoulos. 60d, Director Carolos Koun, stage setting. 100d, Dimitris Rontiris teaching ancient dance, Greek National Theater.

**1987, Dec. 2 Litho. *Perf. 14x13½***

**1606** A539 2d multi .25 .25
**1607** A539 4d multi .25 .25
**1608** A539 7d multi .25 .25
**1609** A539 26d multi .35 .25
**1610** A539 40d multi .55 .25
**1611** A539 50d multi .65 .25
**1612** A539 60d multi .90 .90
**1613** A539 100d multi 1.75 .35
*Nos. 1606-1613 (8)* 4.95 2.75

Christmas — A540

**1987, Dec. 2 *Perf. 13x12½***

**1614** 26d Angel facing right .50 .25
**1615** 26d Angel facing left .50 .25
*a.* Bklt. pane, 5 each #1614-1615 5.00 —
*b.* A540 Pair, #1614-1615 1.00 1.00

Marine Life — A541

**1988, Mar. 2 *Perf. 14x12½***

**1616** A541 30d Codonellina .80 .40
**1617** A541 40d Diaperoecia major 1.25 .60
**1618** A541 50d Artemia 1.75 .90
**1619** A541 60d Posidonia oceanica 4.00 2.00
**1620** A541 100d Padina pavonica 4.00 2.00
*Nos. 1616-1620 (5)* 11.80 5.90

Each denomination sold in booklets containing 20 panes of 5 stamps, perf 12½ vertically only. Value for set of unused booklet stamps $27.50; used booklet stamps sell for somewhat less than the values shown for used sheet stamps.

Europa 1988 — A542

Communication and transport: 60d, Telecommunications satellite, telephone and facsimile machine. 150d, Passenger trains.

**1988, May 6 Litho. *Perf. 12½***

**1621** 60d multi *5.00 3.00*
**1622** 150d multi *5.50 4.00*
*a.* A542 Pair, 60d, 150d *11.50 11.50*
*b.* Bklt. pane of 4, 2 each #1621-1622, perf. 14 vert. *26.00* —
*c.* A542 As "b," pair, 60d, 150d *12.00 12.00*

Nos. 1622b and 1622c perf 14 vertically and imperf horizontally.

1988 Olympics A543

Designs: 4d, Ancient Olympia and Temple of Zeus. 20d, Javelin thrower and and ancient Olympians in open-air gymnasium. 30d, Centenary emblem of the modern Games (cent. in 1996). 60d, Wrestlers, runners and other ancient athletes in training. 170d, Modern torch-bearer.

**1988, May 6 *Perf. 14x12***

**1623** A543 4d multi .50 .35
**1624** A543 20d multi 1.10 .60
**1625** A543 30d multi 2.00 .90
**1626** A543 60d multi 3.75 2.75
**1627** A543 170d multi 5.25 3.25
*a.* Strip of 5, #1623-1627 14.00 14.00
*b.* Bklt. pane of 5, #1623-1627, perf. 12½ vert. 19.00 19.00

Each denomination also sold in bklts. containing 20 panes of 5 stamps, perf. 12½ vert. Value for set of unused booklet stamps $20; used booklet stamps sell for somewhat less than the values shown for used sheet stamps.

See Korea No. B53.

A544

A545

Waterfalls: 10d, Catarractis village falls at the foot of the Tzoumerca Mountain Range. 60d, Edessa Waterfalls. 100d, Edessaios River cascades.

**1988, July 4 Litho. *Perf. 12½x14***

**1628** A544 10d multi 2.00 .40
**1629** A544 60d multi 7.00 2.25
**1630** A544 100d multi 10.00 2.25
*Nos. 1628-1630 (3)* 19.00 4.90

Each denomination also sold in booklets containing 20 panes of 5 stamps, perf. 14 vertically. Value for set of unused booklet stamps $35; used booklet stamps sell for about half the values shown for used sheet stamps.

**1988, July 4 *Perf. 13x12½***

**1631** A545 60d multi 8.00 2.50

20th Pan-European Postal Trade Unions Congress. No. 1631 also sold in booklets containing 20 panes of 5 stamps, perf. 14 vertically. Value of unused booklet stamp $12; the used booklet stamp sells for about half the value shown for the used sheet stamp.

A546

Designs: 30d, Premier Eleutherios Venizelos (1864-1936), natl. flag and map. 70d, Lady liberty, flag and map.

**1988, Oct. 7 Litho. *Perf. 12½x13***

**1632** A546 30d shown .85 .30
**1633** A546 70d multi 1.40 .75

Union of Crete with Greece and liberation of Epirus and Macedonia from Turkish rule, 75th annivs.

Each denomination also sold in booklets containing 20 panes of 5 stamps, perf. 14 horizontally. Value for set of unused booklet stamps $6; used booklet stamps sell for somewhat less than the values shown for used sheet stamps.

A547

Departmental Seats: 2d, Mytilene-Lesbos Harbor, painting by Theophilos. 3d, Alexandroupolis lighthouse. 4d, St. Nicholas bell tower, Kozane. 5d, Labor Center, Hermoupolis. 7d, Sparta Town Hall. 8d, Pegasus of Leukas. 10d, Castle of the Knights, Rhodes. 20d, The Acropolis, Athens. 25d, Kavalla aqueduct. 30d, Statue of Athanasios Diakos and castle, Lamia. 50d, Preveza cathedral bell tower and Venetian clock. 60d, Corfu promenade. 70d, Harbor view of Hagios Nicolaos. 100d, Poligiros public fountains. 200d, Church of the Apostle Paul, Corinth.

**1988, Oct. 7 *Perf. 13***

**1634** A547 2d multi .25 .25
**1635** A547 3d multi .25 .25
**1636** A547 4d multi .25 .25
**1637** A547 5d multi .25 .25
**1638** A547 7d multi .25 .25
**1639** A547 8d multi .25 .25
**1640** A547 10d multi .25 .25
**1641** A547 20d multi .30 .25
*a.* Bklt. pane, 4 each 3d, 5d, 10d, 20d 4.25 —
**1642** A547 25d multi .35 .25
**1643** A547 30d multi .40 .25
**1644** A547 50d multi .60 .25
**1645** A547 60d multi 1.25 .60
**1646** A547 70d multi 1.25 .60
**1647** A547 100d multi 2.00 .40
**1648** A547 200d multi 4.00 .70
*Nos. 1634-1648 (15)* 11.90 5.05

Each denomination was also sold in booklets containing 20 panes of 5 stamps, perf 13 vertically or horizontally. Value for set of unused booklet stamps $12; used booklet stamps sell for slightly less than the values shown for used sheet stamps.

Council of Europe, Rhodes, Dec. 2-3 — A548

Christmas — A549

Designs: 60d, Map and Castle of the Knights, Rhodes. 100d, Head of Helios, Rhodian 2nd-3rd cent. B.C. coin, and flags.

**1988, Dec. 2 Litho. *Perf. 12½***

**1649** A548 60d multi 2.00 1.75
**1650** A548 100d multi 3.00 1.25

Nos. 1649-1650 were also issued in booklets containing 20 panes of 5, perf. 14 horizontally. Value for set of unused booklet stamps $6.50; used booklet stamps sell for somewhat less than the values shown for used sheet stamps.

**1988, Dec. 2 *Perf. 12½***

Paintings: 30d, *Adoration of the Magi*, by El Greco. 70d, *The Annunciation*, by Costas Parthenis, horiz.

**1651** A549 30d multi .80 .40
*a.* Bklt. pane of 10 24.00 —

***Perf. 14***

**1652** A549 70d multi 1.75 .85

No. 1651 was issued in booklets of 10 stamps perf 12½ on three sides. No. 1652 was also issued in booklets containing 20 panes of 5 stamps, perf. 14 vertically. Value for booklet stamp of No. 1651 $2.50; value for booklet stamp of No. 1652 $5; used values for booklet stamps are the same as for sheet stamps.

A550

A551

Athens '96 emblem and: 30d, High jumper and ancient Olympia. 60d, Wrestlers and view of Delphi. 70d, Swimmers and The Acropolis, Athens. 170d, Sports complex.

***Perf. 13¼x13½ Vert.***

**1989, Mar. 17 Litho.**

**1653** A550 30d multi .50 .30
**1654** A550 60d multi 1.00 .90
**1655** A550 70d multi 1.50 1.40
**1656** A550 170d multi 3.00 2.00
*a.* Strip of 4, Nos. 1653-1656 7.00 7.00
*b.* Bklt. pane of 4, #1653-1656, perf 13¼ vert. 10.00 —

**1989, May 22 Litho. *Perf. 12½x14***

Europa: Children's toys.

**1657** A551 60d Whistling bird *4.50 2.50*
**1658** A551 170d Butterfly *5.00 2.50*
*a.* Pair, #1657-1658 *10.00* 10.00
*b.* Bklt. pane, 2 each #1657-1658, perf 13¼ vert. 22.00 *22.00*
*c.* As "b," pair, #1657-1658 *11.00 11.00*

Printed se-tenant in sheets of 16. Nos. 1657-1658 were also issued separately in booklets containing 20 panes of 5 stamps, perf. 13¼ vertically.

Anniversaries — A552

**1989, May 22 *Perf. 14x13½***

**1659** A552 30d Flags .75 .40
**1660** A552 50d Flag, La Liberte .75 .40
**1661** A552 60d Flag, ballot box 1.75 1.10
**1662** A552 70d Coin, emblem 1.75 1.10
**1663** A552 200d Flag, "40" 4.00 1.50
*Nos. 1659-1663 (5)* 9.00 4.50

Six-nation Initiative for Peace and Disarmament, 5th anniv. (30d); French revolution, bicent. (50d); European Parliament Elections in Greece, 10th anniv. (60d); Interparliamentary Union, cent. (70d); and Council of Europe, 40th anniv. (200d).

Nos. 1659-1663 also issued in booklets containing 20 panes of 5 stamps, perf. 13¼ horizontally. Values for unused booklet stamps: No. 1659 $1; 1660 $2.75; 1661 $7.25; 1662 $7.25; 1663 $9. Used booklet stamps sell for up to 5 times the values shown for used sheet stamps.

A553

BALKANFILA XII, Sept. 30-Oct. 8, Salonica — A554

**1989, Sept. 25 Litho. *Perf. 14x12½***

**1664** A553 60d shown .85 .50
**1665** A553 70d Eye, magnifying glass .85 .75

**Souvenir Sheet**

***Perf. 14x13***

**1666** A554 200d shown 3.50 3.50

Wildflowers — A555

**1989, Dec. 8 Litho. *Perf. 14x12½***

**1667** A555 8d Wild rose .25 .25
**1668** A555 10d Common myrtle .25 .25
**1669** A555 20d Field poppy .25 .25
**1670** A555 30d Anemone .40 .25
**1671** A555 60d Dandelion, chicory .80 .40
**1672** A555 70d Mallow .90 .50
**1673** A555 200d Thistle 2.50 1.90
*Nos. 1667-1673 (7)* 5.35 3.80

*Ursus arctos* — A556

Rare and endangered species.

**1990, Mar. 16 Litho. *Perf. 14x12½***

**1674** A556 40d shown .55 .25
**1675** A556 70d *Caretta caretta* 1.90 .45
**1676** A556 90d *Monachus monachus* 2.40 .50
**1677** A556 100d *Lynx lynx* 2.50 1.10
*Nos. 1674-1677 (4)* 7.35 2.30

Europa 1990 — A557

Post offices: 70d, Old Central P.O. interior. 210d, Contemporary p.o. exterior.

**1990, May 11 Litho. *Perf. 13½x12½***

**1678** A557 70d multicolored *3.25 2.75*
**1679** A557 210d multicolored *5.75 4.75*
*a.* Pair, #1678-1679 *9.50 9.50*
*b.* Bklt. pane, 2 each #1678-1679, perf 12½ *20.00*
*c.* As "b," pair, #1678-1679 *10.00 10.00*

Nos. 1678-1679 were printed setenant in sheets of 16 and separately in booklets. Nos. 1679b and 1679c are perf 12½ vertically and imperf horizontally.

Natl. Reconcilation — A558

Political Reformers — A559

**1990, May 11 *Perf. 12½x13½***

**1680** A558 40d Flag, handshake .50 .25
**1681** A558 70d Dove, ribbon .85 .35
**1682** A558 100d Map, gift of flowers 1.25 1.25
*Nos. 1680-1682 (3)* 2.60 1.85

**1990, May 11**

**1683** A559 40d Gregoris Lambrakis (1912-63) .65 .40
**1684** A559 40d Pavlos Bakoyiannis (1935-89) .65 .40

A560

A561

Department Seats: 2d, Karditsa, the commercial-animal fair. 5d, Trikkala fort and clock tower. 8d, Veroia, street with traditional architecture. 10d, Mesolongion, Central Monument of Fallen Heroes in the Exodus. 15d, Chios, view. 20d, Tripolis, street with neoclassical architecture. 25d, Volos, view with town hall, woodcut by A. Tassou. 40d, Kalamata, neoclassical town hall. 50d, Pyrgos, central marketplace. 70d, Ioannina, view of lake and island. 80d, Rethymnon, sculpture at the port. 90d, Argostolion, view before earthquake. 100d, Nauplia, Bourtzi with Palamidi in the background. 200d, Patras, central lighthouse. 250d, Florina, street with neoclassical architecture. Nos. 1685, 1687, 1695, 1698 vert.

**1990, June 20 Litho. *Perf. 12½***

**1685** A560 2d multicolored .25 .25
**1686** A560 5d multicolored .25 .25
**1687** A560 8d multicolored .25 .25
**1688** A560 10d multicolored .25 .25
**1689** A560 15d multicolored .25 .25
**1690** A560 20d multicolored .25 .25
**1691** A560 25d multicolored .40 .25
**1692** A560 40d multicolored .60 .25
**1693** A560 50d multicolored .75 .25
**1694** A560 70d multicolored 1.00 .40
**1695** A560 80d multicolored 1.10 .45
**1696** A560 90d multicolored 1.40 .50
**1697** A560 100d multicolored 2.25 .60
**1698** A560 200d multicolored 4.50 1.10
**1699** A560 250d multicolored 6.00 1.50
*Nos. 1685-1699 (15)* 19.50 6.80

Each denomination was also sold in booklets containing 20 panes of 5 stamps, perf 13½ vertically or horizontally. Value for set of unused booklet stamps $10; used booklet stamps sell for about half of the value of used sheet stamps.

See Nos. 1749-1760, 1792-1801.

**1990, July 13 *Perf. 12½x13½***

**1700** A561 20d Sailing .25 .25
**1701** A561 50d Wrestling .60 .25
**1702** A561 80d Sprinting .90 .90
**1703** A561 100d Basketball 1.25 .90
**1704** A561 250d Soccer 3.00 1.50
*a.* Strip of 5, #1700-1704 7.00 7.00

1996 Summer Olympics. Athens, proposed site for centennial Summer Olympic Games. Exists perf. 13½ vert.

Heinrich Schliemann (1822-1890), Archaeologist — A562

**1990, Oct. 11 Litho. *Perf. 14x13½***

**1705** A562 80d multicolored 5.00 3.00

See Germany No. 1615.

Greco-Italian War, 50th Anniv. — A563

**1990, Oct. 11 *Perf. 12½***

**1706** A563 50d Woman knitting .60 .25
**1707** A563 80d Virgin Mary, soldier 1.00 .80
**1708** A563 100d Women volunteers 1.40 .80
*Nos. 1706-1708 (3)* 3.00 1.85

**Souvenir Sheet**

Stamp Day — A564

**1990, Dec. 14 Litho. *Perf. 14x13***

**1709** A564 300d multicolored *10.00 10.00*

The Muses — A565

Designs: 50d, Calliope, Euterpe, Erato. 80d, Terpsichore, Polyhymnia, Melpomene. 250d, Thalia, Clio, Urania.

**1991, Mar. 11 Litho. *Perf. 12½***

**1710** A565 50d multicolored .60 .25
**1711** A565 80d multicolored .95 .40
**1712** A565 250d multicolored 2.75 1.25
*Nos. 1710-1712 (3)* 4.30 1.90

Battle of Crete by Ioannis Anousakis — A566

300d, Map, flags of participating allied armies.

**1991, May 20 Litho. *Perf. 12½x13½***

**1713** A566 60d multicolored 1.60 .40

**Size: 32x24mm**

***Perf. 12½***

**1714** A566 300d multicolored 3.25 1.50

Battle of Crete, 50th anniv.

Europa
A567

Designs: 80d, Icarus pushing modern satellite. 300d, Chariot of the Sun.

**1991, May 20** *Perf. 12½*

**1715** A567 80d multicolored 4.00 3.00
**1716** A567 300d multicolored 5.50 4.50
*a.* Pair, #1715-1716 10.00 10.00
*b.* Bklt. pane, 2 ea. #1715-1716 22.00 22.00
*c.* As "b," pair, 80d, 300d 11.00 11.00

No. 1716a printed in continuous design in sheets of 16. Nos. 1715-1716 were also issued separately in booklets (#1716b), perf 12½ vertically and imperf horizontally.

A568

A569

**1991, June 25 Litho.** *Perf. 13½x14*

**1717** A568 10d Swimming .25 .25
**1718** A568 60d Basketball .50 .25
**1719** A568 90d Gymnastics .90 .30
**1720** A568 130d Weight lifting 1.25 .50
**1721** A568 300d Hammer throw 3.50 2.00
*Nos. 1717-1721 (5)* 6.40 3.30

1991 Mediterranean Games, Athens.

**1991, Sept. 20 Litho.** *Perf. 13½x14*

**1722** A569 100d multicolored 1.10 .60

Athenian Democracy, 2500th anniv.

Europa Souvenir Sheet

Greek Presidency of CEPT — A570

Europe with Zeus metmorphosed into a bull, from Attic vase, c. 500 B.C.

**1991, Sept. 20** *Perf. 14x13*

**1723** A570 300d multicolored 20.00 20.00

A571

A572

Greek Membership in EEC, 10th anniv.: 50d, Pres. Konstantin Karamanlis signing Treaty of Greek entrance into EEC. 80d, Map showing EEC members, Pres. Karamanlis.

**1991, Dec. 9 Litho.** *Perf. 13x14*

**1724** A571 50d multicolored .55 .25
**1725** A571 80d multicolored .90 .50

**1991, Dec. 9** *Perf. 12½x13½*

**1726** A572 80d Speed skaters .90 .80
**1727** A572 300d Slalom skier 3.25 1.10
*a.* Pair, #1726-1727 4.25 4.25

16th Winter Olympics, Albertville.

A573

1992 Summer Olympics, Barcelona
A574

*Perf. 12½, 14x13½ (90d, 340d)*

**1992, Apr. 3 Litho.**

**1728** A573 10d Javelin .25 .25
**1729** A573 60d Equestrian .90 .30
**1730** A574 90d Runner 1.40 .75
**1731** A573 120d Gymnastics 2.75 .80
**1732** A574 340d Runners 4.50 2.25
*Nos. 1728-1732 (5)* 9.80 4.35

Health — A575

Designs: 60d, Protection against AIDS. 80d, Diseases of digestive system. 90d, Dying flower symbolizing cancer. 120d, Hephaestus at his forge, 6th century BC. 280d, Alexandros S. Onassis Cardiosurgical Center.

**1992, May 22 Litho.** *Perf. 12½*

**1733** A575 60d multicolored .60 .30
**1734** A575 80d multicolored .85 .40
**1735** A575 90d multicolored .90 .45
**1736** A575 120d multicolored 1.50 .65
**1737** A575 280d multicolored 3.25 1.75
*Nos. 1733-1737 (5)* 7.10 3.55

No. 1734, 1st United European Gastroenterology Week. No. 1736, European Year of Social Security, Hygiene and Health in the Workplace.

Discovery of America, 500th Anniv.
A576

Europa: 340d, Map of 15th century Chios, Columbus.

**1992, May 22** *Perf. 13½x12¼*

**1738** A576 90d shown 2.75 2.00
*a.* Perf. 12½ vert. 3.00 2.25
**1739** A576 340d multicolored 6.50 4.75
*a.* Pair, #1738-1739 10.00 10.00
*b.* Perf. 12½ vert. 6.75 5.50
*c.* Bklt. pane, 2 each #1738a, 1739b 20.00 20.00
*d.* Pair, #1738a, 1739b 10.00 10.00

No. 1739a was printed in continuous design in sheets of 16. Nos. 1738-1739 were also issued separately in booklets (#1739c), perf 12¼ vertically and imperf horizontally.

Souvenir Sheet

European Conference on Transportation — A577

**1992, June 8** *Perf. 14x13*

**1740** A577 300d multicolored 8.50 8.50

Macedonian Treasures — A578

Designs: 10d, Head of Hercules wearing lion skin, Vergina treasures. 20d, Bust of Aristotle, map of Macedonia, horiz. 60d, Alexander the Great at Battle of Issus, horiz. 80d, Archaeologist Manolis Andronikos, tomb of King Philip II. 90d, Deer hunt mosaic, Pella. 120d, Macedonian tetradrachm. 340d, St. Paul, 4th century church near Philippi.

**1992, July 17 Litho.** *Perf. 12½*

**1741** A578 10d multicolored .50 .25
**1742** A578 20d multicolored .50 .25
**1743** A578 60d multicolored .60 .25
**1744** A578 80d multicolored 1.60 .25
**1745** A578 90d multicolored 1.90 .25
**1746** A578 120d multicolored 2.40 1.00
**1747** A578 340d multicolored 8.50 2.50
*Nos. 1741-1747 (7)* 16.00 4.75

European Unification — A579

**1992, Oct. 12 Litho.** *Perf. 14x13*

**1748** A579 90d multicolored 1.00 1.00

**Departmental Seat Type of 1990**

Designs: 10d, Piraeus, the old clock. 20d, Amphissa, view of city with citadel. 30d, Samos (Vathy), the Heraion. 40d, Canea, city in 1800s. 50d, Zakinthos (Zante), view in 1800s. 60d, Karpenision, Velouchi and city. 70d, Kilkis, the cave, vert. 80d, Xanthe, door of Town Hall, vert. 90d, Salonika, Macedonian Struggle Museum. 120d, Komotine, Tsanakleous School. 340d, Drama, spring. 400d, Larissa, Pinios bridge.

**1992, Oct. 12** *Perf. 12¾*

**1749** A560 10d multicolored .25 .25
**1750** A560 20d multicolored .25 .25
**1751** A560 30d multicolored .25 .25
**1752** A560 40d multicolored .35 .25
**1753** A560 50d multicolored .40 .25
**1754** A560 60d multicolored .45 .30
**1755** A560 70d multicolored .60 .35
**1756** A560 80d multicolored .60 .35
**1757** A560 90d multicolored 1.25 .40
**1758** A560 120d multicolored 2.50 .65
**1759** A560 340d multicolored 4.00 1.60
**1760** A560 400d multicolored 5.50 2.25
*Nos. 1749-1760 (12)* 16.40 7.15

Each denomination was also sold in booklets containing 20 panes of 5 stamps, perf 10½ vertically or horizontally. Value for set of unused booklet stamps $14.50; used booklet stamps sell for about half the listed values for used sheet stamps.

City of Rhodes, 2400th Anniv. — A580

Designs: 60d, Headstone, 4th cent. B.C. 90d, Bathing Aphrodite, 1st cent. B.C. 120d, St. Irene, Church of St. Catherine, 14th cent. 250d, St. Paul's Gate, 15th cent.

**1993, Feb. 26 Litho.** *Perf. 13x14*

**1761** A580 60d multicolored .65 .35
**1762** A580 90d multicolored 1.10 .80
**1763** A580 120d multicolored 1.25 .70
**1764** A580 250d multicolored 4.00 1.75
*Nos. 1761-1764 (4)* 7.00 3.60

Remembrances of Greek Wars — A581

Designs: 10d, Death of Georgakis Olympios, 1821. 30d, Theodore Kolokotronis in battle, 1821. 60d, Pavlos Melas. 90d, Glory lays wreath over graves of dead from Balkan Wars. 120d, Greek soldiers at Battle of El Alamein, 1942, horiz. 150d, Greek troops in Aegean Islands, 1943-45, horiz. 200d, Kalavryta Massacre Memorial.

*Perf. 13x14, 14x13*

**1993, May 25 Litho.**

**1765** A581 10d multicolored .25 .25
**1766** A581 30d multicolored .40 .25
**1767** A581 60d multicolored .55 .30
**1768** A581 90d multicolored 1.00 .40
**1769** A581 120d multicolored 2.40 1.00
**1770** A581 150d multicolored 2.40 1.60
**1771** A581 200d multicolored 4.75 2.25
*Nos. 1765-1771 (7)* 11.75 6.05

The Benefits of Transportation, by K. Parthenis — A582

Europa: 90d, Tree, three people, ships. 350d, Woman and children, town.

**1993, May 25** *Perf. 13x14*

**1772** 90d multicolored 1.50 1.25
*a.* Perf. 13½ vert. 1.50 1.25
**1773** 350d multicolored 6.75 5.50
*a.* A582 Pair, #1772-1773 9.00 9.00
*b.* Perf. 13½ vert. 6.75 5.50
*c.* Bklt. pane, 2 each #1772a, 1773b 18.00 18.00
*d.* Pair, #1772a, 1773b 9.00 9.00

No. 1773a was printed in continuous design in sheets of 16. Nos. 1772-1773 were also issued separately in booklets (#1773c), perf 13½ vertically and imperf horizontally.

Buildings in Athens
A583

Designs: 30d, Concert Hall. 60d, Numismatic Museum (Iliou Melathron). 90d, Natl. Library of Greece. 200d, Opthalmology Hospital.

**1993, Oct. 4 Litho.** *Perf. 14*

**1774** A583 30d multicolored .85 .25
**1775** A583 60d multicolored .85 .30
**1776** A583 90d multicolored 1.00 .80
**1777** A583 200d multicolored 5.00 2.00
*Nos. 1774-1777 (4)* 7.70 3.35

Souvenir Sheet

Greek Presidency of the European Community Council of Ministers — A584

**1993, Dec. 20 Litho. *Perf. 14***

| | | | | |
|---|---|---|---|---|
| **1778** | A584 | 400d multicolored | *5.00* | *5.00* |

Chariot of Selene Driven by Hermes A585

**1994, Mar. 7 Litho. *Perf. 13x13½***

| | | | | |
|---|---|---|---|---|
| **1779** | A585 | 200d multicolored | 2.25 | 1.50 |

2nd Pan-European Transportation Conference.

Passion of Christ A586

Designs: 30d, Last Supper, 16th cent. icon, St. Catherine's Church, Crete, vert. 60d, Crucifixion, detail from 1552 wall drawing, Great Meteoron, vert. 90d, Burial, 1620-45 icon, Church of the Presentation of the Lord, Patmos. 150d, Resurrection, illustrated manuscript of Mt. Athos, 11th cent.

**1994, Apr. 8 Litho. *Perf. 14***

| | | | | |
|---|---|---|---|---|
| **1780** | A586 | 30d multicolored | .40 | .25 |
| **1781** | A586 | 60d multicolored | .50 | .25 |
| **1782** | A586 | 90d multicolored | .75 | .40 |
| **1783** | A586 | 150d multicolored | 1.60 | .90 |
| | | *Nos. 1780-1783 (4)* | 3.25 | 1.80 |

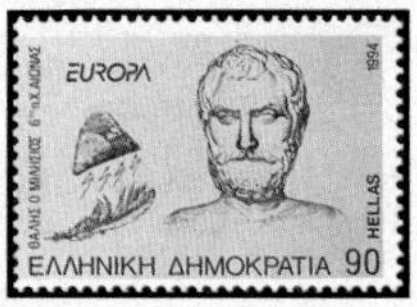


European Inventors, Discoverers A587

Europa: 90d, Thales of Miletus (625?-547? B.C.), philosopher, mathematician. 350d, Konstantinos Karatheodoris (1873-1950).

**1994, May 9 Litho. *Perf. 14x13½***

| | | | | |
|---|---|---|---|---|
| **1784** | A587 | 90d multicolored | *1.75* | *1.50* |
| *a.* | | Perf. 13¾ vert. | *2.00* | *1.75* |
| **1785** | A587 | 350d multicolored | *3.75* | *3.25* |
| *a.* | | Pair, #1784-1785 | *6.00* | *6.00* |
| *b.* | | Perf. 13¾ vert. | *4.00* | *3.50* |
| *c.* | | Bklt. pane, 2 each #1784a-1785b | *13.00* | *13.00* |
| *d.* | | Pair, #1784a, 1785b | *6.50* | *6.50* |

Nos. 1784-1785 was issued in sheets of 16 and in booklets (#1785c), perf 13¾ vertically and imperf horizontally.

Athletic Events, Anniversaries A588

Designs: 60d, Demetrios Vikelas (1835-1908), first president Intl. Olympic Committee, vert. 90, Modern, ancient soccer players. 120d, Volleyball, net, vert. 400d, Statue of Liberty, modern, ancient soccer players.

**1994, June 6 Litho. *Perf. 14***

| | | | | |
|---|---|---|---|---|
| **1786** | A588 | 60d multicolored | .70 | .30 |
| **1787** | A588 | 90d multicolored | .85 | .60 |
| **1788** | A588 | 120d multicolored | 1.75 | .90 |
| | | *Nos. 1786-1788 (3)* | 3.30 | 1.80 |

**Souvenir Sheet**

***Perf. 14x13½***

| | | | | |
|---|---|---|---|---|
| **1789** | A588 | 400d multicolored | 4.50 | 4.50 |

Intl. Olympic Committee, cent. (#1786). 1994 World Cup Soccer Championships, US (#1787, #1789). World Volleyball Championships, Piraeus & Salonika (#1788).

No. 1789 contains one 42x52mm stamp.

Greek Presidency of European Community Council of Ministers A589

Designs: 90d, Winged chariot driven by Greece. 120d, Doric columns, European Community flag.

**1994, June 21 *Perf. 13***

| | | | | |
|---|---|---|---|---|
| **1790** | A589 | 90d multicolored | 1.00 | .90 |
| **1791** | A589 | 120d multicolored | 1.25 | .90 |

**Departmental Seat Type of 1990**

Designs: 10d, Katerine, Tsalopoulou mansion house, vert. 20d, Arta, Byzantine Church Parigoritissas. 30d, Lebadea, medieval bridge, tower of catalanian castle, Krias springs vert. 40d, Kastoria, Church of Panagia Koumbelidkis. 50d, Grevena, outdoor theatre. 60d, Edessa, waterfall. 80d, Chalcis, red house. 90d, Serrai, government house, Merarchias road, Acropolis of Koulas. 120d, Candia (Herakleion), town hall. 150d, Egoumenitsa, Church of Evangelistria, vert.

**1994, Oct. 5 Litho. *Perf. 12¾***

| | | | | |
|---|---|---|---|---|
| **1792** | A560 | 10d multicolored | .25 | .25 |
| **1793** | A560 | 20d multicolored | .25 | .25 |
| **1794** | A560 | 30d multicolored | .30 | .25 |
| **1795** | A560 | 40d multicolored | .40 | .25 |
| **1796** | A560 | 50d multicolored | .50 | .25 |
| **1797** | A560 | 60d multicolored | .65 | .25 |
| **1798** | A560 | 80d multicolored | .75 | .30 |
| **1799** | A560 | 90d multicolored | .80 | .30 |
| **1800** | A560 | 120d multicolored | 1.00 | .40 |
| **1801** | A560 | 150d multicolored | 1.25 | .50 |
| | | *Nos. 1792-1801 (10)* | 6.15 | 3.00 |

Each denomination was also sold in booklets containing 20 panes of 5 stamps, perf 10½ vertically or horizontally. Unused booklet stamps sell for the same price as the sheet stamp values listed; used booklet stamps sell for about half the listed values for the used sheet stamps.

Constitution, 150th Anniv. — A590

Designs: 60d, People, army demonstrating, by Carl Howpt, vert. 150d, Portraits of Ioannis Makriyannis, Andreas Metaxas, Demetrios Kallergis. 200d, Painting of night of Sept. 3, 1843. 340d, Article 107, seal of Greek Parliament, signature of President.

**1994, Nov. 21 Litho. *Perf. 14x13***

| | | | | |
|---|---|---|---|---|
| **1802** | A590 | 60d multicolored | .65 | .40 |
| **1803** | A590 | 150d multicolored | 1.10 | .65 |
| **1804** | A590 | 200d multicolored | 2.25 | 1.00 |
| **1805** | A590 | 340d multicolored | 4.25 | 2.00 |
| | | *Nos. 1802-1805 (4)* | 8.25 | 4.05 |

Melina Mercouri (1925-94), Actress, Politician — A591

**1995, Mar. 7 Litho. *Perf. 14x13***

| | | | | |
|---|---|---|---|---|
| **1806** | A591 | 60d shown | .65 | .25 |
| **1807** | A591 | 90d Portrait, Parthenon | .80 | .40 |
| **1808** | A591 | 100d Portraits as actress | 3.00 | 1.00 |
| **1809** | A591 | 340d Portrait, vert. | 6.75 | 2.25 |
| | | *Nos. 1806-1809 (4)* | 11.20 | 3.90 |

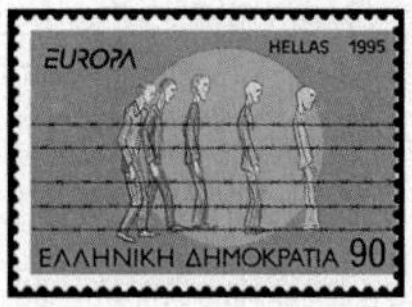


Liberation of Concentration Camps, 50th Anniv. A592

Europa: 90d, Prisoners. 340d, Peace doves, broken barbed wire fence.

**1995, May 3 Litho. *Perf. 14***

| | | | | |
|---|---|---|---|---|
| **1810** | A592 | 90d multicolored | 2.00 | 2.00 |
| *a.* | | Perf. 13½ vert. | 2.00 | 2.00 |
| **1811** | A592 | 340d multicolored | 4.00 | 4.00 |
| *a.* | | Pair, #1810-1811 | 6.50 | 6.50 |
| *b.* | | Perf. 13½ vert. | 4.00 | 4.00 |
| *c.* | | Bklt. pane, 2 each #1810a, 1811b | 13.00 | 13.00 |
| | | Complete booklet, #1811c | 13.00 | |
| *d.* | | Pair, #1810a, 1811b | 6.50 | 6.50 |

Anniversaries & Events — A593

Designs: 10d, Stylized emblem, basketball, vert. 70d, University building. 90d, Architectural ruins, vert. 100d, Flag, soldier, vert. 120d, Statue of Peace, by Kifissodotos, vert. 150d, Dolphins. 200d, Early telephone, push buttons, vert. 300d, Owl, basketball, vert.

***Perf. 13½x13, 13x13½***

**1995, June 21 Litho.**

| | | | | |
|---|---|---|---|---|
| **1812** | A593 | 10d multicolored | .25 | .25 |
| **1813** | A593 | 70d multicolored | 1.00 | .30 |
| **1814** | A593 | 90d multicolored | 1.25 | .40 |
| **1815** | A593 | 100d multicolored | 1.40 | .45 |
| **1816** | A593 | 120d multicolored | 1.75 | .55 |
| **1817** | A593 | 150d multicolored | 2.00 | .65 |
| **1818** | A593 | 200d multicolored | 2.75 | .90 |
| **1819** | A593 | 300d multicolored | 4.50 | 1.25 |
| | | *Nos. 1812-1819 (8)* | 14.90 | 4.75 |

5th World Junior Basketball Championships (#1812). Agricultural University of Athens, 75th anniv. (#1813). UN, 50th anniv. (#1814, #1816). End of World War II, 50th anniv. (#1815). European Nature Conservation Year (#1817). Telephone in Greece, cent. (#1818). 29th European Basketball Championships (#1819).

Book of Revelation, 1900th Anniv. — A594

Visions of the Apocalypse: 80d, First vision, Angels of the Seven Churches of Asia Minor, icon by Thomas Bathas, vert. 110d, Apostle John at Cave of the Apocalypse dictating to Prochoros, miniature from manuscript of Four Gospels, vert. 300d, First Angel with trumpet from silver gilded Gospel cover.

**1995, Sept. 18 Litho. *Perf. 14***

| | | | | |
|---|---|---|---|---|
| **1820** | A594 | 80d multicolored | 2.00 | .35 |
| **1821** | A594 | 110d multicolored | 2.75 | .90 |
| **1822** | A594 | 300d multicolored | 3.75 | 2.00 |
| | | *Nos. 1820-1822 (3)* | 8.50 | 3.25 |

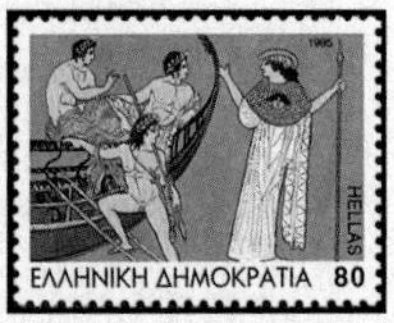

Jason & the Argonauts A595

Designs: 80d, Argonauts, the Argus, goddess Athena setting out for Colchis. 120d, Phineas, Hermes, one of the Voreadae, Harpy. 150d, Jason taming the bull, Medea and Nike. 200d, Jason takes Golden Fleece, kills serpent with Medea's help. 300d, Medea watches, Jason, crowned by Nike, giving Golden Fleece to Pelias.

**1995, Nov. 6 Litho. *Perf. 13x13½***

| | | | | |
|---|---|---|---|---|
| **1823** | A595 | 80d multicolored | .90 | .40 |
| **1824** | A595 | 120d multicolored | .90 | .75 |
| **1825** | A595 | 150d multicolored | 1.10 | .65 |
| **1826** | A595 | 200d multicolored | 1.60 | .75 |
| **1827** | A595 | 300d multicolored | 4.50 | 1.60 |
| | | *Nos. 1823-1827 (5)* | 9.00 | 4.15 |

Lighthouses — A596

**1995, Dec. 18 Litho. *Perf. 14***

| | | | | |
|---|---|---|---|---|
| **1828** | A596 | 80d Psyttaleia | 1.00 | .40 |
| **1829** | A596 | 120d Sapienza | 1.50 | .60 |
| **1830** | A596 | 150d Kastri (Othonoi) | 2.00 | 1.10 |
| **1831** | A596 | 500d Zourva (Hydra) | 7.25 | 2.40 |
| | | *Nos. 1828-1831 (4)* | 11.75 | 4.50 |

Souvenir Sheets

Modern Olympic Games, Cent. — A597

***Perf. 13½x13, 13x13½***

**1996, Mar. 25 Litho.**

| | | | | |
|---|---|---|---|---|
| **1832** | | Sheet of 4 | 15.00 | 15.00 |
| *a.* | A597 | 80d like #117, vert. | 3.00 | 3.00 |
| *b.* | A597 | 120d like #118, vert. | 3.00 | 3.00 |
| *c.* | A597 | 150d like #119, vert. | 3.00 | 3.00 |
| *d.* | A597 | 650d like #120, vert. | 3.00 | 3.00 |
| **1833** | | Sheet of 4 | 15.00 | 15.00 |
| *a.* | A597 | 80d like #122 | 3.00 | 3.00 |
| *b.* | A597 | 120d like #124 | 3.00 | 3.00 |
| *c.* | A597 | 150d like #125 | 3.00 | 3.00 |
| *d.* | A597 | 650d like #128 | 3.00 | 3.00 |
| **1834** | | Sheet of 4 | 15.00 | 15.00 |
| *a.* | A597 | 80d like #121, vert. | 3.00 | 3.00 |
| *b.* | A597 | 120d like #123, vert. | 3.00 | 3.00 |
| *c.* | A597 | 150d like #126, vert. | 3.00 | 3.00 |
| *d.* | A597 | 650d like #127, vert. | 3.00 | 3.00 |

Famous Women — A598

Europa: 120d, Sappho (c.610-580BC), lyric poet. 430d, Amalia Fleming.

**1996, Apr. 22 Litho. *Perf. 14x14½***

| | | | | |
|---|---|---|---|---|
| **1835** | | 120d multicolored | *1.50* | *1.50* |
| *a.* | | Perf. 14½ vert. | *1.50* | *1.50* |
| **1836** | | 430d multicolored | *4.50* | *4.50* |
| *a.* | A598 | Pair, #1835-1836 | *6.25* | *6.25* |
| *b.* | | Perf. 14½ vert. | *4.50* | *4.50* |
| *c.* | | Booklet pane, 2 each #1835a, 1836b | *12.50* | *12.50* |
| | | Complete booklet, #1836c | *12.50* | |
| *d.* | | Pair, #1835a, 1836b | *6.25* | *6.25* |

Modern Olympic Games, Cent. A599

Stylized designs: 10d, Greek runners, vert. 80d, Discus thrower, vert. 120d, Weight lifter, vert. 200d, Wrestlers.

*Perf. 13½x14, 14x13½*

**1996, June 4** **Litho.**

| | | | | | |
|---|---|---|---|---|---|
| **1837** | A599 | 10d | multicolored | .45 | .25 |
| **1838** | A599 | 80d | multicolored | 1.60 | .45 |
| **1839** | A599 | 120d | multicolored | 3.00 | .75 |
| **1840** | A599 | 200d | multicolored | 4.75 | 2.00 |
| | | | *Nos. 1837-1840 (4)* | 9.80 | 3.45 |

First Intl. Medical Olympiad — A600

**1996, July 8** **Litho.** ***Perf. 13½***

| | | | | | |
|---|---|---|---|---|---|
| **1841** | A600 | 80d | Hippocrates | 2.00 | .80 |
| **1842** | A600 | 120d | Galen | 2.50 | 1.25 |

Castles A601

**1996, Oct. 7** **Litho.** ***Perf. 13x13½***

| | | | | | |
|---|---|---|---|---|---|
| **1843** | A601 | 10d | Mytilene | .25 | .25 |
| **1844** | A601 | 20d | Lindos | .25 | .25 |
| **1845** | A601 | 30d | Rethymnon | .30 | .25 |
| **1846** | A601 | 70d | Assos Cephalonia | .65 | .35 |
| **1847** | A601 | 80d | Serbs | .80 | .60 |
| **1848** | A601 | 120d | Monemvasia | 1.00 | .65 |
| **1849** | A601 | 200d | Didimotihon | 1.75 | 1.00 |
| **1850** | A601 | 430d | Vonitsas | 4.25 | 3.00 |
| **1851** | A601 | 1000d | Nikopolis | 10.00 | 6.50 |
| | | | *Nos. 1843-1851 (9)* | 19.25 | 12.85 |

Each denomination was also sold in booklets containing 20 panes of 5 stamps, perf. 13 vertically. Unused sell for the same price as the listed sheet stamps; used booklet stamps sell for about half the values shown for used sheet stamps.

Figures from Shadow Theatre — A602

100d, Four characters, diff. 120d, Three characters. 200d, Two characters, dragon.

**1996, Nov. 15** **Litho.** ***Perf. 14***

| | | | | | |
|---|---|---|---|---|---|
| **1852** | A602 | 80d | multicolored | 1.00 | .45 |
| **1853** | A602 | 100d | multicolored | 1.00 | .55 |
| **1854** | A602 | 120d | multicolored | 2.00 | .70 |
| **1855** | A602 | 200d | multicolored | 3.00 | 1.10 |
| | | | *Nos. 1852-1855 (4)* | 7.00 | 2.80 |

Hellenic Language A603

Designs: 80d, Oldest Hellenic inscription, wine pitcher, 720BC. 120d, Verse IX, 436-445 from Homer's Iliad, 1st-2nd cent. AD. 150d, Psalm of the Holy Apostles, 6th cent. AD. 350d, Reference to Hellenic language, Dionysios Solomos, 1824.

**1996, Dec. 18** **Litho.** ***Perf. 13x13½***

| | | | | | |
|---|---|---|---|---|---|
| **1856** | A603 | 80d | multicolored | .85 | .55 |
| **1857** | A603 | 120d | multicolored | 1.10 | .85 |
| **1858** | A603 | 150d | multicolored | 1.75 | 1.40 |
| **1859** | A603 | 350d | multicolored | 4.25 | 2.10 |
| | | | *Nos. 1856-1859 (4)* | 7.95 | 4.90 |

Andreas G. Papandreou (1919-96), Prime Minister — A604

Papandreou at various ages and: 80d, Graduation cap, books, diploma. 120d, Leaving airplane. 150d, Building. 500d, Greek flag, dove.

**1997, Feb. 12** **Litho.** ***Perf. 13***

| | | | | | |
|---|---|---|---|---|---|
| **1860** | A604 | 80d | multicolored | 1.10 | .30 |
| **1861** | A604 | 120d | multicolored | 1.10 | .45 |
| **1862** | A604 | 150d | multicolored | 1.75 | .85 |
| **1863** | A604 | 500d | multicolored | 4.00 | .95 |
| | | | *Nos. 1860-1863 (4)* | 7.95 | 2.55 |

Thessaloniki, European Cultural Capital A605

Designs: 80d, Frescoe of St. Dimitrios, patron saint of Thessaloniki, Church of Aghios Nikolaos Orphanos, vert. 100d, Hippocratic Hospital. 120d, Marble pedestal with inscription, medallion with woman's head, vert. 150d, Detail of mosaic from Rotunda cupola, vert. 300d, "Iaspis" chalice, 14th cent., Mt. Athos.

**1997, Mar. 26** ***Perf. 13½***

| | | | | | |
|---|---|---|---|---|---|
| **1864** | A605 | 80d | multicolored | .90 | .50 |
| **1865** | A605 | 100d | multicolored | 1.40 | .65 |
| **1866** | A605 | 120d | multicolored | 1.50 | .75 |
| **1867** | A605 | 150d | multicolored | 1.75 | 1.00 |
| **1868** | A605 | 300d | multicolored | 4.50 | 2.00 |
| | | | *Nos. 1864-1868 (5)* | 10.05 | 4.90 |

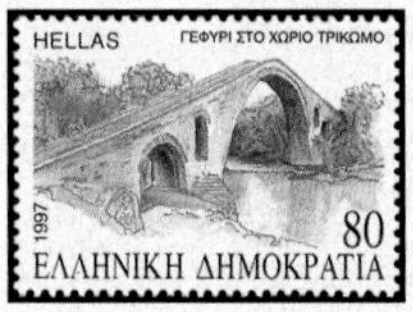


Bridges of Macedonia A606

**1997, Apr. 24** **Litho.** ***Perf. 14***

| | | | | | |
|---|---|---|---|---|---|
| **1869** | A606 | 80d | Village of Trikomo | .70 | .45 |
| **1870** | A606 | 120d | Portitsa | 1.10 | .65 |
| **1871** | A606 | 150d | Village of Ziakas | 2.00 | .85 |
| **1872** | A606 | 350d | Village of Kastro | 5.25 | 1.90 |
| | | | *Nos. 1869-1872 (4)* | 9.05 | 3.85 |

Stories and Legends A607

Europa: 120d, Prometheus, the giver of fire. 430d, Digenis Akritas, Greek swordsmen on horseback.

**1997, May 19** **Litho.** ***Perf. 14***

| | | | | | |
|---|---|---|---|---|---|
| **1873** | A607 | 120d | multicolored | *1.75* | *1.50* |
| *a.* | | | Perf. 13½vert. | *1.75* | *1.50* |
| **1874** | A607 | 430d | multicolored | *4.00* | *3.50* |
| *a.* | | | Pair, #1873-1874 | *5.75* | *5.75* |
| *b.* | | | Perf. 13½vert. | *4.00* | *3.50* |
| *c.* | | | Booklet pane, 2 each #1873a, 1874b | *11.50* | *11.50* |
| | | | Complete booklet, #1874c | *11.50* | |
| *d.* | | | Pair, #1873a, 1874b | *5.75* | *5.75* |

6th IAAF World Track & Field Championships, Athens — A608

Official IAAF emblem, Greek flag and: 20d, Runners. 100d, Nike. 140d, High jump. 170d, Hurdles. 500d, Olympic Stadium, Athens.

**1997, July 11** **Litho.** ***Perf. 13x13½***

| | | | | | |
|---|---|---|---|---|---|
| **1875** | A608 | 20d | multicolored | .25 | .25 |
| **1876** | A608 | 100d | multicolored | .85 | .40 |
| **1877** | A608 | 140d | multicolored | 1.25 | .80 |
| **1878** | A608 | 170d | multicolored | 1.60 | 1.00 |
| **1879** | A608 | 500d | multicolored | 5.25 | 2.50 |
| | | | *Nos. 1875-1879 (5)* | 9.20 | 4.95 |

Famous People A609

Designs: 20d, Alexandros Panagoulis (1939-76), resistance leader, vert. 30d, Grigorios Xenopoulos (1867-1951), novelist, vert. 40d, Odysseus Elytis (1911-96), poet. 50d, Panayiotis Kanellopoulos (1902-86), prime minister, vert. 100d, Harilaos Trikoupis (1832-96), politician. 170d, Maria Callas (1923-77), opera singer. 200d, Rigas Vélestinlis-Feraios (1757-98), revolutionary, vert.

*Perf. 13½x13, 13x13½*

**1997, Oct. 31** **Litho.**

| | | | | | |
|---|---|---|---|---|---|
| **1880** | A609 | 20d | multicolored | .25 | .25 |
| **1881** | A609 | 30d | multicolored | .50 | .25 |
| **1882** | A609 | 40d | multicolored | .60 | .25 |
| **1883** | A609 | 50d | multicolored | .90 | .25 |
| **1884** | A609 | 100d | multicolored | 1.50 | .75 |
| **1885** | A609 | 170d | multicolored | 3.00 | 1.40 |
| **1886** | A609 | 200d | multicolored | 3.50 | 1.60 |
| | | | *Nos. 1880-1886 (7)* | 10.25 | 4.75 |

Film Comedians A610

Designs: 20d, Vassilis Avlonitis. 30d, Vassilis Argyropoulos. 50d, Georgia Vassileiadou. 70d, Lambros Constantaras. 100d, Vassilis Logothetidis. 140d, Dionysis Papagiannopoulos. 170d, Nikos Stavrides. 200d, Mimis Fotopoulos.

**1997, Dec. 17** **Litho.** ***Perf. 13x13½***

| | | | | | |
|---|---|---|---|---|---|
| **1887** | A610 | 20d | multicolored | .25 | .25 |
| **1888** | A610 | 30d | multicolored | .40 | .25 |
| **1889** | A610 | 50d | multicolored | .60 | .45 |
| **1890** | A610 | 70d | multicolored | .85 | .70 |
| **1891** | A610 | 100d | multicolored | 1.10 | .85 |
| **1892** | A610 | 140d | multicolored | 1.60 | 1.60 |
| **1893** | A610 | 170d | multicolored | 2.40 | 1.60 |
| **1894** | A610 | 200d | multicolored | 5.00 | 1.60 |
| | | | *Nos. 1887-1894 (8)* | 12.20 | 7.30 |

Incorporation of the Dodecanese Islands into Greece, 50th Anniv. — A611

100d, German commander signing treaty turning islands over to English and Greek military, Symi (Simi), May 8, 1945. 140d, Greece and Colossus of Rhodes, Greek flag. 170d, English general turns islands over to Greek military command, Rhodes, 3/31/47. 500d, Greek flag raised over Dodecanese, Kasos (Caso), 3/7/47.

**1998, Feb. 27** **Litho.** ***Perf. 13½x13***

| | | | | | |
|---|---|---|---|---|---|
| **1895** | A611 | 100d | multicolored | 1.00 | .65 |
| **1896** | A611 | 140d | multicolored | 1.40 | 1.40 |
| **1897** | A611 | 170d | multicolored | 2.00 | 1.75 |
| **1898** | A611 | 500d | multicolored | 5.50 | 1.25 |
| | | | *Nos. 1895-1898 (4)* | 9.90 | 5.05 |

Hagia Sophia General Children's Hospital, Cent. — A612

Holy Monastery of Xenon, 1000th Anniv. A613

4th World Congress of Thracians, Nea Orestiada A614

16th World Congress of Cardiology Research, Athens — A615

European Movement, 50th Anniv. — A616

*Perf. 13x13½, 13½x13*

**1998, Apr. 30** **Litho.**

| | | | | | |
|---|---|---|---|---|---|
| **1899** | A612 | 20d | multicolored | .25 | .25 |
| **1900** | A613 | 100d | multicolored | .90 | .50 |
| **1901** | A614 | 140d | multicolored | 1.25 | 1.25 |
| **1902** | A615 | 150d | Building, heart, horiz. | 1.25 | 1.25 |
| **1903** | A615 | 170d | multicolored | 2.00 | 1.60 |
| **1904** | A616 | 500d | multicolored | 6.50 | 1.90 |
| | | | *Nos. 1899-1904 (6)* | 12.15 | 6.75 |

Souvenir Sheet

1998 FIBA World Basketball Championships, Greece — A617

**1998, June 15** **Litho.** ***Perf. 14***

| | | | | | |
|---|---|---|---|---|---|
| **1905** | A617 | 300d | multicolored | 3.50 | 3.50 |

Natl. Festivals A618

Europa: 140d, Culture Festival, Grecian Theatre, Epidaurus. 500d, Culture Festival, Herod Atticus Theatre, Athens.

**1998, May 29** **Litho.** ***Perf. 14x13½***

| | | | | | |
|---|---|---|---|---|---|
| **1906** | A618 | 140d | multicolored | *1.50* | *1.50* |
| *a.* | | | Perf. 13 vert. | *1.75* | *1.75* |
| **1907** | A618 | 500d | multicolored | *4.25* | *4.25* |
| *a.* | | | Pair, #1906-1907 | *6.25* | *6.25* |
| *b.* | | | Perf. 13 vert. | *5.00* | *5.00* |
| *c.* | | | Bklt. pane, 2 ea. #1906a, 1907b | *14.50* | *14.50* |
| | | | Complete booklet, #1907c | *14.50* | |
| *d.* | | | Pair, #1906a, 1907b | *7.25* | *7.25* |

Castle Ruins in Greece A619

**1998, July 15** **Litho.** ***Perf. 13½***

| | | | | | |
|---|---|---|---|---|---|
| **1908** | A619 | 30d | Hierapetra | .25 | .25 |
| **1909** | A619 | 50d | Korfu | .40 | .25 |
| **1910** | A619 | 70d | Limnos | .55 | .30 |

| | | | | | |
|---|---|---|---|---|---|
| **1911** | A619 | 100d | Argolis | .75 | .40 |
| **1912** | A619 | 150d | Iraklion | .75 | .65 |
| **1913** | A619 | 170d | Navpaktos, vert. | 1.25 | .90 |
| **1914** | A619 | 200d | Ioannina, vert. | 2.00 | 1.00 |
| **1915** | A619 | 400d | Plataea | 4.50 | 1.50 |
| **1916** | A619 | 550d | Karitainas, vert. | 6.25 | 2.25 |
| **1917** | A619 | 600d | Fragkokastel-lo, Crete | 6.50 | 2.75 |
| | | | *Nos. 1908-1917 (10)* | 23.20 | 10.25 |

Each denomination was also sold in booklets containing 20 panes of stamps, perf. 13⅓ horizontally or vertically. Unused booklet stamps sell for the same price as the listed sheet stamps; used booklet stamps sell for somewhat less than the values shown for used sheet stamps.

Greek Orthodox Community of Venice, 500th Anniv. — A620

Designs: 30d, Cathedral. 40d, Icon, vert. 140d, Illuminated manuscript, vert. 230d, Icon of Madonna and Child surrounded by saints.

**1998, Oct. 26 Litho. *Perf. 14***

| | | | | | |
|---|---|---|---|---|---|
| **1918** | A620 | 30d | multicolored | .30 | .25 |
| **1919** | A620 | 40d | multicolored | .55 | .35 |
| **1920** | A620 | 140d | multicolored | 1.50 | .85 |
| **1921** | A620 | 230d | multicolored | 3.50 | 2.00 |
| | | | *Nos. 1918-1921 (4)* | 5.85 | 3.45 |

Greek Writers of Antiquity — A621

**1998 Litho. *Perf. 13½x13***

| | | | | | |
|---|---|---|---|---|---|
| **1922** | A621 | 20d | Homer | .25 | .25 |
| **1923** | A621 | 100d | Sophocles | 1.60 | 1.60 |
| **1924** | A621 | 140d | Thucydides | 1.90 | 1.90 |
| **1925** | A621 | 200d | Plato | 2.40 | 2.40 |
| **1926** | A621 | 250d | Demosthenes | 3.75 | 3.75 |
| | | | *Nos. 1922-1926 (5)* | 9.90 | 9.90 |

Intl. Year of the Ocean A622

Designs: 40d, Ancient ship, map of Mediterranean Sea. 100d, Sailing ship, Neptune. 200d, Modern ship . 500d, Silver tetradrachm of Antigonos Doson, 229-221 B.C.

**1999, Feb. 19 Litho. *Perf. 13x13½***

| | | | | | |
|---|---|---|---|---|---|
| **1927** | A622 | 40d | multicolored | .30 | .25 |
| **1928** | A622 | 100d | multicolored | .90 | .40 |
| **1929** | A622 | 200d | multicolored | 1.60 | 1.00 |
| **1930** | A622 | 500d | multicolored | 3.25 | 1.50 |
| | | | *Nos. 1927-1930 (4)* | 6.05 | 3.15 |

Pres. Konstantin Karamanlis (1907-98) — A623

Various portraits of Karamanlis and: 100d, Representations of economic development, 1955-63. 170d, People celebrating. 200d, Emblem of European Union. 500d, National flag, vert.

**1999, Apr. 19 Litho. *Perf. 14***

| | | | | | |
|---|---|---|---|---|---|
| **1931** | A623 | 100d | multicolored | .70 | .35 |
| **1932** | A623 | 170d | multicolored | 1.25 | .75 |
| **1933** | A623 | 200d | multicolored | 1.50 | .85 |
| **1934** | A623 | 500d | multicolored | 3.00 | 2.00 |
| | | | *Nos. 1931-1934 (4)* | 6.45 | 3.95 |

Europa A624

Various views Mytikas peak (Mt. Olympus) and wildflowers.

**1999, May 24 Litho. *Perf. 14***

| | | | | |
|---|---|---|---|---|
| **1935** | A624 170d multicolored | | *1.75* | *1.75* |
| *a.* | Perf. 13¼ vert. | | *2.00* | *1.75* |
| **1936** | A624 550d multicolored | | *4.50* | *4.00* |
| *a.* | Pair, #1935-1936 | | *6.75* | *6.75* |
| *b.* | Perf. 13¼ vert. | | *4.75* | *4.00* |
| *c.* | Booklet pane, 2 each #1935a, 1936b | | *14.00* | *14.00* |
| | Complete booklet, #1936c | | *14.00* | |
| *d.* | Pair, #1935a, 1936b | | *7.00* | *7.00* |

Greece-Japan Diplomatic Relations, Cent. — A625

**1999, June 28 Litho. *Perf. 13¾x14***

| | | | | | |
|---|---|---|---|---|---|
| **1937** | A625 | 120d | multicolored | .90 | .75 |

4000 Years of Hellenism — A626

Designs: a, Sanctuary of Apollo Hylates, Kourion. b, Mycenaean "Krater of the Warriors," Athens. c, Mycenaean amphoral krater, Cyprus Museum. d, Sanctuary of Apollo Epikourios, Delphi.

**1999, June 28 Litho. *Perf. 13½x13***

| | | | | | |
|---|---|---|---|---|---|
| **1938** | A626 | 120d | Block of 4, #a.-d. | 3.50 | 3.50 |

See Cyprus No. 936.

Community Support Framework, 5th Anniv. A627

Designs: 20d, Modernization of Greek Railway Organization. 120d, Rio-Antirrio Bridge. 140d, Modernization of Greek Post Office. 250d, Athens Metro train. 500d, Eleftherios Venizelos Airport, Athens.

**1999, Nov. 8 Litho. *Perf. 13x13¼***

| | | | | | |
|---|---|---|---|---|---|
| **1939** | A627 | 20d | multi | .25 | .25 |
| **1940** | A627 | 120d | multi | .75 | .75 |
| **1941** | A627 | 140d | multi | .85 | .85 |
| **1942** | A627 | 250d | multi | 1.50 | 1.50 |
| **1943** | A627 | 500d | multi | 3.00 | 3.00 |
| | | | *Nos. 1939-1943 (5)* | 6.35 | 6.35 |

Armed Forces A628

20d, Exercise with helicopters, rafts. 30d, Patrol boat. 40d, F-16s in flight. 50d, CL-215 dousing forest fire. 70d, Destroyers. 120d, Distribution of goods in Bosnia. 170d, Mirage 2000 in flight. 250d, Exercise with helicopters, tanks. 600d, Submarine Okeanos.

***Perf. 13¾x13½***

**1999, Dec. 13 Litho.**

| | | | | | |
|---|---|---|---|---|---|
| **1944** | A628 | 20d | multi | .25 | .25 |
| **1945** | A628 | 30d | multi | .25 | .25 |
| **1946** | A628 | 40d | multi | .25 | .25 |
| **1947** | A628 | 50d | multi | .30 | .30 |
| **1948** | A628 | 70d | multi | .40 | .40 |
| **1949** | A628 | 120d | multi | .70 | .50 |
| **1950** | A628 | 170d | multi | 1.25 | 1.10 |
| **1951** | A628 | 250d | multi | 1.75 | 1.50 |
| **1952** | A628 | 600d | multi | 3.75 | 3.50 |
| | | | *Nos. 1944-1952 (9)* | 8.90 | 8.05 |

Christianity, 2000th Anniv. A629

Designs: 20d, Birth of Christ, vert. 50d, Inter-religious dialogue, vert. 120d, Angels with instruments, vert. 170d, Dove. 200d, Communion. 500d, Providence, vert.

**2000, Jan. 1 *Perf. 14¼x14***

| | | | | | |
|---|---|---|---|---|---|
| **1953** | A629 | 20d | multi | .25 | .25 |
| **1954** | A629 | 50d | multi | .30 | .30 |
| **1955** | A629 | 120d | multi | .70 | .70 |

***Perf. 14x14¼***

| | | | | | |
|---|---|---|---|---|---|
| **1956** | A629 | 170d | multi | 1.00 | 1.00 |

**Size: 35x35mm**

***Perf. 13¾***

| | | | | | |
|---|---|---|---|---|---|
| **1957** | A629 | 200d | multi | 1.25 | 1.25 |

**Size: 27x57mm**

***Perf. 13½x14***

| | | | | | |
|---|---|---|---|---|---|
| **1958** | A629 | 500d | multi | 3.00 | 3.00 |
| | | | *Nos. 1953-1958 (6)* | 6.50 | 6.50 |

**Europa, 2000**

Common Design Type

**2000, May 9 Litho. *Perf. 13¼x13***

| | | | |
|---|---|---|---|
| **1959** | CD17 170d multi | *3.00* | *3.00* |
| *a.* | Perf. 13 vert. | *3.50* | *3.50* |
| *b.* | Booklet pane, 4 #1959a | *14.00* | *14.00* |
| | Complete booklet, #1959b | *14.00* | |

Ships — A630

Designs: 10d, Steamship Ilissos. 120d, Destroyer Adrias. 170d, Steamship Ia II. 400d, Destroyer Vas. Olga.

***Perf. 14¼x13¾***

**2000, June 26 Litho.**

| | | | | | |
|---|---|---|---|---|---|
| **1960** | A630 | 10d | multi | .30 | .25 |
| **1961** | A630 | 120d | multi | 1.00 | .65 |
| **1962** | A630 | 170d | multi | 1.90 | 1.10 |
| **1963** | A630 | 400d | multi | 4.75 | 3.00 |
| | | | *Nos. 1960-1963 (4)* | 7.95 | 5.00 |

Stampin' the Future Children's Stamp Design Contest Winners A631

Art by: 130d, Spyros Dalakos (rainbow). 180d, Ornella Moshovaki-Chaiger (robots). 200d, Zisis Zariotis (building, tree, vehicles). 620d, Athina Limoudi (rocket).

**2000, June 26**

| | | | | | |
|---|---|---|---|---|---|
| **1964** | A631 | 130d | multi | .70 | .70 |
| **1965** | A631 | 180d | multi | 1.10 | 1.10 |
| **1966** | A631 | 200d | multi | 1.75 | 1.75 |
| **1967** | A631 | 620d | multi | 4.25 | 4.25 |
| | | | *Nos. 1964-1967 (4)* | 7.80 | 7.80 |

Sydney and Athens — A632

Olympic torch, flag and: 200d, Parthenon. 650d, Sydney Opera House.

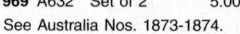

***Perf. 13¼x13¾***

**2000, Sept. 15 Litho.**

| | | | | |
|---|---|---|---|---|
| **1968-1969** | A632 | Set of 2 | 5.00 | 5.00 |

See Australia Nos. 1873-1874.

Emblem of 2004 Athens Olympic Games — A633

Various backgrounds. Denominations: 10d, 50d, 130d, 180d, 200d, 650d.

**2000, Nov. 7 *Perf. 14x14¼***

| | | | | |
|---|---|---|---|---|
| **1970-1975** | A633 | Set of 6 | 8.00 | 8.00 |

Souvenir Sheet

Stamps of the Cretan Government, Cent. — A634

No. 1976: a, 200d, Crete #69. b, 650d, Crete #71.

**2000, Dec. 18 Litho. *Perf. 14x14¼***

| | | | | |
|---|---|---|---|---|
| **1976** | A634 | Sheet of 2, #a-b | 15.00 | 15.00 |

Christianity, 2000th Anniv. A635

Designs: 20d, Sculpture of Christ as Orpheus, vert. 30d, Sculpture of The Good Shepherd, vert. 40d, Mosaic of Christ, vert. 100d, Mural of Christ. 130d, Icon of Christ (green frame), vert. 150d, Icon of Christ with open Bible, vert. 180d, Icon of Christ with closed Bible (dark blue frame), vert. 1000d, Byzantine coin depicting Christ.

**2000, Dec. 18** ***Perf. 14x14¼, 14¼x14***
**1977-1984** A635 Set of 8 10.00 10.00

Post Office Savings Bank, Cent. A636

Designs: 20d, Mother and child, vert. 130d, Emblem and 2-euro coin.

***Perf. 13¼x13¾, 13¾x13¼***
**2001, May 15** **Litho.**
**1985-1986** A636 Set of 2 1.10 1.10

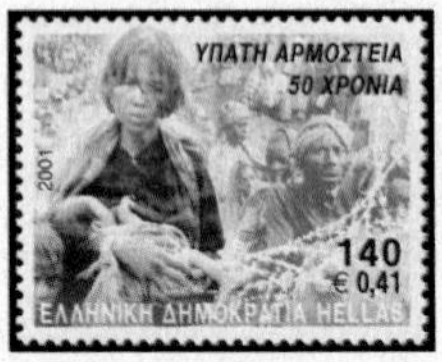


UN High Commissioner for Refugees, 50th Anniv. — A637

**2001, May 15** ***Perf. 13¾x13¼***
**1987** A637 140d multi 1.25 1.25

Thessaloniki Intl. Trade Fair, 75th Anniv. — A638

**2001, May 15** ***Perf. 13¼x13¾***
**1988** A638 180d multi 1.25 1.25

Aristotle University, Thessaloniki, 75th Anniv. — A639

**2001, May 15** ***Perf. 13¾x13¼***
**1989** A639 200d multi 1.50 1.50

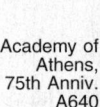

Academy of Athens, 75th Anniv. A640

**2001, May 15**
**1990** A640 500d multi 3.75 3.75

Ioannis Zigdis (1913-97), Politician — A641

**2001, May 15** ***Perf. 13¼x13¾***
**1991** A641 700d multi 5.00 5.00

Europa — A642

Designs: Nos. 1992a, 1992c, Dry leaf, parched earth. Nos. 1992b, 1992d, Water, fresh leaves.

**2001, May 15** ***Perf. 14¼x13¾***

| | | | | |
|---|---|---|---|---|
| **1992** | A642 Horiz. pair | | 8.50 | 8.50 |
| *a.* | 180d multi | | 2.00 | 2.00 |
| *b.* | 650d multi | | 6.50 | 6.50 |
| *c.* | Horiz. pair, perf. 13¼ vert. | | 8.50 | 8.50 |
| *d.* | As "a," perf. 13¼ vert. | | 2.00 | 2.00 |
| *e.* | As "b," perf. 13¼ vert. | | 6.50 | 6.50 |
| *f.* | Booklet pane, 2 # 1992c | | 17.00 | |
| | Booklet, #1992f | | 17.00 | |

Birds and Flowers A643

Designs: 20d, Little egret. 50d, White stork. 100d, Bearded vulture. 140d, Orchid, vert. 150d, Dalmatian pelican, vert. 200d, Lily, Plastira Lake. 700d, Egyptian vulture. 850d, Black vulture.

***Perf. 13¾x13¼, 13¼x13¾***
**2001, June 27**
**1993-2000** A643 Set of 8 17.00 17.00

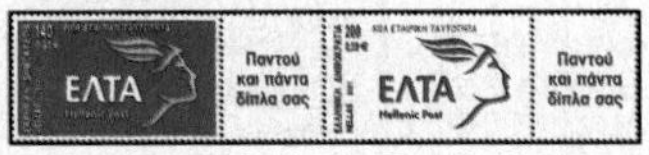


Symbol of Hellenic Post — A644

**2001, Sept. 8** **Litho.** ***Perf. 13x12¾***

| | | | |
|---|---|---|---|
| **2001** | Pair + 2 labels | 2.50 | 2.50 |
| *a.* | A644 140d blue & yellow | 1.00 | 1.00 |
| *b.* | A644 200d blue | 1.50 | 1.50 |

Wording on label varies. No. 2001 could be personalized by adding photos to the labels.

Souvenir Sheet

Christianity in Armenia, 1700th Anniv. — A645

**2001, Dec. 5** ***Perf. 13***
**2002** A645 850d multi 9.50 9.50

Souvenir Sheet

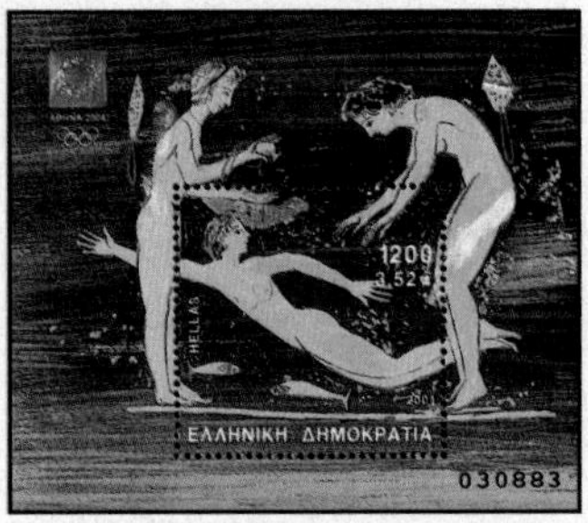


2004 Summer Olympics, Athens — A646

**2001, Dec. 5** ***Perf. 13¾***
**2003** A646 1200d multi 9.50 9.50

100 Cents = 1 Euro (€)

Dances A647

Designs: 2c, Kamakaki. 3c, Bride's dowry. 5c, Zagorissios, vert. 10c, Balos. 15c, Synkathistos. 20c, Tsakonikos, vert. 30c, Pyrrichios. 35c, Fourles, vert. 40c, Apokriatikos. 45c, Kotsari. 50c, Pentozalis, vert. 55c, Karagouna. 60c, Hassapiko. 65c, Zalistos. 85c, Pogonissios. €1, Kalamatianos. €2, Maleviziotis. €2.15, Tsamikos. €2.60, Zeibekikos, vert. €3, Nyfiatikos. €4, Paschaliatikos.

***Perf. 13x13¼, 13¼x13***
**2002, Jan. 2** **Litho.**

| | | | | |
|---|---|---|---|---|
| **2004** | A647 | 2c multi | .25 | .25 |
| **2005** | A647 | 3c multi | .25 | .25 |
| **2006** | A647 | 5c multi | .25 | .25 |
| **2007** | A647 | 10c multi | .30 | .30 |
| **2008** | A647 | 15c multi | .45 | .45 |
| **2009** | A647 | 20c multi | .60 | .60 |
| **2010** | A647 | 30c multi | .90 | .90 |
| **2011** | A647 | 35c multi | 1.00 | 1.00 |
| **2012** | A647 | 40c multi | 1.25 | 1.25 |
| **2013** | A647 | 45c multi | 1.40 | 1.40 |
| **2014** | A647 | 50c multi | 1.50 | 1.50 |
| **2015** | A647 | 55c multi | 1.60 | 1.60 |
| **2016** | A647 | 60c multi | 1.75 | 1.75 |
| **2017** | A647 | 65c multi | 1.90 | 1.90 |
| **2018** | A647 | 85c multi | 2.50 | 2.50 |
| **2019** | A647 | €1 multi | 3.00 | 3.00 |
| **2020** | A647 | €2 multi | 6.00 | 6.00 |
| **2021** | A647 | €2.15 multi | 6.50 | 6.50 |
| **2022** | A647 | €2.60 multi | 7.75 | 7.75 |
| **2023** | A647 | €3 multi | 9.00 | 9.00 |
| **2024** | A647 | €4 multi | 12.00 | 12.00 |
| | *Nos. 2004-2024 (21)* | | 60.15 | 60.15 |

Each denomination also sold in booklets containing 20 panes of stamps, perf 13¼ vertically or horizontally. Unused booklet stamps sell for the same prices as the sheet stamps listed; most used booklet stamps sell for significantly less than the values shown for used sheet stamps.

2004 Summer Olympics, Athens A648

Ancient Olympics: 41c, Runners. 59c, Sculpture of charioteer, vert. 80c, Javelin thrower. €2.05, Doryphoros of Polycleitos, vert. €2.35, Weight lifter.
€5, Stadium archway.

***Perf. 13¾x13¼, 13¼x13¾***
**2002, Mar. 15** **Litho.**
**2025-2029** A648 Set of 5 19.00 19.00

**Souvenir Sheet**
***Perf. 12¾***
**2030** A648 €5 multi 15.00 15.00

No. 2030 contains one 49x28mm stamp.

Europa — A649

**2002, May 9** ***Perf. 13¼x13¾***

| | | | |
|---|---|---|---|
| **2031** | A649 Horiz. pair, #a-b | *8.50* | *8.50* |
| *a.* | 60c Elephant | *1.75* | *1.75* |
| *b.* | €2.60 Equestrian act | *6.75* | *6.75* |
| *c.* | Horiz. pair, perf. 13¼ vert. | *8.50* | *8.50* |
| *d.* | As "a," perf. 13¼ vert. | *1.75* | *1.75* |
| *e.* | As "b," perf. 13¼ vert. | *6.75* | *6.75* |
| *f.* | Booklet pane, 2, #2031c | *17.00* | — |
| | Booklet, #2031f | *17.00* | |

Scouting A650

Designs: 45c, Navy Scout, sailboats. 60c, Scout, emblem of World Conference. 70c, Scouts planting tree. €2.15, Scouts, map and mountain.

**2002, June 26** **Litho.** ***Perf. 13x13½***
**2032-2035** A650 Set of 4 11.50 11.50
*2035a* Miniature sheet, 2 each #2032-2035 + 4 labels 25.00 25.00

Greek Language A651

Designs: 45c, Hieros Nomos, Athens Acropolis, 5th cent. B.C. 60c, Linear B script, 13th cent. B.C., vert. 90c, The Memoirs of General Makriyiannis. €2.15, Byzantine script, 11th cent., vert.

***Perf. 13¾x13¼, 13¼x13¾***
**2002, Sept. 23**
**2036-2039** A651 Set of 4 10.00 10.00

Ancient Olympic Winners With Laurel Wreaths — A652

Head color: 45c, Green. 60c, Dark blue. €2.15, Pink. €2.60, Light blue.

**2002, Oct. 30** **Litho.** ***Perf. 13¼x13¾***
**2040-2043** A652 Set of 4 17.50 17.50
*2043a* Miniature sheet, 2 each #2040-2043 35.00 35.00

Souvenir Sheet

Stadia of First Olympics — A653

**2002, Oct. 30** ***Perf. 12¾***
**2044** A653 €6 multi 18.00 18.00

Archbishops of Athens A654

Archbishop and years of reign: 10c, Chrystostomos I (1923-38). 45c, Chrysanthos (1938-41). €2.15, Damaskinos (1941-49). €2.60, Serapheim (1974-98).

**2002, Dec. 10** ***Perf. 13x13½***

| | | | | |
|---|---|---|---|---|
| **2045-2048** | A654 | Set of 4 | 16.00 | 16.00 |

Olympic Sports Equipment — A655

Designs: 2c, Discus. 5c, Hammer. 47c, Javelin. 65c, Pole vault pole and bar. €2.17, Hurdles. €2.85, Weights.

**2003, Feb. 11** ***Perf. 13¾x14¼***

| | | | | |
|---|---|---|---|---|
| **2049-2054** | A655 | Set of 6 | 19.00 | 19.00 |
| *2054a* | | Sheet, #2049-2054 | 16.00 | 16.00 |

2004 Summer Olympics, Athens.

Souvenir Sheet

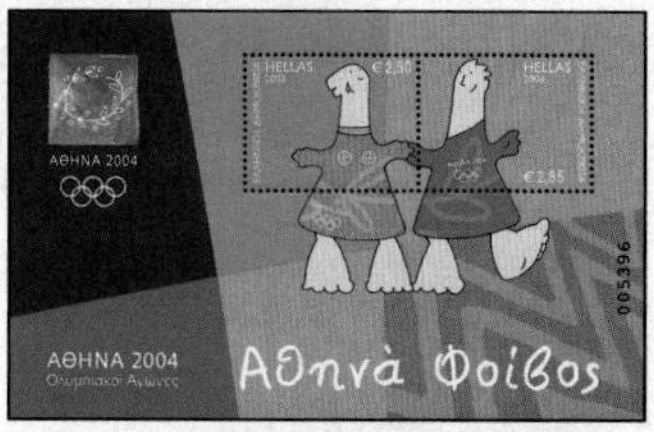


Mascots for 2004 Summer Olympics, Athens — A656

No. 2055: a, €2.50, Mascot with red shirt. b, €2.85, Mascot with blue shirt.

**2003, Feb. 11** ***Perf. 13¼***

| | | | | |
|---|---|---|---|---|
| **2055** | A656 | Sheet of 2, #a-b | 16.00 | 16.00 |

Greetings — A657

No. 2056: a, Globe. b, Athens 2004 Olympic Games emblem and Olympic rings. c, Ancient Greek athlete with laurel wreath. d, Roses and wedding headband. e, Spheres and grid. f, Child's drawing of train. g, Man and woman holding flowers. h, Stone carving of face. i, Acropolis.

**2003, Mar. 18** **Litho.** ***Perf. 14x13¾***

| | | | | |
|---|---|---|---|---|
| **2056** | A657 | Sheet of 9 | 13.50 | 13.50 |
| ***a.-g.*** | | 47c Any single | 1.40 | 1.40 |
| ***h.-i.*** | | 65c Either single | 2.00 | 2.00 |
| ***q.*** | | No. 2056h + label | 3.75 | 3.75 |
| ***r.*** | | #2056a + label | 2.00 | 2.00 |
| ***s.*** | | #2056b + label | 2.00 | 2.00 |
| ***t.*** | | #2056c + label | 2.00 | 2.00 |
| ***u.*** | | #2056d + label | 2.00 | 2.00 |
| ***v.*** | | #2056e + label | 2.00 | 2.00 |
| ***w.*** | | #2056f + label | 2.00 | 2.00 |

No. 2056q was issued in sheets of 15 stamps and 15 labels that sold for €19.50. Labels could be personalized. No. 2056q exists dated "2004." Stamps dated "2004" were issued in sheets of 5 stamps + 5 preprinted labels that sold for €4 per sheet. Additional stamps in this set were available with personalized labels. The editors would like to examine any examples.

Nos. 2056r-2056w were printed in sheets of 15 + 15 labels that sold for €14.10. Labels could be personalized. Two additional personalized stamps exist in this set. The editors would like to examine any examples.

Dove and Stars — A658

White Tower of Thessaloniki in Letters — A659

Fresco of Birds — A660

Jigsaw Puzzle Pieces — A661

**2003, Apr. 16** ***Perf. 14x13¾***

| | | | | |
|---|---|---|---|---|
| **2057** | A658 | 47c multi | 1.40 | 1.40 |
| **2058** | A659 | 65c multi | 2.00 | 2.00 |
| **2059** | A660 | €2.17 multi | 6.50 | 6.50 |
| **2060** | A661 | €2.85 multi | 8.50 | 8.50 |
| *2060a* | | Sheet, 2 each #2057-2060 | 37.50 | 37.50 |
| | | *Nos. 2057-2060 (4)* | 18.40 | 18.40 |

Greek Presidency of European Union.

Europa — A662

Poster art: a, 65c, Abstract. b, €2.85, Tourist poster.

**2003, May 9** **Litho.** ***Perf. 13¼x13¾***

| | | | | |
|---|---|---|---|---|
| **2061** | A662 | Horiz. pair | 10.50 | 10.50 |
| ***a.*** | | 65c multi | 2.00 | 2.00 |
| ***b.*** | | €2.85 multi | 8.50 | 8.50 |
| ***c.*** | | Horiz. pair, perf. 13¼ vert. | 10.50 | 10.50 |
| ***d.*** | | As "a," perf. 13¼ vert. | 2.00 | 2.00 |
| ***e.*** | | As "b," perf. 13¼ vert. | 8.50 | 8.50 |
| ***f.*** | | Booklet pane, 2 #2061c | 21.00 | — |
| | | Complete booklet, #2061f | 21.00 | |

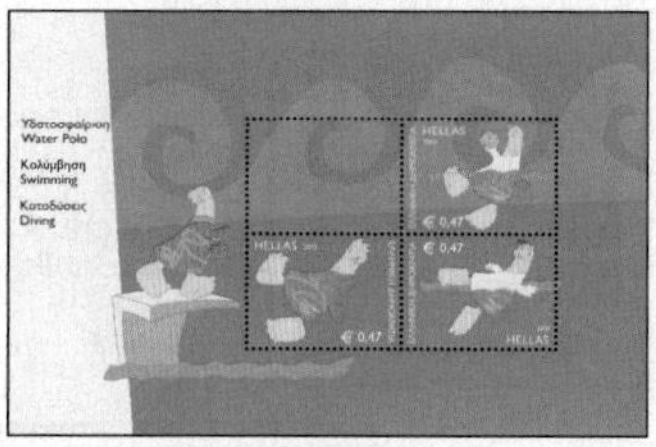

A663

No. 2062: a, Water polo. b, Diving. c, Swimming.

No. 2063, vert.: a, Table tennis. b, Basketball. c, Soccer. d, Handball.

No. 2064: a, Kayak slalom. b, Windsurfing.

No. 2065, vert.: a, Rhythmic gymnastics. b, Judo. c, Archery. d, Trampoline.

No. 2066: a, Kayak (flatwater). b, Rowing (coxswain). c, Rowing (rower).

No. 2067, vert.: a, Badminton. b, Fencing. c, Tennis. d, Taekwondo.

No. 2068: a, Cycling. b, Triathlon.

No. 2069, vert.: a, Baseball. b, Beach volleyball. c, Field hockey. d, Boxing.

No. 2070, vert.: a, Weight lifting (figure in red) b, Weight lifting (figure in blue).

**2003, May 9** **Litho.** ***Perf. 13¼***

| | | | | |
|---|---|---|---|---|
| **2062** | A663 | Booklet pane of 3 + label | 4.75 | — |
| ***a.-c.*** | | 47c Any single | 1.50 | 1.40 |
| **2063** | A663 | Booklet pane of 4 | 6.00 | — |
| ***a.-d.*** | | 47c Any single | 1.50 | 1.40 |
| **2064** | A663 | Booklet pane of 2 | 3.50 | — |
| ***a.-b.*** | | 47c Either single | 1.75 | 1.40 |
| **2065** | A663 | Booklet pane of 4 | 6.00 | — |
| ***a.*** | | 30c multi | 1.25 | 1.00 |
| ***b.-d.*** | | 47c Any single | 1.50 | 1.40 |
| **2066** | A663 | Booklet pane of 3 + label | 4.75 | — |
| ***a.-c.*** | | 47c Any single | 1.50 | 1.40 |
| **2067** | A663 | Booklet pane of 4 | 6.00 | — |
| ***a.*** | | 30c multi | 1.25 | 1.00 |
| ***b.-d.*** | | 47c Any single | 1.50 | 1.40 |
| **2068** | A663 | Booklet pane of 2 | 3.50 | — |
| ***a.-b.*** | | 47c Either single | 1.75 | 1.40 |
| **2069** | A663 | Booklet pane of 4 | 6.00 | — |
| ***a.*** | | 35c multi | 1.25 | 1.10 |
| ***b.-d.*** | | 47c Any single | 1.50 | 1.40 |
| **2070** | A663 | Booklet pane of 2 | 3.50 | — |
| ***a.-b.*** | | 47c Either single | 1.75 | 1.40 |
| | | Complete booklet, #2062-2070 | 50.00 | |

Booklet containing Nos. 2062-2070 sold for €14.99.

Environmental Protection — A664

Designs: 15c, Apple falling from tree. 47c, Apple in water. 65c, Laurel wreath over seacoast. €2.85, Moon over tree.

**2003, June 5** ***Perf. 13¼x13¾***

| | | | | |
|---|---|---|---|---|
| **2071-2074** | A664 | Set of 4 | 12.50 | 12.50 |

Olympic Sports A665

Designs: 5c, High jump. 47c, Wrestling. 65c, Running. 80c, Cycling, vert. €4, Windsurfing, vert.

***Perf. 13¾x13¼, 13¼x13¾***

**2003, Sept. 9**

| | | | | |
|---|---|---|---|---|
| **2075-2079** | A665 | Set of 5 | 18.00 | 18.00 |
| *2079a* | | Miniature sheet, #2075-2079 | 18.00 | 18.00 |

Souvenir Sheet

Mascots for 2004 Summer Olympics, Athens — A666

No. 2080: a, Figure in red. b, Figure in blue.

**2003, Sept. 9** ***Perf. 13¼***

| | | | | |
|---|---|---|---|---|
| **2080** | A666 | Sheet of 2 | 16.00 | 16.00 |
| ***a.*** | | €2.50 multi | 7.50 | 7.50 |
| ***b.*** | | €2.85 multi | 8.50 | 8.50 |

Trades of the Past — A667

Designs: 3c, Stair carving. 10c, Shoemaking. 50c, Blacksmithing. €1, Typesetting by hand. €1.40, Sponge fishing. €4, Weaving.

**2003, Oct. 17** ***Perf. 13¾x13¼***

| | | | | |
|---|---|---|---|---|
| **2081-2086** | A667 | Set of 6 | 21.00 | 21.00 |
| *2086a* | | Miniature sheet, #2081-2086 | 21.00 | 21.00 |

Olympic Athletes — A668

Various athletes: 20c, 30c, 40c, 47c, €2, €2.85.

***Perf. 13¼x13¾***

**2003, Nov. 28** **Litho.**

| | | | | |
|---|---|---|---|---|
| **2087-2092** | A668 | Set of 6 | 19.00 | 19.00 |
| *2092a* | | Miniature sheet, #2087-2092 | 19.00 | 19.00 |

Greek Olympians A669

Athletes: 3c, Spyridon Louis, marathon, 1896 gold medalist. 10c, Aristides Konstantinides, cycling road race, 1896 gold medalist. €2, Ioannis Fokianos, gymnastics coach. €2.17, Ioannis Mitropoulos, rings, 1896 gold medalist. €3.60, Konstantinos Tsiklitiras, standing long jump, 1912 gold medalist.

**Litho. with Foil Application**

**2004, Jan. 15** ***Perf. 13x13½***

| | | | | |
|---|---|---|---|---|
| **2093-2097** | A669 | Set of 5 | 24.00 | 24.00 |

Cities Hosting Events at 2004 Olympics A670

Designs: 1c, Volos. 2c, Patra. 5c, Iraklion. 47c, Athens. €1.40, Thessaloniki. €4, Athens, diff.

**2004, Jan. 15** **Litho.**

| | | | | |
|---|---|---|---|---|
| **2098-2103** | A670 | Set of 6 | 18.00 | 18.00 |

Olympic Sports A671

Designs: 5c, Swimmer. 10c, Gymnast chalking hands. 20c, Kayak. 47c, Relay race. €2, Rhythmic gymnastics, vert. €5, Men's rings, vert.

**2004, Mar. 24** **Litho.** ***Perf. 13¼***

| | | | | |
|---|---|---|---|---|
| **2104-2109** | A671 | Set of 6 | 24.00 | 24.00 |
| *2109a* | | Miniature sheet, #2104-2109 | 24.00 | 24.00 |

Europa — A672

**2004, May 4** ***Perf. 13¼x13¾***

| | | | | |
|---|---|---|---|---|
| **2110** | A672 | Horiz. pair | 10.50 | 10.50 |
| *a.* | | 65c Sailboat | 2.00 | 2.00 |
| *b.* | | €2.85 Balloon | 8.50 | 8.50 |
| *c.* | | Horiz. pair, perf. 13¼ vert. | 10.50 | 10.50 |
| *d.* | | As "a," perf. 13¼ vert. | 2.00 | 2.00 |
| *e.* | | As "b," perf. 13¼ vert. | 8.50 | 8.50 |
| *f.* | | Booklet pane, 2 #2110c | 21.00 | — |
| | | Complete booklet, #2110f | 21.00 | |

## Souvenir Sheets

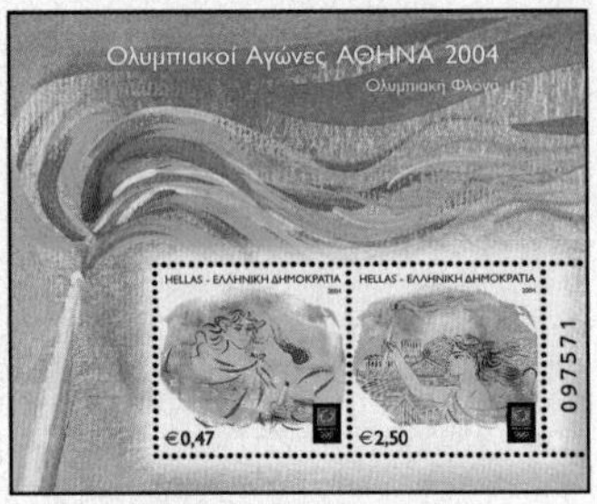


Olympic Flame — A673

Olympic Dove — A674

**2004, May 4** ***Perf. 13¾x14***

| | | | | |
|---|---|---|---|---|
| **2111** | A673 | Sheet of 2 | 9.00 | 9.00 |
| *a.* | | 47c Torch bearer | 1.40 | 1.40 |
| *b.* | | €2.50 Torch bearer, city | 7.50 | 7.50 |
| *c.* | | #2111a + label, perf. 14x13¾ | 2.40 | 2.40 |

***Perf. 13¼***

| | | | | |
|---|---|---|---|---|
| **2112** | A674 | Sheet of 2 | 9.00 | 9.00 |
| *a.* | | 47c Dove, Olympic rings | 1.40 | 1.40 |
| *b.* | | €2.50 Dove, people | 7.50 | 7.50 |

No. 2111c was printed in sheets of 15 + 15 labels that sold for €15. Labels could be personalized.

Olympic Coins — A675

Obverse and reverse of: 47c, Silver three-drachma of Cos, 480-450 BC. 65c, Gold stater of Philip II of Macedonia. €2, Silver two-drachma of Elis, 460 BC. €2.17, Silver four-drachma of Philip II of Macedonia.

**2004, June 15** ***Perf. 13¼***

| | | | | |
|---|---|---|---|---|
| **2113-2116** | A675 | Set of 4 | 16.00 | 16.00 |
| *2116a* | | Miniature sheet, #2113-2116 | 16.00 | 16.00 |

## Souvenir Sheets

Modern Art and the Olympics — A676

**2004, July 23** ***Perf. 13x13¼***

| | | | | |
|---|---|---|---|---|
| **2117** | A676 | Sheet of 2 | 9.00 | 9.00 |
| *a.* | | 50c Wavy lines | 1.50 | 1.50 |
| *b.* | | €2.50 Stripes of color | 7.50 | 7.50 |

***Perf. 13¼x13***

| | | | | |
|---|---|---|---|---|
| **2118** | A676 | Sheet of 2 | 9.00 | 9.00 |
| *a.* | | €1 Paint brush, vert. | 3.00 | 3.00 |
| *b.* | | €2 Paint roller, vert. | 6.00 | 6.00 |
| *c.* | | Miniature sheet, #2117a-2117b, 2118a-2118b | 18.00 | 18.00 |

Greece, 2004 European Soccer Champions A677

Designs: 47c, Greek flag, trophy. 65c, Greek players celebrating. €1, Greek players holding trophy. €2.88, Greek players, trophy.

**2004, July 16 Litho.** ***Perf. 13x13¼***

| | | | | |
|---|---|---|---|---|
| **2119-2122** | A677 | Set of 4 | 15.00 | 15.00 |
| *a.* | | Souvenir sheet, #2119-2122 | 15.00 | 15.00 |

Greek Flag and Trophy — A678

**2004, July Litho.** ***Perf. 14x13¾***

| | | | | |
|---|---|---|---|---|
| **2123** | A678 | 47c multi + label | 1.60 | 1.60 |
| *a.* | | Sheet of 5 + 5 labels | 8.25 | — |
| *b.* | | Sheet of 10 + 10 labels | 16.50 | — |

No. 2123 was printed in sheets of 15 + 15 labels that could be personalized. The sheet sold for €15. Nos. 2123a and 2123b have labels that depict soccer players or emblems, which cannot be personalized. Nos. 2123a and 2123b exist with two different sets of labels, and the set of 4 sheets sold for €20.

2004 Summer Olympics, Athens — A679

Designs: 50c, Hall of Good Harvest, Temple of Heaven, Beijing. 65c, Parthenon, Athens.

**2004, Aug. 9 Litho.** ***Perf. 14***

| | | | | |
|---|---|---|---|---|
| **2124-2125** | A679 | Set of 2 | 4.00 | 4.00 |
| *a.* | | Souvenir sheet, #2124-2125 | 4.00 | 4.00 |

See People's Republic of China Nos. 3376-3377.

## Souvenir Sheet

Olymphilex 2004 Philatelic Exhibition — A680

**2004, Aug. 13** ***Perf. 13½x13¼***

| | | | | |
|---|---|---|---|---|
| **2126** | A680 | €6 multi | 18.00 | 18.00 |

Nikos Syranidis and Thomas Bimis, Synchronized Diving Gold Medalists A681

Leonidas Sampanis, Disqualified Bronze Medalist in 62 Kilogram Weight Lifting — A682

Ilias Iliadis, Judo Gold Medalist A683

Sofia Bekatorou and Emilia Tsoulfa, Women's 470 Sailing Gold Medalists A684

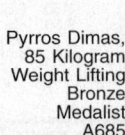

Pyrros Dimas, 85 Kilogram Weight Lifting Bronze Medalist A685

Dimosthenis Tampakos, Rings Gold Medalist A686

Anastasia Kelesidou, Women's Discus Silver Medalist A687

Vasilis Polymeros and Nikos Skiathitis, Lightweight Double Sculls Bronze Medalists A688

Athanasia Tzoumeleka, Women's 20 Kilometer Walk Gold Medalist A689

Chrysopigi Devezi, Women's Triple Jump Silver Medalist A690

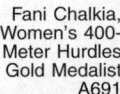

Fani Chalkia, Women's 400-Meter Hurdles Gold Medalist A691

Nikos Kaklamanakis, Men's Mistral Sailing Silver Medalist A692

Artiom Kiouregian, 55 Kilogram Greco-Roman Wrestling Bronze Medalist A693

Women's Water Polo Team, Silver Medalist A694

Mirela Maniani, Women's Javelin Bronze Medalist A695

Elisavet Mystakidou, Women's 67 Kilogram Taekwondo Silver Medalist A696

Alexandros Nikolaidis, Men's 80 Kilogram Taekwondo Silver Medalist A697

## Digitally Printed

**2004, Aug.** ***Perf. 13¼***

| | | | | |
|---|---|---|---|---|
| **2127** | A681 | 65c multi | 1.90 | 1.90 |
| **2128** | A682 | 65c multi | 19.00 | 19.00 |
| **2129** | A683 | 65c multi | 1.90 | 1.90 |
| **2130** | A684 | 65c multi | 1.90 | 1.90 |
| **2131** | A685 | 65c multi | 1.90 | 1.90 |
| **2132** | A686 | 65c multi | 1.90 | 1.90 |
| **2133** | A687 | 65c multi | 1.90 | 1.90 |
| **2134** | A688 | 65c multi | 1.90 | 1.90 |
| **2135** | A689 | 65c multi | 1.90 | 1.90 |
| **2136** | A690 | 65c multi | 1.90 | 1.90 |
| **2137** | A691 | 65c multi | 1.90 | 1.90 |
| **2138** | A692 | 65c multi | 1.90 | 1.90 |

| | | | | | |
|---|---|---|---|---|---|
| **2139** | A693 | 65c multi | | 1.90 | 1.90 |
| **2140** | A694 | 65c multi | | 1.90 | 1.90 |
| **2141** | A695 | 65c multi | | 1.90 | 1.90 |
| **2142** | A696 | 65c multi | | 1.90 | 1.90 |
| **2143** | A697 | 65c multi | | 1.90 | 1.90 |
| | *Nos. 2127-2143 (17)* | | | 49.40 | 49.40 |

### Litho.

| | | | | |
|---|---|---|---|---|
| **2144** | A681 | 65c multi | 1.90 | 1.90 |
| **2145** | A682 | 65c multi | 15.00 | 15.00 |
| **2146** | A683 | 65c multi | 1.90 | 1.90 |
| **2147** | A684 | 65c multi | 1.90 | 1.90 |
| **2148** | A685 | 65c multi | 1.90 | 1.90 |
| **2149** | A686 | 65c multi | 1.90 | 1.90 |
| **2150** | A687 | 65c multi | 1.90 | 1.90 |
| **2151** | A688 | 65c multi | 1.90 | 1.90 |
| **2152** | A689 | 65c multi | 1.90 | 1.90 |
| **2153** | A690 | 65c multi | 1.90 | 1.90 |
| **2154** | A691 | 65c multi | 1.90 | 1.90 |
| **2155** | A692 | 65c multi | 1.90 | 1.90 |
| **2156** | A693 | 65c multi | 1.90 | 1.90 |
| **2157** | A694 | 65c multi | 1.90 | 1.90 |
| **2158** | A695 | 65c multi | 1.90 | 1.90 |
| **2159** | A696 | 65c multi | 1.90 | 1.90 |
| **2160** | A697 | 65c multi | 1.90 | 1.90 |
| *a.* | Souvenir sheet, #2144, 2146-2160 | | 30.00 | 30.00 |
| | *Nos. 2144-2160 (17)* | | 45.40 | 45.40 |

Issued: Nos. 2127-2128, 8/17; No. 2129, 8/18; Nos. 2130-2131, 8/22; Nos. 2132-2134, 8/23, Nos. 2135-2136, 8/24, Nos. 2137-2139, 8/26, No. 2140, 8/27; No. 2141, 8/28; No. 2142, 8/29; No. 2143, 8/30. Nos. 2144-2160 were to have been issued within days of the digitally printed stamp with the same design. The digitally printed stamps have almost illegible lettering above the Olympic rings at upper right, and fuzzy, indistinct details in the emblem above this lettering. These details are clearer and more readable on the lithographed stamps.

Nos. 2128 and 2145 were withdrawn from circulation after the athlete shown was stripped of his medal after failing a drug test.

2004 Paralympics, Athens — A698

Designs: 20c, Horses and riders. 49c, Handicapped runner. €2, Wheelchair basketball. €2.24, Archer in wheelchair.

***Perf. 13¼x13¾***

**2004, Sept. 22** **Litho.**

**2161-2164** A698 Set of 4 12.50 12.50

Island Views — A699

**2004, Dec. 27** ***Perf. 14x13¾***

| | | | | |
|---|---|---|---|---|
| **2165** | A699 | 2c Santorini | .25 | .25 |
| *a.* | Perf. 13¼ horiz. | | .25 | .25 |
| **2166** | A699 | 3c Karpathos | .25 | .25 |
| *a.* | Perf. 13¼ horiz. | | .25 | .25 |
| **2167** | A699 | 5c Crete-Vai | .25 | .25 |
| *a.* | Perf. 13¼ horiz. | | .25 | .25 |
| **2168** | A699 | 10c Mykonos | .30 | .30 |
| *a.* | Perf. 13¼ horiz. | | .30 | .30 |
| **2169** | A699 | 49c Canea | 1.50 | 1.50 |
| *a.* | Perf. 13¼ horiz. | | 1.50 | 1.50 |
| **2170** | A699 | 50c Castellorizo | 1.50 | 1.50 |
| *a.* | Perf. 13¼ horiz. | | 1.50 | 1.50 |
| **2171** | A699 | €1 Astipalaia | 3.00 | 3.00 |
| *a.* | Perf. 13¼ horiz. | | 3.00 | 3.00 |
| **2172** | A699 | €2 Serifos | 6.00 | 6.00 |
| *a.* | Perf. 13¼ horiz. | | 6.00 | 6.00 |
| **2173** | A699 | €2.24 Melos | 6.75 | 6.75 |
| *a.* | Perf. 13¼ horiz. | | 6.75 | 6.75 |
| **2174** | A699 | €4 Skiathos | 12.00 | 12.00 |
| *a.* | Perf. 13¼ horiz. | | 12.00 | 12.00 |
| | *Nos. 2165-2174 (10)* | | 31.80 | 31.80 |

Jewelry A700

Designs: 1c, Necklace, 730 B.C. 15c, Snake-shaped bracelet, 2nd-3rd cent. B.C., vert. 30c, Necklace, 5th cent. 49c, Crown, 2nd cent. €4, Earring, 8th cent. B.C., vert.

***Perf. 13¾x13¼, 13¼x13¾***

**2005, Feb. 25**

**2175-2179** A700 Set of 5 15.00 15.00

State Laboratory, 75th Anniv. — A701

European Diabetes Association, 41st Meeting — A702

European Society for Cardiovascular Surgery, 54th Congress — A703

I. Kondilakis, First President of Athens Journalists Union — A704

Year of Economic Competitiveness — A705

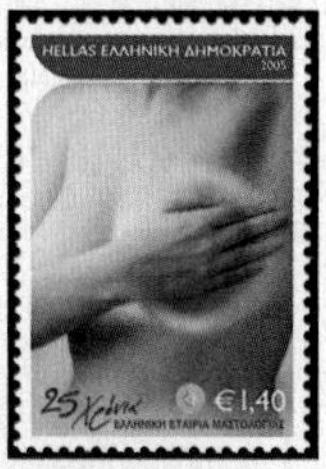

Greek Mastological Society, 25th Anniv. — A706

Angel, by Alekos Kontopoulos — A707

**2005, Apr. 5** ***Perf. 13¼x13, 13x13¼***

| | | | | |
|---|---|---|---|---|
| **2180** | A701 | 1c multi | .25 | .25 |
| **2181** | A702 | 4c multi | .25 | .25 |
| **2182** | A703 | 5c multi | .25 | .25 |
| **2183** | A704 | 40c multi | 1.25 | 1.25 |
| **2184** | A705 | 49c multi | 1.50 | 1.50 |
| **2185** | A706 | €1.40 multi | 4.25 | 4.25 |
| **2186** | A707 | €3.50 multi | 10.50 | 10.50 |
| | *Nos. 2180-2186 (7)* | | 18.25 | 18.25 |

Flowers — A708

Designs: 20c, Gladiolus illyricus. 40c, Crocus sieberi. 49c, Narcissus tazetta. €1.40, Rhododendron luteum. €3, Tulipa boeotica.

**2005, Apr. 5** ***Perf. 13¼x13¾***

**2187-2191** A708 Set of 5 16.00 16.00

Europa — A709

**2005, May 19** ***Perf. 14¼x13¾***

| | | | | |
|---|---|---|---|---|
| **2192** | A709 | Horiz. pair | 9.00 | 9.00 |
| *a.* | 65c Finished dish | | 2.00 | 2.00 |
| *b.* | €2.35 Ingredients | | 7.00 | 7.00 |
| *c.* | Horiz. pair, perf. 13¼ vert. | | 9.00 | 9.00 |
| *d.* | As "a," perf. 13¼ vert. | | 2.00 | 2.00 |
| *e.* | As "b," perf. 13¼ vert. | | 7.00 | 7.00 |
| *f.* | Booklet pane, 2 #2192c | | 18.00 | — |
| | Complete booklet, #2192f | | 18.00 | |

Wine Grapes A710

Designs: 20c, Agiorgitiko grapes and grape pickers, Peloponnisos. 49c, Assyrtiko grapes, Santorini. 65c, Xinomavro grapes and coin, Macedonia. €2.24, Robolla grapes, Cephalonia. €2.40, Moschofilero, Peloponnisos.

**2005, May 19** ***Perf. 13¾x14***

**2193-2197** A710 Set of 5 18.00 18.00

Blackboard A711

Girl Reading — A712

Envelope A713

Stylized People — A714

Grid — A715

Globe and Stylized Stamp — A716

Flowers — A717

Church — A718

**2005, July 15** ***Perf. 14x13¾***

| | | | | |
|---|---|---|---|---|
| **2198** | A711 | 49c multi | 1.50 | 1.50 |
| *a.* | #2198 + label | | 2.50 | 2.50 |
| **2199** | A712 | 49c multi | 1.50 | 1.50 |
| *a.* | #2199 + label | | 2.50 | 2.50 |
| **2200** | A713 | 49c multi | 1.50 | 1.50 |
| **2201** | A714 | 49c multi | 1.50 | 1.50 |
| *a.* | #2201 + label | | 2.50 | 2.50 |
| **2202** | A715 | 49c multi | 1.50 | 1.50 |
| *a.* | #2202 + label | | 2.50 | 2.50 |
| **2203** | A716 | 49c multi | 1.50 | 1.50 |
| **2204** | A717 | 49c multi | 1.50 | 1.50 |
| *a.* | #2204 + label | | 2.50 | 2.50 |
| **2205** | A718 | 65c multi | 1.90 | 1.90 |
| *a.* | #2205 + label | | 3.25 | 3.25 |
| | *Nos. 2198-2205 (8)* | | 12.40 | 12.40 |

Nos. 2198a and 2199a were printed in sheets of 10 + 10 labels that sold for €10. Nos. 2201a, 2202a and 2204a were printed in sheets of 15 + 15 labels that sold for €15. No. 2205a was printed in sheets of 10 + 10 labels that sold for €13. Labels could be personalized. Two additional personalized stamps exist in this set. The editors would like to examine any examples.

Drawing by Fokion Dimitriadis A719

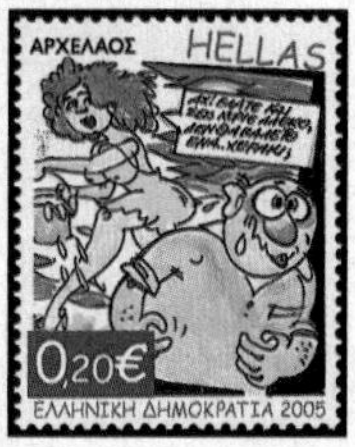

Drawing by Archelaos A720

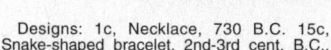

Drawing by Themos Anninos — A721

Drawing by Dimitris Galanis — A722

Drawing by Kostas Mitropoulos A723

Unattributed Odyssey Scene — A724

**2005, Sept. 16** ***Perf. 13¼x13¾***

| | | | |
|---|---|---|---|
| **2206** A719 15c multi | .45 | .45 |
| **2207** A720 20c multi | .60 | .60 |
| **2208** A721 30c multi | .90 | .90 |
| **2209** A722 50c multi | 1.50 | 1.50 |
| **2210** A723 65c multi | 1.90 | 1.90 |
| **2211** A724 €4 multi | 12.00 | 12.00 |
| *Nos. 2206-2211 (6)* | 17.35 | 17.35 |

**Booklet Panes of 1**

**Self-Adhesive**

| | | |
|---|---|---|
| **2212** A719 15c multi | .45 | .45 |
| **2213** A720 20c multi | .60 | .60 |
| **2214** A721 30c multi | .90 | .90 |
| **2215** A722 50c multi | 1.50 | 1.50 |
| **2216** A723 65c multi | 1.90 | 1.90 |
| **2217** A724 €4 multi | 12.00 | 12.00 |
| Complete booklet, #2212-2217 | 17.50 | |
| *Nos. 2212-2217 (6)* | 17.35 | 17.35 |

Greece, 2005 European Basketball Champions A725

Basketball, net and: 30c, Players in game. 50c, Championship bowl. 65c, Fans. €3.55, Players celebrating.

**2005, Oct. 7 Litho.** ***Perf. 13x13¼***

| | | |
|---|---|---|
| **2218-2221** A725 Set of 4 | 15.00 | 15.00 |
| *2221a* Souvenir sheet, #2218-2221 | 15.00 | 15.00 |

Automobiles — A726

Designs: 1c, Mini Cooper. 30c, Fiat 500. 50c, Citroen 2CV. €2.25, Volkswagen Beetle. €2.85, Ford Model T.

**2005, Nov. 4** ***Perf. 13x13¼***

| | | |
|---|---|---|
| **2222-2226** A726 Set of 5 | 17.50 | 17.50 |
| *2226a* As #2226, without inscription "Ford Model T" | 10.00 | 10.00 |
| *2226b* Booklet pane, #2222-2225, 2226a | 20.00 | — |
| Complete booklet, #2226b | 20.00 | |

Panathinaikos Soccer Team Emblem — A727

Panionios Soccer Team Emblem — A728

Iraklis Soccer Team Emblem — A729

PAOK Soccer Team Emblem — A730

Panellinios Sports Club Emblem — A731

Designs: 30c, Ethnikos Sports Club emblem. €4, Omilos Ereton emblem.

**2005, Nov. 30 Litho.** ***Perf. 14x13¾***

| | | |
|---|---|---|
| **2227** A727 30c multi | .90 | .90 |
| **2228** A727 50c multi | 1.50 | 1.50 |
| *a.* #2228 + label | 2.40 | 2.40 |
| **2229** A728 50c multi | 1.50 | 1.50 |
| *a.* #2229 + label | 2.40 | 2.40 |
| **2230** A729 50c multi | 1.50 | 1.50 |
| *a.* #2230 + label | 2.40 | 2.40 |
| **2231** A730 65c multi | 1.90 | 1.90 |
| *a.* #2231 + label | 3.25 | 3.25 |
| **2232** A731 65c multi | 1.90 | 1.90 |
| *a.* #2232 + label | 3.25 | 3.25 |
| **2233** A727 €4 multi | 12.00 | 12.00 |
| *Nos. 2227-2233 (7)* | 21.20 | 21.20 |

Nos. 2228a, 2229a and 2230a were printed in sheets of 10 + 10 labels that sold for €10. Nos. 2231a and 2232a were printed in sheets of 10 + 10 labels that sold for €13. Labels could be personalized.

Christmas A732

Icons: 1c, Hodeghetria Virgin. 20c, Kardiotissa Virgin. 70c, Glykophiloussa Virgin. €3.20, Virgin with Symbols of the Passion.

**Litho. With Foil Application**

**2005, Dec. 20** ***Perf. 13¾***

| | | |
|---|---|---|
| **2234-2237** A732 Set of 4 | 12.50 | 12.50 |

**Souvenir Sheet**

Europa Stamps, 50th Anniv. — A733

**2006, Jan. 10 Litho.** ***Perf. 13x13¼***

| | | |
|---|---|---|
| **2238** A733 Sheet of 2 | 12.00 | 12.00 |
| *a.* €1.50 Greece #1255 | 4.50 | 4.50 |
| *b.* €2.50 Greece #1459 | 7.50 | 7.50 |

Patras, 2006 European Cultural Capital A734

Designs: 1c, Drama masks. 15c, Buildings, sailboat, lighthouse. 20c, Child. 50c, Carnival dragon and clown. 65c, Emblem, vert. €2.25, Jars, containers and boxes. €2.30, Icon, vert.

**2006, Feb. 28** ***Perf. 13x13¼, 13¼x13***

| | | |
|---|---|---|
| **2239-2245** A734 Set of 7 | 18.00 | 18.00 |

Carnival Dragon and Clown — A734a

Emblem — A734b

**2006, Feb. 28 Litho.** ***Perf. 14x13¾***

| | | |
|---|---|---|
| **2245A** A734a 50c multi + label | 2.40 | 2.40 |
| **2245B** A734b 65c multi + label | 3.25 | 3.25 |

Patras, 2006 European Cultural Capital. Nos. 2245A and 2245B were issued in sheets of 10 stamps and 10 labels that could be personalized. Sheets of No. 2245A sold for €10; No. 2245B for €13.

Items in Greek Museums A735

Designs: 5c, Kouros of Anavissos, sculpture, 530 B.C., Natl. Archaeological Museum. 20c, Seated figure, 2800-2300 B.C., Museum of Cycladic Art. 50c, Spiral (28x28mm). 65c, Pediment from Parthenon, Acropolis Museum, horiz. €1.40, Greco-Roman portrait of an Egyptian, 4th cent. €2.25, Concert of the Angels, by El Greco, Natl. Art Gallery, horiz.

**Litho with Foil Application, Litho. (50c)**

**2006, Apr. 7** ***Perf. 14x13¾, 13¾x14***

| | | |
|---|---|---|
| **2246-2251** A735 Set of 6 | 15.00 | 15.00 |
| *2248a* #2248 + label | 2.50 | 2.50 |

No. 2248a was printed in sheets of 10 + 10 labels that sold for €10. Labels could be personalized.

Pediment From Parthenon — A735a

**2006, Apr. 7 Litho.** ***Perf. 14x13¾***

| | | |
|---|---|---|
| **2251A** A735a 65c multi + label | 3.25 | 3.25 |

No. 2251A was printed in sheets of 10 + 10 labels that sold for €13. Labels could be personalized.

**Souvenir Sheets**

Stamps Issued for 1906 Interim Olympic Games — A736

No. 2252: a, 20c, #187. b, 30c, #191. c, 50c, #188. d, €2, #192.

No. 2253: a, 50c, #189. b, 65c, #194. c, 85c, #197. d, €1, #190.

**2006, Apr. 7 Litho.** ***Perf. 13x13¼***

**Sheets of 4, #a-d**

| | | |
|---|---|---|
| **2252-2253** A736 Set of 2 | 18.00 | 18.00 |

Europa — A737

**2006, May 15** ***Perf. 13¾x14¼***

| | | |
|---|---|---|
| **2254** A737 Horiz. pair | 11.00 | 11.00 |
| *a.* 65c Rope and moon | 1.90 | 1.90 |
| *b.* €3 Rope and sun | 9.00 | 9.00 |
| *c.* Horiz. pair, perf. 13¼ vert. | 11.00 | 11.00 |
| *d.* As "a," perf. 13¼ vert. | 1.90 | 1.90 |
| *e.* As "b," perf. 13¼ vert. | 9.00 | 9.00 |
| *f.* Booklet pane, 2 #2254c | 22.50 | — |
| Complete booklet, #2254f | 22.50 | |

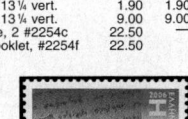

State General Archives — A738

Admission to European Union, 25th Anniv. — A739

2006 Eurovision Song Contest, Athens — A740

Olive and Olive Oil Year — A741

Tinia, Etruscan Sky God — A742

Greek Participation in 2005-06 UN Security Council — A743

**2006, May 15** *Perf. 14x13¾*

| | | | | |
|---|---|---|---|---|
| **2255** | A738 | 15c multi | .45 | .45 |
| **2256** | A739 | 20c multi | .60 | .60 |
| **2257** | A740 | 50c multi | 1.50 | 1.50 |
| *a.* | | #2257 + label | 2.60 | 2.60 |
| **2258** | A741 | 65c multi | 1.90 | 1.90 |
| *a.* | | #2258 + label | 3.50 | 3.50 |
| **2259** | A742 | €1.40 multi | 4.25 | 4.25 |
| **2260** | A743 | €3 multi | 9.00 | 9.00 |
| | | *Nos. 2255-2260 (6)* | 17.70 | 17.70 |

No. 2257a was printed in sheets of 10 + 10 labels that sold for €10. No. 2258a was printed in sheets of 10 + 10 labels that sold for €13. Labels could be personalized.

Island Views A744

**2006, June 16 Litho.** *Perf. 14¼x14*

| | | | | |
|---|---|---|---|---|
| **2261** | A744 | 1c Lesbos | .25 | .25 |
| *a.* | | Perf. 13¼ vert. | .25 | .25 |
| **2262** | A744 | 3c Hydra | .25 | .25 |
| *a.* | | Perf. 13¼ vert. | .25 | .25 |
| **2263** | A744 | 10c Sifnos | .30 | .30 |
| *a.* | | Perf. 13¼ vert. | .30 | .30 |
| **2264** | A744 | 20c Levkas | .60 | .60 |
| *a.* | | Perf. 13¼ vert. | .60 | .60 |
| **2265** | A744 | 40c Samothrace | 1.25 | 1.25 |
| *a.* | | Perf. 13¼ vert. | 1.25 | 1.25 |
| **2266** | A744 | 50c Syros | 1.50 | 1.50 |
| *a.* | | Perf. 13¼ vert. | 1.50 | 1.50 |
| **2267** | A744 | 65c Rhodes | 1.90 | 1.90 |
| *a.* | | Perf. 13¼ vert. | 1.90 | 1.90 |
| **2268** | A744 | 85c Cephalonia | 2.50 | 2.50 |
| *a.* | | Perf. 13¼ vert. | 2.50 | 2.50 |
| **2269** | A744 | €2.25 Corfu | 6.75 | 6.75 |
| *a.* | | Perf. 13¼ vert. | 6.75 | 6.75 |
| **2270** | A744 | €5 Naxos | 15.00 | 15.00 |
| *a.* | | Perf. 13¼ vert. | 15.00 | 15.00 |
| | | *Nos. 2261-2270 (10)* | 30.30 | 30.30 |

Syros — A744a

**2006, June 16 Litho.** *Perf. 14x13¾*

**2270B** A744a 50c multi + label 2.60 2.60

No. 2270B was printed in sheets of 10 + 10 labels that sold for €10. Labels could be personalized. An additional personalized stamp was issued in this set. The editors would like to examine any example.

Ancient Greek Technology A745

Designs: 3c, Trireme "Olympias." 5c, Odometer, by Hero of Alexandria. 50c, Piston water pump, vert. 65c, Antikythera Mechanism, vert. €3.80, Automatic temple gates, by Hero of Alexandria, vert.

**Litho. With Foil Application**

*Perf. 13¾x13¼, 13¼x13¾*

**2006, Sept. 14**

**2271-2275** A745 Set of 5 15.00 15.00

Souvenir Sheet

Second Place Finish of Greek Team at 2006 World Basketball Championships — A746

**Litho. With Foil Application**

**2006, Oct. 16** *Perf. 13¼*

| | | | | |
|---|---|---|---|---|
| **2276** | A746 | Sheet of 3 | 17.00 | 17.00 |
| *a.* | | 50c Silver medal | 1.50 | 1.50 |
| *b.* | | €2 Team | 6.00 | 6.00 |
| *c.* | | €3 Team, medal ribbon | 9.00 | 9.00 |

Soccer Team Emblems A747

Designs: 2c, Apollon Kalamaria. 3c, Atromitos Athinon. 52c, Aris Thessaloniki. €2.27, Ethnikos Piraeus. €3.20, Apollon Smyrnis.

**2006, Nov. 29 Litho.** *Perf. 14x13¾*

| | | | | |
|---|---|---|---|---|
| **2277-2281** | A747 | Set of 5 | 18.00 | 18.00 |
| *2279a* | | #2279 + label | 2.75 | 2.75 |

No. 2279a was printed in sheets of 10 + 10 labels that sold for €10. Labels could be personalized.

Items in Toys, Games and Childhood Section of Benaki Museum A748

Designs: 5c, Doll, chest and clothing from France, c. 1905. 15c, Wooden airplanes, c. 1940. 30c, Dolls made by Skonouchi Karopoulos, c. 1925. 40c, Horses on wheels made by Anestis Romeopoulos, c. 1920. 52c, Dominos, toy cat, duck on wheels. 72c, Parachutist, c. 1950, vert. €2.27, Airplane carousel, 1950s, vert. €4, Puppet theater of the Resistance, 1941-45, vert.

*Perf. 13¾x13¼, 13¼x13¾*

**2006, Dec. 22**

**2282-2289** A748 Set of 8 25.00 25.00

Faces — A749

Globe — A750

Crescents A751

Artemis — A752

Ring Around Earth — A753

Parthenon A754

Phrasikleia Kore — A755

**2007, Mar. 12 Litho.** *Perf. 14x13¾*

| | | | | |
|---|---|---|---|---|
| **2290** | A749 | 52c multi | 1.40 | 1.40 |
| *a.* | | #2290 + label | 2.75 | 2.75 |
| **2291** | A750 | 52c multi | 1.40 | 1.40 |
| *a.* | | #2291 + label | 2.75 | 2.75 |
| **2292** | A751 | 52c multi | 1.40 | 1.40 |
| *a.* | | #2292 + label | 2.75 | 2.75 |
| **2293** | A752 | 52c multi | 1.40 | 1.40 |
| *a.* | | #2293 + label | 2.75 | 2.75 |
| **2294** | A753 | 52c multi | 1.40 | 1.40 |
| *a.* | | #2294 + label | 2.75 | 2.75 |
| **2295** | A754 | 65c multi | 1.75 | 1.75 |
| *a.* | | #2295 + label | 3.50 | 3.50 |
| **2296** | A755 | 65c multi | 1.75 | 1.75 |
| *a.* | | Miniature sheet, #2290-2296 | 10.50 | 10.50 |
| *b.* | | #2296 + label | 3.50 | 3.50 |
| | | *Nos. 2290-2296 (7)* | 10.50 | 10.50 |

Nos. 2290a, 2292a amd 2293a were printed in sheets of 10 + 10 labels that sold for €10. Nos. 2291a and 2294a were printed in sheets of 15 + 15 labels that sold for €15. Nos. 2295a and 2296b were printed in sheets of 10 + 10 labels that sold for € 13. Labels could be personalized.

Kostis Palamas (1859-1943), Poet — A756

Greek Cultural Year in China A757

Symposium of Seven Cardiovascular Surgeons, Athens and Delphi — A758

2nd Union Network International World Postal Conference A759

Treaty of Rome, 50th Anniv. — A760

Georgios Kotzias (1918-77) A761

Rigas Velestinlis (1757-98), Poet — A762

Year of Innovation A763

State Legal Council, 125th Anniv. A764

*Perf. 13¼x13¾, 13¾x13¼*

**2007, Apr. 25**

| | | | | |
|---|---|---|---|---|
| **2297** | A756 | 2c multi | .25 | .25 |
| **2298** | A757 | 10c multi | .30 | .30 |
| **2299** | A758 | 20c multi | .55 | .55 |
| **2300** | A759 | 52c multi | 1.40 | 1.40 |
| **2301** | A760 | 65c multi | 1.75 | 1.75 |
| **2302** | A761 | 85c multi | 2.40 | 2.40 |
| **2303** | A762 | €1 multi | 2.75 | 2.75 |
| **2304** | A763 | €2.27 multi | 6.25 | 6.25 |
| **2305** | A764 | €3 multi | 8.25 | 8.25 |
| | | *Nos. 2297-2305 (9)* | 23.90 | 23.90 |

Europa — A765

No. 2306: a, Scouting fleur-de-lis, dove's tail. b, Scouts, dove's head.

**2007, May 25** ***Perf. 14¼x14***

| | | | | |
|---|---|---|---|---|
| **2306** | A765 | Horiz. pair | 10.50 | 10.50 |
| *a.* | | 65c multi | 1.75 | 1.75 |
| *b.* | | €3.15 multi | 8.75 | 8.75 |
| *c.* | | Horiz. pair, perf. 13¾ vert. | 10.50 | 10.50 |
| *d.* | | As "a," perf. 13¾ vert. | 1.75 | 1.75 |
| *e.* | | As "b," perf. 13¾ vert. | 8.75 | 8.75 |
| *f.* | | Booklet pane, 2 #2306c | 21.00 | — |
| | | Complete booklet, #2306f | 21.00 | |

Scouting, cent.

Signs of the Zodiac A766

**Litho. With Foil Application**

***Perf. 13¾x13¼, 13¼x13¾***

**2007, May 25**

| | | | | | |
|---|---|---|---|---|---|
| **2307** | A766 | 2c | Scorpio | .25 | .25 |
| **2308** | A766 | 3c | Cancer | .25 | .25 |
| **2309** | A766 | 5c | Capricorn | .25 | .25 |
| **2310** | A766 | 10c | Taurus | .30 | .30 |
| **2311** | A766 | 20c | Sagittarius, vert. | .55 | .55 |
| **2312** | A766 | 40c | Leo, vert. | 1.10 | 1.10 |
| **2313** | A766 | 52c | Virgo, vert. | 1.40 | 1.40 |
| **2314** | A766 | 65c | Aries | 1.75 | 1.75 |
| **2315** | A766 | 85c | Aquarius | 2.40 | 2.40 |
| **2316** | A766 | €1 | Libra | 2.75 | 2.75 |
| **2317** | A766 | €2.27 | Pisces | 6.25 | 6.25 |
| **2318** | A766 | €2.80 | Gemini | 7.50 | 7.50 |
| | | | *Nos. 2307-2318 (12)* | 24.75 | 24.75 |

Souvenir Sheet

Statues of Asclepius, Greek God of Medicine — A767

No. 2319: a, Statue from Museum of Ampurias, Spain. b, Statue from National Archaeological Museum, Athens.

**2007, June 28** **Litho.** ***Perf. 13¾***

| | | | | |
|---|---|---|---|---|
| **2319** | A767 | Sheet of 2 | 13.50 | 13.50 |
| *a.-b.* | | €2.50 Either single | 6.75 | 6.75 |

See Spain No. 3521.

Discovery of the Tomb of St. Cyril, 150th Anniv. A768

University of Macedonia, 50th Anniv. — A769

Konstantinos Tsatsos (1899-1987), Politician — A770

**Litho. With Foil Application**

**2007, Sept. 28** ***Perf. 13¾x14***

| | | | | |
|---|---|---|---|---|
| **2320** | A768 | 2c multi | .25 | .25 |

**Litho.**

| | | | | |
|---|---|---|---|---|
| **2321** | A769 | 3c multi | .25 | .25 |

***Perf. 14x13¾***

| | | | | |
|---|---|---|---|---|
| **2322** | A770 | €4 multi | 11.50 | 11.50 |
| | | *Nos. 2320-2322 (3)* | 12.00 | 12.00 |

Sports Team Emblems A771

Designs: 2c, Ergotelis Sports Club. 4c, OFI. 54c, Olympiacos C.F.P. €2.29, Doxa Dramas Sports Club. €5, Nautical Club of Mytilini.

**2007, Nov. 2** **Litho.** ***Perf. 14x13¾***

| | | | | |
|---|---|---|---|---|
| **2323-2327** | A771 | Set of 5 | 23.00 | 23.00 |
| *2325a* | | #2325 + label | 3.00 | 3.00 |

No. 2325a was printed in sheets of 10 + 10 labels that sold for €10. Labels could be personalized.

Busts of Goddesses — A772

Designs: 54c, Bust of Aphrodite. €2.40, Bust of Goddess Anahit, Armenia.

**2007, Dec. 14** ***Perf. 14x14¼***

| | | | | |
|---|---|---|---|---|
| **2328-2329** | A772 | Set of 2 | 8.75 | 8.75 |

See Armenia Nos. 774-775.

Islands A773

**2008, Feb. 27** **Litho.** ***Perf. 14¼x14***

| | | | | | |
|---|---|---|---|---|---|
| **2330** | A773 | 2c | Chios | .25 | .25 |
| *a.* | | | Perf. 13¼ vert. | .25 | .25 |
| **2331** | A773 | 5c | Amorgos | .25 | .25 |
| *a.* | | | Perf. 13¼ vert. | .25 | .25 |
| **2332** | A773 | 10c | Nísiros | .30 | .30 |
| *a.* | | | Perf. 13¼ vert. | .30 | .30 |
| **2333** | A773 | 20c | Paxos | .60 | .60 |
| *a.* | | | Perf. 13¼ vert. | .60 | .60 |
| **2334** | A773 | 40c | Leros | 1.25 | 1.25 |
| *a.* | | | Perf. 13¼ vert. | 1.25 | 1.25 |
| **2335** | A773 | 54c | Kalymnos | 1.75 | 1.75 |
| *a.* | | | Perf. 13¼ vert. | 1.75 | 1.75 |
| **2336** | A773 | 67c | Kos | 2.10 | 2.10 |
| *a.* | | | Perf. 13¼ vert. | 2.10 | 2.10 |
| **2337** | A773 | €1 | Simi | 3.00 | 3.00 |
| *a.* | | | Perf. 13¼ vert. | 3.00 | 3.00 |
| **2338** | A773 | €2.29 | Zákinthos | 7.00 | 7.00 |
| *a.* | | | Perf. 13¼ vert. | 7.00 | 7.00 |
| **2339** | A773 | €4 | Inousses | 12.50 | 12.50 |
| *a.* | | | Perf. 13¼ vert. | 12.50 | 12.50 |
| | | | *Nos. 2330-2339 (10)* | 29.00 | 29.00 |

2008 Summer Olympics, Beijing — A774

Designs: 3c, Discus thrower. 35c, Lighting of Olympic flame. No. 2342, 67c, Torch bearer. No. 2343, 67c, Three cyclists, horiz.

**2008, Mar. 14** ***Perf. 13½x13, 13x13½***

| | | | | |
|---|---|---|---|---|
| **2340-2343** | A774 | Set of 4 | 5.50 | 5.50 |

Letter — A775

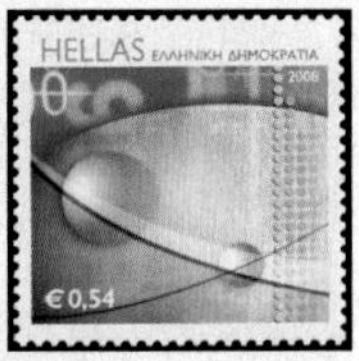


Numbers — A776

Heart — A777

Kites — A778

Pillar — A779

Greek Flag — A780

**2008, Apr. 21** **Litho.** ***Perf. 14x13¾***

| | | | | |
|---|---|---|---|---|
| **2344** | A775 | 54c multi | 1.75 | 1.75 |
| **2345** | A776 | 54c multi | 1.75 | 1.75 |
| **2346** | A777 | 54c multi | 1.75 | 1.75 |
| **2347** | A778 | 54c multi | 1.75 | 1.75 |
| **2348** | A779 | 67c multi | 2.10 | 2.10 |
| **2349** | A780 | 67c multi | 2.10 | 2.10 |
| *a.* | | Miniature sheet, #2344-2349 | 11.50 | 11.50 |
| | | *Nos. 2344-2349 (6)* | 11.20 | 11.20 |

Europa — A781

No. 2350: a, Inkwell, pen and papers. b, Fountain pen and papers.

**2008, May 26** ***Perf. 14¼x14***

| | | | | |
|---|---|---|---|---|
| **2350** | A781 | Horiz. pair | 12.50 | 12.50 |
| *a.* | | 67c multi | 2.25 | 2.25 |
| *b.* | | €3.17 multi | 10.00 | 10.00 |
| *c.* | | Horiz. pair, perf. 13¾ vert. | 12.50 | 12.50 |
| *d.* | | As "a," perf. 13¾ vert. | 2.25 | 2.25 |
| *e.* | | As "b," perf. 13¾ vert. | 10.00 | 10.00 |
| *f.* | | Booklet pane, 2 #2350c | 25.00 | — |
| | | Complete booklet, #2350f | 25.00 | |

Anniversaries A782

Curved lines and: 3c, Emblem of Hellenic Post. 5c, Posthorn, Greek men. 10c, Ioannis Kapodistrias (1776-1831), provisional president of Greece. 57c, M. Karagatsis (1908-60), writer. 70c, Fish. €1.85, Emblem of National Hellenic Research Foundation. €3, Emblem of National Council of Women.

**2008, June 20** ***Perf. 13¼x13¾***

| | | | | |
|---|---|---|---|---|
| **2351-2357** | A782 | Set of 7 | 20.00 | 20.00 |

Hellenic Post, 180th anniv. (#2351-2352); Inauguration of Kapodistrias, 180th anniv. (#2353); Intl. Year of Planet Earth (#2355); National Hellenic Research Foundation, 50th anniv. (#2356), National Council of Women, cent. (#2357).

Greek Products — A783

Designs: 3c, Feta cheese and tomatoes. 5c, Mastic. 20c, Olive, bottle of olive oil, horiz. 57c, Bottle of ouzo, marine life and boat. €1, Pistachio nuts. €4, Bees, rose, jar of honey.

***Perf. 13¼x13¾, 13¾x13¼***

**2008, Sept. 19**

| | | | | |
|---|---|---|---|---|
| **2358-2363** | A783 | Set of 6 | 16.50 | 16.50 |

Sports Team Emblems A784

Designs: 40c, Diagoras Rhodos Sports Club. 57c, A.E.K. soccer team. 70c, Asteras Tripolis soccer team. €2, Panserraoikos soccer team. €3, Kerkiraikos Sports Club.

**2008, Oct. 20** ***Perf. 14x13¾***

| | | | | |
|---|---|---|---|---|
| **2364-2368** | A784 | Set of 5 | 17.00 | 17.00 |

Fairy Tales, Fables and Children's Literature A785

Designs: 10c, The Mermaid and Alexander the Great. 57c, Little Red Riding Hood. €1, The Fairies. €1.85, The Little Match Girl. €3, Arion and the Lyre.

**2008, Dec. 16** ***Perf. 13¾x14***

| | | | | |
|---|---|---|---|---|
| **2369-2373** | A785 | Set of 5 | 18.00 | 18.00 |

Actors and Actresses A786

Designs: 1c, Manos Katrakis (1908-84). 20c, Dinos Iliopoulos (1915-2001). 35c, Elli Lambeti (1926-83). 40c, Alekos Alexandrakis (1928-2005). 50c, Aliki Vougioklaki (1934-96). 57c, Jenny Karezi (1932-92). €1, Dimitris Horn (1921-98). €2.42, Nikos Kourkoulos (1934-2007). €3.50, Thanos Kotsopoulos (1911-94).

**2009, Feb. 9** **Litho.** ***Perf. 13¾x13¼***

| | | | | |
|---|---|---|---|---|
| **2374-2382** | A786 | Set of 9 | 23.00 | 23.00 |
| *2382a* | | Miniature sheet of 9, #2374-2382 | 23.00 | 23.00 |

Compare with type A828.

Souvenir Sheet

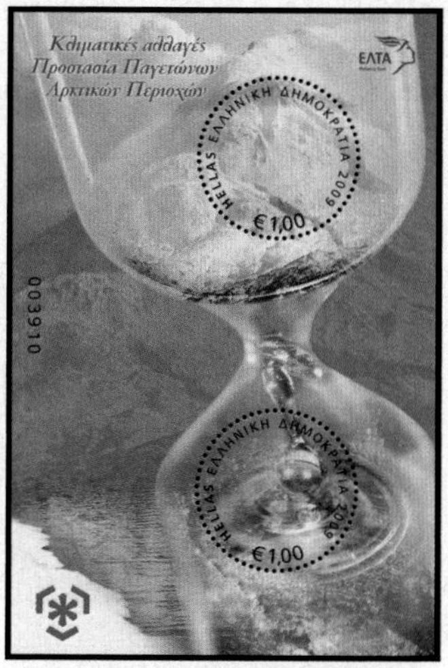


Preservation of Polar Regions and Glaciers — A787

No. 2383: a, Snow-covered mountain. b, Droplet of water.

**2009, Mar. 3** ***Perf.***

| | | | | |
|---|---|---|---|---|
| **2383** | A787 | €1 Sheet of 2, #a-b | 5.75 | 5.75 |

No. 2383 contains two 30mm diameter stamps.

Sivitanidios School, 80th Anniv. A788

University of Piraeus, 70th Anniv. — A789

Natl. Archaeological Museum, 180th Anniv. — A790

Greek Presidency of UPU Postal Operations Council A791

Eye, Braille Script, Hands Touching Braille Book A792

Introduction of Euro, 10th Anniv. A793

Lord Byron (1788-1824), Poet — A794

Natl. Real Estate Registry A795

**Litho., Litho. With Foil Application (10c, 50c), Litho. & Embossed (57c)**

***Perf. 13¾x13¼, 13¼x13¾***

**2009, Mar. 30**

| | | | | | |
|---|---|---|---|---|---|
| **2384** | A788 | 5c | multi | .25 | .25 |
| **2385** | A789 | 10c | multi | .30 | .30 |
| **2386** | A790 | 20c | multi | .60 | .60 |
| **2387** | A791 | 50c | multi | 1.50 | 1.50 |
| **2388** | A792 | 57c | multi | 1.75 | 1.75 |
| **2389** | A793 | 70c | multi | 2.10 | 2.10 |
| **2390** | A794 | €2.42 | multi | 7.25 | 7.25 |
| **2391** | A795 | €3 | multi | 9.00 | 9.00 |
| | *Nos. 2384-2391 (8)* | | | 22.75 | 22.75 |

Louis Braille (1809-52), educator of the blind (#2388), Hellenophile and Intl. Solidarity Day (#2390).

Europa — A796

No. 2392: a, Pulsar diagram. b, Aristarchos Telescope.

**2009, May 11** **Litho.** ***Perf. 14¾x14***

| | | | | |
|---|---|---|---|---|
| **2392** | A796 | Horiz. pair | 11.00 | 11.00 |
| *a.* | | 70c multi | 2.00 | 2.00 |
| *b.* | | €3.20 multi | 9.00 | 9.00 |
| *c.* | | Horiz. pair, perf. 13¾ vert. | 11.00 | 11.00 |
| *d.* | | As "a," perf. 13¾ vert. | 2.00 | 2.00 |
| *e.* | | As "b," perf. 13¾ vert. | 9.00 | 9.00 |
| *f.* | | Booklet pane, 2 #2392c | 22.00 | — |
| | | Complete booklet, #2392f | 22.00 | |

Intl. Year of Astronomy.

UNESCO World Heritage Sites A797

Designs: No. 2393, 57c, Acropolis (denomination at LL). No. 2394, 57c, Meteora (denomination at UR). No. 2395, 70c, Delphi (denomination at UR). No. 2396, 70c, Mycenae (denomination at LL). €2, Mystras. €3, Delos.

**Litho. With Foil Application**

**2009, June 20** ***Perf. 13¾x14***

| | | | | |
|---|---|---|---|---|
| **2393-2398** | A797 | Set of 6 | 21.00 | 21.00 |
| *2398a* | | Miniature sheet of 6, #2393-2398 | 21.00 | 21.00 |

Lighthouses A798

Designs: 1c, Didimi Islet Lighthouse. 57c, Tourlitis Lighthouse. 70c, Chania Lighthouse. €1, Korakas Paros Lighthouse, horiz. €4.20, Strongyli Lighthouse, horiz.

**Litho. With Foil Application**

***Perf. 13¼x13¾, 13¾x13¼***

**2009, Aug. 21**

| | | | | |
|---|---|---|---|---|
| **2399-2403** | A798 | Set of 5 | 19.00 | 19.00 |
| *2403a* | | Souvenir sheet, #2399-2403 | 19.00 | 19.00 |

Greek Mythology A799

Designs: 1c, Theseus against the Minotaur. 5c, Heracles and Triton. 57c, Odysseus and the Sirens, vert. 70c, Talos and the Dioskuroi. €5, Vellerofontis riding Pegasus, vert.

***Perf. 13¾x14, 14x13¾***

**2009, Oct. 20** **Litho.**

| | | | | |
|---|---|---|---|---|
| **2404-2408** | A799 | Set of 5 | 19.00 | 19.00 |

Convention on Rights of the Child, 20th Anniv. — A800

Designs: 20c, Hands of adult and child. 58c, Child standing against wall, horiz. 72c, Clasped hands of children, horiz. €1, Child looking through barred window. €4, Child in darkness.

***Perf. 13¼x13, 13x13¼***

**2009, Dec. 7** **Litho.**

| | | | | |
|---|---|---|---|---|
| **2409-2413** | A800 | Set of 5 | 19.00 | 19.00 |

Souvenir Sheets

Medals For Greek National Basketball Teams — A801

Designs: No. 2414, €2, Gold medal for men's under-20 team at 2009 European Basketball Championships. No. 2415, €2, Silver medal for men's under-19 team at 2009 World Basketball Championships. No. 2416, €2, Bronze medal for men's team at 2009 European Basketball Championships.

**Litho. & Embossed With Foil Application**

**2009, Dec. 15** ***Perf. 13x13¼***

| | | | | |
|---|---|---|---|---|
| **2414-2416** | A801 | Set of 3 | 17.50 | 17.50 |

20th Century Paintings by Greeks — A802

Designs: 1c, Stuffed Head, by Giannis Gaitis. 5c, Orpheus, Hermes and Eurydice, by Nikos Engonopoulos. 50c, Erotic, by Yannis Moralis. 58c, Sailor Sitting at the Table, Pink Background, by Yannis Tsarouchis. €2.43, Wattle Fences, by Nikos Hadjikyriakos-Ghika. €3, The Drawing, by Diamantis Diamantopoulos.

**2010, Feb. 11** **Litho.** ***Perf. 14x13¾***

| | | | | |
|---|---|---|---|---|
| **2417-2422** | A802 | Set of 6 | 18.00 | 18.00 |
| *2422a* | | Sheet of 6, #2417-2422 | 18.00 | 18.00 |

Renewable Energy Development A803

Designs: 1c, Solar energy. 40c, Water energy. 58c, Wind energy, horiz. 72c, Self-contained man. €2.43, Wave energy. €2.50, Bioenergy.

***Perf. 13¼x13¾, 13¾x13¼***

**2010, Apr. 26**

| | | | | |
|---|---|---|---|---|
| **2423-2428** | A803 | Set of 6 | 18.00 | 18.00 |

Europa — A804

No. 2429: a, Boy in balloon, Puss in Boots. b, Girl on books.

**2008, May 26** **Litho.** ***Perf. 14¼x14***

| | | | | |
|---|---|---|---|---|
| **2429** | A804 | Horiz. pair | 9.50 | 9.50 |
| *a.* | | 72c multi | 1.75 | 1.75 |
| *b.* | | €3.22 multi | 7.75 | 7.75 |
| *c.* | | Horiz. pair, perf. 13¾ vert. | 9.50 | 9.50 |
| *d.* | | As "a," perf. 13¾ vert. | 1.75 | 1.75 |
| *e.* | | As "b," perf. 13¾ vert. | 7.75 | 7.75 |
| *f.* | | Booklet pane, 2 #2429c | 19.00 | — |
| | | Complete booklet, #2429f | 19.00 | |

New Acropolis Museum — A805

Designs: 5c, Peplos kore. 58c, Parthenon gallery, horiz. 72c, Fragment of Parthenon frieze, horiz. €1, Entrance to new museum, horiz. €4, Marble sculpture of dog, horiz.

***Perf. 13¼x13¾, 13¾x13¼***

**2010, June 21** **Litho.**

| | | | | |
|---|---|---|---|---|
| **2430-2434** | A805 | Set of 5 | 16.00 | 16.00 |
| *2434a* | | Souvenir sheet, #2430-2434 | 16.00 | 16.00 |

Parthenon Gallery — A805a

Fragment of Parthenon Frieze — A805b

**2010, June 21** **Litho.** ***Perf. 14x13¾***

| | | | | | |
|---|---|---|---|---|---|
| **2435** | A805a | 58c | multi + label | 2.50 | 2.50 |
| **2436** | A805b | 72c | multi + label | 3.25 | 3.25 |

Nos. 2435-2436 each were printed in sheets of 10 stamps + 10 labels that could be personalized. The sheet containing No. 2435 sold for €10, and that of No. 2436 sold for €13.

Battle of Marathon, 2500th Anniv. A806

Designs: 50c, Athenian and Persian fighting. 58c, Phalanx marching into battle. 72c, Battle scene. €3, Bronze Corinthian helmet.

**Litho. With Foil Application**

**2010, June 23** ***Perf. 13¾x14***
**2437-2440** A806 Set of 4 12.50 12.50

Popular Musicians A807

Designs: 10c, Vasilis Tsitsanis (1915-84). 20c, Giorgos Zampetas (1925-92). 58c, Stelios Kazantzidis (1931-2001). 72c, Grigoris Bithikotsis (1922-2005). €1, Vicky Moscholiou (1945-2005). €4.80, Sotiria Bellou (1921-97).

***Perf. 13¾x13¼***

**2010, Sept. 16** **Litho.**
**2441-2446** A807 Set of 6 21.00 21.00
*2446a* Souvenir sheet, #2441-2446 21.00 21.00

Paper Boat — A808

Spiral Staircase — A809

**2010, Oct. 14** ***Perf. 14x13¾***
**2447** A808 (58c) multi 1.75 1.75
*a.* Perf. 12¾ vert. 1.75 1.75
**2448** A809 (72c) multi 2.10 2.10
*a.* Perf. 12¾ vert. 2.10 2.10

Islands A810

**2010, Oct. 14** ***Perf. 14¼x14***
**2449** A810 2c Limnos .25 .25
*a.* Perf. 12¾ vert. .25 .25
**2450** A810 5c Paros .25 .25
*a.* Perf. 12¾ vert. .25 .25
**2451** A810 20c Ithaki .60 .60
*a.* Perf. 12¾ vert. .60 .60
**2452** A810 40c Tinos 1.25 1.25
*a.* Perf. 12¾ vert. 1.25 1.25
**2453** A810 50c Skyros 1.40 1.40
*a.* Perf. 12¾ vert. 1.40 1.40
**2454** A810 €1 Evia-Chalkida 3.00 3.00
*a.* Perf. 12¾ vert. 3.00 3.00
**2455** A810 €2 Samos 5.75 5.75
*a.* Perf. 12¾ vert. 5.75 5.75
**2456** A810 €4 Kassos 11.50 11.50
*a.* Perf. 12¾ vert. 11.50 11.50
*Nos. 2449-2456 (8)* 23.90 23.90

Buildings A811

Designs: 20c, Municipal Theater of Piraeus. 58c, Benaki Museum. €2.43, National Theater. €2.50, National Gallery of Nafplio.

**Litho. With Foil Application**

**2010, Nov. 16** ***Perf. 13¾x14***
**2457-2460** A811 Set of 4 15.50 15.50

Christmas — A812

Designs: 50c, Doves, holly leaves, stars. 58c, Angel with horn. €1, Ship with Christmas decorations. €3.50, Christmas tree, birds, holly leaves.

**2010, Dec. 10** **Litho.** ***Perf. 13¾x14***
**2461-2464** A812 Set of 4 15.00 15.00

**Self-Adhesive**

**Miniature Sheet**

***Die Cut Perf. 13¼***

**2465** Sheet of 4 15.00
*a.* A812 50c multi 1.40 1.40
*b.* A812 58c multi 1.60 1.60
*c.* A812 €1 multi 2.75 2.75
*d.* A812 €3.50 multi 9.25 9.25

20th Century Greek Engraving and Wood-Cut Prints — A813

Designs: 3c, Aigaion V, by Kostas Grammatopoulos (1916-2003). 30c, To Pagoni, by Giannis Kefallinos (1894-1957), horiz. 60c, Maria, by A. Tassos (1914-85). €1, Plastikes Rimes, by Dimitris Galanis (1879-1966), horiz. €4, Mikros Kavalaris, by Vasso Katraki (1914-88).

**Litho. with Foil Application**

**2011, Jan. 20** ***Perf. 14x13¾, 13¾x14***
**2466-2470** A813 Set of 5 16.50 16.50

European Year of Volunteers — A814

Academy of Athens, 85th Anniv. — A815

Alexandros Papadiamantis (1851-1911), Writer — A816

Battle of Crete, 70th Anniv. — A817

Organization for Economic Cooperation and Development, 50th Anniv. — A818

Spyros Samaras (1861-1917), Composer A819

***Perf. 13¾x14, 14x13¾***

**2011, Feb. 23** **Litho.**
**2471** A814 3c multi .25 .25
**2472** A815 10c multi .30 .30
**2473** A816 20c multi .55 .55
**2474** A817 60c multi 1.75 1.75
**2475** A818 €1.50 multi 4.25 4.25
**2476** A819 €3 multi 8.50 8.50
*Nos. 2471-2476 (6)* 15.60 15.60

A820

2011 Special Olympics, Athens — A821

Special Olympics emblem and: 2c, Heart, stylized people, emblem of 2011 Athens Special Olympics. 4c, Stylized person, buildings, emblem of 2011 Athens Special Olympics. No. 2479, 60c, Emblem of 2011 Athens Special Olympics, vert. 75c, Sun, emblem of 2011 Athens Special Olympics, vert. €4.20, Emblem of 2011 Athens Special Olympics.

No. 2482, Emblems of Special Olympics and 2011 Athens Special Olympics.

**2011, Mar. 18** ***Perf. 13¾x14, 14x13¾***
**2477-2481** A820 Set of 5 16.50 16.50

**Booklet Stamp**

***Perf. 14x13¾***

**2482** A821 60c multi + label 2.00 2.00
*a.* Booklet pane of 1 + label 2.00 —
Complete booklet, 24 #2484a 52.50

Complete booklet sold for €18. Each booklet pane in booklet has a label with a different image.

Ancient Greek Ships — A822

Designs: 1c, Ship from a Thera wall painting, 1500 B.C. 20c, Polyreme, 4th-2nd cent. B.C., horiz. 60c, Triaconter, 15th-4th cent. B.C., horiz. 75c, Hellenic trireme, 7th-4th cent. B.C., horiz. €2.47, Macedonian hexareme, 4th-3rd cent. B.C., horiz. €2.50, Byzantine dromond, 5th-11th cent. A.D.

**Litho. With Foil Application**

**2011, Apr. 18** ***Perf. 13¾***
**2483-2488** A822 Set of 6 19.00 19.00
*2488a* Souvenir sheet of 6, #2483-2488 19.00 19.00

Europa — A823

No. 2489 — Leaves and: a, Wildlife. b, Trees.

**2011, May 17** ***Perf. 13¼x13½***
**2489** A823 Horiz. pair 12.00 12.00
*a.* 75c multi 2.25 2.25
*b.* €3.25 multi 9.50 9.50
*c.* Horiz. pair, perf. 12¾ vert. 12.00 12.00
*d.* As "a," perf. 12¾ vert. 2.25 2.25
*e.* As "b," perf. 12¾ vert. 9.50 9.50
*f.* Booklet pane, 2 #2489c 24.00 —
Complete booklet, #2489f 24.00

Intl. Year of Forests.

Tourism A824

Text "www.visitgreece.gr" and: 1c, Stylized waves. 3c, Drama mask. 60c, Paper boat. 75c, Columns. €4, Town on cliff.

**2011, June 22** **Litho.** ***Perf. 13¾***
**2490-2494** A824 Set of 5 15.50 15.50

**Booklet Stamp**
**Self-Adhesive**

***Die Cut Perf. 12x11¼***

**2495** A824 75c multi 2.10 2.10
*a.* Booklet pane of 10 21.00

Primary School Book Cover Art — A825

Book cover art from: 2c, 1954 third grade reading book. 20c, *Little Children,* 1939 first grade reading book. 60c, *Alphavitario,* 1955 first grade reading book. 75c, 1955 second grade reading book. €1, *Krinoloulouda,* 1939 second grade reading book. €3.50, 1955 fifth grade reading book.

**2011, Sept. 5 Litho. *Perf. 14x14¼***

| | | | | |
|---|---|---|---|---|
| **2496-2501** | A825 | Set of 6 | 17.00 | 17.00 |
| *2501a* | | Souvenir sheet of 6, #2496-2501 | 17.00 | 17.00 |

**Booklet Stamp**
**Self-Adhesive**
***Die Cut Perf. 13¼***

| | | | | |
|---|---|---|---|---|
| **2502** | A825 | 60c Like #2498 | 1.75 | 1.75 |
| *a.* | | Booklet pane of 10 | 17.50 | |

First Greek Postage Stamps, 150th Anniv. — A827

Type A1 stamp with original denominations removed in: 15c, Chocolate. 50c, Bister. 60c, Green. 75c, Orange. €1, Blue. €2, Violet. €5, Red.

***Perf. 13¼x13¾***
**2011, Oct. 1 Litho. & Engr.**

| | | | | |
|---|---|---|---|---|
| **2504-2510** | A827 | Set of 7 | 27.50 | 27.50 |
| *2510a* | | Souvenir sheet of 1, #2510 | 14.00 | 14.00 |

Actors and Actresses A828

Designs: 1c, Vassilis Diamantopoulos (1920-99). 5c, Rena Vlachopoulou (1923-2004). 50c, Orestis Makris (1898-1975). 60c, Thanasis Veggos (1927-2011). €2.47, Mary Aroni (1916-92). €2.50, Sapfo Notara (c. 1907-85).

***Perf. 13¾x13½***
**2011, Nov. 22 Litho.**

| | | | | |
|---|---|---|---|---|
| **2511-2516** | A828 | Set of 6 | 16.50 | 16.50 |
| *2516a* | | Souvenir sheet of 6, #2511-2516 | 16.50 | 16.50 |

Compare with type A786.

Souvenir Sheets

Gold Medalists at 2011 FINA World Championships — A829

Designs: No. 2517, €3, Greek flag and medal for Greek women's water polo team. No. 2518, €3, Spyros Gianniotis, swimmer, and gold medal.

**2011, Dec. 15**

| | | | | |
|---|---|---|---|---|
| **2517-2518** | A829 | Set of 2 | 16.00 | 16.00 |

A830

A831

Marine Life A832

Designs: 2c, Palinurus elephas. 3c, Octopus vulgaris. 5c, Anemonia viridis. 20c, Caretta caretta. 35c, Epinephelus marginatus. 50c, Dentex dentex. (60c), Hippocampus guttulatus. €1, Aurelia aurita. (€2.47), Dasyatis pastinaca. €3, Charcharius taurus.

**2012, Feb. 21 *Perf. 14¼x14***

| | | | | |
|---|---|---|---|---|
| **2519** | A830 | 2c multi | .25 | .25 |
| *a.* | | Perf. 12¾ vert. | .25 | .25 |
| **2520** | A830 | 3c multi | .25 | .25 |
| *a.* | | Perf. 12¾ vert. | .25 | .25 |
| **2521** | A830 | 5c multi | .25 | .25 |
| *a.* | | Perf. 12¾ vert. | .25 | .25 |
| **2522** | A830 | 20c multi | .55 | .55 |
| *a.* | | Perf. 12¾ vert. | .55 | .55 |
| **2523** | A830 | 35c multi | .95 | .95 |
| *a.* | | Perf. 12¾ vert. | .95 | .95 |
| **2524** | A830 | 50c multi | 1.40 | 1.40 |
| *a.* | | Perf. 12¾ vert. | 1.40 | 1.40 |
| **2525** | A831 | (60c) multi | 1.60 | 1.60 |
| *a.* | | Perf. 12¾ vert. | 1.60 | 1.60 |
| **2526** | A830 | €1 multi | 2.60 | 2.60 |
| *a.* | | Perf. 12¾ vert. | 2.60 | 2.60 |
| **2527** | A832 | (€2.47) multi | 6.50 | 6.50 |
| *a.* | | Perf. 12¾ vert. | 6.50 | 6.50 |
| **2528** | A830 | €3 multi | 8.00 | 8.00 |
| *a.* | | Perf. 12¾ vert. | 8.00 | 8.00 |
| | | *Nos. 2519-2528 (10)* | 22.35 | 22.35 |

A834

Children's Games — A835

Children and: 2c. Soccer ball. 10c, Scooter, vert. 35c, Jump rope. (60c), Marbles. €2, Tops. €3, Hopscotch.

***Perf. 14¼x14, 14x14¼***
**2012, Apr. 18 Litho.**

| | | | | |
|---|---|---|---|---|
| **2530** | A834 | 2c multi | .25 | .25 |
| **2531** | A834 | 10c multi | .30 | .30 |
| **2532** | A834 | 35c multi | .95 | .95 |
| **2533** | A835 | (60c) multi | 1.60 | 1.60 |
| **2534** | A834 | €2 multi | 5.25 | 5.25 |
| **2535** | A834 | €3 multi | 8.00 | 8.00 |
| | | *Nos. 2530-2535 (6)* | 16.35 | 16.35 |

**Booklet Stamp**
**Self-Adhesive**
***Die Cut Perf. 13¼***

| | | | | |
|---|---|---|---|---|
| **2536** | A835 | (60c) multi | 1.60 | 1.60 |
| *a.* | | Booklet pane of 10 | 16.00 | |

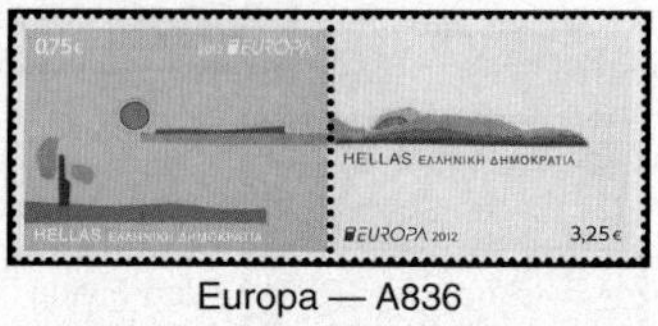

Europa — A836

No. 2537 — Background color: a, Beige. b, White.

**Litho. With Foil Application**
**2012, May 10 *Perf. 13½x13¼***

| | | | | |
|---|---|---|---|---|
| **2537** | A836 | Horiz. pair | 10.00 | 10.00 |
| *a.* | | 75c multi | 1.90 | 1.90 |
| *b.* | | €3.25 multi | 8.00 | 8.00 |
| *c.* | | Horiz. pair, perf. 12¾ vert. | 10.00 | 10.00 |
| *d.* | | As "a," perf. 12¾ vert. | 1.90 | 1.90 |
| *e.* | | As "b," perf. 12¾ vert. | 8.00 | 8.00 |
| *f.* | | Booklet pane, 2 #2537c | 20.00 | — |
| | | Complete booklet, #2537f | 20.00 | |

Nature Tourism A837

Designs: 1c, Tzoumerka Mountains, Epirus, rock climber. 10c, Rope bridge over Evinos River, backpacker. 62c, Samaria Gorge, Crete, hikers. 78c, Acheron River, Epirus, kayaker. €2, Rhodope Mountain stream, backpacker. €2.50, Field near Xanthi, backpacker.

**2012, June 25 Litho. *Perf. 13¾***

| | | | | |
|---|---|---|---|---|
| **2538-2543** | A837 | Set of 6 | 15.00 | 15.00 |

2012 Summer Olympics, London A838

Emblem of 2012 Summer Olympics and: 78c, London landmarks and years London hosted previous Olympic Games. €1.70, Athletes and sporting equipment.

**2012, July 2**

| | | | | |
|---|---|---|---|---|
| **2544-2545** | A838 | Set of 2 | 6.25 | 6.25 |

Souvenir Sheets

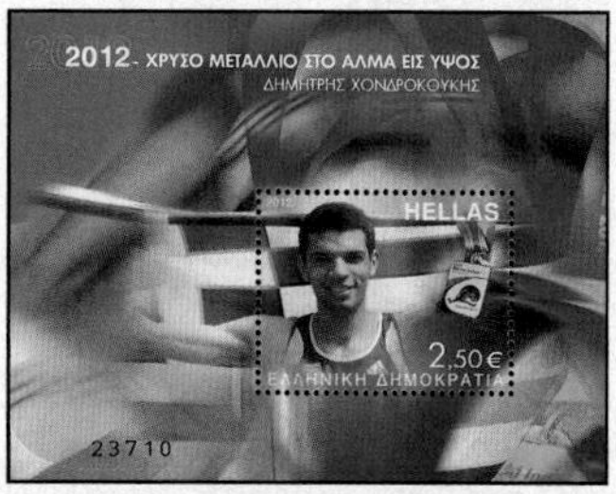

Dimitris Chondrokoukis, 2012 Intl. High Jump Champion — A839

Vlassis Maras, 2001-02 Intl. Horizontal Bar Champion — A840

**2012, July 16 *Perf. 13¾x13¼***

| | | | | |
|---|---|---|---|---|
| **2546** | A839 | €2.50 multi | 6.25 | 6.25 |
| **2547** | A840 | €2.50 multi | 6.25 | 6.25 |

Greek Ships — A841

Designs: 1c, Paron, 1821. 15c, Mistiko, 17th cent. 62c, Corvette, 18th cent. 78c, Ionian-Cretan galley, 16th cent. €2, Sakoleva, 19th cent. €2.40, latinadiko in shipyard, 18th cent.

**Litho. With Foil Application**
**2012, Sept. 12**

| | | | | |
|---|---|---|---|---|
| **2548-2553** | A841 | Set of 6 | 15.50 | 15.50 |

Liberation of Thessalonica, Cent. — A842

Designs: 40c, Battle of Deskati. 62c, Greek Army entering Thessalonica (47x25mm). 85c, Cruiser G. Averof at sea. €2.50, Battle of Sarantaporo.

***Perf. 13¾, 13½x13¼ (62c)***
**2012, Oct. 26**

| | | | | |
|---|---|---|---|---|
| **2554-2557** | A842 | Set of 4 | 11.50 | 11.50 |

Christmas A843

Triangle, beater and Christmas ornament in shape of: 10c, Sphere. 62c, Christmas tree. 78c, Stocking. €3, Gift.

**2012, Dec. 12 *Perf. 14x14¼***

| | | | | |
|---|---|---|---|---|
| **2558-2561** | A843 | Set of 4 | 12.00 | 12.00 |

## SEMI-POSTAL STAMPS

Nos. 440-444 Surcharged in Blue

**1944 Wmk. 252 *Perf. 12½***

| | | | | |
|---|---|---|---|---|
| **B1** | A106 | 100,000d on 15d | .40 | *.90* |
| **B2** | A107 | 100,000d on 25d | .40 | *.90* |
| **B3** | A108 | 100,000d on 50d | .40 | *.90* |
| **B4** | A109 | 100,000d on 75d | .40 | *.90* |
| **B5** | A110 | 100,000d on 100d | .40 | *.90* |
| | | *Nos. B1-B5,CB1-CB5 (10)* | 4.00 | *8.75* |
| | | Set, never hinged | 6.50 | |

The proceeds aided victims of the Piraeus bombing, Jan. 11, 1944. The exceptionally high face value discouraged the use of these stamps.

Nos. 437-441 Surcharged in Blue

**1944, July 20 50,000d + 450,000d**

| | | | | |
|---|---|---|---|---|
| **B11** | A103 | on 2d | .30 | *.65* |
| **B12** | A104 | on 5d | .30 | *.65* |
| **B13** | A105 | on 10d | .30 | *.65* |
| **B14** | A106 | on 15d | .30 | *.65* |
| *a.* | | Pair, one without surcharge | 65.00 | |
| **B15** | A107 | on 25d | .30 | *.65* |
| | | *Nos. B11-B15,CB6-CB10 (10)* | 3.50 | *6.50* |
| | | Set, never hinged | 5.50 | |

The surtax aided children's camps.

## AIR POST STAMPS

### Italy-Greece-Turkey-Rhodes Service

Flying Boat off Phaleron Bay — AP1

Flying Boat over Acropolis — AP2

Flying Boat over Map of Southern Europe — AP3

Flying Boat Seen through Colonnade — AP4

***Perf. 11½***

**1926, Oct. 20 Unwmk. Litho.**

| | | | | |
|---|---|---|---|---|
| **C1** | AP1 2d multicolored | | 1.60 | 1.25 |
| *a.* | Horiz. pair, imperf. vert. | | 725.00 | |
| **C2** | AP2 3d multicolored | | 12.00 | 11.00 |
| **C3** | AP3 5d multicolored | | 1.60 | 1.25 |
| **C4** | AP4 10d multicolored | | 12.00 | 12.00 |
| | *Nos. C1-C4 (4)* | | 27.20 | 25.50 |
| | Set, never hinged | | 80.00 | |

### Graf Zeppelin Issue

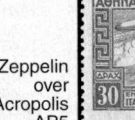

Zeppelin over Acropolis AP5

**1933, May 2** ***Perf. 13½x12½***

| | | | | |
|---|---|---|---|---|
| **C5** | AP5 | 30d rose red | 13.00 | 13.00 |
| **C6** | AP5 | 100d deep blue | 52.50 | 52.50 |
| **C7** | AP5 | 120d dark brown | 52.50 | 52.50 |
| | | *Nos. C5-C7 (3)* | 118.00 | 118.00 |
| | | Set, never hinged | 325.00 | |

Propeller and Pilot's Head AP6

Temple of Apollo, Corinth AP7

Plane over Hermoupolis, Syros — AP8

Allegory of Flight
AP9 AP12

Map of Italy-Greece-Turkey-Rhodes Airmail Route — AP10

Head of Hermes and Airplane — AP11

**1933, Oct. 10 Engr.** ***Perf. 12***

| | | | | |
|---|---|---|---|---|
| **C8** | AP6 | 50 l green & org | .25 | .25 |
| **C9** | AP7 | 1d bl & brn org | .30 | .25 |
| **C10** | AP8 | 3d dk vio & org brn | .50 | .50 |
| **C11** | AP9 | 5d brn org & dk bl | 7.25 | 4.50 |
| **C12** | AP10 | 10d dp red & blk | 1.50 | 1.40 |
| **C13** | AP11 | 20d black & grn | 7.25 | 4.00 |
| **C14** | AP12 | 50d dp brn & dp bl | 50.00 | *55.00* |
| | | *Nos. C8-C14 (7)* | 67.05 | *65.90* |
| | | Set, never hinged | 200.00 | |

By error the 1d stamp is inscribed in the plural "ΔΡΑΧΜΑΙ" instead of the singular "ΔΡΑΧΜΗ." This stamp exists bisected, used as a 50 lepta denomination.

All values of this set exist imperforate but were not regularly issued.

### For General Air Post Service

Airplane over Map of Greece — AP13

Airplane over Map of Icarian Sea — AP14

Airplane over Acropolis AP15

***Perf. 13x13½, 13x12½, 13½x13, 12½x13***

**1933, Nov. 2**

| | | | | |
|---|---|---|---|---|
| **C15** | AP13 | 50 l green | .25 | .25 |
| **C16** | AP13 | 1d red brown | .30 | *.55* |
| **C17** | AP14 | 2d lt violet | .60 | *.85* |
| **C18** | AP15 | 5d ultra | 3.50 | 3.50 |
| *a.* | | Imperf., pair | 650.00 | 550.00 |
| *b.* | | Horiz. pair, imperf. vert. | 650.00 | |
| **C19** | AP14 | 10d car rose | 6.50 | *7.75* |
| **C20** | AP13 | 25d dark blue | 30.00 | 20.00 |
| **C21** | AP15 | 50d dark brown | 30.00 | *42.50* |
| *a.* | | Imperf., pair | 775.00 | 650.00 |
| | | *Nos. C15-C21 (7)* | 71.15 | 75.40 |
| | | Set, never hinged | 225.00 | |

Helios Driving the Sun Chariot AP16

Iris — AP17

Daedalus Preparing Icarus for Flying — AP18

Pallas Athene Holding Pegasus — AP19

Hermes AP20

Zeus Carrying off Ganymede AP21

Triptolemos, King of Eleusis AP22

Bellerophon and Pegasus — AP23

Phrixos and Helle on the Ram Flying over the Hellespont AP24

***Perf. 13x12½, 12½x13***

**1935, Nov. 10 Engr.**

**Grayish Paper**

**Size: 34x23½mm, 23½x34mm**

| | | | | |
|---|---|---|---|---|
| **C22** | AP16 | 1d deep red | 1.50 | 1.50 |
| **C23** | AP17 | 2d dull blue | 1.50 | 1.50 |
| **C24** | AP18 | 5d dk violet | 17.50 | 4.00 |
| **C25** | AP19 | 7d blue violet | 25.00 | 7.25 |
| **C26** | AP20 | 10d bister brown | 5.00 | 5.00 |
| **C27** | AP21 | 25d rose | 6.00 | 5.75 |
| **C28** | AP22 | 30d dark green | 2.00 | 2.00 |
| **C29** | AP23 | 50d violet | 8.00 | 6.00 |
| **C30** | AP24 | 100d brown | 2.50 | 2.25 |
| | | *Nos. C22-C30 (9)* | 69.00 | 35.25 |
| | | Set, never hinged | 150.00 | |

**Re-engraved**

**Size: 34¼x24mm, 24x34¼mm**

**1937-39 White Paper**

| | | | | |
|---|---|---|---|---|
| **C31** | AP16 | 1d red | .30 | .25 |
| **C32** | AP17 | 2d gray blue | .30 | .25 |
| **C33** | AP18 | 5d violet | .30 | .25 |
| **C34** | AP19 | 7d dp ultra | .30 | .25 |
| **C35** | AP20 | 10d brn org | 2.40 | *3.50* |
| | | *Nos. C31-C35 (5)* | 3.60 | *4.50* |
| | | Set, never hinged | 7.00 | |

Issued: #C35, 3/1/39; others 8/3/37.

Postage Due Stamp, 1913, Overprinted in Red

***Serrate Roulette 13½***

**1938, Aug. 8 Litho. Unwmk.**

| | | | |
|---|---|---|---|
| **C36** | D3 50 l violet brown | .25 | .25 |
| | Never hinged | .25 | |
| *a.* | "O" for "P" in word at foot | 30.00 | 30.00 |

**Same Overprint on No. J79 in Red**

**1939, June 26** ***Perf. 13½x12½***

| | | | |
|---|---|---|---|
| **C37** | D3 50 l dark brown | .25 | .25 |
| | Never hinged | .25 | |

Meteora Monasteries, near Trikkala — AP25

Designs: 4d, Simon Peter Monastery. 6d, View of Santorin. 8d, Church of Pantanassa. 16d, Santorin view. 32d, Ponticonissi, Corfu. 45d, Acropolis, Athens. 55d, Erechtheum. 65d, Temple of Nike Apteros. 100d, Temple of the Olympian Zeus, Athens.

**Wmk. Crowns (252)**

**1940, Aug. 3 Litho.** ***Perf. 12½***

| | | | | |
|---|---|---|---|---|
| **C38** | AP25 | 2d red org & blk | .85 | *1.25* |
| **C39** | AP25 | 4d dk grn & blk | 4.00 | 3.50 |
| **C40** | AP25 | 6d lake & blk | 7.25 | 6.50 |
| **C41** | AP25 | 8d dk bl & blk | 18.75 | 16.50 |
| **C42** | AP25 | 16d rose vio & blk | 30.00 | 25.00 |
| **C43** | AP25 | 32d red org & blk | 40.00 | *47.50* |
| **C44** | AP25 | 45d dk grn & blk | 52.50 | 47.50 |
| **C45** | AP25 | 55d lake & blk | 52.50 | 47.50 |
| **C46** | AP25 | 65d dk bl & blk | 52.50 | 47.50 |
| **C47** | AP25 | 100d rose vio & blk | 67.50 | 60.00 |
| | | *Nos. C38-C47 (10)* | 325.85 | 302.75 |
| | | Set, never hinged | 800.00 | |

4th anniv. of the founding of the Greek Youth Organization. The stamps were good for postal duty on Aug. 3-5, 1940, only. They remained on sale until Feb. 3, 1941.

For overprints see Nos. N229-N238.

**Catalogue values for unused stamps in this section, from this point to the end of the section, are for Never Hinged items.**

Postage Due Stamps Nos. J81 and J75 Surcharged in Red

**1941-42 Unwmk. *Perf. 13x12½***

**C48** D3 1d on 2d lt red .25 .25
*a.* Inverted surcharge 45.00

***Serrate Roulette 13½***

**C49** D3 1d on 2d ver ('42) .25 .25
*a.* Inverted surcharge 32.50
*b.* Double surcharge 22.50

Nos. J83, J84, J86, J87 Overprinted in Red

**1941-42 *Perf. 13, 12½x13***

**C50** D3 5d gray bl ('42) .25 .25
*a.* Inverted overprint 45.00
*b.* Double overprint 32.50
*c.* Pair, one without ovpt. 22.50
*d.* Surcharge on back 22.50
*e.* On No. J78 ('42) 140.00 *160.00*
**C51** D3 10d gray grn .30 .30
*a.* Inverted overprint 16.00
*b.* Vert. pair, imperf. btwn. 325.00
**C52** D3 25d lt red .85 .85
*a.* Inverted overprint 110.00
**C53** D3 50d orange 1.50 1.50
*Nos. C50-C53 (4)* 2.90 2.90

Boreas, North Wind — AP35

Winds: 5d, Notus, South. 10d, Apeliotes, East. 20d, Lips, Southwest. 25d, Zephyrus, West. 50d, Kaikias, Northeast.

**Wmk. 252**

**1942, Aug. 15 Litho. *Perf. 12½***

**C55** AP35 2d emerald .25 .25
**C56** AP35 5d red org .25 .25
*a.* Imperf., pair 325.00
*b.* Double impression 55.00 —
**C57** AP35 10d red brown .45 .45
**C58** AP35 20d brt blue .50 .50
**C59** AP35 25d dk red org .50 .50
**C60** AP35 50d gray blk 2.00 2.00
*a.* Double impression 110.00
*Nos. C55-C60 (6)* 3.95 3.95

**1943, Sept. 15**

Winds: 10d, Apeliotes, East. 25d, Zephyrus, West. 50d, Kaikias, Northeast. 100d, Boreas, North. 200d, Eurus, Southeast. 400d, Skiron, Northwest.

**C61** AP35 10d rose red .25 .25
**C62** AP35 25d Prus green .25 .25
**C63** AP35 50d violet blue .25 .25
**C64** AP35 100d slate black .25 .25
**C65** AP35 200d claret .25 .25
**C66** AP35 400d steel blue .25 .25
*Nos. C61-C66 (6)* 1.50 1.50

Double impressions exist of 10d and 400d. Value, each $30.

For surcharges see #472, 473, CB1-CB10.

**Imperf., Pairs**

*C61a* AP35 10d 110.00
*C62a* AP35 25d 110.00
*C63a* AP35 50d 110.00
*C64a* AP35 100d 110.00
*C65a* AP35 200d 110.00
*C66a* AP35 400d 110.00

Priest Blessing Troops on Summit of Mt. Grammos AP36

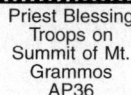

Torchbearer AP37

Designs: 1700d, Victory above Mt. Vitsi. 2700d, Battle Scene. 7000d, Victory leading infantry.

**1952, Aug. 29 Engr. *Perf. 12x13½***

**C67** AP36 1000d deep blue 1.50 .30
**C68** AP36 1700d dp blue grn 5.00 2.00
**C69** AP36 2700d brown 15.00 6.00
**C70** AP36 7000d olive green 45.00 15.00
*Nos. C67-C70 (4)* 66.50 23.30

Greek army's struggle against communism.

**1954, May 15 *Perf. 13***

Designs: 2400dr, Coin of Amphictyonic League. 4000dr, Pallas Athene.

**C71** AP37 1200d dp orange 7.50 .35
**C72** AP37 2400d dk green 37.50 2.50
**C73** AP37 4000d dp ultra 65.00 3.50
*Nos. C71-C73 (3)* 110.00 6.35

5th anniv. of the signing of the North Atlantic Treaty.

Piraeus AP38

Harbors: 15d, Salonika. 20d, Patras. 25d, Hermoupolis (Syra). 30d, Volos. 50d, Cavalla. 100d, Herakleion (Candia).

***Perf. 13½x13***

**1958, July 1 Wmk. 252 Litho.**

**C74** AP38 10d multicolored 12.50 .25
**C75** AP38 15d multicolored 1.75 .40
**C76** AP38 20d multicolored 12.50 .25
**C77** AP38 25d multicolored 2.00 .80
**C78** AP38 30d multicolored 2.25 .80
**C79** AP38 50d multicolored 8.00 .80
**C80** AP38 100d multicolored 40.00 4.00
*Nos. C74-C80 (7)* 79.00 7.30

## AIR POST SEMI-POSTAL STAMPS

**#C61-C65 Surcharged in Blue like #B1-B5**

**1944, June Wmk. 252 *Perf. 12½***

**CB1** AP35 100,000d on 10d .40 *.85*
**CB2** AP35 100,000d on 25d .40 *.85*
**CB3** AP35 100,000d on 50d .40 *.85*
*a.* Inverted overprint 32.50
**CB4** AP35 100,000d on 100d .40 *.85*
**CB5** AP35 100,000d on 200d .40 *.85*
*Nos. CB1-CB5 (5)* 2.00 *4.25*
Set, never hinged 7.00

The exceptionally high face value discouraged the use of these stamps.

The proceeds aided victims of the Piraeus bombing, January 11, 1944.

**#C61-C65 Surcharged in Blue like #B11-B15**

**1944, July 50,000d + 450,000d**

**CB6** AP35 on 10d .40 *.65*
**CB7** AP35 on 25d .40 *.65*
**CB8** AP35 on 50d .40 *.65*
**CB9** AP35 on 100d .40 *.65*
**CB10** AP35 on 200d .40 *.65*
*Nos. CB6-CB10 (5)* 2.00 *3.25*
Set, never hinged 8.00

The surtax aided children's camps. Surcharge exists inverted or double. Value, each $55.

## POSTAGE DUE STAMPS

D1

D2

***Perf. 9, 9½, and 10, 10½ and Compound***

**1875 Litho. Unwmk.**

**J1** D1 1 l green & black 1.50 1.50
**J2** D1 2 l green & black 1.50 1.50
**J3** D1 5 l green & black 1.75 1.25
**J4** D1 10 l green & black 1.75 1.25
**J5** D1 20 l green & black 42.50 30.00
**J6** D1 40 l green & black 8.25 5.50
**J7** D1 60 l green & black 42.50 30.00
**J8** D1 70 l green & black 8.25 5.50
**J9** D1 80 l green & black 17.50 14.50
**J10** D1 90 l green & black 11.00 11.00
**J11** D1 1d green & black 12.00 11.00
**J12** D1 2d green & black 13.00 11.00
*Nos. J1-J12 (12)* 161.50 124.00

Imperforate and part perforated, double and inverted center varieties of Nos. J1-J12 are believed to be printers' waste.

***Perf. 12, 13 and 10½x13***

**J13** D1 1 l green & black 1.60 1.60
**J14** D1 2 l green & black 22.50 22.50
**J15** D1 5 l green & black 2.75 2.75
**J16** D1 10 l green & black 3.25 3.25
**J17** D1 20 l green & black 40.00 27.50
**J18** D1 40 l green & black 10.00 7.75
**J19** D1 60 l green & black 42.50 27.50
**J20** D1 70 l green & black 7.75 7.75
**J21** D1 80 l green & black 12.00 12.00
**J22** D1 90 l green & black 17.50 12.00
**J23** D1 1d green & black 27.50 17.50
**J24** D1 2d green & black 22.50 17.50
*Nos. J13-J24 (12)* 209.85 159.60

**Redrawn**
**"Lepton" or "Lepta" in Larger Greek Letters**

**1876 *Perf. 9, 9½, and 10, 10½***

**J25** D2 1 l green & black 4.50 4.50
**J26** D2 2 l dk grn & blk 6.00 5.75
**J27** D2 5 l dk grn & blk 360.00 275.00
**J28** D2 10 l green & black 3.00 2.10
**J29** D2 20 l green & black 4.00 3.00
**J30** D2 40 l green & black 32.50 25.00
**J31** D2 60 l green & black 27.50 15.00
**J32** D2 70 l green & black 22.50 25.00
**J33** D2 80 l green & black 17.50 15.00
**J34** D2 90 l green & black 17.50 16.00
**J35** D2 100 l green & black 22.50 15.00
**J36** D2 200 l green & black 22.50 15.00
*Nos. J25-J36 (12)* 540.00 416.35

***Perf. 11½ to 13***

**J37** D2 1 l yel grn & blk 1.75 .95
**J38** D2 2 l yel grn & blk 1.75 .95
**J39** D2 5 l yel grn & blk 4.75 1.25
**J40** D2 10 l yel grn & blk 2.75 2.00
*a.* Perf. 10-10½x11½-13 4.00
**J41** D2 20 l yel grn & blk 2.75 2.00
**J42** D2 40 l yel grn & blk 15.00 11.00
**J43** D2 60 l yel grn & blk 9.50 9.50
**J47** D2 100 l yel grn & blk 12.00 12.00
**J48** D2 200 l yel grn & blk 13.50 11.00
*Nos. J37-J48 (9)* 63.75 50.65

Footnote below #J12 applies also to #J25-J48.

D3

**1902 Engr. Wmk. 129 *Perf. 13½***

**J49** D3 1 l chocolate .30 .25
**J50** D3 2 l gray .30 .25
**J51** D3 3 l orange .30 .25
**J52** D3 5 l yel grn .30 .25
**J53** D3 10 l scarlet .30 .25
**J54** D3 20 l lilac .45 .25
**J55** D3 25 l ultra 8.00 4.00
**J56** D3 30 l dp vio .50 .30
**J57** D3 40 l dk brn .60 .50
**J58** D3 50 l red brn .60 .40
**J59** D3 1d black 1.50 .90

**Litho.**

**J60** D3 2d bronze 2.00 1.25
**J61** D3 3d silver 3.00 3.00
**J62** D3 5d gold 6.50 *9.00*
*Nos. J49-J62 (14)* 24.65 20.85

See Nos. J63-J88, J90-J93. For overprints and surcharges see Nos. 383-385, J89, RA56, RA58-RA59, NJ1-NJ31.

**Imperf., Pairs**

*J50a* D3 2 l 90.00
*J51a* D3 3 l 90.00
*J52a* D3 5 l 90.00
*J55a* D3 25 l 150.00
*J56a* D3 30 l 150.00
*J58a* D3 50 l 150.00
*J59a* D3 1d 150.00

***Serrate Roulette 13½***

**1913-26 Unwmk.**

**J63** D3 1 l green .25 .25
**J64** D3 2 l carmine .25 .25
**J65** D3 3 l vermilion .25 .25
**J66** D3 5 l green .25 .25
*a.* Imperf., pair 150.00
*b.* Double impression 60.00
*c.* "o" for "p" in lowest word 5.00 5.00
**J67** D3 10 l carmine .25 .25
**J68** D3 20 l slate .25 .25
**J69** D3 25 l ultra .25 .25
**J70** D3 30 l carmine .25 .25
**J71** D3 40 l indigo .25 .25
**J72** D3 50 l vio brn .30 .25
*a.* "o" for "p" in lowest word 25.00 20.00
**J73** D3 80 l lil brn ('24) .40 .25
**J74** D3 1d blue 8.00 1.25
*a.* 1d ultramarine 12.00 5.00
**J75** D3 2d vermilion 8.00 1.50
**J76** D3 3d carmine 8.00 1.50
**J77** D3 5d ultra 30.00 12.00
**J78** D3 5d gray bl ('26) 8.00 4.00
*Nos. J63-J78 (16)* 64.95 23.00

In 1922-23 and 1941-42 some postage due stamps were used for ordinary postage.

In 1916 Nos. J52, and J63 to J75 were surcharged for the Mount Athos District (see note after No. N166) but were never issued there. By error some of them were put in use as ordinary postage due stamps in Dec., 1924. In 1932 the balance of them was burned.

**Type of 1902 Issue**

***Perf. 13, 13½x12½, 13½x13***

**1930 Litho.**

**J79** D3 50 l dk brown .30 .30
**J80** D3 1d lt blue .30 .30
**J81** D3 2d lt red .30 .30
**J82** D3 3d rose red 27.50 25.00
**J83** D3 5d gray blue .30 .30
**J84** D3 10d gray green .30 .30
**J85** D3 15d red brown .30 .30
**J86** D3 25d light red .70 .65
*Nos. J79-J86 (8)* 30.00 27.45

**Type of 1902 Issue**

**1935 Engr. *Perf. 12½x13***

**J87** D3 50d orange .30 .30
**J88** D3 100d slate green .30 .30

**No. J70 Surcharged with New Value in Black**

**1942**

**J89** D3 50 (l) on 30 l carmine 1.50 1.50

**Type of 1902 Issue**

**1943 Wmk. 252 Litho. *Perf. 12½***

**J90** D3 10d red orange .25 .25
**J91** D3 25d ultramarine .25 .25
**J92** D3 100d black brown .25 .25
**J93** D3 200d violet .25 .25
*Nos. J90-J93 (4)* 1.00 1.00

## POSTAL TAX STAMPS

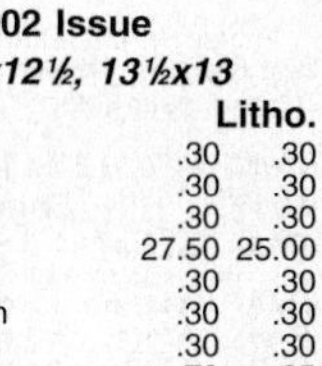

"The Tragedy of War" — PT1

***Serrate Roulette 13½***

**1914 Litho. Unwmk.**

**RA1** PT1 2 l red ('18) .30 .25
*a.* 2 l carmine .35 .25
*b.* Imperf., pair 200.00
**RA2** PT1 5 l blue .50 *.75*
*a.* Imperf., pair 250.00

Red Cross, Nurses, Wounded and Bearers
PT1a

**1915** ***Serrate Roulette 13***

**RA2B** PT1a (5 l) dk bl & red 10.00 2.00

The tax was for the Red Cross.

Women's Patriotic League Badge — PT1b

**1915, Nov.** ***Perf. 11½***

**RA2C** PT1b (5 l) dk bl & car 1.25 1.00
*d.* Horiz. pair, imperf. btwn. 55.00

The tax was for the Greek Women's Patriotic League.

## Nos. 165, 167, 170, 172-175 Surcharged in Black or Brown

a

b

In type "b" the letters, especially those in the first line, are thinner than in type "a," making them appear taller.

***Perf. 11½, 12½, 13½ and Compound***

**1917** **Engr.** **Wmk. 129**

**RA3** A11(a) 1 l on 1 l 1.50 1.50
*a.* Double surcharge 7.00
**RA4** A11(a) 1 l on 1 l (Br) 22.50 22.50
**RA5** A11(a) 1 l on 3 l .30 .30
**RA6** A11(b) 1 l on 3 l .30 .30
*a.* Triple surcharge 5.00
*b.* Dbl. surch., one invtd. 5.00
*c.* "K.M." for "K.Π." 20.00
**RA7** A11(a) 5 l on 1 l 2.00 2.00
*a.* Double surcharge 10.00
*b.* Dbl. surch., one invtd. 10.00
*c.* Inverted surcharge 12.00
**RA8** A11(a) 5 l on 20 l .65 .65
*a.* Double surcharge 12.00
*b.* Dbl. surch., one invtd. 12.00
**RA9** A11(b) 5 l on 40 l .65 .65
*a.* Imperf.
**RA10** A11(b) 5 l on 50 l .65 .65
*a.* Double surcharge 25.00
*b.* Dbl. surch., one invtd. 25.00
**RA11** A13(b) 5 l on 1d 2.25 2.25
*a.* Imperf.
*b.* Inverted surcharge 50.00
**RA12** A11(a) 10 l on 30 l .80 .80
*a.* Imperf.
*b.* Double surcharge 20.00
**RA13** A11(a) 30 l on 30 l .90 .90
*a.* Double surcharge 20.00
*Nos. RA3-RA13 (11)* 32.50 32.50

## Same Surcharge On Occupation Stamps of 1912

***Serrate Roulette 13½***

**1917** **Litho.** **Unwmk.**

**RA14** O2 (b) 5 l on 25 l pale bl .55 .55
*a.* Triple surch., one invtd. 15.00
*b.* Double surcharge 8.00
**RA15** O2 (b) 5 l on 40 l indigo .55 .55
*a.* Double surch., one invtd. 8.00
*b.* Double surcharge 8.00
**RA16** O1 (b) 5 l on 50 l dk bl .55 .55
*a.* Double surcharge 10.00
*b.* Inverted surcharge 10.00
*Nos. RA14-RA16 (3)* 1.65 1.65

There are many wrong font, omitted and misplaced letters and punctuation marks and similar varieties in the surcharges on Nos. RA3 to RA16.

## Revenue Stamps Surcharged in Brown

"Victory"

**1917**

**RA17** R1 1 l on 10 l blue .70 .70
**RA18** R1 1 l on 80 l blue .70 .70
**RA19** R1 5 l on 10 l blue 15.00 *20.00*
**RA20** R1 5 l on 60 l blue 4.00 4.00
*a.* Perf. vert. through middle 6.00 *10.00*
**RA21** R1 5 l on 80 l blue 3.00 3.00
*a.* Perf. vert. through middle 8.00 6.00
*b.* Inverted surcharge
**RA22** R1 10 l on 70 l blue 16.00 12.00
*a.* Perf. vert. through middle 6.00 *8.00*
**RA23** R1 10 l on 90 l blue 12.00 8.00
*a.* Perf. vert. through middle 20.00 *25.00*
**RA24** R1 20 l on 20 l blue 725.00 525.00
**RA25** R1 20 l on 30 l blue 4.00 4.00
**RA26** R1 20 l on 40 l blue 12.00 10.00
**RA27** R1 20 l on 50 l blue 8.00 6.00
**RA28** R1 20 l on 60 l blue 400.00 250.00
**RA29** R1 20 l on 80 l blue 40.00 32.50
**RA30** R1 20 l on 90 l blue 4.00 *6.00*
*a.* Inverted surcharge 70.00
*Nos. RA17-RA30 (14)* 1,244. 881.90

No. RA19 is known only with vertical perforation through the middle.

Counterfeits exist of Nos. RA17-RA43, used.

Surcharged in Brown or Black

**RA31** R1 1 l on 50 l vio (Bk) .80 *1.25*
**RA32** R1 5 l on 10 l bl (Br) .80 *1.25*
*a.* Inverted surcharge 80.00
*b.* Left "5" invert. 80.00
**RA33** R1 5 l on 10 l vio (Br) .80 *1.25*
**RA34** R1 10 l on 50 l vio (Br) 5.50 *10.00*
**RA35** R1 10 l on 50 l vio (Bk) 22.50 20.00
**RA36** R1 20 l on 2d bl (Bk) 8.00 8.00
*a.* Surcharged "20 lept. 30" 65.00 65.00
*b.* Horiz. pair, imperf. btwn.
*Nos. RA31-RA36 (6)* 38.40 41.75

The "T," fourth Greek letter of the denomination in the surcharge ("ΛΕΠΤ."), is normally omitted on Nos. RA31, RA34-RA36.

## Corfu Issue

Surcharged in Black

**1917**

**RA37** R1 1 l on 10 l blue 2.00 2.00
**RA38** R1 5 l on 50 l blue 55.00 *75.00*
**RA39** R1 10 l on 50 l blue 675.00 575.00
**RA40** R1 20 l on 50 l blue 2,850. 1,075.

Surcharged in Black

**RA41** R1 10 l on 50 l blue 12.00 9.00
**RA42** R1 20 l on 50 l blue 26.00 17.50
**RA43** R1 30 l on 50 l blue 17.50 12.00

Surcharged in Black

**RA44** R1 5 l on 10 l vio & red 8.00 *12.00*
*a.* "K" with serifs 12.00 *20.00*

Counterfeits exist of Nos. RA17-RA44.

Similar stamps with denominations higher than 30 lepta were for revenue use.

Wounded Soldier — PT2

**1918** ***Serrate Roulette 13½, 11½***

**RA45** PT2 5 l bl, yel & red 8.00 2.00

Overprinted

**RA46** PT2 5 l blue, yel & red 9.50 2.00

The letters are the initials of Greek words equivalent to "Patriotic Relief Institution." The proceeds were given to the Patriotic League, for the aid of disabled soldiers.

Counterfeits exist of Nos. RA45-RA46.

PT3

## Surcharge in Red

**1922** **Litho.** ***Perf. 11½***

**Dark Blue & Red**

**RA46A** PT3 5 l on 10 l *300.00* 14.00
**RA46B** PT3 5 l on 20 l 95.00 50.00
**RA46C** PT3 5 l on 50 l 275.00 240.00
**RA46D** PT3 5 l on 1d 9.50 *60.00*

Counterfeit surcharges exist. Examples of Nos. RA46A-RA46C without surcharge, each 50 cents.

Red Cross Help to Soldier and Family
PT3a

St. Demetrius
PT4

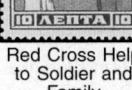

**1924** ***Perf. 11½, 13½ x 12½***

**RA47** PT3a 10 l blue, buff & red .70 .25
*a.* Imperf., pair 40.00
*b.* Horiz. pair, imperf. btwn. 40.00

Proceeds were given to the Red Cross.

**1934** ***Perf. 11½***

**RA48** PT4 20 l brown .40 .25
*a.* Horizontal pair, imperf. between 10.00
*b.* Vertical pair, imperf. between 15.00
*c.* Imperf., pair 20.00

No. RA48 was obligatory as a tax on all interior mail, including air post, mailed from Salonika.

For surcharge see No. RA69.

"Health"
PT5 PT6

**1934, Dec. 28** ***Perf. 13, 13x13½***

**RA49** PT5 10 l bl grn, org & buff .25 .25
*a.* Vert. pair, imperf. horiz.
**RA50** PT5 20 l ultra, org & buff .55 .25
**RA51** PT5 50 l grn, org & buff 2.00 .50
*Nos. RA49-RA51 (3)* 2.80 1.00

For surcharge see No. RA67.

**1935**

**RA52** PT6 10 l yel grn, org & buff .40 .25
**RA53** PT6 20 l ultra, org & buff .40 .25
**RA54** PT6 50 l grn, org & buff 1.25 .65
*Nos. RA52-RA54 (3)* 2.05 1.15

The use of #RA49-RA54 was obligatory on all mail during 4 weeks each year including Christmas, the New Year and Easter, and on parcel post packages at all times. For the benefit of the tubercular clerks and officials of the Post, Telephone and Telegraph Service.

See No. RA64. For surcharge see No. RA68.

No. 364 Overprinted in Red

**1937, Jan. 20** **Engr.** ***Perf. 13x12½***

**RA55** A36 50 l violet 1.40 .25
*a.* Inverted overprint .75 .25

No. RA55a first appeared as an error, then was issued deliberately in quantity to avoid speculation.

## Same Overprint in Blue on No. J67

**Litho.**

***Serrate Roulette 13½***

**RA56** D3 10 l carmine .80 .25
*a.* Inverted overprint 50.00

No. RA56 with blue overprint double exists only with additional black overprint of Ionian Islands No. NRA1a.

## Same Overprint in Green on No. 364

**1937** **Engr.** ***Perf. 13x12½***

**RA57** A36 50 l violet .75 .25

Nos. J66, J68 and 323 Surcharged in Blue or Black

***Serrate Roulette 13½***

**1938** **Litho.** **Unwmk.**

**RA58** D3 50 l on 5 l grn 2.40 .80
*a.* "O" for "P" in lowest word 25.00 25.00
*b.* Vert. pair, imperf. horiz. 55.00
**RA59** D3 50 l on 20 l slate 2.40 .80

**Engr.** ***Perf. 13x12½***

**RA60** A38 50 l on 20 l vio (Bk) .75 .25
*Nos. RA58-RA60 (3)* 5.55 1.85

Surcharge on No. RA60 is 14½x16½mm.

Queens Olga and Sophia
PT7

**1939, Feb. 1 Litho. *Perf. 13½x12***

**RA61** PT7 10 l brt rose, *pale rose* .25 .25
**RA62** PT7 50 l gray grn, *pale grn* .25 .25
**RA63** PT7 1d dl bl, *lt bl* .75 .25
*Nos. RA61-RA63 (3)* .75 .75

For overprints and surcharges see Nos. RA65, RA79-RA81A, NRA1-NRA3.

### "Health" Type of 1935

**1939 *Perf. 12½***

**RA64** PT6 50 l brn & buff .55 .30

No. RA62 Overprinted in Red

**1940 *Perf. 13½x12***

**RA65** PT7 50 l gray grn, *pale grn* .25 .25
*a.* Inverted overprint 35.00
*b.* Pair, one without surcharge 20.00

Proceeds of #RA64-RA65 were used for the benefit of tubercular clerks and officials of the Post, Telephone and Telegraph Service. #RA65 was used in Albania during the Greek occupation, 1940-41 without additional overprint.

No. 321 Surcharged in Carmine

**1941 Unwmk. Engr. *Perf. 13½x13***

**RA66** A36 50 l on 5 l dk grn .25 .25
*a.* Inverted surcharge 15.00

### No. RA49 and Type of 1935 Surcharged with New Value in Black

***Perf. 12½x13, 13x13½***

**Litho.**

**RA67** PT5 50 l on 10 l 2.00 2.00
**RA68** PT6 50 l on 10 l dp bl grn, dl org & buff .25 .25
*a.* Inverted surcharge 40.00
*b.* Double surcharge 40.00

> **Catalogue values for unused stamps in this section, from this point to the end of the section, are for Never Hinged items.**

No. RA48 Surcharged in Green

**1942 *Perf. 11½***

**RA69** PT4 1d on 20 l brn .40 .25
*a.* Pair, one without surcharge 25.00
*b.* Imperf., pair 32.50
*c.* Double surcharge 15.00

Nos. 321, 324 Surcharged In Red or Carmine

**1942-43 Engr. *Perf. 13½x13***

**RA70** A36 10d on 5 l ('43) .25 .25
*a.* Double surcharge 25.00
**RA71** A39 10d on 25 l (C) .25 .25
*a.* Inverted surcharge 25.00

No. 444 Overprinted in Red

**1944 Wmk. 252 Litho. *Perf. 12½***

**RA72** A110 100d black .25 .25
*a.* Double overprint 12.00
*b.* Inverted overprint 9.00

No. 443 Surcharged in Blue

**RA73** A109 5000d on 75d .25 .25
*a.* Double surcharge 25.00

No. 437 Surcharged in Blue

**RA74** A103 25000d on 2d .25 .25
*a.* Double surcharge 25.00
*b.* Additional surcharge on back 17.50

No. 399 Surcharged in Blue or Carmine

**1945 *Perf. 13½x12***

**RA75** A72 1d on 40 l .25 .25
*a.* Double surcharge 17.50
**RA76** A72 2d on 40 l (C) .25 .25
*a.* Vert. pair, one without surch. 20.00
*b.* Surcharged on back 15.00
*c.* Inverted surcharge 22.50

Tax on Nos. RA67, RA68-RA70 to RA76 aided the postal clerks' tuberculosis fund.

Nos. 396 and 399 Surcharged in Carmine

**1946**

**RA77** A72 20d on 40 l .50 .25
*a.* Pair, one without surcharge 25.00
**RA78** A69 20d on 5 l 1.25 .60

### Same Surcharge in Carmine on Nos. RA62 and RA63

**1946-47 Unwmk. *Perf. 13½x12***

**RA79** PT7 50d on 50 l ('47) .50 .25
*a.* Inverted surcharge 27.50
**RA80** PT7 50d on 1d .40 .25
*a.* Violet black surcharge 4.75 3.00

The tax on Nos. RA77 to RA80 was for the Postal Clerks' Welfare Fund.

Nos. RA65 and RA62 Surcharged in Carmine

**1947**

**RA81** 50d on 50 l (RA65) 2.00 .25
**RA81A** 50d on 50 l (RA62) 40.00 40.00

Tax for the postal clerks' tuberculosis fund.

St. Demetrius — PT8

**1948 Litho. *Perf. 12x13½***

**RA82** PT8 50d yellow brown .25 .25

Obligatory on all domestic mail. The tax was for restoration of historical monuments and churches destroyed during World War II.

Nos. 397 and 413 Surcharged in Blue

**1950 Wmk. 252**

**RA83** A70 50d on 10 l (#397) 1.25 .30
*a.* Stamp with double frame *125.00*
*b.* Surcharge reading down 22.50 22.50
**RA84** A70 50d on 10 l (#413) 1.00 .25
*a.* Surcharge reading down 22.50 22.50

Tax for the Postal Clerks' Welfare Fund.

No. 396 Surcharged in Carmine

**1951 *Perf. 13½x12***

**RA85** A69 50d on 5 l 2.00 .25

Tax for the Postal Employees' Welfare Fund.

No. 392 Surcharged in Black

**1951 Wmk. 252 *Perf. 12½x12***

**RA86** A67 50d on 3d red brn 2.00 .25
*a.* Pair, one without surcharge 30.00
*b.* "50" omitted 18.00

Tax for the postal clerks' tuberculosis fund.

No. 393 Surcharged in Carmine

**1952**

**RA87** A67 100d on 8d deep blue 1.00 .25

The tax was for the State Welfare Fund.

Ruins of Church of Phaneromeni, Zante — PT9

500d, Map & scene of destruction, Argostoli.

**1953 Wmk. 252 Litho. *Perf. 12½***

**RA88** PT9 300d indigo & pale grn 1.25 .25
**RA89** PT9 500d dk brn & buff 4.50 .70

The tax was for the reconstruction of Cephalonia, Ithaca, and Zante, Ionian Islands destroyed by earthquake.

Zeus on Macedonian Coin of Philip II — PT10

Design: 1d, Aristotle.

**1956 *Perf. 13½***

**RA90** PT10 50 l dk car rose 1.25 .25
*a.* Imperf., pair 125.00
**RA91** PT10 1d brt blue 4.50 1.25

Tax for archaeological research in Macedonia. The coin on No. RA90 portrays Zeus despite inscription of Philip's name.

## POSTAL TAX SEMI-POSTAL STAMPS

Child — PTSP1

Mother and Child — PTSP2

Virgin and Christ Child — PTSP3

***Perf. 12x13½***

**1943 Wmk. 252 Litho.**

**RAB1** PTSP1 25d + 25d bl grn .25 .25
**RAB2** PTSP2 100d + 50d rose vio .25 .25
**RAB3** PTSP3 200d + 100d red brn .25 .25
*Nos. RAB1-RAB3 (3)* .75 .75

Surtax aided needy children. These stamps were compulsory on domestic mail in Oct. 1943.

## OCCUPATION AND ANNEXATION STAMPS

During the Balkan wars, 1912-13, Greece occupied certain of the Aegean Islands and part of Western Turkey. She subsequently acquired these territories and they were known as the New Greece.

Most of the special issues for the Aegean Islands were made by order of the military commanders.

### For Use in the Aegean Islands Occupied by Greece

### CHIOS

Greece No. 221 Overprinted in Red

### *Serrate Roulette 13½*

**1913** **Litho.** **Unwmk.**

**N1** A25 25 l ultramarine 60.00 *75.00*
*a.* Inverted overprint 225.00 175.00
*b.* Greek "Λ" instead of "Δ" 225.00 175.00

## ICARIA (NICARIA)

Penelope — I1

**1912** **Unwmk.** **Litho.** ***Perf. 11½***

**N2** I1 2 l orange 1.25 *2.40*
**N3** I1 5 l blue green 1.25 *2.40*
**N4** I1 10 l rose 1.25 *2.40*
**N5** I1 25 l ultra 1.25 *2.40*
**N6** I1 50 l gray lilac 1.50 *3.25*
**N7** I1 1d dark brown 2.40 *9.00*
**N8** I1 2d claret 3.25 *15.00*
**N9** I1 5d slate 4.75 *22.50*
*Nos. N2-N9 (8)* 16.90 *59.35*

Counterfeits of Nos. N1-N15 are plentiful.

Stamps of Greece, 1911-23, Overprinted Reading Up

**1913** **On Issue of 1911-21** **Engr.**

**N10** A25 2 l car rose 40.00 30.00
**N11** A24 3 l vermilion 40.00 30.00

**Litho.**

**On Issue of 1912-23**

**N12** A24 1 l green 40.00 30.00
**N13** A24 3 l vermilion 40.00 30.00
**N14** A26 5 l green 40.00 30.00
**N15** A24 10 l carmine 40.00 30.00
*Nos. N10-N15 (6)* 240.00 180.00

## LEMNOS

Regular Issues of Greece Overprinted in Black

**On Issue of 1901**

**1912** **Wmk. 129** **Engr.** ***Perf. 13½***

**N16** A11 20 l red lilac 2.00 2.00

**On Issue of 1911-21**

**Unwmk.**

***Serrate Roulette 13½***

**N17** A24 1 l green .60 .60
**N18** A25 2 l carmine rose .70 .70
**N19** A24 3 l vermilion .70 .70
**N20** A26 5 l green .70 .70
**N21** A24 10 l car rose 1.00 1.00
**N22** A25 20 l gray lilac 1.50 1.50
**N23** A25 25 l ultra 1.75 1.75
**N24** A26 30 l car rose 3.00 3.00
**N25** A25 40 l deep blue 4.50 4.50
**N26** A26 50 l dl violet 4.50 4.50
**N27** A27 1d ultra 6.00 6.00
**N28** A27 2d vermilion 20.00 20.00
**N29** A27 3d car rose 22.50 22.50
**N30** A27 5d ultra 26.00 26.00
**N31** A27 10d deep blue 92.50 92.50
**N32** A28 25d deep blue 150.00 150.00
Never hinged 160.00

**Issues of 1912-23**

**Litho.**

**N33** A24 1 l green .60 .60
*a.* Without period after "ΕΛ-ΛΑΣ" 275.00 275.00
**N34** A26 5 l green .70 .70
**N35** A24 10 l carmine .70 .70
**N36** A25 25 l ultra 3.00 3.00
*Nos. N16-N36 (21)* 342.95 342.95

**Issues of 1911-23 Overprinted in Red**

**Engr.**

**N37** A25 2 l car rose 3.00 3.00
**N38** A24 3 l vermilion 3.00 3.00
**N39** A25 20 l gray lilac 12.00 12.00
**N40** A26 30 l car rose 6.00 6.00
**N41** A25 40 l deep blue 2.00 2.00
**N42** A26 50 l dull violet 2.00 2.00
**N43** A27 1d ultra 3.00 3.00

**Litho.**

**N44** A27 2d vermilion 42.50 42.50
**N45** A27 3d car rose 15.00 15.00
**N46** A27 5d ultra 65.00 65.00
**N47** A27 10d deep blue 120.00 100.00
**N48** A28 25d deep blue 150.00 150.00

**On Issue of 1912-23**

**Litho.**

**N49** A24 1 l green 1.00 1.00
*a.* Without period after "ΕΛ-ΛΑΣ" 150.00 150.00
**N50** A26 5 l green .40 .40
**N51** A24 10 l carmine 4.00 4.00
**N52** A25 25 l ultra 2.00 2.00
*Nos. N37-N52 (16)* 430.90 410.90

The overprint is found inverted or double on many of Nos. N16-N52. There are several varieties in the overprint: Greek "Δ" for "Λ," large Greek "Σ" or "O," and small "o."

**No. N49 with Added "Greek Administration" Overprint, as on Nos. N109-N148, in Black**

**1913**

**N52A** A24 1 l green 29.00 29.00

Counterfeits of #N16-N52A are plentiful.

## MYTILENE (LESBOS)

Turkey Nos. 162, 158 Overprinted in Blue

***Perf. 12, 13½ and Compound***

**1912** **Typo.** **Unwmk.**

**N53** A21 20pa rose 22.50 22.50
**N54** A21 10pi dull red 110.00 110.00

**On Turkey Nos. P68, 151-155, 137, 157-158 in Black**

**N55** A21 2pa olive green 2.00 2.00
**N56** A21 5pa ocher 2.00 2.00
**N57** A21 10pa blue green 2.00 2.00
**N58** A21 20pa rose 2.00 2.00
**N59** A21 1pi ultra 4.00 4.00
**N60** A21 2pi blue black 22.50 22.50
**N61** A19 2½pi dk brown 11.00 11.00
**N62** A21 5pi dk violet 22.50 22.50
**N63** A21 10pi dull red 110.00 110.00
*Nos. N55-N63 (9)* 178.00 178.00

**On Turkey Nos. 161-163, 145 in Black**

**N64** A21 10pa blue green 5.50 5.50
*a.* Double overprint 40.00 40.00
**N65** A21 20pa rose 5.50 5.50
**N66** A21 1pi ultra 5.50 5.50
**N67** A19 2pi blue black 52.50 52.50

**Nos. N55, N58, N65, N59 Surcharged in Blue or Black**

**N68** A21 25 l on 2pa 8.00 8.00
*a.* New value inverted 40.00
**N69** A21 50 l on 20pa 10.00 10.00
*b.* New value inverted 45.00
**N70** A21 1d on 20pa (N65) (Bk) 30.00 30.00
*a.* New value inverted 60.00 60.00
**N71** A21 2d on 1pi (Bk) 22.50 22.50
*a.* New value inverted

**Same Overprint on Turkey No. J49**

**N72** A19 1pi blk, *dp rose* 50.00 50.00

The overprint is found on all values reading up or down with inverted "ι" in the first word and inverted "η" in the third word.

No. N72 was only used for postage.

Counterfeits of Nos. N53-N72 are plentiful.

## SAMOS

**Issues of the Provisional Government**

Map of Samos OS1

**1912** **Unwmk.** **Typo.** ***Imperf.***

**N73** OS1 5 l gray green 20.00 7.00
**N74** OS1 10 l red 20.00 7.00
**N75** OS1 25 l blue 40.00 20.00
*a.* 25 l green (error) *500.00* *600.00*
*Nos. N73-N75 (3)* 80.00 34.00

Nos. N73-N75 exist in tète-bêche pairs. Value per set, $2,000 unused, $1,200 used.

Counterfeits exist of Nos. N73 to N75.

Hermes — OS2

**1912** **Litho.** ***Perf. 11½***

**Without Overprint**

**N76** OS2 1 l gray 3.00 1.50
**N77** OS2 5 l lt green 3.75 1.50
**N78** OS2 10 l rose 4.00 1.50
*b.* Half used as 5 l on cover *200.00*
**N79** OS2 25 l lt blue 7.00 1.50
**N80** OS2 50 l violet brn 12.50 10.00

**With Overprint**

**N81** OS2 1 l gray 1.00 *1.10*
**N82** OS2 5 l blue grn 1.00 *1.10*
**N83** OS2 10 l rose 1.75 1.50
*b.* Half used as 5 l on cover *200.00*
**N84** OS2 25 l blue 2.00 2.00
**N85** OS2 50 l violet brn 11.00 6.50
**N86** OS2 1d orange 10.00 10.00
*Nos. N76-N86 (11)* 57.00 38.20

For overprints and surcharge see Nos. N92-N103.

**Imperf., Pairs**

**Without Overprint**

*N76a* OS2 1 l 40.00
*N77a* OS2 5 l 40.00
*N78a* OS2 10 l 40.00
*N79a* OS2 25 l 40.00
*N80a* OS2 50 l 40.00

**With Overprint**

*N81a* OS2 1 l 100.00
*N82a* OS2 5 l 100.00
*N83a* OS2 10 l 100.00
*N85a* OS2 50 l 100.00 100.00

Church in Savior's Name and Fort Ruins OS3

**Manuscript Initials in Red or Black**

**1913**

**N87** OS3 1d brown (R) 16.00 14.00
**N88** OS3 2d deep blue (R) 16.00 14.00
**N89** OS3 5d gray grn (R) 30.00 25.00
**N90** OS3 10d yellow grn (R) 90.00 80.00
**N91** OS3 25d red (Bk) 80.00 67.50
*Nos. N87-N91 (5)* 232.00 200.50

Victory of the Greek fleet in 1824 and the union with Greece of Samos in 1912. The manuscript initials are those of Pres. Themistokles Sofulis.

Values the same for stamps without initials.

Exist imperf. Counterfeits of Nos. N87-N91 are plentiful.

For overprints see Nos. N104-N108.

Nos. N76 to N80 Overprinted

**1914**

**N92** OS2 1 l gray 4.00 4.00
**N93** OS2 5 l lt green 4.00 4.00
**N94** OS2 10 l rose 4.25 4.00
*a.* Double overprint 60.00
**N95** OS2 25 l lt blue 12.00 12.00
**N96** OS2 50 l violet brn 8.00 8.00
*a.* Double overprint 100.00
*Nos. N92-N96 (5)* 32.25 32.00

**Charity Issues of Greek Administration**

Nos. N81 to N86 Overprinted in Red or Black

**1915**

**N97** OS2 1 l gray (R) 20.00 20.00
*a.* Black overprint 125.00
**N98** OS2 5 l blue grn (Bk) .80 .80
*a.* Red overprint 125.00
*b.* Double overprint 125.00
**N99** OS2 10 l rose (Bk) .90 .90
*a.* Red overprint 125.00
*b.* Inverted overprint 125.00
**N100** OS2 25 l blue (Bk) .80 .80
*a.* Red overprint 125.00
**N101** OS2 50 l violet brn (Bk) 1.00 1.00
*a.* Red overprint 125.00
**N102** OS2 1d orange (R) 2.00 2.00
*a.* Inverted overprint 125.00
*b.* Black overprint 100.00
*c.* Double black overprint 150.00

No. N102 With Additional Surcharge in Black

**N103** OS2 1 l on 1d orange 15.00 15.00
*a.* Black surcharge double 160.00
*b.* Black surcharge inverted 160.00
*Nos. N97-N103 (7)* 40.50 40.50

Issue of 1913 Ovptd. in Red or Black

**1915**

**N104** OS3 1d brown (R) 20.00 20.00
**N105** OS3 2d dp blue (R) 24.00 24.00
*a.* Double overprint
**N106** OS3 5d gray grn (R) 40.00 40.00
**N107** OS3 10d yellow grn (Bk) 60.00 60.00
*a.* Inverted overprint
**N108** OS3 25d red (Bk) 750.00 750.00
*Nos. N104-N108 (5)* 894.00 894.00

Nos. N97 to N108 inclusive have an embossed control mark, consisting of a cross encircled by a Greek inscription.

Most examples of Nos. N104-N108 lack the initials.

Counterfeits of Nos. N104-N108 are plentiful.

## FOR USE IN PARTS OF TURKEY OCCUPIED BY GREECE (NEW GREECE)

Regular Issues of Greece Overprinted

### Black Overprint Meaning "Greek Administration" On Issue of 1901

**1912 Wmk. 129 Engr.** *Perf. 13½*

| | | | | |
|---|---|---|---|---|
| **N109** | A11 | 20 l red lilac | 3.00 | 3.00 |

**On Issue of 1911-21**

**Unwmk.**

*Serrate Roulette 13½*

| | | | | |
|---|---|---|---|---|
| **N110** | A24 | 1 l green | 1.00 | 1.00 |
| **N111** | A25 | 2 l car rose | 1.00 | 1.00 |
| **N112** | A24 | 3 l vermilion | 1.00 | 1.00 |
| **N113** | A26 | 5 l green | 1.00 | 1.00 |
| **N114** | A24 | 10 l car rose | 2.00 | 2.00 |
| **N115** | A25 | 20 l gray lilac | 3.00 | 3.00 |
| **N116** | A25 | 25 l ultra | 3.00 | 3.00 |
| **N117** | A26 | 30 l car rose | 3.00 | 3.00 |
| **N118** | A25 | 40 l deep blue | 5.00 | 5.00 |
| **N119** | A26 | 50 l dl violet | 5.00 | 5.00 |
| **N120** | A27 | 1d ultra | 12.00 | 12.00 |
| **N121** | A27 | 2d vermilion | 50.00 | 25.00 |
| **N122** | A27 | 3d car rose | 60.00 | 35.00 |
| **N123** | A27 | 5d ultra | 25.00 | 35.00 |
| **N124** | A27 | 10d deep blue | 275.00 | 275.00 |
| **N125** | A28 | 25d dp bl, ovpt. horiz. | 340.00 | 340.00 |

**On Issue of 1913-23**

**Litho.**

| | | | | |
|---|---|---|---|---|
| **N126** | A24 | 1 l green | 1.00 | 1.00 |
| *b.* | | Without period after "ΕΛ-ΛΑΣ" | 150.00 | |
| **N127** | A26 | 5 l green | 1.00 | 1.00 |
| **N128** | A24 | 10 l carmine | 3.00 | 3.00 |
| **N129** | A25 | 25 l blue | 5.00 | 5.00 |
| | | *Nos. N109-N129 (21)* | 800.00 | 760.00 |

### Red Overprint

**On Issue of 1911-21**

**Engr.**

| | | | | |
|---|---|---|---|---|
| **N130** | A24 | 1 l green | 1.00 | 1.00 |
| **N131** | A25 | 2 l car rose | 15.00 | 13.00 |
| **N132** | A24 | 3 l vermilion | 15.00 | 13.00 |
| **N133** | A26 | 5 l green | 1.00 | 1.00 |
| **N134** | A25 | 20 l gray lilac | 5.00 | 5.00 |
| **N135** | A25 | 25 l ultra | 100.00 | 95.00 |
| **N136** | A26 | 30 l car rose | 110.00 | 110.00 |
| **N137** | A25 | 40 l deep blue | 2.00 | 3.00 |
| **N138** | A26 | 50 l dl violet | 3.00 | 3.00 |
| **N139** | A27 | 1d ultra | 20.00 | 15.00 |
| **N140** | A27 | 2d vermilion | 95.00 | 100.00 |
| **N141** | A27 | 3d car rose | 40.00 | 50.00 |
| **N142** | A27 | 5d ultra | 550.00 | 400.00 |
| **N143** | A27 | 10d deep blue | 35.00 | 30.00 |
| **N144** | A28 | 25d dp bl, ovpt. horiz. | 55.00 | 55.00 |
| *a.* | | Vertical overprint | 400.00 | 400.00 |

**On Issue of 1913-23**

**Litho.**

| | | | | |
|---|---|---|---|---|
| **N145** | A24 | 1 l green | 10.00 | 12.00 |
| *a.* | | Without period after "ΕΛ-ΛΑΣ" | 450.00 | |
| **N146** | A26 | 5 l green | 2.00 | 1.00 |
| **N147** | A24 | 10 l carmine | 60.00 | 60.00 |
| **N148** | A25 | 25 l blue | 3.00 | 2.00 |
| | | *Nos. N130-N148 (19)* | 1,122. | 969.00 |

The normal overprint is vertical, reading upward on N109-N124, N126-N143, N145-N148. It is often double or reading downward. There are numerous broken, missing and wrong font letters with a Greek "Λ" instead of "Δ" as the first letter of the second word.

Counterfeits exist of Nos. N109-N148.

Cross of Constantine
O1

Eagle of Zeus
O2

**1912** **Litho.**

| | | | | |
|---|---|---|---|---|
| **N150** | O1 | 1 l brown | .25 | .25 |
| **N151** | O2 | 2 l red | .25 | .25 |
| *a.* | | 2 l rose | .80 | .60 |
| **N153** | O2 | 3 l orange | .30 | .25 |
| **N154** | O1 | 5 l green | 1.25 | .25 |
| **N155** | O1 | 10 l rose red | 10.00 | .25 |
| **N156** | O1 | 20 l violet | 21.00 | 4.50 |
| **N157** | O2 | 25 l pale blue | 4.75 | 1.25 |
| **N158** | O1 | 30 l gray grn | 75.00 | 3.25 |
| **N159** | O2 | 40 l indigo | 15.00 | 8.75 |
| **N160** | O1 | 50 l dark blue | 8.00 | 4.50 |
| **N161** | O2 | 1d violet brn | 8.75 | 4.50 |
| **N162** | O1 | 2d gray brn | 60.00 | 12.00 |
| **N163** | O2 | 3d dull blue | 175.00 | 27.50 |
| **N164** | O1 | 5d gray | 175.00 | 32.50 |
| **N165** | O2 | 10d carmine | 250.00 | *350.00* |
| **N166** | O1 | 25d gray blk | 250.00 | *350.00* |
| | | *Nos. N150-N166 (16)* | 1,054. | *800.00* |

Occupation of Macedonia, Epirus and some of the Aegean Islands.

Sold only in New Greece.

Dangerous forgeries of #N165-N166 exist.

In 1916 some stamps of this issue were overprinted in Greek: "Ι (era) Κοινοτισ Αγ (iou) Ορουσ" for the Mount Athos Monastery District. They were never placed in use and most of them were destroyed.

For surcharges and overprints see Nos. 267-276A, RA14-RA16, Thrace 31-33.

**Imperf., Pairs**

**Without Overprint**

| | | | |
|---|---|---|---|
| *N150a* | O1 | 1 l | 500.00 |
| *N151b* | O2 | 2 l | 500.00 |
| *N153a* | O2 | 3 l | 500.00 |
| *N154a* | O1 | 5 l | 200.00 |
| *N155a* | O1 | 10 l | 200.00 |
| *N156a* | O1 | 20 l | 1,750. |
| *N157a* | O2 | 25 l | 1,750. |
| *N158a* | O1 | 30 l | 1,750. |
| *N159a* | O2 | 40 l | 1,750. |
| *N163a* | O2 | 3d | *2,500.* |

## CAVALLA

Bulgaria Nos. 89-97 Surcharged in Red

**1913 Unwmk. Engr.** *Perf. 12*

| | | | | |
|---|---|---|---|---|
| **N167** | A20 | 5 l on 1s | *22.50* | *22.50* |
| **N169** | A25 | 10 l on 15s | *65.00* | *65.00* |
| **N170** | A26 | 10 l on 25s | *32.50* | *32.50* |
| **N171** | A21 | 15 l on 2s | *65.00* | *65.00* |
| **N172** | A22 | 20 l on 3s | *65.00* | *65.00* |
| **N173** | A23 | 25 l on 5s | *20.00* | *12.00* |
| **N174** | A24 | 50 l on 10s | *35.00* | *22.50* |
| **N175** | A25 | 1d on 15s | *225.00* | *200.00* |
| **N176** | A27 | 1d on 30s | *95.00* | *95.00* |
| **N177** | A28 | 1d on 50s | *140.00* | *140.00* |

**Blue Surcharge**

| | | | | |
|---|---|---|---|---|
| **N178** | A24 | 50 l on 10s | *20.00* | *20.00* |
| | | *Nos. N167-N178 (11)* | *785.00* | *739.50* |

The counterfeits and reprints of Nos. N167-N178 are difficult to distinguish from originals. Many overprint varieties exist.

Some specialists question the status of Nos. N167-N178.

## DEDEAGATCH

### (Alexandroupolis)

D1-(10 lepta)

**1913 Unwmk. Typeset** *Perf. 11½*

**Control Mark in Red**

| | | | | |
|---|---|---|---|---|
| **N179** | D1 | 5 l black | 40.00 | 30.00 |
| **N180** | D1 | 10 l black | 5.50 | 4.00 |
| **N181** | D1 | 25 l black | 6.50 | 4.50 |
| *a.* | | Sheet of 8 | 125.00 | 125.00 |
| | | *Nos. N179-N181 (3)* | 52.00 | 38.50 |

Nos. N179-N181 issued without gum in sheets of 8, consisting of one 5 l, three 10 l normal, one 10 l inverted, three 25 l and one blank. The sheet yields se-tenant pairs of 5 l & 10 l, 10 l & 25 l; tete beche pairs of 5 l & 10 l, 10 l & 25 l and 10 l & 10 l.

Also issued imperf., value $200 unused, $150 canceled.

The 5 l reads "ΠΙΝΤΑ ΕΠΤΑ; the 10 l is illustrated; the 25 l carries the numeral "25."

Bulgaria Nos. 89-90, 92-93, 95 Surcharged

**1913 Red Surcharge** *Perf. 12*

| | | | | |
|---|---|---|---|---|
| **N182** | A20 | 5 l on 1s | 65.00 | 42.50 |
| **N183** | A26 | 1d on 25s | 80.00 | 52.50 |

**Blue Surcharge**

| | | | | |
|---|---|---|---|---|
| **N184** | A24 | 10 l on 10s | 30.00 | 25.00 |
| **N185** | A23 | 25 l on 5s | 35.00 | 25.00 |
| **N187** | A21 | 50 l on 2s | 65.00 | 42.50 |
| | | *Nos. N182-N185,N187 (5)* | 275.00 | 187.50 |

The surcharges on Nos. N182 to N187 are printed from a setting of eight, which was used for all, with the necessary changes of value. No. 6 in the setting has a Greek "Λ" instead of "Δ" for the third letter of the third word of the surcharge.

The 25 l surcharge also exists on 8 examples of the 25s, Bulgaria No. 95.

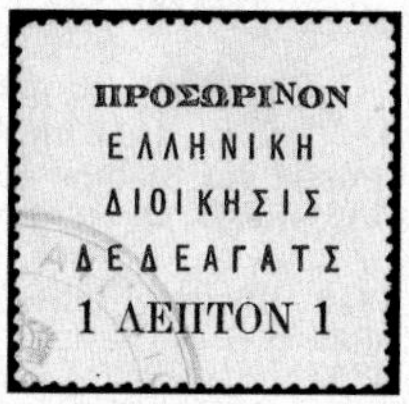


D2

**1913, Sept. 15 Typeset** *Perf. 11½*

**Control Mark in Blue**

| | | | | |
|---|---|---|---|---|
| **N188** | D2 | 1 l blue | *200.00* | 65.00 |
| **N189** | D2 | 2 l blue | *200.00* | 65.00 |
| **N190** | D2 | 3 l blue | *200.00* | 65.00 |
| **N191** | D2 | 5 l blue | *200.00* | 65.00 |
| **N192** | D2 | 10 l blue | *200.00* | 65.00 |
| **N193** | D2 | 25 l blue | *200.00* | 65.00 |
| **N194** | D2 | 40 l blue | *200.00* | 65.00 |
| **N195** | D2 | 50 l blue | *200.00* | 65.00 |
| | | *Nos. N188-N195 (8)* | *1,600.* | |

Issued without gum in sheets of 8 containing all values.

D3

**1913, Sept. 25** **Typeset**

**Control Mark in Blue**

| | | | | |
|---|---|---|---|---|
| **N196** | D3 | 1 l blue, *gray blue* | *160.00* | 50.00 |
| **N197** | D3 | 5 l blue, *gray blue* | *160.00* | 50.00 |
| **N198** | D3 | 10 l blue, *gray blue* | *160.00* | 50.00 |
| **N199** | D3 | 25 l blue, *gray blue* | *160.00* | 50.00 |
| **N200** | D3 | 30 l blue, *gray blue* | *160.00* | 50.00 |
| **N201** | D3 | 50 l blue, *gray blue* | *160.00* | 50.00 |
| | | *Nos. N196-N201 (6)* | *960.00* | |

Nos. N196 to N201 were issued without gum in sheets of six containing all values.

Counterfeits of Nos. N182-N201 are plentiful.

## FOR USE IN NORTH EPIRUS (ALBANIA)

Greek Stamps of 1937-38 Overprinted in Black

*Perf. 13½x12, 12x13½*

**1940 Litho. Wmk. 252**

| | | | | |
|---|---|---|---|---|
| **N202** | A69 | 5 l brn red & bl | .25 | .25 |
| *a.* | | Inverted overprint | 55.00 | |
| **N203** | A70 | 10 l bl & brn red (No. 413) | .25 | .25 |
| *a.* | | Double impression of frame | *160.00* | |
| **N204** | A71 | 20 l blk & grn | .25 | .25 |
| *a.* | | Inverted overprint | 55.00 | |
| **N205** | A72 | 40 l grn & blk | .25 | .25 |
| *a.* | | Inverted overprint | 55.00 | |
| **N206** | A73 | 50 l brn & blk | .25 | .25 |
| **N207** | A74 | 80 l ind & yel brn | .40 | .40 |
| **N208** | A67 | 1d green | .40 | .40 |
| *a.* | | Inverted overprint | *100.00* | |
| **N209** | A75 | 2d ultra | .40 | .40 |
| **N210** | A67 | 3d red brn | .80 | .80 |
| **N211** | A76 | 5d red | .80 | .80 |
| **N212** | A77 | 6d ol brn | .80 | .80 |
| **N213** | A78 | 7d dk brn | .80 | .80 |
| **N214** | A67 | 8d deep blue | .80 | .80 |
| **N215** | A79 | 10d red brn | 2.00 | 2.00 |
| **N216** | A80 | 15d green | 2.00 | 2.00 |
| **N217** | A81 | 25d dark blue | 2.75 | *4.00* |
| *a.* | | Inverted overprint | *90.00* | |

**Engr.**

**Unwmk.**

| | | | | |
|---|---|---|---|---|
| **N218** | A84 | 30d org brn | 5.00 | *8.00* |
| | | *Nos. N202-N218 (17)* | 18.20 | 22.45 |

### Same Overprinted in Carmine on National Youth Issue

**1941 Litho.** *Perf. 12½, 13½x12½*

| | | | | |
|---|---|---|---|---|
| **N219** | A93 | 3d sil, dp ultra & red | 1.00 | 1.00 |
| **N220** | A94 | 5d dk bl & blk | 3.75 | 3.75 |
| **N221** | A94 | 10d red org & blk | 6.00 | 6.00 |
| **N222** | A94 | 15d dk grn & blk | 26.00 | 26.00 |
| **N223** | A94 | 20d lake & blk | 15.00 | 12.00 |
| **N224** | A94 | 25d dk bl & blk | 15.00 | 12.00 |
| **N225** | A94 | 30d rose vio & blk | 15.00 | 12.00 |
| **N226** | A94 | 50d lake & blk | 15.00 | 12.00 |
| **N227** | A94 | 75d dk bl, brn & gold | 20.00 | 12.00 |
| **N228** | A93 | 100d sil, dp ultra & red | 20.00 | 15.00 |
| *a.* | | Inverted overprint | *350.00* | |
| | | *Nos. N219-N228 (10)* | 136.75 | 111.75 |

### Same Overprint in Carmine on National Youth Air Post Stamps

| | | | | |
|---|---|---|---|---|
| **N229** | AP25 | 2d red org & blk | 1.10 | 1.10 |
| *a.* | | Inverted overprint | *150.00* | |
| **N230** | AP25 | 4d dk grn & blk | 4.50 | 4.50 |
| *a.* | | Inverted overprint | *150.00* | |
| **N231** | AP25 | 6d lake & blk | 6.50 | 6.50 |
| *a.* | | Inverted overprint | *150.00* | |
| **N232** | AP25 | 8d dk bl & blk | 6.50 | 6.50 |
| **N233** | AP25 | 16d rose vio & blk | 11.00 | 6.50 |
| **N234** | AP25 | 32d red org & blk | 15.00 | 12.00 |
| **N235** | AP25 | 45d dk grn & blk | 15.00 | 12.00 |
| **N236** | AP25 | 55d lake & blk | 15.00 | 12.00 |
| **N237** | AP25 | 65d dk bl & blk | 15.00 | 12.00 |
| **N238** | AP25 | 100d rose vio & blk | 20.00 | 15.00 |
| | | *Nos. N229-N238 (10)* | 109.60 | 88.10 |

Some specialists have questioned the status of Nos. N230a and N231a.

For other stamps issued by Greece for use in occupied parts of Epirus and Thrace, see the catalogue listings of those countries.

**Catalogue values for unused stamps in this section, from this point to the end of the section, are for Never Hinged items.**

## FOR USE IN THE DODECANESE ISLANDS

Greece, No. 472C, with Additional Overprint in Carmine or Silver

**1947 Wmk. 252 Litho.** *Perf. 12½*

| | | | | |
|---|---|---|---|---|
| **N239** | A113 | 10d on 2,000d (C) | 2.40 | 2.40 |
| **N240** | A113 | 10d on 2,000d (S) | 2.40 | 2.40 |

These stamps sold for 5 lire (100 drachmas) and paid postage for that amount.

### King George II Memorial Issue

Greece, Nos. 484 and 485, With Additional Overprint in Black

**1947 Engr. *Perf. 12½x12***

| | | | | |
|---|---|---|---|---|
| N241 | A67 | 50d on 1d green | 1.60 | 1.60 |
| N242 | A67 | 250d on 3d red brown | 1.60 | 1.60 |

The letters are initials of the Greek words for "Military Administration of the Dodecanese."

Greece, Nos. 501 and 502 Overprinted in Carmine

**1947 Wmk. 252 Litho. *Perf. 12½***

| | | | | |
|---|---|---|---|---|
| N243 | A111 | 20d on 500d dk ol | 2.40 | 2.40 |
| N244 | A104 | 30d on 5d lt bl grn | 2.40 | 2.40 |

Greece, Nos. 437, 406, 407 and 445, Surcharged in Black or Carmine

**1947 *Perf. 12½, 13½x12***

| | | | | |
|---|---|---|---|---|
| N245 | A103 | 50d on 2d | 2.40 | 2.40 |
| | | **Engr.** | | |
| N246 | A79 | 250d on 10d | 7.25 | 7.25 |
| N247 | A80 | 400d on 15d (C) | 8.75 | 8.75 |
| *a.* | | Inverted surcharge | 150.00 | |
| | | **Litho.** | | |
| N248 | A110 | 1000d on 200 (C) | 5.50 | 5.50 |
| *a.* | | Imprint omitted | 40.00 | |
| | | *Nos. N245-N248 (4)* | 23.90 | 23.90 |

## POSTAGE DUE STAMPS

### FOR USE IN PARTS OF TURKEY OCCUPIED BY GREECE (NEW GREECE)

Postage Due Stamps of Greece, 1902, Overprinted

**1912 Wmk. 129 Engr. *Perf. 13½***

**Black Overprint**

| | | | | |
|---|---|---|---|---|
| NJ1 | D3 | 1 l chocolate | .60 | .60 |
| NJ2 | D3 | 2 l gray | .60 | .60 |
| NJ3 | D3 | 3 l orange | .60 | .60 |
| NJ4 | D3 | 5 l yel grn | 1.00 | 1.00 |
| NJ5 | D3 | 10 l scarlet | 1.50 | 1.50 |
| NJ6 | D3 | 20 l lilac | 1.50 | 1.50 |
| NJ7 | D3 | 30 l dp vio | 3.00 | 3.00 |
| NJ8 | D3 | 40 l dk brn | 5.00 | 5.00 |
| NJ9 | D3 | 50 l red brn | 8.00 | 8.00 |
| NJ10 | D3 | 1d black | 45.00 | 45.00 |
| NJ11 | D3 | 2d bronze | 70.00 | 80.00 |
| NJ12 | D3 | 3d silver | 140.00 | 120.00 |
| NJ13 | D3 | 5d gold | 225.00 | 250.00 |
| | | *Nos. NJ1-NJ13 (13)* | 501.80 | 516.80 |

**Red Overprint**

| | | | | |
|---|---|---|---|---|
| NJ14 | D3 | 1 l chocolate | 1.00 | 1.00 |
| NJ15 | D3 | 2 l gray | 1.00 | 1.00 |
| NJ16 | D3 | 3 l orange | 1.00 | 1.00 |
| NJ17 | D3 | 5 l yel grn | 1.00 | 1.00 |
| NJ18 | D3 | 10 l scar, down | 15.00 | 15.00 |
| NJ19 | D3 | 20 l lilac | 1.00 | 1.00 |
| NJ20 | D3 | 30 l dp vio | 5.00 | 5.00 |
| NJ21 | D3 | 40 l dk brn | 1.50 | 1.50 |
| NJ22 | D3 | 50 l red brn | 1.50 | 1.50 |
| NJ23 | D3 | 1d black | 10.00 | 10.00 |
| NJ24 | D3 | 2d bronze | 20.00 | 20.00 |
| NJ25 | D3 | 3d silver | 25.00 | 25.00 |
| NJ26 | D3 | 5d gold | 60.00 | 60.00 |
| | | *Nos. NJ14-NJ26 (13)* | 143.00 | 143.00 |

The normal position of the overprint is reading upward but it is often reversed. Some of the varieties of lettering which occur on the postage stamps are also found on the postage due stamps. Double overprints exist on some denominations.

### FOR USE IN NORTH EPIRUS (ALBANIA)

Postage Due Stamps of Greece, 1930, Surcharged or Overprinted in Black

a

b

***Perf. 13, 13x12½***

**1940 Litho. Unwmk.**

| | | | | |
|---|---|---|---|---|
| NJ27 | D3(a) | 50 l on 25d lt red | .80 | .80 |
| NJ28 | D3(b) | 2d light red | 1.25 | 1.40 |
| *a.* | | Inverted overprint | 52.50 | |
| NJ29 | D3(b) | 5d blue gray | .80 | 1.25 |
| NJ30 | D3(b) | 10d green | 1.25 | 1.40 |
| NJ31 | D3(b) | 15d red brown | 1.25 | 1.60 |
| | | *Nos. NJ27-NJ31 (5)* | 5.35 | 6.45 |

## POSTAL TAX STAMPS

### FOR USE IN NORTH EPIRUS (ALBANIA)

**Postal Tax Stamps of Greece, Nos. RA61-RA63, Overprinted Type "b" in Black**

**1940 Unwmk. Litho. *Perf. 13½x12***

| | | | | |
|---|---|---|---|---|
| NRA1 | PT7 | 10 l | .25 | .30 |
| NRA2 | PT7 | 50 l | .40 | .65 |
| *a.* | | Inverted overprint | 55.00 | |
| NRA3 | PT7 | 1d | .95 | 1.40 |
| | | *Nos. NRA1-NRA3 (3)* | 1.60 | 2.35 |

# MOUNT ATHOS

**Catalogue values for unused stamps in this section are for Never Hinged items.**

All stamps also are available for postage in Greece.

Nikiforos Fokas A1

Ioannis Tsimiskis A2

Map of Mount Athos A3

Church of the Protaton A4

Staff of Protepistates — A5

**Litho. With Foil Application**

***Perf. 13¼x13***

**2008, May 16 Unwmk.**

| | | | | |
|---|---|---|---|---|
| 1 | A1 | 40c multi + label | 1.25 | 1.25 |
| 2 | A2 | 60c multi + label | 1.90 | 1.90 |
| 3 | A3 | 70c multi + label | 2.25 | 2.25 |
| 4 | A4 | €2 multi + label | 6.50 | 6.50 |
| 5 | A5 | €4 multi + label | 13.00 | 13.00 |
| | | *Nos. 1-5 (5)* | 24.90 | 24.90 |

Megiste Lavra Monastery A6

Vatopedis Monastery A7

Koutloumousiou Monastery — A8

Iveron Monastery A9

Chilandari Monastery A10

**2008, June 13**

| | | | | |
|---|---|---|---|---|
| 6 | A6 | 57c multi + label | 1.75 | 1.75 |
| 7 | A7 | 70c multi + label | 2.25 | 2.25 |
| 8 | A8 | €1 multi + label | 3.25 | 3.25 |
| 9 | A9 | €1.85 multi + label | 5.75 | 5.75 |
| 10 | A10 | €3 multi + label | 9.25 | 9.25 |
| | | *Nos. 6-10 (5)* | 22.25 | 22.25 |

Pantokrator Monastery — A11

Xeropotamou Monastery — A12

Karakallou Monastery A13

Zographou Monastery A14

Docheiariou Monastery — A15

**2008, July 4**

| | | | | |
|---|---|---|---|---|
| 11 | A11 | 57c multi + label | 1.90 | 1.90 |
| 12 | A12 | 70c multi + label | 2.25 | 2.25 |
| 13 | A13 | 80c multi + label | 2.50 | 2.50 |
| 14 | A14 | €1.50 multi + label | 4.75 | 4.75 |
| 15 | A15 | €3.50 multi + label | 11.00 | 11.00 |
| | | *Nos. 11-15 (5)* | 22.40 | 22.40 |

Agiou Pavlou Monastery A16

Dionysiou Monastery A17

Stavronikita Monastery — A18

Simonos Petras Monastery A19

Philotheou Monastery A20

**2008, Aug. 22**

| | | | | |
|---|---|---|---|---|
| **16** | A16 | 57c multi + label | 1.75 | 1.75 |
| **17** | A17 | 70c multi + label | 2.10 | 2.10 |
| **18** | A18 | €1.20 multi + label | 3.50 | 3.50 |
| **19** | A19 | €1.80 multi + label | 5.25 | 5.25 |
| **20** | A20 | €3 multi + label | 9.00 | 9.00 |
| | | *Nos. 16-20 (5)* | 21.60 | 21.60 |

Xenophontos Monastery — A21

Gregoriou Monastery A22

Esphigmenou Monastery — A23

Konstamonitou Monastery — A24

Panteleimonos-Rossikou Monastery — A25

**2008, Nov. 7**

| | | | | |
|---|---|---|---|---|
| **21** | A21 | 57c multi + label | 1.50 | 1.50 |
| **22** | A22 | 70c multi + label | 1.90 | 1.90 |
| **23** | A23 | 85c multi + label | 2.25 | 2.25 |
| **24** | A24 | €2.42 multi + label | 6.25 | 6.25 |
| **25** | A25 | €3 multi + label | 7.75 | 7.75 |
| | | *Nos. 21-25 (5)* | 19.65 | 19.65 |

Monk Ringing Talanton A26

Monk in Library A27

Protepistate Konstantinos Prigoumenos Vatopaidinos — A28

Monk Sculpting Wood A29

Monk Packing Mule A30

**2009, May 11**

| | | | | |
|---|---|---|---|---|
| **26** | A26 | 57c multi + label | 1.60 | 1.60 |
| **27** | A27 | 70c multi + label | 2.00 | 2.00 |
| **28** | A28 | 85c multi + label | 2.40 | 2.40 |
| **29** | A29 | €2.42 multi + label | 6.75 | 6.75 |
| **30** | A30 | €3 multi + label | 8.50 | 8.50 |
| | | *Nos. 26-30 (5)* | 21.25 | 21.25 |

Monk Sewing Clothes A31

Monk Binding Book A32

Monk Cooking A33

Monk Watering Flowers A34

Monk Hiking A35

**2009, June 12**

| | | | | |
|---|---|---|---|---|
| **31** | A31 | 57c multi + label | 1.60 | 1.60 |
| **32** | A32 | 70c multi + label | 2.00 | 2.00 |
| **33** | A33 | €1 multi + label | 2.75 | 2.75 |
| **34** | A34 | €1.85 multi + label | 5.25 | 5.25 |
| **35** | A35 | €3.30 multi + label | 9.25 | 9.25 |
| | | *Nos. 31-35 (5)* | 20.85 | 20.85 |

Olive Collecting, by Polykleitos Rengos A36

Old Apostolos with His Lines, by Fotis Kontoglou A37

Shipwright, by Kontoglou A38

Icon Painter on Mount Athos, by Theodoros Rallis A39

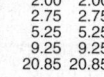

Monk at Study, by Dimitris Gioldasis A40

**2009, Sept. 18**

| | | | | |
|---|---|---|---|---|
| **36** | A36 | 57c multi + label | 1.75 | 1.75 |
| **37** | A37 | 70c multi + label | 2.10 | 2.10 |
| **38** | A38 | 80c multi + label | 2.40 | 2.40 |
| **39** | A39 | €1 multi + label | 3.00 | 3.00 |
| **40** | A40 | €4.50 multi + label | 13.50 | 13.50 |
| | | *Nos. 36-40 (5)* | 22.75 | 22.75 |

Holy Epistiasia of the Holy Community of Mount Athos, 1938 — A41

Athonias School, 1936 — A42

Archimandrite Gabriel Celebrating Feast of the Holy Monastery of Xenophon, 1967 — A43

Holy Community of Mount Athos, 1951 — A44

Archimandrite Vyssarion, 1998 — A45

**2009, Nov. 17** *Perf. 13½*

| | | | | |
|---|---|---|---|---|
| **41** | A41 | 58c multi + label | 1.75 | 1.75 |
| **42** | A42 | 70c multi + label | 2.10 | 2.10 |
| **43** | A43 | €1.20 multi + label | 3.75 | 3.75 |
| **44** | A44 | €1.85 multi + label | 5.50 | 5.50 |
| **45** | A45 | €3 multi + label | 9.00 | 9.00 |
| | | *Nos. 41-45 (5)* | 22.10 | 22.10 |

Flora and Fauna A46

Designs: No. 46, 58c, Pansy. No. 47, 72c, Judas tree. No. 48, €1, Arbutus. No. 49, €2.43, European tree frog. No. 50, €3, Heath.

### Litho. With Foil Application

**2010, May 11** *Perf. 13½x13*

### Stamps + Label

**46-50** A46 Set of 5 18.50 18.50

**2010, June 21** **Stamps + Label**

Designs: No. 51, 50c, Silene orphanidis. No. 52, 58c, Nightingale. No. 53, 72c, European roe deer. No. 54, €2, Laurel. No. 55, €3.50, European green lizard.

**51-55** A46 Set of 5 18.50 18.50

### Flora and Fauna Type of 2010

Designs: No. 56, 58c, Two-tailed pasha butterfly. No. 57, 72c, Golden eagle. No. 58, €1, Mountain tea (white flowers and mountain). No. 59, €2.43, Amaranth (plant). No. 60, €3, Mediterranean monk seal.

### Stamps + Label

### Litho. With Foil Application

**2010, Sept. 16** *Perf. 13½x13*

**56-60** A46 Set of 5 21.50 21.50

**2010, Nov. 16** **Stamps + Label**

Designs: No. 61, 50c, Chestnut. No. 62, 58c, Fir tree. No. 63, 72c, Sage. No. 64, €2, Wild boar. No. 65, €3.50, Spiny puffball mushroom.

**61-65** A46 Set of 5 19.50 19.50

A47

A48

A49

A50

A51

Illuminated Greek Letters — A52

### Litho. With Foil Application

**2011, Mar. 18** *Perf. 13½x13*

| | | | | |
|---|---|---|---|---|
| **66** | A47 | 50c multi + label | 1.50 | 1.50 |
| **67** | A48 | 60c multi + label | 1.75 | 1.75 |
| **68** | A49 | 75c multi + label | 2.25 | 2.25 |
| **69** | A50 | €1 multi + label | 3.00 | 3.00 |
| **70** | A51 | €1.50 multi + label | 4.50 | 4.50 |
| **71** | A52 | €2.15 multi + label | 6.25 | 6.25 |
| | | *Nos. 66-71 (6)* | 19.25 | 19.25 |

A53

A54

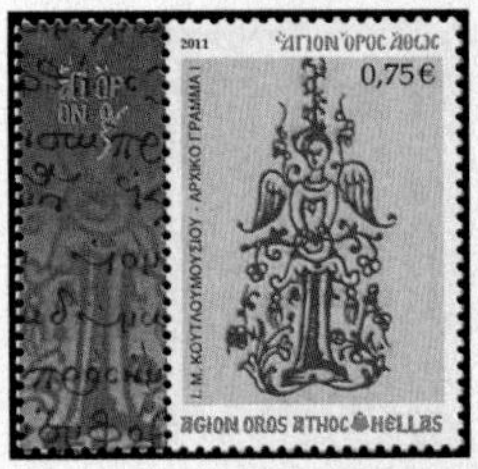

A55

A56

A57

Illuminated Greek Letters — A58

**2011, May 17**

| | | | | |
|---|---|---|---|---|
| **72** | A53 | 50c multi + label | 1.50 | 1.50 |
| **73** | A54 | 60c multi + label | 1.75 | 1.75 |
| **74** | A55 | 75c multi + label | 2.25 | 2.25 |
| **75** | A56 | €1 multi + label | 3.00 | 3.00 |
| **76** | A57 | €1.47 multi + label | 4.25 | 4.25 |
| **77** | A58 | €2 multi + label | 5.75 | 5.75 |
| | | *Nos. 72-77 (6)* | 18.50 | 18.50 |

A59

A60

A61

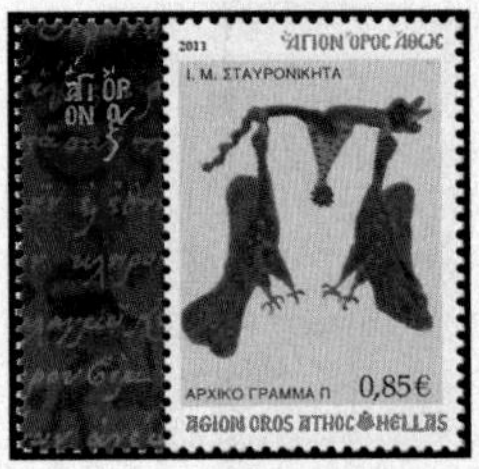

A62

A63

Illuminated Greek Letters — A64

**2011, July 18**

| | | | | |
|---|---|---|---|---|
| **78** | A59 | 50c multi + label | 1.50 | 1.50 |
| **79** | A60 | 60c multi + label | 1.75 | 1.75 |
| **80** | A61 | 75c multi + label | 2.25 | 2.25 |
| **81** | A62 | 85c multi + label | 2.50 | 2.50 |
| **82** | A63 | €1.47 multi + label | 4.25 | 4.25 |
| **83** | A64 | €2 multi + label | 5.75 | 5.75 |
| | | *Nos. 78-83 (6)* | 18.00 | 18.00 |

A65

A66

A67

A68

A69

Illuminated Greek Letters — A70

**2011, Dec. 15**

| | | | | | |
|---|---|---|---|---|---|
| **84** | A65 | 50c | multi + label | 1.40 | 1.40 |
| **85** | A66 | 60c | multi + label | 1.60 | 1.60 |
| **86** | A67 | 85c | multi + label | 2.25 | 2.25 |
| **87** | A68 | €1 | multi + label | 2.60 | 2.60 |
| **88** | A69 | €1.47 | multi + label | 4.00 | 4.00 |
| **89** | A70 | €2 | multi + label | 5.25 | 5.25 |
| | | | *Nos. 84-89 (6)* | 17.10 | 17.10 |

Megiste Lavra Monastery Katholikon A71

Chilandari Monastery Katholikon A72

Iveron Monastery Katholikon A73

Dionysiou Monastery Katholikon A74

Vatopadi Monastery Katholikon A75

Protaton Katholikon A76

**2012, Jan. 26** ***Perf. 13½x13***

| | | | | | |
|---|---|---|---|---|---|
| **90** | A71 | 50c | multi + label | 1.40 | 1.40 |
| **91** | A72 | 60c | multi + label | 1.60 | 1.60 |
| **92** | A73 | 75c | multi + label | 2.00 | 2.00 |
| **93** | A74 | 85c | multi + label | 2.25 | 2.25 |
| **94** | A75 | €1 | multi + label | 2.60 | 2.60 |
| **95** | A76 | €2.20 | multi + label | 5.75 | 5.75 |
| | | | *Nos. 90-95 (6)* | 15.60 | 15.60 |

Kotyloymoysioy Monastery Katholikon — A77

Pantocrator Monastery Katholikon — A78

Xeropotamoy Monastery Katholikon — A79

Zographoy Monastery Katholikon A80

Docheiarioy Monastery Katholikon — A81

**2012, Mar. 20**

| | | | | | |
|---|---|---|---|---|---|
| **96** | A77 | 50c | multi + label | 1.40 | 1.40 |
| **97** | A78 | 60c | multi + label | 1.60 | 1.60 |
| **98** | A79 | €1 | multi + label | 2.60 | 2.60 |
| **99** | A80 | €1.50 | multi + label | 4.00 | 4.00 |
| **100** | A81 | €2 | multi + label | 5.25 | 5.25 |
| | | | *Nos. 96-100 (5)* | 14.85 | 14.85 |

Karakallou Monastery Katholikon A82

Philotheou Monastery Katholikon A83

Simonos Petra Monastery Katholikon A84

Aghiou Pavlou Monastery Katholikon A85

Stavroniketa Monastery Katholikon — A86

**2012, Sept. 12**

| | | | | | |
|---|---|---|---|---|---|
| **101** | A82 | 62c | multi + label | 1.60 | 1.60 |
| **102** | A83 | 78c | multi + label | 2.00 | 2.00 |
| **103** | A84 | 85c | multi + label | 2.25 | 2.25 |
| **104** | A85 | €1 | multi + label | 2.60 | 2.60 |
| **105** | A86 | €2.10 | multi + label | 5.50 | 5.50 |
| | | | *Nos. 101-105 (5)* | 13.95 | 13.95 |

Xenophontos Monastery Katholikon — A87

Gregoriou Monastery Katholikon A88

Esphigmenou Monastery Katholikon — A89

Aghiou Panteleimonos Monastery Katholikon — A90

Konstamonitou Monastery Katholikon — A91

**2012, Nov. 20**

| | | | | | |
|---|---|---|---|---|---|
| **106** | A87 | 50c | multi + label | 1.40 | 1.40 |
| **107** | A88 | 62c | multi + label | 1.60 | 1.60 |
| **108** | A89 | €1 | multi + label | 2.60 | 2.60 |
| **109** | A90 | €1.50 | multi + label | 4.00 | 4.00 |
| **110** | A91 | €2.10 | multi + label | 5.50 | 5.50 |
| | | | *Nos. 106-110 (5)* | 15.10 | 15.10 |

# GREENLAND

'grēn-lənd

LOCATION — North Atlantic Ocean
GOVT. — Danish
AREA — 840,000 sq. mi.
POP. — 56,076 (1998)
CAPITAL — Nuuk (Godthaab)

In 1953 the colony of Greenland became an integral part of Denmark.

100 Ore = 1 Krone

**Catalogue values for unused stamps in this country are for Never Hinged items, beginning with Scott 28 in the regular postage section, Scott B1 in the semi-postal section.**

Christian X — A1

Polar Bear — A2

*Perf. 13x12½*

**1938-46 Unwmk. Engr.**

| | | | | |
|---|---|---|---|---|
| 1 | A1 | 1o olive black | .30 | *.30* |
| 2 | A1 | 5o rose lake | 3.25 | 2.00 |
| 3 | A1 | 7o yellow green | 4.50 | *5.50* |
| 4 | A1 | 10o dk violet | 1.25 | 1.25 |
| 5 | A1 | 15o red | 1.25 | 1.25 |
| 6 | A1 | 20o red ('46) | 1.40 | *2.00* |
| 7 | A2 | 30o blue | 7.25 | *11.00* |
| 8 | A2 | 40o blue ('46) | 27.50 | 12.50 |
| 9 | A2 | 1k light brown | 8.00 | *10.00* |
| | | *Nos. 1-9 (9)* | 54.70 | *45.80* |
| | | Set, never hinged | 135.00 | |

Issued: Nov. 1, 1938; Aug. 1, 1946.

For surcharges see Nos. 39-40.

Harp Seal — A3

Christian X — A4

Dog Team — A5

Designs: 1k, Polar bear. 2k, Eskimo in kayak. 5k, Eider duck.

**1945, Feb. 1** ***Perf. 12***

| | | | | |
|---|---|---|---|---|
| 10 | A3 | 1o ol blk & vio | 27.50 | *50.00* |
| 11 | A3 | 5o rose lake & ol bister | 27.50 | *50.00* |
| 12 | A3 | 7o green & blk | 27.50 | *50.00* |
| 13 | A4 | 10o purple & olive | 27.50 | *50.00* |
| 14 | A4 | 15o red & brt ultra | 27.50 | *50.00* |
| 15 | A5 | 30o dk blue & red brn | 27.50 | *50.00* |
| 16 | A5 | 1k brown & gray blk | 27.50 | *50.00* |
| 17 | A5 | 2k sepia & dp grn | 27.50 | *50.00* |
| 18 | A5 | 5k dk pur & dl brn | 27.50 | *50.00* |
| | | *Nos. 10-18 (9)* | 247.50 | *450.00* |
| | | Set, never hinged | 550.00 | |

Nos. 10-18 Overprinted in Carmine or Blue

**1945**

| | | | | |
|---|---|---|---|---|
| 19 | A3 | 1o (C) | 67.50 | *85.00* |
| 20 | A3 | 5o (Bl) | 67.50 | *85.00* |
| 21 | A3 | 7o (C) | 67.50 | *85.00* |
| 22 | A4 | 10o (Bl) | 125.00 | *150.00* |
| *a.* | | Overprint in carmine | 400.00 | *700.00* |
| 23 | A4 | 15o (C) | 125.00 | *150.00* |
| *a.* | | Overprint in blue | 200.00 | *240.00* |
| 24 | A5 | 30o (Bl) | 125.00 | *150.00* |
| *a.* | | Overprint in carmine | 200.00 | *240.00* |
| 25 | A5 | 1k (C) | 125.00 | *150.00* |
| *a.* | | Overprint in blue | 225.00 | *240.00* |
| 26 | A5 | 2k (C) | 125.00 | *150.00* |
| *a.* | | Overprint in blue | 200.00 | *240.00* |
| 27 | A5 | 5k (Bl) | 125.00 | *150.00* |
| *a.* | | Overprint in carmine | 200.00 | *240.00* |
| | | *Nos. 19-27 (9)* | 952.50 | *1,155.* |
| | | Set, never hinged | 1,450. | |
| | | *Nos. 22a-27a (6)* | 1,425. | *1,900.* |
| | | Set, never hinged | 3,000. | |

Liberation of Denmark from the Germans.

Overprint illustrated as on Nos. 19-21. Larger type and different settings used for Types A4 and A5. Overprint sizes: A3, 11.5 mm; A4, 13 mm; A5, 14.5 mm. A variety of No. 23 exists with overprint measuring 11.5 mm. Value: $3,300. Overprint often smudged.

Nos. 19-27 exist with overprint inverted. Values: 1k and 30o, each $1,200; others, each $1,000.

**Catalogue values for unused stamps in this section, from this point to the end of the section, are for Never Hinged items.**

Frederik IX — A6

Polar Ship "Gustav Holm" — A7

**1950-60 Unwmk. Engr.** ***Perf. 13***

| | | | | |
|---|---|---|---|---|
| 28 | A6 | 1o dark olive green | .30 | .30 |
| 29 | A6 | 5o deep carmine | .30 | .30 |
| 30 | A6 | 10o green | .35 | .35 |
| 31 | A6 | 15o purple | .60 | .40 |
| *a.* | | 15o dull purple | 4.50 | 1.60 |
| 32 | A6 | 25o vermilion | 2.75 | 1.00 |
| 33 | A6 | 30o dark blue | 45.00 | 2.25 |
| 34 | A6 | 30o vermilion | .50 | .35 |
| 35 | A7 | 50o deep blue | 52.50 | 15.00 |
| 36 | A7 | 1k brown | 17.00 | 3.25 |
| 37 | A7 | 2k dull red | 9.25 | 3.25 |
| 38 | A7 | 5k gray | 3.00 | 2.00 |
| | | *Nos. 28-38 (11)* | 131.55 | 28.45 |

Issued: #28-30, 31a, 32, 35-37, 8/15/50; #33, 12/1/53; #38, 8/14/58; #34, 10/29/59; #31, 10/60.

For surcharges see Nos. B1-B2.

Nos. 8 and 9 Surcharged

**1956, Mar. 8**

| | | | | |
|---|---|---|---|---|
| 39 | A2 | 60o on 40o blue | 9.00 | 1.75 |
| 40 | A2 | 60o on 1k lt brown | 67.50 | 8.00 |

Drum Dancer — A8

Designs: 50o, The Boy and the Fox. 60o, The Mother of the Sea. 80o, The Girl and the Eagle. 90o, The Great Northern Diver and the Raven.

**1957-69 Engr.** ***Perf. 13***

| | | | | |
|---|---|---|---|---|
| 41 | A8 | 35o gray olive | 1.40 | 1.00 |
| 42 | A8 | 50o brown red | 1.25 | *1.40* |
| 43 | A8 | 60o blue | 4.00 | 1.40 |
| 44 | A8 | 80o light brown | 1.40 | *1.40* |
| 45 | A8 | 90o dark blue | 4.50 | 4.00 |
| | | *Nos. 41-45 (5)* | 12.55 | 9.20 |

Issued: 35o, 3/16/61; 50o, 9/22/66; 60o, 5/2/57; 80o, 9/18/69; 90o, 11/23/67.

Hans Egede A9

Knud Rasmussen A10

**1958, Nov. 5**

| | | | | |
|---|---|---|---|---|
| 46 | A9 | 30o henna brown | 10.00 | 1.75 |

200th anniv. of death of Hans Egede, missionary to Eskimos in Greenland.

**1960, Nov. 24** ***Perf. 13***

| | | | | |
|---|---|---|---|---|
| 47 | A10 | 30o dull red | 1.60 | 1.10 |

50th anniv. of establishment by Rasmussen of the mission and trading station at Thule (Dundas).

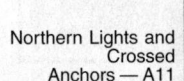

Northern Lights and Crossed Anchors — A11

Frederick IX — A12

Polar Bear — A13

**1963-68 Engr.**

| | | | | |
|---|---|---|---|---|
| 48 | A11 | 1o gray | .30 | *.35* |
| 49 | A11 | 5o rose claret | .30 | *.35* |
| 50 | A11 | 10o green | .40 | *.50* |
| 51 | A11 | 12o yellow grn | .40 | *.40* |
| 52 | A11 | 15o rose vio | 1.00 | *1.25* |
| 53 | A12 | 20o ultra | 4.50 | 3.50 |
| 54 | A12 | 25o lt brown | .75 | *.75* |
| 55 | A12 | 30o green | .30 | *.50* |
| 56 | A12 | 35o dull red | .30 | *.30* |
| 57 | A12 | 40o gray | .35 | *.55* |
| 58 | A12 | 50o grnsh blue | 10.00 | *10.00* |
| 59 | A12 | 50o dark red | .35 | *.45* |
| 60 | A12 | 60o rose claret | .40 | *.45* |
| 61 | A12 | 80o orange | .80 | *.85* |
| 62 | A13 | 1k brown | .65 | .35 |
| 63 | A13 | 2k dull red | 3.50 | 1.10 |
| 64 | A13 | 5k dark blue | 3.00 | 2.25 |
| 65 | A13 | 10k dull slate grn | 5.00 | 1.10 |
| | | *Nos. 48-65 (18)* | 32.30 | 25.00 |

Issued: #48-52, 3/7/63; #53, 61, 7/25/63; #62-65, 9/17/63; #54, 56-58, 3/11/64; #59, 9/9/65; #60, 2/29/68; #55, 11/21/68.

Niels Bohr (1885-1962) and Atom Diagram — A14

**1963, Nov. 21 Unwmk.**

| | | | | |
|---|---|---|---|---|
| 66 | A14 | 35o red brown | .40 | .55 |
| 67 | A14 | 60o dark blue | 4.75 | 4.75 |

50th anniv. of atom theory of Prof. Bohr.

A15

A16

**1964, Nov. 26**

| | | | | |
|---|---|---|---|---|
| 68 | A15 | 35o brown red | .65 | .65 |

Samuel Kleinschmidt (1814-1886), philologist.

**1967, June 10**

| | | | | |
|---|---|---|---|---|
| 69 | A16 | 50o red | 3.50 | 3.50 |

Wedding of Crown Princess Margrethe and Prince Henri de Monpezat.

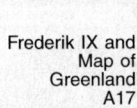

Frederik IX and Map of Greenland A17

**1969, Mar. 11 Engr.** ***Perf. 13***

| | | | | |
|---|---|---|---|---|
| 70 | A17 | 60o dull red | 1.40 | 1.40 |

70th birthday of King Frederik IX.

Musk Ox — A18

Designs: 1k, Right whale diving off Disko Island. 2k, Narwhal. 5k, Polar bear. 10k, Walruses.

**1969-76 Engr.** ***Perf. 13***

| | | | | |
|---|---|---|---|---|
| 71 | A18 | 1k dark blue | .40 | .40 |
| 72 | A18 | 2k gray green | .90 | .60 |
| 73 | A18 | 5k blue | 2.00 | .75 |
| 74 | A18 | 10k sepia | 4.00 | 1.90 |
| 75 | A18 | 25k greenish gray | 11.00 | 4.00 |
| | | *Nos. 71-75 (5)* | 18.30 | 7.65 |

Issued: 1k, 3/5/70; 2k, 2/20/75; 5k, 2/19/76; 10k, 2/15/73; 25k, 11/27/69.

Liberation Celebration at Jakobshaven A19

**1970, May 4**

| | | | | |
|---|---|---|---|---|
| 76 | A19 | 60o red brown | 2.25 | 2.25 |

Hans Egede and Gertrude Rask on the Haabet — A20

**1971, May 6** **Engr.** ***Perf. 13***
**77** A20 60o brown red 1.75 1.75

250th anniv. of arrival of Hans Egede in Greenland and the beginning of its colonization.

Mail-carrying Kayaks — A21

Designs: 70o, Umiak (women's rowboat). 80o, Catalina seaplane dropping mail by parachute. 90o, Dog sled. 1k, Coaster Kununguak and pilot boat. 1.30k, Schooner Sokongen. 1.50k, Longboat off Greenland coast. 2k, Helicopter over mountains.

**1971-77** **Engr.** ***Perf. 13***
**78** A21 50o green .30 .25
**79** A21 70o dull red ('72) .35 .25
**80** A21 80o black ('76) .40 .40
**81** A21 90o blue ('72) .35 .25
**82** A21 1k red ('76) .40 .40
**83** A21 1.30k dull bl ('75) .85 .65
**84** A21 1.50k gray grn ('74) .80 .55
**85** A21 2k blue ('77) 1.00 .85
*Nos. 78-85 (8)* 4.45 3.60

Issued: #78, 11/4; #81, 2/29; #79, 9/21; #84, 2/21; #83, 4/17; #80, 10/11; #85, 2/24.

Queen Margrethe — A22

**1973-79** **Engr.** ***Perf. 13***
**86** A22 5o car rose ('78) .30 .25
**87** A22 10o gray green .30 .25
*a.* 10o emerald ('89) 6.50 6.50
**88** A22 60o sepia .60 .60
**89** A22 80o sepia ('79) .40 .30
**90** A22 90o red brown ('74) .70 .70
**91** A22 1k dark red ('77) .40 .30
*a.* Bklt. pane, 4 #87a, 6 #91b 37.50
*b.* 1k carmine ('89) 5.00 5.00
**92** A22 1.20k dk blue ('74) .70 1.00
**93** A22 1.20k maroon ('78) .75 .50
**94** A22 1.30k dk blue ('77) .60 .60
**95** A22 1.30k red ('79) .60 .50
**96** A22 1.60k blue ('79) .70 .70
**97** A22 1.80k dl green ('78) .85 .70
*Nos. 86-97 (12)* 6.90 6.40

#86, 89, 93, 95-97 inscribed "Kalaallit Nunaat."

The background lines on Nos. 87, 91 are sharp and complete. On No. 87a, 91b they are irregular and broken.

Issue dates: Nos. 87-88, Apr. 16. Nos. 90, 92, Oct. 24. Nos. 91, 94, May 26. Nos. 86, 93, 97, Apr. 17. Nos. 89, 95-96, Mar. 29.

Trawler and Kayaks — A23

2k, Old Trade Buildings, Copenhagen, vert.

**1974, May 16** **Engr.** ***Perf. 13***
**98** A23 1k lt red brown .60 .90
**99** A23 2k sepia .70 .60

Royal Greenland Trade Dept. Bicentennial.

Falcon and Radar — A24

**1975, Sept. 4** **Engr.** ***Perf. 13***
**100** A24 90o red .60 .60

50th anniversary of Greenland's telecommunications system.

Sirius Sled Patrol A25

**1975, Oct. 16** **Engr.** ***Perf. 13***
**101** A25 1.20k sepia .40 .40

Sirius sled patrol in northeast Greenland, 25th anniversary.

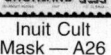

Inuit Cult Mask — A26

Jorgen Bronlund, Jakobshavn, Disko Bay — A27

Designs: 6k, Tupilac, a magical creature, carved whalebone. 7k, Soapstone sculpture. 8k, Eskimo with Family, driftwood sculpture, by Johannes Kreutzmann (1862-1940).

**1977-80**
**102** A26 6k deep rose lilac 2.50 1.90
**103** A26 7k gray olive 2.75 2.40
**104** A26 8k dark blue 3.25 2.50
**105** A26 9k black 3.50 3.25
*Nos. 102-105 (4)* 12.00 10.05

Issue dates: 6k, Oct. 5, 1978. 7k, Sept. 6, 1979. 8k, Feb. 29, 1980. 9k, Sept. 6, 1977.

The 6k, 7k, 8k are inscribed "Kalaallit Nunaat."

**1977, Oct. 20**
**106** A27 1k red brown .40 .25

Jorgen Bronlund, arctic explorer, birth centenary.

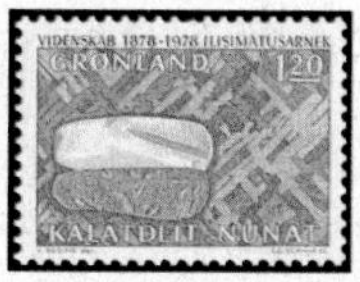


Meteorite — A28

**1978, Jan. 20** **Engr.** ***Perf. 13***
**107** A28 1.20k dull red .55 .50

Scientific Research Commission, centenary.

Sun Rising over Mountains — A29

**1978, June 5** **Engr.** ***Perf. 13***
**108** A29 1.50k dark blue .55 .55

25th anniversary of Constitution.

Hans Egede, Settlers, Troops and Drummer A30

**1978, Aug. 29** **Engr.** ***Perf. 13***
**109** A30 2.50k red brown .95 .70

Founding of Godthaab, 250th anniversary.

A31

A32

**1979, May 1** **Engr.**
**110** A31 1.10k Navigator .40 .40

Establishment of home rule, May 1, 1979.

**1979, Oct. 18** **Engr.** ***Perf. 13***

Eskimo Boy, aurora borealis, IYC emblem.

**111** A32 2k olive green .80 .80

International Year of the Child.

The Legend of the Reindeer and the Larva, by Jens Kreutzmann, 1860 — A33

Designs: 2.70k, Harpooning a Walrus, Jakob Danielsen. No. 114, Life in Thule, c. 1900, by Aninaaq. No. 115, Landscape, Ammassalik Fjord, Eastern Greenland, Peter Rosing (1892-1965). 3k, Footrace, woodcut by Aron from Kagec (1822-1869). 3.70k, Polar Bear Killing Seal Hunter, K. Andreassen (1890-1934). 9k, Hares Hunting, Gerhard Kleist (1855-1931).

**1980-87** **Engr.** ***Perf. 13***
**112** A33 1.60k red .65 .65
**113** A33 2.70k deep violet 1.10 1.00
**114** A33 2.80k lake 1.10 .95
**115** A33 2.80k lake 1.40 1.00
**116** A33 3k black 1.25 1.10
**117** A33 3.70k blue black 1.75 1.50
**118** A33 9k dark green 4.00 2.75
*Nos. 112-118 (7)* 11.25 8.95

Issued: 1.60k, 3/26/81; 2.70k, 6/24/82; #114, 9/4/86; #115, 4/9/87; 3k, 9/4/80; 3.70k, 2/9/84; 9k, 9/5/85.

Queen Margrethe, Map of Greenland A34

**1980-89** **Engr.** ***Perf. 13***
**120** A34 50o purple ('81) .30 .30
*a.* 50o dull purple ('89) 7.50 7.50
**121** A34 80o sepia .40 .40
**122** A34 1.30k red .60 .60
**123** A34 1.50k royal blue ('82) .70 .70
**124** A34 1.60k ultra 1.00 1.00
**125** A34 1.80k dull red ('82) 1.00 .70
**126** A34 2.30k dk grn ('81) 1.00 .75
**127** A34 2.50k red ('83) 1.25 .75
**128** A34 2.80k copper red ('85) 2.00 .80
**129** A34 3k fawn ('88) 2.25 2.00
**130** A34 3.20k rose ('89) 2.25 2.00
*a.* Bklt. pane of 10 (4 #120a, 6 #130) 42.50
**131** A34 3.80k slate blue ('85) 2.00 2.00
**132** A34 4.10k brt blue ('88) 2.25 2.25
**133** A34 4.40k ultra ('89) 4.50 2.75
*Nos. 120-133 (14)* 21.50 17.00

Issued: #121-122, 124, 4/16; #120, 126, 1/29; #123, 125, 5/13; #127, 3/30; #128, 131, 2/7; #129, 132, 2/4; #130, 133, 1/30.

Rasmus Berthelsen (Teacher, Hymnist), in Training College Library, 1830 — A35

**1980, May 29** **Engr.** ***Perf. 13***
**134** A35 2k brown, *cream* .80 .75

Greenland Public Library Service, 150th anniv.

Ejnar Mikkelsen on board Gustav Holm, 1934 — A36

**1980, Oct. 16** **Engr.** ***Perf. 13***
**135** A36 4k slate green 1.40 1.25

Ejnar Mikkelsen, inspector of East Greenland, birth centenary.

Pandalus Borealis — A37

Designs: No. 137, Anarhicas minor. No. 138, Reinhardtius Hippoglossoides. No. 139, Mallotus villosus. 25k, Codfish. 50k, Salmo salar.

**1981-86** **Engr.** ***Perf. 13***
**136** A37 10k multicolored 4.00 2.00
**137** A37 10k dk bl & blk 6.00 4.00
**138** A37 10k multicolored 4.50 4.00
**139** A37 10k grnsh blk & blk 4.75 4.75
**140** A37 25k multicolored 9.75 4.25
**141** A37 50k multicolored 20.00 10.00
*Nos. 136-141 (6)* 49.00 29.00

Issued: 25k, 5/21; #136, 4/1/82; 50k, 1/27/83; #137, 10/11/84; #138, 10/10/85; #139, 10/16/86.

Saqqaq Eskimo in Kayak, Reindeer — A38

5k, Tunit-Dorset hunters hauling seal.

**1981, Oct. 15** **Engr.** ***Perf. 12½***
**146** A38 3.50k dark blue 1.50 1.50
**147** A38 5k brown 2.10 2.10

Thule District Eskimos Catching Whale, 1000AD — A39

Greenland history: No. 149, Bishop Joen Smyrill's house and staff, 12th cent. No. 150, Wooden dolls, 13th cent. No. 151, Eskimo mummy, sacrificial stones, 14th cent. No. 152, Hans Pothorst, explorer, 15th cent. No. 153, Glass pearls, 16th cent. No. 154, Apostle spoons, 17th cent. No. 155, Key, trading station, 18th cent. No. 156, Trade Ship Hvalfisken, masthead, 19th cent. No. 157, Communications satellite, Earth, 20th cent.

**1982, Sept. 30**
**148** A39 2k brown red .90 .90
**149** A39 2.70k dark blue 1.25 1.25

**1983, Sept. 15**
**150** A39 2.50k red 1.00 1.00
**151** A39 3.50k brown 1.50 1.50
**152** A39 4.50k blue 1.75 1.75

**1984, Mar. 29**
**153** A39 2.70k red brown 1.75 1.75
**154** A39 3.70k dark blue 1.75 1.75
**155** A39 5.50k brown 2.25 2.25

**1985, Mar. 21**
**156** A39 2.80k violet 1.75 1.75
**157** A39 6k blue black 2.75 2.75
*Nos. 148-157,B10 (11)* 17.90 17.90

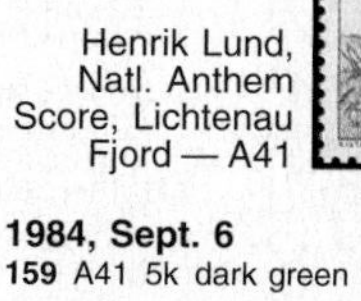

250th Anniv. of Settlement of New Herrnhut — A40

**1983, Nov. 2** **Engr.**
**158** A40 2.50k brown 1.00 1.00

Henrik Lund, Natl. Anthem Score, Lichtenau Fjord — A41

**1984, Sept. 6** **Engr.**
**159** A41 5k dark green 3.25 3.25

Henrik Lund (1875-1948), natl. anthem composer, artist, only Greenlander to win Ingenio et Arti medal.

A42 A43

**1984, June 6** **Engr.** ***Perf. 13***
**160** A42 2.70k dull red 2.25 2.25

Prince Henrik, 50th birthday.

**1984, July 25** **Engr.** ***Perf. 13***
**161** A43 3.70k Danish grenadier, 1734 1.75 1.75

Town of Christianshab, 250th anniv.

Ingrid, Queen Mother of Denmark, Chrysanthemums — A44

**1985, May 21** **Litho. & Engr.**
**162** A44 2.80k multi 1.40 1.40

Arrival in Denmark of Princess Ingrid, 50th anniv. See Denmark No. 775.

Intl. Youth Year — A45

**1985, June 27** **Litho.**
**163** A45 3.80k Emblem, birds nesting, fiord 1.40 1.40

Greenland Port Post Office, Flags — A46

**1986, Mar. 6** **Engr.** ***Perf. 13***
**164** A46 2.80k dark red 1.40 1.40

Transfer of postal control under Greenland Home Rule, Jan. 1, 1986.

Artifacts — A47

**1986-88** **Engr.** ***Perf. 13***
**165** A47 2.80k Sewing needles, case 1.40 .95
**165A** A47 3k Buckets, bowl, scoop 1.25 .90
**166** A47 3.80k Ulos 1.50 1.50
**167** A47 3.80k Masks 1.75 1.75
**168** A47 5k Harpoon points 2.00 1.50
**169** A47 6.50k Lard lamps 2.75 2.75
**172** A47 10k Carved faces 4.50 3.25
*Nos. 165-172 (7)* 15.15 12.60

Issued: #166, 6.50k, May 22. 2.80k, 3.80k, June 11, 1987. 3k, 5k, 10k, Oct. 27, 1988.

Souvenir Sheet

HAFNIA '87 — A48

**1987, Jan. 23** **Litho.** ***Perf. 13***
**175** A48 Sheet of 3 11.00 11.00
*a.* 2.80k Gull in flight 3.00 3.00
*b.* 3.80k Mountain 3.75 3.75
*c.* 6.50k Gulls in water 3.75 3.75

No. 175 sold for 19.50k. See No. 199.

Year of the Fishing, Sealing and Whaling Industries — A49

**1987, Apr. 9** **Litho.** ***Perf. 13***
**176** A49 3.80k multi 1.75 1.50

Lagopus Mutus — A50 Birds of Prey — A51

**1987-90** **Litho.** ***Perf. 13***
**177** A51 3k Falco rusticolus 1.75 1.75
**178** A51 3.20k Clangula hyemalis 2.40 1.40
**179** A51 4k Anser caerulescens 1.75 1.40
**180** A51 4.10k Corvus corax 2.25 2.25
**181** A51 4.40k Plectrophenax nivalis 2.50 2.50
**182** A50 5k shown 3.00 1.90
**183** A51 5.50k Haliaeetus albicilla 3.75 2.50
**184** A51 5.50k Cepphus grylle 3.00 3.25
**185** A51 6.50k Uria lomvia 4.00 2.25
**186** A51 7k Gavia immer 3.75 2.75
**187** A51 7.50k Stercorarius longicaudus 3.25 3.75
**188** A50 10k Nyctea scandiaca 4.50 3.50
*Nos. 177-188 (12)* 35.90 29.20

Issued: 5k, 10k, 9/3; 3k, 4.10k, #183, 7k, 4/14/88; 3.20k, 4.40k, #184, 6.50k, 3/16/89; 4k, 7.50k, 1/15/90.

Plants — A52

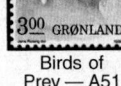

**1989-92** **Litho.** ***Perf. 13***
**189** A52 4k Campanula gieseckiana 1.75 1.50
**190** A52 4k Pedicularis hirsuta 2.25 1.50
**191** A52 5k Eriophorum scheuchzeri 2.75 2.10
**192** A52 5.50k Ledum groenlandicum 2.50 2.25
**193** A52 6.50k Cassiope tetragona 3.25 3.00
**194** A52 7.25k Saxifraga oppositifolia 3.75 3.25
**196** A52 10k Papaver radicatum, vert. 5.25 4.00
*Nos. 189-196 (7)* 21.50 17.60

Issued: 5k, 10k, 10/12/89; #189, 5.50k, 6.50k, 6/7/90; #190, 7.25k, 3/26/92. #189-190 vert.

**HAFNIA type of 1987**
Souvenir Sheet

Uummannaq Mountain in winter, horiz.

**1987, Oct. 16** **Litho.** ***Perf. 13x12½***
**199** A48 2.80k slate blue & lake 3.25 *3.75*

No. 199 sold for 4k.

Greenland Home Rule, 10th Anniv.
A53 A54

**1989, May 1** **Litho.** ***Perf. 13***
**200** A53 3.20k Flag, landscape 1.50 1.40
**201** A54 4.40k Coat of arms 2.50 1.75

Queen Margrethe — A55

and Nos. 214, 217 Surcharged in Red or Blue

**1990-96** **Engr.** ***Perf. 13***
**214** A55 25o green .30 .30
**217** A55 1k brown .55 .45
*a.* Bklt. pane, 4 #214, 6 #217 32.50
*b.* Bklt. pane, 4 each #214, 217 16.00
**224** A55 4k carmine rose 1.75 1.75
Complete booklet, 217a, 10 #224 47.50
**225** A55 4.25k red *2.40* *2.40*
**226** A55 4.25k on 25o #214 (R) *5.00* *5.00*
*a.* Inverted surcharge 1,100.
**227** A55 4.50k on 1k #217 (Bl) 5.00 5.00
**228** A55 6.50k blue 2.75 2.75
**229** A55 7k violet 3.50 3.50
*Nos. 214-229 (8)* *21.25* *21.15*

Issued: #217a, 5/3/90; #217b, 9/9/93; 7k, 2/10/94; #225, 1996; #226-227, 12/31/95; others, 4/5/90.

Frederik Lynge (1889-1957), Politician — A56

25k, Augo Lynge (1899-1959), politician

**1990, Oct. 18** **Engr.** ***Perf. 13x12½***
**231** A56 10k rose brn & dk bl 4.25 4.25
**232** A56 25k vio & dk bl 10.00 10.00

See Nos. 242-243, 249.

Phoca Hispida — A57

Walrus and Seals.

**Litho. & Engr.**

**1991, Mar. 14** ***Perf. 13***
**233** A57 4k shown 1.75 1.75
**234** A57 4k Pagophilus groenlandicus 1.75 1.75
**235** A57 7.25k Cystophora cristata 3.00 3.00
**236** A57 7.25k Odobenus rosmarus 3.00 3.00
**237** A57 8.50k Erignatus barbatus 3.25 3.25
**238** A57 8.50k Phoca vitulina 3.25 3.25
*a.* Miniature sheet of 6, #233-238 18.00 18.00
*Nos. 233-238 (6)* 16.00 16.00

Village of Ilulissat, 250th Anniv. — A58

**1991, May 15** **Litho.** ***Perf. 13***
**239** A58 4k multicolored 1.75 1.75

Tourism — A59

**1991, May 15** ***Perf. 12½x13***
**240** A59 4k Iceberg 1.50 1.50
**241** A59 8.50k Skiers, sled dogs 3.50 3.50

See Nos. 259-260, 289-290.

**Famous Men Type of 1990**

10k, Jonathan Petersen (1881-1961), musician. 50k, Hans Lynge (1906-88), artist & writer. 100k, Lars Moller (1842-1926), newspaper editor.

**1991-92** **Engr.** ***Perf. 13x12½***
**242** A56 10k black & dk blue 4.75 3.50
**243** A56 50k red brn & dk blue 20.00 17.00
**249** A56 100k claret & slate 35.00 30.00
*Nos. 242-249 (3)* 59.75 50.50

Issued: 10k, 50k, 9/5; 100k, 9/15/92.

Settlement of Paamiut, 250th Anniv. A60

**1992, May 14** **Engr.** ***Perf. 13***
**252** A60 7.25k dk bl & ol brn 3.50 3.00

Denmark's Queen Margrethe and Prince Henrik, Silver Wedding Anniv. — A61

**1992, June 10** **Litho.** ***Perf. 12½x13***
**253** A61 4k multicolored 2.40 2.40

See Denmark No. 946.

A62

**1992, Nov. 12** **Litho.** ***Perf. 13***
**254** A62 4k Christmas 2.75 2.10

A63

**1993, Feb. 4 Litho. *Perf. 13***
**255** A63 4k multicolored 2.25 2.00

Intl. Year of Indigenous Peoples.

Crabs — A64

4k, Neolithodes grimaldii. 7.25k, Chionoecetes oiliqo. 8.50k, Hyas coarctatus, Hyas araneus.

**Litho. & Engr.**

**1993, Mar. 25 *Perf. 13***
**256** A64 4k multicolored 1.50 1.50
**257** A64 7.25k multicolored 4.00 4.00
*a.* Chionoecetes opilio 10.50 *13.00*
*b.* Booklet pane, 4 each #256, 257a 50.00
**258** A64 8.50k multicolored 5.00 5.00
*Nos. 256-258 (3)* 10.50 10.50

Issue date: No. 257b, Sept. 9.

**Tourism Type of 1991**

**1993, May 6 Litho. *Perf. 12½x13***
**259** A59 4k Village in winter 2.00 2.00
**260** A59 8.50k Ruins, coastline 4.00 4.00

AIDS Research A66

**1993, Sept. 9 Litho. *Perf. 13***
**261** A66 4k multicolored 2.00 2.00

Native Animals — A67

**Litho. & Engr.**

**1993, Oct. 14 *Perf. 13***
**262** A67 5k Canis lupus 2.50 2.50
**263** A67 8.50k Alopex lagopus 4.00 4.00
**264** A67 10k Rangifer tarandus 4.50 4.50
*Nos. 262-264 (3)* 11.00 11.00

See Nos. 270-272, 296-298.

Christmas A68

**1993, Nov. 11 Litho. *Perf. 13***
**265** A68 4k multicolored 2.25 2.25

Buksefjord Electrical Project — A69

**Litho. & Engr.**

**1994, Mar. 24 *Perf. 13***
**266** A69 4k multicolored 1.50 1.50

Ammassalik, Cent. — A70

**1994, Mar. 24**
**267** A70 7.25k multicolored 3.00 3.00

Expedition to North East Greenland, 1906-08 A71

Europa: 4k, Icebound Danmark. 7.25k, Danmark, expedition car, dogs.

**1994, May 5 Litho. *Perf. 13***
**268** A71 4k multicolored *2.00 2.00*
**269** A71 7.25k multicolored *3.50 3.25*

**Native Animal Type of 1993**

Designs: 5.50k, Mustela erminea. 7.25k, Dicrostonyx torquatus. 9k, Lepus arcticus.

**Litho. & Engr.**

**1994, Sept. 8 *Perf. 13***
**270** A67 5.50k multicolored 2.50 2.50
**271** A67 7.25k multicolored 4.00 4.00
**272** A67 9k multicolored 4.50 4.50
*Nos. 270-272 (3)* 11.00 11.00

Ship's Figureheads — A72

**Litho. & Engr.**

**1994, Oct. 13 *Perf. 13***
**273** A72 4k Ceres 1.50 1.50
**274** A72 8.50k Nordlyset 4.00 4.00

See Nos. 299-300, 309-310.

Christmas Paintings, by Julia Pars — A73

**1994, Nov. 10 Litho. *Perf. 12½x13***
**275** A73 4k shown 2.00 2.00
**276** A73 5k Santa, dogs, igloo 3.25 3.25

Orchids — A74

**Litho. & Engr.**

**1995-96 *Perf. 13x12½***
**279** A74 4k Listera cordata 2.00 2.00
**280** A74 4.25k Corallorhiza trifida 1.75 1.75
**281** A74 4.50k Amerorchis rotundifolia 1.90 1.90
**282** A74 7.25k Leucorchis albida 3.00 3.00
**283** A74 7.50k Plantanthera hyperborea 3.25 3.25
*a.* Booklet pane, #281, 283, 2 ea #225, 280 + 4 labels 12.50
Complete booklet, 2 #283a 25.00
*Nos. 279-283 (5)* 11.90 11.90

No. 283a exists with different labels and stamps in different order. Complete booklet contains one of each type of No. 283a.

Issued: 4k, 7.25k, 2/9/95.

Ilinniarfissuaq Seminarium, Nuuk (The Greenland Training College), 150th Anniv. — A75

**Litho. & Engr.**

**1995, Mar. 23 *Perf. 13***
**287** A75 4k multicolored 2.00 2.00

United Nations, 50th Anniv. — A76

**1995, Mar. 23**
**288** A76 7.25k multicolored 3.50 3.50

**Tourism Type of 1991**

**1995, Apr. 20 Litho. *Perf. 12½x13***
**289** A59 4k Iceberg, inlet 2.25 2.25
**290** A59 8.50k Mountains 4.50 4.50

Peace & Liberty A77

Europa: 4k, Envelope, simulated stamp. 8.50k, Doves flying over Greenland.

**1995, May 5 *Perf. 12½x13***
**291** A77 4k multicolored *1.75 1.75*
**292** A77 8.50k multicolored *4.00 4.00*

Souvenir Sheets
Types A3-A5 Surcharged

America Series — A78

Designs: No. 295a, Dog team. b, Polar bear. c, Eskimo in kayak. d, Eider duck.

**1995, May 5 Litho. *Perf. 13***
**293** A78 Sheet of 2 + 4 labels *6.50 6.50*
*a.* 5k on 10o pur & ol (Type A4) *3.00 3.00*
*b.* 5k on 15o red & vio (Type A4) *3.00 3.00*
**294** A78 Sheet of 3 *7.75 7.75*
*a.* 1k on 1o dk ol & vio bl (Type A3) *.60 .60*
*b.* 5k on 5o rose lake & brn (Type A3) *3.00 3.00*
*c.* 7k on 7o dk grn & blk (Type A3) *4.25 4.25*
**295** A78 Sheet of 4 *10.00 10.00*
*a.* 4k on 30o dk bl & red brn (Type A5) *2.40 2.40*
*b.* 4k on 1k brn & gray blk (Type A5) *2.40 2.40*
*c.* 4k on 2k sep & dp grn (Type A5) *2.40 2.40*
*d.* 4k on 5k dp pur & dl brn (Type A5) *2.40 2.40*

**Native Animal Type of 1993**

**Litho. & Engr.**

**1995, Sept. 7 *Perf. 13***
**296** A67 4k Ursus maritimus 2.00 2.00
**297** A67 7.25k Gulo gulo 3.25 3.25
**298** A67 7.50k Ovibus moschatus 3.25 3.25
*Nos. 296-298 (3)* 8.50 8.50

**Ship's Figureheads Type of 1994**

**Litho. & Engr.**

**1995, Oct. 12 *Perf. 13***
**299** A72 4k Hvalfisken, vert. 1.60 1.60
**300** A72 8.50k Tjalfe 3.75 3.75

Christmas A79

**1995, Nov. 9 Litho. *Perf. 13***
**301** A79 4k Boy running in snow 1.60 1.60
**302** A79 5k Girl running in snow 2.10 2.10

Whales A80

Designs: 25o, Orcinus orca. 50o, Megaptera novaeangliae. 1k, Delphinapterus leucas. 4.50k, Physeter catodon. 6.50k, Balaena mysticetus. 9.50k, Balaenoptera acutorostrata.

**1996, Apr. 25 Litho. *Perf. 13***
**303** A80 25o blue, black & red .25 .25
**304** A80 50o blue, black & red .25 .25
**305** A80 1k blue, black & red .65 .65
**306** A80 4.50k blue, black & red 2.00 2.00
*a.* Bklt. pane, #304, 2 ea #303, 306 6.00
Complete booklet, 2 #306a 13.00
**307** A80 6.50k blue, black & red 3.25 3.25
**308** A80 9.50k blue, black & red 4.50 4.50
*a.* Souvenir sheet, Nos. 303-308 12.00 12.00
*Nos. 303-308 (6)* 10.90 10.90

No. 306a exists with stamps in different order. Issued: No. 306a, 1/1/97.

See Nos. 319-322, 329-334.

**Ship's Figureheads Type of 1994**

**Litho. & Engr.**

**1996, Sept. 5 *Perf. 13***
**309** A72 15k Blaahejren, vert. 6.50 6.50
**310** A72 20k Gertrud Rask 8.50 8.50

Arnarulunnguaq (1896-1933), Member of Thule Expedition — A81

**1996, Sept. 5 Engr.**
**311** A81 4.50k dark blue *1.75 1.75*

Europa.

Christmas A82

Designs: 4.25k, Girl looking through frozen window pane, angels scratched in ice. 4.50k, Paper star, children singing.

**1996, Nov. 7 Litho. *Perf. 13***
**312** A82 4.25k multicolored 2.00 2.00
**313** A82 4.50k multicolored 2.50 2.50
*a.* Booklet pane, 3 each #312-313 13.00
Complete booklet, 2 #313a 26.00

No. 313a was issued in two formats, one with No. 312 at the UL, the other with No. 313 at the UL. The complete booklet contains one of each format.

A83

**Litho. & Engr.**

**1997, Jan. 14** *Perf. 13*
**314** A83 4.50k multicolored 2.50 2.50

Coronation of Queen Margrethe II, 25th anniv.

A84

Butterflies: 2k, Clossiana chariclea. 3k, Colias hecla. 4.75k, Plebejus franklinii. 8k, Lycaena phlaeas.

**1997, Jan. 14**
**315** A84 2k multicolored 1.10 1.10
**316** A84 3k multicolored 1.75 1.75
**317** A84 4.75k multicolored 1.75 1.75
**318** A84 8k multicolored 3.50 3.50
*a.* Booklet pane of 6, 2 #314, 1 ea #315-318 + 2 labels 13.00
Complete booklet, 2 #318a 26.00
*Nos. 315-318 (4)* 8.10 8.10

Issued: No. 318a, 5/5.

No. 318a exists with stamps in two different orders and with two different backgrounds, one of green plants, the other of red flowers. The complete booklet contains one of each type of pane.

**Whale Type of 1996**

Designs: 5k, Balaenoptera musculus. 5.75k, Balaenoptera physalus. 6k, Balaenoptera borealis. 8k, Monodon monoceros.

**1997, May 5** **Litho.** *Perf. 13*
**319** A80 5k blue, black & red 1.90 1.90
**320** A80 5.75k blue, black & red 2.25 2.25
**321** A80 6k blue, black & red 2.25 2.25
**322** A80 8k blue, black & red 3.25 3.25
*a.* Souvenir sheet of 4, #319-322 9.75 9.75
*Nos. 319-322 (4)* 9.65 9.65

Story of the "Bear of the Sea" — A85

**1997, May 5** **Litho. & Engr.** *Perf. 13*
**323** A85 4.75k black & blue black *2.00 2.00*

Europa.

Town of Nanortalik, Bicent. A86

**Litho. & Engr.**

**1997, Aug. 15** *Perf. 13*
**324** A86 4.50k multicolored 2.00 2.00

Paintings by Aage Gitz-Johansen (1897-1977) — A87

Designs: 10k, Native dancer, Thule. 16k, Nude woman, Ammassalik.

**1997, Aug. 15** **Litho.** *Perf. 13x12½*
**325** A87 10k multicolored 4.00 4.00
**326** A87 16k multicolored 6.00 6.00

Christmas A88

Designs: 4.50k, Child with dogs in snow. 4.75k, Family in sled with Christmas presents, tree, father preparing harness.

**1997, Nov. 6** **Litho.** *Perf. 13x12½*
**327** A88 4.50k multicolored 2.00 2.00
**328** A88 4.75k multicolored 2.00 2.00
*a.* Booklet pane, 3 each #327-328 14.00
Complete booklet, 2 #328a 28.00

No. 328a comes in two configurations. One has #327 at UL, the second has #328 at UL. Complete booklet has one of each pane.

**Whale Type of 1996**

Designs: 2k, Phocoena phocoena. 3k, Lagenorhynchus albirostris. No. 331, Globicephala melaena. No. 332, Hyperoodon ampullatus. No. 333, Lagenorhynchus acutus. No. 334, Eubalaena glacialis.

**1998, Feb. 5** **Litho.** *Perf. 13*
**329** A80 2k multicolored .75 .75
**330** A80 3k multicolored 1.50 1.50
**331** A80 4.50k multicolored 2.40 2.40
**332** A80 4.50k multicolored 2.40 2.40
**333** A80 4.75k multicolored 2.40 2.40
**334** A80 4.75k multicolored 2.40 2.40
*a.* Souvenir sheet of 6, #329-334 12.00 12.00
*Nos. 329-334 (6)* 11.85 11.85

Intl. Year of the Ocean.

New Order of 1950 — A89

Design: Augo Lynge, Frederik Lynge, first Greenland politicians in Danish Parliament.

**1998, Feb. 5** **Engr.** *Perf. 13*
**335** A89 4.50k multicolored 2.00 2.00

Europa — A90

Children's drawings of "Children's Day in Greenland:" 4.75k, Happy faces beside lake. 10k, People celebrating across Greenland.

**1998, May 29** **Litho.** *Perf. 13*
**336** A90 4.75k multicolored 1.75 1.75
**337** A90 10k multicolored 4.00 4.00

Ships — A91

**Litho. & Engr.**

**1998, Aug. 20** *Perf. 13*
**338** A91 4.50k Gertrud Rask 2.00 2.00
*a.* Booklet pane of 6 12.00
**339** A91 4.75k Hans Egede 2.00 2.00
*a.* Booklet pane of 6 12.00
Complete booklet, #338a, 339a 24.00

Paintings by Hans Lynge (1906-88) — A92

Designs: 11k, "Brother Gets Breast-fed." 25k, "Refuelling" (men in boat).

**1998, Aug. 20** **Litho.** *Perf. 13*
**340** A92 11k multicolored 4.50 4.50
**341** A92 25k multicolored 9.50 9.50

Christmas A93

**1998, Nov. 5** **Litho.** *Perf. 13*
**342** A93 4.50k Dickey, kamikker 2.00 2.00
*a.* Booklet pane of 6 15.00
**343** A93 4.75k Kamikker, hat 2.50 2.50
*a.* Booklet pane of 6 15.00
Complete booklet, #342a, 343a 30.00

World Wildlife Fund — A94

Nyctea scandiaca (snowy owl): 1k, Nesting with young. 4.75k, In flight. 5.50k, Two adults. 5.75k, Perched on rock.

**Litho. & Engr.**

**1999, Feb. 8** *Perf. 13*
**344** A94 1k multicolored .60 .60
**345** A94 4.75k multicolored 2.00 2.00
*a.* Booklet pane, 3 each #344-345 8.50
**346** A94 5.50k multicolored 2.25 2.25
**347** A94 5.75k multicolored 2.50 2.50
*a.* Booklet pane, 3 each #346-347 14.50
Complete booklet, #345a, 347a 25.00
*Nos. 344-347 (4)* 7.35 7.35

Europa A95

**1999, May 7** **Litho. & Engr.** *Perf. 13*
**348** A95 6k Polar bear *2.25 2.25*

Paintings, by Peter Rosing (1892-1965) — A96

Designs: 7k, The Man from Aluk, 1944. 20k, Homecoming, 1956.

**1999, May 7** **Litho.** *Perf. 12½x13*
**349** A96 7k multicolored 2.50 2.50
**350** A96 20k multicolored 7.50 7.50

Arctic Vikings A97

**1999, Aug. 13** **Engr.** *Perf. 13x13¼*
**351** A97 4.50k Viking ship 2.00 2.00
**352** A97 4.75k Man on drift-wood 2.00 2.00
**353** A97 5.75k Arrowhead, coins 2.50 2.50
**354** A97 8k Tjodhilde's church 3.25 3.25
*a.* Souvenir sheet, #351-354 9.00 9.00
*Nos. 351-354 (4)* 9.75 9.75

See Nos. 358-361, 380-383.

Christmas A98

**1999, Nov. 11** **Litho.** *Perf. 13x13¼*
**355** A98 4.50k Writing letter 1.60 1.60
*a.* Booklet pane of 6 9.75
**356** A98 4.75k Handshake 1.75 1.75
*a.* Booklet pane of 6 10.50
Complete booklet, #355a, 356a 21.00

Millennium A99

**1999, Nov. 11** **Litho.** *Perf. 13x13¼*
**357** A99 5.75k multicolored 2.10 2.10

**Arctic Vikings Type of 1999**

Designs: 25o, Hunter, four walruses. 3k, Storyteller. 5.50k, Dog chasing reindeer. 21k, Man, gyrfalcon, polar bear, narwhal tusk, items made from animals.

**2000, Feb. 21** **Engr.** *Perf. 13x13¼*
**358** A97 25o bl gray & brn .25 .25
**359** A97 3k bl gray & brn 1.40 1.40
**360** A97 5.50k bl gray 2.25 2.25
**361** A97 21k bl gray 9.00 9.00
*a.* Souvenir sheet, #358-361 13.00 13.00
*Nos. 358-361 (4)* 12.90 12.90

Navy Dog Sled Patrol A100

**Litho. & Engr.**

**2000, Feb. 21** *Perf. 12¾*
**362** A100 10k multi 3.25 3.25

## Europa, 2000
Common Design Type

**2000, May 9 Litho.** ***Perf. 13¼x13***

| | | |
|---|---|---|
| **363** CD17 4.75k multi | *1.90* | *1.90* |

Queen Margrethe A101

**2000-01 Engr.** ***Perf. 13x13¼***

| | | |
|---|---|---|
| **364** A101 25o blk & bl gray | .30 | .25 |
| **365** A101 50o red brn & bl gray | .25 | .25 |
| **367** A101 4.50k red & bl gray | 1.75 | 1.75 |
| **368** A101 4.75k bl & bl gray | 1.90 | 1.90 |
| Complete booklet, 4 each #364, #368 | 8.50 | |
| **372** A101 8k yel grn & bl gray | 3.25 | 3.25 |
| **374** A101 10k grn & bl gray | 4.00 | 4.00 |
| **375** A101 12k pur & bl gray | 4.75 | 4.75 |
| *Nos. 364-375 (7)* | 16.20 | 16.15 |

Issued: 4.50k, 4.75k, 8k, 10k, 5/9/00. 25o, 12k, 5/9/01. 50o, 10/21/02.

Cultural Heritage — A102

**2000, Aug. 18 Litho.** ***Perf. 13¼x13***

| | | |
|---|---|---|
| **376** A102 4.50k Wooden map | 1.75 | 1.75 |
| *a.* Booklet pane of 6 + 2 labels | 10.50 | |
| **377** A102 4.75k Sealskin | 1.90 | 1.90 |
| *a.* Booklet pane of 6 + 2 labels | 11.50 | |
| Booklet, #376a, 377a | 22.50 | |

See Nos. 384-385, 392-393, 414-415

Christmas A103

**2000, Nov. 9 Litho.** ***Perf. 13x13¼***

| | | |
|---|---|---|
| **378** A103 4.50k Stars, candles | 1.75 | 1.75 |
| *a.* Booklet pane of 6 | 10.50 | |
| **379** A103 4.75k Star | 1.90 | 1.90 |
| *a.* Booklet pane of 6 | 11.50 | |
| Booklet, #378a, 379a | 22.50 | |

### Arctic Vikings Type of 1999

Designs: 1k, Hunter, dead seals. 4.50k, Mice eating food. 5k, Man and pack animals leaving. 10k, Birds on ruins.

**2001, Feb. 5 Engr.** ***Perf. 13x13¼***

| | | |
|---|---|---|
| **380** A97 1k indigo & red | 1.50 | 1.50 |
| **381** A97 4.50k indigo & blue | 1.75 | 1.75 |
| **382** A97 5k indigo & blue | 3.25 | 3.25 |
| **383** A97 10k indigo & red | 6.50 | 6.50 |
| *a.* Souvenir sheet, #380-383 | 8.25 | 8.25 |
| *Nos. 380-383 (4)* | 13.00 | 13.00 |

### Cultural Heritage Type of 2000

Designs: 4.50k, Smoked fish. 4.75k, Fishing spear.

**2001, May 9 Litho.** ***Perf. 13¼x13***

| | | |
|---|---|---|
| **384** A102 4.50k multi | 1.50 | 1.50 |
| *a.* Booklet pane of 6 + 2 labels | 10.00 | |
| **385** A102 4.75k multi | 2.00 | 2.00 |
| *a.* Booklet pane of 6 + 2 labels | 10.00 | |
| Complete booklet, #384a, 385a | 20.00 | |

Europa A104

**2001, May 9 Litho. & Engr.** ***Perf. 13***

| | | |
|---|---|---|
| **386** A104 15k Krill | *6.00* | *6.00* |

Unissued Stamps from the 1930s — A105

Designs: 5.75k, 5o Northern lights. 8k, 10o Seal. 21k, 15o Polar bear.

**Litho. & Engr.**

**2001, Oct. 16** ***Perf. 12¾***

| | | |
|---|---|---|
| **387** A105 5.75k blk & brn | 2.25 | 2.25 |
| **388** A105 8k blk & brn | 3.25 | 3.25 |
| **389** A105 21k blk & brn | 8.25 | 8.25 |
| *a.* Souvenir sheet, #387-389 + 3 labels | 14.00 | 14.00 |

Christmas A106

Grouse and: 4.50k, Berries. 4.75k, Mountain.

**2001, Oct. 16 Litho.** ***Perf. 13x13¼***

| | | |
|---|---|---|
| **390** A106 4.50k multi | 1.75 | 1.75 |
| *a.* Booklet pane of 6 | 10.50 | — |
| **391** A106 4.75k multi | 1.90 | 1.90 |
| *a.* Booklet pane of 6 | 11.50 | — |
| Complete booklet, #390a, 391a | 22.50 | |

### Cultural Heritage Type of 2000

Designs: 4.50k, Thule drum. 4.75k, Mask.

**2002, Mar. 5 Litho.** ***Perf. 13x13¼***

| | | |
|---|---|---|
| **392** A102 4.50k multi | 1.75 | 1.75 |
| *a.* Minitature sheet of 8 + label | 14.00 | — |
| **393** A102 4.75k multi | 1.90 | 1.90 |
| *a.* Miniature sheet of 8 + label | 15.00 | — |

Sculptures A107

Designs: 1k, Stone and Man, by various sculptors. 31k, Nuuk Snow Festival snow sculpture.

**2002, Mar. 5** ***Perf. 12¾***

| | | |
|---|---|---|
| **394** A107 1k multi | .40 | .40 |
| **395** A107 31k multi | 12.00 | 12.00 |

Europa — A108

**2002, June 24 Litho.** ***Perf. 12¾***

| | | |
|---|---|---|
| **396** A108 11k multi | *4.00* | *4.00* |

Ships A109

**2002, June 24 Engr.** ***Perf. 13x13¼***

| | | |
|---|---|---|
| **397** A109 2k Nordlyset | .80 | .80 |
| **398** A109 4k Hvidbjornen | 1.60 | 1.60 |
| **399** A109 6k Staerkodder | 2.40 | 2.40 |
| *a.* Booklet pane of 4, 2 each #398-399 | 8.00 | — |
| **400** A109 16k Haabet | 6.25 | 6.25 |
| *a.* Booklet pane of 4, 2 each #397, 400 | 14.00 | — |
| Complete booklet, #399a, 400a | 22.50 | |
| *Nos. 397-400 (4)* | 11.05 | 11.05 |

See Nos. 416-419, 434-437, 452-455.

Intl. Council for Exploration of the Seas, Cent. — A110

Designs: 7k, Somniosus microcephalus and iceberg. 19k, Sebastes mentella and exploration ship Paamiut.

**Litho. & Engr.**

**2002, Oct. 21** ***Perf. 13¼x13***

| | | |
|---|---|---|
| **401** A110 7k multi | 2.75 | 2.75 |
| **402** A110 19k multi | 7.50 | 7.50 |
| *a.* Souvenir sheet, #401-402 | 10.50 | 10.50 |

See Denmark Nos. 1237-1238, Faroe Islands No. 426.

Christmas — A111

Designs: 4.50k, Man with gifts, children on sled with tree. 4.75k, Family with gifts near fire.

**2002, Oct. 21 Litho.** ***Perf. 12¾***

| | | |
|---|---|---|
| **403** A111 4.50k multi | 1.90 | 1.90 |
| **404** A111 4.75k multi | 2.00 | 2.00 |

### Booklet Stamps
### Self-Adhesive

***Serpentine Die Cut 14***

| | | |
|---|---|---|
| **405** A111 4.50k multi | 1.90 | 1.90 |
| **406** A111 4.75k multi | 2.00 | 2.00 |
| *a.* Horiz. pair, #405-406 | 4.00 | |
| *b.* Booklet, 6 each #405-406 | 25.00 | |

Danish Literary Greenland Expedition, Cent. — A112

Designs: 15k, Campsite. 21k, Knud Rasmussen.

**2003, Mar. 12 Engr.** ***Perf. 12¾***

| | | |
|---|---|---|
| **407** A112 15k multi | 6.00 | 6.00 |

### Size: 28x21mm

| | | |
|---|---|---|
| **408** A112 21k blue gray | 8.25 | 8.25 |
| *a.* Souvenir sheet, #407-408 + label | 14.50 | 14.50 |

Sled Dogs A113

Designs: 4.50k, Puppies playing. 4.75k, Close-up of dog. 6k, Dog in harness.

**2003, Mar. 12** ***Perf. 13x13¼***

| | | |
|---|---|---|
| **409** A113 4.50k blue gray | 1.75 | 1.75 |
| *a.* Sheet of 8 + central label | 14.00 | 14.00 |
| **410** A113 4.75k blue gray | 1.90 | 1.90 |
| *a.* Sheet of 8 + central label | 15.00 | 15.00 |
| **411** A113 6k blue gray | 2.40 | 2.40 |
| *a.* Booklet pane, 2 each #409-411, with #411 at UL | 12.00 | — |
| *b.* Booklet pane, 2 each #409-411, with #409 at UL | 12.00 | — |
| Complete booklet, #411a, 411b | 24.00 | |

Europa — A114

**2003, June 16 Litho.** ***Perf. 13¼x13***

| | | |
|---|---|---|
| **412** A114 5.50k multi | *2.25* | *2.25* |

Town of Qaanaaq, 50th Anniv. — A115

**2003, June 16** ***Perf. 12¾***

| | | |
|---|---|---|
| **413** A115 15k multi | 6.00 | 6.00 |

### Cultural Heritage Type of 2000

Designs: 25o, Comb. 1k, Ice bucket.

**2003, June 16** ***Perf. 13¼x13***

| | | |
|---|---|---|
| **414** A102 25o multi | .25 | .25 |
| **415** A102 1k multi | .45 | .45 |

### Ship Type of 2002
### Litho. & Engr.

**2003, Oct. 20** ***Perf. 13x13¼***

| | | |
|---|---|---|
| **416** A109 6.75k Emma | 2.75 | 2.75 |
| **417** A109 7.75k Gamle Fox | 3.00 | 3.00 |
| **418** A109 8.75k Godthaab | 3.50 | 3.50 |
| **419** A109 26k Sonja | 10.00 | 10.00 |
| *Nos. 416-419 (4)* | 19.25 | 19.25 |

Christmas A116

Designs: Nos. 420, 422, Christmas tree. Nos. 421, 423, Church.

**2003, Oct. 20 Litho.** ***Perf. 12¾***

| | | |
|---|---|---|
| **420** A116 5k multi | 2.00 | 2.00 |
| **421** A116 5.50k multi | 2.25 | 2.25 |

### Booklet Stamps
### Self-Adhesive

***Serpentine Die Cut 12¼x12¾***

| | | |
|---|---|---|
| **422** A116 5k multi | 2.00 | 2.00 |
| **423** A116 5.50k multi | 2.25 | 2.25 |
| *b.* Booklet pane of 12, 6 each #422-423 | 26.00 | |
| *Nos. 420-423 (4)* | 8.50 | 8.50 |

Polar Air Route, 50th Anniv. — A117

**2004, Mar. 26 Litho.** ***Perf. 13¼x13***

| | | |
|---|---|---|
| **424** A117 8.75k multi | 3.50 | 3.50 |

Home Rule, 25th Anniv. — A118

**2004, Mar. 26** ***Perf. 12¾x12½***

| | | |
|---|---|---|
| **425** A118 11k multi | 4.25 | 4.25 |

Landing Boat From Expedition of Arctic Explorer Otto Sverdrup (1854-1930) — A119

**Litho. & Engr.**

**2004, Mar. 26** ***Perf. 13¼x13***

**426** A119 17.50k multi 7.00 7.00
*a.* Souvenir sheet of 1 + 2 labels 7.00 7.00

See Canada Nos. 2026-2027, Norway Nos. 1398-1399.

Norse Mythology A120

Designs: 5.50k, Moon Man. 6.50k, Northern Lights.

**2004, Mar. 26** **Litho.** ***Perf. 12¾***

**427** A120 5.50k multi 2.50 2.50
**428** A120 6.50k multi 2.75 2.75
*a.* Souvenir sheet, #427-428 5.25 5.25

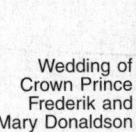

Wedding of Crown Prince Frederik and Mary Donaldson A121

Designs: 5k, Couple facing right. 5.50k, Couple facing left.

**2004, May 14** ***Perf. 13¼***

**429** A121 5k multi 2.00 2.00
**430** A121 5.50k multi 2.25 2.25
*a.* Souvenir sheet, #429-430 + central label 4.25 4.25
*b.* Booklet pane, 3 each #429-430, with #429 at top 13.00 —
*c.* As "b," with #430 at top 13.00 —
Complete booklet, #430b-430c 26.00

Edible Plants A122

Designs: 5k, Angelica archangelica. 5.50k, Thymus praecox. 17k, Empetrum hermaphroditum.

**2004, May 14** ***Perf. 13x13¼***

**431** A122 5k multi 2.00 2.00
*a.* Sheet of 8 + central label 16.00 16.00
**432** A122 5.50k multi 2.25 2.25
*a.* Sheet of 8 + central label 18.00 18.00
**433** A122 17k multi 6.75 6.75
*Nos. 431-433 (3)* 11.00 11.00

See Nos. 459-461

**Ships Type of 2002**

**Litho. & Engr.**

**2004, Oct. 18** ***Perf. 13x13¼***

**434** A109 6.50k Constance 2.50 2.50
**435** A109 8.75k Disko 3.50 3.50
**436** A109 14k Julius Thomsen 5.50 5.50
**437** A109 21.75k Misigssut 8.75 8.75
*Nos. 434-437 (4)* 20.25 20.25

Europa — A123

**2004, Oct. 18** **Litho.** ***Perf. 13¼x13***

**438** A123 6.50k multi *2.50 2.50*

Christmas A124

Designs: 5k, Family, Christmas tree. 5.50k, Carolers with lanterns.

**2004, Oct. 18** ***Perf. 12¾***

**439** A124 5k multi 2.00 2.00
**440** A124 5.50k multi 2.25 2.25

**Booklet Stamps**

**Self-Adhesive**

***Serpentine Die Cut 12¼x12¾***

**441** A124 5k multi 2.00 2.00
**442** A124 5.50k multi 2.25 2.25
*a.* Horiz. pair, #441-442 4.25
*b.* Complete booklet, 6 #442a 26.00
*Nos. 439-442 (4)* 8.50 8.50

Ilulissat Ice Fjord, UNESCO World Heritage Site — A125

**2005, Jan. 17** **Litho.** ***Perf. 12¾***

**443** A125 6k multi 2.40 2.40

Church and School Systems Law, Cent. — A126

**2005, Jan. 17** ***Perf. 12¾***

**444** A126 9.25k multi 3.75 3.75

Europa — A127

**2005, Jan. 17** ***Perf. 13¼x13***

**445** A127 11.75k multi 4.75 4.75

Mushrooms — A128

Designs: 5.25k, Leccinum sp. 6k, Russula subrubens. 7k, Amanita groenlandica.

**2005, Jan. 17** ***Perf. 13x13¼***

**446** A128 5.25k multi 2.10 2.10
*a.* Sheet of 8 + central label 17.00 —
**447** A128 6k multi 2.40 2.40
*a.* Sheet of 8 + central label 19.00 —
**448** A128 7k multi 2.75 2.75
*Nos. 446-448 (3)* 7.25 7.25

**Booklet Stamps**

**Self-Adhesive**

***Serpentine Die Cut 9¾x10¼***

**449** A128 5.25k multi 2.10 2.10
**450** A128 6k multi 2.40 2.40
**451** A128 7k multi 2.75 2.75
*a.* Booklet pane, 2 each #449-451 14.50
Complete booklet, 2 #451a 29.00
*Nos. 449-451 (3)* 7.25 7.25

No. 451a has two different marginal designs.

See Nos. 476-480.

**Ships Type of 2002**

**Litho. & Engr.**

**2005, June 20** ***Perf. 13x13¼***

**452** A109 5.25k Dannebrog 2.10 2.10
**453** A109 6k Kista Arctica 2.40 2.40
**454** A109 18.50k Sarpik Ittuk 7.25 7.25
**455** A109 23k Triton 9.25 9.25
*Nos. 452-455 (4)* 21.00 21.00

Science In Greenland — A129

Designs: 7.25k, Geological map. 9.25k, Diver at limestone columns in Ikka Fjord, horiz. 10k, Limnognathia maerski, horiz.

***Perf. 13¼x13, 13x13¼***

**2005, June 20**

**456** A129 7.25k multi 3.00 3.00
**457** A129 9.25k multi 3.75 3.75
**458** A129 10k multi 4.00 4.00
*Nos. 456-458 (3)* 10.75 10.75

**Edible Plants Type of 2004**

Designs: 75o, Ligusticum scoticum. 6.50k, Rhodiola rosea. 8.25k, Oxyria digyna.

**2005, Oct. 31** **Litho.** ***Perf. 13x13¼***

**459** A122 75o multi .30 .30
**460** A122 6.50k multi 2.50 2.50
**461** A122 8.25k multi 3.25 3.25
*Nos. 459-461 (3)* 6.05 6.05

Admiral Robert E. Peary (1856-1920), Explorer — A130

**Litho. & Engr.**

**2005, Oct. 31** ***Perf. 13***

**462** A130 27.50k multi 11.00 11.00
*a.* Souvenir sheet of 1 11.00 11.00

Parcel Post Stamps, Cent. — A131

**2005-07** **Litho.** ***Perf. 14x13½***

**463** A131 25k #Q3 10.00 10.00

***Perf. 12¾x13***

**464** A131 50k #Q4 20.00 20.00
*a.* Perf. 14x13½, dated "2007" 18.00 18.00

Issued: 25k, 1/16/06; No. 464, 10/3; No. 464a, 2007.

No. 464a is found only in No. 497a, along with an example of No. 463 dated "2007." Issued: No. 464a, 5/21/07.

See No. 497.

Christmas A132

Designs: 5.25k, Boy at left. 6k, Girl at right.

**2005, Oct. 31** ***Perf. 12¾***

**465** A132 5.25k multi 2.10 2.10
**466** A132 6k multi 2.40 2.40

**Booklet Stamps**

**Self-Adhesive**

***Serpentine Die Cut 12¾x13***

**467** A132 5.25k multi 2.10 2.10
**468** A132 6k multi 2.40 2.40
*b.* Booklet pane, 6 each #467-468 27.50

Whale Jaw Gate and Blue Church, Sisimiut — A138

**2006, Jan. 16** ***Perf. 13¾x13¼***

**469** A138 9.75k multi 4.00 4.00

Sisimiut, 250th anniv.

Nordic Union "Norden" Stamps, 50th Anniv. — A139

**2006, Jan. 16**

**470** A139 19.50k multi 7.75 7.75

European Philatelic Cooperation, 50th Anniv. — A140

**2006, Jan. 16** ***Perf. 14x13¼***

**471** A140 26.50k #438 and stars 10.50 10.50

Europa stamps, 50th anniv.

Norse Mythology A141

Designs: 7.50k, The Mother of the Sea. 13.50k, Asiaq, Mistress of the Weather.

***Perf. 13¾x13½***

**2006, Mar. 29** **Litho.**

**472** A141 7.50k multi 3.00 3.00
**473** A141 13.50k multi 5.25 5.25
*a.* Souvenir sheet, #472-473 8.25 8.25

Sheep Farming in Greenland, Cent. A142

**2006, May 22**

**474** A142 7.50k multi 3.00 3.00

Alfred Wegener (1880-1930), Geophysicist A143

**2006, May 22** **Engr.** ***Perf. 13x13¼***

**475** A143 20.75k red & blue 8.25 8.25
*a.* Souvenir sheet of 1 8.25 8.25

**Mushrooms Type of 2005**

Designs: 5.50k, Rozites caperatus. 7k, Lactarius dryadophilus. 10k, Calvatia cretacea.

**2006, May 22 Litho. *Perf. 14x13¼***

| | | | | |
|---|---|---|---|---|
| 476 | A128 5.50k multi | | 2.25 | 2.25 |
| a. | Sheet of 8 + central label | | 18.00 | 18.00 |
| 477 | A128 7k multi | | 2.75 | 2.75 |
| a. | Sheet of 8 + central label | | 22.00 | 22.00 |
| 478 | A128 10k multi | | 4.00 | 4.00 |
| | *Nos. 476-478 (3)* | | 9.00 | 9.00 |

**Self-Adhesive**

**Booklet Stamps**

***Serpentine Die Cut 12¼x12***

| | | | |
|---|---|---|---|
| 479 | A128 5.50k multi | 2.25 | 2.25 |
| 480 | A128 7k multi | 2.75 | 2.75 |
| a. | Booklet pane, 3 each #479-480 | 15.00 | |
| | Complete booklet, 2 #480a | 30.00 | |

No. 480a has two different marginal designs.

Galathea 3 Research Expedition — A144

**2006, Sept. 9 Litho. *Perf. 13½x14***

| | | | |
|---|---|---|---|
| 481 | A144 9.75k multi | 4.00 | 4.00 |

Science — A145

Designs: 50o, Larch tree preserved in Kap Kobenhavn Formation. 8k, Geologist obtaining rock sample from mountains at Isua. 15.50k, Qeqertarsuaq Arctic Station, cent.

**Litho. & Engr.**

**2006, Nov. 6 *Perf. 13¼x13***

| | | | |
|---|---|---|---|
| 482 | A145 50o multi | .25 | .25 |
| 483 | A145 8k multi | 3.25 | 3.25 |
| 484 | A145 15.50k multi | 6.25 | 6.25 |
| | *Nos. 482-484 (3)* | 9.75 | 9.75 |

See Nos. 502-504, 524-526, 552-554.

Christmas A146

Music for hymn and: 5.50k, Angel. 7k, Candle.

**2006, Nov. 6 Litho. *Perf. 13¾x13½***

| | | | |
|---|---|---|---|
| 485 | A146 5.50k multi | 2.25 | 2.25 |
| 486 | A146 7k multi | 2.75 | 2.75 |

**Booklet Stamps**

**Self-Adhesive**

***Serpentine Die Cut 12¼x12***

| | | | |
|---|---|---|---|
| 487 | A146 5.50k multi | 2.00 | 2.00 |
| 488 | A146 7k multi | 2.50 | 2.50 |
| a. | Booklet pane, 3 each #487-488 | 13.50 | — |
| | Complete booklet, 2 #488a | 27.00 | |

Hydroelectric Power — A147

**2007, Jan. 15 Litho. *Perf. 13¾x13½***

| | | | |
|---|---|---|---|
| 489 | A147 5k multi | 1.75 | 1.75 |

West Nordic Council, 10th anniv.

Crown Prince Frederik, Crown Princess Mary and Prince Christian — A148

**2007, Jan. 15 *Perf. 13¼x14***

| | | | |
|---|---|---|---|
| 490 | A148 14.25k multi | 5.00 | 5.00 |

Intl. Polar Year A149

Designs: 7.50k, Scientists drilling ice cores. 8k, Urbanization.

**Litho. & Engr.**

**2007, Jan. 15 *Perf. 13x13¼***

| | | | |
|---|---|---|---|
| 491 | A149 7.50k multi | 2.60 | 2.60 |
| 492 | A149 8k multi | 2.75 | 2.75 |
| a. | Souvenir sheet, #491-492 | 5.50 | 5.50 |

Europa — A150

Scouts: 5.75k, And rock pile. 7.50k, At campsite.

**2007, Jan. 15 Litho. *Perf. 13¾x13¼***

| | | | |
|---|---|---|---|
| 493 | A150 5.75k multi | 2.00 | 2.00 |
| a. | Sheet of 8 + central label | 16.00 | 16.00 |
| 494 | A150 7.50k multi | 2.60 | 2.60 |
| a. | Sheet of 8 + central label | 21.00 | 21.00 |

**Booklet Stamps**

**Self-Adhesive**

***Serpentine Die Cut 12¼x12***

| | | | |
|---|---|---|---|
| 495 | A150 5.75k multi | 2.00 | 2.00 |
| 496 | A150 7.50k multi | 2.60 | 2.60 |
| a. | Booklet pane, 3 each #495-496 | 14.00 | — |
| | Complete booklet, 2 #496a | 28.00 | |

**Parcel Post Stamp Centenary Type of 2005-06**

**2007, May 21 Litho. *Perf. 14x13½***

| | | | |
|---|---|---|---|
| 497 | A131 100k #Q6 | 37.50 | 37.50 |
| a. | Souvenir sheet, #463, 464a, 497 | 65.00 | 65.00 |

Examples of Nos. 463 and 464a in No. 497a are dated "2007."

A151

Contemporary Art — A152

Unnamed paintings by: 3k, Jens Rosing. 8.50k, Anne-Birthe Hove. 10.50k, Linda Riber Sorensen.

**2007, May 21**

| | | | |
|---|---|---|---|
| 498 | A151 3k multi | 1.10 | 1.10 |
| 499 | A152 8.50k multi | 3.25 | 3.25 |
| 500 | A152 10.50k multi | 3.75 | 3.75 |
| | *Nos. 498-500 (3)* | 8.10 | 8.10 |

Greenlandic Landscape — A153

**2007, Oct. 1**

| | | | |
|---|---|---|---|
| 501 | A153 6.50k multi | 2.50 | 2.50 |

**Science Type of 2006**

Designs: 75o, Planting of Greenlandic flag on Tubbiap Queqertaa. 2k, Soapstone bowl and quarry. 10.25k, Cyanobacteria.

**Litho. & Engr.**

**2007, Oct. 1 *Perf. 13¼x13***

| | | | |
|---|---|---|---|
| 502 | A145 75o multi | .30 | .30 |
| 503 | A145 2k multi | .75 | .75 |
| 504 | A145 10.25k multi | 4.00 | 4.00 |
| | *Nos. 502-504 (3)* | 5.05 | 5.05 |

Ship Pourquois-Pas? — A154

Paul-Emile Victor (1907-95), Arctic Explorer — A155

**2007, Nov. 8 Engr. *Perf. 13½***

| | | | |
|---|---|---|---|
| 505 | A154 5.75k multi | 2.25 | 2.25 |
| 506 | A155 7.50k multi | 3.00 | 3.00 |
| a. | Souvenir sheet, #505-506, + label | 5.25 | 5.25 |

See France No. 3369.

Christmas — A156

Snowflakes and: 5.75k, Angel. 7.50k, Star.

**2007, Nov. 8 Litho. *Perf. 13½x13¾***

| | | | |
|---|---|---|---|
| 507 | A156 5.75k multi | 2.25 | 2.25 |
| 508 | A156 7.50k multi | 3.00 | 3.00 |

**Self-Adhesive**

**Booklet Stamps**

***Serpentine Die Cut 12x12¼***

| | | | |
|---|---|---|---|
| 509 | A156 5.75k multi | 2.25 | 2.25 |
| 510 | A156 7.50k multi | 3.00 | 3.00 |
| b. | Booklet pane of 12, 6 each #509-510 | 31.50 | |

Europa — A157

Envelope half and: 5.75k, Man. 7.50k, Woman.

**2008, Jan. 31 Litho. *Perf. 13¾x13½***

| | | | |
|---|---|---|---|
| 511 | A157 5.75k multi | 2.40 | 2.40 |
| a. | Sheet of 8 + central label | 19.50 | 19.50 |
| 512 | A157 7.50k multi | 3.00 | 3.00 |
| a. | Sheet of 8 + central label | 24.00 | 24.00 |

**Booklet Stamps**

**Self-Adhesive**

***Serpentine Die Cut 12¼x12***

| | | | |
|---|---|---|---|
| 513 | A157 5.75k multi | 2.40 | 2.40 |
| 514 | A157 7.50k multi | 3.00 | 3.00 |
| a. | Booklet pane, 6 each #513-514 | 32.50 | |

Contemporary Art — A158

Unnamed paintings by: 5.50k, Ina Rosing. 14.25k, Buuti Pedersen. 30.50k, Aka Hoegh.

**2008, Jan. 31 *Perf. 14x13½***

| | | | |
|---|---|---|---|
| 515 | A158 5.50k multi | 2.25 | 2.25 |
| 516 | A158 14.25k multi | 5.75 | 5.75 |
| 517 | A158 30.50k multi | 12.50 | 12.50 |
| | *Nos. 515-517 (3)* | 20.50 | 20.50 |

Mythical Places — A159

Myths of: 7k, Kayaker and river rocks. 8k, Bear of the Lake.

***Perf. 13¾x13½***

**2008, Mar. 27 Litho.**

| | | | |
|---|---|---|---|
| 518 | A159 7k multi | 3.00 | 3.00 |
| 519 | A159 8k multi | 3.50 | 3.50 |
| a. | Souvenir sheet, #518-519 | 6.50 | 6.50 |

Wedding of Prince Joachim and Marie Cavallier — A160

**2008, May 24 Litho. *Perf. 13½x14***

| | | | |
|---|---|---|---|
| 520 | A160 10.25k multi | 4.50 | 4.50 |

Fossils A161

Designs: 1k, Halkieria evangelista. 20.50k, Ichthyostega stensioei. 25k, Eudimorphodon cromptonellus.

**Litho. & Engr.**

**2008, May 24 *Perf. 13x13¼***

| | | | |
|---|---|---|---|
| 521 | A161 1k multi | .45 | .45 |
| 522 | A161 20.50k multi | 8.75 | 8.75 |
| 523 | A161 25k multi | 10.50 | 10.50 |
| | *Nos. 521-523 (3)* | 19.70 | 19.70 |

See Nos. 553-555.

**Science Type of 2006**

Designs: 6.50k, Scientist, equipment hauler, satellite above Greenland. 10.50k, French station at Scoresbysund. 28k, Danish Arctic station at Nuuk.

**Litho. & Engr.**

**2008, Oct. 20** *Perf. 13¼x13*

| | | | |
|---|---|---|---|
| **524** A145 6.50k multi | 2.25 | 2.25 |
| **525** A145 10.50k multi | 3.75 | 3.75 |
| **526** A145 28k multi | 9.75 | 9.75 |
| *a.* Souvenir sheet, #524-526 | 16.00 | 16.00 |
| *Nos. 524-526 (3)* | 15.75 | 15.75 |

International Geophysical Year, 50th anniv. (#524); French station at Scoresbysund, 75th anniv. (#525); Danish Arctic station at Nuuk, 125th anniv. (#526).

Expedition Ship Sofia — A162

Adolf Erik Nordenskiöld (1832-1901), Arctic Explorer — A163

**2008, Oct. 20** *Perf. 13¼x13*

| | | |
|---|---|---|
| **527** A162 8.50k multi | 3.00 | 3.00 |
| **528** A163 16.25k multi | 5.75 | 5.75 |
| *a.* Souvenir sheet, #527-528, + label | 8.75 | 8.75 |

See Finland No. 1321.

Christmas A164

Designs: 5.75k, Reindeer and house. 7.50k, Christmas tree and houses.

**2008, Oct. 20 Litho.** *Perf. 13¾x13¼*

| | | |
|---|---|---|
| **529** A164 5.75k multi | 2.00 | 2.00 |
| **530** A164 7.50k multi | 2.60 | 2.60 |

**Booklet Stamps**

**Self-Adhesive**

***Serpentine Die Cut 12¼x12***

| | | |
|---|---|---|
| **531** A164 5.75k multi | 2.00 | 2.00 |
| **532** A164 7.50k multi | 2.60 | 2.60 |
| *b.* Booklet pane of 12, 6 each #531-532 | 28.00 | |

**Fossils Type of 2008**

Designs: 2k, Schizoneura carcinoides. 11.50k, Scaphites rosenkrantzi. 22k, Mallotus villosus.

**Litho. & Engr.**

**2009, Jan. 19** *Perf. 13x13¼*

| | | |
|---|---|---|
| **533** A161 2k multi | .70 | .70 |
| **534** A161 11.50k multi | 4.00 | 4.00 |
| **535** A161 22k multi | 7.75 | 7.75 |
| *Nos. 533-535 (3)* | 12.45 | 12.45 |

Preservation of Polar Regions and Glaciers — A165

**2009, Jan. 19 Litho.** *Perf. 14x13¼*

| | | |
|---|---|---|
| **536** A165 5k multi | 1.75 | 1.75 |

Europa — A166

Designs: 6.25k, Ursa Major constellation. 8k, Ursa Major constellation and outline of bear.

**2009, Jan. 19** *Perf. 13¼x13¾*

| | | |
|---|---|---|
| **537** A166 6.25k multi | 2.25 | 2.25 |
| *a.* Sheet of 8 + central label | 18.00 | 18.00 |
| **538** A166 8k multi | 2.75 | 2.75 |
| *a.* Sheet of 8 + central label | 22.00 | 22.00 |

**Booklet Stamps**

**Self-Adhesive**

***Serpentine Die Cut 12x12¼***

| | | |
|---|---|---|
| **539** A166 6.25k multi | 2.25 | 2.25 |
| **540** A166 8k multi | 2.75 | 2.75 |
| *a.* Booklet pane of 12, 6 each #539-540 | 30.00 | |

Intl. Year of Astronomy.

Prince Henri, 75th Birthday — A167

**2009, June 11 Litho.** *Perf. 13¼x14*

| | | |
|---|---|---|
| **541** A167 8k multi | 3.00 | 3.00 |

Self-Governance — A168

**2009, June 21** *Perf. 14x13¼*

| | | |
|---|---|---|
| **542** A168 6.25k multi | 2.40 | 2.40 |

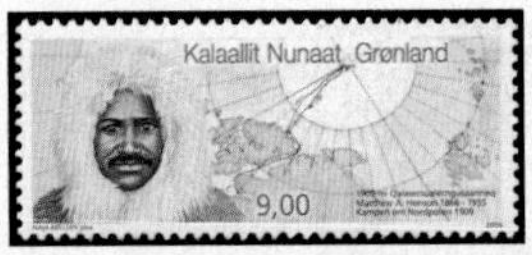


Matthew Henson (1866-1955), Polar Explorer — A169

**2009, June 21** *Perf. 13¼x13¾*

| | | |
|---|---|---|
| **543** A169 9k multi | 3.50 | 3.50 |

First Steps, Comic Strip by Nuka K. Godtfredsen — A170

**2009, June 21** *Perf. 14x13¼*

| | | |
|---|---|---|
| **544** A170 15.50k multi | 6.00 | 6.00 |
| *a.* Souvenir sheet of 1 | 6.00 | 6.00 |

Contemporary Art — A171

Designs: 6k, Two Polar Bears From Above, by Ivalo Abelsen. 18k, Window to the World, by Camilla Nielsen. 33k, Gletscher, by Naja Abelsen.

**2009, June 21**

| | | |
|---|---|---|
| **545** A171 6k multi | 2.25 | 2.25 |
| **546** A171 18k multi | 6.75 | 6.75 |
| **547** A171 33k multi | 12.50 | 12.50 |
| *Nos. 545-547 (3)* | 21.50 | 21.50 |

Greenlandic Landscape — A172

**2009, Sept. 16 Litho.** *Perf. 14x13¼*

| | | |
|---|---|---|
| **548** A172 7k multi | 2.75 | 2.75 |

North Star Mission Station, Thule, Cent. — A173

**2009, Oct. 19 Engr.** *Perf. 13¼x13*

| | | |
|---|---|---|
| **549** A173 15.25k black | 6.25 | 6.25 |

Otto Nordenskjold (1869-1928), Arctic Explorer — A174

**Litho. & Engr.**

**2009, Oct. 19** *Perf. 13¼x13*

**Sans-Serif Inscriptions**

| | | |
|---|---|---|
| **550** A174 30k multi | 12.00 | 12.00 |

**Souvenir Sheet**

**Serifed Inscriptions**

| | | |
|---|---|---|
| **551** A174 30k multi + label | 12.00 | 12.00 |

**Science Type of 2006**

Designs: 1k, Cryolite mine, Ivittuut. 15.50k, Himantolophus groenlandicus. 23.50k, Gold mine, Nalunaq.

**2009, Oct. 19** *Perf. 13¼x14*

| | | |
|---|---|---|
| **552** A145 1k multi | .40 | .40 |
| **553** A145 15.50k multi | 6.25 | 6.25 |
| **554** A145 23.50k multi | 9.50 | 9.50 |
| *a.* Souvenir sheet, #552-554 | 16.50 | 16.50 |
| *Nos. 552-554 (3)* | 16.15 | 16.15 |

Christmas A175

Star and: 6.25k, Family. 8k, Baby.

**2009, Oct. 19 Litho.** *Perf. 13¾x13¼*

| | | |
|---|---|---|
| **555** A175 6.25k multi | 2.50 | 2.50 |
| **556** A175 8k multi | 3.25 | 3.25 |

**Booklet Stamps**

**Self-Adhesive**

***Serpentine Die Cut 12¼x12***

| | | |
|---|---|---|
| **557** A175 6.25k multi | 2.50 | 2.50 |
| **558** A175 8k multi | 3.25 | 3.25 |
| *b.* Booklet pane, 6 each #557-558 | 35.00 | |

Air Greenland, 50th Anniv. — A176

**2010, Jan. 18 Litho.** *Perf. 12½x12¾*

| | | |
|---|---|---|
| **559** A176 16.50kmulti | 6.25 | 6.25 |

Contemporary Art — A177

Designs: 6.50k, Polar Bear, by Maria Panînguak' Kjaerulff. 7.50k, Sun, by Miki Jacobsen, vert. 50k, Greenland Razorbills, by Bolatta Silis-Hoegh.

**2010, Jan. 18** *Perf. 14x13¼, 13¼x14*

| | | |
|---|---|---|
| **560** A177 6.50k multi | 2.50 | 2.50 |
| **561** A177 7.50k multi | 2.75 | 2.75 |
| **562** A177 50k multi | 19.00 | 19.00 |
| *Nos. 560-562 (3)* | 24.25 | 24.25 |

Europa — A178

Designs: 8.50k, Boy reading book. 9.50k, Children reading book.

**2010, Jan. 18** *Perf. 13¾x13¼*

| | | |
|---|---|---|
| **563** A178 8.50k multi | 3.25 | 3.25 |
| *a.* Sheet of 8 + central label | 26.00 | 26.00 |
| **564** A178 9.50k multi | 3.50 | 3.50 |
| *a.* Sheet of 8 + central label | 28.00 | 28.00 |

**Booklet Stamps**

**Self-Adhesive**

***Serpentine Die Cut 12¼x12***

| | | |
|---|---|---|
| **565** A178 8.50k multi | 3.25 | 3.25 |
| **566** A178 9.50k multi | 3.50 | 3.50 |
| *a.* Booklet pane of 12, 6 each #565-566 | 41.00 | |

Intl. Women's Day, Cent. — A179

**2010, Mar. 8 Litho.** *Perf. 13¼x14*

| | | |
|---|---|---|
| **567** A179 12.50k multi | 4.50 | 4.50 |

Life by the Sea — A180

Designs: 7k, Sea ice. 8.50k, Port and sea ice.

**2010, Mar. 24** *Perf. 13¾x13¼*

568 A180 7k multi 2.50 2.50
569 A180 8.50k multi 3.25 3.25
a. Souvenir sheet, #568-569 5.75 5.75

Queen Margrethe II, 70th Birthday — A181

**2010, Apr. 16** *Perf. 13¼x14*

570 A181 35k multi 12.50 12.50

Flag of Greenland, 25th Anniv. — A182

**2010, May 1**

571 A182 7k multi 2.40 2.40

Buuarsikkut, Comic Strip by Robert Holmene — A183

**2010, May 1** *Perf. 14x13¼*

572 A183 23.50k multi 8.00 8.00
a. Souvenir sheet of 1 8.00 8.00

Thule Trading Station, Cent. — A184

**2010, Oct. 18 Engr.** *Perf. 12¼x12½*

573 A184 25k black 9.50 9.50

Hans Sakaeus (c. 1797-1819), Interpreter for Explorer John Ross — A185

Ross Expedition Ships Isabella and Alexander — A186

**2010, Oct. 18** *Perf. 12½x12*

574 A185 25o pur & bl blk .25 .25
575 A186 32k pur & bl blk 12.00 12.00
a. Souvenir sheet, #574-575, + label 12.50 12.50

Mining in Greenland A187

Designs: 50o, King Frederik VII's copper mine. 26.50k, Ivituut cryolite mine.

***Die Cut Perf. 13x13¼***

**2010, Oct. 18** **Litho.**

**Self-Adhesive**

576 A187 50o multi .25 .25
577 A187 26.50k multi 10.00 10.00

See Nos. 601-602, 616-617.

Christmas A188

Santa Claus and: 7k, Two children. 8.50k, One child.

**2010, Oct. 18** *Perf. 13¾x13¼*

578 A188 7k multi 2.75 2.75
579 A188 8.50k multi 3.25 3.25

**Booklet Stamps**

**Self-Adhesive**

***Serpentine Die Cut 12¼x12***

580 A188 7k multi 2.75 2.75
581 A188 8.50k multi 3.25 3.25
b. Booklet pane of 12, 6 each #580-581 36.00

Herbs A189

Designs: 13.50k, Sorbus groenlandica. 25k, Vaccinium vitis-idaea.

**2011, Jan. 17** *Perf. 13*

582 A189 13.50k multi 5.00 5.00
583 A189 25k multi 9.25 9.25

See Nos. 608-609.

Mail Delivery Man in Kamik A190

Atuagagdliutit Newspaper, 150th Anniv. — A191

Greenland Connect Submarine Cable, 2nd Anniv. A192

**2011, Jan. 17** *Perf. 13*

584 A190 2k multi .75 .75
a. Perf. 12¾x12½ .75 .75
585 A191 7.50k multi 2.75 2.75
a. Perf. 12¾x12½ 2.75 2.75
586 A192 46.50k multi 17.00 17.00
a. Perf. 12¾x12½ 17.00 17.00
b. Souvenir sheet of 3, #584a, 585a, 586a 20.50 20.50
*Nos. 584-586 (3)* 20.50 20.50

Communications in Greenland.

Europa — A193

Trees in: 9k, Winter. 10k, Summer.

**2011, Jan. 17** *Perf. 12¾x13*

587 A193 9k multi 3.25 3.25
a. Sheet of 8 + central label 26.00 26.00
588 A193 10k multi 3.75 3.75
a. Sheet of 8 + central label 30.00 30.00

**Booklet Stamps**

**Self-Adhesive**

***Serpentine Die Cut 13x13¼***

589 A193 9k multi 3.25 3.25
590 A193 10k multi 3.75 3.75
b. Booklet pane of 12, 6 each #589-590 42.00

Intl. Year of Forests.

Civil Aircraft — A194

Designs: 8k, Consolidated PBY-5A Catalina. 17.50k, De Havilland DHC-3 Otter.

**2011, May 9 Engr.** *Perf. 12½x12*

591 A194 8k multi 3.00 3.00
592 A194 17.50k multi 6.75 6.75

See Nos. 624-626.

Queen Margrethe II — A195

**2011, May 9 Engr.** *Perf. 13*

593 A195 50o claret *3.00 3.00*
594 A195 1k blue green *6.00 6.00*

Kaassassuk, Comic Strip by Christian Fleischer Rex — A196

**2011, May 9 Litho.** *Perf. 12¾x12½*

595 A196 20k multi 7.75 7.75
a. Souvenir sheet of 1 7.75 7.75

Commonwealth of the Realm Pause, by Julie Edel Hardenberg — A197

Painting by Naja Rosing-Asvid — A198

Painting by Anne-Lise Lovstrom — A199

**2011, May 9**

596 A197 3k multi 1.25 1.25
597 A198 7k multi 2.75 2.75
598 A199 34k multi 13.00 13.00
*Nos. 596-598 (3)* 17.00 17.00

Naomi Uemura (1941-84), Adventurer — A200

**2011, July 28 Engr.** *Perf. 12½x12*

599 A200 36.50k multi 14.00 14.00
a. Souvenir sheet of 1, perf. 12¾x12½ 14.00 14.00

Uemura was, in 1978, the first man to cross Greenland from north to south.

Dogsleds Near Iceberg — A201

**2011, Sept. 28 Litho.** *Perf. 12¾*

600 A201 8k multi 3.00 3.00

**Mining Type of 2010**

Designs: 75o, Shaft tower, Josva's copper mine. 28k, Miners and equipment, Qaarsuarsuk coal mine.

**2011, Oct. 17** ***Die Cut Perf. 13x13¼***

**Self-Adhesive**

601 A187 75o multi .30 .30
602 A187 28k multi 10.50 10.50

Christmas — A202

Girls: 7.50k, Looking at Christmas star through window. 9k, With dogsled carrying gifts, horiz.

**2011, Oct. 17** *Perf. 12½x13*
**603** A202 7.50k multi 2.75 2.75

*Perf. 13x12½*

**604** A202 9k multi 3.50 3.50

**Booklet Stamps**
**Self-Adhesive**

***Serpentine Die Cut 13x13¼***

**605** A202 7.50k multi 2.75 2.75

***Serpentine Die Cut 13¼x13***

**606** A202 9k multi 3.50 3.50
*a.* Booklet pane of 12, 6 each #605-606 37.50

Reign of Queen Margrethe II, 40th Anniv. — A203

**Litho. & Engr.**

**2012, Jan. 4** *Perf. 13¼*
**607** A203 26.50k multi 9.50 9.50
*a.* Souvenir sheet of 1 9.50 9.50

**Herbs Type of 2011**

Designs: 14.50k, Vaccinium uliginosum. 18.50k, Ledum groenlandicum.

**2012, Jan. 16** **Litho.** *Perf. 14x13¼*
**608** A189 14.50k multi 5.25 5.25
**609** A189 18.50k multi 6.50 6.50

Knud Rasmussen Folk High School, Sisimiut, 50th Anniv. — A204

**2012, Jan. 16**
**610** A204 21k multi 7.50 7.50

Painting by Jessie Kleemann — A205

Iceberg by Frederik "Kunngi" Kristensen — A206

Map of Denmark With Ice Sheet, by Inuk Silis Hoegh — A207

**2012, Jan. 16**
**611** A205 8.50k multi 3.00 3.00
**612** A206 9.50k multi 3.50 3.50
**613** A207 38.50k multi 14.00 14.00
*a.* Souvenir sheet of 1 14.00 14.00
*Nos. 611-613 (3)* 20.50 20.50

Marine Life — A208

Iceberg and: 8k, Seal. 9.50k, Whale.

**2012, Mar. 21** *Perf. 13¾x13¼*
**614** A208 8k multi 3.00 3.00
**615** A208 9.50k multi 3.50 3.50
*a.* Souvenir sheet of 2, #614-615 6.50 6.50

**Mining Type of 2010**

Designs: 25o, Eqalussuit graphite mine. 14.50k, Amitsoq graphite mine.

**2012, May 7** *Die Cut Perf. 13x13¼*
**Self-Adhesive**
**616** A187 25o multi .25 .25
**617** A187 14.50k multi 5.00 5.00

Agriculture A209

Designs: 75o, Field of vegetables. 49k, Cattle.

**2012, May 7** *Perf. 12¾x12½*
**618** A209 75o multi .25 .25
**619** A209 49k multi 16.50 16.50

Europa A210

Designs: 9.50k, Aurora Borealis. 10.50k, Ship and sea ice.

**2012, May 7** *Perf. 14x13½*
**620** A210 9.50k multi 3.25 3.25
*a.* Sheet of 8 + central label 26.00 26.00
**621** A210 10.50k multi 3.50 3.50
*a.* Sheet of 8 + central label 28.00 28.00

**Booklet Stamps**
**Self-Adhesive**

***Serpentine Die Cut 13x12¾***

**622** A210 9.50k multi 3.25 3.25
**623** A210 10.50k multi 3.50 3.50
*a.* Booklet pane of 12, 6 each #622-623 41.00

Queen Margrethe II — A211

**Litho. & Engr.**

**2012, Oct. 22** *Perf. 13¼x13*
**627** A211 50o red & blue .25 .25
**628** A211 1k green & blue .35 .35

Hans Hendrik (Suersaq) (1834-89), Polar Explorer — A212

**2012, Oct. 22** *Perf. 13*
**629** A212 29.50k maroon & black 10.00 10.00
*a.* Souvenir sheet of 1 10.00 10.00

Christmas — A213

Heads of Inuit girls: 8k, On Christmas trees. 9.50k, In circles, evergreen branches, flags of Greenland, horiz.

**2012, Oct. 22** **Litho.** *Perf. 13¼x13¾*
**630** A213 8k multi 2.75 2.75

*Perf. 13¾x13¼*

**631** A213 9.50k multi 3.25 3.25

**Booklet Stamps**
**Self-Adhesive**

***Serpentine Die Cut 13x12½***

**632** A213 8k multi 2.75 2.75

***Serpentine Die Cut 12½x13***

**633** A213 9.50k multi 3.25 3.25
*a.* Booklet pane of 12, 6 each #632-633 36.00

**Civil Aircraft Type of 2011**

Designs: 7.50k, Douglas DC-4. 28k, Sikorsky S61N helicopter. 36k, Bell 206 Jet Ranger helicopter.

**Litho. & Engr.**

**2012, Oct. 22** *Perf. 13*
**624** A194 7.50k multi 2.60 2.60
**625** A194 28k multi 9.75 9.75
**626** A194 36k multi 12.50 12.50
*Nos. 624-626 (3)* 24.85 24.85

## SEMI-POSTAL STAMPS

**Catalogue values for unused stamps in this section are for Never Hinged items.**

No. 35 Surcharged in Red

**1958, May 22** **Engr.** *Perf. 13*
**B1** A7 30o + 10o on 50o 6.00 1.90

The surtax was for the campaign against tuberculosis in Greenland.

No. 32 Surcharged

**1959, Feb. 23** **Unwmk.**
**B2** A6 30o + 10o on 25o 5.25 5.25

The surtax was for the benefit of the Greenland Fund.

Two Greenland Boys in Round Tower — SP1

**1968, Sept. 12** **Engr.** *Perf. 13*
**B3** SP1 60o + 10o dark red 1.25 *1.25*

Surtax for child welfare work in Greenland.

Hans Egede Explaining Bible to Natives — SP2

**1971, July 3** **Engr.** *Perf. 13*
**B4** SP2 60o + 10o red brown 2.75 2.75

See footnote after No. 77.

Frederik IX, "Dannebrog" off Umanak — SP3

**1972, Apr. 20**
**B5** SP3 60o + 10o dull red 1.75 1.75

King Frederik IX (1899-1972). The surtax was for humanitarian and charitable purposes.

Heimaey Town and Volcano — SP4

**1973, Oct. 18** **Engr.** *Perf. 13*
**B6** SP4 70o + 20o gray & red 1.75 1.75

The surtax was for the victims of the eruption of Heimaey Volcano.

Arm Pulling, by Hans Egede — SP5

**1976, Apr. 8** **Engr.** *Perf. 12½*
**B7** SP5 100o + 20o multi .70 .70

Surtax for the Greenland Athletic Union.

Rasmussen and Eskimos — SP6

**1979, June 7 Engr. *Perf. 13***
**B8** SP6 1.30k + 20o brown red .95 .95

Knud Rasmussen (1879-1933), arctic explorer and ethnologist.

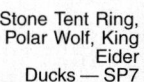

Stone Tent Ring, Polar Wolf, King Eider Ducks — SP7

**1981, Sept. 3 Engr. *Perf. 13***
**B9** SP7 1.60k + 20o lt red brn .90 .90

Surtax was for Peary Land Expeditions.

**History Type of 1982**

Design: Eric the Red sailing for Greenland.

**1982, Aug. 2 Engr. *Perf. 12½***
**B10** A39 2k + 40o dk red brn 1.25 1.25

Surtax was for Cultural House, Julianehab.

Blind Man — SP8

**1983, May 19 Engr.**
**B11** SP8 2.50k + 40o multi 1.40 1.40

Surtax was for the handicapped.

Greenland Sports Union — SP9

**1986, Apr. 17 Litho.**
**B12** SP9 2.80k + 50o Water game 2.00 *2.00*

Surtax for the Sports Union.

Greenland PO, 50th Anniv. — SP10

**1988, Sept. 16 Litho. *Perf. 12½x13***
**B13** SP10 300o +50o multi 3.00 3.00

Surtax for the purchase of postal artifacts.

Sled Dog, Common Eider — SP11

**Litho. & Engr.**

**1990, Sept. 6 *Perf. 13***
**B14** SP11 400o + 50o multi 3.75 3.75

Surtax for the Greenland Environmental Foundation.

SP12

SP13

**1991, Sept. 5 Litho. *Perf. 13***
**B15** SP12 4k +50o multi *15.00 15.00*

Blue Cross of Greenland, 75th Anniv. Surtax benefits Blue Cross of Greenland.

**1992, Oct. 8 Litho. *Perf. 13***
**B16** SP13 4k +50o multi 4.25 4.25

Cancer research in Greenland.

Red Cross — SP14

Boy Scouts in Greenland, 50th Anniv. SP15

**1993, June 17 Litho. *Perf. 13***
**B17** SP14 4k +50o red & blue 2.50 2.50
**B18** SP15 4k +50o multi 2.50 2.50
*a.* Souv. sheet, 2 ea #B17-B18 *20.00 20.00*

1994 Winter Olympics, Lillehammer SP16

**1994, Feb. 10 Litho. *Perf. 13***
**B19** SP16 4k +50o Skiers 3.00 3.00
*a.* Souvenir sheet of 4 12.00 12.00

Surtax to support Greenlandic athletes.

Natl. Flag, 10th Anniv. — SP17

**1995, June 21 Litho. *Perf. 13***
**B20** SP17 4k +50o multi 3.00 3.00
*a.* Souvenir sheet of 4 12.00 12.00

Surtax for benefit of Greenland Flag Society.

Handicapped and Disabled in Greenland — SP18

**1996, Sept. 5 Litho. *Perf. 13***
**B21** SP18 4.25k +50o multi 2.50 2.50
*a.* Souvenir sheet of 4 10.00 10.00

Katuaq Cultural Center, Nuuk SP19

**Litho. & Engr.**

**1997, Jan. 14 *Perf. 13***
**B22** SP19 4.50k +50o multi 2.50 2.50
*a.* Souvenir sheet of 4 10.00 10.00

SP20

SP21

Women's Society of Greenland: Kathrine Chemnitz (1894-1978), first Gen. Secretary.

**1998, May 29 Litho. *Perf. 13***
**B23** SP20 4.50k +50o multi 2.50 2.50
*a.* Souvenir sheet of 4 10.00 10.00

**1999, May 7 Engr. *Perf. 13***
**B24** SP21 4.50k +50o Pincushion, Natl. Museum 1.60 1.60
*a.* Souvenir sheet of 4 7.00 7.00

Surtax for the benefit of Greenland National Museum & Archives.

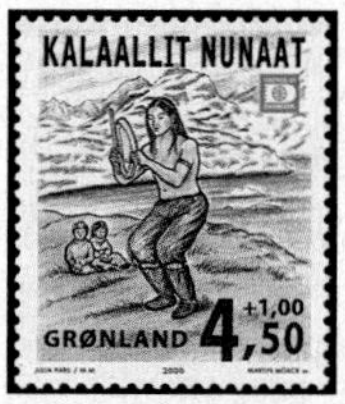

Drum Dance — SP22

**Litho. & Engr.**

**2000, Aug. 18 *Perf. 13¼x13***
**B25** SP22 4.50k + 1k multi 1.75 1.75
*a.* Souvenir sheet of 4 7.00 7.00

Surtax to benefit the Hafnia 01 Philatelic Exhibition, Copenhagen.

2002 Arctic Winter Games — SP23

**2001, Feb. 5 Litho. *Perf. 13¼x13***
**B26** SP23 4.50k +50o multi 1.75 1.75
*a.* Souvenir sheet of 4 7.00 7.00

SP24

**2002, Mar. 5 *Perf. 12¾***
**B27** SP24 4.50k +50o multi 1.75 1.75
*a.* Souvenir sheet of 4 7.00 7.00

Surtax for "Children Are People, Too" Project of Paarisa.

Ornament With Santa Claus, Map of Greenland, House — SP25

**2003, Oct. 20 *Perf. 13¼***
**B28** SP25 5k +50o multi 2.00 2.00
*a.* Souvenir sheet of 4 8.00 8.00

Society of Greenlandic Children, 80th Anniv. — SP26

**2004, May 14 *Perf. 13x13¼***
**B29** SP26 5k +50o multi 2.00 2.00
*a.* Souvenir sheet of 4 8.00 8.00

Surtax for Society of Greenlandic Children.

Child — SP27

**2005, Jan. 17 *Perf. 12¾***
**B30** SP27 5.25k +50o multi 2.10 2.10
*a.* Souvenir sheet of 4 8.50 8.50

Surtax for Save the Children Fund.

Crown Prince Frederik and Crown Princess Mary — SP28

**2006, Mar. 29 *Perf. 13¼x13¾***
**B31** SP28 5.50k +50o multi 2.10 2.10
*a.* Souvenir sheet of 4 8.50 8.50

Surtax for children's charities.

Amnesty Greenland SP29

**2007, Jan. 15 *Perf. 13¾x13¼***
**B32** SP29 575o +50o multi 2.25 2.25
*a.* Souvenir sheet of 4 9.00 9.00

Fight Against Tuberculosis SP30

**2008, May 24 *Perf. 13¾x13½***
**B33** SP30 575o +50o multi 2.75 2.75
*a.* Souvenir sheet of 4 11.00 11.00

Fight Against Cancer — SP31

**2009, Jan. 19** ***Perf. 13¼x14***

**B34** SP31 6.25k +50o blk & red 2.40 2.40
*a.* Souvenir sheet of 4 9.75 9.75

Surtax for Greenlandic Cancer Society.

Performer SP32

**2010, Jan. 18** ***Perf. 14x13¼***

**B35** SP32 7k +50o multi 2.75 2.75
*a.* Souvenir sheet of 4 11.00 11.00

Surtax for Silamiut Theater Group.

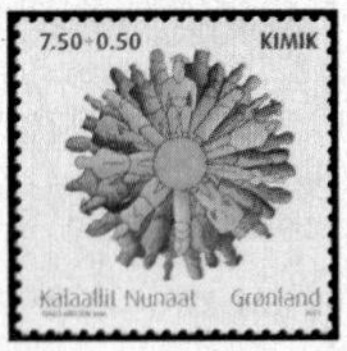


SP33

**2011, Jan. 17 Litho.** ***Perf. 13***

**B36** SP33 7.50k+50o multi 3.00 3.00
*a.* Souvenir sheet of 4 12.00 12.00

Surtax for KIMIK (Association of Artists in Greenland).

Family — SP34

**2012, Jan. 16 Litho.** ***Perf. 12½x12¾***

**B37** SP34 800o+50o multi 3.00 3.00
*a.* Souvenir sheet of 4 12.00 12.00

Surtax for NAKUUSA, a collaborative children's rights project of Naalakersuisut and UNICEF.

---

## PARCEL POST STAMPS

Arms of Greenland PP1

***Perf. 10¾, 11½***

**1905-37 Unwmk. Typo.**

**Q1** PP1 1o ol grn ('16-'26) 57.50 *60.00*
*a.* Perf. 12½ ('05) 775.00 775.00
**Q2** PP1 2o yellow ('16-'24) 350.00 125.00
**Q3** PP1 5o brown ('18-'28) 125.00 125.00
*a.* Perf. 12½ ('05) 750.00 775.00
**Q4** PP1 10o blue ('37) 40.00 *72.50*
*a.* Perf. 12½ ('05) 950.00 625.00
*b.* Perf. 11½ ('16) 60.00 65.00
**Q5** PP1 15o violet ('15-'28) 275.00 275.00
**Q6** PP1 20o red ('15-'33) 17.00 13.00
*a.* Perf. 11 ('37) 40.00 60.00

**Q7** PP1 70o violet ('37) 40.00 *125.00*
*a.* Perf. 11½ ('30) 275.00 275.00
**Q8** PP1 1k yellow ('37) 40.00 *140.00*
*a.* Perf. 11½ ('30) 52.50 65.00
**Q9** PP1 3k brown ('30) 140.00 *175.00*
*Nos. Q1-Q9 (9)* 1,009. *1,035.*

**1937 Litho.** ***Perf. 11***

**Q10** PP1 70o pale violet 42.50 *150.00*
**Q11** PP1 1k yellow 50.00 *77.50*
Nos. Q10-Q11, never hinged 150.00

On lithographed stamps, PAKKE-PORTO is slightly larger, hyphen has rounded ends and lines in shield are fine, straight and evenly spaced.

On typographed stamps, hyphen has squared ends and shield lines are coarse, uneven and inclined to be slightly wavy.

Used values are for stamps postally used from Denmark. Numeral cancels indicate use as postal savings stamps and are worth less. Greenland village cancels are worth more.

Sheets of 25. Certain printings of Nos. Q1-Q2, Q3a, Q4a and Q5-Q6 were issued without sheet margins. Stamps from the outer rows are straight edged. Some of these sheets were reperfed later.

---

# GRENADA

grə-ˈnā-də

LOCATION — Windward Islands, West Indies
GOVT. — Independent nation in the British Commonwealth
AREA — 133 sq. mi.
POP. — 98,600 (1998 est.)
CAPITAL — St. George's

Grenada consists of Grenada Island and the southern Grenadines, including Carriacou. This colony was granted associated statehood with Great Britain in 1967 and became an independent state Feb. 7, 1974.

12 Pence = 1 Shilling
100 Cents = 1 Dollar (1949)

**Catalogue values for unused stamps in this country are for Never Hinged items, beginning with Scott 143 in the regular postage section, Scott B1 in the semi-postal section, Scott C1 in the air post section, Scott J15 in the postage due section, and Scott O1 in the official section.**

Watermarks

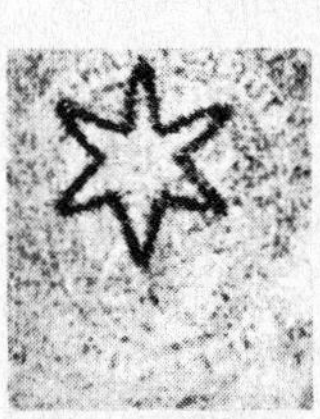

Wmk. 5 — Small Star

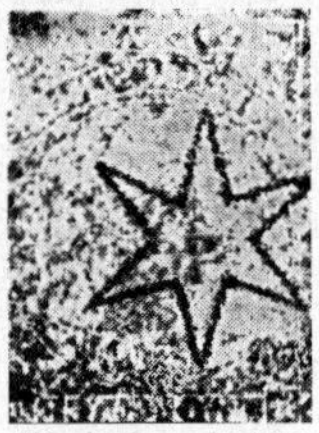

Wmk. 6 — Large Star

Wmk. 7 — Large Star with Broad Points

---

Values for unused stamps are for examples with original gum as defined in the catalogue introduction. Very fine examples of Nos. 1-19, 27-29, and 31-38 will have perforations touching the design on at least one side due to the narrow spacing of the stamps on the plates. Stamps with perfs clear of the design on all four sides are scarce and will command higher prices.

---

Queen Victoria — A1

***Rough Perf. 14 to 16***

**1861 Engr. Unwmk.**

**1** A1 1p green 57.50 50.00
*a.* 1p blue green 5,250. 350.00
*b.* As No. 1, horiz. pair, imperf. btwn.
**2** A1 6p rose 1,050. 110.00
*b.* 6p lake red, perf. 11-12½ 1,000.

No. 2b was not issued. No. 2 imperf is a proof.

**1863-71 Wmk. 5**

**3** A1 1p green ('64) 100.00 15.00
*a.* 1p yellow green 125.00 30.00
**4** A1 6p rose 775.00 20.00
**5** A1 6p vermilion ('71) 875.00 20.00
*a.* 6p dull red 4,000. 275.00
*g.* Double impression 2,350.
*i.* 6p orange red ('66) 750.00 14.00

No. 5a always has sideways watermark. Other colors sometimes have sideways watermark.

**1873-78** ***Clean-Cut Perf. about 15***

**5B** A1 1p deep green 120.00 47.50
*j.* Pair, imperf between *12,000.*
*c.* 1p blue green ('78) 275.00 45.00
*h.* Half used as ½p on cover 11,000.
**5D** A1 6p vermilion ('75) 925.00 40.00
*e.* 6p dull red 950.00 40.00
*f.* Double impression 2,350.

**1873 Wmk. 6**

**6** A1 1p blue green 105.00 22.50
*a.* Diagonal half used as ½p on cover 11,000.
**7** A1 6p vermilion 775.00 35.00

**1875** ***Perf. 14***

**7A** A1 1p yellow green 90.00 9.00
*b.* Half used as ½p on cover 16,000.
*c.* Perf. 15 10,000. *2,600.*

A2

A2a

**Revenue Designs Surcharged in Black**
***Perf. 14, 14½***

**1875-81**

**8** A2 ½p purple ('81) 15.50 7.50
*a.* "OSTAGE" 225.00 150.00
*b.* Imperf., pair 350.00
*c.* "ALF" *4,000.*
*d.* "PEN"
*e.* No hyphen between "HALF" and "PENNY" 225.00 150.00
*f.* Double surcharge 350.00 350.00
**9** A2a 2½p lake ('81) 70.00 10.00
*a.* Imperf., pair 650.00
*b.* Imperf. vertically, pair 5,500.
*c.* "PENCF" 525.00 225.00
*d.* No period after "PENNY" 290.00 90.00
*e.* "PENOE" 175.00
**10** A2 4p blue ('81) 120.00 10.00

**Revenue Designs Surcharged in Dark Blue**

**11** A2 1sh purple 775.00 20.00
*a.* "SHLIING" *6,500.* 800.00
*b.* "NE SHILLING" *3,250.*
*c.* "OSTAGE" 7,250. *3,000.*
*d.* Invtd. "S" in "POSTAGE" *4,500.* *750.00*

See Nos. 27-35.

**1881 Wmk. 7**

**12** A2 2½p lake 200.00 57.50
*a.* 2½p claret 500.00 140.00
*b.* As No. 12, "PENCF" 875.00 325.00
*c.* As No. 12, No period after "PENNY" 650.00 230.00
*d.* As "a," "PENCF" 1,850. 825.00
*e.* As "a," no period after "PENNY" 1,275. 575.00
**13** A2 4p blue 325.00 210.00

**Revenue Stamp Overprinted "POSTAGE" in Black**

A3

A4

A5

**Revenue Stamp Handstamped "POSTAGE" in Manuscript**

A6

**1883 Wmk. 5**

**Denomination & Crown in 2nd Color**

**14** A3 ½p orange & grn 900.00 275.00
*a.* Unsevered pair *5,000.* *1,500.*
*b.* "POSTAGE" inverted 1,500.
**15** A4 ½p orange & grn 325.00 150.00
*a.* Unsevered pair *2,000.* *525.00*
**16** A5 1p orange & grn *400.00* 65.00
*a.* Inverted overprint 3,500. 2,600.
*b.* Double overprint 1,625. 1,275.
*c.* Inverted "S" in "Postage" 1,150. 700.00
*d.* Diagonal half used as ½p on cover *3,500.*

**"Postage" in Manuscript, Red or Black**

**18** A6 1p orange & grn (R) *21,000.*
**19** A6 1p orange & green — *15,000.*

On Nos. 14-19 the words "ONE PENNY" measure from 10-11¼mm in length.

On No. 15, the lower "POSTAGE" is always inverted.

It has been claimed that although Nos. 18 and 19 were used, they were not officially authorized by Grenada's postmaster.

A8

**1883 Wmk. 2** ***Perf. 14***

**20** A8 ½p green 1.75 1.25
*a.* Tete beche pair 5.00 *19.00*
**21** A8 1p rose 90.00 4.00
*a.* Tete beche pair 275.00 *290.00*
**22** A8 2½p ultra 8.00 1.25
*a.* Tete beche pair 30.00 *57.50*
**23** A8 4p slate 9.00 2.25
*a.* Tete beche pair 24.00 *65.00*
**24** A8 6p red lilac 5.00 *6.50*
*a.* Tete beche pair 21.00 *65.00*
**25** A8 8p bister 10.50 *14.00*
*a.* Tete beche pair 40.00 *87.50*
**26** A8 1sh violet 150.00 65.00
*a.* Tete beche pair 1,900. *2,250.*
*Nos. 20-26 (7)* 274.25 94.25

Stamps of types A8, A10 and D2 were printed with alternate horizontal rows inverted.

For surcharges see Nos. 36-38, J4-J7.

Revenue Stamps Surcharged

**1886 Wmk. 6**

**27** A2 1p on 1½ org & grn 55.00 42.50
*a.* Inverted surcharge 350.00 350.00
*b.* Diagonal half used as ½ on cover 2,250.
*c.* Double surcharge 600.00 350.00
*d.* "HALH" instead of "HALF" 300.00 275.00
*e.* "F" for first "E" in "THREE" 300.00 225.00
*f.* "PFNCE" for "PENCE" 300.00 225.00
**28** A2 1p on 1sh org & grn 50.00 40.00
*a.* "SHLLNG" instead of "SHILLING" 525.00 450.00
*b.* No period after "POSTAGE" *500.00*
*c.* Half used as ½p on cover 2,350.

**Wmk. 5**

**29** A2 1p on 4p org & grn 190.00 110.00

A10

**1887 Wmk. 2**

**30** A10 1p rose 3.50 1.75
*a.* Tete beche pair 10.00 *25.00*

### Revenue Stamps Surcharged

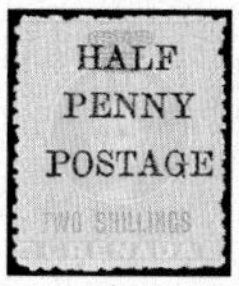

h

i

j

k

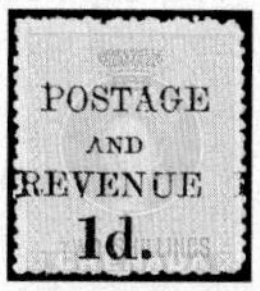

l

**1888-91 Wmk. 5 *Perf. 14½***

| | | | | |
|---|---|---|---|---|
| 31 | A2 (h) | ½p on 2sh org & grn ('89) | 16.00 | *27.00* |
| *a.* | | Double surcharge | 350.00 | *375.00* |
| *b.* | | First "S" in "SHILLINGS" inverted | 325.00 | *350.00* |
| 32 | A2 (i) | 4p on 2sh org & grn | 45.00 | 22.50 |
| *a.* | | "4d" and "POSTAGE" 5mm apart | 80.00 | 37.50 |
| *b.* | | "S" inverted, as in #31b | 550.00 | 400.00 |
| *c.* | | As "a," inverted "S," as in #31b | 750.00 | 650.00 |

**"d" Vertical instead of Slanting**

| | | | | |
|---|---|---|---|---|
| 33 | A2 (j) | 4p on 2sh org & grn | 875.00 | 475.00 |
| 34 | A2 (k) | 1p on 2sh org & grn ('90) | 92.50 | 87.50 |
| *a.* | | Inverted surcharge | 875.00 | — |
| *b.* | | "S" inverted | 825.00 | 750.00 |
| 35 | A2 (l) | 1p on 2sh org & grn ('91) | 70.00 | 70.00 |
| *a.* | | Inverted surcharge | | |
| *b.* | | No period after "d" | 450.00 | — |
| *c.* | | "S" inverted | 575.00 | 575.00 |

### No. 25 Surcharged in Black

**Wmk. 2**

| | | | | |
|---|---|---|---|---|
| 36 | A8 | 1p on 8p bister | 12.00 | *17.00* |
| *a.* | | Tete beche pair | 50.00 | *70.00* |
| *b.* | | Inverted surcharge | 375.00 | 325.00 |
| *c.* | | No period after "d" | 300.00 | 300.00 |

**"2" of "½" Upright**

| | | | | |
|---|---|---|---|---|
| 37 | A8 | 2½p on 8p bister | 11.00 | *14.00* |
| *a.* | | Tete beche pair | 50.00 | *70.00* |
| *b.* | | Inverted surcharge | | |
| *c.* | | Double surcharge | 1,000. | *925.00* |
| *d.* | | Triple surcharge | | 1,100. |
| *e.* | | Double surcharge, one inverted | 650.00 | 575.00 |

**"2" of "½" Italic**

| | | | | |
|---|---|---|---|---|
| 38 | A8 | 2½p on 8p bister | 14.00 | *13.00* |
| *a.* | | Tete beche pair | 50.00 | *70.00* |
| *b.* | | Tete beche pair, #37, 38 | 125.00 | |
| *c.* | | Inverted surcharge | | |
| *d.* | | Double surcharge | 875.00 | *925.00* |
| *e.* | | Triple surcharge | | 1,050. |
| *f.* | | Triple surch., two inverted | | 1,000. |
| *g.* | | Double surcharge, one inverted | 625.00 | 575.00 |

Queen Victoria — A17

**1895-99 Wmk. 2 Typo. *Perf. 14***

| | | | | |
|---|---|---|---|---|
| 39 | A17 | ½p lilac & green | 3.00 | 2.00 |
| 40 | A17 | 1p lilac & car rose | 5.25 | .90 |
| 41 | A17 | 2p lilac & brown | 47.50 | 37.50 |
| 42 | A17 | 2½p lilac & ultra | 7.50 | 1.75 |
| 43 | A17 | 3p lilac & orange | 8.00 | *18.00* |
| 44 | A17 | 6p lilac & green | 20.00 | *55.00* |
| 45 | A17 | 8p lilac & black | 15.00 | *52.50* |
| 46 | A17 | 1sh green & org | 22.50 | *57.50* |
| | | *Nos. 39-46 (8)* | 128.75 | *225.15* |

Numerals of ½p, 3p, 8p and 1sh of type A17 are in color on colorless tablet.

Issue dates: 1p, May, 1896; ½p, 2p, Sept. 1899; others, Sept. 5, 1895.

Columbus' Flagship, La Concepcion
A18

King Edward VII
A19

**1898, Aug. 15 Engr. Wmk. 1**

| | | | | |
|---|---|---|---|---|
| 47 | A18 | 2½p ultra | 19.00 | 8.00 |
| *a.* | | Bluish paper | 37.50 | *47.50* |

Discovery of the island by Columbus, Aug. 15th, 1498.

**1902 Wmk. 2 Typo.**

| | | | | |
|---|---|---|---|---|
| 48 | A19 | ½p violet & grn | 3.75 | 1.50 |
| 49 | A19 | 1p vio & car rose | 5.50 | .35 |
| 50 | A19 | 2p vio & brown | 3.50 | *11.50* |
| 51 | A19 | 2½p vio & ultra | 4.50 | 3.25 |
| 52 | A19 | 3p vio & org | 4.50 | *10.50* |
| 53 | A19 | 6p vio & green | 3.75 | *20.00* |
| 54 | A19 | 1sh green & org | 8.00 | *32.50* |
| 55 | A19 | 2sh grn & ultra | 30.00 | *65.00* |
| 56 | A19 | 5sh grn & car rose | 47.50 | *75.00* |
| 57 | A19 | 10sh green & vio | 140.00 | *300.00* |
| | | *Nos. 48-57 (10)* | 251.00 | *519.60* |

Numerals of ½p, 3p, 1sh, 2sh and 10sh of type A19 are in color on colorless tablet.

**1904-06 Wmk. 3 *Perf. 14***

**Ordinary Paper**

| | | | | |
|---|---|---|---|---|
| 58 | A19 | ½p vio & green | 20.00 | *37.50* |
| 59 | A19 | 1p vio & car rose | 16.00 | 3.00 |
| 60 | A19 | 2p vio & brown | 65.00 | *130.00* |
| 61 | A19 | 2½p vio & ultra | 65.00 | *75.00* |
| 62 | A19 | 3p vio & org | 3.25 | *9.00* |
| *a.* | | Chalky paper | 4.00 | 9.00 |
| 63 | A19 | 6p vio & green | 10.00 | *23.00* |
| *a.* | | Chalky paper | 11.00 | *30.00* |
| 64 | A19 | 1sh green & org | 7.00 | *35.00* |
| 65 | A19 | 2sh grn & ultra | 60.00 | *85.00* |
| *a.* | | Chalky paper | 42.50 | *80.00* |
| 66 | A19 | 5sh grn & car rose | 75.00 | *110.00* |
| 67 | A19 | 10sh green & vio | 180.00 | *300.00* |
| | | *Nos. 58-67 (10)* | 501.25 | *807.50* |

Issued: Nos. 58, 60-62, 64, 1905; Nos. 63, 65-67, 1906.

Seal of Colony — A20

**1906-11 Engr.**

| | | | | |
|---|---|---|---|---|
| 68 | A20 | ½p green | 5.25 | .35 |
| 69 | A20 | 1p carmine | 7.50 | .25 |
| 70 | A20 | 2p yellow | 3.50 | 3.50 |
| 71 | A20 | 2½p blue | 7.00 | 2.00 |
| *a.* | | 2½p ultramarine | 10.00 | 3.75 |

**Typo.**

**Chalky Paper**

**Numerals white on dark ground**

| | | | | |
|---|---|---|---|---|
| 72 | A20 | 3p vio, *yel* ('08) | 5.50 | 1.90 |
| 73 | A20 | 6p violet ('08) | 22.50 | 25.00 |
| 74 | A20 | 1sh blk, *grn* ('11) | 8.00 | 5.00 |
| 75 | A20 | 2sh vio & blue, *blue* ('08) | 26.00 | 14.00 |
| 76 | A20 | 5sh red & green, *yel* ('08) | 67.50 | *80.00* |
| | | *Nos. 68-76 (9)* | 152.75 | *132.00* |

**1908 Wmk. 2**

| | | | | |
|---|---|---|---|---|
| 77 | A20 | 1sh black, *green* | 40.00 | *70.00* |
| 78 | A20 | 10sh red & grn, *grn* | 130.00 | *250.00* |

King George V — A21

**1913 Ordinary Paper Wmk. 3**

| | | | | |
|---|---|---|---|---|
| 79 | A21 | ½p green | 1.25 | 1.60 |
| 80 | A21 | 1p carmine | 2.50 | .35 |
| *a.* | | 1p scarlet ('16) | 10.00 | 2.00 |
| 81 | A21 | 2p orange | 1.90 | .35 |
| 82 | A21 | 2½p ultra | 2.00 | 2.00 |

**Chalky Paper**

| | | | | |
|---|---|---|---|---|
| 83 | A21 | 3p violet, *yel* | .75 | *1.00* |
| 84 | A21 | 6p dull vio & red vio | 1.75 | *10.00* |
| 85 | A21 | 1sh black, *green* | 1.10 | *11.50* |
| *a.* | | 1sh black, *emerald* | 1.75 | *20.00* |
| *b.* | | 1sh blk, *bl grn,* olive back | 52.50 | *90.00* |
| *c.* | | As "a," olive back | 1.75 | *15.00* |
| 86 | A21 | 2sh vio & ultra, *bl* | 7.25 | *14.00* |
| 87 | A21 | 5sh grn & red, *yel* | 20.00 | *67.50* |
| 88 | A21 | 10sh grn & red, *grn* | 62.50 | *100.00* |
| *a.* | | 10sh grn & red, *emer* | 60.00 | *175.00* |
| | | *Nos. 79-88 (10)* | 101.00 | *208.30* |

**1914 Surface-colored Paper**

| | | | | |
|---|---|---|---|---|
| 89 | A21 | 3p violet, *yel* | .70 | *1.60* |
| 90 | A21 | 1sh black, *green* | 1.40 | *8.50* |

**1921-29 Ordinary Paper Wmk. 4**

| | | | | |
|---|---|---|---|---|
| 91 | A21 | ½p green | 1.40 | .35 |
| 92 | A21 | 1p rose red | .90 | .85 |
| 93 | A21 | 1p brown ('23) | 1.75 | .35 |
| 94 | A21 | 1½p rose red ('22) | 1.75 | 1.75 |
| 95 | A21 | 2p orange | 1.40 | .35 |
| 96 | A21 | 2p gray ('26) | 2.75 | *3.00* |
| 97 | A21 | 2½p ultramarine | 5.25 | *10.00* |
| 98 | A21 | 2½p gray ('22) | 1.10 | *10.00* |
| 99 | A21 | 3p ultra ('22) | 1.75 | *12.50* |

**Chalky Paper**

| | | | | |
|---|---|---|---|---|
| 100 | A21 | 3p vio, *yel* ('26) | 3.50 | *5.75* |
| 101 | A21 | 4p blk & red, *yel* ('26) | 1.10 | *4.25* |
| 102 | A21 | 5p gray vio & ol grn ('22) | 1.75 | *4.75* |
| 103 | A21 | 6p dl vio & red vio | 1.50 | *26.00* |
| 104 | A21 | 6p blk & red ('26) | 2.50 | *2.75* |
| 105 | A21 | 9p gray vio & blk ('22) | 2.50 | *11.00* |
| 106 | A21 | 1sh blk, *emer* ('23) | 3.00 | *60.00* |
| 107 | A21 | 1sh org brn ('26) | 4.50 | *11.00* |
| 108 | A21 | 2sh vio & ultra, *bl* ('22) | 7.00 | *19.00* |
| 109 | A21 | 2sh6p blk & red, *bl* ('29) | 8.00 | *22.50* |
| 110 | A21 | 3sh grn & vio ('22) | 6.75 | *30.00* |
| 111 | A21 | 5sh green & red, *yel* ('23) | 14.00 | *40.00* |
| 112 | A21 | 10sh green & red, *emer* ('23) | 57.50 | *150.00* |
| | | *Nos. 91-112 (22)* | 131.65 | *426.15* |

Grand Anse Beach — A22

Seal of the Colony — A23

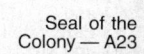

View of Grand Etang — A24

View of St. George's — A25

**1934, Oct. 23 Engr. *Perf. 12½***

| | | | | |
|---|---|---|---|---|
| 114 | A22 | ½p green | .25 | *1.25* |
| *a.* | | Perf. 12½x13 ('36) | 7.00 | *65.00* |

***Perf. 13½x12½***

| | | | | |
|---|---|---|---|---|
| 115 | A23 | 1p blk brn & blk | .65 | .35 |
| *a.* | | Perf 12½ | 1.10 | 3.50 |

***Perf. 12½x13½***

| | | | | |
|---|---|---|---|---|
| 116 | A24 | 1½p car & black | .90 | .45 |
| *a.* | | Perf 12½ ('36) | 5.50 | 4.50 |

***Perf. 12½***

| | | | | |
|---|---|---|---|---|
| 117 | A23 | 2p org & black | 1.10 | .80 |
| 118 | A25 | 2½p deep blue | .55 | .55 |
| 119 | A23 | 3p ol grn & blk | 1.10 | *3.25* |
| 120 | A23 | 6p claret & blk | 2.25 | 2.00 |
| 121 | A23 | 1sh brown & blk | 2.25 | *4.50* |
| 122 | A23 | 2sh6p ultra & blk | 9.00 | *30.00* |
| 123 | A23 | 5sh vio & black | 45.00 | *55.00* |
| | | *Nos. 114-123 (10)* | 63.05 | *98.15* |
| | | Set, never hinged | 125.00 | |

Common Design Types pictured following the introduction.

### Silver Jubilee Issue

Common Design Type

**1935, May 6 *Perf. 11x12***

| | | | | |
|---|---|---|---|---|
| 124 | CD301 | ½p green & blk | 1.10 | *1.50* |
| 125 | CD301 | 1p black & ultra | 1.25 | *2.25* |
| 126 | CD301 | 1½p car & blue | 1.25 | *3.25* |
| 127 | CD301 | 1sh brn vio & ind | 13.00 | *32.50* |
| | | *Nos. 124-127 (4)* | 16.60 | *39.50* |
| | | Set, never hinged | 25.00 | |

### Coronation Issue

Common Design Type

**1937, May 12 Wmk. 4 *Perf. 11x11½***

| | | | | |
|---|---|---|---|---|
| 128 | CD302 | 1p dark purple | .25 | .25 |
| 129 | CD302 | 1½p dark carmine | .25 | .25 |
| 130 | CD302 | 2½p deep ultra | .50 | .35 |
| | | *Nos. 128-130 (3)* | 1.00 | .85 |
| | | Set, never hinged | 1.60 | |

George VI — A26

**1937, July 12 Photo. *Perf. 14½x14***

| | | | | |
|---|---|---|---|---|
| 131 | A26 | ¼p chestnut | .50 | *.75* |

Grand Anse Beach — A27

Seal of the Colony — A28

View of Grand Etang — A29

View of St. George's — A30

Seal of the Colony — A31

**1938, Mar. 16 Engr. *Perf. 12½***

| | | | | |
|---|---|---|---|---|
| 132 | A27 | ½p green | .80 | *1.40* |
| 133 | A28 | 1p blk brn & blk | .55 | .55 |
| 134 | A29 | 1½p scarlet & blk | .25 | *.95* |
| 135 | A28 | 2p orange & blk | .25 | *.55* |

| | | | | |
|---|---|---|---|---|
| 136 | A30 | 2½p ultramarine | .25 | .35 |
| 137 | A28 | 3p olive grn & blk | .25 | 2.10 |
| 138 | A28 | 6p red vio & blk | 1.25 | .45 |
| 139 | A28 | 1sh org brn & blk | 2.50 | .45 |
| 140 | A28 | 2sh ultra & black | 15.00 | 2.00 |
| 141 | A28 | 5sh purple & blk | 2.25 | 2.75 |

**Perf. 14**

| | | | | |
|---|---|---|---|---|
| 142 | A31 | 10sh rose car & gray blue | 20.00 | 13.00 |
| a. | | 10sh deep car & gray blue, perf. 12 ('43) | 700.00 | 1,750. |
| b. | | Perf. 12x13 | 42.50 | 12.00 |
| | | *Nos. 131-142 (12)* | 43.85 | 25.30 |
| | | Set, never hinged | 67.50 | |

**1938-42 Perf. 12½x13½, 13½x12½**

| | | | | |
|---|---|---|---|---|
| 132a | A27 | ½p | 3.50 | .90 |
| 133a | A28 | 1p | .30 | .25 |
| 134a | A29 | 1½p car & blk | 1.25 | .40 |
| 135a | A28 | 2p | 1.40 | .75 |
| 136a | A30 | 2½p | 7,500. | 240.00 |
| 137a | A28 | 3p | 2.50 | 1.00 |
| 138a | A28 | 6p ('42) | 1.25 | .35 |
| 139a | A28 | 1sh ('42) | 2.50 | 1.50 |
| 140a | A28 | 2sh ('41) | 17.50 | 2.00 |
| 141a | A28 | 5sh ('47) | 2.00 | 4.50 |

**Catalogue values for unused stamps in this section, from this point to the end of the section, are for Never Hinged items.**

### Peace Issue
Common Design Type

**1946, Sept. 25 Perf. 13½x14**

| | | | | |
|---|---|---|---|---|
| 143 | CD303 | 1½p carmine | .25 | .25 |
| 144 | CD303 | 3½p deep blue | .25 | .70 |

### Silver Wedding Issue
Common Design Types

**1948, Oct. 27 Photo. Perf. 14x14½**

| | | | | |
|---|---|---|---|---|
| 145 | CD304 | 1½p scarlet | .25 | .25 |

**Engr.; Name Typo.**
**Perf. 11½x11**

| | | | | |
|---|---|---|---|---|
| 146 | CD305 | 10sh gray green | 20.00 | 20.00 |

### UPU Issue
Common Design Types
**Engr.; Name Typo. on 6c, 12c**
**Perf. 13½, 11x11½**

**1949, Oct. 10 Wmk. 4**

| | | | | |
|---|---|---|---|---|
| 147 | CD306 | 5c ultra | .25 | .25 |
| 148 | CD307 | 6c deep olive | 1.50 | 2.25 |
| 149 | CD308 | 12c red lilac | .30 | .50 |
| 150 | CD309 | 24c red brown | .25 | .55 |
| | | *Nos. 147-150 (4)* | 2.30 | 3.55 |

A32

A33

A34

**1951, Jan. 8 Engr. Perf. 11½**
**Center in Black**

| | | | | |
|---|---|---|---|---|
| 151 | A32 | ½c chestnut | .25 | 1.50 |
| 152 | A32 | 1c blue green | .25 | .60 |
| 153 | A32 | 2c dark brown | .25 | .25 |
| 154 | A32 | 3c carmine | .25 | .25 |
| 155 | A32 | 4c deep orange | .40 | .25 |
| 156 | A32 | 5c purple | .50 | .30 |
| 157 | A32 | 6c olive | .50 | .65 |
| 158 | A32 | 7c blue | 2.00 | .30 |
| 159 | A32 | 12c red violet | 2.25 | .75 |

**Perf. 11½x12½**

| | | | | |
|---|---|---|---|---|
| 160 | A33 | 25c dark brown | 2.50 | 1.00 |
| 161 | A33 | 50c ultra | 6.50 | .60 |
| 162 | A33 | $1.50 orange | 8.25 | 8.00 |

**Perf. 11½x13**
**Center in Gray Blue**

| | | | | |
|---|---|---|---|---|
| 163 | A34 | $2.50 deep carmine | 9.50 | 6.50 |
| | | *Nos. 151-163 (13)* | 33.40 | 20.95 |

See #180-183, 202. For overprints see #166-169.

### University Issue
Common Design Types

**1951, Feb. 16 Perf. 14x14½**

| | | | | |
|---|---|---|---|---|
| 164 | CD310 | 3c dp car & gray blk | .55 | 1.00 |
| 165 | CD311 | 6c olive & black | .65 | .60 |

Nos. 154-156 and 159 Overprinted in Black or Carmine

**1951, Sept. 21 Perf. 11½**

| | | | | |
|---|---|---|---|---|
| 166 | A32 | 3c carmine & black | .25 | .40 |
| 167 | A32 | 4c dp orange & black | .25 | .40 |
| 168 | A32 | 5c purple & black (C) | .30 | .65 |
| 169 | A32 | 12c red violet & black | .30 | .90 |
| | | *Nos. 166-169 (4)* | 1.10 | 2.35 |

Adoption of a new constitution for the Windward Islands.

### Coronation Issue
Common Design Type

**1953, June 3 Perf. 13½x13**

| | | | | |
|---|---|---|---|---|
| 170 | CD312 | 3c carmine & black | .30 | .25 |

### Types of 1951 Inscribed "E II R" and

Queen Elizabeth II — A35

**1953-59 Engr. Perf. 11½**
**Center in Black**

| | | | | |
|---|---|---|---|---|
| 171 | A35 | ½c chestnut ('54) | .25 | .25 |
| 172 | A35 | 1c blue green | .25 | .25 |
| 173 | A35 | 2c dark brown | .30 | .25 |
| 174 | A35 | 3c carmine ('54) | .25 | .25 |
| 175 | A35 | 4c dp orange ('54) | .25 | .25 |
| 176 | A35 | 5c purple ('54) | .25 | .25 |
| 177 | A35 | 6c olive | 2.00 | 1.50 |
| 178 | A35 | 7c blue ('55) | 2.50 | .25 |
| 179 | A35 | 12c red violet | .30 | .25 |

**Perf. 11½x12½**

| | | | | |
|---|---|---|---|---|
| 180 | A33 | 25c dark brown ('55) | 1.40 | .35 |
| 181 | A33 | 50c ultra ('55) | 6.00 | 1.00 |
| 182 | A33 | $1.50 orange ('55) | 12.50 | 14.00 |

**Perf. 11½x13**
**Center in Gray Blue**

| | | | | |
|---|---|---|---|---|
| 183 | A34 | $2.50 deep car ('59) | 25.00 | 11.00 |
| | | *Nos. 171-183 (13)* | 51.25 | 29.85 |

See Nos. 195-202.

No. 182 was locally surcharged "2" and two black horizontal lines and issued Dec. 23, 1965, for revenue use. It was used postally, though not authorized for postal use. The "2" is found in two type faces.

### West Indies Federation
Common Design Type
**Perf. 11½x11**

**1958, Apr. 22 Wmk. 314**

| | | | | |
|---|---|---|---|---|
| 184 | CD313 | 3c green | .35 | .25 |
| 185 | CD313 | 6c blue | .55 | .70 |
| 186 | CD313 | 12c carmine rose | .60 | .25 |
| | | *Nos. 184-186 (3)* | 1.50 | 1.20 |

Victoria and Elizabeth II and Mail Truck A36

Queens and: 8c, "La Concepcion" and Dakota plane. 25c, Steam Packet "Solent" and B.O.A.C. plane.

**1961, June 1 Photo. Perf. 14½x14**

| | | | | |
|---|---|---|---|---|
| 187 | A36 | 3c gray & deep car | .30 | .25 |
| 188 | A36 | 8c orange & ultra | .60 | .25 |
| 189 | A36 | 25c blue & maroon | .65 | .25 |
| | | *Nos. 187-189 (3)* | 1.55 | .75 |

Centenary of first Grenada postage stamps.

### Freedom from Hunger Issue
Common Design Type

**1963, June 4 Perf. 14x14½**

| | | | | |
|---|---|---|---|---|
| 190 | CD314 | 8c green | .30 | .25 |

### Red Cross Centenary Issue
Common Design Type

**1963, Sept. 2 Litho. Perf. 13**

| | | | | |
|---|---|---|---|---|
| 191 | CD315 | 3c black & red | .25 | .25 |
| 192 | CD315 | 25c ultra & red | .55 | .25 |

### Types of 1953-55
**Wmk. 314**

**1963-64 Engr. Perf. 11½**
**Center in Black**

| | | | | |
|---|---|---|---|---|
| 195 | A35 | 2c dark brown | .25 | .25 |
| 196 | A35 | 3c carmine | .25 | .25 |
| 197 | A35 | 4c dp orange | .25 | .80 |
| 198 | A35 | 5c purple | .25 | .25 |
| 199 | A35 | 6c olive | 200.00 | 95.00 |
| 201 | A35 | 12c red violet | .30 | .25 |

**Perf. 11½x12½**

| | | | | |
|---|---|---|---|---|
| 202 | A33 | 25c dark brown | 2.50 | 1.00 |
| | | *Nos. 195-198,201-202 (6)* | 3.80 | 2.80 |

Issued: 6c, 1963; others, May 12, 1964.

### ITU Issue
Common Design Type

**1965, May 17 Litho. Perf. 11x11½**

| | | | | |
|---|---|---|---|---|
| 205 | CD317 | 2c vermilion & olive | .25 | .25 |
| 206 | CD317 | 50c yellow & ver | .25 | .25 |

### Intl. Cooperation Year Issue
Common Design Type

**1965, Oct. 25 Litho. Perf. 14½**

| | | | | |
|---|---|---|---|---|
| 207 | CD318 | 1c blue grn & claret | .25 | .25 |
| 208 | CD318 | 25c lt violet & green | .25 | .25 |

### Churchill Memorial Issue
Common Design Type

**1966, Jan. 24 Photo. Perf. 14**
**Design in Black, Gold and Carmine Rose**

| | | | | |
|---|---|---|---|---|
| 209 | CD319 | 1c bright blue | .25 | .25 |
| 210 | CD319 | 3c green | .25 | .25 |
| 211 | CD319 | 25c brown | .25 | .25 |
| 212 | CD319 | 35c violet | .35 | .35 |
| | | *Nos. 209-212 (4)* | 1.10 | 1.10 |

### Royal Visit Issue
Common Design Type

**1966, Feb. 4 Litho. Perf. 11x12**

| | | | | |
|---|---|---|---|---|
| 213 | CD320 | 3c violet blue | .25 | .25 |
| 214 | CD320 | 35c dark car rose | .65 | .25 |

Careenage, St. George's A37

Queen Elizabeth II — A38

Designs: 1c, Hillsborough, Carriacou. 2c, Bougainvillea. 3c, Flamboyant plant. 5c, Levera Beach. 8c, Annandale Falls. 10c, Cacao pods. 12c, Inner Harbor. 15c, Nutmeg. 25c, St. George's. 35c, Grand Anse Beach. 50c, Bananas. $1, Seal of Colony. $3, Map of Grenada.

**Perf. 14½x13½, 14½ (A38)**
**1966, Apr. 1 Photo. Wmk. 314**

| | | | | |
|---|---|---|---|---|
| 215 | A37 | 1c blue, grn & yel | .25 | .80 |
| 216 | A37 | 2c dk grn & dp car rose | .25 | .25 |
| 217 | A37 | 3c multicolored | 1.00 | .90 |
| 218 | A37 | 5c multicolored | 1.25 | .25 |
| 219 | A37 | 6c ultra, grn & car rose | .95 | .25 |
| 220 | A37 | 8c dp grn, ind & yel | .95 | .25 |
| 221 | A37 | 10c yel grn, brn & dk car | .50 | .25 |
| 222 | A37 | 12c multicolored | .30 | .90 |
| 223 | A37 | 15c multicolored | .30 | .90 |
| 224 | A37 | 25c dk bl, grn & car rose | .30 | .25 |
| 225 | A37 | 35c multicolored | .40 | .25 |
| 226 | A37 | 50c violet & green | 1.25 | 2.00 |
| 227 | A38 | $1 brn, ultra & dull grn | 7.00 | 3.50 |
| 228 | A38 | $2 multicolored | 5.00 | 9.00 |
| 229 | A38 | $3 brt grnsh bl, dk bl & dl yel | 4.50 | 15.00 |
| | | *Nos. 215-229 (15)* | 24.20 | 34.75 |

For overprints and surcharges see Nos. 237-261, B1A-B1D.

### World Cup Soccer Issue
Common Design Type

**1966, July 1 Litho. Perf. 14**

| | | | | |
|---|---|---|---|---|
| 230 | CD321 | 5c multicolored | .25 | .25 |
| 231 | CD321 | 50c multicolored | .40 | .70 |

### WHO Headquarters Issue
Common Design Type

**1966, Sept. 20 Litho. Perf. 14**

| | | | | |
|---|---|---|---|---|
| 232 | CD322 | 8c multicolored | .25 | .25 |
| 233 | CD322 | 25c multicolored | .55 | .25 |

### UNESCO Anniversary Issue
Common Design Type

**1966, Dec. 1 Litho. Perf. 14**

| | | | | |
|---|---|---|---|---|
| 234 | CD323 | 2c "Education" | .25 | .25 |
| 235 | CD323 | 15c "Science" | .25 | .25 |
| 236 | CD323 | 50c "Culture" | .60 | .70 |
| | | *Nos. 234-236 (3)* | 1.10 | 1.20 |

### Nos. 216-217, 220 and 224 Overprinted "ASSOCIATED STATEHOOD 1967" in Silver

**Perf. 14½x13½**
**1967, Mar. 3 Photo. Wmk. 314**

| | | | | |
|---|---|---|---|---|
| 237 | A37 | 2c dk grn & dp car rose | .25 | .25 |
| 238 | A37 | 3c multicolored | .25 | .25 |
| 239 | A37 | 8c dp grn, ind & yel | .25 | .25 |
| 240 | A37 | 25c dk bl, grn & car rose | .25 | .25 |
| | | *Nos. 237-240 (4)* | 1.00 | 1.00 |

Nos. 216, 221, 223 and 227-228 Surcharged

**Perf. 14½x13½, 14½ (A38)**
**1967, July 1 Photo. Wmk. 314**

| | | | | |
|---|---|---|---|---|
| 241 | A37 | 1c on 15c multi | .25 | .25 |
| 242 | A37 | 2c dk grn & dp car rose | .25 | .25 |
| 243 | A37 | 3c on 10c multi | .25 | .25 |
| 244 | A38 | $1 multicolored | .25 | .25 |
| 245 | A38 | $2 multicolored | .35 | .35 |
| | | *Nos. 241-245 (5)* | 1.35 | 1.35 |

EXPO '67 Intl. Exhib., Montreal, Apr. 28-Oct. 27.

Nos. 215-229 Ovptd. in Black

**1967-68 Photo. Wmk. 314**

| | | | | |
|---|---|---|---|---|
| 246 | A37 | 1c multicolored | .25 | .25 |
| 247 | A37 | 2c multicolored | .25 | .25 |
| 248 | A37 | 3c multicolored | .25 | .25 |
| 249 | A37 | 5c multicolored | .25 | .25 |
| 250 | A37 | 6c multicolored | .25 | .25 |
| 251 | A37 | 8c multicolored | .25 | .25 |
| 252 | A37 | 10c multicolored | .25 | .25 |
| 253 | A37 | 12c multicolored | .25 | .25 |
| 254 | A37 | 15c multicolored | .25 | .25 |
| 255 | A37 | 25c multicolored | .25 | .25 |
| 256 | A37 | 35c multicolored | .60 | .25 |
| 257 | A37 | 50c multicolored | 1.00 | .30 |
| 258 | A38 | $1 multicolored | 1.40 | .75 |
| 259 | A38 | $2 multicolored | 1.25 | 3.00 |
| 260 | A38 | $3 multicolored | 2.50 | 5.00 |

**Overprinted and Surcharged**

| | | | | |
|---|---|---|---|---|
| 261 | A38 | $5 on $2 multi | 1.75 | 4.50 |
| | | *Nos. 246-261 (16)* | 11.00 | 16.30 |

Issued: $5, 5/18/68; others, 10/19/67.
For surcharges, see Nos. B1A-B1D.

Pres. John F. Kennedy — A39

Pres. Kennedy and: 25c, 50c, Bird-of-paradise flower. 35c, $1, Roses.

*Perf. 14½x14*

**1968, Jan. 13** **Unwmk.**

| | | | | |
|---|---|---|---|---|
| **262** | A39 | 1c lt blue & multi | .25 | .25 |
| **263** | A39 | 15c orange & multi | .25 | .25 |
| **264** | A39 | 25c violet & multi | .25 | .25 |
| **265** | A39 | 35c multicolored | .25 | .25 |
| **266** | A39 | 50c blue & multi | .35 | .25 |
| **267** | A39 | $1 multicolored | .50 | *.70* |
| | | *Nos. 262-267 (6)* | 1.85 | 1.95 |

50th anniv. of the birth of Pres. John F. Kennedy (1917-1963).

Bugler and Jamboree Emblem — A40

Jamboree Emblem and: 2c, 50c, Boy Scouts sitting in tent. 3c, $1, Lord Baden-Powell.

**1968, Feb. 1** **Photo.** ***Perf. 13x14***

| | | | | |
|---|---|---|---|---|
| **268** | A40 | 1c orange & multi | .25 | .25 |
| **269** | A40 | 2c emer & multi | .25 | .25 |
| **270** | A40 | 3c yellow & multi | .25 | .25 |
| **271** | A40 | 35c multicolored | .30 | .25 |
| **272** | A40 | 50c blue & multi | .50 | .40 |
| **273** | A40 | $1 multicolored | .70 | .70 |
| | | *Nos. 268-273 (6)* | 2.25 | 2.10 |

12th Boy Scout Jamboree, Farragut State Park, Idaho, Aug. 1-9, 1967.

Seascape, by Winston Churchill — A41

Paintings: 12c, Pine at the shore. 15c, 35c, Houses at the shore. 50c, Churchill painting a seascape.

*Perf. 14x14½*

**1968, Mar. 23** **Unwmk.**

| | | | | |
|---|---|---|---|---|
| **274** | A41 | 10c multicolored | .25 | .25 |
| **275** | A41 | 12c multicolored | .25 | .25 |
| **276** | A41 | 15c multicolored | .25 | .25 |
| **277** | A41 | 25c multicolored | .25 | .25 |
| **278** | A41 | 35c multicolored | .25 | .25 |
| **279** | A41 | 50c multicolored | .40 | .25 |
| | | *Nos. 274-279 (6)* | 1.65 | 1.50 |

Winston Churchill as a painter.

Edith McGuire, US, 200m. Dash, 1964 A42

Gold Medal Winners: 2c, 50c, Arthur Wint, Jamaica, 400m run, 1948. 3c, 60c, Adhemar Ferreira da Silva, Brazil, hop, step and jump, 1952 & 1956. 10c, Like 1c.

**1968, Sept. 24** **Photo.** ***Perf. 12½***

| | | | | |
|---|---|---|---|---|
| **280** | A42 | 1c ultra & multi | .25 | *.30* |
| **281** | A42 | 2c lilac & multi | .25 | *.30* |
| **282** | A42 | 3c green & multi | .25 | *.30* |
| **283** | A42 | 10c red org & multi | .25 | *.30* |
| **284** | A42 | 50c Prus blue & multi | .45 | *.75* |
| **285** | A42 | 60c orange & multi | .50 | *.85* |
| | | *Nos. 280-285 (6)* | 1.95 | *2.80* |

19th Olympic Games, Mexico City, Oct. 12-27. Nos. 280-282 and 283-285 are printed in sheets of 9 (3 of each denomination).

For surcharges see Nos. 310-315.

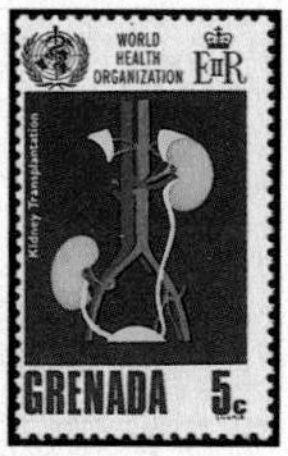


Transplant Operations — A43

*Perf. 13x13½*

**1968, Nov. 25** **Photo.** **Unwmk.**

| | | | | |
|---|---|---|---|---|
| **286** | A43 | 5c Kidney | .25 | .25 |
| **287** | A43 | 25c Heart | .30 | .25 |
| **288** | A43 | 35c Lung | .40 | .25 |
| **289** | A43 | 50c Cornea | .45 | *.60* |
| | | *Nos. 286-289 (4)* | 1.40 | 1.35 |

20th anniv. of WHO.

Adoration of the Magi, by Veronese A44

Paintings: 15c, Madonna and Child with St. John and St. Catherine, by Titian. 35c, Adoration of the Magi, by Botticelli. $1, "A Knight Adoring the Infant Christ" by Vincenzo di Biagio Catena.

**1968, Dec. 3** ***Perf. 12½***

| | | | | |
|---|---|---|---|---|
| **290** | A44 | 5c vio blue & multi | .25 | .25 |
| **291** | A44 | 15c crimson & multi | .25 | .25 |
| **292** | A44 | 35c dk green & multi | .25 | .25 |
| **293** | A44 | $1 dk blue & multi | .25 | .25 |
| | | *Nos. 290-293 (4)* | 1.00 | 1.00 |

Christmas. For overprints see Nos. 341-344.

Hibiscus and "La Concepcion" — A45

Yacht in St. George's Harbour — A45a

Designs: 2c, Bird-of-paradise flower. 3c, Bougainvillea. 5c, Rock hind (fish; horiz.). 6c, Sailfish. 8c, Red snapper, horiz. 10c, Giant toad, horiz. 12c, Yellowfoot tortoise. No. 302, Tree boa, horiz. No. 302A, Thunbergia. 25c, Mouse opossum. 35c Armadillo, horiz. 50c, Mona monkey. $1, Bananaquit (bird). $2, Brown pelican. $3, Magnificent frigate bird. $5, Bare-eyed thrush.

***Perf. 14x14½, 14½x14; 14x13½ (#302A); 13½x14 (#305A)***

**Photo.; Litho. (#302A, 305A)**

**1968-71** **Unwmk.**

| | | | | |
|---|---|---|---|---|
| **294** | A45 | 1c dl yel & multi | .25 | .25 |
| **295** | A45 | 2c brt pink & multi | .25 | .25 |
| **296** | A45 | 3c blue & multi | .25 | .25 |
| **297** | A45 | 5c violet & multi | .25 | .25 |
| **298** | A45 | 6c emer & multi | .25 | .25 |
| **299** | A45 | 8c multicolored | .25 | .25 |
| **300** | A45 | 10c multicolored | .25 | .25 |
| **301** | A45 | 12c ver & multi | .25 | .25 |
| **302** | A45 | 15c emer & multi | .90 | .85 |
| **302A** | A45 | 15c gray & multi | 5.00 | 3.25 |
| **303** | A45 | 25c multicolored | .30 | .25 |
| **304** | A45 | 35c multicolored | .35 | .25 |
| **305** | A45 | 50c ultra & multi | .45 | .25 |
| **305A** | A45a | 75c blue & multi | 10.00 | 8.00 |
| **306** | A45 | $1 multicolored | 3.00 | 2.40 |
| **307** | A45 | $2 multicolored | 4.25 | *10.00* |
| **308** | A45 | $3 yel & multi | 4.25 | 5.00 |
| **309** | A45 | $5 multicolored | 6.00 | *19.00* |
| | | *Nos. 294-309 (18)* | 36.50 | *51.25* |

Nos. 294-309 vary in size from 25x44mm to 29x46mm.

The overprint "VOTE/FEB. 28 1972" was applied to the 2c, 3c, 6c and 25c in Feb., 1972.

Issued: 5c, 10c, 25c, $2, 2/4/69; 3c, 8c, 35c, $5, 7/1/69; #302A, 1970; 75c, 10/9/71; others, 10/68.

For surcharges see Nos. 462-464. For overprints see Nos. 528-541, C3-C19.

### Nos. 280-285 Surcharged in Carmine

**1969, Feb.** ***Perf. 12½***

| | | | | |
|---|---|---|---|---|
| **310** | A42 | 5c on 1c multi | .25 | .25 |
| **311** | A42 | 8c on 2c multi | .25 | .25 |
| **312** | A42 | 25c on 3c multi | .25 | .25 |
| **313** | A42 | 35c on 10c multi | .25 | .25 |
| **314** | A42 | $1 on 50c multi | .25 | .25 |
| **315** | A42 | $2 on 60c multi | .40 | *.60* |
| | | *Nos. 310-315 (6)* | 1.65 | 1.85 |

Gov. Hilda Bynoe and View of St. George's A46

Designs: 15c, Premier Eric M. Gairy, fruits and St. George's. 60c, Emblems of Brussels, New York and Montreal World's Fairs.

**1969, May 1** **Litho.** ***Perf. 13x13½***

| | | | | |
|---|---|---|---|---|
| **316** | A46 | 5c multicolored | .25 | .25 |
| **317** | A46 | 15c multicolored | .25 | .25 |
| **318** | A46 | 50c multicolored | .25 | .25 |
| **319** | A46 | 60c multicolored | .25 | .30 |
| | | *Nos. 316-319 (4)* | 1.00 | 1.05 |

Nos. 310-319 issued to publicize CARIFTA (Caribbean Free Trade Area) Exposition, St. George's, Apr. 5-30.

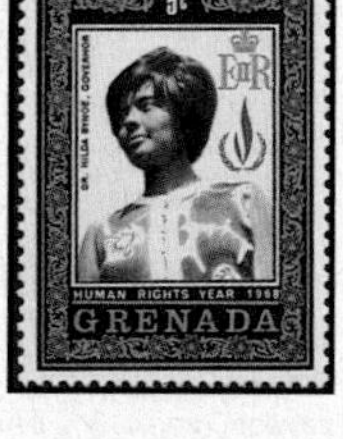


Gov. Hilda Bynoe — A47

Designs: 25c, Dr. Martin Luther King, Jr. $1, Belshazzar's Feast, by Rembrandt, horiz.

***Perf. 13x12½, 12½x13***

**1969, June 8** **Photo.** **Unwmk.**

| | | | | |
|---|---|---|---|---|
| **320** | A47 | 5c multicolored | .25 | .25 |
| **321** | A47 | 25c multicolored | .25 | .25 |
| **322** | A47 | 35c multicolored | .25 | .25 |
| **323** | A47 | $1 multicolored | .30 | .40 |
| | | *Nos. 320-323 (4)* | 1.05 | 1.15 |

International Human Rights Year.

Batsman Playing Off-drive — A48

Cricket: 10c, Batsman playing defensive stroke. 25c, Batsman sweeping ball. 35c, Batsman playing on-drive.

**1969, Aug. 1** ***Perf. 14x14½***

| | | | | |
|---|---|---|---|---|
| **324** | A48 | 3c dk blue & multi | .25 | *.95* |
| **325** | A48 | 10c fawn & multi | .25 | *.40* |
| **326** | A48 | 25c dp green & multi | .50 | *.80* |
| **327** | A48 | 35c brt purple & multi | .65 | *.85* |
| | | *Nos. 324-327 (4)* | 1.65 | *3.00* |

Astronaut Collecting Moon Rocks, Landing Module and Earth — A49

Designs: ½c, like $1. 1c, Apollo 11, moon and earth. 2c, Landing module "Eagle." 3c, Memorial tablet left on moon. 8c, Separation of rocket and spaceship. 25c, Take off from Cape Kennedy, vert. 35c, Apollo 11 circling the moon, vert. 50c, Splashdown, vert. ½c, 2c, 25c, 50c, $1 inscribed: "We came in peace for all mankind." 1c, 3c, 8c, 35c inscribed: "Like the moon it shall be established forever" Psalms 89:37.

***Perf. 13x13½ (½c), 12½***

**1969, Sept. 24** **Litho.** **Unwmk.**

**Size: 56x35mm**

| | | | | |
|---|---|---|---|---|
| **328** | A49 | ½c multicolored | .25 | .25 |

**Size: 44½x28mm, 28x44½mm**

| | | | | |
|---|---|---|---|---|
| **329** | A49 | 1c multicolored | .25 | .25 |
| **330** | A49 | 2c multicolored | .25 | .25 |
| **331** | A49 | 3c multicolored | .25 | .25 |
| **332** | A49 | 8c multicolored | .25 | .25 |
| **333** | A49 | 25c multicolored | .25 | .25 |
| **334** | A49 | 35c multicolored | .25 | .25 |
| **335** | A49 | 50c multicolored | .25 | .25 |
| **336** | A49 | $1 multicolored | .40 | .60 |
| *a.* | | Souvenir sheet of 2 | 2.00 | 2.00 |
| | | *Nos. 328-336 (9)* | 2.40 | 2.60 |

Man's first moonlanding (Apollo 11), July 20, 1969.

No. 336a contains stamps similar to Nos. 331 and 336 with simulated perforations.

For surcharge and overprints see #349, 379-382.

Mahatma Gandhi — A50

Gandhi in various positions. 15c, 25c are vert.

**1969, Oct. 8** ***Perf. 11½x12, 12x11½***

**Queen's Head in Gold**

| | | | | |
|---|---|---|---|---|
| **337** | A50 | 6c multicolored | .25 | .25 |
| **338** | A50 | 15c multicolored | .25 | .25 |
| **339** | A50 | 25c multicolored | .60 | .25 |
| **340** | A50 | $1 multicolored | 1.00 | *1.10* |
| *a.* | | Souvenir sheet of 4 | 4.75 | 4.75 |
| | | *Nos. 337-340 (4)* | 2.10 | 1.85 |

Mohandas K. Gandhi (1869-1948), leader in India's fight for independence.

No. 340a contains stamps similar to Nos. 337-340 with simulated perforation.

Nos. 290-293 Overprinted in Black or Silver

**1969, Dec. 23 Photo. *Perf. 12½***

**341** A44 2c on 15c multi .25 *.75*
**342** A44 5c multi (S) .25 .25
**343** A44 35c multi (S) .25 .25
**344** A44 $1 multi (S) .65 *1.75*
*Nos. 341-344 (4)* 1.40 *3.00*

Christmas.

Edward Teach (Blackbeard) A51

Pirates: 25c, Anne Bonney and sailboats. 50c, Jean Lafitte and sailboats. $1, Mary Read, ships and fighting pirates.

**1970, Feb. 1 Engr. *Perf. 13x13½***

**345** A51 15c black .60 .25
**346** A51 25c emerald 1.00 .25
**347** A51 50c purple 1.90 .25
**348** A51 $1 carmine 3.00 .95
*Nos. 345-348 (4)* 6.50 1.70

**No. 328 Surcharged**

Type I

Type II

**1970, Mar. 18 Litho. *Perf. 13x13½***

**349** A49 5c on ½c multi (I) .40 .40
*a.* Type II 1.25 *1.50*

Christ, from "The Last Supper," by Andrea del Sarto — A52

Paintings: No. 351 (5c), St. John, from Last Supper by Andrea del Sarto. Nos. 352-353 (15c), Christ Crowned with Thorns, by Anthony Van Dyck. Nos. 354-355 (25c), Passion of Christ, by Hans Memling. Nos. 356-357 (60c), Christ in the Tomb, by Peter Paul Rubens. Nos. 350, 352, 354 and 356 have denomination in lower right corner; others in lower left corner. The stamps of the same denomination are printed se-tenant without separating margin, reproducing continuous picture.

**1970, Apr. 13 Litho. *Perf. 11½x11***

**350** 5c rose car & multi .25 .25
**351** 5c rose car & multi .25 .25
*a.* A52 Pair, #350-351 .40 .40
**352** 15c ultra & multi .25 *.25*
**353** 15c ultra & multi .25 *.25*
*a.* A52 Pair, #352-353 .40 *.50*
**354** 25c brt vio & multi .25 *.25*
**355** 25c brt vio & multi .25 *.25*
*a.* A52 Pair, #354-355 .40 .50
**356** 60c dull org & multi .25 *.55*
**357** 60c dull org & multi .25 *.55*
*a.* A52 Pair, #354-355 .40 1.10
*b.* Souvenir sheet of 4, #354-357 1.25 1.25
*Nos. 350-357 (8)* 2.00 *2.60*

Easter.

Girl Pushing Carriage with Kittens — A53

Designs: 15c, Girl playing with puppy and kitten. 30c, Boy fishing and cat. 60c, Children with pets.

**1970, May 27 Litho. *Perf. 11***

**358** A53 5c multicolored .25 .25
**359** A53 15c multicolored .25 .25
**360** A53 30c multicolored .35 .35
*a.* Souvenir sheet of 2 1.50 1.50
**361** A53 60c multicolored .75 *1.00*
*a.* Souvenir sheet of 2 1.50 1.50
*Nos. 358-361 (4)* 1.60 1.85

William Wordsworth (1770-1850). English poet. No. 360a contains stamps similar to Nos. 358 and 360; No. 361a contains stamps similar to Nos. 359 and 361. Sheets have simulated perforations.

Indian Parliament — A54

Commonwealth Parliamentary Association Emblem and: 25c, British Parliament. 50c, Canadian Parliament. 60c, Grenadian Parliament.

**1970, June 15 *Perf. 14½x14***

**362** A54 5c multicolored .25 .25
**363** A54 25c multicolored .25 .25
**364** A54 50c multicolored .25 .25
**365** A54 60c multicolored .25 .25
*a.* Souvenir sheet of 4, #362-365 .85 .85
*Nos. 362-365 (4)* 1.00 1.00

7th Caribbean Regional Conf. of the Commonwealth Parliamentary Assoc., St. George's. June 13-20.

Sun Tower and EXPO Emblem A55

EXPO Emblem and: 2c, Livelihood Industry pavilion, horiz. 3c, Ikenobo, Japanese floral art, vert. 10c, Adam and Eve, by Tintoretto and Italian pavilion, horiz. 25c, UN pavilion and flags reflected in pool, 50c, Peace statue of St. Francis, San Francisco pavilion, cable car and Golden Gate Bridge, $1, Toshiba-Ihi pavilion, horiz.

**1970, Aug. 8 Litho. *Perf. 13½***

**366** A55 1c brt blue & multi .25 .25
**367** A55 2c multicolored .25 .25
**368** A55 3c buff & multi .25 .25
**369** A55 10c multicolored .25 .25
**370** A55 25c gray & multi .25 .25
**371** A55 50c gray & multi .25 *1.00*
*Nos. 366-371 (6)* 1.50 2.25

**Souvenir Sheet**

**372** A55 $1 gold & multi 1.00 *1.75*

EXPO '70 Intl. Exhib., Osaka, Japan, Mar. 15-Sept. 13.

Pres. Roosevelt and Flag-Raising on Iwo Jima — A56

Designs: 5c, Marshal Georgi K. Zhukov and fall of Berlin. 15c, Winston Churchill and evacuation of Dunkirk. 25c, Charles de Gaulle and liberation of Paris. 50c, General Dwight D. Eisenhower and D-Day landing. 60c, Field Marshal Bernard Montgomery and Battle of Alamein.

**1970, Sept. 3 *Perf. 11***

**373** A56 ½c multicolored .25 *.60*
**374** A56 5c multicolored 1.00 .35
**375** A56 15c multicolored 1.50 .55
**376** A56 25c multicolored 1.75 .55
**377** A56 50c multicolored 2.00 1.60
**378** A56 60c multicolored 2.25 *3.00*
*a.* Souv. sheet of 4 #373, 375, 377-378 6.25 6.25
*Nos. 373-378 (6)* 8.75 6.65

End of World War II, 25th anniversary.

**Nos. 333-336 Overprinted in Black or Silver: "PHILYMPIA / LONDON 1970"**

**1970, Sept. 18 *Perf. 12½***

**379** A49 25c multicolored .25 .25
**380** A49 35c multicolored .25 .25
**381** A49 50c multicolored .25 .25
**382** A49 $1 multi (S) .40 .40
*Nos. 379-382 (4)* 1.15 1.15

Philympia 1970, London philatelic exhibition, Sept. 18-26. The overprint on No. 382 is vertical, reading up.

This overprint was applied in silver to No. 336a. Value $47.50.

UPU Headquarters, Emblem and Old Transportation — A57

UPU Headquarters, emblem and: 25c, Jet plane, ship and diesel train. 50c, Rowland Hill, vert. $1, Abraham Lincoln, vert.

**1970, Oct. 17 Litho. *Perf. 14½***

**383** A57 15c orange & multi .65 .25
**384** A57 25c blue & multi .65 .25
**385** A57 50c multicolored .40 .40
**386** A57 $1 rose & multi .60 *2.00*
*a.* Souvenir sheet of 2 1.90 *3.00*
*Nos. 383-386 (4)* 2.30 2.90

Opening of the new UPU Headquarters in Bern. No. 386a contains stamps similar to Nos. 385-386.

Madonna of the Goldfinch, by Tiepolo — A58

Christmas (Paintings): No. 388, 35c, Virgin and Child with Sts. Peter and Paul, by Dirk Bouts. No. 389, $1, Virgin and Child, by Bellini. 3c, Like No. 387. 2c, 50c, Madonna of the Basket, by Correggio.

**1970, Dec. 5 *Perf. 14x13½***

**387** A58 ½c yel grn & multi .25 .25
**388** A58 ½c pink & multi .25 .25
**389** A58 ½c yellow & multi .25 .25
**390** A58 2c lt blue & multi .25 .25
**391** A58 3c dp rose & multi .25 .25
**392** A58 35c dk green & multi .25 .40
**393** A58 50c brown & multi .40 .50
**394** A58 $1 purple & multi .60 1.10
*a.* Souvenir sheet of 2, #393-394 2.25 *3.00*
*Nos. 387-394 (8)* 2.50 3.25

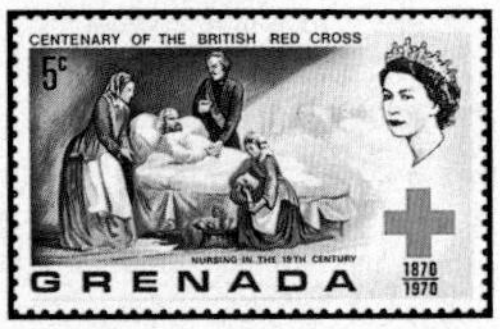


Nursing in 19th Century A59

Designs: 15c, Horse-drawn ambulance, Northern France, 1918. 25c, First aid station, 1941. 60c, Red Cross truck loaded on plane, 1970 emergency aid.

**1970, Dec. 12 Litho. *Perf. 14½x14***

**395** A59 5c red & multi .25 .25
**396** A59 15c red & multi .30 .25
**397** A59 25c red & multi .50 .35
**398** A59 60c red & multi 1.00 *1.25*
*a.* Souvenir sheet of 4, #395-398 2.50 2.25
*Nos. 395-398 (4)* 2.05 2.10

Centenary of the British Red Cross Society.

John Dewey, Children Learning to Paint — A60

Designs: 10c, Jean-Jacques Rousseau and students. 50c, Moses Maimonides and biology student. $1, Bertrand Russell and boys.

**1971, May 8 Litho. *Perf. 13½***

**399** A60 5c multicolored .25 .25
**400** A60 10c multicolored .25 .25
**401** A60 50c multicolored .50 .50
**402** A60 $1 multicolored 1.10 .75
*a.* Souvenir sheet of 2, #401-402 2.00 2.25
*Nos. 399-402 (4)* 2.10 1.75

International Education Year.

Jennifer Hosten and Map of Grenada A61

**1971, June 1 Litho. *Perf. 13½***

**403** A61 5c vio blue & multi .25 .25
**404** A61 10c red lilac & multi .25 .25
**405** A61 15c brt rose & multi .25 .25
**406** A61 25c violet & multi .25 .25
**407** A61 35c blue & multi .30 .45
**408** A61 50c red & multi .65 .65
*a.* Souvenir sheet of 1 1.90 2.00
*Nos. 403-408 (6)* 1.95 2.10

Honoring Miss Jennifer Hosten of Grenada, Miss World, 1971. No. 408a, printed on silk, contains imperf. stamp similar to No. 408.

Nos. 403-408 and 408a were overprinted "INTERPEX/1972" in Mar. 1972. Value $9.50.

For surcharge and overprints #465, C23-C26.

Canadian and French Boy Scouts — A62

Boy Scouts from: 35c, West Germany and US. 50c, Australia and Japan. 75c, Grenada and Great Britain.

**1971, Aug.** **Litho.** ***Perf. 11***

| | | | | |
|---|---|---|---|---|
| **409** | A62 | 5c multicolored | .25 | .25 |
| **410** | A62 | 35c multicolored | .40 | .40 |
| **411** | A62 | 50c multicolored | .50 | .60 |
| **412** | A62 | 75c multicolored | .65 | .90 |
| *a.* | | Souvenir sheet of 2, #411-412 | 2.00 | *2.75* |
| | | *Nos. 409-412 (4)* | 1.80 | 2.15 |

13th Boy Scout World Jamboree, Asagiri Plain, Japan, Aug. 2-10.

Napoleon, by Edouard Détaille A63

Paintings of Napoleon: 15c, Outside Madrid, by Carle Vernet. 35c, Crossing the Alps, by Jacques Louis David. $2, Portrait, by David.

**1971, Sept.** ***Perf. 13x13½***

| | | | | |
|---|---|---|---|---|
| **413** | A63 | 5c multicolored | .25 | .25 |
| **414** | A63 | 15c multicolored | .25 | .25 |
| **415** | A63 | 35c multicolored | .35 | .35 |
| *a.* | | Souvenir sheet of 1 | 2.25 | *3.00* |
| **416** | A63 | $2 multicolored | 1.10 | 1.50 |
| | | *Nos. 413-416 (4)* | 1.95 | 2.35 |

Sesquicentennial of the death of Napoleon Bonaparte (1769-1821).

No. 415a contains stamp similar to No. 415 with simulated perforations.

Grenada No. 1 — A64

15c, Grenada #2 & Queen Elizabeth II. 35c, Grenada #1, 2. 50c, Grenada #1 & scroll.

**1971, Nov. 6** **Litho.** ***Perf. 11***

| | | | | |
|---|---|---|---|---|
| **417** | A64 | 5c dk red & multi | .25 | .25 |
| **418** | A64 | 15c multicolored | .35 | .25 |
| **419** | A64 | 35c dull org & multi | .55 | .25 |
| **420** | A64 | 50c dk green & multi | .75 | *1.75* |
| *a.* | | Souvenir sheet of 2, #419-420 | 1.75 | 1.75 |
| | | *Nos. 417-420 (4)* | 1.90 | *2.50* |

110th anniversary of postal service.

Splashdown, Apollo 13 — A65

Designs: 2c, Capsule and rafts in ocean, Apollo 13. 3c, Separation of landing module from rocket, Apollo 14. 10c, Astronauts collecting moon rocks, Apollo 14. 25c, Astronauts in moon rover, Apollo 15. 50c, $1, Rocket blast-off, Apollo 15, vert.

**1971, Nov.**

| | | | | |
|---|---|---|---|---|
| **421** | A65 | 1c multicolored | .25 | .30 |
| **422** | A65 | 2c multicolored | .25 | .30 |
| **423** | A65 | 3c black & multi | .25 | .30 |
| **424** | A65 | 10c black & multi | .35 | .25 |
| **425** | A65 | 25c multicolored | 1.10 | .35 |
| **426** | A65 | $1 multicolored | 2.25 | *3.50* |
| | | *Nos. 421-426 (6)* | 4.45 | *5.00* |

**Souvenir Sheet**

| | | | | |
|---|---|---|---|---|
| **427** | A65 | 50c multicolored | 2.50 | 2.50 |

US moon missions of Apollo 13, 14 and 15.

67th Regiment of Foot, 1787 — A66

Designs: 1c, 45th Regiment of Foot, 1792. 2c, 29th Regiment of Foot, 1794. 10c, 9th Regiment of Foot, 1801. 25c, 2nd Regiment of Foot, 1815. $1, 70th Regiment of Foot, 1764.

**1971, Dec.** ***Perf. 13½x14***

| | | | | |
|---|---|---|---|---|
| **428** | A66 | ½c red & multi | .25 | .25 |
| **429** | A66 | 1c red & multi | .25 | .25 |
| **430** | A66 | 2c red & multi | .25 | .25 |
| **431** | A66 | 10c red & multi | .50 | .25 |
| **432** | A66 | 25c red & multi | .90 | .30 |
| **433** | A66 | $1 red & multi | 2.75 | 2.75 |
| *a.* | | Souv. sheet of 2, #432-433, perf. 15 | 4.00 | 4.00 |
| | | *Nos. 428-433 (6)* | 4.90 | 4.05 |

Uniforms of British units stationed in Grenada.

For surcharges see Nos. 439, C1-C2.

Adoration of the Kings, by Memling — A67

Christmas: 25c, Madonna and Child, sculpture by Michelangelo. 35c, Madonna and Child, by Murillo. 50c, Madonna with the Apple, by Memling. $1, Adoration of the Kings, by Jan Mostaert.

**1971, Dec.** ***Perf. 14x13½***

| | | | | |
|---|---|---|---|---|
| **434** | A67 | 15c gold & multi | .25 | .25 |
| **435** | A67 | 25c gold & multi | .25 | .25 |
| **436** | A67 | 35c gold & multi | .30 | .25 |
| **437** | A67 | 50c gold & multi | .40 | .75 |
| | | *Nos. 434-437 (4)* | 1.20 | 1.50 |

**Souvenir Sheet**

| | | | | |
|---|---|---|---|---|
| **438** | A67 | $1 gold & multi | 1.10 | 1.10 |

No. 430 Surcharged

**1972, Feb. 3** ***Perf. 13½x14***

| | | | | |
|---|---|---|---|---|
| **439** | A66 | $2 on 2c red & multi | 1.25 | 1.25 |
| *a.* | | Souvenir sheet of 2 | 2.00 | 2.00 |

11th Winter Olympic Games, Sapporo, Japan, Feb. 3-13. See Nos. C1-C2.

No. 439a is overprinted in red on No. 433a (no surcharge); margin inscribed in red: "SAPPORO 1972."

King Arthur, UNICEF Emblem A68

UNICEF Emblem and: 1c, 50c, Robin Hood. 2c, 75c, Robinson Crusoe, vert. 25c, like ½c. $1, Mary and her Little Lamb, vert.

**1972, Mar. 4** ***Perf. 14½x14, 14x14½***

| | | | | |
|---|---|---|---|---|
| **450** | A68 | ½c dp blue & multi | .25 | .25 |
| **451** | A68 | 1c yellow & multi | .25 | .25 |
| **452** | A68 | 2c dp yel & multi | .25 | .25 |
| **453** | A68 | 25c salmon & multi | .25 | .25 |
| **454** | A68 | 50c multicolored | .25 | .35 |
| **455** | A68 | 75c blue & multi | .30 | .60 |
| **456** | A68 | $1 multicolored | .40 | .85 |
| *a.* | | Souvenir sheet of 1 | 1.00 | 1.00 |
| | | *Nos. 450-456 (7)* | 1.95 | 2.80 |

25th anniv. (in 1971) of UNICEF.

Yachting A69

1c, 50c, Equestrian. 2c, 35c, Running, vert.

**1972, Sept. 8** **Litho.** ***Perf. 14***

| | | | | |
|---|---|---|---|---|
| **457** | A69 | ½c multicolored | .25 | .25 |
| **458** | A69 | 1c lt blue & multi | .25 | .25 |
| **459** | A69 | 2c orange & multi | .25 | .25 |
| **460** | A69 | 35c yellow & multi | .40 | .80 |
| **461** | A69 | 50c yel grn & multi | .60 | 1.10 |
| | | *Nos. 457-461,C20-C21 (7)* | 3.15 | 3.70 |

20th Olympic Games, Munich, Aug. 26-Sept. 11. See No. C22.

Nos. 294-296, 403 Surcharged

***Perf. 14x14½, 13½***

**1972, Oct.** **Photo.**

| | | | | |
|---|---|---|---|---|
| **462** | A45 | 12c on 1c multi | .50 | .55 |
| **463** | A45 | 12c on 2c multi | .50 | .55 |
| **464** | A45 | 12c on 3c multi | .50 | .55 |
| **465** | A61 | 12c on 5c multi | .50 | .55 |
| | | *Nos. 462-465 (4)* | 2.00 | 2.20 |

**Silver Wedding Issue, 1972**

Common Design Type

Design: Queen Elizabeth II, Prince Philip, seal of Grenada and myristica fragrans.

***Perf. 14x14½***

**1972, Nov. 20** **Wmk. 314**

| | | | | |
|---|---|---|---|---|
| **466** | CD324 | 8c olive & multi | .25 | .25 |
| **467** | CD324 | $1 multicolored | .45 | .45 |

Boy Scout Saluting A70

Designs: 1c, Two Scouts knotting ropes. 2c, 70c, 75c, Scouts from different nations. 3c, 60c, $1, Lord Baden-Powell.

**Unwmk.**

**1972, Dec. 2** **Litho.** ***Perf. 14***

| | | | | |
|---|---|---|---|---|
| **468** | A70 | ½c yellow & multi | .25 | .25 |
| **469** | A70 | 1c red & multi | .25 | .25 |
| **470** | A70 | 2c yellow & multi | .25 | .25 |
| **471** | A70 | 3c brt lilac & multi | .25 | .25 |
| **472** | A70 | 75c lt blue & multi | .80 | .80 |
| **473** | A70 | $1 multicolored | 1.25 | 1.25 |
| | | *Nos. 468-473,C27-C28 (8)* | 4.05 | 3.95 |

**Souvenir Sheet**

| | | | | |
|---|---|---|---|---|
| **474** | | Sheet of 2 | 2.75 | 2.75 |
| *a.* | | A70 60c ocher & multi | 1.25 | 1.25 |
| *b.* | | A70 70c pale lilac & multi | 1.50 | 1.50 |

Boy Scouts, 65th anniversary.

Virgin and Child, Crosier — A71

Christmas: 3c, 35c, 70c, The Three Kings. 5c, $1, Holy Family. 25c, 60c, Like 1c.

**1972, Dec. 9** **Litho.** ***Perf. 14x13½***

| | | | | |
|---|---|---|---|---|
| **475** | A71 | 1c blue & multi | .25 | .25 |
| **476** | A71 | 3c gray & multi | .25 | .25 |
| **477** | A71 | 5c multicolored | .25 | .25 |
| **478** | A71 | 25c multicolored | .25 | .25 |
| **479** | A71 | 35c lt blue & multi | .25 | .25 |
| **480** | A71 | $1 ocher & multi | .70 | .70 |
| | | *Nos. 475-480 (6)* | 1.95 | 1.95 |

**Souvenir Sheet**

***Perf. 15***

| | | | | |
|---|---|---|---|---|
| **481** | | Sheet of 2 | 1.10 | 1.10 |
| *a.* | | A71 60c blue & multi | .45 | .45 |
| *b.* | | A71 70c bright pink & multi | .60 | .60 |

Flamingos — A72

**1973, Jan. 5** **Litho.** ***Perf. 14***

| | | | | |
|---|---|---|---|---|
| **482** | A72 | 25c shown | 1.00 | .25 |
| **483** | A72 | 35c Tapir | .80 | .25 |
| **484** | A72 | 60c Macaws | 1.75 | 1.75 |
| **485** | A72 | 70c Ocelot | 1.60 | *2.25* |
| | | *Nos. 482-485 (4)* | 5.15 | 4.50 |

National Zoo of Grenada.

Class II Ocean Racing Yacht — A73

**1973, Jan. 26** **Litho.** ***Perf. 13½x14***

| | | | | |
|---|---|---|---|---|
| **486** | A73 | 25c shown | .40 | .35 |
| **487** | A73 | 35c Boats in St. George's Harbour | .55 | .50 |
| **488** | A73 | 60c Yacht "Bloodhound" | .90 | .85 |
| **489** | A73 | 70c St. George's Harbour | .95 | *1.10* |
| | | *Nos. 486-489 (4)* | 2.80 | 2.80 |

Yachting off Grenada.

Sun God Helios, Equinoxes and Solstices — A74

WMO Emblem and: 1c, Poseidon and Nomad automatic storm detector. 2c, Zeus and radarscope. 3c, Goddess Iris, rainbow, weather balloon. 35c, Hermes, ATS 3 satellite. 50c, Zephyr and circulation of atmosphere. 75c, Demeter, space photograph of storm. $1, Selene, globe showing world rainfall. $2, Computer weather map (42x31mm).

**1973, July 6 Litho. *Perf. 13½***

**490** A74 ½c multicolored .25 .25
**491** A74 1c multicolored .25 .25
**492** A74 2c multicolored .25 .25
**493** A74 3c multicolored .25 .25
**494** A74 35c multicolored .30 .25
**495** A74 50c multicolored .45 .25
**496** A74 75c multicolored .55 .45
**497** A74 $1 multicolored .55 .55
*Nos. 490-497 (8)* 2.85 2.50

**Souvenir Sheet**

**498** A74 $2 multicolored 1.75 1.75

Intl. meteorological cooperation, cent.

Racing Class Yachts — A75

**1973, Aug. 3 Litho. *Perf. 13½***

**499** A75 ½c shown .25 .25
**500** A75 1c Cruising class .25 .25
**501** A75 2c Open-decked sloops .25 .25
**502** A75 35c Sloop Mermaid .35 .25
**503** A75 50c St. George's Harbour .45 .25
**504** A75 75c Map of Carriacou .65 .65
**505** A75 $1 Boat building .80 .80
*Nos. 499-505 (7)* 3.00 2.70

**Souvenir Sheet**

**506** A75 $2 End of race 1.50 1.75

Carriacou Regatta, August 1973.

Ignaz Philipp Semmelweiss A76

Designs: Physicians and scientists.

**1973, Sept. 17 Litho. *Perf. 14½***

**507** A76 ½c shown .25 .25
**508** A76 1c Louis Pasteur .25 .25
**509** A76 2c Edward Jenner .25 .25
**510** A76 3c Sigmund Freud .25 .25
**511** A76 25c Emil von Behring .45 .45
**512** A76 35c Carl Jung .60 .60
**513** A76 50c Gharles Calmette .90 .90
**514** A76 $1 William Harvey 1.75 1.75
*Nos. 507-514 (8)* 4.70 4.70

**Souvenir Sheet**

**515** A76 $2 Marie Curie 3.00 3.00

WHO, 25th anniv.

Princess Anne and Mark Phillips — A77

**1973, Nov. 14 Wmk. 314 *Perf. 13½***

**516** A77 25c dp orange & multi .25 .80
**517** A77 $2 green & multi .25 .80
*a.* Souv. sheet of 2 (75c, $1) .60 .60

Wedding of Princess Anne and Capt. Mark Phillips.

Nos. 516-517 were issued only in sheets of 5 plus label. Colors of 75c and $1 are as those of 25c and $2.

Virgin and Child, by Carlo Maratti — A78

Christmas (Paintings): 1c, Virgin and Child, by Carlo Crivelli. 2c, Virgin and Child, by Verrocchio. 3c, Adoration of the Shepherds, by Roberti. 25c, Holy Family, by Federigo Baroccio. 35c, Holy Family, by Bronzino. 75c, Mystic Nativity, by Botticelli. $1, Adoration of the Kings, by Geertgen tot Sint Jans. $2, Adoration of the Kings, by Jan Mostaert (30x45mm).

**1973, Nov. Unwmk. *Perf. 14½***

**519** A78 ½c lt brown & multi .25 .25
**520** A78 1c citron & multi .25 .25
**521** A78 2c blue & multi .25 .25
**522** A78 3c green & multi .25 .25
**523** A78 25c multicolored .25 .25
**524** A78 35c multicolored .25 .25
**525** A78 75c vio blue & multi .25 .80
**526** A78 $1 multicolored .30 1.00
*Nos. 519-526 (8)* 2.05 3.30

**Souvenir Sheet**

***Perf. 13½x14***

**527** A78 $2 red & multi 2.00 2.00

**Nos. 294-297, 299-301, 303-304, 305A-309 Overprinted**

***Perf. 14x14½, 14½x14***

**1974, Feb. 7 Photo.**

**528** A45 1c multicolored .25 .25
**529** A45 2c multicolored .25 .25
**530** A45 3c multicolored .25 .25
**531** A45 5c multicolored .25 .25
**532** A45 8c multicolored .25 .25
**533** A45 10c multicolored .25 .25
**534** A45 12c multicolored .25 .25
**535** A45 25c multicolored .40 .40
**536** A45 35c multicolored .60 .60

**Litho.**

***Perf. 13½x14***

**537** A45a 75c multicolored *2.10* *1.50*

**Photo.**

***Perf. 14x14½***

**538** A45 $1 multicolored *3.75* *1.75*
**539** A45 $2 multicolored *5.75* *6.50*
**540** A45 $3 multicolored *7.25* *8.25*
**541** A45 $5 multicolored *11.50* *18.50*
*Nos. 528-541 (14)* *33.10* *39.25*

Grenada's independence, Feb. 7, 1974. Size of overprint on vertical stamps 16x5mm; on horizontal stamps 20x6mm.

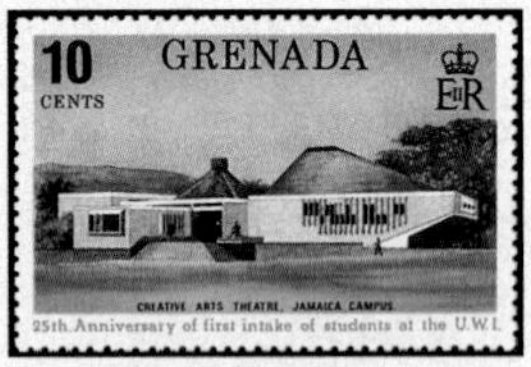

Creative Arts Theater, Jamaica Campus — A79

Designs: 25c, Marryshow House, University Center. 50c, Chapel, vert. $1, $2, University coat of arms, vert.

**1974, Apr. 10 Litho. *Perf. 13½***

**542** A79 10c multicolored .25 .25
**543** A79 25c multicolored .25 .25
**544** A79 50c multicolored .25 .25
**545** A79 $1 multicolored .30 .30
*Nos. 542-545 (4)* 1.05 1.05

**Souvenir Sheet**

**546** A79 $2 multicolored .90 .90

25th anniv. of the University of the West Indies.

Prime Minister Eric M. Gairy — A80

**1974, Aug. 19 Litho. *Perf. 13½***

**547** A80 3c Nutmeg and mace .25 .25
**548** A80 8c Map of Grenada .25 .25
**549** A80 25c shown .30 .30
**550** A80 35c Anse Beach and Flag .45 .30
**551** A80 $1 Coat of arms 1.10 1.10
*Nos. 547-551 (5)* 2.35 2.20

**Souvenir Sheet**

**552** A80 $2 Coat of arms 1.10 1.10

Grenada's independence.

Soccer, Flags of West Germany and Chile — A81

Soccer Games and Flags: 1c, East Germany and Australia. 2c, Yugoslavia and Brazil. 10c, Scotland and Zaire. 25c, Netherlands and Uruguay. 50c, Sweden and Bulgaria. 75c, Italy and Haiti. $1, Poland and Argentina. $2, Flags of participating nations, horiz.

**1974, Sept. 3 Litho. *Perf. 14½***

**553** A81 ½c multicolored .25 .25
**554** A81 1c multicolored .25 .25
**555** A81 2c multicolored .25 .25
**556** A81 10c multicolored .25 .25
**557** A81 25c multicolored .25 .25
**558** A81 50c multicolored .25 .25
**559** A81 75c multicolored .40 .40
**560** A81 $1 multicolored .60 .60
*Nos. 553-560 (8)* 2.50 2.50

**Souvenir Sheet**

***Perf. 13***

**561** A81 $2 multicolored 1.75 1.75

World Cup Soccer Championship, Munich, June 13-July 7.

19th Century US Mail Train, Concorde and UPU Emblem — A82

UPU Emblem and: 1c, Sailing ship "Caesar," 1839, and helicopter. 2c, Zeppelin, jet and early planes. 8c, Pigeon post, 1480, telephone dial. 15c, Bellman, 18th cent. and radar. 25c, German Imperial messenger, 1450, satellite. 35c, French pillar box and ocean liner. $1, German mailman, 18th cent., and futuristic mail train. $2, St. Gotthard mail coach, 1735, vert.

**1974, Oct. 8 Litho. *Perf. 14½***

**562** A82 ½c rose & multi .25 .25
**563** A82 1c gray & multi .25 .25
**564** A82 2c dull pink & multi .25 .25
**565** A82 8c yellow & multi .25 .25
**566** A82 15c yel grn & multi .45 .25
**567** A82 25c dull yel & multi .50 .25
**568** A82 35c lilac & multi .75 .25
**569** A82 $1 lt blue & multi 2.00 1.60
*Nos. 562-569 (8)* 4.70 3.35

**Souvenir Sheet**

***Perf. 13***

**570** A82 $2 multicolored 1.75 *2.25*

UPU, cent.

Sir Winston Churchill — A83

Design: $2, Churchill, different portrait.

**1974, Oct. 28 Litho. *Perf. 13½***

**571** A83 35c multicolored .25 .25
**572** A83 $2 multicolored .65 .65

**Souvenir Sheet**

**573** Sheet of 2 1.10 1.10
*a.* A83 75c like 35c .45 .45
*b.* A83 $1 like $2 .65 .65

Winston Churchill (1874-1965).

Virgin and Child, by Botticelli — A84

Christmas: Paintings of the Virgin and Child.

**1974, Nov. 18 *Perf. 14½***

**574** A84 ½ shown .25 .25
**575** A84 1c Niccolo di Pietro .25 .25
**576** A84 2c Van der Weyden .25 .25
**577** A84 3c Bastiani .25 .25
**578** A84 10c Giovanni .25 .25
**579** A84 25c Van der Weyden .25 .25
**580** A84 50c Botticelli .25 .25
**581** A84 $1 Mantegna .40 .40
*Nos. 574-581 (8)* 2.15 2.15

**Souvenir Sheet**

***Perf. 13½***

**582** A84 $2 Niccolo di Pietro 1.40 1.40

Yachts and Point Saline A85

1c, Grenada Yacht Club race, St. George's. 2c, Careenage taxi (boat). 3c, Large working boats. 5c, Deep Water Dock, St. George's. 6c, Cacao beans in drying trays. 8c, Nutmeg branch. 10c, River Antoine Estate rum distillery, c. 1785. 12c, Cacao branch. 15c, Fishermen landing catch at Fontenoy. 20c, Parliament Building, St. George's. 25c, Fort George cannons. 35c, Pearls Airport. 50c, General Post Office. 75c, Carib Leap, Sauteurs Bay. $1, Careenage, St. George's. $2, St. George's harbor at night. $3, Grand Anse Beach. $5, Canoe Bay and Black Bay from Point Saline Lighthouse. $10, Sugar-loaf Island from Levera Beach.

**1975 Litho. *Perf. 14½***

**Size: 38x25mm**

**583** A85 ½c multicolored .25 *.55*
**584** A85 1c multicolored .25 .25
**585** A85 2c multicolored .25 .25
**586** A85 3c multicolored .25 .25
**587** A85 5c multicolored .25 .25
**588** A85 6c multicolored .25 .25
**589** A85 8c multicolored 1.00 .25
**590** A85 10c multicolored .25 .25
**591** A85 12c multicolored .35 .25
**592** A85 15c multicolored .25 .25
**593** A85 20c multicolored .25 .25
**594** A85 25c multicolored .25 .25
**595** A85 35c multicolored .25 .25
**596** A85 50c multicolored .25 .25

***Perf. 13½x14***

**Size: 45x28mm**

**597** A85 75c multicolored .50 .40
**598** A85 $1 multicolored .55 .60
**599** A85 $2 multicolored .55 *1.25*
**600** A85 $3 multicolored .60 *1.75*
**601** A85 $5 multicolored .70 *2.50*
**602** A85 $10 multicolored 2.00 *5.50*
*Nos. 583-602 (20)* 9.25 15.80

Issue dates: Nos. 583-596, Jan. 13; Nos. 597-601, Jan. 22; No. 602, Mar. 26.

For overprints, see Nos. 965-979.

**1978** *Perf. 13*

| | | | | |
|---|---|---|---|---|
| *584a* | A85 | 1c | .25 | .25 |
| *585a* | A85 | 2c | .25 | .25 |
| *586a* | A85 | 3c | .25 | .25 |
| *587a* | A85 | 5c | .25 | .25 |
| *588a* | A85 | 6c | .25 | .25 |
| *590a* | A85 | 10c | .25 | .25 |
| *592a* | A85 | 15c | .25 | .30 |
| *593a* | A85 | 20c | .25 | .40 |
| *594a* | A85 | 25c | .25 | .50 |
| *596a* | A85 | 50c | .40 | .55 |
| | | *Nos. 584a-596a (10)* | 2.65 | 3.25 |

Sailfish A86

Designs: Big game fish.

**1975, Feb. 3** *Perf. 14½*

| | | | | |
|---|---|---|---|---|
| **603** | A86 | ½c shown | .25 | .25 |
| **604** | A86 | 1c Blue marlin | .25 | .25 |
| **605** | A86 | 2c White marlin | .25 | .25 |
| **606** | A86 | 10c Yellowfin tuna | .25 | .25 |
| **607** | A86 | 25c Wahoo | .35 | .30 |
| **608** | A86 | 50c Dolphin | .60 | .40 |
| **609** | A86 | 70c Grouper | .85 | .40 |
| **610** | A86 | $1 Great barracuda | 1.10 | .50 |
| | | *Nos. 603-610 (8)* | 3.90 | 2.60 |

**Souvenir Sheet**

*Perf. 13*

| | | | | |
|---|---|---|---|---|
| **611** | A86 | $2 Mako shark | 2.40 | 2.40 |

Passiflora Quadrangularis — A87

Designs: Flowers of Grenada.

**1975, Feb. 26** **Litho.** *Perf. 14½*

| | | | | |
|---|---|---|---|---|
| **612** | A87 | ½c shown | .25 | .25 |
| **613** | A87 | 1c Bleeding heart | .25 | .25 |
| **614** | A87 | 2c Poinsettia | .25 | .25 |
| **615** | A87 | 3c Obroma cacao | .25 | .25 |
| **616** | A87 | 10c Gladioli | .25 | .25 |
| **617** | A87 | 25c Red head-yellow head | .45 | .25 |
| **618** | A87 | 50c Plumbago | .65 | .25 |
| **619** | A87 | $1 Orange blossoms | .95 | .45 |
| | | *Nos. 612-619 (8)* | 3.30 | 2.20 |

**Souvenir Sheet**

*Perf. 13½*

| | | | | |
|---|---|---|---|---|
| **620** | A87 | $2 Barbados gooseberry | 1.75 | 1.75 |

Grenada Flag and UN Emblem — A88

Designs: 1c, UN and Grenada flags. 2c, $1, UN emblem and Grenada coat of arms. 35c, UN emblem over map of Grenada. 50c, Grenada flag in front of UN Headquarters. 75c, like ½c. $2, UN emblem and scroll.

**1975, Mar. 19** *Perf. 14½*

| | | | | |
|---|---|---|---|---|
| **621** | A88 | ½c multicolored | .25 | .25 |
| **622** | A88 | 1c multicolored | .25 | .25 |
| **623** | A88 | 2c multicolored | .25 | .25 |
| **624** | A88 | 35c multicolored | .25 | .25 |
| **625** | A88 | 50c multicolored | .25 | .25 |
| **626** | A88 | $2 multicolored | .50 | .50 |
| | | *Nos. 621-626 (6)* | 1.75 | 1.75 |

**Souvenir Sheet**

*Perf. 13½*

| | | | | |
|---|---|---|---|---|
| **627** | | Sheet of 2 | 1.40 | 1.40 |
| *a.* | | A88 75c multicolored | .55 | .55 |
| *b.* | | A88 $1 multicolored | .90 | .90 |

Grenada's admission to the United Nations, Sept. 17, 1974.

> Remainders of Grenada stamps between Scott Nos. 630 and 872, except Nos. 747-748 and 802-804, were later canceled to order and sold at a fraction of their face value. Our used values for these stamps are for c-t-o examples. Postally used stamps are worth the same as unused, never hinged examples.

Midnight Ride of Paul Revere — A89

1c, Crispus Attucks at Boston Massacre. 2c, Patrick Henry. 3c, Franklin visiting Washington at the front. 5c, Lexington-Concord. 10c, John Paul Jones. #634, Arms of Grenada & US. #635, Flags of Grenada & US.

**1975, May 6** **Litho.** *Perf. 14½, 13*

| | | | | |
|---|---|---|---|---|
| **628** | A89 | ½c Prus blue & multi | .25 | *.25* |
| **629** | A89 | 1c buff & multi | .25 | *.25* |
| **630** | A89 | 2c dp org & multi | .25 | *.25* |
| **631** | A89 | 3c orange & multi | .25 | *.25* |
| **632** | A89 | 5c Prus blue & multi | .25 | *.25* |
| **633** | A89 | 10c ultra & multi | .25 | *.25* |
| | | *Nos. 628-633,C29-C32 (10)* | 3.40 | *2.50* |

**Souvenir Sheets**

*Perf. 13½*

| | | | | |
|---|---|---|---|---|
| **634** | A89 | $2 tan & multi | 1.00 | *.45* |
| **635** | A89 | $2 gray & multi | 1.00 | *.45* |

American Revolution Bicentennial. Size of stamps on Nos. 634-635: 47x34mm.

Nos. 628-633 issued in sheets of 40. Each denomination was also printed in sheets of 5 plus label, perf. 13.

Angel Collecting Jesus' Blood in Grail, by Bellini — A90

Easter (Paintings): 1c, Pieta, by Bellini. 2c, The Deposition, by Rogier van der Weyden. 3c, Pieta, by Bellini. 35c, Descent from the Cross, by Bellini. 75c, Jesus Rising from the Tomb, by Bellini. $1, Descent from the Cross, by Procaccini. $2, Pieta, by Botticelli.

**1975, May 21**

| | | | | |
|---|---|---|---|---|
| **636** | A90 | ½c multicolored | .25 | *.25* |
| **637** | A90 | 1c multicolored | .25 | *.25* |
| **638** | A90 | 2c multicolored | .25 | *.25* |
| **639** | A90 | 3c multicolored | .25 | *.25* |
| **640** | A90 | 35c multicolored | .30 | *.25* |
| **641** | A90 | 75c multicolored | .35 | *.25* |
| **642** | A90 | $1 multicolored | .45 | *.25* |
| | | *Nos. 636-642 (7)* | 2.10 | *1.75* |

**Souvenir Sheet**

*Perf. 13½*

| | | | | |
|---|---|---|---|---|
| **643** | A90 | $2 multicolored | 1.40 | *.65* |

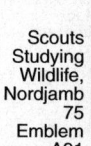

Scouts Studying Wildlife, Nordjamb 75 Emblem A91

Nordjamb 75 Emblem and: 1c, Seamanship; Scouts in sailboat. 2c, Survival; Scouts reading map. 35c, First aid. 40c, Physical fitness; gymnastics. 75c, Mountaineering. $1, Emergency boat building. $2, Scouts singing.

**1975, July 2** **Litho.** *Perf. 14*

| | | | | |
|---|---|---|---|---|
| **644** | A91 | ½c blue & multi | .25 | *.25* |
| **645** | A91 | 1c blue & multi | .25 | *.25* |
| **646** | A91 | 2c blue & multi | .25 | *.25* |
| **647** | A91 | 35c blue & multi | .45 | *.25* |
| **648** | A91 | 40c blue & multi | .50 | *.25* |
| **649** | A91 | 75c blue & multi | .60 | *.25* |
| **650** | A91 | $2 blue & multi | 1.25 | *.35* |
| | | *Nos. 644-650 (7)* | 3.55 | *1.85* |

**Souvenir Sheet**

| | | | | |
|---|---|---|---|---|
| **651** | A91 | $1 blue & multi | 1.60 | *.35* |

Nordjamb 75, 14th Boy Scout World Jamboree, Lillehammer, Norway, July 29-Aug. 7.

Leafy Jewel Box — A92

Designs: Sea shells.

**1975, Aug. 1** **Litho.** *Perf. 14*

| | | | | |
|---|---|---|---|---|
| **652** | A92 | ½c shown | .25 | *.25* |
| **653** | A92 | 1c Emerald nerite | .25 | *.25* |
| **654** | A92 | 2c Yellow cockle | .25 | *.25* |
| **655** | A92 | 25c Purple sea snail | 1.00 | *.25* |
| **656** | A92 | 50c Turkey wing | 2.00 | *.40* |
| **657** | A92 | 75c West Indian fighting conch | 2.75 | *.50* |
| **658** | A92 | $1 Noble wentletrap | 2.75 | *.50* |
| | | *Nos. 652-658 (7)* | 9.25 | *2.40* |

**Souvenir Sheet**

| | | | | |
|---|---|---|---|---|
| **659** | A92 | $2 Music volute | 4.50 | *.90* |

Butterflies — A93

**1975, Sept. 22** **Litho.** *Perf. 14*

| | | | | |
|---|---|---|---|---|
| **660** | A93 | ½c Large tiger | .25 | *.25* |
| **661** | A93 | 1c Five continents | .25 | *.25* |
| **662** | A93 | 2c Large striped blue | .25 | *.25* |
| **663** | A93 | 35c Gonatryx | .85 | *.25* |
| **664** | A93 | 45c Spear-winged cattle heart | 1.00 | *.30* |
| **665** | A93 | 75c Risty nymula | 1.50 | *.40* |
| **666** | A93 | $2 Blue night | 3.75 | *.75* |
| | | *Nos. 660-666 (7)* | 7.85 | *2.45* |

**Souvenir Sheet**

| | | | | |
|---|---|---|---|---|
| **667** | A93 | $1 Lycrophon | 3.00 | *1.00* |

Crew Race A94

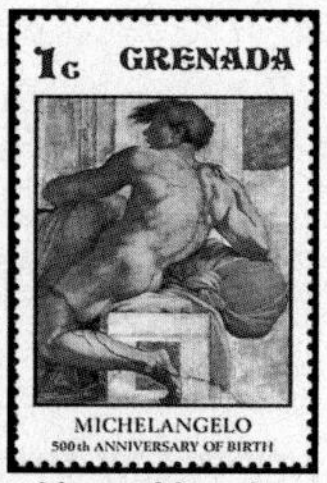

Young Man, by Michelangelo A95

**1975, Oct. 13** **Litho.** *Perf. 14*

| | | | | |
|---|---|---|---|---|
| **668** | A94 | ½c shown | .25 | *.25* |
| **669** | A94 | 1c Women's swimming | .25 | *.25* |
| **670** | A94 | 2c Steeplechase | .25 | *.25* |
| **671** | A94 | 35c Gymnastics | .25 | *.25* |
| **672** | A94 | 45c Soccer | .25 | *.25* |
| **673** | A94 | 75c Boxing | .30 | *.25* |
| **674** | A94 | $2 Bicycling | 1.10 | *.40* |
| | | *Nos. 668-674 (7)* | 2.65 | *1.90* |

**Souvenir Sheet**

| | | | | |
|---|---|---|---|---|
| **675** | A94 | $1 Sailing | 2.00 | *.45* |

7th Pan-American Games, Mexico City, Oct. 13-26.

**1975, Nov. 3**

Works by Michelangelo (except 50c): ½c, David. 2c, Moses. 40c, Zachariah. 50c, St. John the Baptist (sculpture). 75c, Judith and Holofernes (detail). $1, Madonna (head from Pietà). $2, Doni Madonna (detail from Holy Family).

| | | | | |
|---|---|---|---|---|
| **676** | A95 | ½c black & multi | .25 | *.25* |
| **677** | A95 | 1c black & multi | .25 | *.25* |
| **678** | A95 | 2c black & multi | .25 | *.25* |
| **679** | A95 | 40c black & multi | .40 | *.25* |
| **680** | A95 | 50c black & multi | .50 | *.25* |
| **681** | A95 | 75c black & multi | .75 | *.25* |
| **682** | A95 | $2 black & multi | 1.25 | *.45* |
| | | *Nos. 676-682 (7)* | 3.65 | *1.95* |

**Souvenir Sheet**

| | | | | |
|---|---|---|---|---|
| **683** | A95 | $1 black & multi | 2.25 | *.40* |

Michelangelo Buonarroti (1475-1564), Italian painter, sculptor and architect.

Virgin and Child Paintings — A96

Bananaquit — A97

**1975, Dec. 8**

| | | | | |
|---|---|---|---|---|
| **684** | A96 | ½c Filippino Lippi | .25 | *.25* |
| **685** | A96 | 1c Mantegna | .25 | *.25* |
| **686** | A96 | 2c Luis de Morales | .25 | *.25* |
| **687** | A96 | 35c G. M. Morandi | .25 | *.25* |
| **688** | A96 | 50c Antonello da Messina | .25 | *.25* |
| **689** | A96 | 75c Durer | .30 | *.25* |
| **690** | A96 | $1 Velazquez | .35 | *.25* |
| | | *Nos. 684-690 (7)* | 1.90 | *1.75* |

**Souvenir Sheet**

| | | | | |
|---|---|---|---|---|
| **691** | A96 | $2 Bellini | 1.60 | *.45* |

Christmas.

**1976, Jan. 20** **Litho.** *Perf. 14*

Designs: 1c, Orange-rumped agouti. 2c, Hawksbill turtle, horiz. 5c, Dwarf poinciana. 35c, Albacores, horiz. 40c, Cardinal's guard flower. $1, Belted kingfisher. $2, Antillean armadillo, horiz.

| | | | | |
|---|---|---|---|---|
| **692** | A97 | ½c multicolored | .25 | *.25* |
| **693** | A97 | 1c multicolored | .25 | *.25* |
| **694** | A97 | 2c multicolored | .25 | *.25* |
| **695** | A97 | 5c multicolored | .25 | *.25* |
| **696** | A97 | 35c multicolored | 1.10 | *.25* |
| **697** | A97 | 40c multicolored | 1.25 | *.25* |
| **698** | A97 | $2 multicolored | 3.00 | *.75* |
| | | *Nos. 692-698 (7)* | 6.35 | *2.25* |

**Souvenir Sheet**

| | | | | |
|---|---|---|---|---|
| **699** | A97 | $1 multicolored | 7.25 | *1.00* |

Carnival Dancers A98

Designs: 1c, Scuba diving. 2c, Cruise ship in St. George's Harbor. 35c, Game fishing. 50c, St. George's Golf Course. 75c, Tennis. $1, Mount Rich rock carvings. $2, Sailboats.

**1976, Feb. 25** **Litho.** *Perf. 14*

| | | | | |
|---|---|---|---|---|
| **700** | A98 | ½c multicolored | .25 | *.25* |
| **701** | A98 | 1c multicolored | .25 | *.25* |
| **702** | A98 | 2c multicolored | .25 | *.25* |
| **703** | A98 | 35c multicolored | .90 | *.25* |
| **704** | A98 | 50c multicolored | 3.00 | *.25* |
| **705** | A98 | 75c multicolored | 3.25 | *.35* |
| **706** | A98 | $1 multicolored | 3.50 | *.35* |
| | | *Nos. 700-706 (7)* | 11.40 | *1.95* |

**Souvenir Sheet**

| | | | | |
|---|---|---|---|---|
| **707** | A98 | $2 multicolored | 2.75 | *.75* |

Tourist publicity.

Descent from the Cross, by Master of Okolicsno — A99

Easter (Paintings): 1c, Pieta, by Correggio. 2c, Crucifixion, by van der Weyden. 3c, Burial of Christ, by Dürer. 35c, God the Father Holding Crucified Christ, by unknown master (Florence). 75c, Ascension, by Raphael. $1, Burial of Christ, by Raphael. $2, Pieta, by Crespi.

**1976, Mar. 29**

| | | | | |
|---|---|---|---|---|
| **708** | A99 | ½c multicolored | .25 | *.25* |
| **709** | A99 | 1c multicolored | .25 | *.25* |
| **710** | A99 | 2c multicolored | .25 | *.25* |
| **711** | A99 | 3c multicolored | .25 | *.25* |
| **712** | A99 | 35c multicolored | .25 | *.25* |
| **713** | A99 | 75c multicolored | .30 | *.25* |
| **714** | A99 | $1 multicolored | .40 | *.25* |
| | | *Nos. 708-714 (7)* | 1.95 | *1.75* |

**Souvenir Sheet**

| | | | | |
|---|---|---|---|---|
| **715** | A99 | $2 multicolored | 1.25 | *1.25* |

Sharpshooters, 1780 — A100

First Stars and Stripes and: 1c, Defense of Liberty Pole. 2c, Men loading muskets. 35c, 75c, Fight for Liberty. 50c, $2, Peace Treaty, 1783. $1, Drumming march on Breed's Hill. $3, Gunboat, c. 1776.

**1976, Apr. 15 Litho. *Perf. 14***

| | | | | |
|---|---|---|---|---|
| **716** | A100 | ½c multicolored | .25 | *.25* |
| **717** | A100 | 1c multicolored | .25 | *.25* |
| **718** | A100 | 2c multicolored | .25 | *.25* |
| **719** | A100 | 35c multicolored | .40 | *.25* |
| **720** | A100 | 50c multicolored | .50 | *.25* |
| **721** | A100 | $1 multicolored | .80 | *.25* |
| **722** | A100 | $3 multicolored | 2.00 | *.25* |
| | | *Nos. 716-722 (7)* | 4.45 | *1.75* |

**Souvenir Sheet**

| | | | | |
|---|---|---|---|---|
| **723** | | Sheet of 2 | 2.00 | *1.40* |
| ***a.*** | | A100 75c multicolored | .65 | *.55* |
| ***b.*** | | A100 $2 multicolored | 1.40 | *.75* |

American Bicentennial.

Girl Guide Emblems, Nature Study — A101

Volleyball — A102

Various Girl Guide Emblems and: 1c, Cooking. 2c, $2, First aid, diff. 50c, Tenting. 75c, Home economics. $1, Drawing.

**1976, June 1 Litho. *Perf. 14***

| | | | | |
|---|---|---|---|---|
| **724** | A101 | ½c multicolored | .25 | *.25* |
| **725** | A101 | 1c multicolored | .25 | *.25* |
| **726** | A101 | 2c multicolored | .25 | *.25* |
| **727** | A101 | 50c multicolored | .50 | *.25* |
| **728** | A101 | 75c multicolored | .75 | *.25* |
| **729** | A101 | $2 multicolored | 1.75 | *.45* |
| | | *Nos. 724-729 (6)* | 3.75 | *1.70* |

**Souvenir Sheet**

| | | | | |
|---|---|---|---|---|
| **730** | A101 | $1 multicolored | 1.75 | *.80* |

Girl Guides of Grenada, 50th anniv.

**1976, June 21 Litho. *Perf. 14***

Olympic Rings and: 1c, Bicycling. 2c, Rowing. 35c, Judo. 45c, Hockey. 75c, Women's gymnastics. $1, High jump. $3, Equestrian.

| | | | | |
|---|---|---|---|---|
| **731** | A102 | ½c multicolored | .25 | *.25* |
| **732** | A102 | 1c multicolored | .25 | *.25* |
| **733** | A102 | 2c multicolored | .25 | *.25* |
| **734** | A102 | 35c multicolored | .30 | *.25* |
| **735** | A102 | 45c multicolored | .55 | *.25* |
| **736** | A102 | 75c multicolored | .60 | *.40* |
| **737** | A102 | $1 multicolored | .70 | *.40* |
| | | *Nos. 731-737 (7)* | 2.90 | *2.05* |

**Souvenir Sheet**

| | | | | |
|---|---|---|---|---|
| **738** | A102 | $3 multicolored | 1.75 | *1.25* |

21st Olympic Games, Montreal, Canada, July 17-Aug. 1.

Moulin Rouge, by Toulouse-Lautrec A103

Paintings by Toulouse-Lautrec: 1c, Start of the Quadrille. 2c, Woman's Head. 3c, Hall at the Moulin Rouge. 40c, Man Delivering Laundry. 50c, Dancing the Bolero. $1, Lady with Boa. $2, Signor Boileau at the Cafe.

**1976, July 20 Litho. *Perf. 14***

| | | | | |
|---|---|---|---|---|
| **739** | A103 | ½c multicolored | .25 | *.25* |
| **740** | A103 | 1c multicolored | .25 | *.25* |
| **741** | A103 | 2c multicolored | .25 | *.25* |
| **742** | A103 | 3c multicolored | .25 | *.25* |
| **743** | A103 | 40c multicolored | .75 | *.25* |
| **744** | A103 | 50c multicolored | .95 | *.25* |
| **745** | A103 | $2 multicolored | 2.50 | *.50* |
| | | *Nos. 739-745 (7)* | 5.20 | *2.00* |

**Souvenir Sheet**

| | | | | |
|---|---|---|---|---|
| **746** | A103 | $1 multicolored | 4.50 | *1.25* |

Henri de Toulouse-Lautrec (1864-1901), painter, 75th death anniv.

Map of West Indies, Bats, Wicket and Ball A103a

Prudential Cup — A103b

**1976, July 26**

| | | | | |
|---|---|---|---|---|
| **747** | A103a | 35c lt blue & multi | .60 | .60 |
| **748** | A103b | $1 lilac rose & blk | 1.50 | 1.50 |

World Cricket Cup, won by West Indies Team, 1975.

Piper Apache A104

Airplanes: 1c, Beech Twin Bonanza. 2c, D.H. Twin Otter. 40c, Britten Norman Islander. 50c, D.H. Heron. $2, Hawker Siddeley Avro 748. $3, B.A.C. One-Eleven.

**1976, Aug. 18**

| | | | | |
|---|---|---|---|---|
| **749** | A104 | ½c multicolored | .25 | *.25* |
| **750** | A104 | 1c multicolored | .25 | *.25* |
| **751** | A104 | 2c multicolored | .25 | *.25* |
| **752** | A104 | 40c multicolored | .75 | *.25* |
| **753** | A104 | 50c multicolored | .80 | *.25* |
| **754** | A104 | $2 multicolored | 2.50 | *.75* |
| | | *Nos. 749-754 (6)* | 4.80 | *2.00* |

**Souvenir Sheet**

| | | | | |
|---|---|---|---|---|
| **755** | A104 | $3 multicolored | 3.00 | *1.10* |

Helios Mission, Assembly — A105

Designs: 1c, Helios spacecraft in space. 2c, Helios assembled. 15c, Helios, system test and checkout. 45c, Viking nearing Mars, horiz. 75c, Viking on Mars. $2, Viking spacecraft assembled. $3, Helios orbiter and Viking lander.

**1976, Sept. 1 Litho. *Perf. 14***

| | | | | |
|---|---|---|---|---|
| **756** | A105 | ½c multicolored | .25 | *.25* |
| **757** | A105 | 1c multicolored | .25 | *.25* |
| **758** | A105 | 2c multicolored | .25 | *.25* |
| **759** | A105 | 15c multicolored | .25 | *.25* |
| **760** | A105 | 45c multicolored | .25 | *.25* |
| **761** | A105 | 75c multicolored | .35 | *.25* |
| **762** | A105 | $2 multicolored | .65 | *.35* |
| | | *Nos. 756-762 (7)* | 2.25 | *1.85* |

**Souvenir Sheet**

| | | | | |
|---|---|---|---|---|
| **763** | A105 | $3 multicolored | 1.75 | *1.00* |

Helios (solar probe) mission and Viking Mars missions.

S.S. Geestland, Geest Line Flag — A106

Ships: 1c, M.V. Federal Palm, West Indies Shipping Service. 2c, H.M.S. Blake and ship's crest. 25c, M.V. Vistafjord and Norwegian-American Line flag. 75c, S.S. Canberra and P. & O. Line flag. $1, S.S. Regina and Chandris Line flag. $2, Santa Maria and Spanish flag, 1492. $5, S.S. Arandora and Blue Star Line flag.

**1976, Nov. 3 Litho. *Perf. 14½***

| | | | | |
|---|---|---|---|---|
| **764** | A106 | ½c blue & multi | .25 | *.25* |
| **765** | A106 | 1c blue & multi | .25 | *.25* |
| **766** | A106 | 2c blue & multi | .25 | *.25* |
| **767** | A106 | 25c blue & multi | .55 | *.25* |
| **768** | A106 | 75c blue & multi | 1.00 | *.25* |
| **769** | A106 | $1 blue & multi | 1.25 | *.30* |
| **770** | A106 | $5 blue & multi | 2.50 | *.65* |
| | | *Nos. 764-770 (7)* | 6.05 | *2.20* |

**Souvenir Sheet**

| | | | | |
|---|---|---|---|---|
| **771** | A106 | $2 multicolored | 2.50 | *2.50* |

Ships connected with Grenada's development.

Altarpiece of San Barnaba, by Botticelli A107

Christmas (Paintings): 1c, Annunciation, by Botticelli. 2c, Madonna with Chancellor Rolin, by Jan van Eyck. 35c, Annunciation, by Fra Filippo Lippi. 50c, Madonna of the Magnificat, by Botticelli. 75c, Madonna of the Pomegranate, by Botticelli. $2, Gipsy Madonna, by Titian. $3, Madonna with St. Cosmas and Saints, by Botticelli.

**1976, Dec. 8 Litho. *Perf. 14***

| | | | | |
|---|---|---|---|---|
| **772** | A107 | ½c multicolored | .25 | *.25* |
| **773** | A107 | 1c multicolored | .25 | *.25* |
| **774** | A107 | 2c multicolored | .25 | *.25* |
| **775** | A107 | 35c multicolored | .25 | *.25* |
| **776** | A107 | 50c multicolored | .25 | *.25* |
| **777** | A107 | 75c multicolored | .35 | *.25* |
| **778** | A107 | $3 multicolored | .75 | *.40* |
| | | *Nos. 772-778 (7)* | 2.35 | *1.90* |

**Souvenir Sheet**

| | | | | |
|---|---|---|---|---|
| **779** | A107 | $2 multicolored | 1.60 | *.75* |

Globe and Telephone Users A108

Designs: ½c, A. G. Bell, 1876 and modern telephones. 2c, Satellites around globe, world map. 18c, Videophone. 40c, Satellite and ground stations. $1, Satellite and telephone communication with ships. $2, British "Trimphone" and radar station. $5, Flags of the world surrounding globe, and telephone.

**1976, Dec. 17 Litho. *Perf. 14***

| | | | | |
|---|---|---|---|---|
| **780** | A108 | ½c multicolored | .25 | *.25* |
| **781** | A108 | 1c multicolored | .25 | *.25* |
| **782** | A108 | 2c multicolored | .25 | *.25* |
| **783** | A108 | 18c multicolored | .25 | *.25* |
| **784** | A108 | 40c multicolored | .30 | *.25* |
| **785** | A108 | $1 multicolored | .40 | *.25* |
| **786** | A108 | $2 multicolored | .65 | *.45* |
| | | *Nos. 780-786 (7)* | 2.35 | *1.95* |

**Souvenir Sheet**

| | | | | |
|---|---|---|---|---|
| **787** | A108 | $5 multicolored | 2.25 | *.90* |

Centenary of first telephone conversation by Alexander Graham Bell, Mar. 10, 1876.

Coronation of Elizabeth II — A109

Designs: ½c, Coronation. 1c, $1, Orb and scepter. 35c, $3, Trooping of the Guards. 50c, $2, Spoon and ampulla. 35c, (bklt.), $2.50, Elizabeth II and Prince Philip. $5, Royal visit to Grenada.

**1977, Feb. 8 Litho. *Perf. 14, 12***

| | | | | |
|---|---|---|---|---|
| **788** | A109 | ½c multicolored | .25 | *.25* |
| **789** | A109 | 1c multicolored | .25 | *.25* |
| **790** | A109 | 35c multicolored | .25 | *.25* |
| **791** | A109 | $2 multicolored | .30 | *.30* |
| **792** | A109 | $2.50 multicolored | .35 | *.30* |
| ***a.*** | | Booklet pane of 6 (35c) | .95 | |
| ***b.*** | | Booklet pane of 3 (50c, $1, $3) | 3.25 | |
| | | *Nos. 788-792 (5)* | 1.40 | *1.35* |

**Souvenir Sheet**

| | | | | |
|---|---|---|---|---|
| **793** | A109 | $5 multicolored | 1.10 | *1.10* |

Reign of Queen Elizabeth II, 25th anniv.

Nos. 792a-792b are self-adhesive, roulette x imperf. Marginal inscriptions.

Nos. 788-792 were printed in sheets of 40 (10x4), perf. 14, and sheets of 5 plus label, perf. 12, in changed colors.

For overprints see Nos. 821-826.

Water Skiing, One-ski Slalom A110

Designs: 1c, Speedboat racing around Grand Anse. 2c, Crew racing, St. George's. 22c, Swimming, Grand Anse. 35c, Local work boat races. 75c, Water polo, careenage, St. George's. $2, Game fishing. $3, South Coast yacht race.

**1977, Apr. 13 Litho. *Perf. 14***

| | | | | |
|---|---|---|---|---|
| **794** | A110 | ½c multicolored | .25 | *.25* |
| **795** | A110 | 1c multicolored | .25 | *.25* |
| **796** | A110 | 2c multicolored | .25 | *.25* |
| **797** | A110 | 22c multicolored | .25 | *.25* |
| **798** | A110 | 35c multicolored | .35 | *.25* |
| **799** | A110 | 75c multicolored | .55 | *.25* |
| **800** | A110 | $2 multicolored | 1.10 | *.35* |
| | | *Nos. 794-800 (7)* | 3.00 | *1.85* |

**Souvenir Sheet**

| | | | | |
|---|---|---|---|---|
| **801** | A110 | $3 multicolored | 1.75 | *1.25* |

1977 Easter Water Parade.

Tent, OAS Emblem A111

**1977, June 14 Litho. *Perf. 14***

| | | | | |
|---|---|---|---|---|
| **802** | A111 | 35c multicolored | .25 | .25 |
| **803** | A111 | $1 multicolored | .35 | .35 |
| **804** | A111 | $2 multicolored | .60 | .60 |
| | | *Nos. 802-804 (3)* | 1.20 | 1.20 |

7th Regular Session, General Assembly of Organization of American States.

Scouts on Raft A112

Designs: 1c, Tug-of-war. 2c, Boy Scout regatta. 18c, Scouts around camp fire. 40c, Field kitchen. $1, Boy Scouts and Sea Scouts. $2, Hiking and map reading. $3, Semaphore.

**1977, Sept. 6 Litho. *Perf. 14***

| | | | | |
|---|---|---|---|---|
| **805** | A112 | ½c multicolored | .25 | *.25* |
| **806** | A112 | 1c multicolored | .25 | *.25* |
| **807** | A112 | 2c multicolored | .25 | *.25* |
| **808** | A112 | 18c multicolored | .30 | *.25* |
| **809** | A112 | 40c multicolored | .45 | *.25* |
| **810** | A112 | $1 multicolored | 1.10 | *.35* |
| **811** | A112 | $2 multicolored | 2.00 | *.55* |
| | | *Nos. 805-811 (7)* | 4.60 | *2.15* |

**Souvenir Sheet**

| | | | | |
|---|---|---|---|---|
| **812** | A112 | $3 multicolored | 2.75 | *1.25* |

6th Caribbean Jamboree, Kingston, Jamaica, Aug. 5-14.

Annunciation to the Shepherds — A113

Ceiling Paintings, St. Martin's Church, Zillis, Switzerland, 12th Century: 1c, Joseph on his way. 2c, Virgin and Child, Flight into Egypt. 22c, Angel leading the way. 35c, King on way to Herod. 75c, Three horses. $2, Virgin and Child. $3, Adoration of the Kings.

**1977, Nov. 3 Litho. *Perf. 14***

| | | | | |
|---|---|---|---|---|
| **813** | A113 | ½c multicolored | .25 | *.25* |
| **814** | A113 | 1c multicolored | .25 | *.25* |
| **815** | A113 | 2c multicolored | .25 | *.25* |
| **816** | A113 | 22c multicolored | .25 | *.25* |
| **817** | A113 | 35c multicolored | .25 | *.25* |
| **818** | A113 | 75c multicolored | .25 | *.25* |
| **819** | A113 | $2 multicolored | .35 | *.25* |
| | | *Nos. 813-819 (7)* | 1.85 | *1.75* |

**Souvenir Sheet**

| | | | | |
|---|---|---|---|---|
| **820** | A113 | $3 multicolored | 1.60 | *1.00* |

Christmas.

Nos. 788-793 Overprinted

**1977, Nov. 10 *Perf. 12, 14***

| | | | | |
|---|---|---|---|---|
| **821** | A109 | ½c multicolored | .25 | .25 |
| **822** | A109 | 1c multicolored | .25 | .25 |
| **823** | A109 | 35c multicolored | .25 | .25 |
| **824** | A109 | $2 multicolored | .25 | *.35* |
| **825** | A109 | $2.50 multicolored | .25 | *.45* |
| | | *Nos. 821-825 (5)* | 1.25 | *1.55* |

**Souvenir Sheet**

***Perf. 14***

| | | | | |
|---|---|---|---|---|
| **826** | A109 | $5 multicolored | .75 | 1.40 |

Caribbean visit of Queen Elizabeth II. Nos. 821-822 are perf. 12, others perf. 12 and 14.

Christjaan Eijkman — A114

Portraits: 1c, Winston Churchill, Literature, 1953. 2c, Woodrow Wilson, Peace, 1919. 35c, Frederic Passy, Peace 1901. $1, Albert Einstein, Physics, 1921. $2, Alfred Nobel, founder. $3, Carl Bosch, Chemistry, 1931.

**1978, Jan. 25 Litho. *Perf. 14***

| | | | | |
|---|---|---|---|---|
| **827** | A114 | ½c multicolored | .25 | *.25* |
| **828** | A114 | 1c multicolored | .25 | *.25* |
| **829** | A114 | 2c multicolored | .25 | *.25* |
| **830** | A114 | 35c multicolored | .30 | *.25* |
| **831** | A114 | $1 multicolored | .85 | *.30* |
| **832** | A114 | $3 multicolored | 2.25 | *.55* |
| | | *Nos. 827-832 (6)* | 4.15 | *1.85* |

**Souvenir Sheet**

| | | | | |
|---|---|---|---|---|
| **833** | A114 | $2 multicolored | 2.00 | *1.00* |

Nobel Prize winners.

Early Zeppelin and Count Zeppelin A115

Designs: 1c, Lindbergh and Spirit of St. Louis. 2c, "Deutschland" airship. 22c, Lindbergh landing in Paris. 35c, Lindbergh in cockpit. 75c, Lindbergh and Spirit of St. Louis in flight. $1, Zeppelin over Alps. $2, Count Zeppelin and early airship. $3, Zeppelin over Capitol.

**1978, Feb. 13 Litho. *Perf. 14***

| | | | | |
|---|---|---|---|---|
| **834** | A115 | ½c multicolored | .25 | *.25* |
| **835** | A115 | 1c multicolored | .25 | *.25* |
| **836** | A115 | 2c multicolored | .25 | *.25* |
| **837** | A115 | 22c multicolored | .40 | *.25* |
| **838** | A115 | 75c multicolored | .75 | *.25* |
| **839** | A115 | $1 multicolored | .90 | *.25* |
| **840** | A115 | $3 multicolored | 2.00 | *.50* |
| | | *Nos. 834-840 (7)* | 4.80 | *2.00* |

**Souvenir Sheet**

| | | | | |
|---|---|---|---|---|
| **841** | | Sheet of 2 | 3.25 | *1.00* |
| ***a.*** | | A115 35c multicolored | .75 | |
| ***b.*** | | A115 $2 multicolored | 2.50 | |

Aviation history.

Launching of Space Shuttle — A116

Black- headed Gulls — A117

Space Shuttle: 1c, Booster separation. 2c, External tank separation. 18c, In orbit. 75c, Satellite placement. $2, Landing approach. $3, On landing pad.

**1978, Feb. 28**

| | | | | |
|---|---|---|---|---|
| **842** | A116 | ½c multicolored | .25 | *.25* |
| **843** | A116 | 1c multicolored | .25 | *.25* |
| **844** | A116 | 2c multicolored | .25 | *.25* |
| **845** | A116 | 18c multicolored | .40 | *.25* |
| **846** | A116 | 75c multicolored | .90 | *.25* |
| **847** | A116 | $2 multicolored | 1.75 | *.40* |
| | | *Nos. 842-847 (6)* | 3.80 | *1.65* |

**Souvenir Sheet**

| | | | | |
|---|---|---|---|---|
| **848** | A116 | $3 multicolored | 2.10 | *1.00* |

US space shuttle.

**1978, Mar. 8 Litho. *Perf. 14***

Wild Birds of Grenada and Wildlife Fund Emblem: 1c, Wilson's petrels. 2c, Killdeers. 50c, White-necked jacobin and hibiscus. 75c, Blue-faced booby. $1, Broad-winged hawk. $2, Scaley-necked pigeon. $3, Scarlet ibis.

| | | | | |
|---|---|---|---|---|
| **849** | A117 | ½c multicolored | .30 | *.25* |
| **850** | A117 | 1c multicolored | .30 | *.25* |
| **851** | A117 | 2c multicolored | .30 | *.25* |
| **852** | A117 | 50c multicolored | 2.50 | *.40* |
| **853** | A117 | 75c multicolored | 3.00 | *.60* |
| **854** | A117 | $1 multicolored | 4.00 | *.80* |
| **855** | A117 | $2 multicolored | 6.50 | *1.50* |
| | | *Nos. 849-855 (7)* | 16.90 | *4.05* |

**Souvenir Sheet**

| | | | | |
|---|---|---|---|---|
| **856** | A117 | $3 multicolored | 11.00 | *2.00* |

Marquise de Spinola, by Rubens A118

Ludwig van Beethoven A119

Paintings by Peter Paul Rubens (1577-1640): 5c, Reception of Marie de Medicis. 15c, Rubens and Helena Fourment. 25c, Ludovicus Nonnius. 45c, Helena Fourment with her Children. 75c, Child's head. $3, Suzanne Fourment in Velvet Hat.

**1978, Mar. 30 Litho. *Perf. 13½x14***

| | | | | |
|---|---|---|---|---|
| **857** | A118 | 5c lt blue & multi | .30 | *.25* |
| **858** | A118 | 15c lt blue & multi | .30 | *.25* |
| **859** | A118 | 18c lt blue & multi | .30 | *.25* |
| **860** | A118 | 25c lt blue & multi | .30 | *.25* |
| **861** | A118 | 45c lt blue & multi | .55 | *.25* |
| **862** | A118 | 75c lt blue & multi | .80 | *.25* |
| **863** | A118 | $3 lt blue & multi | 1.75 | *.55* |
| | | *Nos. 857-863 (7)* | 4.30 | *2.05* |

**Souvenir Sheet**

| | | | | |
|---|---|---|---|---|
| **864** | A118 | $5 lt blue & multi | 3.75 | *1.00* |

**1978, Apr. 24 *Perf. 14***

Designs: 15c, Woman violinist playing concerto. 18c, Various musical instruments. 22c, Piano. 50c, Two violins. 75c, Beethoven's piano and score. $2, Beethoven and score. $3, Beethoven and his house. 15c, 18c, 22c, 75c, $2, $3, horiz.

| | | | | |
|---|---|---|---|---|
| **865** | A119 | 5c multicolored | .25 | *.25* |
| **866** | A119 | 15c multicolored | .25 | *.25* |
| **867** | A119 | 18c multicolored | .45 | *.25* |
| **868** | A119 | 22c multicolored | .45 | *.25* |
| **869** | A119 | 50c multicolored | .80 | *.35* |
| **870** | A119 | 75c multicolored | 1.40 | *.50* |
| **871** | A119 | $3 multicolored | 2.50 | *.65* |
| | | *Nos. 865-871 (7)* | 6.10 | *2.50* |

**Souvenir Sheet**

| | | | | |
|---|---|---|---|---|
| **872** | A119 | $2 multicolored | 3.25 | *1.25* |

Ludwig van Beethoven (1770-1827), composer, death sesquicentennial.

Elizabeth II with Crown, Scepter and Orb — A120

Trooping of the Colors — A121

Designs: 35c, Coronation. $2.50, St. Edward's crown. $5, Elizabeth II and Prince Philip.

**1978, June 2 Litho. *Perf. 14***

| | | | | |
|---|---|---|---|---|
| **873** | A120 | 35c multicolored | .25 | .25 |
| **874** | A120 | $2 multicolored | .40 | .40 |
| **875** | A120 | $2.50 multicolored | .40 | .40 |
| | | *Nos. 873-875 (3)* | 1.05 | 1.05 |

**Souvenir Sheet**

| | | | | |
|---|---|---|---|---|
| **876** | A120 | $5 multicolored | .80 | .80 |

***Imperf***

**Self-adhesive**

35c, Elizabeth II at Maundy Money distribution ceremony. $5, Elizabeth II and Prince Philip.

| | | | |
|---|---|---|---|
| **877** | Souvenir booklet | 3.25 | |
| ***a.*** | A121 Bklt. pane, 3 each 25c, 35c | 1.00 | |
| ***b.*** | A121 Booklet pane of 1, $5 | 2.50 | |

Coronation of Queen Elizabeth II, 25th anniv.

Nos. 873-875 were printed in sheets of 40 (10x4), perf. 14, and sheets of 3 plus label, perf. 12, in changed colors. Labels show royal insignia.

No. 877 contains 2 booklet panes printed on peelable paper backing showing coins.

Goalkeeper Reaching for Ball — A122

Designs: Goalkeeper reaching for ball, various stages of motion.

**1978, Aug. 1 Litho. *Perf. 15***

| | | | | |
|---|---|---|---|---|
| **878** | A122 | 40c multicolored | .25 | .25 |
| **879** | A122 | 60c multicolored | .25 | .25 |
| **880** | A122 | 90c multicolored | .35 | .35 |
| **881** | A122 | $2 multicolored | .85 | .85 |
| | | *Nos. 878-881 (4)* | 1.70 | 1.70 |

**Souvenir Sheet**

| | | | | |
|---|---|---|---|---|
| **882** | A122 | $2.50 multicolored | 1.75 | 1.75 |

11th World Cup Soccer Championship, Argentina, June 1-25.

Flying Objects, 16th Century Drawing and Flying Saucer, 1962 A123

Designs: 35c, Radar probing skies, and Mars surface. $2, Prime Minister Eric Gairy and UN General Assembly Building. $3, Flying saucer with downwards beam, and UFO photograph.

**1978, Aug. 17**

| | | | | |
|---|---|---|---|---|
| **883** | A123 | 5c multicolored | .25 | .25 |
| **884** | A123 | 35c multicolored | .50 | .35 |
| **885** | A123 | $3 multicolored | 3.25 | 3.00 |
| | | *Nos. 883-885 (3)* | 4.00 | 3.60 |

**Souvenir Sheet**

| | | | | |
|---|---|---|---|---|
| **886** | A123 | $2 multicolored | 3.25 | 3.25 |

Proposal by Prime Minister Eric Gairy of Grenada to the UN General Assembly to study unidentified flying objects, Oct. 7, 1977.

Wright Glider and Allegory of Flight A124

15c, Flyer I, 1903, & eagle. 18c, Flyer III & allegory of flight. 22c, Flyer III & eagle. 50c, Orville Wright, Flyer & allegory of flight. 75c, Flyer, 1908, & eagle. $2, Flyer & allegory of flight. $3, Wilbur Wright, Flyer & allegory of flight.

**1978, Aug. 24** *Perf. 14*

| | | | | |
|---|---|---|---|---|
| **887** | A124 | 5c multicolored | .25 | .25 |
| **888** | A124 | 15c multicolored | .25 | .25 |
| **889** | A124 | 18c multicolored | .25 | .25 |
| **890** | A124 | 22c multicolored | .25 | .25 |
| **891** | A124 | 50c multicolored | .40 | .30 |
| **892** | A124 | 75c multicolored | .50 | .40 |
| **893** | A124 | $3 multicolored | 1.25 | 1.25 |
| | | *Nos. 887-893 (7)* | 3.15 | 2.95 |

**Souvenir Sheet**

| | | | | |
|---|---|---|---|---|
| **894** | A124 | $2 multicolored | 3.00 | 3.00 |

75th anniversary of first powered flight by Wright brothers, Dec. 17, 1903.

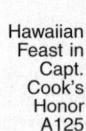

Hawaiian Feast in Capt. Cook's Honor A125

Capt. Cook and: 35c, Hawaiian warriors' dance. 75c, Honolulu harbor. $3, "Resolution." $4, Death scene.

**1978, Dec. 5** **Litho.** *Perf. 14*

| | | | | |
|---|---|---|---|---|
| **895** | A125 | 18c multicolored | .90 | .50 |
| **896** | A125 | 35c multicolored | 1.10 | .60 |
| **897** | A125 | 75c multicolored | 2.00 | 1.90 |
| **898** | A125 | $3 multicolored | 2.75 | *4.50* |
| | | *Nos. 895-898 (4)* | 6.75 | 7.50 |

**Souvenir Sheet**

| | | | | |
|---|---|---|---|---|
| **899** | A125 | $4 multicolored | 5.00 | 5.00 |

Bicentenary of Capt. Cook's arrival in Hawaii and 250th anniversary of his birth.

Detail from Paumgartner Altar, by Dürer — A126

Convention and Cultural Center — A127

Dürer Paintings: 60c, The Three Kings. 90c, Virgin and Child. $2, Head of the Virgin. $4, Virgin and Child.

**1978, Dec. 20** **Litho.** *Perf. 14*

| | | | | |
|---|---|---|---|---|
| **900** | A126 | 40c multicolored | .25 | .25 |
| **901** | A126 | 60c multicolored | .35 | .35 |
| **902** | A126 | 90c multicolored | .40 | .40 |
| **903** | A126 | $2 multicolored | .75 | .75 |
| | | *Nos. 900-903 (4)* | 1.75 | 1.75 |

**Souvenir Sheet**

| | | | | |
|---|---|---|---|---|
| **904** | A126 | $4 multicolored | 2.00 | 2.00 |

Christmas and 450th death anniv. of Albrecht Dürer (1471-1528), German painter.

**1979, Feb. 8** **Litho.** *Perf. 14*

18c, Geodesic Dome. 22c, Rowboat race, Easter parade, St. George's. 35c, Prime Minister Eric M. Gairy. $3, Cross at Fort Frederick at night.

| | | | | |
|---|---|---|---|---|
| **905** | A127 | 5c multicolored | .25 | .25 |
| **906** | A127 | 18c multicolored | .25 | .25 |
| **907** | A127 | 22c multicolored | .25 | .25 |
| **908** | A127 | 35c multicolored | .25 | .25 |
| **909** | A127 | $3 multicolored | .40 | .40 |
| | | *Nos. 905-909 (5)* | 1.40 | 1.40 |

5th anniversary of independence.

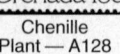

Chenille Plant — A128

Birds in Flight — A129

Native Flowers: 50c, Red hibiscus. $1, Skyflower. $2, Pink pride of India. $3, Rosebay.

**1979, Feb. 26**

| | | | | |
|---|---|---|---|---|
| **910** | A128 | 18c multicolored | .25 | .25 |
| **911** | A128 | 50c multicolored | .30 | .25 |
| **912** | A128 | $1 multicolored | .50 | .45 |
| **913** | A128 | $3 multicolored | 1.25 | 1.10 |
| | | *Nos. 910-913 (4)* | 2.30 | 2.05 |

**Souvenir Sheet**

| | | | | |
|---|---|---|---|---|
| **914** | A128 | $2 multicolored | 1.60 | 1.60 |

**1979, Mar. 15**

$2, Bird in flight & Human Rights emblem.

| | | | | |
|---|---|---|---|---|
| **915** | A129 | 15c multicolored | .25 | .25 |
| **916** | A129 | $2 multicolored | .75 | .75 |

Universal Declaration of Human Rights, 30th anniversary.

Children Playing Cricket — A130

IYC Emblem and: 22c, Boys playing baseball. $4, Children with model spaceship. $5, Three children.

**1979, Apr. 23** **Litho.** *Perf. 14*

| | | | | |
|---|---|---|---|---|
| **917** | A130 | 18c multicolored | 1.00 | .50 |
| **918** | A130 | 22c multicolored | .50 | .30 |
| **919** | A130 | $5 multicolored | 4.50 | *6.00* |
| | | *Nos. 917-919 (3)* | 6.00 | 6.80 |

**Souvenir Sheet**

| | | | | |
|---|---|---|---|---|
| **920** | A130 | $4 multicolored | 2.25 | 2.25 |

Intl. Year of the Child.

Balloon and Space Shuttle A131

Designs: 35c, Octopus holding sailors, nuclear submarine. 75c, Rocket and moon. $3, Imaginary plane and space ship. $4, Multi-propellered ship and US space shuttle.

**1979, May 4**

| | | | | |
|---|---|---|---|---|
| **921** | A131 | 18c multicolored | .40 | .25 |
| **922** | A131 | 35c multicolored | .70 | .25 |
| **923** | A131 | 75c multicolored | .90 | .65 |
| **924** | A131 | $3 multicolored | 2.40 | *3.00* |
| | | *Nos. 921-924 (4)* | 4.40 | 4.15 |

**Souvenir Sheet**

| | | | | |
|---|---|---|---|---|
| **925** | A131 | $4 multicolored | 2.25 | 2.25 |

Jules Verne (1828-1905), science fiction writer.

African Mail Runner A132

Sir Rowland Hill (1795-1879), originator of penny postage, and: 40c, American Pony Express. $1, Oriental pigeon post. $3, European mail coach. $5, Tete-beche stamps with revenue surcharge, 1883.

**1979, July 23** **Litho.** *Perf. 14*

| | | | | |
|---|---|---|---|---|
| **926** | A132 | 20c multicolored | .25 | .25 |
| **927** | A132 | 40c multicolored | .25 | .25 |
| **928** | A132 | $1 multicolored | .25 | .25 |
| **929** | A132 | $3 multicolored | .40 | .40 |
| | | *Nos. 926-929 (4)* | 1.15 | 1.15 |

**Souvenir Sheet**

| | | | | |
|---|---|---|---|---|
| **930** | A132 | $5 multicolored | 1.00 | 1.00 |

Nos. 926-929 were printed in sheets of 40, perf. 14, and in sheets of 5 plus label, perf. 12, in changed colors.

For overprints see Nos. 989A-989D.

Boys, Map of Grenada, Vaccination Gun — A133

**1979, Aug. 2** **Litho.** *Perf. 14*

| | | | | |
|---|---|---|---|---|
| **931** | A133 | 5c multicolored | .25 | .25 |
| **932** | A133 | $1 multicolored | .90 | .90 |

Intl. Year of the Child, immunization of children.

Reef Shark A134

Designs: 45c, Spotted eagle ray. 50c, Many-tooth conger. 60c, Golden olive shells. 70c, West Indian murex. 75c, Giant tuns. 90c, Brown boobies. $1, Magnificent frigate bird. $2.50, Sooty tern.

**1979, Aug. 22** **Litho.** *Perf. 14*

| | | | | |
|---|---|---|---|---|
| **933** | A134 | 40c multicolored | .40 | .35 |
| **934** | A134 | 45c multicolored | .40 | .35 |
| **935** | A134 | 50c multicolored | .45 | .40 |
| **936** | A134 | 60c multicolored | .75 | .60 |
| **937** | A134 | 70c multicolored | .90 | .70 |
| **938** | A134 | 75c multicolored | 1.10 | *1.10* |
| **939** | A134 | 90c multicolored | 1.75 | *2.25* |
| **940** | A134 | $1 multicolored | 1.75 | *2.25* |
| | | *Nos. 933-940 (8)* | 7.50 | 8.00 |

**Souvenir Sheet**

| | | | | |
|---|---|---|---|---|
| **941** | A134 | $2.50 multicolored | 3.25 | 3.25 |

Flight into Egypt, Tapestry A135

Tapestries: 25c, Virgin and Child. 30c, Angel, vert. 40c, Infant Jesus, by Doge Marino Grimani, vert. 90c, Shepherds, vert. $1, Flight into Egypt, vert. $2, Virgin in Glory, vert. $4, Virgin and Child, by Grimani, vert.

**1979, Oct. 16** **Litho.** *Perf. 14*

| | | | | |
|---|---|---|---|---|
| **942** | A135 | 6c multicolored | .25 | .25 |
| **943** | A135 | 25c multicolored | .25 | .25 |
| **944** | A135 | 30c multicolored | .25 | .25 |
| **945** | A135 | 40c multicolored | .25 | .25 |
| **946** | A135 | 90c multicolored | .25 | .25 |
| **947** | A135 | $1 multicolored | .25 | .25 |
| **948** | A135 | $2 multicolored | .30 | .30 |
| | | *Nos. 942-948 (7)* | 1.80 | 1.80 |

**Souvenir Sheet**

| | | | | |
|---|---|---|---|---|
| **949** | A135 | $4 multicolored | 1.25 | 1.25 |

Christmas.

Disney Characters and IYC Emblem A135a

Designs: Sport scenes.

**1979, Nov. 2** **Litho.** *Perf. 11*

| | | | | |
|---|---|---|---|---|
| **950** | A135a | ½c Mickey Mouse, baseball | .25 | .25 |
| **951** | A135a | 1c Donald, high jump | .25 | .25 |
| **952** | A135a | 2c Goofy, basketball | .25 | .25 |
| **953** | A135a | 3c Goofy, hurdles | .25 | .25 |
| **954** | A135a | 4c Donald Duck, golf | .25 | .25 |
| **955** | A135a | 5c Mickey, cricket | .25 | .25 |
| **956** | A135a | 10c Mickey, soccer | .25 | .25 |
| **957** | A135a | $2 Mickey, tennis | 3.00 | *3.50* |
| **958** | A135a | $2.50 Minnie, equestrian | 3.00 | *3.50* |
| | | *Nos. 950-958 (9)* | 7.75 | 8.75 |

**Souvenir Sheet**

*Perf. 13½*

| | | | | |
|---|---|---|---|---|
| **959** | CD329 | $3 Goofy in riding habit | 2.50 | 2.50 |

See Nos. 1031-1032.

Hands, Paul P. Harris, Rotary Emblem — A136

Rotary Emblem and Hands Holding: 30c, Caduceus. 90c, Wheat. $2, Family. $4, Emblem.

**1980, Feb. 25** **Litho.** *Perf. 14*

| | | | | |
|---|---|---|---|---|
| **960** | A136 | 6c multicolored | .25 | .25 |
| **961** | A136 | 30c multicolored | .25 | .25 |
| **962** | A136 | 90c multicolored | .25 | .25 |
| **963** | A136 | $2 multicolored | .60 | .60 |
| | | *Nos. 960-963 (4)* | 1.35 | 1.35 |

**Souvenir Sheet**

| | | | | |
|---|---|---|---|---|
| **964** | A136 | $4 multicolored | 1.60 | 1.60 |

Rotary International, 75th anniversary.

**Nos. 585-586, 588-591, 593-594, 596-602 Overprinted in Black**

**1980** *Perf. 15, 13½*

| | | | | |
|---|---|---|---|---|
| **965** | A85 | 2c multicolored | .25 | .25 |
| **966** | A85 | 3c multicolored | .25 | .25 |
| **967** | A85 | 6c multicolored | .25 | .25 |
| **968** | A85 | 8c multicolored | .25 | .25 |
| **969** | A85 | 10c multicolored | .25 | .25 |
| **970** | A85 | 12c multicolored | .25 | .25 |
| **971** | A85 | 20c multicolored | .25 | .25 |
| **972** | A85 | 25c multicolored | .40 | .60 |
| **973** | A85 | 50c multicolored | .40 | .60 |
| **974** | A85 | 75c multicolored | .65 | .95 |
| **975** | A85 | $1 multicolored | 1.00 | 1.25 |
| **976** | A85 | $2 multicolored | 1.75 | 2.40 |
| **977** | A85 | $3 multicolored | 2.25 | 3.25 |
| **978** | A85 | $5 multicolored | 3.00 | 5.50 |
| **979** | A85 | $10 multicolored | 4.25 | 8.00 |
| | | *Nos. 965-979 (15)* | 15.45 | 24.30 |

Issue dates: 25c, Apr. 7; others, Feb. 28.

Boxing, Kremlin, Olympic Rings A137

**1980, Mar. 24** *Perf. 14*

| | | | | |
|---|---|---|---|---|
| **980** | A137 | 25c shown | .25 | .25 |
| **981** | A137 | 40c Bicycling | .25 | .25 |
| **982** | A137 | 90c Equestrian | .25 | .25 |
| **983** | A137 | $2 Running | .60 | .60 |
| | | *Nos. 980-983 (4)* | 1.35 | 1.35 |

**Souvenir Sheet**

| | | | | |
|---|---|---|---|---|
| **984** | A137 | $4 Yachting | 1.10 | 1.10 |

22nd Summer Olympic Games, Moscow, July 19-Aug. 3.

Tropical Kingbirds — A138

**1980, Apr. 8**

| | | | | |
|---|---|---|---|---|
| **985** | A138 | 20c shown | 1.00 | .80 |
| **986** | A138 | 40c Rufous-breasted hermits | 1.40 | 1.10 |
| **987** | A138 | $1 Troupials | 1.90 | 1.60 |
| **988** | A138 | $2 Ruddy quail doves | 2.25 | *4.00* |
| | | *Nos. 985-988 (4)* | 6.55 | 7.50 |

**Souvenir Sheet**

| | | | | |
|---|---|---|---|---|
| **989** | A138 | $3 Prairie warblers | 5.00 | 5.00 |

**Nos. 926-929 Overprinted: "LONDON 1980"**

**1980, May 6 Litho. *Perf. 12***

| | | | | |
|---|---|---|---|---|
| **989A** | A132 | 20c multicolored | .25 | .25 |
| **989B** | A132 | 40c multicolored | .30 | .30 |
| **989C** | A132 | $1 multicolored | .50 | .50 |
| **989D** | A132 | $3 multicolored | 1.40 | 1.40 |
| | | *Nos. 989A-989D (4)* | 2.45 | 2.45 |

London '80 Intl. Stamp Exhib., May 6-14.

Free School Hot Lunches A139

**1980, May 19 Litho. *Perf. 14***

| | | | | |
|---|---|---|---|---|
| **990** | A139 | 10c shown | .25 | .25 |
| **991** | A139 | 40c Food canning | .25 | .25 |
| **992** | A139 | $1 Health care | .40 | .40 |
| **993** | A139 | $2 Housing projects | .65 | .65 |
| | | *Nos. 990-993 (4)* | 1.55 | 1.55 |

**Souvenir Sheet**

| | | | | |
|---|---|---|---|---|
| **994** | A139 | $5 Prime Minister Bishop, vert. | 1.50 | 1.50 |

People's Revolution, 1st anniv.

Jamb Statues, West Portal, Chartres Cathedral — A140

Masterpieces: 10c, Les Desmoiselles d'Avignon, by Picasso. 40c, Winged Victory of Samothrace. 50c, The Night Watch, by Rembrandt. $1, Edward VI as a Child, by Holbein, the Younger. $3, Queen Nefertiti. $4, Weier Haws, by Dürer, vert.

**1980, June Litho. *Perf. 14***

| | | | | |
|---|---|---|---|---|
| **995** | A140 | 8c multicolored | .25 | .25 |
| **996** | A140 | 10c multicolored | .25 | .25 |
| **997** | A140 | 40c multicolored | .25 | .25 |
| **998** | A140 | 50c multicolored | .25 | .25 |
| **999** | A140 | $1 multicolored | .35 | .35 |
| **1000** | A140 | $3 multicolored | .90 | .90 |
| | | *Nos. 995-1000 (6)* | 2.25 | 2.25 |

**Souvenir Sheet**

| | | | | |
|---|---|---|---|---|
| **1001** | A140 | $4 multicolored | 1.50 | 1.50 |

Carib Canoes A141

Designs: 1c, Boat building. 2c, Small workboat. 4c, "Santa Maria." 5c, West India man barque, 1840. 6c, "Orinoco," 1851. 10c, Schooner. 12c, Trimaran. 15c, "Petite Amie," Spice Island cruising yacht. 20c, Fishing pirogue. 25c, Harbor police launch. 30c, Grand Anse speedboat. 40c, "Seimstrand." 50c, "Ariadne," 3-masted schooner. 90c, "Geestide," banana boat. $1, "Cunard Countess," cruise ship. $3, Rumrunner. $5, "Statendam." $10, Coast Guard patrol boat.

**1980, Sept. 9 Litho. *Perf. 14***

| | | | | |
|---|---|---|---|---|
| **1002** | A141 | ½c multicolored | .25 | .25 |
| **1003** | A141 | 1c multicolored | .25 | .25 |
| **1004** | A141 | 2c multicolored | .25 | .25 |
| **1005** | A141 | 4c multicolored | .40 | .55 |
| **1006** | A141 | 5c multicolored | .40 | .55 |
| **1007** | A141 | 6c multicolored | .40 | .55 |
| **1008** | A141 | 10c multicolored | .45 | .25 |
| **1009** | A141 | 12c multicolored | .90 | .70 |
| **1010** | A141 | 15c multicolored | .50 | .25 |
| **1011** | A141 | 20c multicolored | .90 | .25 |
| **1012** | A141 | 25c multicolored | 1.75 | .45 |
| **1013** | A141 | 30c multicolored | 1.25 | .45 |
| **1014** | A141 | 40c multicolored | 2.00 | .55 |
| **1015** | A141 | 50c multicolored | .60 | .70 |
| **1016** | A141 | 90c multicolored | 1.75 | .70 |
| **1017** | A141 | $1 multicolored | 3.00 | 1.25 |
| **1018** | A141 | $3 multicolored | 2.50 | *4.50* |
| **1019** | A141 | $5 multicolored | 3.50 | *7.25* |
| **1020** | A141 | $10 multicolored | 4.25 | *9.50* |
| | | *Nos. 1002-1020 (19)* | 25.30 | 29.20 |

#1017 reprinted inscribed 1982, #1015, 1984.

For overprints see #O1-O10, O12-O13, O15, O17.

**1982-84 *Perf. 12½x12***

| | | | | |
|---|---|---|---|---|
| *1002a* | A141 | ½c | .25 | .25 |
| *1006a* | A141 | 5c | .60 | .60 |
| *1008a* | A141 | 10c | .65 | .65 |
| *1011a* | A141 | 20c | 1.00 | 1.00 |
| *1012a* | A141 | 25c | 2.00 | 2.00 |
| *1013a* | A141 | 30c | 1.50 | 1.50 |
| *1014a* | A141 | 40c | 2.00 | 2.00 |
| *1015a* | A141 | 50c ('84) | .80 | .80 |
| *1018a* | A141 | $3 | 3.00 | 3.00 |
| *1019a* | A141 | $5 | 4.25 | 4.25 |
| *1020a* | A141 | $10 ('84) | 9.50 | 9.50 |
| | | *Nos. 1002a-1020a (11)* | 25.55 | 25.55 |

Snow White at Well — A142

Christmas: Various scenes from Walt Disney's Snow White and the Seven Dwarfs.

**1980, Sept. 25 Litho. *Perf. 11***

| | | | | |
|---|---|---|---|---|
| **1021** | A142 | ½c multicolored | .25 | .25 |
| **1022** | A142 | 1c multicolored | .25 | .25 |
| **1023** | A142 | 2c multicolored | .25 | .25 |
| **1024** | A142 | 3c multicolored | .25 | .25 |
| **1025** | A142 | 4c multicolored | .25 | .25 |
| **1026** | A142 | 5c multicolored | .25 | .25 |
| **1027** | A142 | 10c multicolored | .25 | .25 |
| **1028** | A142 | $2.50 multicolored | 2.75 | 2.75 |
| **1029** | A142 | $3 multicolored | 3.25 | 3.25 |
| | | *Nos. 1021-1029 (9)* | 7.75 | 7.75 |

**Souvenir Sheet**

| | | | | |
|---|---|---|---|---|
| **1030** | A142 | $4 multicolored | 5.25 | 5.25 |

No. 1030 contains a vertical stamp.

**Disney Type of 1980**

50th anniversary of Pluto character: $2, Pluto and birthday cake. $4, Pluto.

**1981, Jan. 19 Litho. *Perf. 14***

| | | | | |
|---|---|---|---|---|
| **1031** | A135a | $2 multicolored | 2.00 | 2.00 |

**Souvenir Sheet**

| | | | | |
|---|---|---|---|---|
| **1032** | A135a | $4 multicolored | 2.50 | 2.50 |

No. 1031 issued in sheets of 8.

Adult Education — A143

**1981, Mar. 13 Litho. *Perf. 12½***

| | | | | |
|---|---|---|---|---|
| **1033** | A143 | 5c Flags of the Revolution and Grenada | .25 | .25 |
| **1034** | A143 | 10c shown | .25 | .25 |
| **1035** | A143 | 15c Food processing plant | .25 | .25 |
| **1036** | A143 | 25c Agriculture | .25 | .25 |
| **1037** | A143 | 40c Fishing boat, crawfish | .25 | .25 |
| **1038** | A143 | 90c Ships | .65 | .65 |
| **1039** | A143 | $1 Palm trees | .70 | .70 |
| **1040** | A143 | $3 Map | 2.10 | 2.10 |
| | | *Nos. 1033-1040 (8)* | 4.70 | 4.70 |

2nd Festival of the Revolution.

Mickey Mouse and Goofy with Easter Basket A144

Easter: Various Disney characters with Easter baskets.

**1981, Apr. 7 *Perf. 11***

| | | | | |
|---|---|---|---|---|
| **1041** | A144 | 35c multi | .25 | .25 |
| **1042** | A144 | 40c multi | .25 | .25 |
| **1043** | A144 | $2 multi | 1.40 | 1.40 |
| **1044** | A144 | $2.50 multi | 1.75 | 1.75 |
| | | *Nos. 1041-1044 (4)* | 3.65 | 3.65 |

**Souvenir Sheet**

| | | | | |
|---|---|---|---|---|
| **1045** | A144 | $4 multi | 3.00 | 3.00 |

Large Heads, by Picasso — A145

Paintings by Pablo Picasso (1881-1973): 25c, Woman-Flower. 30c, Portrait of Madame. 90c, Cavalier with Pipe. $5, Woman on the Bank of the Seine.

**1981, Apr. 28 *Perf. 14***

| | | | | |
|---|---|---|---|---|
| **1046** | A145 | 25c multicolored | .25 | .25 |
| **1047** | A145 | 30c multicolored | .25 | .25 |
| **1048** | A145 | 90c multicolored | .40 | .40 |
| **1049** | A145 | $4 multicolored | 2.00 | 2.00 |
| | | *Nos. 1046-1049 (4)* | 2.90 | 2.90 |

**Souvenir Sheet**

| | | | | |
|---|---|---|---|---|
| **1050** | A145 | $5 multicolored | 4.50 | 4.50 |

**Royal Wedding Issue**

Common Design Type

**1981, June 16 Litho. *Perf. 15***

| | | | | |
|---|---|---|---|---|
| **1051** | CD331a | 50c Couple | .25 | .25 |
| **1052** | CD331a | $2 Holyrood House | .30 | .30 |
| **1053** | CD331a | $4 Charles | .40 | .40 |
| | | *Nos. 1051-1053 (3)* | .95 | .95 |

**Souvenir Sheet**

| | | | | |
|---|---|---|---|---|
| **1054** | CD331 | $5 Glass coach | .90 | .90 |

**Souvenir Booklet**

| | | | | |
|---|---|---|---|---|
| **1055** | CD331 | | 8.00 | |
| *a.* | | Pane of 6 (3x$1, Lady Diana, 3x$2, Charles) | 5.50 | |
| *b.* | | Pane of 1, $5, Couple | 2.50 | |

No. 1055 contains imperf., self-adhesive stamps.

Sheets of 5 plus label contain 30c, 40c or $4 in changed colors, perf. 14x14½.

For overprints see Nos. O11, O14, O16,

The Bath, by Mary Cassatt (1845-1926) A146

Decade for Women (Paintings by Women): 40c, Mademoiselle Charlotte du Val d'Ognes, by Constance Marie Charpentier. 60c, Self-portrait, by Mary Beale. $3, Woman in White Stockings, by Suzanne Valadon. $5, The Artist Hesitating between the Arts of Music and Painting, horiz.

**1981, Oct. 13 Litho. *Perf. 14***

| | | | | |
|---|---|---|---|---|
| **1058** | A146 | 15c multicolored | .25 | .25 |
| **1059** | A146 | 40c multicolored | .30 | .30 |
| **1060** | A146 | 60c multicolored | .45 | .45 |
| **1061** | A146 | $3 multicolored | 2.00 | 2.00 |
| | | *Nos. 1058-1061 (4)* | 3.00 | 3.00 |

**Souvenir Sheet**

| | | | | |
|---|---|---|---|---|
| **1062** | A146 | $5 multicolored | 3.00 | 3.00 |

Cinderella and Prince Charming Dancing at the Ball — A147

Christmas: Scenes from Walt Disney's Cinderella.

**1981, Nov. 2 Litho. *Perf. 14x13½***

| | | | | |
|---|---|---|---|---|
| **1063** | A147 | ½c multi | .25 | .25 |
| **1064** | A147 | 1c multi | .25 | .25 |
| **1065** | A147 | 2c multi | .25 | .25 |
| **1066** | A147 | 3c multi | .25 | .25 |
| **1067** | A147 | 4c multi | .25 | .25 |
| **1068** | A147 | 5c multi | .25 | .25 |
| **1069** | A147 | 10c multi | .25 | .25 |
| **1070** | A147 | $2.50 multi | 3.00 | 3.00 |
| **1071** | A147 | $3 multi | 3.50 | 3.50 |
| | | *Nos. 1063-1071 (9)* | 8.25 | 8.25 |

**Souvenir Sheet**

| | | | | |
|---|---|---|---|---|
| **1072** | A147 | $5 multi | 6.75 | 6.75 |

Columbia Space Shuttle — A148

Views of the Columbia space shuttle.

**1981, Nov. 12**

| | | | | |
|---|---|---|---|---|
| **1073** | A148 | 30c multicolored | .25 | .25 |
| **1074** | A148 | 60c multicolored | .40 | .40 |
| **1075** | A148 | 70c multicolored | .50 | .50 |
| **1076** | A148 | $3 multicolored | 2.00 | 2.00 |
| | | *Nos. 1073-1076 (4)* | 3.15 | 3.15 |

**Souvenir Sheet**

| | | | | |
|---|---|---|---|---|
| **1077** | A148 | $5 multicolored | 3.25 | 3.25 |

UPU Membership Centenary — A149

**1981, Dec. 10 Litho. *Perf. 15***

| | | | | |
|---|---|---|---|---|
| **1078** | A149 | 25c St. George's P.O. | .25 | .25 |
| **1079** | A149 | 30c No. 1 | .25 | .25 |
| **1080** | A149 | 90c No. 384 | .50 | .50 |
| **1081** | A149 | $4 No. 189 | 2.25 | 2.25 |
| | | *Nos. 1078-1081 (4)* | 3.25 | 3.25 |

**Souvenir Sheet**

| | | | | |
|---|---|---|---|---|
| **1082** | A149 | $5 No. 562 | 4.00 | 4.00 |

Intl. Year of the Disabled (1981) — A150

**1982, Feb. 4** *Perf. 14*

| | | | | | |
|---|---|---|---|---|---|
| **1083** | A150 | 30c | Artist | .25 | .25 |
| **1084** | A150 | 40c | Computer operator | .30 | .30 |
| **1085** | A150 | 70c | Teaching Braille | .50 | .50 |
| **1086** | A150 | $3 | Drummer | 2.00 | 2.00 |
| | | | *Nos. 1083-1086 (4)* | 3.05 | 3.05 |

**Souvenir Sheet**

| | | | | | |
|---|---|---|---|---|---|
| **1087** | A150 | $4 | Auto mechanic | 3.50 | 3.50 |

Scouting Year A151

**1982, Feb. 19** *Perf. 15*

| | | | | | |
|---|---|---|---|---|---|
| **1088** | A151 | 70c | Gardening | .60 | .60 |
| **1089** | A151 | 90c | Map reading | .75 | .75 |
| **1090** | A151 | $1 | Bee keeping | .85 | .80 |
| **1091** | A151 | $4 | Hospital reading | 2.75 | 2.75 |
| | | | *Nos. 1088-1091 (4)* | 4.95 | 4.90 |

**Souvenir Sheet**

| | | | | | |
|---|---|---|---|---|---|
| **1092** | A151 | $5 | Trophy presentation | 3.50 | 3.50 |

Flambeaux A152

**1982, Mar. 24** **Litho.** *Perf. 14*

| | | | | | |
|---|---|---|---|---|---|
| **1093** | A152 | 10c | shown | .70 | .25 |
| **1094** | A152 | 60c | Large orange sulphurs | 2.50 | 1.25 |
| **1095** | A152 | $1 | Red anartias | 3.00 | 2.10 |
| **1096** | A152 | $3 | Polydamas swallowtails | 8.00 | 7.25 |
| | | | *Nos. 1093-1096 (4)* | 14.20 | 10.85 |

**Souvenir Sheet**

| | | | | | |
|---|---|---|---|---|---|
| **1097** | A152 | $5 | Caribbean buckeyes | 8.75 | 8.75 |

Norman Rockwell A153

**1982, Apr. 12** **Litho.** *Perf. 14x13½*

| | | | | | |
|---|---|---|---|---|---|
| **1098** | A153 | 15c | shown | .40 | .25 |
| **1099** | A153 | 30c | Card Tricks | .65 | .25 |
| **1100** | A153 | 60c | Pharmacist | 1.10 | 1.00 |
| **1101** | A153 | 70c | Pals | 1.40 | 1.25 |
| | | | *Nos. 1098-1101 (4)* | 3.55 | 2.75 |

**Princess Diana Issue**

Common Design Type

**1982, July 1** **Litho.** *Perf. 14½x14*

| | | | | | |
|---|---|---|---|---|---|
| **1101A** | CD332 | 50c | Kensington Palace | .55 | *.75* |
| **1102** | CD332 | 60c | like 50c | .60 | .50 |
| **1102A** | CD332 | $1 | Couple in field | .90 | .80 |
| **1103** | CD332 | $2 | like $1 | 2.25 | 1.75 |
| **1103A** | CD332 | $3 | Diana in green dress | 2.50 | 2.50 |
| **1104** | CD332 | $4 | like $3 | 3.25 | 3.25 |
| | | | *Nos. 1101A-1104 (6)* | 10.05 | 9.55 |

**Souvenir Sheet**

| | | | | | |
|---|---|---|---|---|---|
| **1105** | CD332 | $5 | Diana, diff. | 6.00 | 6.00 |

For overprints see Nos. 1115A-1119.

Franklin Roosevelt Birth Centenary A154

Designs: 10c, Mary McLeod Bethune, director of Negro Affairs, 1942. 60c, Leadbelly (Huddie Ledbetter, Works Progress Administration). $1.10, Signing Fair Employment Act, 1941. $3, Farm Security Administration.

**1982, July 27** **Litho.** *Perf. 14*

| | | | | | |
|---|---|---|---|---|---|
| **1106** | A154 | 10c | multi | .25 | .25 |
| **1107** | A154 | 60c | multi | .30 | .30 |
| **1108** | A154 | $1.10 | multi | .50 | .50 |
| **1109** | A154 | $3 | multi | 1.40 | 1.40 |
| | | | *Nos. 1106-1109 (4)* | 2.45 | 2.45 |

**Souvenir Sheet**

| | | | | | |
|---|---|---|---|---|---|
| **1110** | A154 | $5 | multi | 2.50 | 2.50 |

Easter A155

Details from Raphael's "On the Way to Calvary." 70c, $1.10, $4, $5, vert.

**1982, Sept. 2** *Perf. 14½*

| | | | | | |
|---|---|---|---|---|---|
| **1111** | A155 | 40c | multi | .25 | .25 |
| **1112** | A155 | 70c | multi | .30 | .30 |
| **1113** | A155 | $1.10 | multi | .55 | .55 |
| **1114** | A155 | $4 | multi | 1.75 | 1.75 |
| | | | *Nos. 1111-1114 (4)* | 2.85 | 2.85 |

**Souvenir Sheet**

| | | | | | |
|---|---|---|---|---|---|
| **1115** | A155 | $5 | multi | 3.00 | 3.00 |

Nos. 1101A-1105 Overprinted in Black

**1982, Sept. 27** **Litho.** *Perf. 14½x14*

| | | | | | |
|---|---|---|---|---|---|
| **1115A** | CD332 | 50c | multi | .35 | .35 |
| **1116** | CD332 | 60c | multi | .40 | .40 |
| **1116A** | CD332 | $1 | multi | .65 | .65 |
| **1117** | CD332 | $2 | multi | 1.25 | 1.25 |
| **1117A** | CD332 | $3 | multi | 2.00 | 2.00 |
| **1118** | CD332 | $4 | multi | 2.50 | 2.50 |
| | | | *Nos. 1115A-1118 (6)* | 7.15 | 7.15 |

**Souvenir Sheet**

| | | | | | |
|---|---|---|---|---|---|
| **1119** | CD332 | $5 | multi | 4.50 | 4.50 |

Birth of Prince William of Wales, June 21.

Orient Express A156

**1982, Oct. 4**

| | | | | | |
|---|---|---|---|---|---|
| **1120** | A156 | 30c | shown | .35 | *.40* |
| **1121** | A156 | 60c | Trans-Siberian Express | .65 | .65 |
| **1122** | A156 | 70c | Fleche D'or | .75 | .75 |
| **1123** | A156 | 90c | Flying Scotsman | .95 | .95 |
| **1124** | A156 | $1 | German Federal Railways | 1.25 | 1.25 |
| **1125** | A156 | $3 | German Natl. Railways | 3.00 | *4.00* |
| | | | *Nos. 1120-1125 (6)* | 6.95 | *8.00* |

**Souvenir Sheet**

| | | | | | |
|---|---|---|---|---|---|
| **1126** | A156 | $5 | 20th Century Limited, US | 3.75 | 3.75 |

Christmas — A157

Scenes from Walt Disney's Robin Hood.

**1982, Dec. 7** **Litho.** *Perf. 14*

| | | | | | |
|---|---|---|---|---|---|
| **1127** | A157 | ½c | multi | .25 | .25 |
| **1128** | A157 | 1c | multi | .25 | .25 |
| **1129** | A157 | 2c | multi | .25 | .25 |
| **1130** | A157 | 3c | multi | .25 | .25 |
| **1131** | A157 | 4c | multi | .25 | .25 |
| **1132** | A157 | 5c | multi | .25 | .25 |
| **1133** | A157 | 10c | multi | .25 | .25 |
| **1134** | A157 | $2.50 | multi | 2.75 | 2.75 |
| **1135** | A157 | $3 | multi | 3.00 | 3.00 |
| | | | *Nos. 1127-1135 (9)* | 7.50 | 7.50 |

**Souvenir Sheet**

| | | | | | |
|---|---|---|---|---|---|
| **1136** | A157 | $5 | multi | 7.25 | 7.25 |

Italy's Victory in 1982 World Cup A158

**1982, Dec. 2** *Perf. 14x13½*

| | | | | | |
|---|---|---|---|---|---|
| **1137** | A158 | 60c | Stolen ball | .50 | .50 |
| **1138** | A158 | $4 | Captain holding trophy | 3.25 | 3.25 |

**Souvenir Sheet**

| | | | | | |
|---|---|---|---|---|---|
| **1139** | A158 | $5 | Flags | 3.75 | 3.75 |

Killer Whale — A159

**1982, Dec. 15** *Perf. 14*

| | | | | | |
|---|---|---|---|---|---|
| **1140** | A159 | 15c | shown | 1.50 | .50 |
| **1141** | A159 | 40c | Sperm whale | 2.50 | .75 |
| **1142** | A159 | 70c | Blue whale | 3.50 | 2.75 |
| **1143** | A159 | $3 | Common dolphins | 6.00 | 6.00 |
| | | | *Nos. 1140-1143 (4)* | 13.50 | 10.00 |

**Souvenir Sheet**

| | | | | | |
|---|---|---|---|---|---|
| **1144** | A159 | $5 | Humpback whale | 10.00 | 10.00 |

500th Birth Anniv. of Raphael — A160

**1983, Feb. 15** **Litho.** *Perf. 14*

| | | | | | |
|---|---|---|---|---|---|
| **1145** | A160 | 25c | Construction of the Ark | .25 | .25 |
| **1146** | A160 | 30c | Jacob's Vision | .25 | .25 |
| **1147** | A160 | 90c | Joseph Interprets the Dreams | .55 | .55 |
| **1148** | A160 | $4 | Joseph Interprets Pharaoh's Dream | 1.75 | 1.75 |
| | | | *Nos. 1145-1148 (4)* | 2.80 | 2.80 |

**Souvenir Sheet**

| | | | | | |
|---|---|---|---|---|---|
| **1149** | A160 | $5 | Creation of the Animals | 2.75 | 2.75 |

A161

**1983, Mar. 14**

| | | | | | |
|---|---|---|---|---|---|
| **1150** | A161 | 10c | Dental care | .25 | .25 |
| **1151** | A161 | 70c | Airport runway construction | .40 | .40 |
| **1152** | A161 | $1.10 | Beach | .65 | .65 |
| **1153** | A161 | $3 | Boat building | 1.25 | 1.75 |
| | | | *Nos. 1150-1153 (4)* | 2.55 | 3.05 |

Commonwealth Day.

World Communication Year — A162

**1983, Apr. 18**

| | | | | | |
|---|---|---|---|---|---|
| **1154** | A162 | 30c | Ship-satellite communication | .25 | .25 |
| **1155** | A162 | 40c | Rural telephone installation | .25 | .25 |
| **1156** | A162 | $2.50 | Weather map | 1.25 | 1.25 |
| **1157** | A162 | $3 | Airport control tower | 1.50 | 1.50 |
| | | | *Nos. 1154-1157 (4)* | 3.25 | 3.25 |

**Souvenir Sheet**

| | | | | | |
|---|---|---|---|---|---|
| **1158** | A162 | $5 | Satellite | 2.75 | 2.75 |

For overprints see Nos. 1248-1250.

Franklin Sport Sedan, 1928 A163

**1983, May 4** **Litho.** *Perf. 15*

| | | | | | |
|---|---|---|---|---|---|
| **1159** | A163 | 6c | shown | .25 | .25 |
| **1160** | A163 | 10c | Delage D8, 1933 | .25 | .25 |
| **1161** | A163 | 40c | Alvis, 1938 | .25 | .25 |
| **1162** | A163 | 60c | Invicta S-type Tourer, 1931 | .40 | .40 |
| **1163** | A163 | 70c | Alfa-Romeo 1750 Gran Sport, 1930 | .45 | .45 |
| **1164** | A163 | 90c | Isotta Fraschini, 1930 | .65 | .60 |
| **1165** | A163 | $1 | Bugatti Royal Type 41, 1941 | .70 | .70 |
| **1166** | A163 | $2 | BMV 328, 1938 | 1.25 | 1.25 |
| **1167** | A163 | $3 | Marmon V-16, 1931 | 1.75 | 1.75 |
| **1168** | A163 | $4 | Lincoln KB Saloon, 1932 | 2.50 | 2.50 |
| | | | *Nos. 1159-1168 (10)* | 8.45 | 8.40 |

**Souvenir Sheet**

| | | | | | |
|---|---|---|---|---|---|
| **1169** | A163 | $5 | Cougar XR-7, 1972 | 3.25 | 3.25 |

Manned Flight Bicentenary — A164

**1983, July 18** **Litho.** *Perf. 14*

| | | | | | |
|---|---|---|---|---|---|
| **1170** | A164 | 30c | Norge blimp | .60 | .60 |
| **1171** | A164 | 60c | Gloster-VI sea plane | 1.00 | 1.00 |
| **1172** | A164 | $1.10 | Curtiss NC-4 | 1.75 | 1.75 |
| **1173** | A164 | $4 | Dornier Do-18 | 4.25 | 4.25 |
| | | | *Nos. 1170-1173 (4)* | 7.60 | 7.60 |

**Souvenir Sheet**

| | | | | | |
|---|---|---|---|---|---|
| **1174** | A164 | $5 | Hot air balloon-ing, vert. | 4.00 | 4.00 |

Christmas A165

Designs: Walt Disney's It's Beginning to look a lot like Christmas.

**1983, Nov.** *Perf. 11*

| | | | | | |
|---|---|---|---|---|---|
| 1175 | A165 | ½c | Morty and Patches | .25 | .25 |
| 1176 | A165 | 1c | Ludwig von Drake | .25 | .25 |
| 1177 | A165 | 2c | Gyro Gearloose | .25 | .25 |
| 1178 | A165 | 3c | Pluto and Figaro | .25 | .25 |
| 1179 | A165 | 4c | Morty and Ferdy | .25 | .25 |
| 1180 | A165 | 5c | Mickey Mouse and Goofy | .30 | .25 |
| 1181 | A165 | 10c | Chip'n'Dale | .30 | .25 |
| 1182 | A165 | $2.50 | Mickey and Minnie | 2.75 | 2.75 |
| 1183 | A165 | $3 | Donald and Grandma Duck | 2.75 | 2.75 |
| | | | *Nos. 1175-1183 (9)* | 7.35 | 7.25 |

**Souvenir Sheet**

| | | | | | |
|---|---|---|---|---|---|
| 1184 | A165 | $5 | Goofy | 7.50 | 7.50 |

1984 Olympics — A166

Designs: Various Disney characters.

**1983, Dec. 19** **Litho.** *Perf. 13½*

| | | | | | |
|---|---|---|---|---|---|
| 1185 | A166 | ½c | Pommel Horse | .25 | .25 |
| 1186 | A166 | 1c | Boxing | .25 | .25 |
| 1187 | A166 | 2c | Archery | .25 | .25 |
| 1188 | A166 | 3c | Uneven bars | .25 | .25 |
| 1189 | A166 | 4c | Hurdles | .25 | .25 |
| 1190 | A166 | 5c | Weightlifting | .25 | .25 |
| 1191 | A166 | $1 | Kayak | 1.75 | 1.75 |
| 1192 | A166 | $2 | Marathon | 2.50 | 2.50 |
| 1193 | A166 | $3 | Pole Vault | 3.00 | *3.50* |
| | | | *Nos. 1185-1193 (9)* | 8.75 | 9.25 |

**Souvenir Sheet**

| | | | | | |
|---|---|---|---|---|---|
| 1194 | A166 | $5 | Medley Relay, vert. | 8.00 | 8.00 |

**Inscribed with Olympic Rings Emblem**

**1984** *Perf. 12½x12*

| | | | | |
|---|---|---|---|---|
| *1185a* | A166 | ½c | .25 | .25 |
| *1186a* | A166 | 1c | .25 | .25 |
| *1187a* | A166 | 2c | .25 | .25 |
| *1188a* | A166 | 3c | .25 | .25 |
| *1189a* | A166 | 4c | .25 | .25 |
| *1190a* | A166 | 5c | .25 | .25 |
| *1191a* | A166 | $1 | 1.75 | 1.75 |
| *1192a* | A166 | $2 | 2.50 | 2.50 |
| *1193a* | A166 | $3 | 3.00 | *3.50* |
| | | *Nos. 1185a-1193a (9)* | 8.75 | 9.25 |

**Souvenir Sheet**

| | | | | | |
|---|---|---|---|---|---|
| *1194a* | A166 | $5 | Olympic rings emblem inscribed | 8.00 | 8.00 |

Nos. 1185a-1193a printed in sheets of 5.

Banana Boat A167

**1984, July 16** **Litho.** *Perf. 15*

| | | | | | |
|---|---|---|---|---|---|
| 1195 | A167 | 40c | shown | 1.00 | .60 |
| 1196 | A167 | 70c | Queen Elizabeth 2 | 1.50 | 1.00 |
| 1197 | A167 | 90c | Working sailboats | 1.60 | 2.00 |
| 1198 | A167 | $4 | Amerikanis | 6.00 | *8.00* |
| | | | *Nos. 1195-1198 (4)* | 10.10 | 11.60 |

**Souvenir Sheet**

| | | | | | |
|---|---|---|---|---|---|
| 1199 | A167 | $5 | Spanish galleon, flotilla | 6.75 | 6.75 |

King William I, 1066-87 — A168

British Kings or Queens and Years of their reigns: No. 1200b, William II, 1087-1100. c, Henry I, 1100-35. d, Stephen, 1135-54. e, Henry II, 1154-89. f, Richard I, 1189-99. g, John, 1199-1216.

No. 1201a, Henry III, 1216-72. b, Edward I, 1272-1307. c, Edward II, 1307-27. d, Edward III, 1327-77. e, Richard II, 1377-99. f, Henry IV, 1399-1413. g, Henry V, 1413-22.

No. 1202a, Henry VI, 1422-61. b, Edward IV, 1461-83. c, Edward V, 1483. d, Richard III, 1483-85. e, Henry VII, 1485-1509. f, Henry VIII, 1509-47. g, Edward VI, 1547-53.

No. 1203a, Jane Grey, 1553. b, Mary I, 1553-58. c, Elizabeth I, 1558-1603. d, James I, 1603-25. e, Charles I, 1625-49. f, Charles II, 1660-85. g, James II, 1685-88.

No. 1204a, William III, 1688-1702. b, Mary II, 1688-94. c, Anne, 1702-14. d, George I, 1714-27. e, George II, 1727-60. f, George III, 1760-1820. g, George IV, 1820-30.

No. 1205a, William IV, 1830-37. b, Victoria, 1837-1901. c, Edward VII, 1901-10. d, George V, 1910-36. e, Edward VIII, 1936. f, George VI, 1936-52. g, Elizabeth II, since 1952. Size: 141x128mm.

**1984, Jan. 25** **Litho.** *Perf. 14*

| | | | | |
|---|---|---|---|---|
| 1200 | | Sheet of 7 + label | 19.00 | 19.00 |
| *a.-g.* | | A168 $4, any single | 2.75 | 2.75 |
| 1201 | | Sheet of 7 + label | 19.00 | 19.00 |
| *a.-g.* | | A168 $4, any single | 2.75 | 2.75 |
| 1202 | | Sheet of 7 + label | 19.00 | 19.00 |
| *a.-g.* | | A168 $4, any single | 2.75 | 2.75 |
| 1203 | | Sheet of 7 + label | 19.00 | 19.00 |
| *a.-g.* | | A168 $4, any single | 2.75 | 2.75 |
| 1204 | | Sheet of 7 + label | 19.00 | 19.00 |
| *a.-g.* | | A168 $4, any single | 2.75 | 2.75 |
| 1205 | | Sheet of 7 + label | 19.00 | 19.00 |
| *a.-g.* | | A168 $4, any single | 2.75 | 2.75 |

Local Flowers A169

**1984, May** *Perf. 15*

| | | | | | |
|---|---|---|---|---|---|
| 1206 | A169 | 25c | Lantana | .25 | .25 |
| 1207 | A169 | 30c | Plumbago | .30 | .25 |
| 1208 | A169 | 90c | Spider lily | .70 | .60 |
| 1209 | A169 | $4 | Giant alocasia | 2.75 | 2.75 |
| | | | *Nos. 1206-1209 (4)* | 4.00 | 3.85 |

**Souvenir Sheet**

| | | | | | |
|---|---|---|---|---|---|
| 1210 | A169 | $5 | Orange trumpet vine | 3.25 | 3.25 |

For overprints see Nos. 1216-1218.

Coral Reef Fish, World Wildlife Fund Emblem A170

**1984, May** **Litho.** *Perf. 14*

| | | | | | |
|---|---|---|---|---|---|
| 1211 | A170 | 10c | Blue parrot fish | 3.25 | .95 |
| 1212 | A170 | 30c | Flame-back cherub fish | 5.25 | 1.60 |
| 1213 | A170 | 70c | Painted wrasse | 9.00 | 4.00 |
| 1214 | A170 | 90c | Straight-tailed razorfish | 12.00 | 5.25 |
| | | | *Nos. 1211-1214 (4)* | 29.50 | 11.80 |

**Souvenir Sheet**

| | | | | | |
|---|---|---|---|---|---|
| 1215 | A170 | $5 | Spanish hogfish | 10.00 | 10.00 |

**Nos. 1208-1210 Overprinted in Black**

**1984** **Litho.** *Perf. 15*

| | | | | | |
|---|---|---|---|---|---|
| 1216 | A169 | 90c | multi | .70 | .70 |
| 1217 | A169 | $4 | multi | 3.00 | 3.00 |

**Souvenir Sheet**

| | | | | | |
|---|---|---|---|---|---|
| 1218 | A169 | $5 | multi | 3.50 | 3.50 |

AUSIPEX '84 — A171

Correggio & Degas — A171a

**1984, Sept. 21** *Perf. 14*

| | | | | | |
|---|---|---|---|---|---|
| 1219 | A171 | $1.10 | Puffing Billy | 1.25 | 1.25 |
| 1220 | A171 | $4 | Australia II | 5.50 | 5.50 |

**Souvenir Sheet**

| | | | | | |
|---|---|---|---|---|---|
| 1221 | A171 | $5 | Melbourne tram | 7.00 | 7.00 |

**1984, Aug.** **Litho.** *Perf. 14*

Paintings by Correggio: 10c, The Night (detail). 30c, Virgin Adoring the Child. 90c, Mystical Marriage of St. Catherine with St. Sebastian. $4, Madonna and the Fruit Basket. No. 1230, Madonna at the Spring.

Paintings by Degas: 25c, L'Absinthe. 70c, Pouting, horiz. $1.10, The Millinery Shop. $3, The Bellelli Family. No. 1231, The Cotton Market.

| | | | | | |
|---|---|---|---|---|---|
| 1222 | A171a | 10c | multi | .45 | .25 |
| 1223 | A171a | 25c | multi | .60 | .30 |
| 1224 | A171a | 30c | multi | .80 | .40 |
| 1225 | A171a | 70c | multi | 1.25 | 1.00 |
| 1226 | A171a | 90c | multi | 1.50 | 1.00 |
| 1227 | A171a | $1.10 | multi | 1.75 | 1.75 |
| 1228 | A171a | $3 | multi | 3.00 | *4.00* |
| 1229 | A171a | $4 | multi | 4.00 | *5.00* |
| | | | *Nos. 1222-1229 (8)* | 13.35 | 13.70 |

**Souvenir Sheets**

| | | | | | |
|---|---|---|---|---|---|
| 1230 | A171a | $5 | multi | 6.25 | 6.25 |
| 1231 | A171a | $5 | multi | 6.25 | 6.25 |

19th Cent. Locomotives — A172

**1984, Oct.** *Perf. 14½*

| | | | | | |
|---|---|---|---|---|---|
| 1232 | A172 | 30c | Locomotion, 1825 | .80 | .35 |
| 1233 | A172 | 40c | Novelty, 1829 | .90 | .45 |
| 1234 | A172 | 60c | Washington Farmer, 1836 | 1.00 | .70 |
| 1235 | A172 | 70c | French Crampton, 1859 | 1.00 | 1.00 |
| 1236 | A172 | 90c | Dutch State, 1873 | 1.25 | 1.00 |
| 1237 | A172 | $1.10 | Champion, 1882 | 1.50 | *2.00* |
| 1238 | A172 | $2 | Webb Compound, 1893 | 2.40 | *3.00* |
| 1239 | A172 | $4 | Berlin 74, 1900 | 4.75 | *5.00* |
| | | | *Nos. 1232-1239 (8)* | 13.60 | *13.50* |

**Souvenir Sheets**

| | | | | | |
|---|---|---|---|---|---|
| 1240 | A172 | $5 | Crampton Phoenix, 1863 | 4.25 | 4.25 |
| 1241 | A172 | $5 | 2-8-2 Mikado, 1897 | 4.25 | 4.25 |

Christmas and 50th Anniv. of Donald Duck A173

Scenes from various Donald Duck movies.

*Perf. 13½x14, 12 ($2)*

**1984, Nov.** **Litho.**

| | | | | | |
|---|---|---|---|---|---|
| 1242 | A173 | 45c | multicolored | 1.00 | .65 |
| 1243 | A173 | 60c | multicolored | 1.25 | .95 |
| 1244 | A173 | 90c | multicolored | 2.00 | 1.50 |
| 1245 | A173 | $2 | multicolored | 3.25 | 3.25 |
| 1246 | A173 | $4 | multicolored | 6.50 | 6.50 |
| | | | *Nos. 1242-1246 (5)* | 14.00 | 12.85 |

**Souvenir Sheet**

| | | | | | |
|---|---|---|---|---|---|
| 1247 | A173 | $5 | multicolored | 8.50 | 8.50 |

**Nos. 1155. 1157, and 1158 Overprinted**

**1984, Oct. 28** **Litho.** *Perf. 14½x14*

| | | | | | |
|---|---|---|---|---|---|
| 1248 | A162 | 40c | on #1155 | .50 | .50 |
| 1249 | A162 | $3 | on #1157 | 3.00 | 3.00 |

**Souvenir Sheet**

**Same Overprint in Margin in 2 Lines**

| | | | | | |
|---|---|---|---|---|---|
| 1250 | A162 | $5 | on #1158 | 4.50 | 4.50 |

Audubon Birth Bicentenary A174

**1985, Feb.** **Litho.** *Perf. 14*

| | | | | | |
|---|---|---|---|---|---|
| 1251 | A174 | 50c | Clapper Rail | 2.00 | .75 |
| 1252 | A174 | 70c | Hooded Warbler | 2.50 | 1.50 |
| 1253 | A174 | 90c | Flicker | 3.00 | 1.75 |
| 1254 | A174 | $4 | Bohemian Waxwing | 6.50 | *7.50* |
| | | | *Nos. 1251-1254 (4)* | 14.00 | 11.50 |

**Souvenir Sheet**

| | | | | | |
|---|---|---|---|---|---|
| 1255 | A174 | $5 | Pigeon Hawk, horiz. | 11.00 | 11.00 |

See Nos. 1352-1356.

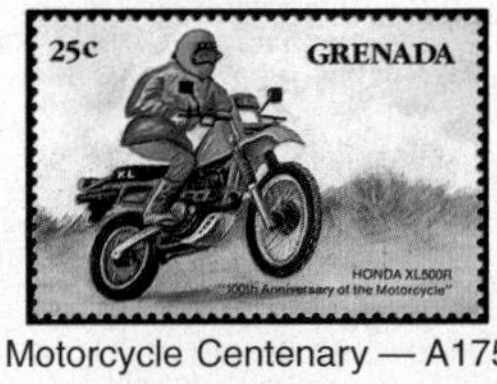


Motorcycle Centenary — A175

**1985, Mar. 11** **Litho.** *Perf. 14*

| | | | | | |
|---|---|---|---|---|---|
| 1256 | A175 | 25c | Honda XL500R | 1.50 | .75 |
| 1257 | A175 | 50c | Suzuki GS1100ES | 1.75 | 1.50 |
| 1258 | A175 | 90c | Kawasaki KZ700 | 2.50 | 1.60 |
| 1259 | A175 | $4 | BMW K100 | 5.75 | *7.50* |
| | | | *Nos. 1256-1259 (4)* | 11.50 | 11.35 |

**Souvenir Sheet**

| | | | | | |
|---|---|---|---|---|---|
| 1260 | A175 | $5 | Yamaha 500CC | 9.00 | 9.00 |

Girl Guides, 75th Anniv. A176

**1985, Apr. 15**

**1261** A176 25c Nature hike .65 .40
**1262** A176 60c Cookout 1.00 .90
**1263** A176 90c Singing around campfire 1.50 1.25
**1264** A176 $3 Public service 4.50 4.50
*Nos. 1261-1264 (4)* 7.65 7.05

**Souvenir Sheet**

**1265** A176 $5 Flags 4.75 4.75

Opening of Point Saline Intl. Airport, Oct. 28, 1984 — A177

Inaugural flights.

**1985, Apr. 30**

**1266** A177 70c From Barbados 2.50 1.40
**1267** A177 $1 From New York 3.50 2.00
**1268** A177 $4 To Miami 7.50 *8.50*
*Nos. 1266-1268 (3)* 13.50 11.90

**Souvenir Sheet**

**1269** A177 $5 Point Saline Intl. Airport 7.75 7.75

Intl. Civil Aviation Org., 40th Anniv. A178

**1985, May 15**

**1270** A178 10c McDonnell Douglas DC-8 .40 .25
**1271** A178 50c Super Constellation 1.00 .65
**1272** A178 60c Vickers Vanguard 1.50 .80
**1273** A178 $4 DeHavilland Twin Otter 5.00 *6.50*
*Nos. 1270-1273 (4)* 7.90 8.20

**Souvenir Sheet**

**1274** A178 $5 Avro 748 Turboprop 5.00 5.00

Water Sports A179

**1985, June 15** ***Perf. 15***

**1275** A179 10c Model boat racing .25 .25
**1276** A179 50c Snorkeling, Sandy Island carriacou .40 .40
**1277** A179 $1.10 Sailing, Grand Anse Beach .90 .90
**1278** A179 $4 Windsurfing 2.75 2.75
*Nos. 1275-1278 (4)* 4.30 4.30

**Miniature Sheet**

**1279** A179 $5 Snorkelers, surfers, sailboats 4.75 4.75

Island Flowers — A180

½c, Strelitzia reginae. 1c, Passiflora coccinea. 2c, Nerium oleander. 4c, Ananas comosus. 5c, Anthurium andraeanum. 6c, Bougainvillea glabra. 10c, Hibiscus rosasinensis. 15c, Alpinia purpurata. 25c, Euphorbia pulcherrima. 30c, Antigonon leptopus. 40c, Datura candida. 50c, Hippeastrum puniceum. 60c, Opuntia megacantha. 70c, Acalypha hispida. 75c, Cordia sebestina. $1, Catharan-thus roseus. $1.10, Ixora macrothyrsa. $3, Justicia brandegeeana. $5, Plumbago capensis. $10, Lantana camara. $20, Jatropha integerrima.

**1985-88** ***Perf. 14***

**1280** A180 ½c multi .25 .25
**1281** A180 1c multi .25 .25
**1282** A180 2c multi .25 .25
**1283** A180 4c multi .25 .25
**1284** A180 5c multi .25 .25
**1285** A180 6c multi .25 .25
**1286** A180 10c multi .25 .25
**1287** A180 15c multi .25 .25
**1288** A180 25c multi .25 .25
**1289** A180 30c multi .25 .25
**1290** A180 40c multi .45 .45
**1291** A180 50c multi .50 .50
**1292** A180 60c multi .60 .60
**1293** A180 70c multi .65 .65
**1293B** A180 75c multi .85 .85
**1294** A180 $1 multi 1.00 1.00
**1295** A180 $1.10 multi 1.10 1.10
**1296** A180 $3 multi 2.75 2.75
**1297** A180 $5 multi 4.50 4.50
**1297A** A180 $10 multi 9.25 9.25
**1297B** A180 $20 multi 18.00 18.00
*Nos. 1280-1297B (21)* 42.15 42.15

Issued: #1280-1293, 1294-1297, 7/1; $10, 11/11; $20, 8/1/86; 75c, 1/12/88.

For overprints see #1357-1358, 1558-1560.

**1986** ***Perf. 12x12½***

**No date inscription**

*1280a* A180 ½c .25 .25
*1281a* A180 1c .25 .25
*1282a* A180 2c .25 .25
*1283a* A180 4c .25 .25
*1284a* A180 5c .25 .25
*1285a* A180 6c .25 .25
*1286a* A180 10c .25 .25
***b.*** Inscribed "1988" 3.00 3.00
*1287a* A180 15c .25 .25
*1288a* A180 25c .25 .25
*1289a* A180 30c .25 .25
*1290a* A180 40c .30 .30
*1291a* A180 50c .35 .35
*1292a* A180 60c .40 .40
*1293a* A180 70c .45 .45
*1294a* A180 $1 .70 .70
*1295a* A180 $1.10 .75 .75
*1296a* A180 $3 3.00 3.00
*1297c* A180 $5 4.25 4.25
*1297d* A180 $10 7.50 7.50
*Nos. 1280a-1297d (19)* 20.20 20.20

Issued: #1280a-1285a, 1287a-1292a, 1294a-1296a, Mar.; 10c, 70c, $5, July; $10, Dec.

**1987** **Inscribed "1987"**

*1289b* A180 30c .95 .65
*1291b* A180 50c 1.25 .80
*1292b* A180 60c 1.60 1.25
*1294b* A180 $1 2.25 1.25
*Nos. 1289b-1294b (4)* 6.05 3.95

Queen Mother, 85th Birthday A181

Photographs: $1, At the Royal Opera, vert. $1.50, Playing pool, London Press Club. $2.50, At Epsom for the Oaks Day races, vert. $5, In open carriage with Prince Charles, Thanksgiving Day, 1980, vert.

**1985, July 5**

**1298** A181 $1 multicolored .60 .60
**1299** A181 $1.50 multicolored .90 .90
**1300** A181 $2.50 multicolored 1.40 1.40
*Nos. 1298-1300 (3)* 2.90 2.90

**Souvenir Sheet**

**1301** A181 $5 multicolored 3.50 3.50

**1986, Jan. 20 Litho.** ***Perf. 12x12½***

**1301A** A181 90c like #1298 .55 .55
**1301B** A181 $1 like #1299 .65 .65
**1301C** A181 $3 like #1300 1.90 1.90
*Nos. 1301A-1301C (3)* 3.10 3.10

#1301A-1301C issued in sheets of 5 + label.

Intl. Youth Year — A182

**1985, Aug. 21** ***Perf. 15***

**1302** A182 25c Gardening .40 .25
**1303** A182 50c At the beach .50 .40
**1304** A182 $1.10 Education 1.00 1.00
**1305** A182 $3 Health care 2.10 2.10
*Nos. 1302-1305 (4)* 4.00 3.75

**Souvenir Sheet**

**1306** A182 $5 Harmonizing 4.00 4.00

4th Caribbean Cuboree, Aug. 17-23 A183

**1985, Sept. 5** ***Perf. 14***

**1307** A183 10c Pitching tents .40 .25
**1308** A183 50c Swimming .80 .65
**1309** A183 $1 Stamp collecting 1.90 1.40
**1310** A183 $4 Bird watching 5.25 5.25
*Nos. 1307-1310 (4)* 8.35 7.55

**Souvenir Sheet**

**1311** A183 $5 Grand Circle ritual 5.75 5.75

Johann Sebastian Bach — A184

Portrait, signature, music from Ciaccona and: 25c, Crumhorn. 70c, Oboe d'amore. $1, Violin. $3, Harpsichord. $5, Portrait.

**1985, Sept. 19**

**1312** A184 25c multicolored .75 .25
**1313** A184 70c multicolored 1.40 .85
**1314** A184 $1 multicolored 1.75 1.25
**1315** A184 $3 multicolored 3.50 3.50
*Nos. 1312-1315 (4)* 7.40 5.85

**Souvenir Sheet**

**1316** A184 $5 multicolored 5.75 5.75

The Prince & the Pauper — A185

Walt Disney characters.

**1985, Oct. 30**

**1317** A185 25c Prince & Pauper meet 1.25 .40
**1318** A185 50c Exchange clothes 1.50 .80
**1319** A185 $1.10 Prince as the Pauper 2.00 1.75
**1320** A185 $1.50 Prince rescued 2.75 2.50
**1321** A185 $2 Pauper as the Prince 4.00 4.00
*Nos. 1317-1321 (5)* 11.50 9.45

**Souvenir Sheet**

**1322** A185 $5 Prince & Pauper celebrate 9.50 9.50

IYY, Mark Twain (1835-1910), author.

Elizabeth II, Royal Visit to Spice Island — A186

**1985, Oct. 31** ***Perf. 14½***

**1323** A186 50c Flags of Grenada, U.K. 1.00 .50
**1324** A186 $1 Elizabeth II, vert. 1.00 1.25
**1325** A186 $4 HMS Britannia 3.50 3.50
*Nos. 1323-1325 (3)* 5.50 5.25

**Souvenir Sheet**

**1326** A186 $5 Map 3.75 3.75

The Brothers Grimm — A187

Disney characters in The Fisherman and His Wife.

**1985, Nov. 4 Litho.** ***Perf. 14***

**1327** A187 30c multicolored 1.00 .50
**1328** A187 60c multicolored 1.50 1.00
**1329** A187 70c multicolored 2.00 1.10
**1330** A187 $1 multicolored 3.00 1.60
**1331** A187 $3 multicolored 5.00 5.00
*Nos. 1327-1331 (5)* 12.50 9.20

**Souvenir Sheet**

**1332** A187 $5 multicolored 9.50 9.50

Indigenous Fish and Coral — A188

**1985, Nov. 15**

**1333** A188 25c Red-spotted hawkfish 1.75 .80
**1334** A188 50c Spotfin butterflyfish 2.75 1.25
**1335** A188 $1.10 Fire coral, orange sponge 5.00 3.25
**1336** A188 $3 Pillar coral 8.75 8.75
*Nos. 1333-1336 (4)* 18.25 14.05

**Souvenir Sheet**

**1337** A188 $5 Bigeye 7.00 7.00

UN, 40th Anniv. A189

UN stamps and famous people: 50c, No. 258, Mary McLeod Bethune (1875-1955), American educator. $2, No. 156, Maimonides (1135-1204), Judaic scholar. $2.50, No. 41, Alexander Graham Bell (1847-1922), inventor of the telephone. $5, Dag Hammarskjold (1905-1961), 2nd UN secretary general.

**1985, Nov. 22** ***Perf. 14½***

**1338** A189 50c multicolored .75 .65
**1339** A189 $2 multicolored 3.25 3.25
**1340** A189 $2.50 multicolored 3.25 3.75
*Nos. 1338-1340 (3)* 7.25 7.65

**Souvenir Sheet**

**1341** A189 $5 multicolored 4.25 4.25

Christmas A190

Religious paintings: 25c, Adoration of the Shepherds, by Andre Mantegna (1431-1506). 60c, Journey of the Magi, by Sassetta (d. 1450). 90c, Madonna and Child Enthroned with Saints, by Raphael (1483-1520). $4, Nativity, by Monaco. $5, Madonna and Child Enthroned with Saints, by Agnolo Gaddi (c. 1350-1396).

**1985, Dec. 23** ***Perf. 15***

| | | | | |
|---|---|---|---|---|
| **1342** | A190 | 25c multicolored | .25 | .25 |
| **1343** | A190 | 60c multicolored | .35 | .35 |
| **1344** | A190 | 90c multicolored | .55 | .55 |
| **1345** | A190 | $4 multicolored | 2.50 | 2.50 |
| | | *Nos. 1342-1345 (4)* | 3.65 | 3.65 |

**Souvenir Sheet**

| | | | | |
|---|---|---|---|---|
| **1346** | A190 | $5 multicolored | 3.25 | 3.25 |

Statue of Liberty, Cent. A191

Views of New York City.

**1986, Jan. 6**

| | | | | |
|---|---|---|---|---|
| **1347** | A191 | 5c Columbus Circle, 1893 | .50 | .25 |
| **1348** | A191 | 25c Circle, 1986 | 1.00 | .45 |
| **1349** | A191 | 40c Central Park Mounted Police, 1895 | 1.75 | 1.25 |
| **1350** | A191 | $4 Mounted Police, 1986 | 6.50 | *8.00* |
| | | *Nos. 1347-1350 (4)* | 9.75 | 9.95 |

**Souvenir Sheet**

| | | | | |
|---|---|---|---|---|
| **1351** | A191 | $5 Statue of Liberty | 4.50 | 4.50 |

Nos. 1347-1348, 1351 vert.

**Audubon Type of 1985**

**1986, Jan. 20** ***Perf. 12x12½***

| | | | | |
|---|---|---|---|---|
| **1352** | A174 | 50c Snowy egret | 2.00 | 1.00 |
| **1353** | A174 | 90c Red flamingo | 2.75 | 1.60 |
| **1354** | A174 | $1.10 Barnacle goose | 3.00 | 2.50 |
| **1355** | A174 | $3 Smew | 5.50 | 5.50 |
| | | *Nos. 1352-1355 (4)* | 13.25 | 10.60 |

**Souvenir Sheet**

***Perf. 14***

| | | | | |
|---|---|---|---|---|
| **1356** | A174 | $5 Brant Goose, horiz. | 16.00 | 16.00 |

Nos. 1291 and 1297 Overprinted in Black

**1986, Feb. 20** ***Perf. 14***

| | | | | |
|---|---|---|---|---|
| **1357** | A180 | 50c multicolored | .45 | .45 |
| **1358** | A180 | $5 multicolored | 4.50 | 4.50 |

St. George Methodist Church, Bicent. A192

**1986, Feb. 24** ***Perf. 15***

| | | | | |
|---|---|---|---|---|
| **1359** | A192 | 60c multicolored | .80 | .80 |

**Souvenir Sheet**

| | | | | |
|---|---|---|---|---|
| **1360** | A192 | $5 multicolored | 3.25 | 3.25 |

Heritage Year.

1986 World Cup Soccer Championships, Mexico — A193

Various soccer plays.

**1986, Mar. 6** ***Perf. 14***

| | | | | |
|---|---|---|---|---|
| **1361** | A193 | 50c multicolored | .80 | .70 |
| **1362** | A193 | 70c multicolored | 1.00 | 1.00 |
| **1363** | A193 | 90c multicolored | 1.50 | 1.50 |
| **1364** | A193 | $4 multicolored | 5.25 | 5.25 |
| | | *Nos. 1361-1364 (4)* | 8.55 | 8.45 |

**Souvenir Sheet**

| | | | | |
|---|---|---|---|---|
| **1365** | A193 | $5 multicolored | 6.00 | 6.00 |

For overprints see Nos. 1399-1403.

Halley's Comet A194

5c, Clyde Tombaugh, discovered Pluto, 1930, & Dudley Observatory. 20c, US X-24B space shuttle prototype, 1973. 40c, Medallic art, Catholic Church, 1618. $4, Lot & his daughters fleeing Sodom & Gomorrah, 1949 B.C. $5, Comet over Grand Anse Beach.

**1986, Mar. 20**

| | | | | |
|---|---|---|---|---|
| **1366** | A194 | 5c multicolored | .50 | .50 |
| **1367** | A194 | 20c multicolored | .75 | .25 |
| **1368** | A194 | 40c multicolored | 1.00 | .40 |
| **1369** | A194 | $4 multicolored | 4.25 | 4.25 |
| | | *Nos. 1366-1369 (4)* | 6.50 | 5.40 |

**Souvenir Sheet**

| | | | | |
|---|---|---|---|---|
| **1370** | A194 | $5 multicolored | 7.75 | 7.75 |

For overprints see Nos. 1416-1420.

**Queen Elizabeth II, 60th Birthday**

Common Design Type

2c, Signing the log, 1951. $1.50, Presenting polo trophy, Windsor, 1965. $4, Derby Day, 1977. $5, Royal family portrait, 1939.

**1986, Apr. 21** ***Perf. 14***

| | | | | |
|---|---|---|---|---|
| **1371** | CD339 | 2c yel & blk | .25 | .25 |
| **1372** | CD339 | $1.50 pale grn & multi | .90 | .90 |
| **1373** | CD339 | $4 dl lil & multi | 2.40 | 2.40 |
| | | *Nos. 1371-1373 (3)* | 3.55 | 3.55 |

**Souvenir Sheet**

| | | | | |
|---|---|---|---|---|
| **1374** | CD339 | $5 tan & blk | 3.25 | 3.25 |

AMERIPEX '86 — A195

Walt Disney characters playing baseball.

**1986, May 22** **Litho.** ***Perf. 11***

| | | | | |
|---|---|---|---|---|
| **1375** | A195 | 1c Pitcher | .25 | .25 |
| **1376** | A195 | 2c Catcher | .25 | .25 |
| **1377** | A195 | 3c Strike | .25 | .25 |
| **1378** | A195 | 4c Force out | .25 | .25 |
| **1379** | A195 | 5c Fly ball | .25 | .25 |
| **1380** | A195 | 6c Third base | .25 | .25 |
| **1381** | A195 | $2 Manager | 2.10 | 1.90 |
| **1382** | A195 | $3 Error | 3.00 | 3.00 |
| | | *Nos. 1375-1382 (8)* | 6.60 | 6.40 |

**Souvenir Sheets**

***Perf. 14***

| | | | | |
|---|---|---|---|---|
| **1383** | A195 | $5 Batter | 6.50 | 6.50 |
| **1384** | A195 | $5 Grand slam | 6.50 | 6.50 |

**Royal Wedding Issue, 1986**

Common Design Type

Designs: 2c, Prince Andrew and Sarah Ferguson. $1.10, Andrew. $4, Andrew in flight suit, helicopter. $5, Couple, diff.

**1986, July 23** ***Perf. 14***

| | | | | |
|---|---|---|---|---|
| **1385** | CD340 | 2c multicolored | .25 | .25 |
| **1386** | CD340 | $1.10 multicolored | .80 | .80 |
| **1387** | CD340 | $4 multicolored | 3.00 | 3.00 |
| | | *Nos. 1385-1387 (3)* | 4.05 | 4.05 |

**Souvenir Sheet**

| | | | | |
|---|---|---|---|---|
| **1388** | CD340 | $5 multicolored | 4.25 | 4.25 |

Seashells A196

Designs: 25c, Gmelin brown-lined latirus. 60c, Lamarck lamellose wentletrap. 70c, Swainson turkey wing. $4, Linne rooster-tail conch. $5, Linne angular triton.

**1986, July 15** **Litho.** ***Perf. 15***

| | | | | |
|---|---|---|---|---|
| **1389** | A196 | 25c multicolored | .50 | .25 |
| **1390** | A196 | 60c multicolored | .75 | .55 |
| **1391** | A196 | 70c multicolored | .90 | .90 |
| **1392** | A196 | $4 multicolored | 3.50 | 3.50 |
| | | *Nos. 1389-1392 (4)* | 5.65 | 5.20 |

**Souvenir Sheet**

| | | | | |
|---|---|---|---|---|
| **1393** | A196 | $5 multicolored | 3.50 | 3.50 |

Mushrooms A197

**1986, Aug. 1** ***Perf. 15***

| | | | | |
|---|---|---|---|---|
| **1394** | A197 | 10c Lepiota roselamellata | .65 | .40 |
| **1395** | A197 | 60c Lentinus bertieri | 1.25 | 1.00 |
| **1396** | A197 | $1 Lentinus retinervis | 2.75 | 2.00 |
| **1397** | A197 | $4 Eccilia cystiophorus | 6.50 | 6.50 |
| | | *Nos. 1394-1397 (4)* | 11.15 | 9.90 |

**Souvenir Sheet**

| | | | | |
|---|---|---|---|---|
| **1398** | A197 | $5 Cystolepiota eriophora | 13.50 | 13.50 |

Nos. 1361-1365 Ovptd. in Gold

**1986, Sept. 15** **Litho.** ***Perf. 14***

| | | | | |
|---|---|---|---|---|
| **1399** | A193 | 50c multicolored | .95 | .95 |
| **1400** | A193 | 70c multicolored | 1.25 | 1.25 |
| **1401** | A193 | 90c multicolored | 1.50 | 1.50 |
| **1402** | A193 | $4 multicolored | 5.50 | 5.50 |
| | | *Nos. 1399-1402 (4)* | 9.20 | 9.20 |

**Souvenir Sheet**

| | | | | |
|---|---|---|---|---|
| **1403** | A193 | $5 multicolored | 5.75 | 5.75 |

Disarmament Week and Intl. Peace Year — A198

60c, Mahatma Gandhi, rifles, dove. $4, Martin Luther King, Jr., hands, olive branch.

**1986, Sept. 15** ***Perf. 15***

| | | | | |
|---|---|---|---|---|
| **1404** | A198 | 60c multi, vert. | .40 | .40 |
| **1405** | A198 | $4 multi | 2.75 | 2.75 |

Christmas — A199

Disney characters. Nos. 1406-1407, 1411-1412 vert.

**1986, Nov. 3** ***Perf. 11***

| | | | | |
|---|---|---|---|---|
| **1406** | A199 | 30c Mickey, hearth | .50 | .30 |
| **1407** | A199 | 45c Mickey, Santa | .75 | .45 |
| **1408** | A199 | 60c Donald, Mickey Mouse phone | .90 | .60 |
| **1409** | A199 | 70c Goofy, toy band | 1.10 | .70 |
| **1410** | A199 | $1.10 Daisy, dolls | 1.25 | 1.10 |
| **1411** | A199 | $2 Goofy as Santa | 1.90 | 1.90 |
| **1412** | A199 | $2.50 Goofy playing piano | 2.10 | 2.10 |
| **1413** | A199 | $3 Train ride | 2.50 | 2.50 |
| | | *Nos. 1406-1413 (8)* | 11.00 | 9.65 |

**Souvenir Sheets**

| | | | | |
|---|---|---|---|---|
| **1414** | A199 | $5 Donald, Goofy, Mickey | 6.75 | 6.75 |
| **1415** | A199 | $5 Dewey | 6.75 | 6.75 |

**Nos. 1366-1370 Ovptd. with Halley's Comet Emblem**

**1986, Oct. 15** **Litho.** ***Perf. 14***

| | | | | |
|---|---|---|---|---|
| **1416** | A194 | 5c multicolored | .60 | .60 |
| **1417** | A194 | 20c multicolored | .80 | .60 |
| **1418** | A194 | 40c multicolored | 1.10 | .70 |
| **1419** | A194 | $4 multicolored | 7.00 | 7.00 |
| | | *Nos. 1416-1419 (4)* | 9.50 | 8.90 |

**Souvenir Sheet**

| | | | | |
|---|---|---|---|---|
| **1420** | A194 | $5 multicolored | 5.00 | 5.00 |

Fauna and Flora A200

**1986, Nov. 17** ***Perf. 14***

| | | | | |
|---|---|---|---|---|
| **1421** | A200 | 10c Chicken, rooster | .25 | .25 |
| **1422** | A200 | 30c Fish-eating bat | .40 | .25 |
| **1423** | A200 | 60c Goat | .85 | .75 |
| **1424** | A200 | 70c Cow | 1.00 | .90 |
| **1425** | A200 | $1 Anthurium | 1.50 | 1.10 |
| **1426** | A200 | $1.10 Royal poinciana | 1.50 | 1.25 |
| **1427** | A200 | $2 Frangipani | 2.50 | 2.50 |
| **1428** | A200 | $4 Orchid | 5.00 | *6.50* |
| | | *Nos. 1421-1428 (8)* | 13.00 | 13.50 |

**Souvenir Sheets**

| | | | | |
|---|---|---|---|---|
| **1429** | A200 | $5 Horse | 4.75 | 4.75 |
| **1430** | A200 | $5 Trees | 4.75 | 4.75 |

Automobile, Cent. — A202

1886 Daimler and modern automobiles.

**1986, Nov. 20** *Perf. 15*

**1431** A202 10c 1984 Maserati Biturbo .25 .25
**1432** A202 30c 1960 AC Cobra .35 .35
**1433** A202 60c 1963 Corvette .55 .55
**1434** A202 70c 1932 Duesenberg SJ7 .65 .65
**1435** A202 90c 1957 Porsche .75 .75
**1436** A202 $1.10 1930 Stoewer 1.00 1.00
**1437** A202 $2 1957 VW Beetle 1.60 1.60
**1438** A202 $3 1963 Mercedes 600 Limo 2.40 *2.75*
*Nos. 1431-1438 (8)* 7.55 7.90

**Souvenir Sheets**

**1439** A202 $5 1914 Stutz 3.75 3.75
**1440** A202 $5 1941 Packard 3.75 3.75

Song of Songs, by Marc Chagall (1887-1984) — A203

Paintings: No. 1441, The Rooster. No. 1442, Lovers in the Moonlight. No. 1443, Woman and Haystack. No. 1444, Snow-Covered Church. No. 1445, Peasant Life. No. 1446, Moses Receiving the Tablets. No. 1447, Vitebsk: From Mt. Zadunuv. No. 1449, Song of Songs, diff. No. 1450, The Creation of Man. No. 1451, Spring. No. 1452, Jacob's Struggle with the Angel. No. 1453, Song of Songs (wedding detail). No. 1454, The Painter to the Moon, 1917. No. 1455, Moses Striking the Rock. No. 1456, To My Betrothed, 1911. No. 1457, Sacrifice of Isaac. No. 1458, Monkey Acting as Judge Over Dispute Between Wolf and Fox, 1925. No. 1459, Song of Songs (bride riding Pegasus). No. 1460, Lovers in the Lilac, 1930. No. 1461, Song of Songs (sun, spirits). No. 1462, Jacob's Dream (figures with ladder). No. 1463, Purim, 1916. No. 1464, Fantastic Horsecart. No. 1465, Listening to the Cock, 1944. No. 1466, Self-portrait, 1914. No. 1467, The Juggler, 1943. No. 1468, Noah and the Rainbow. No. 1469, Moses Before the Burning Bush. No. 1470, Around Her, 1945. No. 1471, The Trough, 1925. No. 1472, The Poet of Half-Past-Three. No. 1473, The Tree of Life, 1948. No. 1474, Bride with the Blue Face, 1932. No. 1475, Chrysanthemums, 1926. No. 1476, Spoonful of Milk, 1912. No. 1477, The Soldier Drinks, 1911. No. 1478, Noah's Ark. No. 1479, Flowers and Fruit. No. 1480, Adam and Eve Expelled fron Paradise. No. 1481. Return from Synagogue. No. 1482, Aleko: A Fantasy of St. Petersburg. No. 1483, The Orchard. No. 1484, Solitude. No. 1485, Paris Through the Window, 1913. No. 1486, The Wedding (bridal couple, musicians), 1910. No. 1487, Paradise. No. 1488, The Dream, 1939. No. 1489, Abraham and the Three Angels. No. 1490, Water Carrier Under the Moon, 1914.

**1986-87**

**1441-1480** A203 $1 Set of 40 40.00 40.00

**Size: 110x95mm**

***Imperf***

**1481-1490** A203 $5 Set of 10 40.00 40.00

Nos. 1441-1446, 1450-1452 1455-1458, 1464-1467 and 1470-1479 vert.

Issued: #1441-1452, 1481-1483, 1986; #1453-1480, 1484-1490, 1987.

A204

America's Cup — A205

**1987, Feb. 5** **Litho.** *Perf. 15*

**1491** A204 10c Columbia, 1958 .25 .25
**1492** A204 60c Resolute, 1920 .45 .45
**1493** A204 $1.10 Endeavor, 1934 .80 .80
**1494** A204 $4 Rainbow, 1934 3.00 3.00
*Nos. 1491-1494 (4)* 4.50 4.50

**Souvenir Sheet**

**1495** A205 $5 Weatherly, 1962 3.75 3.75

Virgin Mary — A206

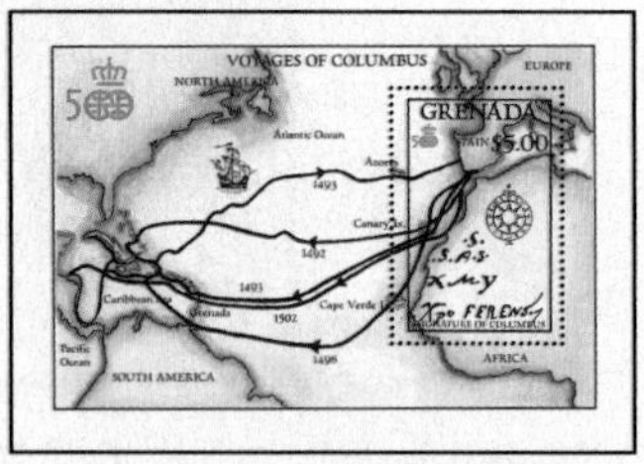


Map of Voyage, Columbus' Signature — A207

**1987, Apr. 27** *Perf. 15*

**1496** A206 10c shown .30 .25
**1497** A206 30c Nina, Pinta, Santa Maria .55 .25
**1498** A206 50c Columbus, map .65 .40
**1499** A206 60c Columbus .75 .45
**1500** A206 90c Isabella, Ferdinand .85 .70
**1501** A206 $1.10 Discovering the Antilles .90 .80
**1502** A206 $2 Carib Indians 1.50 1.50
*a.* Souv. sheet of 3, 30c, 90c, $2 2.40 2.40
**1503** A206 $3 American Indians, 1493 2.25 2.25
*a.* Souv. sheet of 5 + label, 10c, 50c, 60c, $1.10, $3 4.00 4.00
*Nos. 1496-1503 (8)* 7.75 6.60

**Souvenir Sheets**

**1504** A207 $5 shown 3.75 3.75
**1505** A207 $5 Columbus, Christ child 3.75 3.75

Discovery of America 500th anniv. (in 1992). Nos. 1497, 1500 and 1502 horiz.

CAPEX '87 A208

Fish. Nos. 1506, 1508 vert.

**1987, June 15**

**1506** A208 10c Black grouper .40 .25
**1507** A208 30c Blue marlin .60 .25
**1508** A208 60c White marlin .75 .50
**1509** A208 70c Big-eye thresher shark .85 .60
**1510** A208 $1 Bonefish 1.25 1.00
**1511** A208 $1.10 Wahoo 1.50 1.25
**1512** A208 $2 Sailfish 2.25 2.00
**1513** A208 $4 Albacore 3.50 3.50
*Nos. 1506-1513 (8)* 11.10 9.35

**Souvenir Sheets**

**1514** A208 $5 Barracuda 4.50 4.50
**1515** A208 $5 Yellowfin tuna, vert. 4.50 4.50

Transportation Innovations — A209

**1987, May 18** *Perf. 14*

**1516** A209 10c Cornu's Helicopter, 1907 .80 .60
**1517** A209 15c The Monitor and Merrimack, 1862 .80 .60
**1518** A209 30c LZ1 Zeppelin, c. 1900 1.00 .80
**1519** A209 50c S.S. Sirius, 1838 1.10 .85
**1520** A209 60c Trans-Siberian Railway 1.25 1.00
**1521** A209 70c USS Enterprise, 1960 1.40 1.10
**1522** A209 90c Blanchard's Balloon, 1785 1.50 1.40
**1523** A209 $1.50 USS Holland 1, 1900 2.25 2.25
**1524** A209 $2 S.S. Oceanic, 1871 3.00 3.00
**1525** A209 $3 1984 Lamborghini Countach 4.50 4.50
*Nos. 1516-1525 (10)* 17.60 16.10

For overprints see Nos. 1599-1602.

Statue of Liberty, Cent. A210

**1987, Aug. 5**

**1526** A210 10c Computer structural diagrams .25 .25
**1527** A210 25c Fireworks around statue .25 .25
**1528** A210 50c Fireworks in front of statue .50 .50
**1529** A210 60c Statue, boats .65 .60
**1530** A210 70c Structural diagram, close-up .90 .65
**1531** A210 $1 Rear of statue, close-up 1.00 .95
**1532** A210 $1.10 Liberty and Manhattan Isls. 1.10 1.25
**1533** A210 $2 Statue, boats, diff. 2.00 2.25
**1534** A210 $4 Ocean liner, New York Harbor 3.25 *4.50*
*Nos. 1526-1534 (9)* 9.90 11.20

Nos. 1529, 1531-1534 vert.

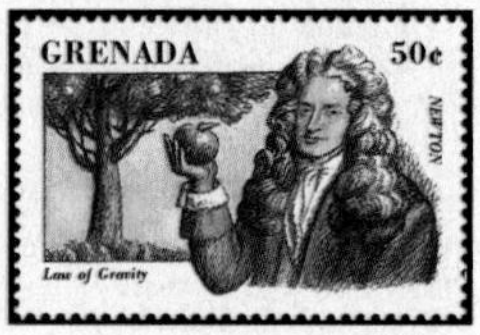


Inventors and Innovators A211

Designs: 50c, Sir Isaac Newton (1642-1727), law of gravity. $1.10, Jons Jakob Berzelius (1779-1848), symbols of chemical elements. $2, Robert Boyle (1627-1691), and Boyle's Law of pressure and volume. $3, James Watt (1736-1819), and diagram of steam engine. $5, Wright Flyer, Voyager.

**1987, Sept. 9**

**1535** A211 50c multicolored .90 .90
**1536** A211 $1.10 multicolored 2.00 2.00
**1537** A211 $2 multicolored 2.75 2.75
**1538** A211 $3 multicolored 5.00 5.00
*Nos. 1535-1538 (4)* 10.65 10.65

**Souvenir Sheet**

**1539** A211 $5 multicolored 5.25 5.25

No. 1536 inscribed with incorrect spelling of inventors name, "John Jacob Berzelius." No. 1538 inscribed with incorrect caption; James Watt and Watt engine are pictured, not Rudolf Diesel and the Diesel engine.

Miniature Sheets

Fairy Tales — A212

Snow White (50th Anniv.): No. 1540a, Snow White scrubs stairs. b, Wicked Queen, looking glass. c, Snow White fleeing. d, Dwarfs, mine. e, Snow White at cottage. f, Snow White, dwarfs. g, Snow White dancing with dwarfs. h, Eating poison apple. i, Prince kissing Snow White.

Sleeping Beauty: No. 1541a, Royal family. b, Maleficent cursing infant (Aurora). c, Merryweather altering curse. d, Three good fairies. e, Briar Rose (Aurora), forest animals. f, Aurora, spinning wheel. g, Sleeping Beauty (Aurora). h, Prince Phillip battling dragon (Maleficent). i, Sleeping Beauty awakes.

Cinderella: No. 1542a, Ella (Cinderella) and father. b, Cinderella sweeping. c, Cinderella, animals in barn. d, Cinderella, stepmother, stepsisters. e, Mice. f, Fairy Godmother. g, Cinderella transformed, coach. h, i, Duke puts glass slipper on Cinderella's foot.

Pinocchio: No. 1543a, Geppetto and puppet. b, Jiminy Cricket. c, Pinocchio, J. Worthington Foulfellow and Gideon. d, Pinocchio, Master Stromboli. e, Blue Fairy rescues Pinocchio. f, Pinocchio, donkeys. g, Pinocchio riding fish. h, Pinocchio and Geppetto at sea. i, Pinocchio transformed into a boy.

Alice in Wonderland: No. 1544a, Alice, rabbit hole. b, Alice in bottle. c, Walrus and Carpenter. d, White Rabbit in pink house. e, Alice, pink butterfly. f, March Hare, Mad Hatter. g, Alice in garden. h, Queen of Hearts. i, Alice on trial.

Peter Pan: No. 1545a, Nana. b, Peter Pan. c, Peter Pan, Tinker Bell, Wendy, John and Michael Darling flying. d, In NeverNever Land. e, Peter Pan and Tiger Lily. f, Captain Hook and First Mate Smee. g, Pater Pan dueling with Captain Hook. h, Tinker Bell, pirate ship. i, Captain Hook, crocodile.

No. 1546, Snow White and Prince riding off into sunset. No. 1547, Aurora and Prince Phillip dancing. No. 1548, Cinderella and Prince Charming marry. No. 1549, Pinocchio, Jiminy Cricket and Gepetto. No. 1550, Alice, cat, mother. No. 1551, Darling children waving goodbye to Peter Pan.

**1987, Sept. 9** *Perf. 14x13½*

**1540** Sheet of 9 4.25 4.25
*a.-i.* A212 30c any single .45 .45
**1541** Sheet of 9 4.25 4.25
*a.-i.* A212 30c any single .45 .45
**1542** Sheet of 9 4.25 4.25
*a.-i.* A212 30c any single .45 .45
**1543** Sheet of 9 4.25 4.25
*a.-i.* A212 30c any single .45 .45
**1544** Sheet of 9 4.25 4.25
*a.-i.* A212 30c any single .45 .45
**1545** Sheet of 9 4.25 4.25
*a.-i.* A212 30c any single .45 .45
*Nos. 1540-1545 (6)* 25.50 25.50

**Souvenir Sheets**

**1546-1551** A212 $5 each 6.75 6.75

Souvenir Sheet

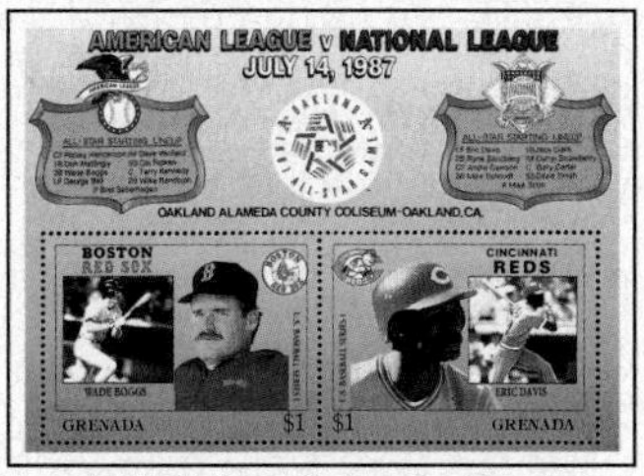


Baseball All-Star Game, Oakland, July 14 — A213

Athletes, team emblems: a, Wade Boggs, Boston Red Sox. b, Eric Davis, Cincinnati Reds.

**1987, Nov. 2** **Litho.** ***Perf. 14***
**1552** A213 Sheet of 2 2.00 2.00
***a.-b.*** $1 any single .95 .95

Massachusetts State Crest — A214

Designs: 15c, Independence Hall, Philadelphia. 50c, Benjamin Franklin. $4, Robert Morris (1734-1806), financier of American Revolution. $5, Pres. James Madison.

**1987, Nov. 2**
**1553** A214 15c multi, vert. .25 .25
**1554** A214 50c multi, vert. .30 .30
**1555** A214 60c shown .40 .40
**1556** A214 $4 multi, vert. 2.50 2.50
*Nos. 1553-1556 (4)* 3.45 3.45

**Souvenir Sheet**

**1557** A214 $5 multi, vert. 3.25 3.25

US Constitution bicent.

Nos. 1286, 1291 and 1296 Overprinted

**1987, Nov. 2**
**1558** A180 10c multicolored .25 .25
**1559** A180 50c multicolored .35 .35
**1560** A180 $3 multicolored 2.00 2.00
*Nos. 1558-1560 (3)* 2.60 2.60

HAFNIA '87 — A215

Disney animated characters in adaptation of fairy tales by Hans Christian Andersen.

**1987, Nov. 16** **Litho.** ***Perf. 14***
**1561** A215 25c The Shadow .50 .30
**1562** A215 30c The Storks .50 .35
**1563** A215 50c The Emperor's New Clothes .75 .60
**1564** A215 60c The Tinderbox 1.00 .65
**1565** A215 70c The Shepherdess and the Chimney Sweep 1.25 .80
**1566** A215 $1.50 The Little Mermaid 2.25 1.75
**1567** A215 $3 The Princess and the Pea 3.25 3.25
**1568** A215 $4 The Marsh King's Daughter 4.25 4.25
*Nos. 1561-1568 (8)* 13.75 11.95

**Souvenir Sheets**

**1569** A215 $5 The Flying Trunk, horiz. 7.50 7.50
**1570** A215 $5 The Sandman, horiz. 7.50 7.50

Christmas — A216

Religious paintings: 15c, The Annunciation, by Fra Angelico. 30c, The Annunciation, attributed to Hubert van Eyck (c. 1370-1426). 60c, Adoration of the Magi, by Januarius Zick (1730-1797). $4, The Flight Into Egypt, by David. $5, The Circumcision, produced by artists of the Giovanni Bellini Studio, 14th cent.

**1987, Dec. 15**
**1571** A216 15c multicolored .55 .45
**1572** A216 30c multicolored 1.00 .50
**1573** A216 60c multicolored 1.75 1.40
**1574** A216 $4 multicolored 6.75 6.75
*Nos. 1571-1574 (4)* 10.05 9.10

**Souvenir Sheet**

**1575** A216 $5 multicolored 8.00 8.00

T. Albert Marryshow (b. 1887) — A217

**1988, Jan. 22** **Litho.** ***Perf. 14***
**1576** A217 25c scarlet, red brn & brn blk .30 .30

40th Wedding Anniv. of Queen Elizabeth II and Prince Philip — A218

**1988, Feb. 15**
**1577** A218 15c Wedding portrait, 1947 .30 .25
**1578** A218 50c Elizabeth, Charles, Anne .60 .45
**1579** A218 $1 Elizabeth, Anne 1.00 1.00
**1580** A218 $4 Elizabeth, c. 1980 3.00 3.00
*Nos. 1577-1580 (4)* 4.90 4.70

**Souvenir Sheet**

**1581** A218 $5 Elizabeth, 1947 3.75 3.75

Disney Animated Characters and 1988 Summer Olympics, Seoul A219

**1988, Apr. 13** **Litho.** ***Perf. 13½x14***
**1582** A219 1c Lighting torch, Olympia .25 .25
**1583** A219 2c Torch bearers .25 .25
**1584** A219 3c Flag bearers .25 .25
**1585** A219 4c Releasing doves .25 .25
**1586** A219 5c Opening ceremony .25 .25
**1587** A219 10c Olympic motto .25 .25
**1588** A219 $6 Tiger character trademark 5.50 5.50
**1589** A219 $7 Oldest Korean p.o. 6.00 5.50
*Nos. 1582-1589 (8)* 13.00 12.50

**Souvenir Sheets**

**1590** A219 $5 Sportsmanship oath 5.50 5.50
**1591** A219 $5 Closing ceremony 5.50 5.50

Boy Scouts A220

**1988, May 3** **Litho.** ***Perf. 14***
**1592** A220 20c Fishing, vert. .40 .25
**1593** A220 70c Hiking 1.25 1.00
**1594** A220 90c First-aid 1.75 1.40
**1595** A220 $3 Canoeing, vert. 4.00 4.00
*Nos. 1592-1595 (4)* 7.40 6.65

**Souvenir Sheet**

**1596** A220 $5 Scout holding koala, vert. 3.75 3.75

Rotary Conference, District 405, St. George, May 5-7 — A221

Rotary Intl. emblem and: $2, Map of District 405 island nations (Grenada, Guyana, Surinam and French Guiana), 15th cent. Spanish galleon Santa Maria, vert. $10, Motto "Service Above Self."

**1988, May 5** ***Perf. 13½x14***
**1597** A221 $2 multicolored 1.50 1.50

**Souvenir Sheet**

***Perf. 14x13½***

**1598** A221 $10 shown 7.25 7.25

**Nos. 1522-1525 Overprinted for Philatelic Exhibitions**

a

b

c

d

**1988, Apr. 19** **Litho.** ***Perf. 14***
**1599** A209 (a) 90c multi 1.25 .85
**1600** A209 (b) $1.50 multi 1.75 1.50
**1601** A209 (c) $2 multi 2.25 2.25
**1602** A209 (d) $3 multi 2.75 2.75
*Nos. 1599-1602 (4)* 8.00 7.35

Birds — A222

**1988, May 31**
**1603** A222 10c Roseate tern .80 .30
**1604** A222 25c Laughing gull 1.00 .30
**1605** A222 50c Osprey 1.25 .60
**1606** A222 60c Rose-breasted grosbeak 1.25 .60
**1607** A222 90c Purple gallinule 1.25 .95
**1608** A222 $1.10 White-tailed tropicbird 1.25 1.10
**1609** A222 $3 Blue-faced booby 3.00 3.00
**1610** A222 $4 Northern shoveler 4.25 4.25
*Nos. 1603-1610 (8)* 14.05 11.10

**Souvenir Sheet**

**1611** A222 $5 Belted kingfisher 5.00 5.00
**1612** A222 $5 Rusty-tailed flycatcher 5.00 5.00

Miniature Sheets

Classic Automobiles — A223

Cars (U.S. unless otherwise stated): No. 1613a, 1934 Tatra Type 77, Czechoslovakia. b, 1938 Rolls-Royce Phantom III, Britain. c, 1947 Studebaker Champion Starlight. d, 1948 Porsche Gmund, Germany. e, 1948 Tucker. f, 1931 Peerless V-16. g, 1931 Minerva AL, Belgium. h, 1933 REO Royale. i, 1933 Pierce-Arrow Silver Arrow. j, 1934 Hupmobile Aerodynamic.

No. 1614a, 1925 Vauxhall Type OE30/98, Britain. b, 1926 Wills Sainte Claire. c, 1928 Bucciali, France. d, 1929 Irving Napier Golden Arrow, Britain. e, 1930 Studebaker President. f, 1907 Thomas Flyer. g, 1908 Isotta-Fraschini Tipo J, Italy. h, 1910 Fiat 10/14HP, Italy. i, 1911 Mercer Type 35 Raceabout. j, 1917 Marmon Model 34 Cloverleaf.

No. 1615a, 1965 Peugeot 404, France. b, 1969 Ford Capri, Britain. c, 1975 Ferrari 312T, Italy. d, 1978 Lotus T-79, Britain. e, 1979 Williams-Cosworth FW07, Britain. f, 1948 H.R.G. 1500 Sports, Britain. g, 1949 Crosley Hotshot. h, 1955 Volvo PV444, Sweden. i, 1960 Maserati Tipo 61, Italy. j, 1963 Saab 96, Sweden.

**1988, June 1** ***Perf. 13x13½***
**1613** Sheet of 10 13.00 13.00
***a.-j.*** A223 $2 any single 1.25 1.25
**1614** Sheet of 10 13.00 13.00
***a.-j.*** A223 $2 any single 1.25 1.25
**1615** Sheet of 10 13.00 13.00
***a.-j.*** A223 $2 any single 1.25 1.25

Paintings by Titian (c. 1488-1576) A224

Paintings by Titian: 10c, Lavinia Vecellio, c. 1546. 20c, Portrait of a Man, c. 1510. 25c, Andrea De Franceschi, 1532. 90c, Head of a Soldier, 1511. $1, Man With a Flute. $2,

Lucrezia and Tarquinius, c. 1515. $3, Duke of Mantua with Dog, 1525. $4, La Bella Di Tiziano, 1536. No. 1624, Allegory of Alfonso D'Avalos. No. 1625, Fall of Man, 1570, horiz.

| 1988, June 15 | | | *Perf. 13½x14* | |
|---|---|---|---|---|
| **1616** | A224 | 10c multicolored | .25 | .25 |
| **1617** | A224 | 20c multicolored | .25 | .25 |
| **1618** | A224 | 25c multicolored | .25 | .25 |
| **1619** | A224 | 90c multicolored | .60 | .60 |
| **1620** | A224 | $1 multicolored | .65 | .65 |
| **1621** | A224 | $2 multicolored | 1.40 | 1.40 |
| **1622** | A224 | $3 multicolored | 2.10 | 2.10 |
| **1623** | A224 | $4 multicolored | 2.50 | 2.50 |
| | | *Nos. 1616-1623 (8)* | 8.00 | 8.00 |

**Souvenir Sheets**

| | | | | |
|---|---|---|---|---|
| **1624** | A224 | $5 multicolored | 3.75 | 3.75 |

*Perf. 14x13½*

| | | | | |
|---|---|---|---|---|
| **1625** | A224 | $5 multicolored | 3.75 | 3.75 |

Zeppelins A225

Designs: 10c, Graf Zeppelin over the Federal Building, Chicago, 1933 World's Fair, vert. 15c, LZ-1 over Lake Constance, 1900. 25c, Washington aerial balloon lifting off the aircraft carrier USS George Washington Parke Custis off Port Royal, South Carolina, 1862, vert. 45c, Hindenburg over a Maybach Zeppelin automobile, Friedrichshaven, 1936. 50c, Goodyear Blimp over the Statue of Liberty, 1986, vert. 60c, Hindenburg passing over the Statue of Liberty during its final flight, 1937. 90c, Experimental docking of aircraft (piloted by Ernst Udet) with the Hindenburg, 1936. $2, Hindenburg over the Olympic stadium, Berlin, 1936, vert. $3, Hindenburg over Christ the Redeemer statue, Rio de Janeiro, 1937, vert. $4, Hindenburg over mail plane catapult ship Bremen, 1936. No. 1636, Zepplin over DLH base, Bathurst, Gambia, 1935. No. 1637, Graf Zeppelin over St. Basil's Cathedral, Moscow, 1930.

| 1988, July 1 | | | *Perf. 14* | |
|---|---|---|---|---|
| **1626** | A225 | 10c multicolored | .50 | .25 |
| **1627** | A225 | 15c multicolored | .60 | .25 |
| **1628** | A225 | 25c multicolored | .70 | .35 |
| **1629** | A225 | 45c multicolored | .75 | .40 |
| **1630** | A225 | 50c multicolored | .80 | .45 |
| **1631** | A225 | 60c multicolored | .85 | .50 |
| **1632** | A225 | 90c multicolored | 1.00 | .80 |
| **1633** | A225 | $2 multicolored | 1.75 | 1.75 |
| **1634** | A225 | $3 multicolored | 2.50 | 2.50 |
| **1635** | A225 | $4 multicolored | 3.50 | 3.50 |
| | | *Nos. 1626-1635 (10)* | 12.95 | 10.75 |

**Souvenir Sheets**

| | | | | |
|---|---|---|---|---|
| **1636** | A225 | $5 multicolored | 3.75 | 3.75 |
| **1637** | A225 | $5 multicolored | 3.75 | 3.75 |

The ship name on No. 1628 is incorrect.

SYDPEX '88, Sydney, Australia — A226

Walt Disney characters in Australian settings: 1c, Camping in the Outback, a howling Tasmanian wolf. 2c, Offering peanuts to wallabies. 3c, With a kangaroo and joey against Ayers Rock. 4c, Riding emus, emu-wrens. 5c, Camp and wombat. 10c, Duck-billed platypuses. No. 1644, Photographing a kookaburra. $6, Koala and Mickey waving flags of Grenada, Australia and the United States, map. No. 1646, Flags and candles atop Cake in the shape of Australia. No. 1647, Mickey, Minnie Pluto and Goofy taking a break during a walkabout.

| 1988, Aug. 1 | | Litho. | *Perf. 14x13½* | |
|---|---|---|---|---|
| **1638** | A226 | 1c multicolored | .25 | .25 |
| **1639** | A226 | 2c multicolored | .25 | .25 |
| **1640** | A226 | 3c multicolored | .25 | .25 |
| **1641** | A226 | 4c multicolored | .25 | .25 |
| **1642** | A226 | 5c multicolored | .25 | .25 |
| **1643** | A226 | 10c multicolored | .25 | .25 |
| **1644** | A226 | $5 multicolored | 5.50 | 5.50 |
| **1645** | A226 | $6 multicolored | 6.50 | 6.50 |
| | | *Nos. 1638-1645 (8)* | 13.50 | 13.50 |

**Souvenir Sheet**

| | | | | |
|---|---|---|---|---|
| **1646** | A226 | $5 multicolored | 6.50 | 6.50 |
| **1647** | A226 | $5 multicolored | 6.50 | 6.50 |

Mickey Mouse, 60th anniversary.

Intl. Fund for Agricultural Development, 10th Anniv. — A227

| 1988, Aug. 11 | | Litho. | *Perf. 14* | |
|---|---|---|---|---|
| **1648** | A227 | 25c Pineapple, vert. | .40 | .40 |
| **1649** | A227 | 75c Banana, vert. | .80 | .80 |
| **1650** | A227 | $3 Mace, nutmeg | 2.50 | 2.25 |
| | | *Nos. 1648-1650 (3)* | 3.70 | 3.45 |

Flowering Trees and Shrubs of the Caribbean A228

| 1988, Sept. 30 | | | Litho. | |
|---|---|---|---|---|
| **1651** | A228 | 15c Lignum vitae | .25 | .25 |
| **1652** | A228 | 25c Saman | .25 | .25 |
| **1653** | A228 | 35c Red frangipani | .25 | .25 |
| **1654** | A228 | 45c Flowering maple | .30 | .30 |
| **1655** | A228 | 60c Yellow poui | .40 | .40 |
| **1656** | A228 | $1 Wild chestnut | .70 | .70 |
| **1657** | A228 | $3 Mountain immortelle | 2.10 | 2.10 |
| **1658** | A228 | $4 Queen of flowers | 2.75 | 2.75 |
| | | *Nos. 1651-1658 (8)* | 7.00 | 7.00 |

**Souvenir Sheets**

| | | | | |
|---|---|---|---|---|
| **1659** | A228 | $5 Flamboyant | 3.50 | 3.50 |
| **1660** | A228 | $5 Orchid tree | 3.50 | 3.50 |

Miniature Sheet

Christmas, Mickey Mouse 60th Anniv. — A229

Designs: a, Huey draping garland. b, Goofy stringing popcorn. c, Chip'n'Dale decorating tree. d, Santa Claus in his sleigh. e, Dewey hanging stockings. f, Louie unpacking decorations. g, Donald Duck. h, Mickey Mouse. No. 1662, Morty and Ferdie leaving milk and cookies for Santa, horiz. No. 1663, Morty and Ferdie dreaming of presents, horiz.

*Perf. 13½x14, 14x13½*

| 1988, Dec. 1 | | | Litho. | |
|---|---|---|---|---|
| **1661** | A229 | Sheet of 8 | 7.50 | 7.50 |
| *a.-h.* | | $1 any single | .90 | .90 |

**Souvenir Sheets**

| | | | | |
|---|---|---|---|---|
| **1662** | A229 | $5 multicolored | 5.00 | 5.00 |
| **1663** | A229 | $5 multicolored | 5.00 | 5.00 |

Miniature Sheets

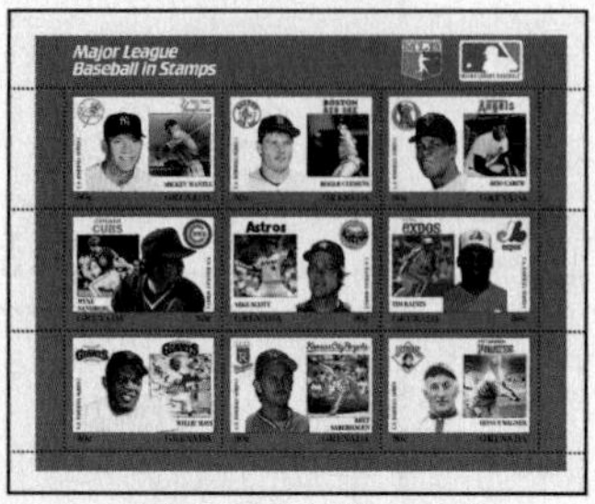

Major League Baseball Players — A230

No. 1664: a, Mickey Mantle. b, Roger Clemens. c, Rod Carew. d, Ryne Sandberg. e, Mike Scott. f, Tim Raines. g, Willie Mays. h, Bret Saberhagen. i, Honus Wagner.

No. 1665: a, Roberto Clemente. b, Cal Ripken, Jr. c, Bob Feller. d, George Bell. e, Mark McGwire. f, Alvin Davis. g, Pete Rose. h, Dan Quisenberry. i, Babe Ruth.

No. 1666: a, Jackie Robinson. b, Dwight Gooden. c, Brooks Robinson, Jr. d, Nolan Ryan. e, Mike Schmidt. f, Gary Gaetti. g, Nellie Fox. h, Tony Gwynn. i, Dizzy Dean.

No. 1667: a, Ernie Banks. b, National League emblem. c, Julio Franco. d, Jack Morris. e, Fernando Valenzuela. f, Lefty Grove. g, Ted Williams. h, Darryl Strawberry. i, Dale Murphy.

No. 1668: a, Johnny Bench. b, Dave Stieb. c, Reggie Jackson. d, Harold Baines. e, Wade Boggs. f, Pete O'Brien. g, Stan Musial. h, Wally Joyner. i, Grover Cleveland Alexander.

No. 1669: a, Jose Cruz. b, American League emblem. c, Al Kaline. d, Chuck Klein. e, Don Mattingly. f, Mike Witt. g, Mark Langston. h, Hubie Brooks. i, Harmon Killebrew.

No. 1670: a, George Brett. b, Joe Carter. c, Frank Robinson. d, Mel Ott. e, Benito Santiago. f, Teddy Higuera. g, Lloyd Moseby. h, Bobby Bonilla. i, Warren Spahn.

No. 1671: a, Gary Carter. b, Hank Aaron. c, Gaylord Perry. d, Ty Cobb. e, Andre Dawson. f, Charlie Hough. g, Kirby Puckett. h, Robin Yount. i, Don Drysdale.

No. 1672: a, Luis Aparicio. b, Paul Molitor. c, Lou Gehrig. d, Jeffrey Leonard. e, Eric Davis. f, Pete Incaviglia. g, Steve Rogers. h, Ozzie Smith. i, Randy Jones.

| 1988, Nov. 28 | | Litho. | *Perf. 14* | |
|---|---|---|---|---|
| **1664** | | Sheet of 9 | 1.75 | 1.75 |
| *a.-i.* | A230 | 30c any single | .25 | .25 |
| **1665** | | Sheet of 9 | 1.75 | 1.75 |
| *a.-i.* | A230 | 30c any single | .25 | .25 |
| **1666** | | Sheet of 9 | 1.75 | 1.75 |
| *a.-i.* | A230 | 30c any single | .25 | .25 |
| **1667** | | Sheet of 9 | 1.75 | 1.75 |
| *a.-i.* | A230 | 30c any single | .25 | .25 |
| **1668** | | Sheet of 9 | 1.75 | 1.75 |
| *a.-i.* | A230 | 30c any single | .25 | .25 |
| **1669** | | Sheet of 9 | 1.75 | 1.75 |
| *a.-i.* | A230 | 30c any single | .25 | .25 |
| **1670** | | Sheet of 9 | 1.75 | 1.75 |
| *a.-i.* | A230 | 30c any single | .25 | .25 |
| **1671** | | Sheet of 9 | 1.75 | 1.75 |
| *a.-i.* | A230 | 30c any single | .25 | .25 |
| **1672** | | Sheet of 9 | 1.75 | 1.75 |
| *a.-i.* | A230 | 30c any single | .25 | .25 |
| | | *Nos. 1664-1672 (9)* | 15.75 | 15.75 |

No. 1665 was reprinted with No. 1665g replaced by a label inscribed "U.S. Baseball Series."

Singers — A231

| 1988, Dec. 5 | | Litho. | *Perf. 14* | |
|---|---|---|---|---|
| **1673** | A231 | 10c Tina Turner | .30 | .25 |
| **1674** | A231 | 25c Lionel Ritchie | .30 | .25 |
| **1675** | A231 | 45c Whitney Houston | .45 | .40 |
| **1676** | A231 | 60c Joan Armatrading | .60 | .50 |
| **1677** | A231 | 75c Madonna | 1.00 | .65 |
| **1678** | A231 | $1 Elton John | 1.25 | .85 |
| **1679** | A231 | $3 Bruce Springsteen | 2.25 | 2.25 |
| **1680** | A231 | $4 Bob Marley | 3.00 | 3.00 |
| | | *Nos. 1673-1680 (8)* | 9.15 | 8.15 |

**Souvenir Sheet**

| | | | | |
|---|---|---|---|---|
| **1681** | | Sheet of 4 (2 55c,2 $1) | 3.50 | 3.50 |
| *a.* | A231 | 55c Yoko Minamino | .75 | .75 |
| *b.* | A231 | $1 Yoko Minamino, diff. | 2.50 | 2.50 |

Armatrading is misspelled "Ammertrading."

**Car Type of 1988**

Miniature Sheets

Locomotives.

No. 1682: a, 1889 Canada Atlantic Railway No. 2 0-6-0, Canada. b, 1875 Virginia & Truckee Railroad J.W. Bowker 2-4-0, US. c, 1872 Philadelphia & Reading Railway Ariel 2-2-2, US. d, 1867 Chicago & Rock Is. Railroad America 4-4-0, US. e, 1866 Lehigh Valley Railroad Consolidation No. 63 2-8-0, US. f, 1860 Great Western Railway Scotia 0-6-0, Canada. g, 1854 Grand Trunk Railway Birkenhead Class 4-4-0, Canada. h, 1837 Camden & Amboy Railroad Monster 0-8-0, US. i, 1834 B&O Railroad Grasshopper Class 0-4-0, US. j, 1829 B&O Railroad Tom Thumb 0-2-2, US.

No. 1683: a, 1925 United Railways of Yucatan Yucatan 4-4-0, Mexico. b, 1924 Canadian Natl. Railways Class T2 2-10-2, Canada. c, 1919 St. Louis-San Francisco Railroad USRA Light Mikado 2-8-2, US. d, 1919 Atlantic Coast Line Railroad USRA Light Pacific 4-6-2, US. e, 1913 Edaville Railroad (Bridgton & Saco River Railroad) No. 7 2-4-4-T, US. f, 1903 Denver & Rio Grande Western Railroad Mudhens Class K27 2-8-2, US. g, 1902 PRR Class E-2 No. 7002 4-4-2, US. h, 1899 PRR Class H6 2-8-0, US. i, 1893 Mohawk & Hudson Railroad De Witt Clinton 0-4-0, US. j, 1891 St. Clair Tunnel Company No. 598 0-10-0, Canada.

No. 1684: a, 1947 Chesapeake & Ohio Railroad M-1 Class No. 500 steam turbine electric, US. b, 1946 Rutland Railroad No. 93 4-8-2, US. c, 1942 PRR Class T1 4-4-4-4, US. d, 1942 Chesapeake & Ohio Railroad Class H-8 2-6-6-6, US. e, 1941 Atchison, Topeka & Santa Fe Railway EMD Model FT Bo-Bo, US. f, 1940 Gulf, Mobile & Ohio Railroad ALCO Models S-1 & S-2 Bo-Bo, US. g, 1937 New York, New Haven & Hartford Railroad Class 15 4-6-4, US. h, 1936 Seaboard Air Line Railroad Class R 2-6-6-4, US. i, 1930 Newfoundland Railway Class R-2 2-8-2, Canada. j, 1928 Canadian Natl. Railway No. 9000 2-Do-1 + 1-Do-2, Canada.

| 1989, Jan. 23 | | Litho. | *Perf. 13x13½* | |
|---|---|---|---|---|
| **1682** | | Sheet of 10 | 14.00 | 14.00 |
| *a.-j.* | A223 | $2 any single | 1.40 | 1.40 |
| **1683** | | Sheet of 10 | 14.00 | 14.00 |
| *a.-j.* | A223 | $2 any single | 1.40 | 1.40 |
| **1684** | | Sheet of 10 | 14.00 | 14.00 |
| *a.-j.* | A223 | $2 any single | 1.40 | 1.40 |

Medalists of the 1988 Summer Olympics, Seoul — A232

Designs: 10c, Jackie Joyner-Kersee, US, long jump. 25c, Steffi Graf, Federal Republic of Germany, women's singles tennis. 45c, Peter Rono, Kenya, 1500m run. 75c, Greg Barton, US, kayak singles. $1, Italy, women's team foil. $2, Kristin Otto, German Democratic Republic, women's 100m freestyle swimming. $3, Holger Behrendt, German Democratic Republic, still rings. $4, Japan, duet synchronized swimming. No. 1693, Yukio Iketani, Japan, men's floor exercise. No. 1694, West Germany, 400m relay, and (Olympic) flame over track.

| 1989, Apr. 6 | | Litho. | *Perf. 14* | |
|---|---|---|---|---|
| **1685** | A232 | 10c multicolored | .30 | .30 |
| **1686** | A232 | 25c multicolored | .70 | .35 |
| **1687** | A232 | 45c multicolored | .80 | .40 |
| **1688** | A232 | 75c multicolored | .90 | .60 |
| **1689** | A232 | $1 multicolored | 1.00 | .75 |
| **1690** | A232 | $2 multicolored | 1.50 | 1.50 |
| **1691** | A232 | $3 multicolored | 2.25 | 2.25 |
| **1692** | A232 | $4 multicolored | 2.75 | 2.75 |
| | | *Nos. 1685-1692 (8)* | 10.20 | 8.90 |

**Souvenir Sheets**

| | | | | |
|---|---|---|---|---|
| **1693** | A232 | $6 multicolored | 4.75 | 4.75 |
| **1694** | A232 | $6 multicolored | 4.75 | 4.75 |

"The Fifty-three Stations on the Tokaido" — A233

Prints by Hiroshige (1797-1858): 10c, Shinagawa on Edo Bay. 25c, Pine Trees on the Road to Totsuka. 60c, Kanagawa on Edo Bay. 75c, Crossing Banyu River to Hiratsuka. $1, Windy Shore at Odawara. $2, Snow-covered Post Station of Mishima. $3, Full Moon at Fuchu. $4, Crossing the Stream at Okitsu. No. 1703, Mt. Uzu at Okabe. No. 1704, Mountain Pass at Nissaka.

| 1989, May 15 | | Litho. | *Perf. 14x13½* | |
|---|---|---|---|---|
| **1695** | A233 | 10c multicolored | .25 | .25 |
| **1696** | A233 | 25c multicolored | .25 | .25 |
| **1697** | A233 | 60c multicolored | .45 | .45 |
| **1698** | A233 | 75c multicolored | .65 | .65 |
| **1699** | A233 | $1 multicolored | 1.00 | .75 |
| **1700** | A233 | $2 multicolored | 1.50 | 1.50 |
| **1701** | A233 | $3 multicolored | 2.25 | 2.25 |
| **1702** | A233 | $4 multicolored | 3.00 | 3.00 |
| | | *Nos. 1695-1702 (8)* | 9.35 | 9.10 |

### Souvenir Sheets

| | | | | | |
|---|---|---|---|---|---|
| **1703** | A233 | $5 multicolored | | 3.75 | 3.75 |
| **1704** | A233 | $5 multicolored | | 3.75 | 3.75 |

Hirohito (1901-1989) and enthronement of Akihito as emperor of Japan.

Indigenous Birds — A234

**1989, June 6 Litho. *Perf. 14***

| | | | | |
|---|---|---|---|---|
| **1705** A234 | 5c | Great blue heron | .75 | *1.00* |
| **1706** A234 | 10c | Green heron | .75 | .60 |
| **1707** A234 | 15c | Ruddy turnstone | .80 | .60 |
| **1708** A234 | 25c | Blue-winged teal | .90 | .30 |
| **1709** A234 | 35c | Ring-necked plover | 1.10 | .30 |
| **1710** A234 | 45c | Emerald-throated hummingbird | 1.10 | .40 |
| **1711** A234 | 50c | Hairy hermit | 1.25 | .45 |
| **1712** A234 | 60c | Lesser Antillean bullfinch | 1.40 | .55 |
| **1713** A234 | 75c | Brown pelican | 1.50 | .65 |
| **1714** A234 | $1 | Black-crowned night heron | 1.60 | 1.00 |
| **1715** A234 | $3 | Sparrow hawk | 2.40 | 2.40 |
| **1716** A234 | $5 | Barn swallow | 4.00 | 4.00 |
| **1717** A234 | $10 | Red-billed tropicbird | 8.00 | 8.00 |
| **1718** A234 | $20 | Barn owl | 21.50 | 21.50 |
| | | *Nos. 1705-1718 (14)* | 47.05 | 41.75 |

Nos. 1709-1718 vert.

**1990-93 Litho. *Perf. 11½x13***

| | | | | |
|---|---|---|---|---|
| *1705a* | A234 | 5c | .70 | .70 |
| *1706a* | A234 | 10c | .70 | .60 |
| *1707a* | A234 | 15c | .75 | .60 |
| *1708a* | A234 | 25c | .85 | .30 |

***Perf. 13x11½***

| | | | | |
|---|---|---|---|---|
| *1709a* | A234 | 35c | 1.00 | .30 |
| *1710a* | A234 | 45c | 1.00 | .35 |
| *1711a* | A234 | 50c | 1.10 | .45 |
| *1712a* | A234 | 60c | 1.25 | .50 |
| *1713a* | A234 | 75c | 1.40 | .55 |
| *1714a* | A234 | $1 | 1.50 | .90 |
| *1715a* | A234 | $3 | 2.40 | 2.40 |
| *1716a* | A234 | $5 | 4.00 | 4.00 |
| *1717a* | A234 | $10 | 8.00 | 8.00 |
| *1718a* | A234 | $20 | 21.50 | 21.50 |
| | | *Nos. 1705a-1718a (14)* | 46.15 | 41.15 |

Issued: #1718a, 1/22/90.

1990 World Cup Soccer Championships, Italy — A235

**1989, June 12 *Perf. 14***

| | | | | |
|---|---|---|---|---|
| **1719** A235 | 10c | Scotland | .50 | .30 |
| **1720** A235 | 25c | England vs. Brazil | .60 | .50 |
| **1721** A235 | 60c | Paolo Rossi, Italy | .80 | .70 |
| **1722** A235 | 75c | Jairzinho of Brazil | 1.00 | .80 |
| **1723** A235 | $1 | Swedish Striker | 1.25 | 1.00 |
| **1724** A235 | $2 | Pele, Brazil | 2.50 | 2.00 |
| **1725** A235 | $3 | Mario Kempes, Argentina | 2.75 | 2.75 |
| **1726** A235 | $4 | Pat Jennings | 3.75 | 3.75 |
| | | *Nos. 1719-1726 (8)* | 13.15 | 11.80 |

### Souvenir Sheets

| | | | | |
|---|---|---|---|---|
| **1727** A235 | $6 | Argentina vs. Holland | 5.50 | 5.50 |
| ***a.*** | | $6 1990 score ovptd. in margin | 7.50 | 7.50 |
| **1728** A235 | $6 | Goalie | 5.50 | 5.50 |

Issue date: No. 1727a, Nov. 30, 1990.

PHILEXFRANCE '89 — A236

19th Cent. ships and cargo: 25c, Chebeck, sugarcane. 75c, Lugger, cotton. $1, Merchantman, cocoa. $4, Ketch, coffee. $6, Vue du Fort et Ville de St. George dans l'Isle de la Grenade et du Morne, 1779.

**1989, July 7 *Perf. 14***

| | | | |
|---|---|---|---|
| **1729** A236 | 25c multicolored | .90 | .30 |
| **1730** A236 | 75c multicolored | 1.10 | .85 |
| **1731** A236 | $1 multicolored | 1.40 | 1.10 |
| **1732** A236 | $4 multicolored | 5.50 | 5.50 |

**Size: 114x71mm**

***Imperf***

| | | | |
|---|---|---|---|
| **1733** A236 | $6 multicolored | 6.00 | 6.00 |
| | *Nos. 1729-1733 (5)* | 14.90 | 13.75 |

First Moon Landing, 20th Anniv. A237

Space achievements: 15c, Alan Shepard, 1st American in space, 1961. 35c, Friendship 7, piloted by John Glenn, 1st manned orbit of the Earth, 1962. 45c, Apollo 8 mission, 1st manned orbit of the Moon, 1968. 70c, Lunar rover on Moon, 1972. $1, Apollo 11 mission emblem and Eagle lunar module on the Moon, 1969. $2, Gemini 8-Agena, 1st space docking, 1969. $3, Edward White, 1st American to walk in space, 1965. $4, Apollo 7 mission emblem. No. 1742, Simple flight plan for the Apollo 11 mission. No. 1743, Raising of the American flag on the Moon.

**1989, July 20 *Perf. 14***

| | | | |
|---|---|---|---|
| **1734** A237 | 15c multicolored | .50 | .40 |
| **1735** A237 | 35c multicolored | .60 | .45 |
| **1736** A237 | 45c multicolored | .80 | .60 |
| **1737** A237 | 70c multicolored | 1.00 | .70 |
| **1738** A237 | $1 multicolored | 1.50 | 1.10 |
| **1739** A237 | $2 multicolored | 2.50 | 2.10 |
| **1740** A237 | $3 multicolored | 3.00 | 3.00 |
| **1741** A237 | $4 multicolored | 4.00 | 4.00 |
| | *Nos. 1734-1741 (8)* | 13.90 | 12.35 |

### Souvenir Sheets

| | | | |
|---|---|---|---|
| **1742** A237 | $5 multicolored | 5.50 | 5.50 |
| **1743** A237 | $5 multicolored | 5.50 | 5.50 |

Mushrooms A238

YWCA, Cent. A239

15c, *Hygrocybe occidentalis scarletina.* 40c, *Marasmius haematocephalus.* 50c, *Hygrocybe hypohaemacta.* 70c, *Lepiota pseudoignicolor.* 90c, *Cookeina tricholoma.* $1.10, *Leucopaxillus gracillimus.* $2.25, *Hygrocybe nigrescens.* $4, *Clathrus crispus.*

#1752, *Mycena holoporphyra.* #1753, *Xeromphalina tenuipes.*

**1989, Aug. 17 Litho. *Perf. 14***

| | | | | |
|---|---|---|---|---|
| **1744-1751** | A238 | Set of 8 | 15.00 | 15.00 |

### Souvenir Sheets

| | | | | |
|---|---|---|---|---|
| **1752-1753** | A238 | $6 Set of 2 | 15.00 | 15.00 |

**1989, Sept. 11 *Perf. 14***

| | | | |
|---|---|---|---|
| **1754** A239 | 50c shown | .70 | .70 |
| **1755** A239 | 75c Emblem, horiz. | .90 | .90 |

Butterflies A240

**1989, Oct. 2 *Perf. 14***

| | | | | |
|---|---|---|---|---|
| **1756** A240 | 6c | Orion | .35 | .35 |
| **1757** A240 | 30c | Southern daggertail | .50 | .50 |
| **1758** A240 | 40c | Soldier | .65 | .65 |
| **1759** A240 | 60c | Silver spot | 1.00 | 1.00 |
| **1760** A240 | $1.10 | Gulf fritillary | 1.60 | 1.60 |
| **1761** A240 | $1.25 | Monarch | 1.90 | 1.90 |
| **1762** A240 | $4 | Polydamas swallowtail | 4.00 | 4.00 |
| **1763** A240 | $5 | Flambeau | 4.75 | 4.75 |
| | | *Nos. 1756-1763 (8)* | 14.75 | 14.75 |

### Souvenir Sheets

| | | | | |
|---|---|---|---|---|
| **1764** A240 | $6 | St. Christopher hairstreak | 6.00 | 6.00 |
| **1765** A240 | $6 | White peacock | 6.00 | 6.00 |

Discovery of America, 500th Anniv. (in 1992) — A241

Anniv. and UPAE emblems and various pre-Columbian petroglyphs.

**1989, Oct. 16 Litho. *Perf. 14***

| | | | |
|---|---|---|---|
| **1766** A241 | 45c multicolored | .90 | .90 |
| **1767** A241 | 60c multi, diff. | 1.10 | 1.10 |
| **1768** A241 | $1 multi, diff. | 1.25 | 1.25 |
| **1769** A241 | $4 multi, diff. | 4.75 | 4.75 |
| | *Nos. 1766-1769 (4)* | 8.00 | 8.00 |

### Souvenir Sheet

| | | | |
|---|---|---|---|
| **1770** A241 | $6 multi, diff. | 5.50 | 5.50 |

World Stamp Expo '89, Scenes from *Ben and Me* — A242

Walt Disney characters, story of the American Revolution: 1c, Amos leaves home. 2c, Amos meets young Benjamin Franklin. 3c, Invention of the Franklin stove. 4c, Invention of bifocals. 5c, *Pennsylvania Gazette.* 6c, Franklin at printing press. 10c, Experimenting with electricity. $5, As an American diplomat in England. No. 1779, Amos's "Document of Agreement." No. 1780, Franklin presiding over meeting of the Ben Franklin Stamp Club. No. 1781, 2nd Continental Congress, Philadelphia, 1775.

***Perf. 14x13½, 13½x14***

**1989, Nov. 17 Litho.**

| | | | |
|---|---|---|---|
| **1771** A242 | 1c multi | .25 | .25 |
| **1772** A242 | 2c multi | .25 | .25 |
| **1773** A242 | 3c multi | .25 | .25 |
| **1774** A242 | 4c multi | .25 | .25 |
| **1775** A242 | 5c multi | .25 | .25 |
| **1776** A242 | 6c multi | .25 | .25 |
| **1777** A242 | 10c multi | .25 | .25 |
| **1778** A242 | $5 multi | 5.50 | 5.50 |
| **1779** A242 | $6 multi | 5.75 | 6.00 |
| | *Nos. 1771-1779 (9)* | 13.00 | 13.25 |

### Souvenir Sheets

| | | | |
|---|---|---|---|
| **1780** A242 | $6 multi, vert. | 5.50 | 5.50 |
| **1781** A242 | $6 multi | 5.50 | 5.50 |

Christmas — A243

Paintings by Rubens: 20c, *Christ in the House of Mary and Martha.* 35c, *The Circumcision.* 60c, *Trinity Adored by Duke of Mantua and Family.* $2, *Holy Family with St. Francis.* $3, *The Ildefonso Altarpiece.* $4, *Madonna and Child with Garland and Putti,* by Rubens and Jan Brueghel. No. 1788, *Adoration of the Magi.* No. 1789, *Virgin and Child Adored by Angels.*

**1990, Jan. 4 Litho. *Perf. 14***

| | | | |
|---|---|---|---|
| **1782** A243 | 20c multicolored | .50 | .25 |
| **1783** A243 | 35c multicolored | .65 | .45 |
| **1784** A243 | 60c multicolored | 1.00 | .65 |
| **1785** A243 | $2 multicolored | 2.00 | 2.00 |
| **1786** A243 | $3 multicolored | 2.50 | 2.50 |
| **1787** A243 | $4 multicolored | 3.50 | 3.50 |
| | *Nos. 1782-1787 (6)* | 10.15 | 9.35 |

### Souvenir Sheets

| | | | |
|---|---|---|---|
| **1788** A243 | $5 multicolored | 4.50 | 4.50 |
| **1789** A243 | $5 multicolored | 4.50 | 4.50 |

Anniversaries and Events (in 1989) — A244

Designs: 10c, Alexander Graham Bell, early telephone, telephone lines. 25c, George Washington, the Capitol Building. 35c, William Shakespeare, birthplace, Stratford-on-Avon. 75c, Jawaharlal Nehru, Mahatma Gandhi. $1, Hugo Eckener, Ferdinand von Zeppelin, zeppelin *Delag.* $2, Charlie Chaplin. $3, Ship in port. $4, Pres. Friedrich Ebert, Heidelberg Gate. No. 1798, Concorde jet. No. 1799, Ship, 13th century, vert.

**1990, Feb. 12 Litho. *Perf. 14***

| | | | |
|---|---|---|---|
| **1790** A244 | 10c multicolored | .35 | .25 |
| **1791** A244 | 25c multicolored | .35 | .25 |
| **1792** A244 | 35c multicolored | 1.10 | .55 |
| **1793** A244 | 75c multicolored | 2.00 | 1.60 |
| **1794** A244 | $1 multicolored | 1.40 | 1.40 |
| **1795** A244 | $2 multicolored | 2.75 | 2.75 |
| **1796** A244 | $3 multicolored | 3.00 | 3.00 |
| **1797** A244 | $4 multicolored | 4.25 | 4.25 |
| | *Nos. 1790-1797 (8)* | 15.20 | 14.05 |

### Souvenir Sheets

| | | | |
|---|---|---|---|
| **1798** A244 | $6 multicolored | 6.00 | 6.00 |
| **1799** A244 | $6 multicolored | 6.00 | 6.00 |

Invention of the telephone, 1876 (10c); American presidency, 200th anniv. (25c); 425th birth anniv. of Shakespeare (35c); birth cent. of Nehru (75c); 1st passenger zeppelin, 80th anniv. ($1); birth cent. of Charlie Chaplin ($2); Hamburg, 800th anniv. ($3, No. 1799); Federal Republic of Germany, 40th anniv. ($4); and test flight of the Concorde supersonic jet, 20th anniv. (No. 1798).

Orchids — A245

**1990, Mar. 6 Litho. *Perf. 14***

| | | | | |
|---|---|---|---|---|
| **1800** A245 | 1c | Odontoglossum triumphans | .25 | .25 |
| **1801** A245 | 25c | Oncidium splendidum | .30 | .30 |
| **1802** A245 | 60c | Laelia anceps | .65 | .65 |
| **1803** A245 | 75c | Cattleya trianaei | .80 | .80 |
| **1804** A245 | $1 | Odontoglossum rossii | 1.25 | 1.25 |
| **1805** A245 | $2 | Brassia gireoudiana | 1.75 | 1.75 |

**1806** A245 $3 Cattleya dowiana 2.50 2.50
**1807** A245 $4 Sobralia macrantha 3.25 3.25
*Nos. 1800-1807 (8)* 10.75 10.75

**Souvenir Sheets**

**1808** A245 $6 Laelia rubescens 5.50 5.50
**1809** A245 $6 Oncidium lanceanum 5.50 5.50

EXPO '90 Intl. Garden and Greenery Exposition, Japan.

America Issue — A246

Butterflies, UPAE and discovery of America 500th anniv. emblems: 15c, Southern dagger tail. 25c, Caribbean buckeye. 75c, Malachite. 90c, Orion. $1, St. Lucia mestra. $2, Red rim. $3, Flambeau. $4, Red anartia. No. 1818, Giant hairstreak. No. 1819, Orange-barred sulphur.

**1990, Mar. 16 Litho. *Perf. 14***

**1810** A246 15c multicolored .65 .25
**1811** A246 25c multicolored .80 .25
**1812** A246 75c multicolored 1.25 .80
**1813** A246 90c multicolored 1.40 .95
**1814** A246 $1 multicolored 1.50 1.00
**1815** A246 $2 multicolored 2.00 2.00
**1816** A246 $3 multicolored 3.00 3.00
**1817** A246 $4 multicolored 4.00 4.00
*Nos. 1810-1817 (8)* 14.60 12.25

**Souvenir Sheets**

**1818** A246 $6 multicolored 7.00 7.00
**1819** A246 $6 multicolored 7.00 7.00

Wildlife A247

**1990, Apr. 3 Litho. *Perf. 14***

**1820** A247 10c Caribbean monk seal .50 .30
**1821** A247 15c Little brown bat .55 .30
**1822** A247 45c Norway rat .65 .50
**1823** A247 60c Old-world rabbit .75 .60
**1824** A247 $1 Water opossum 1.00 .90
**1825** A247 $2 White-nosed ichneumon 1.60 1.60
**1826** A247 $3 Little big-eared bat 2.40 2.40
**1827** A247 $4 Mouse opossums 3.25 3.25
*Nos. 1820-1827 (8)* 10.70 9.85

**Souvenir Sheets**

**1828** A247 $6 Old-world rabbit. diff. 5.50 5.50
**1829** A247 $6 Water opossum 5.50 5.50

No. 1826 is vert. Nos. 1828-1829 have multicolored decorative margins contininuing the designs and picturing little brown bat, prehensile-tailed porcupine and mouse opossum (No. 1828) or four-eyed opossum, West Indies manatee and Norway rat (No. 1829).

World War II A248

Designs: 25c, Operation Battleaxe, June 15, 1941. 35c, Allied landing in southern France, Aug. 15, 1944. 45c, US invasion of Guadalcanal, Aug. 7, 1942. 50c, Allied defeat of Japanese army in New Guinea, Jan. 22, 1943. 60c, US forces secure Leyte, Dec. 11, 1944. 75c, US forces enter Cologne, Mar. 5, 1945. $1, Allied offensive to break out of Anzio, May 23, 1944. $2, Battle of the Bismarck Sea, Mar. 3, 1943. $3, US fleet under Adm. Nimitz, Dec. 17, 1941. $4, Allied landing at Salerno, Sept. 9, 1943. $6, German U-boat.

**1990, Apr. 30 Litho. *Perf. 14x13½***

**1830** A248 25c multicolored .40 .40
**1831** A248 35c multicolored .50 .50
**1832** A248 45c multicolored .60 .60
**1833** A248 50c multicolored .70 .70
**1834** A248 60c multicolored .80 .80
**1835** A248 75c multicolored 1.00 1.00
**1836** A248 $1 multicolored 1.50 1.50
**1837** A248 $2 multicolored 1.75 1.75
**1838** A248 $3 multicolored 2.50 2.50
**1839** A248 $4 multicolored 3.50 3.50
*Nos. 1830-1839 (10)* 13.25 13.25

**Souvenir Sheet**

**1840** A248 $6 multicolored 7.00 7.00

Souvenir Sheet

Penny Black, 150th Anniv. — A249

**1990, May 3 Litho. *Perf. 14***

**1841** A249 $6 violet 5.50 5.50

Stamp World London '90.

Stamp World London '90 — A250

Walt Disney characters and British trains.

**1990, June 21 *Perf. 14***

**1844** A250 5c 1925 King Arthur Class .45 .25
**1845** A250 10c 1813 Puffing Billy .45 .25
**1846** A250 20c 1765 Colliery Tram-wagon .60 .25
**1847** A250 45c 1935 No. 2509 Silver Link 1.00 .55
**1848** A250 $1 1948 No. 60149 Amadis 1.50 1.10
**1849** A250 $2 1830 Liverpool 2.25 2.10
**1850** A250 $4 1870 Flying Scotsman 4.00 4.00
**1851** A250 $5 1972 Advanced Passenger Train 4.75 4.50
*Nos. 1844-1851 (8)* 15.00 13.00

**Souvenir Sheets**

**1852** A250 $6 Stockton & Darlington Railway Opening, 1825, vert. 6.50 6.50
**1853** A250 $6 1809 *Catch-Me-Who-Can* 6.50 6.50

Queen Mother, 90th Birthday — A251

**1990, July 5 Litho. *Perf. 14***

**1854** A251 $2 Wearing black hat 2.10 2.10
**1855** A251 $2 shown 2.10 2.10
**1856** A251 $2 Wearing crown 2.10 2.10
*Nos. 1854-1856 (3)* 6.30 6.30

**Souvenir Sheet**

**1857** A251 $6 Like No. 1855 5.00 5.00

1992 Summer Olympics, Barcelona — A252

Character trademark and: 10c, Men's steeplechase. 15c, Equestrian. 45c, Men's 200 meter butterfly. 50c, Field hockey. 65c, Balance beam. 75c, Flying Dutchman Class yachting. $2, Freestyle wrestling. $3, Men's diving. $4, Women's cycling. $5, Men's basketball. No. 1863, Three-day equestrian event. No. 1863A, Men's 10,000 M race.

**1990, July 9**

**1858** A252 10c multicolored .35 .30
**1858A** A252 15c multicolored .45 .35
**1859** A252 45c multicolored .55 .40
**1859A** A252 50c multicolored .80 .60
**1860** A252 65c multicolored .80 .60
**1860A** A252 75c multicolored 1.00 .80
**1861** A252 $2 multicolored 1.75 1.75
**1861A** A252 $3 multicolored 2.50 2.50
**1862** A252 $4 multicolored 3.75 3.75
**1862A** A252 $5 multicolored 4.00 4.00
*Nos. 1858-1862A (10)* 15.95 15.05

**Souvenir Sheet**

**1863** A252 $8 multicolored 6.00 6.00
**1863A** A252 $8 multicolored 6.00 6.00

Nos. 1858A, 1859A, 1860A, 1861A, 1862A, 1863A were not available until 1991.

US Airborne, 50th Anniv. A253

**1990, July 3**

**1864** A253 75c Mass jump 2.50 2.50

**Souvenir Sheets**

**1865** A253 $2.50 Paratrooper landing 2.50 2.50
**1866** A253 $6 Paratroopers 1940, 1990 5.50 5.50

Yellow Goatfish A254

**1990, Aug. 8**

**1867** A254 10c shown .40 .40
**1868** A254 25c Black margate .60 .60
**1869** A254 65c Bluehead wrasse 1.00 1.00
**1870** A254 75c Puddingwife 1.25 1.25
**1871** A254 $1 Foureye butterflyfish 1.50 1.50
**1872** A254 $2 Honey damselfish 1.90 1.90
**1873** A254 $3 Queen angelfish 2.50 2.50
**1874** A254 $5 Cherubfish 4.50 4.50
*Nos. 1867-1874 (8)* 13.65 13.65

**Souvenir Sheets**

**1875** A254 $6 Smooth trunkfish 6.50 6.50
**1876** A254 $6 Sergeant major 6.50 6.50

Birds A255

**1990, Sept. 10 Litho. *Perf. 14***

**1877** A255 15c Tropical mockingbird .45 .45
**1878** A255 25c Gray kingbird .50 .50
**1879** A255 65c Bare-eyed thrush .80 .80
**1880** A255 75c Antillean crested hummingbird 1.00 1.00
**1881** A255 $1 House wren 1.50 1.50
**1882** A255 $2 Purple martin 1.90 1.90
**1883** A255 $4 Hooded tanager 3.50 3.50
**1884** A255 $5 Common ground dove 4.25 4.25
*Nos. 1877-1884 (8)* 13.90 13.90

**Souvenir Sheets**

**1885** A255 $6 Fork-tailed flycatcher 7.50 7.50
**1886** A255 $6 Smooth-billed ani 7.50 7.50

Crustaceans — A256

**1990, Sept. 17**

**1887** A256 5c Coral crab .25 .25
**1888** A256 10c Smoothtail spiny lobster .25 .25
**1889** A256 15c Flamestreaked box crab .25 .25
**1890** A256 25c Spotted swimming crab .25 .25
**1891** A256 75c Sally lightfoot rock crab .60 .60
**1892** A256 $1 Spotted spiny lobster .80 .80
**1893** A256 $3 Longarm spiny lobster 2.40 2.40
**1894** A256 $20 Caribbean spiny lobster 15.00 15.00
*Nos. 1887-1894 (8)* 19.80 19.80

**Souvenir Sheets**

**1895** A256 $6 Spanish lobster 6.25 6.25
**1896** A256 $6 Copper lobster 6.25 6.25

World Cup Soccer Championships, Italy — A257

Players from participating countries.

**1990, Sept. 24**

**1897** A257 10c Cameroun .25 .25
**1898** A257 25c Spain .25 .25
**1899** A257 $1 West Germany .80 .80
**1900** A257 $5 Scotland 3.75 3.75
*Nos. 1897-1900 (4)* 5.05 5.05

**Souvenir Sheets**

**1901** A257 $6 Uruguay 6.00 6.00
**1902** A257 $6 Italy 6.00 6.00

Christmas A258

Paintings by Raphael: 10c, The Ansidei Madonna. 15c, The Sistine Madonna. $1, Madonna of the Baldacchino. $2, The Large Holy Family. $5, Madonna in the Meadow. No. 1908, Madonna of the Veil. No. 1909, Madonna of the Diadem.

**1990, Dec. 31 Litho. *Perf. 14***

**1903** A258 10c multicolored .30 .25
**1904** A258 15c multicolored .30 .25
**1905** A258 $1 multicolored 1.50 1.00
**1906** A258 $2 multicolored 2.40 2.40
**1907** A258 $5 multicolored 5.00 5.00
*Nos. 1903-1907 (5)* 9.50 8.90

**Souvenir Sheets**

**1908** A258 $6 multicolored 6.75 6.75
**1909** A258 $6 multicolored 6.75 6.75

Peter Paul Rubens (1577-1640), Painter — A259

Entire paintings or different details from: 5c, $1, $4, The Brazen Serpent. 10c, Garden of Love. 25c, Head of Cyrus. 75c, Tournament in Front of a Castle. $2, Judgement of Paris. $5, The Kermesse. No. 1918, The Prodigal Son. No. 1919, Anger of Neptune.

**1991, Jan. 31 Litho. *Perf. 14***

| | | | | |
|---|---|---|---|---|
| **1910** | A259 | 5c multicolored | .35 | .25 |
| **1911** | A259 | 10c multicolored | .35 | .25 |
| **1912** | A259 | 25c multicolored | .60 | .25 |
| **1913** | A259 | 75c multicolored | .80 | .60 |
| **1914** | A259 | $1 multicolored | 1.00 | .80 |
| **1915** | A259 | $2 multicolored | 1.60 | 1.60 |
| **1916** | A259 | $4 multicolored | 3.00 | 3.00 |
| **1917** | A259 | $5 multicolored | 4.00 | 4.00 |
| | | *Nos. 1910-1917 (8)* | 11.70 | 10.75 |

**Souvenir Sheets**

| | | | | |
|---|---|---|---|---|
| **1918** | A259 | $6 multicolored | 6.50 | 6.50 |
| **1919** | A259 | $6 multicolored | 6.50 | 6.50 |

Disney Film *Fantasia,* 50th Anniv. — A260

5c, Mickey as Sorcerer's apprentice, walking broom. 10c, Mushroom Dance Ensemble from The Nutcracker Suite. 20c, Pterodactyls from The Rite of Spring. 45c, Centaurs from The Pastoral Symphony. $1, Bacchus & Jacchus from The Pastoral Symphony. $2, Ostrich ballerina in Dance of the Hours. $4, Elephant dance from Dance of the Hours. $5, Diana, Goddess of the Moon from Dance of the Hours. #1928, Mickey as Sorcerer's apprentice. #1929, Mickey, Leopold Stokowski. $12, Mickey as Sorcerer's Apprentice, vert.

**1991, Feb. 4 Litho. *Perf. 14***

| | | | | |
|---|---|---|---|---|
| **1920** | A260 | 5c multicolored | .75 | .25 |
| **1921** | A260 | 10c multicolored | .75 | .25 |
| **1922** | A260 | 20c multicolored | 1.10 | .25 |
| **1923** | A260 | 45c multicolored | 1.25 | .55 |
| **1924** | A260 | $1 multicolored | 1.75 | 1.75 |
| **1925** | A260 | $2 multicolored | 2.75 | 2.75 |
| **1926** | A260 | $4 multicolored | 5.00 | 5.00 |
| **1927** | A260 | $5 multicolored | 6.50 | 6.50 |
| | | *Nos. 1920-1927 (8)* | 19.85 | 17.30 |

**Souvenir Sheets**

| | | | | |
|---|---|---|---|---|
| **1928** | A260 | $6 multicolored | 8.50 | 8.50 |
| **1929** | A260 | $6 multicolored | 8.50 | 8.50 |
| **1930** | A260 | $12 multicolored | 16.50 | 16.50 |

Butterflies A261

5c, Adelphia iphicla. 10c, Nymphalidae claudina. 15c, Brassolidae polyxena. 20c, Zebra longwing. 25c, Marpesia corinna. 30c, Morpho hecuba. 45c, Morpho rhetenor. 50c, Dismorphia spio. 60c, Prepona omphale. 70c, Morpho anaxibia. 75c, Marpesia iole. $1, Metalmark. $2, Morpho cisseis. $3, Danaidae plexippus. $4, Morpho achilleana. $5, Calliona argenissa. #1947, Anteos clorinde. #1948, Haetera piera. #1949, Papilio cresphontes. #1950, Prepona pheridames.

**1991, Apr. 8 Litho. *Perf. 14***

| | | | | |
|---|---|---|---|---|
| **1931** | A261 | 5c multicolored | .45 | .40 |
| **1932** | A261 | 10c multicolored | .50 | .40 |
| **1933** | A261 | 15c multicolored | .55 | .40 |
| **1934** | A261 | 20c multicolored | .60 | .30 |
| **1935** | A261 | 25c multicolored | .65 | .30 |
| **1936** | A261 | 30c multicolored | .70 | .30 |
| **1937** | A261 | 45c multicolored | .80 | .50 |
| **1938** | A261 | 50c multicolored | .85 | .55 |
| **1939** | A261 | 60c multicolored | 1.00 | .65 |
| **1940** | A261 | 70c multicolored | 1.10 | .80 |
| **1941** | A261 | 75c multicolored | 1.50 | 1.50 |
| **1942** | A261 | $1 multicolored | 1.60 | 1.60 |
| **1943** | A261 | $2 multicolored | 2.25 | 2.25 |
| **1944** | A261 | $3 multicolored | 3.25 | 3.25 |
| **1945** | A261 | $4 multicolored | 4.50 | 4.50 |
| **1946** | A261 | $5 multicolored | 5.75 | 5.75 |
| | | *Nos. 1931-1946 (16)* | 26.05 | 23.45 |

**Souvenir Sheets**

| | | | | |
|---|---|---|---|---|
| **1947** | A261 | $6 multicolored | 7.00 | 7.00 |
| **1948** | A261 | $6 multicolored | 7.00 | 7.00 |
| **1949** | A261 | $6 multicolored | 7.00 | 7.00 |
| **1950** | A261 | $6 multicolored | 7.00 | 7.00 |

Voyages of Discovery A262

Explorer's ships: 5c, Vitus Bering, 1728-1729. 10c, Louis de Bougainville, 1766-1769. 25c, Polynesians. 50c, Alvaro de Mendana, 1567-1569. $1, Charles Darwin, 1831-1835. $2, Capt. James Cook, 1768-1771. $4, Capt. Willem Schouten, 1615-1617. $5, Abel Tasman, 1642-1644. No. 1959, Columbus' ship Santa Maria. No. 1960, Loss of Santa Maria.

**1991, Apr. 29**

| | | | | |
|---|---|---|---|---|
| **1951** | A262 | 5c multicolored | .50 | .40 |
| **1952** | A262 | 10c multicolored | .50 | .40 |
| **1953** | A262 | 25c multicolored | .50 | .30 |
| **1954** | A262 | 50c multicolored | .90 | .50 |
| **1955** | A262 | $1 multicolored | 1.50 | 1.25 |
| **1956** | A262 | $2 multicolored | 2.75 | 2.50 |
| **1957** | A262 | $4 multicolored | 3.75 | 3.75 |
| **1958** | A262 | $5 multicolored | 4.75 | 4.75 |
| | | *Nos. 1951-1958 (8)* | 15.15 | 13.85 |

**Souvenir Sheets**

| | | | | |
|---|---|---|---|---|
| **1959** | A262 | $6 multicolored | 6.50 | 6.50 |
| **1960** | A262 | $6 multicolored | 6.50 | 6.50 |

Discovery of America, 500th anniv. (in 1992).

PHILANIPPON '91 — A263

Walt Disney characters celebrating festivals of Japan: 5c, Daisy Duck and Minnie Mouse, Peach Fete, Festival of the Dolls. 10c, Morty and Ferdie, Tango Festival, Boys' Day Festival. 20c, Mickey, Minnie Mouse, Hoshi-Matsuri, Star Festival. 45c, Minnie, Daisy folk dancing at Bon-Odori Summer Festival. $1, Huey, Dewey and Louie wearing Eboshi headdresses at Yari-Matsuri, Spear Festival of Ohji. $2, Mickey, Goofy pulling Daisy, Minnie in Yamaboko, Gion Festival of Kyoto. $4, Minnie, Daisy preparing rice broth for Nanakusa, Festival of the Seven Plants. $5, Huey, Dewey floating straw boat at O-Bon, Festival of Lanterns. No. 1969, Goofy, Tori-No-Hichi or Rake Festival, vert. No. 1970, Minnie Mouse, Japanese New Year, vert. No. 1971, Mickey, Snow Festival, vert.

**1991, May 6 Litho. *Perf. 13½x14***

| | | | | |
|---|---|---|---|---|
| **1961** | A263 | 5c multicolored | .45 | .25 |
| **1962** | A263 | 10c multicolored | .45 | .25 |
| **1963** | A263 | 20c multicolored | .95 | .25 |
| **1964** | A263 | 45c multicolored | 1.25 | .80 |
| **1965** | A263 | $1 multicolored | 2.25 | 1.25 |
| **1966** | A263 | $2 multicolored | 3.00 | 3.00 |
| **1967** | A263 | $4 multicolored | 4.25 | 4.25 |
| **1968** | A263 | $5 multicolored | 5.00 | 5.00 |
| | | *Nos. 1961-1968 (8)* | 17.60 | 15.05 |

**Souvenir Sheets**

| | | | | |
|---|---|---|---|---|
| **1969** | A263 | $6 multicolored | 5.75 | 5.75 |
| **1970** | A263 | $6 multicolored | 5.75 | 5.75 |
| **1971** | A263 | $6 multicolored | 5.75 | 5.75 |

Paintings by Vincent Van Gogh — A264

Designs: 20c, Blossoming Almond Branch in a Glass, vert. 25c, La Mousme, Sitting, vert. 30c, Still Life with Red Cabbages and Onions. 40c, Japonaiserie: Flowering Plum Tree, vert. 45c, Japonaiserie: Bridge in Rain, vert. 60c, Still Life with Basket of Apples. 75c, Italian Woman (Agostina Segatori), vert. $1, The Painter on His Way to Work, vert. $2, Portrait of Pere Tanguy, vert. $3, Still Life with Plaster Statuette, a Rose and Two Novels, vert. $4, Still Life: Bottle, Lemons and Oranges. $5, Orchard with Blossoming Apricot Trees. No. 1984, Farmhouse in a Wheatfield. No. 1985, The "Roubine du Roi" Canal with Washerwoman, vert. No. 1986, Japonaiserie: Oiran, vert. No. 1987, The Gleize Bridge over the Viguerat Canal. No. 1988, Rocks with Oak Tree.

**1991, May 13 Litho. *Perf. 13½***

| | | | | |
|---|---|---|---|---|
| **1972** | A264 | 20c multicolored | .50 | .25 |
| **1973** | A264 | 25c multicolored | .50 | .25 |
| **1974** | A264 | 30c multicolored | .55 | .30 |
| **1975** | A264 | 40c multicolored | .75 | .40 |
| **1976** | A264 | 45c multicolored | .75 | .50 |
| **1977** | A264 | 60c multicolored | 1.00 | .70 |
| **1978** | A264 | 75c multicolored | 1.10 | 1.00 |
| **1979** | A264 | $1 multicolored | 1.25 | 1.25 |
| **1980** | A264 | $2 multicolored | 1.60 | 1.60 |
| **1981** | A264 | $3 multicolored | 2.40 | 2.40 |
| **1982** | A264 | $4 multicolored | 3.25 | 3.25 |
| **1983** | A264 | $5 multicolored | 4.00 | 4.00 |
| | | *Nos. 1972-1983 (12)* | 17.65 | 15.90 |

**Size: 100x75mm, 75x100mm**

***Imperf***

| | | | | |
|---|---|---|---|---|
| **1984-1988** | A264 | $6 each | 5.00 | 5.00 |

Mushrooms A265

Designs: 15c, Psilocybe cubensis. 25c, Leptonia caeruleocapitata. 65c, Cystolepiota eriophora. 75c, Chlorophyllum molybdites. $1, Xerocomus hypoxanthus. $2, Volvariella cubensis. $4, Xerocomus coccolobae. $5, Pluteus chrysophlebius. No. 1997, Hygrocybe miniata. No. 1998, Psathyrella tuberculata.

**1991, June 1 *Perf. 14***

| | | | | |
|---|---|---|---|---|
| **1989** | A265 | 15c multicolored | .70 | .30 |
| **1990** | A265 | 25c multicolored | .85 | .30 |
| **1991** | A265 | 65c multicolored | 1.25 | .75 |
| **1992** | A265 | 75c multicolored | 1.50 | 1.00 |
| **1993** | A265 | $1 multicolored | 1.75 | 1.00 |
| **1994** | A265 | $2 multicolored | 2.00 | 2.00 |
| **1995** | A265 | $4 multicolored | 4.25 | 4.25 |
| **1996** | A265 | $5 multicolored | 4.75 | 4.75 |
| | | *Nos. 1989-1996 (8)* | 17.05 | 14.35 |

**Souvenir Sheet**

| | | | | |
|---|---|---|---|---|
| **1997** | A265 | $6 multicolored | 8.25 | 8.25 |
| **1998** | A265 | $6 multicolored | 8.25 | 8.25 |

Miniature Sheets

Exploration of Mars — A266

Designs (all different): No. 1999: a, Johannes Kepler, 1571-1630. b, Galileo Galilei, 1564-1642. c, Martian canals drawn by Giovanni Schiaparelli, 1886. d, Sir William Herschel, 1738-1882. e, Mars, planets. f, Percival Lowell at telescope. g, Mariner 4. h, Mars 2. i, Mars 3.

No. 2000: a, e, Profiles of Mars. b, Olympus Mons. c, Dusty face of Mars. d, Martian moon Phobos. f, Martian moon Deimos. g, Nix Olympica. h, Terrain feature resembling human face. i, South Polar Cap.

No. 2001: a, Mars from Phobus. b, Martian dusk. c, "Voyager descent." d, Viking 2 lander on Mars. e, f, Martian landscape. g, h, i, Panorama view from Viking 2 lander.

No. 2002: a, b, Mariner 9. c, Mars. d, Polar cycle. e, Plain of Sinai. f, South pole. g, Nix Olympica. h, Martian surface. i, Outflow channel.

No. 2003, Phobos spacecraft over Mars. No. 2004, Future spacecraft. No. 2005, Future spacecraft, Mars.

**1991, June 21 *Perf. 14x13½***

**Sheets of 9**

| | | | | |
|---|---|---|---|---|
| **1999** | A266 | 75c #a.-i. | 4.25 | 4.25 |
| **2000** | A266 | $1.25 #a.-i. | 6.75 | 6.75 |
| **2001** | A266 | $2 #a.-i. | 11.00 | 11.00 |
| **2002** | A266 | $7 #a.-i. | 37.50 | 37.50 |

**Souvenir Sheets**

| | | | | |
|---|---|---|---|---|
| **2003** | A266 | $6 multicolored | 5.00 | 5.00 |
| **2004** | A266 | $6 multicolored | 5.00 | 5.00 |
| **2005** | A266 | $6 multicolored | 5.00 | 5.00 |

**Royal Family Birthday, Anniversary**

Common Design Type

**1991, July 5 Litho. *Perf. 14***

| | | | | |
|---|---|---|---|---|
| **2006** | CD347 | 10c multicolored | .50 | .25 |
| **2007** | CD347 | 15c multicolored | .50 | .25 |
| **2008** | CD347 | 40c multicolored | .95 | .35 |
| **2009** | CD347 | 50c multicolored | 1.50 | .50 |
| **2010** | CD347 | $1 multicolored | 1.75 | 1.50 |
| **2011** | CD347 | $2 multicolored | 2.75 | 1.75 |
| **2012** | CD347 | $4 multicolored | 3.25 | 3.25 |
| **2013** | CD347 | $5 multicolored | 3.75 | 3.75 |
| | | *Nos. 2006-2013 (8)* | 14.95 | 11.60 |

**Souvenir Sheet**

| | | | | |
|---|---|---|---|---|
| **2014** | CD347 | $5 Philip, Elizabeth | 5.25 | 5.25 |
| **2015** | CD347 | $5 Diana, sons, Charles | 5.25 | 5.25 |

10c, 50c, $1, Nos. 2013, 2015, Charles and Diana, 10th Wedding anniversary. Others, Queen Elizabeth II, 65th birthday.

University of West Indies, 40th Anniv. — A266a

Designs: 45c, Marryshow House, Grenada. 50c, Administrative Building, Barbados.

**1991, July 19**

| | | | | |
|---|---|---|---|---|
| **2016** | A266a | 45c multicolored | .85 | .50 |
| **2017** | A266a | 50c multicolored | .90 | .90 |

Anglican High School, 75th Anniv. A267

**1991, July 29**

| | | | | |
|---|---|---|---|---|
| **2018** | A267 | 10c Existing school | .35 | .25 |
| **2019** | A267 | 25c New school design | .60 | .25 |

Railways of the World — A269

Railways of Great Britain: No. 2020a, Stephenson's first engine, 1814. b, George Stephenson (1781-1848). c, Stephenson's Killingworth engine, 1816. d, Locomotion No. 1, 1825. e, Locomotion in Darlington, 1825. f, Opening of Stockton & Darlington Railway, 1825. g, Royal George No. 5, 1827. h, Northumbrian Rocket, 1829. i, Planet Class engine, 1830.

No. 2021a, Old Ironsides, US, 1832. b, Wilberforce, Stockton & Darlington Railway, Great Britain, 1832. c, Stephenson's Der Adler, Germany, 1835. d, Stephenson's North Star, Great Britain, 1837. e, London & Birmingham No. 1, Great Britain, 1838. f, Stephenson's 1st Austrian locomotive, 1838. g, Mud Digger, US, 1840. h, Standard Norris, US, 1840. i, Fire Fly Class, Great Britain, 1840.

No. 2022a, Lion, Liverpool and Manchester, Great Britain, 1841. b, Beuth 2-2-2, Berlin-Anhalt Railway, Germany, 1843. c, Derwent No. 25, Stockton & Darlington Railway, Great Britain, 1845. d, MKpV, WCB, Vienna, 1846. e, First railway in Hungary, Budapest to Vac, 1846. f, Stockton & Darlington, 1846. g, Stephenson's long boiler type, Paris, 1847. h, Baldwin 4-4-0, US, 1850. i, 2-4-0, Germany, 1850. No. 2023, Boiler of Locomotion No. 1. No. 2024, Liverpool & Manchester Railway, Great Britain, 1833.

**1991-92 Litho. *Perf. 14***

**Sheets of 9**

**2020** A269 75c #a.-i. 6.50 6.50
**2021** A269 $1 #a.-i. 9.00 9.00
**2022** A269 $2 #a.-i. 17.00 17.00

**Souvenir Sheet**

**2023** A269 $6 multicolored 7.50 7.50
**2024** A269 $6 multicolored 7.50 7.50

Issued: 75c, #2023, Dec. 2; others, May 7, 1992.

Miniature Sheet

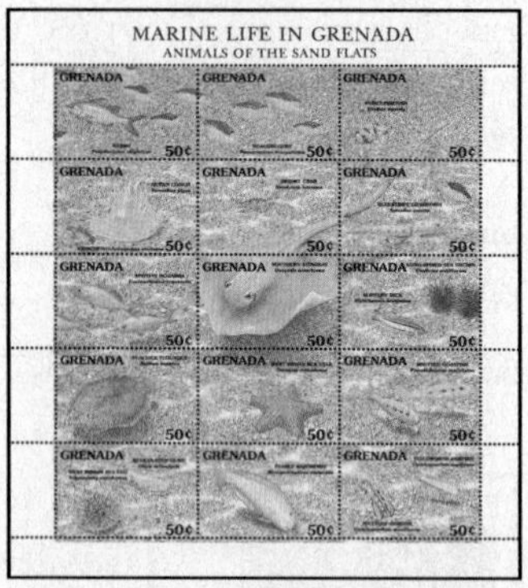


Marine Life in the Sand Flats — A270

Designs: No. 2025a, Barbu. b, Beaugregory. c, Porcupinefish. d, Conchfish, queen conch. e, Hermit crab. f, Bluestripe lizardfish. g, Spotfin mojarra. h, Southern stingray. i, Slippery dick, long-spined sea urchin. j, Peacock flounder. k, West Indian sea star. l, Spotted goatfish. m, West Indian sea egg, reticulated olive. n, Pearly razorfish. o, Mottled and yellowhead jawfish. $6, Shortnose batfish.

**1991, Dec. 5 Litho. *Perf. 14***

**2025** A270 50c Sheet of 15, #a.-o. 12.00 12.00

**Souvenir Sheet**

**2026** A270 $6 multicolored 11.00 11.00

Christmas A271

Details from paintings by Albrecht Durer: 10c, Adoration of the Magi. 35c, The Madonna with the Siskin. 50c, The Feast of the Rose Garlands. 75c, Madonna and Child (Virgin with the Pear). $1, The Virgin in Half-Length. $2, Madonna and Child. $4, Virgin and Child with St. Anne. $5, Virgin and Child, diff. No. 2035, Virgin with a Multitude of Animals. No. 2036, The Nativity.

**1991, Dec. 9 *Perf. 12***

**2027** A271 10c multicolored .40 .25
**2028** A271 35c multicolored .60 .35
**2029** A271 50c multicolored .65 .45
**2030** A271 75c multicolored 1.00 .70
**2031** A271 $1 multicolored 1.10 .90
**2032** A271 $2 multicolored 1.75 1.75
**2033** A271 $4 multicolored 4.00 4.00
**2034** A271 $5 multicolored 4.50 4.50
*Nos. 2027-2034 (8)* 14.00 12.90

**Souvenir Sheets**

***Perf. 14½***

**2035** A271 $6 multicolored 7.00 7.00
**2036** A271 $6 multicolored 7.00 7.00

Thrill Sports — A272

Walt Disney characters enjoying thrill sports.

**1992, Feb. 11 Litho. *Perf. 14x13½***

**2037** A272 5c Windsurfing .45 .35
**2038** A272 10c Skateboarding .55 .35
**2039** A272 20c Gliding .80 .35
**2040** A272 45c Stunt kite flying 1.25 .35
**2041** A272 $1 Mountain biking 1.50 1.00
**2042** A272 $2 Parachuting 2.25 2.25
**2043** A272 $4 Go-carting 4.50 4.50
**2044** A272 $5 Water skiing 5.00 5.00
*Nos. 2037-2044 (8)* 16.30 14.15

**Souvenir Sheets**

**2045** A272 $6 Roller blade hockey 6.00 6.00
**2046** A272 $6 Bungee jumping 6.00 6.00
**2046A** A272 $6 Hang gliding 6.00 6.00
**2046B** A272 $6 River rafting 6.00 6.00

**Queen Elizabeth II's Accession to the Throne, 40th Anniv.**

Common Design Type

**1992, Feb. 6 *Perf. 14***

**2047** CD348 10c multicolored .25 .25
**2048** CD348 50c multicolored .40 .40
**2049** CD348 $1 multicolored .80 .80
**2050** CD348 $5 multicolored 3.50 3.50
*Nos. 2047-2050 (4)* 4.95 4.95

**Souvenir Sheets**

**2051** CD348 $6 Queen at left 5.50 5.50
**2052** CD348 $6 Queen at right 5.50 5.50

Spanish Art — A273

Paintings: 10c, The Corpus Christi Procession in Seville, by Manuel Cabral y Aguado, horiz. 35c, The Mancorbo Channel, by Carlos de Haes. 50c, Countess of Vilches, by Federico de Madrazo y Kuntz. 75c, Countess of Santovenia, by Eduardo Rosales Gallina. $1, Queen Maria Isabel de Braganza, by Bernardo Lopez Piquer. $2, $4, The Presentation of Don John of Austria to Charles V (different details), by Gallina. $5, The Testament of Isabella the Catholic, by Eduardo Rosales Gallina, horiz. No. 2061, Meeting of Poets in Antonio Maria Esquivel's Studio, by Antonio Maria Esquivel y Suarez de Urbina. No. 2062, The Horse Corral in the Old Madrid Bullring, by Manuel Castellano, horiz.

**1992, Apr. 30 Litho. *Perf. 13***

**2053** A273 10c multicolored .35 .25
**2054** A273 35c multicolored .45 .35
**2055** A273 50c multicolored .55 .45
**2056** A273 75c multicolored .80 .65
**2057** A273 $1 multicolored 1.25 .85
**2058** A273 $2 multicolored 1.75 1.75
**2059** A273 $4 multicolored 3.25 3.25
**2060** A273 $5 multicolored 4.00 4.00

**Size: 120x95mm**

***Imperf***

**2061** A273 $6 multicolored 5.50 5.50
**2062** A273 $6 multicolored 5.50 5.50
*Nos. 2053-2062 (10)* 23.40 22.55

Granada '92.

A274

**1992, May 7 Litho. *Perf. 14***

**2063** A274 10c Green-winged parrot .50 .25
**2064** A274 25c Santa Maria .50 .25
**2065** A274 35c Columbus .50 .45
**2066** A274 50c Hourglass .70 .60
**2067** A274 75c Queen Isabella 1.25 1.00
**2068** A274 $4 Cantino map, 1502 4.50 4.50
*Nos. 2063-2068 (6)* 7.95 7.05

**Souvenir Sheets**

**2069** A274 $6 Map, ship, fish 6.75 6.75
**2070** A274 $6 Map, arms, Genoa 6.75 6.75

World Columbian Stamp Expo '92, Chicago.

Discovery of America, 500th Anniv. — A275

**1992 *Perf. 14½***

**2071** A275 $1 Coming ashore 1.40 1.40
**2072** A275 $2 Native, ships 2.50 2.50

Organization of East Caribbean States.

Hummingbirds A276

**1992, May 28**

**2073** A276 10c Ruby-throated .75 .30
**2074** A276 25c Vervain .90 .30
**2075** A276 35c Blue-headed .95 .35
**2076** A276 50c Cuban Emerald 1.25 .50
**2077** A276 75c Antillean Mango 1.50 .75
**2078** A276 $2 Purple-throated carib 1.60 1.60
**2079** A276 $4 Puerto Rican emerald 3.25 3.25
**2080** A276 $5 Green-throated carib 4.00 4.00
*Nos. 2073-2080 (8)* 14.20 11.05

**Souvenir Sheets**

**2081** A276 $6 Rufous-breasted hermit 8.00 8.00
**2082** A276 $6 Antillean crested 8.00 8.00

Genoa '92.

USO, 50th Anniv. — A277

**1992, June 1 *Perf. 14***

**2083** A277 15c Gracie Fields .35 .25
**2084** A277 25c Jack Benny .45 .25
**2085** A277 35c Jinx Falkenburg .50 .40
**2086** A277 50c Frances Langford .65 .50
**2087** A277 75c Joe E. Brown 1.00 1.00
**2088** A277 $1 Phil Silvers 1.25 1.25
**2089** A277 $2 Danny Kaye 2.50 2.50
**2090** A277 $5 Frank Sinatra 5.75 5.75
*Nos. 2083-2090 (8)* 12.45 11.90

**Souvenir Sheets**

**2091** A277 $6 Anna May Wong 6.50 6.50
**2092** A277 $6 Bob Hope 6.50 6.50

1992 Summer Olympics, Barcelona — A278

**1992**

**2093** A278 10c Badminton .50 .30
**2094** A278 25c Women's long jump .50 .25
**2095** A278 35c Women's 100-meter dash .50 .30
**2096** A278 50c Cycling 1.00 .50
**2097** A278 75c Decathlon (pole vault), horiz. 1.00 .70
**2098** A278 $2 Judo, horiz. 1.60 1.60
**2099** A278 $4 Women's gymnastics 3.25 3.25
**2100** A278 $5 Javelin 4.00 4.00
*Nos. 2093-2100 (8)* 12.35 10.90

**Souvenir Sheets**

**2101** A278 $6 Men's floor exercise 5.50 5.50
**2102** A278 $6 Men's vault 5.50 5.50

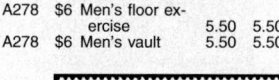

Model Trains A279

Designs: 10c, The Blue Comet, standard gauge, US, 1933. 35c, Switching locomotive, 2-inch gauge, 1906. 40c, B & O Tunnel locomotive, 2-inch gauge, 1905. 75c, Grand Canyon, standard gauge, US, 1931. $1, Lithographed tin streamliner, O gauge, 1930's. $2, Switching locomotive #237, No. 1 gauge, US, 1911. $4, Parlor car, standard gauge, US, 1928. $5, Locomotive #4687 of Improved President's Special, standard gauge, 1927. No. 2111, Engine #3239, No. 1 gauge, US, 1912. No. 2112, Ives engine #1132, 1921.

**1992, Oct. 22 Litho. *Perf. 14***

**2103** A279 10c multicolored .45 .25
**2104** A279 35c multicolored .50 .30
**2105** A279 40c multicolored .50 .35
**2106** A279 75c multicolored .90 .50
**2107** A279 $1 multicolored 1.25 1.00
**2108** A279 $2 multicolored 1.50 1.50
**2109** A279 $4 multicolored 3.00 3.00
**2110** A279 $5 multicolored 3.75 3.75
*Nos. 2103-2110 (8)* 11.85 10.65

**Souvenir Sheet**

***Perf. 13***

**2111** A279 $6 multicolored 6.00 6.00
**2112** A279 $6 multicolored 6.00 6.00

Nos. 2111-2112 contains one 51x40mm stamp.

Souvenir Sheet

Guggenheim Museum, NYC — A280

**1992, Oct. 28 *Perf. 14***

**2113** A280 $6 multicolored 5.00 5.00

Postage Stamp Mega Event '92, NYC.

Christmas
A281

Details or entire paintings: 10c, The Adoration of the Magi, by Fra Filippo Lippi. 15c, Madonna Adoring Child in a Wood, by Fra Filippo Lippi. 25c, Adoration of the Magi, by Botticelli. 35c, The Epiphany-Adoration of the Magi, by Hieronymus Bosch. 50c, Adoration of the Magi, by Giovanni de Paolo. 75c, The Adoration of the Magi, by Gentile da Fabriano. 90c, Adoration of the Magi, by Juan Batista Maino. $1, The Adoration of the Child, by Master of Liesborn. $2, The Adoration of the Kings, by Master of Liesborn. $3, The Adoration of the Three Wise Men, by Pedro Berruguete. $4, The Adoration of the Child, by Filippo Lippi. $5, Adoration of the Child, by Correggio. No. 2126, Adoration of the Magi, by Hans Memling. No. 2127, Adoration of the Magi, by Andrea Mantegna. No. 2128, Adoration of the Shepherds, by De La Tour.

**1992, Nov. 16 Litho. *Perf. 13½x14***

| | | | | | |
|---|---|---|---|---|---|
| **2114** | A281 | 10c | multicolored | .45 | .25 |
| **2115** | A281 | 15c | multicolored | .50 | .25 |
| **2116** | A281 | 25c | multicolored | .55 | .25 |
| **2117** | A281 | 35c | multicolored | .75 | .40 |
| **2118** | A281 | 50c | multicolored | .90 | .50 |
| **2119** | A281 | 75c | multicolored | 1.10 | .80 |
| **2120** | A281 | 90c | multicolored | 1.25 | .90 |
| **2121** | A281 | $1 | multicolored | 1.50 | 1.00 |
| **2122** | A281 | $2 | multicolored | 1.75 | 1.75 |
| **2123** | A281 | $3 | multicolored | 2.75 | 2.75 |
| **2124** | A281 | $4 | multicolored | 3.75 | 3.75 |
| **2125** | A281 | $5 | multicolored | 4.75 | 4.75 |
| | | | *Nos. 2114-2125 (12)* | 20.00 | 17.35 |

**Souvenir Sheet**

| | | | | | |
|---|---|---|---|---|---|
| **2126** | A281 | $6 | multicolored | 6.00 | 6.00 |
| **2127** | A281 | $6 | multicolored | 6.00 | 6.00 |
| **2128** | A281 | $6 | multicolored | 6.00 | 6.00 |

Regattas of the World — A282

Yachts, races: 15c, Matador, Newport News Regatta. 25c, Awesome, Antigua Regatta. 35c, Mistress Quickly, Bermuda Regatta. 50c, Emeraude, St. Tropez Regatta. $1, Diva G, German Admirals Cup. $2, Lady Be, French Admirals Cup. $4, Midnight Sun, Admirals Cup Regatta. $5, Carat, Sardinia Cup Regatta. No. 2137, 1979 Fastnet Race, horiz. No. 2138, Grenada Regatta, horiz.

**1992, Oct. Litho. *Perf. 14***

| | | | | | |
|---|---|---|---|---|---|
| **2129** | A282 | 15c | multicolored | .25 | .25 |
| **2130** | A282 | 25c | multicolored | .25 | .25 |
| **2131** | A282 | 35c | multicolored | .30 | .30 |
| **2132** | A282 | 50c | multicolored | .75 | .40 |
| **2133** | A282 | $1 | multicolored | 1.00 | .75 |
| **2134** | A282 | $2 | multicolored | 1.40 | 1.40 |
| **2135** | A282 | $4 | multicolored | 3.00 | 3.00 |
| **2136** | A282 | $5 | multicolored | 3.75 | 3.75 |
| | | | *Nos. 2129-2136 (8)* | 10.70 | 10.10 |

**Souvenir Sheets**

| | | | | | |
|---|---|---|---|---|---|
| **2137** | A282 | $6 | multicolored | 7.00 | 7.00 |
| **2138** | A282 | $6 | multicolored | 7.00 | 7.00 |

A283

Anniversaries and Events — A284

Designs: 25c, LZ1 on maiden flight, 1900. 50c, Endosat, proposed robot plane. 75c, Konrad Adenauer, factory. $1.50, Golden lion tamarin. No. 2143 Mountain gorilla. No. 2144, WHO emblem and "Heartbeat-the Rhythm of Health." $3, Wolfgang Amadeus Mozart. No. 2146, German flag, map, Adenauer. No. 2147, Voyager 2, Neptune. $5, Count Zeppelin, Graf Zeppelin. $6, Lion's Club emblem, Admiral Richard E. Byrd. No. 2150, Scene from "The Magic Flute." No. 2151, Konrad Adenauer. No. 2152, Earth Summit emblem, northern spotted owl. No. 2153, Count Zeppelin. No. 2154, Satellite rescue, vert.

**1992 Litho. *Perf. 14***

| | | | | | |
|---|---|---|---|---|---|
| **2139** | A283 | 25c | multicolored | 1.50 | 1.50 |
| **2140** | A283 | 50c | multicolored | 1.50 | 1.50 |
| **2141** | A283 | 75c | multicolored | 1.50 | 1.50 |
| **2142** | A283 | $1.50 | multicolored | 3.50 | 3.50 |
| **2143** | A283 | $2 | multicolored | 4.00 | 4.00 |
| **2144** | A283 | $2 | multicolored | 4.75 | 4.75 |
| **2145** | A284 | $3 | multicolored | 5.75 | 5.75 |
| **2146** | A283 | $4 | multicolored | 4.00 | 4.00 |
| **2147** | A283 | $4 | multicolored | 5.50 | 5.50 |
| **2148** | A283 | $5 | multicolored | 8.00 | 8.00 |
| **2149** | A283 | $6 | multicolored | 5.50 | 5.50 |
| | | | *Nos. 2139-2149 (11)* | 45.50 | 45.50 |

**Souvenir Sheets**

| | | | | | |
|---|---|---|---|---|---|
| **2150** | A284 | $6 | multicolored | 6.25 | 6.25 |
| **2151** | A283 | $6 | multicolored | 5.75 | 5.75 |
| **2152** | A283 | $6 | multicolored | 5.50 | 5.50 |
| **2153** | A283 | $6 | multicolored | 5.75 | 5.75 |
| **2154** | A283 | $6 | multicolored | 5.50 | 5.50 |

Count Ferdinand von Zeppelin, 75th anniv. of death (#2139, 2148, 2153). Intl. Space Year (#2140, 2147, 2154). Konrad Adenauer, 25th anniv. of death (#2141, 2146, 2151). Earth Summit, Rio de Janeiro (#2142-2143, 2152). Mozart, bicent. of death (in 1991) (#2145, 2150). Lions Intl., 75th anniv. (#2149).

Issue dates: Nos. 2145, 2150, Oct. Nos. 2140-2141, 2144, 2146-2147, 2149, 2151, 2154, Nov. Nos. 2139, 2142-2143, 2148, 2152-2153, Dec.

Grenada Dove — A285

**1992**

| | | | | | |
|---|---|---|---|---|---|
| **2155** | A285 | 10c | multicolored | 1.00 | 1.00 |

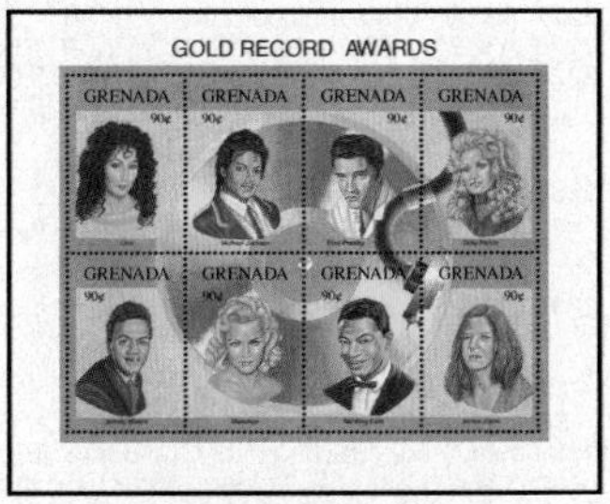


Entertainers — A286

Gold record award winners: No. 2156a, Cher. b, Michael Jackson. c, Elvis Presley. d, Dolly Parton. e, Johnny Mathis. f, Madonna. g, Nat King Cole. h, Janis Joplin.

No. 2157a, Frank Sinatra. b, Perry Como.

No. 2158a, Chuck Berry. b, James Brown.

**1992, Nov. 19 Litho. *Perf. 14***

**Miniature Sheet**

| | | | | | |
|---|---|---|---|---|---|
| **2156** | A286 | 90c | Sheet of 8, #a.-h. | 11.50 | 11.50 |

**Souvenir Sheets**

| | | | | | |
|---|---|---|---|---|---|
| **2157** | A286 | $3 | Sheet of 2, #a.-b. | 7.50 | 7.50 |
| **2158** | A286 | $3 | Sheet of 2, #a.-b. | 7.50 | 7.50 |

Care Bears Promote Conservation — A287

75c, Bear on uncontaminated beachfront. $2, Bear with parasol, butterfly on flower, vert.

**1992, Dec. 15 Litho. *Perf. 14***

| | | | | | |
|---|---|---|---|---|---|
| **2159** | A287 | 75c | multicolored | 1.00 | 1.00 |

**Souvenir Sheet**

| | | | | | |
|---|---|---|---|---|---|
| **2160** | A287 | $2 | multicolored | 4.00 | 4.00 |

Dogs
A288

Designs: 10c, Samoyed, St. Basil's Cathedral, Moscow. 15c, Chow chow, Ling Yin Monastery, China. 25c, Boxer, Traitor's Gate, United Kingdom. 90c, Basenji, Yamma Mosque, Niger. $1, Golden Labrador Retriever, Parliament, Ottawa, Canada. $3, Saint Bernard, Parsenn, Switzerland. $4, Rhodesian ridgeback, Melrose House, South Africa. $5, Afghan, Mazar-i-Sharif, Afghanistan. No. 2169, Alaskan malamute, Alaska. No. 2170, Australian cattle dog, Australia.

**1993, Jan. 20 Litho. *Perf. 14***

| | | | | | |
|---|---|---|---|---|---|
| **2161** | A288 | 10c | multicolored | .70 | .40 |
| **2162** | A288 | 15c | multicolored | .85 | .40 |
| **2163** | A288 | 25c | multicolored | .90 | .40 |
| **2164** | A288 | 90c | multicolored | 1.25 | .75 |
| **2165** | A288 | $1 | multicolored | 1.50 | 1.00 |
| **2166** | A288 | $3 | multicolored | 2.25 | 2.25 |
| **2167** | A288 | $4 | multicolored | 3.00 | 3.00 |
| **2168** | A288 | $5 | multicolored | 3.75 | 3.75 |
| | | | *Nos. 2161-2168 (8)* | 14.20 | 11.95 |

**Souvenir Sheet**

| | | | | | |
|---|---|---|---|---|---|
| **2169** | A288 | $6 | multicolored | 5.75 | 5.75 |
| **2170** | A288 | $6 | multicolored | 5.75 | 5.75 |

Miniature Sheet

Louvre Museum, Bicent. — A289

Paintings by Jean-Antoine Watteau (1684-1721): a, The Faux-Pas. b, A Gentleman. c, Young Lady with Archlute. d, Young Man Dancing. e, Autumn. f, The Judgement of Paris. g-h, Pierrot (diff. details).

No. 2172, The Embarkation for Cythera, horiz.

**1993, Mar. 8 Litho. *Perf. 12***

| | | | | | |
|---|---|---|---|---|---|
| **2171** | A289 | $1 | Sheet of 8, #a.-h. + label | 9.50 | 9.50 |

**Souvenir Sheet**

***Perf. 14½***

| | | | | | |
|---|---|---|---|---|---|
| **2172** | A289 | $6 | multicolored | 7.25 | 7.25 |

No. 2172 contains one 88x55mm stamp.

Moths
A290

**1993, Apr. 13 Litho. *Perf. 14***

| | | | | | |
|---|---|---|---|---|---|
| **2173** | A290 | 10c | Magnificent | .35 | .25 |
| **2174** | A290 | 35c | Metzl's io | .50 | .35 |
| **2175** | A290 | 45c | Owl | .60 | .40 |
| **2176** | A290 | 75c | Pink-spotted hawk | 1.00 | .60 |
| **2177** | A290 | $1 | Faithful beauty | 1.25 | .75 |
| **2178** | A290 | $2 | Green geometrid | 2.50 | 1.50 |
| **2179** | A290 | $4 | Gaudy sphinx | 2.75 | 2.75 |
| **2180** | A290 | $5 | Black witch | 3.50 | 3.50 |
| | | | *Nos. 2173-2180 (8)* | 12.45 | 10.10 |

**Souvenir Sheets**

| | | | | | |
|---|---|---|---|---|---|
| **2181** | A290 | $6 | Titan hawk, vert. | 5.25 | 5.25 |
| **2182** | A290 | $6 | Avocado, vert. | 5.25 | 5.25 |

Flowers — A291

**1993, May 17 Litho. *Perf. 14***

| | | | | | |
|---|---|---|---|---|---|
| **2183** | A291 | 10c | Heliconia | .35 | .25 |
| **2184** | A291 | 35c | Pansy | .50 | .35 |
| **2185** | A291 | 45c | Water lily | .60 | .40 |
| **2186** | A291 | 75c | Bougainvillea | .85 | .60 |
| **2187** | A291 | $1 | Calla lily | 1.00 | .75 |
| **2188** | A291 | $2 | California poppy | 1.50 | 1.50 |
| **2189** | A291 | $4 | Red ginger | 3.00 | 3.00 |
| **2190** | A291 | $5 | Anthurium | 3.75 | 3.75 |
| | | | *Nos. 2183-2190 (8)* | 11.55 | 10.60 |

**Souvenir Sheet**

| | | | | | |
|---|---|---|---|---|---|
| **2191** | A291 | $6 | Christmas rose, horiz. | 5.75 | 5.75 |
| **2192** | A291 | $6 | Moth orchids, horiz. | 5.75 | 5.75 |

Baha'i Shrine, Haifa, Israel — A292

**1993, May Litho. *Perf. 13½x14***

| | | | | | |
|---|---|---|---|---|---|
| **2193** | A292 | 75c | multicolored | 1.90 | 1.90 |

Baha'i faith in Grenada, cent.

Miniature Sheet

Coronation of Queen Elizabeth II, 40th Anniv. — A293

Designs: a, 35c, Official coronation photograph. b, 70c, Queen Consort's Ivory Rod, Queen Consort's Scepter. c, $1, Elizabeth accepting scepter during ceremony. $5, Queen, family, 1960s.

$6, Portrait, by Peter George Greenham, 1965.

**1993, June 2 *Perf. 13½x14***

| | | | | | |
|---|---|---|---|---|---|
| **2194** | A293 | | Sheet, 2 each #a.-d. | 12.00 | 12.00 |

**Souvenir Sheet**

***Perf. 14***

**2195** A293 $6 multicolored 6.25 6.25

No. 2195 contains one 28x42mm stamp.

A294

Anniversaries and Events — A295

Designs: 35c, Telescope. 50c, Willy Brandt, Sen. Edward Kennedy, Mrs. Robert Kennedy, 1973. $4, Astronaut standing on moon. No. 2199, Willy Brandt, Kurt Waldheim. No. 2200, Copernicus. $6, Newspaper headline announcing Brandt's resignation.

**1993, July 1 Litho. *Perf. 14***

**2196** A294 35c multicolored .50 .50
**2197** A295 50c black & brown .75 .75
**2198** A294 $4 multicolored 4.50 4.50
**2199** A295 $5 black & brown 4.25 4.25
*Nos. 2196-2199 (4)* 10.00 10.00

**Souvenir Sheets**

**2200** A294 $5 multicolored 5.50 5.50
**2201** A295 $6 brown & black 5.75 5.75

Nicolaus Copernicus, 450th anniv. of death (#2196, 2198, 2200). Willy Brandt, 1st anniv. of death (#2197, 2199, 2201).

Grenada Carnival, 1992 A296

**1993, July 1**

**2202** A296 35c Public Library, vert. .50 .50
**2203** A296 75c Dancers .95 .95

Public Library, cent. (in 1992) (#2202).

Miniature Sheet

Songbirds — A297

Designs: No. 2204a, 15c, Red-eyed vireo. b, 25c, Scissor-tailed flycatcher (g). c, 35c, Palmchat. d, 35c, Chaffinch. e, 45c, Yellow wagtail. f, 45c Painted bunting. g, 50c, Short-tailed pygmy flycatcher. h, 65c, Rainbow bunting. i, 75c, Red crossbill. j, 75c, Kauai akialoa. k, $1, Yellow-throated wagtail. l, $4, Barn swallow.

No. 2205, Song thrush. No. 2206, White-crested laughing thrush.

**1993, July 13**

**2204** A297 Sheet of 12, #a.-l. 13.00 13.00

**Souvenir Sheets**

**2205** A297 $6 multicolored 5.25 5.25
**2206** A297 $6 multicolored 5.25 5.25

Miniature Sheet

Seashells — A298

Designs: No. 2207a, 15c, Atlantic gray cowrie, Atlantic yellow cowrie. b, 15c, Candy stick tellin, sunrise tellin. c, 25c, Common Atlantic vase. d, 35c, Lightning venus, royal comb venus. e, 35c, Crown cone. f, 45c, Reticulated cowrie-helmet. g, 50c, Barbados miter, variegated turret shell. h, 50c, Common egg cockle, Atlantic strawberry cockle. i, 75c, Measled cowrie. j, 75c, Rooster tail conch. k, $1, Lion's paw, Antillean scallop. l, $4, Dog-head triton.

No. 2208, Dyson's keyhole limpet. No. 2209, Virgin nerite, emerald nerite.

**1993, July 19 Litho. *Perf. 14***

**2207** A298 Sheet of 12, #a.-l. 13.00 13.00

**Souvenir Sheets**

**2208** A298 $6 multicolored 7.00 7.00
**2209** A298 $6 multicolored 7.00 7.00

A299

Picasso (1881-1973): 25c, Woman with Loaves, 1906. 90c, Weeping Woman, 1937. $4, Woman Seated in Armchair, 1947. $6, Three Women at the Spring, 1921.

**1993, July 1 Litho. *Perf. 14***

**2210** A299 25c multicolored .35 .35
**2211** A299 90c multicolored 1.25 1.00
**2212** A299 $4 multicolored 4.00 4.00
*Nos. 2210-2212 (3)* 5.60 5.35

**Souvenir Sheet**

**2213** A299 $6 multicolored 4.75 4.75

A300

1994 Winter Olympics, Lillehammer, Norway: 35c, Gaeten Boucher, speedskating gold medalist, 1984. $5, Norbert Schramm, figure skater. $6, Michela Figini, Sigrid Wolf, Karen Percy, Super G medalists, 1988, horiz.

**1993, July 1**

**2214** A300 35c multicolored .50 .30
**2215** A300 $5 multicolored 4.50 4.50

**Souvenir Sheet**

**2216** A300 $6 multicolored 5.75 5.75

Polska '93 — A301

Paintings: $1, Portrait of Marii Prohaska, by Tytus Czyzewski, 1923. $3, Marysia et Burek a Geylan, by S.I. Wirkiewicz, 1920-21. $6, Parting, by Witold Wojtkiewicz, 1908.

**1993, July 1 Litho. *Perf. 14***

**2217** A301 $1 multicolored 1.25 1.25
**2218** A301 $3 multicolored 3.75 3.75

**Souvenir Sheet**

**2219** A301 $6 multicolored 6.25 6.25

Taipei '93 — A302

Designs: 35c, Fire-breathing dragon, New Year's Fair, Chongqing. 45c, Stone elephant, Spirit Way to Ming Tomb, Nanjing. $2, Marble peifang, Ming Tombs, Beijing. $4, Stone pillar, Nanjing.

Paintings by Han Meilin: No. 2224a, Ornamental cock. b, Tiger cub. c, Owl. d, Cat. e, Gorillas. f, Leopard.

No. 2225, Orangutan.

**1993, Aug. 13 Litho. *Perf. 14***

**2220** A302 35c multicolored .25 .25
**2221** A302 45c multicolored .75 .75
**2222** A302 $2 multicolored 3.25 3.25
**2223** A302 $4 multicolored 6.25 6.25
*Nos. 2220-2223 (4)* 10.50 10.50

**Miniature Sheet**

**2224** A302 $1.50 Sheet of 6, #a.-f. 6.75 6.75

**Souvenir Sheet**

**2225** A302 $6 multicolored 5.50 5.50

**With Bangkok '93 Emblem**

Designs: 35c, Nora Nair, Prasad Phra Thepidon, Wat Phra Kaew. 45c, Stucco deities, Library, Wat Phra Singh. $2, Naga snake, Chiang Mai's Temple. $4, Stucco elephants, Wat Chang Lom.

Thai sculpture: No. 2230a, Horses. b, Wheel of the Law, 7th-8th cent. c, Lanna bronze elephant, 1575. d, Kendi in form of elephant. e, Bronze duck, 14th-15th cent. f, Horseman, 14th-15th cent.

No. 2231, Elephants, horiz.

**1993, Aug. 13**

**2226** A302 35c multicolored .25 .25
**2227** A302 45c multicolored .35 .35
**2228** A302 $2 multicolored 1.50 1.50
**2229** A302 $4 multicolored 3.00 3.00
*Nos. 2226-2229 (4)* 5.10 5.10

**Miniature Sheet**

**2230** A302 $1.50 Sheet of 6, #a.-f. 6.75 6.75

**Souvenir Sheet**

**2231** A302 $6 multicolored 4.50 4.50

**With Indopex '93 Emblem**

35c, Megalithic carving, Sumba Island, Indonesia. 45c, Entrance to Gao Gaja (Elephant Cave), Bali. $2, Loving Mother Bridge, Taroko Gorge Natl. Park. $4, Kala head gateway to Balinese Temple, Northern Bali.

Indonesian sculpture - #2236: a, Kris holder and Kris, 19th cent. b, Hanuman protecting Sita, I. Dojotan of Mas. c, Sendi of Visnu mounted on Garuda, 19th cent. d, Wahana (mini vehicle for votive fig.), 20th cent. e, Mercurial monkey warrior Hanuman, Rodja of Mas. f, Singa (polychrome lion).

No. 2237, Loris.

**1993, Aug. 13 *Perf. 13½x14***

**2232** A302 35c multicolored .25 .25
**2233** A302 45c multicolored .35 .35
**2234** A302 $2 multicolored 1.50 1.50
**2235** A302 $4 multicolored 3.00 3.00
*Nos. 2232-2235 (4)* 5.10 5.10

**Miniature Sheet**

**2236** A302 $1.50 Sheet of 6, #a.-f. 11.00 11.00

**Souvenir Sheet**

**2237** A302 $6 multicolored 5.50 5.50

Miniature Sheet

Italian Soccer Assoc. and Genoa Soccer Club, Cent. — A303

Players for Genoa Soccer Club, each $3: No. 2238a, Vittorio Sardelli. b, Juan Carlos Verdeal. c, Fosco Becattini. d, Julio Cesar Abadie. e, Luigi Meroni. f, Roberto Pruzzo.

No. 2239a, each $3: James K. Spensley. b, Renzo de Vecchi. c, Giovanni de Pra. d, Luigi Burlando. e, Felice Levratto. f, Guglielmo Stabile.

Each $15: No. 2240, 1991 Genoa team photo, horiz. No. 2241, Genoa team emblem.

**1993, Sept. 7 Litho. *Perf. 14***

**Sheets of 6, #a-f**

**2238-2239** A303 Set of 2 40.00 40.00

**Souvenir Sheets**

**2240-2241** A303 Set of 2 37.00 37.00

No. 2240 contains one 48x35mm stamp. No. 2241 contains one 29x45mm stamp.

1994 World Cup Soccer Championships, US — A304

Designs: 10c, Nikolai Larionov, Russia. 25c, Andrea Carnevale, Italy. 35c, Enzo Scifo, Belgium, Soon-Ho Choi, South Korea. 45c, Gary Lineker, England. $1, Diego Maradona, Argentina. $2, Lothar Matthaeus, Germany. $4, Jan Karas, Poland, Julio Cesar Silva, Brazil. $5, Claudio Caniggia, Argentina.

Each $6: No. 2250, Wlodzimierz, Poland. No. 2251, Jose Basualdo, Argentina.

**1993, Sept. 7 Litho. *Perf. 14***

**2242-2249** A304 Set of 8 12.00 12.00

**Souvenir Sheets**

**2250-2251** A304 Set of 2 11.00 11.00

Mickey Mouse, 65th Birthday — A305

Movie clips: 25c, The Band Concert, 1935. 35c, Mickey's Circus, 1936. 50c, Magician Mickey, 1937. 75c, Moose Hunters, 1937. $1, Mickey's Amateurs, 1937. $2, Tugboat Mickey, 1940. $4, Orphan's Benefit, 1941. $5, Mickey's Christmas, 1983.

Each $6: No. 2260, Mickey's Birthday Party, 1942. No. 2261, Mickey's Trailer, 1938.

**1993, Nov. 11 Litho. *Perf. 14x13½***

| | | | | |
|---|---|---|---|---|
| **2252-2259** | A305 | Set of 8 | 12.50 | 12.50 |

**Souvenir Sheets**

| | | | | |
|---|---|---|---|---|
| **2260-2261** | A305 | Set of 2 | 13.00 | 13.00 |

Christmas A306

Woodcuts by Durer: 10c, The Nativity. 25c, "The Annunciation." $1, "Adoration of the Magi." $5, "The Virgin Mary in the Sun."

Paintings by Leonardo Da Vinci: 35c, The Litta Madonna. 60c, Madonna and Child with St. Anne and the Infant St. John. 90c, Madonna with the Carnation. $4, The Benois Madonna.

Each $6: No. 2270, The Holy Family with Three Hares, by Durer. No. 2271, Adoration of the Magi, by Da Vinci.

The 25c actually shows the Adoration of the Magi. The $1 actually shows The Virgin Mary in the Sun. The $5 actually shows The Annunciation.

**1993, Nov. 22 Litho. *Perf. 13½x14***

| | | | | |
|---|---|---|---|---|
| **2262-2269** | A306 | Set of 8 | 10.50 | 10.50 |

**Souvenir Sheets**

| | | | | |
|---|---|---|---|---|
| **2270-2271** | A306 | Set of 2 | 10.50 | 10.50 |

Hugo Eckener (1868-1954) — A307

Graf Zeppelin over: 35c, Vienna. 75c, Pyramids at Giza. $5, Rio de Janeiro. #2275, Flensburg.

**1993, Dec. 21 *Perf. 14***

| | | | | |
|---|---|---|---|---|
| **2272-2274** | A307 | Set of 3 | 5.50 | 5.50 |

**Souvenir Sheet**

| | | | | |
|---|---|---|---|---|
| **2275** | A307 | $6 multicolored | 5.50 | 5.50 |

Royal Air Force, 75th Anniv. A308

**1993, Dec. 21**

| | | | | |
|---|---|---|---|---|
| **2276** | A308 | 50c Lysander | 1.00 | 1.00 |
| **2277** | A308 | $3 Hawker Typhoon | 4.25 | 4.25 |

**Souvenir Sheet**

| | | | | |
|---|---|---|---|---|
| **2278** | A308 | $6 Hawker Hurricane | 5.50 | 5.50 |

Automotive Anniversaries — A309

35c, 1932 Mercedes Benz 370 S Cabriolet. 45c, 1966 Ford Mustang. $3, 1930 Model A Ford Phaeton. $4, Mercedes Benz 300 SL Gullwing.

Each $6: No. 2283, 1903 Ford Model A. No. 2284, 1934 Mercedes Benz 290.

**1993, Dec. 21 Litho. *Perf. 14***

| | | | | |
|---|---|---|---|---|
| **2279-2282** | A309 | Set of 4 | 10.00 | 10.00 |

**Souvenir Sheets**

| | | | | |
|---|---|---|---|---|
| **2283-2284** | A309 | Set of 2 | 10.50 | 10.50 |

1st Benz 4-wheel car, cent. 1st Ford engine, cent.

First Gas Balloon Flight in America, Bicent. A310

Designs: 45c, Lift-off from Philadelphia. $2, Balloon in flight, vert. $6, Blanchard's balloon in flight, diff., vert.

**1993, Dec. 21 Litho. *Perf. 14***

| | | | | |
|---|---|---|---|---|
| **2285-2286** | A310 | Set of 2 | 3.00 | 3.00 |

**Souvenir Sheet**

| | | | | |
|---|---|---|---|---|
| **2287** | A310 | $6 multicolored | 6.50 | 6.50 |

Fine Art — A311

Self-portraits, by Matisse: 15c, 1900. 45c, 1918. $2, 1906. $4, 1900, diff.

Self-portraits, by Rembrandt: 35c, 1629. 50c, 1640. 75c, 1652. $5, 1625-31.

No. 2296, The Painter in His Studio, by Matisse. No. 2297, The Sampling Officials of the Draper's Guild, by Rembrandt, horiz.

**1993, Dec. 31 Litho. *Perf. 13½x14***

| | | | | |
|---|---|---|---|---|
| **2288** | A311 | 15c multicolored | .40 | .25 |
| **2289** | A311 | 35c multicolored | .50 | .25 |
| **2290** | A311 | 45c multicolored | .55 | .40 |
| **2291** | A311 | 50c multicolored | .65 | .45 |
| **2292** | A311 | 75c multicolored | 1.00 | .60 |
| **2293** | A311 | $2 multicolored | 1.75 | 1.60 |
| **2294** | A311 | $4 multicolored | 3.25 | 3.25 |
| **2295** | A311 | $5 multicolored | 4.00 | 4.00 |
| | | *Nos. 2288-2295 (8)* | 12.10 | 10.80 |

**Souvenir Sheets**

| | | | | |
|---|---|---|---|---|
| **2296** | A311 | $6 multicolored | 5.25 | 5.25 |

***Perf. 14x13½***

| | | | | |
|---|---|---|---|---|
| **2297** | A311 | $6 multicolored | 5.25 | 5.25 |

Spice Islands Billfish Tournament, 25th Anniv. — A312

15c, Blue marlin. 25c, Sailfish with angler. 35c, Yellowfin tuna with angler. 50c, White marlin with angler. 75c, Catching a sailfish.

**1993, Dec. Litho. *Perf. 14***

| | | | | |
|---|---|---|---|---|
| **2302-2306** | A312 | Set of 5 | 4.00 | 4.00 |

A313

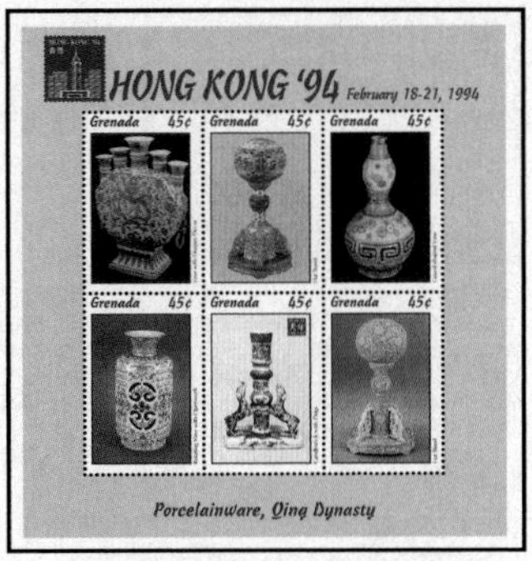


Hong Kong '94 — A314

Stamps, painting, Hong Kong Post Office-1846, by M. Bruce: No. 2307, Hong Kong #263, left detail. No. 2308, Right detail, #1597.

Porcelain ware, Qing Dynasty: No. 2309a, Vase with dragon decor. b, Hat stand. c, Gourd-shaped vase. d, Rotating vase with openwork. e, Candlestick with dogs. f, Hat stand, diff.

**1994, Feb. 18 Litho. *Perf. 14***

| | | | |
|---|---|---|---|
| **2307** | 40c multicolored | .65 | .65 |
| **2308** | 40c multicolored | .65 | .65 |
| *a.* | A313 Pair, #2307-2308 | 1.40 | 1.40 |

**Miniature Sheet**

| | | | | |
|---|---|---|---|---|
| **2309** | A314 | 45c Sheet of 6, #a.-f. | 3.75 | 3.75 |

Nos. 2307-2308 issued in sheets of 5 pairs. No. 2308a is a continuous design.

New Year 1994 (Year of the Dog) (#2309e).

Independence, 20th Anniv. — A315

**1994, Feb. 8 Litho. *Perf. 14***

| | | | | |
|---|---|---|---|---|
| **2310** | A315 | 35c Natl. flag, boat | .80 | .80 |

**Souvenir Sheet**

| | | | | |
|---|---|---|---|---|
| **2311** | A315 | $6 Map of Granada | 6.25 | 6.25 |

Miniature Sheets

Dinosaurs — A316

Jurassic: No. 2312a, Germanodactylus. b, Dimorphodon. c, Ramphorhynchus. d, Apatosaurus (h). e, Pterodactylus. f, Stegosaurus. g, Brachiosaurus. h, Allosaurus (l). i, Plesiosaurus. j, Ceratosaurus. k, Compsognathus. l, Elaphosaurus.

Cretaceous: No. 2313a, Quetzalcoatlus. b, Pteranodon ingens (c). c, Tropeognathus. d, Phobetor. e, Alamosaurus (i). f, Triceratops (e). g, Tyrannosaurus rex (h). h, Tyrannosaurus rex (up close) (l). i, Lambeosaurus. j, Spinosaurus. k, Parasaurolophus (l). l, Hadrosaurus.

No. 2314, Plateosaurus, vert. No. 2315, Pteranodon ingens.

**1994, Apr. 13**

**Sheets of 12**

| | | | | |
|---|---|---|---|---|
| **2312** | A316 | 75c #a.-l. | 7.75 | 7.75 |
| **2313** | A316 | 75c #a.-l. | 7.75 | 7.75 |

**Souvenir Sheets**

| | | | | |
|---|---|---|---|---|
| **2314** | A316 | $6 multicolored | 5.25 | 5.25 |
| **2315** | A316 | $6 multicolored | 5.25 | 5.25 |

Mushrooms A317

Designs: 35c, Hygrocybe acutoconica. 45c, Leucopaxillus gracillimus. 50c, Leptonia caeruleocapitata. 75c, Leucoprinus birnbaumii. $1, Marasmius atrorubens. $2, Boletellus cubensis. $4, Chlorophyllum molybdites. $5, Psilocybe cubensis.

No. 2324, Mycena pura. No. 2325, Pyrrhoglossum lilaceipes.

**1994, Apr. 6**

| | | | | |
|---|---|---|---|---|
| **2316** | A317 | 35c multicolored | .50 | .25 |
| **2317** | A317 | 45c multicolored | .60 | .35 |
| **2318** | A317 | 50c multicolored | .70 | .40 |
| **2319** | A317 | 75c multicolored | .90 | .50 |
| **2320** | A317 | $1 multicolored | 1.25 | .75 |
| **2321** | A317 | $2 multicolored | 1.60 | 1.25 |
| **2322** | A317 | $4 multicolored | 3.25 | 3.25 |
| **2323** | A317 | $5 multicolored | 3.75 | 3.75 |
| | | *Nos. 2316-2323 (8)* | 12.55 | 10.50 |

**Souvenir Sheets**

| | | | | |
|---|---|---|---|---|
| **2324** | A317 | $6 multicolored | 6.00 | 6.00 |
| **2325** | A317 | $6 multicolored | 6.00 | 6.00 |

D-Day, 50th Anniv. A318

Designs: 40c, Sherman Dual-Drive swimming tanks. $2, Churchill "Ark" in operation. $3, Churchill "Bobbin" lays path over soft ground.

$6, Churchill "Avre."

**1994, Aug. 4 Litho. *Perf. 14***

| | | | | |
|---|---|---|---|---|
| **2326-2328** | A318 | Set of 3 | 6.50 | 6.50 |

**Souvenir Sheet**

| | | | | |
|---|---|---|---|---|
| **2329** | A318 | $6 multicolored | 6.25 | 6.25 |

Miniature Sheet

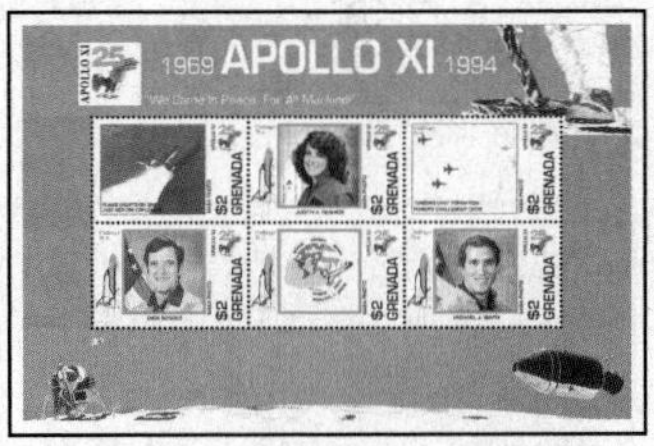


First Manned Moon Landing, 25th Anniv. — A319

Tribute to crew of space shuttle Challenger: No. 2330a, Flame erupting before explosion. b, Judith A. Resnick. c, Aircraft flyover in "Missing Man" formation. d, Dick Scobee. e, Challenger 51-L patch. f, Michael J. Smith.

$6, Crew of mission 51-L.

**1994, Aug. 4**

| | | | | |
|---|---|---|---|---|
| **2330** | A319 | $2 Sheet of 6, #a.-f. | 8.50 | 8.50 |

**Souvenir Sheet**

| | | | | |
|---|---|---|---|---|
| **2331** | A319 | $6 multicolored | 5.25 | 5.25 |

A320

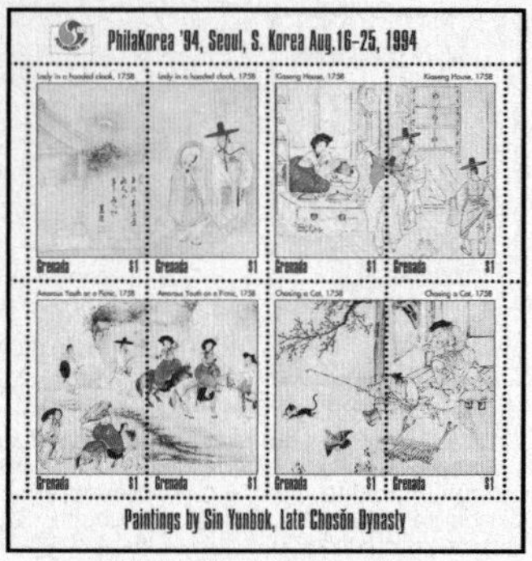


PHILAKOREA '94 — A321

Designs: 40c, Wonson Park & Garden. $1, Port of Pusan. $4, National Theatre, Seoul.

Paintings by Sin Yunbok, Late Choson Dynasty: No. 2335a-2335b, Lady in a Hooded Cloak. c-d, Kiaseng House. e-f, Amorous Youth on a Picnic. g-h, Chasing a Cat.

$6, Roof Tiling, by Kim Hongdo, vert.

**1994, Aug. 4** ***Perf. 14, 13½ (#2335)***

**2332-2334** A320 Set of 3 4.00 4.00

**Miniature Sheet**

**2335** A321 $1 Sheet of 8, #a.-h. 6.00 6.00

**Souvenir Sheet**

**2336** A320 $6 multicolored 4.50 4.50

A322

Orchids: 15c, Brassavola cuculatta. 25c, Comparettia falcata. 45c, Epidendrum ciliare. 75c, Epidendrum cochleatum. $1, Ionopsis utriculariodes. $2, Oncidium ceboletta. $4, Oncidium luridium. $5, Rodriquezia secunda.

Each $6: No. 2345, Ionopis utriculariodes, diff. No. 2346, Onicium luridium, diff.

**1994, Aug. 7** ***Perf. 14***

**2337-2344** A322 Set of 8 11.50 11.50

**Souvenir Sheets**

**2345-2346** A322 Set of 2 12.00 12.00

A323

1994 World Cup Soccer Championships, US: No. 2347a, Tony Meola, US. b, Steve Mark, Grenada. c, Gianluigi Lentini, Italy. d, Belloumi, Algeria. e, Nunoz, Spain. f, Lothar Matthaus, Germany.

Each $6: #2348, Steve Mark, diff. #2349, Poster from 1st World Cup Championships, Uruguay, 1930.

**1994, Aug. 11** ***Perf. 14***

**Miniature Sheet**

**2347** A323 75c Sheet of 6, #a.-f. 5.50 5.50

**Souvenir Sheet**

**2348-2349** A323 Set of 2 10.00 10.00

Fish A324

Designs: 15c, Yellowtail snapper. 20c, Blue tang. 25c, Porkfish, vert. 75c, Foureye butterflyfish. $1, Longsnout seahorse, vert. $2, Spotted moray eel, vert. $4, Fairy basslet. $5, Queen triggerfish, vert.

Each $6: #2358, Queen angelfish. #2359, Squirrelfish.

**1994, Sept. 1**

**2350-2357** A324 Set of 8 9.00 9.00

**Souvenir Sheets**

**2358-2359** A324 Set of 2 10.00 10.00

A325

Intl. Olympic Committee, Cent. — A326

Designs: 50c, Heike Dreschler, Germany, long jump, 1992. $1.50, Nadia Comaneci, Romania, Gymnastics, 1976, 1980.

$6, Dan Jansen, US, 1000-meters long track speed skating, 1994.

**1994, Aug. 4**

**2360** A325 50c multicolored 1.00 1.00
**2361** A325 $1.50 multicolored 2.25 2.25

**Souvenir Sheet**

**2362** A326 $6 multicolored 5.00 5.00

1994, Year of the Dog — A327

Scenes from Disney's Society Dog Show: 2c, Mickey bathing Pluto. 3c, Using atomizer. 4c, Having tail "set." 5c, Putting on mascara. 10c, Having nails done. 15c, Mickey using flea powder on Pluto. 20c, On judge's stand. $4, Judge looking at Pluto. $5, Pluto in chair with first prize.

No. 2372, Pluto wearing "13," first prize ribbon. No. 2373, Little dog beside judge. No. 2374, Pluto with first prize ribbon.

**1994, Sept. 22 Litho.** ***Perf. 14x13½***

**2363-2371** A327 Set of 9 10.00 10.00

**Souvenir Sheets**

**2372-2374** A327 $6 each 4.75 4.75

Butterflies — A328

**1994, Sept. 28** ***Perf. 14***

| | | | | |
|---|---|---|---|---|
| **2375** | A328 | 10c Red anartia | .35 | .25 |
| **2376** | A328 | 15c Ruddy dag-gerwing | .35 | .25 |
| **2377** | A328 | 25c Fiery skipper | .40 | .25 |
| *a.* | | Inscribed "1996" | .40 | .25 |
| **2378** | A328 | 35c Caribbean buckeye | .45 | .40 |
| *a.* | | Inscribed "1996" | .45 | .25 |
| **2379** | A328 | 45c Giant hair-streak | .50 | .40 |
| **2380** | A328 | 50c Zebra longw-ing | .60 | .50 |
| **2381** | A328 | 75c Diadem | .70 | .70 |
| **2382** | A328 | $1 Blue night | 1.25 | 1.25 |
| **2383** | A328 | $2 Orion | 2.25 | 2.25 |
| **2384** | A328 | $3 Orange-barred sulphur | 3.50 | 3.50 |
| **2385** | A328 | $4 Long-tail skipper | 4.50 | 4.50 |
| **2386** | A328 | $5 Polydamas swallowtail | 5.25 | 5.25 |
| **2386A** | A328 | $10 Bamboo page | 10.00 | 10.00 |
| **2386B** | A328 | $20 Queen cracker | 16.50 | 16.50 |
| | | *Nos. 2375-2386B (14)* | 46.60 | 46.00 |

See Nos. 2585-2586.

Intl. Year of the Family A329

**1994, Aug. 4**

**2387** A329 $1 multicolored .90 .90

Order of the Caribbean Community — A330

First award recipients: 15c, Sir Shridath Ramphal, statesman, Guyana. 65c, William Demas, economist, Trinidad & Tobago. $2, Derek Walcott, writer, St. Lucia.

**1994, Sept. 1**

**2388-2390** A330 Set of 3 3.00 3.00

Christmas A331

Paintings, by Zurbaran: 10c, The Virgin and Child with St. John. 15c, The Circumcision. 25c, Adoration of St. Joseph. 35c, Adoration of the Magi. 75c, The Portiuncula. $1, The Virgin and Child with St. John, 1662. $2, The Virgin and Child with St. John, 1658-64. $4, The Flight into Egypt.

Each $6: No. 2399, Adoration of the Shepherds, horiz. No. 2400, Our Lady of Ransom and Two Mercedarians.

**1994, Dec. 5 Litho.** ***Perf. 13½x14***

**2391-2398** A331 Set of 8 7.25 7.25

**Souvenir Sheets**

**2399-2400** A331 Set of 2 10.00 10.00

A332

A333

Birds: 25c, Grenada dove, horiz. 35c, Grenada doves, horiz. 45c, Cuban tody. No. 2404, 75c, Grenada dove, diff. No. 2405, 75c, Painted bunting, horiz. No. 2406, $1, Grenada dove, in flight. No. 2407, $1, Red-legged honeycreeper, horiz. $5, Green jay, horiz.

Each $6: No. 2409, Chestnut-sided shrike-vireo, horiz. No. 2410, Chaffinch, horiz.

**1995, Jan. 10 Litho.** ***Perf. 14***

**2401-2408** A332 Set of 8 13.50 13.50

**Souvenir Sheet**

**2409-2410** A332 Set of 2 11.50 11.50

World Wildlife Fund (#2401-2402, 2404, 2406).

**1995, Jan. 12**

Designs: 25c, Junior Murray, Grenada/W. Indies. 35c, R.B. Richardson, Leeward Isl./W. Indies. $2, A.J. Steward, England, horiz.

No. 2414, West Indies team, horiz.

**2411-2413** A333 Set of 3 3.00 3.00

**Souvenir Sheet**

**2414** A333 $3 multicolored 4.00 4.00

English Touring Cricket, cent.

Water Birds A334

25c, Hooded merganser. 35c, Teal. $1, Harlequin duck. $3, European wigeon.

No. 2419a, King eider. b, Shoveler. c, Long-tailed duck. d, Chiloe wigeon. e, Red-breasted merganser. f, Falcated teal. g, Vericolor teal. h, Smew. i, Red-crested pochard. j, Northern pintail. k, Barrow's goldeneye. l, Stellar's eider.

No. 2420, European wigeon, diff. No. 2421, Egyptian goose.

**1995, Mar. 27 Litho.** ***Perf. 14***

**2415-2418** A334 Set of 4 5.00 5.00

**Miniature Sheet**

**2419** A334 75c Sheet of 12, #a.-l. 9.00 9.00

**Souvenir Sheets**

**2420** A334 $5 multicolored 4.00 4.00
**2421** A334 $6 multicolored 4.50 4.50

New Year 1995 (Year of the Boar) — A335

a, 50c, Pig priest, China. b, 75c, Porcelain pig, Scotland. c, $1, Porcelain pig, Italy.

$2, Jade pig, China.

**1995, Apr. 21 Litho.** ***Perf. 14***

**2422** A335 Strip of 3, #a.-c. 3.00 3.00

**Souvenir Sheet**

**2423** A335 $2 multicolored 3.25 3.25

No. 2422 was issued in miniature sheets containing 3 #2422.

Miniature Sheets of 6 and 8

End of World War II, 50th Anniv. — A336

No. 2423A: b, Great Marianas Turkey Shoot. c, Battle of Midway. d, Battle of the Bismarck Sea. e, Musashi sinks at Leyte Gulf. f, Henderson Field. g, Battle of Guadalcanal.
Fighter planes: No. 2424a, Lavochkin LA7, Soviet Air Force. b, Hawker Hurricane, Royal Air Force (RAF). c, North American P-51D, US Army Air Force (USAAF). d, Messerschmitt ME 109F, Luftwaffe. e, Bristol Beaufighter, RAF. f, Messerschmitt ME 262, Luftwaffe. g, Republic P-47D, USAAF. h, Hawker Tempest V, RAF.
No. 2425, Nose of P-47D. No. 2425A, B-29 bomber.

**1995, May 8**
**2423A** A336 $2 #b.-g. + label 12.00 12.00
**2424** A336 $2 #a.-h. + label 15.00 15.00

**Souvenir Sheets**
**2425** A336 $6 multicolored 7.00 7.00
**2425A** A336 $6 multicolored 6.50 6.50

18th World Scout Jamboree, Holland — A337

Designs: a, 75c, Palm trees, scout. b, $1, Mountain climbing. c, $2, Scout salute, flag.
$6, Canoeing.

**1995, May 8**
**2426** A337 Strip of 3, #a.-c. 3.25 3.25

**Souvenir Sheet**
**2427** A337 $6 multicolored 5.25 5.25
No. 2426 issued in sheets of 9 stamps.

UN, 50th Anniv. — A338

Designs: a, 75c, Man bending sword into plowshare. b, $1, Earth, dove. c, $2, UN Headquarters.
$6, Emblem.

**1995, May 8**
**2428** A338 Strip of 3, #a.-c. 3.25 3.25

**Souvenir Sheet**
**2429** A338 $6 multicolored 5.00 5.00
No. 2428 is a continuous design and was issued in sheets of 9 stamps.

Grenada-Republic of China Friendship — A339

Designs: 75c, Flags of Grenada, Republic of China. $1, Prime Minister Nicholas Brathwaite, Grenada, Pres. Lee Teng-hui, Republic of China.

**1995, Apr. 27 Litho. *Perf. 14***
**2430** A339 75c multicolored 1.25 1.25
**2431** A339 $1 multicolored 1.50 1.50
*a.* Souvenir sheet, #2430-2431 2.75 2.75

Domesticated Animals — A340

Designs: 10c, Cocker spaniel. 15c, Pinto. 25c, Rottweiler. 35c, German shepherd. 45c, Persian. 50c, Snowshoe. 75c, Percheron. $1, Scottish fold. $2, Arabian. $3, Andalusian. $4, C.P. shorthair. $5, Chihuahua.
No. 2444, $5, Manx. No. 2445, $5, Donkey. No. 2446, $6, Shar pei.

**1995, May 3**
**2432-2443** A340 Set of 12 16.00 16.00

**Souvenir Sheets**
**2444-2445** A340 Set of 2 8.00 8.00
**2446** A340 multi 5.25 5.25

Miniature Sheet

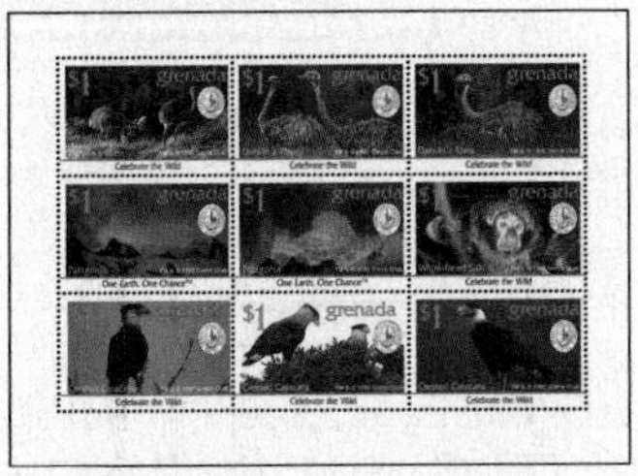

Sierra Club, Cent. — A341

No. 2447, vert, each $1: a, Margay, mouth open. b, Margay seated. c, Margay up close. d, Condor facing left. e, Condor facing right. f, Condor looking back. g, White-faced saki on tree limb. h, White-faced saki, face in light. i, Patagonia Region, South America.
No. 2448, each $1: a, Darwin's rhea, two facing right. b, Darwin's rhea, two facing left. c, One Darwin's rhea. d, Snow covered mountains, Patagonia Region. e, Mountain peaks, Patagonia Region. f, White-faced saki. g, Crested caracara facing right. h, Two crested caracara. i, Crested caracara facing left.

**Sheets of 9, #a.-i.**

**1995, May 5**
**2447-2448** A341 Set of 2 19.00 19.00

FAO, 50th Anniv. — A342

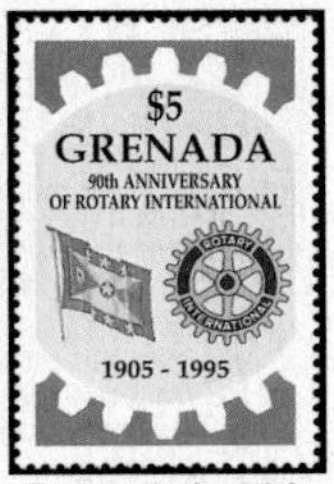


Rotary Intl., 90th Anniv. — A343

No. 2449: a, 75c, Woman with baskets. b, $1, Boy with basket. c, $2, Men working in field.
$6, FAO emblem.

**1995, May 8**
**2449** A342 Strip of 3, #a.-c. 3.25 3.25

**Souvenir Sheet**
**2450** A342 $6 multicolored 5.00 5.00
No. 2449 was issued in sheets of 9 stamps.

**1995, May 8**
**2451** A343 $5 shown 4.25 4.25

**Souvenir Sheet**
**2452** A343 $6 Paul Harris, emblem 5.00 5.00

Queen Mother, 95th Birthday — A344

No. 2453: a, Drawing. b, Holding flower. c, Formal portrait. d, Blue hat, white coat.
$6, As younger woman.

**1995, May 8 *Perf. 13½x14***
**2453** A344 $1.50 Strip or block of 4, #a.-d. 6.75 6.75

**Souvenir Sheet**
**2454** A344 $6 multicolored 6.25 6.25
No. 2453 was issued in sheets of 8 stamps.
Sheets of Nos. 2453 and 2454 exist with black border and text "In Memoriam 1900-2002" overprinted in sheet margins.

1996 Summer Olympics, Atlanta — A345

No. 2455: a, Tian Bingyi, China, badminton. b, Waldemar Leigien, Poland, Frank Wieneke, Germany, judo. c, Nelli Kim, USSR, women's gymnastics. d, Allessandro Andri, Italy, shot put.
No. 2456: a, Jackie Joyner, US, heptathlon. b, Mitsuo Tsukahara, Japan, gymnastics. c, Flo Hyman, US, Zhang Rung Fang, China, volleyball. d, Steffi Graf, Germany, tennis.
Each $6: No. 2457, Sailing. No. 2458, Wilma Rudolph, US, track.

**1995, June 23**
**2455** A345 75c Strip of 4, #a.-d. 3.00 3.00
**2456** A345 $2 Strip of 4, #a.-d. 7.75 7.75

**Souvenir Sheets**
**2457-2458** A345 Set of 2 10.00 10.00

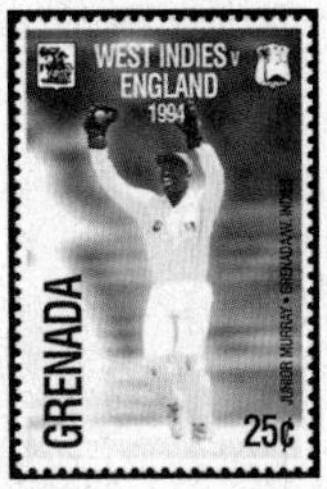


Anniversaries & Events — A346

25c, Junior Murray, cricket player. 75c, Spices. #2461, $1, Sendall Tunnel, cent. #2462, $1, Caribbean Development Bank, 25th anniv.

**1995, Aug. 18 Litho. *Perf. 14***
**2459-2462** A346 Set of 4 3.50 3.50

Miniature Sheet

Trains of the World — A347

No. 2463: a, ETR 450, Italy. b, Isparta to Bozanonu, Turkey. c, TGV, France. d, ICE Inter-City Express, Germany. e, Nishi Nippon Rail, Japan. f, Bullet Train, Japan. g, Standard 4-4-0, Central Pacific RR, US. h, Amatrak 900 Bo-Bo Electric, US. i, Sir Nigel Gresley LNER, Great Britain.
No. 2464: a, Bi Level Vista Dome, Kinki Nippon Rail, Japan. b, Rolios Rail, South Africa. c, Class 460 Bo-Bo, Switzerland. d, The Central, Peru. e, X2000 Tilt Body Train, Sweden. f, Toronto-Vancouver, Canada. g, Talisman 125 Class 31, Great Britain. h, Flying Scotsman, Great Britain. i, Indian Pacific, Australia.
$5, Diesel Hydraulic, Korea. $6, Trans-Mongolian Beijing to Ulan Bator.

**Sheet of 9, #a.-i.**

**1995, Sept. 5**
**2463-2464** A347 $1 #a.-i., each 8.75 8.75

**Souvenir Sheets**
**2465** A347 $5 multicolored 4.25 4.25
**2466** A347 $6 multicolored 5.00 5.00
Singapore '95 (#2463).

Miniature Sheet

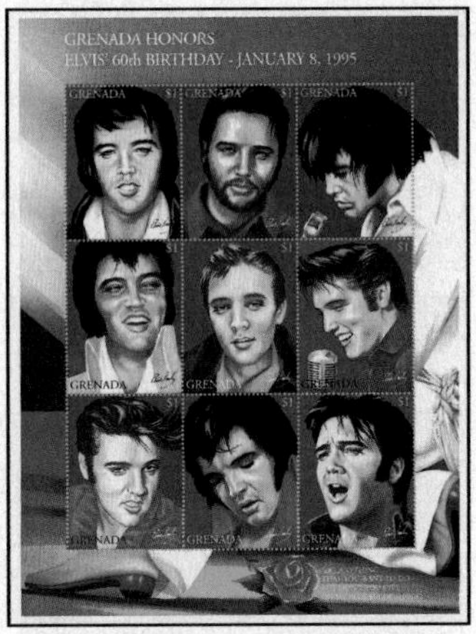


Elvis Presley (1935-77) — A348

Various portraits.

**1995, Sept. 5 *Perf. 13½x14***
**2467** A348 $1 Sheet of 9, #a.-i. 7.50 7.50

A349

Motion Picture, Cent. — A350

No. 2470: a, Film reel, Oscar statuette. b, "HOLLYWOOD" sign. c, Charlie Chaplin. d, Shirley Temple. e, Spencer Tracy, Katherine Hepburn. f, Marilyn Monroe. g, John Wayne. h, Marlon Brando. i, Tom Cruise.
$5, Orson Welles as Citizen Kane, horiz.

**1995, Sept. 5 *Perf. 14***
**2468** A349 75c Marilyn Monroe 1.00 1.00
**2469** A349 75c Elvis Presley 1.00 1.00

**Miniature Sheet**
***Perf. 13½x14***
**2470** A350 $1 Sheet of 9, #a.-i. 8.00 8.00

### Souvenir Sheet
*Perf. 14x13½*

**2471** A350 $5 multicolored 8.75 8.75

Nos. 2468-2469 were each issued in miniature sheets of 16. No. 2470 is a continuous design.

Local Entertainers A351

Designs: No. 2472, 35c, Ajamu, white outfit. No. 2473, 35c, Mighty Sparrow, blue suit. 50c, Mighty Sparrow, black tuxedo. 75c, Ajamu, checkered shirt, sailor hat.

**1995, Sept. 5 Litho. *Perf. 14***
**2472-2475** A351 Set of 4 2.75 2.75

Miniature Sheets

Marine Life — A352

No. 2476: a, Yellowtail damselfish. b, Bluehead wrasse. c, Balloonfish. d, Shy hamlet. e, Orange tube coral. f, Rock beauty.

No. 2477: a, Creole wrasse. b, Queen angelfish. c, Trumpetfish (e, f). d, Barred hamlet. e, Tube sponge (b, f, h, i). f, Porcupine fish. g, Fire coral (d, e, h). h, Fairy basslet. i, Anemone.

Each $6: No. 2478, Elkhorn coral. No. 2479, Common seahorse, gulfweed.

**1995, Apr. 24**
**2476** A352 $1 Sheet of 6, #a.-f. 5.25 5.25
**2477** A352 $1 Sheet of 9, #a.-i. 7.25 7.25

### Souvenir Sheets
**2478-2479** A352 Set of 2 9.00 9.00

Issued: No. 2477, 2478, 4/24/95; Nos. 2476, 2479, 9/19/95.

Mickey's High Sea Adventure A353

Designs: 15c, Mickey sword fighting with pirate. 25c, Mickey with treasure chest. 35c, Minnie trying on jewelry from chest. 75c, Pluto with telescope, Mickey over barrel. $3, Pirate. $5, Mickey holding scarf with Minnie's name.

Each $6: No. 2486, Pirate fox fighting on ratlines. No. 2487, Minnie lowered from pirate ship to Mickey.

**1995, Oct. 2 *Perf. 13½x14***
**2480-2485** A353 Set of 6 8.50 8.50

### Souvenir Sheets
**2486-2487** A353 Set of 2 10.00 10.00

Miniature Sheets

Nobel Prize Fund Established, Cent. — A354

Recipients: No. 2488a, Albert A. Michelson, physics, 1907. b, Ralph Bunche, peace, 1950. c, Edwin Neher, physiology or medicine, 1991. d, Klaus von Klitzing, physics, 1985. e, Johann Deisenhofer, chemistry, 1988. f, Max Delbrück, physiology or medicine, 1969. g, J. Georg Bednorz, physics, 1987. h, Feodor Lynen, physiology or medicine, 1964. i, Walther Bothe, physics, 1954.

No. 2489: a, Hans G. Dehmelt, physics, 1989. b, Heinrich Böll, literature, 1972. c, Georges Köhler, physiology or medicine, 1984. d, Wolfgang Pauli, physics, 1945. e, Sir Bernard Katz, physiology or medicine, 1970. f, Ernest Ruska, physics, 1986. g, William Golding, literature, 1983. h, Hartmut Michel, chemistry, 1988. i, Hans A. Bethe, physics, 1967.

No. 2490: a, James Franck, physics, 1925. b, Gustav Hertz, physics, 1925. c, Friedrich Bergius, chemistry, 1931. d, Otto Loewi, physiology or medicine, 1936. e, Fritz Lipmann, physiology or medicine, 1953. f, Otto Meyerhof, physiology or medicine, 1922. g, Paul Heyse, literature, 1910. h, Jane Addams, peace, 1931. i, Carl F. Braun, physics, 1909.

Each $6: No. 2491, Winston Churchill, literature, 1953. No. 2492, Woodrow Wilson, peace, 1919. No. 2493, Theodore Roosevelt, peace, 1906.

**1995, Oct. 18 Litho. *Perf. 14***
**2488-2490** A354 $1 Sheets of 9, #a.-i., each 8.25 8.25

### Souvenir Sheets
**2491-2493** A354 Set of 3 14.50 14.50

Teresa Teng, Chinese Entertainer A355

Nos. 2495-2496: Various portraits.

**1995, Sept. 29**
**2494** A355 75c shown 1.00 1.00

### Miniature Sheets
**2495** A355 35c Sheet of 16, #a.-p. 5.50 5.50
**2496** A355 75c Sheet of 9, #a.-i. 7.00 7.00

Nos. 2495a-2495p are 24x38mm.

Christmas A356

Details or entire paintings: 15c, The Madonna, by Montagna. 25c, Sacred Conversation Piece, by dei Pitati. 35c, Nativity, by Van Loo. 75c, The Virgin of the Fountain, Van Eyck. $2, Apparition of the Virgin, by Tiepolo. $5, The Holy Family, by Ribera.

Each $6: No. 1503, Madonna with the Christ Child, by Van Dyck. No. 1504, Vision of St. Anthony, by Van Dyck.

**1995, Nov. 28 Litho. *Perf. 13½x14***
**2497-2502** A356 Set of 6 6.50 6.50

### Souvenir Sheets
**2503-2504** A356 Set of 2 10.50 10.50

Liberation of Grenada, 12th Anniv. A357

US Pres. Ronald Reagan and: No. 2505: a, Fort George. b, US, Grenada flags. c, St. George. No. 2506, Island scene, map. No. 2507, Waterfall.

**1995, Dec. 8 *Perf. 14***
**2505** A357 75c Strip of 3, #a.-c. 2.50 2.50

### Souvenir Sheets
**2506** A357 $5 multicolored 5.25 5.25
**2507** A357 $6 multicolored 6.00 6.00

No. 2505 was issued in sheets of 9 stamps.

Pope John Paul II, 1995 Visit to New York City — A358

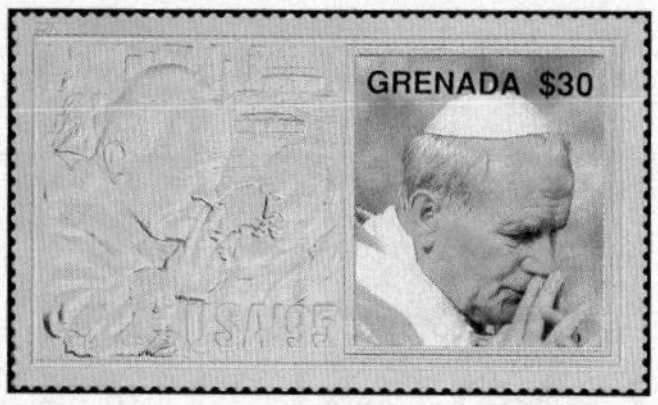


A358a

Pope John Paul II and: No. 2508, Statue of Liberty. No. 2509, St. Patrick's Cathedral.

No. 2510, New York skyline.

**1995, Dec. 13**
**2508** A358 $1 multicolored 1.00 1.00
**2509** A358 $1 multicolored 1.00 1.00

### Souvenir Sheet
**2510** A358 $6 multicolored 5.25 5.25

### Litho. & Embossed
*Perf. 9*

**2510A** A358a $30 gold & multi 30.00

Nos. 2508-2509 were each issued in sheets of 9.

New Year 1996 (Year of the Rat) — A359

Stylized rats: a, green & multi. b, red & multi. c, orange brown & multi.

$1, Two rats, horiz.

**1996, Jan. 2 Litho. *Perf. 14***
**2511** A359 75c Strip of 3, #a.-c. 2.50 2.50

### Miniature Sheet
**2512** A359 75c Sheet of 1 #2511 2.50 2.50

### Souvenir Sheet
**2513** A359 $1 multicolored 1.75 1.75

No. 2511 was issued in sheets of 9 stamps.

Woodcuts by Dürer and Paintings by Rubens A360

Details or entire works: 15c, Young Woman, by Dürer. 25c, Four Horsemen from Apocalypse, by Dürer. 35c, Assumption and Coronation of Virgin, by Dürer. 75c, Mulay Ahmed, by Rubens. $1, Anthony Van Dyck Aged 15, by Rubens. $2, Head of a Young Monk, by Rubens. $3, A Scholar Inspired by Nature, by Rubens. $5, Hanns Dürer, by Dürer.

$5, Martrydom of St. Ursula, by Rubens. $6, The Death and Life of a Virgin, by Dürer.

**1996. Jan. 29 Litho. *Perf. 13½x14***
**2514-2521** A360 Set of 8 10.50 10.50

### Souvenir Sheets
**2522** A360 $5 multicolored 5.00 5.00
**2523** A360 $6 multicolored 5.50 5.50

Disney Dancers — A361

Character, dance: 35c, Goofy, tap dance, vert. 45c, Donald, Mexican hat dance. 75c, Daisy, hula, vert. 90c, Mickey, Minnie, tango. $1, Daisy, Donald, jitterbug, vert. $2, Mickey, Minnie, Ukrainian folk dance. $3, Goofy, Pluto, ballet. $4, Minnie, Mickey, line dancing.

$5, Minnie, the can-can. $6, Scrooge McDuck, Scottish sword dance.

***Perf. 13½x14, 14x 13½***
**1996, Feb. 26 Litho.**
**2524-2531** A361 Set of 8 11.50 11.50

### Souvenir Sheets
**2532** A361 $5 multicolored 5.00 5.00
**2533** A361 $6 multicolored 6.00 6.00

Queen Elizabeth II, 70th Birthday A362

Designs: No. 2534a, 35c, In blue dress. b, 75c, In white hat. c, $4, In black hat.
$6, Younger picture with Prince Phillip.

**1996, May 8 Litho. *Perf. 13½x14***
**2534** A362 Strip of 3, #a.-c. 4.50 4.50

**Souvenir Sheet**

**2535** A362 $6 multicolored 5.25 5.25

No. 2534 was issued in sheets of 9 stamps.

Ferrari Race Cars — A363

Designs: a, 125-F1. b, Tipo 625. c, P4. d, 312P. e, 312, Formula 1. f, 312B.
$6, F333 SP.

**1996, May 8 *Perf. 14***
**2536** A363 $1.50 Sheet of 6, #a.-f. 10.00 10.00

**Souvenir Sheet**

**2537** A363 $6 multicolored 5.75 5.75

China '96, 9th Asian Intl. Philatelic Exhibition (#2536). No. 2537 contains one 85x28mm stamp.

Modern Olympic Games, Cent. A364

Designs: 35c, 1896 Olympic Gold Medal, vert. 75c, Olympic Stadium, Athens, 1896. $2, Ancient Greek Olympic runners. $3, Spiridon Louis, 1896 marathon winner.

**1996, May 8 Litho. *Perf. 14***
**2538-2541** A364 Set of 4 5.00 5.00

See Nos. 2599-2602.

Jerusalem, 3000th Anniv. — A365

Various city gates: 75c, $2, $3.
$5, Buildings inside city, horiz.

**1996, June 26**
**2542-2544** A365 Set of 3 4.75 4.75

**Souvenir Sheet**

**2545** A365 $5 multicolored 4.75 4.75

UNICEF, 50th Anniv. A366

Designs: 35c, Child writing in book. $2, Child planting seedling. $3, Faces of boy, girl.
$5, Boy, vert.

**1996, June 26**
**2546-2548** A366 Set of 3 4.25 4.25

**Souvenir Sheet**

**2549** A366 $5 multicolored 4.00 4.00

Radio, Cent. A367

Entertainers: 35c, Jack Benny. 75c, Gertrude Berg. $1, Eddie Cantor. $2, Groucho Marx.
$6, George Burns, Gracie Allen, horiz.

***Perf. 13½x14, 14x13½***

**1996, June 26**
**2550-2553** A367 Set of 4 4.25 4.25

**Souvenir Sheet**

**2554** A367 $6 multicolored 5.25 5.25

Classic Cars A368

No. 2555: a, 1939 Type 57C Atalante. b, 1900 Cannstatt-Daimler. c, 1925 Delage. d, 1899 Coventry Daimler. e, 1900 Vauxhall. f, 1912 T-15 Hispano-Suza.
No. 2556: a, 35c, 1929 Mercedes-Benz. b, 1935 J. Duesenberg. c, 1914 Mercer. d, 1927 Bugatti Type 35. e, 1929 Alfa Romeo. f, 1910 Rolls Royce.
Each $6: No. 2557, 1915 L-Head Mercer. No. 2558, 1937 Mercedes.

**1996, July 25 Litho. *Perf. 14***
**2555** A368 $1 Sheet of 6, #a.-f. 5.00 5.00
**2556** A368 Sheet of 6, #a.-f. 6.25 6.25

**Souvenir Sheets**

**2557-2558** A368 Set of 2 10.50 10.50

Nos. 2557-2558 each contain one 57x43mm stamp.

Ships A369

War ships, No. 2559, each $1: a, Bounty, Britain, 1788. b, Bismark, Germany, 1941. c, Chuii Apoo, China, 1849. d, F224 Lubeck, Germany, 1970. e, Barbary Corsair, France, 1655. f, Augsburg, Germany, 1970. g, Henri Grace A Dieu, 1514, France. h, Prince of Wales, Britain, 1941. i, Santa Anna, Spain, 1512.
Sailing ships, each $1: No. 2560a, Gorch Fock, Germany, 1916. b, Henry B. Hyde, US, 1886. c, Resolution, Britain, 1652. d, USS Constitution, 1797. e, Nippon Maru, Japan, 1930. f, Preussen, Germany, 1902. g, Taeping, Britain, 1852. h, Chariot of Fame, US, 1853. i, Star of India, US, 1861.
$5, Victory, Britain, 1805. $6, Cutty Sark, Britain, 1869.

**1996, Aug. 14**

**Sheets of 9, #a-i**

**2559-2560** A368 Set of 2 16.00 16.00

**Souvenir Sheets**

**2561** A369 $5 multicolored 4.50 4.50
**2562** A369 $6 multicolored 5.25 5.25

Trains A370

Designs: 35c, C51 Imperial Train, Japan. 75c, Reingold, Germany. $2, Pioneer, US. $3, LA France, France.
Trains of the Orient, each $1: No. 2567: a, C62 4-6-4, Japanese Natl. Railways. b, 4-6-0, Shantung Railways, China. c, C57 Light 4-6-2, Japanese Natl. Railways. d, Diesel Express, Japanese Natl. Railways. e, 4-6-2, Shanghai-Nanking Railway, China. f, 051 2-8-2, Japanese Natl. Railways.
Trains of the world, each $1: No. 2568a, Atlantic Coast Line, US. b, #1619, Pioneer Smith Compound, England. c, 4-8-4 Trans-Siberian Railway. d, "Atlantic type," Palatinate Railway, Germany. e, 4-6-0 Paris, Lyons and Mediterranean Railway, France. f, 0341 Diesel Electric, Italian State Railways.
$5, Baden State Railways, Germany. $6, C11 2-6-4, Japanese National Railways.

**1996, Aug. 28**
**2563-2566** A370 Set of 4 4.50 4.50

**Sheets of 6, #a-f**

**2567-2568** A370 Set of 2 9.00 9.00

**Souvenir Sheets**

**2569** A370 $5 multicolored 4.25 4.25
**2570** A370 $6 multicolored 5.00 5.00

Flowers A371

No. 2571, each $1: a, Winter jasmine. b, Chrysanthemum. c, Lilac. d, Japanese iris. e, Hibiscus. f, Sacred lotus. g, Apple blossom. h, Gladiolus. i, Japanese quince.
No. 2572, vert, each $1: a, Canterbury bell. b, Rose. c, Nasturtium. d, Daffodil. e, Tulip. f, Snapdragon. g, Zinnia. h, Sweetpea. i, Pansy.
$5, Aster. $6, Peony, vert.

**1996, Sept. 9 Litho. *Perf. 14***

**Sheets of 9, #a-i**

**2571-2572** A371 Set of 2 15.00 15.00

**Souvenir Sheets**

**2573** A371 $5 multicolored 5.00 5.00
**2574** A371 $6 multicolored 5.50 5.50

Zeppelins A372

No. 2575: a, 30c, L31, Germany. b, 30c, L35, Germany. c, 50c, L30, Germany. d, 75c, LZ10, Germany. e, $3, L3, Germany. f, $3, Beardmore No. 24, British.
No. 2576: a, Zeppelin L21, Germany. b, Zodiac Type 13 Spiess, France. c, NI "Norge." d, D-LZ 127 "Graf Zeppelin," Germany. e, D-LZ 129 "Hindenburg," Germany. f, Zeppelin NT, Germany, 1996.
Each $6: No. 2577, L13, Germany. No. 2578, Zeppelin ZT, Germany.

**1996, Sept. 9**

**Sheets of 6**

**2575** A372 #a.-f. 7.50 7.50
**2576** A372 $1.50 #a.-f. 8.00 8.00

**Souvenir Sheets**

**2577-2578** A372 Set of 2 10.00 10.00

Birds A373

No. 2579: a, Horned guan. b, St. Lucia parrot. c, Black penelopina. d, Grenada dove. e, St. Vincent parrot. f, White-breasted thrasher.
$5, Barbados yellow warbler. $6, Semper's warbler.

**1996**
**2579** A373 $1.50 Sheet of 6, #a.-f. 8.75 8.75

**Souvenir Sheets**

**2580** A373 $5 multicolored 4.50 4.50
**2581** A373 $6 multicolored 5.25 5.25

Endangered Species — A374

Designs: a, Blue whale. b, Humpback whale. c, Right whale. d, Hawksbill turtle. e, Leatherback turtle. f, Green turtle.

**1996, Sept. 18 Litho. *Perf. 14***
**2582** A374 $1.50 Sheet of 6, #a.-f. 10.00 10.00

Jacqueline Kennedy Onassis (1929-94) — A375

Various portraits.

**1996, Aug. 26**
**2583** A375 $1 Sheet of 9, #a.-i. 8.75 8.75

**Souvenir Sheet**

**2584** A375 $6 multicolored 5.25 5.25

**Butterfly Type of 1994**

90c, Tropical chequered skipper. $1.50, Godman's hairstreak.

**1996, Nov. 7 Litho. *Perf. 12***
**2585** A328 90c multicolored .80 .80
**2586** A328 $1.50 multicolored 1.25 1.25

A376

Sea Creatures: No. 2587, each $1: a, Killer whale. b, Dolphin. c, Dolphins. d, Sea lion, royal angelfish. e, Dolphins, hawksbill turtle. f, Hawksbill turtles (e). g, Royal angelfish. h, Pennant butterflyfish. i, Sea lion, squirrel fish.
No. 2588, each $1: a, Brown pelican. b, Killer whale. c, Whale (c). d, Dolphins, sea lion. e, Shortfin pilot whale, blue ringed octopus, sea lion (d, f, h). f, Hammerhead sharks, sea lion. g, Blue striped grunts. h, Stingray, Van Gogh fusiliers (i). i, Van Gogh fusiliers, golden coney, ribbon moray eel (h).
Each $6: No. 2589, Sea lions, horiz. No. 2590, Dolphins, horiz.

**1996, Nov. 7 *Perf. 14***

**Sheets of 9, #a-i**

**2587-2588** A376 Set of 2 16.00 16.00

**Souvenir Sheets**

**2589-2590** A376 Set of 2 10.00 10.00

Christmas A377

Details or entire paintings: 25c, The Visitation, by Tintoretto. 35c, Virgin with the Child, by Palma Vecchio. 50c, The Adoration of the Magi, by Botticeli. 75c, The Annunciation, by Titian. $1, The Flight into Egypt, by Tintoretto.

$3, The Holy Family with the Infant Saint John, by Andrea Del Sarto.

Each $6: #2597, Adoration of the Magi, by Paolo Schiavo. #2598, Madonna and Child with Saints, by Vincenzo Foppa.

**1996, Nov. 18** *Perf. 13½x14*

**2591-2596** A377 Set of 6 5.50 5.50

**Souvenir Sheets**

**2597-2598** A377 Set of 2 10.50 10.50

**Modern Olympic Games Type of 1996**

Marathon medalists: No. 2599: a, Boughera El Quafi, 1928. b, Gustav Jansson, 1952. c, Spiridon Louis, 1896. d, Basil Heatley, 1964. e, Emil Zatopek, 1952. f, Frank Shorter, 1972. g, Alain Mimoun, 1956. h, Kokichi Tsuburaya, 1964. i, Delfo Cabrera, 1948.

Weight lifting medalists: No. 2600: a, Harald Sakata, 1948. b, Tom Kono, 1952. c, Naim Suleymanoglu, 1988. d, Lee Hyung Kun, 1988. e, Vassily Alexeyev, 1972. f, Chen Weiqiang, 1984. g, Ye Huanming, 1988. h, Manfred Nerlinger, 1984. i, Joseph Depietro, 1948.

$5, Manfred Nerlinger, vert. $6, Thomas Hicks, 1904, vert.

**1996, July 8** **Litho.** *Perf. 14*

**Sheets of 9**

**2599-2600** A364 $1 #a.-i., each 7.75 7.75

**Souvenir Sheets**

**2601** A364 $5 multicolored 4.25 4.25
**2602** A364 $6 multicolored 5.00 5.00

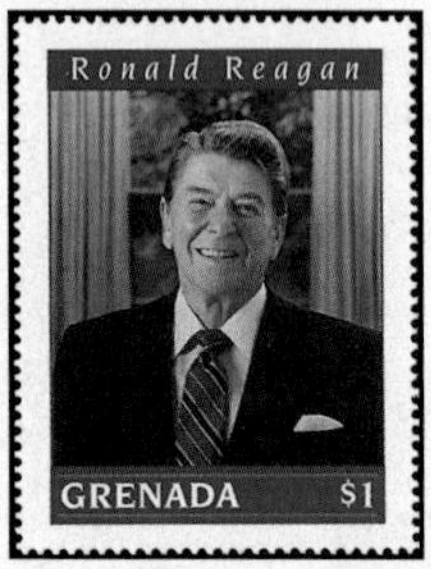


US Pres. Ronald Reagan A378

Various portraits.

**1996, Aug. 26** *Perf. 13½*

**2603** A378 $1 Sheet of 9, #a.-i. 7.25 7.25

Sylvester Stallone in Movie, "Rocky" — A379

**1996, Nov. 21** **Litho.** *Perf. 14*

**2604** A379 $2 Sheet of 3 5.25 5.25

New Year 1997 (Year of the Ox) — A380

Oxen: Nos. 2605a, 2606a, Horns pointed down. Nos. 2605b, 2606b, Horns pointed up. Nos. 2605c, 2606c, Shown.

***Serpentine Die Cut 11***

**1997, Jan. 2** **Litho.**

**Self-Adhesive**

**Sheets of 3**

**2605** A380 $2 #a.-c., gold & multi 4.50 4.50
**2606** A380 $2 #a.-c., sil & multi 4.50 4.50

Mickey Visits Hong Kong — A381

No. 2607: a, Pet birds. b, Kung-fu tea. c, Chinese Wet Market. d, Handmade grasshopper. e, Mid-Autumn Festival. f, Tai-chi.

No. 2608: a, 35c, Tram. b, 50c, Victoria Harbor. c, 75c, Buddha. d, 90c, Bank of China. e, $2, Bottle gas. f, $3, Seafood restaurant.

No. 2609, Mickey at The Peak, vert. $4, Minnie, Mickey, Hong Kong mail, vert. $5, Mickey pulling rickshaw, vert. $6, Mickey at Peking Noodle Show, vert.

**1997, Feb. 12** **Litho.** *Perf. 14x13½*

**2607** A381 $1 Sheet of 6, #a.-f. 7.00 7.00
**2608** A381 Sheet of 6, #a.-f. 8.75 8.75

**Souvenir Sheets**

***Perf. 13½x14***

**2609** A381 $3 multicolored 3.50 3.50
**2610** A381 $4 multicolored 4.25 4.25
**2611** A381 $5 multicolored 5.25 5.25
**2612** A381 $6 multicolored 6.00 6.00

Hong Kong '97.

UNESCO, 50th Anniv. — A382

Designs: 35c, Kyoto, Japan. 75c, Quedlinburg, Germany. 90c, Dubrovnik, Croatia. $1, Ruins, Delphi, Greece. $2, Tomar, Portugal. $3, Palace of Chaillot, Paris, France.

No. 2619, Chinese sites, vert, each $1: a, Entrance to caves, Desert of Taklamakan. b, House, Taklamakan. c, Monument, Taklamakan. d, Palace of Cielos Purpuras, Wudang. e, House, Wudang. f, Stone Guard, Great Wall. g, Ming Dynasty, Wudang. h, Section, Great Wall.

No. 2620, vert, each $1: a, Bryggen Wharf, Bergen, Norway. b, Old City of Bern, Switzerland. c, Warsaw, Poland. d, Fortress Walls, Luxembourg. e, Palace of Drottningholm, Sweden. f, Petäj ävesi Old Church, Finland. g, Vilnius, Lithuania. h, Church of Jelling, Denmark.

No. 2621: a, Cathedral, Segovia, Spain. b, Würzburg, Germany. c, Lakes of Plitvice, Croatia. d, Monastery of Batalha, Portugal. e, River Seine, Paris, France.

Each $6: No. 2622, Monastery of Popocatepetl, Mexico. No. 2623, Shirakami-Sanchi, Japan. No. 2624, Monastery of the Hieronymites and Tower of Belem, Portugal.

**1997, Apr. 3** **Litho.** *Perf. 14*

**2613-2618** A382 Set of 6 7.50 7.50

**Sheets of 8 or 5 + Label**

**2619-2620** A382 Set of 2 15.00 15.00
**2621** A382 $1.50 #a.-e. 7.00 7.00

**Souvenir Sheets**

**2622-2624** A382 Set of 2 11.00 11.00

Cats — A383

Dogs — A384

Cats: 35c, Devon rex. 90c, Japanese bobtail. $2, Cornish rex.

No. 2628: a, Turkish van. b, Ragdoll. c, Siberian. d, Egyptian mau. e, American shorthair. f, Bengal. g, Asian longhair. h, Somali. i, Turkish angora.

**1997, Apr. 10**

**2625-2627** A383 Set of 3 3.50 3.50

**Sheet of 9**

**2628** A383 $1 #a.-i. 8.50 8.50

**Souvenir Sheet**

**2629** A383 $6 Singapura 5.75 5.75

**1997, Apr. 10**

Dogs: 75c, Cavalier King Charles spaniel. $1, Afghan hound. $3, Pekingese.

No. 2633: a, Lhasa apso. b, Rough collie. c, Norwich terrier. d, America cocker spaniel. e, Chinese crested dog. f, Old English sheepdog. g, Standard poodle. h, German shepherd. i, German shorthaired pointer.

No. 2634, Bernese mountain dog.

**2630-2632** A384 Set of 3 4.00 4.00

**Sheet of 9**

**2633** A384 $1 #a.-i. 8.50 8.50

**Souvenir Sheet**

**2634** A384 $6 multicolored 5.75 5.75

Prehistoric Animals — A385

Designs: 35c, Dunkleosteus. 75c, Tyrannosaurus rex. $2, Askeptosaurus, vert. $3, Triceratops, vert.

No. 2639: a, Sordes. b, Dimorphodon. c, Diplodocus. d, Allosaurus. e, Pentaceratops. f, Protoceratops.

Each $6: No. 2640, Maiasaura, vert. No. 2641, Tristychius, Cladoselache, vert.

**1997, Apr. 15**

**2635-2638** A385 Set of 4 6.50 6.50
**2639** A385 $1.50 Sheet of 6, #a.-f. 8.25 8.25

**Souvenir Sheets**

**2640-2641** A385 Set of 2 12.50 12.50

Marine Life A386

Designs: 45c, Porcelain crab. 75c, Humpback whale. 90c, Hermit crab. $1, Great white shark. $3, Green sea turtle. $4, Whale shark.

No. 2648, vert: a, Octopus. b, Lei triggerfish. c, Lionfish. d, Harlequin wrasse. e, Clown fish. f, Moray eel.

Each $6: No. 2649, Pacific barracudas. No. 2650, Scalloped hammerhead shark.

**1997, May 2**

**2642-2647** A386 Set of 6 9.00 9.00
**2648** A386 $1.50 Sheet of 6, #a.-f. 8.50 8.50

**Souvenir Sheets**

**2649-2650** A386 Set of 2 11.50 11.50

Queen Elizabeth II, Prince Philip, 50th Wedding Anniv. A386a

No. 2651: a, Queen, Prince waving. b, Royal Arms. c, Formal portrait in royal attire. d, Formal portrait in street clothes. e, Windsor Castle. f, Prince Philip.

$6, Formal portrait in royal attire, diff.

**1997, May 28** **Litho.** *Perf. 14*

**2651** A386a $1 Sheet of 6, #a.-f. 6.00 6.00

**Souvenir Sheet**

**2652** A386a $6 multicolored 6.00 6.00

Paintings by Hiroshige (1797-1858) A387

No. 2653: a, Nihon Embankment, Yoshiwara. b, Asakusa Ricefields and Torinomachi Festival. c, Senju Great Bridge. d, Dawn Inside the Yoshiwara. e, Tile Kilns and Hasiba Ferry, Sumida River. f, View from Massaki of Suijin Shrine, Uchigawa Inlet and Sekiya.

Each $6: No. 2654, Kinryuzan Temple, Asakusa. No. 2655, Night View of Saruwakamachi.

**1997, May 28** *Perf. 13½x14*

**2653** A387 $1.50 Sheet of 6, #a.-f. 9.50 9.50

**Souvenir Sheets**

**2654-2655** A387 Set of 2 11.50 11.50

Heinrich von Stephan (1831-97), Founder of UPU A388

No. 2656: a, Postal delivery on motorcycle. b, UPU emblem. c, Postal delivery on skis and snowshoes, Rockies, 1900. $6, Chinese long distance carrier.

**1997, May 28** **Litho.** *Perf. 14*

**2656** A388 $2 Sheet of 3, #a.-c. 6.00 6.00

**Souvenir Sheet**

**2657** A388 $6 multicolored 6.00 6.00

PACIFIC 97.

Paul P. Harris (1868-1947), Founder of Rotary, Intl. — A389

Designs: $3, Rotary emblem, vocational training service program, The Philippines, portrait of Harris.

$6, Doves, hands holding globe inscribed "Act with Integrity, Serve with love, Work for Peace".

**1997, May 28**

**2658** A389 $3 multicolored 2.75 2.75

**Souvenir Sheet**

**2659** A389 $6 multicolored 5.25 5.25

Chernobyl Disaster, 10th Anniv. A390

Designs: No. 2660, Chabad's Children of Chernobyl. No. 2661, UNESCO.

**1997, May 28** *Perf. 13½x14*

**2660** A390 $2 multicolored 2.00 2.00
**2661** A390 $2 multicolored 2.00 2.00

Grimm's Fairy Tales A391

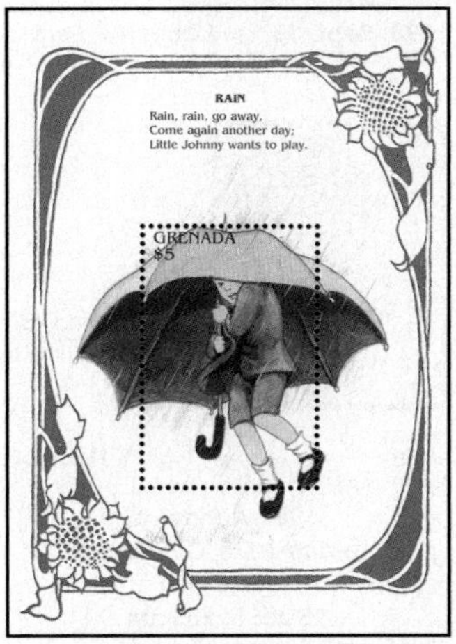

Mother Goose — A392

Scenes from "Snow White and the Seven Dwarfs:" No. 2662: a, Witch as woman looking into mirror. b, Dwarfs looking at Snow White as she sleeps. c, Snow White awakening, Prince. $6, Witch holding out apple for Snow White.

$5, "Little Johnny" walking in rain with umbrella.

**1997, May 28** ***Perf. 13½x14***

**2662** A391 $2 Sheet of 3, #a.-c. 6.25 6.25

**Souvenir Sheets**

***Perf. 14, 13½x14***

**2663** A392 $5 multicolored 4.00 4.00
**2664** A391 $6 multicolored 5.00 5.00

1998 Winter Olympics Games, Nagano A393

Designs: 45c, Luge. 75c, Speed skater in red. $2, Male figure skater. $3, Slalom skier.

No. 2669: a, Luge, diff. b, Ski jumper. c, Downhill skier. d, Speed skater in blue. e, Two-man bobsled. f, Female figure skater. g, Biathlon. h, Hockey. i, Freestyle skier upside down.

Each $6: No. 2670, Downhill skier in air, vert. No. 2671, 4-Man bobsled.

**1997, June 26** ***Perf. 14***

**2665-2668** A393 Set of 4 6.50 6.50
**2669** A393 $1 Sheet of 9, #a.-i. 9.00 9.00

**Souvenir Sheets**

**2670-2671** A393 Set of 2 11.50 11.50

Return of Hong Kong to China — A394

Views of city, Chinese flag as Chinese inscription: 90c, Bank of China, night scene. $1, Skyscrapers. $1.75, "Hong Kong," city in lights, horiz. $2, Deng Xiaoping (1904-97), Hong Kong, horiz.

**1997, July 1**

**2672-2675** A394 Set of 4 7.00 7.00

Nos. 2672-2673 were issued in sheets of 4. Nos. 2674-2675 are 59x28mm and were issued in sheets of 3.

Disney's Hercules A395

No. 2676: a, Hercules. b, Pegasus. c, Megara. d, Philoctetes. e, Nessus. f, Hydra. g, Pain and Panic. h, Hades.

Each $6: No. 2677, Young Hercules. No. 2678, Calliope surrounded by Terpsichore, Melpomene, Clio, Thalia.

**1997, Aug. 7 Litho.** ***Perf. 13½x14***

**2676** A395 $1 Sheet of 8, #a.-h. 7.75 7.75

**Souvenir Sheets**

**2677-2678** A396 Set of 2 13.00 13.00

Butterflies A396

Designs: 45c, Peacock. 75c, Orange flambeau. 90c, Eastern tailed blue. $2, Black and red. $3, Large white. $4, Oriental swallowtail.

No. 2685: a, Brimstone. b, Mocker swallowtail. c, American painted lady. d, Tiger swallowtail. e, Long wing. f, Sunset moth. g, Australian blue mountain swallowtail. h, Bird wing.

Each $5: No. 2686, Monarch. No. 2687, Blue morpho.

**1997, Aug. 12** ***Perf. 14***

**2679-2684** A396 Set of 6 10.00 10.00
**2685** A396 $1 Sheet of 8, #a.-h. 7.50 7.50

**Souvenir Sheets**

**2686-2687** A396 Set of 2 10.50 10.50

1998 World Cup Soccer Championships, France — A397

Various actions scenes from Italy v. West Germany, 1982. 15c, 75c, 90c, $2, $3, $4, vert.

Winning teams: No. 2694, each $1: a, Uruguay. b, Brazil, 1958. c, Germany. d, Argentina. e, Italy. f, West Germany. g, Italy. h, Brazil, 1970.

Soccer players: No. 2695, each $1: a, Seaman, England. b, Klinsmann, Germany. c, Berger, Czech Rep. d, McCoist, Scotland. e, Gascoigne, England. f, Djorkaeff, France. g, Sammer, Germany. h, Futre, Portugal.

Each $6: No. 2696, Beckenbauer, Germany, vert. No. 2697, Moore, England.

**1997** ***Perf. 13½x14***

**2688-2693** A397 Set of 6 10.00 10.00

**Sheets of 8, #a-h**

***Perf. 14x13½***

**2694-2695** A397 Set of 2 14.50 14.50

**Souvenir Sheets**

**2696-2697** A397 Set of 2 12.00 12.00

Minnie Mouse in Hawaiian Holiday — A398

Stamps in flip book sequence showing Minnie doing Hula dance: No. 2698: a, 1. b, 2. c, 3. d, 4. e, 5. f, 6. g, 7. h, 8.

No. 2699: a, 9. b, 10. c, 11. d, 12. e, 13. f, 14. g, 15. h, 16. i, 17.

$6, 18.

**1997, Aug. 7 Litho.** ***Perf. 14x13½***

**Sheets of 8 or 9**

**2698** A398 50c #a.-h. + label 5.50 5.50
**2699** A398 50c #a.-i. 6.00 6.00

**Souvenir Sheet**

**2700** A398 $6 multicolored 8.50 8.50

PACIFIC 97.

Mushrooms — A399

Designs: 35c, Boletus erythropus. 75c, Armillariella mellea. 90c, Amanita flavorubens. $1, Indigo milky. $2, Tylopilus balloui. $4, Boletus parasiticus.

No. 2707, each $1.50: a, Boletus parasiticus, diff. b, Frostis bolete. c, Amanita myscara flavilolvata. d, Volvariella volvacea. e, Stuntz's blue legs. f, Orange-latex milky.

No. 2708, each $1.50: a, Agaricus solidipes. b, Salmon waxy cap. c, Fused marasmius. d, Shellfish-scented russula. e, Red-capped scaber stalk. f, Calocybe tricholoma gambosum.

Each $6: No. 2709, Omphalotus illudens. No. 2710, Agaricus agrenteus.

**1997, Sept. 4** ***Perf. 14***

**2701-2706** A399 Set of 6 8.75 8.75

**Sheets of 6, #a-f**

**2707-2708** A399 Set of 2 16.50 16.50

**Souvenir Sheets**

**2709-2710** A399 Set of 2 11.50 11.50

Orchids A400

Designs: 20c, Paphiopedilum urbanianum. 35c, Trichoceros parviflorus. 45c, Euanthe sanderiana, vert. 75c, Oncidium macranthum, vert. 90c, Psychopsis kramerianum, vert. $1, Oncidium hastatum, vert. $3, Masdevallia saltatrix, vert. $4, Cattleya luteola.

No. 2719, vert, each $2: a, Odontoglossum crispum. b, Cattleya brabantiae. c, Cattleya bicolor. d, Trichopilia suavia. e, Encyclia mariae. f, Angraecum leonis.

No. 2720, vert, each $2: a, Broughtonia sanguinea. b, Anguloa virginalis. c, Dendrobium Bigibbum. d, T. forcia, L. lucasiana. e, Cymbidium, diff.

Each $6: No. 2721, Oncidium onustum. No. 2722, Laelia milleri.

**1997, Sept. 4**

**2711-2718** A400 Set of 8 11.00 11.00

**Sheets of 6, #a-f**

**2719-2720** A400 Set of 2 22.00 22.00

**Souvenir Sheets**

**2721-2722** A400 Set of 2 13.00 13.00

Diana, Princess of Wales (1961-97) — A401

Various portraits.

**1997, Oct. 15 Litho.** ***Perf. 14½***

**2723** A401 $1.50 Sheet of 6, #a.-f. 7.75 7.75

**Souvenir Sheet**

**2724** A401 $5 multicolored 4.75 4.75

Christmas — A402

Works of art, entire paintings, or details: 35c, Angel, by Matthias Grunewald. 50c, Saint Demetrius (icon). 75c, Reliquary in the Form of a Triptych. $1, Angel of the Annunciation, by Jan van Eyck. $3, The Annunciation, by Simone Martini. $4, Saint Michael (mosaic).

Each $6: No. 2731, The Annunciation, by Titian, horiz. No. 2732, The Coronation of the Virgin, by Fra Angelico.

**1997, Dec. 5 Litho.** ***Perf. 14***

**2725-2730** A402 Set of 6 8.75 8.75

**Souvenir Sheets**

**2731-2732** A402 Set of 2 12.50 12.50

New Year 1998 (Year of the Tiger) — A403

Designs: a, shown, b, With mouth open. c, With ears rolled back.

**1998, Jan. 5 Litho.** ***Die Cut Perf. 9***

**Self-Adhesive**

**Sheets of 3, #a.-c.**

**2733** A403 $1.50 gold & multi *25.00*
**2734** A403 $1.50 sil & multi *25.00*

Nos. 2733b, 2734b have point of triangle down.

Fish A404

65c, Black-tailed humbug. 90c, Yellow sweetlips. $1, Common squrrelfish. $2, Powder blue surgeon.

No. 2739, each $1.50: a, Blue tang. b, Porkfish. c, Banded butterflyfish. d, Threadfin butterflyfish. e, Red-headed. f, Emperor angelfish.

No. 2740, each $1.50: a, Scribbled angelfish. b, Lemonpeel angelfish. c, Bandit angelfish. d, Bicolor cherub. e, Regal tang. f, Yellow tang.

Each $6: No. 2741, Two-banded anemonefish. No. 2742, Long-nosed butterflyfish.

**1998, Feb. 10 Litho.** ***Perf. 14***

**2735-2738** A404 Set of 4 5.50 5.50

**Sheets of 6, #a.-f.**

**2739-2740** A404 Set of 2 17.00 17.00

**Souvenir Sheets**

**2741-2742** A404 Set of 2 13.50 13.50

Orchids A405

No. 2743, each $1.50: a, Arachnis clarkei. b, Cymbidium eburneum. c, Dendrobium chrysotoxum. d, Paphiopedilum insigne. e, Paphiopedilum venustum. f, Renanthera imschootiana.

No. 2744, each $1.50: a, Sophronitis grandiflora. b, Phalaenopsis amboinensis. c, Zygopetalum intermedium. d, Paphiopedilum purpuratum. e, Miltonia regnellii. f, Dendrobium parishii.

Each $6: No. 2745, Lycaste aromatica. No. 2746, Pleione maculata.

**1998, Apr. 21 Litho. *Perf. 14***

**Sheets of 6, #a.-f.**

**2743-2744** A405 Set of 2 19.00 19.00

**Souvenir Sheets**

**2745-2746** A405 Set of 2 12.50 12.50

Ships A406

No. 2747, each $1: a, Brig. b, Clipper. c, Caique. d, Mississippi Riverboat. e, Luxury liner. f, The Mayflower. g, Frigate. h, Janggolan. i, Junk.

No. 2748, each $1: a, Dhow. b, Galleon. c, Felucca. d, Schooner. e, Aircraft carrier. f, Knau. g, Destroyer. h, Longship. i, Queen Elizabeth 2.

Each $6: #2749, The Lusitania. #2750, Submarine.

**1998, Apr. 26 Litho. *Perf. 14***

**Sheets of 9, #a-i**

**2747-2748** A406 Set of 2 19.00 19.00

**Souvenir Sheets**

**2749-2750** A406 Set of 2 12.50 12.50

No. 2749 contains one 85x28mm stamp; No. 2750 one 56x42mm stamp.

Disney's Hercules A407

Hercules grows up — #2751: a, Hercules, Zeus. b, Hercules and Pegasus walking past creature. c, Phil, Hercules. d, Hercules swinging through air. e, Centaur carrying captured Meg. f, Hercules attacking centaur. g, Hercules fighting lion. h, Hercules, Pegasus looking at prints.

Birth and childhood of Hercules — #2752, each $1: a, Zeus and Hera with newborn Hercules. b, Hades finds baby. c, Hades in the night. d, Baby sleeping. e, Baby swept away by Pain and Panic. f, Old couple with Baby Hercules. g, Hercules pulling cart. h, Hercules looking into mirror.

Hercules triumphant — #2753, each $1: a, Hercules carrying Meg. b, Meg, Hades. c, Hercules being trained by Phil. d, Hercules meeting Hades. e, Monster coming through city. f, Zeus. g, Hercules lifting column off Meg. h, Hercules diving into water.

Each $6: #2754, Hercules with sword, fighting Hydra. #2755, Hades on fire. #2756, Hercules, Meg on Pegasus, horiz. #2757, Zeus, Hercules, horiz. #2758, Hades. #2759, Zeus with baby Pegasus.

**1998, June 16 Litho. *Perf. 13½x14***

**Sheets of 8**

**2751** A407 10c #a.-h. 3.75 3.75

**2752-2753** A407 Set of 2 19.00 19.00

**Souvenir Sheets**

**2754-2759** A407 Set of 6 40.00 40.00

Sea Birds — A408

Designs: 90c, Arctic skua. $1.10, Humboldt penguin. $2, Herring gull. $3, Red knot.

No. 2764, horiz.: a, Northern fulmar. b, Black-legged kittiwake. c, Cape petrel. d, Mediterranean gull. e, Brandt's cormorant (h). f, Greater shearwater. g, Black-footed albatross. h, Red-necked phalarope. i, Black skimmer (f).

Each $5: No. 2765, Black-browed albatross. No. 2766, King penguin.

**1998, June 30 Litho. *Perf. 14***

**2760-2763** A408 Set of 4 6.00 6.00

**2764** A408 $1 Sheet of 9, #a.-i. 9.25 9.25

**Souvenir Sheets**

**2765-2766** A408 Set of 2 10.50 10.50

Diana, Princess of Wales (1961-97) — A409

Portrait of Diana with rose: No. 2767, Wearing hat. No. 2768, Without hat.

**Litho. & Embossed**

**1998, July 14 *Die Cut 7½***

**2767** A409 $20 gold & multi

**2768** A409 $20 gold & multi

Supermarine Spitfires — A410

No. 2769, each $1.50: a, MK IX. b, MK XIV. c, MK XII. d, MK XI. e, H.F. MK VIII. f, MK VB.

No. 2770, each $1.50: a, MK I. b, MK VIII. c, MK III. d, MK XVI. e, MK V. f, MK XIX.

Each $6: No. 2771, MK IX. No. 2772, MK IA.

**1998, July 20 Litho. *Perf. 14***

**Sheets of 6, #a.-f.**

**2769-2770** A410 Set of 2 15.00 15.00

**Souvenir Sheets**

**2771-2772** A410 Set of 2 12.00 12.00

Nos. 2771-2772 each contain one 57x43mm stamp.

Intl. Year of the Ocean A411

No. 2773: a, Walrus. b, African black footed penguins. c, African black-footed penguin. d, California sea lion. e, Green turtle. f, Redfin anthias. g, Sperm whale. h, French angelfish, Australian sea lion. i, Jellyfish. j, Sawfish. k, Male and female cuckoo wrasse. l, Garibaldi. m, Spinecheek anemonefish. n, Leafy seadragon. o, Blue-spotted goatfish. p, Two-spot gobies.

No. 2774, Atlantic spotted dolphins. No. 2775, Octopus.

**1998, Aug. 19**

**2773** A411 75c Sheet of 16, #a.-p. 13.50 13.50

**Souvenir Sheets**

**2774** A411 $5 multicolored 5.00 5.00

**2775** A411 $6 multicolored 6.25 6.25

CARICOM, 25th Anniv. — A412

**1998, Sept. 15 Litho. *Perf. 13½***

**2776** A412 $1 multicolored 1.10 1.10

Mahatma Gandhi (1869-1948) A413

Design: $6, Portrait, head down.

**1998, Sept. 13 *Perf. 14***

**2777** A413 $1 multicolored 1.50 1.50

**Souvenir Sheet**

**2778** A413 $6 multicolored 6.50 6.50

No. 2777 was issued in sheets of 4.

Paintings by Pablo Picasso (1881-1973) — A414

45c, The Bathers, 1918, vert. $2, Luncheon on the Grass, 1960. $3, The Swimmer, 1929. $5, Woman Reading, 1944, vert.

***Perf. 14½x14, 14x14½***

**1998, Sept. 15**

**2779-2781** A414 Set of 3 5.25 5.25

**Souvenir Sheet**

**2782** A414 $5 multicolored 5.25 5.25

Paintings by Eugéne Delacroix (1798-1863) — A415

No. 2783: a, Horsemen Fighting in the Plain. b, The Assassination of the Bishop of Liege. c, Still-life with Lobsters. d, The Battle of Nancy. e, The Shipwreck of Don Juan. f, The Death of Ophelia. g, Attila and the Barbarians. h, Entertaining the Arabians.

$5, Entry of the Crusaders into Constantinople.

**1998, Sept. 15 *Perf. 14***

**Sheet of 8**

**2783** A415 $1 #a.-h. 7.75 7.75

**Souvenir Sheet**

**2784** A415 $5 multicolored 5.25 5.25

Organization of American States, 50th Anniv. A416

**1998, Sept. 15 Litho. *Perf. 14***

**2785** A416 $1 multicolored 1.10 1.10

Diana, Princess of Wales (1961-97) A417

**1998 *Perf. 14½***

**2786** A417 $1 multicolored 1.25 1.25

**Self-Adhesive**

***Serpentine Die Cut Perf. 11½***

**Sheet of 1**

**Size: 52x65mm**

**2786A** A417 $6 Diana, buildings *6.00*

No. 2786 was issued in sheets of 6.

Soaking in water may affect the multi-layer image of No. 2786A.

Issued: $1, 9/15; $6, 11/5/98.

Enzo Ferrari (1898-1988), Automobile Manufacturer — A418

No. 2787: a, 250 GT Berlinetta Lusso. b, 250 GTO. c, 250 GT Boano/Ellena cabriolet.

$5, Dino 246 GTS.

**1998, Sept. 15 *Perf. 14***

**2787** A418 $2 Sheet of 3, #a.-c. 6.00 6.00

**Souvenir Sheet**

**2788** A418 $5 multicolored 6.00 6.00

No. 2786 was issued in sheets of 6. No. 2788 contains one 91x35mm stamp.

1998 World Scouting Jamboree, Chile — A419

Designs: $2, Scout salute. $3, World Scout flag. $4, Scout first aid. $6, World Scout flag.

**1998, Sept. 15**

**2789-2791** A419 Set of 3 8.75 8.75

**Souvenir Sheet**

**2792** A419 $6 multi, horiz. 7.00 7.00

Royal Air Force, 80th Anniv. A420

No. 2793, each $2: a, Vickers Supermarine Spitfire Mk2a. b, Vickers Supermarine Spitfire HF Mk1XB flying right. c, Vickers Supermarine Spitfire HF Mk1Xb flying left. d, Hawker Hurricane 11C.

No. 2794, each $2: a, EF-2000 Eurofighter prototype. b, Nimrod MR2P. c, Eurofighter 2000, diff. d, C-47 Dakota.

Each $6: No. 2795, Eurofighter 2000, VC10. No. 2796, Biplane, hawk's head. No. 2797, Biplane, hawk. No. 2798, Eurofighter 2000, Jet Provost.

**1998, Sept. 15**

**Sheets of 4, #a-d**

**2793-2794** A420 Set of 2 16.00 16.00

**Souvenir Sheets**

**2795-2798** A420 Set of 4 25.00 25.00

Tennis Stars A421

45c, Arthur Ashe. 75c, Martina Hingis. 90c, Chris Evert. $1, Steffi Graf. $1.50, Arantxa Sanchez Vicario. $3, Martina Navratilova. $2, Monica Seles. $6, Martina Hingis, diff.

**1998, Oct. 28**

**2799-2805** A421 Set of 7 8.75 8.75

**Souvenir Sheet**

**2806** A421 $6 multicolored 7.00 7.00

Peacekeepers, Beirut, Lebanon, 1982-84 — A422

**1998, Nov. 30 Litho. *Perf. 14***

**2807** A422 $1 multicolored 1.25 1.25

Christmas A423

Birds: 45c, Blue-hooded Euphonia. 75c, Black-bellied whistling duck. 90c, Purple martin. $1, Imperial parrot. $2, Adelaide's warbler. $3, Roseate flamingo.

$5, Green-throated carib. $6, Purple-throated carib, Canada #85.

**1998, Dec. 1**

**2808-2813** A423 Set of 6 7.75 7.75

**Souvenir Sheet**

**2814** A423 $5 multicolored 5.25 5.25
**2815** A423 $6 multicolored 8.00 8.00

No. 2815 contains one 38x61mm stamp.

Christmas — A424

Works of art: 35c, Painting, The Angel's Parting from Tobias, by Jean Bilevelt. 45c, Painting, Allegory of Faith, by Moretto da Brescia. 90c, Painting, Cross, with Depiction of the Crucifixion, by Ugolino di Tedice. $1, The Triumphal Entry into Jerusalem, Master of the Thuison Altarpiece.

**1998, Dec. 1**

**2816-2819** A424 Set of 4 2.75 2.75

New Year 1999 (Year of the Rabbit) — A425

Various rabbits, color of country name: a, green. b, orange. c, red.

**1999, Jan. 4 Litho. *Die Cut Perf. 9***

**Self-Adhesive**

**Sheet of 3**

**2820** A425 $1 sil & multi, #a.-c. 4.00 4.00

No. 2820b has point of triangle down.

A426

Famous People: No. 2821: a, Martin Luther King, Jr. (1929-68). b, Socrates (470-399BC). c, Thomas Moore (1478-1535). d, Chaim Weizmann (1874-1952). e, Alexander Solzhenitsyn (1918-2008). f, Galileo Galilei (1564-1642). g, Michael Servetus (1511-53). h, Salman Rushdie (b. 1947).

$6, Mother Teresa (1910-97).

**1999, Mar. 1 Litho. *Perf. 14***

**2821** A426 $1 Sheet of 8, #a.-h. 10.00 10.00

**Souvenir Sheet**

**2822** A426 $6 multicolored 7.00 7.00

Nos. 2821b-2821c, 2821e-2821f are 53x38mm.

A427

Space Exploration — #2823, each $1.50: a, Robert H. Goddard. b, Werner von Braun. c, Yuri Gagarin. d, Freedom 7 rocket. e, Aleksei Leonov. f, Apollo 11 astronauts on moon.

No. 2824, each $1.50: a, Mariner 9. b, Voyager 1. c, Bruce McCandless. d, Giotto probe. e, Space Shuttle. f, Magellan probe.

Each $6: No. 2825, John H. Glenn, Jr. No. 2826, Neil A. Armstrong.

**1999, Mar. 5**

**Sheets of 6, #a-f**

**2823-2824** A427 Set of 2 16.00 16.00

**Souvenir Sheets**

**2825-2826** A427 Set of 2 12.00 12.00

Mickey's Dream Wedding A428

No. 2827: a, Goofy. b, Mickey. c, Minnie. d, Daisy Duck. e, Donald Duck. f, Pluto. g, Huey, Dewey & Louie. h, Dog.

Each $6: No. 2828, Mickey eating cake. No. 2829, Mickey, Minnie in back of carriage, horiz.

**1999, Mar. 12 *Perf. 13½x14, 14x13½***

**2827** A428 $1 Sheet of 8, #a.-h. 8.00 8.00

**Souvenir Sheets**

**2828-2829** A428 Set of 2 14.50 14.50

Mickey Mouse, 70th anniv.

Trains A429

Designs: 25c, Grand Trunk Western. 35c, Louisville & Nashville. 45c, Gulf, Mobile & Ohio. 75c, Missouri Pacific. 90c, RTG, French Natl. Railway. $1, Florida East Coast. $3, Kansas City Southern. $4, New Haven.

No. 2838, each $1.50: a, Western Pacific. b, Union Pacific. c, Chesapeake & Ohio. d, Southern Pacific. e, Baltimore & Ohio. f, Wabash.

No. 2839, each $1.50: a, Burlington Route. b, Texas Special, Missouri, Kansas & Texas. c, City of Los Angeles. d, Northwestern. e, Canadian National. f, Rock Island.

No. 2840, each $1.50: a, Rio Grande. b, Erie Lackawanna. c, New York Central. d, Pennsylvania. e, Milwaukee Road. f, Illinois Central.

No. 2841, each $1.50: a, TGV, French National Railways. b, HST, British Railways. c, TEE, Trans Europe Express. d, Ancona Express Itay. e, XPT, Australia. f, APT-P, British Railways.

Each $6: No. 2842, Bullet Train, Japan. No. 2843, Inter City Express, Germany. No. 2844, Santa Fe. No. 2845, ELD 4, Netherlands.

**1999, Mar. 15 *Perf. 14***

**2830-2837** A429 Set of 8 9.00 9.00

**Sheets of 6, #a-f**

**2838-2841** A429 Set of 4 34.00 34.00

**Souvenir Sheets**

**2842-2845** A429 Set of 4 24.00 24.00

Australia '99, World Stamp Expo A430

Flora and fauna: $1, Orangutan. $2, Dourocouli. $3. Black caiman. $4, Black leopard, vert.

No. 2850, vert, each 75c: a, African binturong. b, Two elephants. c, One elephant. d, Garkulax mitratus. e, Vanda hookeriana (a, f). f, Heron. g, Fur seal (f). h, Pied shag (g). i, Round batfish (e). j, Loggerhead turtle (f, k). k, Three harlequin sweet lips (l). l, Two harlequin sweet lips (k).

No. 2851, each 75c: a, Papilio blumei (d). b, Egret (e). c, Kumarahou (b, f). d, Javan rhinoceros (g). e, Silver eye. f, Kiore (i). g, Cyclorana novaehollandiae. h, Caterpillar. i, Grey duck (h). j, Honey blue-eye. k, Krefft's tortoise. l, Archer fish.

Each $6: No. 2852, Impalas. No. 2853, Ring-tailed lemurs.

**1999, Apr. 12 Litho. *Perf. 14***

**2846-2849** A430 Set of 4 9.50 9.50

**Sheets of 12, #a-l**

**2850-2851** A430 Set of 2 17.50 17.50

**Souvenir Sheets**

**2852-2853** A430 Set of 2 12.50 12.50

Paintings by Hokusai (1760-1849) A431

Entire paintings or details — #2854, each $1.50: a, The Actor Ichikawa Danjuro as Tomoe Gozen. b, E-Tehon drawings (washing clothes). c, The Prostitute of Eguchi. d, Sudden Shower from a Fine Sky. e, E-tehon drawings (hanging clothes up to dry). f, Shimada.

No. 2855, each $1.50: a, Head of Old Man. b, Horse Drawings (with head down). c, Girl Making Cord for Binding Hats. d, Li Po Admiring the Waterfall of Lo-Shan. e, Horse drawings (with head up). f, Potted Dwarf Pine with Basin.

Each $6: No. 2856, Women on the Beach at Enoshima. No. 2857, The Guardian God Fudo Myoo and His Two Young Attendants.

**1999, May 24 Litho. *Perf. 13½x14***

**Sheets of 6, #a-f**

**2854-2855** A431 Set of 2 17.00 17.00

**Souvenir Sheets**

**2856-2857** A431 Set of 2 12.50 12.50

Johann Wolfgang von Goethe (1749-1832), Poet — A432

No. 2858: a, Faust contemplates the moon in his story. b, Portrait of Goethe and Friedrich von Schiller (1759-1805). c, Faust converses with Wagner outside the town gate.

No. 2860, Margaret Muses in "Faust."

**1999, May 24 *Perf. 14***

**2858** A432 $3 Sheet of 3, #a.-c. 8.75 8.75

**Souvenir Sheet**

**2860** A432 $6 multi 6.75 6.75

IBRA '99, World Philatelic Exhibition, Nuremberg — A433

IBRA'99 emblem, 1893 4-4-0 locomotive and: No. 2862, 75c, Prussia #2. No. 2864, $1, Saxony #1.

Emblem, Humboldt sailing ship and: No. 2863, 90c, Mecklenburg-Schwerin #1. No. 2865, $2, Mecklenburg-Strelitz #1.

$6, Saxony #1.

**1999, May 24 Litho. *Perf. 14***

**2862-2865** A433 Set of 4 5.25 5.25

**Souvenir Sheet**

**2866** A433 $6 multicolored 7.75 7.75

Apollo 11 Moon Landing, 30th Anniv. A434

#2867, each $1.50: a, Footprint on moon. b, V2 Rocket. c, Command module, Columbia. d, Lunar rover. e, Lunar lander, Eagle. f, Command module during re-entry.

#2868, each $1.50: a, Moon. b, Edward H. White during first spacewalk. c, Edwin "Buzz" Aldrin. d, Earth. e, Michael Collins. f, Neal A. Armstrong, first man to walk on moon.

Each $6: #2869, Launch of Apollo 11, vert. #2870, US flag, Armstrong on Moon.

**1999, May 24**

**Sheets of 6, #a-f**

**2867-2868** A434 Set of 2 19.00 19.00

**Souvenir Sheets**

**2869-2870** A434 Set of 2 12.50 12.50

Souvenir Sheets

PhilexFrance '99, World Philatelic Exhibition — A435

Designs, each $6: No. 2871, 2-8-0 Heavy freight locomotive, French State Railways. No. 2872, 4 Cylinder Compound Pacific, Paris-Lyons and Mediterranean Railway.

**1999, May 24** ***Perf. 13¾***
**2871-2872** A435 Set of 2 12.50 12.50

A436

Wedding of Prince Edward and Sophie Rhys-Jones — #2873: a, Edward. b, Sophie and Edward. c, Sophie.
$6, Couple, horiz.

**1999, June 18 Litho.** ***Perf. 13½***
**2873** A436 $3 Sheet of 3, #a.-c. 8.75 8.75

**Souvenir Sheet**

**2874** A436 $6 multicolored 7.00 7.00

A437

Children: a, Two with fur hats. b, One with pink hat. c, Boy without shirt, girl with shawl.
$6, Wearing white shirt.

**1999, May 24 Litho.** ***Perf. 14***
**2875** A437 $3 Sheet of 3, #a.-c. 8.75 8.75

**Souvenir Sheet**

**2876** A437 $6 multicolored 7.00 7.00

UN Rights of the Child, 10th anniv.

British Comedy "Carry On" — A438

a, Dick. b, Doctor. c, England. d, Matron. e, Round the Bend. f, Up the Jungle. g, Loving. h, Up the Khyber.
$6, Various characters.

**1999, May 24** ***Perf. 13½x14***
**2877** A438 $1 Sheet of 8, #a.-h. 8.75 8.75

***Perf. 13¾***

**2877I** A438 $6 multicolored 6.75 6.75

Variety Club of Great Britain, 50th anniv.

UPU, 125th Anniv. A439

Mail from space: a, Cosmonaut with letter from home. b, Supply and mail ship, "Progress." c, Postmark of space station Mir. d, Buran shuttle, Mir in space.
$6, Space station Mir.

**1999, May 24** ***Perf. 14***
**2878** A439 $2 Sheet of 4, #a.-d. 8.75 8.75

**Souvenir Sheet**

**2879** A439 $6 multicolored 7.00 7.00

Queen Mother, 100th Birthday (in 2000) — A440

A440a

No. 2880: a, Queen Mother, Prince Charles, 1948. b, Queen Mother, 1970. c, Queen Mother in Australia, 1958. d, Queen Mother.
$6, Queen Mother, 1953.

**1999, Aug. 16 Gold Frames**

**Sheet of 4**

**2880** A440 $2 #a.-d. + label 8.75 8.75

**Souvenir Sheet**

**2881** A440 $6 multicolored 7.00 7.00

**Litho. & Embossed**

***Die Cut Perf. 8¾***

**Without Gum**

**2881A** A440a $20 gold & multi *20.00*

No. 2881 contains one 38x50mm stamp. Margins of sheet are embossed.
See Nos. 3212-3213.

Birth of the Silver Screen A441

Musicians — #2882, each $1: a, George Gershwin, 1929. b, Florence Mills, 1928. c, Sam Beckett, 1925. d, Bessie Smith, 1923. e, Billie Holiday, 1933. f, Bert Williams, 1914. g, Cole Porter, 1934. h, Sophie Tucker, 1915.
Actors — #2883, each $1: a, Lon Chaney, 1930. b, Buster Keaton, 1930. c, Norma Shearer, 1934. d, James Cagney, 1930. e, Hedda Hopper, 1933. f, Jean Harlow, 1931. g, Marlene Dietrich, 1930. h, Ramon Novarro, 1928.
Each $6: No. 2884, Louis Armstrong. No. 2885, Clark Gable, 1932,

**1999, Aug. 18 Sheets of 8, #a-h**
**2882-2883** A441 Set of 2 16.00 16.00

**Souvenir Sheets**

**2884-2885** A441 Set of 2 14.00 14.00

Star Trek A442

Various starships.

**1999, July 20 Litho.** ***Perf. 13¼***
**2886** A442 $1.50 Sheet of 9, #a.-i. 14.50 14.50

Dinosaurs A443

35c, Ouranosaurus. 45c, Struthiomimus, vert. 75c, Parasaurolophus, vert. $2, Triceratops. $3, Stegoceras. $4, Stegosaurus.
No. 2893, each $1: a, Agathaumus. b, Camarosaurus. c, Quetzalcoatlus. d, Alioramus. e, Camptosaurus. f, Albertosaurus. g, Anatosaurus. h, Spinosaurus. i, Centrosaurus.
No. 2894, each $1: a, Archaeopteryx. b, Brachiosaurus. c, Dilophosaurus. d, Dimetrodon. e, Psittacosaurus. f, Acrocanthosaurus. g, Stenonychosaurus. h, Dryosaurus. i, Compsognathus.
Each $6: No. 2895, Velociraptor, vert. No. 2896, Tyrannosaurus, vert.

**1999, Sept. 1 Litho.** ***Perf. 14***
**2887-2892** A443 Set of 6 10.00 10.00

**Sheets of 9, #a-i**

**2893-2894** A443 Set of 2 18.00 18.00

**Souvenir Sheets**

**2895-2896** A443 Set of 2 12.50 12.50

Christmas — A444

Candle and: 20c, Rose. 75c, Tulip. 90c, Pear. $1, Hibiscus. $4, Lily.
$6, The Nativity, by Sandro Botticelli.

**1999, Dec. 7 Litho.** ***Perf. 14***
**2897-2901** A444 Set of 5 6.75 6.75

**Souvenir Sheet**

**2902** A444 $6 multi 7.00 7.00

Flowers A445

Various flowers making up a photomosaic of Princess Diana.

**1999, Dec. 31 Litho.** ***Perf. 13¾***
**2903** A445 $1 Sheet of 8, #a.-h. 8.00 8.00

See No. 3055.

New Year 2000 (Year of the Dragon) — A446

Inscription color: a, Blue green. b, Red. c, Violet.

**2000, Feb. 5** ***Perf. 12½x12¾***
**2904** A446 $2 Sheet of 3, #a.-c. 7.25 7.25

No. 2904b has point of triangle down.

Birds A447

Designs: 75c, Roseate spoonbill. 90c, Scarlet ibis. $1.50, Sparkling violet-ear. $2, Northern jacana.
No. 2909, each $1: a, Blue-headed euphonia. b, Troupial. c, Caribbean parakeet. d, Forest thrush. e, Hooded tanager. f, Stripe-headed tanager. g, Ringed kingfisher. h, Zenaida dove.
No. 2910, each $1: a, Adelaide's warbler. b, Hispaniolan trogon. c, Sun parakeet. d, Black-necked stilt. e, Sora rail. f, Fulvous tree duck. g, Blue-headed parrot. h, Tropical mockingbird.
Each $6: No. 2911, Antillean siskin. No. 2912, Cedar waxwing, vert.

**2000, Mar. 1 Litho.** ***Perf. 14***
**2905-2908** A447 Set of 4 5.00 5.00

**Sheets of 8, #a-h**

**2909-2910** A447 Set of 2 14.00 14.00

**Souvenir Sheets**

**2911-2912** A447 Set of 2 10.00 10.00

No. 2911 contains one 50x37mm stamp. No. 2912 contains one 37x50mm stamp.

Mushrooms A448

Designs: 35c, Clitocybe geotropa. 45c, Psalliota augusta. $1, Amanita rubescens. $4, Boletus satanas.
No. 2917, each $1.50: a, Ungulina marginata. b, Pleurotus ostreatus. c, Flammula penetrans. d, Morchella crassipes. e, Lepiota procera. f, Tricholoma aurantium.
No. 2918, each $1.50: a, Pholiota spectabilis. b, Mycena polygramma. c, Collybia iocephala. d, Corinus cornatus. e, Amanita muscaria. f, Boletus aereus.
Each $6: No. 2919, Lepiota acutesquamosa. No. 2920, Daedala quercina.

**2000, May 1** ***Perf. 14***
**2913-2916** A448 Set of 4 6.25 6.25

**Sheets of 6, #a-f**

**2917-2918** A448 Set of 2 17.00 17.00

**Souvenir Sheets**

**2919-2920** A448 Set of 2 12.00 12.00

Paintings of Anthony Van Dyck
A449

No. 2921, each $1: a, Young Woman Resting Her Head on Her Hand. b, Self-portrait. c, Woman Looking Upwards. d, Head of an Old Man, c. 1621. e, Head of a Boy. f, Head of an Old Man, 1616-18.

No. 2922, each $1: a, Charles I on Horseback with Seigneur de St. Antoine. b, St. Martin Dividing His Cloak. c, Giovanni Paolo Balbi on Horseback. d, Marchese Anton Giulio Brignole-Sale on Horseback. e, Study of a Horse. f, An Oriental on Horseback.

No. 2923, each $1.50: a, Portrait of a Man. b, Portrait of a Man Aged Seventy. c, Portrait of a Woman. d, An Elderly Man. e, Portrait of a Young Man. f, Man with a Glove.

No. 2924, each $1.50: a, St. John the Baptist. b, St. Anthony of Padua and the Ass of Rimini. c, The Stoning of St. Stephen. d, The Martyrdom of St. Sebastian. e, St. Sebastian Bound for Martyrdom. f, St. Jerome.

No. 2925, each $1.50: a, Inscribed "Portrait of Anthony Van Dyck," actually a self-portrait of Rubens. b, Inscribed "Self-portrait (after Peter Paul Rubens)." c, Isabella Brant, Wife of Peter Paul Rubens. d, The Penitent Apostle Peter. e, Head of a Robber. f, The Heads of the Apostles, by Rubens.

Each $5: No. 2926, Prince Thomas-Francis of Savoy-Carignan on Horseback. No. 2927, Charles I on Horseback. No. 2928, The Emperor Theodosius Refused Entry in Milan Cathedral, horiz.

Each $6: No. 2929, St. Jerome (in the Wilderness). No. 2930, St. Martin Dividing His Cloak, horiz. No. 2931, Portrait of a Man and His Wife.

**2000, May 1** ***Perf. 13¾***

**Sheets of 6, #a.-f.**

**2921-2922** A449 Set of 2 10.50 10.50
**2923-2925** A449 Set of 3 22.50 22.50

**Souvenir Sheets**

**2926-2928** A449 Set of 3 13.00 13.00
**2929-2931** A449 Set of 3 14.50 14.50

Millennium
A450

Highlights of 1650-1700: a, Painter Jan Vermeer dies. b, Birth of microbiology. c, Salem Witch Trials. d, Sir Isaac Newton builds first reflecting telescope. e, Voltaire born. f, Ivan V and Peter become joint rulers of Russia. g, First Qing Dynasty Emperor, Shun Zhi, dies. h, Christiaan Huygens discovers rings of Saturn. i, Robert Hooke identifies cells. j, Wang Shih-min paints "Verdant Peaks." k, René Descartes dies. l, Canal du Midi completed. m, Glorious Revolution. n, King William's War ends. o, Gian Domenico Cassini observes polar caps on Mars. p, Newton formulates law of gravitation (60x40mm). q, Ole Roemer discovers that light moves at a finite speed.

**2000, May 1** ***Perf. 12½***

**2932** A450 50c Sheet of 17, #a.-q., + label 8.75 8.75

Orchids — A451

Designs: 75c, Brassolaeliocattleya. 90c, Maxilbera. $1, Isochilius. $2, Oncidium.

No. 2937, each $1.50: a, Laeliocattleya. b, Sophrocattleya (red). c, Epidendrum. d, Cattleya. e, Ionopsis. f, Brassoepidendrum.

No. 2938, each $1.50: a, Lycaste. b, Cochleanthes. c, Brassocattleya. d, Brassolaeliacattleya, diff. e, Iwanagaara. f, Sophrocattleya (orange).

Each $6: No. 2939, Vanilla. No. 2940, Brassocattleya, diff.

**2000, May 15** **Litho.** ***Perf. 14***

**2933-2936** A451 Set of 4 4.25 4.25

**Sheets of 6, #a.-f.**

**2937-2938** A451 Set of 2 17.00 17.00

**Souvenir Sheets**

**2939-2940** A451 Set of 2 11.00 11.00

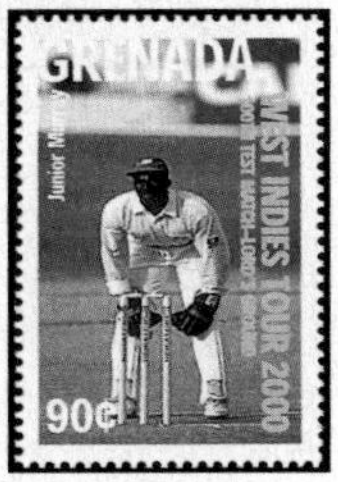


100th Test Match at Lord's Ground — A452

90c, Junior Murray. $5, Rawl Lewis. $6, Lord's Ground, horiz.

**2000, May 15** **Litho.** ***Perf. 14***

**2941-2942** A452 Set of 2 4.75 4.75

**Souvenir Sheet**

**2943** A452 $6 multi 5.25 5.25

Prince William, 18th Birthday — A453

No. 2944: a, In suit. b, In suit, with person in tan suit. c, In suit, waving. d, In ski jacket.
$6, In suit, diff.

**2000, May 15** ***Perf. 14***

**2944** A453 $1.50 Sheet of 4, #a-d 4.50 4.50

**Souvenir Sheet**

***Perf. 13¾***

**2945** A453 $6 multi 4.50 4.50

No. 2944 contains four 28x42mm stamps.

First Zeppelin Flight, Cent. — A454

No. 2946 — Ferdinand von Zeppelin and: a, LZ-130. b, LZ-2. c, LZ-127.
$6, LZ-129.

**2000, May 15** ***Perf. 14***

**2946** A454 $3 Sheet of 3, #a-c 8.00 8.00

**Souvenir Sheet**

**2947** A454 $6 multi 5.25 5.25

No. 2946 contains three 42x28mm stamps.

Berlin Film Festival, 50th Anniv. — A455

No. 2948: a, Alphaville. b, Rod Steiger. c, Os Fuzis. d, Jean-Pierre Leaud. e, Cul-de-sac. f, Ikiru.
$6, Hsi Yen.

**2000, May 15**

**2948** A455 $1.50 Sheet of 6, #a-f 6.75 6.75

**Souvenir Sheet**

**2949** A455 $6 multi 4.50 4.50

Apollo-Soyuz Mission, 25th Anniv. — A456

No. 2950, vert.: a, Soyuz launch vehicle. b, Soyuz 19. c, Apollo 18 and Soyuz 19 docked.
$6, Valeri Kubasov and Thomas Stafford.

**2000, May 15**

**2950** A456 $3 Sheet of 3, #a-c 7.75 7.75

**Souvenir Sheet**

**2951** A456 $6 multi 5.75 5.75

Souvenir Sheets

2000 Summer Olympics, Sydney — A457

No. 2952: a, Archibald Hahn. b, Show jumping. c, Sports Palace, Rome, and Italian flag. d, Ancient Greek chariot racing.

**2000, May 15**

**2952** A457 $2 Sheet of 4, #a-d 7.00 7.00

Public Railways, 175th Anniv. — A458

No. 2953: a, Locomotion No. 1, George Stephenson. b, John Bull.

**2000, May 15**

**2953** A458 $3 Sheet of 2, #a-b 5.75 5.75

Johann Sebastian Bach (1685-1750) — A459

**2000, May 15**

**2954** A459 $6 multi 4.50 4.50

Souvenir Sheet

Albert Einstein (1879-1955) — A460

**2000, May 15** **Litho.** ***Perf. 14¼***

**2955** A460 $6 multi 4.50 4.50

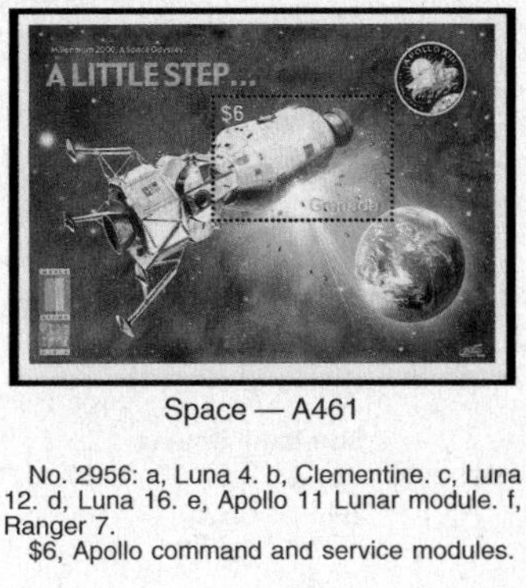


Space — A461

No. 2956: a, Luna 4. b, Clementine. c, Luna 12. d, Luna 16. e, Apollo 11 Lunar module. f, Ranger 7.
$6, Apollo command and service modules.

**2000, May 15 Litho. *Perf. 14***

**2956** A461 $1.50 Sheet of 6, #a-f 7.75 7.75

**Souvenir Sheet**

**2957** A461 $6 multi 5.25 5.25

World Stamp Expo 2000, Anaheim

Marine Life A462

Designs: 45c, Porkfish. 75c, Short bigeye. 90c, Red snapper. $1, Creole wrasse. $2, Indigo hamlet. $3, Blue tang.

No. 2964: a, Juvenile French angelfish. b, Beaugregory. c, Queen angelfish. d, Sergeant major. e, Bank butterflyfish. f, Spanish hogfish. g, Porkfish. h, Banded butterflyfish. i, Long-snout seahorse.

No. 2965: a, Hawksbill turtle. b, Foureye butterflyfish. c, Porcupinefish. d, Yellowtail damselfish. e, Adult French angelfish. f, Yellow goatfish. g, Blue-striped grunt. h, Spanish grunt. i, Queen triggerfish.

No. 2966, Queen angelfish. No. 2967, Blue tang.

**2000, Aug. 8**

**2958-2963** A462 Set of 5 7.00 7.00

**Sheets of 9, #a-i**

**2964-2965** A462 $1 Set of 2 14.50 14.50

**Souvenir Sheets**

**2966-2967** A462 $6 Set of 2 9.00 9.00

Grenada National Stadium A463

Designs: $2, Aerial view.

No. 2969: a, Cricket team photo. b, Cricketers playing.

**2000, Aug. 8**

**2968** A463 $2 multi 1.50 1.50

**Souvenir Sheet**

**2969** A463 $1 Sheet of 2, #a-b 1.50 1.50

European Soccer Championships — A464

No. 2970, horiz. — Belgium: a, Vanderhaege. b, Belgian team. c, Ronny Gaspercic. d, Lorenzo Staelens. e, Stadium Koning Boudewijn. f, Strupar and Mpenza.

No. 2971, horiz. — Spain: a, Sergi Barjuan. b, Spanish team. c, Luis Enrique. d, Hierro. e, De Kuip Stadium. f, Raul Gonzales.

No. 2972, horiz. — Yugoslavia: a, Dejan Savicevic. b, Yugoslavian team. c, Predrag Migatovic. d, Savo Milosevic. e, Jan Breydel Stadium. f, Darko Kovacevic.

No. 2973, Belgian coach Robert Waseige. No. 2974, Spanish coach José Antonio Camacho. No. 2975, Yugoslavian coach Vujadin Boskov.

Illustration reduced.

**2000, Aug. 8 *Perf. 13¾***

**Sheets of 6, #a-f**

**2970-2972** A464 $1.50 Set of 3 20.00 20.00

**Souvenir Sheets**

**2973-2975** A464 $6 Set of 3 13.50 13.50

Ferrari Automobiles — A465

20c, 1953 500 Mondial. 45c, 1948 166 Inter. 75c, 1953 340 MM. 90c, 1964 500 Superfast. $1, 1948 166 MM. $1.50, 1952 250 S. $2, 1957 250 California. $3, 1966 365 California.

**2000, Sept. 5 *Perf. 14***

**2976-2983** A465 Set of 8 8.00 8.00

Antique Automobiles A466

45c, 1921 Marmon Model 34. 75c, 1917 Buick D44. 90c, 1918 Hudson Runabout Landau. $1, 1915 Chevrolet Royal Mail. $2, 1925 Kissel Speedster. $3, 1915 Ford Model T.

No. 2990: a, 1925 Cadillac V63. b, 1939 Plymouth. c, 1934 Franklin Club Sedan. d, 1933 Fiat Ardita. e, 1929 Essex Speedabout. f, 1932 Stutz Bearcat.

No. 2991: a, 1929 Rolls Royce. b, 1932 Graham Convertible. c, 1937 Mercedes-Benz 540K. d, 1948 Jaguar MkV. e, 1939 Lagonda Drophead Coupe. f, 1930 Alfa Romeo Gran Sport.

No. 2992, 1915 Dodge Tourer. No. 2993, 1924 Chrysler.

**2000, Sept. 5**

**2984-2989** A466 Set of 6 6.00 6.00

**Sheets of 6, #a-f**

**2990-2991** A466 $1.50 Set of 2 13.50 13.50

**Souvenir Sheets**

**2992-2993** A466 $6 Set of 2 9.00 9.00

Popes — A467

No. 2994: a, Stephen VIII, 939-42. b, Theodore I, 642-49. c, Theodore II, 897. d, Valentine, 827. e, Vitalian, 657-72. f, Zacharias, 741-52.

$6, Sylvester II, 999-1003.

**2000, Sept. 5 *Perf. 13¾***

**2994** A467 $1.50 Sheet of 6, #a-f 6.75 6.75

**Souvenir Sheet**

**2995** A467 $6 multi 4.50 4.50

Monarchs — A468

No. 2996: a, George III of Great Britain, 1760-1820. b, George IV of Great Britain, 1820-30. c, Duchess Charlotte of Luxembourg, 1964-present. d, Grand Duke Jean of Luxembourg, 1964-present.

$6, Charles VIII of France, 1483-98.

**2000, Sept. 5 *Perf. 13¾***

**2996** A468 $1.50 Sheet of 4, #a-d 4.50 4.50

**Souvenir Sheet**

**2997** A468 $6 multi 4.50 4.50

Shirley Temple in "Heidi" — A469

No. 2998, horiz.: a, With woman holding candle. b, With girl in green dress c, On stairs. d, With Christmas gift.

No. 2999, horiz.: a, Walking with woman. b, Touching bearded man. c, Holding goat. d, With doves. e, With bearded man. f, Seated with woman.

**2000, Oct. 6 Litho. *Perf. 13¾***

**2998** A469 $1.50 Sheet of 4, #a-d 4.50 4.50

**2999** A469 $1.50 Sheet of 6, #a-f 6.75 6.75

**Souvenir Sheet**

**3000** A469 $6 Seated near tree 4.50 4.50

Paintings from the Prado — A470

#3001: a, Monk and king from The Virgin of the Catholic Monarchs, by an Anonymous Castilian. b, Madonna and child from The Virgin of the Catholic Monarchs. c, Monk and queen from The Virgin of the Catholic Monarchs. d, The Flagellation, by Alexo Fernandez. e, The Virgin and Souls in Purgatory, by Pedro Machuca. f, The Holy Trinity, by El Greco.

#3002: a, Playing at Giants, by El Greco. b, The Holy Family Under the Oak Tree, by Raphael. c, Don Gaspar Melchior de Jovellanos, by Francisco de Goya. d, Man with arm on hip from Joseph in the Pharaoh's Palace, by Jacopo Amiconi. e, Man and woman from Joseph in the Pharaoh's Palace. f, Man on bended knee from Joseph in the Pharaoh's Palace.

#3003: a, The Savior Blessing, by Francisco de Zurbarán. b, St. John the Baptist, by Francisco Solimena. c, Noli Me Tangere, by Corregio. d, St. Casilda, by Zurbarán. e, Nicolás Omazur by Bartolomé Esteban Murillo. f, Juan Martínez Montañés, by Diego Velázquez.

#3004, St. Anne, the Virgin, St. Elizabeth, St. John and the Christ child, by Fernando Yáñez de la Almedina. #3005, The Virgin of the Catholic Monarchs. #3006, Joseph in the Pharaoh's Palace, horiz.

Illustration reduced.

**2000, Oct. 19 *Perf. 12x12¼, 12¼x12***

**Sheets of 6, #a-f**

**3001-3003** A470 $1.50 Set of 3 20.00 20.00

**Souvenir Sheets**

**3004-3006** A470 $6 Set of 3 13.50 13.50

Espana 2000 Intl. Philatelic Exhibition.

Battle of Britain, 60th Anniv. — A471

No. 3007: a, Messerschmitt BF 109E and bomb blast. b, Supermarine Spitfire MK XI. c, V1 flying bomb. d, U-boat. e, Ack-ack gun unit. f, Bedford field ambulance.

No. 3008: a, Messerschmitt BF 109E. b, German paratrooper. c, Hawker Hurricane HK 1. d, RAF airfield. e, Heinkel HE 111 H. f, Nose of Supermarine Spitfire MK XI.

No. 3009, Line of Hawker Hurricanes. No. 3010, Supermarine Spitfire MK XI.

**2000, Oct. 30 *Perf. 14***

**Sheets of 6, #a-f**

**3007-3008** A471 $1.50 Set of 2 16.00 16.00

**Souvenir Sheets**

**3009-3010** A471 $6 Set of 2 12.00 12.00

A472 A473

Birds: 25c, Purple gallinule. 40c, Limpkin. 50c, Black-necked stilt. 60c, Painted bunting. 75c, Yellow-breasted warbler. $1, Blackburnian warbler. $1.25, Blue grosbeak. $1.50, Black-and-white warbler. $1.60, Blue whistling thrush. $3, Common yellowthroat. $4, Indigo bunting. $5, Gray catbird. $10, Bananaquit. $20, Blue-gray gnatcatcher.

**2000, Oct. 30 *Perf. 14¾x14***

**3011-3024** A472 Set of 14 37.50 37.50

See No. 3540.

**2000, June 23 Litho. *Perf. 14***

Dogs: $2, Shetland sheepdog. $3, Central Asian sheepdog.

No. 3027, horiz.: a, Labrador retriever. b, Standard poodle. c, Boxer. d, Rough-coated Jack Russell terrier. e, Tibetan terrier. f, Welsh corgi.

$6, Irish red and white setter, horiz.

**3025-3026** A473 Set of 2 3.75 3.75

**3027** A473 $1.50 Sheet of 6, #a-f 6.75 6.75

**Souvenir Sheet**

**3028** A473 $6 multi 4.50 4.50

Butterflies A474

45c, Marpesia eleuchea bahamaensis. 75c, Pterourus palamedes. 90c, Dryas julia framptoni. $1, Hypna clytemnestra iphegenia.
No. 3033, $1.50: a, Danaus plexippus. b, Anartia amathea. c, Colobura dirce. d, Parides gundiachianus. e, Spiroeta stelenes. f, Hammadryas feronia.
No. 3034, $1.50: a, Merchantis isthmia. b, Colias eurytheme. c, Papilio troilus d, Junonia coenia. e, Doxocopa laure. f, Pierella hyalinus.
No. 3035, $6, Agraulis vanilae insularis. No. 3036, $6, Danaus gilippus.

**2000, June 26**
**3029-3032** A474 Set of 4 3.00 3.00

**Sheets of 6, #a-f**

**3033-3034** A474 Set of 2 17.00 17.00

**Souvenir Sheets**

**3035-3036** A474 Set of 2 10.00 10.00

A475

Trains — A476

No. 3037, $1.50: a, Diesel-electric locomotive, Royal State Railway of Thailand. b, Diesel-electric locomotive, Danish Railways. c, French-built Turbo train. d, Diesel, Spanish Railways. e, Virgen del Rosario, Spanish Railways. f, 22 Class Co-Co Diesel-electric locomotive, Malayan Railways.
No. 3038, $1.50: a, Class 87 electric locomotive, British Railways. b, Electric-Diesel locomotive, Iraqi Railway. c, Electric locomotive, Austrian Railways. d, 1.4 meter gauge locomotive, South Australia Railways. e, Automated electric locomotive, Black Mesa & Lake Powell Railroad. f, Diesel-electric, Yugoslav Railways.
No. 3039, $1.50: a, Class 10 4-6-2, German Federal Railway. b, Class E.10 Bo-Bo Electric locomotive, German Federal Railways. c, Class 23 2-6-2, German Federal Railway. d, 2-8-4 locomotive, German Federal Railway. e, Rebuilt 01 Class Pacific, East German State Railway. f, High speed Diesel railcar, Deutschen Reichsbahn.
No. 3040, $1.50: a, Borsig Standard 2-2-2. b, Austerity 2-10-0 Series 52, German Federal Railway. c, Adler, facing right, Nuremburg-Furth Railway. d, Bardenia, Baden State Railways. e, Drache. f, Adler, facing left.
No. 3041, $6, Diesel T.E.E. Parsifal. No. 3042, $6, High speed electric, Netherlands Railway. No. 3043, $6, Electric train, Swiss Railways. No. 3044, $6, Silver Fern, New Zealand Railways. No. 3045, $6, Borsig locomotive, Berlin and Anhalt Railway. No. 3046, $6, Krauss-Maffei V.200 Diesel-hydraulic locomotive, German Federal Railway.
Illustrations reduced.

**2000, Sept. 5** **Sheets of 6, #a-f**
**3037-3038** A475 Set of 2 15.00 15.00
**3039-3040** A476 Set of 2 15.00 15.00

**Souvenir Sheets**

**3041-3044** A475 Set of 4 21.00 21.00
**3045-3046** A476 Set of 2 11.00 11.00

Descriptions of trains are in margins on Nos. 3039-3940, 3045-3046.

Nursery Rhymes — A477

No. 3047, Little Bo Peep, $1.50, vert.: a, Crook, tree, dove. b, Little Bo Peep. c, Sheep. d, Geese. e, Goose, Little Bo Peep's leg. f, Dog.
No. 3048, The Old Woman Who Lived in a Shoe, $1.50, vert.: a, Child, roof. b, Child with hat, rainbow. c, Cow, sun, rainbow. d, Child at door. e, Old woman, child. f, Child on shoe.
No. 3049, Little Boy Blue, $1.50, vert.: a, Sheep, house. b, Sun. c, Cow. d, Geese, path. e, Dog, Little Boy Blue's leg. f, Little Boy Blue.
No. 3050, The Cat and the Fiddle, $1.50, vert. a, Bird, house. b, Cow jumping over moon. c, Spoon. d, Dog, house. e, Cat and fiddle. f, Dish.
No. 3051, $6, Little Bo Peep. No. 3052, $6, The Old Woman Who Lived in a Shoe. No. 3053, $6, Little Boy Blue. No. 3054, Cow jumping over the moon.
Illustration reduced.

**2000, Sept. 9** ***Perf. 13¾x13¼***

**Sheets of 6, #a-f**

**3047-3050** A477 Set of 4 27.50 27.50

**Souvenir Sheets**

***Perf. 13¼x13¾***

**3051-3054** A477 Set of 4 18.00 18.00

**Flower Photomosaic Type of 1999**
**Queen Mother**

Various flowers making up photomosaic.

**2000, Nov. 20** ***Perf. 13¾***
**3055** A445 $1 Sheet of 8, #a-h 6.00 6.00

Cats — A478

75c, Maine Coon cat. 90c, Selkirk Rex.
No. 3058, horiz.: a, Spotted tabby British shorthair. b, Burmilla. c, British blue shorthair. d, Siamese. e, Japanese bobtail. f, Oriental shorthair.

**2000, June 23** **Litho.** ***Perf. 14***
**3056-3057** A478 Set of 2 1.75 1.75
**3058** A478 $1.50 Sheet of 6, #a-f 8.00 8.00

**Souvenir Sheet**

**3059** A478 $6 Scottish Fold 5.75 5.75

Queen Mother, 100th Birthday — A479

**2000, Nov. 20**
**3060** A479 $1.50 multi 1.10 1.10

Printed in sheets of 6.

Christmas — A480

Designs: 15c, 50c, No. 3065b, Angel looking left. 25c, $5, No. 3065a, Angel looking right.

**2000, Dec. 4**
**3061-3064** A480 Set of 4 4.50 4.50
**3065** A480 $2 Sheet, 2 ea #a-b 6.00 6.00

**Souvenir Sheet**

**3066** A480 $6 Baby Jesus 4.50 4.50

Souvenir Sheets

Betty Boop — A481

Designs: No. 3067, $6, Wearing lei. No. 3068, $6, Holding fishing pole and fish. No. 3069, $6, Wearing polka dot hat. No. 3070, $6, Holding castanets. No. 3071, $6, At Japanese tea ceremony. No. 3072, $6, Wearing pink hat. No. 3073, $6, In mountains, wearing flowered hat. No. 3074, $6, Wearing beret. No. 3075, $6, As Statue of Liberty. No. 3076, $6, In Hollywood. No. 3077, $6, On horse. No. 3078, $6, On camel's back.

**2000, Oct. 11** **Litho.** ***Perf. 13¾***
**3067-3078** A481 Set of 12 60.00 60.00

Souvenir Sheet

New Year 2001 (Year of the Snake) — A482

No. 3079: a, Blue green denomination. b, Red denomination. c, Purple denomination.

**2001, Jan. 2** ***Perf. 12½x13***
**3079** A482 $2 Sheet of 3, #a-c 4.50 4.50

Rijksmuseum, Amsterdam, Bicent. — A483

No. 3080, $1.50: a, William I, Prince of Orange, by Adriaen Thomasz Key. b, Rutger Jan Schimmelpennick and Family, by Pierre Paul Prud'hon. c, Johan Rudolf Thorbecke, by Johan Heinrich Neuman. d, St. Sebastian, by Joachim Wtewael. e, St. Sebastian, by Hendrick ter Brugghen. f, Portrait of a Man With a Ring, by Werner Van Den Valckert.
No. 3081, $1.50: a, The Syndics of the Amsterdam Goldsmith's Guild, by Thomas de Keyser. b, Portrait of a Gentleman, by de Keyser. c, Portrait of Eva Wtewael, by Wtewael. d, The Cattle Ferry, by Esaias van de Velde. e, Landscape With the Parable of the Tares Among the Wheat, by Abraham Bloemaert. f, Princess Henrietta Marie Stuart, by Bartholomeus van der Helst.
No. 3082, $1.50: a, The Merry Fiddler, by Gerard van Honthorst. b, The Merry Drinker, by Frans Hals. c, Granida and Daifilo, by van Honthorst. d, Vertumnus and Pomona, by Paulus Moreelse. e, Flutist from The Concert, by ter Brugghen. f, A Young Student at His Desk: Melancholy, by Pieter Codde.
No. 3083, $1.50: a, The Haarlem Painter Abraham Casteleyn and His Wife Margarieta van Bancken, by Jan de Bray. b, Two figures from The Concert. c, The Procuress, by Dirck van Baburen. d, Woman Seated at a Virginal, by Johannes Vermeer. e, Dignified Couples Courting, by Willem Buytewech. f, The Young Flute Player, by Judith Leyster.
No. 3084, $6, Interior of the Portuguese Synagogue in Amsterdam, by Emanuel de Witte. No. 3085, $6, The Denial of St. Peter, by Rembrandt, horiz. No. 3086, $6, Winter Landscape With Skaters, by Hendrick Avercamp, horiz. No. 3087, $6, The Raampoortje, by Wouter Johannes van Troostwijk, horiz.
Illustration reduced.

**2001, Jan. 15** ***Perf. 13¾***

**Sheets of 6, #a-f**

**3080-3083** A483 Set of 4 27.50 27.50

**Souvenir Sheets**

**3084-3087** A483 Set of 4 18.00 18.00

Pokémon — A484

No. 3088: a, Rattata. b, Sandshrew. c, Wartortle. d, Primeape. e, Golduck. f, Persian.

**2001, Feb. 1**
**3088** A484 $1.50 Sheet of 6, #a-f 6.75 6.75

**Souvenir Sheet**

**3089** A484 $6 Jolteon 4.50 4.50

Waterfowl — A485

No. 3090, $1.25: a, African pygmy goose. b, Silver teal. c, Marbled teal. d, Garganey. e, Wandering whistling duck. f, Northern shoveler.
No. 3091, $1.25: a, Female flightless steamer duck. b, Radjah. c, Cape teal. d, Hartlaub's duck. e, Ruddy shelduck. f, White-cheeked pintail.
No. 3092, $1.25, vert.: a, Fulvous whistling duck. b, African black duck. c, Madagascar white-eye. d, Female pygmy goose. e, Female wood duck. f, Male wood duck.
No. 3093, $6, Flightless steamer duck. No. 3094, $6, Flying steamer duck. No. 3095, $6, Australian shelduck, vert.

***Perf. 13¼x13¾, 13¾x13¼***

**2001, Mar. 5** **Litho.**

**Sheets of 6, #a-f**

**3090-3092** A485 Set of 3 17.00 17.00

**Souvenir Sheets**

**3093-3095** A485 Set of 3 13.50 13.50

Hong Kong 2001 Stamp Exhibition.

Cricket Players — A486

No. 3096: Various photos of Sir Donald Bradman swinging bat.
No. 3097, Various photos of Shane Warne bowling.
No. 3098, Various photos of Sir Jack Hobbs.
No. 3099, Various photos of Sir Vivian Richards.
No. 3100, Various photos of Sir Garfield Sobers.
No. 3101, oval vignettes: a, Bradman. b, Sobers. c, Hobbs. d, Warne. e, Richards.

**2001, May 15** ***Perf. 14***

| | | | |
|---|---|---|---|
| **3096** | Sheet of 8, #a-h | 6.00 | 6.00 |
| ***a.-h.*** | A486 $1 Any single | .75 | .75 |
| **3097** | Sheet of 8, #a-h | 6.00 | 6.00 |
| ***a.-h.*** | A486 $1 Any single | .75 | .75 |
| **3098** | Sheet of 4, #a-d | 6.00 | 6.00 |
| ***a.-d.*** | A486 $2 Any single | 1.50 | 1.50 |
| **3099** | Sheet of 4, #a-d | 6.00 | 6.00 |
| ***a.-d.*** | A486 $2 Any single | 1.50 | 1.50 |
| **3100** | Sheet of 4, #a-d | 6.00 | 6.00 |
| ***a.-d.*** | A486 $2 Any single | 1.50 | 1.50 |
| **3101** | Sheet of 5, #a-e | 7.50 | 7.50 |
| ***a.-e.*** | A486 $2 Any single | 1.50 | 1.50 |
| | *Nos. 3096-3101 (6)* | 37.50 | 37.50 |

A487

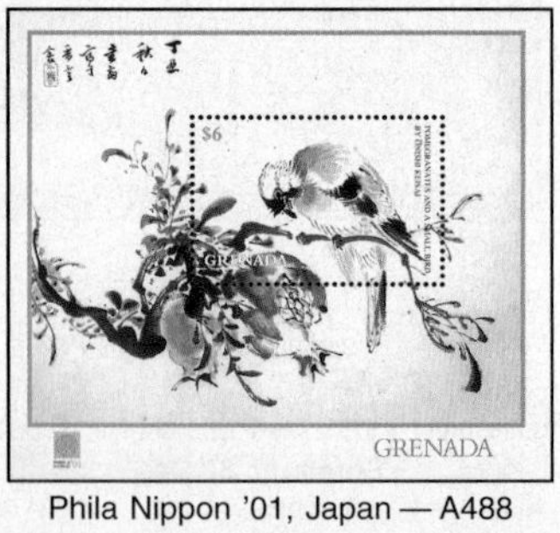


Phila Nippon '01, Japan — A488

Art: 75c, Scenes of Daily Life in Edo, by Miyagawa Choshun. 90c, Twelve Famous Places in Japan, by Kano Isenin Naganobu. $1, After the Rain, by Kawai Gyokudo. $1.25, Ryogoku Bridge Crowded With People, by Kano Kyuei. No. 3106, $2, A Courtesan of Fukagawa, by Katsukawa Shunei. $3, Rite of Bear Killing, by unknown artist.
No. 3108 — Details from the Lotus Sutra, $2, vert.: a, Figure in white at left. b, Figure with flag at lower right. c, Water in center. d, White pagoda at top right.
No. 3109 — Details from the Tale of Genji, $2 (size: 84x28mm): a, Yugao Chapter. b, Suetsumuhana Chapter. c, Wakamurasaki Chapter. d, Momiji-no-ga Chapter.
No. 3110, $6, Pomegranates and a Small Bird, by Onishi Keisai. No. 3111, $6, Bodhisattva from the Lotus Sutra, vert.

**2001, May 1** **Litho.** ***Perf. 14***

**3102-3107** A487 Set of 6 6.75 6.75

**Sheets of 4, #a-d**

**3108-3109** A488 Set of 2 12.00 12.00

**Souvenir Sheets**

**3110-3111** A488 Set of 2 9.00 9.00

Marlene Dietrich — A489

No. 3112: a, With cigarette. b, Behind microphone. c, Seated, showing legs. d, Seated.

**2001, May 15** ***Perf. 13¾***

**3112** A489 $2 Sheet of 4, #a-d 6.00 6.00

Queen Victoria (1819-1901) — A490

No. 3113: a, In white, as young girl. b, Wearing crown as young woman. c, Wearing crown as old woman.
$6, On throne.

**2001, May 15** ***Perf. 14***

**3113** A490 $3 Sheet of 3, #a-c 6.75 6.75

**Souvenir Sheet**

**3114** A490 $6 multi 4.50 4.50

Queen Elizabeth II, 75th Birthday — A491

No. 3115: a, Straw hat. b, Red hat. c, Flowered hat. d, Blue hat.
$6, Blue hat with brim.

**2001, May 15** ***Perf. 14***

**3115** A491 $2 Sheet of 4, #a-d 6.00 6.00

**Souvenir Sheet**

***Perf. 13¾***

**3116** A491 $6 multi 4.50 4.50

No. 3116 contains one 38x51mm stamp.

UN Women's Human Rights Campaign — A492

Designs: 90c, Woman, bird, torch. $1, Woman.

**2001, May 15** **Litho.** ***Perf. 14***

**3117-3118** A492 Set of 2 1.40 1.40

Mao Zedong (1893-1976) — A493

No. 3119 — background colors: a, Deep purple. b, Pinkish gray. c, Mottled red violet.
$6, Mao with cap.

**2001, May 15** ***Perf. 13¾***

**3119** A493 $2 Sheet of 3, #a-c 4.50 4.50

**Souvenir Sheet**

**3120** A493 $3 multi 2.25 2.25

Giuseppe Verdi (1813-1910), Opera Composer — A494

No. 3121: a, Actor with crown. b, Score from Ernani. c, Verdi. d, La Scala Theater, Milan.
$6, Verdi with hat.

**2001, May 15** ***Perf. 14***

**3121** A494 $2 Sheet of 4, #a-d 6.00 6.00

**Souvenir Sheet**

**3122** A494 $6 multi 4.50 4.50

Toulouse-Lautrec Paintings — A495

No. 3123: a, Alone. b, Two Half-naked Women. c, The Toilette. d, Justine Dieuhl.
$6, Mademoiselle Dihau at the Piano.

**2001, May 15** ***Perf. 13¾***

**3123** A495 $2 Sheet of 4, #a-d 6.00 6.00

**Souvenir Sheet**

**3124** A495 $6 multi 4.50 4.50

A496

Ships — A497

Designs: 45c, Phoenician trading ship. 75c, Portuguese caravel. 90c, Marblehead schooner. No. 3128, Mala pansi. $1.50, US corvette. $2, Racing schooner.
No. 3131, $1: a, English carrack. b, Mediterranean carrack. c, Spanish galleon. d, Elizabeth Grumster. e, British East Indiaman. f,

Clipper ship. g, British gunship. h, British flag-ship. i, English hoy.

No. 3132, $1: a, English cog. b, Roman merchantman. c, Greek war galley. d, Greek merchantman. e, Norse Oseberg ship. f, Egyptian sailboat. g, Egyptian oared ship. h, 16th cent. galleass. i, Norman sailing ship.

No. 3133, $1: a, Gloucester fishing schooner. b, Racing sloop. c, Chinese junk. d, Sambuk. e, Baltimore clipper schooner. f, Schooner yacht. g, US Clipper ship. h, US frigate. i Steam naval packet.

No. 3134, $6, Gulf Streamer. No. 3135, $6, Suhaili.

Illustration A497 reduced.

**2001, June 18** ***Perf. 14***

**3125-3130** A496 Set of 6 5.00 5.00

**Sheets of 9, #a-i**

**3131-3133** A496 Set of 3 21.00 21.00

**Miniature Sheets**

**3134-3135** A497 Set of 2 9.00 9.00

Belgica 2001 Intl. Stamp Exhibition, Brussels (Nos. 3131-3133).

A498

Flowers A499

Designs: 25c, Brassavola nodosa. No. 3137, $1, Allamanda cathartica. No. 3138, $2, Aspasia epidendroides. $3, Oncidium splendidum.

35c, Flor de San Miguel. 75c, Red frangipani. No. 3142, $1, Paper flower. No. 3143, $2, Flor de muerto.

No. 3144, $1.50: a, Candlebush. b, Flamingo flower. c, Bush morning glory. d, Laelia anceps. e, Galeandra baueri. f, Chinese hibiscus.

No. 3145, $1.50: a, Red ginger. b, Bird of paradise. c, Psychlis atropurpurea. d, Cattleya velutina. e, Caularthron bicornutum. f, Cattleya warneri.

No. 3146, $1.50, vert.: a, Mandeville. b, Tithonia rotundifolia. c, June rose. d, Columnea argentea. e, Chameleon plant. f, Protlandia albiflora.

No. 3147, $1.50, vert.: a, Wild chestnut. b, Jatropha integerrima. c, Fern tree. d, Geiger tree. e, Golden trumpet. f, Saman.

No. 3148, $6, Ipomoea learii, horiz. No. 3149, $6, Anthurium scherzerianum, horiz.

No. 3150, $6, Ladies eardrops. No. 3151, $6, Heliconia psittacorum, vert.

**2001**

**3136-3139** A498 Set of 4 6.25 6.25
**3140-3143** A499 Set of 4 4.75 4.75

**Sheets of 6, #a-f**

**3144-3145** A498 Set of 2 15.00 15.00
**3146-3147** A499 Set of 2 15.00 15.00

**Souvenir Sheets**

**3148-3149** A498 Set of 2 11.00 11.00
**3150-3151** A499 Set of 2 11.00 11.00

Kane — A500

No. 3152 — Kane: a, In air, above ring ropes. b, On one knee. c, In air. d, With red background. e, With gradiated gray and yellow background. f, Holding up opponent with both hands. g, With spotlight background. h, Holding up shirtless opponent. i, Holding up opponent with one hand.

No. 3153, $5, With red background, diff. No. 3154, $5, With opponent.

**2001** ***Perf. 13¾***

**3152** A500 $1 Sheet of 9, #a-i 6.75 6.75

**Souvenir Sheets**

**3153-3154** A500 Set of 2 7.50 7.50

The Three Stooges — A501

No. 3155, $1: a, Larry, Moe, two cowboys. b, Moe and Shemp with hats, Larry. c, Shemp and Larry in drag, Moe with mustache. d, Moe with gun, Larry, Shemp, woman. e, Larry, Moe, Shemp with certificate. f, Shemp, Moe. g, Larry, picture. h, Moe, picture. i, Shemp.

No. 3156, $1: a, Larry, Curly, Moe with tool. b, Joe DeRita eating hay, horse, Larry, Moe. c, Shemp, Larry with flowers, Moe. d, Moe, Shemp, Larry, reading paper. e, Larry, Moe, Shemp with pots. f, Moe, Shemp, Larry with money. g, Shemp with knight. h, Joe DeRita, horse, Moe, Larry. i, Larry with knight.

No. 3157, $5, Larry, Moe, Shemp, woman from movie poster. No. 3158, $5, Shemp pulling Moe's arm. No. 3159, $5, Joe DeRita and Larry. No. 3160, $5, Larry and Joe DeRita, jet engine. No. 3161, $5, Moe, Larry holding woman's hand. No. 3162, $5, Larry, Moe listening to jet engine, horiz. No. 3163, $5, Larry, Moe, Shemp and cowboy, horiz. No. 3164, $5, Shemp behind bar, cowboys fighting Larry and Moe, horiz. No. 3165, $5, Curly, Moe, Larry and propeller, horiz. No. 3166, $5, Moe, Larry, woman with drink, horiz. No. 3167, $6, Moe, Larry with knight, horiz. No. 3168, $6, Curly in wringer, Moe, horiz.

**2001** **Sheets of 9, #a-i**

**3155-3156** A501 Set of 2 13.50 13.50

**Souvenir Sheets**

**3157-3168** A501 Set of 12 47.50 47.50

Lighthouses A502

Designs: 25c, Montauk Point, NY. 50c, Alcatraz, CA. $1, Barnegat, NJ. $2, St. Augustine, FL.

No. 3173, $1.50: a, Admiralty Head, WA. b, Hooper's Strait, MD. c, Hunting Island, SC. d, Key West Lighthouse Museum, FL. e, Old Point Loma, CA. f, Old Mackinac Moint, MI.

No. 3174, $1.50: a, Point Amour, Canada. b, Inubo-Saki, Japan. c, Belle-Ile. France. d, Faerder, Norway. e, Cape Agulhas, South Africa. f, Minicoy, India.

No. 3175, $1.50: a, Keri, Estonia. b, Anholt, Denmark. c, Porer, Croatia. d, Laotieshan, China. e, Sapientza Methoni, Greece. f, Arkona, Germany.

No. 3176, $6, Boston, MA. No. 3177, $6, Pellworm, Germany. No. 3178, $6, Kvitsoy, Norway. No. 3179, Mahota Pagoda, China.

**2001, Aug. 27** **Litho.** ***Perf. 14***

**3169-3172** A502 Set of 4 2.75 2.75

**Sheets of 6, #a-f**

**3173-3175** A502 Set of 3 20.00 20.00

**Souvenir Sheets**

**3176-3179** A502 Set of 4 18.00 18.00

Marine Mammals A503

Designs: 25c, Commerson's dolphin. 50c, Pacific white-sided dolphin. $2, Northern bottlenosed whale. $3, Baird's beaked whale.

No. 3184, $1.50: a, Risso's dolphin. b, Fraser's dolphin. c, Dall's porpoise. d, Right whale. e, Gray whale. f, Minke whale.

No. 3185, $1.50: a, Common dolphin. b, Antillean beaked whale. c, Killer whale. d, Bryde's whale. e, Cuvier's beaked whale. f, Sei whale.

No. 3186, $1.50: a, Harbor porpoise. b, Beluga. c, White-beaked dolphin. d, Narwhal. e, Bowhead whale. f, Fin whale.

No. 3187, $6, Sperm whale. No. 3188, $6, Blue whale. No. 3189, $6, Southern right whale. No. 3190, $6, Humpback whale.

**2001, Sept. 10**

**3180-3183** A503 Set of 4 4.25 4.25

**Sheets of 6, #a-f**

**3184-3186** A503 Set of 3 20.00 20.00

**Souvenir Sheets**

**3187-3190** A503 Set of 4 18.00 18.00

Monet Paintings — A504

No. 3191, horiz.: a, Boats in Winter Quarters, Etretat. b, Regatta at Sainte Adresse. c, The Bridge at Bougival. d, The Beach at Sainte Adresse.

$6, Monet's Garden at Vétheuil.

**2001, May 15** **Litho.** ***Perf. 13¾***

**3191** A504 $2 Sheet of 4, #a-d 6.00 6.00

**Souvenir Sheet**

**3192** A504 $6 multi 4.50 4.50

2002 World Cup Soccer Championships, Japan and Korea — A505

No. 3193, $1.50: a, Poster, 1950. b, West German championship team, 1954. c, Just Fontaine, 1958. d, Garrincha, Brazil, 1962. e, Bobby Moore, England, 1966. f, Pelé, Brazil, 1970.

No. 3194, $1.50: a, Osvaldo Ardiles, Argentina, 1978. b, Lakhdar Belloumi, Algeria, 1982. c, Diego Maradona, Argentina, 1986. d, Matthaüs and Völler, West Germany, 1990. e, Seo Jung Won, South Korea, 1994. f, Ronaldo, Brazil, 1998.

No. 3195, $6, Face from Jules Rimet trophy. No. 3196, $6, Face and globe from World Cup trophy.

**2001, Nov. 29** ***Perf. 13¾x14¼***

**Sheets of 6, #a-f**

**3193-3194** A505 Set of 2 13.50 13.50

**Souvenir Sheet**

**3195-3196** A505 Set of 2 9.00 9.00

Christmas A506

Santa Claus and: 15c, House, Christmas tree. 50c, Trees, snowman. $1, Tree, ice skates. $4, Children.

$6, Santa eating cookie.

**2001, Dec. 3** ***Perf. 14***

**3197-3200** A506 Set of 4 4.25 4.25

**Souvneir Sheet**

**3201** A506 $6 multi 4.50 4.50

A507

Nobel Prizes, Cent. — A508

1901 Laureates: 75c, Emil A. von Behring, Medicine. 90c, Wilhelm C. Röntgen, Physics. $1, Jacobus H. van't Hoff, Chemistry. No. 3205, $1.50, Frederic Passy, Peace. $2, Jean-Henri Dunant, Peace. $3, René Sully-Prudhomme, Literature.

No. 3208, horiz. — Albert Einstein, 1921 Physics laureate, with: a, Dark hair, black suit. b, Pipe. c, Gray suit. d, Pink sweater. e, Gray hair, black suit. f, Blue sweater.
$6, Einstein wearing hat.

**2001, Dec. 13**

| | | | | |
|---|---|---|---|---|
| **3202-3207** A507 | Set of 6 | | 7.00 | 7.00 |
| **3208** A508 $1.50 | Sheet of 6, #a-f | | 6.75 | 6.75 |

**Souvenir Sheet**

| | | | |
|---|---|---|---|
| **3209** A508 | $6 multi | 4.50 | 4.50 |

Princess Diana (1961-97) — A509

No. 3210: a, Blue gown. b. White gown. c, Red gown.
$6, With pink curtain.

**2001, Dec. 13**

| | | | | |
|---|---|---|---|---|
| **3210** A509 | $1.50 Sheet, 2 each #a-c | | 6.75 | 6.75 |

**Souvenir Sheet**

| | | | |
|---|---|---|---|
| **3211** A509 | $6 multi | 4.50 | 4.50 |

### Queen Mother Type of 1999

No. 3212: a, Queen Mother, Prince Charles, 1948. b, Queen Mother, 1970. c, Queen Mother in Australia, 1958. d, Queen Mother.
$6, Queen Mother, 1953.

**2001, Dec. 13** ***Perf. 14***

**Yellow Orange Frames**

| | | | |
|---|---|---|---|
| **3212** A440 | $2 Sheet of 4, #a-d, + label | 6.00 | 6.00 |

**Souvenir Sheet**

***Perf. 13¾***

| | | | |
|---|---|---|---|
| **3213** A440 | $6 multi | 4.50 | 4.50 |

Queen Mother's 101st birthday. No. 3213 contains one 38x50mm stamp with a redder backdrop than that found on No. 2881. Sheet margins of Nos. 3212-3213 lack embossing and gold arms found on Nos. 2880-2881.

New Year 2002 (Year of the Horse) — A510

Ceramic horses of T'ang dynasty — No. 3214: a, Brown horse with long, tan mane. b, Blue horse with pink hooves. c, Black horse with gray mane. d, Tan horse with round ornaments.
$4, Brown horse with gray and green saddle.

**2001, Dec. 17** ***Perf. 13¾***

| | | | |
|---|---|---|---|
| **3214** A510 | $1.50 Sheet of 4, #a-d | 4.50 | 4.50 |

**Souvenir Sheet**

| | | | |
|---|---|---|---|
| **3215** A510 | $4 multi | 3.00 | 3.00 |

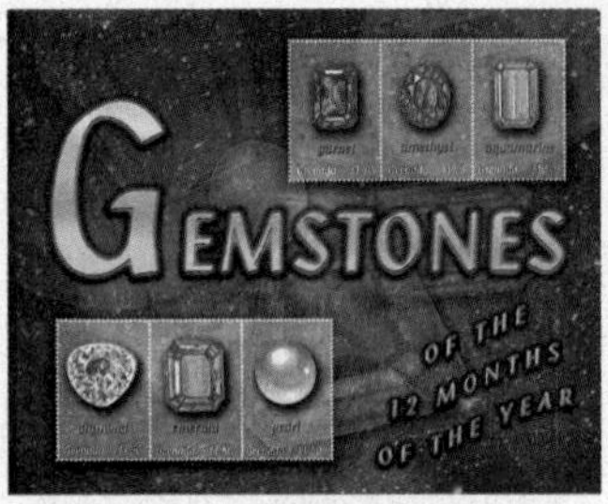


A511

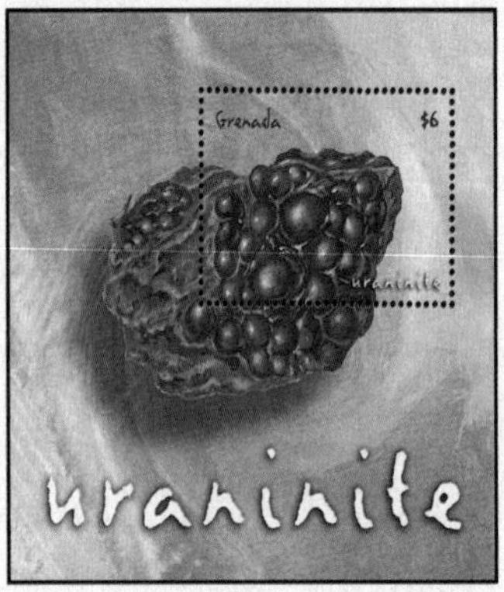


Gemstones and Minerals — A512

Monthly gemstones — No. 3216, $1.50: a, Garnet (January). b, Amethyst (February). c, Aquamarine (March). d, Diamond (April). e, Emerald (May). f, Pearl (June).
No. 3217, $1.50: a, Ruby (July). b, Sardonyx (August). c, Sapphire (September). d, Opal (October). e, Topaz (November). f, Turquoise (December).
Gemstones in mineral form — No. 3218: a, Ruby. b, Diamond. c, Sapphire. d, Opal. e, Turquoise. f, Jade.
No. 3219, $6, Uraninite. No. 3220, $6, Calcite. No. 3221, $6, Quartz, vert.

**2001, Dec. 31** ***Perf. 14***

**Sheets of 6, #a-f**

| | | | |
|---|---|---|---|
| **3216-3217** A511 | Set of 2 | 14.50 | 14.50 |
| **3218** A512 | $1.50 Sheet of 6, #a-f | 7.50 | 7.50 |

**Souvenir Sheets**

| | | | |
|---|---|---|---|
| **3219-3221** A512 | Set of 3 | 14.50 | 14.50 |

US Presidents — A513

No. 3222, $1.50 — John F. Kennedy and: a, Field. b, Flag, building, microphone. c, Airplane.
No. 3223, $1.50 — Ronald Reagan: a, In uniform with binoculars. b, With red tie. c, With flag.
No. 3224, $6, Kennedy. No. 3225, $6, Reagan.

**2001, Dec. 31**

**Sheets, 2 each #a-c**

| | | | |
|---|---|---|---|
| **3222-3223** A513 | Set of 2 | 13.50 | 13.50 |

**Souvenir Sheets**

| | | | |
|---|---|---|---|
| **3224-3225** A513 | Set of 2 | 9.00 | 9.00 |

**Souvenir Sheets**

I Love Lucy — A514

Designs: No. 3226, $6, Ethel watching Lucy and Desi dance. No. 3227, $6, Desi, Lucy, Fred and Ethel near door. No. 3228, $6, Desi holding Lucy. No. 3229, $6, Lucy in plaid shirt.

**2001** ***Perf. 13¾***

| | | | |
|---|---|---|---|
| **3226-3229** A514 | Set of 4 | 18.00 | 18.00 |

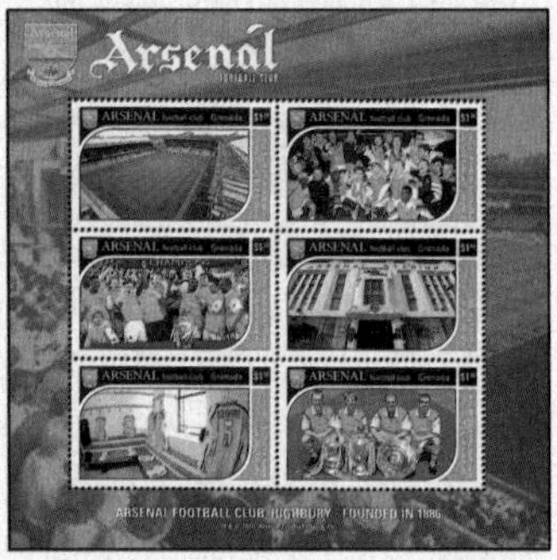


English Soccer Teams — A515

No. 3230, $1.50 — Arsenal: a, Inside of Highbury Stadium. b, Players celebrate 1994 European Cup and Winner's Cup. c, Players celebrate 1998 premiership. d, East stands, Highbury Stadium. e, Locker rooms. f, Four players with trophies, 1998.
No. 3231, $1.50 — Aston Villa: a, Sign on Villa Park. b, Fans watching night game. c, Empty stadium, field at right. d, Empty stadium, field at left. e, Holte End of stadium. f, Fans in stands.
No. 3232, $1.50 — Bolton Wanderers: a, Empty Reebok Stadium. b, Players celebrating 2001 Division 1 playoff win. c, Promotion to Premier League. d, Fans celebrate. e, Players, coaches with trophy. f, Game played in Reebok Stadium.
No. 3233, $1.50 — Everton: a, 2001-02 team. b, Re-signing of Duncan Ferguson. c, Statue of Wiliam Ralph "Dixie" Dean. d, Fans. e, Goodison Park. f, 1969-70 league championship team.
No. 3234, $1.50 — Ipswich Town: a, Players holding banner and trophy after 2000 Division 1 playoff final. b, 2001-02 team. c, Manager George Burley and Chairman David Sheepshanks. d, Pablo Counago fights for ball. e, Captain Matt Holland. f, George Burley receives Manager of the Year award.
No. 3235, $1.50 — Liverpool: a, Anfield. b, 2000-01 Worthington Cup winners. c, 2000-01 FA Cup winners. d, Fans. e, 2000-01 UEFA Cup winners. f, Treble Cup parade.
No. 3236, $1.50 — Manchester United: a, Legends Meredith, Law and Charlton. b, Three 1998-99 trophies. c, Views of Old Trafford, 1948, 1956. d, Recent views of Old Trafford. e, Third premiership in three years, 2000-01. f, Heroes, Best, Robson and Beckham.
No. 3237, $1.50 — Rangers: a, View of Ibrox Stadium from street. b, 1972 European Cup and Winner's Cup team. c, Scottish FA Cup, Scottish Premier League Trophy. d, Aerial view of Ibrox Stadium. e, Fans in stadium. f, Nine consecutive Scottish League wins.

**2001, Sept. 12** **Litho.** ***Perf. 13¼***

**Sheets of 6, #a-f**

| | | | |
|---|---|---|---|
| **3230-3237** A515 | Set of 8 | 55.00 | 55.00 |

See Nos. 3286-3294.

Reign of Queen Elizabeth II, 50th Anniv. — A516

No. 3238: a, With Prince Philip. b, Wearing flowered hat. c, Wearing tiara. d, Wearing gray coat with white collar.
$6, Wearing uniform.

**2002, Feb. 6** ***Perf. 14½***

| | | | |
|---|---|---|---|
| **3238** A516 | $2 Sheet of 4, #a-d | 6.00 | 6.00 |

**Souvenir Sheet**

| | | | |
|---|---|---|---|
| **3239** A516 | $6 multi | 4.50 | 4.50 |

United We Stand — A517

**2002, Feb.** ***Perf. 13¾x13½***

| | | | |
|---|---|---|---|
| **3240** A517 | $2 multi | 1.50 | 1.50 |

Issued in sheets of 4.

Dale Earnhardt, Race Car Driver — A518

Years of Winston Cup Championships: No. 3241, $2, 1980. No. 3242, $2, 1986. No. 3243, $2, 1987. No. 3244, $2, 1990. No. 3245, $2, 1991. No. 3246, $2, 1993. No. 3247, $2, 1994.

**2002, Mar. 4** **Litho.** ***Perf. 14x13¾***

| | | | |
|---|---|---|---|
| **3241-3247** A518 | Set of 7 | 12.00 | 12.00 |

Mickey Mouse A519

No. 3249 — Scenes from: a, The Nifty Nineties, 1941. b, Magician Mickey, 1937. c, Steamboat Willie, 1928. d, Fantasia, 1940. e, Mickey Mouse Club, 1955. f, Cactus Kid, 1930. g, The Prince and the Pauper, 1990. h, Brave Little Tailor, 1938. i, Canine Caddy, 1941.

**2002, Apr. 24** ***Perf. 13¾***

**3248** A519 $1 shown .90 .90
**3249** A519 $1 Sheet of 9, #a-i 8.75 8.75

No. 3248 was printed in sheets of nine.

American Civil War Naval History — A520

No. 3250, $1: a, CSS Teaser. b, US gunboats on the James River. c, USS Tyler. d, USS Maratanza. e, USS Metacomet. f, USS Rattler.

No. 3251, $1.25: a, CSS Tennessee. b, USS Hartford. c, USS Chickasaw. d, USS Ossipee. e, Battle of Mobile Bay. f, USS Chickasaw at Mobile Bay.

No. 3252, $1.50: a, CSS H.L. Hunley. b, USS Cumberland. c, CSS Old Dominion. d, USS Housatonic. e, USS Hartford. f, USS Essex.

No. 3253, $1.50: a, CSS Alabama. b, USS Kearsarge and CSS Alabama. c, USS Hatteras. d, CSS Alabama and decoy. e, CSS Sumter. f, USS Kearsarge.

No. 3254, $6, USS Monitor. No. 3255, $6, CSS Florida. No. 3256, $6, CSS Tennessee. No. 3257, $6, Capt. Raphael Semmes aboard CSS Alabama.

**2002, Apr. 8 Litho.** ***Perf. 13¼x13½***

**Sheets of 6, #a-f**

**3250-3253** A520 Set of 4 28.00 28.00

**Souvenir Sheets**

**3254-3257** A520 Set of 4 22.00 22.00

Chiune Sugihara, Japanese Diplomat Who Saved Jews in World War II — A521

**2002, July 1** ***Perf. 13½x13¾***

**3258** A521 $2 multi 1.50 1.50

Printed in sheets of 4.

2002 Winter Olympics, Salt Lake City A522

Skier with: No. 3259, $2, Red skis. No. 3260, $2, Yellow skis.

**2002, July 1** ***Perf. 13¼x13½***

**3259-3260** A522 Set of 2 3.00 3.00
*a.* Souvenir sheet, #3259-3260 3.00 3.00

Intl. Year of Mountains — A523

No. 3261: a, Mt. Mawensi, Kenya. b, Mt. Stanley, Uganda. c, Mt. Taweche, Nepal. d, Mt. San Exupery, Argentina.

$6, Mt. Aso, Japan.

**2002, July 1**

**3261** A523 $2 Sheet of 4, #a-d 6.00 6.00

**Souvenir Sheet**

**3262** A523 $6 multi 4.50 4.50

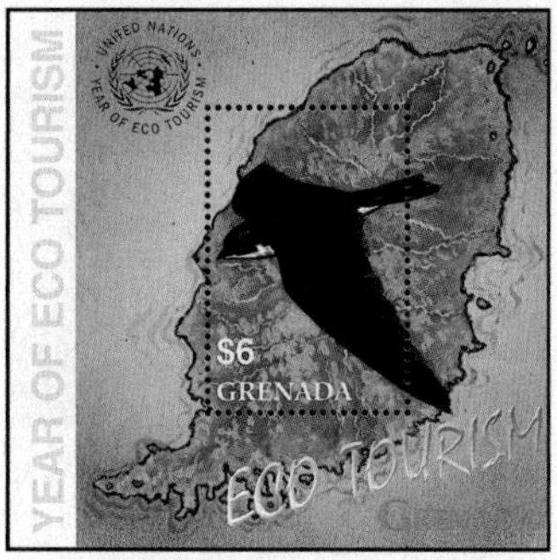


Intl. Year of Ecotourism — A524

No. 3263, horiz.: a, Tower and pennants. b, Bird. c, Flower, vacationer on chair. d, Diver, fish. e, Fish. f, Sailboats.

$6, Map of Grenada, bird.

**2002, July 1** ***Perf. 13¼x13½***

**3263** A524 $1 Sheet of 6, #a-f 4.50 4.50

**Souvenir Sheet**

***Perf. 13½x13¼***

**3264** A524 $6 multi 4.50 4.50

No. 3263 was overprinted in sheet margin "Hurricane Relief 2004" in 2005.

20th World Scout Jamboree, Thailand — A525

No. 3265, horiz.: a, Scout in canoe with oar out of water. b, Scout in canoe with oar in water. c, Bugler. d, Scout making Scout sign.

$6, Scout saluting.

**2002, July 1** ***Perf. 13¼x13½***

**3265** A525 $2 Sheet of 4, #a-d 7.50 7.50

**Souvenir Sheet**

***Perf. 13½x13¼***

**3266** A525 $6 multi 5.00 5.00

Model Heidi Klum — A526

No. 3267: a, Arms up. b, Arms down. c, No arms shown.

**2002, Aug. 16** ***Perf. 14***

**3267** A526 $1.50 Horiz. strip of 3, #a-c 3.50 3.50

Printed in sheets containing two strips.

Elvis Presley (1935-77) A527

**2002, Aug. 26** ***Perf. 13½x13¾***

**3268** A527 $1 multi .75 .75

Printed in sheets of 9.

Pokémon — A528

No. 3269: a, Mareep. b, Sunkern. c, Teddiursa. d, Swinub. e, Murkrow. f, Snubbull.

$6, Togepi.

**2002, Aug. 26** ***Perf. 13¾***

**3269** A528 $1.50 Sheet of 6, #a-f 6.75 6.75

**Souvenir Sheet**

**3270** A528 $6 multi 4.50 4.50

A529

A530

Teddy Bears, Cent. — A531

No. 3271: a, 25c, Bear with red hat, lace collar, cheese wheels. b, $1.25, Bear with black cap. c, $3, Bear with wooden shoes. d, $5, Bear with red hat and ribbon.

No. 3272: a, Army bear. b, Navy bear. c, Air Force bear. d, Marines bear.

No. 3273: a, Basketball bear. b, Martial arts bear. c, Golf bear. d, Baseball bear.

**2002, Aug. 26** ***Perf. 14***

**3271** A529 Sheet of 4, #a-d 7.25 7.25

***Perf. 14¼***

**3272** A530 $2 Sheet of 4, #a-d 6.00 6.00
**3273** A531 $2 Sheet of 4, #a-d 6.00 6.00

Dutch Nobel Prize Winners — A532

Dutch Lighthouses — A533

Traditional Dutch Women's Costumes — A534

No. 3274: a, Jacobus H. van't Hoff, Chemistry, 1901. b, Nobel Peace medal. c, Pieter Zeeman, Physics, 1902. d, Johannes D. van der Waals, Physics, 1910. e, Tobias M. C. Asser, Peace, 1911. f, Heike Kammerlingh-Onnes, Physics, 1913.

No. 3275: a, Schiermonnikoog. b, Texel. c, Egmond. d, Scheveningen. e, Schouwen. f, Hellevoetsluis.

No. 3276: a, Zeeland (woman with red necklace, patterned dress). b, Noord-Brabant (woman with black shawl). c, Noord-Holland (woman with flowered neckpiece).

**2002, Aug. 29** ***Perf. 13½x13¼***

| | | | | |
|---|---|---|---|---|
| **3274** | A532 | $1.50 Sheet of 6, #a-f | 6.75 | 6.75 |
| **3275** | A533 | $1.50 Sheet of 6, #a-f | 6.75 | 6.75 |

***Perf. 13¼***

| | | | | |
|---|---|---|---|---|
| **3276** | A534 | $3 Sheet of 3, #a-c | 6.75 | 6.75 |

Amphilex 2002 Intl. Stamp Exhibition, Amsterdam.

Shirley Temple — A535

Scenes from "Our Little Girl" — No. 3277, horiz.: a, With man. b, With man and woman. c, With dog and man. d, With woman and two men. e, On seesaw with dog. f, With dog.

No. 3278: a, With woman. b, with man and clown. c, Kneeling beside chair. d, With man and woman.

$6, In pink dress.

**2002, Sept. 3** ***Perf. 14¼***

| | | | | |
|---|---|---|---|---|
| **3277** | A535 | $1.50 Sheet of 6, #a-f | 6.75 | 6.75 |
| **3278** | A535 | $2 Sheet of 4, #a-d | 6.00 | 6.00 |

**Souvenir Sheet**

| | | | | |
|---|---|---|---|---|
| **3279** | A535 | $6 multi | 4.50 | 4.50 |

**Souvenir Sheet**

Terrorist Attack on World Trade Center, 1st Anniv. — A536

**2002, Sept. 11** ***Perf. 13¾***

| | | | | |
|---|---|---|---|---|
| **3280** | A536 | $6 multi | 4.50 | 4.50 |

Popeye — A537

No. 3281, vert.: a, Popeye in Florence, Italy. b, Popeye and Brutus in Paris, France. c, Popeye in Athens, Greece. d, Popeye and Olive Oyl in Venice, Italy. e, Popeye in London, England. f, Popeye in Norway.

No. 3282, vert. — At soccer match: a, Swee'Pea. b, Jeep. c, Popeye. d, Brutus.

No. 3283, $6, Popeye playing soccer. No. 3284, $6, Brutus playing soccer. No. 3285, $6, Popeye at Leaning Tower of Pisa, vert.

***Perf. 14¼ (#3281, 3285), 14***

**2002, Sept. 23**

| | | | | |
|---|---|---|---|---|
| **3281** | A537 | $1.50 Sheet of 6, #a-f | 6.75 | 6.75 |
| **3282** | A537 | $2 Sheet of 4, #a-d | 6.00 | 6.00 |

**Souvenir Sheets**

| | | | | |
|---|---|---|---|---|
| **3283-3285** | A537 | Set of 3 | 13.50 | 13.50 |

No. 3218 contains six 38x50mm stamps; No. 3285 contains one 50x75mm stamp.

**English Soccer Teams Type of 2001**

No. 3286, $1.50 — Tottenham Hotspur: a, Fans watching match in White Hart Lane Stadium. b, Sheringham and Anderton in action against Fulham. c, Poyet scoring against Liverpool. d, Tottenham Hotspur wins UEFA Cup, 1972. e, Celebrations after win against Chelsea. f, Fans in stadium, team insignia.

No. 3287, $1.50 — Manchester City: a, Maine Road Stadium from stands. b, Fans celebrate becoming Division One champions. c, Manager Kevin Keegan and trophy. d, Team with trophy. e, Players wearing medals, with trophy. f, Field level view of Maine Road Stadium.

No. 3288, $1.50 — Norwich City: a, Match at the Nest. b, Promotion to the Top Flight, 1971-72. c, Milk Cup win, 1985. d, Carrow Road Stadium. e, Win against Bayern Munich, 1993. f, Action from 1958-59 Cup run.

No. 3289, $1.50 — Arsenal, Double Winners: a, Tony Adams and Patrick Vieira hold FA Cup. b, Team wearing tan shirts, holding championship bannners. c, Team without banners, at Premiership trophy presentation. d, Photo of 2001-02 Premiership team, standing and wearing red shirts. e, Four players celebrate winning goal against Chelsea. f, Manager Arsene Wenger and Tony Adams at Double Winners Parade.

No. 3290, $1.50 — Arsenal, Premiership Winners: a, Inside of Highbury Stadium, team emblem and name in red panels. b, Celebrations after Gilberto scores winning goal. c, Team with FA Community Shield sign. d, Team photo, empty stands. e, Gilberto with FA Community Shield. f, Highbury Stadium with fans, team emblem.

No. 3291, $1.50 — Manchester United: a, David Beckham after free kick. b, Team photo, empty stands. c, Aerial view of Old Trafford Stadium. d, Celebration after Ole Gunnar Solskjaer's 100th goal for Manchester United. e, Fans at Old Trafford Stadium. f, North stand of Old Trafford Stadium.

No. 3292, $1.50 — Liverpool: a, Anfield's Centenary stand, as seen from Main stand. b, 2002-03 team photo. c, Gerard Houllier and Phil Thompson. d, Milan Baros celebrates goal. e, Vladimir Smicer congratulating Danny Murphy. f, The Kop, as seen from Anfield Road end.

No. 3293, $1.50 — Celtic: a, Interior of Celtic Park. b, Martin O'Neill with SPL Trophy. c, Henrik Larsson celebrating goal. d, 2002-03 team photo. e, Players celebrating a goal. f, Exterior of Celtic Park.

No. 3294, $1.50 — Chelsea: a, Night match at Stamford Bridge Stadium. b, Team with 1998 Cup Winners' Cup Final trophy. c, Fans in stadium. d, Sign for the Shed End. e, Field level view of Stamford Bridge Stadium. f, Players celebrating 2000 FA Cup victory.

**2002** ***Perf. 14x13¾***

**Sheets of 6, #a-f**

| | | | | |
|---|---|---|---|---|
| **3286-3294** | A515 | Set of 9 | 60.00 | 60.00 |

Issued: Nos. 3286-3289, 9/23; Nos. 3290-3294, 11/14.

Butterflies, Insects, Mushrooms and Whales — A538

No. 3295, $1.50 — Butterflies: a, Common morpho. b, Blue night. c, Small flambeau. d, Grecian shoemaker. e, Orange-barred sulphur. f, Cramer's mesene.

No. 3296, $1.50 — Insects: a, Honeybees. b, Dragonfly. c, Milkweed bug. d, Bumblebee. e, Migratory grasshopper. f, Monarch caterpillar.

No. 3297, $1.50 — Mushrooms: a, Boletus crocipodius. b, King bolete. c, Velvet shank. d, Death cap. e, Golden cavalier. f, Fly agaric.

No. 3298, $1.50 — Whales: a, Blue. b, Pygmy sperm. c, Humpback. d, Killer. e, Bowhead. f, Gray.

No. 3299, $6, Figure-of-eight butterfly. No. 3300, $6, Hercules beetle. No. 3301, $6, Sharp-scaled parasol mushroom. No. 3302, $6, Blue whale, horiz.

**2002, Oct. 21** ***Perf. 14***

**Sheets of 6, #a-f**

| | | | | |
|---|---|---|---|---|
| **3295-3298** | A538 | Set of 4 | 27.50 | 27.50 |

**Souvenir Sheets**

| | | | | |
|---|---|---|---|---|
| **3299-3302** | A538 | Set of 4 | 18.00 | 18.00 |

Sir Norman Wisdom, British Comedian A539

**2002, Nov. 3** ***Perf. 13¾***

| | | | | |
|---|---|---|---|---|
| **3303** | A539 | $1.50 multi | 1.10 | 1.10 |

Printed in sheets of 6.

Amerigo Vespucci (1454-1512), Explorer — A540

No. 3304, $3: a, Map of South America, ship. b, Compass rose, ship. c, Map of Europe and Africa.

No. 3305, $3, horiz.: a, Sextant, map of northern South America. b, Vespucci, map of central South America. c, Ship, map of southern South America.

No. 3306, $6, Compass rose. No. 3307, $6, Globe.

**2002, Nov. 4** ***Perf. 13¾***

**Sheets of 3, #a-c**

| | | | | |
|---|---|---|---|---|
| **3304-3305** | A540 | Set of 2 | 13.50 | 13.50 |

**Souvenir Sheets**

***Perf. 14***

| | | | | |
|---|---|---|---|---|
| **3306-3307** | A540 | Set of 2 | 9.00 | 9.00 |

No. 3304 contains three 38x50mm stamps; No. 3305 contains three 50x38mm stamps.

Christmas A541

Cimabue paintings: 15c, Madonna and Child, Four Angels and St. Francis, entire. 25c, Madonna and Child and Two Angels, vert. 50c, Madonna Enthroned, detail, vert. $1, Madonna Enthroned, entire, vert. $4, Madonna and Child, Four Angels and St. Francis, detail, vert.

$6, Nativity by Perugino, vert.

**2002, Nov. 4** ***Perf. 14***

| | | | | |
|---|---|---|---|---|
| **3308-3312** | A541 | Set of 5 | 4.50 | 4.50 |

**Souvenir Sheet**

| | | | | |
|---|---|---|---|---|
| **3313** | A541 | $6 multi | 4.50 | 4.50 |

Second Round Matches of 2002 World Cup Soccer Championships, Japan and Korea — A542

No. 3314, $1.50 — Sweden vs. Senegal: a, Johan Mjalby. b, Magnus Hedman. c, Fredrik Ljungberg. d, Khalilou Fadiga. e, El Hadji Diouf. f, Papa Bouba Diop.

No. 3315, $1.50 — Brazil vs. Belgium: a, Roberto Carlos. b, Juninho Paulista. c, Ronaldinho. d, Johan Walem. e, Marc Wilmots. f, Bart Goor.

No. 3316, $3 — Swedish players: a, Henrik Larsson. b, Niclas Alexandersson.

No. 3317, $3 — Senegal players: a, Fadiga. b, Coach Bruno Metsu.

No. 3318, $3 — Brazil players: a, Coach Luiz Felipe Scolari. b, Ronaldo.

No. 3319, $3 — Belgium players: a, Wesley Sonck. b, Coach Robert Waseige.

**2002, Nov. 18** ***Perf. 13¼***

**Sheets of 6, #a-f**

**3314-3315** A542 Set of 2 13.50 13.50

**Souvenir Sheets of 2, #a-b**

**3316-3319** A542 Set of 4 18.00 18.00

Souvenir Sheet

United States Natl. Law Enforcement and Firefighters Children's Foundation — A543

**2002, Nov. 28** ***Perf. 14¼***

**3320** A543 $6 multi 4.50 4.50

Pres. John F. Kennedy (1917-63) — A544

No. 3321, horiz.: a, Meeting with Cabinet. b, Signing bill into law. c, Meeting civil rights leaders. d, With Astronaut John Glenn. e, On campaign trail. f, Arrival in Dallas, Nov. 22, 1963.

$6, At microphone.

**2002, Dec. 4** ***Perf. 14***

**3321** A544 $1.50 Sheet of 6, #a-f 6.75 6.75

**Souvenir Sheet**

**3322** A544 $6 multi 4.50 4.50

Intl. Federation of Stamp Dealers Associations, 50th Anniv. — A545

**2002, Dec. 16** **Litho.**

**3323** A545 $2 multi 1.50 1.50

Princess Diana (1961-97) — A546

No. 3324: a, Wearing bow tie. b, Wearing blue dress. c, Wearing red and white hat. d, Holding flowers.

$6, Wearing earphones and microphone.

**2002** ***Perf. 14***

**3324** A546 $2 Sheet of 4, #a-d 6.00 6.00

**Souvenir Sheet**

**3325** A546 $6 multi 4.50 4.50

**I Love Lucy Type of 2001**

Souvenir Sheets

No. 3326, $6, Lucy standing near fireplace. No. 3327, $6, Lucy and Ethel at desk. No. 3328, $6, Fred and Desi standing. No. 3329, $6, Fred and Desi at desk, horiz.

**2002** ***Perf. 13¾***

**3326-3329** A514 Set of 4 18.00 18.00

New Year 2003 (Year of the Ram) A547

**2003, Jan. 27** ***Perf. 13¾***

**3330** A547 $1.25 multi .95 .95

Printed in sheets of 4.

M-Gears — A548

No. 3331: a, Airplane. b, Vehicle. c, Monster. d, Race car.

**2003, Feb. 16** **Litho.** ***Perf. 14¼***

**3331** A548 $2 Sheet of 4, #a-d 6.00 6.00

Astronauts Killed in Space Shuttle Columbia Accident — A549

No. 3332: a, Mission Specialist 1 David M. Brown. b, Commander Rick D. Husband. c, Mission Specialist 4 Laurel Blair Salton Clark. d, Mission Specialist 4 Kalpana Chawla. e, Payload Commander Michael P. Anderson. f, Pilot William C. McCool. g, Payload Specialist 4 Ilan Ramon.

**2003, Apr. 7** ***Perf. 13¼***

**3332** A549 $1 Sheet of 7, #a-g 6.00 6.00

Paintings of Gustav Klimt (1862-1918) A550

Designs: 15c, Jardin aux Tournesols. 25c, L'allée aux Poulets. 75c, Allée dans le Parc du Schloss Kammer. $1, Portrait of Johanna Staude. $1.25, Portrait of Friederike Maria Beer. $3, Portrait of Mäda Primavesi.

No. 3339: a, La Jeune Fille. b, Les Amies. c, Le Berceau. d, La Vie et la Mort.

$6, Portrait of Margaret Stonborough-Wittgenstein.

**2003, Apr. 28** ***Perf. 14¼***

**3333-3338** A550 Set of 6 5.00 5.00

**3339** A550 $2 Sheet of 4, #a-d 6.00 6.00

**Size: 82x103mm**

***Imperf***

**3340** A550 $6 multi 4.50 4.50

Art of Yoshitoshi Taiso (1839-92) A551

Designs: 75c, A Harlot in Repose. $1, A "Shakuni," or Geisha, Who Serves Wine or Sake. $1.25, A "Joro," or Low Ranking Prostitute, Having a Snack. $3, A Geisha Known as a "Geiko," or Entertainer Relaxing.

No. 3345: a, Enjoying a Cool Evening Breeze in a Pleasure Boat. b, A Fukagawa Waitress Carrying a Wooden Table Laden With Food. c, A Spoiled Unmarried Woman Pretending to Be Displeased With an Admirer. d, A Coy Young Girl, Biting Her Sleeve Pretending to Be Embarrassed.

$6, A Geisha About to Board a Party Boat.

**2003, Apr. 28** ***Perf. 14¼***

**3341-3344** A551 Set of 4 4.50 4.50

**3345** A551 $2 Sheet of 4, #a-d 6.00 6.00

**Souvenir Sheet**

**3346** A551 $6 multi 4.50 4.50

Paintings by Lucas Cranach the Elder (1472-1553) — A552

Details from St. Catherine Altarpiece: 50c, Sts. Dorothy, Agnes and Cunigonde. 75c, St. Margaret, vert. $1.25, St. Barbara, vert. $3, Detail from left wing, vert.

No. 3351 — Painting details: a, Lot and His Daughters. b, David and Bathsheba. c, The Agony in the Garden. d, The Adoration of the Magi.

$6, Detail of Samson and Delilah, vert.

**2003, Apr. 28**

**3347-3350** A552 Set of 4 4.25 4.25

**3351** A552 $2 Sheet of 4, #a-d 6.00 6.00

**Souvenir Sheet**

**3352** A552 $6 multi 4.50 4.50

Teddy Bear A553

**2003, Apr. 29** **Embroidered** ***Imperf.***

**Self-Adhesive**

**3353** A553 $15 multi 11.50 11.50

Issued in sheets of 4.

Reading Rods — A554

No. 3354 — Children and: a, Bulletin board. b, Blackboard. c, Globe. d, Teacher.

**2003, May 5** **Litho.** ***Perf. 13¾***

**3354** A554 $2 Sheet of 4, #a-d 6.00 6.00

Tour de France Bicycle Race, Cent. — A555

No. 3355, $2: a, Sylvére Maes, 1939. b, Jean Lazaridés, 1946. c, Jean Robic, 1947. d, Gino Bartali, 1948.

No. 3356, $2: a, Fausto Coppi, 1949. b, Ferdinand Kubler, 1950. c, Hugo Koblet, 1951. d, Coppi, 1952.

No. 3357, $2: a, Roger Walkowiak, 1956. b, Jacques Anquetil, 1957. c, Charly Gaul, 1958. d, Federico Bahamontes, 1959.

No. 3358, $6, Coppi, 1949, diff. No. 3359, $6, Kubler, 1950, diff. No. 3360, $6, Anquetil, 1964.

**2003, June 17** ***Perf. 13¼***

**Sheets of 4, #a-d**

**3355-3357** A555 Set of 3 18.00 18.00

**Souvenir Sheets**

**3358-3360** A555 Set of 3 13.50 13.50

Powered Flight, Cent. — A556

No. 3361, $2: a: First non-stop transatlantic flight by Alcock & Brown. b, Amelia Earhart, first woman to fly across Atlantic. c, Chuck Yeager, first man to break sound barrier. d, Charles Lindbergh, first solo transatlantic flight.

No. 3362, $2: a, Louis Bleriot, first flight across English Channel. b, Johnnie Johnson, ace pilot in World War II. c, Wright Brothers, first powered flight. d, Jacqueline Cochran, first woman to break sound barrier.

**2003, June 24** ***Perf. 13¼x13½***

**Sheets of 4, #a-d**

**3361-3362** A556 Set of 2 12.00 12.00

Coronation of Queen Elizabeth II, 50th Anniv. — A557

Designs: No. 3363, $2, Enthroning of the Queen. No. 3364, $2, Duke pays homage to the Queen. No. 3365, $2, Celebration of Holy Communion. No. 3366, $2, Floodlit mall. No. 3367, $2, Queen on balcony. No. 3368, $2, St. Edward's Chair. No. 3369, $2, Official coronation portrait. No. 3370, $2, Queen leaves Abbey.

$6, Queen in coach.

**2003, June 30** ***Perf. 13½x14***

**3363-3370** A557 Set of 8 12.00 12.00

**Souvenir Sheet**

**3371** A557 $6 multi 4.50 4.50

No. 3371 contains one 38x51mm stamp.

CARICOM, 30th Anniv. — A558

**2003, July 4** ***Perf. 14***

**3372** A558 $1 multi .75 .75

Intl. Year of Fresh Water — A559

No. 3373: a, Levera Pond. b, Concord Falls. c, Lake Antoine.

$6, Lake Grand Etang.

**2003, July 4** ***Perf. 13½x13¼***

**3373** A559 $2 Sheet of 3, #a-c 4.50 4.50

**Souvenir Sheet**

**3374** A559 $6 multi 4.50 4.50

Circus Performers — A560

No. 3375, $2: a, Clive Andrews. b, Bell Bozo. c, Bumpsy. d, Annie Frattellini.

No. 3376, $2: a, Stag. b, Olga and Regina Kolpensky. c, Brad Byers. d, Tiger.

**2003, July 14** ***Perf. 14***

**Sheets of 4, #a-d**

**3375-3376** A560 Set of 2 12.00 12.00

St. George's University School of Medicine A561

Designs: 75c, Aerial view of campus. $1, Campus buildings.

**2003, July 23**

**3377-3378** A561 Set of 2 1.40 1.40

Prince William, 21st Birthday — A562

No. 3379, vert.: a, With bouquet of flowers. b, Wearing blue shirt. c, Wearing blue shirt, close-up.

$6, Wearing plaid shirt.

**2003, Aug. 25**

**3379** A562 $3 Sheet of 3, #a-c 6.75 6.75

**Souvenir Sheet**

**3380** A562 $6 multi 4.50 4.50

Operation Iraqi Freedom — A563

No. 3381, $1: a, Gazelle helicopter. b, Hovercraft. c, Jaguar. d, HMS Liverpool. e, Harrier GR7. f, Challenger 2 tank. g, Chinook helicopters. h, Tornado F3.

No. 3382, $1: a, Gen. Sir Mike Jackson. b, Air Vice-marshal Glenn Torpy. c, Air Marshal Brian Burridge. d, Maj. Gen. Tony Milton. e, Maj. Gen. Peter Wall. f, Maj. Gen. Barney White-Spunner. g, Adm. Sir Alan West. h, Air Chief Marshal Sir Peter Squire.

**2003, Aug. 29**

**Sheets of 8, #a-h**

**3381-3382** A563 Set of 2 12.00 12.00

Pres. Ronald Reagan — A564

No. 3383: a, On Korean demilitarized zone, 1983. b, With British Prime Minister Margaret Thatcher. c, Speaking at the Berlin Wall, 1987. d, Signing IMF treaty with Soviet Secretary General Mikhail Gorbachev. e, With Egyptian President Anwar Sadat, 1981. f, At home with his horse.

$6, Addressing the nation.

**2003**

**3383** A564 $1.50 Sheet of 6, #a-f 6.75 6.75

**Souvenir Sheet**

**3384** A564 $6 multi 4.50 4.50

Souvenir Sheet

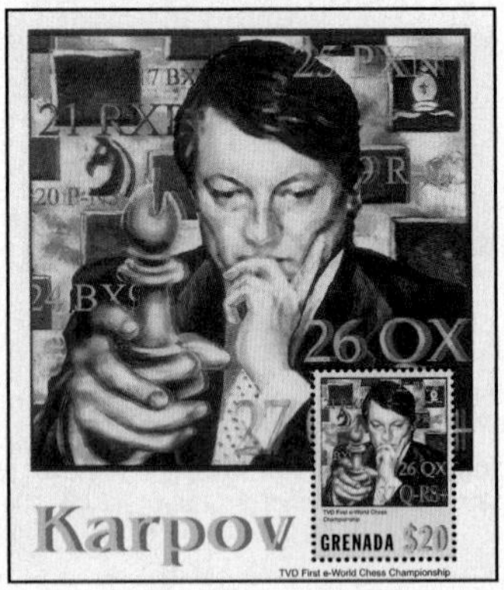


Anatoly Karpov, Chess Champion — A565

**2003** ***Perf. 13¼***

**3385** A565 $20 multi 15.00 15.00

Prehistoric Animals — A566

No. 3386, $2, horiz.: a, Spinosaurus. b, Herrerasaurus. c, Protarchaeopteryx. d, Sinosauropteryx.

No. 3387, $2, horiz.: a, Allosaurus. b, Crylophosaurus. c, Eoraptor. d, Caudipteryx.

No. 3388, $6, Archaeopteryx. No. 3389, $6, Triceratops.

**2003, Oct. 23 Litho.** ***Perf. 13¼x13½***

**Sheets of 4, #a-d**

**3386-3387** A566 Set of 2 14.00 14.00

**Souvenir Sheets**

***Perf. 13½x13¼***

**3388-3389** A566 Set of 2 10.00 10.00

Flowers A567

Designs: 25c, Yellow allamanda. 50c, Queen of the night. 75c, Anthurium. $3, Oleander.

No. 3394: a, Blue passion flower. b, Chinese hibiscus. c, Poinsettia. d, Bird of paradise.

$6, Shrimp flower.

**2003, Oct. 23** ***Perf. 14***

**3390-3393** A567 Set of 4 3.50 3.50

**3394** A567 $2 Sheet of 4, #a-d 6.00 6.00

**Souvenir Sheet**

**3395** A567 $6 multi 4.50 4.50

Fish A568

Designs: No. 3396, $1, Gold coney. No. 3397, $1, Spotfin butterflyfish. No. 3398, $1, Smallmouth grunt. $3, Night sergeant.

No. 3400: a, Cuban hogfish. b, Bluehead wrasse. c, Black cap gramma. d, Cherubfish.

$6, Banded butterflyfish.

**2003, Oct. 23**

**3396-3399** A568 Set of 4 4.50 4.50

**3400** A568 $2 Sheet of 4, #a-d 6.00 6.00

**Souvenir Sheet**

**3401** A568 $6 multi 4.50 4.50

Birds A569

Designs: No. 3402, $1.25, Osprey. No. 3403, $1.25, Northern oriole. No. 3404, $1.25, Red-eyed vireo. $3, Bahama pintail.

No. 3406: a, Slaty-capped shrike vireor. b, Northern flicker. c, Blackburnian warbler. d, Common tody-flycatcher.

$6, Blue grosbeak, vert.

**2003, Oct. 23**

**3402-3405** A569 Set of 4 5.00 5.00

**3406** A569 $2 Sheet of 4, #a-d 6.00 6.00

**Souvenir Sheet**

**3407** A569 $6 multi 4.50 4.50

Christmas A570

Paintings by Giotto: 35c, Madonna and Child, from the Church of the Ognissanti. 75c, Ognissanti Madonna. $1, Madonna of the Angels. $4, Madonna and Child, from the Florentine Church of San Giorgio alla Costa.

$6, Holy Family with John the Baptist and St. Elizabeth, horiz.

**2003, Nov. 17** *Perf. 14¼*

**3408-3411** A570 Set of 4 4.75 4.75

**Souvenir Sheet**

**3412** A570 $6 multi 4.50 4.50

St. Petersburg, Russia, 300th anniv. (#3412).

Paintings by Norman Rockwell (1894-1978) — A571

No. 3413, vert.: a, The Spring Tonic. b, The Facts of Life. c, The Proper Gratuity. d, The Runaway.

$6, Boy with Carriage.

**2003, Dec. 8** *Perf. 13¼*

**3413** A571 $2 Sheet of 4, #a-d 6.00 6.00

**Souvenir Sheet**

**3414** A571 $6 multi 4.50 4.50

Paintings in the Hermitage, St. Petersburg, Russia — A572

Designs: 45c, At the Palmist's, by Jean-Baptiste Le Prince, vert. $1, A Visit to Grandmother, by Louis Le Nain. $1.50, Musicale, by Dirck Hals. $3, A Young Woman in the Morning, by Frans van Mieris the Elder, vert.

No. 3419, vert.: a, Louis, Grand Dauphin de France, by Louis Tocqué. b, Count P. A. Stroganov as a Child, by Jean-Baptiste Greuze. c, A Boy with a Book, by Jean-Baptiste Perronneau. d, A Girl with a Doll, by Greuze.

No. 3420, The Lute Player, by Caravaggio. No. 3421, The Spoiled Child, by Greuze, vert.

**2003, Dec. 8** *Perf. 13¼*

**3415-3418** A572 Set of 4 4.50 4.50

**3419** A572 $2 Sheet of 4, #a-d 6.00 6.00

***Imperf***

**Size: 78x65mm**

**3420** A572 $6 multi 4.50 4.50

**Size: 67x78mm**

**3421** A572 $6 multi 4.50 4.50

Paintings by Pablo Picasso (1881-1973) — A573

No. 3422: a, Claude Drawing. b, Claude and Paloma at Play. c, Paloma at Three Years Old. d, Paloma with an Orange.

$6, Paloma in Blue.

**2003, Dec. 8** **Litho.** *Perf. 13¼*

**3422** A573 $2 Sheet of 4, #a-d 6.00 6.00

***Imperf***

**3423** A573 $6 multi 4.50 4.50

No. 3422 contains four 37x50mm stamps.

New Year 2004 (Year of the Monkey) — A574

No. 3424: a, Buff monkey with brown features. b, Brown monkey. c, Tan monkey. d, Gray monkey.

**2004, Jan. 4** *Perf. 14*

**3424** A574 $1.50 Sheet of 4, #a-d 4.50 4.50

Souvenir Sheet

Training Ship "Lissy" — A575

**2004, Jan. 16** **Litho.** *Perf. 14¼*

**3425** A575 $6 multi 4.50 4.50

Opening of Weser Tunnel, Dedesdorf, Germany.

Paintings by Pu Hsin-yu (1896-1963) — A576

No. 3426: a, Woman. b, Monkeys in tree. c, Landscape. d, Bird in tree. e, Man seated. f, Man standing.

No. 3427: a, Branch. b, Man.

**2004, Jan. 29** *Perf. 13½x13¼*

**3426** A576 $1.50 Sheet of 6, #a-f 6.75 6.75

**3427** A576 $3 Sheet of 2, #a-b 4.50 4.50

2004 Hong Kong Stamp Expo.

Arthur and Friends — A577

No. 3428, $1.50: a, Arthur. b, D. W. with Valentine's Day card. c, Binky. d, Muffy. e, D. W. as Cupid. f, Francine.

No. 3429, $1.50: a, Muffy giving speech about butterflies. b, Francine giving presentation about butterflies. c, Brain with plants. d, D. W. in space. e, Sue Ellen with insects. f, Arthur with model of solar system.

No. 3430, $2: a, Robinson Crusoe. b, Treasure Island. c, Tom Sawyer. d, Jungle Book.

No. 3431, $2: a, Robin Hood. b, Rumplestiltskin. c, How Arthur Drew Forth His Sword. d, King Arthur.

**2004, Jan. 29** *Perf. 13¼*

**Sheets of 6, #a-f**

**3428-3429** A577 Set of 2 13.50 13.50

**Sheets of 4, #a-d**

**3430-3431** A577 Set of 2 12.00 12.00

Cessation of Conorde Flights (in 2003) — A578

No. 3432, $3 — Concorde 210 G-BOAD, British and Singapore flags and: a, Roof line of buildings at UR. b, Curved and jagged lines at UR. c, Dark gray background at UR.

No. 3433, $3 — Concorde 001 F-WTSS, French flag and: a, Concorde above runway. b, Spectators near airport fence. c, Cockpit control panel.

No. 3434, $3 — Concorde 203 F-BVFA and: a, Top of US Capitol. b, Middle part of Capitol dome, head of statue. c, Base of Capitol and statue.

**2004, Feb. 16** *Perf. 13¼x13½*

**Sheets of 3, #a-c**

**3432-3434** A578 Set of 3 21.00 21.00

2004 Summer Olympics, Athens A579

Designs: 75c, Lord Killanin, Intl. Olympic Committee President, 1972-80. $1, 10,000 meter run, 1928 Olympics, horiz. $1.25, Commemorative plaque from 1900 Paris Olympics. $3, Presentation of olive wreath.

**2004, Apr. 8** *Perf. 13¼*

**3435-3438** A579 Set of 4 4.50 4.50

American Indian Chiefs — A580

Paintings of American Indians — A581

No. 3439: a, American Horse. b, Blue Bird. c, Crow King. d, Crow Man. e, Gall. f, Good Horse. g, Goose. h, John Grass. i, Rain-in-the-Face. j, Red Cloud. k, Sitting Bull. l, Wild Horse.

No. 3440: a, Return of the Blackfoot War Party, by Frederic Remington. b, Ridden Down, by Remington. c, Smoke Signal, by Remington. d, Buffalo Hunt, by Charles Russell. e, Scouts, by Russell. f, Piegans, by Russell.

**2004, Apr. 19** *Perf. 13¾*

**3439** A580 75c Sheet of 12, #a-l 6.75 6.75

**3440** A581 $1.25 Sheet of 6, #a-f 5.75 5.75

### Souvenir Sheet

Deng Xiaoping (1904-97), Chinese Communist Party Leader — A582

**2004, May 3** ***Perf. 13½x13¼***
**3441** A582 $6 multi 4.50 4.50

Election of Pope John Paul II, 25th Anniv. — A583

No. 3442: a, Kissing baby. b, With Mikhail Gorbachev. c, Waving to crowd. d, Meeting with Polish deportees. e, Visit to Russia.

**2004, May 3** ***Perf. 13¼x13½***
**3442** A583 $2 Sheet of 5, #a-e 7.50 7.50

Marilyn Monroe (1926-62) — A584

No. 3444: a, Wearing red dress with strap over shoulder, mouth wide open. b, Wearing orange red dress, mouth closed. c, Wearing white dress. d, Wearing red dress, mouth partially open.

**2004, May 3** ***Perf. 14***
**3443** A584 50c shown .60 .60

***Perf. 13½x13¼***
**3444** A584 $2 Sheet of 4, #a-d 7.50 7.50

No. 3443 printed in sheets of 16.

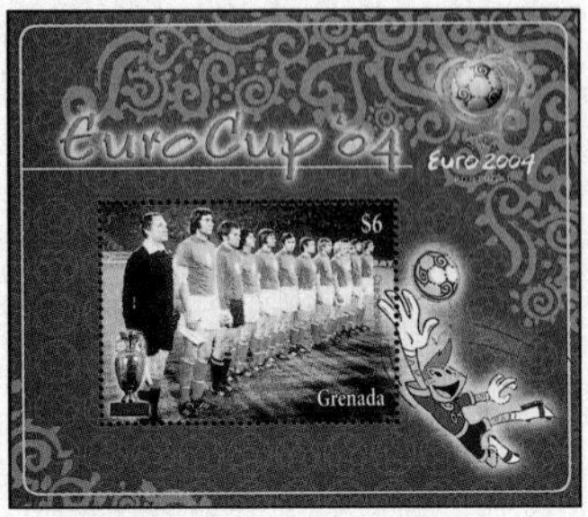


European Soccer Championships, Portugal — A585

No. 3445, vert.: a, Jan Svehlik. b, Franz Beckenbauer. c, Karol Dobias. d, Crvena Zvezda Stadium, Belgrade.
$6, 1976 Czechoslovakian team.

**2004, May 3** ***Perf. 13½x13¼***
**3445** A585 $2 Sheet of 4, #a-d 6.00 6.00

### Souvenir Sheet

***Perf. 13¼***
**3446** A585 $6 multi 4.50 4.50

No. 3445 contains four 28x42mm stamps.

D-Day, 60th Anniv. A586

Designs: 45c, Don Sheppard, Royal Engineers. $1, Air Chief Marshall Sir Arthur Tedder. $1.50, Douglas Kay, 13th/18th Royal Hussars. $3, Gen. Bernard Montgomery.

No. 3451, $2: a, Germans detect Allied invasion. b, Germans prepare to engage Allied invasion fleet. c, Soldier, Merville Battery. d, Paratroopers capture Merville Battery.

No. 3452, $2: a, HMS Belfast fires on German shore batteries. b, Allies pound German coastal defenses. c, Air strikes over Utah Beach. d, Allied troops head towards Omaha Beach.

No. 3453, $6, Fake landing craft. No. 3454, $6, Pipeline under the ocean.

**2004, May 3** ***Perf. 14***

**Stamps + Labels (#3447-3450)**

**3447-3450** A586 Set of 4 4.50 4.50

**Sheets of 4, #a-d**

**3451-3452** A586 Set of 2 12.00 12.00

**Souvenir Sheets**

**3453-3454** A586 Set of 2 9.00 9.00

Locomotives and Famous Men — A587

No. 3455, $1: a, Sir Lord Nelson 4-6-0. b, South African 16CR Class Pacific. c, Florisdorf 0-6-0 Fireless, Austria. d, GWR 57XX Class 0-6-0. e, GWR Castle Class 4-6-0. f, GWR Saint Class 4-6-0. g, GWR Star Class 4-6-0. h, GWR 28XX Class 2-8-0. i, GWR 51XX Class 2-6-2T.

No. 3456, $1, vert.: a, GN Stirling Single 4-2-2. b, Beyer Peacock Mogul 2-6-0. c, Prussian G8 0-8-0. d, George Stephenson. e, James Nasmyth. f, Nasmyth's steam hammer. g, Raven Z Class 4-4-2. h, Sir Vincent Raven. i, Thomas Cook.

No. 3457, $1, vert.: a, SR Schools Class 4-4-0. b, Indian Railways SGS Class 0-6-0. c, Borsig 0-4-0 Tram, Paraguay. d, Richard Trevithick. e, Herbert Garratt. f, Isambard Kingdom Brunel. g, Replica of Trevithick's Coalbrookdale Engine. h, Rhodesian 20th Class Garratt. i, Train on Brunel's Royal Saltash Bridge.

No. 3458, $6, California Zephyr. No. 3459, $6, Indian Pacific. No. 3460, $6, Cumbres and Toltec.

**2004, July 19** **Litho.**

**Sheets of 9, #a-i**

**3455-3457** A587 Set of 3 21.00 21.00

**Souvenir Sheets**

**3458-3460** A587 Set of 3 13.50 13.50

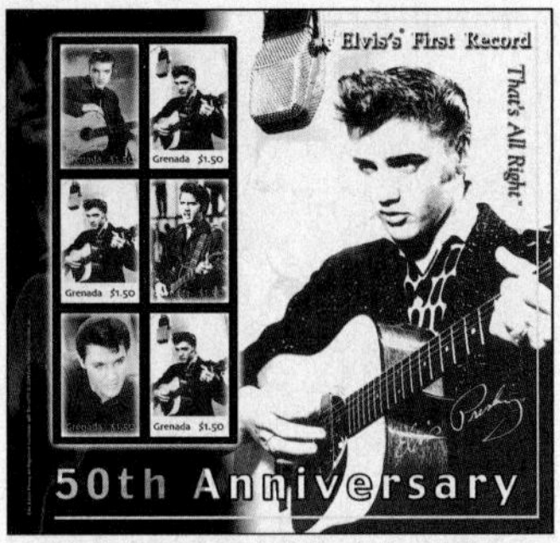


Elvis Presley (1935-77) — A588

No. 3461: a, Holding guitar (brown). b, Playing guitar (green). c, Playing guitar, diff. (red violet). d, Portrait (brown). e, Like #3461b, (blue).

**2004, Aug. 3** ***Perf. 14***
**3461** A588 $1.50 Sheet, #a-d, 2 #e 7.25 7.25

Operation Iraqi Freedom — A589

No. 3462: a, Pres. George W. Bush. b, Paul Bremer. c, Col. James Hickey, US Special Forces. d, A friendly welcome.

**2004, Aug. 25** ***Perf. 13¼x13½***
**3462** A589 $2 Sheet of 4, #a-d 6.00 6.00

Queen Juliana of the Netherlands (1909-2004) — A590

**2004, Aug. 25** **Litho.** ***Perf. 13¼***
**3463** A590 $2 multi 1.50 1.50

Printed in sheets of 6.

### Miniature Sheet

Intl. Year of Peace — A591

No. 3464: a, Jody Williams, 1997 Nobel Peace laureate. b, Protesters against landmines. c, Princess Diana.

**2004, Sept. 7** ***Perf. 14***
**3464** A591 $3 Sheet of 3, #a-c 6.75 6.75

### Miniature Sheet

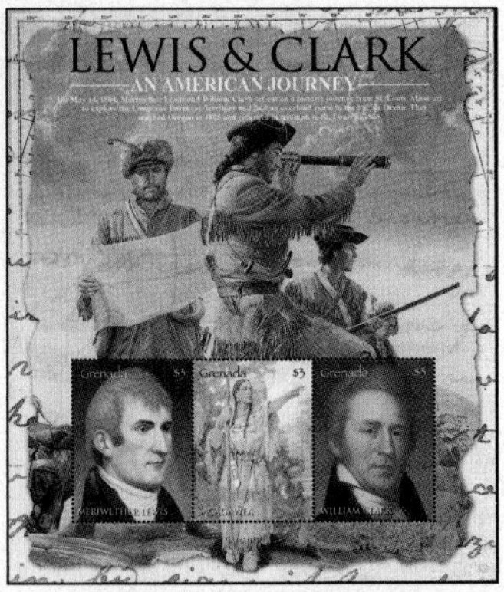


Lewis and Clark Expedition, Bicent. — A592

No. 3465: a, Meriwether Lewis. b, Sacajawea. c, William Clark.

**2004, Sept. 7** ***Perf. 14¼***
**3465** A592 $3 Sheet of 3, #a-c 6.75 6.75

### Miniature Sheet

Mars Rover Mission — A593

No. 3466: a, Delta II rocket blasts off. b, Entering Mars atmosphere. c, Parachute descent. d, Landing on the surface. e, Rover leaving lander. f, Rover on Mars surface.

**2004, Sept. 7**
**3466** A593 $1.50 Sheet of 6, #a-f 6.75 6.75

Ocean Liners — A594

No. 3467, $2: a, RMS Titanic. b, TSS Normandie. c, Mauritania. d, Lusitania.

No. 3468, $2: a, Queen Mary 2. b, Queen Elizabeth II. c, Queen Mary. d, Queen Elizabeth.

$6, Queen Mary 2, diff.

**2004, Sept. 7** ***Perf. 13¼x13***

**Sheets of 4, #a-d**

**3467-3468** A594 Set of 2 12.00 12.00

**Souvenir Sheet**

**3469** A594 $6 multi 4.50 4.50

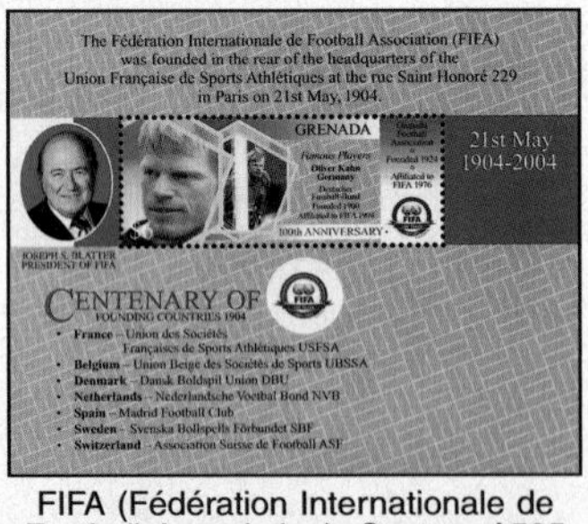


FIFA (Fédération Internationale de Football Association), Cent. — A595

No. 3470: a, Gabriel Batistuta. b, Cafu. c, Michel Platini. d, Gianluca Vialli.
$6, Oliver Kahn.

**2004, Nov. 1** ***Perf. 12¾x12½***
**3470** A595 $2 Sheet of 4, #a-d 6.00 6.00

**Souvenir Sheet**

**3471** A595 $6 multi 4.50 4.50

National Basketball Association Players — A596

Designs: No. 3472, 75c, Pau Gasol, Memphis Grizzlies. No. 3473, 75c, Allen Iverson, Philadelphia 76ers. No. 3474, 75c, Stephon Marbury, New York Knicks.

**2004** ***Perf. 14***
**3472-3474** A596 Set of 3 1.75 1.75

Issued: No. 3472, 11/3; No. 3473, 11/5; No. 3474, 11/6. Each printed in sheets of 12.
See Nos. 3485-3487.

Miniature Sheet

Pres. Ronald Reagan (1911-2004) — A597

No. 3475: a, With Mother Teresa. b, With Colin Powell. c, With Queen Elizabeth II. d, With Brian Mulroney.

**2004** ***Perf. 13½***
**3475** A597 $2 Sheet of 4, #a-d 6.00 6.00

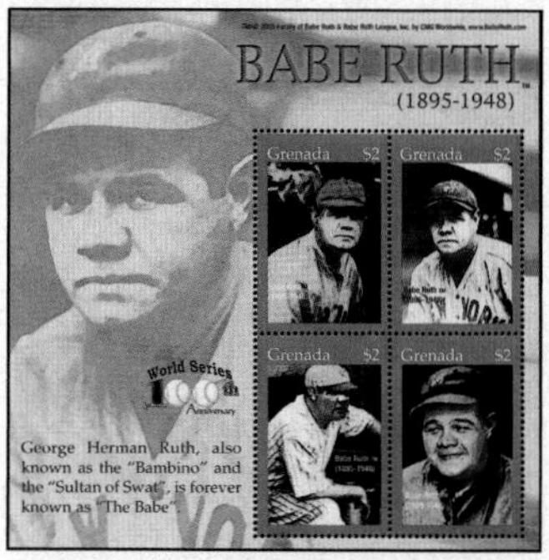


A598

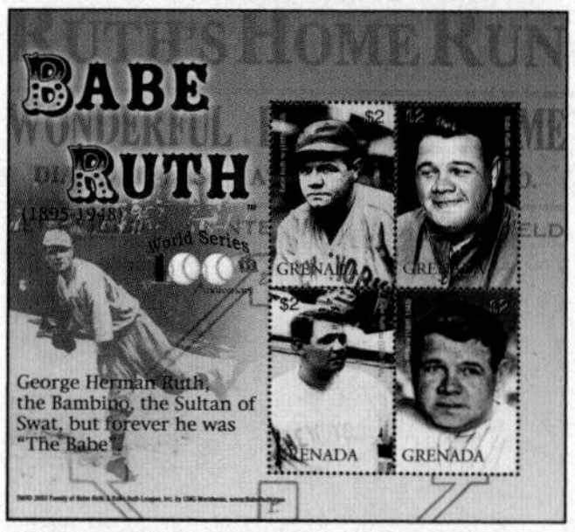


George Herman "Babe" Ruth (1895-1948), Baseball Player — A599

Various portraits.

**2004** ***Perf. 14***
**3476** A598 $2 Sheet of 4, #a-d 6.00 6.00

***Perf. 13¾x13¼***

**3477** A599 $2 Sheet of 4, #a-d 6.00 6.00

Christmas A600

Paintings by Norman Rockwell: 35c, Merry Christmas. 75c, Yuletide Merriment. $1, Dressing Up. $4, Christmas.
$6, The London Coach.

**2004, Dec. 9** ***Perf. 12***
**3478-3481** A600 Set of 4 4.75 4.75

**Souvenir Sheet**

**3482** A600 $6 multi 4.50 4.50

New Year 2005 (Year of the Rooster) — A601

Paintings by Qi Baishi: $1, Chrysanthemums, Cocks and Hens. $4, Taro Leaves and Double Hens.

**2005, Jan. 17 Litho.** ***Perf. 11¾x12¼***
**3483** A601 $1 multi .75 .75

**Souvenir Sheet**

***Perf. 12¾x13***

**3484** A601 $4 multi 3.00 3.00

No. 3483 printed in sheets of 4. No. 3484 contains one 22x76mm stamp.

**Basketball Players Type of 2004**

Designs: No. 3485, 75c, Zydrunas Ilgauskas, Cleveland Cavaliers. No. 3486, 75c, Dwayne Wade, Miami Heat. $3, Tracy McGrady, Orlando Magic.

**2005, Feb. 10** ***Perf. 14***
**3485-3487** A596 Set of 3 3.50 3.50

Souvenir Sheet

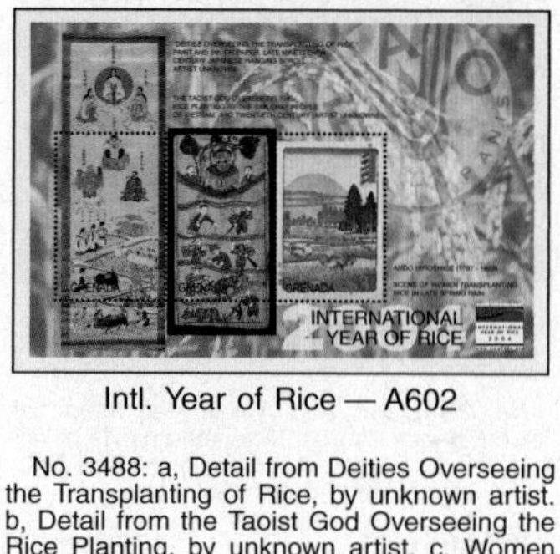


Intl. Year of Rice — A602

No. 3488: a, Detail from Deities Overseeing the Transplanting of Rice, by unknown artist. b, Detail from the Taoist God Overseeing the Rice Planting, by unknown artist. c, Women Transplanting Rice in Late Spring Rain, by Hiroshige.

**2005, Feb. 10**
**3488** A602 $3 Sheet of 3, #a-c 6.75 6.75

Birds, Wild Cats and Butterflies — A603

No. 3489, $1.50, vert. — Birds: a, Turkey vulture. b, Bald eagle. c, Peregrine falcon. d, Prairie falcon. e, Northern goshawk. f, Cooper's hawk.

No. 3490, $1.50, vert. — Wild cats: a, Cheetah. b, Lion. c, White tiger. d, Leopard. e, Bobcat. f, Bengal tiger.

No. 3491, $1.50 — Butterflies: a, Machaonides's swallowtail. b, Viceroy. c, Glasswing satyr. d, Birdwing. e, Ornithoptera goliath procus. f, Ornithoptera priamus alberio.

No. 3492, $6, California condor. No. 3493, $6, Jaguar, vert. No. 3494, $6, Lime butterfly.

**2005, Feb. 10** **Litho.**

**Sheets of 6, #a-f**

**3489-3491** A603 Set of 3 21.00 21.00

**Souvenir Sheets**

**3492-3494** A603 Set of 3 13.50 13.50

A604

Prehistoric Animals — A605

No. 3495: a, Majungatholus. b, Diplodocus. c, Willo. d, Velociraptor.

No. 3496, $2: a, Archelon. b, Ammonite. c, Plesiosaur. d, Xiphactinus.

No. 3497, $2: a, Pteranodon. b, Dimorphodon. c, Pterodactylus. d, Rhamphorhynchus.

No. 3498, Spinosaurus.

No. 3499, $6, Pliosaur. No. 3500, $6, Tapejara imperator.

**2005, Feb. 10**
**3495** A604 $2 Sheet of 4, #a-d 6.00 6.00

**Sheets of 4, #a-d**

**3496-3497** A605 Set of 2 12.00 12.00

**Souvenir Sheets**

**3498** A604 $6 multi 4.50 4.50
**3499-3500** A605 Set of 2 9.00 9.00

Souvenir Sheet

Buildings Damaged in Hurricane Ivan — A606

No. 3501: a, Cathedral of Immaculate Conception. b, Anglican Church. c, York House. d, Springs Sub-office.

**2005, Mar. 8** ***Perf. 12¾***
**3501** A606 $2 Sheet of 4, #a-d 6.00 6.00

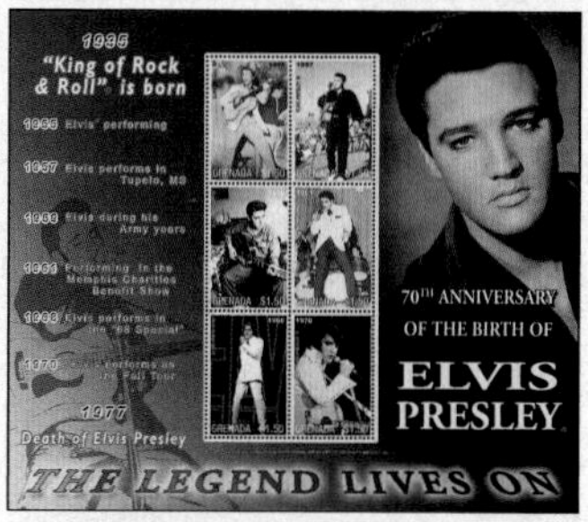


Elvis Presley (1935-77) — A607

No. 3502, $1.50: a, Singing, 1955. b, Holding microphone, 1957. c, Playing guitar, 1959. d, Singing, 1961. e, Singing, 1968. f, With guitar, 1970.

No. 3503, $1.50: a, Dancing, 1957. b, Playing guitar, 1964. c, On saddle, 1965. d, Playing guitar, 1968. e, Playing piano, 1969. f, Singing, 1970.

**2005, Apr. 4** ***Perf. 13¾***

**Sheets of 6, #a-f**

**3502-3503** A607 Set of 2 13.50 13.50

Yasujiro Ozu (1903-63), Film Director — A608

No. 3504: a, Tenement Gentleman, 1947. b, Tokyo Story, 1953. c, A Hen in the Wind, 1948. d, Floating Weeds, 1959.

**2005, Apr. 8** ***Perf. 14¼***
**3504** A608 $2 Sheet of 4, #a-d 6.00 6.00

Dutch Royalty — A609

No. 3505: a, King William I. b, King William II. c, King William III. d, Queen Wilhelmina. e, Queen Juliana. f, Queen Beatrix. g, Prince Willem-Alexander. h, Princess Catharina-Amalia.

**2005, Apr. 14** **Litho.** ***Perf. 12***
**3505** A609 $2 Sheet of 8, #a-h 12.00 12.00

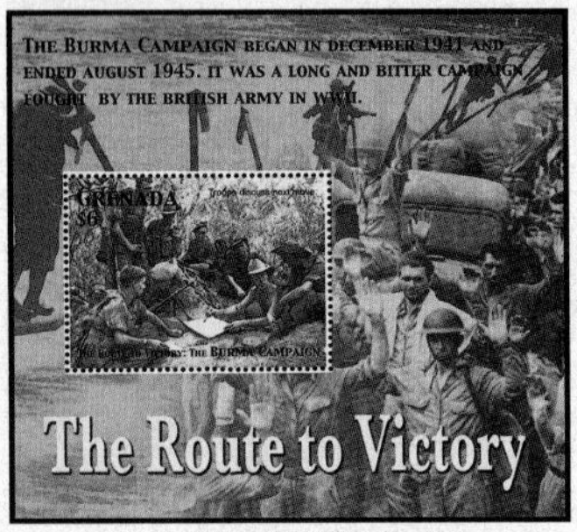


End of World War II, 60th Anniv. — A610

No. 3506, $2 — Burma Campaign: a, "21 Curves" Road. b, British advance through the jungle of Burma. c, Troops at Magwe airstrip. d, Allied troops escorting prisoners.

No. 3507, $2 — Operation Market Garden: a, Allied troops landing behind enemy lines. b, Allied troops fire on German defenders. c, German troops move up to counterattack. d, Bridges still remain in German hands.

No. 3508, $6, Troops discuss next move.

No. 3509, $6, Allied troops meet stiff resistance.

**2005, May 10** ***Perf. 13¼***

**Sheets of 4, #a-d**

**3506-3507** A610 Set of 2 12.00 12.00

**Souvenir Sheets**

**3508-3509** A610 Set of 2 9.00 9.00

V-E Day, 60th Anniv. — A611

No. 3510: a, D-Day. b, Allied troops break through enemy lines. c, German troops begin to surrender. d, The war in Europe is over.

$6, Berlin falls to the armies of the Soviet Union.

**2005, May 10** ***Perf. 14***
**3510** A611 $2 Sheet of 4, #a-d 6.00 6.00

**Souvenir Sheet**

**3511** A611 $6 multi 4.50 4.50

V-J Day, 60th Anniv. — A612

No. 3512: a, Airplanes over islands of the Pacific. b, Allied forces storm the beaches of Japanese-held islands. c, Gen. Douglas MacArthur returns to the Philippines. d, The Japanese armies surrender.

$6, Allies enjoy victory celebration.

**2005, May 10**
**3512** A612 $2 Sheet of 4, #a-d 6.00 6.00

**Souvenir Sheet**

**3513** A612 $6 multi 4.50 4.50

Rotary International, Cent. — A613

No. 3514: a, Child receiving polio vaccination. b, District 7030 Governor David Edwards and wife, Donna. c, Paul P. Harris, Rotary International founder.

$6, 2001-02 Rotary President Richard D. King, children.

**2005, May 10** ***Perf. 14***
**3514** A613 $3 Sheet of 3, #a-c 6.75 6.75

**Souvenir Sheet**

**3515** A613 $6 multi 4.50 4.50

Miniature Sheet

Expo 2005, Aichi, Japan — A614

No. 3516: a, Victoria Falls. b, Bald eagle. c, Caribbean coral reef. d, Childbirth. e, First man on the moon. f, Pollination.

**2005, June 27** ***Perf. 12***
**3516** A614 $1.50 Sheet of 6, #a-f 6.75 6.75

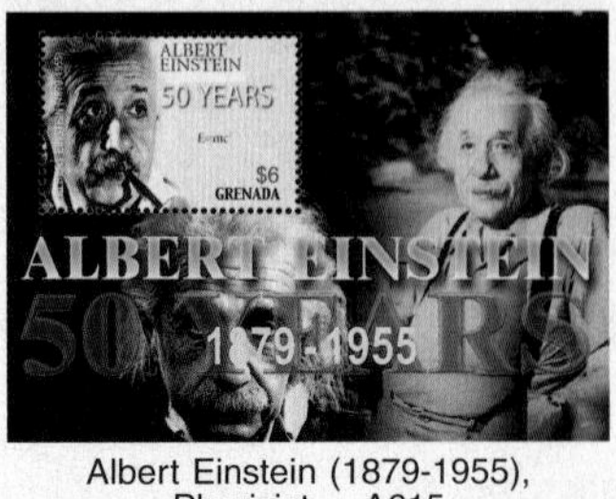


Albert Einstein (1879-1955), Physicist — A615

No. 3517 — Einstein and country name in: a, Blue. b, Black. c, White. d, Red

$6, Einstein with pipe.

**2005, June 27** ***Perf. 12¾***
**3517** A615 $2 Sheet of 4, #a-d 6.00 6.00

**Souvenir Sheet**

**3518** A615 $6 multi 4.50 4.50

Souvenir Sheet

Private Johnson Beharry, Victoria Cross Recipient in Iraq War — A616

**2005, July 11** **Litho.**
**3519** A616 $5 multi 3.75 3.75

Hans Christian Andersen (1805-75), Author — A617

No. 3520: a, Andersen, with hands shown. b, Photograph of Andersen. c, Andersen, with white tie.

$6, Andersen's tombstone, Copenhagen.

**2005, July 11**
**3520** A617 $3 Sheet of 3, #a-c 6.75 6.75

**Souvenir Sheet**

**3521** A617 $6 multi 4.50 4.50

Friedrich von Schiller (1759-1805), Writer — A618

No. 3522, vert.: a, William Tell Memorial, Altdorf, Switzerland. b, Animated movie of William Tell. c, Stage production of William Tell.

$6, Scene from William Tell story.

**2005, July 11** ***Perf. 14***
**3522** A618 $3 Sheet of 3, #a-c 6.75 6.75

**Souvenir Sheet**

**3523** A618 $6 multi 4.50 4.50

Jules Verne (1828-1905), Writer — A619

No. 3524: a, Photograph of Verne. b, Photograph of Verne in oval. c, Drawing of Verne.

$6, From the Earth to the Moon.

**2005, July 11** ***Perf. 12¾***
**3524** A619 $3 Sheet of 3, #a-c 6.75 6.75

**Souvenir Sheet**

**3525** A619 $6 multi 4.50 4.50

Battle of Trafalgar, Bicent. — A620

No. 3526, vert.: a, Admiral Horatio Nelson. b, Napoleon Bonaparte. c, HMS Victory. d, The Nelson Touch.

$6, Sailors on ship.

**2005, July 11** ***Perf. 12¾***
**3526** A620 $2 Sheet of 4, #a-d 6.00 6.00

**Souvenir Sheet**

**3527** A620 $6 multi 4.50 4.50

Miniature Sheets

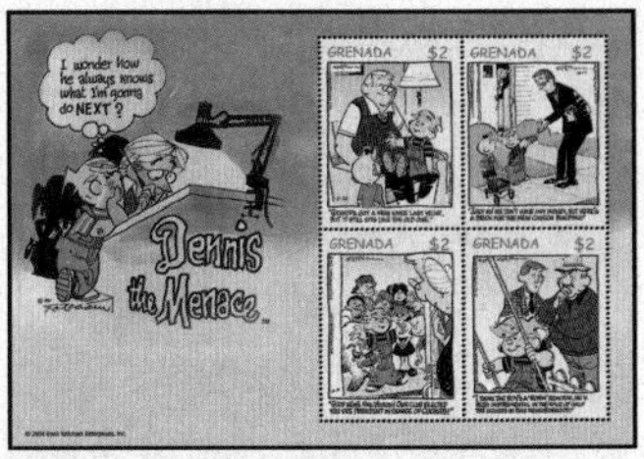


Dennis The Menace, Comic Strip by Hank Ketcham — A621

No. 3528, $2: a, "Grandpa got a new knee. . ." b, "Joey an' me don't have any money. . ." c, "Good news, Mrs. Wilson! . ." d, "I think the boy's. . ."

No. 3529, $2: a, "How 'bout a trade. . ." b, "It's not a good idea. . ." c, "I'll bet you were the top . ." d, "Boy, I'm glad I don't have to. . ."

**2005, July 11** ***Perf. 14¼***

**Sheets of 4, #a-d**

**3528-3529** A621 Set of 2 12.00 12.00

Souvenir Sheet

Taipei 2005 Intl. Stamp Exhibition — A622

No. 3530: a, Shalom Meir Tower, Tel Aviv. b, Empire State Building, New York. c, Taipei 101 Building, Taipei. d, Eiffel Tower, Paris.

**2005, Aug. 19** ***Perf. 14***
**3530** A622 $2 Sheet of 4, #a-d 6.00 6.00

Pope John Paul II (1920-2005) and Lech Walesa — A623

**2005, Aug. 22** ***Perf. 12¾***
**3531** A623 $4 multi 3.00 3.00

Printed in sheets of 4.

Wedding of Prince Charles and Camilla Parker Bowles — A624

Various pictures of couple with oval in: No. 3532, $2, Lemon. No. 3533, $2, Light blue. No. 3534, $2, Pink, horiz.

**2005, Sept. 7** ***Perf. 13½***
**3532-3534** A624 Set of 3 4.50 4.50

Each stamp printed in sheets of 4.

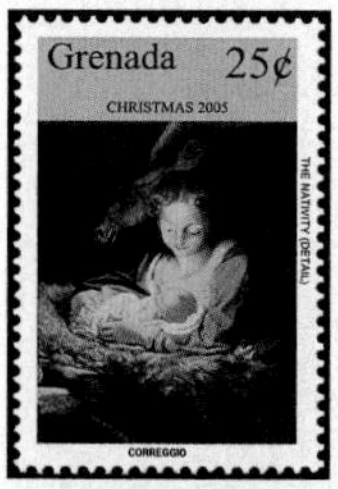


Christmas — A625

Designs: 25c, The Nativity, by Correggio. 75c, Virgin and Child, by Lorenzo Lotto. $1, The Holy Family, by Lotto. $5, Madonna and Child with the Saints, by Lotto.
$6, Allegory of Music, by Fra Filippo Lippi.

**2005, Nov. 15** ***Perf. 12¾***
**3535-3538** A625 Set of 4 5.25 5.25

**Souvenir Sheet**

**3539** A625 $6 multi 4.50 4.50

**Bird Type of 2000**

**2005 Litho.** ***Perf. 12x11¾***
**Size:22x26mm**

**3540** A472 10c Purple-throated Carib .25 .25

Miniature Sheets

Chelsea Soccer Team, Cent. — A626

Liverpool Soccer Team — A627

No. 3541: a, Stadium and field. b, Stadium, field, team emblem and years. c, Players holding English League Championship award. d, Players in bus with cup and flag. e, Fans with flag. f, Aerial view of bus carrying players. g, Players. h, Coach. i, Stadium, field, team emblem. j, Team with award.

No. 3542: a, Crowd watching bus carrying players near stadium. b, Player and coach holding UEFA Cup. c, Gate. d, Aerial view of stadium. e, Banner. f, Players waving. g, Fans. h, Soccer match. i, Players celebrating. j, Crowd cheering players in bus.

**2005, Dec. 28 Litho.** ***Perf. 13¼***
**3541** A626 $1.50 Sheet of 10, #a-j 11.50 11.50
**3542** A627 $1.50 Sheet of 10, #a-j 11.50 11.50

The Two Hounds, by Hui-Tsung A628

**2006, Jan. 3**
**3543** A628 $1 shown .75 .75

**Souvenir Sheet**

**3544** A628 $4 Entire painting 3.00 3.00

No. 3544 contains one 50x37mm stamp.

Pope Benedict XVI — A629

**2006, Jan. 10**
**3545** A629 $2 multi 1.50 1.50

Printed in sheets of 4.

A630

Elvis Presley (1935-77) — A631

No. 3546 — Movie posters: a, Girls! Girls! Girls! b, Jailhouse Rock. c, Paradise - Hawaiian Style. d, It Happened at the World's Fair.

**2006 Litho.** ***Perf. 13¼***
**3546** A630 $3 Sheet of 4, #a-d 9.00 9.00

**Litho. & Embossed**
***Die Cut Perf. 7¾***
**Without Gum**

**3547** A631 $20 shown 15.00 15.00

Issued: No. 3546, 7/11, No. 3547, 2/21.

Queen Elizabeth II, 80th Birthday — A632

No. 3548: a, Wearing necklace, no earrings. b, Wearing blue jacket. c, Portrait. d, Wearing jacket and earrings.
$6, Wearing hat.

**2006, Feb. 21 Litho.** ***Perf. 13¼***
**3548** A632 $3 Sheet of 4, #a-d 9.00 9.00

**Souvenir Sheet**
***Perf. 12¼x12***

**3549** A632 $6 multi 4.50 4.50

Teams Competing in 2006 World Cup Soccer Championships, Germany — A633

Designs: No. 3550, $1.50, Angola. No. 3551, $1.50, Argentina. No. 3552, $1.50, Australia. No. 3553, $1.50, Brazil. No. 3554, $1.50, Costa Rica. No. 3555, $1.50, Croatia. No. 3556, $1.50, Czech Republic. No. 3557, $1.50, Ecuador. No. 3558, $1.50, England. No. 3559, $1.50, France. No. 3560, $1.50, Germany. No. 3561, $1.50, Ghana. No. 3562, $1.50, Iran. No. 3563, $1.50, Italy. No. 3564, $1.50, Ivory Coast. No. 3565, $1.50, Japan. No. 3566, $1.50, Mexico. No. 3567, $1.50, Netherlands. No. 3568, $1.50, Paraguay. No. 3569, $1.50, Poland. No. 3570, $1.50, Portugal. No. 3571, $1.50, Saudi Arabia. No. 3572, $1.50, Serbia and Montenegro. No. 3573, $1.50, South Korea. No. 3574, $1.50, Spain. No. 3575, $1.50, Sweden. No. 3576, $1.50, Switzerland. No. 3577, $1.50, Togo. No. 3578, $1.50, Trinidad and Tobago. No. 3579, $1.50, Tunisia. No. 3580, $1.50, Ukraine. No. 3581, $1.50, United States.

**2006, Mar. 29** ***Perf. 12¼x12***
**3550-3581** A633 Set of 32 36.00 36.00

Nos. 3550-3581 each printed in sheets of 6. Stamps other than Nos. 3550, 3553, 3554, 3560, 3561, 3566, 3575, 3579 and 3581, which have solid color backgrounds, have multicolored backgrounds that vary within the sheet.

Marilyn Monroe (1926-62), Actress — A634

**2006, Mar. 30** ***Perf. 13¼***
**3582** A634 $3 multi 2.25 2.25

Printed in sheets of 4.

2006 Winter Olympics, Turin A635

Designs: No. 3583, Poster for 1980 Lake Placid Winter Olympics. No. 3583A, Poster for 2006 Turin Winter Olympics. No. 3584, Switzerland #B173. No. 3584A, Italy #2722. $2, Poster for 1948 St. Moritz Winter Olympics. $3, Switzerland #B172.

**2006, May 10** ***Perf. 14¼***

| | | | | |
|---|---|---|---|---|
| **3583** | A635 | 75c multicolored | .55 | .55 |
| **3583A** | A635 | 75c multi | .55 | .55 |
| **3584** | A635 | 90c multicolored | .70 | .70 |
| **3584A** | A635 | 90c multi | .70 | .70 |
| **3585** | A635 | $2 multicolored | 1.50 | 1.50 |
| **3586** | A635 | $3 multicolored | 2.25 | 2.25 |
| | | *Nos. 3583-3586 (6)* | 6.25 | 6.25 |

Rosa Parks (1913-2005), American Civil Rights Activist — A636

**2006, May 27** ***Perf. 11½x12***
**3587** A636 $3 multi 2.25 2.25

Printed in sheets of 3.

Flags and Uniforms of World Cup Soccer Champions A637

Designs: 75c, Brazil, 2002. 90c, Germany, 1990. $3, France, 1998.

**2006, June 9** ***Perf. 13¼***
**3588-3590** A637 Set of 3 3.50 3.50

World Cup Trophy — A638

**2006, June 9** ***Die Cut***

**Self-Adhesive**

**3591** A638 $6 multi 4.50 4.50

Rembrandt (1606-69), Painter A639

Designs: 50c, The Little Jewish Bride. $1, Young Man in Velvet Cap. $1.50, Old Woman Sleeping. No. 3595, $3, Woman Reading. No. 3596, $6, Portrait of a Seated Man (70x100mm). No. 3597, $6, Portrait of a Scholar (70x100mm).

No. 3598, $3: a, Young Woman with Flowers in Her Hair. b, Portrait of a Seated Woman. c, Alijdt Adriaensor. d, Amalia van Solms.

***Perf. 12, 12½x12¼ (#3596, 3597)***

**2006, June 16**

**3592-3597** A639 Set of 6 13.50 13.50
*3597a* Imperf. 4.50 4.50

**Miniature Sheet**

***Perf. 13x13¼***

**3598** A639 $3 Sheet of 4, #a-d 9.00 9.00

Souvenir Sheet

Wolfgang Amadeus Mozart (1756-91), Composer — A640

**2006, June 22** ***Perf. 12¾***

**3599** A640 $6 multi 4.50 4.50

Souvenir Sheet

Ludwig Durr (1878-1956), Engineer, and Zeppelins — A641

No. 3600 — Durr and: a, Graf Zeppelin D-LZ-127. b, Graf Zeppelin LT. c, Graf Zeppelin L-26.

**2006, June 22**

**3600** A641 $4 Sheet of 3, #a-c 9.00 9.00

Space — A642

No. 3601, $2 — Sputnik 1: a, Sergei Korolev. b, Sputnik 1 in space. c, Inside Sputnik 1. d, Sputnik 1 capsule.

No. 3602, $2, vert. — Apollo-Soyuz: a, Apollo rocket. b, Apollo command module and adapter. c, Soyuz rocket on launchpad. d, Soyuz.

No. 3603 — Giotto Comet Probe: a, Halley's Comet, round head in yellow at right. b, Tip of Giotto Probe launcher Ariane V14. c, Halley's Comet, head at left, thin tail. d, Halley's Comet, head in white at right. e, Bottom of Giotto Probe launcher Ariane V14. f, Halley's Comet, head at left, wide tail.

No. 3604, $6, Stardust Comet Probe. No. 3605, $6, Comet Tempel 1 Deep Impact Mission. No. 3606, $6, Space Shuttle Discovery's return to space.

**2006, Sept. 14** **Litho.** ***Perf. 12¾***

**Sheets of 4, #a-d**

**3601-3602** A642 Set of 2 12.00 12.00
**3603** A642 $2 Sheet of 6, #a-f 9.00 9.00

**Souvenir Sheets**

**3604-3606** A642 Set of 3 13.50 13.50

Christopher Columbus (1451-1506), Explorer — A643

Designs: $1.50, Sinking of the Santa Maria. $2, Santa Maria, vert. $3, Columbus, sailor and ship, vert. $4, Columbus and ships, vert. $6, Fleet of ships, 1493.

**2006, Oct. 26** ***Perf. 12¾***

**3607-3610** A643 Set of 4 8.00 8.00

**Souvenir Sheet**

**3611** A643 $6 multi 4.50 4.50

Butterflies A644

Designs: 10c, Mourning cloak butterfly. 25c, Snout butterfly. $1, Tithorea pinthias. $2, Diadem butterfly. $4, Red satyr butterfly. $5, Taygetis chrysogone. $10, Pierella hortona. $20, Morpho aega.

**2006, Dec. 1** **Litho.** ***Perf. 12½***

**3612** A644 10c multi .25 .25
**3613** A644 25c multi .25 .25
**3614** A644 $1 multi .75 .75
**3615** A644 $2 multi 1.50 1.50
**3616** A644 $4 multi 3.00 3.00
**3617** A644 $5 multi 3.75 3.75
**3618** A644 $10 multi 7.50 7.50
**3619** A644 $20 multi 15.00 15.00
*Nos. 3612-3619 (8)* 32.00 32.00

Princess Maxima of the Netherlands — A645

No. 3620: a, Head of Princess Maxima. b, Princess Maxima holding purse.

**2006, Dec. 7** ***Perf. 13½***

**3620** A645 $1.50 Pair, #a-b 2.25 2.25

Printed in sheets containing 3 of each stamp.

Christmas — A646

Details of The Adoration of the Shepherds, by Peter Paul Rubens: 25c, Man with hat. 50c, Mary. 75c, Shepherd. $1, Baby Jesus.

No. 3625: a, Like 25c. b, Like 50c. c, Like 75c. d, Like $1.

**2006, Dec. 21** ***Perf. 14***

**3621-3624** A646 Set of 4 1.90 1.90

**Souvenir Sheet**

**3625** A646 $2 Sheet of 4, #a-d 6.00 6.00

Betty Boop — A647

No. 3626 — Betty Boop: a, Sitting on "E." b, With hands on thighs, between "Y" and "B." c, With one leg elevated. d, With hands clasped, Standing behind "E." e, With arms at side, standing in front of "Y." f, With arms raised upwards.

No. 3627: a, With hands clasped, blue circles. b, With arms at side, red and blue circles. c, With arms raised upwards, pink and blue circles. d, At microphone, blue circles.

No. 3628, $3: a, Holding mirror. b, Wearing fruited hat.

No. 3629, $3, horiz.: a, Head and upper torso. b, Lower torso.

**2006, Dec. 22** ***Perf. 14***

**3626** A647 $1.50 Sheet of 6, #a-f 6.75 6.75
**3627** A647 $2 Sheet of 4, #a-d 6.00 6.00

**Souvenir Sheets of 2, #a-b**

**3628-3629** A647 Set of 2 9.00 9.00

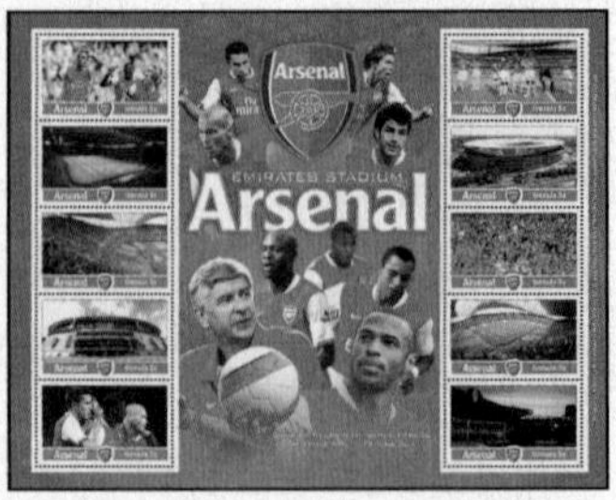


Arsenal Soccer Team — A648

No. 3630: a, $1, Players and crowd. b, $1, Soccer field at night. c, $1, Fans in seats at end of stadium. d, $1, Emirates Stadium exterior. e, $1, Players. f, $2, Players. g, $2, Aerial view of stadium exterior. h, $2, Fans. i, $2, Soccer field and fans. j, $2, Stadium exterior at night.

**2007, Jan. 16**

**3630** A648 Sheet of 10, #a-j 11.50 11.50

Concorde Test Pilots and Flags — A649

No. 3631: a, Amore Turcat, French flag. b, Brian Trubshaw, British flag.

**2007, Feb. 15**

**3631** A649 $2 Pair, #a-b 3.00 3.00

Printed in sheets containing three of each stamp.

Scouting, Cent. — A650

No. 3632 — Scout sign and denomination in: a, Blue. b, Orange. c, Red violet. d, Green $6, Orange.

**2007, Feb. 15**

**3632** A650 $3 Sheet of 4, #a-d 9.00 9.00

**Souvenir Sheet**

**3633** A650 $6 multi 4.50 4.50

Pres. John F. Kennedy (1917-63) — A651

No. 3634, $2 — First meeting with Soviet Premier Nikita Khrushchev: a, Khrushchev at the Simferopol Space Control Center. b, Kennedy greeting Khrushchev. c, Kennedy and Khrushchev on sofa. d, Kennedy and Khrushchev at residence of US Ambassador in Vienna.

No. 3635, $2 — Cuban Missile Crisis: a, Khrushchev and Fidel Castro. b, Kennedy addressing nation. c, Completed SA-2 missile site. d, Kennedy and Khrushchev shaking hands in Vienna.

**2007, Feb. 15**

**Sheets of 4, #a-d**

**3634-3635** A651 Set of 2 12.00 12.00

Souvenir Sheet

New Year 2007 (Year of the Pig) — A652

No. 3636 — Text "Traditional Chinese New Year Paper Cutting" in: a, $1, Black. b, $1, White. c, $2, Beige. d, $2, Yellow.

**2007, Feb. 18** ***Perf. 14***
**3636** A652 Sheet of 4, #a-d 4.50 4.50

Pope Benedict XVI — A653

**2007, June 4 Litho.** ***Perf. 13¼***
**3637** A653 $1 multi .75 .75

Printed in sheets of 8.

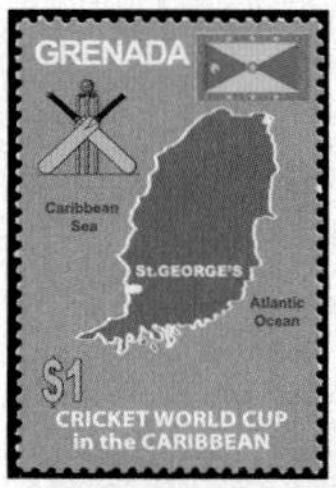


2007 Cricket World Cup, West Indies — A654

Designs: $1, Cricket World Cup emblem, flag and map of Grenada. $2, Rawl Lewis. $3, Queen's Park, horiz.
$6, Cricket World Cup emblem.

**2007, June 18**
**3638-3640** A654 Set of 3 4.50 4.50

**Souvenir Sheet**

**3641** A654 $6 multi 4.50 4.50

Wedding of Queen Elizabeth II and Prince Philip, 60th Anniv. — A655

No. 3642: a, Queen and Prince, orange panel. b, Queen, orange panel. c, Queen, light blue panel. d, Queen and Prince, light blue panel. e, Queen and Prince, lilac panel. f, Queen, lilac panel.
$6, Queen and Prince, diff.

**2007, June 25**
**3642** A655 $2 Sheet of 6, #a-f 9.00 9.00

**Souvenir Sheet**

**3643** A655 $6 multi 4.50 4.50

Princess Diana (1961-97) — A656

No. 3644 — Diana with: a, Red dress. b, Light blue and white dress. c, White gown. d, Green and white dress.
No. 3645, $6, Scarf on head. No. 3646, $6, Red dress, horiz.

**2007, June 25**
**3644** A656 $2 Sheet of 4, #a-d 6.00 6.00

**Souvenir Sheets**

**3645-3646** A656 Set of 2 9.00 9.00

Intl. Polar Year — A657

No. 3647, vert.: a, Adult penguin with head raised. b, Three penguins in distance. c, Adult penguin with head lowered. d, Juvenile penguin, ball. e, Juvenile penguin with wings extended. f, Juvenile penguin with head raised.
$6, Penguin on skis.

**2007, June 25**
**3647** A657 $2 Sheet of 6, #a-f 9.00 9.00

**Souvenir Sheet**

**3648** A657 $6 multi 4.50 4.50

1986 Halley's Comet Merchandising Emblem — A658

No. 3649: a, Orange brown frame. b, Dark blue frame. c, Purple frame. d, Red frame.
$6, Emblem, night sky.

**2007, July 11**
**3649** A658 $2 Sheet of 4, #a-d 6.00 6.00

**Souvenir Sheet**

**3650** A658 $6 multi 4.50 4.50

U.S. Presidents — A659

No. 3651: a, 1c, George Washington. b, 2c, John Adams. c, 3c, Thomas Jefferson. d, 4c, James Madison. e, 5c, James Monroe. f, 6c, John Quincy Adams. g, 7c, Andrew Jackson. h, 8c, Martin Van Buren. i, 9c, William Henry Harrison. j, 10c, John Tyler. k, 11c, James Knox Polk. l, 12c, Zachary Taylor. m, 13c, Millard Fillmore. n, 14c, Franklin Pierce. o, $4, Presidential seal.

No. 3652: a, 15c, James Buchanan. b, 16c, Abraham Lincoln. c, 17c, Andrew Johnson. d, 18c, Ulysses S. Grant. e, 19c, Rutherford B. Hayes. f, 20c, James A. Garfield. g, 21c, Chester A. Arthur. h, 22c, Grover Cleveland. i, 23c, Benjamin Harrison. j, 24c, Grover Cleveland. k, 25c, William McKinley. l, 26c, Theodore Roosevelt. m, 27c, William Howard Taft. n, 28c, Woodrow Wilson. o, $2, Capitol Dome.

No. 3653: a, 29c, Warren G. Harding. b, 30c, Calvin Coolidge. c, 31c, Herbert Hoover. d, 32c, Franklin D. Roosevelt. e, 33c, Harry S Truman. f, 34c, Dwight D. Eisenhower. g, 35c, John F. Kennedy. h, 36c, Lyndon B. Johnson. i, 37c, Richard M. Nixon. j, 38c, Gerald R. Ford. k, 39c, Jimmy Carter. l, 40c, Ronald Reagan. m, 41c, George H. W. Bush. n, 42c, William J. Clinton. o, 43c, George W. Bush.

**2007, July 16** ***Perf. 12***
**3651** A659 Sheet of 15, #a-o 3.75 3.75
**3652** A659 Sheet of 15, #a-o 3.75 3.75
**3653** A659 Sheet of 15, #a-o 4.00 4.00
*Nos. 3651-3653 (3)* 11.50 11.50

Worldwide Fund for Nature (WWF) — A660

No. 3654 — Clymene dolphins with denomination in: a, Orange. b, Bluish green. c, Yellow. d, Aquamarine.

**2007, July 23** ***Perf. 13¼***
**3654** Strip of 4 3.75 3.75
*a.-d.* A660 $1.20 Any single .90 .90
*e.* Miniature sheet, 2 each #3654a-3654d 7.50 7.50

**Souvenir Sheet**

St. George's University, 30th Anniv. — A661

**2007, Oct. 26** ***Perf. 12¾***
**3655** A661 $6 multi 4.50 4.50

**Souvenir Sheet**

Susan Bristol, Painting by Bernard Vidal — A662

**2007, Oct. 26** ***Perf. 13¼***
**3656** A662 $6 multi 4.50 4.50

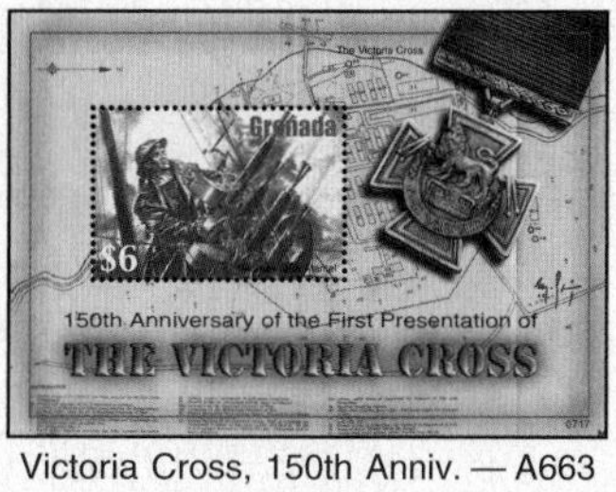


Victoria Cross, 150th Anniv. — A663

No. 3657, vert.: a, Corporal Bryan Budd. b, Brigadier General James Forbes-Robertson. c, Private Johnson Beharry. d, Sergeant William J. Gordon. e, Private Henry Tandey. f, Private Jorgen Christian Jensen.
$6, Seaman Jack Mantel.

**2007, Oct. 26** **Litho.**
**3657** A663 $1.50 Sheet of 6, #a-f 6.75 6.75

**Souvenir Sheet**

**3658** A663 $6 multi 4.50 4.50

First Helicopter Flight, Cent. — A664

No. 3659, horiz.: a, S-65/RH-53D. b, Autogyro and bird. c, BK 117. d, AS-64.
$6, AH-64 Apache.

**2007, Oct. 26**
**3659** A664 $2 Sheet of 4, #a-d 6.00 6.00

**Souvenir Sheet**

**3660** A664 $6 multi 4.50 4.50

**Miniature Sheets**

Intl. Holocaust Remembrance Day — A665

No. 3661 $1.40 — United Nations diplomats and delegates: a, Srgian Kerim, President of 62nd General Assembly. b, Andrei Dapkiunas, Belarus. c, Jean-Marie Ehouzou, Benin. d, Milos Prica, Bosnia & Herzegovina. e, Samuel O. Outlule, Botswana. f, Francis K. Butagira, Uganda. g, Valeriy P. Kuchinsky, Ukraine. h, Jean Ping, President of 59th General Assembly.

No. 3662, $1.40: a, Erasmo Lara-Peña, Dominican Republic. b, Diego Cordovez, Ecuador. c, Carmen M. Gallardo-Hernandez, El Salvador. d, Lino Sima Ekua Avomo, Equatorial Guinea. e, Tina Intelmann, Estonia. f, Dawit Yohannes, Ethiopia. g, Isikia Rabiei Savua, Fiji. h, Lars Wide, Chef de Cabinet of 60th General Assembly.

No. 3663, $1.40: a, Angus Friday, Grenada. b, Alfredo Lopes Cabral, Guinea-Bissau. c, Samuel Rudolph Insanally, Guyana. d, Lèo Mérorès, Haiti. e, Ivan Romero-Martinez, Honduras. f, Gabor Brodi, Hungary. g, Hjalmar W. Hannesson, Iceland. h, Dan Gillerman, Israel.

No. 3664, $1.40: a, Colin Beck, Solomon Islands. b, Dumisani S. Kumalo, South Africa. c, Juan Antonio Yáñez-Barnueva, Spain. d, Anders Liden, Sweden. e, Peter Maurer, Switzerland. f, K. Laxanachantorn Laohaphan, Thailand. g, José Luis Guterres, East Timor. h, Fekitamoeloa 'Utoikamanu, Tonga.

**2007, Oct. 26** **Litho.**

**Sheets of 8, #a-h**

**3661-3664** A665 Set of 4 35.00 35.00

Christmas A666

Various details from Nativity with the Annunciation to the Shepherds, by Follower of Jan Joest: 25c, 50c, 75c, $1.

**2007, Nov. 1** ***Perf. 14¾x14***
**3665-3668** A666 Set of 4 1.90 1.90

New Year 2008 (Year of the Rat) A667

**2007, Dec. 3 Litho. *Perf. 13x13¼***

**3669** A667 $2 multi 1.50 1.50

Printed in sheets of 4.

Souvenir Sheet

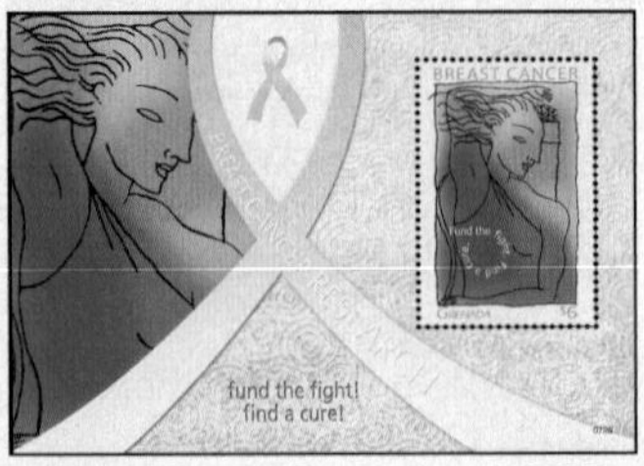


Breast Cancer Prevention — A668

**2007, Dec. 11 *Perf. 14***

**3670** A668 $6 multi 4.50 4.50

Princess Diana (1961-97) — A669

***Serpentine Die Cut 7¾***

**2007, Dec. 11 Litho. & Embossed**

**Without Gum**

**3671** A669 $20 gold & multi 15.00 15.00

Miniature Sheets

A670

Elvis Presley (1935-77) — A671

No. 3672 — Presley: a, Holding guitar at neck. b, Singing, not touching microphone. c, Wearing green shirt. d, Facing right, playing guitar. e, Singing, holding microphone. f, Facing right, playing guitar.

No. 3673 — Presley: a, Holding microphone. b, Wearing necktie. c, Holding guitar over shoulder. d, And guitar head.

**2008 Litho. *Perf. 13¼***

**3672** A670 $1.50 Sheet of 6, #a-f 6.75 6.75

**3673** A671 $2 Sheet of 4, #a-d 6.00 6.00

Issued: No. 3672, 1/14; No. 3673, 6/13.

Muhammad Ali, Boxer — A672

No. 3674, $2 — Ali: a, With towel on head, bank of microphones at left. b, With towel on head, bank of microphone at right. c, With fist raised. d, With towel off head, bank of microphones at right.

No. 3675, $2, horiz. — Ali: a, With arms raised. b, Wearing robe. c, At punching bag. d, Boxing.

No. 3676, $6, Ali wearing protective headgear. No. 3677, $2, Ali with fan's hand on shoulder.

***Perf. 12x11½, 11½ (#3675)***

**2008, Jan. 14**

**Sheets of 4, #a-d**

**3674-3675** A672 Set of 2 12.00 12.00

**Souvenir Sheets**

***Perf. 13¼***

**3676-3677** A672 Set of 2 9.00 9.00

Paintings by Qi Baishi (1864-1957) — A673

No. 3678: a, Magnolias and Bees. b, Mother Hen, Chicks and Banana Leaves. c, Fish, Crabs and Watergrass. d, Crows Returning to Wintry Trees.

$4, Morning Glories.

**2008. Feb. 6 *Perf. 12½***

**3678** A673 $1 Sheet of 4, #a-d 3.00 3.00

**Souvenir Sheet**

***Perf. 11¼x11½***

**3679** A673 $4 multi 3.00 3.00

Miniature Sheet

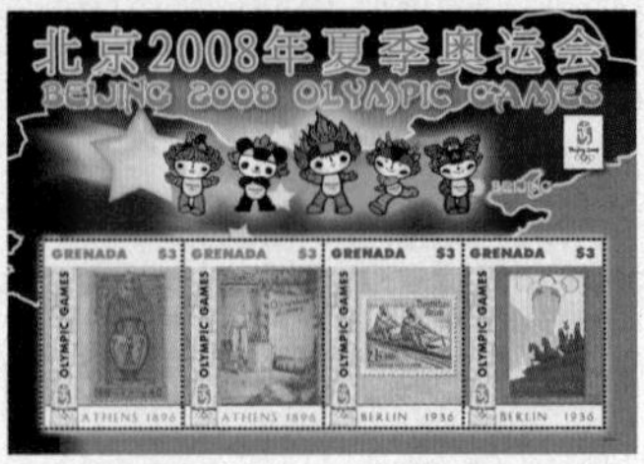


2008 Summer Olympics, Beijing — A674

No. 3680: a, Greece #123. b, Poster for 1896 Olympic Games, Athens. c, Germany #B88. d, Poster for 1936 Olympic Games, Berlin.

**2008, Feb. 6 *Perf. 14¼***

**3680** A674 $3 Sheet of 4, #a-d 9.00 9.00

Flora of Taiwan — A675

No. 3681, horiz.: a, Oolong tea. b, Pink lotus. c, Japanese maple. d, Bitter melon. e, Rice field. f, Lychees.

$5, Shitou Forest.

**2008, May 8 *Perf. 11½***

**3681** A675 $1 Sheet of 6, #a-f 4.50 4.50

**Souvenir Sheet**

***Perf. 13½***

**3682** A675 $5 multi 3.75 3.75

No. 3681 contains six 40x30mm stamps. 2008 Taipei Intl. Stamp Exhibition.

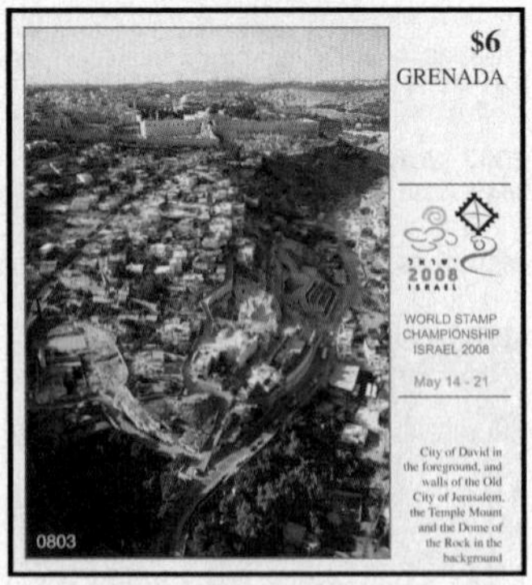


2008 World Stamp Championship, Israel — A676

**2008, May 14 *Imperf.***

**3683** A676 $6 multi 4.50 4.50

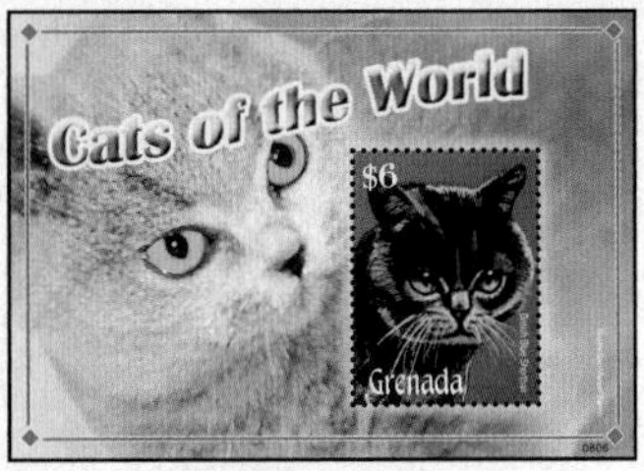


Cats — A677

No. 3684: a, Tortoiseshell. b, Korat. c, Turkish Van. d, Manx.

$6, British blue shorthair.

**2008, June 18 *Perf. 11½***

**3684** A677 $1.40 Sheet of 4, #a-d 4.25 4.25

**Souvenir Sheet**

**3685** A677 $6 multi 4.50 4.50

Miniature Sheet

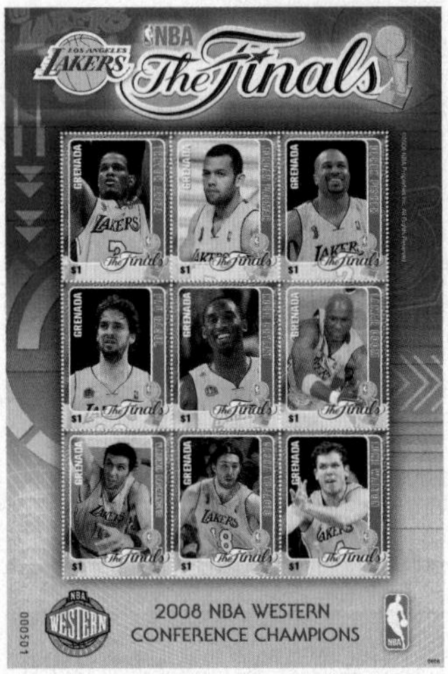


Players on 2008 Los Angeles Lakers Basketball Team — A678

No. 3686: a, Trevor Ariza. b, Jordan Farmar. c, Derek Fisher. d, Pau Gasol. e, Kobe Bryant. f, Lamar Odom. g, Vladimir Radmanovic. h, Sasha Vujacic. i, Luke Walton.

**2008, June 17 Litho. *Perf. 13½***

**3686** A678 $1 Sheet of 9, #a-i 6.75 6.75

Miniature Sheet

Visit of Pope Benedict XVI to United States — A679

No. 3687 — Pope Benedict XVI and faded background showing: a, Bishop's red zucchetto under LL flourish. b, White ceiling tiles at top. c, Bishop's ear at UL. d, Bishop's hands at R.

**2008, June 18 *Perf. 13½***

**3687** A679 $2 Sheet of 4, #a-d 6.00 6.00

Miniature Sheet

Pres. John F. Kennedy (1917-63) — A680

No. 3688 — Kennedy and background designs of: a, Flag's white stripe and blue field. b, Flag's white and red stripes. c, Necktie. d, Flag's red and white stripes, with blue in UL corner.

**2008, Oct. 10** ***Perf. 11½x11¼***

**3688** A680 $1.50 Sheet of 4, #a-d 4.50 4.50

Miniature Sheets

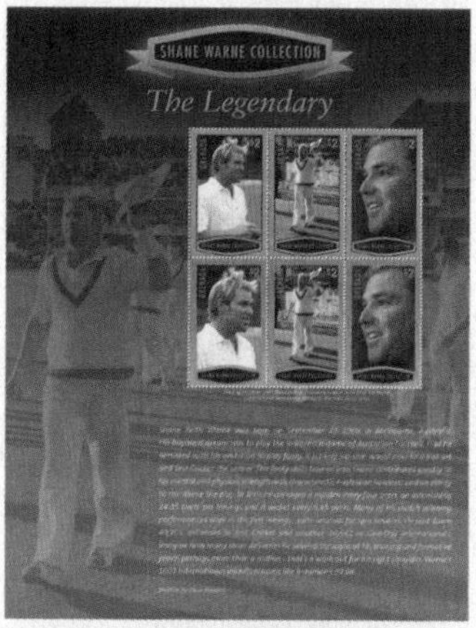


— A681

A682

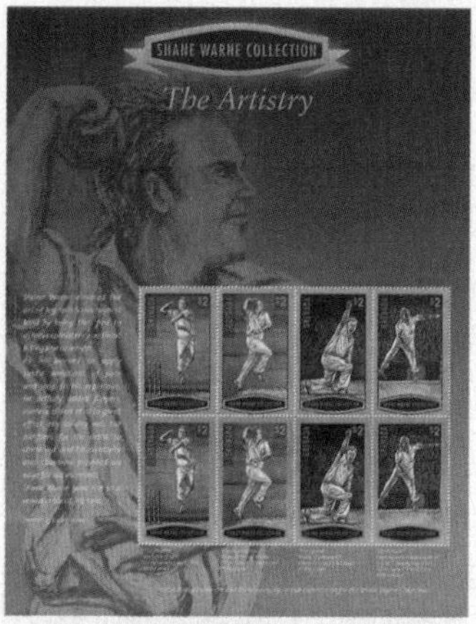


A683

A684

A685

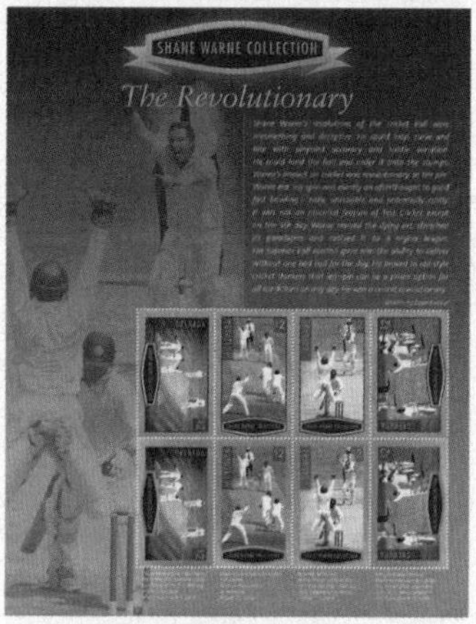


Shane Warne, Cricket Player — A686

No. 3689 — Warne: a, Holding ball, tan frame. b, Waving to crowd, tan frame. c, Close-up, tan frame. d, Wearing white shirt, green frame. e, As "b," green frame. f, As "c," green frame.

No. 3690 — Warne: a, Bowling in Australia uniform, tan frame. b, Holding trophy, tan frame. c, Celebrating, tan frame. d, As "a," green frame. e, As "b," green frame. f, As "c," green frame.

No. 3691 — Drawings of Warne by Phillip Howe: a, The Mastery (tan frame). b, The Revolutionary (tan frame). c, The Appeal (tan frame). d, The Natural (tan frame). e, As "a," green frame. f, As "b," green frame. g, As "c," green frame. h, As "d," green frame. Titles are in sheet margin.

No. 3692 — Warne bowling: a, Left arm horizontal, tan frame. b, Leg lifted, hands even, tan frame. c, Leg lifted, right hand higher than left hand, tan frame. d, Arm above head, tan frame. e, As "a," green frame. f, As "b," green frame. g, As "c," green frame. h, As "d," green frame.

No. 3693 — Warne: a, Celebrating and making fist, tan frame. b, With ball near ear, tan frame. c, After releasing ball, tan frame. d, With arm above head, umpire in background, tan frame. e, As "a," green frame. f, As "b," green frame. g, As "c," green frame. h, As "d," green frame.

No. 3694 — Match scenes: a, Warne bowling against Mike Gatting, tan frame, horiz. b, Warne taking 600th test wicket, tan frame. c, Warne capturing 533rd wicket. d, Warne taking 356th test wicket. e, As "a," green frame. f, As "b," green frame. g, As "c," green frame. h, As "d," green frame. Match descriptions are in sheet margin.

**2008, Dec. 3** ***Perf. 14x14½, 14½x14***

**3689** A681 $2 Sheet of 6, #a-f 9.25 9.25
**3690** A682 $2 Sheet of 6, #a-f 9.25 9.25
**3691** A683 $2 Sheet of 8, #a-h 12.50 12.50
**3692** A684 $2 Sheet of 8, #a-h 12.50 12.50
**3693** A685 $2 Sheet of 8, #a-h 12.50 12.50
**3694** A686 $2 Sheet of 8, #a-h 12.50 12.50
*Nos. 3689-3694 (6)* 68.50 68.50

Miniature Sheet

Pope John Paul II (1920-2005) — A687

No. 3695 — Pope John Paul II: a, As child. b, At coronation. c, Holding books. d, With hands raised. e, Wearing biretta, hand on chin. f, Wearing zucchetto, hand touching face.

**2008, Dec. 8** ***Perf. 13½***

**3695** A687 $2 Sheet of 6, #a-f 9.25 9.25

Coat of Arms — A688

**2008, June 18 Litho.** ***Perf. 14x15***

**3696** A688 250c multi + label 1.90 1.90

Printed in sheets of 8 + 8 labels.

Inauguration of US Pres. Barack Obama — A689

**2009, Jan. 20** ***Perf. 12¼x11¾***

**3697** A689 $2.75 multi 2.10 2.10

Printed in sheets of 4.

Miniature Sheets

Space Exploration, 50th Anniv. (in 2007) — A690

No. 3698, $2: a, Ultraviolet photograph of Sun. b, Buzz Aldrin on Moon. c, Crane lifting Space Shuttle Atlantis at Kennedy Vehicle Assembly Building. d, Mars Orbiter looking at Victoria Crater. e, Cassini Mission to Saturn. f, Engines being installed on Space Shuttle Atlantis.

No. 3699, $2: a, International Space Station. b, Concept for new lunar truck. c, Milky Way over Ontario. d, M16 and the Eagle Nebula. e, Astronaut in space on Expedition 16. f, Dextre robot working on the Space Station.

No. 3700, $2.50, vert.: a, Canadarm 2 (robotic arm on Space Station). b, Space Shuttle Atlantis on launch pad in daylight. c, Cat's Eye Nebula. d, Orion crew capsule.

No. 3701, $2.50, vert.: a, Space Shuttle Atlantis at Kennedy Space Center at night. b, International Space Station as seen from Space Shuttle Discovery. c, Aurora over Saturn. d, Kibo pressurized and logistic modules.

**2009, Jan. 22** ***Perf. 12***

**Sheets of 6, #a-f**

**3698-3699** A690 Set of 2 18.50 18.50

**Sheets of 4, #a-d**

***Perf. 12½***

**3700-3701** A690 Set of 2 15.50 15.50

A691

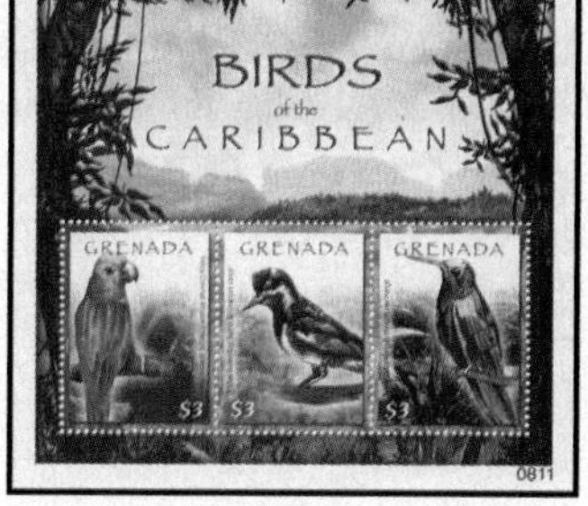


A692

Birds — A693

Designs: $1, White-crowned pigeon. $2, Blue-winged warbler. $4, Bananaquit. $5, Monk parakeet.
No. 3706: a, Yellow-crowned amazon. b, Yellow-bellied sapsucker. c, Jamaican mango.
No. 3707: a, Tree swallow. b, Ringed kingfisher. c, Black-and-white warbler.

**2009, Jan. 22** ***Perf. 12½***
**3702-3705** A691 Set of 4 9.25 9.25
**3706** A692 $3 Sheet of 3, #a-c 7.00 7.00
***Perf. 12¾x13***
**3707** A693 $3 Sheet of 3, #a-c 7.00 7.00

New Year 2009 (Year of the Ox) — A694

**2009, Jan. 26** ***Perf. 12***
**3708** A694 $2.50 multi 1.90 1.90

Printed in sheets of 4.

A695

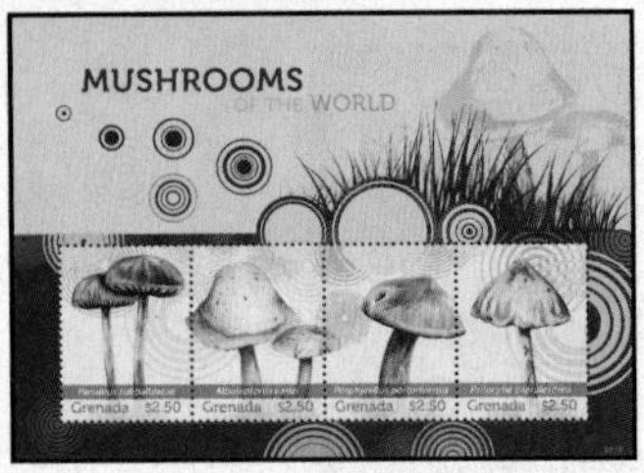


Mushrooms — A696

Designs: 25c, Panaeolus papilionaceus. 50c, Panaeolus cyanescens. 75c, Panaeolus sphintrinus. 90c, Panaeolus fimicola. $1, Copelandia cyanescens. $4, Psilocybe cubensis.
No. 3715: a, Panaleus subbalteatus. b, Alboleptonia earlei. c, Porphyrellus portoricensis. d, Psilocybe caerulescens.

**2009, Feb. 9** ***Perf. 11½***
**3709-3714** A695 Set of 6 5.75 5.75
**3715** A696 $2.50 Sheet of 4, #a-d 7.75 7.75

Miniature Sheet

Marilyn Monroe (1926-62), Actress — A697

No. 3716 — Monroe: a, With arm extended. b, Touching wall. c, With chair in background. d, Resting on arms.

**2009, Feb. 9**
**3716** A697 $2.50 Sheet of 4, #a-d 7.75 7.75

Flag of Grenada, and Designer Anthony C. George — A698

Frame color: 10c, Blue green. 25c, Blue. 50c, Red. 75c, Yellow.
$6, Flag and George, vert.

**2009, Feb. 25** ***Perf. 13¼***
**3717-3720** A698 Set of 4 1.25 1.25

**Souvenir Sheet**
***Perf. 12***
**3721** A698 $6 multi 4.75 4.75

No. 3721 contains one 30x40mm stamp.

Peony on Vase — A699

**2009, Apr. 10** ***Perf. 13¼***
**3722** A699 75c multi .55 .55

**Souvenir Sheet**
**3723** A699 $5 Peony, diff. 3.75 3.75

No. 3723 contains one 44x44mm stamp. No. 3722 was printed in sheets of 12.

Miniature Sheet

Olympic Track and Field Events — A700

No. 3724: a, Pole vault. b, Hurdles. c, Relay race. d, High jump.

**2009, Apr. 29** ***Perf. 12***
**3724** A700 $1.40 Sheet of 4, #a-d 4.25 4.25

China 2009 World Stamp Exhibition, Luoyang.

Miniature Sheet

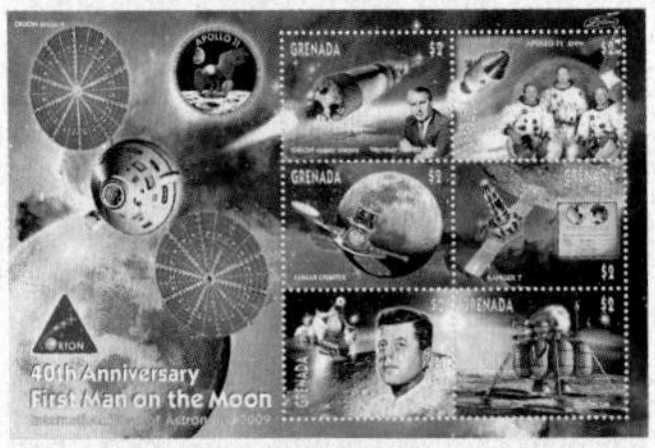


First Man on the Moon, 40th Anniv. — A701

No. 3725: a, Proposed upper stages of Orion spacecraft, Wernher von Braun. b, Crew of Apollo 11. c, Lunar Orbiter. d, Ranger 7. e, Lunar Module, Pres. John F. Kennedy. f, Proposed Orion lunar module.

**2009, Apr. 29** ***Perf. 11½***
**3725** A701 $2 Sheet of 6, #a-f 9.00 9.00

Miniature Sheet

Joseph Haydn (1732-1809), Composer — A702

No. 3726: a, Haydn's birthplace, Rohrau, Austria. b, Johann Peter Salomon, impresario. c, Austro-Hungarian Haydn Orchestra. d, Wolfgang Amadeus Mozart, composer. e, Haydn's house, Vienna. f, Ludwig van Beethoven, composer and student of Haydn.

**2009, Apr. 29**
**3726** A702 $2.25 Sheet of 6, #a-f 10.00 10.00

Miniature Sheet

Elvis Presley (1935-77) — A703

No. 3727 — Presley: a, With guitar strap on both sides. b, Facing left. c, With hand raised. d, With guitar strap at right.

**2009, Apr. 29** ***Perf. 13¼***
**3727** A703 $2.50 Sheet of 4, #a-d 7.50 7.50

Miniature Sheets

Dogs — A704

No. 3728, $2.30 — Golden retriever: a, On outdoor chair. b, On lawn, with pumpkin and gourds. c, On sofa. d, Two dogs in basket.
No. 3729, $2.50 — Beagle: a, On desktop. b, Face. c, On lawn. d, Near stone wall.

**2009, Apr. 29** ***Perf. 11½***
**Sheets of 4, #a-d**
**3728-3729** A704 Set of 2 14.50 14.50

American Kennel Club, 125th anniv.

Miniature Sheet

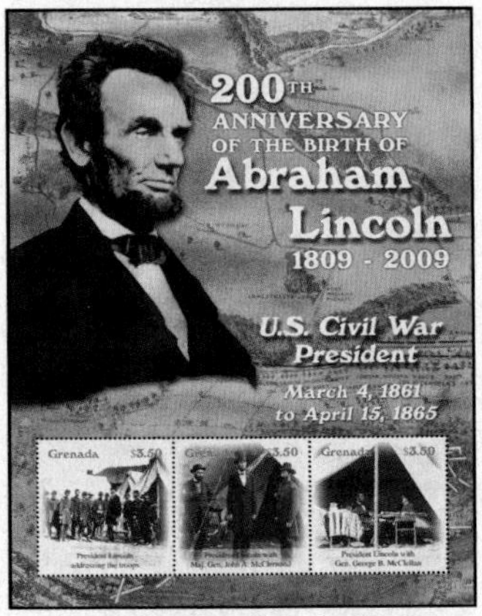


Pres. Abraham Lincoln (1809-65) — A705

No. 3730 — Lincoln: a, Addressing Union troops. b, With Major General John A. McClernand. c, With General George B. McClellan.

**2009, July 21** **Litho.** ***Perf. 13½***
**3730** A705 $3.50 Sheet of 3, #a-c 8.00 8.00

Miniature Sheet

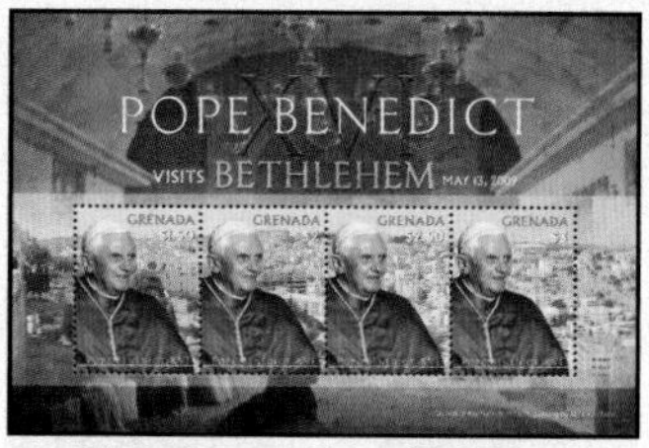


Visit of Pope Benedict XVI to Bethlehem — A706

No. 3731 — Pope Benedict and buildings in Bethlehem: a, $1.50. b, $2. c, $2.50. d, $3.

**2009, July 21** ***Perf. 11½***

**3731** A706 Sheet of 4, #a-d 6.75 6.75

Miniature Sheet

Charles Darwin (1809-82), Naturalist — A707

No. 3732 — Darwin and: a, Bird. b, Wolf. c, Fossil. d, Tortoise.

**2009, July 21**

**3732** A707 $2.50 Sheet of 4, #a-d 7.50 7.50

Chinese Aviation, Cent. — A708

No. 3733: a, J-5. b, J-6. c, J-7G. d, J-7. $6, JF-17.

**2009, Nov. 13** **Litho.** ***Perf. 14***

**3733** A708 $2 Sheet of 4, #a-d 6.50 6.50

**Souvenir Sheet**

***Perf. 14¼***

**3734** A708 $6 multi 4.75 4.75

2009 Aeropex, Beijing. No. 3733 contains four 42x28mm stamps.

Miniature Sheet

Chinese Zodiac Animals — A709

No. 3735: a, Rat. b, Ox. c, Tiger. d, Rabbit. e, Dragon. f, Snake. g, Horse. h, Ram. i, Monkey. j, Cock. k, Dog. l, Pig.

**2010, Jan. 4** ***Perf. 12***

**3735** A709 60c Sheet of 12, #a-l 5.50 5.50

Miniature Sheet

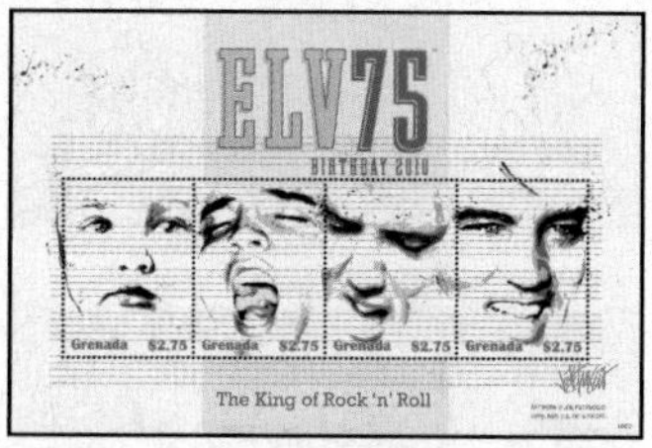


Elvis Presley (1935-77) — A710

Various views of Presley's face.

**2010, Jan. 7** ***Perf. 13¼***

**3736** A710 $2.75 Sheet of 4, #a-d 8.50 8.50

Christmas 2009 A711

Designs: $1, Fish wearing stocking caps. $2, Christmas tree, lights, fruit. $4, Bells. $5, Map of Grenada, stars, Christmas ornaments.

**2010, Jan. 13** ***Perf. 12½***

**3737-3740** A711 Set of 4 9.25 9.25

Orchids — A712

Designs: $1.20, Brassia caudata. $1.80, Epidendrum imatophyllum. No. 3743, $3, Ionopsis utriculoides. $5, Habenaria bractescens.

No. 3745, horiz.: a, Vanilla pompona. b, Caularthron bicornutum. c, Epidendrum nocturnum. d, Aspasia variegata.

No. 3746, $3, horiz.: a, Epidendrum hartii. b, Brassavola cucullata.

**2010, Jan. 13** ***Perf. 13¼x13***

**3741-3744** A712 Set of 4 8.50 8.50

***Perf. 13x13¼***

**3745** A712 $2.75 Sheet of 4, #a-d 8.50 8.50

**Souvenir Sheet**

**3746** A712 $3 Sheet of 2, #a-b 4.75 4.75

Ferrari Automobiles and Their Parts — A713

No. 3747, $1.25: a, Engine of 1989 F1-89. b, 1989 F1-89.

No. 3748, $1.25: a, Engine of 1994 F355 Berlinetta. b, 1994 F355 Berlinetta.

No. 3749, $1.25: a, Wires and parts to 1997 355 F1 Berlinetta. b, 1997 355 F1 Berlinetta.

No. 3750, $1.25: a, Steering wheel of 1997 F310 B. b, 1997 F310 B.

**2010, Mar. 1** ***Perf. 12***

**Vert. Pairs, #a-b**

**3747-3750** A713 Set of 4 7.75 7.75

Miniature Sheet

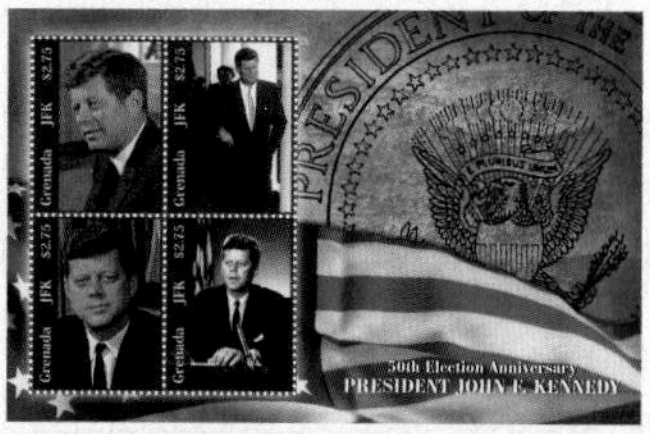


Pres. John F. Kennedy (1917-63), 50th Anniv. of Election — A714

No. 3751: a, Facing left, black and white photograph. b, Standing, black and white photograph. c, Color photograph. d, With flag in background, black and white photograph.

**2010, Apr. 9** ***Perf. 12x11½***

**3751** A714 $2.75 Sheet of 4, #a-d 8.25 8.25

Miniature Sheets

A715

Princess Diana (1961-97) — A716

No. 3752: a, Wearing black hat, gray and white along left margin of stamp. b, Wearing blue hat, with black frame at LL over gray area. c, As "b," with black frame at LL over white area. d, As "a," with hand of Princess Diana (from central illustration) touching black frame at left.

No. 3753: a, Wearing white hat, gray and white along left margin. b, Wearing no hat, with black frame at LL over red area (Diana's jacket from central illustration). c, As "b," with LL corner over gray area. d, As "a," with entire left margin over red area (Diana's jacket from central illustration).

**2010, Apr. 9**

**3752** A715 $2.75 Sheet of 4, #a-d 8.25 8.25

**3753** A716 $2.75 Sheet of 4, #a-d 8.25 8.25

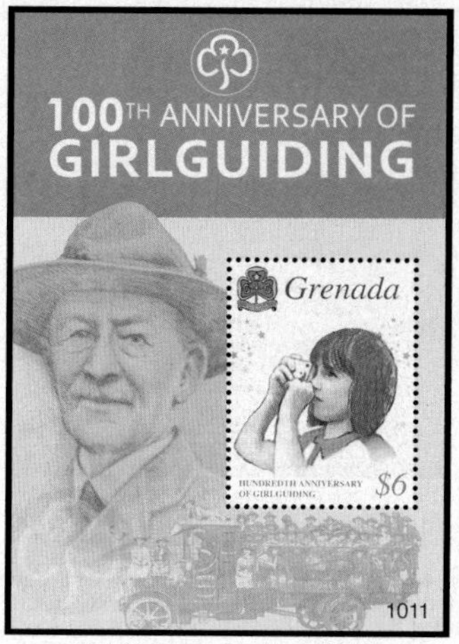


Girl Guides, Cent. — A717

No. 3754, horiz. — Girl Guides: a, Looking at image taken by camera. b, With cameras. c, With movie clapboard. d, Looking at image take by camera with telephoto lens.

$6, Girl Guide with camera.

**2010, June 11** ***Perf. 13x13¼***

**3754** A717 $2.75 Sheet of 4, #a-d 8.25 8.25

**Souvenir Sheet**

***Perf. 13¼x13***

**3755** A717 $6 multi 4.50 4.50

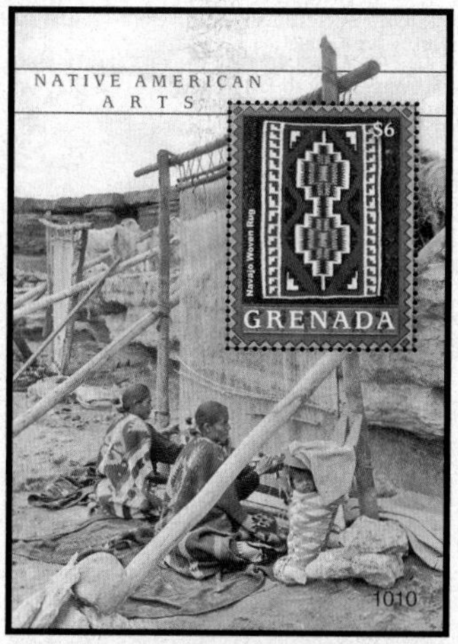


Native American Arts — A718

No. 3756: a, Apache woven basket. b, Sioux beaded moccasins. c, Iroquois cornhusk mask. d, Tlingit totem pole. e, Inuit hunter doll. f, Hopi pottery.

$6, Navajo woven rug.

**2010, June 11** ***Perf. 13¼x13***

**3756** A718 $2 Sheet of 6, #a-f 9.00 9.00

**Souvenir Sheet**

**3757** A718 $6 multi 4.50 4.50

Souvenir Sheet

New Year 2010 (Year of the Tiger) — A719

No. 3758 — Half of tiger's head with denomination at: a, UL. b, UR.

**2010, Jan. 4** **Litho.** ***Perf. 12***

**3758** A719 $5 Sheet of 2, #a-b 7.75 7.75

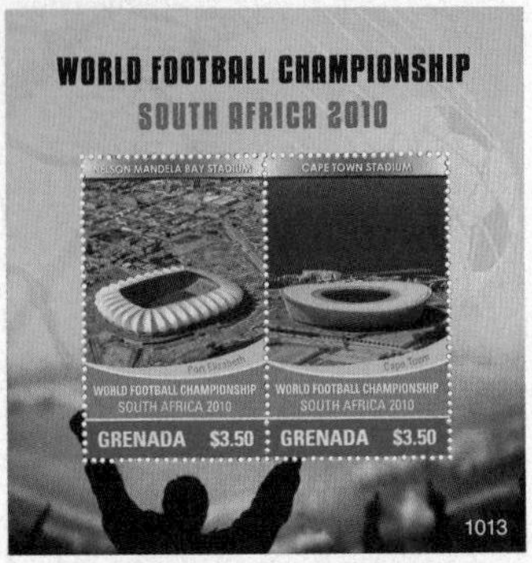


2010 World Cup Soccer Championships, South Africa — A720

No. 3759, $1.50 — Group A first-round matches: a, South Africa vs. Mexico. b, Uruguay vs. France. c, Uruguay vs. South Africa. d, France vs. Mexico. e, Mexico vs. Uruguay. f, France vs. South Africa.

No. 3760, $1.50 — Group B first-round matches: a, South Korea vs. Greece. b, Argentina vs. Nigeria. c, South Korea vs. Argentina. d, Nigeria vs. Greece. e, Nigeria vs. South Korea. f, Greece vs. Argentina.

No. 3761, $1.50 — Group C first-round matches: a, England vs. United States. b, Algeria vs. Slovenia. c, United States vs. Slovenia. d, England vs. Algeria. e, Slovenia vs. England. f, Algeria vs. United States.

No. 3762, $1.50 — Group D first-round matches: a, Serbia vs. Ghana. b, Germany vs. Australia. c, Germany vs. Serbia. d, Ghana vs. Australia. e, Ghana vs. Germany. f, Australia vs. Serbia.

No. 3763, $3.50: a, Nelson Mandela Bay Stadium, Port Elizabeth. b, Cape Town Stadium, Cape Town.

No. 3764, $3.50: a, Soccer City Stadium, Johannesburg. b, Moses Mabhida Stadium, Durban.

**2010, June 11** ***Perf. 13¼***

**Sheets of 6, #a-f**

**3759-3762** A720 Set of 4 27.00 27.00

**Sheets of 2, #a-b**

**3763-3764** A720 Set of 2 10.50 10.50

Miniature Sheet

Carl Edwards, NASCAR Driver — A721

No. 3765 — Edwards: a, Wearing baseball cap, arms not visible. b, Without hat, arms raised. c, Wearing racing helmet. d, Wearing baseball cap, arms visible.

**2010, July 26** ***Perf. 12***

**3765** A721 $2.75 Sheet of 4, #a-d 8.25 8.25

Frédéric Chopin (1810-49), Composer — A722

No. 3766: a, Sketch of Chopin facing left. b, George Sand, writer. c, Chopin, with arms folded. d, Chopin's birthplace.

$6, Chopin and musical notes.

**2010, Sept. 1**

**3766** A722 $2.50 Sheet of 4, #a-d 7.50 7.50

**Souvenir Sheet**

**3767** A722 $6 multi 4.50 4.50

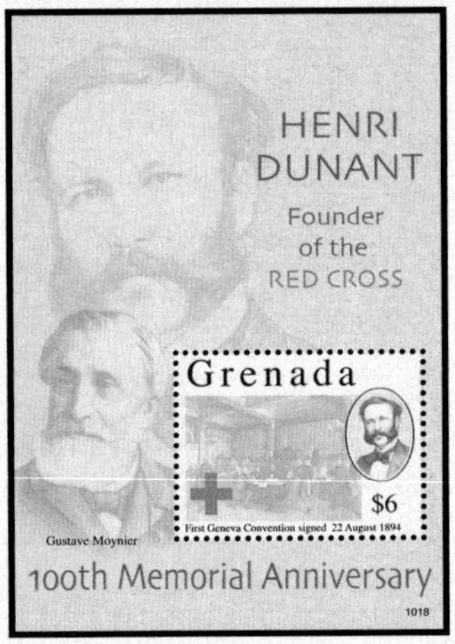


Henri Dunant (1828-1910), Founder of the Red Cross — A723

No. 3768 — Dunant and members of Red Cross "Committee of Five" founding members: a, Louis Appia. b, Gustave Moynier. c, Théodore Maunoir. d, Henri Dufour.

$6, Dunant and the First Geneva Convention, 1894.

**2010, Sept. 1**

**3768** A723 $2.50 Sheet of 4, #a-b 7.50 7.50

**Souvenir Sheet**

**3769** A723 $6 multi 4.50 4.50

Miniature Sheet

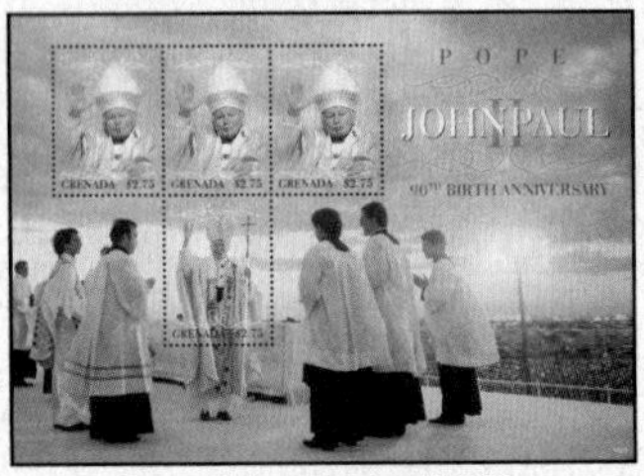


Pope John Paul II (1920-2005) — A724

No. 3770 — Pope John Paul II: a, With crucifix. b, Without crucifix.

**2010, Nov. 4**

**3770** A724 $2.75 Sheet of 4, #3770a, 3 #3770b 8.25 8.25

Boy Scouts of America, Cent. — A725

No. 3771, $2.75: a, Scout saluting. b, Scout rescuing child.

No. 3772, $2.75: a, Scout assisting woman with groceries. b, Scout reading from book.

**2010, Nov. 4** ***Perf. 12½***

**Pairs, #a-b**

**3771-3772** A725 Set of 2 8.25 8.25

Nos. 3771-3772 each were printed in sheets containing two pairs.

A726

Pres. Abraham Lincoln (1809-65) — A727

No. 3773 — Lincoln: a, With mouth to right of "resting." b, With mouth to right of "endure." c, Seated.

No. 3774 — Lincoln: a, Standing. b, With son, Tad. c, Seated.

**2010, Nov. 4**

**3773** A726 $2 Horiz. strip of 3, #a-c 4.50 4.50

**3774** A727 $2 Horiz. strip of 3, #a-c 4.50 4.50

Nos. 3773-3774 each were printed in sheets containing two strips.

Miniature Sheets

Pres. Barack Obama at Nuclear Security Summit — A728

Pres. Obama and Mexican President Felipe Calderón — A729

No. 3775 — Pres. Obama: a, Facing right. b, With Vice-President Joseph Biden. c, Facing left. d, Greeting person.

No. 3776: a, Obama and Calderón shaking hands. b, Calderón. c, Obama. d, Calderón and Obama standing together.

**2010, Nov. 4** ***Perf. 12***

**3775** A728 $2.75 Sheet of 4, #a-d 8.25 8.25

**3776** A729 $2.75 Sheet of 4, #a-d 8.25 8.25

St. George's, 300th Anniv. A730

Photographs from the mid-1900s: 25c, St. George's Lagoon. 50c, Church Street, St. George's, Grenada #91, vert. $1, Market Day, St. George's.

**2010, Dec. 9** **Litho.** ***Perf. 12***

**3777-3779** A730 Set of 3 1.40 1.40

Nos. 3777-3779 each were printed in sheets of 4.

Sickle Cell Association of Grenada — A731

No. 3780 — Flowers, text, orange ribbon: a, 25c. b, 50c. c, $1. d, $2. $6, Flowers, text, blue ribbon.

**2010, Dec. 9**

**3780** A731 Sheet of 4, #a-d 3.00 3.00

**Souvenir Sheet**

**3781** A731 $6 multi 4.50 4.50

Souvenir Sheets

A732

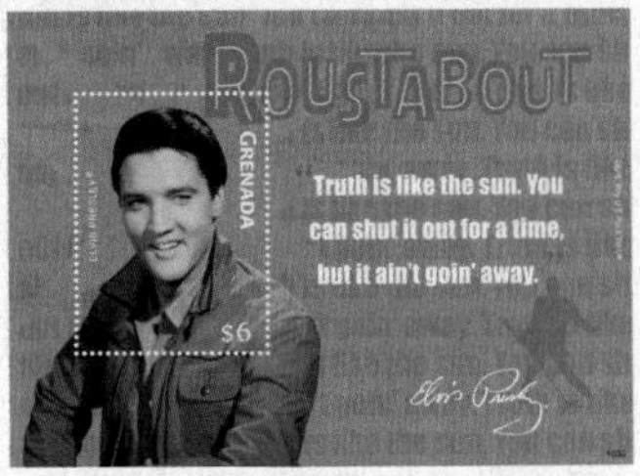


A733

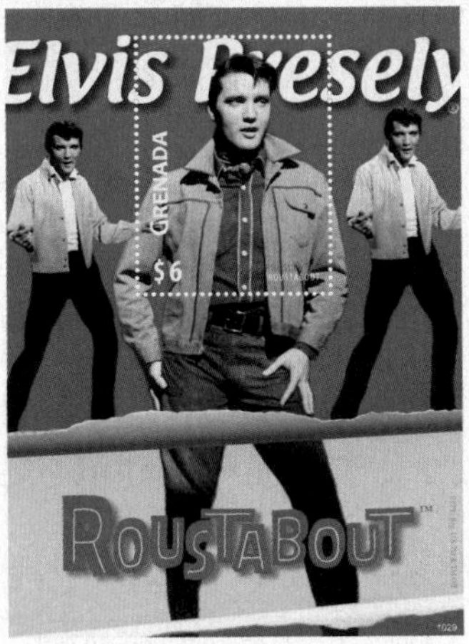


A734

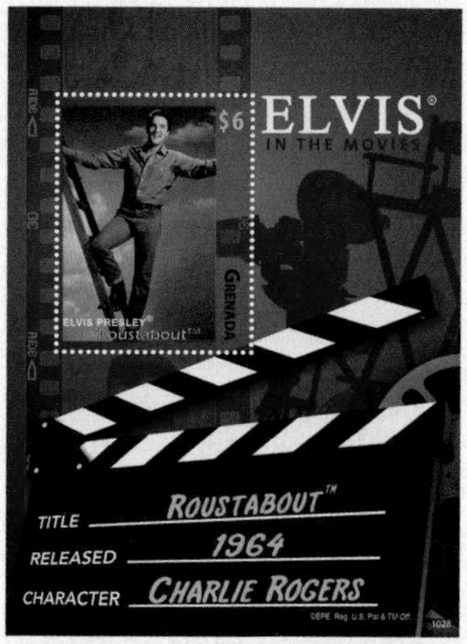


Elvis Presley (1935-77) — A735

**2010, Dec. 9** *Perf. 12½*

| | | | | |
|---|---|---|---|---|
| **3782** A732 $6 multi | | | 4.50 | 4.50 |
| **3783** A733 $6 multi | | | 4.50 | 4.50 |
| **3784** A734 $6 multi | | | 4.50 | 4.50 |
| **3785** A735 $6 multi | | | 4.50 | 4.50 |
| *Nos. 3782-3785 (4)* | | | 18.00 | 18.00 |

Christmas
A736

Designs: 25c, Three Wise Men. 50c, Adoration of the Shepherds, by Guido Reni. $1, Anbetung der Hirten, by Jusepe de Ribera. $2, Star of Bethlehem.
$6, Geburt Christi, by Max Bentele, horiz.

**2010, Dec. 9** *Perf. 12*

**3786-3789** A736 Set of 4 3.00 3.00

**Souvenir Sheet**

*Perf. 12½*

**3790** A736 $6 multi 4.50 4.50

Nos. 3786-3789 each were printed in sheets of 4. No. 3790 contains one 50x38mm stamp.

Souvenir Sheet

New Year 2011 (Year of the Rabbit) — A737

No. 3791 — Background above rabbit's ears in: a, Tan. b, Green.

**2011, Feb. 1** *Perf. 12*

**3791** A737 $2.50 Sheet of 2, #a-b 3.75 3.75

Fish — A738

Designs: 25c, Rock beauty. $1.25, Graysby. $1.50, Beaugregory damselfish. $2, Juvenile Pomacanthus paru.
$100, Longsnout butterflyfish.

**2011, Feb. 1** **Litho.** *Perf. 13¼*

**3792-3795** A738 Set of 4 3.75 3.75

**Souvenir Sheet**

*Perf. 14¾x14*

**3796** A738 $100 multi 75.00 75.00

No. 3796 contains one 40x30mm stamp.

Forbidden City, Beijing — A739

No. 3797: a, Aerial view. b, Ancient sundial. c, Temple roof. d, Canal.
$5, Golden lion, vert.

**2011, Feb. 1** *Perf. 12*

**3797** A739 $2 Sheet of 4, #a-d 6.00 6.00

**Souvenir Sheet**

*Perf. 12½*

**3798** A739 $5 multi 3.75 3.75

2010 Beijing Intl. Stamp and Coin Exhibition. No. 3798 contains one 38x51mm stamp.

Engagement of Prince William and Catherine Middleton
A740

Designs: No. 3799, Couple. No. 3800: a, Prince William. b, Catherine Middleton.

**2011, Feb. 18** *Perf. 13 Syncopated*

**3799** A740 $2.50 multi 1.90 1.90

**3800** A740 $2.50 Horiz. pair, #a-b 3.75 3.75

No. 3799 was printed in sheets of 4; No. 3800, in sheets containing 2 pairs.

Miniature Sheet

Chinese Zodiac Animals — A741

No. 3801: a, Rat. b, Ox. c, Tiger. d, Snake. e, Dragon. f, Rabbit. g, Horse. h, Ram. i, Monkey. j, Pig. k, Dog. l, Rooster.

**2011, Apr. 1** *Perf. 12*

**3801** A741 $1 Sheet of 12, #a-l 9.00 9.00

Miniature Sheets

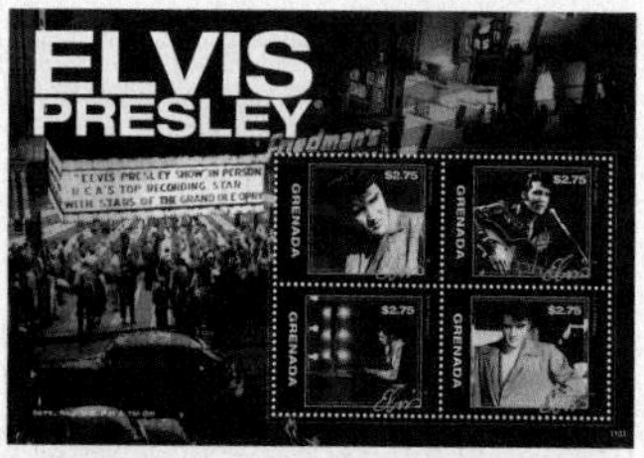


A742

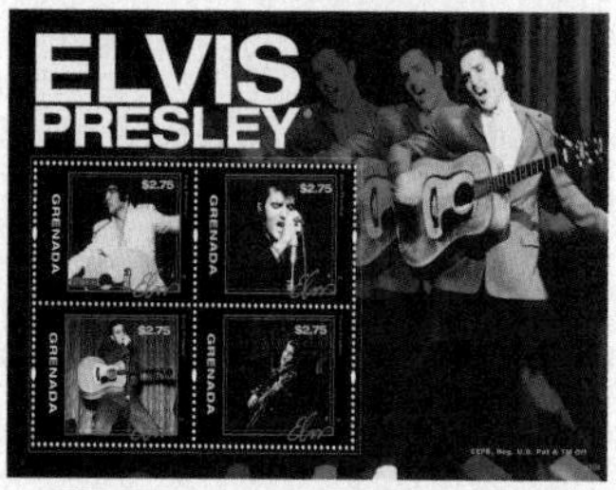


Elvis Presley (1935-77) — A743

No. 3802 — Signature in lilac with Presley: a, Wearing checked jacket, head tilted. b, Playing guitar. c, At dressing room table. d, Wearing checked jacket, head straight.
No. 3803 — Signature in blue with Presley: a, Wearing white jacket. b, Holding microphone, no guitar visible. c, Holding microphone, guitar visible. d, Playing guitar.

**2011, Apr. 6**

**3802** A742 $2.75 Sheet of 4, #a-d 8.25 8.25

*Perf. 13 Syncopated*

**3803** A743 $2.75 Sheet of 4, #a-d 8.25 8.25

Miniature Sheets

A744

Princess Diana (1961-97) — A745

No. 3804 — Princess Diana wearing: a, Black hat and black jacket. b, White and pink hat with veil. c, Gray striped jacket. d, Black hat and white scarf.
No. 3805 — Princess Diana: a, Sniffing flowers. b, Wearing white veil around head. c, Wearing plaid jacket. d, Wearing black hat and black dress with white ruffled collar.

*Perf. 13 Syncopated*

**2011, Apr. 15** **Litho.**

**3804** A744 $2.75 Sheet of 4, #a-d 8.25 8.25

*Perf. 12*

**3805** A745 $2.75 Sheet of 4, #a-d 8.25 8.25

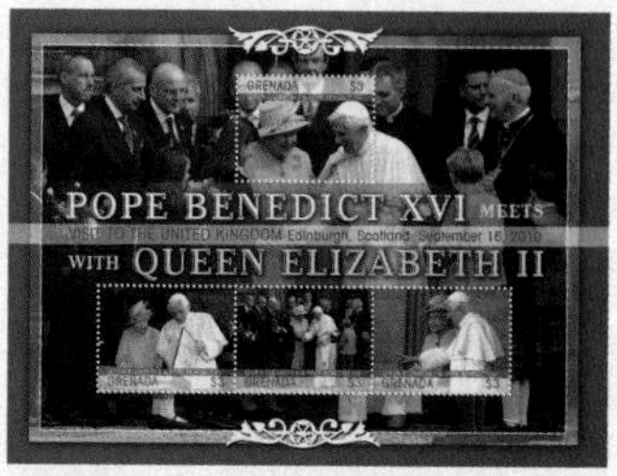


Meeting of Pope Benedict XVI and Queen Elizabeth II — A746

No. 3806: a, Pope Benedict XVI, Queen Elizabeth II and girl. b, Pope and Queen looking at book. c, Pope and Queen with children and dignitaries. d, Pope and Queen, Pope pointing.
No. 3807, vert.: a, Queen. b, Pope.

**2011, Apr. 15** *Perf. 11½x12*

**3806** A746 $3 Sheet of 4, #a-d 9.00 9.00

**Souvenir Sheet**

*Perf. 11½*

**3807** A746 $3.50 Sheet of 2, #a-b 5.25 5.25

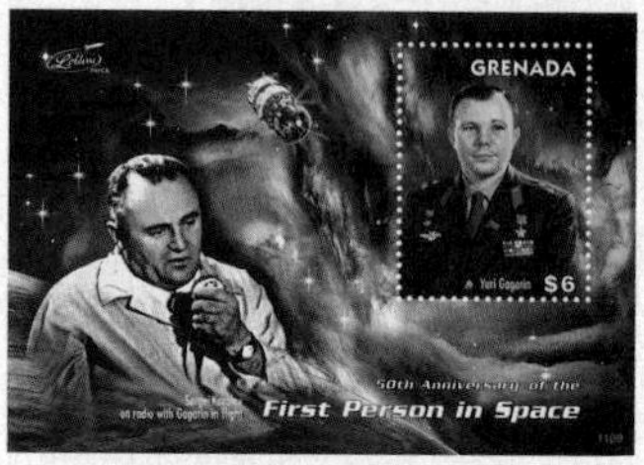


First Man in Space, 50th Anniv. — A747

No. 3808, $2.75: a, Bust of Yuri Gagarin. b, Aluminum medal depicting Gagarin. c, Vostok rocket. d, U.S. astronaut L. Gordon Cooper.
No. 3809, $2.75: a, Monument to the Conquerors of Space, Moscow. b, U.S. astronaut Walter Schirra. c, Gagarin wearing decorations. d, Vostok spaceship.
No. 3810, $6, Gagarin wearing military uniform and decorations, diff. No. 3811, $6, Vostok spaceship, horiz.

**2011, Apr. 15** *Perf. 12x12½*

**Sheets of 4, #a-d**

**3808-3809** A747 Set of 2 16.50 16.50

**Souvenir Sheets**

*Perf. 11¼x11½, 11½x11¼*

**3810-3811** A747 Set of 2 9.00 9.00

Large Hadron Collider, France and Switzerland — A748

No. 3812: a, Galileo Galilei. b, Sir Isaac Newton. c, Large Hadron Collider. d, Albert Einstein. $6, Collider, diff.

**2011, July 22** *Perf. 12*

**3812** A748 $2.75 Sheet of 4, #a-d 8.25 8.25

**Souvenir Sheet**

*Perf. 12½*

**3813** A748 $6 multi 4.50 4.50

No. 3813 contains one 51x38mm stamp.

### Souvenir Sheets

Chinese Civil Engineering Projects — A749

No. 3814, $6, Qingdao Cross-Sea Bridge. No. 3815, $6, Diagram of Qingdao Haozhouwan Tunnel.

**2011, July 22** ***Perf. 12***
**3814-3815** A749 Set of 2 9.00 9.00

Parrots — A750

No. 3816 — Map of Caribbean islands and: a, Scarlet macaw. b, Hyacinth macaw. c, Slender-billed parakeet. d, Blue-and-yellow macaw. e, Olive-throated parakeet. f, Burrowing parrot.
$6, Red-and-green macaw.

**2011, Sept. 15** **Litho.** ***Perf. 12***
**3816** A750 $2 Sheet of 6, #a-f 9.00 9.00

**Souvenir Sheet**

**3817** A750 $6 multi 4.50 4.50

### Miniature Sheets

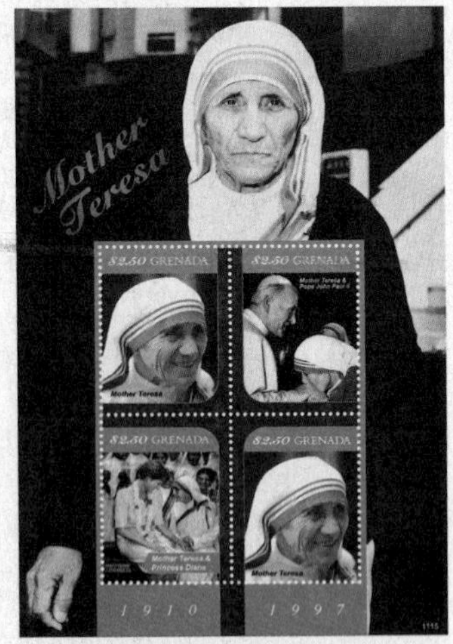


Mother Teresa (1910-97), Humanitarian — A751

No. 3818, $2.50: a, Mother Teresa, curved frame at LR. b, Mother Teresa and Pope John Paul II. c, Mother Teresa and Princess Diana. d, Mother Teresa, curved frame at UL.
No. 3819, $2.50: a, Mother Teresa and Prince Charles. b, Mother Teresa, curved frame at LL. c, Motehr Teresa, curved frame at UR. d, Mother Teresa and Senator Edward M. Kennedy.

**2011, Sept. 15** ***Perf. 12***
**Sheets of 4, #a-d**
**3818-3819** A751 Set of 2 15.00 15.00

### Miniature Sheets

Pres. Abraham Lincoln (1809-65) — A752

No. 3820, $2.75 — Photograph of Lincoln with background color of: a, Green. b, Blue black. c, Gray black. d, Red brown.
No. 3820, $2.75, horiz. — Photograph of Lincoln with background color of: a, Black. b, Dark red. c, Brown. d, Purple.

**2011, Sept. 15** ***Perf. 13 Syncopated***
**Sheets of 4, #a-d**
**3820-3821** A752 Set of 2 16.50 16.50

Chocolate Candy A753

Chocolate Frosting — A754

No. 3822 — Candy with: a, Country name in gray, denomination in pink. b, Country name and denomination in pink. c, "GRE" in pink, "NADA" and denomination in gray.
No. 3823 — Teardrop-shaped swirl in frosting at: a, Left of "NA" in panel at right, above "ho" in "Chocolate," curved frame at UL. b, Left of "A $" in panel at right, above "Ch" in "Chocolate." c, Left of "EN" in panel at right, above "oc" in "Chocolate." d, Left of "RE" in panel at right, above "ho" in "Chocolate." e, Left of "GR" in panel at right, above "e" in "Chocolate." f, Left of "GR" in panel at right, above "oc" in "Chocolate." g, Left of "G" in panel at right (touching edge of stamp), above "ho" in "Chocolate," curved frame at LL. h, Left of "G" in panel at right (touching edge of stamp), above "e" in "Chocolate." i, Left of "G" in panel at right (touching edge of stamp), above "oc" in "Chocolate."

**2011, Oct. 26** **Litho.**
**3822** Horiz. strip of 3 5.25 5.25
***a.-c.*** A753 $2.25 Any single 1.75 1.75
**3823** A754 $2.25 Sheet of 9, #a-i 15.00 15.00

No. 3822 is printed in sheets containing 3 strips. Nos. 3822-3823 are impregnated with a chocolate aroma.

British Monarchs A755

Designs: No. 3824, $2, King William II (c. 1056-1100). No. 3825, $2, King Richard I (1157-99). No. 3826, $2, King Edward III (1312-77). No. 3827, $2, King Edward IV (1442-83). No. 3828, $2, King Henry VIII (1491-1547). No. 3829, $2, King Charles I (1600-49). No. 3830, $2, King George I (1660-1727). No. 3831, $2, King George V (1865-1936).

**2011, Oct. 26** ***Perf. 14***
**3824-3831** A755 Set of 8 12.00 12.00

Nos. 3824-3831 each were printed in sheets of 8 + central label.

Sept. 11, 2011 Terrorist Attacks, 10th Anniv. — A756

No. 3832: a, Tribute in light at World Trade Center site. b, Pentagon Memorial. c, September 11 Memorial, New York. d, September 11 Memorial, New Jersey.
$6, World Trade Center towers, vert.

**2011, Oct. 26** ***Perf. 12***
**3832** A756 $2.75 Sheet of 4, #a-d 8.25 8.25

**Souvenir Sheet**

**3833** A756 $6 multi 4.50 4.50

Mao Zedong (1893-1976), Chinese Leader — A757

**2011, Nov. 8** **Litho.**
**3834** A757 $3 shown 2.25 2.25

**Souvenir Sheet**

**3835** A757 $6 Portrait, diff. 4.50 4.50

China 2011 Intl. Philatelic Exhibition, Wuxi (#3835). No. 3834 was printed in sheets of 3.

### Miniature Sheets

Visit of Pope Benedict XVI to Germany — A758

No. 3836: a, Pope Benedict XVI wearing miter, facing left, building. b, Red City Hall, Berlin. c, Madonna in the Rose Bower, by Stefan Lochner. d, Pope Benedict XVI with arms extended, building.
No. 3837 — Various buildings and Pope Benedict XVI: a, Praying. b, Holding crucifix in his left hand, waving. c, Holding crucifix in his right hand.

**2011, Nov. 8** ***Perf. 13¼x13***
**3836** A758 $2.75 Sheet of 4, #a-d 8.25 8.25
**3837** A758 $3 Sheet of 3, #a-c 6.75 6.75

Chinese Zodiac Animals — A759

New Year 2012 (Year fo the Dragon) — A760

No. 3838: a, Rat. b, Ox. c, Tiger. d, Rabbit. e, Dragon. f, Snake. g, Horse. h, Sheep. i, Monkey. j, Rooster. k, Dog. l, Boar.
$8, Dragon.

**Litho. With Foil Application**
**2011** ***Perf. 13 Syncopated***
**3838** A759 65c Sheet of 12, #a-l 5.75 5.75

**Souvenir Sheet**
**Litho.**
***Perf. 12***

**3839** A760 $8 multi 6.00 6.00

Issued: No. 3838, 11/8; No. 3839, 10/26.

Hummingbirds — A761

No. 3840, horiz.: a, Calliope hummingbird. b, Anna's hummingbird. c, Black-chinned hummingbird. d, Ruby-throated hummingbird. e, Costa's hummingbird. f, Broad-billed hummingbird.
$6, Rufous hummingbird.

**2011, Dec. 16** **Litho.** ***Perf. 12***
**3840** A761 $2 Sheet of 6, #a-f 9.00 9.00

**Souvenir Sheet**

**3841** A761 $6 multi 4.50 4.50

Pres. Barack Obama, 50th Birthday — A762

No. 3842 — Pres. Obama: a, Looking left. b, Close-up. c, Holding hand to face.
$6, Pres. Obama, diff.

**2011, Dec. 16** ***Perf. 12***
**3842** A762 $3.50 Sheet of 3, #a-c 7.75 7.75

**Souvenir Sheet**
***Perf. 12¾***

**3843** A762 $6 multi 4.50 4.50

No. 3843 contains one 51x38mm stamp.

Souvenir Sheets

Pres. John F. Kennedy (1917-63) — A763

No. 3844, $3 — Pres. Kennedy: a, Sitting in rocking chair. b, Standing behind microphone. c, Signing document.
No. 3855, $3 — Pres. Kennedy: a, Close-up photograph of head. b, On campaign posters at convention. c, Standing.

**2011, Dec. 16** ***Perf. 13 Syncopated***
**Sheets of 3, #a-c**

**3844-3845** A763 Set of 2 13.50 13.50

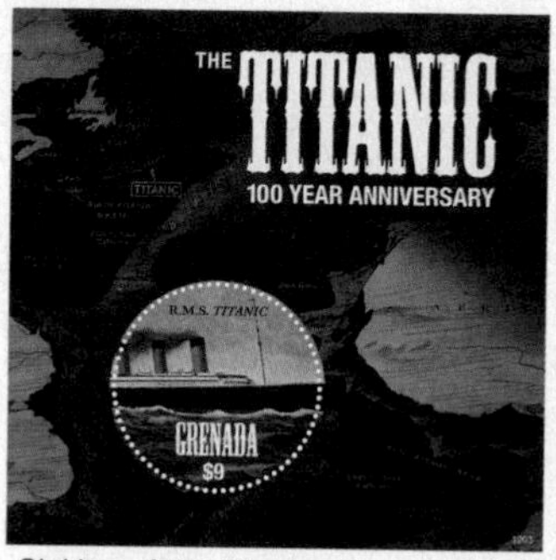


Sinking of the Titanic, Cent. — A764

No. 3846: a, Family waits for survivors. b, Survivors arrive at the docks. c, Captain Edward J. Smith. d, Titanic sinks into the sea.
$9, Titanic at sea.

**2012, Feb. 8** ***Perf.***
**3846** A764 $3.50 Sheet of 4, #a-d 10.50 10.50

**Souvenir Sheet**

**3847** A764 $9 multi 6.75 6.75

Reign of Queen Elizabeth II, 60th Anniv. — A765

No. 3848 — Queen Elizabeth II: a, With Prince Philip. b, In wedding dress. c, Holding infant Prince Charles. d, With young Prince Andrew.
$9, With two children, vert.

**2012, Feb. 8** ***Perf. 12***
**3848** A765 $3.50 Sheet of 4, #a-d 10.50 10.50

**Souvenir Sheet**

**3849** A765 $9 multi 6.75 6.75

Mother Teresa (1910-97), Humanitarian — A766

No. 3850, $4 — Various photos of Mother Teresa with: a, Black denomination, white at UL corner of frame. b, Brown denomination. c, Black denomination, purple at UL corner of frame.
No. 3851, $4, Mother Teresa in truck.

**2012, Apr. 5** ***Perf. 13 Syncopated***
**3850** A766 $4 Sheet of 3, #a-c 9.00 9/00

**Souvenir Sheet**

**3851** A766 $4 multi 3.00 3.00

Souvenir Sheets

A767

A768

A769

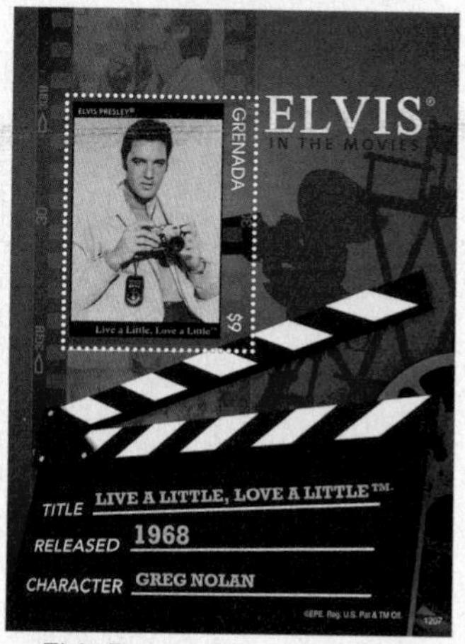


Elvis Presley (1935-77) — A770

**2012, Apr. 5** ***Perf. 12¾***

| | | | | |
|---|---|---|---|---|
| **3852** | A767 $9 multi | | 6.75 | 6.75 |
| **3853** | A768 $9 multi | | 6.75 | 6.75 |
| **3854** | A769 $9 multi | | 6.75 | 6.75 |
| **3855** | A770 $9 multi | | 6.75 | 6.75 |
| | *Nos. 3852-3855 (4)* | | 27.00 | 27.00 |

Dogs — A771

No. 3856, vert.: a, Labrador retriever. b, Bernese mountain dog. c, Bordeaux mastiff. No. 3857: a, Great Dane. b, Chocolate Labrador retriever. c, Chihuahua. d, Miniature pinscher. No. 3858, $9, American cocker spaniel. No. 3859, $9, Shih tzu.

**2012, Apr. 24** ***Perf. 13½x13¼***
**3856** A771 $3.50 Sheet of 3, #a-c 7.75 7.75

***Perf. 12¾***

**3857** A771 $3.50 Sheet of 4, #a-d 10.50 10.50

**Souvenir Sheets**
***Perf. 12***

**3858-3859** A771 Set of 2 13.50 13.50

No. 3856 contains three 30x50mm stamps. No. 3857 contains four 25x25mm stamps.

Emblem of the 2012 Summer Olympics, London A772

No. 3860 — Emblem color: a, Pink. b, Orange. c, Blue. d, Green.

**2012, July 27** ***Perf. 13¼***

| | | | |
|---|---|---|---|
| **3860** | Horiz. strip of 4 | 4.50 | 4.50 |
| ***a.-d.*** | A772 $1.50 Any single | 1.10 | 1.10 |

No. 3860 was printed in sheets containing three strips.

Visit of Pope Benedict XVI to Cuba — A773

No. 3861: a, Pope with arms extended, with other clerics. b, Pope meeting with Fidel Castro. c, Pope meeting with Cuban Pres. Raul Castro and woman. d, Pope kneeling at altar.
$9, Pope carrying crucifix before crowd.

**2012, Nov. 28** ***Perf. 14***
**3861** A773 $3.50 Sheet of 4, #a-d 10.50 10.50

**Souvenir Sheet**
***Perf. 12***

**3862** A773 $9 multi 6.75 6.75

Chinese Zodiac Animals — A774

Designs: No. 3863, 55c, Ram. No. 3864, 55c, Horse.

**2012, Nov. 28** **Litho.** ***Perf. 13¼x13***
**3863-3864** A774 Set of 2 .85 .85

**SEMI-POSTAL STAMPS**

**Catalogue values for unused stamps in this section are for Never Hinged items.**

**Nos. 227-229 Overprinted**

Type I

Type II

**1968**

**Type I**

**B1A** A38 2c + 3c on $2 multi .25 .25
**B1B** A38 3c + 3c on $3 multi .25 .25

**Type II**

**B1C** A38 1c + 3c on $2 multi .25 .25
**B1D** A38 2c + 3c on $3 multi 24.00 *50.00*
*Nos. B1A-B1D (4)* 24.75 *50.75*

Issued: B1A-B1B, 7/22; B1C-B1D, 8/19.

ESPANA '82 World Cup Soccer SP1

Players and Flags of Winning Countries.

**Unwmk.**

**1981, Nov. 30 Litho. *Perf. 14***

**B1** SP1 25c + 10c West Germany, 1974 .50 .50
**B2** SP1 40c + 20c Argentina, 1978 .70 .70
**B3** SP1 50c + 25c Brazil, 1970 1.00 1.00
**B4** SP1 $1 + 50c Grt. Britain, 1966 1.75 1.75
*Nos. B1-B4 (4)* 3.95 3.95

**Souvenir Sheet**

**B5** SP1 $5 + 50c World Cup, ESPANA '82 4.00 4.00

Nos. B1-B4 each issued in sheets of 12 with sheet background showing soccer ball.

1988 Seoul Olympics — SP2

**1986, Dec. 1 Litho. *Perf. 15***

**B6** SP2 10c + 5c Pole vault .25 .30
**B7** SP2 50c + 20c Balance beam .55 *.65*
**B8** SP2 70c + 30c Shot put .85 .85
**B9** SP2 $2 + $1 High jump 1.75 *2.50*
*Nos. B6-B9 (4)* 3.40 *4.30*

**Souvenir Sheet**

**B10** SP2 $3 + $1 Swimming 3.50 3.50

Surtax for natl. Olympic team.

World Philatelic Programs SP3

Halley's Comet or Stamp Collecting emblem and: No. B11, Halley's initial work on nebulae, 1676. No. B12, Experiments at sea (tall ship, manned capsule). No. B13, Halley observes complete lunar cycle, 1720-1738. No. B14, Halley publishes Newton's Principia, 1687. No. B15, Halley charts the southern skies, 1676.

**1989, Apr. 25 Litho. *Perf. 14***

**B11** SP3 25c +5c multi .75 .75
**B12** SP3 75c +5c multi 1.25 1.25
**B13** SP3 90c +5c multi 1.50 1.50
**B14** SP3 $2 +5c multi 2.00 2.00

**Size: 111x78mm**

***Imperf***

**B15** SP3 $5 +5c multi 4.25 4.25
*Nos. B11-B15 (5)* 9.75 9.75

## AIR POST STAMPS

**Catalogue values for unused stamps in this section are for Never Hinged items.**

**Nos. 428-429 Surcharged with New Value, Olympic Rings, "Air Mail" and: "WINTER OLYMPICS / FEB. 3-13, 1972 / SAPPORO, JAPAN"**

***Perf. 13½x14***

**1972, Feb. 3 Litho. Unwmk.**

**C1** A66 35c on ½c multi .40 .40
**C2** A66 50c on 1c multi .60 .60

11th Winter Olympic Games, Sapporo, Japan, Feb. 3-13.

**Nos. 294-300, 302A, 303-309 Surcharged Type "a" or Overprinted Type "b"**

a

b

***Perfs. as Before***

**1972, May 2 Photo.; Litho.**

**C3** A45 5c violet & multi .25 .25
**C4** A45 8c multicolored .25 .25
**C5** A45 10c orange & multi .25 .25
**C6** A45 15c gray & multi .25 .25
**C7** A45 25c multicolored .40 .30
**C8** A45 30c on 1c multi .50 .35
**C9** A45 35c multicolored .55 .40
**C10** A45 40c on 2c multi .60 .45
**C11** A45 45c on 3c multi .65 .50
**C12** A45 50c multicolored .70 .55
**C13** A45 60c on 5c multi .80 .70
**C14** A45 70c on 6c multi .95 .90
**C15** A45 $1 multicolored 6.50 1.25
**C16** A45 $1.35 on 8c multi 3.25 3.00
**C17** A45 $2 multicolored 8.00 7.00
**C18** A45 $3 multicolored 10.00 9.00
**C19** A45 $5 multicolored 13.00 *16.00*
*Nos. C3-C19 (17)* 46.90 41.40

"AIR MAIL" reading down on 5c, 15c, 25c, 35c, 60c and $5.

**Olympic Type of Regular Issue**

Olympic Rings and: 25c, 60c, $1, Boxing. 70c, Equestrian (not inscribed air mail).

**1972, Sept. 8 Litho. *Perf. 14***

**C20** A69 25c blue & multi .50 .30
**C21** A69 $1 green & multi .90 .75

**Souvenir Sheet**

**C22** Sheet of 2 1.50 1.50
*a.* A69 60c blue & multi .50 .50
*b.* A69 70c deep yellow & multi 1.00 1.00

**Nos. 409-412 Overprinted Vertically, Reading Up "AIR MAIL"**

**1972, Oct. Litho. *Perf. 11***

**C23** A62 5c multicolored .60 .25
**C24** A62 35c multicolored 1.50 .60
**C25** A62 50c multicolored 1.75 1.00
**C26** A62 75c multicolored 2.50 2.00
*Nos. C23-C26 (4)* 6.35 3.85

**Boy Scout Type of Regular Issue**

Designs: 25c, Scout saluting. 35c, Two Scouts knotting ropes.

**1972, Nov. *Perf. 14***

**C27** A70 25c dp blue & multi .40 .35
**C28** A70 35c brn org & multi .60 .55

John Hancock — AP1

Designs: 50c, Benjamin Franklin. 75c, John Adams. $1, Marquis de Lafayette.

**1975, May 6 Litho. *Perf. 14½, 13***

**C29** AP1 40c multicolored .25 *.25*
**C30** AP1 50c multicolored .45 *.25*
**C31** AP1 75c multicolored .55 *.25*
**C32** AP1 $1 multicolored .65 *.25*
*Nos. C29-C32 (4)* 1.90 *.85*

American Revolution Bicentennial.
Nos. C29-C32 issued in sheets of 40. Each denomination was also printed in sheets of 5 plus label, perf. 13.

## POSTAGE DUE STAMPS

D1

D2

**1892 Typo. Wmk. 2 *Perf. 14***

**J1** D1 1p black 30.00 2.75
**J2** D1 2p black 225.00 3.25
**J3** D1 3p black 200.00 4.00
*Nos. J1-J3 (3)* 455.00 10.00

**Black Surcharge**

**J4** D2 1p on 6p red lilac 110.00 2.25
*a.* Tete beche pair 2,750. *1,800.*
*b.* Double surcharge 225.00
*c.* Same as "b," tete beche pair
**J5** D2 1p on 8p bister 1,600. 6.00
*a.* Tete beche pair *8,500.* *2,500.*
**J6** D2 2p on 6p red lilac 190.00 4.50
*a.* Tete beche pair *3,500.* 1,800.
**J7** D2 2p on 8p bister 3,200. 12.00
*a.* Tete beche pair *7,500.* 5,000.
*Nos. J4-J7 (4)* 5,100. 24.75

Nos. J4-J7 were printed with alternate horizontal rows inverted.

**1906-11 Wmk. 3**

**J8** D1 1p black ('11) 3.75 *7.50*
**J9** D1 2p black 12.50 3.75
**J10** D1 3p black 15.00 6.50
*Nos. J8-J10 (3)* 31.25 17.75

D3

**1921-22 Wmk. 4**

**J11** D3 1p black 2.00 *1.40*
**J12** D3 1½p black 10.00 *25.00*
**J13** D3 2p black 3.00 *4.50*
**J14** D3 3p black 3.00 *4.75*
*Nos. J11-J14 (4)* 18.00 *35.65*

Issued: 1½p, Dec. 15, 1922, others, Dec. 1921.

**Catalogue values for unused stamps in this section, from this point to the end of the section, are for Never Hinged items.**

**1952, Mar. 1**

**J15** D3 2c black .50 *9.00*
*a.* Wmk. 4a (error) 55.00
**J16** D3 4c black .50 *17.00*
*a.* Wmk. 4a (error) 60.00
**J17** D3 6c black .65 *13.00*
*a.* Wmk. 4a (error) 100.00
**J18** D3 8c black .75 *14.00*
*a.* Wmk. 4a (error) 200.00
*Nos. J15-J18 (4)* 2.40 *53.00*

## WAR TAX STAMPS

Nos. 80a, 80 Overprinted

**1916 Wmk. 3 *Perf. 14***

**MR1** A21 1p carmine 2.50 2.00
*a.* 1p scarlet 3.00 3.00
*b.* Double overprint 325.00
*c.* Inverted overprint 325.00

No. 80 Overprinted

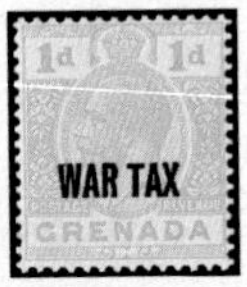


**MR2** A21 1p scarlet .30 .25

## OFFICIAL STAMPS

**Catalogue values for unused stamps in this section are for Never Hinged items.**

**Nos. 1006-1018, 1020, 1051-1053 Overprinted: "P.R.G."**

**1982, July 15 Litho. *Perf. 14, 15***

**O1** A141 5c multicolored .25 .25
**O2** A141 6c multicolored .25 .25
**O3** A141 10c multicolored .25 .25
**O4** A141 12c multicolored .25 .25
**O5** A141 15c multicolored .25 .25
**O6** A141 20c multicolored .25 .25
**O7** A141 25c multicolored .25 .25
**O8** A141 30c multicolored .25 .25
**O9** A141 40c multicolored .30 .30
**O10** A141 50c multicolored .40 .40
**O11** CD331 50c multicolored .40 .40
**O12** A141 90c multicolored .75 .75
**O13** A141 $1 multicolored .80 .80
**O14** CD331 $2 multicolored 1.75 1.75
**O15** A141 $3 multicolored 2.25 2.25
**O16** CD331 $4 multicolored 4.00 4.00
**O17** A141 $10 multicolored 7.00 7.00
*Nos. O1-O17 (17)* 19.65 19.65

PRG stands for People's Revolutionary Government.

## GRENADA GRENADINES

grə-ˈnā-də ˌgre-nə-ˈdēnz

LOCATION — North of Grenada
GOVT. — Part of Grenada
CAPITAL — None

Main islands are Carriacou and Ronde.

**Catalogue values for all unused stamps in this country are for Never Hinged items.**

All stamps are a type of Grenada unless otherwise noted or illustrated. Nos. 15-58 have the additional inscription Grenadines.

**Grenada Nos. 516-517a Overprinted**

***Perf. 13½x14***

**1973, Dec. 23 Litho. Wmk. 314**

**1** A77 25c dp orange & multi .25 .25
**2** A77 $2 green & multi .50 .50
*a.* Souvenir sheet of 2 (75c, $1) .75 .50

Grenada Nos. 294-297, 299-301, 303, 306-309 Overprinted

***Perf. 14x14½, 14½x14***

**1974, May 29 Photo. Unwmk.**

**Size: 25x44mm**

**3** A45 1c multicolored .25 .25
**4** A45 2c multicolored .25 .25
**5** A45 3c multicolored .25 .25
**6** A45 5c multicolored .25 .25
**7** A45 8c multicolored .25 .25
**8** A45 10c multicolored .25 .25
**9** A45 12c multicolored .25 .25
**10** A45 25c multicolored .30 .30

**Size: 25x47mm**

**11** A45 $1 multicolored 2.50 1.40
**12** A45 $2 multicolored 3.75 2.00
**13** A45 $3 multicolored 3.75 2.90
**14** A45 $5 multicolored 4.50 3.50
*Nos. 3-14 (12)* 16.55 11.85

**World Cup Soccer Type**

Designs: Soccer matches and flags. ½c, West Germany-Chile. 1c, East Germany-Australia. 2c, Yugoslavia-Brazil. 10c, Scotland-Zaire. 25c, Netherlands-Uruguay. 50c, Sweden-Bulgaria. 75c, Italy-Haiti. $1, Poland-Argentina. $2, Flags of participating nations.

**1974, Sept. 17 Litho. *Perf. 14½***

**15** A81 ½c multicolored .25 .25
**16** A81 1c multicolored .25 .25
**17** A81 2c multicolored .25 .25
**18** A81 10c multicolored .25 .25
**19** A81 25c multicolored .25 .25
**20** A81 50c multicolored .35 .25
**21** A81 75c multicolored .35 .25
**22** A81 $1 multicolored .40 .30
*Nos. 15-22 (8)* 2.35 2.05

**Souvenir Sheet**

**23** A81 $2 multicolored 2.00 2.00

**UPU Centenary Type**

UPU Emblem and: 8c, Mailboat *Caesar*, 1839, helicopter. 25c, German messenger, 1540, satellite. 35c, Biplanes, zeppelin, jet. No. 27, US Mail train, 19th cent., Concorde. No. 28a, Bellman, 18th cent., radar. $2, German postman, 18th cent., mail train, 1980's.

**1974, Oct. 8 *Perf. 14½***

**24** A82 8c multicolored .25 .25
**25** A82 25c multicolored .25 .25
**26** A82 35c multicolored .25 .25
**27** A82 $1 multicolored .95 .50
*Nos. 24-27 (4)* 1.70 1.25

**Souvenir Sheet**

***Perf. 13***

**28** Sheet of 2 1.75 1.75
*a.* A82 $1 multicolored .50 .50
*b.* A82 $2 multicolored 1.25 1.25

**Churchill Type**

Design: $2, Churchill, different portrait.

**1974, Nov. 11 *Perf. 13½***

**29** A83 35c multicolored .25 .25
**30** A83 $2 multicolored .35 .35

**Souvenir Sheet**

**31** Sheet of 2 .80 .80
*a.* A82 75c like 35c .30 .30
*b.* A82 $1 like $2 .35 .35

**Christmas Type**

Paintings of the Virgin and Child.

**1974, Nov. 27 *Perf. 14½***

**32** A84 ½c Botticelli .25 .25
**33** A84 1c Niccolo di Pietro .25 .25
**34** A84 2c Van der Weyden .25 .25
**35** A84 3c Bastiani .25 .25
**36** A84 10c Giovanni .25 .25
**37** A84 25c Van der Weyden, diff. .25 .25
**38** A84 50c Botticelli .25 .25
**39** A84 $1 Mantegna .30 .25
*Nos. 32-39 (8)* 2.05 2.00

**Souvenir Sheet**

***Perf. 13½***

**40** A84 $2 Niccolo di Pietro 1.00 1.00

**Big Game Fish Type**

**1975, Feb. 17 *Perf. 14½***

**41** A86 ½c Sailfish .25 .25
**42** A86 1c Blue marlin .25 .25
**43** A86 2c White marlin .25 .25
**44** A86 10c Yellowfin tuna .25 .25
**45** A86 25c Wahoo .25 .25
**46** A86 50c Dolphin .25 .25
**47** A86 70c Grouper .40 .30
**48** A86 $1 Great barracuda .60 .50
*Nos. 41-48 (8)* 2.50 2.30

**Souvenir Sheet**

***Perf. 13***

**49** A86 $2 Mako shark 2.50 2.50

**Flowers of Grenada Type**

**1975, Mar. 11 *Perf. 14½***

**50** A87 ½c Grandilla barbadine .25 .25
**51** A87 1c Bleeding heart .25 .25
**52** A87 2c Poinsettia .25 .25
**53** A87 3c Cocoa .25 .25
**54** A87 10c Gladioli .25 .25
**55** A87 25c Red head-yellow head .25 .25
**56** A87 50c Plumbago .35 .35
**57** A87 $1 Orange blossoms .60 .55
*Nos. 50-57 (8)* 2.45 2.40

**Souvenir Sheet**

***Perf. 13½***

**58** A87 $2 Barbados gooseberry 1.50 1.50

Remainders of Grenada Grenadines stamps between Scott Nos. 59 and 269, except Nos. 109-128, 217-220, 237-240 and some souvenir sheets, were later canceled to order and sold at a fraction of their face value. Our used values for these stamps are for c-t-o examples. Postally used stamps are worth the same as unused, never hinged examples.

Christ Crowned with Thorns, by Titian — G1

Easter paintings of the Crucifixion by various artists.

**1975, June 24 *Perf. 14½***

**59** G1 ½c shown .25 .25
**60** G1 1c Giotto .25 .25
**61** G1 2c Tintoretto .25 .25
**62** G1 3c Cranach .25 .25
**63** G1 35c Caravaggio .25 .25
**64** G1 75c Tiepolo .25 .25
**65** G1 $2 Velasquez .30 .25
*Nos. 59-65 (7)* 1.80 1.75

**Souvenir Sheet**

***Perf. 13½***

**66** G1 $1 Titian, diff. 1.10 1.10

Works by Michelangelo (1475-1564) — G2

Butterflies — G3

Designs: ½c, Dawn (sculpture, detail from Medici tomb). 1c, Delphic Sibyl. 2c, Giuliano de Medici (sculpture). 40c, The Creation. 50c, Lorenzo de Medici (sculpture). 75c, Persian Sibyl. $1, The Prophet Jeremiah. $2, Head of Christ (sculpture).

**1975, July 16 *Perf. 14½***

**67** G2 ½c violet & multi .25 .25
**68** G2 1c multicolored .25 .25
**69** G2 2c green & multi .25 .25
**70** G2 40c multicolored .25 .25
**71** G2 50c brt red & multi .30 .25
**72** G2 75c multicolored .45 .25
**73** G2 $2 brt blue & multi .75 .25
*Nos. 67-73 (7)* 2.50 1.75

**Souvenir Sheet**

***Perf. 13½***

**74** G2 $1 multicolored 1.25 .75

**1975, Aug. 12 *Perf. 15***

**75** G3 ½c Emperor .25 .25
**76** G3 1c Queen .25 .25
**77** G3 2c Tiger pierid .25 .25
**78** G3 35c Cracker .55 .25
**79** G3 45c Scarlet bamboo page .70 .25
**80** G3 75c Apricot 1.25 .25
**81** G3 $2 Purple king shoemaker 3.25 .25
*Nos. 75-81 (7)* 6.50 1.75

**Souvenir Sheet**

***Perf. 13½***

**82** G3 $1 Bamboo page 6.00 6.00

Jamboree Scenes and Badges G4

Nordjamb 75 Emblem and: ½c, Progress badge. 1c, Boating badge. 2c, Coxswain badge. 35c. Interpreter badge. 45c, Ambulance badge. 75c, Chief scout's award. $1, Venture award. $2, Queen's scout award.

**1975, Aug. 22 *Perf. 15***

**83** G4 ½c lemon yel & multi .25 .25
**84** G4 1c vio blue & multi .25 .25
**85** G4 2c green & multi .25 .25
**86** G4 35c dull vio & multi .25 .25
**87** G4 45c org brown & multi .25 .25
**88** G4 75c brown & multi .25 .25
**89** G4 $2 green & multi .60 .25
*Nos. 83-89 (7)* 2.10 1.75

**Souvenir Sheet**

***Perf. 13½***

**90** G4 $1 dull vio & multi 1.00 .40

Nordjamb 75, 14th Boy Scout World Jamboree, Lillehammer, Norway, July 29-Aug. 7.

Surrender of Lord Cornwallis G5

Designs: 1c, Minuteman. 2c, Paul Revere's Ride. 3c, Battle of Bunker Hill. 5c, *Spirit of '76.* 45c, Backwoodsman. 75c, Boston Tea Party. No. 98, Naval engagement. No. 99, George Washington. No. 100, White House, flags.

**1975, Sept. 30 *Perf. 14***

**Size: 39x25mm**

**91** G5 ½c multicolored .25 .25
**92** G5 1c multicolored .25 .25
**93** G5 2c multicolored .25 .25
**94** G5 3c multicolored .25 .25
**95** G5 5c multicolored .25 .25
**96** G5 45c multicolored .25 .25
**97** G5 75c multicolored .25 .25
**98** G5 $2 multicolored .45 .45

**Size: 59x39mm**

***Perf. 11***

**99** G5 $2 multicolored, vert. .45 .45
*a.* Souvenir sheet of 1, imperf. 1.00 1.00
**100** G4 $2 multicolored .45 .45
*a.* Souvenir sheet of 1, imperf. 1.00 1.00
*Nos. 91-100 (10)* 3.10 3.10

American Revolution Bicentennial. Nos. 99a, 100a have simulated perfs.

Fencing G6

**1975, Oct. 27 *Perf. 15***

**101** G6 ½c shown .25 .25
**102** G6 1c Hurdling .25 .25
**103** G6 2c Pole vault .25 .25
**104** G6 35c Weightlifting .25 .25
**105** G6 45c Javelin .25 .25
**106** G6 75c Discus .25 .25
**107** G6 $2 Diving .35 .25
*Nos. 101-107 (7)* 1.85 1.75

**Souvenir Sheet**

**108** G6 $1 Sprinter .80 .80

Pan American Games, Mexico City, Oct. 12-26, 1975.

**Type of 1975**

Designs: ½c, Cruising Yachts, Point Saline. 1c, Yacht Club race, St. George's. 2c, Careenage Taxi. 3c, Working boats. 5c, Deep water dock, St. George's. 6c, Cocoa beans drying. 8c, Nutmegs. 10c, Rum distillery, River Antoine Estate. 12c, Cocoa tree. 15c, Landing catch at Fontenoy. 20c, Parliament building, St. George's. 25c, Fort George cannons. 35c, Pearls airport. 50c, General Post Office. 75c, Caribs Leap, Sauteurs Bay. $1, Careenage, St. George's. $2, St. George's harbor at night. $3, Grand Anse beach. $5, Canoe and Black Bays from Point Saline lighthouse. $10, Sugar Loaf Island from Levera beach.

**1975-76 *Perf. 14½***

**Size: 38x25mm**

**109** A85 ½c multicolored .25 *.35*
**110** A85 1c multicolored .25 .25
**111** A85 2c multicolored .25 .25
**112** A85 3c multicolored .25 .25
**113** A85 5c multicolored .25 .25
**114** A85 6c multicolored .25 .25
**115** A85 8c multicolored .25 .25
**116** A85 10c multicolored .25 .25
**117** A85 12c multicolored .25 .25
**118** A85 15c multicolored .25 .25
**119** A85 20c multicolored .25 *.65*
**120** A85 25c multicolored .25 .25
**121** A85 35c multicolored 1.00 .25
**122** A85 50c multicolored .25 *1.00*

***Perf. 13½x14***

**Size: 45x28mm**

**123** A85 75c multicolored .55 *.65*
**124** A85 $1 multicolored .85 *.95*
**125** A85 $2 multicolored 1.25 *2.25*
**126** A85 $3 multicolored 1.50 *2.75*
**127** A85 $5 multicolored 1.75 *5.50*
**128** A85 $10 multicolored 3.00 *6.00*
*Nos. 109-128 (20)* 13.15 22.85

Issued: #109-127, 11/5/75; #128, 1/1/76.
For overprints see Nos. 360-372.

Madonna and Child by Durer — G8

Christmas: Paintings showing Madonna and Child by various artists.

**1975, Dec. 17** *Perf. 14*

| | | | | |
|---|---|---|---|---|
| **129** G8 | ½c | shown | .25 | .25 |
| **130** G8 | 1c | Durer, diff. | .25 | .25 |
| **131** G8 | 2c | Correggio | .25 | .25 |
| **132** G8 | 40c | Botticelli | .25 | .25 |
| **133** G8 | 50c | Niccolo da Cremona | .25 | .25 |
| **134** G8 | 75c | Correggio, diff. | .25 | .25 |
| **135** G8 | $2 | Correggio, diff. | .35 | .25 |
| | | *Nos. 129-135 (7)* | 1.85 | 1.75 |

**Souvenir Sheet**

| | | | | |
|---|---|---|---|---|
| **136** G8 | $1 | Bellini | .80 | .60 |

Sea Shells G9

**1976, Jan. 13**

| | | | | |
|---|---|---|---|---|
| **137** G9 | ½c | Bleeding Tooth | .25 | .25 |
| **138** G9 | 1c | Wedge clam | .25 | .25 |
| **139** G9 | 2c | Hawk wing conch | .25 | .25 |
| **140** G9 | 3c | Distorsio clathrata | .25 | .25 |
| **141** G9 | 25c | Scotch bonnet | .45 | .25 |
| **142** G9 | 50c | King helmet | .90 | .25 |
| **143** G9 | 75c | Queen conch | 1.50 | .25 |
| | | *Nos. 137-143 (7)* | 3.85 | 1.75 |

**Souvenir Sheet**

| | | | | |
|---|---|---|---|---|
| **144** G9 | $2 | Atlantic triton | 2.75 | 1.00 |

Lignum Vitae G10

Designs: 1c, Cocoa thrush. 2c, Tarantula. 35c, Hooded tanager. 50c, Nyctaginaceae. 75c, Grenada dove. $1, Marine toad. $2, Blue-hooded euphonia.

**1976, Feb. 4**

| | | | | |
|---|---|---|---|---|
| **145** G10 | ½c | multicolored | .25 | .25 |
| **146** G10 | 1c | multicolored | .25 | .25 |
| **147** G10 | 2c | multicolored | .25 | .25 |
| **148** G10 | 35c | multicolored | 1.25 | .25 |
| **149** G10 | 50c | multicolored | 1.25 | .25 |
| **150** G10 | 75c | multicolored | 2.50 | .30 |
| **151** G10 | $1 | multicolored | 2.50 | .30 |
| | | *Nos. 145-151 (7)* | 8.25 | 1.85 |

**Souvenir Sheet**

| | | | | |
|---|---|---|---|---|
| **152** G10 | $2 | multicolored | 5.75 | 1.25 |

Hooked Sailfish G11

Designs: 1c, Careened schooner, Carriacou. 2c, Annual regatta. 18c, Boat building. 22c, Workboat race. 75c, Cruising off Petit Martinique. $1, Water skiing. $2, Yacht racing.

**1976, Feb. 17**

| | | | | |
|---|---|---|---|---|
| **153** G11 | ½c | multicolored | .25 | .25 |
| **154** G11 | 1c | multicolored | .25 | .25 |
| **155** G11 | 2c | multicolored | .25 | .25 |
| **156** G11 | 18c | multicolored | .25 | .25 |
| **157** G11 | 22c | multicolored | .25 | .25 |
| **158** G11 | 75c | multicolored | .40 | .25 |
| **159** G11 | $1 | multicolored | .55 | .25 |
| | | *Nos. 153-159 (7)* | 2.20 | 1.75 |

**Souvenir Sheet**

| | | | | |
|---|---|---|---|---|
| **160** G11 | $2 | multicolored | .90 | .90 |

Making a Camp Fire G12

50th anniv. of Girl Guides of Grenada: 1c, First aid. 2c, Nature study. 50c, Cooking. $1, Drawing. $2, Playing guitar.

**1976, Mar. 17**

| | | | | |
|---|---|---|---|---|
| **161** G12 | ½c | multicolored | .25 | .25 |
| **162** G12 | 1c | multicolored | .25 | .25 |
| **163** G12 | 2c | multicolored | .25 | .25 |
| **164** G12 | 50c | multicolored | .45 | .25 |
| **165** G12 | $1 | multicolored | 1.00 | .30 |
| | | *Nos. 161-165 (5)* | 2.20 | 1.30 |

**Souvenir Sheet**

| | | | | |
|---|---|---|---|---|
| **166** G12 | $2 | multicolored | 1.40 | 1.00 |

Christ Mocked by Bosch — G13

Easter Paintings: 1c, Christ Crucified by Messina. 2c, Adoration by Durer. 3c, Lamentation of Christ by Durer. 35c, The Entombment by Van Der Weyden. $2, Blood of the Redeemer by Bellini. $3, The Deposition by Raphael.

**1976, Apr. 28**

| | | | | |
|---|---|---|---|---|
| **167** G13 | ½c | multicolored | .25 | .25 |
| **168** G13 | 1c | multicolored | .25 | .25 |
| **169** G13 | 2c | multicolored | .25 | .25 |
| **170** G13 | 3c | multicolored | .25 | .25 |
| **171** G13 | 35c | multicolored | .25 | .25 |
| **172** G13 | $3 | multicolored | .30 | .30 |
| | | *Nos. 167-172 (6)* | 1.55 | 1.55 |

**Souvenir Sheet**

| | | | | |
|---|---|---|---|---|
| **173** G13 | $2 | multicolored | .80 | .80 |

Frigate South Carolina G14

1c, Schooner Lee. 2c, HMS Roebuck. 35c, Andrew Doria. 50c, Sloop Providence. $1, Flagship Alfred. $2, Frigate Confederacy. $3. Cutter Revenge.

**1976, May 18**

| | | | | |
|---|---|---|---|---|
| **174** G14 | ½c | multicolored | .25 | .25 |
| **175** G14 | 1c | multicolored | .25 | .25 |
| **176** G14 | 2c | multicolored | .25 | .25 |
| **177** G14 | 35c | multicolored | .55 | .25 |
| **178** G14 | 50c | multicolored | .70 | .25 |
| **179** G14 | $1 | multicolored | 1.25 | .25 |
| **180** G14 | $2 | multicolored | 1.75 | .40 |
| | | *Nos. 174-180 (7)* | 5.00 | 1.90 |

**Souvenir Sheet**

| | | | | |
|---|---|---|---|---|
| **181** G14 | $3 | multicolored | 2.25 | 1.25 |

American Revolution Bicentennial.

Piper Apache G15

Designs: 1c, Beech Twin Bonanza. 2c, de Havilland Twin Otter. 40c, Britten Norman Islander. 50c, de Havilland Heron. $2, Hawker Siddeley Avro 748. $3, BAC 1-11.

**1976, June 10**

| | | | | |
|---|---|---|---|---|
| **182** G15 | ½c | multicolored | .25 | .25 |
| **183** G15 | 1c | multicolored | .25 | .25 |
| **184** G15 | 2c | multicolored | .25 | .25 |
| **185** G15 | 40c | multicolored | .40 | .25 |
| **186** G15 | 50c | multicolored | .55 | .25 |
| **187** G15 | $2 | multicolored | 1.25 | .30 |
| | | *Nos. 182-187 (6)* | 2.95 | 1.55 |

**Souvenir Sheet**

| | | | | |
|---|---|---|---|---|
| **188** G15 | $3 | multicolored | 2.25 | 1.50 |

Olympic Games, Montreal G16

**1976, July 1**

| | | | | |
|---|---|---|---|---|
| **189** G16 | ½c | Cycling | .25 | .25 |
| **190** G16 | 1c | Gymnastics | .25 | .25 |
| **191** G16 | 2c | Hurdling | .25 | .25 |
| **192** G16 | 35c | Shot put | .25 | .25 |
| **193** G16 | 45c | Diving | .25 | .25 |
| **194** G16 | 75c | Sprinting | .25 | .25 |
| **195** G16 | $2 | Rowing | .65 | .30 |
| | | *Nos. 189-195 (7)* | 2.15 | 1.80 |

**Souvenir Sheet**

| | | | | |
|---|---|---|---|---|
| **196** G16 | $3 | Sailing | 1.25 | 1.00 |

Virgin and Child by Cima — G17

Christmas: 1c, 2c, The Nativity by Romanino. 35c, Adoration of the Kings by Brueghel. 50c, Madonna and Child by Girolamo. 75c, Adoration of the Magi by Giorgione, horiz. $2, The Adoration of the Kings by Angelico, horiz. $3, The Holy Family by Garofalo.

**1976, Oct. 19**

| | | | | |
|---|---|---|---|---|
| **197** G17 | ½c | multicolored | .25 | .25 |
| **198** G17 | 1c | multicolored | .25 | .25 |
| **199** G17 | 2c | multicolored | .25 | .25 |
| **200** G17 | 35c | multicolored | .25 | .25 |
| **201** G17 | 50c | multicolored | .25 | .25 |
| **202** G17 | 75c | multicolored | .25 | .25 |
| **203** G17 | $2 | multicolored | .75 | .35 |
| | | *Nos. 197-203 (7)* | 2.25 | 1.85 |

**Souvenir Sheet**

| | | | | |
|---|---|---|---|---|
| **204** G17 | $3 | multicolored | 1.60 | 1.60 |

Alexander Graham Bell, First Telephone G18

Portraits of Bell and Telephone from: 1c, 1895. 2c, 1900. 35c, 1915. 75c, 1920. $1, 1929. $2, 1963. $3, 1976.

**1977, Jan. 28**

| | | | | |
|---|---|---|---|---|
| **205** G18 | ½c | multicolored | .25 | .25 |
| **206** G18 | 1c | multicolored | .25 | .25 |
| **207** G18 | 2c | multicolored | .25 | .25 |
| **208** G18 | 35c | multicolored | .25 | .25 |
| **209** G18 | 75c | multicolored | .25 | .25 |
| **210** G18 | $1 | multicolored | .30 | .25 |
| **211** G18 | $2 | multicolored | .55 | .25 |
| | | *Nos. 205-211 (7)* | 2.10 | 1.75 |

**Souvenir Sheet**

| | | | | |
|---|---|---|---|---|
| **212** G18 | $3 | multicolored | 1.75 | 1.00 |

Centenary of 1st telephone conversation, Mar. 10, 1876.

Coronation Coach — G19

Royal Visit — G20

Designs: 50c, Crown of St. Edward. No. 214, Queen entering Abbey. No. 219, Queen and Prince Charles. $4, Queen is crowned. No. 216, Mall on Coronation Night. No. 220, Queen's Flag.

**Litho. and Embossed**

**1977, Feb. 7** *Perf. 13½*

| | | | | |
|---|---|---|---|---|
| **213** G19 | 35c | multicolored | .25 | .25 |
| **214** G19 | $2 | multicolored | .25 | .25 |
| **215** G19 | $4 | multicolored | .35 | .25 |
| | | *Nos. 213-215 (3)* | .85 | .75 |

**Souvenir Sheet**

*Perf. 14*

| | | | | |
|---|---|---|---|---|
| **216** G19 | $5 | multicolored | .90 | .90 |

**Booklet Stamps**

***Roulette x imperf.***

**Self-adhesive**

| | | | | |
|---|---|---|---|---|
| **217** G20 | 35c | multicolored | .25 | .25 |
| *a.* | | Booklet pane of 6 | .75 | |
| **218** G20 | 50c | multicolored | .35 | .35 |
| **219** G20 | $2 | multicolored | .55 | .55 |
| **220** G20 | $5 | multicolored | .65 | .65 |
| *a.* | | Bklt. pane of 3, #218, #219, #220 | 1.25 | |

Reign of Queen Elizabeth II, 25th anniv.

Nos. 213-215, perf. 11, have different background colors and come from sheetlets of 3 stamps plus label.

For overprints see Nos. 237-240.

Easter — G21

Adoration of Jesus by Correggio — G22

Paintings of the Crucifixion by various artists.

**1977, July 5** **Litho.** *Perf. 14*

| | | | | |
|---|---|---|---|---|
| **221** G21 | ½c | Fra Angelico | .25 | .25 |
| **222** G21 | 1c | Fra Angelico, diff. | .25 | .25 |
| **223** G21 | 2c | El Greco | .25 | .25 |
| **224** G21 | 18c | El Greco, diff. | .25 | .25 |
| **225** G21 | 35c | Fra Angelico, diff. | .25 | .25 |
| **226** G21 | 50c | Giottino | .35 | .25 |
| **227** G21 | $2 | da Messina | .25 | .25 |
| | | *Nos. 221-227 (7)* | 1.75 | 1.75 |

**Souvenir Sheet**

| | | | | |
|---|---|---|---|---|
| **228** G21 | $3 | Fra Angelico, diff. | 1.10 | .80 |

**1977, Nov. 17** *Perf. 14*

Christmas: Paintings of the Madonna and Child by various artists.

| | | | | |
|---|---|---|---|---|
| **229** G22 | ½c | shown | .25 | .25 |
| **230** G22 | 1c | Giorgione | .25 | .25 |
| **231** G22 | 2c | Morales | .25 | .25 |
| **232** G22 | 18c | Raphael | .25 | .25 |
| **233** G22 | 35c | Van Dyck | .25 | .25 |
| **234** G22 | 50c | Filippo Lippi | .25 | .25 |
| **235** G22 | $2 | Filippo Lippi, diff. | .25 | .25 |
| | | *Nos. 229-235 (7)* | 1.75 | 1.75 |

**Souvenir Sheet**

| | | | | |
|---|---|---|---|---|
| **236** G22 | $3 | Ghirlandaio | 1.10 | .80 |

**Nos. 213-216 Overprinted**

**1977, Nov. 23** ***Perf. 13½***

**237** G19 35c multicolored .25 .25
**238** G19 $2 multicolored .25 .25
**239** G19 $4 multicolored .55 .55
*Nos. 237-239 (3)* 1.05 1.05

**Souvenir Sheet**

**240** G19 $5 multicolored .80 .80

Caribbean visit of Queen Elizabeth II.
Nos. 237-239 exist perf. 11.

Swimming and Life Saving G23

6th Caribbean Jamboree, Kingston, Jamaica, Aug. 5-14: 1c, Hiking. 2c, Ropes and Knots. 22c, Erecting Tent. 35c, Limbo dance. 75c, Cooking. $2, Pioneer bridge building. $3, Sea Scouts' race.

**1977, Dec. 7** ***Perf. 14***

**241** G23 ½c multicolored .25 .25
**242** G23 1c multicolored .25 .25
**243** G23 2c multicolored .25 .25
**244** G23 22c multicolored .25 .25
**245** G23 35c multicolored .25 .25
**246** G23 75c multicolored .60 .25
**247** G23 $3 multicolored 1.10 .40
*Nos. 241-247 (7)* 2.95 1.90

**Souvenir Sheet**

**248** G23 $2 multicolored 1.75 1.25

Space Shuttle Blast-off G24

Designs: 1c, Booster separation. 2c, External tank separation. 22c, Working in orbit. 50c, Re-entry. $2, Towing in. $3, Landing.

**1978, Feb. 3**

**249** G24 ½c multicolored .25 .25
**250** G24 1c multicolored .25 .25
**251** G24 2c multicolored .25 .25
**252** G24 22c multicolored .25 .25
**253** G24 50c multicolored .25 .25
**254** G24 $3 multicolored 1.25 .50
*Nos. 249-254 (6)* 2.50 1.75

**Souvenir Sheet**

**255** G24 $2 multicolored 1.00 1.00

US Space Shuttle.

Alfred Nobel, Medicine Medal G25

Alfred Nobel and: 1c, Physics, Chemistry Medal. 2c, Peace Medal. 22c, Nobel Institute, Oslo. 75c, Peace Prize committee. $2, Peace Medal, Nobel's will. $3, Literature Medal.

**1978, Feb. 22**

**256** G25 ½c multicolored .25 .25
**257** G25 1c multicolored .25 .25
**258** G25 2c multicolored .25 .25
**259** G25 22c multicolored .30 .25
**260** G25 75c multicolored .70 .25
**261** G25 $3 multicolored 2.25 .40
*Nos. 256-261 (6)* 4.00 1.65

**Souvenir Sheet**

**262** G25 $2 multicolored 2.50 .90

Nobel Prize awards.

Germany No. C37 — G26

15c, France #C43. 25c, Liechtenstein #C8 specimen. 35c, Panama #257. 50c, Russia #C15. 75c, US #C10. $2, Germany #C57. $3, Spain #C56.

**1978, Mar. 15**

**263** G26 5c multicolored .25 .25
**264** G26 15c multicolored .65 .25
**265** G26 25c multicolored .25 .25
**266** G26 35c multicolored .40 .25
**267** G26 50c multicolored .75 .25
**268** G26 $3 multicolored 1.90 .40
*Nos. 263-268 (6)* 4.20 1.65

**Souvenir Sheet**

**269** Sheet of 2 2.50 1.25
*a.* G26 75c multicolored .50 .30
*b.* G26 $2 multicolored 1.50 .80

50th anniv. of Lindbergh's solo trans-Atlantic flight. 75th anniv. of 1st Zeppelin flight.

Coronation Ring — G27

Designs: $2, Queen's Orb. $2.50, Imperial State Crown. $5, Queen Elizabeth II.

**1978, Apr. 12** ***Perf. 14***

**270** G27 50c multicolored .25 .25
**271** G27 $2 multicolored .25 .25
**272** G27 $2.50 multicolored .35 .35
*Nos. 270-272 (3)* .85 .85

**Souvenir Sheet**

**273** G27 $5 multicolored .80 .80

Nos. 270-272, perf 12, printed in sheets of 3 + label, have different background colors. Issue date; June 2, 1978.

G28

Designs: 18c, Drummer, Royal Regiment of Fusiliers. 50c, Drummer, Royal Anglian Regiment. $5, Drum Major, Queen's Regiment.

**1978, Apr. 12** ***Roulette x imperf.***

**Booklet Stamps**

**Self-Adhesive**

**274** Souvenir booklet 2.50 *3.00*
*a.* G28 Pane of 6 (3 ea 18c, 50c) .75 .75
*b.* G28 Pane of 1 ($5) 1.50 1.50

G29

Paintings by Rubens: 5c, Le Chapeau de Paille. 15c, Hector Killed by Achilles. 18c, Helene Fourment and Her Children. 22c, Rubens and Isabella Brandt. 35c, Ildefonso Altarpiece. $2, Self-portrait. $3, Four Negro Heads.

**1978, May 18** ***Perf. 14***

**275** G29 5c multicolored .25 .25
**276** G29 15c multicolored .25 .25
**277** G29 18c multicolored .25 .25
**278** G29 22c multicolored .30 .25
**279** G29 35c multicolored .30 .25
**280** G29 $3 multicolored 2.40 1.50
*Nos. 275-280 (6)* 3.75 2.75

**Souvenir Sheet**

**281** G29 $2 multicolored 1.40 1.40

400th birth anniv. of Rubens.

Wright Flyer G30

Designs: 15c, Orville Wright, vert. 18c, Wilbur Wright, vert. 25c, 35c, 75c, $2, $3, various Wright airplanes.

**1978, Aug. 10**

**282** G30 5c multicolored .25 .25
**283** G30 15c multicolored .25 .25
**284** G30 18c multicolored .25 .25
**285** G30 25c multicolored .25 .25
**286** G30 35c multicolored .25 .25
**287** G30 75c multicolored .25 .25
**288** G30 $3 multicolored 1.00 1.00
*Nos. 282-288 (7)* 2.50 2.50

**Souvenir Sheet**

**289** G30 $2 multicolored 1.75 1.75

75th anniv. of first powered flight by the Wright brothers, Dec. 17, 1903.

Audubon's Shearwater G31

Players, Soccer Ball G32

10c, Northern ring-necked plover. 18c, Garnet-throated hummingbird. 22c, Black-bellied tree duck. 40c, Purple martin. $1, Yellow-bellied tropic bird. $2, Long-billed curlew. $5, Snowy egret.

**1978, Sept. 28**

**290** G31 5c multi *1.00* .25
**291** G31 10c multi *1.25* .25
**292** G31 18c multi, horiz. *1.50* .30
**293** G31 22c multi, horiz. *2.00* .30
**294** G31 40c multi, horiz. *3.00* .50
**295** G31 $1 multi *4.25* .60
**296** G31 $2 multi *5.75* *1.10*
*Nos. 290-296 (7)* *18.75* 3.30

**Souvenir Sheet**

**297** G31 $5 multicolored *17.00 17.00*

**1978, Nov. 2**

Soccer players in action.

**298** G32 15c multicolored .25 .25
**299** G32 35c multicolored .25 .25
**300** G32 50c multicolored .25 .25
**301** G32 $3 multicolored .65 .65
*Nos. 298-301 (4)* 1.40 1.40

**Souvenir Sheet**

**302** G32 $2 multicolored 1.50 1.50

World Cup Soccer Championships, Argentina, June 1-25.

Captain Cook, Kalaniopu (King of Hawaii), 1778 G33

22c, Cook, Hawaiian native. 50c, Cook, death scene, 2/14/79. $3, Cook and offering ceremony. $4, Cook, HMS Resolution.

**1978, Dec. 13**

**303** G33 18c multicolored .50 .25
**304** G33 22c multicolored .65 .25
**305** G33 50c multicolored 1.10 .50
**306** G33 $3 multicolored 2.75 2.00
*Nos. 303-306 (4)* 5.00 3.00

**Souvenir Sheet**

**307** G33 $4 multicolored 3.00 3.00

250th birth anniv. of Captain James Cook and Bicentennial of his discovery of the Hawaiian Islands.

Durer Paintings — G34

Christmas: 40c, The Virgin at Prayer. 60c, Dresden Alterpiece. 90c, Madonna and Child. $2, Madonna and Child. $4, Salvator Mundi.

**1978, Dec 20**

**308** G34 40c multicolored .25 .25
**309** G34 60c multicolored .25 .25
**310** G34 90c multicolored .25 .25
**311** G34 $2 multicolored .70 .70
*Nos. 308-311 (4)* 1.45 1.45

**Souvenir Sheet**

**312** G34 $4 multicolored 1.40 1.40

Strelitzia Reginae — G35

**1979, Feb. 15**

**313** G35 22c shown .25 .25
**314** G35 40c Euphorbia pulcherrima .40 .40
**315** G35 $1 Heliconia humilis .80 .45
**316** G35 $3 Thunbergia alata 1.40 .80
*Nos. 313-316 (4)* 2.85 1.90

**Souvenir Sheet**

**317** G35 $2 Bougainvillea glabra 2.10 2.10

Children with Pig G36

International Year of the Child: 50c, Children with donkey. $1, Children with goats. $3, Children fishing. $4, Child with coconuts.

**1979, Mar. 22**

**318** G36 18c multicolored .25 .25
**319** G36 50c multicolored .25 .25
**320** G36 $1 multicolored .40 .40
**321** G36 $3 multicolored .60 .60
*Nos. 318-321 (4)* 1.50 1.50

**Souvenir Sheet**

**322** G36 $4 multicolored 1.00 1.00

150th Birth Anniv. of Jules Verne G37

Designs: 18c, 20,000 Leagues Under the Sea. 38c, From the Earth to the Moon. 75c, From the Earth to the Moon, diff. $3, Five

Weeks in a Balloon. $4, Around the World in 80 Days.

**1979, Apr. 20**

| | | | | |
|---|---|---|---|---|
| **323** | G37 | 18c multicolored | .65 | .25 |
| **324** | G37 | 38c multicolored | .75 | .25 |
| **325** | G37 | 75c multicolored | .90 | .40 |
| **326** | G37 | $3 multicolored | 1.75 | 1.75 |
| | | *Nos. 323-326 (4)* | 4.05 | 2.65 |

**Souvenir Sheet**

| | | | | |
|---|---|---|---|---|
| **327** | G37 | $4 multicolored | 3.00 | 3.00 |

Sir Rowland Hill, Mail Truck G38

Designs: $1, Ocean liner. $2, Mail train. $3, Concorde. $4, Sir Rowland Hill.

**1979, July 30** *Perf. 14*

| | | | | |
|---|---|---|---|---|
| **328** | G38 | 15c multicolored | .25 | .25 |
| **329** | G38 | $1 multicolored | .25 | .25 |
| **330** | G38 | $2 multicolored | .55 | .55 |
| **331** | G38 | $3 multicolored | .70 | .70 |
| | | *Nos. 328-331 (4)* | 1.75 | 1.75 |

**Souvenir Sheet**

| | | | | |
|---|---|---|---|---|
| **332** | G38 | $4 multicolored | 1.25 | 1.25 |

Death centenary of Sir Rowland Hill.

Nos. 328-331, perf. 12, printed in sheets of 5 + label, have different colored backgrounds.

Virgin and Child Enthroned (Byzantine Era, 11th Cent.) — G39

Christmas sculptures: 25c, Presentation in the Temple by Beauneveu c. 1390. 30c, Flight to Egypt (Utrecht, c. 1510). 40c, Madonna and Child by della Quercia, 1047-48. 90c, Madonna della Mela by della Robbia, c. 1455. $1, Madonna and Child by Rossellino, 1461-66. $2, Madonna (Antwerp, 1700). $4, Virgin (Krumau, c. 1390).

**1979, Oct. 23** *Perf. 14*

| | | | | |
|---|---|---|---|---|
| **333** | G39 | 6c multicolored | .25 | .25 |
| **334** | G39 | 25c multicolored | .25 | .25 |
| **335** | G39 | 30c multicolored | .25 | .25 |
| **336** | G39 | 40c multicolored | .25 | .25 |
| **337** | G39 | 90c multicolored | .25 | .25 |
| **338** | G39 | $1 multicolored | .25 | .25 |
| **339** | G39 | $2 multicolored | .25 | .25 |
| | | *Nos. 333-339 (7)* | 1.75 | 1.75 |

**Souvenir Sheet**

| | | | | |
|---|---|---|---|---|
| **340** | G39 | $4 multicolored | 1.00 | 1.00 |

Great Hammerhead Shark — G40

Designs: 45c, Banded butterflyfish. 50c, Permit. 60c, Threaded turban. 70c, Milk conch. 75c, Great blue heron. 90c, Colored Atlantic natica. $1, Red footed booby. $2.50, Collared plover.

**1979, Nov. 9**

| | | | | |
|---|---|---|---|---|
| **341** | G40 | 40c multicolored | .50 | .50 |
| **342** | G40 | 45c multicolored | .55 | .55 |
| **343** | G40 | 50c multicolored | .65 | .65 |
| **344** | G40 | 60c multicolored | .75 | .75 |
| **345** | G40 | 70c multicolored | .90 | .90 |
| **346** | G40 | 75c multicolored | 1.50 | 1.00 |
| **347** | G40 | 90c multicolored | 1.30 | 1.30 |
| **348** | G40 | $1 multicolored | 1.90 | 1.90 |
| | | *Nos. 341-348 (8)* | 8.05 | 7.55 |

**Souvenir Sheet**

| | | | | |
|---|---|---|---|---|
| **349** | G40 | $2.50 multicolored | 2.00 | 2.00 |

Doctor Goofy G41

International Year of the Child: 1c, Admiral Mickey Mouse. 2c, Fireman Goofy. 3c, Nurse Minnie Mouse. 4c, Drum Major Mickey Mouse. 5c, Policeman Donald Duck. 10c, Pilot Donald Duck. $2, Mailman Goofy, horiz. $2.50 Engineer Donald Duck, horiz. $3, Fireman Mickey Mouse.

**1979, Dec. 12** *Perf. 11*

| | | | | |
|---|---|---|---|---|
| **350** | G41 | ½c multicolored | .25 | .25 |
| **351** | G41 | 1c multicolored | .25 | .25 |
| **352** | G41 | 2c multicolored | .25 | .25 |
| **353** | G41 | 3c multicolored | .25 | .25 |
| **354** | G41 | 4c multicolored | .25 | .25 |
| **355** | G41 | 5c multicolored | .25 | .25 |
| **356** | G41 | 10c multicolored | .25 | .25 |
| **357** | G41 | $2 multicolored | 2.50 | 2.50 |
| **358** | G41 | $2.50 multicolored | 2.75 | 2.75 |
| | | *Nos. 350-358 (9)* | 7.00 | 7.00 |

**Souvenir Sheet**

*Perf. 13½*

| | | | | |
|---|---|---|---|---|
| **359** | G41 | $3 multicolored | 3.50 | 3.50 |

**Nos. 114, 117-128 Overprinted**

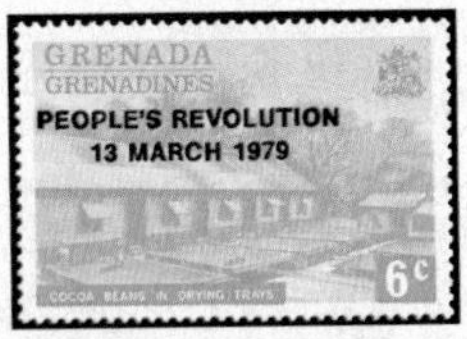


**1980, Mar. 10** *Perf. 15*

| | | | | |
|---|---|---|---|---|
| **360** | A85 | 6c multicolored | .25 | .25 |
| **361** | A85 | 12c multicolored | .25 | .25 |
| **362** | A85 | 15c multicolored | .25 | .25 |
| **363** | A85 | 20c multicolored | .25 | .25 |
| **364** | A85 | 25c multicolored | .25 | .25 |
| **365** | A85 | 35c multicolored | .25 | .25 |
| **366** | A85 | 50c multicolored | .30 | .35 |
| | | ***Perf. 13½x14*** | | |
| **367** | A85 | 75c multicolored | .35 | .40 |
| **368** | A85 | $1 multicolored | .45 | .60 |
| **369** | A85 | $2 multicolored | .70 | .90 |
| **370** | A85 | $3 multicolored | 1.25 | 1.60 |
| **371** | A85 | $5 multicolored | 1.75 | 2.40 |
| **372** | A85 | $10 multicolored | 3.00 | 3.75 |
| | | *Nos. 360-372 (13)* | 9.30 | 11.50 |

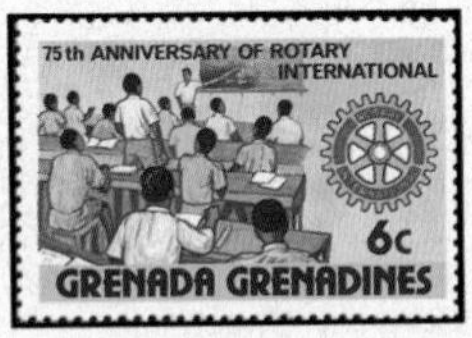


Classroom G42

Rotary Intl., 75th anniv.: 30c, Rotary emblem, people. 60c, Rotary executive making contribution to physician. $3, Young patients, nurses. $4, Paul P. Harris, founder of Rotary.

**1980, Mar. 12** *Perf. 14*

| | | | | |
|---|---|---|---|---|
| **373** | G42 | 6c multicolored | .25 | .25 |
| **374** | G42 | 30c multicolored | .25 | .25 |
| **375** | G42 | 60c multicolored | .45 | .45 |
| **376** | G42 | $3 multicolored | 1.90 | 1.60 |
| | | *Nos. 373-376 (4)* | 2.85 | 2.55 |

**Souvenir Sheet**

| | | | | |
|---|---|---|---|---|
| **377** | G42 | $4 multicolored | 1.25 | 1.25 |

Yellow-bellied Seedeater — G43

40c, Blue-hooded euphonia. 90c, Yellow warbler. $2, Tropical mockingbird. $3, Barn owl.

**1980, Apr. 14**

| | | | | |
|---|---|---|---|---|
| **378** | G43 | 25c multicolored | .65 | .25 |
| **379** | G43 | 40c multicolored | .70 | .25 |
| **380** | G43 | 90c multicolored | 1.50 | .85 |
| **381** | G43 | $2 multicolored | 2.00 | 1.60 |
| | | *Nos. 378-381 (4)* | 4.85 | 2.95 |

**Souvenir Sheet**

| | | | | |
|---|---|---|---|---|
| **382** | G43 | $3 multicolored | 5.50 | 5.50 |

Running G44

Designs: 40c, Soccer. 90c, Boxing. $2, Wrestling. $4, Runners in silhouette.

**1980, Apr. 21**

| | | | | |
|---|---|---|---|---|
| **383** | G44 | 30c multicolored | .25 | .25 |
| **384** | G44 | 40c multicolored | .25 | .25 |
| **385** | G44 | 90c multicolored | .40 | .40 |
| **386** | G44 | $2 multicolored | .85 | .85 |
| | | *Nos. 383-386 (4)* | 1.75 | 1.75 |

**Souvenir Sheet**

| | | | | |
|---|---|---|---|---|
| **387** | G44 | $4 multicolored | .90 | .90 |

22nd Summer Olympic Games, Moscow, July 19-Aug. 3.

**Nos. 328-331 Overprinted**

**1980, May 6** *Perf. 12*

| | | | | |
|---|---|---|---|---|
| **388** | G38 | 15c multicolored | .25 | .25 |
| **389** | G38 | $1 multicolored | 1.10 | .50 |
| **390** | G38 | $2 multicolored | 2.25 | 1.75 |
| **391** | G38 | $3 multicolored | 3.75 | 3.00 |
| | | *Nos. 388-391 (4)* | 7.35 | 5.50 |

Issued in sheets of 5 + label.

Longspine Squirrelfish — G45

Designs: 1c, Blue chromis. 2c, Foureye butterflyfish. 4c, Sergeant major. 5c, Yellowtail snapper. 6c, Mutton snapper. 10c, Cocoa damselfish. 12c, Royal gramma. 15c, Cherubfish. 20c, Blackbar soldierfish. 25c, Comb grouper. 30c, Longsnout butterflyfish. 40c, Pudding wife. 50c, Midnight parrotfish. 90c, Redspotted hawkfish. $1, Hogfish. $3, Beau gregory. $5, Rock beauty. $10, Barred hamlet.

**1980, Aug. 6** *Perf. 14*

**No imprint date below design**

| | | | | |
|---|---|---|---|---|
| **392** | G45 | ½c multicolored | .25 | .25 |
| *a.* | | Perf. 12, inscribed 1982 | 10.00 | 10.00 |
| **393** | G45 | 1c multicolored | .25 | .25 |
| **394** | G45 | 2c multicolored | .25 | .25 |
| **395** | G45 | 4c multicolored | .25 | .25 |
| **396** | G45 | 5c multicolored | .25 | .25 |
| **397** | G45 | 6c multicolored | .25 | .25 |
| **398** | G45 | 10c multicolored | .25 | .25 |
| *a.* | | Inscribed "1984" | .50 | .50 |
| **399** | G45 | 12c multicolored | .25 | .25 |
| **400** | G45 | 15c multicolored | .25 | .25 |
| **401** | G45 | 20c multicolored | .25 | .25 |
| *a.* | | Inscribed "1987" | 1.60 | 1.60 |
| **402** | G45 | 25c multicolored | .25 | .25 |
| **403** | G45 | 30c multicolored | .25 | .25 |
| **404** | G45 | 40c multicolored | .25 | .25 |
| **405** | G45 | 50c multicolored | .30 | .35 |
| **406** | G45 | 90c multicolored | .45 | .50 |
| **407** | G45 | $1 multicolored | .55 | .60 |
| **408** | G45 | $3 multicolored | 1.40 | 1.75 |
| **409** | G45 | $5 multicolored | 1.75 | 2.25 |
| **410** | G45 | $10 multicolored | 3.00 | 3.75 |
| | | *Nos. 392-410 (19)* | 10.70 | 12.45 |

Bambi with Mother — G46

Various scenes from Walt Disney's Bambi.

**1980, Oct. 7** *Perf. 11*

| | | | | |
|---|---|---|---|---|
| **411** | G46 | ½c multicolored | .25 | .25 |
| **412** | G46 | 1c multicolored | .25 | .25 |
| **413** | G46 | 2c multicolored | .25 | .25 |
| **414** | G46 | 3c multicolored | .25 | .25 |
| **415** | G46 | 4c multicolored | .25 | .25 |
| **416** | G46 | 5c multicolored | .25 | .25 |
| **417** | G46 | 10c multicolored | .25 | .25 |
| **418** | G46 | $2.50 multicolored | 1.50 | 1.50 |
| **419** | G46 | $3 multicolored | 1.50 | 1.50 |
| | | *Nos. 411-419 (9)* | 4.75 | 4.75 |

**Souvenir Sheet**

| | | | | |
|---|---|---|---|---|
| **420** | G46 | $4 multicolored | 3.00 | 3.00 |

Christmas.

The Unicorn in Captivity by Unknown 15th Cent. Artist — G47

Designs: 10c, The Fighting Temeraire by J.M.W. Turner. 25c, Sunday Afternoon on the Ile De La Grande-Jatte by Seurat. 90c, Max Schmitt in a Single Scull by Eakins. $2, The Burial of the Count of Orgaz by El Greco. $3, George Washington by Stuart. $5, Kaiser Karl the Great by Durer. Nos. 425-427 are vert.

**1981, Jan. 25** *Perf. 14*

| | | | | |
|---|---|---|---|---|
| **421** | G47 | 6c multicolored | .25 | .25 |
| **422** | G47 | 10c multicolored | .25 | .25 |
| **423** | G47 | 25c multicolored | .25 | .25 |
| **424** | G47 | 90c multicolored | .50 | .50 |
| **425** | G47 | $2 multicolored | .90 | .90 |
| **426** | G47 | $3 multicolored | 1.25 | 1.25 |
| | | *Nos. 421-426 (6)* | 3.40 | 3.40 |

**Souvenir Sheet**

| | | | | |
|---|---|---|---|---|
| **427** | G47 | $5 multicolored | 2.75 | 2.75 |

**Disney Type of 1979**

50th anniv. of Pluto character: $2, Mickey Mouse, Pluto and birthday cake. $4, Pluto.

**1981, Jan. 26**

| | | | | |
|---|---|---|---|---|
| **428** | A135a | $2 multicolored | 1.10 | 1.10 |

**Souvenir Sheet**

| | | | | |
|---|---|---|---|---|
| **429** | A135a | $4 multicolored | 2.50 | 2.50 |

No. 428 issued in sheets of 8.

Chip Coloring Easter Eggs — G48

Easter: Various Disney characters coloring Easter eggs.

**1981, Apr. 14** *Perf. 11*

| | | | | |
|---|---|---|---|---|
| **430** | G48 | 35c multicolored | .25 | .25 |
| **431** | G48 | 40c multicolored | .25 | .25 |
| **432** | G48 | $2 multicolored | .90 | .90 |
| **433** | G48 | $2.50 multicolored | 1.40 | 1.40 |
| | | *Nos. 430-433 (4)* | 2.80 | 2.80 |

### Souvenir Sheet

*Perf. 14*

| | | | | |
|---|---|---|---|---|
| **434** | G48 | $4 multicolored | 2.75 | 2.75 |

Bust of a Woman — G49

Paintings by Pablo Picasso (1881-1973): 40c, Woman (Study for Les Demoiselles d'Avignon). 90c, Nude with Raised Arms (The Dancer of Avignon). $4, The Dryad. $5, Les Demoiselles d'Avignon.

**1981, May 5** *Perf. 14*

| | | | | |
|---|---|---|---|---|
| **435** | G49 | 6c multicolored | .30 | .30 |
| **436** | G49 | 40c multicolored | .30 | .30 |
| **437** | G49 | 90c multicolored | .45 | .45 |
| **438** | G49 | $4 multicolored | 2.25 | 2.25 |

### Size: 103x128mm

*Imperf*

| | | | | |
|---|---|---|---|---|
| **439** | G49 | $5 multicolored | 3.00 | 3.00 |
| | | *Nos. 435-439 (5)* | 6.30 | 6.30 |

Common Design Types pictured following the introduction.

### Royal Wedding Issue

Common Design Type

**1981, June 16** *Perf. 15*

| | | | | |
|---|---|---|---|---|
| **440** | CD331a | 40c Couple | .25 | .25 |
| **441** | CD331a | $2 Balmoral Castle | .25 | .25 |
| **442** | CD331a | $4 Charles | .45 | .45 |
| | | *Nos. 440-442 (3)* | .95 | .95 |

### Souvenir Sheet

| | | | | |
|---|---|---|---|---|
| **443** | CD331a | $5 Royal Coach | 1.40 | 1.40 |

Sheets of 5 plus label contain 30c (like No. 440), 40c (like No. 441), or $4 in changed colors, perf 15x14½.

Diana — G50

$1, Diana. $2, Charles. $5, Diana and Charles.

### Booklet

### Self-Adhesive

***Roulette x imperf. (#444a), Imperf. (#444b)***

**1981, June 16**

| | | | |
|---|---|---|---|
| **444** | G50 | Souvenir Booklet | 4.00 |
| *a.* | | Pane of 6 (3 each $1, $2) | 2.25 |
| *b.* | | Pane of 1, $5 | 1.75 |

Royal wedding.

Amy Johnson, Pilot of 1st Britain-Australia Solo Flight by a Woman, May 1930 — G51

Decade for Women: 70c, Mme. la Baronne de Laroche, 1st qualified aviatrix, May 1910. $1.10, Ruth Nichols. $3, Amelia Earhart, 1st Atlantic solo flight by woman, May 1932. $5, Valentina Tereshkova, 1st woman in space, June 1963.

**1981, Oct. 13** *Perf. 14*

| | | | | |
|---|---|---|---|---|
| **445** | G51 | 30c multicolored | .45 | .45 |
| **446** | G51 | 70c multicolored | .70 | .70 |
| **447** | G51 | $1.10 multicolored | .85 | .85 |
| **448** | G51 | $3 multicolored | 1.75 | 1.75 |
| | | *Nos. 445-448 (4)* | 3.75 | 3.75 |

### Souvenir Sheet

| | | | | |
|---|---|---|---|---|
| **449** | G51 | $5 multicolored | 2.00 | 2.00 |

Lady and the Tramp — G52

Christmas. Various scenes from Walt Disney's film Lady and the Tramp.

**1981, Nov. 2**

| | | | | |
|---|---|---|---|---|
| **450** | G52 | ½c multicolored | .25 | .25 |
| **451** | G52 | 1c multicolored | .25 | .25 |
| **452** | G52 | 2c multicolored | .25 | .25 |
| **453** | G52 | 3c multicolored | .25 | .25 |
| **454** | G52 | 4c multicolored | .25 | .25 |
| **455** | G52 | 5c multicolored | .25 | .25 |
| **456** | G52 | 10c multicolored | .25 | .25 |
| **457** | G52 | $2.50 multicolored | 3.50 | 1.75 |
| **458** | G52 | $3 multicolored | 3.50 | 2.25 |
| | | *Nos. 450-458 (9)* | 8.75 | 5.75 |

### Souvenir Sheet

| | | | | |
|---|---|---|---|---|
| **459** | G52 | $5 multicolored | 7.00 | 6.00 |

747 Carrying Space Shuttle — G53

Designs: 40c, Re-entry. $1.10, External tank separation. $3, Touchdown. $5, Lift-off.

**1981, Nov. 2** *Perf. 14½*

| | | | | |
|---|---|---|---|---|
| **460** | G53 | 10c multicolored | .40 | .25 |
| **461** | G53 | 40c multicolored | .75 | .30 |
| **462** | G53 | $1.10 multicolored | 1.40 | .80 |
| **463** | G53 | $3 multicolored | 2.25 | 1.50 |
| | | *Nos. 460-463 (4)* | 4.80 | 2.85 |

### Souvenir Sheet

| | | | | |
|---|---|---|---|---|
| **464** | G53 | $5 multicolored | 5.00 | 4.00 |

Soccer Player — G54

World Cup Soccer Championships, Spain, 1982: Soccer players in various positions.

**1981, Nov. 30** *Perf. 14*

| | | | | |
|---|---|---|---|---|
| **465** | G54 | 20c multicolored | .25 | .25 |
| **466** | G54 | 40c multicolored | .25 | .25 |
| **467** | G54 | $1 multicolored | .45 | .30 |
| **468** | G54 | $2 multicolored | .90 | .60 |
| | | *Nos. 465-468 (4)* | 1.85 | 1.40 |

### Souvenir Sheet

| | | | | |
|---|---|---|---|---|
| **469** | G54 | $4 multicolored | 1.75 | 1.50 |

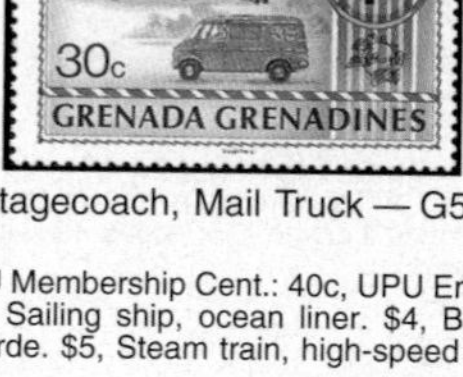

Stagecoach, Mail Truck — G55

UPU Membership Cent.: 40c, UPU Emblem. $2.50, Sailing ship, ocean liner. $4, Biplane, Concorde. $5, Steam train, high-speed trains.

**1982, Jan. 13** *Perf. 15*

| | | | | |
|---|---|---|---|---|
| **470** | G55 | 30c multicolored | .40 | .25 |
| **471** | G55 | 40c multicolored | .40 | .25 |
| **472** | G55 | $2.50 multicolored | 1.75 | 1.00 |
| **473** | G55 | $4 multicolored | 3.00 | 2.00 |
| | | *Nos. 470-473 (4)* | 5.55 | 3.50 |

### Souvenir Sheet

| | | | | |
|---|---|---|---|---|
| **474** | G55 | $5 multicolored | 4.75 | 4.25 |

Sprinting G56

90c, Sea scouts sailing. $1.10, Hand crafts. $3, Animal husbandry. $5, Music around campfire.

**1982, Feb. 19**

| | | | | |
|---|---|---|---|---|
| **475** | G56 | 6c multicolored | .25 | .25 |
| **476** | G56 | 90c multicolored | .70 | .60 |
| **477** | G56 | $1.10 multicolored | .90 | .70 |
| **478** | G56 | $3 multicolored | 1.90 | 1.90 |
| | | *Nos. 475-478 (4)* | 3.75 | 3.45 |

### Souvenir Sheet

| | | | | |
|---|---|---|---|---|
| **479** | G56 | $5 multicolored | 3.00 | 3.00 |

Boy Scouts, 75th anniv. Lord Baden-Powell, 125th birth anniv.

White Peacock G57

Designs: 40c, St. Vincent long-tail skipper. $1.10, Painted lady. $3, Orion. $5, Silver spot.

**1982, Mar. 24** *Perf. 14*

| | | | | |
|---|---|---|---|---|
| **480** | G57 | 30c multicolored | 1.25 | .60 |
| **481** | G57 | 40c multicolored | 1.25 | .85 |
| **482** | G57 | $1.10 multicolored | 3.00 | 2.25 |
| **483** | G57 | $3 multicolored | 5.25 | 5.25 |
| | | *Nos. 480-483 (4)* | 10.75 | 8.95 |

### Souvenir Sheet

| | | | | |
|---|---|---|---|---|
| **484** | G57 | $5 multicolored | 6.50 | 6.50 |

### Princess Diana Issue

Common Design Type

**1982, July 1** *Perf. 14½x14*

| | | | | |
|---|---|---|---|---|
| **485** | CD332 | 50c Blenheim Palace | 1.25 | 1.25 |
| **486** | CD332 | 60c Like 50c | .75 | .75 |
| **487** | CD332 | $1 Couple in field | 1.75 | 1.75 |
| **488** | CD332 | $2 Like $1 | 1.90 | 1.90 |
| **489** | CD332 | $3 Diana | 2.50 | 2.50 |
| **490** | CD332 | $4 Like $3 | 2.50 | 2.50 |
| | | *Nos. 485-490 (6)* | 10.65 | 10.65 |

### Souvenir Sheet

| | | | | |
|---|---|---|---|---|
| **491** | CD332 | $5 Diana, diff. | 7.00 | 7.00 |

50c, $1, $3 issued in sheets of 5 plus label.

Overprinted

**1982, Aug. 30**

| | | | | |
|---|---|---|---|---|
| **492** | CD332 | 50c multicolored | .75 | .75 |
| **493** | CD332 | 60c multicolored | .80 | .80 |
| **494** | CD332 | $1 multicolored | 1.00 | 1.00 |
| **495** | CD332 | $2 multicolored | 1.50 | 1.50 |
| **496** | CD332 | $3 multicolored | 1.90 | 1.90 |
| **497** | CD332 | $4 multicolored | 2.25 | 2.25 |
| | | *Nos. 492-497 (6)* | 8.20 | 8.20 |

### Souvenir Sheet

| | | | | |
|---|---|---|---|---|
| **498** | CD332 | $5 multicolored | 5.25 | 5.25 |

Birth of Prince William of Wales, June 21.

### Roosevelt Type of 1982

Designs: 30c, New Deal soil conservation. 40c, Roosevelt, George Washington Carver. 70c, Civilian Conservation Corps. $3, Roosevelt, Liberian Pres. Edwin Barclay. $5, Roosevelt addressing Howard University.

**1982, July 27** *Perf. 14*

| | | | | |
|---|---|---|---|---|
| **499** | A154 | 30c multicolored | .50 | .25 |
| **500** | A154 | 40c multicolored | .50 | .25 |
| **501** | A154 | 70c multicolored | .60 | .30 |
| **502** | A154 | $3 multicolored | 1.40 | 1.40 |
| | | *Nos. 499-502 (4)* | 3.00 | 2.20 |

### Souvenir Sheet

| | | | | |
|---|---|---|---|---|
| **503** | A154 | $5 multicolored | 3.25 | 3.25 |

Presentation of Christ in the Temple — G58

Easter Paintings by Rembrandt: 60c, Descent from the Cross. $2, Raising of the Cross. $4, Resurrection of Christ. $5, The Risen Christ.

**1982, Sept. 2** *Perf. 14½*

| | | | | |
|---|---|---|---|---|
| **504** | G58 | 30c multicolored | .50 | .25 |
| **505** | G58 | 60c multicolored | .60 | .25 |
| **506** | G58 | $2 multicolored | .80 | .80 |
| **507** | G58 | $4 multicolored | 1.50 | 1.50 |
| | | *Nos. 504-507 (4)* | 3.40 | 2.80 |

### Souvenir Sheet

| | | | | |
|---|---|---|---|---|
| **508** | G58 | $5 multicolored | 3.50 | 3.50 |

G59

**1982, Oct. 4** *Perf. 15*

| | | | | |
|---|---|---|---|---|
| **509** | G59 | 10c Santa Fe | .65 | .25 |
| **510** | G59 | 40c Mistral | .90 | .30 |
| **511** | G59 | 70c Rheingold | 1.00 | .65 |
| **512** | G59 | $1 ET 403 | 1.25 | .70 |
| **513** | G59 | $1.10 Mallard | 1.50 | .75 |
| **514** | G59 | $2 Tokaido | 1.75 | 1.25 |
| | | *Nos. 509-514 (6)* | 7.05 | 3.90 |

### Souvenir Sheet

| | | | | |
|---|---|---|---|---|
| **515** | G59 | $5 Settebello | 3.25 | 3.25 |

Soccer Players G60

Italy, World Cup Soccer Champions: $4, Soccer players, diff. $5, Map of Italy.

**1982, Dec. 2** *Perf. 14*

| | | | | |
|---|---|---|---|---|
| **516** | G60 | 60c multicolored | 1.00 | .45 |
| **517** | G60 | $4 multicolored | 2.75 | 2.75 |

### Souvenir Sheet

| | | | | |
|---|---|---|---|---|
| **518** | G60 | $5 multicolored | 2.50 | 2.50 |

### Christmas Type of 1982

Scenes from Walt Disney's film The Rescuers.

**1982, Dec. 14** *Perf. 13½*

| | | | | |
|---|---|---|---|---|
| **519** | A157 | ½c multicolored | .25 | .25 |
| **520** | A157 | 1c multicolored | .25 | .25 |
| **521** | A157 | 2c multicolored | .25 | .25 |
| **522** | A157 | 3c multicolored | .25 | .25 |
| **523** | A157 | 4c multicolored | .25 | .25 |
| **524** | A157 | 5c multicolored | .25 | .25 |
| **525** | A157 | 10c multicolored | .25 | .25 |
| **526** | A157 | $2.50 multicolored | 3.00 | 3.25 |
| **527** | A157 | $3 multicolored | 3.00 | 3.25 |
| | | *Nos. 519-527 (9)* | 7.75 | 8.25 |

### Souvenir Sheet

| | | | | |
|---|---|---|---|---|
| **528** | A157 | $5 multicolored | 6.75 | 6.75 |

### Whales Type of 1982

Designs: 10c, Pilot whale. 60c, Dall porpoise. $1.10, Humpback whale. $3, Bowfin whale. $5, Spotted dolphin.

**1983, Jan. 10** *Perf. 14*

| | | | | |
|---|---|---|---|---|
| **529** | A159 | 10c multicolored | 1.25 | 1.10 |
| **530** | A159 | 60c multicolored | 3.00 | 2.75 |
| **531** | A159 | $1.10 multicolored | 5.25 | 4.50 |
| **532** | A159 | $3 multicolored | 8.50 | 7.00 |
| | | *Nos. 529-532 (4)* | 18.00 | 15.35 |

**Souvenir Sheet**

| | | | | |
|---|---|---|---|---|
| **533** | A159 | $5 multicolored | 9.00 | 7.50 |

### Raphael Paintings Type

Designs: 25c, David and Goliath. 30c, David Sees Bathsheba. 90c, Triumph of David. $4, Anointing of Solomon. $5, Anointing of David.

**1983, Feb. 15** *Perf. 14*

| | | | | |
|---|---|---|---|---|
| **534** | A160 | 25c multicolored | .25 | .25 |
| **535** | A160 | 30c multicolored | .25 | .25 |
| **536** | A160 | 90c multicolored | .35 | .35 |
| **537** | A160 | $4 multicolored | .80 | .80 |
| | | *Nos. 534-537 (4)* | 1.65 | 1.65 |

**Souvenir Sheet**

| | | | | |
|---|---|---|---|---|
| **538** | A160 | $5 multicolored | 1.25 | 1.25 |

Audio and Video Communication — G61

World Communications Year: 60c, Ambulance. $1.10, Helicopters. $3, Satellite. $5, Diver, bottle-nose porpoise.

**1983, Apr. 7** *Perf. 14*

| | | | | |
|---|---|---|---|---|
| **539** | G61 | 30c multicolored | .25 | .25 |
| **540** | G61 | 60c multicolored | .45 | .45 |
| **541** | G61 | $1.10 multicolored | .80 | .80 |
| **542** | G61 | $3 blk, red & blue | 1.50 | 1.50 |
| | | *Nos. 539-542 (4)* | 3.00 | 3.00 |

**Souvenir Sheet**

| | | | | |
|---|---|---|---|---|
| **543** | G61 | $5 multicolored | 3.50 | 3.00 |

For overprints see Nos. 629-630A.

### Car Type of 1983

Designs: 10c, 1931 Chrysler Imperial Roadster. 30c, 1925 Doble Steam Car. 40c, 1965 Ford Mustang. 60c, 1930 Packard Tourer. 70c, 1913 Mercer Raceabout. 90c, 1963 Corvette Stingray. $1.10, 1935 Auburn 851 Supercharger Speedster. $2.50, 1933 Pierce Arrow Silver Arrow. $3, 1929 Duesenberg Dual Cowl Phaeton. $4, 1928 Mercedes-Benz SSK. $5, 1923 McFarlan Knickerbocker Cabriolet.

**1983, May 4** *Perf. 14½*

| | | | | |
|---|---|---|---|---|
| **544** | A163 | 10c multicolored | .25 | .25 |
| **545** | A163 | 30c multicolored | .35 | .35 |
| **546** | A163 | 40c multicolored | .35 | .35 |
| **547** | A163 | 60c multicolored | .50 | .50 |
| **548** | A163 | 70c multicolored | .50 | .50 |
| **549** | A163 | 90c multicolored | .50 | .50 |
| **550** | A163 | $1.10 multicolored | .50 | .50 |
| **551** | A163 | $2.50 multicolored | .80 | .80 |
| **552** | A163 | $3 multicolored | .90 | .90 |
| **553** | A163 | $4 multicolored | .90 | .90 |
| | | *Nos. 544-553 (10)* | 5.55 | 5.55 |

**Souvenir Sheet**

| | | | | |
|---|---|---|---|---|
| **554** | A163 | $5 multicolored | 3.25 | 3.25 |

### Anniversary of Manned Flight Type

Designs: 40c, Short Solent flying boat. 70c, Curtiss R3C-2 seaplane. 90c, Hawker Nimrod biplane. $4, Montgolfier balloon. $5, Victoria Luise airship.

**1983, July 18** *Perf. 14*

| | | | | |
|---|---|---|---|---|
| **555** | A164 | 40c multicolored | 1.00 | .25 |
| **556** | A164 | 70c multicolored | 1.25 | .50 |
| **557** | A164 | 90c multicolored | 1.50 | 1.50 |
| **558** | A164 | $4 multicolored | 3.75 | 3.25 |
| | | *Nos. 555-558 (4)* | 7.50 | 5.50 |

**Souvenir Sheet**

| | | | | |
|---|---|---|---|---|
| **559** | A164 | $5 multicolored | 3.50 | 3.50 |

Christmas G62

Walt Disney characters in scenes from "Jingle Bells."

**1983, Nov. 7** *Perf. 11*

| | | | | |
|---|---|---|---|---|
| **560** | G62 | ½c multicolored | .25 | .25 |
| **561** | G62 | 1c multicolored | .25 | .25 |
| **562** | G62 | 2c multicolored | .25 | .25 |
| **563** | G62 | 3c multicolored | .25 | .25 |
| **564** | G62 | 4c multicolored | .25 | .25 |
| **565** | G62 | 5c multicolored | .25 | .25 |
| **566** | G62 | 10c multicolored | .25 | .25 |
| **567** | G62 | $2.50 multicolored | 5.25 | 5.25 |
| **568** | G62 | $3 multicolored | 5.75 | 5.75 |
| | | *Nos. 560-568 (9)* | 12.75 | 12.75 |

**Souvenir Sheet**

*Perf. 13½*

| | | | | |
|---|---|---|---|---|
| **569** | G62 | $5 multicolored | 11.00 | 11.00 |

G63

**1984, Jan. 9** *Perf. 14*

| | | | | |
|---|---|---|---|---|
| **570** | G63 | 30c Weightlifting | .25 | .25 |
| **571** | G63 | 60c Gymnastics | .55 | .50 |
| **572** | G63 | 70c Archery | .75 | .60 |
| **573** | G63 | $4 Sailing | 2.25 | 2.25 |
| | | *Nos. 570-573 (4)* | 3.80 | 3.60 |

**Souvenir Sheet**

| | | | | |
|---|---|---|---|---|
| **574** | G63 | $5 Basketball | 3.50 | 3.50 |

Olympic Games, Los Angeles.

G64

Designs: 15c, Frangipani. 40c, Dwarf poinciana. 70c, Walking iris. $4, Lady's slipper. $5, Brazilian glory vine.

**1984, Apr. 9** *Perf. 15*

| | | | | |
|---|---|---|---|---|
| **575** | G64 | 15c multicolored | .25 | .25 |
| **576** | G64 | 40c multicolored | .30 | .30 |
| **577** | G64 | 70c multicolored | .75 | .55 |
| **578** | G64 | $4 multicolored | 2.75 | 2.75 |
| | | *Nos. 575-578 (4)* | 4.05 | 3.85 |

**Souvenir Sheet**

| | | | | |
|---|---|---|---|---|
| **579** | G64 | $5 multicolored | 3.75 | 3.75 |

For overprints see Nos. 598-600.

Easter G65

Walt Disney characters with Easter hats.

**1984, May 1** *Perf. 11*

| | | | | |
|---|---|---|---|---|
| **580** | G65 | ½c multicolored | .25 | .25 |
| **581** | G65 | 1c multicolored | .25 | .25 |
| **582** | G65 | 2c multicolored | .25 | .25 |
| **583** | G65 | 3c multicolored | .25 | .25 |
| **584** | G65 | 4c multicolored | .25 | .25 |
| **585** | G65 | 5c multicolored | .25 | .25 |
| **586** | G65 | 10c multicolored | .25 | .25 |
| **587** | G65 | $2 multicolored | 1.90 | 1.90 |
| **588** | G65 | $4 multicolored | 2.75 | 2.75 |
| | | *Nos. 580-588 (9)* | 6.40 | 6.40 |

**Souvenir Sheet**

| | | | | |
|---|---|---|---|---|
| **589** | G65 | $5 multicolored | 5.25 | 5.25 |

Bobolink G66

Birds: 50c, Eastern kingbird. 60c, Barn swallow. 70c, Yellow warbler. $1, Rose-breasted grosbeak. $1.10, Yellowthroat. $2, Catbird. $5, Fork-tailed flycatcher.

**1984, May 21** *Perf. 14*

| | | | | |
|---|---|---|---|---|
| **590** | G66 | 40c multicolored | 2.50 | 2.00 |
| **591** | G66 | 50c multicolored | 2.90 | 2.25 |
| **592** | G66 | 60c multicolored | 3.25 | 2.90 |
| **593** | G66 | 70c multicolored | 3.25 | 2.90 |
| **594** | G66 | $1 multicolored | 3.50 | 3.50 |
| **595** | G66 | $1.10 multicolored | 4.00 | 4.00 |
| **596** | G66 | $2 multicolored | 5.00 | 5.00 |
| | | *Nos. 590-596 (7)* | 24.40 | 22.55 |

**Souvenir Sheet**

| | | | | |
|---|---|---|---|---|
| **597** | G66 | $5 multicolored | 11.00 | 11.00 |

Nos. 577-579 Overprinted

**1984, June 19** *Perf. 15*

| | | | | |
|---|---|---|---|---|
| **598** | G64 | 70c multicolored | 1.10 | 1.10 |
| **599** | G64 | $4 multicolored | 5.00 | 5.00 |

**Souvenir Sheet**

| | | | | |
|---|---|---|---|---|
| **600** | G64 | $5 multicolored | 4.50 | 4.50 |

Geeststar G67

**1984, July 16** *Perf. 15*

| | | | | |
|---|---|---|---|---|
| **601** | G67 | 30c shown | .85 | .85 |
| **602** | G67 | 60c Daphne | 1.10 | 1.10 |
| **603** | G67 | $1.10 Schooner Southwind | 1.40 | 1.40 |
| **604** | G67 | $4 Oceanic | 2.40 | 2.40 |
| | | *Nos. 601-604 (4)* | 5.75 | 5.75 |

**Souvenir Sheet**

| | | | | |
|---|---|---|---|---|
| **605** | G67 | $5 Privateer | 5.25 | 5.25 |

### Correggio Paintings Type

Designs: 10c, The Hunt — Blowing the Horn. 30c, St. John the Evangelist, horiz. 90c, The Hunt — The Deer's Head. $4, The Virgin Crowned by Christ, horiz. $5, Martyrdom of the Four Saints.

**1984, Aug. 22** *Perf. 14*

| | | | | |
|---|---|---|---|---|
| **606** | A171a | 10c multicolored | .25 | .25 |
| **607** | A171a | 30c multicolored | .25 | .25 |
| **608** | A171a | 90c multicolored | .70 | .70 |
| **609** | A171a | $4 multicolored | 2.50 | 2.50 |
| | | *Nos. 606-609 (4)* | 3.70 | 3.70 |

**Souvenir Sheet**

| | | | | |
|---|---|---|---|---|
| **610** | A171a | $5 multicolored | 3.50 | 3.50 |

The Song of the Dog — G68

Paintings by Edgar Degas: 70c, Cafe-Concert. $1.10, The Orchestra of the Opera. $3, The Dance Lesson. $5, Madame Camus at the Piano.

**1984, Aug. 22**

| | | | | |
|---|---|---|---|---|
| **611** | G68 | 25c multicolored | .45 | .25 |
| **612** | G68 | 70c multicolored | .75 | .60 |
| **613** | G68 | $1.10 multicolored | 1.60 | 1.60 |
| **614** | G68 | $3 multicolored | 3.00 | 3.00 |
| | | *Nos. 611-614 (4)* | 5.80 | 5.45 |

**Souvenir Sheet**

| | | | | |
|---|---|---|---|---|
| **615** | G68 | $5 multicolored | 4.00 | 4.00 |

150th birth anniv. of Degas.

Queen Victoria Gardens G69

$4, Ayers Rock. $5, Yarra River, Melbourne.

**1984, Sept. 21**

| | | | | |
|---|---|---|---|---|
| **616** | G69 | $1.10 multicolored | .85 | .85 |
| **617** | G69 | $4 multicolored | 3.25 | 3.25 |

**Souvenir Sheet**

| | | | | |
|---|---|---|---|---|
| **618** | G69 | $5 multicolored | 4.00 | 4.00 |

AUSIPEX International Stamp Exhibition, Melbourne, Australia.

Colonel Steven's Model, "1825" G70

Locomotives: 50c, Royal George, 1827. 60c, Stourbridge Lion, 1829. 70c, Liverpool, 1830. 90c, South Carolina, 1832. $1.10, Monster, 1836. $2, Lafayette, 1837. $4, Lion, 1838.

**1984, Oct. 3** *Perf. 15*

| | | | | |
|---|---|---|---|---|
| **619** | G70 | 20c multicolored | .80 | .30 |
| **620** | G70 | 50c multicolored | 1.00 | .60 |
| **621** | G70 | 60c multicolored | 1.10 | .75 |
| **622** | G70 | 70c multicolored | 1.25 | 1.25 |
| **623** | G70 | 90c multicolored | 1.40 | 1.40 |
| **624** | G70 | $1.10 multicolored | 1.40 | 1.40 |
| **625** | G70 | $2 multicolored | 1.75 | 1.75 |
| **626** | G70 | $4 multicolored | 2.25 | 2.25 |
| | | *Nos. 619-626 (8)* | 10.95 | 9.70 |

**Souvenir Sheets**

| | | | | |
|---|---|---|---|---|
| **627** | G70 | $5 Sequin's Engine, 1829 | 4.00 | 4.00 |
| **628** | G70 | $5 Der Adler, 1835 | 4.00 | 4.00 |

### Nos. 539, 541, 543 Overprinted

**1984, Oct. 28** *Perf. 14*

| | | | | |
|---|---|---|---|---|
| **629** | G61 | 30c multicolored | .35 | .25 |
| **630** | G61 | $1.10 multicolored | 1.25 | .95 |

**Souvenir Sheet**

| | | | | |
|---|---|---|---|---|
| **630A** | G61 | $5 multicolored | 6.25 | 5.25 |

Opening of the Point Saline International Airport. No. 630A is overprinted in the margin.

### Christmas Type of 1984

Scenes from various Donald Duck movies.

**1984, Nov. 26** *Perf. 13½x14*

| | | | | |
|---|---|---|---|---|
| **631** | A173 | 45c multicolored | .95 | .55 |
| **632** | A173 | 60c multicolored | 1.10 | .75 |
| **633** | A173 | 90c multicolored | 1.50 | 1.25 |
| **634** | A173 | $2 multi, perf. 12 | 2.25 | 2.25 |
| **635** | A173 | $4 multicolored | 4.50 | 4.50 |
| | | *Nos. 631-635 (5)* | 10.30 | 9.30 |

**Souvenir Sheet**

| | | | | |
|---|---|---|---|---|
| **636** | A173 | $5 multicolored | 6.50 | 6.00 |

No. 634 issued in sheets of 8.

### Audubon Type of 1985

Designs: 50c, Blue-winged teal. 90c, White ibis. $1.10, Swallow-tailed kite. $3, Common Gallinule. $5, Mangrove cuckoo.

**1985, Feb. 11** *Perf. 14*

| | | | | |
|---|---|---|---|---|
| **637** | A174 | 50c multicolored | 2.25 | .90 |
| **638** | A174 | 90c multicolored | 2.75 | 1.60 |
| **639** | A174 | $1.10 multicolored | 3.50 | 2.10 |
| **640** | A174 | $3 multicolored | 4.50 | 4.50 |
| | | *Nos. 637-640 (4)* | 13.00 | 9.10 |

**Souvenir Sheet**

| | | | | |
|---|---|---|---|---|
| **641** | A174 | $5 multicolored | 6.00 | 6.00 |

See Nos. 732-736.

Motorcycle Centenary — G71

Anniv. emblem and: 30c, Kawasaki 750, 1972. 60c, Honda Goldwing GL1000, 1974, horiz. 70c, Kawasaki Z650, 1976, horiz. $4, Honda CBX, 1977. $5, BMW R100RS, 1978.

**1985, Mar. 11**

| | | | | |
|---|---|---|---|---|
| **642** | G71 | 30c multicolored | .75 | .50 |
| **643** | G71 | 60c multicolored | 1.00 | 1.00 |
| **644** | G71 | 70c multicolored | 1.25 | 1.25 |
| **645** | G71 | $4 multicolored | 4.50 | 4.50 |
| | | *Nos. 642-645 (4)* | 7.50 | 7.25 |

**Souvenir Sheet**

| | | | | |
|---|---|---|---|---|
| **646** | G71 | $5 multicolored | 5.75 | 5.75 |

Intl. Youth Year G72

Designs: 50c, Folding bandages (health). 70c, Diver, turtle (environment). $1.10, Sailing (leisure). $3, Boys playing chess (education). $5, Hands touching globe.

**1985, Apr. 15**

| | | | | |
|---|---|---|---|---|
| **647** | G72 | 50c multicolored | .65 | .45 |
| **648** | G72 | 70c multicolored | 1.00 | .85 |
| **649** | G72 | $1.10 multicolored | 1.50 | 1.40 |
| **650** | G72 | $3 multicolored | 7.50 | 7.50 |
| | | *Nos. 647-650 (4)* | 10.65 | 10.20 |

**Souvenir Sheet**

| | | | | |
|---|---|---|---|---|
| **651** | G72 | $5 multicolored | 4.75 | 4.75 |

Intl. Civil Aviation Org., 40th Anniv. G73

Designs: 5c, Lockheed Lodestar. 70c, Avro 748 Turboprop. $1.10, Boeing 727. $4, Boeing 707. $5, Pilatus Britten-Norman Islander.

**1985, Apr. 30**

| | | | | |
|---|---|---|---|---|
| **652** | G73 | 5c multicolored | .50 | .25 |
| **653** | G73 | 70c multicolored | 2.10 | .70 |
| **654** | G73 | $1.10 multicolored | 2.50 | 1.10 |
| **655** | G73 | $4 multicolored | 4.25 | 3.25 |
| | | *Nos. 652-655 (4)* | 9.35 | 5.30 |

**Souvenir Sheet**

| | | | | |
|---|---|---|---|---|
| **656** | G73 | $5 multicolored | 5.50 | 5.00 |

**Girl Guides Type**

Designs: 30c, Lady Baden-Powell, Guide leaders. 50c, Botany field trip. 70c, Making camp, vert. $4, Sailing, vert. $5, Lord and Lady Baden-Powell, vert.

**1985, May 30**

| | | | | |
|---|---|---|---|---|
| **657** | A176 | 30c multicolored | .50 | .25 |
| **658** | A176 | 50c multicolored | 1.25 | .35 |
| **659** | A176 | 70c multicolored | 1.25 | .55 |
| **660** | A176 | $4 multicolored | 5.00 | 2.75 |
| | | *Nos. 657-660 (4)* | 8.00 | 3.90 |

**Souvenir Sheet**

| | | | | |
|---|---|---|---|---|
| **661** | A176 | $5 multicolored | 5.50 | 5.50 |

Grenadine Grizzled Skipper G74

Butterflies: 1c, Red anartia. 2c, Lesser Antillean giant hairstreak. 4c, Santa Domingo longtail skipper. 5c, Spotted Manuel's skipper. 6c, Grenada's polydamus swallowtail. 10c, Palmira sulphur. 12c, Pupillated orange sulphur. 15c, Migrant sulphur. 20c, St. Christopher's hairstreak. 25c, St. Lucia mestra. 30c, Insular gulf fritillary. 40c, Michael's Caribbean buckeye. 60c, Frampton's flambeau. 70c, Bamboo page. $1.10, Antillean cracker. $2.50, Red crescent hairstreak. $5, Single colored Antillean white. $10, Lesser whirlabout. $20, Blue night.

**1985-86** *Perf. 14*

| | | | | |
|---|---|---|---|---|
| **662** | G74 | ½c multicolored | .25 | .25 |
| **663** | G74 | 1c multicolored | .25 | .25 |
| **664** | G74 | 2c multicolored | .25 | .25 |
| **665** | G74 | 4c multicolored | .25 | .25 |
| **666** | G74 | 5c multicolored | .25 | .25 |
| **667** | G74 | 6c multicolored | .25 | .25 |
| **668** | G74 | 10c multicolored | .40 | .25 |
| **669** | G74 | 12c multicolored | .60 | .25 |
| **670** | G74 | 15c multicolored | .60 | .25 |
| **671** | G74 | 20c multicolored | .80 | .25 |
| **672** | G74 | 25c multicolored | .80 | .25 |
| **673** | G74 | 30c multicolored | .80 | .30 |
| **674** | G74 | 40c multicolored | 1.00 | .60 |
| **675** | G74 | 60c multicolored | 1.40 | .95 |
| **676** | G74 | 70c multicolored | 1.60 | 1.00 |
| **677** | G74 | $1.10 multicolored | 2.50 | 1.90 |
| **678** | G74 | $2.50 multicolored | 4.50 | 3.75 |
| **679** | G74 | $5 multicolored | 6.75 | 6.25 |
| **680** | G74 | $10 multicolored | 11.00 | 11.00 |
| **681** | G74 | $20 multicolored | 15.50 | 15.50 |
| | | *Nos. 662-681 (20)* | 49.75 | 44.00 |

Issued: #662-679, 6/17; #680, 11/11; #681, 1/8/86.

For overprints see Nos. 737-738.

**1986** *Perf. 12½x12*

| | | | | |
|---|---|---|---|---|
| *662a* | G74 | ½c multicolored | .40 | .40 |
| *663a* | G74 | 1c multicolored | .40 | .40 |
| *664a* | G74 | 2c multicolored | .40 | .40 |
| *665a* | G74 | 4c multicolored | .40 | .40 |
| *666a* | G74 | 5c multicolored | .40 | .40 |
| *667a* | G74 | 6c multicolored | .40 | .40 |
| *668a* | G74 | 10c multicolored | .40 | .40 |
| *669a* | G74 | 12c multicolored | .40 | .40 |
| *670a* | G74 | 15c multicolored | .40 | .40 |
| *671a* | G74 | 20c multicolored | .40 | .40 |
| *672a* | G74 | 25c multicolored | .40 | .40 |
| *673a* | G74 | 30c multicolored | .60 | .60 |
| *674a* | G74 | 40c multicolored | .70 | .70 |
| *675a* | G74 | 60c multicolored | 1.25 | 1.25 |
| *676a* | G74 | 70c multicolored | 1.25 | 1.25 |
| *677a* | G74 | $1.10 multicolored | 2.00 | 2.00 |
| *678a* | G74 | $2.50 multicolored | 7.00 | 7.00 |
| *679a* | G74 | $5 multicolored | 12.00 | 12.00 |
| *680a* | G74 | $10 multicolored | 20.00 | 20.00 |
| *681a* | G74 | $20 multicolored | 26.00 | 26.00 |
| | | *Nos. 662a-681a (20)* | 75.20 | 75.20 |

Issued: #662a-677a, 679a, 1986; #678a, 680a, 9/1986; #681a, 5/1989.

**Queen Mother Birthday Type**

$1, Portrait. $1.50, At Ascot, horiz. $2.50, Queen Mother, Prince Charles. $5, Portrait, diff.

**1985, July 3** *Perf. 14*

| | | | | |
|---|---|---|---|---|
| **682** | A181 | $1 multicolored | .65 | .65 |
| **683** | A181 | $1.50 multicolored | 1.10 | 1.10 |
| **684** | A181 | $2.50 multicolored | 1.75 | 1.75 |
| | | *Nos. 682-684 (3)* | 3.50 | 3.50 |

**Souvenir Sheet**

| | | | | |
|---|---|---|---|---|
| **685** | A181 | $5 multicolored | 3.75 | 3.75 |

**1986, Jan. 28** *Perf. 12x12½*

| | | | | |
|---|---|---|---|---|
| **686** | A181 | 70c like #682 | .60 | .60 |
| **687** | A181 | $1.10 like #683 | .75 | .75 |
| **688** | A181 | $3 like #684 | 2.50 | 2.50 |
| | | *Nos. 686-688 (3)* | 3.85 | 3.85 |

Issued in sheets of 5 plus label.

**Water Sports Type**

Designs: 15c, Scuba diving. 70c, Playing in waterfall. 90c, Water skiing. $4, Swimming. $5, Skin diver, sailboat.

**1985, July 15** *Perf. 15*

| | | | | |
|---|---|---|---|---|
| **689** | A179 | 15c multicolored | .25 | .25 |
| **690** | A179 | 70c multicolored | .55 | .55 |
| **691** | A179 | 90c multicolored | 1.00 | 1.00 |
| **692** | A179 | $4 multicolored | 3.50 | 3.50 |
| | | *Nos. 689-692 (4)* | 5.30 | 5.30 |

**Souvenir Sheet**

| | | | | |
|---|---|---|---|---|
| **693** | A179 | $5 multicolored | 4.50 | 4.50 |

Queen Conch G75

Marine Life: 90c, Porcupine fish, fire coral. $1.10, Ghost crab. $4, West Indies spiny lobster. $5, Long-spined urchin.

**1985, Aug. 1** *Perf. 14*

| | | | | |
|---|---|---|---|---|
| **694** | G75 | 60c multicolored | .85 | .70 |
| **695** | G75 | 90c multicolored | 1.50 | 1.00 |
| **696** | G75 | $1.10 multicolored | 1.75 | 1.25 |
| **697** | G75 | $4 multicolored | 4.25 | 4.25 |
| | | *Nos. 694-697 (4)* | 8.35 | 7.20 |

**Souvenir Sheet**

| | | | | |
|---|---|---|---|---|
| **698** | G75 | $5 multicolored | 8.50 | 8.50 |

**Bach Anniversary Type**

Portrait, signature, music from Invention No. 9 and: 15c, Natural trumpet. 60c, Bass viol. $1.10, Flute. $3, Double flageolet. $5, Portrait.

**1985, Sept. 3** *Perf. 14*

| | | | | |
|---|---|---|---|---|
| **699** | A184 | 15c multicolored | .65 | .25 |
| **700** | A184 | 60c multicolored | 1.10 | .60 |
| **701** | A184 | $1.10 multicolored | 2.00 | 1.00 |
| **702** | A184 | $3 multicolored | 3.00 | 2.50 |
| | | *Nos. 699-702 (4)* | 6.75 | 4.35 |

**Souvenir Sheet**

| | | | | |
|---|---|---|---|---|
| **703** | A184 | $5 multicolored | 4.50 | 4.50 |

**Royal Visit Type**

10c, Arms of Great Britain, Grenada. $1, Queen Elizabeth II. $4, HMY Britannia. $5, Map.

**1985, Nov. 4** *Perf. 14½*

| | | | | |
|---|---|---|---|---|
| **704** | A186 | 10c multicolored | .25 | .25 |
| **705** | A186 | $1 multi, vert. | 1.50 | 1.50 |
| **706** | A186 | $4 multicolored | 4.50 | 4.50 |
| | | *Nos. 704-706 (3)* | 6.25 | 6.25 |

**Souvenir Sheet**

| | | | | |
|---|---|---|---|---|
| **707** | A186 | $5 multicolored | 5.25 | 5.25 |

**UN Anniversary Type**

UN stamps and famous people: $1, #373, Neil Armstrong. $2, #221, Mahatma Gandhi. $2.50, #43, Maimonides. $5, Ralph Bunche.

**1985, Nov. 22**

| | | | | |
|---|---|---|---|---|
| **708** | A189 | $1 multicolored | 1.50 | 1.25 |
| **709** | A189 | $2 multicolored | 4.00 | 4.00 |
| **710** | A189 | $2.50 multicolored | 4.75 | 4.75 |
| | | *Nos. 708-710 (3)* | 10.25 | 10.00 |

**Souvenir Sheet**

| | | | | |
|---|---|---|---|---|
| **711** | A189 | $5 multicolored | 5.00 | 5.00 |

**Twain & Disney Type**

Walt Disney characters in scenes from "Letters From Hawaii": 25c, Mickey, Minnie on beach. 50c, Donald Duck surfing. $1.50, Donald roasting marshmallow. $3, Mickey canoeing. $5, Mickey, cat.

**1985, Nov. 27** *Perf. 14x13½*

| | | | | |
|---|---|---|---|---|
| **712** | A185 | 25c multicolored | .85 | .40 |
| **713** | A185 | 50c multicolored | 1.25 | .90 |
| **714** | A185 | $1.50 multicolored | 3.25 | 3.25 |
| **715** | A185 | $3 multicolored | 5.00 | 5.00 |
| | | *Nos. 712-715 (4)* | 10.35 | 9.55 |

**Souvenir Sheet**

| | | | | |
|---|---|---|---|---|
| **716** | A185 | $5 multicolored | 7.00 | 7.00 |

**Brothers Grimm & Disney Type**

Walt Disney characters in scenes from "The Elves and the Shoemaker": 30c, Mickey as shoemaker. 60c, Elves helping. 70c, Mickey, new shoes. $4, Minnie at sewing machine. $5, Minnie & Mickey.

**1985, Nov. 27** *Perf. 13½x14*

| | | | | |
|---|---|---|---|---|
| **717** | A187 | 30c multicolored | .85 | .45 |
| **718** | A187 | 60c multicolored | 1.25 | 1.00 |
| **719** | A187 | 70c multicolored | 1.60 | 1.25 |
| **720** | A187 | $4 multicolored | 4.75 | 4.75 |
| | | *Nos. 717-720 (4)* | 8.45 | 7.45 |

**Souvenir Sheet**

| | | | | |
|---|---|---|---|---|
| **721** | A187 | $5 multicolored | 7.00 | 7.00 |

Madonna and Child by Titian — G76

Christmas paintings: 70c, Madonna and Child with St. Mary and John the Baptist by Bugiardini. $1.10, Adoration of the Magi by Di Fredi. $3, Madonna and Child with Young St. John the Baptist by Bartolomeo. $5, The Annunciation by Botticelli.

**1985, Dec. 23** *Perf. 15*

| | | | | |
|---|---|---|---|---|
| **722** | G76 | 50c multicolored | .60 | .45 |
| **723** | G76 | 70c multicolored | .70 | .55 |
| **724** | G76 | $1.10 multicolored | 1.10 | .90 |
| **725** | G76 | $3 multicolored | 2.10 | 2.10 |
| | | *Nos. 722-725 (4)* | 4.50 | 4.00 |

**Souvenir Sheet**

| | | | | |
|---|---|---|---|---|
| **726** | G76 | $5 multicolored | 3.50 | 3.50 |

**Statue of Liberty Type of 1985**

Designs: 5c, Croton Reservoir, 1875. 10c, NY Public Library, 1986. 70c, Old Boathouse, Central Park, 1894. $4, Boating, Central Park, 1986. $5, Statue of Liberty, vert.

**1986, Jan. 6** *Perf. 15*

| | | | | |
|---|---|---|---|---|
| **727** | A191 | 5c multicolored | .25 | .25 |
| **728** | A191 | 10c multicolored | .25 | .25 |
| **729** | A191 | 70c multicolored | .40 | .40 |
| **730** | A191 | $4 multicolored | 2.40 | 2.40 |
| | | *Nos. 727-730 (4)* | 3.30 | 3.30 |

**Souvenir Sheet**

| | | | | |
|---|---|---|---|---|
| **731** | A191 | $5 multicolored | 5.00 | 5.00 |

**Audubon Type of 1985**

Designs: 50c, Louisiana heron. 70c, Black-crowned night heron. 90c, Bittern. $4, Glossy ibis. $5, King eider.

**1986, Jan. 28** *Perf. 12½x12*

| | | | | |
|---|---|---|---|---|
| **732** | A174 | 50c multicolored | 2.25 | 1.10 |
| **733** | A174 | 70c multicolored | 2.75 | 1.60 |
| **734** | A174 | 90c multicolored | 3.00 | 2.40 |
| **735** | A174 | $4 multicolored | 5.50 | 5.50 |
| | | *Nos. 732-735 (4)* | 13.50 | 10.60 |

**Souvenir Sheet**

*Perf. 14*

| | | | | |
|---|---|---|---|---|
| **736** | A174 | $5 multicolored | 8.00 | 8.00 |

Nos. 732-735 issued in sheets of 5 plus label.

**Nos. 676, 679 Overprinted**

**1986, Feb. 20** *Perf. 14*

| | | | | |
|---|---|---|---|---|
| **737** | G74 | 70c multicolored | 1.50 | 1.50 |
| **738** | G75 | $5 multicolored | 6.50 | 6.50 |

World Cup Soccer Championships, Mexico — G77

Various soccer plays.

**1986, Mar. 18**

| | | | | |
|---|---|---|---|---|
| **739** | G77 | 10c multicolored | .65 | .40 |
| **740** | G77 | 70c multicolored | 1.75 | 1.40 |
| **741** | G77 | $1 multicolored | 2.10 | 1.90 |
| **742** | G77 | $4 multicolored | 5.00 | 5.00 |
| | | *Nos. 739-742 (4)* | 9.50 | 8.70 |

**Souvenir Sheet**

| | | | | |
|---|---|---|---|---|
| **743** | G77 | $5 multicolored | 6.00 | 6.00 |

For overprints see Nos. 772-776.

### Halley's Comet Type

Designs: 5c, Nicolaus Copernicus, Earl of Rossi's six foot reflector. 20c, Sputnik. 40c, Tycho Brahe's notes, sketch of comet of 1577. $4, Edmond Halley, comet of 1682. $5, Halley's comet. Captions on 40c and $4 are reversed.

**1986, Mar. 26**

**744** A194 5c multicolored .55 .50
**745** A194 20c multicolored .90 .50
**746** A194 40c multicolored 1.10 .75
**747** A194 $4 multicolored 5.25 5.25
*Nos. 744-747 (4)* 7.80 7.00

**Souvenir Sheet**

**748** A194 $5 multicolored 4.50 4.50

"Tycho," on 40c, and "Nicolaus" on 5c misspelled.

For overprints see Nos. 787-791. Compare No. 748 with No. 913.

### Queen Elizabeth II, 60th Birthday
Common Design Type

Designs: 2c, At Windsor Park, 1933. $1.50, Queen Elizabeth II. $4, In Sydney, Australia, 1970. $5, Family portrait, Coronation Day, 1937.

**1986, Apr. 21**

**749** CD339 2c yel & blk .25 .25
**750** CD339 $1.50 pale grn & multi .85 .85
**751** CD339 $4 dl lil & multi 2.40 2.40
*Nos. 749-751 (3)* 3.50 3.50

**Souvenir Sheet**

**752** CD339 $5 tan & blk 3.25 3.25

### AMERIPEX '86 Type

Walt Disney characters visiting: 30c, Grand Canyon. 60c, Golden Gate Bridge. $1, Chicago Watertower. $3, The White House. $5, NY Harbor, Statue of Liberty.

**1986, May 22** ***Perf. 11***

**753** A195 30c multicolored .80 .50
**754** A195 60c multicolored 1.20 1.20
**755** A195 $1 multicolored 2.00 2.00
**756** A195 $3 multicolored 4.00 4.00
*Nos. 753-756 (4)* 8.00 7.70

**Souvenir Sheet**
***Perf. 14***

**757** A195 $5 multicolored 6.00 6.00

### Royal Wedding Issue, 1986
Common Design Type

Designs: 60c, Prince Andrew and Sarah Ferguson. 70c, Andrew. $4, Andrew in dress uniform, helicopter. $5, Couple, diff.

**1986, July 1** ***Perf. 14***

**758** CD340 60c multicolored .45 .45
**759** CD340 70c multicolored .55 .55
**760** CD340 $4 multicolored 3.00 3.00
*Nos. 758-760 (3)* 4.00 4.00

**Souvenir Sheet**

**761** CD340 $5 multicolored 5.00 5.00

Mushrooms
G78

Seashells
G79

Designs: 15c, Hygrocybe firma. 50c, Xerocomus coccolobae. $2, Volvariella cubensis. $3, Lactarius putidus. $5, Leponia caeruleocapitata.

**1986, July 15** ***Perf. 15***

**762** G78 15c multicolored 1.25 .80
**763** G78 50c multicolored 2.60 2.40
**764** G78 $2 multicolored 5.00 5.00
**765** G78 $3 multicolored 6.25 6.25
*Nos. 762-765 (4)* 15.10 14.45

**Souvenir Sheet**

**766** G78 $5 multicolored 13.00 13.00

**1986, Aug. 1**

Designs: 15c, Giant Atlantic pyram. 50c, Beau's murex. $1.10, West Indian fighting conch. $4, Alphabet coral. $5, Brown-lined paper bubble.

**767** G79 15c multicolored 1.25 .60
**768** G79 50c multicolored 3.00 1.75
**769** G79 $1.10 multicolored 3.25 3.25
**770** G79 $4 multicolored 5.75 5.75
*Nos. 767-770 (4)* 13.25 11.35

**Souvenir Sheet**

**771** G79 $5 multicolored 11.50 11.50

Nos. 739-743 Overprinted in Gold

**1986, Sept. 15** ***Perf. 14***

**772** G77 10c multicolored .75 .45
**773** G77 70c multicolored 1.25 1.25
**774** G77 $1 multicolored 1.75 1.50
**775** G77 $4 multicolored 4.25 4.25
*Nos. 772-775 (4)* 8.00 7.45

**Souvenir Sheet**

**776** G77 $5 multicolored 7.50 7.50

Manicou
G80

Wildlife.

**1986, Sept. 15** ***Perf. 15***

**777** G80 10c shown .25 .25
**778** G80 30c Giant toad .50 .50
**779** G80 60c Land tortoise 1.00 1.00
**780** G80 70c Murine opossum 1.10 1.10
**781** G80 90c Burmese mongoose 1.25 1.25
**782** G80 $1.10 Antillean armadillo 1.60 1.60
**783** G80 $2 Agouti 2.50 2.50
**784** G80 $3 Humpback whale 5.75 5.75
*Nos. 777-784 (8)* 13.95 13.95

**Souvenir Sheets**

**785** G80 $5 Mona monkey 6.50 6.50
**786** G80 $5 Iguana 6.50 6.50

### Nos. 744-748 Overprinted in Silver or Black

**1986, Oct. 15** ***Perf. 14***

**787** A194 5c multicolored (Bk) .90 .75
**788** A194 20c multicolored 1.10 .65
**789** A194 40c multicolored (Bk) 1.25 .75
**790** A194 $4 multicolored 6.50 6.50
*Nos. 787-790 (4)* 9.75 8.65

**Souvenir Sheet**

**791** A194 $5 multicolored 8.50 8.50

### Christmas Type of 1986

**1986 Nov. 3** ***Perf. 11***

**792** A199 25c Chip 'n' Dale .55 .25
**793** A199 30c Mickey Mouse .55 .30
**794** A199 50c Piglet, Pooh, Jose Carioca .70 .40
**795** A199 60c Daisy .80 .50
**796** A199 70c A kiss under the mistletoe .95 .60
**797** A199 $1.50 Huey, Dewey, and Louie 1.75 1.75
**798** A199 $3 Mickey Mouse, Morty 2.00 2.00
**799** A199 $4 Kittens on the keys 3.50 3.50
*Nos. 792-799 (8)* 10.80 9.30

**Souvenir Sheets**

**800** A199 $5 Mickey Mouse 5.00 5.00
**801** A199 $5 Bambi 5.00 5.00

Nos. 793, 795-796, 799 vert.

### Automobile Centenary Type

Designs: 10c, 1984 Aston-Martin Volante. 30c, 1948 Jaguar Mk V. 60c, 1956 Nash Ambassador. 70c, 1984 Toyota Supra. 90c, 1985 Ferrari Testarossa. $1, 1955 BMW 501B. $2, 1968 Mercedes-Benz 280SL. $3, 1932 Austro-Daimler ADR8.

**1986, Nov. 20** ***Perf. 15***

**802** A202 10c multicolored .30 .30
**803** A202 30c multicolored .55 .55
**804** A202 60c multicolored .75 .75
**805** A202 70c multicolored .75 .75
**806** A202 90c multicolored .90 .90
**807** A202 $1 multicolored .90 .90
**808** A202 $2 multicolored 1.25 1.25
**809** A202 $3 multicolored 1.60 1.60
*Nos. 802-809 (8)* 7.00 7.00

**Souvenir Sheets**

**810** A202 $5 1977 Morgan +8 4.25 4.25
**811** A202 $5 Checker Taxi 4.25 4.25

### Chagall Type

Paintings.: $1.10 — No. 812, The Mirror. No. 813, Dancer with a Fan. No. 814, The Acrobat. No. 815, Abraham's Sacrifice. No. 816, The Fruit Seller. No. 817, The Rooster, 1947. No. 818, The Wedding. No. 819, Horsewoman. No. 820, The Aged Lion from Fables of La Fontaine. No. 821, The Fruit Basket. No. 822, The Satyr and the Wayfarer. No. 823, Self-portrait with Seven Fingers. No. 824, Fruit and Flowers. No. 825, Lovers and Flowers. No. 826, The Wedded with an Angel. No. 827, In the Cafe, 1936. No. 828, The Equestrian. No. 829, Blue Violinist, 1947. No. 830, Zemphira costume design from Aleko scene I (dancer with red dress). No. 831, Portrait of Vava, 1955. No. 832, I and the Village, 1911. No. 833, The Accordion Player. No. 834, The Violinist, 1913. No. 835, Mother and Child, 1968. No. 836. Sunday, 1953. No. 837, Red and Black World, 1951. No. 838, Double Portrait with Wineglass, 1917. No. 839, Unknown (blonde woman in a blue dress). No. 840, Time is a River without Banks, 1930. No. 841, Homage to Apollinaire. No. 842, Unknown (rooster behind Eiffel tower). No. 843, The Blue Home, 1926, horiz. No. 844, Still-life, 1912, horiz. No. 845, Autumn Village. No. 846, Bonjour Paris. No. 847, The Jew in Pink, 1914. No. 848, Unknown (clown with violin). No. 849, War, 1943. No. 850, The Artist Angel. No. 851, Unknown (vase of flowers, woman at window).

$5 — No. 852, Birthday, 1915. No. 853, Wheatfield on a Summer Afternoon, 1942. No. 854, The Nude Above Vitebsk. No. 855, Aleko and Zemphira by Moonlight. No. 856, The Family Dinner. No. 857, Life (couple with baby, sun, celebrants). No. 858, The Flying Carriage, 1913. No. 859, The Studio. No. 860, Birth. No. 861, Rain.

**1986-87** ***Perf. 14x13½***

**812-851** A203 Set of 40 50.00 50.00

**Size: 110x95mm**
***Imperf***

**852-861** A203 Set of 10 35.00 35.00

Issued: Nos. 824-851, 855-861, 1987.

### America's Cup Type

**1987, Feb. 5** ***Perf. 15***

**862** A204 25c Defender, 1895 .85 .55
**863** A204 45c Caleta, 1886 1.10 .85
**864** A204 70c Azzurra, 1981 1.40 1.40
**865** A204 $4 Australia II, 1983 2.75 2.75
*Nos. 862-865 (4)* 6.10 5.55

**Souvenir Sheet**

**866** A204 $5 Columbia, Shamrock, 1899 6.50 6.50

### Discovery of America Type

**1987, Apr. 27**

**867** A206 15c Columbus .25 .25
**868** A206 30c Queen Isabella .25 .25
**869** A206 50c Santa Maria .40 .40
**870** A206 60c Landing in New World .45 .45
**871** A206 90c Lesser Antilles .75 .75
**872** A206 $1 King Ferdinand .80 .80
**873** A206 $2 Fort of La Navidad 1.75 1.75
**874** A206 $3 Galley off Hispaniola 2.50 2.50
*a.* Sheet of 8 12.00 12.00
*Nos. 867-874 (8)* 7.15 7.15

**Souvenir Sheets**

**875** A207 $5 Native Canoe 6.00 6.00
**876** A207 $5 Santa Maria at anchor 6.00 6.00

### Transportation Innovations Type

Designs: 10c, Saunders Roe SR-N1 Hovercraft, 1959. 15c, Bugatti Royale, 1931. 30c, Aleksei Leonov, 1st space walk, 1965. 50c, CSS Hunley, submarine, 1864. 60c, Rolls Royce Flying Bedstead, VTOL aircraft, 1954. 70c, Jenny Lind, locomotive, 1854. 90c, Duryea, 1893. $1.50, Steam locomotive, London subway, 1863. $2, SS Great Britain, screw-driven steamship, 1843. $3, Budweiser rocket, 1979.

**1987, May 18** ***Perf. 14***

**877** A209 10c multicolored .55 .30
**878** A209 15c multicolored .60 .40
**879** A209 30c multicolored .80 .50
**880** A209 50c multicolored 1.10 .75
**881** A209 60c multicolored 1.25 .90
**882** A209 70c multicolored 1.40 1.25
**883** A209 90c multicolored 1.50 1.25
**884** A209 $1.50 multicolored 2.25 2.25
**885** A209 $2 multicolored 2.75 2.75
**886** A209 $3 multicolored 3.00 3.00
*Nos. 877-886 (10)* 15.20 13.35

### Capex '87 Type

Fish.

**1987, June 15**

**887** A208 6c Yellow chub .25 .25
**888** A208 30c Kingfish .55 .40
**889** A208 50c Mako shark .75 .65
**890** A208 60c Dolphinfish .85 .85
**891** A208 90c Bonito 1.10 1.10
**892** A208 $1.10 Cobia 1.40 1.40
**893** A208 $3 Great tarpon 3.25 3.25
**894** A208 $4 Swordfish 3.50 3.50
*Nos. 887-894 (8)* 11.65 11.40

**Souvenir Sheets**

**895** A208 $5 Jewfish 5.00 5.00
**896** A208 $5 Amberjack 5.00 5.00

### Statue of Liberty Type

10c, Washing statue's face. 15c, Commemorative medals. 25c, Band facing right. 30c, Band facing forward. 45c, Liberty's face. 50c, Washing statue's hair, horiz. 60c, Commemorative statuettes, horiz. 70c, Boats in NY Harbor, horiz. $1, Re-opening. $1.10, Blimps, Liberty & Manhattan Islands. $2, Warship. $3, Commemorative flags.

**1987, Aug. 5**

**897** A210 10c multicolored .25 .25
**898** A210 15c multicolored .30 .30
**899** A210 25c multicolored .45 .45
**900** A210 30c multicolored .50 .50
**901** A210 45c multicolored .55 .55
**902** A210 50c multicolored .60 .60
**903** A210 60c multicolored .70 .70
**904** A210 70c multicolored .80 .80
**905** A210 $1 multicolored .95 .95
**906** A210 $1.10 multicolored 1.00 1.00
**907** A210 $2 multicolored 1.90 1.90
**908** A210 $3 multicolored 2.10 2.10
*Nos. 897-908 (12)* 10.10 10.10

### Inventors Type

Designs: 60c, Isaac Newton, Newton Medal. $1, Louis Daguerre, inventor of Daguerreotype. $2, Antoine Lavoisier, French chemist, apparatus. $3, Rudolf Diesel, German engineer, Diesel engine. $5, Halley's comet.

**1987, Sept. 9**

**909** A211 60c multicolored 1.00 .80
**910** A211 $1 multicolored 1.25 1.25
**911** A211 $2 multicolored 2.60 2.60
**912** A211 $3 multicolored 6.00 6.00
*Nos. 909-912 (4)* 10.85 10.65

**Souvenir Sheet**

**913** A211 $5 multicolored 8.00 8.00

No. 913 inscribed "Great Scientific Discoveries" in margin.

No. 912 incorrectly inscribed "James Watt, Steam Engine." See Grenada No. 1538.

### US Constitution Bicentennial Type

10c, Constitutional Convention, Philadelphia. 50c, Georgia state flag. 60c, Capitol, vert. $4, Thomas Jefferson, vert. $5, Alexander Hamilton, vert.

**1987, Nov. 1**

**914** A214 10c multicolored .25 .25
**915** A214 50c multicolored .85 .75
**916** A214 60c multicolored .85 .80
**917** A214 $4 multicolored 4.50 4.50
*Nos. 914-917 (4)* 6.45 6.30

**Souvenir Sheet**

**918** A214 $5 multicolored 4.00 4.00

### Hafnia '87 Type

Walt Disney characters in adaptations of Hans Christian Andersen Fairy Tales: 25c, The Swineherd. 30c, What the Good Man Does is Always Right. 50c, Little Tuk. 60c, The World's Fairest Rose. 70c, The Garden of Paradise. $1.50, The Naughty Boy. $3, What the Moon

Saw. $4, Thumbelina. No. 927, Hans Clodhopper. No. 928, Elder Tree Mother.

**1987, Nov. 16**

| | | | | | |
|---|---|---|---|---|---|
| **919** | A215 | 25c | multicolored | .55 | .30 |
| **920** | A215 | 30c | multicolored | .60 | .40 |
| **921** | A215 | 50c | multicolored | .80 | .80 |
| **922** | A215 | 60c | multicolored | .80 | .80 |
| **923** | A215 | 70c | multicolored | .85 | .85 |
| **924** | A215 | $1.50 | multicolored | 2.25 | 2.25 |
| **925** | A215 | $3 | multicolored | 3.00 | 3.00 |
| **926** | A215 | $4 | multicolored | 3.50 | 3.50 |
| | | | *Nos. 919-926 (8)* | 12.35 | 11.90 |

### Souvenir Sheets

| | | | | | |
|---|---|---|---|---|---|
| **927** | A215 | $5 | multicolored | 6.25 | 6.25 |
| **928** | A215 | $5 | multicolored | 6.25 | 6.25 |

Christmas — G81

Paintings by El Greco: 10c, Virgin and Child with Saints Martin and Agnes. 50c, Detail from Virgin and Child with Saints Martin and Agnes. 60c, The Annunciation. $4, Holy Family with St. Anne. $5, Adoration of the Shepherds.

**1987, Dec. 15**

| | | | | | |
|---|---|---|---|---|---|
| **929** | G81 | 10c | multicolored | .45 | .25 |
| **930** | G81 | 50c | multicolored | 1.40 | .95 |
| **931** | G81 | 60c | multicolored | 1.40 | 1.10 |
| **932** | G81 | $4 | multicolored | 5.50 | 5.50 |
| | | | *Nos. 929-932 (4)* | 8.75 | 7.80 |

### Souvenir Sheet

| | | | | | |
|---|---|---|---|---|---|
| **933** | G81 | $5 | multicolored | 9.25 | 9.25 |

### Wedding Anniv. Type

**1988, Feb. 15**

| | | | | | |
|---|---|---|---|---|---|
| **934** | A218 | 20c | Elizabeth, Anne | .25 | .25 |
| **935** | A218 | 30c | Wedding portrait | .25 | .25 |
| **936** | A218 | $2 | Elizabeth, Charles, Anne | 1.40 | 1.40 |
| **937** | A218 | $3 | Elizabeth wearing tiara | 2.00 | 2.00 |
| | | | *Nos. 934-937 (4)* | 3.90 | 3.90 |

### Souvenir Sheet

| | | | | | |
|---|---|---|---|---|---|
| **938** | A218 | $5 | Elizabeth in wedding gown | 4.00 | 4.00 |

### 1988 Summer Olympics Type

Walt Disney characters in modern and ancient events.

**1988, Apr. 13** ***Perf. 13½x14, 14x13½***

| | | | | | |
|---|---|---|---|---|---|
| **939** | A219 | 1c | Rhythmic gymnastics | .25 | .25 |
| **940** | A219 | 2c | Pankration | .25 | .25 |
| **941** | A219 | 3c | Synchronized swimming | .25 | .25 |
| **942** | A219 | 4c | Hoplite race | .25 | .25 |
| **943** | A219 | 5c | Baseball | .25 | .25 |
| **944** | A219 | 10c | Horse race | .25 | .25 |
| **945** | A219 | $6 | Windsurfing | 5.00 | 5.00 |
| **946** | A219 | $7 | Chariot race | 5.75 | 5.75 |
| | | | *Nos. 939-946 (8)* | 12.25 | 12.25 |

### Souvenir Sheet

| | | | | | |
|---|---|---|---|---|---|
| **947** | A219 | $5 | Tennis | 5.00 | 5.00 |
| **948** | A219 | $5 | Pentathlon | 5.00 | 5.00 |

### Boy Scout Type

**1988, May 3** ***Perf. 14***

| | | | | | |
|---|---|---|---|---|---|
| **949** | A220 | 50c | Semaphore, vert. | .50 | .50 |
| **950** | A220 | 70c | Canoeing, vert. | .60 | .60 |
| **951** | A220 | $1 | Cook-out | .90 | .90 |
| **952** | A220 | $3 | Campfire | 2.50 | 2.50 |
| | | | *Nos. 949-952 (4)* | 4.50 | 4.50 |

### Souvenir Sheet

| | | | | | |
|---|---|---|---|---|---|
| **953** | A220 | $5 | Pitching tent | 4.50 | 4.50 |

### Bird Type

**1988, May 31**

| | | | | | |
|---|---|---|---|---|---|
| **954** | A222 | 20c | Yellow-crowned night heron | .30 | .30 |
| **955** | A222 | 25c | Brown pelican | .30 | .30 |
| **956** | A222 | 45c | Audubon's shearwater | .45 | .40 |
| **957** | A222 | 60c | Red-footed booby | .65 | .45 |
| **958** | A222 | 70c | Bridled tern | .65 | .60 |
| **959** | A222 | 90c | Red-billed tropicbird | .90 | .90 |
| **960** | A222 | $3 | Blue-winged teal | 2.50 | 2.50 |
| **961** | A222 | $4 | Sora | 3.50 | 3.50 |
| | | | *Nos. 954-961 (8)* | 9.25 | 8.95 |

### Souvenir Sheets

| | | | | | |
|---|---|---|---|---|---|
| **962** | A222 | $5 | Little blue heron | 5.00 | 5.00 |
| **963** | A222 | $5 | Purple-throated carib | 5.00 | 5.00 |

### Titian Type

Paintings by Titian: 15c, Man with Blue Eyes, 1545. 30c, The Three Ages of Man, 1512. 60c, Don Diego Mendoza, 1545. 75c, Emperor Charles V Seated, 1548. $1, A Young Man in a Fur, 1515. $2, Tobias and the Angel, 1543. $3, Pietro Bembo, 1540. $4, Pier Luigi Farnese, 1546. No. 972, Sacred and Profane Love. No. 973, Venus and Adonis.

**1988, June 15** ***Perf. 13½x14***

| | | | | | |
|---|---|---|---|---|---|
| **964** | A224 | 15c | multicolored | .25 | .25 |
| **965** | A224 | 30c | multicolored | .25 | .25 |
| **966** | A224 | 60c | multicolored | .40 | .40 |
| **967** | A224 | 75c | multicolored | .55 | .55 |
| **968** | A224 | $1 | multicolored | .75 | .75 |
| **969** | A224 | $2 | multicolored | 1.40 | 1.40 |
| **970** | A224 | $3 | multicolored | 2.00 | 2.00 |
| **971** | A224 | $4 | multicolored | 2.75 | 2.75 |
| | | | *Nos. 964-971 (8)* | 8.35 | 8.35 |

### Souvenir Sheet

| | | | | | |
|---|---|---|---|---|---|
| **972** | A224 | $5 | multicolored | 5.00 | 5.00 |
| **973** | A224 | $5 | multicolored | 5.00 | 5.00 |

### Airship Type

Historic flights: 10c, Hindenburg over Rio de Janeiro, 1937. 20c, Hindenburg over NYC, 1937. 30c, US Navy airships, WWII convoy to Europe, 1944. 40c, Hindenburg docking at Lakehurst, NJ, 1937, vert. 60c, Joint flight, Hindenburg and Graf Zeppelin, 1936, vert. 70c, DC-3, Hindenburg, Los Angeles at Lakehurst, 1936. $1, Graf Zeppelin II over England, 1939, vert. $2, Deutschland, 1st passenger flight, 1912. $3, Graf Zeppelin over Dome of the Rock, Jerusalem, 1931. $4, Hindenburg Olympic flight, 1936. No. 984, Graf Zeppelin over Vatican City, 1933, vert. No. 985, Graf Zeppelin Polar flight, 1931.

**1988, July 1** ***Perf. 14***

| | | | | | |
|---|---|---|---|---|---|
| **974** | A225 | 10c | multicolored | .25 | .25 |
| **975** | A225 | 20c | multicolored | .25 | .25 |
| **976** | A225 | 30c | multicolored | .25 | .25 |
| **977** | A225 | 40c | multicolored | .35 | .35 |
| **978** | A225 | 60c | multicolored | .80 | .60 |
| **979** | A225 | 70c | multicolored | 1.10 | .80 |
| **980** | A225 | $1 | multicolored | 1.10 | .90 |
| **981** | A225 | $2 | multicolored | 1.75 | 1.75 |
| **982** | A225 | $3 | multicolored | 2.50 | 2.50 |
| **983** | A225 | $4 | multicolored | 3.25 | 3.25 |
| | | | *Nos. 974-983 (10)* | 11.60 | 10.90 |

### Souvenir Sheets

| | | | | | |
|---|---|---|---|---|---|
| **984** | A225 | $5 | multicolored | 6.00 | 6.00 |
| **985** | A225 | $5 | multicolored | 6.00 | 6.00 |

### Fairy Tales Type
Miniature Sheets

*Bambi:* No. 986a, Newborn Bambi, mother and forest animals. b, Bambi, Flower and Thumper. c, Bambi and opossum family hanging from tree. d, Bambi, his mother, and Faline, a female fawn. e, Foraging in a snow storm. f, Meeting his father, the Great Stag. g, Competing for Faline's attention. h, The Great Stag leading animals to safety during forest fire. i, Bambi, grown, becomes the Great Stag.

*The Fox and the Hound:* No. 987a, Big Mama, consoling the orphaned baby fox, Tod. b, Widow Tweed feeding Tod. c, Tod playing with Copper, the hound. d, Copper leashed. e, Copper and Chief. f, Chief barking at Tod, Copper shocked. g, Porcupine. h, Vixey, a female fox. i, Bear attacking Copper.

*101 Dalmatians:* No. 988a, Pongo, Perdita and their masters. b, Pongo and Perdita, courting. c, Three puppies. d, Cruella de Ville and henchmen. e, Captain the Horse, Colonel the Sheepdog and Tibbs the Cat. f, Dalmatians following Tibbs to freedom. g, Cruella racing car in pursuit. h, Dalmatians disguised in soot. i, Nanny dusting off the soot.

*Dumbo:* No. 989a, Stork delivering Dumbo. b, Elephant making fun of Dumbo's large ears. c, Dumbo, Mrs. Jumbo performing. d, Timothy the Mouse. e, Timothy and Dumbo. f, Crows pushing Dumbo off a cliff. g, Dumbo flying away from burning building. h, Dumbo flying with the crows. i, Dumbo and Mrs. Jumbo on train.

*Lady and the Tramp:* No. 990a, Darling holding Lady. b, Lady meets the Tramp. c, Lady looking in bassinet. d, Siamese cats, Lady. e, Lady, Tramp, crocodiles. f, Tramp kisses Lady. g, Lady in dog catcher's carriage. h, Lady and Tramp attacking rat. i, Trusty and Jock overturning dog catcher's carriage where Tramp is imprisoned.

*The Aristocats:* No. 991a, Edgar driving Madame Mornfamille's carriage. b, Dutchess and kittens. c, Edgar feeding the cats cream spiked with sleeping pills. d, Edgar transporting cats on motorcycle. e, Walter O'Malley discovers the abandoned cats. f, Three geese. g, Scat Cat and friends holding a jam session. h, Edgar attacks O'Malley with a pitch fork. i, Frau-Frau kicking Edgar.

No. 992, Faline and newborn twin fawns. No. 993, Tod and Vixey. No. 994, Pongo, Perdita and puppies. No. 995, Dumbo flying with Timothy the Mouse. No. 996, Lady and Tramp's puppies. No. 997, Walter O'Malley, Dutchess and kittens.

**1988, July 25** ***Perf. 14x13½***

| | | | | | |
|---|---|---|---|---|---|
| **986** | | | Sheet of 9 | 4.00 | 4.00 |
| *a.-i.* | A212 | 30c | any single | .40 | .40 |
| **987** | | | Sheet of 9 | 4.00 | 4.00 |
| *a.-i.* | A212 | 30c | any single | .40 | .40 |
| **988** | | | Sheet of 9 | 4.00 | 4.00 |
| *a.-i.* | A212 | 30c | any single | .40 | .40 |
| **989** | | | Sheet of 9 | 4.00 | 4.00 |
| *a.-i.* | A212 | 30c | any single | .40 | .40 |
| **990** | | | Sheet of 9 | 4.00 | 4.00 |
| *a.-i.* | A212 | 30c | any single | .40 | .40 |
| **991** | | | Sheet of 9 | 4.00 | 4.00 |
| *a.-i.* | A212 | 30c | any single | .40 | .40 |
| | | | *Nos. 986-991 (6)* | 24.00 | 24.00 |

### Souvenir Sheets

| | | | | | |
|---|---|---|---|---|---|
| **992-997** | A212 | $5 | each | 6.25 | 6.25 |

### SYDPEX '88 Type

Walt Disney characters: 1c, Conducting at Sydney Opera House. 2c, Climbing Ayers Rock. 3c, Working at a sheep station. 4c, Visiting Lone Pine Koala Sanctuary. 5c, Playing Australian football. 10c, Racing camels. No. 1004, Lawn bowling. $6, America's Cup trophy and Australia II. No. 1006, The Great Barrier Reef. No. 1007, Beach party.

**1988, Aug. 1** ***Perf. 14x13½***

| | | | | | |
|---|---|---|---|---|---|
| **998** | A226 | 1c | multicolored | .25 | .25 |
| **999** | A226 | 2c | multicolored | .25 | .25 |
| **1000** | A226 | 3c | multicolored | .25 | .25 |
| **1001** | A226 | 4c | multicolored | .25 | .25 |
| **1002** | A226 | 5c | multicolored | .25 | .25 |
| **1003** | A226 | 10c | multicolored | .25 | .25 |
| **1004** | A226 | $5 | multicolored | 5.50 | 5.50 |
| **1005** | A226 | $6 | multicolored | 6.50 | 6.50 |
| | | | *Nos. 998-1005 (8)* | 13.50 | 13.50 |

### Souvenir Sheets

| | | | | | |
|---|---|---|---|---|---|
| **1006** | A226 | $5 | multicolored | 5.00 | 5.00 |
| **1007** | A226 | $5 | multicolored | 5.00 | 5.00 |

### Flowering Trees Type

**1988, Sept. 30** ***Perf. 14***

| | | | | | |
|---|---|---|---|---|---|
| **1008** | A228 | 10c | Potato tree, vert. | .25 | .25 |
| **1009** | A228 | 20c | Wild cotton | .25 | .25 |
| **1010** | A228 | 30c | Shower of gold, vert. | .25 | .25 |
| **1011** | A228 | 60c | Napoleon's button, vert. | .50 | .45 |
| **1012** | A228 | 90c | Geiger tree | .75 | .65 |
| **1013** | A228 | $1 | Fern tree | .85 | .85 |
| **1014** | A228 | $2 | French cashew | 1.75 | 1.75 |
| **1015** | A228 | $4 | Amherstia, vert. | 3.00 | 3.00 |
| | | | *Nos. 1008-1015 (8)* | 7.60 | 7.45 |

### Souvenir Sheets

| | | | | | |
|---|---|---|---|---|---|
| **1016** | A228 | $5 | African tulip tree, vert. | 3.75 | 3.75 |
| **1017** | A228 | $5 | Swamp immortelle | 3.75 | 3.75 |

### Car Type
Miniature Sheets

Designs: No. 1018a, 1925 Doble Series E, US. b, 1926 Alvis 12/50, United Kingdom. c, 1927 Sunbeam 3-liter, UK. d, 1928 Franklin Airman, US. e, 1929 Delage D8S, France. f, 1897 Mors, France. g, 1904 Peerless Green Dragon, US. h, 1909 Pope-Hartford, US. i, 1920 Daniels Submarine Speedster, US. j, 1922 McFarlan 9.3 liter, US.

No. 1019a, 1949 Frazer Nash Lemans Replica, UK. b, 1953 Pegaso Z102, Spain. No. 1019c, 1953 Siata Spyder V-8, Italy. d, 1953 Kurtis-Offenhauser, US. No. 1019e, 1954 Kaiser-Darrin, US. f, 1930 Tracta, France. g, 1932 Maybach Zeppelin, Germany. h, 1934 Railton Light Sports, UK. i, 1936 Hotchkiss, France. j, 1939 Mercedes-Benz W163, Germany.

No. 1020a, 1982 Aston Martin Vantage V8, UK. b, 1982 Porsche 956, Germany. No. 1020c, 1983 Lotus Esprit Turbo, UK. d, 1984 McLaren MP4/2, UK. e, 1985 Mercedes-Benz 190E 2-3-16, Germany. f, 1963 Ferrari 250 GT Lusso, Italy. g, 1964 Porsche 904, Germany. h, 1967 Volvo P1800, Sweden. i, 1970 McLaren-Chevrolet M8D, US. j, 1981 Jaguar XJ6, UK.

**1988, Oct. 7** ***Perf. 13x13½***

| | | | | | |
|---|---|---|---|---|---|
| **1018** | | | Sheet of 10 | 15.00 | 15.00 |
| *a.-j.* | A223 | $2 | any single | 1.50 | 1.50 |
| **1019** | | | Sheet of 10 | 15.00 | 15.00 |
| *a.-j.* | A223 | $2 | any single | 1.50 | 1.50 |
| **1020** | | | Sheet of 10 | 15.00 | 15.00 |
| *a.-j.* | A223 | $2 | any single | 1.50 | 1.50 |

### Christmas and Mickey Mouse 60th Anniv. Type
Miniature Sheet

"Mickey's Christmas Parade": No. 1021a, Dumbo. b, Goofy. c, Minnie Mouse. d, Morty, Ferdy and Clarabelle Cow. e, Huey, Dewey and Louie. f, Donald Duck. g, Wooden soldiers marching. h, Mickey Mouse leading parade. No. 1022, Capt. Hook on float. No. 1023, Mickey and Donald on float.

**1988, Dec. 1** ***Perf. 13½x14***

| | | | | | |
|---|---|---|---|---|---|
| **1021** | | | Sheet of 8 | 6.00 | 6.00 |
| *a.-h.* | A229 | $1 | any single | .75 | .75 |

### Souvenir Sheets
***Perf. 14x13***

| | | | | | |
|---|---|---|---|---|---|
| **1022** | A229 | $7 | multicolored | 6.50 | 6.50 |
| **1023** | A229 | $7 | multicolored | 6.50 | 6.50 |

### Japanese Painting Type

"The Fifty-three Stations on the Tokaido" by Hiroshige (1979-1858): 15c, Crossing the Oi at Shimada by Ferry. 20c, Daimyo and Entourage at Arai. 45c, Cargo Portage through Goyu. 75c, Snowfall at Fujigawa. $1, Horses for the Emperor at Chiryu. $2, Rainfall at Tsuchiyama. $3, At Inn of Ishibe. $4, On the Shore of Lake Biwa at Otsu. No. 1032, Pilgrimage to Atsuta Shrine at Miya. No. 1033, Fishing Village of Yokkaichi on the Mie.

**1989, May 15** ***Perf. 14x13½***

| | | | | | |
|---|---|---|---|---|---|
| **1024** | A233 | 15c | multicolored | .30 | .30 |
| **1025** | A233 | 20c | multicolored | .35 | .35 |
| **1026** | A233 | 45c | multicolored | .60 | .60 |
| **1027** | A233 | 75c | multicolored | 1.00 | 1.00 |
| **1028** | A233 | $1 | multicolored | 1.00 | 1.00 |
| **1029** | A233 | $2 | multicolored | 1.75 | 1.75 |
| **1030** | A233 | $3 | multicolored | 2.75 | 2.75 |
| **1031** | A233 | $4 | multicolored | 3.75 | 3.75 |
| | | | *Nos. 1024-1031 (8)* | 11.50 | 11.50 |

### Souvenir Sheets

| | | | | | |
|---|---|---|---|---|---|
| **1032** | A233 | $5 | multicolored | 4.50 | 4.50 |
| **1033** | A233 | $5 | multicolored | 4.50 | 4.50 |

### 1988 Olympic Medalists Type

Designs: 15c, Henry Maske, East Germany, boxing (165 lbs.). 50c, Andreas Schroeder, East Germany, freestyle wrestling (286 lbs.). 60c, East German team, women's gymnastics. 75c, Greg Louganis, US, men's springboard and platform diving. $1, Mitsuru Sato, Japan, freestyle wrestling (115 lbs.). $2, West German team, 4x200m freestyle relay. $3, Dieter Baumann, West Germany, 5000m race. $4, Jackie Joyner-Kersee, US, heptathlon. No. 1042, Joachim Kunz, East Germany, weight lifting (149 lbs.). No. 1043, West German equestrian team, 3-day event.

**1989, Apr. 13** ***Perf. 14***

| | | | | | |
|---|---|---|---|---|---|
| **1034** | A232 | 15c | multicolored | .30 | .25 |
| **1035** | A232 | 50c | multicolored | .40 | .35 |
| **1036** | A232 | 60c | multicolored | .50 | .40 |
| **1037** | A232 | 75c | multicolored | .70 | .55 |
| **1038** | A232 | $1 | multicolored | .85 | .75 |
| **1039** | A232 | $2 | multicolored | 1.50 | 1.50 |
| **1040** | A232 | $3 | multicolored | 2.25 | 2.25 |
| **1041** | A232 | $4 | multicolored | 3.00 | 3.00 |
| | | | *Nos. 1034-1041 (8)* | 9.50 | 9.05 |

### Souvenir Sheets

| | | | | | |
|---|---|---|---|---|---|
| **1042** | A232 | $6 | multicolored | 4.75 | 4.75 |
| **1043** | A232 | $6 | multicolored | 4.75 | 4.75 |

World Cup Soccer Championships, Italy — G82

Designs: 15c, World Cup, vert. 45c, Kaiser Franz, West Germany, vert. 75c, Like 20c, flag of Italy, 1982 champions. $1, Pele, Brazil, vert. $2, Like 20c, flag of West Germany, 1974 champions. $3, Like 20c, flag of Brazil, 1970 champions. $4, Jules Rimet Cup, vert. No. 1052, Pele, Jules Rimet Cup, vert. No. 1053, Goalie.

**1989, June 12**

| | | | | | |
|---|---|---|---|---|---|
| **1044** | G82 | 15c | multicolored | .25 | .25 |
| **1045** | G82 | 20c | multicolored | .25 | .25 |
| **1046** | G82 | 45c | multicolored | .30 | .30 |
| **1047** | G82 | 75c | multicolored | .55 | .55 |
| **1048** | G82 | $1 | multicolored | 1.40 | 1.40 |
| **1049** | G82 | $2 | multicolored | 2.60 | 2.60 |
| **1050** | G82 | $3 | multicolored | 2.10 | 2.10 |
| **1051** | G82 | $4 | multicolored | 2.60 | 2.60 |
| | | | *Nos. 1044-1051 (8)* | 10.05 | 10.05 |

### Souvenir Sheets

| | | | | | |
|---|---|---|---|---|---|
| **1052** | G82 | $6 | multicolored | 4.50 | 4.50 |
| **1053** | G82 | $6 | multicolored | 4.50 | 4.50 |

### Car Type of 1988
Miniature Sheets

North American locomotives: No. 1054a, Morris & Essex, Dover, 1841. No. 1054b, B&O, Memmon No. 57, 1848. No. 1054c, Camden & Amboy, John Stevens, 1849. No. 1054d, Lawrence Machine Shop, Lawrence, 1853. No. 1054e, South Carolina, James S. Corry, 1859. No. 1054f, Mine Hill & Schuylkill Haven, Flexible Beam No. 3, 1860. No. 1054g, DL&W, Montrose, 1861. No. 1054h, Central

Pacific, Pequop No. 68, 1868. No. 1054i, Boston & Providence, Daniel Nason, 1863. No. 1054j, Morris & Essex, Joe Scranton, 1870.

No. 1055a, Central Railroad of New Jersey, No. 124, 1871. No. 1055b, Baldwin Steam Motor for Street Railways, 1876. No. 1055c, Lackawanna & Bloomsburg, Luzerne, 1878. No. 1055d, Central Mexicano, No. 150, 1892. No. 1055e, Denver, South Park & Pacific, Breckenridge No. 15, 1879. No. 1055f, Miles Planting & Manufacturing Co., "Daisy" Plantation locomotive, 1894. No. 1055g, Central of Georgia, Baldwin 854 No. 1136, 1895. No. 1055h, Savannah, Florida & Western, No. 111, 1900. No. 1055i, Douglas, Gilmore, & Co. No. 3, 1902. No. 1055j, Lehigh Valley Coal Co., Compressed Air locomotive No. 900, 1903.

No. 1056a, Morgan's Louisiana & Texas, McKeen Motorcar, 1908. No. 1056b, Clear Lake Lumber Co., Type B Climax, 1910. No. 1056c, Blue Jay Lumber Co., Heisler No. 10, 1912. No. 1056d, Stewartstown, Gasoline Engine No. 6, 1920's. No. 1056e, Bangor & Aroostook, Class G No. 186, 1921. No. 1056f, Hammond Lumber Co., No. 6, 1923. No. 1056g, Central Railroad of New Jersey, No. 1000, 1925. No. 1056h, Atchison, Topeka & Santa Fe, Super Chief No. 1-1A, 1935. No. 1056i, Norfolk & Western, Class Y-6, 1948. No. 1056i, Boston & Maine, Budd Railcar, 1949.

**1989, June 28** ***Perf. 13x13½***

**1054** Sheet of 10 19.00 19.00
*a.-j.* A223 $2 any single 1.60 1.60
**1055** Sheet of 10 19.00 19.00
*a.-j.* A223 $2 any single 1.60 1.60
**1056** Sheet of 10 19.00 19.00
*a.-j.* A223 $2 any single 1.60 1.60

PHILEXFRANCE '89 — G83

Walt Disney characters in Paris.

**1989, July 7** ***Perf. 14x13½, 13½x14***

**1057** G83 1c Military school .25 .25
**1058** G83 2c Conciergerie .25 .25
**1059** G83 3c Hotel de Ville, vert. .25 .25
**1060** G83 4c Genie of the Bastille, vert. .25 .25
**1061** G83 5c The Opera .25 .25
**1062** G83 10c Gardens of Luxembourg .25 .25
**1063** G83 $5 Arche de la Defense, vert. 7.00 7.00
**1064** G83 $6 Place Vendome, vert. 7.00 7.00
*Nos. 1057-1064 (8)* 15.50 15.50

**Souvenir Sheets**

**1065** G83 $6 Riding moped 7.00 7.00
**1066** G83 $6 Hot air ballooning 7.00 7.00

### Moon Landing Anniv. Type

Apollo 11 mission, 1969: 25c, Liftoff, vert. 50c, Splashdown. 60c, Spacecraft approaching moon, vert. 75c, Buzz Aldrin conducting experiment on lunar surface. $1, Leaving Earth orbit. $2, Transport of launch vehicle to pad, vert. $3, Lunar module liftoff. $4, Eagle lands on moon, vert. No. 1075, Footprint on moon. No. 1076, Armstrong stepping onto the moon, vert.

**1989, July 20** ***Perf. 14***

**1067** A237 25c multicolored .30 .30
**1068** A237 50c multicolored .50 .50
**1069** A237 60c multicolored .60 .60
**1070** A237 75c multicolored .75 .75
**1071** A237 $1 multicolored .90 .90
**1072** A237 $2 multicolored 2.00 2.00
**1073** A237 $3 multicolored 2.50 2.50
**1074** A237 $4 multicolored 3.50 3.50
*Nos. 1067-1074 (8)* 11.05 11.05

**Souvenir Sheets**

**1075** A237 $5 multicolored 4.50 4.50
**1076** A237 $5 multicolored 4.50 4.50

### Mushroom Type

**1989, Aug. 17**

**1078** A238 6c Collybia aurea .40 .25
**1079** A238 10c Podaxis pistillaris .40 .25
**1080** A238 20c Hygrocybe firma .65 .50
**1081** A238 30c Agaricus rufoaurantiacus .75 .65
**1082** A238 75c Leptonia howellii 1.60 1.60
**1083** A238 $2 Marasmiellus purpureus 3.00 3.00
**1084** A238 $3 Marasmius trinitatis 3.50 3.50
**1085** A238 $4 Hygrocybe martinicensis 4.00 4.00
*Nos. 1078-1085 (8)* 14.30 13.75

**Souvenir Sheets**

**1086** A238 $6 Lentinus crinitus 8.00 8.00
**1087** A238 $6 Agaricus purpurellus 8.00 8.00

### Butterflies Type

**1989, Oct. 2** ***Perf. 14***

**1088** A239 25c Androgeus swallowtail .85 .85
**1089** A239 35c Cloudless sulpher 1.00 1.00
**1090** A239 45c Cracker 1.10 1.10
**1091** A239 50c Painted lady 1.10 1.10
**1092** A239 75c Great southern white 1.75 1.75
**1093** A239 90c Little sulpher 1.90 1.90
**1094** A239 $2 Migrant sulpher 4.25 4.25
**1095** A239 $3 Mimic 5.00 5.00
*Nos. 1088-1095 (8)* 16.95 16.95

**Souvenir Sheets**

**1096** A239 $6 Giant hairstreak 8.50 8.50
**1097** A239 $6 Red anartia 8.50 8.50

### World Stamp Expo Type

Scenes from Walt Disney animated films and quotes from Poor Richard's Almanack by Benjamin Franklin: 1c, "Beware of little expenses, a small leak will sink a great ship." 2c, "Trust thyself and another shall not betray thee." 3c, "A spoonful of honey will catch more flies than a gallon of vinegar." 4c, "No gain without pain." 5c, "A true friend is the best possession." 6c, "Haste makes waste." 8c, "A quiet conscience sleeps in thunder, but rest and guilt live far asunder." 10c, "The muses love the morning." $5, "An egg today is better than a hen tomorrow." No. 1107, "He that riseth late, must trot all day." No. 1108, "If you'd be belov'd, make yourself amiable." No. 1109, "In Christmas feasting pray take care; let not your table be a snare; but with the poor God's bounty share. Adieu my friends! Till the next year," vert.

**1989, Nov.** **Litho.** ***Perf. 14x13½***

**1098** A242 1c multicolored .25 .25
**1099** A242 2c multicolored .25 .25
**1100** A242 3c multicolored .25 .25
**1101** A242 4c multicolored .25 .25
**1102** A242 5c multicolored .25 .25
**1103** A242 6c multicolored .25 .25
**1104** A242 8c multicolored .25 .25
**1105** A242 10c multicolored .25 .25
**1106** A242 $5 multicolored 4.50 4.50
**1107** A242 $6 multicolored 5.50 5.50
*Nos. 1098-1107 (10)* 12.00 12.00

**Souvenir Sheet**

**1108** A242 $6 multicolored 7.50 7.50
**1109** A242 $6 multicolored 7.50 7.50

World Stamp Expo '89, Washington, D.C.

Shakespearean Actors and Theater Masks — G84

15c, Ethel Barrymore (1879-1959). $1.10, Richard Burton (1925-1984). $2, John Barrymore (1882-1942). $3, Paul Robeson (1898-1976). $6, Bando Tamasaburo & Nakamura Kanzaburo.

**1989, Oct. 9** **Litho.** ***Perf. 14***

**1110** G84 15c multicolored .40 .30
**1111** G84 $1.10 multicolored 1.75 1.50
**1112** G84 $2 multicolored 2.50 2.50
**1113** G84 $3 multicolored 2.75 2.75
*Nos. 1110-1113 (4)* 7.40 7.05

**Souvenir Sheet**

**1114** G84 $6 multicolored 6.50 6.50

20th Century Musicians — G85

**1989, Oct. 9**

**1115** G85 10c Buddy Holly .40 .30
**1116** G85 25c Jimi Hendrix .65 .50
**1117** G85 75c Mighty Sparrow .95 .95
**1118** G85 $4 Katsutoji Kineya 4.25 4.25
*Nos. 1115-1118 (4)* 6.25 6.00

**Souvenir Sheet**

**1119** G85 $6 Lotte Lenya, Kurt Weill 6.25 6.25

Jimi is spelled incorrectly as "Jimmy."

### Discovery of America Type

**1989, Oct. 16**

**1120** A241 15c Canoeing .40 .30
**1121** A241 75c Cooking 1.25 1.25
**1122** A241 90c Using stone tools 1.75 1.75
**1123** A241 $3 Eating 4.50 4.50
*Nos. 1120-1123 (4)* 7.90 7.80

**Souvenir Sheet**

**1124** A241 $6 Building fire 6.25 6.25

### Christmas Type

Religious paintings by Rubens: 10c, The Annunciation. 15c, The Flight of the Holy Family into Egypt. 25c, The Presentation in the Temple. 45c, The Holy Family Under the Apple Tree. $2, Madonna and Child with Saints. $4, The Virgin and Child Enthroned with Saints. No. 1132, The Holy Family. No. 1132, Adoration of the Magi. No. 1133, Adoration of the Magi, diff.

**1990, Jan. 4** ***Perf. 14***

**1125** A243 10c multicolored .40 .25
**1126** A243 15c multicolored .45 .25
**1127** A243 25c multicolored .65 .25
**1128** A243 45c multicolored .85 .40
**1129** A243 $2 multicolored 2.40 2.40
**1130** A243 $4 multicolored 3.50 3.50
**1131** A243 $5 multicolored 3.50 3.50
*Nos. 1125-1131 (7)* 11.75 10.55

**Souvenir Sheets**

**1132** A243 $5 multicolored 7.00 7.00
**1133** A243 $5 multicolored 7.00 7.00

America Issue (Insects) G86

**1990, Mar. 16** ***Perf. 14***

**1134** G86 35c Hercules beetle .45 .45
**1135** G86 40c Click beetle .45 .45
**1136** G86 50c Harlequin beetle .60 .60
**1137** G86 60c Gold rim butterfly 1.10 1.10
**1138** G86 $1 Red skimmer dragonfly 1.25 1.25
**1139** G86 $2 Buprestid beetle 2.40 2.40
**1140** G86 $3 Mimic butterfly 3.50 3.50
**1141** G86 $4 Scarab beetle 3.50 3.50
*Nos. 1134-1141 (8)* 13.25 13.25

**Souvenir Sheets**

**1142** G86 $6 Canna skipper butterfly 6.50 6.50
**1143** G86 $6 Monarch butterfly 6.50 6.50

Orchids — G87

**1990, Mar. 6** **Litho.** ***Perf. 14***

**1144** G87 15c Brassocattleya thalie .35 .35
**1145** G87 20c Odontocidium tigersun .35 .35
**1146** G87 50c Odontioda hambuhren .55 .55
**1147** G87 75c Paphiopedium delrosi .65 .65
**1148** G87 $1 Vuylstekeara yokara 1.10 1.10
**1149** G87 $2 Paphiopedilum geelong 2.10 2.10
**1150** G87 $3 Wilsonara tigerwood 2.75 2.75
**1151** G87 $4 Cymbidium ormoulu 3.50 3.50
*Nos. 1144-1151 (8)* 11.35 11.35

**Souvenir Sheets**

**1152** G87 $6 Odontonia sappho 7.00 7.00
**1153** G87 $6 Cymbidium vieux rose 7.00 7.00

EXPO '90 Intl. Garden and Greenery Exposition, Osaka, Japan.

### Wildlife Type

**1990, Apr. 3**

**1154** A247 5c West Indies giant rice rat .30 .30
**1155** A247 25c Agouti .45 .45
**1156** A247 30c Humpback whale 1.00 1.00
**1157** A247 40c Pilot whale 1.00 1.00
**1158** A247 $1 Spotted dolphin 1.25 1.25
**1159** A247 $2 Mongoose 2.40 2.40
**1160** A247 $3 Prehensile-tailed porcupine 3.25 3.25
**1161** A247 $4 West Indies manatee 3.75 3.75
*Nos. 1154-1161 (8)* 13.40 13.40

**Souvenir Sheets**

**1162** A247 $6 Caribbean monk seal 7.00 7.00
**1163** A247 $6 Mongoose 7.00 7.00

### World War II Type

Designs: 6c, First British troops arrive in France, Sept. 6, 1939. 10c, British launch "Operation Crusader", Nov. 18, 1941. 20c, Rommel begins retreat from El Alamein, Nov. 4, 1942. 45c, US forces land on Aleutian Islands, May 11, 1943. 50c, US Marines land on Tarawa, Nov. 20, 1943. 60c, US 5th Army enters Rome, June 4, 1944. 75c, US troops reach River Seine, Aug. 19, 1944. $1, Battle of the Bulge, Dec. 16, 1944. $5, Allies launch final phase of Italian Campaign, Apr. 9, 1945. No. 1173, Atom bomb dropped on Hiroshima, Aug. 6, 1945. No. 1174, St. Paul's Cathedral during London blitz, Battle of Britain, 1940.

**1990, Apr. 30**

**1164** A248 6c multicolored .40 .40
**1165** A248 10c multicolored .40 .40
**1166** A248 20c multicolored .65 .65
**1167** A248 45c multicolored .70 .70
**1168** A248 50c multicolored .80 .80
**1169** A248 60c multicolored .85 .85
**1170** A248 75c multicolored .95 .95
**1171** A248 $1 multicolored 1.25 1.25
**1172** A248 $5 multicolored 4.00 4.00
**1173** A248 $6 multicolored 5.00 5.00
*Nos. 1164-1173 (10)* 15.00 15.00

**Souvenir Sheets**

**1174** A248 $6 multicolored 7.50 7.50

### Disney Type

Disney characters portraying Shakespearian characters: 15c, Daisy Duck at Ann Hathaway's Cottage, Shottery. 30c, Minnie Mouse and a young Shakespeare walking in Stratford birthplace, vert. 50c, Minnie as Mary Arden, Shakespeare's mother in Wilmcote, vert. 60c, Mickey in front of New Place, Stratford. $1, Mickey walking in Great Garden of New Place. $2, Mickey at Guild Chapel, Scholars Lane, vert. $4, Mickey at the Royal Shakespeare Theater, Stratford, vert. $5, Ludwig von Drake instructing Shakespeare. No. 1183, Mickey at Edge Hill, Stratford, vert. No. 1184, Mickey and Minnie rowing past Holy Trinity Church, Stratford-Upon-Avon.

**1990, May** ***Perf. 14x13½***

**1175** A250 15c multicolored .50 .25
**1176** A250 30c multicolored .65 .45
**1177** A250 50c multicolored .95 .85
**1178** A250 60c multicolored 1.10 1.10
**1179** A250 $1 multicolored 1.50 1.50
**1180** A250 $2 multicolored 2.75 2.75
**1181** A250 $4 multicolored 4.00 4.00
**1182** A250 $5 multicolored 4.00 4.00
*Nos. 1175-1182 (8)* 15.45 14.90

**Souvenir Sheets**

***Perf. 14***

**1183** A250 $6 multicolored 7.50 7.50
**1184** A250 $6 multicolored 7.50 7.50

### Penny Black Type

Souvenir Sheet

**1990, May 3 Litho. *Perf. 14***

**1185** A249 $6 Globe with South America 8.00 8.00

Stamp World London '90.

### Queen Mother, 90th Birthday Type

**1990, July 5**

**1186** A251 $2 Pink hat 1.40 1.40
**1187** A251 $2 With Charles 1.40 1.40
**1188** A251 $2 Blue outfit 1.40 1.40
*Nos. 1186-1188 (3)* 4.20 4.20

**Souvenir Sheet**

**1189** A251 $6 like #1187 4.25 4.25

### Bird Type

**1990, Sept. 10 Litho. *Perf. 14***

**1190** A255 25c Yellow-bellied seedeater .45 .45
**1191** A255 45c Carib grackle .65 .65
**1192** A255 50c Black-whisk-ered vireo .75 .75
**1193** A255 75c Bananaquit .85 .85
**1194** A255 $1 Collared swift 1.25 1.25
**1195** A255 $2 Yellow-bellied elaenia 1.90 1.90
**1196** A255 $3 Blue-hooded euphonia 2.50 2.50
**1197** A255 $5 Eared dove 4.50 4.50
*Nos. 1190-1197 (8)* 12.85 12.85

**Souvenir Sheets**

**1198** A255 $6 Mangrove cuckoo 5.75 5.75
**1199** A255 $6 Scaly-breasted thrasher 5.75 5.75

### Crustaceans Type of 1990

**1990, Sept. 17**

**1200** A256 10c Slipper lobster .25 .25
**1201** A256 25c Green reef crab .35 .35
**1202** A256 65c Caribbean lob-sterette .70 .70
**1203** A256 75c Blind deep sea lobster .80 .80
**1204** A256 $1 Flattened crab 1.10 1.10
**1205** A256 $2 Ridged slipper lobster 2.00 2.00
**1206** A256 $3 Land crab 2.25 2.25
**1207** A256 $4 Mountain crab 2.75 2.75
*Nos. 1200-1207 (8)* 10.20 10.20

**Souvenir Sheets**

**1208** A256 $6 Caribbean king crab 5.00 5.00
**1209** A256 $6 Purse crab 5.00 5.00

G88

G89

Players from participating countries.

**1990, Sept. 24**

**1210** G88 15c England .25 .25
**1211** G88 45c Argentina .50 .50
**1212** G88 $2 Sweden 1.75 1.75
**1213** G88 $4 South Korea 3.00 3.00
*Nos. 1210-1213 (4)* 5.50 5.50

**Souvenir Sheets**

**1214** G88 $6 Yugoslavia 4.50 4.50
**1215** G88 $6 United States 4.50 4.50

World Cup Soccer Championships, Italy.

**1990, Nov. 11 Litho. *Perf. 14***

**1216** G89 10c Boxing .25 .25
**1217** G89 25c Olympic flame .25 .25
**1218** G89 50c Soccer .50 .50
**1219** G89 75c Discus .65 .65
**1220** G89 $1 Pole vault .90 .90
**1221** G89 $2 Equestrian 3-day event 2.00 2.00
**1222** G89 $4 Women's bas-ketball 4.00 4.00
**1223** G89 $5 Men's gymnas-tics 3.50 3.50
*Nos. 1216-1223 (8)* 12.05 12.05

**Souvenir Sheets**

**1224** G89 $6 Sailboarding 6.00 6.00
**1225** G89 $6 Decathlon 6.00 6.00

1992 Summer Olympics, Barcelona.

### Rubens Type

Entire paintings or different details from: 5c, 25c, Adam and Eve, vert. 15c, Esther before Ahasuerus. 50c, Expulsion from Eden. $1, Cain Slaying Abel, vert. $2, Lot's Flight. $4, Samson and Delilah. $5, Abraham and Melchizedek. No. 1234, The Meeting of David and Abigail. No. 1235, Daniel in the Lions Den.

**1991, Jan. 31 Litho. *Perf. 14***

**1226** A259 5c multicolored .25 .25
**1227** A259 15c multicolored .40 .25
**1228** A259 25c multicolored .50 .25
**1229** A259 50c multicolored .85 .65
**1230** A259 $1 multicolored 1.50 1.25
**1231** A259 $2 multicolored 2.00 2.00
**1232** A259 $4 multicolored 3.00 3.00
**1233** A259 $5 multicolored 3.50 3.50
*Nos. 1226-1233 (8)* 12.00 11.15

**Souvenir Sheets**

**1234** A259 $6 multicolored 6.00 6.00
**1235** A259 $6 multicolored 6.00 6.00

### Fish Type of 1990

**1991, Feb. 5**

**1236** A254 15c Barred hamlet .55 .30
**1237** A254 35c Squirrelfish .90 .60
**1238** A254 45c Red-spotted hawkfish 1.00 .70
**1239** A254 75c Bigeye 1.60 1.25
**1240** A254 $1 Spiny puffer 1.90 1.50
**1241** A254 $2 Smallmouth grunt 2.75 2.75
**1242** A254 $3 Harlequin bass 3.50 3.50
**1243** A254 $4 Creole fish 3.75 3.75
*Nos. 1236-1243 (8)* 15.95 14.35

**Souvenir Sheets**

**1244** A254 $6 Fairy basslet 6.50 6.50
**1245** A254 $6 Copper sweep-er 6.50 6.50

Hummel Figurines — G90

Orchids — G91

**1991, Mar. 1 Litho. *Perf. 14***

**1246** G90 10c Angel, star .25 .25
**1247** G90 15c Angel, guitar, Christ Child .35 .25
**1248** G90 25c Shepherd .50 .25
**1249** G90 50c Angel, lantern, horn 1.00 .55
**1250** G90 $1 Angel, children, Christ Child 1.25 1.00
**1251** G90 $2 Angel, candle, Christ Child 2.25 2.25
**1252** G90 $4 Angel with bas-kets 3.25 3.25
**1253** G90 $5 Angels singing 3.50 3.50
*Nos. 1246-1253 (8)* 12.35 11.30

**Souvenir Sheets**

**1254** Sheet of 4 5.00 5.00
*a.* G90 5c like No. 1247 .25 .25
*b.* G90 40c like No. 1249 .30 .30
*c.* G90 60c like No. 1250 .50 .50
*d.* G90 $3 like No. 1253 2.75 2.75
**1255** Sheet of 4 7.00 7.00
*a.* G90 20c like No. 1246 .25 .25
*b.* G90 30c like No. 1248 .25 .25
*c.* G90 75c like No. 1251 .70 .70
*d.* G90 $6 like No. 1252 4.50 4.50

Christmas 1990.

**1991-92 Litho. *Perf. 14***

Designs: 5c, Brassia maculata. 10c, Oncidium lanceanum. 15c, Broughtonia sanguinea. 25c, Diacrium bicornutum. 35c, Cattleya labiata. 45c, Epidendrum fragrans. 50c, Oncidium papilio. 75c, Neocogniauxia monophylla. $1, Epidendrum polybulbon. $2, Spiranthes speciosa. $4, Epidendrum ciliare. $5, Phais tankervilliae. $10, Brassia caudata. $20, Brassavola cordata.

**1256** G91 5c multicolored .70 .70
**1257** G91 10c multicolored .70 .70
**1258** G91 15c multicolored .75 .30
**1259** G91 25c multicolored .90 .30
**1260** G91 35c multicolored .90 .30
**1261** G91 45c multicolored 1.25 .45
**1262** G91 50c multicolored 1.25 .50
**1263** G91 75c multicolored 1.50 .80
**1264** G91 $1 multicolored 2.00 1.25
**1265** G91 $2 multicolored 3.25 3.25
**1266** G91 $4 multicolored 5.25 5.25
**1267** G91 $5 multicolored 5.50 5.50
**1268** G91 $10 multicolored 10.50 10.50
**1269** G91 $20 multicolored 21.00 21.00
*Nos. 1256-1269 (14)* 55.45 50.80

Issued: $20, 6/92; others, 4/1/91.

### Butterfly Type

Designs: 5c, Crimson-patched longwing. 10c, Morpho helena. 15c, Morpho sulkowskyi. 20c, Dynastor napoleon. 25c, Pieridae callinira. 30c, Anartia amathea. 35c, Heliconiidae dido. 45c, Papilionidae columbus. 50c, Nymphalidae praeneste. 60c, Panacea prola. 75c, Julia. $1, Papilionidae orthosilaus. $2, Pyrrhopyge cometes. $3, Papilionidae paeon. $4, Morpho cypris. $5, Choringa. No. 1286, Caligo idomenides. No. 1287, Monarch. No. 1287A, Nymphalidae amydon. No. 1287B, Papilio childrenae.

**1991, Apr. 8 Litho. *Perf. 14***

**1270** A261 5c multicolored .60 .45
**1271** A261 10c multicolored .60 .45
**1272** A261 15c multicolored .85 .50
**1273** A261 20c multicolored .95 .55
**1274** A261 25c multicolored .95 .60
**1275** A261 30c multicolored 1.10 .70
**1276** A261 35c multicolored 1.10 .70
**1277** A261 45c multicolored 1.25 .95
**1278** A261 50c multicolored 1.40 1.00
**1279** A261 60c multicolored 1.60 1.10
**1280** A261 75c multicolored 1.60 1.25
**1281** A261 $1 multicolored 2.00 1.60
**1282** A261 $2 multicolored 2.75 2.75
**1283** A261 $3 multicolored 3.50 3.50
**1284** A261 $4 multicolored 4.00 4.00
**1285** A261 $5 multicolored 5.00 5.00
*Nos. 1270-1285 (16)* 29.25 25.10

**Souvenir Sheets**

**1286** A261 $6 multicolored 6.00 6.00
**1287** A261 $6 multicolored 6.00 6.00
**1287A** A261 $6 multicolored 6.00 6.00
**1287B** A261 $6 multicolored 6.00 6.00

Save Our Planet — G100

Walt Disney characters and ecology themes: 10c, Daisy and Donald, alternate forms of transportation. 15c, Goofy saving water. 25c, Donald, Daisy camping simply. 45c, Donald protecting birds. $1, Donald holding ascending balloons. $2, Minnie, Daisy using natural coolers. $4, Mickey, nephews cleaning beaches. $5, Scrooge McDuck using pedal power. No. 1296, Little Hiawatha and Iron Eyes Cody viewing destroyed forest. No. 1297, Donald, recycling. No. 1298, Minnie, Mickey planting trees.

**1991, Apr. 22 Litho. *Perf. 14***

**1288** G100 10c multicolored .65 .25
**1289** G100 15c multicolored .75 .25
**1290** G100 25c multicolored 1.00 .40
**1291** G100 45c multicolored 1.40 .60
**1292** G100 $1 multicolored 2.25 1.40
**1293** G100 $2 multicolored 3.25 3.00
**1294** G100 $4 multicolored 4.00 4.00
**1295** G100 $5 multicolored 4.00 4.00
*Nos. 1288-1295 (8)* 17.30 13.90

**Souvenir Sheets**

**1296** G100 $6 multicolored 6.50 6.50
**1297** G100 $6 multicolored 6.50 6.50
**1298** G100 $6 multicolored 6.50 6.50

### Voyages of Discovery Type

Discovery of America, 500th anniv. (in 1992).: 15c, Ferdinand Magellan, 1519-1521. 20c, Sir Francis Drake, 1577-1580. 50c, Capt. James Cook, 1768-1771. 60c, Douglas World Cruiser, 1924. $1, Sputnik, 1957. $2, Yuri Gagarin, 1961. $4, John Glenn, 1962. $5, Space Shuttle, 1981. No. 1307, Columbus' fleet. No. 1308, The Pinta, vert.

**1991, Apr. 29 Litho. *Perf. 14***

**1299** A262 15c multicolored .40 .30
**1300** A262 20c multicolored .30 .30
**1301** A262 50c multicolored .60 .60
**1302** A262 60c multicolored .70 .70
**1303** A262 $1 multicolored 1.10 1.10
**1304** A262 $2 multicolored 2.25 2.25
**1305** A262 $4 multicolored 4.25 4.25
**1306** A262 $5 multicolored 5.25 5.25
*Nos. 1299-1306 (8)* 14.85 14.75

**Souvenir Sheets**

**1307** A262 $6 multicolored 6.00 6.00
**1308** A262 $6 multicolored 6.00 6.00

### Disney Phila Nippon '91 Type

Walt Disney characters demonstrating arts, crafts and industries of Japan: 15c, Minnie, silkworms. 30c, Mickey, Minnie, Morty and Ferdie photographing the Torii. 50c, Donald, Mickey, origami. 60c, Mickey, Minnie diving for pearls. $1, Minnie modeling kimono. $2, Mickey making masks. $4, Donald, Mickey making paper. $5, Minnie, Pluto, pottery. #1317, Mickey making prints, vert. #1318, Mickey arranging flowers, vert. #1319, Mickey, tea ceremony, vert. #1320, Mickey carving ivory and wood into netsukes, vert.

**1991, May 6**

**1309** A263 15c multi .50 .25
**1310** A263 30c multi .85 .35
**1311** A263 50c multi 1.00 .55
**1312** A263 60c multi 1.10 .60
**1313** A263 $1 multi 2.00 1.00
**1314** A263 $2 multi 2.75 2.50
**1315** A263 $4 multi 3.75 3.75
**1316** A263 $5 multi 4.50 4.50
*Nos. 1309-1316 (8)* 16.45 13.50

**Souvenir Sheets**

**1317** A263 $6 multi 5.00 5.00
**1318** A263 $6 multi 5.00 5.00
**1319** A263 $6 multi 5.00 5.00
**1320** A263 $6 multi 5.00 5.00

### Mushrooms Type

**1991, June 1 Litho. *Perf. 14***

**1321** A265 5c Pyrrhoglossum pyrrhum .40 .25
**1322** A265 45c Agaricus purpurellus 1.00 .55
**1323** A265 50c Amanita crase-oderma 1.00 .60
**1324** A265 90c Hygrocybe acutoconica 1.75 1.25
**1325** A265 $1 Limacella gut-tata 1.75 1.25
**1326** A265 $2 Lactarius hygropho-roides 2.50 2.50
**1327** A265 $4 Boletellus cubensis 4.00 4.00
**1328** A265 $5 Psilocybe caerulescens 4.00 4.00
*Nos. 1321-1328 (8)* 16.40 14.40

**Souvenir Sheets**

**1329** A265 $6 Marasmius haemato-cephalus 7.50 7.50
**1330** A265 $6 Lepiota spicu-lata 7.50 7.50

### Royal Family Birthday, Anniversary

Common Design Type

**1991, July 5 Litho. *Perf. 14***

**1331** CD347 5c multi .50 .30
**1332** CD347 20c multi .30 .30
**1333** CD347 25c multi .30 .25
**1334** CD347 60c multi 1.00 .75
**1335** CD347 $1 multi 1.00 1.00
**1336** CD347 $2 multi 1.75 1.75
**1337** CD347 $4 multi 3.00 3.00
**1338** CD347 $5 multi 4.50 4.50
*Nos. 1331-1338 (8)* 12.35 11.85

**Souvenir Sheet**

**1339** CD347 $5 Elizabeth, Philip 5.75 5.75
**1340** CD347 $5 Diana, Charles, with sons 5.75 5.75

5c, 60c, $1, Nos. 1338, 1340, Charles and Diana, 10th wedding anniversary. Others, Queen Elizabeth II, 65th birthday.

### Van Gogh Painting Type

Designs: 5c, Two Thistles, vert. 10c, The Baby Marcelle Roulin, vert. 15c, Still Life: Basket with Six Oranges. 25c, Orchard in Blossom, vert. 45c, Portrait of Armand Roulin, vert. 50c, Wood Gatherers in the Snow (detail). 60c, Almond Tree in Blossom, vert. $1, Portrait of an Old Man, vert. $2, The Seine Bridge at Asnieres. $3, Vase with Lilacs, Daisies & Anemones, vert. $4, Self-portrait, vert. $5, Portrait of Patience Escalier, vert. No. 1353, Les Alyscamps, vert. No. 1354, Quay with Men Unloading Sand Barges. No. 1355, Sunset: Wheat Fields Near Arles.

***Perf. 13½x14, 14x13½***

**1991, Nov. 18 Litho.**

**1341** A264 5c multicolored .40 .25
**1342** A264 10c multicolored .40 .25
**1343** A264 15c multicolored .40 .25
**1344** A264 25c multicolored .40 .25
**1345** A264 45c multicolored .50 .40
**1346** A264 50c multicolored .65 .50
**1347** A264 60c multicolored .70 .60
**1348** A264 $1 multicolored 1.25 1.00
**1349** A264 $2 multicolored 2.25 2.25
**1350** A264 $3 multicolored 3.00 3.00
**1351** A264 $4 multicolored 4.25 4.25
**1352** A264 $5 multicolored 4.75 4.75
*Nos. 1341-1352 (12)* 18.95 17.75

**Size: 102x127mm, 127x102mm**

*Imperf*

**1353** A264 $6 multicolored 5.00 5.00
**1354** A264 $6 multicolored 5.00 5.00
**1355** A264 $6 multicolored 5.00 5.00

### Marine Life Type

Miniature Sheet

Marine life of the deeper reef: No. 1356a, Sargassum triggerfish. b, Tobaccofish. c, Longsnout butterflyfish. d, Cherubfish. e, Black jack head. f, Black jack tail, masked goby. g, Spotfin hogfish. h, Fairy basslet. i, Orangeback bass. j, Candy basslet. k, Blackcap basslet. l, Longspine squirrelfish. m, Jackknife fish. n, Bigeye. o, Short Bigeye. $6, Caribbean flashlight fish.

**1991, Dec. 5 Litho. *Perf. 14***

**1356** A270 50c Sheet of 15, #a.-o. 20.00 20.00

**Souvenir Sheet**

**1357** A270 $6 multicolored 14.00 14.00

### Christmas Art Type

Details, entire paintings or engravings by Martin Schongauer: 10c, Angel of the Annunciation. 35c, Madonna of the Rose Hedge. 50c, Madonna of the Rose Hedge, diff. 75c, Nativity. $1, Adoration of the Shepherds. $2, Nativity, diff. $4, Nativity, diff. $5, Symbol of St. Matthew. No. 1366, Nativity, diff. No. 1367, Adoration of the Shepherds.

**1991, Dec. 9 *Perf. 12***

**1358** A271 10c multicolored .45 .25
**1359** A271 35c multicolored .80 .25
**1360** A271 50c multicolored 1.10 .45
**1361** A271 75c multicolored 1.40 .75
**1362** A271 $1 multicolored 1.50 1.25
**1363** A271 $2 multicolored 2.25 2.25
**1364** A271 $4 multicolored 2.75 2.75
**1365** A271 $5 multicolored 2.75 2.75
*Nos. 1358-1365 (8)* 13.00 10.70

**Souvenir Sheets**

***Perf. 14½***

**1366** A271 $6 multicolored 6.25 6.25
**1367** A271 $6 multicolored 6.25 6.25

### Queen Elizabeth II's Accession to the Throne, 40th Anniv.

Common Design Type

**1992, Feb. 6 Litho. *Perf. 14***

**1368** CD348 60c multicolored .90 .35
**1369** CD348 75c multicolored 1.00 .40
**1370** CD348 $2 multicolored 2.10 1.60
**1371** CD348 $4 multicolored 3.00 3.00
*Nos. 1368-1371 (4)* 7.00 5.35

**Souvenir Sheets**

**1372** CD348 $6 Queen, rural scene 5.00 5.00
**1373** CD348 $6 Queen, harbor 5.00 5.00

### Railways of the World Type

Steam locomotives: No. 1379a, Medoc Class, Switzerland, 1857. b, Sterling, Great Britain, 1870. c, No. 90, France, 1877. d, Standard, US, 1880. e, Vittorio Emanuel II, Italy, 1884. f, Johnson Single, Great Britain, 1887. g, No. 999, US, 1893. h, Q1 Class, Great Britain, 1896. i, Claud Hamilton, Great Britain, 1900.

No. 1380a, Class P8, Germany, 1906. b, Class P, Denmark, 1935. c, Class Ps, US, 1926. d, Class 4-4-0, Ireland, 1932. e, Class GS, US, 1937. f, Class 12, Belgium, 1938. g, Class J, US, 1941. h, PA series, US, 1946. i, Class 4E1, South Africa, 1954.

No. 1381a, Tee 4-car train, Europe, 1957. b, FL9B, US, 1960. c, Shin-Kansen 16-car train, Japan, 1964. d, Class 103.1, Germany 1970. e, RTG 4-car train set, France, 1972. f, ETR 401 Pendolino 4-car train, Italy, 1976. g, Class 370, Great Britain, 1981. h, LRC, Canada, 1982. i, Mav BZMOT 601 1B1, Hungary, 1983.

No. 1382, ETR 401 four-car train, Italy, 1976. No. 1382A, Werner von Siemens' first electric locomotive, Germany, 1879.

**1992, Feb. 13 Litho. *Perf. 14***

**Sheets of 9**

**1379** A269 75c #a.-i. 6.00 6.00
**1380** A269 $1 #a.-i. 8.00 8.00
**1381** A269 $2 #a.-i. 16.00 16.00
*Nos. 1379-1381 (3)* 30.00 30.00

**Souvenir Sheets**

**1382** A269 $6 multicolored 5.50 5.50
**1382A** A269 $6 multicolored 5.50 5.50

1992 Summer Olympics, Barcelona — G101

Designs: 10c, Women's 100-meter backstroke. 15c, Women's handball. 25c, 4x100-meter relay. 35c, Hammer throw. 50c, 110-meter hurdles. 75c, Pole vault. $1, Volleyball. $2, Weight lifting. $5, Stationary rings. $6, Soccer. No. 1393, Baseball. No. 1394, Finn class single-handed dinghy.

**1992, Mar. 23 Litho. *Perf. 14***

**1383** G101 10c multicolored .65 .30
**1384** G101 15c multicolored .70 .30
**1385** G101 25c multicolored .80 .30
**1386** G101 35c multicolored .85 .35
**1387** G101 50c multicolored 1.00 .65
**1388** G101 75c multicolored 1.40 .85
**1389** G101 $1 multicolored 1.50 1.10
**1390** G101 $2 multicolored 2.50 2.50
**1391** G101 $5 multicolored 3.50 3.50
**1392** G101 $6 multicolored 3.75 3.75
*Nos. 1383-1392 (10)* 16.65 13.60

**Souvenir Sheets**

**1393** G101 $15 multicolored 10.50 10.50
**1394** G101 $15 multicolored 10.50 10.50

### Spanish Art Type

Paintings: 10c, The Surrender of Seville, by Francisco de Zurbaran. 35c, The Liberation of Saint Peter by an Angel, by Antonio de Pereda. 50c, Joseph Explains the Dreams of the Pharaoh, by Antonio del Castillo Saavedra, horiz. 75c, The Flower Vase, by Juan de Arellano. $1, The Duke of Pastrana, by Juan Carreno de Miranda. $2, $4, The Annunciation (diff. details), by Francisco Rizi. $5, Old Woman Seated, attributed to Antonio Puga. No. 1403, The Triumph of Saint Hermenegildo, by Francisco de Herrera, the Younger, vert. No. 1404, Relief of Genoa by the Second Marquis of Santa Cruz, by de Pereda, horiz.

**1992, Apr. 30 *Perf. 13***

**1395** A273 10c multicolored .30 .25
**1396** A273 35c multicolored .50 .35
**1397** A273 50c multicolored .75 .60
**1398** A273 75c multicolored 1.00 .75
**1399** A273 $1 multicolored 1.10 .90
**1400** A273 $2 multicolored 1.75 1.75
**1401** A273 $4 multicolored 2.75 2.75
**1402** A273 $5 multicolored 2.75 2.75
*Nos. 1395-1402 (8)* 10.90 10.10

**Size: 95x110mm**

*Imperf*

**1403** A273 $6 multicolored 10.00 10.00
**1404** A273 $6 multicolored 10.00 10.00

Granada '92.

Discovery of America, 500th Anniv. G102

Designs: 10c, Don Isaac Abarbanel (1437-1508), Spanish Minister of Finance. 25c, Columbus. 35c, Crewman sighting land. 50c, King Ferdinand and Queen Isabella. 60c, Columbus and Queen Isabella. $5, Santa Maria and map. No. 1411, Portrait of Columbus. No. 1412, Columbus at first landfall.

**1992, May 7 Litho. *Perf. 14***

**1405** G102 10c multicolored .25 .25
**1406** G102 25c multicolored .35 .30
**1407** G102 35c multicolored .55 .45
**1408** G102 50c multicolored .85 .85
**1409** G102 60c multicolored 1.00 1.00
**1410** G102 $5 multicolored 7.00 7.00
*Nos. 1405-1410 (6)* 10.00 9.85

**Souvenir Sheets**

**1411** G102 $6 multicolored 5.25 5.25
**1412** G102 $6 multicolored 5.25 5.25

World Columbian Expo '92, Chicago.

### USO Anniv. Type of 1992

**1992, May 7**

**1413** A277 10c James Cagney .55 .25
**1414** A277 15c Ann Sheridan .55 .25
**1415** A277 35c Jerry Colonna .55 .25
**1416** A277 50c Spike Jones .65 .35
**1417** A277 75c Edgar Bergen, Charlie McCarthy .80 .50
**1418** A277 $1 Andrews Sisters 1.25 .75
**1419** A277 $2 Dinah Shore 1.90 1.90
**1420** A277 $5 Bing Crosby 4.25 4.25
*Nos. 1413-1420 (8)* 10.50 8.50

**Souvenir Sheets**

**1421** A277 $6 Marlene Dietrich 5.25 5.25
**1422** A277 $6 Fred Astaire 5.25 5.25

### Hummingbird Type of 1992

Designs: 5c, Blue-headed male. 10c, Rufous-breasted hermit female. 20c, Blue-headed female. 45c, Green-throated carib male. 90c, Antillean crested male. $2, Purple-throated carib male. $4, Purple-throated carib female. $5, Antillean crested female. No. 1431, Rufous-breated hermit female. No. 1432, Green-throated carib female.

**1992, May 7**

**1423** A276 5c multicolored .25 .25
**1424** A276 10c multicolored .25 .25
**1425** A276 20c multicolored .25 .25
**1426** A276 45c multicolored .40 .40
**1427** A276 90c multicolored .85 .85
**1428** A276 $2 multicolored 2.00 2.00
**1429** A276 $4 multicolored 4.00 4.00
**1430** A276 $5 multicolored 5.00 5.00
*Nos. 1423-1430 (8)* 13.00 13.00

**Souvenir Sheets**

**1431** A276 $6 multicolored 6.00 6.00
**1432** A276 $6 multicolored 6.00 6.00

Genoa '92.

### Discovery of America Type

**1992 *Perf. 14½***

**1433** A275 $1 Coming ashore 1.25 1.25
**1434** A275 $2 Natives, ships 2.75 2.75

Walt Disney's Goofy, 60th Anniv. — G103

Scenes from Disney cartoon films: 5c, Father's Day Off, 1953. 10c, Cold War, 1951. 15c, Home Made Home, 1951. 25c, Get Rich Quick, 1951. 50c, Man's Best Friend, 1952. 75c, Aquamania, 1961. 90c, Tomorrow We Diet, 1951. $1, Teachers Are People, 1952. $2, The Goofy Success Story, 1955. $3, Double Dribble, 1946. $4, Hello Aloha, 1952. $5, Father's Lion, 1952. No. 1447, Father's Weekend, 1953, vert. No. 1448, Motor Mania, 1950. No. 1449, Hold That Pose, 1950, vert.

**1992, Nov. 24 Litho. *Perf. 14x13½***

**1435** G103 5c multicolored .25 .25
**1436** G103 10c multicolored .25 .25
**1437** G103 15c multicolored .25 .25
**1438** G103 25c multicolored .25 .25
**1439** G103 50c multicolored .40 .40
**1440** G103 75c multicolored .60 .60
**1441** G103 90c multicolored .70 .70
**1442** G103 $1 multicolored .75 .75
**1443** G103 $2 multicolored 1.50 1.50
**1444** G103 $3 multicolored 2.25 2.25
**1445** G103 $4 multicolored 2.75 2.75
**1446** G103 $5 multicolored 3.50 3.50
*Nos. 1435-1446 (12)* 13.45 13.45

**Souvenir Sheets**

***Perf. 13½x14***

**1447** G103 $6 multicolored 4.25 4.25
**1448** G103 $6 multicolored 4.25 4.25
**1449** G103 $6 multicolored 4.25 4.25

### Model Trains Type of 1992

Designs: 15c, #2220 Switcher locomotive, 2-inch gauge, US, 1910. 25c, 0-4-0 Engine, Bridge Port Line, O gauge, US, 1907. 50c, First Ives Co. electric toy locomotive, O gauge, US, 1910. 75c, J. C. Penney Special, standard gauge, US, 1920. $1, Cast metal locomotive, O gauge, US, 1916. $2, Copper-plated cast iron locomotive & tender pull toy, US, 1900. $4, Chromium plated locomotive #4689, standard gauge, US, 1928. $5, Ives long cab locomotive of the Olympian set, standard gauge, US, 1929.

No. 1458, Clockwork model, O gauge, US, 1910. No. 1459, American Flyer Statesman passenger train.

**1992, Oct. 22 Litho. *Perf. 14***

**1450** A279 15c multicolored .25 .25
**1451** A279 25c multicolored .40 .25
**1452** A279 50c multicolored .70 .45
**1453** A279 75c multicolored .90 .65
**1454** A279 $1 multicolored 1.00 .90
**1455** A279 $2 multicolored 1.75 1.75
**1456** A279 $4 multicolored 3.25 3.25
**1457** A279 $5 multicolored 3.25 3.25
*Nos. 1450-1457 (8)* 11.50 10.75

**Souvenir Sheet**

***Perf. 13***

**1458** A279 $6 multicolored 5.00 5.00
**1459** A279 $6 multicolored 5.00 5.00

Nos. 1458-1459 contain one 51x40mm stamp.

### New York City Type

Souvenir Sheet

**1992, Oct. 28 *Perf. 14***

**1460** A280 $6 Brooklyn Bridge 5.50 5.50

Postage Stamp Mega Event '92, New York City.

### Christmas Type of 1992

Details or entire paintings of The Annunciation by: 5c, Robert Campin. 15c, Melchior Broederlam. 25c, The Annunciation (2 panels), by Fra Filippo Lippi. 35c, Simone Martini. 50c, Fra Filippo Lippi, detail of angel. 75c, The Annunciation (Mary), by Fra Filippo Lippi. 90c, Albert Bouts. $1, D. Di Michelino. $2, Van der Weyden. $3, Sandro Botticelli, detail of angel. $4, Botticelli, detail of Mary. $5, Bernardo Daddi, horiz. No. 1472, Rogier Van der Weyden, vert. No. 1473, Hubert Van Eyck. No. 1474, Botticelli.

***Perf. 13½x14, 14x13½***

**1992, Nov. 16**

**1461** A281 5c multicolored .25 .25
**1462** A281 15c multicolored .30 .25
**1463** A281 25c multicolored .35 .25
**1464** A281 35c multicolored .45 .30
**1464A** A281 50c multicolored .65 .50
**1465** A281 75c multicolored .85 .70
**1466** A281 90c multicolored .90 .90
**1467** A281 $1 multicolored .90 .90
**1468** A281 $2 multicolored 1.90 1.90
**1469** A281 $3 multicolored 2.50 2.50
**1470** A281 $4 multicolored 3.00 3.00
**1471** A281 $5 multicolored 3.25 3.25
*Nos. 1461-1471 (12)* 15.30 14.70

**Souvenir Sheets**

**1472** A281 $6 multicolored 4.75 4.75
**1473** A281 $6 multicolored 4.75 4.75
**1474** A281 $6 multicolored 4.75 4.75

America's Cup Yacht Race — G104

Designs: 15c, Atalanta, Mischief, 1881. 25c, Valkyrie III, Defender. 35c, Shamrock IV, Resolute. 75c, Endeavour II, Ranger, 1937. $1, Sceptre, Columbia, 1958. $2, Australia II, Liberty. $4, Stars and Stripes, Kookaburra III. $5, New Zealand, Stars and Stripes, 1988. No. 1483, America, Aurora, 1851. No. 1484, Emblems of 1992 participants.

**1992, Oct. *Perf. 14***

**1475** G104 15c multicolored .55 .25
**1476** G104 25c multicolored .70 .25
**1477** G104 35c multicolored .85 .40
**1478** G104 75c multicolored 1.10 .70
**1479** G104 $1 multicolored 1.25 .90
**1480** G104 $2 multicolored 1.75 1.75
**1481** G104 $4 multicolored 2.75 2.75
**1482** G104 $5 multicolored 3.00 3.00
*Nos. 1475-1482 (8)* 11.95 10.00

**Souvenir Sheets**

**1483** G104 $6 multicolored 5.50 5.50
**1484** G104 $6 multicolored 5.50 5.50

Nos. 1483-1484 contains one 58x43mm stamp.

G105

Anniversaries and Events — G106

Designs: 25c, Zeppelin Viktoria Luise over Kiel Harbor. 50c, Space Shuttle Columbia. 75c, Flag, arms of Germany, Konrad Adenauer. $1.50, Giant anteater. No. 1489, Scarlet macaw, vert. No. 1490, Emblem of Intl. Conf. on Nutrition. $3, Wolfgang Amadeus Mozart. No. 1492, Berlin airlift. No. 1493, Space Shuttle Endeavour crew repairing Intelsat VI. $5, Hindenburg disaster. No. 1495, Adm. Richard E. Byrd's Ford Trimotor flying over North Pole, 1926. No. 1496, Map of Federal Republic of Germany, vert. No. 1497, Zeppelin Z.4 above clouds. No. 1498, First flight of space shuttle Endeavour. No. 1499, Scene from "The Marriage of Figaro." No. 1500, Jaguar.

**1992 Litho. Perf. 14**

**1485** G105 25c multicolored .65 .25
**1486** G105 50c multicolored .75 .35
**1487** G105 75c multicolored .75 .60
**1488** G105 $1.50 multicolored 1.10 1.10
**1489** G105 $2 multicolored 2.50 2.00
**1490** G105 $2 multicolored 1.50 1.50
**1491** G106 $3 multicolored 2.25 2.25
**1492** G105 $4 multicolored 3.00 3.00
**1493** G105 $4 multicolored 3.00 3.00
**1494** G105 $5 multicolored 3.75 3.75
**1495** G105 $5 multicolored 3.75 3.75
*Nos. 1485-1495 (11)* 23.00 21.55

**Souvenir Sheets**

***Perf. 13½***

**1496** G105 $6 multicolored 4.75 4.75
**1497** G105 $6 multicolored 4.75 4.75
**1498** G105 $6 multicolored 4.75 4.75

***Perf. 14***

**1499** G106 $6 multicolored 4.75 4.75
**1500** G105 $6 multicolored 4.75 4.75

Count Zeppelin, 75th anniv. of death (#1485, 1494, 1497). Intl. Space Year (#1486, 1493). Konrad Adenauer, 25th anniv. of death (#1487, 1492, 1496).Earth Summit, Rio de Janeiro (#1488-1489, 1500). Intl. Conf. on Nutrition, Rome (#1490). Wolfgang Amadeus Mozart, bicent. of death (in 1991) (#1491, 1499). Intl. Lions Intl., 75th anniv. (#1495). Space Year (#1498).

Issue dates: Nos. 1491, 1499, Oct. Nos. 1485-1486, 1490, 1493-1495, 1497, Nov. Nos. 1487-1489, 1492, 1496, 1500, Dec.

No. 1496 contains one 39x50mm stamp, Nos. 1497-1498 one 50x39mm stamp, No. 1500 one 52x40mm stamp.

## Entertainers Type of 1992

Miniature Sheet

Grammy award winners: No. 1501a, Leonard Bernstein. b, Ray Charles. c, Bob Dylan. d, Barbra Streisand. e, Frank Sinatra. f, Harry Belafonte. g, Aretha Franklin. h, Garth Brooks.

No. 1502a, Johnny Cash. b, Willie Nelson.

No. 1503a, Charlie Parker. b, Miles Davis.

**1992, Nov. 19 Perf. 14**

**1501** A286 90c Sheet of 8, #a.-h. 17.50 17.50

**Souvenir Sheets**

**1502** A286 $3 Sheet of 2, #a.-b. 6.50 6.50
**1503** A286 $3 Sheet of 2, #a.-b. 6.50 6.50

Dogs — G107

Designs: 35c, Irish Setter, Glendalough, Ireland. 50c, Boston terrier, State House, Boston, US. 75c, Beagle, Temple to Athena, Greece. $1, Weimaraner, Nesselwang, Germany. $3, Norwegian elkhound, Urnes Stave Church, Norway. $4, Mastiff, Great Sphinx, Egypt. No. 1510, Akita, Kyoto torii, Japan. No. 1511, Saluki, Rub'al Khali, Saudi Arabia. No. 1512, Shar pei, China. No. 1513, Bulldog, United Kingdom.

**1993, Jan. 20 Litho. Perf. 14**

**1504** G107 35c multicolored .65 .35
**1505** G107 50c multicolored .90 .65
**1506** G107 75c multicolored 1.25 .75
**1507** G107 $1 multicolored 1.60 1.10
**1508** G107 $3 multicolored 3.25 3.25
**1509** G107 $4 multicolored 3.50 3.50
**1510** G107 $5 multicolored 3.50 3.50
**1511** G107 $5 multicolored 3.50 3.50
*Nos. 1504-1511 (8)* 18.15 16.60

**Souvenir Sheets**

**1512** G107 $6 multicolored 4.75 4.75
**1513** G107 $6 multicolored 4.75 4.75

## Louvre Painting Type

Miniature Sheet

Details or entire paintings: No. 1514a, The Virgin and Child with Young St. John the Baptist, by Botticelli. b, The Buffet, by Chardin. c, The Provider, by Chardin. d, Erasmus, by Durer. e, Self-Portrait, by Durer. f, Jeanne of Aragon, by Raphael. g-h, La Belle Jardiniere (diff. details), by Raphael.

$6, Charles I, King of England, Hunting, by Van Dyck.

**1993, Mar. 8 Litho. Perf. 12**

**1514** A289 $1 Sheet of 8, #a.-h. + label 12.00 12.00

**Souvenir Sheet**

***Perf. 14½***

**1515** A289 $6 multicolored 7.75 7.75

No. 1515 contains one 55x88mm stamp.

Butterflies — G108

**1993, Apr. 13 Litho. Perf. 14**

**1516** G108 15c Polydamas swallowtail .35 .35
**1517** G108 35c Guaraguao skipper .50 .50
**1518** G108 45c Giant hair-streak .55 .55
**1519** G108 75c Malachite 1.00 1.00
**1520** G108 $1 Cloudless sulphur 1.25 1.25
**1521** G108 $2 Silver spot 2.50 2.50
**1522** G108 $4 St. Christopher's hair-streak 5.00 5.00
**1523** G108 $5 Common long-tail skipper 6.50 6.50
*Nos. 1516-1523 (8)* 17.65 17.65

**Souvenir Sheets**

**1524** G108 $6 Orion 8.00 8.00
**1525** G108 $6 Zebra 8.00 8.00

## Flowers Type of 1993

**1993, May**

**1526** A291 35c Hibiscus .65 .30
**1527** A291 35c Columbine .65 .30
**1528** A291 45c Red ginger .65 .35
**1529** A291 75c Bougainvillea .90 .60
**1530** A291 $1 Crown imperial 1.00 .75
**1531** A291 $2 Fairy orchid 1.60 1.60
**1532** A291 $4 Heliconia 2.75 2.75
**1533** A291 $5 Tulip 3.00 3.00
*Nos. 1526-1533 (8)* 11.20 9.65

**Souvenir Sheets**

**1534** A291 $6 Balloonflower, horiz. 4.50 4.50
**1535** A291 $6 Blackberry lily, horiz. 4.50 4.50

No. 1536 will not be assigned.

## Coronation of Queen Elizabeth II Type of 1993

Miniature Sheet

Designs: a, 35c, Official coronation photograph. b, 50c, Ampulla, spoon. c, $2, Queen, following coronation. d, $4, Queen, Prince Charles and his family, c. 1984.

$6, Portrait, by Pietro Annigoni, 1954.

**1993, June 2 Litho. Perf. 13½x14**

**1537** A293 Sheet, 2 each #a.-d. 10.50 10.50

**Souvenir Sheet**

***Perf. 14***

**1538** A293 $6 multicolored 5.50 5.50

No. 1538 contains one 28x42mm stamp.

## Anniversaries and Events Types of 1993

Designs: 50c, Telescope. 75c, Willy Brandt, Lyndon Johnson, 1961. $4, Radio telescope. $5, Willy Brandt, Eleanor Hulles, 1957. No. 1543, Copernicus. No. 1544, Willy, Rut Brandt.

**1993, July 1 Litho. Perf. 14**

**1539** A294 50c multicolored 1.40 .50
**1540** A295 75c multicolored 1.60 1.60
**1541** A294 $4 multicolored 4.00 4.00
**1542** A295 $5 multicolored 4.00 4.00
*Nos. 1539-1542 (4)* 11.00 10.10

**Souvenir Sheets**

**1543** A294 $6 multicolored 5.50 5.50
**1544** A295 $6 multicolored 5.50 5.50

Copernicus, 450th death anniv. (#1539, 1541, 1543). Willy Brandt, 1st death anniv. (#1540, 1542, 1544).

## Songbird Type of 1993

Miniature Sheet

Designs: No. 1545a, 15c, Painted bunting. b, 15c, White-throated sparrow. c, 25c, Common grackle. d, 25c, Royal flycatcher. e, 35c, Swallow tanager. f, 35c, Vermilion flycatcher. g, 45c, Black headed bunting. h, 50c, Rosebreasted grosbeak. i, 75c, Corn bunting. j, 75c, Rosebreasted thrush tanager. k, $1, Buff-throated saltator. l, $4, Plush-capped finch.

No. 1546, Bohemian waxwing. No. 1547, Pine grosbeak.

**1993, July 13**

**1545** A297 Sheet of 12, #a.-l. 14.00 14.00

**Souvenir Sheets**

**1546** A297 $6 multicolored 7.25 7.25
**1547** A297 $6 multicolored 7.25 7.25

## Seashell Type of 1993

Miniature Sheet

Designs: No. 1548a, 15c, Hawk wing conch. b, 15c, Music volute. c, 25c, Globe vase, deltoid rock shell. d, 35c, Spiny vase. e, 35c, Common sundial, common purple snail. f, 45c, Caribbean donax, gaudy asaphis. g, 45c, Mouse cone. h, 50c, Gold-mouthed triton. i, 75c, Tulip mussel, trigonal tivela. j, 75c, Common dove shell, chestnut latirus. k, $1, Wide-mouthed purpura. l, $4, Atlantic thorny oyster, Atlantic wing oyster.

No. 1549, Turkey wing. No. 1550, Zebra periwinkle.

**1993, July 19 Litho. Perf. 14**

**1548** A298 Sheet of 12, #a.-l. 13.00 13.00

**Souvenir Sheet**

**1549** A298 $6 multicolored 6.50 6.50
**1550** A298 $6 multicolored 6.50 6.50

## Picasso Type of 1993

Paintings: 15c, Painter and Model, 1928. $1, The Artist and His Model, 1963. $4, The Drawing Lession, 1925. $6, Picasso seated in front of canvas, 1956.

**1993, July 1 Litho. Perf. 14**

**1551** A299 15c multi, horiz. .60 .35
**1552** A299 $1 multi, horiz. 1.50 1.50
**1553** A299 $4 multi, horiz. 3.75 3.75
*Nos. 1551-1553 (3)* 5.85 5.60

**Souvenir Sheet**

**1554** A299 $6 multi, horiz. 5.00 5.00

## Olympics Type of 1993

Design: $6, Emil Zografski, ski jump.

**1993, July 1**

**1554A** A300 35c multi .30 .30
**1554B** A300 $5 multi 3.75 3.75
**1555** A300 $6 multicolored 5.00 5.00
*Nos. 1554A-1555 (3)* 9.05 9.05

## Polska '93 Type of 1993

Paintings: 75c, Gra w Gudziki, by Ludomir Slendzinski, 1928. $2, Pocalunek Mongoskiego Ksiecia, by S.I. Witkiewicz, 1915. $6, Allegory, by Jan Wydra, 1929.

**1993, July 1**

**1556** A301 75c multi, horiz. 1.25 1.25
**1557** A301 $2 multi, horiz. 3.50 3.50

**Souvenir Sheet**

**1558** A301 $6 multicolored 5.25 5.25

## Taipei '93 Type

Designs: 35c, Macao Palace, Hong Kong. 45c, Stone pixie, Ming Tomb, Nanjing. $1, Stone camels, Ming Tomb, Nanjing. $5, Stone lion and elephant, Ming Tomb, Nanjing.

Sculpture: No. 1563a, Nesting quail incense burner. b, Standing quail incense burner. c, Seated qilin incense burner. d, Pottery horse, Han Dynasty. e, Seated caparisoned elephant. f, Cow (imitation delft).

No. 1564, Sumatran tiger.

**1993 Litho. Perf. 14x13½**

**1559** A302 35c multi, horiz. .25 .25
**1560** A302 45c multi, horiz. .35 .35
**1561** A302 $1 multi, horiz. .75 .75
**1562** A302 $5 multi, horiz. 3.75 3.75
*Nos. 1559-1562 (4)* 5.10 5.10

**Miniature Sheet**

**1563** A302 $1.50 Sheet of 6, #a.-f. 11.00 11.00

**Souvenir Sheet**

***Perf. 13½x14***

**1564** A302 $6 multicolored 7.50 7.50

Nos. 1563a-1563f are horiz.

## With Bangkok '93 Emblem

Designs: 35c, Naga snakes, Chiang Mai's Temple, Thailand. 45c, Sri Mariamman Temple, Singapore. $1, Topiary, Hua Hin Resort, Thailand. $5, Pak Tai Temple, Cheung Chau Island.

Thai paintings: No. 1569a, Buddha's victory over Mara. b, Mythological elephant. c, Battle with Mara. d, Untitled work, by Panya Wijinthanasarn, 1984. e, Temple mural. f, Elephants in Pahcekha Buddha's Heaven.

No. 1570, Monkey.

**1993 Perf. 14x13½**

**1565** A302 35c multi, horiz. .25 .25
**1566** A302 45c multi, horiz. .35 .35
**1567** A302 $1 multi, horiz. .75 .75
**1568** A302 $5 multi, horiz. 3.75 3.75
*Nos. 1565-1568 (4)* 5.10 5.10

**Miniature Sheet**

**1569** A302 $1.50 Sheet of 6, #a.-f. 11.00 11.00

**Souvenir Sheet**

***Perf. 13½x14***

**1570** A302 $6 multicolored 6.50 6.50

Nos. 1569a-1569f are horiz.

## Indopex '93 Type

Designs: 35c, Natl. Museum, Central Jakarta, Indonesia. 45c, Sacred Wheel & Deer, Monastery. $1, Ramayana relief, Panataran Temple. $5, Candi Tikus, Trawulan, East Java.

Paintings: No. 1575a, Bullock Carts, bu Batara Lubis, 1951. b, Surat Irsa II, by A.D. Pirous, 1983. c, Self-portrait with Goat, by Kartika, 1987. d, The Cow-est Cow, by Ivan Sagito, 1987. e, Rain Storm, by Sudjana Kerton, 1984. f, Story of Pucuk Flower, by Effendi, 1972.

No. 1576, Banteng cattle.

**1993, Aug. 13 Litho. Perf. 14x13½**

**1571** A302 35c multicolored .25 .25
**1572** A302 45c multicolored .35 .35
**1573** A302 $1 multicolored .75 .75
**1574** A302 $5 multicolored 3.75 3.75
*Nos. 1571-1574 (4)* 5.10 5.10

**Miniature Sheet**

**1575** A302 $1.50 Sheet of 6, #a.-f. 11.00 11.00

**Souvenir Sheet**

**1576** A302 $6 multicolored 5.25 5.25

Nos. 1571-1576 are horiz.

1994 World Cup Soccer Championships, US — G109

Designs: 15c, Stuart McCall, Carlos Verri. 25c, Carlos Verri, Diego Maradona. 35c, S. Schillaci, J.P. Saldana. 45c, Ruud Gullit, Mark Wright. $1, Carlos Verri, Diego Maradona. $2, Zubizarreta, Fernandez, Albert. $4, Gheorghe Hagi, Paul McGrath. $5, Alberto Gorriz, Enzo Scifo. No. 1585, Schaefer Stadium, Foxboro, MA. No. 1586, Rudi Voeller, vert.

**1993, Sept. 7 Litho. *Perf. 14***

**1577** G109 15c multicolored .45 .25
**1578** G109 25c multicolored .45 .25
**1579** G109 35c multicolored .45 .25
**1580** G109 45c multicolored .45 .40
**1581** G109 $1 multicolored .75 .75
**1582** G109 $2 multicolored 1.50 1.50
**1583** G109 $4 multicolored 3.00 3.00
**1584** G109 $5 multicolored 3.75 3.75
*Nos. 1577-1584 (8)* 10.80 10.15

**Souvenir Sheets**

**1585** G109 $6 multicolored 5.00 5.00
**1586** G109 $6 multicolored 5.00 5.00

**Mickey Mouse, 65th Anniv. Type**

Movie clips: 15c, The Worm Turns, 1937. 35c, Mickey's Rival, 1936. 50c, The Pointer, 1939. 75c, Society Dog Show, 1939. $1, A Gentleman's Gentleman, 1941. $2, The Little Whirlwind, 1941. $4, Mickey Down Under, 1948. $5, R'coon Dawg, 1951.
No. 1595, Mickey's Garden, 1935, vert. No. 1596, Lonesome Ghosts, 1937.

***Perf. 13½x14, 14x13½***
**1993, Nov. 11 Litho.**

**1587** A305 15c multicolored .60 .25
**1588** A305 35c multicolored .80 .35
**1589** A305 50c multicolored 1.00 .60
**1590** A305 75c multicolored 1.40 1.00
**1591** A305 $1 multicolored 1.60 1.10
**1592** A305 $2 multicolored 2.25 2.25
**1593** A305 $4 multicolored 3.25 3.25
**1594** A305 $5 multicolored 3.25 3.25
*Nos. 1587-1594 (8)* 14.15 12.05

**Souvenir Sheets**

**1595** A305 $6 multicolored 5.50 5.50
**1596** A305 $6 multicolored 5.50 5.50

**Christmas Type of 1993**

Various details from Adoration of the Shepherds by Durer: 10c, 75c, $1, $4. No. 1605, $6, horiz.
Various details from Oddi Altarpiece by Raphael: 25c, 35c, 50c, $5. No. 1606, $6.

***Perf. 13½x14, 14x13½ (#1605)***
**1993, Nov. 22 Litho.**

**1597-1604** A306 Set of 8 11.00 11.00

**Souvenir Sheets**

**1605-1606** A306 Set of 2 11.00 11.00

**Eckener Type of 1993**

Designs: 50c, Graf Zeppelin over Rio De Janeiro. 75c, Dr. Hugo Eckener. $5, Eckener commanding Graf Zeppelin. $6, Eckener, Pres. Herbert Hoover.

**1993, Dec. 21 Litho. *Perf. 14***

**1607-1609** A307 Set of 3 5.25 5.25

**Souvenir Sheet**

**1610** A307 $6 multicolored 5.00 5.00

**Royal Air Force Anniv. Type of 1993**

Designs: 15c, Avro Lancaster. $5, Short Sunderland. $6, Supermarine Spitfire.

**1993, Dec. 21**

**1611** A308 15c multicolored .35 .25
**1612** A308 $5 multicolored 6.50 6.50

**Souvenir Sheet**

**1613** A308 $6 multicolored 7.00 7.00

**Automobile Anniv. Type**

Designs: 25c, 1955 Mercedes Benz 300SLR. 45c, 1957 Ford Thunderbird. $4, 1929 Ford 150A Station Wagon. $5, Mercedes Benz 540K.
Each $6: No. 1618, 1929 Mercedes Benz SSK. No. 1619, 1924 Ford Model T.

**1993, Dec. 21 Litho. *Perf. 14***

**1614-1617** A309 Set of 4 10.00 10.00

**Souvenir Sheets**

**1618-1619** A309 Set of 2 11.00 11.00

1st Benz 4-wheel car, 1st Ford engine, cent.

**First Gas Balloon Flight in America Type**

Designs: 35c, Blanchard's balloon crossing Delaware River. $3, Blanchard delivering Washington's passport of introduction. $6, Balloon in flight, vert.

**1993, Dec. 21 Litho. *Perf. 14***

**1620-1621** A310 Set of 2 3.50 3.50

**Souvenir Sheet**

**1622** A310 $6 multicolored 5.00 5.00

**Fine Art Type**

Details or entire paintings by Rembrandt: 15c, Hendrickje Stoffels as Flora. 35c, Lady & Gentlemen in Black. 50c, Aristotle with Bust of Homer. $5, Christ & the Woman of Samaria.
Details or entire paintings by Matisse: 75c, Interior: Flowers and Parakeets. $1, Goldfish. $2, The Girl with Green Eyes. $3, Still Life with a Plaster Figure.
Each $6: No. 1631, Anna Accused of Stealing the Kid, by Rembrandt. No. 1632, Tea in the Garden by Matisse, horiz.

***Perf. 13½x14, 14x13½***
**1993, Dec. 31 Litho.**

**1623-1630** A311 Set of 8 11.00 11.00

**Souvenir Sheets**

**1631-1632** A311 Set of 2 11.00 11.00

**Hong Kong '94 Type**

Designs: No. 1633, Hong Kong #426, jet at Kai Tak Airport. No. 1634, Junk, Kwaloon Bay, #975.
Chinese jade: No. 1635a, White jade brush washer. b, Archaic jade brush washer. c, Dark green jade brush washer. d, Green jade alms bowl. e, Archaic jade dog. f, Yellow jade brush washer.

**1994, Feb. 18 Litho. *Perf. 14***

**1633** A313 40c multicolored .90 .90
**1634** A313 40c multicolored .90 .90
*a.* Pair, #1633-1634 2.40 2.40

**Miniature Sheet**

**1635** A314 45c Sheet of 6, #a.-f. 7.50 7.50

Nos. 1633-1634 issued in sheets of of 5 pairs. No. 1634a is a continuous design. Nos. 1635a-1635f are horiz.
New Year 1994 (Year of the Dog) (#1635e).

Dinosaurs G110

15c, Spinosaurus. 35c, Apatosaurus. 45c, Tyrannosaurus rex. 55c, Triceratops. $1, Pachycephalosaurus. $2, Pteranodon. $4, Parasaurolophus. $5, Brachiosaurus.
Each $6: No. 1644, Brachiosaurus, vert. No. 1645, Tyrannosaurus, spinosaurus, vert.

**1994 Litho. *Perf. 14***

**1636-1643** G110 Set of 8 12.50 12.50

**Souvenir Sheets**

**1644-1645** G110 Set of 2 11.00 11.00

Mushrooms G111

Designs: 35c, Hygrocybe hypohaemacta. 45c, Cantherellus cinnabarinus. 50c, Marasmius haematocephalus. 75c, Mycena pura. $1, Gymnopilus russipes. $2, Galocybe cyanocephala. $4, Pleuteus chrysophlebius. $5, Chlorophyllum molybdites.
Each $6: No. 1654, Collybia fibrosipes. No. 1655, Xeromphalina tenuipes.

**1994**

**1646-1653** G111 Set of 8 10.00 10.00

**Souvenir Sheets**

**1654-1655** G111 Set of 2 9.50 9.50

**D-Day Type of 1994**

40c, Churchill bridgelayer in action. $2, Sherman "Firefly" attacks beach. $3, Churchill Crocodile flame thrower. $6, Sherman "Crab" flail tank.

**1994, Aug. 4 Litho. *Perf. 14***

**1656-1658** A318 Set of 3 5.00 5.00

**Souvenir Sheet**

**1659** A318 $6 multicolored 5.25 5.25

**First Manned Moon Landing, 25th Anniv. Type of 1994**

Miniature Sheet of 6

Tribute to Challenger crew: No. 1660a, Slidewire escape training. b, Christa A. McAuliffe. c, Challenger 51-L on pad LC39B. d, Gregory B. Jarvis. e, Ellison S. Onizuka. f, Ronald E. McNair.
$6, Judith A. Resnick, vert.

**1994, Aug. 4**

**1660** A319 $1.10 #a.-f. 7.50 7.50

**Souvenir Sheet**

**1661** A319 $6 multicolored 6.50 6.50

**PHILAKOREA '94 Type**

Designs: 40c, Onung Tomb, Korea. $1, Stone pagoda, Mt. Nansan, Kyongju. $4, Pusan Port.
Paintings, by Sin Yunbok, late Choson Dynasty, 1758: No. 1665a-1665b, Admiring spring in the Country. c-d, Women on Dano Day. e-f, Enjoying Lotuses While Listening to Music. g-h, Women by a Crystal Stream.
$6, Blacksmith's Shop, by Kim Duksin (1754-1822).

**1994, Aug. 4 *Perf. 14, 13½ (#1665)***

**1662-1664** A320 Set of 3 4.25 4.25

**Miniature Sheet of 8**

**1665** A321 $1 #a.-h. 9.50 9.50

**Souvenir Sheet**

**1666** A320 $6 multicolored 5.00 5.00

**Orchid Type of 1994**

15c, Cattleya aurantiaca. 25c, Blettia patula. 45c, Sobralia macrantha. 75c, Encyclia belizensis. $1, Sophrolaeliocattleya. $2, Encyclia frangrans. $4, Schombocattleya. $5, Brassolaeliocattleya.
Each $6: No. 1675, Brassavola nodosa. No. 1676, Orinithidium coccineum.

**1994, Aug. 7 *Perf. 14***

**1667-1674** A322 Set of 8 11.00 11.00

**Souvenir Sheets**

**1675-1676** A322 Set of 2 10.00 10.00

**1994 World Cup Soccer Type**

Miniature Sheet of 6

Designs: No. 1677a, Steve Mark, Grenada. b, Jurgen Kohler, Germany. c, Almir, Brazil. d, Michael Windischmann, US. e, Guiseppe Giannini, Italy. f, Rashidi Yekini, Nigeria.
Each $6: No. 1678, Kemari. No. 1679, The World Cup.

**1994, Aug. 11 *Perf. 14***

**1677** A323 75c #a.-f. 5.25 5.25

**Souvenir Sheets**

**1678-1679** A323 Set of 2 9.50 9.50

Disney's PHILAKOREA '94 — G112

15c, Mickey, Unjin Miruk, Kwanch Ok Temple. 35c, Goofy, statue of Admiral Yi, Chonju. 50c, Cousin Gus, Donald. 75c, Mickey playing flute. $1, Goofy, Tolharubang Grandfather statue. $2, Mickey, Minnie, Hyang-Wonjong. $4, Mickey, Unsan Pyolshin Festival. $5, Minnie, ceremonial fan.
Each $6: No. 1688, Minnie, Buk drum, vert. No. 1689, Mickey, Pugok Hawaii, vert.

**1994, Aug. 16 Litho. *Perf. 14x13½***

**1680-1687** G112 Set of 8 15.00 15.00

**Souvenir Sheets**

***Perf. 13½x14***

**1688-1689** G112 Set of 2 12.00 12.00

This set exists with very low face values.

**Fish Type of 1994**

Designs, each 75c: No. 1690a, Yellowtail snapper (b, e). b, Caribbean reef shark (a). c, Great barracuda. d, Redtail parrotfish. e, Blue tang. f, Queen angelfish. g, Red hind (h). h, Rock beauty. i, Queen parrotfish. j, Spanish hogfish. k, Spotted moray. l, Queen triggerfish (i).
Each 75c: No. 1691a, Pork fish (b). b, Blue chromis (a). c, Caribbean reef shark. d, Longspine squirrelfish. e, Foureye butterflyfish. f, Blue head. g, Royal gramma. h, Sharpnose puffer. i, Longsnout seahorse. j, Blackbar soldierfish (g, k). k, Redlip blenny. l, Rainbow wrasse.
Each $6: No. 1692, Rainbow wrasse, diff. No. 1693, Queen angelfish, diff.

**1994, Sept. 1 *Perf. 14***

**Miniature Sheets of 12**

**1690-1691** A324 Set of 2 24.00 24.00

**Souvenir Sheets**

**1692-1693** A324 Set of 2 12.00 12.00

**Intl. Olympic Committe Type of 1994**

Designs: 50c, Silke Renk, Germany, javelin, 1992. $1.50, Mark Spitz, US, swimming, 1972.
$6, Team Japan, Nordic combined, 1994.

**1994 *Perf. 14***

**1694** A325 50c multi, horiz. .40 .40
**1695** A325 $1.50 multi, horiz. 1.10 1.10

**Souvenir Sheet**

**1696** A326 $6 multicolored 5.00 5.00

**Intl. Year of the Family Type of 1994**

**1994**

**1697** A329 $1 Family of 5 .80 .80

**Order of the Caribbean Community Type**

Designs: 25c, Sir Shridath Ramphal, statesman, Guyana. 50c, William Demas, economist, Trinidad & Tobago. $2, Derek Walcott, writer, St. Lucia.

**1994, Sept. 1**

**1698-1700** A330 Set of 3 3.00 3.00

**Christmas Type of 1994**

Paintings, by Bartolome Murillo: 15c, The Annunciation. 35c, The Adoration of the Shepherds. No. 1703, 50c, Flight into Egypt. No. 1704, 50c, Virgin and Child with St. Rose. 75c, Virgin and Child. $1, Virgin of the Rosary. $4, The Holy Family.
Each $6: No. 1708, Adoration of the Shepherds. No. 1709, The Holy Family with a Little Bird.

**1994, Dec. 5 Litho. *Perf. 13½x14***

**1701-1707** A331 Set of 7 7.50 7.50

**Souvenir Sheets**

**1708-1709** A331 Set of 2 10.00 10.00

**Bird Type of 1995**

25c, Ground dove. 50c, White-winged dove, horiz. $2, Inca dove. $4, Mourning dove, horiz.

**1995, Jan. 10 *Perf. 14***

**1710-1713** A332 Set of 4 9.50 9.50

**English Touring Cricket, Cent. Type**

Designs: 50c, M.A. Atherton, England, horiz. 75c, C.E.L. Ambrose, Leeward Isl./W. Indies. $1, B.C. Lara, Trinidad/W. Indies. $3, West Indies Team, horiz.

**1995, Jan. 12**

**1714-1717** A333 Set of 3 4.00 4.00

**Souvenir Sheet**

**1718** A333 $3 multicolored 4.00 4.00

Capitals of the World — G113

Designs: a, London. b, Cairo. c, Vienna. d, Paris. e, Rome. f, Budapest. g, Moscow. h, Beijing. i, Tokyo. j, Wasington.

**1995, Mar. 10 Litho. *Perf. 14***

**Miniature Sheet of 10**

**1719** G113 $1 #a.-j. 10.00 10.00

New Year 1995 (Year of the Boar) — G114

Various stylized boars with different Chinese inscriptions: a, Smiling, purple legs. b, Smiling, red legs. c, Brown legs. d, Red legs.
$2, Two boars, horiz.

**1995, Apr. 21 Litho. *Perf. 14½***

**1720** G114 75c Block or horiz. strip of 4, #a.-d. 2.25 2.25
*e.* Souvenir sheet of 4, #1720a-1720d 3.00 3.00

**Souvenir Sheet**

**1721** G114 $2 multicolored 2.25 2.25

No. 1720 was issued in miniature sheets of 16 stamps.

**VE Day Type of 1995**

#1721A: b, Mitsubishi G4M1 "Betty." c, Aircraft carrying submarine I-14. d, Mitsubishi G3M1. e, Destroyer Akizuki. f, Battleship Kirishima. g, Cruiser Asigari.
Bombers: #1722: a, Avro Lancaster, Tallboy bomb. b, Junkers JU-88. c, B-25 Mitchell. d, B-17 Flying Fortress. e, Petlyakov Pe-2. f, Martin B-26 Marauder. g, Henkel He-111. h, Consolidated B-24 Liberator.
#1723, Pres. Truman displaying newspaper headline. #1723A, Aichi D3A1 "Val" dive bomber.

**1995, May 8 *Perf. 14***

**Miniature Sheets of 6 and 8**

**1721A** A336 $2 #b.-g. + label 9.50 9.50
**1722** A336 $2 #a.-h. + label 13.00 13.00

**Souvenir Sheets**

**1723** A336 $6 multicolored 5.25 5.25
**1723A** A336 $6 multicolored 6.00 6.00

Inscription in central label of No. 1721A misidentifies a Yokosuka MXY-7 Okha kamikaze plane.
No. 1723 contains one 57x42mm stamp.

**Scout Jamboree Type of 1995**

a, 75c, Beach scene, scout. b, $1, Mountains, sea, scout with pole. c, $2, Flag, scout salute.
$6, Snorkeling, fish.

**1995, May 8**

**1724** A337 Strip of 3, #a.-c. 3.00 3.00

**Souvenir Sheet**

**1725** A337 $6 multicolored 5.50 5.50

No. 1724 was issued in sheets of 9 stamps.

**UN, 50th Anniv. Type of 1995**

Designs: a, 75c, Building, UN flag. b, $1, Trygve Lie (1896-1968), Norway, 1st Secretary General. c, $2, Flag, member of UN peacekeeping force.
$6, Dove, emblem.

**1995, May 8**

**1726** A338 Strip of 3, #a.-c. 3.00 3.00

**Souvenir Sheet**

**1727** A338 $6 multicolored 4.75 4.75

No. 1726 is a continuous design and was issued in sheets of 9 stamps.

Marine Life of the Caribbean G115

No. 1728, each $1: a, Dolphins. b, Scorpion fish. c, Sea turtle, rock beauty. d, Butterflyfish, nurse shark. e, Angel fish. f, Grouper coney. g, Rainbow eel, moray eel. h, Sun flower-star, coral crab. i, Octopus.
No. 1729, each $1: a, Bull shark. b, Big white shark. c, Octopus. d, Barracuda (e). e, Moray eel (f, h, i). f, Spotted eagle ray. g, Gold-spotted snake. h, Stingray. i, Grouper.
$5, French angelfish. $6, Hammerhead shark.

**1995, May 3 Litho. *Perf. 14***

**Miniature Sheets of 9, #a-i**

**1728-1729** G115 Set of 2 18.00 18.00

**Souvenir Sheets**

**1730** G115 $5 multicolored 4.25 4.25
**1731** G115 $6 multicolored 5.00 5.00

Domesticated Animals — G116

Horses: 15c, Suffolk punch. 25c, Shetland pony. $1, Arab. $3, Shire horse.
Dogs, each 75c: No. 1736a, Shetland sheepdog. b, Bull terrier. c, Afghan. d, Scottish terrier. e, Labrador retriever. f, English springer spaniel. g, Samoyed. h, Irish setter. i, Border collie. j, Pekingese. k, Dachshund. l, Weimaraner.
Cats, each 75c: No. 1737a, Blue persian. b, Sorrel abyssinian. c, White angora. d, Brown burmese. e, Red tabby exotic shorthair. f, Seal-point birman. g, Korat. h, Norwegian forest cat. i, Lilac-point Balinese. j, British shorthair. k, Red self longhair. l, Calico manx.
Each $6: No. 1738, English setter. No. 1739, Seal-point colorpoint.

**1995, May 3**

**1732-1735** G116 Set of 4 3.50 3.50

**Miniature Sheets of 12, #a-l**

**1736-1737** G116 Set of 2 14.00 14.00

**Souvenir Sheets**

**1738-1739** G116 Set of 2 11.00 11.00

Sierra Club, Cent. — G117

No. 1740, each $1: a, Brown pelican. b, Northern spotted owl. c, Northern spotted owl in winter. d, Jaguarundi. e, Central American spider monkeys facing forward. f, Two Central American spider monkeys. g, Central American spider monkey. h, Wood stork. i, Maned wolves.
No. 1741, each $1, vert: a, Northern spotted owl. b, Brown pelican. c, Brown pelican up close. d, Jaguarundi up close. e, Jaguarundi. f, Maned wolf. g, Wood stork facing right. h, Wood stork facing left. i, Maned wolf up close.

**Miniature Sheets of 9, #a-i**

**1995, May 5**

**1740-1741** G117 Set of 2 25.00 25.00

FAO, 50th Anniv. — G118

No. 1742: a, 75c, Man working in field. b, $1, Woman working in field. c, $2, Two workers in field.
$6, Child with chopsticks.

**1995, May 8**

**1742** G118 Strip of 3, #a.-c. 3.00 3.00

**Souvenir Sheet**

**1743** G118 $6 multicolored 4.50 4.50

No. 1742 was issued in sheets of 9 stamps.

Rotary Intl., 90th Anniv. G119

**1995, May 8**

**1744** G119 $5 Paul Harris, emblem 3.75 3.75

**Souvenir Sheet**

**1745** G119 $6 Old, new emblems 4.50 4.50

**Queen Mother, 95th Anniv. Type of 1995**

No. 1746: a, Drawing. b, In black outfit. c, Formal portrait. d, In green outfit.
No. 1747, Speaking at Blitz Memorial.

**1995, May 8**

**1746** A344 $1.50 Strip or block of 4, #a.-d. 5.50 5.50

**Souvenir Sheet**

**1747** A344 $6 multicolored 5.50 5.50

No. 1746 was issued in sheets of 8 stamps.
Sheets of Nos. 1746-1747 exist with black border and text "In Memoriam - 1900-2002" in sheet margins.

**1996 Summer Olympics Type**

No. 1748, horiz: a, Rosemary Ackerman, East Germany, high jump. b, Li Ning, China, gymnastics. c, Denise Parker, US, archery.
No. 1749, horiz: a, Terry Carlisle, US, skeet shooting. b, Kathleen Nord, East Germany, 200-meter butterfly. c, Brigit Schmidt, East Germany, kayaking.
Each $6: No. 1750, George Foreman, US, boxing. No. 1751, Dan Gable US, Kikuo Wada, Japan, wrestling.

**1995, June 23**

**1748** A345 15c Strip of 3, #a.-c. .60 .60
**1749** A345 $3 Strip of 3, #a.-c. 9.50 9.50

**Souvenir Sheets**

**1750-1751** A345 Set of 2 11.00 11.00

G120

Designs: 10c, Brown pelican. 15c, Common stilt. 25c, Cuban trogan. 35c, Flamingo. 75c, Parrot. $1, Pintail duck. $2, Ringed kingfisher. $3, Strip-headed tanager.
No. 1760: a, Great blue heron. b, Jamaican tody. c, Laughing gull. d, Purple-throated carib. e, Red-legged thrush. f, Ruddy duck. g, Shoveler duck. h, West Indian red-bellied woodpecker.
Each $5: No. 1761, Blue-hooded Euphonia. No. 1762, Village weaver.

**1995, Sept. 5 Litho. *Perf. 14***

**1752-1759** G120 Set of 8 8.00 8.00

**Miniature Sheet of 8**

**1760** G120 $1 #a.-h. 8.00 8.00

**Souvenir Sheets**

**1761-1762** G120 Set of 2 10.50 10.50

Singapore '95 (#1760-1762). No. 1760d is mis-spelled.

Mickey's High Sea Adventure — G121

10c, Goofy carrying treasure chests, Donald. 35c, Mickey, Minnie at helm. 75c, Mickey, Donald, Goofy opening treasure chest. $1, Pirates confronting Mickey. $2, Mickey, Goofy, Donald in life boat. $5, Goofy using mop to fight enemy.

Each $6: No. 1769, Cannonballs being shot at Goofy, vert. No. 1770, Mickey on island, monkey pinching his nose, vert.

**1995, Oct. 2 Litho. *Perf. 14x13½***

**1763-1768** G121 Set of 6 7.00 7.00

**Souvenir Sheets**

***Perf. 13½x14***

**1769-1770** G121 Set of 2 10.00 10.00

**Nobel Prize Recipients Type of 1995**

No. 1770A, Derek Walcott, literature, 1992. No. 1770B, W. Arthur Lewis, economics, 1979.
No. 1771, each $1: a, Heike Kamerlingh Onnes, physics, 1913. b, Fridtjof Nansen, 1922. c, Sir Ronald Ross, physiology or medicine, 1902. d, Paul Müller, physiology or medicine, 1948. e, Allvar Gullstrand, physiology or medicine, 1911. f, Gerhart Hauptmann, literature, 1912. g, Hans Spemann, physiology or medicine, 1935. h, Cecil F. Powell, physics, 1950. i, Walther Bothe, physics, 1954.
No. 1772, each $1: a, Jules Bordet, physiology or medicine, 1919. b, René Cassin, peace, 1968. c, Verner von Heidenstam, literature, 1916. d, Jose Echegaray, literature, 1904. e, Otto Wallach, chemistry, 1910. f, Corneille Heymans, physiology or medicine, 1938. g, Ivar Giaever, physics, 1973. h, Sir William Cremer, peace, 1903. i, John W. Strutt, physics, 1904.
No. 1773, each $1: a, James Franck, physics, 1925. b, Tobias M.C. Asser, peace, 1911. c, Carl F.G. Spitteler, literature, 1919. d, Christiaan Eijkman, physiology or medicine, 1929. e, Ragnar Granit, physiology or medicine, 1967. f, Frederic Passy, peace, 1901. g, Louis Neel, physics, 1970. h, Sir William Ramsay, chemistry, 1904. i, Philip Noel-Baker, peace, 1959.
Each $6: No. 1774, Albert Schweitzer, peace, 1952. No. 1775, Willy Brandt, peace, 1971. No. 1776, Winston Churchill, literature, 1953.

**1995, Oct. 18 Litho. *Perf. 14***

**1770A** A354 75c multicolored .55 .55
**1770B** A354 75c multicolored .55 .55

**Miniature Sheets of 9, #a-i**

**1771-1773** A354 Set of 3 20.00 20.00

**Souvenir Sheets**

**1774-1776** A354 Set of 3 18.00 18.00

**Miniature Sheets**

Motion Pictures, Cent. — G122

Actresses, each $1: No. 1777a, Marion Davies. b, Marlene Dietrich. c, Lillian Gish. d, Bette Davis. e, Elizabeth Taylor. f, Veronica Lake. g, Ava Gardner. h, Grace Kelly. i, Kim Novak.
Romantic couples, each $1: No. 1778a, Nita Naldi, Rudolph Valentino. b, Ramon Novarro, Alice Terry. c, Frederic March, Joan Crawford. d, Clark Gable, Vivien Leigh. e, Barbara Stanwyck, Burt Lancaster. f, Warren Beatty, Natalie Wood. g, Spencer Tracy, Katharine Hepburn. h, Humphrey Bogart, Lauren Bacall. i, Omar Sharif, Julie Christie.
Each $6: No. 1779, Sophia Loren. No. 1780, Greta Garbo, John Gilbert, horiz.

**1995, Nov. 3 *Perf. 13½x14***

**1777-1778** G122 Set of 2 15.00 15.00

**Souvenir Sheets**

***Perf. 13½x14, 14x13½***

**1779-1780** G122 Set of 2 10.00 10.00

Classic Racing Cars G123

Designs: 10c, 1990's Williams-Renault Formula 1. 25c, 1980's Le Mans Porsche 956. 35c, 1970's Lotus "John Player Special." 75c, 1960's Ford GT 40. $2, 1950's Mercedes Benz W196. $3, 1920's Mercedes SSK.

$6, 1971 Tyrrell-Ford Fourmula 1.

**1995, Nov. 7** *Perf. 14*

**1781-1786** G123 Set of 6 6.75 6.75

**Souvenir Sheet**

**1787** G123 $6 multicolored 6.00 6.00

Local Transportation — G124

**1995, Nov. 7**

**1788** G124 35c Donkey .60 .30
**1789** G124 75c Bus 1.50 1.00

**Miniature Sheet**

Sailing Ships — G125

Designs: No. 1790a, Preussen. b, Japanese junk. c, Pirate ship. d, Mayflower. e, Chinese junk. f, Santa Maria.

$5, Spanish galleon.

**1995, Nov. 7**

**1790** G125 $1 Sheet of 6, #a.-f. 6.00 6.00

**Souvenir Sheet**

**1791** G125 $5 multicolored 5.00 5.00

No. 1791 contains one 57x42mm stamp.

### Christmas Type of 1995

Details or entire paintings: 10c, Immaculate Conception, by De Cosimo. 15c, St. Michel Dedicating Arms to the Madonna, by Le Nain. 35c, Annunciation, by de Credi. 50c, The Holy Family, by Jordaens. $3, Madonna and Child, by Lippi. $5, Madonna and Child with Ten Saints, by Fiorentino.

Each $6: No. 1798, Adoration of the Shepherds, by Van Oost. No. 1799, Holy Family, by Del Sart.

**1995, Nov. 28** *Perf. 13½x14*

**1792-1797** A356 Set of 6 8.00 8.00

**Souvenir Sheets**

**1798-1799** A356 Set of 2 11.00 11.00

New Year 1996 (Year of the Rat) — G126

Stylized rats: No. 1800: a, blue & multi. b, violet & multi. c, red & multi. d, green & multi.

$2, Two rats, horiz.

**1996, Jan. 2** **Litho.** *Perf. 14½*

**1800** G126 75c Block of 4, #a.-d. 2.25 2.25

**Miniature Sheet**

**1801** G126 75c Sheet of 1 #1800 2.25 2.25

**Souvenir Sheet**

**1802** G126 $2 multicolored 1.75 1.75

No. 1800 was issued in sheets of 16 stamps.

### Works by Dürer and Rubens Type of 1996

Details or entire work: 15c, The Centaur Family, by Dürer. 35c, Oriental Ruler Seated, by Dürer. 50c, The Entombment, by Dürer. 75c, Man in Armor, by Rubens. $1, Peace Embracing Plenty, by Rubens. $2, Departure of Lot, by Rubens. $3, The Four Evangelists, by Rubens. No. 1810, $5, Knight, Death and Devil, by Dürer.

No. 1811, The Father of the Church, by Rubens. $6, St. Jerome, 1514 engraving, by Dürer.

**1996, Jan. 29** **Litho.** *Perf. 14*

**1803-1810** A360 Set of 8 10.00 10.00

**Souvenir Sheets**

**1811** A360 $5 multicolored 4.50 4.50
**1812** A360 $6 multicolored 4.50 4.50

Disney Holidays — G127

Disney characters celebrating: 25c, New Year's Day, "Hopping John" Feast. 50c, May Day. 75c, Independence Day. 90c, Halloween. $3, Thanksgiving. $4, Hanukkah.

Each $6: No. 1819, Caribbean Carnival. No. 1820, St. Patrick's Day Parade, vert.

**1996, Apr. 17** **Litho.** *Perf. 14x13½*

**1813-1818** G127 Set of 6 10.00 10.00

**Souvenir Sheets**

*Perf. 14x13½, 13½x14*

**1819-1820** G127 Set of 2 13.00 13.00

Sites in China — G128

No. 1821, each $1: a, Entryway to hall, Imperial Palace. b, Great Wall's eastern end, Shanhaiguan. c, Fortress in Great Wall, Shanhaiguan. d, Gate of Heavenly Peace, Tiananmen, main entrance to Imperial City.

No. 1822, each $1: a, Mausoleum of Dr. Sun Yat-Sen, Nanjing. b, Summer Palace, Beijing. c, Temple of Heaven, Beijing. d, Hall of Supreme Harmony, Forbidden City, Beijing.

Each $6: No. 1823, Great Wall of China. No. 1824, Marble boat, Summer Palace, Beijing. Illustration reduced.

**1996, May 8** *Perf. 13*

**Sheets of 4, #a-d**

**1821-1822** G128 Set of 2 13.00 13.00

**Souvenir Sheets**

**1823-1824** G128 Set of 2 10.50 10.50

China '96, 9th Asian Intl. Philatelic Exhibition (#1821-1822).

No. 1823 contains one 40x51mm stamp, No. 1824 one 51x40mm stamp.

See No. 1881.

### Queen Elizabeth II, 70th Birthday Type of 1996

Designs: a, 35c, Portrait in blue dress. b, $2, Wearing crown. c, $4, Windsor Castle.

$6, Standing in front of palace.

**1996, May 8** **Litho.** *Perf. 13½x14*

**1825** A362 Strip of 3, #a.-c. 4.75 4.75

**Souvenir Sheet**

**1826** A362 $6 multicolored 4.50 4.50

No. 1825 was issued in sheets of 9 stamps with each strip in a different order.

Flowers — G129

35c, Camellia "Apple Blossom." 90c, Camellia japonica "Extravaganza." $1, Chrysanthemum "Primrose Dorothy Else." $2, Dahlia "Brandaris."

No. 1831: a, Odontoglossum. b, Cattleya. c, Paphiopedilum "Venus's Slipper." d, Laeliocattleya "Marysville."

No. 1832: a, Fushcia "Citation." b, Fuchsia "Amy Lye." c, Clysonimus butterfly. d, Digitalis purpurea "Foxglove" (h). e, Lilium martagon "Martagon Lily." f, Tulip "Couleur Cardinal." g, Galanthus nivalis "Snowdrop." h, Rose "Superstar." i, Crocus "Dutch Yellow Mammouth." j, Lilium speciosum Japanese lily. k, Lilium "Joan Evans." l, Rose "Rosemary Harkness."

$5, Narcissus "Rembrandt." $6, Gladiollus "Flowersong."

**1996, June 12** **Litho.** *Perf. 14*

**1827-1830** G129 Set of 4 5.00 5.00
**1831** G129 75c Strip of 4, #a.-d. 3.50 3.50
**1832** G129 75c Sheet of 12, #a.-l. 9.00 9.00

**Souvenir Sheets**

**1833** G129 $5 multicolored 4.50 4.50
**1834** G129 $6 multicolored 5.00 5.00

No. 1831 issued in sheets of 12 stamps.

UNICEF, 50th Anniv. G130

Letters spelling UNICEF and: 75c, Child smiling. $2, Child eating. $3, Child reading.

$6, Child on mother's back.

**1996, June 26**

**1836-1838** G130 Set of 3 4.50 4.50

**Souvenir Sheet**

**1839** G130 $6 multicolored 4.50 4.50

#1838 is unassigned.

Jerusalem, 3000th Anniv. G131

Flowers and: a, $1, Pool of Bethesda. b, $2, Damascus Gate. c, $3, Church of All Nations, Gethsemane.

$6, Church of the Holy Sepulchre.

**1996, June 26**

**1840** G131 Sheet of 3, #a.-c. 4.50 4.50

**Souvenir Sheet**

**1841** G131 $6 multicolored 4.50 4.50

### Radio, Cent. Type of 1996

Entertainers: 35c, Ed Wynn. 75c, Red Skelton. $1, Joe Penner. $3, Jerry Colonna.

$6, Bob Elliott, Ray Goulding, horiz.

**1996, June 26** *Perf. 13½x14*

**1842-1845** A367 Set of 4 3.75 3.75

**Souvenir Sheet**

*Perf. 14x13½*

**1846** A367 $6 multicolored 4.50 4.50

### Olympics Type of 1996

35c, Memorial Coliseum, Los Angeles, 1994. 75c, Connie Carpenter-Phinney, US. $2, Mohamed Bouchighe, Algeria, vert. $3, Jackie Joyner-Kersee, US.

No. 1851, Gymnasts, vert, each $1: a, Julianne McNamara, US. b, Takuti Hayata, Japan. c, Nikolai Andrianov, Russia. d, Mitch Gaylord, US. e, Ludmilla Tourischeva, Russia. f, Karin Janz, Germany. g, Peter Kormann, US. h, Sawao Kato, Japan. i, Nadia Comaneci, Romania.

No. 1852, Equestrian participants, vert, each $1: a, Josef Neckermann, Germany. b, Harry Boldt, Germany. c, Elena Petouchkova, Russia. d, Alwin Schockemoehle, Germany. e, Hans Winkler, Germany. f, Joe Fargis, US. g, David Broome, Great Britain. h, Reiner Klimke, Germany. i, Richard Meade, Great Britain.

No. 1853, Young Japanese girl, vert. No. 1854, William Steinkraus, US.

**1996, July 15** *Perf. 14*

**1847-1850** A364 Set of 4 4.50 4.50

**Sheets of 9, #a-i**

**1851-1852** A364 Set of 2 13.50 13.50

**Souvenir Sheets**

**1853** A364 $5 multicolored 3.75 3.75
**1854** A364 $6 multicolored 4.50 4.50

Classic Cars — G132

No. 1855: a, Delaunay-Belleville HB6, France. b, Bugatti Type-15, Italy. c, Mazda Type 800, Japan. d, Mercedes 24/100/140 Sport, Germany. e, MG K3 Rover, England. f, Plymouth Fury, US.

No. 1856: a, 35c, Chevrolet Belair Convertible, US. b, 75c, Rolls Royce Torpedo, England. c, $1, Nissan Type "Cepric," Japan. d, VIP car. e, Mercedes Benz 500k, Germany. f, Bugatti Type-13, Italy.

$5, Bugatti "Roadster" Type-55. $6, Lincoln Type-L, US.

**1996, July 25** **Litho.** *Perf. 14*

**1855** G132 $1 Sheet of 6, #a.-f. 4.50 4.50
**1856** G132 Sheet of 6, #a.-f. 5.75 5.75

**Souvenir Sheets**

**1857** G132 $5 multicolored 3.75 3.75
**1858** G132 $6 multicolored 4.50 4.50

Nos. 1857-1858 each contain one 51x39mm stamp.

Ships G133

Traditional Grenada schooners: 35c, Red and white. 75c, Blue and white.

No. 1861, Ancient ships, each $1: a, Athenian war triremes, 1000BC. b, Egyptian Nile trader, 30BC. c, Bangladesh dinghi, 3100BC. d, Queen Hatshepsut warship, 1476BC. e, Chinese junk, 200BC. f, Polynesian voyager, 600BC.

No. 1862, Ocean liners, each $1: a, Europa, Germany, 1957. b, Lusitania, England, 1906. c, Queen Mary, England, 1936. d, Bianca C, Italy. e, SS France, 1932. f, Orion, England, 1915.

$5, Queen Elizabeth 2, England, 1969. $6, Viking ship, 610BC.

**1996, Aug. 14**

**1859** G133 35c multicolored .25 .25
**1860** G133 75c multicolored .55 .55

**Sheets of 6, #a-f**

**1861-1862** G133 Set of 2 9.00 9.00

**Souvenir Sheets**

**1863** G133 $5 multicolored 3.75 3.75
**1864** G133 $6 multicolored 4.50 4.50

No. 1863 contains one 51x42mm stamp, No. 1864 one 42x51mm stamp.

Famous Composers G134

Composer, work illustrated: No. 1865, each $1: a, Bèla Bartòk, "Mikrokosmos," 1926. b, Giacomo Puccini, "Madame Butterfly," 1904. c, George Gershwin, "Rhapsody in Blue," 1923. d, Leonard Bernstein, "West Side Story", 1957. e, Kurt Weill, "Three Penny Opera," 1928. f, John Cage, "Music of Changes," 1951. g, Aaron Copland, "El Salón Mexico," 1936. h, Sergei Prokofiev, "Peter and the Wolf," 1936. i, Igor Stravinsky, "Rite of Spring," 1913.

No. 1866, each $1: a, Felix Mendelssohn, overture to "Midsummer Night's Dream," 1826. b, Franz Schubert, "Die Forelle" (The Trout) D.550, 1817. c, Franz Joseph Haydn, "String Quartet in D Major," Op. 64 No. 5 (Lark), 1790. d, Robert Schumann, "Spring," Symphony No. 1, Op. 38, 1841. e, Ludwig Van Beethoven, "Moonlight" sonata Op. 27, No. 2. f, Gioacchino Rossini, "William Tell," 1829. g, George Frederick Handel, "Royal Fireworks Music," 1749. h, Peter Ilyich Tchaikovsky, "Swan Lake," Op.20, 1876. i, Frederic Chopin, "Fantasia," in F minor, Op. 49, 1840-41.

$5, Richard Strauss. $6, Mozart, "Jupiter" symphony in C major.

**1996, Aug. 26 Sheets of 9, #a-i**

**1865-1866** G134 Set of 2 14.00 14.00

**Souvenir Sheets**

**1867** G134 $5 multicolored 3.75 3.75
**1868** G134 $6 multicolored 4.50 4.50

Trains G135

No. 1869, each $1.50: a, Pacific Blue Peter, British Eastern. b, Class P36 4-8-4, Russia. c, Class OJ 2-10-2, China. d, Class 12 4-4-2, Belgium. e, Challenger Class 4-6-6-4, US. f, Class 25 4-8-4 Condenser, South Africa.

No. 1870, each $1.50: a, Federal Railways Class 38 4-6-0, Germany. b, Duchess of Hamilton Class 4-6-2, London & Glasgow. c, Class WP 4-6-2, Indian State Railways. d, Class 141R "L'Americane" 282, France (American-built). e, Class A4 4-6-2 Mallard, England. f, Deutche Reichsbahn Class 18 4-6-2, Germany.

$5, Cornish Rivera Express, King Class 4-6-2, Britain. $6, Caledonian "Royal Scot Class," 4-6-0, Britain.

**1996, Aug. 28 Sheets of 6, #a-f**

**1869-1870** G135 Set of 2 13.50 13.50

**Souvenir Sheets**

**1871** G135 $5 multicolored 3.75 3.75
**1872** G135 $6 multicolored 4.50 4.50

**Christmas Type of 1996**

Details of painting, Suffer Little Children to Come Unto Me, by Van Dyck: 15c, Child with beads over shoulder. 25c, Christ anointing head of child. $1, Mother holding infant, father, children. $1.50, Christ, disciples. $2, Father, infant. $4, Christ, children, family.

Each $6: No. 1879, Entire painting, horiz. No. 1880, Adoration of the Shepherds, by Bernaldo Strozzi, horiz.

**1996, Nov. 18 Litho. *Perf. 13½x14***

**1873-1878** A377 Set of 6 7.00 7.00

**Souvenir Sheets**

**1879-1880** A377 Set of 2 9.00 9.00

Souvenir Sheet

China '96 — G136

Painting depicting scene from "Hong Lou Meng."

**1996, May 8 Litho. *Perf. 13x13½***

**1881** G136 $2 multicolored 4.00 4.00

No. 1881 was not available until March 1997.

Hong Kong Past and Present G137

No. 1882, Man Ho Temple, each $3: a, 1841. b, 1983.

No. 1883, City of Victoria with view of St. John's Cathedral, each $3: a, 1886. b, 1983.

No. 1884, Victoria Harbor, Hong Kong, each $3: a, 1858. b, 1983.

No. 1885, each $3: a, Treaty of Nanking, 1842. b, Margaret Thatcher signing Joint Declaration, 1984.

No. 1886, Victoria Harbor, each $3: a, Older black & white photograph. b, Modern photograph.

**1997, Feb. 12 Litho. *Perf. 14***

**Sheets of 2, #a-b**

**1882-1886** G137 Set of 5 25.00 25.00

Hong Kong '97.

**UNESCO Type of 1997**

Designs: 15c, Kyoto, Japan. 25c, Roman ruins at Trier, Germany. $1, Mount Taishan, China. $1.50, Scandola Nature Reserve, France. $2, Fortress Wall, Dubrovnik, Croatia. $4, Angra Do Heroismo, Portugal.

No. 1893, vert, each $1: a, Sanctuary of Congonhas, Brazil. b, Cartagena, Colombia. c, City of Puebla, Mexico. d, Mayan Ruins, Copan, Honduras. e, Monastery of Popocatepetl, Mexico. f, Galapagos Islands, Ecuador. g, Waterfall, La Amisted Natl. Park, Costa Rica. h, Glaciares Natl. Park, Argentina.

No. 1894, vert, each $1: a, b, c, Kyoto, Japan. d, Ayutthaya, Thailand. e, Temple of Borobudur, Indonesia. f, Monuments, Pattadakal, India. g, Polonnaruwa, Sri Lanka. h, Sagarmatha Natl. Park, Nepal.

No. 1895, each $1.50: a, Cathedral of Notre Dame, France. b, Timbered house, Maulbronn, Germany. c, Himeji-Jo, Japan. d, Ruins, Delphi, Greece. e, Palace of Fontainebleau, France.

Each $6: No. 1896, Temple, Chengde, China. No. 1897, Pre-hispanic city of Teotihuacan, Mexico. No. 1898, Mont St. Michel, France.

**1997, Apr. 3 Litho. *Perf. 14***

**1887-1892** A382 Set of 6 6.75 6.75

**Sheets of 8**

**1893-1894** A382 Set of 2 12.00 12.00

**Sheet of 5 + Label**

**1895** A382 #a.-e. 5.75 5.75

**Souvenir Sheets**

**1896-1898** A382 Set of 3 15.00 15.00

Dogs and Cats G138

Dogs: 35c, Springer spaniel. 75c, Doberman pinscher. $1, Italian spinone, vert. $2, Cocker spaniel, vert.

No. 1903: a, Leonberger. b, Newfoundland. c, Boxer. d, St. Bernard. e, Silky terrier. f, Miniature schnauzer.

No. 1904, Golden retriever puppy.

**1997, Apr. 10**

**1899-1902** G138 Set of 4 3.00 3.00

**Sheet of 6**

**1903** G138 $1.50 #a.-f. 6.75 6.75

**Souvenir Sheet**

**1904** G138 $6 multicolored 6.75 6.75

**1997, Apr. 10**

Cats: 45c, Abyssinian blue. 50c, Bermese cream, vert. 90c, Persian tortoiseshell and white. $3, Oriental shorthair red Agouti tabby, vert.

No. 1909: a, Siamese chocolate point. b, Oriental shorthair white. c, Burmese sable. d, Abysinian tabby. e, Persian shaded silver. f, Tonkinese natural mink.

**1905-1908** G138 Set of 4 3.75 3.75

**Sheet of 6**

**1909** G138 $1.50 #a.-f. 6.75 6.75

**Souvenir Sheet**

**1910** G138 $6 Sphinx, vert. 6.75 6.75

**Prehistoric Animal Type of 1997**

Designs: 45c, Stegosaurus. 90c, Diplodocus. $1, Pteranodon, vert. $2, Deinonychus, ankylasaurus, vert.

No. 1915: a, Rhamphorhynchus, brachiosaurus (c, d, e,). b, Archaeopteryx. c, Anurognathus. d, Albertosaurus (f). e, Herrerasaurus. f, Platyhystrix.

Each $6: No. 1916, Hypacrosaurus. No. 1917, Apatosaurus, allosaurus, vert.

**1997, Apr. 15 Litho. *Perf. 14***

**1911-1914** A385 Set of 4 3.00 3.00
**1915** A385 $1.50 Sheet of 6, #a.-f. 6.75 6.75

**Souvenir Sheets**

**1916-1917** A385 Set of 2 9.00 9.00

**Queen Elizabeth II, Prince Philip, 50th Wedding Anniv. Type of 1997**

No. 1918: a, Colored portrait. b, Royal Arms. c, Black and white portrait. d, Black and white portrait in royal attire. e, Sandringham House. f, Queen in blue dress, Prince in uniform.

$6, Wedding portrait.

**1997, May 28 Litho. *Perf. 14***

**1918** A386a $1 Sheet of 6, #a.-f. 4.75 4.75

**Souvenir Sheet**

**1919** A386a $6 multicolored 4.75 4.75

**Paintings by Hiroshige Type of 1997**

No. 1920: a, Koume Embankment. b, Azuma Shrine and the Entwined Camphor. c, Yanagishima. d, Inside Akiba Shrine, Ukeji. e, Distant View of Kinryuzan Temple and Azuma Bridge. f, Night View of Matsuchiyama and the San'ya Canal.

Each $6: No. 1921, Five Pines, Onagi Canal. No. 1922, Spiral Hall, Five Hundred Rakan Temple.

**1997, May 28 *Perf. 13½x14***

**1920** A387 $1.50 Sheet of 6, #a.-f. 8.50 8.50

**Souvenir Sheets**

**1921-1922** A387 Set of 2 11.00 11.00

**Heinrich von Stephan Type of 1997**

**1997, May 28 Litho. *Perf. 14***

Portrait of Von Stephan and: No. 1923: a, The Pony Express, 1860-61. b, UPU emblem. c, Steam locomotive postal delivery, 1800's.

$6, Camel courier, Baghdad.

**1923** A388 $1.50 Sheet of 3, #a.-c. 2.75 2.75

**Souvenir Sheet**

**1924** A388 $6 multicolored 4.50 4.50

PACIFIC 97.

**Paul P. Harris Type of 1997**

Designs: $3, Women in Burkina Faso pumping well water, portrait of Harris.

$6, Early Rotary parade float.

**1997, May 28**

**1925** A389 $3 multicolored 2.25 2.25

**Souvenir Sheet**

**1926** A389 $6 multicolored 4.50 4.50

**Grimm's Fairy Tale and Mother Goose Types of 1997**

Scenes from "The Fox and the Geese:" No. 1927: a, Fox, geese. b, Geese singing as fox waves knife, fork. c, Fox asleep, geese celebrating. No. 1928, Fox lurking in forest, horiz.

No. 1929, Girl with black sheep.

**1997, May 28 *Perf. 13½x14***

**1927** A391 $2 Sheet of 3, #a.-c. 4.50 4.50

**Souvenir Sheets**

***Perf. 14x13½, 14***

**1928** A391 $6 multicolored 4.50 4.50
**1929** A392 $6 multicolored 4.50 4.50

1998 Winter Olympic Games, Nagano G139

Designs: 90c, Downhill skier. $2, Luge. $3, Male figure skater. $5, Speed skater in blue hat.

No. 1934: a, Downhill skier in air. b, Freestyle skier. c, Curling. d, Ski jumper. e, Bobsled. f, Biathlon. g, Speed skater in yellow and red hat. h, Hockey. i, Cross-country skier.

Each $6: No. 1935, Luge, diff., vert. No. 1936, Female figure skater.

**1997, June 26 *Perf. 14***

**1930-1933** G139 Set of 4 8.25 8.25
**1934** G139 $1 Sheet of 9, #a.-i. 6.75 6.75

**Souvenir Sheets**

**1935-1936** G139 Set of 2 9.50 9.50

**Return of Hong Kong to China Type**

Chinese flag in foreground, "Hong Kong" in English and Chinese with city scene showing through words: $1, Night scene. $1.25, Daytime view of skyscrapers. $1.50, Skyline at night, horiz. $2, View of harbor, horiz.

**1997, July 1**

**1937-1940** A394 Set of 4 4.50 4.50

Nos. 1937-1938 were issued in sheets of 4. Nos. 1939-1940 are 59x28mm and were issued in sheets of 3.

Fish G140

Designs: 10c, Wimplefish. 15c, Clown triggerfish. 25c, Ringed emperor angelfish. 35c, Hooded butterfly fish. 45c, Semicircle angelfish. 75c, Scribbled angelfish. 90c, Threadfin butterfly fish. $1, Clown surgeonfish.

**1997, July 22 Litho. *Perf. 14***

**1941** G140 10c multicolored .25 .25
**1942** G140 15c multicolored .25 .25
**1943** G140 25c multicolored .25 .25
**1944** G140 35c multicolored .25 .25
**1945** G140 45c multicolored .35 .35
**1946** G140 75c multicolored .55 .55
**1947** G140 90c multicolored .70 .70
**1948** G140 $1 multicolored .75 .75
*Nos. 1941-1948 (8)* 3.35 3.35

Winnie the Pooh G141

#1949: a, Winnie the Pooh. b, Kanga & Roo. c, Eeyore. d, Tigger. e, Piglet & Gopher. f, Rabbit.

$6, Christopher Robin.

**1997, Aug. 7 Litho. *Perf. 13½x14***

**1949** G141 $1 Sheet of 6, #a.-f. 6.00 6.00

**Souvenir Sheet**

**1950** G141 $6 multicolored 6.00 6.00

**1998 World Cup Soccer Type of 1997**

Team pictures: 10c, Italy, 1934. 20c, Angola. 45c, Brazil, 1958. $1, Uruguay, 1950. $1.50, West Germany, 1974. $5, Italy, 1938.

World Cup winners: No. 1951: a, England. b, W. Germany, 1954. c, Uruguay. d, West Germany, 1990. e, Argentina, 1986. f, Brazil. g, Argentina, 1978. h, W. Germany 1974.
Tournament stars, vert.: No. 1952: a, Ademir, Brazil. b, Kocsis, Hungary. c, Leonidas, Brazil. d, Nejedly, Czechoslovakia. e, Schiavio, Italy. f, Stabile, Uruguay. g, Pele, Brazil. h, Walter, W. Germany.
Each $6: No. 1953, Shearer, England, vert. No. 1954, Paulao, Angola.

**1997, Aug. 11**
**1950A-1950F** A397 Set of 6 6.25 6.25

**Sheets of 8, #a-h**

**1951-1952** A397 Set of 2 12.50 12.50

**Souvenir Sheets**

**1953-1954** A397 Set of 2 9.50 9.50

### Fish Type of 1997

$2, Tursiops truncatus. $5, Balistes vetula. $10, Pterois volitans. $20, Equetus lanceolatus.

**1997, July 22 Litho. *Perf. 14***
**1955** G140 $2 multicolored 1.50 1.50
**1956** G140 $5 multicolored 3.75 3.75
**1957** G140 $10 multicolored 7.50 7.50
**1958** G140 $20 multicolored 15.00 15.00
*Nos. 1955-1958 (4)* 27.75 27.75

Sealed with a Kiss — G142

Characters from Disney's classic animated films: No. 1959: a, Snow White, 1937. b, Pinocchio, 1940. c, Peter Pan, 1953. d, Cinderella, 1950. e, The Little Mermaid, 1989. f, Beauty and the Beast, 1991. g, Aladdin, 1992. h, Pocahontas, 1995. i, Hunchback of Notre Dame, 1996.
$5, The Artistocats, 1970, vert.

**1997, Aug. 7 Litho. *Perf. 14x13½***
**1959** G142 $1 Sheet of 9, #a.-i. 7.00 7.00

**Souvenir Sheet**
***Perf. 13½x14***

**1960** G142 $5 multicolored 4.00 4.00

Butterflies of the World G143

75c, Polyura dehaani. 90c, Polyura dolon. $1, Charaxes candiope. $1.50, Pantaporia punctata. $2, Charaxes etesippe. $3, Charaxes castor.
No. 1967, Euphaedra, each $1.50: a, Francina. b, Eleus. c, Harpalyce. d, Cyparissa. e, Gausape. f, Imperialis.
No. 1968, each $1.50: a, Euthalia confucius. b, Euthalia kardama. c, Limenitis albomaculata. d, Hestina assimilis. e, Kalima inachus. f, Euthalia teutoides.
Each $6: No. 1969, Charaxes numenes, vert. No. 1970, Charaxes nobilis, vert.

**1997, Aug. 12 *Perf. 14***
**1961-1966** G143 Set of 6 7.25 7.25

**Sheets of 6, #a-f**

**1967-1968** G143 Set of 2 16.00 16.00

**Souvenir Sheets**

**1969-1970** G143 Set of 2 10.00 10.00

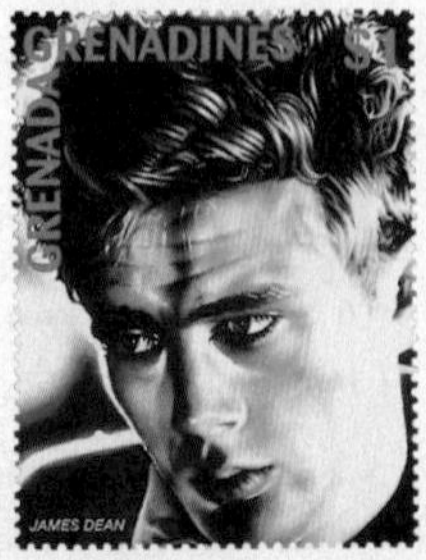

James Dean (1931-55), Actor G144

Various portraits.

**1997, Aug. 22 *Perf. 14x13½***
**1971** G144 $1 Sheet of 9, #a.-i. 7.25 7.25

Mushrooms — G145

Designs: 75c, Clitocybe metachroa. 90c, Clavulinopsis helvola. $1, Lycoperdon pyriforme. $1.50, Auricularia auricula-judae. $2, Clathrus archeri. $3, Lactarius trivialis.
No. 1978: a, Entoloma incanum. b, Coprinus atramentarius. c, Mycena polygramma. d, Lepista nuda. e, Pleurotis cornucopiae. f, Laccaria amethystina.
Each $6: No. 1979, Amanita muscaria. No. 1980, Morchella esculenta.

**1997, Sept. 4 *Perf. 14***
**1972-1977** G145 Set of 6 7.00 7.00
**1978** G145 $1.50 Sheet of 6, #a.-f. 7.00 7.00

**Souvenir Sheets**

**1979-1980** G145 Set of 2 10.00 10.00

G146

Orchids — G147

Designs: 35c, Symphyglossum sanguineum. 45c, Doritaenopsis "Mythic Beauty." 75c, Odontoglossum cervantesii. 90c, Cattleya "Pumpernickel." $1, Vanda "Patricia Law." $1.50, Odontonia "Debutante." $2, Laeliocattleya "Mini Purple." $3, Phragmipedium "Dominiarium."
No. 1989, each $1: a, Cymbidium "Showgirl." b, Disa "Blackii." c, Phalaenopsis aphrodite. d, Iwanagaara "Apple Blossum." e, Masdevallia "Copper Angel." f, Paphiopedilum micranthum. g, Paphiopedilum "Claire de Lune." h, Cattleya forbesii. i, Dendrobium "Dawn Maree."
No. 1990, each $1: a, Lycaste "Aquila." b, Brassolaeliocattleya "Dorothy Bertsch." c, Phalaenopsis "Zuma Urchin." d, Promenaea xanthina. e, Amesiella philippinensis. f, Brassocattleya "Angel Lace." g, Brassoepidsendrum "Peggy Ann." h, Miltonia seine. i, Sophralaeliocattleya "Precious Stones."
No. 1991, each $1.50: a, Miltoniosis "Jean Sabourin." b, Cymbidium "Red Beauty." c, Brassocattleya "Green Dragon." d, Phalaenopsis hybrid. e, Laelio cattleya "Mary Ellen Carter." f, Disa hybrid.
No. 1992, each $1.50: a, Lycaste macrobulbon. b, Cochleanthes discolor. c, Cymbidium "Nang Carpenter." d, Paphiopedilum "Clair de Lune." e, Masdevallia caudata. f, Cymbidium "Showgirl."
$5, Phalenopsis "Medford Star." $6, Brassolaeliocattleya "Mem. Dorothy Bertsch."

**1997, Sept. 4**
**1981-1988** G146 Set of 8 7.50 7.50

**Sheets of 9, #a-i**

**1989-1990** G147 Set of 2 13.50 13.50

**Sheets of 6, #a-f**

**1991-1992** G146 Set of 2 13.50 13.50

**Souvenir Sheets**

**1993** G146 $5 multicolored 3.75 3.75
**1994** G146 $6 multicolored 4.50 4.50

Famous Composers, Musicians G148

No. 1995, each $1: a, Beethoven. b, Tchaikovsky. c, J.S. Bach. d, Chopin. e, Stravinsky. f, Haydn. g, Mahler. h, Rossini.
Each $6: No. 1996, Mozart. No. 1997, Schubert.

**1997, Oct. 10 Litho. *Perf. 14½x14***

**Sheet of 8**

**1995** G148 #a.-h. + label 6.50 6.50

**Souvenir Sheets**

**1996-1997** G148 Set of 2 10.00 10.00

Diana, Princess of Wales (1961-97) G149

Various portraits of Diana wearing various hats, scenes following her death: No. 1998: a, Buckingham Palace. b, Island, Spencer Estate, Althorp. c, Westminster Abbey. d, Gate, Spencer Estate. e, Gate, Kensington Palace. g, Spencer Estate, Althorp.
$6, Diana smelling flowers in front of Kensington Palace.

**1997, Nov. 10 *Perf. 14***
**1998** G149 $1.50 Sheet of 6, #a.-f. 6.75 6.75

**Souvenir Sheet**

**1999** G149 $6 multicolored 4.75 4.75

No. 1999 contains one 60x40mm stamp.

### Christmas Art Type of 1997

Entire paintings, details, or sculptures: 20c, Choir of Angels, by Simon Marmion. 75c, The Annunciation, by Giotto. 90c, Festival of the Rose Garlands, by Albrecht Durer. $1.50, Madonna with Two Angels, by Hans Memling. $2, The Ognissanti Madonna, by Giotto. $3, Angel with Candlestick, by Michelangelo.
Each $6: No. 2006, Cupid Commemorating a Marriage by Incising on a Table, by Jean-Baptiste Huet, horiz. No. 2007, The Rising of the Sun, by Francois Boucher, horiz.

**1997, Dec. 5 Litho. *Perf. 14***
**2000-2005** A402 Set of 6 12.50 12.50

**Souvenir Sheets**

**2006-2007** A402 Set of 2 9.00 9.00

### Marine Life Type of 1997

No. 2008, each $1: a, Holocanthus ciliaris. b, Ballstoides conspicillum. c, Chaetodon quadrimaculatus. d, Microspathodon chrysurus. e, Halichoeres garnoti. f, Gramma loreto. g, Liopropoma carmabi. h, Lactophrys triqueter. i, Cephalopolis miniatus.
Each $6: No. 2009, Carcharhinus melanopterus. No. 2010, Obistognathus aurifrons, vert.

**1997, Dec. 12 Litho. *Perf. 14***
**2008** A386 Sheet of 9, #a.-i. 7.50 7.50

**Souvenir Sheets**

**2009-2010** A386 Set of 2 9.00 9.00

New Year 1998 (Year of the Tiger) — G150

***Die Cut Perf. 11***
**1998, Feb. 10 Litho.**

**Self-Adhesive**

**2011** G150 $1.50 Hologram 3.25

**Souvenir Sheet**

**2012** G150 $3 like #2011 5.50

No. 2011 was issued in sheets of 4. No. 2012 contains one 52x65mm stamp.

Great Ships, Shipwrecks — G151

Ships — #2013: a, CSS Alabama. b, Persia. c, Ariel. d, CSS Florida. e, Great Eastern. f, Jacob Bell. g, Star of India. h, Robert E. Lee. i, US Monitor Passaic. j, Madagascar. k, HMS Devastation. l, General Grant.
"Gone with the Wind," vert. — #2014: a, Clark Gable. b, Blockade runner wrecked on Sullivan's Island, North Carolina, 1863. c, Margaret Mitchell. d, George Alfred Trenholm, model for character Rhett Butler. e, Dock Street Theater, confiscated from Trenholm after Civil War. f, Howlet sinks off Charleston, South Carolina, 1865. g, USS Tecumseh sunk by Confederate gunboats, 1864. h, City jail, where Trenholm was imprisioned, 1865.
Each $6: No. 2015, Nashville sinks the Union clipper, Harvey Birch, vert. No. 2016, Dr. Lee Spence, expert on shipwrecks and sunken treasures, Alabama sinking Hatteras off Texas coast.

**1998, May 7 Litho. *Perf. 14***
**2013** G151 75c Sheet of 12, #a.-l. 7.25 7.25
**2014** G151 $1 Sheet of 8, #a.-h. 6.50 6.50

**Souvenir Sheets**

**2015-2016** G151 Set of 2 9.50 9.50

#2015-2016 contain one 57x43mm stamp.

Modern, Future Aircraft G152

70c, Concept strike fighter. 90c, Concept space shuttle. $2, Concept air & space jet. $3, V Jet II.
No. 2021: a, Velocity 173 RG Elite. b, Davis DA 9. c, Concorde. d, Voyager. e, Factimobile. f, RAF 2000. g, Boomerang. h, N1M Flying Wing.
Each $6: No. 2022, Gee-Bee replica. No. 2023, Concept Aeropod.

**1998, May 13**
**2017-2020** G152 Set of 4 5.50 5.50
**2021** G152 $1 Sheet of 8, #a.-h. 6.50 6.50

**Souvenir Sheets**

**2022-2023** G152 Set of 2 9.00 9.00

No. 2022 is inscribed "Delmar."

Orchids — G153

Designs: $1, Laclia tenebrosa. $1.50, Phragmipedium besseae. $2, Pschopsis papilio. $3, Masdevallia coccinea.
No. 2028, each $1: a, Lycaste deppei. b, Dendrobium victoriae. c, Dendrobium nobile. d, Cymbidium danyanum. e, Cymbidium starbright. f, Cymbidium giganteum. g, Chysis aurea. h, Broughtonia sanguinea. i, Cattleya guttata.
No. 2029, each $1: a, Calanthe vestita. b, Cattleya bicolor. c, Laelia anceps. d, Epidendrum prismatocarpum. e, Coelogyne ochcracea. f, Doritaenopsis eclantant. g, Laelia gouldiana. h, Encyclia vitellina. i, Maxillaria praestans.
Each $6: No. 2030, Masdevallia ignea. No. 2031, Encyclia brassavolae.

**1998, May 19**
**2024-2027** G153 Set of 4 6.25 6.25

**Sheets of 9, #a-i**

**2028-2029** G153 Set of 2 14.00 14.00

**Souvenir Sheets**

**2030-2031** G153 Set of 2 9.50 9.50

### Sea Birds Type of 1998

75c, Bonaparte's gull. 90c, Western sandpiper. $2, Great black-backed gull. $3, Dotterell.
No. 2036, each $1.50: a, Terns. b, Brown pelican. c, Black-legged kittiwake. d, Herring gull. e, Lesser noddy. f, Kittiwake.
No. 2037, each $1.50: a, Whimbrels. b, Golden white-tailed tropic bird. c, Arctic tern. d, Ruddy turnstones. e, Imperial shag. f, Magellan gull.
Each $5: No. 2038, Yellow-nosed albatross, vert. No. 2039, Broad-billed prion.

**1998, June 30 Litho. *Perf. 14***

**2032-2035** A408 Set of 4 6.00 6.00

**Sheets of 6, #a-f**

**2036-2037** A408 Set of 2 15.00 15.00

**Souvenir Sheets**

**2038-2039** A408 Set of 2 9.00 9.00

Diana, Princess of Wales (1961-97) — G155

Diana in front of Kensington Palace: No. 2040, Wearing tiara, ruffled dress. No. 2041, Wearing white dress, pearls.

**Litho. & Embossed**

**1998, July 14 *Die Cut 7½***

**2040** G155 $20 gold
**2041** G155 $20 gold & multi

**Intl. Year of the Ocean Type**

No. 2042: a, Great black-backed gull. b, Common dolphin. c, Seal. d, Amazonian catfish. e, Shark. f, Goldfish. g, Cyathopharynx. h, Whale. i, Telmatochromis. j, Crab. k, Octopus. l, Turtle.

No. 2043: a, Dolphins. b, Seal. c, Turtle. d, Leopard shark. e, Flame angelfish. f, Syndontis. g, Lamprologus. h, Kryptopterus bicirrhus. i, Pterophyllum scalare. j, Swimming pancake. k, Cowfish. l, Sea horse.

Each $6: No. 2044, Tetraodon mbu. No. 2045, Goldfish.

**1998, Aug. 19 Litho. *Perf. 14***

**Sheets of 12**

**2042** A411 75c #a.-l. 7.25 7.25
**2043** A411 90c #a.-l. 8.50 8.50

**Souvenir Sheets**

**2044-2045** A411 Set of 2 9.50 9.50

**Gandhi Type of 1998**

Portraits of Gandhi.

**1998, Sept. 15 Litho. *Perf. 14***

**2046** A413 $1 multicolored .75 .75

**Souvenir Sheet**

**2047** A413 $6 multicolored 4.75 4.75

No. 2046 was issued in sheets of 4.

**Picasso Type of 1998**

Paintings: 45c, Bust of a Woman, 1943, vert. $2, Three Musicians, 1921. $3, Studio at La Californie, 1956.

$5, Woman with a Blue Hat, 1901.

***Perf. 14½x14, 14x14½***

**1998, Sept. 15**

**2048-2050** A414 Set of 3 4.25 4.25

**Souvenir Sheet**

**2051** A414 $5 multicolored 3.75 3.75

**Delacroix Type of 1998**

Paintings — #2052: a, The Natchez. b, Christ and His Disciples Crossing the Sea of Galilee. c, Sunset. d, Moroccans Outside the Walls of Tangier. e, The Fireplace. f, Forest View with a Oak Tree. g, View of the Harbor at Dieppe. h, Arabs Skirmishing in the Mountains.

$5, Orphan Girl in a Cemetary, vert.

**1998, Sept. 15 Litho. *Perf. 14***

**2052** A415 $1 Sheet of 8, #a.-h. 6.50 6.50

**Souvenir Sheet**

**2053** A415 $5 multicolored 4.75 4.75

**Organization of American States Type**

**1998, Sept. 15**

**2054** A416 $1 multicolored .90 .90

**Diana Type of 1998**

**1998 *Perf. 14½***

**2055** A417 $1.50 multicolored 1.25 1.25

**Self-Adhesive**

***Serpentine Die Cut Perf. 11½***

**Sheet of 1**

**Size: 53x65mm**

**2055A** A417 $8 Diana, buildings

No. 2055 was issued in sheets of 6.

Soaking in water may affect the multi-layer image of No. 2055A.

Issued: $1.50, 9/15; $8, 11/5/98.

**Ferrari Type of 1998**

No. 2056: a, 275 GTB. b, 340 MM. c, 250 GT SWB Berlinetta SEFAC "Hot Rod."

$5, First Ferrari Cabriolet (011-S).

**1998, Sept. 15 *Perf. 14***

**2056** A418 $2 Sheet of 3, #a.-c. 4.75 4.75

**Souvenir Sheet**

**2057** A418 $5 multicolored 4.75 4.75

No. 2057 contains one 91x35mm stamp.

**Scout Jamboree Type of 1998**

Designs: 90c, Scout sign. $1.50, Lord Baden-Powell. $5, Scout salute.

$6, Lord Baden-Powell, diff., vert.

**1998, Sept. 15**

**2058-2060** A419 Set of 3 5.75 5.75

**Souvenir Sheet**

**2061** A419 $6 multicolored 4.75 4.75

**Royal Air Force Type of 1998**

No. 2062, each $2: a, Chinook. b, BAe Harrier GR5. c, Panavia Tornado F3 ADV. d, Chinook HC2 carrying 105mm light gun.

No. 2063, each $2: a, Tornado GR1. b, BAe Hawk TIA. c, Sepecat Jaguar GRI. d, Harrier GR7.

Each $6: No. 2064, Eurofighter 2000, Hunter. No. 2065, Biplane, hawk in flight. No. 2066, Head of hawk, biplane. No. 2067, Eurofighter 2000, Tornado.

**1998, Sept. 15 Sheets of 4, #a-d**

**2062-2063** A420 Set of 2 12.00 12.00

**Souvenir Sheets**

**2064-2067** A420 Set of 2 17.00 17.00

Disney Christmas Trains — G156

Silly Symphony Railroad — #2068, each $1: a, Santa in locomotive, rabbit. b, Giraffe, elephant, tiger. c, Wolf, Three Little Pigs. d, Robin Hood blowing horn, Jiminy Cricket, penguins, children. e, Geese, Indian boy, turtle in caboose.

Mickey's Toontown Christmas Train — #2069, each $1: a, Mickey in locomotive. b, Pluto, chipmunks in coal car. c, Donald, Daisy Duck in passenger car. d, Goofy leading Huey, Dewey, & Louie in caroling. e, Minnie in caboose.

Pooh's Railroad — #2070, each $1: a, Piglet as engineer. b, Winnie the Pooh shoveling honey. c, Rabbit, Owl. d, Kanga, Roo, Christopher Robin. e, Eeyore, Tigger.

Each $6: No. 2071, Santa setting up toy train under Christmas tree. No. 2072, Mickey as engineer. No. 2073, Winnie the Pooh reading paper, Rabbit, Piglet.

**1998, Oct. 15 *Perf. 14x13½***

**Sheets of 5, #a-e**

**2068-2070** G156 Set of 3 11.00 11.00

**Souvenir Sheets**

**2071-2073** G156 Set of 3 13.00 13.00

**New Year 1999 (Year of the Rabbit) Type**

Various rabbits, color of country name: a, green. b, orange. c, red.

**Sheet of 3**

**Self-Adhesive**

**1999, Jan. 4 Litho. *Die Cut Perf. 9***

**2074** A425 $1.50 gold & multi, #a.-c. 3.50 3.50

No. 2074b has point of triangle down.

Queen Elizabeth II and Prince Philip, 50th Wedding Anniv. — G157

**Litho. & Embossed**

**1999, Jan. 8 *Die Cut Perf. 7***

**Without Gum**

**2075** G157 $20 gold & multi

Australia '99, World Stamp Expo G158

Dinosaurs — #2076: a, Troodon. b, Camptosaurus. c, Parasaurolophus. d, Dryosaurus. e, Gallimimus. f, Camarasaurus (all vert.).

#2077: a, Duckbill. b, Lambeosaurus. c, Iguanodon. d, Euoplocephalus. e, Triceratops. f, Brachiosaurus. g, Ponoptosaurus. h, Stegosaurus.

Each $6: #2078, Edmontosaurus. #2079, Tyrannosaurus, vert. #2080, Halticosaurus, vert.

**1999, Mar. 1 Litho. *Perf. 14***

**2076** G158 $1 Sheet of 6, #a.-f. 4.50 4.50
**2077** G158 $1.50 Sheet of 8, #a.-h. 9.25 9.25

**Souvenir Sheets**

**2078-2080** G158 Set of 3 13.50 13.50

Trains G159

Designs: 15c, India, 4-4-0 express passenger and mail engine. 75c, Ireland, 4-4-0. 90c, Canada, 4-6-0. $1.50, India, 4-4-0 express. $2, Australia, 4-6-2. $3, Great Britain, Stirling 0-4-2.

No. 2087, each $2: a, Belgium, type 4-4-0. b, Sweden, class "Cc" type 4-4-0. c, Chile, 0-6-4. d, Bolivia, Fairlie-type double engine.

No. 2088, each $2: a, Belgium, 4-cylinder 4-6-0. b, England, 4-cylinder 4-6-0. c, Northern Ireland, 2-cylinder compound 4-4-0. d, Holland, 4-4-0.

No. 2089, each $2: a, Switzerland, 0-8-0. b, Ireland, 0-6-0. c, US 4-6-0. d, Great Britain, Prince of Wales class 4-2-2.

No. 2090, each $2: a, Ireland, narrow gauge 2-4-2. b, Russia, 0-8-0. c, England, Ivatt large-boilered Atlantic. d, Germany, Atlantic type express.

No. 2091, each $2: a, France, 4-6-0. b, New Zealand, 2-6-4. c, Burma, 4-4-4. d, Malaya, 4-6-0.

Each $6: No. 2092, France, 4-4-0. No. 2093, Italy, 0-6-4.

**1999, Apr. 12 Litho. *Perf. 14***

**2081-2086** G159 Set of 6 6.25 6.25

**Sheets of 4, #a-d**

**2087-2091** G159 Set of 5 30.00 30.00

**Souvenir Sheets**

**2092-2093** G159 Set of 2 9.00 9.00

**Flora and Fauna Type of 1999**

Designs: 75c, Porkfish. 90c, Leatherback turtle. $1.50, Ruby-throated hummingbird. $2, Theope eudocia.

No. 2098, vert, each $1: a, White-tailed tropicbird. b, Laughing gull. c, Palm tree. d, Humpback whale. e, Painted bunting. f, Common grackle. g, Green anole. h, Morpho peleides. i, Prepoua meandor.

No. 2099, vert, each $1: a, Common dolphin. b, Catonephele numiti. c, Sooty tern. d, Vermilion flycatcher. e, Blue grosbeak. f, Great egret. g, Actinote pellenea. h, Anteos clorinade. i, Common iguana.

Each $6: No. 2100, Bannaquit. No. 2101, Beay gregory.

**1999, Apr. 26**

**2094-2097** A430 Set of 4 4.00 4.00

**Sheets of 9, #a-i**

**2098-2099** A430 Set of 2 14.00 14.00

**Souvenir Sheets**

**2100-2101** A430 Set of 2 9.25 9.25

**Hokusai Type of 1999**

Entire paintings or details, horiz. — #2102, each $1.50: a, A Breeze on a Fine Day. b, Ejiri. c, Horse drawings (kicking up hind legs). d, Horse drawings (with head down). e, View Along the Bank of the Sumida River. f, Thunderstorm Below the Mountain.

No. 2103. each $1.50: a, Fuchû. b. Doll Fair at Fikkendana. c, Sumo Wrestlers (with arms locked). d, Sumo Wrestlers (one head butting). e, Sôjô Henjô. f, Twin Gardens Gateway of the Asakusa Kannon Temple.

Each $6: No. 2104 Kôbô Daishi Exorcising Demon that Causes Sickness. No. 2105, Stretching Cloth.

**1999, May 24 Litho. *Perf. 14x13½***

**Sheets of 6, #a-f**

**2102-2103** A431 Set of 2 13.50 13.50

**Souvenir Sheet**

**2104-2105** A431 Set of 2 9.00 9.00

John H. Glenn's Return to Space G160

Portraits — #2106: a, Thumbs up, 1998 flight. b, Receiving NASA Service Award from Pres. Kennedy, 1962. c, Talking to Ground Control from Discovery, 1998. d, Climbing out of Friendship 7, 1962. e, Being checked for balance, 1998. f, Climbing into Friendship 7, 1962.

No. 2107, vert.: a, Portrait as Ohio Senator, 1974. b, Official portrait, 1962. c, Suit-up test, 1998. d, Suiting up for Discovery, 1998. e, Meeting press after Discovery flight, 1998. f, Smiling aboard Discovery, 1998. g, Medical research, 1998. h, Official portrait, 1998.

**1999, May 24 *Perf. 14x14½***

**Sheets of 6 and 8**

**2106** G160 $1 #a.-f. 5.00 5.00
**2107** G160 $1 #a.-h. 6.50 6.50

**Goethe Type of 1999**

No. 2108: a, Peasants dancing under the linden tree. b, Faust dreams of soaring above the mortal.

No. 2109, Portrait of Goethe.

**1999, May 24 *Perf. 14***

**2108** A432 $3 Sheet of 3, #a.-b., Grenada #2858b 6.75 6.75

**Souvenir Sheet**

**2109** A432 $6 multi 4.50 4.50

### IBRA '99 World Stamp Expo Type of 1999

IBRA '99 emblem, Luckenbach sailing ship and: No. 2110, 35c, Thurn and Taxis #1. No. 2113, $3, North German Confederation #1.
Emblem, Leipzig-Dresden Railway and: No. 2111, 45c, Schleswig-Holstein #1. No. 2112, $1.50, Oldenburg #4.
$6, Cover showing pair of Thurn & Taxis #1.

**1999, May 24 Litho. *Perf. 14***
**2110-2113** A433 Set of 4 4.00 4.00

**Souvenir Sheet**
**2114** A433 $6 multicolored 4.75 4.75

### Philexfrance '99 Type
Souvenir Sheets

Designs, each $6: No. 2115, Co-co 7000 class high speed electric locomotive. No. 2116, Cha Pelon 4-8-0.

**1999, May 24 Litho. *Perf. 14***
**2115-2116** A435 Set of 2 7.00 7.00

Beginning with Nos. 2117-2118, stamps from Grenada Grenadines will be inscribed GRENADA / Carriacou & Petite Martinique.

### Wedding of Prince Edward and Sophie Rhys-Jones Type

No. 2117: a, Edward. b, Sophie, Edward. c, Sophie.
$6, Couple.

**1999, June 18 Litho. *Perf. 13½***
**2117** A436 $3 Sheet of 3, #a.-c. 6.75 6.75

**Souvenir Sheet**
**2118** A436 $6 multicolored 4.50 4.50

### UN Rights of the Child Type of 1999

No. 2119: a, Boy. b, Liv Ullman, UNICEF's first woman ambassador. c, Woman.
$6, Maurice Pate, founding director of UNICEF.

**1999, May 24 Litho. *Perf. 14***
**2119** A437 $3 Sheet of 3, #a.-c. 6.75 6.75

**Souvenir Sheet**
**2120** A437 $6 multicolored 4.50 4.50

### Queen Mother Type of 1999
**Gold frames**

No. 2121: a, Lady Elizabeth Bowles-Lyon. b, Queen Elizabeth in Rhodesia, 1957. c, Queen Elizabeth, Princess Elizabeth, and Princess Anne, 1950. d, Queen Mother, 1988.

**$6, Queen Mother, Berlin.**

**1999, Aug. 16**
**Sheet of 4**
**2121** A440 $2 #a.-d. + label 6.00 6.00

**Souvenir Sheet**
**2122** A440 $6 multicolored 4.50 4.50

No. 2122 contains one 38x50mm stamp. Margins of sheets are embossed.
See Nos. 2369-2370.

**Litho. & Embossed**
***Die Cut Perf. 8¾***
**Without Gum**
**2122A** A440a $20 gold & multi

### Famous People Type of 1999

Actors — #2123: a, George Raft (1895-1980). b, Raft in movie scene. c, Fatty Arbuckle (1887-1933) in movie scene. d, Portrait of Arbuckle. e, Buster Keaton (1895-1966). f, Keaton in movie scene. g, Harold Lloyd (1893-1971) in movie scene. h, Portrait of Lloyd.
No. 2124: a, James Cagney (1899-1986). b, Cagney in movie scene. c, Edward G. Robinson (1893-1973). d, Robinson in movie scene.
$6, Charlie Chaplin (1889-1977).

**1999, Aug. 20 Litho. *Perf. 14***
**2123** A426 $1 Sheet of 8, #a.-h. 6.00 6.00
**2124** A426 $2 Sheet of 4, #a.-d. 6.00 6.00

**Souvenir Sheet**
**2125** A426 $6 multicolored 4.50 4.50

Space Exploration — G161

No. 2126, each $1.50: a, Sputnik I. b, Explorer I. c, Telstar I. d, Marisat I. e, Long Duration Exposure Facility. f, Hubble Space Telescope.
No. 2127, vert, each $1.50: a, X-15. b, Mercury Redstone 3 rocket, Freedom 7. c, Mercury Atlas 6 rocket, Friendship 7. d, Gemini 4, Edward H. White II. e, Saturn V rocket, Edwin Aldrin. f, Lunar rover.
Each $6: No. 2128, Space Shuttle Columbia. No. 2129, Mars Pathfinder.

**1999, Oct. 8 Litho. *Perf. 14***
**Sheets of 6, #a.-f.**
**2126-2127** G161 Set of 2 13.50 13.50

**Souvenir Sheets**
**2128-2129** G161 Set of 2 9.00 9.00

### Christmas Type of 1999

Christmas plants: 15c, Poinsettia. 35c, Holly. 75c, Fir tree. $1.50, Ivy. $3, Geranium.
$6, The Adoration of the Magi.

**1999, Nov. 23 Litho. *Perf. 13¾***
**2130-2134** A444 Set of 5 4.25 4.25

**Souvenir Sheet**
**2135** A444 $6 multicolored 4.50 4.50

Kirk Douglas (b. 1916), Actor G162

Douglas in various poses.

**1999 Litho. *Perf. 13¾***
**2136** G162 $1.50 Sheet of 6, #a.-f. 6.75 6.75

**Souvenir Sheet**
**2137** G162 $6 multi 4.50 4.50

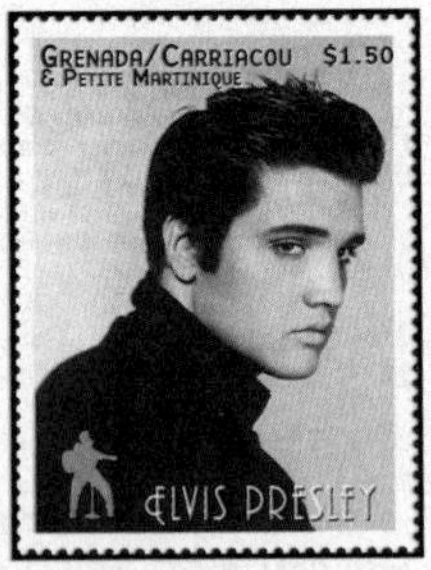

Elvis Presley G163

Presley in various poses.

**1999**
**Sheet of 6**
**2138** G163 $1.50 #a.-f. 6.75 6.75

### Millennium Type of 2000

Highlights of 1970s — No. 2139: a, Salvador Allende elected Pres. of Chile. b, Earth Day. c, CAT scan introduced. d, Pres. Nixon goes to China. e, Massacre at Olympics. f, Gas shortages. g, Sydney Opera House opens. h, Pres. Nixon resigns. i, New theory of black holes. j, US bicentennial. k, 1st "Test tube" baby. l, Pope John Paul II visits Poland. m, Iran's Islamic Revolution. n, Concorde makes 1st flight. o, Charles de Gaulle dies. p, Camp David agreements (60x40mm). q, Mother Teresa wins Nobel Peace Prize.
Highlights of 1300-1350 — No. 2140: a, Robert the Bruce crowned King of Scotland. b, Giotto paints frescoes. c, Mansa Musa rules Mali. d, Dante completes "The Divine Comedy." e, Noh theater developed in Japan. f, Tenochtitlan founded by Aztecs. g, Ibn Battutah journeys to Africa and Asia. h, Munich fire. i, Ivan I of Russia increases Moscow's importance. j, Hundred Years' War begins. k, First use of cannons in Europe. l, Black Death devastates Europe. m, Boccaccio begins writing "Decameron." n, Eyeglasses developed in Italy. o, Plate armor replaces chain mail. p, Grand Canal of China completed. (60x40mm). q, Migration of Maoris to New Zealand.
Sea Exploration — No. 2141: a, Ferdinand Magellan. b, Restless seas. c, Queen Elizabeth I. d, Albatrosses. e, Penguins. f, Tahiti. g, Breadfruit. h, Easter Island. i, Maori carving. j, Lobster. k, Orchid. l, Walrus. m, Kangaroo. n, The Beagle. o, Frigatebird. p, Strait of Magellan (60x40mm). q, Capt. James Cook.

**2000 Litho. *Perf. 12¾x12½***
**Sheets of 17**
**2139** A450 20c #a.-q., + label 2.50 2.50
**2140** A450 50c #a.-q. + label 6.25 6.25
**2141** A450 50c #a.-q., + label 6.25 6.25

Issued: #2139, 3/28; #2140-2141, 2/1.

Souvenir Sheet

New Year 2000 (Year of the Dragon) — G164

**2000, Feb. 5 *Perf. 13¾***
**2142** G164 $4 multi 3.00 3.00

G165

Birds — G166

Designs: 75c, Barn swallow. 90c, Caribbean coot. $2, Common moorhen. $3, Orange-winged parrot.
No. 2147, each $1: a, Red-collared lorikeet. b, Citron-crested cockatoo. c, Stella's lorikeet. d, Leadbeater's cockatoo. e, Golden conure. f, Red-spotted parakeet. g, Nobel macaw. h, Goffins cockatoo. i, Sun conure.
No. 2148, each $1: a, Turquoise parakeet. b, Scarlet-chested parakeet. c, Red-capped parakeet. d, Eastern rosella. e, Budgerigar. f, Orange-flanked parakeet. g, Mallee ringneck. h, Red-rumped parakeet. i, Yellow-fronted parakeet.
No. 2149, each $1.50: a, Puerto Rican emerald. b, Green mango. c, Red-legged thrush. d, Red-crowned parrot. e, Hispaniolan parrot. f, Yellow-crowned parrot.
No. 2150, each $1.50: a, Yellow-shouldered blackbird. b, Troupial. c, Green-throated Carib. d, Black-hooded parakeet. e, Scarlet tanager. f, Yellow-crowned bishop.
Each $6: No. 2151, Puerto Rican lizard-cuckoo. No. 2152, Pin-tailed whydah, vert. No. 2153, Pennant's parakeet. No. 2154, Scarlet macaw, vert.
Illustration G166 reduced.

**2000, Mar. 1 Litho. *Perf. 14***
**2143-2146** G165 Set of 4 5.50 5.50

**Sheets of 9, #a.-i.**
**2147-2148** G166 Set of 2 15.00 15.00

**Sheets of 6, #a.-f.**
**2149-2150** G165 Set of 2 15.00 15.00

**Souvenir Sheets**
***Perf. 13¾***
**2151-2152** G165 Set of 2 10.00 10.00

***Perf. 14***
**2153-2154** G166 Set of 2 10.00 10.00

No. 2151 contains one 48x32mm stamp; No. 2152 contains one 32x48mm stamp.

Tropical Fish G167

35c, Slender mbuna. 45c, Pygoplite diacanthus. #2157, 75c, Siamese fighting fish. #2158, 75c, Pomacanthus semicirclatus. 90c, Zanclus canescens. #2160, $1, Dwarf pencilfish. #2161, $1, Xiphophorus maculatus. #2162, $2, Wimplefish. #2163, $2, Gramma loreto. $3, Zebrasoma xanthurum.
#2165, each $1: a, Emperor angelfish. b, Strawberryfish. c, Jackknife fish. d, Flame angelfish. e, Clarke's anemonefish. f, Flashback dottyback. g, Coral trout. h, Foxface.
#2166, each $1: a, Bumbelbee goby. b, Black-headed blenny. c, Boarfish. d, Achilles tang. e, Swordtail. f, Moorish idol. g, Banded pipefish. h, Striped sea catfish.
#2167, each $1.65: a, Bodianus rufus. b, Coris aygula. c, Centropyge bicolor. d, Balistoides conspicillum. e, Poecilia reticulata. f, Heniochus acuminatus.
#2168, each $1.65: a, Plectorhynchus chaetodonoids. b, Bodianus puchellus. c, Acanthurus leucosternon. d, Chromileptis altivelis. e, Pterophyllum scalare f, Premnas biaculeatus.
Each $6: #2169, Equetus punctatus. #2170, Harlequin tuskfish. #2171, Purplequeen. #2172, Pomacanthius imperator, vert.

**2000, Mar. 28 *Perf. 14***
**2155-2164** G167 Set of 10 9.00 9.00

**Sheets of 8, #a.-h.**
**2165-2166** G167 Set of 2 12.00 12.00

**Sheets of 6, #a.-f.**
**2167-2168** G167 Set of 2 15.00 15.00

**Souvenir Sheets**
**2169-2172** G167 Set of 4 18.00 18.00

### Van Dyck Painting Type of 2000

No. 2173, each $1.50: a, Cardinal Bentivoglio. b, Cardinal Infante Ferdinand. c, Cesare Alessandro Scaglia. d, A Roman Clergyman. e, Jean-Charles della Faille. f, Cardinal Domenico Rivarola.
No. 2174, each $1.50: a, Portrait of an Elderly Woman. b, Head of a Young Woman. c, Portrait of a Man. d, Jan van den Wouwer. e, Portrait of a Young Man. f, Portrait of Everhard Jabach.
No. 2175, each $1.50: a, A Man in Armor. b, Portrait of a Young General. c, Emanuele Filiberto, Prince of Savoy. d, Donna Polixena Spinola Guzman de Leganes. e, Luigia Cattaneo Gentile. f, Portrait of Giovanni Battista Cattaneo.
No. 2176, each $1.50: a, Marchesa Paolina Adorno Brignole-Sale, 1623-25. b, Marchesa Geronima Spinola. c, Marchesa Paolina Adorno Broignole-Sale, 1627. d, Marcello Durazzo. e, Marchesa Grimaldi Cattaneo with a Black Page. f, Young Man of the House of Spinola.
No. 2176G: h, A Man in Armor. i, Portrait of a Young General. j, Emanuele Filiberto, Prince of Savoy. k, Donna Polixena Spinola Guzman de Leganes. l, Luigia Cattaneo Gentile. m, Giovanni Battista Cattaneo.
Each $5: No. 2177, Portrait of Jacques le Roy. No. 2178, Hendrik van der Bergh.
Each $6: No. 2179, Frederik Hendrik, Prince of Orange. No. 2180, Justus van Meerstraeten. No. 2181, The Abbot Scaglia Adoring the Virgin and Child, horiz. No. 2182, Maria Louisa de Tassis, horiz.

**2000, May 1 *Perf. 13¾***
**Sheets of 6, #a.-f.**
**2173-2176** A449 Set of 4 27.00 27.00
**2176G** A449 $1.50 Sheet of 6, #a-f 6.75 6.75

**Souvenir Sheets**
**2177-2178** A449 Set of 2 7.50 7.50
**2179-2182** A449 Set of 4 18.00 18.00

### Prince William Type of 2000

No. 2183: a, Wearing scarf. b, Wearing suit with vest. c, Wearing casual shirt. d, Wearing gray suit.
$6, Wearing sweater.

**2000, May 15 Litho. *Perf. 14***

**2183** A453 $1.50 Sheet of 4, #a-d 4.50 4.50

**Souvenir Sheet**

***Perf. 13¾***

**2184** A453 $6 multi 4.50 4.50

No. 2183 contains four 28x42mm stamps.

### Zeppelin Type of 2000

No. 2185 — Ferdinand von Zeppelin and: a, LZ-3. b, LZ-56. c, LZ-88.
$6, LZ-1.

**2000, May 15 *Perf. 14***

**2185** A454 $3 Sheet of 3, #a-c 6.75 6.75

**Souvenir Sheet**

**2186** A454 $6 multi 4.50 4.50

No. 2185 contains three 42x28mm stamps.

### Berlin Film Festival Type of 2000

No. 2187: a, James Stewart. b, Sachiko Hidari. c, Juliette Mayniel. d, Le Bonheur. e, La Notte. f, Lee Marvin.
$6, The Thin Red Line.

**2000, May 15**

**2187** A455 $1.50 Sheet of 6, #a-f 6.75 6.75

**Souvenir Sheet**

**2188** A455 $6 multi 4.50 4.50

Souvenir Sheets

### Olympics Type of 2000

No. 2189: a, Frantz Reichel. b, Discus throw. c, Seoul Sports Complex and Korean flag. d, Ancient Greek wrestlers.

**2000, May 15**

**2189** A457 $2 Sheet of 4, #a-d 6.00 6.00

### Public Railways Type of 2000

No. 2190: a, Locomotion No. 1 and George Stephenson. b, Rocket.

**2000, May 15**

**2190** A458 $3 Sheet of 2, #a-b 4.50 4.50

### Bach Type of 2000

**2000, May 15**

**2191** A459 $6 Statue of Bach 4.50 4.50

G168

Butterflies and Moths — G169

No. 2192, each $1.50: a, Clara satin moth. b, Spanish festoon. c, Giant silkmoth. d, Oak eggar. e, Common wall. f, Large oak blue.

No. 2193, each $1.50: a, Jersey tiger. b, Boisduval's autumnal moth. c, Orange swallow-tailed moth. d, Regent skipper. e, Hoop pine moth. f, Coppery oysphania.

No. 2194, each $1.50: a, Grecian shoemaker. b, 88. c, Cramer's mesene. d, Salt marsh moth. e, Ruddy dagger wing. f, Blue night.

No. 2195, each $1.50: a, Heliconius charitonius. b, Tiger pierid. c, Hewiton's blue hairstreak. d, Esmeralda. e, California dog-face. f, Orange theope.

No. 2196, each $2: a, Hummingbird glearwing. b, Gold-drop helicopis. c, Great tiger moth. d, Staudinger's longtail.

No. 2197, each $2: a, Common map. b, Papilio machaon. c, Purple emperor. d, Red-lined geometrid.

Each $6: No. 2198, Peacock royal. No. 2199, Queen Alexandra's birdwing. No. 2200, Giant leopard moth. No. 2201, Robin moth, vert.

Illustrations reduced.

**2000, May 29 *Perf. 14***

**Sheets of 6, #a-f**

**2192-2193** G168 Set of 2 13.50 13.50
**2194-2195** G169 Set of 2 13.50 13.50

**Sheets of 4, #a-d**

**2196-2197** G168 Set of 2 12.00 12.00

**Souvenir Sheets**

**2198-2199** G168 Set of 2 9.00 9.00
**2200-2201** G169 Set of 2 9.00 9.00

### Apollo-Soyuz Type

No. 2202, vert.: a, Thomas P. Stafford. b, Mission badge. c, Donald K. Slayton.
$6, Alexei Leonov, vert.

**2000, May 15 Litho. *Perf. 14***

**2202** A456 $3 Sheet of 3, #a-c 6.75 6.75

**Souvenir Sheet**

**2203** A456 $6 Alexei Leonov 4.50 4.50

### Einstein Type

Souvenir Sheet

**2000, May 15 *Perf. 14¼***

**2204** A460 $6 multi 4.50 4.50

### Space Type

Nos. 2205, each $1.50: a, Foton (green and orange background). b, Sub-satellite and comet tail. c, NEAR Eros (green background). d, Explorer 16 and sun. e, Astro Challenger (green and orange background). f, Giotto (green background).

No. 2206, each $1.50: a, Foton and asteroid. b, Sub-satellite and asteroid. c, NEAR Eros and asteroid. d, Explorer 16 and planet surface. e, Space Shuttle. f, Giotto (blue background).

Each $6: No. 2207, Lunar Prospector. No. 2208, Pegasus Saturn.

**2000, May 15 *Perf. 14***

**Sheets of 6, #a-f**

**2205-2206** A461 Set of 2 13.50 13.50

**Souvenir Sheets**

**2207-2208** A461 Set of 2 9.00 9.00

Nos. 2205-2206 depict different satellites, but have the same inscriptions. World Stamp Expo 2000, Anaheim.

Trains G170

Designs: 90c, Golsdorf 2-6-2, Vienna Metropolitan Railways. $1, Forrester 2-2-0, Dublin & Kingstown Railway. $2, Metro-Cammell Co-Co, Nigerian Railways. $3, TGV 001, French Natl. Railways.

No. 2213, each $1.50: a, Braithwait 0-4-0, Eastern Counties Railway. b, The Philadelphia, Austria. c, Stephenson 2-2-2, Russia. d, L'aigle, Western Railway of France. e, Borsig Standard 2-2-2, Germany. f, The Ajax, Great Western Railway.

No. 2214, each $1.50: a, Co-Co locomotive, Norwegian State Railways. b, Diesel-electric locomotive, Jamaica Railway. c, Diesel-electric locomotive, Railway of the People's Republic of China. d, Electric locomotive, Portuguese Railways. e, Re 6/6, Swiss Federal Railways. f, Dual-purpose Electric locomotive, Turkish State Railways.

No. 2215, each $1.50: a, 4-4-0 engine, Perak Government Railway. b, 2-4-2 tank engine, Rhondda & Swansea Railway. c, 2-4-2 tank engine, Lancashire & Yorkshire Railway. d, 2-8-2 tank engine, Northwestern Railway of India. e, 4-2-2 Imperial Yellow Mail engine, Shanghai-Nanking Railway. f, 2-4-2 tank engine, Danish State Railway.

No. 2216, each $1.50: a, Electric railcar, South Jersey Transit. b, Metroliner, US. c, HSST Mag-lev train. d, E60C, Amtrak. e, TEE Express "Parsifal." f, 2-Co-Co-2 electric, Amtrak.

No. 2217, $6, The Experiment, US. No. 2218, 2-8-2 locomotive, Central South African Railway. No. 2219, $6, The Prospector, Western Australian Government Railways. No. 2220, Diesel-electric locomotive, South African Railways.

**2000, June 13**

**2209-2212** G170 Set of 4 5.25 5.25

**Sheets of 6, #a-f**

**2213-2216** G170 Set of 4 26.00 26.00

**Souvenir Sheets**

**2217-2220** G170 Set of 4 18.00 18.00

### European Soccer Championships Type

No. 2221, horiz, each $1.50 — Denmark: a, Tofting. b, Team photo. c, Michael Laudrup. d, Jorgensen. e, Philips Stadium, Eindhoven. f, Moller.

No. 2222, horiz, each $1.50 — France: a, Thuram. b, Team photo. c, Barthez. d, Zidane. e, Jan Breydel Stadium, Brugge. f, Michel Platini.

No. 2223, horiz, each $1.50 — Netherlands: a, Giovanni Van Bronckhorst. b, Team photo. c, Patrick Kluivert. d, Johan Cruyff. e, Amsterdam Arena Stadium. f, Zenden.

Each $6: No. 2224, Denmark coach Bo Johansson. No. 2225, France coach Roger Lemerre. No. 2226, Netherlands coach Frank Rijkaard.

**2000, Aug. 8 *Perf. 13¾***

**Sheets of 6, #a-f**

**2221-2223** A464 Set of 3 20.00 20.00

**Souvenir Sheets**

**2224-2226** A464 Set of 3 13.50 13.50

### Popes Type

No. 2227, each $1.50: a, Adrian VI, 1522-23. b, Paul II, 1464-71. c, Calixtus III, 1455-58. d, Eugenius IV, 1431-47.

**2000, Aug. 22**

**2227** A467 Sheet of 4, #a-d 4.50 4.50

**Souvenir Sheet**

**2228** A467 $6 Gregory IX, 1370-78 4.50 4.50

### Monarchs Type

No. 2229, each $1.50: a, Louis XVI of France, 1774-92. b, Louis XVIII of France, 1814-24. c, Queen of Kublai Khan, China. d, Mary Tudor of England, 1553-58. e, Mohammed Ali of Iran, 1907-09. f, Ch'ien-lung (Qianlong, Hung-li) of China, 1735-96.
$6, Vladimir I, Grand Prince of Kiev, 980-1015.

**2000, Aug. 22**

**2229** A468 Sheet of 6, #a-f 6.75 6.75

**Souvenir Sheet**

**2230** A468 $6 Vladimir I 4.50 4.50

Fauna G171

Designs: 75c, St. Lucia Amazon. 90c, Three-toed sloth. $1, Hispaniolan solenodon. $2,Thick-billed parrot.

No. 2235, each $1.50: a, Jaguarundi. b, Andean condor. c, Darwin's rhea. d, Central American tapir. e, Jaguar. f, Jamaican hutia.

No. 2236, each $1.50: a, Red vakari. b, San Andreas vireo. c, Golden lion tamarin. d, American crocodile. e, Spectacled caiman. f, Rhinoceros iguana.

Each $6: No. 2237, Pronghorn. No. 2238, Kemp Ridley sea turtle.

**2000, Sept. 5 *Perf. 14***

**2231-2234** G171 Set of 4 4.25 4.25

**Sheets of 6, #a-f**

**2235-2236** G171 Set of 2 17.00 17.00

**Souvenir Sheets**

**2237-2238** G171 Set of 2 12.00 12.00

The Stamp Show 2000, London (Nos. 2235-2238).

Souvenir Sheet

David Copperfield, Magician — G172

No. 2239, each $1.50: a, Copperfield's face at L, legs at R. b, Upper torso at L, face at R. c, Legs at L, face at R. d, Face at L, upper torso at R.

**2000, Sept. 14**

**2239** G172 Sheet of 4, #a-d 4.50 4.50

### Prado Paintings Type

#2240, each $1.50: a, St. John the Baptist and the Franciscan Maestro Henricus Werl, by Robert Campin. b, Justice and Peace, by Corrado Giaquinto. c, St. Barbara, by Campin. d, John Fane, 10th Count of Westmoreland, by Thomas Lawrence. e, The Marchioness of Manzanedo, by Jean-Louis-Ernest Meissonier. f, Mr. Storer, by Martin Archer Shee.

#2241, each $1.50: a, Isabella Carla Eugenia, by Alonso Sánchez Coello. b, Portrait of a Nobleman with His Hand on His Chest, by El Greco. c, Philip III, by Juan Pantoja de la Cruz. d, Madonna & child from The Holy Family with Saints Ildefons & John the Evangelist, & the Master Alonso de Villegas, by Blas del Prado. e, The Last Supper, by Bartolomé Carducci. f, Man with goblet from The Holy Family with Saints Ildefons & John the Evangelist, & the Master Alonso de Villegas.

#2242, each $1.50: a, Dominic of Silos, by Bartolomé Bermejo. b, Head of a Prophet, by Jaime Huguet. c, Christ Giving His Blessing, by Fernando Gallego. d, The Mystic Marriage of St. Catherine, by Alonso Sánchez Coello. e, St. Catherine of Alexandria, by Fernando Yáñez de la Almedina. f, Virgin and Child, by Luis de Morales.

Each $6: #2243, The Holy Family with Saints Ildefons & John the Evangelist, & the Master Alonso de Villegas. #2244, The Last Supper, horiz. #2245, The Coronation of the Virgin, by El Greco, horiz.

**2000, Oct. 19 *Perf. 12x12¼, 12¼x12***

**Sheets of 6, #a-f**

**2240-2242** A470 Set of 3 20.00 20.00

**Souvenir Sheets**

**2243-2245** A470 Set of 3 13.50 13.50

Espana 2000, Intl. Philatelic Exhibition.

### Mushroom Type of 2000

No. 2246, $2: a, Cinnabar chanterelle. b, Blackening wax cap. c, Edible cort. d, Orange scaber-stalk bolete.

No. 2247, $2: a, Crab russula. b, Steel blue entoloma. c, Tiger lentinus. d, Yellow-white mycena.

No. 2248, $2, horiz.: a, Le Gal's bolete. b, Emetic russula. c, Silvery violet cort. d, Tree volvariella.

No. 2249, $6, Scaly vase chanterelle, horiz. No. 2250, $6, Common collybia, horiz.

**2000, Mar. 3 Litho. *Perf. 14***

**Sheets of 4, #a-d**

**2246-2248** A448 Set of 3 18.00 18.00

**Souvenir Sheets**

**2249-2250** A448 Set of 2 9.00 9.00

### Dog Type of 2000

Designs: 45c, Irish setter. 90c, Dalmatian. $2, German shepherd.

No. 2254, $1.50: a, Alaskan malamute. b, Golden retriever. c, Afghan hound. d, Long-haired dachshund. e, Irish terrier. f, Miniature poodle.

No. 2255, $1.50: a, Great Dane. b, Newfoundland. c, Rottweiler. d, Bulldog. e, Japanese spitz. f, Bull terrier.

No. 2256, $6, Labrador retriever. No. 2257, $6, Basset hound, horiz.

**2000, June 23**

**2251-2253** A473 Set of 3 2.50 2.50

**Sheets of 6, #a-f**

**2254-2255** A473 Set of 2 13.50 13.50

**Souvenir Sheets**

**2256-2257** A473 Set of 2 9.00 9.00

### Cat Type of 2000

Designs: 75c, Blue point snowshoe. $3, Black and white Maine coon cat. $4, Brown tabby British shorthair.

No. 2261, $1.50: a, California spangled cat. b, Russian blue. c, Seal point Siamese. d, Black Devon rex. e, Silver tabby British shorthair. f, Tricolor Japanese bobtail.

No. 2262, $1.50: a, British white shorthair. b, Blue cream American shorthair. c, Bombay. d, Red Burmese. e, Sorrel Abyssinian. f, Ocicat.

$5, Silver classic tabby Persian, horiz.

No. 2263A, $5, Red-white bicolored British shorthair.

**2000, June 23**

**2258-2260** A478 Set of 3 5.75 5.75

**Sheets of 6, #a-f**

**2261-2262** A478 Set of 2 13.50 13.50

**Souvenir Sheet**

**2263** A478 $5 multi 3.75 3.75
**2263A** A478 $5 multi 3.75 3.75

### Battle of Britain Type of 2000

No. 2264, each $1: a, Women fire fighters, London. b, Family leaving after the Blitz. c, Searchlights, London. d, Winston Churchill in Coventry after German raid. e, Rescue after German bombing. f, Rescue after London bombing. g, Terror hits Buckingham Gate. h, After a German raid on Coventry.

No. 2265, each $1: a, Pilots scramble to their planes. b, Balloons to catch low-flying planes. c, Spitfire B. d, Speech by Princess Elizabeth. e, Fire Watchers, auxiliary fire service. f, Painting stripes to see at night. g, Bombed buildings in Britain. h, Air raid wardens, auxiliary police force.

Each $6: No. 2266, Hawker Hurricane. No. 2267, British family survives German bombing, vert.

**2000, Oct. 30**

**Sheets of 8, #a-h**

**2264-2265** A471 Set of 2 12.00 12.00

**Souvenir Sheets**

**2266-2267** A471 Set of 2 9.00 9.00

### Queen Mother Type of 2000

**2000, Oct. 30**

**2268** A479 $1.50 multi 1.10 1.10

Printed in sheets of 6.

### Photomosaic Type of 1999

No. 2269, $1: Various flowers making up a photomosaic of the Queen Mother.

No. 2270, $1: Various photographs with religious theme making up a photomosaic of Pope John Paul II.

**2000, Oct. 30** ***Perf. 13¾***

**2269-2270** A445 Set of 2 12.00 12.00

Harry Houdini, Magician — G173

**2000** **Litho.** ***Perf. 14***

**2271** G173 $1.50 multi 1.10 1.10

Issued in sheets of 4.

Souvenir Sheet

Barbara Taylor Bradford, Author — G174

**2000** **Litho.** ***Perf. 12¼***

**2272** G174 $6 multi 4.50 4.50

Souvenir Sheet

Hong Kong Comic Strip "The Storm Riders" — G175

No. 2273: a, Character with arms folded. b, Character with sword. c, Character in brown cape. d, Character in green.

**2000** ***Perf. 13½***

**2273** G175 $4 Sheet of 4, #a-d 9.00 9.00

New Year 2001 (Year of the Snake) — G176

No. 2274: a, Rat snake. b, Mangrove snake. c, Boomslang. d, Emerald tree boa. e, African egg-eating snake. f, Chinese green tree viper.

**2001, Jan. 2** ***Perf. 14***

**2274** G176 90c Sheet of 6, #a-f 4.00 4.00

**Souvenir Sheet**

**2275** G176 $4 King cobra 3.00 3.00

### Rijksmuseum Type of 2001

No. 2276, $1.50: a, Person with red shirt from Dune Landcape, by Jan van Goyen. b, The Raampoortje, by Wouter Johannes van Troostwijk. c, House and horse from The Cattle Ferry, by Esaias van de Velde. d, The Departure of a Senior Functionary from Middleburg, by Adriaen van de Venne. e, Steeple and ferry from The Cattle Ferry. f, Four people near rock from Dune Landscape.

No. 2277, $1.50: a, Building, statue and dog from Garden Party, by Dirck Hals. b, Still Life with Gilt Cup, by Willem Claesz Heda. c, Cloud of smoke from Orestes and Pylades Disputing at the Altar, by Pieter Lastman. d, Buildings from Orestes and Pylades Disputing at the Altar. e, Self-portrait in a Yellow Robe, by Jan Lievens. f, Birds in sky from Garden Party.

No. 2278, $1.50: a, Beatrix from Marriage Portrait of Isaac Massa and Beatrix van der Laen, by Frans Hals. b, Winter Landscape With Ice Skaters, by Hendrick Avercamp. c, Man and woman from The Spendthrift, by Cornelis Troost. d, Men in brown from The Spendthrift. e, Men and woman from The Art Gallery of Jan Gildermeester Jansz, by Adriaan de Lelie. f, Three men from The Art Gallery of Jan Gildermeester Jansz.

No. 2279, $1.50: a, Man from A Music Party, by Rembrandt. b, Woman from A Music Party. c, Girl and boy from Rutger Jan Schimmelpennick With His Wife and Children, by Pierre-Paul Prud'hon. d, Girl from Rutger Jan Schimmelpennick With His Wife and Children. e, Two men from The Syndics, by Thomas de Keyser. f, Isaac and Beatrix from Marriage Portrait of Isaac Massa and Beatrix van der Laen.

No. 2280, $6, A Music Party. No. 2281, $6, Anna Accused by Tobit of Stealing a Kid, by Rembrandt. No. 2282, $6, Cleopatra's Banquet, by Gerard Lairesse, horiz. No. 2283, $6, View of Tivoli, by Isaac de Moucheron.

**2001, Jan. 15** ***Perf. 13¾***

**Sheets of 6, #a-f**

**2276-2279** A483 Set of 4 27.50 27.50

**Souvenir Sheets**

**2280-2283** A483 Set of 4 18.00 18.00

### Pokémon Type of 2001

No. 2284, each $1.50: a, Bellsprout. b, Vulpix. c, Dewgong. d, Oddish. e, Dratini. f, Jigglypuff.

**2001, Feb. 1**

**2284** A484 Sheet of 6, #a-f 6.75 6.75

**Souvenir Sheet**

**2285** A484 $6 Pikachu 4.50 4.50

Animals of the Tropics G177

Designs: 75c, Greater flamingo, vert. 90c, Cuban crocodile. $1, Jaguarundi, vert. $2, Wedge-capped capuchin monkey.

No. 2290, $1.50, vert.: a, Cuban pygmy owl. b, Woody spider monkey. c, Bee hummingbirds. d, Dragonfly, poison dart frog. e, Red brocket deer. f, Cuban stream anole.

No. 2291, $1.50, vert.: a, Red-breasted toucan. b, Mexican black howler monkey. c, Fleck's pygmy boa. d, Red-eyed tree frog. e, Caiman. f, Jaguar.

No. 2292, $6, Ocelot, vert. No. 2293, $6, Western knight anole, vert.

**2001, Feb. 1** ***Perf. 14***

**2286-2289** G177 Set of 4 4.25 4.25

**Sheets of 6, #a-f**

**2290-2291** G177 Set of 2 17.00 17.00

**Souvenir Sheets**

**2292-2293** G177 Set of 2 13.00 13.00

Hong Kong 2001 Stamp Exhibition.

### Fish Type of 2000 with Added WWF Emblem

No. 2294: a, Sparisoma rubripinne. b, Scarus vetula. c, Scarus taeniopterus. d, Sparisoma viride.

**2001, Mar. 28** **Litho.** ***Perf. 14***

**2294** G167 75c Strip of 4, #a-d 4.25 4.25

Waterfowl — G178

No. 2295, horiz, each $1.50: a, Falklands streamer duck. b, Black-crowned night heron. c, Muscovy duck. d, Ruddy duck. e, Black-necked screamer. f, White-faced whistling duck.

**2001, Mar. 28**

**2295** G178 Sheet of 6, #a-f 6.75 6.75

**Souvenir Sheet**

**2296** G178 $6 Great egret 4.50 4.50

Scenes From "The Littlest Rebel," Starring Shirley Temple — G179

Temple with — No. 2297, horiz.: a, Pointing soldier. b, Black woman. c, Soldier in carriage. d, Pres. Lincoln.

No. 2298: a, Spoon. b, Woman near tree. c, Soldier with hat. d, Woman. e, Black man and soldier. f, Man.

$6, Black man.

**2001, Apr. 25** ***Perf. 13¾***

**2297** G179 $2 Sheet of 4, #a-d 6.00 6.00
**2298** G179 $2 Sheet of 6, #a-f 9.00 9.00

**Souvenir Sheet**

**2299** G179 $6 multi 4.50 4.50

Clark Gable (1901-60) — G180

No. 2300, $1.50 — Color of photo: a, Purple. b, Sepia (wearing suit and tie). c, Yellow. d, Sepia (wearing sweater). e, Blue. f, Sepia (wearing bow tie).

No. 2301, $1.50 — Signature of Gable and Gable with: a, Cigar. b, Vest. c, Chair. d, Pen. e, Suit and tie. f, Pinstriped suit.

No. 2302, $6, Blue background. No. 2303, $6, Gable in uniform.

**2001, Apr. 25** ***Perf. 14***

**Sheets of 6, #a-f**

**2300-2301** G180 Set of 2 13.50 13.50

**Souvenir Sheets**

**2302-2303** G180 Set of 2 9.00 9.00

### Betty Boop Type of 2000

No. 2304 — Boop: a, With comb. b, With veil. c. With lei. d, At carnival. e, With flower in hair. f, With cowboy hat. g, With beret. h, In automobile. i, As Statue of Liberty.

No. 2305, $6, In sari. No. 2306, $6, In gondola.

**2001, Apr. 25** ***Perf. 13¾***

**2304** A481 $1 Sheet of 9, #a-i 6.75 6.75

**Souvenir Sheets**

**2305-2306** A481 Set of 2 9.00 9.00

### Phila Nippon Type of 2001

Designs: 75c, Scenes of Daily Life in Edo, by Choshun Miyagawa. 90c, Twelve Famous Places in Japan, by Eisenin Naganobu Kano. $1, Scenery Along the Length of the Sumida River, by Kyuei Kano. $1.25, Cranes, by Eisenin Michinobu Kano. No. 2311, $2, A Courtesan of Yoshiwara, by Shunei Katsukawa. $3, Rite of Bear Killing: Praying to the Bear's Spirit, by unknown artist.

No. 2313, $2, vert. — Bodhisattva Samantabhadra from the Lotus Sutra with: a, Surrounding rings, yellow elephant. b, White elephant. c, Temple at left. d, Surrounding rings with rays.

No. 2314, $2 (85x28mm) — Chapter illustrations from Genji Monogatari Emaki, by Ryusetsu Hidenobu Kano: a, Kiritsubo. b, Akashi. c, Hatsune. d, E-Awase.

No. 2315, $6, A Sage Pointing at the Moon, by Ranseki Katagiri. No. 2316, $6, Frontispiece for Devadatta, Lotus Sutra, vert.

**2001, May 1** ***Perf. 14***

**2307-2312** A487 Set of 6 6.75 6.75

**Sheets of 4, #a-d**

**2313-2314** A488 Set of 2 12.00 12.00

**Souvenir Sheets**

**2315-2316** A488 Set of 2 9.00 9.00

### Marlene Dietrich Type of 2001

Dietrich with: a, Microphone. b, Robe. c, Flowered dress. d, Hat.

**2001, May 15** ***Perf. 13¾***

**2317** A489 $2 Sheet of 4, #a-d 6.00 6.00

### Queen Victoria Type of 2001

No. 2318 — Queen Victoria with: a, Scepter. b, Flower. c, Sash.
$6, Sash, diff.

**2001, May 15** ***Perf. 14***

**2318** A490 $3 Sheet of 3, #a-c 6.75 6.75

**Souvenir Sheet**

**2319** A490 $6 multi 4.50 4.50

### Queen Elizabeth II Type of 2001

No. 2320, each $1.25 — Predominant background colors: a, Brown and yellow. b, Green. c, Blue. d, Black. e, Red and violet. f, Red and light blue.
No. 2320G, each $2: h, Green background. i, Purple background. j, Brown background.
$6, Tan.

**2001, May 15** ***Perf. 14***

**2320** A491 Sheet of 6, #a-f 5.75 5.75
**2320G** A491 Sheet of 3, #h-j 4.50 4.50

**Souvenir Sheet**

***Perf. 13¾***

**2321** A491 $6 multi 3.75 3.75

No. 2321 contains one 38x51mm stamp.

### Ship Type of 2001

Designs: 90c, Creole. $1, Britannia. $2, Ariel. $3, Sindia.
No. 2326, $1.25: a, William Fawcett. b, Sirius. c, S.S. Great Britain. d, Oriental. e, Lightning. f, Great Eastern.
No. 2327, $1.25: a, Santa Maria and Christopher Columbus. b, Sao Gabriel and Vasco da Gama. c, Victoria and Ferdinand Magellan. d, Golden Hind and Sir Francis Drake. e, Endeavour and Capt. James Cook. f, HMS Erebus and John Franklin.
No. 2328, $1.25, vert.: a, Mayflower. b, Gabriel. c, Beagle. d, Challenger. e, Vega. f, Fram.
No. 2329, $6, Challenge. No. 2330, $6, Cutty Sark.

**2001, June 18** ***Perf. 14***

**2322-2325** A497 Set of 4 5.25 5.25

**Sheets of 6, #a-f**

**2326-2328** A497 Set of 3 17.00 17.00

**Miniature Sheets**

**2329-2330** A497 Set of 2 9.00 9.00

### Magician Type of Grenada Grenadines of 2000

Designs: No. 2331, $1.50, Howard Thurston. No. 2332, $1.50, Harry Kellar.

**2001**

**2331-2332** G173 Set of 2 2.25 2.25

Issued in sheets of 4.

### Mao Zedong Type of 2001

No. 2333, horiz.: a, Mao on stairs. b, Mao at right, with soldiers. c, Mao at left, with peasants. d, Mao seated, with officers.
$3, Portrait.

**2001, May 15** **Litho.** ***Perf. 14***

**2333** A493 $1.50 Sheet of 4, #a-d 4.50 4.50

**Souvenir Sheet**

**2334** A493 $3 multi 2.25 2.25

### Verdi Type of 2001

No. 2335 — Verdi and score: a, 25c. b, 75c. c, $2. d, $3.
$6, Portrait.

**2001, May 15** ***Perf. 14***

**2335** A494 Sheet of 4, #a-d 4.50 4.50

**Souvenir Sheet**

**2336** A494 $6 multi 4.50 4.50

### Toulouse-Lautrec Type of 2001

No. 2337, horiz.: a, Helene V. b, The Clownesse. c, Madame Berthe Bady. d, The Woman With The Black Boa.
$6, Loie Fuller at the Folies Bergére.

**2001, May 15** ***Perf. 13¾***

**2337** A495 $1 Sheet of 4, #a-d 3.00 3.00

**Souvenir Sheet**

**2338** A495 $6 multi 4.50 4.50

### Monet Type of 2001

No. 2339, horiz.: a, The Magpie. b, La Pointe de la Hève at Low Tide. c, Boats: Regatta at Argenteuil. d, La Grenouillère.
$6, Portrait of J. F. Jaquemart with Parasol.

**2001, May 15**

**2339** A504 $1 Sheet of 4, #a-d 3.00 3.00

**Souvenir Sheet**

**2340** A504 $6 multi 4.50 4.50

Orchids G181

Designs: 25c, Vanda Singapore. 50c, Vanda Joan Warne. 75c, Vanda lamellata. $2, Vanda merrillii.
No. 2345, $1.50: a, Papilionanthe teres. b, Vanda flabellata. c, Vanda tessellata (name at LL). d, Vanda pumila. e, Rhynchostylis gigantea. f, Vandopsis gigantea.
No. 2346, $1.50: a, Vanda tessellata (name at center left). b, Vanda helvola. c, Vanda brunnea. d, Vanda stangeana. e, Vanda limbata. f, Vandopsis tricolor.
No. 2347, $6, Vanda insignis. No. 2348, $6, Vandopsis lissochiloides.

**2001, Oct. 15** ***Perf. 14***

**2341-2344** G181 Set of 4 2.60 2.60

**Sheets of 6, #a-f**

**2345-2346** G181 Set of 2 13.50 13.50

**Souvenir Sheets**

**2347-2348** G181 Set of 2 9.00 9.00

Souvenir Sheets

Richard Petty, Stock Car Racer — G182

Designs: No. 2349, $6, shown. No. 2350, $6, Petty speaking into microphone.

**2001, Oct. 15** ***Perf. 13¾***

**2349-2350** G182 Set of 2 9.00 9.00

Ferrari Formula 1 Racing Cars — G183

No. 2351: a, 1986 F1 86. b, 1989 F1 89. c, 1992 F92A. d, 1993 F1 93. e, 1994 412T1. f, 1996 F310.

**2001, Nov. 19** ***Perf. 13¾***

**2351** G183 $1.50 Sheet of 6, #a-f 6.75 6.75

### World Cup Soccer Championships Type of 2001

No. 2352, $1.50 — World Cup posters and badges from: a, 1950. b, 1954. c, 1958. d, 1962. e, 1966. f, 1970.
No. 2353, $1.50 — World Cup posters and badges from: a, 1978. b, 1982. c, 1986. d, 1990. e, 1994. f, 1998.
No. 2354, $6, World Cup poster and badge, 1930. No. 2355, $6, Head and globe from World Cup trophy.

**2001, Nov. 29** ***Perf. 13¾x14¼***

**Sheets of 6, #a-f**

**2352-2353** A505 Set of 2 13.50 13.50

**Souvenir Sheets**

**2354-2355** A505 Set of 2 9.00 9.00

Christmas — G184

Designs: 25c, Coronation of the Virgin, by Filippo Lippi. 75c, Virgin and Child, by Mantegna. $1.50, Madonna and Child, by Masaccio. $3, Madonna and Child, by Raphael.
$6, Virgin and child Enthroned with Angels, by Mantegna.

**2001, Dec. 3** ***Perf. 14***

**2356-2359** G184 Set of 4 4.25 4.25

**Souvenir Sheet**

**2360** G184 $6 multi 4.50 4.50

Royal Navy Ships — G185

Designs: 75c, HMS Renown in Portsmouth Harbor, 1922. 90c, Battle of the Saintes, 1782. $2, Battle of Trafalgar, 1805. $3, Embarkation at Dover, 1520.
No. 2365, $1.50, horiz.: a, Battle of Solebay, 1672. b, HMS Royal Prince, 1679. c, Battle of Texel, 1673. d, Battle of Scheveningen, 1653. e, Barbary Pirates, 1600s. f, Royal Charles, 1667.
No. 2366, $1.50, horiz.: a, Skirmishing preceding the Battle of the First of June. b, Moonlight Battle, 1780. c, Great ships of the Jacobean Navy, 1623. d, Battle of the Gulf of Genoa, 1795. e, Battle of the Nile, 1798. f, St. Lucia, 1778.
No. 2367, $6, Battle of Navarino, 1827, horiz. No. 2368, $6, HMS Repulse, 1924, horiz.

**2001, Dec. 10** **Litho.**

**2361-2364** G185 Set of 4 5.00 5.00

**Sheets of 6, #a-f**

**2365-2366** G185 Set of 2 13.50 13.50

**Souvenir Sheets**

**2367-2368** G185 Set of 2 9.00 9.00

### Queen Mother Type of 1999 Redrawn

No. 2369: a, Lady Elizabeth Bowles-Lyon. b, In Rhodesia, 1957. c, With Princesses Elizabeth and Anne, 1950. d, In 1988.
$6, In Berlin.

**2001, Dec. 13** ***Perf. 14***

**Yellow Orange Frames**

**2369** A440 $2 Sheet of 4, #a-d, + label 6.00 6.00

**Souvenir Sheet**

***Perf. 13¾***

**2370** A440 $6 multi 4.50 4.50

Queen Mother's 101st birthday. No. 2370 contains one 38x50mm stamp with a slightly darker appearance than that found on No. 2122. Sheet margins of Nos. 2369-2370 lack embossing and gold arms and frames found on Nos. 2121-2122.

### Princess Diana Type of 2001

Souvenir Sheet

Diana in: a, Yellow dress. b, Red jacket. c, White pinstriped suit.

**2001, Feb. 15** ***Perf. 14***

**2371** A509 $1.50 Sheet of 2 each #a-c 6.75 6.75

Pres. John F. Kennedy — G187

No. 2372, vert. — Pres. Kennedy: a, In boat. b, In chair. c, Profile. d, Close-up, smiling. e, Close-up. f, Looking down.
$6, With Nikita Khrushchev.

**2001, Dec. 15** ***Perf. 13¾***

**2372** G187 $1.50 Sheet of 6, #a-f 6.75 6.75

**Souvenir Sheet**

**2373** G187 $6 multi 4.50 4.50

Jacqueline Kennedy Onassis (1929-94) — G188

No. 2374: a, Blue jacket, blue blouse. b, Red jacket, blue blouse. c, Green dress. d, Blue cape. e Pink and blue jacket. f, Blue jacket, yellow blouse.
No. 2375, $6, Mountain in background. No. 2376, $6, Beige background.

**2001, Dec. 15** ***Perf. 14***

**2374** G188 $1.50 Sheet of 6, #a-f 6.75 6.75

**Souvenir Sheets**

**2375-2376** G188 Set of 2 9.00 9.00

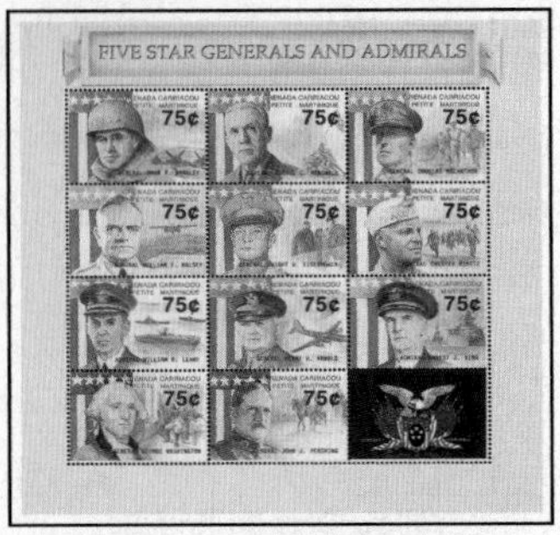


G189

US Generals and Admirals — G190

No. 2377: a, Gen. Omar N. Bradley. b, Gen. George C. Marshall. c, Gen. Douglas MacArthur. d, Adm. William F. Halsey. e, Gen. Dwight D. Eisenhower. f, Adm. Chester Nimitz. g, Adm. William D. Leahy. h, Gen. Henry H. Arnold. i, Adm. Ernest J. King. j, Gen. George Washington. k, Gen. John J. Pershing.

No. 2378: a, Gen. George S. Patton, Jr. b, Gen. Joseph W. Stilwell. c, Adm. Thomas C. Kinkaid. d, Gen. Jonathan Wainwright. e, Lt. Gen. James H. Doolittle. f, Gen. Matthew B. Ridgway. g, Gen. Maxwell D. Taylor. h, Adm. Richmond Kelly Turner. i, Gen. Curtis E. LeMay. j, Gen. Hoyt S. Vandenberg. k, Gen. Carl Spaatz. l, Adm. Raymond Spruance.

No. 2379, $6, Eisenhower. No. 2380, $6, Douglas MacArthur.

**2001, Dec. 15** *Perf. 14*

**2377** G189 75c Sheet of 11, #a-k, + label 6.25 6.25
**2378** G189 75c Sheet of 12, #a-l 6.75 6.75

**Souvenir Sheets**

***Perf. 13¾***

**2379-2380** G190 Set of 2 9.00 9.00

Moths G191

Designs: 75c, Pine emperor. 90c, Inquisitive monkey. $2, Oak eggar. $3, Madagascan sunset moth.

No. 2385, $1.50: a, Spanish moon moth. b, Coppery dysphania. c, Io moth. d, Large agarista. e, Millar's tiger. f, Tropical fruit-piercer.

No. 2386, $1.50: a, Indian moon moth. b, Beautiful tiger. c, Regal moth. d, Great tiger moth. e, Venus moth. f, Zodiac moth.

No. 2387, $6, Diva moth, vert. No. 2388, $6, African moon moth, vert.

**2001, Dec. 17** *Perf. 14*

**2381-2384** G191 Set of 4 5.00 5.00

**Sheets of 6, #a-f**

**2385-2386** G191 Set of 2 13.50 13.50

**Souvenir Sheets**

**2387-2388** G191 Set of 2 9.00 9.00

Vegaspex (#2386).

## Reign of Queen Elizabeth II, 50th Anniv. Type of 2002

No. 2389: a, White hat. b, Red hat. c, Tiara. d, Hatless.

$6, With Princes Philip, Charles, Princess Anne.

**2002, Feb. 6** *Perf. 14¼*

**2389** A516 $2 Sheet of 4, #a-d 6.00 6.00

**Souvenir Sheet**

**2390** A516 $6 multi 4.50 4.50

New Year 2002 (Year of the Horse) — G192

Various horses with background colors of — No. 2391: a, 75c, Light brown and light orange. b, $1.25, Light blue and olive green. c, $2, Tan and bister.

$6, Light orange and orange.

**2002, Mar. 4** **Litho.** *Perf. 13¾*

**2391** G192 Sheet of 3, #a-c 3.00 3.00

**Souvenir Sheet**

**2392** G192 $6 multi 4.50 4.50

United We Stand — G193

**2002, May 21** *Perf. 14*

**2393** G193 80c multi .60 .60

Printed in sheets of 4.

## Chiune Sugihara Type of 2002

Souvenir Sheets

Sugihara and: No. 2394, $6, Map of Asia. No. 2395, $6, Pink background.

**2002, July 1** *Perf. 13½x13¼*

**2394-2395** A521 Set of 2 9.00 9.00

## Winter Olympics Type of 2002

Montages of: No. 2396, $3, Skier in air, course flag, vert. No. 2397, $3, Skier, no flag, vert.

**2002, July 1** *Perf. 13½x13¼*

**2396-2397** A522 Set of 2 4.50 4.50
*2397a* Souvenir sheet, #2396-2397 4.50 4.50

## Intl. Year of Mountains Type of 2002

No. 2398: a, Mt. Kilimanjaro, Tanzania. b, Mt. Kenya, Kenya. c, Mauna Kea, Hawaii. d, Mt. Fuji, Japan.

$6, Koolau Mountains, Hawaii.

**2002, July 1** *Perf. 13¼x13½*

**2398** A523 $2 Sheet of 4, #a-d 6.00 6.00

**Souvenir Sheet**

**2399** A523 $6 multi 4.50 4.50

## Intl. Year of Ecotourism Type of 2002

No. 2400, horiz.: a, Tourists at waterfall. b, Bird. c, Butterfly. d, Fish. e, Cactus. f, Orchid.

$6, Birds, horiz.

**2002, July 1** *Perf. 13¼x13½*

**2400** A524 $1.50 Sheet of 6, #a-f 6.75 6.75

**Souvenir Sheet**

**2401** A524 $6 multi 4.50 4.50

Nos. 2400-2401 were each overprinted in sheet margins "Hurricane Relief 2004" in 2005.

## Scout Jamboree Type of 2002

No. 2402, horiz.: a, Campfire, Scout emblem. b, Scout with walking stick and backpack. c, Scout feeding calf. d, Girl giving Scout sign.

No. 2403, $6, Scout with hat.

**2002, July 1** *Perf. 13¼x13½*

**2402** A525 $2 Sheet of 4, #a-d 6.00 6.00

**Souvenir Sheet**

***Perf. 13½x13¼***

**2403** A525 $2 multi 1.50 1.50

Amerigo Vespucci (1454-1512), Explorer — G194

Various portraits with background colors of: $1, Purple. $2, Orange brown. $3, Green.

$6, Vespucci and map.

**2002, July 1** *Perf. 13½x13¼*

**2404-2406** G194 Set of 3 4.50 4.50

**Souvenir Sheet**

**2407** G194 $6 multi 4.50 4.50

## Butterflies, Insects, Mushrooms and Whales Type of 2002

No. 2408, $1 — Whales: a, Sperm. b, Bottlenose. c, Sei. d, Killer. e, Humpback. f, Pygmy sperm.

No. 2409, $1 — Insects: a, Bumblebee. b, Dragonfly. c, Hercules beetle. d, Ladybug. e, Figure-of-eight butterfly. f, Praying mantis.

No. 2410, $2 — Butterflies: a, White peacock. b, Orange-barred sulphur. c, Blue night. d, Banded king shoemaker. e, Cramer's mesene. f, Common morpho.

No. 2411, $2 — Mushrooms: a, Shaggy mane. b, Shaggy parasol. c, Purple coincap. d, Sharp-scaled parasol. e, Thick-footed morel. f, Rosy-gill fairy helmet.

No. 2412, $6, Blue whale, horiz. No. 2413, $6, Dragonfly, horiz. No. 2414, $6, Blue night butterfly, horiz. No. 2415, $6, Death cap mushroom.

**2002, Aug. 12** *Perf. 14*

**Sheets of 6, #a-f**

**2408-2411** A538 Set of 4 27.50 27.50

**Souvenir Sheets**

**2412-2415** A538 Set of 4 18.00 18.00

## Elvis Presley Type of 2002 and

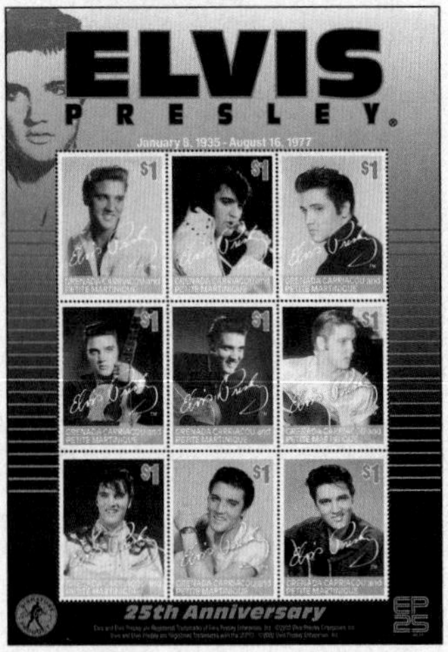


Elvis Presley — G195

No. 2416, Color portrait.

No. 2417: a, Wearing light plaid shirt. b, Holding microphone. c, Wearing dark shirt. d, Holding guitar with neck up. e, Wearing suit, holding guitar. f, Wearing short-sleeve shirt, holding guitar. g, Wearing shirt with flowers on shoulders. h, Wearing wrist watch and short-sleeve shirt. i, Wearing dark plaid shirt, holding guitar.

**2002, Aug. 26** *Perf. 13¾*

**2416** A527 $1 multi .75 .75
**2417** G195 $1 Sheet of 9, #a-i 6.75 6.75

No. 2416 printed in sheets of 9.

## Dutch Nobel Prize Winners, Lighthouses and Women's Costumes Types of 2002

No. 2418 — Nobel Prize winners: a, Paul Crutzen, Chemistry, 1995. b, Nobel Medal for Physics, Chemistry, Physiology or Medicine, and Literature. c, Martinus J. G. Veltman, Physics, 1999. d, Hendrik A. Lorentz, Physics, 1902. e, Christiaan Eijkman, Physiology or Medicine, 1929. f, Gerardus 't Hooft, Physics, 1999.

No. 2419 — Lighthouses: a, Ameland. b, Vlieland. c, Julianadorp. d, Noordwijk. e, Hoek van Holland. f, Goeree.

No. 2420 — Women's costumes: a, Noord-Holland (woman with child). b, Overijssel (woman with blue dress and plaid neckerchief). c, Zeeland (woman with necklace).

**2002, Aug. 29** *Perf. 13½x13¼*

**2418** A532 $1.50 Sheet of 6, #a-f 6.75 6.75
**2419** A533 $1.50 Sheet of 6, #a-f 6.75 6.75

***Perf. 13¼***

**2420** A534 $3 Sheet of 3, #a-c 6.75 6.75

Amphilex 2002 Intl. Stamp Exhibition, Amsterdam.

## Teddy Bear Centenary Types of 2002

No. 2421 — Bear with: a, 15c, Tasseled helmet. b, $2, Black hat with red bullseye. c, $3, Hat and neck ruffle. d, $4, Gray hat.

No. 2422 — Bear with: a, 50c, Happy birthday heart. b, $1, Flower, vest, hat, and violin case. c, $2, Hat and trench coat. d, $5, Shorts.

**2002, Sept. 23** *Perf. 14*

**2421** A529 Sheet of 4, #a-d 7.00 7.00
**2422** A530 Sheet of 4, #a-d 6.50 6.50

## Christmas Type of 2002

Carpaccio paintings: 15c, The Redeemer and the Four Apostles. 25c, The Miracle of the Relic of the Cross, vert. 50c, The Presentation in the Temple. $2, The Visitation. $3, The Birth of the Virgin.

$6, Madonna and Child and Two Angels, by Cimabue, vert.

**2002, Nov. 4** *Perf. 14*

**2423-2427** A541 Set of 5 4.50 4.50

**Souvenir Sheet**

**2428** A541 $6 multi 4.50 4.50

## World Cup Soccer Matches Type of 2002

No. 2429, $1.50: a, Oliver Neuville, Eddie Pope. b, Claudio Reyna, Miroslav Klose. c, Christian Ziege, Frankie Hejduk. d, Nadal, Jung Hwan Ahn. e, Luis Enrique, Chong Gug Song. f, Park Ji Sung, Mendieta Gaizka.

No. 2430, $1.50: a, Danny Mills, Ronaldo. b, Roque Junior, Emile Heskey. c, Sol Campbell, Rivaldo. d, Lamine Diatta, Hakan Sukur. e, Umit Davala, Khalilou Fadiga. f, El Hadji Diouf, Tugay Kerimoglu.

No. 2431, $3: a, Oliver Kahn. b, Brad Friedel.

No. 2432, $3: a, Chun Soo Lee. b, Juan Carlos Valeron.

No. 2433, $3: a, David Beckham, Roberto Carlos. b, Ronaldinho, Nicky Butt.

No. 2434, $3: a, Alpay Ozalan. b, Fadiga.

**2002, Nov. 18** *Perf. 13¼*

**Sheets of 6, #a-f**

**2429-2430** A542 Set of 2 13.50 13.50

**Souvenir Sheets of 2, #a-b**

**2431-2434** A542 Set of 4 18.00 18.00

## Dale Earnhardt Type of 2002

No. 2435: a, $2, 1980 photo. b, $2, 1986 photo. c, $2, 1987 photo. d, $2, 1990 photo. e, $2, 1991 photo. f, $2, 1993 photo. g, $2, 1994 photo. h, $4, Two cars (75x50mm).

**2002** *Perf. 13½x13¾*

**2435** A518 Sheet of 8, #a-h 13.50 13.50

New Year 2003 (Year of the Ram) — G196

**2003, Jan. 27** *Perf. 14*
**2436** G196 $1.25 multi .95 .95

Printed in sheets of 4.

G197

Coronation of Queen Elizabeth II, 50th Anniv. — G198

No. 2437: a, As child. b, In blue dress. c, On horse.
$6, Wearing sash and tiara.
$20, Wearing tiara.

**2003** **Litho.** *Perf. 14*
**2437** G197 $3 Sheet of 3, #a-c 6.75 6.75

**Souvenir Sheet**

**2438** G197 $6 multi 4.50 4.50

**Miniature Sheet**
**Litho. & Embossed**
*Perf. 13¼x13*

**2439** G198 $20 gold & multi 15.00 15.00

Issued: Nos. 2437-2438, 8/25; No. 2439, 2/24.

### Space Shuttle Columbia Type of 2003

No. 2440: a, Mission Specialist 1 David M. Brown. b, Commander Rick D. Husband. c, Mission Specialist 4 Laurel Blair Salton Clark. d, Mission Specialist 4 Kalpana Chawla. e, Payload Commander Michael P. Anderson. f, Pilot William C. McCool. g, Payload Specialist 4 Ilan Ramon.

**2003, Apr. 7** **Litho.** *Perf. 13¼*
**2440** A549 $1 Sheet of 7, #a-g 5.25 5.25

### Klimt Paintings Type of 2003

Designs: 15c, Le Chapeau de Plumes Noires. 25c, Le Schloss Kammer am Attersee. 50c, Malcesine sue le Lac de Garde. 75c, Ferme en Haute Autriche. $1.25, Portrait d'une Dame. $4, La Frise Beethoven.
No. 2447: a, Portrait de la Baronne Elisabeth Bachofen-Echt. b, Portrait d'une Dame, diff. c, Portrait d'Emilie Floge. d, Portrait d'Adele Bloch-Bauer.
$6, Le Baiser.

**2003, Apr. 28** *Perf. 14¼*
**2441-2446** A550 Set of 6 5.25 5.25
*Perf. 13¼*
**2447** A550 $2 Sheet of 4, #a-d 6.00 6.00

**Size: 83x103mm**
*Imperf*

**2448** A550 $6 multi 4.50 4.50

### Japanese Art Type of 2003

Paintings by Kunichika Toyohara: 50c, The Actor Danjuro Ichikawa IX as the Beggar Kagekiyo Akushichibyoe. 75c, The Actor Danjuro Ichikawa IX as the Female Demon Uwanari. $1.25, The Actor Tossho Sawamura II as Sutewakamaru. $3, The Actor Hikosaburo Bando V as Danjo Nikki.
No. 2453: a, The Actor Shikan Nakamura IV as Rokusuke Keyamura. b, The Actor Hikosaburo Bando V as Ichimisair No Musume Osono. c, The Actor Sadanji Ichikawa I as Wada No Shimobe Busuke. d, The Actor Sandanji Ichikawa I as Kiyomizu no Yoshitaka.
$6, The Actor Kikugoro Onoe V as Tsuneemon Torii Retruning to Mikawa, horiz.

**2003, Apr. 28** *Perf. 14¼*
**2449-2452** A551 Set of 4 4.25 4.25
**2453** A551 $2 Sheet of 4, #a-d 6.00 6.00

**Souvenir Sheet**

**2454** A551 $6 multi 4.50 4.50

### Cranach Paintings Type of 2003

Details from paintings by Lucas Cranach the Elder: 25c, The St. Mary Altarpiece, vert. $1, The St. Mary Altarpiece, diff., vert. $1.25, Duke John with St. James the Greater, from Altarpiece of the Princes, vert. $3, Frederick the Wise with St. Bartholomew, vert.
No. 2459: a, Judith at the Table of Holofernes. b, Central panel of St. Catherine Altarpeice. c, Judith Killing Holofernes. d, The Martyrdom of St. Catherine.
$6, Cardinal Albrecht of Brandenbourg as St. Jerome in the Wilderness, vert.

**2003, Apr. 28**
**2455-2458** A552 Set of 4 4.25 4.25
**2459** A552 $2 Sheet of 4, #a-d 6.00 6.00

**Souvenir Sheet**

**2460** A552 $6 multi 4.50 4.50

### Teddy Bear Type of 2003

**2003, Apr. 29** **Embroidered** *Imperf.*
**Self-Adhesive**

**2461** A553 $15 multi 11.50 11.50

Issued in sheets of 4.

### Tour de France Type of 2003

No. 2462, $2: a, Ferdinand Kubler, 1950. b, Hugo Koblet, 1951. c, Fausto Coppi, 1952. d, Louison Bobet, 1953.
No. 2463, $2: a, Bobet, 1954. b, Bobet, 1955. c, Roger Walkowiak, 1956. d, Jacques Anquetil, 1957.
No. 2464, $2: a, Gastone Nencini, 1960. b, Anquetil, 1961. c, Anquetil, 1962. d, Anquetil, 1963.
No. 2465, $6, Bobet, 1953-55. No. 2466, $6, Anquetil, 1957, diff. No. 2467, $6, Eddy Merckx, 1969.

**2003, June 17** *Perf. 13¼*
**Sheets of 4, #a-d**
**2462-2464** A555 Set of 3 18.00 18.00

**Souvenir Sheets**

**2465-2467** A555 Set of 3 13.50 13.50

### John F. Kennedy Type of 2002

No. 2468, $2: a, As Choate graduate, 1935. b, As congressman, 1946. c, With wife, Jacqueline, on tennis court. d, With son, John, Jr.
No. 2469, $2: a, With wife, Jacqueline. b, Announcing Cuban blockade, 1962. c, Seated in White House, 1962. d, Wife and children at funeral, 1963.

**2003, July 1** *Perf. 14*
**Sheets of 4, #a-d**
**2468-2469** A544 Set of 2 12.00 12.00

### Intl. Year of Fresh Water Type of 2003

No. 2470 — Flag and: a, La Sagesse. b, Annadale Falls. c, Grand Etang.
$6, Flag and St. George, horiz.

**2003, July 4** *Perf. 13½x13¼*
**2470** A559 $2 Sheet of 3, #a-c 4.50 4.50

**Souvenir Sheet**
*Perf. 13¼x13½*

**2471** A559 $6 multi 4.50 4.50

### Circus Performers Type of 2003

No. 2472, $2 — Clowns: a, Anton Pilossian. b, Victor Vashnikov. c, Dan Rice. d, Tom Comet.
No. 2473, $2: a, Dog. b, Macaw. c, Monique. d, Vassily Trofimov.

**2003, July 14** *Perf. 14*
**Sheets of 4, #a-d**
**2472-2473** A560 Set of 2 12.00 12.00

### Powered Flight Type of 2003

No. 2474, $2: a, Wright Brothers Flyer. b, NC-4. c, Douglas World Cruiser. d, Fokker Eindecker.
No. 2475, $2: a, Hawker Hart. b, Martin B-10. c, Armstrong Whitworth Siskin IIIA. d, Loening OL-8.
No. 2476, $2: a, Hansa-Brandenberg D.1. b, B.E. 2e. c, Handley Page 0/400. d, Avro 504.
No. 2477, $6, Wright Brothers No. 3 glider. No. 2478, $6, Wright Brothers Flyer No. 2. No. 2479, $6, Gloster Gamecock.

**2003, July 14**
**Sheets of 4, #a-d**
**2474-2476** A556 Set of 3 18.00 18.00

**Souvenir Sheets**

**2477-2479** A556 Set of 3 13.50 13.50

First Nonstop Solo Transatlantic Flight, 75th Anniv. — G199

No. 2480, $2: a, Charles Lindbergh (white denomination, blue background). b, Lindbergh (blue denomination, brown background. c, Lindbergh's arrival in Paris, 1927. d, Lindbergh and Spirit of St. Louis (white denomination, country name in blue)
No. 2481, $2: a, Lindbergh (blue denomination and background). b, Lindbergh and Spirit of St. Louis, blue denomination, red violet background). c, Lindbergh and Spirit of St. Louis (white denomination and country name). d, Lindbergh (white denomination, blue country name).

**2003, July 14**
**Sheets of 4, #a-d**
**2480-2481** G199 Set of 2 12.00 12.00

### Prince William Type of 2003

No. 2482, vert.: a, Looking right. b, Looking forward. c, Looking left.
$6, In ski jacket, vert.

**2003, Sept. 22**
**2482** A562 $3 Sheet of 3, #a-c 6.75 6.75

**Souvenir Sheet**

**2483** A562 $6 multi 4.50 4.50

### Flowers Type of 2003

Designs: 75c, Wild rhododendron, vert. $1, Peony, vert. $1.25, Camellia, vert. No. 2487, $2, Laurel, vert.
No. 2488, $2, vert.: a, Apple blossom. b, Mock orange. c, Wild rose. d, Hibiscus.
$6, Violets, vert.

**2003, Oct. 23** *Perf. 13½*
**2484-2487** A567 Set of 4 3.75 3.75
**2488** A567 $2 Sheet of 4, #a-d 6.00 6.00

**Souvenir Sheet**

**2489** A567 $6 multi 4.50 4.50

ASDA Postage Stamp Mega-event (#2489).

### Fish Type of 2003

Designs: 25c, Domino damsel. 75c, Porcupine fish. $1.25, Damselfish. No. 2493, $2, Clownfish.
No. 2494, $2: a, Triggerfish. b, Half-and-half wrasse. c, Long-fin bannerfish. d, Butterflyfish.
$6, Blue-girdled angelfish.

**2003, Oct. 23**
**2490-2493** A568 Set of 4 3.25 3.25
**2494** A568 $2 Sheet of 4, #a-d 6.00 6.00

**Souvenir Sheet**

**2495** A568 $6 multi 4.50 4.50

### Birds Type of 2003

Designs: 25c, Rose-breasted grosbeak. No. 2497, 50c, Gray catbird. No. 2498, 50c, Bullock's oriole. $1, Blue grosbeak.
No. 2500, $2, vert.: a, Lazuli bunting. b, Indigo bunting. c, Broad-tailed hummingbird. d, Scarlet tanager.
$6, Barn swallow.

**2003, Oct. 23**
**2496-2499** A569 Set of 4 1.75 1.75
**2500** A569 $2 Sheet of 4, #a-d 6.00 6.00

**Souvenir Sheet**

**2501** A569 $6 multi 4.50 4.50

### Christmas Type of 2003

Designs: 35c, Madonna and Child, from Carnesecchi Tabernacle, by Domenico Veneziano. 75c, Madonna and Child, from Magnoli altarpiece, by Veneziano. 90c, Crevole Madonna, by Duccio di Buoninsegna. $3, Madonna and Child, by Veneziano.
$6, Madonna and Child by the Fireplace, by Robert Campin.

**2003, Nov. 17** *Perf. 14¼*
**2502-2505** A570 Set of 4 3.75 3.75

**Souvenir Sheet**

**2506** A570 $6 multi 4.50 4.50

### Hermitage Paintings Type of 2003

Designs: 75c, Abraham and Isaac, by Rembrandt, vert. $1, David and Jonathan, by Rembrandt, vert. $1.25, St. Onuphrius, by Jusepe de Ribera, vert. No. 2510, $2, Pope Paul III, by Titian, vert.
No. 2511, $2: a, Rest on the Flight into Egypt, by Bartolomé Estéban Murillo. b, Esther Before Ahasuerus, by Nicolas Poussin. c, Abraham's Servant and Rebecca, by Jacob Hogers. d, The Prophet Elisha and Naaman, by Lambert Jacobsz.
No. 2512, Hagar Flees Abram's House, by Peter Paul Rubens. No. 2513, The Building of Noah's Ark, by Guido Reni, vert.

**2003, Dec. 8** *Perf. 13½*
**2507-2510** A572 Set of 4 3.75 3.75
**2511** A572 $2 Sheet of 4, #a-d 6.00 6.00

*Imperf*
**Size: 78x65mm**

**2512** A572 $6 multi 4.50 4.50

**Size: 67x78mm**

**2513** A572 $6 multi 4.50 4.50

### Norman Rockwell Type of 2003

No. 2514, vert.: a, The Trumpeter. b, Waiting for the Vet. c, The Diving Board. d, The Discovery.
$6, Day in a Boy's Life.

**2003, Dec. 8** **Litho.** *Perf. 13¼*
**2514** A571 $2 Sheet of 4, #a-d 6.00 6.00

**Souvenir Sheet**

**2515** A571 $6 multi 4.50 4.50

### Pablo Picasso Type of 2003

No. 2516: a, Jacqueline Sitting. b, Jacqueline with Flower. c, Seated Nude. d, Woman in Armchair.
$6, Head of a Woman.

**2003, Dec. 8** *Perf. 13¼*
**2516** A573 $2 Sheet of 4, #a-d 6.00 6.00

*Imperf*

**2517** A573 $6 multi 4.50 4.50

No. 2516 contains four 37x50mm stamps.

**New Year (Year of the Monkey) Type of 2004**

No. 2518: a, White, blue and orange monkey. b, Blue monkey. c, Brown monkey. d, Monkey with orange face.

**2004, Jan. 4** *Perf. 14*
**2518** A574 $1.50 Sheet of 4, #a-d 4.50 4.50

Zhoa Mengfu (1254-1322), Artist — G200

No. 2519: a, The Mind Landscape of Xie Youyu. b, Scroll with green backround and large mountains at left and right. c, Twin Pines. d, Scroll with brown background and large mountain at left.
$6, Autumn.

**2004, Jan. 29 Litho.** *Perf. 13½x13¼*
**2519** G200 $2 Sheet of 4, #a-d 6.00 4.50

**Souvenir Sheet**

**2520** G200 $6 multi 4.50 4.50

**Arthur and Friends Type of 2004**

No. 2521: a, Brain. b, Binky. c, Francine. d, Prunella. e, Arthur. f, Muffy.
No. 2522, $2: a, Francine, diff. b, Buster. c, Muffy, diff. d, Sue Ellen.
No. 2523, $2: a, Francine and butterfly. b, Binky and map. c, Brain and blackboard. d, Arthur and model of solar system.

**2004, Jan. 29** *Perf. 13¼*
**2521** A577 $1.50 Sheet of 6, #a-f 6.75 6.75

**Sheets of 4, #a-d**

**2522-2523** A577 Set of 2 12.00 12.00

**Olympics Type of 2004**

Designs: 25c, Long jumper, 1924 Paris Olympics. 50c, Avery Brundage, Intl. Olympic Committee President, 1952-72. $1, Commemorative medal for 1972 Munich Olympics. $4, Paidotribai.

**2004, Apr. 8** **Litho.**
**2524-2527** A579 Set of 4 4.50 4.50

**Deng Xiaoping Type of 2004**
Souvenir Sheet

**2004, May 3** *Perf. 13½x13¼*
**2528** A582 $6 Wearing cap 4.50 4.50

**Pope John Paul II Type of 2004**

No. 2529: a, With Lech Walesa. b, With Meir Lau, Chief Rabbi of Israel. c, Blessing children. d, At computer. e, Wearing miter.

**2004, May 3** *Perf. 13½*
**2529** A583 $2 Sheet of 5, #a-e 7.50 7.50

**Marilyn Monroe Type of 2004**

Designs: 50c, Portrait, diff.
No. 2531 — Various portraits with color and location of denomination of: a, Black, UL. b, Black, UR. c, White, UR. d, White, UL.

**2004, May 3** *Perf. 13½x13¼*
**2530** A584 50c multi .40 .40
**2531** A584 $2 Sheet of 4, #a-d 6.00 6.00

No. 2530 was printed in sheets of 16.

**D-Day Type of 2004**

Designs: 25c, Admiral Sir Bertram Ramsay. 50c, Lt. Gen. Miles Dempsey. 75c, Bob Shrimpton, Submarine Detector on HMS Belfast. $4, Denis Edwards, 6th Airborne Division.
No. 2536, $2: a, Sir Winston Churchill without hat. b, Churchill with hat. c, British link up with Airborne troops. d, Link up at Orne River.
No. 2537, $2: a, US troops move inland. b, Troops move inland from Omaha Beach. c, Heavy fighting on Sword Beach. d, German generals meet.
No. 2538, $6, Assault landing craft head for invasion beaches. No. 2539, $6, Gunner in a British bomber.

**2004, July 19** *Perf. 14*

**Stamps + Labels (#2532-2535)**

**2532-2535** A586 Set of 4 4.25 4.25

**Sheets of 4, #a-d**

**2536-2537** A586 Set of 2 12.00 12.00

**Souvenir Sheets**

**2538-2539** A586 Set of 2 9.00 9.00

**Locomotives Type of 2004**

No. 2540, $1: a, Liner V2 Class 2-6-2. b, Sudan Railways 2-8-2. c, China Railways DF4 Co-Co. d, LMS 2F 0-6-0 with Black 5 4-6-0. e, LMS Lickey Banker 0-10-0. f, LMS Princess Royal Pacific. g, LMS Reboilered Claughton Class 4-6-0. h, LMS Stanier 8F 2-8-0. i, Midland Railway Compound 4-4-0.
No. 2541, $1: a, Britannia Class 4-6-2. b, Indian Railways XD Class 2-8-2. c, China Railways KD6 2-8-0 (USATC S160). d, SE+CR 01 Class 0-6-0. e, Battle of Britain Light Pacific. f, SR King Arthur Class 4-6-0. g, SR Marsh 13 Class 4-4-2T. h, SR N Class 2-6-0. i, SR School Class 4-4-0.
No. 2542, $1: a, SR Merchant Navy Pacific 4-6-2. b, Gazira Cotton Railway, Sudan. c, Spanish Railways 4-8-4. d, LNER 04-1 Class 2-8-0. e, LNER A1 4-6-2 Pacific. f, LNER A3 Class 4-6-2. g, LNER A4 Class 4-6-2 Pacific. h, LNER B1 Class 4-6-0. i, LNER Ivatt Large Atlantic 4-4-2 A4 Pacific 4-6-2.
No. 2543, $6, Aberdeen to Penzance train. No. 2544, $6, London to Holyhead train. No. 2545, $6, Dublin to Tralee train.

**2004, July 19** *Perf. 14*

**Sheets of 9, #a-i**

**2540-2542** A587 Set of 3 21.00 21.00

**Souvenir Sheets**

**2543-2545** A587 Set of 3 13.50 13.50

**Queen Juliana Type of 2004**

**2004, Aug. 25 Litho.** *Perf. 13¼*
**2546** A590 $2 1937 portrait 1.50 1.50

Printed in sheets of 6.

Carriacou Regatta Festival, 40th Anniv. G201

Designs: 75c, Parade. 90c, People, boats in water. $1, Sailboats, vert.

**2004, Oct. 11** *Perf. 14*
**2547-2549** G201 Set of 3 2.00 2.00

**FIFA Type of 2004**

No. 2550: a, David Beckham. b, Marcel Desailly. c, Guido Buchwald. d, Alfonso.
$6, Bobby Charlton.

**2004, Nov. 1** *Perf. 12¾x12½*
**2550** A595 $2 Sheet of 4, #a-d 6.00 6.00

**Souvenir Sheet**

**2551** A595 $6 multi 4.50 4.50

Ocean Liners — G202

Designs: 25c, Titanic. 75c, Michelangelo. $1, America. $1.25, Vaterland. $2, Deutschland. $3, Mauritania.
$6, Ile de France.

**2004, Nov. 29** *Perf. 14¼*
**2552-2557** G202 Set of 6 6.25 6.25

**Souvenir Sheet**

**2558** G202 $6 multi 4.50 4.50

**Elvis Presley Type of 2004**

No. 2559, $2: a, Wearing purple shirt. b, Playing guitar, wearing polka dot shirt, "Elvis Presley" at right. c, With guitar hanging from neck, "Elvis Presley" at right. d, Wearing patterned shirt.
No. 2560, $2: a, Wearing brown shirt. b, Playing guitar, wearing polka dot shirt, "Elvis Presley" at left. c, With guitar hanging from neck, "Elvis Presley" at left. d, Wearing gray suit and black shirt, playing guitar.

**2004, Nov. 29** *Perf. 13¼*

**Sheets of 4, #a-d**

**2559-2560** A588 Set of 2 12.00 12.00

**Christmas Type of 2004**

Paintings by Norman Rockwell: 35c, Follow Me in Merry Measure. 75c, The Merrie Old Coach Driver. 90c, Joy to the World. $3, Santa Reading His Mail.
$6, Wartime Santa.

**2004, Dec. 9** *Perf. 12*
**2561-2564** A600 Set of 4 3.75 3.75

**Size: 63x81mm**

*Imperf*

**2565** A600 $6 multi 4.50 4.50

**Babe Ruth Type of 2004**

No. 2566: a, Blue background. b, White background.
No. 2567: a, Swinging bat. b, Looking forward. c, Looking to right. d, With glove.

**2004, Jan. 29 Litho.** *Perf. 14*
**2566** A598 50c Pair, #a-b .75 .75
**2567** A598 $2 Sheet of 4, #a-d 6.00 6.00

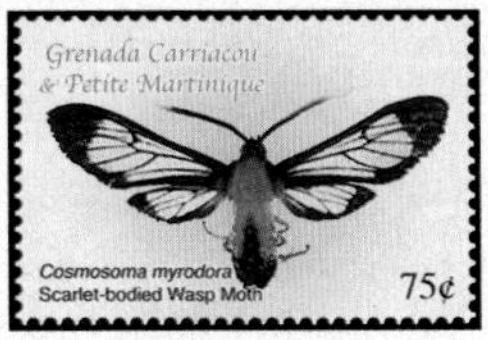


Moths — G202a

Designs: 75c, Scarlet-bodied wasp moth. 90c, Bella moth. $1, Sphinx moth. $3, Faithful beauty moth.
$6, Empyreuma affinis.

**2004, Nov. 17** *Perf. 12¾*
**2568-2571** G202a Set of 4 4.25 4.25

**Souvenir Sheet**

**2572** G202a $6 multi 4.50 4.50

**Ronald Reagan Type of 2004**

No. 2573: a, With Press Secretary James Brady. b, With German Chancellor Helmut Kohl. c, With family. d, With Princess Diana.

**2004, Nov. 29** *Perf. 13¼x13½*
**2573** A597 $2 Sheet of 4, #a-d 6.00 6.00

**Year of the Rooster Type of 2005**

Paintings by Ren Yi: 75c, Double Chickens and Peony. $3, A Rooster, horiz.

**2005, Jan. 17** *Perf. 12¾x13*
**2574** A601 75c multi .60 .60

**Souvenir Sheet**

**2575** A601 $3 multi 2.25 2.25

No. 2574 printed in sheets of 4. No. 2575 contains one 56x35mm stamp.

**Intl. Year of Rice Type of 2005 and**

Screen Panels by Oshen Maruyama — G203

No. 2576 — Various panels depicting rice plants and birds.
$6, Rice Farming in Bali, by unknown artist, horiz.

**2005, Feb. 10** *Perf. 14*
**2576** G203 $1.50 Sheet of 6, #a-f 6.75 6.75

**Souvenir Sheet**

**2577** A602 $6 multi 4.50 4.50

**Prehistoric Animals Type of 2005**

No. 2578: a, Psittacosaurus. b, Deinonychus. c, Suchomimus. d,Smilodon.
$6, Tenotosaurus.

**2005, Feb. 10** *Perf. 13¼x13½*
**2578** A604 $2 Sheet of 4, #a-d 6.00 6.00

**Souvenir Sheet**

**2579** A604 $6 multi 4.50 4.50

See Nos. 2598-2601.

Reptiles and Amphibians — G204

No. 2580: a, Poison dart frog. b, Western Antillean anole. c, Black iguana. d, American crocodile.
$6, Anolis lizard.

**2005, Feb. 10** *Perf. 12¾*
**2580** G204 $2 Sheet of 4, #a-d 8.75 8.75

**Souvenir Sheet**

**2581** G204 $6 multi 6.50 6.50

Carnivorous Plants — G205

No. 2582: a, Heliamphora tatei. b, Sarracenia flava, Genlisea pygmaea. c, Nepenthes bicalcarata. d, Utricularia intermedia.
$6, Dionaea muscipula.

**2005, Feb. 10**
**2582** G205 $2 Sheet of 4, #a-d 6.00 6.00

**Souvenir Sheet**

**2583** G205 $6 multi 4.50 4.50

**Elvis Presley Type of 2005**

No. 2584, $1.50: a, With guitar, 1955. b, Singing, 1956. c, With hand on chin, 1958. d, In suit, 1962. e, With guitar, 1968. f, Singing, 1972.
No. 2585, $1.50: a, In Army uniform, 1958. b, Wearing Hawaiian shirt, 1961. c, Wearing cap, 1963. d, Wearing turban, 1965. e, Sitting on sports car, 1966. f, With stethoscope, 1969.

**2005, Apr. 4** *Perf. 13½*

**Sheets of 6, #a-f**

**2584-2585** A607 Set of 2 13.50 13.50

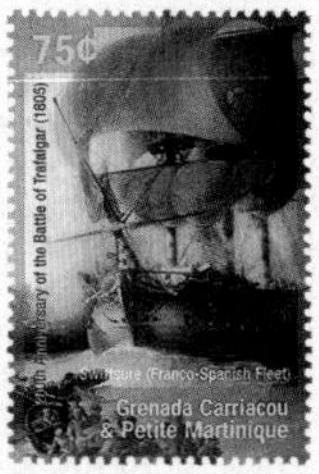


Battle of Trafalgar, Bicent. — G206

Designs: 75c, Swiftsure. $1, British sail near Cape Trafalgar, horiz. $2, Capt. Alexander Ball. $3, Vice-Admiral Francedillaois Brueys d'Aigalliers.
$6, Admiral Aristide du Petit-Thouars.

**2005, Apr. 4** *Perf. 14*
**2586-2589** G206 Set of 4 5.25 5.25

**Souvenir Sheet**

**2590** G206 $6 multi 4.50 4.50

### Yasujiro Ozu Type of 2005

No. 2591: a, A Mother Should Be Loved, 1934. b, An Inn in Tokyo, 1935. c, Dragnet Girl, 1933. d, There Was a Father, 1942.

**2005, Apr. 8** *Perf. 14¼*
**2591** A608 $2 Sheet of 4, #a-d 6.00 6.00

### Basketball Players Type of 2004

Designs: No. 2592, 75c, Steve Francis, Orlando Magic. No. 2593, 75c, Allan Houston, New York Knicks. No. 2594, 75c, Tracy McGrady, Houston Rockets. No. 2595, 75c, Steve Nash, Phoenix Suns. No. 2596, 75c, Shaquille O'Neal, Miami Heat. No. 2597, 75c, Chris Webber, Sacramento Kings.

**2005, Mar. 8 Litho.** *Perf. 14*
**2592-2597** A596 Set of 6 3.50 3.50

Each stamp printed in sheets of 12.

### Prehistoric Animals Type of 2005

No. 2598, $2: a, Eurypholis. b, Ichthyosaurus. c, Plesiosaur. d, Varnerxiphactinus.

No. 2599, $2: a, Pterosaurus. b, Archaeopteryx. c, Pterosaurian. d, Microraptor.

No. 2600, $6, Uintatherium. No. 2601, $6, Mammoth, vert.

*Perf. 13¼x13¾, 13¾x13¼*
**2005, Apr. 15**
**Sheets of 4, #a-d**
**2598-2599** A604 Set of 2 12.00 12.00
**Souvenir Sheets**
**2600-2601** A604 Set of 2 9.00 9.00

### End of World War II Type of 2005

No. 2602, $2 — Battle of El Alamein: a, Field Marshal Bernard Montgomery directs troops forward. b, Field Marshal Erwin Rommel ready for battle. c, Troops move forward into battle. d, Line of German prisoners after battle.

No. 2603, $2 — Fall of Berlin: a, Russians at the gates of Berlin. b, German soldiers surrender. c, Berlin in ruins. d, Picking up the pieces.

No. 2604, $6, Troops attacking. No. 2605, $6, Sign with quote by Adolf Hitler, vert.

**2005, May 10** *Perf. 13¼*
**Sheets of 4, #a-d**
**2602-2603** A610 Set of 2 12.00 12.00
**Souvenir Sheets**
**2604-2605** A610 Set of 2 9.00 9.00

### Albert Einstein Type of 2005

No. 2606, vert.: a, Einstein, planet, diagram of Earth and Moon. b, Einstein. c, Israeli Prime Minister David Ben Gurion.

**2005, June 27** *Perf. 13¼*
**2606** A615 $3 Sheet of 3, #a-c 6.75 6.75

No. 2606 contains three 38x50mm stamps.

### V-J Day Type of 2005

No. 2607, $2: a, P-38J Lightning. b, P-51D Mustang. c, F-4 fighter plane. d, Douglas C-47 Skytrain.

No. 2608, $2: a, Officer reads V-J Day message to his troops. b, Chaplain's prayer. c, Rejoicing the victory. d, USS Missouri in Tokyo Bay.

**2005, July 11** *Perf. 12¾*
**Sheets of 4, #a-d**
**2607-2608** A612 Set of 2 12.00 12.00

### Rotary International Type of 2005

No. 2609, horiz.: a, People in front of National Polio Laboratory. b, People in National Polio Laboratory. c, Rotary International emblem.

**2005, July 11** *Perf. 14*
**2609** A613 $3 Sheet of 3, #a-c 6.75 6.75

Pope John Paul II (1920-2005) — G207

**2005, Sept. 22** *Perf. 13¼x13½*
**2610** G207 $3 multi 2.25 2.25

Printed in sheets of 6.

Maimonides (1135-1204), Philosopher — G208

**2005** *Perf. 12*
**2611** G208 $2 multi 1.50 1.50

### Christmas Type of 2005

Designs: 35c, Madonna and Child, by Andrea del Sarto. 75c, Madonna Pesaro, by Titian. 90c, Madonna and Child, by Titian. $3, Madonna and Child, by Peter Paul Rubens.

$6, Madonna and Child, by Domenico Veneziano.

**2005** *Perf. 12¾*
**2612-2615** A625 Set of 4 3.75 3.75
**Souvenir Sheet**
**2616** A625 $6 multi 4.50 4.50

Dog, by Chang Dai-Chien G209

**2006, Jan. 3 Litho.** *Perf. 11½x11¼*
**2617** G209 $1 multi .75 .75

New Year 2006 (Year of the Dog). Printed in sheets of 4.

### Pope Benedict XVI Type of 2006

**2006, Jan. 10** *Perf. 13¼*
**2618** A629 $2 Pope, diff. 1.50 1.50

Printed in sheets of 4.

### Elvis Presley Type of 2006

*Variable Die Cut Perf.*
**2006, Feb. 21 Litho. & Embossed**
**Without Gum**
**2619** A631 $20 multi 15.00 15.00

### Queen Elizabeth II, 80th Birthday Type of 2006

No. 2620: a, Queen wearing hat, sepia photograph. b, Queen wearing tiara. c, Queen with Princess Anne. d, Queen wearing hat, color photograph.

$6, Portrait of Queen in robe.

**2006, Feb. 21 Litho.** *Perf. 13¼*
**2620** A632 $3 Sheet of 4, #a-d 9.00 9.00
**Souvenir Sheet**
*Perf. 12*
**2621** A632 $6 multi 4.50 4.50

### Marilyn Monroe Type of 2006

**2006, Mar. 30** *Perf. 13½*
**2622** A634 $3 Monroe, diff. 2.25 2.25

Printed in sheets of 4.

### Rembrandt Type of 2006

Designs: 75c, The Strolling Musicians. 90c, The Great Jewish Bride. $1, Old Haaringh. $4, Beggars Receiving Alms at the Door of a House. No. 2627, $6, Young Woman in a Pearl-trimmed Beret (70x100mm). No. 2628, $6, Portrait of a Boy (70x100mm).

No. 2629: a, Man from Lady and Gentleman in Black. b, Woman from Lady and Gentleman in Black. c, Man from The Shipbuilder and His Wife. d, Woman from The Shipbuilder and His Wife.

*Perf. 12, 12½x12¼ (#2627-2628)*
**2006, June 16**
**2623-2628** A639 Set of 6 14.00 14.00
**Miniature Sheet**
**2629** A639 $3 Sheet of 4, #a-d 9.00 9.00

### Mozart Type of 2006

**2006, June 22 Litho.** *Perf. 12¾*
**2630** A640 $6 Don Giovanni 4.50 4.50

### Space Type of 2006

No. 2631 — First Flight of Space Shuttle Columbia: a, Columbia on launchpad. b, Astronauts John W. Young and Robert L. Crippen. c, Liftoff of Columbia. d, Columbia in space. e, Crew in cabin. f, Columbia landing.

No. 2632, $3 — Apollo-Soyuz: a, Liftoff of Soyuz 19. b, Apollo-Soyuz crew. c, Crew in cabin. d, Soyuz 19.

No. 2633, $3 — Space Shuttle Discovery's return to space: a, Discovery on launchpad. b, Crew of Mission STS-114. c, Discovery and International Space Station. d, STS-114 space walk.

No. 2634, $6, Luna 9. No. 2635, $6, Venus Express. No. 2636, $6, Mars Reconnaissance Orbiter.

**2006, Sept. 14**
**2631** A642 $2 Sheet of 6, #a-f 9.00 9.00
**Sheets of 4, #a-d**
**2632-2633** A642 Set of 2 18.00 18.00
**Souvenir Sheets**
**2634-2636** A642 Set of 3 13.50 13.50

### Columbus Type of 2006

Designs: 75c, Pinta, vert. $1.50, Nina, Pinta and Santa Maria set sail. $2, Ship and map. $3, Columbus discovers San Salvador.

$6, Columbus.

**2006, Oct. 26**
**2637-2640** A643 Set of 4 5.50 5.50
**Souvenir Sheet**
**2641** A643 $6 multi 4.50 4.50

### Christmas Type of 2006

Details of St. Willibrod in Adoration Before Mary, Mother of God, by Peter Paul Rubens: 25c, Man. 50c, Angels. 75c, Mary and Jesus. $1, St. Willibrod.

No. 2646: a, Like 25c. b, Like 50c. c, Like 75c. d, Like $1.

**2006, Dec. 21** *Perf. 14*
**2642-2645** A646 Set of 4 1.90 1.90
**Souvenir Sheet**
**2646** A646 $2 Sheet of 4, #a-d 6.00 6.00

Souvenir Sheet

Airships — G210

No. 2647: a, LZ-127. b, Dining room of the Hindenburg. c, Marine airship L53.

**2007, Jan. 16** *Perf. 13¼*
**2647** G210 $3 Sheet of 3, #a-c 6.75 6.75

Souvenir Sheet

Elvis Presley (1935-77) — G211

No. 2648 — Various portraits with: a, Black denomination. b, Red denomination, playing guitar. c, White denomination. d, Red denomination, hands off guitar.

**2007, Jan. 16** *Perf. 14¼*
**2648** G211 $3 Sheet of 4, #a-d 9.00 9.00

Pres. John F. Kennedy (1917-63) — G212

No. 2649, $2: a, On crutches, running for Congress. b, Campaigning for Congress. c, Campaigning in New Hampshire. d, As president.

No. 2650, $2.50: a, Naru Island. b, As Navy lieutenant on Solomon Islands, wearing cap. c, As lieutenant on Solomon Islands, without cap. d, SOS coconut carved by Kennedy.

**2007, Jan. 16** *Perf. 13½*
**Sheets of 4, #a-d**
**2649-2650** G212 Set of 2 13.50 13.50

### Scouting Type of 2007

Scout fleur-de-lis, "100," years "1907 / 2007," and background colors of: $2, Blue and green, horiz. $6, Orange and green, horiz.

**2007, Jan. 16**
**2651** A650 $2 multi 1.50 1.50
**Souvenir Sheet**
**2652** A650 $6 multi 4.50 4.50

No. 2651 printed in sheets of 4.

### Year of the Pig Type of 2007

Miniature Sheet

No. 2653 — Wild Boar, by Liu Jiyou and painting name in: a, $1, Black. b, $1, Brown. c, $2, Black. d, $2, Red.

**2007, Feb. 15 Litho.** *Perf. 14*
**2653** A652 Sheet of 4, #a-d 4.50 4.50

G213

G214

Mushrooms — G215

Designs: 75c, Morchella semilibera. No. 2655, $1, Ganoderma resinaceum. No. 2656, $1, Helvella crispa. $4, Ganoderma sp.

No. 2658, $2: a, Russula sardonia. b, Amanita cruzii. c, Macrocybe titans. d, Amanita microspora.

No. 2659, $2: a, Aleuria aurantia. b, Boletus sp. c, Boletellus russellii. d, Otidea onotica.

No. 2660, $5, Amanita polypyramis. No. 2661, $5, Boletellus ananas. No. 2662, $5, Cantharellus cibarius.

**2007, May 16 Litho. *Perf. 14***
**2654-2657** G213 Set of 4 5.25 5.25

**Sheets of 4, #a-d**
**2658-2659** G214 Set of 2 12.00 12.00

**Souvenir Sheets**
**2660** G214 $5 multi 3.75 3.75
**2661-2662** G215 Set of 2 7.50 7.50

Birds — G216

Designs: 75c, Pied-billed grebe. No. 2664, $1, Black-crowned night heron. No. 2665, $1, Turkey vulture. $4, Green honeycreeper.
No. 2667, $2, horiz.: a, Caspian tern. b, Scarlet tanager. c, Common nighthawk. d, Osprey.
No. 2668, $2, horiz.: a, Hooded warbler. b, Northern flicker. c, Mockingbird. d, Blue tit.
No. 2669, $5, White-winged parakeet. No. 2670, $5, Blackpoll warbler, horiz. No. 2671, $5, Yellow-green vireo, horiz.

**2007, May 16**
**2663-2666** G216 Set of 4 5.25 5.25

**Sheets of 4, #a-d**
**2667-2668** G216 Set of 2 12.00 12.00

**Souvenir Sheets**
**2669-2671** G216 Set of 3 11.50 11.50

Orchids — G217

Designs: 75c, Goodyera tesselata. $1.50, Oncidium floridanum. No. 2674, $2, Hexalectris spicata. $3, Pogonia ophioglossoides.
No. 2676, $2: a, Platanthera blephariglottis. b, Epipactis helleborine. c, Cypripedium alaskanum. d, Zeuxine strateumatica.
No. 2677, $2: a, Platanthera grandiflora. b, Platanthera peramoena. c, Cyrtopodium punctatum. d, Spiranthes odorata.
No. 2678, $6, Platanthera chapmanii. No. 2679, $6, Bletilla striata, horiz. No. 2680, $6, Macradenia lutescens, horiz.

**2007, May 16 *Perf. 12¾***
**2672-2675** G217 Set of 4 5.50 5.50

**Sheets of 4, #a-d**
**2676-2677** G217 Set of 2 12.00 12.00

**Souvenir Sheets**
**2678-2680** G217 Set of 3 13.50 13.50

Betty Boop in "Snow White" — G218

No. 2681, horiz.: a, Queen looking at ring in snow. b, Green witch looking at mirror, dog and clown. c, Dancing ghost. d, Betty Boop asleep, frozen skull.
No. 2682, horiz.: a, $1, Queen looking in mirror. b, $1, Angry queen. c, $1, Knights and tree stump. d, $2, Betty Boop with alarm clock. e, $2, Betty Boop with mirror, dog, clown. f, $2, Betty Boop in snow.
$6, Betty Boop running.

**2007, June 4 *Perf. 13½***
**2681** G218 $2 Sheet of 4, #a-d 6.00 6.00
**2682** G218 Sheet of 6, #a-f 6.75 6.75

**Souvenir Sheet**
**2683** G218 $6 multi 4.50 4.50

**Intl. Polar Year Type of 2007**

No. 2684, vert. — Royal penguins with: a, Country name at UR, denomination at LR. b, Country name at top, denomination at LR. c, Country name at LR, denomination at UL. d, Country name at bottom, denomination at UL. e, Country name at bottom, denomination at UR. f, Country name at UL, denomination at LR.
$6, African penguin, vert.

**2007, June 25 *Perf. 13½***
**2684** A657 $2 Sheet of 6, #a-f 9.00 9.00

**Souvenir Sheet**
**2685** A657 $6 multi 4.50 4.50

**First Helicopter Flight, Cent. Type of 2007**

No. 2686, horiz.: a, BK 117. b, UH-1 Iroquois. c, S-65/RH-53D. d, UH-1B/C Iroquois. e, Autogyro. f, BO 105.
$6, AH-64 Apache, horiz.

**2007, June 25**
**2686** A664 $1.50 Sheet of 6, #a-f 6.75 6.75

**Souvenir Sheet**
**2687** A664 $6 multi 4.50 4.50

**Pope Benedict XVI Type of 2007**

**2007, July 11**
**2688** A653 $1 Pope, diff. .75 .75

Printed in sheets of 8.

Christmas G219

Paintings: 25c, Virgin and Child with Saints Jerome and Bartholomew, by Alessandro Bonvicino. 50c, Virgin and Child Between Saints Thomas and Jerome, by Guido Reni. 75c, Virgin and Child, by Giovanni Batista Salvi. $1, Madonna of Decemviri, by Pietro Perugino.

**2007, Oct. 26 *Perf. 14¼x14¾***
**2689-2692** G219 Set of 4 1.90 1.90

**Wedding of Queen Elizabeth II and Prince Philip, 60th Anniv. Type of 2007**

**Miniature Sheet**

No. 2693: a, Couple, denomination at left, dull maroon panel. b, Queen, denomination at right, dull maroon panel. c, Queen, denomination at left, maroon panel. d, Couple, denomination at right, maroon panel. e, Couple, denomination at left, maroon panel. f, Queen, denomination at right, maroon panel.

**2007, June 25 Litho. *Perf. 13¼***
**2693** A655 $1.50 Sheet of 6, #a-f 6.75 6.75

**Year of the Rat Type of 2007**

**2007, Dec. 3 *Perf. 13x13¼***
**2694** A667 $1 multi .75 .75

Printed in sheets of 4.

**Princess Diana Type of 2007**

No. 2695 — Diana wearing: a, Plaid jacket. b, Purple feathered hat. c, Green dress. d, Plaid jacket, close-up in frame. e, Purple feathered hat, close-up in frame. f, Green dress, close-up in frame.
$6, Princess Diana, Prince Charles and infant, horiz.

**2008, Jan. 14 *Perf. 13¼***
**2695** A656 $1.50 Sheet of 6, #a-f 6.75 6.75

**Souvenir Sheet**
**2696** A656 $6 multi 4.50 4.50

**Elvis Presley Type of 2008**

No. 2697 — Presley: a, Silhouette, holding microphone, gray background. b, Wearing green shirt. c, Silhouette, holding microphone, olive green background. d, Playing guitar. e, Silhouette, playing guitar. f, Wearing orange shirt.

**2008, Jan. 14 *Perf. 13¼***
**2697** A671 $1.50 Sheet of 6, #a-f 6.75 6.75

**World Stamp Championship Type of 2008**

Design: Aerial view of Jerusalem, horiz. (149x125mm).

**2008, May 14 *Imperf.***
**2698** A676 $6 multi 4.50 4.50

**Basketball Type of 2008**

**Miniature Sheet**

No. 2699 — Members of 2008 Boston Celtics basketball team: a, Ray Allen. b, Rajon Rondo. c, Paul Pierce. d, Kendrick Perkins. e, Kevin Garnett. f, Leon Powe. g, James Posey. h, Sam Cassell. i, P. J. Brown.

**2008, June 17 Litho. *Perf. 13½***
**2699** A678 $1 Sheet of 9, #a-i 6.75 6.75

**Cats Type of 2008**

No. 2700: a, Havana. b, Scottish Fold. c, American Curl. d, American Bobtail. e, Balinese. f, Singapura.
$6, Burmese, horiz.

**2008, June 18 *Perf. 11½***
**2700** A677 $1 Sheet of 6, #a-f 4.50 4.50

**Souvenir Sheet**
**2701** A677 $6 multi 4.50 4.50

**Elvis Presley Type of 2008**

**Miniature Sheet**

No. 2702 — Presley: a, Wearing lei, holding microphone in right hand. b, Playing guitar, red striped background. c, Wearing lei, holding microphone in left hand, right arm extended with hand in fist. d, Playing guitar, olive green and black background. e, Wearing lei, holding microphone in left hand, right hand at side. f, Wearing red shirt.

**2008, Oct. 10 *Perf. 13¼***
**2702** A670 $1.50 Sheet of 6, #a-f 6.75 6.75

Christmas G220

Designs: 25c, Christmas ornament washing up on beach. 50c, Gift boxes hanging ornaments and electric Christmas lights. 75c, "Merry Christmas" written on beach. $1, Starfish and shells hanging ornaments, vert.

***Perf. 14¾x14¼, 14¼x14¾***
**2008, Dec. 3 Litho.**
**2703-2706** G220 Set of 4 1.90 1.90

**Space Exploration Type of 2009**

**Miniature Sheets**

No. 2707, $2: a, Venus and Mercury. b, Jupiter. c, Earth and Mars. d, Saturn. e, Neptune. f, Uranus.
No. 2708, $2, vert. — Mariner 9: a, And the Valles Marineris on Mars. b, And technicians. c, And the Olympus Mons on Mars. d, Photograph of Valles Marineris. e, Lifting off on Atlas-Centaur rocket. f, And Phobos.
No. 2709, $2.50, vert. — Mariner 10: a, And Mars at UR. b, Lifting off on Atlas-Centaur rocket. c, And technicians. d, And Moon at UL.
No. 2710, $2.50, vert.: a, Pillars of Creation in Eagle Nebula. b, Orion Nebula. c, Crab Nebula. d, Horsehead Nebula.

**2008, Dec. 24 *Perf. 14***

**Sheets of 6, #a-f**
**2707-2708** A690 Set of 2 18.00 18.00

**Sheets of 4, #a-d**
**2709-2710** A690 Set of 2 15.00 15.00

Fish G221

Designs: $1, Blue chromis. No. 2712, $2, Clown wrasse. No. 2713, $4, Orange-spotted filefish. $5, Palometa.
No. 2715, $2: a, Tiger grouper. b, Bluehead wrasse. c, Squirrel fish. d, Queen parrotfish. e, Yellowtail snapper. f, Barred hamlet.

**2009, Jan. 9 *Perf. 12½***
**2711-2714** G221 Set of 4 9.00 9.00

***Perf. 12***
**2715** G221 $2 Sheet of 6, #a-f 9.00 9.00

G222

Shells — G223

Designs: 25c, True tulip. 50c Twisted plait olive. 75c, Junonia. $1, Royal comb venus.
No. 2720: a, Lion's paw. b, Banded tulip. c, Flame auger. d, Miniature melo, e, West Indian worm shell. f, Mouse cowry.

**2009, Jan. 9 *Perf. 12½***
**2716-2719** G222 Set of 4 1.90 1.90

***Perf. 12***
**2720** G223 $2 Sheet of 6, #a-f 9.00 9.00

**Obama Type of 2009**

No. 2721 — Pres. Barack Obama: a, Pointing. b, Wearing blue tie, hands not shown. c, Touching thumb to index finger. d, Wearing red tie, hands not shown.
$10, Pres. Obama and US Capitol.

**2009, Jan. 20 *Perf. 11½***
**2721** A689 $2.75 Sheet of 4, #a-d 8.50 8.50

**Souvenir Sheet**

***Perf. 13¼***
**2722** A689 $10 multi 7.75 7.75

No. 2722 contains one 38x51mm stamp.

New Year 2009 (Year of the Ox) — G224

**2009, Jan. 26 *Perf. 11½***
**2723** G224 $2.50 multi 1.90 1.90

**Olympic Sports Type of 2009**

**Miniature Sheet**

No. 2724, vert.: a, Archery. b, Track cycling. c, Wrestling. d, Boxing.

**2009, Apr. 26 *Perf. 12***
**2724** A700 $1.40 Sheet of 4, #a-d 4.25 4.25

China 2009 World Stamp Exhibition, Luoyang.

Miniature Sheet

Qianglong (1711-99), Chinese Emperor — G225

No. 2725: a, Qianglong as young man, with chop at UR. b, Qianglong, women, table and tree. c, Qianglong at desk. d, Qianglong as older man.

**2009, Apr. 29** ***Perf. 12***

**2725** G225 $1.40 Sheet of 4, #a-d 4.25 4.25

China 2009 World Stamp Exhibition, Luoyang.

**Elvis Presley Type of 2009**

Miniature Sheet

No. 2726, horiz. — Presley: a, Singing, with hand raised near mouth, denimination in yellow brown. b, Holding microphone, denomination in purple. c, Holding microphone, diff., denomination in red violet. d, Singing and holding microphone, denomination in Prussian blue.

**2009, Apr. 29** ***Perf. 13½***

**2726** A703 $2.50 Sheet of 4, #a-d 7.50 7.50

Worldwide Fund for Nature (WWF) — G226

No. 2727 — Various depictions of Caribbean spiny lobster with denomination in: a, Orange. b, Green. c, Pink. d, Yellow.

**2009, June 23** ***Perf. 13½***

| | | | |
|---|---|---|---|
| **2727** | Strip of 4 | 9.00 | 9.00 |
| ***a.-d.*** | G226 $3 Any single | 2.25 | 2.25 |
| ***e.*** | Sheet of 8 2 each #2727a-2727d | 18.00 | 18.00 |

G227

G228

Mushrooms — G229

Designs: 25c, Psilocybe mexicana. $1, Crinipellis piceae. $2, Psilocybe subcubensis. $5, Psilocybe cubensis.

No. 2732: a, Panacolus fimicola. b, Psilocybe yungensis. c, Panacolus subbalteatus. d, Russula cremeolilacina.

No. 2733: a, Psilocybe guilartensis. b, Psilocybe aztecorum.

**2009, July 2** ***Perf. 14x14¾***

**2728-2731** G227 Set of 4 6.25 6.25

***Perf. 14¼x14¾***

**2732** G228 $2.50 Sheet of 4, #a-d 7.50 7.50

**Souvenir Sheet**

***Perf. 14x14¾***

**2733** G229 $3 Sheet of 2, #a-b 4.50 4.50

Miniature Sheet

Pres. Abraham Lincoln (1809-65) — G230

No. 2734 — Photograph of Lincoln: a, Without beard, ear showing at right. b, Without beard, ear showing at left. c, With beard, wearing vest. d, With beard, without vest.

**2009, July 21** **Litho.** ***Perf. 13¼***

**2734** G230 $2.50 Sheet of 4, #a-d 7.50 7.50

Miniature Sheet

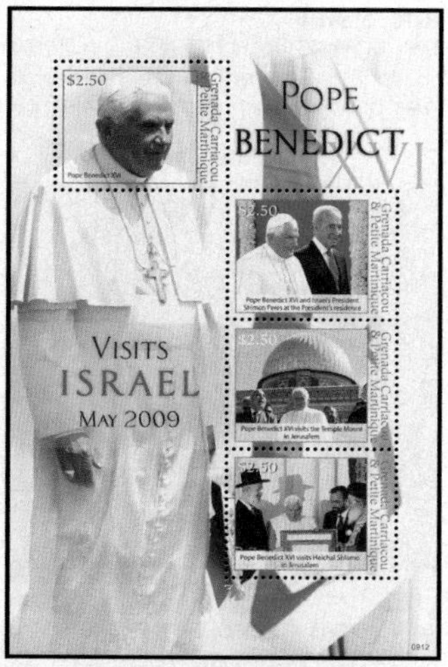


Visit of Pope Benedict XVI to Israel — G231

No. 2735: a, Pope Benedict XVI. b, Pope and Israeli President Shimon Peres. c, Pope at Temple Mount, Jerusalem. d, Pope and Heichal Shlomo.

**2009, Sept. 15** ***Perf. 11½x12***

**2735** G231 $2.50 Sheet of 4, #a-d 7.50 7.50

Miniature Sheet

Teenage Mutant Ninja Turtles, 25th Anniv. — G232

No. 2736: a, Donatello. b, Leonardo. c, Raphael. d, Michelangelo.

**2009, Sept. 15** ***Perf. 12x11½***

**2736** G232 $2.50 Sheet of 4, #a-d 7.50 7.50

Miniature Sheet

John F. Kennedy, Jr. (1960-99), Magazine Publisher — G233

No. 2737: a, As child, with father Pres. John F. Kennedy. b, With mother, Jacqueline. c, Alone. d, As child with mother, father and sister Caroline.

**2009, Dec. 7** **Litho.** ***Perf. 11¼x11½***

**2737** G233 $2.50 Sheet of 4, #a-d 7.75 7.75

**First Man on the Moon, 40th Anniv. Type of 2009**

No. 2738, vert.: a, Saturn, Titan and Voyager I. b, Apollo 11 Lunar Module. c, Voyager I, Europa, Jupiter, Io, Callisto and Ganymede. $6, Apollo 11 Lunar Module, diff., vert.

**2009, Dec. 7** ***Perf. 13¼***

**2738** A701 $2 Horiz. strip of 3, #a-c 4.75 4.75

**Souvenir Sheet**

**2739** A701 $6 multi 4.75 4.75

No. 2738 was printed in sheets containing 2 strips of three stamps.

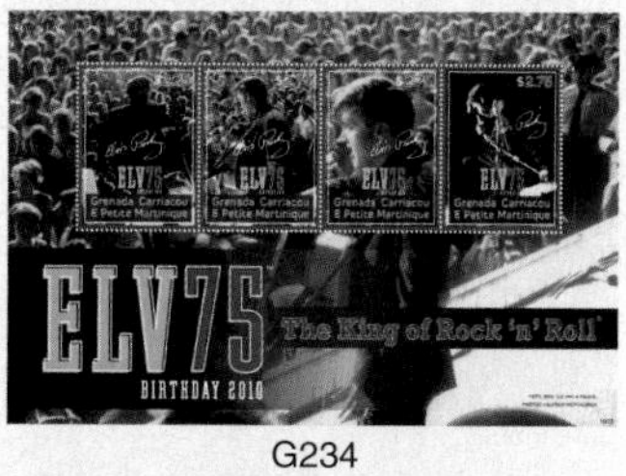


G234

G235

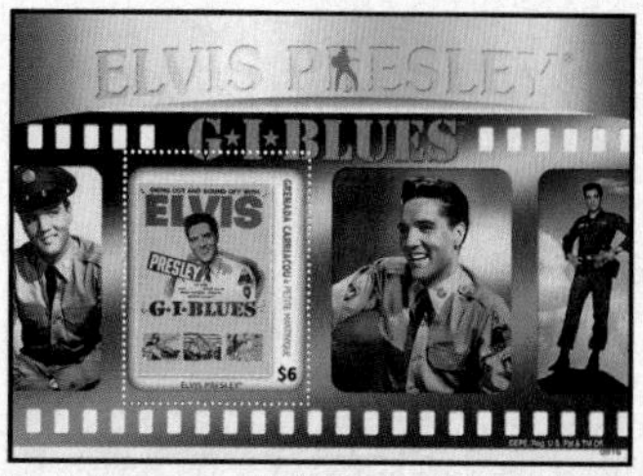


G236

G237

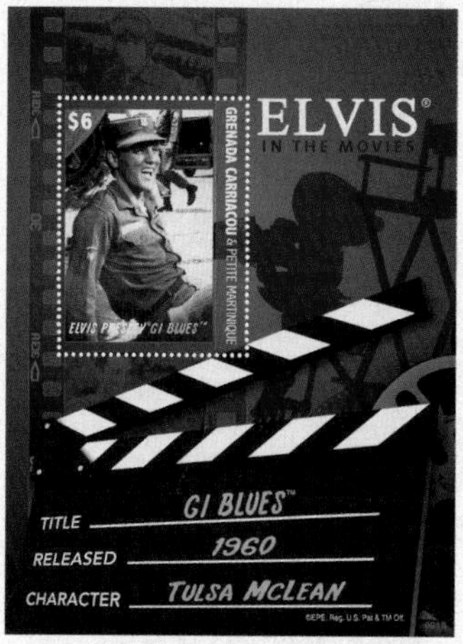


Elvis Presley (1935-77) — G238

No. 2740 — Presley: a, Facing crowd, with guitar at right. b, Facing crowd, with guitar in front of him. c, Close-up with crowd in background. d, Holding microphone, no crowd.

**2010, Jan. 7**

**2740** G234 $2.75 Sheet of 4, #a-d 8.50 8.50

**Souvenir Sheets**

| | | | | |
|---|---|---|---|---|
| **2741** | G235 | $6 multi | 4.75 | 4.75 |
| **2742** | G236 | $6 multi | 4.75 | 4.75 |
| **2743** | G237 | $6 multi | 4.75 | 4.75 |
| **2744** | G238 | $6 multi | 4.75 | 4.75 |
| | *Nos. 2741-2744 (4)* | | 19.00 | 19.00 |

Miniature Sheet

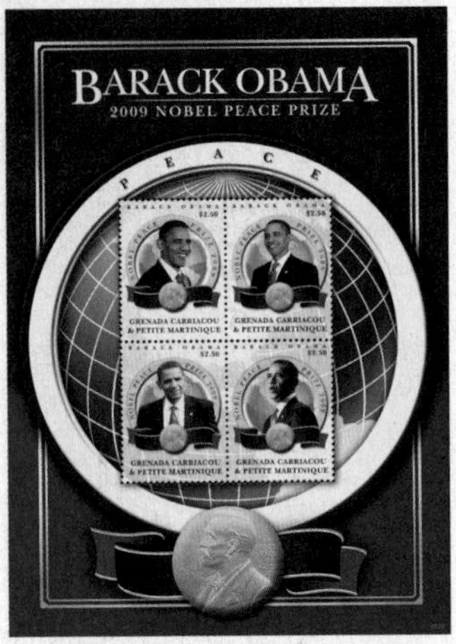


Awarding of 2009 Nobel Peace Prize to Pres. Barack Obama — G239

No. 2745 — Various photographs of Pres. Obama and gray map in background showing: a, Alaska, Western and Central United States. b, Greenland, Northeastern United States, Great Lakes. c, Southwestern United States, Mexico. d, Southeastern United States, Northern South America.

**2010, Mar. 4** *Perf. 12x11½*
**2745** G239 $2.50 Sheet of 4, #a-d 7.75 7.75

Orchids G240

Designs: $1.20, Dendrophylax lindenii. $1.80, Scaphyglottis imbricata. No. 2748, $3, Encyclia ceratistes. $5, Scaphyglottis stellata.
No. 2750: a, Oncidium excavatum. b, Brassavola nodosa. c, Cattleya gaskelliana. d, Phalaenopsis cultivars.
No. 2751, $3: a, Lepanthopsis floripecten. b, Equitant oncidium.

*Perf. 11½x11¼, 11½x12 (#2750)*
**2010, Mar. 4**
**2746-2749** G240 Set of 4 8.50 8.50
**2750** G240 $2.50 Sheet of 4, #a-d 7.75 7.75

**Souvenir Sheet**

**2751** G240 $3 Sheet of 2, #a-b 4.75 4.75

Miniature Sheets

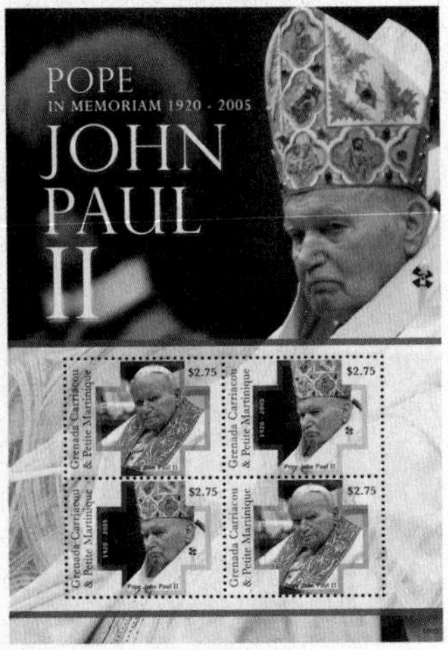


G241

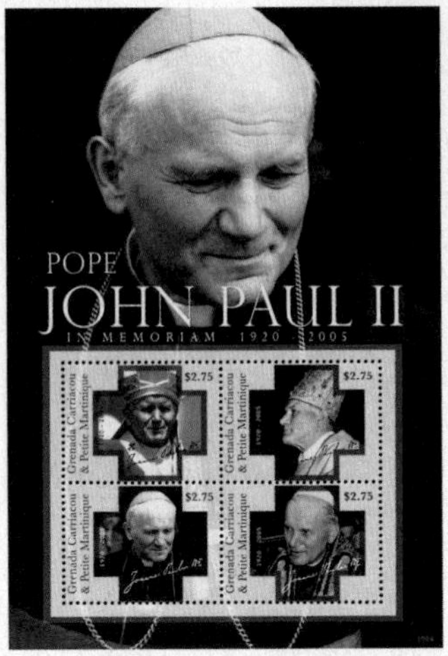


Pope John Paul II (1920-2005) — G242

No. 2752: a, Pope wearing zucchetto, country name over colored area. b, Pope wearing miter, white area under and below denomination. c, As "b," with colored area under and below denomination. d, As "a," country name over white area.
No. 2753: a, Pope wearing miter, looking forward. b, Pope wearing miter, looking left. c, Pope wearing zucchetto, looking right. d, Pope wearing zucchetto, looking left.

**2010, Apr. 9** *Perf. 11½x12*
**2752** G241 $2.75 Sheet of 4, #a-d 8.25 8.25
**2753** G242 $2.75 Sheet of 4, #a-d 8.25 8.25

**Girl Guides Type of 2010**

No. 2754, horiz. — Girl Guides: a, And adult leader. b, In tent. c, Sitting in field of flowers. d, looking at young Girl Guide pointing.
$6, Girl Guides wearing hooded sweatshirts.

**2010, June 11** *Perf. 13x13¼*
**2754** A717 $2.75 Sheet of 4, #a-d 8.25 8.25

**Souvenir Sheet**
***Perf. 13¼x13***

**2755** A717 $6 multi 4.50 4.50

**World Cup Type of 2010**

No. 2756, $1.50 — Group E first-round matches: a, Netherlands vs. Denmark. b, Japan vs. Cameroun. c, Netherlands vs. Japan. d, Denmark vs. Cameroun. e, Japan vs. Denmark. f, Cameroun vs. Netherlands.
No. 2757, $1.50 — Group F first-round matches: a, Italy vs. Paraguay. b, New Zealand vs. Slovakia. c, Slovakia vs. Paraguay. d, New Zealand vs. Italy. e, Slovakia vs. Italy. f, Paraguay vs. New Zealand.
No. 2758, $1.50 — Group G first-round matches: a, Ivory Coast vs. Portugal. b, Brazil vs. North Korea. c, Brazil vs. Ivory Coast. d, Portugal vs. North Korea. e, North Korea vs. Ivory Coast. f, Portugal vs. Brazil.
No. 2759, $1.50 — Group H first-round matches: a, Honduras vs. Chile. b, Spain vs. Switzerland. c, Chile vs. Switzerland. d, Honduras vs. Spain. e, Spain vs. Chile. f, Switzerland vs. Honduras.
No. 2760, $3.50: a, Ellis Park Stadium, Johannesburg. b, Mbombela Stadium, Nelspruit.
No. 2761, $3.50: a, Loftus Versfeld Stadium, Pretoria. b, Free State Stadium, Bloemfontein.
No. 2762, $3.50: a, Peter Mokaba Stadium, Polokwane. b, Royal Bafokeng Stadium, Rustenburg.

**2010, June 11** **Litho.** *Perf. 13¼*

**Sheets of 6, #a-f**

**2756-2759** A720 Set of 4 27.00 27.00

**Sheets of 2, #a-b**

**2760-2762** A720 Set of 3 16.00 16.00

Whales — G243

No. 2763: a, Gervais's beaked whale. b, Cuvier's beaked whale. c, Pygmy sperm whale. d, Melon-headed whale. e, Bryde's whale. f, Sperm whale.
$6, Humpback whale.

**2010, Sept. 1** *Perf. 12*
**2763** G243 $2 Sheet of 6, #a-f 9.00 9.00

**Souvenir Sheet**

**2764** G243 $6 multi 4.50 4.50

Leonardo da Vinci (1452-1519), Artist — G244

No. 2765, vert.: a, Reputed self-portrait. b, Statue of da Vinci outside of Uffizi Gallery, Florence. c, Vitruvian Man. d, La Scapigliata. e, Mona Lisa. f, Study of Horses.
$6, The Last Supper.

**2010, Nov. 4**
**2765** G244 $2 Sheet of 6, #a-f 9.00 9.00

**Souvenir Sheet**

**2766** G244 $6 multi 4.50 4.50

Miniature Sheets

G245

Elvis Presley (1935-77) — G246

No. 2767 — Presley: a, Standing behind microphone. b, With guitar, no microphone visible. c, Holding microphone, no guitar visible. d, With guitar, holding microphone.
No. 2768 — Presley: a, With guitar neck by face. b, Without microphone. c, Holding microphone. d, Playing guitar.

**2010, Nov. 4**
**2767** G245 $2.75 Sheet of 4, #a-d 8.25 8.25
**2768** G246 $2.75 Sheet of 4, #a-d 8.25 8.25

Engagement of Prince William and Catherine Middleton G247

Engagement ring emblem and: No. 2769, Couple.
No. 2770: a, Middleton wearing fur hat. b, Prince William wearing military uniform and beret. c, Middleton without hat. d, Prince William in suit.
No. 2771: a, Middleton wearing beret. b, Prince William.
No. 2772, horiz.: a, Middleton wearing hat. b, Prince William, diff.

**2011, Feb. 18** **Litho.** *Perf. 12*
**2769** G247 $2.50 multi 1.90 1.90
**2770** G247 $2.50 Sheet of 4, #a-d 7.50 7.50

**Souvenir Sheets**
***Perf. 12¾x13 Syncopated***

**2771** G247 $3 Sheet of 2, #a-b 4.50 4.50

***Perf. 13x12¾ Syncopated***

**2772** G247 $3 Sheet of 2, #a-b 4.50 4.50

No. 2769 was printed in sheets of 4.

Miniature Sheet

Pres. Barack Obama in India — G248

No. 2773: a, Obama holding microphone. b, Indian Prime Minister Manmohan Singh, Obama, woman. c, Obama and Singh. d, Obama at lectern.

***Perf. 12¾x13 Syncopated***
**2011, Mar. 30**
**2773** G248 $2.75 Sheet of 4, #a-d 8.25 8.25

Indipex 2011, New Delhi.

Miniature Sheet

Mother Teresa (1910-97), Humanitarian — G249

No. 2774: a, Mother Teresa with hands together in prayer. b, Nobel Prize medal. c, Photographs of Mother Teresa. d, Bharat Ratna award.

**2011, Mar. 30** *Perf. 12*
**2774** G249 $2.75 Sheet of 4, #a-d 8.25 8.25

Indipex 2011, New Delhi.

Miniature Sheets

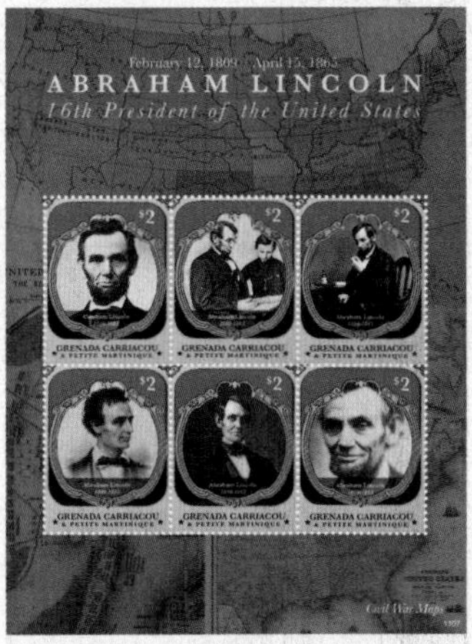


G250

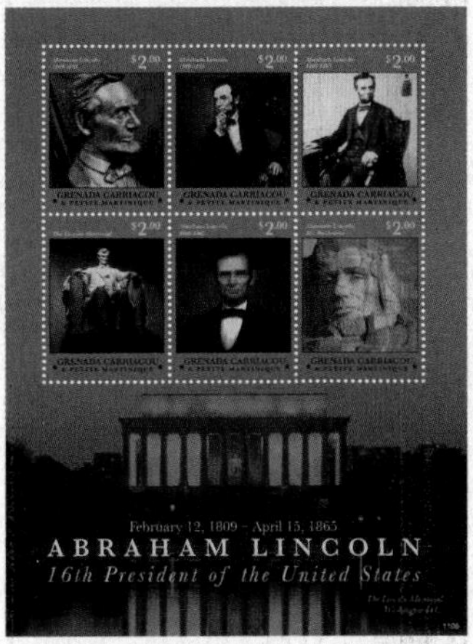


Pres. Abraham Lincoln (1809-65) — G251

No. 2775 — Photographs of Lincoln: a, With beard, both ears visible. b, Reading to son, Tad. c, Sitting in chair. d, Without beard, facing right. e, Without beard, facing forward. f, With beard, one ear visible.

No. 2776: a, Bust of Lincoln. b, Painting of Lincoln with hand at chin. c, Photograph of Lincoln sitting in chair. d, Statue in Lincoln Memorial. e, Painting of Lincoln, hands not visible. f, Mt. Rushmore sculpture of Lincoln.

**2011, Apr. 1** ***Perf. 12***

**2775** G250 $2 Sheet of 6, #a-f 9.00 9.00
**2776** G251 $2 Sheet of 6, #a-f 9.00 9.00

G252

Pres. John F. Kennedy (1917-63) — G253

Designs: No. 2777, Kennedy at desk in Oval Office.

No. 2778: a, Kennedy and family in hallway. b, Kennedy and wife, Jacqueline, in formal wear. c, Kennedy and wife at stadium. d, Kennedy and family on porch.

No. 2779, Kennedy, window at side. No. 2780, Kennedy walking and reviewing papers with aides.

**2011, Apr. 1** ***Perf. 12***

**2777** G252 $2.75 multi 2.10 2.10
**2778** G253 $2.75 Sheet of 4, #a-d 8.25 8.25

**Souvenir Sheets**

***Perf. 12¾x13 Syncopated***

**2779** G252 $6 multi 4.50 4.50
**2780** G253 $6 multi 4.50 4.50

No. 2777 was printed in sheets of 4.

Miniature Sheets

Dogs — G254

No. 2781, $2.50: a, King Charles spaniel. b, Labador retriever. c, German shepherd. d, Weimaraner.

No. 2782, $2.50: a, Border collie. b, Briard. c, Great Dane. d, Afghan hound.

**2011, Apr. 15 Litho.** ***Perf. 12x12½***

**Sheets of 4, #a-d**

**2781-2782** G254 Set of 2 15.00 15.00

Miniature Sheets

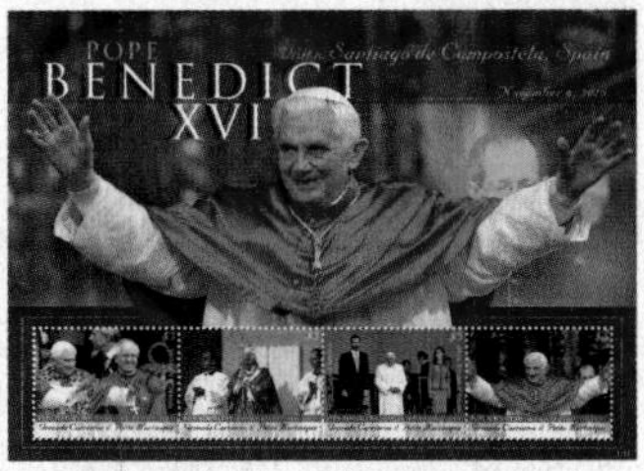


Visit to Spain of Pope Benedict XVI — G255

No. 2783, $3 — Visit to Santiago de Compostela: a, Pope Benedict XVI and Archbishop Julian Barrio. b, Pope holding crucifix, c, Pope with Prince and Princess of Asturias. d, Pope extending arms.

No. 2784, $3 — Visit to Barcelona: a, Pope holding Bible. b, Pope and priest in procession. c, Pope with King Juan Carlos and Queen Sofia. d, Pope at pulpit reading.

***Perf. 11½x12, 11½x11¼ (#2784)***

**2011, Apr. 15**

**Sheets of 4, #a-d**

**2783-2784** G255 Set of 2 18.00 18.00

Beatification of Pope John Paul II — G256

No. 2785 — Pope John Paul II: a, Wearing miter. b, Kneeling in prayer. c, With arm extended.

$6, Pope with arms clasped.

**2011, Apr. 15** ***Perf. 13 Syncopated***

**2785** G256 $3.30 Sheet of 3, #a-c 7.50 7.50

**Souvenir Sheet**

***Perf. 12***

**2786** G256 $6 multi 4.50 4.50

**Princess Diana Type of 2011**

No. 2787 — Princess Diana: a, Wearing hat. b, With children. c, As young girl. d, Walking with Prince Charles. $6, Princess Diana wearing red hat.

**2011, Apr. 15** ***Perf. 12***

**2787** A744 $2.75 Sheet of 4, #a-d 8.25 8.25

**Souvenir Sheet**

***Perf. 13 Syncopated***

**2788** A744 $6 multi 4.50 4.50

Wedding of Prince William and Catherine Middleton — G257

No. 2789, $2.75: a, Couple in coach waving. b, Bride facing left. c, Groom wearing hat. d, Couple holding hands.

No. 2790, $2.75: a, Groom without hat. b, Bride, diff. c, Soldiers on horseback. d, Couple waving.

No. 2791, vert.: a, Bride, diff. b, Groom, diff.

**2011, Sept. 15** ***Perf. 13 Syncopated***

**Sheets of 4, #a-d**

**2789-2790** G257 Set of 2 16.50 16.50

**Souvenir Sheet**

**2791** G257 $3 Sheet of 2, #a-b 4.50 4.50

Birds — G258

No. 2792, $2.50: a, Troupial. b, Green-throated carib. c, Osprey. d, Green heron.

No. 2793, $2.50: a, Village weaver. b, Belted kingfisher. c, Scarlet tanager. d, Semi-palmated plover.

No. 2794, $6, Rose-breasted grosbeak. No. 2795, $6, Merlin.

**2011, Oct. 26** ***Perf. 13 Syncopated***

**Sheets of 4, #a-d**

**2792-2793** G258 Set of 2 15.00 15.00

**Souvenir Sheets**

***Perf. 12***

**2794-2795** G258 Set of 2 9.00 9.00

Chinese Musical Instruments — G259

No. 2796: a, Pipa. b, Guqin. c, Dizi. d, Yangqin. e, Dagu.

$6, Erhu, vert.

**2011, Nov. 8** ***Perf. 13¼***

**2796** G259 $2 Sheet of 5, #a-e 7.50 7.50

**Souvenir Sheet**

***Perf. 13¼x13***

**2797** G259 $6 multi 4.50 4.50

China 2011 Intl. Philatelic Exhibition, Wuxi. No. 2797 contains one 30x80mm stamp.

Christmas G260

Paintings: 25c, Annunciation, by Niccolò di Pietro Gerini. 50c, The Annunciation, by Melchior Broederlam. $1, Coronation of the Virgin, by Giovanni da Milano. $2, Madonna, by André Beauneveu.

**2011, Nov. 1** ***Perf. 12***

**2798-2801** G260 Set of 4 2.75 2.75

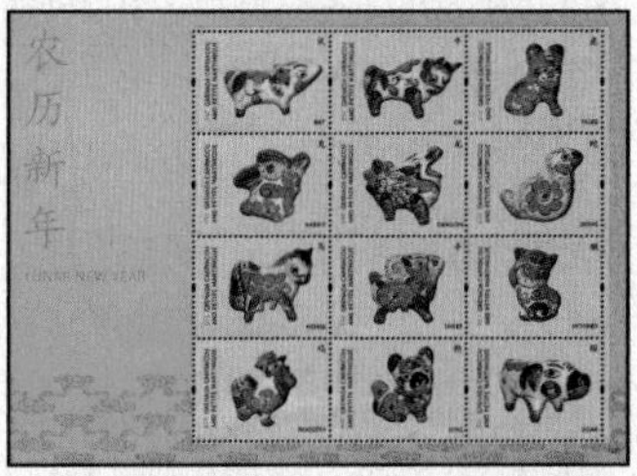


Chinese Zodiac Animals — G261

New Year 2012 (Year of the Dragon) — G262

No. 2802: a, Rat. b, Ox. c, Tiger. d, Rabbit. e, Dragon. f, Snake. g, Horse. h, Sheep. i, Monkey. j, Rooster. k, Dog. l, Boar.

$8, Dragon.

**Litho. With Foil Application**

**2011** ***Perf. 13 Syncopated***

**2802** G261 65c Sheet of 12, #a-l 5.75 5.75

**Souvenir Sheet**

**Litho.**

***Perf. 13¼***

**2803** G262 $8 multi 6.00 6.00

Issued: No. 2802, 11/8; No. 2803, 10/26.

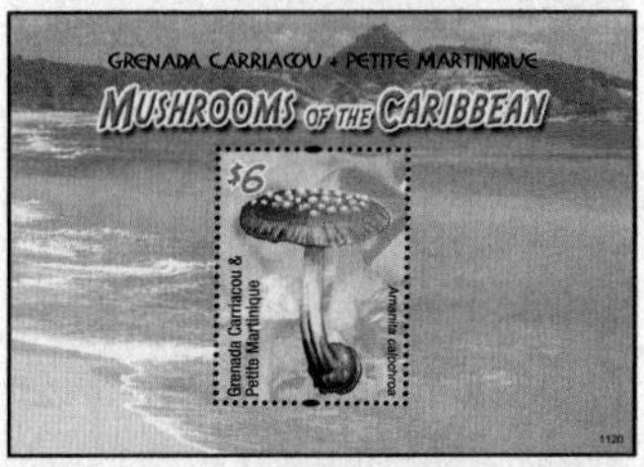


G263

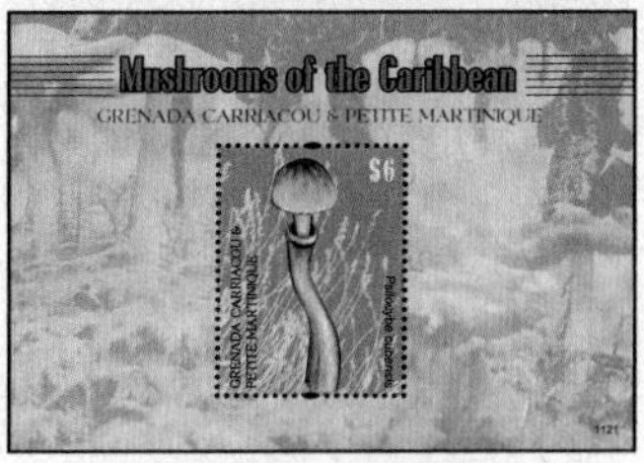


Mushrooms — G264

No. 2804: a, Coltriciella navispora. b, Tylopilus rufonigricans. c, Chroogomphus rutilus. d, Entoloma rugostriatum. e, Xerocomus amazonicus. f, Coltricia oblectabilis.

No. 2805: a, Tylopilus exiguus. b, Mycena acicula. c, Panaeolus papilionaceus. d, Chroomogomphus ochraceus.

No. 2806, Amanita calochroa. No. 2807, Psilocybe cubensis.

**2011, Dec. 16** ***Perf. 13 Syncopated***

| | | | | | |
|---|---|---|---|---|---|
| **2804** | G263 | $2 | Sheet of 6, #a-f | 9.00 | 9.00 |
| **2805** | G264 | $2.50 | Sheet of 4, #a-d | 7.50 | 7.50 |

**Souvenir Sheets**

| | | | | | |
|---|---|---|---|---|---|
| **2806** | G263 | $6 | multi | 4.50 | 4.50 |
| **2807** | G264 | $6 | multi | 4.50 | 4.50 |

Reptiles — G265

No. 2808, $3.50: a, Puerto Rican crested anole. b, Tropical house gecko. c, Dominican ground lizard. d, Eyed anole.

No. 2809, $3.50: a, Giant ditch frog. b, Coqui antillano. c, Gounouj. d, Tink frog.

No. 2810, $9, Lesser Antillean iguana. No. 2811, $9, Red-footed tortoise.

**2012, Feb. 8** ***Perf. 13 Syncopated***

**Sheets of 4, #a-d**

| | | | | |
|---|---|---|---|---|
| **2808-2809** | G265 | Set of 2 | 21.00 | 21.00 |

**Souvenir Sheets**

| | | | | |
|---|---|---|---|---|
| **2810-2811** | G265 | Set of 2 | 13.50 | 13.50 |

Miniature Sheet

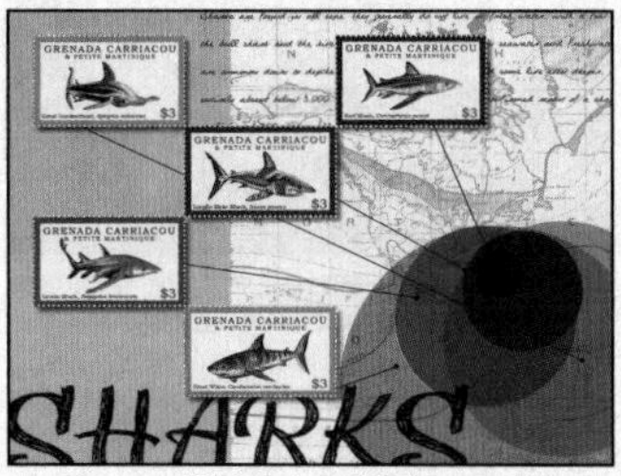


Sharks — G266

No. 2812: a, Great hammerhead shark. b, Reef shark. c, Longfin mako shark. d, Lemon shark. e, Great white shark.

**2012, Apr. 5** ***Perf. 12***

| | | | | | |
|---|---|---|---|---|---|
| **2812** | G266 | $3 | Sheet of 5, #a-e | 11.00 | 11.00 |

Space Exploration — G267

No. 2813: a, Pres. John F. Kennedy. b, Pres. Kennedy looking into space capsule. c, Emblem for NASA's Apollo program. d, Buzz Aldrin on the Moon.

$9, Pres. Kennedy greeting men undeer rocket.

**2012, Apr. 5** ***Perf. 14***

| | | | | | |
|---|---|---|---|---|---|
| **2813** | G267 | $3.50 | Sheet of 4, #a-d | 10.50 | 10.50 |

**Souvenir Sheet**

***Perf. 12***

| | | | | | |
|---|---|---|---|---|---|
| **2814** | G267 | $9 | multi | 6.75 | 6.75 |

No. 2814 contains one 30x50mm stamp.

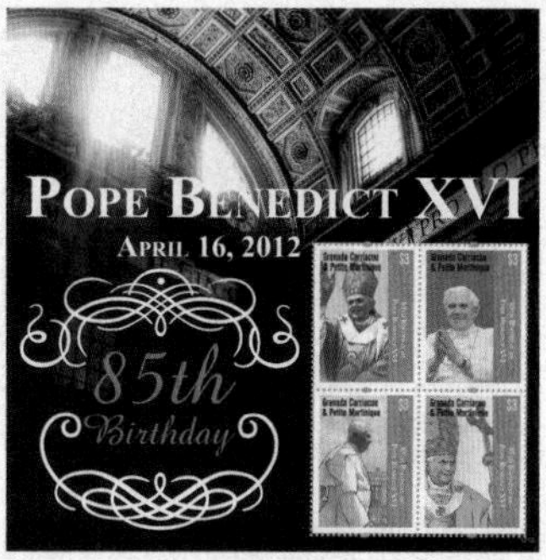


G268

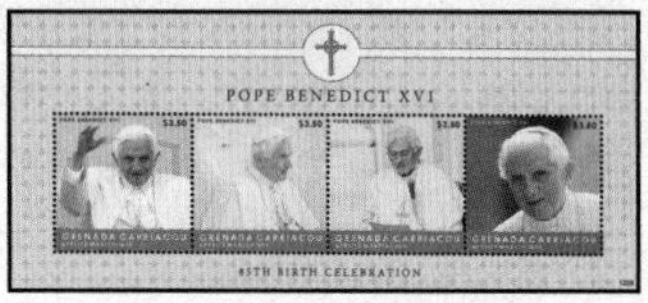


Pope Benedict XVI, 85th Birthday — G269

No. 2815 — Pope Benedict XVI: a, Waving. b, With hands together. c, At Vatican City. d, With crucifix.

No. 2816 — Pope Benedict XVI: a, Waving. b, Facing right. c, In front of microphone. d, Facing forward.

$9, Pope facing right wearing red vestments.

***Perf. 13 Syncopated (G268), 13¾***

**2012, Nov. 28**

| | | | | | |
|---|---|---|---|---|---|
| **2815** | G268 | $3 | Sheet of 4, #a-d | 9.00 | 9.00 |
| **2816** | G269 | $3.50 | Sheet of 4, #a-d | 10.50 | 10.50 |

**Souvenir Sheet**

| | | | | | |
|---|---|---|---|---|---|
| **2817** | G268 | $9 | multi | 6.75 | 6.75 |

**SEMI-POSTAL STAMPS**

**1988 Seoul Olympics Type**

**1986, Dec. 1** ***Perf. 15***

| | | | | | |
|---|---|---|---|---|---|
| **B1** | SP2 | 10c +5c Cycling | | .90 | .45 |
| **B2** | SP2 | 50c +20c Sailing | | .90 | .90 |
| **B3** | SP2 | 70c +30c Uneven Parallel Bars | | .90 | .90 |
| **B4** | SP2 | $2 +$1 Dressage | | 2.40 | 2.40 |
| | | *Nos. B1-B4 (4)* | | 5.10 | 4.65 |

**Souvenir Sheet**

| | | | | |
|---|---|---|---|---|
| **B5** | SP2 | $3 +$1 Marathon | 4.00 | 4.00 |

**OFFICIAL STAMPS**

**Grenada Grenadines Nos. 396-408, 410, 440-442, 465-468 Overprinted "P.R.G."**

**1982, June** ***Perf. 14, 15***

| | | | | | |
|---|---|---|---|---|---|
| **O1** | G45 | 5c | multicolored | .25 | .25 |
| **O2** | G45 | 6c | multicolored | .25 | .25 |
| **O3** | G45 | 10c | multicolored | .25 | .25 |
| **O4** | G45 | 12c | multicolored | .25 | .25 |
| **O5** | G45 | 15c | multicolored | .25 | .25 |
| **O6** | G45 | 20c | multicolored | .25 | .25 |
| **O7** | G54 | 20c | multicolored | .25 | .25 |
| **O8** | G45 | 25c | multicolored | .25 | .25 |
| **O9** | G45 | 30c | multicolored | .25 | .25 |
| **O10** | G45 | 40c | multicolored | .25 | .25 |
| **O11** | CD331 | 40c | multicolored | .25 | .25 |
| **O12** | G54 | 40c | multicolored | .25 | .25 |
| **O13** | G45 | 50c | multicolored | .30 | .30 |
| **O14** | G45 | 90c | multicolored | .55 | .55 |
| **O15** | G45 | $1 | multicolored | .60 | .60 |
| **O16** | G54 | $1 | multicolored | .60 | .60 |
| **O17** | CD331 | $2 | multicolored | 1.10 | 1.10 |
| **O18** | G54 | $2 | multicolored | 1.10 | 1.10 |
| **O19** | G45 | $3 | multicolored | 1.60 | 1.60 |
| **O20** | CD331 | $4 | multicolored | 2.10 | 2.10 |
| **O21** | G45 | $10 | multicolored | 5.75 | 5.75 |
| | | | *Nos. O1-O21 (21)* | 16.70 | 16.70 |

Royal Wedding stamps in changed colors, perf 15x14½ were also overprinted.

## GRIQUALAND WEST

ˈgri-kwə-ˌland ˈwest

LOCATION — In South Africa west of the Orange Free State and north of the Orange River

GOVT. — British Crown Colony

AREA — 15,197 sq. mi.

POP. — 83,375 (1891)

CAPITAL — Kimberley

Originally a territorial division of the Cape of Good Hope Colony, Griqualand West was declared a British Crown Colony in 1873 and together with Griqualand East was annexed to the Cape Colony in 1880.

12 Pence = 1 Shilling

Beware of forgeries.

**Stamps of Cape of Good Hope 1864-65 (Type I, 4p, 6p, 1sh) and 1871-76 (Type II, ½p, 1p, 4p, 5sh) Surcharged or Overprinted**

Type I — With frame line around stamp.
Type II — Without frame line.

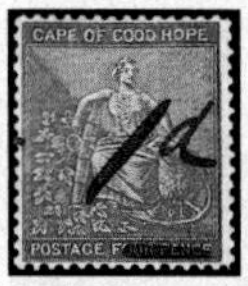


"Hope" — A1

Manuscript Surcharge in Dark Red

**1874** **Wmk. 1** ***Perf. 14***

| | | | | |
|---|---|---|---|---|
| **1** | A1 | 1p on 4p blue (type I) | 1,800. | *2,500.* |

Overprinted

**1877** **Black Overprint**

| | | | |
|---|---|---|---|
| **2** | 1p rose | 700.00 | 100.00 |
| *a.* | Double overprint | | *3,000.* |

**Red Overprint**

| | | | |
|---|---|---|---|
| **3** | 4p blue (type II) | 450.00 | 85.00 |

Overprinted In Black on the One Penny, in Red on the Other Values

a b c d

e f g

| | | | | |
|---|---|---|---|---|
| **4** | (a) | ½p gray black | 35.00 | *37.50* |
| **5** | (a) | 1p rose | 35.00 | 26.00 |
| **6** | (a) | 4p blue (type I) | 325.00 | 45.00 |
| **7** | (a) | 4p blue (type II) | 250.00 | 32.50 |
| **8** | (a) | 6p dull violet | 160.00 | 29.00 |
| **9** | (a) | 1sh green | 190.00 | 27.50 |
| *a.* | | Inverted overprint | | 575.00 |
| **10** | (a) | 5sh orange | 750.00 | 32.50 |
| **11** | (b) | ½p gray black | 35.00 | 40.00 |
| **12** | (b) | 1p rose | 35.00 | 25.00 |
| **13** | (b) | 4p blue (type I) | 425.00 | 50.00 |
| **14** | (b) | 4p blue (type II) | 275.00 | 30.00 |
| **15** | (b) | 6p dull violet | 300.00 | 35.00 |
| **16** | (b) | 1sh green | 375.00 | 27.50 |
| **17** | (b) | 5sh orange | 1,000. | 35.00 |
| **18** | (c) | ½p gray black | 80.00 | *95.00* |
| **19** | (c) | 1p rose | 85.00 | 55.00 |
| **20** | (c) | 4p blue (type I) | *750.00* | 125.00 |
| **21** | (c) | 4p blue (type II) | *500.00* | 80.00 |
| **22** | (c) | 6p dull violet | *350.00* | 85.00 |
| **23** | (c) | 1sh green | *425.00* | 65.00 |
| **24** | (c) | 5sh orange | *1,100.* | 75.00 |
| **25** | (d) | ½p gray black | 47.50 | *55.00* |
| **26** | (d) | 1p rose | 47.50 | 35.00 |
| **27** | (d) | 4p blue (type I) | 500.00 | 65.00 |
| **28** | (d) | 4p blue (type II) | 375.00 | 37.50 |
| **29** | (d) | 6p dull violet | 250.00 | 45.00 |
| **30** | (d) | 1sh green | 350.00 | 37.50 |
| **31** | (d) | 5sh orange | 950.00 | 45.00 |
| **32** | (e) | ½p gray black | 80.00 | *95.00* |
| **33** | (e) | 1p rose | 85.00 | 55.00 |
| **34** | (e) | 4p blue (type I) | 775.00 | 135.00 |
| **35** | (e) | 4p blue (type II) | 500.00 | 85.00 |
| **36** | (e) | 6p dull violet | 375.00 | 90.00 |
| **37** | (e) | 1sh green | 450.00 | 67.50 |
| *a.* | | Inverted overprint | | 950.00 |
| **38** | (e) | 5sh orange | 1,250. | 80.00 |
| **39** | (f) | ½p gray black | 90.00 | *110.00* |
| **40** | (f) | 1p rose | 95.00 | 70.00 |
| **41** | (f) | 4p blue (type I) | 850.00 | 160.00 |
| **42** | (f) | 4p blue (type II) | 625.00 | 110.00 |
| **43** | (f) | 6p dull violet | 450.00 | 110.00 |
| **44** | (f) | 1sh green | 550.00 | 82.50 |
| **45** | (f) | 5sh orange | 1,750. | 95.00 |
| **46** | (g) | ½p gray black | 42.50 | 50.00 |
| **47** | (g) | 1p rose | 35.00 | 24.00 |
| **48** | (g) | 4p blue (type I) | 400.00 | 62.50 |
| **49** | (g) | 4p blue (type II) | 350.00 | 37.50 |
| **50** | (g) | 6p dull violet | 225.00 | 42.50 |
| **51** | (g) | 1sh green | 325.00 | 32.50 |
| *a.* | | Inverted overprint | — | 800.00 |
| **52** | (g) | 5sh orange | 900.00 | 40.00 |

There are minor varieties of types e and f.

Overprinted in Black

i k l m n

o p q r

**1878**

| | | | | |
|---|---|---|---|---|
| **54** | (g) | 4p blue (type II) | 400.00 | 70.00 |
| **55** | (g) | 6p dull violet | 525.00 | 110.00 |
| **56** | (i) | 1p rose | 37.50 | 24.00 |
| **57** | (i) | 4p blue (type II) | 160.00 | 27.50 |
| **58** | (i) | 6p dull violet | 300.00 | 60.00 |
| *a.* | | Double overprint | | — |
| **59** | (k) | 1p rose | 85.00 | 42.50 |
| **60** | (k) | 4p blue (type II) | 375.00 | 57.50 |
| **61** | (k) | 6p dull violet | 500.00 | 95.00 |
| **62** | (l) | 1p rose | 42.50 | 29.00 |
| **63** | (l) | 4p blue (type II) | 175.00 | 29.00 |
| **64** | (l) | 6p dull violet | 400.00 | 75.00 |
| *a.* | | Double overprint | | *1,100.* |
| **65** | (m) | 1p rose | 80.00 | 70.00 |
| **66** | (m) | 4p blue (type II) | 400.00 | 82.50 |
| **67** | (m) | 6p dull violet | 550.00 | 150.00 |
| **68** | (n) | 1p rose | 100.00 | 80.00 |
| **69** | (n) | 4p blue (type II) | 425.00 | 85.00 |
| **70** | (n) | 6p dull violet | 750.00 | 160.00 |
| *a.* | | Double overprint | | *1,400.* |
| **71** | (o) | 1p rose | 90.00 | 55.00 |
| **72** | (o) | 4p blue (type II) | 400.00 | 75.00 |
| **73** | (o) | 6p dull violet | 550.00 | 110.00 |
| **74** | (p) | 1p rose | 90.00 | 70.00 |
| **75** | (p) | 4p blue (type II) | 425.00 | 77.50 |
| **76** | (p) | 6p dull violet | 550.00 | 140.00 |
| **77** | (q) | 1p rose | 150.00 | 110.00 |
| **78** | (q) | 4p blue (type II) | 650.00 | 160.00 |
| **79** | (q) | 6p dull violet | 850.00 | 225.00 |
| **80** | (r) | 1p rose | 500.00 | 350.00 |
| **81** | (r) | 4p blue (type II) | *2,000.* | 475.00 |
| **82** | (r) | 6p dull violet | *2,500.* | 650.00 |

There are two minor varieties of type i and one of type p.

**Overprinted in Red**

s

t

**1878**

| | | | | |
|---|---|---|---|---|
| **83** | (s) | ½p gray black | 22.50 | 22.50 |
| *a.* | | Double overprint | 70.00 | *85.00* |
| *b.* | | Inverted overprint | 25.00 | 25.00 |
| *c.* | | Double overprint, inverted | 140.00 | *160.00* |

**84** (s) 4p blue (type II) 500.00 140.00
*a.* Inverted overprint 550.00 130.00
**85** (t) ½p gray black 24.00 24.00
*a.* Double overprint 110.00 110.00
*b.* Inverted overprint 24.00 *25.00*
**86** (t) 4p blue (type II) — 120.00
*a.* Inverted overprint 500.00 120.00

### Black Overprint

**87** (s) ½p gray black 275.00 150.00
*a.* Inverted overprint 300.00 —
*b.* With 2nd ovpt. *(s)* in red, invtd. 475.00
*c.* With 2nd ovpt. *(t)* in red, invtd. 250.00
**88** (s) 1p rose 22.00 16.00
*a.* Double overprint 275.00 70.00
*b.* Inverted overprint 22.00 22.00
*c.* Double overprint, both inverted 275.00 82.50
*d.* With second overprint *(s)* in red, both inverted 50.00 55.00
**89** (s) 4p blue (type I) 200.00
**90** (s) 4p blue (type II) 180.00 40.00
*a.* Double overprint — 260.00
*b.* Inverted overprint 275.00 97.50
*c.* Double overprint, both inverted — 350.00
**91** (s) 6p dull violet 190.00 37.50
**92** (t) ½p gray black 60.00 60.00
*a.* Inverted overprint 130.00 87.50
*b.* With 2nd ovpt. inverted 225.00
**93** (t) 1p rose 18.00 14.50
*a.* Double overprint — 105.00
*b.* Inverted overprint 100.00 37.50
*c.* Double overprint, both inverted — 130.00
*d.* With 2nd ovpt. *(t)* in red, both invtd. 100.00 100.00
**94** (t) 4p blue (type I) 200.00
**95** (t) 4p blue (type II) 200.00 20.00
*a.* Double overprint — 240.00
*b.* Inverted overprint 350.00 37.50
*c.* Double overprint, both inverted — 325.00
**96** (t) 6p dull violet 37.50

Overprinted in Black

**97** ½p gray black 25.00 9.00
*a.* Double overprint 475.00 300.00
**98** 1p rose 26.00 7.00
*a.* Double overprint — 150.00
*b.* Triple overprint — 275.00
*c.* Inverted overprint — 95.00
**99** 4p blue (type II) 50.00 7.00
*a.* Double overprint — 130.00
**100** 6p brt violet 190.00 11.00
*a.* Double overprint 850.00 200.00
*b.* Inverted overprint — 45.00
**101** 1sh green 180.00 7.50
*a.* Double overprint 450.00 100.00
**102** 5sh orange 600.00 20.00
*a.* Double overprint 800.00 100.00
*b.* Triple overprint — 350.00

These stamps were declared obsolete in 1880 and the remainders were used in Cape of Good Hope offices as ordinary stamps. Prices for used stamps are for examples with such cancels.

## GUADELOUPE

ˈgwä-dəl-ˌüp

LOCATION — In the West Indies lying between Montserrat and Dominica
GOVT. — French colony
AREA — 688 sq. mi.
POP. — 271,262 (1946)
CAPITAL — Basse-Terre

Guadeloupe consists of two large islands, Guadeloupe proper and Grande-Terre, together with five smaller dependencies. Guadeloupe became an integral part of the Republic, acquiring the same status as the departments in metropolitan France, under a law effective Jan. 1, 1947.

100 Centimes = 1 Franc

**Catalogue values for unused stamps in this country are for Never Hinged items, beginning with Scott 168 in the regular postage section, Scott B12 in the semi-postal section, Scott C1 in the air-post section, and Scott J38 in the postage due section.**

**See France Nos. 850, 909, 1280, 1913 for French stamps inscribed "Guadeloupe."**

Stamps of French Colonies Surcharged

**1884** **Unwmk.** ***Imperf.***

**1** A8 20c on 30c brn, *bis* 72.50 60.00
*a.* Large "2" 325.00 260.00
**2** A8 25c on 35c blk, *org* 60.00 60.00
*a.* Large "2" 325.00 260.00
*b.* Large "5" 160.00 125.00

The 5c on 4c (French Colonies No. 40) was not regularly issued. Three examples exist. Value $42,500.

The 5c on 4c also exists as an essay, surcharge similar to the issued values. Value $1,000.

c

d

**1889** ***Perf. 14x13½***

**Surcharged Type c**

**3** A9 3c on 20c red, *grn* 5.25 5.25
**4** A9 15c on 20c red, *grn* 32.50 27.50
**5** A9 25c on 20c red, *grn* 32.50 27.50
*Nos. 3-5 (3)* 70.25 60.25

**Surcharged Type d**

**6** A9 5c on 1c blk, *lil bl* 14.50 13.50
*a.* Inverted surcharge *1,400.*
*b.* Double surcharge *450.00* *450.00*
**7** A9 10c on 40c red, *straw* 40.00 35.00
*a.* Double surcharge 475.00 475.00
**8** A9 15c on 20c red, *grn* 32.50 30.00
*a.* Double surcharge 475.00 475.00
**9** A9 25c on 30c brn, *bis* 52.50 45.00
*a.* Double surcharge 475.00 475.00
*Nos. 6-9 (4)* 139.50 123.50

The word "centimes" in surcharges "b" and "c" varies from 10 to 12½mm.

Issue dates: No. 6, June 25; others, Mar. 22.

Stamps of French Colonies Surcharged

**1891**

**10** A9 5c on 10c blk, *lav* 15.00 12.50
**11** A9 5c on 1fr brnz grn, *straw* 17.00 12.50

Stamps of French Colonies Overprinted in Black

**1891** ***Imperf.***

**12** A7 30c brn, *yelsh* 350.00 *375.00*
*a.* Double overprint 725.00 725.00
**13** A7 80c car, *pnksh* 1,100. *1,300.*

***Perf. 14x13½***

**14** A9 1c blk, *lil bl* 1.75 1.60
*a.* Double overprint 40.00 40.00
*b.* Inverted overprint 150.00 150.00
**15** A9 2c brn, *buff* 2.60 2.00
*a.* Double overprint 45.00 40.00
**16** A9 4c claret, *lav* 6.00 5.25
**17** A9 5c grn, *grnsh* 8.75 7.25
*a.* Double overprint 45.00 40.00
*b.* Inverted overprint 160.00 160.00
**18** A9 10c blk, *lavender* 17.00 13.50
**19** A9 15c blue 52.50 6.00
*a.* Double overprint 110.00
**20** A9 20c red, *grn* 45.00 30.00
*a.* Double overprint 240.00 240.00
**21** A9 25c blk, *rose* 47.50 5.25
*a.* Double overprint 240.00 240.00
*b.* Inverted overprint 225.00 225.00
**22** A9 30c brn, *bister* 45.00 30.00
*a.* Double overprint 240.00 240.00
**23** A9 35c dp vio, *org* 87.50 72.50
*a.* Double overprint 675.00 675.00
**24** A9 40c red, *straw* 65.00 52.50
*a.* Double overprint 675.00 675.00
**25** A9 75c car, *rose* 130.00 125.00
**26** A9 1fr brnz grn, *straw* 92.50 72.50
*Nos. 14-26 (13)* 601.10 423.35

Navigation and Commerce — A7

***Perf. 14x13½***

**1892-1901** **Typo.** **Unwmk.**

**Colony Name in Blue or Carmine**

**27** A7 1c blk, *lil bl* 1.40 1.40
**28** A7 2c brn, *buff* 1.50 1.40
**29** A7 4c claret, *lav* 1.75 1.50
**30** A7 5c grn, *grnsh* 3.50 1.50
**31** A7 5c yel grn ('01) 6.00 1.60
**32** A7 10c blk, *lavender* 10.00 3.25
**33** A7 10c red ('00) 8.75 2.40
*a.* Imperf. 120.00
**34** A7 15c blue, quadrille paper 18.00 1.75
**35** A7 15c gray, *lt gray* ('00) 13.00 1.60
**36** A7 20c red, *grn* 11.00 6.50
**37** A7 25c blk, *rose* 11.00 3.00
**38** A7 25c blue ('00) 100.00 100.00
**39** A7 30c brn, *bister* 24.00 15.00
**40** A7 40c red, *straw* 24.00 15.00
**41** A7 50c car, *rose* 32.50 16.00
**42** A7 50c brn, *az* ('00) 45.00 42.50
**43** A7 75c dp vio, *org* 32.50 22.50
**44** A7 1fr brnz grn, *straw* 32.50 30.00
*Nos. 27-44 (18)* 376.40 266.90

Perf. 13½x14 stamps are counterfeits.
For surcharges see Nos. 45-53, 83-85.

**Nos. 39-41, 43-44 Surcharged in Black**

f

g

h

**1903**

**45** A7 (f) 5c on 30c 4.00 4.00
*a.* "C" instead of "G" 32.50 32.50
*b.* Inverted surcharge 45.00 45.00
*c.* Double surcharge 140.00 140.00
*d.* Double surch., inverted 160.00
**46** A7 (g) 10c on 40c 9.50 9.50
*a.* "C" instead of "G" 40.00 40.00
*b.* "1" inverted 60.00 60.00
*c.* Inverted surcharge 55.00 55.00
*d.* Double surcharge 200.00 200.00
**47** A7 (f) 15c on 50c 13.00 13.00
*a.* "C" instead of "G" 40.00 40.00
*b.* Inverted surcharge 110.00 110.00
*c.* "15" inverted 375.00 375.00
**48** A7 (g) 40c on 1fr 13.00 13.00
*a.* "C" instead of "G" 52.50 52.50
*b.* "4" inverted 120.00 120.00
*c.* Inverted surcharge 110.00 110.00
*d.* Double surcharge 240.00 240.00
*e.* Triple surcharge 450.00 *500.00*
**49** A7 (h) 1fr on 75c 42.50 42.50
*a.* "C" instead of "G" 160.00 160.00
*b.* "1" inverted 160.00 160.00
*c.* Value above "G & D" 300.00 300.00
*d.* Inverted surcharge 125.00 125.00
*Nos. 45-49 (5)* 82.00 82.00

Letters and figures from several fonts were used for these surcharges, resulting in numerous minor varieties.

**Nos. 48-49 With Additional Overprint "1903" in a Frame**

**1904, Mar.**

**Red Overprint**

**50** A7 (g) 40c on 1fr 65.00 72.50
*b.* Inverted surcharge 425.00 425.00
*c.* Double surcharge 1,250. 1,250.
**51** A7 (h) 1fr on 75c 92.50 100.00
*a.* Double surcharge 950.00 1,050.

**Blue Overprint**

**52** A7 (g) 40c on 1fr 52.50 55.00
**53** A7 (h) 1fr on 75c 87.50 95.00
*Nos. 50-53 (4)* 297.50 322.50

The date "1903" may be found in 19 different positions and type faces within the frame. These stamps may also be found with the minor varieties of Nos. 48-49.

The 40c exists with black overprint. Value, $500 unused or used.

Harbor at Basse-Terre — A8

View of La Soufrière A9

Pointe-à-Pitre, Grand-Terre — A10

**1905-27** **Typo.** ***Perf. 14x13½***

**54** A8 1c blk, *bluish* .30 .30
**55** A8 2c vio brn, *straw* .30 .30
**56** A8 4c bis brn, *az* .30 .30
**57** A8 5c green 2.40 .65
**58** A8 5c dp blue ('22) .25 .25
**59** A8 10c rose 2.25 .65
**60** A8 10c green ('22) 1.40 1.25
**61** A8 10c red, *bluish* ('25) .25 .25
**62** A8 15c violet .55 .50
**63** A9 20c red, *grn* .55 .40
**64** A9 20c bl grn ('25) .65 .65
**65** A9 25c blue .95 .55
**66** A9 25c ol grn ('22) .65 .65
**67** A9 30c black 5.00 3.25
**68** A9 30c rose ('22) .70 .70
**69** A9 30c brn ol, *lav* ('25) .55 .55
**70** A9 35c blk, *yel* ('06) .80 .80
**71** A9 40c red, *straw* .80 .80
**72** A9 45c ol gray, *lil* ('07) 1.40 .80
**73** A9 45c rose ('25) .80 .80
**74** A9 50c gray grn, *straw* 5.50 4.00
**75** A9 50c dp bl ('22) 1.25 1.10
**76** A9 50c violet ('25) .70 .70
**77** A9 65c blue ('27) .70 .70
**78** A9 75c car, *bl* .90 .80
**79** A10 1fr blk, *green* 1.75 1.50
**80** A10 1fr lt bl ('25) 1.00 .95
**81** A10 2fr car, *org* 2.25 2.00
**82** A10 5fr dp bl, *org* 7.50 7.50
*Nos. 54-82 (29)* 42.40 33.65

Nos. 57, 59 and 82 exist imperf. Value, Nos. 57 and 59 each $60, No. 82 $140.

For surcharges see #86-95, 167, B1-B2.

**Nos. 29, 39 and 40 Surcharged in Carmine or Black**

**1912, Nov.**

**83** A7 5c on 4c claret, *lav* (C) 1.50 1.50
**84** A7 5c on 30c brn, *bis* (C) 2.00 2.00
**85** A7 10c on 40c red, *straw* 2.25 2.25
*Nos. 83-85 (3)* 5.75 5.75

Two spacings between the surcharaged numerals are found on Nos. 83 to 85. For detailed listings, see the *Scott Classic Specialized Catalogue of Stamps and Covers.*

**Stamps and Types of 1905-27 Surcharged with New Value and Bars**

**1924-27**

**86** A10 25c on 5fr dp bl, *org* .75 .70
**87** A10 65c on 1fr gray grn 1.40 1.25
**88** A10 85c on 1fr gray grn 1.50 1.40
**89** A9 90c on 75c dl red 1.40 1.25
**90** A10 1.05fr on 2fr ver (Bl) 1.00 .85
**91** A10 1.25fr on 1fr lt bl (R) .65 .65
**92** A10 1.50fr on 1fr dk bl 1.25 1.25
**93** A10 3fr on 5fr org brn 1.50 1.50
**94** A10 10fr on 5fr vio rose, *org* 11.00 11.00
**95** A10 20fr on 5fr rose lil, *pnksh* 14.00 13.00
*Nos. 86-95 (10)* 34.45 32.85

Years issued: Nos. 87-88, 1925. Nos. 90-91, 1926. Nos. 89, 92-95, 1927.

Sugar Mill — A11

Saints Roadstead A12

Harbor Scene A13

*Perf. 14x13½*

**1928-40 Unwmk. Typo.**

| | | | | |
|---|---|---|---|---|
| 96 | A11 | 1c yel & vio | .25 | .25 |
| 97 | A11 | 2c blk & lt red | .25 | .25 |
| 98 | A11 | 3c yel & red vio ('40) | .30 | .30 |
| 99 | A11 | 4c yel grn & org brn | .25 | .25 |
| 100 | A11 | 5c ver & grn | .25 | .25 |
| 101 | A11 | 10c bis brn & dp bl | .25 | .25 |
| 102 | A11 | 15c brn red & blk | .30 | .30 |
| 103 | A11 | 20c lil & ol brn | .50 | .50 |
| 104 | A12 | 25c grnsh bl & olvn | .55 | .55 |
| 105 | A12 | 30c gray grn & yel grn | .40 | .40 |
| 106 | A12 | 35c bl grn ('38) | .40 | .40 |
| 107 | A12 | 40c yel & vio | .40 | .40 |
| 108 | A12 | 45c vio brn & slate | .95 | .80 |
| 109 | A12 | 45c bl grn & dl grn ('40) | 1.10 | 1.00 |
| 110 | A12 | 50c dl grn & org | .30 | .30 |
| 111 | A12 | 55c ultra & car ('38) | 1.40 | 1.25 |
| 112 | A12 | 60c ultra & car ('40) | .65 | .65 |
| 113 | A12 | 65c gray blk & ver | .55 | .55 |
| 114 | A12 | 70c gray blk & ver ('40) | .70 | .70 |
| 115 | A12 | 75c dl red & bl grn | .70 | .70 |
| 116 | A12 | 80c car & brn ('38) | .85 | .65 |
| 117 | A12 | 90c dl red & dl rose | 2.00 | 1.75 |
| 118 | A12 | 90c rose red & bl ('39) | 1.25 | 1.10 |
| 119 | A13 | 1fr lt rose & lt bl | 5.25 | 3.75 |
| 120 | A13 | 1fr rose red & org ('38) | 1.75 | 1.50 |
| 121 | A13 | 1fr bl gray & blk brn ('40) | .70 | .70 |
| 122 | A13 | 1.05fr lt bl & rose | 1.25 | 1.10 |
| 123 | A13 | 1.10fr lt red & grn | 4.00 | 2.75 |
| 124 | A13 | 1.25fr bl gray & blk brn ('33) | .65 | .65 |
| 125 | A13 | 1.25fr brt rose & red org ('39) | .95 | .95 |
| 126 | A13 | 1.40fr lt bl & lil rose ('40) | .70 | .70 |
| 127 | A13 | 1.50fr dl bl & bl | .40 | .40 |
| 128 | A13 | 1.60fr lil rose & yel brn ('40) | .70 | .70 |
| 129 | A13 | 1.75fr lil rose & yel brn ('33) | 5.75 | 3.25 |
| 130 | A13 | 1.75fr vio bl ('38) | 6.00 | 4.00 |
| 131 | A13 | 2fr bl grn & dk brn | .40 | .40 |
| 132 | A13 | 2.25fr vio bl ('39) | 1.25 | 1.25 |
| 133 | A13 | 2.50fr pale org & grn ('40) | 1.25 | 1.25 |
| 134 | A13 | 3fr org brn & sl | .65 | .65 |
| 135 | A13 | 5fr dl bl & org | 1.25 | 1.00 |
| 136 | A13 | 10fr vio & ol brn | 1.25 | 1.00 |
| 137 | A13 | 20fr green & mag | 1.50 | 1.40 |
| | | *Nos. 96-137 (42)* | 50.20 | 40.95 |

Nos. 96-103, 110, 119, 123, 134, 137 exist imperf. Values each $30-$60.

For surcharges see Nos. 161-166.

For 10c, type A11, without "RF," see No. 163A.

Common Design Types pictured following the introduction.

**Colonial Exposition Issue**

Common Design Types

**1931, Apr. 13 Engr. *Perf. 12½***

**Name of Country in Black**

| | | | | |
|---|---|---|---|---|
| 138 | CD70 | 40c deep green | 4.75 | 4.75 |
| 139 | CD71 | 50c violet | 4.75 | 4.75 |
| 140 | CD72 | 90c red orange | 4.75 | 4.75 |
| 141 | CD73 | 1.50fr dull blue | 4.75 | 4.75 |
| | | *Nos. 138-141 (4)* | 19.00 | 19.00 |

Cardinal Richelieu Establishing French Antilles Co., 1635 — A14

Victor Hugues and his Corsairs — A15

**1935 *Perf. 13***

| | | | | |
|---|---|---|---|---|
| 142 | A14 | 40c gray brown | 10.00 | 10.00 |
| 143 | A14 | 50c dull red | 10.00 | 10.00 |
| 144 | A14 | 1.50fr dull blue | 10.00 | 10.00 |
| 145 | A15 | 1.75fr lilac rose | 10.00 | 10.00 |
| 146 | A15 | 5fr dark brown | 10.00 | 10.00 |
| 147 | A15 | 10fr blue green | 10.00 | 10.00 |
| | | *Nos. 142-147 (6)* | 60.00 | 60.00 |

Tercentenary of the establishment of the French colonies in the West Indies.

**Paris International Exposition Issue**

Common Design Types

**1937 *Perf. 13***

| | | | | |
|---|---|---|---|---|
| 148 | CD74 | 20c deep violet | 1.90 | 1.90 |
| 149 | CD75 | 30c dark green | 1.75 | 1.75 |
| 150 | CD76 | 40c car rose | 1.50 | 1.50 |
| 151 | CD77 | 50c dk brn & blk | 1.50 | 1.50 |
| 152 | CD78 | 90c red | 1.50 | 1.50 |
| 153 | CD79 | 1.50fr ultra | 1.90 | 1.90 |
| | | *Nos. 148-153 (6)* | 10.05 | 10.05 |

**Colonial Arts Exhibition Issue**

Souvenir Sheet

Common Design Type

**1937 *Imperf.***

| | | | | |
|---|---|---|---|---|
| 154 | CD75 | 3fr dark blue | 9.50 | *11.00* |

**New York World's Fair Issue**

Common Design Type

**1939 Engr. *Perf. 12½x12***

| | | | | |
|---|---|---|---|---|
| 155 | CD82 | 1.25fr car lake | 1.25 | 1.25 |
| 156 | CD82 | 2.25fr ultra | 1.25 | 1.25 |

For surcharges see Nos. 159-160.

La Soufrière View and Marshal Pétain A16

**1941 Engr. *Perf. 12½x12***

| | | | |
|---|---|---|---|
| 157 | A16 | 1fr lilac | .80 |
| 158 | A16 | 2.50fr blue | .80 |

Nos. 157-158 were issued by the Vichy government in France, but were not placed on sale in Guadeloupe.

For surcharges, see Nos. B11A-B11B.

**Nos. 155, 156, 113, 117 and 118 Surcharged in Black**

**1943 *Perf. 14x13½, 12½x12***

| | | | | |
|---|---|---|---|---|
| 159 | CD82 | 40c on 1.25fr | .80 | .80 |
| 160 | CD82 | 40c on 2.25fr | 1.60 | 1.60 |
| 161 | A12 | 50c on 65c | 1.00 | 1.00 |
| 162 | A12 | 1fr on 90c (#117) | 1.40 | 1.40 |
| 163 | A12 | 1fr on 90c (#118) | 1.25 | 1.25 |
| | | *Nos. 159-163 (5)* | 6.05 | 6.05 |

**Type of 1928 Without "RF"**

**1943 *Perf. 14x13½***

| | | | |
|---|---|---|---|
| 163A | A11 | 10c bis brn & dp blue | .65 |

No. 163A was issued by the Vichy government in France, and was not placed on sale in Guadeloupe.

**Nos. 104, 106, 113 and 90 Surcharged in Black**

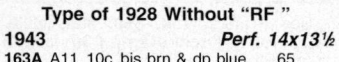

**1944 *Perf. 14x13½***

| | | | | |
|---|---|---|---|---|
| 164 | A12 | 40c on 35c | 1.10 | 1.10 |
| 165 | A12 | 50c on 25c | .30 | .30 |
| 166 | A12 | 1fr on 65c | 1.25 | 1.25 |
| *a.* | | Double surcharge | 200.00 | 150.00 |
| 167 | A10 | 4fr on 1.05fr on 2fr | 1.75 | 1.75 |
| | | *Nos. 164-167 (4)* | 4.40 | 4.40 |

The surcharge on No. 166 is spelled out.

**Catalogue values for unused stamps in this section, from this point to the end of the section, are for Never Hinged items.**

Dolphins A17

**1945 Unwmk. Photo. *Perf. 11½***

| | | | | |
|---|---|---|---|---|
| 168 | A17 | 10c chlky bl & red org | .30 | .25 |
| 169 | A17 | 30c lt yel grn & red | .30 | .25 |
| 170 | A17 | 40c lt bl & car | .85 | .65 |
| 171 | A17 | 50c red org & yel grn | .40 | .30 |
| 172 | A17 | 60c ol bis & lt bl | .40 | .30 |
| 173 | A17 | 70c lt gray & yel grn | .85 | .65 |
| 174 | A17 | 80c lt bl grn & yel | .85 | .65 |
| 175 | A17 | 1fr brn vio & grn | .40 | .30 |
| 176 | A17 | 1.20fr brt red vio & yel grn | .40 | .30 |
| 177 | A17 | 1.50fr dl brn & car | .90 | .55 |
| 178 | A17 | 2fr cer & bl | .90 | .55 |
| 179 | A17 | 2.40fr sal & yel grn | 1.50 | .95 |
| 180 | A17 | 3fr gray brn & bl vio | .85 | .55 |
| 181 | A17 | 4fr ultra & buff | .70 | .30 |
| 182 | A17 | 4.50fr brn org & grn | .90 | .55 |
| 183 | A17 | 5fr dk vio & grn | 1.10 | .65 |
| 184 | A17 | 10fr gray grn & red vio | 1.10 | .65 |
| 185 | A17 | 15fr sl gray & org | 1.50 | .85 |
| 186 | A17 | 20fr pale gray & dl org | 2.50 | 1.00 |
| | | *Nos. 168-186 (19)* | 16.70 | 10.25 |

**Eboue Issue**

Common Design Type

**1945 Engr. *Perf. 13***

| | | | | |
|---|---|---|---|---|
| 187 | CD91 | 2fr black | .65 | .50 |
| 188 | CD91 | 25fr Prussian green | 1.40 | 1.10 |

Basse-Terre Harbor and Woman A18

Cutting Sugar Cane — A19

Pineapple Bearer — A20

Guadeloupe Woman — A21

Gathering Coffee — A22

Guadeloupe Woman — A23

**1947 Unwmk. Engr. *Perf. 13***

| | | | | |
|---|---|---|---|---|
| 189 | A18 | 10c red brown | .30 | .25 |
| 190 | A18 | 30c sepia | .30 | .25 |
| 191 | A18 | 50c blue grn | .40 | .30 |
| 192 | A19 | 60c black brn | .75 | .50 |
| 193 | A19 | 1fr dp carmine | 1.00 | .65 |
| 194 | A19 | 1.50fr dk gray bl | 1.50 | .85 |
| 195 | A20 | 2fr blue grn | 1.50 | .85 |
| 196 | A20 | 2.50fr dp car | 1.40 | .95 |
| 197 | A20 | 3fr deep blue | 1.50 | .95 |
| 198 | A21 | 4fr violet | 1.40 | .95 |
| 199 | A21 | 5fr blue grn | 1.40 | .95 |
| 200 | A21 | 6fr red | 1.40 | .95 |
| 201 | A22 | 10fr deep blue | 1.50 | 1.00 |
| 202 | A22 | 15fr dk vio brn | 2.50 | 1.25 |
| 203 | A22 | 20fr rose red | 2.75 | 1.50 |
| 204 | A23 | 25fr blue green | 7.00 | 3.00 |
| 205 | A23 | 40fr red | 8.00 | 4.00 |
| | | *Nos. 189-205 (17)* | 34.60 | 19.15 |

## SEMI-POSTAL STAMPS

Nos. 59 and 62 Surcharged in Red

**1915-17 Unwmk. *Perf. 14 x 13½***

| | | | | |
|---|---|---|---|---|
| B1 | A8 | 10c + 5c rose | 5.25 | 3.50 |
| B2 | A8 | 15c + 5c violet | 5.25 | 3.50 |
| *a.* | | Double surcharge | 225.00 | 225.00 |
| *b.* | | Triple surcharge | 240.00 | 240.00 |
| *c.* | | Inverted surcharge | 240.00 | 240.00 |
| *d.* | | In pair with unovptd. stamp | 275.00 | |

**Curie Issue**

Common Design Type

**1938, Oct. 24 *Perf. 13***

| | | | | |
|---|---|---|---|---|
| B3 | CD80 | 1.75fr + 50c brt ultra | 11.00 | 10.50 |

**French Revolution Issue**

Common Design Type

Name and Value Typo. in Black

**1939, July 5 Photo. *Perf. 13***

| | | | | |
|---|---|---|---|---|
| B4 | CD83 | 45c + 25c green | 10.00 | 10.00 |
| B5 | CD83 | 70c + 30c brown | 10.00 | 10.00 |
| B6 | CD83 | 90c + 35c red org | 10.00 | 10.00 |
| B7 | CD83 | 1.25fr + 1fr rose pink | 10.00 | 10.00 |
| B8 | CD83 | 2.25fr + 2fr blue | 10.00 | 10.00 |
| | | *Nos. B4-B8 (5)* | 50.00 | 50.00 |

**Common Design Type and**

Colonial Artillery SP1

Colonial Infantry — SP2

**1941** **Photo.** ***Perf. 13½***

| | | | | |
|---|---|---|---|---|
| **B9** | SP1 | 1fr + 1fr red | 1.00 | |
| **B10** | CD86 | 1.50fr + 3fr maroon | 1.00 | |
| **B11** | SP2 | 2.50fr + 1fr blue | 1.50 | |
| | | *Nos. B9-B11 (3)* | 3.50 | |

Nos. B9-B11 were issued by the Vichy government in France, but were not placed on sale in Guadeloupe.

Nos. 157-158 Surcharged in Black or Red

**1944** **Engr.** ***Perf. 12½x12***

| | | | |
|---|---|---|---|
| **B11A** | 50c + 1.50fr on 2.50fr blue (R) | .80 | |
| **B11B** | + 2.50fr on 1fr lilac | .80 | |

Colonial Development Fund.

Nos. B11A-B11B were issued by the Vichy government in France, but were not placed on sale in Guadeloupe.

**Catalogue values for unused stamps in this section, from this point to the end of the section, are for Never Hinged items.**

### Red Cross Issue

Common Design Type

**1944** ***Perf. 14½x14***

| | | | | |
|---|---|---|---|---|
| **B12** | CD90 | 5fr + 20fr ultra | 1.40 | 1.00 |

The surtax was for the French Red Cross and national relief.

## AIR POST STAMPS

**Catalogue values for unused stamps in this section are for Never Hinged items.**

Common Design Type

**1945** **Unwmk.** **Photo.** ***Perf. 14½x14***

| | | | | |
|---|---|---|---|---|
| **C1** | CD87 | 50fr green | 1.50 | 1.00 |
| **C2** | CD87 | 100fr deep plum | 2.25 | 1.50 |

### Victory Issue

Common Design Type

**1946, May 8** **Engr.** ***Perf. 12½***

| | | | | |
|---|---|---|---|---|
| **C3** | CD92 | 8fr redsh brn | 1.25 | 1.00 |

### Chad to Rhine Issue

Common Design Types

**1946, June 6**

| | | | | |
|---|---|---|---|---|
| **C4** | CD93 | 5fr dk slate grn | 2.00 | 1.60 |
| **C5** | CD94 | 10fr deep blue | 2.00 | 1.60 |
| **C6** | CD95 | 15fr brt violet | 2.00 | 1.60 |
| **C7** | CD96 | 20fr brown car | 2.00 | 1.60 |
| **C8** | CD97 | 25fr black | 2.00 | 1.60 |
| **C9** | CD98 | 50fr red brown | 2.00 | 1.60 |
| | | *Nos. C4-C9 (6)* | 12.00 | 9.60 |

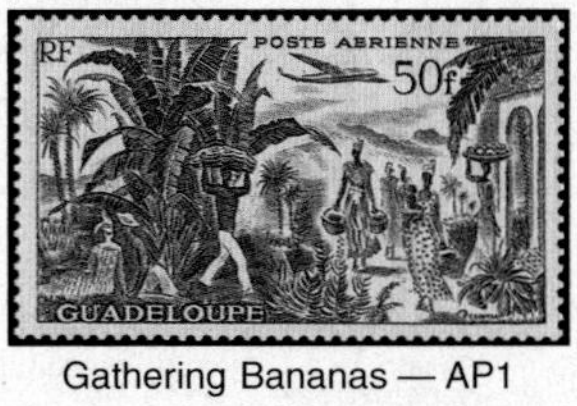

Gathering Bananas — AP1

Seaplane at Roadstead — AP2

Pointe-a-Pitre Harbor and Guadeloupe Woman — AP3

**1947** **Unwmk.** ***Perf. 13***

| | | | | |
|---|---|---|---|---|
| **C10** | AP1 | 50fr dk brown violet | 6.00 | 2.75 |
| **C11** | AP2 | 100fr deep blue | 8.75 | 5.25 |
| **C12** | AP3 | 200fr red | 11.50 | 5.50 |
| | | *Nos. C10-C12 (3)* | 26.25 | 13.50 |

## AIR POST SEMI-POSTAL STAMPS

Mother & Nurse with Children — SPAP1

**1942, June 22** **Engr.** ***Perf. 13***

| | | | | |
|---|---|---|---|---|
| **CB1** | SPAP1 | 1.50fr + 3.50fr green | 1.00 | |
| **CB2** | SPAP1 | 2fr + 6fr brown & red | 1.00 | |

Native children's welfare fund.

Nos. CB1-CB2 were issued by the Vichy government in France, but were not placed on sale in Guadeloupe.

### Colonial Education Fund

Common Design Type

**1942, June 22**

| | | | | |
|---|---|---|---|---|
| **CB3** | CD86a | 1.20fr + 1.80fr blue & red | 1.10 | |

No. CB3 was issued by the Vichy government in France, but was not placed on sale in Guadeloupe.

## POSTAGE DUE STAMPS

D1

D2

D3

**1876** **Unwmk.** **Typeset** ***Imperf.***

| | | | | |
|---|---|---|---|---|
| **J1** | D1 | 25c black | 1,350. | 925. |
| **J2** | D2 | 40c black, *blue* | | *37,500.* |
| **J3** | D3 | 40c black | 1,500. | 1,200. |

Twenty varieties of each.

*Nos. J1 and J3 have been reprinted on thinner and whiter paper than the originals.*

D4

D5

**1879**

| | | | | |
|---|---|---|---|---|
| **J4** | D4 | 15c black, *blue* | 55.00 | 52.50 |
| *a.* | | Period after "c" omitted | 175.00 | 175.00 |
| **J5** | D4 | 30c black | 110.00 | 87.50 |
| *a.* | | Period after "c" omitted | 240.00 | 225.00 |

Twenty varieties of each.

**1884**

| | | | | |
|---|---|---|---|---|
| **J6** | D5 | 5c black | 35.00 | 35.00 |
| *a.* | | Double impression | 100.00 | 100.00 |
| **J7** | D5 | 10c black, *blue* | 75.00 | 65.00 |
| *a.* | | Double impression | 150.00 | 150.00 |
| **J8** | D5 | 15c black, *violet* | 110.00 | 87.50 |
| *a.* | | Double impression | 225.00 | 225.00 |
| **J9** | D5 | 20c black, *rose* | 160.00 | 100.00 |
| *a.* | | Italic "2" in "20" | 1,000. | 950.00 |
| **J10** | D5 | 30c black, *yellow* | 160.00 | 160.00 |
| *a.* | | Double impression | 450.00 | 450.00 |
| **J11** | D5 | 35c black, *gray* | 60.00 | 52.50 |
| *a.* | | Double impression | 225.00 | 225.00 |
| **J12** | D5 | 50c black, *green* | 32.50 | 27.50 |
| *a.* | | Double impression | 200.00 | 200.00 |
| | | *Nos. J6-J12 (7)* | 632.50 | 527.50 |

There are ten varieties of the 35c, and fifteen of each of the other values, also numerous wrong font and missing letters.

Postage Due Stamps of French Colonies Surcharged in Black

Two surcharge types: I, wide font, "3" with rounded top; II, narrow font, "3" with flat top.

**1903**

**Type I**

| | | | | |
|---|---|---|---|---|
| **J13** | D1 | 30c on 60c brn, *cr* | 325.00 | 325.00 |
| *a.* | | Inverted surcharge | 1,100. | 1,100. |
| *b.* | | Bee corner ornament turned | 1,150. | 1,150. |
| *c.* | | As "b," inverted surcharge | 1,700. | |
| *d.* | | "G" omitted | 800.00 | 800.00 |
| *e.* | | As "d," inverted surcharge | 1,250. | |
| *f.* | | Corrected surcharge, "30" over "33" | 10,500. | 10,500. |
| **J14** | D1 | 30c on 1fr rose, *cr* | 400.00 | 400.00 |
| *a.* | | Inverted surcharge | 1,200. | 1,200. |
| *b.* | | "30" sideways | 10,500. | 10,500. |
| *c.* | | As "b," inverted surcharge | 10,500. | 10,500. |

**Type II**

| | | | | |
|---|---|---|---|---|
| **J13A** | D1 | 30c on 60c brn, *cr* | 1,000. | 1,000. |
| *a.* | | Inverted surcharge | 1,100. | 1,100. |
| *b.* | | Bee corner ornament turned | 1,600. | 1,600. |
| *c.* | | As "b," inverted surcharge | 2,200. | |
| *d.* | | "G" omitted | 1,000 | 1,000. |
| *e.* | | As "d," inverted surcharge | 1,500. | |
| *f.* | | Corrected surcharge, "30" over "33" | 10,500. | 10,500. |
| **J14A** | D1 | 30c on 1fr rose, *cr* | 400.00 | 400.00 |
| *a.* | | Inverted surcharge | 1,200. | 1,200. |
| *b.* | | "30" sideways | 10,500. | 10,500. |
| *c.* | | As "b," inverted surcharge | 10,500. | 10,500. |

Gustavia Bay — D6

**1905-06** **Typo.** ***Perf. 14x13½***

| | | | | |
|---|---|---|---|---|
| **J15** | D6 | 5c blue | .55 | .55 |
| **J16** | D6 | 10c brown | .55 | .55 |
| **J17** | D6 | 15c green | 1.00 | 1.00 |
| **J18** | D6 | 20c black, *yel* ('06) | 1.00 | 1.00 |
| **J19** | D6 | 30c rose | 1.25 | 1.25 |
| **J20** | D6 | 50c black | 3.25 | 3.25 |
| **J21** | D6 | 60c brown orange | 1.75 | 1.75 |
| **J22** | D6 | 1fr violet | 3.25 | 3.25 |
| | | *Nos. J15-J22 (8)* | 12.60 | 12.60 |

Type of 1905-06 Issue Surcharged

**1926-27**

| | | | | |
|---|---|---|---|---|
| **J23** | D6 | 2fr on 1fr gray | 2.00 | 2.00 |
| **J24** | D6 | 3fr on 1fr ultra ('27) | 2.75 | 2.75 |

Avenue of Royal Palms — D7

**1928, June 18**

| | | | | |
|---|---|---|---|---|
| **J25** | D7 | 2c olive brn & lil | .25 | .25 |
| **J26** | D7 | 4c bl & org brn | .25 | .25 |
| **J27** | D7 | 5c gray grn & dk brn | .25 | .25 |
| **J28** | D7 | 10c dl vio & yel | .30 | .30 |
| **J29** | D7 | 15c rose & olive grn | .30 | .30 |
| **J30** | D7 | 20c brn org & ol grn | .50 | .50 |
| **J31** | D7 | 25c brn red & bl grn | .50 | .50 |
| **J32** | D7 | 30c slate & olivine | .80 | .80 |
| **J33** | D7 | 50c ol brn & lt red | .80 | .80 |
| **J34** | D7 | 60c dp bl & blk | .80 | .80 |
| **J35** | D7 | 1fr green & orange | 3.00 | 2.60 |
| **J36** | D7 | 2fr bis brn & lt red | 2.25 | 1.90 |
| **J37** | D7 | 3fr vio & bl blk | 1.25 | 1.10 |
| | | *Nos. J25-J37 (13)* | 11.25 | 10.35 |

### Type of 1928 Without "RF"

**1944**

| | | | | |
|---|---|---|---|---|
| **J37A** | D7 | 60c dp bl & blk | .30 | |
| **J37B** | D7 | 1fr green & orange | .65 | |
| **J37C** | D7 | 2fr bis brn & lt red | .65 | |
| | | *Nos. J37A-J37C (3)* | 1.60 | |

Nos. J37A-J37C were issued by the Vichy government in France, but were not placed on sale in Guadeloupe.

**Catalogue values for unused stamps in this section, from this point to the end of the section, are for Never Hinged items.**

D8

***Perf. 14x13***

**1947, June 2** **Unwmk.** **Engr.**

| | | | | |
|---|---|---|---|---|
| **J38** | D8 | 10c black | .30 | .25 |
| **J39** | D8 | 30c dull blue green | .40 | .30 |
| **J40** | D8 | 50c bright ultra | .40 | .30 |
| **J41** | D8 | 1fr dark green | .65 | .50 |
| **J42** | D8 | 2fr dark blue | .85 | .70 |
| **J43** | D8 | 3fr black brown | 1.25 | 1.00 |
| **J44** | D8 | 4fr lilac rose | 1.40 | 1.25 |
| **J45** | D8 | 5fr purple | 1.90 | 1.60 |
| **J46** | D8 | 10fr red | 2.60 | 2.10 |
| **J47** | D8 | 20fr dark violet | 3.00 | 2.25 |
| | | *Nos. J38-J47 (10)* | 12.75 | 10.25 |

# GUATEMALA

ˌgwä-lə-ˈmä-lə

LOCATION — Central America, bordering on Atlantic and Pacific Oceans
GOVT. — Republic
AREA — 42,042 sq. mi.
POP. — 12,335,580 (1999 est.)
CAPITAL — Guatemala City

100 Centavos = 8 Reales = 1 Peso
100 Centavos de Quetzal = 1 Quetzal (1927)

**Catalogue values for unused stamps in this country are for Never Hinged items, beginning with Scott 316 in the regular postage section, Scott B5 in the semi-postal section, Scott C137 in the air post section, Scott CB5 in the air post semi-postal section and Scott E2 in the special delivery section.**

Coat of Arms
A1 A2

Two types of 10c:
Type I — Both zeros in "10" are wide.
Type II — Left zero narrow.

***Perf. 14x13½***

**1871, Mar. 1 Typo. Unwmk.**

| | | | | |
|---|---|---|---|---|
| **1** | A1 | 1c ocher | .80 | *10.50* |
| *a.* | | Imperf., pair | 5.00 | |
| *b.* | | Printed on both sides, imperf. | 75.00 | |
| **2** | A1 | 5c lt bister brn | 4.00 | *8.00* |
| *a.* | | Imperf. pair | 35.00 | |
| *b.* | | Tête bêche pair | 150.00 | |
| *c.* | | Tête bêche pair, imperf. | 2,600. | |
| **3** | A1 | 10c blue (I) | 5.00 | *8.00* |
| *a.* | | Imperf., pair (I) | 45.00 | |
| *b.* | | Type II | 8.00 | *10.50* |
| *c.* | | Imperf. pair (II) | 60.00 | |
| **4** | A1 | 20c rose | 4.00 | *8.00* |
| *a.* | | Imperf., pair | 45.00 | |
| *b.* | | 20c blue (error) | 125.00 | 125.00 |
| *c.* | | As "b," imperf. | *800.00* | |
| | | *Nos. 1-4 (4)* | 13.80 | *34.50* |

Forgeries exist. Forged cancellations abound. See No. C458.

**1873 Litho. *Perf. 12***

| | | | | |
|---|---|---|---|---|
| **5** | A2 | 4r dull red vio | 325.00 | 85.00 |
| **6** | A2 | 1p dull yellow | 175.00 | 115.00 |

Forgeries exist.

Liberty
A3 A4

A5 A6

**1875, Apr. 15 Engr.**

| | | | | |
|---|---|---|---|---|
| **7** | A3 | ¼r black | 1.00 | *3.50* |
| **8** | A4 | ½r blue green | 1.00 | *3.00* |
| **9** | A5 | 1r blue | 1.00 | *3.00* |
| *a.* | | Half used as ½r on cover | | *1,700.* |
| **10** | A6 | 2r dull red | 1.00 | *3.00* |
| | | *Nos. 7-10 (4)* | 4.00 | *12.50* |

Nos. 7-10 normally lack gum. Unused values are for examples without gum.

Forgeries and forged cancellations exist.

Indian Woman — A7 Quetzal — A8

**Typographed on Tinted Paper**

**1878, Jan. 10 *Perf. 13***

| | | | | |
|---|---|---|---|---|
| **11** | A7 | ½r yellow grn | .80 | *3.25* |
| **12** | A7 | 2r carmine rose | 1.25 | *4.00* |
| **13** | A7 | 4r violet | 1.25 | *4.75* |
| **14** | A7 | 1p yellow | 2.00 | *9.00* |
| *c.* | | Half used as 4r on cover | | *2,200.* |
| | | *Nos. 11-14 (4)* | 5.30 | *21.00* |

Some sheets of Nos. 11-14 have papermaker's watermark, "LACROIX FRERES," in double-lined capitals appearing on six stamps.

Part perforate pairs of Nos. 11, 12 and 14 exist. Value for each, about $100.

Forgeries of Nos. 11-14 are plentiful. Forged cancellations exist.

For surcharges see Nos. 18, 20.

**Imperf., Pairs**

| | | | |
|---|---|---|---|
| *11a* | A7 | ½r yellow green | 50.00 |
| *12a* | A7 | 2r carmine rose | 50.00 |
| *13a* | A7 | 4r violet | 50.00 |
| *14a* | A7 | 1p yellow | 50.00 |

**1879 Engr. *Perf. 12***

| | | | | |
|---|---|---|---|---|
| **15** | A8 | ¼r brown & green | 7.25 | *9.50* |
| **16** | A8 | 1r black & green | 10.50 | *13.50* |

For similar types see A11, A72, A103, A121, A146. For surcharges see Nos. 17, 19.

Nos. 11, 12, 15, 16 Surcharged in Black

**1881 *Perf. 12 and 13***

| | | | | |
|---|---|---|---|---|
| **17** | A8 | 1c on ¼r brn & grn | 12.00 | *16.00* |
| *a.* | | "ecntavo," | 40.00 | *47.50* |
| *b.* | | Pair, one without surcharge | 200.00 | |
| **18** | A7 | 5c on ½r yel grn | 5.50 | *8.00* |
| *a.* | | "ecntavos," | 35.00 | *40.00* |
| *b.* | | "5" omitted | 100.00 | |
| *c.* | | Double surcharge | 95.00 | *120.00* |
| **19** | A8 | 10c on 1r blk & grn | 17.50 | *24.00* |
| *a.* | | "s" of "centavos" missing | 75.00 | 75.00 |
| *b.* | | "ecntavos" | 57.50 | *87.50* |
| **20** | A7 | 20c on 2r car rose | 32.50 | *87.50* |
| *a.* | | Horiz. pair, imperf. between | 425.00 | |
| | | *Nos. 17-20 (4)* | 67.50 | *135.50* |

The 5c had three settings.

Surcharge varieties found on Nos. 17-20 include: Period omitted; comma instead of period; "ecntavo." or "ecntavos."; "s" omitted; spaced "centavos."; wider "0" in "20."

Counterfeits of Nos. 17-20 are plentiful.

Quetzal — A11

**1881, Nov. 7 Engr. *Perf. 12***

| | | | | |
|---|---|---|---|---|
| **21** | A11 | 1c black & grn | 3.00 | 2.00 |
| **22** | A11 | 2c brown & grn | 3.00 | 2.00 |
| *a.* | | Center inverted | 400.00 | 250.00 |
| **23** | A11 | 5c red & grn | 6.00 | 2.60 |
| *a.* | | Center inverted | *3,250.* | 1,300. |
| **24** | A11 | 10c gray vio & grn | 2.75 | 2.00 |
| **25** | A11 | 20c yellow & grn | 2.75 | 2.40 |
| *a.* | | Center inverted | 500.00 | |
| | | *Nos. 21-25 (5)* | 17.50 | 11.00 |

**Surcharged in Black**

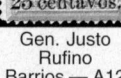

Gen. Justo Rufino Barrios — A12 A12a

A12b

**1886, Mar. 6**

| | | | | |
|---|---|---|---|---|
| **26** | A12 | 25c on 1p ver | .70 | .70 |
| *a.* | | "centovos" | 1.50 | |
| *b.* | | "centanos" | 1.50 | |
| *c.* | | "255" instead of "25" | 150.00 | |
| *d.* | | Inverted "S" in "Nacionales" | 20.00 | |
| *f.* | | "cen avos" | 20.00 | |
| *h.* | | "Corre cionales" | 20.00 | |
| *i.* | | Inverted surcharge | 75.00 | |
| **27** | A12 | 50c on 1p ver | .70 | .70 |
| *a.* | | "centovos" | 1.50 | |
| *b.* | | "centanos" | 1.50 | |
| *c.* | | "Carreos" | 1.50 | |
| *d.* | | Inverted surcharge | 50.00 | |
| *e.* | | Double surcharge | 75.00 | |
| *f.* | | Inverted "S" in "Nacionales" | 10.00 | |
| *g.* | | "centavo" | 20.00 | |
| *h.* | | "cen avos" | 20.00 | |
| **28** | A12 | 75c on 1p ver | .70 | .70 |
| *a.* | | "centovos" | 1.50 | |
| *b.* | | "centanos" | 1.50 | |
| *c.* | | "Carreos" | 1.50 | |
| *d.* | | "50" for "75" at upper right | 2.00 | |
| *e.* | | Inverted "S" in "Nacionales" | 10.00 | |
| *f.* | | Double surcharge | 75.00 | |
| *g.* | | "ales" inverted | 100.00 | |
| **29** | A12a | 100c on 1p ver | 1.40 | 1.40 |
| *a.* | | "110" at upper left and "á" at lower left, instead of "100" | 5.00 | |
| *b.* | | Inverted surcharge | 75.00 | |
| *c.* | | "Guatemala" bolder; 23mm instead of 18½mm wide | 2.25 | |
| *d.* | | Double surcharge, one diagonal | 100.00 | |
| **30** | A12b | 150c on 1p ver | 1.40 | 1.40 |
| *a.* | | Inverted "G" | 5.00 | |
| *b.* | | "Guetemala" and italic "5" in upper 4 numerals | 5.00 | |
| *d.* | | Inverted surcharge | 90.00 | |
| *e.* | | Pair, one without surcharge | 100.00 | |
| *f.* | | Double surcharge | 100.00 | |
| | | *Nos. 26-30 (5)* | 4.90 | 4.90 |

There are many other minor varieties, such as wrong font letters, etc.

Used values of Nos. 26-30 are for canceled to order stamps. Postally used sell for much more.

National Emblem — A13

**1886, July 1 Litho. *Perf. 12***

| | | | | |
|---|---|---|---|---|
| **31** | A13 | 1c dull blue | 5.00 | 2.00 |
| **32** | A13 | 2c brown | 5.00 | 3.00 |
| **33** | A13 | 5c purple | 37.50 | .75 |
| **34** | A13 | 10c red | 10.00 | .75 |
| **35** | A13 | 20c emerald | 15.00 | 1.25 |
| **36** | A13 | 25c orange | 15.00 | 1.50 |
| **37** | A13 | 50c olive green | 10.00 | 2.00 |
| **38** | A13 | 75c carmine rose | 10.00 | 3.00 |
| **39** | A13 | 100c red brown | 10.00 | 3.00 |
| **40** | A13 | 150c dark blue | 15.00 | 3.75 |
| **41** | A13 | 200c orange yellow | 18.50 | 4.75 |
| | | *Nos. 31-41 (11)* | 151.00 | 25.75 |

Used values of Nos. 38-41 are for canceled to order stamps. Postally used sell for more.

See Nos. 43-50, 99-107. For surcharges see Nos. 42, 51-59, 75-85, 97-98, 108-110, 124-130.

No. 32 Surcharged in Black

Two settings:
I — "1886" (no period).
II — "1886." (period).

**1886, Nov. 12**

| | | | | |
|---|---|---|---|---|
| **42** | A13 | 1c on 2c brown, I | 2.00 | *2.50* |
| *a.* | | Date inverted, I | 75.00 | |
| *b.* | | Date double, I | 75.00 | |
| *c.* | | Date omitted, I | 60.00 | |
| *d.* | | Date double, one invtd., I | 100.00 | |
| *e.* | | Date triple, one inverted, I | 100.00 | |
| *f.* | | Setting II | 1.50 | 1.00 |
| *g.* | | Inverted surcharge, II | 4.00 | |
| *h.* | | Double surcharge, II | 100.00 | |

Forgeries exist.

Type I Type II

Two types of 5c:
I — Thin "5"
II — Larger, thick "5"

**1886-95 Engr. *Perf. 12***

| | | | | |
|---|---|---|---|---|
| **43** | A13 | 1c blue | .80 | .25 |
| **44** | A13 | 2c yellow brn | 2.40 | .25 |
| *a.* | | Half used as 1c on cover | | 100.00 |
| **45** | A13 | 5c purple (I) | 52.50 | 1.00 |
| **46** | A13 | 5c vio (II) ('88) | 1.60 | .25 |
| **47** | A13 | 6c lilac ('95) | .65 | .25 |
| **48** | A13 | 10c red ('90) | 1.60 | .25 |
| **49** | A13 | 20c green ('93) | 3.25 | .75 |
| **50** | A13 | 25c red org ('93) | 8.00 | 1.25 |
| | | *Nos. 43-44,46-50 (7)* | 18.30 | 3.25 |

The impression of the engraved stamps is sharper than that of the lithographed. On the engraved stamps the top four lines at left are heavier than those below them. (This is also true of the 1c litho., which is distinguished from the engraved only by a slight color difference and the impression.)

The "2" and "5" (I) are more open than the litho. numerals. The "10" of the engraved is wider. The 20c and 25c of the engraved have a vertical line at right end of the "centavos" ribbon.

No. 38 Surcharged in Blue Black

"1894" 14½mm wide

**1894, Apr. 25**

| | | | | |
|---|---|---|---|---|
| **51** | A13 | 10c on 75c car rose | 4.50 | 4.50 |
| *a.* | | Double surcharge | 75.00 | |
| *b.* | | Inverted surcharge | 100.00 | |

Same on Nos. 38-41 in Blue or Red
"1894" 14mm wide

**1894, June 13**

| | | | | |
|---|---|---|---|---|
| **52** | A13 | 2c on 100c | 7.50 | 4.25 |
| **53** | A13 | 6c on 150c (R) | 7.50 | 3.50 |
| **54** | A13 | 10c on 75c | 550.00 | 500.00 |
| **55** | A13 | 10c on 200c | 7.50 | 4.25 |
| *c.* | | Inverted surcharge | 75.00 | |

Nos. 54-55 exist with thick or thin "1" in new value.

Same on Nos. 39-41 in Black or Red
"1894" 12mm wide

**1894, July 14**

| | | | | |
|---|---|---|---|---|
| *52a* | A13 | 2c on 100c red brn (Bk) | 4.00 | 3.50 |
| *b.* | | Vert. pair, one without surcharge | 150.00 | |
| *53a* | A13 | 6c on 150c dk bl (R) | 4.50 | 3.50 |
| *55a* | A13 | 10c on 200c org yel (Bk) | 5.00 | 3.50 |
| *d.* | | Inverted surcharge | 100.00 | |
| *e.* | | Vert. pair, one without surcharge | 150.00 | |

**Nos. 44 and 46 Surcharged in Black, Blue Black, or Red**

b c

d e

**1894-96**

| | | | | |
|---|---|---|---|---|
| **56** | A13 (b) | 1c on 2c (Bk) | .75 | .30 |
| *a.* | | "Centav" | 5.00 | 5.00 |
| *b.* | | Double surcharge | 75.00 | |
| *c.* | | As "a," dbl. surcharge | 150.00 | |
| *d.* | | Blue black surcharge | 20.00 | 20.00 |
| *e.* | | Dbl. surch., one inverted | 150.00 | |
| **57** | A13 (c) | 1c on 5c (R) ('95) | .50 | .25 |
| *a.* | | Inverted surcharge | 3.00 | 3.00 |
| *b.* | | "1894" instead of "1895" | 3.50 | 3.00 |
| *c.* | | Double surcharge | | 50.00 |

**58** A13 (d) 1c on 5c (R) ('95) .75 .25
*a.* Inverted surcharge 50.00 50.00
*b.* Double surcharge 50.00
**59** A13 (e) 1c on 5c (R) ('96) 1.25 .40
*a.* Inverted surcharge 50.00 50.00
*b.* Double surcharge 50.00
*Nos. 56-59 (4)* 3.25 1.20

Nos. 56-58 may be found with thick or thin "1" in the new value.

National Arms and President J. M. Reyna Barrios A21

**1897, Jan. 1 Engr. Unwmk.**
**60** A21 1c blk, *lil gray* .55 .55
**61** A21 2c blk, *grnsh gray* .55 .55
**62** A21 6c blk, *brn org* .55 .55
**63** A21 10c blk, *dl bl* .55 .55
**64** A21 12c blk, *rose red* .55 .55
**65** A21 18c blk, *grysh white* 9.50 9.50
**66** A21 20c blk, *scarlet* 1.00 1.00
**67** A21 25c blk, *bis brn* 1.60 1.00
**68** A21 50c blk, *redsh brn* 1.00 1.00
**69** A21 75c blk, *gray* 52.50 52.50
**70** A21 100c blk, *bl grn* 1.00 1.00
**71** A21 150c blk, *dl rose* 105.00 *135.00*
**72** A21 200c blk, *magenta* 1.00 1.00
**73** A21 500c blk, *yel grn* 1.00 1.00
*Nos. 60-73 (14)* 176.35 *205.75*

Issued for Central American Exposition.

Stamps often sold as Nos. 65, 69 and 71 are examples with telegraph overprint removed.

Used values for Nos. 60-73 are for canceled-to-order stamps. Postally used examples are worth more.

The paper of Nos. 64 and 66 was originally colored on one side only, but has "bled through" on some examples.

No. 64 Surcharged in Violet

**1897, Nov.**
**74** A21 1c on 12c *rose red* 1.00 1.00
*a.* Inverted surcharge 30.00 30.00
*b.* Pair, one without surcharge 75.00
*c.* Dbl. surch., one invtd. 100.00

### Stamps of 1886-93 Surcharged in Red

f

g

**1898**
**75** (f) 1c on 5c violet 1.00 1.00
*a.* Inverted surcharge 75.00
**76** (f) 1c on 50c ol grn 1.50 1.25
*a.* Inverted surcharge 100.00 100.00
**77** (f) 6c on 5c violet 4.50 1.50
**78** (f) 6c on 150c dk bl 4.50 3.25
**79** (g) 10c on 20c emerald 5.00 4.00
*a.* Double surch., one inverted 125.00 125.00
*Nos. 75-79 (5)* 16.50 11.00

### Black Surcharge

**80** (f) 1c on 25c red org 2.00 2.00
**81** (f) 1c on 75c car rose 1.50 1.50
*a.* Double surcharge 100.00
**82** (f) 6c on 10c red 10.00 9.00
**83** (f) 6c on 20c emer 5.00 4.00
**84** (f) 6c on 100c red brn 5.00 4.00
**85** (f) 6c on 200c org yel 5.00 4.00
*a.* Inverted surcharge 50.00 50.00
*Nos. 80-85 (6)* 28.50 24.50

Information indicates that No. 77 inverted and double surcharges are counterfeits.

National Emblem — A24

### Revenue Stamp Overprinted or Surcharged in Carmine

***Perf. 12, 12x14, 14x12***

**1898, Oct. 8 Litho.**
**86** A24 1c dark blue 1.40 1.40
*a.* Inverted overprint 12.50 12.50
**87** A24 2c on 1c dk bl 2.25 2.25
*a.* Inverted surcharge 12.50 12.50

Counterfeits exist.

See type A26.

National Emblem — A25

### Revenue Stamps Surcharged in Carmine

**1898 Engr. *Perf. 12½ to 16***
**88** A25 1c on 10c bl gray .75 .75
*a.* "ENTAVO" 5.00 5.00
**89** A25 2c on 5c pur 1.25 1.00
**90** A25 2c on 10c bl gray 6.50 *7.00*
*a.* Double surch., car & blk 100.00 75.00
**91** A25 2c on 50c dp bl 9.25 *9.25*
*a.* Double surch., car & blk 100.00 100.00
*Nos. 88-91 (4)* 17.75 *18.00*

### Black Surcharge

**92** A25 2c on 1c lil rose 3.50 2.00
**93** A25 2c on 25c red 7.50 8.00
**94** A25 6c on 1p purple 4.00 4.50
**95** A25 6c on 5p gray vio 7.50 7.50
**96** A25 6c on 10p emer 7.50 7.50
*Nos. 92-96 (5)* 30.00 29.50

Nos. 88 and 90 are found in shades ranging from Prussian blue to slate blue.

Varieties other than those listed are bogus.

Counterfeits exist of No. 92.

Soaking in water causes marked fading.

See type A27.

No. 46 Surcharged in Red

**1899, Sept. *Perf. 12***
**97** A13 1c on 5c violet .40 .25
*a.* Inverted surcharge 7.50 7.50
*b.* Double surcharge 15.00 15.00
*c.* Double surcharge, one inverted 15.00 15.00

No. 48 Surcharged in Black

**1900, Jan.**
**98** A13 1c on 10c red .65 .50
*a.* Inverted surcharge 10.00 10.00
*b.* Double surcharge 75.00 75.00

### Quetzal Type of 1886

**1900-02 Engr.**
**99** A13 1c dark green .60 .25
**100** A13 2c carmine .60 .25
**101** A13 5c blue (II) 2.25 1.25
**102** A13 6c lt green .75 .25
**103** A13 10c bister brown 7.50 1.00
**104** A13 20c purple 7.50 7.50
**105** A13 20c bister brn ('02) 7.50 7.50
**106** A13 25c yellow 7.50 7.50
**107** A13 25c blue green ('02) 7.50 7.50
*Nos. 99-107 (9)* 41.70 33.00

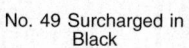

No. 49 Surcharged in Black

**1901, May**
**108** A13 1c on 20c green .50 .50
*a.* Inverted surcharge 22.50 22.50
*b.* Double surch., one diagonal 50.00
**109** A13 2c on 20c green 1.50 1.50

No. 50 Surcharged in Black

**1901, Apr.**
**110** A13 1c on 25c red org .60 .60
*a.* Inverted surcharge 25.00 25.00
*b.* Double surcharge 50.00 50.00

A26

A27

### Revenue Stamps Surcharged in Carmine or Black

**1902, July *Perf. 12, 14x12, 12x14***
**111** A26 1c on 1c dk blue 1.10 1.10
*a.* Double surcharge 20.00
*b.* Inverted surcharge 20.00
**112** A26 2c on 1c dk blue 1.10 1.10
*a.* Double surcharge 90.00
*b.* Inverted surcharge 25.00

***Perf. 14, 15***

**113** A27 6c on 25c red (Bk) 2.50 2.50
*a.* Double surch., one invtd. 75.00 75.00
*Nos. 111-113 (3)* 4.70 4.70

National Emblem — A28

Statue of Justo Rufino Barrios — A29

"La Reforma" Palace — A30

Temple of Minerva — A31

Lake Amatitlán — A32

Cathedral in Guatemala — A33

Columbus Theater — A34

Artillery Barracks — A35

Monument to Columbus — A36

School for Indians — A37

**1902 Engr. *Perf. 12 to 16***
**114** A28 1c grn & claret .25 .25
*a.* Horiz. pair, imperf. vert. 100.00
**115** A29 2c lake & blk .25 .25
*a.* Horiz. or vert. pair, imperf. btwn. 150.00
**116** A30 5c blue & blk .30 .25
*a.* 5c ultra & blk .75 .40
*b.* Imperf., pair 100.00 100.00
*c.* Horiz. pair, imperf. vert. 100.00
**117** A31 6c bister & grn .30 .25
*a.* Horiz. pair, imperf. btwn. 150.00
**118** A32 10c orange & bl .40 .40
*a.* Horiz. pair, imperf. vert. 100.00
**119** A33 20c rose lil & blk .60 .40
*a.* Horiz. pair, imperf. vert. 100.00
**120** A34 50c red brn & bl .45 .40
*a.* Vert. pair, imperf. btwn. 350.00
**121** A35 75c gray lil & blk .55 .40
*a.* Horiz. pair, imperf. btwn. 150.00
*b.* Horiz. pair, imperf. vert. 100.00
**122** A36 1p brown & blk .85 .40
*a.* Horiz. pair, imperf. btwn. 150.00
**123** A37 2p ver & blk 1.00 .85
*Nos. 114-123 (10)* 4.95 3.85

See Nos. 210, 212-214, 219, 223, 239-241, 243. For overprints and surcharges see Nos. 133, 135-139, 144-157, 168, 170-171, 178, 192-194, 298-299, 301, C19, C27, C123.

Issues of 1886-1900 Surcharged in Black or Carmine

**1903, Apr. 18 *Perf. 12***
**124** A13 25c on 1c dk grn 1.25 .55
*a.* Inverted surcharge 50.00 50.00
**125** A13 25c on 2c carmine 1.50 .55
**126** A13 25c on 6c lt grn 2.50 1.75
*a.* Inverted surcharge 40.00 40.00
**127** A13 25c on 10c bis brn 7.50 7.00
**128** A13 25c on 75c rose 10.00 10.00
**129** A13 25c on 150c dk bl (C) 9.00 9.00
**130** A13 25c on 200c yellow 10.00 10.00
*Nos. 124-130 (7)* 41.75 38.85

Forgeries and bogus varieties exist.

Declaration of Independence A38

**1907, Jan. 1 *Perf. 13½ to 15***
**132** A38 12½c ultra & blk .45 .45
*a.* Horiz. pair, imperf. btwn. 150.00

For surcharge see No. 134.

Nos. 118, 119 and 132 Surcharged in Black or Red

**1908, May**
**133** A32 1c on 10c org & bl .30 .30
*a.* Double surcharge 25.00
*b.* Inverted surcharge 15.00 15.00
*c.* Pair, one without surcharge 50.00

**134** A38 2c on 12½c ultra & blk (R) .25 .25
- *a.* Horiz. or vert. pair, imperf. btwn. 100.00
- *b.* Inverted surcharge 15.00 10.00
- *c.* Double surcharge 30.00

**135** A33 6c on 20c rose lil & blk .45 .25
- *a.* Inverted surcharge 20.00 20.00

*Nos. 133-135 (3)* 1.00 .80

## Similar Surcharge, Dated 1909, in Red or Black on Nos. 121 and 120

**1909, Apr.**

**136** A35 2c on 75c (R) .55 .55
**137** A34 6c on 50c (R) 62.50 62.50
- *a.* Double surcharge 125.00 125.00

**138** A34 6c on 50c (Bk) .30 .30
*Nos. 136-138 (3)* 63.35 63.35

Counterfeits exist of Nos. 137, 137a.

No. 123 Surcharged in Black

**139** A37 12½c on 2p ver & blk .30 .30
- *a.* Inverted surcharge 25.00 25.00
- *b.* Period omitted after "1909" 12.50 12.50

Counterfeits exist.

Gen. Miguel García Granados, Birth Cent. (in 1909) — A39

**1910, Feb. 11** *Perf. 14*

**140** A39 6c bis & indigo .55 .40
- *a.* Imperf., pair 55.00

Some sheets used for this issue contained a two-line watermark, "SPECIAL POSTAGE PAPER / LONDON." For surcharge see No. 143.

General Post Office — A40

Pres. Manuel Estrada Cabrera — A41

**1911, June** *Perf. 12*

**141** A40 25c bl & blk .55 .25
- *a.* Center inverted *1,750.* 900.00

**142** A41 5p red & blk .65 .65
- *a.* Center inverted 30.00 27.50

## Nos. 116, 118 and 140 Surcharged in Black or Red

h

i

j

**1911** *Perf. 14*

**143** A39 (h) 1c on 6c 25.00 9.75
- *a.* Double surcharge 75.00 75.00

**144** A30 (i) 2c on 5c (R) 1.60 .85
**145** A32 (j) 6c on 10c 1.25 1.25
- *a.* Double surcharge 50.00

*Nos. 143-145 (3)* 27.85 11.85

See watermark note after No. 140. Forgeries exist.

## Nos. 119-121 Surcharged in Black

k

l

m

**1912, Sept.**

**147** A33 (k) 1c on 20c .40 .40
- *a.* Inverted surcharge 12.50 12.50
- *b.* Double surcharge 15.00 15.00

**148** A34 (l) 2c on 50c .40 .40
- *a.* Inverted surcharge 12.50 12.50
- *b.* Double surcharge 12.50
- *c.* Double inverted surcharge 25.00

**149** A35 (m) 5c on 75c .80 .80
- *a.* "191" for "1912" 7.50 7.50
- *b.* Double surcharge 15.00 15.00
- *c.* Inverted surcharge 10.00

*Nos. 147-149 (3)* 1.60 1.60

Forgeries exist.

## Nos. 120, 122 and 123 Surcharged in Blue, Green or Black

n

o

p

**1913, July**

**151** A34 (n) 1c on 50c (Bl) .25 .25
- *a.* Inverted surcharge 10.00
- *b.* Double surcharge 17.50
- *c.* Horiz. pair, imperf. btwn. 100.00

**152** A36 (o) 6c on 1p (G) .30 .30
**153** A37 (p) 12½c on 2p (Bk) .30 .30
- *a.* Inverted surcharge 15.00 15.00
- *b.* Double surcharge 40.00
- *c.* Horiz. pair, imperf. btwn. 100.00

*Nos. 151-153 (3)* .85 .85

Forgeries exist.

## Nos. 114 and 115 Surcharged in Black

q

r

s

t

**1916-17**

**154** A28 (q) 2c on 1c ('17) .25 .25
**155** A28 (r) 6c on 1c .25 .25
**156** A28 (s) 12½c on 1c .25 .25
**157** A29 (t) 25c on 2c .25 .25
*Nos. 154-157 (4)* 1.00 1.00

Numerous errors of value and color, inverted and double surcharges and similar varieties are in the market. They were not regularly issued, but were surreptitiously made and sold.

Counterfeit surcharges abound.

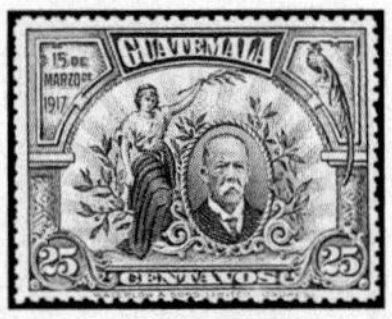

"Liberty" and President Estrada Cabrera — A51

**1917, Mar. 15** *Perf. 14, 15*

**158** A51 25c dp blue & brown .25 .25

Re-election of President Estrada Cabrera.

Estrada Cabrera and Quetzal — A52

**1918** *Perf. 12*

**161** A52 1.50p dark blue .30 .25

Radio Station — A54

"Joaquina" Maternity Hospital — A55

"Estrada Cabrera" Vocational School — A56

National Emblem — A57

**1919, May 3** *Perf. 14, 15*

**162** A54 30c red & blk 2.75 .75
**163** A55 60c ol grn & blk .80 .50
**164** A56 90c red brn & blk .80 .75
**165** A57 3p dp grn & blk 1.75 .50
*Nos. 162-165 (4)* 6.10 2.50

See Nos. 215, 227. For surcharges see Nos. 166-167, 179-185, 188, 195-198, 245-246, C8-C11, C21-C22.

No. 162 Ovptd. in Blue & Srchd. in Black

**1920, Jan.** **Unwmk.**

**166** A54 2c on 30c red & blk .30 .25
- *a.* Inverted surcharge 12.50 12.50
- *b.* "1920" double 10.00 10.00
- *c.* "1920" omitted 15.00 15.00
- *d.* "2 centavos" omitted 20.00
- *e.* Imperf, pair 100.00
- *f.* Pair, imperf. btwn. 100.00

## Nos. 123 and 163 Surcharged

u

v

**1920**

**167** A55 2c on 60c (Bk & R) .25 .25
- *a.* Inverted surcharge 10.00 10.00
- *b.* "1920" inverted 7.50 7.50
- *c.* "1920" omitted 10.00 10.00
- *d.* "1920" only 10.00
- *e.* Double surcharge 25.00

**168** A37 25c on 2p (Bk) .30 .25
- *a.* "35" for "25" 10.00 10.00
- *b.* Large "5" in "25" 10.00 10.00
- *c.* Inverted surcharge 15.00 15.00
- *d.* Double surcharge 25.00

A61

**1920**

**169** A61 25c green .25 .25
- *a.* Double overprint 50.00
- *b.* Double overprint, inverted 75.00

See types A65-A66.

No. 119 Surcharged

**1921, Apr.**

**170** A33 12½c on 20c .25 .25
- *a.* Double surcharge 15.00
- *b.* Inverted surcharge 15.00

No. 121 Surcharged

**1921, Apr.**

**171** A35 50c on 75c lil & blk .50 .30
- *a.* Double surcharge 22.50
- *b.* Inverted surcharge 25.00 25.00

Mayan Stele at Quiriguá — A62

Monument to President Granados — A63

"La Penitenciaria" Bridge — A64

**1921, Sept. 1** *Perf. 13½, 14, 15*

**172** A62 1.50p blue & org .85 .25
**173** A63 5p brown & grn 2.75 1.25
**174** A64 15p black & ver 22.50 12.50
*Nos. 172-174 (3)* 26.10 14.00

See Nos. 216, 228, 229. For surcharges see Nos. 186-187, 189-191, 199-201, 207, 231, 247-251, C1-C5, C12, C23-C24.

### Telegraph Stamps Overprinted or Surcharged in Black or Red

A65

A66

**1921** *Perf. 14*

| | | | | |
|---|---|---|---|---|
| 175 | A65 | 25c green | .25 | .25 |
| 176 | A66 | 12½c on 25c grn (R) | .25 | .25 |
| 177 | A66 | 12½c on 25c grn | 15.00 | 15.00 |
| | | *Nos. 175-177 (3)* | 15.50 | 15.50 |

### Nos. 119, 163 and 164 Surcharged in Black or Red

w

x

**1922, Mar.**

| | | | | |
|---|---|---|---|---|
| 178 | A33(w) | 12½c on 20c | .25 | .25 |
| *a.* | | Inverted surcharge | 10.00 | |
| 179 | A55(w) | 12½c on 60c (R) | .50 | .50 |
| *a.* | | Inverted surcharge | 25.00 | |
| 180 | A56(w) | 12½c on 90c | .50 | .50 |
| *a.* | | Inverted surcharge | 25.00 | |
| 181 | A55(x) | 25c on 60c | 1.00 | 1.00 |
| *a.* | | Inverted surcharge | 20.00 | |
| 182 | A55(x) | 25c on 60c (R) | 125.00 | 125.00 |
| 183 | A56(x) | 25c on 90c | 1.00 | 1.00 |
| *a.* | | Inverted surcharge | 25.00 | |
| 184 | A56(x) | 25c on 90c (R) | 4.00 | 4.00 |
| | | *Nos. 178-181,183-184 (6)* | 7.25 | 7.25 |

Counterfeits exist.

Nos. 165, 173-174 Surcharged in Red or Dark Blue

**1922, May**

| | | | | |
|---|---|---|---|---|
| 185 | A57 | 12½c on 3p grn & blk (R) | .25 | .25 |
| 186 | A63 | 12½c on 5p brn & grn | .50 | .45 |
| 187 | A64 | 12½c on 15p blk & ver | .50 | .45 |
| | | *Nos. 185-187 (3)* | 1.25 | 1.15 |

### Nos. 165, 173-174 Surcharged in Red or Black

Type I

Type II

Type III

Type IV

**1922**

| | | | | |
|---|---|---|---|---|
| 188 | A57 | 25c on 3p (I) (R) | .25 | .25 |
| *a.* | | Type II | .60 | .60 |
| *b.* | | Type III | .60 | .60 |
| *c.* | | Type IV | .30 | .30 |
| *d.* | | Inverted surcharge | 40.00 | |
| *e.* | | Horiz. or vert. pair, imperf. btwn. (I) | 125.00 | |
| 189 | A63 | 25c on 5p (I) | 1.00 | 2.00 |
| *a.* | | Type II | 2.00 | 3.00 |
| *b.* | | Type III | 2.00 | 3.00 |
| *c.* | | Type IV | 1.00 | 2.00 |
| 190 | A64 | 25c on 15p (I) | 1.00 | 1.50 |
| *a.* | | Type II | 2.00 | 3.00 |
| *b.* | | Type III | 2.00 | 3.00 |
| *c.* | | Type IV | 1.00 | 1.50 |
| 191 | A64 | 25c on 15p (I) (R) | 22.50 | 30.00 |
| *a.* | | Type II | 40.00 | 45.00 |
| *b.* | | Type III | 45.00 | 45.00 |
| *c.* | | Type IV | 30.00 | 35.00 |
| | | *Nos. 188-191 (4)* | 24.75 | 33.75 |

### Stamps of 1902-21 Surcharged in Dark Blue or Red

Type V

Type VI

Type VII

Type VIII

Type IX

**1922, Aug.** **On Nos. 121-123**

| | | | | |
|---|---|---|---|---|
| 192 | A35 | 25c on 75c (V) | .40 | .40 |
| *a.* | | Type VI | .40 | .40 |
| *b.* | | Type VII | 1.75 | 1.75 |
| *c.* | | Type VIII | 5.50 | 4.75 |
| *d.* | | Type IX | 6.50 | 6.00 |
| 193 | A36 | 25c on 1p (V) | .30 | .30 |
| *a.* | | Type VI | .30 | .30 |
| *b.* | | Type VII | 1.25 | 1.25 |
| *c.* | | Type VIII | 2.50 | 2.50 |
| *d.* | | Type IX | 4.00 | 3.50 |
| *e.* | | Inverted surcharge | 40.00 | |
| 194 | A37 | 25c on 2p (V) | .45 | .45 |
| *a.* | | Type VI | .45 | .45 |
| *b.* | | Type VII | 1.25 | 1.25 |
| *c.* | | Type VIII | 4.00 | 4.00 |
| *d.* | | Type IX | 6.50 | 6.50 |

**On Nos. 162-165**

| | | | | |
|---|---|---|---|---|
| 195 | A54 | 25c on 30c (V) | .45 | .45 |
| *a.* | | Type VI | .45 | .45 |
| *b.* | | Type VII | 1.25 | 1.25 |
| *c.* | | Type VIII | 5.50 | 5.50 |
| *d.* | | Type IX | 6.50 | 6.50 |
| 196 | A55 | 25c on 60c (V) | 1.00 | 1.50 |
| *a.* | | Type VI | 1.25 | 1.50 |
| *b.* | | Type VII | 6.25 | 7.75 |
| *c.* | | Type VIII | 8.50 | 9.50 |
| *d.* | | Type IX | 10.00 | 11.00 |
| 197 | A56 | 25c on 90c (V) | 1.00 | 1.50 |
| *a.* | | Type VI | 1.50 | 2.00 |
| *b.* | | Type VII | 6.00 | 6.75 |
| *c.* | | Type VIII | 8.50 | 9.50 |
| *d.* | | Type IX | 10.00 | 11.00 |
| 198 | A57 | 25c on 3p (R) (V) | .40 | .40 |
| *a.* | | Type VI | .40 | .40 |
| *b.* | | Type VII | 1.25 | 1.00 |
| *c.* | | Type VIII | 6.00 | 4.50 |
| *d.* | | Type IX | 6.50 | 6.00 |
| *e.* | | Inverted surcharge | 50.00 | |

**On Nos. 172-174**

| | | | | |
|---|---|---|---|---|
| 199 | A62 | 25c on 1.50p (V) | .30 | .30 |
| *a.* | | Type VI | .30 | .30 |
| *b.* | | Type VII | 1.25 | 1.00 |
| *c.* | | Type VIII | 3.00 | 3.00 |
| *d.* | | Type IX | 4.50 | 4.50 |
| *e.* | | Inverted surcharge | 40.00 | |
| 200 | A63 | 25c on 5p (V) | .75 | .90 |
| *a.* | | Type VI | .80 | 1.00 |
| *b.* | | Type VII | 3.00 | 3.50 |
| *c.* | | Type VIII | 5.50 | 6.00 |
| *d.* | | Type IX | 8.00 | 8.50 |
| 201 | A64 | 25c on 15p (V) | .85 | .90 |
| *a.* | | Type VI | 1.50 | 1.50 |
| *b.* | | Type VII | 5.00 | 5.50 |
| *c.* | | Type VIII | 6.50 | 6.50 |
| *d.* | | Type IX | 12.00 | 12.00 |
| | | *Nos. 192-201 (10)* | 5.90 | 7.10 |

Centenary Palace — A69

National Palace at Antigua — A70

### Printed by Waterlow & Sons

**1922** *Perf. 14, 14½*

| | | | | |
|---|---|---|---|---|
| 202 | A69 | 12½c green | .30 | .25 |
| *a.* | | Horiz. or vert. pair, imperf. btwn. | 100.00 | |
| 203 | A70 | 25c brown | .30 | .25 |

See Nos. 211, 221, 234.

Columbus Theater A71

Quetzal A72

Granados Monument — A73

### Litho. by Castillo Bros.

**1924, Feb.** *Perf. 12*

| | | | | |
|---|---|---|---|---|
| 204 | A71 | 50c rose | .50 | .25 |
| *a.* | | Imperf., pair | 7.50 | |
| *b.* | | Horiz. or vert. pair, imperf. btwn. | 25.00 | |
| 205 | A72 | 1p dark green | 2.25 | .25 |
| *a.* | | Imperf. vertically | 15.00 | |
| *b.* | | Vert. pair, imperf. btwn. | 20.00 | |
| *c.* | | Imperf., pair | 7.50 | |
| 206 | A73 | 5p orange | 1.25 | .50 |
| *a.* | | Imperf., pair | 8.50 | |
| *b.* | | Horiz. pair, imperf. btwn. | 20.00 | |
| | | *Nos. 204-206 (3)* | 4.00 | 1.00 |

For surcharges see Nos. 208-209.

Nos. 172 and 206 Surcharged

**1924, July**

| | | | | |
|---|---|---|---|---|
| 207 | A62 | 1p on 1.50p bl & org | .30 | .25 |
| 208 | A73 | 1.25p on 5p orange | .50 | .50 |
| *a.* | | "UN PESO 25 Cents." omitted | 40.00 | |
| *b.* | | Horiz. pair, imperf. btwn. | 25.00 | |

No. 208 Overprinted

**1924**

| | | | | |
|---|---|---|---|---|
| 209 | A73 | 1p on 5p orange | .50 | .50 |

### Types of 1902-22 Issues Engr. by Perkins Bacon & Co.

**1924, Aug.** **Re-engraved** *Perf. 14*

| | | | | |
|---|---|---|---|---|
| 210 | A31 | 6c bister | .25 | .25 |
| 211 | A70 | 25c brown | .25 | .25 |
| 212 | A34 | 50c red | .25 | .25 |
| 213 | A36 | 1p orange brn | .25 | .25 |
| 214 | A37 | 2p orange | .35 | .25 |
| 215 | A57 | 3p deep green | 2.00 | .50 |
| 216 | A64 | 15p black | 5.00 | 2.75 |
| | | *Nos. 210-216 (7)* | 8.35 | 4.50 |

The designs of the stamps of 1924 differ from those of the 1902-22 issues in many details which are too minute to illustrate. The re-engraved issue may be readily distinguished by the imprint "Perkins Bacon & Co. Ld. Londres."

Pres. Justo Rufino Barrios A74

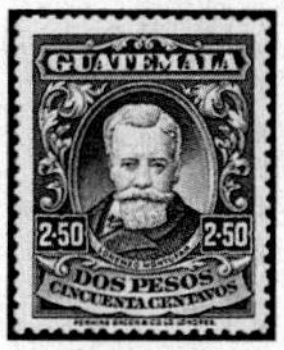
Lorenzo Montúfar A75

**1924, Aug.**

| | | | | |
|---|---|---|---|---|
| 217 | A74 | 1.25p ultra | .25 | .25 |
| 218 | A75 | 2.50p dk violet | 1.00 | .25 |

See Nos. 224, 226. For surcharges see Nos. 232, C6, C20.

Aurora Park — A76

National Post Office — A77

National Observatory A78

### Types of 1921-24 Re-engraved and New Designs Dated 1926

### Engraved by Waterlow & Sons, Ltd.

**1926, July-Aug.** *Perf. 12½*

| | | | | |
|---|---|---|---|---|
| 219 | A31 | 6c ocher | .25 | .25 |
| 220 | A76 | 12½c green | .25 | .25 |
| 221 | A70 | 25c brown | .25 | .25 |
| 222 | A77 | 50c red | .25 | .25 |
| 223 | A36 | 1p orange brn | .25 | .25 |
| 224 | A74 | 1.50p dk blue | .25 | .25 |
| 225 | A78 | 2p orange | 1.25 | 1.00 |
| 226 | A75 | 2.50p dk violet | 1.50 | 1.25 |
| 227 | A57 | 3p dark green | .45 | .25 |
| 228 | A63 | 5p brown vio | 1.00 | .40 |
| 229 | A64 | 15p black | 6.00 | 2.75 |
| | | *Nos. 219-229 (11)* | 11.70 | 7.15 |

These stamps may be distinguished from those of the same designs in preceding issues by the imprint "Waterlow & Sons, Limited, Londres," the date, "1926," and the perforation.

See Nos. 233, 242. For surcharge see No. 230.

Nos. 225-226, 228 Surcharged in Various Colors

**1928**

| | | | | |
|---|---|---|---|---|
| 230 | A78 | ½c on 2p (Bl) | .65 | .50 |
| *a.* | | Inverted surcharge | 12.50 | |
| 231 | A63 | ½c on 5p (Bk) | .35 | .25 |
| *a.* | | Inverted surcharge | 10.00 | 10.00 |
| *b.* | | Double surcharge | 50.00 | |
| *c.* | | Blue surcharge | 45.00 | 45.00 |
| *d.* | | Blue and black surcharge | 50.00 | 50.00 |
| 232 | A75 | 1c on 2.50p (R) | .35 | .25 |
| *b.* | | Double surcharge | 50.00 | |
| | | *Nos. 230-232 (3)* | 1.35 | 1.00 |

Barrios — A79

Montúfar — A80

Granados A81

General Orellana A82

Coat of Arms of Guatemala City — A83

**Engraved by T. De la Rue & Co.**

**1929, Jan.** ***Perf. 14***

| | | | | |
|---|---|---|---|---|
| **233** | A78 | ½c yellow grn | .75 | .25 |
| **234** | A70 | 1c dark brown | .25 | .25 |
| **235** | A79 | 2c deep blue | .25 | .25 |
| **236** | A80 | 3c dark violet | .25 | .25 |
| **237** | A81 | 4c orange | .25 | .25 |
| **238** | A82 | 5c dk carmine | .50 | .25 |
| **239** | A31 | 10c brown | .40 | .25 |
| **240** | A36 | 15c ultra | .50 | .25 |
| **241** | A29 | 25c brown org | 1.00 | .25 |
| **242** | A76 | 30c green | .90 | .30 |
| **243** | A32 | 50c pale rose | 2.00 | .60 |
| **244** | A83 | 1q black | 3.00 | .40 |
| | | *Nos. 233-244 (12)* | 10.05 | 3.55 |

Nos. 233, 234 and 239 to 243 differ from the illustrations in many minor details, particularly in the borders.

See No. 300 for bisect of No. 235. For overprints and surcharges see Nos. 297, C13, C17-C18, C25-C26, C28, E1, RA17-RA18.

No. 227 Surcharged in Black or Red

**1929, Dec. 28** ***Perf. 12½, 13***

| | | | | |
|---|---|---|---|---|
| **245** | A57 | 3c on 3p dk grn (Bk) | 1.25 | *1.90* |
| *a.* | | Inverted surcharge | 15.00 | 15.00 |
| **246** | A57 | 5c on 3p dk grn (R) | 1.25 | *1.90* |
| *a.* | | Inverted surcharge | 15.00 | 15.00 |

Inauguration of the Eastern Railroad connecting Guatemala and El Salvador.

No. 229 Surcharged in Red

**1930, Mar. 30** **Unwmk.**

| | | | | |
|---|---|---|---|---|
| **247** | A64 | 1c on 15p black | 1.25 | *1.40* |
| **248** | A64 | 2c on 15p black | 1.25 | *1.40* |
| **249** | A64 | 3c on 15p black | 1.25 | *1.40* |
| **250** | A64 | 5c on 15p black | 1.25 | *1.40* |
| **251** | A64 | 15c on 15p black | 1.25 | 1.40 |
| | | *Nos. 247-251 (5)* | 6.25 | *7.00* |

Opening of Los Altos electric railway.

Hydroelectric Dam — A85

Los Altos Railway A86

Railroad Station A87

**1930, Mar. 30** **Typo.** ***Perf. 12***

| | | | | |
|---|---|---|---|---|
| **252** | A85 | 2c brn vio & blk | 1.40 | *1.90* |
| *a.* | | Horiz. pair, imperf. btwn. | 125.00 | |
| **253** | A86 | 3c dp red & blk | 2.75 | *2.75* |
| *a.* | | Vert. pair, imperf. btwn. | 125.00 | |
| **254** | A87 | 5c buff & dk bl | 2.75 | *2.75* |
| | | *Nos. 252-254 (3)* | 6.90 | *7.40* |

Opening of Los Altos electric railway. Exist imperf.

Mayan Stele at Quiriguá — A91

**1932, Apr. 8** **Engr.**

| | | | | |
|---|---|---|---|---|
| **258** | A91 | 3c carmine rose | 1.90 | .40 |

See Nos. 302-303.

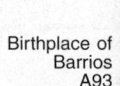

Flag of the Race, Columbus and Tecum Uman A92

**1933, Aug. 3** **Litho.** ***Perf. 12½***

| | | | | |
|---|---|---|---|---|
| **259** | A92 | ½c dark green | .75 | *.75* |
| **260** | A92 | 1c dull brown | 1.25 | 1.10 |
| **261** | A92 | 2c deep blue | 1.25 | 1.10 |
| **262** | A92 | 3c dull violet | 1.25 | .75 |
| **263** | A92 | 5c rose | 1.25 | 1.10 |
| | | *Nos. 259-263 (5)* | 5.75 | *4.80* |

Day of the Race and 441st anniv. of the sailing of Columbus from Palos, Spain, Aug. 3, 1492, on his 1st voyage to the New World.

The 3c and 5c exist imperf.

Birthplace of Barrios A93

View of San Lorenzo A94

Justo Rufino Barrios A95

National Emblem and Locomotive A96

General Post Office — A97

Telegraph Building and Barrios A98

Military Academy A99

National Police Headquarters — A100

Jorge Ubico and J. R. Barrios A101

**1935, July 19** **Photo.**

| | | | | |
|---|---|---|---|---|
| **264** | A93 | ½c yel grn & mag | .40 | *.45* |
| **265** | A94 | 1c org red & pck bl | .40 | *.45* |
| **266** | A95 | 2c orange & blk | .40 | *.55* |
| **267** | A96 | 3c car rose & pck bl | 4.50 | 2.25 |
| **268** | A97 | 4c pck bl & org red | 4.50 | *10.00* |
| **269** | A98 | 5c bl grn & brn | 3.25 | *4.25* |
| **270** | A99 | 10c slate grn & rose lake | 4.50 | *5.50* |
| **271** | A100 | 15c ol grn & org brn | 4.50 | *4.75* |
| **272** | A101 | 25c scarlet & bl | 4.50 | *4.75* |
| | | *Nos. 264-272 (9)* | 26.95 | *32.95* |

General Barrios. See Nos. C29-C31.

Lake Atitlán A102

Quetzal A103

Legislative Building — A104

**1935, Oct. 10**

| | | | | |
|---|---|---|---|---|
| **273** | A102 | 1c brown & crim | .25 | .25 |
| **274** | A103 | 3c rose car & pck grn | .70 | .25 |
| **275** | A103 | 3c red org & pck grn | .70 | .25 |
| **276** | A104 | 4c brt bl & dp rose | .35 | .25 |
| | | *Nos. 273-276 (4)* | 2.00 | 1.00 |

See No. 277. For surcharges see Nos. B1-B3.

**No. 273 perforated diagonally through the center**

**1936, June** ***Perf. 12½x12***

| | | | | |
|---|---|---|---|---|
| **277** | A102 | (½c) brown & crimson | .25 | .25 |
| *a.* | | Unsevered pair | .50 | .60 |

Bureau of Printing — A105

Map of Guatemala A106

**1936, Sept. 24** ***Perf. 12½***

| | | | | |
|---|---|---|---|---|
| **278** | A105 | ½c green & pur | .25 | .25 |
| **279** | A106 | 5c blue & dk brn | .90 | .25 |

For surcharge see No. B4.

Quetzal A107

Union Park, Quezaltenango A108

Gen. Jorge Ubico on Horseback A109

1c, Tower of the Reformer. 3c, National Post Office. 4c, Government Building, Retalhuleu. 5c, Legislative Palace entrance. 10c, Custom House. 15c, Aurora Airport Custom House. 25c, National Fair. 50c, Residence of Presidential Guard. 1.50q, General Ubico, portrait standing, no cap.

**1937, May 20**

| | | | | |
|---|---|---|---|---|
| **280** | A107 | ½c pck bl & car rose | .70 | *.45* |
| **281** | A107 | 1c ol gray & red brn | .70 | .35 |
| **282** | A108 | 2c vio & car rose | .60 | .35 |
| **283** | A108 | 3c brn vio & brt bl | .50 | .25 |
| **284** | A108 | 4c yel & dl ol grn | 3.00 | *3.00* |
| **285** | A107 | 5c crim & brt vio | 3.00 | 3.00 |
| **286** | A107 | 10c mag & brn blk | 4.00 | *4.00* |
| **287** | A108 | 15c ultra & cop red | 3.00 | *3.00* |
| **288** | A108 | 25c red org & vio | 4.00 | *4.00* |
| **289** | A108 | 50c dk grn & org red | 6.00 | *6.00* |
| **290** | A109 | 1q magenta & blk | *50.00* | *50.00* |
| **291** | A109 | 1.50q red brn & blk | *50.00* | *50.00* |
| | | *Nos. 280-291 (12)* | 125.50 | 124.40 |

Second term of President Ubico.

Mayan Calendar A119

Natl. Flower (White Nun Orchid) A120

Quetzal — A121

Map of Guatemala
A122

**1939, Sept. 7** ***Perf. 13x12, 12½***
**292** A119 ½c grn & red brn *.85* .25
**293** A120 2c bl & gray blk *5.00* 1.00
**294** A121 3c red org & turq grn *6.50* 1.75
**295** A121 3c ol bis & turq grn *6.50* 1.75
**296** A122 5c blue & red *5.75* 5.75
*Nos. 292-296 (5)* 24.60 10.50

For overprints see Nos. 324, C157.

No. 235 Surcharged in Red

**1939, Sept.** ***Perf. 14***
**297** A79 1c on 2c deep blue .25 .25

**Stamps of 1929 Surcharged in Blue**

y

z

**1940, June**
**298** A29 (y) 1c on 25c brn org .25 .25
**299** A32 (z) 5c on 50c pale rose (bar 10x¾mm) .25 .25
*a.* Bar 12½x2mm .30 .25
*b.* Bar 12½x1mm 50.00 5.00

No. 235 perforated diagonally through the center

**1941, Aug. 16** ***Perf. 14x11½***
**300** A79 (1c) deep blue .30 .25
*a.* Unsevered pair .80 .80

No. 241 Surcharged in Black

**1941, Dec. 24** ***Perf. 14***
**301** A29 ½c on 25c brn org .30 .30

**Type of 1932 Inscribed "1942"**

**1942** **Engr.** ***Perf. 12***
**302** A91 3c green .95 .25
**303** A91 3c deep blue .95 .25

Issued to publicize the coffee of Guatemala.

Vase of Guastatoya
A123

Home for the Aged
A124

**1942, July 13** **Unwmk.**
**304** A123 ½c red brown .35 .25
**305** A124 1c carmine rose .35 .25

National Printing Works
A125

Rafael Maria Landivar
A126

**1943, Jan. 25** **Engr.** ***Perf. 11, 12***
**307** A125 2c scarlet .25 .25
*a.* Vert. pair, imperf. horiz. 35.00

**1943, Aug.** ***Perf. 11***
**308** A126 5c brt ultra .25 .25

Death of Rafael Landivar, poet, 150th anniv.

National Palace
A127

**1944, June 30** ***Perf. 11***
**309** A127 3c dk blue green .30 .30

Inauguration of the Natl. Palace, Nov. 10, 1943.
See Nos. C137A-C139. For overprints see Nos. 311-311A, C133.

Ruins of Zakuleu
A128

**1945, Jan. 6**
**310** A128 ½c black brown .25 .25

**Type of 1944 Overprinted in Blue**

**1945, Jan. 15**
**311** A127 3c deep blue .30 .25

**Overprint Bar 1mm Thick**
**311A** A127 3c deep blue 1.00 .70

Allegory of the Revolution
A129

Torch
A130

**1945, Feb. 20**
**312** A129 3c grayish blue .30 .25
*Nos. 312,C128-C131 (5)* 2.30 1.25

Revolution of 10/20/44.

**1945, Oct. 20**
**313** A130 3c deep blue .25 .25

1st anniv. of the Revolution of Oct. 20, 1944. See No. C135-C136.

José Milla y Vidaurre
A131

Payo Enriquez de Rivera
A132

**1945** ***Perf. 11, 12½***
**314** A131 1c deep green .25 .25
**315** A132 2c dull lilac .25 .25
*Nos. 314-315,C134-C134A (4)* 2.20 1.80

See Nos. 343-346, 379, C137, C269, C311-C315.

**Catalogue values for unused stamps in this section, from this point to the end of the section, are for Never Hinged items.**

José Batres y Montufar
A133

UPU Monument Bern, Switzerland
A134

**1946** **Unwmk.**
**316** A133 ½c sepia .25 .25
**317** A133 3c deep blue .25 .25

See Nos. 319, C142.

**1946, Aug. 5** **Photo.** ***Perf. 14x13***
**318** A134 1c vio & gray brn .30 .25
*Nos. 318,C140-C141 (3)* 1.45 .80

Centenary of the first postage stamp.

**Batres Type of 1946**

**1947, Nov. 11** **Engr.** ***Perf. 11, 12½***
**319** A133 3c dull green .25 .25

Symbolical of Labor — A135

**1948, May 14** **Unwmk.** ***Perf. 11***
**320** A135 1c deep green .40 .25
*a.* Perf. 12½ 5.00
**321** A135 2c sepia .40 .25
*a.* Perf. 12½ 5.00
**322** A135 3c deep ultra .40 .25
*a.* Perf. 12½ 5.00
**323** A135 5c rose carmine .40 .25
*a.* Perf. 12½ 5.00
*Nos. 320-323 (4)* 1.60 1.00

Labor Day, May 1, 1948. Other perfs. and compound perfs. exist.

**No. 296 Overprinted in Carmine at Lower Right**

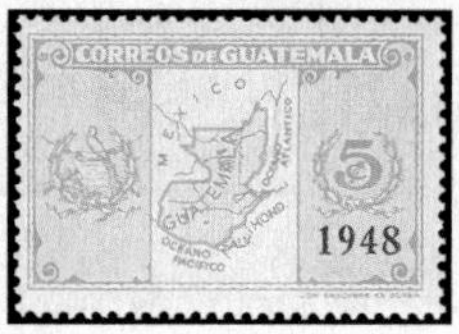


**1948, May 14** ***Perf. 12½***
**324** A122 5c blue & red .40 .30

Bartolomé de las Casas and Indian — A136

**1949, Oct. 8** **Engr.** ***Perf. 12½, 13½***
**325** A136 ½c red .25 .25
**326** A136 1c black brown .25 .25
**327** A136 2c dk blue grn .25 .25
*a.* 2c green, perf. 11, 11½ ('60) .25 .25
**328** A136 3c rose pink .25 .25
*a.* 3c car, perf. 11, 12½, 13½ ('64) .30 .25
**329** A136 4c ultra .25 .25
*Nos. 325-329 (5)* 1.25 1.25

See Nos. 384-386.

Gathering Coffee — A137

1c, Poptun Agricultural Colony. 2c, Banana trees. 3c, Sugar cane field. 6c, Intl. Bridge.

**1950, Feb.** **Photo.** ***Perf. 14***
**330** A137 ½c vio bl, pink & ol gray .25 .25
**331** A137 1c red brn, yel & grnsh gray .25 .25
**332** A137 2c ol grn, pink & bl gray .25 .25
**333** A137 3c pur, bl & org brn .25 .25
**334** A137 6c dp org, aqua & vio .50 .25
*Nos. 330-334 (5)* 1.50 1.25

See Nos. 347-349.

Badge of Public and Social Assistance Ministry — A138

Nurse — A139

Map Showing Hospitals — A140

**1950-51** **Litho.** ***Perf. 12, 12½x12***
**335** A138 1c car rose & bl .25 .25
**336** A139 3c dl grn & rose red .35 .25

***Perf. 12***
**337** A140 5c dk bl & choc ('51) .50 .25
*a.* Souvenir sheet, #335-337 8.00 8.00
*Nos. 335-337 (3)* 1.10 .75

Issued to publicize the National Hospitals Fund.
No. 337a exists perf. and imperf., same values.
A perforated souvenir sheet is known which is similar to No. 337a, but with the 5c stamp like the basic stamp of No. C232 (with "BRITISH HONDURAS" inscription).
See #C177-C180a. For overprint see #C232.

Motorcycle Messenger
A141

**1951, May 22** *Perf. 14x12½*
**337B** A141 4c bl grn & gray blk .55 .25

Issued for regular postage, although inscribed "Expreso." See No. E2.

Souvenir Sheet

A142

### Typographed and Engraved

**1951, Oct. 22** *Imperf.*
**338** A142 Sheet of 2 5.00 5.00
*a.* 1c rose carmine 2.00 1.50
*b.* 10c deep ultramarine 2.00 1.50

75th anniv. (in 1949) of the UPU.
For overprint see No. 419.

A143

Modern Model Schools
A144

**1951, Oct. 22 Photo.** *Perf. 13½x14*
**339** A143 ½c purple & sepia .35 .25
**340** A144 1c brn car & dl grn .35 .25
**341** A143 2c grnsh bl & red brn .35 .25
**342** A144 4c blk brn & rose vio .35 .25
*Nos. 339-342 (4)* 1.40 1.00

### Enriquez de Rivera Type of 1945 Re-engraved

**1952, June 4** *Perf. 12½*
**343** A132 ½c violet .25 .25
**344** A132 1c rose carmine .25 .25
**345** A132 2c green .25 .25
**346** A132 4c orange .45 .25
*Nos. 343-346 (4)* 1.20 1.00

A panel containing the dates "1660-1951" has been added below the portrait.

### Produce Type of 1950

Designs: ½c, Sugar cane field. 1c, Banana trees. 2c, Poptun Agricultural Colony.

**1953, Feb. 11 Photo.** *Perf. 13½*
**347** A137 ½c dk brn & dp bl .70 .25
**348** A137 1c red org & ol grn .70 .25
**349** A137 2c dk car & gray blk .70 .25
*Nos. 347-349 (3)* 2.10 .75

Issued to publicize farming.

Rafael Alvarez Ovalle and José Joaquin Palma
A145

**1953, May 13**
**350** A145 ½c purple & blk .55 .40
**351** A145 1c dk grn & org brn .55 .40
**352** A145 2c org brn & ol grn .55 .40
**353** A145 3c dk bl & ol brn .55 .40
*Nos. 350-353 (4)* 2.20 1.60

Authors of Guatemala's national anthem.
For overprints see Nos. 374-378.

Quetzal — A146

**1954, Sept. 27 Engr.** *Perf. 12½, 11*
**354** A146 1c dp violet blue 1.75 .25

See Nos. 367-373, 380-382A, 434-444. For overprint see No. 395.

Mario Camposeco — A147

10c, Carlos Aguirre Matheu. 15c, Goalkeeper.

**1955-56 Unwmk.** *Perf. 12½*
**355** A147 4c violet 1.00 .25
**356** A147 4c carmine ('56) 1.00 .25
**357** A147 4c blue grn ('56) 1.00 .25
**358** A147 10c bluish grn 3.25 .75
**359** A147 15c dark blue 3.25 2.00
*Nos. 355-359 (5)* 9.50 3.50

50 years of Soccer in Guatemala.

Globe and Red Cross — A148

Designs: 3c, Red Cross, Telephone and "5110." 4c, Nurse, patient and Red Cross flag.

**1956, May 23** *Perf. 13x12½*
**360** A148 1c brown & car .25 .25
**361** A148 3c dk green & red .25 .25
**362** A148 4c dk sl grn & red .30 .25
*Nos. 360-362 (3)* .80 .75

Red Cross. See Nos. B5-B7, CB5-CB7. For surcharges see Nos. CB8-CB10.

Dagger-Cross of the Liberation — A149

1c, Map showing 2,000 km. (1,243 miles) of new roads. 3c, Oil production.

**1956 Engr.** *Perf. 12½*
**363** A149 ½c violet .25 .25
**364** A149 1c dk blue grn .25 .25

*Perf. 11*

**365** A149 3c sepia .25 .25
*Nos. 363-365 (3)* .75 .75

Liberation of 1954-55. Issue dates: ½c, 1c, July 27; 3c, Oct. 31. See Nos. C210-C218.

### Quetzal Type of 1954

**1957-58** *Perf. 11, 12½*
**367** A146 2c violet .85 .25
**368** A146 3c carmine rose 1.00 .25
**369** A146 3c ultra 1.00 .25
*a.* 3c dark blue, perf. 11½ ('72) — —
**370** A146 4c orange 1.25 .25
**371** A146 5c brown 1.75 .25
**372** A146 5c org ver ('58) 1.75 .25
**373** A146 6c yellow grn 2.25 .25
*Nos. 367-373 (7)* 9.85 1.75

No. 368 is only perf. 12½. The 2c, 4c and No. 369 are found in perf. 11 and 12½. Other values are only perf. 11.

### No. 350 Ovptd. in Blue, Black, Carmine, Red Orange or Green

**1958, Nov.-Dec. Photo.** *Perf. 13½*
**374** A145 ½c purple & blk (Bl) .65 *.65*
**375** A145 ½c purple & blk (Bk) .65 *.65*
**376** A145 ½c purple & blk (C) .65 *.65*
**377** A145 ½c purple & blk (RO) .65 *.65*
**378** A145 ½c purple & blk (G) .65 *.65*
*Nos. 374-378 (5)* 3.25 *3.25*

Cent. of the birth of Rafael Alvarez Ovalle, composer of Guatemala's national anthem.

### Re-engraved Rivera Type of 1945

**1959, Sept. 12 Engr.** *Perf. 11, 12½*
**379** A132 4c gray blue .30 .25

See note after No. 346.

### Quetzal Type of 1954

**1960-63 Unwmk.** *Perf. 11*
**380** A146 2c brown ('61) .90 .35
**381** A146 4c lt violet 1.50 .35
**382** A146 5c blue green 1.75 .35

*Perf. 12½*

**382A** A146 5c slate gray ('63) 2.75 .55
*Nos. 380-382A (4)* 6.90 1.60

Romulus and Remus Statue, Rome — A150

**1961 Photo.** *Perf. 14*
**383** A150 3c blue .65 .25

Inauguration of the Plaza Italia.

### Las Casas Type of 1949

*Perf. 11, 11½, 12½, 13½*

**1962-64 Engr.**
**384** A136 ½c blue .25 .25
**385** A136 1c brt violet ('64) .25 .25
**386** A136 4c brown ('64) .25 .25
*Nos. 384-386 (3)* .75 .75

1871 Stamp — A151

**1963-66 Unwmk.** *Perf. 11*
**387** A151 10c carmine .40 .25
**388** A151 10c slate ('64) .40 .25

*Perf. 11½*

**389** A151 10c olive brn ('66) .40 .25
**390** A151 20c dp purple ('64) .65 .30
**391** A151 20c dk blue ('65) .65 .30
*Nos. 387-391 (5)* 2.50 1.35

For souvenir sheet, see No. C310.

Pedro Bethancourt Comforting Sick Man — A152

**1964, Jan. 6 Engr.** *Perf. 11*
**394** A152 2½c olive bister .45 .25

Beatification (1962-63) of Pedro Bethancourt (1626-67). See Nos. C319-C322. For overprints see Nos. C381-C382.

Quetzal Type of 1957-58 Overprinted in Blue

**1964, Dec. 29 Engr.** *Perf. 12½*
**395** A146 4c orange .45 .25

15th anniv. (in 1963) of the Intl. Soc. of Guatemala Collectors.

Map of Guatemala and British Honduras
A153

**1967, Apr. 28 Litho.** *Perf. 14x13½*
**396** A153 4c ol, vio bl & dp rose .55 .30
**397** A153 5c ocher, vio bl & dp org .45 .30
**398** A153 6c dp org, vio bl & gray .45 .30
*Nos. 396-398 (3)* 1.45 .90

Issued to state Guatemala's claim to British Honduras.
For overprints see Nos. C411-C413.

Quetzal, Mayan Ball Game Goal — A154

### Lithographed and Engraved

**1968, Oct. 15** *Perf. 11½*
**399** A154 1c blk, lt grn & red .40 .25
**400** A154 5c yel, lt grn & red .55 .25
**401** A154 8c org, lt grn & red .65 .25
**402** A154 15c bl, lt grn & red 1.10 .25
**403** A154 30c lt vio, lt grn & red 2.00 1.10
*Nos. 399-403 (5)* 4.70 2.10

19th Olympic Games, Mexico City, 10/12-27.
The 1c, 5c, 8c, 15c also exist perf 12½, 1c, 8c, perf 13½.
See Nos. 412-415. For overprints see Nos. 408-411, C431-C435.

Child and Poinsettia — A155

**1968-70 Typo.** *Perf. 13½*
**404** A155 2½c grn, dp bis & car .30 .25
**405** A155 2½c grn, org & car ('70) .45 *.55*
**406** A155 5c green, gray & car .45 .25
**407** A155 21c green, lil & car 1.00 .85
*Nos. 404-407 (4)* 2.20 1.90

Issued to help abandoned children.

Type of 1968 Overprinted in Black or Red

**1970, Mar. 19 Litho. *Perf. 13½***

| | | | | |
|---|---|---|---|---|
| 408 | A154 | 8c org, lt grn & red | .50 | *1.25* |
| 409 | A154 | 8c org, lt grn & red (R) | .50 | *1.25* |
| | | ***Perf. 12½*** | | |
| 410 | A154 | 15c bl, lt grn & red | .75 | *1.25* |
| 411 | A154 | 15c bl, lt grn & red (R) | .75 | *1.25* |
| | | *Nos. 408-411 (4)* | 2.50 | *5.00* |

50th anniv. of ILO. Gold overprint believed to be a trial color.

**Type of 1968**

**1971 Typo. & Engr. *Perf. 11½***

| | | | | |
|---|---|---|---|---|
| 412 | A154 | 1c gray, yel grn & red | .30 | .25 |
| | | **Typo.** | | |
| 413 | A154 | 5c brt pink, yel grn & red | .55 | .25 |
| 414 | A154 | 5c brown, grn & red | .55 | .25 |
| 415 | A154 | 5c dk bl, grn & red | .55 | .55 |
| | | *Nos. 412-415 (4)* | 1.95 | 1.30 |

Mayas and CARE Package — A156

**1971-72 Typo. *Perf. 13½***

| | | | | |
|---|---|---|---|---|
| 416 | A156 | 1c black & multi | .25 | .25 |
| | | ***Perf. 11½*** | | |
| 417 | A156 | 1c violet & multi ('72) | .25 | .25 |
| 418 | A156 | 1c brown & multi ('72) | .25 | .25 |
| | | *Nos. 416-418 (3)* | .75 | .75 |

10th anniv. of CARE in Guatemala, a US-Canadian Cooperative for American Relief Everywhere. Exist imperf. See No. C459.

**No. 338 (trimmed) Overprinted in Orange**

Souvenir Sheet

**Typo. & Engr.**

**1972, Oct. 23 *Imperf.***

| | | | | |
|---|---|---|---|---|
| 419 | A142 | Sheet of 2 | 1.50 | *1.50* |
| *a.* | | 1c rose carmine ("Munich") | .40 | *.40* |
| *b.* | | 10c deep ultra ("1972") | .50 | *.50* |

20th Olympic Games, Munich, Aug. 26-Sept. 11. Commemorative inscriptions on No. 338 at left, top and right have been trimmed off. Size: 61x45mm (approximately). Many varieties exist. Gold overprints probably are proofs.

Pres. Carlos Arana Osorio A157

Designs: 3c, 5c, President Osorio seated, vert. 8c, Pres. Osorio standing, vert.

**1973-74 Typo. *Perf. 12½***

| | | | | |
|---|---|---|---|---|
| 420 | A157 | 2c blue & blk | .80 | .25 |
| 421 | A157 | 3c orange & brn | 1.00 | .25 |
| 422 | A157 | 5c rose car & blk | 1.25 | .25 |
| 423 | A157 | 8c black & brt grn | 1.50 | .25 |
| *a.* | | Lithographed ('74) | 1.00 | .25 |
| | | *Nos. 420-423 (4)* | 4.55 | 1.00 |

8th population and 3rd dwellings census, Mar. 26-Apr. 7, 1973.

Francisco Ximenez — A158

**Typographed, Lithographed (#426)**

**1973-77 *Perf. 11½, 13½ (#426)***

| | | | | |
|---|---|---|---|---|
| 424 | A158 | 2c black & emer | .25 | .25 |
| 425 | A158 | 3c dk brn & org | .25 | .25 |
| 426 | A158 | 3c black & yellow | .45 | .25 |
| 427 | A158 | 6c black & brt bl | .45 | .25 |
| | | *Nos. 424-427 (4)* | 1.40 | 1.00 |

Brother Francisco Ximenez, discoverer and translator of National Book of Guatemala. No. 427 issued for Intl. Book Year 1972.

Issued: 6c, 8/2; 2c, 1/14/75; #425, 3/5/75; #426, 9/26/77.

Sculpture of Christ, by Pedro de Mendoza, 1643 — A159

8c, Sculpture by Lanuza Brothers, 18th century.

**1977, Apr. 4 Litho. *Perf. 11***

| | | | | |
|---|---|---|---|---|
| 428 | A159 | 6c purple & multi | .40 | .25 |
| 429 | A159 | 8c purple & multi | .40 | .25 |
| | | *Nos. 428-429,C614-C619 (8)* | 4.65 | 2.80 |

Holy Week 1977.

INTERFER 77 Emblem — A160

**1977, Oct. 31 Litho. *Perf. 11½***

| | | | | |
|---|---|---|---|---|
| 430 | A160 | 7c black & multi | .40 | .25 |

INTERFER 77, 4th International Fair, Guatemala, Oct. 31-Nov. 13.

Rotary Intl., 75th Anniv. A161

**1980, July 31 Litho. *Perf. 11½***

| | | | | |
|---|---|---|---|---|
| 431 | A161 | 4c shown | .80 | .25 |
| 432 | A161 | 6c Diamond and Quetzal | .80 | .25 |
| 433 | A161 | 10c Paul P. Harris | .95 | .60 |
| | | *Nos. 431-433 (3)* | 2.55 | 1.10 |

**Quetzal Type of 1954**

**1984-86 Engr. *Perf. 12½***

| | | | | |
|---|---|---|---|---|
| 434 | A146 | 1c deep green | *2.75* | .90 |
| 435 | A146 | 2c deep blue | *2.75* | .90 |
| 436 | A146 | 3c olive green | *2.75* | *2.75* |
| 437 | A146 | 3c sepia | *2.75* | .90 |
| 438 | A146 | 3c blue | *2.75* | .90 |
| 439 | A146 | 3c red | *2.75* | *2.75* |
| 440 | A146 | 3c orange | *2.75* | *2.75* |
| 441 | A146 | 3c vermilion | *2.75* | *2.75* |
| 442 | A146 | 4c lt red brn | *2.75* | .90 |
| 443 | A146 | 5c magenta | *2.75* | .90 |
| 444 | A146 | 6c deep blue | *2.75* | *2.75* |
| | | *Nos. 434-444 (11)* | *30.25* | *19.15* |

Issued: #436-439, 2/20; #441, 6c, 4/25/86; 1c, 4c, 5c, 2/16/87; 2c, 3/25/87.

Miguel Angel Asturias Cultural Center — A162

***Perf. 12½, 11½ (5c, 9c), 12½x11½ (4c), 13x12½ (6c)***

**1987-96 Litho.**

| | | | | |
|---|---|---|---|---|
| 445 | A162 | 1c light blue | .25 | .25 |
| 446 | A162 | 2c bister brown | .25 | .25 |
| 447 | A162 | 3c ultra | .25 | .25 |
| 448 | A162 | 4c bright pink | .25 | .25 |
| 449 | A162 | 5c orange | .25 | .25 |
| 450 | A162 | 6c pale green | .25 | .25 |
| 451 | A162 | 7c vermilion | .25 | .25 |
| 452 | A162 | 8c brt pink | .25 | .25 |
| 453 | A162 | 9c black | .25 | .25 |
| 454 | A162 | 10c pale green | .30 | .25 |
| | | *Nos. 445-454 (10)* | 2.55 | 2.50 |

Miguel Angel Asturias (1899-1974), 1967 Nobel laureate in literature.

Issued: 3c, 11/24; 7c, 11/17; 8c, 11/27; 10c, 12/8; 2c, 3/2/88; 5c, 3/23/90; 9c, 10/1/91; 4c, 6c, 3/16/93; 1c, 7/9/96.

For surcharge see No. 573.

Central American and Caribbean University Games A163

Toucan as a participant in various events.

**1990 Litho. *Perf. 12½***

| | | | | |
|---|---|---|---|---|
| 455 | A163 | 15c shown | .30 | .25 |
| 456 | A163 | 20c Torch bearer, vert. | .45 | .25 |
| 457 | A163 | 25c Volleyball | .65 | .25 |
| 458 | A163 | 30c Soccer | .70 | .25 |
| 459 | A163 | 45c Karate | 1.10 | .30 |
| 460 | A163 | 1q Baseball | 2.50 | .70 |
| 461 | A163 | 2q Basketball | 4.50 | 1.50 |
| 462 | A163 | 3q Hurdles | 7.50 | 2.50 |
| | | *Nos. 455-462 (8)* | 17.70 | 6.00 |

Issued: 20c, 8/22; 30c, 3q, 7/10; others, 4/25.

A164

Oct. 20 Revolution, 50th Anniv. A165

A166

Designs: 1q, Student holding book, rifle. 2q, Constitution, city buildings, San Carlos University, social security building.

**1994, Nov. 8 Litho. *Perf. 11½***

| | | | | |
|---|---|---|---|---|
| 463 | A164 | 40c multicolored | .30 | .25 |
| 464 | A165 | 60c multicolored | .50 | .35 |
| 465 | A164 | 1q multicolored | .95 | .65 |
| 466 | A166 | 2q multicolored | 1.75 | 1.25 |
| 467 | A166 | 3q multicolored | 3.00 | 1.75 |
| | | *Nos. 463-467 (5)* | 6.50 | 4.25 |

UNICEF, 50th Anniv. — A167

Designs: 10c, Soldier hugging child, vert. 20c, Children flying on doves.

**1997, May 21 Litho. *Perf. 12½***

| | | | | |
|---|---|---|---|---|
| 468 | A167 | 10c multicolored | .25 | .25 |
| | | ***Perf. 11½x12½*** | | |
| 469 | A167 | 20c multicolored | .25 | .25 |

Landmark Buildings A168

Designs: 50c, Paraninfo University. 1q, Central American Brewery Building, vert.

**1997, Mar. 6 *Perf. 12½***

| | | | | |
|---|---|---|---|---|
| 470 | A168 | 50c multicolored | .30 | .30 |
| 471 | A168 | 1q multicolored | .65 | .65 |

Famous Guatemalans With 1999 Birth Anniversaries A169

Designs: 3q, Francisco Marroquin (b. 1499), first Guatemalan bishop. 4q, Jacinto Rodriguez Diaz (b. 1899), aviator. 8.75q, Miguel Angel Asturias (1899-1974), 1967 Nobel Laureate for Literature. 10q, Cesar Brañas (b. 1899), writer.

**2001, Oct. 9 Litho. *Perf. 12½x11½***

| | | | | |
|---|---|---|---|---|
| 472-475 | A169 | Set of 4 | 20.00 | 10.00 |

Visit of Pope John Paul II and Canonization of St. Peter of San José Betancur (1626-67) — A170

Designs: Nos. 476, 483a, 20c, Saint and churches, vert. Nos. 477, 483b, 25c, Saint and bell, vert. Nos. 478, 483c, 50c, Pope, Saint and church. Nos. 479, 483d, 1q, Saint, painting of nativity, and bell, vert. Nos. 480, 483e, 2q, Pope and Guatemala Archbishop Quezada Toruño. Nos. 481, 483f, 5q, Pope, fountain and church decoration. Nos. 482, 483g, 8.75q, Pope and churches.

**2002, July 16 Litho. *Perf. 12½***

| | | | | |
|---|---|---|---|---|
| 476-482 | A170 | Set of 7 | 13.50 | 6.00 |

**Souvenir Sheet**

***Rouletted 8½***

| | | | | |
|---|---|---|---|---|
| 483 | A170 | Sheet of 7, #a-g | 13.50 | 13.50 |

Universal Postal Union, 125th Anniv. (in 1999) — A171

Designs: 20c, Quetzal, air mail envelopes, globe, flags. 2q, UPU emblem, quetzal, envelopes. 3q, Globe, quetzal, UPU emblem. 5q, Map of Guatemala, globe, envelopes and flags.

**2002, Oct. 31 Litho. *Perf. 12½***
**484-487** A171 Set of 4 6.00 3.00

2001 Ascent of Mt. Everest by Jaime Viñals — A172

**2002, Nov. 22**
**488** A172 3q multi 1.75 .85

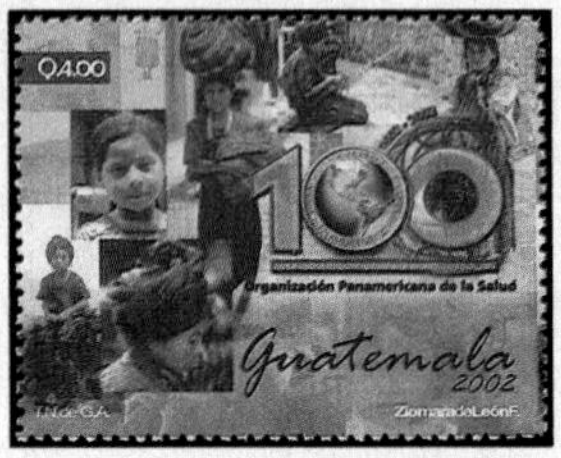

Pan-American Health Organization, Cent. — A173

**2002, Dec. 18**
**489** A173 4q multi 2.25 1.10

St. Josemaría Escrivá de Balaguer (1902-75) A174

Balaguer and: 20c, Farmer. 50c, Fisherman with boatful of fish. 3q, Fisherman, mountain. 10q, Church.

**2003 Litho. *Perf. 12¼***
**490-493** A174 Set of 4 8.00 4.00

Masks for Dances — A175

Mask for: 20c, Dance of the Conquest. 2q, Dance of the Moors and Christians. 3q, Dance of the Deer. 4q, Dance of the Jaguar.
5q, Dance of Paabanc.

**2003, July 9 Litho. *Perf. 12½***
**494-497** A175 Set of 4 6.00 2.75

**Souvenir Sheet**

***Rouletted 8½***

**498** A175 5q multi 3.50 3.50

No. 498 was issued in sheets of 18 and has perf. 12½ margins.

Regional Sanitary Agricultural Organization, 50th Anniv. — A176

Designs: 20c, Banana picker. 1q, Hands in corn. 2q, Cow. 4q, Cultivated field. 5q, Sliced meat. 10q, Eye, map, ear of corn.
3q, Basket of vegetables.

**2003, Dec. 8 Litho. *Perf. 12½***
**499-504** A176 Set of 6 11.00 5.25

**Souvenir Sheet**

***Rouletted 8¼***

**505** A176 3q multi 1.50 .70

Tourist Attractions of Izabal Department A177

Designs: 20c, Punta de Manabique. 50c, Siete Altares. 1q, Las Escobas. 1.50q, View between Barrios and Pichilingo. 2q, Acropolis, Quiriguá. 3q, Livingston on the Río Dulce. No. 512, 4q, Castle of San Felipe. 5q, El Estor. 8.75q, Agua Caliente. 10q, Río Polochic.
No. 516, Quiriguá.

**2004, Jan. 30 *Perf. 12½***
**506-515** A177 Set of 10 18.00 8.00

**Souvenir Sheet**

***Rouletted 6½***

**516** A177 4q multi 2.75 1.25

Elevation to Cardinal of Archbishop Rodolfo Quezada Toruño A178

Designs: 20c, Cardinal, cathedral. 25c, Cardinal holding crucifix, cathedral. 50c, Cardinal wearing biretta kneeling before Pope John Paul II. 1q, Cardinal wearing zucchetto kneeling before Pope. 2q, Cardinal holding biretta, wearing zucchetto. No. 522, 3q, Cardinal wearing zucchetto. 4q, Cardinal wearing miter. 5q, Cardinal kissing hand of Pope. 8.75q, Cardinal and bishops. 10q, Coat of arms
No. 527, 3q, Statue of Virgin Mary.

**2004, Nov. 5 Litho. *Perf. 12½***
**517-526** A178 Set of 10 17.00 8.50

**Souvenir Sheet**

***Rouletted 6½***

**527** A178 3q multi 1.50 .75

America Issue, Flora and Fauna — A179

Designs: 50c, Sarcoranphus papa. 3q, Heliconia collinsiana, vert. 5q, Felis concolor. 10q, Heliconius petiveranus.
12q, Tapirus vairdii.

**2005, Apr. 29 Litho. *Perf. 12½***
**528** A179 50c multi .25 .25
**529** A179 3q multi 1.50 1.50
**530** A179 5q multi 2.75 2.75
**531** A179 10q multi 5.50 5.50

**Souvenir Sheet**

***Rouletted 6½***

**532** A179 12q multi 6.50 6.50

Diplomatic Relations Between Guatemala and Japan A180

Flags of Guatemala and Japan and: 1q, Child, flowing well pipe, San Pedro La Laguna. 8q, Child, hospital, Puerto Barrios.
14q, Mt. Fuji.

**2005, July 29 Litho. *Perf. 12½***
**533-534** A180 Set of 2 4.50 4.50

**Souvenir Sheet**

***Rouletted 8½***

**535** A180 14q multi 7.00 7.00

Majolica A181

Designs: 1q, Incense burner. 2q, Jars. 6.50q, Bowls. 8q, Lantern.
12q, Covered jar and sugar bowls.

**2005, Oct. 4 *Perf. 12½***
**536-539** A181 Set of 4 8.50 8.50

**Souvenir Sheet**

***Rouletted 8½***

**540** A181 12q multi 6.00 6.00

Rotary International, Cent. — A182

Designs: 2q, Emblem, handshake, Western Hemisphere. 6.50q, Emblem, Polio Plus emblem.
8q, Emblem.

**2005, Nov. 15 *Perf. 12½***
**541-542** A182 Set of 2 4.00 4.00

**Souvenir Sheet**

***Rouletted 8½***

**543** A182 8q multi 4.00 4.00

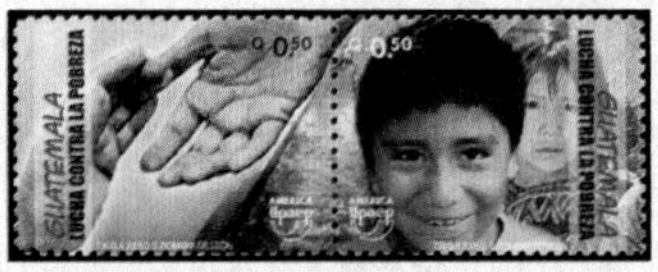

America Issue, Fight Against Poverty — A183

No. 544, 50c: a, Open hands. b, Two children
No. 545, 5q: a, Clasped hands. b, Two children, diff.

**2006, Feb. 22 *Perf. 12½***

**Horiz. Pairs, #a-b**

**544-545** A183 Set of 2 5.50 5.50

Prof. José Joaquín Pardo, Historian, Cent. of Birth — A184

**2006, Feb. 28**
**546** A184 3q multi 1.50 1.50

Churches A185

Designs: 50c, Santa Cruz Hermitage, Antigua Guatemala. 1q, San Jacinto Church, Salcajá. 2q, San Andres Xecul Church, Totonicapan, vert. 3q, El Calvario Church, Chichicastenango, vert. 4q, San Cristobal Acasaguastlán, El Progreso, vert. 5q, Antigua Cathedral, Antigua Guatemala. 8q, San Pedro Church and Hospital, Antigua Guatemala. 10q, San Pedro Las Huertas Church, Antigua Guatemala.
14q, Metropolitan Cathedral, Guatemala City.

**2006, Mar. 15 *Perf. 12½***
**547-554** A185 Set of 8 16.00 16.00

**Souvenir Sheet**

***Rouletted 8½***

**555** A185 14q multi 7.00 7.00

Christmas A186

Various ceramic creche figurines: 20c, 6.50q.

**2006, Nov. 27 Litho. *Perf. 12½***
**556-557** A186 Set of 2 3.25 3.25

Coffee Growing Regions A187

Designs: 50c, Acatenango. 1q, Antigua. 2q, Atitlán. 6.50q, Cobán. 8q, Fraijanes. 10q, Huehue.
No. 564: a, 5q, Oriente. b, 20q, San Marcos.

**2006, Nov. 29 *Perf. 12½***
**558-563** A187 Set of 6 14.00 14.00

**Souvenir Sheet**

***Rouletted 6½***

**564** A187 Sheet of 2, #a-b 12.50 12.50

America Issue, Energy Conservation A188

Designs: 3q, Oil wells, gasoline pump nozzle. 10q, Light switch, solar panels.

**2006, Dec. 7 *Perf. 12½***
**565-566** A188 Set of 2 6.50 6.50

Diplomatic Relations Between Guatemala and Brazil, Cent. — A189

No. 567: a, Baile de la Conquista dancers. b, Maracatu dancers.

**2006, Dec. 12**
**567** A189 4q Horiz. pair, #a-b 4.00 4.00

**Nos. 453, C850-C852, C863, C865, C870-C871 Surcharged**

**Methods and Perfs As Before**

**2007, Jan. 23**

| | | | | | |
|---|---|---|---|---|---|
| **568** | AP186 | 50c on 40c #C850 | .25 | .25 |
| **569** | AP188 | 50c on 40c #C863 | .25 | .25 |
| **570** | AP186 | 1q on 60c #C851 | .40 | .40 |
| **571** | AP191 | 2q on 80c #C871 | .95 | .95 |
| **572** | AP188 | 3q on 60c #C865 | 1.50 | 1.50 |

**573** A162 5q on 9c #453 3.00 3.00
**574** AP186 8q on 80c #C852 4.00 4.00
**575** AP191 10q on 60c #C870 4.75 4.75
*Nos. 568-575 (8)* 15.10 15.10

"Aereo" on Nos. 568-572, 574-575 is not obliterated.

Year of Transparency (in 2006) — A190

Designs: 20c, Hand holding ball with map of Guatemala. 6.50q, Magnifying glass, fingerprint (45x25mm)

**2007, Jan. 23 Litho. *Perf. 12½***
**576-577** A190 Set of 2 3.25 3.25

Dated 2006.

Guatemala Philatelic Association, 75th Anniv. — A191

Designs: 1q, Guatemala #21. 3q, Guatemala #22. 6.50q, Guatemala #23. 8q, Guatemala #24.
25q, Guatemala #25.

**2007, July 19 Litho. *Perf. 12½***
**578-581** A191 Set of 4 9.00 9.00

**Souvenir Sheet**

**582** A191 25q multi 12.00 12.00

Diplomatic Relations Between Guatemala and Uruguay, Cent. — A192

No. 583: a, Santa Catarina Arch, Antigua, Guatemala. b, City gate, Colonia del Sacramento, Uruguay.

**2007, Sept. 7**
**583** A192 4q Horiz. pair, #a-b 4.00 4.00

See Uruguay No. 2205.

America Issue, Education For All — A193

No. 584 — Stick figure children and: a, Blue panel. b, Red panel. c, Yellow orange panel. d, Green panel.

**2007, Oct. 25**
**584** A193 4q Block of 4, #a-d 8.00 8.00

Christmas A194

Scouting, Cent. A195

Creche figures: 20c, Holy Family. 6.50q, Magi, horiz. (36x31mm).

**2007, Dec. 4**
**585-586** A194 Set of 2 3.25 3.25

**2007, Dec. 5**
**587** A195 20c multi .25 .25

Institute For Municipal Development, 50th Anniv. (in 2007) — A196

**2008, Jan. 30**
**588** A196 3q multi 1.50 1.50

Dated 2007.

Monsignor Juan Gerardi Conedera (1922-98) A197

**2008, Apr. 25 Litho. *Perf. 12½***
**589** A197 8q multi 2.25 2.25

19th Cent. Defensive Bulwarks of Guatemala City — A198

No. 590: a, San Rafael de Matamoros. b, San José de Buena Vista.

**2008, June 27**
**590** A198 1q Horiz. pair, #a-b .55 .55

2008 Summer Olympics, Beijing — A199

Birds — A200

**2008, Oct. 17 Litho. *Perf. 12½***
**591** A199 6.50q multi 1.75 1.75

**2008, Nov. 14**

Designs: 50c, Trogon violaceus braccatus. 1q, Amarilia beryllina viola. 2q, Turdus rufitorques. 4q, Glaucidium brasilianum ridgwayi. 20q, Brotogeris jugularis.

**592-595** A200 Set of 4 2.10 2.10

**Souvenir Sheet**

**596** A200 20q multi 6.25 6.25

Christmas — A201

Needlepoint: 20c, Flower. 8q, Christmas tree.

**2008, Dec. 2 Litho.**
**597-598** A201 Set of 2 2.25 2.25

Franciscan Order, 800th Anniv. (in 2009) — A202

**2008, Dec. 16**
**599** A202 3q multi .85 .85

Consecration of Basilica of Esquipulus, 250th Anniv. A203

**2009, Jan. 3**
**600** A203 50c multi .25 .25

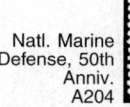

Natl. Marine Defense, 50th Anniv. A204

**2009, Jan. 12**
**601** A204 1q multi .30 .30

America Issue, National Festivals — A205

Designs: 50c, Dancers, Comalapa. 2q, All Saints Day Festival, Santiago Sacatepequez. 3q, Dancers and marimba players. 5q, Dancers.
8q, Cofrades y Capitanas.

**2009, Feb. 6**
**602-605** A205 Set of 4 2.75 2.75

**Souvenir Sheet**

**606** A205 8q multi 2.25 2.25

Native Costumes A206

Designs: 50c, San Juan Atitán man. 1q, San Juan Sacatepéquez woman. 2q, Tamahú woman. 3q, San Rafael Petzal woman. 4q, Totonicapán man. 5q, Patzicia woman. 8q, San Pedro San Marcos woman.
10q, San Juan Cotzal man and woman.

**2009, Apr. 14 Litho. *Perf. 12½***
**607-613** A206 Set of 7 6.50 6.50

**Souvenir Sheet**

**614** A206 10q multi 2.75 2.75

See Nos. 645-648.

Marimbas A207

Designs: 3q, Gourd marimba. 4q, 18th cent. marimba. 5q, Double marimba. 8q, Concert marimba. 10q, Man playing marimba.

**2009, Oct. 30**
**615-619** A207 Set of 5 8.25 8.25

Louis Braille (1809-52), Educator of the Blind — A208

**2009, Nov. 13 Litho. & Embossed**
**620** A208 1q multi .30 .30

Christmas A209

Beaded ornaments: 20c, Spheres. 50c, Reindeer. 1q, Angels. 6.50q, Star.

**2009, Dec. 4 Litho.**
**621-624** A209 Set of 4 2.40 2.40

Battle of La Arada, 150th Anniv. (in 2011) — A210

No. 625: a, Sword and arms. b, Pres. Rafael Carrera.
10q, Carrera, vert.

**2010, Feb. 12 *Perf. 12½***
**625** A210 5q Horiz. pair, #a-b 2.60 2.60

**Souvenir Sheet**

**626** A210 10q multi 2.60 2.60

America Issue A211

Traditional toys and games: 50c, Capitucho. 1q, Barillete (kite). 6.50q, Yo-yo. 8q, Trompo (top).

**2010, Mar. 17**
**627-630** A211 Set of 4 4.25 4.25

Dated 2009.

José Ernesto Monzón (1917-2003), Musician — A212

**2010, Aug. 6 Litho. *Perf. 12½***

**631** A212 2q multi .55 .55

Tourist Sites in Chiquimula Department — A213

No. 632: a, Ipala Volcano. b, Ipala Lake.

**2010, Sept. 11**

**632** A213 8q Vert. pair, #a-b 4.25 4.25

Christmas — A214

No. 633: a, Joseph. b, Infant Jesus and Star of Bethlehem. c, Mary.

**2010, Dec. 2**

**633** A214 3q Horiz. strip of 3, #a-c 2.40 2.40

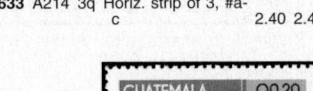

Textile Art by Priscilla Bianchi A215

Various designs.

**2010, Dec. 15 *Perf. 12½***

**634** A215 20c multi .25 .25
**635** A215 50c multi .25 .25
**636** A215 1q multi .25 .25
**637** A215 2q multi .50 .50
**638** A215 3q multi .75 .75
**639** A215 4q multi 1.00 1.00
**640** A215 5q multi 1.25 1.25
**641** A215 6.50q multi 1.75 1.75
**642** A215 8q multi 2.00 2.00
**643** A215 10q multi 2.50 2.50
*Nos. 634-643 (10)* 10.50 10.50

Postal Union of the Americas, Spain and Portugal (UPAEP), Cent. — A216

**2011, Mar. 23 Litho. *Perf. 12½***

**644** A216 2q multi .55 .55

**Native Costumes Type of 2009**

Designs: 50c, San Mateo Ixtatán woman. 5q, Almolonga man. 6.50q, Tecpán woman. 10q, Palín man and women.

**2011, May 17**

**645-647** A206 Set of 3 3.25 3.25

**Souvenir Sheet**

**648** A206 10q multi 2.60 2.60

National Journalism Library, 50th Anniv. — A217

**2011, May 17 Litho. *Perf. 12½***

**649** A217 5q multi 1.25 1.25

Phragmipedium Humboltii — A218

**2011, June 29**

**650** A218 5q multi 1.25 1.25

Alexander von Humboldt (1769-1859), naturalist.

America Issue, National Symbols A219

Designs: 20c, Ceiba tree. 10q, White nun orchids.

**2011, Sept. 14 Litho. *Perf. 12½***

**651-652** A219 Set of 2 2.60 2.60

Republic of China, Cent. — A220

**2011, Oct. 3**

**653** A220 2q multi .50 .50

Civil Aviation in Guatemala, Cent. — A221

**2011, Dec. 8**

**654** A221 8q multi 2.10 2.10

Christmas A222

Creche scenes from: 4q, Señora de las Misericordias Church. 10q, Merced Parish Church.

**2011, Dec. 9**

**655-656** A222 Set of 2 3.75 3.75

José Joaquín Palma (1844-1911), Poet — A223

**2011, Dec. 23**

**657** A223 1q multi .25 .25

---

## SEMI-POSTAL STAMPS

Regular Issues of 1935-36 Surcharged in Blue or Red similar to illustration

**1937, Mar. 15 Unwmk. *Perf. 12½***

**B1** A102 1c + 1c brn & crim .75 *1.00*
**B2** A103 3c + 1c rose car & pck grn .75 *1.00*
**B3** A103 3c + 1c red org & pck grn .75 *1.00*
**B4** A106 5c + 1c bl & dk brn (R) .75 *1.00*
*Nos. B1-B4 (4)* 3.00 *4.00*

1st Phil. Exhib. held in Guatemala, Mar. 15-20.

**Catalogue values for unused stamps in this section, from this point to the end of the section, are for Never Hinged items.**

**Type of Regular Issue, 1956**

Designs: 5c+15c, Nurse, Patient and Red Cross Flag. 15c+50c, Red Cross, telephone and "5110." 25c+50c, Globe and Red Cross.

**1956, June 19 Engr. *Perf. 13x12½***

**B5** A148 5c + 15c ultra & red 1.00 *1.40*
*a.* Imperf., pair 75.00
**B6** A148 15c + 50c dk vio & red 2.25 *2.75*
**B7** A148 25c + 50c bluish blk & car 2.25 *2.75*
*Nos. B5-B7 (3)* 5.50 *6.90*

The surtax was for the Red Cross.

Jesus and Esquipulas Cathedral — SP1

**1957, Oct. 29 *Perf. 13***

**B8** SP1 1½c + ½c blk & brn .55 .25

The surtax was for the Esquipulas highway. See Nos. CB12-CB14.

**Type of Air Post Semi-Postal Stamps and**

Arms — SP2

3c+3c, Wounded man, Battle of Solferino.

**1960, Apr. 9 Photo. *Perf. 13½x14***

**Cross in Rose Red**

**B9** SP2 1c + 1c red brn & bl .30 .25
**B10** SPAP2 3c + 3c lil, bl & pink .30 .25
**B11** SP2 4c + 4c blk & bl .30 .25
*Nos. B9-B11 (3)* .90 .75

Cent. (in 1959) of the Red Cross idea. The surtax went to the Red Cross. Exist imperf. See Nos. CB15-CB21.

---

## AIR POST STAMPS

Surcharged in Red on No. 229

**1929, May 20 Unwmk. *Perf. 12½***

**C1** A64 3c on 15p blk 1.10 *1.40*
**C2** A64 5c on 15p blk .55 .45
**C3** A64 15c on 15p blk 1.50 .45
*a.* Double surcharge (G & R) 100.00
**C4** A64 20c on 15p blk 2.25 2.25
*a.* Inverted surcharge 100.00
*b.* Double surcharge 100.00

Surcharged in Red on No. 216

**1929, May 20 *Perf. 14***

**C5** A64 5c on 15p black 3.25 2.25
*Nos. C1-C5 (5)* 8.65 6.80

Surcharged in Black on No. 218

**1929, Oct. 9**

**C6** A75 3c on 2.50p dk vio 1.00 1.00

Airplane and Mt. Agua AP3

**1930, June 4 Litho. *Perf. 12½***

**C7** AP3 6c rose red *4.50* *4.50*
*a.* Double impression 25.00 25.00
*b.* Imperf., pair 350.00

For overprint see No. C14.

Nos. 227, 229 Surcharged in Black or Red

**1930, Dec. 9 *Perf. 12½***

**C8** A57 1c on 3p grn (Bk) .40 .40
*a.* Double surcharge 100.00
**C9** A57 2c on 3p grn (Bk) 1.10 *1.50*
**C10** A57 3c on 3p grn (R) 1.10 *1.50*
**C11** A57 4c on 3p grn (R) 1.10 *1.50*
**C12** A64 10c on 15p blk (R) 5.00 *5.00*
*a.* Double surcharge 125.00
*Nos. C8-C12 (5)* 8.70 *9.90*

No. 237 Overprinted

**1931, May 19** *Perf. 14*

| | | | | |
|---|---|---|---|---|
| **C13** | A81 | 4c orange | .40 | .30 |
| *a.* | | Double overprint | 40.00 | *50.00* |

**No. C7 Overprinted**

*Perf. 12½*

| | | | | |
|---|---|---|---|---|
| **C14** | AP3 | 6c rose red | *2.00* | *2.00* |
| *a.* | | On No. C7a | 30.00 | 30.00 |
| *b.* | | Inverted overprint | 7.00 | *7.00* |

Nos. 240, 242 Overprinted in Red

**1931, Oct. 21** *Perf. 14*

| | | | | |
|---|---|---|---|---|
| **C15** | A36 | 15c ultra | 2.00 | .25 |
| *a.* | | Double overprint | 125.00 | 125.00 |
| **C16** | A76 | 30c green | 3.00 | .95 |
| *a.* | | Double overprint | 75.00 | 75.00 |

Nos. 235-236 Overprinted in Red or Green

**1931, Dec. 5**

| | | | | |
|---|---|---|---|---|
| **C17** | A79 | 2c dp bl (R) | 2.50 | *3.00* |
| **C18** | A80 | 3c dk vio (G) | 2.50 | *3.00* |

No. 240 Overprinted in Red

| | | | | |
|---|---|---|---|---|
| **C19** | A36 | 15c ultra | 2.75 | *3.00* |

Nos. C17-C19 were issued in connection with the 1st postal flight from Barrios to Miami.

No. 224 Surcharged in Red

**1932-33** *Perf. 12½*

| | | | | |
|---|---|---|---|---|
| **C20** | A74 | 2c on 1.50p dk bl | .80 | .55 |

Nos. 227, 229 Surcharged in Violet, Red or Blue

| | | | | |
|---|---|---|---|---|
| **C21** | A57 | 3c on 3p grn (V) | .80 | .25 |
| *a.* | | Inverted surcharge | 45.00 | 45.00 |
| *b.* | | Vert. pair, imperf. horiz. | 900.00 | |
| **C22** | A57 | 3c on 3p grn (R) | .80 | .25 |
| **C23** | A64 | 10c on 15p blk (R) | 7.75 | 6.25 |
| *b.* | | First "I" of "Interior" missing | 10.00 | 10.00 |
| **C24** | A64 | 15c on 15p blk (Bl) | 9.00 | 8.50 |
| *a.* | | First "I" of "Interior" missing | 15.00 | 15.00 |
| | | *Nos. C20-C24 (5)* | 19.15 | 15.80 |

Issued: #C22, 1/1/33; others, 2/11/32.

No. 237 Overprinted in Green

**1933, Jan. 1** *Perf. 14*

| | | | | |
|---|---|---|---|---|
| **C25** | A81 | 4c orange | .40 | .35 |
| *a.* | | Double overprint | 40.00 | 40.00 |

Nos. 235, 238 and 240 Overprinted in Red or Black

**1934, Aug. 7**

| | | | | |
|---|---|---|---|---|
| **C26** | A82 | 5c dk car (Bk) | 1.50 | .25 |
| **C27** | A36 | 15c ultra (R) | 1.50 | .25 |

Overprinted in Red

| | | | | |
|---|---|---|---|---|
| **C28** | A79 | 2c deep blue | .55 | .25 |

View of Port Barrios — AP7

Designs: 15c, Tomb of Barrios. 30c, Equestrian Statue of Barrios.

**1935, July 19** **Photo.** *Perf. 12½*

| | | | | |
|---|---|---|---|---|
| **C29** | AP7 | 10c yel brn & pck grn | 6.00 | 4.50 |
| **C30** | AP7 | 15c gray & brn | 1.50 | *1.75* |
| **C31** | AP7 | 30c car rose & bl vio | 1.50 | 1.25 |
| | | *Nos. C29-C31 (3)* | 9.00 | 7.50 |

Birth cent. of Gen. Justo Rufino Barrios.

Lake Amatitlán AP10

Designs: Nos. C36, C37, C45, C46. Different views of Lake Amatitlan. 3c, Port Barrios. No. C34, C35, Ruins of Fort San Felipe. 10c, Port Livingston. No. C39, C40, Port San Jose. No. C41, C42, View of Atitlan. No. C43, C44, Aurora Airport.

**Overprinted with Quetzal in Green**

**1935-37** **Size: 37x17mm**

| | | | | |
|---|---|---|---|---|
| **C32** | AP10 | 2c org brn | .25 | .25 |
| **C33** | AP10 | 3c blue | .25 | .25 |
| **C34** | AP10 | 4c black | .25 | .25 |
| **C35** | AP10 | 4c ultra ('37) | .25 | .25 |
| **C36** | AP10 | 6c yel grn | .25 | .25 |
| **C37** | AP10 | 6c blk vio ('37) | 4.00 | .25 |
| **C38** | AP10 | 10c claret | .50 | .25 |
| **C39** | AP10 | 15c red org | .65 | .40 |
| **C40** | AP10 | 15c yel grn ('37) | .65 | .65 |
| **C41** | AP10 | 30c olive grn | 6.00 | 6.50 |
| **C42** | AP10 | 30c ol bis ('37) | .75 | .50 |
| **C43** | AP10 | 50c rose vio | 17.50 | 15.00 |
| **C44** | AP10 | 50c Prus bl ('36) | 4.00 | 3.00 |
| **C45** | AP10 | 1q scarlet | 17.50 | 20.00 |
| **C46** | AP10 | 1q car ('36) | 4.50 | 3.00 |
| | | *Nos. C32-C46 (15)* | 57.30 | 50.80 |

Issue dates follow No. C69.

For overprints and surcharges see Nos. C70-C79, CB1-CB2.

Central Park, Antigua AP11

Designs: 1c, Guatemala City. 2c, Central Park, Guatemala City. 3c, Monastery. Nos. C50-C51, Mouth of Dulce River. Nos. C52-C53, Plaza Barrios. Nos. C54-C55, Los Proceres Monument. No. C56, Central Park, Antigua. No. C57, Dulce River. Nos. C58-C59, Quezaltenango. Nos. C60-C61, Ruins at Antigua. Nos. C62-C63, Dock at Port Barrios. Nos. C64-C65, Port San Jose. Nos. C66-C67, Aurora Airport. 2.50q, Island off Atlantic Coast. 5q, Atlantic Coast view.

**Overprinted with Quetzal in Green**

**Size: 34x15mm**

| | | | | |
|---|---|---|---|---|
| **C47** | AP11 | 1c yel brn | .25 | .25 |
| **C48** | AP11 | 2c vermilion | .25 | .25 |
| **C49** | AP11 | 3c magenta | .50 | .25 |
| **C50** | AP11 | 4c org yel ('36) | 1.75 | 1.40 |
| **C51** | AP11 | 4c car lake ('37) | 1.00 | .75 |
| **C52** | AP11 | 5c dl bl | .25 | .25 |
| **C53** | AP11 | 5c org ('37) | .25 | .25 |
| **C54** | AP11 | 10c red brn | .50 | .35 |
| **C55** | AP11 | 10c ol grn ('37) | .50 | .30 |
| **C56** | AP11 | 15c rose red | .25 | .25 |
| **C57** | AP11 | 15c ver ('37) | .25 | .25 |
| **C58** | AP11 | 20c ultra | 2.50 | *3.00* |
| **C59** | AP11 | 20c dp cl ('37) | .50 | .25 |
| **C60** | AP11 | 25c gray blk | 3.00 | *3.50* |
| **C61** | AP11 | 25c bl grn ('37) | .45 | .25 |
| *a.* | | Quetzal omitted | | *1,100.* |
| **C62** | AP11 | 30c yel grn | 1.50 | 1.50 |
| **C63** | AP11 | 30c rose red ('37) | 1.00 | .25 |
| **C64** | AP11 | 50c car rose | 7.00 | *8.00* |
| **C65** | AP11 | 50c pur ('36) | 6.50 | *7.50* |
| **C66** | AP11 | 1q dk bl | 22.50 | *25.00* |
| **C67** | AP11 | 1q dk grn ('36) | 7.50 | 7.50 |

**Size: 46x20mm**

| | | | | |
|---|---|---|---|---|
| **C68** | AP11 | 2.50q rose red & ol grn ('36) | 5.00 | 3.00 |
| **C69** | AP11 | 5q org & ind ('36) | 7.00 | 4.00 |
| *a.* | | Quetzal omitted | 1,500. | 1,250. |
| | | *Nos. C47-C69 (23)* | 70.20 | *68.30* |

Issued: #C32-C69, 11/1/35; 10/1/36; 1/1/37.

Value for No. C61a is for a sound stamp.

For overprints and surcharges see Nos. C80-C91, CB3-CB4.

**Types of Air Post Stamps, 1935 Overprinted with Airplane in Blue**

2c, Quezaltenango. 3c, Lake Atitian. 4c, Progressive Colony, Lake Amatitlan. 6c, Carmen Hill. 10c, Relief map. 15c, National University. 30c, Espana Plaza. 50c, Police Station, Aurora Airport. 75c, Amphitheater, Aurora Airport. 1q, Aurora Airport.

**1937, May 18**

**Center in Brown Black**

| | | | | |
|---|---|---|---|---|
| **C70** | AP10 | 2c carmine | .25 | .25 |
| **C71** | AP10 | 3c blue | 1.00 | *1.25* |
| **C72** | AP10 | 4c citron | .25 | .25 |
| **C73** | AP10 | 6c yel grn | .35 | .25 |
| **C74** | AP10 | 10c red vio | 2.00 | *2.25* |
| **C75** | AP10 | 15c orange | 1.50 | 1.00 |
| **C76** | AP10 | 30c ol grn | 3.75 | 3.00 |
| **C77** | AP10 | 50c pck bl | 5.00 | 4.25 |
| **C78** | AP10 | 75c dk vio | 10.00 | *11.00* |
| **C79** | AP10 | 1q dp rose | 11.00 | *12.00* |
| | | *Nos. C70-C79 (10)* | 35.10 | *35.50* |

**Overprinted with Airplane in Black**

1c, 7th Ave., Guatemala City. 2c, Los Proceres Monument. 3c, Natl. Printing Office. 5c, Natl. Museum. 10c, Central Park. 15c, Escuintla. 20c, Motorcycle Police. 25c, Slaughterhouse, Escuintla. 30c, Exhibition Hall. 50c, Barrios Plaza. 1q, Polytechnic School. 1.50q, Aurora Airport.

**Size: 33x15mm**

| | | | | |
|---|---|---|---|---|
| **C80** | AP11 | 1c yel brn & brt bl | .25 | .25 |
| **C81** | AP11 | 2c crim & dp vio | .25 | .25 |
| **C82** | AP11 | 3c red vio & red brn | .50 | .50 |
| **C83** | AP11 | 5c pck grn & cop red | 4.00 | 3.00 |
| **C84** | AP11 | 10c car & grn | 1.25 | 1.00 |
| **C85** | AP11 | 15c rose & dl ol grn | .50 | .25 |
| **C86** | AP11 | 20c ultra & blk | 3.00 | 1.75 |
| **C87** | AP11 | 25c dk gray & scar | 2.50 | 2.50 |
| **C88** | AP11 | 30c grn & dp vio | 1.25 | 1.25 |
| **C89** | AP11 | 50c magenta & ultra | 10.00 | *12.00* |

**Size: 42x19mm**

| | | | | |
|---|---|---|---|---|
| **C90** | AP11 | 1q ol grn & red vio | 10.00 | *12.00* |
| **C91** | AP11 | 1.50q scar & ol brn | 10.00 | *12.00* |
| | | *Nos. C80-C91 (12)* | 43.50 | *46.75* |

Second term of President Ubico.

Souvenir Sheet

AP12

**1938, Jan. 10** *Perf. 12½*

| | | | | |
|---|---|---|---|---|
| **C92** | AP12 | Sheet of 4 | 8.00 | 8.00 |
| *a.* | | 15c George Washington | 1.50 | 1.50 |
| *b.* | | 4c Franklin D. Roosevelt | 1.50 | 1.50 |
| *c.* | | 4c Map of the Americas | 1.50 | 1.50 |
| *d.* | | 15c Pan American Union Building, Washington, DC | .75 | .75 |

150th anniv. of US Constitution.

President Arosemena, Panama AP13

Flags of Central American Countries — AP19

Designs: 2c, Pres. Cortés Castro, Costa Rica. 3c, Pres. Somoza, Nicaragua. 4c, Pres. Carias Andino, Honduras. 5c, Pres. Martinez, El Salvador. 10c, Pres. Ubico, Guatemala.

**1938, Nov. 20** **Unwmk.**

| | | | | |
|---|---|---|---|---|
| **C93** | AP13 | 1c org & ol brn | .25 | .25 |
| **C94** | AP13 | 2c scar, pale pink & sl grn | .30 | .25 |
| **C95** | AP13 | 3c grn, buff & ol brn | .40 | .30 |
| **C96** | AP13 | 4c dk cl, pale lil & brn | .55 | .35 |
| **C97** | AP13 | 5c bis, pale grn & ol brn | .50 | *.60* |
| **C98** | AP13 | 10c ultra, pale bl & brn | 1.00 | *1.25* |
| | | *Nos. C93-C98 (6)* | 3.00 | *3.00* |

**Souvenir Sheet**

| | | | | |
|---|---|---|---|---|
| **C99** | AP19 | Sheet of 6 | 8.00 | 8.00 |
| *a.* | | 1c Guatemala | .80 | .80 |
| *b.* | | 2c El Salvador | .80 | .80 |
| *c.* | | 3c Honduras | 1.10 | 1.10 |
| *d.* | | 4c Nicaragua | 1.40 | 1.40 |
| *e.* | | 5c Costa Rica | 1.40 | 1.40 |
| *f.* | | 10c Panama | 2.40 | 2.40 |

1st Central American Phil. Exhib., Guatemala City, Nov. 20-27.

For overprints see Nos. CO1-CO7.

La Merced Church, Antigua AP20

Designs: 2c, Ruins of Christ School, Antigua. 3c, Aurora Airport. 4c, Drill ground, Guatemala City. 5c, Cavalry barracks. 6c, Palace of Justice. 10c, Customhouse, San José. 15c, Communications Building, Retalhuleu. 30c, Municipal Theater, Quezaltenango. 50c, Customhouse, Retalhuleu. 1q, Departmental Building.

**Inscribed "Aéreo Interior" Overprinted with Quetzal in Green**

**1939, Feb. 14**

| | | | | |
|---|---|---|---|---|
| **C100** | AP20 | 1c ol bis & chnt | .25 | .25 |
| **C101** | AP20 | 2c rose red & sl grn | .25 | .25 |
| **C102** | AP20 | 3c dl bl & bis | .25 | .25 |
| **C103** | AP20 | 4c rose pink & yel grn | .25 | .25 |
| **C104** | AP20 | 5c brn lake & brt ultra | .30 | .25 |
| **C105** | AP20 | 6c org & gray brn | .35 | .25 |
| **C106** | AP20 | 10c bis brn & gray blk | .50 | .25 |
| **C107** | AP20 | 15c dl vio & blk | .75 | .25 |
| **C108** | AP20 | 30c dp bl & dk car | 1.10 | .25 |
| **C109** | AP20 | 50c org & brt vio | 1.50 | .40 |
| *a.* | | Quetzal omitted | | *1,750.* |
| **C110** | AP20 | 1q yel grn & brt ultra | 2.50 | 1.25 |
| | | *Nos. C100-C110 (11)* | 8.00 | 3.90 |

See Nos. C111-C122. For overprint and surcharge see No. C124, C132.

**1939, Feb. 14**

Designs: 1c, Mayan Altar, Aurora Park. 2c, Sanitation Building. 3c, Lake Amatitlan. 4c, Lake Atitlan. 5c, Tamazulapa River bridge. 10c, Los proceres Monument. 15c, Palace of Captains General. 20c, Church on Carmen Hill. 25c, Barrios Park. 30c, Mayan Altar. 50c, Charles III fountain. 1q, View of Antigua.

**Inscribed "Aéreo Internacional" or "Aérea Exterior"**

**Overprinted with Quetzal in Green**

| | | | | |
|---|---|---|---|---|
| **C111** | AP20 | 1c ol grn & gldn brn | .25 | .25 |
| **C112** | AP20 | 2c lt grn & blk | .30 | .25 |
| **C113** | AP20 | 3c ultra & cob bl | .25 | .25 |
| **C114** | AP20 | 4c org brn & yel grn | .25 | .25 |
| **C115** | AP20 | 5c sage grn & red org | .35 | .25 |
| **C116** | AP20 | 10c lake & sl blk | 1.75 | .25 |
| **C117** | AP20 | 15c ultra & brt rose | 1.75 | .25 |
| **C118** | AP20 | 20c yel grn & ap grn | .60 | .25 |
| **C119** | AP20 | 25c dl vio & lt ol grn | .60 | .25 |
| **C120** | AP20 | 30c dl rose & blk | .80 | .25 |
| **C121** | AP20 | 50c scar & brt yel | 1.50 | .25 |
| **C122** | AP20 | 1q org & yel grn | 2.50 | .35 |
| | | *Nos. C111-C122 (12)* | 10.90 | 3.10 |

No. 240 Overprinted in Carmine

**1940, Apr. 14** ***Perf. 14***

**C123** A36 15c ultra .60 .25

Pan American Union, 50th anniversary.

No. C112 Overprinted in Carmine

**1941, Dec. 2** ***Perf. 12½***

**C124** AP20 2c lt grn & blk .40 .25

Second Pan American Health Day.

San Carlos University, Antigua AP21

**1943, June 25** **Engr.** ***Perf. 11***

**C125** AP21 15c dk red brn .55 .25
*a.* Imperf., pair 100.00

Don Pedro de Alvarado AP22

Type I — Diagonal shading lines running from lower left to upper right at inner edges of commemorative tablet.

Type II — Additional diagonal shading lines running from upper left to lower right added throughout tablet, resulting in crosshatched lines at inner edges.

**1943, Mar. 10** **Unwmk.** ***Perf. 11½***

**C126** AP22 15c dp ultra (II) .55 .25
*a.* Type I 25.00 17.50

400th anniv. of the founding of Antigua.

National Police Building AP23

**1943, Aug. 3** ***Perf. 11***

**C127** AP23 10c dp rose vio .35 .25

**Allegory of Revolution Type**

**1945, Apr. 27** **Engr.**

| | | | | |
|---|---|---|---|---|
| **C128** | A129 | 5c dp rose | .50 | .25 |
| **C129** | A129 | 6c dk bl grn | .50 | .25 |
| *a.* | | Imperf., pair | 110.00 | |
| **C130** | A129 | 10c violet | .50 | .25 |
| **C131** | A129 | 15c aqua | .50 | .25 |
| | | *Nos. C128-C131 (4)* | 2.00 | 1.00 |

No. C113 Surcharged in Red

**1945, July 25** ***Perf. 12½***

**C132** AP20 2½c on 3c *5.00 5.00*

The 1945 Book Fair.

**Type of 1944 Overprinted in Carmine**

**1945, Aug.** **Engr.** ***Perf. 11***

**C133** A127 5c rose car .30 .25
*a.* Triple ovpt., one inverted 50.00 25.00
*b.* Double ovpt., one inverted 65.00

See Nos. C137A-C139.

**José Milla y Vidaurre Type**

**1945**

**C134** A131 7½c sepia 1.10 1.00
**C134A** A131 7½c dark blue .60 .30

Issued: #C134, Sept. 28; #C134A, Dec. 6.
For overprint see No. C230.

**Torch Type**

**1945, Oct. 19**

**C135** A130 5c brt red vio .40 .25

**Souvenir Sheet**

***Imperf***

**C136** A130 Sheet of 2 5.00 4.00
*a.* 5c bright red violet .40 .40

1st anniv. of the Revolution of Oct. 20, 1944.
See Nos. C147-C150.

**Catalogue values for unused stamps in this section, from this point to the end of the section, are for Never Hinged items.**

**Payo Enriquez de Rivera Type**

**1946, Jan. 22** **Unwmk.** ***Perf. 11***

**C137** A132 5c rose pink .50 .25

See Nos. C269, C311-C315.

**Palace Type of 1944**

**1946-47**

| | | | | |
|---|---|---|---|---|
| **C137A** | A127 | 5c rose car ('47) | .55 | .25 |
| **C138** | A127 | 10c deep lilac | .25 | .25 |
| *a.* | | Imperf., pair | 100.00 | |
| **C139** | A127 | 15c blue | .55 | .25 |
| *a.* | | Imperf., pair | 100.00 | |
| | | *Nos. C137A-C139 (3)* | 1.35 | .75 |

See No. C133 for #C137A without overprint.

Sir Rowland Hill — AP30

Globes, Quetzal — AP31

**1946, Aug. 5** **Photo.** ***Perf. 14x13***

**C140** AP30 5c slate & brn (blk ovpt.) .50 .25
*a.* Without "AEREO" ovpt. *400.00 400.00*
**C141** AP31 15c car lake, ultra & emer .65 .30

Centenary of the first postage stamp.

José Batres y Montufar — AP32

**1946, Sept. 16** **Engr.** ***Perf. 11***

**C142** AP32 10c Prus grn .45 .25
*a.* Perf. 12½ 10.00 .25

Signing the Declaration of Independence AP33

**1946, Dec. 19** ***Perf. 11***

| | | | | |
|---|---|---|---|---|
| **C143** | AP33 | 5c rose car | .25 | .25 |
| **C144** | AP33 | 6c ol brn | .25 | .25 |
| **C145** | AP33 | 10c violet | .30 | .25 |
| **C146** | AP33 | 20c blue | .40 | .25 |
| | | *Nos. C143-C146 (4)* | 1.20 | 1.00 |

125th anniv. of the signing of the Declaration of Independence.

**Torch Type of 1945**

Dated 1944-1946

**1947, Feb. 3** **Engr.**

| | | | | |
|---|---|---|---|---|
| **C147** | A130 | 1c green | .40 | .25 |
| **C148** | A130 | 2c carmine | .40 | .25 |
| **C149** | A130 | 3c violet | .40 | .25 |
| **C150** | A130 | 5c dp bl | .40 | .25 |
| | | *Nos. C147-C150 (4)* | 1.60 | 1.00 |

Inscribed "II Aniversario de la Revolucion." "Aereo" in color on a white background.
2nd anniv. of the Revolution of 10/20/44.

Franklin D. Roosevelt — AP34

**1947, June 6**

| | | | | |
|---|---|---|---|---|
| **C151** | AP34 | 5c rose car | .25 | .25 |
| **C152** | AP34 | 6c blue | .25 | .25 |
| **C153** | AP34 | 10c dp ultra | .35 | .25 |
| **C154** | AP34 | 30c gray blk | 1.60 | .90 |
| **C155** | AP34 | 50c lt violet | 2.50 | 2.25 |
| *a.* | | Imperf., pair | 125.00 | |
| **C156** | AP34 | 1q gray grn | 4.25 | 3.75 |
| *a.* | | Imperf., pair | 125.00 | |
| | | *Nos. C151-C156 (6)* | 9.20 | 7.65 |

**No. 296 Overprinted in Carmine**

**1948, May 14** ***Perf. 12½***

**C157** A122 5c blue & red .35 .25

Soccer Game AP35

**1948, Aug. 31** **Engr.**

**Center in Black**

| | | | | |
|---|---|---|---|---|
| **C158** | AP35 | 3c brt carmine | .75 | .30 |
| **C159** | AP35 | 5c blue green | .90 | .40 |
| **C160** | AP35 | 10c dk violet | 1.00 | .95 |
| **C161** | AP35 | 30c dp blue | 2.25 | *3.50* |
| **C162** | AP35 | 50c bister | 4.50 | 4.50 |
| | | *Nos. C158-C162 (5)* | 9.40 | 9.65 |

4th Central American and Caribbean Soccer Championship, Mar. 1948.

Seal, University of Guatemala — AP36

**1949, Nov. 29** ***Perf. 12½***

**Center in Blue**

| | | | | |
|---|---|---|---|---|
| **C163** | AP36 | 3c carmine | .70 | .40 |
| **C164** | AP36 | 10c green | 1.00 | .75 |
| **C165** | AP36 | 50c yellow | 3.75 | 3.25 |
| | | *Nos. C163-C165 (3)* | 5.45 | *4.40* |

1st Latin American Cong. of Universities.

Lake Atitlan — AP37

Tecum Uman Monument — AP38

Designs: 8c, San Cristobal Church. 13c, Weaver. 35c, Momostenango Cliffs.

**1950, Feb. 17** **Photo.** ***Perf. 14***

**Multicolored Centers**

| | | | | |
|---|---|---|---|---|
| **C166** | AP37 | 3c car rose | .35 | .25 |
| **C167** | AP38 | 5c red brn | .35 | .25 |
| **C168** | AP37 | 8c dk sl grn | .40 | .25 |
| **C169** | AP38 | 13c brown | .70 | .25 |
| **C170** | AP37 | 35c purple | 2.50 | *3.00* |
| | | *Nos. C166-C170 (5)* | 4.30 | 4.00 |

See No. C181.

Soccer — AP39

Pole Vault — AP40

Designs: 3c, Foot race. 8c, Tennis. 35c, Diving. 65c, Stadium.

**1950, Feb. 25 Engr. *Perf. 12½***

**Center in Black**

| | | | | |
|---|---|---|---|---|
| **C171** | AP39 | 1c purple | .65 | .25 |
| **C172** | AP39 | 3c carmine | .70 | .25 |
| **C173** | AP40 | 4c orange brn | .95 | .30 |
| **C174** | AP39 | 8c red violet | 1.10 | .40 |
| **C175** | AP40 | 35c lt blue | 2.50 | *3.25* |

**Center in Green**

| | | | | |
|---|---|---|---|---|
| **C176** | AP40 | 65c dk slate grn | 5.00 | *5.50* |
| | | *Nos. C171-C176 (6)* | 10.90 | 9.95 |

6th Central American and Caribbean Games.

Nurse and Patient AP41

Designs: 10c, School of Nurses. 50c, Zacapa Hospital. 1q, Roosevelt Hospital.

**1950, Sept. 6 Litho. *Perf. 12***

**Quetzal in Blue Green**

| | | | | |
|---|---|---|---|---|
| **C177** | AP41 | 5c rose vio & car | .25 | .25 |
| *a.* | | Double impression (frame) | 25.00 | |
| **C178** | AP41 | 10c ol brn & emer | .70 | .35 |
| **C179** | AP41 | 50c ver & red vio | 3.50 | *3.50* |
| **C180** | AP41 | 1q org yel & sage grn | 5.00 | *5.00* |
| *a.* | | Souv. sheet, #C177-C180 | 12.00 | *12.00* |
| | | *Nos. C177-C180 (4)* | 9.45 | *9.10* |

National Hospital Fund.

Nos. C177-C180 exist with colors reversed, perf. and imperf. These are proofs.

No. C168 Perf. 12½ or 12 diagonally through center

**1951, Apr. *Perf. 14***

| | | | | |
|---|---|---|---|---|
| **C181** | AP37 | (4c) multi | 15.00 | 9.00 |
| *a.* | | Unservered pair | 36.00 | 22.50 |

Counterfeits of diagonal perforation exist.

Ceremonial Stone Ax — AP42

**1953, Feb. 11 Photo. *Perf. 14x13½***

| | | | | |
|---|---|---|---|---|
| **C182** | AP42 | 3c dk bl & ol gray | .45 | .45 |
| **C183** | AP42 | 5c dk gray & hn brn | .55 | .45 |
| **C184** | AP42 | 10c dk pur & slate | .75 | .45 |
| | | *Nos. C182-C184 (3)* | 1.75 | 1.35 |

National Flag and Emblem — AP43

**1953, Mar. 14 *Perf. 13½***

**Multicolored Center**

| | | | | |
|---|---|---|---|---|
| **C185** | AP43 | 1c maroon | .25 | .25 |
| **C186** | AP43 | 2c slate green | .25 | .25 |
| **C187** | AP43 | 4c dark brown | .30 | .25 |
| | | *Nos. C185-C187 (3)* | .80 | .75 |

Issued to mark the passing of the presidency from J. J. Arevalo to Col. Jacobo Arbenz Guzman.

Regional Dance — AP44

Horse Racing AP45

Designs: 4c, White nun — national flower. 5c, Allegory of the fair. 20c, Zakuleu ruins. 30c, Symbols of Agriculture. 50c, Champion bull. 65c, Bicycle racing. 1q, Quetzal.

**1953, Dec. 18 Engr. *Perf. 12½***

| | | | | |
|---|---|---|---|---|
| **C188** | AP44 | 1c dp ultra & car | .25 | .25 |
| **C189** | AP44 | 4c org & grn | 1.25 | .30 |
| **C190** | AP44 | 5c emer & choc | .80 | .40 |
| **C191** | AP45 | 15c choc & dk pur | 1.10 | 1.00 |
| **C192** | AP45 | 20c car & ultra | 1.00 | 1.00 |
| **C193** | AP44 | 30c dp ultra & choc | 1.25 | *1.25* |
| **C194** | AP45 | 50c pur & blk | 1.25 | 1.25 |
| **C195** | AP45 | 65c lt bl & dk grn | 2.50 | *2.50* |
| **C196** | AP44 | 1q dk bl grn & dk red | 25.00 | *15.00* |
| | | *Nos. C188-C196 (9)* | 34.40 | *22.95* |

National Fair, Oct. 20, 1953.

Indian — AP46

**1954, Apr. 21 Unwmk. *Perf. 12½***

| | | | | |
|---|---|---|---|---|
| **C197** | AP46 | 1c carmine | .30 | .25 |
| **C198** | AP46 | 2c dp blue | .30 | .25 |
| **C199** | AP46 | 4c yellow grn | .30 | .25 |
| **C200** | AP46 | 5c aqua | .55 | .25 |
| **C201** | AP46 | 6c orange | .55 | .25 |
| **C202** | AP46 | 10c violet | 1.10 | .30 |
| **C203** | AP46 | 20c black brn | 3.25 | 3.25 |
| | | *Nos. C197-C203 (7)* | 6.35 | 4.80 |

Guatemala and ODECA Flags — AP47

**1954, Oct. 13 Photo. *Perf. 14x13½***

| | | | | |
|---|---|---|---|---|
| **C204** | AP47 | 1c multicolored | .55 | .50 |
| **C205** | AP47 | 2c multicolored | .55 | .50 |
| **C206** | AP47 | 4c multicolored | .55 | .50 |
| | | *Nos. C204-C206 (3)* | 1.65 | 1.50 |

3rd anniv. of the formation of the Organization of Central American States.

Rotary Emblem, Map of Guatemala AP48

**1956, Sept. 8 Engr.**

| | | | | |
|---|---|---|---|---|
| **C207** | AP48 | 4c bl & dl yel | .30 | .25 |
| **C208** | AP48 | 6c lt bl grn & dl yel | .30 | .25 |
| **C209** | AP48 | 35c pur & dl yel | 1.50 | *1.75* |
| | | *Nos. C207-C209 (3)* | 2.10 | *2.25* |

50th anniv. of Rotary Intl. (in 1955).

Mayan Warrior Holding Dagger Cross of the Liberation AP49

4c, Family looking into the sun. 5c, The dagger of the Liberation destroying communist symbols. 6c, Hands holding cogwheel & map of Guatemala. 20c, Monument to the victims of communism & flag. 30c, Champerico harbor. 65c, Radio tower, Mercury & map of Guatemala. 1q, Flags of the American nations. 5q, Pres. Carlos Castillo Armas.

**1956, Oct. 10 Photo. *Perf. 14x13½***

| | | | | |
|---|---|---|---|---|
| **C210** | AP49 | 2c dp grn, red, bl & brn | .25 | .25 |
| **C211** | AP49 | 4c dp car & gray blk | .25 | .25 |
| **C212** | AP49 | 5c bl & red brn | .25 | .25 |
| **C213** | AP49 | 6c dk brn & dp ultra | .30 | .25 |
| **C214** | AP49 | 20c vio, brn & bl | 1.40 | *1.75* |
| **C215** | AP49 | 30c dp bl & ol | 1.75 | *2.00* |
| **C216** | AP49 | 65c chnt brn & grn | 2.50 | *3.00* |
| **C217** | AP49 | 1q dk brn & multi | 3.50 | *4.00* |
| **C218** | AP49 | 5q multi | 14.00 | *15.00* |
| | | *Nos. C210-C218 (9)* | 24.20 | *26.75* |

Liberation of 1954-55.

For overprints see Nos. C233, C243, C265-C266, C417.

Red Cross, Map and Quetzal AP50

Designs: 2c, José Ruiz Angulo and woman with child, vert. 3c, Pedro de Bethancourt with sick man. 4c, Rafael Ayau.

***Perf. 13½x14, 14x13½***

**1958, May 13 Unwmk.**

| | | | | |
|---|---|---|---|---|
| **C219** | AP50 | 1c multicolored | .75 | .40 |
| **C220** | AP50 | 2c multicolored | .45 | .25 |
| **C221** | AP50 | 3c multicolored | .45 | .25 |
| **C222** | AP50 | 4c multicolored | .45 | .25 |
| | | *Nos. C219-C222 (4)* | 2.10 | 1.15 |

Issued in honor of the Red Cross.

For overprints and surcharges see Nos. C235-C242, C251-C254, C283-C298, C390-C395.

Col. Carlos Castillo Armas — AP51

**1959, Feb. 27 *Perf. 14x13½***

**Center in Dark Blue and Yellow**

| | | | | |
|---|---|---|---|---|
| **C223** | AP51 | 1c black | .30 | .25 |
| **C224** | AP51 | 2c rose red | .30 | .25 |
| **C225** | AP51 | 4c brown | .30 | .25 |
| **C226** | AP51 | 6c dk bl grn | .30 | .25 |
| **C227** | AP51 | 10c dk purple | .45 | .30 |
| **C228** | AP51 | 20c blue grn | 1.25 | .75 |
| **C229** | AP51 | 35c gray | 1.75 | 1.40 |
| | | *Nos. C223-C229 (7)* | 4.65 | 3.45 |

Pres. Carlos Castillo Armas (1914-1957).

No. C134A Overprinted in Carmine

**1959, Mar. 4 Engr. *Perf. 11***

| | | | | |
|---|---|---|---|---|
| **C230** | A131 | 7½c dk blue | 1.25 | *1.25* |

Issued to honor the United Nations.

Galleon of 1532 and Freighter "Quezaltenango" AP52

**1959, May 15 Litho. *Perf. 11***

| | | | | |
|---|---|---|---|---|
| **C231** | AP52 | 6c ultra & rose red | 1.00 | .30 |

Issued to honor the formation of the Guatemala-Honduras merchant fleet.

For overprint see No. C467.

Type of 1950 Overprinted in Dark Blue

**1959, Oct. 9 *Perf. 12***

| | | | | |
|---|---|---|---|---|
| **C232** | A140 | 5c dk bl & lt brn | .65 | .25 |
| *a.* | | Inverted overprint | 200.00 | 35.00 |

Issued to state Guatemala's claim to British Honduras. Overprint reads: "Belize is ours." Map includes "BRITISH HONDURAS" and its borderline, and excludes bit extending above "A" of "GUATEMALA" on No. 337.

No. C232 is known without overprint in multiples.

No. C213 Overprinted in Red

**1959, Oct. 26 Photo. *Perf. 14x13½***

| | | | | |
|---|---|---|---|---|
| **C233** | AP49 | 6c dk brn & dp ultra | .60 | .30 |

Centenary of coffee export.

Pres. and Mrs. Villeda of Honduras AP53

**1959, Nov. 3 Litho. *Perf. 11***

| | | | | |
|---|---|---|---|---|
| **C234** | AP53 | 6c pale brown | .40 | .30 |

Visit of President Ramon Villeda Morales of Honduras, Oct. 12, 1958.

For overprint see No. C415.

Nos. C219-C222 Overprinted in Green, Violet, Blue or Brown

*Perf. 13½x14, 14x13½*

**1960, Apr. 23 Photo. Unwmk.**

| | | | | |
|---|---|---|---|---|
| **C235** | AP50 | 1c multi (G) | 2.00 | 1.75 |
| **C236** | AP50 | 2c multi (V) | .95 | .95 |
| **C237** | AP50 | 3c multi (Bl) | .95 | .95 |
| **C238** | AP50 | 4c multi (Br) | .95 | .95 |

Nos. C219-C222 Overprinted

| | | | | |
|---|---|---|---|---|
| **C239** | AP50 | 6c on 1c multi | 5.00 | 2.50 |
| **C240** | AP50 | 7c on 2c multi | 2.50 | 2.25 |
| **C241** | AP50 | 10c on 3c multi | 4.00 | 4.25 |
| **C242** | AP50 | 20c on 4c multi | 4.50 | 4.50 |
| | | *Nos. C235-C242 (8)* | 20.85 | 18.10 |

Nos. C235-C242 issued to publicize World Refugee Year, July 1, 1959-June 30, 1960.

No. C213 Overprinted in Red

**1960, Apr. 30** *Perf. 14x13½*

| | | | | |
|---|---|---|---|---|
| **C243** | AP49 | 6c dk brn & dp ultra | 1.25 | 1.25 |

Founding of the city of Melchor de Mencos.

UNESCO and Eiffel Tower, Paris AP54

**1960, Nov. 4 Photo.** *Perf. 12½*

| | | | | |
|---|---|---|---|---|
| **C244** | AP54 | 5c dp mag & vio | .25 | .25 |
| **C245** | AP54 | 6c ultra & vio brn | .25 | .25 |
| **C246** | AP54 | 8c emer & magenta | .40 | .25 |
| **C247** | AP54 | 20c red brn & dl bl | 1.40 | 1.40 |
| | | *Nos. C244-C247 (4)* | 2.30 | 2.15 |

Issued to honor UNESCO.
For overprints see Nos. C258, C267-C268.

Abraham Lincoln — AP55

**1960, Oct. 29 Engr.** *Perf. 11*

| | | | | |
|---|---|---|---|---|
| **C248** | AP55 | 5c violet blue | .25 | .25 |
| **C249** | AP55 | 30c violet | 1.10 | *1.40* |
| **C250** | AP55 | 50c gray | 5.50 | *6.50* |
| | | *Nos. C248-C250 (3)* | 6.85 | *8.15* |

Sesquicentenary of the birth of Abraham Lincoln.

An 8c was also printed, but was not issued and all copies were destroyed.

Nos. C219-C222 Overprinted in Green, Blue or Brown

*Perf. 13½x14, 14x13½*

**1961, Apr. 20 Photo. Unwmk.**

| | | | | |
|---|---|---|---|---|
| **C251** | AP50 | 1c multi (G) | .60 | .45 |
| **C252** | AP50 | 2c multi (Bl) | .60 | .45 |
| **C253** | AP50 | 3c multi (Bl) | .60 | .45 |
| **C254** | AP50 | 4c multi (Br) | .60 | .45 |
| | | *Nos. C251-C254 (4)* | 2.40 | 1.80 |

Issued to honor the Red Cross.

Proclamation of Independence — AP56

**1962 Engr.** *Perf. 11*

| | | | | |
|---|---|---|---|---|
| **C255** | AP56 | 4c sepia | .25 | .25 |
| **C256** | AP56 | 5c violet blue | .40 | .25 |
| **C257** | AP56 | 15c brt violet | 1.40 | .65 |
| | | *Nos. C255-C257 (3)* | 2.05 | 1.15 |

140th anniv. of Independence (in 1961).
Issue dates: 4c, 5c, May 23; 15c, Aug. 10.

No. C245 Overprinted in Red

**1962, Oct. 4 Photo.** *Perf. 12½*

| | | | | |
|---|---|---|---|---|
| **C258** | AP54 | 6c ultra & vio brn | 1.00 | *1.40* |

WHO drive to eradicate malaria.

Dr. José Luna — AP57

Guatemalan physicians: 4c, Rodolfo Robles. 5c, Narciso Esparragoza y Gallardo. 6c, Juan J. Ortega. 10c, Dario Gonzalez. 20c, José Felipe Flores.

**1962, Dec. 12 Photo.** *Perf. 14x13½*

| | | | | |
|---|---|---|---|---|
| **C259** | AP57 | 1c ol bis & dl pur | .80 | .25 |
| **C260** | AP57 | 4c org yel & gray ol | .80 | .25 |
| **C261** | AP57 | 5c pale bl & red brn | .80 | .25 |
| **C262** | AP57 | 6c salmon & blk | .80 | .25 |
| **C263** | AP57 | 10c pale grn & red brn | 1.10 | .25 |
| **C264** | AP57 | 20c pale pink & bl | 1.25 | .80 |
| | | *Nos. C259-C264 (6)* | 5.55 | 2.05 |

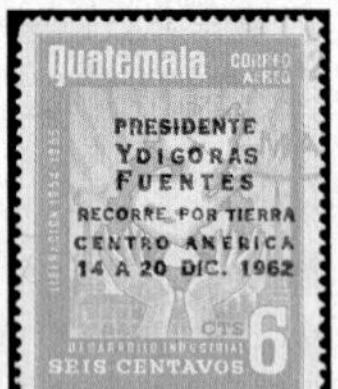


No. C213 Overprinted in Red

**1962, Dec. Photo.** *Perf. 14x13½*

| | | | | |
|---|---|---|---|---|
| **C265** | AP49 | 6c dk brn & dp ultra | 1.10 | .80 |

Pres. Ydigoras' tour of Central America, Dec. 14-20, 1962.

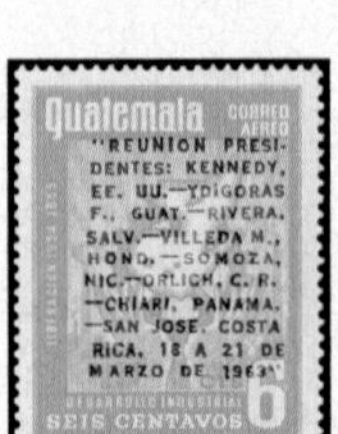


No. C213 Overprinted in Vermilion

*Perf. 14x13½*

**1963, Mar. 18 Unwmk.**

| | | | | |
|---|---|---|---|---|
| **C266** | AP49 | 6c dk brn & dp ultra | 6.00 | 3.00 |

Meeting of Pres. John F. Kennedy with the Presidents of the Central American Republics, San Jose, Costa Rica, Mar. 18-21.

Nos. C245-C246 Overprinted in Magenta or Black

**1963, Mar. 14** *Perf. 12½*

| | | | | |
|---|---|---|---|---|
| **C267** | AP54 | 6c ultra & vio brn (M) | .50 | .25 |
| **C268** | AP54 | 8c emerald & mag | .55 | .25 |

Signing of the new charter of the Organization of Central American States (ODECA).

**Enriquez de Rivera Type of 1946**

*Perf. 11, 11½, 12½*

**1963, Mar. 26 Engr.**

| | | | | |
|---|---|---|---|---|
| **C269** | A132 | 5c olive bister | .30 | .25 |

Woman Carrying Fruit Basket — AP58

**1963, Mar. 14 Litho.** *Perf. 11, 12½*

| | | | | |
|---|---|---|---|---|
| **C270** | AP58 | 1c multicolored | .25 | .25 |

Spring Fair, 1960.

Reaper — AP59

**1963, July 25 Photo.** *Perf. 14*

| | | | | |
|---|---|---|---|---|
| **C271** | AP59 | 5c Prus green | .30 | .25 |
| **C272** | AP59 | 10c dark blue | .60 | .30 |

FAO "Freedom from Hunger" campaign.

Ceiba Tree — AP60

**1963 Unwmk.** *Perf. 12*

| | | | | |
|---|---|---|---|---|
| **C273** | AP60 | 4c brown & green | 1.40 | .25 |

Patzun Palace AP61

Buildings: 3c, Coban. 4c, Retalhuleu. 5c, San Marcos. 6c, Captains General of Antigua.

**1964, Jan. 15** *Perf. 13½x14*

| | | | | |
|---|---|---|---|---|
| **C274** | AP61 | 1c rose red & brn | .50 | .25 |
| **C275** | AP61 | 3c rose cl & Prus grn | .50 | .25 |
| **C276** | AP61 | 4c vio bl & rose lake | .50 | .25 |
| **C277** | AP61 | 5c brown & blue | .65 | .25 |
| **C278** | AP61 | 6c green & slate | .65 | .25 |
| | | *Nos. C274-C278 (5)* | 2.80 | 1.25 |

City Hall, Guatemala City AP62

Design: 4c, Social Security Institute.

**1964, Jan. 15 Photo.** *Perf. 12x11½*

| | | | | |
|---|---|---|---|---|
| **C279** | AP62 | 3c brt bl & brn | .40 | .25 |
| **C280** | AP62 | 4c brn & brt bl | .50 | .25 |

See Nos. C281-C282A. For overprints see Nos. C360-C361, C421.

**1964-65 Engr.** *Perf. 11½*

Designs: 3c, Social Security Institute. 4c, University administration building. No. C282, City Hall, Guatemala City. No. C282A, Engineering School.

**Different Frames**

| | | | | |
|---|---|---|---|---|
| **C281** | AP62 | 3c dull green | .55 | .25 |
| **C281A** | AP62 | 4c gray ('65) | .55 | .25 |
| **C282** | AP62 | 7c blue | .60 | .25 |
| **C282A** | AP62 | 7c olive bis ('65) | .60 | .25 |
| | | *Nos. C281-C282A (4)* | 2.30 | 1.00 |

Nos. C219-C222 Ovptd. in Green, Blue or Black

**1964 Photo.** *Perf. 13½x14, 14x13½*

| | | | | |
|---|---|---|---|---|
| **C283** | AP50 | 1c multi (G) | 1.25 | *1.40* |
| **C284** | AP50 | 2c multi (Bl) | 1.25 | *1.40* |
| **C285** | AP50 | 3c multi (G) | 1.25 | *1.40* |
| **C286** | AP50 | 4c multi (Bk) | 1.25 | *1.40* |
| | | *Nos. C283-C286 (4)* | 5.00 | *5.60* |

18th Olympic Games, Tokyo, 10/10-25/64.

Nos. C219-C222 Surcharged in Green, Blue or Black

**1964**

| | | | | |
|---|---|---|---|---|
| **C287** | AP50 | 7c on 1c multi (G) | .30 | .25 |
| **C288** | AP50 | 9c on 2c multi (Bl) | .40 | *.40* |
| **C289** | AP50 | 13c on 3c multi (Bl) | .55 | .45 |
| **C290** | AP50 | 21c on 4c multi (Bk) | 1.00 | *.85* |
| | | *Nos. C287-C290 (4)* | 2.25 | *1.95* |

Nos. C219-C222 Ovptd. in Green, Blue or Black

**1964, June 25**

| | | | | |
|---|---|---|---|---|
| **C291** | AP50 | 1c multi (G) | .80 | *.85* |
| **C292** | AP50 | 2c multi (Bl) | .80 | *.85* |
| **C293** | AP50 | 3c multi (G) | .80 | *.85* |
| **C294** | AP50 | 4c multi (Bk) | .80 | *.85* |
| | | *Nos. C291-C294 (4)* | 3.20 | *3.40* |

New York World's Fair.

**Nos. C219-C222 Ovptd. in Green, Blue or Black**

**1964**

| | | | | |
|---|---|---|---|---|
| **C295** | AP50 | 1c multi (G) | 1.60 | *1.40* |
| **C296** | AP50 | 2c multi (Bl) | 1.60 | *1.40* |
| **C297** | AP50 | 3c multi (G) | 1.60 | *1.40* |
| **C298** | AP50 | 4c multi (Bk) | 2.50 | *2.25* |
| | | *Nos. C295-C298 (4)* | 7.30 | *6.45* |

Eighth Bicycle Race.

Pres. John F. Kennedy — AP63

**1964 Engr. *Perf. 11½***

| | | | | |
|---|---|---|---|---|
| **C299** | AP63 | 1c violet | 1.10 | .70 |
| **C300** | AP63 | 2c yellow grn | 1.10 | .70 |
| **C301** | AP63 | 3c brown | 1.10 | .70 |
| **C302** | AP63 | 7c deep blue | 1.10 | .70 |
| **C303** | AP63 | 50c dk gray | 8.50 | *7.50* |
| | | *Nos. C299-C303 (5)* | 12.90 | *10.30* |

Minute letters "TEOK" are in lower right corner of 1c, 2c, 3c and 50c.

Issue dates: 7c, July 10; others, Aug. 21.

Centenary Emblem — AP64

***Perf. 11x12***

**1964, Sept. 9 Unwmk. Photo.**

| | | | | |
|---|---|---|---|---|
| **C304** | AP64 | 7c ultra, sil & red | .90 | .25 |
| **C305** | AP64 | 9c org, sil & red | .90 | .40 |
| **C306** | AP64 | 13c pur, sil & red | 1.40 | .55 |
| **C307** | AP64 | 21c brt grn, sil & red | 1.10 | *1.00* |
| **C308** | AP64 | 35c brn, sil & red | 2.10 | *1.40* |
| **C309** | AP64 | 1q lem, sil & red | 3.75 | 3.00 |
| | | *Nos. C304-C309 (6)* | 10.15 | *6.60* |

Centenary (in 1963) of the Intl. Red Cross.

For overprints see Nos. C323-C327, C395-C400.

### Type of Regular Issue 1963

Souvenir Sheet

**1964 Engr. *Imperf.***

| | | | |
|---|---|---|---|
| **C310** | Sheet of 2 | 9.50 | *10.00* |
| *a.* | A151 10c violet blue | 4.00 | 4.00 |
| *b.* | A151 20c carmine | 4.00 | 4.00 |

15th UPU Congress, Vienna, May-June, 1964.

### Enriquez de Rivera Type of 1946

**1964, Dec. 18 Engr. *Perf. 11½***

| | | | | |
|---|---|---|---|---|
| **C311** | A132 | 5c gray | .30 | .25 |
| **C312** | A132 | 5c orange | .30 | .25 |
| **C313** | A132 | 5c lt green | .30 | .25 |
| **C314** | A132 | 5c lt ultra | .30 | .25 |
| **C315** | A132 | 5c dull violet | .30 | .25 |
| | | *Nos. C311-C315 (5)* | 1.50 | 1.25 |

Bishop Francisco Marroquin AP65

**1965, Jan. 21 Photo. Unwmk.**

| | | | | |
|---|---|---|---|---|
| **C316** | AP65 | 4c lilac & brn | .25 | .25 |
| **C317** | AP65 | 7c gray & sepia | .60 | .25 |
| **C318** | AP65 | 9c vio bl & blk | .70 | .25 |
| | | *Nos. C316-C318 (3)* | 1.55 | .75 |

Issued to honor Bishop Francisco Marroquin.

### Bethancourt Type of Regular Issue, 1964

**1965, Apr. 20 Engr. *Perf. 11½***

| | | | | |
|---|---|---|---|---|
| **C319** | A152 | 2½c violet blue | .25 | .25 |
| **C320** | A152 | 3c orange | .25 | .25 |
| **C321** | A152 | 4c purple | .25 | .25 |
| **C322** | A152 | 5c yellow grn | .30 | .25 |
| | | *Nos. C319-C322 (4)* | 1.05 | 1.00 |

For overprints see Nos. C381-C382.

Nos. C304-C308 Overprinted in Red

**1965, June 18 Photo. *Perf. 11x12***

| | | | | |
|---|---|---|---|---|
| **C323** | AP64 | 7c ultra, sil & red | .45 | .45 |
| **C324** | AP64 | 9c org, sil & red | .55 | .55 |
| **C325** | AP64 | 13c pur, sil & red | .60 | .55 |
| **C326** | AP64 | 21c brt grn, sil & red | .85 | .80 |
| **C327** | AP64 | 35c brn, sil & red | 1.00 | *1.25* |
| | | *Nos. C323-C327 (5)* | 3.45 | 3.60 |

Guatemalan Boy Scout Emblem — AP66

Designs: 9c, Campfire and Scouts. 10c, Scout emblem and Scout carrying torch and flag. 15c, Scout emblem, flags and Scout giving Scout sign. 20c, Lord Baden-Powell.

**1966, Mar. 3 Photo. *Perf. 14x13½***

| | | | | |
|---|---|---|---|---|
| **C328** | AP66 | 5c multicolored | .60 | .55 |
| **C329** | AP66 | 9c multicolored | .75 | .70 |
| **C330** | AP66 | 10c multicolored | .95 | .85 |
| **C331** | AP66 | 15c multicolored | 1.25 | 1.10 |
| **C332** | AP66 | 20c multicolored | 1.75 | 1.50 |
| | | *Nos. C328-C332 (5)* | 5.30 | 4.70 |

5th Interamerican Regional Training Conf., Guatemala City, Mar. 1-3.

For overprints see Nos. C376-C380.

### Central American Independence Issue

Flags of Central American States — AP67

**1966, Mar. 9 *Perf. 12½x13½***

| | | | | |
|---|---|---|---|---|
| **C333** | AP67 | 6c multicolored | .40 | .25 |

Queen Nefertari Temple, Abu Simbel AP68

**1966, Oct. 3 Photo. *Perf. 12***

| | | | | |
|---|---|---|---|---|
| **C334** | AP68 | 21c violet & ocher | .85 | .45 |

UNESCO world campaign to save historic monuments in Nubia.

Coat of Arms — AP69

**1966-70 Engr. *Perf. 13½***

| | | | | |
|---|---|---|---|---|
| **C335** | AP69 | 5c orange | .90 | .30 |
| **C336** | AP69 | 5c green | .90 | .30 |
| *a.* | | 5c yel grn, perf. 11½ ('69) | .90 | .30 |

***Perf. 11½***

| | | | | |
|---|---|---|---|---|
| **C337** | AP69 | 5c blue ('67) | .90 | .30 |
| *a.* | | 5c dk bl, perf. 12½ ('69) | .90 | .30 |

***Perf. 12½***

| | | | | |
|---|---|---|---|---|
| **C338** | AP69 | 5c gray ('67) | .90 | .30 |
| **C339** | AP69 | 5c purple ('67) | .90 | .30 |
| *a.* | | 5c bright violet ('69) | .90 | .30 |

***Perf. 11½***

| | | | | |
|---|---|---|---|---|
| **C339B** | AP69 | 5c dp mag ('70) | 1.50 | .30 |
| **C339C** | AP69 | 5c grn, *yel* ('70) | 1.75 | .30 |
| | | *Nos. C335-C339C (7)* | 7.75 | 2.10 |

Issued: #C335, 10/31; #C336, 12/15/66; #C337, 2/9/67; #C338-C339, 4/28/67; #C336a, 12/3/69; #C339a, 12/11/69; #C339B, 7/8/70; #C339C, 10/16/70.

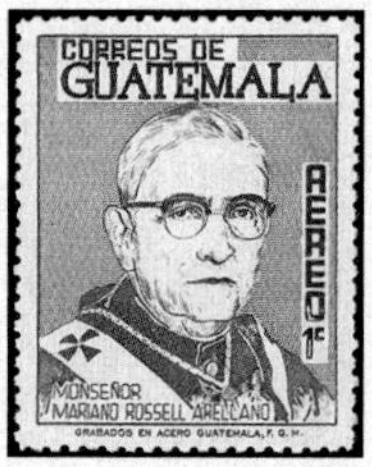

Msgr. Mariano Rossell y Arellano AP70

**1966, Nov. 3 Engr. *Perf. 13½***

| | | | | |
|---|---|---|---|---|
| **C340** | AP70 | 1c dp violet | .25 | .25 |
| **C341** | AP70 | 2c green | .30 | .25 |
| **C342** | AP70 | 3c brown | .30 | .25 |
| **C343** | AP70 | 7c blue | .45 | .40 |
| **C344** | AP70 | 50c gray | 2.00 | 2.00 |
| | | *Nos. C340-C344 (5)* | 3.30 | 3.15 |

Issued to honor Msgr. Mariano Rossell y Arellano, apostolic delegate.

Mario Mendez Montenegro AP71

**1966-67 *Perf. 13½***

| | | | | |
|---|---|---|---|---|
| **C345** | AP71 | 2c rose red ('67) | .25 | .25 |
| **C346** | AP71 | 3c orange ('67) | .30 | .25 |
| **C347** | AP71 | 4c rose claret ('67) | .40 | .25 |
| **C348** | AP71 | 5c gray | .55 | .25 |
| **C349** | AP71 | 5c lt ultra ('67) | .55 | .25 |
| **C350** | AP71 | 5c green ('67) | .55 | .25 |
| **C351** | AP71 | 5c bluish blk ('67) | .55 | .25 |
| | | *Nos. C345-C351 (7)* | 3.15 | 1.75 |

Mario Mendez Montenegro (1910-65), founder of the Revolutionary Party.

Morning Glory and Map of Guatemala AP72

Flowers: 8c, Bird of paradise, horiz. 10c, White nun orchid, national flower, horiz. 20c, Nymphs of Amatitlan.

**1967, Jan. 12 Photo. *Perf. 12***

**Flowers in Natural Colors**

| | | | | |
|---|---|---|---|---|
| **C352** | AP72 | 4c orange | 1.40 | .60 |
| **C353** | AP72 | 8c green | 1.40 | .60 |
| **C354** | AP72 | 10c dk blue | 1.60 | 1.10 |
| **C355** | AP72 | 20c dk red | 3.50 | 2.40 |
| | | *Nos. C352-C355 (4)* | 7.90 | 4.70 |

Pan-American Institute Emblem — AP73

**1967, Apr. 13 Photo. *Perf. 13½***

| | | | | |
|---|---|---|---|---|
| **C356** | AP73 | 4c lt brn, lil & blk | .40 | .25 |
| **C357** | AP73 | 5c ol, bl & blk | .75 | .25 |
| **C358** | AP73 | 7c org yel, bl & blk | 1.10 | .40 |
| | | *Nos. C356-C358 (3)* | 2.25 | .90 |

8th Gen. Assembly of the Pan-American Geographical and Historical Institute in 1965.

No. C281 Overprinted

**1967, Apr. 28 Engr. *Perf. 11½***

| | | | | |
|---|---|---|---|---|
| **C360** | AP62 | 3c dull green | 1.60 | 1.10 |

Guatemala's victory in the 3rd Norceca Soccer Games (Caribbean, Central and North American).

No. C281A Overprinted in Red

**1967, June 28 Engr. *Perf. 11½***

| | | | | |
|---|---|---|---|---|
| **C361** | AP62 | 4c gray | 1.10 | 1.10 |

Meeting of American Presidents, Punta del Este, Apr. 10-12.

Handshake AP74

**1967, June 28 Photo. *Perf. 12***

| | | | | |
|---|---|---|---|---|
| **C362** | AP74 | 7c pink, brn & grn | .55 | .25 |
| **C363** | AP74 | 21c lt bl, grn & brn | .85 | .55 |

"Peace and Progress through Cooperation."

For overprint see No. C416.

Church of Santo Domingo AP75

1c, Yurrita Church, vert. 3c, Church of St. Francis. 4c, Antonio José de Irisarri, vert. 5c, Church of the Convent, vert. 7c, Mercy Church, Antigua. 10c, Metropolitan Cathedral.

**1967, Aug. *Perf. 11½x12, 12x11½***

| | | | | |
|---|---|---|---|---|
| **C364** | AP75 | 1c grn, lt bl & dk brn | .40 | .25 |
| **C365** | AP75 | 2c plum, sal pink & brn | .45 | .25 |
| **C366** | AP75 | 3c brt rose, gray & blk | .45 | .25 |
| **C367** | AP75 | 4c mar, sl grn & org | .45 | .25 |
| **C368** | AP75 | 5c lil, pale grn & dk brn | .45 | .25 |
| **C369** | AP75 | 7c ultra, lil rose & blk | .55 | .25 |
| **C370** | AP75 | 10c pur, yel & blk | .95 | .30 |
| | | *Nos. C364-C370 (7)* | 3.70 | 1.80 |

Abraham Lincoln (1809-1865) AP76

**1967 Engr. *Perf. 13½, 11½ (9c)***

| | | | | |
|---|---|---|---|---|
| **C371** | AP76 | 7c gray & dp org | .45 | .25 |
| **C372** | AP76 | 9c dk grn & grysh | .55 | .25 |
| **C373** | AP76 | 11c brn org & slate | .45 | .30 |
| **C374** | AP76 | 15c ultra & vio brn | .65 | .40 |
| **C375** | AP76 | 30c magenta & grn | 1.50 | 1.50 |
| | | *Nos. C371-C375 (5)* | 3.60 | 2.70 |

Issued: 7c, 9c, Oct. 9; others, Dec. 12.
For surcharge see No. C554.

Nos. C328-C332 Overprinted

**1967, Dec. 1 Photo. *Perf. 14x13½***

| | | | | |
|---|---|---|---|---|
| **C376** | AP66 | 5c multicolored | .40 | .40 |
| **C377** | AP66 | 9c multicolored | .65 | .65 |
| **C378** | AP66 | 10c multicolored | .85 | .85 |
| **C379** | AP66 | 15c multicolored | .85 | .85 |
| **C380** | AP66 | 20c multicolored | 1.00 | 1.00 |
| | | *Nos. C376-C380 (5)* | 3.75 | 3.75 |

Issued to commemorate the 8th Central American Boy Scout Camporee, Dec. 1-8.

Nos. C320-C321 Overprinted

**1967, Dec. 11 Engr. *Perf. 11½***

| | | | | |
|---|---|---|---|---|
| **C381** | A152 | 3c orange | .55 | .55 |
| **C382** | A152 | 4c purple | .55 | .55 |

Awarding of the Nobel Prize for Literature to Miguel Angel Asturias, Guatemalan writer.

Institute Emblem — AP77

**1967, Dec. 12 Engr. *Perf. 11½***

| | | | | |
|---|---|---|---|---|
| **C383** | AP77 | 9c black & grn | 3.75 | 3.75 |
| **C384** | AP77 | 25c car & brn | 5.00 | 5.00 |
| **C385** | AP77 | 1q ultra & bl | 17.50 | *19.00* |
| | | *Nos. C383-C385 (3)* | 26.25 | 27.75 |

Inter-American Agriculture Institute, 25th anniv.

UNESCO Emblem and Children AP78

**1967, Dec. 12**

| | | | | |
|---|---|---|---|---|
| **C386** | AP78 | 4c blue green | .30 | .25 |
| **C387** | AP78 | 5c blue | .35 | .25 |
| **C388** | AP78 | 7c gray | .50 | .35 |
| **C389** | AP78 | 21c brt rose lil | 1.10 | 1.10 |
| | | *Nos. C386-C389 (4)* | 2.25 | 1.95 |

20th anniv. (in 1966) of UNESCO.

Nos. C219-C221 and C304-C308 Ovptd. in Black or Yellow Green

***Perf. 13½x14, 14x13½, 11x12***

**1968, Jan. 23 Photo.**

| | | | | |
|---|---|---|---|---|
| **C390** | AP50 | 1c multi | .80 | .55 |
| **C391** | AP50 | 1c multi (G) | .80 | .80 |
| **C392** | AP50 | 2c multi | .80 | .80 |
| **C393** | AP50 | 2c multi (G) | .80 | .80 |
| **C394** | AP50 | 3c multi | .80 | .80 |
| **C395** | AP50 | 3c multi (G) | .80 | .80 |
| **C396** | AP64 | 7c multi | .80 | .80 |
| **C397** | AP64 | 9c multi | 1.10 | 1.10 |
| **C398** | AP64 | 13c multi | 1.60 | 1.10 |
| **C399** | AP64 | 21c multi | 2.25 | 1.10 |
| **C400** | AP64 | 35c multi | 1.90 | 1.90 |
| | | *Nos. C390-C400 (11)* | 12.45 | 10.55 |

3rd meeting of Central American Presidents, Nov. 15-18, 1967.

Our Lady of the Coro — AP79

**1968-74 Engr. *Perf. 13½, 11½***

| | | | | |
|---|---|---|---|---|
| **C403** | AP79 | 4c ultra | .55 | .25 |
| **C404** | AP79 | 7c slate | .50 | .25 |
| **C405** | AP79 | 9c green | .50 | .25 |
| **C406** | AP79 | 9c lilac ('74) | .55 | .25 |
| **C407** | AP79 | 10c brick red | .95 | .25 |
| **C408** | AP79 | 10c gray | .60 | .25 |
| **C408A** | AP79 | 10c vio bl ('74) | .40 | .25 |
| **C409** | AP79 | 1q vio brn | 4.00 | 3.50 |
| **C410** | AP79 | 1q org yel | 4.00 | 3.50 |
| | | *Nos. C403-C410 (9)* | 12.05 | 8.75 |

Perf. 13½ applies to 4c and Nos. C407, C409-C410; perf. 11½ to 4c, 7c, 9c and Nos. C408, C408A.

Nos. 396-398 Overprinted

**1968, Mar. 25 Litho. *Perf. 14x13½***

| | | | | |
|---|---|---|---|---|
| **C411** | A153 | 4c multicolored | .85 | .85 |
| **C412** | A153 | 5c multicolored | .85 | .85 |
| **C413** | A153 | 6c multicolored | .70 | .70 |
| | | *Nos. C411-C413 (3)* | 2.40 | 2.40 |

The 11th Bicycle Race.

Miguel Angel Asturias, Flags of Guatemala and Sweden — AP80

**1968, June 18 Engr. *Perf. 11½***

| | | | | |
|---|---|---|---|---|
| **C414** | AP80 | 20c ultra | *5.00* | *5.00* |

Awarding of the Nobel Prize for Literature to Miguel Angel Asturias.

**No. C234 Overprinted in Carmine**

**1968, July 18 Litho. *Perf. 11***

| | | | | |
|---|---|---|---|---|
| **C415** | AP53 | 6c pale brown | .75 | .40 |

International Human Rights Year.

No. C362 Overprinted

**1968, July 18 Photo. *Perf. 12***

| | | | | |
|---|---|---|---|---|
| **C416** | AP74 | 7c pink, brn & grn | .65 | .40 |

Issued to publicize forest conservation.

No. C213 Overprinted in Brown

**1968, Aug. 23 Photo. *Perf. 14x13½***

| | | | | |
|---|---|---|---|---|
| **C417** | AP49 | 6c dk brn & dp ultra | .65 | .65 |

Nahakin scientific expedition along the route of the Mayas undertaken jointly with Peru.

Views, Quetzal and White Nun Orchid — AP81

**1968, Aug. 23 Engr. *Perf. 13½***

| | | | | |
|---|---|---|---|---|
| **C418** | AP81 | 10c dp cl & grn | 3.00 | 2.00 |
| **C419** | AP81 | 20c dp org & blk | 4.00 | 3.00 |
| **C420** | AP81 | 50c ultra & car | 5.00 | 5.00 |
| | | *Nos. C418-C420 (3)* | 12.00 | 10.00 |

Issued for tourist publicity.

No. C281A Overprinted in Carmine

**1968, Nov. 4 *Perf. 11½***

| | | | | |
|---|---|---|---|---|
| **C421** | AP62 | 4c gray | .55 | .55 |

20th anniv. of the Federation of Central American Universities.

Presidents Gustavo Diaz Ordaz and Julio Cesar Mendez Montenegro AP82

**1968, Dec. 3 Litho. *Perf. 14x13½***

| | | | | |
|---|---|---|---|---|
| **C422** | AP82 | 5c multicolored | .25 | .25 |
| **C423** | AP82 | 10c multicolored | .40 | .25 |
| **C424** | AP82 | 25c multicolored | .95 | .85 |
| | | *Nos. C422-C424 (3)* | 1.60 | 1.35 |

Mutual visits of the Presidents of Mexico and Guatemala.

ITU Emblem, Old and New Communication Equipment — AP83

**Engraved and Photogravure**

**1968-74 *Perf. 11½, 12½ (21c)***

| | | | | |
|---|---|---|---|---|
| **C425** | AP83 | 7c violet blue | .25 | .25 |
| **C426** | AP83 | 15c gray & emer | .45 | .25 |
| **C426A** | AP83 | 15c vio brn & org ('74) | .55 | .25 |
| **C427** | AP83 | 21c magenta | .70 | .45 |
| **C428** | AP83 | 35c rose red & emer | .95 | .45 |
| **C429** | AP83 | 75c green & red | 2.40 | 2.40 |
| **C430** | AP83 | 3q brown & red | 9.25 | 7.75 |
| | | *Nos. C425-C430 (7)* | 14.55 | 11.80 |

Cent. (in 1965) of the ITU.

Nos. C425, C427 are engr. only; on others denominations are photo. No. C426A is on thin, toned paper.

Issued: #C426A, 2/18/74; others 12/13/68.

For surcharges see Nos. C454, C516.

Nos. 399-403 Overprinted in Red, Black or Gold

**Lithographed and Engraved**

**1969 *Perf. 11½, 13½ (1c)***

| | | | | |
|---|---|---|---|---|
| **C431** | A154 | 1c blk, lt grn & red (R) | .80 | *2.00* |
| **C432** | A154 | 5c yel, lt grn & red | 1.10 | *2.00* |
| **C433** | A154 | 8c org, lt grn & red | 1.25 | *4.00* |
| **C434** | A154 | 15c bl, lt grn & red | 1.40 | *4.00* |
| **C435** | A154 | 30c lt vio, lt grn & red (G) | 1.75 | *4.00* |
| | | *Nos. C431-C435 (5)* | 6.30 | *16.00* |

Dante Alighieri — AP84

**1969, July 17 Engr. *Perf. 12½***

| | | | | |
|---|---|---|---|---|
| **C436** | AP84 | 7c rose vio & ultra | .40 | .25 |
| **C437** | AP84 | 10c dk blue | .45 | .25 |
| **C438** | AP84 | 20c green | .70 | .25 |
| **C439** | AP84 | 21c gray & brn | 1.10 | .80 |
| **C440** | AP84 | 35c pur & brt grn | 2.75 | 1.75 |
| | | *Nos. C436-C440 (5)* | 5.40 | 3.30 |

Dante Alighieri (1265-1321), Italian poet.

Map of Latin America — AP85

Design: 9c, Seal of University.

**1969, Oct. 29 Typo. *Perf. 13***

**Size: 44x27mm**

| | | | | |
|---|---|---|---|---|
| **C441** | AP85 | 2c brt pink & blk | .25 | .25 |

**Size: 35x27mm**

C442 AP85 9c gray & blk .55 .25

**Souvenir Sheet**

***Imperf***

C443 AP85 Sheet of 2 1.40 1.40
 *a.* 2c light blue & black .60 .60
 *b.* 9c orange & black .60 .60

20th anniv. of the Union of Latin American Universities.

**Moon Landing Issue**

Moon Landing — AP86

**1969-70 Engr. *Perf. 11½***

C444 AP86 50c maroon & blk 2.75 2.75
C445 AP86 1q ultra & blk 4.75 4.75

**Souvenir Sheet**

***Imperf***

C446 AP86 1q yel grn & ultra 6.75 6.75

See note after US No. C76. No. C446 contains one stamp with simulated perforations.

Issued: #C445-C446, 12/19/69; #C444, 1/6/70.

Giant Grebe Family on Lake Atitlan AP87

Designs: 4c, Lake Atitlan. 20c, Grebe chick, eggs atop floating nest, vert.

**1970, Mar. 31 Litho. *Perf. 13½***

C447 AP87 4c red & multi .95 .25
C448 AP87 9c red & multi 1.40 .30
 *a.* Souv. sheet of 2, #C447-C448 15.00 15.00
C449 AP87 20c red & multi 2.40 .85
 *Nos. C447-C449 (3)* 4.75 1.40

Protection of zambullidor ducks.

Dr. Victor Manuel Calderon — AP88

**1970 Litho. & Engr. *Perf. 13, 12½***

C450 AP88 1c lt bl & blk .25 .25
C451 AP88 2c pale grn & blk .25 .25

***Perf. 13***

C452 AP88 9c yellow & blk .55 .25
 *Nos. C450-C452 (3)* 1.05 .75

Dr. Victor Manuel Calderon (1889-1969), who described microfilaria, a blood parasite.

Hand Holding Bible — AP89

**1970 Litho. & Typo. *Perf. 13x13½***

C453 AP89 5c red & multi .30 .25

Fourth centenary of the Bible in Spanish.

No. C430 Surcharged

**1971, Mar. 11 Engr. *Perf. 11½***

C454 AP83 50c on 3q brn & red 2.00 2.00

Arms of Guatemala, Newspapers — AP90

Official Decree of First Issue — AP91

**1971 Litho. *Perf. 11½, 12½***

C455 AP90 2c dk bl & red .25 .25
C456 AP90 5c brn & red .25 .25
C457 AP90 25c brt bl & red .65 .40
 *Nos. C455-C457 (3)* 1.15 .90

**Souvenir Sheet**

**Lithographed and Engraved**

***Imperf***

C458 AP91 Sheet of 5 2.00 2.00

Cent. of Guatemala's postage stamps.

Nos. C456-C457 have white value tablet.

No. C458 contains a litho. 4c black and engr. reproductions of Nos. 1-4 in colors similar to 1871 issue. Simulated perforations.

In 1974 No. C458 was overprinted "Conmemorativa / al Campeonato Mundial de Foot Ball / Munich 1974" and Munich Games emblem in black. Value $12. Overprint in gold or other colors was not authorized.

See Nos. C569-C570.

Mayas with CARE Package — AP92

**1971 Typo. *Perf. 11½***

C459 AP92 5c multi .40 .40
 *a.* Souv. sheet of 2 2.50 2.50

25th anniversary of CARE, a US-Canadian Cooperative for American Relief Everywhere.

No. C459a contains imperf. stamps similar to Nos. 416 and C459.

J. Rufino Barrios, M. Garcia Granados, Map of Guatemala, Quetzal — AP93

**1971, June 30 *Perf. 11½***

C460 AP93 2c multi, perf 13½ .80 .25
 *a.* Value in pink ('72) .70 .25
C461 AP93 10c multi 1.50 .30
 *a.* Value in pink, perf. 12½ ('72) 1.50 .30
C462 AP93 50c multi 8.00 3.25
C463 AP93 1q multi 12.00 6.50
 *Nos. C460-C463 (4)* 22.30 10.30

Centenary of the liberal revolution of 1871.

Chavarry Arrué and León Bilak — AP94

***Perf. 11½, 11x12½, 12½***

**1971-72 Engr.**

C464 AP94 1c grn & blk ('72) .25 .25
C465 AP94 2c lt brn & blk ('72) .30 .25
C466 AP94 5c org & blk .45 .30
 *Nos. C464-C466 (3)* 1.00 .80

Honoring J. Arnoldo Chavarry Arrué, stamp engraver; León Bilak, philatelist.

No. C231 Overprinted

**1971, Oct. 25 Litho. *Perf. 11½***

C467 AP52 6c ultra & rose red *5.00* 3.00

INTERFER 71, Intl. Fair, Guatemala, Oct. 30-Nov. 21.

Flag and Map of Guatemala AP95

***Perf. 13½ (1c), 12½ (3c, 9c), 11 (5c)***

**1971-75 Typo.**

C468 AP95 1c blk, bl & lil .25 .25
 *a.* Lithographed ('75) .25 .25
C469 AP95 3c brn, brt pink & bl .25 .25
C470 AP95 5c brn, org & bl .25 .25
 *a.* Lithographed, perf. 12½ ('74) .25 .25
C471 AP95 9c blk, emer & bl .25 .25
 *Nos. C468-C471 (4)* 1.00 1.00

Central American independence, sesqui.
Date of issue: #C469-C471, July 10, 1972.

UNICEF Emblem and Mayan Figure — AP96

**1971-75 Engr. *Perf. 11½***

C472 AP96 1c yel grn .25 .25
C472A AP96 2c purple .25 .25
C473 AP96 50c vio brn 1.90 1.90
C474 AP96 1q ultra 3.00 3.00
 *Nos. C472-C474 (4)* 5.40 5.40

25th anniv. UNICEF.
Issued: 2c, 2/24/75; others, 11/71.

Early Boeing Planes — AP97

Design: 10c, Bleriot's plane.

**1972 Typo. *Perf. 11½***

C475 AP97 5c lt brn & brt bl .75 .30
C476 AP97 10c dark blue 1.25 .30

Military aviation in Guatemala, 50th anniv.

Arches, Antigua — AP98

**1972-73 Typo. *Perf. 11½***

**Dark Blue and Light Blue**

C480 AP98 1c shown .25 .25
C481 AP98 1c Cathedral .25 .25
C482 AP98 1c Fountain, Central Park .25 .25
C483 AP98 1c Capuchin Monastery .25 .25
C484 AP98 1c Fountain and Santa Clara .25 .25
C485 AP98 1c Portal of San Francisco .25 .25
 *a.* Block of 6, #C480-C485 1.75 1.60

**Black, Lilac Rose, and Silver**

C486 AP98 2½c shown .45 .25
C487 AP98 2½c Cathedral .45 .25
C488 AP98 2½c Fountain and Santa Clara .45 .25
C489 AP98 2½c Portal of San Francisco .45 .25
C490 AP98 2½c Fountain .45 .25
C491 AP98 2½c Capuchin Monastery .45 .25
 *a.* Block of 6, #C3486-C491 3.00 1.60

**Blue, Orange and Black**

C492 AP98 5c shown .95 .25
C493 AP98 5c Cathedral .95 .25
C494 AP98 5c Santa Clara .95 .25
C495 AP98 5c Portal of San Francisco .95 .25
C496 AP98 5c Fountain .95 .25
C497 AP98 5c Capuchin Monastery .95 .25
 *a.* Block of 6, #C492-C497 6.00 3.00

Nos. C492-C497 exist perf. 12½, same value.

***Perf. 12½***

**Red, Blue and Black**

C498 AP98 1q Fountain 4.75 2.50
C499 AP98 1q Capuchin Monastery 4.75 2.50
C500 AP98 1q shown 4.75 2.50
C501 AP98 1q Cathedral 4.75 2.50
C502 AP98 1q Fountain and Santa Clara 4.75 2.50
C503 AP98 1q Portal of San Francisco 4.75 2.50
 *a.* Block of 6, #C498-C503 27.50 15.00
 *Nos. C480-C503 (24)* 38.40 19.50

Earthquake ruins of Antigua. 1c printed se-tenant in sheets of 90 (10x9); 2½c, 5c se-tenant in sheets of 30 (5x6); 1q se-tenant in sheets of 6 (3x2).

On Nos. C498-C503 the inks were applied by a thermographic process giving a shiny raised effect.

Issued: #C480-C485, 12/14; #C486-C491, 1/22/73; #C492-C497, 3/12/73; #C498-C503, 8/22/73.

Nos. C480-C485 were overprinted "II Feria Internacional / INTERFER/73 / 31 Octubre — Noviembre 18 / 1973 / GUATEMALA" in black or lilac rose and issued 11/3/73. Value $3.

The same overprint exists in black on Nos. C480-C485, but these stamps were not decreed or issued.

See Nos. C528-C545, C770-C775F. For overprints see Nos. C517-C523.

Simon Bolivar and Map of Americas AP99

**1973-74** *Perf. 11½*

| | | | | |
|---|---|---|---|---|
| **C504** | AP99 | 3c brt lil rose & blk | .25 | .25 |
| **C505** | AP99 | 3c org & dk bl ('74) | *5.00* | *2.00* |
| **C506** | AP99 | 5c yel & multi | .25 | .25 |
| **C507** | AP99 | 5c brt grn & blk | .25 | .25 |
| | | *Nos. C504-C507 (4)* | 5.75 | 2.75 |

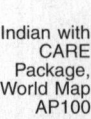

Indian with CARE Package, World Map AP100

CARE Package AP101

**1973, June 14** **Typo.** *Perf. 12½*

| | | | | |
|---|---|---|---|---|
| **C508** | AP100 | 2c blk & multi | .25 | .25 |
| **C509** | AP101 | 10c blk & multi | .55 | .40 |
| *a.* | | Souvenir sheet of 2 | 1.50 | 1.50 |

25th anniversary of CARE (in 1971), a US-sponsored relief organization and 10th anniversary of its work in Guatemala.

No. C509a contains 2 stamps similar to Nos. C508-C509 with simulated perforations.

Guatemala No. 1, Laurel AP102

**1973-74** **Engr.** *Perf. 12½, 11½ (1q)*

| | | | | |
|---|---|---|---|---|
| **C510** | AP102 | 1c yel brn ('74) | .25 | .25 |
| **C511** | AP102 | 1q rose claret | 3.00 | 2.50 |

Centenary (in 1971) of Guatemala postage stamps. See Nos. C574-C576A.

Oak Wreath and Star AP103

**1973, Aug. 22** **Typo.** *Perf. 12½*

| | | | | |
|---|---|---|---|---|
| **C512** | AP103 | 5c brn, yel & bl | .30 | .25 |

Centenary of Escuela Politecnica, Guatemala's military academy.

See Nos. C552-C553.

Eleanor Roosevelt AP104

*Perf. 11½, 12½*

**1973, Sept. 11** **Engr.**

| | | | | |
|---|---|---|---|---|
| **C513** | AP104 | 7c blue | .40 | .25 |

Eleanor Roosevelt (1884-1962), lecturer, writer, UN delegate.

Boys' School, Chiquimula AP105

**1973-74** **Typo.** *Perf. 12½*

| | | | | |
|---|---|---|---|---|
| **C514** | AP105 | 3c blk & bl | .30 | .25 |
| **C515** | AP105 | 5c blk & dp lil rose | .30 | .25 |

Centenary of the Instituto Varones in Chiquimula.

Issued: 5c, 12/5/73; 3c, 6/13/74.

### No. C430 Surcharged in Red

**1974** **Engr. & Photo.** *Perf. 11½*

| | | | | |
|---|---|---|---|---|
| **C516** | AP83 | 50c on 3q brn & red | 2.00 | 2.00 |

### Nos. C480-C485 and C509a Overprinted

**1974, June 13** **Typo.** *Perf. 11½*

| | | | | |
|---|---|---|---|---|
| **C517** | AP98 | 1c dk bl & lt bl | .40 | .30 |
| **C518** | AP98 | 1c dk bl & lt bl | .40 | .30 |
| **C519** | AP98 | 1c dk bl & lt bl | .40 | .30 |
| **C520** | AP98 | 1c dk bl & lt bl | .40 | .30 |
| **C521** | AP98 | 1c dk bl & lt bl | .40 | .30 |
| **C522** | AP98 | 1c dk bl & lt bl | .40 | .30 |
| | | *Nos. C517-C522 (6)* | 2.40 | 1.80 |

### Souvenir Sheet

| | | | | |
|---|---|---|---|---|
| **C523** | | Sheet of 2 | 13.50 | 13.50 |

Centenary of Universal Postal Union.

No. C523 consists of an overprint on No. C509a, including "UNIVERSAL POSTAL UNION" instead of "UPU."

The overprint on No. C523 in red was not authorized by the Post Office. Value $28.

### Antigua Type of 1972-73

**1974, Oct. 8** **Typo.** *Perf. 11½*

**Black and Light Brown**

| | | | | |
|---|---|---|---|---|
| **C528** | AP98 | 2c Capuchin Monastery | .25 | .25 |
| **C529** | AP98 | 2c Arches | .25 | .25 |
| **C530** | AP98 | 2c Cathedral | .25 | .25 |
| **C531** | AP98 | 2c Fountain and Santa Clara | .25 | .25 |
| **C532** | AP98 | 2c Portal of San Francisco | .25 | .25 |
| **C533** | AP98 | 2c Fountain | .25 | .25 |
| | | *Nos. C528-C533 (6)* | 1.50 | 1.50 |

**1974, Sept. 24** **Black and Yellow**

| | | | | |
|---|---|---|---|---|
| **C540** | AP98 | 20c Capuchin Monastery | .55 | .55 |
| **C541** | AP98 | 20c Arches | .55 | .55 |
| **C542** | AP98 | 20c Cathedral | .55 | .55 |
| **C543** | AP98 | 20c Fountain and Santa Clara | .55 | .55 |
| **C544** | AP98 | 20c Portal of San Francisco | .55 | .55 |
| **C545** | AP98 | 20c Fountain | .55 | .55 |
| | | *Nos. C540-C545 (6)* | 3.30 | 3.30 |

Earthquake ruins of Antigua. Each group of six printed se-tenant in sheets of 30 (5x6). Value $2.

Nos. C528-C533 were printed in 1975 in black and bister se-tenant in sheets of 24 (4x6) on whiter paper. Value $5.

Generals Justo Rufino Barrios and M. Garcia Granados — AP106

Polytechnic School AP107

**1974-75** **Typo.** *Perf. 12½, 11½ (25c)*

| | | | | |
|---|---|---|---|---|
| **C552** | AP106 | 6c red, gray & bl | .25 | .25 |
| **C553** | AP107 | 25c multi | .45 | .30 |

Centenary (in 1973) of Escuela Politecnica, Guatemala's military academy.

Issued: 6c, 9/17; 25c, 1/1/75.

No. C373 Surcharged in Black and Green

**1974, Dec. 3** **Engr.** *Perf. 13½*

| | | | | |
|---|---|---|---|---|
| **C554** | AP76 | 10c on 11c multi | 1.10 | .50 |

Nature protection. The quetzal, Guatemala's national bird.

Costume San Martin Sacatepequez AP108

Costumes of Women: 2c, Solola. 9c, Coban. 20c, Chichicastenango.

**1974-75** **Typo.** *Perf. 12½*

| | | | | |
|---|---|---|---|---|
| **C556** | AP108 | 2c car & multi | .25 | .25 |
| **C557** | AP108 | 2½c bl, car & brn | .25 | .25 |
| **C559** | AP108 | 9c bl & multi | .30 | .25 |
| *a.* | | Perf. 12½x13½ | .30 | .25 |
| **C561** | AP108 | 20c red & multi | .55 | .25 |
| | | *Nos. C556-C561 (4)* | 1.35 | 1.00 |

Issue dates: 2½c, Dec. 16, 1974; 20c, Jan. 14, 1975; 2c, 9c, May 19, 1975.

Quetzals and Maya Quekchi Woman Wearing Huipil — AP109

**1975, June 25** **Litho.** *Perf. 13½*

| | | | | |
|---|---|---|---|---|
| **C565** | AP109 | 8c bl & multi | .70 | .25 |
| **C566** | AP109 | 20c red & multi | 1.25 | .40 |

International Women's Year 1975.

Rotary Emblem AP110

**1975-76** **Typo.** *Perf. 13½*

| | | | | |
|---|---|---|---|---|
| **C567** | AP110 | 10c bl & multi | .40 | .25 |

*Perf. 11½*

| | | | | |
|---|---|---|---|---|
| **C568** | AP110 | 15c bl & multi | .45 | .25 |

Guatemala City Rotary Club, 50th anniv. Issued: 10c, 10/1; 15c, 12/21/76.

### Gaceta Type of 1971 Redrawn

**1975-76** **Typo.** *Perf. 12½*

| | | | | |
|---|---|---|---|---|
| **C569** | AP90 | 5c brn & red | .25 | .25 |
| **C570** | AP90 | 50c brt rose & brn | 1.40 | .55 |

The white background around numeral and on right of arms has been filled in.

Issued: 5c, 12/12; 50c, 12/1/76.

IWY Emblem and White Nun Orchid — AP111

**1975-76** *Perf. 12½x13½, 11½ (8c)*

| | | | | |
|---|---|---|---|---|
| **C571** | AP111 | 1c multi | .30 | .25 |
| **C572** | AP111 | 8c yel & multi | .40 | .25 |
| **C573** | AP111 | 26c rose & multi | .95 | .30 |
| | | *Nos. C571-C573 (3)* | 1.65 | .80 |

International Women's Year 1975.

Issued: 1c, 12/19; 8c, 12/12; 26c, 5/10/76.

### Stamp Centenary Type of 1973

**1975-77** **Engr.** *Perf. 11½*

| | | | | |
|---|---|---|---|---|
| **C574** | AP102 | 6c orange | .25 | .25 |
| **C575** | AP102 | 6c green ('76) | .25 | .25 |
| **C576** | AP102 | 6c gray ('77) | .25 | .25 |
| **C576A** | AP102 | 6c vio bl ('77) | .25 | .25 |
| | | *Nos. C574-C576A (4)* | 1.00 | 1.00 |

Issued: #C574, 12/31; #C575, 5/10; others, 8/10.

Destroyed Joyabaj Village — AP112

Designs (Guatemala Flag and): 3c, Emergency food distribution. 5c, Jaguar Temple, Tikal. 10c, Destroyed bridge. 15c, Outdoors emergency hospital. 20c, Sugar cane harvest. 25c, Destroyed house. 30c, New building, Tecpan. 50c, Destroyed Cerro del Carmen church. 75c, Cleaning up debris. 1q, Military help. 2q, Lake Atitlan.

**1976, June 4** **Litho.** *Perf. 12½*

| | | | | |
|---|---|---|---|---|
| **C577** | AP112 | 1c red & multi | .25 | .25 |
| **C578** | AP112 | 3c multi | .25 | .25 |
| **C579** | AP112 | 5c pink & multi | .25 | .25 |
| **C580** | AP112 | 10c red & multi | .30 | .25 |
| **C581** | AP112 | 15c multi | .45 | .25 |
| **C582** | AP112 | 20c pink & multi | .45 | .30 |
| **C583** | AP112 | 25c red & multi | .80 | .35 |
| **C584** | AP112 | 30c multi | .95 | .50 |
| **C585** | AP112 | 50c red & multi | 1.25 | 1.00 |
| **C586** | AP112 | 75c multi | 2.00 | 1.75 |
| **C587** | AP112 | 1q multi | 3.00 | 2.50 |
| **C588** | AP112 | 2q multi | 5.75 | 5.75 |
| | | *Nos. C577-C588 (12)* | 15.70 | 13.40 |

Earthquake of Feb. 4, 1976, and gratitude for foreign help. Inscriptions in colored panels vary. 3 imperf. souvenir sheets exist (50c, 1q, 2q). Size: 112x83mm. Value, each $15.

Allegory of Independence — AP113

Designs: 2c, Boston Tea Party. 3c, Thomas Jefferson, vert. 4c, 20c, 35c, Allegory of Independence (each different; 4c, 35c, vert.). 5c, Warren's Death at Bunker Hill. 10c, Washington at Valley Forge. 15c, Washington at Monmouth. 25c, The Generals at Yorktown. 30c, Washington Crossing the Delaware. 40c, Declaration of Independence. 45c, Patrick Henry, vert. 50c, Congress Voting Independence. 1q, Washington, vert. 2q, Lincoln, vert. 3q, Franklin, vert. 5q, John F. Kennedy, vert. The historical designs and portraits are after paintings.

**1976, July 30 Litho. *Perf. 12½***

**Size: 46x27mm, 27x46mm**

| | | | | |
|---|---|---|---|---|
| **C592** | AP113 | 1c multicolored | .25 | .25 |
| **C593** | AP113 | 2c multicolored | .25 | .25 |
| **C594** | AP113 | 3c multicolored | .25 | .25 |
| **C595** | AP113 | 4c multicolored | .25 | .25 |
| **C596** | AP113 | 5c multicolored | .25 | .25 |
| **C597** | AP113 | 10c multicolored | .25 | .25 |
| **C598** | AP113 | 15c multicolored | .30 | .25 |
| **C599** | AP113 | 20c multicolored | .45 | .25 |
| **C600** | AP113 | 25c multicolored | .45 | .25 |
| **C601** | AP113 | 30c multicolored | .80 | .25 |
| **C602** | AP113 | 35c multicolored | .85 | .45 |
| **C603** | AP113 | 40c multicolored | .85 | .55 |
| **C604** | AP113 | 45c multicolored | 1.00 | .65 |
| **C605** | AP113 | 50c multicolored | 1.40 | .45 |
| **C606** | AP113 | 1q multicolored | 2.40 | 2.00 |
| *a.* | | Souvenir sheet | 2.75 | 2.75 |
| **C607** | AP113 | 2q multicolored | 4.00 | 4.00 |
| *a.* | | Souvenir sheet | 5.00 | 5.00 |
| **C608** | AP113 | 3q multicolored | 5.50 | 5.50 |
| *a.* | | Souvenir sheet | 6.25 | 6.25 |

**Size: 35x55mm**

| | | | | |
|---|---|---|---|---|
| **C609** | AP113 | 5q multicolored | 9.50 | 3.50 |
| *a.* | | Souvenir sheet | 12.00 | 12.00 |
| | | *Nos. C592-C609 (18)* | 29.00 | 19.60 |

American Bicentennial. Souvenir sheets contain one imperf. stamp each.

1974 Quetzal Coin AP114

**Lithographed and Engraved**

**1976, Dec. 1 *Perf. 11½***

| | | | | |
|---|---|---|---|---|
| **C610** | AP114 | 8c org, blk & bl | .25 | .25 |

***Perf. 13½***

| | | | | |
|---|---|---|---|---|
| **C611** | AP114 | 20c brt rose, bl & blk | .70 | .25 |

50th anniv. of introduction of Quetzal currency.

Engineers at Work AP115

**1976, Dec. 21 Engr. *Perf. 11½***

| | | | | |
|---|---|---|---|---|
| **C612** | AP115 | 9c ultra | .30 | .25 |
| **C613** | AP115 | 10c green | .30 | .25 |

School of Engineering, Guatemala City, centenary.

**Holy Week Type of 1977**

Designs: Sculptures of Christ from various Guatemalan churches. 4c, 7c, 9c, 20c, vert.

**1977, Apr. 4 Litho. *Perf. 11***

| | | | | |
|---|---|---|---|---|
| **C614** | A159 | 3c pur & multi | .40 | .25 |
| **C615** | A159 | 4c pur & multi | .40 | .25 |
| **C616** | A159 | 7c pur & multi | .40 | .25 |
| **C617** | A159 | 9c pur & multi | .45 | .25 |
| **C618** | A159 | 20c pur & multi | .95 | .60 |
| **C619** | A159 | 26c pur & multi | 1.25 | .70 |
| | | *Nos. C614-C619 (6)* | 3.85 | 2.30 |

**Souvenir Sheet**

***Roulette 7½***

| | | | | |
|---|---|---|---|---|
| **C620** | A159 | 30c pur & multi | 4.00 | 4.00 |

Holy Week 1977.

City Hall and Bank of Guatemala — AP116

Designs: 6c, Deed to original site, vert. 8c, Church and farm house, site of first legislative session. 9c, Coat of arms of Pedro Cortes, first archbishop. 22c, Arms of Guatemala City, vert.

***Perf. 13½ (6c); 11½ (others)***

**1977, Aug. 10 Litho.**

| | | | | |
|---|---|---|---|---|
| **C621** | AP116 | 6c multicolored | .40 | .25 |
| **C622** | AP116 | 7c multicolored | .40 | .25 |
| **C623** | AP116 | 8c multicolored | .40 | .25 |
| **C624** | AP116 | 9c multicolored | .55 | .25 |
| *a.* | | Souvenir sheet | .80 | .80 |
| **C625** | AP116 | 22c multicolored | .85 | .25 |
| *a.* | | Souvenir sheet | 1.10 | 1.10 |
| | | *Nos. C621-C625 (5)* | 2.60 | 1.25 |

Bicentenary of the founding of Nueva Guatemala de la Asuncion (Guatemala City). Nos. C624a-C625a contain one stamp each with simulated perforations.

Arms of Quetzaltenango AP117

City Hall and Torch AP118

**1977, Sept. 11 Litho. *Perf. 11½***

| | | | | |
|---|---|---|---|---|
| **C626** | AP117 | 7c blk & sil | .25 | .25 |
| **C627** | AP118 | 30c bl & yel | .85 | .30 |

Founding of Quetzaltenango, 150th anniv.

Mayan Bas-relief — AP119

**1977, Nov. 7**

| | | | | |
|---|---|---|---|---|
| **C628** | AP119 | 10c brt car & blk | .30 | .25 |

14th Intl. Cong. of Latin Notaries.

Children Bringing Gifts to Christ Child — AP120

Christmas: 1c, Mother and children, horiz. 4c, Guatemalan children's Nativity scene.

**1977, Dec. 16 Litho. *Perf. 11½***

| | | | | |
|---|---|---|---|---|
| **C629** | AP120 | 1c multicolored | .25 | .25 |
| **C630** | AP120 | 2c multicolored | .25 | .25 |
| **C631** | AP120 | 4c multicolored | .25 | .25 |
| | | *Nos. C629-C631 (3)* | .75 | .75 |

Almolonga Costume, Cancer League Emblem — AP121

Regional Costumes after Paintings by Carlos Mérida and Cancer League Emblem: 2c, Nebaj woman. 5c, San Juan Cotzal couple. 6c, Todos Santos couple. 20c, Regidores men. 30c, San Cristobal woman.

***Perf. 14 (1c, 5c, No. C636); Perf. 12 (2c, 6c, No. C636a, 30c)***

**1978, Apr. 3 Litho.**

| | | | | |
|---|---|---|---|---|
| **C632** | AP121 | 1c gold & multi | .25 | .25 |
| **C633** | AP121 | 2c gold & multi | .25 | .25 |
| **C634** | AP121 | 5c gold & multi | .25 | .25 |
| **C635** | AP121 | 6c gold & multi | .30 | .25 |
| **C636** | AP121 | 20c gold & multi | 1.10 | .25 |
| *a.* | | Souv. sheet of 1 | 3.00 | 3.00 |
| **C637** | AP121 | 30c gold & multi | 1.10 | .30 |
| | | *Nos. C632-C637 (6)* | 3.25 | 1.55 |

Part of proceeds from sale of stamps went to National League to Fight Cancer.

Virgin of Sorrows, Antigua — AP122

Statues from Various Churches: 4c, Virgin of Mercy, Antigua. 5c, Virgin of Anguish, Yurrita. 6c, Virgin of the Rosary, Santo Domingo. 8c, Virgin of Sorrows, Santo Domingo. 9c, Virgin of the Rosary, Quetzaltenango. 10c, Virgin of the Immaculate Conception, Church of St. Francis. 20c, Virgin of the Immaculate Conception, Cathedral Church.

**1978 Litho. *Perf. 11½***

| | | | | |
|---|---|---|---|---|
| **C638** | AP122 | 2c multicolored | .45 | .30 |
| **C639** | AP122 | 4c multicolored | .45 | .30 |
| **C640** | AP122 | 5c multicolored | .45 | .30 |
| **C641** | AP122 | 6c multicolored | .45 | .30 |
| **C642** | AP122 | 8c multicolored | .45 | .30 |
| **C643** | AP122 | 9c multicolored | .45 | .30 |
| **C644** | AP122 | 10c multicolored | .45 | .30 |
| **C645** | AP122 | 20c multicolored | 1.25 | .30 |
| | | *Nos. C638-C645 (8)* | 4.40 | 2.40 |

Holy Week 1978. A 30c imperf. souvenir sheet shows the Pietà from Calvary Church, Antigua. Size: 71x101mm. Value $4.50.

Issued: 6c, 10c, 20c, 9/28; others, 5/22.

Soccer Player, Argentina '78 Emblem AP123

**1978, July 3 Litho. *Perf. 12***

| | | | | |
|---|---|---|---|---|
| **C646** | AP123 | 10c multicolored | .50 | .25 |

11th World Cup Soccer Championship, Argentina, June 1-25.

Gymnastics AP124

**1978, Sept. 4 *Perf. 12***

| | | | | |
|---|---|---|---|---|
| **C647** | AP124 | 6c shown | .25 | .25 |
| **C648** | AP124 | 6c Volleyball | .25 | .25 |
| **C649** | AP124 | 6c Target shooting | .25 | .25 |
| **C650** | AP124 | 6c Weight lifting | .25 | .25 |
| *a.* | | Block of 4, #C647-C650 | 4.00 | 4.00 |
| **C651** | AP124 | 8c Track & field | .25 | .25 |
| | | *Nos. C647-C651 (5)* | 1.25 | 1.25 |

13th Central American and Caribbean Games, Medellin, Colombia.

Cattleya Pachecoi AP125

Designs: Orchids.

**1978, Dec. 7 Litho. *Perf. 12***

| | | | | |
|---|---|---|---|---|
| **C652** | AP125 | 1c shown | 1.40 | 1.40 |
| **C653** | AP125 | 1c Sobralia | 1.40 | 1.40 |
| **C654** | AP125 | 1c Cypripedium | 1.40 | 1.40 |
| **C655** | AP125 | 1c Oncidium | 1.40 | 1.40 |
| *a.* | | Block of 4, #C652-C655 | 20.00 | 20.00 |
| **C656** | AP125 | 3c Cattleya bowrigiana | 1.60 | 1.60 |
| **C657** | AP125 | 3c Encyclia | 1.60 | 1.60 |
| **C658** | AP125 | 3c Epidendrum | 1.60 | 1.60 |
| **C659** | AP125 | 3c Barkeria | 1.60 | 1.60 |
| *a.* | | Block of 4, #C656-C659 | 20.00 | 20.00 |
| **C660** | AP125 | 8c Spiranthes | 8.00 | 3.00 |
| **C661** | AP125 | 20c Lycaste | 12.50 | 10.50 |
| | | *Nos. C652-C661 (10)* | 32.50 | 25.50 |

Seal of University AP126

Students of Different Departments AP127

Designs: 12c, Student in 17th cent. clothes. 14c, Students, 1978, and molecular model.

**1978, Dec. 7**

| | | | | |
|---|---|---|---|---|
| **C662** | AP126 | 6c multicolored | .25 | .25 |
| **C663** | AP127 | 7c multicolored | .25 | .25 |
| **C664** | AP126 | 12c multicolored | .30 | .25 |
| **C665** | AP126 | 14c multicolored | .45 | .25 |
| | | *Nos. C662-C665 (4)* | 1.25 | 1.00 |

San Carlos University of Guatemala, tercentenary.

Brown and White Children AP128

A Helping Hand — AP129

Designs: 7c, Child at play. 14c, Hands sheltering Indian girl.

**1978, Dec. 7**

| | | | | |
|---|---|---|---|---|
| **C666** | AP128 | 6c multicolored | .25 | .25 |
| **C667** | AP128 | 7c multicolored | .25 | .25 |
| **C668** | AP129 | 12c multicolored | .30 | .25 |
| **C669** | AP129 | 14c multicolored | .45 | .25 |
| | | *Nos. C666-C669 (4)* | 1.25 | 1.00 |

Year of the Children of Guatemala.

Tree Planting and FAO Emblem — AP130

Forest protection: 8c, Burnt forest. 9c, Watershed, river and trees. 10c, Sawmill. 26c, Forests, river and cultivated terraces.

**1979, Apr. 16 Litho. *Perf. 13½***

| | | | | |
|---|---|---|---|---|
| **C670** | AP130 | 6c multicolored | .30 | .25 |
| **C671** | AP130 | 8c multicolored | .30 | .25 |
| **C672** | AP130 | 9c multicolored | .30 | .25 |
| **C673** | AP130 | 10c multicolored | .30 | .25 |
| **C674** | AP130 | 26c multicolored | .55 | .25 |
| *a.* | | Souv. sheet of 5, #C670-C674 | 9.50 | *9.50* |
| | | *Nos. C670-C674 (5)* | 1.75 | 1.25 |

Peten Wild Turkey — AP131

Wildlife conservation: 3c, White-tailed deer, horiz. 5c, King buzzard. 7c, Horned owl. 9c, Young wildcat. 30c, Quetzal.

**1979, June 14 Litho. *Perf. 13½***

| | | | | |
|---|---|---|---|---|
| **C675** | AP131 | 1c multicolored | 1.90 | .70 |
| **C676** | AP131 | 3c multicolored | 1.10 | .70 |
| **C677** | AP131 | 5c multicolored | 5.75 | .70 |
| **C678** | AP131 | 7c multicolored | 12.50 | 2.75 |
| **C679** | AP131 | 9c multicolored | 2.75 | .70 |
| | | *Nos. C675-C679 (5)* | 24.00 | 5.55 |

**Souvenir Sheet**

| | | | | |
|---|---|---|---|---|
| **C680** | AP131 | 30c multicolored | 16.00 | 16.00 |

Clay Jar, 50-100 A.D. — AP132

Archaeological Treasures from Tikal: 3c, Mayan woman, ceramic head, 900 A.D. 4c, Earring, 50-100 A.D. 5c, vase, 700 A.D. 6c, Boy, 200-50 B.C. 7c, Bone carving, 700 A.D. 8c, Striped vase, 700 A.D. 10c, Covered vase on tripod, 450 B.C.

**1979, Sept. 19 Litho. *Perf. 13***

| | | | | |
|---|---|---|---|---|
| **C681** | AP132 | 2c multi | .40 | .25 |
| **C682** | AP132 | 3c multi | .55 | .40 |
| **C683** | AP132 | 4c multi | .80 | .55 |
| **C684** | AP132 | 5c multi | .95 | .55 |
| **C685** | AP132 | 6c multi | 1.25 | .80 |
| **C686** | AP132 | 7c multi | 1.25 | .95 |
| **C687** | AP132 | 8c multi | 1.50 | 1.00 |
| **C688** | AP132 | 10c multi | 2.00 | 1.25 |
| | | *Nos. C681-C688 (8)* | 8.70 | 5.75 |

Presidential Guard Patches AP133

Presidential Guard, 30th anniv.: 10c, Guard Headquarters.

**1979, Dec. 6 Litho. *Perf. 11½***

| | | | | |
|---|---|---|---|---|
| **C689** | AP133 | 8c multi | .25 | .25 |
| **C690** | AP133 | 10c multi | .25 | .25 |

National Coat of Arms — AP134

Arms of Guatemalan Municipalities.

**1979, Dec. 27 Litho. *Perf. 13½***

| | | | | |
|---|---|---|---|---|
| **C691** | AP134 | 8c shown | .45 | .25 |
| **C692** | AP134 | 8c Alta Verapaz | .45 | .25 |
| **C693** | AP134 | 8c Baja Verapaz | .45 | .25 |
| **C694** | AP134 | 8c Chimal Tenango | .45 | .25 |
| **C695** | AP134 | 8c Chiquimula | .45 | .25 |
| **C696** | AP134 | 8c Escuintla | .45 | .25 |
| **C697** | AP134 | 8c Flores | .45 | .25 |
| **C698** | AP134 | 8c Guatemala | .45 | .25 |
| **C699** | AP134 | 8c Huehuetenango | .45 | .25 |
| **C700** | AP134 | 8c Izabal | .45 | .25 |
| **C701** | AP134 | 8c Jalapa | .45 | .25 |
| **C702** | AP134 | 8c Jutiapa | .45 | .25 |
| **C703** | AP134 | 8c Mazatenango | .45 | .25 |
| **C704** | AP134 | 8c Progreso | .45 | .25 |
| **C705** | AP134 | 8c Quezaltenan-go | .45 | .25 |
| **C706** | AP134 | 8c Quiche | .45 | .25 |
| **C707** | AP134 | 8c Retalhuleu | .45 | .25 |
| **C708** | AP134 | 8c Sacatepequez | .45 | .25 |
| **C709** | AP134 | 8c San Marcos | .45 | .25 |
| **C710** | AP134 | 8c Santa Rosa | .45 | .25 |
| **C711** | AP134 | 8c Solola | .45 | .25 |
| **C712** | AP134 | 8c Totonicapan | .45 | .25 |
| **C713** | AP134 | 8c Zacapa | .45 | .25 |
| | | *Nos. C691-C713 (23)* | 10.35 | 5.75 |

**Miniature Sheet**

***Imperf***

| | | | | |
|---|---|---|---|---|
| **C714** | AP134 | 50c 1st & current natl. arms | 3.50 | 3.50 |

No. C714 is horizontal.

Scenes from Popul Vuh (Sacred Book of the Ancient Quiches of Guatemala) AP135

Designs: No. C715, Creation of the World. No. C716, Origin of the Twin Semi-gods. No. C717, Populating the earth. No. C718, Balam Quitze. No. C719, Quiche monarch Cotuha. No. C720, Birth of the Stick Men. No. C721, Princess Xquic's punishment. No. C722, Caha Paluma. No. C723, Cotuha and Iztayul invincible. No. C724, Odyssey of Hun Ahpu and Xbalanque. No. C725, Balam Acab. No. C726, Chief of all Nations. No. C727, Destruction of the Stick Men. No. C728, The Test in Xibalba. No. C729, Chomiha. No. C730, Warrior with captive. No. C731, Creation of the Corn Men. No. C732, Multiplication of the Prodigies. No. C733, Mahucutah. No. C734, Undefeatable king. No. C735, Thanksgiving. No. C736, Deification of Hun Ahpu and Xbalanque. No. C737, Tzununiha. No. C738, Greatness of the Quiches (battle scene).

**1981 Litho. *Perf. 12***

**Background Color**

| | | | | |
|---|---|---|---|---|
| **C715** | AP135 | 1c lilac | .40 | .75 |
| **C716** | AP135 | 1c pink | .40 | .75 |
| **C717** | AP135 | 2c green | .40 | .75 |
| **C718** | AP135 | 2c brt lilac | .40 | .75 |
| **C719** | AP135 | 3c blue | .50 | .75 |
| **C720** | AP135 | 4c dk blue | .95 | .75 |
| **C721** | AP135 | 4c blue vio | .95 | .75 |
| **C722** | AP135 | 4c blue | .95 | .75 |
| **C723** | AP135 | 4c lilac | .95 | .75 |
| **C724** | AP135 | 6c brown | .95 | .75 |
| **C725** | AP135 | 6c pink | .80 | .75 |
| **C726** | AP135 | 6c org brn | .50 | .50 |
| **C727** | AP135 | 8c citron | 1.25 | 1.00 |
| **C728** | AP135 | 8c green | 1.25 | 1.00 |
| **C729** | AP135 | 8c yel grn | 1.25 | 1.00 |
| **C730** | AP135 | 8c gray | 1.25 | 1.00 |
| **C731** | AP135 | 10c orange | 1.25 | 1.00 |
| **C732** | AP135 | 10c brt yellow | 1.25 | 1.00 |
| **C733** | AP135 | 10c blue green | 1.25 | 1.00 |
| **C734** | AP135 | 10c dull green | 1.25 | 1.00 |
| **C735** | AP135 | 22c brown | 1.25 | 1.25 |
| **C736** | AP135 | 26c dull bl grn | 1.40 | 1.25 |
| **C737** | AP135 | 30c gray grn | 2.25 | 1.50 |
| **C738** | AP135 | 50c red violet | 3.50 | 2.00 |
| | | *Nos. C715-C738 (24)* | 26.55 | 22.75 |

Issued: #C715, C717, 3c, C727, C731, 22c, 1/29; #C716, C718, C721-C722, C724-C725, C728-C729, C732-C733, 26c, 30c, 3/16; others, 1981.

Thomas Edison (Phonograph Centenary) AP136

Talking Movies, 50th Anniv. — AP137

Telephone Centenary (1976) — AP138

Lindbergh's Atlantic Flight, 50th Anniv. (1977) AP139

12c, Jose Cecilio del Valle, patriot. 25c, Jesus Castillo (1877-1949), composer.

***Perf. 11½, 12½ (25c)***

**1981, June 1 Litho.**

| | | | | |
|---|---|---|---|---|
| **C739** | AP136 | 3c multi | .25 | .25 |
| **C740** | AP137 | 5c multi | .30 | .25 |
| **C741** | AP138 | 6c multi | .40 | .25 |
| **C742** | AP139 | 7c multi | .45 | .30 |
| **C743** | AP139 | 12c multi | .80 | .45 |
| **C744** | AP139 | 25c multi | 1.50 | 1.00 |
| | | *Nos. C739-C744 (6)* | 3.70 | 2.50 |

First Police Chief Roderico Toledo and Present Chief German Chupina AP140

**1981, Sept. 12 Litho. *Perf. 11½***

| | | | | |
|---|---|---|---|---|
| **C745** | AP140 | 2c shown | .40 | .25 |
| **C746** | AP140 | 4c Headquarters | .40 | .25 |

Mayan Rock of the Sun Calendar AP141

**1981, Oct. 9**

| | | | | |
|---|---|---|---|---|
| **C747** | AP141 | 1c multi | .25 | .25 |

Gen. Jose Gervasio Artigas of Uruguay AP142

Liberators of the Americas: 2c, Bernardo O'Higgins (Chile). 4c, Jose de San Martin (Argentina). 10c, Miguel Garcia Granados. 2c, 4c, 10c, 31x47mm.

**1982, Apr. 2 Litho. *Perf. 11½***

| | | | | |
|---|---|---|---|---|
| **C748** | AP142 | 2c multi | *1.00* | *1.00* |
| **C749** | AP142 | 3c multi | .25 | .25 |

***Perf. 12½***

| | | | | |
|---|---|---|---|---|
| **C750** | AP142 | 4c multi | *1.00* | *1.00* |
| **C751** | AP142 | 10c tan & blk | .25 | .25 |
| | | *Nos. C748-C751 (4)* | 2.50 | 2.50 |

Occidents Bank Centenary (1981) AP143

1c, Justo Rufino Barrios (1st pres.), Main Office, Quezaltenango. 2c, Main Office, 3c, Emblem, vert. 4c, Commemorative medals, vert.

**1982, July 28 Litho. *Perf. 11½***

| | | | | |
|---|---|---|---|---|
| **C752** | AP143 | 1c multi | .30 | .25 |
| **C753** | AP143 | 2c multi | .30 | .25 |
| **C754** | AP143 | 3c multi | .30 | .25 |
| **C755** | AP143 | 4c multi | .30 | .25 |
| | | *Nos. C752-C755 (4)* | 1.20 | 1.00 |

50th Anniv. of Natl. Mortgage Bank (1980) AP144

Various emblems. 5c vert.

**1982, Oct. 18 Litho. *Perf. 11½***

| | | | | |
|---|---|---|---|---|
| **C756** | AP144 | 1c multi | .30 | .25 |
| **C757** | AP144 | 2c multi | .30 | .25 |
| **C758** | AP144 | 5c multi | .30 | .25 |
| **C759** | AP144 | 10c multi | .30 | .25 |
| | | *Nos. C756-C759 (4)* | 1.20 | 1.00 |

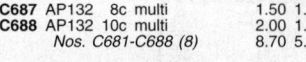

AP145

**1983, May 16 Litho. *Perf. 11½***

| | | | | |
|---|---|---|---|---|
| **C760** | AP145 | 1c Portrait | .25 | .25 |
| **C761** | AP145 | 20c Aparition, horiz. | .60 | .40 |

20th Anniv. of Beatification of Pedro Bethancourt (1626-1667).

AP146

**1983, July 25 Litho. *Perf. 11½***

| | | | | |
|---|---|---|---|---|
| **C762** | AP146 | 10c multi | .50 | .25 |

World Telecommunications and Health Day, May 17, 1981

Evangelical Church Centenary (1982) — AP147

**1983, Aug. 9**

| | | | | |
|---|---|---|---|---|
| **C763** | AP147 | 3c Hands holding bible | .40 | .25 |
| **C764** | AP147 | 5c Church | .40 | .25 |

Natl. Railroad Centenary — AP148

10c, 1st locomotive crossing Puenta de Las Vacas. 25c, General Justo Rufino Barrios, Railroad Yard. 30c, Spanish Diesel, Amatitlan crossing.

**1983, Sept. 28 Litho. *Perf. 11½***

| | | | | |
|---|---|---|---|---|
| **C765** | AP148 | 10c multi | 1.00 | .80 |
| **C766** | AP148 | 25c multi | 2.75 | 1.75 |
| **C767** | AP148 | 30c multi | 3.00 | 2.00 |
| | | *Nos. C765-C767 (3)* | 6.75 | 4.55 |

World Food Day AP149

**1983, Oct. 16 Photo. *Perf. 11½***

| | | | | |
|---|---|---|---|---|
| **C768** | AP149 | 8c Globe, wheat, vert. | 1.25 | .75 |
| **C769** | AP149 | 1q shown | 8.00 | 4.00 |

**Architecture Type of 1972**

**1984, Feb. 20 Typo. *Perf. 12½***

**Black and Green**

| | | | | |
|---|---|---|---|---|
| **C770** | AP98 | 1c like #C480 | .25 | .25 |
| **C771** | AP98 | 1c like #C481 | .25 | .25 |
| **C772** | AP98 | 1c like #C482 | .25 | .25 |
| **C773** | AP98 | 1c like #C483 | .25 | .25 |
| **C774** | AP98 | 1c like #C484 | .25 | .25 |
| **C775** | AP98 | 1c like #C485 | .25 | .25 |
| *g.* | | Strip of 6, #C770-C775 | 1.00 | 1.00 |

**Black, Brown and Orange Brown**

| | | | | |
|---|---|---|---|---|
| **C775A** | AP98 | 5c like #C484 | .25 | .25 |
| **C775B** | AP98 | 5c like #C485 | .25 | .25 |
| **C775C** | AP98 | 5c like #C482 | .25 | .25 |
| **C775D** | AP98 | 5c like #C483 | .25 | .25 |
| **C775E** | AP98 | 5c like #C480 | .25 | .25 |
| **C775F** | AP98 | 5c like #C481 | .25 | .25 |
| *h.* | | Strip of 6, #C775A-C775F | 1.75 | 1.75 |

Visit of Pope John Paul II, Mar. 8-9, 1983 AP150

**1984, Mar. 26 Litho. *Perf. 11½***

| | | | | |
|---|---|---|---|---|
| **C776** | AP150 | 4c Pope, arms | .45 | .35 |
| **C777** | AP150 | 8c Receiving Mayan indian | .45 | .35 |

Rafael Landivar (1731-93), Poet — AP151

**1984, Aug. 6 Litho. *Perf. 11½***

| | | | | |
|---|---|---|---|---|
| **C778** | AP151 | 2c Portrait, vert. | .30 | .25 |
| **C779** | AP151 | 4c Tomb | .30 | .25 |

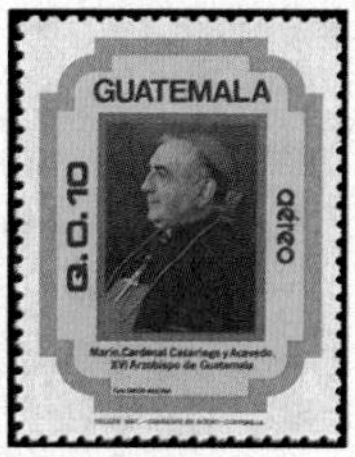

Cardinal Mario Casariego y Acevedo AP152

**1984, Aug. 6**

| | | | | |
|---|---|---|---|---|
| **C780** | AP152 | 10c 16th archbishop of Guat. (1909-83) | .40 | .25 |

Central American Bank for Economic Integration, 20th Anniv. — AP153

**1984, Sept. 10 Litho. *Perf. 11½***

| | | | | |
|---|---|---|---|---|
| **C781** | AP153 | 30c Bank emblem, map | 1.10 | .60 |

Coffee Production, 1870 AP154

Modern Coffee Production AP155

Designs: 1c, Planting coffee. 2c, Harvesting. 3c, Drying beans. 4c, Loading beans on steamer. 5c, Reyna plant grafting method. 10c, Picking beans, coffee cup. 12c, Drying unripened beans, Gardiola Freeze-drying machine. 25c, Cargo transports.

**1984, Dec. 19 *Perf. 11½***

| | | | | |
|---|---|---|---|---|
| **C782** | AP154 | 1c sep & pale brn | .25 | .25 |
| **C783** | AP154 | 2c sep & pale org brn | .25 | .25 |
| **C784** | AP154 | 3c sep & beige | .25 | .25 |
| **C785** | AP154 | 4c sep & pale yel brn | .25 | .25 |
| **C786** | AP155 | 5c multi | .30 | .25 |
| **C787** | AP155 | 10c multi | .60 | .40 |
| **C788** | AP155 | 12c multi | .80 | .45 |
| **C789** | AP155 | 25c multi | 1.50 | 1.00 |
| | | *Nos. C782-C789 (8)* | 4.20 | 3.10 |

Natl. coffee production and export. An 86x112mm 25c stamp of Type AP154 and a 105x85mm 30c stamp of Type AP155 exist, value $80. and $110. respectively.

Natl. Scouting Assoc. — AP156

Scouting emblems and: 5c, Beaver scout, Pyramid of Tikal. 6c, Wolf scout, Palace of the Captains-General and Ahua Volcano. 8c, Scout, San Pedro Volcano and Marimba player. 10c, Rover scout and conquest mask dance. 20c, Lord Baden-Powell and Col. Carlos Cipriani, natl. founder.

**1985, July 1**

| | | | | |
|---|---|---|---|---|
| **C792** | AP156 | 5c multi | .30 | .25 |
| **C793** | AP156 | 6c multi | .40 | .25 |
| **C794** | AP156 | 8c multi | .45 | .30 |
| **C795** | AP156 | 10c multi | .45 | .40 |
| **C796** | AP156 | 20c multi | 1.25 | .85 |
| | | *Nos. C792-C796 (5)* | 2.85 | 2.05 |

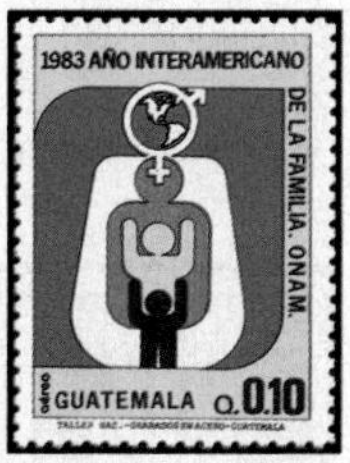

Inter-American Family Unity Year — AP157

**1985, Oct. 16**

| | | | | |
|---|---|---|---|---|
| **C797** | AP157 | 10c multi | .45 | .30 |

Central American Aeronautics Admin., 25th Anniv. — AP158

**1985, Nov. 11**

| | | | | |
|---|---|---|---|---|
| **C798** | AP158 | 10c multi | .40 | .25 |

Natl. Telegraph, Cent. — AP159

Portraits: Samuel Morse, telegraph inventor, and Justo Rufino Barrios, communications pioneer.

**1985, Nov. 20 *Perf. 12***

| | | | | |
|---|---|---|---|---|
| **C799** | AP159 | 4c brn & blk | .25 | .25 |

Intl. Olympic Committee, 90th Anniv. — AP160

Designs: 8c, Mayan bust of ancient sportsman. 10c, Baron Pierre de Coubertin (1863-1937), father of modern Games, 1st committee president.

**1986, Jan. 28 Litho. *Perf. 11½***

| | | | | |
|---|---|---|---|---|
| **C800** | AP160 | 8c multi | .55 | .45 |
| **C801** | AP160 | 10c multi | .75 | .45 |

Volunteer Fire Department AP161

**1986, Feb. 6 Litho. *Perf. 11½***

| | | | | |
|---|---|---|---|---|
| **C802** | AP161 | 6c multi | .65 | .25 |

Temple of Minerva — AP162

Quetzaltenango Coat of Arms, City Hall — AP163

**1986, July 16 Litho. *Perf. 12½, 11½***

| | | | | |
|---|---|---|---|---|
| **C803** | AP162 | 8c multi | .25 | .25 |
| **C804** | AP163 | 10c multi | .30 | .25 |

Quetzaltenango Independence Fair, cent.

Volunteer Fire Department AP164

**1986, Oct. 10 Litho. *Perf. 11½***

| | | | | |
|---|---|---|---|---|
| **C805** | AP164 | 8c Rescue | .85 | .30 |
| **C806** | AP164 | 10c Ruins | .85 | .30 |

Assoc. of Telegraphers and Radio-Telegraph Operators, 25th Anniv. — AP165

**1986, Oct. 10 *Perf. 12***

| | | | | |
|---|---|---|---|---|
| **C807** | AP165 | 6c multi | .50 | .25 |

San Carlos University School of Architecture, 25th Anniv. — AP166

**1987, Feb. 16 Litho. *Perf. 11½***
**C808** AP166 10c multi .50 .25

ICAO, 40th Anniv. (in 1984) AP167

**1987, Apr. 2 Litho. *Perf. 11½***
**C809** AP167 8c Aviateca Airlines jet .25 .25
**C810** AP167 10c Jet, vert. .30 .25

Chixoy Hydroelectric Power Plant — AP168

**1987, May 18 Litho. *Perf. 11½***
**C811** AP168 2c multi .40 .40

Nat'l. Electrification Institute inauguration (in 1985).

San Jose de los Infantes College, 200th Anniv. (in 1981) AP169

8c, Portrait of Archbishop Cayetano Francos y Monroy, founder. 10c, College crest.

**1987, June 10**
**C812** AP169 8c multi, vert. .25 .25
**C813** AP169 10c multi .30 .25

Promotion of Literacy in Latin America and Caribbean AP170

**1987, Aug. 20 Litho. *Perf. 11½***
**C814** AP170 12c apple grn, blk & brt org .40 .25

19th Natl. Folklore Carnival of Coban, Alta Verapaz, July 25 — AP171

**1987, Oct. 12**
**C815** AP171 1q Three girls from Tamahu 5.50 2.00

**1987, Dec. 8**
**C816** AP171 50c Girl weaving 2.75 .95

See No. C831.

9th Pan American Games, Caracas AP172

**1987, Nov. 5 *Perf. 12½***
**C817** AP172 10c blk & sky blue *9.50 5.00*

Writers and Historians AP173

Designs: 1c, Flavio Herrera, poet, novelist. 2c, Rosendo Santa Cruz, novelist. 3c, Werner Ovalle Lopez, poet. 4c, Enrique A. Hidalgo, poet, humorist. 5c, Enrique Gomez Carrillo (1873-1927), novelist. 6c, Cesar Branas (1899-1976), journalist. 7c, Clemente Marroquin Rojas, historian. 8c, Rafael Arevalo Martinez (1884-1975), poet. 9c, Jose Milla y Vidaurre (1822-1882), historian. 10c, Miguel Angel Asturias, Nobel laureate for literature.

**1987-90 *Perf. 11½***
**C818** AP173 1c blk & lil .30 .25
**C819** AP173 2c blk & dl org .30 .25
**C820** AP173 3c blk & brt bl .30 .25
**C821** AP173 4c blk & ver .30 .25
**C822** AP173 5c blk & org brn .30 .25
**C823** AP173 6c blk & org .30 .25
**C824** AP173 7c blk & grn .30 .25
**C825** AP173 8c blk & brt red .30 .25
**C826** AP173 9c blk & brt rose lil .30 .25
**C827** AP173 10c blk & yel .30 .25
*Nos. C818-C827 (10)* 3.00 2.50

Issued: 6c, 8c, 9c, 11/5/87; 4c, 5c, 1/13/88; 7c, 3/23/90; 1c, 2c, 3c, 10c, 4/9/90.

Esquipulas II — AP174

**1988, Jan. 15 *Perf. 12½***
**C828** AP174 10c dark olive grn .40 .25
**C829** AP174 40c plum 1.50 1.00
**C830** AP174 60c deep blue vio 2.40 1.50
*Nos. C828-C830 (3)* 4.30 2.75

2nd Meeting of the Central American Peace Plan. Nos. C828-C829 horiz.

**Folklore Festival Type of 1987 Souvenir Sheet**

**1988, Dec. 6 Litho. *Imperf.***
**C831** AP171 2q Music ensemble, horiz. 10.00 10.00

St. John Bosco (1815-1888), Educator AP175

**1989, Feb. 1 Litho. *Perf. 11½***
**C832** AP175 40c gold & blk .95 .55

French Revolution, Bicent. AP176

**1989, Oct. 18 Litho. *Perf. 11½***
**C833** AP176 1q dark red, blk & deep blue 5.00 2.00

America Issue — AP177

UPAE emblem and: 10c, Detail of the *Madrid Codex.* 20c, Temple of the Gran Jaguar of Tikal, Tikal Natl. Park.

**1990, Jan. 25 Litho. *Perf. 11½***
**C834** AP177 10c shown 1.75 1.10
**C835** AP177 20c brown & multi 3.50 2.40

Institute of Nutrition of Central America and Panama, 40th Anniv. AP178

**1990, May 18**
**C837** AP178 20c multicolored .55 .25

Red Cross, Red Crescent Societies, 125th Anniv. AP179

**1990, June 8**
**C838** AP179 50c multicolored 1.25 .40

Defense Ministry General Staff, Cent. AP180

**1991, May 8 Litho. *Perf. 11½***
**C839** AP180 20c multicolored .45 .25

America AP181

UPAE: 10c, Pacaya Volcano Erupting at Night. 60c, Lake Atitlan.

**1991, July 30 Litho. *Perf. 11½***
**C840** AP181 10c multicolored .25 .25
**C841** AP181 60c multicolored 2.25 .50

America Issue AP182

Designs: 40c, Pinzon brothers, Nina. 60c, Columbus, Santa Maria, vert.

**1992, July 27 Litho. *Perf. 11½***
**C842** AP182 40c green & black .95 .45
**C843** AP182 60c green & black 1.40 .70

AP183

**1992, Oct. 6 Litho. *Perf. 12½***
**C844** AP183 10c multicolored *5.00 5.00*

Interamerican Institute for Agricultural Cooperation, 50th anniv.

AP184

**1992, Dec. 1 Photo. *Perf. 11½***
**C845** AP184 1q multicolored 2.50 .80

World campaign against AIDS.

Orchids — AP185

20c, Phragmipedium caudatum. 50c, Encyclia cochleata. 1q, Encyclia vitellina. 1.50q, Odontoglossum laeve 2q, Odontoglossum uroskinneri.

**1994, Aug. 9 Litho. *Perf. 11½***
**C845A** AP185 20c multi .60 .60
**C846** AP185 50c multi 1.10 .80
**C847** AP185 1q multi 2.40 .80
**C847A** AP185 1.50q multi 4.75 4.75
**C848** AP185 2q multi 4.25 1.50
*Nos. C845A-C848 (5)* 13.10 8.45

#C845A, C847A put on sale 8/16/96.

Tourism — AP186

Designs: 20c, Rafting. 40c, Water sports. 60c, Boats on Lake Atitlan, volcanic mountain.

80c, Tourist boat on Lake Atitlan. 1q, Mt. Pacaya erupting. 2q, Guatemala City. 3q, Macaws, vert. 4q, Temple of the Gran Jaguar, vert. 5q, Holy Week procession from Antigua, carpet of colored saw dust, vert.

**1995-96 Litho. *Perf. 12½***

| | | | | |
|---|---|---|---|---|
| **C849** | AP186 | 20c multicolored | .40 | .25 |
| **C850** | AP186 | 40c multicolored | .40 | .25 |
| **C851** | AP186 | 60c multicolored | .55 | .30 |
| **C852** | AP186 | 80c multicolored | .60 | .40 |
| **C853** | AP186 | 1q multicolored | .60 | .30 |
| **C854** | AP186 | 2q multicolored | 1.25 | .60 |
| **C855** | AP186 | 3q multicolored | 1.75 | .85 |
| **C856** | AP186 | 4q multicolored | 2.50 | 1.25 |
| **C857** | AP186 | 5q multicolored | 3.00 | 1.75 |
| | | *Nos. C849-C857 (9)* | 11.05 | 5.95 |

Issued: #C850, 7/5/96; #C852, 7/9/96.

For surcharges see Nos. 568-570, 574.

Visit of Pope John Paul II — AP187

Papal arms, quotation, Pope John Paul II: 10c, With arms outstreached, dove, "That all the people join hands for peace." 1q, Kissing infant, "Let the children come unto me." 1.75q, Holding crucifix, "The house of the Lord is my house." 1.90q, Looking forward, "Blessed is he who comes in the name of the Lord." 2.90q, Waving hand, "Remember that all men are our brothers."

**1996, Jan. 5 Litho. *Perf. 12½***

| | | | | |
|---|---|---|---|---|
| **C858** | AP187 | 10c multicolored | .25 | .25 |
| **C859** | AP187 | 1q multicolored | .45 | .45 |
| **C860** | AP187 | 1.75q multicolored | .85 | .85 |
| **C861** | AP187 | 1.90q multicolored | .95 | .95 |
| **C862** | AP187 | 2.90q multicolored | 1.50 | 1.50 |
| | | *Nos. C858-C862 (5)* | 4.00 | 4.00 |

Distinguished Guatemalans AP188

Designs: 40c, Carlos Merida (Self-portrait). 50c, José Eulalio Samayoa. 60c, Manuel Montufar y Coronado.

**1996, Oct. 21 Litho. *Perf. 12½***

| | | | | |
|---|---|---|---|---|
| **C863** | AP188 | 40c multicolored | .25 | .25 |
| **C864** | AP188 | 50c multicolored | .25 | .25 |
| **C865** | AP188 | 60c multicolored | .30 | .30 |
| | | *Nos. C863-C865 (3)* | .80 | .80 |

For surcharge see No. 572.

Mother Breastfeeding — AP190

**1997, Mar. 6 *Perf. 11½***

| | | | | |
|---|---|---|---|---|
| **C868** | AP190 | 1q multicolored | .60 | .60 |

Public Finance Projects — AP191

Designs: 20c, Education. 60c, Health care. 80c, Road construction. 1q, Family security.

**1997, Oct. 6 Litho. *Perf. 11½x12½***

| | | | | |
|---|---|---|---|---|
| **C869** | AP191 | 20c multicolored | .25 | .25 |
| **C870** | AP191 | 60c multicolored | .30 | .25 |
| **C871** | AP191 | 80c multicolored | .45 | .40 |
| **C872** | AP191 | 1q multicolored | .60 | .45 |
| | | *Nos. C869-C872 (4)* | 1.60 | 1.35 |

For surcharges see Nos. 571, 575.

Jorge Rybar and Machine — AP192

**1998 Litho. *Perf. 12½***

| | | | | |
|---|---|---|---|---|
| **C873** | AP192 | 10c multi | .25 | .25 |

Plastics industry in Guatemala, 50th anniv.

Intl. Society of Guatemala Collectors, 50th Anniv. — AP193

**1999, May 14 Litho. *Perf. 11½x12½***

| | | | | |
|---|---|---|---|---|
| **C874** | AP193 | 1q Quetzel note | .60 | .60 |

1993 Census AP194

**2001, Dec. 6 Litho. *Perf. 11½***

| | | | | |
|---|---|---|---|---|
| **C875** | AP194 | 10c multi | 50.00 | 50.00 |

No. C875 was withdrawn from sale 12/11/01.

## AIR POST SEMI-POSTAL STAMPS

Air Post Stamps of 1937 Surcharged in Red or Blue

**1937, Mar. 15 Unwmk. *Perf. 12½***

| | | | | |
|---|---|---|---|---|
| **CB1** | AP10 | 4c + 1c ultra (R) | .90 | *1.25* |
| **CB2** | AP10 | 6c + 1c blk vio (R) | .90 | *1.25* |
| **CB3** | AP11 | 10c + 1c ol grn (Bl) | .90 | *1.25* |
| **CB4** | AP11 | 15c + 1c ver (Bl) | .90 | *1.25* |
| | | *Nos. CB1-CB4 (4)* | 3.60 | *5.00* |

1st Phil. Exhib. held in Guatemala, Mar. 15-20.

**Catalogue values for unused stamps in this section, from this point to the end of the section, are for Never Hinged items.**

### Type of Regular Issue, 1956

Designs: 35c+1q, Red Cross, Ambulance and Volcano. 50c+1q, Red Cross, Hospital and Nurse. 1q+1q, Nurse and Red Cross.

***Perf. 13x12½***

**1956, June 19 Engr. Unwmk.**

| | | | | |
|---|---|---|---|---|
| **CB5** | A148 | 35c + 1q red & ol grn | 5.50 | *5.75* |
| **CB6** | A148 | 50c + 1q ultra & red | 5.50 | *5.75* |
| **CB7** | A148 | 1q + 1q dk grn & dk red | 5.50 | *5.75* |
| | | *Nos. CB5-CB7 (3)* | 16.50 | *17.25* |

The surtax was for the Red Cross.

Nos. B5-B7 Overprinted

**1957, May 11**

| | | | | |
|---|---|---|---|---|
| **CB8** | A148 | 5c + 15c | 7.00 | *8.00* |
| *a.* | | Imperf., pair | 225.00 | |
| **CB9** | A148 | 15c + 50c | 7.00 | *8.00* |
| *a.* | | Overprint inverted | 275.00 | |
| **CB10** | A148 | 25c + 50c | 7.00 | *8.00* |
| | | *Nos. CB8-CB10 (3)* | 21.00 | *24.00* |

The surtax was for the Red Cross.

Type of Semi-Postal Stamps, 1957 and

Esquipulas Cathedral SPAP1

15c+1q, Cathedral & crucifix. 20c+1q, Christ with crown of thorns and part of globe. 25c+1q, Archbishop Mariano Rossell y Arellano.

***Perf. 13½x14½, 13***

**1957, Oct. 29 Engr. Unwmk.**

| | | | | |
|---|---|---|---|---|
| **CB11** | SPAP1 | 10c + 1q choc & emer | 7.00 | *7.50* |
| **CB12** | SP1 | 15c + 1q dl grn & sep | 7.00 | *7.50* |
| **CB13** | SP1 | 20c + 1q bl gray & brn | 7.00 | *7.50* |
| **CB14** | SP1 | 25c + 1q lt vio & car | 7.00 | *7.50* |
| | | *Nos. CB11-CB14 (4)* | 28.00 | *30.00* |

The tax was for the Esquipulas highway.

Wounded Man, Battle of Solferino SPAP2

Designs: 6c+6c, 20c+20c, Flood disaster. 10c+10c, 25c+25c, Earth, moon and stars. 15c+15c, 30c+30c, Red Cross headquarters.

**1960, Apr. 9 Photo. *Perf. 13½x14***

| | | | | |
|---|---|---|---|---|
| **CB15** | SPAP2 | 5c + 5c multi | 2.50 | *2.75* |
| **CB16** | SPAP2 | 6c + 6c multi | 2.50 | *2.75* |
| **CB17** | SPAP2 | 10c + 10c multi | 2.50 | *2.75* |
| **CB18** | SPAP2 | 15c + 15c multi | 2.50 | *2.75* |
| **CB19** | SPAP2 | 20c + 20c multi | 2.50 | *2.75* |
| **CB20** | SPAP2 | 25c + 25c multi | 2.50 | *2.75* |
| **CB21** | SPAP2 | 30c + 30c multi | 2.50 | *2.75* |
| | | *Nos. CB15-CB21 (7)* | 17.50 | *19.25* |

Cent. (in 1959) of the Red Cross idea. The surtax went to the Red Cross. Exist imperf.

## AIR POST OFFICIAL STAMPS

Nos. C93-C98 Overprinted in Black

**1939, Apr. 29 Unwmk. *Perf. 12½***

| | | | | |
|---|---|---|---|---|
| **CO1** | AP13 | 1c org & ol brn | 1.10 | 1.10 |
| **CO2** | AP13 | 2c multi | 1.10 | 1.10 |
| **CO3** | AP13 | 3c multi | 1.10 | 1.10 |
| **CO4** | AP13 | 4c multi | 1.10 | 1.10 |
| **CO5** | AP13 | 5c multi | 1.10 | 1.10 |
| **CO6** | AP13 | 10c multi | 1.10 | 1.10 |
| | | *Nos. CO1-CO6 (6)* | 6.60 | 6.60 |

### No. C99 Overprinted in Black

**1939**

| | | | | |
|---|---|---|---|---|
| **CO7** | AP19 | Sheet of 6 | 3.75 | 3.75 |
| *a.* | | 1c yel org, blue & blk | .60 | .60 |
| *b.* | | 2c lake, org, blue & blk | .60 | .60 |
| *c.* | | 3c olive, blue & orange | .60 | .60 |
| *d.* | | 4c dk claret, bl, org & blk | .60 | .60 |
| *e.* | | 5c grnsh bl, bl, red, org & blk | .60 | .60 |
| *f.* | | 10c olive bister, red & org | .60 | .60 |

## SPECIAL DELIVERY STAMPS

No. 237 Overprinted in Red

**1940, June Unwmk. *Perf. 14***

| | | | | |
|---|---|---|---|---|
| **E1** | A81 | 4c orange | 1.50 | .35 |

No. E1 paid for express service by motorcycle messenger between Guatemala City and Coban.

**Catalogue values for unused stamps in this section, from this point to the end of the section, are for Never Hinged items.**

Motorcycle Messenger SD1

**Black Surcharge**

**1948, Sept. 3 Photo. *Perf. 14x12½***

| | | | | |
|---|---|---|---|---|
| **E2** | SD1 | 10c on 4c bl grn & gray blk | 3.25 | .85 |

No. E2 without surcharge was issued for regular postage, not special delivery. See No. 337B.

## OFFICIAL STAMPS

O1

**1902, Dec. 18 Typeset *Perf. 12***

| | | | | |
|---|---|---|---|---|
| **O1** | O1 | 1c green | 9.00 | 5.50 |
| **O2** | O1 | 2c carmine | 9.00 | 5.50 |
| **O3** | O1 | 5c ultra | 9.00 | 4.50 |
| **O4** | O1 | 10c brown violet | 12.00 | 4.50 |
| **O5** | O1 | 25c orange | 12.00 | 4.50 |
| *a.* | | Horiz. pair, imperf. between | 125.00 | |
| | | *Nos. O1-O5 (5)* | 51.00 | 24.50 |

Nos. O1-O5 printed on thin paper with sheet watermark "AMERICAN LINEN BOND." Nos. O1-O3 also printed on thick paper with sheet watermark "ROYAL BANK BOND." Values are for copies that do not show the watermark. Counterfeits of Nos. O1-O5 exist.

During the years 1912 to 1926 the Post Office Department perforated the word "OFICIAL" on limited quantities of the following stamps: Nos. 114-123, 132, 141-149, 151-153, 158, 202, 210-229 and RA2. The perforating was done in blocks of four stamps at a time and was of two types.

A rubber handstamp "OFICIAL" was also used during the same period and was applied in violet, red, blue or black to stamps No. 117-118, 121-123, 163-165, 172 and 202-218.

Both perforating and handstamping were done in the post office at Guatemala City and use of the stamps was limited to that city.

National Emblem — O2

**1929, Jan. Engr. *Perf. 14***

| | | | | |
|---|---|---|---|---|
| **O6** | O2 | 1c pale grnsh bl | .30 | .30 |
| **O7** | O2 | 2c dark brown | .30 | .30 |
| **O8** | O2 | 3c green | .30 | .30 |
| **O9** | O2 | 4c deep violet | .40 | .35 |
| **O10** | O2 | 5c brown car | .40 | .35 |
| **O11** | O2 | 10c brown orange | .70 | .70 |
| **O12** | O2 | 25c dark blue | 1.40 | 1.10 |
| | | *Nos. O6-O12 (7)* | 3.80 | 3.40 |

## POSTAL TAX STAMPS

National Emblem — PT1

***Perf. 13½, 14, 15***

**1919, May 3 Engr. Unwmk.**

**RA1** PT1 12½c carmine .30 .25

Tax for rebuilding post offices.

G. P. O. and Telegraph Building — PT2

**1927, Nov. 10 Typo. *Perf. 14***

**RA2** PT2 1c olive green .55 .25

Tax to provide a fund for building a post office in Guatemala City.

No. RA2 Overprinted in Green

**1936, June 30**

**RA3** PT2 1c olive green *5.75 4.00*

Liberal revolution, 65th anniversary.

No. RA2 Overprinted in Blue

**1936, Sept. 15**

**RA4** PT2 1c olive green .55 .55

115th anniv. of the Independence of Guatemala.

No. RA2 Overprinted in Red Brown

**1936, Nov. 15**

**RA5** PT2 1c olive green .55 .45

National Fair.

No. RA2 Overprinted in Red

**1937, Mar. 15**

**RA6** PT2 1c olive green .55 .55

No. RA2 Overprinted in Blue

**1938, Jan. 10 *Perf. 14x14½***

**RA7** PT2 1c olive green .30 .25

*a.* "1937-1939" omitted 110.00

150th anniv. of the US Constitution.

No. RA2 Overprinted in Blue or Red

**1938 *Perf. 14***

**RA8** PT2 1c olive green (Bl) .40 .30

**RA9** PT2 1c olive green (R) .40 .30

No. RA2 Overprinted in Violet

**1938, Nov. 20**

**RA10** PT2 1c olive green .40 .25

1st Central American Philatelic Exposition.

No. RA2 Overprinted in Green or Black

**1939**

**RA11** PT2 1c olive green (G) .40 .25

**RA12** PT2 1c olive green (Bk) .40 .25

No. RA2 Overprinted in Violet or Brown

**1940**

**RA13** PT2 1c olive green (V) .40 .25

**RA14** PT2 1c olive green (Br) .40 .25

No. RA2 Overprinted in Red

**1940, Apr. 14**

**RA15** PT2 1c olive green .40 .25

Pan American Union, 50th anniversary.

No. RA2 Overprinted in Red

**1941**

**RA16** PT2 1c olive green .55 .25

No. 235 Surcharged in Red

**RA17** A79 1c on 2c deep blue .30 .25

No. 235 Surcharged in Carmine

**1942, Jan.**

**RA18** A79 1c on 2c deep blue .55 .25

PT3

**With Imprint Below Design**

**1942, June 3 Engr. *Perf. 11, 12x11***

**RA19** PT3 1c black brown 14.50 8.00

**No imprint; Thin Paper**

***Perf. 11, 12x11, 11x12, 11x12x11x11***

**1942, July 18**

**RA20** PT3 1c black brown .40 .25

Arch of Communications Building — PT4

**1943 *Perf. 11, 12x11, 12***

**RA21** PT4 1c orange .40 .25

PT5

***Perf. 11, 12½ and Compound***

**1945, Feb. Unwmk.**

**RA22** PT5 1c orange .30 .25

**1949 *Perf. 12½***

**RA23** PT5 1c deep ultra .30 .25

# GUINEA

'gi-nē

LOCATION — Coast of West Africa, between Guinea-Bissau and Sierra Leone

GOVT. — Republic

AREA — 94,926 sq. mi.

POP. — 7,538,953 (1999 est.)

CAPITAL — Conakry

This former French Overseas Territory of French West Africa proclaimed itself an independent republic on October 2, 1958.

100 Centimes = 1 Franc

100 Caury = 1 Syli (1973)

100 Centimes = 1 Guinean Franc (1986)

**Catalogue values for all unused stamps in this country are for Never Hinged items.**

Common Design Types pictured following the introduction.

French West Africa No. 79 Overprinted

**1959 Unwmk. Photo. *Perf. 12x12½***

**168** CD104 10fr multi 3.00 2.50

French West Africa No. 78 Surcharged in Red

**Engr.**

***Perf. 13***

**169** A33 45fr on 20fr multi 3.50 2.25

Map, Dove and Pres. Sékou Touré A12

**1959 Unwmk. Engr. *Perf. 13***

| | | | | |
|---|---|---|---|---|
| **170** | A12 | 5fr rose car | .30 | .25 |
| **171** | A12 | 10fr ultramarine | .40 | .25 |
| **172** | A12 | 20fr orange | .70 | .30 |
| **173** | A12 | 65fr slate green | 2.10 | .95 |
| **174** | A12 | 100fr violet | 3.50 | 2.10 |
| | | *Nos. 170-174 (5)* | 7.00 | 3.85 |

Proclamation of independence, Oct. 2, 1958.

Bananas — A13

**1959 Litho. *Perf. 11½***

| | | | | |
|---|---|---|---|---|
| **175** | A13 | 10fr shown | .25 | .25 |
| **176** | A13 | 15fr Grapefruit | .40 | .25 |
| **177** | A13 | 20fr Lemons | .70 | .25 |
| **178** | A13 | 25fr Avocados | .80 | .25 |
| **179** | A13 | 50fr Pineapple | 1.75 | .25 |
| | | *Nos. 175-179 (5)* | 3.90 | 1.25 |

For overprints see Nos. 209-213.

Fishing Boats and Tamara Lighthouse A14

5fr, Coco palms & sailboat, vert. 10fr, Launching fishing pirogue. 15fr, Elephant's head. 20fr, Pres. Sékou Touré & torch, vert. 25fr, Elephant.

**1959 Engr. *Perf. 13½***

| | | | | |
|---|---|---|---|---|
| **180** | A14 | 1fr rose | .25 | .25 |
| **181** | A14 | 2fr green | .25 | .25 |
| **182** | A14 | 3fr brown | .25 | .25 |
| **183** | A14 | 5fr blue | .50 | .25 |
| **184** | A14 | 10fr claret | .55 | .25 |
| **185** | A14 | 15fr light brn | .70 | .25 |
| **186** | A14 | 20fr claret | 1.00 | .25 |
| **187** | A14 | 25fr red brown | 1.25 | .25 |
| | | *Nos. 180-187 (8)* | 4.75 | 2.00 |

Flag Raising, Labé — A15

**1959 Litho. *Perf. 12***

| | | | | |
|---|---|---|---|---|
| **188** | A15 | 50fr multicolored | 1.10 | .25 |
| **189** | A15 | 100fr multicolored | 2.00 | .50 |

For overprints see Nos. 201-202.

UN Headquarters, New York, and People of Guinea — A16

**1959 *Perf. 12***

| | | | | |
|---|---|---|---|---|
| **190** | A16 | 1fr vio blue & org | .25 | .25 |
| **191** | A16 | 2fr red lil & emer | .25 | .25 |
| **192** | A16 | 3fr brn & crimson | .25 | .25 |
| **193** | A16 | 5fr brn & grnsh bl | .25 | .25 |
| | | *Nos. 190-193,C22-C23 (6)* | 3.40 | 2.65 |

Guinea's admission to the UN, first anniv.
For overprints see Nos. 205-208, C27-C28.

Uprooted Oak Emblem — A17

**1960 Photo. *Perf. 11½***
**Granite Paper**

| | | | | |
|---|---|---|---|---|
| **194** | A17 | 25fr multicolored | .80 | .25 |
| **195** | A17 | 50fr multicolored | 1.10 | .25 |

World Refugee Year, 7/1/59-6/30/60.
For surcharges see Nos. B17-B18.

UPU Monument, Bern — A18

**1960 Granite Paper Unwmk.**

| | | | | |
|---|---|---|---|---|
| **196** | A18 | 10fr gray brn & blk | .25 | .25 |
| **197** | A18 | 15fr lil & purple | .45 | .25 |
| **198** | A18 | 20fr ultra & dk blue | .65 | .25 |
| **199** | A18 | 25fr yel grn & sl grn | .85 | .25 |
| **200** | A18 | 50fr red org & brown | .90 | .25 |
| | | *Nos. 196-200 (5)* | 3.10 | 1.25 |

Nos. 199-200 are vertical.
Admission to the UPU, first anniv.

Nos. 188-189 Overprinted in Black, Orange or Carmine: "Jeux Olympiques Rome 1960" and Olympic Rings

**1960 Litho. *Perf. 12***

| | | | | |
|---|---|---|---|---|
| **201** | A15 | 50fr multi (Bk) | 8.00 | 6.00 |
| **202** | A15 | 100fr multi (O or C) | 12.50 | 9.00 |
| | | *Nos. 201-202,C24-C26 (5)* | 92.25 | 67.25 |

17th Olympic Games, Rome, 8/25-9/11. See note after No. C26.

Map and Flag of Guinea — A19

**1960 Photo. *Perf. 11½***

| | | | | |
|---|---|---|---|---|
| **203** | A19 | 25fr multicolored | .60 | .30 |
| **204** | A19 | 30fr multicolored | .80 | .30 |

Second anniversary of independence.

**Nos. 190-193 Overprinted**

**1961 Litho. *Perf. 12***

| | | | | |
|---|---|---|---|---|
| **205** | A16 | 1fr vio blue & org | .25 | .25 |
| **206** | A16 | 2fr red lil & emer | .25 | .25 |
| **207** | A16 | 3fr brn & crimson | .25 | .25 |
| **208** | A16 | 5fr brn & grnsh bl | .25 | .25 |

Nos. 175-179 Overprinted in Black or Orange

***Perf. 11½***
**Fruits in Natural Colors**

| | | | | |
|---|---|---|---|---|
| **209** | A13 | 10fr red | .25 | .25 |
| **210** | A13 | 15fr grn & pink | .40 | .25 |
| **211** | A13 | 20fr red brn & bl | .50 | .25 |
| **212** | A13 | 25fr bl & yel (O) | .50 | .25 |
| **213** | A13 | 50fr dk vio blue | 1.00 | .40 |
| | | *Nos. 205-213,C27-C28 (11)* | 6.15 | 3.35 |

15th anniversary of United Nations.

Defassa Waterbuck A20

**1961, Sept. 1 Photo. *Perf. 11½***
**Multicolored Design; Granite Paper**

| | | | | |
|---|---|---|---|---|
| **214** | A20 | 5fr bright grn | .25 | .25 |
| **215** | A20 | 10fr emerald | .35 | .25 |
| **216** | A20 | 25fr lilac | .40 | .25 |
| **217** | A20 | 40fr orange | .75 | .25 |
| **218** | A20 | 50fr red orange | 1.75 | .30 |
| **219** | A20 | 75fr ultramarine | 2.50 | .30 |
| | | *Nos. 214-219 (6)* | 6.00 | 1.60 |

For surcharges see Nos. B19-B24.

Exhibition Hall — A21

**1961, Oct. 2 *Perf. 11½***
**Flag in Red, Yellow & Green**
**Granite Paper**

| | | | | |
|---|---|---|---|---|
| **220** | A21 | 5fr ultra & red | .30 | .25 |
| **221** | A21 | 10fr brown & red | .30 | .25 |
| **222** | A21 | 25fr gray grn & red | .30 | .25 |
| | | *Nos. 220-222 (3)* | .90 | .75 |

First Three-Year Plan.

Gray-breasted Helmet Guinea Fowl — A22

**1961 Unwmk. *Perf. 13x14***

| | | | | |
|---|---|---|---|---|
| **223** | A22 | 5fr rose lil, sepia & bl | .30 | .25 |
| **224** | A22 | 10fr dp org, sepia & bl | .35 | .25 |
| **225** | A22 | 25fr cerise, sepia & bl | .55 | .25 |
| **226** | A22 | 40fr ocher, sepia & bl | .95 | .25 |
| **227** | A22 | 50fr lemon, sepia & bl | 1.25 | .25 |
| **228** | A22 | 75fr apple grn, sep & bl | 2.50 | .30 |
| | | *Nos. 223-228 (6)* | 5.90 | 1.55 |

For surcharges see Nos. B30-B35.

Patrice Lumumba and Map of Africa — A23

**1962, Feb. 13 Photo. *Perf. 11½***

| | | | | |
|---|---|---|---|---|
| **229** | A23 | 10fr multicolored | .65 | .25 |
| **230** | A23 | 25fr multicolored | .80 | .25 |
| **231** | A23 | 50fr multicolored | .50 | .25 |
| | | *Nos. 229-231 (3)* | 1.95 | .75 |

Death anniv. (on Feb. 12, 1961) of Patrice Lumumba, Premier of the Congo Republic.

King Mohammed V of Morocco and Map of Africa — A24

**1962, Mar. 15 Litho. *Perf. 13***

| | | | | |
|---|---|---|---|---|
| **232** | A24 | 25fr multicolored | .90 | .25 |
| **233** | A24 | 75fr multicolored | 2.25 | .60 |

First anniv. of the conference of African heads of state at Casablanca.
For surcharges see Nos. B36-B37.

**African Postal Union Issue**

Map of Africa and Post Horn — A25

**1962, Apr. 23 Photo. *Perf. 13½x13***

| | | | | |
|---|---|---|---|---|
| **234** | A25 | 25fr org, blk & grn | .80 | .25 |
| **235** | A25 | 100fr deep brn & org | 1.90 | .55 |

Establishment of African Postal Union.

Bolon Player A26

Musical Instruments: 30c, 25fr, 50fr, Bote, vert. 1fr, 10fr, Flute, vert. 1.50fr, 3fr, Koni. 2fr, 20fr, Kora. 40fr, 75fr, Bolon.

***Perf. 13½x13, 13x13½***
**1962, June 15**

| | | | | |
|---|---|---|---|---|
| **236** | A26 | 30c bl, dk grn & red | .25 | .25 |
| **237** | A26 | 50c sal, brn & brt grn | .25 | .25 |
| **238** | A26 | 1fr yel grn, grn & lil | .25 | .25 |
| **239** | A26 | 1.50fr yel, red & bl | .25 | .25 |
| **240** | A26 | 2fr rose lil, red lil & grn | .25 | .25 |
| **241** | A26 | 3fr brn grn, grn & lil | .25 | .25 |
| **242** | A26 | 10fr org, brn & bl | .25 | .25 |
| **243** | A26 | 20fr ol, dk ol & car | .45 | .25 |
| **244** | A26 | 25fr ol, dk ol & lil | .55 | .25 |
| **245** | A26 | 40fr bl, grn & red lil | .80 | .25 |
| **246** | A26 | 50fr rose, dp rose & Prus bl | 1.10 | .25 |
| **247** | A26 | 75fr dl yel, brn & Prus bl | 1.50 | .60 |
| | | *Nos. 236-247,C32-C34 (15)* | 16.10 | 9.10 |

Hippopotamus — A27

25fr, 75fr, Lion. 30fr, 100fr, Leopard.

**1962, Aug. 25 Litho. *Perf. 13x13½***

| | | | | |
|---|---|---|---|---|
| **248** | A27 | 10fr org, grn & brn | .35 | .25 |
| **249** | A27 | 25fr emer, blk & brn | .90 | .25 |
| **250** | A27 | 30fr yel grn, dk brn & yel | 1.00 | .25 |
| **251** | A27 | 50fr vio bl, dk brn & grn | 1.25 | .30 |
| **252** | A27 | 75fr lil, lt lil & red brn | 1.90 | .40 |
| **253** | A27 | 100fr grnsh bl, dk brn & yel | 2.40 | .60 |
| | | *Nos. 248-253 (6)* | 7.80 | 2.05 |

See Nos. 340-345

Child at Blackboard — A28

Designs: 10fr, 20fr, Adult class.

**1962, Sept. 19 Photo. *Perf. 13½x13***

| | | | | |
|---|---|---|---|---|
| **254** | A28 | 5fr yel, dk brn & org | .25 | .25 |
| **255** | A28 | 10fr org & dk brn | .25 | .25 |
| **256** | A28 | 15fr yel grn, dk brn & red | .30 | .25 |
| **257** | A28 | 20fr bl & dk brn | .40 | .25 |
| | | *Nos. 254-257 (4)* | 1.20 | 1.00 |

Campaign against illiteracy.

> Imperforates
> From late 1962 onward, most Guinea stamps exist imperforate.

Alfa Yaya — A29

30fr, King Behanzin. 50fr, King Ba Bemba. 75fr, Almamy Samory. 100fr, Tierno Aliou.

**1962, Oct. 2 *Perf. 13½***
**Gold Frame**

| | | | | |
|---|---|---|---|---|
| **258** | A29 | 25fr brt bl & sepia | .35 | .25 |
| **259** | A29 | 30fr yel & sepia | .60 | .25 |
| **260** | A29 | 50fr brt pink & sepia | .70 | .30 |
| **261** | A29 | 75fr yel grn & sepia | 1.75 | .45 |
| **262** | A29 | 100fr org, red & sepia | 2.10 | .70 |
| | | *Nos. 258-262 (5)* | 5.50 | 1.95 |

Heroes and martyrs of Africa.

Gray Parrot
A30

Birds: 30c, 3fr, 50fr, Crowned crane (vert). 1fr, 20fr, Abyssinian ground hornbill. 1.50fr, 25fr, White spoonbill. 2fr, 40fr, Bateleur eagle.

**1962, Dec.** ***Perf. 13½x13, 13x13½***

| | | | | | |
|---|---|---|---|---|---|
| **263** | A30 | 30c | multicolored | .25 | .25 |
| **264** | A30 | 50c | multicolored | .25 | .25 |
| **265** | A30 | 1fr | multicolored | .25 | .25 |
| **266** | A30 | 1.50fr | multicolored | .25 | .25 |
| **267** | A30 | 2fr | multicolored | .25 | .25 |
| **268** | A30 | 3fr | multicolored | .65 | .25 |
| **269** | A30 | 10fr | multicolored | .80 | .25 |
| **270** | A30 | 20fr | multicolored | .90 | .25 |
| **271** | A30 | 25fr | multicolored | .95 | .25 |
| **272** | A30 | 40fr | multicolored | 1.10 | .25 |
| **273** | A30 | 50fr | multicolored | 1.60 | .35 |
| **274** | A30 | 75fr | multicolored | 2.10 | .50 |
| | | | *Nos. 263-274,C41-C43 (15)* | 27.10 | 11.60 |

Wheat Emblem and Globe
A31

**1963, Mar. 21** **Photo.** ***Perf. 13x14***

| | | | | | |
|---|---|---|---|---|---|
| **275** | A31 | 5fr | red & yellow | .25 | .25 |
| **276** | A31 | 10fr | emerald & yel | .25 | .25 |
| **277** | A31 | 15fr | brown & yel | .25 | .25 |
| **278** | A31 | 25fr | dark ol & yel | .25 | .25 |
| | | | *Nos. 275-278 (4)* | 1.00 | 1.00 |

FAO "Freedom from Hunger" campaign.

Basketball — A32

50c, 4fr, 30fr, Boxing. 1fr, 5fr, Running. 1.50fr, 10fr, Bicycling. 2fr, 20fr, Single sculls.

**1963, Mar. 16** **Unwmk.** ***Perf. 14***

| | | | | | |
|---|---|---|---|---|---|
| **279** | A32 | 30c | ver, dp claret & grn | .25 | .25 |
| **280** | A32 | 50c | lilac & blue | .25 | .25 |
| **281** | A32 | 1fr | dl org, sep & grn | .25 | .25 |
| **282** | A32 | 1.50fr | org, ultra & mag | .25 | .25 |
| **283** | A32 | 2fr | aqua, dk bl & mag | .25 | .25 |
| **284** | A32 | 3fr | ol, dp cl & grn | .25 | .25 |
| **285** | A32 | 4fr | car rose, pur & bl | .25 | .25 |
| **286** | A32 | 5fr | brt grn, ol & mag | .25 | .25 |
| **287** | A32 | 10fr | lil rose, ultra & mag | .25 | .25 |
| **288** | A32 | 20fr | red org, dk bl & crim | .25 | .25 |
| **289** | A32 | 25fr | emer, dp cl & dk grn | .25 | .25 |
| **290** | A32 | 30fr | gray, pur & bl | .30 | .25 |
| | | | *Nos. 279-290,C44-C46 (15)* | 15.40 | 9.55 |

For overprints and surcharges see Nos. 312-314, C58-C60.

A33

Various Butterflies.

**1963, May 10** **Photo.** ***Perf. 12***

| | | | | | |
|---|---|---|---|---|---|
| **291** | A33 | 10c | dp rose, blk & gray | .25 | .25 |
| **292** | A33 | 30c | rose, blk & yel | .25 | .25 |
| **293** | A33 | 40c | yel grn, brn & yel | .25 | .25 |
| **294** | A33 | 50c | pale vio, blk & grn | .25 | .25 |
| **295** | A33 | 1fr | yel, blk & emer | .40 | .25 |
| **296** | A33 | 1.50fr | bluish grn, blk & sep | .40 | .25 |
| **297** | A33 | 2fr | multi | .40 | .25 |
| **298** | A33 | 3fr | multi | 1.10 | .25 |
| **299** | A33 | 10fr | rose lil, blk & grn | 1.25 | .25 |
| **300** | A33 | 20fr | gray, blk & grn | 1.40 | .25 |
| **301** | A33 | 25fr | yel grn, blk & gray | 1.60 | .25 |
| **302** | A33 | 40fr | multi | 2.00 | .45 |
| **303** | A33 | 50fr | ultra, blk & yel | 2.50 | .55 |
| **304** | A33 | 75fr | yel, blk & grn | 3.25 | .80 |
| | | | *Nos. 291-304,C47-C49 (17)* | 30.40 | 11.80 |

Handshake, Map and Dove — A34

**1963, May 22** ***Perf. 13½x14***

| | | | | | |
|---|---|---|---|---|---|
| **305** | A34 | 5fr | bluish grn & dk brn | .25 | .25 |
| **306** | A34 | 10fr | org yel & dk brn | .25 | .25 |
| **307** | A34 | 15fr | ol & dk brn | .25 | .25 |
| **308** | A34 | 25fr | bis brn & dk brn | .30 | .25 |
| | | | *Nos. 305-308 (4)* | 1.05 | 1.00 |

Conference of African heads of state for African Unity, Addis Ababa.

Globe Encircled by Satellite — A35

**1963, July 25** **Engr.** ***Perf. 10½***

| | | | | | |
|---|---|---|---|---|---|
| **309** | A35 | 5fr | green & car | .25 | .25 |
| **310** | A35 | 10fr | vio bl & car | .40 | .25 |
| **311** | A35 | 15fr | yellow & car | .50 | .25 |
| | | | *Nos. 309-311,C50 (4)* | 1.90 | 1.00 |

Centenary of the International Red Cross.

**Nos. 279-281 Surcharged in Carmine, Yellow or Orange**

**1963, Nov. 20** **Photo.** ***Perf. 14***

| | | | | | |
|---|---|---|---|---|---|
| **312** | A32 | 40fr | on 30c (C or Y) | 1.40 | 1.10 |
| **313** | A32 | 50fr | on 50c (C or O) | 2.10 | 1.75 |
| **314** | A32 | 75fr | on 1fr (C or O) | 3.50 | 2.50 |
| | | | *Nos. 312-314,C58-C60 (6)* | 18.00 | 13.75 |

Meeting of the Olympic Games Preparatory Commission at Conakry. The overprint is in a circular line on #312, in 3 lines on each side on #313-314.

Jewelfish
A36

Fish: 40c, 30fr, Golden pheasant. 50c, 40fr, Blue gularis. 1fr, 75fr, Banded Jewelfish. 1.50fr, African lyretail. 2fr, Six-barred epiplatys. 5fr, Jewelfish.

**1964, Feb. 15** **Litho.** ***Perf. 14x13½***

| | | | | | |
|---|---|---|---|---|---|
| **315** | A36 | 30c | car rose & multi | .25 | .25 |
| **316** | A36 | 40c | pur & multi | .25 | .25 |
| **317** | A36 | 50c | car rose & multi | .25 | .25 |
| **318** | A36 | 1fr | blue & multi | .25 | .25 |
| **319** | A36 | 1.50fr | blue & multi | .25 | .25 |
| **320** | A36 | 2fr | pur & multi | .60 | .25 |
| **321** | A36 | 5fr | blue & multi | .65 | .25 |
| **322** | A36 | 30fr | grn & multi | .85 | .25 |
| **323** | A36 | 40fr | pur & multi | 1.75 | .40 |
| **324** | A36 | 75fr | multi | 2.50 | .55 |
| | | | *Nos. 315-324,C54-C55 (12)* | 17.60 | 4.90 |

John F. Kennedy
A37

**1964, Mar. 5** **Engr.** ***Perf. 10½***

**Flag in Red and Blue**

| | | | | | |
|---|---|---|---|---|---|
| **325** | A37 | 5fr | blk & pur | .25 | .25 |
| **326** | A37 | 25fr | grn & pur | .40 | .25 |
| **327** | A37 | 50fr | brn & pur | .85 | .30 |
| | | | *Nos. 325-327,C56 (4)* | 3.25 | 1.60 |

Issued in sheets of 20 with marginal quotations in English and French. Two sheets for each denomination. See No. C56.

Workers Welding Pipe — A38

5fr, Pipe line over mountains, vert. 10fr, Waterworks. 30fr, Transporting pipe. 50fr, Laying pipe.

**1964, May 1** **Photo.** ***Perf. 11½***

| | | | | | |
|---|---|---|---|---|---|
| **328** | A38 | 5fr | deep mag | .25 | .25 |
| **329** | A38 | 10fr | bright pur | .25 | .25 |
| **330** | A38 | 20fr | org red | .50 | .25 |
| **331** | A38 | 30fr | ultra | .65 | .25 |
| **332** | A38 | 50fr | yel grn | .75 | .25 |
| | | | *Nos. 328-332 (5)* | 2.40 | 1.25 |

Completion of the water-supply pipeline to Conakry, Mar. 1964.

Ice Hockey — A39

**1964, May 15** ***Perf. 13x12½***

| | | | | | |
|---|---|---|---|---|---|
| **333** | A39 | 10fr | shown | .40 | .25 |
| **334** | A39 | 25fr | Ski jump | .60 | .25 |
| **335** | A39 | 50fr | Slalom | 1.10 | .40 |
| | | | *Nos. 333-335,C57 (4)* | 4.35 | 1.30 |

9th Winter Olympic Games, Innsbruck, Jan. 29-Feb. 9, 1964.

Eleanor Roosevelt Reading to Children — A40

**1964, June 1** **Engr.** ***Perf. 10½***

| | | | | | |
|---|---|---|---|---|---|
| **336** | A40 | 5fr | green | .25 | .25 |
| **337** | A40 | 10fr | red org | .25 | .25 |
| **338** | A40 | 15fr | bright bl | .25 | .25 |
| **339** | A40 | 25fr | car rose | .25 | .25 |
| | | | *Nos. 336-339,C61 (5)* | 1.90 | 1.25 |

Eleanor Roosevelt, 15th anniv. of the Universal Declaration of Human Rights (in 1963).

**Animal Type of 1962**

Designs: 5fr, 30fr, Striped hyenas. 40fr, 300fr, Black buffaloes. 75fr, 100fr, Elephants.

**1964, Oct. 8** **Litho.** ***Perf. 13x13½***

| | | | | | |
|---|---|---|---|---|---|
| **340** | A27 | 5fr | yellow & blk | .25 | .25 |
| **341** | A27 | 30fr | light bl & blk | .45 | .25 |
| **342** | A27 | 40fr | lil rose & blk | 1.00 | .25 |
| **343** | A27 | 75fr | yel grn & blk | 2.25 | .40 |
| **344** | A27 | 100fr | bister & blk | 2.50 | .75 |
| **345** | A27 | 300fr | orange & blk | 6.50 | 2.75 |
| | | | *Nos. 340-345 (6)* | 12.95 | 4.65 |

Guinea Exhibit, World's Fair — A41

**1964, Oct. 26** **Engr.** ***Perf. 10½***

| | | | | | |
|---|---|---|---|---|---|
| **346** | A41 | 30fr | vio & emerald | .35 | .25 |
| **347** | A41 | 40fr | red lil & emer | .50 | .25 |
| **348** | A41 | 50fr | sepia & emer | .70 | .25 |
| **349** | A41 | 75fr | rose red & dk bl | 1.10 | .25 |
| | | | *Nos. 346-349 (4)* | 2.65 | 1.00 |

New York World's Fair, 1964-65.
See Nos. 372-375, C62-C63, C69-C70.

Queen Nefertari Crowned by Isis and Hathor — A42

Designs: 25fr, Ramses II in battle. 50fr, Submerged sphinxes, sailboat, Wadies-Sebua. 100fr, Ramses II holding crook and flail, Abu Simbel. 200fr, Feet and legs of Ramses statues, Abu Simbel.

**1964, Nov. 19** **Photo.** ***Perf. 12***

| | | | | | |
|---|---|---|---|---|---|
| **350** | A42 | 10fr | dk bl, red brn & cit | .25 | .25 |
| **351** | A42 | 25fr | blk, dl red & brn | .60 | .25 |
| **352** | A42 | 50fr | dk brn, bl & vio | .75 | .25 |
| **353** | A42 | 100fr | dk brn, yel & pur | 1.25 | .40 |
| **354** | A42 | 200fr | pur, dl grn & buff | 2.75 | .75 |
| | | | *Nos. 350-354,C64 (6)* | 9.60 | 3.30 |

UNESCO campaign to preserve Nubian monuments.
For overprint see No. 415.

Weight Lifter and Caucasian, Japanese and Negro Children — A43

10fr, Runner carrying torch. 25fr, Pole vaulting and flags. 40fr, Runners. 50fr, Judo. 75fr, Japanese woman, flags and stadium.

**1965, Jan. 18 Photo. *Perf. 13x12½***

| | | | | |
|---|---|---|---|---|
| **355** | A43 | 5fr gold, claret & blk | .25 | .25 |
| **356** | A43 | 10fr gold, blk, ver & bl | .40 | .25 |
| **357** | A43 | 25fr gold, blk, yel grn & red | .45 | .25 |
| **358** | A43 | 40fr gold, blk, brn & yel | .50 | .25 |
| **359** | A43 | 50fr gold, blk & grn | .80 | .30 |
| **360** | A43 | 75fr gold & multi | 1.50 | .40 |
| | | *Nos. 355-360,C65 (7)* | 5.65 | 2.05 |

18th Olympic Games, Tokyo, 10/10-25/64.
For overprints see Nos. 410-414.

Doudou Mask, Boké — A44

Designs: 40c, 1fr, 15fr, Various Niamou masks, N'Zérékoré region. 60c, "Yoki," wood-carved statuette of a girl, Boke. 80c, Masked woman dancer from Guekedou. 2fr, Masked dancer from Macenta. 20fr, Beater from Tam-tam. 60fr, Bird dancer from Macenta. 80fr, Bassari dancer from Koundara. 100fr, Sword dancer from Karana.

**1965, Feb. 15 Unwmk. *Perf. 14***

| | | | | |
|---|---|---|---|---|
| **361** | A44 | 20c multicolored | .25 | .25 |
| **362** | A44 | 40c multicolored | .25 | .25 |
| **363** | A44 | 60c multicolored | .25 | .25 |
| **364** | A44 | 80c multicolored | .25 | .25 |
| **365** | A44 | 1fr multicolored | .25 | .25 |
| **366** | A44 | 2fr multicolored | .25 | .25 |
| **367** | A44 | 15fr multicolored | .50 | .25 |
| **368** | A44 | 20fr multicolored | .55 | .25 |
| **369** | A44 | 60fr multicolored | 1.25 | .40 |
| **370** | A44 | 80fr multicolored | 1.25 | .50 |
| **371** | A44 | 100fr multicolored | 1.75 | .50 |
| | | *Nos. 361-371,C68 (12)* | 13.05 | 6.15 |

**World's Fair Type of 1964 Inscribed "1965"**

**1965, Mar. 24 Engr. *Perf. 10½***

| | | | | |
|---|---|---|---|---|
| **372** | A41 | 30fr grn & orange | .40 | .25 |
| **373** | A41 | 40fr car & brt grn | .50 | .25 |
| **374** | A41 | 50fr brt grn & vio | .70 | .25 |
| **375** | A41 | 75fr brown & vio | 1.00 | .35 |
| | | *Nos. 372-375 (4)* | 2.60 | 1.10 |

See Nos. C69-C70.

Blacksmith A45

Handicrafts: 20fr, Potter. 60fr, Cloth dyers. 80fr, Basketmaker.

**1965, May 1 Photo. *Perf. 14***

| | | | | |
|---|---|---|---|---|
| **376** | A45 | 15fr multicolored | .25 | .25 |
| **377** | A45 | 20fr multicolored | .50 | .25 |
| **378** | A45 | 60fr multicolored | .80 | .30 |
| **379** | A45 | 80fr multicolored | .95 | .40 |
| | | *Nos. 376-379,C71-C72 (6)* | 9.25 | 2.80 |

ITU Emblem, Old and New Communication Equipment — A46

**1965, May 17 Unwmk.**

| | | | | |
|---|---|---|---|---|
| **380** | A46 | 25fr yel, gray, gold & blk | .45 | .25 |
| **381** | A46 | 50fr yel, grn, gold & blk | .70 | .25 |
| | | *Nos. 380-381,C73-C74 (4)* | 4.75 | 1.55 |

ITU centenary.

Maj. Virgil I. Grissom — A47

Moon from 258mi. — A48

Sputnik Over Earth A49

American Achievements in Space: 10fr, Lt. Com. John W. Young. 25fr, Moon from 115mi. 30fr, Moon from 58mi. 100fr, Grissom and Young in Gemini 2 spaceship.

**1965, July 19 Photo. *Perf. 13***

**Size: 21x29mm**

| | | | | |
|---|---|---|---|---|
| **382** | A47 | 5fr dk red & multi | .25 | .25 |
| **383** | A47 | 10fr dk red & multi | .25 | .25 |
| **384** | A48 | 15fr gold, bl & dk bl | .25 | .25 |

**Size: 39x28mm**

| | | | | |
|---|---|---|---|---|
| **385** | A48 | 25fr gold, bl & dk bl | .25 | .25 |

**Size: 21x29mm**

| | | | | |
|---|---|---|---|---|
| **386** | A48 | 30fr gold, bl & dk bl | .25 | .25 |

**Size: 39x28mm**

| | | | | |
|---|---|---|---|---|
| **387** | A47 | 100fr multi & dk red | .50 | .40 |
| *a.* | | Sheet of 15, #382-387 | 9.00 | |

Russian Achievements in Space: 5fr, Col. Pavel Belyayev. 10fr, Lt. Col. Alexei Leonov. 15fr, Vostoks 3 & 4 in space. 30fr, Vostoks 5 & 6 over Earth. 100fr, Leonov floating in space.

**Size: 21x29mm**

| | | | | |
|---|---|---|---|---|
| **388** | A47 | 5fr bl & multi | .25 | .25 |
| **389** | A47 | 10fr bl & multi | .25 | .25 |
| **390** | A49 | 15fr bl & multi | .25 | .25 |

**Size: 39x28mm**

| | | | | |
|---|---|---|---|---|
| **391** | A49 | 25fr bl & multi | .25 | .25 |

**Size: 21x29mm**

| | | | | |
|---|---|---|---|---|
| **392** | A49 | 30fr bl & multi | .25 | .25 |

**Size: 39x28mm**

| | | | | |
|---|---|---|---|---|
| **393** | A47 | 100fr blk, dk red & gold | .50 | .40 |
| *a.* | | Sheet of 15, #388-393 | 9.00 | |
| | | *Nos. 382-393 (12)* | 3.50 | 3.30 |

American and Russian achievements in space. Nos. 387a and 393a contain five triptychs each: four rows with 5fr, 100fr and 10fr, and a center row with 15fr, 25fr and 30fr stamps each.

ICY Emblem, UN Headquarters and Skyline, New York — A50

**1965, Sept. 8 *Perf. 10½***

| | | | | |
|---|---|---|---|---|
| **394** | A50 | 25fr yel grn & ver | .35 | .25 |
| **395** | A50 | 45fr vio & orange | .40 | .25 |
| **396** | A50 | 75fr red brn & org | .65 | .25 |
| | | *Nos. 394-396,C75 (4)* | 2.65 | 1.10 |

Intl. Cooperation Year, 1965.

Polytechnic Institute, Conakry — A51

New Projects, Conakry: 30fr, Hotel Camayenne. 40fr, Gbessia Airport. 75fr, Stadium "28 September."

**1965, Oct. 2 Photo. *Perf. 13½***

| | | | | |
|---|---|---|---|---|
| **397** | A51 | 25fr multicolored | .30 | .25 |
| **398** | A51 | 30fr multicolored | .35 | .25 |
| **399** | A51 | 40fr multicolored | .60 | .30 |
| **400** | A51 | 75fr multicolored | .75 | .40 |
| | | *Nos. 397-400,C76-C77 (6)* | 8.75 | 5.20 |

Seventh anniversary of independence.

Photographing Far Side of Moon — A52

10fr, Trajectories of Ranger VII on flight to moon. 25fr, Relay satellite. 45fr, Vostoks I & II & globe.

**1965, Nov. 15 Litho. *Perf. 14x13½***

| | | | | |
|---|---|---|---|---|
| **401** | A52 | 5fr blk, pur & ocher | .25 | .25 |
| **402** | A52 | 10fr red brn, lt grn & yel | .25 | .25 |
| **403** | A52 | 25fr blk, bl & bis | .50 | .25 |
| **404** | A52 | 45fr blk, lt ultra & bis | 1.00 | .25 |
| | | *Nos. 401-404,C78-C79 (6)* | 5.50 | 2.50 |

For overprints and surcharges see Nos. 529-530, C112-C112B.

Sword Dance, Karana — A53

Designs: 30c, Dancing girls, Lower Guinea. 50c, Behore musicians of Tiekere playing "Eyoro," horiz. 5fr, Doundouba dance of Kouroussa. 40fr, Bird man's dance of Macenta.

**1966, Jan. 5 Photo. *Perf. 13½***

**Size: 26x36mm**

| | | | | |
|---|---|---|---|---|
| **405** | A53 | 10c multicolored | .25 | .25 |
| **406** | A53 | 30c multicolored | .25 | .25 |

**Size: 36x28½mm**

| | | | | |
|---|---|---|---|---|
| **407** | A53 | 50c multicolored | .45 | .25 |

**Size: 26x36mm**

| | | | | |
|---|---|---|---|---|
| **408** | A53 | 5fr multicolored | .45 | .25 |
| **409** | A53 | 40fr multicolored | .75 | .25 |
| | | *Nos. 405-409,C80 (6)* | 3.40 | 1.75 |

Festival of African Art and Culture. See Nos. 436-441.

Engraved Overprint in Red or Orange on Nos. 355-356 and Nos. 358-360

**1966, Mar. 14 *Perf. 13x12½***

| | | | | |
|---|---|---|---|---|
| **410** | A43 | 5fr multi (R) | .40 | .25 |
| **411** | A43 | 10fr multi (R) | .50 | .25 |
| **412** | A43 | 40fr multi (O) | .85 | .25 |
| **413** | A43 | 50fr multi (R) | 1.10 | .40 |
| **414** | A43 | 75fr multi (R) | 2.00 | .65 |
| | | *Nos. 410-414,C81 (6)* | 6.10 | 2.25 |

4th Pan Arab Games, Cairo, Sept. 2-11, 1965. The same overprint was also applied to imperf. sheets of No. 357.

Engraved Red Orange Overprint on No. 352

**1966, Mar. 14 *Perf. 12***

| | | | | |
|---|---|---|---|---|
| **415** | A42 | 50fr dk brn, bl & vio | 1.00 | .50 |

1st Egyptian postage stamps, cent. See #C82.

Vonkou Rock, Telimélé — A54

Views: 25fr, Artificial lake, Coyah. 40fr, Kalé waterfalls. 50fr, Forécariah bridge. 75fr, Liana bridge.

**1966, Apr. 4 Photo. *Perf. 13½***

| | | | | |
|---|---|---|---|---|
| **416** | A54 | 20fr multicolored | .25 | .25 |
| **417** | A54 | 25fr multicolored | .45 | .25 |
| **418** | A54 | 40fr multicolored | .50 | .25 |
| **419** | A54 | 50fr multicolored | .70 | .25 |
| **420** | A54 | 75fr multicolored | .90 | .30 |
| | | *Nos. 416-420,C83 (6)* | 4.20 | 1.90 |

See Nos. 475-478, C90-C91. For overprints see Nos. 482-488, C93-C95.

UNESCO Emblem A55

**1966, May 2 Photo. Unwmk.**

| | | | | |
|---|---|---|---|---|
| **421** | A55 | 25fr multicolored | .70 | .25 |

20th anniv. of UNESCO. See Nos. C84-C85.

Woman of Guinea and Morning Glory — A56

Symbolic Water Cycle and UNESCO Emblem — A57

Designs: Women and Flowers of Guinea.

**1966, May 30 Photo. *Perf. 13½***

**Size: 23x34mm**

| | | | | |
|---|---|---|---|---|
| **422** | A56 | 10c multicolored | .25 | .25 |
| **423** | A56 | 20c multicolored | .25 | .25 |
| **424** | A56 | 30c multicolored | .25 | .25 |
| **425** | A56 | 40c multicolored | .25 | .25 |
| **426** | A56 | 3fr multicolored | .25 | .25 |
| **427** | A56 | 4fr multicolored | .25 | .25 |
| **428** | A56 | 10fr multicolored | .25 | .25 |
| **429** | A56 | 25fr multicolored | .65 | .25 |

**Size: 28x43mm**

| | | | | |
|---|---|---|---|---|
| **430** | A56 | 30fr multicolored | .80 | .25 |
| **431** | A56 | 50fr multicolored | 1.00 | .35 |
| **432** | A56 | 80fr multicolored | 1.50 | .45 |
| | | *Nos. 422-432,C86-C87 (13)* | 14.20 | 5.85 |

**1966, Sept. 26 Engr. *Perf. 10½***

| | | | | |
|---|---|---|---|---|
| **433** | A57 | 5fr bl & dp org | .30 | .25 |
| **434** | A57 | 25fr grn & dp org | .35 | .25 |
| **435** | A57 | 100fr brt rose lil & dp org | .95 | .35 |
| | | *Nos. 433-435 (3)* | 1.60 | .85 |

Hydrological Decade (UNESCO), 1965-74.

### Dance Type of 1966

Various folk dances. 25fr, 75fr, horizontal.

**1966, Oct. 24 Photo. *Perf. 13½***
**Sizes: 26x36mm, 36x28½mm**

| | | | | |
|---|---|---|---|---|
| **436** | A53 | 60c multicolored | .25 | .25 |
| **437** | A53 | 1fr multicolored | .25 | .25 |
| **438** | A53 | 1.50fr multicolored | .25 | .25 |
| **439** | A53 | 25fr multicolored | .75 | .25 |
| **440** | A53 | 50fr multicolored | .95 | .25 |
| **441** | A53 | 75fr multicolored | 1.40 | .50 |
| | | *Nos. 436-441 (6)* | 3.85 | 1.75 |

Guinean National Dancers.

Child's Drawing and UNICEF Emblem — A58

Children's Drawings: 2fr, Elephant. 3fr, Girl. 20fr, Village, horiz. 25fr, Boy playing soccer. 40fr, Still life. 50fr, Bird in a tree.

**1966, Dec. 12 Photo. *Perf. 13½***

| | | | | |
|---|---|---|---|---|
| **442** | A58 | 2fr multicolored | .25 | .25 |
| **443** | A58 | 3fr multicolored | .25 | .25 |
| **444** | A58 | 10fr multicolored | .25 | .25 |
| **445** | A58 | 20fr multicolored | .25 | .25 |
| **446** | A58 | 25fr multicolored | .40 | .25 |
| **447** | A58 | 40fr multicolored | .45 | .25 |
| **448** | A58 | 50fr multicolored | .65 | .25 |
| | | *Nos. 442-448 (7)* | 2.50 | 1.75 |

20th anniv. of UNICEF. Printed in sheets of 10 stamps and 2 labels with ornamental borders and inscriptions.

Laboratory Technician — A59

WHO Emblem and: 50fr, Physician examining infant. 75fr, Pre-natal care & instruction. 80fr, WHO Headquarters, Geneva.

**1967, Jan. 20 Photo. *Perf. 13½***

| | | | | |
|---|---|---|---|---|
| **449** | A59 | 30fr multicolored | .30 | .25 |
| **450** | A59 | 50fr multicolored | .40 | .25 |
| **451** | A59 | 75fr multicolored | .60 | .25 |
| **452** | A59 | 80fr multicolored | .70 | .35 |
| | | *Nos. 449-452 (4)* | 2.00 | 1.10 |

Inauguration (in 1966) of WHO Headquarters, Geneva.

Niamou Mask, N'Zerekore — A60

Designs: 10c, 1fr, 30fr, Small Banda mask, Kanfarade, Boké region. 1.50fr, 50fr, Like 30c. 50c, 5fr, 75fr, Bearded Niamou mask. 60c, 25fr, 100fr, Horned Yinadjinkele mask, Kankan region.

**1967, Mar. 25 Photo. *Perf. 14x13***

| | | | | |
|---|---|---|---|---|
| **453** | A60 | 10c org & multi | .25 | .25 |
| **454** | A60 | 30c cit & brn blk | .25 | .25 |
| **455** | A60 | 50c dp lil rose, blk & red | .25 | .25 |
| **456** | A60 | 60c dp org, blk & bis | .25 | .25 |
| **457** | A60 | 1fr yel grn & multi | .25 | .25 |
| **458** | A60 | 1.50fr sal pink & brn blk | .25 | .25 |
| **459** | A60 | 5fr ap grn, blk & red | .25 | .25 |
| **460** | A60 | 25fr red lil, blk & bis | .45 | .25 |
| **461** | A60 | 30fr bis & multi | .50 | .25 |
| **462** | A60 | 50fr grnsh bl & brn blk | .70 | .25 |
| **463** | A60 | 75fr yel, blk & red | 1.00 | .35 |
| **464** | A60 | 100fr lt ultra, blk & bis | 1.60 | .55 |
| | | *Nos. 453-464 (12)* | 6.00 | 3.40 |

Ball Python — A61

20c, Pastoria Research Institute. 50c, 75fr, Extraction of snake venom. 1fr, 50fr, Rock python. 2fr, Men holding rock python. 5fr, 30fr, Gaboon viper. 20fr, West African mamba.

**1967, May 15 Litho. *Perf. 13½***
**Size: 43½x20mm**

| | | | | |
|---|---|---|---|---|
| **465** | A61 | 20c multicolored | .25 | .25 |
| **466** | A61 | 30c multicolored | .25 | .25 |
| **467** | A61 | 50c multicolored | .25 | .25 |
| **468** | A61 | 1fr multicolored | .25 | .25 |
| **469** | A61 | 2fr multicolored | .25 | .25 |
| **470** | A61 | 5fr multicolored | .25 | .25 |

**Size: 56x26mm**

| | | | | |
|---|---|---|---|---|
| **471** | A61 | 20fr multicolored | .65 | .25 |
| **472** | A61 | 30fr multicolored | .90 | .25 |
| **473** | A61 | 50fr multicolored | 1.00 | .25 |
| **474** | A61 | 75fr multicolored | 1.60 | .25 |
| | | *Nos. 465-474,C88-C89 (12)* | 12.65 | 6.00 |

Research Institute for Applied Biology of Guinea (Pastoria). For souvenir sheet see No. C88a.

### Scenic Type of 1966

Views: 5fr, Loos Island. 30fr, Tinkisso Waterfalls. 70fr, "The Elephant's Trunk" Hotel, Mt. Kakoulima. 80fr, Evening at the shore, Ratoma.

**1967, June 20 Photo. *Perf. 13½***

| | | | | |
|---|---|---|---|---|
| **475** | A54 | 5fr multicolored | .25 | .25 |
| **476** | A54 | 30fr multicolored | .25 | .25 |
| **477** | A54 | 70fr multicolored | .60 | .25 |
| **478** | A54 | 80fr multicolored | .85 | .25 |
| | | *Nos. 475-478,C90-C91 (6)* | 4.30 | 2.55 |

People's Palace, Conakry — A62

Elephant A63

**1967, Sept. 28 Photo. *Perf. 13½***

| | | | | |
|---|---|---|---|---|
| **479** | A62 | 5fr silver & multi | .25 | .25 |
| **480** | A63 | 30fr silver & multi | .30 | .25 |
| **481** | A62 | 55fr gold & multi | .50 | .25 |
| | | *Nos. 479-481 (3)* | 1.05 | .75 |

20th anniv. of the Democratic Party of Guinea and the opening of the People's Palace, Conakry. See No. C92.

Nos. 418-420 and 475-478 Overprinted

**1967, Nov. 6**

| | | | | |
|---|---|---|---|---|
| **482** | A54 | 5fr multicolored | .45 | .25 |
| **483** | A54 | 30fr multicolored | .90 | .25 |
| **484** | A54 | 40fr multicolored | .75 | .25 |
| **485** | A54 | 50fr multicolored | .80 | .25 |
| **486** | A54 | 70fr multicolored | 1.00 | .30 |
| **487** | A54 | 75fr multicolored | 1.45 | .50 |
| **488** | A54 | 80fr multicolored | 1.90 | .50 |
| | | *Nos. 482-488,C93-C95 (10)* | 12.90 | 5.60 |

50th anniversary of Lions International.

WHO Office for Africa — A64

**1967, Dec. 4 Photo. *Perf. 13½***

| | | | | |
|---|---|---|---|---|
| **489** | A64 | 30fr lt ol grn, bis & dk grn | .45 | .25 |
| **490** | A64 | 75fr red org, bis & dk bl | .80 | .30 |

Inauguration of the WHO Regional Office for Africa in Brazzaville, Congo.

Human Rights Flame — A65

**1968, Jan. 15 Photo. *Perf. 13½***

| | | | | |
|---|---|---|---|---|
| **491** | A65 | 30fr ocher, grn & dk car | .50 | .25 |
| **492** | A65 | 40fr vio, grn & car | .60 | .25 |

International Human Rights Year, 1968.

Coyah, Dubréka Region A66

Homes and People: 30c, 30fr, Kankan Region. 40c, Kankan, East Guinea. 50c, 15fr, Woodlands Region. 60c, Fulahmori, Gaoual Region. 5fr, Cognagui, Kundara Region. 40fr, Fouta Djallon, West Guinea. 100fr, Labé, West Guinea.

**1968, Apr. 1 Photo. *Perf. 13½x14***
**Size: 36x27mm**

| | | | | |
|---|---|---|---|---|
| **493** | A66 | 20c gold & multi | .25 | .25 |
| **494** | A66 | 30c gold & multi | .25 | .25 |
| **495** | A66 | 40c gold & multi | .25 | .25 |
| **496** | A66 | 50c gold & multi | .25 | .25 |

***Perf. 14x13½***
**Size: 57x36mm**

| | | | | |
|---|---|---|---|---|
| **497** | A66 | 60c gold & multi | .25 | .25 |
| **498** | A66 | 5fr gold & multi | .25 | .25 |
| **499** | A66 | 15fr gold & multi | .25 | .25 |
| **500** | A66 | 20fr gold & multi | .35 | .25 |
| **501** | A66 | 30fr gold & multi | .40 | .25 |
| **502** | A66 | 40fr gold & multi | .55 | .25 |
| **503** | A66 | 100fr gold & multi | 1.50 | .30 |
| | | *Nos. 493-503,C100 (12)* | 9.05 | 4.05 |

The Storyteller — A67

African Legends: 15fr, The Little Genie of Mt. Nimba. No. 506, The Legend of the Moons and the Stars. No. 507, Lan, the Child Buffalo, vert. 40fr, Nianablas and the Crocodiles. 50fr, Leuk the Hare Playing the Drum, vert. 75fr, Leuk the Hare Selling his Sister, vert. 80fr, The Hunter and the Antelope-woman. The designs are from paintings by students of the Academy of Fine Arts in Bellevue.

**1968 Photo. *Perf. 13½***

| | | | | |
|---|---|---|---|---|
| **504** | A67 | 15fr multicolored | .25 | .25 |
| **505** | A67 | 25fr multicolored | .25 | .25 |
| **506** | A67 | 30fr multicolored | .25 | .25 |
| **507** | A67 | 30fr multicolored | .25 | .25 |
| **508** | A67 | 40fr multicolored | .40 | .25 |
| **509** | A67 | 50fr multicolored | .65 | .25 |
| *a.* | | Souv. sheet of 4 | 5.50 | 5.50 |
| **510** | A67 | 75fr multicolored | .65 | .25 |
| **511** | A67 | 80fr multicolored | 1.10 | .25 |
| | | *Nos. 504-511,C101-C104 (12)* | 12.85 | 4.80 |

Issued in sheets of 10 plus 2 labels. No. 509a contains 4 imperf. stamps similar to Nos. 508-509, C101 and C104. "Poste Aerienne" omitted on the 70fr and 300fr of the souvenir sheet.

Issued: #505-506, 510-511, 5/16; #504, 507-509, 9/16.

Anubius Baboon — A68

African Animals: 10fr, Leopards. 15fr, Hippopotami. 20fr, Nile crocodile. 30fr, Ethiopian wart hog. 50fr, Defassa waterbuck. 75fr, Cape buffaloes.

**1968, Nov. 25 Photo. *Perf. 13½***
**Size: 44x31mm**

| | | | | |
|---|---|---|---|---|
| **512** | A68 | 5fr gold & multi | .25 | .25 |
| **513** | A68 | 10fr gold & multi | .60 | .25 |
| **514** | A68 | 15fr gold & multi | .65 | .25 |
| *a.* | | Souv. sheet of 3, #512-514 | 1.50 | 1.50 |
| **515** | A68 | 20fr gold & multi | .75 | .25 |
| **516** | A68 | 30fr gold & multi | .75 | .25 |
| **517** | A68 | 50fr gold & multi | .90 | .25 |
| *a.* | | Souv. sheet of 3, #515-517 | 3.75 | 3.75 |
| **518** | A68 | 75fr gold & multi | 1.45 | .30 |
| *a.* | | Souv. sheet of 3 | 10.50 | 10.50 |
| | | *Nos. 512-518,C105-C106 (9)* | 10.60 | 4.45 |

No. 518a contains one No. 518 and one each similar to Nos. C105-C106 without "POSTE AERIENNE" inscription. The three souvenir sheets contain 3 stamps and one green and gold label inscribed "FAUNE AFRICAINE."

Senator Robert F. Kennedy A69

Portraits: 75fr, Rev. Martin Luther King, Jr. 100fr, Pres. John F. Kennedy.

**1968, Dec. 16**

| | | | | |
|---|---|---|---|---|
| **519** | A69 | 30fr yel & multi | .55 | .25 |
| **520** | A69 | 75fr multicolored | 1.00 | .25 |
| **521** | A69 | 100fr multicolored | 1.40 | .30 |
| | | *Nos. 519-521,C107-C109 (6)* | 9.75 | 2.55 |

Robert F. Kennedy, John F. Kennedy and Martin Luther King, Jr., martyrs for freedom.

The stamps are printed in sheets of 15 (3x5) containing 10 stamps and five yellow-green and gold center labels. Sheets come either with English or French inscriptions on label.

Sculpture and Runner A70

Sculpture and Soccer — A71

Designs (Sculpture and): 10fr, Boxing. 15fr, Javelin. 30fr, Steeplechase. 50fr, Hammer throw. 75fr, Bicycling.

**1969, Feb. 18 Photo. *Perf. 13½***

| | | | | |
|---|---|---|---|---|
| **522** | A70 | 5fr multicolored | .25 | .25 |
| **523** | A70 | 10fr multicolored | .25 | .25 |
| **524** | A70 | 15fr multicolored | .40 | .25 |
| **525** | A71 | 25fr multicolored | .40 | .25 |
| **526** | A70 | 30fr multicolored | .40 | .25 |
| **527** | A70 | 50fr multicolored | .50 | .25 |
| **528** | A70 | 75fr multicolored | .75 | .25 |
| | | *Nos. 522-528,C110-C111A (10)* | 11.45 | 4.05 |

19th Olympic Games, Mexico City, 10/12-27.

No. 404 Srchd. and Ovptd. in Red

**1969, Mar. 17 Litho. *Perf. 14x13½***

| | | | | |
|---|---|---|---|---|
| **529** | A52 | 30fr on 45fr multi | .60 | .35 |
| **530** | A52 | 45fr multicolored | .60 | .35 |
| | | *Nos. 529-530,C112-C112B (5)* | 4.60 | 2.60 |

US Apollo 8 mission, the first men in orbit around the moon, Dec. 21-27, 1968.

Nos. 529-530 also exist with surcharge and overprint in black. These sell for about 10% more.

Tarzan — A72

Designs: 30fr, Tarzan sitting in front of Pastoria Research Institute gate. 75fr, Tarzan and his family. 100fr, Tarzan sitting in a tree.

**1969, June 6 Photo. *Perf. 13½***

| | | | | |
|---|---|---|---|---|
| **531** | A72 | 25fr orange & multi | .45 | .25 |
| **532** | A72 | 30fr bl grn & multi | .60 | .25 |
| **533** | A72 | 75fr yel grn & multi | 1.25 | .25 |
| **534** | A72 | 100fr yellow & multi | 1.90 | .35 |
| | | *Nos. 531-534 (4)* | 4.20 | 1.10 |

Tarzan was a Guinean chimpanzee with superior intelligence and ability.

Campfire A73

25fr, Boy Scout & tents. 30fr, Marching Boy Scouts. 40fr, Basketball. 45fr, Senior Scouts, thatched huts & mountain. 50fr, Guinean Boy Scout badge.

**1969, July 1**

| | | | | |
|---|---|---|---|---|
| **535** | A73 | 5fr gold & multi | .25 | .25 |
| **536** | A73 | 25fr gold & multi | .30 | .25 |
| **537** | A73 | 30fr gold & multi | .30 | .25 |
| **538** | A73 | 40fr gold & multi | .45 | .25 |
| **539** | A73 | 45fr gold & multi | .60 | .25 |
| **540** | A73 | 50fr gold & multi | .65 | .25 |
| *a.* | | Min. sheet of 6, #535-540 | 3.50 | 3.50 |
| | | *Nos. 535-540 (6)* | 2.55 | 1.50 |

Issued to honor the Boy Scouts of Guinea.

Launching Apollo 11 — A74

Designs: 30fr, Earth showing Africa as seen from moon. 50fr, Separation of lunar landing module and spaceship. 60fr, Astronauts and module on moon. 75fr, Module on moon and earth. 100fr, Module leaving moon. 200fr, Splashdown. "a" stamps are inscribed in French. "b" stamps are inscribed in English.

**1969, Aug. 20 Photo. *Perf. 13½***

**Size: 34x55mm**

| | | | | |
|---|---|---|---|---|
| **541** | A74 | 25fr Pair, #541a, 541b | .40 | .25 |
| **542** | A74 | 30fr Pair, #542a, 542b | .50 | .25 |
| **543** | A74 | 50fr Pair, #543a, 543b | .75 | .25 |
| **544** | A74 | 60fr Pair, #544a, 544b | 1.25 | .35 |
| **545** | A74 | 75fr Pair, #545a, 545b | 1.50 | .40 |

**Size: 34x71mm**

| | | | | |
|---|---|---|---|---|
| **546** | A74 | 100fr Pair, #546a, 546b | 2.50 | .60 |

**Size: 34x55mm**

| | | | | |
|---|---|---|---|---|
| **547** | A74 | 200fr Pair, #547a, 547b | 5.00 | 1.50 |
| | | *Nos. 541-547 (7)* | 11.90 | 3.60 |

Man's 1st landing on the moon, 7/20/69.

Harvest and ILO Emblem A75

ILO, 50th Anniv.: 25fr, Power lines and blast furnaces. 30fr, Women in broadcasting studio. 200fr, Potters.

**1969, Oct. 28 Photo. *Perf. 13½***

| | | | | |
|---|---|---|---|---|
| **548** | A75 | 25fr gold & multi | .25 | .25 |
| **549** | A75 | 30fr gold & multi | .30 | .25 |
| **550** | A75 | 75fr gold & multi | .65 | .25 |
| **551** | A75 | 200fr gold & multi | 1.90 | .60 |
| | | *Nos. 548-551 (4)* | 3.10 | 1.35 |

Mother and Sick Child — A76

25fr, Sick child. 40fr, Girl receiving vaccination. 50fr, Boy receiving vaccination. 60fr, Mother receiving vaccination. 200fr, Edward Jenner, M.D.

**1970, Jan. 15 Photo. *Perf. 13½***

| | | | | |
|---|---|---|---|---|
| **552** | A76 | 25fr multicolored | .25 | .25 |
| **553** | A76 | 30fr multicolored | .35 | .25 |
| **554** | A76 | 40fr multicolored | .40 | .25 |
| **555** | A76 | 50fr multicolored | .50 | .25 |
| **556** | A76 | 60fr multicolored | .60 | .25 |
| **557** | A76 | 200fr multicolored | 2.00 | 1.00 |
| | | *Nos. 552-557 (6)* | 4.10 | 2.25 |

Campaign against smallpox and measles.

Map of Africa — A77

**1970, Feb. 3 Litho. *Perf. 14½x14***

| | | | | |
|---|---|---|---|---|
| **558** | A77 | 30fr lt bl & multi | .25 | .25 |
| **559** | A77 | 200fr lt vio & multi | 1.75 | .75 |

Meeting of statesmen of countries bordering on Senegal River: Mali, Guinea, Senegal and Mauritania.

Open Book and Radar A78

**1970, July 6 Litho. *Perf. 14***

| | | | | |
|---|---|---|---|---|
| **560** | A78 | 5fr lt bl & blk | .25 | .25 |
| **561** | A78 | 10fr rose & blk | .25 | .25 |
| **562** | A78 | 50fr yellow & blk | .60 | .25 |
| **563** | A78 | 200fr lilac & blk | 2.10 | .90 |
| | | *Nos. 560-563 (4)* | 3.20 | 1.65 |

International Telecommunications Day.

Lenin — A79

Designs: 20fr, Meeting with Lenin, by V. Serov. 30fr, Lenin Addressing Workers, by V. Serov. 40fr, Lenin with Red Guard Soldier and Sailor, by P. V. Vasiliev. 100fr, Lenin Speaking from Balcony, by P. V. Vasiliev. 200fr, Like 5fr.

**1970, Nov. 16 Photo. *Perf. 13***

| | | | | |
|---|---|---|---|---|
| **564** | A79 | 5fr gold & multi | .25 | .25 |
| **565** | A79 | 20fr gold & multi | .40 | .25 |
| **566** | A79 | 30fr gold & multi | .50 | .25 |
| **567** | A79 | 40fr gold & multi | .80 | .25 |
| **568** | A79 | 100fr gold & multi | 1.60 | .30 |
| **569** | A79 | 200fr gold & multi | 3.25 | .75 |
| | | *Nos. 564-569 (6)* | 6.80 | 2.05 |

Lenin (1870-1924), Russian communist leader.

Phenecogrammus Interruptus — A80

Designs: Various fish from Guinea.

**1971, Apr. 1 Photo. *Perf. 13***

| | | | | |
|---|---|---|---|---|
| **570** | A80 | 5fr gold & multi | .25 | .25 |
| **571** | A80 | 10fr gold & multi | .25 | .25 |
| **572** | A80 | 15fr gold & multi | .30 | .25 |
| **573** | A80 | 20fr gold & multi | .30 | .25 |
| **574** | A80 | 25fr gold & multi | .30 | .25 |
| **575** | A80 | 30fr gold & multi | .45 | .25 |
| **576** | A80 | 40fr gold & multi | .60 | .25 |
| **577** | A80 | 45fr gold & multi | .70 | .25 |
| **578** | A80 | 50fr gold & multi | 1.00 | .25 |
| **579** | A80 | 75fr gold & multi | 1.75 | .55 |
| **580** | A80 | 100fr gold & multi | 2.25 | .65 |
| **581** | A80 | 200fr gold & multi | 5.00 | 1.10 |
| | | *Nos. 570-581 (12)* | 13.15 | 4.55 |

Violet-crested Touraco — A81

Birds: 20fr, European golden oriole. 30fr, Blue-headed coucal. 40fr, Northern shrike. 75fr, Vulturine guinea fowl. 100fr, Southern ground hornbill.

**1971, June 18 Photo. *Perf. 13***

**Size: 34x34mm**

| | | | | |
|---|---|---|---|---|
| **582** | A81 | 5fr gold & multi | .25 | .25 |
| **583** | A81 | 20fr gold & multi | .35 | .25 |
| **584** | A81 | 30fr gold & multi | .55 | .25 |
| **585** | A81 | 40fr gold & multi | .65 | .25 |
| **586** | A81 | 75fr gold & multi | 2.00 | .55 |
| **587** | A81 | 100fr gold & multi | 2.50 | .80 |
| | | *Nos. 582-587,C113-C113B (9)* | 14.15 | 4.80 |

UNICEF Emblem, Map of Africa — A82

**1971, Dec. 24 *Perf. 12x12½***

**Map in Olive**

| | | | | |
|---|---|---|---|---|
| **588** | A82 | 25fr orange & blk | .25 | .25 |
| **589** | A82 | 30fr pink & black | .35 | .25 |
| **590** | A82 | 50fr gray grn & blk | .60 | .25 |
| **591** | A82 | 60fr gray bl & blk | .70 | .25 |
| **592** | A82 | 100fr lil rose & blk | 1.10 | .25 |
| | | *Nos. 588-592 (5)* | 3.00 | 1.25 |

UNICEF, 25th anniv.

For overprints see Nos. 625-629.

Imaginary Prehistoric Space Creature — A83

Various imaginary prehistoric space creatures.

**1972, Apr. 1 *Perf. 13½x13***

| | | | | |
|---|---|---|---|---|
| **593** | A83 | 5fr multicolored | .25 | .25 |
| **594** | A83 | 20fr multicolored | .25 | .25 |
| **595** | A83 | 30fr multicolored | .45 | .25 |
| **596** | A83 | 40fr multicolored | .50 | .25 |
| **597** | A83 | 100fr multicolored | 1.10 | .35 |
| **598** | A83 | 200fr multicolored | 2.75 | .75 |
| | | *Nos. 593-598 (6)* | 5.30 | 2.10 |

Black Boy, Men of 4 Races, Emblem — A84

Designs: 20fr, Oriental boy. 30fr, Indian youth. 50fr, Caucasian girl. 100fr, Men of 4 races and Racial Equality emblem.

**1972, May 14 *Perf. 13x13½***

| | | | | |
|---|---|---|---|---|
| **599** | A84 | 15fr gold & multi | .25 | .25 |
| **600** | A84 | 20fr gold & multi | .25 | .25 |
| **601** | A84 | 30fr gold & multi | .25 | .25 |

**602** A84 50fr gold & multi .40 .25
**603** A84 100fr gold & multi .75 .30
*Nos. 599-603,C119 (6)* 3.00 2.30

Intl. Year Against Racial Discrimination, 1971.

Map of Africa, Syncom Satellite — A85

Designs (Map of Africa and Satellites): 30fr, Relay. 75fr, Early Bird. 80fr, Telstar.

**1972, May 17 Litho. *Perf. 13***

**604** A85 15fr multicolored .25 .25
**605** A85 30fr red org & multi .25 .25
**606** A85 75fr grn & multi 1.00 .25
**607** A85 80fr multicolored 1.10 .45
*Nos. 604-607,C120-C121 (6)* 7.00 3.30

4th World Telecommunications Day.

Carrier Pigeon, UPAF Emblem — A86

**1972, July 10**

**608** A86 15fr brt bl & multi .25 .25
**609** A86 30fr multicolored .25 .25
**610** A86 75fr lil & multi .75 .25
**611** A86 80fr multicolored .90 .45
*Nos. 608-611,C122-C123 (6)* 5.05 3.00

Book Year Emblem, Reading Child — A87

Designs (Book Year Emblem and): 15fr, Book as sailing ship. 40fr, Young woman with flower and book. 50fr, Book as key. 75fr, Man reading and globe. 200fr, Book and laurel.

**1972, Aug. 2 Photo. *Perf. 14x13½***

**612** A87 5fr red & multi .25 .25
**613** A87 15fr multicolored .25 .25
**614** A87 40fr yel & multi .45 .25
**615** A87 50fr blue & multi .65 .25
**616** A87 75fr dk red & multi .75 .45
**617** A87 200fr org & multi 1.50 .90
*Nos. 612-617 (6)* 3.85 2.35

International Book Year 1972.

Javelin, Olympic Emblems, Arms of Guinea A88

**1972, Aug. 26 Photo. *Perf. 13***

**618** A88 5fr shown .25 .25
**619** A88 10fr Pole vault .25 .25
**620** A88 25fr Hurdles .40 .25
**621** A88 30fr Hammer throw .60 .25
**622** A88 40fr Boxing .75 .25
**623** A88 50fr Vaulting .80 .35
**624** A88 75fr Running 1.90 .45
*Nos. 618-624,C124-C125 (9)* 11.10 3.75

20th Olympic Games, Munich, 8/26-9/11.

Nos. 588-592 Overprinted

**1972, Sept. 28 Photo. *Perf. 12x12½***
**Map in Olive**

**625** A82 25fr org & blk .40 .25
**626** A82 30fr pink & blk .60 .25
**627** A82 50fr gray grn & blk .90 .25
**628** A82 60fr gray bl & blk 1.50 .25
**629** A82 100fr lil rose & blk 2.10 .80
*Nos. 625-629 (5)* 5.50 1.80

UN Conference on Human Environment, Stockholm, June 5-16.

Dimitrov at Leipzig Trial — A89

**1972, Sept. 28 *Perf. 13***
**Gold, Dark Green & Black**

**630** A89 5fr shown .25 .25
**631** A89 25fr In Moabit Prison, 1933 .45 .25
**632** A89 40fr Writing his memoirs .50 .25
**633** A89 100fr Portrait 1.25 .30
*Nos. 630-633 (4)* 2.45 1.05

George Dimitrov (1882-1949), Bulgarian Communist party leader and Premier.

Emperor Haile Selassie — A90

Design: 200fr, Emperor facing right.

**1972, Oct. 2**

**634** A90 40fr blk & multi .55 .25
**635** A90 200fr multicolored 3.25 .95

Syntomeida Epilais — A91

Designs: Various insects.

**1973, Mar. 5 Photo. *Perf. 14x13½***

**636** A91 5fr shown .35 .25
**637** A91 15fr Ladybugs .45 .25
**638** A91 30fr Green locust 1.50 .30
**639** A91 40fr Honey bee 2.00 .40
**640** A91 50fr Photinus pyralis 2.50 .60
**641** A91 200fr Ancyluris formosissima 7.00 1.75
*Nos. 636-641 (6)* 13.80 3.55

Kwame Nkrumah A92

Various portraits of Kwame Nkrumah.

**1973, May 25 Photo. *Perf. 13½***

**642** A92 1.50s lt grn, gold & brn .25 .25
**643** A92 2.50s lt grn, gold & brn .35 .25
**644** A92 5s lt grn, gold & brn .60 .25
**645** A92 10s gold & dark vio 1.75 .45
*Nos. 642-645 (4)* 2.95 1.20

OAU, 10th anniversary.

Institute for Applied Biology, Kindia A93

WHO Emblem and: 2.50s, Technicians inoculating egg. 3s, Filling vaccine into ampules. 4s, Sterilization of vaccine. 5s, Assembling of vaccine and vaccination gun. 10s, Inoculation of steer. 20s, Vaccination of woman.

**1973, Nov. 16 Photo. *Perf. 13½***
**Size: 40x36mm**

**646** A93 1s gold & multi .25 .25
**647** A93 2.50s gold & multi .40 .25
**648** A93 3s gold & multi .55 .25
**649** A93 4s gold & multi .75 .25

**Size: 47½x31mm**

**650** A93 5s gold & multi .90 .25
**651** A93 10s gold & multi 1.40 .40
**652** A93 20s gold & multi 3.25 1.00
*Nos. 646-652 (7)* 7.50 2.65

WHO, 25th anniversary.

Copernicus, Heliocentric System, Primeval Landscape — A94

Nicolaus Copernicus — A95

Designs (Copernicus and): 2s, Sun rising over volcanic desert, and spacecraft. 4s, Earth, moon and spacecraft. 5s, Moon scape and spacecraft. 10s, Jupiter and spacecraft. 20s, Saturn and heliocentric system.

**1973, Dec. 17 Photo. *Perf. 13½***

**653** A94 50c gold & multi .25 .25
**654** A94 2s gold & multi .30 .25
**655** A94 4s gold & multi .40 .25
**656** A94 5s gold & multi .60 .25
**657** A94 10s gold & multi 1.50 .40
**658** A94 20s gold & multi 3.00 .90
*Nos. 653-658 (6)* 6.05 2.30

**Souvenir Sheet**

**659** Sheet of 4 20.00 20.00
*a.* A95 20s Single stamp 3.25 3.25

Nicolaus Copernicus (1473-1543), Polish astronomer. No. 659 contains center label showing rocket and heliocentric system in gold margin.

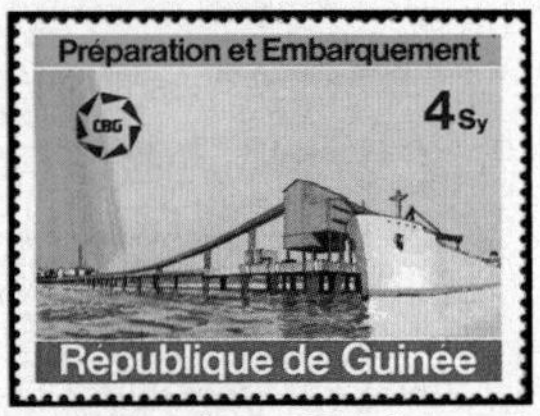

Loading Bauxite on Freighter — A96

**1974, Mar. 1 Litho. *Perf. 13½***

**660** A96 4s shown .60 .25
**661** A96 6s Freight train 1.60 .25
**662** A96 10s Mining 2.75 .65
*Nos. 660-662 (3)* 4.95 1.15

Bauxite mining, Boke.

Clappertonia Ficifolia — A97

**1974, May 20 Photo. *Perf. 13***
**Size: 25x36mm**

**663** A97 50c shown .25 .25
**664** A97 1s Rothmannia longiflora .25 .25
**665** A97 2s Oncoba spinosa .25 .25
**666** A97 3s Venidium fastuosum .30 .25

**Size: 31x42mm**

**667** A97 4s Bombax costatum .40 .25
**668** A97 5s Clerodendrum splendens .75 .25
**669** A97 7.50s Combretum grandiflorum .85 .30
**670** A97 10s Mussaendra erythrophylla 1.00 .35

**Size: 38x38mm (Diamond)**

**671** A97 12s Argemone mexicana 1.25 .45
*Nos. 663-671,C127-C129 (12)* 18.80 7.40

Drummers, Pigeon, UPAF and UPU Emblems — A98

Designs (Carrier Pigeon, African Postal Union and UPU Emblems): 6s, Runner with letter stick. 7.50s, Monorail and mail truck. No. 675, Jet and ocean liner. No. 676, Balloon and dugout canoe. 20s, Satellites over earth.

**1974, Oct. 16 Photo. *Perf. 13½x14***

**672** A98 5s mag & multi .60 .25
**673** A98 6s grn & multi .80 .25
**674** A98 7.50s ver & multi 1.25 .35
**675** A98 10s Prus bl & multi 1.75 .60
*Nos. 672-675 (4)* 4.40 1.45

**Souvenir Sheets**
***Perf. 13½***

**676** A98 10s ocher & multi 6.00 6.00
**677** Sheet of 4, multi 12.00 12.00
*a.* A98 20s Single stamp 1.60 1.60

Centenary of Universal Postal Union. No. 676 contains one 70x60mm stamp.

Rope Bridge — A99

Designs (Pioneers): 2s, Field observation. 4s, Communication. 5s, Cooking in camp. 7.50s, Salute. 10s, Basketball.

**1974, Nov. 22 Photo.** ***Perf. 14x13½***

**678** A99 50c multicolored .25 .25
**679** A99 2s multicolored .35 .25
**680** A99 4s multicolored .45 .25
**681** A99 5s multicolored .75 .25
**682** A99 7.50s multicolored 1.10 .25
**683** A99 10s multicolored 1.90 .45
*a.* Souv. sheet of 2, #682-683 4.00 4.00
*Nos. 678-683 (6)* 4.80 1.70

National Pioneer Movement.

Souvenir Sheet

Fruit — A100

**1974, Nov. 22 Photo.** ***Perf. 13x14***

**684** A100 Sheet of 5 *12.00* 12.00
*a.* 4s Limes 1.00 .75
*b.* 4s Oranges 1.00 .85
*c.* 5s Bananas 1.50 1.25
*d.* 5s Mangos 1.50 1.25
*e.* 12s Pineapple 2.75 2.50

Chimpanzee — A101

**1975, May 14 Photo.** ***Perf. 13½***

**685** A101 1s shown .45 .25
**686** A101 2s Impala .65 .25
**687** A101 3s Wart hog .75 .25
**688** A101 4s Kobus defassa .75 .25
*a.* Souv. sheet of 4, #685-688 9.00 9.00
**689** A101 5s Leopard 1.40 .25
**690** A101 6s Greater kudu 1.40 .25
**691** A101 6.50s Zebra 1.60 .25
**692** A101 7.50s Cape buffalo 2.00 .25
*a.* Souv. sheet of 4, #689-692 4.00 9.00
**693** A101 8s Hippopotamus 3.25 .85
**694** A101 10s Lion 3.25 .85
**695** A101 12s Black rhinoceros 4.00 1.00
**696** A101 15s Elephant 6.00 1.50
*a.* Souv. sheet of 4, #693-696 26.50 26.50
*Nos. 685-696 (12)* 25.50 6.20

Sheets exist perf. and imperf.

Stamps in Nos. 692a, 696a are inscribed "Poste Aerienne."

Lions, Pipe Line and ADB Emblem A102

Designs (African Development Bank Emblem, Pipe Line and): 7s, Elephants. 10s, Male lions. 20s, Elephant and calf.

**1975, June 16 Photo.** ***Perf. 13½***

**697** A102 5s gold & multi .90 .25
**698** A102 7s gold & multi 1.25 .25
**699** A102 10s gold & multi 1.60 .35
**700** A102 20s gold & multi 3.25 .70
*Nos. 697-700 (4)* 7.00 1.55

African Development Bank, 10th anniv.

Women Musicians, IWY Emblem A103

IWY Emblem and: 7s, Women banjo & guitar players. 9s, Woman railroad shunter & train. 15s, Woman physician examining infant. 20s, Male & female symbols.

**1976, Apr. 12 Photo.** ***Perf. 13½***

**701** A103 5s multicolored .60 .25
**702** A103 7s multicolored .90 .25
**703** A103 9s blue & multi 1.50 .45
**704** A103 15s multicolored 2.25 .75
*a.* Souvenir sheet 3.00 3.00
**705** A103 20s vio bl & multi 2.75 1.00
*a.* Souvenir sheet of 4 13.00 13.00
*Nos. 701-705 (5)* 8.00 2.70

International Women's Year 1975. No. 704a contains one stamp similar to No. 704 with gold frame. No. 705a contains 4 stamps similar to No. 705 with gold frame.

Woman Gymnast A104

Montreal Olympic Games Emblem and: 4s, Long jump. 5s, Hammer throw. 6s, Discus. 6.50s, Hurdles. 7s, Javelin. 8s, Running. 8.50s, Bicycling. 10s, High jump. 15s, Shot put. 20s, Pole vault. #717, Soccer. #718, Swimming.

**1976, May 17 Photo.** ***Perf. 13½***

**Size: 38x38mm**

**706** A104 3s multicolored .40 .25
**707** A104 4s grn & multi .60 .25
**708** A104 5s yel & multi .60 .25
**709** A104 6s multicolored .70 .25
**710** A104 6.50s plum & multi .70 .25
**711** A104 7s blue & multi .95 .30
**712** A104 8s ultra & multi .95 .30
**713** A104 8.50s org & multi 1.50 .35
**714** A104 10s multicolored 1.60 .40
**715** A104 15s multicolored 2.50 .75
**716** A104 20s multicolored 3.25 .95
**717** A104 25s grn & multi 3.75 1.00
*Nos. 706-717 (12)* 17.50 5.30

**Souvenir Sheet**

**718** A104 25s multicolored 5.00 5.00

21st Olympic Games, Montreal, Canada, July 17-Aug. 1. No. 718 contains one 32x32mm stamp. See No. C130.

A. G. Bell, Telephone, 1900 — A105

7s, Wall telephone, 1910. 12s, Syncom telecommunications satellite. #722, Telstar satellite. #723, Telephone switchboard operator, 1914.

**1976, Nov. 15 Photo.** ***Perf. 13***

**719** A105 5s multicolored .65 .25
**720** A105 7s multicolored 1.00 .25
**721** A105 12s multicolored 1.60 .45
**722** A105 15s multicolored 2.25 .60
*a.* Souvenir sheet of 4, #719-722 7.00 7.00
*Nos. 719-722 (4)* 5.50 1.55

**Souvenir Sheet**

**723** A105 15s multicolored 2.50 2.50

Centenary of first telephone call by Alexander Graham Bell, Mar. 10, 1876.

Collybia Fusipes — A106

Mushrooms: 7s, Lycoperdon perlatum. 9s, Boletus edulis. 9.50s, Lactarius deliciosus. 11.50s, Agaricus campestris.

**1977, Feb. 6 Photo.** ***Perf. 13***

**Size: 48x26mm**

**724** A106 5s multicolored 1.90 .25
**725** A106 7s multicolored 3.00 .25
**726** A106 9s multicolored 3.50 .55
*a.* Souvenir sheet of 2, #724, 726 7.50 7.50
**727** A106 9.50s multicolored 3.50 .65

**Size: 48x31mm**

**728** A106 11.50s multicolored 6.25 1.10
*Nos. 724-728,C131-C133 (8)* 35.15 6.50

Hexaplex Hoplites — A107

Sea Shells: 2s, Perrona lineata. 4s, Marginella pseudofaba. 5s, Tympanotonos radula. 7s, Marginella strigata. 8s, Harpa doris. 10s, Demoulia pinguis. 20s, Bursa scrobiculator. 25s, Marginella adansoni.

**1977, Apr. 25 Photo.** ***Perf. 13***

**Size: 50x25mm**

**729** A107 1s gold & multi .25 .25
**730** A107 2s gold & multi .30 .25
**731** A107 4s gold & multi .75 .30
**732** A107 5s gold & multi 1.15 .35
**733** A107 7s gold & multi 1.60 .40
**734** A107 8s gold & multi 1.90 .60

**Size: 50x30mm**

**735** A107 10s gold & multi 2.50 .90
**736** A107 20s gold & multi 5.00 1.25
**737** A107 25s gold & multi 6.50 1.75
*Nos. 729-737 (9)* 19.95 6.05

Farmers and Ox Plow A108

Designs: 5s, Pres. Touré addressing rally. 20s, Soldier driving farm tractor. 25s, Pres. Touré addressing UN General Assembly. 30s, 40s, Pres. Sékou Touré, vert.

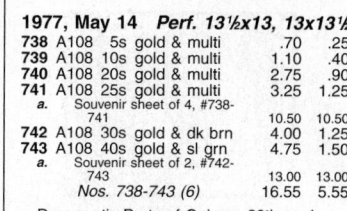

**1977, May 14** ***Perf. 13½x13, 13x13½***

**738** A108 5s gold & multi .70 .25
**739** A108 10s gold & multi 1.10 .40
**740** A108 20s gold & multi 2.75 .90
**741** A108 25s gold & multi 3.25 1.25
*a.* Souvenir sheet of 4, #738-741 10.50 10.50
**742** A108 30s gold & dk brn 4.00 1.25
**743** A108 40s gold & sl grn 4.75 1.50
*a.* Souvenir sheet of 2, #742-743 13.00 13.00
*Nos. 738-743 (6)* 16.55 5.55

Democratic Party of Guinea, 30th anniv.

Nile Monitor — A109

Reptiles and Snakes: 4s, Frogs. 5s, Lizard (uromastix). 6s, Sand skink. 6.50s, Agama. 7s, Black-lipped spitting cobra. 8.50s, Ball python. 20s, Toads.

**1977, Oct. 10 Photo.** ***Perf. 13½***

**Size: 46x20mm**

**744** A109 3s multi .50 .25
**745** A109 4s multi .70 .25
**746** A109 5s multi .70 .25

**Size: 46x30mm**

**747** A109 6s multi 1.15 .25
**748** A109 6.50s multi 1.45 .25
**749** A109 7s multi 1.90 .55
**750** A109 8.50s multi 2.10 .65
**751** A109 20s multi 5.00 1.40
*Nos. 744-751,C134-C136 (11)* 28.50 7.35

Eland — A110

Endangered Animals: 2s, Chimpanzee. 2.50s, Pygmy elephant. 3s, Lion. 4s, Palm squirrel. 5s, Hippopotamus. Each animal shown male, female and young.

**1977, Dec. 12 Photo.** ***Perf. 14x13½***

**752** A110 Strip of 3 .95 .25
*a.-c.* 1s any single .25
**753** A110 Strip of 3 1.50 .25
*a.-c.* 2s any single .35
**754** A110 Strip of 3 1.90 .30
*a.-c.* 2.50s any single .50
**755** A110 Strip of 3 2.50 .40
*a.-c.* 3s any single .60
**756** A110 Strip of 3 3.00 .55
*a.-c.* 4s any single .95
**757** A110 Strip of 3 4.00 .65
*a.-c.* 5s any single 1.25
*Nos. 752-757,C137-C142 (12)* 50.60 22.40

Russian October Revolution, 60th Anniv. — A111

Designs: 2.50s, First Lenin debate, Moscow. 5s, Lenin speaking, 1917. 7.50s, Lenin and people. 8s, Lenin in first parade on Red Square.

**1978, Feb. 27 Photo.** ***Perf. 14***

**758** A111 2.50s gold & multi .60 .25
**759** A111 5s gold & multi 1.00 .25
**760** A111 7.50s gold & multi 1.50 .30
**761** A111 8s gold & multi 1.60 .35
*Nos. 758-761,C143-C144 (6)* 14.10 4.05

Pres. Giscard d'Estaing at Microphones — A112

Pres. Valery Giscard d'Estaing of France and Pres. Sekou Toure of Guinea: 5s, 10s, In conference. 6.50s, Signing agreement. 7s, Attending official meeting. 8.50s, With their wives. 20s, Drinking a toast.

**1979, Sept. 14 Photo. *Perf. 13***

| | | | | | |
|---|---|---|---|---|---|
| **762** | A112 | 3s | lt brn & brn | .85 | .25 |
| **763** | A112 | 5s | green & brn | 1.50 | .25 |
| **764** | A112 | 6.50s | red lil & brn | 1.75 | .25 |
| **765** | A112 | 7s | ultra & brn | 1.90 | .30 |
| **766** | A112 | 8.50s | dk red & brn | 2.40 | .55 |
| **767** | A112 | 10s | vio & brown | 2.75 | .80 |
| **768** | A112 | 20s | yel grn & brn | 4.00 | 1.10 |
| | | | *Nos. 762-768,C145 (8)* | 20.15 | 5.50 |

Visit of Pres. Valery Giscard d'Estaing to Guinea.

Twenty Thousand Leagues Under the Sea — A113

Jules Verne Stories: 3s, Children of Capt. Grant. 5s, Mysterious Island. 7s, A Captain at Fifteen. 10s, The Borsac Mission.

**1979, Nov. 8 Litho. *Perf. 12x12½***

| | | | | | |
|---|---|---|---|---|---|
| **769** | A113 | 1s | multicolored | .40 | .25 |
| **770** | A113 | 3s | multicolored | .45 | .25 |
| **771** | A113 | 5s | multicolored | .85 | .25 |
| **772** | A113 | 7s | multicolored | 1.25 | .30 |
| **773** | A113 | 10s | multicolored | 1.75 | .40 |
| | | | *Nos. 769-773,C146-C147 (7)* | 11.70 | 3.95 |

Jules Verne (1828-1905), French science fiction writer.

"Aerial Steam Carriage," 1842 — A114

Aviation Retrospect: 5s, Wright's Flyer 1 1903. 6.50s, Caudron, 1934. 7s, Spirit of St. Louis, 1927. 8.50s, Bristol Beaufighter, 1940. 10s, Bleriot XI, 1909. #780, Concorde. #781, Boeing 727, 1963.

**1979, Nov. 22 Photo. *Perf. 14***

| | | | | | |
|---|---|---|---|---|---|
| **774** | A114 | 3s | multi | .50 | .25 |
| **775** | A114 | 5s | multi | .90 | .25 |
| **776** | A114 | 6.50s | multi | 1.10 | .35 |
| **777** | A114 | 7s | multi | 1.25 | .35 |
| **778** | A114 | 8.50s | multi | 1.50 | .45 |
| **779** | A114 | 10s | multi | 1.75 | .45 |
| **780** | A114 | 20s | multi | 3.50 | .95 |
| **781** | A114 | 20s | multi | 3.50 | .95 |
| | | | *Nos. 774-781 (8)* | 14.00 | 4.00 |

Hafia Soccer Team — A115

Designs: 2s, Players and Sekou Touré cup, vert. 5s, Pres. Touré presenting cup. 7s, Pres. Touré and player holding cup, vert. 8s, Sekou Touré cup, vert. 10s, Team captains and referees, vert. 20s, The winning goal.

***Perf. 12½x12, 12x12½***

**1979, Dec. 18 Litho.**

| | | | | | |
|---|---|---|---|---|---|
| **782** | A115 | 1s | multicolored | .25 | .25 |
| **783** | A115 | 2s | multicolored | .25 | .25 |
| **784** | A115 | 5s | multicolored | .80 | .25 |
| **785** | A115 | 7s | multicolored | 1.10 | .35 |
| **786** | A115 | 8s | multicolored | 1.25 | .40 |
| **787** | A115 | 10s | multicolored | 1.75 | .45 |
| **788** | A115 | 20s | multicolored | 3.25 | .75 |
| | | | *Nos. 782-788 (7)* | 8.65 | 2.70 |

Hafia Soccer Team, African triple champions, 1977.

Train, IYC Emblem A116

IYC Emblem and: 2s, Children dancing around tree, vert. 4s, "1979" and leaves, vert. 7s, Village. 10s, Boy climbing tree. 25s, Boys of different races, flowers, sun.

**1980, Jan. 14 *Perf. 13x13½, 13½x13***

| | | | | | |
|---|---|---|---|---|---|
| **789** | A116 | 2s | multicolored | .30 | .25 |
| **790** | A116 | 4s | multicolored | .65 | .25 |
| **791** | A116 | 5s | multicolored | .80 | .25 |
| **792** | A116 | 7s | multicolored | 1.00 | .30 |
| **793** | A116 | 10s | multicolored | 1.75 | .40 |
| **794** | A116 | 25s | multicolored | 4.00 | 1.10 |
| | | | *Nos. 789-794 (6)* | 8.50 | 2.55 |

International Year of the Child (1979).

Butterflyfish — A117

**1980, Apr. 1 *Perf. 12½x12, 12x12½***

| | | | | | |
|---|---|---|---|---|---|
| **795** | A117 | 1s | shown | .30 | .25 |
| **796** | A117 | 2s | Porgy | .50 | .25 |
| **797** | A117 | 3s | Zeus conchifer, vert. | .55 | .25 |
| **798** | A117 | 4s | Grouper | .70 | .25 |
| **799** | A117 | 5s | Sea horse, vert. | 1.00 | .25 |
| **800** | A117 | 6s | Hatchet fish | 1.15 | .35 |
| **801** | A117 | 7s | Pisodonophis semicinctus | 1.25 | .40 |
| **802** | A117 | 8s | Flying gurnard, vert. | 1.60 | .50 |
| **803** | A117 | 9s | Squirrelfish | 2.00 | .65 |
| **804** | A117 | 10s | Psettus sebae, vert. | 2.25 | .65 |
| **805** | A117 | 12s | Abudefuf hoeffleri | 2.75 | .75 |
| **806** | A117 | 15s | Triggerfish | 4.00 | 1.00 |
| | | | *Nos. 795-806 (12)* | 18.05 | 5.55 |

Apollo 11 Take-Off — A118

**1980, July 20 Photo. *Perf. 14***

| | | | | | |
|---|---|---|---|---|---|
| **807** | A118 | 1s | shown | .25 | .25 |
| **808** | A118 | 2s | Earth from moon | .25 | .25 |
| **809** | A118 | 4s | Armstrong leaving module | .75 | .25 |
| **810** | A118 | 5s | Armstrong on moon | .90 | .25 |
| **811** | A118 | 7s | Collecting samples | 1.25 | .35 |
| **812** | A118 | 8s | Re-entry | 1.40 | .45 |
| **813** | A118 | 12s | Recovery | 2.25 | .75 |
| **814** | A118 | 20s | Crew | 3.50 | 1.10 |
| | | | *Nos. 807-814 (8)* | 10.55 | 3.65 |

Apollo 11 moon landing, 10th anniv. (1979).

Intl. Palestinian Solidarity Day — A119

**1981, Nov. 21 Photo. *Perf. 13½***

| | | | | | |
|---|---|---|---|---|---|
| **815** | A119 | 8s | multicolored | 1.50 | .45 |
| **816** | A119 | 11s | multicolored | 2.25 | .60 |

Soccer — A120

**1982 Litho. *Perf. 12½x12***

| | | | | | |
|---|---|---|---|---|---|
| **817** | A120 | 1s | shown | .25 | .25 |
| **818** | A120 | 2s | Basketball | .25 | .25 |
| **819** | A120 | 3s | Diving | .50 | .25 |
| **820** | A120 | 4s | Gymnast | .65 | .25 |
| **821** | A120 | 5s | Boxing | .90 | .25 |
| **822** | A120 | 6s | Pole vault | 1.10 | .30 |
| **823** | A120 | 7s | Running | 1.25 | .35 |
| **824** | A120 | 8s | Long jump | 1.50 | .40 |
| | | | *Nos. 817-824,C148-C152 (13)* | 20.90 | 6.25 |

22nd Summer Olympic Games, Moscow, July 19-Aug. 3, 1980.

5th Anniv. of West African Economic Community — A121

**1982, May 14 *Perf. 13½***

| | | | | | |
|---|---|---|---|---|---|
| **825** | A121 | 6s | multicolored | 1.10 | .25 |
| **826** | A121 | 7s | multicolored | 1.50 | .35 |
| **827** | A121 | 9s | multicolored | 2.00 | .55 |
| | | | *Nos. 825-827 (3)* | 4.60 | 1.15 |

Kemal Ataturk Birth Centenary A122

**1982, July 19 Photo. *Perf. 13½***

| | | | | | |
|---|---|---|---|---|---|
| **828** | A122 | 7s | multi | 1.25 | .35 |
| **829** | A122 | 10s | multi, diff. | 2.00 | .45 |
| **830** | A122 | 25s | multi, horiz. | 4.75 | 1.10 |
| | | | *Nos. 828-830,C153 (4)* | 13.00 | 3.15 |

1982 World Cup A123

Designs: Various soccer players.

**1982, Aug. 23**

| | | | | | |
|---|---|---|---|---|---|
| **831** | A123 | 6s | multicolored | 1.25 | .30 |
| **832** | A123 | 8s | multicolored | 1.75 | .40 |
| **833** | A123 | 9s | multicolored | 1.90 | .45 |
| **834** | A123 | 10s | multicolored | 2.10 | .45 |
| | | | *Nos. 831-834,C154-C156 (7)* | 21.60 | 7.40 |

**Nos. 831-834 Overprinted in Red and Green**

**1982, Aug. 23 Photo. *Perf. 13½***

| | | | | | |
|---|---|---|---|---|---|
| **835** | A123 | 6s | multicolored | 1.25 | .30 |
| **836** | A123 | 8s | multicolored | 1.75 | .40 |
| **837** | A123 | 9s | multicolored | 1.90 | .45 |
| **838** | A123 | 10s | multicolored | 2.10 | .45 |
| | | | *Nos. 835-838,C157-C159 (7)* | 20.40 | 6.10 |

Italy's victory in 1982 World Cup.

23rd Olympic Games, Los Angeles, July 28-Aug. 12, 1984 A124

**1983, July 1 Litho. *Perf. 13½***

| | | | | | |
|---|---|---|---|---|---|
| **839** | A124 | 5s | Wrestling | 1.10 | .25 |
| **840** | A124 | 7s | Weightlifting | 1.40 | .30 |
| **841** | A124 | 10s | Gymnastics | 2.00 | .55 |
| **842** | A124 | 15s | Discus | 3.25 | .95 |
| **843** | A124 | 20s | Kayak | 4.50 | 1.40 |
| **844** | A124 | 25s | Equestrian | 5.00 | 1.60 |
| | | | *Nos. 839-844 (6)* | 17.25 | 5.05 |

**Litho. & Embossed**

**Size: 39x58mm**

| | | | | | |
|---|---|---|---|---|---|
| **844A** | A124 | 100s | Running | 45.00 | 37.50 |

**Souvenir Sheets**

**Litho.**

| | | | | | |
|---|---|---|---|---|---|
| **845** | A124 | 30s | Running | 5.00 | 1.60 |

**Litho. & Embossed**

| | | | | | |
|---|---|---|---|---|---|
| **845A** | A124 | 100s | Show jumping | 15.00 | 12.50 |

Nos. 844A, 845A are airmail. No. 845A contains one 58x39mm stamp.

First Manned Balloon Flight, 200th Anniv. — A125

Designs: 5s, Marquis D'Arlandes, Pilatre de Rozier. 7s, Marie Antoinette Balloon, Rozier. 10s, Dirigible, Dupuy De Lome, horiz. 15s, Dirigible, Major A. Perseval, horiz.

**1983, Aug. 1 Litho. *Perf. 13½***

**846** A125 5s multicolored .80 .25
**847** A125 7s multicolored 1.10 .30
**848** A125 10s multicolored 1.50 .55
**849** A125 15s multicolored 2.40 .65
*Nos. 846-849,C160-C161 (6)* 12.80 4.75

Intl. Year of the Handicapped — A126

**1983, Aug. 24 Litho.**

**850** A126 10s multicolored 2.50 .80
**851** A126 20s multicolored 5.50 1.40

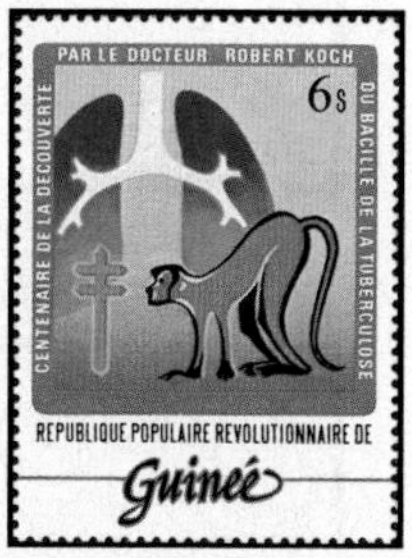


Dr. Robert Koch (1843-1910), TB Bacillus A127

Various phases of research.

**1983, Aug. 24 Litho.**

**852** A127 6s multicolored 1.10 .25
**853** A127 10s multicolored 1.75 .40
**854** A127 11s multicolored 1.90 .40
**855** A127 12s multicolored 2.25 .80
**856** A127 15s multicolored 2.75 .95
**857** A127 20s multicolored 3.75 1.10
**858** A127 25s multicolored 4.25 1.40
*Nos. 852-858 (7)* 17.75 5.30

Mosque, Conakry A128

**1983, Oct. 2 Litho. *Perf. 13½***

**859** A128 1s multicolored .40 .25
**860** A128 2s multicolored .55 .25
**861** A128 5s multicolored .95 .25
**862** A128 10s multicolored 1.90 .55
*Nos. 859-862 (4)* 3.80 1.30

**Souvenir Sheet**

**863** A128 25s multicolored 4.00 1.90

Natl. independence, 25th anniv. No. 863 airmail.

Mano River Union, 10th Anniv. A129

2s, Development program graduates. 7s, Emblem. 8s, Pres. Toure of Guinea, Stevens of Sierra Leone, Doe of Liberia. 10s, 20s, Signing treaty.

**1983, Oct. 3**

**864** A129 2s multicolored .40 .25
**865** A129 7s multicolored .85 .25
**866** A129 8s multicolored 1.25 .30
**867** A129 10s multicolored 1.50 .35
*Nos. 864-867 (4)* 4.00 1.15

**Souvenir Sheet**

**868** A129 20s multicolored 3.25 1.75

No. 868 airmail.

14th Winter Olympics, Sarajevo, Feb. 8-19, 1984 — A130

**1983, Dec. 5 Litho. *Perf. 13½***

**869** A130 5s Biathlon .75 .25
**870** A130 7s Bobsledding .95 .30
**871** A130 10s Downhill skiing 1.40 .40
**872** A130 15s Speed skating 2.25 .65
**873** A130 20s Ski jumping 3.00 .85
**874** A130 25s Figure skating 3.50 1.10
*Nos. 869-874 (6)* 11.85 3.55

**Litho. & Embossed**

**Size: 58x39mm**

**874A** A130 100s Downhill skiing 40.00 32.50

**Souvenir Sheets**

**Litho.**

**875** A130 30s Hockey 5.00 1.60

**Litho. & Embossed**

**875A** A130 100s 4-man bobsled 15.00 12.50

Nos. 873-875A airmail. No. 875A contains one 58x39mm stamp.

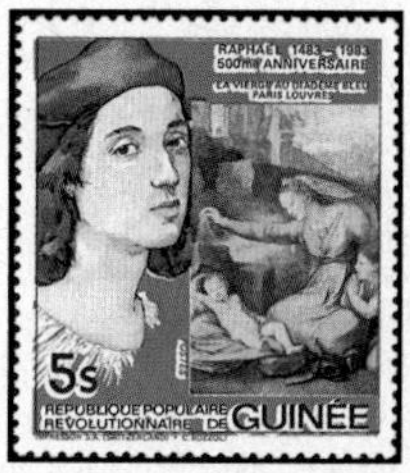


Self-portrait and Virgin with Blue Diadem, by Raphael A131

Designs: 7s, Self-portrait and Holy Family, by Rubens. 10s, Self-portrait and Portrait of Saskia, by Rembrandt. 15s, Portrait of Goethe and scene from Young Werther. 20s, Scouting Year. 25s, Paul Harris, Rotary emblem. 30s, J.F. Kennedy, Apollo XI. 100s, Paul Harris, 3 other men in Rotary meeting.

**1984, Jan 2 Litho. *Perf. 13***

**876** A131 5s multicolored 2.00 .35
**877** A131 7s multicolored 2.50 .45
**878** A131 10s multicolored 2.50 .60
**879** A131 15s multicolored 2.50 .75
**880** A131 20s multicolored 2.50 .85
**881** A131 25s multicolored 3.00 1.25
*Nos. 876-881 (6)* 15.00 4.25

**Souvenir Sheets**

**882** A131 30s multicolored 6.00 2.75

**Litho. & Embossed**

***Perf. 13½***

**882A** A131 100s gold & multi 12.00 8.00

Nos. 880-882A airmail. No. 882A contains one 51x42mm stamp.
For overprints see Nos. C164-C165.

Transportation — A132

**1984, May 7 Litho. *Perf. 13½***

**883** A132 5s Congo River steamer .75 .25
**884** A132 7s Graf Zeppelin LZ 127 1.25 .25
**885** A132 10s Daimler automobile, 1886 1.60 .30
**886** A132 15s E. African RR Beyer-Garrat 2.25 .50
**887** A132 20s Latecoere 28, 1929 3.25 .65
**888** A132 25s Sial Marchetti S.M. 73, 1934 4.25 .85
*Nos. 883-888 (6)* 13.35 2.80

**Souvenir Sheet**

**889** A132 30s Series B locomotive 6.00 3.00

Nos. 887-889 airmail.

Anniversaries and Events — A133

Famous men: 5s, Abraham Lincoln, log cabin, the White House. 7s, Jean-Henri Dunant, Red Cross at Battle of Solferino. 10s, Gottlieb Daimler, 1892 Motor Carriage. 15s, Louis Bleriot, monoplane. 20s, Paul Harris, Rotary Intl. 25s, Auguste Piccard, bathyscaphe Trieste. 30s, Anatoly Karpov, world chess champion, chessboard and knight. 100s, Paul Harris, Rotary Intl. emblem.

**1984, Aug. 20 Litho. *Perf. 13½***

**890** A133 5s multicolored .80 .25
**891** A133 7s multicolored 1.10 .25
**892** A133 10s multicolored 1.60 .35
**893** A133 15s multicolored 2.40 .50
**894** A133 20s multicolored 3.00 .65
**895** A133 25s multicolored 4.00 .80
*Nos. 890-895 (6)* 12.90 2.80

**Litho. & Embossed**

**Size: 60x30mm**

**895A** A133 100s gold & multi 16.00 —
*b.* Min. sheet of 1, 91x70mm 60.00 —
*c.* Min. sheet of 1, 121x70mm 16.00 12.50

**Souvenir Sheet**

**896** A133 30s multicolored 6.00 2.40

Nos. 894-896 are airmail.
For overprints see Nos. C163, C166.

The Holy Family, by Durer — A134

Painting details: 5s, The Mystic Marriage of St. Catherine and St. Sebastian, by Correggio. 10s, The Veiled Woman, by Raphael. 15s, Portrait of a Young Man, by Durer. 20s, Portrait of Soutine, by Modigliani. 25s, Esterhazy Madonna, by Raphael. 30s, Impannata Madonna, by Raphael.

**1984, Aug. 23**

**897** A134 5s multicolored .75 .25
**898** A134 7s multicolored 1.25 .30
**899** A134 10s multicolored 1.75 .35
**900** A134 15s multicolored 2.25 .75
**901** A134 20s multicolored 3.50 1.10
**902** A134 25s multicolored 4.50 1.25
*Nos. 897-902 (6)* 14.00 4.00

**Souvenir Sheet**

**903** A134 30s multicolored 6.00 2.40

Nos. 901-903 airmail.

1984 Winter Olympics, Sarajevo A135

Gold medalists: 5s, East German two-man bobsled. 7s, Thomas Wassberg, Sweden, 50-kilometer cross-country. 10s, Gaetan Boucher, Canada, 1000 and 1500-meter speed skating. 15s, Katarina Witt, DDR, singles figure skating. 20s, Bill Johnson, US, men's downhill. 25s, Soviet Union, ice hockey. 30s, Jens Weissflog, DDR, 70-meter ski jump. No. 909A, Phil Mahre, US, slalom skiing. No. 910A, Jayne Torvill & Christopher Dean, Great Britain, ice dancing.

**1985, Sept. 23 Litho. *Perf. 13½***

**904** A135 5s multicolored .60 .25
**905** A135 7s multicolored .75 .25
**906** A135 10s multicolored 1.20 .30
**907** A135 15s multicolored 1.75 .45
**908** A135 20s multicolored 2.25 .60
**909** A135 25s multicolored 3.00 .75
*Nos. 904-909 (6)* 9.55 2.60

**Litho. & Embossed**

**Size: 51x36mm**

**909A** A135 100s gold & multi 60.00 30.00

**Souvenir Sheets**

**Litho.**

**910** A135 30s multicolored 6.00 2.10

**Litho. & Embossed**

**910A** A135 100s gold & multi 18.00 15.00

Nos. 908A-910A are airmail. No. 910A contains one 51x36mm stamp.

1984 Los Angeles Summer Olympics — A136

Medalists and various satellites: 5s, T. Ruiz and C. Costie, US, synchronized swimming. 7s, West Germany, team dressage. 10s, US, yachting, flying Dutchman class. 15s, Mark Todd, New Zealand, individual 3-day equestrian event. 20s, Daley Thompson, G.B., decathlon. 25s, US, team jumping. 30s, Carl Lewis, US, long jump, 100 and 200-meter run, 4x100 relay.

**1985, Mar. 18 Litho. *Perf. 13½***

**911** A136 5s multicolored .45 .25
**912** A136 7s multicolored .70 .25
**913** A136 10s multicolored .90 .25
**914** A136 15s multicolored 1.40 .40
**915** A136 20s multicolored 1.60 .45
**916** A136 25s multicolored 2.40 .60
*Nos. 911-916 (6)* 7.45 2.20

**Souvenir Sheet**

**917** A136 30s multicolored 6.00 2.10

Nos. 915-917 airmail.

Fungi — A137

**1985, Mar. 21 Litho. *Perf. 13½***

**918** A137 5s Rhodophyllus callidermus .70 .25
**919** A137 7s Agaricus niger 1.25 .25
**920** A137 10s Thermitomyces globulus 1.75 .45
**921** A137 15s Amanita robusta 2.75 .60
**922** A137 20s Lepiota subradicans 3.75 .90
**923** A137 25s Cantharellus rhodophyllus 4.75 1.25
*Nos. 918-923 (6)* 14.95 3.70

**Souvenir Sheet**

**924** A137 30s Phlebopus sylvaticus 5.50 4.00

Nos. 922-924 airmail.
For surcharges see Nos. 962-968.

Scientist Herman J. Oberth, and Two-Stage Rocket A138

Space achievements: 10s, Lunik 1, USSR, 1959. 15s, Lunik 2 on the Moon, 1959. 20s, Lunik 3 photographing the Moon, 1959. 30s, US astronauts Armstrong, Aldrin, Collins and Apollo 11, 1969. 35s, Sally Ride, 1st American woman in space, 1983. 50s, Recovering a Palapa B satellite, 1984. No. 930A, Guion S. Bluford, 1st black American astronaut. No. 931A, Viking probe on Mars.

**1985, May 26 Litho. *Perf. 13½***

**925** A138 7s multicolored .90 .25
**926** A138 10s multicolored 1.10 .25
**927** A138 15s multicolored 1.75 .40
**928** A138 20s multicolored 1.90 .45
**929** A138 30s multicolored 3.75 .85
**930** A138 35s multicolored 4.50 .90
*Nos. 925-930 (6)* 13.90 3.10

**Litho. & Embossed**

**Size: 51x36mm**

**930A** A138 200s gold & multi 37.50 —

**Souvenir Sheet**

**Litho.**

**931** A138 50s multicolored 6.50 3.25

**Litho. & Embossed**

**931A** A138 200s gold & multi 27.50 —

Nos. 929-931A are airmail. No. 931A contains one 51x36mm stamp.

Maimonides (1135-1204), Jewish Scholar, Cordoba Jewish Quarter — A139

Anniversaries and events: 10s, Christopher Columbus departing from Palos for New World, 1492. 15s, Frederic Auguste Bartholdi (1834-1904), sculptor, architect, and Statue of Liberty, cent. 20s, Queen Mother, 85th birthday. 30s, Ulf Merbold, German physicist, US space shuttle Columbia. 35s, Wedding of Prince Charles and Lady Diana, 1981. 50s, Charles, Diana, Princes Henry and William. 100s, Queen Mother Elizabeth's 85th birthday.

**1985, Sept. 23**

**932** A139 7s multicolored .80 .25
**933** A139 10s multicolored 1.10 .25
**934** A139 15s multicolored 1.75 .40
**935** A139 20s multicolored 2.25 .55
**936** A139 30s multicolored 3.25 .80
**937** A139 35s multicolored 4.00 .90
*Nos. 932-937 (6)* 13.15 3.15

**Litho. & Embossed**

**Size: 42x51mm**

**937A** A139 100s gold & multi 13.00 12.50

**Souvenir Sheet**

**Litho.**

**938** A139 50s multicolored 6.50 3.25

Nos. 936-938 airmail. No. 938 contains one 51x36mm stamp. Nos. 934 and 937A exist in souvenir sheets of one.

Audubon Birth Bicent. — A140

Illustrations of bird species from Birds of America.

**1985, Sept. 23 Litho. *Perf. 13½***

**939** A140 7s Coccyzus erythrophtalmus .75 .25
**940** A140 10s Conuropsis carolinensis 1.20 .30
**941** A140 15s Anhinga anhinga 2.00 .50
**942** A140 20s Buteo lineatus 2.50 .70
**943** A140 30s Otus asio 4.25 1.25
**944** A140 35s Toxostoma rufum 4.50 1.50
*Nos. 939-944 (6)* 15.20 4.50

**Souvenir Sheet**

**945** A140 50s Zenaidura macroura 6.50 3.00

Nos. 941, 944 vert. Nos. 943-945 are airmail. No. 945 contains one 51x36mm stamp. Nos. 939-944 exist in souvenir sheets of one. Value, set $90.

1986 World Cup Soccer Championships, Mexico — A141

Famous soccer players: 7s, Bebeto, Brazil. 10s, Rinal Dassaev, USSR. 15s, Phil Neal, Great Britain. 20s, Jean Tigana, France. 30s, Fernando Chalana, Portugal. 35s, Michel Platini, France. 50s, Karl Heinz Rummenigge, West Germany.

**1985, Oct. 26**

**946** A141 7s multicolored .95 .25
**947** A141 10s multicolored 1.25 .25
**948** A141 15s multicolored 1.90 .40
**949** A141 20s multicolored 2.50 .60
**950** A141 30s multicolored 3.50 .85
**951** A141 35s multicolored 4.50 .95
*Nos. 946-951 (6)* 14.60 3.30

**Souvenir Sheet**

**952** A141 50s multicolored 7.50 3.00

Nos. 950-952 airmail.

Cats and Dogs A142

**1985, Oct. 26**

**953** A142 7s Blue-point Siamese 1.10 .25
**954** A142 10s Cocker spaniel 1.50 .25
**955** A142 15s Poodles 2.25 .40
**956** A142 20s Blue Persian 3.00 .60
**957** A142 25s European red-and-white tabby 3.75 .70
**958** A142 30s German shepherd 4.25 .85
**959** A142 35s Abyssinians 5.50 .95
**960** A142 40s Boxer 6.50 1.25
*Nos. 953-960 (8)* 27.85 5.25

**Souvenir Sheet**

**961** A142 50s Pyrenean mountain dog, chartreux cat 7.50 3.00

Nos. 958-961 airmail. No. 961 contains one 51x30mm stamp.

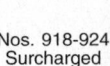

Nos. 918-924 Surcharged

**1985, Nov. 15**

**962** A137 1s on 5s multi .80 .25
**963** A137 2s on 7s multi .85 .25
**964** A137 8s on 10s multi 1.75 .40
**965** A137 30s on 15s multi 6.50 1.60
**966** A137 35s on 20s multi 7.50 2.25
**967** A137 40s on 25s multi 9.00 2.75
*Nos. 962-967 (6)* 26.40 7.50

**Souvenir Sheet**

**968** A137 50s on 30s multi 9.50 4.00

Nos. 966-968 airmail.

Locomotives — A143

Designs: 7s, 8F Class steam, Great Britain. 15s, Bobo 5500 Series III electric, German Fed. Railways. 25s, Pacific A Mazout No. 270, African Railways. 35s, Serie 420 electric train set, Suburban S-Bahn, Germany. 50s, ICE high-speed train, German Fed. Railways.

**1985, Dec. 18 Litho. *Perf. 13½***

**969** A143 7s multicolored 1.10 .25
**970** A143 15s multicolored 2.40 .70
**971** A143 25s multicolored 4.00 .90
**972** A143 35s multicolored 5.50 1.25
*Nos. 969-972 (4)* 13.00 3.10

**Souvenir Sheet**

**973** A143 50s multicolored 6.50 3.25

Nos. 972-973 airmail.
For surcharges see Nos. 991-995.

Columbus Discovering America, 1492 — A144

**1985, Dec. 18**

**974** A144 10s Pinta 1.25 .25
**975** A144 20s Santa Maria 2.50 .65
**976** A144 30s Nina 4.00 .95
**977** A144 40s Santa Maria, sighting land 5.75 1.25
*Nos. 974-977 (4)* 13.50 3.10

**Souvenir Sheet**

**978** A144 50s Columbus and Nina 6.50 3.00

Nos. 976-978 airmail.

Intl. Youth Year — A145

**1986, Jan. 21**

**979** A145 10s Chopin 1.40 .40
**980** A145 20s Botticelli 2.75 .85
**981** A145 25s Picasso 3.50 1.10
**982** A145 35s Rossini 5.00 1.50
*Nos. 979-982 (4)* 12.65 3.85

**Souvenir Sheet**

**983** A145 50s Michelangelo 7.50 3.00

Nos. 981, 983 airmail.
For surcharges see Nos. 996-1000.

Halley's Comet — A146

Sightings: 5fr, Bayeux Tapestry (detail), c. 1092, France. 30fr, Arab, astrolabe, 1400. 40fr, Montezuma II, Aztec deity. 50fr, Edmond Halley, trajectory diagram. 300fr, Halley, Sir Isaac Newton. 500fr, Giotto, Soviet and NASA space probes, comet. 600fr, Hally commemorative medal, Giotto probe.

**1986, July 1 Litho. *Perf. 13½***

**5fr-500fr Surcharged with New Currency in Silver or Black**

**984** A146 5fr multi .25 .25
**985** A146 30fr multi .35 .25
**986** A146 40fr multi .40 .25
**987** A146 50fr multi .50 .25
**988** A146 300fr multi 2.75 1.00
**989** A146 500fr multi 4.75 1.75
*Nos. 984-989 (6)* 9.00 3.75

**Souvenir Sheet**

**990** A146 600fr multi 6.50 2.50

Nos. 988-990 are airmail. Nos. 984-989 not issued without surcharge.

**No. 969 Surcharged**

**Nos. 970-973 Surcharged**

**1986, Aug. 25 Litho. *Perf. 13½***

**991** A143 2fr on 7s multi (B on S) .40 .25
**992** A143 25fr on 15s multi .50 .25
**993** A143 50fr on 25s multi .75 .25
**994** A143 90fr on 35s multi 1.25 .55
*Nos. 991-994 (4)* 2.90 1.30

**Souvenir Sheet**

**995** A143 500fr on 50s multi 5.00 2.10

**Nos. 979-983 Surcharged**

**1986, Aug. 25**

**996** A145 5fr on 10s multi .40 .25
**997** A145 35fr on 20s multi .50 .25
**998** A145 50fr on 25s multi .75 .25
**999** A145 90fr on 35s multi 1.25 .40
*Nos. 996-999 (4)* 2.90 1.15

**Souvenir Sheet**

**1000** A145 500fr on 50s multi 6.00 2.10

Locomotives — A147

Designs: 20fr, Dietrich 640 CV. 100fr, T.13 7906. 300fr, Vapeur 01220. 400fr, ABH Type 3 5020. 600fr, Renault ABH 3 (300 CV).

**1986, Nov. 1**

**1001** A147 20fr multi .35 .25
**1002** A147 100fr multi 1.00 .35
**1003** A147 300fr multi 3.00 .95
**1004** A147 400fr multi 4.25 1.25
*Nos. 1001-1004 (4)* 8.60 2.80

**Souvenir Sheet**

**1005** A147 600fr multi 7.00 2.50

Nos. 1004-1005 are airmail.

Discovery of America, 500th Anniv. (in 1992) — A148

Designs: 40fr, Columbus at Ft. Navidad construction, Santa Maria, 1492. 70fr, Landing at Hispaniola, 2nd voyage, 1494. 200fr, Aboard ship, 3rd voyage, 1498. 500fr, Trading with Indians. 600fr, At court of Ferdinand and Isabella, 1493.

**1986, Nov. 1**

**1006** A148 40fr multi .50 .25
**1007** A148 70fr multi .80 .25
**1008** A148 200fr multi 2.25 .70
**1009** A148 500fr multi 5.50 1.75
*Nos. 1006-1009 (4)* 9.05 2.95

**Souvenir Sheet**

**1010** A148 600fr multi 7.00 2.50

Nos. 1009-1010 are airmail.

Anniversaries & Events A149

30fr, Prince Charles and Diana, 5th wedding anniv. 40fr, Alain Prost, San Marino, 1985 Formula 1 Grand Prix world champion. 100fr, Wedding of Prince Andrew and Sarah Ferguson. 300fr, Elvis Presley. 500fr, Michael Jackson. 600fr, M. Dassault (1892-1986), aerospace engineer.

**1986, Nov. 12**

**1011** A149 30fr multi .35 .25
**1012** A149 40fr multi .45 .25
**1013** A149 100fr multi 1.10 .40
**1014** A149 300fr multi 3.00 1.25
**1015** A149 500fr multi 5.00 2.40
*Nos. 1011-1015 (5)* 9.90 4.55

**Souvenir Sheet**

**1016** A149 600fr multi 6.50 2.75

Nos. 1015-1016 are airmail.

1986 World Cup Soccer Championships — A150

Various players and final scores.

**1986, Nov. 12**

**1017** A150 100fr Pfaff 1.00 .35
**1018** A150 300fr Platini 3.00 .95
**1019** A150 400fr Matthaus 4.00 1.50
**1020** A150 500fr D. Maradona 5.00 2.10
*Nos. 1017-1020 (4)* 13.00 4.90

**Souvenir Sheet**

**1021** A150 600fr Maradona, trophy 7.00 2.50

Nos. 1020-1021 are airmail. No. 1021 contains one 51x42mm stamp.
For surcharge see No. 1182A.

1988 Summer Olympics, Seoul — A151

Pierre de Coubertin (1863-1937), Seoul Stadium, Telecommunications Satellite — A151a

**1987, Jan. 17** **Litho.** ***Perf. 13½***

**1022** A151 20fr Judo .25 .25
**1023** A151 30fr High jump .35 .25
**1024** A151 40fr Team handball .45 .25
**1025** A151 100fr Women's gymnastics 1.00 .25
**1026** A151 300fr Javelin 3.00 .90
**1027** A151 500fr Equestrian 5.00 2.10
*Nos. 1022-1027 (6)* 10.05 4.00

**Souvenir Sheet**

**1028** A151a 600fr multi 6.50 2.50

Dated 1986. Nos. 1026-1028 are airmail.

1988 Winter Olympics, Calgary — A152

**1987, Mar. 23** **Litho.** ***Perf. 13½***

**1029** A152 50fr on 40fr Biathlon .50 .25
**1030** A152 100fr Cross-country skiing 1.00 .35
**1031** A152 400fr Ski jumping 4.00 2.50
**1032** A152 500fr Two-man bobsled 5.00 2.10
*Nos. 1029-1032 (4)* 10.50 5.20

**Souvenir Sheet**

**1033** A152 600fr Woman skater, satellite 6.50 2.50

No. 1029 not issued without overprint. Nos. 1031-1033 are airmail.

1988 Winter Olympics, Calgary A153

Telecommunications satellite, athletes and emblem.

**1987, May 1**

**1034** A153 25fr Women's slalom .30 .25
**1035** A153 50fr Hockey .50 .25
**1036** A153 100fr Men's figure skating .95 .30
**1037** A153 150fr Men's downhill skiing 1.50 .45
**1038** A153 300fr Speed skating 3.00 1.25
**1039** A153 500fr Four-man bobsled 4.75 2.10
*Nos. 1034-1039 (6)* 11.00 4.60

**Souvenir Sheet**

**1040** A153 600fr Ski jumping 6.50 2.50

Nos. 1038-1040 are airmail.

Famous Men — A154

Intl. Cardiology Congresses in Chicago, Washington and New York — A155

Designs: 50fr, Lafayette, military leader during American and French revolutions. 100fr, Ettore Bugatti (1881-1947), Italian automobile manufacturer, 200fr, Garri Kasparov, Russian chess champion. 300fr, George Washington. 400fr, Boris Becker, 1987 Wimbledon tennis champion. 500fr, Sir Winston Churchill.

**1987, Nov. 1** **Litho.** ***Perf. 13½***

**1041** A154 50fr multi .45 .25
**1042** A154 100fr multi 1.00 .40
**1043** A154 200fr multi 1.90 .80
**1044** A154 300fr multi 2.75 1.25
**1045** A154 400fr multi 3.75 1.60
**1046** A154 500fr multi 4.75 2.00
*Nos. 1041-1046 (6)* 14.60 6.30

**Souvenir Sheet**

**1047** A155 1500fr multi 16.00 12.50

Nos. 1045-1047 are airmail. Stamp in No. 1047 divided into three sections by simulated perforations.
For surcharge see No. 1182B.

Cave Bear — A156

Prehistoric Animals — A157

**1987, Nov. 1**

**1048** A156 50fr Dimetrodon .60 .25
**1049** A156 100fr Iguanodon 1.25 .50
**1050** A156 200fr Tylosaurus 2.40 1.00
**1051** A156 300fr shown 3.50 1.50
**1052** A156 400fr Saber-tooth tiger 4.75 2.10
**1053** A156 500fr Stegosaurus 6.25 2.50
*Nos. 1048-1053 (6)* 18.75 7.85

**Souvenir Sheet**

**1054** A157 600fr Triceratops 7.00 2.75

Nos. 1052-1054 are airmail.
For surcharge see No. 1182C.

1988 Summer Olympics, Seoul — A158

Male and female tennis players in action.

**1987, Nov. 28**

**1055** A158 50fr multi .45 .25
**1056** A158 100fr multi, diff. 1.00 .35
**1057** A158 150fr multi, diff. 1.50 .60
**1058** A158 200fr multi, diff. 1.90 .75
**1059** A158 300fr multi, diff. 3.00 1.25
**1060** A158 500fr multi, diff. 5.00 1.90
*Nos. 1055-1060 (6)* 12.85 5.10

**Souvenir Sheet**

**1061** A158 600fr multi 7.00 2.75

Reintroduction of tennis as an Olympic event. Nos. 1059-1061 are airmail.

1992 Summer Olympics, Barcelona A159

Athletes participating in events, Barcelona highlights: 50fr, Discus, courtyard of St. Croix and St. Paul Hospital. 100fr, High jump, Pablo Casals playing cello. 150fr, Long jump, Labyrinth of Horta. 170fr, Javelin, lizard from Guell Park. 400fr, Gymnastics, Mercy Church. 500fr, Tennis, Picasso Museum. 600fr, Running, tapestry by Miro.

**1987, Dec. 28** **Litho.** ***Perf. 13½***

**1062** A159 50fr multi .50 .25
**1063** A159 100fr multi 1.00 .35
**1064** A159 150fr multi 1.50 .55
**1065** A159 170fr multi 1.75 .60
**1066** A159 400fr multi 3.75 1.40
**1067** A159 500fr multi 5.00 1.75
*Nos. 1062-1067 (6)* 13.50 4.90

**Souvenir Sheet**

**1068** A159 600fr multi 6.50 4.50

Nos. 1066-1068 are airmail.
For surcharges see Nos. 1182D-1182E.

Wildlife A160

**1987, Dec. 28**

**1069** A160 50fr African wild dog pups 1.75 .75
**1070** A160 70fr Adult 2.25 1.00
**1071** A160 100fr Adults circling gazelle 2.75 1.25
**1072** A160 170fr Chasing gazelle 3.25 1.50
**1073** A160 400fr Crown cranes 4.75 1.40
**1074** A160 500fr Derby elands 5.75 2.50
*Nos. 1069-1074 (6)* 20.50 8.40

**Souvenir Sheet**

**1075** A160 600fr Vervet monkeys 7.00 5.50

Nos. 1069-1072 picture World Wildlife Fund emblem; Nos. 1073, 1075, picture Scouting trefoil and No. 1074 pictures Rotary Intl. emblem. Nos. 1073-1075 are airmail.
For surcharges see Nos. 1182F-1182G.

Reconciliation Summit Conference, July 11-12, 1986 — A161

Heads of state and natl. flags: Dr. Samuel Kanyon Doe of Liberia, Colonel Lansana Conte of Guinea and Maj.-Gen. Joseph Saidu Momoh of Sierra Leone.

**1987** **Litho.** ***Perf. 13½***

**1076** A161 40fr multi .30 .25
**1077** A161 50fr multi .40 .25
**1078** A161 75fr multi .70 .40
**1079** A161 100fr multi .85 .55
**1080** A161 150fr multi 1.25 .85
*Nos. 1076-1080 (5)* 3.50 2.30

Space Exploration — A162

**1988, Apr. 16**

**1081** A162 50fr Galaxie-Grasp .60 .25
**1082** A162 150fr Energia-Mir 1.50 .50
**1083** A162 200fr NASA Space Station 2.00 .70
**1084** A162 300fr Ariane 5-E.S.A. 3.00 1.00
**1085** A162 400fr Mars-Rover 3.75 1.40
**1086** A162 450fr Venus-Vega 5.00 1.60
*Nos. 1081-1086 (6)* 15.85 5.45

**Souvenir Sheet**

**1087** A162 500fr Mars-Phobos 8.00 6.00

Nos. 1085-1087 are airmail.

A163

Boy Scouts watching birds and butterflies.

**1988, July 5** **Litho.** ***Perf. 13½***

**1088** A163 50fr Spermophaga ruficapilla .50 .25
**1089** A163 100fr Medon nymphalidae 1.05 .35
**1090** A163 150fr Euplecte orix 1.45 .60
**1091** A163 300fr Nectarinia pulchella 3.00 1.25
**1092** A163 400fr Sophia nymphalidae 3.75 1.50
**1093** A163 450fr Rumia nymphalidae 4.50 1.75
*Nos. 1088-1093 (6)* 14.25 5.70

**Souvenir Sheet**

**1094** A163 750fr Opis nymphalidae, Psittacula krameri 7.50 6.50

A163a

**1990, Aug. 3** **Litho. & Embossed**

**1094A** A163a 1500fr Druya antimachus 20.00 12.50

Nos. 1092-1094A are airmail. No. 1094 contains one 35x50mm stamp.
#1094A exists in souvenir sheet of 1. Value $45.
For surcharge and overprints see Nos. 1182H, 1240-1246.

A164

Famous People: 200fr, Queen Elizabeth II, Prince Philip and crown jewels. 250fr, Fritz von Opel (1899-1971), German automotive industrialist, and 1928 RAK 2 Opel. 300fr, Wolfgang Amadeus Mozart, composer, and Masonic emblem. 400fr, Steffi Graf, tennis champion. 450fr, Buzz Aldrin and Masonic emblem. 500fr, Paul Harris, Rotary Intl. founder, and organization emblem. 750fr, Thomas Jefferson, horiz.

**1988, July 5**

**1095** A164 200fr multi 2.00 .75
**1096** A164 250fr multi 2.50 .95
**1097** A164 300fr multi 3.25 1.25
**1098** A164 400fr multi 4.25 1.50
**1099** A164 450fr multi 4.75 1.60
**1100** A164 500fr multi 5.25 1.90
*Nos. 1095-1100 (6)* 22.00 7.95

**Souvenir Sheet**

**1101** A164 750fr multi 8.00 2.75

40th wedding anniv. of Queen Elizabeth II and Prince Philip (200fr).
Nos. 1099-1101 are airmail. No. 1101 contains one 42x36mm stamp.
For surcharges see Nos. 1182I, 1182Q.

1988 Winter Olympics Gold Medalists A165

Designs: 50fr, Vreni Schneider, Switzerland, women's giant slalom and slalom. 100fr, Frank-Peter Roetsch, East Germany, 10 and 20-kilometer biathlon. 150fr, Matti Nykaenen, Finland, 70 and 90-meter ski jumping. 250fr, Marina Kiehl, West Germany, women's downhill. 400fr, Frank Piccard, France, super giant slalom. 450fr, Katarina Witt, East Germany, women's figure skating. 750fr, Pirmin Zurbriggen, Switzerland, men's downhill.

**1988, Oct. 2** **Litho.** ***Perf. 13½***

**1102** A165 50fr multi, vert. .45 .25
**1103** A165 100fr multi, vert. .90 .35
**1104** A165 150fr multi, vert. 1.50 .60
**1105** A165 250fr multi, vert. 2.50 .95
**1106** A165 400fr multi, vert. 3.75 1.50
**1107** A165 450fr multi, vert. 4.50 1.60
*Nos. 1102-1107 (6)* 13.60 5.25

**Souvenir Sheet**

**1108** A165 750fr multi 8.00 2.75

Nos. 1103, 1107-1108 are airmail.
For surcharge see No. 1182J.

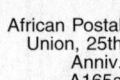

African Postal Union, 25th Anniv. A165a

**1988** **Litho.** ***Perf. 13½***

**1108A** A165a 50fr multicolored .45 .25
**1108B** A165a 75fr multicolored .75 .35
**1108C** A165a 100fr multicolored 1.00 .40
**1108D** A165a 150fr multicolored 1.60 .65
*Nos. 1108A-1108D (4)* 3.80 1.65

World Health Day — A165b

**1988, Oct. 2** **Litho.** ***Perf. 13½***

**1108E** A165b 50fr Medical research .50 .25
**1108F** A165b 150fr Immunization 1.50 .65
**1108G** A165b 500fr Dentistry 4.75 2.25
*Nos. 1108E-1108G (3)* 6.75 3.15

For surcharge see No. 1182K.

Opening of MT 20 Intl. Communications Center — A165c

**1988, Dec. 8** **Litho.** ***Perf. 13½***

**1108H** A165c 50fr multicolored .50 .25
**1108I** A165c 100fr multicolored 1.00 .25
**1108J** A165c 150fr multicolored 1.50 .65

Pierre de Coubertin, Founder of Intl. Olympic Committee A165d

**1988** **Litho.** ***Perf. 13½y***

**1108K** A165d 50fr multi .45 .40
**1108L** A165d 100fr multi .95 .80
**1108M** A165d 150fr multi 1.50 1.40
**1108N** A165d 500fr multi 5.00 4.00
*Nos. 1108K-1108N (4)* 7.90 6.60

For surcharge see No. 1182L.

1992 Summer Olympics, Barcelona — A166

**1989, May 3** **Litho.** ***Perf. 13½***

**1109** A166 50fr Diving .45 .25
**1110** A166 100fr Running, vert. 1.00 .55
**1111** A166 150fr Shooting 1.75 .95
**1112** A166 250fr Tennis, vert. 2.75 1.50
**1113** A166 400fr Soccer 4.25 2.40
**1114** A166 500fr Equestrian, vert. 5.25 3.00
*Nos. 1109-1114 (6)* 15.45 8.65

**Souvenir Sheet**

**1115** A166 750fr Yachting, vert. 7.50 2.50

Nos. 1113-1115 are airmail.
For surcharge see No. 1182M.

French Revolution, Bicent. — A167

Personalities of and scenes from the revolution: 250fr, Jean-Sylvain Bailly (1736-1793) leading proceedings in Tennis Court, June 20, 1789. 300fr, Count Mirabeau (1749-1791) at royal session, June 23, 1789. 400fr, Lafayette (1757-1834), federation anniversary celebration, July 18, 1790. 450fr, Jerome Petion de Villeneuve (1756-1794), king's arrest at Varennes-en-Argonne, June 21, 1791. 750fr, Camille Desmoulins (1760-1794), destruction of the Bastille, July 1789.

**1989, July 7** **Litho.** ***Perf. 13½***

**1116** A167 250fr multi 3.00 .80
**1117** A167 300fr multi 3.50 1.00
**1118** A167 400fr multi 4.50 1.40
**1119** A167 450fr multi 5.00 1.50
*Nos. 1116-1119 (4)* 16.00 4.70

**Souvenir Sheet**

**1120** A167 750fr multi 8.00 2.50

Nos. 1119-1120 airmail.

Nos. 1116-1119 exist in souvenir sheets of 1. Sold for 100fr extra.
For surcharge and overprints see Nos. 1182N, 1216-1220.

Planting A168

**1989** **Litho.** ***Perf. 13½***

**1121** A168 25fr shown .25 .25
**1122** A168 50fr Irrigation .50 .25
**1123** A168 75fr Milking .70 .25
**1124** A168 100fr Fishing .95 .35
**1125** A168 150fr Farmers in corn field 1.40 .55
**1126** A168 300fr Public well 3.00 1.10
*Nos. 1121-1126 (6)* 6.80 2.75

Natl. Campaign for Self-sufficiency in Food Production and 10th anniv. of the Intl. Fund for Agricultural Development (in 1988). Dated 1988.

African Development Bank, 25th Anniv. — A169

**1989, Nov. 4** **Litho.** ***Perf. 13½***

**1127** A169 300fr multicolored 3.00 1.10

Mano River Union, 15th Anniv. A170

Design: 300fr, Map of Guinea, Sierra Leone and Liberia, leaders' portraits.

**1989, Nov. 4**

**1128** A170 150fr multicolored 1.50 .65
**1129** A170 300fr multicolored 3.00 1.25

World Cup Soccer, Italy — A171

Various soccer plays and: 200fr, Spire of San Domenico, Naples. 250fr, Piazza San Carlo, Turin. 300fr, Church of San Cataldo. 450fr, Church of San Francesco, Utine. 750fr, Statue of Dante, Florence and World Cup Soccer Trophy.

**1990, Aug. 3 Litho. *Perf. 13½***

| | | | | | |
|---|---|---|---|---|---|
| **1130** | A171 | 200fr | multicolored | 1.50 | .80 |
| **1131** | A171 | 250fr | multicolored | 2.00 | 1.00 |
| **1132** | A171 | 300fr | multicolored | 2.50 | 1.25 |
| **1133** | A171 | 450fr | multicolored | 4.00 | 1.90 |
| | | | *Nos. 1130-1133 (4)* | 10.00 | 4.95 |

**Souvenir Sheet**

| | | | | | |
|---|---|---|---|---|---|
| **1134** | A171 | 750fr | multicolored | 7.25 | 2.75 |

No. 1133-1134 airmail.
For overprints see Nos. 1221-1225.

Concorde, TGV Atlantic — A172

**1990, Aug. 3**

| | | | | | |
|---|---|---|---|---|---|
| **1135** | A172 | 400fr | multicolored | 4.00 | 1.50 |

No. 1135 exists in a souvenir sheet of 1.
For surcharge see No. 1182O.

Pope John Paul II, Pres. Gorbachev — A173

**1990, Aug. 3**

| | | | | | |
|---|---|---|---|---|---|
| **1136** | A173 | 300fr | multicolored | 3.25 | 1.10 |

Summit Meeting, Dec. 2, 1989. No. 1136 exists in a souvenir sheet of 1. Value $10.

1992 Winter Olympics, Albertville — A174

**1990, Aug. 3**

| | | | | | |
|---|---|---|---|---|---|
| **1137** | A174 | 150fr | Downhill skiing | 1.40 | .65 |
| **1138** | A174 | 250fr | Cross country skiing | 2.50 | 1.10 |
| **1139** | A174 | 400fr | Two-man bob-sled | 3.75 | 1.60 |
| **1140** | A174 | 500fr | Speedskating | 5.00 | 2.00 |
| | | | *Nos. 1137-1140 (4)* | 12.65 | 5.35 |

**Souvenir Sheet**

| | | | | | |
|---|---|---|---|---|---|
| **1141** | A174 | 750fr | Slalom skiing | 8.00 | 3.00 |

Nos. 1140-1141 airmail. Nos. 1137-1140 exist in souvenir sheets of 1.
For overprints and surcharge see Nos. 1182P, 1225-1230.

Pres. Bush, Pres. Gorbachev — A175

**1990, Aug. 3 Litho. *Perf. 13½***

| | | | | | |
|---|---|---|---|---|---|
| **1142** | A175 | 200fr | multicolored | 1.75 | .75 |

Summit Meeting Dec. 3, 1989. No. 1142 exists in a souvenir sheet of 1.

De Gaulle's Call for French Resistance, 50th Anniv. — A176

**1990**

| | | | | | |
|---|---|---|---|---|---|
| **1143** | A176 | 250fr | multi | 2.50 | 1.00 |

No. 1143 exists in a souvenir sheet of 1.

A177

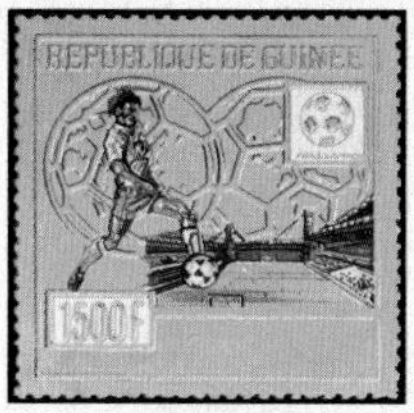

World Cup Soccer Championships, Italy 1990 — A178

No. 1152, Player, Chateau Saint-Ange.

**1991, Apr. 1 Litho. *Perf. 13½***

| | | | | | |
|---|---|---|---|---|---|
| **1144** | A177 | 200fr | Rudi Voller | 1.75 | .80 |
| **1145** | A177 | 250fr | Uwe Bein | 2.25 | 1.00 |
| **1146** | A177 | 300fr | Pierre Littbarski | 2.75 | 1.25 |
| **1147** | A177 | 400fr | Jurgen Klinsmann | 4.00 | 1.90 |
| **1148** | A177 | 450fr | Lothar Matthaus | 4.00 | 1.90 |
| **1149** | A177 | 500fr | Andreas Brehme | 4.50 | 2.00 |
| | | | *Nos. 1144-1149 (6)* | 19.25 | 8.85 |

**Litho. & Embossed**

| | | | | | |
|---|---|---|---|---|---|
| **1150** | A178 | 1500fr | gold & multi | 24.00 | 18.00 |

**Souvenir Sheets**

**Litho.**

| | | | | | |
|---|---|---|---|---|---|
| **1151** | A177 | 750fr | Brehme, diff. | 8.00 | 3.00 |

**Litho. & Embossed**

| | | | | | |
|---|---|---|---|---|---|
| **1152** | A178 | 1500fr | gold & multi | 16.00 | 12.50 |

Nos. 1148-1152 are airmail. Nos. 1144-1150 exist in souvenir sheets of 1.

Christmas A179

Paintings by Raphael: 50fr, Della Tenda Madonna. 100fr, Cowper Madonna. 150fr, Tempi Madonna. 250fr, Niccolini Madonna. 300fr, Orleans Madonna. 500fr, Solly Madonna. 750fr, Madonna of the Fish.

**1991, Apr. 1 Litho.**

| | | | | | |
|---|---|---|---|---|---|
| **1153** | A179 | 50fr | multi | .50 | .25 |
| **1154** | A179 | 100fr | multi | .85 | .45 |
| **1155** | A179 | 150fr | multi | 1.40 | .65 |
| **1156** | A179 | 250fr | multi | 2.25 | 1.00 |
| **1157** | A179 | 300fr | multi | 2.75 | 1.25 |
| **1158** | A179 | 500fr | multi | 4.50 | 2.00 |
| | | | *Nos. 1153-1158 (6)* | 12.25 | 5.60 |

**Souvenir Sheet**

| | | | | | |
|---|---|---|---|---|---|
| **1159** | A179 | 750fr | multi | 8.00 | 3.00 |

Nos. 1157-1159 are airmail. Nos. 1153-1158 exist in souvenir sheets of 1.

A180

World War II Battles — A181

Designs: No. 1160, Sinking of the Bismarck, May 27, 1941, Adm. Raeder and Adm. Tovey. No. 1161, Battle of Midway, June 3, 1942, Adm. Yamamoto and Adm. Nimitz. 200fr, Guadalcanal, Oct. 7, 1942, Adm. Kondo and Adm. Halsey. 250fr, Battle of El Alamein, Oct. 23, 1942, Field Marshal Erwin Rommel, Field Marshal Montgomery. 300fr, Battle of the Bulge, Dec. 16, 1944, Gen. Guderian and Gen. Patton. 450fr, Sinking of the Yamato, Apr., 7, 1945, Adm. Kogo and Gen. MacArthur. No. 1166, Review of Free French Forces, July 14, 1940, Gen. Charles De Gaulle. 750fr, Boeing B-17G, Gen. Dwight Eisenhower. No. 1168, De Gaulle's Call for French Resistance, June 18, 1940.

**1991, Apr. 8 Litho. *Perf. 13½***

| | | | | | |
|---|---|---|---|---|---|
| **1160** | A180 | 100fr | multicolored | .90 | .45 |
| **1161** | A180 | 150fr | multicolored | 1.25 | .70 |
| **1162** | A180 | 200fr | multicolored | 1.75 | .90 |
| **1163** | A180 | 250fr | multicolored | 2.25 | 1.10 |
| **1164** | A180 | 300fr | multicolored | 2.75 | 1.25 |
| **1165** | A180 | 450fr | multicolored | 6.00 | 3.00 |
| *a.* | | | Sheet of 6, #1160-1165 | 16.00 | 8.00 |

**Litho. & Embossed**

| | | | | | |
|---|---|---|---|---|---|
| **1166** | A181 | 1500fr | gold & multi | 17.00 | 11.00 |

**Souvenir Sheets**

**Litho.**

| | | | | | |
|---|---|---|---|---|---|
| **1167** | A180 | 750fr | multicolored | 8.00 | 3.00 |

**Litho. & Embossed**

| | | | | | |
|---|---|---|---|---|---|
| **1168** | A181 | 1500fr | gold & multi | 15.00 | 10.00 |

Nos. 1164-1168 are airmail. No. 1160-1166 exist in souvenir sheets of 1. Value, set $32.
For overprint see No. C177.

Doctors Without Borders A182

**1991, Feb. 22 Litho. *Perf. 13½***

| | | | | | |
|---|---|---|---|---|---|
| **1169** | A182 | 300fr | multicolored | 3.25 | 1.50 |

Telecom '91 A183

**1991, Jan. 15**

| | | | | | |
|---|---|---|---|---|---|
| **1170** | A183 | 150fr | multi, vert. | 1.50 | 1.25 |
| **1171** | A183 | 300fr | shown | 2.75 | 2.40 |

6th World Forum and Exposition on Telecommunications, Geneva, Switzerland.

American Entertainers and Films — A184

Designs: 100fr, Nat King Cole Trio. 150fr, Yul Brynner, The Magnificent Seven. 250fr, Judy Garland, The Wizard of Oz. 300fr, Steve McQueen, Papillon. 500fr, Gary Cooper, Sergeant York. 600fr, Bing Crosby, High Society. 750fr, John Wayne, How the West Was Won.

**1991, Oct. 2 Litho. *Perf. 13½***

| | | | | | |
|---|---|---|---|---|---|
| **1172** | A184 | 100fr | multicolored | .75 | .45 |
| **1173** | A184 | 150fr | multicolored | 1.10 | .60 |
| **1174** | A184 | 250fr | multicolored | 2.00 | 1.00 |
| **1175** | A184 | 300fr | multicolored | 2.40 | 1.25 |
| **1176** | A184 | 500fr | multicolored | 4.00 | 2.00 |
| **1177** | A184 | 600fr | multicolored | 8.75 | 4.25 |
| | | | *Nos. 1172-1177 (6)* | 19.00 | 9.55 |

**Souvenir Sheet**

| | | | | | |
|---|---|---|---|---|---|
| **1178** | A184 | 750fr | multicolored | 8.00 | 3.00 |

Nos. 1176-1178 are airmail. No. 1172-1177 exist in souvenir sheets of 1.

Care Bears Promoting Environmental Protection — A184a

Designs: 50fr, Care Bears circling earth, vert. 100fr, Save water, vert. 200fr, Recycle, vert. 300fr, Control noise, vert. 400fr, Elephant. 500fr, Care Bear emblem, end of rainbow. 600fr, Scout, tent, Lord Baden-Powell.

**1991 Litho. *Perf. 13½***

| | | | | | |
|---|---|---|---|---|---|
| **1178A** | A184a | 50fr | multi | .40 | .25 |
| **1178B** | A184a | 100fr | multi | .85 | .40 |
| **1178C** | A184a | 200fr | multi | 1.75 | .85 |
| **1178D** | A184a | 300fr | multi | 2.50 | 1.25 |
| **1178E** | A184a | 400fr | multi | 3.50 | 1.75 |
| | | | *Nos. 1178A-1178E (5)* | 9.00 | 4.50 |

**Souvenir Sheets**

| | | | | | |
|---|---|---|---|---|---|
| **1178F** | A184a | 500fr | multi | 4.25 | 2.25 |
| **1178G** | A184a | 600fr | multi | 5.00 | 2.50 |

Nos. 1178F-1178G each contain one 39x27mm stamp. No. 1178G is airmail.

African Tourism Year A185

**1991, Aug. 16 Litho. *Perf. 13½***

| | | | | | |
|---|---|---|---|---|---|
| **1179** | A185 | 100fr Dancer, vert. | 1.25 | .60 |
| **1180** | A185 | 150fr Baskets | 2.00 | .90 |
| **1181** | A185 | 250fr Drum | 3.25 | 1.25 |
| **1182** | A185 | 300fr Flute player, vert. | 3.50 | 1.60 |
| | | *Nos. 1179-1182 (4)* | 10.00 | 4.35 |

**Stamps of 1986-92 Surcharged in Black or Silver**

Nos. 1182A, 1182M, 1182P, 1182R Surcharged

Nos. 1182B, 1182D, 1182H, 1182I, 1182N Surcharged

Nos. 1182C, 1182E, 1182G, 1182O Surcharged

Nos. 1182F, 1182J, 1182K, 1182L, 1182Q Surcharged

**1991 Litho. *Perfs. as Before***

| | | | | |
|---|---|---|---|---|
| **1182A** A150 | 100fr on 400fr #1019 | .85 | .40 |
| **1182B** A154 | 100fr on 400fr #1045 | .85 | .40 |
| **1182C** A156 | 100fr on 400fr #1052 | .85 | .40 |
| **1182D** A159 | 100fr on 170fr #1065 | .85 | .40 |
| **1182E** A159 | 100fr on 400fr #1066 | .85 | .40 |
| **1182F** A160 | 100fr on 170fr #1072 | 125.00 | — |
| **1182G** A160 | 100fr on 400fr #1073 | 4.00 | 1.00 |
| **1182H** A163 | 100fr on 400fr #1092 | .85 | .40 |
| **1182I** A164 | 100fr on 400fr #1098 | .85 | .40 |
| **1182J** A165 | 100fr on 400fr #1106 | .85 | .40 |
| **1182K** A165b | 100fr on 500fr #1108G | .85 | .40 |
| **1182L** A165d | 100fr on 500fr #1108N | .85 | .40 |
| **1182M** A166 | 100fr on 400fr #1113 | .85 | .40 |
| **1182N** A167 | 100fr on 250fr #1116 | .85 | .40 |
| **1182O** A172 | 100fr on 400fr #1135 | .85 | .40 |
| **1182P** A174 | 100fr on 400fr #1139 | .85 | .40 |
| **1182Q** A164 | 300fr on 450fr #1099 | 2.50 | 1.25 |
| **1182R** AP14 | 300fr on 450fr #C170 | 2.50 | 1.25 |
| | *Nos. 1182A-1182R (18)* | 145.90 | 9.10 |

Nos. 1182B-1182C, 1182E, 1182G, 1182M, 1182Q-1182R are airmail.

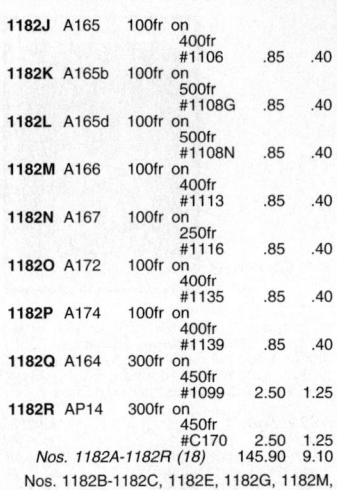

Visit by Pope John Paul II — A185a

**1992, Feb. 24 Litho. *Perf. 13½***

| | | | | |
|---|---|---|---|---|
| **1182S** | A185a 150fr multicolored | 3.00 | 1.75 |

1994 World Cup Soccer, US — A186

A186a

Player, World Cup Trophy and scenes of Atlanta: 100fr, Little Five Points. 300fr, Fulton County Stadium. 400fr, Inman Park. 500fr, High Museum of Art. 1000fr, Intelsat VI, Capitol.

#1187A, Player in white shirt. #1187B, Player in red.

**1992, Apr. 27 Litho. *Perf. 13½***

| | | | | |
|---|---|---|---|---|
| **1183** | A186 | 100fr multi | 1.25 | .40 |
| **1184** | A186 | 300fr multi | 4.00 | 1.25 |
| **1185** | A186 | 400fr multi | 5.75 | 1.75 |
| **1186** | A186 | 500fr multi | 7.00 | 2.25 |
| | | *Nos. 1183-1186 (4)* | 18.00 | 5.65 |

**Souvenir Sheets**

| | | | | |
|---|---|---|---|---|
| **1187** | A186 | 1000fr multi | 10.00 | 6.00 |

**Litho. & Embossed**

| | | | | |
|---|---|---|---|---|
| **1187A** | A186a | 1500fr gold & multi | 24.00 | 14.00 |

**Souvenir Sheet**

| | | | | |
|---|---|---|---|---|
| **1187B** | A186a | 1500fr gold & multi | 20.00 | 12.00 |

Nos. 1186-1187B are airmail. Nos. 1183-1187A exist in souvenir sheets of 1.

Lions Intl., 75th Anniv. — A187

**1992, May 22 Litho. *Perf. 13½***

| | | | | |
|---|---|---|---|---|
| **1188** | A187 | 150fr blue & multi | 1.50 | .75 |
| **1188A** | A187 | 400fr lilac rose & multi | 4.00 | 2.00 |

Anniversaries and Events — A188

Designs: 100fr, Satellite ERS-1 in orbit. 150fr, Vase with Fourteen Sunflowers, by Vincent van Gogh. 200fr, Napoleon Bonaparte. 250fr, Henri Dunant, Red Cross workers. 300fr, Brandenburg Gate. 400fr, Pope John Paul II. 450fr, Garry Kasparov, Anatoly Karpov, chess pieces. 500fr, African child, dove, emblems of Rotary and Lions Clubs.

**1992, Nov. 10 Litho. *Perf. 13½***

| | | | | |
|---|---|---|---|---|
| **1189** | A188 | 100fr multicolored | 1.00 | .45 |
| **1190** | A188 | 150fr multicolored | 1.50 | .75 |
| **1191** | A188 | 200fr multicolored | 2.25 | 1.00 |
| **1192** | A188 | 250fr multicolored | 2.50 | 1.25 |
| **1193** | A188 | 300fr multicolored | 3.25 | 1.50 |
| **1194** | A188 | 400fr multicolored | 4.25 | 2.10 |
| **1195** | A188 | 450fr multicolored | 4.75 | 2.25 |
| **1196** | A188 | 500fr multicolored | 5.50 | 2.50 |
| | | *Nos. 1189-1196 (8)* | 25.00 | 11.80 |

Intl. Space Year (#1189). Vincent van Gogh, cent. of death (in 1990) (#1190). Napolean Bonaparte, 170th anniv. of death (in 1991) (#1191). Founding of Red Cross (in 1864) (#1192). Brandenburg Gate, bicent. (#1193). Pope John Paul II's visit to Africa in 1989 (#1194). World Chess Championships (#1195). Lions Intl., 75th anniv. (#1196).

Nos. 1195-1196 are airmail. Nos. 1189-1196 exist in souvenir sheets of one.

For overprint see No. C178.

Anniversaries and Events — A189

Designs: 200fr, The Devil and Kate, Antonin Dvorak. 300fr, Antonio Vivaldi. 350fr, Graf Zeppelin, flying boat, Count Ferdinand von Zeppelin. 400fr, English Channel Euro-Tunnel Train. 450fr, Konrad Adenauer, Brandenburg Gate. 500fr, Japanese naval ensign, Emperor Hirohito. 750fr, Tunnel Train, diff.

**1992, Nov. 10**

| | | | | |
|---|---|---|---|---|
| **1197** | A189 | 200fr multicolored | 2.25 | .90 |
| **1198** | A189 | 300fr multicolored | 3.25 | 1.40 |
| **1199** | A189 | 350fr multicolored | 3.75 | 1.50 |
| **1200** | A189 | 400fr multicolored | 4.00 | 1.90 |
| **1201** | A189 | 450fr multicolored | 5.00 | 2.00 |
| *a.* | | Souvenir sheet of 2, #1199, 1201 | 8.00 | 3.25 |
| **1202** | A189 | 500fr multicolored | 5.50 | 2.25 |
| | | *Nos. 1197-1202 (6)* | 23.75 | 9.95 |

**Souvenir Sheet**

| | | | | |
|---|---|---|---|---|
| **1203** | A189 | 750fr multicolored | 8.00 | 3.75 |

Antonin Dvorak, 90th anniv. of death (in 1994) (#1197). Antonio Vivaldi, 250th anniv. of death (in 1991) (#1198). Count Ferdinand von Zeppelin, 75th anniv. of death (#1199). Opening of English Channel Tunnel (in 1994) (#1200, 1203). Konrad Adenauer, 25th anniv. of death, Brandenburg Gate, bicent. (#1201). Death of Emperor Hirohito (in 1989) (#1202).

Nos. 1201-1203 are airmail. Nos. 1197-1202 exist imperf. and in souvenir sheets of one. No. 1203 exists imperf. and contains one 60x42mm stamp.

Anniversaries and Events A190

Designs: 50fr, Modern Times, film by Charlie Chaplin. 100fr, Expo '92 Seville, Columbus. 150fr, St. Peter's Square, Rome. 200fr, Marlene Dietrich, roses. 250fr, Michael Schumacher, Benetton Ford B192. 300fr, Mercury rocket, John Glenn. 400fr, Bill Koch, America 3. 450fr, Mark Rypien, quarterback of Washington Redskins. 500fr, Rescue of Intelsat VI by shuttle Endeavour.

**1992, Dec. 3**

| | | | | |
|---|---|---|---|---|
| **1204** | A190 | 50fr multicolored | .45 | .25 |
| **1205** | A190 | 100fr multicolored | .90 | .40 |
| **1206** | A190 | 150fr multicolored | 1.40 | .65 |
| **1207** | A190 | 200fr multicolored | 1.90 | .85 |
| **1208** | A190 | 250fr multicolored | 2.25 | 1.10 |
| **1209** | A190 | 300fr multicolored | 2.75 | 1.25 |
| **1210** | A190 | 400fr multicolored | 3.50 | 1.75 |
| **1211** | A190 | 450fr multicolored | 4.00 | 1.90 |
| **1212** | A190 | 500fr multicolored | 4.50 | 2.10 |
| | | *Nos. 1204-1212 (9)* | 21.65 | 10.25 |

Discovery of America, 500th anniv. (#1205). First US orbital space flight, 30th anniv. (#1209). Americas Cup yacht race (#1210). Super Bowl XXVI football game (#1211).

Nos. 1210-1212 are airmail. Nos. 1204-1212 exist in souvenir sheets of one.

Intl. Conference on Nutrition, Rome — A191

**1992, Nov. 10 Litho. *Perf. 13½***

| | | | | |
|---|---|---|---|---|
| **1213** | A191 | 150fr multi | 1.50 | .70 |
| **1214** | A191 | 400fr multi | 3.50 | 1.90 |
| **1215** | A191 | 500fr multi | 4.50 | 2.25 |
| | | *Nos. 1213-1215 (3)* | 9.50 | 4.85 |

**Nos. 1116-1120 Ovptd. in Silver**

**1992, Feb. 24 Litho. *Perf. 13½***

| | | | | |
|---|---|---|---|---|
| **1216** | A167 | 250fr multicolored | 2.50 | 1.10 |
| **1217** | A167 | 300fr multicolored | 3.00 | 1.40 |
| **1218** | A167 | 400fr multicolored | 4.00 | 1.75 |
| **1219** | A167 | 450fr multicolored | 4.75 | 2.00 |
| | | *Nos. 1216-1219 (4)* | 14.25 | 6.25 |

**Souvenir Sheet**

| | | | | |
|---|---|---|---|---|
| **1220** | A167 | 750fr multicolored | 9.00 | 4.50 |

Nos. 1219-1220 are airmail. Nos. 1216-1219 exist in souvenir sheets of 1. Sold for 100fr extra.

Nos. 1130-1134 Ovptd. in Gold

**1992, Feb. 24 Litho. *Perf. 13½***

| | | | | |
|---|---|---|---|---|
| **1221** | A171 | 200fr multicolored | 2.00 | .80 |
| **1222** | A171 | 250fr multicolored | 2.50 | 1.00 |
| **1223** | A171 | 300fr multicolored | 3.00 | 1.25 |
| **1224** | A171 | 450fr multicolored | 5.00 | 2.00 |
| | | *Nos. 1221-1224 (4)* | 12.50 | 5.05 |

**Souvenir Sheet**

| | | | | |
|---|---|---|---|---|
| **1225** | A171 | 750fr multicolored | 8.00 | 3.00 |

Nos. 1137 Ovptd. in Gold

Nos. 1138 Ovptd. in Gold

Nos. 1139 Ovptd. in Gold

Nos. 1141 Ovptd. in Gold

**1992 Litho. *Perf. 13½***

| | | | | |
|---|---|---|---|---|
| **1226** | A174 | 150fr multicolored | 1.45 | .70 |
| **1227** | A174 | 250fr multicolored | 2.00 | 1.10 |
| **1228** | A174 | 400fr multicolored | 3.25 | 1.75 |
| **1229** | A174 | 500fr multicolored | 4.25 | 2.10 |
| | | *Nos. 1226-1229 (4)* | 10.95 | 5.65 |

**Souvenir Sheet**

| | | | | |
|---|---|---|---|---|
| **1230** | A174 | 750fr multicolored | 6.25 | 3.00 |

Overprints read: 150fr, "SLALOM GEANT / Alberto Tomba, Italie." 250fr, "SKI NORDIQUE / Vegard Ulvang, Norvege." 400fr, "BOB A DEUX / G. Weder / D Acklin, Suisse." 500fr, "PATINAGE DE VITESSE / Olaf Zinke 1000m., Allemagne."

A192

1994 World Cup Soccer Championships, US — A192a

Soccer player, city skyline: 100fr, San Francisco. 300fr, Washington, DC. 400fr, Detroit. 500fr, Dallas. 1000fr, New York.

**1993, Sept. 24 Litho. *Perf. 13½***

| | | | | |
|---|---|---|---|---|
| **1233** | A192 | 100fr multicolored | .95 | .45 |
| **1234** | A192 | 300fr multicolored | 3.25 | 1.50 |
| **1235** | A192 | 400fr multicolored | 4.00 | 1.90 |
| **1236** | A192 | 500fr multicolored | 5.25 | 2.40 |
| | | *Nos. 1233-1236 (4)* | 13.45 | 6.25 |

**Souvenir Sheet**

| | | | | |
|---|---|---|---|---|
| **1237** | A192 | 1000fr multicolored | 10.00 | 5.50 |

**Litho. & Embossed**

| | | | | |
|---|---|---|---|---|
| **1237A** | A192a | 1500fr gold & multi | 16.00 | 12.50 |

Nos. 1236-1237A are airmail. No. 1237A exists in a souvenir sheet of 1.

Miniature Sheet

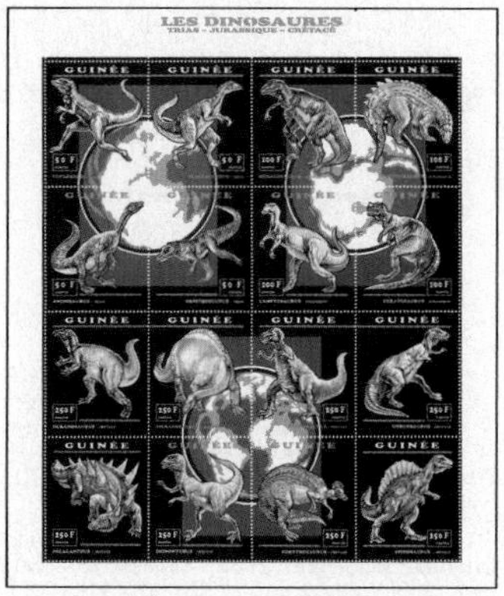


Dinosaurs — A193

No. 1238: a, 50fr, Euparkeria. b, 50fr, Plateosaurus. c, 50fr, Anchisaurus. d, 50fr, Ornithosuchus. e, 100fr, Megalosaurus. f, 100fr, Scelidosaurus. g, 100fr, Camptosaurus. h, 100fr, Ceratosaurus. i, 250fr, Ouranosaurus. j, 250fr, Dicraeosaurus. k, 250fr, Tarbosaurus. l, 250fr, Gorgosaurus. m, 250fr, Polacanthus. n, 250fr, Deinonychus. o, 250fr, Corythosaurus. p, 250fr, Spinosaurus.
1000fr, Tyrannosaurus rex.

**1993, Oct. 27**

| | | | | |
|---|---|---|---|---|
| **1238** | A193 | Sheet of 16, #a.-p. | 25.00 | 15.00 |

**Souvenir Sheet**

| | | | | |
|---|---|---|---|---|
| **1239** | A193 | 1000fr multicolored | 10.00 | 4.50 |

No. 1239 is airmail and contains one 50x60mm stamp.

Nos. 1088-1094 Ovptd. in Silver

**1993, Feb. 24 Litho. *Perf. 13½***

| | | | | |
|---|---|---|---|---|
| **1240** | A163 | 50fr multicolored | .45 | .25 |
| **1241** | A163 | 100fr multicolored | 1.10 | .50 |
| **1242** | A163 | 150fr multicolored | 1.75 | .65 |
| **1243** | A163 | 300fr multicolored | 3.25 | 1.40 |
| **1244** | A163 | 400fr multicolored | 3.75 | 1.90 |
| **1245** | A163 | 450fr multicolored | 4.75 | 2.00 |
| | | *Nos. 1240-1245 (6)* | 15.05 | 6.70 |

**Souvenir Sheet**

| | | | | |
|---|---|---|---|---|
| **1246** | A163 | 750fr multicolored | 8.00 | 3.25 |

Nos. 1244-1246 are airmail.

A194

1994 Winter Olympic Games, Lillehammer A195

Views of Lillehammer: 150fr, Ice hockey. 250fr, Bobsled. 400fr, Biathlon. 450fr, Ski jump.
1000fr, Slalom skiing. 1500fr, Ice skating.

**1993, July 16 Litho. *Perf. 13½***

| | | | | |
|---|---|---|---|---|
| **1247** | A194 | 150fr multicolored | 1.25 | .65 |
| **1248** | A194 | 250fr multicolored | 2.75 | 1.25 |
| **1249** | A194 | 400fr multicolored | 4.25 | 2.10 |
| **1250** | A194 | 450fr multicolored | 4.75 | 2.25 |
| | | *Nos. 1247-1250 (4)* | 13.00 | 6.25 |

**Souvenir Sheet**

| | | | | |
|---|---|---|---|---|
| **1251** | A194 | 1000fr multicolored | 10.00 | 5.00 |

**Litho. & Embossed**

| | | | | |
|---|---|---|---|---|
| **1252** | A195 | 1500fr gold & multi | 16.00 | 12.50 |

Nos. 1249-1252 are airmail.
For overprints see #1267A-1267E.

A196

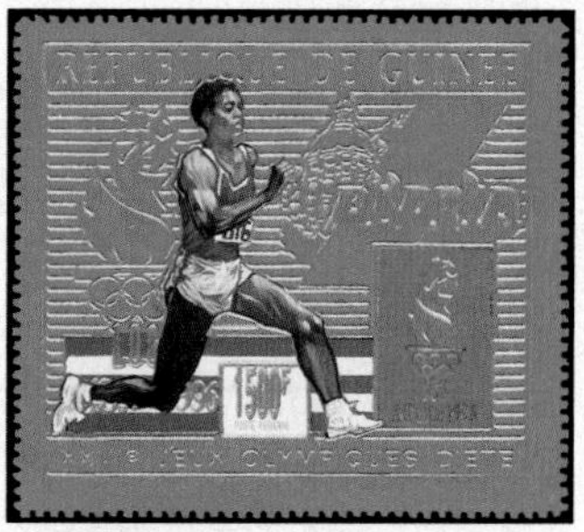


1996 Summer Olympic Games, Atlanta — A197

Event, scenes of Atlanta: 150fr, Soccer, "Little White House." 250fr, Cycling, Georgia World Congress Center. 400fr, Basketball, underground Atlanta. 500fr, Baseball, new Georgia Railroad.
1000fr, Table tennis, Atlanta at night. 1500fr, Running, Georgia State Capitol, Olympic torch.

**1993, July 16 Litho. *Perf. 13½***

| | | | | |
|---|---|---|---|---|
| **1253** | A196 | 150fr multi | 1.50 | .65 |
| **1254** | A196 | 250fr multi | 2.75 | 1.25 |
| **1255** | A196 | 400fr multi | 4.75 | 2.10 |
| **1256** | A196 | 500fr multi | 6.00 | 2.50 |
| | | *Nos. 1253-1256 (4)* | 15.00 | 6.50 |

**Souvenir Sheet**

| | | | | |
|---|---|---|---|---|
| **1257** | A196 | 1000fr multi | 10.00 | 5.00 |

**Litho. & Embossed**

| | | | | |
|---|---|---|---|---|
| **1257A** | A197 | 1500fr gold & multi | 16.00 | 12.50 |

Nos. 1256-1257A are airmail.
#1253-1256 exist in souvenir sheets of 1.

First Manned Moon Landing, 25th Anniv. — A197a

d, Luna 3, 1959. e, Ranger 7, 1964. f, Luna 9, 1966. g, Surveyor 1, 1966. h, Lunar Orbiter 1, 1966. i, Launch of Apollo 11, Neil Armstrong, 1969. j, Michael Collins, Apollo 11 command module. k, Apollo 11 landing on Moon, "Buzz" Aldrin. l, Apollo 12, 1969. m, Apollo 13, 1969. n, Luna 16, 1970. o, Luna 17, 1970. p, Apollo 14, 1971. q, Apollo 15, 1971. r, Apollo 16, 1972. s, Apollo 17, 1972.

**1993, July 27 Litho. *Perf. 13½***

**Sheet of 16**

| | | | | |
|---|---|---|---|---|
| **1257B** | A197a | 150fr #d.-s. | 25.00 | 12.25 |

D-Day Landings, Normandy, 50th Anniv. — A198

Battle scenes and: No. 1258a, 150fr, Field Marshal Irwin Rommel (1891-1944), Germany. b, 600fr, Gen. Dwight D. Eisenhower (1890-1969), Allies. c, 150fr, Gen. George S. Patton, Jr. (1885-1945), Allies.
Battle of the Bulge, 1944: No. 1259a, 150fr, Lt. Gen. William H. Simpson. b, 600fr, Battle scene. c, 150fr, Gen. Heinz Guderian (1888-1954).
Austerlitz, Dec. 2, 1805: No. 1260a, 150fr, John I, Prince of Liechtenstein (1760-1836). b, 600fr, Napoleon I. c, 150fr, Marshal Joachim Murat (1767-1815).
Battle of Borodino, Sept. 7, 1812: No. 1261a, 150fr, Marshal Michael Ney (1769-1815). b, 600fr, Battle scene. c, 150fr, Prince Pyotr Ivanovich Bagration (1765-1812).

**1994, Jan. 26 Litho. *Perf. 13½***

| | | | | |
|---|---|---|---|---|
| **1258** | A198 | Strip of 3, #a.-c. | 11.00 | 4.75 |
| **1259** | A198 | Strip of 3, #a.-c. | 11.00 | 4.75 |
| **1260** | A198 | Strip of 3, #a.-c. | 11.00 | 4.75 |
| **1261** | A198 | Strip of 3, #a.-c. | 11.00 | 4.75 |
| | | *Nos. 1258-1261 (4)* | 44.00 | 19.00 |

No. 1258b, 1259b, 1260b, 1261b are 60x46mm. Nos. 1258-1261 are each a continuous design.

Astronomers and Spacecraft — A199

Designs: a, 300fr, Johannes Kepler, Pluto probe. b, 500fr, Copernicus, Galileo probe. b, 300fr, Sir Isaac Newton, Voyager.

**1994, Jan. 26**

**1262** A199 Strip of 3, #a.-c. 15.00 6.75

No. 1262b is 60x46mm. No. 1262 has a continuous design.

Nos. 1233-1237 Ovptd. in Silver

| **1994, Sept. 14** | **Litho.** | | *Perf. 13½* | |
|---|---|---|---|---|
| **1263** A192 | 100fr | multicolored | 1.00 | .50 |
| **1264** A192 | 300fr | multicolored | 3.00 | 1.75 |
| **1265** A192 | 400fr | multicolored | 4.00 | 2.25 |
| **1266** A192 | 500fr | multicolored | 4.75 | 2.50 |
| | *Nos. 1263-1266 (4)* | | 12.75 | 7.00 |

**Souvenir Sheet**

**1267** A192 1000fr multicolored 10.00 5.00

Nos. 1266-1267 are airmail.

No. 1247 Overprinted in Gold

No. 1248 Overprinted in Gold

No. 1249 Overprinted in Gold

No. 1250 Overprinted in Gold

| **1994, Sept. 14** | **Litho.** | | *Perf. 13½* | |
|---|---|---|---|---|
| **1267A** | A194 | 150fr multi | 1.25 | .65 |
| **1267B** | A194 | 250fr multi | 2.40 | 1.25 |
| **1267C** | A194 | 400fr multi | 3.75 | 1.90 |
| **1267D** | A194 | 450fr multi | 4.50 | 2.10 |
| | *Nos. 1267A-1267D (4)* | | 11.90 | 5.90 |

**Souvenir Sheet**

**1267E** A194 1000fr multi 10.00 5.00

Overprints read: 1000fr, T. MOE / U.S.A. Nos. 1267C-1267E are airmail.

Birds — A200

150fr, Carduelis carduelis. 250fr, Luscinia megarhynchos. #1270, Serinus canaria. #1271, Fringilla coelebs. #1272, Carduelis chloris.
No. 1273, Erithacus rubecula.

| **1995, Aug. 31** | **Litho.** | | *Perf. 13* | |
|---|---|---|---|---|
| **1268** A200 | 150fr | multicolored | .50 | .25 |
| **1269** A200 | 250fr | multicolored | .80 | .35 |
| **1270** A200 | 500fr | multicolored | 1.60 | .80 |
| **1271** A200 | 500fr | multicolored | 1.60 | .80 |
| **1272** A200 | 500fr | multicolored | 1.60 | .80 |
| | *Nos. 1268-1272 (5)* | | 6.10 | 3.00 |

**Souvenir Sheet**

**1273** A200 1000fr multicolored *6.00 3.00*

No. 1273 contains one 32x40mm stamp.

1996 Summer Olympics, Atlanta — A201

| **1995, Aug. 5** | | | | |
|---|---|---|---|---|
| **1274** A201 | 150fr | Javelin | .50 | .25 |
| **1275** A201 | 250fr | Boxing | .80 | .40 |
| **1276** A201 | 500fr | Basketball | 1.60 | .80 |
| **1277** A201 | 500fr | Weight lifting | 1.60 | .80 |
| **1278** A201 | 500fr | Soccer | 1.60 | .80 |
| | *Nos. 1274-1278 (5)* | | 6.10 | 3.05 |

**Souvenir Sheet**

**1279** A201 1000fr Archery *4.75 2.50*

No. 1279 contains one 32x40mm stamp.

African Animals A202

Designs: 150fr, Cercopithecus mona, vert. 250fr, Cercopithecus aethiops, vert. No. 1282, Galagoides demidovi, vert. No. 1283, Manis gigantea. No. 1284, Lepus crawshayi.
1000fr, Aonyx capensis, vert.

| **1995, Sept. 25** | | | | |
|---|---|---|---|---|
| **1280** A202 | 150fr | multicolored | .50 | .25 |
| **1281** A202 | 250fr | multicolored | .80 | .35 |
| **1282** A202 | 500fr | multicolored | 1.60 | .80 |
| **1283** A202 | 500fr | multicolored | 1.60 | .80 |
| **1284** A202 | 500fr | multicolored | 1.60 | .80 |
| | *Nos. 1280-1284 (5)* | | 6.10 | 3.00 |

**Souvenir Sheet**

**1285** A202 1000fr multicolored *6.00 3.00*

1998 World Cup Soccer Championships, France — A203

Opposing two players wearing: No. 1288, Yellow shirt & blue shorts, red shirt & white shorts. No. 1289, Red & white uniform, red shirt & white shorts. No. 1290, Striped shirt & blue shorts, red & yellow shirt & green shorts.
1000fr, Three players.

| **1995, Oct. 30** | **Litho.** | | *Perf. 13* | |
|---|---|---|---|---|
| **1286** A203 | 150fr | multicolored | .50 | .25 |
| **1287** A203 | 250fr | multicolored | .80 | .35 |
| **1288** A203 | 500fr | multicolored | 1.60 | .80 |
| **1289** A203 | 500fr | multicolored | 1.60 | .80 |
| **1290** A203 | 500fr | multicolored | 1.60 | .80 |
| | *Nos. 1286-1290 (5)* | | 6.10 | 3.00 |

**Souvenir Sheet**

**1291** A203 1000fr multicolored *6.00 3.00*

No. 1291 contains one 32x40mm stamp.

Domestic Cats A204

150fr, Tortoiseshell. 250fr, Tabby and white. #1294, Tortoiseshell and white longhair. #1295, Red tabby. #1296, Smoke long-haired.
1000fr, Chinchilla.

| **1995, July 25** | | | | |
|---|---|---|---|---|
| **1292** A204 | 150fr | multicolored | .80 | .40 |
| **1293** A204 | 250fr | multicolored | 1.25 | .55 |
| **1294** A204 | 500fr | multicolored | 2.50 | 1.25 |
| **1295** A204 | 500fr | multicolored | 2.50 | 1.25 |
| **1296** A204 | 500fr | multicolored | 2.50 | 1.25 |
| | *Nos. 1292-1296 (5)* | | 9.55 | 4.70 |

**Souvenir Sheet**

***Perf. 12½***

**1297** A204 1000fr multicolored *6.00 3.00*

No. 1297 contains one 40x32mm stamp.

Production of Electrical Power — A205

Designs: 100fr, Banéa Dam. 150fr, Water Chamber, Donkea. 200fr, Tinkisso Spillway, vert. 250fr, Cascades of Grand Falls. 500fr, Building, Kinkon.

| **1995, July 18** | | | *Perf. 12½* | |
|---|---|---|---|---|
| **1298** A205 | 100fr | multicolored | .50 | .25 |
| **1299** A205 | 150fr | multicolored | .75 | .35 |
| **1300** A205 | 200fr | multicolored | 1.00 | .50 |
| **1301** A205 | 250fr | multicolored | 1.25 | .65 |
| **1302** A205 | 500fr | multicolored | 2.50 | 1.25 |
| | *Nos. 1298-1302 (5)* | | 6.00 | 3.00 |

FAO, 50th Anniv. A206

Designs: 200fr, Man, oxen, boy. 750fr, Instructing women, children on nutrition.

| **1995, Oct. 16** | | | *Perf. 13* | |
|---|---|---|---|---|
| **1303** A206 | 200fr | multicolored | 1.00 | .55 |
| **1304** A206 | 750fr | multicolored | 4.00 | 2.00 |

Light Aircraft — A207

100fr, Pup-150, UK. 150fr, Gardan GY-80 Horizon, France. 250fr, Piper Cub J-3, US. No. 1308, Valmet L-90TP Redigo, Finland. No. 1309, Pilatus PC-6 Porter, Switzerland. No. 1310, Piper PA-28 Cherokee Arrow, US.
1000fr, Stol DO-27, Germany.

| **1995, Oct. 1** | | | *Perf. 12½* | |
|---|---|---|---|---|
| **1305** A207 | 100fr | multicolored | .45 | .25 |
| **1306** A207 | 150fr | multicolored | .75 | .35 |
| **1307** A207 | 250fr | multicolored | 1.25 | .65 |
| **1308** A207 | 500fr | multicolored | 2.40 | 1.10 |
| **1309** A207 | 500fr | multicolored | 2.40 | 1.10 |
| **1310** A207 | 500fr | multicolored | 2.40 | 1.10 |
| | *Nos. 1305-1310 (6)* | | 9.65 | 4.55 |

**Souvenir Sheet**

**1311** A207 1000fr multicolored *5.50 2.75*

No. 1311 contains one 40x32mm stamp.

Flowers — A208

100fr, Sprekelia formosissima. 150fr, Rudbeckia purpurea. 250fr, Meconopsis betonicifolia. #1314, Gail Borden rose. #1315, Lathyrus odoratus. #1316, Iris starshine.
1000fr, Cypripedium alma gaevert.

| **1995, Oct. 12** | | | | |
|---|---|---|---|---|
| **1312** A208 | 100fr | multicolored | .45 | .25 |
| **1313** A208 | 150fr | multicolored | .75 | .35 |
| **1314** A208 | 250fr | multicolored | 1.25 | .60 |
| **1315** A208 | 500fr | multicolored | 2.40 | 1.10 |
| **1316** A208 | 500fr | multicolored | 2.40 | 1.10 |
| **1317** A208 | 500fr | multicolored | 2.40 | 1.10 |
| | *Nos. 1312-1317 (6)* | | 9.65 | 4.50 |

**Souvenir Sheet**

**1318** A208 1000fr multicolored *5.50 2.75*

No. 1318 contains one 32x40mm stamp.

Historic Buses — A209

250fr, 1832 Omnibus. 300fr, 1898 Daimler. 400fr, 1904 V.H. Bussing. 450fr, 1906 Autobus M.A.N. 500fr, 1904 Autocar M.A.N.

| **1995, Dec. 3** | **Litho.** | | *Perf. 12½* | |
|---|---|---|---|---|
| **1319** A209 | 250fr | multicolored | .75 | .35 |
| **1320** A209 | 300fr | multicolored | .90 | .45 |
| **1321** A209 | 400fr | multicolored | 1.25 | .60 |
| **1322** A209 | 450fr | multicolored | 1.40 | .70 |
| **1323** A209 | 500fr | multicolored | 1.50 | .75 |
| | *Nos. 1319-1323 (5)* | | 5.80 | 2.85 |

Arabian Horses A210

Various horses.

| **1995** | | **Background Colors** | | |
|---|---|---|---|---|
| **1324** A210 | 100fr | dk bl, vert. | .30 | .25 |
| **1325** A210 | 150fr | tan, vert. | .55 | .25 |
| **1326** A210 | 250fr | lt bl, vert. | .90 | .40 |
| **1327** A210 | 500fr | pink, vert. | 1.75 | .90 |
| **1328** A210 | 500fr | lilac, vert. | 1.75 | .90 |
| **1329** A210 | 500fr | sage | 1.75 | .90 |
| | *Nos. 1324-1329 (6)* | | 7.00 | 3.60 |

**Souvenir Sheet**

**1330** A210 1000fr white & gray *6.00 3.00*

No. 1330 contains one 32x40mm stamp.

Mushrooms
A211

150fr, Leccinum nigrescens. 250fr, Boletus rhodoxanthus. #1333, Paxillus involutus. #1334, Cantharellus lutescens. #1335, Xerocomus rubellus.
1000fr, Gymnopilus junonius.

**1995 Litho. *Perf. 12½***

| | | | | | |
|---|---|---|---|---|---|
| **1331** | A211 | 150fr | multicolored | .45 | .25 |
| **1332** | A211 | 250fr | multicolored | .75 | .40 |
| **1333** | A211 | 500fr | multicolored | 1.50 | .75 |
| **1334** | A211 | 500fr | multicolored | 1.50 | .75 |
| **1335** | A211 | 500fr | multicolored | 1.50 | .75 |
| | | | *Nos. 1331-1335 (5)* | 5.70 | 2.90 |

**Souvenir Sheet**

| | | | | | |
|---|---|---|---|---|---|
| **1336** | A211 | 1000fr | multicolored | *6.00* | *3.00* |

No. 1336 contains one 32x40mm stamp.

Tourism — A212

**1996, Sept. 5 Litho. *Perf. 12½***

| | | | | | |
|---|---|---|---|---|---|
| **1337** | A212 | 200fr | Mountain cliff | 1.00 | .50 |
| **1338** | A212 | 750fr | Young child | 3.75 | 1.75 |
| **1339** | A212 | 1000fr | Women carrying wood | 4.75 | 2.50 |
| | | | *Nos. 1337-1339 (3)* | 9.50 | 4.75 |

Dogs — A213

**1996, Oct. 20**

| | | | | | |
|---|---|---|---|---|---|
| **1340** | A213 | 200fr | Bull terrier | .85 | .50 |
| **1341** | A213 | 250fr | Elkhound | 1.10 | .70 |
| **1342** | A213 | 300fr | Akita | 1.40 | .75 |
| **1343** | A213 | 400fr | Collie | 1.75 | 1.00 |
| **1344** | A213 | 450fr | Rottweiler | 2.00 | 1.00 |
| **1345** | A213 | 500fr | Boxer | 2.40 | 1.10 |
| | | | *Nos. 1340-1345 (6)* | 9.50 | 5.05 |

**Souvenir Sheet**

***Perf. 13***

| | | | | | |
|---|---|---|---|---|---|
| **1346** | A213 | 1000fr | German pointer | 5.00 | 2.50 |

No. 1346 contains one 32x40mm stamp.

Mushrooms
A214

**1996, Dec. 20 Litho. *Perf. 12½***

| | | | | | |
|---|---|---|---|---|---|
| **1347** | A214 | 200fr | Chestnut | .60 | .45 |
| **1348** | A214 | 250fr | Granular | .80 | .55 |
| **1349** | A214 | 300fr | Destroying angel | 1.00 | .70 |
| **1350** | A214 | 400fr | Milky blue | 1.25 | .95 |
| **1351** | A214 | 450fr | Violet cortinarius | 1.50 | 1.00 |
| **1352** | A214 | 500fr | Rough-stemmed | 1.75 | 1.10 |
| | | | *Nos. 1347-1352 (6)* | 6.90 | 4.75 |

**Souvenir Sheet**

***Perf. 13***

| | | | | | |
|---|---|---|---|---|---|
| **1353** | A214 | 1000fr | Hygrophorus | *5.00* | *2.50* |

No. 1353 contains one 32x40mm stamp.

Locomotives — A215

Designs: 200fr, Tom Thumb, 1829. 250fr, Genf, 1858. 300fr, Dübs and Company, 1873. 400fr, W.G. Bagnall of Castle Engine Works, 1932. 450fr, Werner von Siemens, 1879. 500fr, North London Tramways Co., 1885-89.
1000fr, General, 1862.

**1996, Aug. 30 *Perf. 12½***

| | | | | | |
|---|---|---|---|---|---|
| **1354** | A215 | 200fr | multicolored | .85 | .45 |
| **1355** | A215 | 250fr | multicolored | 1.10 | .60 |
| **1356** | A215 | 300fr | multicolored | 1.40 | .70 |
| **1357** | A215 | 400fr | multicolored | 2.00 | .95 |
| **1358** | A215 | 450fr | multicolored | 2.25 | 1.00 |
| **1359** | A215 | 500fr | multicolored | 2.40 | 1.10 |
| | | | *Nos. 1354-1359 (6)* | 10.00 | 4.80 |

**Souvenir Sheet**

| | | | | | |
|---|---|---|---|---|---|
| **1360** | A215 | 1000fr | multicolored | *5.50* | *2.75* |

Nos. 1355, 1358 are each 68x27mm. No. 1360 contains one 40x32mm stamp.

Cats
A216

200fr, Tortoiseshell short-hair. 250fr, Black and white short-hair. 300fr, Japanese. 400fr, Himalayan. 450fr, Brown long-hair. 500fr, Blue Persian.
1000fr, Tortoiseshell long-hair.

**1996, Nov. 15 *Perf. 12½***

| | | | | | |
|---|---|---|---|---|---|
| **1361** | A216 | 200fr | multicolored | .85 | .45 |
| **1362** | A216 | 250fr | multicolored | 1.10 | .60 |
| **1363** | A216 | 300fr | multicolored | 1.40 | .70 |
| **1364** | A216 | 400fr | multicolored | 2.00 | .95 |
| **1365** | A216 | 450fr | multicolored | 2.25 | 1.00 |
| **1366** | A216 | 500fr | multicolored | 2.40 | 1.10 |
| | | | *Nos. 1361-1366 (6)* | 10.00 | 4.80 |

**Souvenir Sheet**

| | | | | | |
|---|---|---|---|---|---|
| **1367** | A216 | 1000fr | multicolored | *5.00* | *2.50* |

No. 1367 contains one 32x40mm stamp.

Birds — A217

Designs: 200fr, Carduelis cucullata. 250fr, Uraeginthus bengalus. 300fr, Lonchura castaneothorax. 400fr, Amadina erythrocephala. 450fr, Chloebia gouldiae. 500fr, Euplectes orix.
1000fr, Poephila guttata.

**1996, Sept. 28 *Perf. 12½***

| | | | | | |
|---|---|---|---|---|---|
| **1368** | A217 | 200fr | multicolored | .85 | .45 |
| **1369** | A217 | 250fr | multicolored | 1.10 | .60 |
| **1370** | A217 | 300fr | multicolored | 1.40 | .70 |
| **1371** | A217 | 400fr | multicolored | 2.00 | .95 |
| **1372** | A217 | 450fr | multicolored | 2.25 | 1.00 |
| **1373** | A217 | 500fr | multicolored | 2.40 | 1.10 |
| | | | *Nos. 1368-1373 (6)* | 10.00 | 4.80 |

**Souvenir Sheet**

| | | | | | |
|---|---|---|---|---|---|
| **1374** | A217 | 1000fr | multicolored | *5.00* | *2.50* |

No. 1374 contains one 32x40mm stamp.

Orchids
A218

Designs: 200fr, Paphiopedilum millmoore. 250fr, Paphiopedilum ernest read. 300fr, Paphiopedilum harrisianum. 400fr, Paphiopedilum gaudianum. 450fr, Paphiopedilum papa röhl. 500fr, Paphiopedilum sea cliffl.
1000fr, Paphiopedilum gowenanum.

**1997, Mar. 3 Litho. *Perf. 12½***

| | | | | | |
|---|---|---|---|---|---|
| **1375** | A218 | 200fr | multicolored | .90 | .50 |
| **1376** | A218 | 250fr | multicolored | 1.10 | .60 |
| **1377** | A218 | 300fr | multicolored | 1.25 | .65 |
| **1378** | A218 | 400fr | multicolored | 1.75 | .90 |
| **1379** | A218 | 450fr | multicolored | 2.25 | 1.00 |
| **1380** | A218 | 500fr | multicolored | 2.50 | 1.10 |
| | | | *Nos. 1375-1380 (6)* | 9.75 | 4.75 |

**Souvenir Sheet**

| | | | | | |
|---|---|---|---|---|---|
| **1381** | A218 | 1000fr | multicolored | 5.00 | 2.50 |

No. 1381 contains one 32x40mm stamp.

1998 World Cup Soccer Championships, France — A219

Various soccer plays.

**1997, Jan. 15**

| | | | | | |
|---|---|---|---|---|---|
| **1382** | A219 | 200fr | multi, vert. | .90 | .50 |
| **1383** | A219 | 250fr | multi, vert. | 1.10 | .60 |
| **1384** | A219 | 300fr | multi, vert. | 1.25 | .65 |
| **1385** | A219 | 400fr | multicolored | 1.75 | .90 |
| **1386** | A219 | 450fr | multicolored | 2.25 | 1.00 |
| **1387** | A219 | 500fr | multicolored | 2.50 | 1.10 |
| | | | *Nos. 1382-1387 (6)* | 9.75 | 4.75 |

**Souvenir Sheet**

| | | | | | |
|---|---|---|---|---|---|
| **1388** | A219 | 1000fr | Goalie at net | 5.00 | 2.50 |

No. 1388 contains one 32x40mm stamp.

Wild
Animals
A220

Designs: 200fr, Giraffa camelopardalis. 250fr, Cerothoterium simun, vert. 300fr, Phacochoerus aethiopicus. 400fr, Acinonyx jubatus. 450fr, Loxodonta africana, vert. 500fr, Choeropsis liberiensis.
1000fr, Okapia johnstoni.

**1997, Apr. 15 Litho. *Perf. 12½***

| | | | | | |
|---|---|---|---|---|---|
| **1389** | A220 | 200fr | multicolored | .65 | .45 |
| **1390** | A220 | 250fr | multicolored | .85 | .55 |
| **1391** | A220 | 300fr | multicolored | 1.00 | .75 |
| **1392** | A220 | 400fr | multicolored | 1.35 | .95 |
| **1393** | A220 | 450fr | multicolored | 1.45 | 1.00 |
| **1394** | A220 | 500fr | multicolored | 1.75 | 1.25 |
| | | | *Nos. 1389-1394 (6)* | 7.05 | 4.95 |

**Souvenir Sheet**

| | | | | | |
|---|---|---|---|---|---|
| **1395** | A220 | 1000fr | multicolored | *10.00* | *4.00* |

19th Century Warships — A221

Designs: 200fr, Captain, England, 1870. 250fr, Konig Wilhelm, Germany, 1869. 300fr, Téméraire, England, 1877. 400fr, Mouillage, Italy, 1866. 450fr, Inflexible, England, 1881. 500fr, Magenta, France, 1862.
1000fr, Redoutable, France, 1878.

**1997, May 20 Litho. *Perf. 12½***

| | | | | | |
|---|---|---|---|---|---|
| **1396** | A221 | 200fr | multicolored | .65 | .45 |
| **1397** | A221 | 250fr | multicolored | .75 | .55 |
| **1398** | A221 | 300fr | multicolored | 1.00 | .75 |
| **1399** | A221 | 400fr | multicolored | 1.35 | .95 |
| **1400** | A221 | 450fr | multicolored | 1.45 | 1.00 |
| **1401** | A221 | 500fr | multicolored | 1.75 | 1.10 |
| | | | *Nos. 1396-1401 (6)* | 6.95 | 4.80 |

**Souvenir Sheet**

| | | | | | |
|---|---|---|---|---|---|
| **1402** | A221 | 1000fr | multicolored | 3.50 | 2.50 |

No. 1402 contains one 32x40mm stamp.

Fish
A222

Designs: 200fr, Siganus trispilos. 250fr, Scarus niger. 300fr, Choerodon fasciata. 400fr, Naso lituratus. 450fr, Hypoplectrus gemma. 500fr, Acanthurus achilles.
1000fr, Zebrasoma flavescens.

**1997, June 15 Litho. *Perf. 13***

| | | | | | |
|---|---|---|---|---|---|
| **1403** | A222 | 200fr | multicolored | .35 | .25 |
| **1404** | A222 | 250fr | multicolored | .80 | .50 |
| **1405** | A222 | 300fr | multicolored | 1.00 | .60 |
| **1406** | A222 | 400fr | multicolored | 1.50 | .80 |
| **1407** | A222 | 450fr | multicolored | 1.75 | .90 |
| **1408** | A222 | 500fr | multicolored | 1.75 | .95 |
| | | | *Nos. 1403-1408 (6)* | 7.15 | 4.00 |

**Souvenir Sheet**

***Perf. 12½***

| | | | | | |
|---|---|---|---|---|---|
| **1409** | A222 | 1000fr | multicolored | 3.50 | 2.50 |

No. 1409 contains one 40x32mm stamp.

Chess Pieces
A222a

200fr, Thailand, 14th cent. 250fr, China, 1930. 300fr, Portugal, 1920. 400fr, Germany. 450fr, Russia. 500fr, Pieces by Max Ernst.
1000fr, France, 18th cent.

**1997, Oct. 20 Litho. *Perf. 13***

| | | | | | |
|---|---|---|---|---|---|
| **1409A** | A222a | 200fr | multi | .65 | .45 |
| **1409B** | A222a | 250fr | multi | .75 | .55 |
| **1409C** | A222a | 300fr | multi | 1.00 | .70 |
| **1409D** | A222a | 400fr | multi | 1.25 | .90 |
| **1409E** | A222a | 450fr | multi | 1.50 | 1.00 |
| **1409F** | A222a | 500fr | multi | 1.75 | 1.10 |
| | | | *Nos. 1409A-1409F (6)* | 6.90 | 4.70 |

**Souvenir Sheet**

***Perf. 12½***

| | | | | | |
|---|---|---|---|---|---|
| **1409G** | A222a | 1000fr | multi | 3.50 | 2.75 |

No. 1409G contains one 32x40mm stamp.

Dogs
A223

**1997, Nov. 10 Litho. *Perf. 12½***

**Stamp plus Label**

| | | | | | |
|---|---|---|---|---|---|
| **1410** | A223 | 200fr | Siberian husky | .70 | .35 |
| **1411** | A223 | 250fr | Dachshund | .85 | .45 |
| **1412** | A223 | 300fr | Boston terrier | 1.00 | .50 |
| **1413** | A223 | 400fr | Basset hound | 1.40 | .70 |

**1414** A223 450fr Dalmatian 1.50 .75
**1415** A223 500fr Rottweiler 1.70 .85
*Nos. 1410-1415 (6)* 7.15 3.60

### Souvenir Sheet

**1416** A223 1000fr Golden retriever 5.50 2.75

Nos. 1410-1415 are each printed with se-tenant label.

Prehistoric Animals — A224

200fr, Dilophosaurus. 250fr, Psittacosaurus. 300fr, Dromiceiomimus. 400fr, Stenonychosaurus. 450fr, Opisthocoelicaudia. 500fr, Ornitholestes.
1000fr, Anchiceratops.

**1997 Litho. *Perf. 12½***

**1417** A224 200fr multi .65 .40
**1418** A224 250fr multi, vert. .80 .50
**1419** A224 300fr multi 1.00 .55
**1420** A224 400fr multi, vert. 1.35 .75
**1421** A224 450fr multi 1.45 .80
**1422** A224 500fr multi 1.75 .90
*Nos. 1417-1422 (6)* 7.00 3.90

### Souvenir Sheet

**1423** A224 1000fr multicolored 4.00 2.10

No. 1423 contains one 40x32mm stamp.

UNICEF — A224a

Design: 200fr, Children at school, horiz. 300fr, Baby receiving inoculation, horiz. 750fr, Mother nursing child. 1500fr, Women reading, horiz.

**1997 Litho. *Perf. 13¼***

**1423A** A224a 200fr multi — —
**1423B** A224a 300fr multi — —
**1423C** A224a 750fr multi — —
**1423D** A224a 1500frmulti — —

Butterflies — A225

200fr, Eueides cleobaea. 250fr, Danaus cleophile. 300fr, Dryas julia. 400fr, Dismorphia cubana. 450fr, Pyrrhocalles antiga. 500fr, Phoebis orbis.
1000fr, Morpho adonis.

**1998**

**1424** A225 200fr multicolored .75 .40
**1425** A225 250fr multicolored .90 .50
**1426** A225 300fr multicolored 1.10 .55
**1427** A225 400fr multicolored 1.50 .75
**1428** A225 450fr multicolored 1.60 .80
**1429** A225 500fr multicolored 1.90 .90
*Nos. 1424-1429 (6)* 7.75 3.90

### Souvenir Sheet

**1430** A225 1000fr multicolored 4.25 2.10

No. 1430 contains one 40x32mm stamp.

Environmental Protection Week A225a

Mount Nimba and frame in: 200fr, Brown. 300fr, Blue. 750fr, Green.

**1998 Litho. *Perf. 13¼x13½***

**1430A-1430C** A225a Set of 3 — —

Domestic Cats — A226

200fr, English shorthair bicolor. 250fr, Scottish fold. 300fr, Birman. 400fr, American coarse hair. 450fr, Snowshoe. 500fr, Maine coon.
1000fr, Malaysian.

**1998 Litho. *Perf. 12½***

**1431** A226 200fr multicolored .65 .30
**1432** A226 250fr multicolored 1.00 .45
**1433** A226 300fr multicolored 1.10 .60
**1434** A226 400fr multicolored 1.50 .75
**1435** A226 450fr multicolored 1.75 .90
**1436** A226 500fr multicolored 2.00 1.00
*Nos. 1431-1436 (6)* 8.00 4.00

### Souvenir Sheet
***Perf. 13***

**1437** A226 1000fr multicolored 4.25 2.10

No. 1437 contains one 32x40mm stamp.

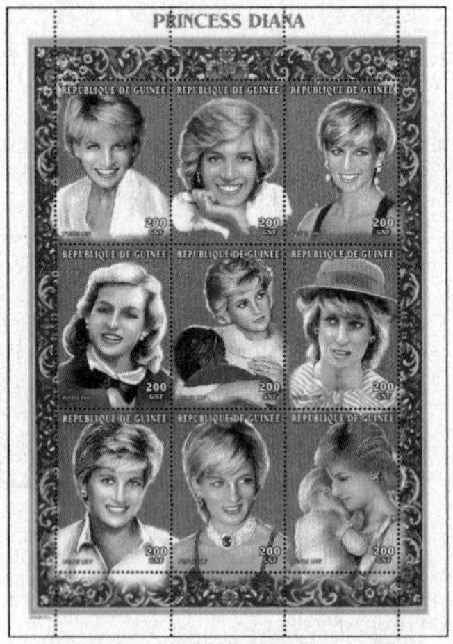


Diana, Princess of Wales (1961-97) — A227

Various portraits.

**1998 Litho. *Perf. 13½***

### Sheets of 9

**1438** A227 200fr #a.-i. 8.00 4.00
**1439** A227 300fr #a.-i 12.00 6.00
**1440** A227 750fr #a.-i. 30.00 15.00

### Souvenir Sheets

**1441** A227 1500fr multicolored 10.00 5.00
**1442** A227 2000fr multicolored 10.00 5.00

Dated 1997.

1998 World Cup Soccer Championships, France — A228

Various soccer plays.

**1998 Litho. *Perf. 12½***

**1443** A228 200fr multi, vert. .75 .40
**1444** A228 250fr multi, vert. .90 .50
**1445** A228 300fr multi, vert. 1.10 .55
**1446** A228 400fr multi, vert. 1.50 .75
**1447** A228 450fr multi 1.60 .80
**1448** A228 500fr multi 1.90 .90
*Nos. 1443-1448 (6)* 7.75 3.90

### Souvenir Sheet
***Perf. 13***

**1449** A228 1000fr multi 5.50 2.75

No. 1449 contains one 32x40mm stamp.

Old Germanic Military Uniforms A228a

Designs: 200fr, Officer, Von Witerfeldt's Regiment. 250fr, Non-commissioned officer, Von Kanitz's Regiment. 300fr, Private, Prince Franz von Anhalt-Dessau's Regiment. 400fr, Private, Von Kalnein's Regiment. 450fr, Grenadier, Duke Ferdinand of Brunswick's Regiment. 500fr, Musician, Rekow's Guards Battalion.
1000fr, Pioneer.

**1997, Aug. 17 Litho. *Perf. 12½***

**1449A-1449F** A228a Set of 6 8.00 5.00

### Souvenir Sheet

**1449G** A228a 1000fr multi 4.00 2.25

No. 1449G contains one 32x40mm stamp.

Steam Locomotives — A229

200fr, Baldwin Locomotive Works, 0-4-2. 250fr, American Locomotive Co., 0-6-0. 300fr, Vulcan Iron Works, 0-6-0. 400fr, Baldwin Locomotive Works, 0-6-0. 450fr, H.K. Porter Co., 0-6-0. 500fr, Vulcan Iron Works, 0-6-0, diff.
1000fr, Baldwin Locomotive Works, 0-6-0, diff.

**1997, Sept. 10 Litho. *Perf. 12½***

**1450-1455** A229 Set of 6 8.00 4.75

### Souvenir Sheet

**1456** A229 1000fr multicolored 6.00 3.50

No. 1456 contains one 40x32mm stamp.

Nectophrynoides Occidentalis — A230

Color of border: 200fr, green. 300fr, blue. 750fr, pale rose.

**1998 *Perf. 13½***

**1457-1459** A230 Set of 3 5.50 2.75

Intl. Year of the Ocean A231

Marine life — #1460: a, Physeter macrocephalus, neophova cinerea. b, Melanogrammus aeglefinus. c, Delphinapterus leucas. d, Megaptera novaengliae. e, Notorhynchus cependianus. f, Manta birostris. g, Delphinaterusleucas, macrozoarces americanus. h, Physalia physalis, pollachius virens. i, Manta birostris. j, Odontapis taurus. k, Thalassoma ruppelli, octopus vulgaris. l, Sebestes marinus.
1500fr, Megaptera novaengliae, diff.

**1998**

**1460** A231 200fr Sheet of 12, #a.-l. 11.00 11.00

### Souvenir Sheet

**1461** A231 1500fr multicolored 9.00 4.25

Antique Cars A232

200fr, 1932 Chrysler, 8 cylinders, US. 300fr, 1907 Napier, 60HP, England. 450fr, 1903 Mercedes, 60HP, Germany. 750fr, 1925 Fiat 509, Italy.
No. 1466: a, 1929 Alfa Romeo 6C 1750 Zagato, Italy. b, 1932 Hispano-Suiza Type 68, Spain. c, 1931 Horsch V12, Germany. d, 1909 Rolland Pilain, 16hp, France. e, 1920 McLaughlin, Canada. f, 1930 Walter 6B, Czechoslovakia.
No. 1467: a, 1914 Fischer SS, Switzerland. b, 1922 Excelsior Adex C, Belgium. c, 1912 Pilain Torpedo, France. d, 1932 Franklin, 6 cylinders, US. e, 1912 Abadal 18/24hp, Spain. f, 1923 Alvis 12/50, England.
Each 1500fr: No. 1468, 1925 Rolls Royce Phantom 1, England. No. 1468A, 1932 Ford V8, US.

**1998, Aug. 21**

**1462-1465** A232 Set of 4 8.50 4.25

### Sheets of 6

**1466** A232 450fr #a.-f. 13.00 6.50
**1467** A232 750fr #a.-f. 24.00 11.50

### Souvenir Sheets

**1468-1468A** A232 Set of 2 18.00 8.50

Nos. 1468-1468A each contain one 56x42mm stamp.

Greenpeace — A233

Designs: a, Albatross looking left. b, Albatross in flight. c, Stern of Greenpeace ship, helicopter. d, Bow of Greenpeace ship. e, Albatross nesting. f, Albatross looking right.
2000fr, Albatross with chick.

**1998 Litho. *Perf. 13½***

**1469** A233 450fr Sheet of 6, #a.-f. 10.00 8.00

**Souvenir Sheet**

**1470** A233 2000fr multicolored 9.50 4.75

No. 1470 contains one 40x46mm stamp.

Endangered Species — A234

Designs, vert: 200fr, Lynx pardellus. 300fr, Lepilemur mustelinus. 450fr, Canis rufus. 750fr, Bison bonasus.

No. 1475: a, Leopard. b, Civet (f). c, Bird (d). d, Hawk. e, Rhinoceros, impala. f, Okapi (e, h, i). g, Lion. h, Chimpanzee. i, Gorilla. j, Bird (long, curved beak). k, Hippopotamus (l). l, Antelope (h).

No. 1476: a, Falco pereginus. b, Acinonyx jubatus. c, Antilocapre americana. d, Mustela nigripes. e, Ursus maritimus. f, Rhinoceros unicornis.

No. 1477: a, Gymnobelideus leadbeater. b, Felis concolor. c, Felis pardalis. d, Panthera pardus. e, Bufo hemiophyrs. f, Mustela rutorius.

Each 1500fr: No. 1478, Muscardinus avellanarius. No. 1479, Aepyceros melampus, vert. No. 1480, Panthera uncia.

**1998, Sept. 8**

**1471-1474** A234 Set of 4 9.00 4.50

**Sheets of 12 & 6**

**1475** A234 200fr #a.-l. 10.00 5.00
**1476** A234 450fr #a.-f. 12.00 5.75
**1477** A234 750fr #a.-f. 18.00 9.00

**Souvenir Sheets**

**1478-1480** A234 Set of 3 24.00 12.00

**Sheets of 8**

Locomotives of the World — A235

No. 1481: a, Sir Nigel Gresley, England. b, Switzerland. c, Canada. d, EMU 102-6 Tobu Railway Spacia, Japan. e, Krauss Maffei V200, Germany. f, IC 580 Portugal. g, Amtrak No. 5, US. h, TGV, France.

No. 1482: a, Nippon Pacific No. 82, Middle East. b, Russia. c, Freight train, Albania. d, Dart No. 8319, Ireland. e, No. 141-F-177, France. f, EMU No. 69625, Norway. g, Bo-Bo, New Zealand. h, Azusa, Japan.

No. 1483: a, Syrian Railways 2-8-0, Iraq. b, The Irish Mail, England. c, Four car EMU, Italy. d, Sprinter, England. e, Van Golu Express, Turkey. f, No. 11.2110, Norway. g, Two-car EMU, New Zealand. h, Grey Mouse, France.

No. 1484: a, The Flying Scotman, United Kingdom. b, National Railways, Japan. c, North Africa. d, F-40M Winnebago, US. e, Federal Railways Class 10, three cylinder 4-6-2, Germany. f, DX5500, New Zealand. g, CIE, Ireland. h, Intercity class 43, England.

Each 1500fr: No. 1485, D2157, New Zealand. No. 1486, 140.7410, German Railways. No. 1487, JR Shinkansen 221-204, Japan. No. 1488, Egyptian Railways, Bo-Bo.

**1998, Oct. 30**

**1481** A235 200fr #a.-h. 8.00 3.75
**1482** A235 300fr #a.-h. 12.00 5.75
**1483** A235 450fr #a.-h. 16.00 7.75
**1484** A235 750fr #a.-h. 24.00 12.00

**Souvenir Sheets**

**1485-1488** A235 Set of 4 30.00 15.00

**Sheets of 8 & 6**

Aircraft — A236

Amphibians & flying boats — #1489: a, Boeing Model 1, 1916. b, Grumman G-21 Goose, 1937. c, Latecoere 631, 1942. d, Cessna Model 205. e, Sikorsky S-42, 1934. f, Boeing Model 314 Clipper. g, De Havilland Canada DHC-2 Beaver, 1947. h, Lake Buccaneer, 1979.

Balloons and Dirigibles — #1490: a, Henri Giffard, 1852. b, Santos-Dumont "Baladeuse," 1903. c, Zeppelin L37. d, R101, 1930. e, Santos-Dumont, 1898. f, Baldwin, 1908. g, Norge, 1926. h, Hindenburg, 1936.

Helicopters — #1491: a, Sikorsky VS-300, 1940. b, Sikorsky S-61, 1957. c, Bell Long Ranger, 1966. d, Dauphin SA 365, 1972. e, Bell 47, 1946. f, Boeing Vertol 243LR, 1958. g, Aerospatial SA 315 Blama. h, Bell Model 222, 1981.

Spacecraft — #1492: a, Mercury Capsule, 1961. b, Gemini 8, 1966. c, Apollo Lunar Module, 1968. d, Soviet Vostok, 1961. e, Apollo Command Module, 1968. f, Soviet Soyuz, 1975.

Each 1500fr: No. 1493, Cessna 208 Caravan, 1980. No. 1494, Goodyear Blimp. No. 1495, Miles Mi-26, 1983. No. 1496, Space Shuttle Columbia, 1981.

**1998, Oct. 30**

**1489** A236 200fr #a.-h. 9.00 4.25
**1490** A236 300fr #a.-h. 13.00 6.25
**1491** A236 450fr #a.-h. 18.00 9.00
**1492** A236 750fr #a.-f. 22.50 11.00

**Souvenir Sheets**

**1493-1496** A236 Set of 4 20.00 10.00

No. 1489a incorrectly inscribed "1961."

Dinosaurs — A237

No. 1497: a, Dicraeosaurus. b, Parasaurolophus. c, Sauronithoides. d, Dilophosaurus. e, Titanosaurus, bagaceratops. f, Iguanodon. g, Tenontosaurus. h, Dryosaurus. i, Ceratosaurus.

1500fr, Yangchuanosaurus, brachiosaurus.

**1998 Litho. *Perf. 13½***

**1497** A237 750fr Sheet of 9, #a.-i. 27.50 13.50

**Souvenir Sheet**

**1498** A237 1500fr multicolored 6.00 3.00

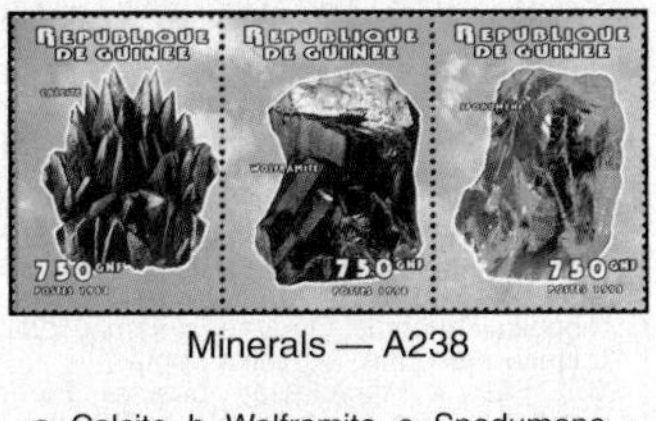


Minerals — A238

a, Calcite. b, Wolframite. c, Spodumene.

#1500D: e, Psilomelane. f, Heterosite. g, Columbo-tantalite.

**1998 Litho. *Perf. 13½***

**Strip of 3**

**1499** A238 750fr Green background, #a.-c. 10.50 5.25

**Souvenir Sheets of 3**

**1500** A238 750fr Gray blue background, #a.-c. 10.50 5.25
**1500D** A238 1500fr #e-g 21.00 21.00

Sailing Ships — A239

No. 1501, each 450fr: a, "Theseus." b, "Euphrates." c, Phoenician War Galley. d, Chinese Junk.

No. 1502, each 450fr: a, "Juan Sebastian." b, "Santa Maria." c, Frigate. d, Madurese Jukung rig.

No. 1503, vert, each 750fr: a, Windjammer, "Wavertree." b, British frigate, "Rose." c, Tromp's flagship, "Golden Leeuw." d, Danish Timber Barque.

No. 1504, vert, each 750fr: a, Kraeck. b, Clipper ship, "Golden State." c, English ship, "Resolution." d, "Eagle."

Each 1500fr: No. 1505, British barque, "Garthpool." No. 1506, HMS Victory.

**1998, Nov. 10 *Perf. 14***

**Sheets of 4, #a.-d.**

**1501-1502** A239 Set of 2 16.00 7.75
**1503-1504** A239 Set of 2 30.00 15.00

**Souvenir Sheets**

**1505-1506** A239 Set of 2 15.00 15.00

Novotel Hotel, Conakry — A239a

**1998 Litho. *Perf. 13x13½***

**1506A** A239a 200fr multi
**1506B** A239a 750fr multi — —

The editors suspect that additional stamps may have been issued in this set and would like to examine any examples. Numbers may change.

Modern Guinean Arts

A239b

A239c

A239d

A239e

A239f

A239g

A239h

A239i

**1998, Dec. 8 Litho. *Perf. 13¼x13***

**1506D** A239b 750fr Dance — —
**1506E** A239c 750fr Painting — —
**1506F** A239d 750fr Ceramics — —
**1506G** A239e 750fr Sculpture — —
**1506H** A239f 750fr Sculpture — —
**1506I** A239g 750fr Dance — —
**1506J** A239h 750fr Painting — —
**1506K** A239i 750fr Painting — —

Horses A240

Designs: 150fr, Trotteur Russe. 200fr, Brabant. 300fr, Camargue. No. 1510, 450fr, Unidentified breed. No. 1511, 450fr, Dales pony. No. 1512, 750fr, Fjord.

No. 1513, vert.: a, Kabardin. b, Shire. c, Arabian. d, Mustang. e, Quarter horse. f, Appaloosa.

No. 1514, vert.: a, Thoroughbred. b, Lipizaner. c, Belgian. d, Palomino. e, Haflinger. f, Fjord, diff.

Each 1500fr: No. 1515, Mustang, diff. No. 1516, Thorougbred colt.

**1999, May 1 Litho. *Perf. 14***

**1507-1512** A240 Set of 6 11.00 11.00

**Sheets of 6**

**1513** A240 450fr #a.-f. 12.00 12.00
**1514** A240 750fr #a.-f. 21.00 21.00

**Souvenir Sheets**

**1515-1516** A240 Set of 2 17.00 17.00

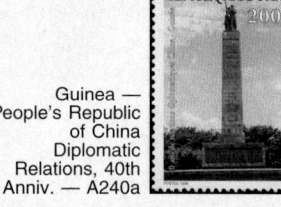

Guinea — People's Republic of China Diplomatic Relations, 40th Anniv. — A240a

Designs: 200fr, Shown. 300fr, Building with flat roof, horiz. 750fr, Building with slanted roof, horiz.

**1999 Litho.** ***Perf. 13¼x13***

**1516A** A240a 200fr multi — —
**1516B** A240a 300fr multi — —
**1516C** A240a 750fr multi — —

Dogs A241

Designs: 200fr, Newfoundland. No. 1518, 750fr, St. Bernard.

No. 1519, vert.: a, Bulldog. b, Miniature schnauzer. c, Dachshund. d, Beagle. e, Bloodhound. f, Miniature pinscher.

1500fr, Irish setter.

**1999, May 1**

**1517-1518** A241 Set of 2 5.00 5.00

**Sheet of 6**

**1519** A241 750fr #a.-f. 18.00 18.00

**Souvenir Sheet**

**1520** A241 1500fr multi 8.00 8.00

Modern Guinean Sculptures — A241a

Various sculptures.

**1999, Aug. 9 Litho.** ***Perf. 13¼x13***

**1520A** A241a 200fr multi 2.40 2.40
**1520B** A241a 250fr multi 2.40 2.40
**1520C** A241a 300fr multi 2.40 2.40
**1520D** A241a 500fr shown 2.40 2.40
**1520E** A241a 750fr multi 2.40 2.40

PhilexFrance '99.

A242

Dinosaurs & Prehistoric Animals — A243

Designs: 300fr, Ouranosaurus. No. 1522, 450fr, Centrosaurus. No. 1523, 450fr, Dilophosaurus, vert.

No. 1524: a, Cymbospondylus. b, Kronosaurus. c, Ichthyosaurus. d, Eurhinosaurus. e, Stenopterygius. f, Ophthalmosaurus. g, Shonisaurus. h, Temnodontosaurus. i, Mixosaurus.

No. 1525, vert.: a, Eudimorphodon. b, Sordes. c, Dimorphodon. d, Albertosaurus. e, Triceratops. f, Alioramus. g, Mesosaurus. h, Labidosaurus. i, Struthiomimus.

No. 1526: a, Saltosaurus. b, Corythosaurus. c, Protoceratops. d, Baryonyx. e, Pachycephalosaurus. f, Maiasaurus. g, Spinosaurus. h, Lambeosaurus.

2500fr, Elasmosaurus, vert. No. 1528, Tyrannosaurus Rex. No. 1529, Utahraptor. No. 1530, Parasaurolophus, vert.

**1999, Aug. 12**

**1521-1523** A242 Set of 3 5.00 5.00

**Sheets of 9**

**1524** A243 350fr #a.-i. 15.00 15.00
**1525** A243 450fr #a.-i. 18.00 18.00

**Sheet of 8**

**1526** A242 450fr #a.-h 18.00 18.00

**Souvenir Sheets**

**1527** A243 2500fr multi 13.00 13.00
**1528** A243 3000fr multi 13.00 13.00
**1529-1530** A242 3000fr Set of 2 28.00 28.00

No. 1527 contains one 42x56mm stamp. No. 1528 contains one 56x42mm stamp.

Return of Macao to People's Republic of China, Dec. 20, 1999 A244

No. 1531, each 650fr: a, Current view of Nam Van (tall buildings). b, Nam Van in 1850s (hilltop and bay). c, Current view of Largo de Senado. d, Largo de Senado in 1900s.

No. 1532, each 650fr: a, Current view of Nam Van (highway). b, Nam Van in 1850s (buildings at water's edge). c, Current view of Nam Van (boat). d, Nam Van in 1850s (ships).

**1999, Aug. 20** ***Perf. 14¼x14½***

**Sheets of 4, #a.-d.**

**1531-1532** A244 Set of 2 24.00 24.00

China 1999 World Philatelic Exhibition.

Paintings of Zhang Daqian (1899-1983) — A245

No. 1533: a, Ink Lotus. b, Ink Peony. c, Red Cliff Excursion at Night. d, Poetic Landscape. e, Landscape in the Evening. f, Spring Landscape. g, Chatting at Leisure in Mountains. h, Pine Nesting. i, Pine in Thunder. j, Blue and Green Landscape.

No. 1534: a, Landscape. b, Versing in the Landscape.

**1999, Aug. 20 Litho.** ***Perf. 13¼***

**1533** A245 330fr Sheet of 10, #a.-j. 15.00 15.00

**Souvenir Sheet of 2**

***Perf. 13***

**1534** A245 1150fr #a.-b. 4.50 4.50

No. 1534 contains two 51x39mm stamps. China 1999 World Philatelic Exhibition

First French Postage Stamp, 150th Anniv. — A245a

**Litho. with Hologram Applied**

**1999, Sept. 10** ***Perf. 13***

**1534C** A245a 750fr multi *4.75 4.75*

Trains A246

100fr, Diesel TGV, East Germany. No. 1536, 200fr, 1900 horsepower Diesel-electric, Finland. No. 1537, 200fr, Type MLW 3000 horsepower Diesel-electric. No. 1538, 250fr, A-4, Britain. No. 1539, 250fr, Class R 4-6-4. No. 1540, 250fr, Class M, 4-6-2, Tasmania. No. 1541, 450fr, Class 68000 Diesel-electric, France. No. 1542, 450fr, 4-8-4 Daylight Express. No. 1543, 450fr, Electric TGV, Italy. No. 1544, 450fr, Western Class Hydraulic-Diesel.

No. 1545: a, Class 10 3-cylinder 4-6-2. b, SD18 Diesel-electric. c, Hikari Super Express Train, Japan. d, Diesel-electric No. 10000. e, PA-1 Diesel-electric. f, 2500 horsepower experimental gas turbine locomotive.

No. 1546: a, YP Class, India. b, Class 47, Standard Type 4 Diesel-electric. c, DSI Class 2-8-2, Japan. d, Class D-341 Diesel-electric. e, S1 Class 2-6-4. f, 3600 horsepower electric, India.

No. 1547: a, 2000 horsepower GP-20 Diesel-electric. b, Class C-53 3-cylinder, Japan. c, Multiple-unit Diesel, Japan. d, Royal Scot Class 4-6-0. e, Deltic electric prototype. f, W.P. Standard 4-6-2.

No. 1548: 2500fr, Class 40 electric, England.

Each 3000fr: No. 1549, GP-40 Diesel-electric. No. 1550, 9780 horsepower DM-3, Sweden. No. 1551, 1750 horsepower Diesel-electric, Denmark.

**1999, Oct. 25** ***Perf. 14***

**1535-1544** A246 Set of 10 13.00 13.00

**Sheets of 6**

**1545** A246 300fr #a.-f. 8.50 8.50
**1546** A246 450fr #a.-f. 12.00 12.00
**1547** A246 750fr #a.-f. 21.00 21.00

**Souvenir Sheets**

**1548** A246 2500fr multi 11.00 11.00
**1549-1551** A246 Set of 3 40.00 40.00

Mushrooms and Insects — A247

Mushrooms and unidentified insects: No. 1552, 100fr, Lentinellus cochleatus. No. 1553, 100fr, Lactarius blennius. No. 1554, Lactarius sanguifluus. No. 1555, 150fr, Leucocortinarius bulbiger. No. 1556, 300fr, Clitocybe phyllophila. No. 1557, 300fr, Calocybe ionides. No. 1558, 300fr, Lactarius porninsis. No. 1559, 300fr, Cystoderma amianthinum. No. 1560, 300fr, Limacella guttata. No. 1561, 450fr, Suillus placidus. No. 1562, 450fr, Suillus grevillei. No. 1563, 450fr, Suillus luteus. No. 1564, 450fr, Suillus granulatus. No. 1565, 450fr, Pleurotus cornuscopiae. No. 1566, 450fr, Calocybe carnea. No. 1567, 450fr, Panus tigrinus.

Mushrooms and insects — No. 1568: a, Hygrocybe nigreseens, Argynnis paphia. b, Hygrocybe subglobispora, Pterophoridae. c, Oudemansiella mucida, Tettigonia viridissima. d, Amanita rubescens, unidentified insect. e, Amanita muscaria, Oedipoda caerulescens. f, Suillus luteus, Happarchia fagi. g, Coprinus picaceus, Aphantopus hyperantus. h, Gymnopilus junonius, Ourapteryx sambucaria. i, Amanita muscaria, Catocala nupta.

No. 1569: a, Macrolepiota procera, Pieris brassicae. b, Lactarius britannicus, Pyrochroa cocci. c, Cortinarius sanguineus, Tabicina haematodes. d, Amanita muscaria, Sympetrum. e, Aerocomus badius, Issoria lathonia. f, Laccaria amethystea, Sympetrum. g, Paxillus atrotomentosus, Inachis io. h, Armillaria mellea, Chrystoxum cautum. i, Amanita echinocephala, Vanessa atalanta.

Each 2500fr: No. 1570, Lactarius britanticus, Coccinella punctala. No. 1571, Amanita phalloides, Ochlodes venatus. No. 1572, Coprinus atramentarius, unidentified insect.

Each 3000fr: No. 1573, Amanita citrina, unidentified insect. No. 1574, Amanita pantherina, Aperia syringaria.

**1999, Nov. 11**

**1552-1567** A247 Set of 16 24.00 24.00

**Sheets of 9**

**1568** A247 300fr #a.-i. 12.00 12.00
**1569** A247 450fr #a.-i. 18.00 18.00

**Souvenir Sheets**

**1570-1572** A247 Set of 3 35.00 35.00
**1573-1574** A247 Set of 2 24.00 24.00

Birds

A248 A249

Designs: No. 1575, 200fr, Catamblyrhychus diadema. No. 1576, 200fr, Tichodrome. No. 1577, 300fr, Turtle dove. No. 1578, 300fr, Flamingo. No. 1579, 300fr, Duck. No. 1580, 300fr, Woodpecker. No. 1581, 450fr, Warbler. No. 1582, 450fr, Bullfinch.

No. 1583: a, Wild turkey. b, Ring-necked pheasant. c, Gray partridge. d, Woodcock. e, Capercaillie. f, Rock partridge.

No. 1584: a, Cuban hummingbird. b, Rufous-breated hermit. c, Green-throated hummingbird. d, Bee-eater. e, Puerto Rican hummingbird. f, Antillean hummingbird.

No. 1585: a, Gould's finch. b, Oriole. c, Psarismus dalhousiae. d, Woodchat shrike. e, Pitta guajana. f, Neodreponis coruscans.

No. 1586, horiz.: a, Purple-throated Carib. b, Bahamas hummingbird. c, Blue-bearded hummingbird. d, Green hummingbird. e, Jamaican hummingbird. f, Vervaine.

Each 2500fr: No. 1587, Spotted waxwing. No. 1588, Red-banded bee-eater.

Each 2500fr: No. 1589, Bahamas hummingbird, horiz. No. 1590, Antillean crested hummingbird.

No. 1591, 3000fr, Emerald hummingbird.

**1999, Nov. 22**

**1575-1582** A248 Set of 8 10.00 10.00

**Sheets of 6**

**1583** A248 450fr #a.-f. 12.00 12.00
**1584** A249 500fr #a.-f. 15.00 15.00
**1585** A248 600fr #a.-f. 16.00 16.00
**1586** A249 750fr #a.-f. 20.00 20.00

**Souvenir Sheets**

**1587-1588** A248 Set of 2 24.00 24.00
**1589-1590** A249 Set of 2 24.00 24.00
**1591** A249 3000fr multi 14.00 14.00

Butterflies A250

Designs: No. 1592, 300fr, Acraea acerata. No. 1593, 300fr, Charaxes protoclea. No. 1594, 300fr, Charaxes hadrianus. No. 1595, 300fr, Colotis halimede. No. 1596, 300fr, Colotis eucharis. No. 1597, Papilio dardanus.

No. 1598, vert.: a, Papilio charopus. b, Papilio dardanus. c, Acraea zetes. d, Hypolimnas salmacis. e, Cymothoe beckeri. f, Papilio nobilis.

No. 1599, vert.: a, Iolaus lalos. b, Graphium gudenusi. c, Hewitsonia boisduvali. d, Graphium ucalegon. e, Danaus chrysippus. f, Acraea satis.

Each 2500fr: No. 1600, Euxanthe tiberius. No. 1601, Colotis danae.

**1999, Nov. 22**

**1592-1597** A250 Set of 6 7.50 7.50

**Sheets of 6**

**1598** A250 450fr #a.-f. 12.00 12.00
**1599** A250 750fr #a.-f. 20.00 20.00

**Souvenir Sheets**

**1600-1601** A250 Set of 2 24.00 24.00

Wedding of Prince Edward and Sophie Rhys-Jones
A251

No. 1602: a, Edward in blue striped shirt. b, Sophie with scarf. c, Edward looking left. d, Sophie looking right. e, Edward with blue checked shirt. f, Sophie with black blouse.
3000fr, Couple.

**1999, Dec. 6**

**1602** A251 750fr Sheet of 6, #a.-f. 21.00 21.00

**Souvenir Sheet**

**1603** A251 3000fr multi 14.00 14.00

Hokusai Paintings
A252

No. 1604, each 750fr: a, Actor Ichikawa Ebizo. b, Drawings (man with fan). c, Actor Sakata Hangoro. d, Geisha and Madam. e, Drawings (man with sword). f, Kabuki Actor Hanshiro IV.
No. 1605, each 750fr: a, Kintaro and Wild Animals. b, Drawings (man with clasped hands). c, Lady Walking in the Snow. d, Lady and Maiden on an Outing. e, Drawings (man with incense burner). f, Girls at Their Toilette.
Each 3000fr: No. 1606, Sumo Wrestlers. No. 1607, Geisha House and Madam at Leisure with Child.

**1999, Dec. 6** ***Perf. 12¼***

**Sheets of 6, #a.-f.**

**1604-1605** A252 Set of 2 35.00 35.00

**Souvenir Sheets**

**1606-1607** A252 Set of 2 27.50 27.50

Johann Wolfgang von Goethe (1749-1832), German Poet — A253

No. 1608, each 1000fr: a, Mephistopheles tempts Faust with Margaret. b, Goethe and Friedrich von Schiller. c, The witches' kitchen, a potion brewed.
3000fr, Euphorion.

**1999, Dec. 6** ***Perf. 14***

**1608** A253 Sheet of 3, #a.-c. 14.00 14.00

**Souvenir Sheet**

**1609** A253 3000fr multi 14.00 14.00

A254

A255

Space Exploration — A256

Designs: No. 1610, 300fr, Pioneer 10. No. 1611, 300fr, Viking 1.
No. 1612: a, Takao Doi. b, Frank Borman. c, Alan B. Shepard, Jr. d, M. Scott Carpenter. e, Ulf Merbold. f, David R. Scott. g, Mamoru Mohri. h, Gherman Titov. i, Sally K. Ride. j, Walter M. Schirra. k, John L. Swigert, Jr. l, Yuri A. Gagarin.
No. 1613, each 500fr: a, Venus. b, Neptune. c, Jupiter. d, Uranus. e, Saturn. f, Mercury.
No. 1614, each 500fr: a, Mariner 4. b, HL-20. c, Mariner 2. d, Voyager 1. e, Venture Star. f, Phobos.
No. 1615, each 750fr: a, 1961 drawing of lunar ferry. b, 1960 drawing of lunar lander. c, 1959 drawing of lunar lander. d, 1962 drawing of lunar lander. e, 1962 drawing of lunar lander trainer. f, 1961 drawing of lunar lander.
No. 1616, vert, each 750fr: a, Apollo 5. b, Apollo 6, c, Apollo 7. d, Apollo escape test. e, Apollo "Little Joe." f, Apollo 4.
No. 1617, 1500fr, John Glenn.
Each 1500fr: No. 1618, Apollo 11 command module, vert. No. 1619, Collecting moon rocks.
Each 2000fr: No. 1620, Viking, diff. No. 1621, Mars Global Surveyor. No. 1622, Sojourner.

**1999, Dec. 9**

**1610-1611** A254 Set of 2 3.00 3.00

**Sheet of 12, #a.-l.**

**1612** A255 450fr multi 27.50 27.50

**Sheets of 6, #a.-f.**

**1613-1614** A254 Set of 2 24.00 24.00
**1615-1616** A256 Set of 2 40.00 40.00

**Souvenir Sheets**

**1617** A255 1500fr multi 8.00 8.00
**1618-1619** A256 Set of 2 15.00 15.00
**1620-1622** A254 Set of 3 26.50 26.50

Nos. 1620-1622 each contain one 50x37mm stamp.

Queen Mother (b. 1900) — A257

No. 1623: a, In 1934. b, With tiara. c, Lady of the Garter. d, In 1997.
3000fr, With tiara, diff.

**1999, Dec. 6** ***Perf. 14***

**1623** A257 1000fr Sheet of 4, #a.-d., + label 19.00 19.00

**Souvenir Sheet**

***Perf. 13¾***

**1624** A257 3000fr multi 14.00 14.00

No. 1624 contains one 38x50mm stamp.

Cats
A257a

Designs: 300fr, Ragdoll. No. 1626, 400fr, Egyptian Mau.
No. 1627, vert.: a, Tonkinese. b, Korat. c, Siamese. d, British Shorthair. e, Bengal. f, Persian.
1500fr, Calico Shorthair, vert.

**1999** ***Perf. 14***

**1625-1626** A257a Set of 2 3.25 3.25

**Sheet of 6**

**1627** A257a 450fr #a.-f. 12.00 12.00

**Souvenir Sheet**

**1628** A257a 1500fr multi 8.00 8.00

Romance of the Three Kingdoms
A258

No. 1629, each 460fr: a, Archer and four men. b, Two men and tea pot. c, Spear carrier, man, woman. d, Horsemen jousting. e, Four men.
No. 1630, each 460fr: a, Swordsman on white horse. b, Spear carrier on black horse. c, Bed chamber. d, Man being speared. e, At sea.
2000fr, Three men with tea cups.

**1999** ***Perf. 13¼***

**Sheets of 5, #a.-e.**

**1629-1630** A258 Set of 2 20.00 20.00

**Souvenir Sheet**

**1631** A258 2000fr multi 9.00 9.00

No. 1631 contains one 48x58mm stamp.

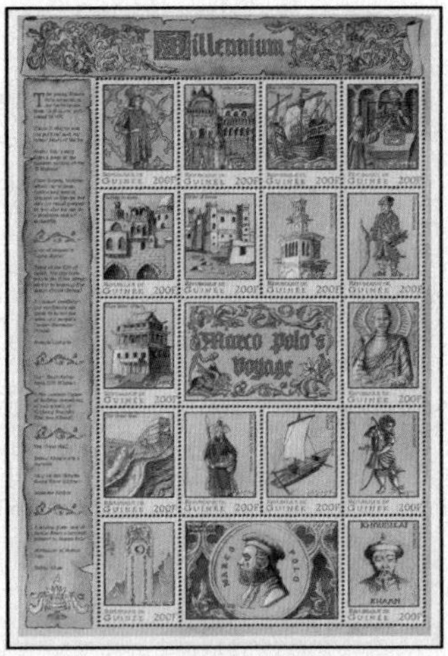


Millennium — A354

No. 1823 — Marco Polo's Voyages: a, Young Marco Polo. b, Piazza San Marco. c, Polo's ship. d, Priest buying incense. e, Houses in Syria. f, Ruins of Saveh. g, Persian ventilator. h, Moncia costume. i, Ulan Bator Abbey. j, Buddha, 5th cent. k, Great Wall of China. l, Warrior of Kublai Khan's Army. m, Ship on the Yangtze. n, Japanese archer. o, Golden plate. p, Medallion of Marco Polo, horiz. (60x40mm). q, Kublai Khan.
No. 1824 — Expansion of Knowledge: a, Election of King Sigismund I of Hungary as Holy Roman Emperor, 1411. b, Filippo Brunelleschi wins architectural contest to build the dome of the Santa Maria de Fiore, 1420. c, Lorenzo Ghiberti sculpts human forms on doors of the Florence Baptistry, 1425. d, Death of Juliana of Norwich, c. 1443. e, Chinese Ming capital moves from Nanjing to Beijing, 1420. f, Europeans begin to use Chinese method of black printing, 1423. g, King Henry V of England defeats French at Battle of Agincourt, 1415. h, Tamerlane defeats Ottomans at Battle of Ankyra, 1402. i, Joan of Arc leads French forces at Siege of Orleans, 1429. j, Korea prospers under rule of King Sejong, 1419. k, Thomas à Kempis writes *The Imitation of Christ,* 1427. l, King Casimir IV of Poland unites Polish Kingdom with Grand Duchy of Lithuania, 1447. m, End of the Great Schism, 1417. n, John Hus burnt at the stake, 1415. o, Medici family dominates the government of Florence, 1434. p, Chaucer completes *Canterbury Tales,* 1400, horiz. (60x40mm). q, Shogun Yoshima Ashikaga begins rule in Japan, 1449.
No. 1825 — Across the Continents: a, Engraving, c. 1598. b, Caribbean warriors. c, Viking ship, 12th cent. d, Ship of Vasco da Gama. e, Detail from Italian engraving. f, Columbus's letter of 1493. g, Kokyrboom tree, h, Megalzina virens. i, Details from a map, Moon between Earth and Sun. j, Details from a map, Earth between Sun and Moon. k, Maori wood carving. l, Astrolabes. m, Frilled lizard (inscribed "Gila monster"). n, White ibises. o, Tahitian utensils. p, Ocean monsters, horiz. (60x40mm). q, Samoan boat.

***Perf. 12¾x12½***

**2000, Feb. 18** **Litho.**

**Sheets of 17, #a-q, + Label**

**1823** A354 200fr multi 16.00 16.00
**1824** A354 250fr multi 21.00 21.00
**1825** A354 300fr multi 24.00 24.00
*Nos. 1823-1825 (3)* 61.00 61.00

New Year 2000 (Year of the Dragon) — A355

No. 1826 — Dragon with background in: a, Red, claws near "Office." b, Green. c, Blue. d, Red, tail near "Office."
2000fr, Light blue.

**2000, Feb. 18** ***Perf. 13¾***

**1826** A355 400fr Sheet of 4, #a-d 7.50 7.50

**Souvenir Sheet**

**1827** A355 2000fr multi 9.50 9.50

No. 1826 contains four 48x32mm stamps.

Miniature Sheet

Vacation Photographs — A356

No. 1828: Various photographs making up a photomosaic of the Titanic.

**2000, Feb. 18**

**1828** A356 750fr Sheet of 8, #a-h 24.00 24.00

2000 Summer Olympics, Sydney — A357

No. 1829: a, Women's discus. b, Javelin. c, Men's discus. d, Shot put. e, Hammer throw.

No. 1830: a, Women's volleyball. b, Water polo. c, Women's beach volleyball. d, Handball. e, Women's soccer.

No. 1831: a, Women's judo. b, Wrestling. c, Men's judo. d, Boxing, pink background. e, Boxing, green background.

No. 1832: a, Women's diving. b, Synchronized swimming. c, Women's swimming. d, Women's sailing. e, Kayaking.

No. 1833: a, Badminton. b, Field hockey. c, Baseball. d, Fencing. e, Weight lifting.

No. 1834: a, Dressage. b, Archery. c, Show jumping. d, Rifle shooting. e, Pistol shooting.

No. 1835: a, Table tennis, two men. b, Table tennis, one man, blue and purple background. c, Table tennis, one man, green and yellow background. d, Women's table tennis. e, Table tennis, four players.

No. 1836: a, Women's tennis, blue background. b, Men's tennis, green background. c, Women's tennis, bister background. d, Men's tennis, gray background. e, Men's tennis, blue background.

No. 1837: a, Women's basketball. b, Men's basketball (Michael Jordan dunking basketball). c, Men's basketball, two players. d, Men's basketball (Jordan dribbling). e, Men's basketball, blue background.

No. 1838: a, Cycling Road Race (Route). b, Cycling Sprint Race (Vitesse). c, Cycling Team Pursuit. d, Cycling Points Race (Kilometre). e, Cycling Time Trial (Contre la montre).

**2000, Nov. 14** ***Perf. 13¼***

**Sheets of 5, #a-e, + Label**

| | | | | | |
|---|---|---|---|---|---|
| **1829** | A357 | 150fr multi | | 3.50 | 3.50 |
| **1830** | A357 | 150fr multi | | 3.50 | 3.50 |
| **1831** | A357 | 200fr multi | | 4.50 | 4.50 |
| **1832** | A357 | 200fr multi | | 4.50 | 4.50 |
| **1833** | A357 | 300fr multi | | 7.00 | 7.00 |
| **1834** | A357 | 300fr multi | | 7.00 | 7.00 |
| **1835** | A357 | 600fr multi | | 13.50 | 13.50 |
| **1836** | A357 | 600fr multi | | 13.50 | 13.50 |
| **1837** | A357 | 750fr multi | | 17.00 | 17.00 |
| **1838** | A357 | 750fr multi | | 17.00 | 17.00 |
| | *Nos. 1829-1838 (10)* | | | 91.00 | 91.00 |

Sports and Chess — A358

No. 1839 — Golf: a, Golfer with purple cap. b, Golfer with white pants. c, Golfer with white cap. d, Golfer with green shirt.

No. 1840 — Soccer: a, Marcel Dessally. b, Zinedine Zidane. c, Youri Djorkaeff. d, Thierry Henry.

No. 1841 — Auto racing: a, Ayrton Senna. b, Mika Hakkinen. c, Alain Prost. d, Michael Schumacher.

No. 1842 — Chess: a, Player with hands on forehead. b, Player with blue jacket. c, Player with gray jacket. d, Female player.

**2000, Nov. 14** **Sheets of 4, #a-d**

| | | | | |
|---|---|---|---|---|
| **1839** | A358 | 450fr multi | 8.00 | 8.00 |
| **1840** | A358 | 450fr multi | 8.00 | 8.00 |
| **1841** | A358 | 750fr multi | 14.00 | 14.00 |
| **1842** | A358 | 750fr multi | 14.00 | 14.00 |
| | *Nos. 1839-1842 (4)* | | 44.00 | 44.00 |

Locomotives — A359

No. 1843, horiz.: a, De Witt Clinton. b, American 220. c, Triplet Mallet. d, Philadelphia & Reading 422 Baldwin. e, Mason Bogie. f, Promontory Point 220 No. 119. g, Mogul. h, Best Friend of Charleston. i, John Bull.

No. 1844, horiz.: a, Union Pacific Bo-Bo-Bo-Bo. b, Bipolar No. 2. c, Burlington Northern-Series SD 40-2 No. 7044. d, Amtrak Metroliner No. 880. e, Rio Grande Western Series F. f, Union Pacific Series DD 40AX. g, Lake Superior & Ishpeming Co-Co 025C No. 2500. h, Chicago, Milwaukee, St. Paul & Pacific Bipolar 3000V No. 4. i, Southern Pacific Krauss-Maffei C-C No. 9006.

No. 1845, horiz.: a, Southern Pacific GM-EMD Series F No. 98. b, Union Pacific M-10001. c, Union Pacific Switcher No. 4466. d, Chesapeake & Ohio Series M No. 500. e, Amtrak Series P32 No. 513. f, Southern Pacific EMD SD 40-2 No. 9368. g, Great Northern Series W-1 No. 5018. h, Grand Canyon 140. i, Pennsylvania Railroad 6100.

No. 1846, horiz.: a, Burlington Northern Santa Fe No. 4326. b, Conrail Series GP EMD No. 8194. c, Kansas City Southern No. 6639. d, Southern Pacific No. 9800. e, Pennsylvania Railroad 661 No. 4835. f, Union Pacific No. 8182. g, Burlington Northern No. 2917. h, Gulf, Mobile & Ohio Railroad Series F. i, Santa Fe No. 627.

No. 1847, horiz.: a, Norfolk Southern No. 6627. b, Grand Trunk No. 6219. c, Soo Line No. 6401. d, Santa Fe BNSF No. 2512. e, Chessie System No. 6035. f, Utah Railway No. 9010. g, Chicago & Northwestern No. 6866. h, Norfolk Southern No. 3328. i, Canadian National No. 4634.

No. 1848, horiz.: a, Canadian Pacific Budd Autorail Diesel No. 9112. b, New York Central 2-Do-2 No. 113. c, British Columbia Railway Series C630 No. 703. d, Chesapeake & Ohio Series GP9 No. 6137. e, Amtrak 661 No. 902. f, Santa Fe GP9 No. 2293. g, Trainmaster Type Co-Co. h, Chicago, Burlington & Quincy Pioneer Zephyr. i, Denver & Rio Grande Western No. 5350.

No. 1849, 2000fr, Tom Thumb, 2-2-0. No. 1850, 2000fr, Norfolk & Western Class J. No. 1851, 2000fr, Royal Gorge CC No. 403. No. 1852, 2000fr, Hudson 4-6-4 No. 490.

**2000, Dec. 7** **Sheets of 9, #a-i**

| | | | | |
|---|---|---|---|---|
| **1843** | A359 | 200fr multi | 5.25 | 5.25 |
| **1844** | A359 | 300fr multi | 8.00 | 8.00 |
| **1845** | A359 | 350fr multi | 10.00 | 10.00 |
| **1846** | A359 | 400fr multi | 11.00 | 11.00 |
| **1847** | A359 | 450fr multi | 12.00 | 12.00 |
| **1848** | A359 | 500fr multi | 14.00 | 14.00 |
| | *Nos. 1843-1848 (6)* | | 60.25 | 60.25 |

**Souvenir Sheets**

| | | | | |
|---|---|---|---|---|
| **1849-1852** | A359 | Set of 4 | 22.50 | 22.50 |

Nos. 1843-1848 each contain nine 51x36mm stamps.

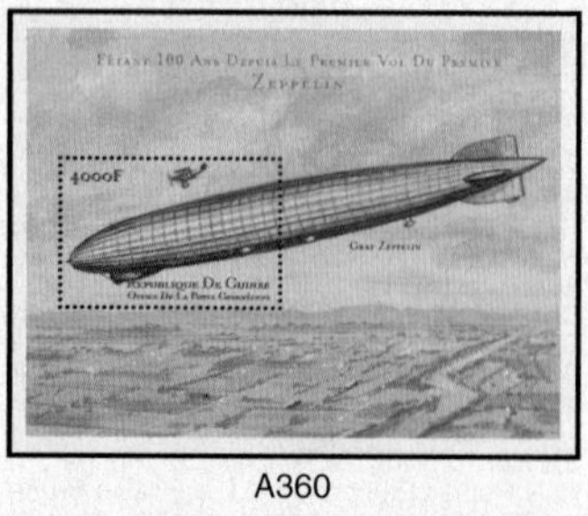

A360

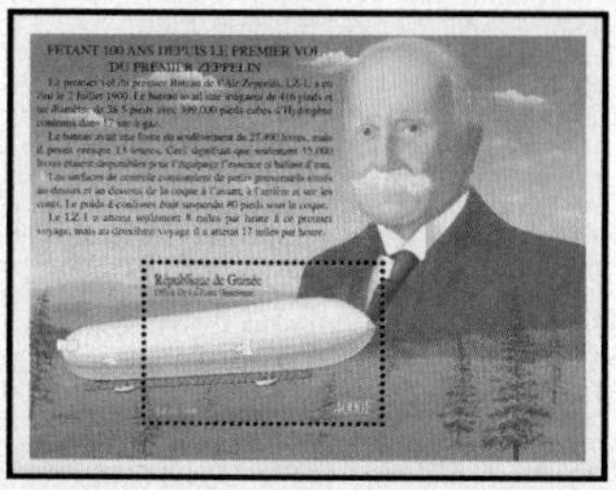

First Zeppelin flight, Cent. — A361

No. 1853: a, Zeppelin LZ-11 Viktoria Luise. b, E. T. Willows. c, Hindenburg. d, Astra-Torres 1. e, Beta. f, Schutte-Lanz SL3.

No. 1854: a, Gross-Basenach M1. b, Schutte-Lanz SL1. c, Parseval PL25. d, Siemens-Schuckert. e, Delta. f, Parseval PL VIII.

No. 1855: a, LZ-9. b, LZ-10 Schwaben. c, LZ-11 Viktoria Luise, diff. d, LZ-127 Graf Zeppelin. e, LZ-129 Hindenburg. f, LZ-130.

No. 1856: a, LZ-1. b, LZ-2. c, LZ-3. d, LZ-4. e, LZ-5. f, LZ-6.

No. 1857, Graf Zeppelin and airplane. No. 1858, LZ-1, diff.

**2000, Dec. 11** ***Perf. 14***

**Sheets of 6, #a-f**

| | | | | |
|---|---|---|---|---|
| **1853** | A360 | 300fr multi | 8.50 | 8.50 |
| **1854** | A360 | 450fr multi | 12.00 | 12.00 |
| **1855** | A361 | 1000fr multi | 27.50 | 27.50 |
| **1856** | A361 | 1000fr multi | 27.50 | 27.50 |
| | *Nos. 1853-1856 (4)* | | 75.50 | 75.50 |

**Souvenir Sheets**

| | | | | |
|---|---|---|---|---|
| **1857** | A360 | 4000fr multi | 20.00 | 20.00 |
| **1858** | A361 | 4000fr multi | 20.00 | 20.00 |

Miniature Sheet

Flowers — A362

No. 1859: Various photographs making up a photomosaic of Queen Mother Elizabeth.

**2000, Dec. 11**

| | | | | |
|---|---|---|---|---|
| **1859** | A362 | 750fr Sheet of 8, #a-h | 20.00 | 20.00 |

Prince William of Wales, 18th Birthday — A363

No. 1860: a, Wearing red tie. b, Wearing black and white checked tie. c, With Prince Harry. d, Wearing blue sweater.

4000fr, Wearing scarf.

**2000, Dec. 11** ***Perf. 14***

| | | | | |
|---|---|---|---|---|
| **1860** | A363 | 1000fr Sheet of 4, #a-d | 18.00 | 18.00 |

**Souvenir Sheet**

***Perf. 13¾***

| | | | | |
|---|---|---|---|---|
| **1861** | A363 | 4000fr multi | 19.00 | 19.00 |

History of Space Exploration — A364

No. 1862, 200fr: a, Discovery of gunpowder. b, Fire arrows. c, Wan Hu's rocket glider. d, Konstantin Tsiolkovsky. e, Telescope of William Herschel. f, Galileo Galilei. g, Nicolaus Copernicus. h, Robert H. Goddard. i, Paper hot air balloons. j, Wernher von Braun. k, Launch of first rocket by Goddard. l, V-1 missile buzz-bomb.

No. 1863, 200fr: a, First American spacewalk by Ed White, Gemini 4. b, First man on the Moon, Apollo 11. c, Space Shuttle Atlantis. d, Voskhod 2. e, Sputnik 1. f, Apollo-Soyuz. g, John Glenn, first American to orbit Earth. h, Valentina Tereshkova, first woman in space. i, Yuri Gagarin, first man in space. j, Apollo 17. k, Robotic lunar explorer. l, Hubble Space Telescope.

No. 1864, 4000fr, Atlas-Centaur launch vehicle. No. 1865, 4000fr, International Space Station.

**2000, Dec. 11** ***Perf. 14***

**Sheets of 12, #a-l**

| | | | | |
|---|---|---|---|---|
| **1862-1863** | A364 | Set of 2 | 17.00 | 17.00 |

**Souvenir Sheets**

| | | | | |
|---|---|---|---|---|
| **1864-1865** | A364 | Set of 2 | 12.00 | 12.00 |

Apollo-Soyuz Mission, 25th Anniv. — A365

No. 1866, 1000fr: a, Saturn IB rocket. b, Apollo 18 command and service modules with docking adapter. c, Apollo 18 Commander Thomas P. Stafford. d, A-2 Soyuz rocket. e, Soyuz 19 spacecraft. f, Soyuz 19 Commander Alexei Leonov.

No. 1867, 1000fr, vert.: a, Lunar Module Eagle, upside-down. b, Lunar Module Eagle, with thrusters firing. c, Apollo 11 command module Columbia. d, Edwin E. Aldrin, Jr. on lunar module ladder. e, Apollo 11 Saturn V rocket. f, Re-entry of Apollo 11 capsule.

4000fr, Aldrin and lunar module on Moon.

**2000, Dec. 11** **Sheets of 6, #a-f**

| | | | | |
|---|---|---|---|---|
| **1866-1867** | A365 | Set of 2 | 42.50 | 42.50 |

**Souvenir Sheet**

| | | | | |
|---|---|---|---|---|
| **1868** | A365 | 4000fr multi | 6.00 | 6.00 |

Marine Life — A367

Designs: No. 1873, 400fr, Coral grouper. No. 1874, 400fr, Candy cane sea star. 450fr, Hippocampus kuda.

No. 1876, 750fr: a, Chromis caerulea. b, Brittle star. c, Calloplesiops altivelis. d, Ewa blenny. e, Coral polyp. f, Butterflyfish.

No. 1877, 750fr: a, Chelonia mydas. b, Ptereleotris evides. c, Halichoeres iridis. d, Sea fan. e, Florometra serratissima. f, Gramma loreto.

No. 1878, 5000fr, Clownfish. No. 1879, 5000fr, Bigeye scad, horiz.

***Perf. 13½x13¼, 13¼x13½***

**2001, Feb. 28**

**1873-1875** A367 Set of 3 5.50 5.50

**Sheets of 6, #a-f**

**1876-1877** A367 Set of 2 40.00 40.00

**Souvenir Sheets**

**1878-1879** A367 Set of 2 42.50 42.50

Marine Life A368

Designs: No. 1880, 400fr, Chaetodon semilarvatus. No. 1881, 400fr, Amphiprion ocellarus. No. 1882, 450fr, Gramma malecara. No. 1883, 450fr, Amphiprion bicinctuc.

No. 1884, 200fr: a, Diodon hystrix. b, Synchiropus splendidos. c, Lactoria cornuta. d, Canthigaster solandri. e, Gymnothorax tesselatus. f, Gramma loreto.

No. 1885, 200fr: a, Synchiropus picturatus. b, Pygoplytes diacanthus. c, Pomocanthus imperator. d, Holocanthus ciliaris. e, Phinecanthus aculeatus. f, Lienardella fasciatus.

No. 1886, 5000fr, Pterois antennata, vert. No. 1887, 5000fr, Hippocampus kuda, vert.

***Perf. 13¼x13½, 13½x13¼***

**2001, Feb. 28**

**1880-1883** A368 Set of 4 6.00 6.00

**Sheets of 6, #a-f**

**1884-1885** A368 Set of 2 9.00 9.00

**Souvenir Sheets**

**1886-1887** A368 Set of 2 35.00 35.00

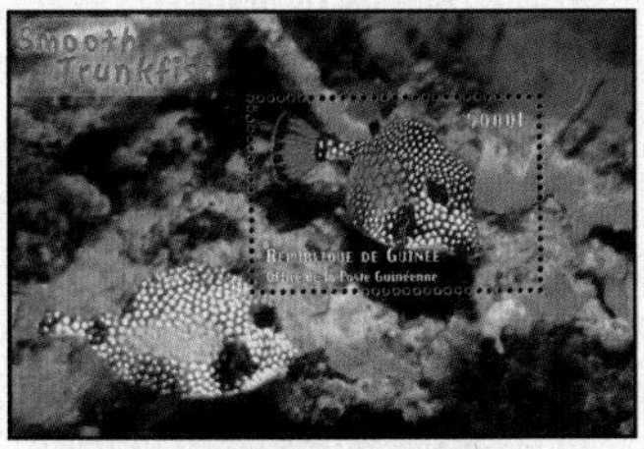

Marine Life — A369

No. 1888, 1000fr: a, Jackknife fish. b, Requiem shark. c, Great white shark (Grand blanc). d, Holocanthus ciliaris. e, Brain coral. f, Bluehead wrasse.

No. 1889, 1000fr: a, Sergeant major. b, Bottlenose dolphin. c, Swordfish. d, Sea horse. e, Slate pencil urchin. f, Gold-spotted snake eel.

No. 1890, 1000fr: a, Great white shark (Grand requin blanc). b, Baird's beaked whale. c, Butterflyfish. d, Turtle. e, Solenostomus paradoxus. f, Australian pineapple fish.

No. 1891, 1000fr: a, Hawksbill turtle. b, Killer whale. c, Manta ray. d, Filefish. e, Graysby. f, Striped-eel catfish.

No. 1892, 5000fr, Smooth trunkfish. No. 1879, 5000fr, Dolphin.

**2001, Feb. 28** ***Perf. 13¼x13½***

**Sheets of 6, #a-f**

**1888-1891** A369 Set of 4 80.00 80.00

**Souvenir Sheets**

**1892-1893** A369 Set of 2 35.00 35.00

Flora and Fauna — A370

No. 1894, 300fr — Bears: a, Spectacled bear. b, Giant panda. c, Silver bear. d, Cannelle (Pyreneean bear). e, Syrian bear. f, Grizzly bear.

No. 1895, 300fr — Primates: a, Howler monkey. b, Macaque. c, Drill. d, Yellow baboon. e, Anubis baboon. f, Gelada.

No. 1896, 300fr, vert. — Lemurs: a, Crowned lemur (couronné). b, Black lemur (macao). c, Albifrons lemur. d, Mongoz lemur. e, Sanfordi lemur. f, Fulvus lemur.

No. 1897, 300fr, vert. — Fish: a, Sebastes nigrocinctus. b, Lampris guttatus. c, Cyclopterus lumpus. d, Carnegiella strigata. e, Parosphromenus dreissneri. f, Syncniropus splendidus.

No. 1898, 300fr, vert. — Flowers: a, Peony (Pivoine des rocheuses). b, Hypericum richeri. c, Flamboyant. d, Bird of paradise (oiseau du paradis). e, Hesperantha petitiana. f, Moraea neopavonia.

No. 1899, 750fr — Lemurs: a, Lepilemur leucopus. b, Wooly avahi (avahi laineux). c, Black lemur (macao). d, Verreaux's sifaka (Propithecus verreauxi deckeni). e, Phaner. f, Verreaux's sifaka (Propithecus verrauxi majori).

No. 1900, 750fr — Flowers: a, Thunia alba. b, Eulophia guineensis. c, Polystacha bella. d, Oeceoclades maculata. e, Serapias cordigera. f, Angraecum distichum.

No. 1901, 750fr — Birds: a, Black cockatoo. b, Rosalbin cockatoo. c, Leadbetter's cockatoo. d, Goffin's cockatoo. e, Gray parrot. f, Senegal parrot.

No. 1902, 750fr, vert. — Owls: a, Hibou des marais. b, Hibou petit duc. c, Grand duc American. d, Chouette chevechette perlée. e, Hibou grand duc. f, Harphang des neiges.

No. 1903, 750fr, vert. — Insects: a, Giant Himalayan bee. b, Phyllium. c, Magicicada septemdecim. d, Petasida ephippigera. e, Graphosoma semipunctatum. f, Honeybee.

**2001, Mar. 28** **Litho.** ***Perf. 13¼***

**Sheets of 6, #a-f**

**1894-1903** A370 Set of 10 125.00 125.00

Guinean Railways Locomotive A371

Design: 200fr, Front view. 300fr, Side view, horiz. 750fr, Rear view.

**2001, May 16**

**1904-1906** A371 Set of 3 5.50 5.50

Nos. 1904-1906 each exist in souvenir sheets of 1, containing stamps lacking printer's inscription.

Locomotives — A372

Designs: 300fr, Union Pacific Jupiter. 400fr, No. 7200 Philadelphia. 600fr, C-28 Type 2-8-0. 800fr, Wainwright P Type 0-6-0. 1300fr, Union Pacific Rogers 119. 1600fr, Northwestern 4-6-0 steam engine.

No. 1913, 950fr: a, Oliver Cromwell. b, Big Boy 4-8-8-4 No. 4019. c, 1858 Rogers. d, Gray Lady. e, Old No. 1. f, Jones Goods 4-6-0.

No. 1914, 950fr: a, Jubilee Type No. SS96. b, Iron Horse. c, 4-6-0. d, Type OS2 2-10-0. e, Single Driver 1887 Johnson. f, King George V 4-6-0.

No. 1915, 950fr: a, Hardwicke Western 2-4-0, No. 790. b, High-wheeled Pacific, Texas State Railroad. c, Longhorne. d, City of Truro 4-4-0 No. 3440. e, Leander Type Jubilee. f, The American.

No. 1916, 4000fr, Stanier Black 5-4-6-0. No. 1917, 4000fr, LMS 5305. No. 1918, 4000fr, Duchess of Hamilton.

**2001, June 8** ***Perf. 13¼x13½***

**1907-1912** A372 Set of 6 21.00 21.00

**Sheets of 6, #a-f**

**1913-1915** A372 Set of 3 70.00 70.00

**Souvenir Sheets**

**1916-1918** A372 Set of 3 55.00 55.00

Locomotives — A373

Designs: 500fr, Ae 6/6 Co-Co electric. 750fr, Hikari Super Express. 1000fr, Krauss-Maffei V200 Diesel-electric. 1250fr, 46 Type electric.

No. 1923, 950fr: a, EW Type Bo-Bo-Bo electric. b, 68000 Type Diesel-electric. c, Type Ge 6/6 electric. d, 19,000 horsepower Diesel-electric. e, Express Co-Co electric. f, AL6 Bo-Bo electric.

No. 1924, 950fr: a, 1,750 horsepower Diesel-electric. b, 7000 Co-Co electric. c, Type E10 Bo-Bo electric. d, D341 Type Diesel-electric. e, Diesel-hydraulic express. f, 5E1 electric.

No. 1925, 4000fr, Santa Fe F9 Diesel-electric. No. 1926, 4000fr, Type SSI Co-Co electric. No. 1918, 4000fr, Union Pacific electric.

**2001, June 8**

**1919-1922** A373 Set of 4 15.00 15.00

**Sheets of 6, #a-f**

**1923-1924** A373 Set of 2 45.00 45.00

**Souvenir Sheets**

**1925-1927** A373 Set of 3 55.00 55.00

Belgica 2001 Intl. Stamp Exhibition, Brussels.

Locomotives — A374

Designs: 750fr, Type 18 4-6-2. 1000fr, ICE. 1250fr, Type G.

No. 1931, 950fr: a, Type WP 4-6-2. b, ETR 450. c, EU-07 Bo-Bo. d, Type 25 4-8-4. e, TGV. f, Type 345 Bo-Bo.

No. 1932, 950fr: a, Type SY 2-6-2. b, GM F7 War Bonnet. c, Type 4-4-0. d, Type A2/1 4-6-2. e, Type BB 22200. f, Type OL-49 4-6-2.

No. 1933, 4000fr, VT601. No. 1934, 4000fr, Type QJ 2-10-2.

**2001, June 8**

**1928-1930** A374 Set of 3 13.00 13.00

**Sheets of 6, #a-f**

**1931-1932** A374 Set of 2 45.00 45.00

**Souvenir Sheets**

**1933-1934** A374 Set of 2 37.50 37.50

Belgica 2001 Intl. Stamp Exhibition, Brussels.

Famous People — A375

No. 1935 — Explorers: a, Vasco da Gama. b, Sir Francis Drake. c, Ferdinand Magellan. d, Capt. James Cook. e, Jacques Cartier. f, Christopher Columbus.

No. 1936: a, Albert Einstein. b, Albert Schweitzer. c, Henri Dunant. d, Sir Alexander Fleming. e, Marie Curie. f, Louis Pasteur.

No. 1937 — Space pioneers: a, Yuri Gagarin. b, John Glenn. c, Edward White. d, Neil Armstrong. e, John Young. f, Thomas Stafford and Alexei Leonov.

No. 1938 — Pope John Paul II: a, As baby, with mother and dove. b, Wearing miter and holding crucifix. c, In garden. d, Kneeling. e, Holding crucifix, with dove. f, With arms raised.

No. 1939 — Lord Robert Baden-Powell, Scouts and: a, Psittacus enthacus. b, Charaxes eupale. c, Pluvianus aegyptius. d, Catacroptera cloanthe. e, Merops albicollis. f, Euphaedra eupalus.

**2001, June 14** ***Perf. 13¼***

**Sheets of 6, #a-f**

| | | | | | |
|---|---|---|---|---|---|
| **1935** | A375 | 350fr multi | | 10.00 | 10.00 |
| **1936** | A375 | 450fr multi | | 12.00 | 12.00 |
| **1937** | A375 | 475fr multi | | 13.00 | 13.00 |
| **1938** | A375 | 600fr multi | | 16.00 | 16.00 |
| **1939** | A375 | 750fr multi | | 21.00 | 21.00 |
| | | *Nos. 1935-1939 (5)* | | 72.00 | 72.00 |

Nos. 1936a-1936f and 1939a-1939f each exist in souvenir sheets of one.

Birds — A377

Designs: 200fr, Guinea fowl (pintade vulturine). 250fr, African fish eagle (pygarve vocifer). 300fr, Striped hoopoe (huppe fasciée). 350fr, Jacana. 400fr, Secretary bird (serpentaire). 450fr, Wild Guinea fowl (pintade sauvage).

No. 1948, 950fr: a, Verreaux's eagle (aigle de verreaux). b, White pelican. c, Swallow (hirondelle de rivage). d, Egyptian geese (ouette d'Egypte). e, Crane (grue cendrée). f, Heron.

No. 1949, 950fr: a, Swallow (hirondelle de fenetre). b, Dwarf bee-eater (guepier nain). c, Blue rock thrush (merle solitaire rouge). d, Senegal jabiru. e, Ibis. f, Purple swamphen (talève sultane).

No. 1950, 950fr: a, Vulture (vautour chaugoun). b, Red and yellow barbet (barbican à tete rouge). c, Buzzard (buse rounoir). d, Tufted lark (cochevis). e, Gray wagtail (bergeronnette des ruisseaux). f, Red-heades shrike (pie grieche à tete rouge).

No. 1951, 4000fr, Flamingo (petit flamant). No. 1952, 4000fr, Anhinga. No. 1953, 4000fr, Marabout. No. 1954, 4000fr, Ostrich (autriche).

**2001, Aug. 27** ***Perf. 13½x13¼***

**1942-1947** A377 Set of 6 8.50 8.50

**Sheets of 6, #a-f**

**1948-1950** A377 Set of 3 52.50 52.50

**Souvenir Sheets**

**1951-1954** A377 Set of 4 16.50 16.50

Phila Nippon '01, Japan (#1948-1954).

Birds — A378

Designs: 200fr, Heron. 300fr, Ibis. 500fr, Stonechat (tarier patre). 550fr, Sparrow (hirondelle striée). 600fr, Egyptian courser (pluvian fluviatile). 650fr, Jacana.

No. 1961, 750fr: a, Variable sunbird (souimanga à ventre jaune). b, Long-tailed sunbird (soui-manga à longue queue). c, Scarlet-chested sunbird (soui-manga à poitrine rouge). d, Abyssinian roller (rollier d'Abyssinie). e, Blue-breasted roller (rollier à ventre bleu). f, Broad-billed roller (rolle violet).

No. 1962, 750fr: a, Black bee-eater (guepier noir). b, Blue-headed bee-eater (guepier à tete bleue). c, White-throated bee-eater (guepier à gorge blanche). d, Red-throated bee-eater (guepier à gorge rouge). e, Rosy bee-eater (guepier gris-rose). f, Carmine bee-eater (guepier supreme).

No. 1963, 750fr: a, Blue-breasted kingfisher (martin-chasseur à poitrine bleue). b, Gray-headed kingfisher (martin-chasseur à tete grise). c, Chocolate-backed kingfisher (martin-chasseur marron). d, Dwarf kingfisher (martin-pécheur à tete rousse). e, Malachite kingfisher (martin-pécheur huppé). f, Giant kingfisher (alcyon géant).

No. 1964, 4000fr, Touraco. No. 1965, 4000fr, White-faced whistling duck (dendrocygne veuf). No. 1966, 4000fr, Denham's bustard (outarde du Denham).

**2001, Aug. 27**

**1955-1960** A378 Set of 6 11.00 11.00

**Sheets of 6, #a-f**

**1961-1963** A378 Set of 3 55.00 55.00

**Souvenir Sheets**

**1964-1966** A378 Set of 3 52.50 52.50

Phila Nippon '01, Japan (#1961-1966).

A379

Butterflies — A380

Designs: 700fr, Icolotis zoe. 750fr, Catopsilia florella. 800fr, Kallimoides rumia. 850fr, Charaxes eupale. No. 1971, 950fr, Physcaeneura leda. 1000fr, Mylothris chloris.

No. 1973, 900fr: a, Papilio demodocus. b, Anaphaeis auroto. c, Charaxes superbus. d, Amauris echeria. e, Euxanthe wakefieldi. f, Papilio dardanus.

No. 1974, 900fr: a, Hypolimnas salmacis. b, Myrena silenus. c, Charaxes smagardus. d, Papilio zalmoxis. e, Salamis parnassus. f, Charaxes bohemani.

No. 1975, 900fr: a, Charaxes fournierae. b, Eurema floricola. c, Mimacraea marshalli. d, Charaxes candiope. e, Catacroptera cloanthe. f, Danaus chrysippus.

No. 1976, 950fr: a, Castalius isis. b, Axiocera amanga. c, Eurema brenda. d, Epamera stenogrammica. e, Pseudaletis agrippina. f, Alaena margaritalea.

No. 1977, 950fr: a, Papilio dardanus, diff. b, Charaxes eupale, diff. c, Acraea cerasa. d, Precis clelia. e, Colotis celimene. f, Pseudacraea poggei.

No. 1978, 4000fr, Papilio antimachus. No. 1979, 4000fr, Acraea zetes. No. 1980, 4000fr, Colotis danae.

No. 1981, 4000fr, Hypolimnas deceptor. No. 1982, 4000fr, Euphaedra perseis.

**2001, Aug. 27** ***Perf. 13¼x13½***

**1967-1972** A379 Set of 6 20.00 20.00

**Sheets of 6, #a-f**

**1973-1975** A379 Set of 3 21.00 21.00
**1976-1977** A380 Set of 2 35.00 35.00

**Souvenir Sheets**

**1978-1980** A379 Set of 3 52.50 52.50
**1981-1982** A380 Set of 2 35.00 35.00

Phila Nippon '01, Japan (#1973-1982). Rectangles replace the accented "e's" on all stamps of type A280.

Hummingbirds — A387

Designs: No. 2038, 900fr, Anthracothorax manga. No. 2039, 900fr, Eulampis holosericeus. No. 2040, 1000fr, Archilochus colubris. No. 2041, 1000fr, Chlorostilbon ricordii.

No. 2042, 1000fr: a, Selasphorus rufus. b, Mellisuga helenae. c, Eutoxeres aquila. d, Anthracothorax viridis. e, Allamanda catharica. f, Orthorhynchus cristatus.

No. 2043, 1000fr: a, Archilochus alexandri. b, Calliphlox evelynae. c, Chlorostilbon maugaeus. d, Musta ornata. e, Phaethornis superciliosus. f, Eulampis jugularis.

No. 2044, 1000fr: a, Cyanophaia bicolor. b, Glaucis hirsuta. c, Chlorostilbon swainsonn. d, Heliconia. e, Heliconia bihai. f, Anthracothorax dominicus.

No. 2045, 4000fr, Amazilia violiceps. No. 2046, 4000fr, Trochilus scitulus. No. 2047, 4000fr, Trochilus polytmus, vert.

***Perf. 13¼x13½, 13½x13¼***

**2001** **Litho.**

**2038-2041** A387 Set of 4 14.00 14.00

**Sheets of 6, #a-f**

**2042-2044** A387 Set of 3 65.00 65.00

**Souvenir Sheets**

**2045-2047** A387 Set of 3 47.50 47.50

Trains of Africa A390

Designs: No. 2050, 750fr, 0-6-4, Z.A.S.M, Transvaal, 1858. No. 2051, 750fr, 4-6-2, Central South Africa, 1858. No. 2052, 750fr, 4-4-0, Cape Province, 1903. No. 2053, 750fr, 4-8-2 Class 12, South Africa, 1920. No. 2054, 750fr, 4-6-2 Class 10 RB, South Africa, 1950. No. 2055, 750fr, 4-8-2, Benguela, 1951. No. 2056, 750fr, 4-6-4+4-6-4 Class 15A, South Africa, 1952. No. 2057, 750fr, 4-8-4 Class 25 NC, South Africa, 1953.

No. 2058, 200fr: a, Cape Province locomotive, 1895. b, 2-8-2, Central South Africa, 1920. c, 4-4-2, Cape Province, 1898. d, 4-8-2 Class 23, South Africa, 1930. e, Natal Province locomotive, 1901. f, 2-8-4 Class 24, South Africa, 1940.

No. 2059, 300fr: a, 4-6-2 Class 16E, South Africa, 1935. b, 4-8-4 Class 25, South Afirca, 1953. c, 2-D-1+1-D-2 Class 20, South Africa, 1954. d, 4-8-2+2-8-4 Class 59, East Africa, 1955. e, 1-Co-Co-1 Class 92, East Africa, 1971. f, 2-D-2 Class 26, South Africa, 1982.

No. 2060, 750fr: a, 4-8-2 Class 15F, South Africa, 1948. b, 4-8-2+2-8-4 GEA Beyer-Garret, South Africa, 1950. c, 4-8-2 Class 11, South Africa, 1951. d, 4-8-2+2-8-4 GEA Beyer-Garret, South Africa, 1954. e, 1-Co-Co-1 Class 4E, South Africa, 1954. f, Co-Co Class 9E, South Africa, 1978.

No. 2061, 4000fr, Umtali-Salisbury Class 4-4-0, 1897. No. 2062, 4000fr, Bo-Bo Class 5E, Blue Train, South Africa, 1969.

**2002, Feb. 8** **Litho.** ***Perf. 13¼x13½***

**2050-2057** A390 Set of 8 21.00 21.00

**Sheets of 6, #a-f**

**2058-2060** A390 Set of 3 26.50 26.50

**Souvenir Sheets**

**2061-2062** A390 Set of 2 12.00 12.00

Watercraft — A391

Designs: No. 2063, 750fr, Three-masted schooner, 1866. No. 2064, 750fr, Two-masted schooner, 1932. No. 2065, 750fr, Bark, 1968. No. 2066, 750fr, Sailboard. No. 2067, 750fr, Galleass, 16th cent., horiz. No. 2068, 750fr, Sailboat, horiz.

No. 2069, 750fr: a, Galleon, 16th cent. b, 17th cent. ship. c, Corvette, 18th cent. d, Gaff-rig yacht. e, Dinghy. f, Catamaran.

No. 2070, 4000fr, Full-rigged ship, 20th cent., horiz. No. 2071, 4000fr, Pinnace, 17th cent., horiz.

***Perf. 13½x13¼, 13¼x13½***

**2002, Feb. 8**

**2063-2068** A391 Set of 6 16.00 16.00
**2069** A391 750fr Sheet of 6, #a-f 17.00 17.00

**Souvenir Sheets**

**2070-2071** A391 Set of 2 12.00 12.00

Nos. 2070-2071 each contain one 56x42mm stamp.

Airplanes and Ships — A392

No. 2072, 750fr: a, Wright Brothers Flyer. b, Super Sabre F-100. c, Junkers J1. d, De Havilland Comet. e, Douglas DC-3. f, Boeing 747.

No. 2073, 750fr: a, Egyptian wooden boat. b, 18th cent. sailboat. c, Viking longboat. d, Great Eastern. e, Spanish galleon, 16th cent. f, Savannah.

No. 2074, 4000fr, Concorde. No. 2075, 4000fr, Ocean Princess.

**2002, Feb. 8** ***Perf. 13¼x13½***

**Sheets of 6, #a-f**

**2072-2073** A392 Set of 2 9.25 9.25

**Souvenir Sheets**

**2074-2075** A392 Set of 2 8.25 8.25

First Zeppelin Flight, Cent. — A393

No. 2076: a, LZ-3. b, LZ-5. c, USS Macon. d, Zeppelin NT.

No. 2077, 4000fr, LZ-4. No. 2078, 4000fr, LZ-129.

**2002, Feb. 8**

**2076** A393 750fr Sheet of 4, #a-d 12.00 12.00

**Souvenir Sheets**

**2077-2078** A393 Set of 2 12.00 12.00

Airplanes — A394

No. 2079: a, Lockheed Streamliner. b, Dornier Do-X. c, Lockheed Vega. d, Boeing 707. e, Douglas DC-3. f, De Havilland Comet. 4000fr, Concorde.

**2002, Feb. 8**

**2079** A394 750fr Sheet of 6, #a-f 17.00 17.00

**Souvenir Sheet**

**2080** A394 4000fr multi 6.00 6.00

Airplanes A395

Designs: No. 2081, 750fr, Tupelov TU-144. No. 2082, 750fr, Tri-star L-1011. No. 2083, 750fr, Airbus A-300-B. No. 2084, 750fr, Boeing 777-200.

No. 2085, 750fr: a, Junkers G-24. b, Armstrong Whitworth XV Atalanta. c, Aerospatiale SE 210 Caravelle III. d, De Havilland D. H. 106 Comet 4B. e, Armstrong Whitworth 650 Argosy 100. f, Douglas DC-9.

No. 2086, 750fr: a, Wright Brothers Flyer. b, Vickers Vimy. c, Spirit of St. Louis. d, Junkers G-38. e, Douglas DC-3. f, Vickers-Armstrong Viscount 700.

No. 2087, 4000fr, Boeing 747. No. 2088, 4000fr, Airbus A-3XX.

**2002, Feb. 8**

**2081-2084** A395 Set of 4 11.00 11.00

**Sheets of 6, #a-f**

**2085-2086** A395 Set of 2 32.50 32.50

**Souvenir Sheets**

**2087-2088** A395 Set of 2 12.00 12.00

Military Aircraft A396

Designs: No. 2089, 750fr, Sopwith Camel. No. 2090, 750fr, Fokker Dr-1. No. 2091, 750fr, Messerschmitt Bf-109 E. No. 2092, 750fr, Mitsubishi Zero. No. 2093, 750fr, Northrop F-20 Tigershark. No. 2094, 750fr, Dassault-Breguet Mirage 2000.

No. 2095, 750fr: a, S.E. 5A. b, Fokker D-VII. c, Thomas Morse S4C. d, De Havilland D.H. 2. e, Boeing PW-9D. f, Spad XIII.

No. 2096, 750fr: a, Mustang P-51. b, Junkers Ju-87R. c, Curtiss Hawk 75A. d, Hawker Hurricane. e, Nakajima Ki-43 Hayabusa. f, Macchi M.C. 200 Saetta.

No. 2097, 750fr: a, Panavia Tornado Gr. Mk1. b, Mikoyan-Gurevich MiG-15. c, Vought A-7D Corsair 11. d, BAe Sea Harrier FRS Mk1. e, General Dynamics F-111. f, Dassault/Breguet Dornier Alpha Jet.

No. 2098, 4000fr, Saab Draken J35. No. 2099, 4000fr, Supermarine Spitfire.

**2002, Feb. 8**

**2089-2094** A396 Set of 6 16.00 16.00

**Sheets of 6, #a-f**

**2095-2097** A396 Set of 3 52.50 52.50

**Souvenir Sheets**

**2098-2099** A396 Set of 2 12.00 12.00

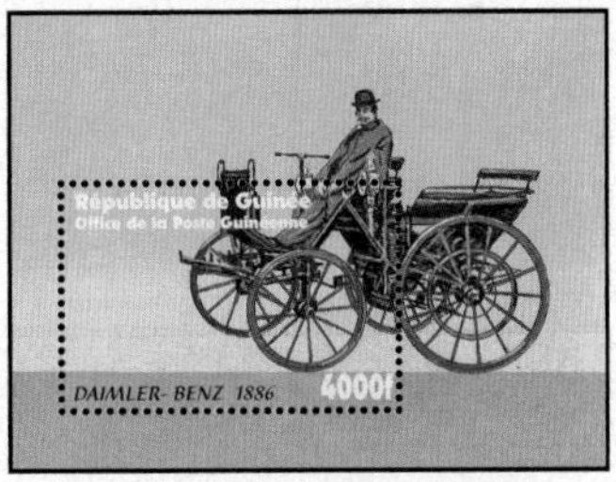


Antique Automobiles — A397

No. 2100, 1000fr: a, 1920 Rolls-Royce. b, 1896 Ford. c, 1930 Hispano-Suiza. d, 1924 Stoewer Allemagne D10 D12. e, 1924 Chrysler. f, 1912 Hudson.

No. 2101, 1000fr: a, 1930 Bugatti SIA. b, 1901 Mercedes. c, 1926 Jordan Playboy. d, 1936 Cadillac V-16. e, 1914 Stutz Bearcat. f, 1904 Daimler.

No. 2102, 4000fr, 1886 Daimler-Benz. No. 2103, 4000fr, 1903 Ford Model A.

**2002, Feb. 8** ***Perf. 13¼x13½***

**Sheets of 6, #a-f**

**2100-2101** A397 Set of 2 42.50 42.50

**Souvenir Sheets**

**2102-2103** A397 Set of 2 12.00 12.00

Race Cars A398

Designs: No. 2104, 750fr, Marmon Wasp, 1911 Indianapolis 500. No. 2105, 750fr, Ferrari Dino 246, 1958 French Grand Prix. No. 2106, 750fr, Lotus 49, 1967 German Grand Prix. No. 2107, Tyrell 003, 1971 American Grand Prix.

No. 2108, 750fr: a, Mercedes, 1914 French Grand Prix. b, Duesenberg, 1921 French Grand Prix. c, Bugatti, 1924 French Grand Prix. d, Alfa Romeo P3, 1934 French Grand Prix. e, Auto Union, 1937 Nürburgring Rally. f, Maserati 8C, 1939 German Grand Prix.

No. 2109, 750fr: a, Vanwall, 1957 British Grand Prix. b, Cooper T43, 1958 Argentine Grand Prix. c, Lotus 25, 1965 British Grand Prix. d, Brabham-Repro BT-19, 1966 French Grand Prix. e, Renault RS 01, 1977 British Grand Prix. f, Ferrari 640, 1989 Brazilian Grand Prix.

No. 2110, 4000fr, Coventry Daimler, 1899 Paris-Ostende Race. No. 2111, 4000fr, Penske PC-23, 1994 Portland Race.

**2002, Feb. 8**

**2104-2107** A398 Set of 4 11.00 11.00

**Sheets of 6, #a-f**

**2108-2109** A398 Set of 2 17.00 17.00

**Souvenir Sheets**

**2110-2111** A398 Set of 2 12.00 12.00

Pres. John F. Kennedy (1917-63) — A400

No. 2113: a, With ship's wheel. b, With doves. c, With arch.

4000fr, At podium with flag and map.

***Perf. 13½x13¼***

**2002, Feb. 20** **Litho.**

**2113** A400 750fr Horiz. strip of 3, #a-c 8.00 8.00

**Souvenir Sheet**

**2114** A400 4000fr multi 7.00 7.00

No. 2113 printed in sheets of 2 strips.

Pres. Ronald Reagan (1911-2004) — A401

No. 2115: a, With stars. b, With curtain. c, With US Capitol.

4000fr, With Statue of Liberty and Presidential seal.

**2002, Feb. 20**

**2115** A401 750fr Horiz. strip of 3, #a-c 8.00 8.00

**Souvenir Sheet**

**2116** A401 4000fr multi 7.00 7.00

No. 2115 printed in sheets of 2 strips.

Princess Diana (1961-97) — A402

No. 2117: a, Wearing tiara. b, Holding flowers. c, Wearing hat.

4000fr, Wearing black dress.

**2002, Feb. 20**

**2117** A402 750fr Horiz. strip of 3, #a-c 8.00 8.00

**Souvenir Sheet**

**2118** A402 4000fr multi 7.00 7.00

No. 2117 printed in sheets of 2 strips.

Prince William of Wales — A403

No. 2119, 750fr: a, Wearing brown checked shirt. b, Wearing jacket and bow tie. c, Wearing green sweater. d, Wearing lilac sweater. e, Wearing brown suit, white shirt and blue tie. f, Wearing brown suit, striped shirt and blue gray tie.

No. 2120, 750fr: a, Wearing blue shirt. b, Wearing blue suit, blue background. c, Wearing riding helmet. d, Wearing blue suit, white background. e, Wearing blue sweater. f, Wearing ski gear.

No. 2121, 4000fr, With Prince Harry. No. 2122, 4000fr, With Prince Charles, horiz.

***Perf. 13½x13¼, 13¼x13½***

**2002, Feb. 20**

**Sheets of 6, #a-f**

**2119-2120** A403 Set of 2 32.50 32.50

**Souvenir Sheets**

**2121-2122** A403 Set of 2 14.00 14.00

Queen Elizabeth II, 50th Anniv. of Reign — A404

No. 2123: a, Wearing blue coat and gloves. b, With Prince Philip. c, Wearing gray coat and hat. d, Wearing yellow suit and hat.

4000fr, Wearing red uniform.

**2002, Feb. 20** ***Perf. 14¼***

**2123** A404 1400fr Sheet of 4, #a-d 12.00 12.00

**Souvenir Sheet**

**2124** A404 4000fr multi 7.00 7.00

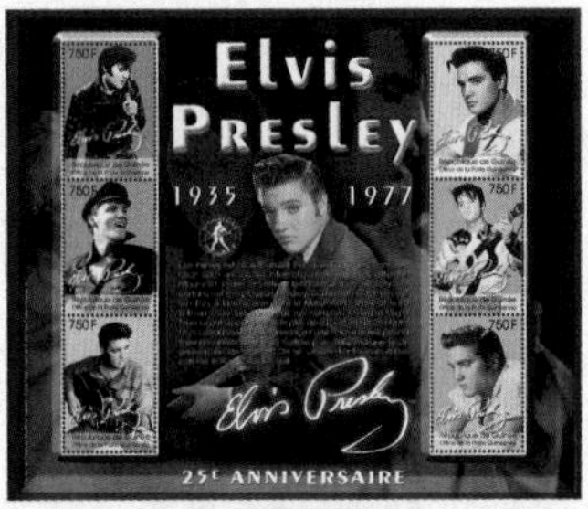


A405

A406

Elvis Presley (1935-77) — A407

No. 2125 — Background color: a, Blue. b, Yellow. c, Red. d, Pink. e, Lilac. f, Yellow green.

No. 2126: a, Red and white shirt. b, Blue shirt. c, Black and brown shirt. d, Purple shirt. e, Red jacket with neckerchief. f, Red shirt.

No. 2127: a, Wearing red and white shirt with scarf. b, Wearing black jacket and gray shirt. c, Holding guitar on shoulder. d, With hands resting on guitar. e, Singing. f, Wearing army uniform.

**2002, Feb. 20** ***Perf. 13½x13¼***

**2125** A405 750fr Sheet of 6, #a-f 18.00 18.00

**2126** A406 750fr Sheet of 6, #a-f 18.00 18.00

**2127** A407 750fr Sheet of 6, #a-f 18.00 18.00

Nobel Prize Physics Laureates — A408

No. 2128, each 750fr: a, Hendrik Lorentz, 1902. b, Pieter Zeeman, 1902. c, Sir Joseph Thomson, 1906. d, Gabriel Lippman, 1908. e, Max von Laue, 1914. f, Jean B. Perrin, 1926.

No. 2129, each 750fr: a, Owen Richardson, 1928. b, Sir Chandrasekhara Venkata Raman, 1930. c, Victor F. Hess, 1936. d, Carl D. Anderson, 1936. e, Sir George Thompson, 1937. f, Clinton Davisson, 1937.

No. 2130, each 750fr: a, Enrico Fermi, 1938. b, Ernest Lawrence, 1939. c, Isidor I. Rabi, 1944. d, Patrick Blackett, 1948. e, Fritz Zernike, 1953. f, Donald A. Glaser, 1960.

No. 2131, each 750fr: a, Alfred Kastler, 1966. b, Luis W. Alvarez, 1968. c, Murray Gell-Mann, 1969. d, John Bardeen, 1972. e, Leon N. Cooper, 1972. f, John R, Schrieffer, 1972.

No. 2132: 4000fr, Wilhelm Röntgen, 1901. No. 2133, 4000fr, Marie Curie, 1903. No. 2134, 4000fr, Pierre Curie, 1903. No. 2135, 4000fr, Antoine Henri Becquerel, 1903.

**2002, Feb. 20** **Litho.**

**Sheets of 6, #a-f**

**2128-2131** A408 Set of 4 72.50 72.50

**Souvenir Sheets**

**2132-2135** A408 Set of 4 27.50 27.50

Nobel Prizes, cent. (in 2001).

Albert Einstein (1879-1955), Physicist — A409

No. 2136: a, Smoking pipe. b, Wearing black jacket and tie, facing left. c, Wearing blue sweater. d, Wearing black jacket and tie, facing right. e, Wearing black sweater. f, Wearing brown jacket.

4000fr, With wife, Elsa.

**2002, Feb. 20**

**2136** A409 750fr Sheet of 6, #a-f 17.00 17.00

**Souvenir Sheet**

**2137** A409 4000fr multi 7.00 7.00

Pres. Theodore Roosevelt (1858-1919) — A410

No. 2138: a, As Assistant Navy Secretary. b, In Cuba, 1898. c, In Yellowstone Park, 1903. d, As President, 1901-09. e, Campaigning for war preparedness, 1916. f, In 1917.
4000fr, As colonel in Rough Riders.

**2002, Feb. 20** ***Perf. 13¼***

**2138** A410 950fr Sheet of 6, #a-f 21.00 21.00

**Souvenir Sheet**

**2139** A410 4000fr multi 7.00 7.00

Jacqueline Kennedy Onassis (1929-94), First Lady — A411

Designs: No. 2140, 1000fr, Wearing white blouse, yellow background. 2000fr, With Pres. John F. Kennedy, horiz. No. 2142, 4000fr, Wearing Inaugural Ball gown.
No. 2143: a, Wearing necklace, shoulders showing, green background. b, Wearing hat. c, Facing left, green background. d, Wearing necklace, orange background. e, Wearing necklace, shoulders covered, green background. f, Wearing sunglasses.
No. 2144, 4000fr, As child.

***Perf. 13½x13¼, 13¼x13½***

**2002, Feb. 20**

**2140-2142** A411 Set of 3 26.00 26.00

**2143** A411 1000fr Sheet of 6, #a-f 24.00 24.00

**Souvenir Sheet**

**2144** A411 4000fr multi 7.00 7.00

Famous People — A412

Designs: No. 2145, 750fr, Pres. John F. Kennedy (1917-63). No. 2146, 750fr, Pres. Ronald Reagan (1911-2004). No. 2147, 750fr, Chiune Sugihara, Japanese diplomat who saved Jews in World War II. No. 2148, 750fr, Queen Elizabeth II as younger woman, denomination at right. No. 2149, 750fr, Queen Elizabeth II wearing tiara, denomination at left. No. 2150, 750fr, Princess Diana (1961-97). No. 2151, 750fr, Queen Mother Elizabeth (1900-2002). No. 2152, 750fr, Prince William of Wales, denomination in red. No. 2153, 750fr, Prince William of Wales, denomination in yellow. No. 2154, 750fr, Prince William of Wales, denomination in violet. No. 2155, 750fr, Hereditary Prince Haakon and Princess Mette-Marie of Norway, horiz. No. 2156, 750fr, Prince Philippe and Princess Mathilde of Belgium, horiz.

**2002, Feb. 20** ***Perf. 14***

**2145-2156** A412 Set of 12 32.50 32.50

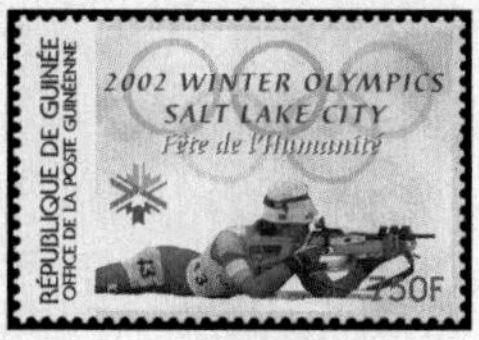


2002 Winter Olympic Games, Salt Lake City A413

Designs: No. 2157, 750fr, Biathlon. No. 2158, 750fr, Luge. No. 2159, 750fr, Skiing. No. 2160, 750fr, Snowboarding, vert.

***Perf. 13¼x13½, 13½x13¼***

**2002, Feb. 20**

**2157-2160** A413 Set of 4 11.00 11.00

Japanese Entertainment — A414

No. 2161, 750fr — Film stars: a, Miyoshi Umeki. b, Kimiko Ikegami. c, Masahiro Takashima. d, Sessue Hayakawa. e, Toshiro Mifune. f, Kaho Minami.
No. 2162, 750fr — Kabuki actors: a, Shinnosuke as Sukeroku. b, Kikugoro as Genkuro Kitsune. c, Ganjiro as Izaemon. d, Kikunosuke as Shiratama. e, Kikunosuke as Keisei. f, Shinnosuke as Matsuomaru.
No. 2163, 4000fr, Akira Kurosawa, film director. No. 2164, 4000fr, Danjuro as Kampei and Tamasaburo as Okaru, horiz.

***Perf. 13½x13¼, 13¼x13½***

**2002, Feb. 20**

**Sheets of 6, #a-f**

**2161-2162** A414 Set of 2 32.50 32.50

**Souvenir Sheets**

**2163-2164** A414 Set of 2 14.00 14.00

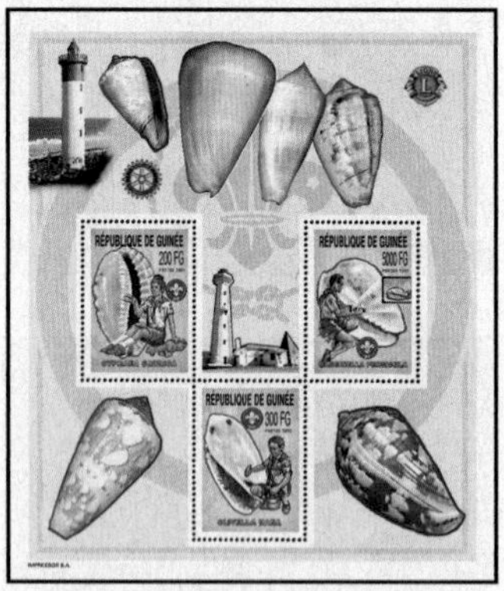


Scouts — A422

No. 2208 — Scouts and shells: a, 200fr, Cypraea caurica. b, 300fr, Olivella nana. c, 5000fr, Marginella persicula.
No. 2209 — Scouts and sea mammals: a, 200fr, Balaena mysticetus. b, 300fr, Tursiops truncatus. c, 5000fr, Delphinus delphis.
No. 2210 — Scouts and dinosaurs: a, 200fr, Spinosaurus. b, 300fr, Ouranosaurus. c, 5000fr, Kentrosaurus.
No. 2211 — Scouts and dogs: a, 200fr, Bouvier Bernois. b, 750fr, Chihuahua. c, 5000fr, Irish wolfhound.
No. 2212 — Scouts and meteorites from: a, 200fr, Tatahouine. b, 750fr, Gao-Guenie. c, 5000fr, Great Sand Sea.
No. 2213 — Scouts and cats: a, 300fr, Japanese bobtail. b, 750fr, Egyptian Mau. c, 5000fr, Bombay.
No. 2214 — Scouts and minerals: a, 300fr, Anglesite. b, 750fr, Brucite. c, 5000fr, Beudantite.
No. 2215 — Scouts and mushrooms: a, 300fr, Aseroe rubra. b, 750fr, Boletus edulis. c, 5000fr, Hygrocybe punicea.
No. 2216 — Scouts and butterflies: a, 300fr, Anaphe panda. b, 750fr, Eurema brigitta. c, 5000fr, Acraea zetes.

**2002, Dec. 27** **Litho.** ***Perf. 13¼***

**Sheets of 3, #a-c**

**2208-2216** A422 Set of 9 62.50 62.50

Each stamp exists in souvenir sheet of 1.

Nicolaus August Otto (1832-91), Engineer A423

Wright Brothers and Wright Flyer A424

Astronaut Spacewalking — A425

Pierre de Coubertin (1863-1937), Intl. Olympic Committee President A426

Winston Churchill, Franklin D. Roosevelt and Joseph Stalin A427

Newspaper Mastheads A428

Ferris Wheels on Film A429

**2002** ***Perf. 13½x13¼, 13¼x13½***

| | | | | | |
|---|---|---|---|---|---|
| **2217** | A423 | 200fr | multi | 1.60 | 1.60 |
| **2218** | A424 | 300fr | multi | 1.60 | 1.60 |
| **2219** | A425 | 750fr | multi | 1.60 | 1.60 |
| **2220** | A426 | 1000fr | multi | 1.60 | 1.60 |
| **2221** | A427 | 1250fr | multi | 1.60 | 1.60 |
| **2222** | A428 | 1500fr | multi | 1.60 | 1.60 |
| **2223** | A429 | 2000fr | multi | 1.60 | 1.60 |

Space — A430

Designs: No. 2224, 3000fr, Multi-scout Mars Lander. No. 2225, 3000fr, Stardust Probe. No. 2226, 3000fr, Mars Rover. No. 2227, 3000fr, Ceres-Vesta Probe. No. 2228, 3000fr, Deep Space Probe. No. 2229, 3000fr, NGST Space Telescope. No. 2230, 3000fr, Rosetta Probe. No. 2231, 3000fr, NEAR Probe.
No. 2232, 1500fr, horiz.: a, Newton Space Telescope. b, Darwin Space Telescope. c, Kepler Space Telescope. d, Herschel Space Telescope. e, Plank Space Telescope. f, Xeus Space Telescope. g, Mars Orbiter. h, Net Lander.
No. 2233, 1500fr, horiz.: a, Mission Specialist 4 Kalpana Chawla. b, Payload Commander Michael P. Anderson. c, Mission Specialist 1 David M. Brown. d, Pilot William C. McCool. e, Mission Specialist 4 Laurel B. Clark. f, Payload Specialist 4 Ilan Ramon. g, Commander Rick D. Husband. h, Columbia Space Shuttle.
No. 2234, 3000fr, Chawla, diff. No. 2235, 3000fr, Anderson, diff. No. 2236, 3000fr, Brown, diff. No. 2237, 3000fr, McCool, diff. No. 2238, 3000fr, Clark, diff. No. 2239, 3000fr, Ramon, diff. No. 2240, 3000fr, Husband, diff. No. 2241, 3000fr, Columbia Space Shuttle, diff. No. 2242, 6000fr, Corot Space Telescope, horiz. No. 2243, 6000fr, Crew of ill-fated Columbia Space Shuttle mission STS-107, horiz.

**2003, Mar. 3** ***Perf. 13¼***

**2224-2231** A430 Set of 8 25.00 25.00

**Sheets of 8, #a-h**

**2232-2233** A430 Set of 2 30.00 30.00

**Souvenir Sheets**

**2234-2243** A430 Set of 10 37.50 37.50

Nos. 2242 and 2243 each contain one 50x41mm stamp. Nos. 2224-2231 each exist in souvenir sheets of 1.

2004 Summer Olympics, Athens — A431

Designs: No. 2244, 750fr, No. 2252, 3000fr, Triathlon and Pentathlon. No. 2245, 750fr, No. 2253, 3000fr, Archery. No. 2246, 1500fr, No. 2254, 3000fr, Table tennis. No. 2247, 1500fr, No. 2255, 3000fr, Taekwondo and Judo. No. 2248, 1500fr, No. 2256, 3000fr, Equestrian. No. 2249, 1500fr, No. 2257, 3000fr, Women's tennis. No. 2250, 1500fr, No. 2258, 3000fr, Swimming. No. 2251, 1500fr, No. 2259, 3000fr, Track and field.
No. 2260, 6000fr, Soccer.

**2003, Nov. 12** ***Perf. 13¼***

**2244-2251** A431 Set of 8 15.00 15.00

**Souvenir Sheets**

**2252-2260** A431 Set of 9 30.00 30.00

*2259a* Souvenir sheet, #2252, 2257-2259 12.00 12.00

No. 2260 contains one 36x51mm stamp.

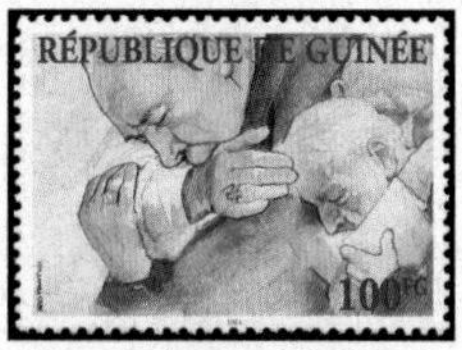


Pope John Paul II (1920-2005) — A433

Pope: 100fr, Hugging man. 150fr, In vestments, with open arms. 200fr, Face. 300fr, Praying at microphone. 350fr, Praying. 400fr, Holding crucifix. 450fr, Blessing bishop. 500fr, Kissing ground and with arms raised. 550fr, With Black Madonna of Czestochowa. 600fr,

Wounded in assassination attempt. 650fr, With man. 1000fr, With children and Virgin Mary. 1500fr, Handshake. 2000fr, With Lech Walesa. 2500fr, With people tearing down Berlin Wall. 7500fr, With crowd.

**2004 Litho. *Perf. 13x13¼***

| | | | | |
|---|---|---|---|---|
| **2263** | A433 | 100fr multi | — | — |
| **2264** | A433 | 150fr multi | — | — |
| **2265** | A433 | 200fr multi | — | — |
| **2266** | A433 | 300fr multi | — | — |
| **2267** | A433 | 350fr multi | | — |
| **2268** | A433 | 400fr multi | | — |
| **2269** | A433 | 450fr multi | — | — |
| **2270** | A433 | 500fr multi | — | — |
| **2271** | A433 | 550fr multi | — | — |
| **2272** | A433 | 600fr multi | — | — |
| **2273** | A433 | 650fr multi | — | — |
| **2274** | A433 | 1000fr multi | — | — |
| **2275** | A433 | 1500fr multi | — | — |
| **2276** | A433 | 2000fr multi | — | — |
| **2277** | A433 | 2500fr multi | — | — |
| **2278** | A433 | 7500fr multi | — | — |

Eleven additional stamps exist in this set. The editors would like to examine any examples.

## SEMI-POSTAL STAMPS

Eye Examination — SP1

Microscopic Examination SP2

#B13, Medical laboratory. #B14, Insect control. #B16, Surgical operation.

**Engraved and Lithographed**

**1960 Unwmk. *Perf. 11½***

| | | | | |
|---|---|---|---|---|
| **B12** | SP1 | 20fr + 10fr ultra & car | .95 | .60 |
| **B13** | SP1 | 30fr + 20fr brn org & violet | .95 | .60 |
| **B14** | SP1 | 40fr + 20fr rose lil & blue | 1.25 | .80 |
| **B15** | SP2 | 50fr + 50fr grn & brn | 1.90 | 1.25 |
| **B16** | SP2 | 100fr + 100fr lil & grn | 2.25 | 1.50 |
| | | *Nos. B12-B16 (5)* | 7.30 | 4.75 |

Issued for national health propaganda.
For overprints see Nos. B25-B29.

Nos. 194-195 Surcharged in Red or Orange

**1961, June 6 Photo.**

| | | | | |
|---|---|---|---|---|
| **B17** | A17 | 25fr + 10fr (R or O) | 5.50 | 3.50 |
| **B18** | A17 | 50fr + 20fr (R or O) | 5.50 | 3.50 |

Nos. B17-B18 exist with orange surcharges transposed: "1961 + 10FRS." on 50fr and "1961 + 20FRS." on 25fr.

**Nos. 214-219 Surcharged in Green, Lilac, Orange or Blue**

**Photo., Surcharge Engr.**

**1961, Dec. 8**

**Multicolored Design; Granite Paper**

| | | | | |
|---|---|---|---|---|
| **B19** | A20 | 5fr + 5fr brt grn (G) | .70 | .25 |
| **B20** | A20 | 10fr + 5fr emer (G) | .75 | .25 |
| **B21** | A20 | 25fr + 5fr lilac (L) | 1.90 | .35 |
| **B22** | A20 | 40fr + 5fr org (O) | 2.50 | .45 |
| **B23** | A20 | 50fr + 5fr red org (O) | 3.50 | .65 |
| **B24** | A20 | 75fr + 5fr ultra (B) | 4.75 | .90 |
| | | *Nos. B19-B24 (6)* | 14.10 | 2.85 |

The surtax was for animal protection.

Nos. B12-B16 Overprinted in Red or Orange

**Engr. & Litho.**

**1962, Feb. *Perf. 11½***

| | | | | |
|---|---|---|---|---|
| **B25** | SP1 | 20fr + 10fr (R or O) | .35 | .25 |
| **B26** | SP1 | 30fr + 20fr (R or O) | .50 | .35 |
| **B27** | SP1 | 40fr + 20fr (R or O) | .60 | .40 |
| **B28** | SP2 | 50fr + 50fr (R or O) | 1.25 | .80 |
| **B29** | SP2 | 100fr + 100fr (R or O) | 2.40 | 1.60 |
| | | *Nos. B25-B29 (5)* | 5.10 | 3.40 |

WHO drive to eradicate malaria.
No. B25 also exists with black overprint.

Nos. 223-228 Srchd. in Red

**Photo., Surcharge Engr.**

**1962, May 14 *Perf. 13x14***

| | | | | |
|---|---|---|---|---|
| **B30** | A22 | 5fr + 5fr multi | .40 | .25 |
| **B31** | A22 | 10fr + 5fr multi | .50 | .25 |
| **B32** | A22 | 25fr + 5fr multi | .65 | .25 |
| **B33** | A22 | 40fr + 5fr multi | .90 | .45 |
| **B34** | A22 | 50fr + 5fr multi | 1.50 | .75 |
| **B35** | A22 | 75fr + 5fr multi | 3.50 | 1.75 |
| | | *Nos. B30-B35 (6)* | 7.45 | 3.70 |

The surtax was for bird protection.

Nos. 232-233 Surcharged & Overprinted in Orange or Red

**1962, Nov. 1 Litho. *Perf. 13***

| | | | | |
|---|---|---|---|---|
| **B36** | A24 | 25fr + 15fr multi | .60 | .45 |
| **B37** | A24 | 75fr + 25fr multi | 1.40 | .90 |

Issued to help Algerian refugees.

Astronomers and Space Phenomena — SP3

**1989, Mar. 7 Litho. *Perf. 13½***

| | | | | |
|---|---|---|---|---|
| **B38** | SP3 | 100fr +25fr Helical nebula | 1.00 | .40 |
| **B39** | SP3 | 150fr +25fr Orion nebula | 1.50 | .80 |
| **B40** | SP3 | 200fr +25fr Eagle nebula | 2.25 | 1.00 |
| **B41** | SP3 | 250fr +25fr Trifide nebula | 2.75 | 1.10 |
| **B42** | SP3 | 300fr +25fr Eta-carinae nebula | 3.25 | 1.50 |
| **B43** | SP3 | 500fr +25fr NGC-2264 nebula | 5.25 | 2.40 |
| | | *Nos. B38-B43 (6)* | 16.00 | 7.20 |

**Souvenir Sheet**

| | | | | |
|---|---|---|---|---|
| **B44** | SP3 | 750fr +50fr Horse's Head nebula | 7.25 | 3.00 |

Nos. B42-B44 are airmail.

## AIR POST STAMPS

Lockheed Constellation — AP1

Design: 500fr, Plane on ground.

**Lithographed and Engraved**

**1959, July 13 Unwmk. *Perf. 11½***

**Size: 52½x24mm**

| | | | | |
|---|---|---|---|---|
| **C14** | AP1 | 100fr dp car, ultra & emer | 2.10 | 1.00 |
| **C15** | AP1 | 200fr emer, brn & lil | 2.75 | 2.00 |

**Size: 56½x26mm**

| | | | | |
|---|---|---|---|---|
| **C16** | AP1 | 500fr multicolored | 7.25 | 3.50 |
| | | *Nos. C14-C16 (3)* | 12.10 | 6.50 |

For overprints see Nos. C24-C26, C52-C53.

Doves with Letter and Olive Twig — AP2

**1959, Oct. 16 Engr. *Perf. 13½***

| | | | | |
|---|---|---|---|---|
| **C17** | AP2 | 40fr blue | .30 | .25 |
| **C18** | AP2 | 50fr emerald | .60 | .40 |
| **C19** | AP2 | 100fr dk car rose | 1.00 | 1.00 |
| **C20** | AP2 | 200fr rose red | 1.90 | 1.75 |
| **C21** | AP2 | 500fr red orange | 5.25 | 3.00 |
| | | *Nos. C17-C21 (5)* | 9.05 | 6.40 |

For overprints see Nos. C35-C38.

**Admission to UN Type of 1959**

**Engr. & Litho.**

**1959, Dec. 12 *Perf. 12***

**Size: 44x26mm**

| | | | | |
|---|---|---|---|---|
| **C22** | A16 | 50fr multicolored | 1.00 | .75 |
| **C23** | A16 | 100fr multicolored | 1.40 | .90 |

For overprints see Nos. C27-C28.

**Nos. C14-C16 Overprinted in Carmine, Orange or Blue**

**1960 Litho. & Engr. *Perf. 11½***

**Size: 52½x24mm**

| | | | | |
|---|---|---|---|---|
| **C24** | AP1 | 100fr multi (C or O) | 9.75 | 4.25 |
| **C25** | AP1 | 200fr multi (Bl) | 17.00 | 8.00 |

**Size: 56½x26mm**

| | | | | |
|---|---|---|---|---|
| **C26** | AP1 | 500fr multi (C or O) | 45.00 | 40.00 |
| | | *Nos. C24-C26 (3)* | 71.75 | 52.25 |

17th Olympic Games, Rome, 8/25-9/11.

No. 201 overprinted in green and Nos. C24 and C26 overprinted in black were included in a souvenir gift booklet celebrating Guinea's 3rd anniversary of independence. The booklet was sold at the NY World's Fair, but the stamps were not valid for postage.

**Nos. C22-C23 Overprinted**

**Engr. & Litho.**

**1961, Oct. 24 *Perf. 12***

| | | | | |
|---|---|---|---|---|
| **C27** | A16 | 50fr multicolored | 1.00 | .40 |
| **C28** | A16 | 100fr multicolored | 1.50 | .55 |

United Nations, 15th anniversary.

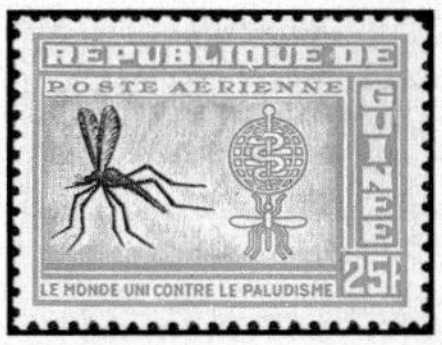


Mosquito and Malaria Eradication Emblem AP3

**1962, Apr. 7 Engr. *Perf. 10½***

| | | | | |
|---|---|---|---|---|
| **C29** | AP3 | 25fr orange & blk | .50 | .25 |
| **C30** | AP3 | 50fr car rose & blk | .80 | .35 |
| **C31** | AP3 | 100fr green & blk | 1.40 | .60 |
| | | *Nos. C29-C31 (3)* | 2.70 | 1.20 |

WHO drive to eradicate malaria.

A souvenir sheet exists containing a 100fr green & sepia stamp, imperf. Sepia coat of arms in margin. Size: 102x76mm. Value $10.

**Musician Type of Regular Issue**

Musical Instruments: 100fr, 200fr, Kora. 500fr, Balafon.

**1962, June 15 Photo. *Perf. 13x13½***

| | | | | |
|---|---|---|---|---|
| **C32** | A26 | 100fr brt pink, dk car & Prus bl | 1.10 | .50 |
| **C33** | A26 | 200fr lt & dk ultra & car rose | 2.10 | 1.25 |
| **C34** | A26 | 500fr dl org, pur & Prus bl | 6.75 | 4.00 |
| | | *Nos. C32-C34 (3)* | 13.15 | 5.75 |

Nos. C17-C20 Ovptd. in Carmine, Orange or Black

***Perf. 13½***

**1962, Nov. 15 Unwmk. Engr.**

| | | | | |
|---|---|---|---|---|
| **C35** | AP2 | 40fr blue (C or O) | .60 | .25 |
| **C36** | AP2 | 50fr emer (C or O) | .60 | .35 |
| **C37** | AP2 | 100fr dk car rose (B) | 1.35 | .70 |
| **C38** | AP2 | 200fr rose red (B) | 2.40 | 1.25 |
| | | *Nos. C35-C38 (4)* | 4.95 | 2.55 |

The conquest of space. Two types of overprint: Straight lines on 40fr and 50fr in carmine, 100fr (black). Curved lines on 40fr and 50fr in orange, 200fr (black).

**Bird Type of Regular Issue**

Birds: 100fr, Hornbill. 200fr, White spoonbill. 500fr, Bateleur eagle.

**1962, Dec. Photo. *Perf. 13x13½***

| | | | | |
|---|---|---|---|---|
| **C41** | A30 | 100fr multicolored | 2.50 | 1.10 |
| **C42** | A30 | 200fr multicolored | 4.25 | 2.40 |
| **C43** | A30 | 500fr multicolored | 11.00 | 4.75 |
| | | *Nos. C41-C43 (3)* | 20.50 | 8.25 |

**Sports Type of Regular Issue, 1963**

Designs: 100fr, Running. 200fr, Bicycling. 500fr, Single sculls.

**1963, Mar. 16 *Perf. 14***

| | | | | |
|---|---|---|---|---|
| **C44** | A32 | 100fr dp rose, sep & grn | 1.60 | .80 |
| **C45** | A32 | 200fr ol bis, ultra & mag | 3.50 | 2.00 |
| **C46** | A32 | 500fr ocher, dk bl & red | 7.25 | 3.75 |
| | | *Nos. C44-C46 (3)* | 15.50 | 6.55 |

**Butterfly Type of Regular Issue**

Various Butterflies.

**1963, May 10 Unwmk. *Perf. 12***

C47 A33 100fr cit, dk brn & gray 1.60 .35
C48 A33 200fr sal pink, blk & green 5.00 2.40
C49 A33 500fr multicolored 8.50 4.50
*Nos. C47-C49 (3)* 18.75 7.25

### Red Cross Type of Regular Issue

**1963, July 25 Engr. *Perf. 10½***

C50 A35 25fr black & car .75 .25

### Souvenir Sheet

***Imperf***

C51 A35 100fr green & car 4.00 3.00

### Nos. C14-C15 Overprinted

### Lithographed and Engraved

**1963, Oct. 28 *Perf. 11½***

C52 AP1 100fr dp car, ultra & emer 1.60 .70
C53 AP1 200fr emer, brn & lil 3.75 1.25

1st Pan American air service from Conakry to New York, July 30, 1963.

### Fish Type of Regular Issue, 1964

100fr, African lyretail. 300fr, Six-barred epiplatys.

**1964, Feb. 15 Litho. *Perf. 14x13½***

C54 A36 100fr grn & multi 2.25 .55
C55 A36 300fr brn & multi 7.75 1.40

### Kennedy Type of Regular Issue, 1964

**1964, Mar. 5 Engr. *Perf. 10½***

C56 A37 100fr multicolored 1.75 .80

See note after No. 327.

### Olympic Type of Regular Issue

Design: 100fr, Women's ice skating.

**1964, May 15 Photo. *Perf. 13x12½***

C57 A39 100fr gold, brn org & ind 2.25 .40

### Nos. C44-C46 Overprinted in Carmine or Orange

**1964, May 15 Unwmk. *Perf. 14***

C58 A32 100fr (C or O) 1.75 1.40
C59 A32 200fr (C or O) 2.75 2.00
C60 A32 500fr (C or O) 6.50 5.00
*Nos. C58-C60 (3)* 11.90 8.40

18th Olympic Games, Tokyo, Oct. 10-25.

### Mrs. Roosevelt Type of Regular Issue

**1964, June 1 Engr. *Perf. 10½***

C61 A40 50fr violet .90 .25

### Souvenir Sheets

Unisphere, "Rocket Thrower" and Guinea Pavilion — AP4

**1964, Oct. 26 Engr. *Imperf.***

C62 AP4 100fr dk bl & org 1.60 .80
C63 AP4 200fr rose red & emer 3.75 1.90

NY World's Fair, 1964-65. See Nos. C69-C70.

### Nubian Monuments Type of Regular Issue

300fr, Queen Nefertari, Abu Simbel.

**1964, Nov. 19 Photo. *Perf. 12***

C64 A42 300fr gold, dl red brn & sal 4.00 1.40

For overprint see No. C82.

Japanese Hostess, Plane and Map of Africa AP5

**1965, Jan. 18 *Perf. 12½x13***

C65 AP5 100fr gold, blk & red lil 1.75 .35

18th Olympic Games, Tokyo, Oct. 10-25, 1964. Two multicolored souvenir sheets (200fr vert. and 300fr horiz.) exist, showing different views of Mt. Fuji. Sizes: 86x119mm, 119x86mm. Value, both: $12.50 perf; $40 imperf.
For overprint see No. C81.

### Mask Type of Regular Issue

300fr, Niamou mask from N'Zérékoré.

**1965, Feb. 15 Photo. *Perf. 14***

C68 A44 300fr multicolored 6.25 2.75

### World's Fair Type of 1964

Souvenir Sheets

**1965, Mar. 24 Engr. *Imperf.***

C69 AP4 100fr green & brn 2.40 1.00
C70 AP4 200fr grn & car rose 4.75 2.50

### Handicraft Type of Regular Issue

100fr, Cabinetmaker. 300fr, Ivory carver.

**1965, May 1 Photo. *Perf. 14***

C71 A45 100fr multicolored 1.50 .35
C72 A45 300fr multicolored 5.25 1.25

### ITU Type of Regular Issue, 1965

**1965, May 17 Unwmk.**

C73 A46 100fr multicolored 1.10 .30
C74 A46 200fr multicolored 2.50 .75

Exist imperf.

### ICY Type of Regular Issue, 1965

**1965, Sept. 8 Engr. *Perf. 10½***

C75 A50 100fr bl & yel org 1.25 .35

West Facade, Polytechnic Institute — AP6

Design: 200fr, North facade.

**1965, Oct. 2 Photo. *Perf. 13½***

C76 AP6 200fr gold & multi 1.75 1.00
C77 AP6 500fr gold & multi 5.00 3.00

Seventh anniversary of independence.

For overprints see Nos. C84-C85.

### Moon Type of 1965

100fr, Ranger VII approaching moon, vert. 200fr, Launching of Ranger VII, Cape Kennedy, vert.

**1965, Nov. 15 Litho. *Perf. 13½x14***

C78 A52 100fr rose red, yel & dk brown 1.00 .50
C79 A52 200fr multicolored 2.50 1.00

For overprints & surcharge see #C112-C112B.

### Dancer Type of Regular Issue, 1966

100fr, Kandia Kouyate, national singer.

**1966, Jan. 5 Photo. *Perf. 13½***
**Size: 36x28½mm**

C80 A53 100fr multi, horiz. 1.25 .50

Engraved Overprint on No. C65

**1966, Mar. 14 Photo. *Perf. 12½x13***

C81 AP5 100fr gold, blk & red lil 1.25 .45

Fourth Pan Arab Games, Cairo, Sept. 2-11, 1965. The same overprint was applied to two souvenir sheets noted after No. C65 (red ovpt. on 200fr, black ovpt. on 300fr).

Engraved Dark Blue Overprint on No. C64

**1966, Mar. 14 *Perf. 12***

C82 A42 300fr gold, dl red brn & sal 2.75 1.50

Centenary of first Egyptian postage stamp.

### Scenic Type of Regular Issue

View: Boulbinet Lighthouse.

**1966, Apr. 4 *Perf. 13½***

C83 A54 100fr multicolored 1.40 .60

See #C90-C91. For overprints see #C93-C95.

### Nos. C76-C77 Ovptd. in Blue or Yellow

**1966, May 2 Photo. *Perf. 13½***

C84 AP6 200fr multi (Bl) 2.25 1.10
C85 AP6 500fr multi (Y) 5.00 2.75

UNESCO, 20th anniv.

### Woman-Flower Type of Regular Issue

Designs: Women and flowers of Guinea.

**1966, May 30 Photo. *Perf. 13½***
**Size: 28x34mm**

C86 A56 200fr multicolored 3.50 .70
C87 A56 300fr multicolored 5.00 2.10

### Snake Type of Regular Issue

Designs: 200fr, Pastoria Research Institute. 300fr, Men holding rock python.

**1967, May 15 Litho. *Perf. 13½***
**Size: 56x20mm**

C88 A61 200fr multicolored 2.50 1.25
*a.* Souv. sheet of 3, #471, 474, C88 9.00 6.50
C89 A61 300fr multicolored 4.50 2.25

### Scenic Type of Regular Issue

Views: 100fr, House of explorer Olivier de Sanderval. 200fr, Conakry.

**1967, June 20 Photo. *Perf. 13½***

C90 A54 100fr multicolored .75 .45
C91 A54 200fr multicolored 1.60 1.10

For overprints see Nos. C94-C95.

### Elephant Type of Regular Issue, 1967

**1967, Sept. 28 Photo. *Perf. 13½***

C92 A63 200fr gold & multi 1.60 .75

Nos. C83 and C90-C91 Overprinted

**1967, Nov. 6**

C93 A54 100fr multi (#C83) 1.45 .90
C94 A54 100fr multi (#C90) 1.45 .90
C95 A54 200fr multi (#C91) 2.75 1.50
*Nos. C93-C95 (3)* 10.00 3.30

50th anniversary of Lions International.

Detail from Mural by José Vela Zanetti — AP7

Family, Mural by Per Krohg — AP8

The designs of the 30fr, 50fr and 200fr show mankind's struggle for a lasting peace after the mural in the lobby of the UN Conference Building, NY. The designs of the 100fr and of Nos. C98a-C98b show mankind's hope for the future after a mural in the UN Security Council Chamber.

**1967, Nov. 11**

C96 AP7 30fr multicolored .30 .25
C97 AP7 50fr multicolored .40 .25
C98 AP8 100fr multicolored .85 .35
*a.* Souv. sheet of 3, English inscription 2.25 2.25
*b.* As "a," French inscription 2.25 2.25
C99 AP7 200fr multi 1.90 .50
*Nos. C96-C99 (4)* 3.45 1.35

Nos. C98a and C98b each contain a 100fr stamp similar to No. C98 and two 50fr stamps showing festival scenes. The 50fr stamps have not been issued individually.

### People and Dwellings Type of Regular Issue

Design: 300fr, People and village of Les Bassari, Kundara Region.

**1968, Apr. 1 Photo. *Perf. 14x13½***
**Size: 57x36mm**

C100 A66 300fr gold & multi 4.50 1.25

### Legends Type of Regular Issue

70fr, The Girl and the Hippopotamus. 100fr, Old Faya's Inheritance, vert. 200fr, Soumangourou Kante Killed by Djegue (woman on horseback). 300fr, Little Gouné, Son of the Lion, vert.

**1968 Photo. *Perf. 13½***

**C101** A67 70fr multicolored .90 .25
**C102** A67 100fr multicolored 1.40 .30
**C103** A67 200fr multicolored 2.75 1.00
*a.* Souv. sheet of 4 7.00 7.00
**C104** A67 300fr multicolored 4.00 1.25
*Nos. C101-C104 (4)* 9.05 2.75

Issued in sheets of 10 plus 2 labels. No. C103a contains 4 imperf. stamps similar to Nos. 510-511 and C102-C103.;

For souvenir sheet see No. 509a.

Issued: #C102-C103, 5/16; #C101, C104, 9/16.

### African Animal Type of Regular Issue

**1968, Nov. 25 Photo. *Perf. 13½***
**Size: 49x35mm**

**C105** A68 100fr Lions 1.75 .55
**C106** A68 200fr Elephant 3.50 2.10

For souvenir sheet see No. 518a.

### Robert F. Kennedy Type of Regular Issue, 1968

Portraits: 50fr, Senator Robert F. Kennedy. 100fr, Rev. Martin Luther King, Jr. 200fr, Pres. John F. Kennedy.

**1968, Dec. 16**

**C107** A69 50fr yel & multi .90 .25
**C108** A69 100fr multicolored 1.90 .25
**C109** A69 200fr multicolored 4.00 1.25
*Nos. C107-C109 (3)* 8.35 1.65

The stamps are printed in sheets of 15 (3x5) containing 10 stamps and five green and gold center labels. Sheets come either with English or French inscriptions on label.

### Olympic Type of Regular Issue

Sculpture &: 100fr, Gymnast on vaulting horse. 200fr, Gymnast on rings. 300fr, High jump.

**1969, Feb. 1 Photo. *Perf. 13½***

**C110** A71 100fr multicolored 1.25 .30
**C111** A71 200fr multicolored 2.75 .90
**C111A** A71 300fr multicolored 4.50 1.10
*Nos. C110-C111A (3)* 8.50 2.30

Nos. C78-C79 Surcharged and Overprinted in Red

**1969, Mar. 17 Litho. *Perf. 13½x14***

**C112** A52 25fr on 200fr multi .40 .25
**C112A** A52 100fr multicolored 1.00 .65
**C112B** A52 200fr multicolored 2.00 1.00
*Nos. C112-C112B (3)* 4.15 1.85

See note after No. 530.

Nos. C112-C112B also exist with surcharge and overprint in orange (25fr, 200fr) or black (100fr). These sell for a small premium.

### Bird Type of Regular Issue

Birds: 50fr, Violet-crested touraco. 100fr, European golden oriole. 200fr, Vulturine guinea fowl.

**1971, June 18 Photo. *Perf. 13***
**Size: 41x41mm**

**C113** A81 50fr gold & multi 1.10 .40
**C113A** A81 100fr gold & multi 2.25 .80
**C113B** A81 200fr gold & multi 4.50 1.25
*Nos. C113-C113B (3)* 10.15 2.45

John and Robert Kennedy, Martin Luther King, Jr. — AP9

### Embossed on Metallic Foil

**1972 *Die Cut Perf. 10½***

**C114** AP9 300fr silver *35.00 35.00*

### Embossed & Typo.

**C114A** AP9 1500fr gold, cream & green *55.00 55.00*

Jules Verne, Moon Rocket — AP10

### Embossed on Metallic Foil

**1972 *Die Cut Perf. 10½***

**C115** AP10 300fr silver *35.00 35.00*
**C115A** AP10 1200fr gold *85.00 85.00*

Richard Nixon — AP11

Nixon and Mao — AP12

Nixon's Trip to People's Republic of China: a, Nixon. b, Chinese table tennis player. c, American table tennis player, Capitol dome. d, Mao Tse-tung.

### Embossed on Metallic Foil

**1972 *Die Cut Perf. 10½***

**C116** AP11 90fr Block of 4, #a.-d., silver *27.50 27.50*
**C117** AP11 290fr Block of 4, #a.-d., gold *45.00 45.00*

### Embossed & Typo.

**C118** AP12 1200fr gold & red *70.00 70.00*

Perforations within blocks of 4 are perf. 11.

### Racial Equality Year Type of Regular Issue

Design: 100fr, Men of 4 races and racial equality emblem (like No. 603).

**1972, May 14 Photo. *Perf. 13x13½***

**C119** A84 100fr gold & multi 1.10 1.00

### Satellite Type of Regular Issue

Designs: 100fr, Map of Africa and Relay. 200fr, Map of Africa and Early Bird.

**1972, May 17 Litho. *Perf. 13***

**C120** A85 100fr yel & multi 1.40 .70
**C121** A85 200fr multicolored 3.00 1.40

### African Postal Union Type of Regular Issue

Air mail envelope and UPAF emblem.

**1972, July 10**

**C122** A86 100fr multicolored 1.00 .55
**C123** A86 200fr multicolored 1.90 1.25

### Olympic Type of Regular Issue

**1972, Aug. 26 Photo. *Perf. 13***

**C124** A88 100fr Gymnast on rings 2.40 .60
**C125** A88 200fr Bicycling 3.75 1.10

### Souvenir Sheet

**C126** A88 300fr Soccer 7.00 7.00

### Flower Type of 1974

**1974, May 20 Photo. *Perf. 13***
**Size: 38x38mm (Diamond)**

**C127** A97 20s Thunbergia alata 2.75 .95
**C128** A97 25s Diascia barberae 3.50 1.10
**C129** A97 50s Kigelia africana 7.25 2.75
*Nos. C127-C129 (3)* 17.75 4.80

### Olympic Games Type of 1976
Souvenir Sheet

**1976, May 17 Photo. *Perf. 13½***

**C130** Sheet of 4 16.00 12.50
*a.* A104 25s Soccer 2.50 2.50

No. C130 contains 32x32mm stamps.

### Mushroom Type of 1977

Mushrooms: 10s, Morchella esculenta. 12s, Lepiota procera. 15s, Cantharellus cibarius.

**1977, Feb. 6 Photo. *Perf. 13***
**Size: 48x31mm**

**C131** A106 10s multicolored 4.00 .70
**C132** A106 12s multicolored 5.50 .90
**C133** A106 15s multicolored 7.50 2.10
*Nos. C131-C133 (3)* 19.00 3.70

### Reptile Type of 1977

Reptiles: 10s, Flap-necked chameleon. 15s, Nile crocodiles. 25s, Painted tortoise.

**1977, Oct. 10 Photo. *Perf. 13½***
**Size: 46x30mm**

**C134** A109 10s multicolored 3.50 .80
**C135** A109 15s multicolored 4.50 1.10
**C136** A109 25s multicolored 7.00 1.60
*Nos. C134-C136 (3)* 17.75 3.50

### Animal Type of 1977

Endangered Animals: 5s, Eland. 8s, Pygmy elephant. 9s, Hippopotamus. 10s, Chimpanzee. 12s, Palm squirrel. 13s, Lion. Male, female and young of each animal shown.

**1977, Dec. 12 Photo. *Perf. 14x13½***

**C137** A110 Strip of 3 3.50 1.75
*a.-c.* 5s any single .95
**C138** A110 Strip of 3 5.50 2.75
*a.-c.* 8s any single 1.60
**C139** A110 Strip of 3 5.75 3.00
*a.-c.* 9s any single 1.75
**C140** A110 Strip of 3 6.00 3.50
*a.-c.* 10s any single 1.75
**C141** A110 Strip of 3 7.50 4.00
*a.-c.* 12s any single 2.25
**C142** A110 Strip of 3 8.50 5.00
*a.-c.* 13s any single 2.50
*Nos. C137-C142 (6)* 42.25 20.00

### Russian Revolution Type, 1978

10s, Russian ballet. 30s, Pushkin Monument.

**1978, Feb. 27 Photo. *Perf. 14***

**C143** A111 10s gold & multi 2.40 .80
**C144** A111 30s gold & multi 7.00 2.10

### Giscard d'Estaing Type of 1979

Pres. Valery Giscard d'Estaing of France, vert.

**1979, Sept. 14 Photo. *Perf. 13***

**C145** A112 25s multicolored 5.00 2.00

### Jules Verne Type of 1979

Designs: 20s, Five Weeks in a Balloon. 25s, Robur the Conqueror.

**1979, Nov. 8 Litho. *Perf. 12x12½***

**C146** A113 20s multicolored 3.50 1.25
**C147** A113 25s multicolored 3.50 1.25

### Olympic Type of 1982

**1982 Litho. *Perf. 12½x12, 12x12½***

**C148** A120 9s Fencing 1.60 .45
**C149** A120 10s Soccer, vert. 1.90 .45
**C150** A120 11s Basketball, vert. 2.25 .45
**C151** A120 20s Diving, vert. 4.00 1.10
**C152** A120 25s Boxing, vert. 4.75 1.50
*Nos. C148-C152 (5)* 14.50 3.95

### Ataturk Type of 1982

**1982, July 19 Photo. *Perf. 13½***

**C153** A122 25s like #830 5.00 1.25

### World Cup Type of 1982

Designs: Various soccer players.

**1982, Aug. 23**

**C154** A123 10s multicolored 2.60 .95
**C155** A123 20s multicolored 5.50 2.10
**C156** A123 25s multicolored 6.50 2.75
*Nos. C154-C156 (3)* 14.60 5.80

### Nos. C154-C156 Overprinted

**1982, Aug. 23 Photo. *Perf. 13½***

**C157** A123 10s multicolored 2.40 .75
**C158** A123 20s multicolored 5.00 1.75
**C159** A123 25s multicolored 6.00 2.00
*Nos. C157-C159 (3)* 13.40 4.50

Location of flag in overprint varies.

### Balloon Type

Designs: 20s, Graf Zeppelin, Airship, horiz. 25s, Double Eagle II, L. Newman, B. Abruzzo, M. Anderson. 30s, Le Geant Hot Air Balloon, Nadar; Dirigible, Dumont.

**1983, Aug. 1 Litho. *Perf. 13½***

**C160** A125 20s multicolored 3.25 1.25
**C161** A125 25s multicolored 3.75 1.75

### Souvenir Sheet

**C162** A125 30s multicolored 5.00 1.90

### Nos. 894, 880-881 & 896 Overprinted

No. C163

No. C164

**1985, Nov. 5 Litho. *Perf. 13½***

**C163** A133 20s multi 2.75 1.25
**C164** A131 20s multi 2.75 1.25
**C165** A131 25s Overprint like #C163 3.50 1.50
*Nos. C163-C165 (3)* 9.00 4.00

### Souvenir Sheet

**C166** A133 30s "Kasparov / champion / du Monde" 15.00 10.00

US Space Shuttle Challenger Explosion, Jan. 28, 1986 — AP13

Designs: 100fr, Lift-off, crew names. 170fr, Shuttle design, Christa McAuliffe holding shuttle model. 600fr, Lift-off, vert.

**1986, July 1**
**100fr, 170fr Surcharged in Silver and Black**

**C167** AP13 100fr multicolored 1.10 .30

| | | | | |
|---|---|---|---|---|
| **C168** | AP13 | 170fr multicolored | 1.60 | .50 |

**Souvenir Sheet**

| | | | | |
|---|---|---|---|---|
| **C169** | AP13 | 600fr multicolored | 7.00 | 2.75 |

#C167-C168 not issued without surcharge.

Souvenir sheets of one exist containing Nos. C167 and C168.

Robin Yount, Milwaukee Brewers Baseball Player — AP14

**1990, Aug. 3 Litho. *Perf. 13½***

| | | | | |
|---|---|---|---|---|
| **C170** | AP14 | 450fr multicolored | 5.00 | 2.10 |

No. C170 exists in a souvenir sheet of 1.

For surcharge see No. 1182R.

Souvenir Sheet

Armstrong, Aldrin, Collins and Apollo 11 Emblem — AP15

**1990, Aug. 3 Litho. *Perf. 13½***

| | | | | |
|---|---|---|---|---|
| **C171** | AP15 | 750fr multicolored | 8.00 | 3.25 |

Galileo Spacecraft — AP16

**1990, Aug. 3**

| | | | | |
|---|---|---|---|---|
| **C172** | AP16 | 500fr multicolored | 5.25 | 2.25 |

No. C172 exists as a souvenir sheet of 1.

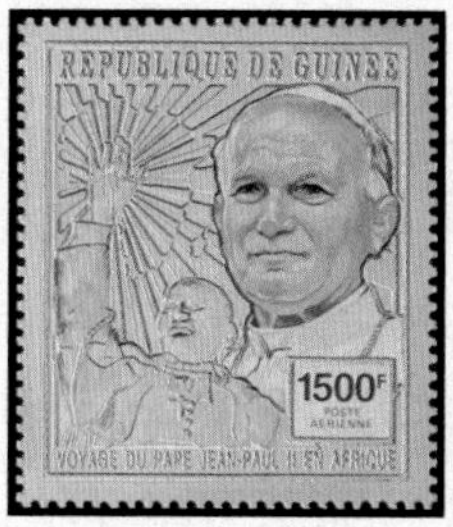


Pope John Paul II, Visit to Africa AP18

Portrait and: No. C174, Raising hand in benediction. No. C175, Child.

**Litho. & Embossed**

**1992, Oct. 26 *Perf. 13½***

| | | | | |
|---|---|---|---|---|
| **C174** | AP18 | 1500fr gold & multi | 24.00 | 19.00 |

**Souvenir Sheet**

| | | | | |
|---|---|---|---|---|
| **C175** | AP18 | 1500fr gold & multi | 18.00 | 15.00 |

No. C175 exists imperf.

Elvis Presley, 15th Anniv. of Death — AP19

**1992, Nov. 10**

| | | | | |
|---|---|---|---|---|
| **C176** | AP19 | 1500fr gold & multi | 24.00 | 20.00 |

No. C176 exists in miniature sheet of one.

De Gaulle Type of 1991 Overprinted "6 JUNE 1944 / DEBARQUEMENT"

**1994 Litho. & Embossed *Perf. 13½***

| | | | | |
|---|---|---|---|---|
| **C177** | A181 | 1500fr like #1168 | 15.00 | 12.50 |

No. 1195 Overprinted in Silver

**1993, Feb. 24 Litho. *Perf. 13½***

| | | | | |
|---|---|---|---|---|
| **C178** | A188 | 450fr multicolored | 4.50 | 2.25 |

No. C178 exists in souvenir sheet of 1.

---

## POSTAGE DUE STAMPS

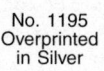

D5

D6

**1959 Unwmk. Litho. *Perf. 11½***

| | | | | |
|---|---|---|---|---|
| **J36** | D5 | 1fr emerald | .30 | .25 |
| **J37** | D5 | 2fr lilac rose | .30 | .25 |
| **J38** | D5 | 3fr brown | .55 | .25 |
| **J39** | D5 | 5fr blue | 1.40 | .25 |
| **J40** | D5 | 10fr orange | 2.10 | .55 |
| **J41** | D5 | 20fr rose lilac | 4.25 | .95 |
| | | *Nos. J36-J41 (6)* | 8.90 | 2.50 |

**1960 Engr. *Perf. 13½***

| | | | | |
|---|---|---|---|---|
| **J42** | D6 | 1fr dark carmine | .25 | .25 |
| **J43** | D6 | 2fr brown orange | .25 | .25 |
| **J44** | D6 | 3fr dark car rose | .30 | .25 |
| **J45** | D6 | 5fr bright green | .70 | .35 |
| **J46** | D6 | 10fr dark brown | 1.50 | .55 |
| **J47** | D6 | 20fr dull blue | 3.00 | 1.25 |
| | | *Nos. J42-J47 (6)* | 6.00 | 2.90 |

---

# GUINEA-BISSAU

'gi-nē-bi-'sau̇ⁿ

LOCATION — West coast of Africa between Senegal and Guinea
GOVT. — Republic
AREA — 13,948 sq. mi.
POP. — 1,234,555 (1999 est.)
CAPITAL — Bissau

Guinea-Bissau, the former Portuguese Guinea, attained independence September 10, 1974. The state includes the Bissagos Islands.

100 Centavos = 1 Escudo
100 Centavos = 1 Peso

**Catalogue values for all unused stamps in this country are for Never Hinged items.**

Amilcar Cabral, Map of Africa and Flag — A27

Design: Flag of the PAIGC (African Party of Independence of Guinea-Bissau and Cape Verde) shows location of Guinea-Bissau on map of Africa.

***Perf. 11x10½***

**1974, Sept. 10 Litho. Unwmk.**

| | | | | |
|---|---|---|---|---|
| **345** | A27 | 1p brown & multi | 1.00 | .55 |
| **346** | A27 | 2.50p brown & multi | 1.40 | .80 |
| **347** | A27 | 5p brown & multi | *15.00* | *7.50* |
| **348** | A27 | 10p brown & multi | 3.75 | 2.10 |
| | | *Nos. 345-348 (4)* | *21.15* | *10.95* |

First anniv. of Proclamation of Independence, Sept. 24, 1973.

WMO Emblem — A28

Portuguese Guinea No. 344 Overprinted in Black

**1975 Litho. *Perf. 13***

| | | | | |
|---|---|---|---|---|
| **349** | A28 | 2c brown & multi | 1.20 | 1.20 |

No. 349 exists with overprint in brown. Value, $5.

Amilcar Cabral, Map of Africa, Flag — A29

**1975, Sept. Litho. *Perf. 11***

| | | | | |
|---|---|---|---|---|
| **350** | A29 | 1p brown & multi | .75 | .75 |
| **351** | A29 | 2.50p brown & multi | 1.25 | 1.25 |
| **352** | A29 | 5p brown & multi | 7.00 | 7.00 |
| **353** | A29 | 10p brown & multi | 7.00 | 7.00 |
| | | *Nos. 350-353 (4)* | 16.00 | 16.00 |

Nos. 350-353 are dated Sept. 24, 1973, in the design. Also exist dated Sept. 21, 1973. Value of latter set, $14.

Flag and Arms of Guinea-Bissau and Amilcar Cabral — A30

Flag, Arms and: 2e, #358, Family. 3e, 5e, Pres. Luiz Cabral. #359, like 1e.

**1975, Sept. *Perf. 14***

| | | | | |
|---|---|---|---|---|
| **354** | A30 | 1e yel & multi | 1.50 | 1.00 |
| **355** | A30 | 2e multicolored | 1.50 | 1.25 |
| **356** | A30 | 3e red & multi | 2.25 | 1.50 |
| **357** | A30 | 5e yel & multi | 6.25 | 4.00 |
| **358** | A30 | 10e red & multi | 9.25 | 5.00 |
| **359** | A30 | 10e brt grn & multi | 9.25 | 5.00 |
| | | *Nos. 354-359 (6)* | 30.00 | 17.75 |

Amilcar Cabral's 51st birth anniv. (1e, No. 359); African Party of Independence of Guinea-Bissau and Cape Verde, 19th anniv. (2e, No. 358); Proclamation of Independence, 2nd anniv. (3e, 5e).

For surcharges see Nos. 367-367E.

Henry Knox, Cannons of Ticonderoga — A30a

Designs: 10e, Israel Putnam, Battle of Bunker Hill. 15e, Washington crossing the Delaware. 20e, Tadeusz Kosciuszko, Battle of Saratoga. 30e, Von Steuben, winter at Valley Forge. 40e, Lafayette, Washington rallying troops at Monmouth. 50e, Signing the Declaration of Independence.

**1976, May 5 Litho. *Perf. 13½***

| | | | | |
|---|---|---|---|---|
| **360** | A30a | 5e multicolored | .50 | .25 |
| **360A** | A30a | 10e multicolored | .50 | .25 |
| **360B** | A30a | 15e multicolored | 1.00 | .40 |
| **360C** | A30a | 20e multicolored | 2.25 | .85 |
| **360D** | A30a | 30e multicolored | 2.75 | 1.00 |
| **360E** | A30a | 40e multicolored | 3.00 | 1.10 |
| | | *Nos. 360-360E (6)* | 10.00 | 3.85 |

**Souvenir Sheet**

| | | | | |
|---|---|---|---|---|
| **360F** | A30a | 50e multicolored | 13.50 | |

American Revolution, bicentennial. Nos. 360D-360F are airmail. Nos. 360-360E exist in miniature sheets of 1, perf. and imperf. No. 360F contains one 75x45mm stamp and exists imperf.

See Nos. 371-371A.

Masked Dancer A30b

**1976, May 10 *Perf. 11***

**Denomination in Black on Silver Block**

| | | | | |
|---|---|---|---|---|
| **361** | A30b | 2p shown | .35 | .25 |
| **361A** | A30b | 3p Dancer, drummer | .40 | .25 |
| **361B** | A30b | 5p Dancers on stilts | .60 | .25 |
| **361C** | A30b | 10p Dancer with spear, bow | .65 | .25 |
| **361D** | A30b | 15p Masked dancer, diff. | 2.00 | .75 |
| **361E** | A30b | 20p Dancer with striped cloak | 4.00 | 1.25 |
| | | *Nos. 361-361E (6)* | 8.00 | 3.00 |

**Souvenir Sheet**

| | | | | |
|---|---|---|---|---|
| **361F** | A30b | 50p Like No. 361E | 7.00 | 7.00 |

Nos. 361C-361F are airmail. Silver block obliterates original denomination. Not issued without surcharge.

Nos. 361-361F Ovptd. in Black

**1976, June 8** *Perf. 11*

| | | | | |
|---|---|---|---|---|
| **362** | A30b | 2p on No. 361 | .50 | .25 |
| **362A** | A30b | 3p on No. 361A | .60 | .25 |
| **362B** | A30b | 5p on No. 361B | .90 | .25 |
| **362C** | A30b | 10p on No. 361C | 1.25 | .45 |
| **362D** | A30b | 15p on No. 361D | 1.75 | .65 |
| **362E** | A30b | 20p on No. 361E | 2.50 | .95 |
| | | *Nos. 362-362E (6)* | 7.50 | 2.80 |

**Souvenir Sheet**

| | | | | |
|---|---|---|---|---|
| **362F** | A30b | 50p on No. 361F | 4.25 | 4.25 |

Nos. 362C-362F are airmail. UPU cent. (in 1974). Nos. 362-362F exist imperf, and Nos. 362-362E in imperf miniature sheets of 1, all with black or red overprints.

Cabral, Guinean Mother and Children — A31

**1976, Aug. Litho.** *Perf. 13½*

| | | | | |
|---|---|---|---|---|
| **363** | A31 | 3p multicolored | .25 | .25 |
| **364** | A31 | 5p multicolored | .25 | .25 |
| **365** | A31 | 6p multicolored | .45 | .25 |
| **366** | A31 | 10p multicolored | .55 | .25 |
| | | *Nos. 363-366 (4)* | 1.50 | 1.00 |

3rd anniv. of assassination of Amilcar Cabral (1924-1973), revolutionary leader.

**Nos. 354-359 Surcharged in Black on Silver**

**1976, Sept. 12 Litho.** *Perf. 14*

| | | | | |
|---|---|---|---|---|
| **367** | A30 | 1p on 1e No. 354 | .40 | .25 |
| **367A** | A30 | 2p on 2e No. 355 | .40 | .25 |
| **367B** | A30 | 3p on 3e No. 356 | .40 | .25 |
| **367C** | A30 | 5p on 5e No. 357 | 1.40 | .25 |
| **367D** | A30 | 10p on 10e No. 358 | 1.45 | .25 |
| **367E** | A30 | 10p on 10e No. 359 | 1.45 | .25 |
| | | *Nos. 367-367E (6)* | 5.50 | 1.50 |

1876 Bell Telephone and Laying First Trans-Atlantic Cable — A31a

Telephones of: 3p, France, 1890, and first telephone booth, 1893. 5p, Germany, 1903, and automatic telephone, 1898. 10p, England, 1910, and relay station, 1963. 15p, France, 1924, and communications satellite. 20p, Modern telephone, 1970, and Molniya satellite. 50p, Picture phone.

**1976, Oct. 18** *Perf. 13½*

| | | | | |
|---|---|---|---|---|
| **368** | A31a | 2p multicolored | .25 | .25 |
| **368A** | A31a | 3p multicolored | .25 | .25 |
| **368B** | A31a | 5p multicolored | .25 | .25 |
| **368C** | A31a | 10p multicolored | .75 | .45 |
| **368D** | A31a | 15p multicolored | 1.25 | .70 |
| **368E** | A31a | 20p multicolored | 1.75 | .85 |
| | | *Nos. 368-368E (6)* | 4.50 | 2.75 |

**Souvenir Sheet**

| | | | | |
|---|---|---|---|---|
| **368F** | A31a | 50p multicolored | 6.00 | 6.00 |

Nos. 368C-368F are airmail. No. 368F contains one 68x42mm stamp. No. 368F exists imperf. Nos. 368-368E exist in souvenir sheets of one, perf. and imperf.

1976 Winter Olympics, Innsbruck — A31b

**1976, Nov. 3** *Perf. 14x13½*

| | | | | |
|---|---|---|---|---|
| **369** | A31b | 1p Women's figure skating | .25 | .25 |
| **369A** | A31b | 3p Ice hockey | .25 | .25 |
| **369B** | A31b | 5p Two-man bobsled | .40 | .25 |
| **369C** | A31b | 10p Pairs figure skating | .90 | .25 |
| **369D** | A31b | 20p Cross country skiing | 1.45 | .65 |
| **369E** | A31b | 30p Speed skating | 1.75 | .85 |
| | | *Nos. 369-369E (6)* | 5.00 | 2.50 |

**Souvenir Sheet**

| | | | | |
|---|---|---|---|---|
| **369F** | A31b | 50p Downhill skiing | 4.50 | 4.50 |

Nos. 369C-369F are airmail. No. 369F exists imperf. Nos. 369-369E exist in souvenir sheets of one, perf. and imperf.

1976 Summer Olympics, Montreal A31c

**1976, Nov. 24** *Perf. 13½*

| | | | | |
|---|---|---|---|---|
| **370** | A31c | 1p Soccer | .25 | .25 |
| **370A** | A31c | 3p Pole vault | .25 | .25 |
| **370B** | A31c | 5p Women's hurdles | .40 | .25 |
| **370C** | A31c | 10p Discus | .75 | .40 |
| **370D** | A31c | 20p Sprinting | 1.60 | .50 |
| **370E** | A31c | 30p Wrestling | 2.75 | .60 |
| | | *Nos. 370-370E (6)* | 6.00 | 2.25 |

**Souvenir Sheet**

| | | | | |
|---|---|---|---|---|
| **370F** | A31c | 50p Cycling, horiz. | 5.50 | 5.50 |

Nos. 370E-370F are airmail. No. 370F contains one 47x38mm stamp. No. 370F exists imperf. Nos. 370-370E exist in souvenir sheets of one, perf. and imperf.

**American Revolution Type of 1976**

Designs: 3.50p, Crispus Attucks, Boston Massacre. 5p, Martin Luther King, US Capitol.

**1977, Jan. 27** *Perf. 13½*

**Denomination in Black on Gold Block**

| | | | | |
|---|---|---|---|---|
| **371** | A30a | 3.50p multicolored | .35 | .25 |
| **371A** | A30a | 5p multicolored | .45 | .25 |
| | | *Nos. 371-371A (2)* | .80 | .50 |

Gold block obliterates original denomination. Not issued without surcharge. Exist in souvenir sheets of one, perf. and imperf.

Cabral Addressing UN General Assembly — A32

Design: 50c, Cabral and guerrilla fighters.

**1977, July Litho.** *Perf. 13½*

| | | | | |
|---|---|---|---|---|
| **372** | A32 | 50c multicolored | .25 | .25 |
| **373** | A32 | 3.50p multicolored | .30 | .25 |

For surcharges see Nos. C12-C13.

Henri Dunant, Nobel Peace Prize, 1901 A32a

Nobel Prize Winners: 5p, Einstein, Physics, 1921. 6p, Irene and Frederic Joliot-Curie, Chemistry, 1935. 30p, Fleming, Medicine, 1945. 35p, Hemingway, Literature, 1954. 40p, J. Tinbergen, Economics, 1969. 50p, Nobel Prize Medal.

**1977, July 27**

| | | | | |
|---|---|---|---|---|
| **374** | A32a | 3.50p multicolored | .35 | .25 |
| **374A** | A32a | 5p multicolored | .40 | .25 |
| **374B** | A32a | 6p multicolored | .75 | .25 |
| **374C** | A32a | 30p multicolored | 2.75 | 1.20 |
| **374D** | A32a | 35p multicolored | 5.00 | 1.40 |
| **374E** | A32a | 40p multicolored | 7.75 | 1.90 |
| | | *Nos. 374-374E (6)* | 17.00 | 5.25 |

**Souvenir Sheet**

| | | | | |
|---|---|---|---|---|
| **374F** | A32a | 50p multicolored | 6.00 | 6.00 |

Nos. 374D-374F are airmail. No. 374F contains one 57x39mm stamp. No. 374F exists imperf. Nos. 374-374E exist in souvenir sheets of one, perf. and imperf.

Postal Runner, Telstar Satellite — A32b

UPU Centenary (in 1974): 5p, Biplane, satellites encircle globe. 6p, Mail truck, satelite control room. 30p, Stagecoach, astronaut canceling letters on Moon. 35p, Steam locomotive, communications satellite. 40p, Space shuttle, Apollo-Soyuz link-up. 50p, Semaphore signalling system, satellite dish.

**1977, Sept. 30**

| | | | | |
|---|---|---|---|---|
| **375** | A32b | 3.50p multicolored | .25 | .25 |
| **375A** | A32b | 5p multicolored | .25 | .25 |
| **375B** | A32b | 6p multicolored | .35 | .25 |
| **375C** | A32b | 30p multicolored | 2.25 | .75 |
| **375D** | A32b | 35p multicolored | 2.40 | 1.25 |
| **375E** | A32b | 40p multicolored | 3.00 | 1.50 |
| | | *Nos. 375-375E (6)* | 8.50 | 4.25 |

**Souvenir Sheet**

| | | | | |
|---|---|---|---|---|
| **375F** | A32b | 50p multicolored | 4.25 | 4.25 |

Nos. 375D-375F are airmail. No. 375F exists imperf. Nos. 375-375E exist in souvenir sheets of one, perf. and imperf.

Torch and Party Emblem — A33

**1977, Sept. Litho.** *Perf. 14*

| | | | | |
|---|---|---|---|---|
| **376** | A33 | 3p yel & multi | .25 | .25 |
| **377** | A33 | 15p sal & multi | .95 | .60 |
| **378** | A33 | 50p lt grn & multi | 2.25 | 1.50 |
| | | *Nos. 376-378 (3)* | 3.45 | 2.35 |

African Party of Independence of Guinea-Bissau and Cape Verde, 20th anniversary.

Queen Elizabeth II, Silver Jubilee — A33a

Designs: 5p, Coronation ceremony. 10p, Yeoman of the Guard, Crown Jewels. 20p, Trumpeter. 25p, Royal Horse Guard. 30p, Royal Family. 50p, Queen Elizabeth II.

**1977, Oct. 15**

| | | | | |
|---|---|---|---|---|
| **379** | A33a | 3.50p multicolored | .35 | .25 |
| **379A** | A33a | 5p multicolored | .40 | .25 |
| **379B** | A33a | 10p multicolored | .85 | .25 |
| **379C** | A33a | 20p multicolored | 1.90 | .40 |
| **379D** | A33a | 25p multicolored | 2.75 | .60 |
| **379E** | A33a | 30p multicolored | 3.25 | 1.00 |
| | | *Nos. 379-379E (6)* | 9.50 | 2.75 |

**Souvenir Sheet**

| | | | | |
|---|---|---|---|---|
| **379F** | A33a | 50p multicolored | 4.25 | 4.25 |

Nos. 379D-379F are airmail. No. 379F contains one 42x39mm stamp. No. 379F exists imperf. Nos. 379-379E exist in souvenir sheets of one, perf. and imperf.

Massacre of the Innocents by Rubens A33b

Paintings by Peter Paul Rubens: 5p, Rape of the Daughters of Leukippos. 6p, Lamentation of Christ, horiz. 30p, Francisco IV Gonzaga, Prince of Mantua. 35p, The Four Continents. 40p, Marquise Brigida Spinola Doria. 50p, The Wounding of Christ.

**1977, Nov. 15**

| | | | | |
|---|---|---|---|---|
| **380** | A33b | 3.50p multicolored | .40 | .25 |
| **380A** | A33b | 5p multicolored | .60 | .25 |
| **380B** | A33b | 6p multicolored | .70 | .30 |
| **380C** | A33b | 30p multicolored | 2.50 | 1.20 |
| **380D** | A33b | 35p multicolored | 3.00 | 1.40 |
| **380E** | A33b | 40p multicolored | 4.25 | 1.60 |
| | | *Nos. 380-380E (6)* | 11.45 | 5.00 |

**Souvenir Sheet**

| | | | | |
|---|---|---|---|---|
| **380F** | A33b | 50p multicolored | 4.50 | 4.50 |

Nos. 380D-380F are airmail. Nos. 380-380F exist imperf. Nos. 380-380E exist in souvenir sheets of one, perf. and imperf.

Congress Emblem — A34

**1977, Nov. 15 Litho.** *Perf. 14*

| | | | | |
|---|---|---|---|---|
| **381** | A34 | 3.50p multicolored | .30 | .25 |

3rd PAIGC Congress, Bissau, Nov. 15-20.

Santos-Dumont's Airship, 1901 — A34a

Airships: 5p, R-34 crossing the Atlantic, 1919. 10p, Norge over North Pole, 1926. 20p, Graf Zeppelin over Abu Simbel, 1931. 25p, Hindenburg over New York, 1937. 30p, Graf Zeppelin, Concorde, space shuttle. 50p, Ferdinand von Zeppelin, horiz.

**1978, Feb. 27**

| | | | | | |
|---|---|---|---|---|---|
| **382** | A34a | 3.50p | multicolored | .25 | .25 |
| **382A** | A34a | 5p | multicolored | .35 | .25 |
| **382B** | A34a | 10p | multicolored | 1.00 | .25 |
| **382C** | A34a | 20p | multicolored | 2.00 | .50 |
| **382D** | A34a | 25p | multicolored | 2.50 | 1.00 |
| **382E** | A34a | 30p | multicolored | 2.75 | 1.50 |
| | | | *Nos. 382-382E (6)* | 8.85 | 3.75 |

**Souvenir Sheet**

| | | | | | |
|---|---|---|---|---|---|
| **382F** | A34a | 50p | multicolored | 6.75 | 5.50 |

Nos. 382D-382F are airmail. No. 382F exists imperf. Nos. 382-382E exist in souvenir sheets of one, perf. and imperf.

World Cup Soccer Championships, Argentina — A34b

Soccer players and posters from previous World Cup Championships: 3.50p, 1930. 5p, 1938. 10p, 1950. 20p, 1962. 25p, 1970. 30p, 1974. 50p, Argentina '78 emblem.

**1978, Mar. 15**

| | | | | | |
|---|---|---|---|---|---|
| **383** | A34b | 3.50p | multicolored | .25 | .25 |
| **383A** | A34b | 5p | multicolored | .25 | .25 |
| **383B** | A34b | 10p | multicolored | .65 | .25 |
| **383C** | A34b | 20p | multicolored | 1.45 | .50 |
| **383D** | A34b | 25p | multicolored | 1.90 | 1.00 |
| **383E** | A34b | 30p | multicolored | 2.25 | 1.50 |
| | | | *Nos. 383-383E (6)* | 6.75 | 3.75 |

**Souvenir Sheet**

| | | | | | |
|---|---|---|---|---|---|
| **383F** | A34b | 50p | multicolored | 4.25 | 4.25 |

Nos. 383D-383F are airmail. Nos. 383-383F exist imperf. Nos. 383-383E exist in miniature sheets of one, perf. and imperf.

For surcharges see Nos. 393-393F.

Endangered Species — A34c

**1978, Apr. 17**

| | | | | | |
|---|---|---|---|---|---|
| **384** | A34c | 3.50p | Black antelope | .25 | .25 |
| **384A** | A34c | 5p | Fennec | .40 | .25 |
| **384B** | A34c | 6p | Secretary bird | .60 | .30 |
| **384C** | A34c | 30p | Hippopotami | 3.00 | 1.45 |
| **384D** | A34c | 35p | Cheetahs | 3.25 | 1.75 |
| **384E** | A34c | 40p | Gorillas | 3.50 | 2.00 |
| | | | *Nos. 384-384E (6)* | 11.00 | 6.00 |

**Souvenir Sheet**

| | | | | | |
|---|---|---|---|---|---|
| **384F** | A34c | 50p | Cercopithecus erythotis | 5.50 | 5.50 |

Nos. 384D-384F are airmail. No. 384F contains one 39x42mm stamp. No. 384F exists imperf. Nos. 384-384E exist in souvenir sheets of one, perf. and imperf.

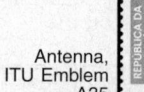

Antenna, ITU Emblem A35

**1978, May 17 Litho. *Perf. 13½***

| | | | | | |
|---|---|---|---|---|---|
| **385** | A35 | 3.50p | silver & multi | .25 | .25 |
| **386** | A35 | 10p | gold & multi | .65 | .30 |

10th World Telecommunications Day.

Boy — A36

3p, Infant and grandfather. 5p, Boys. 30p, Girls.

**1978 *Perf. 14***

| | | | | | |
|---|---|---|---|---|---|
| **387** | A36 | 50c | yel grn & dk bl | .25 | .25 |
| **388** | A36 | 3p | claret & car rose | .25 | .25 |
| **389** | A36 | 5p | ocher & brown | .30 | .25 |
| **390** | A36 | 30p | car & ocher | 2.10 | .80 |
| | | | *Nos. 387-390 (4)* | 2.90 | 1.55 |

Children's Day.

Queen Elizabeth II, Silver Jubilee A36a

Elizabeth, Imperial State Crown — A36b

Designs: 5p, Queen, Prince Philip in Coronation Coach. 10p, Queen, Prince Philip. 20p, Mounted drummer. 25p, Imperial State Crown, St. Edward's Crown. 30p, Queen holding orb and scepter. 50p, Queen on Throne flanked by Archbishops. No. 391H, Coronation Coach.

**1978, June 15**

| | | | | | |
|---|---|---|---|---|---|
| **391** | A36a | 3.50p | multicolored | .25 | .25 |
| **391A** | A36a | 5p | multicolored | .25 | .25 |
| **391B** | A36a | 10p | multicolored | .60 | .25 |
| **391C** | A36a | 20p | multicolored | 1.25 | .40 |
| **391D** | A36a | 25p | multicolored | 1.75 | .60 |
| **391E** | A36a | 30p | multicolored | 1.90 | 1.00 |
| | | | *Nos. 391-391E (6)* | 6.00 | 2.75 |

**Litho. & Embossed**

| | | | | | |
|---|---|---|---|---|---|
| **391F** | A36b | 100p | gold & multi | 17.50 | — |

**Souvenir Sheets**

| | | | | | |
|---|---|---|---|---|---|
| **391G** | A36a | 50p | multicolored | 4.25 | 4.25 |

**Litho. & Embossed**

| | | | | | |
|---|---|---|---|---|---|
| **391H** | A36b | 100p | gold & multi | 12.00 | — |

Nos. 391D-391H are airmail. Nos. 391-391E exist in souvenir sheets of one, perf. and imperf. Nos. 391F-391H exist imperf.

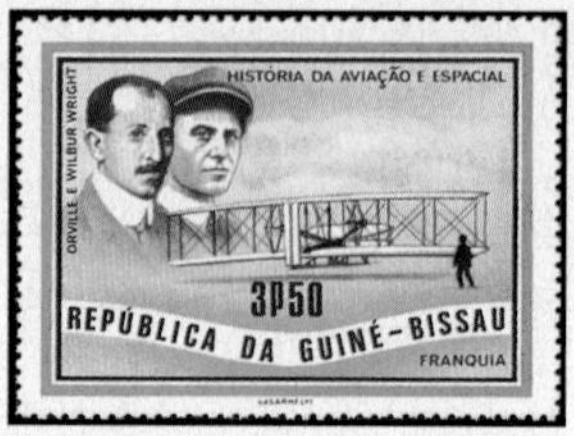

History of Aviation — A36c

**1978, June 15 Litho. *Perf. 13½***

| | | | | | |
|---|---|---|---|---|---|
| **392** | A36c | 3.50p | Wright Brothers | .25 | .25 |
| **392A** | A36c | 10p | Santos-Dumont | .70 | .25 |
| **392B** | A36c | 15p | Bleriot | 1.00 | .45 |
| **392C** | A36c | 20p | Lindbergh, Spirit of St. Louis | 1.45 | .60 |
| **392D** | A36c | 25p | Lunar module | 1.75 | .70 |
| **392E** | A36c | 30p | Space shuttle | 2.10 | .95 |
| | | | *Nos. 392-392E (6)* | 7.25 | 3.20 |

**Souvenir Sheet**

| | | | | | |
|---|---|---|---|---|---|
| **392F** | A36c | 50p | Concorde | 4.75 | 4.75 |

Nos. 392D-392F are airmail. Nos. 392-392E exist in souvenir sheets of one, perf. and imperf. No. 392F exists imperf.

**Nos. 383-383F Ovptd. in Gold**

**1978, Oct. 2**

| | | | | | |
|---|---|---|---|---|---|
| **393** | A34b | 3.50p | on No. 383 | .25 | .25 |
| **393A** | A34b | 5p | on No. 383A | .25 | .25 |
| **393B** | A34b | 10p | on No. 383B | .65 | .45 |
| **393C** | A34b | 20p | on No. 383C | 1.45 | .60 |
| **393D** | A34b | 25p | on No. 383D | 1.90 | .70 |
| **393E** | A34b | 30p | on No. 383E | 2.50 | .95 |
| | | | *Nos. 393-393E (6)* | 7.00 | 3.20 |

**Souvenir Sheet**

| | | | | | |
|---|---|---|---|---|---|
| **393F** | A34b | 50p | on No. 383F | 4.25 | 4.25 |

Nos. 393D-393F are airmail. Nos. 393-393F exist imperf. Nos. 393-393E exist in miniature sheets of 1 perf. and imperf. No. 393F exists overprinted in silver.

Virgin and Child by Albrecht Durer — A36d

Different Paintings of the Virgin and Child (Virgin only on 30p) by Durer.

**1978, Nov. 14**

| | | | | | |
|---|---|---|---|---|---|
| **394** | A36d | 3.50p | multicolored | .25 | .25 |
| **394A** | A36d | 5p | multicolored | .35 | .25 |
| **394B** | A36d | 6p | multicolored | .40 | .25 |
| **394C** | A36d | 30p | multicolored | 2.25 | .75 |
| **394D** | A36d | 35p | multicolored | 2.50 | 1.10 |
| **394E** | A36d | 40p | multicolored | 3.00 | 1.40 |
| | | | *Nos. 394-394E (6)* | 8.75 | 4.00 |

**Souvenir Sheet**

| | | | | | |
|---|---|---|---|---|---|
| **394F** | A36d | 50p | multicolored | 4.75 | 4.75 |

Nos. 394D-394F are airmail. No. 394F contains one 51x56mm stamp. Nos. 394-394E exist in souvenir sheets of one, perf. and imperf. No. 394F exists imperf.

Sir Rowland Hill (1795-1879), Wurttemberg No. 53 — A36e

Hill and: 5p, Belgium #1. 6p, Monaco #10. 30p, Spain 2r stamp of 1851 in blue. 35p, Switzerland #5. 40p, Two Sicilies #8. 50p, Portuguese Guinea #13 in brown.

**1978, Dec. 15**

| | | | | | |
|---|---|---|---|---|---|
| **395** | A36e | 3.50p | multicolored | .25 | .25 |
| **395A** | A36e | 5p | multicolored | .50 | .25 |
| **395B** | A36e | 6p | multicolored | .75 | .25 |
| **395C** | A36e | 30p | multicolored | 3.00 | .25 |
| **395D** | A36e | 35p | multicolored | 4.50 | .30 |
| **395E** | A36e | 40p | multicolored | 5.50 | .70 |
| | | | *Nos. 395-395E (6)* | 14.50 | 2.00 |

**Souvenir Sheet**

| | | | | | |
|---|---|---|---|---|---|
| **395F** | A36e | 50p | multicolored | 4.75 | 4.75 |

Nos. 395D-395F are airmail. No. 395F contains one 51x42mm stamp. Nos. 395-395E exist in souvenir sheets of one, perf. and imperf. No. 395F exists imperf.

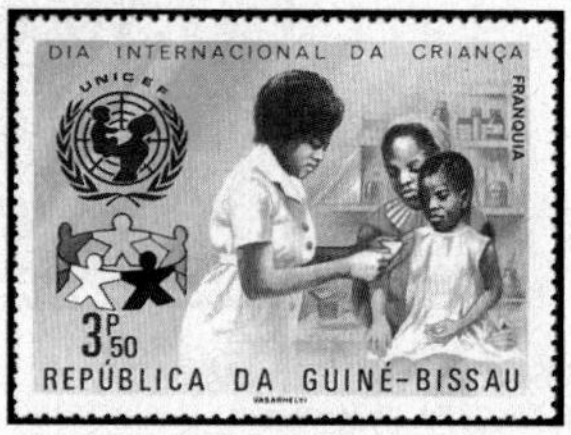

Intl. Day of the Child — A36f

**1979, Jan. 15 *Perf. 14***

| | | | | | |
|---|---|---|---|---|---|
| **396** | A36f | 3.50p | shown | .25 | .25 |
| **396A** | A36f | 10p | Children drinking | .75 | .25 |
| **396B** | A36f | 15p | Child with book | 1.10 | .55 |
| **396C** | A36f | 20p | Space plane | 1.40 | .65 |
| **396D** | A36f | 25p | Skylab | 1.75 | .85 |
| **396E** | A36f | 30p | Children playing chess | 2.00 | .95 |
| | | | *Nos. 396-396E (6)* | 7.25 | 3.50 |

**Souvenir Sheet**

| | | | | | |
|---|---|---|---|---|---|
| **396F** | A36f | 50p | Children watching spaceship | 4.75 | 4.75 |

Nos. 396C-396F are airmail. Nos. 396-396E exist in souvenir sheets of one, perf. and imperf. No. 396F exists imperf.

A36g

A36h

**1979 Litho. *Perf. 13***

| | | | | | |
|---|---|---|---|---|---|
| **397** | A36g | 4.50p | multicolored | .45 | .25 |

Massacre of Pindjiguiti, 20th anniv.

**1979 Litho. *Perf. 14***

| | | | | | |
|---|---|---|---|---|---|
| **397A** | A36h | 50c | shown | .25 | .25 |
| **397B** | A36h | 4p | People, rainbow, diff. | .30 | .25 |

World Telecommunications Day.

Family A37

**1979, May Litho. *Perf. 12x11½***

| | | | | | |
|---|---|---|---|---|---|
| **398** | A37 | 50c | multicolored | .40 | .25 |
| **399** | A37 | 2p | multicolored | .80 | .25 |
| **400** | A37 | 4p | multicolored | .40 | .25 |
| | | | *Nos. 398-400 (3)* | 1.60 | .75 |

General population census, Apr. 16-30.

Cassaca Conference, 16th Anniv. — A37a

**1980, Feb. 13 Litho. *Perf. 14x14¼***

| | | | | | |
|---|---|---|---|---|---|
| **400A** | A37a | 3.50p | multi | .25 | .25 |
| **400B** | A37a | 6.50p | multi | .30 | .25 |

An additional stamp was issued in this set. The editors would like to examine any examples.

Ernst Udet and Fokker D.VII — A38

**1980 Litho. *Perf. 13½***

| | | | | | |
|---|---|---|---|---|---|
| **401** | A38 | 3.50p | shown | .35 | .25 |
| **401A** | A38 | 5p | Charles Nungesser, Nieuport 17 | .35 | .25 |
| **401B** | A38 | 6p | von Richthofen, Fokker DR.1 | .45 | .25 |
| **401C** | A38 | 30p | Francesco Baracca, Spad XIII | 1.90 | .70 |
| | | | *Nos. 401-401C,C14-C14A (6)* | 8.30 | 3.70 |

Lake Placid Emblem, Speed Skating — A39

**1980**

| | | | | | |
|---|---|---|---|---|---|
| **402** | A39 | 3.50p | shown | .45 | .25 |
| **402A** | A39 | 5p | Downhill skiing | .45 | .25 |
| **402B** | A39 | 6p | Luge | .55 | .25 |
| **402C** | A39 | 30p | Cross-country skiing | 2.25 | .70 |
| | | | *Nos. 402-402C,C15-C16 (6)* | 9.95 | 3.70 |

13th Winter Olympic Games, Lake Placid, NY, Feb. 12-24.

Shot-put A40

**1980, Aug. Litho. *Perf. 13½***

| | | | | | |
|---|---|---|---|---|---|
| **403** | A40 | 3.50p | shown | .25 | .25 |
| **403A** | A40 | 5p | Athlete on rings | .60 | .25 |
| **403B** | A40 | 6p | Running | .80 | .25 |
| **403C** | A40 | 30p | Fencing | 3.00 | .70 |
| | | | *Nos. 403-403C,C18-C19 (6)* | 12.90 | 3.70 |

22nd Summer Olympic Games, Moscow, 7/19-8/3.

Pres. Luis Cabral, Children and Workers A41

5p, Pres. Cabral holding books.

**1980, Aug. Litho. *Perf. 13½***

| | | | | | |
|---|---|---|---|---|---|
| **404** | A41 | 3.50p | multicolored | .35 | .25 |
| **405** | A41 | 5p | multicolored | .60 | .25 |

Literacy campaign. See Nos. C21-C22.

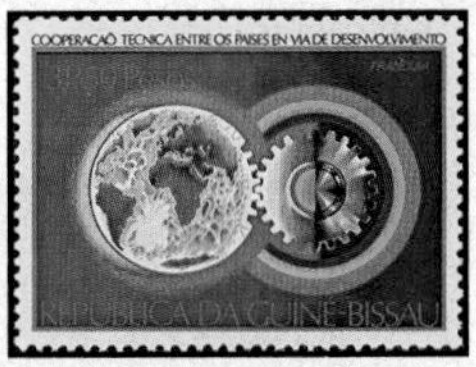


Cooperation Among Developing Countries — A42

**1980, Aug.**

| | | | | | |
|---|---|---|---|---|---|
| **406** | A42 | 3.50p | multicolored | .70 | .25 |
| **407** | A42 | 6p | multicolored | .70 | .25 |
| **408** | A42 | 10p | multicolored | 1.35 | .25 |
| | | | *Nos. 406-408 (3)* | 2.75 | .75 |

Baskets — A43

**1980, Aug. Litho. *Perf. 13½***

| | | | | | |
|---|---|---|---|---|---|
| **409** | A43 | 3p | Bird, family wood statues, vert. | .25 | .25 |
| **410** | A43 | 6p | shown | .25 | .25 |
| **411** | A43 | 20p | Head, doll carvings | 1.10 | .45 |
| | | | *Nos. 409-411 (3)* | 1.60 | .95 |

Infant and Toy Train, Locomotive, IYC Emblem A44

**1980**

| | | | | | |
|---|---|---|---|---|---|
| **412** | A44 | 6p | Classroom, horiz. | .40 | .30 |
| **412A** | A44 | 10p | Boy reading Jules Verne story | .75 | .55 |
| **412B** | A44 | 25p | shown | 1.50 | .80 |
| **412C** | A44 | 35p | Archer, boy with bow | 2.40 | 1.25 |
| | | | *Nos. 412-412C (4)* | 5.05 | 2.90 |

**Souvenir Sheet**

| | | | | | |
|---|---|---|---|---|---|
| **412D** | A44 | 50p | Students in lab | 4.50 | 4.50 |

International Year of the Child (1979).

Columbia Space Shuttle and Crew — A45

Space Exploration: 3.50p, Galileo, satellites. 5p, Wernher von Braun. 6p, Jules Verne, rocket.

**1981, May Litho. *Perf. 13½***

| | | | | | |
|---|---|---|---|---|---|
| **413** | A45 | 3.50p | multicolored | .35 | .25 |
| **413A** | A45 | 5p | multicolored | .40 | .25 |
| **413B** | A45 | 6p | multicolored | .45 | .25 |
| **413C** | A45 | 30p | multicolored | 2.10 | .90 |
| | | | *Nos. 413-413C,C23-C24 (6)* | 9.55 | 4.40 |

Soccer Players, World Cup, Argentina '78 and Espana '82 Emblems — A46

Soccer scenes and famous players: 3.50p, Platini, France. 5p, Bettega, Italy. 6p, Rensenbrink, Netherlands. 30p, Rivelino, Brazil.

**1981, May**

| | | | | | |
|---|---|---|---|---|---|
| **414** | A46 | 3.50p | multicolored | .35 | .25 |
| **414A** | A46 | 5p | multicolored | .40 | .25 |
| **414B** | A46 | 6p | multicolored | .45 | .25 |
| **414C** | A46 | 30p | multicolored | 2.10 | .80 |
| | | | *Nos. 414-414C,C26-C27 (6)* | 9.55 | 4.30 |

Prince Charles and Lady Diana, St. Paul's Cathedral A47

Royal Wedding (Couple and): 3.50p, Diana leading horse. 5p, Charles crowned Prince of Wales. 6p, Diana with kindergarten children.

**1981 Litho. *Perf. 13½***

| | | | | | |
|---|---|---|---|---|---|
| **415** | A47 | 3.50p | multicolored | .40 | .25 |
| **415A** | A47 | 5p | multicolored | .55 | .25 |
| **415B** | A47 | 6p | multicolored | .60 | .25 |
| **415C** | A47 | 30p | multicolored | 2.10 | .90 |
| | | | *Nos. 415-415C,C29-C30 (6)* | 12.40 | 4.40 |

Woman Before a Mirror, by Picasso (1881-1973) A48

Picasso Birth Cent.: Various paintings.

**1981, Dec. Litho. *Perf. 13½***

| | | | | | |
|---|---|---|---|---|---|
| **416** | A48 | 3.50p | multi | .30 | .25 |
| **417** | A48 | 5p | multi | .45 | .25 |
| **418** | A48 | 6p | multi | .65 | .25 |
| **419** | A48 | 30p | multi | 3.00 | .90 |
| | | | *Nos. 416-419,C32-C33 (6)* | 15.15 | 4.50 |

Henrique Vermelho and his Ship, Drakkar A49

Navigators and their ships: 5p, Vasco de Gama, St. Gabriel. 6p, Ferdinand Magellan, Victoria. 30p, Jacques Cartier, Emerillon.

**1981 Litho. *Perf. 13½***

| | | | | | |
|---|---|---|---|---|---|
| **420** | A49 | 3.50p | multicolored | .30 | .25 |
| **421** | A49 | 5p | multicolored | .45 | .25 |
| **422** | A49 | 6p | multicolored | .65 | .25 |
| **423** | A49 | 30p | multicolored | 3.00 | 1.00 |
| | | | *Nos. 420-423,C35-C36 (6)* | 13.15 | 4.90 |

Christmas — A50

Designs: Virgin and Child paintings.

**1981**

| | | | | | |
|---|---|---|---|---|---|
| **424** | A50 | 3.50p | Mantegna | .30 | .25 |
| **425** | A50 | 5p | Bellini | .45 | .25 |
| **426** | A50 | 6p | Mantegna, diff. | .65 | .25 |
| **427** | A50 | 25p | Correggio | 3.00 | 1.00 |
| | | | *Nos. 424-427,C38-C39 (6)* | 13.15 | 4.90 |

Scouting Year — A51

**1982, June 9 Litho. *Perf. 13½***

| | | | | | |
|---|---|---|---|---|---|
| **428** | A51 | 3.50p | Archery | .35 | .25 |
| **429** | A51 | 5p | First aid training | .35 | .25 |
| **430** | A51 | 6p | Bugler | .45 | .25 |
| **431** | A51 | 30p | Cub scouts | 2.50 | .65 |
| | | | *Nos. 428-431,C41-C42 (6)* | 10.15 | 3.50 |

1982 World Cup — A52

Various soccer players and cup.

**1982, June 13 Litho. *Perf. 13½***

| | | | | | |
|---|---|---|---|---|---|
| **432** | A52 | 3.50p | Keegan | .35 | .25 |
| **433** | A52 | 5p | Rossi | .35 | .25 |
| **434** | A52 | 6p | Zico | .45 | .25 |
| **435** | A52 | 30p | Arconada | 2.50 | .65 |
| | | | *Nos. 432-435,C44-C45 (6)* | 10.15 | 3.50 |

21st Birthday of Princess Diana — A53

Portraits and scenes of Diana.

**1982**

**436** A53 3.50p multicolored .35 .25
**437** A53 5p multicolored .35 .25
**438** A53 6p multicolored .45 .25
**439** A53 30p multicolored 2.50 .65
*Nos. 436-439,C47-C48 (6)* 10.15 3.50

For overprints see Nos. 450-456.

Visit by Portuguese President Eanes — A54

4.50p, Portugal and Guinea-Bissau flags.

**1982** **Litho.** ***Perf. 13½***

**440** A54 4.50p multicolored .40 .25
**441** A54 20p multicolored 1.60 1.10

Manned Flight Bicentenary — A55

Various hot air balloons.

**1983, Jan. 15** **Litho.** ***Perf. 11***

**442** A55 50c multicolored .25 .25
**443** A55 2.50p multicolored .25 .25
**444** A55 3.50p multicolored .30 .25
**445** A55 5p multicolored .50 .25
**446** A55 10p multicolored .55 .25
**447** A55 20p multicolored 1.35 .35
**448** A55 30p multicolored 1.90 .45
*Nos. 442-448 (7)* 5.10 2.05

**Souvenir Sheet**

***Perf. 12½***

**449** A55 50p multicolored 4.75 .90

No. 449 contains one 47x47mm stamp.

**Nos. 436-439, C47-C48, C49A-C49B Overprinted**

**1982** **Litho.** ***Perf. 13½***

**450** A53 3.50p multicolored .45 .25
**451** A53 5p multicolored .55 .25
**452** A53 6p multicolored .65 .25
**453** A53 30p multicolored 3.00 .65
**454** A53 35p multicolored 3.50 .80
**455** A53 40p multicolored 4.00 1.10
*Nos. 450-455 (6)* 12.15 3.30

**Souvenir Sheet**

**456** A53 50p multicolored 8.00 1.25

**Litho. & Embossed**

**456A** A53a 200p gold & multi 18.00

**Souvenir Sheet**

**456B** A53a 200p gold & multi, vert. 35.00

Nos. 454-456A are airmail.

African Apes and Monkeys A56

**1983, Mar. 15** **Litho.** ***Perf. 13½***

**457** A56 1p Comopithecus hamadryas .25 .25
**458** A56 1.50p Gorilla gorilla .25 .25
**459** A56 3.50p Theropithecus gelada .30 .25
**460** A56 5p Mandrillus sphinx .40 .25
**461** A56 8p Pan trogladytes .90 .25
**462** A56 20p Colobus abyssinicus 1.45 .30
**463** A56 30p Cercopithecus diana 2.00 .45
*Nos. 457-463 (7)* 5.55 2.00

Souvenir Sheet

TEMBAL '83, Stamp Exhibition, Basel — A57

**1983, May 21**

**464** A57 50p Space shuttle 4.25 1.10

A58

Designs: Various telecommunications satellites and space shuttles.

**1983, May 25** **Litho.** ***Perf. 13½***

**465** A58 1p multicolored .25 .25
**466** A58 1.50p multicolored .25 .25
**467** A58 3.50p multicolored .25 .25
**468** A58 5p multicolored .35 .25
**469** A58 8p multicolored .50 .25
**470** A58 20p multicolored 1.25 .40
**471** A58 30p multicolored 1.90 .65
*Nos. 465-471 (7)* 4.75 2.30

**Souvenir Sheet**

**472** A58 50p multicolored 3.75 .90

History of Chess — A59

Early Chess Game — A60

Various chess pieces.

**1983, June 13** **Litho.** ***Perf. 12***

**473** A59 1p multicolored .25 .25
**474** A59 1.50p multicolored .25 .25
**475** A59 3.50p multicolored .25 .25
**476** A59 5p multicolored .35 .25
**477** A59 10p multicolored .80 .25
**478** A59 20p multicolored 1.50 .25
**479** A59 40p multicolored 3.50 .60
*Nos. 473-479 (7)* 6.90 2.10

**Souvenir Sheet**

**480** A60 50p brown & blk 4.25 .85

Raphael, 500th Birth Anniv. A61

Various paintings.

**1983, June 30** **Litho.** ***Perf. 12½***

**481** A61 1p gold & multi .25 .25
**482** A61 1.50p gold & multi .25 .25
**483** A61 3.50p gold & multi .25 .25
**484** A61 5p gold & multi .40 .25
**485** A61 8p gold & multi .55 .25
**486** A61 15p gold & multi 1.05 .25
**487** A61 30p gold & multi 2.00 .45
*Nos. 481-487 (7)* 4.75 1.95

**Souvenir Sheet**

**488** A61 50p gold & multi 3.75 1.25

1984 Summer Olympics, Los Angeles — A62

**1983, July 20** **Litho.** ***Perf. 12½***

**489** A62 1p Swimming .25 .25
**490** A62 1.50p Jumping .25 .25
**491** A62 3.50p Fencing .40 .25
**492** A62 5p Weightlifting .40 .25
**493** A62 10p Running .55 .25
**494** A62 20p Equestrian 1.20 .25
**495** A62 40p Bicycling 2.40 .70
*Nos. 489-495 (7)* 5.45 2.20

**Souvenir Sheet**

**496** A62 50p Stadium 4.00 1.25

Souvenir Sheet

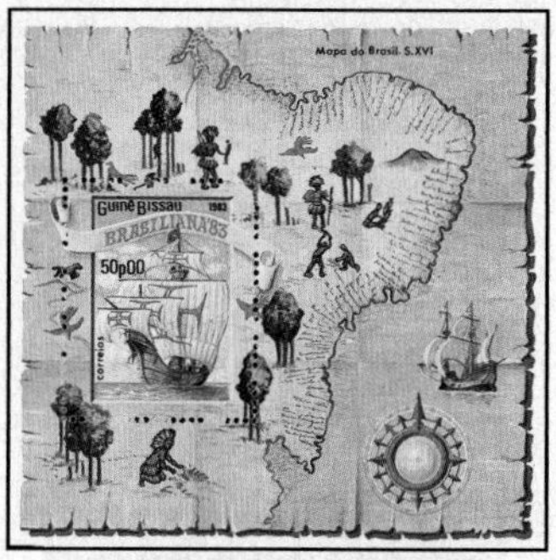


BRASILIANA '83, Philatelic Exhibition — A63

**1983, July 29** **Litho.** ***Perf. 13***

**497** A63 50p multicolored *8.00* *7.50*

Local Fish — A64

***Perf. 12x11½, 11½x12***

**1983, Dec. 8** **Litho.**

**498** A64 1p Monodactylus sebae, vert. .25 .25
**499** A64 1.50p Botia macracanthus .25 .25
**500** A64 3.50p Ctenopoma acutirostre .30 .25
**501** A64 5p Roloffia bertholdi .35 .25
**502** A64 8p Aphyosemion bualanum .50 .25
**503** A64 10p Aphyosemion bivittatum .75 .25
**504** A64 30p Aphyosemion australe 2.25 .95
*Nos. 498-504 (7)* 4.65 2.45

1984 Winter Olympics, Sarajevo — A65

**1983, Oct. 10** **Litho.** ***Perf. 13***

**505** A65 1p Speed skating .25 .25
**506** A65 1.50p Ski jumping .25 .25
**507** A65 3p Biathlon .40 .25
**508** A65 5p Bobsledding .55 .25
**509** A65 10p Hockey .65 .25
**510** A65 15p Figure skating 1.25 .25
**511** A65 20p Luge 1.75 .30
*Nos. 505-511 (7)* 5.10 1.80

**Souvenir Sheet**

**512** A65 50p Downhill skiing 4.25 4.25

No. 512 contains one 31x40mm stamp.

A66

**1983, Nov. 7** ***Perf. 12½***

**513** A66 4.50p Emblem .50 .25
**514** A66 7.50p Woman, flag .70 .25
**515** A66 9p Sewing .95 .25
**516** A66 12p Farm workers 1.25 .25
*Nos. 513-516 (4)* 3.40 1.00

First anniv. of Women's Federation.

A67

Designs: Local flowers.

**1983, Nov. 12 Litho. *Perf. 13***

| | | | | | |
|---|---|---|---|---|---|
| **517** | A67 | 1p | Canna coccinea | .25 | .25 |
| **518** | A67 | 1.50p | Bouganville litoral-is | .25 | .25 |
| **519** | A67 | 3.50p | Euphorbia milii | .30 | .25 |
| **520** | A67 | 5p | Delonix regia | .35 | .25 |
| **521** | A67 | 8p | Bauhinia varie-gata | .60 | .25 |
| **522** | A67 | 10p | Spathodea campanulata | .80 | .25 |
| **523** | A67 | 30p | Hibiscus rosa sinensis | 2.25 | .80 |
| | | | *Nos. 517-523 (7)* | 4.80 | 2.30 |

JAAC Congress, Sept. 8-12 — A68

**1983, Sept. 1 Litho. *Perf. 13***

| | | | | | |
|---|---|---|---|---|---|
| **524** | A68 | 4p | shown | 1.00 | .25 |
| **524A** | A68 | 5p | Emblem | 1.00 | .25 |

World Food Day A69

**1983, Oct. 16 Litho. *Perf. 12½x12***

| | | | | | |
|---|---|---|---|---|---|
| **525** | A69 | 1.50p | multicolored | .25 | .25 |
| **526** | A69 | 2p | multicolored | .30 | .25 |
| **527** | A69 | 4p | multicolored | .40 | .25 |

***Imperf***

**Size: 61x62mm**

| | | | | | |
|---|---|---|---|---|---|
| **528** | A69 | 10p | Hoeing | *2.50* | *1.00* |
| | | | *Nos. 525-528 (4)* | *3.45* | *1.75* |

1984 Winter Olympics, Sarajevo A70

**1984, Feb. 8 *Perf. 12***

| | | | | | |
|---|---|---|---|---|---|
| **529** | A70 | 50c | Ski jumping | .25 | .25 |
| **530** | A70 | 2.50p | Speed skating | .30 | .25 |
| **531** | A70 | 3.50p | Hockey | .40 | .25 |
| **532** | A70 | 5p | Biathlon | .45 | .25 |
| **533** | A70 | 6p | Downhill skiing | .50 | .25 |
| **534** | A70 | 20p | Figure skating | 1.40 | .40 |
| **535** | A70 | 30p | Bobsledding | 2.25 | .45 |
| | | | *Nos. 529-535 (7)* | 5.55 | 2.10 |

**Souvenir Sheet**

***Perf. 11½***

| | | | | | |
|---|---|---|---|---|---|
| **536** | A70 | 50p | Skiing | 4.25 | 3.25 |

No. 536 contains one 32x43mm stamp.

World Communications Year — A71

**1983, Aug. 30 Litho. *Perf. 12½***

| | | | | | |
|---|---|---|---|---|---|
| **537** | A71 | 50c | Rowland Hill | .35 | .25 |
| **538** | A71 | 2.50p | Samuel Morse | .45 | .25 |
| **539** | A71 | 3.50p | H.R. Hertz | .50 | .25 |
| **540** | A71 | 5p | Lord Kelvin | .65 | .25 |
| **541** | A71 | 10p | Alex. Graham Bell | 1.25 | .25 |
| **542** | A71 | 20p | G. Marconi | 2.50 | .60 |
| **543** | A71 | 30p | V. Zworykin | 3.75 | .75 |
| | | | *Nos. 537-543 (7)* | 9.45 | 2.60 |

**Souvenir Sheet**

| | | | | | |
|---|---|---|---|---|---|
| **544** | A71 | 50p | Satellites | 4.00 | 3.25 |

No. 544 contains one stamp 31x39mm.

Vintage Cars A72

**1984, Mar. 20 *Perf. 12***

| | | | | | |
|---|---|---|---|---|---|
| **545** | A72 | 5p | Duesenberg, 1928 | .25 | .25 |
| **546** | A72 | 8p | MG Midget, 1932 | .40 | .25 |
| **547** | A72 | 15p | Mercedes, 1928 | .55 | .25 |
| **548** | A72 | 20p | Bentley, 1928 | .65 | .30 |
| **549** | A72 | 24p | Alfa Romeo, 1929 | .75 | .35 |
| **550** | A72 | 30p | Datsun, 1932 | 1.10 | .50 |
| **551** | A72 | 35p | Lincoln, 1932 | 1.25 | .55 |
| | | | *Nos. 545-551 (7)* | 4.95 | 2.45 |

**Souvenir Sheet**

| | | | | | |
|---|---|---|---|---|---|
| **552** | A72 | 100p | Gottlieb Daimler | 5.00 | 4.25 |

No. 552 contains one stamp 50x42mm.

Madonna and Child, by Morales — A73

Paintings by Spanish Artists (Espana '84): 6p, Dona Tadea Arias de Enriquez, by Goya. 10p, Santa Cassilda, by Zurbaran. 12p, Saints Andrew and Francis, by El Greco. 15p, Infanta Isabel Clara Eugenia, by Coello. 35p, Queen Maria of Austria, by Velazquez. 40p, Holy Trinity, by El Greco. 100p, Clothed Maja, by Goya.

**1984, Apr. 20**

| | | | | | |
|---|---|---|---|---|---|
| **553** | A73 | 3p | multicolored | .25 | .25 |
| **554** | A73 | 6p | multicolored | .25 | .25 |
| **555** | A73 | 10p | multicolored | .25 | .25 |
| **556** | A73 | 12p | multicolored | .45 | .25 |
| **557** | A73 | 15p | multicolored | .60 | .25 |
| **558** | A73 | 35p | multicolored | 1.45 | .60 |
| **559** | A73 | 40p | multicolored | 1.75 | .65 |
| | | | *Nos. 553-559 (7)* | 5.00 | 2.50 |

**Souvenir Sheet**

| | | | | | |
|---|---|---|---|---|---|
| **560** | A73 | 100p | multicolored | 5.00 | 4.75 |

No. 560 contains one stamp 29x50mm.

Carnivorous Animals — A74

**1984, June 28**

| | | | | | |
|---|---|---|---|---|---|
| **561** | A74 | 3p | Panthera tigris | .25 | .25 |
| **562** | A74 | 6p | Panthera leo | .40 | .25 |
| **563** | A74 | 10p | Neofelis nebulosa | .45 | .25 |
| **564** | A74 | 12p | Acinonyx jubatus | .60 | .25 |
| **565** | A74 | 15p | Lynx lynx | .65 | .25 |
| **566** | A74 | 35p | Panthera pardus | 1.75 | .45 |
| **567** | A74 | 40p | Uncia uncia | 1.90 | .45 |
| | | | *Nos. 561-567 (7)* | 6.00 | 2.15 |

Intl. Civil Aviation Org., 40th Anniv. — A75

**1984, Apr. 4 Litho. *Perf. 12½***

| | | | | | |
|---|---|---|---|---|---|
| **568** | A75 | 8p | Caravelle | .40 | .25 |
| **569** | A75 | 22p | DC-6B | .85 | .35 |
| **570** | A75 | 80p | IL-76 | 3.00 | 1.25 |
| | | | *Nos. 568-570 (3)* | 4.25 | 1.85 |

1984 Summer Olympics, Los Angeles — A76

**1984, May 24 *Perf. 12***

| | | | | | |
|---|---|---|---|---|---|
| **571** | A76 | 6p | Soccer | .25 | .25 |
| **572** | A76 | 8p | Dressage | .25 | .25 |
| **573** | A76 | 15p | Yachting | .55 | .25 |
| **574** | A76 | 20p | Field hockey | .70 | .25 |
| **575** | A76 | 22p | Women's team handball | .75 | .25 |
| **576** | A76 | 30p | Canoeing | 1.10 | .40 |
| **577** | A76 | 40p | Boxing | 1.40 | .80 |
| | | | *Nos. 571-577 (7)* | 5.00 | 2.45 |

**Souvenir Sheet**

***Perf. 11½***

| | | | | | |
|---|---|---|---|---|---|
| **578** | A76 | 100p | Windsurfing | 10.00 | 3.75 |

World Heritage — A77

Wood sculptures: 3p, Pearl throne, Cameroun and Central Africa. 6p, Antelope, South Sudan. 10p, Kneeling woman, East Africa. 12p, Mask, West African coast. 15p, Leopard, Guinea coast. 35p, Standing woman, Zaire. 40p, Funerary statues, Southeast Africa and Madagascar.

**1984, Aug. 15 *Perf. 12½***

| | | | | | |
|---|---|---|---|---|---|
| **579** | A77 | 3p | multicolored | .35 | .25 |
| **580** | A77 | 6p | multicolored | .40 | .25 |
| **581** | A77 | 10p | multicolored | .45 | .25 |
| **582** | A77 | 12p | multicolored | .75 | .25 |
| **583** | A77 | 15p | multicolored | .95 | .30 |
| **584** | A77 | 35p | multicolored | 1.90 | .65 |
| **585** | A77 | 40p | multicolored | 2.10 | .70 |
| | | | *Nos. 579-585 (7)* | 6.90 | 2.65 |

Amilcar Cabral, 60th Birth Anniv. — A78

**1984, Sept. 12 *Perf. 13***

| | | | | | |
|---|---|---|---|---|---|
| **586** | A78 | 5p | Public speaking | .50 | .25 |
| **587** | A78 | 12p | In combat fatigues | .55 | .25 |
| **588** | A78 | 20p | Memorial building, Bafata | 1.00 | .35 |
| **589** | A78 | 50p | Mausoleum, Bis-sau | 2.50 | .80 |
| | | | *Nos. 586-589 (4)* | 4.55 | 1.65 |

Independence, 11th Anniv. — A79

**1984, Sept. 24**

| | | | | | |
|---|---|---|---|---|---|
| **590** | A79 | 3p | Mechanic | .30 | .25 |
| **591** | A79 | 6p | Student | .35 | .25 |
| **592** | A79 | 10p | Mason | .45 | .25 |
| **593** | A79 | 12p | Health care, vert. | .60 | .30 |
| **594** | A79 | 15p | Seamstress, vert. | .75 | .30 |
| **595** | A79 | 35p | Telecommunica-tions | 1.50 | .70 |
| **596** | A79 | 40p | PAIGC building | 1.75 | .75 |
| | | | *Nos. 590-596 (7)* | 5.70 | 2.80 |

Whales A80

**1984, Sept. 30 *Perf. 12***

| | | | | | |
|---|---|---|---|---|---|
| **597** | A80 | 5p | Eschrichtius gib-bosus | .45 | .25 |
| **598** | A80 | 8p | Balaenoptera mus-culus | .60 | .25 |
| **599** | A80 | 15p | Tursiops truncatus | .90 | .35 |
| **600** | A80 | 20p | Physeter macrocephalus | 1.25 | .35 |
| **601** | A80 | 24p | Orcinus orca | 1.75 | .45 |
| **602** | A80 | 30p | Balaena mys-ticetus | 2.00 | .55 |
| **603** | A80 | 35p | Balaenoptera borealis | 2.10 | .60 |
| | | | *Nos. 597-603 (7)* | 9.05 | 2.80 |

Butterflies A81

**1984, Oct. 6 *Perf. 12½x13***

| | | | | | |
|---|---|---|---|---|---|
| **604** | A81 | 3p | Hypolimnas dex-ithea | .35 | .25 |
| **605** | A81 | 6p | Papilio arcturus | .45 | .25 |
| **606** | A81 | 10p | Morpho menelaus terrestris | .50 | .25 |
| **607** | A81 | 12p | Apaturina erminea papuana | .65 | .25 |
| **608** | A81 | 15p | Prepona praeneste | .85 | .35 |
| **609** | A81 | 35p | Ornithoptera paradisea | 1.40 | .65 |
| **610** | A81 | 40p | Morpho hecuba obidona | 1.90 | .75 |
| | | | *Nos. 604-610 (7)* | 6.10 | 2.75 |

1984 Olympic Winners — A82

National flag, medal and: 6p, Carl Lewis, 4x100 relay, US. 8p, Koji Gushiken, gymnastics, Japan. 15p, Reiner Klimke, equestrian,

Federal Republic of Germany. 20p, Tracie Ruiz, synchronized swimming, US. 22p, Mary Lou Retton, gymnastics, US. 30p, Michael Gross, swimming, Federal Republic of Germany. 40p, Edwin Moses, hurdler, US. 100p, Daley Thompson, decathlon, Great Britain.

**1984, Nov. 27** *Perf. 13*

**611** A82 6p multicolored .25 .25
**612** A82 8p multicolored .30 .25
**613** A82 15p multicolored .50 .25
**614** A82 20p multicolored .75 .25
**615** A82 22p multicolored .80 .30
**616** A82 30p multicolored 1.25 .45
**617** A82 40p multicolored 1.60 .65
*Nos. 611-617 (7)* 5.45 2.40

**Souvenir Sheet**

*Perf. 12½*

**618** A82 100p multicolored 5.50 3.75

No. 618 contains one stamp 32x40mm.

Locomotives — A83

**1984, Dec. 15** *Perf. 13*

**619** A83 5p White Mountain Central No. 4 .30 .25
**620** A83 8p Kessler 2-6-OT, 1886 .35 .25
**621** A83 15p Langen tram, 1901 .45 .30
**622** A83 20p Gurjao No. 6 .60 .35
**623** A83 24p Achenseebahn .75 .40
**624** A83 30p Vitznau-Rigi steam locomotive .95 .55
**625** A83 35p Riggenbach rackrail, 1873 1.05 .85
*Nos. 619-625 (7)* 4.45 2.95

**Souvenir Sheet**

*Perf. 12½*

**625A** A83 100p like #621 5.50 3.25

No. 625A contains one stamp 40x32mm.

Native Crafts — A83a

LUBRAPEX '84: a, Numbe mask. b, Sono statue. c, Erande statue. d, Kokumba arms. e, Oma mask. f, Koni mask.

**1984** **Litho.** *Perf. 13½*

**626** A83a 7.50p Strip of 6, #a.-f. *5.00* 3.50

Motorcycle Cent. — A84

**1985, Feb. 20** *Perf. 13x12½*

**627** A84 5p Harley-Davidson *.30* .25
**628** A84 8p Kawasaki *.45* .25
**629** A84 15p Honda *.70* .25
**630** A84 20p Yamaha *1.10* .35
**631** A84 25p Suzuki *1.60* .40
**632** A84 30p BMW *1.90* .55
**633** A84 35p Moto Guzzi *2.75* .60
*Nos. 627-633 (7)* *8.80* 2.65

**Souvenir Sheet**

*Perf. 12½*

**634** A84 100p Daimler Motorized Bicycle, 1885, vert. *8.00* 5.50

No. 634 contains one 32x40mm stamp.

Miniature Sheet

Mushrooms — A85

**1985, May 15** *Perf. 13*

**635** Sheet of 6 6.00 2.10
*a.* A85 7p Clitocybe gibba .35 .25
*b.* A85 9p Morchella elata .40 .25
*c.* A85 12p Lepista nuda .55 .30
*d.* A85 20p Lactarius deliciosus .95 .35
*e.* A85 30p Russula virescens 1.35 .45
*f.* A85 35p Chroogomphus rutilus 1.50 .55

Henri Dunant (1828-1910), Red Cross Founder, Plane — A87

**1985, June 12** *Perf. 12½*

**643** A87 20p shown .50 .25
**644** A87 25p Ambulance .60 .25
**645** A87 40p Helicopter 1.25 .45
**646** A87 80p Speed boat 2.75 .65
*Nos. 643-646 (4)* 5.10 1.60

Cats — A88

**1985, July 5** *Perf. 13*

**647** A88 7p multicolored *.25* .25
**648** A88 10p multicolored *.25* .25
**649** A88 12p multicolored *.35* .25
**650** A88 15p multicolored *.55* .25
**651** A88 20p multicolored *.80* .25
**652** A88 40p multicolored *1.15* .25
**653** A88 45p multicolored *1.75* .40
*Nos. 647-653 (7)* *5.10* 1.90

**Souvenir Sheet**

**654** A88 100p multicolored *5.50* 4.00

ARGENTINA '85. No. 654 contains one 40x32mm stamp.

Composers and Musical Instruments A89

Designs: 4p, Vincenzo Bellini (1801-1835), harp, 1820, and descant viol, 16th cent. 5p, Schumann (1810-1856) and Viennese pyramid piano, 1829. 7p, Chopin (1810-1849) and piano-forte, 1817. 12p, Luigi Cherubini (1760-1842) and 18th cent. Baryton violin and Quinton viol. 20p, G. B. Pergolesi (1710-1736) and double-manual harpsichord, 1734. 30p, Handel (1685-1759), valve trumpet, 1825, and timpani drum, 18th cent. 50p, Heinrich Schutz (1585-1672), bass viol and two-stop oboe, 17th cent. 100s, Bach (1685-1750) and St. Thomas Church organ, Leipzig.

**1985, Aug. 5** *Perf. 12*

**655** A89 4p multicolored .25 .25
**656** A89 5p multicolored .30 .25
**657** A89 7p multicolored .45 .25
**658** A89 12p multicolored .70 .25
**659** A89 20p multicolored 1.00 .25
**660** A89 30p multicolored 1.60 .30
**661** A89 50p multicolored 2.50 .60
*Nos. 655-661 (7)* 6.80 2.15

**Souvenir Sheet**

*Perf. 11½*

**662** A89 100p multicolored 6.50 4.25

No. 662 contains one 30x50mm stamp.

Santa Maria, 15th Cent., Spain — A90

Ships: 15p, Carack, 16th cent., Netherlands. 20p, Mayflower, 17th cent., Great Britain. 30p, St. Louis, 17th cent., France. 35p, Royal Sovereign, 1635, Great Britain. 45p, Soleil Royal, 17th cent., France. 80p, English brig, 18th-19th cent.

**1985, Sept. 12** *Perf. 13*

**663** A90 8p multicolored .30 .25
**664** A90 15p multicolored .45 .25
**665** A90 20p multicolored .60 .25
**666** A90 30p multicolored 1.00 .30
**667** A90 35p multicolored 1.15 .30
**668** A90 45p multicolored 1.50 .45
**669** A90 80p multicolored 3.00 .75
*Nos. 663-669 (7)* 8.00 2.55

UN, 40th Anniv. A91

**1985, Oct. 17**

**670** A91 10p Emblem, doves, vert. .80
**671** A91 20p Emblem, 40 1.60

Venus and Mars, by Sandro Botticelli (1445-1510) A92

Botticelli paintings (details): 7p, Virgin with Child and St. John. 12p, St. Augustine in the Work Hall. 15p, Awakening of Spring. 20p, Virgin and Child. 40p, Virgin with Child and St. John, diff. 45p, Birth of Venus. 100p, Virgin and Child with Two Angels.

**1985, Oct. 25** *Perf. 12½x13*

**672** A92 7p multicolored .35 .25
**673** A92 10p multicolored .40 .25
**674** A92 12p multicolored .50 .25
**675** A92 15p multicolored .55 .25
**676** A92 20p multicolored .75 .25
**677** A92 40p multicolored 1.50 .40
**678** A92 45p multicolored 1.90 .45

**Size: 73x106mm**

***Imperf***

**679** A92 100p multicolored 7.00 5.50
*Nos. 672-679 (8)* 12.95 7.60

ITALIA '85.

Intl. Youth Year A93

**1985, Nov. 29** **Litho.** *Perf. 12½*

**680** A93 7p Dance .25 .25
**681** A93 13p Wind surfing .30 .25
**682** A93 15p Rollerskating .35 .25
**683** A93 25p Hang gliding .65 .25
**684** A93 40p Surfing 1.00 .30
**685** A93 50p Skateboarding 1.25 .50
**686** A93 80p Parachuting 2.25 .70
*Nos. 680-686 (7)* 6.05 2.50

**Souvenir Sheet**

*Perf. 13*

**687** A93 100p Self-defense 7.00 5.50

No. 687 contains one 40x32mm stamp.

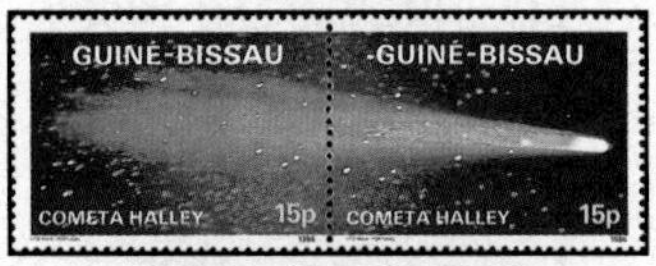


Halley's Comet — A94

1986 World Cup Soccer Championships, Mexico — A95

24th Summer Olympics, Seoul, 1988 A96

Italian Automobile Industry, Cent. A97

German Railways, 150th Anniv. A98

Discovery of America, 500th Anniv. (in 1992) A99

First American Manned Space Flight, 25th Anniv. — A100

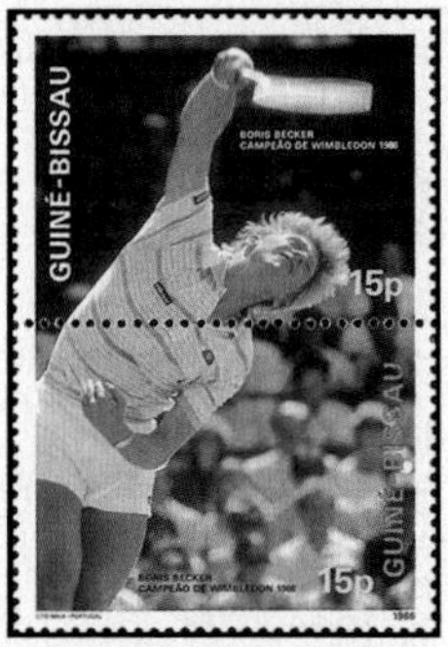


1986 Wimbledon Tennis Championships — A101

1986 Masters Tennis Championships — A102

Giotto Space Probe — A103

Designs: a, Comet tail. b, Comet. c, Trophy. d, Trophy base. e, Five-ring Olympic emblem. f, Alfa Tourer, Italy, c. 1905. g, Railway station, Frankfurt-on Main, c. 1914. h, Barcelona, site of Discovery of America exhibition and 1992 Olympics. i, Space station solar panels and tanks. j, Space station. k, Removing cargo from space shuttle. l, Docking facility, station panels. m, Boris Becker swinging tennis racket. n, Becker, diff. o, Ivan Lendl holding racket. p, Lendl, diff.

**Miniature Sheet**

**1986, Dec. 30 Litho. *Perf. 13½***
**688** Sheet of 16 *100.00*
***a.-p.*** A94-A102 15p any single 6.00 3.25

**Souvenir Sheet**

**689** A103 100p multicolored 14.00 10.00

Nos. 688a-688b, 688c-688d, 688i-688l, 688m-688n, 688o-688p are se-tenant in continuous designs. Inscription on Nos. 688i-688l incorrect; should read "TRIPULADO MERCURY / 5-5-1961."

Discovery of America, 500th Anniv. (in 1992) — A104

Designs: No. 690, Christopher Columbus aboard caravelle. No. 691, Guadalquivir Port, Seville, c. 1490. No. 692, Pedro Alvars Cabral landing at Bahia, Brazil. No. 693, Bridge over the Guadalquivir River, Seville. No. 694, Port, Lisbon, 15th cent.

**1987, Feb. 27**
**690** A104 50p multicolored 3.50 1.00
**691** A104 50p multicolored 3.50 1.00
**692** A104 50p multicolored 3.50 .70
**693** A104 50p multicolored 3.50 1.00
*Nos. 690-693 (4)* 14.00 3.70

**Souvenir Sheet**

**694** A104 150p multicolored 15.00 10.00

No. 694 exists with pink or yellow anniv. emblem pictured in vignette. Values are the same.

Portuguese Guinea Nos. 306-309, 313, 316-317, Ovptd., Guinea-Bissau No. 349 Srchd.

**1987, July Litho. *Perf. 13½***
**696** A21 100p on 20c #306 *1.75* *.60*
**697** A21 200p on 35c #307 *3.25* *1.25*
**698** A21 300p on 70c #308 *5.00* *1.60*
**699** A21 400p on 80c #309 *5.50* *2.00*
**700** A21 500p on 3.50e #313 *7.75* *2.75*
**701** A21 1000p on 15e #316 *20.00* *5.50*
**702** A21 2000p on 20e #317 *40.00* *13.50*

***Perf. 13***

**703** CD61 2500p on 2e #349 *50.00* 14.50
*Nos. 696-703 (8)* *133.25* 41.70

Placement of "Bissau," new denomination and obliterating bar varies.

1988 Winter Olympics, Calgary — A106

**1988, Jan. 15 Litho. *Perf. 13***
**704** A106 5p Pairs figure skating .30 .25
**705** A106 10p Luge .50 .25
**706** A106 50p Skiing .60 .25
**707** A106 200p Slalom skiing .75 .35
**708** A106 300p Skibobbing 1.35 .50
**709** A106 500p Ski jumping, vert. 2.00 .65
**710** A106 800p Speed skating, vert. 3.50 2.25
*Nos. 704-710 (7)* 9.00 4.50

**Souvenir Sheet**

**710A** A106 900p Two-man luge 7.00 3.25

No. 710A contains one 40x32mm stamp.

Soccer — A107

Various soccer plays.

**1988, Apr. 14 Litho. *Perf. 13***
**711** A107 5p multi .25 .25
**712** A107 10p multi, diff. .25 .25
**713** A107 50p multi, diff. .55 .25
**714** A107 200p multi, diff. 1.20 .40
**715** A107 300p multi, diff. 1.90 .50
**716** A107 500p multi, diff. 2.50 .65
**717** A107 800p multi, diff. 4.50 1.60
*Nos. 711-717 (7)* 11.15 3.90

**Souvenir Sheet**

**718** A107 900p multi, diff. 7.00 4.25

ESSEN '88 stamp exhibition. No. 718 contains one 32x40mm stamp.

1988 Summer Olympics, Seoul — A108

***Perf. 12½x12, 12x12½***

**1988, Feb. 26 Litho.**
**719** A108 5p Yachting, vert. .25 .25
**720** A108 10p Equestrian .25 .25
**721** A108 50p High jump .40 .25
**722** A108 200p Shooting 1.35 .40
**723** A108 300p Long jump, vert. 2.10 .50
**724** A108 500p Tennis, vert. 3.25 .65
**725** A108 800p Women's archery, vert. 5.25 1.25
*Nos. 719-725 (7)* 12.85 3.55

**Souvenir Sheet**

***Perf. 12½***

**726** A108 900p Soccer 5.00 2.25

No. 726 contains one 40x32mm stamp.

Ancient Ships — A109

Designs: 5p, Egyptian, c. 3300 B.C. 10p, Pharaoh Sahure's ship, c. 2700 B.C. 50p, Queen Hatsepsowe's ship, c. 1500 B.C. 200p, Ramses III's ship, c. 1200 B.C. 300p, Greek trireme, 480 B.C. 500p, Etruscan bireme, 600 B.C. 800p, Venetian galley, 12th cent.

**1988 Litho. *Perf. 13x12½***
**727** A109 5p multi .25 .25
**728** A109 10p multi .25 .25
**729** A109 50p multi .45 .25
**730** A109 200p multi 1.10 .25
**731** A109 300p multi 1.50 .30
**732** A109 500p multi 2.50 .50
**733** A109 800p multi 4.00 .85
*Nos. 727-733 (7)* 10.05 2.65

FINLANDIA '88 — A110

Chess champions, board and chessmen.

**1988 Litho. *Perf. 12x12½***
**734** A110 5p Philidor .25 .25
**735** A110 10p Staunton .25 .25
**736** A110 50p Anderssen .50 .25
**737** A110 200p Morphy 1.25 .25
**738** A110 300p Steinitz 1.60 .30
**739** A110 500p Lasker 3.00 .40
**740** A110 800p Capablanca 4.50 .65
*Nos. 734-740 (7)* 11.35 2.35

**Souvenir Sheet**

***Perf. 13***

**741** A110 900p Ruy Lopez 7.00 4.50

No. 741 contains one 40x32mm stamp.

Dogs A111

**1988 *Perf. 13x12½***
**742** A111 5p Basset hound .25 .25
**743** A111 10p Great blue of Gascony .35 .25
**744** A111 50p Sabujo of Italy .35 .25
**745** A111 200p Yorkshire terrier .85 .55
**746** A111 300p Small munsterlander 1.40 .80
**747** A111 500p Pointer 2.25 1.40
**748** A111 800p German setter 3.50 2.25
*Nos. 742-748 (7)* 8.95 5.75

**Souvenir Sheet**

***Perf. 12½***

**749** A111 900 German shepherd 5.50 2.50

No. 749 contains one 40x32mm stamp.

Intl. Red Cross and Red Crescent Organizations, 125th Annivs. — A112

**1988 *Perf. 13***
**750** A112 10p Jean-Henri Dunant .55 .25
**751** A112 50p Dr. T. Maunoir .25 .25
**752** A112 200p Dr. Louis Appia 1.00 .25
**753** A112 800p Gustave Moynier 4.75 .65
*Nos. 750-753 (4)* 6.55 1.40

Maps and Fauna — A113

**1988 *Perf. 12½x13, 13x12½***
**754** A113 5p Panthera leo .25 .25
**755** A113 10p Glaucidium brasilianum .25 .25
**756** A113 50p Upupa epops .55 .25
**757** A113 200p Equus burchelli antiquorum 1.20 .25

**758** A113 300p Loxodonta africana 1.75 .30
**759** A113 500p Acryllium vulturinum 2.75 1.60
**760** A113 800p Diceros bicornis 4.75 .65
*Nos. 754-760 (7)* 11.50 3.55

Nos. 754-755, 758-760 vert. The genus *"Upupa"* is misspelled on the 50p and *"Loxodonta"* is misspelled on the 300p.

Samora Machel (1933-1986), Pres. of Mozambique
A114

**1988** *Perf. 13*
**761** A114 10p shown .25 .25
**762** A114 50p Raising fist .40 .25
**763** A114 200p With sentry 1.25 .25
**764** A114 300p Wearing earphones at UN 2.10 .25
*Nos. 761-764 (4)* 4.00 1.00

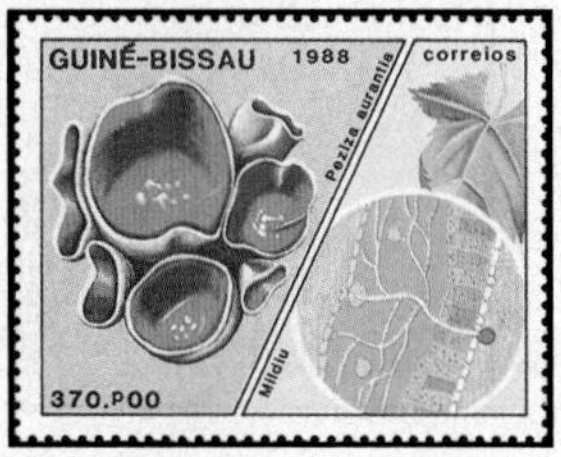


Mushrooms — A115

**1988** **Litho.** *Perf. 13x12½*
**765** A115 370p Peziza aurantia 1.60 .35
**766** A115 470p Morchella 2.00 .40
**767** A115 600p Amanita caesarea 3.00 .60
**768** A115 780p Amanita muscaria 4.50 .70
**769** A115 800p Amanita phalloides 4.50 .70
**770** A115 900p Agaricus bisporus 5.25 .90
**771** A115 945p Cantharellus cibarius 4.75 .95
*Nos. 765-771 (7)* 25.60 4.60

1992 Winter Olympics, Albertville — A116

**1989, Oct. 12** **Litho.** *Perf. 12½x12*
**772** A116 50p Speed skating .40 .25
**773** A116 100p Women's figure skating .55 .25
**774** A116 200p Ski jumping 1.10 .25
**775** A116 350p Skiing 1.25 .40
**776** A116 500p Skiing, diff. 2.10 .55
**777** A116 800p Bobsled 3.25 .95
**778** A116 1000p Ice hockey 4.25 1.10
*Nos. 772-778 (7)* 12.90 3.75

**Souvenir Sheet**
*Perf. 12½*
**779** A116 1500p Ice hockey, diff. 6.00 5.00

No. 779 contains one 32x40mm stamp.

World Cup Soccer Championships, Italy — A117

Various soccer players.

**1989** **Litho.** *Perf. 12½*
**780** A117 50p multicolored .25 .25
**781** A117 100p multicolored .45 .25
**782** A117 200p multicolored .60 .25
**783** A117 350p multicolored 1.00 .35
**784** A117 500p multicolored 1.20 .45
**785** A117 800p multicolored 2.50 .80
**786** A117 1000p multicolored 3.00 .90
*Nos. 780-786 (7)* 9.00 3.25

**Souvenir Sheet**
*Perf. 13*
**786A** A117 1500p multicolored 4.50 2.75

No. 786A contains one 40x32mm stamp.

Lilies (Lilium) — A118

**1989** *Perf. 12½*
**787** A118 50p Limelight .25 .25
**788** A118 100p Candidum .40 .25
**789** A118 200p Pardalinum .70 .35
**790** A118 350p Auratum 1.15 .65
**791** A118 500p Canadense 1.35 .70
**792** A118 800p Enchantment 2.75 1.50
**793** A118 1000p Black Dragon 3.50 1.90
*Nos. 787-793 (7)* 10.10 5.60

**Souvenir Sheet**
**794** A118 1500p Lilium pyrenaicum 5.00 2.75

No. 794 contains one 32x40mm stamp.

Trains
A119

Various railroad engines.

**1989, May 24** **Litho.** *Perf. 13*
**795** A119 50p multicolored .25 .25
**796** A119 100p multicolored .35 .25
**797** A119 200p multicolored .60 .35
**798** A119 350p multicolored 1.25 .70
**799** A119 500p multicolored 1.75 .95
**800** A119 800p multicolored 2.50 1.60

*Perf. 12½*
**Size: 68x27mm**
**801** A119 1000p multicolored 3.25 .85
*Nos. 795-801 (7)* 9.95 4.95

**Souvenir Sheet**
*Perf. 12½*
**802** A119 1500p multicolored 5.00 3.25

No. 802 contains one 32x40mm stamp.

La Marseillaise by Francois Rude — A120

Paintings: 100p, Armed mob. 200p, Storming the Bastille. 350p, Lafayette, Liberty, vert. 500p, Dancing around the Liberty tree. 800p, Rouget de Lisle singing La Marseillaise by Pils. 1000p, Storming the Bastille, diff. 1500p, Arms of the Republic of France.

*Perf. 12½, 12x12½ (350p)*
**1989, July 5**
**803** A120 50p shown .25 .25
**804** A120 100p multicolored .25 .25
**805** A120 200p multicolored .55 .40
**806** A120 350p multicolored, 27x44mm 1.10 .75
**807** A120 500p multicolored 1.60 1.00
**808** A120 800p multicolored 2.50 1.60
**809** A120 1000p multicolored 3.00 2.00
*Nos. 803-809 (7)* 9.25 6.25

**Souvenir Sheet**
*Perf. 13*
**810** A120 1500p multicolored 5.00 2.75

Birds
A121

Designs: 50p, Alectroenas pulcherrima. 100p, Streptopelia senegalensis. 200p, Oena capensis. 350p, Claravis mondetoura. 500p, Streptopelia roseogrisea. 800p, Otidiphaps nobilis. 1000p, Chalcophaps indica. 1500p, Reinwardtoena Reinwardtsi.

**1989** **Litho.** *Perf. 12½*
**811** A121 50p multicolored .25 .25
**812** A121 100p multicolored .30 .25
**813** A121 200p multicolored .60 .40
**814** A121 350p multicolored 1.10 .65
**815** A121 500p multicolored 1.60 .90
**816** A121 800p multicolored 2.50 1.60
**817** A121 1000p multicolored 3.00 1.90
*Nos. 811-817 (7)* 9.35 5.95

**Souvenir Sheet**
**818** A121 1500p multicolored 6.00 3.50

Pioneers Organization — A122

**1989** *Perf. 13*
**819** A122 10p Children presenting flag, vert. .25 .25
**820** A122 50p Children saluting, vert. .60 .25
**821** A122 200p shown 2.50 .95
**822** A122 300p Children playing ball 3.50 1.50
*Nos. 819-822 (4)* 6.85 2.95

Town of Cacheu, 400th Anniv.
A123

**1989, Nov. 30**
**823** A123 10p Monument, vert. .25 .25
**824** A123 50p shown .25 .25
**825** A123 200p Old building .85 .25
**826** A123 300p Church 1.35 .30
*Nos. 823-826 (4)* 2.70 1.05

Dated 1988.

A124

Designs: Prehistoric creatures.

*Perf. 13, 12½x12 (100p)*
**1989, Sept. 15**
**827** A124 50p Trachodon .25 .25
**828** A124 100p Edaphosaurus, 68x27mm .35 .25
**829** A124 200p Mesosaurus .60 .35
**830** A124 350p Elephas primigenius 1.05 .65
**831** A124 500p Tyrannosaurus 1.75 .90
**832** A124 800p Stegosaurus 2.75 1.50
**833** A124 1000p Cervus megaceros 3.25 1.75
*Nos. 827-833 (7)* 10.00 5.65

Nos. 828, 831-833 horiz.

A125

Designs: Musical instruments.

**1989, Apr. 10** **Litho.** *Perf. 13*
**834** A125 50p Bombalon .30 .25
**835** A125 100p Flauta .45 .25
**836** A125 200p Tambor .90 .30
**837** A125 350p Dondon 1.45 .40
**838** A125 500p Balafon 1.75 .45
**839** A125 800p Kora 2.25 .60
**840** A125 1000p Nhanhero 2.40 .70
*Nos. 834-840 (7)* 9.50 2.95

A126

Designs: Indian artifacts.

**1989, July 13** *Perf. 12x12½*
**841** A126 50p Teotihuacan .25 .25
**842** A126 100p Mochica .30 .25
**843** A126 200p Jaina .55 .35
**844** A126 350p Nayarit 1.25 .70
**845** A126 500p Inca 1.75 1.00
**846** A126 800p Hopewell 2.75 1.60
**847** A126 1000p Taina 3.25 1.90
*Nos. 841-847 (7)* 10.10 6.05

**Souvenir Sheet**
*Perf. 12½*
**848** A126 1500p Indian statuette 5.00 2.50

Brasiliana '89 Philatelic Exhibition. Nos. 841-847 printed se-tenant with multicolored label showing scenes of colonization. No. 848 contains one 32x40mm stamp.

1992 Summer Olympics, Barcelona
A127

**1989, June 3** *Perf. 12½x13*
**849** A127 50p Hurdles .30 .25
**850** A127 100p Boxing .40 .25
**851** A127 200p High jump .60 .25
**852** A127 350p Sprinters in the blocks .95 .35

**853** A127 500p Woman sprinter 1.60 .55
**854** A127 800p Gymnastics 2.50 .95
**855** A127 1000p Pole vault 3.25 1.25
*Nos. 849-855 (7)* 9.60 3.85

**Souvenir Sheet**

**856** A127 1500p Soccer 4.50 2.40

No. 856 contains one 32x40mm stamp.

Wild Animals — A128

**1989, Nov. 24** *Perf. 12½*

**857** A128 50p Syncerus caffer .30 .25
**858** A128 100p Equus quagga .45 .25
**859** A128 200p Diceros bicornis .60 .25
**860** A128 350p Okapia johnstoni 1.00 .40
**861** A128 500p Macaca mulatta 1.25 .60
**862** A128 800p Hippopotamus amphibius 2.10 1.00
**863** A128 1000p Acinonyx jubatus 2.40 1.25
**864** A128 1500p Panthera leo 3.75 1.75
*Nos. 857-864 (8)* 11.85 5.75

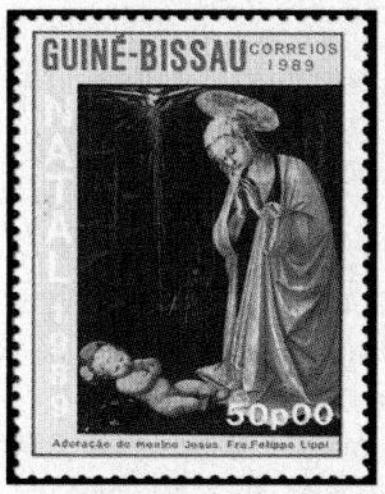


Christmas A129

Paintings of the Madonna and Child (50p) and the Adoration of the Magi.

**1989, Dec. 10** *Perf. 13*

**865** A129 50p Fra Filippo Lippi .35 .25
**866** A129 100p Pieter Brueghel .45 .25
**867** A129 200p Mostaert .60 .25
**868** A129 350p Durer .95 .35
**869** A129 500p Rubens 1.60 .60
**870** A129 800p Van der Weyden 2.75 .90
**871** A129 1000p Francia, horiz. 3.25 1.25
*Nos. 865-871 (7)* 9.95 3.85

Womens' Hairstyles A130

Various hairstyles.

**1989, Mar. 8** *Perf. 12½x13*

**872** A130 50p multicolored .25 .25
**873** A130 100p multicolored .40 .25
**874** A130 200p multicolored .65 .35
**875** A130 350p multicolored 1.15 .65
**875A** A130 500p multicolored 1.50 .90
**876** A130 800p multicolored 2.75 1.50
**877** A130 1000p multicolored 3.25 1.75
*Nos. 872-877 (7)* 9.95 5.65

Vegetables — A131

**1989, May 20** *Perf. 12½*

**878** A131 50p Capisium annum .25 .25
**879** A131 100p Solanium .25 .25
**880** A131 200p Curcumis peco .85 .25
**881** A131 350p Solanium licopersicum 1.50 .40
**882** A131 500p Solanium itiopium 2.10 .60
**883** A131 800p Hibiscus esculentus 3.25 .95
**884** A131 1000p Oseille de guine 4.25 1.25
*Nos. 878-884 (7)* 12.45 3.95

Visit of Pope John Paul II — A132

**1990, Jan. 27** **Litho.** *Perf. 13½*

**885** A132 500p shown 1.75 1.60
**886** A132 1000p multi, diff. 3.25 3.25

**Souvenir Sheet**

**887** A132 1500p multi, diff., vert. 4.00 6.25

Souvenir Sheet

Belgica '90 — A133

**1990, June 1** *Perf. 14½*

**888** A133 3000p multicolored 6.00 3.50

World Meteorology Day — A134

**1990, Oct. 1** **Litho.** *Perf. 13*

**889** A134 1000p Radar weather map 1.75 .70
**890** A134 3000p Heliograph 7.25 2.50

LUBRAPEX '90 — A135

**1990, Sept. 21** *Perf. 14*

**891** A135 500p Rooster, hen 1.10 .50
**892** A135 800p Turkey 1.90 .75
**893** A135 1000p Duck, ducklings 2.50 .90
*Nos. 891-893 (3)* 5.50 2.15

**Souvenir Sheet**

*Perf. 13½*

**894** A135 1500p Rooster, turkey, ducks 6.00 2.40

UN Development Program, 40th Anniv. — A136

**1990** **Litho.** *Perf. 14*

**895** A136 1000p multicolored 2.50 .75

Fight against AIDS.

Textile Manufacturing A137

No. 896: a, Gossypium hirsutum. b, Processing cotton. c, Spinning thread. d, Picking cotton. e, Moth, silkworms. f, Dyeing thread. g, Weaving. h, Animal design. i, Multicolored stripes design. j, Stripes, dots design.

**1990**

**896** Sheet of 10 2.00
*a.-j.* A137 150p any single .25 .25
**897** A137 400p like #896a .35 .25
**898** A137 500p like #896g .45 .25
**899** A137 600p like #896h .55 .35
*Nos. 896-899 (4)* 3.35 .85

Carnival Masks A138

**1990** **Litho.** *Perf. 14*

**900** A138 200p Mickey Mouse .45 .25
**901** A138 300p Hippopotamus .65 .25
**902** A138 600p Bull 1.25 .35
**903** A138 1200p Bull, diff. 2.50 .50
*Nos. 900-903 (4)* 4.85 1.35

Fish A139

Designs: 300p, Pentanemus quinquarius. 400p, Psettias sabae. 500p, Chaetodipterus goreensis. 600p, Trachinotus goreensis.

**1991, Mar. 10** **Litho.** *Perf. 14*

**904** A139 300p multicolored .65 .35
**905** A139 400p multicolored 1.00 .45
**906** A139 500p multicolored 1.10 .55
**907** A139 600p multicolored 1.25 .70
*Nos. 904-907 (4)* 4.00 2.05

Fire Trucks A140

**1991, Aug. 19** **Litho.** *Perf. 14*

**908** A140 200p shown .40 .25
**909** A140 500p Ladder truck .85 .45
**910** A140 800p Rescue vehicle 1.25 .70
**911** A140 1500p Ambulance 2.50 1.25
*Nos. 908-911 (4)* 5.00 2.65

Birds — A141

Designs: 100p, Kaupifalco monogrammicus. 250p, Balearica pavonina. 350p, Bucorvus abyssinicus. 500p, Ephippiorhynchus senegalensis. 1500p, Kaupifalco monogrammicus, diff.

**1991, Sept. 10**

**912** A141 100p multicolored .75 .25
**913** A141 250p multicolored 1.10 .25
**914** A141 350p multicolored 1.75 .55
**915** A141 500p multicolored 2.40 .75
*Nos. 912-915 (4)* 6.00 1.80

**Souvenir Sheet**

*Perf. 14½*

**916** A141 1500p multicolored 5.00 5.00

No. 916 contains one 40x50mm stamp.

Messages A142

**1991, Oct. 28** **Litho.** *Perf. 14*

**917** A142 250p Congratulations .40 .25
**918** A142 400p With love .75 .40
**919** A142 800p Happiness 1.25 .80
**920** A142 1000p Seasons Greetings 1.60 .95
*Nos. 917-920 (4)* 4.00 2.40

Fruits — A143

Designs: 500p, Landolfia owariensis. 1500p, Dialium guineensis. 2000p, Adansonia digitata. 3000p, Parkia biglobosa.

**1992, Mar. 25** **Litho.** *Perf. 14*

**921** A143 500p multicolored .30 .30
**922** A143 1500p multicolored .75 .75
**923** A143 2000p multicolored 1.10 1.10
**924** A143 3000p multicolored 1.75 1.75
*Nos. 921-924 (4)* 3.90 3.90

Healthy Hearts — A144

Designs: 1500p, Cigarette butts, healthy heart. 4000p, Heart running over junk food.

**1992, Apr. 7**

**925** A144 1500p multicolored 1.75 .80
**926** A144 4000p multicolored 3.75 2.10

Traditional Costumes
A145

Designs: a, 400p, Fula. b, 600p, Balanta. c, 1000p, Fula, diff. d, 1500p, Manjaco.

**1992, Feb. 28** **Litho.** ***Perf. 14***
**927** A145 Strip of 4, #a.-d. 3.00 2.10

Canoes
A146

Designs: Nos. 928-931, Various types of canoes. No. 932, Alcedo cristata galerita.

**1992, May 10**
**928** A146 750p multicolored .40 .40
**929** A146 800p multicolored .55 .55
**930** A146 1000p multicolored .70 .70
**931** A146 1300p multicolored .90 .90
*Nos. 928-931 (4)* 2.55 2.55

**Souvenir Sheet**
***Perf. 13½***
**932** A146 1500p multicolored 6.00 6.00

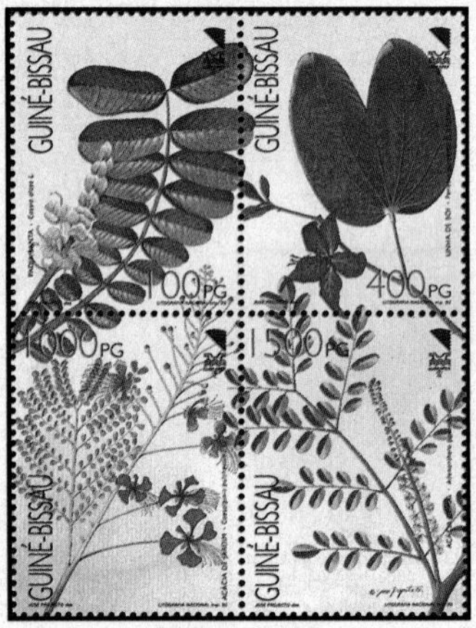


Trees — A147

a, 100p, Cassia alata. b, 400p, Perlebia purpurea. c, 1000p, Caesalpina pulcherrima. d, 1500p, Adenanthera pavonina. 3000p, Caesalpina pulcherrima, diff.

**1992, May 8** ***Perf. 14***
**933** A147 Block of 4, #a.-d. 5.50 5.50

**Souvenir Sheet**
***Perf. 13½***
**934** A147 3000p multicolored 5.00 5.00

1992 Summer Olympics, Barcelona
A148

**1992, July 28** **Litho.** ***Perf. 14***
**935** A148 600p Basketball .25 .25
**936** A148 1000p Volleyball .60 .25
**937** A148 1500p Team handball .90 .25
**938** A148 2000p Soccer 1.25 .25
*Nos. 935-938 (4)* 3.00 1.00

Trees
A149

Designs: 1000p, Afzelia africana Smith. 1500p, Kaya senegalenses. 2000p, Militia regia. 3000p, Pterocarpus erinaceus.

**1992, Sept. 11** ***Perf. 12***
**939** A149 1000p multicolored .50 .45
**940** A149 1500p multicolored .65 .60
**941** A149 2000p multicolored .95 .80
**942** A149 3000p multicolored 1.40 1.25
*Nos. 939-942 (4)* 3.50 3.10

Souvenir Sheet

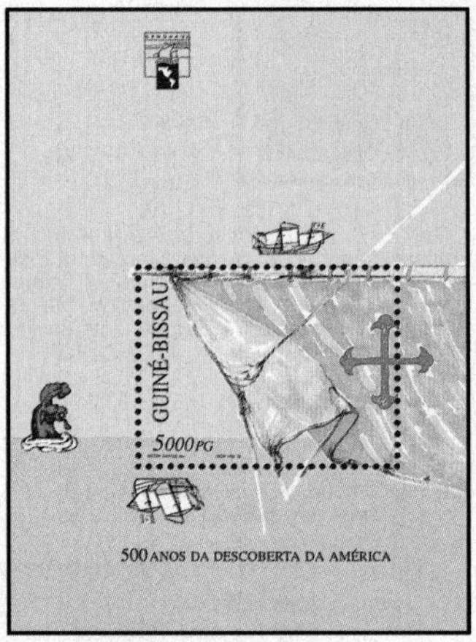


Discovery of America, 500th Anniv. — A150

**1992, Sept. 18**
**943** A150 5000p multicolored 3.50 3.50

Genoa '92.

Procolobus Badius Temminckii
A151

Designs: a, Pair in tree. b, Adult seated in vegetation c, Adult seated in tree fork. d, Female with young.

**1992** **Litho.** ***Perf. 12x11½***
**944** A151 2000p Strip of 4, #a.-d. 5.25 5.25

World Wildlife Fund.

Reptiles
A152

**1993, May 18** **Litho.** ***Perf. 14***
**945** A152 1500p Bitis sp. .50 .25
**946** A152 3000p Osteolaemus tetraspis 1.10 .55
**947** A152 4000p Varanus nitolicus 1.50 .70
**948** A152 5000p Agama agama 1.90 .85
*a.* Souvenir sheet of 4, #945-948 6.00 2.50
*Nos. 945-948 (4)* 5.00 2.35

Souvenir Sheet

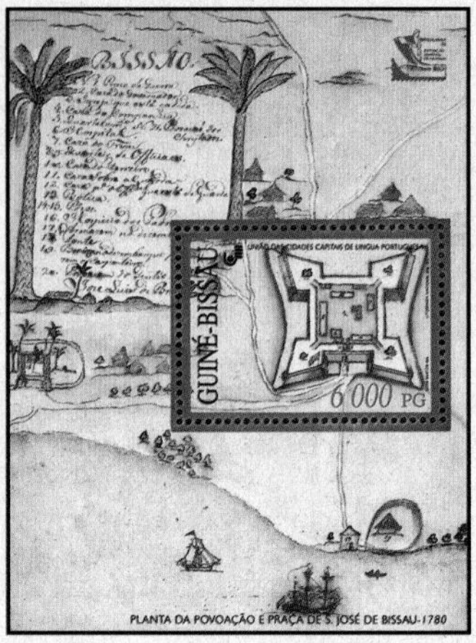


Union of Portuguese Speaking Capitals — A153

**1993, July 30** **Litho.** ***Perf. 13½***
**949** A153 6000p Fort 1.50 1.50

Brasiliana '93.

Tourism — A154

Designs: a, 1000p. b, 2000p. c, 4000p. d, 5000p.

**1993, Nov. 15** **Litho.** ***Perf. 14***
**950** A154 Block of 4, #a.-d. 4.00 4.00

Traditional Jewelry
A155

**1993, Nov. 30** ***Perf. 14½***
**951** A155 1500p Bracelet .45 .25
**952** A155 3000p Mask pendant 1.10 .50
**953** A155 4000p Circle pendant 1.50 .65
**954** A155 5000p Filigree pendant 1.75 .80
*Nos. 951-954 (4)* 4.80 2.20

**1994, Nov. 30** **Souvenir Sheet**
**955** A155 18,000p like #952 8.00 8.00

Hong Kong '94 (No. 955). No. 955 has continuous design.

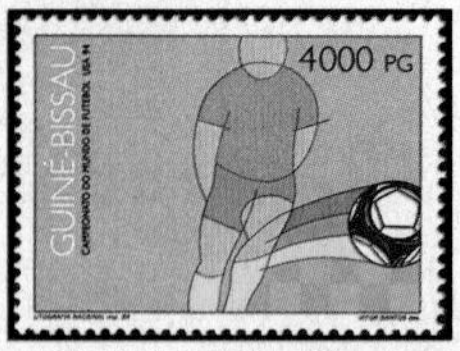


1994 World Cup Soccer Championships, US — A156

Various stylized designs of player, ball, net.

**1994, June 17** **Litho.** ***Perf. 14***
**956** A156 4000p multicolored 1.00 .85
**957** A156 5000p multicolored 1.25 1.10
**958** A156 5500p multicolored 1.60 1.25
**959** A156 6500p multicolored 2.00 1.60
*Nos. 956-959 (4)* 5.85 4.80

Flowering Plants — A157

Designs: 2000p, Erythrina senegalensis. 3000p, Cassia occidentalis. 4000p, Gardenia ternifolia. 6000p, Cochlospermum tinctorium.

**1994, May 30** **Litho.** ***Perf. 14***
**960** A157 2000p multicolored .90 .45
**961** A157 3000p multicolored 1.25 .70
**962** A157 4000p multicolored 1.60 .90
**963** A157 6000p multicolored 2.75 1.50
*Nos. 960-963 (4)* 6.50 3.55

Snakes — A158

#964: a, Dasypeltis scabra. b, Philothamnus. c, Naja melanoleuca. d, Python sebae.

15,000p, Thelotornis kirtlandii.

**1994, Aug. 16** **Litho.** ***Perf. 14***
**964** A158 5000p Block of 4, #a.-d. 8.00 8.00

**Souvenir Sheet**
***Perf. 13½***
**965** A158 15,000p multicolored 6.50 6.50

PHILAKOREA '94, SINGPEX '94. No. 965 contains one 60x50mm stamp.

Palmeira Dendem — A159

3000p, Climbing tree to pick fruit. 6500p, Hand processing palm fruit into baskets. 7500p, Mechanical processing. 8000p, Palm oil, uses.

**1995, Feb. 27** **Litho.** ***Perf. 14***
**966** A159 3000p multicolored .75 .35
**967** A159 6500p multicolored 1.50 .70
**968** A159 7500p multicolored 1.75 .80
**969** A159 8000p multicolored 2.00 .85
*Nos. 966-969 (4)* 6.00 2.70

FAO, 50th Anniv.
A160

**1995** **Litho.** ***Perf. 13½***
**970** A160 3000p Net fishing .75 .45
**971** A160 6500p Disking field 1.50 .85
**972** A160 7500p Hands holding fruit 1.75 1.00
**973** A160 8000p Vendors along road 2.00 1.10
*a.* Souvenir sheet of 2, #972-973 4.50 2.25
*Nos. 970-973 (4)* 6.00 3.40

UN, 50th Anniv. — A161

**1995, Oct. 24 Litho. *Perf. 13½***

**974** A161 4000p shown 1.00 .55
**975** A161 5500p UN flag 1.25 .75
**976** A161 7500p Natl. flag 1.75 1.00
**977** A161 8000p Hand on dove 2.00 1.10
*Nos. 974-977 (4)* 6.00 3.40

**Souvenir Sheet**

**978** A161 15,000p UN emblem 5.00 5.00

100 Centimes = 1 Franc (1997)

Endangered Animals — A166

No. 995: a, 5000p, Hippopotamus. b, 7500p, Crocodile. c, 10,000p, Chelonia mydas. d, 12,000p, Trichechus senegalensis.

**1997 Litho. *Perf. 12x11¾***

**995** A166 Block of 4, #a-d — —

Despite change to franc currency on May 2, 1997, Nos. 995-997 have denominations in pesos.

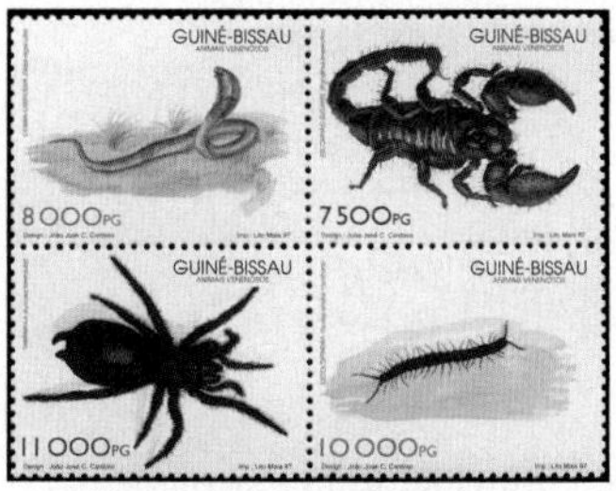


Venomous Animals — A167

No. 996: a, 7500p, Pandinus imperator. b, 8000p, Naja nigricollis. c, 10,000p, Scolopendra morsitans. d, 11,000p, Lycosa tarentula.

**1997**

**996** A167 Block of 4, #a-d *15.00 15.00*

Economic Community of West African States, 20th Anniv. (in 1995) — A168

**1997, Dec. 26**

**997** A168 25,000p multi *5.00 5.00*

Native Foods A169

Designs: 100fr, Caldo branco. 120fr, Siga. 160fr, Caldo de amendoin. 190fr, Caldo de chabeu.

**1998, June 1**

**998-1001** A169 Set of 4 *5.00 5.00*

**No. 1001 Overprinted in Brown**

**1998, Sept. 4 Litho. *Perf. 12x11¾***

**1002** A169 190fr on No. 1001 *2.00 2.00*

Maritime Discoveries — A170

**1998, Oct. 9 *Perf. 12x11¾***

**1003** A170 200fr multi *2.00 2.00*
*a.* Souvenir sheet of 1, perf. 12½ *5.00 5.00*

Marine Life A171

Designs: 150fr, Cultellus tenuis. 170fr, Penaeus keraethurus. 200fr, Periophthalmus papilio. 250fr, Istiophorus albicans.

**1998, Dec. 28 *Perf. 12x11¾***

**1004-1007** A171 Set of 4 *6.00 6.00*
*1007a* Souvenir sheet, #1004-1007, perf. 12½ *6.00 6.00*

**Souvenir Sheet**

España 2000 World Philatelic Exhibition — A174

**2000 Litho. *Perf. 13x12¾***

**1016** A174 1000fr multi — —

No. 924 Surcharged

**Methods and Perfs As Before**

**2000 ?**

**1027** A143 1000fr on 3000p #924 —

At least 12 other surcharges were issued in this set. The editors would like to examine any examples.

---

## AIR POST STAMPS

Liftoff of Soyuz Spacecraft AP1

Apollo-Soyuz mission: 10p, Launch of Apollo spacecraft. 15p, Leonov, Stafford and meeting in space. 20p, Eclipse of the sun. 30p, Infra-red photo of Earth. 40p, Return to Earth. 50p, Apollo and Soyuz docked, horiz.

**1976, Oct. 4 *Perf. 13½***

**C10** AP1 5p multicolored
**C10A** AP1 10p multicolored
**C10B** AP1 15p multicolored
**C10C** AP1 20p multicolored
**C10D** AP1 30p multicolored
**C10E** AP1 40p multicolored
*Nos. C10-C10E (6)* 11.50 6.50

**Souvenir Sheet**

**C10F** AP1 50p multicolored 5.00 5.00

No. C10F contains one 60x42mm stamp. Nos. C10-C10E exist in souvenir sheets of one, perf. and imperf.

Viking Spacecraft Orbiting Mars AP2

35p, Viking gathering Martian soil samples.

**1977, Jan. 27**

**C11** AP2 25p multicolored 3.75 1.00
**C11A** AP2 35p multicolored 3.75 1.00

**Nos. 372-373 Surcharged in Black on Silver Panels**

**1978 Litho. *Perf. 13½***

**C12** A32 15p on 3.50p multi .95 .40
**C13** A32 30p on 50c multi 1.45 .60

**History of Aviation Type of 1980**

**1980 Litho. *Perf. 13½***

**C14** A38 35p Willy de Houthulst, Hanriot HD.1 2.25 1.00
**C14A** A38 40p Charles Guynemer, Spad S. VII 3.00 1.25

**Souvenir Sheet**

**C14B** A38 50p Comdr. de Rose, Nieuport 5.50 4.50

No. C14B contains one stamp 37x55mm.

**Winter Olympics Type of 1980**

**1980**

**C15** A39 35p Slalom 2.75 1.00
**C16** A39 40p Figure skating 3.50 1.25

**Souvenir Sheet**

**C17** A39 50p Ice hockey, horiz. 6.00 4.50

**Summer Olympics Type of 1980**

**1980, Aug. Litho. *Perf. 13½***

**C18** A40 35p Somersault 3.75 1.00
**C19** A40 40p Running 4.50 1.25

**Souvenir Sheet**

**C20** A40 50p Emblem 6.00 4.50

**Literacy Type of 1980**

**1980, Aug. Litho. *Perf. 13½***

**C21** A41 15p like #404 1.75 .50
**C22** A41 25p like #405 2.75 .60

**Space Type of 1981**

35p, Viking 1 & 2. 40p, Apollo-Soyuz craft & crew. 50p, Apollo 11 crew, craft & emblem.

**1981, May Litho. *Perf. 13½***

**C23** A45 35p multicolored 3.00 1.25
**C24** A45 40p multicolored 3.25 1.50

**Souvenir Sheet**

**C25** A45 50p multicolored 7.50 6.00

No. C25 contains one stamp 60x42mm.

**Soccer Type of 1981**

Designs: 35p, Rummenigge, Germany. 40p, Kempes, Argentina. 50p, Juanito, Spain.

**1981, May**

**C26** A46 35p multicolored 3.00 1.25
**C27** A46 40p multicolored 3.25 1.50

**Souvenir Sheet**

**C28** A46 50p multicolored 9.50 7.25

No. C28 contains one stamp 56x40mm.

**Royal Wedding Type of 1981**

**1981 Litho. *Perf. 13½***

**C29** A47 35p Palace 4.00 1.25
**C30** A47 40p Prince of Wales arms 4.75 1.50

**Souvenir Sheet**

**C31** A47 50p Couple 9.00 6.00

**Picasso Type of 1981**

**1981, Dec. Litho. *Perf. 13½***

**C32** A48 35p multicolored 4.75 1.25
**C33** A48 40p multicolored 6.00 1.60

**Souvenir Sheet**

**C34** A48 50p multicolored 7.75 6.00

No. C34 contains one stamp 41x50mm.

**Navigator Type of 1981**

35p, Francis Drake, Golden Hinde. 40p, James Cook, Endeavor. 50p, Columbus, Santa Maria.

**1981 Litho. *Perf. 13½***

**C35** A49 35p multicolored 3.75 1.40
**C36** A49 40p multicolored 5.00 1.75

**Souvenir Sheet**

**C37** A49 50p multicolored 12.00 7.50

**Christmas Type of 1981**

**1981**

**C38** A50 30p Memling 4.00 1.40
**C39** A50 35p Bellini, diff. 4.75 1.75

**Souvenir Sheet**

**C40** A50 50p Fra Angelico 9.00 6.00

No. C40 contains one 35x59mm stamp.

**Scout Type of 1982**

**1982, June 9 Litho. *Perf. 13½***

**C41** A51 35p Canoeing 3.00 .85
**C42** A51 40p Flying model planes 3.50 1.25

**Souvenir Sheet**

**C43** A51 50p Playing chess 15.00 8.25

No. C43 contains one 48x38mm stamp.

**Soccer Type of 1982**

**1982, June 13 Litho. *Perf. 13½***

**C44** A52 35p Kempes 3.00 .85

**C45** A52 40p Kaltz 3.50 1.25

**Souvenir Sheet**

**C46** A52 50p Stadium 8.00 3.75

**Diana Type of 1982 and**

Princess Diana, 21st Birthday — AP3

**1982**

**C47** A53 35p multicolored 3.00 .85
**C48** A53 40p multicolored 3.50 1.25

**Souvenir Sheet**

**C49** A53 50p multi, vert. 8.00 3.75

**1982, Oct. 1 Litho. & Embossed**

**C49A** AP3 200p gold & multi 15.50

**Souvenir Sheet**

**C49B** AP3 200p gold & multi, vert. 35.00

For overprints see Nos. 456A-456B.

Audubon Birth Bicent. — AP4

**1985, Apr. 16 Litho.** ***Perf. 12***

**C50** AP4 5p Brown pelican .60
**C51** AP4 10p American white pelican 1.00
**C52** AP4 20p Great blue heron 1.25
**C53** AP4 40p American flamingo 2.50
*Nos. C50-C53 (4)* 5.35

# GUYANA

gī-ˈa-nə

LOCATION — Northeast coast of South America
GOVT. — Republic
AREA — 83,000 sq. mi.
POP. — 705,156 (1999 est.)
CAPITAL — Georgetown

The former Crown Colony of British Guiana became an independent member of the British Commonwealth May 26, 1966, taking the name Guyana. On February 23, 1970, Guyana became a republic, remaining a Commonwealth nation.

100 Cents = 1 Dollar

**Catalogue values for all unused stamps in this country are for Never Hinged items.**

**Watermark**

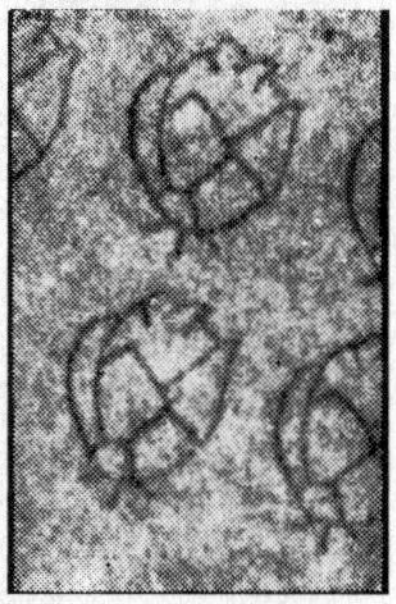

Wmk. 364 — Lotus Bud Multiple

British Guiana #254-256, 258-260, 267 Overprinted

***Perf. 12½x13, 13***

| 1966, May 26 | | Wmk. 4 | Engr. | |
|---|---|---|---|---|
| **1** | A60 | 2c dark green | .35 | *.45* |
| **1A** | A60 | 3c red brn & ol | 3.00 | *7.00* |
| **2** | A61 | 4c violet | 1.75 | .90 |
| **3** | A60 | 6c yellow green | .45 | .25 |
| **4** | A60 | 8c ultra | 1.75 | 1.75 |
| **5** | A61 | 12c brn & blk | 1.75 | 1.40 |
| **6** | A61 | $5 blk & ultra | 27.50 | *57.50* |
| | | *Nos. 1-6 (7)* | 36.55 | *69.25* |

Same Overprint on British Guiana Stamps and Types of 1954

**Engr.; Center Litho. on $1**

| 1966-67 | | Wmk. 314 Upright | | |
|---|---|---|---|---|
| **7** | A60 | 1c black ('67) | .25 | *.40* |
| **8** | A60 | 3c red brn & ol (#279) | 2.00 | .25 |
| **9** | A61 | 4c violet ('67) | .35 | *.75* |
| **10** | A60 | 5c blk & red (#280) | .50 | .25 |
| **10A** | A60 | 6c yel green ('67) | .35 | .30 |
| **11** | A60 | 8c ultra ('67) | 1.00 | *1.90* |
| **12** | A61 | 12c brn & blk (#281) | .25 | .25 |
| **13** | A60 | 24c org & blk (#282) | 5.00 | .25 |
| **14** | A60 | 36c blk & rose (#283) | .40 | .40 |
| **15** | A61 | 48c red brn & ultra (#284) | 4.00 | *9.00* |
| **16** | A61 | 72c emer & rose (#285) | .75 | .75 |
| **17** | A60 | $1 blk & multi (#286) | 4.50 | .50 |
| **18** | A60 | $2 mag (#287) | 2.00 | 1.25 |
| **19** | A61 | $5 black & ultra | 1.50 | 3.00 |
| | | *Nos. 7-19 (14)* | 22.85 | 19.25 |

For surcharges see Nos. 543, 544A, 625-626, 1446.

| 1966-67 | | Wmk. 314 Sideways | | |
|---|---|---|---|---|
| *7a* | A60 | 1c black | .25 | .25 |
| *9a* | A61 | 4c violet | .25 | .25 |
| *11a* | A60 | 8c ultramarine | .25 | .25 |
| *12a* | A61 | 12c brown & black ('67) | .25 | .25 |
| *13a* | A60 | 24c orange & black | 3.50 | 1.25 |
| *14a* | A60 | 36c black & rose ('67) | .55 | *3.00* |
| *15a* | A61 | 48c red brown & ultra | .55 | .55 |
| *16a* | A61 | 72c emerald & rose ('67) | 3.25 | *6.75* |
| *17a* | A60 | $1 black & multi ('67) | 5.00 | *6.75* |
| *18a* | A60 | $2 magenta ('67) | 5.75 | *6.75* |
| *19a* | A61 | $5 black & ultra ('67) | 2.75 | *6.00* |
| | | *Nos. 7a-19a (11)* | 22.35 | 32.05 |

See Nos. 32-32T and note. For surcharges see Nos. 544, 627-628, 1447.

Flag and Map of Guyana — A1

Designs: 25c, $1, Arms of Guyana.

**Unwmk.**

| 1966, May 26 | | Photo. | *Perf. 14* | |
|---|---|---|---|---|
| **20** | A1 | 5c violet & multi | .30 | .30 |
| **21** | A1 | 15c dk red brown & multi | .30 | .30 |
| **22** | A1 | 25c brt blue & multi | .35 | .35 |
| **23** | A1 | $1 sepia & multi | 1.00 | 1.00 |
| | | *Nos. 20-23 (4)* | 1.95 | 1.95 |

Guyana's independence, May 26, 1966.

Bank of Guyana A2

| 1966, Oct. 11 | | | *Perf. 13½x14* | |
|---|---|---|---|---|
| **24** | A2 | 5c yel grn, blue, blk & gold | .25 | .25 |
| **25** | A2 | 25c blue, black & gold | .25 | .25 |

Establishment of the Bank of Guyana.

British Guiana No. 13 — A3

| 1967, Feb. 23 | | Litho. | *Perf. 12½* | |
|---|---|---|---|---|
| **26** | A3 | 5c multicolored | .25 | .25 |
| | *a.* | Imperf., pair | | |
| **27** | A3 | 25c multicolored | .25 | .25 |

Issued to honor the unique British Guiana 1c black on magenta stamp of 1856.

Canceled to Order

Remainders of Nos. 26-30, 33-38 and 54-67 were canceled and sold by the Post Office in 1969. Values are for these canceled to order stamps. Postally used examples do not command a significant premium.

Chateau Margot — A4

Designs: 15c, Independence Arch. 25c, Guyana Fort, Fort Island, horiz. $1, Parliament, National Assembly Hall, horiz.

***Perf. 14, 14½x14, 14x14½***

| 1967, May 26 | | Photo. | Unwmk. | |
|---|---|---|---|---|
| **28** | A4 | 6c multicolored | .25 | .25 |
| **29** | A4 | 15c multicolored | .25 | .25 |
| **30** | A4 | 25c multicolored | .25 | .25 |
| **31** | A4 | $1 multicolored | .25 | .25 |
| | | *Nos. 28-31 (4)* | 1.00 | 1.00 |

First anniversary of independence.

British Guiana Stamps and Types of 1954 Locally Overprinted

| 1967 | | | Wmk. 4 | |
|---|---|---|---|---|
| **32** | A60 | 1c black | .25 | .25 |
| **32A** | A60 | 2c dark green | .25 | .25 |
| **32B** | A60 | 3c red brown & ol | .90 | .25 |
| **32C** | A61 | 4c violet | .30 | .25 |
| **32D** | A60 | 6c yellow green | .30 | .25 |
| **32E** | A60 | 8c ultramarine | .30 | .25 |
| **32F** | A61 | 12c brown & black | .30 | .25 |
| **32G** | A60 | $2 magenta | 3.25 | 2.50 |
| **32H** | A61 | $5 black & ultra | 4.25 | 2.75 |
| | | *Nos. 32-32H (9)* | 10.10 | 7.00 |

The 24c with Wmk. 4 also exists with this overprint. Value: unused $450; used $110.

| 1967-68 | | Wmk. 314 Upright | | |
|---|---|---|---|---|
| **32I** | A60 | 1c black ('68) | .25 | *.70* |
| **32J** | A60 | 2c dk green ('68) | .45 | *1.40* |
| **32K** | A60 | 3c red brown & ol | .35 | .25 |
| **32L** | A61 | 4c violet ('68) | .25 | *1.25* |
| **32M** | A60 | 5c black & red | 1.50 | *2.00* |
| **32N** | A60 | 6c yel green ('68) | .40 | *.90* |
| **32O** | A60 | 24c orange & blk | 3.25 | .25 |
| **32P** | A60 | 36c black & rose | 1.25 | .25 |
| **32Q** | A61 | 48c red brn & ultra | 1.25 | .75 |
| **32R** | A61 | 72c emer & rose | 2.50 | .85 |
| **32S** | A60 | $1 black & multi | 4.75 | 1.00 |
| **32T** | A60 | $2 magenta | 5.00 | 4.00 |
| | | *Nos. 32I-32T (12)* | 21.20 | 13.60 |

The 1c, 4c, 6c, 8c and $5 with Wmk. 314 were not issued without overprint.
For surcharges see Nos. 540, 542, 543A.

"Millie," the Bilingual Macaw — A5

**Christmas Issues**

| 1967, Nov. 6 | | | *Perf. 14½x14* | |
|---|---|---|---|---|
| **33** | A5 | 5c olive green & multi | .25 | .25 |
| **33A** | A5 | 25c purple & multi | .25 | .25 |

| 1968, Jan. 22 | | | | |
|---|---|---|---|---|
| **34** | A5 | 5c red & multi | .25 | .25 |
| **35** | A5 | 25c yel green & multi | .25 | .25 |

Wicketkeeper, Emblem of West Indies Cricket Team — A6

Designs: 6c, Batsman and emblem of Marylebone Cricket Club. 25c, Bowler and emblem of West Indies Cricket Team.

| 1968, Jan. 8 | | Photo. | *Perf. 14* | |
|---|---|---|---|---|
| **36** | A6 | 5c multicolored | .25 | .25 |
| **37** | A6 | 6c multicolored | .25 | .25 |
| **38** | A6 | 25c multicolored | .35 | .25 |
| | *a.* | Strip of 3, #36-38 | 1.00 | 1.00 |

Visit of the Marylebone Cricket Club to the West Indies, Jan.-Feb. 1968. Printed in sheets of 9.

Pike Cichlid — A7

Marail Guan — A8

Designs: 2c, Piranha. 3c, Cichla ocellaris (fish). 5c, Armored catfish. 6c, Two-spotted cichlid. 15c, Harpy eagle. 20c, Hoatzin. 25c, Andean cock-of-the-rock. 40c, Great kiskadee. 50c, Agouti. 60c, Peccary. $1, Paca. $2, Armadillo. $5, Ocelot.

***Perf. 14x14½, 14½x14***

| 1968, Mar. 4 | | Photo. | Unwmk. | |
|---|---|---|---|---|
| **39** | A7 | 1c chalky blue & multi | .25 | .25 |
| **40** | A7 | 2c gray & multi | .25 | .25 |
| **41** | A7 | 3c grnsh bl & multi | .25 | .25 |
| **42** | A7 | 5c ultra & multi | .25 | .25 |
| **43** | A7 | 6c brt olive & multi | .80 | .25 |
| **44** | A8 | 10c yel green & multi | .90 | .25 |
| **45** | A8 | 15c green & multi | 1.90 | .25 |
| **46** | A8 | 20c ap grn & multi | 1.00 | .25 |
| **47** | A8 | 25c brt green & multi | 1.00 | .25 |
| **48** | A8 | 40c pale brn & multi | 1.75 | .80 |
| **49** | A7 | 50c rose brn & multi | 1.40 | .75 |
| **50** | A7 | 60c lilac rose & multi | 1.50 | .25 |
| **51** | A7 | $1 dp orange & multi | 1.90 | .25 |
| **52** | A7 | $2 ocher & multi | 2.50 | *3.50* |
| **53** | A7 | $5 red & multi | 3.50 | *4.25* |
| | | *Nos. 39-53 (15)* | 19.15 | 12.05 |

See Nos. 68-82.
For overprints & surcharges see #357, 410-413, 603, 752, 756, 761a, 1463, 1501, 1839, 2045.

Christ of St. John of the Cross, by Salvador Dali — A9

| 1968, Mar. 25 | | | *Perf. 14x14½* | |
|---|---|---|---|---|
| **54** | A9 | 5c car rose & multi | .25 | .25 |
| **55** | A9 | 25c brt violet & multi | .25 | .25 |

Easter.

"Efficiency Year" — A10

Designs: 30c, 40c, "Savings bonds."

| 1968, July 22 | | Litho. | *Perf. 14* | |
|---|---|---|---|---|
| **56** | A10 | 6c green & multi | .25 | .25 |
| **57** | A10 | 25c fawn & multi | .25 | .25 |
| **58** | A10 | 30c multicolored | .25 | .25 |
| **59** | A10 | 40c multicolored | .25 | .25 |
| | | *Nos. 56-59 (4)* | 1.00 | 1.00 |

Issued to promote the sale of savings bonds and to publicize Efficiency Year.

Open Koran A11

***Perf. 14x13½***

| 1968, Oct. 9 | | Photo. | Unwmk. | |
|---|---|---|---|---|
| **60** | A11 | 6c sal pink, gold & blk | .25 | .25 |
| **61** | A11 | 25c pale vio, gold & blk | .25 | .25 |
| **62** | A11 | 30c pale yel grn, gold & blk | .25 | .25 |
| **63** | A11 | 40c pale blue, gold & blk | .25 | .25 |
| | | *Nos. 60-63 (4)* | 1.00 | 1.00 |

Koran's 1400th anniversary.
For overprints & surcharges see #354, 355, 441, 445, 487-488, 575, 630, 1464-1465.

Dish Aerials, Thomas Lands, Guyana — A12

Designs: 30c, 40c, Map showing connection between Guyana and Trinidad. All stamps are inscribed: "Guyana Sends Christmas Greetings to the World."

**Wmk. 364**

**1968, Nov. 11 Litho. *Perf. 14***

**64** A12 6c blue, gray, ocher & emer .25 .25
**65** A12 25c brt rose lil, brn & emer .25 .25
**66** A12 30c blue grn & dk blue grn .25 .25
**67** A12 40c blue grn & red .25 .25
*Nos. 64-67 (4)* 1.00 1.00

Christmas; communications link with Trinidad by the tropospheric scatter system.

**Types of 1968**

Designs as before.

***Perf. 14x14½, 14½x14***

**1968 Photo. Wmk. 364**

**68** A7 1c chalky bl & multi .25 .25
**69** A7 2c gray & multi .25 *.25*
**70** A7 3c grnsh bl & multi .25 *.55*
**71** A7 5c ultra & multi .25 .25
**72** A7 6c brt olive & multi .25 *.55*
**73** A8 10c yel grn & multi .65 .55
**74** A8 15c green & multi .65 .25
**75** A8 20c apple grn & multi .65 .65
**76** A8 25c brt green & multi .65 .25
**77** A8 40c pale brn & multi 1.25 .65
**78** A7 50c rose brn & multi .70 .25
**79** A7 60c lilac rose & multi .75 *.90*
**80** A7 $1 dp org & multi 1.50 1.10
**81** A7 $2 ocher & multi 2.10 *3.00*
**82** A7 $5 red & multi 2.10 *4.50*
*Nos. 68-82 (15)* 12.25 13.95

For overprints & surcharges see #373, 376-377, 413D, 565-566, 633, 635, 704-705, 744, 749, 752a, 757-758, 761-762, 1862-1863, 1981, 4107, 4164, O2.

Celebrants Spraying Perfumed Powder — A13

Phagwah (Holi) Hindu Festival: 25c, 40c, Two celebrants spraying colored water.

**1969, Feb. 26 Litho. *Perf. 13½***

**83** A13 6c multicolored .25 .25
**84** A13 25c multicolored .25 .25
**85** A13 30c multicolored .25 .25
**86** A13 40c multicolored .25 .25
*Nos. 83-86 (4)* 1.00 1.00

The Last Supper, by Salvador Dali A14

**1969, Mar. 10 Photo. *Perf. 13***

**87** A14 6c dp carmine & multi .25 .25
**88** A14 25c green & multi .25 .25
**89** A14 30c org brown & multi .25 .25
**90** A14 40c dp violet & multi .25 .25
*Nos. 87-90 (4)* 1.00 1.00

Easter. For overprints and surcharges see Nos. 393-394, 482-485, 572, 576, 634, 765, 772, 1407-1410, 1813, 1815-1817, 2050, 4108.

Map of Caribbean — A15

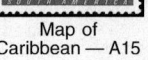

Prow of Aluminum Ship — A16

Design: 25c, "Strength in Unity," horiz.

**Wmk. 364**

**1969, Apr. 30 Litho. *Perf. 13½***

**91** A15 6c violet blue & multi .25 .25
**92** A15 25c brt rose, yel & brown .25 .25

1st anniv. of CARIFTA (Caribbean Free Trade Area).

**1969, Apr. 30 *Perf. 12x11, 11x12***

50th Anniv. of the ILO: 40c, Bauxite processing plant, horiz.

**93** A16 30c black, blue & silver .40 .25
**94** A16 40c multicolored .50 .25

Flag Raising A17

Designs: 8c, 30c, Campfire.

**1969, Aug. 13 Litho. *Perf. 13½x13***

**95** A17 6c pale green & multi .25 .25
**96** A17 8c orange & multi .25 .25
**97** A17 25c pale brown & multi .25 .25
**98** A17 30c multicolored .25 .25
**99** A17 50c rose & multi .25 .25
*Nos. 95-99 (5)* 1.25 1.25

60th anniv. of Scouting in Guyana; 3rd Caribbean Scout Jamboree, Georgetown, Aug. 13-22. For overprints and surcharges see Nos. 392, 395, 397, 402, 404-405, 453.

Gandhi and Spinning Wheel A18

**1969, Oct. 1 *Perf. 14½x14***

**100** A18 6c olive, blk & lt brn .30 *.65*
**101** A18 15c rose lilac, blk & lt brn 1.00 .65

Mohandas K. Gandhi (1868-1948), leader in India's fight for independence.

Mother Sally Troupe — A19

City Hall, Georgetown — A20

**1969, Nov. 17 *Perf. 14x13½***

**102** A19 5c multicolored .25 .25
**103** A20 6c blue & multi .25 .25
**104** A19 25c multicolored .25 .25
**105** A20 60c orange & multi .25 .25
*Nos. 102-105 (4)* 1.00 1.00

Christmas. The 5c, 6c, and 25c exist without the "Christmas 1969" overprint.

Prime Minister Forbes Burnham and Map — A21

Descent from the Cross, by Rubens — A22

6c, "Rural Self Help Project" (man & woman building house). 15c, University of Guyana, horiz. 25c, President's Residence, horiz.

**1970, Feb. 23 Litho. *Perf. 14***

**106** A21 5c blue, brn & ocher .25 .25
**107** A21 6c blue, blk ocher & brn .25 .25
**108** A21 15c apple grn & multi .25 .25
**109** A21 25c multicolored .25 .25
*Nos. 106-109 (4)* 1.00 1.00

Issued for Republic Day, Feb. 23, 1970.

**1970, Mar. 24 *Perf. 14x14½***

Easter: 6c, 25c, Christ on the Cross, by Rubens.

**110** A22 5c blue & multi .25 .25
**111** A22 6c rose lilac & multi .25 .25
**112** A22 15c dark red & multi .25 .25
**113** A22 25c yellow & multi .25 .25
*Nos. 110-113 (4)* 1.00 1.00

"Peace" and UN Emblem A23

UN 25th Anniv.: 6c, 25c, UN emblem, panning for gold and drilling for minerals.

**1970, Oct. 26 *Perf. 14½x14***

**114** A23 5c red & multi .25 .25
**115** A23 6c blue & multi .25 .25
**116** A23 15c multicolored .25 .25
**117** A23 25c brown & multi .25 .25
*Nos. 114-117 (4)* 1.00 1.00

Mother and Child, by Philip Moore — A24

**1970, Dec. 8 Litho. *Perf. 13½***

**118** A24 5c violet & multi .25 .25
**119** A24 6c brown & multi .25 .25
**120** A24 15c dk green & multi .25 .25
**121** A24 25c maroon & multi .25 .25
*Nos. 118-121 (4)* 1.00 1.00

Christmas.

National Cooperative Bank — A25

**1971, Feb. 23 Wmk. 364 *Perf. 14***

**122** A25 6c red & multi .25 .25
**123** A25 15c yellow & multi .25 .25
**124** A25 25c ultra & multi .25 .25
*Nos. 122-124 (3)* .75 .75

Republic Day.

"Togetherness, Vision, Understanding" A26

**1971, Mar. 22 *Perf. 14½x14***

**125** A26 5c yel grn & multi .25 .25
**126** A26 6c lil rose & multi .25 .25
**127** A26 15c multicolored .25 .25
**128** A26 25c yellow & multi .25 .25
*Nos. 125-128 (4)* 1.00 1.00

Intl. year against racial discrimination.

Volunteer Felling Tree, by John Criswick — A27

**1971, July 19 *Perf. 14***

**129** A27 5c blue & multi .25 .25
**130** A27 20c green & multi .25 .25
**131** A27 25c yellow & multi .25 .25
**132** A27 50c brown & multi .40 *1.25*
*Nos. 129-132 (4)* 1.15 2.00

1st anniv. of the Natl. Self-help Road Project.

Yellow Allamanda — A28

Flora: 1c, Pitcher plant of Mt. Roraima. 3c, Hanging heliconia. 5c, Annatto tree. 6c, Cannonball tree. 10c, Cattleya violacea. 15c, Christmas orchid. 20c, Paphinia cristata. 25c, Gongora quinquinervis. 40c, Tiger beard. 50c, Guzmania lingulata. 60c, Soldier's cap. $1, Chelonanthus uliginoides. $2, Norantea guianensis. $5, Odontadenia grandiflora.

**1971-76 Litho. *Perf. 13x13½***

**133** A28 1c multi ('72) .25 .25
**134** A28 2c lilac & multi .25 .25
**135** A28 3c multicolored .25 .25
**136** A28 5c lt blue & multi .25 .25
**137** A28 6c dull rose & multi .25 .25

***Perf. 13½***

**138** A28 10c multi ('72) 4.25 .25
*a.* Perf. 13 5.25 .25
**139** A28 15c multi ('72) 1.00 .25
*a.* Perf. 13 ('76) .75 .25
**140** A28 20c multi ('72) 4.00 .40
*a.* Perf. 13 7.00 .40
**141** A28 25c multi, 25c at center ('72) 6.50 *9.00*
**141A** A28 25c multi, 25c right of center ('73) .45 .55
*b.* Perf. 13 ('76) .45 .30
**142** A28 40c multi ('72) 4.50 .25
**143** A28 50c multi ('73) .50 *.80*
**144** A28 60c multi ('73) .40 *.65*
**145** A28 $1 multi ('73) .40 .40
**146** A28 $2 multi ('73) .60 .60
**147** A28 $5 multi ('73) 1.00 1.00
*Nos. 133-147 (16)* 24.85 15.40

No. 141 has 2 blossoms at left, 3 at right; this is reversed on No. 141A.

The overprint "REVENUE / ONLY" between rules was applied to Nos. 134-136, 141A, 142-147 in 1975. Postal use was permitted in Nov.-Dec., 1975. Value, set $20.

See Nos. 433-434, 731-732, 4125-4126.

For overprints and surcharges see Nos. 192, 209, 234, 331-335, 351, 358-359, 367, 370, 372, 374-375A, 379-383, 385-390A, 401, 407, 422-425, 433-434, 438-440, 447, 450, 451, 457-458, 460-461, 464-466, 497-500, 545-546, 550, 563-564, 597, 602, 618, 631-632, 641-642, 666-667, 727, 747-748, 750-751, 753-754, 759-760, 803, 805, 807-808, 810-812, 847-848, 910-911, 995, 1361, 1382-1383, 1385-1386, 1391-1392, 1452, 1454,

1456-1460, 1466, 1499, 1778-1779, 1781-1784, 1837-1838, 1870-1872, 1898-1900, 2046-2049, 2225-2227, 4165, C2-C4, O1, O3-O5, O7, O13-O14, Q1-Q4, QO1.

The Lord's Prayer, by School Girl Veronica Bassoo — A29

Guyana Masker, by School Boy Michael Austin — A30

***Perf. 13½x14, 14x13½***

**1971, Nov. 15 Litho. Wmk. 364**

| | | | | | |
|---|---|---|---|---|---|
| **148** | A29 | 5c brt green & multi | .25 | .25 |
| **149** | A29 | 20c brt green & multi | .25 | .25 |
| **150** | A30 | 25c multicolored | .25 | .25 |
| **151** | A30 | 50c multicolored | .30 | .30 |
| | | *Nos. 148-151 (4)* | 1.05 | 1.05 |

Christmas.

Guyana Dollar — A31

**1972, Feb. 23 Litho. *Perf. 14½x14***

| | | | | |
|---|---|---|---|---|
| **152** | A31 | 5c blk, dp org & silver | .25 | .25 |
| **153** | A31 | 20c blk, dp lil rose & sil | .25 | .25 |
| **154** | A31 | 25c black, ultra & silver | .25 | .25 |
| **155** | A31 | 50c black, emerald & silver | .25 | .25 |
| | | *Nos. 152-155 (4)* | 1.00 | 1.00 |

Republic Day.

Handclasp and Mosque — A32

**1972, Apr. 3 *Perf. 14***

| | | | | |
|---|---|---|---|---|
| **156** | A32 | 5c brown & multi | .25 | .25 |
| **157** | A32 | 25c blue & multi | .25 | .25 |
| **158** | A32 | 30c green & multi | .25 | .25 |
| **159** | A32 | 60c yellow brn & multi | .25 | .25 |
| | | *Nos. 156-159 (4)* | 1.00 | 1.00 |

Youman Nabi (Peaceful Prophet), Mohammedan festival.

Map of South America, Emblem of Non-aligned Countries — A33

**1972, July 20**

| | | | | |
|---|---|---|---|---|
| **160** | A33 | 8c violet & multi | .25 | .25 |
| **161** | A33 | 25c yellow grn & multi | .25 | .25 |
| **162** | A33 | 40c orange & multi | .25 | .25 |
| **163** | A33 | 50c red brown & multi | .25 | .25 |
| | | *Nos. 160-163 (4)* | 1.00 | 1.00 |

Conf. of Foreign Ministers of Nonaligned Countries, Georgetown, Aug. 7-12.

For overprints & surcharges see #573, 611, O17.

CARIFESTA '72 Emblem — A34

**1972, Aug. 25**

| | | | | |
|---|---|---|---|---|
| **164** | A34 | 8c orange & multi | .25 | .25 |
| **165** | A34 | 25c orange & multi | .25 | .25 |
| **166** | A34 | 40c orange & multi | .25 | .25 |
| **167** | A34 | 50c orange & multi | .25 | .35 |
| | | *Nos. 164-167 (4)* | 1.00 | 1.10 |

Caribbean Festival of Arts (CARIFESTA), Georgetown, Aug. 25-Sept. 15.

Holy Family — A35

**1972, Oct. 18 Litho. *Perf. 13x13½***

| | | | | |
|---|---|---|---|---|
| **168** | A35 | 8c blue & multi | .25 | .25 |
| **169** | A35 | 25c blue & multi | .25 | .25 |
| **170** | A35 | 40c blue & multi | .25 | *.25* |
| **171** | A35 | 50c blue & multi | .25 | *.30* |
| | | *Nos. 168-171 (4)* | 1.00 | 1.05 |

Christmas.

Umana Yana (Meeting Place of Wai Wai Chiefs) — A36

Designs: 25c, 40c, Bethel Chapel.

**1973, Feb. 23 Litho. *Perf. 14x14½***

| | | | | |
|---|---|---|---|---|
| **172** | A36 | 8c brt blue & multi | .25 | .25 |
| **173** | A36 | 25c rose red & multi | .25 | .25 |
| **174** | A36 | 40c emerald & multi | .25 | .25 |
| **175** | A36 | 50c black & multi | .35 | .25 |
| | | *Nos. 172-175 (4)* | 1.10 | 1.00 |

Republic Day.

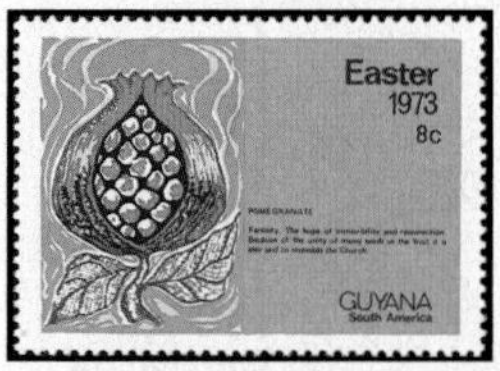


Pomegranate, Fertility and Church Symbol — A37

Map of Guyana and People Looking to the Cross — A38

**1973, Apr. 19 *Perf. 14x14½, 13½***

| | | | | |
|---|---|---|---|---|
| **176** | A37 | 8c pink & multi | .25 | .25 |
| **177** | A38 | 25c yellow & multi | .25 | .25 |
| **178** | A38 | 40c ultra & multi | .25 | .25 |
| **179** | A37 | 50c yellow & multi | .25 | .25 |
| | | *Nos. 176-179 (4)* | 1.00 | 1.00 |

Easter.

Symbolic of Blood Donation — A39

***Perf. 14x14½***

**1973, Oct. 1 Wmk. 364**

| | | | | |
|---|---|---|---|---|
| **180** | A39 | 8c red & black | .25 | .25 |
| **181** | A39 | 25c red & lilac | .25 | .25 |
| **182** | A39 | 40c red & vio blue | .40 | *.50* |
| **183** | A39 | 50c red & brown | .65 | *.90* |
| | | *Nos. 180-183 (4)* | 1.55 | 1.90 |

Guyana Red Cross, 25th anniversary.

Steel Band, Star, Pegasus Hotel — A40

Madonna and Child, St. Philip's Anglican Church, Georgetown A41

**1973, Nov. 20 Litho. *Perf. 14x14½***

| | | | | |
|---|---|---|---|---|
| **184** | A40 | 8c lilac & multi | .25 | .25 |
| **185** | A40 | 25c lilac & multi | .25 | .25 |

***Perf. 13½x14***

| | | | | |
|---|---|---|---|---|
| **186** | A41 | 40c violet blue & multi | .40 | *.70* |
| **187** | A41 | 50c violet blue & multi | .40 | *.70* |
| | | *Nos. 184-187 (4)* | 1.30 | 1.90 |

Christmas.

"One People, One Nation, One Destiny" A42

Designs: 25c, 50c, Wai Wai Indian.

**1974, Feb. 23 Litho. *Perf. 13½***

| | | | | |
|---|---|---|---|---|
| **188** | A42 | 8c multicolored | .25 | .25 |
| **189** | A42 | 25c multicolored | .25 | .25 |
| **190** | A42 | 40c multicolored | .25 | *.30* |
| **191** | A42 | 50c multicolored | .25 | *.40* |
| | | *Nos. 188-191 (4)* | 1.00 | 1.20 |

Republic Day.

No. 137 Surcharged with New Value and 2 Bars

***Perf. 13x13½***

**1974, Mar. 18 Wmk. 364**

| | | | | |
|---|---|---|---|---|
| **192** | A28 | 8c on 6c multi | .50 | .50 |

For overprints and surcharges see Nos. 424, 459, 474-478, 1453, 1500, 1780.

Crucifix Super-imposed on Eddy Bow Kite — A43

Crucifix in Pre-Columbian Timehri Style — A44

**1974, Apr. 8 *Perf. 13½x14***

| | | | | |
|---|---|---|---|---|
| **193** | A43 | 8c green & multi | .25 | .25 |
| **194** | A44 | 25c black, green & gray | .25 | .25 |
| **195** | A44 | 40c black, gray & car | .25 | .25 |
| **196** | A43 | 50c gold & multi | .25 | .25 |
| | | *Nos. 193-196 (4)* | 1.00 | 1.00 |

Easter.

UPU Emblem and British Guiana Type of 1863 — A45

Mailman and UPU Emblem A46

**1974, June 18 Litho. *Perf. 14, 14½***

| | | | | |
|---|---|---|---|---|
| **197** | A45 | 8c rose & multi | .50 | .25 |
| **198** | A46 | 25c yellow green & multi | .60 | .25 |
| **199** | A45 | 40c blue & multi | .60 | .40 |
| **200** | A46 | 50c yellow green & multi | .80 | .55 |
| | | *Nos. 197-200 (4)* | 2.50 | 1.45 |

Centenary of Universal Postal Union.

Girl Guides Holding Banner A47

Designs: 25c, 40c, Guides in camp cooking and carrying water. 50c, Like 8c.

**1974, Aug. 1** ***Perf. 14½***

| | | | | |
|---|---|---|---|---|
| **201** | A47 | 8c multicolored | .25 | .25 |
| **202** | A47 | 25c multicolored | .35 | .25 |
| **203** | A47 | 40c multicolored | .50 | .40 |
| **204** | A47 | 50c multicolored | .50 | .50 |
| *a.* | | Souvenir sheet of 4, #201-204 | 2.00 | 2.00 |
| | | *Nos. 201-204 (4)* | 1.60 | 1.40 |

Girl Guides of Guyana, 50th anniv. For overprints see Nos. 574, 1352.

Buck Toyeau — A48

Christmas (Fruit): 35c, Carambola (starfruit) and awaras. 50c, Pawpaw and tangerine. $1, Pineapple and sapodillas.

**1974, Nov. 18 Litho.** ***Perf. 14x13½***

| | | | | |
|---|---|---|---|---|
| **205** | A48 | 8c multicolored | .25 | .25 |
| **206** | A48 | 35c multicolored | .25 | .25 |
| **207** | A48 | 50c multicolored | .25 | .25 |
| **208** | A48 | $1 multicolored | .40 | .75 |
| *a.* | | Souvenir sheet of 4, #205-208 | 1.00 | *3.00* |
| | | *Nos. 205-208 (4)* | 1.15 | 1.50 |

For overprints & surcharges see #551, 612, 716, 4173.

No. 135 Surcharged with New Value and Two Bars

**1975, Jan. 20 Litho.** ***Perf. 13x13½***

| | | | | |
|---|---|---|---|---|
| **209** | A28 | 8c on 3c multi | .25 | .25 |

For surcharge see No. 423.

Golden Arrow of Courage — A49

Republic Day: 35c, Cacique's Crown of Honour. 50c, Cacique's Crown of Valour. $1, Order of Excellence.

**1975, Feb. 23** ***Perf. 13x13½***

| | | | | |
|---|---|---|---|---|
| **210** | A49 | 10c brown & multi | .25 | .25 |
| **211** | A49 | 35c brown red & multi | .25 | .25 |
| **212** | A49 | 50c green & multi | .25 | .35 |
| **213** | A49 | $1 violet bl & multi | .50 | .65 |
| | | *Nos. 210-213 (4)* | 1.25 | 1.50 |

For overprints and surcharges see Nos. 360, 368, 398, 637, 1359.

Old Sluice Gate — A50

Modern Sluice Gate A51

**1975, May 2** ***Perf. 14***

| | | | | |
|---|---|---|---|---|
| **214** | A50 | 10c bister & multi | .25 | .25 |
| **215** | A51 | 35c brown & multi | .25 | .25 |
| **216** | A50 | 50c bister & multi | .25 | .40 |
| **217** | A51 | $1 green & multi | .50 | .75 |
| *a.* | | Souvenir sheet of 4, #214-217 | 1.25 | *3.50* |
| | | *Nos. 214-217 (4)* | 1.25 | 1.65 |

Intl. Commission on Irrigation and Drainage, 25th anniv.

For overprints see Nos. 361, 592, 794-795, 1374-1375.

IWY Emblem, Symbolic Man and Woman A52

Designs: IWY emblem and petroglyph designs of men and women.

**1975, July 1 Litho. Wmk. 364**

| | | | | |
|---|---|---|---|---|
| **218** | A52 | 10c yellow & dull grn | .25 | .25 |
| **219** | A52 | 35c Prus blue & pur | .25 | .25 |
| **220** | A52 | 50c orange & dk blue | .25 | .25 |
| **221** | A52 | $1 ultra & brown | .40 | *.50* |
| *a.* | | Souvenir sheet of 4, #218-221, perf. 14½ | 1.50 | *3.50* |
| | | *Nos. 218-221 (4)* | 1.15 | 1.25 |

Intl. Women's Year. For overprints and surcharges see Nos. 362, 399, 555.

Freedom Monument, Georgetown A53

"GNS," Flower and Clasped Hands A54

Designs: Various views of Freedom Monument, Georgetown.

**1975, Aug. 26 Litho.** ***Perf. 14***

| | | | | |
|---|---|---|---|---|
| **222** | A53 | 10c gray & multi | .25 | .25 |
| **223** | A53 | 35c yellow & multi | .25 | .25 |
| **224** | A53 | 50c lilac & multi | .30 | .30 |
| **225** | A53 | $1 olive & multi | .40 | .40 |
| | | *Nos. 222-225 (4)* | 1.20 | 1.20 |

Namibia Day (independence for South-West Africa).

For overprints and surcharges see Nos. 330, 582, 593, 619, 1360.

**1975, Oct. 2 Wmk. 364** ***Perf. 14***

"GNS" and Clasped hands: 35c, Wheel. 50c, Soccer ball. $1, Uniform cap.

| | | | | |
|---|---|---|---|---|
| **226** | A54 | 10c violet, yel & grn | .25 | .25 |
| **227** | A54 | 35c brt bl, org & grn | .25 | .25 |
| **228** | A54 | 50c lt brn, brt bl & grn | .25 | .25 |
| **229** | A54 | $1 grn, vio & brt grn | .40 | .40 |
| *a.* | | Souvenir sheet of 4, #226-229 | 1.25 | *3.00* |
| | | *Nos. 226-229 (4)* | 1.15 | 1.15 |

Guyana National Service, 1st anniv. For overprint & surcharges see #448, 636, 638.

Foresters' Building and Badge A55

35c, Rock painting of hunter. 50c, Crossed axes and hunting horn. $1, Bow and arrow.

**1975, Nov. 14 Litho. Wmk. 364**

| | | | | |
|---|---|---|---|---|
| **230** | A55 | 10c red, black & gold | .25 | .25 |
| **231** | A55 | 35c red, black & gold | .25 | .25 |
| **232** | A55 | 50c gold & multi | .25 | .25 |
| **233** | A55 | $1 gold & multi | .45 | .45 |
| *a.* | | Souvenir sheet of 4, #230-233 | 1.00 | *3.00* |
| | | *Nos. 230-233 (4)* | 1.20 | 1.20 |

Ancient Order of Foresters, centenary. For overprints and surcharges see Nos. 356, 363, 400, 422, 583, 4170.

No. 144 Surcharged

**1976, Feb. 10** ***Perf. 13½***

| | | | | |
|---|---|---|---|---|
| **234** | A28 | 35c on 60c multi | .40 | .40 |

For overprints see Nos. 703-703b, 852.

St. John Ambulance Emblem — A56

Independence Arch, 1966 — A57

**1976, Mar. 29 Litho.** ***Perf. 14***

| | | | | |
|---|---|---|---|---|
| **235** | A56 | 8c black, lil rose & sil | .25 | .25 |
| **236** | A56 | 15c black, orange & sil | .25 | .25 |
| **237** | A56 | 35c black, emer & silver | .25 | .25 |
| **238** | A56 | 40c black, blue & sil | .30 | .30 |
| | | *Nos. 235-238 (4)* | 1.05 | 1.05 |

Guyana St. John Ambulance, 50th anniv. For surcharges see Nos. 715, 717, 1411.

**1976, May 25** ***Perf. 13½***

Stylized Designs: 15c, Victoria regia. 35c, Letter "S" for socialism. 40c, Worker with pitchfork.

| | | | | |
|---|---|---|---|---|
| **239** | A57 | 8c silver & multi | .25 | .25 |
| **240** | A57 | 15c silver & multi | .25 | .25 |
| **241** | A57 | 35c silver & multi | .25 | .25 |
| **242** | A57 | 40c silver & multi | .25 | .25 |
| *a.* | | Souvenir sheet of 4, #239-242, perf. 14 | 1.00 | *1.50* |
| | | *Nos. 239-242 (4)* | 1.00 | 1.00 |

10th anniv. of independence. For surcharges see Nos. 567, 639, 1444.

Map of West Indies, Bats, Wicket and Ball A57a

Prudential Cup — A57b

**Unwmk.**

**1976, Aug. 3 Litho.** ***Perf. 14***

| | | | | |
|---|---|---|---|---|
| **243** | A57a | 15c light blue & multi | 1.25 | *1.75* |
| **244** | A57b | 15c lilac rose & black | 1.25 | *1.75* |

World Cricket Cup, won by West Indies Team, 1975.

For overprints & surcharges see #352-353, 653-654.

Lamp — A58

Guitar-Sitar, Benin Head — A59

Designs: 15c, Hand and flame. 35c, Flame. 40c, Lakshmi, Hindu goddess of wealth.

**1976, Oct. 21** ***Perf. 14***

| | | | | |
|---|---|---|---|---|
| **245** | A58 | 8c multicolored | .25 | .25 |
| **246** | A58 | 15c orange & multi | .25 | .25 |
| **247** | A58 | 35c purple & multi | .25 | .25 |
| **248** | A58 | 40c ultra & multi | .30 | .30 |
| *a.* | | Souvenir sheet of 4, #245-248 | 1.25 | *1.75* |
| | | *Nos. 245-248 (4)* | 1.05 | 1.05 |

Deepavali, Hindu Festival of Lights. For surcharges see Nos. 719-721.

**1977, Feb. 1 Litho.** ***Perf. 14½***

| | | | | |
|---|---|---|---|---|
| **249** | A59 | 10c gold & multi | .25 | .25 |
| **250** | A59 | 35c gold & multi | .25 | .25 |
| **251** | A59 | 50c gold & multi | .35 | .35 |
| **252** | A59 | $1 gold & multi | .50 | .50 |
| *a.* | | Souvenir sheet of 4, #249-252 | 1.60 | *3.50* |
| | | *Nos. 249-252 (4)* | 1.35 | 1.35 |

2nd World Black and African Festival, Lagos, Nigeria, Jan. 15-Feb. 12. Nos. 249-252a were not issued without black bar.

For overprints see Nos. 364, 369, 584.

1c and 5c Coins A60

Coins (Obverse): 15c, 10c and 25c. 35c, 50c and $1. 40c, $5 and $10. $1, $50 and $100. $2, Reverse, Coat of arms.

**1977, May 26** ***Perf. 14***

| | | | | |
|---|---|---|---|---|
| **253** | A60 | 8c multicolored | .35 | .35 |
| **254** | A60 | 15c multicolored | .40 | .40 |
| **255** | A60 | 35c multicolored | .70 | .70 |
| **256** | A60 | 40c multicolored | .85 | .85 |
| **257** | A60 | $1 multicolored | 1.25 | 1.25 |
| **258** | A60 | $2 multicolored | 2.00 | 2.00 |
| | | *Nos. 253-258 (6)* | 5.55 | 5.55 |

New coinage. For overprints and surcharges see Nos. 539, 541A, 568, 594, O18, O20, Q5.

Hand Pump, c. 1850 A61

National Fire Prevention Week: 15c, Steam engine, c. 1860. 35c, Fire engine, c. 1930. 40c, Fire engine, 1977.

***Perf. 14x14½***

**1977, Nov. 15 Litho. Wmk. 364**

| | | | | |
|---|---|---|---|---|
| **259** | A61 | 8c multicolored | 1.25 | .25 |
| **260** | A61 | 15c multicolored | 2.00 | .25 |
| **261** | A61 | 35c multicolored | 2.25 | 1.10 |
| **262** | A61 | 40c multicolored | 2.50 | 1.25 |
| | | *Nos. 259-262 (4)* | 8.00 | 2.85 |

For surcharges see Nos. 1370-1371.

Cuffy Monument — A62

8c, 35c, Cuffy statue from monument.

**1977, Dec. 7 Litho. *Perf. 14***

**263** A62 8c multicolored .25 .25
**264** A62 15c multicolored .25 .25
**265** A62 35c multicolored .25 .25
**266** A62 40c multicolored .25 .25
*Nos. 263-266 (4)* 1.00 1.00

Cuffy, Guyana's national hero, led a slave revolution in 1763. The monument was unveiled in 1976. For overprints see Nos. 446, 569, 613.

Wildlife Protection — A63

**1978, Feb. 15 *Perf. 14***

**267** A63 8c Manatee 1.25 .25
**268** A63 15c Giant sea turtle 1.50 .40
**269** A63 35c Harpy eagle 6.25 2.75
**270** A63 40c Iguana 6.00 2.75
*Nos. 267-270 (4)* 15.00 6.15

8c, 15c are horiz. For overprints and surcharges see Nos. 443, 722-723, 1416.

Parliament and Prime Minister Burnham — A64

Prime Minister and: 15c, Student and school children. 35c, Bauxite mine. 40c, Cooperative village.

**1978, Apr. 27 Litho. *Perf. 13½x14***

**271** A64 8c violet & black .25 .25
**272** A64 15c gray, blk & bl .25 .25
**273** A64 35c multicolored .25 .25
**274** A64 40c gray, blk & org .25 .25
*a.* Souvenir sheet of 4, #271-274 1.10 *1.75*
*Nos. 271-274 (4)* 1.00 1.00

Prime Minister Linden Forbes Burnham, 25th anniv. of his entry into parliament. For surcharges see Nos. 648-649.

Dr. George Giglioli, Anopheles Mosquito — A65

Agrias Claudina — A66

30c, Institute of Applied Science & Technology, proposed for University of Guyana. 50c, Map of Guyana & National Science Research Council emblem. 60c, Commonwealth Science Council emblem.

***Perf. 13½x14, 14x13½***

**1978, Sept. 4 Litho. Wmk. 364**

**275** A65 10c multi .25 .25
**276** A65 30c multi, horiz. .25 .25
**277** A65 50c multi .30 .30
**278** A65 60c multi, horiz. .30 .30
*Nos. 275-278 (4)* 1.10 1.10

For overprints see Nos. 577, 585, 590.

**1978-80 *Perf. 14x13½***

**Size: 22x16mm**

**279** A66 5c Prepona pheridamas 2.50 .25
**280** A66 10c Archonias bellona 2.50 .25
**281** A66 15c Eryphanis polyxena 2.50 .25
**282** A66 20c Helicopis cupido 2.50 .25
**283** A66 25c Nessaea batesli 2.50 .25
**283A** A66 30c Nymphidium mantus ('80) 2.00 *3.25*
**284** A66 35c Siderone galanthis 2.50 .25
**285** A66 40c Morpho rhetenor, male 2.50 .25
**286** A66 50c Hamadryas amphinone 2.50 .30
**286A** A66 60c Papilio androgeus ('80) 2.25 1.75

***Perf. 13½x13***

**287** A66 $1 Agrias claudina 6.00 .35
**288** A66 $2 Morpho rhetenor, female 8.75 .70
**289** A66 $5 Morpho deidamia 9.75 1.50
**289A** A66 $10 Elbella patrobas, perf. 14 ('80) 7.50 6.25
*Nos. 279-289A (14)* 56.25 15.85

Issued: #279-283, 284-286, 287-289, 10/1/78. For overprints and surcharges see Nos. 391, 406, 436-436A, 481, 486, 554, 668-670, 733-743, 871, 936-939, 944, 969, 1373, 1418, 1455, 1786, 1812, 1814, 1832-1833, 1873, 1901, 1912-1913, 1984-1988, 2051, 2053, 2054C, 2055, 2057, 2057B-2057C, 2058-2059, 2082-2111, C5-C6, O15-O16, O23-O29.

Indian Making Stone Chip Grater — A67

UNESCO Emblem and: 30c, Arawak Cassiri jar and decorated Amerindian jar. 50c, Gate to old Dutch fort, Kykover-al. 60c, Fort Island, Dutch ruins.

**1978, Dec. 27 Wmk. 364 *Perf. 14***

**290** A67 10c green & multi .25 .25
**291** A67 30c green & multi .25 .25
**292** A67 50c green & multi .25 .25
**293** A67 60c green & multi .25 .25
*Nos. 290-293 (4)* 1.00 1.00

National and International Heritage Year. For surcharges see Nos. 604-606.

Earth Station at Dawn, Georgetown A68

Designs: 30c, Earth Station in daylight, Georgetown. 50c, Intelsat V. $3, Intelsat IVa.

**1979, Feb. 7 Litho. *Perf. 14x14½***

**294** A68 10c multicolored .25 .25
**295** A68 30c multicolored .25 .25
**296** A68 50c multicolored .40 .25
**297** A68 $3 multicolored 1.40 1.00
*Nos. 294-297 (4)* 2.30 1.75

For surcharges see Nos. 384, 655, 714, 1376-1377, 1380, O9.

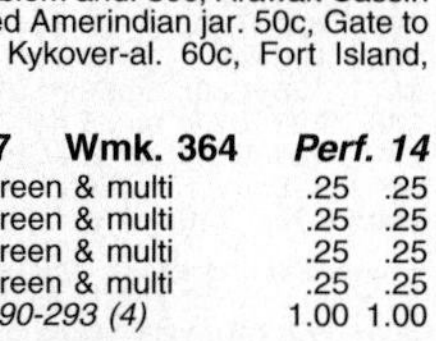

British Guyana No. 5 — A69

Designs: 30c, British Guiana No. 13, vert. 50c, British Guiana No. 152. $3, Printing press used for 1c Magenta, vert.

**1979, June 11 Wmk. 364 *Perf. 14***

**298** A69 10c multicolored .25 .25
**299** A69 30c multicolored .30 .25
**300** A69 50c multicolored .40 .25
**301** A69 $3 multicolored .60 .60
*Nos. 298-301 (4)* 1.55 1.35

Sir Rowland Hill (1795-1879), originator of penny postage.
For overprints & surcharges see #409, 426, 428, 449, 479, 480, 578, 586, 598, 614, O6.

"Fun with the Fowls" and IYC Emblem — A70

Children's Drawings and IYC Emblem: 10c, "Me and my sister," vert. 50c, "Two boys catching ducks." $3, "Mango season."

**1979, Aug. 20 Litho. *Perf. 13½***

**302** A70 10c multicolored .25 .25
**303** A70 30c multicolored .25 .25
**304** A70 50c multicolored .25 .25
**305** A70 $3 multicolored .60 *1.75*
*Nos. 302-305 (4)* 1.35 2.50

Intl. Year of the Child. For overprints and surcharges see Nos. 435, 579, 587, 599, 615, 943.

H. N. Critchlow, Worker Hauling Sack — A71

Critchlow and: 30c, Baker, horiz. 50c, Flag and crowd. $3, Portrait only.

**1979, Sept. 27 Litho. *Perf. 14***

**306** A71 10c multicolored .25 .25
**307** A71 30c multicolored .25 .25
**308** A71 50c multicolored .25 .25
**309** A71 $3 multicolored .60 *.90*
*Nos. 306-309 (4)* 1.35 1.65

Guyana Labor Union, 60th anniversary. For surcharges see Nos. 403, 429, 718.

Cooperative Republic, 10th Anniv. — A72

**Wmk. 364**

**1980, Feb. 23 Litho. *Perf. 14***

**313** A72 10c shown .25 .25
**314** A72 35c Demerara River Bridge .30 .25
**315** A72 60c Kaieteur Falls .50 .25
**316** A72 $3 Makanaima, American Indian .75 .75
*Nos. 313-316 (4)* 1.80 1.50

For overprints and surcharges see Nos. 365, 371, 450A, 442, 591, 656.

Miniature Sheet

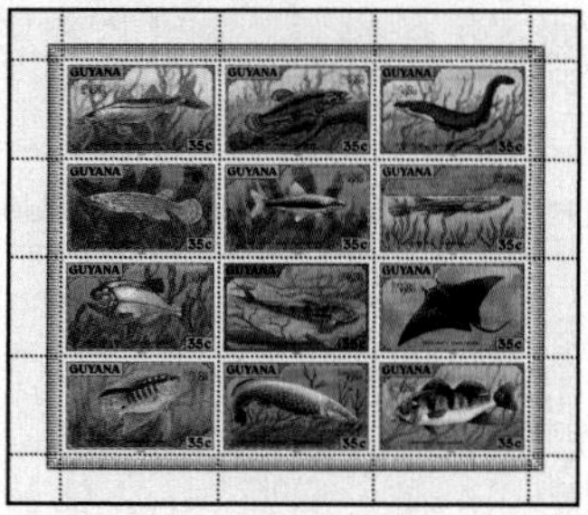

Snoek, London 1980 Emblem — A73

London 80 Emblem and Fish; a, Snoek. b, Haimara. c, Electric eel. d, Golden rivulus. e, Pencil fish. f, Four-eyed fish. g, Pirai. h, Smoking hassar. i, Devil ray. j, Flying patwa. k, Arapaima. l, Lukanani.

**1980, May 6 Wmk. 373 *Perf. 14***

**317** Sheet of 12 6.00 6.00
*a.-l.* A73 35c any single .40 .40

London 1980 Intl. Stamp Exhib., May 6-14. For overprints & surcharges see #444, 725-726, 1414.

Children's Convalescent Home, Rotary Emblem — A74

Rotary International, 75th anniversary (Emblem and): 30c, Georgetown club emblem. 50c, District 404 emblem (hibiscus), vert. $3, Anniversary emblem, vert.

***Perf. 14x14½, 14½x14***

**1980, June 23 Litho. Wmk. 364**

**318** A74 10c multicolored .25 .25
**319** A74 30c multicolored .25 .25
**320** A74 50c multicolored .35 .35
**321** A74 $3 multicolored 1.00 1.00
*Nos. 318-321 (4)* 1.85 1.85

For overprints and surcharges see Nos. 552, 580, 601, C1.

Emblem and Caduceus A75

**Wmk. 364**

**1980, Sept. 23 Litho. *Perf. 13½***

**322** A75 10c shown .25 .25
**323** A75 60c Scientist, beach scene .60 .30
**324** A75 $3 Emblems over island 1.50 1.25
*Nos. 322-324 (3)* 2.35 1.80

Commonwealth Caribbean Medical Research Council, 25th anniversary. For overprints and surcharges see Nos. 366, 427, 430, 494, 553.

Virola Surinamensis (Christmas 1980) — A76

**1980, Nov. 1 Wmk. 373 *Perf. 14***

**325** A76 10c shown .25 .25
**326** A76 30c Hymenaea courbaril .30 .25
**327** A76 50c Mora excelsa .40 .25
**328** A76 $3 Peltogyne venosa 1.25 *1.60*
*Nos. 325-328 (4)* 2.20 2.35

For overprints and surcharges see Nos. 431, 773, 790, 792-793, 4169, 4175.

Miniature Sheet

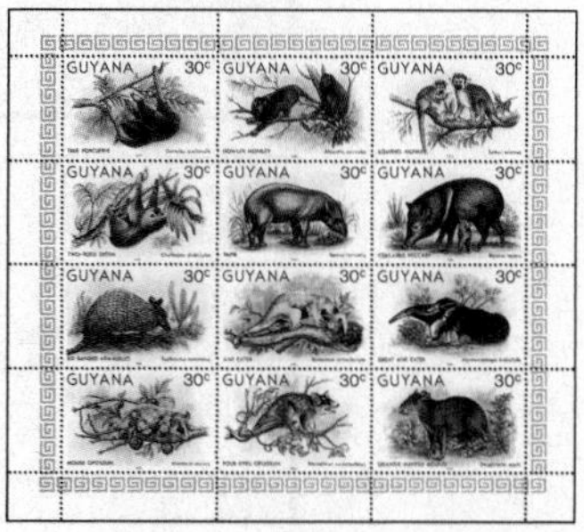

A77

Designs: a, Tree porcupine. b, Howler monkeys. c, Squirrel monkeys. d, Two-toed sloth. e, Tapir. f, Collared peccary. g, Six-banded armadillo. h, Anteater. i, Great anteaters. j, Mouse opossums. k, Four-eyed opossum. l, Orange-rumped agouti.

**1981, Mar. 2 Wmk. 364 *Perf. 14***

**329** Sheet of 12 6.00 6.00
*a.-l.* A77 30c any single .35 .35
*m.* As #329g, perf. 12 3.00 .40

For overprints see #581, 819, 1399, 1503, 1844.

During 1981-91, there were numerous sources creating stamps for Guyana, with as many as 5-7 parties being active at any given time.

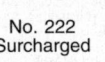

No. 222 Surcharged

**1981, May 4**

**330** A53 $1.05 on 10c multi 1.25

For surcharges see Nos. 396, 620.

**Nos. 135, 145-147 Surcharged**

No. 331

No. 332

No. 333

No. 334

No. 335

**1981 Litho. Wmk. 364 *Perf. 13½***

**331** A28 60c on 3c #135 3.00
**332** A28 75c on $5 #147 3.00
**333** A28 $1.10 on $2 #146 3.00
**334** A28 $3.60 on $5 #147 (Blk) 4.00
*a.* Blue overprint 4.00
**335** A28 $7.20 on $1 #145 (Bl) 4.00
*a.* Black overprint 6.00

No. 333 is airmail. Issue dates: $3.60, $7.20, May 6. Others July 22. Diagonal overprint on No. 332. Vertical overprint on No. 333. Location of surcharge varies.

See Nos. 621, 666-667, Q4, QO5. For overprints and surcharges see Nos. 378, 489-496, 547, 549, 646, 818, 867-868, O11, Q3, QO3.

Map of Guyana — A78

**1981, May 11 Photo. *Perf. 13½***

**336** A78 10c on 3c multi 1.00
**337** A78 30c on 2c multi 1.00
**338** A78 50c on 2c multi 1.00
**339** A78 60c on 2c multi 1.00
**340** A78 75c on 3c multi 1.00
*Nos. 336-340 (5)* 5.00

Revenue stamps surcharged for postal use. For similar stamp, see #934a. For surcharge see #503.

**Nos. J5-J8 Surcharged in Red, Black, or Brown**

a

b

**Type "a"**

**1981, June 8 Typo. *Perf. 13½x14***

**341** D1 10c on 2c #J6
**342** D1 15c on 12c #J8 (Blk)
**343** D1 20c on 1c #J5
**344** D1 45c on 2c #J6
**345** D1 55c on 4c #J7
**346** D1 60c on 4c #J7 (Brn)
**347** D1 65c on 2c #J6
**348** D1 70c on 4c #J7
**349** D1 80c on 4c #J7
*Nos. 341-349 (9)* 11.00

**Type "b"**

*341a* D1 10c on 2c #J6
*342a* D1 15c on 12c #J8 (Blk)
*343a* D1 20c on 1c #J5
*344a* D1 45c on 2c #J6
*345a* D1 55c on 4c #J7
*347a* D1 65c on 2c #J6
*348a* D1 70c on 4c #J7
*349a* D1 80c on 4c #J7
*Nos. 341a-349a (8)* 11.00

Pairs with types a and b exist for all values except the 60c.

Nos. 48, 61-62, 74, 139, 142-143, 145-147, 212-213, 216, 220, 231-232, 243-244, 251-252, 315-316, and 323 Overprinted in Black or Red

**1981 *Perfs. as Before***
**Watermarks & Printing Methods as Before**

**350** A8 15c on #74 (R) 17.50
**351** A28 15c on #139
*a.* Red overprint 7.00
*b.* On #139a, red overprint 8.00
**352** A57a 15c on #243 8.50
**353** A57b 15c on #244 5.00
**354** A11 25c on #61 (R) .75
**355** A11 30c on #62 (R) .75
**356** A55 35c on #231 (R) 3.00
**357** A8 40c on #48 12.00
**358** A28 40c on #142
**359** A28 50c on #143 4.00
**360** A49 50c on #212 3.25
**361** A50 50c on #216 1.50
**362** A52 50c on #220 26.00
**363** A55 50c on #232 3.25
**364** A59 50c on #251 15.00
**365** A72 60c on #315 .90
**366** A75 60c on #323 .90
**367** A28 $1 on #145 3.50
*a.* Red overprint 2.00
**368** A49 $1 on #213 7.50
**369** A59 $1 on #252 6.50
**370** A28 $2 on #146 8.00
*a.* Red overprint 2.00
*b.* Black ovpt. with serifs 25.00
**371** A72 $3 on #316 3.00
**372** A28 $5 on #147 4.25
*Nos. 350-372 (23)* 50.00

Issued: #354-356, 367, 6/8; #350, 357, 370, 7/1; #351-353, 359-366, 368-369, 371-372, 7/7.

Location and size of overprint varies. Refer to second paragraph in footnote following No. 147 for Nos. 358-359.

For surcharges and overprints see Nos. 556, 607, 659, 745, 849-850, 1362.

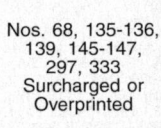

Nos. 68, 135-136, 139, 145-147, 297, 333 Surcharged or Overprinted

**1981 Litho. *Perfs. as Before***
**Watermarks & Printing Methods as Before**

**373** A7 15c on 1c #68 1.10
**374** A28 50c on 5c #136 2.50
**375** A28 75c on 5c #136 30.00
**375A** A28 80c on 15c #139
**376** A7 100c on 1c #68 1.00
**377** A7 110c on 1c #68 1.00
*a.* Strip of 3, #373, 376-377 7.00
**378** A28 $1.10 on #333 17.50
**379** A28 120c on $1 #145 2.50
**380** A28 140c on $1 #145 2.50
**381** A28 150c on $2 #146 2.50
**382** A28 210c on $5 #147 30.00
**383** A28 220c on 5c #136 30.00
**384** A68 220c on $3 #297 5.00
**385** A28 250c on $5 #147 2.75
**386** A28 280c on $5 #147 2.75
**387** A28 360c on $2 #146 3.50
**388** A28 375c on $5 #147 3.00
**389** A28 $7.20 on 3c #135 100.00
**390** A28 720c on 60c #144 3.75
**390A** A28 $20 on 5c #136

Location and size of surcharge and obliterator varies. Obliterator is an "X" on Nos. 381-388, 390, two solid boxes on Nos. 379-380, and five bars on No. 389. Numeral "7" is placed before 5 make surcharge on No. 375. "Royal Wedding 1981" obliterated by three bars on No. 378. New denomination on No. 375A does not have cent sign. Obliterator on No. 390A is three horizontal bars.

Refer to second paragraph in footnote following No. 147 for Nos. 381, 387 and 390. Nos. 376-378 are airmail.

Issued: #375, 382, 6/8; #373-374, 376-388, 390, 7/1.

For overprint and surcharges see Nos. 408, 788, 859-860, 863-864, 1379, 1417.

No. 281 Overprinted "ESSEQUIBO / IS OURS"

**1981, July Litho. *Perf. 14x13½***

**391** A66 15c on #281 6.75
*a.* Ovpt. without serifs

**Nos. 87, 95-96, 142, 146, 210, 218, 230, 309, 330, O15 Surcharged**

**1981 *Perfs. as Before***
**Watermarks & Printing Methods as Before**

**392** A17 55c on 6c #95 4.50
**393** A14 70c on 6c #87 1.25
**394** A14 100c on 6c #87 1.50
**395** A17 100c on 8c #96 4.50
**396** A53 100c on #330 (surcharge reading down) 40.00
*a.* Surcharge reading up 50.00
**397** A17 110c on 6c #95 3.00
**398** A49 110c on 10c #210 3.00
**399** A52 110c on 10c #218 7.00
**400** A55 110c on 10c #230 7.00
**401** A28 125c on $2 #146 15.00
**402** A17 180c on 6c #95 4.50
**403** A71 240c on $3 #309 12.00
**404** A17 400c on 6c #95 4.50
**405** A17 $4.40 on 6c #95 2.25
*a.* Fours same size 11.00
**406** A66 550c on $10 #O15 10.00
**407** A28 625c on 40c #142 17.50

Issued: #392, 394-395, 397-399, 405, 405a, 407, July 7; #393, 402-404, 406, Sept. 15. Refer to 2nd paragraph in footnote following #147 for #407. For overprints and surcharges see #651-652, 996, 1858-1859, 1861, O8, O10, O12.

No. 383 Ovptd. "Espana 82"
No. 301 Surcharged "1831-1981 / Von Stephan"

***Perfs. as Before***

**1981, July 22 Litho. Wmk. 364**

**408** A28 220c on #383 2.00
**409** A69 330c on $3 #301 10.00

For surcharges see Nos. 616, 622.

Nos. 43, 72 Surcharged

**1981 Photo. Unwmk. *Perf. 14x14½***

**410** A7 12c on 12c on 6c #43
**411** A7 Pair, #a.-b.
*a.* 15c on 10c on 6c #43
*b.* 15c on 30c on 6c #43
**412** A7 Pair, #a.-b.
*a.* 15c on 50c on 6c #43
*b.* 15c on 60c on 6c #43
**413** A7 Strip of 3, #a.-c.
*a.* 12c On 6c #43
*b.* 50c On 6c #43
*c.* $1 On 6c #43

**Wmk. 364**

**413D** A7 Strip of 3, #e.-g.
*e.* 12c On 6c #72
*f.* 50c On 6c #72
*g.* $1 On 6c #72

Issue dates: Nos. 410-412, Aug. 24. No. 413-413D, Nov. 10.

Nos. 410-412 were not issued without large numeral surcharges. Obliterator is black box on Nos. 410-412, "X" on Nos. 413a & 413De. Nos. 413b-413c, 413Df-g are airmail.

For overprints and surcharges see Nos. 728-728a, 914, 994, 994a, 1400-1401, 4174.

16th Anniv. of the Guyana Defense Force — A79

**1981, Oct. 1 Wmk. 364 *Perf. 13½***

**414** A79 15c on 10c Armed Ranger, 1772 .30 .25
**415** A79 50c Private, Foot Regiment, 1825 .75 .45
**416** A79 $1 on 30c Marine Private, 1775 1.40 1.40
**417** A79 $1.10 on $3 Defense Force officers, 1966 1.60 1.60
*Nos. 414-417 (4)* 4.05 3.70

Nos. 414, 416-417 not issued without surcharge. For overprints see Nos. 570, 588, 595, 1368-1369.

Louis Braille and Boy Reading Braille — A80

Intl. Year of the Disabled: 50c, Helen Keller and Rajkumari Singh. $1, Beethoven and Sonny Thomas. $1.10, Renoir and painting.

**1981, Nov. 2 *Perf. 13½x14***

**418** A80 15c on 10c multi .50 .50
**419** A80 50c multi 1.50 1.50
**420** A80 $1 on 60c multi 2.50 2.50
**421** A80 $1.10 on $3 multi 4.00 4.00
*Nos. 418-421 (4)* 8.50 8.50

Nos. 418, 420-421 not issued without surcharge. For overprints and surcharge see #571, 589, 596, 1913A.

Nos. 192, 209, 230, 298, 301, 309, 322, 324, 328, O1 Surcharged in Blue or Red

**1981, Nov. 14** ***Perfs. as Before***
**Watermarks & Printing Methods as Before**

**422** A55 110c on 10c #230 4.00
**423** A28 110c on #209 5.00
**424** A28 110c on #192 5.00
**425** A28 110c on #O1 5.00
**426** A69 110c on 10c #298 (R) 3.00
**427** A75 110c on 10c #322 15.00
**428** A69 110c on $3 #301 (R) 3.00
**429** A71 110c on $3 #309 8.00
**430** A75 110c on $3 #324 5.00
*a.* Red surcharge 8.00
**431** A76 110c on $3 #328 8.00
*a.* Red surcharge 60.00
*Nos. 422-431 (10)* 61.00

Nos. 423-424 were issued with two 110c surcharges of different sizes. Refer to second paragraph in footnote below No. 147 for No. 425. For overprints and surcharges see Nos. 791, 820, 855, 1000, 1364-1366.

Flower Type of 1971-76 Surcharged

**1981, Nov. 24 Photo.** ***Perf. 15x14***
**Size: 20x23mm**
**Coil Stamps**

**433** A28 15c on 2c like #134 .35
**434** A28 15c on 8c Mazaruni Pride .35
*a.* Pair, #433-434 1.10

Nos. 433-434 were not issued without surcharge. See Nos. 731-732.

No. 305 Surcharged "U.N.I.C.E.F. / 1946-1981"

**Wmk. 364**
**1981, Nov. 14 Litho.** ***Perf. 13½***
**435** A70 125c on $3 #305 4.00

For surcharge see No. 942.

No. 279 Surcharged "Nov. 81" (#436) or "Cancun 81" (#436A)

**1981, Nov. 14** ***Perf. 14x13½***
**436** A66 50c on 5c #279
**436A** A66 50c on 5c #279 6.50

Conversion to Metric System, Jan. 2 — A81

a, Tape measure. b, Juggler. c, Man, envelope. d, Baby on scale. e, Canje Bridge. f, Liter bucket.

***Perf. 14½x14***
**1982, Jan. 18** **Wmk. 364**
**437** A81 15c Sheet of 6, #a.-f. 3.25 3.25

For surcharge see No. 557.

Nos. 61, 63, 139, 140, 141A, 143-144, 146-147, 228, 266, 269, 300, 314 and 316-317 Ovptd. "1982" Vertically or Horizontally in Blue or Violet

**1982-83** ***Perfs. as Before***
**Watermarks & Printing Methods as Before**

**438** A28 15c on #139 8.00
*a.* On #139a 65.00
**439** A28 20c on #140 4.00
**440** A28 25c on #141A 7.50
**441** A11 25c on #61 (V) 2.00
**442** A72 35c on #314 1.00
**443** A63 35c on #269 6.00
**444** A73 35c on block of 6, #317a-317f 20.00
**445** A11 40c on #63 (V) 1.00
**446** A62 40c on #266 1.00
**447** A28 50c on #143 3.00
**448** A54 50c on #228 2.00
**449** A69 50c on #300 1.00
**449A** A28 60c on #144 7.00
**450** A28 $2 on #146 1.50
**450A** A72 $3 on #316 2.25
**451** A28 $5 on #147 1.50
*Nos. 438-451 (16)* 68.75

Issued: #439-441, 2/8; #450-451, 4/23; #445-446, 4/27; #438, 6/17; #443-444, 8/16; #442, 9/15; #447-449, 10/11; #449A, 7/1/83; #450A, 11/3/83.

For other stamps overprinted "1982" only, see Nos 482-483, 555.

For overprints and surcharges see Nos. 806, 809, 813-814, 851, 999, 1354, 1415, 4171.

Nos. 97, O3, O4, O9-O10 Ovptd. "POSTAGE" in Blue

**1982** ***Perfs. as Before***
**Watermarks and Printing Methods as Before**

**452** A28 15c on #O3 10.00
**453** A17 25c on #97 *6.00*
**454** A28 50c on #O4 1.50
**455** A68 100c on #O9 2.50
**456** A17 110c on #O10 *3.00*

For surcharge see No. 853. For similar overprints see Nos. 729-730. Refer to second paragraph in footnote following No. 147 for No. 454.

Nos. 133, 137, 142, and 192 Surcharged in Blue or Green

***Perfs. as Before***
**1982 Litho. Wmk. 364**

**457** A28 20c on 6c #137 1.00
**458** A28 20c on 6c #137 (G) 1.00
**459** A28 125c on #192 1.00
**460** A28 180c on #142 ovpt. "1982" 6.00
**461** A28 220c on 1c #133 2.00
*Nos. 457-461 (5)* 11.00

No. 458 has no obliterator, "20c" is 23mm long.

Issued: #457-459, 2/8; #460, 4/8; #461, 4/23.

Refer to 2nd paragraph in footnote following #147 for #460.

For overprints see #755, 856, 862.

Savings Campaign A81a

**1982 Litho.** ***Perf. 14½***
**462** A81a $1 Soldier & flag 1.00
**463** A81a $1.10 on $5, two soldiers, flag 7.50
*a.* Inverted comma before "OURS"

Size of obliterator differs on Nos. 463 and 463a. Nos. 462-463a are revenue stamps ovptd. for postal use.

Issued: #462, 2/8; #463, 3/3; #463a, 7/13.

Nos. 134, 136, & 192 Surcharged in Black or Green "BADEN-POWELL / 1857-1982" (#464a, 465a, 466a) "Scout Movement / 1907-1982" (#464b, 465b, 466b) "1907-1982" (#464c, 465c, 466c) "1857-1982" (#464d, 465d, 466d) "1982" (#464e, 465e, 466e)

***Perf. 13x13½***
**1982, Feb. 22 Litho. Wmk. 364**
**Sheets of 25**

**464** 8 #a.-b., 4 #c.-d., 1 #e. 20.00
*a.-e.* A28 15c on 2c #134, any single .70
**465** 8 #a.-b., 4 #c.-d., 1 #e. 35.00
*a.-e.* A28 110c on 5c #136, any single 1.00
**466** 8 #a.-b., 4 #c.-d., 1 #e. 35.00
*a.-e.* A28 125c on #192, any single (G) 1.00

Lord Robert Baden-Powell, 125th anniv. of birth. Boy Scout Movement, 75th anniv.

For overprints and surcharges see Nos. 558, 778-784, 836-837, 1347.

**Nos. 289, 299, 301 Surcharged or Overprinted in Black or Blue**

***Perfs. as Before***
**1982, Feb. 15 Litho. Wmk. 364**

**479** A69 100c on $3 #301 2.00 1.00
**480** A69 400c on 30c #299 3.00 2.00
**481** A66 $5 #289 (Bl) 15.00 10.00
*Nos. 479-481 (3)* 20.00 13.00

For surcharges see Nos. 617, 904-906, 937-939, O22-O29.

Nos. 88-89 Ovptd. "1982" in Blue and Nos. 87, 90 Surcharged in Blue or Red

**1982, Mar. 15 Photo.** ***Perf. 13***
**482** A14 25c on #88
**483** A14 30c on #89
**484** A14 45c on 6c #87
**485** A14 75c on 40c #90 (R)
*Nos. 482-485 (4)* 3.00

For overprints see Nos. 766-767.

Nos. 60, 284, 324, and 331-333 Surcharged in Black or Blue

**1982** ***Perfs. as Before***
**Watermarks & Printing Methods as Before**

**486** A66 20c on 35c #284 7.50
**487** A11 80c on 6c #60 (Bl) 3.00
**488** A11 85c on 6c #60 (Bl) 3.00
**489** A28 85c on #331 6.00
**490** A28 130c on #331 4.00
**491** A28 160c on #333 (Bl) 3.00
*a.* Black surcharge 5.00
**492** A28 170c on #333 15.00
**493** A28 210c on #332 (Bl) 3.00
**494** A75 210c on $3 #324 (Bl) 4.00
**495** A28 235c on #332 5.00
*a.* Blue surcharge 9.00
**496** A28 330c on #333 4.00
*Nos. 486-496 (11)* 57.50

Nos. 491-491a, 492, & 496 are airmail. Obliterators differ.

Issue dates: #486, Mar. 15. Others, Apr. 27.

For surcharges see Nos. 647, 1367.

Nos. 135, 137, 144 & 145 Overprinted or Surcharged in Blue or Black "ESPANA / 1982" or "ESPANA / 1982" and "ITALY" (#499)

**Wmk. 364**
**1982, May 15 Litho.** ***Perf. 13½***
**497** A28 $1 on #145 (Blk) 1.50
**498** A28 110c on 3c #135 1.50
**499** A28 $2.35 on 180c on 60c #144 *14.00*
**500** A28 250c on 6c #137 2.00

Refer to second paragraph in footnote below No. 147 for No. 499.

#499 not issued without $2.35 surcharge.

See No. 597 for stamp with one-line Espana 1982 overprint. For surcharges see #774-777.

Map Revenue Type A78 Surcharged in Black, Blue, or Red

**1982-83 Photo. Wmk. 364** ***Perf. 13***
**501** A78 15c on 2c (Bl)
**502** A78 20c on 2c (Bl)
**503** A78 20c on 10c #336 (Bl)
**504** A78 25c on 2c
*a.* Blue surcharge
*b.* Red surcharge 1.00
**505** A78 30c on 2c (Bl)
**506** A78 40c on 2c
*a.* Blue surcharge
**507** A78 45c on 2c (Bl)
**508** A78 50c on 2c (Bl)
**509** A78 60c on 2c (Bl)
**510** A78 75c on 2c (Bl)
**511** A78 80c on 2c (Bl)
**512** A78 85c on 2c (Bl)
**513** A78 $1.00 on 3c
**514** A78 $1.10 on 3c
**515** A78 $1.20 on 3c
**516** A78 $1.25 on 3c
**517** A78 $1.30 on 3c
**518** A78 $1.50 on 3c
**519** A78 $1.60 on 3c
**520** A78 $1.70 on 3c
**521** A78 $1.75 on 3c
**522** A78 $1.80 on 3c
**523** A78 $2.00 on 3c
**524** A78 $2.10 on 3c
**525** A78 $2.20 on 3c
**526** A78 $2.35 on 3c
**527** A78 $2.40 on 3c
**528** A78 $2.50 on 3c
**529** A78 $3.00 on 3c
**530** A78 $3.30 on 3c
**531** A78 $3.75 on 3c
**532** A78 $4.00 on 3c
**533** A78 $4.40 on 3c
**534** A78 $5.00 on 3c
**535** A78 $5.50 on 3c
**536** A78 $6.25 on 3c
**537** A78 $15 on 2c (R)
**538** A78 $20 on 2c (R)
*Nos. 501-538 (38)* 210.00

Revenue stamps surcharged for postal use. Issue dates: Nos. 501-502, 504-538, May 17, 1982; No. 503, Mar. 14, 1983.

For surcharge see No. 935.

British Guiana Nos. 254, 255, 279, Guyana 10A, 13, 13a, 32J, 32K, 32N Surcharged "H.R.H. / Prince William / 21st June 1982" in Blue

British Guiana stamps also have "GUYANA."

**1982, July 12** ***Perfs. as Before***
**Watermarks & Printing Methods as Before**

**539** A60 50c on 2c #254 1.00 .45
**540** A60 50c on 2c #32J 10.00 4.50
**541** A66 $1.10 on 5c #279 3.00 .65
**541A** A60 $1.10 on 3c #255 2.00 .55
**542** A60 $1.10 on 3c #32K 32.50 4.50
**543** A60 $1.25 on 6c #10A

**543A** A60 $1.25 on 6c #32N .85 .85
**544** A60 $2.20 on 24c #13a 4.00
**544A** A60 $2.20 on 24c #13 2.00 2.00

For surcharges see Nos. 797-800.

### Nos. 133-134 Surcharged "C.A. & CARIB / Games / 1982"

***Perf. 13x13½***

**1982, Aug. 16 Litho. Wmk. 364**

**545** A28 50c on 2c #134 2.25 .40
**546** A28 60c on 1c #133 2.75 .25
*Nos. 545-546 (2)* 5.00

Central American and Caribbean Games, Havana. For overprint see No. 816.

### Nos. 331, C2 Surcharged

**1982, Sept. 15**

**547** A28 130c on #331 3.00
**548** A28 170c on #C2 4.00
**549** A28 440c on #331 ovptd. "1982" 3.50
*a.* Without "1982" 80.00
*Nos. 547-549 (3)* 10.50

For surcharge see No. 802.

### No. 137 Surcharged "Commonwealth / GAMES / AUSTRALIA / 1982" in Blue

**1982, Sept. 27**

**550** A28 $1.25 on 6c #137 2.25 .50

For surcharge see No. 789.

### No. 207 Ovptd. "INT. / FOOD DAY / 1982" in Dark Blue

No. 320 Ovptd. "INT. YEAR / OF THE / ELDERLY" in Dark Blue
No. 323 Ovptd. "Dr. R. KOCH / CENTENARY / TBC BACILLUS / DISCOVERY" in Dark Blue
No. 287 Ovptd. "F.D. ROOSEVELT / 1882-1982 " in Green
No. 221 Ovptd. "1982" in Blue
No. 332 Surcharged "GAC Inaug. Flight / Georgetown- / Boa Vista, Brasil" in Blue and "1982" in Blue Green

**1982, Oct. 15 *Perfs. as Before***

**Watermarks & Printing Methods as Before**

**551** A48 50c on #207 21.00 1.00
**552** A74 50c on #320 14.00 1.00
**553** A75 60c on #323 5.00 .55
**554** A66 $1 on #287 6.00 1.00
**555** A52 $1 on #221 6.00 1.25
**556** A28 200c on #332 20.00 2.75
*Nos. 551-556 (6)* 72.00 7.55

For surcharges see Nos. 895, 902, 936, 1363.

### No. 437 Surcharged "CARICOM / Heads of Gov't / Conference / July 1982"

***Perf. 14½x14***

**1982, Jan. 18 Litho. Wmk. 364**

**557** Sheet of 6 15.00 12.50
*a.-f.* A81 50c on 15c, any single 2.25 .50

### Nos. 464 Ovptd. "CHRISTMAS / 1982" in Red

**1982, Dec. 1 *Perf. 13x13½***

**558** Sheet of 25, 8 #a.-b., 4 #c.-d., 1 #e. 32.50 32.50
*a.-b.* A28 15c on #464a-464b, either single .90 .45
*c.-d.* A28 15c on #464c-464d, either single 2.10 .45
*e.* A28 15c on #464e 24.00 24.00

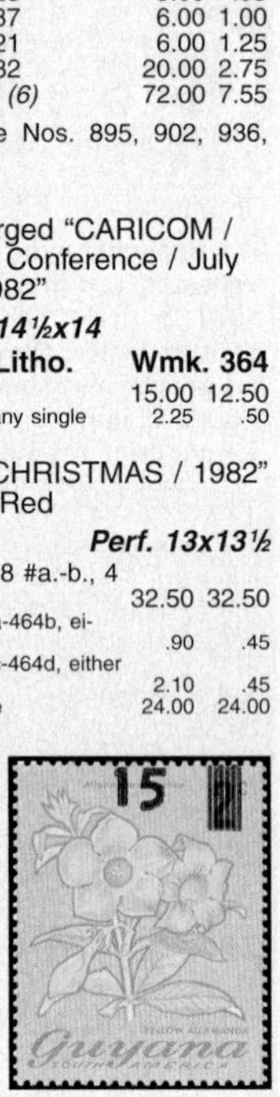


Nos. 134, 137 Surcharged

***Perf. 13x13½***

**1982-83 Litho. Wmk. 364**

**563** A28 15c on 2c #134 (Bl) .75
*a.* Red surcharge 2.00
*b.* Black surcharge .75
**564** A28 20c on 6c #137 (Bk) .75
*a.* Green surcharge .75

Issued: #563, Dec. 15; #564, Jan. 5, 1983.
Compare No. 564 with Nos. 631-632. For surcharges see Nos. 846, 846a, 846b.

### No. 72 Surcharged

**1982, Dec. 15 Photo. *Perf. 14x14½***

**565** A7 50c on 6c #72 .75 .25
**566** A7 $1.00 on 6c #72 1.25 .45
*Nos. 565-566 (2)* 2.00 .70

### Nos. 62, 88-89, 144, 161, 202, 217, 224-225, 232, 240, 251, 254, 257, 264, 276-278, 299-301, 303-305, 315, 319, 321, 329m, 414-416, and 418-420 Ovptd. "1983" Vertically or Horizontally

**1983 *Perfs. as Before***

**Watermarks & Printing Methods as Before**

**567** A57 15c on #240 6.00
**568** A60 15c on #254 1.50
**569** A62 15c on #264 1.00
**570** A79 15c on 10c #414 1.00
**571** A80 15c on 10c #418 .25
**572** A14 25c on #88 .50
**573** A33 25c on #161 14.00
**574** A47 25c on #202 1.50
**575** A11 30c on #62 1.50
**576** A14 30c on #89 .50
**577** A65 30c on #276 12.50
**578** A69 30c on #299 5.00
**579** A70 30c on #303 10.00
**580** A74 30c on #319 6.00
**581** A77 30c on #329m 3.00
**582** A53 50c on #224 2.00
**583** A55 50c on #232 5.00
**584** A59 50c on #251 7.00
**585** A65 50c on #277 5.00
**586** A69 50c on #300 2.00
**587** A70 50c on #304 30.00
**588** A79 50c on #415 1.00
**589** A80 50c on #419 2.00
**590** A65 60c on #278 5.50
**591** A72 60c on #315 7.00
**592** A51 $1 on #217 10.00
**593** A53 $1 on #225 10.00
**594** A60 $1 on #257 6.00
**595** A79 $1 on 30c #416 2.75
**596** A80 $1 on 60c #420 7.50
**597** A28 180c on 60c #144 2.00
**598** A69 $3 on #301 12.00
**599** A70 $3 on #305 15.00
**601** A74 $3 on #321 75.00
**602** A28 360c on $2 #146 2.25

Issued: #567-571, 583, 585-586, 2/1; #596, 3/7; #573, 3/11; #572, 576, 3/17; #582, 584, 587, 588, 589, 592-595, 598-599, 601, 4/1; #574, 5/23; #575, 577-580, 590-591, 7/1; #602, 11/3; #581, 11/15; #597, 12/14.
Refer to the second paragraph in footnote under No. 147 for Nos. 597 & 602. No. 597 contains unissued overprint, "ESPANA 1982."
For overprints and surcharges see Nos. 724, 901, 940, 943A.

### No. O2 Ovptd. "POSTAGE" in Red

***Perf. 14½x14***

**1983, Feb. 1 Photo. Wmk. 364**

**603** A8 15c on #O2 16.00 .50

For surcharge see Nos. 746-746a.

### Nos. 291-293, 356 Surcharged in Blue or Black

**Wmk. 364**

**1983, Feb. 8 Litho. *Perf. 14***

**604** A67 90c on 30c #291 (Blk) 2.00 1.00
**605** A67 90c on 50c #292 1.25 .30
**606** A67 90c on 60c #293 2.00 1.00
**607** A55 90c on #356 4.75 .50
*Nos. 604-607 (4)* 10.00 2.80

For overprints and surcharges see Nos. 763-764, 768-769, 770-771.

Flag A82

Cooperative Youth Palace — A83

**1983, Feb. 19 *Perf. 14½x14***

**608** A82 Pair 1.00 1.00
*a.* 25c Flag flying right .40 .40
*b.* 25c Flag flying left .40 .40

***Perf. 13½***

**609** A83 $1.30 shown 1.00 1.00

**Size: 43x25mm**

***Perf. 14½***

**610** A83 $6 Map 3.75 3.75

60th birthday of Pres. Linden Forbes Burnham. No. 608a inscribed for birthday; No. 608b for Burnham's 30th anniv. of election to parliament.
See #660, 913. For overprints & surcharges see #826-835, 924-926, 1404-1406.

Nos. 160, 205, 222, 263, 298, 302, 330, 333, 408-409, 480, C4, O1 and Q3 Ovptd. in Blue or Red

**1983 Litho. *Perfs. as Before***

**Watermarks & Printing Methods as Before**

**611** A33 50c on 8c #160 (R) 25.00
**612** A48 50c on 8c #205 2.25
**613** A62 50c on 8c #263 8.00
**614** A69 50c on 10c #298 (R) 1.50
**615** A70 50c on 10c #302 4.00
**616** A69 50c on #409 4.50
**617** A69 50c on #480 2.00
**618** A28 50c on #O1 5.00
**619** A53 $1 on #222 8.50
**620** A53 $1 on #330 5.00
**621** A28 $1 on #333 5.00
**622** A28 $1 on #408 10.00
**623** A28 $1 on #C4 1.50
**624** A28 $1 on #Q3 25.00

#621 has Royal Wedding ovpt. similar to #331. #624 also ovptd. "1982." See #648-649 for similar surcharges. For overprint see #815, 941. Issued: #614, 617, 619-624, 3/7; #611, 3/11; others, 4/1.

### Nos. 10A, 13a Surcharged "Commonwealth / Day / 14 March 1983" and Emblem in Blue or Black

**Wmk. 314 Upright**

**1983, Mar. 14 Engr. *Perf. 12½x13***

**625** A60 25c on 6c #10A
**626** A60 $1.20 on 6c #10A (Bl)

**Wmk. 314 Sideways**

**627** A60 $1.30 on 24c #13a
**628** A60 $2.40 on 24c #13a (Bl)
*Nos. 625-628 (4)* 5.00

For overprints see Nos. 1823-1825.

Intl. Maritime Organization, 25th Anniv. — A84

**Red Overprint on British Guiana Revenue Stamp**

***Perf. 14***

**1983, Mar. 17 Typo. Wmk. 3**

**629** A84 $4.80 grn & blue 10.00

### Nos. 60, 72, 87 & 137 Surcharged in Black or Blue

**1983 *Perfs. as Before***

**Watermarks & Printing Methods as Before**

**630** A11 15c on 6c #60 .75
*a.* Blue surcharge 1.00
**631** A28 20c on 6c #137, two obliterators 1.00
**632** A28 20c on 6c #137 1.00
**633** A7 50c on 6c #72 .75
**634** A14 50c on 6c #87 1.00
*Nos. 630-634 (5)* 4.50

Issued: #630, 632-633, 5/23; #630a, 631, 634, 5/2.
Surcharge on No. 632 has "c" after value. No. 564 does not.
For surcharge see No. 916.

### No. 72 Surcharged in Black or Red

***Perf. 14x14½***

**1983 Photo. Wmk. 364**

**635** A7 $1 on 6c #72 1.60
*a.* Red overprint, 4mm high 1.60

Issue dates: #635, May 2. #635a, May 23.
For surcharge see No. 916A.

### Nos. 142, 147, 211, 226-227, 239 & 249 Surcharged in Blue

**1983 *Perfs. as Before***

**Watermarks & Printing Methods as Before**

**636** A54 110c on 10c #226 3.00
**637** A49 120c on 35c #211 4.50
**638** A54 120c on 35c #227 4.50
**639** A57 120c on 8c #239 4.50
**640** A59 120c on 10c #249 4.50
**641** A28 250c on 40c #142 12.00
**642** A28 400c on $5 #147 9.00
*Nos. 636-642 (7)* 42.00

Issue dates: Nos. 636, 641-642, May 2. Others, July 1. For surcharge see No. 865.

### Nos. 332, 495a, C3 Surcharged in Red or Blue

"ITU / 1983" or (#643)
"WHO / 1983" or (#644)
"17 MAY '83 / ITU/WHO /" (#645)
"ITU/WHO / 17 MAY / 1983" (#646-647)

**1983, May 17 *Perfs. as Before***

**Watermarks & Printing Methods as Before**

**643** A28 25c on #C3 4.00 .90
**644** A28 25c on #C3 4.00 .90
**645** A28 25c on #C3 4.00 .90
*a.* Strip of 3, #643-645 22.50 10.00
**646** A28 $4.50 on #332 (Bl) 16.00 2.00
**647** A28 $4.50 on #495a (Bl) 16.00

Nos. 643-645 issued in sheets of 25 with 8 each Nos. 643-644 and 9 No. 645.

### Nos. 272, 274 Surcharged in Dark Blue

***Perf. 13½x14***

**1983, May 18 Litho. Wmk. 364**

**648** A64 $1 on 15c #272 7.50 1.00
**649** A64 $1 on 40c #274 12.50 1.00
*Nos. 648-649 (2)* 20.00 2.00

Surcharge on No. 648 also contains overprint "1983."

### Nos. 402, 404, O8 Surcharged or Overprinted "CANADA 1983"

**1983, June 15 *Perf. 13½x13***

**650** A17 $1.30 on #O8 4.50 3.00
**651** A17 180c on #402 4.50 4.50
**652** A17 $3.90 on #404 10.00 10.00
*Nos. 650-652 (3)* 19.00 17.50

For surcharge see No. 1860.

### Nos. 243-244 Surcharged

**1983, June 22 Unwmk. *Perf. 14***

**653** A57a 60c on 15c #243 15.00 1.00
**654** A57b $1.50 on 15c #244 22.50 2.50
*Nos. 653-654 (2)* 37.50 3.50

### Nos. 297, 313 Surcharged

***Perfs. as Before***

**1983, July 1 Wmk. 364**

**655** A68 120c on #297 7.50 1.25
**656** A72 120c on 10c #313 (R) 7.50 1.25

No. 655 has unissued surcharge, "INTERNATIONAL / SCIENCE YEAR / 375."

### British Guiana No. J1 and Guyana No. J5 Surcharged "120 / GUYANA" in Dark Blue

**1983, July 1 Wmk. 4 *Perf. 13½x14***

**657** D1 120c on 1c #J1 6.00 1.25

**Wmk. 364**

**658** D1 120c on 1c #J5 6.00 1.25

### No. 371 Surcharged in Red "CARICOM DAY 1983"

**1983, July 1 Wmk. 364 *Perf. 14***

**659** A72 60c on $3 #371 3.00

**Type A82 Without Inscription**

**1983, July 1 Litho. *Perf. 14½x14***

**660** A82 Pair 1.00 1.00
*a.* 25c, Flag flying right .40 .40
*b.* 25c, Flag flying left .40 .40

River Steamers A85

**1983, July 11 Litho. *Perf. 14***
**661** A85 30c Kurupukari .25 .25
*a.* Tete-beche pair — —
**662** A85 60c Makouria .50 .50
*a.* Tete-beche pair
**663** A85 120c Powis 1.00 1.00
*a.* Tete-beche pair
**664** A85 130c Pomeroon 1.25 1.25
**665** A85 150c Lukanani 1.50 1.50
*a.* Tete-beche pair — —
*Nos. 661-665 (5)* 4.50 4.50

For surcharge, see No. 4020J.

No. 146 Surcharged in Dark Blue

**1983, July 22 *Perf. 13½***
**666** A28 $2.30 on $1.10 on $2
**667** A28 $3.20 on $1.10 on $2
*Nos. 666-667 (2)* 8.00

Nos. 666-667 have unissued surcharge of "$1.10 / Royal Wedding / 1981" similar to No. 331.

Nos. 282-283 & 283A Overprinted as Shown or with Various Initials in Red or Blue

Overprints: No. 668a, BW. b, LM. c, GY 1963 / 1983. d, JW. e, CU. f. Mont Golfier / 1783-1983.

No. 669a, BGI. b, GEO. c, MIA. d, BVB. e, PBM. f, Mont Golfier / 1783-1983. g, POS. h, JFK.

No. 670a, AHL. b, BCG. c, BMJ. d, EKE. e, GEO. f, GFO. g, IBM. h, Mont Golfier / 1783-1983. i, KAI. j, KAR. k, KPG. l, KRG. m, KTO. n, LTM. o, MHA. p, MWI. q, MYM. r, NAI. s, ORJ. t, USI. u, VEG.

**1983, Sept. 5 *Perf. 14x13½***
**Sheets of 25**
**668** A66 20c 4 each #a.-e., 5 #f *30.00*
**669** A66 25c 2 each #a., c.-e., g.-h., 8 #b., 5 #f. *45.00*
**670** A66 30c #a.-e., g.-u., 5 #f., (Bl) *40.00*

Manned flight, bicentennial and Guyana Airways, 20th anniv. For ovpts. see #871, 969.

No. 234 Surcharged in Dark Blue

**1983, Sept. 14 *Perf. 13½***
**703** A28 240c on #234 3.00 1.25
*a.* "4" with serif 3.50 1.50

Nos. 703, 703a appear in same sheet.

Nos. 68, 70 Surcharged "FAO 1983" in Red

***Perf. 14x14½***
**1983, Sept. 15 Photo. Wmk. 364**
**704** A7 30c on 1c #68 .50 .25
**705** A7 $2.60 on 3c #70 2.50 2.50
*Nos. 704-705 (2)* 3.00 2.75

For overprints see Nos. 1497-1498.

Great Britain, Postal Use In British Guiana, 150th Anniv. — A86

Stamps: a, #20. b, #26. c, #27. d, #28.

**1983, Oct. 1 Litho. *Perf. 14***
**Inscribed in Black**
**706** A86 25c #20 .25 .25
**707** A86 30c #26 .25 .25
**708** A86 60c #27 .45 .45
**709** A86 120c #28 1.00 1.00
**Inscribed in Blue**
**710** Block of 4 .80 .80
*a.-d.* A86 25c any single .25 .25
**711** Block of 4 1.00 1.00
*a.-d.* A86 30c any single .25 .25
**712** Block of 4 1.75 1.75
*a.-d.* A86 45c any single .40 .40
**713** Block of 4 5.00 5.00
*a.* A86 120c #20 .80 .80
*b.* A86 130c #26, Demerara .85 .85
*c.* A86 150c #27, Berbice 1.00 1.00
*d.* A86 200c #28, Essequibo 1.50 1.50
*Nos. 706-713 (8)* 10.50 10.50

Nos. 706-709 printed in sheets with bottom two rows inverted. Nos. 710-712 printed in sheets of 60. No. 713 printed in sheets with blue marginal text.

For overprints and surcharges see Nos. 796, 903, 912, 1448, 1982.

#235 & 238 Surcharged
#297 Surcharged "INT. / COMMUNICATIONS / YEAR"
#206 Surcharged "Int. Food Day / 1983"
#309 Surcharged "1918-1983 / I.L.O."

**1983, Oct. 15 *Perfs. as Before***
**Watermarks & Printing Methods as Before**
**714** A68 50c on 375c on $3 #297 6.00
**715** A56 75c on 8c #235 7.00
**716** A48 $1.20 on 35c #206 1.75
**717** A56 $1.20 on 40c #238 7.00
**718** A71 240c on $3 #309 2.00
*Nos. 714-718 (5)* 23.75

No. 714 was not issued without 375c surcharge. For overprint see No. 821.

Nos. 245, 247-248 Surcharged

**Unwmk.**
**1983, Nov. 1 Litho. *Perf. 14***
**719** A58 25c on 8c #245 .35 .25
**720** A58 $1.50 on 35c #247 2.40 1.00
**721** A58 $1.50 on 40c #248 1.25 1.00
*Nos. 719-721 (3)* 4.00 2.20

Nos. 268 & 270 Surcharged

**1983, Nov. 15 Wmk. 364**
**722** A63 60c on 15c #268 2.50 .50
**723** A63 $1.20 on 40c #270 2.50 .90

No. 601 Ovptd. "Human Rights / Day"

**1983, Dec. 1 *Perf. 14½x14***
**724** A74 $3 on #601 3.50 1.75

For surcharge see footnote following No. 998.

Nos. 317 and 726 Surcharged "LOS ANGELES / 1984"

**1983, Dec. 6 Wmk. 373**
**725** Sheet of 12 80.00
*a.-l.* A73 55c on 125c on 35c #726a-726l, any single —
**726** Sheet of 12 120.00
*a.-l.* A73 125c on 35c #317a-317l, any single —

For surcharge see No. 1897.

No. 133 Surcharged "COMMONWEALTH / HEADS OF GOV'T / MEETING--INDIA / 1983"

***Perf. 13x13½***
**1983, Dec. 14 Litho. Wmk. 364**
**727** A28 150c on 1c #133 4.00 1.00

Nos. 413a, 413e Surcharged "CHRISTMAS / 1983"

**1983, Dec. 14 Photo. *Perf. 14x14½***
**Watermarks as before**
**728** A7 20c on #413a 1.50 .25
*a.* 20c on #413De .50 .25

Nos. 146, O15 Ovptd. "POSTAGE" in Blue

**1984, Jan. 8 *Perfs. as before***
**729** A28 $2 on #146 4.25 1.00
**730** A66 550c on $10 #O15 22.00 10.00

Refer to second paragraph in footnote following No. 147 for No. 729.

Flower Type of 1971-76 Surcharged in Blue

***Perf. 15x14***
**1984, Jan. Photo. Unwmk.**
**Size: 20x23mm**
**Coil Stamps**
**731** A28 17c on 2c, like #134 4.50 2.75
**732** A28 17c on 8c, Mazaruni Pride 4.50 2.75
*a.* Pair, #731-732 10.00 10.00

Nos. 731-732 were intended for use on 8c envelopes to increase postage rate to 25c and were not issued without surcharge.

Nos. 284, 286A Surcharged in Black or Overprinted in Dark Blue
(1) "ALL / OUR HERITAGE"
(2) "1984" 7mm long
(3) "REPUBLIC / DAY"
(4) "BERBICE"
(5) "DEMERARA"
(6) "ESSEQUIBO"
(7) "1984" 18mm long

***Perf. 14x13½***
**1984, Feb. 24 Litho. Wmk. 364**
**733** A66 25c on 35c (1) .75 .25
**734** A66 25c on 35c (2) 1.25 .50
**735** A66 25c on 35c (3) 1.25 .50
**736** A66 25c on 35c #284 1.25 .50
**737** A66 25c on 35c (4) 6.00 4.50
**738** A66 25c on 35c (5) 6.00 4.50
**739** A66 25c on 35c (6) 6.00 4.50
**740** A66 25c on 35c (7) 14.00 14.00
**741** A66 60c on #286A (1) (DBl) 3.50 1.00
**742** A66 60c on #286A (3) (DBl) 3.50 1.00
**743** A66 60c on #286A (2) (DBl) 3.50 1.00

Nos. 733-740 were issued in sheets of 25, 6 #733, 4 each #734-736, 2 each #737-739, 1 #740. Nos. 741-743 were issued in sheets of 25, 8 each #741-742, 9 #743.

Nos. 49-50, 52, 73-74, 77-80, 82, 139, 141A-143, 350, 603 Surcharged or Overprinted in Black and/or Blue "Protecting Our Heritage"

**1984, Mar. 5 *Perfs. as Before***
**Watermarks & Printing Methods as Before**
**744** A8 20c on 15c #74 8.00 .50
*a.* Blue surcharge (value and words) 20.00
**745** A8 20c on 15c #350 8.50 .50
**746** A8 20c on 15c #603 (Bl) 15.00 2.00
*a.* "Protecting our Heritage" in black 40.00
**747** A28 25c on #141A 12.50 .50
*a.* 25c on #141b 65.00 .60
**748** A28 30c on 15c #139 24.00 .60
**749** A8 40c on #77 10.00 .60
**750** A28 50c on #143 1.50 .60
**751** A28 50c on #143 (Revenue Ovpt.) 1.50 .60
**752** A7 60c on #50 15.00 .60
*a.* 60c on #79 90.00
**753** A28 90c on 40c #142 16.00 .90
**754** A28 90c on 40c #142 (Revenue ovpt.) 125.00
**755** A28 180c on #460 12.50 1.50
**756** A7 $2 on #52 70.00 2.25
**757** A8 225c on 10c on #73 21.00 1.75
**758** A7 260c on $1 #80 15.00 1.50
**759** A28 320c on 40c #142 15.00 3.25
**760** A28 350c on 40c #142 20.00 4.25
**761** A7 390c on 50c #78 8.00 4.00
*a.* 390c on #49 125.00
**762** A7 450c on $5 #82 10.00 4.00
*Nos. 744-762 (19)* 408.50

Nos. 748, 753-754, 759-760 use row of "X", 6mm high, as obliterator. Nos. 744-746, 757 have new value printed vertically over old value. Nos. 758, 761-762 have new value printed horizontally over old value. Refer to second paragraph in footnote under No. 147 for Nos. 751, 754-755.

Nos. 89, 484-485, 606 Overprinted or Surcharged in Dark Blue "1984"
No. 87 Surcharged
No. 606 Surcharged "INT. / CHESS / FED. / 1924-1984" in Dark Blue (#764a, 769a, 771a)

**1984 *Perfs. as Before***
**Watermarks & Printing Methods as Before**
**763** A67 25c on #606 2.00
**764** A67 25c on #606 4.00
*a.* Pair, #763-764 10.00
**765** A14 30c on #89 .75
**766** A14 45c on 6c #484 .75
**767** A14 75c on 40c #485 .75
**768** A67 75c on #606 1.00
**769** A67 75c on #606 3.00
*a.* Pair, #768-769 8.00
**770** A67 90c on #606 1.00
**771** A67 90c on #606 3.00
*a.* Pair, #770-771 9.00
**772** A14 130c on 6c #87 .50
**773** A76 $3 on #328 3.00
*Nos. 763-773 (11)* 19.75

Issued: #765-767, 772, Mar. 17; #773, June 15; #763-764, 768-769, 770-771, July 20.

No. 767 exists with surcharge either above old value or in center of stamp.

Nos. 497-500 Surcharged

**1984, Apr. 2 Litho. *Perf. 13½***
**774** A28 75c on #497 11.00 .55
**775** A28 75c on #498 13.00 .55
**776** A28 225c on #500 3.50 1.75
**777** A28 230c on #499 4.00 1.25
*Nos. 774-777 (4)* 31.50 4.10

Nos. 464e, 465a, 465b, 465e, 466a, 466b, 466e Surcharged Like No. 748

**1984, May 2**
**778** A28 20c on #464e 2.25 .50
**779** A28 75c on #465e 11.50 1.00
**780** A28 90c on #465a 7.00 1.25
**781** A28 90c on #465b 9.50 1.25
**782** A28 120c on #466a 11.00 1.50
**783** A28 120c on #466e 11.00 1.50
**784** A28 120c on #466b 3.50 1.50

No. C3 Surcharged "ITU DAY / 1984" (#785)
No. C3 Surcharged "WHO DAY / 1984" (#786)
Nos. C3, 386 Surcharged "ITU/WHO / DAY / 1984" (#787-788)

**1984, May 17**
**785** A28 25c on #C3 1.60 1.60
**786** A28 25c on #C3 1.60 1.60
**787** A28 25c on #C3 1.60 1.60
**788** A28 $4.50 on #386 2.50 2.50
*Nos. 785-788 (4)* 7.30 7.30

The surcharge is vertical on Nos. 785-787, horizontal on No. 788.

No. 550 Surcharged

**1984, June 11**
**789** A28 120c on #550 8.75 1.00

Nos. 325-327, 431 Surcharged in Blue or Black

**Wmk. 373**
**1984, June 15 Litho. *Perf. 14***
**790** A76 55c on 30c #326 (Blk) 5.00 .50
**791** A76 75c on #431 1.10 .75
**792** A76 160c on 50c #327 1.50 1.25
**793** A76 260c on 10c #325 2.50 1.75
*Nos. 790-793 (4)* 10.10 4.25

No. 214 Surcharged

**1984, June 18 Litho. Wmk. 364**
**794** A50 55c on 110c on 10c 1.25 .50
**795** A50 90c on 110c on 10c 1.50 .75

No. 214 surcharged 110c only was never issued.

No. 713 Ovptd. "UPU / Congress 1984 / Hamburg"

**1984, June 19**
**796** Block of 4 5.00 5.00
*a.* A86 120c on #713a .75 .75
*b.* A86 130c on #713b .90 .90
*c.* A86 150c on #713c 1.00 1.00
*d.* A86 200c on #713d 1.25 1.25

Nos. 539, 541, 543-544 Surcharged in Black, Blue or Dark Green

**1984, June 21 *Perfs. as Before***
**Watermarks & Printing Methods as Before**
**797** A60 45c on #539 .50 .50
**798** A66 60c on #541 (DkG) 2.50 .60
*a.* 60c on British Guiana #255 (DkG)
**799** A60 120c on #543 .75 .55
**800** A60 200c on #544 (Bl) 6.75 1.50
*Nos. 797-800 (4)* 10.50 3.15

Nos. 135, 548, C2-C3 Surcharged in Blue or Black
No. C4 Overprinted "1984"

***Perf. 13x13½***
**1984, June 30 Litho. Wmk. 364**
**801** A28 75c on #C2 (Blk) 1.50 .50
**802** A28 120c on #548 (Blk) 1.90 .75
**803** A28 150c on #135 1.60 .80
**804** A28 200c on #C3 17.50 2.50
**804A** A28 330c on #C4 3.00 3.00
*Nos. 801-804A (5)* 25.50 7.55

Surcharge on Nos. 801-802, 804 is like No. 748. Surcharge on No. 803 is like No. 457.

No. 135 Surcharged "CARICOM / HEADS OF GOV'T / CONFERENCE / JULY 1984"
No. 450A Surcharged "CARICOM DAY 1984"

**1984, June 30 *Perfs. as Before***
**Watermarks & Printing Methods as Before**
**805** A28 60c on 3c #135 .75 .60
**806** A72 60c on #450A .75 .60

Nos. 140-141, 141A, 329, 334, 427, 439a-440, 546, 611, 718, O13 Ovptd. "1984" in Black or Blue

**1984** ***Perfs. as Before***

**Watermarks & Printing Methods as Before**

**807** A28 20c on #140 12.50
a. On #140a 150.00
**808** A28 20c on #140 55.00
a. On #140a 150.00
**809** A28 20c on #439, 1984 omitted 60.00
**810** A28 25c on #141 100.00
a. 1984 omitted 100.00
**811** A28 25c on #141 (Revenue Only) 6.00
**812** A28 25c on #141A
**813** A28 25c on #141, 1982 ovpt., 1984 omitted 40.00
**814** A28 25c on #440, 1984 omitted 40.00
**815** A33 50c on #611 (Bl) 10.00
**816** A28 60c on #546 (Bl) 1.00
**817** A28 $2 on #O13 (Bl) 2.50
**818** A28 $3.60 on #334 10.00
c. As #818, fleur-de-lis omitted 5.00
d. On #334a (Bl) 5.00
e. As "d," fleur-de-lis omitted 5.00
**819** Sheet of 12 6.00
a.-l. A77 30c on #329a-329l, any single
**820** A71 240c on #429 4.75
**821** A71 240c on #718 4.75

Overprint on Nos. 808-814, 818 contains fleur-de-lis. Refer to second paragraph in footnote below No. 147 for Nos. 811-812, 817.

Issued: #819, Sept. 15; #820-821, Oct. 15.

Teachers' Assoc. Centenary — A87

**1984, July 16** **Wmk. 364** ***Perf. 14***

**822** A87 25c Children dancing .25 .25
**823** A87 25c Torch, graduate .25 .25
**824** A87 25c Torch concentric circles .25 .25
**825** A87 25c Teachers, school .25 .25
a. Block of 4 1.00 1.00

No. 609 Surcharged in Blue:
"CYCLING" (#826, 831)
"TRACK / AND / FIELD" (#827, 832)
"OLYMPIC / GAMES / 1984" (#828, 833)
"BOXING" (#829, 834)
"OLYMPIC / GAMES / 1984 / LOS ANGELES" (#830, 835)

***Perf. 14½x14***

**1984, July 28** **Litho.** **Wmk. 364**

**826** A83 25c on $1.30 1.00 .80
**827** A83 25c on $1.30 1.00 .80
**828** A83 25c on $1.30 1.00 .80
**829** A83 25c on $1.30 3.75 2.00
**830** A83 25c on $1.30 3.75 2.25
**831** A83 $1.20 on $1.30 3.00 2.50
**832** A83 $1.20 on $1.30 3.00 2.50
**833** A83 $1.20 on $1.30 3.00 2.50
**834** A83 $1.20 on $1.30 5.50 3.00
**835** A83 $1.20 on $1.30 5.50 4.00

Nos. 826-828 and 831-833 exist in strips of 3. Nos. 827, 829-830 and 832, 834-835 exists in booklets.

Nos. 465-466 Surcharged "GIRL / GUIDES / 1924-1984" in Blue

**1984, Aug. 15** ***Perf. 13x13½***

**Sheets of 25**

**836** 8 #a.-b., 4 #c.-d., 1 #e.
a.-e. A28 25c on #465a-465e, any single
**837** 8 #a.-b., 4 #c.-d., 1 #e.
a.-e. A28 25c on #466a-466e, any single
*Nos. 836-837 (2)* 35.00

Nos. 138-139, 234, 335, 351, 378, 380, 388, 401, 423, 438, 452, 459, 461, 563, 642, O3, O11-O12, O14 Surcharged

**1984** ***Perfs. as Before***

**Watermarks & Printing Methods as Before**

**846** A28 20c on #563 1.00
a. 20c on #563a (Blk over R) 1.00
b. 20c on #563b (Blk over Bl) 1.00
**847** A28 25c on #138 27.50
a. 25c on #138a 55.00
**848** A28 25c on #139 150.00
**849** A28 25c on #351a 20.00
a. 25c on #351 70.00
**850** A28 25c on #351b 8.50
**851** A28 25c on #438 8.00
a. 25c on #438a 150.00
**852** A28 25c on #234 100.00
**853** A28 25c on #452 8.00
**854** A28 25c on #O3 8.00
**855** A28 60c on #423, two obliterators, small 110 only 45.00
a. Single obliterator, small 110 only
**856** A28 120c on #459 5.00
**857** A28 120c on #401 35.00
**858** A28 120c on #O12 2.00
**859** A28 120c on #380 6.00
**860** A28 130c on #378 100.00
**861** A28 130c on #O11 12.50
**862** A28 200c on #461 5.00
**863** A28 320c on #378 5.50
**864** A28 350c on #388 5.00
**865** A28 390c on #642 6.00
**866** A28 450c on #O14 5.75
**867** A28 600c on #335 15.00
a. 600c on #335a 10.00
**868** A28 600c on #335a 17.50
a. 600c on #335 4.00
*Nos. 846-868 (23)* 596.25

Nos. 860-861 are airmail. Obliterator on Nos. 846, 856-859, 862-866 is row of "X", on Nos. 847, 850, 852 is single line, on Nos. 848-849, 851, 853-854 is fleur-de-lis, on No. 855 is a block of 6 lines, on No. 867 is 3 lines, on No. 868 is 3 lines and fleur-de-lis.

Nos. 556, 670, C4 Overprinted in Blue or Surcharged in Blue and Black

Overprints: #a-f, ICAO on #670a-670f. g, IMB/ICAO on #g. h, KCV/ICAO on #h. i, KAI/ICAO on #i. j-k, ICAO on #670j-670k. l, 1984 on #h. m, KPM/ICAO on #h. n-p, ICAO on #670 l-670n. q, PMT/ICAO on #h. r-x, ICAO on #670o-670u.

***Perf. 14x13½***

**1984, Sept. 6** **Litho.** **Wmk. 364**

**871** A66 30c Sheet of 25, #a.-k., m.-x., 2 #l 65.00 65.00
**895** A28 200c ICAO on #556 5.50 2.25
**896** A28 200c ICAO on #C4 (Bl & Blk) 3.00 2.00

No. 896 is airmail with unissued "GAC" overprint. For surcharge see No. 1470.

Nos. J3-J4, J7-J8 Surcharged "120 / GUYANA" in Blue

***Perf. 13½x14***

**1984, Oct. 1** **Typo.** **Wmk. 314**

**897** D1 120c on 4c #J3 7.50 .80
**898** D1 120c on 12c #J4 7.50 .80

**Wmk. 364**

**899** D1 120c on 4c #J7 25.00 .80
**900** D1 120c on 12c #J8 7.00 1.25
*Nos. 897-900 (4)* 47.00 3.65

Nos. 551, 571 Surcharged in Black or Blue

***Perfs. as Before***

**1984, Oct. 15** **Wmk. 364**

**901** A80 $1.50 on #571 (Bl) 14.00 1.50
**902** A48 150c on 50c #551 4.00 1.00

Obliterator is "X" on No. 901. Surcharge on No. 902 places "1" before existing 50c value, obliterates "1982" and adds "1984."

Nos. 712, 479-481 Surcharged

**1984, Oct. 22** ***Perf. 14***

**903** Block of 4 1.25 1.25
a.-d. A86 25c on 45c on #712a-712d, any single .25 .25
**904** A69 120c on #479 9.50 .75
**905** A69 120c on #480 1.25 .75
**906** A66 320c on #481 20.00 2.75
*Nos. 903-906 (4)* 32.00 5.50

Nos. 135-136 Surcharged "MAHA SABHA / 1934-1984" in Blue

**1984, Nov. 1** ***Perf. 13x13½***

**910** A28 25c on 5c #136 .75 .25
**911** A28 $1.50 on 3c #135 4.25 1.50
*Nos. 910-911 (2)* 5.00 1.75

No. 713 Ovptd. "Philatelic Exhibition / New York 1984" in Red

**1984, Nov. 15** ***Perf. 14***

**912** Block of 4 5.00 5.00
a. A86 120c on No. 713a 1.00 .80
b. A86 130c on No. 713b 1.10 .90
c. A86 150c on No. 713c 1.25 1.00
d. A86 200c on No. 713d 1.50 1.25

Type A83 Inscribed with Olympic Rings and "OLYMPIC GAMES 1984 / LOS ANGELES"

**1984, Nov. 16** ***Perf. 13½***

**913** A83 $1.20 multicolored 5.00 5.00

Copies with numbers stamped on back are coils.

For similar stamp overprinted see No. 923.

For surcharges see Nos. 1953-1957.

Nos. 410, 413e, 633, 635a Surcharged

**1984, Nov. 24** **Photo.** ***Perf. 14x14½***

**Watermarks as Before**

**914** A7 20c on #410 1.00 .25
**915** A7 20c on #413De 92.50 7.50
**916** A7 25c on #633 .50 .25
**916A** A7 60c on #635a .70 .45

No. 914 has an "X" obliterating a "1" and no obliterating lines. No. 1400 has obliterating lines and small "20" in UR.

Elanoides Forficatus A88

Designs: a, Pair in tree. b, Landing on branch. c, In flight, wings up. d, In flight, wings down. e, In flight, wings outstretched.

**1984, Dec. 3** **Wmk. 364** ***Perf. 14½***

**917** A88 60c Strip of 5, #a.-e. 22.50 22.50

Inscribed "Christmas 1982."

For surcharges see Nos. 1502, 1840.

High Street Architecture — A89

Designs: 25c, St. George's Cathedral, 1892, Colonial Life Insurance Co. 60c, No. 920a, Demerara Mutual Life Assurance Soc., Ltd. No. 920b, 200c, Town Hall, 1888, City Engineers Office. No. 920c, 300c, Victoria Law Courts, 1887.

**1985, Feb. 8** ***Perf. 14***

**918** A89 25c multi .25 .25
**919** A89 60c multi .40 .40
**920** Triptych 1.40 1.40
a.-c. A89 120c, any single .45 .45
d. Triptych, unwmkd. 1.75 1.75
e.-g. As "d," any single .60 .60
**921** A89 200c multi 1.25 1.25
**922** A89 300c multi 1.75 1.75
*Nos. 918-922 (5)* 5.05 5.05

For surcharge see No. 1850.

Type A83 Ovptd. "INTERNATIONAL / YOUTH YEAR 1985"

**Wmk. 364**

**1985, Feb. 15** **Litho.** ***Perf. 14½***

**923** A83 $1.20 multi 3.00 .75

Bars obliterate Olympic Games inscription with second line spelled "LOS ANGELLES." No. 913 spells "Los Angeles" correctly.

Nos. 608, 610 Ovptd. in Red "Republic / Day / 1970-1985" or "1970 / 1985 / Republic / Day"

**1985, Feb. 22** ***Perfs. as Before***

**924** A82 25c on #608
**925** A83 120c on $6 #610
**926** A83 130c on $6 #610
*Nos. 924-926 (3)* 3.00 2.25

Ocelot Cub Xica — A90

Macaw Nena — A90a

***Perf. 12½x13***

**1985, Mar. 11** **Wmk. 364**

**927** A90 25c multi 2.00 .30
**928** A90 60c multi .60 .60
**929** Triptych 3.50 3.50
a.-c. A90 120c, like #927-928, 930 1.10 1.10
**930** A90 130c multi 1.25 1.25

***Perf. 14½***

**931** A90a 320c shown 4.25 2.00
**932** A90a 330c Cub on hind legs 2.50 2.00
*Nos. 927-932 (6)* 14.10 9.65

No. 929, perf. 14, inscribed "1986," were from the liquidation of stock held by the printer, value 75c.

For overprints see #1903-1905, 1983, 2032.

Map Revenue Type A78 and Nos. 481, 501, 554, O6 Surcharged in Black or Blue

**1985** ***Perfs as Before***

**Watermarks & Printing Methods as Before**

**933** A69 30c on 50c on #O6 (Bl) 1.00 .25
**934** A78 55c on 2c multi 1.00 .25
a. "ESSEQUIBO IS OURS" omitted 15.00
**935** A78 55c on #501 1.00 .40
**936** A66 90c on #554 (Bl) 7.00 .65
**937** A66 225c on #481 10.00 2.00
**938** A66 230c on #481 (Bl) 10.00 2.25
**939** A66 260c on #481 (Bl) 10.00 2.50
*Nos. 933-939 (7)* 40.00 8.30

Issued: #933-936, 938-939, 3/11; #937, 4/11.

Obliterator on Nos. 934-935 is fleur-de-lis.

Nos. 305, 435, 587, 599, & 615 Ovptd. "INTERNATIONAL / YOUTH YEAR / 1985" in Blue

**Wmk. 364**

**1985, Apr. 15** **Litho.** ***Perf. 13½***

**940** A70 50c on #587 2.00 .30
**941** A70 50c on #615 7.00 .30
**942** A70 120c on #435 2.25 .55
**943** A70 $3 on #305 15.00 —
**943A** A70 $3 on #599 2.25 1.25
*Nos. 940-943A (5)* 28.50 2.40

No. 280 Surcharged with Names of 1860 Post Offices or Postal Agencies in Blue

Overprints: a, Airy Hall. b, Belfield / Arab. Coast. c, Belfield / E.C. Dem. d, Belladrum. e, Beterver- / wagting. f, Blairmont / Ferry. g, Boeraserie. h, Brahn. i, Bushlot. j, De / Kinderen. k, Fort / Wellington. l, Georgetown. m, Hague. n, Leguan. o, Mahaica. p, Mahaicony. q, New / Amsterdam. r, Plaisance. s, No. 6 Police / Station. t, Queenstown. u, Vertenoegen. v, Vigilance. w, Vreed-en- / Hoop. x, Wakenaam. y, Windsor / Castle.

***Perf. 14x13½***

**1985, May 2** **Litho.** **Wmk. 364**

**Sheet of 25**

**944** A66 25c on 10c, #a.-y. 27.50 27.50

Colonial Post Office, 125th anniv.

Nos. 670 Ovptd. "1985" or with Letters in Red

Overprints: a-f, 1985 on #670a-670f. g, I on #670g. h, T on #670h. i, U on #670i. j-k, 1985 on #670j-670k. l, W on #670h. m, H on #670h. n, O on #670h. o-p, 1985 on #670 l-670m. q, D on #670n. r, A on #670h. s, Y on #670o. t-y, 1985 on #670p-#670u.

**1985, May 17**

**Sheet of 25**

**969** A66 30c #a.-y. 20.00 20.00

Nos. 413a & 413e Surcharged

**1985, May 21 Photo.** ***Perf. 14x14½***
**Watermarks as Before**

**994** A7 20c on #413a 10.00 .30
*a.* 20c on #413De 14.00 2.00

#994a has "20" at left and 11 obliterating lines. #1401 has "20" at right and 12 lines.

No. 135 Surcharged "CARDI / 1975-1985"

***Perf. 13x13½***
**1985, May 29 Litho. Wmk. 364**

**995** A28 60c on 3c #135 1.75 .40

Caribbean Agricultural Research Development Institute, 10th anniv.

No. 407 Surcharged

**1985, June 3**

**996** A28 600c on #407 40.00 5.00

Nos. 288, 724, C1 Surcharged "ROTARY / INTERNATIONAL / 1905-1985" in Red

**1985, June 21** ***Perfs. as Before***
**Watermarks & Printing Methods as Before**

**997** A74 120c on #C1 14.50 1.00
**998** A66 300c on #288 10.00 3.50

No. 724 with a similar surcharge is usually found on first day covers.

No. 450A Surcharged "CARICOM DAY / 1985" and
No. 426 Surcharged "135th Anniversary / Cotton Reel / 1850-1985" in Red

**1985, June 28** ***Perfs. as Before***
**Watermarks & Printing Methods as Before**

**999** A72 60c on #450A 1.00 .50
**1000** A69 120c on #426 1.00 .50

Orchids from Reichenbachia, by Sanders — A91

**Wmk. 364 (#1027, 1031, 1036, 1046, 1049, 1052, 1054, 1071, 1074, 1076, 1079, 1084, 1091, 1108), Unwmkd.**

**1985-87** ***Perf. 14***
**Series 1**

**1021** A91 120c Plate No. 1 .90 .60
**1022** A91 60c Plate No. 2 .50 .50
**1023** A91 130c Plate No. 3 1.00 .65
**1024** A91 200c Plate No. 4 1.75 1.00
**1025** A91 60c Plate No. 5 .60 .60
**1026** A91 75c like #1025 .60 .60
*a.* Wmk. 364 ('87) 12.50 12.50
**1027** A91 100c Plate No. 6 .90 .90
**1028** A91 130c like #1027 1.00 .65
*a.* Wmk. 364 ('86) 1.25 1.25
**1029** A91 60c Plate No. 7 .60 .60
**1030** A91 25c Plate No. 8 .60 .60
**1031** A91 50c Plate No. 9 .60 .60
**1032** A91 55c like #1031 .60 .60
*a.* Wmk. 364 ('86) .60 .60
**1033** A91 60c Plate No. 10 .60 .60
**1034** A91 120c Plate No. 11 .90 .60
**1035** A91 25c Plate No. 12 .60 .60
**1036** A91 100c Plate No. 13 .90 .90
**1037** A91 130c like #1036 1.00 .65
*a.* Wmk. 364 ('86) 5.00 3.00
**1038** A91 200c Plate No. 14 1.75 1.00
**1039** A91 55c Plate No. 15 .60 .60
**1040** A91 180c like #1039 1.60 .90
*a.* Wmk. 364 ('87) 11.00 9.00
*Nos. 1021-1040 (20)* 17.60 13.75

Issued: #1022-1024, 1028-1029, 1033, 1035, 1037, 7/9; #1032, 8/12; #1021, 1030, 1034, 1038, 9/16; #1026, 2/26/86; #1040, 7/24/86; #1025, 1027, 1031, 1036, 1039, 8/21/86.
Nos. 1021, 1034 horiz.

**1041** A91 130c Plate No. 16 1.00 .65
**1042** A91 55c Plate No. 17 .60 .60
*a.* Wmk. 364 ('87) 7.50 7.50
**1043** A91 80c like #1042 .70 .70
**1044** A91 130c Plate No. 18 1.00 .65
**1045** A91 60c Plate No. 19 .60 .60
**1046** A91 100c Plate No. 20 .90 .90
**1047** A91 130c like #1046 1.00 .65
*a.* Wmk. 364 ('86) 4.00 2.50
**1048** A91 200c Plate No. 21 1.75 1.00
**1049** A91 50c Plate No. 22 .60 .60
**1050** A91 55c like #1049 .60 .60
*a.* Wmk. 364 ('86) .60 .60
**1051** A91 25c Plate No. 23 .60 .60
**1052** A91 50c Plate No. 24 .60 .60
**1053** A91 225c like #1052 2.00 1.10
*a.* Wmk. 364 ('86) 6.50 4.00
**1054** A91 100c Plate No. 25 .90 .90
**1055** A91 130c like #1054 1.00 .65
*a.* Wmk. 364 ('86) 6.50 4.00
**1056** A91 150c Plate No. 26 1.40 .75
**1057** A91 120c Plate No. 27 .90 .60
**1058** A91 120c Plate No. 28 .90 .60
**1059** A91 130c Plate No. 29 1.00 .65
**1060** A91 130c Plate No. 30 1.00 .65
*Nos. 1041-1060 (20)* 19.05 14.05

Issued: #1044-1045, 1047, 1055, 1057, 1059-1060, 7/9; #1041, 1050, 8/12; #1048, 1051, 1058, 9/16; #1042, 1053, 1056, 7/10/86; #1046, 1049, 1052, 1054, 8/21/86; #1043, 11/25/86.
Nos. 1048, 1058 horiz.

**1061** A91 60c Plate No. 31 .60 .60
**1062** A91 150c Plate No. 32 1.25 .75
**1063** A91 200c Plate No. 33 1.75 1.00
**1064** A91 150c Plate No. 34 1.40 .75
**1065** A91 150c Plate No. 35 1.40 .75
**1066** A91 120c Plate No. 36 .90 .60
**1067** A91 120c Plate No. 37 .90 .60
**1068** A91 130c Plate No. 38 .90 .65
**1069** A91 80c Plate No. 39 .60 .60
**1070** A91 260c like #1069 2.50 1.25
*a.* Wmk. 364 ('87) 6.50 5.50
**1071** A91 100c Plate No. 40 .80 .80
**1072** A91 150c like #1071 1.25 .75
*a.* Wmk. 364 ('86) 6.50 3.50
**1073** A91 150c Plate No. 41 1.25 .75
**1074** A91 100c Plate No. 42 .90 .90
**1075** A91 150c like #1075 1.25 .75
*a.* Wmk. 364 ('86) 6.50 3.50
**1076** A91 100c Plate No. 43 .80 .80
**1077** A91 200c like #1076 1.75 1.00
*a.* Wmk. 364 ('86) 6.50 3.25
**1078** A91 60c Plate No. 44 1.00 1.00
**1079** A91 100c Plate No. 45 .90 .90
**1080** A91 150c like #1079 1.25 .75
*a.* Wmk. 364 ('86) 6.50 3.50
*Nos. 1061-1080 (20)* 23.35 15.95

Issued: #1061, 7/9; #1062, 1064-1066, 1068, 1073, 1078, 8/12; #1072, 1075, 1077, 1080, 9/16; #1063, 1067, 1070, 7/10/86; #1069, 1071, 1074, 1076, 1079, 8/21/86.
Nos. 1063, 1071-1072, 1074-1077, 1079-1080 horiz.

**1081** A91 120c Plate No. 46 .80 .60
**1082** A91 60c Plate No. 47 .60 .60
**1083** A91 150c Plate No. 48 1.25 .75
**1084** A91 50c Plate No. 49 1.25 1.25
**1085** A91 55c like #1084 .60 .60
*a.* Wmk. 364 ('86) 4.00 4.00
**1086** A91 60c Plate No. 50 .60 .60
**1087** A91 320c like #1086 4.00 2.10
*a.* Wmk. 364 ('87) 10.00 9.50
**1088** A91 25c Plate No. 51 .60 .60
**1089** A91 25c Plate No. 52 1.00 1.00
**1090** A91 30c Plate No. 53 .60 .60
*a.* Wmk. 364 ('86) 3.25 3.25
**1091** A91 50c like #1090 .60 .60
**1092** A91 45c Plate No. 54 .60 .60
*a.* Wmk. 364 ('87) 10.00 10.00
**1093** A91 60c like #1092 .60 .60
**1094** A91 50c Plate No. 55 1.10 1.10
**1095** A91 60c like #1094 1.40 1.40
**1096** A91 75c like #1094 .60 .60
*a.* Wmk. 364 3.25 3.25
**1097** A91 120c Plate No. 56 1.00 .70
**1098** A91 60c Plate No. 57 .60 .60
**1099** A91 120c Plate No. 58 1.00 .70
**1100** A91 25c Plate No. 59 .50 .50
*a.* Dark red flowers ('86) 4.00 4.00
*Nos. 1081-1100 (20)* 19.30 16.10

Issued: #1082-1083, 1085, 1089, 8/12; #1088, 9/16; #1095, 10/7; #1087, 1092, 2/26/86; #1081, 1090, 1096-1100, 7/10/86; #1086, 1091, 1093, 8/21/86; #1084, 12/22/86; #1094, 1/16/87.
No. 1098 horiz.

**1101** A91 75c Plate No. 60 .70 .70
**1102** A91 225c like #1101 2.00 1.10
*a.* Wmk. 364 ('87) 13.00 13.00
**1103** A91 25c Plate No. 61 .60 .60
**1104** A91 150c Plate No. 62 1.25 .75
**1105** A91 25c Plate No. 63 .60 .60
**1106** A91 50c Plate No. 64 1.25 1.25
*a.* Wmk. 364 — —
**1107** A91 55c like #1106 .60 .60
*a.* Wmk. 364 ('86) 4.25 4.25
**1108** A91 50c Plate No. 65 .60 .60
**1109** A91 100c like #1108 .60 .60
*a.* Wmk. 364 4.00 4.00
**1110** A91 130c Plate No. 66 1.00 .65
**1111** A91 120c Plate No. 67 .90 .60
**1112** A91 40c Plate No. 68 1.00 1.00
**1113** A91 100c like #1112 .60 .60
*a.* Wmk. 364 ('87) 6.50 6.50
**1114** A91 60c Plate No. 69 .60 .60
**1115** A91 120c like #1114 .90 .60
*a.* Wmk. 364 ('87) 14.00 14.00
**1116** A91 25c Plate No. 70 .60 .60
**1117** A91 25c Plate No. 71 .60 .60
*a.* Wmk. 364 ('87) 15.00 15.00
**1118** A91 60c like #1117 .70 .70
**1119** A91 25c Plate No. 72 .60 .60
**1120** A91 60c Plate No. 73 .60 .60
*Nos. 1101-1120 (20)* 16.30 13.95

Issued: #1104, 1107, 8/12; #1103, 1105, 1116, 1119, 9/16; #1102, 1115, 1117, 4/4/86; #1109-1111, 1113, 1120, 7/10/86; #1101, 1108, 1114, 1118, 8/21/86; #1112, 11/25/86.
No. 1114-1115, 1117-1118, 1120 horiz.

**1121** A91 80c Plate No. 74 .70 .70
**1122** A91 250c like #1121 2.25 1.25
*a.* Wmk. 364 ('87) 6.50 6.50
**1123** A91 60c Plate No. 75 .60 .60
**1124** A91 65c Plate No. 76 .60 .60
**1125** A91 150c like #1124 1.25 .75
*a.* Wmk. 364 ('87) 14.00 14.00
**1126** A91 40c Plate No. 77 .60 .60
*a.* Wmk. 364 ('87) 12.00 12.00
**1127** A91 45c like #1126 .60 .60
**1128** A91 45c Plate No. 78 .60 .60
**1129** A91 150c like #1128 1.25 .75
*a.* Wmk. 364 ('87) 14.00 14.00
**1130** A91 60c Plate No. 79 .60 .60
**1131** A91 200c like #1130 1.75 1.00
*a.* Wmk. 364 ('87) 14.00 14.00
**1132** A91 65c Plate No. 80 .60 .60
**1133** A91 330c like #1132 3.00 1.60
*a.* Wmk. 364 ('87) 15.00 15.00
**1134** A91 45c Plate No. 81 .50 .50
*a.* Wmk. 364 ('87) 15.00 15.00
**1135** A91 55c like #1134 .60 .60
**1136** A91 55c Plate No. 82 .60 .60
**1137** A91 320c like #1136 3.00 1.60
*a.* Wmk. 364 ('87) 15.00 15.00
**1138** A91 75c Plate No. 83 .70 .70
**1139** A91 300c like #1138 2.75 1.50
*a.* Wmk. 364 ('87) 15.00 15.00
**1140** A91 45c Plate No. 84 .60 .60
**1141** A91 90c like #1140 .60 .60
*a.* Wmk. 364 ('87) 14.00 14.00
*Nos. 1121-1141 (21)* 23.75 16.95

Issued: #1126, 1129, 1131, 1139, 1141, 2/26/86; #1122-1123, 7/10/86; #1125, 1133-1134, 1137, 7/24/86; #1121, 1124, 1127-1128, 1130, 1132, 1135-1136, 1138, 1140, 8/21/86.
No. 1123 horiz.

**1142** A91 45c Plate No. 85 .60 .60
**1143** A91 360c like #1142 3.00 1.75
*a.* Wmk. 364 ('87) 15.00 15.00
**1144** A91 30c Plate No. 86 .60 .60
*a.* Wmk. 364 ('87) 7.50 7.50
**1145** A91 40c like #1144 1.10 1.10
**1146** A91 60c Plate No. 87 .60 .60
**1147** A91 150c like #1146 1.25 .75
*a.* Wmk. 364 ('87) 17.50 17.50
**1148** A91 65c Plate No. 88 .60 .60
**1149** A91 100c like #1148 .65 .65
*a.* Wmk. 364 ('87) 15.00 15.00
**1150** A91 55c Plate No. 89 .60 .60
**1151** A91 90c like #1150 .60 .60
*a.* Wmk. 364 ('87) 15.00 15.00
**1152** A91 40c Plate No. 90 .60 .60
**1153** A91 375c like #1152 2.50 2.50
*a.* Wmk. 364 ('87) 8.00 8.00
**1154** A91 40c Plate No. 91 2.50 2.50
**1155** A91 130c like #1154 1.25 .65
*a.* Wmk. 364 ('87) 7.50 7.50
**1156** A91 50c Plate No. 92 .60 .60
*a.* Wmk. 364 ('87) 15.00 15.00
**1157** A91 75c like #1156 .70 .70
**1158** A91 60c Plate No. 93 .60 .60
*a.* Wmk. 364 ('87) 7.50 7.50
**1159** A91 80c like #1158 .70 .70
**1160** A91 60c Plate No. 94 .60 .60
**1161** A91 350c like #1160 3.25 1.75
*a.* Wmk. 364 ('87) 15.00 15.00
**1162** A91 60c Plate No. 95 .70 .70
*a.* Wmk. 364 ('87) 15.00 15.00
**1163** A91 75c like #1162 .70 .70
**1164** A91 40c Plate No. 96 .60 .60
*a.* Wmk. 364 ('87) 14.00 14.00
**1165** A91 65c like #1164 .70 .70
*Nos. 1142-1165 (24)* 25.60 21.75

See note below #1341. Issued: #1143, 1156, 1162, 2/26/86; #1147, 1161, 4/4/86; #1144, 1153, 1155, 1158, 7/10/86; #1149, 1151, 1164, 7/24/86; #1142, 1146, 1148, 1150, 1152, 1157, 1159-1160, 1163, 1165, 8/21/86; #1154, 9/26/86; #1145, 10/23/86.
Some stamps printed in sheets of 25, blocks of 4 each of different stamps separated by gutter containing 2 #1337 and strip of 5 #1339. Margin contains separation marks for #1337, 1339.
Nos. 1146-1147, 1160-1161 horiz.
Nos. 1025, 1027, 1031, 1036, 1039, 1046, 1049, 1052, 1054, 1069, 1071, 1074, 1076, 1079, 1086, 1091, 1093, 1101, 1108, 1114, 1118, 1121, 1124, 1127-1128, 1130, 1132, 1135-1136, 1138, 1140, 1142, 1146, 1148, 1150, 1152, 1157, 1159-1160, 1163, 1165 sold as singles in booklets only. Two booklets of 48 stamps each contain these numbers and previous values issued in the series. Value, each booklet, $80.
See #1372. For overprints and surcharges see #1342-1346, 1393, 1402-1403, 1412-1413, 1494, 1511-1670F, 1731-1740, 1742-1750, 1755-1759, 1761, 1764-1773, 1785, 1845-1849, 1906-1909, 1914-1933, 1939-1941, 1943-1947, 1958-1959, 1960-1979, 2000, C7, C9-C12, E2, E4.

**1986-89 Litho. Unwmk.** ***Perf. 14***
**Series 2**

**1166** A91 175c Plate No. 1 1.50 .65
**1167** A91 560c like #1166 4.50 1.60
**1168** A91 90c Plate No. 2 1.25 1.25
**1169** A91 200c like #1168 2.25 1.25
**1170** A91 50c Plate No. 3 .50 .50
**1171** A91 90c like #1170 .60 .60
**1172** A91 90c Plate No. 4 .60 .60
**1173** A91 140c like #1172 1.25 .50
**1174** A91 130c Plate No. 5 1.10 .50
**1175** A91 160c like #1174 1.50 .80
**1176** A91 50c Plate No. 6 .50 .50
**1177** A91 390c like #1176 3.50 2.00
**1178** A91 30c Plate No. 7 .50 .50
**1179** A91 40c like #1178 .50 .50
**1180** A91 70c Plate No. 8 .50 .50
**1181** A91 75c like #1180 .60 .60
**1182** A91 70c Plate No. 9 .50 .50
**1183** A91 200c like #1182 1.75 1.00
**1184** A91 90c Plate No. 10 1.25 1.25
**1185** A91 320c like #1184 3.00 1.75
*Nos. 1166-1185 (20)* 27.65 17.35

Issued: #1172, 1175, 1181, 1183, 9/23; #1184, 10/23; #1177, 1185, 10/31; #1169, 11/25; #1171, 1179, 12/27; #1168, 1/5/87; #1167, 4/24/87; #1166, 1170, 1173-1174, 1176, 1178, 1180, 1182, 8/23/88.
Nos. 1174-1175 horiz.

**1186** A91 200c Plate No. 11 1.75 .75
**1187** A91 70c Plate No. 12 .50 .50
**1188** A91 320c like #1187 2.75 1.60
**1189** A91 50c Plate No. 13 1.50 1.50
**1190** A91 90c like #1189 .60 .60
**1191** A91 30c Plate No. 14 .60 .60
**1192** A91 120c like #1191 1.00 .60
**1193** A91 50c Plate No. 15 4.25 4.25
**1194** A91 85c like #1193 .50 .50
**1195** A91 260c Plate No. 16 2.25 .60
**1196** A91 320c like #1195 3.25 1.40
**1197** A91 45c Plate No. 17 .50 .50
**1198** A91 70c like #1197 .50 .50
**1199** A91 85c Plate No. 18 .60 .60
**1200** A91 320c like #1199 3.00 1.60
**1201** A91 175c Plate No. 19 1.50 .65
**1202** A91 450c like #1201 3.75 1.25
**1203** A91 25c Plate No. 20 .50 .50
**1204** A91 50c like #1203 .50 .50
**1205** A91 45c Plate No. 21 2.00 2.00
*Nos. 1186-1205 (20)* 31.80 21.00

Issued: #1188, 1205, 9/23; #1190, 1197, 10/31; #1189, 12/3; #1192, 1194, 1200, 1203, 12/27; #1193, 1199, 1/5/87; #1202, 4/24/87; #1196, 6/1/88; #1186-1187, 1191, 1198, 1201, 1204, 8/23/88; #1195, 7/7/89.
Nos. 1201-1202, 1205, horiz.

**1206** A91 30c Plate No. 22 .50 .50
**1207** A91 150c like #1206 1.25 .75
**1208** A91 200c Plate No. 23 1.75 .75
**1209** A91 85c Plate No. 24 1.60 1.60
**1210** A91 225c like #1209 4.75 4.75
**1211** A91 140c Plate No. 25 1.25 .55
**1212** A91 230c like #1211 2.25 .70
**1213** A91 200c Plate No. 26 1.75 .75
**1214** A91 60c Plate No. 27 .50 .50
**1215** A91 90c like #1214 1.10 1.10
**1216** A91 30c Plate No. 28 .50 .50
**1217** A91 330c like #1216 3.00 1.60
**1218** A91 130c Plate No. 29 1.00 .50
**1219** A91 350c like #1218 3.25 1.75
**1220** A91 30c Plate No. 30 3.25 3.25
**1221** A91 875c Plate No. 31 6.00 3.50
**1222** A91 50c Plate No. 32 .50 .50
**1223** A91 130c like #1222 1.00 .65
**1224** A91 50c Plate No. 33 .50 .50
**1225** A91 100c like #1224 .90 .90
*Nos. 1206-1225 (20)* 36.60 25.60

Issued: #1219, 1220, 9/23; #1214, 1224, 10/31; #1210, 11/25; #1209, 1215, 12/15; #1207, 1217, 1223, 12/27; #1212, 2/14/87; #1221, 6/15/88; #1206, 1208, 1211, 1213, 1216, 1218, 1222, 1225, 8/23/88.
Nos. 1218-1219 horiz.

**1226** A91 140c Plate No. 34 1.10 .50
**1227** A91 360c like #1226 3.00 1.75
**1228** A91 380c Plate No. 35 3.25 1.40
**1229** A91 525c Plate No. 36 4.00 2.25
**1230** A91 175c Plate No. 37 1.25 .65
**1231** A91 390c like #1230 3.00 1.25
**1232** A91 130c Plate No. 38 1.00 .65
**1233** A91 140c like #1232 1.10 .50
**1234** A91 175c Plate No. 39 1.50 .65
**1235** A91 260c like #1234 2.00 .75
**1236** A91 250c Plate No. 40 4.50 1.90
**1237** A91 $10 like #1236 7.50 5.75
**1238** A91 140c Plate No. 41 1.10 .50
**1239** A91 180c like #1238 1.40 .45
**1240** A91 80c Plate No. 42 .50 .50
**1241** A91 130c like #1240 1.10 .50
**1242** A91 200c Plate No. 43 1.75 .55
**1243** A91 100c Plate No. 44 .80 .80
**1244** A91 200c like #1243 1.75 1.00
**1245** A91 35c Plate No. 45 .50 .50
**1246** A91 85c like #1245 .60 .60
*Nos. 1226-1246 (21)* 42.70 23.40

Issued: #1227, 1232, 1240, 9/23; #1244, 1246, 10/31; #1245, 1/5/87; #1239, 2/14/87; #1231, 1235, 4/24/87; #1242, 9/29/87; #1237, 3/24/88; #1229, 6/1/88; #1226, 1228, 1230, 1233-1234, 1236, 1238, 1241, 1243, 8/23/88.
Nos. 1230-1231, 1240-1241 horiz.

**1247** A91 225c Plate No. 46 1.50 .80
**1248** A91 175c Plate No. 47 1.25 .65
**1249** A91 240c like #1248 1.75 .70
**1250** A91 200c Plate No. 48 1.40 .55
**1251** A91 200c Plate No. 49 1.40 .55
**1252** A91 720c like #1251 5.00 3.75
**1253** A91 160c Plate No. 50 1.00 .55
**1254** A91 300c like #1253 2.00 1.50
**1255** A91 175c Plate No. 51 1.10 .60

**1256** A91 500c like #1255 3.00 1.50
**1257** A91 140c Plate No. 52 1.00 .40
**1258** A91 590c like #1257 3.25 1.60
**1259** A91 200c Plate No. 53 1.25 .55
**1260** A91 290c like #1259 2.00 1.25
**1261** A91 175c Plate No. 54 1.25 .60
**1261A** A91 460c like #1261 2.75 1.40
**1262** A91 120c Plate No. 55 .90 .35
**1263** A91 75c Plate No. 56 .50 .50
**1264** A91 100c like #1263 .50 .50
**1265** A91 225c Plate No. 57 1.25 .60
*Nos. 1247-1265 (20)* 34.05 18.90

Issued: #1254, 1263, 10/31; #1258, 2/14/87; #1249, 1256, 1261A, 4/24/87; #1250, 9/29/87; #1252, 1260, 11/23/87; #1247-1248, 8/23/88; #1253, 1255, 11/3/88; #1251, 1257, 1259, 1261-1262, 1264-1265, 1/3/89.

Nos 1261, 1261A horiz.

**1266** A91 175c Plate No. 58 1.25 .50
**1267** A91 275c like #1266 2.00 .85
**1268** A91 775c Plate No. 59 4.00 3.25
**1269** A91 200c Plate No. 60 1.50 .55
**1270** A91 575c like #1269 2.75 1.50
**1271** A91 255c Plate No. 61 2.00 1.00
**1272** A91 280c Plate No. 62 1.40 .95
**1273** A91 700c like #1272 4.75 4.25
**1274** A91 285c Plate No. 63 1.40 1.00
**1275** A91 200c Plate No. 64 1.00 .55
**1276** A91 680c like #1275 3.75 3.25
**1277** A91 140c Plate No. 65 .70 .40
**1278** A91 650c like #1277 3.00 1.60
**1279** A91 280c Plate No. 66 1.25 .75
**1280** A91 750c like #1279 4.75 4.25
**1281** A91 280c Plate No. 67 1.25 .75
**1282** A91 $15 like #1281 8.50 7.50
**1283** A91 325c Plate No. 68 1.75 .85
**1284** A91 530c Plate No. 69 3.00 2.75
**1285** A91 550c Plate No. 70 3.75 3.75
*Nos. 1266-1285 (20)* 53.75 40.25

Issued: #1278, 2/14/87; #1267, 4/24/87; #1270, 1283, 10/26/87; #1271, 1276, 1280, 11/23/87; #1282, 1284, 6/1/88; #1268, 1273, 6/15/88; #1285, 8/15/88; #1272, 1274, 11/3/88; #1266, 1269, 1275, 1277, 1279, 1281, 1/3/89.

No. 1266-1267, 1283, 1285 horiz.

**1286** A91 670c Plate No. 71 4.50 4.25
**1287** A91 300c Plate No. 72 1.50 .80
**1288** A91 $25 like #1287 9.50 8.50
**1289** A91 130c Plate No. 73 .80 .25
**1290** A91 475c like #1289 2.75 2.50
**1291** A91 350c Plate No. 74 2.25 2.00
**1291A** A91 900c like #1291 6.50 6.00
**1291B** A91 600c on 900c #1291A
**1292** A91 200c Plate No. 75 1.00 .70
**1293** A91 250c Plate No. 76 1.25 .65
**1294** A91 850c like #1293 4.75 4.25
**1295** A91 300c Plate No. 77 1.50 .80
**1296** A91 480c like #1295 2.25 1.25
**1297** A91 280c Plate No. 78 1.40 .75
**1298** A91 950c like #1298 6.50 6.00
**1299** A91 250c Plate No. 79 1.25 .90
**1300** A91 800c like #1299 5.00 4.00
**1301** A91 300c Plate No. 80 1.50 .80
**1302** A91 400c like #1301 2.00 1.10
**1303** A91 305c Plate No. 81 1.50 .80
**1304** A91 250c Plate No. 82 1.25 .65
**1305** A91 330c like #1304 1.60 .85
*Nos. 1286-1291A,1292-1305 (21)* 60.55 47.80

Issued: #1305, 2/14/87; #1288, 1296, 1302, 7/22/87; #1291A-1291B, 10/9/87; #1294, 1300, 11/23/87; #1290, 6/1/88; #1298, 6/15/88; #1291, 6/22/88; #1286, 8/15/88; #1292, 1299, 11/3/88; #1287, 1293, 1295, 1297, 1301, 1303-1304, 1/3/89; #1289, 7/7/89.

No. 1286 horiz.

**1306** A91 350c Plate No. 83 1.75 .95
**1307** A91 $20 like #1306 7.50 5.25
**1308** A91 360c Plate No. 84 2.25 2.00
**1309** A91 250c Plate No. 85 1.25 .65
**1310** A91 300c like #1309 1.50 .75
**1311** A91 350c Plate No. 86 1.75 .95
**1312** A91 500c like #1311 2.25 1.25
**1313** A91 250c Plate No. 87 1.25 .65
**1314** A91 425c like #1313 2.00 1.00
**1315** A91 250c Plate No. 88 1.25 .65
**1316** A91 440c like #1315 2.00 1.10
**1317** A91 350c Plate No. 89 1.75 .95
**1318** A91 520c like #1317 2.60 1.40
**1319** A91 270c Plate No. 90 1.25 1.25
**1320** A91 250c Plate No. 91 1.10 .65
**1321** A91 $12 like #1320 7.50 7.00
**1322** A91 200c Plate No. 92 1.00 .55
**1323** A91 200c Plate No. 93 1.00 .70
**1324** A91 300c Plate No. 94 1.50 .80
**1325** A91 600c like #1324 2.75 1.60
**1326** A91 420c Plate No. 95 2.25 1.40
**1327** A91 200c Plate No. 96 1.00 .40
**1328** A91 375c like #1327 2.25 2.00
*Nos. 1306-1328 (23)* 50.70 33.90

Issued: #1310, 1314, 1316, 2/14/87; #1307, 1312, 1318, 6/2/87; #1325, 7/22/87/ #1322, 9/29/87; #1326, 10/26/87; #1328, 11/23/87; #1321, 3/24/88; #1308, 1319, 8/15/88; #1323, 11/3/88; #1306, 1309, 1311, 1313, 1315, 1317, 1320, 1324, 1/3/89; #1327, 7/7/89.

No. 1326, horiz.

Nos. 1166, 1170, 1174, 1176, 1178, 1180, 1182, 1187, 1191, 1193, 1198, 1201, 1204, 1206, 1211, 1216, 1218, 1222, 1225-1226, 1230, 1233-1234, 1236, 1238, 1248, 1257, 1261, 1264, 1266, 1277, 1279, 1281, 1287, 1293, 1295, 1297, 1301, 1304, 1306, 1308-1309, 1311, 1313, 1315, 1317, 1320, 1324 sold as singles in booklets only. Two booklets of 48 stamps each contain these numbers and previous values issued in the series. Value, each booklet, $80.

### Miniature Sheets of 4

Designs: Nos. 1329a, 1330b, 1331b, like #1303. Nos. 1329b, 1330a, 1332a, like #1265. Nos. 1329c, 1330c, 1332b, like #1247. Nos. 1330d, 1331a, 1332c, like #1262.

**1329** #1262, 1329a-1329c 4.50 4.50
*a.-c.* A91 120c any single 1.00 1.00
**1330** #a.-d. 4.50 4.50
*a.-d.* A91 150c any single 1.00 1.00
**1331** #1247, 1265, 1331a-1331b 5.00 5.00
*a.-b.* A91 225c any single .95 .95
**1332** #1303, 1332a-1332c 5.00 5.00
*a.-c.* A91 305c any single .95 .95
**1333** 7.00 7.00
*a.* A91 320c like #1262 1.25 1.25
*b.* A91 330c like #1247 1.25 1.25
*c.* A91 350c like #1303 1.50 1.50
*d.* A91 500c like #1265 2.40 2.40
**1334** 7.00 7.00
*a.* A91 320c like #1247 1.25 1.25
*b.* A91 330c like #1262 1.25 1.25
*c.* A91 350c like #1265 1.50 1.50
*d.* A91 500c like #1303 2.40 2.40
**1335** 7.00 7.00
*a.* A91 320c like #1303 1.25 1.25
*b.* A91 330c like #1265 1.25 1.25
*c.* A91 350c like #1262 1.50 1.50
*d.* A91 500c like #1247 2.40 2.40
**1336** 7.00 7.00
*a.* A91 320c like #1265 1.25 1.25
*b.* A91 330c like #1303 1.25 1.25
*c.* A91 350c like #1247 1.50 1.50
*d.* A91 500c like #1262 2.40 2.40

Issued: #1329-1332, 7/7/89; others, 2/26/88.

For surcharges & overprints see #1671-1727, 1776-1777, 1834-1835, 1942, 1948-1952, 1998-1999, 2031, 2033-2044, 2064, 2619A-2619D, 2578A-2578C, 2907A-2907G, 2928A-2928D, E3, E5, O40-O56.

Natl. Arms — A92

**1985-87** ***Perf. 14 Vert.***
**1337** A92 25c multi .50 .50
**1338** A92 25c multi ('87) 1.25 .75

***Perf. 14 Horiz.***
**1339** A92 25c multi .25 .25
**1340** A92 25c multi ('87) 1.25 .75
*Nos. 1337-1340 (4)* 3.25 2.25

***Perf. 14***
**1341** A92 25c multi

Nos. 1337-1340 were cut from orchid sheet gutters. Stamps vary considerably in size.

Nos. 1338, 1340 are Nos. 1337 and 1339 redrawn to include black border.

Issue dates: Nos. 1337, 1339, 1341, July 1985. No. 1338, 1340 June 2, 1987.

See Nos. 1467-1468. For surcharges see Nos. 1777A-1777C, 4166-4168.

### Nos. 1024, 1044, 1047, 1059, 1060 Surcharged or Overprinted in Blue or Black "QUEEN MOTHER 1900-1985" on 1 or 2 Lines

**1985** ***Perfs. as Before***
**1342** A91 130c on #1044
**1343** A91 130c on #1059
**1344** A91 130c on #1060
*Nos. 1342-1344 (3)* 6.25

### Miniature sheets

**1345** Sheet of 4 7.50
*a.-d.* A91 200c on #1024, any single
**1346** Sheet of 4 12.00
*a.-d.* A91 200c on 130c #1047, any single (Bk)

Issued: #1342-1345, July 9; #1346, Sept. 12.

Nos. 1345a, 1346a overprinted "LADY BOWES-LYON 1900-1923". Nos. 1345b, 1346b overprinted "DUCHESS OF YORK 1923-1937". Nos. 1345c, 1346c overprinted "QUEEN ELIZABETH 1937-1952". Surcharge on No. 1346 sans serif.

For overprints see #1741, 1751-1754, 1774-1775.

### Nos. 465 Surcharged in Red "INTERNATIONAL / YOUTH YEAR / 1985"

***Perf. 13x13½***

**1985, July 18 Litho. Wmk. 364**
**1347** Sheet of 25, 8 #a.-b., 4 #c.-d., 1 #e. 175.00
*a.-e.* A28 25c on #465a-465e, any single

### No. 203 Surcharged

### No. 443 Surcharged

**1985, July 26** ***Perfs. as Before***
**Watermarks & Printing Methods as Before**
**1352** A47 225c on #203 30.00 4.00
**1354** A63 240c on #443 12.00 5.00

Girl Guides, 75th anniv. (#1352), John J. Audubon, bicentennial of birth. No. 203 surcharged only with 350c, $2.25 or surcharged with both was not issued.

Abolition of Slavery, Sesquicent. — A93

Designs: 25c, Revolution leaders, 1763. 60c, Damon's execution, 1834. 130c, Demerara Uprising, 1823. 150c Den Arendt slave ship.

**Unwmk.**

**1985, July 29 Litho.** ***Perf. 14***
**1355** A93 25c gray & black .25 .25
**1356** A93 60c pink & black .75 .75
**1357** A93 130c blue grn & blk 1.40 1.40
**1358** A93 150c lilac & blk 1.60 1.60
*Nos. 1355-1358 (4)* 4.00 4.00

See Nos. 1994-1997 for changed colors.

### No. 210 Surcharged "Guyana/Libya / Friendship 1985"
### No. 223 Surcharged in Brown
### No. 135 Surcharged "Mexico / 1986"

**1985, Aug. 16** ***Perfs. as Before***
**Watermarks and Printing Methods as Before**
**1359** A49 150c on #210 9.00 3.00
**1360** A53 150c on #223 2.75 .85
**1361** A28 275c on 3c #135 9.00 1.75
*Nos. 1359-1361 (3)* 20.75 5.60

Refer to 2nd paragraph under No. 147 for No. 1361. See No. 1452 for 225c Mexico 1986 surcharge.

### Nos. 366, 427, 430, 430a, 494, & 553 Ovptd. or Surcharged "1955-1985" Vertically or Horizontally

**Wmk. 364**

**1985, Sept. 23 Litho.** ***Perf. 13½***
**1362** A75 60c on #366 .50 .50
**1363** A75 60c on #553 .50 .50
**1364** A75 120c on #427 1.00 1.00
**1365** A75 120c on #430 1.00 1.00
**1366** A75 120c on #430a 1.00 1.00
**1367** A75 120c on #494 1.00 1.00
*Nos. 1362-1367 (6)* 5.00 5.00

### No. 417 Surcharged "1965-1985" Vertically

**1985, Sept. 30**
**1368** A79 25c on #417 .75 .30
**1369** A79 225c on #417 2.50 1.50

### Nos. 260 & 262 Surcharged "1985"

**1985, Oct. 5 Litho.** ***Perf. 14x14½***
**1370** A61 25c on 40c #262 11.00 .40
**1371** A61 320c on 15c #260 20.00 3.75

### Orchid Type of 1985 Surcharged in Red "CRISTOBAL COLON / 1492-1992"

**1985, Oct. 12** ***Perf. 14***
**1372** A91 350c on 120c like #1108 8.00 3.25

No. 1372 not issued without surcharge. For overprint see No. E1. For surcharge see No. 1591A.

### No. 288 Overprinted "SIR WINSTON CHURCHILL / 1965-1985"

**1985, Oct. 15** ***Perf. 13½x13***
**1373** A66 $2 on #288 12.00 3.75

### No. 214 Surcharged "1950-1985"

**1985, Oct. 15** ***Perf. 14***
**1374** A50 25c on 110c on 10c .40 .25
**1375** A50 200c on 110c on 10c 1.40 1.40

#214 with 110c surcharge only was not issued.

### Nos. 295-297, 384, and O9 Overprinted or Surcharged "United / Nations / 1945-1985"

**1985, Oct. 28** ***Perf. 14x14½***
**1376** A68 30c on #295 1.75 .25
**1377** A68 50c on #296 1.75 .30
**1378** A68 100c on #O9 1.75 .50
**1379** A68 225c on #384 18.50 1.25
**1380** A68 $3 on #297 4.00 2.75
*Nos. 1376-1380 (5)* 27.75 5.05

### Nos. 142-144, 289A, O4-O5, O7, O15, and QO1-QO2 Ovptd. "POSTAGE"

**1985, Oct. 29** ***Perfs. as Before***
**Watermarks and Printing Methods as Before**
**1381** A28 30c on #O4 1.00 .30
**1382** A28 40c on #142 60.00 .90
**1383** A28 50c on #143 1.00 .50
**1384** A28 50c on #O5 1.00 .40
**1385** A28 60c on #144 4.25 .50
**1386** A28 60c on #144 (Revenue Only) 1.00 .35
**1387** A28 60c on #O7 3.00 .40
**1388** A66 $10 on #O15 17.50 7.00
**1389** A28 $15 on #QO1 17.50 12.00
**1390** A28 $20 on #QO2 17.50 13.00
*Nos. 1381-1390 (10)* 123.75 35.35

Refer to 2nd paragraph in footnote following No. 147 for Nos. 1381, 1384, 1386-1387.

### Nos. 133-134 Surcharged "Deepavali / 1985"

**1985, Nov. 1**
**1391** A28 25c on 2c #134 1.00 .35
**1392** A28 150c on 1c #133 2.50 1.00

### Miniature Sheet
### No. 1050 Ovptd. in Red

Overprinted: a, "Christmas 1985." b, "Happy New Year." c, "Merry Christmas." d, "Happy Holidays."

**1985, Nov. 3 Unwmk.** ***Perf. 14***
**1393** A91 55c Sheet of 4, #a.-d. 12.00 7.00

For surcharge see No. 1670F.

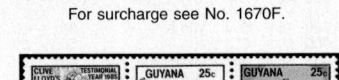

Clive Lloyd, Cricketer — A94

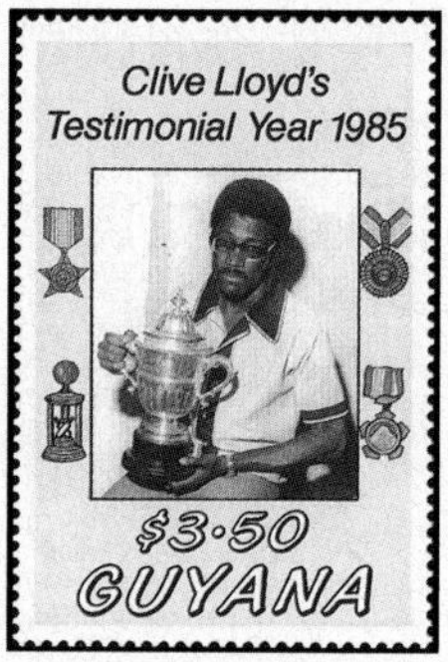


Lloyd Holding Intl. Cup — A95

Designs: #a, $2.25, Lloyd playing cricket. #b, $1.30, Lloyd, bat and wicket. #c, 60c, Gloves, wicket, bat, natl. flag.

**1985, Nov. 7** ***Perf. 14½x14***

**1394** Triptych .75 .75
*a.-c.* A94 25c any single .25 .25

**Size: 30x38mm**

***Perf. 14x14½***

**1395** A94 60c multi .45 .45
**1396** A94 $1.30 multi .90 .90
**1397** A94 $2.25 multi 1.60 1.60
**1398** A95 $3.50 multi 2.60 2.60
*Nos. 1394-1398 (5)* 6.30 6.30

For surcharge see No. 1504.

Miniature Sheet

No. 329 Ovptd. "1985" in Red

**Wmk. 364**

**1985, Nov. 15 Litho.** ***Perf. 14***

**1399** A77 30c Sheet of 12, #a.-l. 17.50 17.50

Nos. 410 and 413e Surcharged

**1985, Dec. 23 Photo.** ***Perf. 14x14½***

**Watermarks as Before**

**1400** A7 20c on #410 3.00 .50
**1401** A7 20c on #413De 3.00 .50

Compare No. 1400 with No. 914 and 1401 with No. 994a.

Nos. 1075, 1077 Ovptd. "REICHENBACHIA 1886-1986" in Purple

**1986, Jan. 13 Litho.** ***Perf. 14***

**1402** A91 150c on #1075 9.00 1.00
**1403** A91 200c on #1077 9.00 1.10

For surcharge and overprints see Nos. 1553, 1760, 1762-1763.

Nos. 608, 610 Surcharged "Republic Day / 1986"

***Perfs. as Before***

**1986, Feb. 22** **Wmk. 364**

**1404** A82 25c on #608
**1405** A83 120c on $6 #610
**1406** A83 225c on $6 #610
*Nos. 1404-1406 (3)* 2.00

No. 87 Surcharged "1986"

**1986, Mar. 24 Photo.** ***Perf. 13***

**1407** A14 25c on 6c #87 .30 .25
**1408** A14 50c on 6c #87 .50 .45
**1409** A14 100c on 6c #87 .90 .85
**1410** A14 200c on 6c #87 1.75 1.50
*Nos. 1407-1410 (4)* 3.45 3.05

No. 237 Surcharged "1926 / 1986"

**1986, Mar. 27 Litho.** ***Perf. 14***

**1411** A56 150c on 35c #237 5.50 1.00

St. John Ambulance, 60th anniv.

Nos. 1028, 1037 Surcharged "Queen Elizabeth / 1926 1986"

**1986, Apr. 21** **Unwmk.**

**1412** A91 Sheet of 4 7.00 7.00
*a.* 130c on 130c #1028 1.75 1.50
*b.* 200c on 130c #1028 1.75 1.50
*c.* 260c on 130c #1028 1.75 1.50
*d.* 330c on 130c #1028 1.75 1.50
**1413** A91 130c on #1037 1.75 .75

Location of overprint on No. 1413 differs from No. 1412.

For overprints & surcharges see #1670A, 1738B.

Nos. 267, 317g-317 l, 444a-444f Surcharged "Protect the"

**Wmk. 373**

**1986, May 3 Litho.** ***Perf. 14***

**1414** A73 60c on 35c #317g-317l, block of 6, #a.-f. 3.00 3.00
**1415** A73 60c on 35c #444, block of 6, #a.-f. — —

**Wmk. 364**

**1416** A63 $6 on 8c #267 5.00 4.00

No. 390 Surcharged

**1986, May 5 Litho.** ***Perf. 13***

**1417** A28 600c on #390 15.00 1.25

No. 283A Surcharged

Overprints: a, Abary. b, Anna Regina. c, Aurora. d, Bartica Grove. e, Bel Air. f, Belle Plaine. g, Clonbrook. h, T.P.O. Dem. / Railway. i, Enmore. j, Fredericks / burg. k, Good Success. l, 1986. m, Mariabba. n, Massaruni. o, Nigg. p, No. 50. q, No. 63 / Benab. r, Philadelphia. s, Sisters. t, Skeldon. u, Suddie. v, Taymouth / Manor. w, Wales. x, Whim.

***Perf. 14x13½***

**1986, May 15 Litho.** **Wmk. 364**

**1418** Sheet of 25, #a.-k., m.-x., 2 #l. 27.50 27.50
*a.-x.* A66 25c on 30c, any single 1.00 .75

British Guiana No. 254 Surcharged "GUYANA / INDEPENDENCE 1966-1986"

Nos. 10A and 13a Surcharged "1986"

No. 237 Surcharged

No. 713a-713d Surcharged "INDEPENDENCE / 1966-1986"

**1986, May 26** ***Perfs. as Before***

**Watermarks and Printing Methods as Before**

**1443** A60 25c on 2c British Guiana #254 .25 .25
**1444** A57 25c on 35c #241 .25 .25
**1445** A60 60c on 2c British Guiana #254 .45 .30
**1446** A60 120c on 6c #10A .50 .35
**1447** A60 130c on 24c #13a 9.00 .75
**1448** Block of 4 1.75 1.75
*a.* A86 25c on 120c #713a .35 .25
*b.* A86 25c on 130c #713b .35 .25
*c.* A86 25c on 150c #713c .35 .25
*d.* A86 225c on 200c #713d .70 .70
*Nos. 1443-1448 (6)* 12.20

No. 135 Surcharged "MEXICO / 1986" in Blue

***Perf. 13x13½***

**1986, May 31 Litho.** **Wmk. 364**

**1452** A28 225c on 3c #135 20.00 3.75

World Cup Soccer Championships, Mexico City.

Nos. 135 and 192 Surcharged "CARICOM HEADS OF GOV'T / CONFERENCE / JULY 1986" in Blue

No. 286A Ovptd. "CARICOM / DAY 1986" in Blue

**1986** ***Perfs. as Before***

**Watermarks and Printing Methods as Before**

**1453** A28 25c on #192 2.75 .75
**1454** A28 60c on 3c #135 3.50 .30
**1455** A66 60c on #286A 11.00 .75
*Nos. 1453-1455 (3)* 17.25

Issued: #1455, June 28; #1453-1454, July 1.

Nos. 133 and 137 Surcharged "INT. YEAR / OF PEACE" in Black or Blue

**1986, July 14 Litho.** ***Perf. 13x13½***

**1456** A28 25c on 1c #133 (Bl) .75 .45
**1457** A28 60c on 6c #137 1.75 1.75
**1458** A28 120c on 6c #137 1.75 1.75
**1459** A28 130c on 6c #137 1.75 1.75
**1460** A28 150c on 6c #137 1.75 1.75
*Nos. 1456-1460 (5)* 7.75

Halley's Comet — A96

Designs: a, Br. Guiana #172. b, Guyana #931.

**1986, July 19** ***Perf. 14***

**1461** A96 320c Pair, #a.-b. 3.00 3.00
*c.* Imperf. 7.50

No. 1461 has continuous design. No. 1461 exists imperf. between. Most were overprinted.

For overprints and surcharges see Nos. 1822, 1836, 2029, E5-E6, E11, E14.

No. 43 Surcharged

**1986, July 28 Photo.** ***Perf. 14x14½***

**1463** A7 20c on 6c #43 8.00 .40

Nos. 60-61 Surcharged "GUSIA / 1936-1986"

***Perf. 14x13½***

**1986, Aug. 15 Photo.** **Unwmk.**

**1464** A11 25c on #61 5.25 .45
**1465** A11 $1.50 on 6c #60 10.00 3.25

No. 136 Surcharged "REGIONAL / PHARMACY / CONFERENCE / 1986" in Blue

***Perf. 13x13½***

**1986, Aug. 15 Litho.** **Wmk. 364**

**1466** A28 130c on 5c #136 12.00 1.75

Nos. 1337, 1339, 1341 Inscribed "1966-1986"

***Perfs. as Before***

**1986, Sept. 23** **Unwmk.**

**1467** A92 25c on #1337 2.50 .30
**1468** A92 25c on #1339 2.50 .30
**1469** A92 25c on #1341 2.50 .30
*Nos. 1467-1469 (3)* 7.50 .90

No. 871 Surcharged

***Perf. 14x13½***

**1986, Oct. 1 Litho.** **Wmk. 364**

**Sheet of 25**

**1470** #a.-k., m.-x., 2 #l 55.00 40.00
*a.-x.* A66 120c any single 2.00 1.25

No. 1145 Surcharged "12th World Orchid Conference" / "TOKYO JAPAN MARCH 1987"

**Unwmk.**

**1986, Oct. 6 Litho.** ***Perf. 14***

**1494** A91 650c on 40c #1145 17.50 6.00

For overprint see No. 1851.

Orchid Type like No. 1052 Surchd. "1492-1992" and "CHRISTOPHER COLUMBUS" in Black and Red or Red

**1986, Oct.**

**1495** A91 320c on 150c 11.50 3.00
**1496** A91 320c on 150c (R) 11.50 3.00

Issued: #1495, 10/10; #1496, 10/30. #1495-1496 not issued without surcharge.

Nos. 704 and 705 Surcharged "1986"

***Perf. 14x14½***

**1986, Oct. 15 Photo.** **Wmk. 364**

**1497** A7 50c on #704 4.75 .60
**1498** A7 225c on #705 13.50 3.25

Nos. 134, 192 Surcharged "Deepavali /1986"

**1986, Nov. 3 Litho.** ***Perf. 13x13½***

**1499** A28 25c on 2c #134 3.00 .50
**1500** A28 200c on #192 10.00 3.00

No. 43 Surcharged "CHRISTMAS / 1986" in Red

No. 917 Surcharged in Red

**1986, Nov. 26** ***Perfs. as Before***

**Watermarks and Printing Methods as Before**

**1501** A7 20c on 6c #43 4.75 .30

**Miniature Sheet**

**1502** A88 120c on 60c on #a.-e. 8.50 8.50

No. 1502 is surcharged on an unissued miniature sheet containing No. 917.

No. 329 Ovptd. "1986" in Blue

**Wmk. 364**

**1986, Nov. 26 Litho.** ***Perf. 14***

**1503** A77 30c Sheet of 12, #a.-l. 25.00 25.00

No. 1398 Surcharged in Red

**1986, Dec. 1 Litho.** ***Perf. 14x14½***

**1504** A95 $15 on $3.50 #1398 45.00 20.00

L.F.S. Burnham, President 1980-85 A97

**1986, Dec. 13 Litho.** ***Perf. 12½x13***

**1505** A97 25c Tomb .25 .25
**1506** A97 120c Flags, map .35 .35
**1507** A97 130c Government building .45 .45
**1508** A97 $6 Portrait, necklace, vert. 2.00 2.00
*Nos. 1505-1508 (4)* 3.05 3.05

Orchid Type of 1985-87 Surcharged "GPOC / 1977 - 1987"

**1987, Jan. 19** ***Perf. 14***

**1509** A91 225c on 25c like #1090 4.50 1.00
**1510** A91 $10 on 50c like #1052 11.00 11.00

Nos. 1509-1510 not issued without surcharge. No. 1509 adds "2" to 25c value, No. 1510 uses flower as obliterator.

**Stamps of Type A91 Surcharged in Black or Red**

a

b

c

d

e

f

g

h

i

j

k

l

**1987-89** ***Perfs. as Before***

**Design A91**

**Series 1**

**(Plate Number in Parentheses)**

**On Nos. 1022-1039**

**1511** (a) 120c on 60c (2) 2.75
**1512** (b) 120c on 60c (2) 1.10
**1513** (a) 120c on 60c (5) 2.10
**1514** (c) 200c on 60c (5) 1.10
**1515** (c) 200c on 75c (5) 1.10

Obliterator invtd. in surch. on #1514-1515.

**1516** (d) 200c on 60c (7) 1.10
**1517** (d) 200c on 25c (8) 1.60
**1518** (e) 200c on 25c (8) 1.10
**1519** (a) 120c on 50c (9) 1.10
**1520** (b) 120c on 50c (9)
**1521** (f) 120c on 50c (9) 1.10
**1522** (g) 120c on 50c (9)
**1523** (a) 120c on 55c (9) 2.25
**1524** (f) 120c on 55c (9) 1.60
*a.* 120c on 55c #1032a 2.00
**1525** (g) 120c on 55c (9) 1.10
**1526** (a) 120c on 60c (10) 2.25
**1527** (d) 200c on 60c (10) 1.10
**1528** (h) $2 on 25c (12) 1.10

Surcharge on No. 1528 lacks obliterator.

**1529** (f) 120c on 55c (15) 1.40
**1530** (a) 200c on 55c (15) 5.50

Issued: #1518, 1528, 3/6; #1514-1515, 3/17; #1516-1517, 1522, 1525, 1527, 3/87; #1521, 1524, 1529, 7/87; #1511, 1513, 1519, 1523, 1526, 1530, 9/87; #1512, 1520, 7/88.

**On Nos. 1042-1061**

**1531** (b) 120c on 55c (17)
**1532** (d) 200c on 55c (17) 1.60
**1533** (a) 600c on 80c (17) 3.25
**1534** (a) 120c on 60c (19) 2.25
**1535** (d) 200c on 60c (19) 1.10
**1536** (a) 120c on 50c (22)
**1537** (b) 120c on 50c (22)
**1538** (f) 120c on 50c (22) 1.10
**1539** (c) 200c on 50c (22) 1.10
**1540** (i) 225c on 50c (22) 1.60
**1541** (a) 120c on 55c #1050a (22) 2.25
**1542** (f) 120c on 55c #1050a (22) 1.75
**1543** (c) 200c on 55c #1050a (22) 1.10
**1544** (h) $2 on 25c (23) 1.40
**1545** (a) 120c on 50c (24) 2.25
**1546** (a) 200c on 50c (24)
**1547** (d) 200c on 50c (24) 1.10
**1548** (a) 120c on 60c (31) 2.25
**1549** (d) 200c on 60c (31) 1.10

Issued: #1544, 3/6; #1539, 1543, 3/17; #1532, 1535, 1547, 1549, 3/87; #1540, 6/87; #1538, 1542, 7/87; #1533-1534, 1536, 1541, 1545-1546, 1548, 9/87; #1531, 1537, 7/88.

**On Nos. 1069-1091**

**1550** (b) 120c on 80c (39)
**1551** (a) 600c on 80c (39) 3.25
**1552** (g) $15 on 80c (39) 4.50
**1553** (i) 225c on #1402 (42) 1.60
**1554** (d) 200c on 60c (44) 1.10
**1555** (d) 200c on 60c (47) 1.10
**1556** (a) 120c on 50c (49)
**1557** (f) 120c on 50c (49) 1.50
**1558** (a) 120c on 55c #1085a (49) 2.25
**1559** (f) 120c on 55c (49) 1.40
*a.* 120c on 55c on #1085a 2.50
**1560** (d) 200c on 55c (49) 1.25
*a.* 200c on 55c on #1085a 4.50
**1561** (a) 120c on 60c (50) 2.25
**1562** (b) 120c on 60c (50)
**1563** (e) 200c on 25c (51) 1.40
**1564** (d) 200c on 25c (52) 1.10
**1565** (b) 120c on 30c (53) 1.10
*a.* 120c on 30c on #1090a
**1566** (a) 120c on 50c (53) 2.25
**1567** (d) 200c on 30c #1090a (53) 1.10
**1568** (a) 200c on 50c (53)
**1569** (d) 200c on 50c (53) 1.10
**1570** (g) $10 on 25c (53) 3.25
**1571** (g) $25 on 25c (53) 6.50

Surcharge on #1571 lacks obliterator and places a "$" in front of original denomination. #1570-1571 not issued without surcharge.

Issued: #1563, 3/6; #1552, 1554-1555, 1560, 1564, 1567, 1569-1571, 3/87; #1553, 6/87; #1557, 1559, 7/87; #1551, 1556, 1558, 1561, 1566, 1568, 9/87; #1550, 1562, 1565, 7/88.

**On Nos. 1092-1108, 1372**

**1572** (b) 120c on 45c (54)
**1573** (a) 120c on 60c (54) 2.25
**1574** (b) 120c on 60c (54) 1.10
**1575** (a) 200c on 50c (55)
**1576** (i) 225c on 60c (55) 1.60
**1577** (b) 120c on 60c (57) 1.10
*a.* New value at bottom
**1578** (d) 200c on 60c (57) 1.10
**1579** (b) 120c on 25c (59) 1.10
**1580** (a) 120c on 75c (60) 2.25
**1581** (c) 200c on 75c (60) 2.75
**1582** (b) 120c on 25c (61)
**1583** (b) 120c on 25c (63) 1.10
**1584** (a) 120c on 50c (64)
**1585** (f) 120c on 50c (64) 1.60
**1586** (a) 120c on 55c, wmkd. (64) 2.25
**1587** (f) 120c on 55c (64) 1.10
*a.* 120c on 55c on #1107a 1.40
**1588** (g) 120c on 55c (64) 1.10
*a.* 120c on 55c on #1107a 1.25

Surcharge on Nos. 1522, 1525, 1588-1588a does not contain date.

**1589** (a) 120c on 50c (65) 2.25
**1590** (a) 200c on 50c (65)
**1591** (d) 200c on 50c (65) 1.10
**1591A** (i) 225c on #1372 (65)

Issued: #1581, 3/17; #1578, 1588, 1591, 3/87; #1576, 6/87; #1585, 1587, 7/87; #1573, 1575, 1580, 1584, 1586, 1589-1590, 9/87; #1591A, 10/9/87; #1572, 1574, 1577, 1579, 1582-1583, 7/88.

**On Nos. 1112-1124**

**1592** (b) 120c on 40c (68) 1.10
*a.* New value at LL
**1593** (c) 200c on 40c (68) 1.10
*a.* Obliterator inverted 1.25
**1594** (a) 225c on 40c (68) 2.75
**1595** (a) 120c on 60c (69)
**1596** (b) 120c on 60c (69) 1.10
**1597** (b) 120c on 25c (70)
**1598** (b) 120c on 25c (71)
**1599** (a) 120c on 60c (71) 2.25
**1600** (d) 200c on 25c (71) 1.10
**1601** (d) 200c on 60c (71) 1.10
**1602** (j) 120c on 25c (72)
**1603** (d) 200c on 25c (72) 1.10
**1604** (b) 120c on 60c (73)
**1605** (d) 200c on 60c (73) .80
**1606** (b) 120c on 80c (74)
**1607** (a) 600c on 80c (74) 3.25
**1608** (g) $12 on 80c (74) 3.75
**1609** (b) 120c on 60c (75)
*a.* New value at bottom
**1610** (d) 200c on 60c (75) 1.10
**1611** (a) 225c on 65c (76) 2.75

Issued: #1593, 3/17; #1600-1601, 1603, 1605, 1608, 1610, 3/87; #1594-1595, 1599, 1611, 9/87; #1592, 1596-1598, 1604, 1606-1607, 1609, 7/88; #1602, 9/88.

**On Nos. 1126-1142**

**1612** (b) 120c on 40c (77)
*a.* New value at UL
**1613** (d) 200c on 40c (77) 1.10
**1614** (a) 200c on 45c (77) 3.25
**1615** (d) 200c on 45c (77) 1.10
**1616** (a) 200c on 45c (78) 3.25
**1617** (d) 200c on 45c (78) 1.10
**1618** (a) 120c on 60c (79) 3.25
**1619** (b) 120c on 60c (79)
**1620** (a) 225c on 65c (80) 3.25
**1621** (b) 120c on 45c (81)
**1622** (f) 120c on 55c (81) 1.40
**1623** (d) 200c on 45c (81) 1.10
**1624** (a) 200c on 55c (81) 4.50
**1625** (f) 120c on 55c (82) 1.75
**1626** (a) 200c on 55c (82) 11.50
**1627** (a) 120c on 75c (83) 3.25
**1628** (b) 120c on 90c (84)
**1629** (a) 200c on 45c (84) 3.25
**1630** (a) 200c on 45c (85) 3.25
**1631** (d) 200c on 45c (85) 1.10

Issued: #1613, 1615, 1617, 1623, 1631, 3/87; #1622, 1625, 7/87; #1614, 1616, 1618, 1620, 1624, 1626-1627, 1629-1630, 9/87; #1612, 1619, 1621, 1628, 7/88.

**On Nos. 1144-1153**

**1632** (b) 120c on 30c (86)
**1633** (b) 120c on 40c (86) 1.10
**1634** (d) 200c on 30c (86) 1.10
**1635** (d) 200c on 40c (86)
**1636** (a) 225c on 40c (86) 3.25
*a.* Inscribed "ONTOGLOS-SUM" 2.75
**1637** (a) 120c on 60c (87) 2.25
*a.* Surcharge reading up
**1638** (d) 200c on 60c (87) 1.10
**1639** (a) 225c on 65c (88) 2.75
**1640** (f) 120c on 55c (89) 1.40
**1641** (b) 120c on 90c (89)
**1642** (a) 200c on 55c (89) 5.25
**1643** (d) 225c on 90c (89) 1.10
**1644** (a) 120c on 40c (90) 2.25
**1645** (b) 120c on 40c (90) 1.10
**1646** (c) 200c on 40c (90) 1.10
**1647** (d) 200c on 40c (R) (90) 1.40
**1648** (c) 200c on 375c (90) 1.10
*a.* 200c on 375c #1153a 4.50
**1649** (a) 225c on 40c (90) 2.75
**1650** (i) 225c on 40c (90) 1.75
**1651** (k) 260c on 375c (90) 1.10

Issued: #1647, 2/9/87; #1646, 1648, 3/17/87; #1634-1635, 1638, 1643, 3/87; #1650, 6/87; #1640, 7/87; #1636-1637, 1639, 1642, 1644, 1649, 9/87; #1632-1633, 1641, 1645, 7/88; #1651, 10/88.

Surcharge on #1651 is placed over original value and has no obliterator.

**On Nos. 1154-1165**

**1652** (a) 120c on 40c (91) 2.25
**1653** (b) 120c on 40c (91) 1.10
*a.* New value at LR
**1654** (a) 225c on 40c (91) 3.25
**1655** (i) 225c on 40c (91) 1.60
**1656** (b) 120c on 50c (92)
**1657** (a) 120c on 75c (92) 2.75
**1658** (c) 200c on 50c (92)
**1659** (c) 200c on 75c (92) 1.10
**1660** (b) 120c on 60c (93)
**1661** (b) 120c on 80c (93)
**1662** (i) 225c on 60c (93) 1.75
**1663** (i) 225c on 80c (93) 1.75
**1664** (a) 600c on 80c (93)
**1665** (a) 120c on 60c (94)
**1666** (b) 120c on 60c (94)
**1667** (b) 120c on 60c (95) 1.10
**1668** (a) 120c on 75c (95) 3.50
**1669** (b) 120c on 40c (96)
**1670** (a) 225c on 65c (96) 2.75

**Miniature Sheets**

**1670A** Sheet of 4 27.50
*b.* (a) 600c on 130c #1412a (6)
*c.* (a) 600c on 200c #1412b (6)
*d.* (a) 600c on 260c #1412c (6)
*e.* (a) 600c on 330c #1412d (6)
**1670F** Sheet of 4 15.00
*g.* (i) 225c on #1393a (22)
*h.* (i) 225c on #1393b (22)
*i.* (i) 225c on #1393c (22)
*j.* (i) 225c on #1393d (22)

Issued: #1658-1659, 3/17/87; #1655, 1662-1663, 6/87; #1652, 1654, 1657, 1664-1665, 1668, 1670, 9/87; #1670F, 11/9/87; #1670A, 11/20/87; #1653, 1656, 1660-1661, 1666-1667, 1669, 7/88.

For overprints see Nos. 1975, 1979.

**Series 2**

**On Nos. 1168-1204**

**1671** (b) 120c on 90c (2) 1.10
**1672** (b) 120c on 50c (3) 1.10
**1673** (f) 120c on 50c (3) 1.10
**1674** (b) 200c on 90c (4)
**1675** (b) 120c on 50c (6) 1.10
**1676** (f) 120c on 50c (6) 1.10
**1677** (b) 120c on 30c (7) 1.10
**1678** (b) 120c on 70c (8) 1.10
**1679** (b) 120c on 70c (9) 1.10
*a.* New value at LR
**1680** (b) 120c on 90c (10) 1.10
**1681** (b) 120c on 70c (12) 1.10
*a.* New value at LL
**1682** (b) 120c on 50c (13) 1.10
**1683** (b) 120c on 90c (13)
**1684** (b) 120c on 30c (14) 1.10
*a.* New value at UR
**1685** (b) 120c on 50c (15) 1.10
**1686** (b) 120c on 85c (15)
**1687** (b) 120c on 70c (17) 13.50
**1688** (b) 120c on 85c (18) 1.10
**1689** (c) 200c on 85c (18)
**1690** (b) 120c on 50c (20) 1.10
**1691** (f) 120c on 50c (20) 1.75

Issued: #1689, 3/17/87; #1673, 1676, 1691, 7/87; #1671-1672, 1674-1675, 1677-1688, 1690, 7/88.

**On Nos. 1205-1240**

**1692** (b) 120c on 45c (21) 1.10
**1693** (b) 120c on 30c (22) 1.10
**1694** (l) 350c on 330c #O52 (23) 1.10
**1695** (b) 120c on 85c (24) 1.10
**1696** (j) 120c on 140c (R) (25) 1.10
**1697** (l) 250c on 225c #O46 (26) 1.10
*a.* New value at UL
**1698** (b) 120c on 60c (27) 2.25
**1699** (b) 120c on 90c (27)

**1700** (b) 120c on 30c (28) 1.10
*a.* New value at UL 2.25
**1701** (b) 120c on 30c (30) 1.10
**1702** (k) 240c on 140c (30) 1.10

No. 1702 not issued without surcharge.

**1703** (l) 150c on 175c #O44 (31) 1.10
**1704** (b) 120c on 50c (32) 1.10
**1705** (f) 120c on 50c (32) 1.10
**1706** (k) 240c on 140c (34) 1.10
**1707** (l) 125c on 140c #O42 (36) 1.10
**1708** (k) 120c on 140c (38) 1.10
**1709** (k) 120c on 140c (41) 1.10
**1710** (b) 200c on 80c (42) 1.10
**1711** (l) 150c on #O43 (43) 1.10

Issued: #1705, 7/87; #1692-1693, 1695, 1698-1701, 1704, 1710, 7/88; #1702, 1706, 10/88; #1696, 1708-1709, 2/22/89; #1694, 1697, 1703, 1707, 1711, 3/89.

**On Nos. 1245-1314**

**1712** (b) 120c on 35c (45) 1.10
**1713** (b) 120c on 85c (45)
**1714** (j) 120c on 140c (R) (52) 1.10
**1715** (k) 300c on 290c (53) 1.10
**1716** (j) 120c on 175c (R) (54) 1.10
**1717** (k) 170c on 175c (58) 1.10
**1718** (l) 250c on #O48 (59) 1.10
**1719** (j) 120c on 140c (R) (65) 1.10
**1720** (k) 250c on 280c (66) 1.10
**1721** (k) 250c on 280c (67) 1.10
**1722** (l) 250c on 230c #O47 (68) 1.10
**1723** (l) 250c on 260c #O49 (69) 1.10
*a.* New value at UR 1.10
**1724** (l) 600c on #O54 (70) 1.10
**1725** (l) $12 on #O55 (71) 1.10
**1726** (l) $15 on #O56 (84) 1.10
**1727** (k) 240c on 425c (87) 1.10
**1728** (l) 300c on 275c #O50 (90) 1.10
**1729** (l) 125c on 130c #O41 (92) 1.10
**1730** (l) 350c on #O53 (95) 1.10

On No. 1730 "Postage" reads up or down.
Issued: #1712-1713, 7/88; #1727, 10/88; #1714, 1716, 1719, 2/22/89; #1715, 1717-1718, 1720-1726, 1728-1730, 3/89.
Obliterator on Nos. 1708-1709, 1715, 1717, 1720-1721 has two thick bars.

**Stamps of Type A91 Overprinted**

p

m

n

o

**1987** ***Perfs. as Before***

**Series 1**

**1731** (m) 120c on #1021 (1) 5.25
**1732** (n) 130c on #1023 (3) 2.50
**1733** (m) 130c on #1028a (6) 5.00
**1734** (n) 130c on #1028 (6) 2.50
*a.* 130c on #1028a 2.50
**1735** (m) 120c on #1034 (11) 3.25
**1736** (m) 130c on #1037a (13) 3.25
**1737** (n) 130c on #1413 (13) 5.00
**1738** (o) 130c on #1037 (13) 1.10
*a.* 130c on #1037a 1.10
**1738B** (p) 130c on #1413 (13)
**1739** (n) 200c on #1038 (14) 2.50
**1740** (n) 130c on #1041 (16) 1.10
**1741** (n) 130c on #1342 (18) 1.10
**1742** (p) 130c on #1342 (18) 1.10
**1743** (m) 130c on #1047a (20) 2.25
**1744** (n) 130c on #1047a (20) 2.50
*a.* 130c on #1047 4.00
**1745** (m) 200c on #1048 (21) 2.25
**1746** (n) 200c on #1048 (21)
**1747** (m) 130c on #1055a (25) 4.50
**1748** (o) 130c on #1055 (25) 1.10
*a.* 130c on #1055a 1.10
**1749** (p) 150c on #1056 (26) 1.10
**1750** (m) 120c on #1058 (28) 5.00
**1751** (n) 130c on #1343 (29) 1.10
**1752** (p) 130c on #1343 (29) 1.10

Issued: #1732, 1734, 1737-1741, 1744, 1746, 1748, 1751, Mar; #1731, 1733, 1735-1736, 1743, 1745, 1747, 1750, July; #1738B, Nov. 20; #1742, 1749, 1752, Dec.

**1753** (n) 130c on #1344 (30) 1.10
**1754** (p) 130c on #1344 (30) 1.10
**1755** (n) 200c on #1063 (33) 1.10
**1756** (m) 120c on #1067 (37) 1.60
**1757** (n) 260c on #1070 (39) 2.25
**1758** (m) 150c on #1072a, ovpt. reading up (40) 2.00
*a.* 150c on #1072 3.25
**1759** (m) 150c on #1075a (42) 3.50
**1760** (m) 150c on #1402 (42) 5.50
**1761** (m) 200c on #1077a (43) 5.50
**1762** (m) 200c on #1403 (43) 5.50
**1763** (n) 200c on #1403 (43) 3.50
**1764** (m) 150c on #1080 reading down (45) 2.25
*a.* 150c on #1080a reading up 3.25
**1765** (m) 120c on #1081 (46) 8.50
**1766** (m) 120c on #1097 (56) 3.25
**1767** (m) 120c on #1099 (58) 3.25
**1768** (n) 130c on #1110 (66) 3.25
**1769** (p) 130c on #1110 (66) 1.10
**1770** (p) 120c on #1111 (67) 1.10
**1771** (n) 250c on #1122 (74) 1.40
**1772** (n) 200c on #1131 (79) 1.10
**1773** (o) 130c on #1155 (91) 1.60

**Miniature Sheets of 4**

**1774** (n) 200c on #1345 (4) 4.00
**1775** (n) 200c on 130c #1346 (20) 5.50

**Series 2**

**1776** (n) 200c on #1169 (2) 7.00
**1777** (n) 200c on #1183 (9) 1.75

Issued: #1753, 1755, 1757, 1763, 1768, 1771-1777, Mar.; #1756, 1758, 1759-1762, 1764-1767, July. #1754, 1769-1770, Dec.
Overprint reads up on #1759, 1761. Overprint reads down on #1731, 1735, 1745, 1750, 1755, 1758a, 1760, 1762, 1763, 1764.
See Nos. 1813-1814, 1844 for other stamps overprinted "1987" only.

**Nos. 1337, 1339, 1341 Surcharged**

**1987, Mar. 6** ***Perfs. as Before***

**1777A** A92 200c on #1337 6.00 2.00
**1777B** A92 200c on #1339 6.00 2.00
**1777C** A92 200c on #1341 6.00 2.00
*Nos. 1777A-1777C (3)* 18.00 6.00

See note following No. 1341.

**Nos. 134, 136, 139a, and 192 Surcharged "Post Office / Corp. / 1977-1987" in Blue**

***Perfs. as Before***

**1987, Feb. 17 Litho. Wmk. 364**

**1778** A28 25c on 2c #134 .25 .25
**1779** A28 25c on 5c #136 .25 .25
**1780** A28 25c on #192 .25 .25
**1781** A28 25c on 15c #139a 5.00 .50
**1782** A28 60c on 15c #139a 10.00 .40
**1783** A28 $1.20 on 2c #134 .85 .85
**1784** A28 $1.30 on 15c #139a 11.00 2.75
*Nos. 1778-1784 (7)* 27.60 5.25

**Nos. 1032, 1032a Surcharged "12th World Orchid Conference" and "TOKYO JAPAN"**

**1987, Mar. 12 Unwmk.** ***Perf. 14***

**1785** A91 650c on 55c #1032 11.00 6.50
*a.* 650c on 55c #1032a 12.00 7.00

**No. 280 Surcharged with Names of Post Offices Operating in 1885**

Overprints: a, AGRICOLA. b, BAGOTVILLE. c, BOURDA. d, BUXTON. e, CABACABURI. f, CAR- / MICHAEL STREET. g, COTTON / TREE. h, DUNOON. i, FELLOW- / SHIP. j, GROVE. k, HACKNEY. l, LEONORA. m, 1987. n, MALLALI. o, PROVI- / DENCE. p, RELIANCE. q, SPARTA. r, STEWART- / VILLE. s, TARLOGY. t, T.P.O. / BERBICE RIV. u, T.P.O. / DEM. RIV. v, T.P.O. / ESSEQ. RIV. w, T.P.O. / MASSARUNI / RIV. x, TUSCHEN / (De / VRIENDEN). y, ZORG.

***Perf. 14x13½***

**1987, Mar. 17 Wmk. 364**

**1786** Sheet of 25, #a.-y. 42.50 35.00
*a.-y.* A66 25c on 10c, any single 1.50 1.25

British Guiana Post Office, 125th Anniv.

Columbus' Discovery of America, 500th Anniv. (in 1992) — A98

Paintings: 120c, Discovery of America, by Dali. 225c, Preparations Before the Journey, by unknown artist. 360c, Catholic Kings from Prado Museum.
$6, Columbus' Fleet, by R. Monleon.

**1987, Mar. 30 Litho.** ***Perf. 13½***

**1787** A98 120c multicolored 1.75 1.00
**1788** A98 225c multicolored 4.00 3.00
**1789** A98 360c multicolored 6.25 3.00
*a.* Strip of 3, #1787-1789 13.50 13.50

**Souvenir Sheet**

**1790** A98 $6 gold & multi 15.00 15.00

No. 1790 exists with silver border.

**No. 289A Ovptd. "28 MARCH 1927 / PAA / GEO-POS"**

**1987, Mar. 28** ***Perf. 13½x13***

**1811** A66 $10 on #289A 24.00 13.00

First Georgetown to Port-of-Spain Flight, 50th Anniv.

**No. 285 Surcharged**

**1987, Apr. 6** ***Perf. 14x13½***

**1812** A66 25c on 40c #285 12.50 .40

**Nos. 87-88, 90, 287 Surcharged or Overprinted "1987"**

**1987, Apr.** ***Perfs. as Before***

**Watermarks and Printing Methods as Before**

**1813** A14 25c on #88 .75 .10
**1814** A66 $1 on #287 15.00 1.00
**1815** A14 120c on 6c #87 .90 .25
**1816** A14 320c on 6c #87 1.50 .75
**1817** A14 500c on 40c #90 2.00 1.40
*Nos. 1813-1817 (5)* 20.15 3.50

Issued: #1813, 1815-1817, Apr. 21; #1814, Apr.

**No. 1461 Ovptd. "CAPEX '87"**

**1987, June 10 Litho.** ***Perf. 14***

**1822** A96 320c Pair, #a.-b. 5.50 5.50
*c.* on #1461, imperf. between 11.00

For surcharges see Nos. 2030, E15.

**Nos. 626-628 Ovptd. "1987"**

**Wmk. 314 Upright**

**1987, July 15 Engr.** ***Perf. 12½x13***

**1823** A60 $1.20 on #626 .90 .25

**Wmk. 314 Sideways**

**1824** A60 $1.30 on #627 10.00 .75
**1825** A60 $2.40 on #628 12.00 3.75
*Nos. 1823-1825 (3)* 22.90 4.75

A99

A100

Locomotives — A101

#1826a, 1827a, Alexandra 4. #1826b, 1827b, Diesel locomotive facing right. #1826c, 1827c, Steam locomotive facing right. #1826d, 1827d, Diesel locomotive No. 21 facing left.
#1829a, 1830b, Alexandra 4. #1829b, 1830a, Diesel locomotive. #1829c, 1830d, Steam locomotive facing right. #1829d, 1830c, Diesel locomotive No. 21. #1830e, Photograph of trains in Georgetown Station. #1831, Steam locomotive pulling cattle cars, map of routes from Parika to Vreedenhoop and from Georgetown to Rosignol.

**1987, Aug. 3** ***Perf. 15***

**1826** Block of 4 2.00 2.00
*a.-d.* A99 $1.20 green, any single .40 .40
**1827** Block of 5 5.00 5.00
*a.-d.* A99 $3.20 blue, any single .85 .85
*e.* A100 $3.20 blue .85 .85
**1828** A101 $12 shown 4.00 4.00
*Nos. 1826-1828 (3)* 11.00 11.00

**1987, Dec. 4**

**1829** Block of 4 2.40 2.40
*a.-d.* A99 $1.20 rose lake, any single .50 .50
**1830** Block of 5 6.25 6.25
*a.-d.* A99 $3.30 blk, any single 1.10 1.10
*e.* A100 $3.30 black 1.10 1.10
**1831** A101 $10 multi 4.50 4.50
*Nos. 1829-1831 (3)* 13.15 13.15

Sizes: #1827e, 1830e, 84x57mm. #1828, 1831, 90x40mm.
For surcharges see #E12-E13. For overprints see #1910-1911, 1935-1938, 2024-2028F, 2054, 2056.

**No. 287 Ovptd. "FAIREY NICHOLL / 15 AUG 1927 / GEO-MAB" or "FAIREY NICHOLL / 8 AUG 1927 / GEO-MAZ"**

**1987, Aug. 7 Litho.** ***Perf. 13½x13***

**1832** A66 $1 "MAB" on #287 12.00 11.00
**1833** A66 $1 "MAZ" on #287 12.00 11.00
*a.* Pair, #1832-1833 30.00 27.50

**No. 1291A Surcharged "CRISTOVAO COLOMBO / 1492 — 1992" (#1834) or "CHRISTOPHE COLOMB / 1492 — 1992" (#1835)**

**No. 1461c Surcharged "THE PASSING OF HALLEY'S COMET: / PROPHESY OF THE ARRIVAL OF / HERNAN CORTES 1519. / V CENTENARY OF THE LANDING OF / CHRISTOPHER COLUMBUS / IN THE AMERICAS"**

**Unwmk.**

**1987, Oct. 9 Litho.** ***Perf. 14***

**1834** A91 950c on 900c #1291A 3.00 3.00
**1835** A91 950c on 900c #1291A 3.00 3.00
*a.* Pair, #1834-1835 7.00 7.00

***Imperf***

**1836** A96 $20 on 320c #1461c 8.50 8.50

**Nos. 135-136 Surcharged "DEEPAVALI / 1987"**

**1987, Nov. 2 Litho.** ***Perf. 13x13½***

**1837** A28 25c on 3c #135 2.25 .40
**1838** A28 $3 on 5c #136 8.00 3.50

No. 43 Surcharged "CHRISTMAS / 1987" in Red

No. 1502 Surcharged "1987" in Blue

**1987, Nov. 9** *Perfs. as Before*

**Watermarks and Printing Methods as Before**

**1839** A7 20c on 6c #43

**Miniature Sheet**

**1840** A88 120c on 60c #1502

No. 329 Overprinted "1987"

No. 920 Surcharged "Protect Our Heritage '87" in Red

Nos. 1037, 1040, 1056, 1110-1111, 1494 Surcharged "PROTECT OUR HERITAGE '87"

**1987, Dec. 9** *Perfs. as Before*

**Watermarks and Printing Methods as Before**

**1844** A77 30c Sheet of 12, #a.-l, on #329 7.00 7.00
**1845** A91 120c on #1111 1.50 1.50
**1846** A91 130c on #1110 1.75 1.75
**1847** A91 150c on #1056 2.25 2.25
**1848** A91 180c on #1040 2.50 2.50
**1849** A91 320c on #1137 3.00 3.00
**1850** A89 320c Triptych, #a.-c, on 120c #920 9.00 9.00
**1851** A91 650c on #1494 5.00 5.00
*Nos. 1844-1851 (8)* 32.00 32.00

1988 Summer Olympics, Seoul — A102

**1987, Dec. 30 Litho.** *Perf. 13½x14*

**1852** A102 $2 Jumping 2.50 2.25
**1853** A102 $3 Discus 3.75 3.25
**1854** A102 $5 Vase 6.50 5.50
*a.* Strip of 3, #1852-1854 13.50 13.50

**Souvenir Sheet**

***Perf. 14***

**1855** A102 $3.50 Olympic Rings, horiz. 10.00 10.00

Christmas 1987 — A103

Paintings: #a, The Virgin of the Rocks, by Da Vinci. #b, Virgin with Grapes, by Mignard. #c, Sacred Family, by Raphael. #d, Virgin Mary, by Lucas Cranach. No. 1857, Adoration of Three Kings, by Rubens.

**1988, Jan. 7 Litho.** *Perf. 14*

**1856** A103 $2 Strip of 4, #a.-d. 7.75 7.75

**Souvenir Sheet**

**1857** A103 $10 Sheet of 1 13.50 13.50

Dated 1987.

Nos. 397, 405 and 651 Ovptd. or Surcharged "*AUSTRALIA* / 1987 JAMBOREE 1988" in Red

**1988, Jan. 7 Litho.** *Perf. 13½x13*

**1858** A17 $4.40 on #405
**1859** A17 $10 on #397
**1860** A17 $10 on #651
**1861** A17 $10 on #405
*a.* $10 on #405a
Nos. 1858-1861 (4) 10.00

Obliterator on Nos. 1859-1861 is red fleur-de-lis. Size and location of overprint varies.

Nos. 68 and 70 Surcharged "IFAD / For a World / Without Hunger"

***Perf. 14x14½***

**1988, Jan. 26 Photo. Wmk. 364**

**1862** A7 25c on 1c #68 2.00 .30
**1863** A7 $5 on 3c #70 7.00 3.00
*Nos. 1862-1863 (2)* 9.00 3.30

No. 1862 uses new denomination as obliterator and No. 1863 uses "X."

Flora and Fauna — A104

Mushrooms — #1864: a, Corprinus comatus. b, Amanita muscaria. c, Pholiota aurivella. d, Laccaria amethstina.

Birds — #1865: a, Starling. b, Reed warbler. c, Kingfisher. d, Goldcrest.

Cats — #1866: a, Himalayan. b, American shorthaired. c, Maine coon. d, Abyssinian.

Cactus flowers — #1866: e, Sulcorebutia densiseta. f, Subutia hyalacantha. g, Echinopsis. h, Lobivia polycephala.

Nos. 1866a-1866h horiz.

**1988, Jan. 28** *Perf. 14*

**1864** A104 $2 Strip of 4, #a.-d. 10.50 10.50
**1865** A104 $2 Strip of 4, #a.-d. 9.50 9.50

**Miniature Sheet**

***Perf. 14x13½***

**1866** A104 $2 Sheet of 8, #a.-h. 13.00 13.00

Dated 1987.

Santa Maria — A105

Ships: a, Santa Maria. b, Grande Francoise. #1869, San Martin, horiz.

**1988, Feb. 10 Litho.** *Perf. 13½x14*

**1867** A105 $7 Pair, #a.-b., pale yel & multi 6.00 6.00
**1868** A105 $7 Pair, #a.-b., bl & multi 6.00 6.00

**Souvenir Sheet**

***Perf. 14***

**1869** A105 $7 silver & multi 12.00 12.00

Discovery of America, 500th anniv. (in 1992). Nos. 1867-1868 printed checkerwise with se-tenant labels describing ship dimensions. No. 1869 exists with gold border.

Nos. 136, 139a, and 146 Surcharged "Republic / Day / 1988" in Blue

***Perfs. as Before***

**1988, Feb. 23 Litho. Wmk. 364**

**1870** A28 25c on 5c #136 .25 .25
**1871** A28 120c on 15c #139a 6.50 .75
**1872** A28 $10 on $2 #146 2.00 2.00
*Nos. 1870-1872 (3)* 8.75 3.00

No. 283A Surcharged with Names of Post Offices Operating in 1900

Overprints: a, Albouystown. b, Anns Grove. c, Amacura. d, Arakaka. e, Baramanni. f, Cuyuni. g, Hope Placer. h, HMPS. i, Kitty. j, M'M'Zorg. k, Maccaseema. l, 1988. m, Morawhanna. n, Naamryck. o, Purini. p, Potaro / Landing. q, Rockstone. r, Rosignol. s, Stanleytown. t, Santa Rosa. u, Tumatumari. v, Weldaad. w, Wismar. x, TPO Berbice / Railway.

**1988, Apr. 5** *Perf. 14x13½*

**1873** A66 25c Sheet of 25, #a.-k., m.-x., 2 #l. 32.50 32.50

British Guiana Post Office, 125th Anniv.

No. 725 Surcharged "Olympic / Games / 1988"

***Perf. 14½x14***

**1988, May 3 Litho. Wmk. 373**

**1897** A73 120c Sheet of 12, #a.-l. 18.00 18.00

Nos. 136-137 and 146 Surcharged "Caricom Day / 1988"

***Perf. 13x13½***

**1988, June 15 Litho. Wmk. 364**

**1898** A28 25c on 5c #136 .90 .25
**1899** A28 $1.20 on 6c #137 .90 .25
**1900** A28 $10 on $2 #146 4.50 4.00
*Nos. 1898-1900 (3)* 6.30 4.50

No. 286A Overprinted

Overprints: a, 1988. b, WHO / 1948-1988.

**1988, June 17 Litho.** *Perf. 14x13½*

**1901** Sheet of 25, 24 #a., 1 #b. 27.50 25.00
*a.* A28 60c any single .40 .25
*b.* A28 60c 17.50 17.50

World Health Day, 40th anniv.

No. 929d Overprinted as Indicated

Nos. 1053a, 1063, 1131, and 1161 Overprinted "CONSERVE / WATER"

Overprints: No. 1903, "CONSERVE TREES" on ocher stamp, "CONSERVE ELECTRICITY on green stamp, "CONSERVE WATER on brown stamp. No. 1904, "CONSERVE ELECTRICITY" on ocher stamp, "CONSERVE WATER on green stamp, "CONSERVE TREES on brown stamp. No. 1905, "CONSERVE WATER" on ocher stamp, "CONSERVE TREES on green stamp, "CONSERVE ELECTRICITY on brown stamp.

***Perfs. as Before***

**1988, July 15 Litho.**

**Watermarks as Before**

**1903** Triptych 3.50 3.50
*a.-c.* A90 120c any single .90 .60
**1904** Triptych 3.50 3.50
*a.-c.* A90 120c any single .90 .60
**1905** Triptych 3.50 3.50
*a.-c.* A90 120c any single .90 .90
**1906** A91 200c on #1063 1.10 1.10
**1907** A91 200c on #1131 1.10 1.10
**1908** A91 225c on #1053a 1.10 1.10
**1909** A91 350c on #1161 1.10 1.10
*Nos. 1903-1909 (7)* 14.90 14.90

Location and size of overprint varies.

Nos. 1826a and 1829a Ovptd. "BEWARE / OF ANIMALS" (a.)

Nos. 1826b and 1829b Ovptd. "BEWARE / OF CHILDREN" (b.)

Nos. 1826c and 1829c Ovptd. "DRIVE SAFELY" (c.)

Nos. 1826d and 1829d Ovptd. "DO NOT / DRINK AND DRIVE" (d.)

**Unwmk.**

**1988, July 15 Litho.** *Perf. 15*

**Block of 4, #a.-d.**

**1910** A99 $1.20 on #1826 7.50 7.50
**1911** A99 $1.20 on #1829 7.50 7.50
*Nos. 1910-1911 (2)* 15.00 15.00

No. 287 Ovptd. or Surcharged

***Perf. 13½x13***

**1988, July Litho. Wmk. 364**

**1912** A66 $1 "1988" on #287 8.00 1.50
**1913** A66 120c on $1 #287 8.00 1.50

No. 421 Surcharged with New Value and "1988"

**1988? Litho.** *Perf. 13½x14*

**1913A** A80 $1.20 on $1.10 on $3 #421

Nos. 1037a, 1047a, 1056-1057, 1066-1068, 1097, 1099, 1109-1109a, 1110-1111, 1113, 1115, 1122, 1125, 1129, 1147, 1149, and 1155 Ovptd. "CONSERVE / OUR RESOURCES"

**1988, July** *Perf. 14*

**Watermarks as Before**

**Series 1**

**Plate Numbers in Parentheses**

**1914** 130c on #1037a (13) 1.00 .75
*a.* Overprint inverted 7.50

#1914a probably is as common as #1914.

**1915** A91 130c on #1047a (20) 1.00 .75
**1916** A91 150c on #1056 (26) 1.00 .75
**1917** A91 120c on #1057 (27) 1.00 .75
**1918** A91 120c on #1066 (36) 1.00 .75
**1919** A91 120c on #1067 (37) 1.00 .75
**1920** A91 130c on #1068 (38) 1.00 .75
**1921** A91 120c on #1097 (56) 1.00 .75
**1922** A91 120c on #1099 (58) 1.00 .75
**1923** A91 100c on #1109 (65) 1.00 .75
*a.* 100c on #1109a
**1924** A91 130c on #1110 (66) 1.00 .75
**1925** A91 120c on #1111 (67) 1.00 .75
**1926** A91 100c on #1113 (68) 1.00 .75
**1927** A91 120c on #1115 (69) 1.00 .75
**1928** A91 250c on #1122 (74) 1.00 .75
**1929** A91 150c on #1125 (76) 1.00 .75
**1930** A91 150c on #1129 (78) 1.00 .75
**1931** A91 150c on #1147 (87) 1.00 .75
**1932** A91 100c on #1149 (88) 1.00 .75
**1933** A91 130c on #1155 (91) 1.00 .75

Nos. 1827a-1827d and 1830a-1830d Ovptd. with Red Cross

**1988, Aug. 3 Litho.** *Perf. 15*

**1935** A99 $3.20 Pair, #a.-b., on #1827a, 1827c 3.50 3.50
**1936** A99 $3.20 Pair, #a.-b., on #1827b, 1827d 3.50 3.50
**1937** A99 $3.30 Pair, #a.-b., on #1830a, 1830c 3.50 3.50
**1938** A99 $3.30 Pair, #a.-b., on #1830b, 1830d 3.50 3.50
*Nos. 1935-1938 (4)* 14.00 14.00

Nos. 1038, 1131 Ovptd. and Nos. 1147, 1175 Surcharged "1928-1988 / CRICKET / JUBILEE"

**1988, Sept. 5 Litho.** *Perf. 14*

**Watermarks as Before**

**Plate Numbers in Parentheses**

**1939** A91 200c on #1038 (14) 22.50 22.50
**1940** A91 200c on #1131 (79) 1.25 .50
**1941** A91 800c on 150c #1147 (87) 9.50 9.50
**1942** A91 800c on 160c #1175 (5) 3.75 3.75
*Nos. 1939-1942 (4)* 37.00 36.25

**Series 1**

**Plate Numbers in Parentheses**

Nos. 1063, 1081, 1139, 1147, 1161, 1185, 1219, 1232, and 1305 Ovptd. and No. 1227 Surcharged "OLYMPIC GAMES / 1988"

**1988, Sept. 16 Unwmk.**

**1943** A91 200c on #1063 (33) .70 .70
**1944** A91 120c on #1081 (46) .70 .70
**1945** A91 300c on #1139 (83) .70 .70
**1946** A91 150c on #1147 (87) .70 .70
**1947** A91 350c on #1161 (94) .90 .90

**Series 2**

**1948** A91 320c on #1185 (10) .90 .90
**1949** A91 350c on #1219 (29) .90 .90
**1950** A91 300c on 360c #1227 (34) .90 .90
**1951** A91 130c on #1232 (38) .90 .90
**1952** A91 330c on #1305 (82) .90 .90

Overprint reads up on No. 1947.

Type A83 Ovptd. or Surcharged "OLYMPICS 1988" (a.) or "KOREA 1988" (b.)

**1988 Litho. Wmk. 364** *Perf. 13½*

**1953** A83 $1.20 Pair, #a.-b. 1.25 1.25
**1954** A83 130c on $1.20, pair, #a.-b. 1.25 1.25
**1955** A83 150c on $1.20, pair, #a.-b. 1.25 1.25
**1956** A83 200c on $1.20, pair, #a.-b. 1.50 1.50
**1957** A83 350c on $1.20, pair, #a.-b. 1.75 1.75
*c.* Strip of 5, #1953a-1957a 7.00 7.00
*d.* Strip of 5, #1953b-1957b 7.00 7.00

Overprint obliterates inscription spelled "LOS ANGELLES."

No. 1087 Ovptd. and No. 1143 Surcharged "V CENTENARY OF / THE LANDING OF / CHRISTOPHER COLUMBUS / IN THE AMERICAS"

**Unwmk.**

**1988, Oct. 12 Litho.** *Perf. 14*

**1958** A91 320c on #1087 2.75 .75
**1959** A91 $15 on 360c #1143 5.00 5.00
*Nos. 1958-1959 (2)* 7.75 5.75

Nos. 1027, 1036, 1040, 1046, 1054, 1062, 1070, 1071, 1074, 1076, 1079, 1102, 1104, 1133, 1137 and 1143 Surcharged "SEASON'S / GREETINGS" in Blue or Black

Nos. 1053, 1053a, 1102, 1591A and 1670F Ovptd. or Surcharged "SEASON'S / GREETINGS / 1988" in Blue

**1988, Nov. 10** *Perfs. as Before*

**Watermarks and Printing Methods as Before**

**Plate Numbers in Parentheses**

**1960** A91 120c on 100c #1027 (6) 2.00
**1961** A91 120c on 100c #1036 (13) 2.00
**1962** A91 240c on 180c #1040 (15) (Bk) 1.00
**1963** A91 120c on 100c #1046 (20) 2.00
**1964** A91 225c on #1053 (24) 1.00
*a.* 225c on #1053a 2.50

**1965** A91 120c on 100c #1054 (25) 2.00
**1966** A91 150c on #1062 (32) (Bk) 1.00
**1967** A91 260c on #1070 (39) (Bk) 1.00
**1968** A91 120c on 100c #1071 (40) 2.00
**1969** A91 120c on 100c #1074 (42) 2.00
**1970** A91 120c on 100c #1076 (43) 2.00
**1971** A91 120c on 100c #1079 (45) 2.00
**1972** A91 225c on #1102 (60) (Bk) 1.00
**1973** A91 225c on #1102 (60) 1.00
**1974** A91 150c on #1104 (62) (Bk) 1.00
**1975** A91 225c on #1591A (65) 1.50
**1976** A91 330c on #1133 (80) (Bk) 1.00
**1977** A91 320c on #1137 (82) (Bk) 1.00
**1978** A91 360c on #1143 (85) (Bk) 1.00
*Nos. 1960-1978 (19)* 27.50

**Miniature Sheet**

**1979** A91 225c on #1670F (22) 4.75 4.75

Size and location of overprint varies.

Nos. 72, 713 and 932 Surcharged or Ovptd. "CHRISTMAS / 1988" in Red or Black

**1988, Nov. 16** ***Perfs. as Before***

**Watermarks and Printing Methods as Before**

**1981** A7 20c on 6c #72 .30 .25
**1982** A86 Block of 4 (Bk) 2.25 2.25
*a.* 120c on #713a .50 .50
*b.* 120c on 130c #713b .50 .50
*c.* 120c on 150c #713c .50 .50
*d.* 120c on 200c #713d .50 .50
**1983** A90a 500c on 330c #932 2.50 2.50
*Nos. 1981-1983 (3)* 5.05 5.00

Overprint reads up on No. 1983.

Nos. 288, 289, and 289A Surcharged or Ovptd. for Prevention of AIDS

Beginnning of overprint reads: Nos. 1984a, 1985e, "Get information..." Nos. 1984b, 1985a, "Get the facts..." Nos. 1984c, 1985b, "Say no to drugs..." Nos. 1984d, 1985c, $2, $5, $10, "Protect yourself..." Nos. 1984e, 1985d, "Be compassionate..."

***Perf. 13½x13***

**1988, Dec. 1 Litho. Wmk. 364**

**1984** A66 120c Strip of 5, #a.-e., on #289 18.50 18.50
**1985** A66 120c Strip of 5, #a.-e., on #289A 18.50 18.50
**1986** A66 $2 on #288 12.00 3.00
**1987** A66 $5 on #289 14.00 7.50
**1988** A66 $10 on #289A 16.00 12.00
*Nos. 1984-1988 (5)* 79.00 59.50

For surcharge, see No. 4176.

1988 Winter Olympics, Calgary A106

Design: $3.50, Olympic rings.

**1988, Dec. 1** ***Perf. 14***

**1989** A106 $7 Downhill skiing 11.00 11.00

**Souvenir Sheet**

**1990** A106 $3.50 Sheet of 1 6.00 6.00

No. 1989 exists in souvenir sheet of 1. Value $40.

Christmas — A107

Paintings: No. 1991a, Virgin and Child Between St. George and St. Catherine, by Titian. b, Adoration of the Magi, by Titian.
No. 1992a, Holy Family, by Rubens. b, Adoration of the Shepherds, by Rubens.
$8, The Madonna, by Titian.

***Perf. 14x13½, 13½x14***

**1988, Dec. 15 Litho.**

**1991** A107 $2 Pair, #a.-b. 7.00 7.00
**1992** A107 $2 Pair, #a.-b. 7.00 7.00

**Souvenir Sheet**

***Perf. 13½x14***

**1993** A107 $8 multicolored 17.50 17.50

Nos. 1991a-1991b, 1992a-1992b exist in souvenir sheets of 1.

**Abolition of Slavery Type of 1985**

**1988, Dec. 16 Litho.** ***Perf. 14***

**Designs as Before**

**1994** A93 25c brown & black .25 .25
**1995** A93 60c magenta & black .50 .50
**1996** A93 130c green & black 1.00 1.00
**1997** A93 150c blue & black 1.25 1.25
*Nos. 1994-1997 (4)* 3.00 3.00

Nos. 1087, 1167, and 1200 Surcharged "SALUTING WINNERS / OLYMPIC GAMES / 1988"

**Unwmk.**

**1989, Jan. 3 Litho.** ***Perf. 14***

**1998** A91 $5.50 on 560c #1167 1.75 1.25
**1999** A91 $9 on 320c #1200 2.25 2.25
**2000** A91 $10.50 on 320c #1087 3.00 3.00
*Nos. 1998-2000 (3)* 7.00 6.50

Miniature Sheets

Red Cross, 125th Anniv. — A108

Designs: No. 2001, Henri Dunant, vert. No. 2002, First maritime ambulance. No. 2003, Red Cross hospital ship in African War. No. 2004, Red Cross air ambulance. No. 2005, Red Cross train.
Nos. 2001-2004 printed with red cross in center of sheet. Each stamp contains part of the red cross at the: a, LR. b, LL. c, UR. d, UL.

***Perf. 13½x14, 14x13½***

**1989, Jan. 5 Litho.**

**2001** A108 $2 Sheet of 4, #a.-d. 10.00 10.00
**2002** A108 $2 Sheet of 4, #a.-d. 10.00 10.00
**2003** A108 $2 Sheet of 4, #a.-d. 10.00 10.00
**2004** A108 $2 Sheet of 4, #a.-d. 10.00 10.00
*Nos. 2001-2004 (4)* 40.00 40.00

**Souvenir Sheet**

***Perf. 14x13½***

**2005** A108 $7 Sheet of 1 11.00 11.00

Dated 1988.

Trains — A109

Designs: a, Hernalser sleeping carriage. b, 5 Forney locomotive. c, Austrian sleeping carriage. d, Pacific 231 locomotive.
$10, First Japanese imperial train.

**1989, Jan. 5 Litho.** ***Perf. 14***

**2006** A109 $2 Sheet of 4, #a.-d. 15.00 15.00

**Souvenir Sheet**

**2007** A109 $10 multicolored 11.00 11.00

Nos. 2006a-2006d exist in souvenir sheets of 1. Value, each $3.75.

Dated 1988.

Naval Airship LZ 92, 1916 — A110

#2008: a, Astronaut on moon. b, Graf Zeppelin over San Francisco Bay, 1929. c, Testu-Brissy on horseback ascending in balloon, 1798.
#2009, Graf Zeppelin LZ 127.

**1989, Jan. 26** ***Perf. 14***

**2007A** A110 $2 black 3.00 3.00
**2008** A110 $2 Strip of 3, #a.-c. 8.00 8.00

**Souvenir Sheet**

**2009** A110 $2 Sheet of 1 10.00 6.00

Nos. 2007A, 2008b, 2009, Ferdinand von Zeppelin, 150th birth anniv. in 1988. No. 2008a, 1st moon landing, 20th anniv. in 1989. The inscriptions on Nos. 2007A and 2009 are in error. Dated 1988.

Mushrooms — A111

#2010: a, Cortinarius bolaris. b, Cortinarius laniger. c, Tricholoma sulphureum. d, Lepiota cristata.
#2011, Sarcoscypha coccinea, vert.

**1989, Feb. 1** ***Perf. 14x13½***

**2010** A111 $2 Block of 4, #a.-d. 15.00 15.00

**Souvenir Sheet**

***Perf. 13½x14***

**2011** A111 $5 Sheet of 1 11.00 11.00

Dated 1988.

Boy Scout Jamboree, Australia — A112

Design: $8, Scouts of different races.

**1989, Feb. 10**

**2012** A112 $10 grn, black & yel 15.00 15.00

**Souvenir Sheet**

**2013** A112 $8 Sheet of 1 15.00 15.00

Dated 1988. #2012 exists in souvenir sheet of 1.

1988 Summer Olympics, Seoul — A113

Emblem of South American Soccer Federation — A113a

Designs: No. 2014, Florence Griffith-Joyner. No. 2015, Carl Lewis. No. 2016, Equestrian. No. 2017, Runners, horiz. No. 2018, City skyline, Olympic Rings, horiz. No. 2019, 1988 & 1992 Olympic mascots, horiz. No. 2022, Griffith-Joyner, Lewis, horiz. No. 2023, Cosmic Athlete by Dali, horiz.

**1989, Feb. 15 Litho.** ***Perf. 14***

**2014** A113 $2 multicolored 3.50 3.50
**2015** A113 $2 multicolored 3.50 3.50
**2016** A113 $2 multicolored 3.50 3.50
**2017** A113 $2 multicolored 3.50 3.50
**2018** A113 $2 multicolored 3.50 3.50
**2019** A113 $2 multicolored 3.50 3.50
**2020** A113a $2 multicolored 3.50 3.50

**Souvenir Sheets**

**2022** A113 $3.50 multicolored 15.00 15.00
**2023** A113 $3.50 multicolored 15.00 15.00

No. 2023 exists with gold border and inscriptions. Nos. 2014-2020 inscribed 1988.
An additional stamp was issued in this set. The editors would like to examine any examples.

Nos. 1826, 1829 and 1831 Ovptd. "REPUBLIC DAY 1989" in Red

**1989, Feb. 22 Litho.** ***Perf. 15***

**2024** A99 $1.20 Block of 4, #a.-d., on #1826 4.50 4.50
**2025** A99 $1.20 Block of 4, #a.-d., on #1829 4.50 4.50
**2026** A101 $10 on #1831 7.50 7.50
*Nos. 2024-2026 (3)* 16.50 16.50

Nos. 1827a-1827d and 1830a-1830d Surcharged in Red

**1989, Feb. 22**

**2027** A99 $5 Pair, #a.-b., on $3.20 #a., c. 7.50 7.50
**2028** A99 $5 Pair, #a.-b., on $3.20 #b., d. 7.50 7.50
**2028C** A99 $5 Pair, #d.-e., on $3.30 #a., c. 7.50 7.50
**2028F** A99 $5 Pair, #g-h., on $3.30 #b., d. 7.50 7.50

Nos. 1461, 1822 Surcharged in Red

**1989, Feb. 22 Litho.** ***Perf. 14***

**2029** A96 $10 #a.-b. on #1461 10.00 10.00
**2030** A96 $10 #a.-b. on #1822 10.00 10.00

No. 1188 Surcharged "EASTER"

**1989, Mar. 22** ***Perf. 14***

**2031** A91 Sheet of 4 on #1188 5.00 5.00
*a.* 125c on 320c #1188 .50 .50
*b.* 250c on 320c #1188 1.00 1.00
*c.* 300c on 320c #1188 1.25 1.25
*d.* 350c on 320c #1188 1.50 1.50

No. 927 Surcharged

**1989, Mar. Wmk. 364 *Perf. 14***
2032 A90 250c on 25c #927 6.00 1.25

Inscribed "1986."

No. 1197 Surcharged "RED CROSS / 1948 / 1988"

**1989, Apr. Unwmk. *Perf. 14***
2033 A91 375c on 45c #1197 5.50 5.50
2034 A91 425c on 45c #1197 5.50 5.50

Guyana Red Cross, 40th anniv.

#1263 & 1252 Surcharged in Pairs "ALL FOR / HEALTH" (a.) or "HEALTH / FOR ALL" (b.)

**1989, Apr. 3**
2035 A91 250c on 75c #1263 (56), pair 8.00 8.00
2036 A91 675c on 720c #1252 (49), pair 10.00 10.00

For surcharge see No. 2052.

Nos. 1224-1225, and 1254 Overprinted or Surcharged "BOY SCOUTS / 1909 1989" (a.) or "GIRL GUIDES / 1924 1989" (b.) Nos. 1272-1273 Surcharged "LADY BADEN POWELL / 1889-1989"

**1989, Apr. 11**
2037 A91 250c on 100c, pair, #a.-b. 5.00 5.00
2038 A91 $2.50 on 50c, pair, #a.-b. 5.00 5.00
2039 A91 300c Pair, #a.-b. 5.00 5.00
*c.* Pair, #d.-e., Prussian bl ovpt.
2040 A91 $25 on 280c #1272 7.00 7.00
*a.* Prussian blue overprint
2041 A91 $25 on 700c #1273 7.00 7.00
*a.* Prussian blue overprint
*Nos. 2037-2041 (5)* 29.00 29.00

Nos. 2037-2039, Boy Scouts in Guyana, 80th anniversary and Girl Guides, 65th anniversary. Nos. 2040-2041, Lady Baden Powell, birth centenary.

No. 1177 Surcharged "PHOTOGRAPHY / 1839-1989"

**1989, Apr. 15**
2042 A91 550c on 390c 7.00 7.00
2043 A91 650c on 390c, 2 bar obliterator 7.00 7.00
*a.* 6 bar obliterator 7.00 7.00
*Nos. 2042-2043, 2043a (3)* 21.00 21.00

Nos. 2042-2043 printed in sheets of 4 with alternating overprints.

No. 1263 Surcharged "I.L.O. / 1919-1989"

**1989, May 2**
2044 A91 300c on 75c #1263 12.00 2.25

Intl. Labor Organization, 70th anniversary.

**Nos. 43, 87, 134-137, 279-280, 284-285, and 286A 288, 1827, 1830, and 2035-2036 Surcharged in Black or Blue**

q

s

r

t

**1989-92 *Perfs. as Before***
**Watermarks and Printing Methods as Before**

2045 A7(q) 80c on 6c #43 .60 .35
*a.* A7 80c on 6c #43 .60 .35
2046 A28(q) $1 on 2c #134 .60 .35
*a.* A28(r) $1 on 2c #134 .60 .35
2047 A28(q) $2.05 on 3c #135 .60 .35
2048 A28(q) $2.55 on 5c #136 .60 .35
*a.* A28(r) $2.55 on 5c #136 .60 .35
2049 A28(q) $3.25 on 6c #137 .60 .40
*a.* A28(r) $3.25 on 6c #137 .60 .40
2050 A14(q) $5 on 6c #87 .60 .35
*a.* A14(s) $5 on 6c #87 .60 .35
*b.* A14(r) $5 on 6c #87 —
2051 A66(q) $6 on 5c #279
2052 A91 640c Pair, #2036 5.00 5.00
2053 A66(q) $6.40 on 10c #280 6.00 .90
*a.* A66 $6.40 on 10c #280 6.00 .90
*b.* A66(r) $6.40 on 10c #280 6.00 .90
2054 Block of 5, #a.-e. on #1830 42.50 42.50
*a.-d.* A99(t) $6.40 on $3.30 #a.-d. 5.00 2.00
*e.* A100(t) $190 on $3.30 #e. 22.50 20.00
2054F A66(r) $7.65 on 35c #284 7.25 1.50
2055 A66 $7.65 on 40c #285 8.25 1.50
2056 Block of 5, #a.-e. on #1827 42.50 42.50
*a.-d.* A99(t) $7.65 on $3.20 #a.-d. 5.00 2.00
*e.* A100(t) $225 on $3.20 #e. 22.50 20.00
2057 A66(q) $8.90 on 60c #286A 9.00 1.50
*a.* A66 $8.90 on 60c #286A 9.00 1.50
2057B A66(q) $30 on 10c #280
2057C A66(q) $35 on 35c #284
2058 A66(r) $50 on $2 #288 (Bl) 20.00 10.00
2059 A66(r) $100 on $2 #288 27.50 20.00

Issued: #2045a, 2053-2053a, 2054F, 2055, May 18; #2057, May 26; #2058-2059, June 5; #2045, 2049, 2046a, 2048a, 2049a, June 15; #2050-2050a, 2051, 2052, 2054, 2056, Aug. 16; #2050b, 1992.

Nos. 2045a, 2053a, 2055, 2057a have no obliterator. New denominations are larger on Nos. 2045a, 2053a and 2057a. No. 2045a has no cent sign. Denomination on No. 2050b is above "X" obliterator.

Nos. 2054e, 2056b additionally overprinted "SPECIAL DELIVERY."

No. 1244 Surcharged "CARICOM / DAY"

**Unwmk.**
**1989, June 26 Litho. *Perf. 14***
2064 A91 125c on 200c #1244, 2 bar obliterator 8.00 1.50
*a.* 6 bar obliterator 10.00 1.75

No. 280 Ovptd. in Gold or Silver for Gold Medalists at 1988 Summer Olympics

Overprints read: Nos. 2082a, 2083a, "SEOUL / OLYMPICS." Nos. 2082b, 2083b, "Men's 800M / Ereng / Kenya." Nos. 2082c, 2083c, "KOREA." Nos. 2082d, 2083d, "Men's / Gymnastics / Artemov / USSR." Nos. 2082e, 2083e, "Men's / Swimming / Louganis / USA." Nos. 2082f, 2083f, "Woman's / Swimming / Otto / DDR." Nos. 2082g, 2083g, "Men's Fencing / Lamour / France." Nos. 2082h, 2083h, "Men's / Gymnastics / Lou / China." Nos. 2082i, 2083i, "Women's / Cycling / Knol / Holland." Nos. 2082j, 2083j, "Men's / Swimming / Szabo / Hungary." Nos. 2082k, 2083k, "1988." Nos. 2082l, 2083l, "Men's / Swimming / Nesty / Suriname." Nos. 2082m, 2083m, "Men's Boxing / Lewis / Canada." Nos. 2082n, 2083n, "Men's Javelin / Korjus / Finland." Nos. 2082o, 2083o, "Basketball / USA." Nos. 2082p, 2083p, "Men's / Equestrian / Klimke / W. Germany." Nos. 2082q, 2083q, "Men's Boxing / Park / Korea." Nos. 2082r, 2083r, "Women's / Marathon / Mota / Portugal." Nos. 2082s, 2083s, "Men's / Swimming / Suzuki / Japan."

Nos. 2084a, 2085a, "Men's 100M / Lewis / USA." Nos. 2084b, 2085b, "Men's / Pole Vault / Bubka / USSR." Nos. 2084c, 2085c, "Women's / 100-200m / Joyner / USA." Nos. 2084d, 2085d, "Men's Pentathlon / Martinek / Hungary." Nos. 2084e, 2085e, "Men's Wrestling / Sako / Japan." Nos. 2084f, 2085f, "Men's Judo / Saito / Japan." Nos. 2084g, 2085g, "Women's 800M / Wodars / DDR." Nos. 2084h, 2085h, "Men's Boxing / Gross / W. Germany." Nos. 2084i, 2085i, "Men's Boxing / Maske / DDR." Nos. 2084j, 2085j, "Men's Boxing / Kim / Korea." Nos. 2084k, 2085k, "Woman's / Swimming / Evans / USA." Nos. 2084l, 2085l, "Soccer / USSR." Nos. 2084m, 2085m, "Woman's / Gymnastics / Silivas / Romania." Nos. 2084n, 2085n, "Men's Boxing / Mercer / USA." Nos. 2084o, 2085o, "Men's Marathon / Bordin / Italy." Nos. 2084p, 2085p, "Women's Tennis / Graf / W. Germany."

***Perf. 14x13½***
**1989, Apr. Litho. Wmk. 364**
**Sheets of 25**

2082 5 #a., 3 #c., #b., d.-s. 12.50 12.50
*a.-s.* A66 10c on #280, any single .45 .45
2083 5 #a., 3 #c., #b., d.-s. (S) 12.50 12.50
*a.-s.* A66 10c on #280, any single .45 .45
2084 #a.-p., 5 #2082a, 3 #2082c, #2082k 12.50 12.50
*a.-p.* A66 10c on #280, any single .45 .45
2085 #a.-p., 5 #2083a, 3 #2083c, #2083k (S) 12.50 12.50
*a.-p.* A66 10c on #280, any single .45 .45

No. 280 Ovptd. in Gold or Silver for Gold Medalists at 1988 Winter Olympics

Overprints read: Nos. 2086a, 2087a, "Gold Medal / Winners." Nos. 2086b, 2087b, "Ice Hockey / USSR." Nos. 2086c, 2087c, "CALGARY / OLYMPICS." Nos. 2086d, 2087d, "Bobsled / Kipours-Kozlov / USSR." Nos. 2086e, 2087e, "Women's Skating / 1500-3000-5000M / Gennip / Netherlands." Nos. 2086f, 2087f, "Men's / Speed / Skating / 5000-10000M / Gustafson / Sweden." Nos. 2086g, 2087g, "Men's Figure / Skating / Boitano / USA." Nos. 2086h, 2087h, "Women's / 500M Skating / Blair / USA." Nos. 2086i, 2087i, "Women's / Figure Skating / Witt / DDR." Nos. 2086j, 2087j, "Men's Giant / Slalom / Tomba / Italy." Nos. 2086k, 2087k, "CANADA." Nos. 2086l, 2087l, "Men's Super / Giant Slalom / Picard / France." Nos. 2086m, 2087m, "Women's / Downhill Skiing / Kiehl / W. Germany." Nos. 2086n, 2087n, "Men's 50km Skiing Svan / Sweden." Nos. 2086o, 2087o, "Men's Nordic / Combined Skiing / Mueller-Pohl / Schwarz / W. Germany." Nos. 2086p, 2087p, "Women's / Giant Slalom / Schneider / Switzerland." Nos. 2086q, 2087q, "Women's / 5-km Skiing / Matikainen / Finland." Nos. 2086r, 2087r, "Men's Downhill / Alpine Skiing / Zurbriggen / Switzerland." Nos. 2086s, 2087s, "Men's Ski / Jumping / Nykanen / Finland."

**1989, Apr.**
2086 4 #a., 3 #c., #b., d.-s., #2082k 12.50 12.50
*a.-s.* A66 10c on #280, any single .45 .45
2087 4 #a., 3 #c., #b., d.-s., #2083k (S) 12.50 12.50
*a.-s.* A66 10c on #280, any single .45 .45

No. 281 Ovptd. in Gold or Silver in Memory of Hirohito, Emperor of Japan

Overprints read: Nos. 2088a, 2089a, "Emperor / Hirohito." Nos. 2088b, 2089b, "Showa / Era." Nos. 2088c, 2089c, "Chrysanthemum / Dynasty." Nos. 2088d, 2089d, "Emperor / of Japan." Nos. 2088e, 2089e, "1901." Nos. 2088f, 2089f, "1989." Nos. 2088g, 2089g, "Emperor / Hirohito / 1901-1989."

**1989, Apr.**
2088 5 #a., 4 #c.-d., 9 #b., #e.-g. 12.50 12.50
*a.-g.* A66 15c on #281, any single .45 .45
2089 5 #a., 4 #c.-d., 9 #b., #e.-g. (S) 12.50 12.50
*a.-g.* A66 15c on #281, any single .45 .45

No. 280 Ovptd. in Gold or Silver for Enthronment of Akihito, Emperor of Japan

Overprints reads: Nos. 2090a, 2091a, "Honoring / His / Majesty." Nos. 2090b, 2091b, "Emperor / of / Japan." Nos. 2090c, 2091c, "1989." Nos. 2090d, 2091d, "HEISI / ERA."

**1989, Apr.**
2090 12 #a, 8 #b., 4 #c., #d. 12.50 12.50
*a.-d.* A66 10c on #280, any single .45 .45
2091 12 #a., 8 #b., 4 #c., #d. (S) 12.50 12.50
*a.-d.* A66 10c on #280, any single .45 .45

Overprint is 10mm long on #2090c, 2091c.

Nos. 280-281 and 283 Ovptd. with Emblems of Scouts, Rotary Intl., and Lions Intl. in Gold, Silver, Metallic Red, Metallic Green and Black

Overprints: Nos. 2092a, 2093a, 2094a, 2095a, 2096b, 2097b, 2098b, 2099b, 2100c, 2101c, 2102c, 2103c, Scouting emblem. Nos. 2092b, 2093b, 2094b, 2095b, 2096a, 2097a, 2098a, 2099a, 2100b, 2101b, 2102b, 2103b, Rotary emblem. Nos. 2092c, 2093c, 2094c, 2095c, 2096c, 2097c, 2098c, 2099c, 2100a, 2101a, 2102a, 2103a, Lions emblem. Nos. 2092d, 2093d, 2094d, 2095d, 2096d, 2097d, 2098d, 2099d, 2100d, 2101d, 2102d, 2103d, "1989." Nos. 2092e, 2093e, 2094e, 2095e, Large scouting emblem. Nos. 2096e, 2097e, 2098e, 2099e, Large Rotary emblem. Nos. 2100e, 2101e, 2102e, 2103e, Large Lions emblem.

**1989, Apr.**
2092 8 #a.-b., 6 #c., 2 #d., #e. 12.50 12.50
*a.-e.* A66 10c on #280, any single .45 .45
2093 8 #a.-b., 6 #c., 2 #d., #e. (S) 12.50 12.50
*a.-e.* A66 10c on #280, any single .45 .45
2094 8 #a.-b., 6 #c., 2 #d., #e. (R) 12.50 12.50
*a.-e.* A66 10c on #280, any single .45 .45
2095 8 #a.-b., 6 #c., 2 #d., #e. (Bk) 12.50 12.50
*a.-e.* A66 10c on #280, any single .45 .45
2096 8 #a.-b., 6 #c., 2 #d., #e. 12.50 12.50
*a.-e.* A66 15c on #281, any single .45 .45
2097 8 #a.-b., 6 #c., 2 #d., #e. (S) 12.50 12.50
*a.-e.* A66 15c on #281, any single .45 .45
2098 8 #a.-b., 6 #c., 2 #d., #e. (R) 12.50 12.50
*a.-e.* A66 15c on #281, any single .45 .45
2099 8 #a.-b., 6 #c., 2 #d., #e. (Gr) 12.50 12.50
*a.-e.* A66 15c on #281, any single .45 .45
2100 8 #a.-b., 6 #c., 2 #d., #e. 12.50 12.50
*a.-e.* A66 25c on #283, any single .45 .45
2101 8 #a.-b., 6 #c., 2 #d., #e. (S) 12.50 12.50
*a.-e.* A66 25c on #283, any single .45 .45
2102 8 #a.-b., 6 #c., 2 #d., #e. (R) 12.50 12.50
*a.-e.* A66 25c on #283, any single .45 .45
2103 8 #a.-b., 6 #c., 2 #d., #e. (Gr) 12.50 12.50
*a.-e.* A66 25c on #283, any single .45 .45

"1989" overprints are 7½mm long.

No. 280 Ovptd. in Gold or Silver for Halley's Comet

Overprints read: Nos. 2104a, 2105a, "Halley's / Comet." Nos. 2104b, 2105b, "Famous / Space Event." Nos. 2104c, 2105c, "Edmund / Halley / 1656-1742." Nos. 2104d, 2105d, "1910." Nos. 2104e, 2105e, "1986."

**1989, Apr.**
2104 11 #a., 6 #b., 4 #c., 2 #d.-e. 12.50 12.50
*a.-e.* A66 10c on #280, any single .45 .45
2105 11 #a., 6 #b., 4 #c., 2 #d.-e. (S) 12.50 12.50
*a.-e.* A66 10c on #280, any single .45 .45

No. 280 Ovptd. in Gold or Silver for Space Achievements

Overprints read: Nos. 2106a, 2107a, "Sputnik I / Oct. 4, 1957." Nos. 2106b, 2107b, "Explorer I / Jan. 31, 1958." Nos. 2106c, 2107c, "Sputnik II / Laika / Spacedog / Nov. 3, 1957." Nos. 2106d, 2107d, "Alan Shepard, Jr. / Mercury III / May 5, 1961." Nos. 2106e, 2107e, "Yuri Gagarin / Vostok I / April 12, 1961." Nos. 2106f, 2107f, "John Glenn / Mercury VI / Feb. 20, 1962." Nos. 2106g, 2107g, "Vostok III / Vostok IV / Aug. 12, 1962." Nos. 2106h, 2107h, "Grissom-Young / Gemini III / March 23, 1965." Nos. 2106i, 2107i, "Luna III / Oct. 4, 1959." Nos. 2106j, 2107j, "Edward H. White II / Gemini IV / June 3, 1965." Nos. 2106k, 2107k, "V. Tereshkova / First Woman / in Space / June 16-19, 1963." Nos. 2106 l, 2107 l, "Surveyor I / June 2, 1966." Nos. 2106m, 2107m, "Space / Achievements." Nos. 2106n, 2107n, "Voskod I / First 3 Man Crew / Oct. 12-13, 1964." Nos. 2106o, 2107o, "Apollo I / Jan. 27, 1967." Nos. 2106p, 2107p, "Alexei A. Leonov / First Walk in Space / March 18-19, 1965." Nos. 2106q, 2107q, "Apollo VIII / Dec. 21-27, 1968." Nos. 2106r, 2107r, "V. Komarov / Soyuz I / April 24, 1967." Nos. 2106s, 2107s, "Apollo XI / First Man on Moon / July 20, 1969." Nos. 2106t, 2107t, "Lunokhod I / Dec. 10, 1970." Nos. 2106u, 2107u, "Apollo XIII / April 11-17, / 1970." Nos. 2106v, 2107v, "Soyuz XI / June 30, 1971." Nos. 2106w, 2107w, "Viking I / July 20, 1976." Nos. 2106x, 2107x, "Vega I / March 6, 1986." Nos. 2106y, 2107y, "Columbia Sts-1 / April 12-14, / 1981."

**1989, Apr.**
2106 #a.-y. 12.50 12.50
*a.-y.* A66 10c on #280, any single .45 .45
2107 #a.-y. (S) 12.50 12.50
*a.-y.* A66 10c on #280, any single .45 .45

No. 280 Ovptd. in Gold or Silver

Overprints read: Nos. 2108a, 2109a, "1969- / 1989." Nos. 2108b, 2109b, "Apollo XI." Nos. 2108c, 2109c, "First Man / on Moon." Nos. 2108d, 2109d, "USA." Nos. 2108e, 2109e, "Neil A. / Armstrong." Nos. 2108f, 2109f, "Col.

Edwin E. / Aldrin, Jr." Nos. 2108g, 2109g, "Lt. Col. / Michael / Collins."

**1989, Apr.**

**2108** 5 #a, 7 b, 4 c, 6 d, e-g 12.50 12.50
*a.-g.* A66 10c on #280, any single .45 .45
**2109** 5 #a, 7 b, 4 c, 6 d, e-g (S) 12.50 12.50
*a.-g.* A66 10c on #280, any single .45 .45

Moon Landing, 20th anniv.

### No. 281 Ovptd. in Gold or Silver for Space Shuttle Program

Overprints read: Nos. 2110a, 2111a, "Enterprise / Aug. 12, 1977." Nos. 2110b, 2111b, "Columbia / April 12, 1981." Nos. 2110c, 2111c, "Space / Shuttles." Nos. 2110d, 2111d, "Discovery / Aug. 30, 1984." Nos. 2110e, 2111e, "Atlantis / Oct. 3, 1985." Nos. 2110f, 2111f, "Challenger / Heroes." Nos. 2110g, 2111g, "Resnik / McAuliffe / Jarvis." Nos. 2110h, 2111h, "In Memoriam / Challenger / Jan. 28, 1986." Nos. 2110i, 2111i, "Onizuka / Smith / McNair / Scobee."

**1989, Apr.**

**2110** 4 #a.-e., 2 #f., #g.-i. 12.50 12.50
*a.-i.* A66 15c on #281, any single .45 .45
**2111** 4 #a.-e., 2 #f., #g.-i. (S) 12.50 12.50
*a.-i.* A66 15c on #281, any single .45 .45

Butterflies — A115 A116

**1989, Sept. 7 Litho. *Perf. 14***

**2208** A115 80c Stalachtis calliope .50 .25
**2209** A115 $2.25 Morpho rhetenor .60 .25
**2210** A115 $5 Agrias claudia .75 .40
**2211** A115 $6.40 Marpesia marcella .85 .70
**2212** A115 $7.65 Papilio zagreus 1.00 .90
**2213** A115 $8.90 Chorinea faunus 1.25 1.10
**2214** A115 $25 Cepheuptychia cephus 4.00 3.00
**2215** A115 $100 Nessaea regina 13.50 12.50
*Nos. 2208-2215 (8)* 22.45 19.10

See Nos. E16-E17. For overprints see Nos. 2251-2254, 2256-2257, 2260-2261, 2283-2290, E19-E22, E24, E26-E27, E31.

**1989, Nov. 8**

Women in Space, 25th Anniv. (in 1988): $6.40, Kathryn Sullivan, 1st US woman to walk in space. $12.80, Svetlana Savitskaya, 1st Soviet woman to walk in space. $15.30, Judy Resnik & Christa McAuliffe, astronauts killed in Challenger explosion. $100, Sally Ride, 1st US woman astronaut.

**2216** A116 $6.40 multicolored 1.00 .25
**2217** A116 $12.80 multicolored 1.75 1.25
**2218** A116 $15.30 multicolored 2.00 1.50
**2219** A116 $100 multicolored 11.50 11.50
*Nos. 2216-2219 (4)* 16.25 14.50

See No. E18. For overprints see Nos. 2255, 2258-2259, 2262, E23, E25, E28, E32.

1990 World Cup Soccer Championships, Italy — A117

Various soccer players.

***Perf. 14x13½, 13½x14***

**1989, Nov. 20**

**2220** A117 $2.55 shown 5.00 5.00
**2221** A117 $2.55 Yellow shirt, vert. 5.00 5.00
**2222** A117 $2.55 Goalie 5.00 5.00
**2223** A117 $2.55 Green shirt, vert. 5.00 5.00
Nos. 2220-2223 (4) 20.00 20.00

**Souvenir Sheet**

**2224** A117 $20 Championships emblem, vert. 17.50 17.50

#2220-2223 exist in souvenir sheets of 1. For surcharges see Nos. 2263-2267.

### No. 134-136 Surcharged "AHMADIYYA / CENTENARY / 1889-1989"

***Perf. 13x13½***

**1989, Nov. 22 Litho. Wmk. 364**

**2225** A28 80c on 2c #134 4.50 .60
**2226** A28 $6.40 on 3c #135 13.50 5.50
**2227** A28 $8.90 on 5c #136 15.00 8.00
Nos. 2225-2227 (3) 33.00 14.10

1992 Summer Olympics, Barcelona A118

**1989, Dec. 5 *Perf. 13½x14, 14x13½***

**2228** A118 $2.55 shown 4.00 4.00
**2229** A118 $2.55 Boxing, horiz. 4.00 4.00
**2230** A118 $2.55 Chariot racing, horiz. 4.00 4.00
**2231** A118 $2.55 Javelin, horiz. 4.00 4.00
**2232** A118 $2.55 Running, horiz. 4.00 4.00
**2233** A118 $2.55 Wrestling 4.00 4.00
*Nos. 2228-2233 (6)* 24.00 24.00

**Souvenir Sheets**

**2234** A118 $10 Running, horiz., diff. 15.00 15.00
**2235** A118 $10 Columbus Walk by Picasso 15.00 15.00
*Nos. 2234-2235 (2)* 30.00 30.00

#2228-2233 exist in souvenir sheets of 1.

Christmas — A119

Paintings: No. 2236, Child Declaring in Favor of His Mother, by Titian. No. 2237, The Sacred Family, by Rubens. No. 2238, Saint Anne, the Virgin and Child, by Durer. No. 2239, Madonna Enthroned, Surrounded by Saints, by Rubens. $20, Saint Ildefonso, by Rubens.

**1989, Dec. 26 *Perf. 14x13½, 13½x14***

**2236** A119 $2.55 multi 4.00 4.00
**2237** A119 $2.55 multi, vert. 4.00 4.00
**2238** A119 $2.55 multi, vert. 4.00 4.00
**2239** A119 $2.55 multi, vert. 4.00 4.00
*Nos. 2236-2239 (4)* 16.00 16.00

**Souvenir Sheet**

**2240** A119 $20 multi, vert. 20.00 20.00

#2236-2239 exist in souvenir sheets of 1.

Harpy Eagle — A120

Channel-billed Toucan — A121

**1990, Jan. 23 Litho. *Perf. 14***

**2241** A120 $2.25 Eagle's head 1.25 .50
**2242** A120 $5 Eagle with prey 1.75 .75
**2243** A120 $8.90 Eagle facing right 2.75 1.00
**2244** A121 $15 shown 1.75 .90
**2245** A121 $25 Blue & yellow macaw 2.25 1.00
**2246** A120 $30 Eagle facing left 5.25 4.50
**2247** A121 $50 Wattled jacana, horiz. 4.00 3.00
**2248** A121 $60 Hoatzin, horiz. 4.50 3.25
*Nos. 2241-2248 (8)* 23.50 14.90

**Souvenir Sheets**

**2249** A121 $100 Great kiskadee, horiz. 7.00 7.00
**2250** A121 $100 Amazon kingfisher, horiz. 7.00 7.00

Nos. 2241-2243, 2246, World Wildlife Fund.

### Nos. 2208-2184 Ovptd. in Silver with Rotary Emblem and "ROTARY INTERNATIONAL 1905-1990" on 2 or 3 Lines

**1990, Mar. 15**

**2251** A115 80c on #2208
**2252** A115 $2.25 on #2209
**2253** A115 $5 on #2210
**2254** A115 $6.40 on #2211
**2255** A116 $6.40 on #2216
**2256** A115 $7.65 on #2212
**2257** A115 $8.90 on #2213
**2258** A116 $12.80 on #2217
**2259** A116 $15.30 on #2218
**2260** A115 $25 on #2214
**2261** A115 $100 on #2215
**2262** A116 $100 on #2219
Nos. 2251-2262 (12) 37.50

### Nos. 2220-2222, 2224 Surcharged "GERMANY / CHAMPION"

### No. 2223 Surcharged "GERMANY / CHAMPION / ARGENTINA / SUB-CHAMPION"

**1990 *Perfs. as Before***

**2263** A117 $75 on #2220
**2264** A117 $75 on #2221
**2265** A117 $75 on #2222
**2266** A117 $75 on #2223
*Nos. 2263-2266 (4)* 10.00

**Souvenir Sheet**

**2267** A117 $225 on #2224 8.00

#2263-2266 exist in souvenir sheets of 1.

Miniature Sheets

Penny Black, 150th Anniv., 500th Anniv. of Thurn & Taxis Postal Service — A122

No. 2268: a, Banghy Post runner, 1832. b, Penny Black, Sir Rowland Hill. c, Dutch mail ship. d, Paddle steamer Monarch, 1830. e, Paddle steamer Hindostan, 1842. f, Mail steamer Chusan. g, Sailing ship Madagascar, 1853. h, Paddle steamer Orinoco, 1855. i, Packet Orpheus, 1835.

No. 2269: a, Imperial postal messenger. b, Swiss messenger, 1499. c, River messenger, 15th century. d, Russian courier, Middle Ages. e, Oldenburg postilions, 1820. f, Indian mail coach, 1829. g, Baden mail coach postilions, 1820. h, Pony Express, 1860. i, Camel rider.

No. 2270: a, Mail coach, 1840. b, Danish Ball Post, 1815. c, Australian Bush mailman, 1838. d, Japanese postmen, 1870. e, Mail cart, 1857. f, Russian mail troika. g, Wells, Fargo Overland Express. h, Phantoms of the Night, 1853. i, Cobb & Co. coach, Australia.

No. 2271: a, Postilions, 1850. b, Mounted postilion, Holland. c, Paddle steamer Arctic, 1850. d, Peruvian swimming couriers. e, First London post box, 1855. f, Indian mail cart, 1870. g, Balloon post, 1870. h, Bath Mail Coach. i, Postrider, 1837.

No. 2272: a, Northeastern Railway post office. b, Traveling post office, 1838. c, American Express. d, Graf Zeppelin. e, Columbia Post airplane, 1925. f, Calcutta flying boat. g, Junkers JU-52/3M mail plane. h, Douglas M2 mail plane. i, US air mail service, DH-4.

No. 2273: a, First Atlantic Airways. b, Morris post office van, 1931. c, Swiss post-passenger bus. d, Westland-Sikorsky S51 helicopter mail flight. e, Union Pacific Railway. f, Boeing Model 314 flying boat, Yankee Clipper. g, Boeing 747. h, Concorde. i, Apollo 11, US #C76.

No. 2274, Mounted postilion. No. 2275, Thurn & Taxis #7. No. 2276, Thurn & Taxis #45.

**1990, May 3**

**2268** A122 $15.30 Sheet of 9, #a.-i. 9.00 9.00
**2269** A122 $15.30 Sheet of 9, #a.-i. 9.00 9.00
**2270** A122 $15.30 Sheet of 9, #a.-i. 9.00 9.00
**2271** A122 $17.80 Sheet of 9, #a.-i. 10.00 10.00
**2272** A122 $20 Sheet of 9, #a.-i. 11.00 11.00
**2273** A122 $20 Sheet of 9, #a.-i. 11.00 11.00
*Nos. 2268-2273 (6)* 59.00 59.00

**Souvenir Sheets**

**2274** A122 $150 multi 7.50 7.50
**2275** A122 $150 multi 7.50 7.50
**2276** A122 $150 multi 7.50 7.50

For overprint see No. 2551.

### Nos. 1028, 1032, 1055, 1085, 1107 Surcharged "ROTARY / DISTRICT 405 / 9th CONFERENCE / MAY 1990 / GEORGETOWN"

**Unwmk.**

**1990, May 8 Litho. *Perf. 14***

**Design A91**

**Plate Numbers in Parentheses**

**2277** 80c on 55c #1032 (9)
**2278** 80c on 55c #1085 (49)
**2279** 80c on 55c #1107 (64)
**2280** $6.40 on 130c #1028 (6)
**2281** $6.40 on 130c #1055 (25)
**2282** $7.65 on 130c #1055 (25)
Nos. 2277-2282 (6) 10.00

Nos. 2208-2215 Overprinted

**1990, June 8 Litho. *Perf. 14***

**2283** A115 80c on #2208 1.75 .45
**2284** A115 $2.25 on #2209 2.00 .45
**2285** A115 $5 on #2210 2.50 .65
**2286** A115 $6.40 on #2211 2.75 .65
**2287** A115 $7.65 on #2212 3.00 .90
**2288** A115 $8.90 on #2213 3.25 1.00
**2289** A115 $25 on #2214 6.00 6.00
**2290** A115 $100 on #2215 15.00 15.00
*Nos. 2283-2290 (8)* 36.25 25.10

See Nos. E26-E27.

Locomotives — A123

**1990, July 15 *Perf. 14x13½***

**2291** A123 $2.55 Class 3F
**2292** A123 $2.55 Class A4
**2293** A123 $2.55 Liner Class A34
**2294** A123 $2.55 Pacific Class

**2295** A123 $2.55 Grange Class
*Nos. 2291-2295 (5)* 13.50

### Souvenir Sheets

***Perf. 13½x14, 14x13½***

**2296** A123 $20 Castle Class, vert.
**2297** A123 $20 Southern Railway
*Nos. 2296-2297 (2)* 22.50

Still Life with Guitar, by Picasso — A124

Paintings: No. 2299, Horseman, by Velazquez. No. 2300, Sunflowers, by Van Gogh, vert. No. 2301, Man Wearing Striped Shirt, by Miro, vert. No. 2302, Franz von Taxis, by Durer, vert. No. 2303, Virgin and Child, by Titian, vert. No. 2304, Presentation of Marie de Medici, by Rubens, vert.

***Perf. 14x13½, 13½x14***

**1990, Aug. 1** **Litho.**

**2298** A124 $2.55 multicolored
**2299** A124 $2.55 multicolored
**2300** A124 $2.55 multicolored
**2301** A124 $2.55 multicolored
**2302** A124 $2.55 multicolored
*Nos. 2298-2302 (5)* 11.50

### Souvenir Sheets

**2303** A124 $20 multicolored
**2304** A124 $20 multicolored
*Nos. 2303-2304 (2)* 18.00

Postal System of Thurn and Taxis, 500th anniv. (#2302). Titian, 500th birth anniv. (#2303). Rubens, 350th death anniv. (#2304).

Birds — A125

Designs: 80c, Guiana partridge, horiz. $2.55, Collared trogon. $3.25, Derby aracari. $5, Black-necked aracari. $5.10, Green aracari. $5.80, Ivory-billed aracari. $6.40, Guiana toucanet. $6.50, Sulphur-breasted toucan. $7.55, Red-billed toucan. $7.65, Toco toucan. $8.25, Natterers toucanet. $8.90, Welcome trogon. $9.75, Doubtful trogon. $11.40, Banded aracari. $12.65, Golden-headed train bearer. $12.80, Rufus-breasted hermit. $13.90, Band-tail barbthroat. $15.30, White-tipped sickle bill. $17.80, Black jacobin. $19.20, Fiery topaz. $22.95, Tufted coquette. $26.70, Ecuadorian pied-tail. $30, Quetzal. $50, Green-crowned brilliant. $100, Emerald-chinned hummingbird. $190, Lazuline sabre-wing. $225, Berylline hummingbird.

**1990, Sept. 12** **Litho.** ***Perf. 14***

**2305** A125 80c multi .25 .25
**2306** A125 $2.55 multi .25 .25
**2307** A125 $3.25 multi .25 .25
**2308** A125 $5 multi .25 .25
**2309** A125 $5.10 multi .25 .25
**2310** A125 $5.80 multi .25 .25
**2311** A125 $6.40 multi .25 .25
**2312** A125 $6.50 multi .25 .25
**2313** A125 $7.55 multi .35 .35
**2314** A125 $7.65 multi .45 .45
**2315** A125 $8.25 multi .55 .55
**2316** A125 $8.90 multi .65 .65
**2317** A125 $9.75 multi .65 .65
**2318** A125 $11.40 multi .70 .70
**2319** A125 $12.65 multi .75 .75
**2320** A125 $12.80 multi .80 .80
**2321** A125 $13.90 multi .90 .90
**2322** A125 $15.30 multi 1.10 1.10
**2323** A125 $17.80 multi 1.25 1.25
**2324** A125 $19.20 multi 1.40 1.40
**2325** A125 $22.95 multi 1.60 1.60
**2326** A125 $26.70 multi 1.90 1.90
**2327** A125 $30 multi 2.00 2.00
**2328** A125 $50 multi 3.25 3.25
**2329** A125 $100 multi 6.00 6.00
**2330** A125 $190 multi 11.50 11.50
**2331** A125 $225 multi 14.00 14.00
*Nos. 2305-2331 (27)* 51.80 51.80

For surcharge, see No. 4020M.

Butterflies — A126

No. 2340: a, Thecla falerina. b, Pheles heliconides. c, Echenais leucocyana. d, Heliconius xanthocles. e, Mesopthalma idotea. f, Parides aeneas. g, Heliconius numata. h, Thecla critola. i, Themone pais. j, Nymula agle. k, Adelpha cocala. l, Anaea eribotes. m, Prepona demophon. n, Selenophanes cassiope. o, Consul hippona. p, Antirrhaea avernus.

No. 2341: a, Thecla telemus. b, Thyridia confusa. c, Heliconius burneyi. d, Parides lysander. e, Eunica orphise. f, Adelpha melona. g, Morpho menelaus. h, Nymula phylleus. i, Stalachtis phlegia. j, Theope barea. k, Morpho perseus. l, Lycorea ceres. m, Archonias bellona. n, Caerois chorinaeus. o, Vila azeca. p, Nessaea batesii.

No. 2342: a, Heliconius silvana. b, Eunica alcmena. c, Mechanitis polymnia. d, Mesosemia ephyne. e, Thecla erema. f, Callizona acesta. g, Stalachtis phaedusa. h, Battus belus. i, Nymula phliasus. j, Parides childrenae. k, Stalachtis euterpe. l, Dysmathia portia. m, Tithorea hermias. n, Prepona pheridamas. o, Dismorphia fortunata. p, Hamadryas amphinome.

No. 2343: a, Heliconius vetustus. b, Mesosemia eumene. c, Parides phosphorus. d, Polystichtis emylius. e, Xanthocleis aedesia. f, Doxocopa agathina. g, Adelpha plesaure. h, Heliconius wallacei. i, Notheme eumeus. j, Melinaea mediatrix. k, Theritas coronata. l, Dismorphia orise. m, Phyciodes ianthe. n, Morpho aega. o, Zaretis isidora. p, Pierella lena.

Nos. 2340-2341 are horiz.

**1990, Sept. 26** **Litho.** ***Perf. 14***

**2332** A126 80c Melinaea idae .85 .85
**2333** A126 $2.55 Rhetus dysonii .85 .85
**2334** A126 $5 Actinote anteas .85 .85
**2335** A126 $6.40 Heliconius tales .85 .85
**2336** A126 $7.65 Thecla telemus .85 .85
**2337** A126 $8.90 Theope eudocia 1.10 1.10
**2338** A126 $50 Heliconius vicini 4.50 4.50
**2339** A126 $100 Amarynthis meneria 9.50 9.50
*Nos. 2332-2339 (8)* 19.35 19.35

### Miniature Sheets

**2340** A126 $10 Sheet of 16, #a.-p. 16.00 16.00
**2341** A126 $10 Sheet of 16, #a.-p. 16.00 16.00
**2342** A126 $10 Sheet of 16, #a.-p. 16.00 16.00
**2343** A126 $10 Sheet of 16, #a.-p. 16.00 16.00

### Souvenir Sheets

**2344** A126 $150 Heliconius aoede 10.00 10.00
**2345** A126 $150 Phyciodes clio, horiz. 10.00 10.00
**2346** A126 $190 Nymphidium caricae 15.00 15.00
**2347** A126 $190 Thecla hemon 15.00 15.00

For surcharges see #2415-2425, 2596-2606.

Mushrooms A127

**1990, Oct. 12**

**2348** A127 $2.55 Oudemanseilla mucida
**2349** A127 $2.55 Pholiota squarosa
**2350** A127 $2.55 Coprinus comatus
**2351** A127 $2.55 Anellaria semiovaja
*Nos. 2348-2351 (4)* 14.00

### Souvenir Sheet

**2352** A127 $20 Phallus impudicus 14.00

Sailing Ships — A128

**1990, Oct. 12**

**2353** A128 $2.55 Brig century
**2354** A128 $2.55 Dutch marine ship
**2355** A128 $2.55 Galleon, 1588
**2356** A128 $2.55 Warship, 16th cent.
**2357** A128 $2.55 Hulk, 17th cent.
*Nos. 2353-2357 (5)* 13.00

### Souvenir Sheet

**2358** A128 $20 Dutch ships, 16th-17th cent. 14.00

No. 2358 printed in continuous design. Discovery of America, 500th anniv. (in 1992).

Flora — A129

Orchids: $7.65, Vanilla inodora. $8.90, Epidendrum ibaguense. No. 858, Maxillaria parkeri. $15.30, Epidendrum nocturnum. $17.80, Catasetum discolor. $20, Scuticaria hadwenii. $25, Epidendrum fragrans. $100, Epistephium parviflorum.

No. 2367: a, Dichea muricata. b, Octomeria erosilabia. c, Spiranthes orchiodes. d, Brassavola nodosa. e, Epidendrum rigidum. f, Brassia caudata. g, Pleurothallis diffusa. h, Aspasia variegata. i, Stenia pallida. j, Cyrtopodium punctatum. k, Cattleya deckeri. l, Cryptarrhena lunata. m, Cattleya violacea. n, Caularthron bicornutum. o, Oncidium carthagenense. p, Galeandra devoniana.

No. 2368: a, Bifrenaria aurantiaca. b, Epidendrum ciliare. c, Dichaea picta. d, Scaphyglottis violacea. e, Cattleya percivaliana. f, Map of Guyana (no flower). g, Epidendrum difforme. h, Eulophia maculata. i, Spiranthes tenuis. j, Peristeria guttata. k, Pleurothallis pruinosa. l, Cleistes rosea. m, Maxillaria variabilis. n, Brassavola cucullata. o, Epidendrum moyobambae. p, Oncidium orthostates.

No. 2369: a, Brassavola martiana. b, Paphinia cristata. c, Aganisia pulchella. d, Oncidium lanceanum. e, Lockhartia imbricata. f, Caularthron bilamellatum. g, Oncidium nanum. h, Pleurothallis ovalifolia. i, Galeandra dives. j, Cycnoches loddigesii. k, Ada aurantiaca. l, Catasetum barbatum. m, Palmorchis pubescens. n, Epidendrum anceps. o, Huntleya meleagris. p, Sobralia sessilis.

No. 2370: a, Maxillaria camaridii. b, Vanilla pompona. c, Stanhopea grandiflora. d, Oncidium pusillum. e, Polycycnis vittata. f, Cattleya lawrenceana. g, Menadenium labiosum. h, Rodriguezia secunda. i, Mormodes buccinator. j, Otostylis brachystalix. k, Maxillaria discolor. l, Liparis elata. m, Gongora maculata. n, Koellensteinia graminea. o, Rudolfiella aurantiaca. p, Scuticaria steelei.

Flowering Trees: No. 2371: a, Cochlospermum vitifolium. b, Eugenia malaccensis. c, Plumiera rubra. d, Erythrina glauca. e, Spathodea campanulata. f, Jacaranda filicifolia. g, Samanea saman. h, Cassia fistula. i, Abutilon integerrimum. j, Lagerstroemia speciosa. k, Tabebuia serratifolia. l, Guaiacum officinale. m, Solanum macranthum. n, Peltophorum roxburghii. o, Bauhinia variegata. p, Plumiera alba.

Flowering Vines: No. 2372: a, Gloriosa rothschildiana. b, Pseudocalymma alliaceum. c, Callichlamys latifolia. d, Distictis riversii. e, Maurandya barclaiana. f, Beaumontia fragrans. g, Phaseolus caracalla. h, Mandevilla splendens. i, Solandra longiflora. j, Passiflora coccinea. k, Allamanda cathartica. l, Bauhinia galpini. m, Verbena maritima. n, Mandevilla suaveolens. o, Phryganocydia corymbosa. p, Jasminum sambac.

**1990, Oct. 16** **Litho.** ***Perf. 14***

**2359** A129 $7.65 multicolored .40 .40
**2360** A129 $8.90 multicolored .55 .55
**2361** A129 $12.80 multicolored .85 .85
**2362** A129 $15.30 multicolored .90 .90
**2363** A129 $17.80 multicolored 1.00 1.00
**2364** A129 $20 multicolored 1.25 1.25
**2365** A129 $25 multicolored 1.50 1.50
**2366** A129 $100 multicolored 6.50 6.50
*Nos. 2359-2366 (8)* 12.95 12.95

### Miniature Sheets

**2367** A129 $10 Sheet of 16, #a.-p. 8.00 8.00
**2368** A129 $10 Sheet of 16, #a.-p. 8.00 8.00
**2369** A129 $12.80 Sheet of 16, #a.-p. 12.00 12.00
**2370** A129 $12.80 Sheet of 16, #a.-p. 12.00 12.00
**2371** A129 $12.80 Sheet of 16, #a.-p. 12.00 12.00
**2372** A129 $12.80 Sheet of 16, #a.-p. 12.00 12.00
*Nos. 2367-2372 (6)* 64.00 64.00

### Souvenir Sheets

**2373** A129 $150 Galeandra devoniana 9.00 9.00
**2374** A129 $150 Delonix regia 9.00 9.00
**2375** A129 $150 Hexisea bidentata 9.00 9.00
**2376** A129 $150 Lecythis ollaria 9.00 9.00
**2377** A129 $190 Ionopsis utricularioides 11.00 11.00
*Nos. 2373-2377 (5)* 47.00 47.00

Nos. 2370-2375 are horiz. For surcharges see Nos. 2593-2595, 4020N, 4119, 4120, 4121, 4178, 4179.

Souvenir Sheet

Cenozoic Era Wildlife — A130

Designs: a, Palaelodus. b, Archaeotrogon. c, Vulture. d, Bradyrus tridactylus. e, Natalus stramineus bat. f, Cebidae. g, Cuvieronius. h, Phororhacos. i, Smilodectes. j, Megatherium. k, Titanotylopus. l, Teleoceras. m, Macrauchenia. n, Mylodon. o, Smilodon. p, Glyptodon. q, Protohydrocherus. r, Archaeohyrax. s, Pyrotherium. t, Platypittamys.

**1990, Nov. 6**

**2378** A130 $12.80 Sheet of 20, #a.-t. 15.00 15.00

### Miniature Sheets

Endangered Wildlife — A131

#2379: a, Ivory-billed woodpecker. b, Cauca guan. c, Sun conure. d, Quetzal. e, Long-wattled umbrellabird. f, Banded cotinga. g, Blue-chested parakeet. h, Rufous-bellied chachalaca. i, Yellow-faced amazon. j, Toucan barbet. k, Red siskin. l, Cock-of-the-rock. m, Hyacinth macaw. n, Yellow cardinal. o, Bare-necked umbrellabird. p, Saffron toucanette. q, Red-billed curassow. r, Spectacled parrotlet. s, Lovely cotinga. t, Black-breasted gnateater.

#2380: a, Swallow-tailed kite. b, Hoatzin. c, Ruby topaz hummingbird. d, Black vulture. e, Rufous-tailed jacamar. f, Scarlet macaw. g, Rose-breasted thrush tanager. h, Toco toucan. i, Bearded bellbird. j, Blue-crowned motmot. k, Green oropendola. l, Pompadour cotinga. m, Vermilion flycatcher. n, Blue and yellow macaw. o, White-barred piculet. p, Great razor-billed curassow. q, Ruddy quail-dove. r, Paradise tanager. s, Anhinga. t, Greater flamingo.

#2381: a, Harpy eagle. b, Andean condor. c, Amazonian umbrellabird. d, Spider monkeys. e, Hyacinth macaw, diff. f, Red siskin, diff. g, Toucan barbet, diff. h, Three-toed sloth. i, Guanaco. j, Spectacled bear. k, White-lipped peccary. l, Maned wolf. m, Jaguar. n, Spectacled caiman. o, Giant armadillo. p, Giant anteater. q, South American river otter. r, Yapok. s, Central American river turtle. t, Cauca guan, diff.

***Perf. 14x13½, 13½x14***

**1990, Nov. 6** **Litho.**

**2379** A131 $12.80 Sheet of 20, #a.-t. 22.50 22.50
**2380** A131 $12.80 Sheet of 20, #a.-t. 22.50 22.50
**2381** A131 $12.80 Sheet of 20, #a.-t. 22.50 22.50

#2381a-2381t are horiz. #2380s incorrectly inscribed Anhigna. See #E29-E30.

Numbers have been reserved for additional values in this set.

Independence, 25th Anniv. — A132

**1991, June 25** **Litho.** ***Imperf.***

**2389** A132 $225 multicolored 10.00 10.00

### Miniature Sheets

Olympic Gold Medal Winners — A133

No. 2390: a, Ramon Fonst. b, Lucien Gaudin. c, Ole A. Lilloe-Olsen. d, Morris Fisher. e, Ray C. Ewry. f, Hubert Van Innes. g, Alvin Kraenzlein. h, Johnny Weissmuller. i, Hans Winkler.

No. 2391: a, Viktor Chukarin. b, Agnes Keleti. c, Barbel Wochel. d, Eric Heiden. e, Alvodar Gerevich. f, Guiseppe Delfino. g, Alexander Tikhonov. h, C.F. Pahud de Mortanges. i, Patricia McCormick.

No. 2392: a, Nelli Kim. b, Viktor Krovopuskov. c, Viktor Sidiak. d, Nikolai Andrianov. e, Nadia Comaneci. f, Mitsuo Tsukahara. g, Yelena Novikova-Belova. h, John Naber. i, Kornelia Ender.

No. 2393: a, Olga Korbut. b, Lyudmila Turischeva. c, Lasse Viren. d, George Miez. e, Roland Matthes. f, Pal Kovaks. g, Jesse Owens. h, Mark Spitz. i, Eduardo Mangiarotti.

No. 2394: a, Sawao Kato. b, Rudolf Karpati. c, Jeno Fuchs. d, Emil Zatopek. e, Fanny Blankers-Koen. f, Melvin Sheppard. g, Gert Fredriksson. h, Paul Elvstrom. i, Harrison W. Dillard.

No. 2395: a, Lydia Skoblikova. b, Ivar Ballangrud. c, Clas Thunberg. d, Anton Heida. e, Akinori Nakayama. f, Sixten Jernberg. g, Yevgeniy Grischin. h, Paul Radmilovic. i, Charles Daniels.

No. 2396: a, Betty Cuthbert. b, Vera Caslavska. c, Galina Kulakova. d, Yukio Endo. e, Vladimir Morozov. f, Boris Shaklin. g, Don Schollander. h, Gyozo Kulscar. i, Christian D'Oriola.

No. 2397: a, Al Oerter. b, Polina Astakhova. c, Takashi Ono. d, Valentin Muratov. e, Henri St. Cyr. f, Iain Murray Rose. g, Larissa Latynina. h, Carlo Pavesi. i, Dawn Fraser.

No. 2398, Paavo Nurmi, vert. No. 2399, Johannes Kolehmainen, vert. $190. Nedo Nadi, vert.

**1991, Aug. 12** **Litho.** ***Perf. 14x13½***

**2390** A133 $15.30 Sheet of 9, #a.-i. 5.75 5.75
**2391** A133 $17.80 Sheet of 9, #a.-i. 6.75 6.75
**2392** A133 $20 Sheet of 9, #a.-i. 7.25 7.25
**2393** A133 $20 Sheet of 9, #a.-i. 7.25 7.25
**2394** A133 $25 Sheet of 9, #a.-i. 9.50 9.50
**2395** A133 $25 Sheet of 9, #a.-i. 9.50 9.50
**2396** A133 $30 Sheet of 9, #a.-i. 11.50 11.50
**2397** A133 $30 Sheet of 9, #a.-i. 11.50 11.50
*Nos. 2390-2397 (8)* 69.00 69.00

### Souvenir Sheets

***Perf. 13x13½***

**2398** A133 $150 multicolored 5.50 5.50
**2399** A133 $150 multicolored 5.50 5.50
**2400** A133 $190 multicolored 7.00 7.00

For overprints see Nos. 2552-2557.

Discovery of America, 500th Anniv. (in 1992) — A134

Birds: $6.40, Phoenicopterus ruber. $7.65, Ostinops decumanus. $50, Falco peregrinus. $100, Nymphicus hollandicus. $190, Vultur feriphus. $260, Merganetta armata, horiz.

**1991, Sept. 15** **Litho.** ***Perf. 13½x14***

**2401** A134 $6.40 multicolored
**2402** A134 $7.65 multicolored
**2403** A134 $50 multicolored
**2404** A134 $100 multicolored
**2405** A134 $190 multicolored
*Nos. 2401-2405 (5)* 16.50

### Souvenir Sheet

***Perf. 14x13½***

**2406** A134 $360 multicolored 15.00

A135

Various orchids.

***Perf. 13½x14, 14x13½***

**1991, Sept. 30**

**2407** A135 $6.40 multicolored
**2408** A135 $7.65 multi, horiz.
**2409** A135 $50 multicolored
**2410** A135 $100 multicolored
**2411** A135 $190 Odontoglossum
Nos. 2407-2411 (5) 8.00

### Souvenir Sheets

**2412** A135 $360 multicolored
**2413** A135 $360 Cycnoches ventricosum
**2414** A135 $360 Miltonia hibrida, horiz.
Nos. 2412-2414 (3) 22.50

### Nos. 2332-2339, 2343-2345 Ovptd. or Surcharged

Overprints: 80c, $2.55, Nos. 2421-2422, 2423a, 2423p, Rotary emblem and "1905-1990." $5.00, $6.40, $7.65, Nos. 2420, 2423d, 2423m, Rotary emblem and "Paul Percy Harris Founder 1868-1947" on 2 or 3 lines. Nos. 2423b, 2423l, 2423n, Boy Scout emblem and "1907-1992." Nos. 2423c, 2423i, 2423o, Lions Intl. emblem and "1917-1992." Nos. 2423e, 2423h, Red Cross emblem and "125 Years / Red Cross." Nos. 2423f-2423g, 2423j-2423k have parts of larger Rotary emblem. Nos. 2424-2425 ovptd. with service emblems in sheet margins.

**1991, Oct. 29** ***Perfs. as Before***

**2415** A126 80c on #2332 .25 .25
**2416** A126 $2.55 on #2333 .25 .25
**2417** A126 $5 on #2334 .25 .25
**2418** A126 $6.40 on #2335 .25 .25
**2419** A126 $7.65 on #2336 .25 .25
**2420** A126 $100 on $8.90 #2337 2.75 2.75
**2421** A126 $190 on $50 #2338 5.00 5.00
**2422** A126 $225 on $100 #2339 5.75 5.75
*Nos. 2415-2422 (8)* 14.75 14.75

### Miniature Sheet

**2423** A126 Sheet of 16 12.00 12.00
*a.-l.* $10 any single .25 .25
*m.* $50 on $10 #2343m 1.25 1.25
*n.* $75 on $10 #2343n 1.75 1.75
*o.* $100 on $10 #2343o 2.25 2.25
*p.* $190 on $10 #2343p 4.25 4.25

### Souvenir Sheets

**2424** A126 $400 on $150 #2344 12.00 12.00
**2425** A126 $500 on $150 #2345 14.00 14.00

Swiss Confederation, 700th Anniv. — A136

Designs: $6.40, Painting by Diego Giacometti. $7.65, Swiss puppets. $50, Man in top hat by Goya. $100, Stained glass window of Mary & Joseph. $190, Stained glass window of Jesus healing the sick.

No. 2431, Ship's cross-section, by Le Corbusier. No. 2432, Portrait of Giovanna Tornabuoni.

**1991, Oct. 30** ***Perf. 13½x14***

**2426** A136 $6.40 multicolored
**2427** A136 $7.65 multicolored
**2428** A136 $50 multicolored
**2429** A136 $100 multicolored
**2430** A136 $190 multicolored
*a.* Sheet of 5 + label, #2426-2430 12.00

### Souvenir Sheets

**2431** A136 $360 multicolored
**2432** A136 $360 multicolored
Nos. 2431-2432 (2) 25.00

Phila Nippon '91 — A137

Trains: $6.40, Class 581 12-car. $7.65, Class EF-81. $50, Class 381 9-car. $100, Kodama 8-car. $190, Shin-Kansen 16-car. No. 2438, Shin-Kansen 16-car, diff. No. 2439, Japanese locomotives in Calcutta.

**1991, Nov. 16** ***Perf. 14x13½***

**2433** A137 $6.40 multicolored
**2434** A137 $7.65 multicolored
**2435** A137 $50 multicolored
**2436** A137 $100 multicolored
**2437** A137 $190 multicolored
*Nos. 2433-2437 (5)* 16.50

### Souvenir Sheets

**2438** A137 $360 multicolored
**2439** A137 $360 multicolored
*Nos. 2438-2439 (2)* 32.50

Swiss Confederation, 700th anniv., #2439.

---

Common Design Types pictured following the introduction.

---

### Royal Family Birthday, Anniversary

Common Design Type

**1991, Nov.** **Litho.** ***Perf. 14***

**2440** CD347 $8.90 multi .35 .25
**2441** CD347 $12.80 multi .35 .30
**2442** CD347 $15.30 multi .35 .30
**2443** CD347 $50 multi 1.25 1.10
**2444** CD347 $75 multi 1.75 1.75
**2445** CD347 $100 multi 2.50 2.50
**2446** CD347 $130 multi 3.00 3.00
**2447** CD347 $150 multi 3.75 3.75
**2448** CD347 $190 multi 5.00 5.00
**2449** CD347 $200 multi 5.25 5.25
*Nos. 2440-2449 (10)* 23.55 23.20

### Souvenir Sheets

**2450** CD347 $225 Elizabeth 6.50 6.50
**2451** CD347 $225 Charles, Diana, sons 7.00 7.00

$8.90, $50, $75, $190, No. 2451, Charles and Diana, 10th wedding anniversary. $130, $150, Prince Philip, 70th birthday. Others, Queen Elizabeth II, 65th birthday.

### Miniature Sheet

Japanese Attack on Pearl Harbor, 50th Anniv. — A138

No. 2452: a, Akagi launches attack planes. b, Sakamaki's midget submarine beached. c, Mistubishi ASM Zero fighter. d, USS Arizona under attack. e, Aichi D3A1 Val dive bomber. f, USS California. g, P40 defends Pearl Harbor. h, USS Cassin and Downes hit at dry dock. i, B17 crash lands at Bellows Field. j, USS Nevada burns at Hospital Point.

**1991, Dec. 7** ***Perf. 14½x15***

**2452** A138 $50 Sheet of 10, #a.-j. 17.00 17.00

1992 Winter Olympics, Albertville — A139

Walt Disney characters at the Olympics: $6.40, Gus Gander playing ice hockey. $7.65, Mickey, Minnie in bobsled. $8.90, Huey, Dewey, Louie pretending to luge. $12.80, Goofy freestyle skiing. $50, Goofy ski jumping. $100, Donald, Daisy Duck speed skating. $130, Pluto cross-country skiing. $190, Mickey, Minnie ice dancing. No. 2461, Scrooge McDuck slalom skiing. No. 2462, Huey curling.

**1991, Dec. 12** ***Perf. 13½x13***

| | | | | | |
|---|---|---|---|---|---|
| **2453** | A139 | $6.40 multi | .40 | .40 |
| **2454** | A143 | $7.65 multi | .45 | .45 |
| **2455** | A139 | $8.90 multi | .50 | .50 |
| **2456** | A143 | $12.80 multi | .70 | .70 |
| **2457** | A143 | $50 multi | 1.50 | 1.50 |
| **2458** | A139 | $100 multi | 2.50 | 2.50 |
| **2459** | A139 | $130 multi | 3.00 | 3.00 |
| **2460** | A143 | $190 multi | 4.50 | 4.50 |
| | | *Nos. 2453-2460 (8)* | 13.55 | 13.55 |

**Souvenir Sheets**

| | | | | |
|---|---|---|---|---|
| **2461** | A139 | $225 multi | 7.00 | 7.00 |
| **2462** | A143 | $225 multi | 7.00 | 7.00 |

Mushrooms — A140

Designs: $6.40, Boletus satanoides. $7.65, Russula nigricans. $50, Cortinarius glaucopus. $100, Lactarius camphoratus. $190, Cortinarius callisteus. No. 2468, Russula integra. No. 2469, Coprinus micaceus, vert.

**1991, Dec. 16** **Litho.** ***Perf. 14x13½***

| | | | | |
|---|---|---|---|---|
| **2463** | A140 | $6.40 multicolored | | |
| **2464** | A140 | $7.65 multicolored | | |
| **2465** | A140 | $50 multicolored | | |
| **2466** | A140 | $100 multicolored | | |
| **2467** | A140 | $190 multicolored | | |
| | | *Nos. 2463-2467 (5)* | 16.00 | 16.00 |

**Souvenir Sheets**

***Perf. 14x13½, 13½x14***

| | | | |
|---|---|---|---|
| **2468** | A140 | $360 multicolored | |
| **2469** | A140 | $360 multicolored | |
| | | *Nos. 2468-2469 (2)* | 30.00 |

Walt Disney Christmas Cards — A141

Designs and year of issue: 80c, Mickey, friends singing carols, 1989. $2.55, Mickey, friends riding trolley car, 1962. $5, Donald, Pluto wrapping package, 1971. $6.40, Mickey holding candle, 1948. $7.65, Mickey with Santa mask, 1947. $8.90, Pinocchio's shadow, 1939. $50, Three Little Pigs, dancing on wolf's back, 1933. $200, Mickey, mice singing carols, 1949.

No. 2478: a, Conductor, Donald. b, Elephant with book. c, Goofy, centaurs. d, Snow White, dwarfs. e, Pluto, dinosaur.

No. 2479: a, Mickey in sleigh. b, Three little pigs, Winnie-the-Pooh, Bambi. c, Dalmatian, bear, monkey, Lady and the Tramp. d, Alice, Goofy, Mad Hatter. e, Pinocchio, Tinker Bell, Peter Pan, Seven Dwarfs, Donald Duck. f, Pluto, 1974.

No. 2480, Mickey and friends riding in coach, 1932. No. 2481, Mickey, Pluto greeting friends, 1935. No. 2482, Donald, Jose Carioca, 1944. No. 2483, Couple dancing, baseball batter, 1945. No. 2484, Mickey, Donald, Goofy, 1946. No. 2485, Santa in chimney, 1969. No. 2486, Portrait of Winnie-the-Pooh hanging on wall, 1969. No. 2487, Mickey, 1978.

**1991, Dec. 17** ***Perf. 14x13½***

| | | | | |
|---|---|---|---|---|
| **2470** | A141 | 80c multi | .25 | .25 |
| **2471** | A141 | $2.55 multi | .25 | .25 |
| **2472** | A141 | $5 multi | .25 | .25 |
| **2473** | A141 | $6.40 multi | .35 | .25 |
| **2474** | A141 | $7.65 multi | .35 | .25 |
| **2475** | A141 | $8.90 multi | .35 | .25 |
| **2476** | A141 | $50 multi | 1.40 | 1.40 |
| **2477** | A141 | $200 multi | 5.25 | 5.25 |
| **2478** | A141 | $50 Strip of 5, #a.-e. | 7.00 | 7.00 |
| **2479** | A141 | $50 Strip of 6, #a.-f. | 8.50 | 8.50 |
| | | *Nos. 2470-2479 (10)* | 23.95 | 23.65 |

**Souvenir Sheets**

| | | | | |
|---|---|---|---|---|
| **2480** | A141 | $260 multi | 6.00 | 6.00 |
| **2481** | A141 | $260 multi | 6.00 | 6.00 |
| **2482** | A141 | $260 multi | 6.00 | 6.00 |
| **2483** | A141 | $260 multi | 6.00 | 6.00 |
| **2484** | A141 | $260 multi | 6.00 | 6.00 |
| **2485** | A141 | $260 multi | 6.00 | 6.00 |
| **2486** | A141 | $260 multi | 6.00 | 6.00 |
| **2487** | A141 | $260 multi | 6.00 | 6.00 |
| | | *Nos. 2480-2487 (8)* | 48.00 | 48.00 |

Nos. 2478a-2478e, 2479a-2479f, 2480-2481, 2485 and 2487 are vert.

**No. 2377 Surcharged**

**1991, Dec. 19** **Litho.** ***Perf. 14***

**2487B** A129 $600 on $190 #2377 — —

An additional sheet was issued in this set. The editors would like to examine it.

Christmas A142

Paintings: $6.40, Madonna and Child with Angels, by Titian, horiz. $7.65, Madonna and Child with Angels, by Rubens. $50, Madonna and Child, by Raphael. $100, Madonna and Child, by Durer. $190, Madonna, by Durer. No. 2493, Madonna and Child, by Rubens, horiz. No. 2494, Madonna, by Durer, diff.

**1991, Dec. 30** ***Perf. 14x13½, 13½x14***

| | | | |
|---|---|---|---|
| **2488** | A142 | $6.40 multicolored | |
| **2489** | A142 | $7.65 multicolored | |
| **2490** | A142 | $50 multicolored | |
| **2491** | A142 | $100 multicolored | |
| **2492** | A142 | $190 multicolored | |
| | | *Nos. 2488-2 92(5)* | 15.00 |

**Souvenir Sheets**

| | | | |
|---|---|---|---|
| **2493** | A142 | $360 multicolored | |
| **2494** | A142 | $360 multicolored | |
| | | *Nos. 2493-2494 (2)* | 35.00 |

Brandenburg Gate, Bicent. — A143

Designs: $10, Map of Berlin. $25, US Pres. George Bush, Polish Pres. Lech Walesa. $100, German Chancellor Helmut Kohl, Foreign Minister Hans-Dietrich Genscher. $190, Armored helmet.

**1991, Dec.** ***Perf. 14***

| | | | | |
|---|---|---|---|---|
| **2495** | A143 | $10 multicolored | .40 | .40 |
| **2496** | A143 | $25 multicolored | .90 | .90 |
| **2497** | A143 | $100 multicolored | 3.25 | 3.25 |
| | | *Nos. 2495-2497 (3)* | 4.55 | 4.55 |

**Souvenir Sheet**

**2498** A143 $190 multicolored 6.50 6.50

Wolfgang Amadeus Mozart, Death Bicent. A144

Portrait of Mozart and: $75, Laxenburg. $80, Death of Leopold II. $100, Mozart's birthplace, Salzburg.

**1991, Dec.**

| | | | | |
|---|---|---|---|---|
| **2499** | A144 | $75 multicolored | 2.50 | 2.50 |
| **2500** | A144 | $80 multicolored | 2.75 | 2.75 |
| **2501** | A144 | $100 multicolored | 3.00 | 3.00 |
| | | *Nos. 2499-2501 (3)* | 8.25 | 8.25 |

**Souvenir Sheet**

**2502** A144 $190 Bust of Mozart, vert. 6.00 6.00

17th World Scout Jamboree, Korea — A145

Designs: $30, Scouts hiking. $40, Emblems, flag. $100, Lord Baden-Powell, vert. $190, Rocket cover with US No. 1145.

**1991, Dec.**

| | | | | |
|---|---|---|---|---|
| **2503** | A145 | $25 multicolored | 1.00 | 1.00 |
| **2504** | A145 | $30 multicolored | 1.10 | 1.10 |
| **2505** | A145 | $40 multicolored | 1.25 | 1.25 |
| **2506** | A145 | $100 multicolored | 3.25 | 3.25 |
| | | *Nos. 2503-2506 (4)* | 6.60 | 6.60 |

**Souvenir Sheet**

**2507** A145 $190 multicolored 6.50 6.50

Charles de Gaulle A146

De Gaulle: $60, In Venice, 1944. $75, With Khrushchev, 1960. $80, In Algiers, 1958. $100, With Pope Paul VI, 1967.

**1991, Dec.**

| | | | | |
|---|---|---|---|---|
| **2508** | A146 | $60 multicolored | 2.00 | 2.00 |
| **2509** | A146 | $75 multicolored | 2.50 | 2.50 |
| **2510** | A146 | $80 multicolored | 2.75 | 2.75 |
| **2511** | A146 | $100 multicolored | 3.25 | 3.25 |
| | | *Nos. 2508-2511 (4)* | 10.50 | 10.50 |

**Souvenir Sheets**

| | | | | |
|---|---|---|---|---|
| **2512** | A146 | $150 Portrait, vert. | 7.50 | 7.50 |
| **2513** | A146 | $190 Portrait, diff, vert. | 9.75 | 9.75 |

Anniversaries and Events — A147

Designs: No. 2515, Caroline Herschel, astronomer, Old Town Hall, Hanover. No. 2516, Map of Switzerland, woman in traditional dress. $80, Otto Lilienthal's glider No. 3. $100, Locomotive. $190, Arms of Bern and Solothurn.

**1991, Dec.**

| | | | | |
|---|---|---|---|---|
| **2515** | A147 | $75 multicolored | 4.00 | 4.00 |
| **2516** | A147 | $75 multicolored | 3.25 | 3.25 |
| **2517** | A147 | $80 multicolored | 3.75 | 3.75 |
| **2518** | A147 | $100 multicolored | 5.00 | 5.00 |
| | | *Nos. 2515-2518 (4)* | 16.00 | 16.00 |

**Souvenir Sheet**

**2519** A147 $190 multicolored 5.75 5.75

Hanover, 750th anniv. (#2515), Swiss Confederation, 700th anniv. (#2516, 2519), first glider flight, cent. (#2517), Trans-Siberian Railway, cent. (#2518).

Discovery of America, 500th Anniv. A148

Designs: $6.40, Columbus lands on Trinidad. $7.65, Columbus, globe. $8.90, Ships blown off course by hurricane. $12.80, Map, hands in chains. $15.30, Land sighted. $50, Nina, Pinta. $75, Santa Maria. $100, Columbus trading with natives. $125, Superstitions & sea monsters. $130, Map, Columbus ashore. $140, Priest & natives. $150, Columbus kneeling before King Ferdinand and Queen Isabella. #2532, Map of New World. #2533, One of Columbus' ships, vert. #2534, Columbus.

**1992, Jan. 2** ***Perf. 14***

| | | | | |
|---|---|---|---|---|
| **2520** | A148 | $6.40 multi | .40 | .35 |
| **2521** | A148 | $7.65 multi | .45 | .40 |
| **2522** | A148 | $8.90 multi | .50 | .45 |
| **2523** | A148 | $12.80 multi | .55 | .50 |
| **2524** | A148 | $15.30 multi | .60 | .55 |
| **2525** | A148 | $50 multi | 1.75 | 1.75 |
| **2526** | A148 | $75 multi | 2.25 | 2.25 |
| **2527** | A148 | $100 multi | 3.00 | 3.00 |
| **2528** | A148 | $125 multi | 3.75 | 3.75 |
| **2529** | A148 | $130 multi | 4.00 | 4.00 |
| **2530** | A148 | $140 multi | 4.25 | 4.25 |
| **2531** | A148 | $150 multi | 4.50 | 4.50 |
| | | *Nos. 2520-2531 (12)* | 26.00 | 25.75 |

**Souvenir Sheets**

| | | | | |
|---|---|---|---|---|
| **2532** | A148 | $280 multi | 8.50 | 8.50 |
| **2533** | A148 | $280 multi | 8.50 | 8.50 |
| **2534** | A148 | $280 multi | 8.50 | 8.50 |

Movie Posters — A149

Designs: $8.90, The Great K & A Train Robbery. $12.80, Cimarron. $15.30, Buzzin' Around. $25, Adventures of Captain Marvel. $30, The Mummy. $50, A Sainted Devil. $75, A Tale of Two Cities. $100, A Tugboat Romeo. $130, Thief of Bagdad. $150, Bacon Grabbers. $190, A Night at the Opera. $200, Citizen Kane. No. 2547, She Done Him Wrong. No. 2548, The Circus. No. 2549, Babe Comes Home. No. 2550, Zeppelin, horiz.

**1992, Mar. 11** **Litho.** ***Perf. 14***

| | | | | |
|---|---|---|---|---|
| **2535** | A149 | $8.90 multi | .60 | .50 |
| **2536** | A149 | $12.80 multi | .65 | .55 |
| **2537** | A149 | $15.30 multi | .70 | .65 |
| **2538** | A149 | $25 multi | .80 | .75 |
| **2539** | A149 | $30 multi | .90 | .85 |
| **2540** | A149 | $50 multi | 1.50 | 1.40 |
| **2541** | A149 | $75 multi | 2.25 | 2.00 |
| **2542** | A149 | $100 multi | 3.00 | 2.75 |
| **2543** | A149 | $130 multi | 3.75 | 3.50 |
| **2544** | A149 | $150 multi | 4.50 | 4.25 |
| **2545** | A149 | $190 multi | 5.75 | 5.50 |
| **2546** | A149 | $200 multi | 6.00 | 5.75 |
| | | *Nos. 2535-2546 (12)* | 30.40 | 28.45 |

**Size: 70x100mm, 100x70mm**

***Imperf***

| | | | | |
|---|---|---|---|---|
| **2547** | A149 | $225 multi | 6.75 | 6.75 |
| **2548** | A149 | $225 multi | 6.75 | 6.75 |
| **2549** | A149 | $225 multi | 6.75 | 6.75 |
| **2550** | A149 | $225 multi | 6.75 | 6.75 |

No. 2273 Overprinted or Surcharged with Olympic Rings and "ALBERTVILLE '92" or "XVIth Olympic Winter / Games in Albertville" (No. 2551e)

**1992** *Perfs. as Before*

**2551** A122 Sheet of 9
*a.-f.* $20 on #2273a-2273f
*g.* $70 on $20 #2273g
*h.* $100 on $20 #2273h
*i.* $190 on $20 #2273i

Nos. 2391g, 2395c, 2396c, 2398, 2400 Ovptd. "ALBERTVILLE '92"
No. 2399 Ovptd. "Barcelona '92" and emblems in Sheet Margin

**1992** *Perfs. as Before*

**2552** A133 $17.80 on #2391g 12.00 12.00
**2553** A133 $25 on #2395c 12.00 12.00
**2554** A133 $30 on #2396c 12.00 12.00

**Souvenir Sheets**

**2555** A133 $150 on #2398 7.00 7.00
**2556** A133 $150 on #2399 7.00 7.00
**2557** A133 $190 on #2400 7.00 7.00

Nos. 2552-2554 printed in sheets of 9, overprint applied to only one stamp per sheet. Overprint on Nos. 2555, 2557 applied to sheet margin.

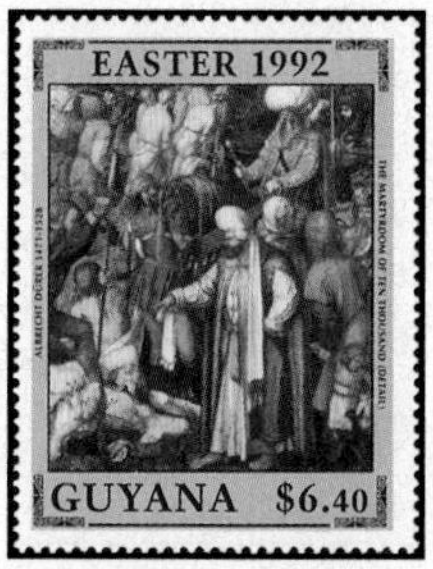


Easter
A150

Various details from paintings by Durer: $6.40, $12.80, $50, $130, No. 2567, The Martyrdom of Ten Thousand. $7.65, $15.30, $100, $190, No. 2566, Adoration of the Trinity.

**1992** **Litho.** *Perf. 13½x14*

**2558** A150 $6.40 multi .30 .25
**2559** A150 $7.65 multi .30 .25
**2560** A150 $12.80 multi .45 .25
**2561** A150 $15.30 multi .55 .45
**2562** A150 $50 multi 1.50 1.25
**2563** A150 $100 multi 2.75 2.75
**2564** A150 $130 multi 3.75 3.75
**2565** A150 $190 multi 5.75 5.75
*Nos. 2558-2565 (8)* 15.35 14.70

**Souvenir Sheets**

**2566** A150 $225 multi 6.75 6.75
**2567** A150 $225 multi 6.75 6.75

Queen Elizabeth II's Accession to the Throne, 40th Anniv.
A151

Queen Elizabeth II: $8.90, With Prince Philip. $12.80, In uniform. $100, At coronation. $130, Wearing black cape and hat. No. 2572, Coronation portrait. No. 2573, Fortieth anniv. portrait.

**1992** **Litho.** *Perf. 14*

**2568** A151 $8.90 multicolored 1.00 .50
**2569** A151 $12.80 multicolored 1.50 .60
**2570** A151 $100 multicolored 5.25 4.00
**2571** A151 $130 multicolored 6.25 5.00
*Nos. 2568-2571 (4)* 14.00 10.10

**Souvenir Sheets**

**2572** A151 $225 multicolored 7.25 7.25
**2573** A151 $225 multicolored 7.25 7.25

Diocese of Guyana, 150th Anniv.
A152

Designs: $6.40, Holy Cross Church, Annai Bupununi. $50, St. Peter's Church. $100, St. George's Cathedral, interior, vert. $190, Map, vert. $225, Religious symbols.

**1992** **Litho.** *Perf. 14*

**2574** A152 $6.40 multicolored .40 .30
**2575** A152 $50 multicolored 1.25 1.10
**2576** A152 $100 multicolored 2.75 2.75
**2577** A152 $190 multicolored 4.50 4.50
*Nos. 2574-2577 (4)* 8.90 8.65

**Souvenir Sheet**

**2578** A152 $225 multicolored 7.00 7.00

Nos. 1033, 1045 and 1061 Surcharged

**Method, Perfs, and Watermarks As Before**

**1992, May 29**

**2578A** A91 $6.40 on 60c #1033 — —
**2578B** A91 $7.65 on 60c #1061 — —
**2578C** A91 $8.90 on 60c #1045 — —

An additional stamp was issued in this set. The editors would like to examine any example of it.

Miniature Sheet

Horses — A153

No. 2579: a, Palomino. b, Appaloosa. c, Clydesdale. d, Arab. e, Morgan. f, Friesian. g, Pinto. h, Thoroughbred. No. 2580, Lipizzaner.

**1992, Aug. 10**

**2579** A153 $190 Sheet of 8, #a.-h. 37.50 37.50

**Souvenir Sheet**

**2580** A153 $190 multicolored 8.00 8.00

No. 2580 contains one 58x29mm stamp.

Cats — A154

No. 2588A: b, Russian blue. c, Havana brown. d, Himalayan. e, Manx. f, Cornish rex. g, Black Persian. h, Scottish fold. i, Siamese.

**1992, Aug. 10** *Perf. 14½x14*

**2581** A154 $5 Burmese .30 .25
**2582** A154 $6.40 Turkish van .30 .25
**2583** A154 $12.80 American shorthair .40 .35
**2584** A154 $15.30 Egyptian .55 .50
**2585** A154 $50 Egyptian mau 1.75 1.50
**2586** A154 $100 Japanese bobtail 3.25 3.25
**2587** A154 $130 Abyssinian 4.00 4.00
**2588** A154 $225 Oriental shorthair 7.50 7.50
*Nos. 2581-2588 (8)* 18.05 17.60

**Miniature Sheet**

*Perf. 14x13½*

**2588A** A154 $50 Sheet of 8, #b.-i. 12.00 12.00

**Souvenir Sheets**

*Perf. 14x14½*

**2589** A152 $250 Chartreuse, vert. 7.25 7.25
**2590** A154 $250 Turkish angora 7.25 7.25
**2591** A154 $250 Maine coon 7.25 7.25
**2592** A154 $250 Chinchilla 7.25 7.25

No. 2589 has continuous design. Nos. 2590-2592 are vert. and have continous design.

Nos. 2368-2369 Surcharged on 4 stamps and Overprinted in Red "PHILA NIPPON '91 / WORLD STAMP EXHIBITION NIPPON '91" and Show Emblem in Sheet Margin
No. 2376 Surcharged in Red

**1992** *Perfs. as Before*

**2593** A129 Sheet of 12, #a.-d., #2368a-2368l 19.00
*a.* $25 on $10 #2368m
*b.* $50 on $10 #2368n
*c.* $75 on $10 #2368o
*d.* $130 on $10 #2368p
**2594** A129 Sheet of 16, #a.-d., 2369a-2369l 19.00
*a.* $25 on $12.80 #2369m
*b.* $50 on $12.80 #2369n
*c.* $75 on $12.80 #2369o
*d.* $100 on $12.80 #2369p

**Souvenir Sheet**

**2595** A129 $250 on $150 #2376

Nos. 2332-2340, 2346-2347 Overprinted or Surcharged

Overprints: 80c, $2.55, Nos. 2602-2603, Lions emblem and "Lions International / 1917-1992." $5, $6.40, $7.65, Nos. 2601, 2604d, 2604m, Lions emblem and "Melvin Jones Founder 1880-1961" on 2 or 3 lines. Nos. 2604a, 2604p, Lions emblem and "1917-1992." Nos. 2604b, 2604i, 2604o, Rotary emblem and "1905-1990." Nos. 2604c, 2604l, 2604n, Boy Scout emblem and "1907-1992." Nos. 2604e, 2604h, Red Cross emblem and "125 Years Red Cross." Nos. 2604f-2604g, 2604j-2604k have parts of larger Lions emblem. Nos. 2605-2606 have service organization emblems in sheet margins.

**1992** *Perfs. as Before*

**2596** A126 80c on #2332
**2597** A126 $2.55 on #2333
**2598** A126 $5 on #2334
**2599** A126 $6.40 on #2335
**2600** A126 $7.65 on #2336
**2601** A126 $100 on $8.90 #2337
**2602** A126 $190 on $50 #2338
**2603** A126 $225 on $100 #2339

**Miniature Sheet**

**2604** Sheet of 16 45.00
*a.-l.* A126 $10 any single
*m.* A126 $50 on $10 #2340m
*n.* A126 $75 on $10 #2340n
*o.* A126 $100 on $10 #2340o
*p.* A126 $190 on $10 #2340p

**Souvenir Sheets**

**2605** A126 $400 on $190 #2346
**2606** A126 $500 on $190 #2347

Elephants — A155

No. 2607: a, Mammoth, Oligocene Epoch. b, Stegodon, mid- Miocene Epoch. c, Mammoth, Pliocene Epoch. d, Hannibal's army crossing Alps. e, Royal elephant of the Maharaja of Mysore, India. f, Elephant pulling tree trunks, Burma. g, Tiger hunt, India. h, Elephant towing raft on River Kwai, Thailand.
$225, African elephants, Kenya.

**1992, Aug. 10** **Litho.** *Perf. 14*

**2607** A155 $50 Sheet of 8, #a.-h. 16.00 16.00

**Souvenir Sheet**

**2608** A155 $225 multicolored 11.00 11.00

No. 2607 has continuous design.

Animals of Guyana
A156

**1992, Aug. 10**

**2609** A156 $8.90 Red howler monkey .25 .25
**2610** A156 $12.80 Ring-tailed coati .30 .25
**2611** A156 $15.30 Jaguar .40 .35
**2612** A156 $25 Two-toed sloth .65 .60
**2613** A156 $50 Giant armadillo 1.40 1.25
**2614** A156 $75 Giant anteater 2.00 2.00
**2615** A156 $100 Capybara 2.75 2.75
**2616** A156 $130 Ocelot 3.50 3.50
*Nos. 2609-2616 (8)* 11.25 10.95

**Souvenir Sheets**

**2617** A156 $225 Wooly opossum, vert. 7.00 7.00
**2618** A156 $225 Night monkey, vert. 7.00 7.00

Souvenir Sheet

Statue of Liberty, New York — A157

**1992, Oct. 28**

**2619** A157 $325 multicolored 11.00 11.00

Postage Stamp Mega Event '92, New York City.

**Nos. 1072a, 1075a, 1077a and 1080a Surcharged**

**Methods, Perfs, and Watermarks As Before**

**1992, Nov. 2**

| | | | | |
|---|---|---|---|---|
| **2619A** | A91 | $6.40 on 150c #1080a | — | — |
| **2619B** | A91 | $7.65 on 150c #1075a | — | — |
| **2619C** | A91 | $8.90 on 150c #1072a | — | — |
| **2619D** | A91 | $10 on 200c #1077a | — | — |

An additional stamp was issued in this set. The editors would like to examine any example of it.

Miniature Sheets

Model Trains — A158

Marklin toy locomotives: No. 2620a, 2-4-4-2 Crocodile locomotive, 1 gauge, 1933. b, French prototype streetcar, 1 gauge, 1933. c, British prototype Flatiron 2-4-4 tank engine, O gauge, 1913. d, German National Railways 0-6-0 switching engine, Z gauge, 1970. e, Smoking/non-smoking third class car, 1 gauge, 1909. f, American style 0-4-0 locomotive, O gauge, 1904. g, Zurich, Switzerland prototype streetcar, O gauge, 1928. h, Central London Railway Bo-Bo, 1 gauge, 1904. i, "The Great Bear" Pacific, 1 gauge, 1909.

No. 2621: a, 0-4-4 American style locomotive, 2 gauge, 1907. b, German first and second class passenger car, 1 gauge, 1908. c, British Great Eastern Railway 4-4-0, 1 gauge, 1908. d, English prototype steeplecab, O gauge, 1904. e, Santa Fe Railroad diesel, 1962. f, British Great Northern 4-4-0, 3 gauge, live steam model, 1903. g, Caledonian Railway "Cardean" of Scotland, 1 gauge, 1904. h, British LNWR passenger car, 1 gauge, 1903. i, Swiss Gotthard Rwy. 0-4-0 locomotive, O gauge, 1920.

No. 2622: a, British LB & SCR tank engine, O gauge, 1920. b, Central London Railway, tunnel locomotive, 1 gauge, 1904. c, "Borsig" 4-6-4 streamliner, O gauge, 1935. d, French PLM first class car, 1 gauge, 1929. e, American style 0-4-0 locomotive #1021, 1 gauge, 1904. f, "Paris-Orsay" long-nose steeplecab, 1 gauge, 1920. g, British "Cock O' The North," 1 gauge, 1936. h, Prussian State Railways P8 4-6-0 live steam model, 1 gauge, 1975. i, 1937 German "Schnell Treibwagen," O gauge, 1937.

No. 2623: a, Marklin North British Railway "Atlantic," 1 gauge, 1913. b, Bing British London & Western Railway 4-4-2 "Precursor," O gauge, clockwork model, 1916. c, Marklin British Great Western "King George V," O gauge, 1937. d, Marklin passenger car, "Kaiser Train," 1 gauge, 1901. e, Bing 4-4-0 side tank engine, 1 gauge, live steam model, 1904. f, Marklin short-nose steeplecab, 1 gauge, 1912. g, Marklin "Der Adler", 1 gauge, 1935. h, Bing British Great Western Railway "County of Northampton," 1 gauge, live steam model, 1909. i, Bing British Midland Railway "Black Prince," 3 gauge, live steam model, 1908.

Bing toy locomotives: No. 2624: a, Midland Railway "Deeley Type" 4-4-0, 1 gauge clockwork model, 1909. b, No. 2631, British Midland Railway 0-4-0, 3 gauge clockwork model, 1903. c, German 4-6-2 Pacific, O gauge clockwork model, 1927. d, British Great Western Railway, third class coach, O gauge, 1926. e, British London & Southwestern "M7" 0-4-4, 1 gauge clockwork model, 1909. f, "Pilot" 4-4-0 side tank engine, 3 gauge live steam model, 1901. g, British London & Northwestern Railway Webb "Cauliflower," O gauge clockwork model, 1912. h, No. 112, 4-4-0 side tank locomotive, 1 gauge live steam model, 1910. i, British Great Northern Railway, "Stirling Single," 2 gauge live steam model, 1904.

Carette toy locomotives: No. 2625: a, Lithographed tin "Penny Bazaar" train, 1904. b, Winteringham 0-4-0 locomotive, O gauge, 1917. c, British Northeastern Railway, Smith Compound, 3 gauge, 1905. d, SE & CR 2-2-4 steam railcar, 1 gauge, live steam model, 1908. e, No. 776 British Great Northern Railway Stirling "Single," 3 gauge, live steam model, 1903. f, British Midland Railway 4-4-0, O gauge, clockwork model, 1911. g, London Metropolitan Railway "Westinghouse," 1 gauge, 1908. h, Clestory coach, 1 gauge, 1907. i, Steam railcar No. 1, O gauge, live steam model, 1906.

Marklin toy locomotives: No. 2626: a, LMS "Precursor" 4-4-2 tank engine, O gauge clockwork model, 1923. b, American "Congressional Limited" passenger car, 1 gauge, 1908. c, Swiss prototype "Ae 3/6" locomotive, O gauge, 1934. d, German National Railways class 80, 0-6-0, 1 gauge, 1975. e, British Southern Railway third class coach, O gauge, 1926. f, "Bowen-Cooke" 4-6-2 tank engine, O gauge, 1913. g, First electric prototype model, "Two Penny Tube," London, 1 gauge clockwork model, 1901. h, "Paris-Orsay" steeplecab, 1 gauge, 1920. i, 0-2-2 Passenger engine, O gauge clockwork model, 1895.

Bing toy locomotives: No. 2627: a, 2-2-0 engine and tender, 2 gauge live steam model, 1895. b, British Midland Railway "single," O gauge clockwork model, 1913. c, #524/510 reversible express passenger locomotive, 1 gauge, 1916. d, "Kaiser Train" passenger car with Gothic windows, 1 gauge, 1902. e, Tinplate model, British rural station, 1 gauge, 1915. f, British LSMR "M7" side tank locomotive, O gauge clockwork model, 1909. g, 4-4-4 "Windcutter," 1 gauge live steam model, 1912. h, British Great Central Railway "Sir Sam Fay," 1 gauge clockwork model, 1914. i, "Dunalastair" locomotive Caledonian Railway, 1 gauge clockwork model, 1910.

No. 2628, German National Railroad class 0-1 Pacific, O gauge, 1937. No. 2629, Bing 0-4-0 Contractor's locomotive, 4 gauge, 1904. No. 2630, Rack Railway "Steeplecab" locomotive, 2 gauge, 1908. No. 2631, Bing Pabst Blue Ribbon Beer refrigerator car, O gauge, 1925. No. 2632, Marklin "Commodore Vanderbilt," O gauge, 1937. No. 2633, Bing British Great Western Railway "County of Northampton," 1 gauge, live steam model, 1909. No. 2634, Marklin French Prototype PLM Pacific, 1 gauge, live steam model, 1912. No. 2635, Marklin "Mountain Etat" second series, O gauge, 1933.

**1992, Nov. 19** ***Perf. 14***

| | | | | | |
|---|---|---|---|---|---|
| **2620** | A158 | $45 | Sheet of 9, #a.-i. | 8.00 | 8.00 |
| **2621** | A158 | $45 | Sheet of 9, #a.-i. | 8.00 | 8.00 |
| **2622** | A158 | $45 | Sheet of 9, #a.-i. | 8.00 | 8.00 |
| **2623** | A158 | $45 | Sheet of 9, #a.-i. | 8.00 | 8.00 |
| **2624** | A158 | $45 | Sheet of 9, #a.-i. | 8.00 | 8.00 |
| **2625** | A158 | $45 | Sheet of 9, #a.-i. | 8.00 | 8.00 |
| **2626** | A158 | $45 | Sheet of 9, #a.-i. | 8.00 | 8.00 |
| **2627** | A158 | $45 | Sheet of 9, #a.-i. | 8.00 | 8.00 |

**Souvenir Sheets**

| | | | | | |
|---|---|---|---|---|---|
| **2628** | A158 | $350 | multicolored | 7.00 | 7.00 |
| **2629** | A158 | $350 | multicolored | 7.00 | 7.00 |

***Perf. 14x13½***

| | | | | | |
|---|---|---|---|---|---|
| **2630** | A158 | $350 | multicolored | 7.00 | 7.00 |

***Perf. 13x13½, 13½x13***

| | | | | | |
|---|---|---|---|---|---|
| **2631** | A158 | $350 | multicolored | 7.00 | 7.00 |
| **2632** | A158 | $350 | multicolored | 7.00 | 7.00 |
| **2633** | A158 | $350 | multicolored | 7.00 | 7.00 |
| **2634** | A158 | $350 | multicolored | 7.00 | 7.00 |
| **2635** | A158 | $350 | multicolored | 7.00 | 7.00 |

Genoa '92. Nos. 2628-2635 each contain one 50x39mm stamp.

While Nos. 2622-2623 & 2631 have the issue date as Nos. 2620-2621 & 2628-2630, the face value of Nos. 2622-2623 & 2631 was lower when they were released.

Anniversaries and Events — A159

Designs: $12.80, Zeppelin over Lake Constance, 1909. No. 2638, Voyager 1, Jupiter. No. 2639, Konrad Adenauer, John F. Kennedy. No. 2640, Aeromedical airlift. No. 2641, Amazon dolphins. No. 2642, Lift-off of Voyager 1, 1977. No. 2643, Baby gorilla. No. 2644, America's Cup yacht Stars and Stripes. No. 2644A, Eye screening van, doctor with patient. $190, Adenauer, Charles de Gaulle. $225, Zeppelin preparing for takeoff. No. 2647, Count Zeppelin, vert. No. 2648 View of Earth from space, vert. No. 2649, Konrad Adenauer, vert. No. 2650, Tree frog, vert.

**1993, Jan.** **Litho.** ***Perf. 14***

| | | | | | |
|---|---|---|---|---|---|
| **2637** | A159 | $12.80 | multi | .75 | .75 |
| **2638** | A159 | $50 | multi | 1.75 | 1.75 |
| **2639** | A159 | $50 | multi | 2.00 | 2.00 |
| **2640** | A159 | $100 | multi | 4.50 | 4.50 |
| **2641** | A159 | $100 | multi | 3.00 | 3.00 |
| **2642** | A159 | $130 | multi | 4.25 | 4.25 |
| **2643** | A159 | $130 | multi | 3.75 | 3.75 |
| **2644** | A159 | $130 | multi | 4.75 | 4.75 |
| **2644A** | A159 | $130 | multi | 4.75 | 4.75 |
| **2645** | A159 | $190 | multi | 6.00 | 6.00 |
| **2646** | A159 | $225 | multi | 6.50 | 6.50 |
| | | | *Nos. 2637-2646 (11)* | 42.00 | 42.00 |

**Souvenir Sheets**

| | | | | | |
|---|---|---|---|---|---|
| **2647** | A159 | $225 | multi | 7.50 | 7.50 |
| **2648** | A159 | $225 | multi | 7.00 | 7.00 |
| **2649** | A159 | $225 | multi | 7.00 | 7.00 |
| **2650** | A159 | $225 | multi | 7.00 | 7.00 |

Count Zeppelin, 75th anniv. of death (#2637, 2646-2647). Intl. Space Year (#2638, 2642, 2648). Konrad Adenaurer, 25th anniv. of death (#2639, 2645, 2649). World Health Organization (#2640). Earth Summit, Rio (#2641, 2643, 2650). America's Cup Yacht Race (#2644). Lions Intl., 75th anniv. (#2644A).

Miniature Sheet

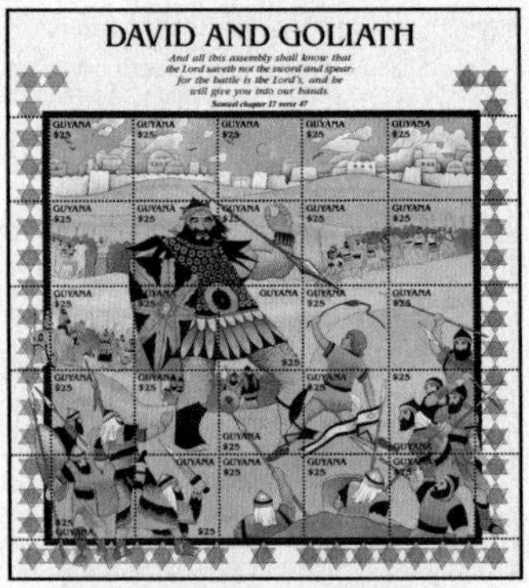


Biblical Story of David and Goliath — A160

No. 2651: a, City of Jerusalem, two birds in flight. b, City, bird in flight at right. c, City, sun above. d, City, bird in flight at left. e, City with clouds above. f, Philistine army (i-k, q-r). g, Goliath. h, Goliath's arm, spear shaft (b, i, n). l, Goliath's leg (m, q-s), shield. n, David (r-t, w) with slingshot. o, Jewish soldiers with spears or swords (p-y).

**1992, Dec. 29** **Litho.** ***Perf. 14***

| | | | | | |
|---|---|---|---|---|---|
| **2651** | A160 | $25 | Sheet of 25, #a.-y. | 19.00 | 19.00 |

No. 2651 has a continuous design.

Parrots A161

**1993, Mar. 10**

| | | | | | |
|---|---|---|---|---|---|
| **2652** | A161 | 80c | Hyacinth macaw | .35 | .25 |
| **2653** | A161 | $6.40 | Scarlet macaw | .60 | .30 |
| **2654** | A161 | $7.65 | Green macaw, vert. | .60 | .30 |
| **2655** | A161 | $15.30 | Tovi parakeet | .80 | .60 |
| **2656** | A161 | $50 | Blue & yellow macaw | 1.25 | .95 |
| **2657** | A161 | $100 | Military macaw, vert. | 2.50 | 2.40 |
| **2658** | A161 | $130 | Red & green macaw, vert. | 3.25 | 3.25 |
| **2659** | A161 | $190 | Severa macaw | 3.75 | 3.75 |
| | | | *Nos. 2652-2659 (8)* | 13.10 | 11.80 |

**Souvenir Sheet**

| | | | | | |
|---|---|---|---|---|---|
| **2660** | A161 | $225 | Scarlet macaw, diff. | 6.00 | 6.00 |
| **2661** | A161 | $225 | Green parakeet, vert. | 6.00 | 6.00 |

While Nos. 2654-2656, 2659, 2661 have the same issue date as Nos. 2652-2653, 2657-2658, 2660, the value of Nos. 2654-2656, 2659, 2661 was lower when released.

For surcharge, see No. 4172.

Miniature Sheets

Dinosaurs — A162

No. 2662: a, Archaeopteryx. b, Pteranodon. c, Quetzalcoatlus. d, Protoavis. e, Dicraeosaurus. f, Moschops. g, Lystrosaurus. h, Dimetrondon. i, Staurikosaurus. j, Cacops. k, Diarthrognathus. l, Estemmenosuchus.

No. 2663: a, Pteranodon. b, Cearadactylus. c, Eudimorphodon. d, Pterodactylus. e, Stauirkosaurus. f, Euoplocephalus. g, Tuojiangosaurus. h, Oviraptor. i, Protoceratops. j, Panaoplosaurus. k, Psittacosaurus. l, Corythosaurus.

No. 2664: a, Sordes. b, Quetzalcoatlus. c, Archaeopteryx. d, Rhamphorynchus. e, Spinosaurus. f, Anchisaurus. g, Stegosaurus. h, Leaellynosaurus. i, Minmi. j, Heterdontosaurus. k, Lesothosaurus. l, Deninonychus.

**1993, Mar. 10** **Litho.** ***Perf. 14***

| | | | | | |
|---|---|---|---|---|---|
| **2662** | A162 | $30 | Sheet of 12, #a.-l. | 8.75 | 8.75 |
| **2663** | A162 | $30 | Sheet of 12, #a.-l. | 8.75 | 8.75 |
| **2664** | A162 | $30 | Sheet of 12, #a.-l. | 8.75 | 8.75 |

For surcharge, see No. 4117.

Miniature Sheet

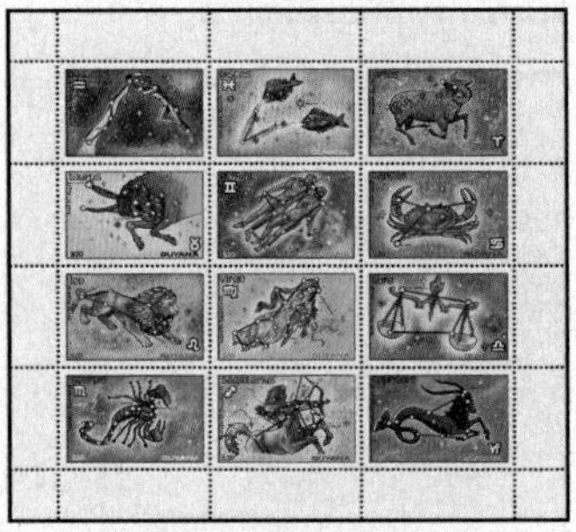

Signs of the Zodiac — A163

No. 2665: a, Aquarius. b, Pisces. c, Aries. d, Taurus. e, Gemini. f, Cancer. g, Leo. h, Virgo. i, Libra. j, Scorpio. k, Sagittarius. l, Capricorn.

**1992, Dec. 29** **Litho.** ***Perf. 14x13½***

**Sheet of 12**

| | | | | | |
|---|---|---|---|---|---|
| **2665** | A163 | $30 | Sheet of 12, #a.-l. | 19.00 | 19.00 |

Caribbean Manatee A164

Designs: $6.40, Adult sticking head out of water. $7.65, Adult, eating, with young. $8.90, Adult swimming underwater. $50, Adult swimming with young.

**1993, Mar. 10** **Litho.** ***Perf. 15x14½***

| | | | | | |
|---|---|---|---|---|---|
| **2666** | A164 | $6.40 | multicolored | 1.25 | 1.10 |
| **2667** | A164 | $7.65 | multicolored | 1.25 | 1.10 |
| **2668** | A164 | $8.90 | multicolored | 1.25 | 1.10 |
| **2669** | A164 | $50 | multicolored | 4.75 | 4.75 |
| | | | *Nos. 2666-2669 (4)* | 8.50 | 8.05 |

World Wildlife Federation. Exists imperf. Value, set $36.

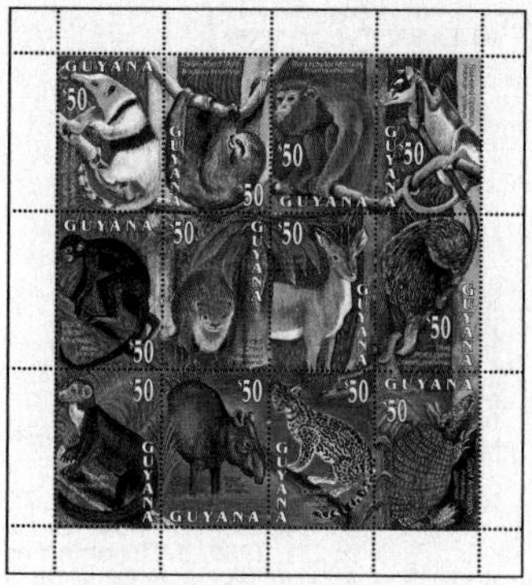

Fauna — A165

No. 2670: a, Southern tamandua. b, Three-toed sloth. c, Red howler monkey. d, Four-eyed opossum. e, Black spider monkey. f, Giant otter. g, Red brocket. h, Tree porcupine. i, Tayra. j, Tapir. k, Ocelot. l, Giant armadillo.

No. 2671: a, Crimson topaz hummingbird. b, Bearded bellbird (f). c, Amazonian umbrellabird. d, Paradise jacamar (h). e, Paradise tanager. f, White-tailed trogon (i-j). g, Scarlet macaw (k). h, Red fan parrot. i, Red-billed toucan. j, White plumed antbird. k, Crimson-hooded manakin. l, Guyanan cock-of-the-rock.

No. 2672, Paca. No. 2673, Tufted coquettes, horiz.

**1993, Mar. 10** ***Perf. 14***

| | | | | | |
|---|---|---|---|---|---|
| **2670** | A165 | $50 | Sheet of 12, #a.-l. | 14.00 | 14.00 |
| **2671** | A165 | $50 | Sheet of 12, #a.-l. | 13.75 | 13.75 |

**Souvenir Sheets**

| | | | | | |
|---|---|---|---|---|---|
| **2672** | A165 | $325 | multicolored | 8.25 | 8.25 |
| **2673** | A165 | $325 | multicolored | 9.00 | 9.00 |

Coronation of Queen Elizabeth II, 40th Anniv. A166

No. 2674: a, $25, Official coronation photograph. b, $50, Gems from royal collection. c, $75, Queen, Duke of Edinburgh. d, $130, Queen opening Parliament.

$325, State Portrait, by Sir James Gunn, 1954-56.

**1993, June 2** **Litho.** ***Perf. 13½x14***

| | | | | |
|---|---|---|---|---|
| **2674** | A166 | Sheet, 2 each #a.-d. | 16.00 | 16.00 |

**Souvenir Sheet**

***Perf. 14***

| | | | | | |
|---|---|---|---|---|---|
| **2675** | A166 | $325 | multicolored | 10.00 | 10.00 |

No. 2675 contains one 28x42mm stamp.
For overprints see Nos. 2793-2795.

A167

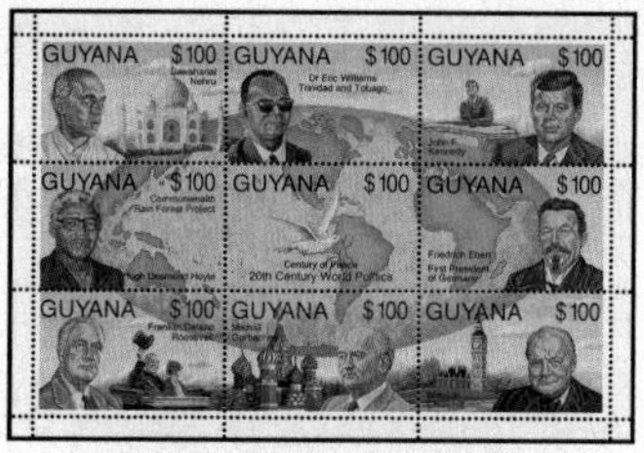

Famous People — A168

Athletes: No. 2676: a, O. J. Simpson, football. b, Rohan B. Kanhai, cricket. c, Gabriela Sabatini, tennis. d, Severiano Ballesteros, golf. e, Peace dove, blue background. f, Franz Beckenbauer, soccer. g, Pele, soccer. h, Wilt Chamberlain, basketball, i, Nadia Comaneci, gymnastics.

Scientists: No. 2677: a, Louis Leakey, archaeology. b, Jonas Salk, polio vaccine. c, Hideyo Noguchi, yellow fever. d, Karl Landsteiner, blood transfusions. e, Peace dove, blue green background. f, Sigmund Freud, psychoanalysis. g, Louis Pasteur. h, Madame Curie, radium tubes. i, Jean Baptiste Perrin, physics.

Artists, entertainers: No. 2678: a, Gabriel Marquez, writer. b, Pablo Picasso, artist. c, Cecil DeMille, film director. d, Martha Graham, dance. e, Peace dove, purple background. f, Charles Chaplin, actor. g, Paul Robeson, singer. h, Rudolph Dunbar, musician. i, Louis Armstrong, musician.

Politicians: No. 2679: a, Jawaharlal Nehru. b, Dr. Eric Williams, first prime minister of Trinidad and Tobago. c, John F. Kennedy. d, Hugh Desmond Hoyte, president of Guyana. e, Peace dove over map. f, Friedrich Ebert. g, Franklin D. Roosevelt. h, Mikhail Gorbachev. i, Winston Churchill.

Humanitarians: No. 2680: a, Gandhi. b, Dalai Lama. c, Michael Manley, prime minister of Jamaica. d, Javier Perez de Cuellar, former UN Secretary General. e, Peace dove, globe. f, Mother Teresa. g, Martin Luther King, Jr. h, Nelson Mandela. i, Raoul Wallenberg.

Transportation, communication: No. 2681: a, DC-3 cargo plane. b, Space shuttle. c, Concorde. d, Ferdinand von Zeppelin. e, Peace dove. f, Guglielmo Marconi. g, Adrian Thompson, mountaineer. h, Bullet train, Japan. i, John von Neumann, mathematician.

No. 2682, UN Flag, natl. flags. No. 2683, Jackie Robinson. No. 2684, Einstein's formula. No. 2685, Elvis Presley. No. 2686, Nobel Peace Prize certificate. No. 2687, Apollo Moon Landing.

**1993, July 26** **Litho.** ***Perf. 14***

| | | | | | |
|---|---|---|---|---|---|
| **2676** | A167 | $50 | Sheet of 9, #a.-i. | 16.00 | 16.00 |
| **2677** | A167 | $50 | Sheet of 9, #a.-i. | 16.00 | 16.00 |
| **2678** | A167 | $50 | Sheet of 9, #a.-i. | 16.00 | 16.00 |
| **2679** | A168 | $100 | Sheet of 9, #a.-i. | 16.00 | 16.00 |
| **2680** | A168 | $100 | Sheet of 9, #a.-i. | 16.00 | 16.00 |
| **2681** | A168 | $100 | Sheet of 9, #a.-i. | 16.00 | 16.00 |

**Souvenir Sheets**

| | | | | | |
|---|---|---|---|---|---|
| **2682** | A168 | $250 | multi, vert. | 8.00 | 8.00 |
| **2683** | A167 | $250 | multi, vert. | 8.00 | 8.00 |
| **2684** | A167 | $250 | multi, vert. | 8.00 | 8.00 |
| **2685** | A167 | $250 | multi, vert. | 8.00 | 8.00 |
| **2686** | A168 | $250 | multi, vert. | 8.00 | 8.00 |
| **2687** | A168 | $250 | multi | 8.00 | 8.00 |

Willy Brandt (1913-1992), German Chancellor — A169

Designs: $25, Brandt, Golda Meir, 1969. $190, Brandt at steel mill, 1969. $325, Brandt.

**1993, Aug. 16** **Litho.** ***Perf. 14***

| | | | | | |
|---|---|---|---|---|---|
| **2688** | A169 | $25 | multicolored | .90 | .90 |
| **2689** | A169 | $190 | multicolored | 6.50 | 6.50 |

**Souvenir Sheet**

| | | | | | |
|---|---|---|---|---|---|
| **2690** | A169 | $325 | multicolored | 9.00 | 9.00 |

Armillary Sphere — A170

Copernicus (1473-1543): $190, Satellite antenna. $300, Copernicus.

**1993, Aug. 16**

| | | | | | |
|---|---|---|---|---|---|
| **2691** | A170 | $50 | multicolored | 1.75 | 1.75 |
| **2692** | A170 | $190 | multicolored | 6.25 | 6.25 |

**Souvenir Sheet**

| | | | | | |
|---|---|---|---|---|---|
| **2693** | A170 | $300 | multicolored | 8.00 | 8.00 |

Georg Hackl, Luge Gold Medalist, 1992 — A171

1994 Winter Olympics, Lillehammer, Norway: $130, Karen Magnussen, figure skater, 1972. $325, German bobsled team, 1992.

**1993, Aug. 16**

| | | | | | |
|---|---|---|---|---|---|
| **2694** | A171 | $50 | multicolored | 1.75 | 1.75 |
| **2695** | A171 | $130 | multicolored | 4.25 | 4.25 |

**Souvenir Sheet**

| | | | | | |
|---|---|---|---|---|---|
| **2696** | A171 | $325 | multicolored | 9.50 | 9.50 |

A172

World War II — A173

Designs: $6.40, Audie Murphy. $7.65, British, US forces link up in France, June 8, 1944. $8.90, Monte Cassino falls to Allies, May 18, 1944. $12.80, Battleship Yamato attacked by US in Battle of East China Sea, Apr. 7, 1945. $15.30, St. Basil's Cathedral, Moscow, Foreign Ministers Conf., Oct. 19, 1943. $50, US forces cross Rhine River, Mar. 7, 1945. $100, B-29s begin bombing raids on Japan from China, June 15, 1944. $130, Gen. George S. Patton, Jr., Battle of Sicily ends, Aug. 17, 1943. $190, Battleship Tirpitz sunk, Nov. 12, 1944. $200, US Sherman tank, US forces enter Brittany after taking Normandy, Aug. 1, 1944. $225, End of fighting in Italy, May 2, 1945.

No. 2708 — War at Sea, 1943: a, Adm. Yamamoto launches air offensive, Apr. 7. b, PT-109 in Blackett Strait, Aug. 1. c, USS Enterprise. d, Allied ships attack Rabaul, Oct. 12. e, US troops land at Cape Gloucester, Dec. 26. f, USS Bogue enters service, Feb. g, Wildcat fighters sink U-118. h, Battle of Atlantic reaches peak, U-boats sink 108 ships. i, Italian fleet surrenders at Malta, Sept. 10. j, Battleship Duke of York sinks Scharnhorst, Dec. 26.

No. 2709 — War in the Air, 1943: a, Royal Australian Air Force Beaufighter, Battle of Bismark Sea, Mar. 2-4. b, P-38 Lightening shoots down Adm. Yamamoto's plane over Bougainville, Apr. 7. c, B-24 Liberators bomb Tarawa prior to landings, Sept. 17-19. d, B-25 Mitchell of Fifth Air Force bombs Rabaul, Oct. 12. e, US Navy aircraft attack Makin, Nov. 19. f, US Army Air Force's first daylight raid over Germany, Jan. 27. g, Royal Air Force Mosquito bombers make first daylight raid on Berlin, Jan. 30. h, Allies devastate Hamburg with first firestorm, July 24-30. i, B-24 bombers raid Ploesti oil refineries in Romania, Aug. 1. j, Battle of Berlin begins, Nov. 18.

No. 2710, $325, US, Russian infantry meeting at Elbe River, Apr. 25, 1945.

**1993, Oct. 18** **Litho.** ***Perf. 14***

| | | | | | |
|---|---|---|---|---|---|
| **2697** | A172 | $6.40 | multicolored | .80 | .30 |
| **2698** | A172 | $7.65 | multicolored | .85 | .35 |
| **2699** | A172 | $8.90 | multicolored | .90 | .40 |
| **2700** | A172 | $12.80 | multicolored | .95 | .60 |
| **2701** | A172 | $15.30 | multicolored | 1.00 | .70 |
| **2702** | A172 | $50 | multicolored | 1.75 | 1.25 |
| **2703** | A172 | $100 | multicolored | 2.75 | 2.50 |
| **2704** | A172 | $130 | multicolored | 4.00 | 4.00 |
| **2705** | A172 | $190 | multicolored | 5.50 | 5.50 |
| **2706** | A172 | $200 | multicolored | 5.75 | 5.75 |
| **2707** | A172 | $225 | multicolored | 6.50 | 6.50 |
| | | | *Nos. 2697-2707 (11)* | 30.75 | 27.85 |

**Miniature Sheets**

***Perf. 15***

| | | | | | |
|---|---|---|---|---|---|
| **2708** | A173 | $50 | Sheet of 10, #a.-j. | 14.00 | 14.00 |
| **2709** | A172 | $50 | Sheet of 10, #a.-j. | 14.00 | 14.00 |

Nos. 2709a-2709j are 35½x22mm.

**Souvenir Sheet**

***Perf. 14***

| | | | | | |
|---|---|---|---|---|---|
| **2710** | A172 | $325 | multicolored | 12.00 | 12.00 |

1994 World Cup Soccer Championships, U.S. — A174

Player, country: $5, Stuart Pearce, England. $6.40, Ronald Koeman, Holland. $7.65, Gianluca Vialli, Italy. $12.80, McStay, Scotland, Alemao, Brazil. $15.30, Ceulemans, Belgium, Butcher, England. $50, Dragan Stojkovic, Yugoslovia. $100, Ruud Gullit, Holland. $130, Miloslav Kadlec, Czechoslovakia. $150, Ramos, Uruguay, Berthold, Germany. $190, Baggio, Italy; Wright, England. $200, Yarentchuck, Russia, Renquin, Belgium. $225, Timofte, Romania; Aleinikov, Russia. No. 2724, Rene Higuita, Colombia. No. 2723, Salvatore Schillaci, Italy, horiz.

**1993, Oct. 18** **Litho.** ***Perf. 14***

| | | | | | |
|---|---|---|---|---|---|
| **2711** | A174 | $5 | multicolored | .25 | .25 |
| **2712** | A174 | $6.40 | multicolored | .25 | .25 |
| **2713** | A174 | $7.65 | multicolored | .35 | .25 |
| **2714** | A174 | $12.80 | multicolored | .40 | .25 |
| **2715** | A174 | $15.30 | multicolored | .45 | .30 |
| **2716** | A174 | $50 | multicolored | 1.60 | .90 |
| **2717** | A174 | $100 | multicolored | 2.50 | 2.50 |
| **2718** | A174 | $130 | multicolored | 3.00 | 3.00 |
| **2719** | A174 | $150 | multicolored | 3.50 | 3.50 |
| **2720** | A174 | $190 | multicolored | 4.25 | 4.25 |
| **2721** | A174 | $200 | multicolored | 5.00 | 5.00 |
| **2722** | A174 | $225 | multicolored | 5.25 | 5.25 |
| | | | *Nos. 2711-2722 (12)* | 26.80 | 25.70 |

**Souvenir Sheets**

| | | | | | |
|---|---|---|---|---|---|
| **2723** | A174 | $325 | multicolored | 8.50 | 8.50 |
| **2724** | A174 | $325 | multicolored | 8.50 | 8.50 |

Order of the Caribbean Community A175

**1993, Sept. 27** **Litho.** ***Perf. 14***

| | | | | | |
|---|---|---|---|---|---|
| **2725** | A175 | $7.65 | William Demas | 1.00 | .75 |
| **2726** | A175 | $7.65 | Derek Walcott | 1.00 | .75 |
| **2727** | A175 | $7.65 | Sir Shridath Ramphal | 2.00 | 1.00 |
| | | | *Nos. 2725-2727 (3)* | 4.00 | 2.50 |

Christmas
A176

Christmas
A177a

Details from Holy Family Under the Apple Tree, by Rubens: No. 2728, $6.40, No. 2730, $12.80, No. 2733, $130, No. 2734, $190.

Details from The Virgin in Glory, by Durer: No. 2729, $7.65, No. 2731, $15.30, No. 2732, $50, No. 2735, $250.

No. 2736, Holy Family Under the Apple Tree (entire). No. 2737, The Virgin in Glory (entire).

**1993, Dec. 1** *Perf. 13½x14*

**2728-2735** A176 Set of 8 14.00 14.00

**Souvenir Sheets**

**2736** A174 $325 multicolored 7.00 7.00
**2737** A174 $325 multicolored 7.00 7.00

For surcharge, see No. 4177.

Louvre Museum, Bicent.
A177

Details or entire paintings: No. 2738, Mona Lisa, by Da Vinci.

No. 2739, $50: a, La Femme à la Puce, by Crespi. b, La Femme Hydropique, by Dou. c, Portrait d'un Couple, by Ittenbach. d, Cléopâtre Assise, Demi Face, sur un Trône Élevé , by Moreau. e, La Richesse, by Vouet. f, Vieillard et Jeune Garçon, by Ghirlandaio. g, Louis XIV, by Rigaud. h, La Buveuse, by Pieter De Hooch.

No. 2740, $50: a, Autoportrait aux Besicles, by Chardin. b, L'Infante Marie-Thérèse, by Velasquez. c, Le Printemps, by Arcimboldo. d, La Vierge de Douleur, by Bouts. e, L'Etude, by Fragonard. f. François 1er, by Clouet. g, Le Condottière, by Antonello Da Messina. h, La Bohémienne, by Hals.

No. 2741, $50: a, La Femme à la Puce, entire, by Crespi. b, Autoportrait au Chevalet, by Rembrandt. c, Femmes d'Alger dans Leur Appartement, by Delacroix. d, Tête de Jeune Homme, by Raphael. e, Vénus et les Grâces, by Botticelli. f, Nature Morte à l'Échiquier, by Lubin Baugin. g, Lady MacBeth Somnambule, by Fussli. h, La Tabagie, by Chardin.

Nos. 2742, $50: a-c, L'Accordée de Village (left, center, right), by Greuze. d, Autoportrait, by Melendez. e, Le Chevalier, La Jeune Fille et La Mont, by Baldung-Grien. f, Le Jeune Mendiant, by Murillo. g-h, Les Pèlerins d'Emmaus (left, right), by Mathieu Le Nain.

No. 2743, $50: a-b, Le Vierge au Lapin (diff. details), by Titian. c, La Belle Jardinière, by Raphael. d, La Dentellière, by Vermeer. e, Jeanne d'Aragon, by Raphael. f, L'Astronome, by Vermeer. g, Le Pont du Rialto, by Canaletto. h, Sigismond Malatesta, by Piero Della Francesca.

No. 2744, $325, Cour de Ferme, by Jan Brueghel, the Younger. No. 2745, $325, Le Pont du Rialto, by Canaletto. No. 2746, $325, Le Sacre de Napoléon 1er, by David. No. 2747, $325, Details and painting of Mona Lisa. No. 2748, $325, Le Diseuse de Bonne Aventure, by Caravaggio. No. 2749, $325, Les Noces de Cana, by Veronese.

**1993, Dec. 6 Litho.** *Perf. 13½x14*

**2738** A177 $50 multicolored .90 .90
*a.* Sheet of 8 + label 8.00 8.00

**Sheets of 8, #a-h, + Label**

**2739-2743** A177 Set of 5 40.00 40.00

**Souvenir Sheets**

*Perf. 12*

**2744-2749** A177 Set of 6 37.50 37.50

Nos. 2744-2746 each contain one 80x47mm stamp. Nos. 2747-2749 one 80x53mm stamp.

Entire paintings or details: $7.65, St. Anne with Mary and the Child Jesus, by Dürer. $8.90, Mary Being Crowned by Two Angels, by Dürer. $50, Pentecost, by Titian. $100, Samson and Delilah, by Rubens. $250, Origin of the Milky Way, by Rubens.

No. 2749F, $500, The Descent from the Cross, by Rubens, horiz. No. 2749G, $500, The Descent from the Cross, by Dürer, horiz.

**1993 Litho.** *Perf. 13½x14, 14x13½*

**2749A-2749E** A177a Set of 5 13.50 13.50

**Souvenir Sheets**

**2749F-2749G** A177a Set of 2 16.00 16.00

Polska '93 (Paintings) — A178

Designs: $50, $130, Pantaloons, by Tadeusz Brzozowski, 1966. $75, Photo of fortress in Miedzyrecz. $325, Children in the Garden, by Wladyslaw Podkowinski, 1892, horiz.

**1993** *Perf. 14*

**2750** A178 $50 multicolored 1.75 1.75
**2751** A178 $75 multicolored 2.25 2.25
**2752** A178 $130 multicolored 4.00 4.00
*a.* Pair, #2750, #2752 6.00 6.00
*Nos. 2750-2752 (3)* 8.00 8.00

**Souvenir Sheet**

**2753** A178 $325 multicolored 8.00 8.00

Picasso (Paintings) — A179

Designs: $15.30, Bather, Paris, 1909. $100, Two Nudes, 1906. $190, Nude Seated on a Rock, 1921. $325, The Rescue, 1922.

**1993, Nov. Litho.** *Perf. 14*

**2754** A179 $15.30 multicolored .40 .40
**2755** A179 $100 multicolored 2.60 2.60
**2756** A179 $190 multicolored 5.00 5.00
*Nos. 2754-2756 (3)* 8.00 8.00

**Souvenir Sheet**

**2756A** A179 $325 multicolored 8.00 8.00

Rebirth of Democracy, 1st Anniv. — A180

Designs: $6.40, Dr. Cheddie B. Jagan, Guyana Pres. $325, Sunburst, "REBIRTH OF DEMOCRACY," horiz.

**1993, Dec. 17 Litho.** *Perf. 13½x14*

**2757** A180 $6.40 multicolored .80 .80

**Souvenir Sheet**

*Perf. 13*

**2757A** A180 $325 multicolored 7.50 7.50

Aladdin — A181

Nos. 2758: a-h, Various characters from Disney animated film, vert.

Nos. 2759: a-i, Various film scenes.

Nos. 2760: a-i, Various scenes from Disney animated film.

No. 2761, Genie, Jasmine, and Aladdin. No. 2762, Aladdin, the Genie, Abu, Magic Carpet. No. 2763, Aladdin as Prince Ali Ababwa. No. 2764, Aladdin, Abu, Jasmine.

**1993, Dec. 20 Litho.** *Perf. 14x13½*

**2758** A181 $7.65 Sheet of 8, #a.-h. 2.00 2.00
**2759** A181 $50 Sheet of 9, #a.-i. 12.00 12.00
**2760** A181 $65 Sheet of 9, #a.-i. 14.00 14.00
*Nos. 2758-2760 (3)* 28.00 28.00

**Souvenir Sheets**

**2761** A181 $325 multicolored 7.50 7.50
**2762** A181 $325 multicolored 7.50 7.50
**2763** A181 $325 multicolored 7.50 7.50
**2764** A181 $325 multicolored 7.50 7.50

A182

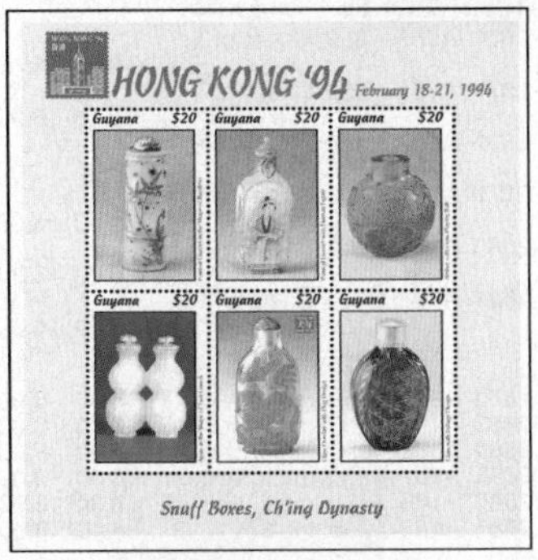


Hong Kong '94 — A183

Stamps, photograph of Happy Valley Horse Race Course: No. 2765, Hong Kong #437, scoreboard. No. 2766, Track, horses, #2545.

No. 2767 — Snuff boxes, Qing Dynasty: a, Painted enamel in shape of bamboo. b, Painted enamel with human figure. c, Amber with lions playing ball. d, Agate in shape of two gourds. e, Glass overlay with dog. f, Glass, foliage design.

No. 2768 — Porcelain, Ch'ing Dynasty: a, Covered jar with dragon. b, Rotating brush holder. c, Covered jar with horses. d, Amphora vase with bats & peaches. e, Tea caddy with Fo dogs. f, Vase with wild camellia & peaches.

**1994, Feb. 18** *Perf. 14*

**2765** A182 $50 multicolored .80 .80
**2766** A182 $50 multicolored .80 .80
*a.* Pair, #2765-2766 1.60 1.60

**Miniature Sheets**

**2767** A183 $20 Sheet of 6, #a.-f. 8.00 8.00
**2768** A183 $20 Sheet of 6, #a.-f. 8.00 8.00

Nos. 2765-2766 issued in sheets of 5 pairs. No. 2766a is continuous design.

New Year 1994 (Year of the Dog) (#2767e, #2768e).

Vintage Donald Duck — A184

No. 2769, $60 — Movie posters: a, Donald's Better Self, 1938. b, Donald's Golf Game, 1938. c, Sea Scouts, 1939. d, Donald's Penguin, 1939. e, A Good Time for a Dime, 1941. f, Truant Officer Donald. g, Orphan's Benefit, 1941. h, Chef Donald, 1941.

No. 2770, $60: a, The Village Smithy, 1942. b, Donald's Snow Fight, 1942. c, Donald's Garden, 1942. d, Donald's Gold Mine, 1942. e, The Vanishing Private, 1942. f, Sky Trooper, 1942. g, Bellboy Donald, 1942. h, The New Spirit, 1942.

No. 2771, $60: a, Saludos Amigos, 1943. b, The Eyes Have It, 1945. c, Donald's Crime, 1945. d, Straight Shooters, 1947. e, Donald's Dilemma, 1947. f, Bootle Beetle, 1947. g, Daddy Duck, 1948. h, Soup's On, 1948.

No. 2772 — Story boards from Pirate Gold, horiz.: a, Pirate ship. b, Carrying treasure chest. c, Donald Duck with map. d, Donald, souvenir shop. e, Donald following Aracuan bird. f, Angry Donald.

No. 2773, $80 — Movie posters: a, Donald's Happy Birthday, 1949. b, Sea Salts, 1949. c, Honey Harvester, 1949. d, All in a Nutshell, 1949. e, The Greener Yard, 1949. f, Slide, Donald, Slide, 1949. g, Lion Around, 1950. h, Trailer Horn, 1950.

No. 2774, $80: a, Bee at the Beach, 1950. b, Out on a Limb, 1950. c, Corn Chips, 1951. d, Test Pilot Donald, 1951. e, Lucky Number, 1951. f, Out of Scale, 1951. g, Bee on Guard, 1951. h, Let's Stick Together, 1952.

No. 2775, $80: a, Trick or Treat, 1952. b, Don's Fountain of Youth, 1953. c, Rugged Bear, 1953. d, Canvas Back Duck, 1953. e, Dragon Around, 1954. f, Grin and Bear It, 1954. g, The Flying Squirrel, 1954. h, Up a Tree, 1955.

No. 2776, Studio Fan Card, Melody Time, 1948.

No. 2777, $500, Scene from picture book of first movie, The Wise Little Hen, 1944, horiz. No. 2778, $500, Sketch for closing scene of Timber, 1941. No. 2779, $500, Donald Duck, horiz. No. 2780, $500, Studio fan card, The Three Caballeros, 1945, horiz.

Movie posters contained in No. 2780A are listed as designs for Nos. 2769-2771, 2774-2775, 2777, 2780.

*Perf. 14x13½, 13½x14*

**1993, Dec. 6** **Litho.**

**Sheets of 8, #a-h**

**2769-2771** A184 Set of 3 28.50 28.50
**2772** A184 $80 Sheet of 6, #a.-f. 9.00 9.00

**Sheets of 8, #a-h**

**2773-2775** A184 Set of 3 34.50 34.50

**Size: 130x104mm**

*Imperf*

**2776** A184 $500 multi 10.00 10.00

**Souvenir Sheets**

*Perf. 14x13½, 13½x14*

**2777-2780** A184 Set of 4 40.00 40.00

*Imperf*

**Self-Adhesive**

**Size: 64x89mm**

**2780A** A184 $60 Set of 50 70.00

No. 2780A exists with backing labels printed in English or French. Value is for either set. No. 2780A was printed on thin card and sold in sealed cellophane packages containing 10 stamps. To affix stamps, backing containing film information must be removed.

#2769-2771, 2773-2775 exist in sheets of 7 $5 stamps + label. The label replaces #2769f, 2770b, 2771h, 2773a, 2774d, 2775e. These sheets became available Nov. 20, 1996.

Tropical Flowers
A185

Designs: $6.40, Cestrum parqui. $7.65, Brunfelsia calycina. $12.80, Datura rosei. $15.30, Ruellia macrantha. No. 2785, $50, Portlandia albiflora. $130, Pachystachys coccinea. $190, Beloperone guttata. $250, Ferdinandusa speciosa.

No. 2789, $50: a, Clusia grandiflora. b, Begonia haageana. c, Fuchsia simplicicaulis. d, Guaiacum officinale (a). e, Pithecoctenium cynanchoides. f, Sphaeralcea umbellata. g, Erythrina poeppigiana. h, Steriphoma paradoxa. i, Allemanda violacea (f). j, Centropogon cornutus (g). k, Passiflora quadrangularis. l, Victoria amazonica.

No. 2790, $50: a, Cobaea scandens. b, Pyrostegia venusta (c). c, Petrea kohautiana (b). d, Hippobroma longiflora (a). e, Cleome hassleriana (b, d, f, h, i). f, Verbena peruviana (c). g, Tropaeolum peregrinum. h, Plumeria rubra (g, i). i, Selenicereus grandiflorus. j, Mandevilla splendens (g). k, Pereskia aculeata. l, Ipomoea learii.

No. 2791, $325, Columnea fendleri. No. 2792, $325, Lophospermum erubescens.

**1994, Feb. 10 Litho. *Perf. 13½***

**2781-2788** A185 Set of 8 13.75 13.75

**Sheets of 12, #a-l**

***Perf. 14***

**2789-2790** A185 Set of 2 27.00 27.00

**Souvenir Sheets**

***Perf. 13***

**2791-2792** A185 Set of 2 14.00 14.00

For surcharges, see Nos. 4110, 4111, 4113, 4114.

Nos. 2674-2675 Ovptd. "ROYAL VISIT FEB 19-22, 1994" in One or Two Lines

**1994 Litho. *Perf. 13½x14***

**2793** A166 Sheet, 2 each #a.-d. 14.00 14.00

**Souvenir Sheet**

***Perf. 14***

**2794** A166 $325 multicolored 9.00 9.00

Hummel Figurines — A186

Designs: No. 2795, $20, No. 2803a, $30, Girl holding basket and heart. No. 2796, $25, Boy holding heart. No. 2797, $35, No. 2804a, $20, Chef holding dessert. No. 2798, $50, No. 2804b, $130, Girl holding planter of mushrooms. No. 2799, $60, Girl holding plant, horn. No. 2800, $130, No. 2803b, $6, Four girls. No. 2801, $190, Two girls, boy and puppy. No. 2802, $250, No. 2804c, $35, Boy holding covered dish, puppy.

**1994, May 5 Litho. *Perf. 14***

**2795-2802** A186 Set of 8 18.00 18.00

**Souvenir Sheets**

**2803** A186 Sheet of 4, #a.-b, #2796, 2801 5.50 5.50

**2804** A186 Sheet of 4, #a.-c, #2799 5.50 5.50

Sierra Club, Cent. A187

No. 2805 — Various animals or scenic places: a-b, American alligator. c-d, Italian Alps. e-f, Mono Lake.

No. 2806: a, Red kangaroo. b-d, Whooping crane. e-f, Alaskan brown bear. g, Bald eagle. h, Giant panda.

No. 2807, vert.: a-b, Red kangaroo. c, American alligator. d, Alaskan brown bear. e-f, Bald eagle. g-h, Giant panda.

No. 2808, vert.: a-c, Sea lion. d, Mono Lake. e, Sierra Club centennial emblem. f, Italian Alps. g-i, Matterhorn.

**1994, May 20 Litho. *Perf. 14***

**2805** A187 $70 Sheet of 6, #a.-f. 8.50 8.50

**2806** A187 $70 Sheet of 8, #a.-h. 11.50 11.50

**2807** A187 $70 Sheet of 8, #a.-h. 11.50 11.50

**2808** A187 $70 Sheet of 9, #a.-i. 14.50 14.50

*Nos. 2805-2808 (4)* 46.00 46.00

First Manned Moon Landing, 25th Anniv. A188

No. 2809, $60: a, Robert R. Gilruth, Apollo 16. b, Ernst Stuhlinger, Apollo 17. c, Christopher C. Kraft, X-30 National Aero-Space Plane. d, Rudolf Opitz, Me-163, July 24, 1943. e, Clyde W. Tombaugh, "Face on Mars." f, Hermann Oberth, Scene from "The Girl in the Moon."

No. 2810, $60: a, Wernher von Braun, Apollo 11. b, Rocco A. Petrone, Apollo 11. c, Eberhard Rees, Apollo 12. d, Charles A. Berry, Apollo 13. e, Thomas O. Paine, Apollo 14. f, A.F. Staats, Apollo 15.

No. 2811, $60: a, Walter Dornberger, 1st A-4 launch. b, Rudolph Nebel, Surveyor 1. c, Robert H. Goddard, Apollo 7. d, Kurt Debus, Apollo 8. e, James T. Webb, Apollo 9. f, George E. Mueller, Apollo 10.

No. 2812, Frank J. Everest, Jr.

**1994, July 20 Litho. *Perf. 14***

**Sheets of 6, #a-f**

**2809-2811** A188 Set of 3 22.00 22.00

**Souvenir Sheet**

**2812** A188 $325 multicolored 8.50 8.50

A189

World War II — A190

Designs: $6, Photo reconnaissance Spitfire. $35, 226 Squadron B-25. $190, 76 Squadron P-47 Thunderbolts.

No. 2816 — Europe and North Africa, 1944: a, Allied landings, Anzio, Jan. 22. b, RAF bombs Amiens prison, Feb. 18. c, Sevastopol falls to Red Army, May 9. d, Allies breach Gustav Line, May 19. e, D-Day, June 6. f, V-1 attacks on London begin, June 13. g, Cease fire declared for Paris, Aug. 19. h, Germany launches V-2 rockets, Sept. 8. i, German battleship Tirpitz sunk, Nov. 12. j, Siege of Bastogne lifted, Dec. 29.

No. 2817 — D-Day: a, Paratroops drop behind enemy lines. b, Glider-born commandos land behind enemy lines. c, USS Arkansas shells Omaha beach defenses. d, Allied aircraft attack enemy movements. e, Allied landing craft hit the beach. f, Allied troops pinned down by enemy fire. g, Commandos exit landing craft. h, Specialized Allied tanks destroy enemy mines. i, Allies break through beach defenses. j, Consolidation of position.

No. 2818, RAF Lancaster bomber.

**1994, June 20 *Perf. 14***

**2813** A189 $6 multicolored .40 .40

**2814** A189 $35 multicolored 1.10 1.10

**2815** A189 $190 multicolored 5.00 5.00

*Nos. 2813-2815 (3)* 6.50 6.50

***Perf. 13***

**2816** A190 $60 Sheet of 10, #a.-j. 14.00 14.00

**2817** A190 $60 Sheet of 10, #a.-j. 14.00 14.00

**Souvenir Sheet**

***Perf. 14***

**2818** A189 $325 multicolored 9.00 9.00

A191

Butterflies A192

Designs: $6, Heliconius melpomene. $20, Helicopius cupido. $25, Agrias claudina. $30, Parides coelus. $50, Heliconius hecale. $60, Morpho diana. $190, Dismorphia orise. $250, Morpho deidamia.

No. 2827: a, Anaea marthesia. b, Brassolis astyra. c, Heliconius melpomene. d, Haetera piera. e, Morpho diana dixey. f, Parides coelus. g, Catagramma pitheas. h, Nessaea obrinus. i, Automeris janus. j, Papilio torquatus. k, Eunica sophonisba. l, Ceratinia nise. m, Panacea procilla. n, Pyrrhogyra neaerea. o, Morpho deidamia. p, Dismorphia orise.

No. 2829, $325, Eunica sophonisba. No. 2830, $325, Anaea eribotes.

No. 2831, $325, Hamadryas velutina. No. 2832, $325, Agrias claudina.

**1994, July 5 Litho. *Perf. 14***

**2819-2826** A191 Set of 8 16.00 16.00

**2827** A192 $50 Sheet of 16, #a.-p. 22.00 22.00

**Souvenir Sheets**

**2829-2830** A191 Set of 2 15.00 15.00

**2831-2832** A192 Set of 2 15.00 15.00

Nos. 2829-2830 each contain one 43x28mm stamp.

Bible Stories — A193

No. 2833 — Story of Ruth and Naomi: a-f: Ruth & Naomi preparing to leave Moab & return to Israel. g-l: Ruth harvesting grain in fields of Boaz. m-r: Boaz receives a man's sandal, finalizing sale of Naomi's field. s-x: Naomi, Boaz, Ruth and Obed, who was David's grandfather.

No. 2834 — Story of Joseph: a-d, Jacob made Joseph a coat of many colors. e-h, Joseph's brothers take his coat and cast him into pit. i-l, Joseph is sold to the Ishmaelites. m-p, Joseph is accused by Potiphar's wife and thrown into prison. q-t, Joseph interprets Pharoah's dreams. u-x, Joseph is reunited with his brothers.

No. 2835 — Parting of the Red Sea: a-x, Moses leading Israelites through sea, Pharoah's army drowning.

No. 2836 — Daniel and the Lions: a-x, Daniel in lion's den surrounded by various animals, angel.

**1994, Aug. 4 Litho. *Perf. 14***

**Sheets of 24, #a-x**

**2833-2836** A193 $20 Set of 4 52.00 52.00

Nos. 2835-2836 have continuous design.

A194 A195

Philakorea '94: $6, Statues of socialist ideals, Pyongyang. $25, Statue of Adm. Yi Sunsin. $120, Sokkat'ap Pagoda, Pulguksa. $130, Village guardian, Chejudo Island.

No. 2841, $60 — Ten-fold screens: a, Shown. b-e, Cranes. h-i, Deer. j, Deer, mushrooms, waterfall.

No. 2842, $60: b-d, Cranes. f-h, Deer. c, h, Waterfalls. i-j, Mushrooms.

No. 2843, $325, Falled Rock, horiz. No. 2844, $325, Westerners at Korean Court, horiz.

**1994, June 20 Litho. *Perf. 14***

**2837-2840** A194 Set of 4 6.00 6.00

**Sheets of 10, #a-j**

***Perf. 13***

**2841-2842** A195 Set of 2 26.00 26.00

**Souvenir Sheets**

***Perf. 14***

**2843-2844** A194 Set of 2 14.00 14.00

Nos. 2841-2842 have continuous design.

Entertainers of Takarazuka Revue, Japan A196

No. 2845: a, $60, Mira Anju. b, $60, Yuki Amami. c, $60, Maki Ichiro. d, $60, Yu Shion. e, $20, Miki Maya. f, $20, Fubuki Takane. g, $20, Seika Juze. h, $20, Saki Asaji.

**1994 *Perf. 14½***

**2845** A196 Sheet of 8, #a.-h. + 4 labels 9.00 9.00

Nos. 2845a-2845d are 34x47mm.

A197

Intl. Olympic Committee, Cent. — A198

Designs: $20, Nancy Kerrigan, US, figure skating, 1994. $35, Sawao Kato, Japan, gymnastics, 1976. $130, Florence Griffith-Joyner, US, 100-, 200-meters, 1988.

$325, Mark Wasmeier, Germany, super giant & giant slalom, 1994.

**1994, June 20**

**2846-2848** A197 Set of 3 4.50 4.50

**Souvenir Sheet**

**2849** A198 $325 multicolored 8.00 8.00

1994 World Cup Soccer Championships, U.S. — A199

Player, country: $6, Paulo Futre, Portugal. $35, Lyndon Hooper, Canada. $60, Enzo Francescoli, Uruguay. $190, Freddy Rincon, Colombia.

No. 2854, $60: a, Paolo Maldini, Italy. b, Guyana player. c, Bwalya Kalusha, Zambia. d, Diego Maradona, Argentina. e, Andreas Brehme, Germany. f, Eric Wynalda, US.

No. 2855, $60: a, John Doyle, US. b, Eric Wynalda, US, diff. c, Thomas Dooley, US. d, Ernie Stewart, US. f, Marcelo Balboa, US. g, Coach Bora Milutinovic, US.

No. 2856, $325, 1994 World Cup program cover. No. 2857, $325,Oiler Watson.

**1994, Aug. 8**

**2850-2853** A199 Set of 4 7.00 7.00

**Sheets of 6, #a-f**

**2854-2855** A199 Set of 2 18.00 18.00

**Souvenir Sheets**

**2856-2857** A199 Set of 2 17.00 17.00

Birds — A200

No. 2858, $35: a, Goshawk. b, Lapwing. c, Ornate umbrellabird. d, Slatey-headed parakeet. e, Regent bowerbird. f, Egytian goose. g, White-winged crossbill. h, Waxwing. i, Ruff. j, Hoopoe. k, Superb starling. l, Great jacamar.

No. 2859, $35: a, Peregrine falcon. b, Great spotted woodpecker. c, White-throated kingfisher. d, Peruvian cock-of-the-rock. e, Yellow-headed Amazon. f, Victoria crowned pigeon. g, Little owl. h, Pheasant. i, Goldfinch. j, Jay. k, Sulphur-brasted toucan. l, Japanese blue flycatcher.

No. 2860, $325, Gould's violet-ear. No. 2861, $325, Bald eagle.

**1994, Sept. 15**

**Sheets of 12, #a.-i.**

**2858-2859** A200 Set of 2 22.00 22.00

**Souvenir Sheets**

**2860-2861** A200 Set of 2 19.00 19.00

PHILAKOREA '94. For surcharge, see No. 4118.

1996 Summer Olympics, Atlanta — A201

German athletes: $6, Anja Fichtel, fencing, 1988, horiz. $25, Annegret Richter, 100-meter dash, 1976. $30, Heike Henkel, high jump, 1982. $35, Armin Hary, 100-meter dash, 1960. $50, Heide Rosendahl, long jump, 1972. $60, Josef Neckermann, equestrian grand prix, 1968. $130, Heike Drechsler, long jump, 1988. $190, Ulrike Mayfarth, high jump, 1984. $250, Michael Gross, swimming, 1984, horiz.

No. 2870A: b, $135, Markus Wasmeier, skiing, 1994. c, $190, Katja Seizinger, skiing, 1994.

No. 2871, $325, Franziska van Almsick, swimming, 1992. No. 2872, $325, Steffi Graf, tennis, 1992.

**1994, Sept. 28**

**2862-2870** A201 Set of 9 18.00 18.00

**Souvenir Sheets**

**2870A** A201 Sheet of 2, #b.-c. 7.25 7.25

**2871-2872** A201 Set of 2 14.50 14.50

Space Missions, First Manned Moon Landing, 25th Anniv. A202

No. 2873, $60: a, Laika, first dog in space. b, Yuri Gagarin, first man in space. c, John Glenn, first American to orbit earth. d, Edward White, first American to walk in space. e, Neil Armstrong, first to step foot onto moon. f, Luna 16. g, Luna 17. h, Skylab 1. i, 1975 Apollo-Soyuz.

No. 2874, $60 — Unmanned probes: a, Mars 3, Mars. b, Mariner 10, Mercury. c, Voyager, planetary grand tour. d, Pioneer, Venus. e, Giotto, Halley's Comet. f, Megellan, Venus. g, Galileo, Jupiter. h, Ulysses, Sun. i, Cassini, Titan.

No. 2875, $325, "Buzz" Aldrin, Neil Armstrong, Michael Collins. No. 2876, $325, Pioneer 1, 2.

**1994, Nov. 10 Litho. *Perf. 13½***

**Sheets of 9, #a-i**

**2873-2874** A202 Set of 2 26.00 26.00

**Souvenir Sheets**

**2875-2876** A202 Set of 2 17.00 17.00

Steam Locomotives — A203

Designs: No. 2877, $25, South Eastern Railway #285, 1882. No. 2878, $25, West Point Foundry, 1830. No. 2879, $300, Mt. Washington Cog Railway, 1886. No. 2880, $300, Stroudley-Brighton, 1872.

No. 2881, $30: a, "John Bull," 1831. b, Stephenson, 1837. c, "Atlantic," 1832. d, Stourbridge Lion, 1829. e, Polonceau, 1854. f, Rogers, 1856. g, "Vulcan," 1858. h, "Namur," 1846.

No. 2882, $30: a, West Point Foundry, 1832. b, Sequin, 1830. c, Stephenson's Planet, 1830. d, Norris 4-2-0, 1840. e, Union Iron Works os San Francisco, 1867. f, Andrew Jackson, 1832. g, Herald, 1831. h, Cumberland, 1845.

No. 2883, $30: a, Pennsylvania's Class K, 1880. b, Cooke, 1885. c, John B. Turner, 1867. d, Baldwin, 1871. e, Richard Trevithick, 1804. f, John Stephens, 1825. g, John Blenkinsop, 1814. h, Pennsylvania, 1803.

$250, Est Railway, 1878. $300, "Claud Hamilton," 1840.

**1994, Nov. 15 *Perf. 14***

**2877-2880** A203 Set of 4 15.00 15.00

**Sheets of 8, #a-h, + Label**

**2881-2883** A203 Set of 3 19.00 19.00

**Souvenir Sheets**

**2884** A203 $250 multicolored 8.00 8.00

**2885** A203 $300 multicolored 10.00 10.00

For surcharge, see No. 4116.

English Touring Cricket, Cent. A204

Designs: $20, C.H. Lloyd, Guyana/West Indies, vert. $35, C.W. Hooper, Guyana/West Indies, Wisden Trophy. $60, G.A. Hick, England, Wisden Trophy.

$200, First English Team, 1895.

**1994, June 20 Litho. *Perf. 14***

**2886-2888** A204 Set of 3 4.00 4.00

**Souvenir Sheet**

**2889** A204 $200 multicolored 6.00 6.00

Christmas A205

Paintings: $6, Joseph with the Christ Child, by Guido Reni. $20, Adoration of the Christ Child, by Girolamo Romanino. $25, Adoration of the Christ Child with St. Barbara and St. Martin, by Raffaello Botticini. $30, Holy Family, by Pompeo Girolam Batoni. $35, Flight into Egypt, by Bartolommeo Carducci. $60, Holy Family and the Baptist, by Andrea del Sarto. $120, Sacred Conversation, by Cesare de Sesto. $190, Madonna and Child with Sts. Joseph & John the Baptist, by Pontormo.

No. 2898, $325, Holy Family and St. Elizabeth and St. John the Baptist, by Francisco Primaticcio. No. 2899, $325, Presentation of Christ in the Temple, by Fra Bartolommeo.

**1994, Dec. 5 *Perf. 13½x14***

**2890-2897** A205 Set of 8 13.50 13.50

**Souvenir Sheets**

**2898-2899** A205 Set of 2 18.00 18.00

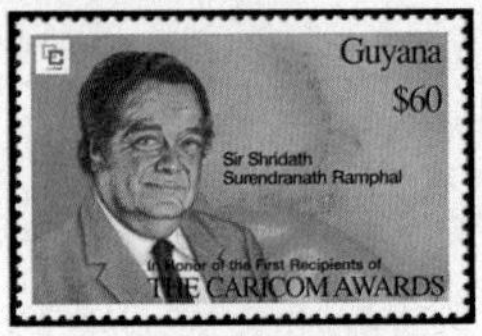


Order of the Caribbean Community — A206

First award recipients: No. 2900, $60, Sir Shridath Ramphal, statesman, Guyana. No. 2901, $60, William Demas, economist, Trinidad & Tobago. No. 2902, $60, Derek Walcott, writer, St. Lucia.

**1994 *Perf. 14***

**2900-2902** A206 Set of 3 5.00 5.00

Motion Picture, Star Trek Generations A207

A207a

No. 2903, "Boldly Go," Starship Enterprise.

No. 2904, $100: a, Capt. Picard. b, Cmdr. Riker. c, Capt. Kirk. d, Villain with phaser. e, Kirk, Picard on horseback. f, Klingons L'rsa and B'tor. g, Kirk, Picard, diff. h, Counselor Troi. i, Picard, Lt. Cmdr. Data.

No. 2905, $100: a, Troi, Riker. b, Worf. c, Picard. d, Worf, Lt. Cmdr. LaForge. e, Sailing ship, Enterprise. f, Picard, Riker. g. Data. h, Worf. i, Dr. Crusher.

No. 2906, Like No. 2903, horiz.

$1000, Kirk and Picard.

No. 2906D: e, Capt. Picard. f, Capt. Kirk.

**1994 Litho. *Perf. 13½x14***

**2903** A207 $100 multicolored 3.25 3.25

**Sheets of 9, #a-i**

**2904-2905** A207 Set of 2 58.50 58.50

**Souvenir Sheet**

***Perf. 14x13½***

**2906** A207 $500 multicolored 12.00 12.00

**Litho. & Embossed**

***Die Cut Perf. 9***

**2906C** A207a $1000 gold & multi *30.00 30.00*

**Souvenir Sheet**

***Die Cut Perf. 9 on Outside***

**2906D** A207a $500 Sheet of 2, #e.-f. *30.00 30.00*

Issued: No. 2906C, 11/18, others 12/7. No. 2903 was issued in sheets of 9. Nos. 2906e-2906f are imperf.

Sisters of Mercy of Guyana, Cent. — A208

**1994, Dec. 12 *Perf. 14***

**2907** A208 $60 multicolored 1.90 1.90

Nos. 1037a, 1097, 1099 Surcharged "ILO / 75th Anniversary / 1919-1994"

***Perfs & Printing Methods as Before***

**1994**

**2907A** A91 $6 on 130c #1037a

**2907B** A91 $30 on 120c #1099

**2907C** A91 $35 on 120c #1097

Nos. 1063, 1098, 1120, 1123 Surcharged in Blue "CENTENARY / Sign For The / MAHDI / 1894-1994"

***Perfs. & Printing Methods as Before***

**1994**

**2907D** A91 $6 on 60c #1120

**2907E** A91 $20 on 200c #1063

**2907F** A91 $30 on 60c #1098

**2907G** A91 $35 on 60c #1123

Cricket A209

Designs: $20, Sobers congratulates Lara. $30, Brian Lara setting world record, vert. $375, Lara, Chanderpaul.

$300, Brian Lara walking under "avenue of bats," vert.

**1995, Feb. 3 Litho. *Perf. 14***

**2908-2910** A209 Set of 3 8.25 8.25

**Souvenir Sheet**

**2911** A209 $300 multicolored 7.00 7.00

A210

A211

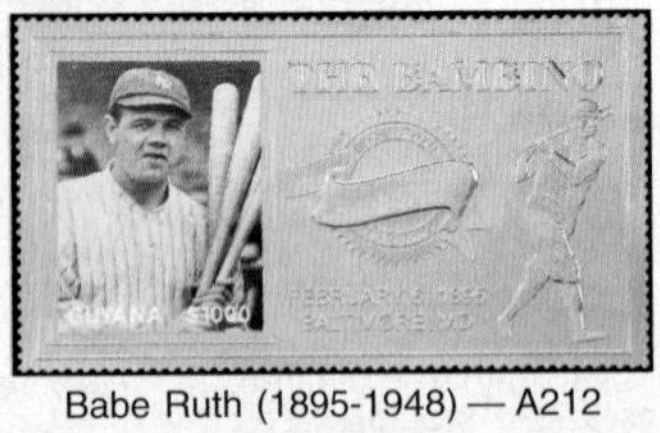


Babe Ruth (1895-1948) — A212

Type A211 various portraits like #2914.

$2000, Portrait, Ruth holding bat, vert.

**1995, Feb. 6 Litho. *Perf. 14***

**2912** A210 $65 multi 1.40 1.40

**Self-Adhesive (#2913)**

**Size: 64x89mm (#2913)**

**2913** A211 $350 Set of 12 70.00 70.00

**Litho. & Embossed**

***Perf. 12***

**2914** A212 $1000 gold & sep *25.00*

**Embossed**

**2914A** A212 $2000 gold *29.00*

**Litho.**

***Perf. 14***

**2915** A211 $65 Sheet of 12, #a.-l. 14.00 14.00

**Souvenir Sheet**

**2916** A211 $500 like #2912a, horiz. 12.00 12.00

No. 2912 issued in sheets of 9. Portraits of Babe Ruth in No. 2913 are same as in No. 2915, but surrounded by gold frame, gold autograph, baseballs, and simulated perfs. No. 2913 was sold in sealed celophane package. To affix stamps, backing containing biographical information must be removed.

Disney Characters at Work — A213

No. 2917, $30 — Animal workers: a, Veterinarian. b, Animal trainer. c, Animal psychiatrist. d, Ornithologist. e, Dog groomer. f, Herpetologist. g, Pet shop keeper. h, Park ranger. i, Aquarist.

No. 2918, $30 — Arts & crafts: a, Mickey the animator, Pluto. b, Goofy the tailor, Mickey. c, Pete the glass blower, Morty. d, Clarabelle modeling for Minnie the artist. e, Daisy sculpts Donald. f, Donald, nephews working with clay. g, Watchmakers, Chip & Dale. h, Locksmith Donald, nephews. i, Grandma Duck makes a quilt.

No. 2919, $30 — Medical group: a, Family doctor. b, Optometrist. c, Nurse. d, Psychiatrist. e, Physical therapist. f, Dentist. g, Radiologist. h, Pharmacist. i, Chiropractor.

No. 2920, $35 — Hard hat & company, vert.: a, Mickey, Pluto in truck. b, Mickey at work. c, Goofy jackhammer. d, Minnie at work. e, Forklifters. f, Construction contractor. g, Carpenter. h, Bulldozer.

No. 2921, $35 — Home services, vert.: a, Mickey, plumber. b, Mickey, paperboy. c, Huey, Dewey, Louie, moving service. d, Pete, handyman. e, Donald, newphews' house painting service. f, Goofy, washer repairman. g, Minnie, babysitter. h, Daisy cares for Grandma Duck.

No. 2922, $35 — Public service workers, vert.: a, Policeman. b, Fireman. c, Ambulance driver. d, Crossing guard. e, Museum docent. f, Census taker. g, Street maintenance workers. h, Sanitation worker.

No. 2923, $200, Goofy, zoo keeper. No. 2924, $200, Camera, Pluto, vert. No. 2925, $200, Goofy, surgeon. No. 2926, $200, Minnie, pups, tool chest. No. 2927, $200, Minnie, maid. No. 2928, $200, Horace, politician.

**1995, Feb. 23 Litho. *Perf. 13½x14***

**Sheets of 9, #a-i**

**2917-2919** A213 Set of 3 18.00 18.00

**Sheets of 8, #a-h**

***Perf. 14x13½***

**2920-2922** A213 Set of 3 19.00 19.00

**Souvenir Sheets**

**2923-2928** A213 Set of 6 39.00 39.00

Nos. 2917-2922 exist in sheets of 7 or 8 $5 stamps + label. The label replaces Nos. 2917e, 2918e, 2919g, 2920h, 2921h, 2922e. These sheets became available Nov. 20, 1996.

For sucharges, see Nos. 4122, 4123, 4124.

Nos. 1022, 1033, 1045, 1061 Surcharged in Red "SALVATION / ARMY / 1895-1995"

**1995, Apr. 24 Litho. *Perf. 14***

**2928A** A91 $6 on 60c #1033

**2928B** A91 $20 on 60c #1045

**2928C** A91 $30 on 60c #1022

**2928D** A91 $35 on 60c #1061

New Year 1995 (Year of the Boar) — A214

No. 2929 — Stylized boars: a, $20. b, $30. c, $50, Facing forward. denomination LR. d, $100. f, $50, "Abundant Year of the Pig." g, $50, "Fortunate Year of the Pig." h, $50, Facing forward, denomination LL.

$150, Face, Chinese inscriptions.

**1995, May 4 Litho. *Perf. 14½***

**2929** A214 Block of 4, #a.-d. 6.00 6.00

*e.* Souvenir sheet of 4, #c, f.-h. 8.00 8.00

**Souvenir Sheet**

**2930** A214 $150 multicolored 6.00 6.00

No. 2929 was issued in miniature sheets of 4.

A215

Birds: $5, Goshawk. $6, Lapwing. $8, Ornate umbrellabird. $15, Slatey-headed parakeet. $19, Regent bowerbird. $20, Egyptian goose. $25, White-winged crossbill. $30, Waxwing. $35, Ruff. $60, Hoopoe. $100, Superb starling. $500, Great jacamar.

**1995, May 8 Litho. *Perf. 14½x13½***

| | | | | | |
|---|---|---|---|---|---|
| **2931** | A215 | $5 | multicolored | .25 | .25 |
| **2932** | A215 | $6 | multicolored | .30 | .25 |
| **2933** | A215 | $8 | multicolored | .35 | .25 |
| **2934** | A215 | $15 | multicolored | .45 | .30 |
| **2935** | A215 | $19 | multicolored | .55 | .30 |
| **2936** | A215 | $20 | multicolored | .60 | .40 |
| **2937** | A215 | $25 | multicolored | .70 | .45 |
| **2938** | A215 | $30 | multicolored | .80 | .50 |
| **2939** | A215 | $35 | multicolored | 1.00 | .60 |
| **2940** | A215 | $60 | multicolored | 1.25 | 1.10 |
| **2941** | A215 | $100 | multicolored | 2.00 | 2.00 |
| **2942** | A215 | $500 | multicolored | 9.00 | 8.50 |
| | *Nos. 2931-2942 (12)* | | | 17.25 | 14.90 |

For surcharges, see Nos. 4020K, 4020O, 4112.

Lapwing — A215a

**1995 ? Litho. *Perf. 13¼***

**2942A** A215a $6 multi —

For surcharges see Nos. 4020L, 4020P.

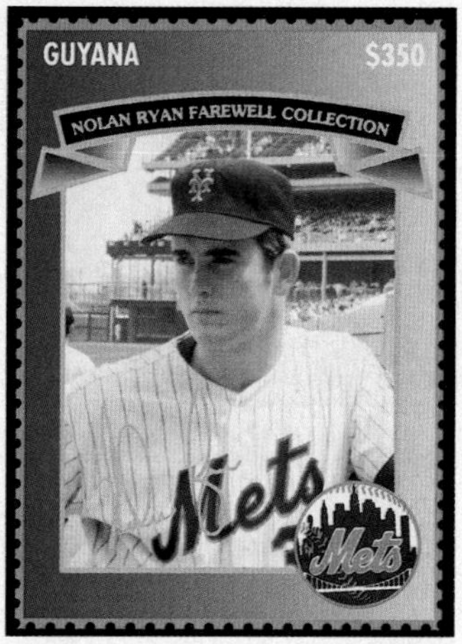


Nolan Ryan, Baseball Player — A216

No. 2943: a, Looking left, Mets. b, With bat, Mets. c, Pitching, Mets. d, Looking toward home plate, Angels. e, Pitching, Angels. f, Without hat, Angels. g, In red cap, Astros. h, Pitching, Astros. i, In black cap, Astros. j, Pitching, Rangers. k, Getting ready to pitch, Rangers. l, Up close, Rangers.

**1995 Litho. *Imperf.***

**Self-Adhesive**

**Size: 64x89mm**

**2943** A216 $350 Set of 12, #a.-l. 70.00 70.00

Nos. 2943a-2943l are printed on thin cards, distributed in boxed sets containing certificate of aunthenticity and sealed in celophane packages. To affix stamps, backing containing biographical information must be removed.

Miniature Sheets

Singapore '95 — A217

No. 2944, $35 — Dogs: a, Gordon setter. b, Long-haired chihuahua. c, Dalmation. d, Afghan. e, English bulldog. f, Miniature schnauzer. g, Clumber spaniel. h, Pekingese. i, St. Bernard. j, English cocker spaniel. k, Alaskan malamute. l, Rottweiler.

No. 2945, $35 — Cats: a, Norwegian forest cat. b, Scottish fold. c, Red burmese. d, British blue-hair. e, Abyssinian. f, Siamese. g, Exotic shorthair. h, Turkish van cat. i, Black Persian. j, Black-tipped burmilla. k, Singapura. l, Calico shorthair.

No. 2946, $35 — Horses: a, Chestnut thoroughbred colt. b, Liver chestnut quarter horse. c, Black Freisian. d, Chestnut Belgian. e, Appaloosa. f, Lipizzanas. g, Chestnut hunter. h, British shire. i, Palomino. j, Seal brown point. k, Arab. l, Afghanistan Kabardin.

No. 2947, $300, Golden retriever. No. 2948, $300, Maine coon. No. 2949, $300, American Anglo-Arab.

**1995, June 1 *Perf. 14***

**Sheets of 12, #a-l**

**2944-2946** A217 Set of 3 30.00 30.00

**Souvenir Sheets**

**2947-2949** A217 Set of 3 18.00 18.00

Pocahontas A218

No. 2950 — Characters from Disney animated film: a, Pocahontas, Meeko. b, John Smith. c, Chief Powhatan. d, Kocoum. e, Ratcliffe. f, Wiggins. g, Nakoma. h, Thomas.

No. 2951, Meeko, horiz.

**1995, June 23 Litho. *Perf. 13½x14***

**2950** A218 $50 Sheet of 8, #a.-h. 17.00 17.00

**Souvenir Sheet**

***Perf. 14x13½***

**2951** A218 $300 multicolored 10.00 10.00

See Nos. 2985-2990.

UN, 50th Anniv. — A219

No. 2952 — Map of: a, $35, North, South America. b, $60, Europe, Africa. c, $200, Asia, Australia.

$300, Secretary General Boutros Boutros-Ghali.

**1995, July 6 *Perf. 14***

**2952** A219 Strip of 3, #a.-c. 5.50 5.50

**Souvenir Sheet**

**2953** A219 $300 multicolored 5.00 5.00

End of World War II, 50th Anniv. A220

No. 2954: a, P61 Black Widow. b, PT boat. c, B26 Marauder. d, Cruiser USS San Juan. e, US Gato class submarine. f, US destroyer.

No. 2955: a, Jan. 1945, Battle of Bulge is over. b, Sigfried Line is breached. c, Liberation of concentration camps. d, Operation "Manna," Allies drop food to starving Dutch. e, GIs looking for snipers at end of Italian campaign. f, Newspaper headline announces Hitler's suicide. g, Soviet tanks pour into Berlin. h, U-858, first German warship to surrender in US waters.

No. 2956, $300, Battleship, aircraft carrier. No. 2957, $300, Top of Brandenburg Gate.

**1995, July 6**

**2954** A220 $60 Sheet of 6, #a.-f. + label 7.25 7.25

**2955** A220 $60 Sheet of 8, #a.-h. + label 9.50 9.50

**Souvenir Sheets**

**2956-2957** A220 Set of 2 10.00 10.00

No. 2957 contains one 57x42mm stamp.

FAO, 50th Anniv. — A221

No. 2958: a, $35, Girl carrying sack on head. b, $60, Man carrying sack, woman sorting sacks. c, $200, Woman lifting sack.
$300, Pouring from ladle into bowl.

**1995, July 6** **Litho.** ***Perf. 14***
**2958** A221 Strip of 3, #a.-c. 5.75 5.75

**Souvenir Sheet**

**2959** A221 $300 multicolored 5.00 5.00

No. 2958 is a continuous design.

Rotary Intl., 90th Anniv. A222

Designs: $200, Paul Harris, Rotary emblem. $300, Old, new Rotary emblems.

**1995, July 6**
**2960** A222 $200 multicolored 4.50 4.50

**Souvenir Sheet**

**2961** A222 $300 multicolored 5.25 5.25

1995 Boy Scout Jamboree, Netherlands — A223

Slogan, emblem, and: $20, Campfire. $25, Scout, beach. $30, Hiking. $35, Snorkeling. $60, Natl. flag, scout salute. $200, Fishing from boat.
No. 2968, $300, Canoeing. No. 2969, $300, Camping.

**1995, July 6**
**2962-2967** A223 Set of 6 7.00 7.00

**Souvenir Sheets**

**2968-2969** A223 Set of 2 10.00 10.00

Queen Mother, 95th Birthday A224

No. 2970: a, Drawing. b, Violet hat. c, Formal portrait. d, Green blue hat.
$325, As younger woman.

**1995, July 6** ***Perf. 13½x14***
**2970** A224 $100 Strip or block of 4, #a.-d. 8.25 8.25

**Souvenir Sheet**

**2971** A224 $325 multicolored 7.00 7.00

No. 2970 issued in sheets of 2.
Sheets of Nos. 2970 and 2971 exist with black border in margin with text "In Memoriam/1900-2002."

Holidays of the World A225

No. 2972: a, Thanksgiving, US. b, Christmas, Germany. c, Hanukkah, Israel. d, Easter, Spain. e, Carnivale, brazil. f, Bastill Day, France. g, Independence Day, India. h, St. Patrick's Day, Ireland.
$300, Chinese New Year, China.

**1995, Aug. 8** **Litho.** ***Perf. 14***
**2972** A225 $60 Sheet of 8, #a.-h. 9.75 9.75

**Souvenir Sheet**

**2973** A225 $300 multicolored 5.00 5.00

Marine Life A226

No. 2974, vert: a, Cocoa damselfish. b, Sergeant major. c, Beau gregory. d, Yellowtail damselfish.
No. 2975: a, $30, Butterflyfish. b, $35, Bluehead. c, $60, Yellow damselfish. d, $200, Clown wrasse.
No. 2976: a, $30, Lemon shark. b, $35, Green turtle. c, $60 Sawfish. d, $200, Stingray.
No. 2977, $60: a, Tiger shark. b, Needlefish. c, Horse-eye jack. d, Princess parrotfish. e, Yellowtail snapper. f, Spotted snake eel. g, Trunkfish. h, Cherubfish. i, French angelfish.
No. 2978, $60: a, Sei whale. b, Barracuda. c, Mutton snapper. d, Hawksbill turtle. e, Spanish hogfish. f, Queen angelfish. g, Porkfish. h, Trumpetfish. i, Electric ray.
No. 2979, $300, Carcharodon carcharias. No. 2980, $300, Dermochelys coriacea.

**1995, Sept. 5** **Litho.** ***Perf. 14***
**2974** A226 $80 Strip of 4, #a.-d. 6.00 6.00

**Sheets of 4, #a-d**

**2975-2976** A226 Set of 2 12.00 12.00

**Sheets of 9, #a-i**

**2977-2978** A226 Set of 2 26.00 26.00

**Souvenir Sheets**

**2979-2980** A226 Set of 2 16.00 16.00

No. 2974 was issued in sheets of 4.

Miniature Sheets

1996 Summer Olympics, Atlanta — A227

No. 2981 $60: a, Shot put. b, Relay. c, Balance beam. d, Cycling. e, Synchronized swimming. f, Hurdles. g, Pommel horse. h, Discus thrower, head down.
No. 2982, $60: a, Pole vault. b, Long jump. c, Track. d, Wrestling. e, Discus thrower, head up. f, Basketball. g, Boxing. h, Weight lifting.
No. 2983, $300, Long jump. No. 2984, $300, Runners.

**1995, Oct. 2** **Litho.** ***Perf. 14***

**Sheets of 8, #a-h**

**2981-2982** A227 Set of 2 16.00 16.00

**Souvenir Sheets**

**2983-2984** A227 Set of 2 10.00 10.00

**Pocahontas Type of 1995**

Miniature Sheets

Nos. 2985-2987: Various scenes from Disney animated film, horiz.
No. 2988, $325, Pocahontas behind tree branch, horiz. No. 2989, Pocahontas, Powhatan, horiz. No. 2990, $325, Pocahontas kneeling.

***Perf. 14x13½, 13½x14 (#2990)***
**1995, Oct. 9** **Litho.**
**2985** A218 $8 Sheet of 9, #a.-i. 3.50 3.50
**2986** A218 $30 Sheet of 9, #a.-i. 11.50 11.50
**2987** A218 $35 Sheet of 9, #a.-i. 15.00 15.00

**Souvenir Sheets**

**2988-2990** A218 Set of 3 32.50 32.50

Fauna — A228

No. 2991: a, $35, House martin. b, $60. Hobby. c, $20, Sand martin (a). d, $200, Long-tailed skua (b).
No. 2992: a, Olive colobus. b, Violet-backed starling. c, Diana monkey. d, African palm civet. e, Giraffe, zebras. f, African linsang. g, Royal antelope (fawn). h, Royal antelope (adult, fawn) (g, i). i, Palm squirrel.
No. 2993, $300, Brush pig. No. 2994, $300, Chimpanzee.

**1995, Oct. 18** **Litho.** ***Perf. 14***
**2991** A228 Block of 4, #a.-d. 7.00 7.00
**2992** A228 $60 Sheet of 9, #a.-i. 9.00 9.00

**Souvenir Sheets**

**2993-2994** A228 Set of 2 10.00 10.00

No. 2991 was issued in sheets of 16 stamps.

Queenstown Holy Mosque, Georgetown, Cent. — A229

**1995, Dec. 1** **Litho.** ***Perf. 14***
**2995** A229 $60 multicolored 1.00 1.00

Christmas A230

Details or entire paintings, by Carracci: $25, The Angel of Annunciation. $30, Annunciation of the Virgin. $35, Assumption of the Virgin. $60, Baptism of Christ. $100, Madonna and Child. $300, Birth by the Virgin.
No. 3002, $325, Madonna and Ten Saints, by Fiorentino. No. 3003, $325, Mystical Marriage of St. Catherine, by Carracci.

**1995, Dec. 4** ***Perf. 13½x14***
**2996-3001** A230 Set of 6 9.25 9.25

**Souvenir Sheets**

**3002-3003** A230 Set of 2 11.00 11.00

Guyana Defense Force, 30th Anniv. — A231

**1995, Dec. 7** ***Perf. 14***
**3004** A231 $6 Woman with gun .25 .25
**3005** A231 $60 Man with gun .90 .90

For surcharge, see No. 4109.

John Lennon (1940-80) — A232

**1995**
**3006** A232 $35 multicolored 1.00 1.00

No. 3006 was issued in sheets of 16.

Nobel Prize Fund Established, Cent. — A233

No. 3007, $35: a, Henri Becquerel, physics, 1903. b, Igor Tamm, physics, 1958. c, Georges Köhler, medicine, 1984. d, Gerhard Domagk, medicine, 1939. e, Yasunari Kawabata, literature, 1968. f, Maurice Allais, economics, 1988. g, Aristide Briand, peace, 1926. h, Pavel Cherenkov, physics, 1958. i, Feodor Lynen, medicine, 1964.
No. 3008 $35: a, Adolf von Baeyer, chemistry, 1905. b, Hideki Yukawa, physics, 1949. c, George W. Beadle, medicine, 1958. d, Edwin M. McMillian, chemistry, 1951. e, Samuel C.C. Ting, physics, 1976. f, Saint-John Perse, literature, 1960. g, John F. Enders, medicine, 1954. h, Felix Bloch, physics, 1952. i, P.B. Medawar, medicine, 1960.
No. 3009, $35: a, Albrecht Kossel, medicine, 1910. b, Arthur H. Compton, physics, 1927. c, N.M. Butler, peace, 1931. d, Charles Laveran, medicine, 1907. e, George R. Minot, medicine, 1934. f, Henry H. Dale, medicine, 1936. g, Jacques Monod, medicine, 1965. h, Alfred Hershey, medicine, 1969. i, Pär Lagerkvist, literature, 1951.
No. 3010, $35: a, Francis Crick, medicine, 1962. b, Manne Siegbahn, physics, 1924. c, Eisaku Sato, peace, 1974. d, Robert Koch, medicine, 1905. e, Edgar D. Adrian, medicine, 1932. f, Erwin Neher, medicine, 1991. g, Henry Taube, chemistry, 1983. h, Norman Angell, peace, 1933. i, Robert Robinson, chemistry, 1947.
No. 3011 $35: a, Nikolai Basov, physics, 1964. b, Klas Arnoldson, peace, 1908. c, René Sully-Prudhomme, literature, 1901. d, Robert W. Wilson, physics, 1978. e, Hugo Theorell, medicine, 1955. f, Nelly Sachs, literature, 1966. g, Hans von Euler-Chelpin, chemistry, 1929. h, Mairead Corrigan, peace, 1976. i, Willis E. Lamb, Jr, physics, 1955.
No. 3012 $35: a, Norman F. Ramsey, physics, 1989. b, Chen Ning Yang, physics, 1957. c, Earl W. Sutherland, Jr., medicine, 1971. d, Paul Karrer, chemistry, 1937. e, Harmut Michel, chemistry, 1988. f, Richard Kuhn, chemistry, 1938. g, P.A.M. Dirac, physics, 1933. h, Victor Grignard, chemistry, 1912. i, Richard Willstätter, chemistry, 1915.
No. 3013, $300, Le Duc Tho, peace, 1973. No. 3014, $300, Yasunari Kawabata, literature, 1968. No. 3015, $300, Heinrich Böll, literature, 1972. No. 3016, $300, Henry Kissinger, peace, 1973. No. 3017, $300, Kenichi Fukui, chemistry, 1981. No. 3018, $300, Lech Walesa, peace, 1983.

**1995, Dec. 20** **Litho.** ***Perf. 14***

**Sheets of 9, #a-i**

**3007-3012** A233 Set of 6 57.00 57.00

**Souvenir Sheets**

**3013-3018** A233 Set of 6 36.00 36.00

Caribbean Development Bank, 25th Anniv. — A234

**1995, Dec. 29** **Litho.** ***Perf. 14***
**3019** A234 $60 multicolored 1.00 1.00

Marilyn Monroe (1926-62) A235

No. 3020, Various portraits. No. 3021, Portrait, horiz.

**1995, Dec. 29** *Perf. 13½x14*
**3020** A235 $60 Sheet of 9, #a.-i. 9.00 9.00

**Souvenir Sheet**
*Perf. 14x13½*
**3021** A235 $300 multicolored 5.00 5.00

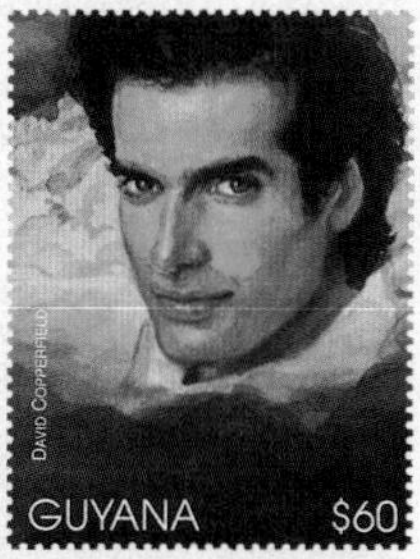


David Copperfield, Magician A236

Nos. 3022-3023, Various portraits, magic acts.

**1995, Dec. 29** *Perf. 13½x14*
**3022** A236 $60 Sheet of 9, #a.-i. 10.00 10.00

**Souvenir Sheet**
**3023** A236 $300 multicolored 5.00 5.00

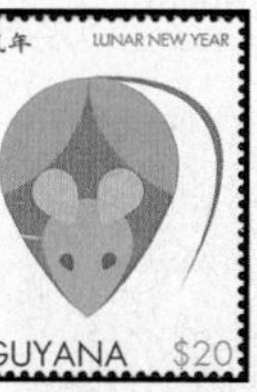


New Year 1996 (Year of the Rat) — A237

No. 3024 — Stylized rats: a, $20. b, $30. c, $50, light brown & multi. d, $100.
No. 3025: a, Like #3024a, b, Like #3024b. c, Like #3024c, darker brown & multi. d, Like #3024d.
No. 3026, Rat facing forward.

**1996, Jan. 2** *Perf. 14½*
**3024** A237 Block of 4, #a.-d. 4.00 4.00

**Miniature Sheet**
**3025** A237 $50 Sheet of 4, #a.-d. 3.50 3.50

**Souvenir Sheet**
**3026** A237 $150 multicolored 3.50 3.50

No. 3024 was issued in sheets of 16 stamps.

UNICEF, 50th Anniv. A238

No. 3027: a, Children, building in background. b, Man, boy, tree in background. c, Children behind tree. d, Man, children.

**1996, Jan. 2** *Perf. 14*
**3027** A238 $1100 Sheet of 4, #a.-d. *22.50 22.50*

No. 3027 is a continuous design.
Extreme speculation might have occurred with this issue.

Paintings by Peter Paul Rubens A239

Details or entire paintings: $6, The Garden of Love. $10, Two Sleeping Children. $20, All Saints Day. $25, Sacrifice of Abraham. $30, The Last Supper. $35, The Birth of Henry of Navarre. $40, Standing Female Saint Study. $50, $60, The Garden of Love, each diff. No. 3037, $200, The Martyrdom of St. Livinus. No. 3038, $200, Der Heilige Franz Von Paula. $300, The Union of Maria de Medici and Henry IV.
No. 3039, $325, The Three Crosses. No. 3040, $325, Decius Mus Addressing the Legions, horiz. No. 3041, $325, Triumph of Henry IV, horiz.

**1996, Jan. 29** **Litho.** *Perf. 14*
**3028-3038A** A239 Set of 11 19.00 19.00

**Souvenir Sheets**
**3039-3041** A239 Set of 3 18.50 18.50

Nos. 3039-3041 each contain one 57x85mm or 85x57mm stamp.

Miniature Sheets

A240

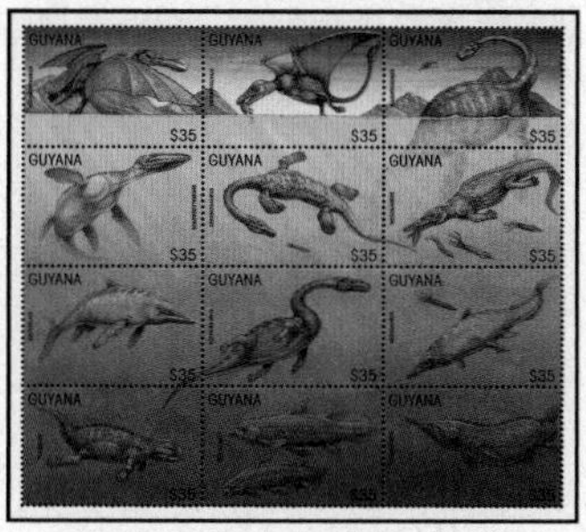

Prehistoric Animals — A241

No. 3042: a, Tarbosaurus. b, Hadrosaurus. c, Polacanthus. d, Psittacosaurus. e, Ornitholestes. f, Yangchuanosaurus. g, Scelidosaurus. h, Kentrosaurus. i, Coelophysis. j, Lesothosaurus. k, Plateosaurus. l, Staurikosaurus.
No. 3043, $35: a, Eudimorphodon. b, Criorynchus. c, Elasmosaurus. d, Rhomaleosaurus. e, Ceresiosaurus. f, Mesosaurus. g, Grendelius. h, Nothosaurus. i, Mixosaurus. j, Placodus. k, Coelacanth. l, Mosasaurus.
No. 3044, $35: a, Ornithomimus. b, Pteranodon. c, Rhamphorynchus. d, Ornitholestes. e, Brachiosaurus. f, Parasaurolophus. g, Ceratosaurus. h, Camarasaurus. i, Euoplocephalus. j, Scutellosaurus. k, Compsognathus. l, Stegoceras.
No. 3045, $35: a, Apatosaurus. b, Archaeopteryx. c, Dimorphodon. d, Deinonychus. e, Coelophysis. f, Tyrannosaurus. g, Triceratops. h, Anatosaurus. i, Saltasaurus. j, Allosaurus. k, Oviraptor. l, Stegosaurus.
No. 3046, $60: a, Heterodontosaurus (b). b, Compsognathus (c). c, Ornithomimus (b).
No. 3047, $60: a, Saurolophus. b, Muttaburrasaurus (a). c, Dicraeosaurus (b).
No. 3048, $300, Apatosaurus, allosaurus, horiz. No. 3049, $300, Tyrannosaurus rex.
No. 3050, $300, Quetzalcoatlus. No. 3051, $300, Lagosuchus. No. 3052, $300Struthiomimus.

**1996, Feb. 12**
**3042** A240 $35 Sheet of 12, #a.-l. 8.00 8.00

**Sheets of 12, #a-l**
**3043-3045** A241 Set of 3 24.00 24.00

**Sheets of 3, #a-c**
**3046-3047** A240 Set of 2 7.00 7.00

**Souvenir Sheets**
**3048-3049** A240 Set of 2 12.00 12.00
**3050-3052** A241 Set of 3 18.00 18.00

Pandas — A242

No. 3053 — In tree: a, Lying on back, looking right. b, Arms, legs around branch. c, Paws holding onto tree. d, Sitting, looking left.
No. 3054 — On rocks by stream: a, Standing. b, Sitting, holding bamboo stick. c, Holding bamboo to mouth. d, Lying on stomach.

**1996, Apr. 12** **Litho.** *Perf. 14*
**3053** A242 $60 Sheet of 4, #a.-d. 5.00 5.00
**3054** A242 $60 Sheet of 4, #a.-d. 5.00 5.00

China '96, 9th Asian Intl. Philatelic Exhbition.

Mushrooms, Insects and Coral — A243

Designs: $20, Yellow morce, leaf beetle. $25, Green spored mushroom. $30, Leaf beetle, common mushroom. $35, Monarch caterpillars, pine cone mushroom.
No. 3059, $60: a, Green-beaded jelly club. b, Aspic puffball. c, Stalkless paxillus. d, Stout-stalked amanita.
No. 3060, $60: a, Fly agaric. b, Graying yellow russula, click beetle. c, Netted stinkhorn, housefly. d, Butterfly hunter, stropharia.
No. 3061, $60: a, Cockle-shell lentinus. b, Parasitic volvariella. c, Deadly lepiota. d, Shaggy-stalked boleta.
No. 3062: a, Armillauella mellea. b, Sealy vase chanterelle. c, Bitter pholiota. d, Flute white helvella. e, Fading scarlet waxy cap. f, Jask's lantern. g, Hygzocybe acutoconica. h, Mycena viscosa.
No. 3063, $300, Orange mycena. No. 3064, $300, Violet-branched coral, Red raspberry slime, yellow-tipped coral, horiz.

**1996, May 3** **Litho.** *Perf. 14*
**3055-3058** A243 Set of 4 3.50 3.50

**Strips of 4, #a-d**
**3059-3061** A243 Set of 3 13.50 13.50
**3062** A243 $60 Sheet of 8, #a.-h. 9.00 9.00

**Souvenir Sheets**
**3063-3064** A243 Set of 2 11.50 11.50

Nos. 3059-3061 were issued in sheets of 8 stamps.

Deng Xiaoping, Chinese Communist Leader — A244

No. 3065: a, Painting inscription. b, With dignitaries, waving. c, Signing autograph. d, Waving.
$300, Wearing white shirt, vert.

**1996** *Perf. 13*
**3065** A244 $30 Strip or block of 4, #a.-d. 2.00 2.00

**Souvenir Sheet**
**3066** A244 $300 multicolored 5.00 5.00

No. 3065 issued in sheets of 16 stamps.

Queen Elizabeth II, 70th Birthday A245

No. 3067: a, Portrait wearing blue dress. b, Wearing blue green dress, hat. c, On throne, opening Parliament.
$325, In ceremonial attire.

**1996, May 3** **Litho.** *Perf. 13½x14*
**3067** A245 $100 Strip of 3, #a.-c. 5.00 5.00

**Souvenir Sheet**
**3068** A245 $325 multicolored 5.25 5.25

No. 3067 was issued in sheets of 9 stamps, with each strip having a different order.

Jerusalem, 3000th Anniv. — A246

No. 3069: a, $30. The Hulda Gates. b, $35, Old City, View from Mt. of Olives. c, $200, Absalom's Memorial, Kidron Valley.
$300, Children's Memorial.

**1996** **Litho.** *Perf. 14*
**3069** A246 Sheet of 3, #a.-d. 5.00 5.00

**Souvenir Sheet**
**3070** A246 $300 multicolored 5.00 5.00

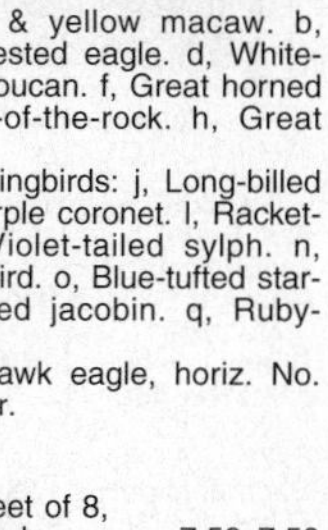


Birds — A247

No. 3071: a, Blue & yellow macaw. b, Andean condor. c, Crested eagle. d, White-tailed trogon. e, Toco toucan. f, Great horned owl. g, Andean cock-of-the-rock. h, Great curassow.
No. 3071I — Hummingbirds: j, Long-billed starthroat. k, Velvet-purple coronet. l, Racket-tailed coquette. m, Violet-tailed sylph. n, Broad-tailed hummingbird. o, Blue-tufted starthroat. p, White-necked jacobin. q, Ruby-throated hummingbird.
No. 3072, Ornate hawk eagle, horiz. No. 3073, Gould's violet-ear.

**1996, July 10**
**3071** A247 $60 Sheet of 8, #a.-h. 7.50 7.50
**3071I** A247 $60 Sheet of 8, #j.-q. 7.50 7.50

**Souvenir Sheets**
**3072** A247 $300 multicolored 5.50 5.50
**3073** A247 $300 multicolored 5.50 5.50

Radio, Cent. A248

Entertainers: $20, Frank Sinatra. $35, Gene Autry. $60, Groucho Marx. $200, Red Skelton. $300, Burl Ives.

**1996, July 25**

**3074-3077** A248 Set of 4 5.00 5.00

**Souvenir Sheet**

**3078** A248 $300 multicolored 5.00 5.00

1996 Summer Olympic Games, Atlanta A249

Designs: $20, Pancratium. $30, Olympic Stadium, 1956. $60, Leonid Spirin, 20k walk, 1956, vert. $200, Lars Hall, modern pentathlon, 1952, 1956, vert.

No. 3083, $50, vert.: a, Florence Griffith-Joyner. b, Ines Geissler. c, Nadia Comaneci. d, Tatiana Gutsu. e, Olga Korbut. f, Barbara Krause. g, Olga Bryzgina. h, Fanny Blankers-Koen. i, Irena Szewinska.

No. 3084, $50, vert.: a, Gerd Wessig. b, Jim Thorpe. c, Norman Read. d, Lasse Viren. e, Milt Campbell. f, Abebe Bikila. g, Jesse Owens. h, Viktor Saneev. i, Waldemer Cierpinski.

No. 3085, $50, vert.: a, Dietmar Schmidt. b, Pam Shriver. c, Zina Garrison. d, Hyun Jung-Hwa. e, Steffi Graf. f, Michael Jordan. g, Karch Kiraly. h, "Magic" Johnson. i, Ingolf Wiegert.

No. 3086, $50: a, Volleyball. b, Basketball. c, Tennis. d, Table tennis. e, Baseball. f, Handball. g, Field hockey. h, Water polo. i, Soccer.

No. 3087, $50, vert.: a, Cycling. b, Hurdles. c, High jump. d, Diving. e, Weight lifting. f, Canoeing. g, Wrestling. h, Gymnastics. i, Running.

No. 3088, $300, Carl Lewis, track and field gold medalist. No. 3089, $300, US defeats Korea for gold medal in baseball, 1988.

**1996, July 25**

**3079-3082** A249 Set of 4 5.00 5.00

**Sheets of 9, #a-i**

**3083-3087** A249 Set of 5 35.00 35.00

**Souvenir Sheets**

**3088-3089** A249 Set of 2 9.75 9.75

Olymphilex '96 (#3088).

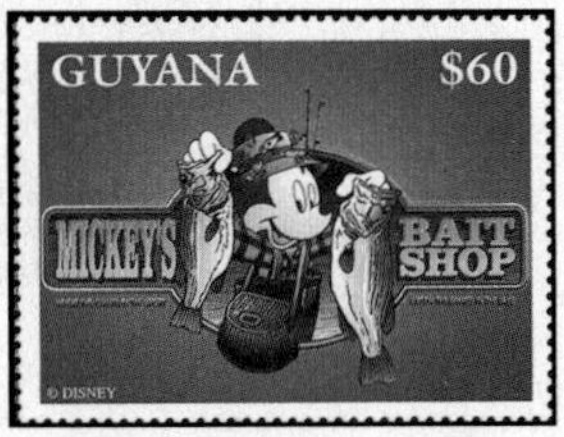


Disney Cartoons — A250

No. 3090 — Mickey outdoors: a, Mickey's Bait Shop. b, Ol' Mickey, The Lumbercamp Legend and Pluto the Yellow Dog. c, For All Men Are Equal Before Fish.

No. 3091, vert. — Super sports: a, BMX Championships. b, Goofy, Hockey Superstar. c, Malibu Surf City.

No. 3092, vert. — Nautical Mickey: a, The Path to Adventure is Shown in the Stars. b, Captain Mickey's Steamship School. c, Ahoy, Follow the Wind on Waves of Fortune.

No. 3093, $250, M. Mouse, ESQ, Lawman, vert.: No. 3094, $250, All Aboard, Ride the Great American Transcontinental Railroad. No. 3095, $250, Mouse and Pinkerton, Wild West Detective Agency, vert.

$300, Donald's Rock & Ice Mountaineers. $325, Guided by The Great Spirit, vert.

**1996, July 26** ***Perf. 14x13½, 13½x14***

**3090** A250 $60 Strip of 3, #a.-c. 4.50 4.50

**3091** A250 $80 Strip of 3, #a.-c. 6.00 6.00

**3092** A250 $100 Strip of 3, #a.-c. 8.50 8.50

**Souvenir Sheets**

**3093-3095** A250 Set of 3 22.50 22.50

**3096** A250 $300 multi 7.50 7.50

**3097** A250 $325 multi 8.50 8.50

Nos. 3090-3092 were issued in sheets of 9 stamps.

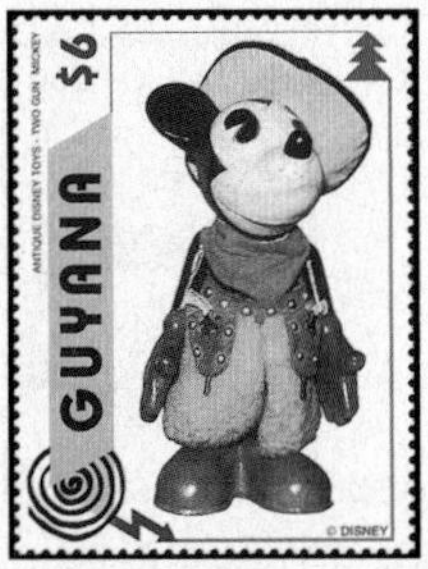


Disney Antique Toys — A251

No. 3098: a, Two-Gun Mickey. b, Wood-jointed Mickey doll. c, Donald Jack-in-the Box. d, Rocking Minnie. e, Fireman Donald Duck. f, Long-billed Donald Duck. g, Painted wood Mickey doll. h, Wind-up Jiminy Cricket.

No. 3099, $300, Mickey doll. No. 3100, $300, Carousel train.

**1996, July 26** ***Perf. 13½x14***

**3098** A251 $6 Sheet of 8, #a.-h. 7.00 7.00

**Souvenir Sheets**

**3099-3100** A251 Set of 2 18.00 18.00

Elvis Presley's First "Hit" Year, 40th Anniv. A252

Various portraits.

**1996, Sept. 8** **Litho.** ***Perf. 13½x14***

**3101** A252 $100 Sheet of 6, #a.-f. 11.00 11.00

Domestic Cats A253

No. 3102, $60: a, Birman. b, American curl. c, Turkish Angora. d, European shorthair. e, Persian. f, Scottish fold. g, Sphynx. h, Malayan. i, Cornish rex.

No. 3103, $60, vert: a, Norwegian forest. b, Russian shorthair. c, European shorthair. d, Birman. e, Ragdoll. f, Egyptian mau. g, Persian. h, Angora. i, Siamese.

No. 3104, $300, Maine coon, vert. No. 3105, $300, Himalayan.

**1996, Sept. 18** ***Perf. 14***

**Sheets of 9, #a-i**

**3102-3103** A253 Set of 2 19.00 19.00

**Souvenir Sheets**

**3104-3105** A253 Set of 2 11.00 11.00

Deep Ocean Exploration — A254

No. 3106: a, Goblin shark, coelacanth. b, Remote operated vehicle, JASON. c, Deep water invertebrates. d, Submarine NR1 (e). e, Giant squid (b, c, f, g, h, j, m). f, Sperm whale (b, c). g, Volcanic vents, submersible ALVIN. h, Air-recycling pressure suit, shipwreck. i, Bacteria survey, submersible SHINKAI 6500. j, Giant tube worms. k, Anglerfish. l, Six-gill shark (k). m. Autonomous underwater vehicle ABE. n, Viperfish. o, Swallower, hatchetfish.

$300, Sea anemone.

**1996, Dec. 2** **Litho.** ***Perf. 14***

**3106** A254 $30 Sheet of 15, #a.-o. 7.50 7.50

**Souvenir Sheet**

**3107** A254 $300 multicolored 5.25 5.25

Characters from Disney's Snow White in Christmas Scenes A255

Designs: $6, Snow White. $20, Doc. $25, Dopey, Sneezy. $30, Sleepy, Happy, Bashful. $35, Dopey, Santa. $60, Dopey, fireplace. $100, Dopey, Grumpy. $200, Dopey as Santa.

No. 3116, $300, Snow White looking at squirrel in box. No. 3117, $300, Dopey placing star on tree.

**1996, Dec. 16** ***Perf. 13½x14***

**3108-3115** A255 Set of 8 17.50 17.50

**Souvenir Sheets**

**3116-3117** A255 Set of 2 22.00 22.00

Marine Life A256

No. 3118: a, Red gorgonians. b, Plexaura homomalla, butterflyfish (a, c). c, Dendronephtbya. d, Common clownfish, anemone, mushroom coral (a). e, Anemone, horse-eyed jack (d, g-h). f, Slender snappers (c), splendid coral trout. g, Anemones. h, Brain coral, Indo-Pacific hard coral. i, Cup coral (f, h).

**1996, Dec. 2** **Litho.** ***Perf. 14***

**3118** A256 $60 Sheet of 9, #a.-i. 11.00 11.00

New Year 1997 (Year of the Ox) — A257

No. 3119 — Denomination at: a, $20, LR. b, $30, LL. c, $35, UR. d, $50, UL.

No. 3120: a, Like #3119a. b, Like #3119b. c, Like #3119c.

$150, Ox, facing.

**1997, Jan. 2** **Litho.** ***Perf. 14½***

**3119** A257 Block of 4, #a.-d. 3.75 3.75

**3120** A257 $50 Sheet of 4, #a.-c. + #3119d 4.00 4.00

**Souvenir Sheet**

**3121** A257 $150 multicolored 3.00 3.00

No. 3119 was issued in sheets of 16 stamps.

Mickey and Friends Celebrate Chinese Lunar New Year — A258

No. 3122: a, $6, Mickey. b, $20, Home visit. c, $25, Fortune lantern. d, $30, Silhouette. e, $35, Flower market. f, $60, Harmonious man, woman.

No. 3123: a, Red-pocket money. b, Lion dance. c, Calligraphy. d, Surplus every year. e, Fireworks. f, Ox.

$150, Mickey marching, vert. $200, Mickey, ox.

**1997, Jan. 2** ***Perf. 14x13½***

**3122** A258 Sheet of 6, #a.-f. 6.00 6.00

**3123** A258 $30 Sheet of 6, #a.-f. 6.50 6.50

**Souvenir Sheets**

***Perf. 13½x14, 14x13½***

**3124** A258 $150 multicolored 5.50 5.50

**3125** A258 $200 multicolored 6.00 6.00

Marine Life A259

No. 3126, $6, Angelfish. No. 3127, $6, Hyed snapper. $20, Box fish. $25, Golden damselfish. $35, Clown triggerfish. $200, Harlequin tuskfish.

$300, Caribbean flower coral.

**1996** **Litho.** ***Perf. 14***

**3126-3131** A259 Set of 6 8.50 8.50

**Souvenir Sheet**

**3132** A259 $300 multicolored 7.00 7.00

Hotel Tower, 50th Anniv. — A260

**1996, Dec. 28**

**3133** A260 $30 multicolored 1.00 1.00

For surcharge, see No. 4180.

**Souvenir Sheet**

The Summer Palace, Beijing — A261

**1996, Apr. 12** **Litho.** ***Perf. 13***

**3134** A261 $60 multicolored 2.00 2.00

China '96. No. 3134 was not available until March 1997.

Transfer of Hong Kong — A262

No. 3135, $80: a, Tortoise. b, Dragon. c, Unicorn. d, Phoenix.
No. 3136, $80, vert.: a, Swallow & willow. b, Kingfisher & chrysanthemum. c, Crane & pine. d, Peacock & peony.
No. 3137, $80, vert.: a-d, Various kites.
No. 3138, vert.: a-b, Paintings of mountains and lakes.

**1997, Feb. 12** ***Perf. 14***

**Sheets of 4 , #a-d**

**3135-3137** A262 Set of 3 15.00 15.00
**3138** A262 $200 Sheet of 2, #a.-b. 6.00 6.00

Hong Kong '97. No. 3138 contains two 70x44mm stamps.

Motion Pictures, Cent. A263

No. 3139 — Movie star, World War II films: a, Burgess Meredith, "The Story of GI Joe." b, M.E. Clifton-James, "I Was Monty's Double." c, Audie Murphy, "To Hell and Back." d, Gary Cooper, "The Story of Dr. Wassell." e, James Mason, "The Desert Fox." f, Manart Kippen, "Mission to Moscow." g, Robert Taylor, "Above and Beyond." h, James Cagney, "The Gallant Hours." i, John Garfield, "Pride of the Marines."
$300, George C. Scott, "Patton," horiz.

**1997, Feb. 21** ***Perf. 13½x14***

**3139** A263 $50 Sheet of 9, #a.-i. 10.00 10.00

**Souvenir Sheet**

***Perf. 14x13½***

**3140** A263 $300 multicolored 9.00 9.00

Pres. John F. Kennedy (1917-63) — A264

**1997, Mar. 14** **Litho.** ***Perf. 14***

**3141** A264 $50 blue 1.25 1.25

George Washington A265

Designs from works of art: No. 3142: a, Washington in battle. b, Washington taking oath. c, Washington Seated in Armchair, from engraving after Chappel. d, Col. Washington of Virginia Militia, by Charles W. Peale. e, George Washington, by Rembrandt Peale. f, Washington Addressing Constitutional Convention, by Junius Brutus Stearns. g, Washington on His Way to the Continental Congress. h, Washington on a White Charger, by John Faed. i, Washington as a Surveyor, from an engraving by G.R. Hall after Darley's drawing. j, Bas-relief of Washington Praying at Valley Forge. k, Death of Gen. Mercer at Battle of Princeton, by John Trumbull. l, Washington Taking Command of the Continental Army at Cambridge. m, George Washington, by Gilbert Stuart.
No. 3143: a, Washington Before the Battle of Trenton, by John Trumbull. b, Washington, His Family at Mt. Vernon, by Alonzo Chappel. c, Inauguration of Washington in New York City, by Chappel. d, Washington, by Adolph Ulrich Wertmuller. e, Washington Accepts His Commission as Commander-in-Chief, June 1775, Currier & Ives lithograph. f, Washington from a mezzotint by Sartain. g, On the Lawn at Mt. Vernon after the War. h, Washington Conversing with a Farmhand During the Baling Season with Nelly and Washington Custus Playing Nearby, from anonymous print after Junius Brutus Stearns. i, Nellie Custis' Wedding on Washington's Last Birthday, by Ogden. j, Washington Crossing the Delaware, by Leutze. k, Washington Receives Orders from Mortally Wounded Gen. Braddock at 1755 Battle of Monongahela. l, Washington Birthplace (supposed) on the Potomac, Currier & Ives lithograph. m, Washington at Yorktown, by James Peale.

**1997, Mar. 14** **Litho.** ***Perf. 14***

**3142** Sheet of 13 17.50 17.50
*a.-l.* A265 $60 any single 1.00 1.00
*m.* A265 $300 imperf. 5.00 5.00
**3143** Sheet of 13 17.50 17.50
*a.-l.* A265 $60 any single 1.00 1.00
*m.* A265 $300 imperf. 5.00 5.00

Nos. 3142m, 3143m are each 66x91mm and have simulated perforations.
No. 3142m exists perf. 14½.

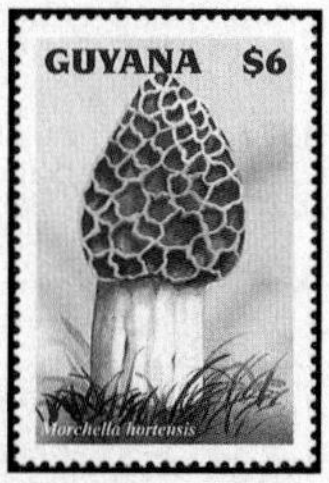


Mushrooms A266

Designs: $6, Morchella hortensis. $20, Boletus chyrsenteron. $25, Hygrophorus agathosmus. $30, Cortinarius violaceus. $35, Acanthocystis geogenius. $60, Mycena polygramma. $200, Hebeloma radicosum. $300, Coprinus comatus.
No. 3152, $80: a, Coprinus picaceus. b, Stropharia umbonatescens. c, Paxillus involutus. d, Amanita inaurata. e, Lepiota rhacodes. f, Russula amoena.
No. 3153, $80: a, Volvaria volvacea. b, Psalliota augusta. c, Tricholoma aurantium. d, Pholiota spectabilis. e, Cortinarius armillatus. f, Agrocybe dura.
No. 3154, $300, Pholiota mutabilis. No. 3155, $300, Amanita muscaria.

**1997, Apr. 2** **Litho.** ***Perf. 14***

**3144-3151** A266 Set of 8 10.50 10.50

**Sheets of 6, #a-f**

**3152-3153** A266 Set of 2 16.00 16.00

**Souvenir Sheets**

**3154-3155** A266 Set of 2 10.00 10.00

Flowers — A267

Designs: No. 3156, $6, Pineapple lily. No. 3157, $6, Blue columbine. $20, Petunia. $25, Lily of the Nile. $30, Bird of Paradise. $35, African daisy. $60, Cape daisy. $80, Gazania. $100, Cape water lily. $200, Insigne lady's slipper.
No. 3166: a, Monarch supperwart. b, Passion flower. c, Butterfly iris. d, Red-hot poker. e, Dir. G.T. Moore water lily. f, Superbissima painted tongue. g, Orchid. h, Annual chrysanthemum.
No. 3167: a, Tulips. b, Liatris. c, Roses. d, Gerber daisies. e, Sunflowers. f, Chrysanthemums.
No. 3168, Petunia.

**1997, Apr. 2**

**3156-3165** A267 Set of 10 9.00 9.00
**3166** A267 $60 Sheet of 8, #a.-h. 8.50 8.50
**3167** A267 $80 Sheet of 6, #a.-f. 8.50 8.50

**Souvenir Sheet**

**3168** A267 $300 multicolored 5.00 5.00

Deng Xiaoping (1904-97) — A268

**1997, May 1**

**3169** A268 $100 shown 1.75 1.75

**Souvenir Sheet**

**3170** A268 $150 Portrait, diff. 2.75 2.75

No. 3169 was issued in sheets of 3.

UNESCO, 50th Anniv. — A269

Designs: $20, Horyu-Ji, Japan. $25, Scandola Nature Reserve, France. $30, Great Wall Defenses, China. $35, Wurzburg, Germany. $60, Monastery of Batalha, Portugal. $200, Dubrovnik, Croatia.
No. 3177, $60, vert. — Sites in Germany: a, Cathedral of Aquisgran, Aachen. b, Cathedral at Trier. c, Column of Augusta Treveror, Trier. d, f, Residences, Wurzburg. e, Church interior, Wurzburg. g, House of the River at Inselstadt, Bamberg. h, Cathedral interior, Speyer.
No. 3178, $60, Sites in Greece, vert: No. 3178: a, Monastery of Thessaloniki. b, d, e, Monastery at Mystras. c, Church of Santa Sofia, Thessaloniki. f, City, Thessaloniki. g, Painting, Mystras. h, Museum of Byzantine Art, Thessaloniki.
No. 3179, $60, vert.: a, Monastery of Poblet Catalonia, Spain. b, Old City of Salamanca, Spain. c, Toledo, Spain. d, Cathedral of Florence, Italy. e, Tower of Pisa, Italy. f, g, h, Convent of Christ, Tomar, Portugal.
No. 3180, $80 — Sites in Japan: a, d, e, Horyu-Ji. b, c, Kyoto.
No. 3181, $80 — Sites in the Americas: a, Cuzco, Peru. b, Potosi, Bolivia. c, Fortress, San Lorenzo, Panama. d, Sangay Natl. Park, Ecuador. e, Los Glaciares Natl. Park, Argentina.
No. 3182, $80 — Sites in US: a, Monticello. b, Yosemite Natl. Park. c, Yellowstone Natl. Park. d, Olympic Natl. Park. e, Everglades.
No. 3183, $300, Mount Taishan Shrine, China. No. 3184, $300, Monastery of Batalha, Portugal. No. 3185, $300, Bamberg Cathedral (detail), Germany. No. 3186, $300, Monastery, Mount Athos, Greece.

**1997, May 20**

**3171-3176** A269 Set of 6 9.00 9.00

**Sheets of 8, #a-h + Label**

**3177-3179** A269 Set of 3 22.50 22.50

**Sheets of 5**

**3180-3182** A269 Set of 3 17.50 17.50

**Souvenir Sheets**

**3183-3186** A269 Set of 4 18.50 18.50

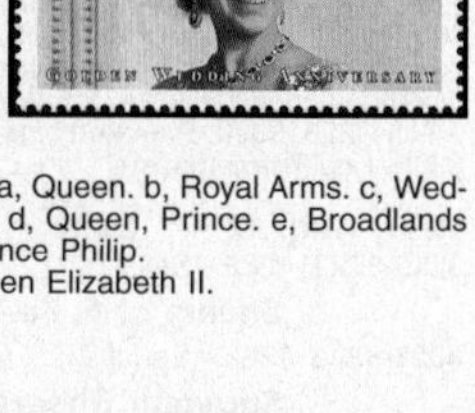

Queen Elizabeth II, Prince Philip, 50th Wedding Anniv. A270

No. 3187: a, Queen. b, Royal Arms. c, Wedding portrait. d, Queen, Prince. e, Broadlands House. f, Prince Philip.
$300, Queen Elizabeth II.

**1997, May 20** **Litho.** ***Perf. 14***

**3187** A270 $60 Sheet of 6, #a.-f. 7.00 7.00

**Souvenir Sheet**

**3188** A270 $300 multicolored 5.50 5.50

Paintings, by Hiroshige (1797-1858) A271

No. 3189: a, Oumayagashi. b, Ryogoku Ekoin & Moto-Yanagibashi Bridge. c, Pine of Success and Oumayagashi Asakusa River. d, Fireworks at Ryogoku. e, Dyers' Quarter, Kanda. f, Cotton-goods Lane, Ōdenma-cho.
No. 3190, $300, Suruga-cho. No. 3191, $300, Yatsukoji, inside Sujikai Gate.

**1997, May 20** ***Perf. 13½x14***

**3189** A271 $80 Sheet of 6, #a.-f. 6.75 6.75

**Souvenir Sheets**

**3190-3191** A271 Set of 2 10.00 10.00

Heinrich von Stephan (1831-97), Founder of UPU A272

No. 3192: a, Frieze of Roman post service. b, UPU emblem. c, Cable car, Boston, 1907.
$300, Von Stephan, Egyptian messenger.

**1997, May 20** **Litho.** ***Perf. 14***

**3192** A272 $100 Sheet of 3, #a.-c. 8.00 8.00

**Souvenir Sheet**

**3193** A272 $300 multicolored 9.00 9.00

PACIFIC 97.

Paul P. Harris (1868-1947), Founder of Rotary, Intl. — A273

Designs: $200, Health, hunger and humanity, portrait of Harris. $300, Mutual respect among all faiths, races and cultures.

**1997, May 20**

**3194** A273 $200 multicolored 2.75 2.75

**Souvenir Sheet**

**3195** A273 $300 multicolored 4.25 4.25

Chernobyl Disaster, 10th Anniv. A274

Designs: No. 3196, Chabad's Children of Chernobyl. No. 3197, UNESCO.

**1997, May 20** ***Perf. 13½x14***

**3196** A274 $200 multicolored 3.00 3.00
**3197** A274 $200 multicolored 3.00 3.00

Grimm's Fairy Tales — A275

Mother Goose — A276

Scenes from "Hansel & Gretel:" No. 3198: a, Hansel & Gretel in forest. b, Gingerbread house. c, Wicked witch. $500, Witch trying to capture Gretel, horiz.
$300, Rooster from "Cock-A-Doodle-Doo."

**1997, May 20** ***Perf. 13½x14***
**3198** A275 $100 Sheet of 3, #a.-c. 5.50 5.50

**Souvenir Sheets**
***Perf. 14, 14x13½***
**3199** A276 $300 multicolored 5.00 5.00
**3200** A275 $500 multicolored 8.25 8.25

US Pres. Bill Clinton's Visit to Caribbean, May 1997 — A277

Designs: $30, Guyana Pres. Cheddi Jagan, Pres. Clinton, map of Caribbean, vert. $100, Clinton, Jagan, flags of US, Guyana, palm trees, beach.

***Perf. 13½x14, 14x13½***
**1997, June 23**
**3201** A277 $30 multicolored .50 .50
**3202** A277 $100 multicolored 1.50 1.50

Nos. 3201-3202 each issued in sheets of 9. See Nos. 3237-3238.

1998 Winter Olympic Games, Nagano
A278 A279

Medalists: $30, Georg Thoma. $35, Katja Seizinger. $60, Georg Hackl. $200, Katarina Witt.
No. 3207, $60: a, Gunda Niemann, 3000- & 5000-m speed skating, 1992. b, Tony Nash, Robin Dixon, 2-man bobsled, 1964. c, Switzerland 4-man bobsled, 1988. d, Piet Kleine, speed skating, 1976.
No. 3208, $60: a, Oksana Baiul, figure skating, 1994. b, Cathy Turner, 500-m short track speed skating, 1994. c, Brian Boitano, figure skating, 1988. d, Nancy Kerrigan, figure skating, 1994.
No. 3209: a, Markus Wasmeier. b, Jens Weissflog. c, Erhard Keller. d, Rosi Mittermaier. e, Gunda Niemann. f, Peter Angerer.
No. 3210, Swiss 4-Man bobsled team.
No. 3211, $300, Jean-Claude Killy, slalom, 1968. No. 3212, $300, Chen Lu, figure skating, 1992.

**1997, July 1** ***Perf. 14***
**3203-3206** A278 Set of 4 4.75 4.75

**Strips or Blocks of 4, #a-d**
**3207-3208** A279 Set of 2 12.00 12.00
**3209** A278 $30 Sheet of 6, #a.-f. 3.00 3.00

**Souvenir Sheets**
**3210** A278 $300 multicolored 6.00 6.00
**3211-3212** A279 Set of 2 12.00 12.00

Nos. 3207-3208 issued in sheets of 8 stamps.

Souvenir Sheet

Return of Hong Kong to China — A280

**Litho. & Embossed**
**1997, July 1** ***Perf. 14***
**3213** A280 $500 gold & multi 7.50 7.50

Domestic Cats A281

Designs, vert.: $30, Norwegian forest cat. $35, Oriental spotted tabby. $200, Asian smoke.
No. 3217: a, Abyssinian. b, Chocolate colorpoint shorthair. c, Silver tabby. d, Persian. e, Maine coon cat & kitten. f, Brown shaded Burmese. g, Persian kitten. h, Siamese. i, British shorthair.
$300, Manx, vert.

**1997, July 29**
**3214-3216** A281 Set of 3 4.25 4.25
**3217** A281 $60 Sheet of 9, #a.-i. 8.50 8.50

**Souvenir Sheet**
**3218** A281 $300 multi 5.50 5.50

Birds A282

Designs: $25, Verdin. $30, Wood thrush, vert. $60, Rofous-sided towhee. $200, Pygmy nuthatch, vert.
No. 3223, $80: a, Groove-billed ani. b, Green honeycreeper. c, Toucanet. d, Wire-tailed manakin. e, Hoatzin. f, Tiger heron.
No. 3224, $80 — Hummingbirds: a, Magenta-throated woodstar. b, Long-tailed hermit. c, Red-footed plumeleteer. d, Anna's. e, White-tipped sicklebill. f, Fiery-throated.
No. 3225, $300, Pinnated bittern. No. 3226, $300, Keel-billed toucan.

**1997, Aug. 12** **Litho.** ***Perf. 14***
**3219-3222** A282 Set of 4 6.00 6.00

**Sheets of 6, #a-f**
**3223-3224** A282 Set of 2 16.00 16.00

**Souvenir Sheets**
**3225-3226** A282 Set of 2 12.00 12.00

Dogs — A283

Designs: $20, Chihuahua. $25, Norfolk terrier. $60, Welsh terrier.
No. 3230: a, Shar-pei. b, Chihuahua. c, Chow chow. d, Sealyham terrier. e, Collie. f, German shorthair pointer. g, Bulldog. h, German shepherd. i, Old English sheepdog.
$300, Tibetan spaniel.

**1997, July 29** **Litho.** ***Perf. 14***
**3227-3229** A283 Set of 3 3.75 3.75
**3230** A283 $60 Sheet of 9, #a.-i. 8.50 8.50

**Souvenir Sheet**
**3231** A283 $300 multicolored 5.50 5.50

Pres. Cheddi Jagan's 1st Election to Parliament, 50th Anniv. — A284

**1997, Oct. 6** **Litho.** ***Perf. 14***
**3232** A284 $6 green & multi .25 .25
**3233** A284 $30 pale yellow & multi 4.25 4.25

Nos. 3232-3233 each issued in sheets of 9.

Diana, Princess of Wales (1961-97) — A285

No. 3234: a-f, Various portraits.
No. 3235, $300, Wearing red dress. No. 3236, $300, With longer hair.

**1997, Oct. 15**
**3234** A285 $80 Sheet of 6, #a.-f. 8.25 8.25

**Souvenir Sheets**
***Perf. 14½***
**3235-3236** A285 Set of 2 10.00 10.00

Nos. 3235-3236 each contain one 34x52mm stamp.

**US Pres. Bill Clinton's Visit Type of 1997**

Designs: $6, Like #3201. No. 3238, Clinton, Jagan, flags, sun on horizon.

***Perf. 13½x14, 14x13½***
**1997, Nov. 10**
**3237** A277 $6 multi .25 .25
**3238** A277 $30 multi .50 .50

Nos. 3237-3238 each issued in sheets of 9. For surcharge, see No. 4115.

Souvenir Sheets

Chinese Pres. Jiang Zemin's Visit to New York — A286

Pres. Zemin, New York skyline, and: $200, Flags of China, UN, US. $300, Flags of China, US.

**1997, Nov. 10** ***Perf. 14***
**3239** A286 $200 multicolored 3.00 3.00
**3240** A286 $300 multicolored 4.50 4.50

Buildings in Guyana — A287

**1997, Dec. 8** **Litho.** ***Perf. 14***
**3241** A287 $6 W. Fogarty #1 .25 .25
**3242** A287 $30 Public building .60 .60

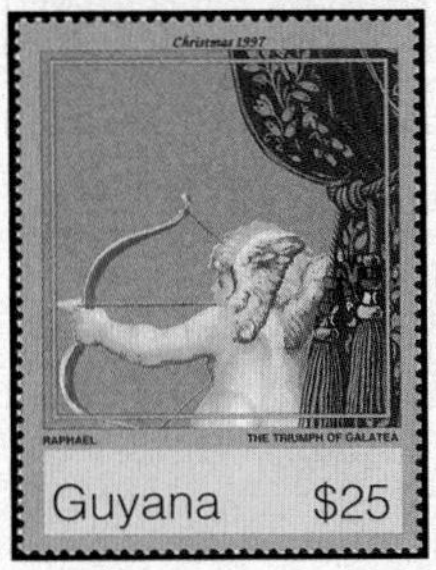


Christmas A288

Entire paintings, details, or sculptures: $24, $30, Diff. angels from The Triumph of Galatea, by Raphael. $35, Primavera, by Botticelli. $60, Angel Musicians, by Agostino di Duccio, (bas relief). $100, From cover of Life Magazine, #1212, 1906. $200, Madonna and Saints, by Rosso Fiorentino.
No. 3249, $300, The Gardens of Love, by Rubens. No. 3250, $300, Cherubs, by Philippe de Champaigne.

**1997, Dec. 8**
**3243-3248** A288 Set of 6 7.50 7.50

**Souvenir Sheets**
**3249-3250** A288 Set of 2 12.00 12.00

Historical Events A289

Designs: No. 3251, $60, Explorers discover tomb of Tutankhamun, 1922. No. 3252, $60, Lincoln Memorial dedicated, Washington, DC, 1922. No. 3253, $60, Alexander Graham Bell dies, 1922. No. 3254, $60, Calvin Coolidge becomes President, 1923. No. 3255, $60, John L. Baird develops 1st experimental television, 1923. No. 3256, $60, Warren G. Harding dies, 1923. No. 3257, $60, First Winter Olympic Games, Chamonix, France, 1924. No. 3258, $60, Tennessee bans teaching of evolution in schools, 1925. No. 3259, $60, Chinese leader Sun Yat-Sen dies, 1925. No. 3260, $60, Robert Goddard launches 1st liquid fuel rocket, 1926. No. 3261, $60, Richard E. Byrd is 1st to fly over North Pole, 1926. No.

3262, $60, Sesquicentennial Exposition, Philadelphia, 1926.

**1997. Dec. 8**
**3251-3262** A289 Set of 12 12.50 12.50

New Year 1998 (Year of the Tiger) — A290

No. 3263 — Various stylized tigers with denomination in: a, LR. b, LL. c, UR. d, UL. $150, Tiger, red background.

**1998, Jan. 5 Litho. *Perf. 14½***
**3263** A290 $50 Sheet of 4, #a.-d. 5.00 5.00

**Souvenir Sheet**
**3264** A290 $150 multicolored 4.25 4.25

Prehistoric Wildlife — A291

Designs: $25, Kentrosaurus. $30, Lesothosaurus. $35, Stegoceras. $60, Lagosuchus. $100, Herrerasaurus. $200, Iguanodon.

No. 3271, $55: a, Quetzalcoatlus (d). b, Pteranodon (a, c). c, Peteinosaurus. d, Criorhychus (g). e, Pterodaustro. f, Eudimorphodon. g, Archeopteryx. h, Dimorphodon. i, Sharovipteryx.

No. 3272, $55: a, Ceresiosaurus. b, Nothosaurus. c, Rhomaleosaurus. d, Grendelius. e, Mixosaurus. f, Mesosaurus. g, Placodus. h, Stethacanthus. i, Coelacanth.

No. 3273, $300, Styracosaurus, vert. No. 3274, $300, Yangchuanosaurus, vert.

**1998, Feb. 23 Litho. *Perf. 14***
**3265-3270** A291 Set of 6 7.00 7.00

**Sheets of 9, #a-i**
**3271-3272** A291 Set of 2 16.00 16.00

**Souvenir Sheets**
**3273-3274** A291 Set of 2 8.50 8.50

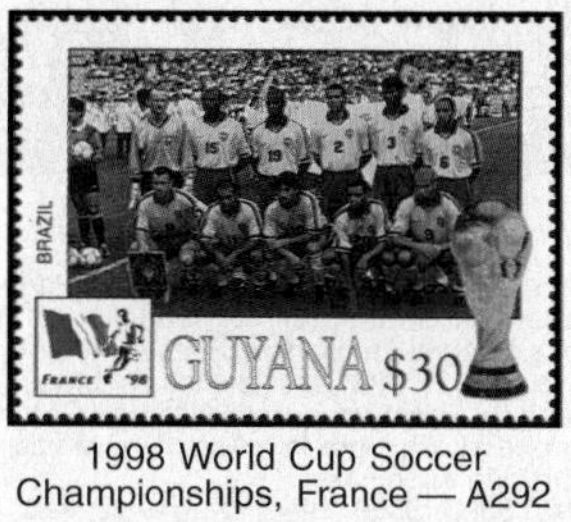

1998 World Cup Soccer Championships, France — A292

Group A: No. 3275, $30, Brazil. No. 3276, $30, Morocco. No. 3277, $30, Norway. No. 3278, $30, Scotland.

Group B: No. 3279, $30, Austria. No. 3280, $30, Cameroun. No. 3281, $30, Chile. No. 3282, $30, Italy.

Group C: No. 3283, $30, Denmark. No. 3284, $30, France. No. 3285, $30, Saudi Arabia. No. 3286, $30, South Africa.

Group D: No. 3287, $30, Bulgaria. No. 3288, $30, Nigeria. No. 3289, $30, Paraguay. No. 3290, $30, Spain.

Group E: No. 3291, $30, Belgium. No. 3292, $30, Holland. No. 3293, $30, S. Korea. No. 3294, $30, Mexico.

Group F: No. 3295, $30, Germany. No. 3296, $30, Iran. No. 3297, $30, US. No. 3298, $30, Yugoslavia.

Group G: No. 3299, $30, Colombia. No. 3300, $30, England. No. 3301, $30, Romania. No. 3302, $30, Tunisia.

Group H: No. 3303, $30, Argentina. No. 3304, $30, Croatia. No. 3305, $30, Jamaica. No. 3306, $30, Japan.

Japanese players, vert.: No. 3306A, $300, Okada. No. 3306B, $300, Nakata.

**1998, Apr. 8 Litho. *Perf. 14x13½***
**3275-3306** A292 Set of 32 14.00 14.00

***Perf. 13½x14***

**Souvenir Sheets**
**3306A-3306B** A292 Set of 2 8.50 8.50

Nos. 3275-3306 were each issued in sheets of 8 + 1 label.

For overprints see Nos. 3317-3324.

The Titanic A293

No. 3307: a, J. Bruce Ismay, managing director, White Star Line. b, Jack Phillips, radio operator. c, Margaret "Unsinkable Molly" Brown, passenger. d, Capt. Edward J. Smith. e, Frederick Fleet, lookout. f, Thomas Andrews, managing director of Harland and Wolff.

$300, Titanic sinking.

**1998, June 17 Litho. *Perf. 14***
**3307** A293 $80 Sheet of 6, #a.-f. 6.75 6.75

**Souvenir Sheet**
**3308** A293 $300 multicolored 4.25 4.25

Sailing Ships A294

No. 3309, $80: a, Viking double-ended ship, 14th cent. b, Portuguese caravel. c, "Nina." d, Fannie, 1896. e, "Victoria," 1519. f, Arab sambook.

No. 3310, $80: a, "Dutch Fluyt." b, "Alastor." c, "Falcon." d, "Red Rover." e, "British Anglesey." f, "Archibald Russel."

No. 3311, $300, Oseberg ship. No. 3312, $300, "Half Moon," 1609.

**1998, June 17 Litho. *Perf. 14***

**Sheets of 6, #a-f**
**3309-3310** A294 Set of 2 13.50 13.50

**Souvenir Sheets**
**3311-3312** A294 Set of 2 8.50 8.50

Diana, Princess of Wales (1961-97) — A295

Designs: No. 3313, $1500, Diana in black and brown fur trimmed hat and coat. No. 3314, $1500, Diana wearing suit and hat.

**Litho. & Embossed**

**1998, Aug. 3 *Die Cut 7½***
**3313-3314** A295 $1500 Set of 2 150.00

Queen Mother A296

**1998, Aug. 4 *Perf. 13½***
**3315** A296 $90 multicolored 1.40 1.40

CARICOM, 25th Anniv. — A297

**1998, July 4 Litho. *Perf. 13½***
**3316** A297 $20 multicolored .40 .40

**Nos. 3275, 3282-3286, 3289, 3304 Ovptd. "FRANCE WINNERS" in Gold**

**1998, Aug. 20 Litho. *Perf. 14x13½***

| | | | | |
|---|---|---|---|---|
| **3317** | A292 $30 on #3275 | .45 | .45 |
| **3318** | A292 $30 on #3282 | .45 | .45 |
| **3319** | A292 $30 on #3283 | .45 | .45 |
| **3320** | A292 $30 on #3284 | .45 | .45 |
| **3321** | A292 $30 on #3285 | .45 | .45 |
| **3322** | A292 $30 on #3286 | .45 | .45 |
| **3323** | A292 $30 on #3289 | .45 | .45 |
| **3324** | A292 $30 on #3304 | .45 | .45 |
| | *Nos. 3317-3324 (8)* | 3.60 | 3.60 |

Nos. 3317-3324 were each issued in sheets of 8+label. Each sheet contains additional overprints in sheet margins.

National Hockey League Players — A298

No. 3325: a, Bryan Berard. b, Ray Bourque. c, Martin Brodeur. d, Pavel Bure. e, Chris Chelios. f, Sergei Fedorov. g, Peter Forsberg. h, Wayne Gretzky. i, Dominik Hasek. j, Brett Hull. k, Jarome Iginla. l, Jaromir Jagr. m, Paul Kariya. n, Saku Koivu. o, John LeClair. p, Brian Leetch. q, Eric Lindros. r, Patrick Marleau. s, Mark Messier. t, Mike Modano. u, Chris Osgood. v, Zigmund Palffy. w, Felix Potvin. x, Jeremy Roenick. y, Patrick Roy. z, Joe Sakic. aa, Sergei Samsonov. ab, Teemu Selanne. ac, Brendan Shanahan. ad, Ryan Smyth. ae, Jocelyn Thibault. af, Joe Thornton. ag, Keith Tkachuk. ah, John Vanbiesbrouck. ai, Steve Yzerman. aj, Dainius Zubrus.

**1998, Apr. 1 Litho. *Perf. 13½***
**3325** A298 $35 Sheet of 36, #a.-aj. 18.00 18.00

Aircraft A299

No. 3326, $80 — Military aircraft: a, A7K Corsair II. b, A6E Intruder. c, U2 Spy plane. d, Blackhawk. e, F-16. f, Phantom II.

No. 3327, $80 — Pioneers of aviation: a, Wright Brothers, 1903. b, Bleriot, 1911. c, Curtiss Jenny, 1919. d, Airship Schwaben, 1911. e, W-8B, 1923. f, DH-66, 1926.

No. 3328, $300, A-10 Warthog. No. 3329, $300HH-65A Dolphin.

**1998, Sept. 28 *Perf. 14***

**Sheets of 6, #a-f**
**3326-3327** A299 Set of 2 13.50 13.50

**Souvenir Sheets**
**3328-3329** A299 Set of 2 8.50 8.50

Endangered Species — A300

Nos. 3330, $80, 3332, $300, Various pictures of the giant panda.

Nos. 3331, $80, 3333, $300, Various pictures of the mountain gorilla.

**1998, Oct. 8 Sheets of 6, a-f**
**3330-3331** A300 Set of 2 17.00 17.00

**Souvenir Sheets**
**3332-3333** A300 Set of 2 18.00 18.00

Donald Duck Adventures, Christmas on Bear Mountain — A301

No. 3334 — Cartoon panels: a, 1-8. b, 9-16. c, 17-24. d, 25-32. e, 33-40. f, 41-48. g, 49-56. h, 57-64. i, 65-72. j, 73-80. k, Pane of 2, Carl Barks, vert., bears and duck.

**1998, Oct. 15 *Perf. 14x13½, 13½x14***
**3334** Complete booklet 45.00 45.00
*a.-j.* A301 $35 Any pane of 4 2.75 2.75
*k.* A301 $300 Pane of 2 10.00 10.00

Disney's Uncle Scrooge, by Carl Barks, 50th anniv.

Organization of American States, 50th Anniv. A302

**1998, Oct. 29 *Perf. 14***
**3335** A302 $40 multicolored .55 .55

Ferrari Automobiles — A302a

No. 3335A: c, 212 Export. d, 410 Superamerica chassis. e, 125 S.

$300, 512 S Racer.

**1998, Oct. 29 Litho. *Perf. 14***
**3335A** A302a $100 Sheet of 3, #c-e 5.00 5.00

**Souvenir Sheet**
**3335B** A302a $300 multi 5.00 5.00

No. 3335A contains three 39x25mm stamps.

Diana, Princess of Wales (1961-97) A303

**1998, Oct. 29**

**3336** A303 $60 multicolored 1.00 1.00

**Self-Adhesive**

***Serpentine Die Cut Perf. 11½***

**Sheet of 1**

**Size: 53x65mm**

**3336A** A303 $300 Diana, buildings, bridge 65.00

No. 3336 was issued in sheets of 6.

Soaking in water may affect the multi-layer image of No. 3336A.

Issued: $60, 10/29; $300, 11/5/98.

Grand Prix Champion Racing Cars and Drivers—A304 — 3337

No. 3337, $80: a, 1914 Grand Prix Mercedes, Christian Lautenschlager. b, 1930 Bugati Type 35B, P. Etancelin. c, 1934 Alfa Romeo P3, Louis Chiron. d, 1938 Mercedes Benz W154, Richard Seaman. e, 1938 Auto Union D Type, Tazio Nuvolari. f, 1951 Alfa Romeo 158, Juan Manuel Fangio.

No. 3338, $80: a, 1955 Mercedes Benz W196, Stirling Moss. b, 1960 Ferrari Dino 246, Phil Hill. c, 1966 Brabham-Repco BT19, Jack Brabham. d, 1970 Lotus Ford 72, John Miles. e, 1983 Renault RE40, Alain Prost. f, 1998 McLaren Mercedes MP4/13, David Coulthard.

No. 3339, $300, 1906 Grand Prix Renault, Ferenc Szisz. No. 3340, $300, 1956 Maserati 250F, Stirling Moss.

**1998, Oct. 29** **Sheets of 6, #a-f**

**3337-3338** A304 Set of 2 13.50 13.50

**Souvenir Sheets**

**3339-3340** A304 Set of 2 8.50 8.50

Nos. 3339-3340 contain one 57x42mm stamp.

Tigger's Happy New Year — A304a

No. 3340A, vert. — Tigger: d, Giving gift to Winnie the Pooh. e, With fireworks. f, Giving flowers to Kanga. g, With Piglet. h, At door. i, With Eeyore.

No. 3340B, $300,Tigger beating drum. No. 3340C, $300, Tigger carrying staff for dragon.

**1998, Oct. 29** **Litho.** ***Perf. 13¼***

**3340A** A304a $60 Sheet of 6, #a-f 5.75 5.75

**Souvenir Sheets**

**3340B-3340C** A304a Set of 2 8.50 8.50

Gandhi — A305

No. 3341: a, Age 37, 1906. b, Age 77, 1946. c, Age 78, 1948. d, Age 77, 1947.

$300, Age 76, 1946, horiz.

**1998, Oct. 29**

**3341** A305 $100 Sheet of 4, #a.-d. 5.50 5.50

**Souvenir Sheet**

**3342** A305 $300 multicolored 4.25 4.25

No. 3341b-3341c are each 53x38mm.

Pablo Picasso A306

Paintings, details: $25, Sleeping Peasants, 1919. $60, Large Nude in Red Armchair, 1929, vert. $200, Sculpture, "Female Head," 1931, vert.

$300, Man and Woman, 1971, vert.

**1998, Oct. 29** ***Perf. 14½***

**3343-3345** A306 Set of 3 4.00 4.00

**Souvenir Sheet**

**3346** A306 $300 multicolored 4.50 4.50

Royal Air Force, 80th Anniv. A307

No. 3347, $100: a, Avro Lancaster B2. b, PBY-5A Catalina Amphibian. c, BAe Hawk TIA trainers (Red Arrows). d, Avro Lancaster, DeHavilland Mosquito.

No. 3348, $100: a, BAe Hawk TIA. b, C130 Hercules. c, Panavia Tornado GRI. d, BAe Hawk 200.

No. 3349 $150: a, BAe Nimrod RIP. b, Panavia Tornado F3 ADV. c, CH-47 Chinook helicopter. d, Panavia Tornado GRIA.

No. 3350, $200, Biplane, hawks in flight. No. 3351, $200, Eurofighter, Spitfire. No. 3352, $300, Eurofighters. No. 3353, $300, Head of hawk, hawk spreading wings, biplane. No. 3354, $300, Tiger Moth, Eurofighter. No. 3355, $300, Hawk spreading wings, biplane.

**1998, Oct. 29** ***Perf. 14***

**Sheets of 4, #a.-d.**

**3347-3349** A307 Set of 3 20.00 20.00

**Souvenir Sheets**

**3350-3355** A307 Set of 6 22.50 22.50

1998 World Scout Jamboree, Chile — A308

No. 3356: a, James E. West, 1st scout executive with early Eagle Scouts. b, Pres. Kennedy greets Explorers, 51st Scouts anniv., 1961. c, Astronaut Walter Schirra receives a special merit badge, 1962.

**1998, Oct. 29** **Litho.** ***Perf. 14***

**3356** A308 $160 Sheet of 3, #a.-c. 7.00 7.00

Paintings by Eugene Delacroix (1798-1863) A309

No. 3357, $60: a, The Sultan of Morocco Receives the Count de Mornay. b, Armed Indian with a Gurkha Scimitar. c, Portrait presumed to be of the Singer Baroihet in Turkish Dress. d, Moroccan Notebook: Studies of Jewish Women. e, Arab Horseman Giving a Signal. f, Arab Cavalry Practicing a Charge. g, A Seated Moor. h, Jewish Woman in Traditional Dress.

No. 3358, $60: a, Corner of the Studio; the Stove. b, Room in the Apartment the Count de Mornay. c, Hamlet and Horatio in the Graveyard. d, George Sand. e, The Bride of Abydos. f, Elysian Fields. g, A Lioness Standing by a Tree. h, Monsieur Alfred Bruyas.

No. 3359, $300, Moroccan Jewish Wedding, horiz. No. 3360, $300, Death of Sardanapulus, horiz.

**1998, Oct. 29** **Sheets of 8, #a.-h.**

**3357-3358** A309 Set of 2 13.50 13.50

**Souvenir Sheets**

**3359-3360** A309 Set of 2 8.50 8.50

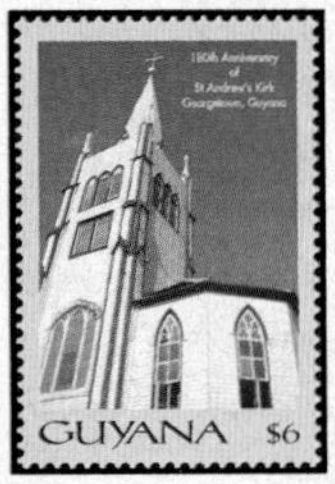

St. Andrew's Church, Georgetown, 180th Anniv. — A310

Various views of front of church: $6, $30, $60.

**1998** **Litho.** ***Perf. 14***

**3361-3363** A310 Set of 3 1.25 1.25

New Year 1999 (Year of the Rabbit) — A311

No. 3364 — Various stylized rabbits with denomination at: a, LR. b, LL. c, UR. d, UL.

$150, Red background, Chinese inscription.

**1999, Jan. 4** **Litho.** ***Perf. 14½***

**3364** A311 $50 Sheet of 4, #a.-d. 3.00 3.00

**Souvenir Sheet**

**3365** A311 $150 multicolored 2.25 2.25

Disney Characters in Sporting Activities A312

No. 3366, $80 — Skateboarding: a, Huey. b, Mickey. c, Dewey. d, Louie. e, Goofy. f, Donald.

No. 3367, $80 — Rollerblading: a, Minnie. b, Goofy. c, Daisy. d, Baby Duck. e, Donald. f, Mickey.

No. 3368, $80 — Skateboarding, rollerblading, red, white & blue background:: a, Baby Duck. b, Daisy. c, Mickey. d, Goofy. e, Dewey. f, Donald.

No. 3369, $300, Dewey. No. 3370, $300, Daisy. No. 3371, $300, Goofy, horiz.

***Perf. 13½x14, 14X13½***

**1999, Mar. 1** **Litho.**

**Sheets of 6, #a-f**

**3366-3368** A312 Set of 3 25.00 25.00

**Souvenir Sheets**

**3369-3371** A312 Set of 3 18.50 18.50

Mickey Mouse, 70th anniv.

Disney Characters in Trains — A313

No. 3372, $100 — 101 Dalmatians Express: a, Locomotive. b, Flatcar. c, Car with pillars. d, "Basket" car. e, Caboose.

No. 3373, $100 — Robin Hood Train: a, Engine. b, Marian, Robin Hood. c, Royal coach. d, Flatcar. e, Caboose.

No. 3374, $100 — Snow White, Diamond Mine Railroad: a, Engine. b, Flatcar. c, Snow White, Prince Charming. d, Passenger car. e, Pump car.

No. 3375, $100 — Little Mermaid Railroad: a, Engine. b, Fish holding pearls. c, Little Mermaid. d, Various marine life in car. e, "Bah Hum Bug!"

No. 3376: a, Dwarf from Diamond Mine Railroad driving locomotive. b, Dwarf on pump car.

No. 3377, $300, Bandits, Cruela De Vil. No. 3378, $300, Robin Hood, Bear. No. 3379, $300, Little Mermaid kissing Prince under mistletoe. No. 3380, $300, Little Mermaid holding starfish.

**1999, Mar. 1** ***Perf. 13½x14***

**Sheets of 5, #a-e**

**3372-3375** A313 Set of 4 36.00 36.00

**3376** A313 $200 Sheet of 2, #a.-b. 9.00 9.00

**Souvenir Sheets**

**3377-3380** A313 Set of 4 22.00 22.00

Caribbean Butterflies — A314

No. 3381, $80: a, Scarce Bamboo Page. b, Spicebush swallowtail. c, Isabella. d, The mosaic. e, Gulf fritillary. f, Figure-of-eight.

No. 3382, $80: a, Hewitson's blue hairstreak. b, Polydamas swallowtail. c, Common morpho. d, Blue-green reflector. e, Malachite. f, Grecian shoemaker.

No. 3383, $300, Giant swallowtail, vert. No. 3384, $300, Pipevine swallowtail, vert.

**1999, Mar. 15** ***Perf. 14***

**Sheets of 6, #a-f**

**3381-3382** A314 Set of 2 14.50 14.50

**Souvenir Sheets**

**3383-3384** A314 Set of 2 9.00 9.00

Flowers A315

No. 3385, $60: a, Geranium. b, Oncidium macranthum. c, Bepi orchidglades. d, Sunflowers (2). e, Cattleya walkeriana. f, Cattleya frasquita. g, Helianthus maximilani (one). h, Paphiopedilum insigne sanderae, lily. i, Lily (2).

No. 3386, $60: a, Dendrobium nobile. b, Phalaenopsis schilleriana. c, Cymbidium alexette. d, Rhododendron. e, Phragmipedium besseae, laelia cinnabarina. f, Masdevallia veitchiana. g, Calochortus nuttallii. h, Brassolaeliocattleya pure gold. i, Laelia cinnabarina.

No. 3387: a, Leptotes bicolor, masdevallia ignea. b, Sophrolaeliocattleya, anguloa clowesii. c, Laelia pumila. d, Masdevallia ignea. e, Dendrobium phalaenopsis. f, Anguloa clowesii.

No. 3388, $300, Asocentrum miniatum, vert. No. 3389, $300, Iris pseudacorus.

**1999, Mar. 15 Litho. *Perf. 14***

**Sheets of 9, #a-i**

**3385-3386** A315 Set of 2 16.00 16.00
**3387** A315 $90 Sheet of 6, #a.-f. 7.50 7.50

**Souvenir Sheet**

**3388-3389** A315 Set of 2 8.50 8.50

Akira Kurosawa (1910-98), Film Director — A316

No. 3390 — Films, vert.: a, "The Dream." b, "Rashomon." c, "Kagemusha." d, "Red Beard." e, "Seven Samurai." f, "Yojimbo."

No. 3391 — Portraits: a, Pointing. b, Hand on face. c, Standing. d, With camerman.

$300, Scene from "Dreams."

**1999, Mar. 22**

**3390** A316 $80 Sheet of 6, #a.-f. 6.75 6.75
**3391** A316 $130 Sheet of 4, #a.-d. 7.25 7.25

**Souvenir Sheet**

**3392** A316 $300 multicolored 4.25 4.25

Mushrooms A317

Designs: $25, Coprinus atramentarius. $35, Hebeloma crustuliniforme. $100, Russula nigricans. $200, Tricholoma aurantium.

No. 3397, $60: a, Boletus aereus. b, Coprinus comatus. c, Inocybe godeyi. d, Morchella crassipes. e, Lepiota acutesquamosa. f, Amanita phalloides. g, Boletus spadiceus. h, Cortinarius collinitus. i, Lepiota procera.

No. 3398, $60: a, Russula ochroleuca. b, Hygrophorus hypotheius. c, Amanita rubescens. d, Boletus satanas. e, Amanita echinocephala. f, Amanita muscaria. g, Boletus badius. h, Hebeloma radicosum. i, Mycena polygramma.

No. 3399, $300, Lepiota acutequamoso. No. 3400, $300, Pluteus cervinus.

**1999, May 6 Litho. *Perf. 14***

**3393-3396** A317 Set of 4 4.25 4.25

**Sheets of 9, #a-i**

***Perf. 14½***

**3397-3398** A317 Set of 2 16.50 16.50

**Souvenir Sheet**

**3399-3400** A317 Set of 2 9.00 9.00

Nos. 3397-3398 each contain nine 32x41mm stamps. Nos. 3399-3400 each contain one 32x41mm stamp.

Trains — A318

No. 3401, $80: a, Burlington Northern GP 39-2, 1974. b, CSX GP40-2, 1967. c, Erie Lackawana Railroad GP 9, 1956. d, Amtrak P 42 Genesis, 1993. e, Erie Railroad S-2, 1948. f, Pennsylvania Railroad S-1, 1947.

No. 3402, $80: a, Northern and Western #610, c. 1933. b, Pennsylvania Railroad M1B Mountain, 1930. c, Reading Railroad FP7A, 1951. d, New York Central 2-8-4, c. 1940. e, Union Pacific Challenger Big Boy, 1963. f, GP 15-15-1, 1956.

No. 3403, $80: a, Shinkansen Bullet 100 series, 1984, Japan. b, Ukranian Diesel ZMGR, 1983, Russia. c, Rhatische Bahn GE 6/6 II, Germany. d, Eurostar TGV, 1986, France. e, Atlantique TGV, 1989, France. f, Class 86-6, UK.

No. 3404, $80: a, Joseph Clark 0-4-0, 1868. b, Diamond Stack Bethel 4-4-0, 1863. c, New York Central #999, 1890. d, Boston & Maine Ballardville 0-4-0, 1876. e, Atlantic 4-4-0 Portland Rochester Railroad, 1863. f, America 4-4-0 Baltimore & Ohio Railroad, 1881.

Railroad pioneers: No. 3405, $300, George Stephen, vert. No. 3406, $300, Alfred de Glehn, vert. No. 3407, $300, George Nagelmackers, vert. No. 3408, $300, R.F. Trevithick, vert.

**1999, May 10 *Perf. 14***

**Sheets of 6, #a.-f.**

**3401-3404** A318 Set of 4 29.00 29.00

**Souvenir Sheets**

**3405-3408** A318 Set of 4 17.00 17.00

Australia '99 World Stamp Expo.

Wedding of Prince Edward and Sophie Rhys-Jones — A319

Various portraits: Nos. 3409, $150, 3411, $300, rose lilac sheet margin. Nos. 3410, $150, 3412, $300, yellow brown sheet margin.

**1999, June 19 Litho. *Perf. 14¼***

**Sheets of 4, #a.-d.**

**3409-3410** A319 Set of 2 17.00 17.00

**Souvenir Sheets**

**3411-3412** A319 Set of 2 8.50 8.50

Nos. 3411-3412 are horiz.

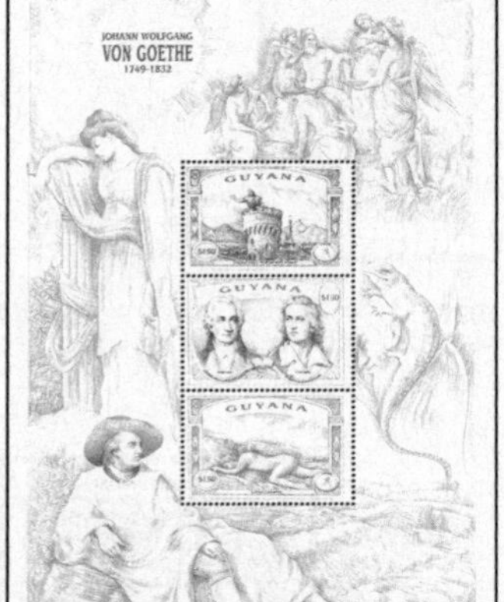


Johann Wolfgang von Goethe (1749-1832), Poet — A320

No. 3413: a, Lynceus sings from the watchtower. b, Portaits of Von Goethe and Friedrich von Schiller (1759-1805), poet. c, The fallen Icarus.

$300, Mephistopheles appears as salamander, vert.

**1999, June 22 Litho. *Perf. 14***

**3413** A320 $150 Sheet of 3, #a.-c. 6.25 6.25

**Souvenir Sheet**

**3414** A320 $300 multicolored 4.25 4.25

IBRA '99, World Philatelic Exhibition, Nuremberg — A321

Designs: $60, Class E10 Bo-bo electric locomotive, BMW offices, Munich, 1952, vert. $200, Class 01, 4-6-2 steam express train, 1926.

**1999, June 22**

**3415** A321 $60 multicolored .90 .90
**3416** A321 $200 multicolored 2.75 2.75

Apollo 11 Moon Landing, 30th Anniv. — A322

No. 3417, $80: a, Blast off. b, Command Module docked with Lunar Lander. c, First man on moon. d, Seismic experiments package. e, Back to the orbiter. f, Astronauts being picked up.

No. 3418, $80, vert: a, Sputnik, 1959, Konstantin Tsiolkovsky. b, Apollo 11 liftoff. c, On the moon. d, Collecting samples of lunar rocks. e, Apollo 11 Lunar Module. f, Splashdown.

No. 3419, $300, Salute to the flag. No. 3420, $300, Michael Collins.

**1999, June 22 Sheets of 6, #a-f**

**3417-3418** A322 Set of 2 13.00 13.00

**Souvenir Sheet**

**3419-3420** A322 Set of 2 8.50 8.50

Souvenir Sheets

PhilexFrance '99, World Philatelic Exhibition — A323

Designs: No. 3421, $300, Co-Co 7000 Class High Speed 1949-55. No. 3422, $300, 241-P Class 4-8-2 Express 1947-49.

**1999, June 22**

**3421-3422** A323 Set of 2 9.00 9.00

Paintings by Hokusai (1760-1849) — A324

No. 3423, $80: a, Travelers Climbing a Mountain Path. b, Washing in a River. c, The Blind (eyes & mouth open). d, The Blind (eyes & mouth shut). e, Convolvulus and Tree-Frog. f, Fishermen Hauling a Net.

No. 3424, $80: a, Hibiscus and Sparrow. b, Hydrangea and Swallow. c, The Blind (eyes shut, mouth open). d, The Blind (eyes open, mouth shut). e, Irises. f, Lilies.

No. 3425, $300, Flowering Cherries at Mount Yoshino, vert. No. 3426, $300, A View of a Stone Causeway, vert.

**1999, June 22 Litho. *Perf. 14x13¾***

**Sheets of 6, #a-f**

**3423-3424** A324 Set of 2 13.50 13.50

**Souvenir Sheets**

***Perf. 13¾x14***

**3425-3426** A324 Set of 2 8.50 8.50

Pope John Paul II — A325

**1999, June 22 *Perf. 14***

**3427** A325 $80 Sheet of 6, #a.-f. 7.50 7.50

John Glenn's Return to Space — A326

No. 3428: a, In space suit, 1962. b, After landing, 1962. c, As Senator. d, With helmet, 1998. e, Without helmet, 1998.

**1999, June 22 *Perf. 14½x14¼***

**3428** A326 $100 Sheet of 5, #a.-e. 7.00 7.00

Parrots and Parakeets — A327

No. 3429, $60: a, Hyacinth macaw. b, Blue and gold macaw. c, Blue-fronted Amazon parrot. d, Amazon parrot. e, Sun Conure. f, Tivi parakeet. g, Bavaria's conure. h, Fairy lorikeet.
No. 3430, $60: a, Marron macaw. b, Thick-billed parrot. c, Golden-crowned canure. d, Yellow-naped macaw. e, Double yellow-headed parrot. f, Golden-fronted parakeet. g, Maroon-billed conure. h, Nandaya conure.
No. 3431, $300, Jendaya conure, horiz. No. 3432, $300, Gray-cheeked parakeet.

**1999, Aug. 3** ***Perf. 14***
**Sheets of 8, #a.-h.**
**3429-3430** A327 Set of 2 14.00 14.00
**Souvenir Sheets**
**3431-3432** A327 Set of 2 8.50 8.50

Queen Mother, 100th Birthday (in 2000) — A328

No. 3433: a, Duchess of York, Princess Elizabeth, 1928. b, Lady Elizabeth Bowles-Lyon, 1914. c, Queen Elizabeth, Princess Elizabeth, 1940. d, Queen Mother, Venice, 1984.
$400, Queen Mother, Canada, 1988.

**1999, Aug. 4** **Gold Frames**
**3433** A328 $130 Sheet of 4, #a.-d. + label 8.00 8.00
**Souvenir Sheet**
***Perf. 13¾***
**3434** A328 $400 multicolored 5.50 5.50

No. 3434 contains one 38x50mm stamp. Margins of sheets are embossed.
See Nos. 3689-3690.

China Soccer League Superstars A329

Nos. 3435a-3435g, 3436a-3436g, Various players. Nos. 3435h, 3436h, League emblem.

**1999, Aug. 16** ***Perf. 14½x14¼***
**3435** A329 $50 Sheet of 8, #a.-h. 5.25 5.25
**3436** A329 $60 Sheet of 8, #a.-h. 6.25 6.25

Rights of the Child — A330

No. 3437: a, Denomination at LL, flag at UR. b, Denomination at UL, flag at LL. c, Denomination at UL, flag at UR.
$300, Prince Talal.

**1999, June 22** **Litho.** ***Perf. 14***
**3437** A330 $150 Sheet of 3, #a.-c. 5.50 5.50
**Souvenir Sheet**
**3438** A330 $300 multicolored 4.00 4.00

Intl. Year of the Elderly — A331

No. 3439: a, Kurt Masur. b, Rupert Murdoch. c, Margaret Thatcher. d, Pope John Paul II. e, Mikhail Gorbachev. f, Ted Turner. g, Sophia Loren. h, Nelson Mandela. i, John Glenn. j, Luciano Pavarotti. k, Queen Mother. l, Jimmy Carter.
No. 3440 — Ronald Reagan: a, As young man. b, In uniform. c, Feeding chimp. d, With campaign poster. e, With cowboy hat. f, With wine glass.
$300, Reagan in star.

**1999, June 22** **Litho.** ***Perf. 14***
**3439** A331 $50 Sheet of 12, #a.-l. 8.50 8.50
**3440** A331 $100 Sheet of 6, #a.-f. 7.00 7.00
**Souvenir Sheet**
**3441** A331 $300 multicolored 3.50 3.50

Souvenir Sheet

Mei Lan Fang, Chinese Actor — A332

**1999, Aug. 16** **Litho.** ***Perf. 13¾***
**3442** A332 $400 multicolored 4.50 4.50

First Balloon Flight Around the World — A333

No. 3443: a, Orbiter 3. b, Emblem. c, Bertrand Piccard. d, Brian Jones.
$300, Orbiter 3, flight path.

**1999, Aug. 16** **Litho.** ***Perf. 14***
**3443** A333 $150 Sheet of 4, #a.-d. 7.25 7.25
**Souvenir Sheet**
**3444** A333 $300 multicolored 4.00 4.00

The Kennedy Family A334

No. 3445: a, Jacqueline and John, Jr. b. John and John, Jr. c, John and Jacqueline. d, Jacqueline. e, John, Jr. and Caroline. f, John.
No. 3445G: h, John, Jr. as adult and child. i, John, Jr. and Jacqueline. j, John Jr.

**1999, Oct. 4** **Litho.** ***Perf. 13¾***
**3445** A334 $80 Sheet of 6, #a.-f. 6.25 6.25
**3445G** A334 $160 Sheet of 3, #h.-j. 5.75 5.75

Inter-American Development Bank, 40th Anniv. — A335

**1999, Nov. 15** **Litho.** ***Perf. 14***
**3446** A335 $30 multicolored .40 .40

Ferrari Automobiles — A336

Designs: $30, 312 T2. $35, 553 F.1. $60, D 50. $200, 246 F.1. $300, 126/C2. $400, 312/B2.

**1999** **Litho.** ***Perf. 14***
**3447-3452** A336 Set of 6 11.50 11.50

Sidney Sheldon, Novelist — A337

**1999** **Litho.** ***Perf. 14***
**3453** A337 $80 multicolored 1.00 1.00

Issued in sheets of 4.

A338

No. 3454: a, During World War II. b, Wedding photo. c, As child. d, At coronation of George VI. e, In 1971. f, In 1991. g, In 1914. h, In 1988. i, At Royal Agricultural show. j, On 60th birthday.
$1,000, Portrait.

**1999** **Litho.** ***Perf. 12***
**3454** A338 $60 Sheet of 10, #a.-j. 8.75 8.75
***Imperf***
**Size: 51x76mm**
**3455** A338 $1000 multicolored 12.00 12.00

Sheets of #3454 exist with black border in margin with text "In Memoriam/1900-2002."

Queen Mother (b. 1900) — A339

**Litho. & Embossed**
**1999, Aug. 4** ***Die Cut Perf. 8¾***
**3456** A339 $1500 gold & multi *35.00*

Millennium A340

No. 3457, Founding of first university, 1088.
No. 3458 — Highlights of the 11th Century: a, Anasazi trade center. b, "Black Virgin." c, Seljuk warrior. d, Appearance of Halley's Comet. e, Battle of Hastings. f, William of Normandy crowned King of England. g, Power of the Fujiwara is checked. h, Holy Roman Emperor Henry IV. i, Muslims build Timbuktu. j, Like No. 3457. k, Gondolas come into use in Venice. l, El Cid. m, First crusade. n, Crusaders capture Jerusalem. o, Chinese statue of Guanyin. p, Rubiayat of Omar Khayyam (60x40mm). q, Syrian storage jar.
No. 3459 — Highlights of the 1910s: a, Manet and Post-impressionists show, Grafton Gallery, London. b, Standard Oil loses Supreme Court antitrust suit. c, Harriet Quimby, 1st female pilot in US d, US enters World War I. e, Titanic sinks. f, Pu Yi resigns as Chinese Emperor. g, Grand Central Station built in NYC. h, Assassination of Archduke Francis Ferdinand. i, Panama Canal opens. j, Lawrence of Arabia. k, Easter Uprising, Ireland. l, 1917 Russian Revolution. m, Execution of the Romanovs. n, Treaty of Versailles ends World War I. o, Influenza epidemic. p, Leo Tolstoy & Mark Twain die (60x40mm). q, Bauhaus opens, Weimar, Germany.

**1999, Dec. 20** **Litho.** ***Perf. 13¼x13***
**3457** A340 $35 multi .50 .50
***Perf. 12¾x12½***
**3458** A340 $35 Sheet of 17, #a.-q. 7.50 7.50
**3459** A340 $35 Sheet of 17, #a.-q., + label 7.50 7.50

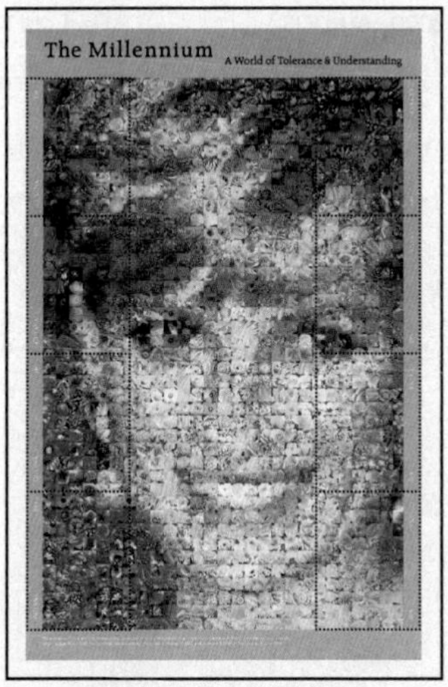


Flowers — A341

#3460: Various flowers making up a photomosaic of Princess Diana.
#3461: Various details of paper money of the world making up a photomosaic of George Washington's portrait on $1 bill.

**1999-2000 Litho. *Perf. 13¾***

**3460** A341 $80 Sheet of 8, #a.-h. 12.00 12.00
**3461** A341 $80 Sheet of 8, #a.-h. 10.00 10.00

Issued: #3460, 12/31; #3461, 3/27/00.
See Nos. 3568-3569.

New Year 2000 (Year of the Dragon) — A342

No. 3462 — Dragons with denomination in: a, LR. b, LL. c, UR, d, UL.
$300, LR.

**2000, Feb. 5 *Perf. 14¾***

**3462** A342 $100 Sheet of 4, #a.-d. 5.00 5.00

**Souvenir Sheet**

**3463** A342 $300 multi 3.50 3.50

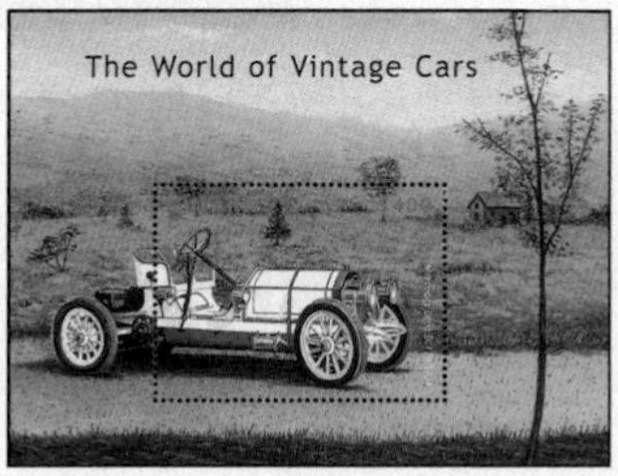


A343

Automobiles — A344

No. 3464, $100: a, Nicholas Cugnot's steam-powered Fardier, 1769. b, Siegfried Marcus's motor carriage, 1875. c, Karl Benz's Velo, 1894. d, Virgilio Bordino's steam carriage, 1854. e, 1886 Benz. f, 1908 Ford Model T.
No. 3465, $100: a,1926 Duesenberg Model A Phaeton. b, 1927 Mercedes-Benz Model K. c, 1928, Rolls-Royce Phantom I limousine. d, 1935 Auburn 851 Speedster. e, 1936 Mercedes-Benz 540K Cabriolet B. f, 1949, Volkswagen Cabriolet Beetle.
No. 3466, $100: a, 1957 Ford Thunderbird. b, 1957 Jaguar XK150. c, 1968 Chevrolet Corvette Stingray. d, 1973 BMW 2002 Turbo. e, 1975 Porsche 911 Turbo. f, 1999 Volkswagen Beetle.
No. 3467, $100: a, 1886 Daimler motor car. b, 1898 Opel Luzman. c, 1899 Benz Landaulet coupe. d, 1892 Peugeot Vis-a-vis. e, 1886 Benz. f, 1894 Benz Velo, diff.
No. 3468, $100: a, 1896 Ford. b, 1903 De Dion-Bouton Populare. c, 1900 Adler. d, 1904 Vauxhall. e, 1908 Rolls-Royce Silver Ghost. f, 1908 Ford Model T, diff.
No. 3469, $400, 1904 Mercedes-Benz 60/70. No. 3470, $400, 1939 Mercedes-Benz Type 320 Cabriolet. No. 3471, $400, 1954 Mercedes-Benz 300SL Gullwing.
No. 3472, $400, 1904 Turner-Miesse. No. 3473, $400, 1910 Runabout.

**2000, Mar. 13 Litho. *Perf. 13½***

**Sheets of 6, #a.-f.**

**3464-3466** A343 Set of 3 22.00 22.00

***Perf. 14***

**3467-3468** A344 Set of 2 14.00 14.00

**Souvenir Sheets**

***Perf. 14½***

**3469-3471** A343 Set of 3 13.50 13.50

***Perf. 14¼***

**3472-3473** A344 Set of 2 9.00 9.00

Size of stamps from Nos. 3463-3466, 41x25mm; from Nos. 3467-3468, 42x28mm.

No. 1341 Surcharged in Red

**2000 ? Litho. Unwmk. *Perf. 14***

**3473A** A92 $6 on 25c #1341 —

Marine Life A345

Designs: $30, Lachnolaimus maximus. $35, Cyphoma gibbosum. $60, Trachinotus falcatus. $100, Bodianus pulchellus. $200, Anisotremus virginicus. $300, Etheostoma spectabile.
No. 3480, $80: a, Hypoplectrus indigo. b, Chlamys hastata. c, Sebastes rubrivinctus. d, Selene vomer. e, Marginella carnea. f, Phoca vitulina. g, Coryphaena hippurus. h, Epinephelus fulvus.
No. 3481, $80: a, Sphyraena barracuda. b, Saccopharynx sp. c, Chromodoris amoena. d, Makaira nigricans. e, Orcinus orca. f, Hippocampus reidi. g, Chelonia mydas. h, Emblemaria pandionis.
No. 3482, $80, vert.: a, Pterois volitans. b, Tursiops truncatus. c, Diplulmaris antarctica. d, Pomacanthus arcuatus. e, Aetobatus narinari. f, Carcharhinus amblyrhynchos. g, Sacura margaritacea. h, Octopus dolfeini.
No. 3483, $400, Asteroschema tenue, vert. No. 3484, $400, Apodichthys flavidus, vert. No. 3485, $400, Periclimenes pedersoni.

**2000, May 15 *Perf. 14***

**3474-3479** A345 Set of 6 8.50 8.50

**Sheets of 8, #a.-h.**

**3480-3482** A345 Set of 3 25.00 25.00

**Souvenir Sheets**

**3483-3485** A345 Set of 3 14.00 14.00

No. 3485 contains one 57x42mm stamp.

Souvenir Sheet

1999 Return of Macao to People's Republic of China — A346

No. 3486: a, Flag. b, Skyline.

**2000, May 15**

**3486** A346 $150 Sheet of 2, #a.-b. 3.75 3.75

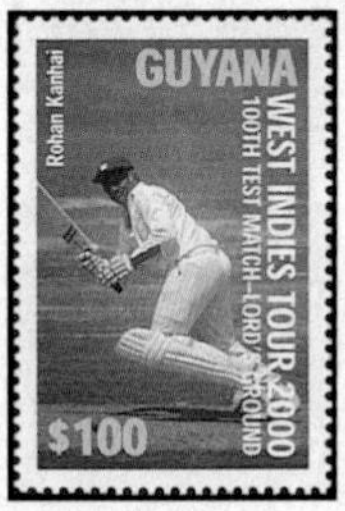


100th Test Match at Lord's Ground — A347

Designs: $100, Rohan Kanhai. $300, Clive Lloyd.
$400, Lord's Ground, horiz.

**2000, May 15 Litho. *Perf. 14***

**3487-3488** A347 Set of 2 5.00 5.00

**Souvenir Sheet**

**3489** A347 $400 multi 5.25 5.25

Prince William, 18th Birthday — A348

No. 3490: a, With Prince Harry. b, Wearing sweater. c, In profile. d, In suit.
$400, In ski wear.

**2000, May 15 *Perf. 14***

**3490** A348 $100 Sheet of 4, #a-d 5.50 5.50

**Souvenir Sheet**

***Perf. 13¾***

**3491** A348 $400 multi 5.25 5.25

No. 3490 contains four 28x42mm stamps. It exists imperf.

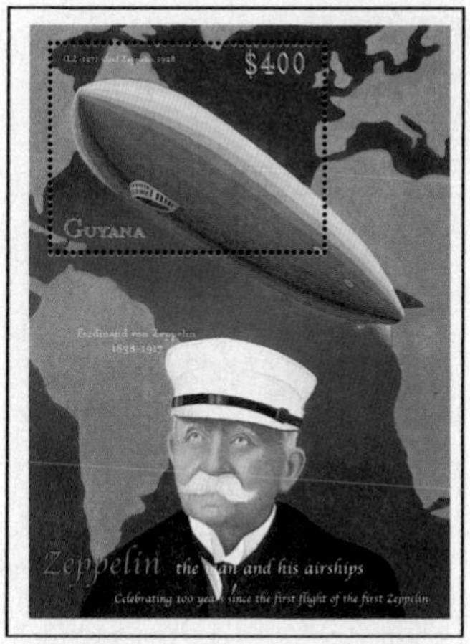


First Zeppelin Flight, Cent. — A349

No. 3492 — Ferdinand von Zeppelin and: a, LZ-1. b, LZ-2. c, LZ-9.
$400, LZ-127.

**2000, May 15 *Perf. 14***

**3492** A349 $200 Sheet of 3, #a-c 7.25 7.25

**Souvenir Sheet**

**3493** A349 $400 multi 4.75 4.75

No. 3492 contains three 40x24mm stamps.

Berlin Film Festival, 50th Anniv. — A350

No. 3494: a, Das Boot Ist Voll. b, David. c, Hong Gao Liang (Red Sorghum). d, Die Ehe der Maria Braun. e, Edith Evans. f, Michel Simon.
$400, Love Streams.

**2000, May 15**

**3494** A350 $100 Sheet of 6, #a-f 7.00 7.00

**Souvenir Sheet**

**3495** A350 $400 multi 4.50 4.50

Apollo-Soyuz Mission, 25th Anniv. — A351

No. 3496: a, Vance D. Brand, Thomas P. Stafford. b, Apollo 18, docking adapter. c, Stafford, Valeri Kubasov.
$400, Stafford, Donald K. Slayton.

**2000, May 15**
**3496** A351 $200 Sheet of 3, #a-c 7.25 7.25

**Souvenir Sheet**

**3497** A351 $400 multi 4.50 4.50

Souvenir Sheets

2000 Summer Olympics, Sydney — A352

No. 3498: a, Henry Robert Pearce. b, Volleyball. c, Olympic Park, Montreal, and Canadian flag. d, Ancient Greek runners.

**2000, May 15**
**3498** A352 $160 Sheet of 4, #a-d 7.50 7.50

Public Railways, 175th Anniv. — A353

No. 3499: a, Timothy Hackworth. b, Sans Pareil. c, Branhope Tunnel.

**2000, May 15**
**3499** A353 $200 Sheet of 3, #a-c 7.00 7.00

Johann Sebastian Bach (1685-1750) — A354

**2000, May 15**
**3500** A354 $400 multi 4.75 4.75

Souvenir Sheet

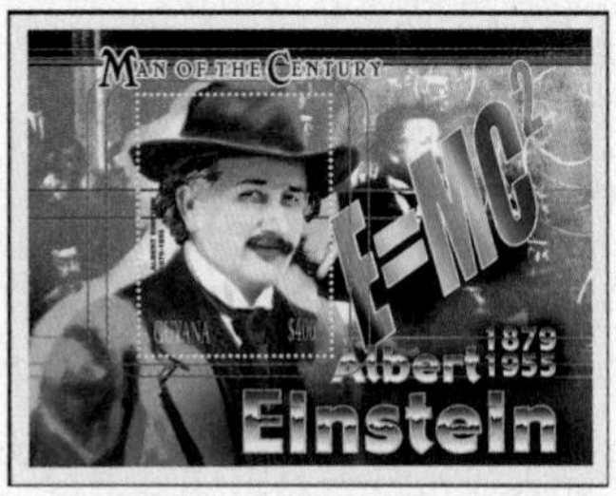


Albert Einstein (1879-1955) — A355

**2000, May 15 Litho. *Perf. 14¼***
**3501** A355 $400 multi 5.00 5.00

Space — A356

No. 3502, $100: a, Amsat IIIc. b, SRET. c, Inspector. d, Stardust. e, Temisat. f, Arsene.

No. 3503, $100, horiz.: a, Sun and Echo satellite (inscribed Apollo 11). b, Saturn, and Pioneer. c, Moon and Apollo 11 (inscribed Echo satellite). d, Mars and Mars Explorer. e, Space Shuttle, Intl. Space Station. f, Halley's Comet and Giotto.

No. 3504, $100, horiz.: a, Cesar, Argentine, Spanish flags. b, Sirio 2, Italian flag. c, Taos S.80, French flag. d, Viking, Swedish flag. e, SCD 1, Brazilian flag. f, Offeq 1, Israeli flag.

No. 3505, $400, Clementine. No. 3506, $400, Solar Max, horiz.

**2000, May 15 Litho. *Perf. 14***

**Sheets of 6, #a-f**

**3502-3504** A356 Set of 3 22.00 22.00

**Souvenir Sheets**

**3505-3506** A356 Set of 2 9.25 9.25

World Stamp Expo 2000, Anaheim.

The Three Stooges — A357

No. 3507: a, Shemp, Moe, Larry, man with glasses. b, Skeleton, Larry, Moe. c, Shemp. d, Stooges with fingers in mouths. e, Stooges reading book. f, Stooges attacking man. g, Stooges with candle. h, Stooges, man, fire bucket. i, Moe, Shemp, man in window.

No. 3508, $400, Moe in doorway. No. 3509, $400, Larry, skeleton.

**2000, July 27 *Perf. 13¾***
**3507** A357 $80 Sheet of 9, #a-i 8.75 8.75

**Souvenir Sheets**

**3508-3509** A357 Set of 2 9.00 9.00

See Nos. 3542-3544.

Betty Boop — A358

No. 3510: a, In striped blouse. b, With shopping bags. c, On cushion. d, As belly dancer. e, In red lingerie. f, In cutoff shorts. g, With musical notes. h, In flowered pants. i, In black dress.

No. 3511, $400, In fur coat. No. 3512, $400, In polka dot bathing suit, with flamingos.

**2000, July 27 *Perf. 13¾***
**3510** A358 $80 Sheet of 9, #a-i 9.00 9.00

**Souvenir Sheets**

**3511-3512** A358 Set of 2 9.00 9.00

See Nos. 3545-3552.

Third Annual Caribbean Media Conference A359

**2000, Aug. 14 *Perf. 14***
**3513** A359 $100 multi 1.25 1.25

European Soccer Championships — A360

No. 3514, $80, horiz.: a, Denmark. b, Germany. c, Italy. d, Netherlands. e, Portugal. f, Romania. g, Czech Republic. h, Norway.

No. 3515, $80, horiz.: a, Turkey. b, Slovenia. c, Yugoslavia. d, Sweden. e, Belgium. f, Spain. g, France. h, England.

No. 3516, $400, Jurgen Klinsmann. No. 3517, $400, Stefan Kuntz.

**2000, Aug. 21 *Perf. 13¾***

**Sheets of 8, #a-h, + label**

**3514-3515** A360 Set of 2 16.00 16.00

**Souvenir Sheets**

**3516-3517** A360 Set of 2 9.50 9.50

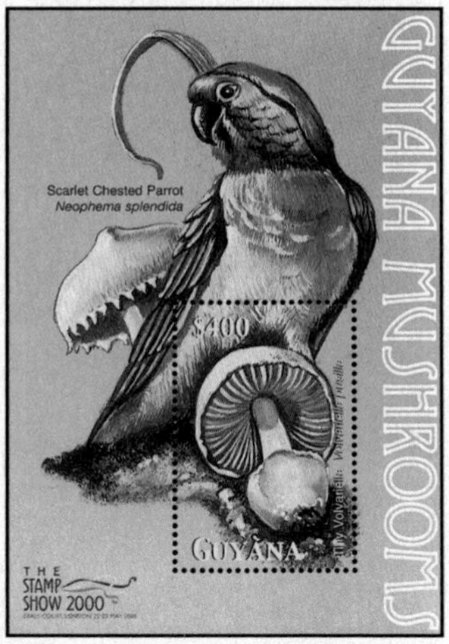


Mushrooms — A361

No. 3518, $100, horiz.: a, Sealy vase chanterelle. b, Caesar's mushroom. c, Green-headed jelly club. d, Salmon unicorn entoloma. e, White oysterette. f, Variable cort.

No. 3519, $100, horiz.: a, Coccora. b, Winter polypore. c, Turpentine waxy cap. d, Aeryginosa. e, Fly agaric. f, Honey mushroom.

No. 3520, $100, horiz: a, Salmon waxy cap. b, Shellfish-scented russula. c, Scarlet waxy cap. d, Stuntz's blue legs. e, Netted rhodotus. f, Indigo milky.

No. 3521, $400, Tiny volvariella. No. 3522, $400, Turkey tail, horiz. No. 3523, $400, Pinwheel marasmius, horiz.

**2000, Oct. 4 *Perf. 14***

**Sheets of 6, #a-f**

**3518-3520** A361 Set of 3 22.50 22.50

**Souvenir Sheets**

**3521-3523** A361 Set of 3 14.00 14.00

The Stamp Show 2000, London.

A362

Flowers — A363

Designs: No. 3524, $35, Bougainvillea spectabilis. No. 3525, $60, Euphorbia milii. No. 3526, $200, Catharanthus roseus. No. 3527, $300, Ipomoea carnea.

No. 3528, $35, Russelia equisetiformis. No. 3529, $60, Sprekelia formosissima. No. 3530, $200, Passiflora quadrangularis. No. 3531, $300, Mirabilis jalapa.

No. 3532, $100: a, Lantana camara. b, Jatropha integerrima. c, Plumeria alba. d, Strelitzia reginae. e, Clerodendrum splendens. f, Thunbergia grandiflora.

No. 3533, $100, vert.: a, Cordia sebestena. b, Heliconia wagneriana. c, Dendrobium phalaenopsis. d, Passiflora caerulea. e, Oncidium nubigenum. f, Hibiscus rosa-sinensis.

No. 3534, $100: a, Ipomoea tricolor. b, Lantana camara (inscribed canara). c, Cantua buxifolia. d, Fuchsia. e, Eichornia crassipes. f, Cosmos sulphureus.

No. 3535, $100: a, Bignonia capreolata. b, Calceolaria herbeo-hybrida. c, Canna generalis. d, Bauhinia grandiflora. e, Amaranthus caudatus. f, Abutilon megapotamicum.

No. 3536, $400, Guzmania lingulata. No. 3537, $400, Cattleya granulosa, vert.
No. 3538, $400, Tacsonia van-volxemii. No. 3539, $400, Oeceoclades maculata.

**2000, Oct. 30** ***Perf. 14***

**3524-3527** A362 Set of 4 6.75 6.75
**3528-3531** A363 Set of 4 6.75 6.75

**Sheets of 6, #a-f**

**3532-3533** A362 Set of 2 14.00 14.00
**3534-3535** A363 Set of 2 14.00 14.00

**Souvenir Sheets**

**3536-3537** A362 Set of 2 9.50 9.50
**3538-3539** A363 Set of 2 9.50 9.50

Munich Olympics Massacre — A364

No. 3540: a, Yaakov Springer. b, Andrei Schpitzer. c, Amitsur Shapira. d, David Berger. e, Ze'ev Friedman. f, Joseph Gottfreund. g, Moshe Weinberg. h, Kahat Shor. i, Mark Slavin. j, Eliezer Halfin. k, Joseph Romano. l, Poster of Munich Olympics.

**2000, Oct. 30**

**3540** A364 $40 Sheet of 12, #a-l 7.00 7.00

**Souvenir Sheet**

**3541** A364 $400 Torch bearer 5.50 5.50

**Three Stooges Type of 2000**

No. 3542: a, Moe with seltzer bottle, Shemp, Larry. b, As cave men trying to break rock. c, Moe with cow. d, Two women, Shemp, Moe. e, As cave men, seated. f, As cave men, Shemp holding large rock. g, Stooges wearing pith helmets. h, Stooges, picture frames. i, Stooges with fake beards.
No. 3543, $400, Larry, woman, vert. No. 3544, $400, Moe in plaid shirt, vert.

**2000, July 27** **Litho.** ***Perf. 13¾***

**3542** A357 $80 Sheet of 9, #a-i 8.75 8.75

**Souvenir Sheets**

**3543-3544** A357 Set of 2 9.00 9.00

**Betty Boop Type of 2000**

Souvenir Sheets

#3545, At football field. #3546, With tennis racquet. #3547, With ankh earrings, winking. #3548, With red swimsuit. #3549, As portrait of queen. #3550, As Can-can girl. #3551, Standing on shell. #3552, As Mona Lisa, horiz.

**2000, July 27**

**3545-3552** A358 $400 Set of 8 40.00 40.00

I Love Lucy — A365

No. 3553: a, Lucy reading book. b, Ricky, Lucy with book. c, Ricky kissing Lucy. d, Lucy near window. e, Lucy grabbing Ethel. f, Ricky holding scarf, Lucy in bed. g, Ethel, Lucy, frying pan. h, Ricky with frying pan. i, Lucy, Ethel, coffee table.
No. 3554, $400, Lucy in pink robe. No. 3555, $400, Lucy with garbage can lid.

**2000, July 27**

**3553** A365 $60 Sheet of 9, #a-i 6.75 6.75

**Souvenir Sheets**

**3554-3555** A365 Set of 2 9.00 9.00

FIN. K. L — A366

No. 3556: a, Lee Hyo-Ri. b, Ok Ju-Hyun. c, Lee Jin. d, Lee Jin. e, Group. f, Sung Yu-Ri. g, Lee Hyo-Ri. h, Sung Yu-Ri. i, Ok Ju-Hyun. #d, f, i, full color, others, sepia tone.

**2000, Sept. 7** ***Perf. 13½***

**3556** A366 $80 Sheet of 9, #a-i 9.00 9.00

Queen Mother, 100th Birthday — A367

**2000, Dec. 1** ***Perf. 14***

**3557** A367 $100 multi 1.40 1.40

Printed in sheets of 6.

Christmas — A368

$60, #3562b, Heads of 2 angels, org background. $90, #3562a, 2 full angels, bl background. $120, #3562c, Heads of 2 angels, bl background. #3561, $400, #3562d, 2 full angels, org background.
No. 3563, Baby Jesus, horiz.

**2000, Dec. 18**

**3558-3561** A368 Set of 4 8.50 8.50
**3562** A368 $180 Sheet of 4, #a-d 8.25 8.25

**Souvenir Sheet**

**3563** A368 $400 multi 4.75 4.75

New Year 2001 (Year of the Snake) — A369

No. 3564: a, Green snake head. b, Red snake head. c, Blue snake head. d, Yellow snake head.
$250, Purple snake head, vert.

**2001, Jan. 2** **Litho.** ***Perf. 13½x13***

**3564** A369 $80 Sheet of 4, #a-d 4.25 4.25

**Souvenir Sheet**

***Perf. 13x13½***

**3565** A369 $250 multi 3.00 3.00

Tourist Attractions — A370

Designs: No. 3566, $90, Prime Minister's residence. No. 3567, $90, Kaiteur Falls, vert.

**2001, Jan. 30** ***Perf. 13¼***

**3566-3567** A370 Set of 2 2.25 2.25

**Flower Photomosaic Type of 1999**

No. 3568, $80: Various photographs of flowers making up a photomosaic of the Queen Mother.
No. 3569, $100: Various photographs of religious sites making up a photomosaic of Pope John Paul II.

**2001, Feb. 13** ***Perf. 13¾***

**Sheets of 8, #a-h**

**3568-3569** A341 Set of 2 19.00 19.00

**Souvenir Sheet**

Chow Yun-Fat, Actor — A371

Background color: a, Blue green. b, Dark red. c, Olive brown. d, Red violet. e, Dark blue. f, Purple.

**2001, Feb. 13** ***Perf. 13¾x13¼***

**3570** A371 $60 Sheet of 6, #a-f 4.25 4.25

Pokémon — A372

No. 3571: a, Staryu. b, Seaking. c, Tentacool. d, Magikarp. e, Seadra. f, Goldeen.

**2001, Feb. 13** ***Perf. 13¾***

**3571** A372 $100 Sheet of 6, #a-f 7.50 7.50

**Souvenir Sheet**

**3572** A372 $400 Horsea 4.50 4.50

**Betty Boop Type of 2000**

Designs: No. 3573, $400, In pink hat. No. 3574, $400, As singer on stage. No. 3575, $400, With red top and necklace, on beach. No. 3576, $400, In orange and black hat, horiz.

**2001 ?** **Litho.** ***Perf. 13¾***

**3573-3576** A358 Set of 4 18.00 18.00

**I Love Lucy Type of 2000**

Designs: No. 3577, $400, Dressed like Carmen Miranda. No. 3578, $400, With blue hat and gloves. No. 3579, $400, As knife thrower's target. No. 3580, $400, At table, wearing blue hat. No. 3581, $400, Wearing glasses with thick black frames.

**2001 ?**

**3577-3581** A365 Set of 5 22.50 22.50

A373

A374

Cats and Dogs — A375

Designs: No. 3582, $35, Boxer. No. 3583, $60, Cinnamon ocicat. No. 3584, $100, Smooth dachshund. $300, White Manx.
No. 3586, $35, Chihuahua. No. 3587, $60, Persian tabby. No. 3588, $100, Colorpoint shorthair. $200, Cocker spaniel.
No. 3590 — Names of dogs (border color and location of denomination), $100: a, Pup (pink, bottom). b, Yogi (orange, bottom). c, Hooch (yellow, bottom) d, Huxley Blu (orange, top) e, Snowflake (yellow, top). f, Red (pink, top).
No. 3591 — Names of cats (border color and location of denomination), $100: a, Tom (orange, bottom). b, Puff (yellow, bottom). c, Jag (pink, bottom). d, Fritz (yellow, top). e, Smokey (pink, top). f, Thor, (orange, top).
No. 3592, $60: a, Devon rex. b, Egyptian mau. c, Turkish angora. d, Sphynx. e, Persian. f, American wirehair. g, Exotic shorthair. h, American curl.
No. 3593, $80: a, Airedale terrier. b, Greyhound. c, Afghan hound. d, Samoyed. e, Field spaniel. f, Scottish terrier. g, Brittany spaniel. h, Boston terrier.
No. 3594, $80: a, American shorthair. b, Somali. c, Singapura. d, Balinese. e, Egyptian mau. f, Scottish fold. g, Sphynx. h, Korat.
No. 3595, $80: a, Rottweiler. b, German shepherd. c, Bernese mountain dog. d, Sharpei. e, Dachshund. f, Jack Russell terrier. g, Boston terrier. h, Welsh corgi.
No. 3596, $400, Dalmatian. No. 3597, $400, Birman. No. 3598, $400, Abyssinian. No. 3599, $400, Beagle. No. 3600, $400, German shepherd named Baron of Fillmore. No. 3601, $400, Cat named Spike.

**2001, Mar. 1** ***Perf. 14***

**3582-3585** A373 Set of 4 6.25 6.25
**3586-3589** A374 Set of 4 5.25 5.25

**Sheets of 6, #a-f**

**3590-3591** A375 Set of 2 16.00 16.00

**Sheets of 8, #a-h**

**3592-3593** A373 Set of 2 15.00 15.00
**3594-3595** A374 Set of 2 16.50 16.50

**Souvenir Sheets**

**3596-3597** A373 Set of 2 9.50 9.50
**3598-3599** A374 Set of 2 9.50 9.50
**3600-3601** A375 Set of 2 9.50 9.50

Hong Kong 2001 Stamp Exhibition (Nos. 3592-3593, 3596-3597).

Souvenir Sheets

Hello Kitty — A376

Western children's stories with Hello Kitty characters: No. 3602, $400, Cinderella. No. 3603, $400, The Wizard of Oz. No. 3604, $400, Little Red Riding Hood. No. 3605, $400, Peter Pan. No. 3606, $400, Heidi. No. 3607, $400, Alice in Wonderland.

Oriental children's stories with Hello Kitty characters: No. 3608, $400, The Fishermen. No. 3609, $400, In the Snow. No. 3610, $400, Bamboo Princess. No. 3611, $400, Three in a Boat. No. 3612, $400, Up a Tree. No. 3613, $400, On a Bear.

**2001, Mar. 28 Litho. *Perf. 13¾***
**3602-3613** A376 Set of 12 55.00 55.00

Phila Nippon '01, Japan — A377

Designs: No. 3614, $25, Hanaogi with Maid-servant, by Eisho Chokosai. No. 3615, $25, Girl at a Hot Spring Resort, by Goyo Hashiguchi. No. 3616, $30, Morokoshi of the Echizenya, by Eiri Rekisentei. No. 3617, $30, Courtesan Receiving Letter of Invitation, by Harunobu Suzuki. No. 3618, $35, Two Girls on Their Way to or from the Bathhouse, by Suzuki. No. 3619, $35, Mother and Daughter on an Outing, by Hokusai. No. 3620, $60, Matron in Love, by Utamaro. No. 3621, $60, Girl and Frog, by Suzuki. No. 3622, $100, The Courtesan Midorigi, by Eisho Chokosai. No. 3623, $100, Three Beauties of High Fame, by Utamaro. No. 3624, $200, Maiko, by Bakusen Tsuchida. No. 3625, $200, Girl Breaking Off the Branch of a Flowering Tree, by Suzuki.

No. 3626 — Paintings by Jakuchu Ito (28x84mm): a, Insects, Reptiles and Amphibians at a Pond. b, Rose Mallows and Fowl. c, Rooster, Sunflower and Morning Glories. d, A Group of Roosters. e, Black Rooster and Nandina. f, Birds and Autumn Maples. g, Wagtail and Roses. h, Cockatoos in a Pine.

No. 3627 — Predominate features of sections of Procession to the Shugakuin Imperial Villa, by Sesshin Kakimoto (28x84mm): a, Bridge. b, High mountain, road and bridge. c, Large tree in foreground. d, Small island in foreground. e, Building at bottom. f, Building and large tree at bottom.

No. 3628 — Paintings of Women (28x84mm): a, Girls After the Bath, by Utamaro. b, Summer Evening on the Riverbank at Hama-cho, by Kiyonaga Torii. c, A Beauty in the Wind, by Ando Kaigetsudo. d, Sisters by Shoen Uemura. e, Kasamori Osen, by Suzuki.

No. 3629 — Details from Backstage at a Kabuki Theater, by Moronobu Hishikawa (30x38mm): a, Top of screen. b, Man with red kimono. c, Man with stringed instrument. e, Man on chair.

No. 3630, $400, Portrait of Senseki Takami, by Kazan Watanabe. No. 3631, $400, Fish and Octopus From the Colorful Realm of Living Beings, by Ito. No. 3632, $400, Woman Holding a Flower, by Hisako Kajiwara, horiz. No. 3633, $400, Palace of Immortals in an Autumn Valley, by Yako Okochi, horiz. No. 3634, $400, Wintry Sky, by Hosen Higashibara, horiz.

**2001, June 18 *Perf. 14***
**3614-3625** A377 Set of 12 11.00 11.00
**3626** A377 $80 Sheet of 8, #a-h 8.25 8.25
**3627** A377 $100 Sheet of 6, #a-f 7.50 7.50
**3628** A377 $120 Sheet of 5, #a-e 6.75 6.75
**3629** A377 $160 Sheet of 4, #a-d 7.50 7.50

**Sizes: 90x120mm, 120x90mm**

***Imperf***

**3630-3634** A377 Set of 5 22.50 22.50

Giuseppe Verdi (1813-1901), Opera Composer — A378

No. 3635: a, Verdi, score at LR. b, Actor, score from Rigoletto. c, Actor, score from Ernani. d, Verdi, scores at left.
$400, Verdi and scores.

**2001, June 18 *Perf. 14***
**3635** A378 $160 Sheet of 4, #a-d 8.25 8.25

**Souvenir Sheet**

**3636** A378 $400 multi 5.50 5.50

Toulouse-Lautrec Paintings — A379

No. 3637, horiz.: a, Maurice Joyant in the Baie de Somme. b, Monsieur Boileau. c, Monsieur, Madame and the Dog.
$300, Man from Monsieur, Madame and the Dog.

**2001, June 18 *Perf. 13¾***
**3637** A379 $160 Sheet of 3, #a-c 5.50 5.50

**Souvenir Sheet**

**3638** A379 $300 multi 5.25 5.25

Monet Paintings — A380

No. 3639, horiz.: a, Village Street in Normandy, Near Honfleur. b, The Road to Chailly. c, Train in the Countryside. d, The Quai du Louvre.
$400, Flowering Garden.

**2001, June 18**
**3639** A380 $150 Sheet of 4, #a-d 7.50 7.50

**Souvenir Sheet**

**3640** A380 $400 multi 5.25 5.25

Queen Victoria (1819-1901) — A381

Pictures of Victoria from — No. 3641, $200: a, 1829. b, 1837. c, 1840. d, 1897 (with crown).
No. 3642, $200: a, 1850. b, 1843. c, 1859. d, 1897 (with hat).
No. 3643, $400, 1885 (with crown). No. 3644, $400, Undated.

**2001, June 18 *Perf. 14***

**Sheets of 4, #a-d**

**3641-3642** A381 Set of 2 19.00 19.00

**Souvenir Sheets**

**3643-3644** A381 Set of 2 9.50 9.50

Queen Elizabeth II, 75th Birthday — A382

No. 3645: a, Pink hat. b, Red hat. c, White hat. d, Tiara.

**2001, June 18 *Perf. 14***
**3645** A382 $150 Sheet of 4, #a-d 7.50 7.50

**Souvenir Sheet**

***Perf. 13¾***

**3646** A382 $400 shown 5.25 5.25

No. 3645 contains four 28x42mm stamps.

Photomosaic of Queen Elizbeth II — A383

**2001, June 18 *Perf. 14***
**3647** A383 $80 multi .90 .90

Printed in sheets of 8, with and without inscription reading "In Celebration of the 50th Anniversary of H.M. Queen Elizabeth II's Accession to the Throne."

**Flower Photomosaic Type of 1999-2000**

No. 3648: Various pictures of American scenes making up a photomosaic of Pres. John F. Kennedy.

**2001, June 18**
**3648** A341 $80 Sheet of 8, #a-h 7.50 7.50

Pres. Ronald Reagan — A384

Reagan: a, In checked shirt. b, With Bonzo. c, With cowboy hat. d, With dark tie. e, With wife, Nancy. f, With striped tie. g, Waving. h, Signing treaty with Mikhail Gorbachev. i, With hammer and chisel. j, With Pres. Clinton.

**2001, June 18**
**3649** A384 $60 Sheet of 10, #a-j 8.25 8.25

**Betty Boop Type of 2000**

Designs: No. 3650, $400, With swimsuit and sunglasses. No. 3651, $400, With lilac headdress. No. 3652, $400, With purple top and pirate's hat. No. 3653, $400, Dancing on radio, horiz.

**2001 *Perf. 13¾***
**3650-3653** A358 Set of 4 18.00 18.00

**Betty Boop Type of 2000**

Designs: No. 3654, $400, In orange and yellow polka dot swimsuit, holding gift. No. 3655, $400, Holding on to anchor. No. 3556, $400, In red bikini, surfing. No. 3557, $400, Wearing birthday hat, horiz.

**2001 Litho. *Perf. 13¾***
**3654-3657** A358 Set of 4 18.00 18.00

**Historical Events Type of 1997**

No. 3658: a, Securities and Exchange Commission formed, 1934. b, Herbert Hoover is elected president, 1928. c, The Jazz Singer is first talking movie, 1927. d, J. Edgar Hoover becomes director of FBI, 1924. e, Alexander Fleming discovers penicillin, 1928. f, FCC established to regulate broadcasting, 1934. g, Lindbergh becomes first to fly solo across

Atlantic, 1927. h, Albert Einstein is awarded Nobel Prize for Physics, 1921. i, Hindenburg dies and Hitler becomes German Führer, 1934. j, Social Security Act provides safety for Americans, 1935. k, Earhart is first to fly solo from Hawaii to California, 1935. l, Marcus Garvey's prison sentence is commuted, 1927.

**2001, Mar. 28** ***Perf. 14¼x14¾***

**3658** A289 $60 Sheet of 12, #a-l 9.50 9.50

Prehistoric Animals — A385

Designs: $20, Allosaurus. $30, Spinosaurus. $35, Pteranodon. $60, Cetiosaurus. $200, Archaeopteryx. $300, Parasaurolophus.

No. 3665, $100, horiz.: a, Alamosaurus. b, Archaeopteryx, diff. c, Pachycephalosaurus. d, Parasaurolophus, diff. e, Edmontosaurus. f, Triceratops.

No. 3666, $100, horiz.: a, Brachiosaurus and two palm trees. b, Dimorphodon. c, Coelophysis. d, Velociraptor. e, Antrodemus. f, Euparkeria.

No. 3667, $100, horiz.: a, Ichthyostega. b, Eryops. c, Ichthyosaur. d, Pliosaur. e, Dunklosteus. f, Eogyrinus.

No. 3668, $100, horiz.: a, Brachiosaurus and palm tree. b, Pteranodon, diff. c, Compsognathus. d, Corythosaurus. e, Allosaurus, diff. f, Torosaurus.

No. 3669, $400, Brachiosaurus, diff. No. 3670, $400, Torosaurus, diff., horiz. No. 3671, $400, Ichthyosaur, diff., horiz. No. 3672, $400, Pteranodon, diff., horiz.

**2001, Oct. 15** ***Perf. 14***

**3659-3664** A385 Set of 6 7.25 7.25

**Sheets of 6, #a-f**

**3665-3668** A385 Set of 4 27.50 27.50

**Souvenir Sheets**

**3669-3672** A385 Set of 4 18.00 18.00

Vegaspex (#3665-3672).

Animals of Tropical Rainforests A386

Designs: $35, Mandrill, vert. $100, Leaf cutting ants.

No. 3675, $80: a, Elephant. b, Impala. c, Leopard. d, Gray parrot. e, Hippopotamus. f, Pygmy chimp. g, African green python. h, Mountain gorilla.

No. 3676, $80: a, Three-toed sloth. b, Lion tamarin. c, Ringtail lemur. d, Sugar glider. e, Toucan. f, Trogons. g, Pygmy marmoset. h, Poison arrow frog.

No. 3677, $400, Tapir, vert. No. 3678, $400, Sable antelope, vert.

**2001, Oct. 15**

**3673-3674** A386 Set of 2 1.50 1.50

**Sheets of 8, #a-h**

**3675-3676** A386 Set of 2 14.50 14.50

**Souvenir Sheets**

**3677-3678** A386 Set of 2 9.00 9.00

Tropical Birds — A387

No. 3679, $100, horiz.: a, Rainbow lorikeet. b, King bird of paradise. c, Yellow-chevroned parakeet. d, Masked lovebird. e, Scarlet ibis. f, Toco toucan.

No. 3680, $100, horiz.: a, Hyacinth macaw. b, Wire-tailed manakin. c, Scarlet macaw. d, Sun parakeet. e, Roseate spoonbill. f, Red-billed toucan.

No. 3681, $400, Eclectus parrot. No. 3682, $400, Sulfur-crested cockatoo.

**2001, Oct. 15** **Litho.**

**Sheets of 6, #a-f**

**3679-3680** A387 Set of 2 15.00 15.00

**Souvenir Sheets**

**3681-3682** A387 Set of 2 11.00 11.00

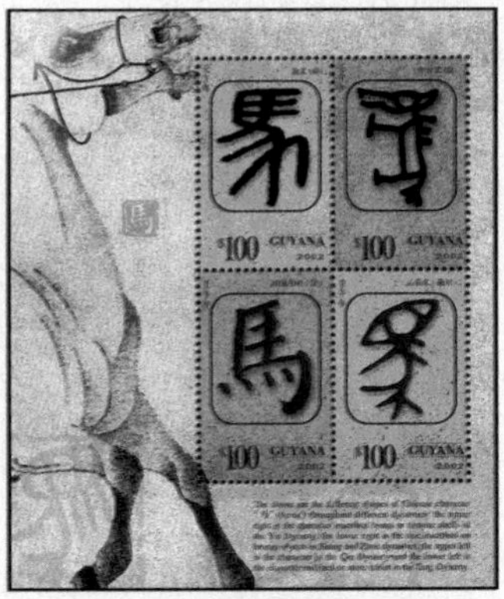


New Year 2002 (Year of the Horse) — A388

No. 3683 — Evolution of Chinese character for "horse": a, Two characters outside, one character inside parentheses at UR. b, Three characters outside, one character inside parentheses at UR. c, Four characters outside, one character inside parentheses at UR. d, Three characters outside, two characters inside parentheses at UR.

No. 3684 — Figure on horse: a, Denomination at UL. b, Denomination at UR.

**2001, Oct. 15** ***Perf. 13***

**3683** A388 $100 Sheet of 4, #a-d 6.50 6.50

***Perf. 13¼***

**3684** A388 $150 Sheet of 2, #a-b 5.50 5.50

No. 3684 contains two 38x50mm stamps.

2002 World Cup Soccer Championships, Japan and Korea — A389

No. 3685, $100 — Posters from: a, 1950, and player. b, 1954, and Jules Rimet. c, 1958, Pelé and teammates. d, 1962, and Zito scoring goal. e, 1966, and English players celebrating. f, 1970, and Jairzinho.

No. 3686, $100 — Posters from: a, 1978, and Daniel Passarella. b, 1982, and Paolo Rossi. c, 1986, and Diego Maradona. d, 1990, and German players celebrating. e, 1994, and Brazilian players celebrating. f, 1998, and Zinedine Zidane.

No. 3687, $400, 1930 poster, head from Jules Rimet Trophy. No. 3688, $400, Head and globe from World Cup trophy.

**2001, Dec. 26** ***Perf. 13¾x14¼***

**Sheets of 6, #a-f**

**3685-3686** A389 Set of 2 14.00 14.00

**Souvenir Sheets**

***Perf. 14¼***

**3687-3688** A389 Set of 2 9.00 9.00

**Queen Mother Type of 1999 Redrawn**

No. 3689: a, With Princess Elizabeth, 1928. b, Lady Elizabeth-Bowles Lyon, 1914. c, With Princess Elizabeth, 1950. d, In Venice, 1984.

$400, In Canada, 1988.

**2001, Dec.** ***Perf. 14***

**Yellow Orange Frames**

**3689** A328 $130 Sheet of 4, #a-d, + label 5.75 5.75

**Souvenir Sheet**

***Perf. 13¾***

**3690** A328 $400 multi 4.50 4.50

Queen Mother's 101st birthday. No. 3690 contains one 38x50mm stamp with a bluer cast than that found on No. 3434. Sheet margins of Nos. 3689-3690 lack embossing and gold arms and frames found on Nos. 3433-3434.

**I Love Lucy Type of 2000**

Souvenir Sheets

Designs: No. 3691, $400, Lucy wearing leis, with hands up. No. 3692, $400, Lucy with checked shirt and apron, with mouth open.

**2001 ?** ***Perf. 13¾***

**3691-3692** A365 Set of 2 9.00 9.00

Wedding of Netherlands Prince Willem-Alexander and Máxima Zorreguieta — A390

No. 3693: a, Couple (Máxima at left), flag colors at left. b, Couple (heads apart), flag colors at right. c, Couple (Máxima at right), flag colors at left. d, Couple (heads together), flag colors at right. e, Willem-Alexander. f, Máxima.

**2002, Jan. 7** **Litho.** ***Perf. 14¾x14¼***

**3693** A390 $120 Sheet of 6, #a-f 8.00 8.00

United We Stand — A391

**2002, Feb. 6** ***Perf. 13½x13¼***

**3694** A391 $200 multi 2.25 2.25

Printed in sheets of four.

Reign of Queen Elizabeth II, 50th Anniv. — A392

No. 3695: a, Blue hat. b, Feathered hat. c, Waving. d, With horse at right.

$400, With horse at left.

**2002, Feb. 6** ***Perf. 14½***

**3695** A392 $150 Sheet of 4, #a-d 6.75 6.75

**Souvenir Sheet**

**3696** A392 $400 multi 4.50 4.50

**Flower Photomosaic Type of 1999-2000**

No. 3697: Various science photographs making up a photomosaic of Albert Einstein.

**2002, Feb. 25** ***Perf. 13¾***

**3697** A341 $80 Sheet of 8, #a-h 7.25 7.25

Nobel Prizes, Cent. (in 2001) — A393

No. 3698, $100 — Chemistry laureates: a, Harold C. Urey, 1934. b, Willard F. Libby, 1960. c, Frederick Sanger, 1958 and 1980. d, Theodor Svedberg, 1926. e, Cyril N. Hinshelwood, 1956. f, Nikolai Semenov, 1956.

No. 3699, $100: a, Alexander Todd, Chemistry, 1957. b, John Steinbeck, Literature, 1962. c, Edward C. Kendall, Physiology or Medicine, 1950. d, Frederick G. Banting, Physiology or Medicine, 1923. e, Charles Nicolle, Physiology or Medicine, 1928. f, Charles Richet, Physiology or Medicine, 1913.

No. 3700, $400, International Red Cross, Peace, 1917. No. 3701, $400, John J. R. MacLeod, Physiology or Medicine, 1923. No. 3702, $400, Derek H. R. Barton, Chemistry, 1969.

**2002, Feb. 25** ***Perf. 14***

**Sheets of 6, #a-f**

**3698-3699** A393 Set of 2 13.50 13.50

**Souvenir Sheets**

**3700-3702** A393 Set of 3 13.50 13.50

2002 Winter Olympics, Salt Lake City A394

Designs: No. 3703, $200, Skier. No. 3704, $200, Figure skater.

**2002, July 1 Litho. *Perf. 13¼x13½***

| | | | | |
|---|---|---|---|---|
| **3703-3704** A394 | Set of 2 | | 4.50 | 4.50 |
| *a.* | Souvenir sheet, #3703-3704 | | 4.50 | 4.50 |

Guyana — People's Republic of China Diplomatic Relations, 30th Anniv. — A395

Designs: No. 3705, $100, Chinese flag, Kaieteur Falls, Guyana. No. 3706, $100, Guyanese flag, Great Wall of China.

**2002, July 1** ***Perf. 14***

| | | | |
|---|---|---|---|
| **3705-3706** A395 | Set of 2 | 2.25 | 2.25 |

Intl. Volunteers Year (in 2001) A396

Emblem, Guyanese flag and: $35, Person on ladder touching Guyana on map. $60, Map of Guyana and IVY emblem. $300, People.

**2002, July 1**

| | | | |
|---|---|---|---|
| **3707-3709** A396 | Set of 3 | 4.50 | 4.50 |

Intl. Year of Ecotourism — A397

No. 3710: a, Owl. b, Waterfall and tourists. c, Baboon. d, Butterfly. e, Flower. f, Otter.
$400, Leopard.

**2002, July 1** ***Perf. 13¼x13***

| | | | |
|---|---|---|---|
| **3710** A397 $100 Sheet of 6, #a-f | | 6.75 | 6.75 |

**Souvenir Sheet**

| | | | |
|---|---|---|---|
| **3711** A397 $400 multi | | 4.50 | 4.50 |

Intl. Year of Mountains — A398

No. 3712: a, Devil's Tower, US. b, Schreckhorn, Switzerland. c, Mt. Rainier, US. d, Mt. Everest, Nepal and Tibet. No. 3713: Mt. McKinley. U.S.

**2002, July 1** ***Perf. 13½x13¼***

| | | | |
|---|---|---|---|
| **3712** A398 $200 Sheet of 4, #a-d | | 14.00 | 14.00 |

**Souvenir Sheet**

| | | | |
|---|---|---|---|
| **3713** A398 $400 multi | | 7.00 | 7.00 |

See Nos. 3848-3851.

20th World Scout Jamboree, Thailand — A399

No. 3714: a, Environmental Science merit badge. b, Citizenship in the World merit badge. c, Life Saving merit badge.
$400, Mascot, Scout emblem.

**2002, July 1**

| | | | |
|---|---|---|---|
| **3714** A399 $200 Sheet of 3, #a-c | | 6.75 | 6.75 |

**Souvenir Sheet**

| | | | |
|---|---|---|---|
| **3715** A399 $400 multi | | 4.50 | 4.50 |

Flora and Fauna — A400

No. 3716, $100 — Butterflies: a, Sweet oil. b, Swallowtail. c, Southern white admiral. d, Prepona pheridamas. e, Plain tiger. f, Common eggfly.
No. 3717, $100 — Moths: a, Burgena varia. b, Lime hawkmoth. c, Spurge hawkmoth. d, Eligma laetipicta. e, Io moth. f, Pine hawkmoth.
No. 3718, $100 — Birds: a, Flycatcher. b, Barbary shrike. c, Red-faced mousebird. d, Red-footed booby. e, White-fronted goose. f, Great crested grebe.
No. 3719, $100 — Whales: a, Sperm. b, Pygmy sperm. c, Blue. d, Bottlenose. e, Killer. f, True's beaked.
No. 3720, $100, vert. — Orchids: a, Masdevallia tovarensis. b, Encyclia vitellina. c, Dendrobium nobile. d, Masdevallia falcata. e, Calanthe vestita. f, Brassolaeliacattleya Rising Sun.
No. 3721, $400, Zebra butterfly. No. 3722, $400, Callimorpha quadripuntaria. No. 3723, $400, Whiskered tern. No. 3724, $400, Beluga whale. No. 3725, $400, Brassavola nodosa.

**2002, Aug. 7** ***Perf. 14***

**Sheets of 6, #a-f**

| | | | |
|---|---|---|---|
| **3716-3720** A400 | Set of 5 | 47.50 | 47.50 |

**Souvenir Sheets**

| | | | |
|---|---|---|---|
| **3721-3725** A400 | Set of 5 | 35.00 | 35.00 |

Elvis Presley (1935-77) A401

Designs: No. 3726, $60, In army uniform. No. 3727, $60, Singing.

**2002, Aug. 16** ***Perf. 13¾***

| | | | |
|---|---|---|---|
| **3726-3727** A401 | Set of 2 | 2.25 | 2.25 |

Each stamp was printed in a sheet of nine.

Popeye — A402

No. 3728: a, Popeye. b, Olive Oyl. c, Wimpy. d, Jeep. e, Swee'Pea and Olive Oyl. f, Swee'Pea.
$400, Popeye, diff.

**2002, Oct. 7** ***Perf. 14***

| | | | |
|---|---|---|---|
| **3728** A402 $100 Sheet of 6, #a-f | | 8.50 | 8.50 |

**Souvenir Sheet**

| | | | |
|---|---|---|---|
| **3729** A402 $400 multi | | 6.50 | 6.50 |

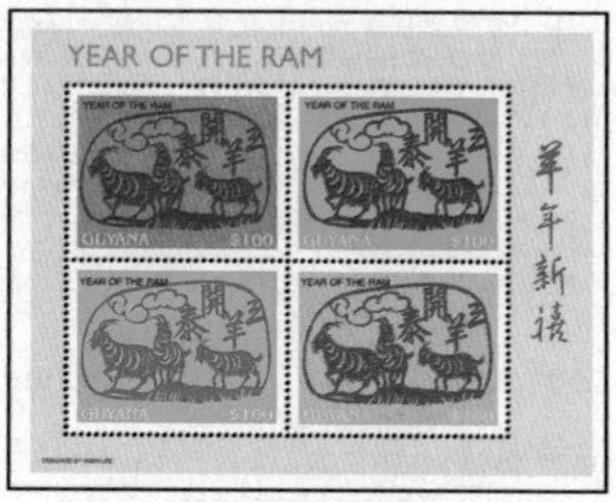


New Year 2003 (Year of the Ram) — A403

Rams and background color of: a, Red. b, Orange. c, Bright pink. d, Yellow green.

**2003, Jan. 27 Litho. *Perf. 14¼x14½***

| | | | |
|---|---|---|---|
| **3730** A403 $100 Sheet of 4, #a-d | | 6.50 | 6.50 |

Pres. John F. Kennedy (1917-63) — A404

No. 3731, vert.: a, Pres. Kennedy, Presidential seal. b, Pres. Kennedy, Dr. Martin Luther King, Jr. c, Pres. Kennedy, space capsule. d, Pres. Kennedy, US flag, White House. e, Pres. Kennedy, map of Cuba, missile. f, Jacqueline and John F. Kennedy, Jr., US flag.
$400, Pres. Kennedy and wife, Jacqueline.

**2003, Jan. 27** ***Perf. 14***

| | | | |
|---|---|---|---|
| **3731** A404 $100 Sheet of 6, #a-f | | 8.00 | 8.00 |

**Souvenir Sheet**

| | | | |
|---|---|---|---|
| **3732** A404 $400 multi | | 6.50 | 6.50 |

Pres. Ronald Reagan — A405

No. 3733, vert. — Pres. Reagan: a, And eagle. b, As actor. c, And Mt. Rushmore. d, And wife Nancy. e, And White House. f, Riding horse.
$400, With Mikhail Gorbachev.

**2003, Jan. 27**

| | | | |
|---|---|---|---|
| **3733** A405 $100 Sheet of 6, #a-f | | 8.00 | 8.00 |

**Souvenir Sheet**

| | | | |
|---|---|---|---|
| **3734** A405 $400 multi | | 7.00 | 7.00 |

Princess Diana (1961-97) — A406

No. 3735: a-f, Various depictions of Princess wearing tiaras or bridal veils.
$400, Wearing pink and yellow dress.

**2003, Jan. 27**

| | | | |
|---|---|---|---|
| **3735** A406 $100 Sheet of 6, #a-f | | 7.00 | 7.00 |

**Souvenir Sheet**

| | | | |
|---|---|---|---|
| **3736** A406 $400 multi | | 5.00 | 5.00 |

Paintings of Lucas Cranach the Elder (1472-1553) A407

Designs: $35, Portrait of a Man. $60, Portrait of a Woman. $100, Duchess Catherine of Mecklenburg. $200, Portrait of Duke Henry of Saxony.
No. 3741: a, The Virgin, c. 1518. b, The Virgin and Child Under the Apple Tree. c, The Virgin, c, 1535. d, The Virgin, c. 1525.
$400, The Virgin and Child Holding a Piece of Bread.

**2003, June 17 Litho. *Perf. 14¼***

| | | | |
|---|---|---|---|
| **3737-3740** A407 | Set of 4 | 4.50 | 4.50 |
| **3741** A407 $150 Sheet of 4, #a-d | | 6.75 | 6.75 |

**Souvenir Sheet**

| | | | |
|---|---|---|---|
| **3742** A407 $400 multi | | 4.50 | 4.50 |

Art by Kunichika Toyohara (1835-1900) A408

Designs: $60, The Actor Shikan Nakamura IV. $80, The Actor Danjuro Ichikawa IX as Sukeroku, 1883. $100, The Actor Tatsunosuke Onoe. $300, The Actor Sadanji Ichikawa I as Kyusuke.
No. 3747: a, The Actor Sansho Kawarazaki as Watonai. b, The Actor Danjuro Ichikawa IX as Gongoru Kagemasa Kamakura. c, The Actor Sadanji Ichikawa I as Sadakuro. d, The Actor Danjuro Ichikawa IX as Sukeroku, 1898.
$400, The Actor Danjuro Ichikawa IX as Shukeigashira Kiyomasa Kato, horiz.

**2003, June 17**

| | | | |
|---|---|---|---|
| **3743-3746** A408 | Set of 4 | 6.00 | 6.00 |
| **3747** A408 $150 Sheet of 4, #a-d | | 6.75 | 6.75 |

**Souvenir Sheet**

| | | | |
|---|---|---|---|
| **3748** A408 $400 multi | | 4.50 | 4.50 |

Paintings by Wassily Kandinsky (1866-1944) — A409

Designs: $25, Tension in Red. $30, Black Accompaniment. $35, Calm Tension. $60, Hard and Soft. $100, Yellow Point, horiz. $300, Composition VIII, horiz.

No. 3755: a, Red Oval. b, On the White II. c, Mutual Agreement. d, Inclination.

No. 3756, $400, White Center, horiz. No. 3757, $400, Black Weft, horiz.

**2003, June 17**

**3749-3754** A409 Set of 6 6.25 6.25
**3755** A409 $150 Sheet of 4, #a-d 6.75 6.75

**Size: 104x84mm**

***Imperf***

**3756-3757** A409 Set of 2 9.00 9.00

Caribbean Community, 30th Anniv. — A410

Anniversary emblem and: $20, Map of Guyana, vert. $60, Bank of Guyana Building. $100, Hands with torch, vert. $160, Stethoscope and AIDS ribbon, vert.

**2003, July 7** ***Perf. 14***

**3758-3761** A410 Set of 4 3.75 3.75

A411

Teddy Bears, Cent. (in 2002) — A412

No. 3762 — Background color: a, Lilac. b, Dull greenish blue. c, Light blue. d, Dull yellow green. e, Dull blue green. f, Dull gray green. h, Gray. i, Dull green. j, Gray blue.

No. 3763 — Bear with: a, Red dress. b, Menorah. c, Christmas lights. d, Blue dress.

**2003, Aug. 25**

**3762** A411 $80 Sheet of 9, #a-i 8.50 8.50
**3763** A412 $150 Sheet of 4, #a-d 7.00 7.00

Intl. Year of Fresh Water — A413

No. 3764 — Kaieteur Falls: a, Top. b, Middle. c, Base.

$400, Amazon River.

**2003, Aug. 25** ***Perf. 13¾***

**3764** A413 $200 Sheet of 3, #a-c 8.25 8.25

**Souvenir Sheet**

**3765** A413 $400 multi 6.00 6.00

Tour de France Bicycle Race, Cent. — A414

No. 3766: a, Jacques Anquetil, 1964. b, Felice Gimondi, 1965. c, Lucien Aimar, 1966. d, Roger Pingeon, 1967.

$400, Jan Janssen, 1968.

**2003, Aug. 25** ***Perf. 13½x13***

**3766** A414 $150 Sheet of 4, #a-d 7.25 7.25

**Souvenir Sheet**

**3767** A414 $400 multi 5.00 5.00

Coronation of Queen Elizabeth II, 50th Anniv. — A415

No. 3768: a, Wearing tiara. b, Wearing dark blue dress. c, Wearing lilac dress.

$400, Wearing crown.

**2003, Aug. 25** ***Perf. 14***

**3768** A415 $200 Sheet of 3, #a-c 6.75 6.75

**Souvenir Sheet**

**3769** A415 $400 multi 4.50 4.50

Prince William, 21st Birthday — A416

No. 3770: a, As toddler. b, As adult. c, As infant.

$400, As young boy.

**2003, Aug. 25**

**3770** A416 $200 Sheet of 3, #a-c 7.00 7.00

**Souvenir Sheet**

**3771** A416 $400 multi 5.50 5.50

Powered Flight, Cent. — A417

Designs: $100, Airplane of Sir Alliot Verdon Roe. $160, Airplane of Samuel Franklin Cody.

No. 3772, $150: a, Wright Flyer. b, Spad 13. c, Sopwith F-1. d, Albatros D.II.

No. 3773, $150: a, Nieuport 17. b, S. E. 5a. c, D. H. 4. d, German biplane.

No. 3774, $400, Wright Flyer making first flight. No. 3775, $400, Fokker D.VIIs.

**2003, Aug. 25**

**3771A** A417 $100 multi 1.10 1.10
**3771B** A417 $160 multi 1.75 1.75

**Sheets of 4, #a-d**

**3772-3773** A417 Set of 2 13.50 13.50

**Souvenir Sheets**

**3774-3775** A417 Set of 2 10.00 10.00

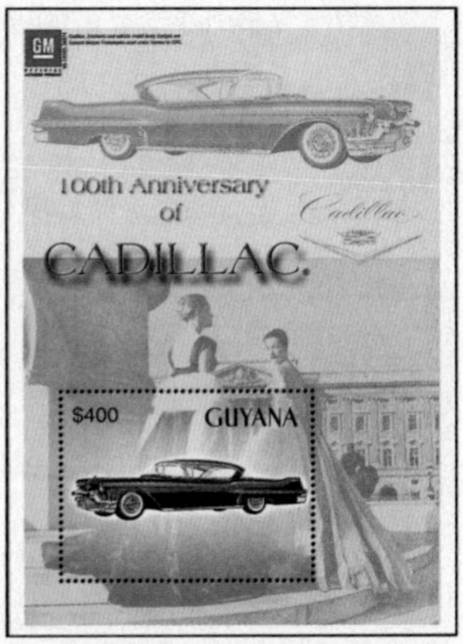


General Motors Automobiles — A418

No. 3776, $150 — Cadillacs: a, 1948 Sixty Special. b, 1966 Fleetwood Sixty Special. c, 1967 Eldorado. d, 1976 Eldorado convertible.

No. 3777, $150 — Corvettes: a, 1964 Stingray. b, 1963 Stingray. c, 1966 Stingray. 4. d, 1969.

No. 3778, $400, Undescribed Cadillac (1957 Coupe de Ville). No. 3779, $400, 1971 Corvette.

**2003, Aug. 25** **Sheets of 4, #a-d**

**3776-3777** A418 Set of 2 14.50 14.50

**Souvenir Sheets**

**3778-3779** A418 Set of 2 9.50 9.50

Butterflies — A419

Designs: $20, Grecian shoemaker. $55, Clorinde. $80, Orange-barred sulphur. $100, Atala. $160, White peacock. $200, Polydamus swallowtail. $300, Giant swallowtail. $400, Banded king shoemaker. $500, Blue night. $1000, Orange theope. $2000, Small lacewing. $3000, Common morpho.

**2003, Nov. 4** **Litho.** ***Perf. 13¼***

| | | | | | |
|---|---|---|---|---|---|
| **3780** | A419 | $20 | multi | .30 | .30 |
| **3781** | A419 | $55 | multi | .85 | .85 |
| **3782** | A419 | $80 | multi | 1.25 | 1.25 |
| **3783** | A419 | $100 | multi | 1.50 | 1.50 |
| **3784** | A419 | $160 | multi | 2.25 | 2.25 |
| **3785** | A419 | $200 | multi | 3.00 | 3.00 |
| **3786** | A419 | $300 | multi | 4.25 | 4.25 |
| **3787** | A419 | $400 | multi | 5.75 | 5.75 |
| **3788** | A419 | $500 | multi | 7.25 | 7.25 |
| **3789** | A419 | $1000 | multi | 13.50 | 13.50 |
| **3790** | A419 | $2000 | multi | 27.50 | 27.50 |
| **3791** | A419 | $3000 | multi | 40.00 | 40.00 |
| | *Nos. 3780-3791 (12)* | | | 107.40 | 107.40 |

Worldwide Fund for Nature (WWF) — A420

No. 3792: a, Head of channel-billed toucan. b, Two toco toucans on branch. c, Channel-billed toucan on branch. d, Toco toucan and chick.

**2003, Dec. 1** ***Perf. 14***

**3792** Horiz. strip of 4, #a-d 5.00 5.00
*a.-d.* A420 $100 Any single 1.20 1.20
*e.* Souvenir sheet, 2 each #3792a-3792d 10.50 10.50

Mushrooms — A421

Designs: No. 3793, $20, Clitocybe gibba. No. 3794, $20, Clitocybe clavipes. $30, Calocybe carnea. $300, Marasmius.

No. 3797: a, Amanita spissa. b, Boletus aestivalis. c, Boletus rubellus. d, Clathrus archeri.
$400, Volvariella bombycina.

**2003, Dec. 1**

| | | | | | |
|---|---|---|---|---|---|
| **3793-3796** | A421 | | Set of 4 | 4.50 | 4.50 |
| **3797** | A421 | $150 | Sheet of 4, #a-d | 7.25 | 7.25 |

**Souvenir Sheet**

| | | | | | |
|---|---|---|---|---|---|
| **3798** | A421 | $400 | multi | 5.75 | 5.75 |

Mammals A422

Designs: $25, Common tenrec. $60, Humboldt's woolly monkey, vert. $100, Gundi. $200, Harbor seal.
No. 3803: a, Prevost's squirrel. b, Mountain tapir. c, Sea otter. d, Indus dolphin.
$400, Peter's disk-winged bat, vert.

**2003, Dec. 1**

| | | | | | |
|---|---|---|---|---|---|
| **3799-3802** | A422 | | Set of 4 | 4.25 | 4.25 |
| **3803** | A422 | $150 | Sheet of 4, #a-d | 6.75 | 6.75 |

**Souvenir Sheet**

| | | | | | |
|---|---|---|---|---|---|
| **3804** | A422 | $400 | multi | 4.50 | 4.50 |

Flowers — A423

Designs: $20, Begonia sedeni. $30, Dahlia. $35, Eschecholzia californica. $300, Lupinus perennis.
No. 3809: a, Agapanthus africanus. b, Hyacinth cultivars. c, Protea linearis. d, Hippestrum aulicum.
$400, Crocus sativus, horiz.

**2003, Dec. 1**

| | | | | | |
|---|---|---|---|---|---|
| **3805-3808** | A423 | | Set of 4 | 4.25 | 4.25 |
| **3809** | A423 | $150 | Sheet of 4, #a-d | 6.75 | 6.75 |

**Souvenir Sheet**

| | | | | | |
|---|---|---|---|---|---|
| **3810** | A423 | $400 | multi | 5.00 | 5.00 |

Fish A424

Designs: $25, Regal tang. $60, Pajama tang. $100, Coral beauty. $200, Emperor angelfish.
No. 3815: a, High hat. b, Regal angelfish. c, Fire clown. d, Domino damselfish.
$400, Tomato clown.

**2003, Dec. 1**

| | | | | | |
|---|---|---|---|---|---|
| **3811-3814** | A424 | | Set of 4 | 4.75 | 4.75 |
| **3815** | A424 | $150 | Sheet of 4, #a-d | 9.00 | 9.00 |

**Souvenir Sheet**

| | | | | | |
|---|---|---|---|---|---|
| **3816** | A424 | $400 | multi | 5.50 | 5.50 |

Guyana — Brazil Diplomatic Relations, 35th Anniv. A425

**2003, Dec. 18**

| | | | | | |
|---|---|---|---|---|---|
| **3817** | A425 | $20 | multi | .25 | .25 |

New Year 2004 (Year of the Monkey) — A426

No. 3818: a, Dark brown monkey with orange face. b, Dark brown and white monkey with brown face. c, Brown monkey. d, Orange monkey with black face.

**2004, Jan. 5**

| | | | | | |
|---|---|---|---|---|---|
| **3818** | A426 | $100 | Sheet of 4, #a-d | 4.75 | 4.75 |

Paintings by Tang Yin (1470-1524) — A427

No. 3819, vert.: a, Concubines of Emperor Chu. b, Lady. c, Untitled painting depicting woman. d, Untitled painting depicting landscape.
$400, Mountain Scene.

**2004, Jan. 21 Litho. *Perf. 13¼***

| | | | | | |
|---|---|---|---|---|---|
| **3819** | A427 | $150 | Sheet of 4, #a-d | 6.75 | 6.75 |

**Souvenir Sheet**

| | | | | | |
|---|---|---|---|---|---|
| **3820** | A427 | $400 | multi | 4.50 | 4.50 |

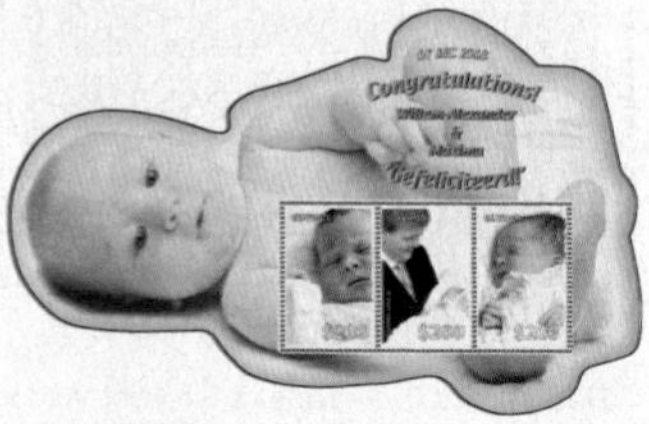


Birth of Princess Catherina Amalia of the Netherlands — A428

No. 3821: a, Princess, one hand shown. b, Princess and father, Prince Willem-Alexander. c, Princess, two hands shown.

**2004, Feb. 15 *Perf. 14¼***

| | | | | | |
|---|---|---|---|---|---|
| **3821** | A428 | $200 | Sheet of 3, #a-c | 7.00 | 7.00 |

FIFA (Fédération Internationale de Football Association), Cent. — A429

World Cup championship teams: No. 3822, $80, Uruguay, 1930. No. 3823, $80, Italy, 1934. No. 3824, $80, Italy, 1938. No. 3825, $80, Uruguay, 1950. No. 3826, $80, Germany, 1954. No. 3827, $80, Brazil, 1958. No. 3828, $80, Brazil, 1962. No. 3829, $80, England, 1966. No. 3830, $80, Brazil, 1970.

**2004, Feb. 16 *Perf. 13¼***

| | | | | | |
|---|---|---|---|---|---|
| **3822-3830** | A429 | | Set of 9 | 8.25 | 8.25 |

Paintings by Norman Rockwell (1894-1978) — A430

No. 3831, vert.: a, Doctor and Doll. b, Babysitter with Screaming Infant. c, Girl with Black Eye. d, Checkup.
$400, Girl Running with Wet Canvas (Wet Paint).

**2004, Feb. 16 *Perf. 14¼***

| | | | | | |
|---|---|---|---|---|---|
| **3831** | A430 | $150 | Sheet of 4, #a-d | 6.75 | 6.75 |

**Souvenir Sheet**

| | | | | | |
|---|---|---|---|---|---|
| **3832** | A430 | $400 | multi | 4.50 | 4.50 |

Paintings by Pablo Picasso (1881-1973) — A431

No. 3833: a, Woman in Yellow Hat. b, Seated Woman, 1962. c, Head of a Woman. d, Large Profile.
$400, Seated Woman, 1971.

**2004, Feb. 16 *Perf. 14¼***

| | | | | | |
|---|---|---|---|---|---|
| **3833** | A431 | $150 | Sheet of 4, #a-d | 6.75 | 6.75 |

***Imperf***

| | | | | | |
|---|---|---|---|---|---|
| **3834** | A431 | $400 | multi | 4.50 | 4.50 |

No. 3833 contains four 38x50mm stamps.

Rembrandt Paintings A432

Designs: $35, A Woman Bathing. $60, Flora. $100, The Poet, Jan Hermansz Krul. $200, Portrait of a Young Man.
No. 3839: a, The Apostle James. b, The Apostle Bartholemew. c, The Evangelist Matthew Inspired by an Angel. d, The Apostle Peter Standing.
$400, Balaam and the Ass.

**2004, Feb. 16 *Perf. 14¼***

| | | | | | |
|---|---|---|---|---|---|
| **3835-3838** | A432 | | Set of 4 | 4.50 | 4.50 |
| **3839** | A432 | $150 | Sheet of 4, #a-d | 6.75 | 6.75 |

**Souvenir Sheet**

| | | | | | |
|---|---|---|---|---|---|
| **3840** | A432 | $400 | multi | 4.75 | 4.75 |

Paintings in the Hermitage, St. Petersburg, Russia — A433

Designs: $35, Mercury Giving Bacchus to Nymphs to Raise, by Laurent de La Hyre. $60, Satyr and Bacchante, by Nicolas Poussin, vert. $100, Parting of Abelard and Eloisa, by Angelica Kauffmann. $200, Pastoral Scene, by François Boucher.
No. 3845, vert.: a, The Union of Earth and Water, by Peter Paul Rubens. b, Hercules Between Love and Wisdom, by Pompeo Girolano Batoni. c, Innocence Choosing Love Over Wealth, by Pierre-Paul Prud'hon. d, Mars and Venus, by Joseph Marie Vien.
No. 3846, Allegory of Virtuous Life, by Hendrik Van Balen. No. 3847, Statue of Ceres, by Rubens, vert.

**2004, Feb. 16 *Perf. 14¼***

| | | | | | |
|---|---|---|---|---|---|
| **3841-3844** | A433 | | Set of 4 | 4.50 | 4.50 |
| **3845** | A433 | $150 | Sheet of 4, #a-d | 7.00 | 7.00 |

***Imperf***

**Size: 77x55mm**

| | | | | | |
|---|---|---|---|---|---|
| **3846** | A433 | $400 | multi | 5.50 | 5.50 |

**Size: 56x77mm**

| | | | | | |
|---|---|---|---|---|---|
| **3847** | A433 | $400 | multi | 5.50 | 5.50 |

**Intl. Year of Mountains Type of 2002**

Designs: $80, Mt. Kosciuszko, Australia. $100, Mt. Elbrus, Russia. $150, Mt. Vinson, Antarctica.
$400, Mt. Everest, Nepal.

**2004 *Perf. 14***

| | | | | | |
|---|---|---|---|---|---|
| **3848-3850** | A398 | | Set of 3 | 3.75 | 3.75 |

**Souvenir Sheet**

| | | | | | |
|---|---|---|---|---|---|
| **3851** | A398 | $400 | multi | 4.50 | 4.50 |

Miniature Sheet

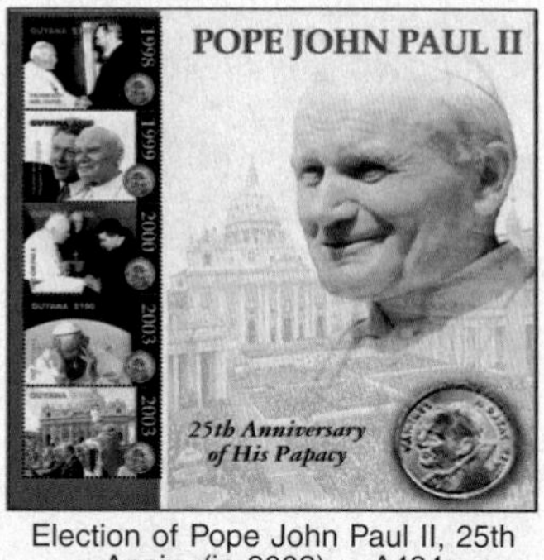


Election of Pope John Paul II, 25th Anniv. (in 2003) — A434

No. 3852: a, With Fidel Castro, 1998. b, With Pres. Bill Clinton, 1999. c, With bishop and man, 2000. d, With hands on head, 2003. e, In Popemobile, 2003.

**2004, Sept. 27 Litho. *Perf. 14***

| | | | | | |
|---|---|---|---|---|---|
| **3852** | A434 | $100 | Sheet of 5, #a-e | 5.75 | 5.75 |

2004 Summer Olympics, Athens A435

Designs: $60, Poster for 1912 Stockholm Olympics. $80, High jump, 1932 Los Angeles Olympics, horiz. $100, Commemorative medal for 1932 Olympics. $200, Ancient Greek runners, horiz.

**2004, Sept. 27 *Perf. 14¼***

| | | | | | |
|---|---|---|---|---|---|
| **3853-3856** | A435 | | Set of 4 | 6.75 | 6.75 |

European Soccer Championships, Portugal — A436

No. 3857, vert.: a, Michel Platini. b, Luis Arconada. c, Bruno Bellone. d, Parc des Princes, Paris.
$400, 1984 France team.

**2004, Sept. 27** **Litho.**

**3857** A436 $150 Sheet of 4, #a-d 8.00 8.00

**Souvenir Sheet**

**3858** A436 $400 multi 5.00 5.00

No. 3857 contains four 28x47mm stamps.

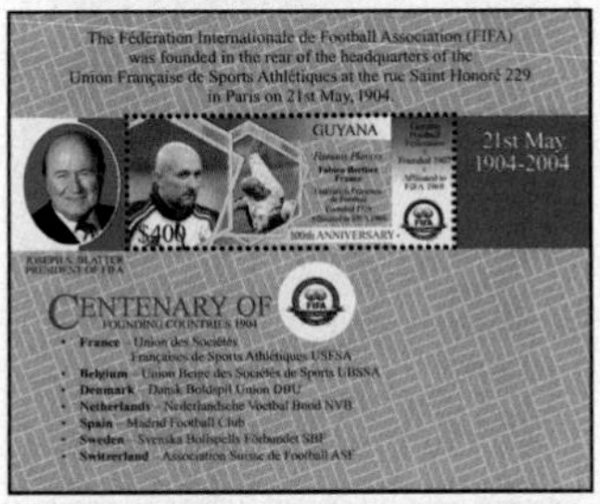


FIFA (Fédération Internationale de Football Association), Cent. — A437

No. 3859: a, Alf Ramsey. b, Pele. c, Lothar Matthaus. d, Dennis Bergkamp.
$400, Fabien Barthez.

**2004, Sept. 27** ***Perf. 12¾x12½***

**3859** A437 $150 Sheet of 4, #a-d 7.00 7.00

**Souvenir Sheet**

**3860** A437 $400 multi 5.00 5.00

A438

D-Day, 60th Anniv. — A439

No. 3861, $150: a, Operation Overlord begins. b, Troops in landing craft storm the beaches of Normandy. c, Troops deep behind enemy lines. d, Churchill announces landings a success.

No. 3862, $150: a, Royal Scots Fusiliers. b, 2nd Company, 101st Heavy Tank Battalion. c, Anti-tank gun of 7th Green Howards. d, 229th Engineer Combat Battalion.

No. 3863, $150, vert.: a, Michael Wittmann. b, Lt. Robert Edlin. c, CSM Stanley Hollis. d, Kurt Meyer.

No. 3864, vert.: a, Rear Admiral John L. Hall. b, Rear Admiral Carlton F. Bryant. c, General Dwight D. Eisenhower. d, General Hap Arnold.

No. 3865, $400, Tank battle, Cotentin Peninsula. No. 3866, $400, Seaforth Highlanders of Canada. No. 3867, $400, Sgt. Clifton Barker. No. 3868, Major General Maxwell D. Taylor.

**2004, Sept. 27** ***Perf. 13½***

**Sheets of 4, #a-d**

**3861-3863** A438 Set of 3 21.00 21.00
**3864** A439 $150 Sheet of 4, #a-d 7.00 7.00

**Souvenir Sheets**

**3865-3867** A438 Set of 3 15.00 15.00
**3868** A439 $400 multi 5.00 5.00

A440

A441

A442

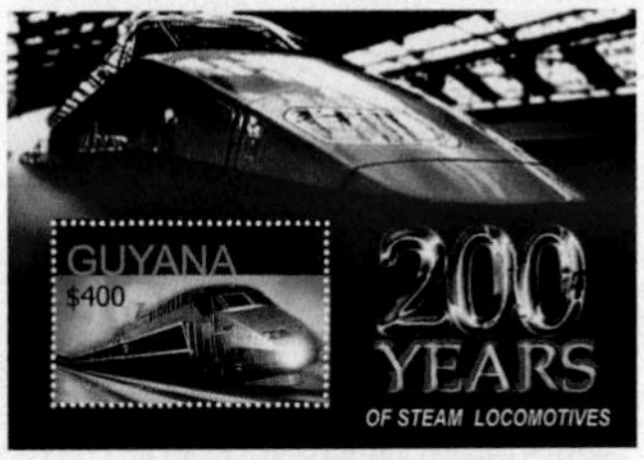


Locomotives — A443

No. 3869: a, Santa Fe Depot. b, LD Porta. c, D9000 Royal Scots Gray. d, TGV.

No. 3870, $150: a, Hercules 4-4-0. b, Sterling 8 ft Single Class 4-2-2. c, Class YP 4-6-2. d, Class 01.10 4-6-2.

No. 3871, $150: a, GWR King Class 4-6-0. b, 4500 Class 4-6-2. c, Class F 4-6-2. d, Class 231C 4-6-2.

No. 3872, $150: a, Western Railway, France, 1856. b, Dutch State Railway, 1880. c, Southern Railway, England, 1890. d, Madras and Southern Mahratta Railway, India, 1891.

No. 3873, $150: a, Baltimore and Ohio Railroad, US, 1856. b, Utica and Schenectady Railroad, US, 1837. c, Great Southern Railway, Spain, 1913. d, Victorian Government Railway, Australia, 1906.

No. 3874, $150: a, Shantung Railway, China, 1919. b, Great Indian Peninsula Railway, 1898. c, Cumberland Valley Railroad, US, 1851. d, Central Pacific Railroad, US, 1863.

No. 3875, $150: a, Great Northern Railway, Ireland, 1876. b, London and Northwestern Railways, 1873. c, Shanghai-Nanking Railway, China, 1910. d, London, Brighton and South Coast Railway, 1846.

No. 3876, $400, No. 990, 4-4-0. No. 3877, $400, Northumbrian 0-2-2, vert.

No. 3878, $400, Netherlands State Railway, 1888. No. 3879, $400, Austrian State Railway, 1868. No. 3880, $400, London, Midland and Scottish Railway, 1923. No. 3881, $400, Pennsylvania Railroad, 1848.

No. 3882, TGV Atlantique.

**2004, Sept. 27** ***Perf. 13½***

**3869** A440 $150 Sheet of 4, #a-d 7.00 7.00

**Sheets of 4, #a-d**

**3870-3871** A441 Set of 2 14.00 14.00
**3872-3875** A442 Set of 4 30.00 30.00

**Souvenir Sheets**

**3876-3877** A441 Set of 2 10.00 10.00
**3878-3881** A442 Set of 4 20.00 20.00
**3882** A443 $400 multi 5.00 5.00

Souvenir Sheet

Deng Xiaoping (1904-97), Chinese Leader — A444

**2004** ***Perf. 14***

**3883** A444 $400 multi 4.75 4.75

South American Reptiles, Fish, Bats and Flowers — A445

No. 3884, $160 — Reptiles: a, Red-foot tortoise. b, Emerald tree boa. c, Green iguana. d, Cuvier's dwarf caiman.

No. 3885, $160 — Fish: a, Velvet cichlid. b, Freshwater sting ray. c, Splash tetra. d, Red piranha.

No. 3886, $160 — Bats: a, Mexican funnel-eared bat. b, Greater bulldog bat. c, Vampire bat. d, Doffroy's tailless bat.

No. 3887, $160, vert. — Flowers: a, Blue passion flower. b, Scarlet passion flower. c, Passion vine. d, Bromeliad flower.

No. 3888, $400, Eyelash viper. No. 3889, $400, Tambaqui, vert. No. 3890, $400, Short-tailed fruit bat, vert. No. 3891, $400, Epiphytic blueberry, vert.

***Perf. 13¼x13½, 13½x13¼***

**2005, Jan. 10** **Litho.**

**Sheets of 4, #a-d**

**3884-3887** A445 Set of 4 36.00 36.00

**Souvenir Sheets**

**3888-3891** A445 Set of 4 19.50 19.50

New Year 2005 (Year of the Rooster) — A446

No. 3892: a, Rooster with dark feathers. b, Rooster with white feathers.

**2005, Jan. 24** ***Perf. 12¾***

**3892** A446 $50 Pair, #a-b 1.40 1.40

Printed in sheets containing two pairs.

Prehistoric Animals — A447

No. 3893, $150: a, Eustreptospondylus. b, Rhamphorhynchus. c, Utahraptor. d, Entelodonts.

No. 3894, $150: a, Moeritherium. b, Deinonychus. c, Ophthalmosaurus. d, Grendelius.

No. 3895, $150: a, Spinosaurus. b, Tarbosaurus. c, Coelophysis. d, Sinosauropteryx prima.

No. 3896, $400, Velociraptor babies. No. 3897, $400, Ophthalmosaurus baby. No. 3898, $400, Iguanodon bernissartensis, vert.

**2005, Jan. 24** **Litho.** ***Perf. 12¾***

**Sheets of 4, #a-d**

**3893-3895** A447 Set of 3 20.00 20.00

**Souvenir Sheets**

**3896-3898** A447 Set of 3 15.00 15.00

Eddy Grant, Musician — A448

Designs: $20, Grant at UR. $80, Grant at UL.

No. 3901 — Portrait in: a, Blue. b, Yellow green. c, Blue violet. d, Red violet.
$400, Grant with guitar.

**2005, Feb. 17** ***Perf. 12¾***

**3899-3900** A448 Set of 2 1.25 1.25
**3901** A448 $190 Sheet of 4, #a-d 9.75 9.75

**Souvenir Sheet**

**3902** A448 $400 multi 4.75 4.75

Pope John Paul II (1920-2005) and Pres. Ronald Reagan (1911-2004) A449

**2005, Aug. 12** **Litho.** ***Perf. 13½***

**3903** A449 $300 multi 3.25 3.25

Battle of Trafalgar, Bicent. A450

Designs: $25, Vice-admiral Cuthbert Collingwood. $35, Admiral Horatio Nelson injured at Battle of Santa Cruz. $60, Nelson's funeral car arriving at St. Paul's Cathedral, horiz. $80, Nelson and Flag Captain Thomas M. Hardy. $100, First shots of Battle of Trafalgar, horiz. $300, British ship hoists signals to begin pincer movement.

$400, Nelson.

**2005, Aug. 12** ***Perf. 13¼***

**3904-3909** A450 Set of 6 6.50 6.50

**Souvenir Sheet**

***Perf. 12***

**3910** A450 $400 multi 5.00 5.00

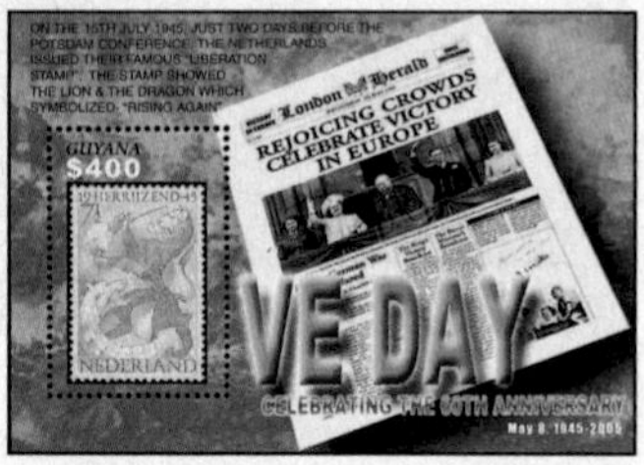


V-E Day, 60th Anniv. — A451

No. 3911, horiz.: a, Neville Chamberlain makes peace with Adolf Hitler, 1938. b, The Royal Air Force hits back. c, Victory, 1945.

$400, Netherlands #277.

**2005, Aug. 12** ***Perf. 12¾***

**3911** A451 $200 Sheet of 3, #a-c 7.25 7.25

**Souvenir Sheet**

**3912** A451 $400 multi 5.00 5.00

V-J Day, 60th Anniv. — A452

No. 3913: a, Japan attacks Pearl Harbor, 1941. b, Iwo Jima War Memorial, Harlington, Texas. c, Newspaper announcing Japanese surrender, 1945.

$400, Seebees celebrate Japanese surrender.

**2005, Aug. 12**

**3913** A452 $200 Sheet of 3, #a-c 7.25 7.25

**Souvenir Sheet**

**3914** A452 $400 multi 5.00 5.00

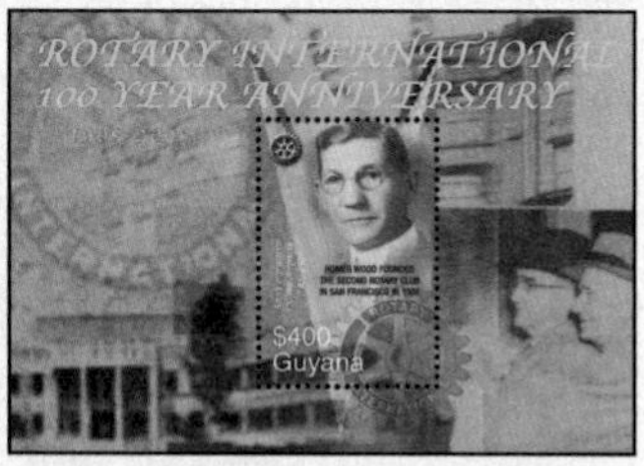


Rotary International, Cent. — A453

No. 3915: a, Dentist examining patient's mouth. b, 2005 Rotary President-elect Carl-Wilhelm Stenhammar. c, Rotary District of Guyana first couple.

$400, Homer Wood, founder of second Rotary Club.

**2005, Aug. 12**

**3915** A453 $150 Sheet of 3, #a-c 6.25 6.25

**Souvenir Sheet**

**3916** A453 $400 multi 4.75 4.75

Friedrich von Schiller (1759-1805), Writer — A454

Designs: $400, Schiller and Ludwig van Beethoven.

No. 3918: a, Schiller. b, Schiller and his house. c, Beethoven.

**2005, Aug. 12**

**3917** A454 $400 multi 4.75 4.75

**Souvenir Sheet**

**3918** A454 $200 Sheet of 3, #a-c 7.00 7.10

No. 3918 contains three 42x28mm stamps.

Hans Christian Andersen (1805-75), Author — A455

No. 3919: a, The Traveling Companion. b, The Shadow. c, The Drop of Water.

$400, The Emperor's New Suit.

**2005, Aug. 12** ***Perf. 12¾***

**3919** A455 $200 Sheet of 3, #a-c 7.00 7.00

**Souvenir Sheet**

***Perf. 12***

**3920** A455 $400 multi 4.75 4.75

No. 3919 contains three 42x28mm stamps.

Jules Verne (1828-1905), Writer — A456

No. 3921, vert.: a, Verne. b, Book illustration. c, Space capsule as imagined by Verne. d, Space capsule.

$400, Man on the Moon.

**2005, Aug. 12** ***Perf. 12¾***

**3921** A456 $150 Sheet of 4, #a-d 6.50 6.50

**Souvenir Sheet**

**3922** A456 $400 multi 5.00 5.00

World Cup Soccer Championships, 75th Anniv. — A457

No. 3923: a, 1954 Germany team. b, Final goal in 1954 German victory over Hungary. c, Wankdorf Stadium. d, Helmut Rahn.

$400, German players celebrating victory.

**2005, Aug. 12** ***Perf. 12***

**3923** A457 $150 Sheet of 4, #a-d 8.00 8.00

**Souvenir Sheet**

**3924** A457 $400 multi 4.75 4.75

Space — A458

No. 3925: a, Luna 9 in space. b, Luna 9 capsule. c, Oceanus Procellarum region of Moon. d, Sergei Korolev. e, First images of the Moon. f, Launch of Molniya 8K78M rocket.

No. 3926, $200: a, Space Shuttle Discovery docked with International Space Station Destiny Laboratory, b, Astronaut Stephen K. Robinson attached to Canadarm 2. c, View of Discovery during docking operation. d, Discovery and stairway truck.

No. 3927, $200, vert.: a, First launch of Space Shuttle Columbia. b, Astronaut Robert C. Crippen. c, Astronaut John W. Young. d, Mission control.

No. 3928, $200, vert.: a, Launch vehicle MV-5 rocket. b, Hayabusa satellite. c, Composite color image of Itokawa asteroid. d, Projected return to Earth of satellite.

No. 3929, $400, Venus Express. No. 3930, $400, Lunar Reconnaissance Orbiter. No. 3931, $400, Calipso satellite. No. 3932, $400, Hayabusa satellite over Itokawa asteroid.

**2006** **Litho.** ***Perf. 14***

**3925** A458 $160 Sheet of 6, #a-f 12.50 12.50

**Sheets of 4, #a-d**

**3926-3928** A458 Set of 3 28.00 28.00

**Souvenir Sheets**

**3929-3932** A458 Set of 4 17.00 17.00

Issued: Nos. 3925, 3926, 3930, 7/10, Nos. 3928, 3932, 7/27.

Souvenir Sheet

"Penny Magenta" Stamp, 150th Anniv. — A459

**2006, July 27** ***Perf. 12x11½***

**3933** A459 $400 multi 4.50 4.50

Souvenir Sheet

Christopher Columbus (1451-1506), Explorer — A460

No. 3934: a, Nina. b, Pinta. c, Santa Maria.

**2006, July 27** ***Perf. 13¼***

**3934** A460 $300 Sheet of 3, #a-c 11.00 11.00

Airships — A461

No. 3935: a, De Beers Zeppelin NT. b, Lockheed Martin LTA 2004. c, Strattelite concept airship.

$400, Skybus Airship.

**2006, July 27** ***Perf. 13¼***

**3935** A461 $200 Sheet of 3, #a-c 7.25 7.25

**Souvenir Sheet**

**3936** A461 $400 multi 4.50 4.50

Rembrandt (1606-69), Painter — A462

No. 3937 — Details from The Music Makers: a, Man with viola. b, Woman with shawl. c, Man with harp. d, Woman with tiara.

$400, Old Man with a Jewelled Cross.

**2006, July 27** ***Perf. 13¼***

**3937** A462 $160 Sheet of 4, #a-d 8.25 8.25

***Imperf***

**3938** A462 $400 shown 4.50 4.50

No. 3937 contains four 37x50mm stamps.

Queen Elizabeth II, 80th Birthday — A463

No. 3939: a, Queen and Guyana Parliament Building. b, Queen wearing black and white hat.

$400, Queen and flags of Guyana and Great Britain.

**2006, July 27** ***Perf. 13¼***

**3939** A463 $200 Pair, #a-b 4.50 4.50

**Souvenir Sheet**

**3940** A463 $400 multi 5.25 5.25

No. 3939 printed in sheets containing two pairs.

Souvenir Sheet

2006 World Cup Soccer Championships, Germany — A464

No. 3941 — 2006 World Cup emblem, World Cup and: a, $80, Man in Japanese clothing. b, $100, Kemari players. c, $160, Tsu chu players. d, $300, People's Republic of China #2073.

**2006, Sept. 14 Litho. *Perf. 13¼***
**3941** A464 Sheet of 4, #a-d 7.00 7.00

Betty Boop — A465

No. 3942, vert.: a, With top hat and cane. b, Holding mirror. c, Holding flower bouquet. d, In city. e, At microphone. f, Lifting dress.
No. 3943: a, Sitting with legs crossed. b, In car.

**2006, Dec. 14 Litho. *Perf. 14***
**3942** A465 $100 Sheet of 6, #a-f 6.50 6.50

**Souvenir Sheet**

**3943** A465 $200 Sheet of 2, #a-b 4.25 4.25

Marilyn Monroe (1926-62), Actress — A466

No. 3944: a, Wearing beret. b, Wearing red dress, horizontal post at both sides of neck. c, Wearing red dress, horizontal post at left of neck. d, With eyes closed.
$400, With eyes partially closed.

**2007, Feb. 15 *Perf. 13¼***
**3944** A466 $200 Sheet of 4, #a-d 8.00 8.00

**Souvenir Sheet**

**3945** A466 $400 multi 4.00 4.00

Dogs — A467

No. 3946: a, Papillon. b, Dogue de Bordeaux. c, Cavalier King Charles spaniel. d, Neapolitan mastiff.
$400, Basset hound.

**2007, Feb. 15 *Perf. 14***
**3946** A467 $160 Sheet of 4, #a-d 6.50 6.50

**Souvenir Sheet**

**3947** A467 $400 multi 4.00 4.00

Cats A468

Designs: $25, Chartreux. $35, Seal snowshoe. $60, Maine coon cat. $300, Turkish Angora.
$400, Blue Burmese, vert.

**2007, Feb. 15**
**3948-3951** A468 Set of 4 4.25 4.25

**Souvenir Sheet**

**3952** A468 $400 multi 4.00 4.00

Birds A469

Designs: $25, Summer tanager. $35, Gray-cheeked thrush. $60, Blackpoll warbler. $300, Thick-billed parrot.
No. 3957, vert.: a, Golden-tailed warbler. b, Blue-crowned parakeet. c, White-winged parakeet. d, Yellow-green vireo.
No. 3958, $400, Pacific golden plover, vert. No. 3959, $400, Bobolink, vert.

**2007, Feb. 15**
**3953-3956** A469 Set of 4 4.25 4.25
**3957** A469 $160 Sheet of 4, #a-d 6.50 6.50

**Souvenir Sheets**

**3958-3959** A469 Set of 2 8.00 8.00

For overprint, see No. 4025.

Butterflies A470

Designs: $25, Morpho vitrea. $35, Rothschildia hesperus. $60, Anaea nessus. $300, Dryas iulia.
No. 3964: a, Callithea sapphira. b, Prepona buckleyana. c, Lycorea pasinutia. d, Danaus eresimus.
No. 3965, $400, Cithaerias aurorina. No. 3966, $400, Eurytides protesilaus.

**2007, Feb. 15**
**3960-3963** A470 Set of 4 4.25 4.25
**3964** A470 $160 Sheet of 4, #a-d 6.50 6.50

**Souvenir Sheets**

**3965-3966** A470 Set of 2 8.00 8.00

Orchids — A471

Designs: $25, Bletia florida. $35, Basiphyllaea corallicola. $60, Calopogon multiflorus. $300, Bletia purpurea.
No. 3971: a, Cypripedium acaule. b, Calopogon tuberosus. c, Calopogon pallidus. d, Bletia patula.
$400, Cypripedium reginae.

**2007, Feb. 15**
**3967-3970** A471 Set of 4 4.25 4.25
**3971** A471 $160 Sheet of 4, #a-d 6.50 6.50

**Souvenir Sheet**

**3972** A471 $400 multi 4.00 4.00

Souvenir Sheet

New Year 2007 (Year of the Pig) — A472

No. 3973 — Pig at: a, $55, Right. b, $80, Left. c, $100, Right. d, $160, Left.

**2007, Mar. 21 *Perf. 13¼***
**3973** A472 Sheet of 4, #a-d 4.00 4.00

Souvenir Sheet

Wolfgang Amadeus Mozart (1756-91), Composer — A473

No. 3974 — Mozart: a, In 1770. b, In 1762. c, Circa 1789. d, Portrait by Joseph Grassi.

**2007, Mar. 21**
**3974** A473 $190 Sheet of 4, #a-d 7.50 7.50

Scouting, Cent. — A474

No. 3975, horiz.: a, Lord Robert Baden-Powell and dove. b, Scouts on raft. c, Scouts pulling tug-of-war rope.
$400, Dove and hand of Baden-Powell.

**2007, Mar. 21**
**3975** A474 $180 Sheet of 3, #a-c 5.50 5.50

**Souvenir Sheet**

**3976** A474 $400 multi 4.00 4.00

Souvenir Sheets

Pres. John F. Kennedy (1917-63) — A475

No. 3977: a, $80, Taking oath of office. b, $100, Giving inaugural speech. c, $160, Portrait. d, $190, With wife at inaugural ball.
No. 3978: a, $80, Peace Corps. b, $100, Space program. c, $160, Civil rights. d, $190, Portrait, diff.

**2007, Mar. 21 *Perf. 13¼***

**Sheets of 4, #a-d**

**3977-3978** A475 Set of 2 10.50 10.50

Elvis Presley (1935-77) — A476

No. 3979, $160: a, Wearing glasses, blue panel at top. b, Without glasses, red background.
No. 3980, $160: a, With glasses, orange panel at bottom. b, With glasses, red background.

**2007, Mar. 21 *Perf. 14***

**Pairs, #a-b**

**3979-3980** A476 Set of 2 6.50 6.50

Nos. 3979-3980 each were printed in sheets containing two pairs.

2007 Cricket World Cup, West Indies — A477

Designs: $100, Cricket World Cup emblem, map and flag of Guyana. $200, Guyana cricket team, horiz.
$500, Cricket World Cup emblem.

**2007, Mar. 28** ***Perf. 13¼***
**3981-3982** A477 Set of 2 3.00 3.00

**Souvenir Sheet**

**3983** A477 $500 multi 5.00 5.00

A478

Pope Benedict XVI — A479

**2007, Apr. 17** **Litho.** ***Perf. 13¼***
**3984** A478 $80 multi .80 .80

**Litho. & Embossed**
***Serpentine Die Cut***
**Without Gum**

**3985** A479 $1500 multi 15.00 15.00

No. 3984 was printed in sheets of 8.

Concorde
A480

No. 3986, $100: a, Concorde Prototype 002 and towing vehicle. b, Concorde Prototype 002 and stairway.
No. 3987, $100: a, Concorde and Royal Air Force Red Arrows. b, Concorde, Red Arrows and Queen Elizabeth 2.

**2007, Apr. 17** **Litho.** ***Perf. 13¼***
**Pairs, #a-b**

**3986-3987** A480 Set of 2 4.00 4.00

Nos. 3986-3987 were each printed in sheets containing 3 pairs.

Miniature Sheet

2008 Summer Olympics, Beijing — A481

No. 3988: a, Field hockey. b, Basketball. c, Judo. d, Shooting.

**2008, Apr. 22** **Litho.** ***Perf. 13¼x13***
**3988** A481 $100 Sheet of 4, #a-d 4.00 4.00

10th Caribbean Festival of Arts — A482

Map in: $20, Yellow and white, frame in red. $55, White, frame in green. $80, Yellow and white, frame in blue green. $160, Green, frame in white and yellow.

**2008, Aug. 19** ***Perf. 14¼***
**3989-3992** A482 Set of 4 3.25 3.25

Jesuits in Guyana, 150th Anniv. A483

Designs: $80, St. Stanislaus College. $100, Sacred Heart Church. $160, Father Cuthbert Cary-Elwes, missionary, and indigenous people.

**2008. Aug. 25** **Litho.** ***Perf. 13x13¼***
**3993-3995** A483 Set of 3 3.50 3.50

Souvenir Sheet

Sir James Douglas (1803-77), First Governor of British Columbia — A484

**2008, Aug. 25** ***Perf. 13¼***
**3996** A484 $160 multi 1.60 1.60

Peony
A485

**2009, Apr. 10** **Litho.**
**3997** A485 $80 multi .80 .80

Printed in sheets of 8.

Miniature Sheet

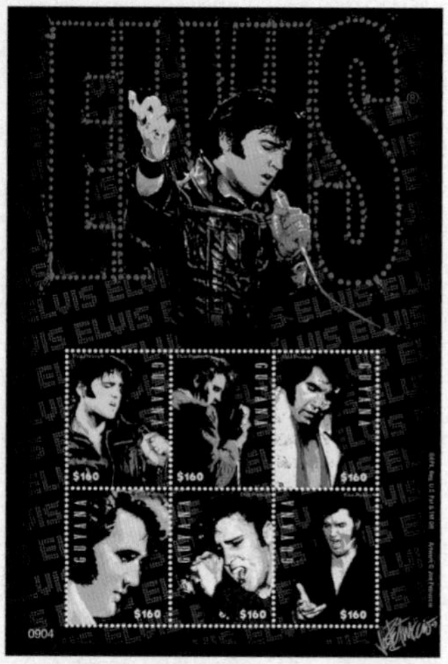

Elvis Presley (1935-77) — A486

No. 3998 — Presley with: a, Red and blue jacket, bright yellow face, holding microphone. b, Brown jacket, holding microphone. c, White jacket and red shirt. d, Tan and white shirt. e, Gray face, holding microphone. f, With hand open.

**2009, July 7** ***Perf. 12***
**3998** A486 $160 Sheet of 6, #a-f 9.50 9.50

Miniature Sheet

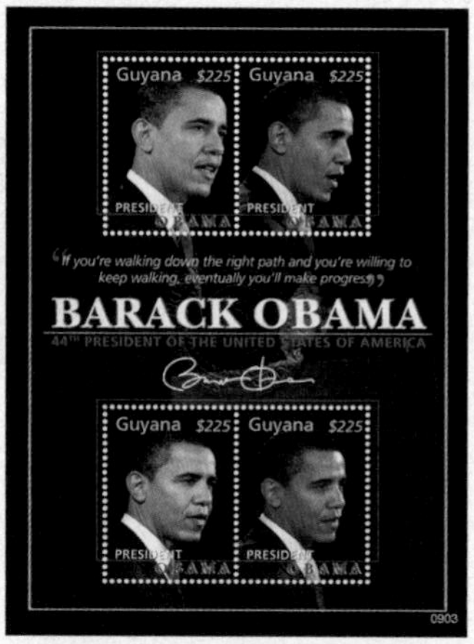


US Pres. Barack Obama — A487

No. 3999 — Pres. Obama with: a, Gray tie, with "O" on jacket and shirt collar and "B" on shirt collar and tie. b, Gray tie, with "O" on jacket and shirt collar and "B" on tie and jacket. c, Red tie. d, Gray tie, with "O" on jacket and "B" on tie and shirt collar.

**2009, July 7**
**3999** A487 $225 Sheet of 4, #a-d 9.00 9.00

Miniature Sheet

China 2009 World Stamp Exhibition, Luoyang — A488

No. 4000 — Unnamed works of art by Wang Hui (1632-1717): a, Flowers. b, Mountain at right. c, Mountain at left in clouds, part of show emblem at LR. d, Mountain in center, part of show emblem at LL.

**2009, Apr. 10** **Litho.** ***Perf. 12***
**4000** A488 $100 Sheet of 4, #a-d 4.00 4.00

Miniature Sheet

Georgetown Rotary Club, 50th Anniv. — A489

No. 4001 — Map of Guyana, Rotary International emblem and: a, $80, 50th anniversary commemorative magazine. b, $80, Santa Claus visiting the elderly. c, $160, Poster showing people in wheelchairs. d, $160, Man and boy in front of canopy.

**2009, July 22** ***Perf. 11½***
**4001** A489 Sheet of 4, #a-d 4.75 4.75

Miniature Sheet

Ferrari Race Cars — A490

No. 4002: a, 1952 500 F2. b, 1953, 500 F2. c, 1958, 246 F1. d, 1976 312 T2.

**2009, July 22** ***Perf. 14¼***
**4002** A490 $200 Sheet of 4, #a-d 8.00 8.00

Souvenir Sheet

Takutu Bridge — A491

**2009, Sept. 14** ***Perf. 13¼***
**4003** A491 $400 multi 4.00 4.00

Scouting
A492

Designs: No. 4004, $55, Parade for Guyana Scouting centenary. No. 4005, $55, Scout shooting arrow at 14th Caribbean Jamboree, vert. No. 4006, $80, Scout leader, Scout and tent. No. 4007, $80, Scouts lashing logs together. No. 4008, $160, Guyana Scouting Centenary emblem. No. 4009, $160, Emblem of 14th Caribbean Jamboree.

***Perf. 14¾x14, 14x14¾***

**2009, Sept. 29**
**4004-4009** A492 Set of 6 5.75 5.75

Miniature Sheets

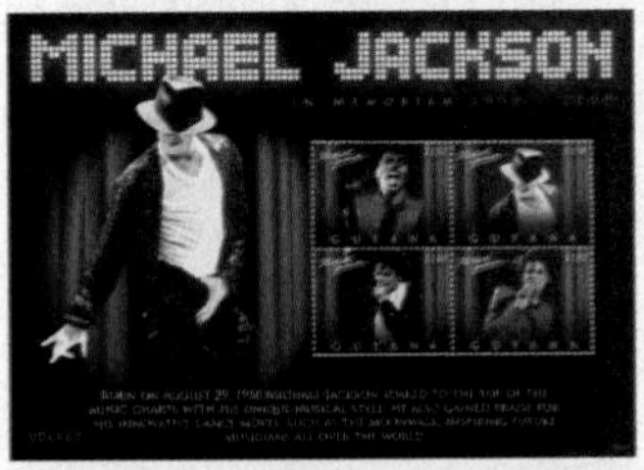


A493

Michael Jackson (1958-2009), Singer — A494

No. 4010: a, Wearing jacket with red collar. b, Wearing hat. c, Wearing black jacket, with microphone at mouth. d, Wearing red and black shirt, with microphone at mouth.

No. 4011: a, Facing forward, with microphone at mouth. b, Facing right, with microphone at waist. c, Facing left, with microphone at mouth. d, Facing forward with arms at side, with microphone at waist.

**2009, Oct. 9** ***Perf. 11½x11¼***

**4010** A493 $180 Sheet of 4, #a-d 7.25 7.25

***Perf. 11¼x11½***

**4011** A494 $180 Sheet of 4, #a-d 7.25 7.25

Miniature Sheets

Teams in 2009 National Basketball Association Finals — A495

No. 4012, $90 — Los Angeles Lakers: a, Trevor Ariza. b, Shannon Brown. c, Jordan Farmar. d, Andrew Bynum. e, Kobe Bryant. f, Derek Fisher. g, Pau Gasol. h, Lamar Odom. i, Luke Walton.

No. 4013, $90 — Orlando Magic: a. Rafer Alston. b, Marcin Gortat. c, Rashard Lewis. d, Courtney Lee. e, Dwight Howard. f, Jameer Nelson. g, Mickael Pietrus. h, J. J. Redick. i, Hedo Türkoglu.

**2009, Oct. 9** ***Perf. 14¼***

**Sheets of 9, #a-i**

**4012-4013** A495 Set of 2 16.00 16.00

British Commonwealth, 60th Anniv. — A496

**2009, Nov. 25 Litho.** ***Perf. 12x11½***

**4014** A496 $60 multi .60 .60

Printed in sheets of 6.

Miniature Sheet

National Library, Cent. — A497

No. 4015: a, Building exterior, black and white photograph. b, Building exterior, color photograph. c, Interior, color photograph. d, Interior, black and white photograph.

**2009, Dec. 15** ***Perf. 11½x12***

**4015** A497 $100 Sheet of 4, #a-d 4.00 4.00

Chinese Aviation, Cent. — A498

No. 4016: a, J-8II. b, J-11. c, J-10 with landing gear visible. d, J-10 with landing gear retracted.

$100, J-10, diff.

**2009, Dec. 15** ***Perf. 14***

**4016** A498 $150 Sheet of 4, #a-d 6.00 6.00

**Souvenir Sheet**

***Perf. 14¼***

**4017** A498 $100 multi 1.00 1.00

Aeropex 2009, Beijing. No. 4016 contains four 42x28mm stamps.

Pope Benedict XVI and Pope John Paul II — A499

No. 4018 — Pope Benedict XVI (while Cardinal) and Pope John Paul II with: a, Part of dome of St. Peter's Basilica at LL. b, Upper section of Basilica entablature at bottom. c, Columns of Basilica at bottom, with dark grayish yellow area next to denomination. d, As "c," with smaller light grayish yellow area next to denomination.

No. 4019: a, Pope Benedict XVI (while Cardinal). b, Pope John Paul II.

**2009, Dec. 15** ***Perf. 11½***

**4018** A499 $200 Sheet of 4, #a-d 8.00 8.00

**Souvenir Sheet**

***Perf. 11½x12***

**4019** A499 $400 Sheet of 2, #a-b 8.00 8.00

Miniature Sheet

Chinese Zodiac Animals — A500

No. 4020: a, Rat. b, Ox. c, Tiger. d, Rabbit. e, Dragon. f, Snake. g, Horse. h, Ram. i, Monkey. j, Cock. k, Dog. l, Pig.

**2010, Jan. 4** ***Perf. 12***

**4020** A500 $45 Sheet of 12, #a-l 5.25 5.25

No. 661 Srchd.

**Method, Perf and Watermark As Before**

**2010**

**4020J** A85 $20 on 30c #661 —

Obliterator is a marker line over old denomination.

Nos. 2316, 2363, 2932, 2935 and 2942A Handstamped Surcharged in Violet Black

**Methods, Perfs and Watermarks As Before**

**2010**

**4020K** A215 $20 on $6 #2932 — —

**4020L** A215a $20 on $6 #2942A — —

**4020M** A125 $20 on $8.90 #2316 —

**4020N** A129 $20 on $17.80 #2363 — —

**4020O** A215 $20 on $19 #2935 — —

Obliterators are marker lines over old denominations.

No. 2942A Surcharged

**2010 Method and Perf As Before**

**4020P** A215a $20 on $6 #2942A — —

Obliterator is a printed rectangle, which was augmented with a marker line when the rectangle missed the old denomination.

Miniature Sheet

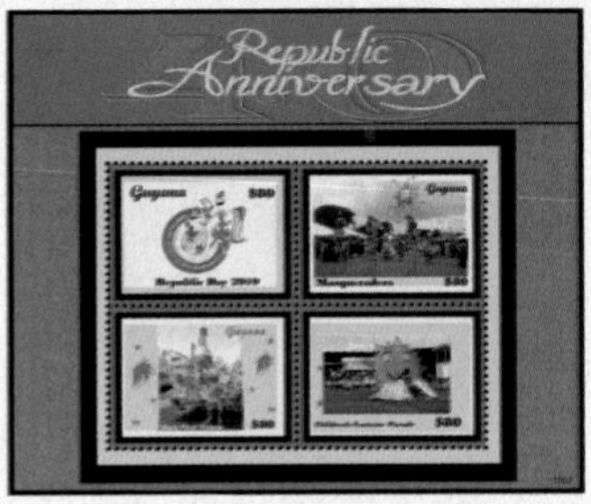


Republic of Guyana, 40th Anniv. — A501

No. 4021: a, 2010 Republic Day emblem. b, Masqueraders. c, Mash float parade. d, Children's costume parade.

**2010, Mar. 17** ***Perf. 11½x12***

**4021** A501 $80 Sheet of 4, #a-d 3.25 3.25

Personalizable Stamp — A502

**2010, Apr. 26 Litho.** ***Perf. 14¾x14***

**4022** A502 $160 gray & black 1.60 1.60

The image shown is generic. No. 4022 was available in sheets of 12 without any image ("Guyana $160" only), and vignette portions could be personalized.

Pope Benedict XVI — A503

**Litho. & Embossed**

**2010, Apr. 26** ***Die Cut Perf. 8½***

**Without Gum**

**4023** A503 $2000 multi 20.00 20.00

Souvenir Sheet

Presidents of the United States and People's Republic of China — A504

No. 4024: a, Pres. Barack Obama. b, Pres. Hu Jintao.

**2010, Apr. 26 Litho.** ***Perf. 11½***

**4024** A504 $300 Sheet of 2, #a-b 6.00 6.00

**No. 3957 Overprinted**
Miniature Sheet

**Methods and Perfs As Before**

**2010, Apr. 26**

**4025** A469 $160 Sheet of 4, #a-d 6.25 6.25

Miniature Sheets

Princess Diana (1961-97) — A505

No. 4026, $225 — Diana wearing: a, Tiara. b, Red and black hat. c, Blouse with red collar and cuffs. d, Sailor's hat.

No. 4027, $225 — Diana wearing: a, Black hat. b, Beige hat. c, White dress. d, Blue hat.

**2010, Apr. 26** **Litho.** ***Perf. 12***

**Sheets of 4, #a-d**

**4026-4027** A505 Set of 2 18.00 18.00

Souvenir Sheets

A506

A507

A508

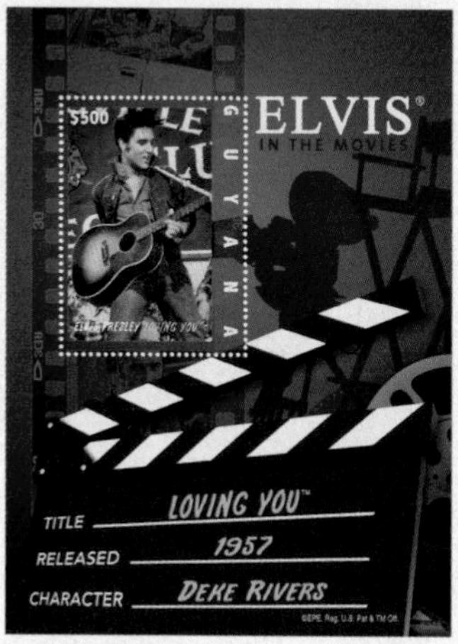


Elvis Presley (1935-77) — A509

**2010, Apr. 26** ***Perf. 13¼***

| | | | | |
|---|---|---|---|---|
| **4028** | A506 $500 multi | | 5.00 | 5.00 |
| **4029** | A507 $500 multi | | 5.00 | 5.00 |
| **4030** | A508 $500 multi | | 5.00 | 5.00 |
| **4031** | A509 $500 multi | | 5.00 | 5.00 |
| | *Nos. 4028-4031 (4)* | | 20.00 | 20.00 |

Souvenir Sheet

New Year 2010 (Year of the Tiger) — A510

No. 4032 — Tiger with denomination in: a, Green. b, White.

**2010, Jan. 4** **Litho.** ***Perf. 12***

**4032** A510 $450 Sheet of 2, #a-b 9.00 9.00

Girl Guides, Cent. — A511

No. 4033, horiz.: a, Three Girl Guides wearing rabbit ears. b, Two Girl Guides. c, Three Girl Guides wearing blue uniforms. d, Four Girl Guides holding rope.

$450, Girl Guide saluting.

**2010, July 14** ***Perf. 11½x12***

**4033** A511 $275 Sheet of 4, #a-d 11.00 11.00

**Souvenir Sheet**

***Perf. 11¼x11½***

**4034** A511 $450 multi 4.50 4.50

Miniature Sheet

Winning Entries In Children's Postage Stamp Design Contest — A512

No. 4035 — Slogan: a, Don't Be a Joker - Drugs Kill. b, The Right Not to be Mistreated. c, The Right to Live With a Family. d, Your Right Not to Witness Domestic Violence.

**2010, Sept. 2** ***Perf. 12***

**4035** A512 $100 Sheet of 4, #a-d 4.00 4.00

Miniature Sheet

Porkknocker Day, 10th Anniv. — A513

No. 4036: a, Map of area near Bartica. b, Cyrilda de Jesus, female porkknocker (miner). c, Dick Manning, male porkknocker. d, Mazaruni diamonds and gold nuggets.

**2010, Oct. 14**

**4036** A513 $100 Sheet of 4, #a-d 4.00 4.00

2010 World Cup Soccer Championships, South Africa — A514

No. 4037, $120: a, Joan Capdevila. b, Arjen Robben. c, Pedro. d, Gregory Van Der Wiel. e, Xabi Alonso. f, Wesley Sneijder.

No. 4038, $120: a, Dennis Aogo. b, Diego Forlan. c, Bastian Schweinsteiger. d, Martin Caceres. e, Stefan Kiessling. f, Maximiliano Pereira.

No. 4039, $550, Andres Iniesta. No. 4040, $550, Thomas Mueller.

**2011, Feb. 21** **Litho.** ***Perf. 12***

**Sheets of 6, #a-f**

**4037-4038** A514 Set of 2 14.00 14.00

**Souvenir Sheets**

**4039-4040** A514 Set of 2 11.00 11.00

Miniature Sheets

Qin Shi Huang (259 B.C-210 B.C), First Emperor of China — A515

Deng Xiaoping (1904-97), Paramount Leader of People's Republic of China — A516

Jiang Zemin, President of People's Republic of China, 1993-2003 — A517

No. 4041: a, 21x22mm painting of Qin Shi Huang. b, Sculpture. c, 16x28 painting of Qin Shi Huang. d, Text.

No. 4042: Various photographs of Deng Xiaoping, as shown.

No. 4043: Various photographs of Jiang Zemin, as shown.

**2011, Feb. 21**

| | | | | |
|---|---|---|---|---|
| **4041** | A515 $150 Sheet of 4, #a-d | | 6.00 | 6.00 |
| **4042** | A516 $150 Sheet of 4, #a-d | | 6.00 | 6.00 |
| **4043** | A517 $150 Sheet of 4, #a-d | | 6.00 | 6.00 |
| | *Nos. 4041-4043 (3)* | | 18.00 | 18.00 |

Beijing 2010 Intl. Stamp Exhibition.

Souvenir Sheet

New Year 2011 (Year of the Rabbit) — A518

No. 4044 — Rabbit: a, Leaping. b, Sitting.

**2011, Feb. 21 Litho. *Perf. 12***
**4044** A518 $200 Sheet of 2, #a-b 4.00 4.00

Christmas 2010 — A519

Paintings: $80, The Adoration of the Magi, by Hieronymus Bosch. $100, The Adoration of the Magi, by Peter Paul Rubens. $225, Madonna and Child, by Carlo Crivelli. $500, The Flight into Egypt, by Lucas Cranach the Elder.

**2011, Mar. 9 Litho. *Perf. 12¾x12½***
**4045-4048** A519 Set of 4 9.00 9.00

Miniature Sheets

A520

Pope John Paul II (1920-2005) — A521

No. 4049: With "G" of "Guyana" on Papal Arms: a, Orange denomination, wearing vestments without clerical collar. b, Wearing white vestments and zucchetto. c, Wearing miter. d, Orange denomination, wearing vestments with clerical collar.

No. 4050: With "G" of Guyana to right of Papal Arms: a, Black denomination, praying. b, Wearing white vestments. c, Holding crucifix. d, White denomination, praying.

**2011, Mar. 9 *Perf. 13x13¼***
**4049** A520 $225 Sheet of 4, #a-d 9.00 9.00
**4050** A521 $225 Sheet of 4, #a-d 9.00 9.00

Text on Nos. 4049a-4049d is incorrectly placed on stamps.

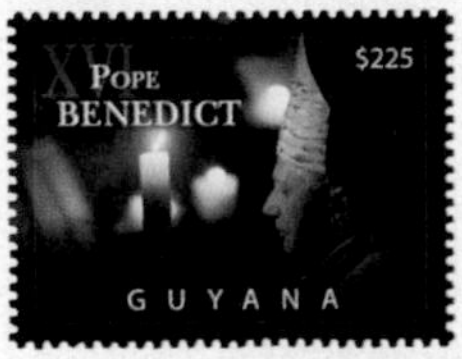


A522

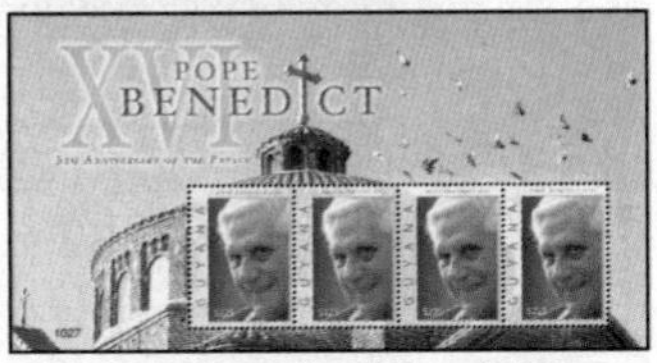


Pope Benedict XVI — A523

No. 4052: a, Blue sky at UL. b, Blue sky at UR. c, Part of bird above "XVI." d, Birds above "N" and last "A" in "Guyana."

**2011, Mar. 9 *Perf. 13x13¼***
**4051** A522 $225 multi 2.25 2.25

***Perf. 12***

**4052** A523 $225 Sheet of 4, #a-d 9.00 9.00

Souvenir Sheets

Popes and Their Coats of Arms — A524

No. 4053, $725: a, Pope Benedict XV (1854-1922). b, Arms of Pope Benedict XV.

No. 4054, $725: a, Pope Pius XI (1857-1939). b, Arms of Pope Pius XI.

**2011, Mar. 9 Litho. *Imperf.***
**Sheets of 2, #a-b**
**Without Gum**
**4053-4054** A524 Set of 2 29.00 29.00

Miniature Sheets

Intl. Year of Astronomy (in 2009) — A525

No. 4055, $225: a, UNITEC-1. b, IKAROS. c, KSAT Negai. d, Waseda-sat 2.

No. 4056, $255: a, Phobos-Grunt arrival. b, Phobos-Grunt landing. c, Mars Reconnaissance Orbiter. d, Phobos-Grunt liftoff.

**2011, Mar. 9 Litho. *Perf. 13x13¼***
**Sheets of 4, #a-d**
**4055-4056** A525 Set of 2 19.00 19.00

A526

U.S. Pres. Abraham Lincoln (1809-65) — A527

No. 4057 — Lincoln: a, With beard. b, Without beard.

No. 4058 — Background color above shoulder at right: a, Gray. b, Pink. c, Greenish gray. d, Lilac.

**2011, Mar. 9 Litho. *Perf. 13¼x13***
**4057** A526 $225 Pair, #a-b 4.50 4.50

***Perf. 12½***

**4058** A527 $225 Sheet of 4, #a-d 9.00 9.00

No. 4057 was printed in sheets containing two pairs.

Miniature Sheets

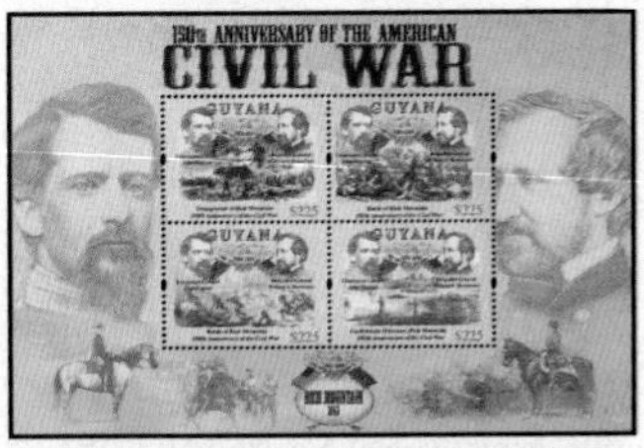


United States Civil War, 150th Anniv. — A528

No. 4059, $225 — Eagle, shield, Union and Confederate flags, Lieutenant Colonel John Pegram and Brigadier General William S. Rosecrans of Battle of Rich Mountain, July 11, 1861, and: a, Engagement at Rich Mountain. b, Battle of Rich Mountain (purple vignette). c, Battle of Rich Mountain (red brown vignette). d, Confederate prisoners.

No. 4060, $225 — Eagle, shield, Union and Confederate flags, Brigadier General James Longstreet and General Daniel Tyler of Battle of Blackburn's Ford, July 18, 1861, and: a, Blackburn's Ford. b, Members of Longstreet's brigade. c, Fairfax County Courthouse. d, Battle of Blackburn's Ford.

No. 4061, $225 — Eagle, shield, Union and Confederate flags, Brigadier General Joseph E. Johnston and Brigadier General Irvin McDowell of First Battle of Bull Run, July 21, 1861, and: a, First Battle of Bull Run. b, Confederate fortifications, Manassas. c, Union charge at Bull Run. d, Henry House in ruins.

**2011, Apr. 4 *Perf. 13 Syncopated***
**Sheets of 4, #a-d**
**4059-4061** A528 Set of 3 27.00 27.00

Engagement of Prince William and Catherine Middleton A529

Designs: No. 4062, Couple (black-and-white photo).

No. 4063 — Color photographs: a, Couple holding hands. b, Couple, Middleton wearing hat. c, Middleton. d, Prince William.

No. 4064 — Black-and-white photographs: a, Prince William. b, Middleton.

$450, Couple, Middleton at left.

**2011, Apr. 4 *Perf. 12***
**4062** A529 $200 multi 2.00 2.00
**4063** A529 $200 Sheet of 4, #a-d 8.00 8.00

**Souvenir Sheets**

***Perf. 13 Syncopated***

**4064** A529 $225 Sheet of 2, #a-b 4.50 4.50
**4065** A529 $450 multi 4.50 4.50

No. 4062 was printed in sheets of 4.

Mother Teresa (1910-97), Humanitarian A530

**2011, Apr. 4 *Perf. 12***
**4066** A530 $225 multi 2.25 2.25

Printed in sheets of 4.

Indipex 2011 Intl. Philatelic Exhibition, New Delhi — A531

No. 4067, $225 — Taj Mahal, Agra: a, Interior hallway. b, Large and small domes. c, Mausoleum, minarets and reflecting pool. d, Exterior wall and arches.

No. 4068, $225: a, Temple of Shiva, Varanasi. b, Ramnagar Fort. c, Kangra Valley. d, Khajuraho Temple.

$450, Statue of Lord Shiva.

***Perf. 13 Syncopated***
**2011, Apr. 4 Litho.**
**Sheets of 4, #a-d**
**4067-4068** A531 Set of 2 17.50 17.50

**Souvenir Sheet**

***Perf. 12¾***

**4069** A531 $450 multi 4.50 4.50

No. 4069 contains one 38x51mm stamp.

Worldwide Fund for Nature (WWF) — A532

No. 4070 — Bush dogs: a, Three at water hole. b, Four at water hole. c, Three in den. d, Head of adult.

**2011, June 6 Litho. *Perf. 13¼***

| | | | |
|---|---|---|---|
| **4070** | Block of 4 | 6.00 | 6.00 |
| *a.-d.* | A532 $150 Any single | 1.50 | 1.50 |
| *e.* | Souvenir sheet of 8, 2 each #4070a-4070d | 12.00 | 12.00 |

Tenth World Cricket Cup Championships, India, Sri Lanka and Bangladesh — A533

Designs: $100, Shivnarine Chanderpaul. $150, Sardar Patel Stadium, Ahmedabad, India, horiz.

$300, Cricket World Cup.

**2011, June 20** ***Perf. 12¾***
**4071-4072** A533 Set of 2 2.50 2.50

**Souvenir Sheet**

***Perf. 13 Syncopated***

**4073** A533 $300 multi 3.00 3.00

U.S. Pres. Barack Obama — A534

No. 4074, $225: a, Black background. b, Blue background.
No. 4075, $225: a, Bister background. b, Red background.

**2011, June 20** ***Perf. 13 Syncopated***

**Pairs, #a-b**

**4074-4075** A534 Set of 2 8.75 8.75

Nos. 4074-4075 each were printed in sheets containing two pairs.

A535

U.S. Pres. John F. Kennedy (1917-63) — A536

No. 4076: a, Head of Kennedy. b, Kennedy at lectern in stadium. c, Kennedy at lectern (black-and-white photo).
No. 4077: a, Kennedy and wife, Jacqueline (black-and-white photo). b, Kennedy presidential campaign button. c, Kennedy talking to person. d, Kennedy and wife (color photo).

**2011, June 20** ***Perf. 13 Syncopated***
**4076** A535 $175 Horiz. strip of 3, #a-c 5.25 5.25
**4077** A536 $225 Sheet of 4, #a-d 8.75 8.75

No. 4076 was printed in sheet containing two strips.

Wedding of Prince William and Catherine Middleton — A537

No. 4078, $250 — Black-and-white photos of: a, Prince William. b, Couple. c, Procession in streets. d, Middleton.
No. 4079, $275, vert. — Color photos of: a, Couple holding hands (30x40mm. b, Couple in coach. c, Couple (60x40mm, with perforations in middle of stamp).
$500, Couple kissing, vert.

**2011, Sept. 19** ***Perf. 12½x12***
**4078** A537 $250 Sheet of 4, #a-d 10.00 10.00

***Perf. 12x12½***
**4079** A537 $275 Sheet of 3, #a-c 8.25 8.25

**Souvenir Sheet**

***Perf. 13¼***

**4080** A537 $500 multi 5.00 5.00

No. 4080 contains one 38x51mm stamp.

Souvenir Sheet

Visit to Germany of Pope Benedict XVI — A538

**Litho. & Embossed**

**2011, Sept. 19** ***Microrouletted***

**Without Gum**

**4081** A538 $3000 multi 30.00 30.00

Princess Diana (1961-97) — A539

No. 4082 — Princess Diana wearing: a, Pink hat and dress. b, White dress and veil. c, Striped sweater.
$450, Princess Diana wearing black hat, horiz.

**2011, Oct. 12 Litho.** ***Perf. 12x12½***
**4082** A539 $275 Sheet of 3, #a-c 8.25 8.25

**Souvenir Sheet**

***Perf. 13¼***

**4083** A539 $450 multi 4.50 4.50

No. 4083 contains one 51x38mm stamp.

Miniature Sheets

A540

A541

Elvis Presley (1935-77) — A542

No. 4084 — Presley: a, Outdoors wearing leis. b, Holding microphone with hand even with his neck. c, Holding microphone with hand below his neck. d, Waving.
No. 4085 — Presley: a, With hand touching head. b, Playing guitar, figures in background out of focus. c, Playing guitar, figures in background in focus. d, Dancing, with jail bars in background.
No. 4086 — Presley albums: a, Viva Las Vegas. b, Elvis (curved lettering). c, Elvis (block letters in lights). d, I Got Stung.
No. 4087 — Presley albums: a, Blue Hawaii. b, Elvis' Gold Records. c, Elvis Presley. d, Moody Blue.

**2011, Oct. 12** ***Perf. 12x12½***
**4084** A540 $225 Sheet of 4, #a-d 9.00 9.00
**4085** A541 $225 Sheet of 4, #a-d 9.00 9.00

***Perf. 12½x12***
**4086** A542 $225 Sheet of 4, #a-d 9.00 9.00
**4087** A542 $225 Sheet of 4, #a-d 9.00 9.00
*Nos. 4084-4087 (4)* 36.00 36.00

Mushrooms — A543

No. 4088: a, Pseudotulostoma volvata. b, Inocybe ayangannae. c, Amanita perphaea. d, Entoloma olivaceacoloratum. e, Panaeolus cyanescens. f, Tylopilus vinaceipallidus.
No. 4089: a, Boletellus dicymbophilus. b, Inocybe epidendron. c, Tylopilus pakaraimensis. d, Amanita aurantiobrunnea.
No. 4090, $475, Amauroderma gusmanianum. No. 4091, $475, Craterellus excelsus.

**2011, Oct. 12** ***Perf. 11½***
**4088** A543 $150 Sheet of 6, #a-f 9.00 9.00
**4089** A543 $225 Sheet of 4, #a-d 9.00 9.00

**Souvenir Sheets**

**4090-4091** A543 Set of 2 9.50 9.50

Intl. Year of Forests.

Miniature Sheet

Chinese Zodiac Animals — A544

No. 4092: a, Rat. b, Ox. c, Tiger. d, Rabbit. e, Dragon. f, Snake. g, Horse. h, Sheep. i, Monkey. j, Rooster. k, Dog. l, Boar.

**Litho. With Foil Application**

**2012, Jan. 9** ***Perf. 13 Syncopated***
**4092** A544 $50 Sheet of 12, #a-l 6.00 6.00

King Edward VIII (1894-1972) A545

King Edward VIII wearing: $300, Top hat. $700, Uniform, horiz.

**2012, May 30 Litho.** ***Perf. 12***
**4093** A545 $300 multi 3.00 3.00
*a.* Inscribed "King Edward VIII" 3.00 3.00

**Souvenir Sheet**

**4094** A545 $700 multi 7.00 7.00
*a.* Inscribed "King Edward VIII" 7.00 7.00

No. 4094 contains one 50x30mm stamp. Nos. 4093-4094 are incorrectly inscribed "King Edward XIII."

A546

Birds — A547

No. 4095, $160: a, Anhinga. b, Least grebe. c, Scarlet ibis. d, Neotropic cormorant.
No. 4096, $1.60: a, Northern caracara. b, Cocoi heron. c, Tricolored heron. d, Jabiru.
No. 4097, $400, Glossy ibis. No. 4098, $400, White-tailed kite, vert.

**2012, May 30** ***Perf. 14***

**Sheets of 4, #a-d**

**4095-4096** A546 Set of 2 13.00 13.00

**Souvenir Sheets**

***Perf. 12***

**4097-4098** A547 Set of 2 8.00 8.00

Butterflies — A548

No. 4099, $250, horiz.: a, Iphiclus sister. b, Gaudy altinote. c, Gulf fritillary. d, Tiger crescent.
No. 4100, $250, horiz.: a, Orange-banded gem. b, Red-barred amarynthis. c, Thesprotia sister. d, Orange-barred sister.
No. 4101, $500, White-barred sister. No. 4102, $500, Blue duskywing.

**2012, May 30** *Perf. 14*

**Sheets of 4, #a-d**

**4099-4100** A548 Set of 2 20.00 20.00

**Souvenir Sheets**

***Perf. 12½***

**4101-4102** A548 Set of 2 10.00 10.00

Nos. 4099-4100 each contain four 40x30mm stamps.

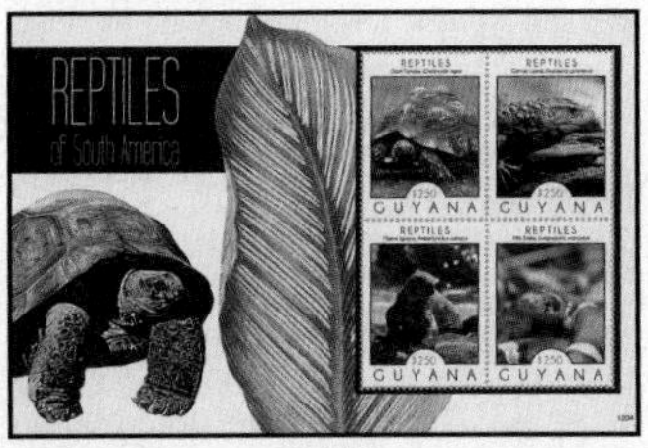


A549

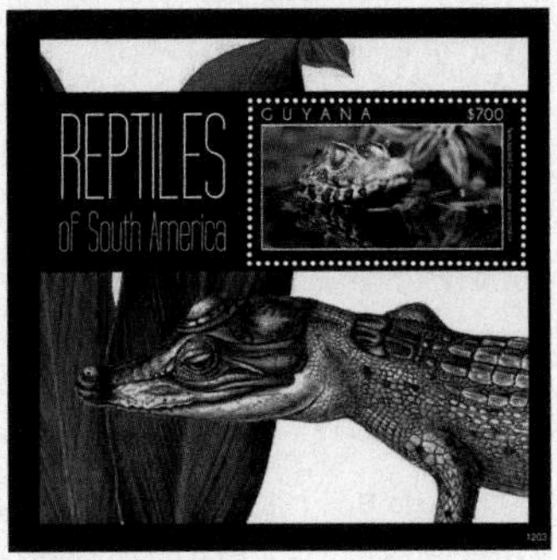


Reptiles — A550

No. 4103, $250: a, Giant tortoise. b, Caiman lizard. c, Marine iguana. d, Milk snake.
No. 4104, $250: a, Rainbow whiptail. b, Emerald tree boa. c, Green vine snake. d, Green iguana.
No. 4105, $700, Spectacled caiman. No. 4106, $700, Boa constrictor, vert.

**2012, May 30** *Perf. 14*

**Sheets of 4, #a-d**

**4103-4104** A549 Set of 2 20.00 20.00

**Souvenir Sheets**

***Perf. 12***

**4105-4106** A550 Set of 2 14.00 14.00

No. 4106 contains one 30x80mm stamp.

**Nos. 70, 89, 2367, 2368, 2370, 2662, 2781, 2782, 2783, 2784, 2859, 2883, 2933, 3004, and 3238 Handstamp Surcharged in Violet Black Like No. 4020K**

**Methods, Perfs and Watermarks As Before**

**2012**

**4107** A7 $20 on 3c #70 — —
**4108** A14 $20 on 30c #89 — —
**4109** A231 $20 on $6 #3004 — —
**4110** A185 $20 on $6.40 #2781 — —
**4111** A185 $20 on $7.65 #2782 — —
**4112** A215 $20 on $8 #2933 — —
**4113** A185 $20 on $12.80 #2783 — —
**4114** A185 $20 on $15.30 #2784 — —
**4115** A277 $20 on $30 #3238 — —

**Miniature Sheet of 8, #a-h**

**4116** A203 $20 on $30 #2883 — —

**Miniature Sheets of 12, #a-l**

**4117** A162 $20 on $30 #2662 — —
**4118** A200 $20 on $35 #2859 — —

**Miniature Sheets of 16, #a-p**

**4119** A129 $20 on $10 #2367 — —
**4120** A129 $20 on $10 #2368 — —
**4121** A129 $20 on $12.80 #2370 — —

**Footnoted Disney Types of 1995 Surcharged Like No. 4020K in Violet Black**

**Methods and Perfs As Before**

**2012**

**Miniature Sheets of 8, #a-h, + Label**

**4122** A217 $20 on $5 #2917 footnote — —
**4123** A213 $20 on $5 #2918 footnote — —

**Miniature Sheet of 7, #a-g, + Label**

**4124** A213 $20 on $5 #2920 footnote — —

**Flower Type of 1971-76 Surcharged Like No. 4020K in Violet Black**

**4125** A28 $20 on 2c Yellow allamanda — —
**4126** A28 $20 on 8c Mazaruni Pride — —
*a.* Pair, #4125-4126 — —

Nos. 4125-4126 were not issued without surcharge.

Ferry and Guyana Flag A551

**2012** **Litho.** *Perf. 13¼x13¾*

**4127** A551 $20 on $30 multi — —

The editors would like to examine an example of this stamp without the surcharge.

Souvenir Sheet

Diplomatic Relations Between Guyana and People's Republic of China, 40th Anniv. — A552

No. 4128: a, Tiananmen, Beijing, China. b, Guyana International Conference Center.

**2012, June 27** **Litho.** *Perf. 12½x12*

**4128** A552 $350 Sheet of 2, #a-b 7.00 7.00

2012 Summer Olympics, London — A553

No. 4129 — Mascots: a, Wenlock (with torch). b, Mandeville (without torch).

**2012, June 27** *Perf. 14*

**4129** A553 $125 Horiz. pair, #a-b 2.50 2.50

No. 4129 was printed in sheets containing four pairs.

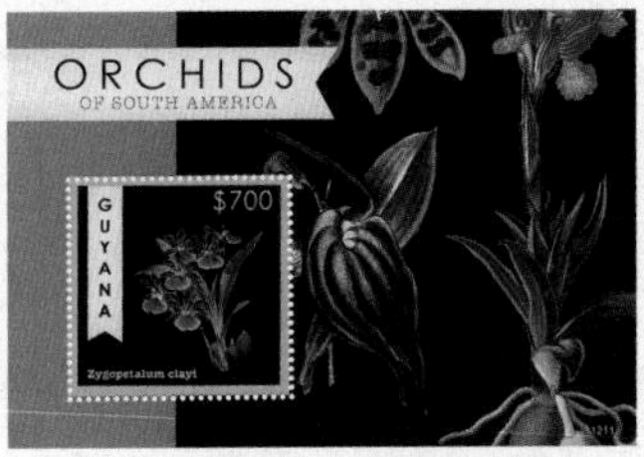


Orchids — A554

No. 4130: a, Ada aurantiaca. b, Cattleya labiata. c, Masdevallia haryana. d, Masdevallia davisii.
$700, Zygopetalum clayi.

**2012, Aug. 28** *Perf. 13¾*

**4130** A554 $250 Sheet of 4, #a-d 10.00 10.00

**Souvenir Sheet**

**4131** A554 $700 multi 7.00 7.00

**No. 357 Handstamp Surcharged Like No. 4020K**

**Method and Perf. As Before**

**2012 ?**

**4132** A8 $20 on 40c #357 — —

Nos. 142 With "Revenue Only" Overprint, 445 and 506 Handstamp Surcharged in Black

**2012 ?** **Litho.**

**4133** A28 $20 on 40c #142 with "Revenue Only" Overprint — —
**4134** A11 $20 on 40c #445 — —
**4135** A78 $20 on 40c on 2c #506 — —

No. 2937 Surcharged

**Method and Perf. As Before**

**2012 ?**

**4136** A215 $55 on $25 #2937 —

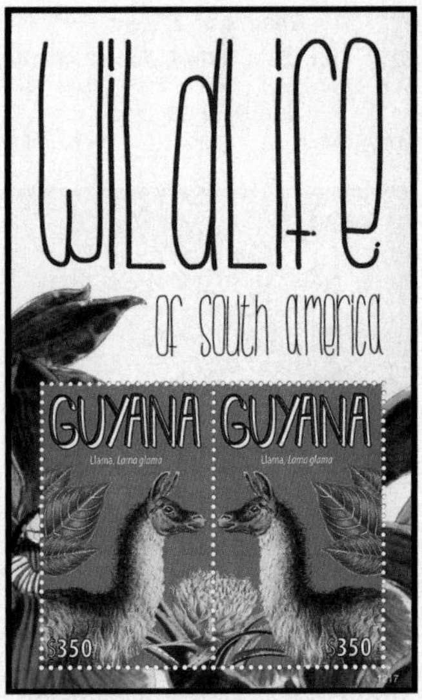


South American Wildlife — A555

No. 4137: a, Jaguar. b, Toucan. c, Chinchilla.
No. 4138: a, Llama facing right. b, Llama facing left.

**2012, Oct. 23** **Litho.** *Perf. 12*

**4137** A555 $300 Sheet of 3, #a-c 9.00 9.00

**Souvenir Sheet**

**4138** A555 $350 Sheet of 2, #a-b 7.00 7.00

A556

Whales — A557

No. 4139: a, Killer whale. b, Humpback whale. c, Blue whale.
$700, Beluga whale.

**2012, Oct. 23**

**4139** A556 $300 Sheet of 3, #a-c 9.00 9.00

**Souvenir Sheet**

**4140** A557 $700 multi 7.00 7.00

Dolphins — A558

No. 4141, $300: a, Spinner dolphin. b, Atlantic spotted dolphin. c, Amazon River dolphin.
No. 4142, $300: a, Clymene dolphin. b, Dusky dolphin. c, White-sided dolphin.
No. 4143, $700, Common dolphin. No. 4144, $700, Bottlenose dolphin, vert.

**Sheets of 3, #a-c**

**2012, Oct. 23** ***Perf. 14, 12 (#4144)***
**4141-4142** A558 Set of 2 18.00 18.00

**Souvenir Sheets**

**4143-4144** A558 Set of 2 14.00 14.00

Shells — A559

No. 4145: a, Melampus coffeus coffeus. b, Nerita fulgurans. c, Nerita peloronta. d, Littorina nebulosa. e, Tectarius muricatus. f, Hyalina avena.
No. 4146: a, Cassis flammea. b, Liguus virgineus. c, Trigonostoma rugosum. d, Neritina virginea.
No. 4147, $500, Cymatium raderi. No. 4148, $500, Cassis madagascariensis.

**2012, Oct. 23** ***Perf. 13 Syncopated***
**4145** A559 $175 Sheet of 6, #a-f 10.50 10.50
**4146** A559 $225 Sheet of 4, #a-d 9.00 9.00

**Souvenir Sheets**

**4147-4148** A559 Set of 2 10.00 10.00

Dogs and Their Evolution — A560

No. 4149, horiz.: a, Gray wolf. b, Canaan dog. c, Maltese. d, Greyhound. e, Golden retriever.
No. 4150, horiz.: a, Coyote. b, Alaskan husky. c, Red fox. d, Yorkshire terrier.
No. 4151, $700, Bull mastiff. No. 4152, $700, Dalmatian.

**2012, Oct. 23** ***Perf. 12***
**4149** A560 $225 Sheet of 5, #a-e 11.00 11.00
**4150** A560 $250 Sheet of 4, #a-d 10.00 10.00

**Souvenir Sheets**

***Perf. 14***

**4151-4152** A560 Set of 2 14.00 14.00

Completion of Painting of the Sistine Chapel Ceiling by Michelangelo, 500th Anniv. — A561

No. 4153, horiz. — Painting details: a, Joel. b, Daniel. c, The Libyan Sibyl.
No. 4154: a, Michelangelo. b, Detail of Ancestors of Christ.

**2012, Oct. 29** ***Perf. 12***
**4153** A561 $225 Sheet of 3, #a-c 6.75 6.75

**Souvenir Sheet**

**4154** A561 $350 Sheet of 2, #a-b 7.00 7.00

No. 4153 contains three 40x30mm stamps.

Miniature Sheets

Princess Diana (1961-97) — A562

No. 4155, $250 — Stamps with blue panels with Princess Diana: a, Holding flowers. b, Wearing white hat. c, Wearing tiara. b, Wearing beige hat with ribbon.
No. 4156, $250 — Stamps with yellow green panels with Princess Diana wearing: a, Red jacket and lei. b, Patterned dress and necklace. c, Jacket and tie. d, White jacket and leis.

**Sheets of 4, #a-d**

**2012, Oct. 29** ***Perf. 14, 12 (#4156)***
**4155-4156** A562 Set of 2 20.00 20.00

Souvenir Sheets

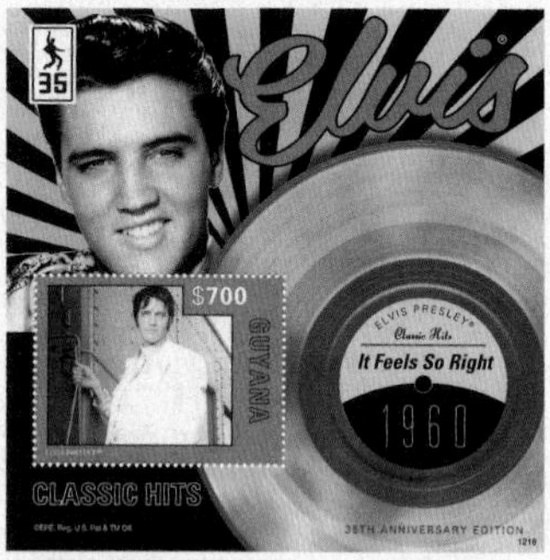


Elvis Presley (1935-77) — A563

Designs: No. 4157, $700, Color photograph of Presley, red frame with country name outlined in black. No. 4158, $700, Black-and-white photograph of Presley, red frame with country name outlined in white. No. 4159, $700, Color photograph of Presley, black frame. No. 4160, $700, Color photograph of Presley, gray frame. No. 4161, $700, Black-and-white photograph of Presley, purple frame.

**2012, Oct. 29** ***Perf. 12¾***
**4157-4161** A563 Set of 5 35.00 35.00

Chinese Zodiac Animals — A564

Designs: No. 4162, $50, Rabbits. No. 4163, $50, Tiger.

**2012, Dec. 5** ***Perf. 13¼x13***
**4162-4163** A564 Set of 2 1.00 1.00

**Nos. 68, 136, 208, 231, 326, 328, 413Dg, 442, 1337-1339, 1987, 2360, 2361, 2652, 2728, 3133 Surcharged in Violet Black Like No. 4020K**

**Methods, Perfs and Watermarks As Before**

**2012**

| | | | | | |
|---|---|---|---|---|---|
| **4164** | A7 | $20 on 1c #68 | — | — |
| **4165** | A28 | $20 on 5c #136 | — | — |
| **4166** | A92 | $20 on 25c #1337 | | — |
| **4167** | A92 | $20 on 25c #1338 | | — |
| **4168** | A92 | $20 on 25c #1339 | — | — |
| **4169** | A76 | $20 on 30c #326 | — | — |
| **4170** | A55 | $20 on 35c #231 | — | — |
| **4171** | A72 | $20 on 35c #442 | — | — |
| **4172** | A161 | $20 on 80c #2652 | | — |
| **4173** | A48 | $20 on $1 #208 | — | — |
| **4174** | A7 | $20 on $1 on 6c #413Dg | — | — |
| **4175** | A76 | $20 on $3 #328 | — | — |
| **4176** | A66 | $20 on $5 #1987 | — | — |
| **4177** | A176 | $20 on $6.40 #2728 | | — |
| **4178** | A129 | $20 on $8.90 #2360 | | — |
| **4179** | A129 | $20 on $12.80 #2361 | | — |
| **4180** | A260 | $20 on $30 #3133 | | — |

**AIR POST STAMPS**

No. 321 Surcharged in Blue "HUMAN RIGHTS / DAY / 1981 / 110 AIR"

**1981, Nov. 14** ***Perfs. as Before***
**C1** A74 110c on $3 No. 321 6.00

For surcharge see No. 997.

Nos. 133, 136 and 146 Surcharged in Red, Black or Blue "AIR / Princess / of Wales / 1961-1982"

**1982, June 25** ***Perfs. as Before***

**Printing Methods as Before**

**C2** A28 110c on 5c No. 136 (R) 4.00 .40
**C3** A28 220c on 1c No. 133 4.00 1.00
**C4** A28 330c on $2 No. 146 (Bl) 4.00 1.60
*Nos. C2-C4 (3)* 12.00 3.00

For surcharges see Nos. 623, 785-787, 801, 804-804A, O19, O21, O30-O39.

No. 287 Surcharged in Dark Blue "UNICEF / 1946-1986 / AIR" or "UNESCO / 1946-1986 / AIR"

***Perfs. as Before***

**1986, Oct. 24** **Litho.**
**C5** A66 120c on $1 UNICEF 11.00
**C6** A66 120c on $1 UNESCO 11.00
*a.* Pair, #C5-C6 24.00

Nos. 1026, 1095, 1096, 1096a, 1100, 1138, 1163 Surcharged "AIR"

**1987-88** **Litho.** ***Perf. 14***

**Design A91**

**Plate Numbers in Parentheses**

**C7** 75c on 25c No. 1100 (59) 13.50 1.50
**C8** 60c on No. 1095 (55) 11.00 10.00
**C9** 75c on No. 1026 (5) 1.25 .65
**C10** 75c on No. 1096 (55) 1.25 .65
*a.* 75c on No. 1096a
**C11** 75c on No. 1138 (83) 1.25 .65
**C12** 75c on No. 1163 (95) 1.25 .65

Issued: #C7, 11/87; #C8, 12/87; #C9-C12, 8/88.

**SPECIAL DELIVERY STAMPS**

Orchid Type of 1985 Overprinted or Surcharged "EXPRESS"

**1986-87** **Litho.** ***Perf. 14***

**Plate Numbers in Parentheses**

**E1** A91 $12 on #1372 (65) 12.00 12.00
**E2** A91 $15 on 40c #1145 (86) 12.00 12.00
**E3** A91(p) $15 on #E2 (86) 11.00 11.00
**E4** A91 $25 on 25c like #1090 (53) 15.00 15.00
*Nos. E1-E4 (4)* 50.00

Issue dates: $12, $25, #E2, Nov. 10. #E3, Dec. 1987. #E4 not issued without surcharge.

No. 1461c Surcharged "EXPRESS"

**1986-87** **Litho.** ***Imperf.***
**E5** A96 $20 on 320c #1461c 12.00 12.00

No. E5 Ovptd. with Maltese Cross

**1987, Mar. 3**
**E6** A96 $20 on No. E5 12.00 12.00

**Orchid Type of 1985 Inscribed "Express"**

**1987-88** **Litho.** ***Perf. 14***

**Series 2**

**Plate Numbers in Parentheses**

**E7** A91 $15 like #1186 (11) 4.00 4.00
**E8** A91 $20 like #1323 (93) 7.50 7.50
**E9** A91 $25 like #1274 (63) 6.50 6.50
**E10** A91 $45 like #1228 (35) 12.00 12.00
*Nos. E7-E10 (4)* 30.00 30.00

Issued: $45, 9/1; $15, 9/29; $25, 10/26; $20, 5/17/88.

No. "1461" Surcharged "EXPRESS / FORTY DOLLARS"

**1987, Nov.** ***Perf. 14***
**E11** A96 $40 on 320c No. 1461, imperf. btwn. 15.00 15.00

A five-pointed star appears between the lines of the surcharge on #E11. See #E14.

Nos. 1827e, 1830e Surcharged in Red "SPECIAL DELIVERY"

**1988, Aug. 10** ***Perf. 15***
**E12** A100 $40 on $3.20 #1827e 12.00 12.00
**E13** A100 $45 on $3.30 #1830e 12.00 12.00

See Nos. 2054b, 2056b.

Nos. "1461," 1822c Surcharged in Red "EXPRESS / FORTY DOLLARS"

**1989, Mar.** ***Perf. 14***
**E14** A96 $40 on 320c #1461, imperf. btwn. 7.00 7.00
**E15** A96 $40 on 320c #1822c, imperf. btwn. 7.00 7.00

**Butterflies Type of 1989 Inscribed "EXPRESS"**

Souvenir Sheets

**1989, Sept. 7** **Litho.** ***Perf. 14***
**E16** A115 $130 Phareas coeleste 7.75 7.75
**E17** A115 $190 Papilio torquatus 12.50 12.50

For overprints see #E19-E22, E24, E26-E27, E31.

**Women in Space Type of 1989 Inscribed "EXPRESS"**

Souvenir Sheets

**1989, Nov. 8**
**E18** A116 $190 Valentina Tereshkova 5.00 5.00

For overprints see No. E23, E25, E28, E32.

Nos. E16-E17 Ovptd. with World Stamp Expo '89 Emblem

**1989, Nov. 17**
**E19** A115 $130 on No. E16 7.00 7.00
**E20** A115 $190 on No. E17 7.00 7.00

Nos. E16-E18 Ovptd. in Sheet Margin "Stamp World London 90" and Show Emblem

**1990, May 3**
**E21** A115 $130 on No. E16
**E22** A115 $190 on No. E17
**E23** A116 $190 on No. E18
*Nos. E21-E23 (3)* 20.00

Nos. E17-E18 Ovptd. in Sheet Margin with Rotary Emblem and "ROTARY / INTERNATIONAL / 1905-1990"

**1990, Mar.**
**E24** A115 $190 on No. E17
**E25** A116 $190 on No. E18
*Nos. E24-E25 (2)* 22.50

Nos. E16-E18 Ovptd. in Sheet Margin "90th BIRTHDAY / H.M. THE / QUEEN MOTHER"

**1990, June 8** **Litho.** ***Perf. 14***
**E26** A115 $130 on No. E16 7.75 7.75
**E27** A115 $190 on No. E17 12.50 12.50
**E28** A116 $190 on No. E18 12.50 12.50
*Nos. E26-E28 (3)* 32.75 32.75

**Endangered Wildlife Type**

Souvenir Sheets

**1990, Nov. 6** **Litho.** ***Perf. 14***
**E29** A131 $130 Harpy eagle 7.00 7.00
**E30** A131 $150 Ocelot 7.50 7.50

Nos. E29-E30 each contain one 43x57mm stamp.

Nos. E16, E18 Ovptd. in Sheet Margin with "BELGICA PHILATELIC / EXPOSITION 1990" and Scout, Lions, Rotary and Show Emblems

**1990, June 2**
**E31** A115 $130 on No. E16 7.50 7.50
**E32** A116 $190 on No. E18 7.50 7.50

No. E31 has Scout and Lions emblems. No. E32 has Scout and Rotary emblems.

## POSTAGE DUE STAMPS

**Type of British Guiana Inscribed "Guyana"**

***Perf. 13½x14***

| **1967-68** | | **Wmk. 314** | **Typo.** | |
|---|---|---|---|---|
| **J2** | D1 | 2c black ('68) | 1.00 | 1.00 |
| **J3** | D1 | 4c ultramarine | .50 | .50 |
| **J4** | D1 | 12c carmine | .75 | .75 |
| | | *Nos. J2-J4 (3)* | 2.25 | 2.25 |

For surcharges see Nos. 897-898.

| **1973** | | | **Wmk. 364** | |
|---|---|---|---|---|
| **J5** | D1 | 1c green | .35 | *2.00* |
| **J6** | D1 | 2c black | .35 | *2.00* |
| **J7** | D1 | 4c ultramarine | .35 | *2.00* |
| **J8** | D1 | 12c carmine | .40 | *2.00* |
| | | *Nos. J5-J8 (4)* | 1.45 | 8.00 |

For surcharges see #341-349, 658, 899-900.

## OFFICIAL STAMPS

Nos. 74, 139, 141, 143-144, 146-147, 289A, 297, 300, 333, 395, 397, 401 Srchd. in Black, Red, or Black and Red

| **1981-82** | | ***Perfs. as Before*** | | |
|---|---|---|---|---|
| | | **Printing Methods as Before** | | |
| **O1** | A28 | 10c on 25c #141 (Bk & R) | 4.00 | 2.25 |
| **O2** | A8 | 15c on #74 | 10.00 | 2.00 |
| **O3** | A28 | 15c on #139 | 13.50 | 1.00 |
| **O4** | A28 | 30c on $2 #146 (Bk & R) | 1.00 | .50 |
| **O5** | A28 | 50c on #143 (R) | 2.00 | .75 |
| **O6** | A69 | 50c on #300 | 1.50 | .40 |
| **O7** | A28 | 60c on #144 (R) | 1.50 | .25 |
| **O8** | A17 | 100c on #395 | 2.00 | 2.00 |
| **O9** | A68 | 100c on $3 #297 (Bk & R) | 5.00 | .75 |
| **O10** | A17 | 110c on #397 | 4.00 | 2.00 |
| **O11** | A28 | $1.10 on #333 (R) | | |
| **O12** | A28 | 125c on #401 (R) | 4.50 | .80 |
| **O13** | A28 | $2 on #146 (R) | 12.50 | |
| **O14** | A28 | $5 on #147 (R) | 6.00 | 6.00 |
| **O15** | A66 | $10 on #289A | 20.00 | |

Issued: #O1, O5, O7, O15, 6/8; #O2, O4, O9, O11-O12, 7/1; #O13, 7/12/82; others, 7/7.

Surcharge on Nos. O3, O6, O8, O10, O13-O14 have no obliterator. No. O11 is airmail.

Refer to 2nd paragraph in footnote following #147 for #O1, O4-O5, O7 and O13.

For overprints and surcharges see No. 406, 425, 452, 454-456, 603, 618, 650, 817, 854, 861, 866, 933, 1378, 1381, 1384, 1387-1388.

Nos. 162, 256, 258, 282, 480, C2-C3 Srchd. in Blue or Black

| **1982** | | ***Perfs. as Before*** | | |
|---|---|---|---|---|
| | | **Printing Methods as Before** | | |
| **O16** | A66 | 20c on #282 | 10.00 | 1.25 |
| **O17** | A33 | 40c on #162 | 3.00 | 1.50 |
| **O18** | A60 | 40c on #256 | 2.00 | 1.00 |
| **O19** | A28 | 110c on #C2 (Bk) | 6.00 | 2.00 |
| **O20** | A60 | $2 on #258 | 18.00 | 3.50 |
| **O21** | A28 | 220c on #C3 | 4.00 | 1.00 |
| **O22** | A69 | 250c on #480 | 2.00 | 1.00 |
| | | *Nos. O16-O22 (7)* | 45.00 | |

Issue dates: 110c, Sept. 15; others, May 17. Nos. O19, O21 are airmail.

No. 481 Surcharged "OPS" Reading Up in Blue Violet or Blue Violet and Black

| **1984, Apr. 2** | | ***Perfs. as Before*** | | |
|---|---|---|---|---|
| **O23** | A66 | 150c on $5 | 6.00 | 3.00 |
| **O24** | A66 | 200c on $5 | 6.50 | 3.25 |
| **O25** | A66 | 225c on $5 (BV & Bk) | 6.50 | 3.25 |
| **O25A** | A66 | 230c on $5 | 6.75 | 3.50 |
| **O26** | A66 | 260c on $5 | 7.00 | 3.75 |
| **O27** | A66 | 320c on $5 | 7.00 | 3.75 |
| **O28** | A66 | 350c on $5 | 7.50 | 3.75 |
| **O29** | A66 | 600c on $5 | 8.00 | 4.25 |
| | | *Nos. O23-O29 (8)* | 10.00 | 6.00 |

Nos. C2-C3 Surcharged "OPS" in Black and Blue, Black or Blue

| **1984, June 25** | | ***Perfs. as Before*** | | |
|---|---|---|---|---|
| **O30** | A28 | 25c on No. C2 (Bk) | | |
| **O31** | A28 | 30c on No. C2 | 1.00 | .50 |
| **O32** | A28 | 45c on No. C3 | 1.00 | .50 |
| **O33** | A28 | 55c on No. C2 (Bk) | 1.25 | .50 |
| **O34** | A28 | 60c on No. C3 | 1.50 | .60 |
| **O35** | A28 | 75c on No. C3 | 2.00 | .70 |
| **O36** | A28 | 90c on No. C3 (Bl) | 2.00 | .70 |
| **O37** | A28 | 120c on No. C3 | 2.25 | .90 |
| **O38** | A28 | 130c on No. C3 (Bl) | 2.25 | 1.25 |
| **O39** | A28 | 330c on No. C3 (Bl) | 4.00 | 1.25 |
| | | *Nos. O30-O39 (10)* | 17.25 | |

Overprint reads up on No. O39.

**Orchid Type of 1985**
**Series 2**
**Plate Numbers in Parentheses**

| **1987-88** | **Litho.** | **Unwmk.** | ***Perf. 14*** | |
|---|---|---|---|---|
| **O40** | A91 | 120c like #1250 (48) | 1.50 | .40 |
| **O41** | A91 | 130c like #1322 (92) | 1.50 | .40 |
| **O42** | A91 | 140c like #1229 (36) | 1.00 | .40 |
| **O43** | A91 | 150c like #1242 (43) | 1.50 | .50 |
| **O44** | A91 | 175c like #1221 (31) | 1.00 | .50 |
| **O45** | A91 | 200c like #1271 (61) | 1.50 | .60 |
| **O46** | A91 | 225c like #1213 (26) | 1.50 | .60 |
| **O47** | A91 | 230c like #1283 (68) | .75 | .60 |
| **O48** | A91 | 250c like #1268 (59) | .75 | .60 |
| **O49** | A91 | 260c like #1284 (69) | .75 | .60 |
| **O50** | A91 | 275c like #1319 (90) | 1.75 | .75 |
| **O51** | A91 | 320c like #1292 (75) | 1.75 | .85 |
| **O52** | A91 | 330c like #1208 (23) | 2.00 | 1.00 |
| **O53** | A91 | 350c like #1326 (95) | 1.00 | 1.00 |
| **O54** | A91 | 600c like #1285 (70) | 1.50 | 1.50 |
| **O55** | A91 | $12 like #1286 (71) | 2.50 | 2.50 |
| **O56** | A91 | $15 like #1308 (84) | 3.00 | 3.00 |
| | | *Nos. O40-O56 (17)* | 25.25 | 15.80 |

Nos. O47, O53-O56 horiz.

Issued: #O42, O44, O48, O49, 10/5/88; others, 10/5/87.

For overprints & surcharges see #1694, 1697, 1703, 1707, 1722-1726, 1728-1730.

## PARCEL POST STAMPS

No. 145 Surcharged "PARCEL POST"

| **1981, June 8** | | ***Perf. 13½*** | | |
|---|---|---|---|---|
| **Q1** | A28 | $15 on $1 No. 145 | 19.50 | 3.50 |
| **Q2** | A28 | $20 on $1 No. 145 | 19.00 | 7.00 |
| | | *Nos. Q1-Q2 (2)* | 38.00 | |

For overprints see Nos. QO1-QO2.

No. 333 Surcharged "PARCEL POST" in Blue

| **1983, Jan. 15** | | | | |
|---|---|---|---|---|
| **Q3** | A28 | $12 on No. 333 | 12.50 | 2.00 |

For surcharge see No. 624.

No. 146 Surcharged "Parcel Post"

| **1983, Sept. 14** | | | | |
|---|---|---|---|---|
| **Q4** | A28 | $12 on $1.10 on $2 | 3.00 | 3.00 |

No. Q4 has a horizontal Royal Wedding / 1981 surcharge similar to No. 331. For overprint see No. QO5.

No. 255 Surcharged in Red "TWENTY FIVE DOLLARS / PARCEL POST 25.00"

| **1985, Apr. 25** | | ***Perf. 14*** | | |
|---|---|---|---|---|
| **Q5** | A60 | $25 on 35c No. 255 | 33.00 | 27.50 |

## PARCEL POST OFFICIAL STAMPS

Nos. Q1-Q2 Overprinted "OPS" in Red

| **1981, June 8** | | | | |
|---|---|---|---|---|
| **QO1** | A28 | $15 on No. Q1 | 18.00 | 2.50 |
| **QO2** | A28 | $20 on No. Q2 | 17.00 | 3.25 |

For surcharges see Nos. 1389-1390.

No. 333 Surcharged in Blue "OPS / 1982 / Parcel Post / $12.00"

| **1983, Jan. 15** | | | | |
|---|---|---|---|---|
| **QO3** | A28 | $12 on No. 333 | 115.00 | 20.00 |

No. QO3 Overprinted "OPS" in Black

| **1983, Aug. 22** | | | | |
|---|---|---|---|---|
| **QO4** | A28 | $12 on No. QO3 | 42.50 | 4.00 |

No. Q4 Overprinted "OPS" in Blue

| **1983, Nov. 3** | | | | |
|---|---|---|---|---|
| **QO5** | A28 | $12 on No. Q4 | 15.00 | 4.00 |

# HAITI

'hā-tē

LOCATION — Western part of Hispaniola
GOVT. — Republic
AREA — 10,714 sq. mi.
POP. — 6,884,264 (1999 est.)
CAPITAL — Port-au-Prince

100 Centimes = 1 Piaster (1906)
100 Centimes = 1 Gourde

**Catalogue values for unused stamps in this country are for Never Hinged items, beginning with Scott 370 in the regular postage section, Scott B2 in the semi-postal section, Scott C33 in the air post section, Scott CB9 in the air post semi-postal section, Scott CO6 in the air post official section, Scott CQ1 in the air post parcel post seciton, Scott E1 in the special delivery section, Scott J21 in the postage due section, Scott Q1 in the parcel post section, Scott RA1 in the postal tax section, and Scott RAC1 in the air post postal tax section.**

## ISSUES OF THE REPUBLIC

**Watermark**

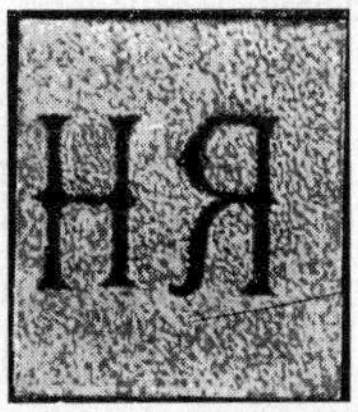

Wmk. 131 — RH

Liberty Head — A1

A3

A4

On A3 (#18, 19) there are crossed lines of dots on face. On A4 the "5" is 3mm wide, on A1 2½mm wide.

| **1881** | | **Unwmk. Typo.** | ***Imperf.*** | |
|---|---|---|---|---|
| **1** | A1 | 1c vermilion, *yelsh* | 9.00 | 5.50 |
| **2** | A1 | 2c violet, *pale lil* | 11.00 | 5.50 |
| **3** | A1 | 3c gray bister, *pale bis* | 20.00 | 8.00 |
| **4** | A1 | 5c yel green, *grnsh* | 32.50 | 16.00 |
| **5** | A1 | 7c deep blue, *grysh* | 22.00 | 4.00 |
| **6** | A1 | 20c red brown, *yelsh* | 82.50 | 30.00 |
| | | *Nos. 1-6 (6)* | 177.00 | 69.00 |

Nos. 1-6 were printed from plate I, Nos. 7-13 from plates II and III.

| **1882** | | ***Perf. 13½*** | | |
|---|---|---|---|---|
| **7** | A1 | 1c dp ver, *dp yelsh* ('83) | 5.75 | 2.10 |
| *a.* | | Vert. pair imperf. btwn. | 200.00 | *250.00* |
| **8** | A1 | 2c dp purple, *pale lil* ('83) | 11.00 | 3.25 |
| *a.* | | 2c dark violet, *white* ('84) | 12.00 | 6.50 |
| *b.* | | As "a," vert. pair, imperf between | 175.00 | *250.00* |
| *c.* | | As "a.," horiz. pair, imperf between | 175.00 | *250.00* |
| *d.* | | 2c red violet, *pale lilac* ('85) | 7.25 | 2.60 |
| *e.* | | As "d," vert. pair, imperf between | 175.00 | *275.00* |
| *f.* | | As "d," horiz. pair, imperf between | 175.00 | *275.00* |
| **9** | A1 | 3c gray bister, *pale bis* | 11.50 | 3.25 |
| **10** | A1 | 5c blue grn, *grnsh* | 8.25 | 1.60 |
| *a.* | | 5c yellow green, *greenish* ('85) | 7.75 | 1.40 |
| *b.* | | 5c deep green, *greenish* ('85) | 7.75 | 1.40 |
| *c.* | | As "b," horiz. pair, imperf between | 190.00 | *275.00* |
| **11** | A1 | 7c deep blue, *grysh* ('85) | 10.50 | 2.10 |
| *a.* | | Horiz. pair, imperf. between | 150.00 | *250.00* |
| **12** | A1 | 7c ultra, *grysh* ('85) | 16.00 | 3.25 |
| *a.* | | Vert. pair, imperf. between | 150.00 | *250.00* |
| **13** | A1 | 20c pale brn, *yelsh* ('86) | 15.00 | 4.50 |
| *a.* | | Vert. pair, imperf between | 175.00 | *275.00* |
| *b.* | | 20c red brown, *yellowish* ('84) | 20.00 | 8.00 |
| *c.* | | As "b," vert. pair, imperf between | 150.00 | *300.00* |
| *d.* | | As "b," horiz. pair, imperf between | 150.00 | *300.00* |
| | | *Nos. 7-13 (7)* | 78.00 | 20.05 |

Stamps perf. 14, 16 are postal forgeries.

| **1886-87** | | ***Perf. 13½*** | | |
|---|---|---|---|---|
| **18** | A3 | 1c vermilion, *yelsh* | 5.75 | 2.00 |
| *a.* | | Horiz. pair, imperf. vert. | | 175.00 |
| *b.* | | Horiz. pair, imperf. between | 200.00 | 190.00 |
| **19** | A3 | 2c dk violet, *lilac* | 42.50 | 7.00 |
| **20** | A4 | 5c green ('87) | 20.00 | 2.75 |
| | | *Nos. 18-20 (3)* | 68.25 | 11.75 |

General Louis Etienne Félicité Salomon — A5

| **1887** | | **Engr.** | ***Perf. 14*** | |
|---|---|---|---|---|
| **21** | A5 | 1c lake | .40 | .30 |
| **22** | A5 | 2c violet | 1.00 | .70 |
| **23** | A5 | 3c blue | .70 | .45 |
| **24** | A5 | 5c green | 50.00 | .55 |
| *a.* | | Double impression | *300.00* | |
| | | *Nos. 21-24 (4)* | 52.10 | 2.00 |

Imperfs. of Nos. 21-24 are plate proofs. Value per pair, $50.

Nos. 21-22 are known overprinted "R:S:" and postally used. Neither is known unused. Overprint is of a provisional or revolutionary government.

No. 23 Handstamp Surcharged in Red

| **1890** | | | | |
|---|---|---|---|---|
| **25** | A5 | 2c on 3c blue | 3.50 | 3.00 |
| *a.* | | Inverted surcharge | 12.00 | *16.00* |
| *b.* | | Double surcharge | 12.00 | *14.00* |
| *c.* | | Double surcharge, one inverted | — | *20.00* |

Missing letters are frequently found. This applies to succeeding surcharged issues.

Coat of Arms A7

Coat of Arms (Leaves Drooping) A9

| **1891** | | ***Perf. 13*** | | |
|---|---|---|---|---|
| **26** | A7 | 1c violet | 1.00 | .30 |
| **27** | A7 | 2c blue | 1.50 | .30 |
| **28** | A7 | 3c gray lilac | 2.00 | .45 |
| *a.* | | 3c slate | 1.75 | .55 |
| **29** | A7 | 5c orange | 5.50 | .50 |
| **30** | A7 | 7c red | 20.00 | 2.75 |
| | | *Nos. 26-30 (5)* | 30.00 | 4.30 |

Nos. 26-30 exist imperf. Value of unused pairs, each $50.

The 2c, 3c and 7c exist imperf. vertically.

No. 28 Surcharged Like No. 25 in Red

| **1892** | | | | |
|---|---|---|---|---|
| **31** | A7 | 2c on 3c gray lilac | 3.00 | 2.00 |
| *a.* | | 2c on 3c slate | 3.50 | 2.25 |
| *b.* | | Inverted surcharge | 24.00 | |
| *c.* | | Double surcharge | 32.50 | |
| *d.* | | Pair, one without surcharge | 32.50 | |

| **1892-95** | | **Engr., Litho. (20c)** | ***Perf. 14*** | |
|---|---|---|---|---|
| **32** | A9 | 1c lilac | .40 | .25 |
| *b.* | | Double impression | | *350.00* |
| **33** | A9 | 2c deep blue | .50 | .25 |
| **34** | A9 | 3c gray | .70 | .45 |
| **35** | A9 | 5c orange | 2.75 | .50 |

| | | | | |
|---|---|---|---|---|
| **36** | A9 | 7c red | .50 | .25 |
| *a.* | | Imperf., pair | 30.00 | |
| **37** | A9 | 20c brown | 1.40 | 1.00 |
| | | *Nos. 32-37 (6)* | 6.25 | 2.70 |

Nos. 32, 33, 35 exist in horiz. pairs, imperf. vert., Nos. 33, 35, in vert. pairs, imperf. horiz. No. 32 exists imperf. It is a proof.

**1896 Engr. *Perf. 13½***

| | | | | |
|---|---|---|---|---|
| **38** | A9 | 1c light blue | .55 | *.70* |
| **39** | A9 | 2c red brown | .65 | *1.20* |
| **40** | A9 | 3c lilac brown | .55 | *1.20* |
| **41** | A9 | 5c slate green | .65 | *1.20* |
| **42** | A9 | 7c dark gray | .90 | *1.75* |
| **43** | A9 | 20c orange | 1.10 | *2.25* |
| | | *Nos. 38-43 (6)* | 4.40 | 8.30 |

Nos. 32-37 are 23¾mm high, Nos. 38-43 23¼mm to 23½mm. The "C" is closed on Nos. 32-37, open on Nos. 38-43. Other differences exist. The stamps of the two issues may be readily distinguished by their colors and perfs.

Nos. 38-43 exist imperf. and in horiz. pairs, imperf. vert. The 1c, 3c, 5c, 7c exist in vert. pairs, imperf. horiz. or imperf. between. The 5c, 7c exist in horiz. pairs, imperf. between. Value of unused pairs, $9 and up.

#37, 43 Surcharged Like #25 in Red

**1898**

| | | | | |
|---|---|---|---|---|
| **44** | A9 | 2c on 20c brown | 3.00 | *6.00* |
| *a.* | | Inverted surcharge | 27.50 | |
| *b.* | | Double surcharge | 32.50 | |
| **45** | A9 | 2c on 20c orange | 1.75 | 1.40 |
| *a.* | | Inverted surcharge | 18.00 | |
| *b.* | | Double surcharge | 27.50 | |
| *c.* | | Double surcharge, one inverted | 35.00 | |

No. 45 exists in various part perf. varieties.

Coat of Arms — A11

**1898 Wmk. 131 *Perf. 11***

| | | | | |
|---|---|---|---|---|
| **46** | A11 | 1c ultra | 2.50 | 2.50 |
| **47** | A11 | 2c brown carmine | .55 | .40 |
| **48** | A11 | 3c dull violet | 2.50 | 2.50 |
| **49** | A11 | 5c dark green | .55 | .40 |
| *a.* | | Double impression | *350.00* | |
| **50** | A11 | 7c gray | 5.00 | 5.00 |
| **51** | A11 | 20c orange | 10.00 | 10.00 |
| | | *Nos. 46-51 (6)* | 21.10 | 20.80 |

All values exist imperforate. They are plate proofs.

Pres. T. Augustin Simon Sam — A12

Coat of Arms — A13

**1898-99 Unwmk. *Perf. 12***

| | | | | |
|---|---|---|---|---|
| **52** | A12 | 1c ultra | .25 | .25 |
| **53** | A13 | 1c yel green ('99) | .25 | .25 |
| **54** | A12 | 2c deep orange | .25 | .25 |
| **55** | A13 | 2c car lake ('99) | .25 | .25 |
| **56** | A12 | 3c green | .25 | .25 |
| **57** | A13 | 4c red | .25 | .25 |
| **58** | A12 | 5c red brown | .25 | .25 |
| **59** | A13 | 5c pale blue ('99) | .25 | .25 |
| **60** | A12 | 7c gray | .25 | .25 |
| **61** | A13 | 8c carmine | .25 | .25 |
| **62** | A13 | 10c orange red | .25 | .25 |
| **63** | A13 | 15c olive green | .60 | .45 |
| **64** | A12 | 20c black | .60 | .45 |
| **65** | A12 | 50c rose brown | 1.00 | .50 |
| **66** | A12 | 1g red violet | 2.25 | 2.00 |
| | | *Nos. 52-66 (15)* | 7.20 | 6.15 |

For overprints see Nos. 67-81, 110-124, 169, 247-248.

Stamps of 1898-99 Handstamped in Black

**1902**

| | | | | |
|---|---|---|---|---|
| **67** | A12 | 1c ultra | .60 | *1.50* |
| *a.* | | Inverted overprint | 1.75 | |
| *b.* | | Pair, one without overprint | *40.00* | |
| **68** | A13 | 1c yellow green | .45 | .30 |
| *a.* | | Inverted overprint | 1.75 | |
| *b.* | | Double overprint | 6.00 | |
| *c.* | | Pair, one without overprint | 25.00 | |
| **69** | A12 | 2c deep orange | .80 | *1.50* |
| *a.* | | Inverted overprint | 2.00 | |
| *b.* | | Double overprint | 6.00 | |
| *c.* | | Pair, one without overprint | *40.00* | |
| **70** | A13 | 2c carmine lake | .45 | .30 |
| *a.* | | Inverted overprint | 2.00 | |
| *b.* | | Double overprint | 6.00 | |
| **71** | A12 | 3c green | .45 | .45 |
| *a.* | | Inverted overprint | 2.00 | |
| **72** | A13 | 4c red | .60 | *.90* |
| *a.* | | Inverted overprint | 2.00 | |
| *b.* | | Double overprint | 6.00 | |
| **73** | A12 | 5c red brown | 1.25 | *5.00* |
| *a.* | | Inverted overprint | 6.00 | |
| **74** | A13 | 5c pale blue | .45 | .45 |
| *a.* | | Inverted overprint | 2.00 | |
| *b.* | | Double overprint | 6.00 | |
| **75** | A12 | 7c gray | .95 | .95 |
| *a.* | | Inverted overprint | 2.50 | |
| *b.* | | Double overprint | 6.00 | |
| **76** | A13 | 8c carmine | .95 | *7.50* |
| *a.* | | Inverted overprint | 5.00 | |
| *b.* | | Double overprint | 6.00 | |
| **77** | A13 | 10c orange red | .95 | *1.50* |
| *a.* | | Inverted overprint | 6.00 | |
| *b.* | | Double overprint | 6.00 | |
| **78** | A13 | 15c olive green | 4.50 | *6.00* |
| *a.* | | Inverted overprint | 8.00 | |
| *b.* | | Double overprint | 10.00 | |
| **79** | A12 | 20c black | 4.50 | *5.00* |
| *a.* | | Inverted overprint | 14.00 | |
| *b.* | | Double overprint | 16.00 | |
| **80** | A12 | 50c rose brown | 14.50 | *35.00* |
| *a.* | | Inverted overprint | 20.00 | |
| **81** | A12 | 1g red violet | 20.00 | *55.00* |
| *a.* | | Inverted overprint | 40.00 | |
| *b.* | | Pair, one without overprint | 75.00 | |
| | | *Nos. 67-81 (15)* | 51.40 | 121.35 |

Many forgeries exist of this overprint.

**Centenary of Independence Issues**

Coat of Arms — A14

Francois-Dominique Toussaint L'Ouverture — A15

Emperor Jean Jacques Dessalines A16

Pres. Alexandre Sabes Pétion A17

**1903, Dec. 31 Engr. *Perf. 13¼, 14***

| | | | | |
|---|---|---|---|---|
| **82** | A14 | 1c green | .35 | .35 |

**Center Engr., Frame Litho.**

| | | | | |
|---|---|---|---|---|
| **83** | A15 | 2c rose & blk | 1.25 | *3.00* |
| **84** | A15 | 5c dull blue & blk | 1.25 | *3.00* |
| **85** | A16 | 7c plum & blk | 1.25 | *3.00* |
| **86** | A16 | 10c yellow & blk | 1.25 | *3.00* |
| **87** | A17 | 20c slate & blk | 1.25 | *3.00* |
| **88** | A17 | 50c olive & blk | 1.25 | *3.00* |
| | | *Nos. 82-88 (7)* | 7.85 | 18.35 |

Nos. 82 to 88 exist imperforate.

Nos. 83-88 exist with centers inverted. Some are known with head omitted.

Forgeries exist both perforated and imperf and constitute the great majority of Nos. 83-88 offered in the marketplace. Stamps perforated 13½ are forgeries. Many forgeries exist with heads lithographed instead of engraved.

Same Handstamped in Blue

**1904**

| | | | | |
|---|---|---|---|---|
| **89** | A14 | 1c green | .50 | 1.50 |
| **90** | A15 | 2c rose & blk | .50 | 1.50 |
| **91** | A15 | 5c dull blue & blk | .50 | 1.50 |
| **92** | A16 | 7c plum & blk | .50 | 1.50 |
| **93** | A16 | 10c yellow & blk | .50 | 1.50 |
| **94** | A17 | 20c slate & blk | .50 | 1.50 |
| **95** | A17 | 50c olive & blk | .50 | 1.50 |
| | | *Nos. 89-95 (7)* | 3.50 | 10.50 |

Two dies were used for the handstamped overprint on Nos. 89-95. Letters and figures are larger on one than on the other. All values exist imperforate.

Pres. Pierre Nord-Alexis — A18

**1904 Engr. *Perf. 13¼, 14***

| | | | | |
|---|---|---|---|---|
| **96** | A18 | 1c green | .35 | .35 |
| **97** | A18 | 2c carmine | .35 | .35 |
| **98** | A18 | 5c dark blue | .35 | .35 |
| **99** | A18 | 10c orange brown | .35 | .35 |
| **100** | A18 | 20c orange | .35 | .35 |
| **101** | A18 | 50c claret | .35 | .35 |
| *a.* | | Tête bêche pair | *500.00* | |
| | | *Nos. 96-101 (6)* | 2.10 | 2.10 |

Used values are for c-t-o's. Postally used examples are worth considerably more.

Nos. 96-101 exist imperforate. Value, set $10.

This issue, and the overprints and surcharges, exist in horiz. pairs, imperf. vert., and in vert. pairs, imperf. horiz.

For overprints and surcharges see Nos. 102-109, 150-161, 170-176, 217-218, 235-238, 240-242, 302-303.

Forgeries of Nos. 96, 101, 101a exist.

*Reprints or very accurate imitations of this issue exist, including No. 101a. Some are printed in very bright colors on very white paper and are found both perforated and imperforate. The original stamps are perf. 13¼ or 14, the reprints (forgeries) perf 13½, as well as numerous other perforations, including compound perfs.*

Same Handstamped in Blue like #89-95

**1904**

| | | | | |
|---|---|---|---|---|
| **102** | A18 | 1c green | .60 | 1.50 |
| **103** | A18 | 2c carmine | .60 | 1.50 |
| **104** | A18 | 5c dark blue | .60 | 1.50 |
| **105** | A18 | 10c orange brown | .60 | 1.50 |
| **106** | A18 | 20c orange | .60 | 1.50 |
| **107** | A18 | 50c claret | .60 | 1.50 |
| | | *Nos. 102-107 (6)* | 3.60 | 9.00 |

The note after No. 95 applies also to Nos. 102-107. All values exist imperf.

Forgeries exist.

**Regular Issue of 1904 Handstamp Surcharged in Black**

**1906, Feb. 20**

| | | | | |
|---|---|---|---|---|
| **108** | A18 | 1c on 20c orange | .35 | .25 |
| *a.* | | 1c on 50c claret | *950.00* | |
| **109** | A18 | 2c on 50c claret | .35 | .25 |

No. 108a is known only with inverted surcharge.

Forgeries exist.

Nos. 52-66 Handstamped in Red

**1906**

| | | | | |
|---|---|---|---|---|
| **110** | A12 | 1c ultra | 1.40 | .95 |
| **111** | A13 | 1c yellow green | .75 | .75 |
| **112** | A12 | 2c deep orange | 2.50 | 2.25 |
| **113** | A13 | 2c carmine lake | 1.50 | 1.25 |
| **114** | A12 | 3c green | 1.50 | 1.25 |
| **115** | A13 | 4c red | 5.75 | 4.50 |
| **116** | A12 | 5c red brown | 7.00 | 5.50 |
| **117** | A13 | 5c pale blue | 1.10 | .60 |
| **118** | A12 | 7c gray | 5.00 | 4.50 |
| **119** | A13 | 8c carmine | 1.10 | 1.00 |
| **120** | A13 | 10c orange red | 2.00 | 1.25 |
| **121** | A13 | 15c olive green | 2.50 | 1.25 |
| **122** | A12 | 20c black | 5.75 | 4.50 |
| **123** | A12 | 50c rose brown | 5.50 | 3.50 |
| **124** | A12 | 1g red violet | 12.00 | 7.25 |
| | | *Nos. 110-124 (15)* | 55.35 | 40.30 |

Forgeries of this overprint are plentiful.

Coat of Arms — A19

President Nord-Alexis A20

Market at Port-au-Prince A21

Sans Souci Palace — A22

Independence Palace at Gonaives — A23

Entrance to Catholic College at Port-au-Prince A24

Monastery and Church at Port-au-Prince A25

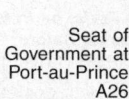

Seat of Government at Port-au-Prince A26

Presidential Palace at Port-au-Prince A27

**For Foreign Postage (centimes de piastre)**

**1906-13 *Perf. 12***

| | | | | |
|---|---|---|---|---|
| **125** | A19 | 1c de p green | .35 | .25 |
| **126** | A20 | 2c de p ver | .45 | .25 |
| **127** | A21 | 3c de p brown | .60 | .25 |
| **128** | A21 | 3c de p org yel ('11) | 6.00 | 6.00 |
| **129** | A22 | 4c de p car lake | .60 | .35 |
| **130** | A22 | 4c de p lt ol grn ('13) | 25.00 | 25.00 |
| **131** | A20 | 5c de p dk blue | 2.50 | .30 |
| **132** | A23 | 7c de p gray | 1.75 | .85 |
| **133** | A23 | 7c de p org red ('13) | 65.00 | 65.00 |

134 A24 8c de p car rose 1.75 .80
135 A24 8c de p ol grn ('13) 55.00 35.00
136 A25 10c de p org red 1.25 .30
137 A25 10c de p red brn ('13) 27.50 22.50
138 A26 15c de p sl grn 2.25 .90
139 A26 15c dp p yel ('13) 20.00 12.00
140 A20 20c de p blue grn 2.25 .90
141 A19 50c de p red 3.25 2.25
142 A19 50c de p org yel ('13) 20.00 12.00
143 A27 1p claret 7.25 4.50
144 A27 1p red ('13) 13.00 11.00
*Nos. 125-144 (20)* 255.75 200.40

All 1906 values exist imperf. These are plate proofs.

For overprints and surcharges see Nos. 177-195, 213-216, 239, 245, 249-260, 263, 265-277, 279-284, 286-301, 304.

Nord-Alexis
A28

Coat of Arms — A29

**For Domestic Postage (centimes de gourde)**

**1906-10**

145 A28 1c de g blue .35 .25
146 A29 2c de g org yel .45 .25
147 A29 2c de g lemon ('10) .65 .25
148 A28 3c de g slate .40 .25
149 A29 7c de g green 1.25 .45
*Nos. 145-149 (5)* 3.10 1.45

For overprints see Nos. 196-197.

Regular Issue of 1904 Handstamp Surcharged in Red like #108-109

**1907**

150 A18 1c on 5c dk bl .40 .35
151 A18 1c on 20c org .40 .25
152 A18 2c on 10c org brn .40 .40
153 A18 2c on 50c claret .50 .40

**Black Surcharge**

154 A18 1c on 5c dk bl .50 .40
155 A18 1c on 10c org brn .50 .25
156 A18 2c on 20c org .40 .40

**Brown Surcharge**

157 A18 1c on 5c dk bl 1.50 1.25
158 A18 1c on 10c org brn 1.50 1.25
159 A18 2c on 20c org 5.00 4.00
160 A18 2c on 50c claret 27.50 22.50

**Violet Surcharge**

161 A18 1c on 20c org 150.00

The handstamps are found sideways, diagonal, inverted and double.

Forgeries exist.

A30

President Antoine T. Simon — A31

**1910 For Foreign Postage**

162 A30 2c de p rose red & blk .65 .50
163 A30 5c de p bl & blk 13.00 1.00
164 A30 20c de p yel grn & blk 12.50 12.50

**For Domestic Postage**

165 A31 1c de g lake & blk .30 .25
*Nos. 162-165 (4)* 26.45 14.25

For overprint and surcharges see Nos. 198, 262, 278, 285.

A32

A33

Pres. Cincinnatus Leconte — A34

**1912**

166 A32 1c de g car lake .40 .40
167 A33 2c de g dp org .50 .40

**For Foreign Postage**

168 A34 5c de p dp blue .90 .40
*Nos. 166-168 (3)* 1.80 1.20

For overprints see Nos. 199-201.

Stamps of Preceding Issues Handstamped Vertically

**1914 On No. 61**

169 A13 8c carmine 13.00 10.00

**On Nos. 96-101**

170 A18 1c green 35.00 30.00
171 A18 2c carmine 35.00 30.00
172 A18 5c dk blue .65 .40
173 A18 10c orange brn .65 .40
174 A18 20c orange 1.10 .50
175 A18 50c claret 2.50 1.25
*Nos. 170-175 (6)* 74.90 62.55

Perforation varieties of Nos. 172-175 exist.

No. 175 overprinted "T. M." is a revenue stamp. The letters are the initials of "Timbre Mobile."

**On No. 107**

176 A18 50c claret *10,000. 13,000.*

**Horizontally on Stamps of 1906-13**

177 A19 1c de p green .55 .45
178 A20 2c de p ver .75 .45
179 A21 3c de p brown 1.25 .65
180 A21 3c de p org yel .55 .45
181 A22 4c de p car lake 1.25 .65
182 A22 4c de p lt ol grn 3.00 1.60
183 A23 7c de p gray 2.75 2.75
184 A23 7c de p org red 7.25 6.75
185 A24 8c de p car rose 5.00 4.50
186 A24 8c de p ol grn 9.25 9.00
187 A25 10c de p org red 1.50 .65
188 A25 10c de p red brn 4.00 2.50
189 A26 15c de p sl grn 4.25 3.75
190 A26 15c de p yellow 3.00 1.60
191 A20 20c de p bl grn 3.75 1.40
192 A19 50c de p red 6.50 6.00
193 A19 50c de p org yel 11.00 10.00
194 A27 1p claret 6.50 6.00
195 A27 1p red 12.00 11.00
196 A29 2c de g lemon .55 .45
197 A28 3c de g slate .55 .45
*Nos. 177-197 (21)* 85.20 71.05

**On No. 164**

198 A30 20c de p yel grn & blk 3.75 3.50

**Vertically on Nos. 166-168**

199 A32 1c de g car lake .50 .40
200 A33 2c de g dp org .65 .50
201 A34 5c de p dp blue 1.10 .40
*Nos. 199-201 (3)* 2.25 1.30

Two handstamps were used for the overprints on Nos. 169-201. They may be distinguished by the short and long foot of the "L" of "GL" and the position of the first "1" in "1914" with regard to the period above it. Both handstamps are found on all but #176, 294, 295, 306, 308.

Handstamp Surcharged

**On Nos. 141 and 143**

213 A19 1c de p on 50c de p red .50 .40
214 A27 1c de p on 1p claret .65 .50

**On Nos. 142 and 144**

215 A19 1c de p on 50c de p org yel .65 .50
216 A27 1c de p on 1p red .65 .50

Handstamp Surcharged

**On Nos. 100 and 101**

217 A18 7c on 20c orange .50 .25
218 A18 7c on 50c claret .45 .25

The initials on the preceding handstamps are those of Gen. Oreste Zamor; the date is that of his triumphal entry into Port-au-Prince.

Pres. Oreste Zamor

Coat of Arms

Pres. Tancrède Auguste

Owing to the theft of a large quantity of this 1914 issue, while in transit from the printers, the stamps were never placed on sale at post offices. A few stamps have been canceled through carelessness of favor. Value, set of 10, $8.50.

Preceding Issues Handstamp Surcharged in Carmine or Blue

**1915-16 On Nos. 98-101**

235 A18 1c on 5c dk bl (C) 2.00 2.25
236 A18 1c on 10c org brn .60 .75
237 A18 1c on 20c orange .60 .75
238 A18 1c on 50c claret .60 .75

**On No. 132**

239 A23 1c on 7c de p gray (C) .60 .75

**On Nos. 106-107**

240 A18 1c on 20c orange 1.50 1.50
241 A18 1c on 50c claret 3.50 1.50
242 A18 1c on 50c cl (C) *125.00 125.00*
*Nos. 235-242 (8)* 134.40 133.25

Nos. 240-242 are known with two types of the "Post Paye" overprint. No. 237 with red surcharge and any stamps with violet surcharge are unofficial.

Values for Nos. 245-308 are for examples with the boxed "Gourde" surcharge partially on the stamp. Examples upon which this surcharge is fully present on the stamp command substantial premiums.

No. 143 Handstamp Surcharged in Red

**1917-19**

245 A27 2c on 1p claret .50 .50

**Stamps of 1906-14 Handstamp Surcharged in Various Colors**

1c, 5c

**On Nos. 123-124**

247 A12 1c on 50c (R) 90.00 40.00
248 A12 1c on 1g (R) 90.00 40.00

**On #127, 129, 134, 136, 138, 140-141**

249 A22 1c on 4c de p (Br) .65 *.75*
250 A25 1c on 10c de p (Bl) .65 *.75*
252 A20 1c on 20c de p (R) .65 *.75*
253 A20 1c on 20c de p (Bk) .65 *.75*
254 A19 1c on 50c de p (R) .65 *.75*
255 A19 1c on 50c de p (Bk) .65 *.75*
256 A21 2c on 3c de p (R) .65 *.75*
257 A24 2c on 8c de p (R) .65 *.75*
258 A24 2c on 8c de p (Bk) .65 *.75*
259 A26 2c on 15c de p (R) .65 *.75*
260 A20 2c on 20c de p (R) .65 *.75*
*Nos. 249-260 (11)* 7.15 8.25

The 1c on 10c de p stamp in black is actually a blue ink which bled into the stamps.

**On Nos. 164, 128**

262 A30 1c on 20c de p (Bk) 3.75 3.50
263 A21 2c on 3c de p (R) .60 .75

**On #130, 133, 135, 137, 139, 142, 144**

265 A22 1c on 4c de p (R) .70 *.85*
266 A23 1c on 7c de p (Br) .70 *.85*
267 A26 1c on 15c de p (R) .70 *.85*
268 A19 1c on 50c de p (Bk) 2.25 *2.75*
269 A27 1c on 1p (Bk) 2.25 *2.75*
270 A24 2c on 8c de p (R) .70 *.85*
271 A25 2c on 10c de p (Br) .70 *.85*
272 A26 2c on 15c de p (R) .70 *.85*
273 A25 5c on 10c de p (Bl) 2.25 *2.75*
274 A25 5c on 10c de p (VBk) .70 *.85*
275 A26 5c on 15c de p (R) 5.50 *6.75*
*Nos. 265-275 (11)* 17.15 *20.95*

"O. Z." Stamps of 1914 Handstamp Surcharged in Red or Brown

**276** A26 1c on 15c de p sl grn .70 *.85*
**277** A20 1c on 20c de p bl grn .70 *.85*
**278** A30 1c on 20c de p yel grn & blk .70 *.85*
**279** A27 1c on 1p claret (Br) .70 *.85*
**280** A27 1c on 1p claret 2.25 *2.75*
**281** A27 5c on 1p red (Br) .70 *.85*
*Nos. 276-281 (6)* 5.75 *7.00*

Srchd. in Violet, Green, Red, Magenta or Black 1 ct and 2 cts as in 1917-19 and

**1919-20**

**282** A22 2c on 4c de p car lake (V) .70 *.85*
**283** A24 2c on 8c de p car rose (G) .70 *.85*
**284** A24 2c on 8c de p ol grn (R) .70 *.85*
**285** A30 2c on 20c de p yel grn & blk (R) .85 *1.10*
**286** A19 2c on 50c de p red (G) .70 *.85*
**288** A19 2c on 50c de p red (R) .70 *.85*
**289** A19 2c on 50c de p org yel (R) .70 *.85*
**290** A27 2c on 1pi claret (R) 3.50 *4.00*
**291** A27 2c on 1pi red (R) 2.25 *2.75*
**292** A21 3c on 3c de p brn (R) .70 *.85*
**293** A23 3c on 7c de p org red (R) .70 *.85*
**294** A21 5c on 3c de p brn (R) .70 *.85*
**295** A21 5c on 3c de p org yel (R) 2.25 *2.75*
**296** A22 5c on 4c de p car lake (R) .70 *.85*
**297** A22 5c on 4c de p ol grn (R) .70 *.85*
**298** A23 5c on 7c de p gray (V) .70 *.85*
**299** A23 5c on 7c de p org red (V) .70 *.85*
**300** A25 5c on 10c de p org red (V) .70 *.85*
**301** A26 5c on 15c de p yel (M) .70 *.85*
*Nos. 282-301 (19)* 19.35 *23.35*

Nos. 217 and 218 Handstamp Surcharged with New Value in Magenta

**302** A18 5c on 7c on 20c orange .60 .75
**303** A18 5c on 7c on 50c claret 3.50 4.00

No. 187 Handstamp Surcharged in Magenta

**304** A25 5c de p on 10c de p .60 .75

Postage Due Stamps of 1906-14 Handstamp Surcharged in Black or Magenta (#308)

**On Stamp of 1906**

**305** D2 5c on 50c ol gray 15.00 15.00

**On Stamp of 1914**

**306** D2 5c on 10c violet .60 .75
**307** D2 5c on 50c olive gray .60 .75
**308** D2 5c on 50c ol gray (M) 2.50 2.00
*Nos. 305-308 (4)* 18.70 18.50

Nos. 299 with red surcharge and 306-307 with violet are trial colors or essays.

Allegory of Agriculture A40

Allegory of Commerce A41

**1920, Apr. Engr. *Perf. 12***

**310** A40 3c deep orange .40 .40
**311** A40 5c green .40 .40
**312** A41 10c vermilion .50 .40
**313** A41 15c violet .50 .40
**314** A41 25c deep blue .65 .50
*Nos. 310-314 (5)* 2.45 2.10

Nos. 311-313 overprinted "T. M." are revenue stamps. The letters are the initials of "Timbre Mobile."

President Louis J. Borno — A42

Christophe's Citadel — A43

Old Map of West Indies — A44

Borno — A45

National Capitol — A46

**1924, Sept. 3**

**315** A42 5c deep green .40 .25
**316** A43 10c carmine .40 .25
**317** A44 20c violet blue .90 .40
**318** A45 50c orange & blk .90 .40
**319** A46 1g olive green 1.60 .50
*Nos. 315-319 (5)* 4.20 1.80

For surcharges see Nos. 359, C4A.

Coffee Beans and Flowers — A47

**1928, Feb. 6**

**320** A47 35c deep green 3.75 .60

For surcharge see No. 337.

Pres. Louis Borno — A48

**1929, Nov. 4**

**321** A48 10c carmine rose .50 .40

Signing of the "Frontier" treaty between Haiti and the Dominican Republic.

Presidents Salomon and Vincent — A49

Pres. Sténio Vincent — A50

**1931, Oct. 16**

**322** A49 5c deep green 1.30 .50
**323** A50 10c carmine rose 1.30 .50

50th anniv. of Haiti's joining the UPU.

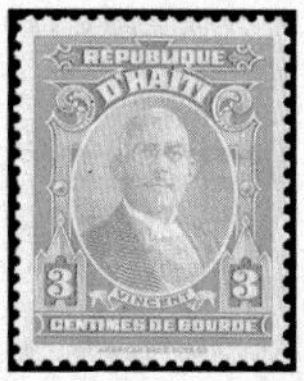

President Vincent — A52

Aqueduct at Port-au-Prince A53

Fort National — A54

Palace of Sans Souci — A55

Christophe's Chapel at Milot — A56

King's Gallery Citadel — A57

Vallières Battery — A58

**1933-40**

**325** A52 3c orange .30 .25
**326** A52 3c dp ol grn ('39) .30 .25
**327** A53 5c green .30 .25
*a.* 5c emerald ('38) .30 .25
*b.* 5c bright green ('39) .30 .25
*c.* 5c brown olive ('40) .50 .25
**329** A54 10c rose car .50 .25
*a.* 10c vermilion .65 .25
**330** A54 10c red brn ('40) .50 .25
**331** A55 25c blue .90 .25
**332** A56 50c brown 2.50 .55
**333** A57 1g dark green 2.50 .55
**334** A58 2.50g olive bister 4.50 .90
*Nos. 325-334 (9)* 12.30 3.50

For surcharges see Nos. 357-358, 360.

Alexandre Dumas, His Father and Son — A59

**1935, Dec. 29 Litho. *Perf. 11½***

**335** A59 10c rose pink & choc .90 .40
**336** A59 25c blue & chocolate 1.60 .50
*Nos. 335-336,C10 (3)* 7.00 3.40

Visit of a delegation from France to Haiti.
No. 335 exists imperf and in horiz. pair, imperf. between. #336 exists as pair, imperf horiz.

**No. 320 Surcharged in Red**

**1939, Jan. 24 *Perf. 12***

**337** A47 25c on 35c dp grn .90 .40

Statue of Liberty, Map of Haiti and Flags of American Republics A60

**1941, June 30 Engr. *Perf. 12***

**338** A60 10c rose carmine 1.00 .50
**339** A60 25c dark blue .90 .40
*Nos. 338-339,C12-C13 (4)* 8.40 2.40

3rd Inter-American Caribbean Conf., held at Port-au-Prince.

Patroness of Haiti, Map and Coat of Arms — A61

**1942, Dec. 8 Size: 26x36¼mm**

**340** A61 3c dull violet .40 .25
**341** A61 5c brt green .50 .25
**342** A61 10c rose car .50 .25
**343** A61 15c orange .65 .50
**344** A61 20c brown .65 .50
**345** A61 25c deep blue 1.40 .50
**346** A61 50c red orange 1.75 .70
**347** A61 2.50g olive black 4.75 1.10

**Size: 32x45mm**

**348** A61 5g purple 14.00 4.50
*Nos. 340-348,C14-C18 (14)* 30.30 10.60

Issued in honor of Our Lady of Perpetual Help, patroness of Haiti.
For surcharges see Nos. 355-356.

Adm. Hammerton Killick and Destruction of "La Crête-à-Pierrot" — A62

**1943, Sept. 6**

**349** A62 3c orange .40 .25
**350** A62 5c turq green .50 .40
**351** A62 10c carmine rose .50 .40
**352** A62 25c deep blue .65 .40
**353** A62 50c olive 1.40 .50
**354** A62 5g brown black 5.75 3.00
*Nos. 349-354,C22-C23 (8)* 11.45 6.95

Nos. 343 and 345 Surcharged with New Value and Bars in Red

**1944, July 19**

**355** A61 10c on 15c orange .40 .25
**356** A61 10c on 25c dp blue .40 .25

Nos. 319, 326 and 334 Surcharged with New Values and Bars in Red

**1944-45**

**357** A52 2c on 3c dp ol grn .30 .25
**358** A52 5c on 3c dp ol grn .40 .40
**359** A46 10c on 1g ol grn .50 .40
*a.* Surcharged "01.0" 1.50 *3.00*
**360** A58 20c on 2.50g ol bis .50 .40
*Nos. 357-360 (4)* 1.70 1.45

Nurse and Wounded Soldier on Battlefield — A63

**1945, Feb. 20** **Cross in Rose**

**361** A63 3c gray black .25 .25
**362** A63 5c dk blue grn .25 .25
**363** A63 10c red orange .30 .25
**364** A63 20c black brn .30 .25
**365** A63 25c deep blue .40 .25
**366** A63 35c orange .50 .25
**367** A63 50c car rose .50 .25
**368** A63 1g olive green .90 .40
**369** A63 2.50g pale violet 2.50 .50
*Nos. 361-369,C25-C32 (17)* 18.75 7.55

Issued to honor the Intl. Red Cross.

20c, 1g, 2.50g, Aug. 14. Others, Feb. 20.

For overprints and surcharges see Nos. 456-457, C153-C160.

**Catalogue values for unused stamps in this section, from this point to the end of the section, are for Never Hinged items.**

Col. François Capois A64

Jean Jacques Dessalines A65

**Unwmk.**

**1946, July 18** **Engr.** ***Perf. 12***

**370** A64 3c red orange .25 .25
**371** A64 5c Prus green .25 .25
**372** A64 10c red .25 .25
**373** A64 20c olive black .25 .25
**374** A64 25c deep blue .30 .25
**375** A64 35c orange .40 .25
**376** A64 50c red brown .50 .40
**377** A64 1g olive brown .50 .40
**378** A64 2.50g gray 1.30 .50
*Nos. 370-378,C35-C42 (17)* 9.60 6.15

For surcharges see Nos. 383, 392, C43-C45, C49-C51, C61-C62. For overprint see No. Q4.

**1947-54**

**379** A65 3c orange yel .25 .25
**380** A65 5c green .25 .25
**380A** A65 5c dp vio ('54) .65 .25
**381** A65 10c carmine rose .25 .25
**382** A65 25c deep blue .40 .25
*Nos. 379-382,C46 (6)* 2.20 1.50

No. 375 Surcharged with New Value and Rectangular Block in Black

**1948**

**383** A64 10c on 35c orange .40 .25

Arms of Port-au-Prince A66

**Engraved and Lithographed**

**1950, Feb. 12** ***Perf. 12½***

**384** A66 10c multicolored .40 .25
*Nos. 384,C47-C48 (3)* 2.20 1.25

200th anniv. (in 1949) of the founding of Port-au-Prince.

**Nos. RA10-RA12 and RA16 Surcharged or Overprinted in Black**

**1950, Oct. 4** **Unwmk.** ***Perf. 12***

**385** PT2 3c on 5c ol gray .25 .25
**386** PT2 5c green .40 .25
**387** PT2 10c on 5c car rose .40 .25
**388** PT2 20c on 5c blue .50 .50
*Nos. 385-388,C49-C51 (7)* 4.30 3.55

75th anniv. (in 1949) of the UPU.

Exist with inverted or double surcharge and 10c on 5c green.

Cacao — A67

**1951, Sept. 3** **Photo.** ***Perf. 12½***

**389** A67 5c dark green .40 .25
*Nos. 389,C52-C54 (4)* 27.15 4.75

Pres. Paul E. Magloire and Day Nursery, Saline — A68

Design: 10c, Applying asphalt.

**1953, May 4** **Engr.** ***Perf. 12***

**390** A68 5c green .25 .25
**391** A68 10c rose carmine .30 .25
*Nos. 390-391,C57-C60 (6)* 3.80 2.35

No. 375 Surcharged in Black

**1953, Apr. 7**

**392** A64 50c on 35c orange .50 .40

Gen. Pierre Dominique Toussaint L'Ouverture, 1743-1803, liberator.

J. J. Dessalines and Paul E. Magloire — A69

Alexandre Sabes Pétion — A70

Battle of Vertieres — A71

Design: No. 395, Larmartiniere. No. 396, Boisrond-Tonnerre. No. 397, Toussaint L'Ouverture. No. 399, Capois. No. 401, Marie Jeanne and Lamartiniere leading attack.

**1954, Jan. 1** **Photo.** ***Perf. 11½***

**Portraits in Black**

**393** A69 3c blue gray .25 .25
**394** A70 5c yellow green .30 .25
**395** A70 5c yellow green .30 .25
**396** A70 5c yellow green .40 .30
**397** A70 5c yellow green .30 .25
**398** A69 10c crimson .30 .25
**399** A70 15c rose lilac .40 .25

***Perf. 12½***

**400** A71 25c dark gray .40 .25
**401** A71 25c deep orange .40 .25
*Nos. 393-401 (9)* 3.05 2.30
*Nos. 393-401,C63-C70,C71-C74 (21)* 14.90 10.65

150th anniv. of Haitian independence.

See Nos. C95-C96.

Mme. Yolette Magloire — A72

**1954, Jan. 1** ***Perf. 11½***

**402** A72 10c orange .30 .25
**403** A72 10c blue .30 .25
*Nos. 402-403,C75-C80 (8)* 6.75 5.20

Henri Christophe, Paul Magloire and Citadel A73

Tomb and Arms of Henri Christophe — A74

***Perf. 13½x13***

**1954, Dec. 6** **Litho.** **Unwmk.**

**404** A73 10c carmine .25 .25

***Perf. 13***

**405** A74 10c red, blk & car .30 .25
*Nos. 404-405,C81-C90 (12)* 15.10 8.85

Restoration of Christophe's Citadel.

J. J. Dessalines A75

Pres. Magloire and Dessalines Memorial, Gonaives A76

**1955-57** **Photo.** ***Perf. 11½***

**406** A75 3c ocher & blk .25 .25
**407** A75 5c pale vio & blk ('56) .25 .25
**408** A75 10c rose & blk .25 .25
*a.* 10c salmon pink & black ('57) .25 .25
**409** A75 25c chalky bl & blk ('56) .30 .25
*a.* 25c blue & black ('57) .30 .25
*Nos. 406-409,C93-C94 (6)* 1.55 1.50

For surcharges, see Nos. 454-455.

**1955, Aug. 1**

**410** A76 10c deep blue & blk .40 .25
**411** A76 10c crimson & blk .40 .25
*Nos. 410-411,C97-C98 (4)* 2.10 1.00

21st anniv. of the new Haitian army.

Nos. 410-411 were printed in a single sheet of 20 (5x4). The two upper rows are of No. 410, the two lower No. 411, providing five se-tenant pairs. Value 85 cents.

Flamingo A77

Mallard A78

**1956, Apr. 14** **Photo.** ***Perf. 11½***

**Granite Paper**

**412** A77 10c blue & ultra 2.25 .30
**413** A78 25c dk grn & bluish grn 3.25 .45
*Nos. 412-413,C99-C104 (8)* 43.40 6.80

Immanuel Kant — A79

**1956, July 19** ***Perf. 12***

**Granite Paper**

**414** A79 10c brt ultra .30 .25
*Nos. 414,C105-C107 (4)* 2.45 1.40

10th anniv. of the 1st Inter-American Philosophical Congress.

Zim Waterfall A80

J. J. Dessalines and Dessalines Memorial, Gonaives A81

**1957, Dec. 16 Unwmk. *Perf. 11½***
**Granite Paper**

| | | | |
|---|---|---|---|
| **415** | A80 10c orange & blue | .30 | .25 |
| | *Nos. 415,C108-C111 (5)* | 4.70 | 3.00 |

For surcharge & overprint see #CB49, CQ2.

**1958, July 1 Photo.**

| | | | |
|---|---|---|---|
| **416** | A81 5c yel grn & blk | .25 | .25 |

Bicentenary of birth of J. J. Dessalines.
See Nos. 470-471, C112, C170. For overprints see Nos. 480-482, C183-C184, CQ1, Q1-Q3.

"Atomium" — A82

View of Brussels Exposition A83

***Perf. 13x13½, 13½x13***
**1958, July 22 Litho. Unwmk.**

| | | | |
|---|---|---|---|
| **417** | A82 50c brown | .40 | .25 |
| **418** | A83 75c brt green | .40 | .25 |
| **419** | A82 1g purple | .75 | .25 |
| **420** | A83 1.50g red orange | .75 | .40 |
| | *Nos. 417-420,C113-C114 (6)* | 5.05 | 2.50 |

Issued for the Universal and International Exposition at Brussels.
For surcharges see Nos. B2-B3, CB9.

Sylvio Cator — A84

U. S. Satellite — A85

**1958, Aug. 16 Photo. *Perf. 11½***
**Granite Paper**

| | | | |
|---|---|---|---|
| **421** | A84 5c green | .25 | .25 |
| **422** | A84 10c brown | .25 | .25 |
| **423** | A84 20c lilac | .25 | .25 |
| | *Nos. 421-423,C115-C118 (7)* | 4.15 | 2.50 |

30th anniversary of the world championship record broad jump of Sylvio Cator.

**1958, Oct. 8 *Perf. 14x13½***

Designs: 20c, Emperor penguins. 50c, Modern observatory. 1g, Ocean exploration.

| | | | |
|---|---|---|---|
| **424** | A85 10c brt bl & brn red | .30 | .25 |
| **425** | A85 20c black & dp org | 1.40 | .50 |
| **426** | A85 50c grn & rose brn | .75 | .30 |
| **427** | A85 1g black & blue | .80 | .30 |
| | *Nos. 424-427,C119-C121 (7)* | 9.35 | 2.75 |

Issued for the International Geophysical Year 1957-58.

President François Duvalier — A86

**Engraved and Lithographed**
**1958, Oct. 22 Unwmk. *Perf. 11½***
**Commemorative Inscription in Ultramarine**

| | | | |
|---|---|---|---|
| **428** | A86 10c blk & dp pink | .30 | .25 |
| **429** | A86 50c blk & lt grn | .40 | .25 |
| **430** | A86 1g blk & brick red | .50 | .40 |
| **431** | A86 5g blk & sal | 2.40 | 1.50 |
| | *Nos. 428-431,C122-C125 (8)* | 10.90 | 6.50 |

1st anniv. of the inauguration of Pres. Dr. François Duvalier. See note on souvenir sheets after No. C125.

**1958 Nov. 20**
**Without Commemorative Inscription**

| | | | |
|---|---|---|---|
| **432** | A86 5c blk & lt vio bl | .25 | .25 |
| **433** | A86 10c blk & dp pink | .25 | .25 |
| **434** | A86 20c blk & yel | .25 | .25 |
| **435** | A86 50c blk & lt grn | .30 | .25 |
| **436** | A86 1g blk & brick red | .50 | .40 |
| **437** | A86 1.50g blk & rose pink | .65 | .50 |
| **438** | A86 2.50g blk & gray vio | .90 | .50 |
| **439** | A86 5g blk & sal | 1.60 | 1.10 |
| | *Nos. 432-439,C126-C132 (15)* | 13.35 | 8.15 |

For surcharges see Nos. B13, B22-B24.

Map of Haiti — A87

**1958, Dec. 5 Photo. *Perf. 11½***
**Granite Paper**

| | | | |
|---|---|---|---|
| **440** | A87 10c rose pink | .25 | .25 |
| **441** | A87 25c green | .30 | .25 |
| | *Nos. 440-441,C133-C135 (5)* | 1.85 | 1.40 |

Tribute to the UN. See No. C135a. For overprints and surcharges see Nos. 442-443, B4-B5, CB11-CB12.

Nos. 440-441 Overprinted "10th ANNIVERSARY OF THE / UNIVERSAL DECLARATION / OF HUMAN RIGHTS" in English (a), French (b), Spanish (c) or Portuguese (d)

**1959, Jan. 28**

| | | | |
|---|---|---|---|
| **442** | Block of 4 | .35 | .35 |
| **a.-d.** | A87 10c any single | .25 | .25 |
| **443** | Block of 4 | .90 | .70 |
| **a.-d.** | A87 25c any single | .25 | .25 |
| | *Nos. 442-443,C136-C138 (5)* | 14.75 | 14.55 |

10th anniv. of the signing of the Universal Declaration of Human Rights.

Pope Pius XII and Children — A88

50c, Pope praying. 2g, Pope on throne.

**1959, Feb. 28 Photo. *Perf. 14x13½***

| | | | |
|---|---|---|---|
| **444** | A88 10c vio bl & ol | .25 | .25 |
| **445** | A88 50c green & dp brn | .40 | .25 |
| **446** | A88 2g dp claret & dk brn | .90 | .50 |
| | *Nos. 444-446,C139-C141 (6)* | 3.45 | 2.05 |

Issued in memory of Pope Pius XII.
For surcharges see Nos. B6-B8.

Abraham Lincoln — A89

**1959, May 12 Photo. *Perf. 12***

| | | | |
|---|---|---|---|
| **447** | A89 50c lt bl & deep claret | .40 | .25 |
| | *Nos. 447,C142-C144 (4)* | 2.50 | 1.55 |

Sesquicentennial of the birth of Abraham Lincoln. Imperf. pairs exist.
For surcharges see #B9, CB16-CB18.

Chicago's Skyline and Dessables House — A90

Jean Baptiste Dessables and Map of American Midwest, c. 1791 — A91

Design: 50c, Discus thrower and flag of Haiti.

**1959, Aug. 27 Unwmk. *Perf. 14***

| | | | |
|---|---|---|---|
| **448** | A90 25c blk brn & lt bl | .40 | .25 |
| **449** | A90 50c multicolored | .50 | .40 |
| **450** | A91 75c brown & blue | .65 | .50 |
| | *Nos. 448-450,C145-C147 (6)* | 4.70 | 2.30 |

3rd Pan American Games, Chicago, 8/27-9/7.
For surcharges see #B10-B12, CB19-CB21.

**No. 449 Overprinted**

**1960, Feb. 29**

| | | | |
|---|---|---|---|
| **451** | A90 50c multicolored | 1.60 | 1.20 |
| | *Nos. 451,C148-C150 (4)* | 7.65 | 7.25 |

8th Olympic Winter Games, Squaw Valley, Calif., Feb. 18-29, 1960.

Uprooted Oak Emblem and Hands — A92

**1960, Apr. 7 Litho. *Perf. 12½x13***

| | | | |
|---|---|---|---|
| **452** | A92 10c salmon & grn | .25 | .25 |
| **453** | A92 50c violet & mag | .40 | .25 |
| | *Nos. 452-453,C151-C152 (4)* | 1.55 | 1.15 |

World Refugee Year, July 1, 1959-June 30, 1960. See Nos. 489-490, C191-C192. For surcharges see Nos. B14-B17, B28-B29, CB24-CB27, CB45-CB46.

No. 406 Surcharged with New Values

**1960, Apr. 27 Photo. *Perf. 11½***

| | | | |
|---|---|---|---|
| **454** | A75 5c on 3c ocher & blk | .25 | .25 |
| **455** | A75 10c on 3c ocher & blk | .35 | .25 |

No. 369 Surcharged or Overprinted in Red: "28eme ANNIVERSAIRE"

**1960, May 8 Engr. *Perf. 12***
**Cross in Rose**

| | | | |
|---|---|---|---|
| **456** | A63 1g on 2.50g pale vio | .90 | .50 |
| **457** | A63 2.50g pale violet | 1.40 | 1.00 |
| | *Nos. 456-457,C153-C160 (10)* | 7.30 | 5.35 |

28th anniversary of the Haitian Red Cross.

Claudinette Fouchard, Miss Haiti, Sugar Queen — A93

Sugar Queen and: 20c, Sugar harvest. 50c, Beach. 1g, Sugar plantation.

***Perf. 11½***
**1960, May 30 Photo. Unwmk.**
**Granite Paper**

| | | | |
|---|---|---|---|
| **458** | A93 10c ol bis & vio | .25 | .25 |
| **459** | A93 20c red brn & blk | .30 | .25 |
| **460** | A93 50c brt bl & brn | .75 | .25 |
| **461** | A93 1g green & brn | 1.75 | .25 |
| | *Nos. 458-461,C161-C162 (6)* | 6.20 | 1.75 |

Haitian sugar industry.

Olympic Victors, Athens, 1896, Melbourne Stadium and Olympic Flame A94

Designs: 20c, Discus thrower and Rome stadium. 50c, Pierre de Coubertin and victors, Melbourne, 1956. 1g, Athens stadium, 1896.

**1960, Aug. 18 Photo. *Perf. 12***

| | | | |
|---|---|---|---|
| **462** | A94 10c black & org | .25 | .25 |
| **463** | A94 20c dk blue & crim | .25 | .25 |
| **464** | A94 50c green & ocher | .65 | .25 |
| **465** | A94 1g dk brn & grnsh bl | .80 | .65 |
| | *Nos. 462-465,C163-C165 (7)* | 5.60 | 2.50 |

17th Olympic Games, Rome, Aug. 25-Sept. 11. For surcharges see Nos. B18-B19, CB28-CB29.

Occide Jeanty and Score from "1804" A95

20c, Occide Jeanty and National Capitol.

**1960, Oct. 19 *Perf. 14x14½***

| | | | |
|---|---|---|---|
| **466** | A95 10c orange & red lilac | .25 | .25 |
| **467** | A95 20c blue & red lilac | .35 | .25 |
| **468** | A95 50c green & sepia | .50 | .40 |
| | *Nos. 466-468,C166-C167 (5)* | 2.35 | 1.40 |

Cent. of the birth of Occide Jeanty, composer. Printed in sheets of 12 (3x4) with commemorative inscription and opening bars of "1804," Jeanty's military march, in top margin.

UN Headquarters, NYC — A96

**1960, Nov. 25 Engr. *Perf. 10½***

| | | | |
|---|---|---|---|
| **469** | A96 1g green & blk | .50 | .40 |
| | *Nos. 469,C168-C169 (3)* | 1.40 | 1.05 |

15th anniv. of the UN. For surcharges see Nos. B20-B21, CB30-CB31, CB35-CB36.
Exists with center inverted.

**Dessalines Type of 1958**

*Perf. 11½*

**1960, Nov. 5 Unwmk. Photo.**

**Granite Paper**

**470** A81 10c red org & blk .25 .25
**471** A81 25c ultra & blk .35 .25
*Nos. 470-471,C170 (3)* .85 .75

Alexandre Dumas Père and Musketeer — A97

5c, Map of Haiti & birthplace of General Alexandre Dumas, horiz. 50c, Alexandre Dumas, father & son, French & Haitian flags, horiz.

**1961, Feb. 10** *Perf. 11½*

**Granite Paper**

**472** A97 5c lt blue & choc .25 .25
**473** A97 10c rose, blk & sep .25 .25
**474** A97 50c dk blue & crim .40 .25
*Nos. 472-474,C177-C179 (6)* 3.35 1.60

Gen. Dumas (Alexandre Davy de la Pailleterie), born in Jeremie, Haiti, and his son and grandson, French authors.

Three Pirates — A98

Tourist publicity: 5c, Map of Tortuga. 15c, Pirates. 20c, Privateer in battle. 50c, Pirate with cutlass in rigging.

**1961, Apr. 4 Litho. *Perf. 12***

**475** A98 5c blue & yel .25 .25
**476** A98 10c lake & yel .25 .25
**477** A98 15c ol grn & org .25 .25
**478** A98 20c choc & org .30 .25
**479** A98 50c vio bl & org .40 .25
*Nos. 475-479,C180-C182 (8)* 2.75 2.15

For surcharges and overprints see Nos. 484-485, C186-C187.

Nos. 416, 470-471 and 378 Overprinted: "Dr. F. Duvalier / Président / 22 Mai 1961"

**1961, May 22 Photo. *Perf. 11½***

**480** A81 5c yel grn & blk .25 .25
**481** A81 10c red org & blk .25 .25
**482** A81 25c ultra & blk .25 .25

**Engr.**

***Perf. 12***

**483** A64 2.50g gray 1.10 .60
*Nos. 480-483,C183-C185 (7)* 2.75 2.25

Re-election of Pres. Francois Duvalier.

No. 475 Surcharged: "EXPLORATION SPATIALE JOHN GLENN," Capsule and New Value

**1962, May 10 Litho.**

**484** A98 50c on 5c bl & yel .50 .40
**485** A98 1.50g on 5c bl & yel 1.40 1.00
*Nos. 484-485,C186-C187 (4)* 3.80 2.80

U.S. achievement in space exploration and for the 1st orbital flight of a US astronaut, Lt. Col. John H. Glenn, Jr., Feb. 20, 1962.

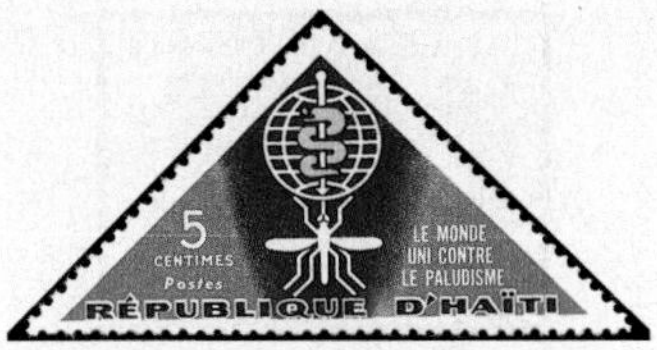


Malaria Eradication Emblem — A99

Design: 10c, Triangle pointing down.

**Unwmk.**

**1962, May 30 Litho. *Perf. 12***

**486** A99 5c crimson & dp bl .25 .25
**487** A99 10c red brn & emer .25 .25
**488** A99 50c blue & crimson .40 .25
*Nos. 486-488,C188-C190 (6)* 2.05 1.65

WHO drive to eradicate malaria.
Sheets of 12 with marginal inscription.
For surcharges see Nos. B25-B27, CB42-CB44.

**WRY Type of 1960 Dated "1962"**

**1962, June 22** *Perf. 12½x13*

**489** A92 10c lt blue & org .25 .25
**490** A92 50c rose lil & ol grn .40 .40
*Nos. 489-490,C191-C192 (4)* 1.40 1.30

Issued to publicize the plight of refugees. For souvenir sheet see note after #C191-C192.

Haitian Scout Emblem — A100

5c, 50c, Scout giving Scout sign. 10c, Lord and Lady Baden-Powell, horiz.

***Perf. 14x14½, 14½x14***

**1962, Aug. 6 Photo.**

**491** A100 3c blk, ocher & pur .25 .25
**492** A100 5c cit, red brn & blk .25 .25
**493** A100 10c ocher, blk & grn .25 .25
**494** A100 25c maroon, ol & bl .25 .25
**495** A100 50c violet, grn & red .40 .25
*Nos. 491-495,C193-C195 (8)* 2.80 2.30

22nd anniv. of the Haitian Boy Scouts.
For surcharges and overprints see Nos. B31-B34, C196-C199.

TIMBRE MOBILE, etc.

From 1970 through 1979 postage and airmail stamps were overprinted for use as revenue stamps. The overprints used were: "TIMBRE MOBILE," "TIMBRE DE SOLIDARITE," "SOLIDARITE," "TIMBRE SOLIDARITE," "OBLIGATION PELIGRE."

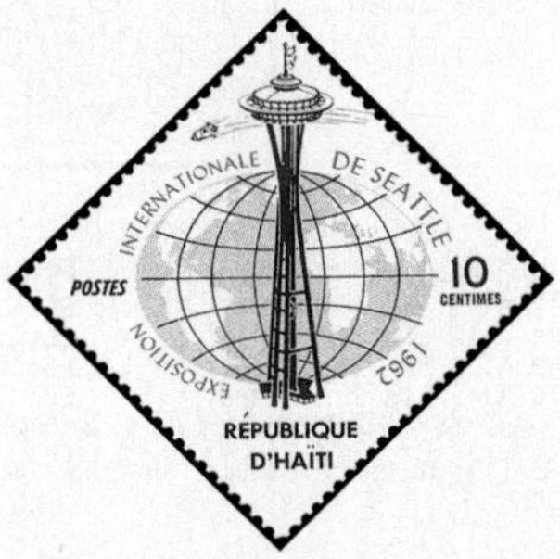


Space Needle, Space Capsule and Globe — A101

**1962, Nov. 19 Litho. *Perf. 12½***

**496** A101 10c red brn & lt bl .25 .25
**497** A101 20c vio bl & pink .25 .25
**498** A101 50c emerald & yel .40 .25
**499** A101 1g car & lt grn .50 .40
*Nos. 496-499,C200-C202 (7)* 3.10 2.20

"Century 21" International Exposition, Seattle, Wash., Apr. 21-Oct. 21.
For overprints see #503-504, C206-C207.

Plan of Duvalier Ville and Stamp of 1904 — A102

**1962, Dec. 10 Photo. *Perf. 14x14½***

**500** A102 5c vio, yel & blk .25 .25
**501** A102 10c car rose, yel & blk .25 .25
**502** A102 25c bl gray, yel & blk .35 .25
*Nos. 500-502,C203-C205 (6)* 3.25 1.90

Issued to publicize Duvalier Ville.
For surcharge see No. B30.

**Nos. 498-499 with Vertical Overprint in Black**

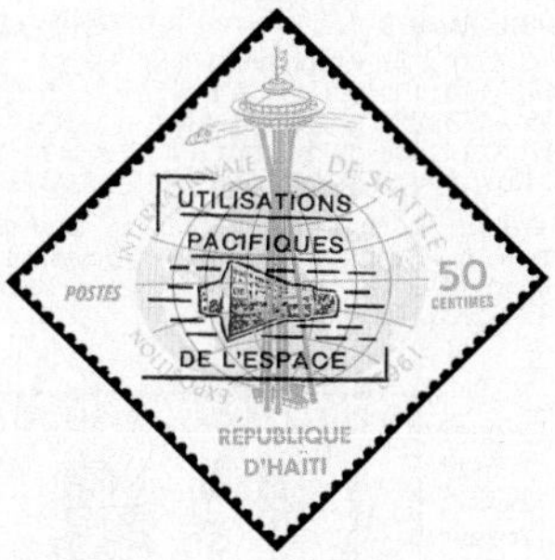


**1963, Jan. 23 Litho. *Perf. 12½***

**503** A101 50c emerald & yel .65 .40
*a.* Claret overprint, horiz. .65 .40
**504** A101 1g car & lt grn 1.40 .50
*a.* Claret overprint, horiz. 1.40 .50
*Nos. 503-504,C206-C207 (4)* 5.20 2.60
*Nos. 503a-504a,C206a-C207a (4)* 5.20 2.60

"Peaceful Uses of Outer Space." The black vertical overprint has no outside frame lines and no broken shading lines around capsule. Nos. 503a and 504a were issued Feb. 20.

Symbolic Harvest A103

**1963, July 12 Photo. *Perf. 13x14***

**505** A103 10c orange & blk .25 .25
**506** A103 20c bluish grn & blk .25 .25
*Nos. 505-506,C208-C209 (4)* 1.40 1.15

FAO "Freedom from Hunger" campaign.

J. J. Dessalines A104

Weight Lifter A105

**1963, Oct. 17** *Perf. 14x14½*

**507** A104 5c tan & ver .25 .25
**508** A104 10c yellow & blue .25 .25
*Nos. 507-508,C214-C215 (4)* 1.00 1.00

For overprints see Nos. 509, C216-C217.

No. 508 Overprinted: "FETE DES MERES / 1964"

**1964, July 22**

**509** A104 10c yellow & blue .25 .25
*Nos. 509,C216-C218 (4)* 1.65 1.15

Issued for Mother's Day, 1964.

**1964, Nov. 12 Photo. *Perf. 11½***

**Granite Paper**

Design: 50c, Hurdler.

**510** A105 10c lt bl & dk brn .25 .25
**511** A105 25c salmon & dk brn .25 .25
**512** A105 50c pale rose lil & dk brn .40 .25
*Nos. 510-512,C223-C226 (7)* 2.85 2.15

18th Olympic Games, Tokyo, Oct. 10-25. Printed in sheets of 50 (10x5), with map of Japan in background extending over 27 stamps.
For surcharges see #B35-B37, CB51-CB54.

Madonna of Haiti and International Airport, Port-au-Prince A106

**1964, Dec. 15** *Perf. 14½x14*

**513** A106 10c org yel & blk .25 .25
**514** A106 25c bl grn & blk .25 .25
**515** A106 50c brt yel grn & blk .40 .25
**516** A106 1g vermilion & blk .50 .40
*Nos. 513-516,C227-C229 (7)* 3.85 2.45

Same Overprinted "1965"

**1965, Feb. 11**

**517** A106 10c org, yel & blk .25 .25
**518** A106 25c blue grn & blk .25 .25
**519** A106 50c brt yel grn & blk .40 .25
**520** A106 1g vermilion & blk .50 .40
*Nos. 517-520,C230-C232 (7)* 3.45 2.50

Unisphere, NY World's Fair — A107

20c, "Rocket Thrower" by Donald De Lue.

**1965, Mar. 22 Photo. *Perf. 13½***

**521** A107 10c grn, yel ol & dk red .25 .25
**522** A107 20c plum & orange .25 .25
**523** A107 50c dk brn, dk red, yel & grn .40 .25
*Nos. 521-523,C233-C235 (6)* 4.20 3.30

New York World's Fair, 1964-65.

Merchantmen — A108

**1965, May 13 Unwmk. *Perf. 11½***

**524** A108 10c blk, lt grn & red .25 .25
**525** A108 50c blk, lt bl & red .40 .25
*Nos. 524-525,C236-C237 (4)* 1.80 1.25

The merchant marine.

ITU Emblem, Old and New Communication Equipment — A109

**1965, Aug. 16 Litho. *Perf. 13½***

**526** A109 10c gray & multi .25 .25
**527** A109 25c multicolored .40 .25
**528** A109 50c multicolored .50 .25
*Nos. 526-528,C242-C245 (7)* 4.55 2.50

Cent. of the ITU.
For overprints see #537-539, C255-C256.

Statue of Our Lady of the Assumption A110

Designs: 5c, Cathedral of Port-au-Prince, horiz. 10c, High altar.

***Perf. 14x13, 13x14***

**1965, Nov. 19 Photo.**

**Size: 39x29mm, 29x39mm**

**529** A110 5c multicolored .25 .25
**530** A110 10c multicolored .25 .25
**531** A110 25c multicolored .30 .25
*Nos. 529-531,C246-C248 (6)* 4.60 3.65

200th anniv. of the Metropolitan Cathedral of Port-au-Prince.

Passionflower A111

Flowers: 5c, 15c, American elder. 10c, Okra.

**1965, Dec. 20 Photo. *Perf. 11½***

**Granite Paper**

**532** A111 3c dk vio, lt vio bl & grn .25 .25
**533** A111 5c grn, lt bl & yel .25 .25
**534** A111 10c multicolored .25 .25
*a.* "0.10" omitted
**535** A111 15c grn, pink & yel .70 .25
**536** A111 50c dk vio, yel & grn 1.40 1.10
*Nos. 532-536,C249-C254 (11)* 15.45 7.15

For surcharges see Nos. 566, B38-B40, CB55-CB56.

Nos. 526-528 Overprinted in Red: "20e. Anniversaire / UNESCO"

**1965, Aug. 27 Litho. *Perf. 13½***

**537** A109 10c gray & multi .30 .25
**538** A109 25c yel brn & multi .35 .35
**539** A109 50c pale grn & multi .70 .70
*Nos. 537-539,C255-C256 (5)* 5.35 2.65

20th anniversary of UNESCO.

Amulet — A112

Ceremonial Stool — A113

***Perf. 14x½x14, 14x14½***

**1966, Mar. 14 Photo. Unwmk.**

**540** A112 5c grnsh bl, blk & yel .25 .25
**541** A113 10c multi .25 .25
**542** A112 50c scar, yel & blk .40 .25
*Nos. 540-542,C257-C259 (6)* 3.45 2.35

For overprints and surcharges see Nos. 543, 567-570, C260-C261, C280-C281.

No. 541 Overprinted in Red: "Hommage / a Hailé Sélassiéler / 24-25 Avril 1966"

**1966, Apr. 24**

**543** A113 10c multi .30 .25
*Nos. 543,C260-C262 (4)* 2.35 1.70

Visit of Emperor Haile Selassie of Ethiopia, Apr. 24-25.

Space Rendezvous of Gemini VI and VII, Dec. 15, 1965 A114

**1966, May 3 *Perf. 13½***

**544** A114 5c vio bl, brn & lt bl .25 .25
**545** A114 10c pur, brn & lt bl .25 .25
**546** A114 25c grn, brn & lt bl .30 .25
**547** A114 50c dk red, brn & lt bl .40 .25
*Nos. 544-547,C263-C265 (7)* 2.75 2.15

Walter M. Schirra, Thomas P. Stafford, Frank A. Borman, James A. Lovell and Gemini VI.

For overprint see No. 584.

Soccer Ball within Wreath and Pres. Duvalier A115

Design: 10c, 50c, Soccer player within wreath and Duvalier.

**Lithographed and Photogravure**

**1966, June 16 *Perf. 13x13½***

**Portrait in Black; Gold Inscription; Green Commemorative Inscription in Two Lines**

**548** A115 5c pale sal & grn .25 .25
**549** A115 10c lt ultra & grn .25 .25
**550** A115 15c lt grn & grn .25 .25
**551** A115 50c pale lil rose & grn .40 .25

**Green Commemorative Inscription in 3 Lines; Gold Inscription Omitted**

**552** A115 5c pale sal & grn .25 .25
**553** A115 10c lt ultra & grn .25 .25
**554** A115 15c lt grn & grn .25 .25
**555** A115 50c pale lil rose & grn .40 .25
*Nos. 548-555,C266-C269 (12)* 4.40 3.65

Caribbean Soccer Festival, June 10-22. Nos. 548-551 also for the Natl. Soccer Championships, May 8-22.

For surcharges and overprint see Nos. 578-579, C288, CB57.

"ABC," Boy and Girl — A116

10c, Scout symbols. 25c, Television set, book and communications satellite, horiz.

***Perf. 14x13½, 13½x14***

**1966, Oct. 18 Litho. & Engr.**

**556** A116 5c grn, sal pink & brn .25 .25
**557** A116 10c red brn, lt brn & blk .25 .25
**558** A116 25c grn, bl & dk vio .25 .25
*Nos. 556-558,C270-C272 (6)* 2.30 1.90

Issued to publicize education through literacy, Scouting and by audio-visual means.

Dr. Albert Schweitzer, Maps of Alsace and Gabon — A117

Designs: 10c, Dr. Schweitzer and pipe organ. 20c, Dr. Schweitzer and Albert Schweitzer Hospital, Deschapelles, Haiti.

***Perf. 12½x13***

**1967, Apr. 20 Photo. Unwmk.**

**559** A117 5c pale lil & multi .25 .25
**560** A117 10c buff & multi .25 .25
**561** A117 20c gray & multi .40 .25
*Nos. 559-561,C273-C276 (7)* 3.45 2.75

Issued in memory of Dr. Albert Schweitzer (1875-1965), medical missionary to Gabon, theologian and musician.

Watermelon and J. J. Dessalines — A118

**1967, July 4 Photo. *Perf. 12½***

**562** A118 5c shown .25 .25
**563** A118 10c Cabbage .25 .25
**564** A118 20c Tangerine 1.25 .25
**565** A118 50c Chayote 2.00 .25
*Nos. 562-565,C277-C279 (7)* 11.25 5.75

No. 532 Surcharged

**1967, Aug. 21 Photo. *Perf. 11½***

**566** A111 50c on 3c multi .30 .25
*Nos. 566,B38-B40,CB55-CB56 (6)* 2.25 1.90

12th Boy Scout World Jamboree, Farragut State Park, Idaho, Aug. 1-9.

Nos. 540-542 Overprinted and Surcharged

***Perf. 14½x14, 14x14½***

**1967, Aug. 30 Photo.**

**567** A112 5c grnsh bl, blk & yel .25 .25
**568** A113 10c multi .25 .25
**569** A112 50c scar, yel & blk .25 .25
**570** A112 1g on 5c multi .50 .40
*Nos. 567-570,C280-C281 (6)* 2.60 2.10

EXPO '67 Intl. Exhibition, Montreal, 4/28-10/27.

Pres. Duvalier and Brush Turkey A119

**1967, Sept. 22 Photo. *Perf. 14x13***

**571** A119 5c car rose & gold .25 .25
**572** A119 10c ultra & gold .25 .25
**573** A119 25c dk red brn & gold .25 .25
**574** A119 50c dp red lil & gold .40 .25
*Nos. 571-574,C282-C284 (7)* 3.40 2.60

10th anniversary of Duvalier revolution.

Writing Hands A120

Designs: 10c, Scout emblem and Scouts, vert. 25c, Audio-visual teaching of algebra.

**1967, Dec. 11 Litho. *Perf. 11½***

**575** A120 5c multicolored .25 .25
**576** A120 10c multicolored .25 .25
**577** A120 25c dk grn, lt bl & yel .25 .25
*Nos. 575-577,C285-C287 (6)* 2.15 1.90

Issued to publicize the importance of education.

For surcharges see Nos. CB58-CB60.

**Nos. 552 and 554 Surcharged**

**Lithographed and Photogravure**

**1968, Jan. 18 *Perf. 13x13½***

**578** A115 50c on 15c .85 .25
**579** A115 1g on 5c 1.00 .85
*Nos. 578-579,C288,CB57 (4)* 6.50 4.60

19th Olympic Games, Mexico City, Oct. 12-27.

The 1968 date is missing on 2 stamps in every sheet of 50.

Caiman Woods, by Raoul Dupoux A121

**1968, Apr. 22 Photo. *Perf. 12***

**Size: 36x26mm**

**580** A121 5c multi .25 .25
**581** A121 10c rose red & multi .25 .25
**582** A121 25c multi .25 .25
**583** A121 50c dl lil & multi .40 .25
*Nos. 580-583,C289-C295 (11)* 6.60 5.00

Caiman Woods ceremony during the Slaves' Rebellion, Aug. 14, 1791.

**No. 547 Overprinted**

**1968, Apr. 19 Photo. *Perf. 13½***

**584** A114 50c dk red, brn & lt bl .90 .80
*Nos. 584,C296-C298 (4)* 5.40 2.90

10th Winter Olympic Games, Grenoble, France, Feb. 6-18, 1968.

Monument to the Unknown Maroon — A122

Palm Tree and Provincial Coats of Arms — A123

Madonna, Papal Arms and Arms of Haiti — A124

**1968, May 22** *Perf. 11½*

**Granite Paper**

**585** A122 5c bl & blk .25 .25
**586** A122 10c rose brn & blk .25 .25
**587** A122 20c vio & blk .25 .25
**588** A122 25c lt ultra & blk .25 .25
**589** A122 50c brt bl grn & blk .40 .25
*Nos. 585-589,C299-C301 (8)* 3.10 2.40

Unveiling of the monument to the Unknown Maroon, Port-au-Prince.

For surcharges see Nos. 610 and C324-C325.

*Perf. 13x14, 12½x13½*

**1968, Aug. 16** **Photo.**

Design: 25c, Cathedral, arms of Pope Paul VI and arms of Haiti.

**590** A123 5c grn & multi .25 .25
**591** A124 10c brn & multi .25 .25
**592** A124 25c multi .25 .25
*Nos. 590-592,C302-C305 (7)* 3.70 3.00

Consecration of the Bishopric of Haiti, 10/28/66.

Air Terminal, Port-au-Prince — A125

**1968, Sept. 22** **Photo.** *Perf. 11½*

**Portrait in Black**

**593** A125 5c brn & lt ultra .25 .25
**594** A125 10c brn & lt bl .25 .25
**595** A125 25c brn & pale lil .25 .25
*Nos. 593-595,C306-C308 (6)* 2.70 2.30

Inauguration of the Francois Duvalier Airport in Port-au-Prince.

Slave Breaking Chains, Map of Haiti, Torch, Conch — A126

**1968, Oct. 28** **Litho.** *Perf. 14½x14*

**596** A126 5c brn, lt bl & brt pink .25 .25
**597** A126 10c brn, lt ol & brt pink .25 .25
**598** A126 25c brn, bis & brt pink .25 .25
*Nos. 596-598,C310-C313 (7)* 3.10 2.50

Slaves' Rebellion, of 1791.

Children Learning to Read A127

10c, Children watching television. 50c, Hands setting volleyball and sports medal.

**1968, Nov. 14** *Perf. 11½*

**599** A127 5c multi .25 .25
**600** A127 10c multi .25 .25
**601** A127 50c multi .40 .25
*Nos. 599-601,C314-C316 (6)* 2.45 1.90

Issued to publicize education through literacy, audio-visual means and sport.

For surcharges see #B41-B42, CB61-CB62.

Winston Churchill — A128

Churchill: 5c, as painter. 10c, as Knight of the Garter. 15c, and soldiers at Normandy. 20c, and early seaplane. 25c, and Queen Elizabeth II. 50c, and Big Ben, London.

**1968, Dec. 23** **Photo.** *Perf. 13*

**602** A128 3c gold & multi .25 .25
**603** A128 5c gold & multi .25 .25
**604** A128 10c gold & multi .25 .25
**605** A128 15c gold & multi .25 .25
**606** A128 20c gold & multi .25 .25
**607** A128 25c gold & multi .25 .25
**608** A128 50c gold & multi .40 .25
*Nos. 602-608,C319-C322 (11)* 4.25 3.50

Exist imperf. For surcharge see No. 828.

1968 Winter Olympics, Grenoble A128a

Designs: 5c, 1.50g, Peggy Fleming, US, figure skating. 10c, Harold Groenningen, Norway, cross-country skiing. 20c, Belousova & Protopopov, USSR, pairs figure skating. 25c, Toini Gustafsson, Sweden, cross country skiing. 50c, Eugenio Monti, Italy, 4-man bobsled. 2g, Erhard Keller, Germany, speed skating. 4g, Jean-Claude Killy, France, downhill skiing.

**1968, Nov. 11** **Litho.** *Perf. 14x13½*

**609** A128a 5c brt bl & multi .25 .25
**609A** A128a 10c bl grn & multi .25 .25
**609B** A128a 20c brt rose & multi .25 .25
**609C** A128a 25c sky bl & multi .25 .25
**609D** A128a 50c ol bis & multi .45 .30
**609E** A128a 1.50g vio & multi 1.10 .65

**Size: 36x65mm**

*Perf. 12x12½*

**609F** A128a 2g emer grn & multi 2.25 2.25
*Nos. 609-609F (7)* 4.80 4.20

**Souvenir Sheet**

**609G** A128a 4g brn & multi 20.00 20.00

No. 609G contains one 36x65mm stamp. Nos. 609F-609G are airmail. No. 609G exists imperf. with green, brown and blue margin.

No. 589 Surcharged

**1969, Feb. 21** **Photo.** *Perf. 11½*

**610** A122 70c on 50c .50 .40
*Nos. 610,C324-C325 (3)* 1.80 1.30

Blue-headed Euphonia — A129

Birds of Haiti: 10c, Hispaniolan trogon. 20c, Palm chat. 25c, Stripe-headed tanager. 50c, Like 5c.

**1969, Feb. 26** *Perf. 13½*

**611** A129 5c lt grn & multi 2.00 .50
**612** A129 10c yel & multi 2.00 .50
**613** A129 20c cream & multi 2.25 .50
**614** A129 25c lt lil & multi 2.50 .60
**615** A129 50c lt gray & multi 3.50 .60
*Nos. 611-615,C326-C329 (9)* 28.50 9.45

For overprints see Nos. C344A-C344D.

Olympic Marathon Winners, 1896-1968 — A130

Designs: Games location, date, winner, country and time over various stamp designs. Souvenir sheets do not show location, date, country or time.

**1969, May 16** *Perf. 12½x12*

**Size: 66x35mm (Nos. 616, 616C, 616F, 616O)**

**616** A130 5c like Greece #124 .25 .25
**616A** A130 10c like France #124 .25 .25
**616B** A130 15c US #327 .25 .25
**616C** A130 20c like Great Britain #142 .50 .25
**616D** A130 20c Sweden #68 .50 .25
**616E** A130 25c Belgium #B49 .80 .35
**616F** A130 25c like France #198 .80 .35
**616G** A130 25c Netherlands #B30 .80 .35
**616H** A130 30c US #718 .90 .40
**616I** A130 50c Germany #B86 1.40 .60
**616J** A130 60c Great Britain #274 1.75 .85
**616K** A130 75c like Finland #B110 2.50 1.25
**616L** A130 75c like Australia #277 2.50 1.25
**616M** A130 90c Italy #799 2.75 1.40
**616N** A130 1g like Japan #822 3.75 1.60
**616O** A130 1.25g like Mexico #C328 5.00 2.50
*Nos. 616-616O (16)* 24.70 12.15

**Souvenir Sheets**

**616P** A130 1.50g US #718, diff. 16.00 9.00

***Imperf***

**616Q** A130 1.50g Germany #B86, diff. 16.00 9.00

Nos. 616H-616O are airmail. Nos. 616P-616Q contain one 66x35mm stamp. A 2g souvenir sheet exists, perf. & imperf. Value, each $9.

Power Lines and Light Bulb — A131

**1969, May 22** **Litho.** *Perf. 13x13½*

**617** A131 20c lilac & blue .25 .25

Issued to publicize the Duvalier Hydroelectric Station. See Nos. C338-C340.

Learning to Write — A132

Designs: 10c, children playing, vert. 50c, Peace poster on educational television, vert.

**1969, Aug. 12** **Litho.** *Perf. 13½*

**618** A132 5c multi .25 .25
**619** A132 10c multi .25 .25
**620** A132 50c multi .25 .25
*Nos. 618-620,C342-C344 (6)* 2.35 1.90

Issued to publicize national education.

ILO Emblem A133

**1969, Sept. 22** *Perf. 14*

**621** A133 5c bl grn & blk .25 .25
**622** A133 10c brn & blk .25 .25
**623** A133 20c vio bl & blk .25 .25
*Nos. 621-623,C345-C347 (6)* 3.10 1.95

50th anniv. of the ILO.

Apollo Space Missions — A133a

Designs: 10c, Apollo 7 rendezvous of command module, third stage. 15c, Apollo 7, preparation for re-entry. 20c, Apollo 8, separation of third stage. 25c, Apollo 8, mid-course correction. 70c, Apollo 8, approaching moon. 1g, Apollo 8, orbiting moon, Christmas 1968, vert. 1.25, Apollo 8, leaving moon. 1.50g, Apollo 8, crew, vert. 1.75g, 2g, Apollo 11, first lunar landing.

**1969, Oct. 6** *Perf. 12x12½*

**624** A133a 10c brt rose & multi .25 .25
**624A** A133a 15c vio & multi .25 .25
**624B** A133a 20c ver & multi .25 .25
**624C** A133a 25c emer grn & multi .25 .25
**624D** A133a 70c brt bl & multi .25 .25
**624E** A133a 1g bl grn & multi .55 .30
**624F** A133a 1.25g dk bl & multi .65 .40
**624G** A133a 1.50g dp rose lil & multi .80 .50

**Souvenir Sheets**

**624H** A133a 1.75g grn & multi 12.00 8.00
**624I** A133a 2g sky bl & multi 12.00 8.00
*Nos. 624-624I (10)* 27.25 18.45

Nos. 624D-624I are airmail. Nos. 624-624I exist imperf. in different colors.

Papilio Zonaria — A134

Butterflies: 20c, Zerene cesonia cynops. 25c, Papilio machaonides.

**1969, Nov. 14 Photo. *Perf. 13½***

**625** A134 10c pink & multi *2.75* .90
**626** A134 20c gray & multi *5.00* 2.50
**627** A134 25c lt bl & multi *7.50* 2.75
*Nos. 625-627,C348-C350 (6)* 69.25 19.15

Martin Luther King, Jr. A135

**1970, Jan. 12 Litho. *Perf. 12½x13½***

**628** A135 10c bis, red & blk .25 .25
**629** A135 20c grnsh bl, red & blk .25 .25
**630** A135 25c brt rose, red & blk .25 .25
*Nos. 628-630,C351-C353 (6)* 3.20 2.45

Martin Luther King, Jr. (1929-1968), American civil rights leader.

Laeliopsis Dominguensis A136

UPU Monument and Map of Haiti A137

Haitian Orchids: 20c, Oncidium Haitiense. 25c, Oncidium calochilum.

**1970, Apr. 3 Litho. *Perf. 13x12½***

**631** A136 10c yel, lil & blk .25 .25
**632** A136 20c lt bl grn, yel & brn 2.00 2.00
**633** A136 25c bl & multi 2.50 2.00
*Nos. 631-633,C354-C356 (6)* 15.50 10.50

**1970, June 23 Photo. *Perf. 11½***

Designs: 25c, Propeller and UPU emblem, vert. 50c, Globe and doves.

**634** A137 10c blk, brt grn & ol bis .25 .25
**635** A137 25c blk, brt rose & ol bis .25 .25
**636** A137 50c blk & bl .35 .25
*Nos. 634-636,C357-C359 (6)* 2.80 2.10

16th Cong. of the UPU, Tokyo, Oct. 1-Nov. 16, 1970.

For overprints see Nos. 640, C360-C362.

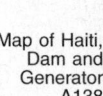

Map of Haiti, Dam and Generator A138

Design: 25c, Map of Haiti, dam and pylon.

**1970 Litho. *Perf. 14x13½***

**637** A138 20c lt grn & multi .25 .25
**638** A138 25c lt bl & multi .25 .25

François Duvalier Central Hydroelectric Plant.

For surcharges see #B43-B44, RA40-RA41.

Apollo 12 — A138a

**1970, Sept. 7 *Perf. 13½x14***

**639** A138a 5c Lift-off .25 .25
**639A** A138a 10c 2nd stage ignition .25 .25
**639B** A138a 15c Docking preparations .25 .25
**639C** A138a 20c Heading for moon .35 .25
**639D** A138a 25c like 639B .45 .25
**639E** A138a 25c Lunar exploration .25 .25
**639F** A138a 30c Landing on Moon .65 .25
**639G** A138a 30c Lift-off from Moon .45 .25
**639H** A138a 40c 3rd stage separation .90 .35
**639I** A138a 40c Lunar module, crew .55 .25
**639J** A138a 50c Lunar orbital activities 1.10 .35
**639K** A138a 50c Leaving Moon orbit .65 .35
**639L** A138a 75c In Earth orbit 1.10 .40
**639M** A138a 1g Re-entry 1.50 .50
**639N** A138a 1.25g Landing at sea 2.25 .75
**639O** A138a 1.50g Docking with lunar module 2.40 .75
*Nos. 639-639O (16)* 13.35 5.70

Nos. 639E, 639G, 639I, 639K-639O are airmail. Nos. 639-639O exist imperf. with brighter colors. Value, unused $16.

For overprints see Nos. 656-656O.

No. 636 Overprinted in Red with UN Emblem and: "XXVe ANNIVERSAIRE / O.N.U."

**1970, Dec. 14 Photo. *Perf. 11½***

**640** A137 50c blk & bl .35 .25
*Nos. 640,C360-C362 (4)* 2.30 1.60

UN, 25th anniv.

Fort Nativity, Drawing by Columbus — A139

Ascension, by Castera Bazile — A140

**1970, Dec. 22**

**641** A139 3c dk brn & buff .25 .25
**642** A139 5c dk grn & pale grn .30 .25

Christmas 1970.

**1971, Apr. 29 Litho. *Perf. 12x12½***

Paintings: 5c, Man with Turban, by Rembrandt. 20c, Iris in a Vase, by Van Gogh. 50c, Baptism of Christ, by Castera Bazile. No. 647, Young Mother Sewing, by Mary Cassatt. No. 648, The Card Players, by Cezanne.

**Size: 20x40mm**

**643** A140 5c multi .25 .25
**644** A140 10c multi .25 .25

***Perf. 13x12½***

**Size: 25x37mm**

**645** A140 20c multi .25 .25

***Perf. 12x12½***

**Size: 20x40mm**

**646** A140 50c multi .50 .25
*Nos. 643-646,C366-C368 (7)* 3.65 2.70

**Souvenir Sheets**

***Imperf***

**647** A140 3g multi 5.00 5.00
**648** A140 3g multi 5.00 5.00

No. 647 contains one stamp, size: 20x40mm, No. 648 size: 25x37mm.

Nos. 643-646, C366-C368 exist imperf in changed colors.

Soccer Ball — A141

Design: No. 651, 1g, 5g, Jules Rimet cup.

**1971, June 14 Photo. *Perf. 11½***

**649** A141 5c salmon & blk .25 .25
**650** A141 50c tan & blk .50 .35
**651** A141 50c rose pink, blk & gold .50 .35
**652** A141 1g lil, blk & gold .65 .45
**653** A141 1.50g gray & blk .80 .55
**654** A141 5g gray, blk & gold 2.40 1.60
*Nos. 649-654 (6)* 5.10 3.55

**Souvenir Sheet**

***Imperf***

**655** Sheet of 2 12.00 8.50
*a.* A141 70c light violet & black 4.00 3.00
*b.* A141 1g light green, blue & gold 4.00 3.00

9th World Soccer Championships for the Jules Rimet Cup, Mexico City, May 30-June 21, 1970. The surface tint of the sheets of 50 (10x5) of Nos. 649-654 includes a map of Brazil covering 26 stamps. Positions 27, 37 and 38 inscribed "Brasilia," "Santos," "Rio de Janeiro" respectively. On soccer ball design the 4 corner stamps are inscribed "Pele."

Nos. 655a and 655b have portions of map of Brazil in background; No. 655a inscribed "Pele" and "Santos," No. 655b "Brasilia."

**Nos. 639-639O Ovptd. in Gold**

**1971, Mar. 15**

**656** A138a 5c multi .25 .25
**656A** A138a 10c multi .25 .25
**656B** A138a 15c multi .25 .25
**656C** A138a 20c multi .35 .25
**656D** A138a 25c multi .45 .25
**656E** A138a 25c multi .25 .25
**656F** A138a 30c multi .65 .25
**656G** A138a 30c multi .45 .25
**656H** A138a 40c multi .90 .35
**656I** A138a 40c multi .55 .35
**656J** A138a 50c multi 1.10 .35
**656K** A138a 50c multi .65 .35
**656L** A138a 75c multi 1.10 .40
**656M** A138a 1g multi 1.50 .50
**656N** A138a 1.25g multi 2.25 .75
**656O** A138a 1.50g multi 2.40 .75
*Nos. 656-656O (16)* 13.35 5.80

Nos. 656E, 656G, 656I, 656K-656O are airmail.

Exist overprinted in silver. Value, unused $16.

J. J. Dessalines — A142

**1972, Apr. 28 Photo. *Perf. 11½***

**657** A142 5c grn & blk .25 .25
**658** A142 10c brt bl & blk .25 .25
**659** A142 25c org & blk .25 .25
*Nos. 657-659,C378-C379 (5)* 2.20 1.65

See Nos. 697-700, C448-C458, 727, C490-C493, C513-C514. For surcharges see Nos. 692, 705-709, 724-726, C438, C512.

"Sun" and EXPO '70 Emblem — A143

**1972, Oct. 27 Photo. *Perf. 11½***

**660** A143 10c ocher, brn & grn .25 .25
**661** A143 25c ocher, brn & mar .25 .25
*Nos. 660-661,C387-C390 (6)* 3.00 2.10

EXPO '70 International Exposition, Osaka, Japan, Mar. 15-Sept. 13, 1970.

Gold Medalists, 1972 Summer Olympics, Munich — A143a

Designs: 5c, L. Linsenhoff, dressage, W. Ruska, judo. 10c, S. Kato, gymnastics, S.Gould, women's swimming. 20c, M. Peters, women's pentathlon, K. Keino, steeplechase. 25c, L. Viren, 5,000, 10,000m races, R. Milburn, 110m hurdles. No. 662D, D. Morelon, cycling, J. Akii-Bua, 400m hurdles. No. 662E, R. Williams, long jump. 75c, G. Mancinelli, equestrian. 1.50g, W. Nordwig, pole vault. 2.50g, K. Wolferman, javelin. 5g, M. Spitz, swimming.

**1972, Dec. 29 *Perf. 13½***

**662** A143a 5c multicolored .25 .25
**662A** A143a 10c multicolored .25 .25
**662B** A143a 20c multicolored .25 .25
**662C** A143a 25c multicolored .25 .25
**662D** A143a 50c multicolored .25 .25
**662E** A143a 50c multicolored .70 .25
**662F** A143a 75c multicolored 1.00 .25
**662G** A143a 1.50g multicolored 1.50 .70
**662H** A143a 2.50g multicolored 3.00 1.10
**662I** A143a 5g multicolored 5.75 1.60
*Nos. 662-662I (10)* 13.20 5.15

Nos. 662E-662I are airmail.

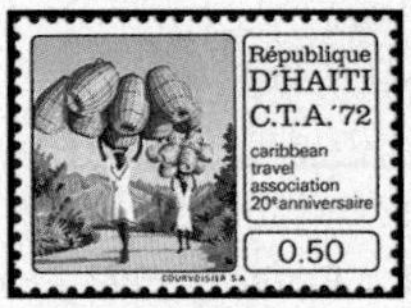

Basket Vendors A144

Designs: 80c, 2.50g, Postal bus.

**1973, Jan. Photo. *Perf. 11½***

**665** A144 50c blk & multi .35 .25
**666** A144 80c blk & multi .45 .35
**667** A144 1.50g blk & multi .70 .45
**668** A144 2.50g blk & multi 1.50 .80
*Nos. 665-668 (4)* 3.00 1.85

20th anniv. of Caribbean Travel Assoc.

Space Exploration

A set of 12 stamps for US-USSR space exploration, the same overprinted for the centenary of the UPU and 3 overprinted in silver for Apollo 17 exist but we have no evidence that they were printed with the approval of the Haitian postal authorities. Value, $10 and $6, respectively.

Micromelo Undata A145

Designs: Marine life; 50c horizontal.

**1973, Sept. 4 Litho. *Perf. 14***

**669** A145 5c *shown* .25 .25
**670** A145 10c *Nemaster rubiginosa* .25 .25
**671** A145 25c *Cyerce cristallina* .50 .25
**672** A145 50c *Desmophyllum riisei* 1.00 .25
*Nos. 669-672,C395-C398 (8)* 8.90 2.20

For surcharge see No. C439.

Gramma Loreto — A146

**1973 *Perf. 13½***

**673** A146 10c *shown* .50 .25
**674** A146 50c *Acanthurus coeruleus* .65 .50
*Nos. 673-674,C399-C402 (6)* 8.00 4.55

For surcharges see Nos. 693, C440.

Soccer Stadium A147

Design: 20c, Haiti No. 654.

**1973, Nov. 29 *Perf. 14x13***

**675** A147 10c bis, blk & emer .25 .25
**676** A147 20c rose lil, blk & tan .25 .25
*Nos. 675-676,C407-C410 (6)* 5.50 3.80

Caribbean countries preliminary games of the World Soccer Championships, Munich, 1974.

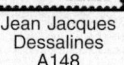

Jean Jacques Dessalines A148

Nicolaus Copernicus A149

**1974, Apr. 22 Photo. *Perf. 14***

**677** A148 10c lt bl & emer .25 .25
**678** A148 20c rose & blk .25 .25
**679** A148 25c yel & vio .25 .25
*Nos. 677-679,C411-C414 (7)* 3.05 2.35

For surcharges see Nos. 694, C443.

**1974, May 24 Litho. *Perf. 14x13½***

Design: 10c, Symbol of heliocentric system.

**680** A149 10c multi .25 .25
**681** A149 25c brt grn & multi .25 .25
*Nos. 680-681,C415-C419 (7)* 3.15 2.35

For overprint and surcharges see Nos. 695, C444, C460-C463.

Pres. Jean-Claude Duvalier — A151

**1974 Photo. *Perf. 14x13½***

**689** A151 10c grn & gold .25 .25
**690** A151 20c car rose & gold .30 .25
**691** A151 50c bl & gold .40 .25
*Nos. 689-691,C421-C426 (9)* 7.40 4.60

For surcharge and overprints see Nos. C445, C487-C489.

---

Audubon Birds

In 1975 or later various sets of bird paintings by Audubon were produced by government employees without official authorization. They were not sold by the Haiti post office and were not valid for postage. The first set consisted of 23 values and was sold in 1975. A second set containing some of the original stamps and some new stamps appeared unannounced several years later. More sets may have been printed as there are 75 different stamps. These consist of 5 denominations each for the 15 designs.

Perf and imperf souvenir sheets picturing Audubon were also produced.

---

Nos. 659, 673 and 679-680 Surcharged with New Value and Bar

***Perf. 11½, 13½, 14, 14x13½***

**1976 Photo.; Litho.**

**692** A142 80c on 25c .55 .35
**693** A146 80c on 10c .55 .35
**694** A148 80c on 25c .55 .35
**695** A149 80c on 10c .55 .35
*Nos. 692-695 (4)* 2.20 1.40

Haiti No. C11 and Bicentennial Emblem — A152

**1976, Apr. 22 Photo. *Perf. 11½***

**Granite Paper**

**696** A152 10c multi .25 .25
*Nos. 696,C434-C437 (5)* 4.70 3.30

American Bicentennial.

**Dessalines Type of 1972**

**1977 Photo. *Perf. 11½***

**697** A142 10c rose & blk .25 .25
**698** A142 20c lemon & blk .25 .25
**699** A142 50c vio & blk .35 .25
**700** A142 50c tan & blk .35 .25
*Nos. 697-700 (4)* 1.20 1.00

Dessalines Type of 1972 Surcharged in Black or Red

**1978 Photo. *Perf. 11½***

**705** A142 1g on 20c (#698) .65 .35
**706** A142 1g on 1.75g (#C454) .65 .35
**707** A142 1.25g on 75c (#C448) .65 .35
**708** A142 1.25g on 1.50g (#C453) .65 .35
**709** A142 1.25g on 1.50g (#C453; R) .65 .35
*Nos. 705-709 (5)* 3.25 1.75

Rectangular bar obliterates old denomination on Nos. 705-709 and "Par Avion" on Nos. 706-709.

J. C. Duvalier Earth Telecommunications Station — A153

Designs: 20c, Video telephone. 50c, Alexander Graham Bell, vert.

**1978, June 19 Litho. *Perf. 13½***

**710** A153 10c multi .25 .25
**711** A153 20c multi .25 .25
**712** A153 50c multi .35 .25
*Nos. 710-712,C466-C468 (6)* 2.70 2.10

Centenary of first telephone call by Alexander Graham Bell, Mar. 10, 1876.

Athletes' Inaugural Parade — A154

**1978, Sept. 4 Litho. *Perf. 13½x13***

**713** A154 5c shown .25 .25
**714** A154 25c Bicyclists .25 .25
**715** A154 50c Pole Vault .40 .25
*Nos. 713-715,C469-C471 (6)* 6.60 4.10

21st Olympic Games, Montreal, 7/17-8/1/76.

Mother Nursing Child — A155

Mother Feeding Child — A156

**1979, Jan. 15 Photo. *Perf. 14x14½***

**716** A155 25c multi .25 .25
*Nos. 716,C472-C473 (3)* 1.60 1.15

Inter-American Children's Inst., 50th anniv.

**1979, May 11 Photo. *Perf. 11½***

**717** A156 25c multi .25 .25
**718** A156 50c multi .35 .25
*Nos. 717-718,C474-C476 (5)* 3.60 2.55

30th anniversary of CARE (Cooperative for American Relief Everywhere).

Human Rights Emblem — A157

**1979, July 20 Litho. *Perf. 14***

**719** A157 25c multi .30 .25
*Nos. 719,C477-C479 (4)* 3.30 2.30

30th anniversary of declaration of human rights.

Anti-Apartheid Year Emblem, Antenor Firmin, "On the Equality of Human Races" A158

**1979, Nov. 22 Photo. *Perf. 12x11½***

**720** A158 50c tan & black .50 .25
*Nos. 720,C480-C482 (4)* 4.35 2.30

Anti-Apartheid Year (1978).

Children Playing, IYC Emblem A159

**1979, Dec. 19 Photo. *Perf. 12***

**721** A159 10c multi .25 .25
**722** A159 25c multi .25 .25
**723** A159 50c multi .40 .25
*Nos. 721-723,C483-C486 (7)* 8.50 4.65

International Year of the Child.

Nos. C379, C449, C454 Surcharged

**1980 Photo. *Perf. 11½***

**Granite Paper**

**724** A142 1g on 2.50g lil & blk .55 .45
**725** A142 1.25g on 80c emer & blk .65 .55
**726** A142 1.25g on 1.75g rose & blk .65 .55
*Nos. 724-726 (3)* 1.85 1.55

**Dessalines Type of 1972**

**1980, Aug. 27 Photo. *Perf. 11½***

**Granite Paper**

**727** A142 25c org yel & blk .30 .25
*Nos. 727,C490-C493 (5)* 5.10 3.70

Henry Christophe Citadel — A160

**1980, Dec. 2 Litho. *Perf. 12½x12***

**728** A160 5c shown .25 .25
**729** A160 25c Sans Souci Palace .25 .25
**730** A160 50c Vallieres market .35 .25
*Nos. 728-730,C494-C498 (8)* 5.60 4.25

World Tourism Conf., Manila, Sept. 27.

For surcharges see Nos. 738, C511.

Soccer Players, World Cup, Flag of Uruguay (1930 Champion) — A161

**1980, Dec. 30 Litho. *Perf. 14***

**731** A161 10c shown .25 .25
**732** A161 20c Italy, 1934 .25 .25
**733** A161 25c Italy, 1938 .25 .25
*Nos. 731-733,C499-C506 (11)* 10.25 6.90

World Cup Soccer Championship, 50th anniv.

For surcharges see Nos. 741, 829.

Going to Church, by Gregoire Etienne A162

Paintings: 5c, Woman with Birds and Flowers, by Hector Hyppolite, vert. 20c, Street Market, by Petion Savain. 25c, Market Vendors, by Michele Manuel.

**1981, May 12 Photo. *Perf. 11½***

734 A162 5c multi .25 .25
735 A162 10c multi .25 .25
736 A162 20c multi .25 .25
737 A162 25c multi .25 .25
*Nos. 734-737,C507-C510 (8)* 5.65 4.25

For surcharges see Nos. 739-740.

Nos. 728, 734-735, 732 Surcharged

***Perf. 12½x12, 14, 11½***

**1981, Dec. 30 Litho., Photo.**

738 A160 1.25g on 5c multi .65 .55
739 A162 1.25g on 5c multi .65 .55
740 A162 1.25g on 10c multi .65 .55
741 A161 1.25g on 20c multi .65 .55
*Nos. 738-741,C511-C512 (6)* 4.45 3.60

10th Anniv. of Pres. Duvalier Reforms — A163

**1982, June 21 Photo. *Perf. 11½x12***
**Granite Paper**

742 A163 25c yel grn & blk .25 .25
743 A163 50c olive & blk .35 .25
744 A163 1g rose & blk .55 .45
745 A163 1.25g bl & blk .65 .55
746 A163 2g org red & blk 1.10 .85
747 A163 5g org & blk 2.40 1.60
*Nos. 742-747 (6)* 5.30 3.95

Nos. 742, 744-746 Overprinted in Blue: "1957-1982 / 25 ANS DE REVOLUTION"

**1982, Nov. 29 Photo. *Perf. 11½x12***
**Granite Paper**

748 A163 25c yel grn & blk .25 .25
749 A163 1g rose & blk .55 .45
750 A163 1.25g blue & blk .65 .55
751 A163 2g org red & blk 1.10 .85
*Nos. 748-751 (4)* 2.55 2.10

25th anniv. of revolution.

Scouting Year A164

***Perf. 13½x14, 14x13½***

**1983, Feb. 26 Litho.**

752 A164 5c Building campfire .25 .25
753 A164 10c Baden-Powell, vert. .25 .25
754 A164 25c Boat building .25 .25
755 A164 50c like 10c .50 .25
756 A164 75c like 25c 1.25 .25
757 A164 1g like 5c 1.50 .30
758 A164 1.25g like 25c 2.00 .35
759 A164 2g like 10c 2.75 .60
*Nos. 752-759 (8)* 8.75 2.50

Nos. 756-759 airmail.
For surcharge see No. 827.

Patroness of Haiti — A165

**1983, Mar. 9 Litho. *Perf. 14***

760 A165 10c multi .25 .25
761 A165 20c multi .25 .25
762 A165 25c multi .25 .25
763 A165 50c multi .25 .25
764 A165 75c multi .35 .25
765 A165 1g multi .60 .25
766 A165 1.25g multi .70 .30
767 A165 1.50g multi 1.00 .35
768 A165 1.75g multi 1.40 .40
769 A165 2g multi 1.75 .50
770 A165 5g multi 2.75 1.00
a. Souvenir sheet, 116x90mm 11.00 11.00
j. Souvenir sheet, 90x116mm 11.00 11.00
*Nos. 760-770 (11)* 9.55 4.05

Centenary of the Miracle of Our Lady of Perpetual Help. Nos. 764-770 airmail.
For surcharge see No. 875.

UPU Admission, 100th Anniv. A165a

**1983, June 10 Litho. *Perf. 15x14***

770B A165a 5c shown .50 .25
770C A165a 10c L.F. Salomon, J.C. Duvalier .50 .25
770D A165a 25c No. 1, UPU emblem .50 .25
770E A165a 50c like 5c .50 .25
770F A165a 75c like 10c .60 .25
770G A165a 1g like 5c .80 .25
770H A165a 1.25g like 25c 1.00 .30
770I A165a 2g like 25c 1.60 .40
*Nos. 770B-770I (8)* 6.00 2.20

Nos. 770F-770I airmail.
For surcharge see No. 825.

1982 World Cup — A166

Games and scores. Nos. 776-780 airmail, horiz.

**1983, Nov. 22 Litho. *Perf. 14***

771 A166 5c Argentina, Belgium .25 .25
772 A166 10c Northern Ireland, Yugoslavia .25 .25
773 A166 20c England, France .25 .25
774 A166 25c Spain, Northern Ireland .25 .25
775 A166 50c Italy (champion) .35 .25
776 A166 1g Brazil, Scotland .55 .45
777 A166 1.25g Northern Ireland, France .65 .55
778 A166 1.50g Poland, Cameroun .95 .65
779 A166 2g Italy, Germany 1.10 .85
780 A166 2.50g Argentina, Brazil 1.40 1.10
*Nos. 771-780 (10)* 6.00 4.85

For surcharge see No. 826.

Haiti Postage Stamp Centenary — A167

**1984, Feb. 28 Litho. *Perf. 14½***

781 A167 5c #1 .30 .25
782 A167 10c #2 .30 .25
783 A167 25c #3 .30 .25
784 A167 50c #5 .30 .25
785 A167 75c Liberty, Salomon .45 .25
786 A167 1g Liberty, Salomon .60 .35
787 A167 1.25g Liberty, Duvalier .70 .40
788 A167 2g Liberty, Duvalier 1.10 .75
*Nos. 781-788 (8)* 4.05 2.75

Nos. 785-788 airmail.
For surcharge see No. 826A.

A168

A169

**1984, May 30 Photo. *Perf. 11½***
**Granite Paper**

789 A168 25c Broadcasting equipment, horiz. .25 .25
790 A168 50c like 25c .35 .25
791 A168 1g Drum .55 .45
792 A168 1.25g like 1g .65 .55
793 A168 2g Globe 1.10 .85
794 A168 2.50g like 2g 1.40 1.10
*Nos. 789-794 (6)* 4.30 3.45

World Communications Year.

**1984, July 27 Granite Paper**

795 A169 5c Javelin, running, pole vault, horiz. .25 .25
796 A169 10c like 5c .25 .25
797 A169 25c Hurdles, horiz. .25 .25
798 A169 50c like 25c .75 .25
799 A169 1g Long jump 1.25 .95
800 A169 1.25g like 1g 1.75 1.25
801 A169 2g like 1g 2.40 1.75
*Nos. 795-801 (7)* 6.90 4.95

**Souvenir Sheet**

802 A169 2.50g like 1g 15.00 10.00

1984 Summer Olympics. No. 802 exists imperf. Value $15.
For surcharge see No. 874.

Arrival of Europeans in America, 500th Anniv. — A170

The Unknown Indian, detail or full perspective of statue. Nos. 807-809 are vert. and airmail.

**1984, Dec. 5 Litho. *Perf. 14***

803 A170 5c multi .55 .45
804 A170 10c multi .55 .45
805 A170 25c multi .55 .45
806 A170 50c multi .90 .60
807 A170 1g multi 1.10 .60
808 A170 1.25g multi 1.75 .90
809 A170 2g multi 6.00 3.00
a. Souvenir sheet of #806, 809 16.00 16.00
*Nos. 803-809 (7)* 11.40 6.45

For surcharge see No. 881.

Simon Bolivar and Alexander Petion — A171

Designs: 25c, 1.25g, 7.50g, Portraits reversed. 50c, 4.50g, Bolivar, flags of Grand Colombian Confederation member nations.

**1985, Aug. 30 *Perf. 13½x14***

810 A171 5c multi .30 .25
811 A171 25c multi .30 .25
812 A171 50c multi .35 .25
813 A171 1g multi .55 .30
814 A171 1.25g multi .60 .45
815 A171 2g multi 1.10 .85
816 A171 7.50g multi 3.25 2.10
*Nos. 810-816 (7)* 6.45 4.45

**Souvenir Sheet**
***Imperf***

817 A171 4.50g multi 3.50 2.50

Nos. 813-817 airmail.
For surcharge see No. 876.

Arrival of Europeans in America, 500th Anniv. — A172

Designs: 10c, 25c, 50c, Henri, cacique of Bahoruco, hero of the Spanish period, 1492-1625. 1g, 1.25g, 2g, Henri in tropical forest.

**1986, Apr. 11 Litho. *Perf. 14***

818 A172 10c multi 1.00 .35
819 A172 25c multi 1.00 .35
820 A172 50c multi 1.00 .35
821 A172 1g multi 1.75 .45
822 A172 1.25g multi 2.50 .50
823 A172 2g multi 3.75 .75
*Nos. 818-823 (6)* 11.00 2.75

Nos. 821-823 are airmail. A 3g souvenir sheet exists picturing Henri in tropical forest. Value $16.
For surcharge see No. 883.

Nos. 770B, 771, 781, 756, C322, C500 Surcharged

**1986, Apr. 18**

825 A165a 25c on 5c No. 770B .30 .25
826 A166 25c on 5c No. 771 .30 .25
826A A167 25c on 5c No. 781 .30 .25
827 A164 25c on 75c No. 756 .30 .25
828 A128 25c on 1.50g No. C322 .30 .25
829 A161 25c on 75c No. C500 .30 .25
*Nos. 825-829 (6)* 1.80 1.50

Intl. Youth Year — A173

**1986, May 20 Litho. *Perf. 14x15***

830 A173 10c Afforestation .25 .25
831 A173 25c IYY emblem .25 .25
832 A173 50c Girl Guides .35 .25
833 A173 1g like 10c .55 .45
834 A173 1.25g like 25c .65 .55
835 A173 2g like 50c 1.10 .85
*Nos. 830-835 (6)* 3.15 2.60

**Souvenir Sheet**

836 A173 3g multi *12.50 12.50*

Nos. 833-836 are airmail.
For surcharge see No. 873.

UNESCO, 40th Anniv. (in 1986) — A174

**1987, May 29 Photo. *Perf. 11½***
**Granite Paper**

837 A174 10c multi .25 .25
838 A174 25c multi .25 .25
839 A174 50c multi .35 .25
840 A174 1g multi .55 .45
841 A174 1.25g multi .70 .55
842 A174 2.50g multi 1.40 1.10
*Nos. 837-842 (6)* 3.50 2.85

**Souvenir Sheet**
**Granite Paper**

843 A174 2g multi *3.00 3.00*

Nos. 840-842 are airmail.
For surcharge see No. 882.

Charlemagne Peralte, Resistance Leader — A175

**1988, Oct. 18 Litho. *Perf. 14***

**844** A175 25c multi .25 .25
**845** A175 50c multi .35 .25
**846** A175 1g multi .55 .45
**847** A175 2g multi 1.10 .85
*a.* Souvenir sheet of 1 7.50 7.50
**848** A175 3g multi 1.75 1.40
*Nos. 844-848 (5)* 4.00 3.20

Nos. 846-848, 847a are airmail.

Slave Rebellion, 200th Anniv. A176

Design: 1g, 2g, 3g, Slaves around fire, vert.

**1991, Aug. 22 Litho. *Perf. 12x11½***

**849** A176 25c brt green & multi .60 .30
**850** A176 50c pink & multi 1.00 .50

***Perf. 11½x12***

**851** A176 1g blue & multi 2.00 1.00
**852** A176 2g yellow & multi 4.00 2.00
*a.* Souv. sheet of 2, #850 & 852 *27.50 27.50*
**853** A176 3g buff & multi 7.50 3.50
*Nos. 849-853 (5)* 15.10 7.30

Nos. 851-853 are airmail.

Discovery of America, 500th Anniv. A177

Designs: 25c, 50c, Ships at anchor, men coming ashore, native. 1g, 2g, 3g, Ships, beached long boats, vert.

**1993, July 30 Litho. *Perf. 11½***

**854** A177 25c green & multi .60 .35
**855** A177 50c yellow & multi .85 .40
**856** A177 1g blue & multi 1.25 .75
**857** A177 2g pink & multi 2.75 1.25
*a.* Souvenir sheet of 2, #856-857 — —
**858** A177 3g orange yellow & multi 6.00 3.75
*Nos. 854-858 (5)* 11.45 6.50

Nos. 856-858, 857a are airmail.

25th Genl. Assembly of the Organization of American States A178

Designs: 50c, 75c, 7.50g, Emblem, map of Haiti. 1g, 2g, 3g, 5g, Emblems, map of North, South America, vert.

***Perf. 14x12½, 12½x14***
**1995, June 25 Litho.**

**859** A178 50c violet & multi .40 .25
**860** A178 75c green & multi .60 .30
**861** A178 1g gray blue & multi .75 .45
**862** A178 2g lilac rose & multi 1.50 .85
**863** A178 3g green & multi 2.00 1.40
**864** A178 5g violet & multi 3.25 1.90
*Nos. 859-864 (6)* 8.50 5.15

**Souvenir Sheet**
***Imperf***

**865** A178 7.50g green blue & multi *10.00 10.00*

UN, 50th Anniv. A179

Designs: 50c, 75c, Dove holding UN, Haitian flags. 1g, 2g, 3g, 5g, Haitian, UN flags, dove carrying olive branch.

**1995, Nov. 24 Litho. *Perf. 12x11½***

**866** A179 50c blue & multi *.50 .30*
**867** A179 75c lilac & multi *.75 .40*
**868** A179 1g apple green & multi *1.00 .60*
**869** A179 2g yellow & multi *2.25 1.00*
**870** A179 3g orange brown & multi *3.50 1.50*
**871** A179 5g blue green & multi *5.75 3.00*
*Nos. 866-871 (6) 13.75 6.80*

**Souvenir Sheet**

**872** A179 5g multicolored *16.50 16.50*

Nos. 868-872 are airmail.

Nos. 766, 800, 814, 834 Surcharged

**1996 *Perfs., Etc., as Before***

**873** A173 1g on 1.25g #834 *.75 .60*
**874** A169 2g on 1.25g #800 *1.50 1.00*
**875** A165 3g on 1.25g #766 *2.25 1.50*
**876** A171 3g on 1.25g #814 *2.50 1.50*
*Nos. 873-876 (4) 7.00 4.60*

Size and location of surcharge varies. Nos. 873, 875-876 are airmail.

1996 Summer Olympic Games, Atlanta — A180

**1996, Aug. 2 Litho. *Perf. 14***

**877** A180 3g Hurdler .75 .45
**878** A180 10g Athlete up close 2.50 1.60

Volleyball Federation, 1996 Summer Olympics, Atlanta — A181

#879: a, 50c, Three players in yellow shirts. b, 75c, Three players in red shirts. c, 1g, Two players in white shirts, torch. d, 2g, Players in yellow, in red.
15g, Player in red.

**1996, Aug. 2**

**879** A181 Sheet of 4, #a.-d. 17.50 17.50

**Souvenir Sheet**

**880** A181 15g multicolored 17.50 17.50

Volleyball, cent. (#880).

**Nos. 803, 818, 837 Surcharged**

**1996, Nov. Litho. *Perfs. as Before***

**881** A170 1g on 5c #803 *.75 .60*
**882** A174 4g on 10c #837 *3.00 2.00*
**883** A172 6g on 10c #818 *4.00 3.00*
*Nos. 881-883 (3) 7.75 5.60*

Size and location of surcharge varies.

Christmas A182

Paintings: 2g, The Virgin and Infant, by Jacopo Bellini. 3g, Adoration of the Shepherds, by Strozzi. 6g, Virgin and the Infant, by Giovanni Bellini. 10g, Virgin and the Infant, by Francesco Mazzola. #888, Adoration of the Magi, by Gentile da Fabriano.
#889 The Nativity, by Jan de Beer, horiz.

**1996, Dec. 16 Litho. *Perf. 13½x14***

**884** A182 2g multicolored *.50 .30*
**885** A182 3g multicolored *.75 .60*
**886** A182 6g multicolored *1.50 1.25*
**887** A182 10g multicolored *3.00 1.50*
**888** A182 25g multicolored *6.50 4.25*
*Nos. 884-888 (5) 12.25 7.90*

**Souvenir Sheet**
***Perf. 14x13½***

**889** A182 25g multicolored *10.00 10.00*

UNICEF, 50th Anniv. — A183

**1997, Jan. 28 *Perf. 14***

**890** A183 4g green & multi *1.25 .75*
**891** A183 5g pink & multi *1.75 1.00*
**892** A183 6g blue & multi *2.25 1.50*
**893** A183 10g brown & multi *3.75 2.00*
**894** A183 20g bister & multi *7.00 3.50*
*Nos. 890-894 (5)* 16.00 8.75

**Souvenir Sheet**

**895** A183 25g like #890-894, vert. *10.00 10.00*

#890-894 were each issued in sheets of 6.

Grimm's Fairy Tales — A184

2g, #902a, Sleeping Beauty. 3g, #902b, Snow White. 4g, #902c, Prince awakening Sleeping Beauty. 6g, #902d, Old man sleeping from "The Drink of Life." 10g, #902e, Cinderella. 20g, #902f, Old man awakened after taking drink.
No. 903, Cottage of the Seven Dwarfs, horiz.

**1998, Jan. 5 Litho. *Perf. 13½***

**896-901** A184 Set of 6 *30.00 30.00*

**Size: 38x50mm**
***Perf. 14***

**902** A184 Sheet of 6, #a.-f. *35.00 35.00*

**Souvenir Sheet**

**903** A184 25g multicolored *27.50 27.50*

Abstract paintings A185

2g, "Coconut on Pastel Stairs," by Luce Turnier. 3g, "Ogou," by Rose Marie Desruisseau. 5g, "Lantern," by Hilda Williams. 6g, Woman using artist's brush and palette.
15g, Fish, flower and geometric design with faces, snakes by Philippe Dodard.

**1998, Oct. 30 Litho. *Perf. 12½***

**904** A185 2g multicolored *3.00 1.50*
**905** A185 3g multicolored *5.00 2.00*
**906** A185 5g multicolored *7.00 2.75*
**907** A185 6g multicolored *12.00 4.00*
*Nos. 904-907 (4) 27.00 10.25*

**Souvenir Sheet**
***Perf. 13***

**908** A185 15g multicolored *40.00 35.00*

Tourism. Nos. 904-907 exist in imperf. souvenir sheet of 4. No. 908 contains one 28x36mm stamp.

Birds A186

Designs: 2g, Priotelus roseigaster. 4g, Xenoligeo mantana. 10g, Phoenicophilus poliocephalus. 20g, Phoenicopterus ruber.

**1999, Aug. 27 Litho. *Perf. 14***

**909** A186 2g multicolored *.75 .75*
**910** A186 4g multicolored *1.50 1.50*
**911** A186 10g multicolored *4.00 4.00*
**912** A186 20g multicolored *7.00 7.00*
*a.* Souvenir sheet, #909-912 *15.00 15.00*
*Nos. 909-912 (4) 13.25 13.25*

Nos. 911-912 are airmail.

Worldwide Fund for Nature — A187

No. 913: a, 2g, Hyla vasta. b, 4g, Head of Hyla vasta. c, 2g, Cyclura ricordii. d, 4g, Head of Cyclura ricordii.

**1999, Aug. 27 Litho. *Perf. 14***

**913** A187 Block of 4, #a.-d. 3.00 3.00

Issued in sheets of 16 (4x4) and 8 (2x4).

Souvenir Sheet

Protection of Natural Resources — A188

**1999 Litho. *Perf. 13¾***

**914** A188 20g multicolored 7.50 7.50

Christmas
A188a A188b

**1999 Photo. *Perf. 11¾***
**Panel Color**

**914A** A188a 1g Prussian blue .35 .35
**914B** A188a 3g red brown .65 .65
**914C** A188a 5g dark blue *1.75 1.75*
**914D** A188b 10g dk purple *3.25 3.25*
**914E** A188b 15g red *4.00 4.00*
**914F** A188b 20g blue *6.00 6.00*
*g.* Souvenir sheet, #915A-915F *16.00 16.00*
*Nos. 914A-914F (6)* 14.45 14.45

Nos. 914D-914F are airmail.

Chinese Inventions — A189

No. 915, 2g, Movable type. No. 916, 3g, Paper. No. 917, 6g, Gunpowder, cannon. No. 918, 10g, Compass.

**1999, Dec. 20 Litho. *Perf. 13¾***

**915-918** A189 Set of 4 *30.00 30.00*
*a.* Souv. sheet, #915-918 *20.00 20.00*

UPU, 125th anniv.

Tourism
A190

Designs: 2g, Pirogue. 3g, Smiling girl. 4g, Zim Pond, vert. 5g, Ardadins Island, vert. 6g, Gingerbread House. 10g, National Palace.20g, Peligre Reservoir, vert.

***Perf. 14¼x14½, 14½x14¼***
**2000, June 5 Litho.**

**919-925** A190 Set of 7 *11.00 11.00*
*a.* Souv. sheet, #919-925 + label *12.50 12.50*

**Souvenir Sheet**

**926** A190 25g Boat "Pays," vert. *12.00 12.00*

1801 Constitution, Bicent.
A191

Designs: 1g, 2g, 5g, 10g, 25g, 50g, Toussaint L'Ouverture and 1801 Constitution.
No. 933: a, Toussaint L'Ouverture. b, 1801 Constitution.

**2001 Litho. *Perf. 13¾x13¼***

**927** A191 1g multi *.50 .50*
**928** A191 2g multi *.50 .50*
**929** A191 5g multi *.50 .50*
**930** A191 10g multi *1.25 1.25*
**931** A191 25g multi *2.25 2.25*
**932** A191 50g multi *3.75 3.75*
*Nos. 927-932 (6)* 8.75 8.75

**Souvenir Sheet**
***Perf. 12¾***

**933** A191 25g Sheet of 2, #a-b *4.00 4.00*

Nos. 929-932 are airmail. No. 933 contains two 25x29mm stamps.

Toussaint L'Ouverture (c. 1743-1803)
A192

Background color: 1g, Green. 2g, Brown. 3g, Yellow green. 5g, Red brown. 6g, blue. 10g, Violet.

**2003, Apr. 7 Litho. *Perf. 13***

**934-939** A192 Set of 6 *30.00 30.00*

**Souvenir Sheet**
***Imperf***

**940** A192 15g multi *20.00 20.00*

---

**Pope John Paul II and Pope Benedict XVI Stamps**

In 2005 a set of 8 face-different stamps with the image of John Paul II and 8 face different stamps with the image of Benedict XVI were printed without official authorization. They were printed in sheetlets numbered 1-40, with either three or six stamps per sheet. Selvage of various sheets containing the same stamps bear text in either French, English, Latin, Polish, Italian or Spanish. They were not sold by the Haiti post office and were not valid for postage.

---

The following items inscribed "Republic of Haiti" have been declared "illegal" by Haitian postal authorities:

Sheets of six 8g stamps depicting Pope John Paul II, and Pope Benedict XVI.

Sheets of six 10g stamps depicting Pope John Paul II, and Pope Benedict XVI.

Sheets of six 15g stamps depicting Pope John Paul II, and Pope Benedict XVI.

Sheet of three 20g stamps depicting Pope John Paul II.

Sheet of three 30g stamps depicting Pope John Paul II.

Sheets of two 25g stamps depicting Pope Benedict XVI (2 different).

---

A sheet of seven stamps of various denominations and two labels and a sheet of eight 25g stamp and one label commemorating the Jan. 12, 2010 Haiti earthquake have been determined to be bogus issues.

---

## SEMI-POSTAL STAMPS

Pierre de Coubertin
SP1

**Engraved & Litho (flag)**
**1939, Oct. 3 Unwmk. *Perf. 12***

**B1** SP1 10c + 10c multi 27.50 27.50
*Nos. B1,CB1-CB2 (3)* 77.50 77.50

Pierre de Coubertin, organizer of the modern Olympic Games. The surtax was used to build a Sports Stadium at Port-au-Prince.

**Catalogue values for unused stamps in this section, from this point to the end of the section, are for Never Hinged items.**

Nos. 419-420 Surcharged in Deep Carmine

***Perf. 13x13½, 13½x13***
**1958, Aug. 30 Litho. Unwmk.**

**B2** A82 1g + 50c purple 2.50 2.40
**B3** A83 1.50g + 50c red org 2.50 2.40
*Nos. B2-B3,CB9 (3)* 7.50 7.20

The surtax was for the Red Cross. Overprint arranged horizontally on No. B3.

Similar Surcharge in Red on One Line on Nos. 440-441

**1959, Apr. 7 Photo. *Perf. 11½***
**Granite Paper**

**B4** A87 10c + 25c rose pink .40 .25
**B5** A87 25c + 25c green .40 .35

Nos. 444-446 Surcharged Like Nos. B2-B3 in Red
***Perf. 14x13½***

**B6** A88 10c + 50c vio bl & ol .75 .50
**B7** A88 50c + 50c grn & dp brn .75 .60
**B8** A88 2g + 50c dp cl & dk brn 1.25 1.00
*Nos. B6-B8,CB10-CB15 (9)* 7.65 7.00

The surtax was for the Red Cross.

**No. 447 Surcharged Diagonally**

**Unwmk.**
**1959, July 23 Photo. *Perf. 12***

**B9** A89 50c + 20c lt bl & dp cl .85 .85
*Nos. B9,CB16-CB18 (4)* 4.05 4.05

Issued for the World Refugee Year, July 1, 1959-June 30, 1960.

**Nos. 448-450 Surcharged in Dark Carmine**

**1959, Oct. 30 *Perf. 14***

**B10** A90 25c + 75c blk brn & lt bl .65 .60
**B11** A90 50c + 75c multi .90 .60
**B12** A91 75c + 75c brn & bl .90 .60
*Nos. B10-B12,CB19-CB21 (6)* 5.45 4.80

The surtax was for Haitian athletes.
On No. B12, surcharge lines are spaced to total depth of 16mm.

No. 436 Surcharged in Red: "Hommage a l'UNICEF +G. 0,50"

**Engraved and Lithographed**
**1960, Feb. 2 *Perf. 11½***

**B13** A86 1g + 50c blk & brick red .90 .90
*Nos. B13,CB22-CB23 (3)* 3.65 3.65

UNICEF.

Nos. 452-453 Surcharged with Additional Value and Overprinted "ALPHABETISATION" in Red or Black

***Perf. 12½x13***
**1960, July 12 Litho. Unwmk.**

**B14** A92 10c + 20c sal & grn (R) .35 .25
**B15** A92 10c + 30c sal & grn .40 .25
**B16** A92 50c + 20c vio & mag (R) .40 .25
**B17** A92 50c + 30c vio & mag .55 .50
*Nos. B14-B17,CB24-CB27 (8)* 4.55 3.70

**Olympic Games Issue**

Nos. 464-465 Surcharged with Additional Value

**1960, Sept. 9 Photo. *Perf. 12***

**B18** A94 50c + 25c grn & ocher .40 .25
**B19** A94 1g + 25c dk brn & grnsh bl .50 .40
*Nos. B18-B19,CB28-CB29 (4)* 1.95 1.45

No. 469 Surcharged: "UNICEF +25 centimes"

**1961, Jan. 14 Engr. *Perf. 10½***

**B20** A96 1g + 25c grn & blk .50 .40
*Nos. B20,CB30-CB31 (3)* 1.55 1.20

UNICEF.

No. 469 Surcharged: "OMS SNEM +20 CENTIMES"

**1961, Dec. 11**

**B21** A96 1g + 20c grn & blk .55 .50
*Nos. B21,CB35-CB36 (3)* 4.40 4.35

Haiti's participation in the UN malaria eradication drive.

Nos. 434, 436 and 438 Surcharged in Black or Red

(Surcharge arranged to fit shape of stamp.)

**1961-62 Engr. & Litho. *Perf. 11½***

**B22** A86 20c + 25c blk & yel .30 .25
**B23** A86 1g + 50c blk & brick red (R) ('62) .50 .50
**B24** A86 2.50g + 50c blk & gray vio (R) ('62) .90 .60
*Nos. B22-B24,CB37-CB41 (8)* 5.55 5.20

The surtax was for the benefit of the urban rehabilitation program in Duvalier Ville.

Nos. 486-488 Surcharged: "+25 centimes"

**1962, Sept. 13 Litho. *Perf. 12***

**B25** A99 5c + 25c crim & dp bl .30 .25
**B26** A99 10c + 25c red brn & emer .30 .25
**B27** A99 50c + 25c bl & crim .40 .25
*Nos. B25-B27,CB42-CB44 (6)* 2.15 1.65

Nos. 489-490 Surcharged in Red: "+0.20"

**1962 Unwmk. *Perf. 12½x13***

**B28** A92 10c + 20c bl & org .30 .25
**B29** A92 50c + 20c rose lil & ol grn .40 .40
*Nos. B28-B29,CB45-CB46 (4)* 1.60 1.45

No. 502 Surcharged: "ALPHABETISATION" and "+0,10"

**1963, Mar. 15 Photo. *Perf. 14x14½***

**B30** A102 25c + 10c bl gray, yel & blk .25 .25
*Nos. B30,CB47-CB48 (3)* 1.15 .90

Nos. 491-494 Surcharged and Overprinted in Black or Red With Olympic Emblem and: "JEUX OLYMPIQUES / D'HIVER / INNSBRUCK 1964"

***Perf. 14x14½, 14½x14***

**1964, July 27 Unwmk.**

**B31** A100 50c + 10c on 3c (R) .60 .40
**B32** A100 50c + 10c on 5c .60 .40
**B33** A100 50c + 10c on 10c (R) .60 .40
**B34** A100 50c + 10c on 25c .60 .40
*Nos. B31-B34,CB49 (5)* 3.30 2.40

9th Winter Olympic Games, Innsbruck, Austria, Jan. 20-Feb. 9, 1964. The 10c surtax went for charitable purposes.

Nos. 510-512 Surcharged: "+ 5c." in Black

**1965, Mar. 15 Photo. *Perf. 11½***

**Granite Paper**

**B35** A105 10c + 5c lt bl & dk brn .25 .25
**B36** A105 25c + 5c sal & dk brn .30 .25
**B37** A105 50c + 5c pale rose lil & dk brn .50 .40
*Nos. B35-B37,CB51-CB54 (7)* 3.15 2.45

Nos. B35-B37 and CB51-CB54 also exist with this surcharge (without period after "c") in red. They also exist with a similar black surcharge which lacks the period and is in a thinner, lighter type face.

Nos. 533 and 535-536 Surcharged and Overprinted with Haitian Scout Emblem and "12e Jamboree / Mondial 1967" Like Regular Issue

**1967, Aug. 21 Photo. *Perf. 11½***

**B38** A111 10c + 10c on 5c multi .25 .25
**B39** A111 15c + 10c multi .25 .25
**B40** A111 50c + 10c multi .30 .25
*Nos. B38-B40,CB55-CB56 (5)* 1.85 1.50

12th Boy Scout World Jamboree, Farragut State Park, Idaho, Aug. 1-9. The surcharge on No. B38 includes 2 bars through old denomination.

Nos. 600-601 Surcharged in Red with New Value, Red Cross and: "50ème. Anniversaire / de la Ligue des / Sociétés de la / Croix Rouge"

**1969, June 25 Litho. *Perf. 11½***

**B41** A127 10c + 10c multi .25 .25
**B42** A127 50c + 20c multi .50 .40
*Nos. B41-B42,CB61-CB62 (4)* 2.15 1.55

50th anniv. of the League of Red Cross Societies.

Nos. 637-638 Surcharged with New Value and: "INAUGURATION / 22-7-71"

**1971, Aug. 3 Litho. *Perf. 14x13½***

**B43** A138 20c + 50c multi .45 .35
**B44** A138 25c + 1.50g multi .80 .45

Inauguration of the François Duvalier Central Hydroelectric Plant, July 22, 1971.

## AIR POST STAMPS

Plane over Port-au-Prince — AP1

**1929-30 Unwmk. Engr. *Perf. 12***

**C1** AP1 25c dp grn ('30) .50 .40
**C2** AP1 50c dp vio .65 .40
**C3** AP1 75c red brn ('30) 1.75 1.25
**C4** AP1 1g dp ultra 1.90 1.60
*Nos. C1-C4 (4)* 4.80 3.65

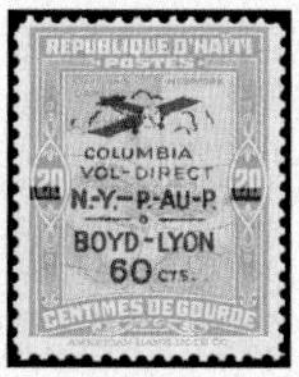


AP1a

**1933, July 6 Red Surcharge**

**C4A** AP1a 60c on 20c blue 75.00 80.00

Non-stop flight of Capt. J. Errol Boyd and Robert G. Lyon from New York to Port-au-Prince.

Plane over Christophe's Citadel — AP2

**1933-40**

**C5** AP2 50c org brn 5.25 1.00
**C6** AP2 50c ol grn ('35) 4.00 1.00
**C7** AP2 50c car rose ('37) 3.50 2.00
**C8** AP2 50c blk ('38) 2.00 1.00
**C8A** AP2 60c choc ('40) 1.10 .50
**C9** AP2 1g ultra 1.75 .50
*Nos. C5-C9 (6)* 17.60 6.00

For surcharge see No. C24.

**Dumas Type of Regular Issue**

**1935, Dec. 29 Litho. *Perf. 11½***

**C10** A59 60c brt vio & choc 4.50 2.50

Visit of delegation from France to Haiti.

Arms of Haiti and Portrait of George Washington — AP4

**1938, Aug. 29 Engr. *Perf. 12***

**C11** AP4 60c deep blue .70 .40

150th anniv. of the US Constitution.

**Caribbean Conference Type of Regular Issue**

**1941, June 30**

**C12** A60 60c olive 3.25 .85
**C13** A60 1.25g purple 3.25 .65

**Madonna Type of Regular Issue**

**1942, Dec. 8 *Perf. 12***

**C14** A61 10c dk olive .40 .25
**C15** A61 25c brt ultra .50 .40
**C16** A61 50c turq grn .90 .40
**C17** A61 60c rose car 1.40 .50
**C18** A61 1.25g black 2.50 .50
*Nos. C14-C18 (5)* 5.70 2.00

**Souvenir Sheets**

**C19** A61 Sheet of 2, #C14, C16 5.00 5.00
*a.* Imperf 25.00 25.00
**C20** A61 Sheet of 2, #C15, C17 5.00 5.00
*a.* Imperf 25.00 25.00
**C21** A61 Sheet of 1, #C18 5.00 5.00
*a.* Imperf 25.00 25.00

Our Lady of Perpetual Help, patroness of Haiti.

**Killick Type of Regular Issue**

**1943, Sept. 6**

**C22** A62 60c purple .65 .40
**C23** A62 1.25g black 1.60 1.60

No. C8A Surcharged with New Value and Bars in Red

**1944, Nov. 25**

**C24** AP2 10c on 60c choc .50 .40
*a.* Bars at right vertical 2.40
*b.* Double surcharge 75.00

**Red Cross Type of Regular Issue**

**1945 Cross in Rose**

**C25** A63 20c yel org .40 .25
**C26** A63 25c brt ultra .40 .25
**C27** A63 50c ol blk .40 .25
**C28** A63 60c dl vio .50 .25
**C29** A63 1g yellow 1.40 .40
**C30** A63 1.25g carmine 1.25 .40
**C31** A63 1.35g green 1.25 .60
**C32** A63 5g black 7.25 2.50
*Nos. C25-C32 (8)* 12.85 4.70

Issue dates: 1g, Aug. 14; others, Feb. 20.
For surcharges see Nos. C153-C160.

**Catalogue values for unused stamps in this section, from this point to the end of the section, are for Never Hinged items.**

Franklin D. Roosevelt — AP11

**1946, Feb. 5 Unwmk. *Perf. 12***

**C33** AP11 20c black .40 .25
**C34** AP11 60c black .50 .25

**Capois Type of Regular Issue**

**1946, July 18 Engr.**

**C35** A64 20c car rose .25 .25
**C36** A64 25c dk grn .25 .25
**C37** A64 50c orange .25 .25
**C38** A64 60c purple .40 .25
**C39** A64 1g gray blk .50 .25
**C40** A64 1.25g red vio .75 .40
**C41** A64 1.35g black .80 .50
**C42** A64 5g rose car 2.40 1.20
*Nos. C35-C42 (8)* 5.50 3.10

For surcharges see Nos. C43-C45, C49-C51, C61-C62.

Nos. C37 and C41 Surcharged with New Value and Bar or Block in Red or Black

**1947-48**

**C43** A64 5c on 1.35g (R) ('48) .60 .40
**C44** A64 30c on 50c .50 .40
**C45** A64 30c on 1.35g (R) .50 .40
*Nos. C43-C45 (3)* 1.60 1.20

**Dessalines Type of 1947-54 Regular Issue**

**1947, Oct. 17 Engr.**

**C46** A65 20c chocolate .40 .25

Christopher Columbus and Fleet — AP14

Pres. Dumarsais Estimé and Exposition Buildings — AP15

**1950, Feb. 12 *Perf. 12½***

**C47** AP14 30c ultra & gray .90 .50
**C48** AP15 1g black .90 .50

200th anniversary (in 1949) of the founding of Port-au-Prince.

Nos. C36, C39 and C41 Surcharged or Overprinted in Carmine

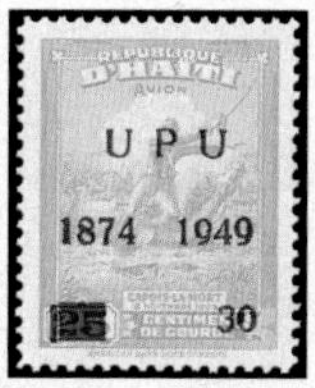


**1950, Oct. 4 *Perf. 12***

**C49** A64 30c on 25c dk grn .40 .30
*a.* 30c on 1g gray black 75.00
**C50** A64 1g gray blk .60 .50
*a.* "P" of overprint omitted 65.00 60.00
**C51** A64 1.50g on 1.35g blk 1.75 1.50
*Nos. C49-C51 (3)* 2.75 2.30

75th anniv. (in 1949) of the UPU.

Bananas AP16

Coffee AP17

Sisal AP18

Isabella I AP19

**1951, Sept. 3 Photo. *Perf. 12½***

**C52** AP16 30c dp org 2.25 .40
**C53** AP17 80c dk grn & sal pink 5.50 .60
**C54** AP18 5g gray 19.00 3.50
*Nos. C52-C54 (3)* 26.75 4.50

For surcharge see No. C218.

**1951, Oct. 12 *Perf. 13***

**C55** AP19 15c brown .30 .25
**C56** AP19 30c dull blue .40 .40

Queen Isabella I of Spain, 500th birth anniv.

**Type of Regular Issue**

**1953, May 4 Engr. *Perf. 12***

20c, Cap Haitien Roadstead. 30c, Workers' housing, St. Martin. 1.50g, Restored cathedral. 2.50g, School lunchroom.

**C57** A68 20c dp bl .25 .25
**C58** A68 30c red brn .40 .25
**C59** A68 1.50g gray blk .85 .50
**C60** A68 2.50g violet 1.75 .85
*Nos. C57-C60 (4)* 3.25 1.75

Nos. C38 and C41 Surcharged in Black

**1953, May 18**
C61 A64 50c on 60c pur .40 .25
a. Double surcharge 50.00 50.00
C62 A64 50c on 1.35g blk .40 .25
a. Double surcharge 50.00

150th anniv. of the adoption of the natl. flag.

### Dessalines and Magloire Type and

Henri Christophe — AP21

**1954, Jan. 1 Photo. *Perf. 11½***
C63 AP21 50c shown .50 .25
C64 AP21 50c Toussaint L'Ouverture .50 .25
C65 AP21 50c Dessalines .50 .25
C66 AP21 50c Petion .50 .25
C67 AP21 50c Boisrond-Tonerre .50 .25
C68 AP21 1g Petion .80 .50
C69 AP21 1.50g Lamartiniere 1.50 1.00
C70 A69 7.50g shown 5.50 5.00
*Nos. C63-C70 (8)* 10.30 7.75

See Nos. C95-C96.

Marie Jeanne and Lamartinière Leading Attack — AP23

Design: Nos. C73, C74, Battle of Vertieres.

**1954, Jan. 1 *Perf. 12½***
C71 AP23 50c black .40 .25
C72 AP23 50c carmine .40 .25
C73 AP23 50c ultra .40 .25
C74 AP23 50c sal pink .40 .25
*Nos. C71-C74 (4)* 1.60 .80

150th anniv. of Haitian independence.

### Mme. Magloire Type of Regular Issue

**1954, Jan. 1 *Perf. 11½***
C75 A72 20c red org .25 .25
C76 A72 50c brown .40 .40
C77 A72 1g gray grn .50 .40
C78 A72 1.50g crimson .75 .50
C79 A72 2.50g bl grn 1.25 .90
C80 A72 5g gray 3.00 2.25
*Nos. C75-C80 (6)* 6.10 4.65

### Christophe Types of Regular Issue

**1954, Dec. 6 Litho. *Perf. 13½x13***
**Portraits in Black**
C81 A73 50c orange .40 .25
C82 A73 1g blue .80 .50
C83 A73 1.50g green 1.10 .65
C84 A73 2.50g gray 1.75 .90
C85 A73 5g rose car 3.25 1.90

***Perf. 13***
**Flag in Black and Carmine**
C86 A74 50c orange .40 .25
C87 A74 1g dp bl .75 .45
C88 A74 1.50g bl grn 1.10 .65
C89 A74 2.50g gray 1.75 .90
C90 A74 5g red org 3.25 1.90
*Nos. C81-C90 (10)* 14.55 8.25

Fort Nativity, Drawing by Christopher Columbus — AP27

**1954, Dec. 14 Engr. *Perf. 12***
C91 AP27 50c dk rose car .65 .50
C92 AP27 50c dk gray .65 .50

### Dessalines Type of 1955-57 Issue

***Perf. 11½***
**1955, July 14 Unwmk. Photo.**
C93 A75 20c org & blk .25 .25
C94 A75 20c yel grn & blk .25 .25

For overprint see No. C183a.

### Portrait Type of 1954
Dates omitted

Design: J. J. Dessalines.

**1955, July 19**
**Portrait in Black**
C95 AP21 50c gray .40 .25
C96 AP21 50c blue .40 .25

### Dessalines Memorial Type of Regular Issue

**1955, Aug. 1**
C97 A76 1.50g gray & blk .65 .25
C98 A76 1.50g grn & blk .65 .25

### Types of 1956 Regular Issue and

Car and Coastal View — AP30

Designs: No. C100, 75c, Plane, steamship and Haiti map. 1g, Car and coastal view. 2.50g, Flamingo. 5g, Mallard.

**1956, Apr. 14 Unwmk. *Perf. 11½***
**Granite Paper**
C99 AP30 50c hn brn & lt bl .70 .25
C100 AP30 50c blk & gray .45 .25
C101 AP30 75c dp grn & bl grn .95 .50
C102 AP30 1g ol grn & lt bl .80 .30
C103 A77 2.50g dp org & org 14.00 1.75
C104 A78 5g red & buff 21.00 3.00
*Nos. C99-C104 (6)* 37.90 6.05

For overprint see No. C185.

### Kant Type of Regular Issue

**1956, July 19 Photo. *Perf. 12***
**Granite Paper**
C105 A79 50c chestnut .40 .25
C106 A79 75c dp yel grn .50 .40
C107 A79 1.50g dp magenta 1.25 .50
a. Miniature sheet of 3 8.00 5.00
*Nos. C105-C107 (3)* 2.15 1.10

No. C107a exists both perf. and imperf. Each sheet contains Nos. C105, C106 and a 1.25g gray black of same design.

### Waterfall Type of Regular Issue

**1957, Dec. 16 *Perf. 11½***
**Granite Paper**
C108 A80 50c grn & grnsh bl .25 .25
C109 A80 1.50g ol grn & grnsh bl .65 .40
C110 A80 2.50g dk bl & brt bl 1.00 .60
C111 A80 5g bluish blk & saph 2.50 1.50
*Nos. C108-C111 (4)* 4.40 2.70

For surcharge and overprint see Nos. CB49, CQ2.

### Dessalines Type of Regular Issue

**1958, July 2**
C112 A81 50c org & blk .65 .40

For overprints see Nos. C184, CQ1.

### Brussels Fair Types of Regular Issue, 1958

***Perf. 13x13½, 13½x13***
**1958, July 22 Litho. Unwmk.**
C113 A82 2.50g pale car rose 1.25 .50
C114 A83 5g bright blue 1.50 .85
a. Souv. sheet of 2, #C113-C114, imperf. 5.50 5.00

For surcharge see No. CB9.

Sylvio Cator — AP33

**1958, Aug. 16 Photo. *Perf. 11½***
**Granite Paper**
C115 AP33 50c green .25 .25
C116 AP33 50c blk brn .25 .25
C117 AP33 1g org brn .50 .40
C118 AP33 5g gray 2.40 .85
*Nos. C115-C118 (4)* 3.40 1.65

30th anniversary of the world championship record broad jump of Sylvio Cator.

### IGY Type of Regular Issue, 1958

Designs: 50c, US Satellite. 1.50g, Emperor penguins. 2g, Modern observatory.

**1958, Oct. 8 *Perf. 14x13½***
C119 A85 50c dp ultra & brn red .60 .25
C120 A85 1.50g brn & crim 3.25 .75
C121 A85 2g dk bl & crim 2.25 .40
a. Souv. sheet of 4, #427, C119-C121, imperf. 8.00 7.50
*Nos. C119-C121 (3)* 6.10 1.40

President Francois Duvalier AP34

### Commemorative Inscription in Ultramarine

**Engraved and Lithographed**
**1958, Oct. 22 Unwmk. *Perf. 11½***
C122 AP34 50c blk & rose 1.00 .25
C123 AP34 2.50g blk & ocher 1.40 .60
C124 AP34 5g blk & rose lil 1.90 1.25
C125 AP34 7.50g blk & lt bl grn 3.00 2.00
*Nos. C122-C125 (4)* 7.30 4.05

See note after No. 431.

Souvenir sheets of 3 exist, perf. and imperf., containing one each of Nos. C124-C125 and No. 431. Sheets measure 132x77mm. with marginal inscription in ultramarine. Value, $6.25 each.

For surcharges see Nos. CB37-CB39.

### Same Without Commemorative Inscription

**1958, Nov. 20**
C126 AP34 50c blk & rose .40 .25
C127 AP34 1g blk & vio .50 .25
C128 AP34 1.50g blk & pale brn .75 .40
C129 AP34 2g blk & rose pink 1.00 .40
C130 AP34 2.50g blk & ocher 1.00 .50
C131 AP34 5g blk & rose lil 2.00 1.25
C132 AP34 7.50g blk & lt bl grn 3.00 1.60
*Nos. C126-C132 (7)* 8.65 4.60

For surcharges see #CB22-CB23, CB40-CB41.

### Type of Regular Issue and

Flags of Haiti and UN — AP35

***Perf. 11½***
**1958, Dec. 5 Unwmk. Photo.**
**Granite Paper**
C133 AP35 50c pink, car & ultra .40 .25
C134 A87 75c brt bl .40 .25
C135 A87 1g brown .50 .40
a. Souv. sheet of 2, #C133, C135, imperf. 3.50 3.50
*Nos. C133-C135 (3)* 1.30 .80

For surcharges see Nos. CB10-CB12.

Nos. C133-C135 Overprinted: "10th ANNIVERSARY OF THE UNIVERSAL DECLARATION OF HUMAN RIGHTS," in English (a), French (b), Spanish (c) or Portuguese (d)

**1959, Jan. 28**
C136 Block of 4 2.75 2.75
a.-d. AP35 50c any single .60 .60
C137 Block of 4 3.75 3.75
a.-d. A87 75c any single .80 .80
C138 Block of 4 7.00 7.00
a.-d. A87 1g any single 1.50 1.50
*Nos. C136-C138 (3)* 13.50 13.50

Pope Pius XII — AP36

1.50g, Pope praying. 2.50g, Pope on throne.

**1959, Feb. 28 Photo. *Perf. 14x13½***
C139 AP36 50c grn & lil .25 .25
C140 AP36 1.50g ol & red brn .65 .40
C141 AP36 2.50g pur & dk bl 1.00 .40
*Nos. C139-C141 (3)* 1.90 1.00

Issued in memory of Pope Pius XII.
For surcharges see Nos. CB13-CB15.

### Lincoln Type of Regular Issue, 1959

Designs: Various Portraits of Lincoln.

**1959, May 12 *Perf. 12***
C142 A89 1g lt grn & chnt .50 .40
C143 A89 2g pale lem & sl grn .75 .50
C144 A89 2.50g buff & vio bl .85 .40
a. Min. sheet of 4, #447, C142-C144, imperf. 3.00 2.75
*Nos. C142-C144 (3)* 2.10 1.30

Imperf. pairs exist.
For surcharges see Nos. CB16-CB18.

### Pan American Games Types of Regular Issue

Designs: 50c, Jean Baptiste Dessables and map of American Midwest, c. 1791. 1g, Chicago's skyline and Dessables house. 1.50g, Discus thrower and flag of Haiti.

**Unwmk.**
**1959, Aug. 27 Photo. *Perf. 14***
C145 A91 50c hn brn & aqua .75 .25
C146 A90 1g lil & aqua 1.00 .40
C147 A90 1.50g multi 1.40 .50
*Nos. C145-C147 (3)* 3.15 1.15

For surcharges see Nos. CB19-CB21.

Nos. C145-C147 Overprinted like No. 451

**1960, Feb. 29**
C148 A91 50c hn brn & aqua 1.40 1.40
C149 A90 1g lil & aqua 1.90 1.90
C150 A90 1.50g multi 2.75 2.75
*Nos. C148-C150 (3)* 6.05 6.05

### WRY Type of Regular Issue, 1960

**1960, Apr. 7 Litho. *Perf. 12½x13***
C151 A92 50c bl & blk .40 .25
C152 A92 1g lt grn & mar .50 .40
a. Souv. sheet of 4, #452-453, C151-C152, imperf. 6.50 6.00

See Nos. C191-C192. For surcharges see Nos. CB24-CB27, CB45-CB46.

Nos. C31, C28 and 369 Surcharged or Overprinted in Red: "28ème ANNIVERSAIRE"

**1960, May 8 Engr. *Perf. 12***
**Cross in Rose**
C153 A63 20c on 1.35g grn .40 .25
C154 A63 50c on 60c dl vio .65 .40
C155 A63 50c on 1.35g grn .40 .40
C156 A63 50c on 2.50g pale vio .40 .40
C157 A63 60c dl vio .40 .40
C158 A63 1g on 1.35g grn .70 .50
C159 A63 1.35g green .65 .50
C160 A63 2g on 1.35g grn 1.40 1.00
*Nos. C153-C160 (8)* 5.00 3.80

28th anniv. of the Haitian Red Cross. Additional overprint "Avion" on No. C156.

### Sugar Type of Regular Issue

Miss Fouchard &: 50c, Harvest. 2.50g, Beach.

***Perf. 11½***
**1960, May 30 Unwmk. Photo.**
**Granite Paper**
C161 A93 50c lil rose & brn .90 .25
C162 A93 2.50g ultra & brn 2.25 .50

### Olympic Type of Regular Issue

Designs: 50c, Pierre de Coubertin, Melbourne stadium and Olympic Flame. 1.50g, Discus thrower and Rome stadium. 2.50g, Victors' parade, Athens, 1896, and Melbourne, 1956.

**1960, Aug. 18 *Perf. 12***
C163 A94 50c mar & bis .65 .25
C164 A94 1.50g rose car & yel grn 1.40 .40
C165 A94 2.50g sl grn & mag 1.60 .45
a. Souv. sheet of 2, #465, C165, imperf. 5.50 5.50
*Nos. C163-C165 (3)* 3.65 1.05

For surcharges see Nos. CB28-CB29.

### Jeanty Type of Regular Issue

50c, Occide Jeanty and score from "1804." 1.50g, Occide Jeanty and National Capitol.

**1960, Oct. 19** ***Perf. 14x14½***
**C166** A95 50c yel & bl .50 .25
**C167** A95 1.50g lil rose & sl grn .75 .25

Printed in sheets of 12 (3x4) with inscription and opening bars of "1804," Jeanty's military march, in top margin.

### UN Type of Regular Issue, 1960

**1960, Nov. 25** **Engr.** ***Perf. 10½***
**C168** A96 50c red org & blk .40 .25
**C169** A96 1.50g dk bl & blk .50 .40
*a.* Souv. sheet of 3, #469, C168-C169, imperf. 3.25 3.25

For surcharges see #CB30-CB31, CB35-CB36.
Nos. C168-C169 exist with centers inverted.

### Dessalines Type of Regular Issue

**1960, Nov. 5** **Photo.** ***Perf. 11½***
**Granite Paper**
**C170** A81 20c gray & blk .25 .25

For overprint see No. C183.

Sud-Caravelle Jet Airliner and Orchid — AP37

Designs: 50c, Boeing 707 jet airliner, facing left, and Kittyhawk. 1g, Sud-Caravelle jet airliner and Orchid. 1.50g, Boeing 707 jet airliner and air post stamp of 1933.

**1960, Dec. 17** **Photo.** **Unwmk.**
**Granite Paper**
**C171** AP37 20c dp ultra & car .25 .25
**C172** AP37 50c rose brn & grn .50 .25
**C173** AP37 50c brt grnsh bl & ol grn .50 .25
**C174** AP37 50c gray & grn .50 .25
**C175** AP37 1g gray ol & ver 1.60 .25
**C176** AP37 1.50g brt pink & dk bl 1.25 .30
*a.* Souv. sheet of 3, #C174-C176, imperf. 4.00 4.00
*Nos. C171-C176 (6)* 4.60 1.55

Issued for Aviation Week, Dec. 17-23.
#C172-C174 are dated 17 Decembre 1903.
For overprints and surcharges see Nos. CB32-CB34, CO1-CO5.

### Dumas Type of Regular Issue

Designs: 50c, The Three Musketeers and Dumas père, horiz 1g, The Lady of the Camellias and Dumas fils. 1.50g, The Count of Monte Cristo and Dumas père.

**1961, Feb. 10** **Photo.** ***Perf. 11½***
**Granite Paper**
**C177** A97 50c brt bl & blk .60 .25
**C178** A97 1g blk & red .75 .25
**C179** A97 1.50g brt grn & bl blk 1.10 .35
*Nos. C177-C179 (3)* 2.45 .80

### Type of Regular Issue, 1961

Tourist publicity: 20c, Privateer in Battle. 50c, Pirate with cutlass in rigging. 1g, Map of Tortuga.

**1961, Apr. 4** **Litho.** ***Perf. 12***
**C180** A98 20c dk bl & yel .30 .25
**C181** A98 50c brt pur & org .55 .25
**C182** A98 1g Prus grn & yel .45 .40
*Nos. C180-C182 (3)* 1.30 .85

For overprint and surcharge see #C186-C187.

Nos. C170, C112 and C101 Overprinted: "Dr. F. Duvalier Président 22 Mai 1961"

**1961, May 22** **Photo.** ***Perf. 11½***
**C183** A81 20c gray & blk .25 .25
*a.* On No. C93
**C184** A81 50c org & blk .25 .25
**C185** AP30 75c dp grn & bl grn .40 .40
*Nos. C183-C185 (3)* .85 .80

Re-election of Pres. Francois Duvalier.

No. C182 Overprinted or Surcharged: "EXPLORATION SPATIALE JOHN GLENN" and Capsule

**1962, May 10** **Litho.** ***Perf. 12***
**C186** A98 1g Prus grn & yel .50 .40
**C187** A98 2g on 1g Prus grn & yel 1.40 1.00

See note after No. 485.

### Malaria Type of Regular Issue

Designs: 20c, 1g, Triangle pointing down. 50c, Triangle pointing up.

**1962, May 30** **Unwmk.**
**C188** A99 20c lilac & red .25 .25
**C189** A99 50c emer & rose car .40 .25
**C190** A99 1g org & dk vio .50 .40
*a.* Souv. sheet of 3 3.00 3.00
*Nos. C188-C190 (3)* 1.10 .80

Sheets of 12 with marginal inscription.
No. C190a contains stamps similar to Nos. 488 and C189-C190 in changed colors and imperf. Issued July 16.
A similar sheet without the "Contribution . . ." inscription was issued May 30.
For surcharges see Nos. CB42-CB44.

### WRY Type of 1960 Dated "1962"

**1962, June 22** ***Perf. 12½x13***
**C191** A92 50c lt bl & red brn .35 .25
**C192** A92 1g bister & blk .40 .40

A souvenir sheet exists containing one each of #489-490, C191-C192, imperf. Value, $5.50.
For surcharges see Nos. CB45-CB46.

### Boy Scout Type of 1962

Designs: 20c, Scout giving Scout sign. 50c, Haitian Scout emblem. 1.50g, Lord and Lady Baden-Powell, horiz.

***Perf. 14x14½, 14½x14***
**1962, Aug. 6** **Photo.** **Unwmk.**
**C193** A100 20c multi .25 .25
**C194** A100 50c multi .50 .40
**C195** A100 1.50g multi .65 .40
*Nos. C193-C195 (3)* 1.35 1.00

A souvenir sheet contains one each of Nos. C194-C195 imperf. Value, $5.50.
A similar sheet inscribed in gold, "Epreuves De Luxe," was issued Dec. 10. Value $3.

Nos. 495 and C193-C195 Overprinted: "AEROPORT INTERNATIONAL 1962"

**1962, Oct. 26** ***Perf. 14x14½, 14½x14***
**C196** A100 20c multi, #C193 .25 .25
**C197** A100 50c multi, #495 .40 .25
**C198** A100 50c multi, #C194 .40 .25
**C199** A100 1.50g multi, #C195 .60 .40
*Nos. C196-C199 (4)* 1.65 1.15

Proceeds from the sale of Nos. C196-C199 were for the construction of new airport at Port-au-Prince. The overprint on No. C197 has "Poste Aérienne" added.

### Seattle Fair Type of 1962

Design: Denomination at left, "Avion" at right.

**1962, Nov. 19** **Litho.** ***Perf. 12½***
**C200** A101 50c blk & pale lil .40 .25
**C201** A101 1g org brn & gray .60 .40
**C202** A101 1.50g red lil & org .70 .40
*Nos. C200-C202 (3)* 1.70 1.00

An imperf. sheet of two exists containing one each of Nos. C201-C202 with simulated gray perforations. Size: 133x82mm. Value, $5.50.

Street in Duvalier Ville and Stamp of 1881 — AP38

**1962, Dec. 10** **Photo.** ***Perf. 14x14½***
**Stamp in Dark Brown**
**C203** AP38 50c orange .50 .25
**C204** AP38 1g blue .90 .40
**C205** AP38 1.50g green 1.00 .50
*Nos. C203-C205 (3)* 2.40 1.10

Issued to publicize Duvalier Ville.
For surcharges see Nos. CB47-CB48.

### Nos. C201-C202 Overprint in Black

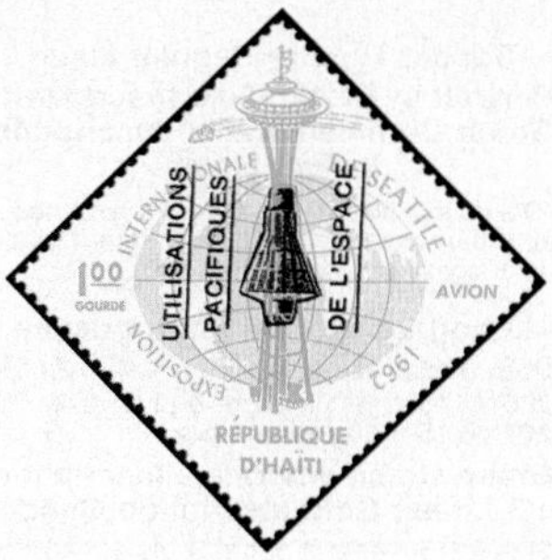


**1963, Jan. 23** **Litho.** ***Perf. 12½***
**C206** A101 1g org brn & gray 1.40 .60
*a.* Claret overprint, horiz. 1.40 .60
**C207** A101 1.50g red lil & org 1.75 1.10
*a.* Claret overprint, horiz. 1.75 1.10

"Peaceful Uses of Outer Space." The black vertical overprint has no outside frame lines and no broken shading lines around capsule. Nos. C206a and C207a were issued Feb. 20.

### Hunger Type of Regular Issue

***Perf. 13x14***
**1963, July 12** **Unwmk.** **Photo.**
**C208** A103 50c lil rose & blk .40 .25
**C209** A103 1g lt ol grn & blk .50 .40

Dag Hammarskjold and UN Emblem — AP39

**Lithographed and Photogravure**
**1963, Sept. 28** ***Perf. 13½x14***
**Portrait in Slate**
**C210** AP39 20c buff & brn .25 .25
**C211** AP39 50c lt bl & car .40 .25
*a.* Souvenir sheet of 2 3.50 3.50
**C212** AP39 1g pink & bl .40 .25
**C213** AP39 1.50g gray & grn .65 .50
*Nos. C210-C213 (4)* 1.70 1.25

Dag Hammarskjold, Sec. Gen. of the UN, 1953-61. Printed in sheets of 25 (5x5) with map of Sweden extending over 9 stamps in second and third vertical rows. No. C211a contains 2 imperf. stamps: 50c blue and carmine and 1.50g ocher and brown with map of southern Sweden in background.
For overprints see Nos. C219-C222, C238-C241, CB50.

### Dessalines Type of Regular Issue, 1963

**1963, Oct. 17** **Photo.** ***Perf. 14x14½***
**C214** A104 50c bl & lil rose .25 .25
**C215** A104 50c org & grn .25 .25

Nos. C214-C215 and C53 Overprinted in Black or Red: "FETE DES MERES / 1964"

**1964, July 22** ***Perf. 14x14½, 12½***
**C216** A104 50c bl & lil rose .40 .25
**C217** A104 50c org & grn .40 .25
**C218** AP17 1.50g on 80c dk grn & sal pink (R) .60 .40
*Nos. C216-C218 (3)* 1.40 .80

Issued for Mother's Day, 1964.

### Nos. C210-C213 Overprinted in Red

**Lithographed and Engraved**
**1964, Oct. 2** ***Perf. 13½x14***
**Portrait in Slate**
**C219** AP39 20c buff & brn .40 .25
**C220** AP39 50c lt bl & car .40 .25
**C221** AP39 1g pink & bl .60 .40
**C222** AP39 1.50g gray & grn .70 .50
*Nos. C219-C222,CB50 (5)* 3.50 2.65

Cent. (in 1963) of the Intl. Red Cross.

### Olympic Type of Regular Issue

#C223, Weight lifter. #C224-C226, Hurdler.

**1964, Nov. 12** **Photo.** ***Perf. 11½***
**Granite Paper**
**C223** A105 50c pale lil & dk brn .40 .25
**C224** A105 50c pale grn & dk brn .40 .25
**C225** A105 75c buff & dk brn .50 .40
**C226** A105 1.50g gray & dk brn .65 .50
*a.* Souv. sheet of 4 2.60 2.50
*Nos. C223-C226 (4)* 1.95 1.30

Printed in sheets of 50 (10x5), with map of Japan in background extending over 27 stamps.
No. C226a contains four imperf. stamps similar to Nos. C223-C226 in changed colors and with map of Tokyo area in background.
For surcharges see Nos. CB51-CB54.

### Airport Type of Regular Issue, 1964

**1964, Dec. 15** ***Perf. 14½x14***
**C227** A106 50c org & blk .40 .25
**C228** A106 1.50g brt lil rose & blk .65 .45
**C229** A106 2.50g lt vio & blk 1.40 .60
*Nos. C227-C229 (3)* 2.45 1.25

Same Overprinted "1965"

**1965, Feb. 11** **Photo.**
**C230** A106 50c org & blk .40 .25
**C231** A106 1.50g brt lil rose & blk .65 .40
**C232** A106 2.50g lt vio & blk 1.00 .70
*Nos. C230-C232 (3)* 2.05 1.30

### World's Fair Type of Regular Issue, 1965

Designs: 50c, 1.50g, "Rocket Thrower" by Donald De Lue. 5g, Unisphere, NY World's Fair.

**1965, Mar. 22** **Unwmk.** ***Perf. 13½***
**C233** A107 50c dp bl & org .40 .25
**C234** A107 1.50g gray & org .50 .40
**C235** A107 5g multi 2.40 1.90
*Nos. C233-C235 (3)* 3.30 2.50

### Merchant Marine Type of Regular Issue, 1965

**1965, May 13** **Photo.** ***Perf. 11½***
**C236** A108 50c blk, lt grnsh bl & red .40 .25
**C237** A108 1.50g blk, lt vio & red .75 .50

### Nos. C210-C213 Overprinted

**Lithographed and Photogravure**
**1965, June 26** ***Perf. 13½x14***
**Portrait in Slate**
**C238** AP39 20c buff & brn .25 .25
**C239** AP39 50c lt bl & car .40 .25
**C240** AP39 1g pink & bl .50 .40
**C241** AP39 1.50g gray & grn .65 .50
*Nos. C238-C241 (4)* 1.80 1.40

20th anniversary of the United Nations.

### ITU Type of Regular Issue

***Perf. 13½***
**1965, Aug. 16** **Unwmk.** **Litho.**
**C242** A109 50c multi .40 .25
**C243** A109 1g multi .50 .40
**C244** A109 1.50g bl & multi 1.00 .50
**C245** A109 2g pink & multi 1.50 .60
*Nos. C242-C245 (4)* 3.40 1.70

A souvenir sheet, released in 1966, contains 50c and 2g stamps resembling Nos. C242 and C245, with simulated perforations. Value $15.00.
For overprints see Nos. C255-C256.

### Cathedral Type of Regular Issue, 1965

Designs: 50c, Cathedral, Port-au-Prince, horiz. 1g, High Altar. 7.50g, Statue of Our Lady of the Assumption.

*Perf. 14x13, 13x14*

**1965, Nov. 19 — Photo.**

**Size: 39x29mm, 29x39mm**

**C246** A110 50c multi .40 .25
**C247** A110 1g multi .65 .40

**Size: 38x52mm**

**C248** A110 7.50g multi 2.75 2.25
*Nos. C246-C248 (3)* 3.80 2.85

### Flower Type of Regular Issue

#C249, 5g, Passionflower. #C250, C252, Okra. #C251, C253, American elder.

**1965, Dec. 20 — Photo. — *Perf. 11½***

**Granite Paper**

**C249** A111 50c dk vio, yel & grn 1.10 .25
**C250** A111 50c multi 1.10 .25
**C251** A111 50c grn, gray & yel 1.10 .25
**C252** A111 1.50g multi 1.90 1.40
**C253** A111 1.50g grn, tan & yel 1.90 1.40
**C254** A111 5g dk vio, yel grn & grn 5.50 1.50
*Nos. C249-C254 (6)* 12.60 4.90

For surcharges see Nos. CB55-CB56.

Nos. C242-C243 Overprinted in Red: "20e. Anniversaire / UNESCO"

**1965, Aug. 27 — Litho. — *Perf. 13½***

**C255** A109 50c lt vio & multi 1.40 .50
**C256** A109 1g citron & multi 2.10 .85

20th anniversary of UNESCO.

The souvenir sheet noted below No. C245 was also overprinted "20e. Anniversaire / UNESCO" in red. Value, $20.

### Culture Types of Regular Issue and

Modern Painting — AP40

Designs: 50c, Ceremonial stool. 1.50g, Amulet.

*Perf. 14x14½, 14½x14, 14*

**1966, Mar. 14 — Photo. — Unwmk.**

**C257** A113 50c lil, brn & brnz .40 .25
**C258** A112 1.50g brt rose lil, yel & blk .65 .50
**C259** AP40 2.50g multi 1.50 .85
*Nos. C257-C259 (3)* 2.55 1.55

For overprints and surcharge see Nos. C260-C262, C280-C281.

Nos. C257-C259 Overprinted in Black or Red: "Hommage / a Hailé Sélassié Ier / 24-25 Avril 1966"

**1966, Apr. 24**

**C260** A112 50c (R) .40 .25
**C261** A113 1.50g (vert. ovpt.) .65 .50
**C262** AP40 2.50g (R) 1.00 .70
*Nos. C260-C262 (3)* 2.05 1.40

See note after No. 543.

Walter M. Schirra, Thomas P. Stafford, Frank A. Borman, James A. Lovell and Gemini VI and VII — AP41

**1966, May 3 — *Perf. 13½***

**C263** AP41 50c vio bl, brn & lt bl .40 .25
**C264** AP41 1g grn, brn & lt bl .50 .40
**C265** AP41 1.50g car, brn & bl .65 .50
*Nos. C263-C265 (3)* 1.55 1.10

See No. 547.

For overprints see Nos. C296-C298.

### Soccer Type of Regular Issue Portrait in Black; Gold Inscription; Green Commemorative Inscription in Two Lines

Designs: 50c, Pres. Duvalier and soccer ball within wreath. 1.50g, President Duvalier and soccer player within wreath.

**Lithographed and Photogravure**

**1966, June 16 — *Perf. 13x13½***

**C266** A115 50c lt ol grn & plum .40 .25
**C267** A115 1.50g rose & plum .65 .50

**Green Commemorative Inscription in 3 Lines; Gold Inscription Omitted**

**C268** A115 50c lt ol grn & plum .40 .40
**C269** A115 1.50g rose & plum .65 .50
*Nos. C266-C269 (4)* 2.10 1.60

Caribbean Soccer Festival, June 10-22. Nos. C266-C267 also for the National Soccer Championships, May 8-22.

For overprint and surcharge see Nos. C288, CB57.

### Education Type of Regular Issue

Designs: 50c, "ABC", boy and girl. 1g, Scout symbols. 1.50g, Television set, book and communications satellite, horiz.

*Perf. 14x13½, 13½x14*

**Litho. and Engraved**

**1966, Oct. 18**

**C270** A116 50c grn, yel & brn .40 .25
**C271** A116 1g dk brn, org & blk .50 .40
**C272** A116 1.50g grn, bl grn & dk bl .65 .50
*Nos. C270-C272 (3)* 1.55 1.10

### Schweitzer Type of Regular Issue

Designs (Schweitzer and): 50c, 1g, Albert Schweitzer Hospital, Deschapelles, Haiti. 1.50g, Maps of Alsace and Gabon. 2g, Pipe organ.

*Perf. 12½x13*

**1967, Apr. 20 — Photo. — Unwmk.**

**C273** A117 50c multi .50 .40
**C274** A117 1g multi .50 .40
**C275** A117 1.50g lt bl & multi .65 .50
**C276** A117 2g multi .90 .70
*Nos. C273-C276 (4)* 2.55 2.00

### Fruit-Vegetable Type of Regular Issue, 1967

**1967, July 4 — Photo. — *Perf. 12½***

**C277** A118 50c Watermelon 2.00 .25
**C278** A118 1g Cabbage 2.50 2.00
**C279** A118 1.50g Tangerine 3.00 2.50
*Nos. C277-C279 (3)* 7.50 4.70

No. C258 Overprinted or Surcharged Like EXPO '67 Regular Issue

**1967, Aug. 30 — Photo. — *Perf. 14½x14***

**C280** A112 1.50g multi .60 .40
**C281** A112 2g on 1.50g multi .75 .55

Issued to commemorate EXPO '67 International Exhibition, Montreal, Apr. 28-Oct. 27.

### Duvalier Type of Regular Issue, 1967

**1967, Sept. 22 — Photo. — *Perf. 14x13***

**C282** A119 1g brt grn & gold .50 .40
**C283** A119 1.50g vio & gold .65 .50
**C284** A119 2g org & gold 1.10 .70
*Nos. C282-C284 (3)* 2.25 1.60

### Education Type of Regular Issue, 1967

50c, Writing hands. 1g, Scout emblem and Scouts, vert. 1.50g, Audio-visual teaching of algebra.

**1967, Dec. 11 — Litho. — *Perf. 11½***

**C285** A120 50c multi .25 .25
**C286** A120 1g multi .50 .40
**C287** A120 1.50g multi .65 .50
*Nos. C285-C287 (3)* 1.40 1.10

For surcharges see Nos. CB58-CB60.

### No. C269 Overprinted

**Lithographed and Photogravure**

**1968, Jan. 18 — *Perf. 13x13½***

**C288** A115 1.50g rose & plum 1.40 1.00

See note after No. 579.

### Caiman Woods Type of Regular Issue

**1968, Apr. 22 — Photo. — *Perf. 12***

**Size: 36x26mm**

**C289** A121 50c multi .40 .25
**C290** A121 1g multi .50 .40

*Perf. 12½x13½*

**Size: 49x36mm**

**C291** A121 50c multi .40 .25
**C292** A121 1g multi .50 .40
**C293** A121 1.50g multi .75 .60
**C294** A121 2g gray & multi .90 .70
**C295** A121 5g multi 2.00 1.40
*Nos. C289-C295 (7)* 5.45 3.90

Nos. C263-C265 Overprinted

**1968, Apr. 19 — *Perf. 13½***

**C296** AP41 50c multi .70 .40
**C297** AP41 1g multi 1.40 .60
**C298** AP41 1.50g multi 2.40 1.10
*Nos. C296-C298 (3)* 4.50 2.10

See note after No. 584.

### Monument Type of Regular Issue

**1968, May 22 — *Perf. 11½***

**Granite Paper**

**C299** A122 50c ol bis & blk .40 .25
**C300** A122 1g brt rose & blk .50 .40
**C301** A122 1.50g org & blk .80 .50
*Nos. C299-C301 (3)* 1.70 1.10

For surcharges see Nos. C324-C325.

### Types of Regular Bishopric Issue

50c, Palm tree & provincial coats of arms. 1g, 2.50g, Madonna, papal arms & arms of Haiti. 1.50g, Cathedral, arms of Pope Paul VI & arms of Haiti.

*Perf. 13x14, 12½x13½*

**1968, Aug. 16 — Photo.**

**C302** A123 50c lil & multi .40 .25
**C303** A124 1g multi .50 .40
**C304** A124 1.50g multi .65 .50
**C305** A124 2.50g multi 1.40 1.10
*Nos. C302-C305 (4)* 2.95 2.20

### Airport Type of Regular Issue

50c, 1.50g, 2.50g, Front view of air terminal.

**1968, Sept. 22 — Photo. — *Perf. 11½***

**Portrait in Black**

**C306** A125 50c rose lake & pale vio .40 .25
**C307** A125 1.50g rose lake & bl .65 .50
**C308** A125 2.50g rose lake & lt grnsh bl .90 .80
*Nos. C306-C308 (3)* 1.95 1.50

Pres. Francois Duvalier — AP42

### Embossed & Typo. on Gold Foil

**1968, Sept. 22 — *Die Cut Perf. 14***

**C309** AP42 30g black & red *40.00 50.00*

### Freed Slaves' Type of Regular Issue

**1968, Oct. 28 — Litho. — *Perf. 14½x14***

**C310** A126 50c brn, lil & brt pink .40 .25
**C311** A126 1g brn, yel grn & brt pink .50 .40
**C312** A126 1.50g brn, lt vio bl & brt pink .65 .50
**C313** A126 2g brn, lt grn & brt pink .80 .60
*Nos. C310-C313 (4)* 2.35 1.70

### Education Type of Regular Issue, 1968

50c, 1.50g, Children watching television. 1g, Hands throwing ball, and sports medal.

**1968, Nov. 14 — *Perf. 11½***

**C314** A127 50c multi .40 .25
**C315** A127 1g multi .50 .40
**C316** A127 1.50g multi .65 .50
*Nos. C314-C316 (3)* 1.55 1.10

For surcharges see Nos. CB61-CB62.

Jan Boesman and his Balloon — AP43

**1968, Nov. 28 — Litho. — *Perf. 13½***

**C317** AP43 70c lt yel grn & sepia .65 .50
**C318** AP43 1.75g grnsh bl & sepia 1.40 1.00

Dr. Jan Boesman's balloon flight, Mexico City, Nov. 1968.

Miniature Sheet

Cachet of May 2, 1925 Flight — AP44

### Black Cachets, Magenta Inscriptions and Rose Lilac Background

**1968, Nov. 28 — Litho. — *Perf. 13½x14***

**C318A** Sheet of 12 13.00 *13.00*
*b.* AP44 70c 2 Mai 1925 .70 *.80*
*c.* AP44 70c 2 Septembre 1925 .70 *.80*
*d.* AP44 70c 28 Mars 1927 .70 *.80*
*e.* AP44 70c 12 Juillet 1927 .70 *.80*
*f.* AP44 70c 13 Septembre 1927 .70 *.80*
*g.* AP44 70c 6 Fevrier 1928 .70 *.80*

Galiffet 1784 balloon flight and pioneer flights of the 1920's. No. C318A contains 2 each of Nos. C318b-C318g. The background of the sheet shows in white outlines a balloon and the inscription "BALLON GALIFFET 1784." The design of each stamp shows a different airmail cachet, date of a special flight and part of the white background design.

### Churchill Type of Regular Issue

Churchill: 50c, and early seaplane. 75c, and soldiers at Normandy. 1g, and Queen Elizabeth II. 1.50g, and Big Ben, London. 3g, and coat of arms, horiz.

**1968, Dec. 23 — Photo. — *Perf. 13***

**C319** A128 50c gold & multi .40 .25
**C320** A128 75c gold & multi .50 .40
**C321** A128 1g gold & multi .65 .50
**C322** A128 1.50g gold & multi .80 .60
*Nos. C319-C322 (4)* 2.35 1.70

**Souvenir Sheet**

*Perf. 12½x13, Imperf.*

**C323** A128 3g sil, blk & red 6.00 6.00

Nos. C319-C322 exist imperf. Value, $6.

No. C323 contains one horizontal stamp.

For surcharge, see No. C515. size: 38x25½mm.

Nos. C299-C300 Surcharged

**1969, Feb. 21 Photo. *Perf. 11½***

**C324** A122 70c on 50c .50 .40
**C325** A122 1.75g on 1g .80 .50

### Bird Type of Regular Issue

Birds of Haiti: 50c, Hispaniolan trogon. 1g, Black-cowled oriole. 1.50g, Stripe-headed tanager. 2g, Striated woodpecker.

**1969, Feb. 26 *Perf. 13½***

**C326** A129 50c multi 3.00 .85
**C327** A129 1g lt bl & multi 3.75 1.40
**C328** A129 1.50g multi 4.50 2.00
**C329** A129 2g gray & multi 5.00 2.50
*Nos. C326-C329 (4)* 16.25 6.75

For overprints see Nos. C344A-C344D.

### Electric Power Type of 1969

**1969, May 22 Litho. *Perf. 13x13½***

**C338** A131 20c dk bl & lil .25 .25
**C339** A131 25c grn & rose red .25 .25
**C340** A131 25c rose red & grn .25 .25
*Nos. C338-C340 (3)* .75 .75

### Education Type of 1969

Designs: 50c, Peace poster on educational television, vert. 1g, Learning to write. 1.50g, Playing children, vert.

**1969, Aug. 12 Litho. *Perf. 13½***

**C342** A132 50c multi .30 .25
**C343** A132 1g multi .50 .40
**C344** A132 1.50g multi .80 .50
*Nos. C342-C344 (3)* 1.60 1.10

Nos. C326-C329 Overprinted

**1969, Aug. 29 Photo. *Perf. 13½***

**C344A** A129 50c multi 1.25 1.25
**C344B** A129 1g lt bl & multi 2.40 2.40
**C344C** A129 1.50g multi 4.50 4.50
**C344D** A129 2g gray & multi 5.75 5.75
*Nos. C344A-C344D (4)* 13.90 13.90

### ILO Type of Regular Issue

**1969, Sept. 22 *Perf. 14***

**C345** A133 25c red & blk .30 .25
**C346** A133 70c org & blk .65 .25
**C347** A133 1.75g brt pur & blk 1.40 .70
*Nos. C345-C347 (3)* 2.35 1.10

### Butterfly Type of Regular Issue

50c, Danaus eresimus kaempfferi. 1.50g, Anaea marthesia nemesis. 2g, Prepona antimache.

**1969, Nov. 14 Photo. *Perf. 13½***

**C348** A134 50c multi *9.00* 3.00
**C349** A134 1.50g multi *17.50* 4.00
**C350** A134 2g yel & multi *27.50* 6.00
*Nos. C348-C350 (3)* *54.00* 13.00

### King Type of Regular Issue

**1970, Jan. 12 Litho. *Perf. 12½x13½***

**C351** A135 50c emer, red & blk .45 .25
**C352** A135 1g brick red, red & blk .80 .60
**C353** A135 1.50g brt bl, red & blk 1.20 .85
*Nos. C351-C353 (3)* 2.45 1.65

### Orchid Type of Regular Issue

Haitian Orchids: 50c, Tetramicra elegans. 1.50g, Epidendrum truncatum. 2g, Oncidium desertorum.

**1970, Apr. 3 Litho. *Perf. 13x12½***

**C354** A136 50c buff, brn & mag 2.00 .25
**C355** A136 1.50g multi 3.50 2.50
**C356** A136 2g lilac & multi 5.25 3.50
*Nos. C354-C356 (3)* 10.75 6.20

### UPU Type of Regular Issue

Designs: 50c, Globe and doves. 1.50g, Propeller and UPU emblem, vert. 2g, UPU Monument and map of Haiti.

**1970, June 23 Photo. *Perf. 11½***

**C357** A137 50c blk & vio .35 .25
**C358** A137 1.50g multi .65 .45
**C359** A137 2g multi .95 .65
*a.* Souvenir sheet of 3, #C357-C359, imperf. 2.50 2.25
*Nos. C357-C359 (3)* 1.95 1.30

Nos. C357-C359a Overprinted in Red with UN Emblem and: "XXVe ANNIVERSAIRE / O.N.U."

**1970, Dec. 14 Photo. *Perf. 11½***

**C360** A137 50c blk & vio .35 .25
**C361** A137 1.50g multi .65 .45
**C362** A137 2g multi .95 .65
*a.* Souvenir sheet of 3 3.50 3.00
*Nos. C360-C362 (3)* 1.95 1.30

United Nations, 25th anniversary.

Haitian Nativity AP45

**1970, Dec. 22**

**C363** AP45 1.50g sepia & multi .65 .45
**C364** AP45 1.50g ultra & multi .65 .45
**C365** AP45 2g multi 1.10 .65
*Nos. C363-C365 (3)* 2.40 1.55

Christmas 1970.

### Painting Type of Regular Issue

Paintings: 50c, Nativity, by Rigaud Benoit. 1g, Head of a Negro, by Rubens. 1.50g, Ascension, by Castera Bazile (like No. 648).

**1971, Apr. 29 Litho. *Perf. 12x12½***

**Size: 20x40mm**

**C366** A140 50c multi .50 .25
**C367** A140 1g multi .80 .65
**C368** A140 1.50g multi 1.10 .80
*Nos. C366-C368 (3)* 2.40 1.65

Nos. C366-C368 exist imperf in changed colors.

Balloon and Haiti No. C2 — AP46

No. C370, as #C369. No. C373, Haiti #C2. 1g, 1.50g, Supersonic transport & Haiti #C2.

**1971, Dec. 22 Photo. *Perf. 11½***

**C369** AP46 20c bl, red org & blk .30 .25
**C370** AP46 50c ultra, red org & blk .50 .25
**C371** AP46 1g org & blk 1.25 .35
**C372** AP46 1.50g lil rose & blk 1.90 .45
*Nos. C369-C372 (4)* 3.95 1.30

### Souvenir Sheet

***Imperf***

**C373** AP46 50c brt grn & blk 9.00 4.50

40th anniv. (in 1969) of air post service in Haiti.

For overprints see #C374-C377, C380-C386.

### Nos. C369-C372 Overprinted

**1972, Mar. 17 *Perf. 11½***

**C374** AP46 20c multi .25 .25
**C375** AP46 50c multi .35 .35
**C376** AP46 1g org & blk .55 .45
**C377** AP46 1.50g lil rose & blk .65 .55
*Nos. C374-C377 (4)* 1.80 1.60

14th INTERPEX, NYC, Mar. 17-19.

### Dessalines Type of Regular Issue

**1972, Apr. 28 Photo. *Perf. 11½***

**C378** A142 50c yel grn & blk .35 .25
**C379** A142 2.50g lil & blk 1.10 .65

For surcharge see No. C438.

### Nos. C369-C372 Overprinted

**1972, May 4**

**C380** AP46 20c multi .25 .25
**C381** AP46 50c multi .35 .25
**C382** AP46 1g org & blk .45 .35
**C383** AP46 1.50g lil rose & blk .65 .45
*Nos. C380-C383 (4)* 1.70 1.30

HAIPEX, 5th Congress.

### Nos. C370-C372 Overprinted

**1972, July**

**C384** AP46 50c multi .35 .25
**C385** AP46 1g org & blk .45 .35
**C386** AP46 1.50g lil rose & blk .65 .45
*Nos. C384-C386 (3)* 1.45 1.05

Belgica '72, International Philatelic Exhibition, Brussels, June 24-July 9.

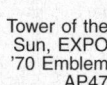

Tower of the Sun, EXPO '70 Emblem AP47

**1972, Oct. 27**

**C387** AP47 50c bl, plum & dk bl .35 .25
**C388** AP47 1g bl, plum & red .55 .35
**C389** AP47 1.50g bl, plum & blk .65 .45
**C390** AP47 2.50g bl, plum & grn .95 .55
*Nos. C387-C390 (4)* 2.50 1.55

EXPO '70 International Exposition, Osaka, Japan, Mar. 15-Sept. 13, 1970.
For surcharges see Nos. C447-C447A.

### Souvenir Sheets

1972 Summer Olympics, Munich — AP47a

Designs: 2.50g, Israeli delegation, opening ceremony in Munich Stadium. 5g, Assassinated Israeli athlete David Berger.

**1973 *Perf. 13½***

**C390A** AP47a 2.50g multi 2.00 2.00
**C390B** AP47a 5g multi 2.25 1.50

No. C390B contains one 22½x34mm stamp.

Headquarters and Map of Americas — AP48

**1973, May 11 Litho. *Perf. 14½***

**C391** AP48 50c dk bl & multi .35 .25
**C392** AP48 80c multi .50 .35
**C393** AP48 1.50g vio & multi .60 .45
**C394** AP48 2g brn & multi .85 .55
*Nos. C391-C394 (4)* 2.30 1.60

70th anniversary (in 1972) of the Panamerican Health Organization.

### Marine Life Type of Regular Issue

50c, 1.50g horizontal.

**1973, Sept. 4 *Perf. 14***

**C395** A145 50c Platypodia spectabilis 1.00 .25
**C396** A145 85c Goniaster tessellatus 1.40 .25
**C397** A145 1.50g Stephanocyathus diadema 2.00 .30
**C398** A145 2g Phyllangia americana 2.50 .40
*Nos. C395-C398 (4)* 6.90 1.10

For surcharge see No. C439.

### Fish Type of Regular Issue

Designs: Tropical fish.

**1973 *Perf. 13½***

**C399** A146 50c Gramma melacara .65 .50
**C400** A146 85c Holacanthus tricolor .80 .65
**C401** A146 1.50g Liopropoma rubre 1.40 .75
**C402** A146 5g Clepticus parrai 4.00 1.90
*Nos. C399-C402 (4)* 6.85 3.80

For surcharge see No. C440.

Haitian Flag AP49

Nos. C404, C405, Haitian flag and coat of arms. No. C406, Flag and Pres. Jean-Claude Duvalier.

**1973, Nov. 18 *Perf. 14½x14***

**Size: 35x22½mm**

**C403** AP49 80c blk & red .45 .35
**C404** AP49 80c red & blk .45 .35

***Perf. 14x13½***

**Size: 42x27mm**

**C405** AP49 1.85g blk & red .95 .65
**C406** AP49 1.85g red & blk .95 .65
*Nos. C403-C406 (4)* 2.80 2.00

For overprints and surcharges see Nos. C427-C428, C432-C433, C441-C442.

### Soccer Type of Regular Issue

50c, 80c, Soccer Stadium. 1.75g, 10g, Haiti #654.

**1973, Nov. 29 *Perf. 14x13***

**C407** A147 50c multi .35 .25
**C408** A147 80c multi .45 .35
**C409** A147 1.75g multi .95 .45
**C410** A147 10g multi 3.25 2.25
*Nos. C407-C410 (4)* 5.00 3.25

**Dessalines Type of 1974**

**1974, Apr. 22 Photo. *Perf. 14***

**C411** A148 50c brn & grnsh bl .35 .25
**C412** A148 80c gray & brn .45 .35
**C413** A148 1g lt grn & mar .55 .45
**C414** A148 1.75g lil & ol brn .95 .55
*Nos. C411-C414 (4)* 2.30 1.55

For surcharge see No. C443.

**Copernicus Type of 1974**

Designs: No. C415, 80c, 1.50g, 1.75g, Symbol of heliocentric system. No. C416, 1g, 2.50g, Nicolaus Copernicus.

**1974, May 24 Litho. *Perf. 14x13½***

**C415** A149 50c org & multi .35 .25
**C416** A149 50c yel & multi .35 .25
**C417** A149 80c multi .45 .35
**C418** A149 1g multi .55 .45
**C419** A149 1.75g brn & multi .95 .55
*Nos. C415-C419 (5)* 2.65 1.75

**Souvenir Sheet**

***Imperf***

**C420** Sheet of 2 2.50 2.50
*a.* A149 1.50g light green & multi .90 .90
*b.* A149 2.50g deep orange & multi 1.40 1.40

For overprint and surcharges see Nos. C444, C460-C463.

**Pres. Duvalier Type of 1974**

**1974 Photo. *Perf. 14x13½***

**C421** A151 50c vio brn & gold .35 .25
**C422** A151 80c rose red & gold .45 .35
**C423** A151 1g red lil & gold .65 .45
**C424** A151 1.50g Prus bl & gold 1.00 .65
**C425** A151 1.75g brt vio & gold 1.25 .65
**C426** A151 5g ol grn & gold 2.75 1.50
*Nos. C421-C426 (6)* 6.45 3.80

For surcharge and overprints see Nos. C445, C487-C489.

**Nos. C405-C406 Surcharged in Violet Blue**

**1975, July 15 Litho. *Perf. 14x13½***

**C427** AP49 80c on 1.85g, #C405 1.50 1.50
**C428** AP49 80c on 1.85g, #C406 1.50 1.50

**Nos. C405-C406 Overprinted in Blue**

**1975, July 15 Litho. *Perf. 14x13½***

**C432** AP49 1.85g blk & red .95 .65
**C433** AP49 1.85g red & blk .95 .65

Centenary of Universal Postal Union. "100 ANS" in 2 lines on No. C433.

Names of Haitian Participants at Siege of Savannah — AP50

**1976, Apr. 22 Photo. *Perf. 11½***

**Granite Paper**

**C434** AP50 50c multi .35 .25
**C435** AP50 80c multi .55 .35
**C436** AP50 1.50g multi .80 .55
**C437** AP50 7.50g multi 2.75 1.90
*Nos. C434-C437 (4)* 4.45 3.00

American Bicentennial.

Stamps of 1972-74 Surcharged with New Value and Bar in Black or Violet Blue

**Photogravure; Lithographed**

**1976 *Perf. 11½, 13½, 14x13½, 14***

**C438** A142 80c on 2.50g, #C379 .55 .35
**C439** A145 80c on 85c, #C396 .55 .35
**C440** A146 80c on 85c, #C400 .55 .35
**C441** AP49 80c on 1.85g, #C405 .55 .35
**C442** AP49 80c on 1.85g, #C406 .55 .35
**C443** A148 80c on 1.75g, #C414 (VB) .55 .35
**C444** A149 80c on 1.75g, #C419 (VB) .55 .35
**C445** A151 80c on 1.75g, #C425 .55 .35
**C446** AP50 80c on 1.50g, #C436 .55 .35
**C447** AP47 80c on 1.50g, #C389 .55 .35
**C447A** AP47 80c on 2.50g #C390 .55 .35
*Nos. C438-C447A (11)* 6.05 3.85

Black surcharge of Nos. C441-C442 differs from the violet blue surcharge of Nos. C427-C428 in type face, arrangement of denomination and bar, and size of bar (10x6mm).

**Dessalines Type of 1972**

**1976-77 Photo. *Perf. 11½***

**Granite Paper**

**C448** A142 75c yel & blk .35 .35
**C449** A142 80c emer & blk .35 .35
**C450** A142 1g bl & blk .45 .35
**C451** A142 1g red brn & blk .55 .45
**C452** A142 1.25g yel grn & blk .45 .35
**C453** A142 1.50g bl gray & blk .45 .35
**C454** A142 1.75g rose & blk .55 .45
**C455** A142 2g yel & blk .65 .55
**C457** A142 5g bl grn & blk 1.75 1.10
**C458** A142 10g ocher & blk 3.50 2.10
*Nos. C448-C458 (10)* 9.05 6.40

Issued: 75c, 80c, #C451, 1,75g, 5g, 10g, 1977.

Nos. C415-C416, C418-C419 Overprinted or Surcharged in Black, Dark Blue or Green

**1977, July 6 Litho. *Perf. 14x13½***

**C460** A149 1g (Bk) .45 .35
**C461** A149 1.25g on 50c (DB) .55 .45
**C462** A149 1.25g on 50c (G) .55 .45
**C463** A149 1.25g on 1.75g (Bk) .55 .45
*Nos. C460-C463 (4)* 2.10 1.70

Charles A. Lindbergh's solo transatlantic flight from NY to Paris, 50th anniv.

**Telephone Type of 1978**

Designs: 1g, Telstar over globe. 1.25g, Duvalier Earth Telecommunications Station. 2g, Wall telephone, 1890, vert.

**1978, June 19 Litho. *Perf. 13½***

**C466** A153 1g multi .45 .35
**C467** A153 1.25g multi .55 .45
**C468** A153 2g multi .85 .55
*Nos. C466-C468 (3)* 1.85 1.35

**Olympic Games Type of 1978**

Montreal Olympic Games' Emblem and: 1.25g, Equestrian. 2.50g,Basketball. 5g, Yachting.

**1978, Sept. 4 Litho. *Perf. 13½x13***

**C469** A154 1.25g multi .70 .60
**C470** A154 2.50g multi 1.50 1.25
**C471** A154 5g multi 3.50 1.50
*Nos. C469-C471 (3)* 5.70 3.35

**Children's Institute Type, 1979**

Designs: 1.25g, Mother nursing child. 2g, Nurse giving injection.

**1979, Jan. 15 Photo. *Perf. 14x14½***

**C472** A155 1.25g multi .55 .35
**C473** A155 2g multi .80 .55

Haitians Spinning Cotton, CARE Workshop AP51

**1979, May 11 Photo. *Perf. 11½***

**C474** AP51 1g multi .65 .55
**C475** AP51 1.25g multi .95 .65
**C476** AP51 2g multi 1.40 .85
*Nos. C474-C476 (3)* 3.00 2.05

30th anniversary of CARE.

**Human Rights Type of 1979**

**1979, July 20 Litho. *Perf. 14***

**C477** A157 1g multi .65 .55
**C478** A157 1.25g multi .95 .65
**C479** A157 2g multi 1.40 .85
*Nos. C477-C479 (3)* 3.00 2.05

**Anti-Apartheid Year Type of 1979**

**1979, Nov. 22 Photo. *Perf. 12x11½***

**C480** A158 1g yel grn & blk 1.00 .55
**C481** A158 1.25g bl & blk 1.10 .65
**C482** A158 2g gray olive 1.75 .85
*Nos. C480-C482 (3)* 3.85 2.05

**IYC Type of 1979**

**1979, Dec. 19 Photo. *Perf. 12***

**C483** A159 1g multi .65 .55
**C484** A159 1.25g multi .95 .65
**C485** A159 2.50g multi 2.50 1.10
**C486** A159 5g multi 3.50 1.60
*Nos. C483-C486 (4)* 7.60 3.90

Nos. C421, C424-C425 Overprinted

**1980, May 17 Photo. *Perf. 14x13½***

**C487** A151 50c multi .35 .25
**C488** A151 1.50g multi .95 .45
**C489** A151 1.75g multi 1.20 .55
*Nos. C487-C489 (3)* 2.50 1.25

Wedding of Pres. Duvalier, May 27.

**Dessalines Type of 1972**

**1980, Aug. 27 Photo. *Perf. 11½***

**Granite Paper**

**C490** A142 1g gray vio & blk .55 .45
**C491** A142 1.25g sal pink & blk .65 .55
**C492** A142 2g pale grn & blk 1.20 .85
**C493** A142 5g lt bl & blk 2.40 1.60
*Nos. C490-C493 (4)* 4.80 3.45

For surcharge see No. C512.

**Tourism Type**

**1980, Dec. 2 Litho. *Perf. 12½x12***

**C494** A160 1g like #728 .55 .45
**C495** A160 1.25g like #729 .65 .55
**C496** A160 1.50g Carnival dancers .95 .55
**C497** A160 2g Vendors 1.20 .85
**C498** A160 2.50g like #C497 1.40 1.10
*Nos. C494-C498 (5)* 4.75 3.50

For surcharge see No. C511.

**Soccer Type of 1980**

**1980, Dec. 30 Litho. *Perf. 14***

**C499** A161 50c Uruguay, 1950 .35 .25
**C500** A161 75c Germany, 1954 .45 .35
**C501** A161 1g Brazil, 1958 .65 .45
**C502** A161 1.25g Brazil, 1962 .80 .55
**C503** A161 1.50g Gt. Britain, 1966 1.10 .65
**C504** A161 1.75g Brazil, 1970 1.25 .85
**C505** A161 2g Germany, 1974 1.40 .95
**C506** A161 5g Argentina, 1978 3.50 2.10
*Nos. C499-C506 (8)* 9.50 6.10

**Painting Type of 1981**

**1981, May 12 Photo. *Perf. 11½***

**C507** A162 50c like #734 .35 .25
**C508** A162 1.25g like #735 .65 .55
**C509** A162 2g like #736 1.25 .85
**C510** A162 5g like #737 2.40 1.60
*Nos. C507-C510 (4)* 4.65 3.20

Nos. C496, C493 Surcharged

***Perf. 12½x12, 11½***

**1981, Dec. 30 Litho., Photo.**

**C511** A160 1.25g on 1.50g multi .65 .55
**C512** A142 2g on 5g multi 1.20 .85

**Dessalines Type of 1972**

**1982, Jan. 25 Photo. *Perf. 11½***

**Granite Paper**

**C513** A142 1.25g lt brn & blk .65 .55
**C514** A142 2g lilac & blk 1.20 .85

**No. C320 Surcharged**

**2000? Photo. *Perf. 13***

**C515** A128 3g on 75c #C320 — —

**AIR POST SEMI-POSTAL STAMPS**

**Coubertin Semipostal Type of 1939**

**Unwmk.**

**1939, Oct. 3 Engr. *Perf. 12***

**CB1** SP1 60c + 40c multi 25.00 25.00
**CB2** SP1 1.25g + 60c multi 25.00 25.00

Mosquito and National Sanatorium — SPAP2

**1949, July 22 Cross in Carmine**

**CB3** SPAP2 20c + 20c sep 11.00 6.00
**CB4** SPAP2 30c + 30c dp grn 11.00 6.00
**CB5** SPAP2 45c + 45c lt red brn 11.00 6.00
**CB6** SPAP2 80c + 80c pur 11.00 6.00
**CB7** SPAP2 1.25g + 1.25g car rose 11.00 6.00
*a.* Souvenir sheet 40.00 25.00
**CB8** SPAP2 1.75g + 1.75g bl 11.00 6.00
*a.* Souvenir sheet 40.00 25.00
*Nos. CB3-CB8 (6)* 66.00 36.00

The surtax was used for fighting tuberculosis and malaria.

**Catalogue values for unused stamps in this section, from this point to the end of the section, are for Never Hinged items.**

No. C113 Surcharged in Deep Carmine

**1958, Aug. 30 Litho. *Perf. 13x13½***

**CB9** A82 2.50g + 50c 2.50 2.40

The surtax was for the Red Cross.

**Similar Surcharge in Red on One Line on Nos. C133-C135**

**1959, Apr. 7 Photo. *Perf. 11½***

**Granite Paper**

**CB10** AP35 50c + 25c pink, car & ultra .40 .40
**CB11** A87 75c + 25c brt bl .50 .50
**CB12** A87 1g + 25c brn .75 .75

**Nos. C139-C141 Surcharged Like No. CB9 in Red**

**CB13** AP36 50c + 50c grn & lil 1.00 1.00
**CB14** AP36 1.50g + 50c ol & red brn 1.00 1.00
**CB15** AP36 2.50g + 50c pur & dk bl 1.25 1.25
*Nos. CB10-CB15 (6)* 4.90 4.90

Surtax for the Red Cross.

**Nos. C142-C144 Surcharged Diagonally**

**1959, July 23 Unwmk. *Perf. 12***

**CB16** A89 1g + 20c 1.00 1.00
**CB17** A89 2g + 20c 1.10 1.10
**CB18** A89 2.50g + 20c 1.10 1.10
*Nos. CB16-CB18 (3)* 3.20 3.20

World Refugee Year, July 1, 1959-June 30, 1960. A similar surcharge of 50c was applied horizontally to stamps in No. C144a. Value $25.

**C145-C147 Surcharged in Dark Carmine**

**1959, Oct. 30 Photo. *Perf. 14***

**CB19** A91 50c + 75c hn brn & aqua 1.00 1.00
**CB20** A90 1g + 75c lil & aqua 1.00 1.00
**CB21** A90 1.50g + 75c multi 1.00 1.00
*Nos. CB19-CB21 (3)* 3.00 3.00

The surtax was for Haitian athletes.
On No. CB19, surcharge lines are spaced to total depth of 16mm.

Nos. C129-C130 Surcharged in Red: "Hommage a l'UNICEF +G. 0,50"

**Engraved and Lithographed**

**1960, Feb. 2 *Perf. 11½***

**CB22** AP34 2g + 50c 1.00 1.00
**CB23** AP34 2.50g + 50c 1.75 1.75

Issued to honor UNICEF.

Nos. C151-C152 Surcharged and Overprinted: "ALPHABETISATION" in Red or Black.

**1960, July 12 Litho. *Perf. 12½x13***

**CB24** A92 50c + 20c (R) .40 .40
**CB25** A92 50c + 30c .65 .55
**CB26** A92 1g + 20c (R) .90 .75
**CB27** A92 1g + 30c .90 .75
*Nos. CB24-CB27 (4)* 2.85 2.45

**Olympic Games Issue**

Nos. C163-C164 Surcharged

**1960, Sept. 9 Photo. *Perf. 12***

**CB28** A94 50c + 25c .40 .25
**CB29** A94 1.50g + 25c .65 .55

Nos. C168-C169 Surcharged: "UNICEF +25 centimes"

**1961, Jan. 14 Engr. *Perf. 10½***

**CB30** A96 50c + 25c red org & blk .40 .25
**CB31** A96 1.50g + 25c dk bl & blk .65 .55

Nos. C171, C175-C176 Surcharged with Additional Value, Scout Emblem and: "18e Conference Internationale du Scoutisme Mondial Lisbonne Septembre 1961"

**1961, Sept. 30 Photo. *Perf. 11½***

**CB32** AP37 20c + 25c .40 .30
**CB33** AP37 1g + 25c .50 .40
**CB34** AP37 1.50g + 25c .60 .60
*Nos. CB32-CB34 (3)* 1.50 1.30

Issued to commemorate the 18th Boy Scout World Conference, Lisbon, Sept. 19-24, 1961. The surtax was for the Red Cross. Additional proceeds from the sale of Nos. CB32-CB34 benefited the Port-au-Prince airport project.
The same surcharge was also applied to No. C176a. Value $3.

Nos. C168-C169 Surcharged: "OMS SNEM +20 CENTIMES"

**1961, Dec. 11 Engr. *Perf. 10½***

**CB35** A96 50c + 20c 1.60 1.60
**CB36** A96 1.50g + 20c 2.25 2.25

Issued to publicize Haiti's participation in the UN malaria eradication drive.

**Nos. C123, C126-C127 and C131-C132 Surcharged in Black or Red**

**Engraved and Lithographed**

**1961-62 *Perf. 11½***

**CB37** AP34 50c + 25c .25 .25
**CB38** AP34 1g + 50c .35 .35
**CB39** AP34 2.50g + 50c (R) ('62) .65 .65
**CB40** AP34 5g + 50c 1.10 1.10
**CB41** AP34 7.50g + 50c (R) ('62) 1.50 1.50
*Nos. CB37-CB41 (5)* 3.85 3.85

The surtax was for the benefit of the urban rehabilitation program in Duvalier Ville.

Nos. C188-C190 Surcharged: "+25 centimes"

**1962, Sept. 13 Litho. *Perf. 12***

**CB42** A99 20c + 25c .25 .25
**CB43** A99 50c + 25c .40 .25
**CB44** A99 1g + 25c .50 .40
*Nos. CB42-CB44 (3)* 1.15 .80

#C191-C192 Surcharged in Red: "+0.20"

**1962 *Perf. 12½x13***

**CB45** A92 50c + 20c .40 .40
**CB46** A92 1g + 20c .50 .40

Nos. C203 and C205 Surcharged: "ALPHABETISATION" and "+0, 10"

**1963, Mar. 15 Photo. *Perf. 14x14½***

**CB47** AP38 50c + 10c .40 .25
**CB48** AP38 1.50g + 10c .50 .40

No. C110 Surcharged in Red with Olympic Emblem and: "JEUX OLYMPIQUES / D'HIVER / INNSBRUCK 1964"

**1964, July 27 Photo. *Perf. 11½***

**CB49** A80 2.50g + 50c + 10c .90 .80

See note after No. B34. The 50c+10c surtax went for charity.

**No. C213 Surcharged in Red**

**Engraved and Photogravure**

**1964, Oct. 2 *Perf. 13½x14***

**CB50** AP39 2.50g + 1.25g on 1.50g 1.40 1.25

Issued to commemorate the centenary (in 1963) of the International Red Cross.

Nos. C223-C226 Surcharged: "+ 5c."

**1965, Mar. 15 Photo. *Perf. 11½***

**CB51** A105 50c + 5c pale lil & dk brn .40 .25
**CB52** A105 50c + 5c pale grn & dk brn .40 .25
**CB53** A105 75c + 5c buff & dk brn .50 .40
**CB54** A105 1.50g + 5c gray & dk brn .80 .65
*Nos. CB51-CB54 (4)* 2.10 1.45

The souvenir sheet No. C226a was surcharged "+25c." Value, $8.
See note following No. B37.

Nos. C251 and C253 Surcharged and Overprinted with Haitian Scout Emblem and "12e Jamboree / Mondial 1967" Like Regular Issue

**1967, Aug. 21 Photo. *Perf. 11½***

**CB55** A111 50c + 10c multi .50 .40
**CB56** A111 1.50g + 50c multi .65 .50

See note after No. B40.

No. C269 Surcharged Like Regular Issue

**Lithographed and Photogravure**

**1968, Jan. 18 *Perf. 13x13½***

**CB57** A115 2.50g + 1.25g on 1.50g 3.25 2.50

See note after No. 579.

#C285-C287 Surcharged "CULTURE + 10"

**1968, July 4 Litho. *Perf. 11½***

**CB58** A120 50c + 10c multi .40 .25
**CB59** A120 1g + 10c multi .50 .40
**CB60** A120 1.50g + 10c multi .65 .50
*Nos. CB58-CB60 (3)* 1.55 1.15

Nos. C314 and C316 Surcharged in Red with New Value, Red Cross and: "50ème. Anniversaire / de la Ligue des / Sociétés de la / Croix Rouge"

**1969, June 25 Litho. *Perf. 11½***

**CB61** A127 50c + 20c multi .50 .40
**CB62** A127 1.50g + 25c multi .90 .50

League of Red Cross Societies, 50th anniv.

## AIR POST OFFICIAL STAMPS

Nos. C172-C176 and C176a Overprinted: "OFFICIEL"

***Perf. 11½***

**1961, Mar. Unwmk. Photo.**

**CO1** AP37 50c rose brn & grn .60
**CO2** AP37 50c brt grnsh bl & ol grn .60
**CO3** AP37 50c gray & grn .60
**CO4** AP37 1g gray ol & ver .85
**CO5** AP37 1.50g brt pink & dk bl 1.40
*a.* Sheet of 3 3.75
*Nos. CO1-CO5 (5)* 4.05

Nos. CO1-CO5a only available canceled.

**Catalogue values for unused stamps in this section, from this point to the end of the section, are for Never Hinged items.**

Jean Jacques Dessalines — OA1

**1962, Mar. 7 Photo. *Perf. 14x14½***

**Size: 20½x38mm**

**CO6** OA1 50c dk bl & sepia .50 .40
**CO7** OA1 1g lt bl & maroon .80 .50
**CO8** OA1 1.50g bister & bl 1.00 .70

**Size: 30x40mm**

**CO9** OA1 5g rose & ol grn 2.75 2.40
*Nos. CO6-CO9 (4)* 5.05 4.00

Inscription at bottom of #CO9 is in 2 lines.

## AIR POST PARCEL POST STAMPS

**Catalogue values for unused stamps in this section are for Never Hinged items.**

Nos. C112 and C111 Overprinted in Red

***Perf. 11½***

**1960, Nov. 21 Unwmk. Photo.**

**CQ1** A81 50c orange & black .50 .40
**CQ2** A80 5g bluish blk & saph 3.50 2.60

**Type of Parcel Post Stamps, 1961**

Inscribed "Poste Aerienne"

**1961, Mar. 24 *Perf. 14***

**CQ3** PP1 2.50g yel grn & mar 2.00 1.40
**CQ4** PP1 5g org & green 2.50 1.60

## SPECIAL DELIVERY STAMP

**The catalogue value for the unused stamp in this section is for Never Hinged.**

Postal Administration Building — SD1

**Unwmk.**

**1953, May 4 Engr. *Perf. 12***

**E1** SD1 25c vermilion .70 .50

## POSTAGE DUE STAMPS

D1

**1898, Aug. Unwmk. Engr. *Perf. 12***

**J1** D1 2c black 1.00 .75
**J2** D1 5c red brown 1.50 1.00
**J3** D1 10c brown orange 2.00 1.50
**J4** D1 50c slate 3.00 2.50
*Nos. J1-J4 (4)* 7.50 5.75

For overprints see Nos. J5-J9, J14-J16.

Stamps of 1898 Handstamped like #67-81

**1902 Black Overprint**

**J5** D1 2c black 2.50 1.50
**J6** D1 5c red brown 2.50 1.50
**J7** D1 10c brown orange 2.50 1.50
**J8** D1 50c slate 12.00 7.00

**Red Overprint**

**J9** D1 2c black 3.50 3.50
*Nos. J5-J9 (5)* 23.00 15.00

D2

**1906**

**J10** D2 2c dull red 1.50 1.00
**J11** D2 5c ultra 2.75 2.50
**J12** D2 10c violet 2.75 2.50
**J13** D2 50c olive gray 11.50 7.50
*Nos. J10-J13 (4)* 18.50 13.50

For surcharges and overprints see Nos. 305-308, J17-J20.

Preceding Issues Handstamped like #169-201

**1914 On Stamps of 1898**

**J14** D1 5c red brown 1.50 1.10
**J15** D1 10c brown orange 1.50 1.10
**J16** D1 50c slate 6.00 5.50
*Nos. J14-J16 (3)* 9.00 7.70

**On Stamps of 1906**

**J17** D2 2c dull red 1.25 1.00
**J18** D2 5c ultra 2.25 2.25
**J19** D2 10c violet 7.50 5.50
**J20** D2 50c olive gray 45.00 45.00
*Nos. J17-J20 (4)* 56.00 53.75

The note after No. 201 applies to Nos. J14-J20 also.

Unpaid Letter — D3

**1951, July Litho. *Perf. 11½***

**J21** D3 10c carmine .25 .25
**J22** D3 20c red brown .25 .25
**J23** D3 40c green .40 .40
**J24** D3 50c orange yellow .50 .50
*Nos. J21-J24 (4)* 1.40 1.40

**PARCEL POST STAMPS**

**Catalogue values for unused stamps in this section are for Never Hinged items.**

Nos. 416, 470-471 and 378 Overprinted in Red

**Photogravure, Engraved**
***Perf. 11½, 12***

**1960, Nov. 21 Unwmk.**

**Q1** A81 5c yel grn & blk .25 .25
**Q2** A81 10c red org & blk .25 .25
**Q3** A81 25c ultra & black .40 .25
**Q4** A64 2.50g gray 2.75 2.40
*Nos. Q1-Q4 (4)* 3.65 3.15

Coat of Arms — PP1

**Unwmk.**

**1961, Mar. 24 Photo. *Perf. 14***

**Q5** PP1 50c bister & purple .50 .40
**Q6** PP1 1g pink & dark blue .80 .50

See Nos. CQ3-CQ4.

**POSTAL TAX STAMPS**

**Catalogue values for unused stamps in this section, are for Never Hinged items.**

Haitian Woman, War Invalids and Ruined Buildings PT1

**Unwmk.**

**1944, Aug. 16 Engr. *Perf. 12***

**RA1** PT1 5c dull purple 1.40 .60
**RA2** PT1 5c dark blue 1.40 .60
**RA3** PT1 5c olive green 1.40 .60
**RA4** PT1 5c black 1.40 .60

**1945, Dec. 17**

**RA5** PT1 5c dark green 1.40 .60
**RA6** PT1 5c sepia 1.40 .60
**RA7** PT1 5c red brown 1.40 .60
**RA8** PT1 5c rose carmine 1.40 .60
*Nos. RA1-RA8 (8)* 11.20 4.80

The proceeds from the sale of Nos. RA1 to RA8 were for United Nations Relief.

George Washington, J.J. Dessalines and Simón Bolivar — PT2

**1949, Sept. 20**

**RA9** PT2 5c red brown .50 .40
**RA10** PT2 5c olive gray .50 .40
**RA11** PT2 5c blue .50 .40
**RA12** PT2 5c green .50 .40
**RA13** PT2 5c violet .50 .40
**RA14** PT2 5c black .50 .40
**RA15** PT2 5c orange .50 .40
**RA16** PT2 5c carmine rose .50 .40
*Nos. RA9-RA16 (8)* 4.00 3.20

Bicentenary of Port-au-Prince.
For overprint and surcharges see #385-388.

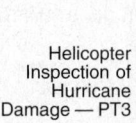

Helicopter Inspection of Hurricane Damage — PT3

**1955, Jan. 3 Photo. *Perf. 11½***

**RA17** PT3 10c bright green .25 .25
**RA18** PT3 10c bright blue .25 .25
**RA19** PT3 10c gray black .25 .25
**RA20** PT3 10c orange .25 .25
**RA21** PT3 20c rose carmine .35 .25
**RA22** PT3 20c deep green .35 .25
*Nos. RA17-RA22 (6)* 1.70 1.50

Helicopter — PT4

**1955, May 3**

**RA23** PT4 10c black, *gray* .25 .25
**RA24** PT4 20c violet blue, *blue* .30 .25

The surface tint of the sheets of 50, (10x5) of #RA23-RA24, RAC1-RAC2 includes a map of Haiti's southern peninsula which extends over the three center rows of stamps.
The tax was for reconstruction.
See Nos. RAC1-RAC2.

PT5

**1959-60 Unwmk. Photo. *Perf. 11½***
**Size: 38x22½mm**

**RA25** PT5 5c green .25 .25
**RA26** PT5 5c black ('60) .25 .25
**RA27** PT5 10c red .25 .25
*Nos. RA25-RA27 (3)* .75 .75

**1960-61 Size: 28x17mm**

**RA28** PT5 5c green .25 .25
**RA29** PT5 10c red .25 .25
**RA30** PT5 10c blue ('61) .25 .25
*Nos. RA28-RA30 (3)* .75 .75

PT6

**1963, Sept. *Perf. 14½x14***
**Size: 13½x21mm**

**RA31** PT6 10c red orange .25 .25
**RA32** PT6 10c bright blue .25 .25
**RA33** PT6 10c olive .25 .25
*Nos. RA31-RA33,RAC6-RAC8 (6)* 1.50 1.50

**1966-69 Photo. *Perf. 14x14½***
**Size: 17x25mm**

**RA34** PT6 10c bright green .25 .25
**RA35** PT6 10c violet .25 .25
**RA36** PT6 10c violet blue .25 .25
**RA37** PT6 10c brown ('69) .25 .25
*Nos. RA34-RA37,RAC9-RAC15 (11)* 2.75 2.75

Nos. RA25-RA37 represent a tax for a literacy campaign.
See Nos. RA42-RA45, RAC20-RAC22.

Duvalier de Peligre Hydroelectric Works — PT7

**1970-72**

**RA38** PT7 20c violet & olive .25 .25
**RA39** PT7 20c ultra & blk ('72) .25 .25

See Nos. RA46, RAC16-RAC19, RAC23.

Nos. 637-638 Surcharged: "ALPHABETISATION +10"

**1971, Dec. 23 Litho. *Perf. 14x13½***

**RA40** A138 20c + 10c multi .35 .25
*a.* Inverted surcharge 2.00
**RA41** A138 25c + 10c multi .35 .25

Tax was for the literacy campaign.

**"CA" Type of 1963**

**1972-74 Photo. *Perf. 14x14½***
**Size: 17x25mm**

**RA42** PT6 5c violet blue .25 .25
**RA43** PT6 5c deep carmine .25 .25
**RA44** PT6 5c ultra ('74) .25 .25
**RA45** PT6 5c carmine rose ('74) .25 .25
*Nos. RA42-RA45 (4)* 1.00 1.00

Tax was for literacy campaign.

**Hydroelectric Type of 1970**

**1980 Photo. *Perf. 14x14½***

**RA46** PT7 25c choc & green .25 .25

**AIR POST POSTAL TAX STAMPS**

**Catalogue values for unused stamps in this section, are for Never Hinged items.**

**Helicopter Type of 1955**

**1955 Unwmk. Photo. *Perf. 11½***

**RAC1** PT4 10c red brn, *pale sal* .30 .25
**RAC2** PT4 20c rose pink, *pink* .35 .25

See note after No. RA24.

**Type of Postal Tax Stamps, 1960-61**

**1959 Size: 28x17mm**

**RAC3** PT5 5c yellow .25 .25
**RAC4** PT5 10c dull salmon .25 .25
**RAC5** PT5 10c blue .25 .25
*Nos. RAC3-RAC5 (3)* .75 .75

**Type of Postal Tax Stamps, 1963**

**1963, Sept. *Perf. 14½x14***
**Size: 13½x21mm**

**RAC6** PT6 10c dark gray .25 .25
**RAC7** PT6 10c violet .25 .25
**RAC8** PT6 10c brown .25 .25
*Nos. RAC6-RAC8 (3)* .60 .60

**1966-69 *Perf. 14x14½***
**Size: 17x25mm**

**RAC9** PT6 10c orange .25 .25
**RAC10** PT6 10c sky blue .25 .25
**RAC11** PT6 10c yellow ('69) .25 .25
**RAC12** PT6 10c carmine ('69) .25 .25
**RAC13** PT6 10c gray grn ('69) .25 .25
**RAC14** PT6 10c lilac ('69) .25 .25
**RAC15** PT6 10c dp claret ('69) .25 .25
*Nos. RAC9-RAC15 (7)* 1.40 1.40

Nos. RAC3-RAC15, RAC20-RAC21 represent a tax for a literacy campaign.

**Hydroelectric Type of 1970**

**1970-74**

**RAC16** PT7 20c tan & slate .25 .25
**RAC17** PT7 20c brt bl & dl vio .25 .25
**RAC18** PT7 25c sal & bluish blk ('74) .25 .25
**RAC19** PT7 25c yel ol & bluish blk ('74) .25 .25
*Nos. RAC16-RAC19 (4)* 1.00 1.00

**"CA" Type of 1963**

**1973 Photo. *Perf. 14x14½***
**Size: 17x26mm**

**RAC20** PT6 10c brn & blue .35 .25
**RAC21** PT6 10c brn & green .35 .25
**RAC22** PT6 10c brn & orange .35 .25
*Nos. RAC20-RAC22 (3)* 1.05 .75

**Hydroelectric Power Type of 1970**

**1979(?) Photo. *Perf. 14x14½***

**RAC23** PT7 25c blue & vio brn .25 .25

## HATAY

hä-ˈtī

LOCATION — Northwest of Syria, bordering on Mediterranean Sea
GOVT. — Semi-independent republic
AREA — 10,000 sq. mi. (approx.)
POP. — 273,350 (1939)
CAPITAL — Antioch

Alexandretta, a semi-autonomous district of Syria under French mandate, was renamed Hatay in 1938 and transferred to Turkey in 1939.

100 Santims = 1 Kurush
40 Paras = 1 Kurush (1939)

**Stamps of Turkey, 1931-38, Surcharged in Black**

On A77

On A78

**1939 Unwmk. *Perf. 11½x12***

| | | | | |
|---|---|---|---|---|
| 1 | A77 | 10s on 20pa dp org | 1.75 | .35 |
| a. | | "Sent" instead of "Sant" | 125.00 | 22.50 |
| 2 | A78 | 25s on 1ku dk sl grn | 2.00 | .35 |
| a. | | Small "25" | 12.50 | 1.50 |
| 3 | A78 | 50s on 2ku dk vio | 2.00 | .35 |
| a. | | Small "50" | 6.00 | 2.00 |
| 4 | A77 | 75s on 2½ku green | 1.75 | .40 |
| 5 | A78 | 1ku on 4ku slate | 10.00 | 4.25 |
| 6 | A78 | 1ku on 5ku rose red | 5.50 | 1.40 |
| 7 | A78 | 1½ku on 3ku brn org | 2.75 | .80 |
| 8 | A78 | 2½ku on 4ku slate | 3.75 | 1.00 |
| 9 | A78 | 5ku on 8ku brt blue | 6.00 | 1.25 |
| 10 | A77 | 12½ku on 20ku ol grn | 7.00 | 2.00 |
| 11 | A77 | 20ku on 25ku Prus bl | 13.00 | 7.00 |
| | | *Nos. 1-11 (11)* | 55.50 | 19.15 |
| | | Set, never hinged | 130.00 | |

Map of Hatay — A1

Lions of Antioch A2

Flag of Hatay A3

Post Office A4

**1939 Unwmk. Typo. *Perf. 12***

| | | | | |
|---|---|---|---|---|
| 12 | A1 | 10p orange & aqua | 2.50 | .75 |
| 13 | A1 | 30p lt vio & aqua | 2.50 | .75 |
| 14 | A1 | 1½ku olive & aqua | 2.50 | .75 |
| 15 | A2 | 2½ku turq grn | 3.00 | 1.00 |
| 16 | A2 | 3ku light blue | 3.00 | 1.00 |
| 17 | A2 | 5ku chocolate | 3.00 | 1.00 |
| 18 | A3 | 6ku brt blue & car | 3.75 | 1.25 |
| 19 | A3 | 7½ku dp green & car | 4.25 | 1.40 |
| 20 | A3 | 12ku violet & car | 5.00 | 1.40 |
| 21 | A3 | 12½ku dk blue & car | 4.00 | 1.50 |
| 22 | A4 | 17½ku brown car | 8.00 | 3.00 |
| 23 | A4 | 25ku olive brn | 9.00 | 3.50 |
| 24 | A4 | 50ku slate blue | 18.00 | 8.50 |
| | | *Nos. 12-24 (13)* | 68.50 | 25.80 |
| | | Set, never hinged | 175.00 | |

Stamps of 1939 Overprinted in Black

**1939**

| | | | | |
|---|---|---|---|---|
| 25 | A1 | 10p orange & aqua | 1.75 | .75 |
| a. | | Overprint reading up | 22.50 | |
| 26 | A1 | 30p lt vio & aqua | 1.75 | .75 |
| 27 | A1 | 1½ku ol & aqua | 2.50 | .80 |
| 28 | A2 | 2½ku turq grn | 2.50 | .80 |
| 29 | A2 | 3ku light blue | 2.75 | .80 |
| 30 | A2 | 5ku chocolate | 3.50 | 1.25 |
| a. | | Overprint inverted | 22.50 | |
| 31 | A3 | 6ku brt bl & car | 3.75 | 1.25 |
| 32 | A3 | 7½ku dp grn & car | 4.00 | 1.25 |
| 33 | A3 | 12ku vio & car | 4.00 | 1.25 |
| 34 | A3 | 12½ku dk bl & car | 4.50 | 1.25 |
| 35 | A4 | 17½ku brn car | 5.50 | 2.25 |
| a. | | Overprint inverted | 22.50 | |
| 36 | A4 | 25ku olive brn | 9.00 | 4.25 |
| 37 | A4 | 50ku slate blue | 19.00 | 10.00 |
| | | *Nos. 25-37 (13)* | 64.50 | 26.65 |
| | | Set, never hinged | 150.00 | |

The overprint reads "Date of annexation to the Turkish Republic, June 30, 1939."

On Nos. 25-27, the overprint reads down. On Nos. 28-37, it is horizontal.

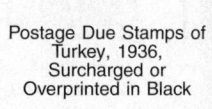

### POSTAGE DUE STAMPS

Postage Due Stamps of Turkey, 1936, Surcharged or Overprinted in Black

**1939 Unwmk. *Perf. 11½***

| | | | | |
|---|---|---|---|---|
| J1 | D6 | 1ku on 2ku lt bl | 3.75 | .70 |
| J2 | D6 | 3ku bright violet | 4.25 | 1.25 |
| J3 | D6 | 4ku on 5ku Prus bl | 4.25 | 1.25 |
| J4 | D6 | 5ku on 12ku brt rose | 4.75 | 1.25 |
| J5 | D6 | 12ku bright rose | 52.50 | 35.00 |
| | | *Nos. J1-J5 (5)* | 69.50 | 39.45 |
| | | Set, never hinged | 170.00 | |

Castle at Antioch D1

**1939 Typo. *Perf. 12***

| | | | | |
|---|---|---|---|---|
| J6 | D1 | 1ku red orange | 4.50 | 1.50 |
| J7 | D1 | 3ku dk olive brown | 5.00 | 1.75 |
| J8 | D1 | 4ku turquoise green | 5.50 | 2.00 |
| J9 | D1 | 5ku slate black | 6.50 | 2.50 |
| | | *Nos. J6-J9 (4)* | 21.50 | 7.75 |
| | | Set, never hinged | 42.50 | |

Nos. J6-J9 Overprinted in Black like Nos. 25-37

**1939**

| | | | | |
|---|---|---|---|---|
| J10 | D1 | 1ku red orange | 4.25 | 1.50 |
| J11 | D1 | 3ku dk olive brown | 5.00 | 1.75 |
| J12 | D1 | 4ku turquoise green | 5.00 | 2.00 |
| J13 | D1 | 5ku slate black | 7.25 | 2.50 |
| a. | | Overprint inverted | 22.50 | |
| | | *Nos. J10-J13 (4)* | 21.50 | 7.75 |
| | | Set, never hinged | 52.50 | |

## HELIGOLAND

ˈhe-lə-gō-ˌland

LOCATION — An island in the North Sea near the northern coast of Germany
GOVT. — Former British Possession
AREA — ¼ sq. mi.
POP. — 2,307 (1900)

Great Britain ceded Heligoland to Germany in 1890. It became part of Schleswig-Holstein province. Stamps of Heligoland were superseded by those of the German Empire.

16 Schillings = 1 Mark
100 Pfennig = 1 Mark = 1 Schilling (1875)

**REPRINTS**

Most Heligoland issues were extensively reprinted between 1875 and 1895, and these comprise the great majority of Heligoland stamps in the marketplace. Such reprints sell for much less than the originals, usually for $1-$2 each. Expertization of Heligoland issues is strongly recommended by the editors.

Queen Victoria
A1 A2

A3

A4

HALF SCHILLING
A1: Curl below chignon is rounded.
A2: Curl resembles hook or comma.

**Typo., Head Embossed**

**1867-68 Unwmk. *Rouletted***

| | | | | |
|---|---|---|---|---|
| 1 | A1 | ½sch bl grn & rose | 325.00 | *1,000.* |
| 1A | A2 | ½sch bl grn & rose | 800.00 | *1,700.* |
| 2 | A1 | 1sch rose & dp grn | 190.00 | *200.00* |
| 3 | A3 | 2sch rose & pale grn | 15.00 | *60.00* |
| 4 | A3 | 6sch gray grn & rose | 17.00 | *475.00* |

*Reprints of No. 2 lack the large curl, those of No. 1A are not in blue green, and those of Nos. 3 and 4 are on slightly porous paper and the colors are either too deep or too bright. The 2sch and 6sch perforated exist only as reprints.*

**1869-71 *Perf. 13½x14½***

**Thick Soft Paper**

| | | | | |
|---|---|---|---|---|
| 5 | A2 | ½sch ol grn & car rose | 125.00 | *160.00* |
| a. | | ½sch blue green & rose | 240.00 | *250.00* |
| b. | | ½sch yellow green & rose | 475.00 | *450.00* |
| 6 | A2 | 1sch rose & yel grn | 175.00 | *300.00* |

*Reprints are on thinner paper and in too dark colors.*

**1873 Thick Quadrille Paper**

| | | | | |
|---|---|---|---|---|
| 7 | A4 | ¼sch pale rose & pale grn | 32.50 | *2,250.* |
| a. | | ¼sch deep rose & pale grn | 325.00 | *2,250.* |
| 8 | A4 | ¼sch yel grn & rose | 135.00 | *3,600.* |
| 9 | A2 | ½sch brt grn & rose | 125.00 | *210.00* |
| 10 | A4 | ¾sch gray grn & pale rose | 35.00 | *2,250.* |
| a. | | ¾sch gray green & dp rose | 35.00 | *2,250.* |
| 11 | A2 | 1sch rose & pale grn | 210.00 | *425.00* |
| 12 | A4 | 1½sch yel grn & rose | 72.50 | *325.00* |

*Reprints are never on quadrille paper.*

**1874 Thin Wove Paper**

| | | | | |
|---|---|---|---|---|
| 13 | A4 | ¼sch rose & yel grn | 17.50 | |

*Originals have the large curl. The early reprints have the small curl. The later reprints are on thin hard paper with smooth white gum and the colors are too bright.*

A5

A6

A7

Coat of Arms — A8

**1875 Wove Paper**

| | | | | |
|---|---|---|---|---|
| 14 | A5 | 1pf dk rose & dk grn | 16.00 | *600.00* |
| 15 | A5 | 2pf yel grn & dk rose | 17.00 | *875.00* |
| 16 | A6 | 5pf dk rose & dk grn | 20.00 | *21.00* |
| 17 | A6 | 10pf blue grn & red | 15.00 | *37.50* |
| a. | | 10pf yel green & dark rose | 110.00 | *27.50* |
| b. | | 10pf lt green & pale red | 140.00 | *25.00* |
| 18 | A7 | 25pf rose & dk green | 16.50 | *30.00* |
| a. | | 25pf dk rose & dk green | 16.50 | *30.00* |
| 19 | A7 | 50pf grn & brick red | 22.50 | *85.00* |
| a. | | 50pf dl grn & dk rose | 65.00 | *37.50* |

*The 1pf and 2pf have been reprinted on very white paper with white gum. The colors are too bright and too light.*

**1876-88 Typo.**

| | | | | |
|---|---|---|---|---|
| 20 | A8 | 3pf dp grn & dl red | 275.00 | *1,600.* |
| a. | | 3pf green & bright red ('77) | 175.00 | *1,000.* |
| 21 | A8 | 20pf ver & brt grn ('88) | 20.00 | *32.50* |
| a. | | 20pf brn org & grn ('87) | 425.00 | *47.50* |
| b. | | 20pf vio car & yel grn ('80) | 240.00 | *125.00* |
| c. | | 20pf anil rose & dk grn ('85) | 425.00 | *65.00* |
| d. | | 20pf lil rose & dk grn ('76) | 240.00 | *125.00* |
| e. | | 20pf rose red & dk grn ('80) | 240.00 | *125.00* |

The coat-of-arms on Nos. 20, 21 and sub-varieties is printed in three colors: varying shades of yellow, red and green.

*The 3pf has been reprinted. The colors are usually too pale, especially the red, which is either orange or orange red.*

A9

A10

**1879 Typo.**

| | | | | |
|---|---|---|---|---|
| 22 | A9 | 1m dp green & car | 225.00 | *225.00* |
| a. | | 1m blue green & salmon | 225.00 | *240.00* |
| b. | | 1m dark green & ver | 80.00 | |
| 23 | A10 | 5m blue grn & sal | 200.00 | *1,200.* |
| | | ***Perf. 11½*** | | |
| 24 | A9 | 1m dp grn & car | 1,500. | *5,500.* |
| 25 | A10 | 5m bl grn & rose red | 1,500. | *12,000.* |
| a. | | Horiz. pair, imperf. vert. | *5,000.* | |

Nos. 13, 20a, 22b, 24 and 25 were never placed in use. Forged cancellations of Nos. 1-23 are plentiful.

Heligoland stamps were replaced by those of the German Empire in 1890.

# HONDURAS

hän-ˈdur-əs

LOCATION — Central America, between Guatemala on the north and Nicaragua on the south
GOVT. — Republic
AREA — 43,277 sq. mi.
POP. — 5,997,327 (1999 est.)
CAPITAL — Tegucigalpa

8 Reales = 1 Peso
100 Centavos = 1 Peso (1878)
100 Centavos = 1 Lempira (1933)

**Catalogue values for unused stamps in this country are for Never Hinged items, beginning with Scott 344 in the regular postage section, Scott B1 in the semi-postal section, Scott C144 in the airpost section, Scott CB5 in the airpost semi-postal section, Scott CE3 in the airpost special delivery section, Scott CO110 in the airpost official section, and Scott RA6 in the postal tax section.**

Values for unused stamps are for examples with original gum as defined in the catalogue introduction. Very fine examples of the locally printed Nos. 95-110, 127, 140, 151-210C, and 218-279 will have margins clear of the perforations but will be noticeably off center.

**Watermark**

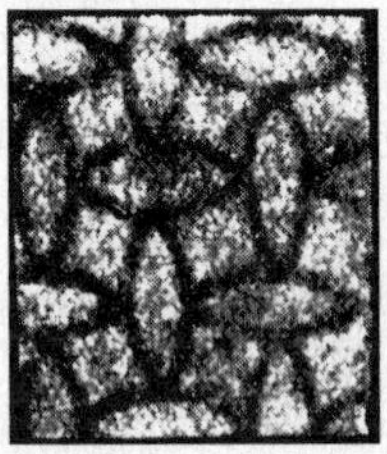

Wmk. 209 — Multiple Ovals

Coat of Arms — A1

**1865, Dec. Unwmk. Litho. *Imperf.***

| | | | | |
|---|---|---|---|---|
| 1 | A1 | 2r black, *green* | .65 | — |
| 2 | A1 | 2r black, *pink* | .65 | — |

Comayagua

Tegucigalpa

Medio real = ½ real
Un real = 1 real
Dos reales = 2 reales

**Comayagua Issue**

**1877, May Red Surcharge**

| | | | | |
|---|---|---|---|---|
| 3 | A1 | ½r on 2r blk, *grn* | 70.00 | |

**Blue Surcharge**

| | | | | |
|---|---|---|---|---|
| 5 | A1 | 2r on 2r blk, *grn* | 150.00 | — |
| 6 | A1 | 2r on 2r blk, *pink* | *475.00* | — |

**Black Surcharge**

| | | | | |
|---|---|---|---|---|
| 7 | A1 | 1r on 2r blk, *grn* | 150.00 | |
| 8 | A1 | 2r on 2r blk, *grn* | *800.00* | |
| 9 | A1 | 2r on 2r blk, *pink* | 500.00 | |

No. 5 may exist only as the base for No. 13a.

**Tegucigalpa Issue**

**1877, July Black Surcharge**

| | | | | |
|---|---|---|---|---|
| 13 | A1 | 1r on 2r blk, *grn* | 15.00 | *35.00* |
| *a.* | | Surcharged on #5 | *1000.* | |
| 14 | A1 | 1r on 2r blk, *pink* | *80.00* | |
| 16 | A1 | 2r on 2r blk, *pink* | — | |

**Blue Surcharge**

| | | | | |
|---|---|---|---|---|
| 18 | A1 | ½r on 2r blk, *grn* | *80.00* | |
| 19 | A1 | ½r on 2r blk, *pink* | *25.00* | |
| 20 | A1 | 1r on 2r blk, *pink* | *35.00* | |
| 23 | A1 | 2r on 2r blk, *pink* | 15.00 | *25.00* |

**Red Surcharge**

| | | | | |
|---|---|---|---|---|
| 24 | A1 | ½r on 2r blk, *grn* | 15.00 | *35.00* |
| 25 | A1 | ½r on 2r blk, *pink* | 60.00 | |

Only the stamps valued or dashed used are known to have been postally used. Nos. 3 and 7 may have been postally used, but to date no examples are recorded used. The other listed stamps were sold as remainders. No covers bearing Nos. 3 to 25 are known.

The blue surcharges range from light blue to violet black. The black surcharge has no tinge of blue. The red surcharges range from light to dark carmine. Some exist double or inverted, but genuine errors are rare. Normal cancel is a blue or black 7-bar killer. Target cancels on Nos. 1-24 are forgeries. Surcharges and cancels have been extensively forged.

**Regular Issue**

President Francisco Morazán — A4

**Printed by National Bank Note Co. of N.Y.**
**Thin, hard paper, colorless gum**
**Various Frames**

**1878, July Engr. *Perf. 12***

| | | | | |
|---|---|---|---|---|
| 30 | A4 | 1c violet | .50 | .50 |
| 31 | A4 | 2c brown | .50 | .50 |
| 32 | A4 | ½r black | 5.00 | .50 |
| 33 | A4 | 1r green | 25.00 | .50 |
| 34 | A4 | 2r deep blue | 3.00 | *5.00* |
| 35 | A4 | 4r vermilion | 5.00 | *10.00* |
| 36 | A4 | 1p orange | 6.00 | *25.00* |
| | | *Nos. 30-36 (7)* | 45.00 | *42.00* |

Various counterfeit cancellations exist on Nos. 30-36. Most used copies of Nos. 35-36 offered are actually 35a-36a with fake or favor cancels.

**Printed by American Bank Note Co. of N.Y.**
**Re-Issue Soft paper, yellowish gum**
**Various Frames**

**1889**

| | | | | |
|---|---|---|---|---|
| *30a* | A4 | 1c deep violet | *10.00* | |
| *31a* | A4 | 2c red brown | .25 | |
| *32a* | A4 | ½r black | .25 | |
| *33a* | A4 | 1r blue green | .25 | |
| *34a* | A4 | 2r ultramarine | *5.00* | |
| *35a* | A4 | 4r scarlet vermilion | .25 | |
| *36a* | A4 | 1p orange yellow | .25 | |
| | | *Nos. 30a-36a (7)* | 16.25 | |

Although Nos. 30a-36a were not intended for postal use, they were valid, and genuine cancels are known on Nos. 31a-34a.

Arms of Honduras — A5

**1890, Jan. 6**

| | | | | |
|---|---|---|---|---|
| 40 | A5 | 1c yellow green | .30 | .30 |
| 41 | A5 | 2c red | .30 | .30 |
| 42 | A5 | 5c blue | .30 | .30 |
| 43 | A5 | 10c orange | .35 | *.40* |
| 44 | A5 | 20c ocher | .35 | *.40* |
| 45 | A5 | 25c rose red | .35 | *.40* |
| 46 | A5 | 30c purple | .50 | *.60* |
| 47 | A5 | 40c dark blue | .50 | *.80* |
| 48 | A5 | 50c brown | .55 | *.80* |
| 49 | A5 | 75c blue green | .55 | *2.00* |
| 50 | A5 | 1p carmine | .70 | *2.25* |
| | | *Nos. 40-50 (11)* | 4.75 | *8.55* |

The tablets and numerals of Nos. 40 to 50 differ for each denomination.
For overprints see Nos. O1-O11.

**Used values of Nos. 1-110 are for stamps with genuine cancellations applied while the stamps were valid. Various counterfeit cancellations exist.**

A6

President Luis Bográn — A7

**1891, July 31**

| | | | | |
|---|---|---|---|---|
| 51 | A6 | 1c dark blue | .30 | .30 |
| 52 | A6 | 2c yellow brown | .30 | .30 |
| 53 | A6 | 5c blue green | .30 | .30 |
| 54 | A6 | 10c vermilion | .30 | .30 |
| 55 | A6 | 20c brown red | .30 | .30 |
| 56 | A6 | 25c magenta | .40 | *.55* |
| 57 | A6 | 30c slate | .40 | *.55* |
| 58 | A6 | 40c blue green | .40 | *.55* |
| 59 | A6 | 50c black brown | .50 | *.80* |
| 60 | A6 | 75c purple | .50 | *1.25* |
| 61 | A6 | 1p brown | .75 | *1.60* |
| 62 | A7 | 2p brn & black | 2.25 | *5.00* |
| *a.* | | Head inverted | 225.00 | |
| 63 | A7 | 5p pur & black | 2.00 | *5.75* |
| *a.* | | Head inverted | 60.00 | |
| 64 | A7 | 10p green & blk | 2.00 | *5.75* |
| *a.* | | Head inverted | 75.00 | |
| | | *Nos. 51-64 (14)* | 10.70 | *23.30* |

#62, 64 exist with papermakers watermark.
For overprints see Nos. O12-O22.

Columbus Sighting Honduran Coast — A8

General Trinidad Cabanas — A9

**1892, July 31**

| | | | | |
|---|---|---|---|---|
| 65 | A8 | 1c slate | .40 | *.45* |
| 66 | A8 | 2c deep blue | .40 | *.45* |
| 67 | A8 | 5c yellow green | .40 | *.45* |
| 68 | A8 | 10c blue green | .40 | *.45* |
| 69 | A8 | 20c red | .40 | *.45* |
| 70 | A8 | 25c orange brown | .50 | *.55* |
| 71 | A8 | 30c ultramarine | .50 | *.60* |
| 72 | A8 | 40c orange | .50 | *.90* |
| 73 | A8 | 50c brown | .60 | *.85* |
| 74 | A8 | 75c lake | .60 | *1.25* |
| 75 | A8 | 1p purple | .60 | *1.40* |
| | | *Nos. 65-75 (11)* | 5.30 | *7.80* |

Discovery of America by Christopher Columbus, 400th anniv.

**1893, Aug.**

| | | | | |
|---|---|---|---|---|
| 76 | A9 | 1c green | .25 | *1.50* |
| 77 | A9 | 2c scarlet | .25 | *1.50* |
| 78 | A9 | 5c dark blue | .25 | *1.50* |
| 79 | A9 | 10c orange brn | .25 | *1.50* |
| 80 | A9 | 20c brown red | .25 | *1.50* |
| 81 | A9 | 25c dark blue | .30 | *1.50* |
| 82 | A9 | 30c red orange | .50 | *1.50* |
| 83 | A9 | 40c black | .50 | *1.50* |
| 84 | A9 | 50c olive brn | .50 | *1.50* |
| 85 | A9 | 75c purple | .75 | *1.50* |
| 86 | A9 | 1p deep magenta | .75 | *1.75* |
| | | *Nos. 76-86 (11)* | 4.55 | *16.75* |

"Justice" A10

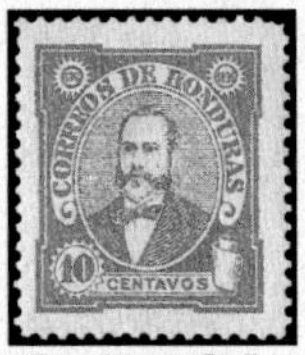

President Celio Arias A11

**1895, Feb. 15**

| | | | | |
|---|---|---|---|---|
| 87 | A10 | 1c vermilion | .30 | .30 |
| 88 | A10 | 2c deep blue | .30 | .30 |
| 89 | A10 | 5c slate | .35 | *.50* |
| 90 | A10 | 10c brown rose | .45 | *.50* |
| 91 | A10 | 20c violet | .45 | *.50* |
| 92 | A10 | 30c deep violet | .45 | *.85* |
| 93 | A10 | 50c olive brown | .55 | *1.25* |
| 94 | A10 | 1p dark green | .60 | *1.60* |
| | | *Nos. 87-94 (8)* | 3.45 | *5.80* |

The tablets and numerals of Nos. 76-94 differ for each denomination.

**1896, Jan. 1 Litho. *Perf. 11½***

| | | | | |
|---|---|---|---|---|
| 95 | A11 | 1c dark blue | .30 | *.35* |
| 96 | A11 | 2c yellow brn | .30 | *.35* |
| 97 | A11 | 5c purple | 1.10 | .30 |
| *a.* | | 5c red violet | .60 | *1.10* |
| 98 | A11 | 10c vermilion | .40 | .40 |
| *a.* | | 10c red | 4.50 | *4.50* |
| 99 | A11 | 20c emerald | .75 | .50 |
| *a.* | | 20c deep green | | |
| 100 | A11 | 30c ultramarine | .65 | *.70* |
| 101 | A11 | 50c rose | .90 | *1.00* |
| 102 | A11 | 1p black brown | 1.25 | *1.50* |
| | | *Nos. 95-102 (8)* | 5.65 | *5.10* |

Counterfeits are plentiful. Nos. 95-102 exist imperf. between horiz. or vertically.
*Originals of Nos. 95 to 102 are on both thin, semi-transparent paper and opaque paper; reprints are on thicker, opaque paper and usually have a black cancellation "HONDURAS" between horizontal bars.*

Railroad Train — A12

**1898, Aug. 1**

| | | | | |
|---|---|---|---|---|
| 103 | A12 | 1c brown | .50 | .25 |
| 104 | A12 | 2c rose | .50 | .25 |
| 105 | A12 | 5c dull ultra | 1.00 | .25 |
| *b.* | | 5c red violet (error) | 1.50 | .70 |
| 106 | A12 | 6c red violet | .90 | .25 |
| *b.* | | 6c dull rose (error) | | |
| 107 | A12 | 10c dark blue | 1.00 | .30 |
| 108 | A12 | 20c dull orange | 1.25 | .75 |
| 109 | A12 | 50c orange red | 2.00 | 1.25 |
| 110 | A12 | 1p blue green | 4.00 | 3.00 |
| | | *Nos. 103-110 (8)* | 11.15 | 6.30 |

Excellent counterfeits of Nos. 103-110 exist.
For overprints see Nos. O23-O27.

**Laid Paper**

| | | | | |
|---|---|---|---|---|
| *103a* | A12 | 1c | 1.00 | .50 |
| *104a* | A12 | 2c | 1.25 | .50 |
| *105a* | A12 | 5c | 1.60 | .50 |
| *106a* | A12 | 6c | 1.60 | .75 |
| *107a* | A12 | 10c | 1.60 | 1.00 |
| | | *Nos. 103a-107a (5)* | 7.05 | 3.25 |

General Santos Guardiola A13

President José Medina A14

**1903, Jan. 1 Engr. *Perf. 12***

| | | | | |
|---|---|---|---|---|
| 111 | A13 | 1c yellow grn | .35 | .25 |
| 112 | A13 | 2c carmine rose | .35 | .30 |
| 113 | A13 | 5c blue | .35 | .30 |
| 114 | A13 | 6c dk violet | .35 | .30 |
| 115 | A13 | 10c brown | .40 | .30 |
| 116 | A13 | 20c dull ultra | .45 | .40 |
| 117 | A13 | 50c vermilion | 1.25 | 1.10 |
| 118 | A13 | 1p orange | 1.25 | 1.10 |
| | | *Nos. 111-118 (8)* | 4.75 | 4.05 |

"PERMITASE" handstamped on stamps of 1896-1903 was applied as a control mark by the isolated Pacific Coast post office of Amapala to prevent use of stolen stamps.

**1907, Jan. 1 *Perf. 14***

| | | | | |
|---|---|---|---|---|
| 119 | A14 | 1c dark green | .25 | .25 |
| 120 | A14 | 2c scarlet | .25 | .25 |
| 120A | A14 | 2c carmine | 9.00 | 5.50 |
| 121 | A14 | 5c blue | .30 | .30 |
| 122 | A14 | 6c purple | .35 | .30 |
| *a.* | | 6c dark violet | .80 | .60 |
| 123 | A14 | 10c gray brown | .40 | .35 |
| 124 | A14 | 20c ultra | .90 | .85 |
| *a.* | | 20c blue violet | 110.00 | 110.00 |

125 A14 50c deep lake 1.10 1.10
126 A14 1p orange 1.50 1.50
*a.* 1p orange yellow —
*Nos. 119-126 (9)* 14.05 10.40

All values of the above set exist imperforate, imperforate horizontally and in horizontal pairs, imperforate between. No. 124a imperf is worth only 10% of the listed perforated variety.
For surcharges see Nos. 128-130.

**1909 Typo. *Perf. 11½***
127 A14 1c green 1.25 1.00
*a.* Imperf., pair 4.00 4.00
*b.* Printed on both sides 7.50 10.00

The 1909 issue is roughly typographed in imitation of the 1907 design. It exists pin perf. 8, 13, etc.

### No. 124 Handstamp Surcharged in Black, Green or Red

**1910, Nov. *Perf. 14***
128 A14 1c on 20c ultra 8.50 6.00
129 A14 5c on 20c ultra (G) 8.50 6.00
130 A14 10c on 20c ultra (R) 8.50 6.00
*Nos. 128-130 (3)* 25.50 18.00

As is usual with handstamped surcharges inverts and double exist.

Honduran Scene — A15

**1911, Jan. Litho. *Perf. 14, 12 (1p)***
131 A15 1c violet .35 .25
132 A15 2c green .35 .25
*a.* Perf. 12 5.00 1.25
133 A15 5c carmine .40 .25
*a.* Perf. 12 8.00 3.50
134 A15 6c ultramarine .50 .30
135 A15 10c blue .60 .40
136 A15 20c yellow .60 .50
137 A15 50c brown 2.00 1.75
138 A15 1p olive green 2.50 2.00
*Nos. 131-138 (8)* 7.30 5.70

For overprints and surcharges see Nos. 139, 141-147, O28-O47.

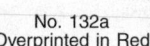

No. 132a Overprinted in Red

**1911, Sept. 19 *Perf. 12***
139 A15 2c green 20.00 18.00
*a.* Inverted overprint 24.00 22.50

90th anniversary of Independence.
Counterfeit overprints on perf. 14 stamps exist.

President Manuel Bonilla — A16

**1912, Feb. 1 Typo. *Perf. 11½***
140 A16 1c orange red 12.00 12.00

Election of Pres. Manuel Bonilla.

### Stamps of 1911 Surcharged in Black, Red or Blue

a

b

**1913 Litho. *Perf. 14***
141 A15(a) 2c on 1c violet 1.25 .75
*a.* Double surcharge 3.25
*b.* Inverted surcharge 4.50
*c.* Double surch., one invtd. 6.75
*d.* Red surcharge 40.00 40.00
142 A15(b) 2c on 1c violet 7.00 5.75
*a.* Inverted surcharge 14.00
143 A15(b) 2c on 10c blue 2.75 2.25
*a.* Double surcharge 5.75 5.75
*b.* Inverted surcharge
144 A15(b) 2c on 20c yellow 7.00 6.75
145 A15(b) 5c on 1c violet 2.50 .75
146 A15(b) 5c on 10c bl (Bl) 2.75 1.50
147 A15(b) 6c on 1c violet 2.75 2.25
*Nos. 141-147 (7)* 26.00 20.00

Counterfeit surcharges exist.

Terencio Sierra — A17

Bonilla — A18

ONE CENTAVO:
Type I — Solid border at sides below numerals.
Type II — Border of light and dark stripes.

**1913-14 Typo. *Perf. 11½***
151 A17 1c dark brn, I .25 .25
*a.* 1c brown, type II .75 .45
152 A17 2c carmine .25 .25
153 A18 5c blue .40 .25
154 A18 5c ultra ('14) .40 .25
155 A18 6c gray vio .50 .25
156 A18 6c purple ('14) .40 .25
*a.* 6c red lilac .60 .35
157 A17 10c blue .75 .75
158 A17 10c brown ('14) 1.25 .50
159 A17 20c brown 1.00 .75
160 A18 50c rose 2.00 2.00
161 A18 1p gray green 2.25 2.25
*Nos. 151-161 (11)* 9.45 7.75

For overprints and surcharges see Nos. 162-173, O48-O57.

Surcharged in Black or Carmine

**1914**
162 A17 1c on 2c carmine .75 .75
163 A17 5c on 2c carmine 1.25 .90
164 A18 5c on 6c gray vio 2.00 2.00
165 A17 10c on 2c carmine 2.00 2.00
166 A18 10c on 6c gray vio 2.00 2.00
*a.* Double surcharge 10.00
167 A18 10c on 6c gray vio (C) 2.00 2.00
168 A18 10c on 50c rose 6.50 5.00
*Nos. 162-168 (7)* 16.50 14.65

No. 158 Surcharged

**1915**
173 A17 5c on 10c brown 2.50 1.75

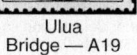

Ulua Bridge — A19

Bonilla Theater — A20

**1915-16 Typo.**
174 A19 1c chocolate .25 .25
175 A19 2c carmine .25 .25
*a.* Tête bêche pair 1.00 1.00
176 A20 5c bright blue .25 .25
177 A20 6c deep purple .35 .25
178 A19 10c dull blue .75 .25
179 A19 20c red brown 1.25 1.00
*a.* Tête bêche pair 4.00 4.00
180 A20 50c red 1.50 1.50
181 A20 1p yellow grn 2.50 2.50
*Nos. 174-181 (8)* 7.10 6.25

For overprints & surcharges see #183, 231-232, 237, 239-240, 285, 292, C1-C13, C25, C28, C31, C36, C57, CO21, CO30-CO32, CO42, O58-O65.

**Imperf., Pairs**

*174a* A19 1c 2.00 2.00
*175b* A19 2c 2.00 2.00
*176a* A20 5c 3.50
*178a* A19 10c 3.50
*179b* A19 20c 5.25
*180b* A20 50c 7.00
*181a* A20 1p 8.75 8.75

Francisco Bertrand — A21

**1916, Feb. 1**
182 A21 1c orange 2.00 2.00

Election of Pres. Francisco Bertrand.
Unauthorized reprints exist.

Official Stamp No. O60 Overprinted

**1918**
183 A20 5c bright blue 2.00 1.50
*a.* Inverted overprint 5.00 5.00

Statue to Francisco Morazán — A22

**1919 Typo.**
184 A22 1c brown .25 .25
*a.* Printed on both sides 2.00
*b.* Imperf., pair .70
185 A22 2c carmine .25 .25
186 A22 5c lilac rose .25 .25
187 A22 6c brt violet .25 .25
188 A22 10c dull blue .25 .25
189 A22 15c light blue .75 .25
190 A22 15c dark violet .60 .25
191 A22 20c orange brn 1.00 .30
*a.* 20c gray brown 10.00 .30
*b.* Imperf., pair 2.75
192 A22 50c light brown 4.00 2.50
*a.* Imperf. pair 15.00
193 A22 1p yellow green 7.50 *20.00*
*a.* Imperf., pair 20.00
*b.* Printed on both sides 9.00
*c.* Tête bêche pair 15.00
*Nos. 184-193 (10)* 15.10 24.55

See note on handstamp following No. 217.
Unauthorized reprints exist.
For overprints and surcharges see Nos. 201-210C, 230, 233, 235-236, 238, 241-243, 287, 289, C58, C61, CO23, CO25, CO33, CO36-CO38, CO39, CO40, O66-O74.

"Dawn of Peace" — A23

**1920, Feb. 1 Size: 27x21mm**
194 A23 2c rose 2.50 2.50
*a.* Tête bêche pair 15.00 12.50
*b.* Imperf., pair 15.00 12.50

**Size: 51x40mm**
195 A23 2c gold 10.00 10.00
196 A23 2c silver 10.00 10.00
197 A23 2c bronze 10.00 10.00
198 A23 2c red 12.00 12.00
*Nos. 194-198 (5)* 44.50 44.50

Assumption of power by Gen. Rafael Lopez Gutierrez.
Nos. 195-198 exist imperf.
Unauthorized reprints of #195-198 exist.

### Type of 1919, Dated "1920"

**1921**
201 A22 6c dark violet 10.00 *5.00*
*a.* Tête bêche pair 15.00
*b.* Imperf., pair 15.00

Unauthorized reprints exist.

No. 185 Surcharged in Antique Letters

**1922**
202 A22 6c on 2c carmine .40 .40
*a.* "ALE" for "VALE" 2.00 2.00
*b.* Comma after "CTS" 2.00 2.00
*c.* Without period after "CTS" 2.00 2.00
*d.* "CT" for "CTS" 2.00 2.00
*e.* Double surcharge 4.25
*f.* Inverted surcharge 4.25

Stamps of 1919 Surcharged in Roman Figures and Antique Letters in Green

**1923**
203 A22 10c on 1c brown 1.50 1.50
204 A22 50c on 2c carmine 2.00 2.00
*a.* Inverted surcharge 10.00 10.00
*b.* "HABILITADO" 6.00 6.00

Surcharged in Black or Violet Blue

205 A22 1p on 5c lil rose (Bk) 3.50 3.50
*a.* "PSEO" 20.00 20.00
*b.* Inverted surcharge 20.00 20.00
206 A22 1p on 5c lil rose (VB) 20.00 20.00
*a.* "PSEO" 70.00

On Nos. 205-206, "Habilitado Vale" is in Antique letters, "Un Peso" in Roman.

No. 185 Surcharged in Roman Letters in Green

207 A22 6c on 2c carmine 3.50 2.75

Nos. 184-185 Surcharged in Roman Letters in Green

**208** A22 10c on 1c brown 1.75 1.25
- *a.* "DIES" 6.00
- *b.* "DEIZ" 6.00
- *c.* "DEIZ CAS" 6.00
- *d.* "TTS" for "CTS" 6.00
- *e.* "HABILTADO" 6.00
- *f.* "HABILITAD" 6.00
- *g.* "HABILITA" 6.00
- *h.* Inverted surcharge 30.00

**209** A22 50c on 2c carmine 3.75 2.75
- *a.* "CAT" for "CTA" 10.00
- *b.* "TCA" for "CTA" 10.00
- *c.* "TTS" for "CTS" 10.00
- *d.* "CAS" for "CTS" 10.00
- *e.* "HABILTADO" 10.00

Surcharge on No. 209 is found in two spacings between value and HABILITADO: 5mm (illustrated) and 1½mm.

No. 186 Surcharged in Antique Letters in Black

**$ 1.00**
**HABILITADO**
**VALE**
**UN PESO**

**210** A22 1p on 5c lil rose 25.00 *25.00*
- *a.* "PFSO" 75.00

In the surcharges on Nos. 202 to 210 there are various wrong font, inverted and omitted letters.

No. 184 Surcharged in Large Antique Letters in Green

**210C** A22 10c on 1c brown 15.00 15.00
- *d.* "DIFZ" 55.00 55.00

Dionisio de Herrera A24

Pres. Miguel Paz Baraona A25

**1924, June Litho. *Perf. 11, 11½***

**211** A24 1c olive green .30 .25
**212** A24 2c deep rose .35 .25
**213** A24 6c red violet .40 .25
**214** A24 10c blue .40 .25
**215** A24 20c yellow brn .80 .35
**216** A24 50c vermilion 1.75 1.10
**217** A24 1p emerald 4.00 2.75
*Nos. 211-217 (7)* 8.00 5.20

In 1924 a facsimile of the signatures of Santiago Herrera and Francisco Caceres, covering four stamps, was handstamped in violet to prevent the use of stamps that had been stolen during a revolution.

Imperfs exist.

For overprints and surcharges see Nos. 280-281, 290-291, C14-C24, C26-C27, C29-C30, C32-C35, C56, C60, C73-C76, CO1-CO5, CO22, CO24, CO28-CO29, CO34-CO35, CO38A, CO39A, CO41, CO43, O75-O81.

**1925, Feb. 1 Typo. *Perf. 11½***

**218** A25 1c dull blue 2.00 2.00
- *a.* 1c dark blue 2.00 2.00

**219** A25 1c car rose 5.00 5.00
- *a.* 1c brown carmine 5.00 5.00

**220** A25 1c olive brn 14.00 14.00
- *a.* 1c orange brown 14.00 14.00
- *b.* 1c dark brown 14.00 14.00
- *c.* 1c black brown 14.00 14.00

**221** A25 1c buff 12.00 12.00
**222** A25 1c red 60.00 60.00
**223** A25 1c green 40.00 40.00
*Nos. 218-223 (6)* 133.00 133.00

***Imperf***

**225** A25 1c dull blue 5.50 5.50
- *a.* 1c dark blue 5.50 5.50

**226** A25 1c car rose 8.75 8.75
- *a.* 1c brown carmine 8.75 8.75

**227** A25 1c olive brn 8.75 8.75
- *a.* 1c orange brown 8.75 8.75
- *b.* 1c deep brown 8.75 8.75
- *c.* 1c black brown 8.75 8.75

**228** A25 1c buff 8.75 8.75
**229** A25 1c red 60.00 60.00
**229A** A25 1c green 27.50 27.50
*Nos. 225-229A (6)* 119.25 119.25

Inauguration of President Baraona. Counterfeits and unauthorized reprints exist.

No. 187 Overprinted in Black and Red

**1926, June *Perf. 11½***

**230** A22 6c bright violet 1.50 1.25

Many varieties of this two-part overprint exist: one or both inverted or double, and various combinations. Value, each $10.

Nos. 177 and 187 Overprinted in Black or Red

**1926**

**231** A20 6c deep pur (Bk) 2.00 2.00
- *a.* Inverted overprint 5.50 5.50
- *b.* Double overprint 5.50 5.50

**232** A20 6c deep pur (R) 2.50 2.50
- *a.* Double overprint 5.00 5.00

**233** A22 6c lilac (Bk) .60 .60
- *a.* 6c violet .75 .75
- *b.* Inverted overprint 5.00 5.00
- *c.* Double overprint 5.00 5.00
- *d.* Double ovpt., one inverted 5.00 5.00
- *e.* "192" 7.50 7.50
- *f.* Double ovpt., both inverted 7.50 7.50

**Same Overprint on No. 230**

**235** A22 6c violet 20.00 20.00
- *a.* "1926" inverted 20.00 20.00
- *b.* "Habilitado" triple, one invtd. 20.00 20.00

No. 188 Surcharged in Red or Black

**236** A22 6c on 10c blue (R) .50 .25
- *c.* Double surcharge 5.00 4.00
- *d.* Without bar
- *e.* Inverted surcharge 4.00 3.50
- *f.* "Vale" omitted
- *g.* "6cts" omitted
- *h.* "cts" omitted
- *k.* Black surcharge *55.00 55.00*

Nos. 175 and 185 Overprinted in Green

**237** A19 2c carmine .25 .25
- *a.* Tête bêche pair 4.00 4.00
- *b.* Double overprint 2.00 1.40
- *c.* "HARILITADO" 2.00 1.40
- *d.* "1926" only 2.75 2.75
- *e.* Double overprint, one inverted 2.75 2.75
- *f.* "1926" omitted 3.50 3.50
- *g.* Triple overprint, two inverted 5.25 5.25
- *h.* Double on face, one on back 5.25 5.25

**238** A22 2c carmine .25 .25
- *a.* "HARILITADO" .90 .90
- *b.* Double overprint 1.40 1.40
- *c.* Inverted overprint 2.00 2.00

No. 177 Overprinted in Red

**1927 Large Numerals, 12x5mm**

**239** A20 6c deep purple 25.00 25.00
- *a.* "1926" over "1927" 35.00 35.00
- *b.* Invtd. ovpt. on face of stamp, normal ovpt. on back 30.00

No. 179 Surcharged

**1927**

**240** A19 6c on 20c brown .75 .75
- *a.* Tête bêche pair 2.75 2.75
- *c.* Interted surcharge 2.50 2.50
- *d.* Double surcharge 8.50 8.50

Nos. 8 and 10 in the setting have no period after "cts" and No. 50 has the "t" of "cts" inverted.

Same Surcharge on Nos. 189-191

**241** A22 6c on 15c blue 27.50 27.50
- *a.* "c" of "cts" omitted

**242** A22 6c on 15c vio .70 .70
- *a.* Double surcharge 1.75 1.75
- *b.* Double surch., one invtd. 2.00 2.00
- *c.* "L" of "Vale" omitted

**243** A22 6c on 20c yel brn .60 .60
- *a.* 6c on 20c deep brown
- *b.* "6" omitted 1.75 1.75
- *c.* "Vale" and "cts" omitted 3.50 3.50

*Nos. 240-243 (4)* 29.55 29.55

On Nos. 242 and 243 stamps Nos. 12, 16 and 43 in the setting have no period after "cts" and No. 34 often lacks the "s." On No. 243 the "c" of "cts" is missing on stamp No. 38. On No. 241 occur the varieties "ct" or "ts" for "cts." and no period.

Southern Highway — A26

Ruins of Copán — A27

Pine Tree — A28

Presidential Palace — A29

Ponciano Leiva — A30

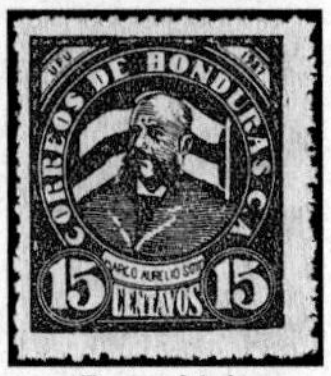

Pres. M.A. Soto — A31

Lempira — A32

Map of Honduras — A33

President Juan Lindo — A34

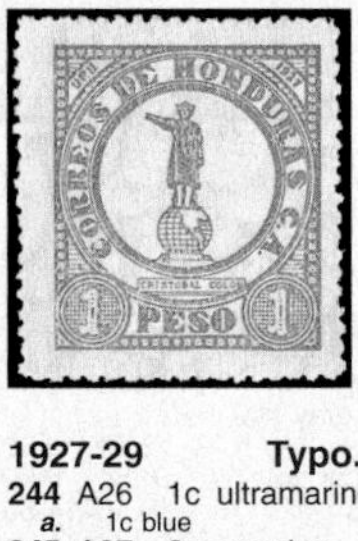

Statue of Columbus — A35

**1927-29 Typo. Wmk. 209**

**244** A26 1c ultramarine .30 .25
- *a.* 1c blue .30 .25

**245** A27 2c carmine .30 .25
**246** A28 5c dull violet .30 .25
**247** A28 5c bl gray ('29) 25.00 7.00
**248** A29 6c blue black .75 .50
- *a.* 6c gray black .75 .50

**249** A29 6c dark bl ('29) .40 .25
- *a.* 6c light blue .40 .25

**250** A30 10c blue .70 .25
**251** A31 15c deep blue 1.00 .50
**252** A32 20c dark blue 1.25 .60
**253** A33 30c dark brown 1.50 1.00
**254** A34 50c light blue 2.50 1.50
**255** A35 1p red 5.00 2.50
*Nos. 244-255 (12)* 39.00 14.85

In 1929 a quantity of imperforate sheets of No. 249 were stolen from the Litografia Nacional. Some of them were perforated by sewing machine and a few copies were passed through the post. To prevent the use of stolen stamps of the 1927-29 issues they were declared invalid and the stock on hand was overprinted "1929 a 1930."

For overprints and surcharges see Nos. 259-278, CO19-CO20B.

Pres. Vicente Mejia Colindres and Vice-Pres. Rafael Diaz Chávez — A36

President Mejia Colindres — A37

**1929, Feb. 25**

**256** A36 1c dk carmine 3.00 3.00
**257** A37 2c emerald 3.00 3.00

Installation of Pres. Vicente Mejia Colindres. Printed in sheets of ten.

Nos. 256 and 257 were surreptitiously printed in transposed colors. They were not regularly issued.

Stamps of 1927-29 Overprinted in Various Colors

**1929, Oct.**

**259** A26 1c blue (R) .25 .25
- *a.* 1c ultramarine (R) .50 .25
- *b.* Double overprint 2.50 1.75
- *c.* As "a", double overprint 2.50 1.75

**260** A26 1c blue (Bk) 6.50 6.50
- *a.* 1c ultramarine (Bk)

**261** A27 2c car (R Br) 3.50 3.50
- *a.* Double overprint

**262** A27 2c car (Bl Gr) 1.00 1.00
- *a.* Double overprint

**263** A27 2c car (Bk) 1.00 .50
**264** A27 2c car (V) .50 .25
- *a.* Double overprint
- *b.* Double ovpt., one inverted

**265** A27 2c org red (V) 1.50
**266** A28 5c dl vio (R) .40 .30
- *a.* Double overprint (R+V)

**267** A28 5c bl gray (R) 1.00 .75
- *a.* Double overprint (R+Bk)

**269** A29 6c gray blk (R) 2.50 2.00
- *a.* Double overprint 6.00 6.00

**272** A29 6c dk blue (R) .40 .25
- *a.* 6c light blue (R) .40 .25
- *b.* Double overprint 2.00 2.00
- *c.* Double overprint (R+V)

**273** A30 10c blue (R) .40 .25
- *a.* Double overprint 2.50 1.75

**274** A31 15c dp blue (R) .50 .25
- *a.* Double overprint 3.50 2.50

**275** A32 20c dark bl (R) .50 .35
**276** A33 30c dark brn (R) .75 .60
- *a.* Double overprint 3.50 2.50

**277** A34 50c light bl (R) 2.00 1.00
**278** A35 1p red (V) 5.00 2.50
*Nos. 259-278 (17)* 27.70 20.25

Nos. 259-278 exist in numerous shades. There are also various shades of the red and violet overprints. The overprint may be found reading upwards, downwards, inverted, double, triple, tête bêche or combinations.

Status of both 6c stamps with overprint in black is questioned.

A38

**1929, Dec. 10**

**279** A38 1c on 6c lilac rose .70 .70
- *a.* "1992" for "1929"
- *b.* "9192" for "1929"
- *c.* Surcharge reading down 8.00
- *d.* Dbl. surch., one reading down

Varieties include "1992" reading down and pairs with one surcharge reading down, double or with "1992."

No. 214 Surcharged in Red

***Perf. 11, 11½***

**1930, Mar. 26** **Unwmk.**

**280** A24 1c on 10c blue .35 .30
- *a.* "1093" for "1930" 1.40
- *b.* "tsc" for "cts" 1.40

**281** A24 2c on 10c blue .35 .30
- *a.* "tsc" for "cts" 2.00
- *b.* "Vale 2" omitted

Official Stamps of 1929 Overprinted in Red or Violet

**1930, Mar.** **Wmk. 209** ***Perf. 11½***

**282** O1 1c blue (R) .50 .50
- *a.* Double overprint 2.00 2.00

**284** O1 2c carmine (V) .90 .90

Stamps of 1915-26 Overprinted in Blue

**On No. 174**

**1930, July 19** **Unwmk.**

**285** A19 1c chocolate .30 .25
- *a.* Double overprint 1.00 1.00
- *b.* Inverted overprint 1.40 1.40
- *c.* Dbl. ovpt., one inverted 1.40 1.40

**On No. 184**

**287** A22 1c brown 15.00 15.00
- *a.* Double overprint
- *c.* Inverted overprint

**On No. 204**

**289** A22 50c on 2c carmine 100.00 90.00
- *b.* Inverted surcharge

**On Nos. 211 and 212**

**290** A24 1c olive green .25 .25
- *a.* Double overprint 1.75 1.75
- *b.* Inverted overprint 1.75 1.75
- *d.* On No. O75 12.00

**291** A24 2c carmine rose .25 .25
- *a.* Double overprint 1.75 1.75
- *b.* Inverted overprint 1.75 1.75

**On No. 237**

**292** A19 2c car (G & Bl) 100.00 100.00

From Title Page of Government Gazette, First Issue — A39

**1930, Aug. 11** **Typo.** **Wmk. 209**

**295** A39 2c orange 2.00 2.00
**296** A39 2c ultramarine 2.00 2.00
**297** A39 2c red 2.00 2.00
*Nos. 295-297 (3)* 6.00 6.00

Publication of the 1st newspaper in Honduras, cent. The stamps were on sale and available for postage on Aug. 11th, 1930, only. Not more than 5 examples of each color could be purchased by an applicant.

Nos. 295-297 exist imperf. and part-perforate. Unauthorized reprints exist.

For surcharges see Nos. CO15-CO18A.

Paz Baraona — A40

Manuel Bonilla — A41

Lake Yojoa — A42

View of Palace at Tegucigalpa A43

City of Amapala A44

Mayan Stele at Copán A45

Christopher Columbus A46

Discovery of America A47

Loarque Bridge A48

**Unwmk.**

**1931, Jan. 2** **Engr.** ***Perf. 12***

**298** A40 1c black brown .75 .25
**299** A41 2c carmine rose .75 .25
**300** A42 5c dull violet 1.00 .25
**301** A43 6c deep green 1.00 .25
**302** A44 10c brown 1.50 .25
**303** A45 15c dark blue 2.00 .30
**304** A46 20c black 3.50 .40
**305** A47 50c olive green 4.50 1.50
**306** A48 1p slate black 9.00 2.50
*Nos. 298-306 (9)* 24.00 5.95

Regular Issue of 1931 Overprinted in Black or Various Colors

**1931**

**307** A40 1c black brown .40 .30
**308** A41 2c carmine rose .60 .30
**309** A45 15c dark blue 1.00 .30
**310** A46 20c black 2.50 .40

Overprinted

**311** A42 5c dull violet .50 .30
**312** A43 6c deep green .50 .30
**315** A44 10c brown 1.50 .35
**316** A47 50c olive green 8.00 5.00
**317** A48 1p slate black 10.00 7.50
*Nos. 307-317 (9)* 25.00 14.75
*Nos. 307-317,C51-C55 (14)* 50.00 35.75

The overprint is a control mark. It stands for "Tribunal Superior de Cuentas" (Superior Tribunal of Accounts).

Overprint varieties include: inverted; double; double, one or both inverted; on back; pair, one without overprint; differing colors (6c exists with overprint in orange, yellow and red).

President Carías and Vice-President Williams — A49

**1933, Apr. 29**

**318** A49 2c carmine rose .50 .35
**319** A49 6c deep green .75 .40
**320** A49 10c deep blue 1.00 .50
**321** A49 15c red orange 1.25 .75
*Nos. 318-321 (4)* 3.50 2.00

Inauguration of Pres. Tiburcio Carias Andino and Vice-Pres. Abraham Williams, Feb. 1, 1933.

Columbus' Fleet and Flag of the Race — A50

**Wmk. 209**

**1933, Aug. 3** **Typo.** ***Perf. 11½***

**322** A50 2c ultramarine 1.00 .65
**323** A50 6c yellow 1.00 .65
**324** A50 10c lemon 1.40 .85

***Perf. 12***

**325** A50 15c violet 2.00 1.50
**326** A50 50c red 4.00 3.50
**327** A50 1 l emerald 7.00 7.00
*Nos. 322-327 (6)* 16.40 14.15

"Day of the Race," an annual holiday throughout Spanish-American countries. Also for the 441st anniv. of the sailing of Columbus to the New World, Aug. 3, 1492.

Masonic Temple, Tegucigalpa — A51

Designs: 2c, President Carias. 5c, Flag. 6c, Tomás Estrada Palma.

**Unwmk.**

**1935, Jan. 12** **Engr.** ***Perf. 12***

**328** A51 1c green .40 .25
**329** A51 2c carmine .40 .25
**330** A51 5c dark blue .40 .25
**331** A51 6c black brown .40 .25
- *a.* Vert. pair, imperf. btwn. 20.00 20.00

*Nos. 328-331 (4)* 1.60 1.00
*Nos. 328-331,C77-C83 (11)* 15.20 6.50

Gen. Carías Bridge — A55

**1937, June 4**

**332** A55 6c car & ol green .90 .40
**333** A55 21c grn & violet 1.50 .65
**334** A55 46c orange & brn 2.10 1.50
**335** A55 55c ultra & black 3.00 2.40
*Nos. 332-335 (4)* 7.50 4.95

Prolongation of the Presidential term to Jan. 19, 1943.

Seal of Honduras A56

Central District Palace — A57

Designs: 3c, Map of Honduras. 5c, Bridge of Choluteca. 8c, Flag.

**1939, Mar. 1** ***Perf. 12½***

**336** A56 1c orange yellow .25 .25
**337** A57 2c red orange .25 .25
**338** A57 3c carmine .30 .25
**339** A57 5c orange .30 .25
**340** A56 8c dark blue .50 .25
*Nos. 336-340 (5)* 1.60 1.25
*Nos. 336-340,C89-C98 (15)* 15.35 8.65

Nos. 336-340 exist imperf.

For overprints see #342-343.

Nos. 336 and 337 Overprinted in Green

**1944** ***Perf. 12½***

**342** A56 1c orange yellow .30 .30
- *a.* Inverted overprint 5.00 5.00

**343** A57 2c red orange 1.25 .75
- *a.* Inverted overprint 5.00 5.00

**Catalogue values for unused stamps in this section, from this point to the end of the section, are for Never Hinged items.**

International Peace Movement — A58

**1984, Feb. 15** **Litho.** ***Perf. 12***

**344** A58 78c multi .85 .65
**345** A58 85c multi .95 .30
**346** A58 95c multi 1.00 .35
**347** A58 1.50 l multi 1.75 .55
**348** A58 2 l multi 2.10 .70
**349** A58 5 l multi 5.50 1.75
*Nos. 344-349 (6)* 12.15 4.30

Central American Aeronautics Corp., 25th Anniv. — A59

Designs: 2c, Edward Warner Award issued by the Intl. Civil Aviation Organization, vert. 5c, Corp. emblem, flags of Guatemala, Honduras, El Salvador, Costa Rica and Panama. 60c, Transmission tower, plane. 75c, Corp. emblem, vert. 1 l, 1.50 l, Emblem, flags, diff.

**1987, Feb. 26 Litho. *Perf. 12***

**350** A59 2c multi .25 .25
**351** A59 5c multi .25 .25
**352** A59 60c multi .75 .35
**353** A59 75c multi .95 .40
**354** A59 1 l multi 1.25 .55
*Nos. 350-354 (5)* 3.45 1.80

**Souvenir Sheet**

**355** A59 1.50 l multi 3.00 3.00

Housing Institute (INVA), 30th Anniv. A60

**1987, Oct. 9 Litho. *Perf. 13½***

**356** A60 5c shown .30 .25
**357** A60 95c Map, emblem, text 1.00 .40

EXFILHON '88 — A61

**1988, Sept. 11 Litho. *Imperf.***

**358** A61 3 l dull red brn & brt ultra 4.50 4.50

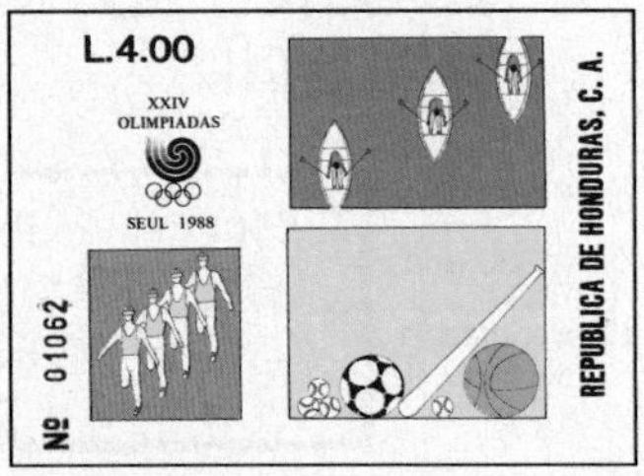


1988 Summer Olympics, Seoul — A62

**1988, Sept. 30 Litho. *Imperf.***

**359** A62 4 l multi 4.75 4.75
*Nos. 359,C772-C773 (3)* 7.05 5.65

Luis Bogran Technical Institute, Cent. A63

85c, Cogwheel, map, flag of Honduras.

**1990, Sept. 28 Litho. *Perf. 10½***

**360** A63 20c multicolored .25 .25
**361** A63 85c multicolored .65 .40

**Size: 114x82mm**

***Imperf***

**362** A63 2 l like #360 2.00 1.40
*Nos. 360-362 (3)* 2.90 2.05

Nos. 360-361 are airmail.

America Issue A64

UPAE emblem, land and seascapes showing produce and fish.

**1990, Oct. 31 Litho. *Perf. 13½***

**363** A64 20c multi, vert. .30 .25
**364** A64 1 l multicolored .80 .30

A65

**1992, Feb. 17**

**365** A65 50c shown .40 .25
**366** A65 3 l Cross-country skiing 2.00 1.25

1992 Winter Olympics, Albertville.

A66

Mother's Day (Paintings): 20c, Saleswoman, by Manuel Rodriguez. 50c, The Grandmother and Baby, by Rodriguez. 5 l, Saleswomen, by Maury Flores.

**1992, May 21 Litho. *Perf. 13½***

**367** A66 20c shown .25 .25
**368** A66 50c multicolored .40 .25
**369** A66 5 l multicolored 3.25 2.00
*Nos. 367-369 (3)* 3.90 2.50

Butterflies A67

Designs: 25c, Melitaeinae chlosyne janais. 85c, Heliconiinae agrilus vanillae. 3 l, Morphinae morpho granadensis. 5 l, Heliconiinae dryadula phalusa.

**1992, June 22**

**370** A67 25c multicolored .50 .25
**371** A67 85c multicolored 1.25 .40
**372** A67 3 l multicolored 4.50 1.25

**Size: 108x76mm**

***Imperf***

**373** A67 5 l multicolored 6.00 5.25
*Nos. 370-373 (4)* 12.25 7.15

1992 Summer Olympics, Barcelona — A68

**1992, Mar. 16 Litho. *Perf. 13½***

**374** A68 20c Running .25 .25
**375** A68 50c Tennis .30 .25
**376** A68 85c Soccer .55 .40
*Nos. 374-376 (3)* 1.10 .90

Japanese Overseas Cooperation Volunteers in Honduras, 20th Anniv. — A69

Designs: 1.40 l, Volunteers working on Japanese letter, vert. 4.30 l, Folding screen showing Mayan Gods. 5.40 l, Men, women of Honduras in traditional costumes, volunteer.

**1995, Sept. 20 Litho. *Perf. 13½***

**377** A69 1.40 l multicolored .50 .40
**378** A69 4.30 l multicolored 1.50 1.25
**379** A69 5.40 l multicolored 1.75 1.50
*Nos. 377-379 (3)* 3.75 3.15

Nos. 378-379 are airmail.

Birds — A70

Designs: 1.40 l, Buteo jamaicensis. 1.50 l, Ramphastos sulfuratus. 2 l, Dendrocygna autumnalis. 2.15 l, Micrastur semitorquatus. 3 l, Polyporus plancus. 5.40 l, 10 l, Sarcoramphus papa.

**1997, Apr. 29 Litho. *Perf. 13½***

**380** A70 1.40 l multicolored .55 .55
**381** A70 1.50 l multicolored .60 .60
**382** A70 2 l multicolored .80 .80
**383** A70 2.15 l multicolored .90 .90
*a.* Pair, #382, 383 3.00 3.00
**384** A70 3 l multicolored 1.25 1.25
*a.* Pair, #380, 384 3.00 3.00
**385** A70 5.40 l multicolored 2.00 2.00
*a.* Pair, #381, 385 4.00 4.00
*Nos. 380-385 (6)* 6.10 6.10

**Size: 50x73mm**

***Imperf***

**386** A70 20 l multicolored 6.50 6.00

Nos. 380-385 were printed in panes of 30 (5x6), with one value compring the top three rows and another the bottom three rows. Thus, each pane contains five setenant pairs.

No. 386 is airmail.

No. RA8 Surcharged in Gold

**1999, June 25 Litho. *Perf. 13½***

**387** PT6 2.60 l on 1c .65 .35
**388** PT6 7.85 l on 1c 1.90 .95
**389** PT6 10.65 l on 1c 2.60 1.25
**390** PT6 11.55 l on 1c 2.75 1.40
**391** PT6 12.45 l on 1c 3.00 1.50
**392** PT6 13.85 l on 1c 3.50 1.75
*Nos. 387-392 (6)* 14.40 7.20

For surcharges, see C1199//C1206.

## SEMI-POSTAL STAMPS

**Catalogue values for unused stamps in this section are for Never Hinged items.**

Indiginous Musical Instruments SP1

No. B1: a, Garífuna drum. b, Flutes. c, Toltec drum. d, Hornpipe. e, Maya drum. f, Conch shell.

**2000, Apr. 7 Litho. *Perf. 13¼***

**B1** Sheet of 6, "Pro filatelia" in black 16.00 16.00
*a.-f.* SP1 10 l + 1 l Any single 2.50 2.50
*g.* As #B1, "Pro filatelia" in gold 17.50 17.50

See Nos. C1073, C1209.

## AIR POST STAMPS

Regular Issue of 1915-16 Overprinted in Black, Blue or Red

**1925 Unwmk. *Perf. 11½***

**C1** A20 5c lt blue (Bk) 87.50 87.50
**C2** A20 5c lt blue (Bl) 300.00 300.00
*a.* Inverted overprint *400.00*
*b.* Vertical overprint *600.00*
*c.* Double overprint *800.00*
**C3** A20 5c lt blue (R) *7,250.*

Value for No. C3 is for an example without gum.

**C4** A19 10c dk blue (R) 175.00
*a.* Inverted overprint 325.00
*b.* Overprint tête bêche, pair *800.00*
**C5** A19 10c dk blue (Bk) *1,100.*
**C6** A19 20c red brn (Bk) 175.00 175.00
*a.* Inverted overprint 250.00
*b.* Tête bêche pair 400.00
*c.* Overprint tête bêche, pair *725.00*
*d.* "AFRO" *1,400.*
*e.* Double overprint *600.00*
**C7** A19 20c red brn (Bl) 175.00 175.00
*a.* Inverted overprint *700.00*
*b.* Tête bêche pair *1,000*
*c.* Vertical overprint 900.00
**C8** A20 50c red (Bk) 450.00 300.00
*a.* Inverted overprint *550.00*
*b.* Overprint tête bêche, pair *900.00*
**C9** A20 1p yel grn (Bk) 600.00 600.00

Surcharged in Black or Blue

**C10** A19 25c on 1c choc 125.00 125.00
*a.* Inverted surcharge 700.00
**C11** A20 25c on 5c lt bl (Bl) 225.00 225.00
*a.* Inverted surcharge 700.00
*b.* Double inverted surcharge *675.00*
**C12** A19 25c on 10c dk bl *125,000.*
**C13** A19 25c on 20c brn (Bl) 200.00 200.00
*a.* Inverted surcharge 325.00
*b.* Tête bêche pair 450.00

Counterfeits of Nos. C1-C13 are plentiful.

Monoplane and Lisandro Garay AP1

**1929, June 5 Engr. *Perf. 12***

**C13C** AP1 50c carmine 2.00 1.75

No. 216 Surcharged in Blue

**1929 *Perf. 11, 11½***

**C14** A24 25c on 50c ver 5.00 3.50

In the surcharges on Nos. C14 to C40 there are various wrong font and defective letters and numerals, also periods omitted.

Nos. 215-217 Surcharged in Green, Black or Red

**1929, Oct.**

C15 A24 5c on 20c yel brn (G) 1.40 1.40
*a.* Double surcharge (R+G) 45.00
C16 A24 10c on 50c ver (Bk) 2.25 1.90
C17 A24 15c on 1p emer (R) 3.50 3.50
*Nos. C15-C17 (3)* 7.15 6.80

**Nos. 214 and 216 Surcharged Vertically in Red or Black**

a

b

**1929, Dec. 10**

C18 A24(a) 5c on 10c bl (R) .60 .60
C19 A24(b) 20c on 50c ver 1.00 1.00
*a.* "1299" for "1929" 190.00
*b.* "cts. cts." for "cts. oro." 190.00
*c.* "r" of "Aereo" omitted 2.00
*d.* Horiz. pair, imperf. btwn. 20.00

Nos. 214, 215 and 180 Surcharged in Various Colors

**1930, Feb.**

C20 A24 5c on 10c (R) .50 .50
*a.* "1930" reading down 3.50
*b.* "1903" for "1930" 3.50
*c.* Surcharge reading down 10.00
*d.* Double surcharge 14.00
*e.* Dbl. surch., one downward 14.00
C21 A24 5c on 10c (Y) *450.00 450.00*
C22 A24 5c on 20c (Bl) 125.00 125.00
C23 A24 10c on 20c (Bk) .70 .70
*a.* "0" for "10" 3.50
*b.* Double surcharge 8.75
*c.* Dbl. surch., one downward 12.00
*d.* Horiz. pair, imperf. btwn. 70.00
C24 A24 10c on 20c (V) *750.00 750.00*
*a.* "0" for "10" *1,600.*
C25 A20 25c on 50c (Bk) .95 .95
*a.* "Internaoicnal" 3.50
*b.* "o" for "oro" 3.50
*c.* Inverted surcharge 17.50
*d.* As "a," invtd. surch. *175.00*
*e.* As "b," invtd. surch. *175.00*

Surcharge on Nos. C20-C24 are vertical.

Nos. 214, 215 and 180 Surcharged

**1930, Apr. 1**

C26 A24 5c on 10c blue .50 .50
*a.* Double surcharge 9.50
*b.* "Servicioa" 3.50
C27 A24 15c on 20c yel brn .55 .55
*a.* Double surcharge 7.00
C28 A20 20c on 50c red, surch. reading down .95 .95
*a.* Surcharge reading up 7.00
*Nos. C26-C28 (3)* 2.00 2.00

Nos. C22 and C23 Surcharged Vertically in Red

**1930**

C29 A24 10c on 5c on 20c (Bl+R) .90 .90
*a.* "1930" reading down 9.00 9.00
*b.* "1903" for "1930" 9.00 9.00
*c.* Red surcharge, reading down 14.00

C30 A24 10c on 10c on 20c (Bk+R) 87.50 87.50
*a.* "0" for "10" 190.00

No. 181 Surcharged as No. C25 and Re-surcharged

C31 A20 50c on 25c on 1p grn 4.25 4.25
*a.* "Internaoicnal" 7.00
*b.* "o" for "oro" 7.00
*c.* 25c surcharge inverted 17.50 17.50
*d.* 50c surcharge inverted 17.50 17.50
*e.* As "a" and "c"
*f.* As "a" and "d"
*g.* As "b" and "c"
*h.* As "b" and "d"
*Nos. C29-C31 (3)* 92.65 92.65

No. 215 Surcharged in Dark Blue

**1930, May 22**

C32 A24 5c on 20c yel brn 1.25 1.00
*a.* Double surcharge 5.25 5.25
*b.* Horiz. pair, imperf. btwn. 60.00 60.00
*c.* Vertical pair, imperf. between 20.00 20.00

Nos. O78-O80 Surcharged like Nos. C20 to C25 in Various Colors

**1930**

C33 A24 5c on 10c (R) 450.00 350.00
*a.* "1930" reading down *1,500.*
*b.* "1903" for "1930" *1,500.*
C34 A24 5c on 20c (Bl) 400.00 400.00
C35 A24 25c on 50c (Bk) 225.00 225.00
*a.* 55c on 50c vermilion 325.00 325.00

No. C35 exists with inverted surcharge.

No. O64 Surcharged like No. C28

C36 A20 20c on 50c red, surcharge reading down *350.00 350.00*
*a.* Surcharge reading up *350.00 350.00*
*b.* Dbl. surch., reading down *350.00 350.00*
*c.* Dbl. surch., reading up *350.00 350.00*

No. O87 Overprinted

**1930, Feb. 21 Wmk. 209 *Perf. 11½***

C37 O1 50c yel, grn & blue 1.40 1.25
*a.* "Internacional" 5.25
*b.* "luternacional" 5.25
*c.* Double overprint 5.25

Nos. O86-O88 Overprinted in Various Colors

**1930, May 23**

C38 O1 20c dark blue (R) 1.10 .85
*a.* Double overprint 8.75
*b.* Triple overprint 12.00
C39 O1 50c org, grn & bl (Bk) 1.10 .90
C40 O1 1p buff (Bl) 1.40 1.25
*a.* Double overprint 10.50
*Nos. C38-C40 (3)* 3.60 3.00

National Palace AP3

**Unwmk.**

**1930, Oct. 1 Engr. *Perf. 12***

C41 AP3 5c yel orange .50 .30
C42 AP3 10c carmine .75 .60
C43 AP3 15c green 1.00 .75
C44 AP3 20c dull violet 1.25 .60
C45 AP3 1p light brown 4.00 4.00
*Nos. C41-C45 (5)* 7.50 6.25

**Overprinted in Various Colors**

**1931 *Perf. 12***

C51 AP3 5c yel orange (R) *2.00 1.50*
C52 AP3 10c carmine (Bk) *3.00 2.50*
C53 AP3 15c green (Br) *5.00 4.00*
C54 AP3 20c dull vio (O) *5.00 4.25*
C55 AP3 1p lt brown (G) *10.00 8.75*
*Nos. C51-C55 (5)* *25.00 21.00*

See note after No. 317.

Stamps of Various Issues Surcharged in Blue or Black (#C59)

**1931, Oct. *Perf. 11½***

**On No. 215**

C56 A24 15c on 20c yel brn 3.50 2.75
*a.* Horiz. pair, imperf. btwn. 42.50
*b.* Green surcharge 20.00 20.00

**On No. O64**

C57 A20 15c on 50c red 4.25 3.50
*a.* Inverted surcharge 10.50 10.50

**On No. O72**

C58 A22 15c on 20c brn 4.25 4.25
*a.* Vert. pair, imperf. between 12.00

On Nos. C57 and C58 the word "OFICIAL" is canceled by two bars.

**On No. O88**

**Wmk. 209**

C59 O1 15c on 1p buff 4.25 4.25
*a.* Vert. pair, imperf. horiz. 25.00
*b.* "Sevricio" 14.00 14.00

The varieties "Vaie" for "Vale," "aereo" with circumflex accent on the first "e" and "Interior" with initial capital "I" are found on #C56, C58-C59. #C57 is known with initial capital in "Interior."

A similar surcharge, in slightly larger letters and with many minor varieties, exists on Nos. 215, O63, O64 and O73. The authenticity of this surcharge is questioned.

Nos. 215, O73, O87-O88 Surcharged in Green, Red or Black

**1931, Nov. Unwmk.**

C60 A24 15c on 20c (G) 3.50 2.75
*a.* Inverted surcharge 6.25
*b.* "XI" omitted 6.25
*c.* "X" for "XI" 6.25
*d.* "PI" for "XI" 6.25
C61 A22 15c on 50c (R) 3.50 2.75
*a.* "XI" omitted 6.75
*b.* "PI" for "XI" 6.75
*c.* Double surcharge 20.00 20.00

On No. C61 the word "OFICIAL" is not barred out.

**Wmk. 209**

C62 O1 15c on 50c (Bk) 2.75 2.50
*a.* "1391" for "1931" 10.50 10.50
*b.* Double surcharge 8.75 8.75
C63 O1 15c on 1p (Bk) 2.50 2.25
*a.* "1391" for "1931" 12.50
*b.* Surcharged on both sides 7.00

Nos. O76-O78 Surcharged in Black or Red

**1932 Unwmk. *Perf. 11, 11½***

C73 A24 15c on 2c .80 .80
*a.* Double surcharge 5.50
*b.* Inverted surcharge 4.25
*c.* "Ae" of "Aero" omitted 1.00
*d.* On No. 212 (no "Official")
C74 A24 15c on 6c .80 .80
*a.* Double surcharge 3.50
*b.* Horiz. pair, imperf. btwn. 17.50
*c.* "Aer" omitted
*d.* "A" omitted 1.00
*e.* Inverted surcharge 3.50
C75 A24 15c on 10c (R) .80 .80
*a.* Double surcharge 5.50
*b.* Inverted surcharge 3.50
*c.* "r" of "Aereo" omitted 1.00

**Same Surcharge on No. 214 in Red**

C76 A24 15c on 10c dp bl *150.00 100.00*

There are various broken and missing letters in the setting.

A similar surcharge with slightly larger letters exists.

Post Office and National Palace AP4

View of Tegucigalpa — AP5

Designs: 15c, Map of Honduras. 20c, Mayol Bridge. 40c, View of Tegucigalpa. 50c, Owl. 1 l, Coat of Arms.

**1935, Jan. 10 *Perf. 12***

C77 AP4 8c blue .25 .25
C78 AP5 10c gray .25 .25
C79 AP5 15c olive gray .40 .25
C80 AP5 20c dull green .50 .25
C81 AP5 40c brown .70 .25
C82 AP4 50c yellow 8.25 1.60
C83 AP4 1 l green 3.25 2.75
*Nos. C77-C83 (7)* 13.55 5.35

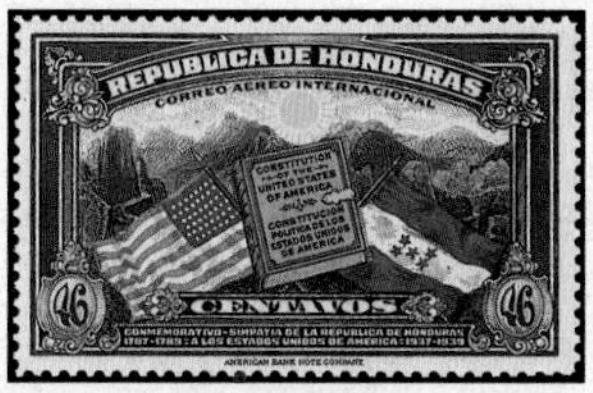


Flags of US and Honduras — AP11

**Engr. & Litho.**

**1937, Sept. 17 Unwmk.**

C84 AP11 46c multicolored 2.75 1.40

US Constitution, 150th anniv.

Comayagua Cathedral AP12

Founding of Comayagua AP13

Alonzo Cáceres and Pres. Carías — AP14

Lintel of Royal Palace
AP15

**1937, Dec. 7** **Engr.**

| | | | | | |
|---|---|---|---|---|---|
| **C85** | AP12 | 2c copper red | .25 | .25 |
| **C86** | AP13 | 8c dark blue | .35 | .25 |
| **C87** | AP14 | 15c slate black | .70 | .70 |
| **C88** | AP15 | 50c dark brown | 4.25 | 2.75 |
| | | *Nos. C85-C88 (4)* | 5.55 | 3.95 |

City of Comayagua founding, 400th anniv.
For surcharges see Nos. C144-C146.

Mayan Stele at Copán
AP16

Mayan Temple, Copán
AP17

Designs: 15c, President Carias. 30c, José C. de Valle. 40c, Presidential House. 46c, Lempira. 55c, Church of Our Lady of Suyapa. 66c, J. T. Reyes. 1 l, Hospital at Choluteca. 2 l, Ramón Rosa.

**1939, Mar. 1** ***Perf. 12½***

| | | | | |
|---|---|---|---|---|
| **C89** AP16 | 10c orange brn | .25 | .25 |
| **C90** AP16 | 15c grnsh blue | .30 | .25 |
| **C91** AP17 | 21c gray | .50 | .25 |
| **C92** AP16 | 30c dk blue grn | .55 | .25 |
| **C93** AP17 | 40c dull violet | 1.00 | .25 |
| **C94** AP16 | 46c dk gray brn | 1.00 | .65 |
| **C95** AP16 | 55c green | 1.25 | 1.00 |
| *a.* | Imperf., pair | 22.50 | |
| **C96** AP16 | 66c black | 1.75 | 1.25 |
| **C97** AP16 | 1 l olive grn | 3.00 | 1.00 |
| **C98** AP16 | 2 l henna red | 4.25 | 2.50 |
| | *Nos. C89-C98 (10)* | 13.80 | 7.45 |

For surcharges see Nos. C118-C119, C147-C152.

Souvenir Sheets

AP26

14c, Francisco Morazan. 16c, George Washington. 30c, J. C. de Valle. 40c, Simon Bolivar.

**1940, Apr. 13** **Engr.** ***Perf. 12***
**Centers of Stamps Lithographed**

| | | | |
|---|---|---|---|
| **C99** AP26 Sheet of 4 | 10.00 | 10.00 |
| *a.* 14c black, yellow, ultra & rose | 1.40 | 1.40 |
| *b.* 16c black, yellow, ultra & rose | 1.75 | 1.75 |
| *c.* 30c black, yellow, ultra & rose | 2.40 | 2.40 |
| *d.* 40c black, yellow, ultra & rose | 2.75 | 2.75 |

***Imperf***

| | | |
|---|---|---|
| **C100** AP26 Sheet of 4 | 16.00 | 16.00 |
| *a.* 14c black, yellow, ultra & rose | 2.25 | 2.25 |
| *b.* 16c black, yellow, ultra & rose | 2.75 | 2.75 |
| *c.* 30c black, yellow, ultra & rose | 4.00 | 4.00 |
| *d.* 40c black, yellow, ultra & rose | 4.50 | 4.50 |

Pan American Union, 50th anniv.
For overprints see Nos. C153-C154, C187.

Air Post Official Stamps of 1939 Overprinted in Red

**1940, Oct. 12** ***Perf. 12½***

| | | | | |
|---|---|---|---|---|
| **C101** OA2 | 2c dp bl & green | .25 | .25 |
| **C102** OA2 | 5c dp blue & org | .25 | .25 |
| **C103** OA2 | 8c deep bl & brn | .30 | .30 |
| **C104** OA2 | 15c dp blue & car | .50 | .50 |
| **C105** OA2 | 46c dp bl & ol grn | .80 | .80 |
| **C106** OA2 | 50c dp bl & vio | .90 | .90 |
| **C107** OA2 | 1 l dp bl & red brn | 3.75 | 3.75 |
| **C108** OA2 | 2 l dp bl & red org | 7.50 | 7.50 |
| | *Nos. C101-C108 (8)* | 14.25 | 14.25 |

Erection and dedication of the Columbus Memorial Lighthouse.

Air Post Official Stamps of 1939 Overprinted in Black

**1941, Aug. 2**

| | | | | |
|---|---|---|---|---|
| **C109** OA2 | 5c deep bl & org | 3.00 | .25 |
| **C110** OA2 | 8c dp blue & brn | 5.00 | .25 |
| *a.* | Overprint inverted | | 225.00 |

Nos. CO44, CO47-CO51 Surcharged in Black

**1941, Oct. 28**

| | | | | |
|---|---|---|---|---|
| **C111** OA2 | 3c on 2c | .40 | .25 |
| **C112** OA2 | 8c on 2c | .50 | .50 |
| **C113** OA2 | 8c on 15c | .50 | .25 |
| **C114** OA2 | 8c on 46c | .60 | .60 |
| **C115** OA2 | 8c on 50c | .75 | .50 |
| **C116** OA2 | 8c on 1 l | 1.25 | .70 |
| **C117** OA2 | 8c on 2 l | 2.00 | 1.50 |
| | *Nos. C111-C117 (7)* | 6.00 | 4.30 |

Once in each sheet a large "h" occurs in "ocho."

Nos. C90, C94 Surcharged in Red

**1942, July 14**

| | | | | |
|---|---|---|---|---|
| **C118** AP16 | 8c on 15c | .70 | .30 |
| *a.* | "Cerreo" | 2.00 | 2.00 |
| *b.* | Double surcharge | 25.00 | 25.00 |
| *c.* | As "a," double surcharge | 175.00 | |
| **C119** AP16 | 16c on 46c | .70 | .30 |
| *a.* | "Cerreo" | 2.00 | 2.00 |

Plaque
AP27

Morazán's Tomb, San Salvador — AP28

Designs: 5c, Battle of La Trinidad. 8c, Morazán's birthplace. 16c, Statue of Morazán. 21c, Church where Morazán was baptized. 1 l, Arms of Central American Federation. 2 l, Gen. Francisco Morazán.

**1942, Sept. 15** ***Perf. 12***

| | | | | |
|---|---|---|---|---|
| **C120** AP27 | 2c red orange | .25 | .25 |
| **C121** AP27 | 5c turq green | .25 | .25 |
| **C122** AP27 | 8c sepia | .25 | .25 |
| **C123** AP28 | 14c black | .40 | .30 |
| **C124** AP27 | 16c olive gray | .25 | .25 |
| **C125** AP27 | 21c light blue | 1.00 | .65 |
| **C126** AP27 | 1 l brt ultra | 3.00 | 2.25 |
| **C127** AP28 | 2 l dl ol brn | 7.50 | 7.25 |
| | *Nos. C120-C127 (8)* | 12.90 | 11.45 |

Gen. Francisco Morazan (1799-1842).
For surcharges see Nos. C349-C350.

Coat of Arms
AP35

Cattle
AP36

Bananas — AP37 Pine Tree — AP38

Tobacco Plant
AP39

Orchid
AP40

Coco Palm — AP41

Map of Honduras
AP42

Designs: 2c, Flag. 8c, Rosario. 16c, Sugar cane. 30c, Oranges. 40c, Wheat. 1 l, Corn. 2 l, Map of Americas.

**1943, Sept. 14** ***Perf. 12½***

| | | | | |
|---|---|---|---|---|
| **C128** AP35 | 1c light grn | .25 | .25 |
| **C129** AP35 | 2c blue | .25 | .25 |
| **C130** AP36 | 5c green | .30 | .25 |
| **C131** AP37 | 6c dark bl grn | .25 | .25 |
| **C132** AP36 | 8c lilac | .30 | .25 |
| **C133** AP38 | 10c lilac brn | .30 | .25 |
| **C134** AP39 | 15c dp claret | .35 | .25 |
| **C135** AP38 | 16c dark red | .35 | .25 |
| **C136** AP40 | 21c deep blue | .75 | .25 |
| **C137** AP39 | 30c org brown | .60 | .25 |
| **C138** AP40 | 40c red orange | .60 | .25 |
| **C139** AP41 | 55c black | 1.10 | .60 |
| **C140** AP41 | 1 l dark olive | 1.75 | 1.40 |
| **C141** AP37 | 2 l brown red | 5.25 | 4.00 |
| **C142** AP42 | 5 l orange | 13.00 | 13.00 |
| *a.* | Vert. pair, imperf. btwn. | 150.00 | |
| | *Nos. C128-C142 (15)* | 25.40 | 21.75 |

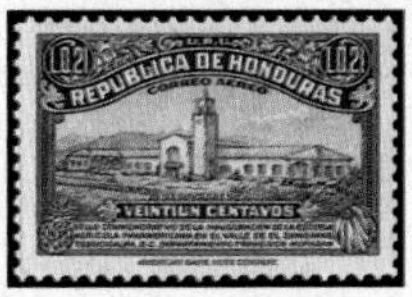


Pan-American School of Agriculture
AP50

**1944, Oct. 12** ***Perf. 12***

| | | | |
|---|---|---|---|
| **C143** AP50 | 21c dk blue grn | .40 | .25 |

Inauguration of the Pan-American School of Agriculture, Tegucigalpa.

**Catalogue values for unused stamps in this section, from this point to the end of the section, are for Never Hinged items.**

Air Post Stamps of 1937-39 Surcharged in Red or Green

**1945, Mar. 13** ***Perf. 11, 12½***

| | | | | |
|---|---|---|---|---|
| **C144** AP15 | 1c on 50c dk brn | .25 | .25 |
| **C145** AP12 | 2c on 2c cop red | .25 | .25 |
| **C146** AP14 | 8c on 15c sl blk | .25 | .25 |
| **C147** AP16 | 10c on 10c org brown (G) | .45 | .30 |
| **C148** AP16 | 15c on 15c grnsh blue (G) | .30 | .25 |
| **C149** AP17 | 30c on 21c gray (G) | 4.50 | 3.00 |
| **C150** AP17 | 40c on 40c dull violet (G) | 2.25 | 1.25 |
| **C151** AP16 | 1 l on 46c dk gray brown (G) | 2.25 | 1.75 |
| **C152** AP16 | 2 l on 66c blk (G) | 4.50 | 3.00 |
| | *Nos. C144-C152 (9)* | 15.00 | 10.30 |

**Nos. C99 and C100 Overprinted in Red**

Souvenir Sheets

**1945, Oct. 1** ***Perf. 12***

| | | | | |
|---|---|---|---|---|
| **C153** AP26 | Sheet of 4 | 4.00 | 3.00 |

***Imperf***

| | | | | |
|---|---|---|---|---|
| **C154** AP26 | Sheet of 4 | 6.50 | 4.25 |

Allied Nations' victory and Germany's unconditional surrender, May 8, 1945.

Seal of Honduras
AP51

Arms of Gracias and Trujillo
AP52

Franklin D. Roosevelt ("F.D.R." under Column)
AP53

Arms of San Miguel de Heredia de Tegucigalpa AP54

Designs (Coats of Arms): 5c, Comayagua and San Jorge de Olancho. 15c, Province of Honduras and San Juan de Puerto Caballas. 21c, Comayagua and Tencoa. 1 l, Jerez de la Frontera de Choluteca and San Pedro de Zula.

***Perf. 12½***

**1946, Oct. 15 Unwmk. Engr.**

| | | | | |
|---|---|---|---|---|
| **C155** | AP51 | 1c red | .25 | .25 |
| *a.* | | Vert. pair, imperf. between | 17.50 | |
| *b.* | | Imperf., pair | 70.00 | |
| **C156** | AP52 | 2c red orange | .25 | .25 |
| *a.* | | Imperf., pair | 70.00 | |
| **C157** | AP52 | 5c violet | .45 | .25 |
| **C158** | AP53 | 8c brown | 1.60 | .50 |
| *a.* | | Horiz. pair, imperf. btwn. | 70.00 | |
| **C159** | AP52 | 15c sepia | .80 | .25 |
| **C160** | AP52 | 21c deep blue | .90 | .30 |
| *a.* | | Horiz. pair, imperf. btwn. | 15.00 | |
| *b.* | | Imperf., pair | 70.00 | |
| **C161** | AP52 | 1 l green | 3.25 | 1.25 |
| **C162** | AP54 | 2 l dark grn | 5.00 | 2.00 |
| | | *Nos. C155-C162 (8)* | 12.50 | 5.05 |

No. C158 commemorates the death of Franklin D. Roosevelt and the Allied victory over Japan in World War II.

Type AP53 Redrawn ("Franklin D. Roosevelt" under Column) AP59

**1947, Oct.** ***Perf. 12½***

| | | | | |
|---|---|---|---|---|
| **C163** | AP59 | 8c brown | .50 | .35 |
| *a.* | | Vert. pair, imperf. between | 87.50 | |
| *b.* | | Horiz. pair, imperf. btwn. | 175.00 | |
| *c.* | | Perf. 12x6 | *175.00* | |

Map, Ancient Monuments and Conference Badge AP60

**1947, Oct. 20** ***Perf. 11x12½***

**Various Frames**

| | | | | |
|---|---|---|---|---|
| **C164** | AP60 | 16c green | .40 | .25 |
| **C165** | AP60 | 22c orange yel | .30 | .25 |
| **C166** | AP60 | 40c orange | .65 | .35 |
| **C167** | AP60 | 1 l deep blue | 1.10 | .90 |
| **C168** | AP60 | 2 l lilac | 4.00 | 3.50 |
| **C169** | AP60 | 5 l brown | 10.50 | 8.00 |
| | | *Nos. C164-C169 (6)* | 16.95 | 13.25 |

1st Intl. Archeological Conf. of the Caribbean.

For overprints and surcharges see Nos. C181-C186, C351, C353-C354, C379, C544.

Flag and Arms of Honduras AP61

Juan Manuel Galvez AP62

J. M. Galvez, Gen. Tiburcio Carias A. and Julio Lozano AP63

National Stadium AP64

Designs: 5c, 15c, Julio Lozano. 9c, Juan Manuel Galvez. 40c, Custom House. 1 l, Recinto Hall. 2 l, Gen. Tiburcio Carias A. 5 l, Galvez and Lozano.

Various frames inscribed: "Conmemorativa de la Sucesion Presidencial para el Periodo de 1949-1955."

**1949, Sept. 17 Engr.** ***Perf. 12***

| | | | | |
|---|---|---|---|---|
| **C170** | AP61 | 1c deep blue | .25 | .25 |
| **C171** | AP62 | 2c rose car | .25 | .25 |
| **C172** | AP62 | 5c deep blue | .25 | .25 |
| **C173** | AP62 | 9c sepia | .25 | .25 |
| **C174** | AP62 | 15c red brown | .25 | .25 |
| **C175** | AP63 | 21c gray black | .45 | .25 |
| **C176** | AP64 | 30c olive gray | .60 | .25 |
| **C177** | AP64 | 40c slate gray | .90 | .25 |
| **C178** | AP61 | 1 l red brown | 1.40 | .40 |
| **C179** | AP62 | 2 l violet | 3.25 | 1.50 |
| **C180** | AP64 | 5 l rose car | 9.25 | 5.50 |
| | | *Nos. C170-C180 (11)* | 17.10 | 9.40 |

Presidential succession for the 1949-1955 term.

For overprints and surcharges see Nos. C188-C197, C206-C208, C346, C355, C419-C420, C478, C545.

Nos. C164-C169 Overprinted in Carmine

**1951, Feb. 26** ***Perf. 11x12½***

| | | | | |
|---|---|---|---|---|
| **C181** | AP60 | 16c green | .50 | .40 |
| *a.* | | Inverted overprint | 45.00 | 45.00 |
| **C182** | AP60 | 22c orange yel | .65 | .55 |
| *a.* | | Inverted overprint | 45.00 | |
| **C183** | AP60 | 40c orange | .65 | .55 |
| **C184** | AP60 | 1 l deep blue | 2.00 | 1.75 |
| **C185** | AP60 | 2 l lilac | 3.75 | 3.25 |
| *a.* | | Inverted overprint | 60.00 | |
| **C186** | AP60 | 5 l brown | 32.50 | 29.00 |
| | | *Nos. C181-C186 (6)* | 40.05 | 35.50 |

**Souvenir Sheets**

**Same Overprint in Carmine on Nos. C99 and C100**

***Perf. 12***

| | | | | |
|---|---|---|---|---|
| **C187** | AP26 | Sheet of 4 | 8.00 | 4.75 |
| *a.* | | Imperf. | *250.00* | *250.00* |

UPU, 75th anniv. (in 1949).

Nos. C170 to C179 Overprinted in Carmine

**1951, Feb. 27** ***Perf. 12***

| | | | | |
|---|---|---|---|---|
| **C188** | AP61 | 1c deep blue | .25 | .25 |
| **C189** | AP62 | 2c rose car | .25 | .25 |
| **C190** | AP62 | 5c deep blue | .25 | .25 |
| **C191** | AP62 | 9c sepia | .25 | .25 |
| **C192** | AP62 | 15c red brown | .25 | .25 |
| **C193** | AP63 | 21c gray black | .25 | .25 |
| **C194** | AP64 | 30c olive gray | .60 | .30 |
| **C195** | AP64 | 40c slate gray | .90 | .60 |
| **C196** | AP61 | 1 l red brown | 2.25 | 1.50 |
| **C197** | AP62 | 2 l violet | 7.25 | 5.00 |
| | | *Nos. C188-C197 (10)* | 12.50 | 8.90 |

Founding of Central Bank, July 1, 1950.

Discovery of America AP65

Queen Isabella I — AP66

2c, 1 l, Columbus at court. 8c, Surrender of Granada. 30c, Queen Isabella offering her jewels.

***Perf. 13½x14, 14x13½***

**1952, Oct. 11 Engr. Unwmk.**

| | | | | |
|---|---|---|---|---|
| **C198** | AP65 | 1c red org & blk | .25 | .25 |
| **C199** | AP65 | 2c bl & red brn | .25 | .25 |
| **C200** | AP65 | 8c dk grn & dk brown | .25 | .25 |
| **C201** | AP66 | 16c dk bl & blk | .40 | .25 |
| **C202** | AP65 | 30c pur & dk grn | .70 | .70 |
| **C203** | AP65 | 1 l dp car & blk | 1.75 | 1.40 |
| **C204** | AP65 | 2 l brn & vio | 4.25 | 3.50 |
| **C205** | AP66 | 5 l rose lil & ol | 9.25 | 8.75 |
| | | *Nos. C198-C205 (8)* | 17.10 | 15.35 |

500th birth anniv. of Isabella I of Spain.

For overprints and surcharges see Nos. C209-C221, C377-C378, C404-C406, C489, CO52-CO59.

**No. C175 Surcharged in Carmine**

**1953, May 13** ***Perf. 12***

| | | | | |
|---|---|---|---|---|
| **C206** | AP63 | 5c on 21c gray blk | .25 | .25 |
| **C207** | AP63 | 8c on 21c gray blk | .55 | .25 |
| **C208** | AP63 | 16c on 21c gray blk | .95 | .25 |
| | | *Nos. C206-C208 (3)* | 1.75 | .75 |

Nos. CO52-CO54 Surcharged "HABILITADO 1953" and New Value in Red

**1953, Dec. 8** ***Perf. 13½x14, 14x13½***

| | | | | |
|---|---|---|---|---|
| **C209** | AP65 | 10c on 1c | .25 | .25 |
| *a.* | | Inverted surcharge | 50.00 | 50.00 |
| **C210** | AP65 | 12c on 1c | .25 | .25 |
| **C211** | AP65 | 15c on 2c | .30 | .25 |
| **C212** | AP65 | 20c on 2c | .50 | .30 |
| **C213** | AP65 | 24c on 2c | .50 | .30 |
| *a.* | | Inverted surcharge | 50.00 | 50.00 |
| **C214** | AP65 | 25c on 2c | .50 | .30 |
| **C215** | AP65 | 30c on 8c | .60 | .30 |
| **C216** | AP65 | 35c on 8c | .70 | .45 |
| **C217** | AP65 | 50c on 8c | .80 | .45 |
| **C218** | AP65 | 60c on 8c | 1.00 | .90 |

**Same Overprint on Nos. CO57-CO59**

| | | | | |
|---|---|---|---|---|
| **C219** | AP65 | 1 l dk grn & dk brown | 3.00 | 2.25 |
| **C220** | AP65 | 2 l bl & red brn | 6.75 | 5.50 |
| **C221** | AP66 | 5 l red org & blk | 16.00 | 13.00 |
| *a.* | | Date inverted | 150.00 | |
| | | *Nos. C209-C221 (13)* | 31.15 | 24.50 |

Flags of UN and Honduras AP67

2c, UN emblem. 3c, UN building. 5c, Shield. 15c, Juan Manuel Galvez. 30c, UNICEF. 1 l, UNRRA. 2 l, UNESCO. 5 l, FAO.

**Engraved; Center of 1c Litho.**

**1953, Dec. 18** ***Perf. 12½***

**Frames in Black**

| | | | | |
|---|---|---|---|---|
| **C222** | AP67 | 1c ultra & vio bl | .25 | .25 |
| **C223** | AP67 | 2c blue | .25 | .25 |
| **C224** | AP67 | 3c rose lilac | .25 | .25 |
| **C225** | AP67 | 5c green | .25 | .25 |
| **C226** | AP67 | 15c red brown | .40 | .25 |
| **C227** | AP67 | 30c brown | .85 | .50 |
| **C228** | AP67 | 1 l dp carmine | 6.75 | 4.50 |
| **C229** | AP67 | 2 l orange | 8.75 | 6.25 |
| **C230** | AP67 | 5 l blue green | 19.00 | 15.00 |
| | | *Nos. C222-C230 (9)* | 36.75 | 27.50 |

Issued to honor the United Nations.

For overprints and surcharges see Nos. C231-C249, C331-C335, C472, C490, CO60-CO68.

Nos. CO60-CO66 Overprinted in Red

**1955, Feb. 23 Unwmk.** ***Perf. 12½***

**Frames in Black**

| | | | | |
|---|---|---|---|---|
| **C231** | AP67 | 1c ultra & vio bl | .25 | .25 |
| **C232** | AP67 | 2c dp blue grn | .25 | .25 |
| **C233** | AP67 | 3c orange | .25 | .25 |
| **C234** | AP67 | 5c dp carmine | .25 | .25 |
| **C235** | AP67 | 15c dk brown | .35 | .35 |
| **C236** | AP67 | 30c purple | 1.00 | .90 |
| **C237** | AP67 | 1 l olive gray | 20.00 | 15.00 |

Overprint exists inverted on 1c, 3c.

Nos. C231 to C233 Surcharged in Black

| | | | | |
|---|---|---|---|---|
| **C238** | AP67 | 8c on 1c | .25 | .25 |
| **C239** | AP67 | 10c on 2c | .25 | .25 |
| **C240** | AP67 | 12c on 3c | .25 | .25 |
| | | *Nos. C231-C240 (10)* | 23.10 | 18.00 |

50th anniv. of the founding of Rotary International (Nos. C231-C240).

**Nos. CO60-CO63, C226-C230 Overprinted**

**1956, July 14 Unwmk.** ***Perf. 12½***

**Frames in Black**

| | | | | |
|---|---|---|---|---|
| **C241** | AP67 | 1c ultra & vio bl | .25 | .25 |
| **C242** | AP67 | 2c dp bl grn | .25 | .25 |
| **C243** | AP67 | 3c orange | .25 | .25 |
| **C244** | AP67 | 5c dp car | .30 | .25 |
| **C245** | AP67 | 15c red brn | .35 | .30 |
| **C246** | AP67 | 30c brown | .55 | .40 |
| **C247** | AP67 | 1 l dp car | 4.00 | 2.75 |
| **C248** | AP67 | 2 l orange | 5.75 | 4.75 |
| **C249** | AP67 | 5 l bl grn | 15.00 | 14.00 |
| | | *Nos. C241-C249 (9)* | 26.70 | 23.20 |

10th anniv. of UN (in 1955). The red "OFICIAL" overprint was not obliterated.

The "ONU" overprint exists inverted on 1c, 3c, 5c and 1-lempira.

Basilica of Suyapa AP68

Pres. Julio Lozano Diaz — AP69

3c, Southern Highway. 4c, Genoveva Guardiola de Estrada Palma. 5c, Maria Josefa

Lastiri de Morazan. 8c, Landscape and cornucopia (5-Year Plan). 10c, National Stadium. 12c, US School. 15c, Central Bank. 20c, Legislative Palace. 25c, Development Bank (projected). 30c, Toncontin Airport. 40c, Juan Ramon Molina Bridge. 50c, Peace Monument. 60c, Treasury Palace. 1 l, Blood bank. 2 l, Communications Building. 5 l, Presidential Palace.

**Engraved; #C255 Litho.**

**1956, Oct. 3 *Perf. 13x12½, 12½x13***

**C250** AP68 1c black & vio bl .25 .25
**C251** AP69 2c black & dk bl .25 .25
**C252** AP68 3c black & brown .25 .25
**C253** AP69 4c black & lilac .25 .25
**C254** AP69 5c black & dk red .25 .25
**C255** AP68 8c brown & multi .25 .25
**C256** AP68 10c black & emer .25 .25
**C257** AP68 12c black & green .25 .25
**C258** AP69 15c dk red & blk .30 .25
**C259** AP68 20c black & ultra .30 .25
**C260** AP69 24c black & lil .35 .25
**C261** AP68 25c black & green .40 .25
**C262** AP68 30c black & car rose .40 .25
**C263** AP68 40c black & red brn .50 .25
**C264** AP69 50c black & bl grn .60 .35
**C265** AP68 60c black & orange .80 .45
**C266** AP68 1 l black & rose vio 2.00 1.00
**C267** AP69 2 l black & mag 3.75 2.25
**C268** AP69 5 l black & brn car 9.00 5.00
*Nos. C250-C268 (19)* 20.40 12.55

Issued to publicize the Five-Year Plan.
For overprints and surcharges see Nos. C414-C418, C491-C493, C537-C538, C542, C550.
Types AP68 and AP69 in different colors, overprinted "OFICIAL," see Nos. CO69-CO87.

Flag of Honduras AP70

Designs: 2c, 8c, Monument and mountains. 10c, 15c, 1 l, Lempira. 30c, 2 l, Coat of arms.

**1957, Oct. 21 Litho. *Perf. 13***
**Frames in Black**

**C269** AP70 1c buff & ultra .25 .25
**C270** AP70 2c org, pur & emerald .25 .25
**C271** AP70 5c pink & ultra .25 .25
**C272** AP70 8c org, vio & ol .25 .25
**C273** AP70 10c violet & brown .25 .25
**C274** AP70 12c lt grn & ultra .25 .25
**C275** AP70 15c green & brown .30 .25
**C276** AP70 30c pink & slate .45 .25
**C277** AP70 1 l blue & brown 2.00 1.50
**C278** AP70 2 l lt grn & slate 3.75 3.00
*Nos. C269-C278 (10)* 8.00 6.50

First anniv. of the October revolution.
For overprints and surcharge, see Nos. C551, CO88-CO97.

---

Control marks were handstamped in violet on many current stamps in July and August, 1958, following fire and theft of stamps at Tegucigalpa in April.

All post offices were ordered to honor only stamps overprinted with the facsimile signature of their departmental revenue administrator. Honduras has 18 departments.

---

Flags of Honduras and US — AP71

**1958, Oct. 2 Engr. *Perf. 12***
**Flags in National Colors**

**C279** AP71 1c light blue .25 .25
**C280** AP71 2c red .25 .25
**C281** AP71 5c green .25 .25
**C282** AP71 10c brown .25 .25
**C283** AP71 20c orange .40 .25
**C284** AP71 30c deep rose .45 .25
**C285** AP71 50c gray .60 .40
**C286** AP71 1 l orange yel 1.25 1.00
**C287** AP71 2 l gray olive 2.40 2.00
**C288** AP71 5 l vio blue 5.50 4.00
*Nos. C279-C288 (10)* 11.60 8.90

Honduras Institute of Inter-American Culture. The proceeds were intended for the Binational Center, Tegucigalpa.
For overprints see Nos. C320-C324.

Abraham Lincoln — AP72

Lincoln's Birthplace AP73

Designs: 3c, 50c, Gettysburg Address. 5c, 1 l, Freeing the slaves. 10c, 2 l, Assassination. 12c, 5 l, Memorial, Washington.

**1959, Feb. 12 Unwmk. *Perf. 13½***
**Flags in National Colors**

**C289** AP72 1c green .25 .25
**C290** AP73 2c dark blue .25 .25
**C291** AP73 3c purple .25 .25
**C292** AP73 5c dk carmine .25 .25
**C293** AP73 10c black .30 .25
**C294** AP73 12c dark brown .30 .25
**C295** AP72 15c red orange .40 .25
**C296** AP73 25c dull pur .60 .40
**C297** AP73 50c ultra .75 .65
**C298** AP73 1 l red brown 1.50 1.40
**C299** AP73 2 l gray olive 2.40 1.75
**C300** AP73 5 l ocher 5.50 5.00
*a.* Miniature sheet 10.00 10.00
*Nos. C289-C300 (12)* 12.75 10.95

Birth sesquicentennial of Abraham Lincoln.
No. C300a contains one each of the 1c, 3c, 10c, 25c, 1 l and 5 l, imperf.
For overprints and surcharges see Nos. C316-C319, C325-C330, C345, C347-C348, C352, C356-C364, C494-C495, C539-C541, C552-C553.
Types AP72 and AP73 in different colors, overprinted "OFICIAL," see Nos. CO98-CO109.

Constitution AP74

Designs: 2c, 12c, Inauguration of Pres. Villeda Morales, horiz. 3c, 25c, Pres. Ramon Villeda Morales. 5c, 50c, Allegory of Second Republic (Torch and olive branches).

**Engr.; Seal Litho. on 1c, 10c**

**1959, Dec. 21 *Perf. 13½***

**C301** AP74 1c red brn, car & ultra .25 .25
**C302** AP74 2c bister brn .25 .25
**C303** AP74 3c ultra .25 .25
**C304** AP74 5c orange .25 .25
**C305** AP74 10c dull green, car & ultra .25 .25
**C306** AP74 12c rose red .35 .25
**C307** AP74 25c dull lilac .85 .25
**C308** AP74 50c dark blue 1.40 .50
*Nos. C301-C308 (8)* 3.85 2.25

Second Republic of Honduras, 2nd anniv.
For surcharge see No. C543.

King Alfonso XIII and Map AP75

Designs: 2c, 1906 award of King Alfonso XIII of Spain. 5c, Arbitration commission delivering its award, 1907. 10c, Intl. Court of Justice. 20c, Verdict of the Court, 1960. 50c, Pres. Morales, Foreign Minister Puerto and map. 1 l, Pres. Davila and Pres. Morales.

**1961, Nov. 18 Engr. *Perf. 14½x14***

**C309** AP75 1c dark blue .25 .25
**C310** AP75 2c magenta .25 .25
**C311** AP75 5c deep green .25 .25
**C312** AP75 10c brn orange .25 .25
**C313** AP75 20c vermilion .40 .35
**C314** AP75 50c brown 1.00 .55
**C315** AP75 1 l vio black 1.50 1.00
*Nos. C309-C315 (7)* 3.90 2.90

Judgment of the Intl. Court of Justice at The Hague, Nov. 18, 1960, returning a disputed territory to Honduras from Nicaragua.

Nos. C295-C297 and CO105 Surcharged

**1964, Apr. 7 *Perf. 13½***
**Flags in National Colors**

**C316** AP72 6c on 15c red org .25 .25
**C317** AP73 8c on 25c dull pur .25 .25
**C318** AP73 10c on 50c ultra .30 .25
**C319** AP73 20c on 25c black .75 .40
*Nos. C316-C319 (4)* 1.55 1.15

The red "OFICIAL" overprint on No. C319 was not obliterated.
See Nos. C345-C355, C419-C421.

Nos. C279-C281, C284 and C287 Overprinted: "FAO / Lucha Contra / el Hambre"

**1964, Mar. 23 Unwmk. *Perf. 12***
**Flags in National Colors**

**C320** AP71 1c light blue .25 .25
**C321** AP71 2c red .25 .25
**C322** AP71 5c green .25 .25
**C323** AP71 30c deep rose 1.10 .75
**C324** AP71 2 l gray olive 5.75 5.50
*Nos. C320-C324 (5)* 7.60 7.00

FAO "Freedom from Hunger Campaign" (1963).

Nos. CO98-CO101, CO104 and CO106 Overprinted in Blue or Black: "IN MEMORIAM / JOHN F. KENNEDY / 22 NOVEMBRE 1963"

**1964, May 29 *Perf. 13½***
**Flags in National Colors**

**C325** AP72 1c ocher (Bl) .25 .25
**C326** AP73 2c gray ol (Bl) .25 .25
**C327** AP73 3c red brn (Bl) .35 .25
**C328** AP73 5c ultra (Bk) .50 .30
**C329** AP72 15c dk brn (Bl) 2.00 1.25
**C330** AP73 50c dk car (Bl) 10.50 6.25
*Nos. C325-C330 (6)* 13.85 8.55

Pres. John F. Kennedy (1917-63). The red "OFICIAL" overprint was not obliterated. The same overprint was applied to the stamps in miniature sheet No. C300a and seal of Honduras and Alliance for Progress emblem added in margin. Value $65.

Nos. C222-C224, C226 and CO67 Overprinted with Olympic Rings and "1964"

**Engr.; Center of 1c Litho.**

**1964, July 23 *Perf. 12½***
**Frames in Black**

**C331** AP67 1c ultra & vio bl .25 .25
**C332** AP67 2c blue .25 .25
**C333** AP67 3c rose lilac .25 .25
**C334** AP67 15c red brown .50 .50
**C335** AP67 2 l lilac rose 6.25 6.25
*Nos. C331-C335 (5)* 7.50 7.50

18th Olympic Games, Tokyo, Oct. 10-25. The red "OFICIAL" overprint on No. C335 was not obliterated.
The same overprint was applied in black to the 6 stamps in #CO108a, with additional rings and "1964" in margins of souvenir sheet. Value $50.

View of Copan AP76

Designs: 2c, 12c, Stone marker from Copan. 5c, 1 l, Mayan ball player (stone). 8c, 2 l, Olympic Stadium, Tokyo.

**Unwmk.**

**1964, Nov. 27 Photo. *Perf. 14***
**Black Design and Inscription**

**C336** AP76 1c yellow grn .25 .25
**C337** AP76 2c pale rose lil .25 .25
**C338** AP76 5c light ultra .25 .25
**C339** AP76 8c bluish green .30 .25
**C340** AP76 10c buff .40 .30
**C341** AP76 12c lemon .60 .35
**C342** AP76 1 l light ocher 1.60 1.25
**C343** AP76 2 l pale ol grn 4.25 3.50
**C344** AP76 3 l rose 4.75 4.00
*Nos. C336-C344 (9)* 12.65 10.40

18th Olympic Games, Tokyo, Oct. 10-25.
Perf. and imperf. souvenir sheets of four exist containing one each of Nos. C338-C339, C341 and C344. Size: 129x110mm. Values: perf $40; imperf $50.
For overprints, see Nos. CO111-CO119.

Nos. C292, C174, CO106, CO104, C124-C125, C165, CO105, C167-C168 and C178 Surcharged

**1964-65**

**C345** AP73 4c on 5c dk car, bl & red .25 .25
**C346** AP62 10c on 15c red brn .25 .25
**C347** AP73 10c on 50c dk car, bl & red .25 .25
**C348** AP72 12c on 15c dk brn, bl & red .30 .25
**C349** AP27 12c on 16c ol gray .30 .25
**C350** AP27 12c on 21c lt blue .30 .25
**C351** AP60 12c on 22c org yel .30 .25
**C352** AP73 12c on 25c blk, bl & red .30 .25
**C353** AP60 30c on 1 l dp blue .50 .25
**C354** AP60 40c on 2 l lilac ('65) .70 .50
**C355** AP61 40c on 1 l red brown ('65) .70 .30
*Nos. C345-C355 (11)* 4.15 3.05

The red "OFICIAL" overprint on Nos. C347-C348 and C352 was not obliterated.

Nos. C289, CO99, C291-C292, C295-C296, CO106 and C299-C300 Overprinted in Black or Green: "Toma de Posesión / General / Oswaldo López A. / Junio 6, 1965"

**1965, June 6 Engr. *Perf. 13½***
**Flags in National Colors**

**C356** AP72 1c green .25 .25
**C357** AP73 2c gray ol (G) .25 .25
**C358** AP73 3c purple (G) .25 .25
**C359** AP73 5c dk car (G) .25 .25
**C360** AP72 15c red orange .35 .35
**C361** AP73 25c dull pur (G) .50 .50
**C362** AP73 50c dk carmine (G) 1.00 1.00
**C363** AP73 2 l gray olive (G) 4.00 4.00
**C364** AP73 5 l ocher (G) 9.50 9.50
*Nos. C356-C364 (9)* 16.35 16.35

Inauguration of Gen. Oswaldo López Arellano as president. The red "OFICIAL" overprint on Nos. C357 and C362 was not obliterated.

Ambulance and Maltese Cross AP77

Designs (Maltese Cross and): 5c, Hospital of Knights of Malta. 12c, Patients treated in village. 1 l, Map of Honduras.

**1965, Aug. 30 Litho. *Perf. 12x11***
**C365** AP77 1c ultra .35 .25
**C366** AP77 5c dark green .40 .30
**C367** AP77 12c dark brown .55 .50
**C368** AP77 1 l brown 2.25 1.90
*Nos. C365-C368 (4)* 3.55 2.95

Knights of Malta; campaign against leprosy.

Father Manuel de Jesus Subirana — AP78

Designs: 1c, Jicaque Indian. 2c, Preaching to the Indians. 10c, Msgr. Juan de Jesus Zepeda. 12c, Pope Pius IX. 20c, Tomb of Father Subirana, Yore. 1 l, Mission church. 2 l, Jicaque mother and child.

***Perf. 13½x14***

**1965, July 27 Litho. Unwmk.**
**C369** AP78 1c multicolored .25 .25
**C370** AP78 2c multicolored .25 .25
**C371** AP78 8c multicolored .25 .25
**C372** AP78 10c multicolored .25 .25
**C373** AP78 12c multicolored .25 .25
**C374** AP78 20c multicolored .45 .30
**C375** AP78 1 l multicolored 2.00 1.50
**C376** AP78 2 l multicolored 4.00 3.00
*a.* Souv. sheet of 4, #C371, C373, C375-C376 20.00 20.00
*Nos. C369-C376 (8)* 7.70 6.05

Centenary (in 1964) of the death of Father Manuel de Jesus Subirana (1807-64), Spanish missionary to the Central American Indians.

For overprints and surcharges see Nos. C380-C386, C407-C413, C487-C488, C554.

Nos. C198-C199 and C168 Overprinted: "IN MEMORIAM / Sir Winston Churchill / 1874-1965."

**1965, Dec. 20 Engr. *Perf. 13½x14***
**C377** AP65 1c red org & blk .30 .30
**C378** AP65 2c blue & red brn .80 .80
**C379** AP60 2 l lilac 7.00 7.00
*Nos. C377-C379 (3)* 8.10 8.10

Sir Winston Spencer Churchill (1874-1965), statesman and World War II leader.

Nos. C369-C375 Overprinted

**1966, Mar. 10 Litho. *Perf. 13½x14***
**C380** AP78 1c multicolored .25 .25
**C381** AP78 2c multicolored .25 .25
**C382** AP78 8c multicolored .25 .25
**C383** AP78 10c multicolored .25 .25
**C384** AP78 12c multicolored .30 .25
**C385** AP78 20c multicolored .35 .35
**C386** AP78 1 l multicolored 3.25 3.25
*Nos. C380-C386 (7)* 4.90 4.85

Visit of Pope Paul VI to the UN, New York City, Oct. 4, 1965.

Stamp of 1866, #1 — AP79

Tomas Estrada Palma — AP80

Post Office, Tegucigalpa AP81

Designs: 2c, Air post stamp of 1925, #C1. 5c, Locomotive. 6c, 19th cent. mail transport with mules. 7c, 19th cent. mail room. 8c, Sir Rowland Hill. 9c, Modern mail truck. 10c, Gen. Oswaldo Lopez Arellano. 12c, Postal emblem. 15c, Heinrich von Stephan. 20c, Mail plane. 30c, Flag of Honduras. 40c, Coat of Arms. 1 l, UPU monument, Bern. 2 l, José Maria Medina.

***Perf. 14½x14, 14x14½***

**1966, May 31 Litho. Unwmk.**
**C387** AP79 1c gold, blk & grnsh gray .25 .25
**C388** AP79 2c org, blk & lt bl .25 .25
**C389** AP80 3c brt rose, gold & dp plum .25 .25
**C390** AP81 4c bl, gold & blk .25 .25
**C391** AP81 5c pink, gold & blk .75 .25
**C392** AP81 6c lil, gold & blk .25 .25
**C393** AP81 7c lt bl grn, gold & black .25 .25
**C394** AP80 8c lt bl, gold & blk .25 .25
**C395** AP81 9c lt ultra, gold & black .25 .25
**C396** AP80 10c cit, gold & blk .25 .25
**C397** AP79 12c gold, blk, yel & emerald .25 .25
**C398** AP80 15c brt pink, gold & dp claret .40 .40
**C399** AP81 20c org, gold & blk .45 .45
**C400** AP79 30c gold & bl .55 .55
**C401** AP79 40c multi .90 .80
**C402** AP79 1 l emer, gold & dk green 2.00 1.50
**C403** AP80 2 l gray, gold & black 4.25 4.25
*a.* Souv. sheet of 6, #C387-C388, C396-C397, C402-C403 6.75 6.75
*Nos. C387-C403 (17)* 11.80 10.70

Centenary of the first Honduran postage stamp. #C403a exists perf. and imperf. See #CE3. For surcharges see #C473-C474, C479, C486, C496.

Nos. CO53, C201 and C204 Overprinted: "CAMPEONATO DE FOOTBALL Copa Mundial 1966 Inglaterra-Alemania Wembley, Julio 30"

***Perf. 13½x14, 14x13½***

**1966, Nov. 25 Engr.**
**C404** AP65 2c brown & vio .25 .25
**C405** AP66 16c dk bl & blk .30 .30
**C406** AP65 2 l brn & vio 8.50 8.50
*Nos. C404-C406 (3)* 9.05 9.05

Final game between England and Germany in the World Soccer Cup Championship, Wembley, July 30, 1966. The overprint on the 2c and 2 l is in 5 lines, it is in 8 lines on the 16c. There is no hyphen between "Inglaterra" and "Alemania" on the 16c.

Nos. C369-C371 and C373-C376 Overprinted in Red: "CONMEMORATIVA / del XX Aniversario / ONU 1966"

**1967, Jan. 31 Litho. *Perf. 13½x14***
**C407** AP78 1c multicolored .25 .25
**C408** AP78 2c multicolored .25 .25
**C409** AP78 8c multicolored .30 .30
**C410** AP78 12c multicolored .50 .40
**C411** AP78 20c multicolored .65 .55
**C412** AP78 1 l multicolored 1.50 1.50
**C413** AP78 2 l multicolored 3.50 3.25
*Nos. C407-C413 (7)* 6.95 6.50

UN, 20th anniversary.

Nos. C250, C252, C258, C261 and C267 Overprinted in Red: "Siméon Cañas y Villacorta / Libertador de los esclavos / en Centro America / 1767-1967"

**1967, Feb. 27 Engr.**
**C414** AP68 1c blk & vio bl .25 .25
**C415** AP68 3c blk & brown .25 .25
**C416** AP68 15c dk red & blk .35 .35
**C417** AP68 25c blk & grn 1.00 .70
**C418** AP69 2 l blk & mag 2.75 2.50
*Nos. C414-C418 (5)* 4.60 4.05

Birth bicentenary of Father José Siméon Canas y Villacorta, D.D. (1767-1838), emancipator of the Central American slaves. The overprint is in 6 lines on the 2 l, in 4 lines on all others.

Nos. C178-C179 and CE2 Surcharged

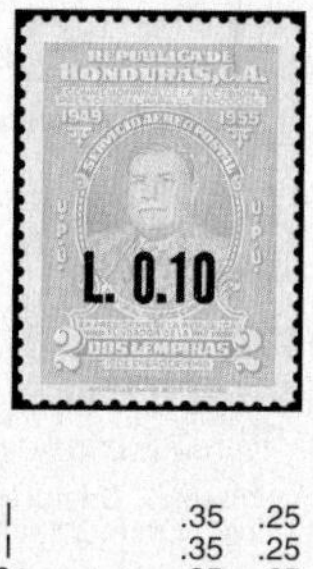


**1967**
**C419** AP61 10c on 1 l .35 .25
**C420** AP62 10c on 2 l .35 .25
**C421** APSD1 10c on 20c .35 .25
*Nos. C419-C421 (3)* 1.05 .75

José Cecilio del Valle, Honduras AP82

Designs: 12c, Ruben Dario, Nicaragua. 14c, Batres Montufar, Guatemala. 20c, Francisco Antonio Gavidia, El Salvador. 30c, Juan Mora Fernandez, Costa Rica. 40c, Federation Emblem with map of Americas. 50c, Map of Central America.

**1967, Aug. 4 Litho. *Perf. 13***
**C422** AP82 11c gold, ultra & blk .25 .25
**C423** AP82 12c lt bl, yel & blk .25 .25
**C424** AP82 14c sil, grn & blk .25 .25
**C425** AP82 20c pink, grn & blk .25 .25
**C426** AP82 30c bluish lil, yel & black .40 .35
**C427** AP82 40c pur, lt bl & gold .70 .70
**C428** AP82 50c lem, grn & car rose .70 .70
*Nos. C422-C428 (7)* 2.80 2.75

Founding of the Federation of Central American Journalists.

For surcharges see Nos. C475-C476.

Olympic Rings, Flags of Mexico and Honduras AP83

Olympic Rings and Winners of 1964 Olympics: 2c, Like 1c. 5c, Italian flag and boxers. 10c, French flag and women skiers. 12c, German flag and equestrian team. 50c, British flag and women runners. 1 l, US flag and runners (Bob Hayes).

**1968, Mar. 4 Litho. *Perf. 14x13½***
**C429** AP83 1c gold & multi .25 .25
**C430** AP83 2c gold & multi .25 .25
**C431** AP83 5c gold & multi .25 .25
**C432** AP83 10c gold & multi .30 .25
**C433** AP83 12c gold & multi .50 .25
**C434** AP83 50c gold & multi 3.25 3.25
**C435** AP83 1 l gold & multi 6.25 6.25
*Nos. C429-C435 (7)* 11.05 10.75

19th Olympic Games, Mexico City, Oct. 12-27.

Exist imperf. Value $45.

Perf. and imperf. souvenir sheets of 2 exist containing 20c and 40c stamps in design of 1c. Values: perf $8; imperf $16.

For surcharge see No. C499.

John F. Kennedy, Rocket at Cape Kennedy AP84

ITU Emblem and: 2c, Radar and telephone. 3c, Radar and television set. 5c, Radar and globe showing Central America. 8c, Communications satellite. 10c, 20c, like 1c.

**1968, Nov. 28 *Perf. 14x13½***
**C436** AP84 1c vio & multi .25 .25
**C437** AP84 2c sil & multi .25 .25
**C438** AP84 3c multicolored .35 .35
**C439** AP84 5c org & multi .40 .40
**C440** AP84 8c multicolored .50 .50
**C441** AP84 10c olive & multi .55 .55
**C442** AP84 20c multicolored .70 .70
*Nos. C436-C442 (7)* 3.00 3.00

ITU, cent. A 30c in design of 2c, a 1 l in design of 5c and a 1.50 l in design of 1c exist; also two souvenir sheets, one containing 10c, 50c and 75c, the other one 1.50 l.

For overprints see Nos. C446-C453.

Nos. C436, C441-C442 Overprinted: "In Memoriam / Robert F. Kennedy / 1925-1968"

**1968, Dec. 23**
**C446** AP84 1c vio & multi .25 .25
**C447** AP84 10c olive & multi .50 .50
**C448** AP84 20c multicolored .80 .80
*Nos. C446-C448 (3)* 1.55 1.55

In memory of Robert F. Kennedy. Same overprint was also applied to a 1.50 l and to a souvenir sheet containing one 1.50 l. Value, souvenir sheet $6.

Nos. C437-C440 Overprinted in Blue or Red with Olympic Rings and: "Medalias de Oro / Mexico 1968"

**1969, Mar. 3**
**C450** AP84 2c multi (Bl) .50 .50
**C451** AP84 3c multi (Bl) 1.00 1.00
**C452** AP84 5c multi (Bl) 1.50 1.50
**C453** AP84 8c multi (R) 2.00 2.00
*Nos. C450-C453 (4)* 5.00 5.00

Gold medal winners in 19th Olympic Games, Mexico City. The same red overprint was also applied to a 30c and a 1 l. The souvenir sheet of 3 noted after No. C442 exists with this overprint in black. Value, souvenir sheet $6.

Rocket Blast-off AP85

Designs: 10c, Close-up view of moon. 12c, Spacecraft, horiz. 20c, Astronaut and module on moon, horiz. 24c, Lunar landing module.

***Perf. 14½x13½, 13½x14***

**1969, Oct. 29**
**C454** AP85 5c multicolored .25 .25
**C455** AP85 10c multicolored .30 .30
**C456** AP85 12c multicolored .40 .40
**C457** AP85 20c multicolored .50 .50
**C458** AP85 24c multicolored 1.00 1.00
*Nos. C454-C458 (5)* 2.45 2.45

Man's first landing on the moon, July 20, 1969. A 30c showing re-entry of capsule, a 1 l in design of 20c and a 1.50 l in design of 24c exist. Two souvenir sheets exist, one containing #C454-C455 and 1.50 l, and the other #C456, 30c and 1 l.

For the safe return of Apollo 13, overprints were applied in 1970 to #C454-C458, the 3 unlisted denominations and the 2 souvenir sheets. Value of 2 souvenir sheets $20.

For overprints and surcharges see Nos. C500-C504, C555.

Nos. C224, C393, C395, C422, C424, CE2 and C178 Surcharged with New Value

**1970, Feb. 20** **Engr.; Litho.**

**C472** AP67 4c on 3c blk & rose lil .25 .25
**C473** AP81 5c on 7c multi .25 .25
**C474** AP81 10c on 9c multi .30 .25
**C475** AP82 10c on 11c multi .30 .25
**C476** AP82 12c on 14c multi .35 .25
**C477** APSD1 12c on 20c blk & red .35 .25
**C478** AP61 12c on 1 l red brn .35 .25
*Nos. C472-C478 (7)* 2.15 1.75

No. CE3 Overprinted "HABILITADO"

**1970** **Litho.** ***Perf. 14x14½***

**C479** AP81 20c bis brn, brn & gold .75 .35

Julio Adolfo Sanhueza AP86

Emblems, Map and Flag of Honduras — AP87

Designs: 8c, Rigoberto Ordoñez Rodriguez. 12c, Forest Fire Brigade emblem (with map of Honduras) and emblems of fire fighters, FAO and Alliance for Progress, horiz. 1 l, Flags of Honduras, UN and US, Arms of Honduras and emblems as on 12c.

***Perf. 14½x14, 14x14½***

**1970, Aug. 15** **Litho.**

**C480** AP86 5c gold, emer & ind .30 .25
**C481** AP86 8c gold, org brn & indigo .40 .25
**C482** AP87 12c bl & multi .50 .25
**C483** AP87 20c yel & multi .70 .25
**C484** AP87 1 l gray & multi 3.50 1.75
*a.* Souvenir sheet of 5 3.00 2.00
*Nos. C480-C484 (5)* 5.40 2.75

Campaign against forest fires and in memory of the men who lost their lives fighting forest fires. No. C484a contains 5 imperf. stamps with simulated perforations and without gum similar to Nos. C480-C484. Sold for 1.45 l.

For surcharges see Nos. C497-C498.

Hotel Honduras Maya AP88

**1970, Oct. 24** **Litho.** ***Perf. 14***

**C485** AP88 12c sky blue & blk .30 .25

Hotel Honduras Maya, Tegucigalpa, opening.

Stamps of 1952-1968 Surcharged

**1971** **Litho.; Engr.**

**C486** AP79 4c on 1c (#C387) .25 .25
**C487** AP78 5c on 1c (#C369) .30 .25
**C488** AP78 8c on 2c (#C370) .65 .30
**C489** AP65 10c on 2c (#C251) .80 .40
**C490** AP67 10c on 3c (#C224) .80 .40
*a.* Inverted surcharge .80 .40
**C491** AP68 10c on 3c (#C252) .80 .40
**C492** AP68 10c on 3c (#CO71) .80 .40
**C493** AP69 10c on 2c (#C251) .80 .40
**C494** AP73 10c on 2c (#CO99) .80 .40
**C495** AP73 10c on 3c (#CO100) .80 .40
**C496** AP80 10c on 3c (#C389) .80 .40
**C497** AP87 15c on 12c (#C482) 1.00 .55
**C498** AP87 30c on 12c (#C482) 1.25 .80
**C499** AP83 40c on 50c (#C434) 2.10 1.60
**C500** AP85 40c on 24c (#C458) 2.10 1.60
*Nos. C486-C500 (15)* 14.05 8.55

Red "OFICIAL" overprint was not obliterated on Nos. C492, C494-C495.

No. C491 exists with inverted surcharge.

**Nos. C454, C456-C458 Ovptd. & Srchd.**

***Perf. 14½x13½, 13½x14½***

**1972, May 15** **Litho.**

**C501** AP85 5c multi .70 .40
**C502** AP85 12c multi 1.50 .75
**C503** AP85 1 l on 20c multi 3.50 3.00
**C504** AP85 2 l on 24c multi 6.00 5.00
*Nos. C501-C504 (4)* 11.70 9.15

Masonic Grand Lodge of Honduras, 50th anniv. Overprint varies to fit stamp shape.

Soldier's Bay, Guanaja AP89

Designs: 5c, 7c, 9c, 10c, 2 l, vertical.

**1972, May 19** ***Perf. 13***

**C505** AP89 4c shown .25 .25
**C506** AP89 5c Taps .25 .25
**C507** AP89 6c Yojoa Lake .25 .25
**C508** AP89 7c Banana Carrier, by Roberto Aguilar .25 .25
**C509** AP89 8c Military parade .25 .25
**C510** AP89 9c Orchid, national flower .25 .25
**C511** AP89 10c like 9c .25 .25
**C512** AP89 12c Soldier with machine gun .25 .25
**C513** AP89 15c Sunset over beach .30 .25
**C514** AP89 20c Litter bearers .30 .25
**C515** AP89 30c Landscape, by Antonio Velasquez .50 .25
**C516** AP89 40c Ruins of Copan .75 .40
*a.* Souv. sheet of 4, #C508, C513, C515-C516 2.00 2.00
**C517** AP89 50c Girl from Huacal, by Pablo Zelaya Sierra .60 .35
*a.* Souv. sheet of 4, #C506-C507, C514, C517 2.00 2.00
**C518** AP89 1 l Trujillo Bay 1.50 1.00
*a.* Souv. sheet of 4, #C505, C509, C512, C518 2.75 2.75
**C519** AP89 2 l Orchid, national flower 4.00 3.00
*a.* Souv. sheet of 3, #C510-C511, C519 6.50 6.50
*Nos. C505-C519,CE4 (16)* 10.65 7.85

Sesquicentennial of independence (stamps inscribed 1970).

For surcharge see No. CE5.

Sister Maria Rosa and Child — AP90

Designs: 15c, SOS Children's Village emblem, horiz. 30c, Father José Trinidad Reyes. 40c, Kennedy Center, first SOS village in Central America, horiz. 1 l, Boy.

***Perf. 13½x13, 13x13½***

**1972, Nov. 10** **Photo.**

**C520** AP90 10c grn, gold & brn .25 .25
**C521** AP90 15c grn, gold & brn .25 .25
**C522** AP90 30c grn, gold & brn .40 .25
**C523** AP90 40c grn, gold & brn .50 .25
**C524** AP90 1 l grn, gold & brn 2.00 1.50
*Nos. C520-C524 (5)* 3.40 2.50

Children's Villages in Honduras (Intl. SOS movement to save homeless children).

For overprints and surcharges see #C531, C534-C536, C546-C549, C556, C560-C561.

Map of Honduras and Society Emblem AP91

Design: 12c, Map of Honduras, emblems of National Geographic Institute and Interamerican Geodesic Service.

**1973, Mar. 27** **Litho.** ***Perf. 13***

**C525** AP91 10c multicolored .55 .30
**C526** AP91 12c multicolored .65 .30

25th annivs. of Natl. Cartographic Service (10c) and of joint cartographic work (12c).

For overprints and surcharges see Nos. C532-C533, C557-C558.

Juan Ramón Molina AP92

Designs: 8c, Illustration from Molina's book "Habitante de la Osa." 1 l, Illustration from "Tierras Mares y Cielos." 2 l, "UNESCO."

**1973, Apr. 17** **Litho.** ***Perf. 13½***

**C527** AP92 8c brn org, blk & red brn .25 .25
**C528** AP92 20c brt bl & multi .65 .25
**C529** AP92 1 l green & multi 1.50 1.00
**C530** AP92 2 l org & multi 3.25 2.75
*a.* Sheet of 4 6.00 6.00
*Nos. C527-C530 (4)* 5.65 4.25

Molina (1875-1908), poet, and 25th anniv. (in 1971) of UNESCO. #C530a contains 4 stamps similar to #C527-C530. Exists perf. & imperf.

For surcharge see No. C559.

Nos. C520-C523, C525-C526 Overprinted in Red or Black: "Censos de Población y Vivienda, marzo 1974. 1974, Año Mundial de Población"

***Perf. 13½x13, 13x13½, 13***

**1973, Dec. 28** **Photo; Litho.**

**C531** AP90 10c multi (R) .25 .25
**C532** AP91 10c multi (B) .25 .25
**C533** AP91 12c multi (B) .25 .25
**C534** AP90 15c multi (R) .25 .25
**C535** AP90 30c multi (R) .30 .25
**C536** AP90 40c multi (R) .35 .35
*Nos. C531-C536 (6)* 1.65 1.60

1974 population and housing census; World Population Year. The overprint is in 7 lines on vertical stamps, in 5 lines on horizontal.

Issues of 1947-59 Surcharged in Red or Black

***Perf. 13x12½, 13½, 11x12½, 12***

**1974, June 28** **Engr.**

**C537** AP68 2c on 1c (#C250) (R) .25 .25
**C538** AP68 2c on 1c (#CO69) .25 .25
**C539** AP72 2c on 1c (#C289) .25 .25
**C540** AP72 2c on 1c (#CO98) .25 .25
**C541** AP72 3c on 1c (#C289) .25 .25
**C542** AP68 3c on 1c (#C250) (R) .25 .25
**C543** AP74 1 l on 50c (#C308) 1.40 1.40
**C544** AP60 1 l on 2 l (#C168) 1.40 1.40
**C545** AP62 1 l on 2 l (#C179) (R) 1.40 1.40
*Nos. C537-C545 (9)* 5.70 5.70

Red "OFICIAL" overprint was not obliterated on Nos. C538 and C540.

Nos. C520-C523 Overprinted in Bright Green: "1949-1974 SOS Kinderdorfer International Honduras-Austria"

**1974, July 25** **Photo.**

**C546** AP90 10c grn, gold & brn .25 .25
**C547** AP90 15c grn, gold & brn .25 .25
**C548** AP90 30c grn, gold & brn .25 .25
**C549** AP90 40c grn, gold & brn .35 .35
*Nos. C546-C549 (4)* 1.10 1.10

25th anniversary of Children's Villages in Honduras. Overprint in 6 lines on 10c and 30c, in 4 lines on 15c and 40c.

Stamps of 1956-73 Surcharged

**1975, Feb. 24** **Litho.; Engr.**

**C550** AP68 16c on 1c (#C250) .25 .25
**C551** AP70 16c on 1c (#C269) .25 .25
**C552** AP72 16c on 1c (#C289) .25 .25
**C553** AP72 16c on 1c (#CO98) .25 .25
**C554** AP78 16c on 1c (#C369) .30 .30
**C555** AP85 18c on 12c (#C456) .40 .25
**C556** AP90 18c on 10c (#C520) .25 .25
**C557** AP91 18c on 10c (#C525) .25 .25
**C558** AP91 18c on 12c (#C526) .25 .25
**C559** AP92 18c on 8c (#C527) .25 .25
**C560** AP90 50c on 30c (#C522) .75 .50
**C561** AP90 1 l on 30c (#C522) 1.25 .90
*Nos. C550-C561,CE5 (13)* 5.70 4.60

Denominations not obliterated on Nos. C551, C553-C558, C560-C561; "OFICIAL" overprint not obliterated on No. C553.

For surcharges, see Nos. C1197, C1198, C1200.

Flags of Germany and Austria AP93

Designs (Flags): 2c, Belgium & Denmark. 3c, Spain & France. 4c, Hungary & Russia. 5c, Great Britain & Italy. 10c, Norway & Sweden. 12c, Honduras. 15c, US & Switzerland. 20c, Greece & Portugal. 30c, Romania & Serbia. 1 l, Egypt & Netherlands. 2 l, Luxembourg & Turkey.

**1975, June 18** **Litho.** ***Perf. 13***

**Gold & Multicolored; Colors Listed are for Shields**

**C562** AP93 1c lilac .25 .25
**C563** AP93 2c gold .25 .25
**C564** AP93 3c rose gray .25 .25
**C565** AP93 4c light blue .25 .25
**C566** AP93 5c yellow .25 .25
**C567** AP93 10c gray .25 .25
**C568** AP93 12c lilac rose .25 .25
**C569** AP93 15c bluish green .35 .35
**C570** AP93 20c bright blue .40 .40
**C571** AP93 30c pink .75 .75
**C572** AP93 1 l salmon 1.75 1.75
**C573** AP93 2 l yellow green 3.75 3.75
*Nos. C562-C573 (12)* 8.75 8.75

**Souvenir Sheet**

**C574** AP93 Sheet of 12 *12.00 12.00*

UPU, cent. (in 1974). No. C574 contains 12 stamps similar to Nos. C562-C573 with shields in different colors.

Humuya Youth Center and Mrs. Arellano AP94

Designs (Portrait of First Lady, Gloria de Lopez Arellano, IWY Emblem and): 16c, Jalteva Youth Center. 18c, Mrs. Arellano (diff. portrait) and IWY emblem. 30c, El Carmen de San Pedro Sula Youth Center. 55c, Flag of National Social Welfare Organization, vert. 1 l, La Isla sports and recreational facilities. 2 l, Women's Social Center.

**1976, Mar. 5** **Litho.** ***Perf. 13½***

**C575** AP94 8c sal & multi .25 .25
**C576** AP94 16c yel & multi .25 .25
**C577** AP94 18c pink & multi .25 .25
**C578** AP94 30c org & multi .45 .45
**C579** AP94 55c multicolored .70 .70
**C580** AP94 1 l multicolored 1.50 1.50
**C581** AP94 2 l multicolored 2.75 2.75
*Nos. C575-C581 (7)* 6.15 6.15

International Women's Year (1975).

For surcharges see Nos. C736-C737, C781, C798, C886, C887, C919, C1203.

"CARE" and Globe
AP95

Designs: 1c, 16c, 30c, 55c, 1 l, Care package and globe, vert. Others like 5c.

**1976, May 24 Litho. *Perf. 13½***

| | | | | |
|---|---|---|---|---|
| **C582** | AP95 | 1c blk & lt blue | .25 | .25 |
| **C583** | AP95 | 5c rose brn & blk | .25 | .25 |
| **C584** | AP95 | 16c black & org | .25 | .25 |
| **C585** | AP95 | 18c lemon & blk | .25 | .25 |
| **C586** | AP95 | 30c blk & blue | .35 | .35 |
| **C587** | AP95 | 50c yel grn & blk | .50 | .50 |
| **C588** | AP95 | 55c blk & buff | .50 | .50 |
| **C589** | AP95 | 70c brt rose & blk | .70 | .70 |
| **C590** | AP95 | 1 l blk & lt grn | 1.25 | 1.25 |
| **C591** | AP95 | 2 l ocher & blk | 2.40 | 2.40 |
| | | *Nos. C582-C591 (10)* | 6.70 | 6.70 |

20th anniversary of CARE in Honduras.
For surcharges see Nos. C735, C738, C788, C888, C922, C1105.

Fawn in Burnt-out Forest — AP96

Forest Protection: 16c, COHDEFOR emblem (Corporacion Hondureña de Desarollo Forestal). 18c, Forest, horiz. 30c, 2 l, Live and burning trees. 50c, like 10c. 70c, Emblem. 1 l, Young forest, horiz.

**1976, May 28 Litho. *Perf. 13½***

| | | | | |
|---|---|---|---|---|
| **C592** | AP96 | 10c multicolored | .25 | .25 |
| **C593** | AP96 | 16c multicolored | .25 | .25 |
| **C594** | AP96 | 18c multicolored | .25 | .25 |
| **C595** | AP96 | 30c grn & multi | .50 | .25 |
| **C596** | AP96 | 50c multicolored | .75 | .30 |
| **C597** | AP96 | 70c brn & multi | 1.00 | .40 |
| **C598** | AP96 | 1 l yel & multi | 2.00 | .75 |
| **C599** | AP96 | 2 l vio & multi | 3.50 | 3.50 |
| | | *Nos. C592-C599,CE6 (9)* | 9.25 | 6.45 |

For surcharges see Nos. C784, C787, C917, C1100.

"Sons of Liberty" — AP97

American Bicentennial: 2c, Raising flag of "Liberty and Union." 3c, Bunker Hill flag. 4c, Washington's Cruisers' flag. 5c, 1st Navy Jack. 6c, Flag of Honduras over Presidential Palace, Tegucigalpa. 18c, US flag over Capitol. 55c, Grand Union flag. 2 l, Bennington flag. 3 l, Betsy Ross and her flag.

**1976, Aug. 29 Litho. *Perf. 12***

| | | | | |
|---|---|---|---|---|
| **C601** | AP97 | 1c multicolored | .25 | .25 |
| **C602** | AP97 | 2c multicolored | .25 | .25 |
| **C603** | AP97 | 3c multicolored | .25 | .25 |
| **C604** | AP97 | 4c multicolored | .25 | .25 |
| **C605** | AP97 | 5c multicolored | .25 | .25 |
| **C606** | AP97 | 6c multicolored | .25 | .25 |
| **C607** | AP97 | 18c multicolored | .30 | .35 |
| **C608** | AP97 | 55c multicolored | .75 | .70 |
| *a.* | | Souv. sheet of 4, #C603, C606-C608 | 2.00 | 2.00 |
| **C609** | AP97 | 2 l multicolored | 2.25 | 2.25 |
| *a.* | | Souv. sheet of 3, #C601, C604, C609 | 4.50 | 4.50 |
| **C610** | AP97 | 3 l multicolored | 4.75 | 4.75 |
| *a.* | | Souv. sheet of 3, #C602, C605, C610 | 5.50 | 5.50 |
| | | *Nos. C601-C610 (10)* | 9.55 | 9.55 |

For surcharges see Nos. C883-C884, C885, C889, C1102.

King Juan Carlos of Spain — AP98

Designs: 16c, Queen Sophia. 30c, Queen Sophia and King Juan Carlos. 2 l, Arms of Honduras and Spain, horiz.

**1977, Sept. 13 Litho. *Perf. 14***

| | | | | |
|---|---|---|---|---|
| **C611** | AP98 | 16c multicolored | .25 | .25 |
| **C612** | AP98 | 18c multicolored | .25 | .25 |
| **C613** | AP98 | 30c multicolored | .30 | .25 |
| **C614** | AP98 | 2 l multicolored | 2.10 | 2.10 |
| | | *Nos. C611-C614 (4)* | 2.90 | 2.85 |

Visit of King and Queen of Spain.
For surcharges see Nos. C890, C918, C1107.

Mayan Steles, Exhibition Emblems
AP99

Designs: 18c, Giant head. 30c, Statue. 55c, Sun god. 1.50 l, Mayan pelota court.

**1978, Apr. 28 Litho. *Perf. 12***

| | | | | |
|---|---|---|---|---|
| **C615** | AP99 | 15c multi | .25 | .25 |
| **C616** | AP99 | 18c multi | .45 | .45 |
| **C617** | AP99 | 30c multi | .65 | .65 |
| **C618** | AP99 | 55c multi | 1.25 | 1.25 |

***Imperf***

| | | | | |
|---|---|---|---|---|
| **C619** | AP99 | 1.50 l multi | 4.00 | 4.00 |
| | | *Nos. C615-C619 (5)* | 6.60 | 6.60 |

Honduras '78 Philatelic Exhibition.
For overprints and surcharges see Nos. C642-C645, C786, C920, C924, CB6.

Del Valle's Birthplace
AP100

Designs: 14c, La Merced Church, Choluteca, where del Valle was baptized. 15c, Baptismal font, vert. 20c, Del Valle reading independence acts. 25c, Portrait, documents, map of Central America. 40c, Portrait, vert. 1 l, Monument, Central Park, Choluteca, vert. 3 l, Bust, vert.

**1978, Apr. 11 Litho. *Perf. 14***

| | | | | |
|---|---|---|---|---|
| **C620** | AP100 | 8c multicolored | .25 | .25 |
| **C621** | AP100 | 14c multicolored | .25 | .25 |
| **C622** | AP100 | 15c multicolored | .25 | .25 |
| **C623** | AP100 | 20c multicolored | .25 | .25 |
| **C624** | AP100 | 25c multicolored | .30 | .30 |
| **C625** | AP100 | 40c multicolored | .40 | .40 |
| **C626** | AP100 | 1 l multicolored | 1.25 | 1.25 |
| **C627** | AP100 | 3 l multicolored | 4.00 | 4.00 |
| | | *Nos. C620-C627 (8)* | 6.95 | 6.95 |

Bicentenary of the birth of José Cecilio del Valle (1780-1834), Central American patriot and statesman.
For surcharges see Nos. C739, C793, C795, C886A, C1098.

Rural Health Center
AP101

Designs: 6c, Child at water pump. 10c, Los Laureles Dam, Tegucigalpa. 20c, Rural aqueduct. 40c, Teaching hospital, Tegucigalpa. 2 l, Parents and child. 3 l, National vaccination campaign. 5 l, Panamerican Health Organization Building, Washington, DC.

**1978, May 10 Litho. *Perf. 14***

| | | | | |
|---|---|---|---|---|
| **C628** | AP101 | 5c multicolored | .25 | .25 |
| **C629** | AP101 | 6c multicolored | .25 | .25 |
| **C630** | AP101 | 10c multicolored | .25 | .25 |
| **C631** | AP101 | 20c multicolored | .25 | .25 |
| **C632** | AP101 | 40c multicolored | .45 | .45 |
| **C633** | AP101 | 2 l multicolored | 1.90 | 1.90 |
| **C634** | AP101 | 3 l multicolored | 3.00 | 3.00 |
| **C635** | AP101 | 5 l multicolored | 4.50 | 4.50 |
| | | *Nos. C628-C635 (8)* | 10.85 | 10.85 |

75th anniv. of Panamerican Health Organization (in 1977).
For surcharges see Nos. C783, C783A.

Luis Landa and his "Botanica"
AP102

Designs (Luis Landa and): 16c, Map of Honduras showing St. Ignacio. 18c, Medals received by Landa. 30c, Landa's birthplace in St. Ignacio. 2 l, Brassavola (orchid), national flower. 3 l, Women's Normal School.

**1978, Aug. 29 Photo. *Perf. 13x13½***

| | | | | |
|---|---|---|---|---|
| **C636** | AP102 | 14c multicolored | .25 | .25 |
| **C637** | AP102 | 16c multicolored | .25 | .25 |
| **C638** | AP102 | 18c multicolored | .25 | .25 |
| **C639** | AP102 | 30c multicolored | .40 | .25 |
| **C640** | AP102 | 2 l multicolored | 3.00 | 1.00 |
| **C641** | AP102 | 3 l multicolored | 3.50 | 3.50 |
| | | *Nos. C636-C641 (6)* | 7.65 | 5.50 |

Prof. Luis Landa (1875-1975), botanist.
For surcharges see Nos. C740, C794, C888A, C923, C1099.

Nos. C615-C618 Overprinted in Red with Argentina '78 Soccer Cup Emblem and: "Argentina Campeon / Holanda Sub-Campeon / XI Campeonato Mundial / de Football"

**1978, Sept. 6 Litho. *Perf. 12***

| | | | | |
|---|---|---|---|---|
| **C642** | AP99 | 15c multicolored | .25 | .25 |
| **C643** | AP99 | 18c multicolored | .35 | .25 |
| **C644** | AP99 | 30c multicolored | .45 | .40 |
| **C645** | AP99 | 55c multicolored | 1.00 | .65 |
| | | *Nos. C642-C645 (4)* | 2.05 | 1.55 |

Argentina's victory in World Cup Soccer Championship. Same overprint was applied to No. C619. Value $45.
For surcharges, see No. C924, C1079.

Central University and Coat of Arms — AP103

Designs show for each denomination a 19th century print and a contemporary photograph of the same area (except 1.50 l, 5 l): No. C647, University City. 8c, Manuel Bonilla Theater. No. C650, Court House, vert. No. C651, North Boulevard highway intersection, vert. No. C652, Natl. Palace. No. C653, Presidential Palace. 20c, Hospital. 40c, Cathedral. 50c, View of Tegucigalpa. 1.50 l, Aerial view of Tegucigalpa. No. C660, Arms of San Miguel de Tegucigalpa, 18th cent., vert. No. C661, Pres. Marco Aurelio Soto (1846-1908) (painting), vert.

**1978, Sept. 29**

| | | | | |
|---|---|---|---|---|
| **C646** | AP103 | 6c black & brn | .25 | .25 |
| **C647** | AP103 | 6c multicolored | .25 | .25 |
| *a.* | | Pair, #C646-C647 | .25 | .25 |
| **C648** | AP103 | 8c black & brn | .25 | .25 |
| **C649** | AP103 | 8c multicolored | .25 | .25 |
| *a.* | | Pair, #C648-C649 | .25 | .25 |
| **C650** | AP103 | 10c black & brn | .25 | .25 |
| **C651** | AP103 | 10c multicolored | .25 | .25 |
| *a.* | | Pair, #C650-C651 | .30 | .30 |
| **C652** | AP103 | 16c black & brn | .25 | .25 |
| **C653** | AP103 | 16c multicolored | .25 | .25 |
| *a.* | | Pair, #C652-C653 | .50 | .50 |
| **C654** | AP103 | 20c black & brn | .30 | .25 |
| **C655** | AP103 | 20c multicolored | .30 | .25 |
| *a.* | | Pair, #C654-C655 | .60 | .60 |
| **C656** | AP103 | 40c black & brn | .75 | .45 |
| **C657** | AP103 | 40c multicolored | .75 | .45 |
| *a.* | | Pair, #C656-C657 | 1.60 | 1.60 |
| **C658** | AP103 | 50c black & brn | 1.00 | .50 |
| **C659** | AP103 | 50c multicolored | 1.00 | .50 |
| *a.* | | Pair, #C658-C659 | 2.10 | 2.10 |
| **C660** | AP103 | 5 l black & brn | 6.75 | 6.75 |
| **C661** | AP103 | 5 l multicolored | 6.75 | 6.75 |
| *a.* | | Pair, #C660-C661 | 14.00 | 14.00 |
| | | *Nos. C646-C661 (16)* | 19.60 | 17.90 |

**Souvenir Sheet**

| | | | | |
|---|---|---|---|---|
| **C662** | AP103 | 1.50 l multi | 2.75 | 2.75 |

400th anniv. of the founding of Tegucigalpa.
In the listing the first number is for the 19th cent. design, the second for the 20th cent. design.
For overprints and surcharges see #C724-C725, C740A-C746, C766-C769, C779-C780, C1094-C1095, C1103-C1104.

Goalkeeper — AP104

Designs: Various soccer scenes.

**1978, Nov. 26 Litho. *Perf. 12***

| | | | | |
|---|---|---|---|---|
| **C663** | AP104 | 15c multi, vert. | .25 | .25 |
| **C664** | AP104 | 30c multi | .30 | .30 |
| **C665** | AP104 | 55c multi, vert. | .60 | .60 |
| **C666** | AP104 | 1 l multi | 1.40 | 1.40 |
| **C667** | AP104 | 2 l multi | 2.50 | 2.50 |
| | | *Nos. C663-C667 (5)* | 5.05 | 5.05 |

7th Youth Soccer Championship, Nov. 26.
For surcharge see No. C797.

UPU Emblem — AP105

2c, Postal emblem of Honduras. 25c, Dr. Ramon Rosa, vert. 50c, Pres. Marco Aurelio Soto, vert.

**1979, Apr. 1 Litho. *Perf. 12***

| | | | | |
|---|---|---|---|---|
| **C668** | AP105 | 2c multicolored | .25 | .25 |
| **C669** | AP105 | 15c multicolored | .25 | .25 |
| **C670** | AP105 | 25c multicolored | .25 | .25 |
| **C671** | AP105 | 50c multicolored | .40 | .40 |
| | | *Nos. C668-C671 (4)* | 1.15 | 1.15 |

Centenary of Honduras joining UPU.

Rotary Emblem and "50"
AP106

**1979, Apr. 26 Litho. *Perf. 14***

| | | | | |
|---|---|---|---|---|
| **C672** | AP106 | 3c multi | .25 | .25 |
| **C673** | AP106 | 5c multi | .25 | .25 |
| **C674** | AP106 | 50c multi | .50 | .50 |
| **C675** | AP106 | 2 l multi | 1.75 | 1.75 |
| | | *Nos. C672-C675 (4)* | 2.75 | 2.75 |

Rotary Intl. of Honduras, 50th anniv.
For surcharge see No. C884A, C1096.

Map of Caratasca Lagoon
AP107

Designs: 10c, Fort San Fernando de Omoa. 24c, Institute anniversary emblem, vert. 5 l, Map of Santanilla islands.

**1979, Sept. 15** **Litho.** ***Perf. 13½***

**C676** AP107 5c multi .25 .25
**C677** AP107 10c multi .25 .25
**C678** AP107 24c multi .25 .25
**C679** AP107 5 l multi 4.00 4.00
*Nos. C676-C679 (4)* 4.75 4.75

Panamerican Institute of History and Geography, 50th anniversary.

For surcharge see No. C891.

General Post Office, 1979 — AP108

UPU Membership Cent.: 3 l, Post Office, 19th cent.

**1980, Feb. 20** **Litho.** ***Perf. 12***

**C680** AP108 24c multi .25 .25
**C681** AP108 3 l multi 2.75 2.75

For surcharge see No. C925.

Workers in the Field, IYC Emblem AP109

**1980, Dec. 9** **Litho.** ***Perf. 14½***

**C682** AP109 1c shown .25 .25
**C683** AP109 5c Landscape, vert. .25 .25
**C684** AP109 15c Sitting boy, vert. .25 .25
**C685** AP109 20c IYC emblem, vert. .25 .25
**C686** AP109 30c Beach scene .45 .45
*Nos. C682-C686 (5)* 1.45 1.45

**Souvenir Sheet**

**C687** AP109 1 l UNICEF and IYC emblems, vert. 1.50 1.50

International Year of the Child (1979).

Maltese Cross, Hill AP110

**1980, Dec. 17**

**C688** AP110 1c shown .25 .25
**C689** AP110 2c Penny Black .25 .25
**C690** AP110 5c Honduras type A1 .25 .25
**C691** AP110 10c Honduras type A1 .25 .25

**Size: 47x34mm**

**C692** AP110 15c Postal emblem .25 .25
**C693** AP110 20c Flags of Honduras, Gt. Britain .25 .25
*Nos. C688-C693 (6)* 1.50 1.50

**Souvenir Sheet**

**C694** AP110 1 l Honduras #C402 2.50 2.50

Sir Rowland Hill (1795-1879), originator of penny postage. No. C694 contains one stamp 47x34mm.

Intibucana Mother and Child — AP111

Inter-American Women's Commission, 50th Anniv.: 2c, Visitacion Padilla, Honduras Section founder. 10c, Maria Trinidad del Cid, Section member. 1 l, Emblem, horiz.

**1981, June 15** **Litho.** ***Perf. 14½***

**C695** AP111 2c multicolored .25 .25
**C696** AP111 10c multicolored .25 .25
**C697** AP111 40c multicolored .30 .30
**C698** AP111 1 l multicolored .80 .80
*Nos. C695-C698 (4)* 1.60 1.60

Bernardo O'Higgins, by Jose Gil de Castro — AP112

Paintings of O'Higgins: 16c, Liberation of Chile, by Cosme San Martin, horiz. 20c, Portrait of Ambrosio O'Higgins (father). 1 l, Abdication of Office, by Antonio Caro, horiz.

**1981, June 29**

**C699** AP112 16c multicolored .25 .25
**C700** AP112 20c multicolored .25 .25
**C701** AP112 30c multicolored .25 .25
**C702** AP112 1 l multicolored 1.00 .50
*Nos. C699-C702 (4)* 1.75 1.25

For surcharges see Nos. C785, C888B, C1106.

CONCACAF 81 Soccer Cup — AP113

**1981, Dec. 30** **Litho.** ***Perf. 14***

**C703** AP113 20c Emblem .60 .25
**C704** AP113 50c Player 1.25 .35
**C705** AP113 70c Flags 1.90 1.00
**C706** AP113 1 l Stadium 2.75 1.50
*Nos. C703-C706 (4)* 6.50 3.10

**Souvenir Sheet**

**C707** AP113 1.50 l like #C703 1.75 1.75

For overprint see No. C797.

50th Anniv. of Air Force (1981) AP114

Designs: 3c, Curtiss CT-32 Condor. 15c, North American NA-16. 25c, Chance Vought F4U-5. 65c, Douglas C47. 1 l Cessna A37-B. 2 l, Super Mystere SMB-11.

**1983, Jan. 14** **Litho.** ***Perf. 12***

**C708** AP114 3c multi .25 .25
**C709** AP114 15c multi .25 .25
**C710** AP114 25c multi .35 .25
**C711** AP114 65c multi .65 .35
**C712** AP114 1 l multi 1.00 .50
**C713** AP114 2 l multi 2.00 1.75
*Nos. C708-C713 (6)* 4.50 3.35

**Souvenir Sheet**

**C714** AP114 1.55 l Helicopter 4.00 4.00

For surcharges see Nos. C884B, C1097.

UPU Executive Council Membership, 3rd Anniv. — AP115

**1983, Jan. 14**

**C715** AP115 16c UPU monument .25 .25
**C716** AP115 18c 18th UPU Congress emblem .25 .25
**C717** AP115 30c Natl. Postal Service emblem .35 .35
**C718** AP115 55c Rio de Janeiro .50 .50
**C719** AP115 2 l Dove on globe 2.00 2.00
*Nos. C715-C719 (5)* 3.35 3.35

**Souvenir Sheet**

**C720** AP115 1 l like 2 l 2.50 2.50

For surcharges see Nos. C921, C1204.

Natl. Library and Archives Centenary (1980) AP116

**1983, Feb. 11** **Litho.** ***Perf. 12***

**C721** AP116 9c Library .30 .25
**C722** AP116 1 l Books 1.10 .40

For surcharge see No. C1101.

Intl. Year of the Disabled (1979) AP117

**1983, Feb. 11**

**C723** AP117 25c Emblem .40 .25

No. C657a Overprinted in Red: "CONMEMORATIVA DE LA VISITA / DE SS. JUAN PABLO II / 8 de marzo de 1983"

**1983, Mar. 8**

**C724** AP103 40c multicolored 3.00 2.50
**C725** AP103 40c multicolored 3.00 2.50
*a.* Pair, #C724-C725 6.00 5.00

Visit of Pope John Paul II.

Literacy Campaign (1980) — AP118

**1983, May 18** **Litho.** ***Perf. 12***

**C726** AP118 40c Hands, open book .50 .45
**C727** AP118 1.50 l People holding books 2.00 1.90

World Food Day, Oct. 16, 1981 — AP119

**1983, May 18**

**C728** AP119 65c Produce, emblem 1.00 1.00

20th Anniv. of Inter-American Development Bank (1980) — AP120

**1983, June 17** **Litho.** ***Perf. 12***

**C729** AP120 1 l Comayagua River Bridge 1.50 .50
**C730** AP120 2 l Luis Bogran Technical Institute of Physics 2.75 1.00

2nd Anniv. of Return to Constitutional Government — AP121

**1984, Jan. 27** **Litho.** ***Perf. 12***

**C731** 20c Arms, text .25 .25
**C732** 20c Pres. Suazo Cordova .25 .25
*a.* AP121 Pair, #C731-C732 .65 .55

La Gaceta Newspaper Sesquicentenary (1980) — AP122

**1984, May 25** **Litho.** ***Perf. 12***

**C733** AP122 10c multicolored .35 .35
**C734** AP122 20c multicolored .35 .35

Nos. C582 and C575-C576 Surcharged

**1985, June 26** **Litho.** ***Perf. 13½***

**C735** AP95 5c on 1c #C582 .25 .25
**C736** AP94 10c on 8c #C575 .25 .25
**C737** AP94 20c on 16c #C576 .25 .25
**C738** AP95 1 l on 1c #C582 1.00 .40
*Nos. C735-C738 (4)* 1.75 1.15

Nos. C621, C636, C647a Surcharged

**Litho., Photo. (No. C740)**

**1986, Aug. 21** ***Perfs. as before***

**C739** AP100 50c on 14c #C621 .45 .25
**C740** AP102 60c on 14c #C636 .55 .30
**C740A** AP103 85c on 6c #C646 .80 .55
**C740B** AP103 85c on 6c #C647 .80 .55
*c.* Pair, #C740A-C740B 1.75 1.50
**C741** AP103 95c on 6c #C646 .90 .60
**C742** AP103 95c on 6c #C647 .90 .60
*a.* Pair, #C741-C742 2.00 1.75
*Nos. C739-C742 (6)* 4.40 2.85

Black bar obliterating old values on #C739-C740 also cover "aereo."

**Nos. C656-C657 Overprinted in Red**

No. C743

No. C744

No. C745

No. C746

**1986, Sept. 12 Litho. *Perf. 12***

C743 AP103 40c No. C656 .40 .25
C744 AP103 40c No. C657 .40 .25
C745 AP103 40c No. C657 .40 .25
C746 AP103 40c No. C656 .40 .25
a. Block of 4, #C743-C746 2.00

AP123

San Fernando de Omoa Castle — AP124

20c, Phulapanzak Falls. 78c, Bahia Isls. beach. 85c, Bahia Isls. cove. 95c, Yojoa Lake. 1 l, Woman painting pottery.

***Perf. 13½x14, 14x13½***

**1986, Nov. 10 Litho.**

C747 AP123 20c multi, vert. .25 .25
C748 AP123 78c multi 1.10 .55
C749 AP123 85c multi 1.25 .55
C750 AP123 95c multi, vert. 1.40 .65
C751 AP123 1 l multi, vert. 1.50 .70

**Size: 84x59mm**

***Imperf***

C752 AP124 1.50 l multi 2.75 2.75
*Nos. C747-C752 (6)* 8.25 5.45

For overprint see No. C782.

AP125

National flag, Pres. Jose Azcona Hoyo.

**1987, Feb. 2 Litho. *Perf. 13½***

C753 AP125 20c multicolored .30 .25
C754 AP125 85c multicolored 1.25 .85

Democratic government, 1st anniv.

Flora — AP126

**1987, July 8 Litho. *Perf. 13½x14***

C755 AP126 10c Eupatorium cyrillinelsonii .25 .25
C756 AP126 20c Salvia ernesti-vargasii .45 .45
C757 AP126 95c Robinsonella erasmi-sosae 1.40 .75
*Nos. C755-C757 (3)* 2.10 1.45

Birds — AP127

**1987, Sept. 10 Litho. *Perf. 13½x14***

C758 AP127 50c Eumomota superciliosa 1.75 .50
C759 AP127 60c Ramphastos sulfuratus 2.00 .50
C760 AP127 85c Amazona autumnalis 3.50 1.10
*Nos. C758-C760 (3)* 7.25 2.10

AP128

**1987, Dec. 10 Litho. *Perf. 13½***

C761 AP128 1 l blk, brt yel & dark red 1.25 .50

Natl. Autonomous University of Honduras, 30th anniv.

AP129

**1987, Dec. 23 Litho. *Perf. 13½***

C762 AP129 20c red & dk ultra .50 .25

Natl. Red Cross, 50th anniv.

AP130

**1988, Jan. 27 Litho. *Perf. 13½***

C763 AP130 95c brt blue & org yel 1.10 .45

17th regional meeting of Lions Intl.

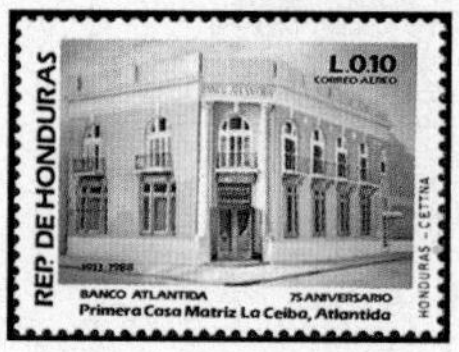


Atlantida Bank, 75th Anniv. AP131

Main offices: 10c, La Ceiba, Atlantida, 1913. 85c, Tegucigalpa, 1988.

**1988, Feb. 10**

C764 AP131 10c multi .25 .25
C765 AP131 85c mutli .90 .40
a. Souv. sheet of 2, #358-359, imperf. 1.25 1.25

No. C765a sold for 1 l.

**No. C649a Surcharged**

**1988, June 9 Litho. *Perf. 12***

C766 AP103 20c on 8c #C648 .90 .90
C767 AP103 20c on 8c #C649 .90 .90
a. Pair, #C766-C767 2.00 2.00

**No. C647a Surcharged**

**1988, July 8 Litho. *Perf. 12***

C768 AP103 5c on 6c #C646 .30 .30
C769 AP103 5c on 6c #C647 .30 .30
a. Pair, #C768-C769 .80 .80

Postman AP132

Tegucigalpa Postmark on Stampless Cover, 1789 — AP133

**1988, Sept. 11 Litho. *Perf. 13½***

C770 AP132 85c dull red brn 1.10 .40
C771 AP133 2 l dull red brn & ver 2.50 1.00

EXFILHON '88.

**Summer Olympics Type of 1988**

**1988, Sept. 30 Litho. *Perf. 13½***

**Size: 28x33mm**

C772 A62 85c Running, vert. 1.10 .40

**Size: 36x27mm**

C773 A62 1 l Baseball, soccer, basketball 1.20 .50

Discovery of America, 500th Anniv. (in 1992) AP134

Pre-Colombian pottery artifacts: 10c, Footed vase, vert. 25c, Bowl. 30c, Footed bowl. 50c, Pitcher, vert. 1 l, Rectangular footed bowl.

**1988 Litho. *Perf. 13½***

C774 AP134 10c multicolored .30 .25
C775 AP134 25c multicolored .75 .25
C776 AP134 30c multicolored .90 .30
C777 AP134 50c multicolored 1.50 .50
*Nos. C774-C777 (4)* 3.45 1.30

**Size: 115x83mm**

***Imperf***

C778 AP134 1 l multicolored 3.25 3.25

Nos. C653a and C576 Surcharged

**1988 Litho. *Perf. 12, 13½***

C779 AP103 10c on 16c #C652 .25 .25
C780 AP103 10c on 16c #C653 .25 .25
a. Pair, #C779-C780 .50 .50
C781 AP94 50c on 16c #C576 .80 .40
*Nos. C779-C781 (3)* 1.30 .90

Nos. C779-C780 exist with double surcharge. Issued: 10c, Apr. 7, 50c, May 25.

**No. C752 Overprinted**

**1989, July 14 Litho. *Imperf.***

C782 AP124 1.50 l multi 2.75 2.75

French revolution, bicent.

**Nos. C629 and C593 Surcharged**

I

II

**1989 Litho. *Perf. 14, 13½***

C783 AP101 15c on 6c, I .40 .25
C783A AP101 15c on 6c, II 1.00 .25
C784 AP96 1 l on 16c 1.25 .95
*Nos. C783-C784 (3)* 2.65 1.45

Issue date: 1 l, June 15.

Nos. C699 and C616 Surcharged

**1989, Dec. 15 Litho. *Perf. 14½, 12***

C785 AP112 20c on 16c #C699 .40 .25
C786 AP99 95c on 18c #C616 1.40 .50

No. C786 exists with inverted surcharge. Issued: #C785, Dec. 15; #C786, Dec. 28.

Nos. C594 and C585 Surcharged with New Denomination and "IV Juegos / Olimpicos / Centroamericanos"

**1990, Jan. 12 *Perf. 13½***

C787 AP96 75c on 18c #C594 (S) 1.10 .85
C788 AP95 85c on 18c #C585 1.25 .95

No. C787 exists with double and inverted surcharge.

World Wildlife Fund — AP135

Various *Mono ateles.*

**1990, Apr. 18 Litho. *Perf. 13½***

C789 AP135 10c shown 3.75 2.50
C790 AP135 10c Adult, young 3.75 2.50
C791 AP135 20c Adult hanging, diff. 6.00 4.00
C792 AP135 20c Adult, young, diff. 6.50 4.50
*Nos. C789-C792 (4)* 20.00 13.50

No. C621 Surcharged

**1990, Feb. 8 Litho. *Perf. 14***

**C793** AP100 20c on 14c multi .25 .25

Nos. C621 and C636 Surcharged "50 Aniversario / IHCI" / 1939-1989

**1990, Mar. 29**

**C794** AP102 20c on 14c No. 636 .25 .25
**C795** AP100 1 l on 14c No. 621 .65 .40

No. C665 Surcharged

**1990, June 14 Litho. *Perf. 12***

**C796** AP104 1 l on 55c multi .75 .40

World Cup Soccer Championships, Italy.

No. C707 Ovptd. in Margin "CAMPEONATO MUNDIAL DE FUTBOL Italia '90," and Character Trademark

Souvenir Sheet

**1990, June 14 *Perf. 14***

**C797** AP113 1.50 l multi .80 .80

No. C577 Surcharged in Black

**1990, Feb. 22 Litho. *Perf. 13½***

**C798** AP94 20c on 18c multi .40 .25

FAO, 45th Anniv. — AP136

**1990, Oct. 16 Litho. *Perf. 13½***

**C799** AP136 95c yel, blk, bl, grn .85 .75

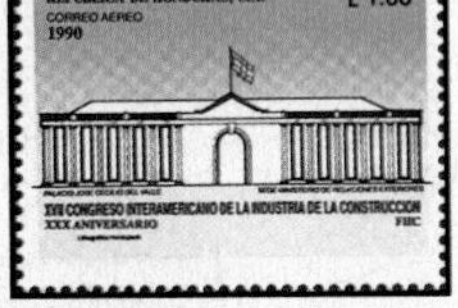


17th Interamerican Congress of Industry and Construction — AP137

**1990, Nov. 21 Litho. *Perf. 13½***

**C800** AP137 20c Map, vert. .25 .25
**C801** AP137 1 l Jose Cecilio Del Valle Palace .65 .45

AP138

Christmas — AP139

**1990, Nov. 30 Litho. *Perf. 13½***

**C802** AP138 20c shown .40 .25
**C803** AP138 95c Madonna and Child, vert. .80 .40

**Size: 112x82mm**

***Imperf***

**C804** AP139 3 l Poinsettia 2.50 2.00
*Nos. C802-C804 (3)* 3.70 2.65

Salesian Order in Honduras, 80th Anniv. AP140

**1990, Dec. 28 Litho. *Perf. 13½***

**C805** AP140 75c St. John Bosco .50 .30
**C806** AP140 1 l Natl. Youth Sanctuary .70 .50

Pres. Rafael Leonardo Callejas — AP141

**1991, Jan. 31**

**C807** AP141 30c Taking oath .25 .25
**C808** AP141 2 l Portrait 1.25 .90

Moths and Butterflies AP142

**1991, Feb. 28 Litho. *Perf. 13½***

**C809** AP142 85c Strymon melinus 1.25 .40
**C810** AP142 90c Diorina sp. 1.50 .50
**C811** AP142 1.50 l Hyalophora cecropia 2.50 .70

**Size: 114x82mm**

***Imperf***

**C812** AP142 5 l Papilio polixenes 4.00 4.00
*Nos. C809-C812 (4)* 9.25 5.60

Notary Day — AP143

**1991, May 22 Litho. *Perf. 13½***

**C813** AP143 50c multicolored .40 .25

Rafael Heliodoro Valle, Birth Cent. — AP144

**1991, July 26 Litho. *Perf. 13½***

**C815** AP144 2 l pale pink & blk 1.40 .90

Churches AP145

Discovery of America, 500th Anniv. emblem and: 30c, Church of St. Manuel of Colohete, Gracias. 95c, Church of Our Lady of Mercy, Gracias. 1 l, Comayagua Cathedral.

**1991, Aug. 30 Litho. *Perf. 13½***

**C816** AP145 30c multicolored .25 .25
**C817** AP145 95c multicolored .70 .25
**C818** AP145 1 l multicolored .85 .45
*Nos. C816-C818 (3)* 1.80 .95

Latin American Institute, 25th Anniv. AP146

**1991, June 20**

**C819** AP146 1 l multicolored .70 .40

Flowers AP147

**1991, Apr. 30**

**C820** AP147 30c Rhyncholaelia glauca .25 .25
**C821** AP147 50c Oncidium splendidum, vert. .50 .40
**C822** AP147 95c Laelia anceps, vert. .75 .70
**C823** AP147 1.50 l Cattleya skinneri 1.25 1.10
*Nos. C820-C823 (4)* 2.75 2.45

Espamer '91, Buenos Aires AP148

**1991, July 1**

**C824** AP148 2 l multicolored 2.25 .80

**Size: 101x82mm**

***Imperf***

**C825** AP148 5 l like #C824 3.50 3.50

Discovery of America, 500th anniv. (in 1992).

11th Pan American Games, Havana AP149

**1991, Aug. 8**

**C826** AP149 30c Equestrian .25 .25
**C827** AP149 85c Judo .60 .40
**C828** AP149 95c Men's swimming .75 .40

**Size: 114x83mm**

***Imperf***

**C829** AP149 5 l Women's swimming 3.50 3.50
*Nos. C826-C829 (4)* 5.10 4.55

Pre-Columbian Culture — AP150

UPAEP emblem, artifacts and: 25c, ears of corn. 40c, ear of corn, map. 1.50 l, map.

**1991, Sept. 30 Litho. *Perf. 13½***

**C830** AP150 25c multicolored .25 .25
**C831** AP150 40c multicolored .75 .40
**C832** AP150 1.50 l multicolored 1.50 .60
*Nos. C830-C832 (3)* 2.50 1.25

4th Intl. Congress on Control of Insect Pests AP151

Designs: 30c, Tactics to control pests. 75c, Integration of science. 1 l, Cooperation between farmers and scientists. 5 l, Pests and biological controls.

**1991, Nov. 22**

**C833** AP151 30c multicolored .40 .25
**C834** AP151 75c multicolored 1.10 .55
**C835** AP151 1 l multicolored 2.10 .85

**Size: 115x83mm**

***Imperf***

**C836** AP151 5 l multicolored 3.25 3.25
*Nos. C833-C836 (4)* 6.85 4.90

America Issue AP152

**1992, Jan. 27 Litho. *Perf. 13½***

**C837** AP152 90c Sighting land .75 .60
**C838** AP152 1 l Columbus' ships .85 .75
**C839** AP152 2 l Ship, map, birds 1.60 1.25
*Nos. C837-C839 (3)* 3.20 2.60

Christmas AP153

**1991, Dec. 19**

**C840** AP153 1 l shown .65 .40
**C841** AP153 2 l Poinsettias in rooster vase 1.40 .90

Honduran Savings Insurance Company, 75th Anniv. AP154

**1992, Jan. 17**

| | | | | |
|---|---|---|---|---|
| **C842** | AP154 85c multicolored | | .55 | .30 |
| **C843** | AP154 1 l Priest saying mass | | .65 | .40 |

**Size: 115x83mm**

***Imperf***

| | | | | |
|---|---|---|---|---|
| **C844** | AP154 5 l like #C842 | | 3.25 | 3.25 |
| | *Nos. C842-C844 (3)* | | 4.45 | 3.95 |

First mass in New World, 490th anniv. (No. C843). Taking possession of new continent, 490th anniv. (Nos. C842, C844).

Pres. Rafael Leonardo Callejas, 2nd Year in Office AP155

Callejas with: 20c, Italian president Francesco Cossiga. 2 l, Pope John Paul II.

**1992, Jan. 27 Litho. *Perf. 13½***

| | | | |
|---|---|---|---|
| **C845** | AP155 20c black & purple | .25 | .25 |
| **C846** | AP155 2 l black & multi | 1.40 | .80 |

Flowers AP156

**1992, July 25 Litho. *Perf. 13½***

| | | | |
|---|---|---|---|
| **C847** | AP156 20c Bougainvillea glabra | .25 | .25 |
| **C848** | AP156 30c Canna indica | .25 | .25 |
| **C849** | AP156 75c Epiphyllum | .70 | .45 |
| **C850** | AP156 95c Sobralia macrantha | .90 | .65 |
| | *Nos. C847-C850 (4)* | 2.10 | 1.60 |

Gen. Francisco Morazan Hydroelectric Complex — AP157

**1992, Aug. 17**

| | | | |
|---|---|---|---|
| **C851** | AP157 85c Dam face, vert. | .50 | .30 |
| **C852** | AP157 4 l Rear of dam | 2.40 | 1.60 |

AP158

**1992, Aug. 24**

| | | | |
|---|---|---|---|
| **C853** | AP158 95c black & multi | .65 | .55 |
| **C854** | AP158 95c multicolored | .65 | .55 |

Intl. Conference on Agriculture, 50th anniv.

AP159

Gen. Francisco Morazan (1792-1842): 5c, Morazan mounted on horseback. 10c, Statue of Morazan. 50c, Watch and sword, horiz. 95c, Portrait of Josefa Lastiri de Morazan. 5 l, Portrait of Morazan in uniform.

**1992, Sept. 18 Litho. *Perf. 13½***

| | | | |
|---|---|---|---|
| **C855** | AP159 5c multicolored | .25 | .25 |
| **C856** | AP159 10c multicolored | .25 | .25 |
| **C857** | AP159 50c multicolored | .35 | .25 |
| **C858** | AP159 95c multicolored | .60 | .30 |

**Size: 76x108mm**

***Imperf***

| | | | |
|---|---|---|---|
| **C859** | AP159 5 l multicolored | 3.00 | 2.25 |
| | *Nos. C855-C859 (5)* | 4.45 | 3.30 |

Children's Day — AP160

Paintings of children: 25c, Musicians. 95c, Boy, dog standing in doorway. 2 l, Flower girl.

**1992, Sept. 7**

| | | | |
|---|---|---|---|
| **C860** | AP160 25c multicolored | .25 | .25 |
| **C861** | AP160 95c multicolored | .60 | .30 |
| **C862** | AP160 2 l multicolored | 1.25 | .80 |
| | *Nos. C860-C862 (3)* | 2.10 | 1.35 |

Intl. Conference on Nutrition AP161

**1992, Sept. 30 Litho. *Perf. 13½***

| | | | |
|---|---|---|---|
| **C863** | AP161 1.05 l multicolored | .70 | .45 |

Pan-American Agricultural School, 50th Anniv. — AP162

**1992, Oct. 9**

| | | | |
|---|---|---|---|
| **C864** | AP162 20c Bee keepers | .25 | .25 |
| **C865** | AP162 85c Woman, goats | .50 | .30 |
| **C866** | AP162 1 l Plowing | .60 | .40 |
| **C867** | AP162 2 l Man with tool, vert. | 1.25 | .80 |
| | *Nos. C864-C867 (4)* | 2.60 | 1.75 |

Exfilhon '92 — AP163

Birds: 1.50 l, F. triquilidos. 2.45 l, Ara macao. 5 l, Quetzal pharomachrus mocinno.

**1992, Oct. 2**

| | | | |
|---|---|---|---|
| **C868** | AP163 1.50 l multicolored | 1.75 | 1.50 |
| **C869** | AP163 2.45 l multicolored | 2.75 | 2.40 |

**Size: 76x108mm**

***Imperf***

| | | | |
|---|---|---|---|
| **C870** | AP163 5 l multicolored | 3.25 | 3.25 |
| | *Nos. C868-C870 (3)* | 7.75 | 7.15 |

Discovery of America, 500th anniv.

America Issue — AP164

UPAEP emblem and: 35c, Native settlement. 5 l, Explorers meeting natives in boats.

**1992, Oct. 30 Litho. *Perf. 13½***

| | | | |
|---|---|---|---|
| **C871** | AP164 35c multicolored | .25 | .25 |
| **C872** | AP164 5 l multicolored | 2.75 | 2.00 |

Printed on both thick and thin paper.

Discovery of America, 500th Anniv. — AP165

Details from First Mass, by Roque Zelaya: 95c, Ships off-shore. 1 l, Holding services with natives, horiz. 2 l, Natives, countryside, temples, horiz.

**1992, Oct. 30**

| | | | |
|---|---|---|---|
| **C873** | AP165 95c multicolored | .50 | .40 |
| **C874** | AP165 1 l multicolored | .65 | .45 |
| **C875** | AP165 2 l multicolored | 1.25 | 1.00 |
| | *Nos. C873-C875 (3)* | 2.40 | 1.85 |

City of El Progreso, Cent. AP166

**1992, Oct. 17**

| | | | |
|---|---|---|---|
| **C876** | AP166 1.55 l multicolored | .90 | .55 |

First Road Conservation Congress of Panama and Central America — AP167

**1992, Nov. 16 *Perf. 13½***

| | | | |
|---|---|---|---|
| **C878** | AP167 20c shown | .25 | .25 |
| **C879** | AP167 85c Bulldozer on highway | .45 | .30 |

Pan-American Health Organization, 90th Anniv. — AP168

**1992, Nov. 27**

| | | | |
|---|---|---|---|
| **C880** | AP168 3.95 l multicolored | 2.25 | 1.75 |

Christmas AP169

Paintings by Roque Zelaya: 20c, Crowd watching people climb pole in front of church, vert. 85c, Nativity scene.

**1992, Nov. 24**

| | | | |
|---|---|---|---|
| **C881** | AP169 20c multicolored | .25 | .25 |
| **C882** | AP169 85c multicolored | .65 | .30 |

**Surcharges on**

No. C601

Nos. C606-C607

Nos. C584, C612, C637

Nos. C672, C678, C708

Nos. C575-C576, C603, C620, C699

**1992-93**

**Perfs. and Printing Methods as Before**

| | | | | |
|---|---|---|---|---|
| **C883** | AP97 | 20c on 1c #C601 | .40 | .25 |
| **C884** | AP97 | 20c on 3c #C603 | .40 | .25 |
| **C884A** | AP106 | 20c on 3c #C672 | .40 | .25 |
| **C884B** | AP114 | 20c on 3c #C708 | .40 | .25 |
| **C885** | AP97 | 20c on 6c #C606 | .40 | .25 |
| **C886** | AP94 | 20c on 8c #C575 | .40 | .25 |
| **C886A** | AP100 | 20c on 8c #C620 | .25 | .25 |
| **C887** | AP94 | 50c on 16c #C576 | .40 | .25 |
| **C888** | AP95 | 50c on 16c #C584 | .40 | .25 |
| **C888A** | AP102 | 50c on 16c #C637 | .40 | .25 |
| **C888B** | AP112 | 50c on 16c #C699 | .40 | .25 |
| **C889** | AP97 | 85c on 18c #C607 | .50 | .30 |
| **C890** | AP98 | 85c on 18c #C612 | .50 | .30 |
| **C891** | AP107 | 85c on 24c #C678 | .40 | .30 |
| | | *Nos. C883-C891 (14)* | 5.65 | 3.65 |

Size and location of surcharge varies.

Issued: #C883, 12/18/92; #C889, 1/22/93; #C885, 3/8/93; #C888A, 9/7/93; #C888, 9/13/93; #C890, 9/24/93; #C891, 10/1/93; #C884A, 10/5/93; #C884B, 10/8/93; #C884, C886A, 10/21/93; #C886, 10/29/93; #C887, C888B, 11/3/93.

Intl. Court of Justice Decision on Border Dispute Between Honduras & El Salvador
AP170

Designs: 90c, Pres. of El Salvador and Pres. Callejas of Honduras, vert. 1.05 l, Country flags, map of Honduras and El Salvador.

**1993, Feb. 24 Litho. *Perf. 13½***

**C893** AP170 90c multicolored .50 .30
**C894** AP170 1.05 l multicolored .65 .40

Third year of Pres. Callejas' term.

Mother's Day — AP171

Paintings of a mother and child, by Sandra Pendrey.

**1993, May 5 Litho. *Perf. 13½***

**C895** AP171 50c Red blanket .30 .25
**C896** AP171 95c Green blanket .55 .30

Endangered Animals — AP172

**1993, May 14 *Perf. 13½***

**C897** AP172 85c Manatee, horiz .65 .50
**C898** AP172 2.45 l Puma, horiz. 1.75 1.25
**C899** AP172 10 l Jaguar 6.50 4.00
*Nos. C897-C899 (3)* 8.90 5.75

Natl. Symbols AP173

**1993, June 25 Litho. *Perf. 13½***

**C900** AP173 25c Ara macao 1.10 .95
**C901** AP173 95c Odocoileus virginianus 1.50 1.25

First Brazilian Postage Stamps, 150th Anniv. AP174

**1993, Sept. 10 Litho. *Perf. 13½***

**C902** AP174 20c Brazil No. 1 .25 .25
**C903** AP174 50c Brazil No. 2 .30 .25
**C904** AP174 95c Brazil No. 3 .55 .40
*Nos. C902-C904 (3)* 1.10 .90

Departments in Honduras — AP175

Various scenes, department name: No. C905a, Atlantida. b, Colon. c, Cortes. d, Choluteca. e, El Paraiso. f, Francisco Morazan.

No. C906a, Comayagua. b, Copan. c, Intibuca. d, Islas de la Bahia. e, Lempira. f, Ocotepeque.

No. C907a, La Paz. b, Olancho. c, Santa Barbara. d, Valle. e, Yoro. f, Gracias a Dios.

**1993, Sept. 20 Litho. *Perf. 13½***

**C905** AP175 20c Strip of 6, #a.-f. .65 .65
**C906** AP175 50c Strip of 6, #a.-f. 1.50 1.50
**C907** AP175 1.50 l Strip of 6, #a.-f. 4.25 4.25
*Nos. C905-C907 (3)* 6.40 6.40

No. C906 is vert.

Endangered Birds — AP176

**1993, Oct. 11 Litho. *Perf. 13½***

**C908** AP176 20c Spizaetus ornatus .25 .25
**C909** AP176 80c Cairina moschata, horiz. 1.00 .50
**C910** AP176 2 l Harpia harpija, horiz. 2.25 1.50
*Nos. C908-C910 (3)* 3.50 2.25

UN Development Program AP177

**1993, Oct. 19**

**C911** AP177 95c multicolored .50 .35

Christmas AP178

**1993, Nov. 5**

**C912** AP178 20c Church .25 .25
**C913** AP178 85c Woman, flowers .45 .30

Nos. C577, C585, C593, C611, C616, C638, C643, C680, C716 Surcharged

**1993**

**Perfs. and Printing Methods as Before**

**C917** AP96 50c on 16c #C593 .25 .25
**C918** AP98 50c on 16c #C611 .25 .25
**C919** AP94 50c on 18c #C577 .25 .25
**C920** AP99 50c on 18c #C616 .25 .25
**C921** AP115 50c on 18c #C716 .40 .40
**C922** AP95 85c on 18c #C585 .40 .40
**C923** AP102 85c on 18c #C638 .40 .40
**C924** AP99 85c on 18c #C643 .40 .40
**C925** AP108 85c on 24c #C680 .40 .40
*Nos. C917-C925 (9)* 3.00 3.00

Size and location of surcharge varies.
Issued: #C917-C918, 11/12; #C920, C924, 11/23; #C921, C925, 11/30; #C922-C923, 12/3; #C919, 12/10.

Fish AP179

**1993, Dec. 7 Litho. *Perf. 13½***

**C931** AP179 20c Pomacanthus arcuatus .30 .25
**C932** AP179 85c Holacanthus ciliaris .80 .50
**C933** AP179 3 l Chaetodon striatus 2.50 1.90
*Nos. C931-C933 (3)* 3.60 2.65

Famous Men — AP180

**1993, Nov. 17**

**C934** AP180 25c Ramon Rosa .25 .25
**C935** AP180 65c Jesus Aguilar Paz .30 .25
**C936** AP180 85c Augusto C. Coello .40 .30
*Nos. C934-C936 (3)* .95 .80

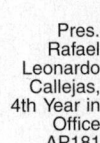

Pres. Rafael Leonardo Callejas, 4th Year in Office AP181

95c, Wife, Norma, planting tree, vert.

**1994, Jan. 21 Litho. *Perf. 13½***

**C937** AP181 95c multicolored .45 .30
**C938** AP181 1 l multicolored .50 .30

AP182

**1994, Mar. 8 Litho. *Perf. 13 ½***

**C939** AP182 1 l multicolored .45 .30

Intl. Year of the Family.

AP183

**1994, Oct. 24 Litho. *Perf. 13½***

**C940** AP183 1 l multicolored .45 .30

Intl. Conference on Peace and Development in Central America, Tegucigalpa.

Christmas AP184

Paintings by Gelasio Gimenez: 95c, Madonna and Child. 1 l, Holy Family.

**1994, Dec. 15 Litho. *Perf. 13½***

**C941** AP184 95c multicolored .45 .30
**C942** AP184 1 l multicolored .55 .40

UN, 50th Anniv. — AP185

Designs: 1 l, The Sowing: Ecological Family, by Elisa Dulcey. 2 l, Family Scene, by Delmer Mejia. 3 l, UN emblem, "50."

**1995, Jan. 17**

**C943** AP185 1 l multicolored .50 .50
**C944** AP185 2 l multicolored .85 .85
**C945** AP185 3 l multicolored 1.25 1.25
*Nos. C943-C945 (3)* 2.60 2.60

Pres. Carlos Roberto Reina, 1st Anniv. of Taking Office AP186

Designs: 80c, Beside flag, vert. 1 l, Summit meeting of area presidents & vice presidents.

**1995, Jan. 27**

**C946** AP186 80c multicolored .30 .30
**C947** AP186 95c multicolored .35 .30
**C948** AP186 1 l multicolored .40 .40
*Nos. C946-C948 (3)* 1.05 1.00

America Issue AP187

Postal vehicles.

**1995, Feb. 28 Litho. *Perf. 13½***

**C949** AP187 1.50 l Van .65 .55
**C950** AP187 2 l Motorcycle .80 .70

Miniature Sheet

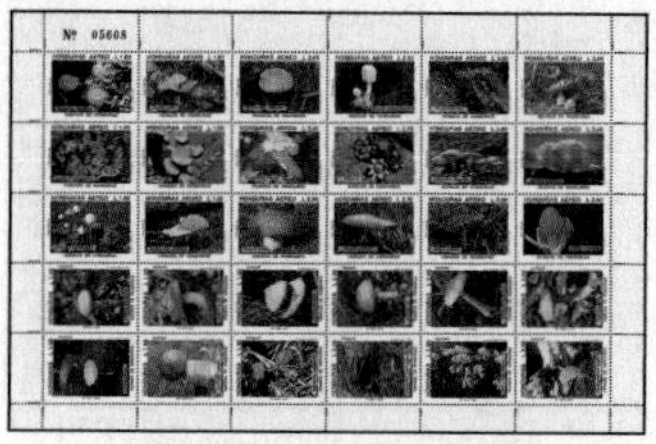

Mushrooms — AP188

1 l: a, Marasmius cohaerens. b, Lepista nuda. c, Polyporus pargamenus. d, Fomes. e, Paneolus sphinctrinus. f, Hygrophorus aurantiaca.

1.50 l, vert: g, Psathyrella. h, Amanita rubescens. i, Boletellus russelli. j, Boletus frostii. k, Marasmius spegazzinii. l, Fomes annosus.

2 l, vert: m, Craterellus cornucopioides. n, Amanita. o, Auricularia delicata. p, Psllocybe cubensis. q, Clavariadelphus pistilaris. r, Boletus regius.

2.50 l: s, Scleroderma aurantium. t, Amanita praegraveolens. u, Cantharellus cibarius. v, Geastrum triplex. w, Russula emetica. x, Boletus pinicola.

3 l: y, Fomes versicolor. z, Cantharellus pupurascens. aa, Lyophyllum decastes. ab, Pleurotus ostreatus. ac, Boletus ananas. ad, Amanita caesarea.

**1995, Apr. 7**

**C951** AP188 Sheet of 30, #a.-ad. 35.00 35.00

FAO, 50th Anniv. AP189

**1995, May 25 Litho. *Perf. 13½***

**C952** AP189 3 l multicolored .70 .40

CARE, 50th Anniv. AP190

Designs: 1.40 l, Family, farm. No. C954, Orchid, wildlife, couple working in soil. No. C955, Couple in vegetable garden.

**1995, Aug. 4 Litho. *Perf. 13½***

**C953** AP190 1.40 l multicolored .50 .50
**C954** AP190 5.40 l multicolored 2.10 2.10
**C955** AP190 5.40 l multicolored 2.10 2.10
*Nos. C953-C955 (3)* 4.70 4.70

El Puente Archaeological Park — AP191

**1995, Aug. 8 *Imperf.***

**C956** AP191 20 l multicolored 6.25 6.25

America Issue AP192

1.40 l, Kinosternon scorpioides. 4.54 l, Alpinia purpurata, vert. 10 l, Polyborus plancus, vert.

**1995, Oct. 10 Litho. *Perf. 13½***

**C957** AP192 1.40 l multicolored .50 .50
**C958** AP192 4.54 l multicolored 1.60 1.60
**C959** AP192 10 l multicolored 3.50 3.50
*Nos. C957-C959 (3)* 5.60 5.60

Reptiles and Amphibians — AP193

**1995, Nov. 10 Litho. *Perf. 13***

**C960** AP193 5.40 l Iguana iguana 2.10 2.00
**C961** AP193 5.40 l Agalychnis 2.10 2.00

Christmas AP194

**1995, Dec. 4 Litho. *Perf. 13½***

**C962** AP194 1.40 l Bell, vert. .50 .60
**C963** AP194 5.40 l Nativity figurines 2.25 2.25
**C964** AP194 6.90 l Carved deer, vert. 2.50 2.50
*Nos. C962-C964 (3)* 5.25 5.35

Integration System of Central America AP195

1.40 l, Map of Central America, Tegucigalpa Protocol, 1991. 4.30 l, Functions listed, 1993. 5.40 l, 17th Summit of Presidents of Central America.

**1996, Feb. 19 Litho. *Perf. 13½***

**C965** AP195 1.40 l multicolored .50 .50
**C966** AP195 4.30 l multicolored 1.60 1.60
**C967** AP195 5.40 l multicolored 2.00 2.00
*Nos. C965-C967 (3)* 4.10 4.10

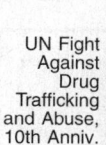

UN Fight Against Drug Trafficking and Abuse, 10th Anniv. AP196

Designs: 1.40 l, Stylized picture of minds on drugs. 5.40 l, Person with butterfly for brain, vert. 10 l, Musical score, "Viva la Vida."

**1996, May 3**

**C968** AP196 1.40 l multicolored .40 .40
**C969** AP196 5.40 l multicolored 1.75 1.75
**C970** AP196 10 l multicolored 2.75 2.75
*Nos. C968-C970 (3)* 4.90 4.90

Arrival of the Garifunas in Honduras, Bicent. AP197

Designs: 1.40 l, Headdress, vert. 5.40 l, Dancers, men playing drums. 10 l, Drums.

**1996, June 13 Litho. *Perf. 13½***

**C971** AP197 1.40 l multicolored .40 .25
**C972** AP197 5.40 l multicolored 1.50 1.00
**C973** AP197 10 l multicolored 2.75 1.50
*Nos. C971-C973 (3)* 4.65 2.75

EXFILHON '96, 7th Philatelic Exhibition AP198

**1996, July 12 Litho. *Perf. 13½***

**C974** AP198 5.40 l Steam locomotive 2.00 2.00
**C975** AP198 5.40 l Passenger railcar 2.00 2.00

**73x52mm**

***Imperf***

**C976** AP198 20 l +2 l like #C974 7.50 7.50
*Nos. C974-C976 (3)* 11.50 11.50

6th Central American Games AP199

**1996, Aug. 30 Litho. *Perf. 13½***

**C977** AP199 4.30 l Soccer 1.40 .60
**C978** AP199 4.54 l Volleyball 1.40 .65
**C979** AP199 5.40 l Mascot, vert. 1.60 .75
*Nos. C977-C979 (3)* 4.40 2.00

Scouting in Honduras, 75th Anniv. AP200

**1996, Oct. 25 Litho. *Perf. 13½***

**C980** AP200 2.15 l Emblems .50 .25
**C981** AP200 5.40 l Emblem, vert. 1.40 .60
**C982** AP200 6.90 l Scout feeding deer, vert. 2.10 .80
*Nos. C980-C982 (3)* 4.00 1.65

Christmas AP201

Poinsettia and: 1.40 l, Candles. 5.40 l, Candles, vert.

**1996, Dec. 23 Litho. *Perf. 13½***

**C983** AP201 1.40 l multicolored .65 .25
**C984** AP201 3 l shown 1.25 .50
**C985** AP201 5.40 l multicolored 2.10 .95
*Nos. C983-C985 (3)* 4.00 1.70

Traditional Costumes AP202

America issue: 4.55 l, Man in costume. 5.40 l, Woman in costume. 10 l, Couple in costumes.

**1997, Jan. 17 Litho. *Perf. 13½***

**C986** AP202 4.55 l multicolored 1.10 .50
**C987** AP202 5.40 l multicolored 1.40 .65
**C988** AP202 10 l multicolored 3.50 1.10
*Nos. C986-C988 (3)* 6.00 2.25

Honduras Plan, 20th Anniv., Intl. Plan, 60th Anniv. AP203

Children's paintings: 1.40 l, Outdoor scene, children swimming, vert. 5.40 l, Girl standing beside lake, fish. 9.70 l, People working between buildings.

**1997, Feb. 7 Litho. *Perf. 13½***

**C989** AP203 1.40 l multicolored .50 .25
**C990** AP203 5.40 l multicolored 1.50 .70
**C991** AP203 9.70 l multicolored 3.00 2.50
*Nos. C989-C991 (3)* 5.00 3.45

Heinrich von Stephan (1831-97) AP205

**1997, May 9 Litho. *Perf. 13½***

**C995** AP205 5.40 l multicolored 1.25 .55

World Population Day AP206

Designs: 6.90 l, Child's drawing of people outside, trees, houses.

**1997, July 11 Litho. *Perf. 13½***

**C996** AP206 1.40 l shown .50 .50
**C997** AP206 6.90 l multicolored 2.50 1.25

Butterflies AP207

Designs: 1 l, Rothchildia forbesi. 1.40 l, Parides photinus. 2.15 l, Morpho peleides. 3 l, Eurytides marcellus. 4.30 l, Parides iphidamas. 5.40 l, Danaus plexippus. 20 l+2 l, Hamadryas arinome.

**1997, July 31**

**C998** AP207 1 l multi .50 .25
**C999** AP207 1.40 l multi .50 .25
**C1000** AP207 2.15 l multi .90 .25
**C1001** AP207 3 l multi 1.25 .25
**C1002** AP207 4.30 l multi 1.60 .65
**C1003** AP207 5.40 l multi 2.25 .85

***Imperf***

**Size: 80x53mm**

**C1004** AP207 20 l +2 l multi 7.50 5.50
*Nos. C998-C1004 (7)* 14.50 8.00

For surcharge see No. C1175.

St. Teresa of Jesus, Death Cent. — AP208

**1997, Aug. 20 Litho. *Perf. 13½***

**C1005** AP208 1.40 l shown .30 .25
**C1006** AP208 5.40 l Portrait, diff. 1.25 .60

Astronomical Observatory AP209

Designs: 5.40 l, Statue of Father Jose Trinidad Reyes. 10 l, Woman with book leading child up steps.

**1997, Sept. 19 Litho. *Perf. 13½***

| | | | | |
|---|---|---|---|---|
| **C1007** AP209 | 1.40 l multicolored | .30 | .25 |
| **C1008** AP209 | 5.40 l multicolored | 1.25 | .60 |
| **C1009** AP209 | 10 l multicolored | 2.25 | 1.10 |
| *Nos. C1007-C1009 (3)* | | 3.80 | 1.95 |

Alma Mater Foundation, 150th anniv., Autonomous University, 40th anniv.

Alcoholics Anonymous in Honduras, 37th anniv. — AP210

**1997, Oct. 27**

**C1010** AP210 5.40 l multicolored 1.60 .60

Diana, Princess of Wales (1961-97) AP211

1.40 l, Portrait, vert. 5.40 l, Diana dressed to walk through mine field, warning sign.
20 l, Mother Teresa, Princess Diana.

**1997, Oct. 15**

| | | | |
|---|---|---|---|
| **C1011** AP211 | 1.40 l multi | .40 | .25 |
| **C1012** AP211 | 5.40 l multi | 1.60 | .70 |

**Size: 51x78mm**

***Imperf***

| | | | |
|---|---|---|---|
| **C1013** AP211 | 20 l multicolored | 6.00 | 4.25 |
| *Nos. C1011-C1013 (3)* | | 8.00 | 5.20 |

Christmas AP212

**1997, Dec. 2 Litho. *Perf. 13½***

| | | | |
|---|---|---|---|
| **C1014** AP212 | 1.40 l Christ of Picacho | .40 | .40 |
| **C1015** AP212 | 5.40 l Virgin of Suyapa | 1.60 | .85 |

Mascot — AP213

C1016: a, Basketball. b, At bat, baseball. c, Soccer. d, Racquetball. e, Spiking volleyball. f, Setting volleyball. g, Bowling. h, Table tennis. i, Rings over map of Central America. j, Pitching, baseball.

No. C1017: a, Kicking, karate. b, Chopping, karate. c, Bowing, karate. d, Wrestling. e, Weight lifting. f, Boxing. g, Body building. h, Fencing. i, Program cover. j, Shooting.

No. C1018: a, Riding bicycle. b, Riding bicycle by shoreline. c, Swimming. d, Water polo. e, Hurdles. f, Gymnastics. g, Riding horse. h, Tennis. i, Program cover with mascot. j, Chess.

**1997 Sheets of 10**

| | | | |
|---|---|---|---|
| **C1016** AP213 | 1.40 l #a.-j. | 3.50 | 3.50 |
| **C1017** AP213 | 1.50 l #a.-j. | 3.75 | 3.75 |
| **C1018** AP213 | 2.15 l #a.-j. | 5.00 | 5.00 |

6th Central American Games, San Pedro Sula.

Fish AP214

1.40 l, Cichlasoma dovii. 2 l, Cichlasoma spilurum. 3 l, Cichlasoma spilurum facing right. 5.40 l, Astyanay fasciatus.

**1997 Litho. *Perf. 13½***

| | | | |
|---|---|---|---|
| **C1019** AP214 | 1.40 l multicolored | .30 | .30 |
| **C1020** AP214 | 2 l multicolored | .40 | .40 |
| **C1021** AP214 | 3 l multicolored | .60 | .50 |
| **C1022** AP214 | 5.40 l multicolored | 1.10 | .90 |
| *Nos. C1019-C1022 (4)* | | 2.40 | 2.10 |

Marine Life, Islas de la Bahía (Bay Islands) — AP215

Designs: a, Balistes vetula. b, Haemudon plumieri. c, Pomacanthus paru. d, Juvenile halichoeres garnoti. e, Pomacanthus arcuatus. f, Holacanthus ciliaris. g, Diver's face, pseud opterogorgia. h, Diver's oxygen tanks, pseud opterogorgia. i, Dendrogya cylindrus. j, Holocentrus adscensionis. k, Dendrogya cylindrus, diff. l, Stegastes fuscus. m, Gorgonia mariae. n, Pillar coral. o, Pomacanthus arcuatus, diff. p, Holocentrus adscensionis, diff. q, Eusmilia fastigiata. r, Scarus coelestinus. s, Pillar coral, diff. t, Lachnolaimus masimus.

**1998, Mar. 13 Litho. *Perf. 13½***

**Sheet of 20**

**C1023** AP215 2.50 l #a.-t. 16.00 16.00

Bancahsa, 50th anniv.
Exists imperf.

America Issue AP216

**1998, May 29 Litho. *Perf. 13½***

| | | | |
|---|---|---|---|
| **C1024** AP216 | 5.40 l Post Office headquarters | 1.60 | .80 |
| **C1025** AP216 | 5.40 l Postman on motorcycle | 1.60 | .80 |

Maya Artifacts — AP217

Designs: 1 l, Large carving on temple. 1.40 l, Stele of Mayan king. 2.15 l, Large stelae. 5.40 l, Small ornamental carving.
20 l, Maya Ruins, Copán.

**1998, June 19 Litho. *Perf. 13½***

| | | | |
|---|---|---|---|
| **C1026** AP217 | 1 l multi | .25 | .25 |
| **C1027** AP217 | 1.40 l multi | .55 | .25 |
| **C1028** AP217 | 2.15 l multi | .90 | .25 |
| **C1029** AP217 | 5.40 l multi | 2.10 | .55 |

**Size: 78x52mm**

***Imperf***

| | | | |
|---|---|---|---|
| **C1030** AP217 | 20 l multicolored | 6.50 | 3.00 |
| *Nos. C1026-C1030 (5)* | | 10.30 | 4.30 |

1998 World Cup Soccer Championships, France — AP218

No. C1033: a, Stadium, Tegucigalpa. b, St. Denis Stadium, France.

**1998, July 3 Litho. *Perf. 13½***

| | | | |
|---|---|---|---|
| **C1031** AP218 | 5.40 l shown | 1.50 | .70 |
| **C1032** AP218 | 10 l Players, vert. | 3.00 | 1.50 |

***Imperf***

**C1033** AP218 10 l Pair, #a.-b. 8.25 7.00

No. C1033 contains two 53x42mm stamps. No. C1033 also issued rouletted between the stamps; value the same.

Reptiles AP219

Designs: 1.40 l, Green iguana. 2 l, Rattlesnake. 3 l, Two iguanas. 5.40 l, Coral snake.
20 l + 2 l, Marine turtle.

**1998, July 31 Litho. *Perf. 13½***

| | | | |
|---|---|---|---|
| **C1034** AP219 | 1.40 l multi | .40 | .35 |
| **C1035** AP219 | 2 l multi | .75 | .60 |
| **C1036** AP219 | 3 l multi | .95 | .75 |
| **C1037** AP219 | 5.40 l multi | 1.90 | 1.25 |

**Size: 77x52mm**

***Imperf***

| | | | |
|---|---|---|---|
| **C1038** AP219 | 20 l +2 l multi | 7.00 | 4.50 |
| *Nos. C1034-C1038 (5)* | | 11.00 | 7.45 |

Christmas AP220

Designs: 3 l, Girl taking ornament from bird, vert. 5.40 l, Christ Child asleep on bed of holly, dove, stars. 10 l, Boy with lantern leading donkey, cabin in the snow, vert.

**1998, Dec. 8 Litho. *Perf. 13½***

| | | | |
|---|---|---|---|
| **C1039** AP220 | 3 l multicolored | .70 | .30 |
| **C1040** AP220 | 5.40 l multicolored | 1.25 | .60 |
| **C1041** AP220 | 10 l multicolored | 2.25 | 1.25 |
| *Nos. C1039-C1041 (3)* | | 4.20 | 2.15 |

Pres. Carlos Roberto Flores, 1st Anniv. of Taking Office AP221

Designs: 5.40 l, Pres. and Mrs. Flores, Pope John Paul II. 10 l, Portrait of Pres., Mrs. Flores, vert.

**1999, Jan. 27 Litho. *Perf. 13½***

| | | | |
|---|---|---|---|
| **C1042** AP221 | 5.40 l multicolored | 1.10 | .55 |
| **C1043** AP221 | 10 l multicolored | 2.00 | 1.00 |

Hurricane Mitch — AP222

No. C1044: a, Men working to clean up. b, Helicopter distributing aid. c, Vehicles under water, North Zone. d, Tipper Gore, Mary de Flores cleaning. e, Working to save banana crop. f, Destruction of Tegucigalpa. g, Cars, buses, trucks blocked by rock slide. h, Destruction of Comayagüela. i, Streets of Comayagüela. j, Oriental Zone. k, Loading debris, help from Mexico. l, Streets of Limpieza. m, Pres. Flores with Pres. Chirac of Fance. n, Business district of Comayagüela. o, Flooding, Tegucigalpa. p, Car in street, Comayagüela.

No. C1045: a, Central Zone. b, South Zone. c, Prince Felipe de Borbon, Mary de Flores. d, Small child crying. e, Cleaning up debris, Comayagüela. f, Families, man carrying baby, North Zone. g, Two men looking at destruction of building, Tegucigalpa. h, Man, child, woman wading in water, North Zone. i, Destruction in rural area. j, Cars piled up, concrete abutment along roadway. k, Cars, buildings along roadway. l, Mexican troops, airplane. m, Boys swimming. n, Pres. & Mrs. Flores, Hillary Clinton. o, People walking over rubble and debris, South Zone. p, Pres. Flores, former US Pres. George Bush.

**1999, Feb. 19 *Rouletted***

**Sheets of 16**

| | | | |
|---|---|---|---|
| **C1044** AP222 | 5.40 l #a.-p. | 18.00 | 18.00 |
| **C1045** AP222 | 5.40 l #a.-p. | 18.00 | 18.00 |

For surcharges, see Mos. C1207, C1208.

Famous Honduran Women — AP223

America Issue: 2.60 l, Maria del Pilar Salinas (b. 1914), scholar. 7.30 l, Clementina Suarez (1902-91), poet, writer. 10.65 l, Mary Flake de Flores, first lady of Honduras.

**1999, Apr. 20 Litho. *Perf. 13½***

| | | | |
|---|---|---|---|
| **C1046** AP223 | 2.60 l multi | .55 | .25 |
| **C1047** AP223 | 7.30 l multi | 1.50 | .75 |
| **C1048** AP223 | 10.65 l multi | 2.25 | 1.10 |
| *Nos. C1046-C1048 (3)* | | 4.30 | 2.10 |

Dated 1998.

Mother's Day AP224

Designs: 20 l, Police officer Orellana breastfeeding baby, vert. 30 l, Paphiopedilum urbanianum. 50 l, Miltoniopsis vexillaria.

**1999, May 14 Litho. *Perf. 13½***

| | | | |
|---|---|---|---|
| **C1049** AP224 | 20 l multicolored | 4.25 | 3.50 |
| **C1050** AP224 | 30 l multicolored | 6.25 | 4.25 |
| **C1051** AP224 | 50 l multicolored | 10.50 | 7.25 |
| *Nos. C1049-C1051 (3)* | | 21.00 | 15.00 |

Endangered Birds — AP225

No. C1052, 5 l: a, Sarcorampohus papa. b, Leucopternis albicollis. c, Harpia harpyja. d, Pulsatrix perspicallata. e, Spizaetus ornatus. f, Pharomarchrus mocinno. g, Aulacorhynchus prasinus. h, Amazilia luciae. i, Ara macao. j, Centurus pygmaeus.

3 l: k, Aratinga canicularis. l, Amazona albifrons. m, Amazona auropalliata. n, Amazona autumnalis. o, Eurypyga helias. p, Crax rubra. q, Brotogeris jugularis. r, Pionus senilis. s, Aratinga rubritorques. t, Tinamus major.

No. C1053: a, Jaberu mycteria. b, Chondrohierax uncinatus. c, Pharomachrus mocinno. d, Ramphastos sulfuratus.

**1999, July 8**

| | | | | |
|---|---|---|---|---|
| **C1052** | AP225 | Sheeet of 20, #a.-t. | 17.50 | 17.50 |
| **C1053** | AP225 | 10 l Sheet of 4, #a.-d. | 9.00 | 7.50 |

Banco Sogerin, 30th anniv.

Inter-American Development Bank, 40th Anniv. — AP226

**1999, Nov. 22 Litho. *Perf. 13½***

| | | | | |
|---|---|---|---|---|
| **C1054** | AP226 18.30 l multi | | 3.75 | 2.00 |

For surcharge see No. C1249.

Blessed Josemaría Escrivá de Balaguer (1902-75), Founder of Opus Dei — AP227

**1999, Nov. 29**

| | | | | |
|---|---|---|---|---|
| **C1055** | AP227 | 2.60 l multi | .60 | .30 |
| **C1056** | AP227 | 16.40 l multi | 3.25 | 2.00 |

Millennium AP228

Designs: 2 l, Salvador Moncada, discoverer of nitric oxide in blood, vert. 8.65 l, Albert Einstein, vert. 10 l, Wilhelm Röntgen, vert. 14.95 l, George Stephenson and locomotive "Rocket."

**1999, Oct. 18**

| | | | | |
|---|---|---|---|---|
| **C1057** | AP228 | 2 l multi | .40 | .25 |
| **C1058** | AP228 | 8.65 l multi | 1.60 | .80 |
| **C1059** | AP228 | 10 l multi | 1.90 | .95 |
| **C1060** | AP228 | 14.95 l multi | 2.75 | 1.40 |
| | | *Nos. C1057-C1060 (4)* | 6.65 | 3.40 |

National Congress, 175th Anniv. AP229

Designs: 4.30, Statue of Francisco Morazán. 10 l, Congress President Rafael Pineda Ponce, Congress Building.

**1999, Dec. 17 Litho. *Perf. 13¼***

| | | | | |
|---|---|---|---|---|
| **C1061** | AP229 | 4.30 l multi | 1.00 | .50 |
| **C1062** | AP229 | 10 l multi | 2.25 | 1.10 |

AP230

Holy Year 2000 — AP231

Holy Year Emblem and: 4 l, Pope John Paul II, people. 4.30 l, St. Peter. 6.90 l, Jesus, Jerusalem, horiz. 7.30 l, John Paul II, crowd, horiz. 10 l, John Paul II giving blessing. 14 l, Pres. Carlos Roberto Flores, John Paul II.

**2000, Jan. 1 Litho. *Perf. 13¼***

| | | | | |
|---|---|---|---|---|
| **C1063** | AP230 | 4 l multi | .90 | .40 |
| **C1064** | AP230 | 4.30 l shown | 1.40 | .70 |
| **C1065** | AP230 | 6.90 l multi | 1.50 | .80 |
| **C1066** | AP230 | 7.30 l multi | 1.60 | .85 |
| **C1067** | AP230 | 10 l multi | 2.25 | 1.10 |
| **C1068** | AP231 | 14 l shown | 4.25 | 1.75 |

**Nos. C1064, C1068 Redrawn**

| | | | | |
|---|---|---|---|---|
| **C1069** | AP230 | 4.30 l multi | 1.25 | .50 |
| **C1070** | AP231 | 14 l multi | 3.50 | 1.50 |
| | | *Nos. C1063-C1070 (8)* | 16.65 | 7.60 |

#C1067 issued in sheets of 6, with picture of John Paul II in selvage. #C1069 has "HONDURAS" in yellow; #C1064 in white. #C1070 has "HONDURAS" at right, reading up; #C1068 at top.

2nd Anniv. of Inauguration of Pres. Flores — AP232

Pres. Flores and: 10 l, Conference delegates. 10.65 l, Mario Hung Pacheco.

**2000, Jan. 27**

| | | | | |
|---|---|---|---|---|
| **C1071** | AP232 | 10 l multi | 2.50 | 1.25 |
| **C1072** | AP232 | 10.65 l multi | 3.00 | 1.40 |

**Musical Instruments Type of Semi-postals of 2000**

No. 1073, vert.: a, 1.40 l, Marimba, denomination at L. b, 1.40 l, Marimba, denomination at L. c, 1.40 l, Ayotl. d, 10 l, Maya drum. e, 10 l, Teponaxtle. f, 2.60 l, Maracas. g, 2.60 l, Güiro. h, 2.60 l, Chinchín. i, 2.60 l, Raspador. j, 2.60 l, Horse's jawbone. k, 3 l, Green zoomorphic whistle. l, 3 l, Aztec drum. m, 3 l, One-tone zoomorphic whistle. n, 3 l, Two-tone zoomorphic whistle. o, 3 l, Tun. p, 4 l, Gourd. q, 4 l, Deer hide drum. r, 4 l, Guacalitos. s, 4 l, Five musicians, marimba. t, 4 l, Four musicians, marimba.

**2000, Apr. 7 Litho. *Perf. 13¼***

| | | | | |
|---|---|---|---|---|
| **C1073** | SP1 | Sheet of 20, #a-t | 21.00 | 21.00 |

Paintings of Pablo Zelaya Sierra — AP233

No. C1074: a, 2 l, Green City (building and tree). b, 2 l, Old Woman With Rosary. c, 2 l, Rural Women (women with jars). d, 2 l, Woman With Green Robe. e, 2 l, City. f, 1.40 l, Shoulders of a Man. g, 1.40 l, Goat. h, 1.40 l, Spanish City. i, 1.40 l, Woman With Chignon. j, 1.40 l, Woman With Calabash. k, 2.60 l, Goat and Birds. l, 2.60 l, Tree Trunks. m, 2.60 l, Nuns. n, 2.60 l, Archers. o, 2.60 l, Moon and Boats. p, 2.60 l, Bust. q, 10 l, Still-life. r, 10 l, Composition With Books. s, 2.60 l, Landscape. t, 2.60 l, Head, Fan and Book.

**2000, July 1**

| | | | | |
|---|---|---|---|---|
| **C1074** | AP233 | Sheet of 20, #a-t | 22.50 | 22.50 |

**Airmail Anniv. Type of Semi-postals**

Designs: 7.30 l, #C12. 10 l, Thomas Canfield Pounds, owner of Central American Airline, vert. 10.65 l, Pres. Rafael López Gutiérrez, signer of first airmail contract, vert.

**2000, July 7**

**Size: 35x25mm**

| | | | | |
|---|---|---|---|---|
| **C1075** | SP2 | 7.30 l multi | 1.60 | .85 |

**Size: 25x35mm**

| | | | | |
|---|---|---|---|---|
| **C1076** | SP2 | 10 l multi | 2.25 | 1.10 |
| **C1077** | SP2 | 10.65 l multi | 2.40 | 1.25 |
| | | *Nos. C1075-C1077 (3)* | 6.25 | 3.20 |

America Issue, A New Millennium Without Arms — AP234

Designs: 10 l, Sobralia macrantha, No guns, vert. 10.65 l, Peace dove, No soldiers, vert. 14 l, Train, No bombs, no more terrorism.

**2000, July 28 Litho. *Perf. 13¼***

| | | | | |
|---|---|---|---|---|
| **C1078-C1080** | AP234 | Set of 3 | 9.00 | 7.00 |

2000 Summer Olympics, Sydney AP235

Designs: 2.60 l, Soccer players Ivan Guerrero, Mario Chirinos. 10.65 l, Swimmer Ramon Valle, vert. 12.45 l, Runner Gina Coello.

No. C1084: a, 4.30 l, Swimmer. b, 4.30 l, Soccer player Danilo Turcios. c, 10.65 l, Runner Pedro Ventura. d, 12.45 l, Soccer player David Suazo.

**2000, Sept. 13**

| | | | | |
|---|---|---|---|---|
| **C1081-C1083** | AP235 | Set of 3 | 10.00 | 8.50 |

**Souvenir Sheet**

| | | | | |
|---|---|---|---|---|
| **C1084** | AP235 | Sheet of 4, #a-d | 11.00 | 11.00 |

No. C1084 exists imperf.

Intl. Voluntarism Year — AP236

Emblem, people and: 2.60 l, White-crowned parrot. 10.65 l, Telipogon ampliflorus.

**2000, Dec. 5**

| | | | | |
|---|---|---|---|---|
| **C1085-C1086** | AP236 | Set of 2 | 3.25 | 2.25 |

Christmas AP237

Designs: 2.60 l, Madonna and child. 7.30 l, Nativity, vert. 14 l, Carpet painter.

**2000, Dec. 18**

| | | | | |
|---|---|---|---|---|
| **C1087-C1089** | AP237 | Set of 3 | 5.00 | 3.25 |

America Issue, Birds — AP238

Designs: 2.60 l, Amazona auropalliata caribea. 4.30 l, Columbina passerina, horiz. 10.65 l, Ara macao. 20 l, Aguila harpia.

**2001, Feb. 16 Litho. *Perf. 13¼***

| | | | | |
|---|---|---|---|---|
| **C1090-C1093** | AP238 | Set of 4 | 10.00 | 8.25 |

Nos. C584, C593, C606, C611, C646-C647, C652-C653, C699 Surcharged — c

Nos. C620, C672, C708, C721 Surcharged — d

No. C637 Surcharged — e

**Methods and Perfs. as Before**

**2001**

| | | | | |
|---|---|---|---|---|
| **C1094** | AP103(c) | 2 l on 16c #C652 | .35 | .25 |
| **C1095** | AP103(c) | 2 l on 16c #C653 | .35 | .25 |
| *a.* | | Pair, #C1094-C1095 | .70 | .35 |
| **C1096** | AP106(d) | 2.60 l on 3c #C672 | .45 | .25 |
| **C1097** | AP114(d) | 2.60 l on 3c #C708 | .45 | .25 |
| **C1098** | AP100(d) | 2.60 l on 8c #C620 | .45 | .25 |
| **C1099** | AP102(e) | 2.60 l on 16c #C637 | .45 | .25 |
| **C1100** | AP96(c) | 3 l on 16c #C593 | .55 | .25 |
| **C1101** | AP116(d) | 4 l on 9c #C721 | .70 | .35 |
| **C1102** | AP97(c) | 4.30 l on 6c #C606 | .75 | .35 |
| **C1103** | AP103(c) | 7.30 l on 6c #C646 | 1.25 | .60 |
| **C1104** | AP103(c) | 7.30 l on 6c #C647 | 1.25 | .60 |
| *a.* | | Pair, #C1103-C1104 | 2.50 | 1.20 |

**C1105** AP95(c) 10 l on 16c #C584 1.75 .90
**C1106** AP112(c) 10.65 l on 16c #C699 1.90 .95
**C1107** AP98(c) 14 l on 16c #C611 3.00 1.25
*Nos. C1094-C1107 (14)* 13.65 6.75

Size and location of surcharge varies. Issued: Nos. C1096-C1099, 3/26; others, 4/3.

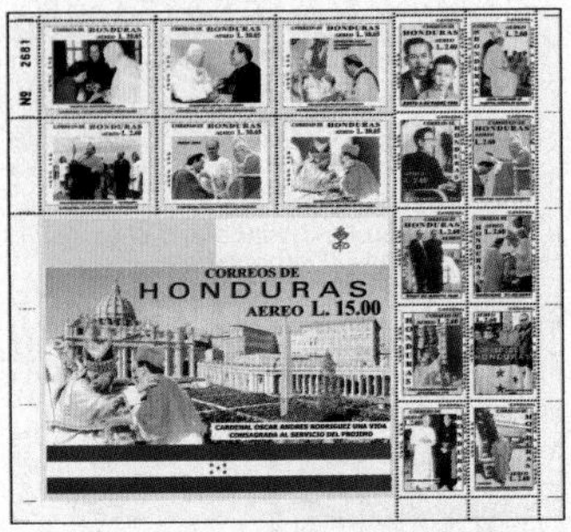

Oscar Cardinal Rodriguez — AP239

No. C1108: a, 2.60 l, With father, 1946. b, 2.60 l, In Sanctuary of Our Lady of Suyapa. c, 2.60 l, As seminarian, 1964. d, 2.60 l, Installation as archbishop. e, 2.60 l, Ordination, 1960. f, 2.60 l, At Vatican, Feb. 21, 2001. g, 2.60 l, At mass in Guatemala, 1970. h, 2.60 l, Standing behind Honduran flag. i, 2.60 l, With Pope John Paul II, 1993. j, 2.60 l, Returning to Honduras as Cardinal. k, 2.60 l, Giving address as Cardinal, Mar. 10, 2001. l, 10.65 l, With Pope and woman, 1993. m, 10.65 l, Papal audience, Feb. 23, 2001. n, 10.65 l, Celebration of the Eucharist. o, 10.65 l, Kneeling before Pope, 1993. p, 10.65 l, Installation as Cardinal, Feb. 21, 2001. q, 15 l, Installation as Cardinal, St. Peter's Square.

**2001, May 9 Litho. *Perf. 13¼***
**C1108** AP239 Sheet of 17, #a-q 30.00 30.00

Stamp sizes: Nos. C1108a-C1108j, 29x40mm; C1108k-C1108p, 49x40mm; C1108q, 163x131mm. No. C1108 exists imperf. Value $30.

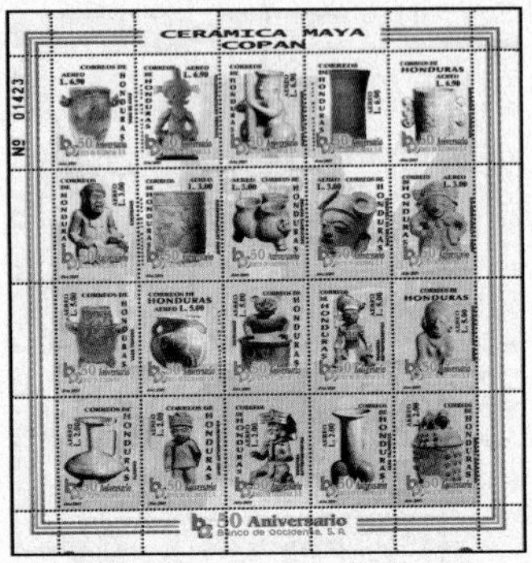

Banco de Occidente, S.A., 50th Anniv. — AP240

Mayan ceramics: a, 2 l, Flower pot. b, 2 l, Anthropomorphic jar. c, 2 l, Anthropomorphic cover. d, 2 l, Cylindrical vase. e, 2 l, Censer tripod. f, 3 l, Scribe. g, 3 l, Cylindrical jar with anthropomorphic figures. h, 3 l, Three-part container. i, 3 l, Ceramic face. j, 3 l, Anthropomorphic jar, diff. k, 5 l, Three-legged vessel. l, 5 l, Pot with handles. m, 5 l, Censer. n, 5 l, Anthropomorphic cover. o, 5 l, Anthropomorphic jar, diff. p, 6.90 l, Pot with handles, diff. q, 6.90 l, Anthropomorphic cover, diff. r, 6.90 l, Anthropomorphic jar, diff. s, 6.90 l, Red cylindrical container. t, 6.90 l, Decorated container.

**2001, Sept. 1 Litho. *Perf. 13¼***
**C1109** AP240 Sheet of 20, #a-t 26.00 26.00

UN High Commissioner for Refugees, 50th Anniv. — AP241

Designs: 2.60 l, Refugee and child, vert. 10.65 l, Refugees running.

**2001**
**C1110-C1111** AP241 Set of 2 4.00 3.00

**Souvenir Sheet**

Juan Ramon Molina Bridge — AP242

No. C1112: a, 2.60 l, Aerial view from end. b, 10 l, Close-up view from side. c, 10.65 l, Aerial view from side. d, 13.65 l, Side view showing river.

**2001, Dec. 20 Litho. *Rouletted 6½***
**C1112** AP242 Sheet of 4, #a-d 15.00 15.00

Stamp sizes: No. C1112b, 152x93mm; others, 40x30mm.

America Issue — Wildlife AP243

Designs: 10 l, Bird, Yojoa Lake. 10.65 l, Iguana, Cisne Islands. 20 l, Chrysina quetzalcoatli, Morpho sp., Pulaphanzhak Cataracts.

**2002, Jan. 31 *Perf. 13¼***
**C1113-C1115** AP243 Set of 3 13.00 13.00

Pan-American Health Organization, Cent. — AP244

**2002, Apr. 7**
**C1116** AP244 10 l multi 3.25 3.25

Miguel R. Pastor, Central District Mayor — AP245

Central District emblem and: a, 1.40 l, Cathedral of San Miguel, statues, birds (57x35mm). b, 1.40 l, Chimpanzee throwing banana peel in trash can (57x35mm). c, 1.40 l, Municipal building (57x35mm). d, 2.60 l, Mayor Pastor, flags (27x35mm). e, 2.60 l, Mayor Pastor under tree (27x35mm). f, 2.60 l, Mayor Pastor with old woman (27x35mm). g, 2.60 l, Mayor Pastor with crowd (27x35mm). h, 2.60 l, Mayor Pastor planting seedling (27x35mm). i, 2.60 l, Mayor Pastor and family (27x35mm). j, 10 l, Municipal council (57x35mm). k, 10 l, Mayor with guests (57x35mm). l, 10.65 l, Cathedral of San Miguel, statues, birds (114x75mm).

**2002, June 13 Litho. *Perf. 13¼***
**C1117** AP245 Sheet of 12, #a-l 16.00 16.00

**Souvenir Sheet**

Discovery of Honduras, 500th Anniv. — AP246

No. C1118: a, 10.65 l, Boat on shore, jungle. b, 12.45 l, Natives on shore. c, 13.65 l, Spaniards coming ashore. d, 20 l, Spanish ship.

**2002, Aug. 14**
**C1118** AP246 Sheet of 4, #a-d 9.00 9.00

Exfilhon 2002.

**Souvenir Sheet**

Christianity in Honduras, 500th Anniv. — AP247

No. C1119: a, 2.60 l, Natives and cross. b, 3 l, Santa Barbara Trujillo Fort. c, 10 l, 400 Years of History, by Mario Castillo. d, 10 l, Spaniards on shore, ships at sea.

**2002, Aug. 14**
**C1119** AP247 Sheet of 4, #a-d 5.00 5.00

America issue.

Banco del Pais, 10th Anniv. AP248

**2002, Sept. 5 Litho. *Perf. 13¼***
**C1120** AP248 2 l multi .25 .25
*a.* Block of 10 3.00 3.00
**C1121** AP248 2.60 l multi .50 .50
*a.* Block of 10 4.25 4.25
**C1122** AP248 10 l multi 1.75 1.75
*a.* Sheet of 30 45.00 45.00
**C1123** AP248 10.65 l multi 2.00 2.00
*a.* Sheet of 30 50.00 50.00
*Nos. C1120-C1123 (4)* 4.50 4.50

Backgrounds of Nos. C1120-C1123 show a flag on a staff and clouds in the blocks and and the flag on the sheets, giving each stamp a different background.

Orchids AP249

Designs: 1.40 l, Vanilla planifolia. 2.60 l, Lycaste viriginalis. 3 l, Coelia bella. 4.30 l, Chysis laevis. 8.65 l, Myrmecophila bryslana. 10 l, Rhyncolaelia digbyana.
20 l, Mormodes aromatica.

**2002, Sept. 25 Litho. *Perf. 13¼***
**C1124-C1129** AP249 Set of 6 7.00 7.00

**Size: 96x66mm**
***Imperf***
**C1130** AP249 20 l multi 6.00 6.00

for surcharges see Nos. C1241, C1243, C1252-C1253.

Christmas AP250

Designs: 2.60 l, Creche scene. 10.65 l, Holy Family. 14 l, People at recreation of nativity scene.

**2002, Nov. 25**
**C1131-C1133** AP250 Set of 3 4.00 4.00

National Children's Foundation AP251

Designs: 2.60 l, Children. 10 l, Elderly people. 10.65 l, Symbols of Honduras, vert.

**2002, Dec. 6**
**C1134-C1136** AP251 Set of 3 3.50 3.50

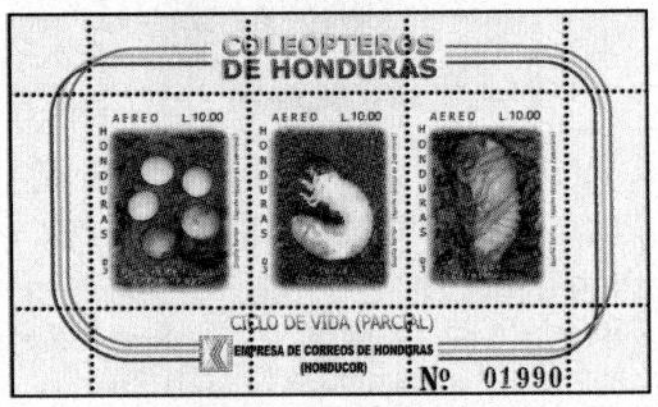

Insects — AP252

No. C1137: a, 2 l, Chrysina spectabilis. b, 2 l, Chrysina strasseni. c, 2 l, Viridimicus omoaensis. d, 2 l, Hoplopyga liturata. e, 2.60 l, Chrysina cusuquensis. f, 2.60 l, Calomacraspis haroldi. g, 2.60 l, Pelidnota strigosa. h, 2.60 l, Odontocheila tawahka. i, 3 l, Chrysina cavei. j, 3 l, Macropoides crassipes. k, 3 l, Pelidnota velutipes. l, 3 l, Tragidion cyanovestis. m, 4 l, Chrysina pastori. n, 4 l, Platycoelia humeralis. o, 4 l, Phanaeus eximius. p, 4 l, Acanthoderes cavei. q, 10.65 l, Chrysina quetzalcoatli. r, 10.65 l, Cyclocephala abrelata. s, 10.65 l, Aegithus rufipennis. t, 10.65 l, Callipogon barbatum.
No. C1138 — Chrysina spp.: a, Eggs. b, Larva. b, Pupa.

**2003, Feb. 20**
**C1137** AP252 Sheet of 20, #a-t 17.00 17.00

**Souvenir Sheet**
**C1138** AP252 10 l Sheet of 3, #a-c 6.00 6.00

Banco Atlantida, 90th anniv. (#C1137).

World Food Program AP253

Designs: 2.60 l, Children with food. 6.90 l, Child with food. 10.65 l, Child with bowl and spoon.

**2003, May 15**
**C1139-C1141** AP253 Set of 3 3.50 3.50

For surcharge see No. C1196.

Souvenir Sheet

Pontificate of John Paul II, 25th Anniv., and 20th Anniv. of Visit to Honduras — AP254

No. C1142: a, 13.65 l, Pope giving blessing. b, 14.55 l, Pope at airport. c, 15.45 l, Pope with staff. d, 16.65 l, Pope with rosary beads.

**2003, Oct. 10** ***Perf. 10½***
**C1142** AP254 Sheet of 4, #a-d 11.00 11.00

For surcharges, See Nos. C1299-C1300.

Regional Sanitary Agricultural Organization, 50th Anniv. — AP255

Designs: 2.60 l, Eggs, sliced meat. 10 l, Eye, map of Central America, corn. 10.65 l, Emblem, map of Central America. 14 l, Vegetables. 20 l, Corn, tomato, fish.

**2003, Oct. 24** ***Perf. 13¼***
**C1143-C1147** AP255 Set of 5 10.00 10.00

Bridges Built by Japan — AP256

No. C1148: a, 3 l, Ilama Bridge, Santa Bárbara. b, 3 l, Sol Naciente Bridge, Choluteca. c, 4.30 l, Río Hondo Bridge, Francisco Morazán. d, 4.30 l, El Chile Bridge, Central District. e, 4.30 l, Iztoca Bridge, Choluteca. f, 10 l, La Democracia Bridge, near El Progreso. g, 10 l, Guasaule Bridge, Honduras-Nicaragua border. 20 l, Juan Ramón Molina Bridge, Tegucigalpa (168x109mm).

**2003, Nov. 25** **Litho.** ***Perf. 13¼***
**C1148** AP256 Sheet of 7, #a-h + label 10.00 10.00

Telethon Honduras AP257

Telethon emblem and: 1.40 l, Flag on staff. 2.60 l, Hand, flag in light blue. 7.30 l, Hand, flag in dark blue. 10 l, Map.

**2003, Dec. 4**
**C1149-C1152** AP257 Set of 4 3.50 3.50

For surcharges see Nos. C1244-C1245, C1247.

Christmas AP258

Designs: 10.65 l, Angel. 14 l, Holy Family in manger.

**2003, Dec. 8**
**C1153-C1154** AP258 Set of 2 4.00 4.00

**Souvenir Sheet**

Endangered Birds — AP259

No. C1155: a, 10 l, Arantinga strenua. b, 10.65 l, Falco deiroleucus. c, 14 l, Spizaetus melanoleucos. d, 20 l, Amazona xantholora.

**2004, May 13**
**C1155** AP259 Sheet of 4, #a-d 10.00 10.00
Exfilhon 2004.

Endangered Animals — AP260

Designs: 85c, Pecari tajacu. 1.40 l, Mazama americana. 2 l, Tamandua mexicana, vert. 2.60 l, Felis concolor. No. C1160, Tamandua mexicana, vert. No. C1161, Felis concolor. No. C1162, Mazama americana. No. C1163, Bradypus variegatus. 4.30 l, Pecari tajacu. 7.85 l, Agalychinis challidryas, vert. 10.65 l, Bradypus variegatus. 14.95 l, Agalchinis challidryas, vert.

No. C1168, vert.: a, Mono titi. b, Cebus capucinus. c, Ateles geoffroyi. d, Alouatta palliata.

**2004, May 24** **Litho.** ***Perf. 13¼***

| | | | | |
|---|---|---|---|---|
| **C1156** | AP260 | 85c multi | .25 | .25 |
| **C1157** | AP260 | 1.40 l multi | .25 | .25 |
| **C1158** | AP260 | 2 l multi | .40 | .40 |
| **C1159** | AP260 | 2.60 l multi | .45 | .45 |
| **C1160** | AP260 | 3 l multi | .55 | .55 |
| **C1161** | AP260 | 3 l multi | .55 | .55 |
| **C1162** | AP260 | 4 l multi | .60 | .60 |
| **C1163** | AP260 | 4 l multi | .60 | .60 |
| **C1164** | AP260 | 4.30 l multi | .65 | .65 |
| **C1165** | AP260 | 7.85 l multi | 1.40 | 1.40 |
| **C1166** | AP260 | 10.65 l multi | 2.10 | 2.10 |
| **C1167** | AP260 | 14.95 l multi | 3.00 | 3.00 |
| | *Nos. C1156-C1167 (12)* | | 10.80 | 10.80 |
| **C1168** | AP260 | 10 l Sheet of 4, #a-d | 7.50 | 7.50 |

Nos. C1156-C1158, C1161, C1163, and C1165 were each printed in souvenir sheets of 4.

For surcharges see Nos. C1239-C1240, C1242, C1254-C1255.

Shells AP261

Designs: Nos. C1169, C1174f, Voluta polypleura. Nos. C1170, C1174d, Strombus gallus. Nos. C1171, C1174a, Charonia variegata, Terebra taurina. Nos. C1172, C1174e, Spondylus americanus. Nos. C1173, C1174c, Strombus raninus. No. C1174b, Man blowing conch shell.

**2004, July 19** **Litho.** ***Perf. 13¼***

| | | | | |
|---|---|---|---|---|
| **C1169** | AP261 | 85c multi | .25 | .25 |
| **C1170** | AP261 | 1.40 l multi | .25 | .25 |
| **C1171** | AP261 | 2 l multi | .25 | .25 |
| **C1172** | AP261 | 2.60 l multi | .55 | .55 |
| **C1173** | AP261 | 10.65 l multi | 2.10 | 2.10 |
| | *Nos. C1169-C1173 (5)* | | 3.40 | 3.40 |

**Miniature Sheet**

| | | | |
|---|---|---|---|
| **C1174** | Sheet of 6 | 11.00 | 11.00 |
| *a.-b.* | AP261 4 l Either single | .75 | .75 |
| *c.-d.* | AP261 5 l Either single | .95 | .95 |
| *e.-f.* | AP261 20 l Either single | 3.75 | 3.75 |

For surcharges see Nos. C1246, C1248, C1250-C1251.

**No. C1004 Surcharged in Red**

**2004, Aug. 13** **Litho.** ***Imperf.***
**C1175** AP207 50 l on 20 l+2 l multi 9.00 9.00

Miniature Sheet

Banco Fichosa, Sponsor of National Soccer Team — AP262

No. C1176: a, 4.30 l, Players, Honduras flag. b, 10.65 l, Team. c, 14 l, Saúl Martinez, David Suazo. d, 20 l, Amado Guevara.

**2004, Sept. 3** **Litho.** ***Perf. 13¼***
**C1176** AP262 Sheet of 4, #a-d 6.50 6.50

Christmas AP263

Designs: 2.60 l, Flight into Egypt. 7.85 l, Santa Claus on ornament. 10.65 l, Three Kings. 20 l, Holy Family.

**2004, Nov. 23** **Litho.** ***Perf. 13¼***
**C1177-C1180** AP263 Set of 4 7.50 7.50
*C1178a* Sheet of 4 #C1178 6.50 6.50

For surcharges see Nos. C1224-C1227.

AP264

National Unity — AP265

**2005, Feb. 3**
**C1181** AP264 10 l multi 1.10 1.10
**C1182** AP265 20 l multi 2.25 2.25

Rotary International, Cent. — AP266

Rotary International emblem and: 2.60 l, Rafael Diaz Chávez, Paul Harris and Jorge Fidel Durón. 5 l, "100 años," vert. 8 l, Globe and arrows. 10.65 l, Map of Honduras, PolioPlus emblem. 14 l, Mayan sculpture.

**2005, Feb. 23**
**C1183-C1187** AP266 Set of 5 5.25 5.25

Pope John Paul II (1920-2005) AP267

Pope: 10 l, Wearing white vestments. 15 l, Wearing colored vestments.
20 l, Holding crucifix.

**2005, Apr. 15** **Litho.** ***Perf. 13¼***
**C1188-C1189** AP267 Set of 2 3.25 3.25

**Souvenir Sheet**

**C1190** Sheet of 2 #C1190a 5.25 5.25
*a.* AP267 20 l multi, 29x42mm 2.50 2.50

Honduran Medical Review, 75th Anniv. — AP268

Designs: 3 l, House. 5 l, Bird. 12 l, Jaguar. 30 l, Flowers.

No. C1195: a, Macaws. b, Macaw in banana tree. c, Rooster. d, Turkeys and hens.

**2005, May 18**
**C1191-C1194** AP268 Set of 4 6.50 6.50

**Souvenir Sheet**

**C1195** AP268 25 l Sheet of 4, #a-d 13.00 13.00

**Nos. 390-392, B1, C550, C552, C553, C576, C715, C1044-C1045, C1140 and RA8 Surcharged**

"X" Obliterators — f

Box Obliterator and "Aereo" — g

Box Obliterator — h

**Methods and Perfs as Before**

**2005, June 3**

| | | | | |
|---|---|---|---|---|
| **C1196** | AP253(f) | 3 l on 6.90 l #C1140 | .30 | .30 |
| **C1197** | AP72(f) | 5 l on 16c on 1c #C552 | .55 | .55 |
| **C1198** | AP72(f) | 5 l on 16c on 1c #C553 | .55 | .55 |
| **C1199** | PT6(g) | 10 l on 13.85 l on 1c #392 | 1.10 | 1.10 |
| **C1200** | AP68(f) | 14 l on 16c on 1c #C550 | 1.50 | 1.50 |
| **C1201** | PT6(g) | 20 l on 13.85 l on 1c #392 | 2.10 | 2.10 |
| **C1202** | PT6(g) | 25 l on 11.55 l on 1c #390 | 2.75 | 2.75 |
| **C1203** | AP94(f) | 30 l on 16c #C576 | 3.25 | 3.25 |
| **C1204** | AP115(f) | 35 l on 16c #C715 | 3.75 | 3.75 |
| **C1205** | PT6(g) | 40 l on 11.55 l on 1c #390 | 4.25 | 4.25 |
| **C1206** | PT6(g) | 50 l on 12.45 l on 1c #391 | 5.50 | 5.50 |
| | *Nos. C1196-C1206 (11)* | | 25.60 | 25.60 |

**Sheets**

| | | | |
|---|---|---|---|
| **C1207** | Sheet of 16 (#C1044) | 15.00 | 15.00 |
| *a.-p.* | AP222(h) 8 l on 5.40 l any single | .90 | .90 |
| **C1208** | Sheet of 16 (#C1045) | 15.00 | 15.00 |
| *a.-p.* | AP222(h) 8 l on 5.40 l any single | .90 | .90 |
| **C1209** | Sheet of 6 (#B1) | 10.00 | 10.00 |
| *a.-f.* | SP1(f) 15 l on 10 l +1 l any single | 1.60 | 1.60 |
| *g.* | As No. C1209, on No. B1a | 10.00 | 10.00 |

Size, location and font of surcharges and obliterators vary on types "f" and "h."

Honduras — Japan Diplomatic Relations, 70th Anniv. AP269

Designs: 8 l, Actors in play. 15 l, Emblem of Japanese-Central American Year. 30 l, National Congress, Japanese Princess Sayako.

No. C1213: a, Japanese ceramics. b, Flowers. c, Mayan ceramics. d, Mount Fuji, Japan and Pico Bonito National Park, Honduras.

**2005, Aug. 9 Litho. *Perf. 13¼***

**C1210-C1212** AP269 Set of 3 7.00 7.00

**Souvenir Sheet**

**C1213** AP269 25 l Sheet of 4, #a-d 13.00 13.00

Gen. José Trinidad Cabañas (1805-71) AP270

Cabañas: 3 l, With green panel at bottom. 8 l, With university buildings, horiz. 15 l, In oval frame.

**2005, Sept. 12**

**C1214-C1216** AP270 Set of 3 3.25 3.25

Honduras, Water Capital — AP271

Water droplet and: 30 l, Heart, butterfly, Sanaa and Ras-hon emblems. 50 l, Heart.

**2005, Sept. 28**

**C1217** AP271 30 l multi 4.00 4.00

**Souvenir Sheet**

**C1218** AP271 50 l multi 7.00 7.00

**Souvenir Sheet**

America Issue — Endangered Mushrooms — AP272

No. C1219: a, 20 l, Hygrophorus marzuolus. b, 25 l, Lactarius deliciosus. c, 30 l, Boletus pinophilus. d, 50 l, Gyromitra esculenta.

**2005**

**C1219** AP272 Sheet of 4, #a-d 17.00 17.00

AP273

Mail Transport AP274

Designs: 5 l, Charles Lindbergh, PAA emblem. 25 l, Postal rail car, 1920. 30 l, First Honduran postal car, 1914.

50 l, Sikorsky S-38 airplane, PAA emblem, horiz.

**2005, Dec. 6 Litho. *Perf. 13¼***

| | | | | |
|---|---|---|---|---|
| **C1220** | AP273 | 5 l multi | .65 | .65 |
| **C1221** | AP274 | 25 l multi | 3.00 | 3.00 |
| **C1222** | AP274 | 30 l multi | 3.75 | 3.75 |
| | *Nos. C1220-C1222 (3)* | | 7.40 | 7.40 |

***Imperf***

**Size: 89x64mm**

**C1223** AP273 50 l multi 6.50 6.50

Nos. C1177-C1179 Surcharged

**2005 Litho. *Perf. 13¼***

| | | | | |
|---|---|---|---|---|
| **C1224** | AP263 | 3 l on 2.60 l #C1177 | .35 | .35 |
| **C1225** | AP263 | 15 l on 7.85 l #C1178 | 1.90 | 1.90 |
| **C1226** | AP263 | 25 l on 7.85 l #C1178 | 3.50 | 3.50 |
| **C1227** | AP263 | 50 l on 10.65 l #C1179 | 6.75 | 6.75 |
| | *Nos. C1224-C1227 (4)* | | 12.50 | 12.50 |

No. C1226 has a thick wavy line obliterator and was issued in sheets of four.

2006 Winter Olympics, Turin — AP275

Skier and: 20 l, Turin Olympics emblem, Olympic rings. 50 l, Olympic rings.

**2006, Jan. 24**

**C1228-C1229** AP275 Set of 2 9.00 9.00

Forgiveness of Honduran Debts by Foreign Nations — AP276

Designs: 14 l, Structure 4, Copán Ruins. 15 l, Flags of nations forgiving debts. 30 l, Honduras Pres. Ricardo Maduro, vert.

**2006, Jan. 26**

**C1230-C1232** AP276 Set of 3 12.50 12.50

Cortés Chamber of Commerce and Industry, 75th Anniv. — AP277

Anniversary and Chamber of Commerce emblem and: 20 l, Gears. 35 l, The Forger, sculpture by J. Zelaya, horiz. 50 l, El Industrial, mural by A. Martínez.

**2006**

**C1233-C1235** AP277 Set of 3 13.00 13.00

Diplomatic Relations Between Honduras and Brazil, Cent. AP278

Designs: 20 l, Flags of Honduras and Brazil. 30 l, Baron of Rio Branco (1845-1912) Brazilian diplomat, vert.

**2006 Litho. *Perf. 13¼***

**C1236-C1237** AP278 Set of 2 6.50 6.50

**Miniature Sheet**

Honduran Friendship With Japan — AP279

No. C1238: a, 10 l, Children learning about Chagas disease. b, 15 l, Teacher and children. c, 20 l, Japanese naval vessels and flag. d, 25 l, Sailors in dress uniforms.

**2006**

**C1238** AP279 Sheet of 4, #a-d 7.50 7.50

**Nos. C1054, C1124-C1125, C1127-C1128, C1149-C1151, C1159, C1162, C1164, C1166-C1167, C1169-C1170, C1172-C1173 Surcharged**

**Methods and Perfs As Before**

**2007 ?**

| | | | | |
|---|---|---|---|---|
| **C1239** | AP260 | 2 l on 2.60 l #C1159 | .25 | .25 |
| **C1240** | AP260 | 2 l on 4 l #C1162 | .25 | .25 |
| **C1241** | AP249 | 2 l on 8.65 l #C1128 | .25 | .25 |
| **C1242** | AP260 | 2 l on 10.65 l #C1166 | .25 | .25 |
| **C1243** | AP249 | 3 l on 1.40 l #C1124 | .35 | .35 |
| **C1244** | AP257 | 3 l on 1.40 l #C1149 | .35 | .35 |
| **C1245** | AP257 | 3 l on 2.60 l #C1150 | .35 | .35 |
| **C1246** | AP261 | 3 l on 2.60 l #C1172 | .35 | .35 |
| **C1247** | AP257 | 3 l on 7.30 l #C1151 | .35 | .35 |
| **C1248** | AP261 | 3 l on 10.65 l #C1173 | .35 | .35 |
| **C1249** | AP226 | 3 l on 18.30 l #C1054 | .35 | .35 |
| **C1250** | AP261 | 5 l on 85c #C1169 | .55 | .55 |
| **C1251** | AP261 | 5 l on 1.40 l #C1170 | .55 | .55 |
| **C1252** | AP249 | 5 l on 2.60 l #C1125 | .55 | .55 |
| **C1253** | AP249 | 5 l on 4.30 l #C1127 | .55 | .55 |
| **C1254** | AP260 | 5 l on 4.30 l #C1164 | .55 | .55 |
| **C1255** | AP260 | 5 l on 14.95 l #C1167 | .55 | .55 |
| | *Nos. C1239-C1255 (17)* | | 6.75 | 6.75 |

Constitution, 25th Anniv. — AP280

Designs: 5 l, Leaders of the Legislative, Executive and Judicial branches of government. 10 l, 1824 Constituent Assembly Building. 15 l, Presidential House, 1922-91, vert. 20 l, Legislative Building.

**2007 Litho. *Perf. 13¼***
**C1256-C1259** AP280 Set of 4 5.50 5.50

Miniature Sheet

Central Bank of Honduras, 50th Anniv. — AP281

No. C1260 — Central Bank of Honduras emblem and paintings: a, 5 l, Holocausto, by César Rendón. b, 10 l, La Novia, by Miguel Angel Ruiz Matute. c, 15 l, Ayer, Hoy y Mañana, by Felipe Bouchard. d, 20 l, Paisaje de Tegucigalpa, by Mario Castillo. e, 25 l, Dinamismo, by Benigno Gómez. f, 30 l, Guitarras en Descanso, by Dante Lazzaroni.

**2007**
**C1260** AP281 Sheet of 6, #a-f 11.50 11.50

Adjudication of "Four Cardinal Points" Police Torture Case — AP282

**2007, Oct. 18 Litho. *Perf. 13¼***
**C1261** AP282 50 l multi 5.50 5.50

Printed in sheets of 2.

Miniature Sheets

Launch of Sputnik I, 50th Anniv. — AP283

No. C1262: a, 25 l, Sputnik launch vehicle, pale blue background (30x40mm). b, 35 l, Sputnik I, yellow background (30x40mm). c, 50 l, Sputnik orbiting Earth, pale green background (60x40mm).

No. C1263: a, 25 l, As #C1262a, pale green background. b, 35 l, As #C1262b, pale blue background. c, 50 l, As #C1262c, yellow background.

**2007, Nov. 30**
**C1262** AP283 Sheet of 3, #a-c 12.00 12.00
**C1263** AP283 Sheet of 3, #a-c 12.00 12.00

Miniature Sheet

Paintings by Gaye-Darléne Bidart de Satulsky — AP284

No. C1264: a, 3 l, Medusa de las Islas. b, 3 l, Nido de Amor. c, 3 l, Guitarrista Isleño. d, 5 l, "M" Hombre Cruz. e, 5 l, Amor a Martillazos. f, 5 l, Sor María Rosa. g, 5 l, Isleña, Luna y Mar. h, 5 l, Clementina Suárez. i, 5 l, La Naranjera.

**2008**
**C1264** AP284 Sheet of 9, #a-i 4.25 4.25

Miniature Sheet

America Issue — AP285

No. C1265: a, 2 l, Factory workers and sewing machine. b, 3 l, Energy savings mascot. c, 5 l, School children. d, 10 l, Children in native costumes.

**2008**
**C1265** AP285 Sheet of 4, #a-d 2.10 2.10

2008 Summer Olympics, Beijing AP286

Designs: 3 l, Olympic torch. No. C1267, 5 l, Judo. No. C1268, 5 l, Runners. 25 l, Soccer.

**2008, July 30**
**C1266-C1269** AP286 Set of 4 4.00 4.00

Juan Ramón Molina (1875-1908), Poet — AP287

Designs: 10 l, Molina, mermaid and ship. 25 l, Molina.

**2008, Oct. 30**
**C1270-C1271** AP287 Set of 2 3.75 3.75

Miniature Sheet

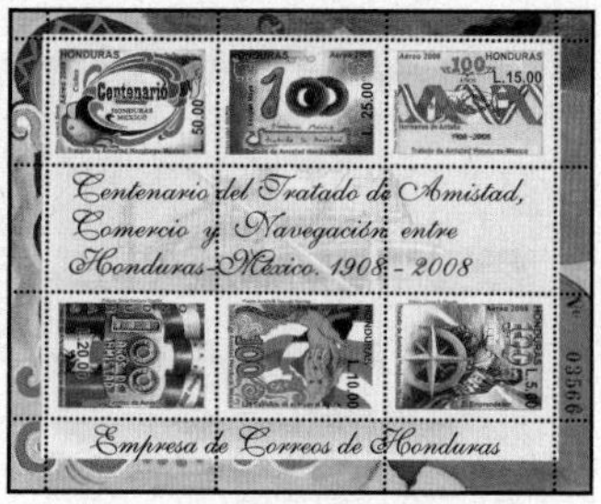


Treaty of Amity, Commerce and Navigation Between Honduras and Mexico, Cent. — AP288

No. C1272: a, 5 l, Sailor and ship. b, 10 l, Hands, flags and maps. c, 15 l, Handshake, double helix of flags, horiz. d, 20 l, Flags and "100 Años de Amistad." e, 25 l, "100" and colors of flags, horiz. f, 50 l, Parrot and eagle, horiz.

**2008 Litho. *Perf. 13¼***
**C1272** AP288 Sheet of 6, #a-f + 3 labels 13.50 13.50

España Normal School, Villa Ahumada, 58th Anniv. AP289

Designs: 2 l, School. 5 l, School emblem.

**2009, Aug. 28 Litho. *Perf. 13¼***
**C1273-C1274** AP289 Set of 2 .75 .75

America Issue AP290

Traditional toys and games: 3 l, Hopscotch. 10 l, Kite. 20 l, Top. 50 l, Children playing soccer, jumping rope and flying kite.

**2009, Aug. 28**
**C1275-C1278** AP290 Set of 4 8.75 8.75

President's House AP291

Dove, Map of Honduras AP292

Interim President Roberto Micheletti Baín — AP293

**2009, Dec. 3**
**C1279** AP291 3 l multi .35 .35
**C1280** AP292 15 l multi 1.60 1.60
**C1281** AP293 20 l multi 2.10 2.10
*Nos. C1279-C1281 (3)* 4.05 4.05

2010 World Cup Soccer Championships, South Africa — AP294

Designs: 5 l, Child playing soccer. 20 l, Honduras soccer team. 25 l, Emblem of Honduras soccer team.

**2009, Dec. 3**
**C1282-C1284** AP294 Set of 3 5.25 5.25

2010 World Cup Soccer Championships, South Africa — AP295

2010 World Cup emblem, Ficohsa Bank emblem, stadium and flag of: 3 l, Chile. 5 l, Switzerland. 14 l, Spain.

No. C1288, vert.: a, 2010 World Cup emblem, World Cup trophy. b, 2010 World Cup emblem.

**2010, May Litho. *Perf. 13¼***
**C1285-C1287** AP295 Set of 3 2.40 2.40

**Souvenir Sheet**

**C1288** AP295 20 l Sheet of 2, #a-b 4.25 4.25

America Issue, National Symbols AP296

Designs: 5 l, Flag and coat of arms of Honduras. 25 l, Odocoileus virginianus. 50 l, Ara macao.

**2010, Nov.**
**C1289-C1291** AP296 Set of 3 8.50 8.50

Maria Auxiliadora Institute, Cent. — AP297

Designs: 10 l, Virgin Mary and Jesus, "100" with hearts replacing zeroes. 50 l, Virgin Mary and Jesus.

**2010, Nov.**
**C1292-C1293** AP297 Set of 2 6.50 6.50

Christmas AP298

Designs: 3 l, Angel and lamb. 20 l, Adoration of the Magi.

50 l, Locomotive with Christmas decorations, horiz.

**2010, Nov.** *Perf. 13¼*
**C1294-C1295** AP298 Set of 2 2.50 2.50

*Imperf*

**Size: 90x63mm**

**C1296** AP298 50 l multi 5.50 5.50

Postal Union of the Americas, Spain and Portugal (UPAEP), Cent. — AP299

Designs: 5 l, Mayan sculpture. 25 l, Yum Kax, Mayan agricultural deity.

**2011, Mar. 23** *Perf. 13½x13¼*
**C1297-C1298** AP299 Set of 2 3.25 3.25

**No. C1142 Surcharged**

**Method and Perf. As Before**

**2011, May**

**C1299** Sheet of 4 3.25 3.25
*a.* AP254 5 l on 13.65 l #C1142a .50 .50
*b.* AP254 5 l on 14.55 l #C1142b .50 .50
*c.* AP254 10 l on 15.45 l #C1142c 1.10 1.10
*d.* AP254 10 l on 16.65 l #C1142d 1.10 1.10
**C1300** Sheet of 4 7.50 7.50
*a.* AP254 15 l on 13.65 l #C1142a 1.60 1.60
*b.* AP254 15 l on 14.55 l #C1142b 1.60 1.60
*c.* AP254 20 l on 15.45 l #C1142c 2.10 2.10
*d.* AP254 20 l on 16.65 l #C1142d 2.10 2.10

Inscribed across the stamps of the sheet is the text "Beato Juan Pablo 01/05/2011" on No. C1299 and "Beatificacion 01/05/2011" on No. C1300.

AP300

Diplomatic Relations Between Honduras and South Korea, 50th Anniv. — AP301

Designs: 5 l, Presidents and flags of Honduras and South Korea.

No. C1302: a, Korean vase. b, Mayan calendar. c, Korean statue of Buddha. d, Honduran bowl. e, Korean sundial. f, Mayan stele.

**2012, Apr. 25** **Litho.** *Perf. 13¼*
**C1301** AP300 5 l multi .55 .55

**Miniature Sheet**

**C1302** AP301 2 l Sheet of 6, #a-f 1.25 1.25

## AIR POST SEMI-POSTAL STAMPS

No. C13C Surcharged in Black

**Unwmk.**

**1929, June 5** **Engr.** *Perf. 12*
**CB1** AP1 50c + 5c carmine .65 .30
**CB2** AP1 50c + 10c carmine .70 .35
**CB3** AP1 50c + 15c carmine .95 .55
**CB4** AP1 50c + 20c carmine 1.40 .75
*Nos. CB1-CB4 (4)* 3.70 1.95

**Catalogue values for unused stamps in this section, from this point to the end of the section, are for Never Hinged items.**

Souvenir Sheet

Airmail Pilot Sumner B. Morgan and Airplane — SP2

**2000, July 7**
**CB5** SP2 50 l + 5 l multi 11.00 11.00

First airmail flight in Honduras, 75th anniv., EXFILHON 2000. See Nos. C1075-C1077.

No. C619 Surcharged With New Value in Black and 2000 Sydney Olympics Emblem in Red

**2000, Sept. 13** **Litho.** *Imperf.*
**CB6** AP99 48.50 l +1.50 l multi 10.00 10.00

## AIR POST SPECIAL DELIVERY STAMPS

No. CO52 Surcharged in Red

*Perf. 13½x14*

**1953, Dec. 8** **Engr.** **Unwmk.**
**CE1** AP65 20c on 1c 3.00 1.50

Transport Plane APSD1

**1956, Oct. 3** *Perf. 13x12½*
**CE2** APSD1 20c black & red .80 .50

Surcharges on No. CE2 (see Nos. C421, C477) eliminate its special delivery character.

**Catalogue values for unused stamps in this section, from this point to the end of the section, are for Never Hinged items.**

**Stamp Centenary Type of Air Post Issue**

Design: 20c, Mailman on motorcycle.

**1966, May 31** **Litho.** *Perf. 14x14½*
**CE3** AP81 20c bis brn, brn & gold 1.00 .50

Centenary (in 1965) of the first Honduran postage stamp.

The "HABILITADO" overprint on No. CE3 (see No. C479) eliminates its special delivery character.

**Independence Type of Air Post Issue**

**1972, May 19** **Litho.** *Perf. 13*
**CE4** AP89 20c Corsair plane .70 .35

No. CE4 Surcharged

**1975**
**CE5** AP89 60c on 20c 1.00 .65

**Forest Protection Type of Air Post**

**1976, May 28** **Litho.** *Perf. 13½*
**CE6** AP96 60c Stag in forest .75 .50

## AIR POST OFFICIAL STAMPS

Official Stamps Nos. O78 to O81 Overprinted in Red, Green or Black

**1930** *Perf. 11, 11½*
**CO1** A24 10c deep blue (R) 1.25 1.25
**CO2** A24 20c yellow brown 1.25 1.25
*a.* Vert. pair, imperf. btwn. 14.00
**CO3** A24 50c vermilion (Bk) 1.40 1.40
**CO4** A24 1p emerald (R) 1.25 1.25
*Nos. CO1-CO4 (4)* 5.15 5.15

OA1

**Green Surcharge**

**CO5** OA1 5c on 6c red vio 1.00 1.00
*a.* "1910" for "1930" 2.75 2.75
*b.* "1920" for "1930" 2.75 2.75

The overprint exists in other colors and on other denominations but the status of these is questioned.

Official Stamps of 1931 Overprinted

**1931** **Unwmk.** *Perf. 12*
**CO6** O2 1c ultra .35 .35
**CO7** O2 2c black brown .85 .85
**CO8** O2 5c olive gray 1.00 1.00
**CO9** O2 6c orange red 1.00 1.00
*a.* Inverted overprint 24.00 24.00
**CO10** O2 10c dark green 1.25 1.25
**CO11** O2 15c olive brown 2.00 1.75
*a.* Inverted overprint 20.00 20.00
**CO12** O2 20c red brown 2.00 1.75
**CO13** O2 50c gray violet 1.40 1.40
**CO14** O2 1p deep orange 2.00 1.75
*Nos. CO6-CO14 (9)* 11.85 11.10

In the setting of the overprint there are numerous errors in the spelling and punctuation, letters omitted and similar varieties.

This set is known with blue overprint. A similar overprint is known in larger type, but its status has not been fully determined.

**Postage Stamps of 1918-30 Surcharged Type "a" or Type "b" (#CO22-CO23) in Green, Black, Red and Blue**

a

b

**1933** **Wmk. 209, Unwmk.**
**CO15** A39 20c on 2c #295 (G) 3.25 3.25
**CO16** A39 20c on 2c #296 (G) 3.25 3.25
**CO17** A39 20c on 2c #297 (G) 3.25 3.25
**CO17A** A39 40c on 2c #295 2.00 2.00
**CO18** A39 40c on 2c #297 (G) 7.00 7.00
**CO18A** A39 40c on 2c #297 4.25 4.25
**CO19** A28 40c on 5c #246 4.25 4.25
**CO19A** A28 40c on 5c #247 7.00 7.00
**CO20** A28 40c on 5c #266 15.00 15.00
**CO20A** A28 40c on 5c #267 9.00 9.00
**CO20B** A28 40c on 5c #267 (R) 14.00 14.00
**CO21** A20 70c on 5c #183 3.00 3.00
**CO22** A24 70c on 10c #214 (R) 3.25 3.25
**CO23** A22 1 l on 20c #191 (Bl) 3.25 3.25
**CO24** A24 1 l on 50c #216 (Bl) 14.00 14.00
**CO25** A22 1.20 l on 1p #193 (Bl) 1.00 1.00
*Nos. CO15-CO25 (16)* 96.75 96.75

**Official Stamps of 1915-29 Surcharged Type "a" or Type "b" (#CO28-CO29, CO33-CO41, CO43) in Black, Red, Green, Orange, Carmine or Blue**

**CO26** O1 40c on 5c #O84 (Bk) 1.00 1.00
**CO27** O1 40c on 5c #O84 (R) 25.00 25.00
**CO28** A24 60c on 6c #O77 (Bk) .70 .70
**CO29** A24 60c on 6c #O77 (G) 25.00 25.00
**CO30** A20 70c on 5c #O60 (Bk) 5.25 5.25
**CO31** A19 70c on 10c #O62 (R) 9.00 9.00
**CO32** A19 70c on 10c #O62 (Bk) 7.75 7.75
**CO33** A22 70c on 10c #O70 (R) 4.50 4.00
**CO34** A24 70c on 10c #O78 (O) 3.50 3.50
**CO35** A24 70c on 10c #O78 (C) 4.50 4.50
**CO36** A22 70c on 15c #O71 (R) 87.50 87.50
**CO37** A22 90c on 10c #O70 (R) 5.25 5.25
**CO38** A22 90c on 15c #O71 (R) 8.00 8.00
**CO38A** A24 1 l on 2c #O76 1.40 1.40
**CO39** A22 1 l on 20c #O72 2.50 2.50
**CO39A** A24 1 l on 20c #O79 3.75 3.75
**CO40** A22 1 l on 50c #O73 1.90 1.90
**CO41** A24 1 l on 50c #O80 4.25 4.25
**CO42** A20 1.20 l on 1p #O65 9.00 7.00
**CO43** A24 1.20 l on 1p #O81 3.00 3.00
*Nos. CO26-CO43 (20)* 212.75 210.25

Varieties of foregoing surcharges exist.

Merchant Flag and Seal of Honduras OA2

**1939, Feb. 27** **Unwmk.** *Perf. 12½*
**CO44** OA2 2c dp blue & grn .25 .25
**CO45** OA2 5c dp blue & org .25 .25
**CO46** OA2 8c dp blue & brn .25 .25
**CO47** OA2 15c dp blue & car .30 .25
**CO48** OA2 46c dp blue & ol grn .40 .30
**CO49** OA2 50c dp blue & vio .50 .30

CO50 OA2 1 l dp blue & red brn 1.75 1.25
CO51 OA2 2 l dp blue & red org 3.75 2.25
*Nos. CO44-CO51 (8)* 7.45 5.10

For overprints and surcharges see #C101-C117.

**Types of Air Post Stamps of 1952 Ovptd. in Red**

***Perf. 13½x14, 14x13½***

**1952 Engr. Unwmk.**
CO52 AP65 1c rose lil & ol .25 .25
CO53 AP65 2c brown & vio .25 .25
CO54 AP65 8c dp car & blk .25 .25
CO55 AP66 16c pur & dk grn .25 .25
CO56 AP65 30c dk bl & blk .50 .50
CO57 AP65 1 l dk grn & dk brown 1.75 1.75
CO58 AP65 2 l bl & red brn 3.50 3.50
CO59 AP66 5 l red org & blk 8.50 8.50
*Nos. CO52-CO59 (8)* 15.25 15.25

Queen Isabella I of Spain, 500th birth anniv.
For overprints and surcharge, see Nos. CE1, CO110.

No. C222 and Types of Air Post Stamps of 1953 Overprinted in Red

**Engraved; Center of 1c Litho.**
**1953, Dec. 18 *Perf. 12½***
**Frames in Black**
CO60 AP67 1c ultra & vio bl .25 .25
CO61 AP97 2c dp blue grn .25 .25
CO62 AP67 3c orange .25 .25
CO63 AP67 5c dp carmine .25 .25
CO64 AP67 15c dk brown .25 .25
CO65 AP67 30c purple .45 .35
CO66 AP67 1 l olive gray 4.00 2.25
CO67 AP67 2 l lilac rose 5.00 3.00
CO68 AP67 5 l ultra 11.50 7.00
*Nos. CO60-CO68 (9)* 22.20 13.85

Issued to honor the United Nations.

Types of Air Post Stamps Overprinted in Red

**Engraved; 8c Lithographed**
**1956, Oct. 3 *Perf. 13x12½***
CO69 AP68 1c blk & brn car .25 .25
CO70 AP69 2c black & mag .25 .25
CO71 AP68 3c blk & rose vio .25 .25
CO72 AP69 4c black & org .25 .25
CO73 AP69 5c black & bl grn .25 .25
CO74 AP68 8c violet & multi .25 .25
CO75 AP68 10c blk & red brn .25 .25
CO76 AP68 12c blk & car rose .25 .25
CO77 AP68 15c carmine & blk .25 .25
CO78 AP68 20c black & ol brn .25 .25
CO79 AP69 24c black & blue .25 .25
CO80 AP68 25c blk & rose vio .25 .25
CO81 AP68 30c black & grn .25 .25
CO82 AP68 40c blk & red org .25 .25
CO83 AP69 50c blk & brn red .30 .30
CO84 AP68 60c blk & rose vio .40 .40
CO85 AP68 1 l black & brn 1.40 1.10
CO86 AP69 2 l black & dk bl 2.75 2.25
CO87 AP69 5 l black & vio bl 5.75 5.25
*Nos. CO69-CO87 (19)* 14.10 12.80

**Nos. C269-C278 Overprinted Vertically in Red (Horizontally on Nos. CO89 and CO91)**

**1957, Oct. 21 Litho. *Perf. 13***
**Frames in Black**
CO88 AP70 1c buff & aqua .25 .25
CO89 AP70 2c org, pur & emer .25 .25
CO90 AP70 5c pink & ultra .25 .25
*a.* Inverted overprint
CO91 AP70 8c orange, vio & ol .25 .25
CO92 AP70 10c violet & brn .25 .25
CO93 AP70 12c lt grn & ultra .25 .25
CO94 AP70 15c green & brn .25 .25
CO95 AP70 30c pink & sl .55 .25
CO96 AP70 1 l blue & brn 1.40 1.00
CO97 AP70 2 l lt grn & sl 2.75 2.25
*Nos. CO88-CO97 (10)* 6.45 5.25

Types of Lincoln Air Post Stamps 1959 Overprinted in Red

**1959 Engr. *Perf. 13½***
**Flags in National Colors**
CO98 AP72 1c ocher .25 .25
CO99 AP73 2c gray olive .25 .25
*a.* Inverted overprint
CO100 AP73 3c red brown .25 .25
CO101 AP73 5c ultra .25 .25
CO102 AP73 10c dull purple .25 .25
*a.* Overprint omitted
CO103 AP73 12c red orange .25 .25
CO104 AP72 15c dark brown .25 .25
CO105 AP73 25c black .25 .25
CO106 AP73 50c dark car .30 .25
CO107 AP73 1 l purple .75 .65
CO108 AP73 2 l dark blue 1.40 1.10
*a.* Min. sheet of 6, 2c, 5c, 12c, 15c, 50c, 2 l, imperf. 3.00 3.00
CO109 AP73 5 l green 4.50 3.75
*Nos. CO98-CO109 (12)* 8.95 7.75

**Catalogue values for unused stamps in this section, from this point to the end of the section, are for Never Hinged items.**

No. CO55 Overprinted: "IN MEMORIAM / Sir Winston / Churchill / 1874-1965"

**1965, Dec. 20 *Perf. 14x13½***
CO110 AP66 16c purple & dk grn 1.00 1.00

See note after No. C379.

**Nos. C336-C344 Ovptd. in Red**

**1965 Photo. *Perf. 14***
**Black Design and Inscription**
CO111 AP76 1c yellow green .25 .25
CO112 AP76 2c pale rose lil .25 .25
CO113 AP76 5c light ultra .25 .25
CO114 AP76 8c bluish grn .25 .25
CO115 AP76 10c buff .30 .30
CO116 AP76 12c lemon .35 .35
CO117 AP76 1 l light ocher 4.00 4.00
CO118 AP76 2 l pale olive grn 8.75 8.75
CO119 AP76 3 l rose 11.00 11.00
*Nos. CO111-CO119 (9)* 25.40 25.40

---

## OFFICIAL STAMPS

Type of Regular Issue of 1890 Overprinted in Red

**1890 Unwmk. *Perf. 12***
O1 A5 1c pale yellow .25
O2 A5 2c pale yellow .25
O3 A5 5c pale yellow .25
O4 A5 10c pale yellow .25
O5 A5 20c pale yellow .25
O6 A5 25c pale yellow .25
O7 A5 30c pale yellow .25
O8 A5 40c pale yellow .25
O9 A5 50c pale yellow .25
O10 A5 75c pale yellow .25
O11 A5 1p pale yellow .25
*Nos. O1-O11 (11)* 2.75

Type of Regular Issue of 1891 Overprinted in Red

**1891**
O12 A6 1c yellow .25
O13 A6 2c yellow .25
O14 A6 5c yellow .25
O15 A6 10c yellow .25
O16 A6 20c yellow .25
O17 A6 25c yellow .25
O18 A6 30c yellow .25
O19 A6 40c yellow .25
O20 A6 50c yellow .25
O21 A6 75c yellow .25
O22 A6 1p yellow .25
*Nos. O12-O22 (11)* 2.75

Nos. O1 to O22 were never placed in use. Cancellations were applied to remainders. They exist with overprint inverted, double, triple and omitted; also, imperf. and part perf.

Regular Issue of 1898 Overprinted

**1898-99 *Perf. 11½***
O23 A12 5c dl ultra .40
O24 A12 10c dark bl .80
O25 A12 20c dull org 1.25
O26 A12 50c org red 2.40
O27 A12 1p blue grn 3.00
*Nos. O23-O27 (5)* 7.85

Counterfeits of basic stamps and of overprint exist.

Regular Issue of 1911 Overprinted

**1911-15 *Perf. 12, 14***
**Carmine Overprint**
O28 A15 1c violet 1.50 .65
*a.* Inverted overprint 2.40 2.40
*b.* Double overprint 2.00
O29 A15 6c ultra 2.50 2.00
*a.* Inverted overprint 2.75 2.75
O30 A15 10c blue 1.50 1.25
*a.* "OFICAIL" 2.50
*b.* Double overprint 3.50
O31 A15 20c yellow 15.00 12.00
O32 A15 50c brown 8.00 7.00
O33 A15 1p ol grn 12.00 10.00
*Nos. O28-O33 (6)* 40.50 32.90

**Black Overprint**
O34 A15 2c green 1.00 .70
*a.* "CFICIAL" 5.00
O35 A15 5c carmine 1.50 1.00
*a.* Perf. 12 7.50 5.00
O36 A15 6c ultra 4.50 4.50
O37 A15 10c blue 4.00 4.00
O38 A15 20c yellow 5.00 5.00
O39 A15 50c brown 5.50 4.00
*Nos. O34-O39 (6)* 21.50 19.20

Counterfeits of overprint of Nos. O28-O39 exist.

With Additional Surcharge

**1913-14**
O40 A15 1c on 5c car 1.75 1.50
O41 A15 2c on 5c car 2.00 1.50
O42 A15 10c on 1c vio 4.00 3.50
*a.* "OFICIAL" inverted 7.50
O43 A15 20c on 1c vio 3.00 2.50
*Nos. O40-O43 (4)* 10.75 9.00

On No. O40 the surcharge reads "1 cent."
Nos. O40-O43 exist with double surcharge.

No. O43 Surcharged Vertically in Black, Yellow or Maroon

**1914**
O44 A15 10c on 20c on 1c 20.00 20.00
*a.* Maroon surcharge 20.00 20.00
O45 A15 10c on 20c on 1c (Y) 40.00 40.00

No. O35 Surcharged

**1915**
O46 A15 10c on 5c car *20.00 20.00*

No. O39 Surcharged

O47 A15 20c on 50c brn 5.00 5.00

Regular Issues of 1913-14 Overprinted in Red or Black

**1915 *Perf. 11½***
O48 A17 1c brn (R) .40 .40
*a.* "OFICAIL" 5.00
O49 A17 2c car (Bk) .40 .40
*a.* "OFICAIL" 5.00
*b.* Double overprint 4.00
O50 A18 5c ultra (Bk) .45 .45
*a.* "OFIC" 4.00
O51 A18 5c ultra (R) 1.00 1.00
*a.* "OFIC"
*b.* "OFICAIL" 5.00
O52 A18 6c pur (Bk) 1.50 1.50
*a.* 6c red lil (Bk)
O53 A17 10c brn (Bk) 1.25 1.25
O54 A17 20c brn (Bk) 3.00 3.00
O55 A17 20c brn (R) 3.00 3.00
*a.* Double overprint (R+Bk) 10.00
*b.* "OFICAIL" 5.00
O56 A18 50c rose (Bk) 6.00 6.00
*Nos. O48-O56 (9)* 17.00 17.00

The 10c blue has the overprint "OFICIAL" in different type from the other stamps of the series. It is stated that forty stamps were overprinted for the Postmaster General but the stamp was never put in use or on sale at the post office.

No. 152 Surcharged

O57 A17 1c on 2c car 2.00 2.00
*a.* "0.10" for "0.01" 4.25 4.25
*b.* "0.20" for "0.01" 4.25 4.25
*c.* Double surcharge 8.50 8.50
*d.* As "a," double surcharge 77.50
*e.* As "b," double surcharge 77.50

Regular Issue of 1915-16 Overprinted in Black or Red

**1915-16**

| | | | | |
|---|---|---|---|---|
| **O58** | A19 | 1c choc (Bk) | .25 | .25 |
| **O59** | A19 | 2c car (Bk) | .25 | .25 |
| *a.* | | Tête bêche pair | 1.25 | 1.25 |
| *b.* | | Double overprint | 2.00 | |
| *c.* | | Double overprint, one inverted | 2.00 | |
| *d.* | | "b" and "c" in tête bêche pair | | |
| **O60** | A20 | 5c brt blue (R) | .30 | .30 |
| *a.* | | Inverted overprint | 3.00 | |
| **O61** | A20 | 6c deep pur (R) | .40 | .40 |
| *a.* | | Black overprint | 3.00 | |
| *b.* | | Inverted overprint | 2.00 | 2.00 |
| **O62** | A19 | 10c dl bl (R) | .40 | .40 |
| **O63** | A19 | 20c red brn (Bk) | .60 | .60 |
| *a.* | | Tête bêche pair | 2.50 | |
| **O64** | A20 | 50c red (Bk) | 1.75 | 1.75 |
| **O65** | A20 | 1p yel grn (C) | 3.75 | 3.75 |
| | | *Nos. O58-O65 (8)* | 7.70 | 7.70 |

The 6c, 10c and 1p exist imperf.

Regular Issue of 1919 Overprinted

**1921**

| | | | | |
|---|---|---|---|---|
| **O66** | A22 | 1c brown | *2.25* | *2.25* |
| *a.* | | Inverted overprint | 3.00 | 3.00 |
| **O67** | A22 | 2c carmine | *6.50* | *6.50* |
| *a.* | | Inverted overprint | 3.00 | 3.00 |
| **O68** | A22 | 5c lilac rose | *6.50* | *6.50* |
| *a.* | | Inverted overprint | 3.00 | |
| **O69** | A22 | 6c brt vio | .50 | .50 |
| *a.* | | Inverted overprint | | |
| **O70** | A22 | 10c dull blue | .60 | .60 |
| *a.* | | Double overprint | | |
| **O71** | A22 | 15c light blue | .70 | .70 |
| *a.* | | Inverted overprint | 2.00 | |
| *b.* | | Double ovpt., one inverted | 4.00 | |
| **O72** | A22 | 20c brown | 1.00 | 1.00 |
| **O73** | A22 | 50c light brown | 1.50 | 1.50 |
| **O74** | A22 | 1p yellow green | 3.00 | 3.00 |
| | | *Nos. O66-O74 (9)* | 22.55 | 22.55 |

Regular Issue of 1924 Overprinted

**1924** ***Perf. 11, 11½***

| | | | | |
|---|---|---|---|---|
| **O75** | A24 | 1c olive brn | .25 | .25 |
| **O76** | A24 | 2c deep rose | .25 | .25 |
| **O77** | A24 | 6c red vio | .30 | .30 |
| **O78** | A24 | 10c deep bl | .45 | .45 |
| **O79** | A24 | 20c yel brn | .60 | .60 |
| **O80** | A24 | 50c vermilion | 1.25 | 1.25 |
| **O81** | A24 | 1p emerald | 2.00 | 2.00 |
| | | *Nos. O75-O81 (7)* | 5.10 | 5.10 |

J. C. del Valle — O1

Designs: 2c, J. R. Molina. 5c, Coffee tree. 10c, J. T. Reyes. 20c, Tegucigalpa Cathedral. 50c, San Lorenzo Creek. 1p, Radio station.

**1929 Litho. Wmk. 209** ***Perf. 11½***

| | | | | |
|---|---|---|---|---|
| **O82** | O1 | 1c blue | .25 | .25 |
| **O83** | O1 | 2c carmine | .25 | .25 |
| *a.* | | 2c rose | .25 | .25 |
| **O84** | O1 | 5c purple | .35 | .35 |
| **O85** | O1 | 10c emerald | .50 | .35 |
| **O86** | O1 | 20c dk bl | .60 | .60 |
| **O87** | O1 | 50c org, grn & bl | 1.00 | 1.00 |
| **O88** | O1 | 1p buff | 1.75 | 1.75 |
| | | *Nos. O82-O88 (7)* | 4.70 | 4.55 |

Nos. O82-O88 exist imperf.

For overprints and surcharges see Nos. 282, 284, C37-C40, C59, C62-C63, CO26-CO27.

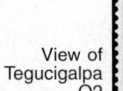

View of Tegucigalpa O2

**1931 Unwmk. Engr.** ***Perf. 12***

| | | | | |
|---|---|---|---|---|
| **O89** | O2 | 1c ultra | .30 | .25 |
| **O90** | O2 | 2c black brn | .30 | .25 |
| **O91** | O2 | 5c olive gray | .35 | .25 |
| **O92** | O2 | 6c orange red | .40 | .30 |
| **O93** | O2 | 10c dark green | .50 | .35 |
| **O94** | O2 | 15c olive brn | .65 | .40 |
| **O95** | O2 | 20c red brown | .75 | .50 |
| **O96** | O2 | 50c gray vio | 1.00 | .65 |
| **O97** | O2 | 1p dp orange | 1.75 | 1.75 |
| | | *Nos. O89-O97 (9)* | 6.00 | 4.70 |

For overprints see #CO6-CO14, O98-O105.

Official Stamps of 1931 Overprinted in Black

**1936-37**

| | | | | |
|---|---|---|---|---|
| **O98** | O2 | 1c ultra | .25 | .25 |
| **O99** | O2 | 2c black brn | .25 | .25 |
| *a.* | | Inverted overprint | 10.00 | |
| **O100** | O2 | 5c olive gray | .30 | .30 |
| **O101** | O2 | 6c red orange | .40 | .40 |
| **O102** | O2 | 10c dark green | .40 | .40 |
| **O103** | O2 | 15c olive brown | .50 | .50 |
| *a.* | | Inverted overprint | 5.00 | |
| **O104** | O2 | 20c red brown | 1.00 | 1.00 |
| *a.* | | "1938-1935" | | |
| **O105** | O2 | 50c gray violet | 4.00 | 3.00 |
| | | *Nos. O98-O105 (8)* | 7.10 | 6.10 |

Double overprints exist on 1c and 2c. No. O97 with this overprint is fraudulent.

## POSTAL TAX STAMPS

Red Cross PT1

Francisco Morazán PT2

**Engr.; Cross Litho.**

**1941, Aug. 1 Unwmk.** ***Perf. 12***

| | | | | |
|---|---|---|---|---|
| **RA1** | PT1 | 1c blue & carmine | .25 | .25 |

Obligatory on all domestic or foreign mail, the tax to be used by the Honduran Red Cross.

**1941, Aug. 1 Engr.**

| | | | | |
|---|---|---|---|---|
| **RA2** | PT2 | 1c copper brown | .40 | .25 |

Francisco Morazan, 100th anniv. of death.

Mother and Child — PT3

**1945 Engr.; Cross Litho.**

| | | | | |
|---|---|---|---|---|
| **RA3** | PT3 | 1c ol brn, car & bl | .25 | .25 |

The tax was for the Honduran Red Cross.

**Similar to Type of 1945**
Large Red Cross

**1950**

| | | | | |
|---|---|---|---|---|
| **RA4** | PT3 | 1c olive brn & red | .25 | .25 |

The tax was for the Honduran Red Cross.

Henri Dunant — PT4

**1959** ***Perf. 13x13½***

| | | | | |
|---|---|---|---|---|
| **RA5** | PT4 | 1c blue & red | .25 | .25 |

The tax was for the Red Cross.

**Catalogue values for unused stamps in this section, from this point to the end of the section, are for Never Hinged items.**

Henri Dunant — PT5

No. RA7, as PT5, but redrawn; country name panel at bottom, value at right, "El poder . . ." at top.

**1964, Dec. 15 Litho.** ***Perf. 11***

| | | | | |
|---|---|---|---|---|
| **RA6** | PT5 | 1c brt grn & red | .25 | .25 |
| **RA7** | PT5 | 1c brown & red | .25 | .25 |

The tax was for the Red Cross.

Nurse and Patient — PT6

**1969, June Litho.** ***Perf. 13½***

| | | | | |
|---|---|---|---|---|
| **RA8** | PT6 | 1c light blue & red | .25 | .25 |

The tax was for the Red Cross.

For surcharges see Nos. 387-391, C1199, C1201-C1202, C1205-C1206.

# HONG KONG

'häŋ,käŋ

LOCATION — A peninsula and island in southeast China at the mouth of the Canton River

GOVT. — Special Administrative Area of China (PRC) (as of 7/1/97)

AREA — 426 sq. mi.

POP. — 6,847,125 (1999 est.)

CAPITAL — Victoria

100 Cents = 1 Dollar

**Catalogue values for unused stamps in this country are for Never Hinged items, beginning with Scott 174 in the regular postage section, Scott B1 in the semi-postal section and Scott J13 in the postage due section.**

**Watermark**

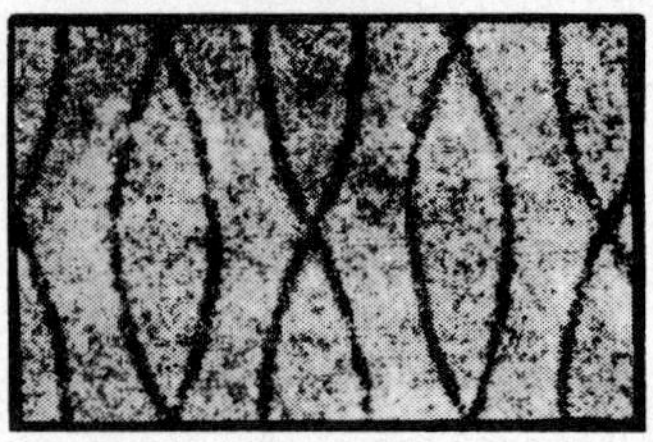

Wmk. 340

Values for unused stamps are for examples with original gum as defined in the catalogue introduction. Very fine examples of Nos. 1-25, 29-48, 61-66d and 69-70a will have perforations touching the design on at least one side due to the narrow spacing of the stamps on the plates. Stamps with perfs clear of the design on all four sides are scarce and will command higher prices.

Queen Victoria — A1

**Unwmk.**

**1862, Dec. 8 Typo.** ***Perf. 14***

| | | | | |
|---|---|---|---|---|
| **1** | A1 | 2c pale brown | 550.00 | 125.00 |
| *a.* | | 2c deep brown | 750.00 | 160.00 |
| **2** | A1 | 8c buff | 775.00 | 85.00 |
| **3** | A1 | 12c blue | 700.00 | 72.50 |
| **4** | A1 | 18c lilac | 700.00 | 67.50 |
| **5** | A1 | 24c green | 1,200. | 140.00 |
| **6** | A1 | 48c rose | 3,000. | 450.00 |
| **7** | A1 | 96c gray | 4,000. | 525.00 |

**1863-80 Wmk. 1**

| | | | | |
|---|---|---|---|---|
| **8** | A1 | 2c brown ('65) | 145.00 | 8.50 |
| *a.* | | 2c deep brown ('64) | 350.00 | 35.00 |
| **9** | A1 | 2c dull rose ('80) | 225.00 | 35.00 |
| *a.* | | 2c rose | 250.00 | 35.00 |
| **10** | A1 | 4c slate | 135.00 | 9.00 |
| *a.* | | 4c greenish grey | 350.00 | 55.00 |
| *b.* | | 4c bluish slate | 525.00 | 25.00 |
| **11** | A1 | 5c ultra ('80) | 650.00 | 55.00 |
| **12** | A1 | 6c lilac | 475.00 | 19.00 |
| *a.* | | 6c violet | 600.00 | 20.00 |
| **13** | A1 | 8c org buff ('65) | 600.00 | 12.50 |
| *a.* | | 8c bright orange | 475.00 | 15.00 |
| *b.* | | 8c brownish orange | 525.00 | 15.00 |
| **14** | A1 | 10c violet ('80) | 750.00 | 19.00 |
| **15** | A1 | 12c light blue | 37.50 | 7.50 |
| *a.* | | 12c light greenish blue | 1,600. | 37.50 |
| *b.* | | 12c deep blue | 300.00 | 14.00 |
| **16** | A1 | 16c yellow ('77) | 2,200. | 77.50 |
| **17** | A1 | 18c lilac ('66) | 7,750. | 350.00 |
| **18** | A1 | 24c green ('65) | 650.00 | 12.50 |
| *a.* | | 24c deep green | 1,300. | 35.00 |
| **19** | A1 | 30c vermilion | 1,000. | 17.50 |
| **20** | A1 | 30c violet ('71) | 300.00 | 7.00 |
| **21** | A1 | 48c rose carmine | 1,100. | 55.00 |
| **22** | A1 | 48c brown ('80) | 1,600. | 120.00 |
| **23** | A1 | 96c bister ('65) | *85,000.* | 800.00 |
| **24** | A1 | 96c gray ('66) | 1,750. | 65.00 |

Imperfs. are plate proofs.

**1874** ***Perf. 12½***

| | | | | |
|---|---|---|---|---|
| **25** | A1 | 4c slate | 13,500. | 300.00 |

See Nos. 36-49. For surcharges or overprints on stamps of type A1 see Nos. 29-35B, 51-56, 61-66, 69-70.

A2

A3

A4

**1874 Engr. Wmk. 1** ***Perf. 15½x15***

| | | | | |
|---|---|---|---|---|
| **26** | A2 | $2 sage green | 400.00 | 70.00 |
| **27** | A3 | $3 violet | 375.00 | 55.00 |
| **28** | A4 | $10 rose | 8,250. | 800.00 |

Nos. 26-28 are revenues which were used postally. Used values are for postally canceled examples. Black "Paid All" cancels are fiscal usage.

See Nos. 57-59. For surcharges see Nos. 50, 67. For type surcharged see No. 60.

### Nos. 17 and 20 Surcharged in Black

**1876** *Perf. 14*

**29** A1 16c on 18c lilac 2,500. 185.00
**30** A1 28c on 30c violet 1,750. 62.50

Stamps of 1863-80 Surcharged in Black

**1879-80**

**31** A1 5c on 8c org ('80) 1,100. 110.00
*a.* Inverted surcharge *20,000.*
*b.* Double surcharge *21,000.*
**32** A1 5c on 18c lilac 1,050. 70.00
**33** A1 10c on 12c blue 1,100. 65.00
**34** A1 10c on 16c yellow 4,750. 175.00
*a.* Inverted surcharge *90,000.*
*b.* Double surcharge *85,000.*
**35** A1 10c on 24c green ('80) 1,550. 95.00

Most examples of No. 31a are damaged.

### Nos. 16-17, 35B Surcharged in Black

A5

A6

**1879**

**35A** A5 3c on 16c on card 425. *2,200.*
Stamp off card 475.
**35B** A5 5c on 18c on card 425. *2,600.*
Stamp off card 550.
**35C** A6 3c on 5c on 18c on card 8,000. *9,500.*
Stamp off card 6,500. *8,250.*

Nos. 35A-35C were sold affixed to postal cards. Most used examples are found off card so values are given for these.

### Type of 1862

**1882-1902** **Wmk. 2** *Perf. 14*

**36b** A1 2c carmine ('84) 50.00 2.75
**37** A1 2c green ('00) 32.50 1.10
**38** A1 4c slate ('96) 22.50 3.00
**39** A1 4c car rose ('00) 22.50 1.25
**40** A1 5c ultramarine 40.00 1.25
**41** A1 5c yellow ('00) 27.50 8.00
**42** A1 10c lilac 950.00 21.00
**43** A1 10c green 180.00 2.25
*a.* 10c blue green 2,000. 45.00
**44** A1 10c vio, *red* ('91) 40.00 2.25
**45** A1 10c ultra ('00) 57.50 2.50
**46** A1 12c blue ('02) 55.00 *67.50*
**47** A1 30c gray grn ('91) 100.00 27.50
*a.* 30c yellow green 150.00 45.00
**48** A1 30c brown ('01) 60.00 27.50
*Nos. 36b-48 (13)* 1,579. 166.60

No. 47 has fugitive ink. Both colors will turn dull green upon soaking.

The 2c rose, perf 12, is a proof.

No. 28 Surcharged in Black

**1880** **Wmk. 1** *Perf. 15½x15*

**50** A4 12c on $10 rose 1,000. 375.00

Surcharged in Black

**1885-91** **Wmk. 2** *Perf. 14*

**51** A1 20c on 30c ver 200.00 7.00
*a.* Double surcharge —
**52** A1 20c on 30c gray grn ('91) 125.00 *175.00*
*a.* 20c on 30c yellow green 200.00 200.00
**53** A1 50c on 48c brown 450.00 45.00
**54** A1 50c on 48c lil ('91) 300.00 *325.00*
**55** A1 $1 on 96c ol gray 825.00 90.00
**56** A1 $1 on 96c vio, *red* ('91) 900.00 400.00

For overprints see Nos. 61-63.

### Types of 1874 and

A7

**1890-1902** **Wmk. 2** *Perf. 14*

**56A** A7 2c dull purple 150.00 30.00

**Wmk. 1**

**57** A2 $2 gray green 475.00 300.00
**58** A3 $3 lilac ('02) 625.00 525.00
**59** A4 $10 gray grn ('92) *12,000.* *12,000.*

Due to a shortage of 2c postage stamps, No. 56A was authorized for postal use December 24-30, 1890.

Fake postmarks are known on No. 59. Beware also of fiscal cancels altered to resemble postal cancels.

For surcharge see No. 68.

Type of 1874 Surcharged in Black

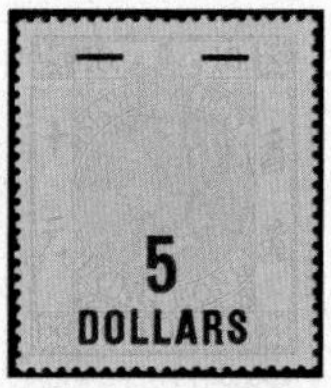


**1891, Jan. 1** **Wmk. 2**

**60** A4 $5 on $10 vio, *red* 360.00 115.00

### Nos. 36b, 44 Overprinted

a

b

**1891, Jan. 1**

**60A** A1 2c carmine (a) 1,100. 425.00
**60B** A1 2c carmine (b) 1,050. 425.00
*a.* Inverted overprint 6,500.
**60C** A1 10c vio, *red* (a) 1,900. 475.00

Nos. 60A-60C were overprinted for use as fiscal stamps, "S.O." denoting "Stamp Office" and "S.D." denoting "Stamp Duty." They were authorized for postal use Jan. 1, 1891-1893. Examples of No. 60A with "O" changed to "D" in manuscript are known.

Forged overprints are often encountered. Expertization is required.

### Nos. 52, 54 and 56 Handstamped with Chinese characters

g

h

i

**61** A1 (g) 20c on 30c 55.00 8.50
*a.* 20c on 30c dull green 62.50 11.00
*b.* "20 CENTS" double 25,000. 25,000.
**62** A1 (h) 50c on 48c 95.00 6.25
**63** A1 (i) $1 on 96c 525.00 27.50

No. 61 may be found with Chinese character 2mm, 2½mm or 3mm high.

The handstamped Chinese surcharges on Nos. 61-63 exist in several varieties including inverted, double, triple, misplaced, omitted and (on No. 63) on both front and back.

Nos. 43 and 20 Surcharged

**1891**

**64** A1 7c on 10c green 90.00 10.00
*a.* Double surcharge *6,500.* *1,500.*

**Wmk. 1**

**65** A1 14c on 30c violet 200.00 80.00

Beware of faked varieties.

No. 36 Overprinted in Black

**1891, Jan. 22** **Wmk. 2**

**66** A1 2c rose *575.00* 140.00
*a.* Double overprint *17,500.* *13,000.*
*b.* "U" of "JUBILEE" shorter *800.00* 200.00
*c.* "J" of "JUBILEE" shorter *800.00* 200.00
*d.* Tall "K" in "KONG" *1,300.* 500.00

50th anniversary of the colony.

Beware of faked varieties.

No. 26 Surcharged (Chinese Handstamped)

**1897, Sept.** **Wmk. 1** *Perf. 15½x15*

**67** A2 $1 on $2 sage green 300.00 150.00
*a.* Without Chinese surcharges 5,000. 4,500.
*b.* Diagonal Chinese surcharge omitted *33,000.*

**On No. 57**

*Perf. 14*

**68** A2 $1 on $2 gray green 300.00 150.00
*a.* Without Chinese surcharges 2,100. 2,000.
*b.* Diagonal Chinese surcharge omitted *16,000.*
*c.* Vertical Chinese surcharge omitted

Handstamp Surcharged in Black

**1898** **Wmk. 2**

**69** A1 10c on 30c gray grn 60.00 *90.00*
*a.* Large Chinese surcharge 1,600. 1,600.
*b.* Without Chinese surcharge 600.00 *1,200.*
**70** A1 $1 on 96c black 200.00 32.50
*a.* Without Chinese surcharge 3,000. *4,000.*

The Chinese surcharge is added separately.

See notes below Nos. 61-63. The small Chinese surcharge is illustrated.

King Edward VII — A10

**1903** **Wmk. 2**

**71** A10 1c brown & lilac 2.25 .55
**72** A10 2c gray green 18.00 1.75
**73** A10 4c violet, *red* 22.00 .45
**74** A10 5c org & gray grn 20.00 10.00
**75** A10 8c violet & black 13.00 1.75
**76** A10 10c ultra & lil, *bl* 55.00 2.00
**77** A10 12c red vio & gray grn, *yel* 10.00 5.50
**78** A10 20c org brn & blk 55.00 4.25
**79** A10 30c blk & gray grn 57.50 24.00
**80** A10 50c red vio & gray green 60.00 55.00
**81** A10 $1 olive grn & lil 110.00 25.00
**82** A10 $2 scar & black 325.00 325.00
**83** A10 $3 dp blue & blk 400.00 *425.00*
**84** A10 $5 blue grn & lil 550.00 550.00
**85** A10 $10 org & blk, *bl* 1,300. 500.00
*Nos. 71-85 (15)* 2,997. 1,930.

**1904-11** **Wmk. 3**

**Ordinary or Chalky Paper**

**86** A10 1c brown ('10) 6.75 1.10
*a.* Booklet pane of 4
**87** A10 2c gray green 16.00 2.25
**88** A10 2c deep green 32.50 1.90
*a.* Booklet pane of 4
*b.* Booklet pane of 12
**89** A10 4c violet, *red* 21.00 .50
**90** A10 4c carmine 15.00 .50
*a.* Booklet pane of 4
*b.* Booklet pane of 12
**91** A10 5c org & gray grn 32.50 10.00
**92** A10 6c red vio & org ('07) 27.50 5.25
**93** A10 8c vio & blk ('07) 16.00 2.25
**94** A10 10c ultra & lil, *bl* 27.50 1.50
**95** A10 10c ultramarine 40.00 .50
**96** A10 12c red vio & gray grn, *yel* ('07) 18.00 6.00
**97** A10 20c org brn & blk 50.00 3.00
**98** A10 20c ol grn & vio ('11) 50.00 50.00
**99** A10 30c blk & gray grn 50.00 25.00
**100** A10 30c org & vio ('11) 60.00 32.50
**101** A10 50c red vio & gray green 90.00 12.50
**102** A10 50c blk, *grn* ('11) 47.50 18.00
**103** A10 $1 ol grn & lil 150.00 32.50
**104** A10 $2 scar & black 290.00 130.00
**105** A10 $2 blk & car ('10) 360.00 360.00
**106** A10 $3 dp bl & blk 325.00 250.00
**107** A10 $5 bl grn & lil 525.00 425.00
**108** A10 $10 org & blk, *bl* 2,000. 1,300.
*Nos. 86-108 (23)* 4,250. 2,670.

Nos. 86, 88, 90, 94 and 95 are on ordinary paper only. Nos. 92, 93, 96, 98, 100, 102, 105, 106 and 107 are on chalky paper and the others of the issue are on both papers.

The 4c, 5c, 8c, 12c 20c, 50c, $2 and $5 denominations of type A10 are expressed in colored letters or numerals and letters on a colorless background.

King George V
A11 A12

A13

A14

A15

Type I— No. 117

Type II— No. 128

Two Types of 25c:

I: A short vertical stroke crosses the bottom of the top Chinese character in the left label.

II: The vertical stroke is absent from the character.

**1912-14** **Ordinary Paper**

**109** A11 1c brown 4.50 .60
*a.* Booklet pane of 12
**110** A11 2c deep green 12.00 .40
*a.* Booklet pane of 12
**111** A12 4c carmine 6.50 .40
*a.* Booklet pane of 12
*b.* Booklet pane of 4
**112** A13 6c orange 6.00 2.25
**113** A12 8c gray 27.50 8.00
**114** A11 10c ultramarine 37.50 .35

**Chalky Paper**

**115** A14 12c vio, *yel* 9.00 *10.00*
**116** A14 20c ol grn & vio 12.00 1.50
**117** A15 25c red vio & dl vio (I) ('14) 32.50 *32.50*
**118** A13 30c org & violet 29.00 9.00
**119** A14 50c black, *bl grn*, white back 25.00 2.00
*a.* 50c black, *emerald* 27.50 10.00
*b.* 50c black, *bl grn*, ol back 1,400. 32.50
*c.* 50c black, *emer*, ol back 32.50 10.00
**120** A11 $1 blue & vio, *bl* 55.00 6.00
**121** A14 $2 black & red 180.00 70.00
**122** A13 $3 vio & green 275.00 100.00
**123** A14 $5 red & grn, *grn* 725.00 400.00
*a.* $5 red & grn, *bl grn*, ol back 1,300. 375.00
**124** A13 $10 blk & vio, *red* 675.00 95.00
*Nos. 109-124 (16)* 2,111. 738.00

For overprints see British Offices in China Nos. 1-27.

**1914, May** **Surface-colored Paper**

**125** A14 12c violet, *yel* 10.00 *18.00*
**126** A14 50c black, *green* 25.00 5.00
**127** A14 $5 red & grn, *grn* 675.00 350.00
*Nos. 125-127 (3)* 710.00 373.00

**Stamp of 1912-14 Redrawn (Type II)**

**1919, Aug.** **Chalky Paper**

**128** A15 25c red vio & dl vio 250.00 80.00

**Types of 1912-14 Issue**

**1921-37** **Wmk. 4**

**Ordinary Paper**

**129** A11 1c brown 1.25 .50
**130** A11 2c deep green 4.00 .75
**131** A11 2c gray ('37) 22.50 8.00
**132** A12 3c gray ('31) 10.00 1.50
**133** A12 4c rose red 5.50 1.00
**134** A12 5c violet ('31) 18.00 .40
**135** A12 8c gray 21.00 *40.00*
**136** A12 8c orange 5.75 2.00
**137** A11 10c ultramarine 7.50 .45

**Chalky Paper**

**138** A14 12c vio, *yel* ('33) 20.00 4.00
**139** A14 20c ol grn & dl vio 8.50 .40
**140** A15 25c red vio & dl vio, redrawn 7.50 1.50
**141** A13 30c yel & violet 12.00 1.75
**142** A14 50c blk, *emerald* 24.00 .45
**143** A11 $1 ultra & vio, *bl* 45.00 .60
**144** A14 $2 black & red 140.00 7.50
**145** A13 $3 dl vio & grn ('26) 200.00 70.00
**146** A14 $5 red & grn, *emer* ('25) 550.00 85.00
*Nos. 129-146 (18)* 1,102. 225.80

Common Design Types pictured following the introduction.

**Silver Jubilee Issue**

Common Design Type

**1935, May 6** **Engr.** ***Perf. 11x12***

**147** CD301 3c black & ultra 4.00 4.00
**148** CD301 5c indigo & grn 10.00 3.00
**149** CD301 10c ultra & brn 22.50 4.00
**150** CD301 20c brn vio & ind 40.00 10.00
*Nos. 147-150 (4)* 76.50 21.00
Set, never hinged 200.00

**Coronation Issue**

Common Design Type

**1937, May 12** ***Perf. 11x11½***

**151** CD302 4c deep green 4.00 4.00
**152** CD302 15c dark carmine 10.00 4.00
**153** CD302 25c deep ultra 13.00 4.50
*Nos. 151-153 (3)* 27.00 12.50
Set, never hinged 40.00

King George VI — A16

**1938-48** **Typo.** ***Perf. 14***

**Ordinary Paper**

**154** A16 1c brown .75 *1.00*
**155** A16 2c gray 1.25 .25
**156** A16 4c orange 2.50 3.25
**157** A16 5c green 1.10 .25
**157B** A16 8c brown red ('41) 1.00 *2.75*
*c.* Imperf., pair 30,000. —
**158** A16 10c violet 3.50 .60
**159** A16 15c carmine 1.00 .30
**159A** A16 20c gray ('46) .60 .30
**159B** A16 20c rose red ('48) 3.75 .45
**160** A16 25c ultramarine 17.00 3.50
**160A** A16 25c gray ol ('46) 2.25 *2.75*
**161** A16 30c olive bister 110.00 4.00
**161B** A16 30c lt ultra ('46) 3.50 .25

**Chalky Paper**

**162** A16 50c red violet 4.50 .40
*b.* Ordinary paper 32.50 .75
**162C** A16 80c lilac rose ('48) 2.50 1.00
**163** A16 $1 lilac & ultra 4.50 3.75
*a.* Ordinary paper 8.00 *17.50*
**163B** A16 $1 dp org & grn ('46) 27.50 1.25
*c.* Ordinary paper 12.50 .35
**164** A16 $2 dp org & grn 52.50 27.50
**164A** A16 $2 vio & red ('46) 25.00 1.10
*b.* Ordinary paper 25.00 8.25
**165** A16 $5 lilac & red 40.00 *50.00*
**165A** A16 $5 grn & vio ('46) 60.00 4.75
*b.* Ordinary paper 45.00 16.00
**166** A16 $10 grn & vio 325.00 130.00
**166A** A16 $10 vio & ultra ('46) 110.00 20.00
*b.* Ordinary paper 80.00 50.00
*Nos. 154-166A (23)* 799.70 259.40
Set, never hinged 1,200.

**Coarse Impressions**

Ordinary Rough-Surfaced Paper

**1941-46** ***Perf. 14½x14***

*155a* A16 2c gray 1.50 *6.00*
*156a* A16 4c orange ('46) 3.00 3.25
*157a* A16 5c green 1.75 *5.25*
*158a* A16 10c violet 6.00 .25
*161a* A16 30c dull olive bister 18.00 9.50
*162a* A16 50c red lilac 20.00 2.00
*Nos. 155a-162a (6)* 50.25 26.25
Set, never hinged 85.00

A17

**1938, Jan. 11** **Wmk. 4**

**167** A17 5c green 50.00 20.00

No. 167 is a revenue stamp officially authorized to be sold and used for postal purposes. Used Jan. 11-20, 1938. The used price is for the stamp on cover. CTO covers exist.

Street Scene — A18

Hong Kong Bank — A22

Liner and Junk — A19

University of Hong Kong — A20

Harbor — A21

China Clipper and Seaplane A23

***Perf. 13½x13, 13x13½***

**1941, Feb. 26** **Engr.** **Wmk. 4**

**168** A18 2c sepia & org 3.50 2.00
**169** A19 4c rose car & vio 4.00 4.50
**170** A20 5c yel grn & blk 1.75 .35
**171** A21 15c red & black 4.00 2.50
**172** A22 25c dp blue & dk brn 9.00 8.00
**173** A23 $1 brn org & brt bl 29.00 12.00
*Nos. 168-173 (6)* 51.25 29.35
Set, never hinged 100.00

Centenary of British rule.

**Catalogue values for unused stamps in this section, from this point to the end of the section, are for Never Hinged items.**

**Peace Issue**

Phoenix Rising from Flames A24

**1946, Aug. 29** ***Perf. 13x12½***

**174** A24 30c car & dp blue 4.00 2.00
**175** A24 $1 car & brown 6.25 1.00
Set, hinged 5.00

Return to peace after WWII.

**Silver Wedding Issue**

Common Design Types

***Perf. 14x14½***

**1948, Dec. 22** **Photo.** **Wmk. 4**

**178** CD304 10c purple 3.50 1.00

**Engr.; Name Typo.**

***Perf. 11½x11***

**179** CD305 $10 rose car 400.00 110.00
Set, hinged 275.00

**UPU Issue**

Common Design Types

**Engr.; Name Typo. on 20c & 30c**

**1949, Oct. 10** ***Perf. 13½, 11x11½***

**180** CD306 10c violet 4.25 1.00
**181** CD307 20c deep car 18.00 4.50
**182** CD308 30c indigo 15.00 4.25
**183** CD309 80c red violet 35.00 10.00
*Nos. 180-183 (4)* 72.25 19.75
Set, hinged 25.00

**Coronation Issue**

Common Design Type

**1953, June 2** **Engr.** ***Perf. 13½x13***

**184** CD312 10c purple & black 7.00 .35
Hinged 2.50

Elizabeth II A25

Arms of University A26

**1954-60** **Typo.** ***Perf. 13½x14***

**185** A25 5c orange 1.75 .25
*a.* Imperf., pair 1,350.
**186** A25 10c violet 2.50 .25
**187** A25 15c green 4.50 1.00
**188** A25 20c brown 6.00 .30
**189** A25 25c rose red 4.75 3.00
**190** A25 30c gray 5.00 .25
**191** A25 40c blue 6.00 .40
**192** A25 50c red violet 6.50 .25
**193** A25 65c lt gray ('60) 21.00 13.00
**194** A25 $1 org & green 8.00 .25
**195** A25 $1.30 bl & ver ('60) 26.50 .85
**196** A25 $2 violet & red 13.50 .50
**197** A25 $5 green & vio 90.00 2.50
**198** A25 $10 violet & ultra 75.00 10.00
*Nos. 185-198 (14)* 271.00 32.80
Set, hinged 125.00

Nos. 185-187 are on ordinary paper; Nos. 188-198 on chalky paper.

***Perf. 11½x12***

**1961, Sept. 11** **Photo.** **Wmk. 314**

**199** A26 $1 bl, blk, red, grn & gold 8.00 2.00
*a.* Gold omitted 2,000.

University of Hong Kong, 50th anniv.

Queen Victoria Statue, Victoria Park, Hong Kong — A27

**1962, May 4** ***Perf. 14***

**200** A27 10c car rose & black .65 .25
**201** A27 20c blue & black 2.00 *2.25*
**202** A27 50c bister & black 4.50 .45
*Nos. 200-202 (3)* 7.15 2.95

1st postage stamps of Hong Kong, cent.

Queen Elizabeth II — A28

**Wmk. 314 Upright**

**1962, Oct. 4** **Photo.** ***Perf. 14½x14***

**Size: 17x21mm**

**203** A28 5c red orange .80 .60
*a.* Booklet pane of 4 3.00
**204** A28 10c purple 1.50 .25
*a.* Booklet pane of 4 6.50
**205** A28 15c green 3.50 2.75
**206** A28 20c red brown 2.50 .25
*a.* Booklet pane of 4 13.00
**207** A28 25c lilac rose 3.25 *4.00*
**208** A28 30c dark blue 2.50 .25
**209** A28 40c Prus green 4.00 .70
**210** A28 50c crimson 1.75 .30
*a.* Booklet pane of 4 25.00
**211** A28 65c ultramarine 18.50 2.00
**212** A28 $1 dark brown 19.00 .40

***Perf. 14x14½***

**Size: 25½x30½mm**

**Portrait in Natural Colors**

**213** A28 $1.30 sky blue 5.00 .25
*a.* Ocher (sash) omitted 42.50
*b.* Yellow omitted 57.50
**214** A28 $2 fawn 7.00 1.00
*a.* Yellow and ocher (sash) omitted 225.00
*b.* Yellow omitted 57.50
**215** A28 $5 orange 17.50 1.50
*a.* Ocher (sash) omitted 57.50
**216** A28 $10 green 30.00 3.00
**217** A28 $20 violet blue 150.00 27.50
*Nos. 203-217 (15)* 266.80 44.75

**1966-72** **Wmk. 314 Sideways**

*203b* A28 5c ('67) .60 .60
*204b* A28 10c ('67) .75 .50
*205a* A28 15c ('67) 2.00 2.00
*206b* A28 20c 1.75 2.50
*207a* A28 25c ('67) 3.00 3.00
*208a* A28 30c ('70) 10.00 4.00
*209a* A28 40c ('67) 4.00 3.00
*210b* A28 50c ('67) 3.00 2.00
*211a* A28 65c ('67) 8.00 2.75
*212a* A28 $1 ('67) 18.50 1.75
*213c* A28 $1.30 ('72) 11.00 2.75

*214c* A28 $2 ('71) 18.00 3.00
*215b* A28 $5 ('71) 75.00 24.50
*217a* A28 $20 ('72) 200.00 75.00
*Nos. 203b-217a (14)* 355.60 127.35

**Freedom from Hunger Issue**
Common Design Type
***Perf. 14x14½***

**1963, June 4 Photo. Wmk. 314**
**218** CD314 $1.30 green 57.50 8.75

**Red Cross Centenary Issue**
Common Design Type

**1963, Sept. 2 Litho. *Perf. 13***
**219** CD315 10c black & red 4.50 .35
**220** CD315 $1.30 ultra & red 35.00 8.50

**ITU Issue**
Common Design Type

**1965, May 17 *Perf. 11x11½***
**221** CD317 10c red lil & yel 4.50 .30
**222** CD317 $1.30 apple grn & turq blue 27.50 4.25

**Intl. Cooperation Year Issue**
Common Design Type

**1965, Oct. 25 *Perf. 14½***
**223** CD318 10c blue grn & cl 3.50 .35
**224** CD318 $1.30 lt violet & grn 22.50 3.75

**Churchill Memorial Issue**
Common Design Type

**1966, Jan. 24 Photo. *Perf. 14***
**Design in Black, Gold and Carmine Rose**
**225** CD319 10c bright blue 3.00 .25
**226** CD319 50c green 3.50 .40
**227** CD319 $1.30 brown 24.00 3.50
**228** CD319 $2 violet 37.50 8.00
*Nos. 225-228 (4)* 68.00 12.15

**WHO Headquarters Issue**
Common Design Type

**1966, Sept. 20 Litho. *Perf. 14***
**229** CD322 10c multicolored 3.25 .30
**230** CD322 50c multicolored 11.00 2.00

**UNESCO Anniversary Issue**
Common Design Type

**1966, Dec. 1 Litho. *Perf. 14***
**231** CD323 10c "Education" 4.00 .25
**232** CD323 50c "Science" 20.00 1.25
**233** CD323 $2 "Culture" 65.00 18.50
*Nos. 231-233 (3)* 89.00 20.00

Three Rams' Heads A29

Lunar New Year: $1.30, Three rams.

**1967, Jan. 17 Photo. *Perf. 14***
**234** A29 10c red, citron & grn 2.50 .60
**235** A29 $1.30 red, cit & brt grn 37.50 11.00

Outline of Telephone with Map of South East Asia and Australia A30

**1967, Mar. 30 Photo. *Perf. 12½***
**236** A30 $1.30 dk red & blue 21.00 4.75

Completion of the Hong Kong-Malaysia link of the South East Asia Commonwealth Cable, SEACOM.

Monkeys A31

Lunar New Year: $1.30, Two monkey families.

**1968, Jan. 23 Wmk. 314 *Perf. 14***
**237** A31 10c crim, blk & gold 2.25 .50
**238** A31 $1.30 crim, blk & gold 37.50 8.50

Liner and New Sea Terminal A32

Seacraft: 20c, Pleasure launch and sailing cruiser. 40c, Vehicle ferry. 50c, Passenger ferry. $1, Sampan. $1.30, Junk.

***Perf. 13x12½***

**1968, Apr. 24 Litho. Unwmk.**
**239** A32 10c multicolored 2.25 .25
**240** A32 20c sky blue, bis & black 3.75 .80
**241** A32 40c org, rose lil & black 11.00 9.00
**242** A32 50c brt red, emer & black 7.50 .65
**243** A32 $1 yel, cop red & black 17.50 5.50
**244** A32 $1.30 dk bl, brt pink & black 47.50 5.50
*Nos. 239-244 (6)* 89.50 21.70

Bauhinia Blakeana — A33

***Perf. 14x14½***

**1968, Sept. 25 Photo. Wmk. 314**
**245** A33 65c shown 11.00 .60
*a.* Wmkd. sideways ('72) 55.00 17.50
**246** A33 $1 Coat of Arms 11.00 .55
*a.* Wmkd. sideways ('71) 11.00 2.50

Human Rights Flame and "Lamp of Life" A34

**1968, Nov. 20 Litho. *Perf. 13½***
**247** A34 10c green, org & blk 2.25 .85
**248** A34 50c magenta, yel & blk 6.50 2.50

International Human Rights Year.

Cock A35

Design: $1.30, Cock, vert.

***Perf. 13x13½, 13½x13***

**1969, Feb. 11 Photo. Unwmk.**
**249** A35 10c brown, blk, org & red *8.00* 1.25
*a.* Red omitted *350.00*
**250** A35 $1.30 ocher, blk, org & red *70.00* *15.00*

Lunar New Year, Feb. 17, 1969.

Chinese University Seal — A36

**1969, Aug. 26 Unwmk. *Perf. 13***
**251** A36 40c multicolored 9.00 4.00

Chinese University of Hong Kong, founded 1963.

Radar, Globe and Satellite A37

***Perf. 14x14½***

**1969, Sept. 24 Photo. Wmk. 314**
**252** A37 $1 scar, blk, sil & bl 27.50 5.50

Opening of the satellite earth station (connected through the Indian Ocean satellite Intelsat III) on Stanley Peninsula, Hong Kong.

Chow — A38

Emblem — A39

Lunar New Year (Year of the Dog): $1.30, Chow, horiz.

**1970, Jan. 28 *Perf. 14***
**253** A38 10c black & multi *5.00* .60
**254** A38 $1.30 green & multi *70.00* 13.00

***Perf. 13½x13, 13x13½***

**1970, Mar. 14 Litho. Wmk. 314**

25c, Emblem and Chinese junks, horiz.

**255** A39 15c multicolored .90 .90
**256** A39 25c multicolored 2.00 2.00

EXPO '70 Intl. Exposition, Osaka, Japan, Mar. 15-Sept. 13.

"A Compassionate Ship on the Bitter Sea" — A40

**1970, Apr. 9 Photo. *Perf. 14***
**257** A40 10c yel green & multi 1.25 .30
**258** A40 50c scarlet & multi 4.50 1.75

Centenary of the Tung Wah Group of Hospitals (including schools and various charitable organizations).

A.P.Y. Emblem — A41

**1970, Aug. 5 Litho. Wmk. 314**
**259** A41 10c yellow & multi 1.50 .65

Issued for Asian Productivity Year.

Boar A42

***Perf. 13x13½***

**1971, Jan. 20 Photo. Unwmk.**
**260** A42 10c yel grn, gold & black *6.00* 1.25
**261** A42 $1.30 vio, gold & blk *40.00* *12.00*

Lunar New Year.

Scout Emblem and "60" — A43

***Perf. 14x14½***

**1971, July 23 Litho. Wmk. 314**
**262** A43 10c red, yellow & black .90 .25
**263** A43 50c blue, emer & black 4.25 1.25
**264** A43 $2 vio, lil rose & blk 25.00 12.00
*Nos. 262-264 (3)* 30.15 13.50

60th anniversary of Hong Kong Boy Scouts.

Festival Emblem A44

Symbolic Flower A45

Festival of Hong Kong: 50c, Dancers, horiz.

**1971, Nov. 2 *Perf. 14***
**265** A44 10c lilac & orange 1.75 .25

***Perf. 14½***

**266** A45 50c lilac & multi 3.50 1.10
**267** A45 $1 lilac & multi 10.00 7.75
*Nos. 265-267 (3)* 15.25 9.10

Rats A46

***Perf. 13½x13***

**1972, Feb. 8 Photo. Unwmk.**
**268** A46 10c black, red & gold *4.00* .60
**269** A46 $1.30 black, gold & red *37.50* 13.50

Lunar New Year.

Cross Harbor Tunnel Entrance — A47

***Perf. 14x14½***

**1972, Oct. 20 Litho. Wmk. 314**
**270** A47 $1 multicolored 7.50 2.25

Inauguration of Cross Harbor Tunnel linking Victoria and Kowloon.

**Silver Wedding Issue, 1972**
Common Design Type

Design: Queen Elizabeth II, Prince Philip, phoenix and dragon.

**1972, Nov. 20 Photo. *Perf. 14x14½***
**271** CD324 10c citron & multi 1.10 .25
**272** CD324 50c gray & multi 1.00 *1.50*

Ox
A48

Lunar New Year: 10c, Ox, vert.

**1973, Feb. 3** ***Perf. 14***
**273** A48 10c dk brown & red 3.50 .60
**274** A48 $1.30 dk brn, yel & org 10.00 8.00

Elizabeth II — A49

**Wmk. 314 Upright; Sideways (15c, 30c, 40c)**

**1973, June 12 Photo.** ***Perf. 14½x14***

**Size: 20x24mm**

**275** A49 10c orange 1.00 .60
*d.* Watermark sideways (coil) 1.75 1.75
**276** A49 15c olive green 8.00 8.00
**277** A49 20c bright purple 1.75 .30
**278** A49 25c deep brown 12.50 8.00
**279** A49 30c ultramarine 1.10 .60
**280** A49 40c blue green 3.25 3.25
**281** A49 50c red 1.50 .60
**282** A49 65c dp bister 16.50 12.50
**283** A49 $1 dk slate green 2.50 .75

***Perf. 14x14½***

**Wmk. 314 Sideways**

**Size: 28x32mm**

**284** A49 $1.30 dk pur & yel 7.75 .90
**285** A49 $2 dp brn & lt grn 9.00 1.25
**286** A49 $5 dk vio bl & rose 14.00 3.50

**Photo. & Embossed**

**287** A49 $10 dk sl green & pink 20.00 9.00
**288** A49 $20 black & rose 32.50 32.50
*Nos. 275-288 (14)* 131.35 81.75

**1975-78 Wmk. 373** ***Perf. 14½x14***

**Size: 20x24mm**

*275a* A49 10c orange .50 .30
*c.* Booklet pane of 4 ('76) 2.00
*276a* A49 15c olive green 17.50 13.00
*c.* Booklet pane of 4 70.00
*277a* A49 20c bright purple .50 .25
*c.* Booklet pane of 4 ('76) 2.00
*278a* A49 25c deep brown 20.00 17.50
*279a* A49 30c ultramarine .75 .70
*280a* A49 40c blue green 1.25 1.25
*281a* A49 50c red 2.75 .75
*c.* Booklet pane of 4 11.00
Complete booklet, 2 #275c, 276c, 2 #277c, 281c 90.00
*282a* A49 65c deep bister 22.50 12.50
*283a* A49 $1 dark slate green 3.50 1.00

***Perf. 14x14½***

**Size: 28x32mm**

*284a* A49 $1.30 dark purple & yel 3.00 .90
*285a* A49 $2 dp brn & lt grn 5.00 1.60
*286a* A49 $5 dk vio bl & rose ('78) 12.50 3.00
*287a* A49 $10 dk sl grn & pink ('78) 14.50 7.50
*288a* A49 $20 black & rose ('78) 17.50 14.00
*Nos. 275a-288a (14)* 121.75 74.25

No. 288a exists imperf. Value, pair $750.
See Nos. 316-327.

**Princess Anne's Wedding Issue**

Common Design Type

**Wmk. 314**

**1973, Nov. 14 Litho.** ***Perf. 14***
**289** CD325 50c ocher & multi .75 .25
**290** CD325 $2 lilac & multi 2.50 2.00

Chinese Character "Hong" — A50

Designs: 50c, "Kong." $1, "Festival."

**1973, Nov. 23 Litho.** ***Perf. 14½x14***
**291** A50 10c red & green .60 .25
**292** A50 50c plum & red 2.50 1.00
**293** A50 $1 emerald & plum 5.50 4.00
*Nos. 291-293 (3)* 8.60 5.25

Festival of Hong Kong 1973.

Tiger
A51

Lunar New Year: $1.30, Tiger, vert.

***Perf. 14½x14, 14x14½***

**1974, Jan. 8** **Wmk. 314**
**294** A51 10c green & multi 3.00 .50
**295** A51 $1.30 lilac & multi 13.00 12.00

Chinese Opera Mask — A52

Designs: Chinese opera masks.

**1974, Feb. 1 Photo.** ***Perf. 12x12½***
**296** A52 10c black, red & org .60 .25
**297** A52 $1 multicolored 6.00 4.50
**298** A52 $2 black, org & gold 12.00 9.50
*a.* Souvenir sheet of 3, #296-298, perf. 14x13 65.00 55.00
*Nos. 296-298 (3)* 18.60 14.25

Hong Kong Arts Festival.

Carrier Pigeons
A53

Cent. of UPU: 50c, Symbolic globe in envelope. $2, Hands holding letters.

**1974, Oct. 9 Litho.** ***Perf. 14***
**299** A53 10c blue, grn & blk .50 .25
*a.* Unwatermarked 35.00
**300** A53 50c magenta & multi 2.25 .40
**301** A53 $2 violet & multi 5.50 4.00
*Nos. 299-301 (3)* 8.25 4.65

Rabbit
A54

Lunar New Year: $1.30, Two rabbits.

**1975, Feb. 5 Wmk. 314** ***Perf. 14***
**302** A54 10c silver & red 1.50 .50
*a.* Unwatermarked 1.60 1.00
**303** A54 $1.30 gold & green 7.75 7.75
*a.* Unwatermarked 8.00 11.00

Queen Elizabeth II, Prince Philip, Hong Kong Arms — A55

**Wmk. 373**

**1975, Apr. 30 Litho.** ***Perf. 13½***
**304** A55 $1.30 blue & multi 3.50 1.50
**305** A55 $2 yellow & multi 4.75 4.50

Royal Visit 1975.

Mid-Autumn Festival — A56

Brown Laughing Thrush — A57

Abstract Designs: $1, Dragon Boat Festival (boats). $2, Tin Hau Festival (ships with flags).

**1975, July 31 Unwmk.** ***Perf. 14***
**306** A56 50c rose lil & multi 3.00 .75
**307** A56 $1 brt grn & multi 11.00 2.75
**308** A56 $2 orange & multi 32.50 11.00
*a.* Souv. sheet of 3, #306-308 *125.00 65.00*
*Nos. 306-308 (3)* 46.50 14.50

Hong Kong Festivals, 1975.

**1975, Oct. 29 Litho. Wmk. 373**

Birds: $1.30, Chinese bulbul. $2, Black-capped kingfisher.

**309** A57 50c lt blue & multi 2.75 .75
**310** A57 $1.30 pink & multi 11.00 6.00
**311** A57 $2 yellow & multi 19.50 12.50
*Nos. 309-311 (3)* 33.25 19.25

Dragon
A58

Lunar New Year: $1.30, like 20c, pattern reversed.

**1976, Jan. 21 Litho.** ***Perf. 14½***
**312** A58 20c gold, pur & lilac 1.25 .50
**313** A58 $1.30 gold, red & grn 8.00 3.50

**Queen Elizabeth Type of 1973**

**Wmk. 373 (#320-323), Unwmkd.**

**1976-81 Photo.** ***Perf. 14½x14***

**Size: 20x24mm**

**316** A49 20c bright purple 3.50 1.25
**318** A49 30c ultramarine 8.00 2.25
**320** A49 60c lt violet ('77) 1.75 1.75
**321** A49 70c yellow ('77) 1.75 .75
**322** A49 80c brt magenta ('77) 2.25 2.25
**323** A49 90c sepia ('81) 9.00 2.25

**Size: 28x32mm**

***Perf. 14x14½***

**324** A49 $2 dp brn & lt grn 10.50 4.00
**325** A49 $5 dk vio bl & rose 14.00 7.50

**Photo. & Embossed**

**326** A49 $10 dk sl grn & pink 90.00 40.00
**327** A49 $20 black & rose 175.00 60.00
*Nos. 316-327 (10)* 315.75 122.00

"60" and Girl Guides Emblem
A59

$1.30, "60," tents and Girl Guides emblem.

**1976, Apr. 23 Wmk. 314** ***Perf. 14½***
**328** A59 20c silver & multi 1.25 .25
**329** A59 $1.30 silver & multi 6.50 4.50

60th anniv. of Hong Kong Girl Guides.

"Postal Services" (in Chinese) — A60

Designs: $1.30, General Post Office, 1911-1976. $2, New G.P.O., 1976.

**1976, Aug. 11 Litho. Wmk. 373**
**330** A60 20c gray, green & black .90 .25
**331** A60 $1.30 gray, red & black 4.00 1.75
**332** A60 $2 gray, yel & black 7.00 4.00
*Nos. 330-332 (3)* 11.90 6.00

Opening of new GPO building.

Snake
A61

Lunar New Year: $1.30, Snake & branch face left.

**1977, Jan. 6** ***Perf. 13½***
**333** A61 20c multicolored .90 .25
**334** A61 $1.30 multicolored 5.75 4.00

Queen Dotting Eye of Dragon, 1975 Visit — A62

20c, Presentation of the orb. $2, Orb, vert.

**1977, Feb. 7** **Litho.**
**335** A62 20c multicolored .60 .25
**336** A62 $1.30 multicolored 1.50 1.00
**337** A62 $2 multicolored 2.00 1.50
*Nos. 335-337 (3)* 4.10 2.75

25th anniv. of the reign of Elizabeth II.

Streetcars — A63

Designs: 60c, Star ferryboat. $1.30, Funicular railway. $2, Junk and sampan.

**1977, June 30 Wmk. 373** ***Perf. 13½***
**338** A63 20c multicolored .70 .25
**339** A63 60c multicolored 1.75 1.75
**340** A63 $1.30 multicolored 3.25 2.25
**341** A63 $2 multicolored 3.75 3.25
*Nos. 338-341 (4)* 9.45 7.50

Tourist publicity.

Buttercup Orchid — A64

$1.30, Lady's-slipper. $2, Susan orchid.

**1977, Oct. 12 Litho. *Perf. 14***

| | | | | |
|---|---|---|---|---|
| **342** | A64 | 20c blue & multi | 1.50 | .35 |
| **343** | A64 | $1.30 yellow & multi | 4.50 | 1.75 |
| **344** | A64 | $2 green & multi | 7.50 | 4.50 |
| | | *Nos. 342-344 (3)* | 13.50 | 6.60 |

Horse and Chinese Character "Ma" — A65

**1978, Jan. 26 Litho. *Perf. 14½***

| | | | | |
|---|---|---|---|---|
| **345** | A65 | 20c multicolored | .75 | .25 |
| **346** | A65 | $1.30 multicolored | 5.00 | 4.50 |

Lunar New Year.

Elizabeth II — A66

**1978, June 2 Litho. *Perf. 14x14½***

| | | | | |
|---|---|---|---|---|
| **347** | A66 | 20c carmine & dk blue | .50 | .25 |
| **348** | A66 | $1.30 dk blue & carmine | 1.75 | 1.75 |

25th anniv. of coronation of Elizabeth II.

Boy and Girl A67

Design: $1.30, Ring-around-a-rosy.

**1978, Nov. 8 Wmk. 373 *Perf. 14½***

| | | | | |
|---|---|---|---|---|
| **349** | A67 | 20c multicolored | .25 | .25 |
| **350** | A67 | $1.30 multicolored | 1.50 | 1.00 |

Centenary of Po Leung Kuk, society for help and education of orphans and poor children.

Electronics — A68

Industries: $1.30, Toy (bear and drum). $2, Garment (mannequins).

**1979, Jan. 9 Litho. *Perf. 14½***

| | | | | |
|---|---|---|---|---|
| **351** | A68 | 20c multicolored | .30 | .25 |
| **352** | A68 | $1.30 multicolored | 1.10 | 1.00 |
| **353** | A68 | $2 multicolored | 1.25 | 1.25 |
| | | *Nos. 351-353 (3)* | 2.65 | 2.50 |

Precis Orithya — A69

Butterflies: $1, Graphium sarpedon. $1.30, Heliophorus epicles phoenicoparyphus. $2, Danaus genutia.

**1979, June 20 Photo. Unwmk.**

| | | | | |
|---|---|---|---|---|
| **354** | A69 | 20c multicolored | 1.10 | .25 |
| **355** | A69 | $1 multicolored | 2.00 | .85 |
| **356** | A69 | $1.30 multicolored | 2.25 | 1.90 |
| **357** | A69 | $2 multicolored | 2.50 | 2.50 |
| | | *Nos. 354-357 (4)* | 7.85 | 5.50 |

Cross Section of Station A70

Mass Transit Railroad: $1.30, Front, rear and side views of train. $2, Map of routes.

**1979, Oct. 1 Litho. *Perf. 13½***

| | | | | |
|---|---|---|---|---|
| **358** | A70 | 20c multicolored | .50 | .25 |
| **359** | A70 | $1.30 multicolored | 1.75 | .55 |
| **360** | A70 | $2 multicolored | 2.25 | 2.50 |
| | | *Nos. 358-360 (3)* | 4.50 | 3.30 |

Ching Chung Koon Temple, Tuen Mun — A71

Rural Architecture: 20c, Tsui Shing Lau Pagoda, Sheung Cheung Wai, vert. $1.30, Village house, Sai O.

***Perf. 13x13½, 13½x13***

**1980, May 14 Litho. Wmk. 373**

| | | | | |
|---|---|---|---|---|
| **361** | A71 | 20c multicolored | .35 | .25 |
| **362** | A71 | $1.30 multicolored | 1.40 | 1.10 |
| **363** | A71 | $2 multicolored | 1.75 | 1.75 |
| | | *Nos. 361-363 (3)* | 3.50 | 3.10 |

**Queen Mother Elizabeth Birthday Issue**

Common Design Type

**1980, Aug. 4 Litho. *Perf. 14***

| | | | | |
|---|---|---|---|---|
| **364** | CD330 | $1.30 multicolored | 1.10 | 1.00 |

Botanical Gardens — A72

**1980, Nov. 12 Litho. *Perf. 13½***

| | | | | |
|---|---|---|---|---|
| **365** | A72 | 20c shown | .30 | .25 |
| **366** | A72 | $1 Ocean Park | .65 | .35 |
| **367** | A72 | $1.30 Kowloon Park | .75 | .75 |
| **368** | A72 | $2 Country Park | 1.40 | 1.40 |
| | | *Nos. 365-368 (4)* | 3.10 | 2.75 |

Epinephelus Akaara — A73

**1981, Jan. 28 Litho. *Perf. 13½***

| | | | | |
|---|---|---|---|---|
| **369** | A73 | 20c shown | .25 | .25 |
| **370** | A73 | $1 Nemipterus virgatus | .65 | .45 |
| **371** | A73 | $1.30 Choerodon azurio | .80 | .60 |
| **372** | A73 | $2 Scarus ghobban | 1.25 | 1.25 |
| | | *Nos. 369-372 (4)* | 2.95 | 2.55 |

**Royal Wedding Issue**

Common Design Type

**1981, July 29 Photo. *Perf. 14***

| | | | | |
|---|---|---|---|---|
| **373** | CD331 | 20c Bouquet | .25 | .25 |
| **374** | CD331 | $1.30 Charles | .55 | .35 |
| **375** | CD331 | $5 Couple | 2.50 | 2.50 |
| | | *Nos. 373-375 (3)* | 3.30 | 3.10 |

Public Housing Development A74

Various public housing developments.

**1981, Oct. 14 Litho. *Perf. 13½***

| | | | | |
|---|---|---|---|---|
| **376** | A74 | 20c multicolored | .25 | .25 |
| **377** | A74 | $1 multicolored | .70 | .40 |
| **378** | A74 | $1.30 multicolored | 1.00 | .65 |
| **379** | A74 | $2 multicolored | 1.25 | 1.25 |
| *a.* | | Souvenir sheet of 4, #376-379 | 6.50 | 6.50 |
| | | *Nos. 376-379 (4)* | 3.20 | 2.55 |

Port of Hong Kong A75

Various views of Port of Hong Kong.

**1982, Jan. 12 Litho. *Perf. 14½***

| | | | | |
|---|---|---|---|---|
| **380** | A75 | 20c multicolored | .60 | .25 |
| **381** | A75 | $1 multicolored | 1.75 | 1.10 |
| **382** | A75 | $1.30 multicolored | 2.00 | 1.60 |
| **383** | A75 | $2 multicolored | 2.25 | 2.25 |
| | | *Nos. 380-383 (4)* | 6.60 | 5.20 |

Five-banded Civet — A76

**1982, May 4 Litho. *Perf. 14½***

| | | | | |
|---|---|---|---|---|
| **384** | A76 | 20c shown | .30 | .25 |
| **385** | A76 | $1 Pangolin | .60 | .45 |
| **386** | A76 | $1.30 Chinese porcupine | 1.25 | .85 |
| **387** | A76 | $5 Barking deer | 3.50 | 3.50 |
| | | *Nos. 384-387 (4)* | 5.65 | 5.05 |

Queen Elizabeth II
A77 A78

***Perf. 14½x14***

**1982, Aug. 30 Photo. Wmk. 373**

| | | | | |
|---|---|---|---|---|
| **388** | A77 | 10c yellow & dk red | .80 | .60 |
| **389** | A77 | 20c blue vio & vio | 1.00 | 1.00 |
| **390** | A77 | 30c orange & pur | 1.50 | .30 |
| **391** | A77 | 40c lt blue & red | 1.50 | .30 |
| **392** | A77 | 50c pale grn & brn | 1.50 | .30 |
| **393** | A77 | 60c gray & brt mag | 2.75 | 2.00 |
| **394** | A77 | 70c brt org & dk grn | 2.75 | .90 |
| **395** | A77 | 80c gray ol & brn ol | 2.75 | 3.00 |
| **396** | A77 | 90c grnsh bl & grn | 4.50 | .60 |
| **397** | A77 | $1 brt pink & brn org | 2.50 | .30 |
| **398** | A77 | $1.30 rose vio & dk bl | 4.00 | .30 |
| **399** | A77 | $2 buff & blue | 6.50 | 1.00 |

**Photo. & Embossed**

***Perf. 14x14½***

| | | | | |
|---|---|---|---|---|
| **400** | A78 | $5 lemon & lake | 8.00 | 2.50 |
| **401** | A78 | $10 brn & blk brn | 9.00 | 5.00 |
| **402** | A78 | $20 lt blue & lake | 15.00 | 15.00 |
| **403** | A78 | $50 gray & lake | 36.00 | 30.00 |
| | | *Nos. 388-403 (16)* | 100.05 | 63.10 |

Nos. 388 and 397 also issued in coils.

**1985-87 Unwmk.**

| | | | | |
|---|---|---|---|---|
| *388a* | A77 | 10c | .75 | .75 |
| *389a* | A77 | 20c | 18.50 | 10.00 |
| *391a* | A77 | 40c | 1.00 | 1.00 |
| *392a* | A77 | 50c | 1.00 | .30 |
| *393a* | A77 | 60c | 1.60 | 1.00 |
| *394a* | A77 | 70c | 3.50 | .50 |
| *395a* | A77 | 80c | 3.75 | 2.75 |
| *396a* | A77 | 90c | 4.25 | .50 |
| *397a* | A77 | $1 | 1.90 | .40 |
| *398b* | A77 | $1.30 | 2.50 | .35 |
| **398A** | A77 | $1.70 brt yel grn & dp bl | 4.25 | 1.50 |
| *399a* | A77 | $2 | 4.00 | 1.50 |
| *400a* | A78 | $5 | 9.00 | 3.00 |
| *401a* | A78 | $10 | 9.00 | 4.00 |
| *402a* | A78 | $20 | 11.00 | 7.00 |
| *403a* | A78 | $50 | 32.50 | 25.00 |
| | | *Nos. 388a-403a (16)* | 108.50 | 59.55 |

Issued: $1.30, 6/13/86; $1.70, 9/2/86; 20c, 6/87; others, 10/10/85.

3rd Far East and South Pacific Games for the Disabled A79

***Perf. 14x14½***

**1982, Oct. 31 Litho. Wmk. 373**

| | | | | |
|---|---|---|---|---|
| **404** | A79 | 30c Table tennis | .50 | .25 |
| **405** | A79 | $1 Racing | 1.10 | 1.00 |
| **406** | A79 | $1.30 Basketball | 3.25 | 1.75 |
| **407** | A79 | $5 Archery | 5.25 | 5.25 |
| | | *Nos. 404-407 (4)* | 10.10 | 8.25 |

Performing Arts — A80

**1983, Jan. 26 Litho. *Perf. 14½x14***

| | | | | |
|---|---|---|---|---|
| **408** | A80 | 30c Dancing | .50 | .25 |
| **409** | A80 | $1.30 Theater | 2.00 | 1.50 |
| **410** | A80 | $5 Music | 5.25 | 5.25 |
| | | *Nos. 408-410 (3)* | 7.75 | 7.00 |

A81

**1983, Mar. 14 *Perf. 14½x13½***

| | | | | |
|---|---|---|---|---|
| **411** | A81 | 30c Aerial view | .75 | .25 |
| **412** | A81 | $1 Liverpool Bay | 1.75 | 1.10 |
| **413** | A81 | $1.30 Flag | 2.00 | 1.25 |
| **414** | A81 | $5 Queen Elizabeth II | 4.50 | 4.50 |
| | | *Nos. 411-414 (4)* | 9.00 | 7.10 |

Commonwealth Day.

Views by Night A82

**1983, Aug. 17 Litho. *Perf. 14½***

| | | | | |
|---|---|---|---|---|
| **415** | A82 | 30c Victoria Harbor | 1.50 | .75 |
| **416** | A82 | $1 Space Museum | 4.50 | 2.25 |
| **417** | A82 | $1.30 Chinese New Year Fireworks | 5.50 | 2.50 |
| **418** | A82 | $5 Jumbo Restaurant | 16.50 | 14.00 |
| | | *Nos. 415-418 (4)* | 28.00 | 19.50 |

Royal Observatory Centenary — A83

**1983, Nov. 23 Litho. *Perf. 14½***

| | | | | |
|---|---|---|---|---|
| **419** | A83 | 40c Technical facilities | .90 | .30 |
| **420** | A83 | $1 Wind measurement | 2.50 | 1.50 |
| **421** | A83 | $1.30 Temperature measurement | 2.75 | 1.75 |

| | | | | | |
|---|---|---|---|---|---|
| 422 | A83 | $5 | Earthquake measurement | 8.50 | 8.50 |
| | | | *Nos. 419-422 (4)* | 14.65 | 12.05 |

Training Plane, Dorado A84

**1984, Mar. 7 Wmk. 373 *Perf. 13½***

| | | | | | |
|---|---|---|---|---|---|
| 423 | A84 | 40c | shown | 1.50 | .30 |
| 424 | A84 | $1 | Hong Kong Clipper seaplane | 2.75 | 1.75 |
| 425 | A84 | $1.30 | Jumbo jet, Kai Tak Airport | 3.00 | 1.75 |
| 426 | A84 | $5 | Baldwin Brothers balloon, vert. | 8.50 | 8.50 |
| | | | *Nos. 423-426 (4)* | 15.75 | 12.30 |

Map of Hong Kong, 19th Cent. A85

Various maps.

**1984, June 21 Litho. *Perf. 14***

| | | | | | |
|---|---|---|---|---|---|
| 427 | A85 | 40c | multicolored | 1.25 | .35 |
| 428 | A85 | $1 | multicolored | 2.00 | 1.40 |
| 429 | A85 | $1.30 | multicolored | 3.25 | 2.00 |
| 430 | A85 | $5 | multicolored | 11.00 | 11.00 |
| | | | *Nos. 427-430 (4)* | 17.50 | 14.75 |

Chinese Lanterns A86

**1984, Sept. 6 Litho. *Perf. 13½x13***

| | | | | | |
|---|---|---|---|---|---|
| 431 | A86 | 40c | Rooster | 1.25 | .50 |
| 432 | A86 | $1 | Bull | 3.00 | 1.75 |
| 433 | A86 | $1.30 | Butterfly | 4.00 | 2.00 |
| 434 | A86 | $5 | Fish | 12.00 | 12.00 |
| | | | *Nos. 431-434 (4)* | 20.25 | 16.25 |

Jockey Club Centenary — A87

**1984, Nov. 21 Litho. *Perf. 14½***

| | | | | | |
|---|---|---|---|---|---|
| 435 | A87 | 40c | Supporting health care | 1.50 | .50 |
| 436 | A87 | $1 | Supporting disabled | 3.00 | 1.50 |
| 437 | A87 | $1.30 | Supporting the arts | 4.00 | 2.25 |
| 438 | A87 | $5 | Supporting Ocean Park | 9.00 | 9.00 |
| *a.* | | | Souvenir sheet of 4, #435-438 | 30.00 | 30.00 |
| | | | *Nos. 435-438 (4)* | 17.50 | 13.25 |

Historic Buildings A88

***Perf. 13½***

**1985, Mar. 14 Unwmk. Litho.**

| | | | | | |
|---|---|---|---|---|---|
| 439 | A88 | 40c | Hung Sing Temple | 1.00 | .30 |
| 440 | A88 | $1 | St. John's Cathedral | 2.00 | 1.75 |
| 441 | A88 | $1.30 | Old Supreme Court Building | 2.50 | 2.00 |
| 442 | A88 | $5 | Wan Chai Post Office | 7.00 | 7.00 |
| | | | *Nos. 439-442 (4)* | 12.50 | 11.05 |

Intl. Dragon Boat Festival A89

***Perf. 13½x13***

**1985, June 19 Wmk. 373 Litho.**

| | | | | | |
|---|---|---|---|---|---|
| 443 | A89 | 40c | multicolored | .75 | .30 |
| 444 | A89 | $1 | multicolored | 2.25 | 1.50 |
| 445 | A89 | $1.30 | multicolored | 3.50 | 1.75 |
| 446 | A89 | $5 | multicolored | 11.00 | 9.00 |
| *a.* | | | Strip of 4, #443-446 | 32.50 | 30.00 |
| *b.* | | | Souvenir sheet of 4, #443-446, perf. 13x12½ | 32.50 | 32.50 |
| | | | *Nos. 443-446 (4)* | 17.50 | 12.55 |

Nos. 443-446 when placed together form a continuous design.

### Queen Mother 85th Birthday Issue

Common Design Type

**1985, Aug. 7 Litho. *Perf. 14½x14***

| | | | | | |
|---|---|---|---|---|---|
| 447 | CD336 | 40c | At Glamis Castle, age 9 | .65 | .25 |
| 448 | CD336 | $1 | On balcony with Princes William and Charles | 1.60 | 1.25 |
| 449 | CD336 | $1.30 | Photograph by Cecil Beaton,1980 | 2.25 | 1.25 |
| 450 | CD336 | $5 | Holding Prince Henry | 5.75 | 5.75 |
| | | | *Nos. 447-450 (4)* | 10.25 | 8.50 |

Indigenous Flowers — A90

**1985, Sept. 25 Litho. *Perf. 13½***

| | | | | | |
|---|---|---|---|---|---|
| 451 | A90 | 40c | Melastoma | 2.00 | .60 |
| 452 | A90 | 50c | Chinese lily | 2.25 | .70 |
| 453 | A90 | 60c | Grantham's camellia | 2.75 | 1.75 |
| 454 | A90 | $1.30 | Narcissus | 3.75 | 1.75 |
| 455 | A90 | $1.70 | Bauhinia | 4.25 | 2.00 |
| 456 | A90 | $5 | Chinese New Year flower | 8.00 | 8.00 |
| | | | *Nos. 451-456 (6)* | 23.00 | 14.80 |

See No. 898.

Modern Architecture — A91

**1985, Nov. 27 *Perf. 15***

| | | | | | |
|---|---|---|---|---|---|
| 457 | A91 | 50c | Hong Kong Academy for Performing Arts | .80 | .30 |
| 458 | A91 | $1.30 | Exchange Square, vert. | 1.50 | 1.00 |
| 459 | A91 | $1.70 | Hong Kong Bank Hdqtrs., vert. | 2.25 | 1.25 |
| 460 | A91 | $5 | Hong Kong Coliseum | 7.50 | 7.50 |
| | | | *Nos. 457-460 (4)* | 12.05 | 10.05 |

Halley's Comet A92

**1986, Feb. 26 Litho. *Perf. 13½x13***

| | | | | | |
|---|---|---|---|---|---|
| 461 | A92 | 50c | Comet, solar system | 1.50 | .25 |
| 462 | A92 | $1.30 | Edmond Halley | 2.25 | 1.25 |
| 463 | A92 | $1.70 | Hong Kong, trajectory | 3.50 | 1.50 |
| 464 | A92 | $5 | Comet, Earth | 10.00 | 10.00 |
| *a.* | | | Souvenir sheet of 4, #461-464 | 32.50 | 32.50 |
| | | | *Nos. 461-464 (4)* | 17.25 | 13.00 |

### Queen Elizabeth II 60th Birthday

Common Design Type

Designs: 50c, At the wedding of Cecillia Bowes-Lyon, Brompton Parish Church, 1939. $1, Most Noble Order of the Garter, service at St. George's Chapel, Windsor Castle, 1977. $1.30, State visit, 1975. $1.70, Queen Mother's 80th birthday celebration, Royal Lodge, Windsor, 1980. $5, Visiting Crown Agents' offices, 1983.

**1986, Apr. 21 *Perf. 14½***

| | | | | | |
|---|---|---|---|---|---|
| 465 | CD337 | 50c | scar, blk & sil | .50 | .25 |
| 466 | CD337 | $1 | ultra & multi | 1.10 | .35 |
| 467 | CD337 | $1.30 | green & multi | 1.40 | .50 |
| 468 | CD337 | $1.70 | violet & multi | 1.60 | .75 |
| 469 | CD337 | $5 | rose vio & multi | 5.00 | 5.00 |
| | | | *Nos. 465-469 (5)* | 9.60 | 6.85 |

EXPO '86, Vancouver — A93

**1986, July 18 Litho. *Perf. 13½***

| | | | | | |
|---|---|---|---|---|---|
| 470 | A93 | 50c | Transportation | 1.00 | .30 |
| 471 | A93 | $1.30 | Finance | 1.75 | 1.00 |
| 472 | A93 | $1.70 | Trade | 2.75 | 1.50 |
| 473 | A93 | $5 | Communications | 7.50 | 7.50 |
| | | | *Nos. 470-473 (4)* | 13.00 | 10.30 |

Fishing Vessels A94

**1986, Sept. 24 Litho.**

| | | | | | |
|---|---|---|---|---|---|
| 474 | A94 | 50c | Hand-liner sampan | .90 | .30 |
| 475 | A94 | $1.30 | Stern trawler | 1.75 | 1.25 |
| 476 | A94 | $1.70 | Long liner junk | 3.50 | 1.50 |
| 477 | A94 | $5 | Junk trawler | 7.50 | 7.50 |
| | | | *Nos. 474-477 (4)* | 13.65 | 10.55 |

19th Cent. Paintings — A95

50c, Possibly, Second puan khequa, by Spoilum. $1.30, Chinese woman, artist unknown. $1.70, Self-portrait at age 52, by Kwan Kiu Chin. $5, Possibly, Wife of a merchant, by George Chinnery.

**1986, Dec. 9 Litho. *Perf. 14***

| | | | | | |
|---|---|---|---|---|---|
| 478 | A95 | 50c | multicolored | .50 | .25 |
| 479 | A95 | $1.30 | multicolored | 1.60 | 1.25 |
| 480 | A95 | $1.70 | multicolored | 1.90 | 1.50 |
| 481 | A95 | $5 | multicolored | 5.25 | 5.25 |
| | | | *Nos. 478-481 (4)* | 9.25 | 8.25 |

New Year (Year of the Hare) A96

Embroideries of various rabbits.

**1987, Jan. 21 Litho. *Perf. 13½x14***

| | | | | | |
|---|---|---|---|---|---|
| 482 | A96 | 50c | multicolored | 1.00 | .30 |
| 483 | A96 | $1.30 | multicolored | 1.60 | 1.25 |
| 484 | A96 | $1.70 | multicolored | 2.00 | 1.25 |
| 485 | A96 | $5 | multicolored | 7.00 | 7.00 |
| *a.* | | | Souvenir sheet of 4, #482-485 | 45.00 | 45.00 |
| | | | *Nos. 482-485 (4)* | 11.60 | 9.80 |

19th Century Paintings in the Hong Kong Museum of Art and Shanghai Banking Corp. A97

Scenes: 50c, A Village Square, Hong Kong Island, 1838, by Auguste Borget (1809-1877). $1.30, Boat Dwellers in Kowloon Bay, 1838, by Borget. $1.70, Flagstaff House, Lt. Governor D'Aguilar's Residence, 1846, by Murdoch Bruce. $5, A View of Wellington Street, late 19th century, by C. Andrasi.

**1987, Apr. 23 Litho. *Perf. 14***

| | | | | | |
|---|---|---|---|---|---|
| 486 | A97 | 50c | multicolored | 1.00 | .25 |
| 487 | A97 | $1.30 | multicolored | 2.50 | 1.40 |
| 488 | A97 | $1.70 | multicolored | 3.00 | 1.50 |
| 489 | A97 | $5 | multicolored | 9.00 | 9.00 |
| | | | *Nos. 486-489 (4)* | 15.50 | 12.15 |

Elizabeth II, Hong Kong Waterfront A98

Queen, Natl. Landmarks A99

Type I — Darker Shading Under Chin

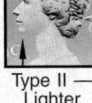

Type II — Lighter Shading Under Chin

Designs: $5, Tsim Shah Tsui, Kowloon. $10, Victoria Harbor. $20, Legislative Council Building. $50, Government House.

**1987, July 13 Litho. *Perf. 14½x14***

**Type I**

**No date inscription below design**

| | | | | | |
|---|---|---|---|---|---|
| 490 | A98 | 10c | yel grn, gray & blk | .50 | .25 |
| 491 | A98 | 40c | bluish grn, lt yel & blk | 1.25 | .25 |
| 492 | A98 | 50c | brn org, buff & blk | 1.00 | .25 |
| 493 | A98 | 60c | lt blue, pale rose & blk | 1.00 | .25 |
| 494 | A98 | 70c | vio, pale rose & blk | 1.25 | .25 |
| 495 | A98 | 80c | brt rose lil, lt blue & blk | 1.50 | 1.00 |
| 496 | A98 | 90c | pink, pale beige & blk | 1.25 | 1.00 |
| 497 | A98 | $1 | brt lem & blk | 1.25 | .40 |
| 498 | A98 | $1.30 | rose claret, brt yel grn & blk | 1.25 | 1.25 |
| 499 | A98 | $1.70 | lt blue & blk | 1.25 | .80 |
| 500 | A98 | $2 | yel grn, cream & blk | 1.40 | .70 |

***Perf. 14***

| | | | | | |
|---|---|---|---|---|---|
| 501 | A99 | $5 | grn, lt grn & blk | 3.50 | 2.00 |
| 502 | A99 | $10 | brn, yel brn & blk | 8.00 | 5.00 |
| 503 | A99 | $20 | rose vio, lil & blk | 17.50 | 10.00 |
| 504 | A99 | $50 | sep, gray & blk | 42.50 | 32.50 |
| | | | *Nos. 490-504 (15)* | 84.40 | 55.90 |

**Type II**

**No date inscription below design**

**1988, Sept. 1**

| | | | | |
|---|---|---|---|---|
| *490a* | A98 | 10c | .60 | .25 |
| *491a* | A98 | 40c | 1.25 | .25 |
| *492a* | A98 | 50c | 1.25 | .25 |
| *493a* | A98 | 60c | 1.25 | .25 |
| *494a* | A98 | 70c | 1.50 | 1.00 |
| *495a* | A98 | 80c | 1.50 | 1.00 |
| *496a* | A98 | 90c | 1.50 | 1.00 |
| *497a* | A98 | $1 | 1.50 | .45 |
| *498a* | A98 | $1.30 | 2.25 | 1.50 |
| *499a* | A98 | $1.70 | 1.50 | 1.00 |
| *500a* | A98 | $2 | 1.75 | .75 |
| *501a* | A99 | $5 | 5.50 | 2.25 |
| *502a* | A99 | $10 | 10.00 | 6.00 |
| *503a* | A99 | $20 | 20.00 | 12.00 |
| *504a* | A99 | $50 | 45.00 | 35.00 |
| | | *Nos. 490a-504a (15)* | 96.35 | 62.95 |

See Nos. 532-533, 592-593, 629.

**1989, Aug. 1** **Inscribed "1989"**

| | | | | |
|---|---|---|---|---|
| *490b* | A98 | 10c | .75 | *1.00* |
| *491b* | A98 | 40c | 1.75 | *2.00* |
| *492b* | A98 | 50c | 1.25 | .55 |
| *493b* | A98 | 60c | 1.60 | .30 |
| *494b* | A98 | 70c | 2.00 | 1.60 |
| *495b* | A98 | 80c | 2.00 | 1.25 |
| *496b* | A98 | 90c | 1.50 | 1.00 |
| *497b* | A98 | $1 | 2.00 | .65 |
| *498b* | A98 | $1.30 | 3.75 | *4.00* |
| *500b* | A98 | $2 | 2.25 | .75 |
| *501b* | A99 | $5 | 5.50 | 2.25 |
| *502b* | A99 | $10 | 8.00 | 6.50 |
| *503b* | A99 | $20 | 13.50 | 12.00 |
| *504b* | A99 | $50 | 21.00 | *22.50* |
| | | *Nos. 490b-504b (14)* | 66.85 | 56.35 |

**1990** **Inscribed "1990"**

| | | | | |
|---|---|---|---|---|
| *490c* | A98 | 10c | .75 | *1.00* |
| *491c* | A98 | 40c | 1.75 | *2.00* |
| *492c* | A98 | 50c | 1.25 | .55 |
| *493c* | A98 | 60c | 1.60 | .30 |
| *494c* | A98 | 70c | 2.00 | 1.60 |
| *495c* | A98 | 80c | 2.00 | 1.25 |
| *496c* | A98 | 90c | 1.50 | 1.00 |
| *497c* | A98 | $1 | 2.00 | .65 |
| *498c* | A98 | $1.30 | 3.75 | *4.00* |
| *500c* | A98 | $2 | 2.25 | .75 |
| *501c* | A99 | $5 | 5.50 | 2.25 |
| *502c* | A99 | $10 | 8.00 | 6.50 |
| *e.* | | Souv. sheet of 1 | 110.00 | |
| *503c* | A99 | $20 | 13.50 | 12.00 |
| *504c* | A99 | $50 | 21.00 | *22.50* |
| | | *Nos. 490c-504c (14)* | 66.85 | 56.35 |

No. 502e was issued in conjunction with the New Zealand 1990 World Stamp Exhibition with NZ 1990 inscriptions and related design in the sheet selvage.

No. 502e issued 8/24.

**1991** **Inscribed "1991"**

| | | | | |
|---|---|---|---|---|
| *490d* | A98 | 10c | 1.10 | *1.00* |
| *492d* | A98 | 50c | 2.00 | .55 |
| *493d* | A98 | 60c | 2.50 | .30 |
| *494d* | A98 | 70c | 3.25 | 1.60 |
| *495d* | A98 | 80c | 3.25 | 1.25 |
| *496d* | A98 | 90c | 2.40 | 1.00 |
| *497d* | A98 | $1 | 3.25 | .65 |
| *499d* | A98 | $1.70 | 2.40 | 1.00 |
| *500d* | A98 | $2 | 3.50 | .75 |
| *501d* | A99 | $5 | 8.75 | 2.25 |
| *502d* | A99 | $10 | 13.00 | 6.50 |
| *f.* | | Souv. sheet of 1, PHILANIPPON selvage | 55.00 | 30.00 |
| *g.* | | As "f," Olympics selvage | 27.50 | 17.50 |
| *503d* | A99 | $20 | 22.50 | 12.00 |
| *504d* | A99 | $50 | 22.50 | 25.00 |
| | | *Nos. 490d-504d (13)* | 90.40 | 53.85 |

Nos. 502f-502g were were issued to commemorate Hong Kong's participation in PHILANIPPON ' and the sponsorship of the 1992 Olympics Games by the Hong Kong Post Office, respectively. The selvage of each sheets bears a distinctive design and inscriptions. See No. 629.

Issued: No. 502f, 11/16; 502g, 12/4.

Nethersole Hospital, Cent. — A100

**1987, Sept. 8** ***Perf. 14½***

| | | | | |
|---|---|---|---|---|
| **505** | A100 | 50c Hospital, 1887 | 1.25 | .25 |
| **506** | A100 | $1.30 Patients, staff | 2.75 | 1.40 |
| **507** | A100 | $1.70 Technology, 1987 | 3.25 | 1.50 |
| **508** | A100 | $5 Treatment | 10.00 | 10.00 |
| | | *Nos. 505-508 (4)* | 17.25 | 13.15 |

Natl. Flag A101

Map of Hong Kong A101a

**Coil Stamps**

**1987, July 13** ***Perf. 15x14***

**No date inscription below design**

| | | | | |
|---|---|---|---|---|
| **509** | A101 | 10c shown | *1.75* | *1.75* |
| *b.* | | Inscribed "1990" | 1.50 | 1.50 |
| *c.* | | Inscribed "1991" | 1.50 | 1.50 |
| **510** | A101a | 50c blk, dull olive & lake | *2.00* | *2.00* |

See Nos. 611-614.

**1989, Aug. 1** **Inscribed "1989"**

| | | | | |
|---|---|---|---|---|
| **509a** | A101 | 10c multicolored | *1.00* | *1.25* |
| **510a** | A101a | 50c multicolored | *1.75* | *1.25* |

Folk Costumes — A102

**1987, Nov. 18** ***Perf. 13½***

| | | | | |
|---|---|---|---|---|
| **511** | A102 | 50c multicolored | .65 | .25 |
| **512** | A102 | $1.30 multi, diff. | 1.75 | 1.25 |
| **513** | A102 | $1.70 multi, diff. | 2.00 | 1.60 |
| **514** | A102 | $5 multi, diff. | 6.25 | 6.25 |
| | | *Nos. 511-514 (4)* | 10.65 | 9.35 |

New Year (Year of the Dragon) A103

**1988, Jan. 27** **Litho.** ***Perf. 13½***

| | | | | |
|---|---|---|---|---|
| **515** | A103 | 50c multicolored | .90 | .30 |
| **516** | A103 | $1.30 multi, diff. | 2.25 | 1.00 |
| **517** | A103 | $1.70 multi, diff. | 2.50 | 1.50 |
| **518** | A103 | $5 multi, diff. | 5.00 | 5.00 |
| *a.* | | Souv. sheet of 4, #515-518 | *20.00* | *20.00* |
| | | *Nos. 515-518 (4)* | 10.65 | 7.80 |

See No. 838e.

Indigenous Birds — A104

**1988, Apr. 20** ***Perf. 13½x14***

| | | | | |
|---|---|---|---|---|
| **519** | A104 | 50c White-breasted kingfisher | 1.25 | .30 |
| **520** | A104 | $1.30 Fukien niltava | 2.50 | 1.50 |
| **521** | A104 | $1.70 Black kite | 3.00 | 1.75 |
| **522** | A104 | $5 Pied kingfisher | 6.50 | 6.50 |
| | | *Nos. 519-522 (4)* | 13.25 | 10.05 |

Indigenous Trees — A105

**1988, June 16** **Litho.** ***Perf. 13½***

| | | | | |
|---|---|---|---|---|
| **523** | A105 | 50c Chinese banyan | .35 | .25 |
| **524** | A105 | $1.30 Bauhinia blakeana | 1.10 | .75 |
| **525** | A105 | $1.70 Cotton tree | 1.40 | .85 |
| **526** | A105 | $5 Schima | 3.75 | 3.75 |
| *a.* | | Souv. sheet of 4, #523-526 | *16.00* | *12.00* |
| | | *Nos. 523-526 (4)* | 6.60 | 5.60 |

See No. 923. See note after No. 940.

Peak Tramway, Victoria, Cent. — A106

Various views of Hong Kong and the tram line.

**1988, Aug. 4** **Litho.** ***Perf. 15***

| | | | | |
|---|---|---|---|---|
| **527** | A106 | 50c multicolored | .55 | .25 |
| **528** | A106 | $1.30 multi, diff. | 1.10 | 1.00 |
| **529** | A106 | $1.70 multi, diff. | 1.25 | 1.25 |
| **530** | A106 | $5 multi, diff. | 3.75 | 3.75 |
| *a.* | | Souvenir sheet of 4, #527-530 | *12.00* | *12.00* |
| | | *Nos. 527-530 (4)* | 6.65 | 6.25 |

Catholic Cathedral, Caine Road, Cent. — A107

**1988, Sept. 30** **Litho.** ***Perf. 14***

| | | | | |
|---|---|---|---|---|
| **531** | A107 | 60c multicolored | 1.60 | 1.60 |

**Queen and Waterfront Type of 1987 Type II**

**1988, Sept. 1** **Litho.** ***Perf. 14½x14***

**No date inscription below design**

| | | | | |
|---|---|---|---|---|
| **532** | A98 | $1.40 multicolored | 3.00 | .60 |
| *a.* | | Inscribed "1989" | 3.00 | .60 |
| *b.* | | Inscribed "1990" | 3.00 | .60 |
| **533** | A98 | $1.80 multicolored | 4.50 | .75 |
| *a.* | | Inscribed "1989" | 4.50 | .75 |
| *b.* | | Inscribed "1990" | 4.50 | .75 |
| *c.* | | Inscribed "1991" | 4.50 | .75 |

Issued: No. 532a, 533a, 8/1/89; 532b, 533b, 1990; No. 533c, 4/2/91.

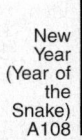

New Year (Year of the Snake) A108

**1989, Jan. 18** **Litho.** ***Perf. 13½x14***

| | | | | |
|---|---|---|---|---|
| **534** | A108 | 60c multicolored | .75 | .25 |
| **535** | A108 | $1.40 multi, diff. | 1.75 | .70 |
| **536** | A108 | $1.80 multi, diff. | 2.00 | .90 |
| *a.* | | Bklt. pane, 5 each #534, 536 | 14.00 | |
| **537** | A108 | $5 multi, diff. | 6.25 | 6.25 |
| *a.* | | Souv. sheet of 4, #534-537 | *18.00* | *13.00* |
| | | *Nos. 534-537 (4)* | 10.75 | 8.10 |

See No. 838g.

Cheung Chau Bun Festival — A109

**1989, May 4** **Unwmk.** ***Perf. 13½***

| | | | | |
|---|---|---|---|---|
| **538** | A109 | 60c Girl, doll | .65 | .25 |
| **539** | A109 | $1.40 Girl | 1.40 | .80 |
| **540** | A109 | $1.80 Festival paper god | 1.90 | .90 |
| **541** | A109 | $5 Bun tower gate | 4.75 | 4.75 |
| | | *Nos. 538-541 (4)* | 8.70 | 6.70 |

Modern Art — A110

Hong Kong People — A111

60c, Twin, sculpture by Cheung Yee (b. 1936). $1.40, Figures, painted by Luis Chan (b. 1905). $1.80, Lotus, sculpture by Van Lau (b. 1933). $5, Zen, painted by Lui Shou-kwan (1919-1975).

**1989, July 19** ***Perf. 12x13***

| | | | | |
|---|---|---|---|---|
| **542** | A110 | 60c multicolored | .65 | .25 |
| **543** | A110 | $1.40 multicolored | 1.50 | .80 |
| **544** | A110 | $1.80 multicolored | 1.90 | .95 |
| **545** | A110 | $5 multicolored | 4.00 | 4.00 |
| | | *Nos. 542-545 (4)* | 8.05 | 6.00 |

**1989, Sept. 6** ***Perf. 13x14½***

Designs: 60c, Youth holding autumn festival decoration, lunar year festival dragon. $1.40, Shadow boxer, horse racing. $1.80, Office and construction workers. $5, Two women, two men (ethnic multiplicity).

| | | | | |
|---|---|---|---|---|
| **546** | A111 | 60c multicolored | .75 | .25 |
| **547** | A111 | $1.40 multicolored | 2.25 | .80 |
| **548** | A111 | $1.80 multicolored | 2.50 | .90 |
| **549** | A111 | $5 multicolored | 5.25 | 5.25 |
| | | *Nos. 546-549 (4)* | 10.75 | 7.20 |

See No. 762.

Construction Projects A112

**1989, Oct. 5** **Unwmk.** ***Perf. 13***

| | | | | |
|---|---|---|---|---|
| **550** | A112 | 60c University of Science and Technology | .55 | .25 |
| **551** | A112 | 70c Cultural center | .60 | .40 |
| **552** | A112 | $1.30 Eastern Harbor Crossing | 1.10 | 1.10 |
| **553** | A112 | $1.40 Bank of China | 1.25 | .85 |
| **554** | A112 | $1.80 Convention center | 1.40 | 1.25 |
| **555** | A112 | $5 Light rail transit | 6.50 | 6.50 |
| | | *Nos. 550-555 (6)* | 11.40 | 10.35 |

Visit of the Prince and Princess of Wales — A113

Portraits and view of Hong Kong: 60c, Charles and Diana. $1.40, Diana. $1.80, Charles. $5, Couple wearing formal attire.

**1989, Nov. 8** **Wmk. 340** ***Perf. 14½***

| | | | | |
|---|---|---|---|---|
| **556** | A113 | 60c multicolored | 1.50 | .30 |
| **557** | A113 | $1.40 multicolored | 2.50 | 1.10 |
| **558** | A113 | $1.80 multicolored | 1.90 | 1.10 |
| **559** | A113 | $5 multicolored | 7.50 | 7.50 |
| *a.* | | Souvenir sheet of 1 | 17.50 | 15.00 |
| | | *Nos. 556-559 (4)* | 13.40 | 10.00 |

New Year 1990 (Year of the Horse) A114

***Perf. 13½x12½***

**1990, Jan. 23** **Unwmk.**

| | | | | |
|---|---|---|---|---|
| **560** | A114 | 60c multicolored | .90 | .35 |
| **561** | A114 | $1.40 multi, diff. | 2.00 | 1.25 |
| **562** | A114 | $1.80 multi, diff. | 2.25 | 1.25 |
| *a.* | | Bklt. pane, 3 each 60c, $1.80 | 15.00 | |
| | | Complete booklet, 2 #562a | 30.00 | |
| **563** | A114 | $5 multi, diff. | 6.50 | 6.50 |
| *a.* | | Souvenir sheet of 4, #560-563 | 20.00 | 15.00 |
| | | *Nos. 560-563 (4)* | 11.65 | 9.35 |

Examples of No. 562a ovptd. with marginal inscription were released on May 3 to publicize Stamp World London '90.

See No. 838k.

Intl. Cuisine — A115

Pollutants — A116

**1990, Apr. 26 Litho. *Perf. 12½x13***

564 A115 60c Chinese .70 .25
565 A115 70c Indian .70 .50
566 A115 $1.30 Chinese, diff. 1.25 1.25
567 A115 $1.40 Thai 1.25 .70
568 A115 $1.80 Japanese 1.50 1.10
569 A115 $5 French 4.75 4.75
*Nos. 564-569 (6)* 10.15 8.55

**Wmk. 340**

**1990, June 5 Litho. *Perf. 14½***

570 A116 60c Air .45 .25
571 A116 $1.40 Noise .95 .80
572 A116 $1.80 Water 1.60 .80
573 A116 $5 Land 3.50 3.50
*Nos. 570-573 (4)* 6.50 5.35

World Environment Day.

Electrification of Hong Kong, Cent. — A117

Views of Hong Kong and streetlights.

**1990, Oct. 2 Litho. *Perf. 14½***

574 A117 60c 1890 .60 .25
575 A117 $1.40 1940 1.40 1.00
576 A117 $1.80 1960 1.50 1.00
577 A117 $5 1980 3.25 3.25
*a.* Souvenir sheet of 2, #575, 577 7.50 7.50
Complete booklet, 4 #577a 30.00
*Nos. 574-577 (4)* 6.75 5.50

Christmas — A118

**1990, Nov. 8**

578 A118 50c shown .30 .25
579 A118 60c Dove, holly .40 .25
580 A118 $1.40 Skyline, snowman 1.00 .45
581 A118 $1.80 Santa Claus' hat, skyscraper 1.10 .55
582 A118 $2 Children, Santa Claus 1.60 1.40
583 A118 $5 Candy cane, skyline 3.75 3.75
*Nos. 578-583 (6)* 8.15 6.65

New Year 1991 (Year of the Sheep) A119

Different embroidered rams.

**1991, Jan. 24 Litho. *Perf. 13½x12½***

584 A119 60c multicolored .40 .25
585 A119 $1.40 multicolored .95 .60
586 A119 $1.80 multicolored 1.10 .75
*a.* Bklt. pane, 3 each #584, 586 7.50
Complete booklet, 2 #586a 15.00
587 A119 $5 multicolored 3.50 3.50
*a.* Souv. sheet of 4, #584-587 9.00 9.00
*Nos. 584-587 (4)* 5.95 5.10

See No. 838j.

Education — A120

***Perf. 13½x13***

**1991, Apr. 18 Litho. Unwmk.**

588 A120 80c Kindergarten .40 .25
589 A120 $1.80 Primary & secondary 1.25 .80
590 A120 $2.30 Vocational 1.50 1.25
591 A120 $5 Tertiary 4.00 4.00
*Nos. 588-591 (4)* 7.15 6.30

**Queen and Waterfront Type of 1987**
**Type II**

**1991, Apr. 2 Litho. *Perf. 14½x14***

592 A98 $1.20 multicolored .45 .30
593 A98 $2.30 multicolored .90 .60

Transportation A121

**1991, June 6 Unwmk. *Perf. 14***

594 A121 80c Rickshaw .55 .30
595 A121 90c Bus .75 .60
596 A121 $1.70 Ferry 1.25 1.00
597 A121 $1.80 Tram 1.50 .80
598 A121 $2.30 Mass transit railway 2.25 2.00
599 A121 $5 Hydrofoil 4.25 3.75
*Nos. 594-599 (6)* 10.55 8.45

A122

Royal postboxes with contemporary envelopes: 80c, Stamp of Type A1, Queen Victoria. $1.70, Stamps of Type A10, King Edward VII. $1.80, #149, King George V. $2.30, Stamps of Type A16, King George VI. $5, $10, Stamp of Type A98, Queen Elizabeth II.

**1991, Aug. 25 Litho. *Perf. 14***

600 A122 80c multicolored .60 .30
601 A122 $1.70 multicolored 1.25 1.00
602 A122 $1.80 multicolored 1.75 .80
603 A122 $2.30 multicolored 1.50 1.25
604 A122 $5 multicolored 4.00 3.00
*Nos. 600-604 (5)* 9.10 6.35

**Souvenir Sheet**

605 A122 $10 multicolored 15.00 15.00

Hong Kong Post Office, 150th anniv.
See No. 792.

Historic Landmarks A123

**1991, Oct. 24**

606 A123 80c Bronze Buddha .65 .25
607 A123 $1.70 Peak Pavilion 1.10 .55
608 A123 $1.80 Clock Tower 1.25 .60
609 A123 $2.30 Catholic Cathedral 1.75 .75
610 A123 $5 Wong Tai Sin Temple 4.25 1.75
*Nos. 606-610 (5)* 9.00 3.90

**Map of Hong Kong Type**

**1992, Mar. 26 Photo. *Perf. 14½x14***
**Coil Stamps**
**Color of Map**

611 A101a 80c red lilac .50 .40
612 A101a 90c blue .75 .60
613 A101a $1.80 brt yel grn 1.40 1.00
614 A101a $2.30 red brown 1.60 1.40
*Nos. 611-614 (4)* 4.25 3.40

Inscribed 1991.

New Year 1992 (Year of the Monkey) A125

Various embroidery designs of monkeys.

**1992, Jan. 22 Litho. *Perf. 14½***

615 A125 80c multicolored .35 .25
616 A125 $1.80 multicolored .90 .50
617 A125 $2.30 multicolored 1.50 .75
*a.* Bklt. pane, 3 ea #615, 617 6.25
Complete booklet, 2 #617a 14.00
618 A125 $5 multicolored 3.50 3.00
*a.* Sheet of 4, #615-618 10.50 12.00
*Nos. 615-618 (4)* 6.25 4.50

See No. 838i.

**Queen Elizabeth II's Accession to the Throne, 40th Anniv.**
Common Design Type
**Unwmk.**

**1992, Feb. 11 Litho. *Perf. 14***

619 CD349 80c multicolored .35 .25
620 CD349 $1.70 multicolored .70 .35
621 CD349 $1.80 multicolored .75 .40
622 CD349 $2.30 multicolored 1.10 .55
623 CD349 $5 multicolored 2.75 1.10
*Nos. 619-623 (5)* 5.65 2.65

1992 Summer Olympics, Barcelona — A126

**1992, Apr. 2 Litho. *Perf. 14½***
**Black Inscription**

624 A126 80c Running .40 .25
625 A126 $1.80 Swimming and javelin 1.00 .80
626 A126 $2.30 Cycling 1.50 1.25
627 A126 $5 High jump 3.00 2.50
*Nos. 624-627 (4)* 5.90 4.80

**Souvenir Sheet**

628 Sheet of 4 7.50 7.50
*a.* A126 80c red inscription .25 .25
*b.* A126 $1.80 green inscription .60 .60
*c.* A126 $2.30 blue inscription 1.00 1.00
*d.* A126 $5 orange yellow inscription 1.75 1.75
*e.* Sheet of 4 with inscription in margin 5.75 5.75

Issue date: No. 628e, July 25. New inscription on No. 628e sheet margin reads "To Commemorate the Opening of the 1992 Summer Olympic Games 25 July 1992" in English and Chinese.

**Queen and Landmarks Type of 1987**
Souvenir Sheet
***Perf. 14***

**1992, May 22 Litho. Type II**

629 A99 $10 lt violet & black 6.00 4.75

World Columbian Stamp Expo '92.

A127

***Perf. 15x14***

**1992-97 Photo. Unwmk.**
**Color of Chinese Inscription**

630 A127 10c pink .30 .30
630A A127 20c black 1.00 1.00
631 A127 50c red orange .30 .25
632 A127 60c blue 1.50 .40
633 A127 70c red lilac 1.50 .55
634 A127 80c rose .30 .25
635 A127 90c gray green .30 .25
636 A127 $1 orange brown .35 .25
637 A127 $1.10 carmine 1.00 .45
638 A127 $1.20 violet .35 .25
639 A127 $1.30 dark blue 1.50 .65
640 A127 $1.40 apple green 1.00 .25
641 A127 $1.50 brown 1.00 .80
642 A127 $1.60 green 1.00 .45
643 A127 $1.70 ultramarine .80 .80
644 A127 $1.80 rose lilac 1.50 .55
645 A127 $1.90 green .80 .80
646 A127 $2 blue green 1.00 .50
647 A127 $2.10 claret 1.50 1.10
648 A127 $2.30 gray 1.50 .65
649 A127 $2.40 dark blue 2.50 1.25
650 A127 $2.50 olive green 1.00 .55
*a.* Sheet of 6, 2 #647, 4 #650 9.00
*d.* Booklet pane, 2 #647, 4 #650 7.50
651 A127 $2.60 dark brown 1.50 1.50
651A A127 $3.10 salmon 1.25 .65
*l.* Sheet of 6, 2 #642, 4 #651A 8.00
*o.* Booklet pane, 2 #642, 4 #651A 7.50
651B A127 $5 bright green 3.00 2.00
*k.* Souvenir sheet of 1 7.00 2.00
*m.* Sheet of 6, 4 #639, 2 #651B 12.50
*n.* Booklet pane, 4 #639, 2 #651B 18.00
*p.* Souvenir booklet, #650d, 651Ao, 651Bn 35.00

**Size: 25x30mm**
***Perf. 14½x14***

651C A127 $10 brown 4.00 2.50
*h.* Souvenir sheet of 1 6.00 2.50
651D A127 $20 orange red 6.00 4.00
651E A127 $50 gray 12.50 10.00
*Nos. 630-651E (28)* 50.25 32.95

Issued: 20c, $1.30, $1.90, $2.40, 11/1/93; No. 651Bk, 2/18/94; No. 651Ch, 8/16/94; $1.10, $1.50, $2.10, $2.60, 6/1/95; $1.40, $1.60, $2.50, $3.10, 9/2/96; No. 651Bp, 2/14/97; others, 6/16/92.

10c, 50c, 80c, 90c, $1, $1.20, $1.30, $1.50, $1.60, $1.80, $1.90, $2.10, 2.30, $2.40, $2.50, $2.60, $3.10 also issued in coils. These have numbers on the back of every fifth stamp.

No. 651Bk issued for Hong Kong '94; No. 651Ch for Conference of Commonwealth Postal Administrations.

Nos. 650a, 651Al, 651Bm are 130x85mm.

Nos. 650d, 651Ao, 651Bn are 180x130mm and are rouletted at left.

See Nos. 656, 677-678, 683, 688, 724, 729, 738, 743, 756-757.

**1993-96 Litho. *Perf. 15x14***

*636a* A127 $1 Litho. .75 .75
*b.* As "a," bklt. pane of 10 7.50
*638a* A127 $1.20 Litho. .75 .75
*b.* As "a," bklt. pane of 10 7.50
Complete booklet, #638b 7.50
*639a* A127 $1.30 Litho. .50 .50
*b.* As "a," booklet pane of 10 5.00
*645a* A127 $1.90 Litho. 1.00 1.00
*b.* As "a," bklt. pane of 10 10.00
*647a* A127 $2.10 Litho. 1.00 1.00
*b.* As "a," bklt. pane of 10 10.00
Complete booklet, #647b 10.00
*649a* A127 $2.40 Litho. 1.00 1.00
*b.* As "a," bklt. pane of 10 10.00
*650b* A127 $2.50 Litho. 1.00 1.00
*c.* As "b," booklet pane of 10 10.00
*651f* A127 $2.60 Litho. 1.00 1.00
*g.* As "f," bklt. pane of 10 10.00
Complete booklet, #651g 10.00
*651Ai* A127 $3.10 Litho. 1.00 1.00
*j.* As "i," booklet pane of 10 10.00
*Nos. 636a-651Ai (9)* 8.00 8.00

Chinese characters on Nos. 636a, 638a, 645a, 647a, 649a, 651f are lighter in shade and contrast less with the background color than characters on Nos. 636, 638, 645, 647, 649, 651.

Issued: No. 636a, 12/14/93; Nos. 645a, 649a, 12/28/93; Nos. 638a, 647a, 651f, 6/1/95; Nos. 639a, 650a, 651Ai, 9/2/96.

Stamp Collecting — A128

Stamps and: 80c, Perforation gauge, #559, 586a. $1.80, Canceler, #66, stamp tongs. $2.30, Magnifying glass, #174, 180, 181. $5, Watermark detector, Type A1.

**1992, July 15 Litho. *Perf. 14½***

**652** A128 80c multicolored .35 .25
**653** A128 $1.80 multicolored .75 .40
**654** A128 $2.30 multicolored 1.10 .90
**655** A128 $5 multicolored 2.25 1.75
*Nos. 652-655 (4)* 4.45 3.30

See note after No. 940.

**Queen Type of 1992**
Souvenir Sheet
***Perf. 14½x14***

**1992, Sept. 1 Photo. Unwmk.**
**Background Color**

**656** A127 $10 blue 6.50 6.50

Kuala Lumpur Philatelic Exhibition '92. Size of stamp: 25x30mm.

Chinese Opera — A129

**1992, Sept. 24 Litho. *Perf. 13½***

**657** A129 80c Principal male role 1.10 .30
**658** A129 $1.80 Martial role 1.90 1.40
**659** A129 $2.30 Principal female role 2.25 1.60
**660** A129 $5 Comic role 4.25 3.25
*Nos. 657-660 (4)* 9.50 6.55

Greetings Stamps — A130

**1992, Nov. 19 Litho. *Perf. 14½***

**661** A130 80c Hearts .35 .25
**662** A130 $1.80 Stars .70 .35
**663** A130 $2.30 Presents .80 .80
**664** A130 $5 Balloons 1.90 1.40
*a.* Bklt. pane of 6, #662-664, 3 #661 6.00 5.00
Complete booklet, 2 #664a 12.00
*Nos. 661-664 (4)* 3.75 2.80

New Year 1993 (Year of the Rooster) A131

Various embroidery designs of a rooster.

**1993, Jan. 7 Litho. *Perf. 13½***

**665** A131 80c multicolored .25 .25
**666** A131 $1.80 multicolored .65 .50
**667** A131 $2.30 multicolored 1.10 1.00
*a.* Bklt. pane, 3 ea #665, 667 4.75
Complete booklet, 2 #667a 9.50
**668** A131 $5 multicolored 2.75 2.75
*a.* Souvenir sheet of 4, #665-668 8.50 8.50
*Nos. 665-668 (4)* 4.75 4.50

See No. 838h.

Chinese String Instruments A132

**1993, Apr. 14 Litho. *Perf. 14½***

**669** A132 80c Pipa .40 .25
**670** A132 $1.80 Erhu .75 .70
**671** A132 $2.30 Ruan 1.10 1.00
**672** A132 $5 Gehu 2.25 2.00
*Nos. 669-672 (4)* 4.50 3.95

Coronation of Queen Elizabeth II, 40th Anniv. A133

Different views of Hong Kong with portraits of Queen that appear on Types A25, A28, A49 and A127.

**1993, June 3 Litho. *Perf. 14***

**673** A133 80c multicolored .40 .25
**674** A133 $1.80 multicolored .80 .75
**675** A133 $2.30 multicolored 1.25 1.10
**676** A133 $5 multicolored 3.00 2.50
*Nos. 673-676 (4)* 5.45 4.60

**Queen Type of 1992**
Souvenir Sheets

**1993, July 6 Litho. *Perf. 14½x14***
**Background Color**

**677** A127 $10 brown 7.00 7.00

**1993, Aug. 12 Background Color**

**678** A127 $10 bright blue 6.50 6.50

Hong Kong '94 Stamp Exhibition. Nos. 677-678 contain a 25x30mm stamp.

No. 678 exists with gold, silver or red overprints with the Hong Kong Philatelic Society emblem and Chinese characters. These sheets were sold only at various philatelic exhibitions.

Science and Technology — A134

Designs: 80c, Education, Hong Kong University of Science and Technology. $1.80, Public presentation, Hong Kong Science Museum. $2.30, Achievement regognition, Governor's Award. $5, World class telecommunications, telecommunications industry.

**1993, Sept. 8 *Perf. 14½***

**679** A134 80c multicolored .25 .25
**680** A134 $1.80 multicolored .60 .50
**681** A134 $2.30 multicolored .80 .70
**682** A134 $5 multicolored 1.90 1.40
*Nos. 679-682 (4)* 3.55 2.85

**Queen Type of 1992**
Souvenir Sheet

**1993, Oct. 5 Litho. *Perf. 14½x14***
**Background Color**

**683** A127 $10 bright green 4.00 4.50

Bangkok '93 Stamp Exhibition. No. 683 contains one 25x30mm stamp.

Goldfish A135

**1993, Nov. 17 Litho. *Perf. 14½***

**684** A135 $1 Red calico egg-fish .40 .35
**685** A135 $1.90 Red cap oranda .80 .50
**686** A135 $2.40 Red & white fringetail 1.25 1.10
**687** A135 $5 Black & gold dragon-eye 2.75 2.50
*a.* Souvenir sheet of 4, #684-687 10.00 10.00
*Nos. 684-687 (4)* 5.20 4.45

**Queen Type of 1992**
***Perf. 15x14***

**1994, Jan. 27 Photo. Wmk. 373**

**688** Souvenir booklet 20.00 20.00
*a.* A127 Sheet of #630, 5 #646 6.50 6.50
*b.* A127 Sheet of #643, 5 #644 6.50 6.50
*c.* A127 Sheet of 5 #636, #651B 6.50 6.50

First Hong Kong stamps, 130th anniv. No. 688 sold for $38.

Year of the Dog A136

Various embroidery designs of dogs.

**1994, Jan. 27 Litho. *Perf. 14½***

**689** A136 $1 multicolored .35 .25
**690** A136 $1.90 multicolored .75 .50
**691** A136 $2.40 multicolored 1.00 .80
*a.* Bklt. pane, 3 ea #689, 691 6.50
Complete booklet, 2 #691a 13.00
**692** A136 $5 multicolored 2.25 2.00
*a.* Souvenir sheet of 4, #689-692 12.00 12.00
*Nos. 689-692 (4)* 4.35 3.55

See No. 838f.

Royal Hong Kong Police Force, 150th Anniv. — A137

Designs: $1, Traffic policeman, woman. $1.20, Marine policeman. $1.90, Male, female officers of 1950. $2, Policeman holding M-16. $2.40, Policemen, 1906, pre-1920. $5, Policemen, 1900.

**1994, May 4 Litho. *Perf. 13½***

**693** A137 $1 multicolored .35 .30
**694** A137 $1.20 multicolored .45 .35
**695** A137 $1.90 multicolored .65 .55
**696** A137 $2 multicolored 1.00 .60
**697** A137 $2.40 multicolored 1.50 1.25
**698** A137 $5 multicolored 3.25 3.00
*Nos. 693-698 (6)* 7.20 6.05

Traditional Chinese Festivals — A138

Designs: $1, Dragon Boat Festival. $1.90, Lunar New Year. $2.40, Seven Sisters Festival. $5, Mid-Autumn Festival.

**1994, June 8 Litho. *Perf. 14***

**699** A138 $1 multicolored .35 .25
**700** A138 $1.90 multicolored .75 .75
**701** A138 $2.40 multicolored 1.25 1.25
**702** A138 $5 multicolored 2.25 2.25
*Nos. 699-702 (4)* 4.60 4.50

XV Commonwealth Games, Victoria, BC, Canada — A139

**Unwmk.**

**1994, Aug. 25 Litho. *Perf. 14***

**703** A139 $1 Swimming .25 .25
**704** A139 $1.90 Lawn bowling .90 .50
**705** A139 $2.40 Gymnastics 1.10 .60
**706** A139 $5 Weight lifting 2.00 1.25
*Nos. 703-706 (4)* 4.25 2.60

Dr. James Legge (1815-97), Religious Leader, Translator — A140

**1994, Oct. 5 Litho. *Perf. 14***

**707** A140 $1 multicolored 1.00 1.00

Corals — A141

**1994, Nov. 17 Litho. *Perf. 14***

**708** A141 $1 Alcyonium .30 .25
**709** A141 $1.90 Zoanthus .50 .45
**710** A141 $2.40 Tubastrea .65 .55
**711** A141 $5 Platygyra 1.50 1.10
*a.* Souv. sheet of 4, #708-711 6.50 6.50
*Nos. 708-711 (4)* 2.95 2.35

See No. 916.

New Year 1995 (Year of the Boar) A142

Various embroidery designs of pigs.

**1995, Jan. 17 Litho. *Perf. 14½***

**712** A142 $1 multicolored .40 .35
**713** A142 $1.90 multicolored .85 .65
**714** A142 $2.40 multicolored 1.10 .75
*a.* Bklt. pane, 3 each #712, 714 6.00
Complete booklet, 2 #714a 12.00
**715** A142 $5 multicolored 2.50 2.50
*a.* Souvenir sheet of 4, #712-715 7.50 7.50
*Nos. 712-715 (4)* 4.85 4.25

See No. 838d.

Intl. Sporting Events A143

Designs: $1, Hong Kong Rugby Sevens. $1.90, China Sea Race. $2.40, Intl. Dragon Boat Races. $5, Hong Kong Intl. Horse Races.

**1995, Mar. 22 Litho. *Perf. 14½***

**716** A143 $1 multicolored .50 .25
**717** A143 $1.90 multicolored .80 .80
**718** A143 $2.40 multicolored 1.25 1.25
**719** A143 $5 multicolored 2.50 2.50
*Nos. 716-719 (4)* 5.05 4.80

Traditional Buildings — A144

**Litho. & Engr.**

**1995, May 24 *Perf. 13½***

**720** A144 $1 Tsui Shing Lau .40 .25
**721** A144 $1.90 Sam Tung UK .75 .45
**722** A144 $2.40 Lo Wai .85 .50
**723** A144 $5 Man Shek Tong 2.00 1.10
*Nos. 720-723 (4)* 4.00 2.30

**Queen Type of 1992**
Souvenir Sheet

**1995, Aug. 25 Litho. *Perf. 14***
**Background Color**

**724** A127 $10 carmine 6.00 2.50

Singapore '95 World Stamp Exhibition. No. 724 contains one 25x30mm stamp.

Royal Hong Kong Regiment (1854-1995) — A145

$1.20, Modern Regimental Badge, vert. $2.10, Current flag. $2,60, Former flag. $5, Royal Hong Kong Defense Force, 1951 soldier's badge, vert.

**1995, Aug. 16 Litho. *Perf. 14½***

**725** A145 $1.20 multicolored .30 .30
**726** A145 $2.10 multicolored .50 .50
**727** A145 $2.60 multicolored .80 .80
**728** A145 $5 multicolored 2.00 2.00
*Nos. 725-728 (4)* 3.60 3.60

**Queen Type of 1992**
Souvenir Sheet

**1995, Oct. 9 Litho. *Perf. 14***
**Background Color**

**729** A127 $10 brown 6.75 6.75

End of World War II, 50th anniv. No. 729 contains one 25x30mm stamp.

Hong Kong Movie Stars A146

**1995, Nov. 15 Litho. *Perf. 13½***

**730** A146 $1.20 Bruce Lee 2.00 1.00
**731** A146 $2.10 Leung Sing-Por 3.00 1.50
**732** A146 $2.60 Yam Kim-Fai 4.00 2.50
**733** A146 $5 Lin Dai 6.00 6.00
*Nos. 730-733 (4)* 15.00 11.00

New Year 1996 (Year of the Rat) A147

Various embroidery designs of rats.

**1996, Jan. 31 Litho. *Perf. 13½***

**734** A147 $1.20 multicolored .30 .30
**735** A147 $2.10 multicolored .55 .55
**736** A147 $2.60 multicolored .70 .70
*a.* Bklt. pane, 3 ea #734, 736 3.75
Complete booklet, 2 #736a 7.50
**737** A147 $5 multicolored 1.25 1.25
*a.* Souvenir sheet of 4, #734-737 5.00 5.00
*Nos. 734-737 (4)* 2.80 2.80

See No. 838a.

**Queen Type of 1992**
Souvenir Sheet
**Unwmk.**

**1996, Feb. 23 Litho. *Perf. 14***

**738** A127 $10 org & grn 7.00 7.00

Hong Kong '97 Stamp Exhibition. No. 738 contains one 25x30mm stamp.

1996 Summer Olympics, Atlanta — A148

**1996, Mar. 20 Litho. *Perf. 13½***

**739** A148 $1.20 Gymnastics .30 .30
**740** A148 $2.10 Diving .70 .70
**741** A148 $2.60 Running .90 .90
**742** A148 $5 Basketball 1.60 1.60
*Nos. 739-742 (4)* 3.50 3.50

**Souvenir Sheet**

**742A** Sheet of 4, #742b-742e 4.00 4.00
*f.* As #742A, different sheet margin 4.75 4.75

No. 742Af shows Olympic gold medal at top of sheet margin.

Nos. 748-751 have denominations in color and Olympic rings in gold. Nos. 739-742 have denominations in black, Olympic rings in different colors. No. 742Ab-742Ae have gold Olympic rings.

No. 742f issued 7/19/96.

**Queen Type of 1992**
Souvenir Sheet
**Unwmk.**

**1996, May 18 Litho. *Perf. 14***

**743** A127 $10 brt grn & bl vio 4.00 4.00

Hong Kong '97 Stamp Exhibition. No. 743 contains one 25x30mm stamp.

Archaeological Finds — A149

**1996, June 26 Litho. *Perf. 13½***

**744** A149 $1.20 Painted pottery basin .30 .30
**745** A149 $2.10 Stone "Yue" .55 .55
**746** A149 $2.60 Stone "GE" .80 .80
**747** A149 $5 Pottery tripod 1.50 1.50
*Nos. 744-747 (4)* 3.15 3.15

**1996 Summer Olympic Games Type**

**1996, July 19 Litho. *Perf. 14x14½***
**Color of Denomination**

**748** A148 $1.20 like #739, red .30 .25
**749** A148 $2.10 like #740, blue .40 .40
**750** A148 $2.60 like #741, green .75 .75
**751** A148 $5 like #742, org 1.50 1.50
*Nos. 748-751 (4)* 2.95 2.90

Nos. 748-751 have denominations in color and Olympic rings in gold. Nos. 739-742 have denonminations in black, Olympic rings in different colors.

Mountains in Hong Kong — A150

**Unwmk.**

**1996, Sept. 24 Litho. *13½x14***

**752** A150 $1.30 Pat Sing Leng .50 .45

***Perf. 14x14½, 14½x14***

**753** A150 $2.50 Ma On Shan 1.00 1.00
**754** A150 $3.10 Lion Rock, vert. 1.25 1.25

***Perf. 14x13½***

**755** A150 $5 Lantau Peak, vert. 1.90 1.90
*Nos. 752-755 (4)* 4.65 4.60

No. 753 is 40x36mm, No. 754 36x40mm.
See Nos. 899, 905.

**Queen Type of 1992**
Souvenir Sheets

**1996 Photo. Unwmk. *Perf. 14***

**756** A127 $10 red & grn 3.50 3.50
**757** A127 $10 brn & dk brn 4.00 4.00

Issued: No. 756, 10/16; No. 757, 10/29.

Visit Hong Kong '97 Stamp Exhibition (No. 756). 1996 Summer Olympic Games, Atlanta (No. 757). Nos. 756-757 each contain one 25x30mm stamp.

Urban Heritage A151

Designs: $1.30, Main building, University of Hong Kong, 1912. $2.50, Western Market, 1906. $3.10, Old Pathological Institute, 1905. $5, Flagstaff House, 1846.

**Litho. & Engr.**

**1996, Nov. 20 *Perf. 13½***

**758** A151 $1.30 multicolored .45 .45
**759** A151 $2.50 multicolored .75 .75
**760** A151 $3.10 multicolored .90 .90
**761** A151 $5 multicolored 1.50 1.50
*Nos. 758-761 (4)* 3.60 3.60

**Hong Kong People Type of 1989**
Souvenir Sheet
***Perf. 13x13½***

**1997, Jan. Photo. Unwmk.**

**762** A111 $5 like No. 549 1.50 1.50

No. 762 contains one 23x33mm stamp that has darker colors and a different perf. than No. 549.

Panoramic Views of Hong Kong Skyline — A152

Nos. 763-775: Various daytime views from harbor.

Nos. 776-778, Various nighttime views from harbor.

***Perf. 13½x13***

**1997, Jan. 26 Litho. Unwmk.**
**Background Color**

**763** A152 10c pink .25 .25
**764** A152 20c vermilion .25 .25
**765** A152 50c orange .25 .25
**766** A152 $1 orange yellow .25 .25
**767** A152 $1.20 olive .30 .30
**768** A152 $1.30 apple green .35 .35
*a.* Booklet pane of 10 3.50
Complete booklet, #768a 3.50
**769** A152 $1.40 green .35 .35
**770** A152 $1.60 blue green .40 .40
**771** A152 $2 green blue .55 .55
**772** A152 $2.10 blue .55 .55
**773** A152 $2.50 purple .65 .65
*a.* Booklet pane of 10 6.50
Complete booklet, #773a 6.50
**774** A152 $3.10 rose .80 .80
*a.* Booklet pane of 10 8.00
Complete booklet, #774a 8.00
*c.* Sheet of 4, #771-774 2.50 2.50
**775** A152 $5 orange 1.25 1.25
*a.* Sheet of 13, #763-775 5.75 5.75

**Size: 28x33mm**
***Perf. 14x13½***

**776** A152 $10 blue 2.50 2.50
*a.* Souv. sheet of 1 (Series #4) *8.00*
*b.* Souv. sheet of 1 (Series #5) *8.00*
*c.* Souv. Sheet of 1 (Sheet #12) 3.00 3.00
*d.* Souv. sheet of 1, perf14x13¼ (Sheet #14) 2.60 2.60
**777** A152 $20 bl, pur & rose 5.25 5.25
**778** A152 $50 purple & rose 13.00 13.00
*a.* Sheet of 3, #776-778 *21.00*
*Nos. 763-778 (16)* 26.95 26.95

Hong Kong '97 (Nos. 776a-776b). 1996 Atlanta Paralympic Games (No. 776c). 13th Asian Games, Bangkok, Thailand (No. 774c). China 1999 World Philatelic Exhibition (No. 776d).

Perforations are alternating small and large holes.

Nos. 775a and 778a are continuous designs.

Issued: No. 776a, 2/12; No. 776b, 2/16; No. 774c, 3/27/99; No. 776d, 8/21/99.

See note after No. 940.

**Coil Stamps**

**Photo. *Perf. 14½x14***

*763a* A152 10c .25 .25
*765a* A152 50c .25 .25
*768b* A152 $1.30 .45 .45
*770a* A152 $1.60 .50 .50
*773b* A152 $2.50 .80 .80
*774b* A152 $3.10 1.00 1.00
*Nos. 763a-774b (6)* 3.25 3.25

These have numbers on back of every fifth stamp.

Perforations are the same size.

New Year 1997 (Year of the Ox) A153

Various designs of oxen.

***Perf. 14½***

**1997, Feb. 27 Litho. Unwmk.**
**Background Color**

**780** A153 $1.30 pink .30 .30
**781** A153 $2.50 orange yellow .65 .65
**782** A153 $3.10 green .80 .80
*a.* Booklet pane, 3 each #780a, 782b 6.00
Complete booklet, 2 #782a 12.00
**783** A153 $5 blue 1.25 1.25
*a.* Souvenir sheet of 4, #780-783 4.50 4.50
*Nos. 780-783 (4)* 3.00 3.00

See Nos. 838b, 838c.

***Perf. 13½***

*780a* A153 $1.30 .50 .50
*781a* A153 $2.50 .90 .90
*782b* A153 $3.10 1.10 1.10
*783b* A153 $5 1.75 1.75
*c.* Souvenir sheet of 4, #780a-781a, 782b-783b 4.50 4.50

Migratory Birds — A154

$1.30, Yellow-breasted bunting. $2.50, Great knot. $3.10, Falcated teal. $5, Black-faced spoonbill.

***Perf. 13½***

**1997, Apr. 27 Unwmk. Photo.**

**784** A154 $1.30 multicolored .30 .30
**785** A154 $2.50 multicolored .65 .65
**786** A154 $3.10 multicolored .80 .80
**787** A154 $5 multicolored 1.25 1.25
*Nos. 784-787 (4)* 3.00 3.00

Landmarks — A155

$1.30, Hong Kong Stadium. $2.50, The Peak Tower. $3.10, Hong Kong Convention & Exhibition Center. $5, The Lantau Link (bridge).

**1997, May 18 *Perf. 13½***

**788** A155 $1.30 multicolored .30 .30
**789** A155 $2.50 multicolored .75 .75
**790** A155 $3.10 multicolored 1.00 1.00
**791** A155 $5 multicolored 1.75 1.75
*a.* Souvenir sheet of 1 2.25 2.25
*Nos. 788-791 (4)* 3.80 3.80

Opening of the Lantau Link (bridge) (No. 791a).

Nos. 788-791 and 791a also exist perf 14x14½. Values are the same.

**Royal Postbox Type of 1991**
Souvenir Sheet

**1997, June 30 Litho. *Perf. 11½***

**792** A122 $5 like No. 604 1.50 1.50

No. 792 contains one 19x29mm stamp.

**Special Administrative Region of People's Republic of China**

First Issue Under Chinese Administration A156

Sights and symbols of Hong Kong: $1.30, Chinese architecture. $1.60, Modern buildings, methods of transportation. $2.50, Skyscrapers, Hong Kong Convention & Exhibition Center. $2.60, Cargo ship entering port. $3.10, Chinese junks, dolphins jumping in water. $5, Hibiscus flower.

**1997, July 1 Litho. *Perf. 12x12½***

| | | | | |
|---|---|---|---|---|
| **793** | A156 $1.30 multicolored | .35 | .35 |
| **794** | A156 $1.60 multicolored | .40 | .40 |
| **795** | A156 $2.50 multicolored | .65 | .65 |
| **796** | A156 $2.60 multicolored | .70 | .70 |
| **797** | A156 $3.10 multicolored | .80 | .80 |
| **798** | A156 $5 multicolored | 1.25 | 1.25 |
| *a.* | Souvenir sheet of 1 | 1.25 | 1.25 |
| | *Nos. 793-798 (6)* | 4.15 | 4.15 |

1997 World Bank Group/Intl. Monetary Fund Annual Meetings — A157

Designs: $1.30, Finance, banking. $2.50, Investment, stock exchange. $3.10, Trade, telecommunications. $5, Infrastructure, transport.

***Perf. 14½***

**1997, Sept. 21 Litho. Unwmk.**

| | | | |
|---|---|---|---|
| **799** | A157 $1.30 multicolored | .30 | .30 |
| **800** | A157 $2.50 multicolored | .65 | .65 |
| **801** | A157 $3.10 multicolored | .80 | .80 |
| **802** | A157 $5 multicolored | 1.25 | 1.25 |
| | *Nos. 799-802 (4)* | 3.00 | 3.00 |

Shells — A158

**1997, Nov. 9 Photo. *Perf. 13½***

| | | | |
|---|---|---|---|
| **803** | A158 $1.30 Clam | .35 | .35 |
| **804** | A158 $2.50 Cowrie | .65 | .65 |
| **805** | A158 $3.10 Cone | .80 | .80 |
| **806** | A158 $5 Murex | 1.25 | 1.25 |
| | *Nos. 803-806 (4)* | 3.05 | 3.05 |

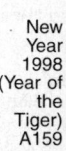

New Year 1998 (Year of the Tiger) A159

Various embroidery designs of tigers.

**1998, Jan. 4 Litho. *Perf. 13½***

| | | | |
|---|---|---|---|
| **807** | A159 $1.30 multicolored | .35 | .35 |
| **808** | A159 $2.50 multicolored | .75 | .75 |
| **809** | A159 $3.10 multicolored | .95 | .95 |
| *a.* | Bklt. pane, 6 ea #807, 809 | 9.00 | |
| | Complete booklet, #809a | 8.00 | |
| **810** | A159 $5 multicolored | 1.50 | 1.50 |
| *a.* | Souvenir sheet, #807-810 | 4.00 | 4.00 |
| | *Nos. 807-810 (4)* | 3.55 | 3.55 |

See No. 838.

Star Ferry, Cent. A160

Star Ferry during: $1.30, 1900's. $2.50, 1910's-1920's. $3.10, 1920's-1950's. $5, Mid-1950's on.

**1998, Apr. 26 Photo. *Perf. 13½***

| | | | |
|---|---|---|---|
| **811** | A160 $1.30 multicolored | .40 | .40 |
| **812** | A160 $2.50 multicolored | .85 | .85 |
| **813** | A160 $3.10 multicolored | 1.05 | 1.05 |
| **814** | A160 $5 multicolored | 1.60 | 1.60 |
| | *Nos. 811-814 (4)* | 3.90 | 3.90 |

Nos. 811-814 also exist perf 14½ from a booklet of one each sold only at "Australia '99" International Stamp Exhibition for $25.

Souvenir Sheet

The Closing of Kai Tak Airport — A161

**1998, July 5 Photo. *Perf. 13½***

| | | | |
|---|---|---|---|
| **815** | A161 $5 multicolored | 2.25 | 2.25 |

New Hong Kong Airport A162

$1.30, Passengers on terminal's moving sidewalks. $1.60, Couple entering Automated People Mover. $2.50, Airport Railway, Tsing Ma Bridge. $2.60, Terminal building, Airmail Center. $3.10, Aircraft gates. $5, Terminal departure level.

**1998, July 5 *Perf. 14***

| | | | |
|---|---|---|---|
| **816** | A162 $1.30 multicolored | .35 | .35 |
| **817** | A162 $1.60 multicolored | .40 | .40 |
| **818** | A162 $2.50 multicolored | .65 | .65 |
| **819** | A162 $2.60 multicolored | .70 | .70 |
| **820** | A162 $3.10 multicolored | .80 | .80 |
| **821** | A162 $5 multicolored | 1.25 | 1.25 |
| *a.* | Souvenir sheet of 1 | 1.50 | 1.50 |
| *b.* | Block of 6, #816-821 | 4.75 | 4.75 |

See note after No. 940.

A163

A164

Scouting in Hong Kong: Rope tied in various knots, different scouting divisions: $1.30, Grasshopper Scouts, Cub Scouts. $2.50, Tower, tents, Boy Scouts, Girl Scouts. $3.10, Helicopter, sailboats, Venture Scouts. $5, City buildings, Rover Scouts, adult leaders.

**Unwmk.**

**1998, July 26 Litho. *Perf. 14***

| | | | |
|---|---|---|---|
| **822** | A163 $1.30 multicolored | .40 | .40 |
| **823** | A163 $2.50 multicolored | .70 | .70 |
| **824** | A163 $3.10 multicolored | 1.00 | 1.00 |
| **825** | A163 $5 multicolored | 1.50 | 1.50 |
| | *Nos. 822-825 (4)* | 3.60 | 3.60 |

**1998, Sept. 20 Litho. *Perf. 13½***

Hong Kong designs.

| | | | |
|---|---|---|---|
| **826** | A164 $1.30 Graphic | .40 | .40 |
| **827** | A164 $2.50 Product | .75 | .75 |
| **828** | A164 $3.10 Interior | .95 | .95 |
| **829** | A164 $5 Fashion | 1.40 | 1.40 |
| | *Nos. 826-829 (4)* | 3.50 | 3.50 |

Kites — A165

**1998, Nov. 15 Litho. *Perf. 13½***

| | | | |
|---|---|---|---|
| **830** | A165 $1.30 Dragonfly | .40 | .40 |
| **831** | A165 $2.50 Dragon | .85 | .85 |
| **832** | A165 $3.10 Butterfly | 1.10 | 1.10 |
| **833** | A165 $5 Goldfish | 1.60 | 1.60 |
| *a.* | Souvenir sheet, #830-833 | 4.00 | 4.00 |
| | *Nos. 830-833 (4)* | 3.95 | 3.95 |

A166

New Year 1999 (Year of the Rabbit): White rabbit with flower designs in various positions.

**1999, Jan. 31 Photo. *Perf. 14x13½***

| | | | |
|---|---|---|---|
| **834** | A166 $1.30 yel org & multi | .40 | .40 |
| | Scratched panel | | .40 |
| *a.* | Sheet of 10 | 4.00 | |
| **835** | A166 $2.50 green & multi | .75 | .75 |
| | Scratched panel | | .40 |
| *a.* | Sheet of 10 | 7.50 | |
| **836** | A166 $3.10 orange & multi | .90 | .90 |
| | Scratched panel | | .40 |
| *a.* | Sheet of 10 | 9.25 | |
| **837** | A166 $5 red lilac & multi | 1.45 | 1.45 |
| | Scratched panel | | .40 |
| *a.* | Sheet of 10 | 14.50 | |
| | *Nos. 834-837 (4)* | 3.50 | 3.50 |

Nos. 834-837 are printed with a layering of gold "scratch off" ink, which, when removed, reveals a Chinese greeting.

**New Year Types of 1987-98**

Designs: a, Like #734. b, Like #780. c, Like #783. d, Like #712. e Like 515. f, LIke #691. g, Like #534. h, Like #668. i, Like #615. j, Like #584. k, Like #560. #a.-k. have 4 Chinese characters at UL instead of crown and ER.

**1999, Feb. 21 Litho. *Perf. 13½***

**Sheet of 12**

| | | | |
|---|---|---|---|
| **838** | $1.30 #a.-k., #807 + label | 7.50 | 7.50 |

Design in label and sheet selvage is engraved.

Intl. Year of Older Persons — A167

***Perf. 14½***

**1999, Mar. 14 Litho. Unwmk.**

| | | | |
|---|---|---|---|
| **839** | A167 $1.30 Calligraphy | .40 | .40 |
| **840** | A167 $2.50 Bird raising | .75 | .75 |
| **841** | A167 $3.10 Playing Go | .90 | .90 |
| **842** | A167 $5 Voluntary services | 1.45 | 1.45 |
| | *Nos. 839-842 (4)* | 3.50 | 3.50 |

Souvenir Sheet

Giant Pandas in Hong Kong — A168

**1999, Apr. 25 Litho. *Perf. 14¼***

| | | | |
|---|---|---|---|
| **843** | A168 $10 multicolored | 3.50 | 3.50 |

No. 843 contains one circular stamp 38mm in diameter.

Public Transport — A169

**1999, May 23**

| | | | |
|---|---|---|---|
| **844** | A169 $1.30 Bus | .45 | .45 |
| **845** | A169 $2.40 Minibus | .90 | .90 |
| **846** | A169 $2.50 Tram | .95 | .95 |
| **847** | A169 $2.60 Taxi | 1.00 | 1.00 |
| **848** | A169 $3.10 Airport express | 1.15 | 1.15 |
| | *Nos. 844-848 (5)* | 4.45 | 4.45 |

Hong Kong and Singapore Tourism — A170

Designs: $1.20, Hong Kong Harbor. $1.30, Singapore Skyline. $2.50, Giant Buddha, Hong Kong. $2.60, Merlion, Sentosa Island, Singapore. $3.10, Hong Kong street scene. $5, Bugis Junction, Singapore.

***Perf. 13¼***

**1999, July 1 Litho. Unwmk.**

| | | | |
|---|---|---|---|
| **849** | A170 $1.20 multicolored | .35 | .35 |
| **850** | A170 $1.30 multicolored | .40 | .40 |
| **851** | A170 $2.50 multicolored | .70 | .70 |
| **852** | A170 $2.60 multicolored | .70 | .70 |
| **853** | A170 $3.10 multicolored | .85 | .85 |
| **854** | A170 $5 multicolored | 1.50 | 1.50 |
| *a.* | Souvenir sheet, #849-854 | 4.50 | 4.50 |
| | *Nos. 849-854 (6)* | 4.50 | 4.50 |

See Singapore Nos. 896-902.

People's Republic of China, 50th Anniv. — A171

Designs: $1.30, Flags of People's Republic and Hong Kong Special Administrative District. $2.50 Bauhinia blakeana flower, Hong Kong skyline. $3.10, Dragon dance. $5, Fireworks.

***Perf. 14¼ Syncopated***

**1999, Oct. 1 Photo.**

**Granite Paper**

| | | | |
|---|---|---|---|
| **855** | A171 $1.30 multicolored | .50 | .50 |
| **856** | A171 $2.50 multicolored | 1.00 | 1.00 |
| **857** | A171 $3.10 multicolored | 1.10 | 1.10 |
| **858** | A171 $5 multicolored | 1.90 | 1.90 |
| *a.* | Block or strip of 4, #855-858 | 4.50 | 4.50 |

Issued in sheets of 4 blocks or strips and individually in sheets of 20.

Landmarks — A172

10c, Museum of Tea Ware. 20c, St. John's Cathedral. 50c, Legislative Council building. $1, Tai Fu Tai. $1.20, Wong Tai Sin Temple. $1.30, Victoria Harbor. $1.40, Hong Kong Railway Museum. $1.60, Tsim Sha Tsui Clock Tower. $2, Happy Valley Racecourse. $2.10, Kowloon-Canton Railway. $2.50, Chi Lin Nunnery. $3.10, Buddha at Po Lin Monastery. $5, Aw Boon Haw Gardens. $10, Tsing Ma Bridge. $20, Hong Kong Convention & Exhibition Center. $50, Hong Kong Intl. Airport.

***Perf. 13x13¾ Syncopated***

**1999, Oct. 18** **Photo.**

**Granite Paper**

**859** A172 10c blue & multi .25 .25
*a.* Booklet pane of 1 .20
**860** A172 20c blue & multi .25 .25
*a.* Booklet pane of 1 .20
**861** A172 50c blue & multi .25 .25
*a.* Booklet pane of 1 .25
**862** A172 $1 blue & multi .25 .25
*a.* Booklet pane of 1 .50
**863** A172 $1.20 blue & multi .30 .30
*a.* Booklet pane of 1 .60
**864** A172 $1.30 blue & multi .35 .35
*a.* Booklet pane of 1 .70
**865** A172 $1.40 blue & multi .35 .35
*a.* Booklet pane of 1 .70
*b.* Booklet pane of 10 3.50 —
Booklet, #865b 3.50
**866** A172 $1.60 blue & multi .40 .40
*a.* Booklet pane of 1 .80
**867** A172 $2 blue & multi .50 .50
*a.* Booklet pane of 1 1.00
**868** A172 $2.10 blue & multi .55 .55
*a.* Booklet pane of 1 1.10
**869** A172 $2.50 blue & multi .60 .60
*a.* Booklet pane of 1 1.25
**870** A172 $3.10 blue & multi .75 .75
*a.* Booklet pane of 1 1.50
**871** A172 $5 blue & multi 1.25 1.25
*a.* Booklet pane of 1 2.50
Souv. booklet, #859a-871a 12.00
*b.* Sheet of 13, #859-871 5.50 5.50
*c.* Souvenir sheet of 1 (Definitive #4) 1.25 1.25
*d.* Souv. sheet of 1 (Definitive #6) 1.25 1.25

**Size: 26x32mm**

***Perf. 13¼***

**872** A172 $10 blue & multi 2.50 2.50
*a.* Souv. sheet of 1 (Definitive #1) 2.50 2.50
*b.* Souv. sheet of 1 (Exhibition #1) 3.50 3.50
*c.* Souv. sheet of 1 (Exhibition #2) 2.50 2.50
*d.* Souv. sheet of 1 (Definitive #2) 2.50 2.50
*e.* Souv. sheet of 1 (Definitive #5) 2.50 2.50
**873** A172 $20 blue & multi 5.00 5.00
**874** A172 $50 blue & multi 12.50 12.50
*a.* Sheet of 3, #872-874 20.00 20.00
*Nos. 859-874 (16)* 26.05 26.05

**Coil Stamps**

***Perf. 15x13½ Syncopated***

**Size: 18x22mm**

**874B** A172 10c blue & multi .25 .25
**874C** A172 50c blue & multi .25 .25
**874D** A172 $1.30 blue & multi .35 .35
**874E** A172 $1.60 blue & multi .40 .40
**874F** A172 $2.50 blue & multi .60 .60
**874G** A172 $3.10 blue & multi .75 .75
*Nos. 874B-874G (6)* 2.60 2.60

Nos. 872a-872b are Syncopated perf 14x14¼. No. 872c is Syncopated perf 13¼x13. No. 872d is Syncopated perf 14x14½. No. 872e is Syncopated perf. 13¼x13.

Issued: No. 872a, 1/31/00; No. 872b, 2/10/00; No. 872c, 4/15/00; No. 872d, 12/2/00; No. 871c, 4/21/01; No. 872e, 8/1/01; Nos. 874B-874E, 874G, 10/18/99; No. 874F, 10/18/99; No. 871d, 1/19/02. No. 865b, 4/1/02.

See note after No. 940.

See also Nos. 917, 965-973, 991-993, 1083

Chinese White Dolphin — A173

Various views of dolphin.

**1999, Nov. 14** **Litho.** ***Perf. 14½***

**Granite Paper**

**875** A173 $1.30 green & multi .60 .60
**876** A173 $2.50 bl grn & multi 1.00 1.00
**877** A173 $3.10 blue & multi 1.25 1.25
**878** A173 $5 pur & multi 1.75 1.75

**Souvenir Sheet**

**879** Sheet of 4, #a.-d. 5.00 5.00

Nos. 875-878 have Worldwide Fund for Nature (WWF) emblem; Nos. 879a-879d do not.

See No. 900.

Souvenir Sheet

Millennium — A174

No. 880: a, Dragon boat races, skyline. b, Bridge, birds.

***Perf. 14¼ Syncopated***

**1999, Dec. 31** **Photo.**

**Granite Paper**

**880** A174 $5 Sheet of 2, #a.-b. 4.00 4.00

New Millennium Children's Stamp Design Contest Winners — A175

Designs: $1.30, Scales. $2.50, Children planting tree on planet. $3.10, Planets. $5, Inhabited planets, space shuttle, rocket.

**2000, Jan. 1** **Granite Paper**

**881** A175 $1.30 multi .40 .30
**882** A175 $2.50 multi .75 .75
**883** A175 $3.10 multi .85 .85
**884** A175 $5 multi 1.50 1.50
*Nos. 881-884 (4)* 3.50 3.40

Victoria Harbor A176

**Litho. & Embossed with Foil Application**

**2000, Jan. 1** ***Perf. 13¼***

**885** A176 $50 gold & multi 24.00 24.00

New Year 2000 (Year of the Dragon) — A177

Various dragons.

***Perf. 14¼ Syncopated***

**2000, Jan. 23** **Litho.**

**Granite Paper**

**886** A177 $1.30 multi .40 .40
**887** A177 $2.50 multi .75 .75
**888** A177 $3.10 multi .85 .85
**889** A177 $5 multi 1.45 1.45
*a.* Souvenir sheet of 1, imperf. 15.00 15.00
*b.* Souvenir sheet, #886-889 4.00 4.00
*Nos. 886-889 (4)* 3.45 3.45

See Nos. 1030a, 1431a, 1479a, 1480a.

Museums and Libraries — A178

Designs: $1.30, Heritage Museum. $2.50, Central Library. $3.10, Museum of Coastal Defense. $5 Museum of History.

***Perf. 14½x14¼***

**2000, Mar. 26** **Photo.**

**Granite Paper**

**890** A178 $1.30 multi .70 .35
**891** A178 $2.50 multi 1.25 .95
**892** A178 $3.10 multi 1.50 1.00
**893** A178 $5 multi 2.25 2.25
*a.* Block, #890-893 6.00 6.00
*Nos. 890-893 (4)* 5.70 4.55

Nos. 890-893 issued in sheets of 24. No. 893a issued only in sheet containing 4 blocks.

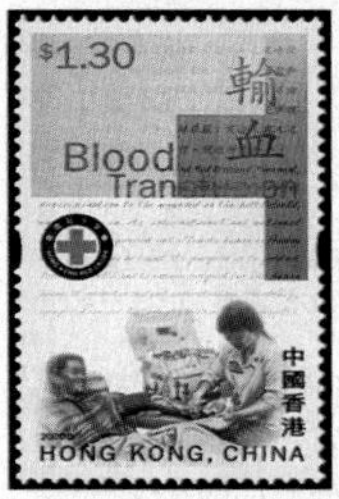


Red Cross — A179

Designs: $1.30, Blood transfusion. $2.50, Special education. $3.10, Disaster relief. $5, Voluntary service.

***Perf. 14¼ Syncopated***

**2000, May 7** **Photo.**

**Granite Paper**

**894** A179 $1.30 multi .45 .35
**895** A179 $2.50 multi .85 .85
**896** A179 $3.10 multi .95 .95
**897** A179 $5 multi 1.75 1.75
*a.* Souvenir sheet, #894-897 4.00 4.00
*Nos. 894-897 (4)* 4.00 3.90

**Flower Type of 1989, Mountain Type of 1996 Inscribed "Hong Kong, China," and Dolphin Type of 1999**

***Perf. 14¼ Syncopated***

**2000, June 17** **Photo.**

**Granite Paper**

**898** A90 $5 Booklet pane of 1, like #455 4.00 4.00
**899** A150 $5 Booklet pane of 1, like #755 4.00 4.00
**900** A173 $5 Booklet pane of 1, like #879d 4.00 4.00
Booklet, #898-900 12.00

Hong Kong 2001 Stamp Exhibition. Booklet sold for $35.

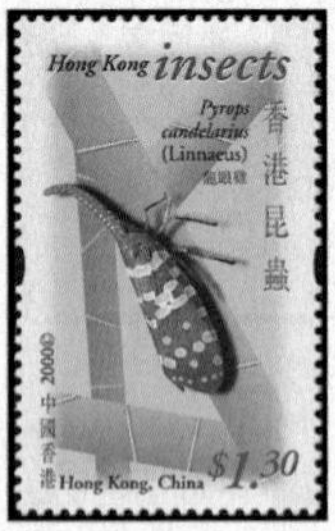


Insects — A180

Designs: $1.30, Pyrops candelarius. $2.50, Macromidia ellenae. $3.10, Troides helena spilotia. $5, Chiridopsis bowringi.

***Perf. 13½x13¼ Syncopated***

**2000, July 16** **Litho.**

**Granite Paper**

**901-904** A180 Set of 4 4.00 3.50
*904a* Souvenir sheet, #901-904 4.00 4.00

**Mountain Type of 1996 Inscribed "Hong Kong, China"**

Souvenir Sheet

***Perf. 13¼ Syncopated***

**2000, Aug. 12** **Photo.**

**Granite Paper**

**905** A150 $10 Like #754 4.00 3.50

Hong Kong 2001 Stamp Exhibition.

2000 Summer Olympics, Sydney — A181

Designs: $1.30, Cycling, badminton. $2.50, Table tennis, running. $3.10, Judo, rowing. $5, Swimming, sailboarding.

***Perf. 14¼ Syncopated***

**2000, Aug. 27** **Litho.**

**Granite Paper**

**906-909** A181 Set of 4 4.25 3.50

Birds A182

**2000, Sept. 30** **Photo.**

**Granite Paper**

**910** Booklet pane of 2 3.25
*a.* A182 $1.30 Yellow-breasted bunting 1.15 1.15
*b.* A182 $2.50 Great knot 2.10 2.10
**911** Booklet pane of 2 4.75
*a.* A182 $3.10 Falcated teal 1.75 1.75
*b.* A182 $5 Black-faced spoonbill 3.00 3.00
Booklet, #910-911 7.00

Booklet containing Nos. 910-911 sold for $25.

Chinese General Chamber of Commerce, Cent. — A183

Designs: $1.30, Hong Kong in 1900. $2.50, Headquarters buildings. $3.10, People reading notice for distribution of relief funds. $5, Hand with computer mouse, currency symbols.

***Perf. 13¾ Syncopated***

**2000, Oct. 22** **Litho.**

**Granite Paper**

**912-915** A183 Set of 4 4.25 3.50

**Coral Type of 1994 Inscribed "Hong Kong, China"**

Souvenir Sheet

***Perf. 13¼ Syncopated***

**2000, Nov. 25** **Photo.**

**Granite Paper**

**916** A141 $10 Like #709 4.00 3.00

**Landmarks Type of 1999**

Souvenir Sheet

**Litho. & Holography**

**2000, Dec. 31**

**917** A172 $20 Like #873 6.50 6.50

Soaking in water may affect hologram.

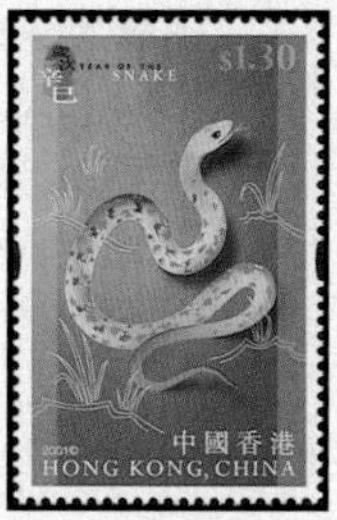

New Year 2001 (Year of the Snake) — A184

Various snakes. Denominations: $1.30, $2.50, $3.10, $5.

*Perf. 14½ Sync.*

**2001, Jan. 1** **Photo.**

| | | | | |
|---|---|---|---|---|
| **918-921** | A184 | Set of 4 | 3.50 | 3.00 |
| *921a* | | Souvenir sheet of 1, imperf. | 1.75 | 1.75 |
| *921b* | | Souvenir sheet, #918-921 | 4.00 | 4.00 |

See Nos. 1030b, 1431b, 1479b, 1480b.

Souvenir Sheet

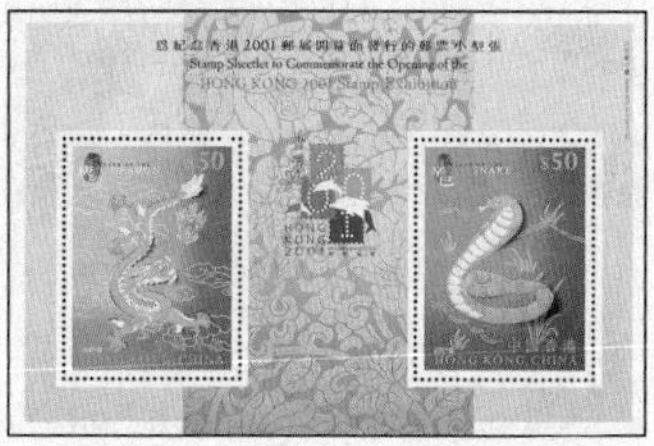

Opening of Hong Kong 2001 Stamp Exhibition — A185

No. 922: a, Year of the Dragon. b, Year of the Snake.

**Litho. & Embossed with Foil Application**

**2001, Feb. 1** ***Perf. 13¼***

**922** A185 $50 Sheet of 2, #a-b 45.00 45.00

**Indiginous Trees Type of 1988 Inscribed "Hong Kong, China"**

**2001 Photo. *Perf. 14¼ Syncopated***

**Granite Paper**

| | | | | |
|---|---|---|---|---|
| **923** | A105 | $5 multi, sheetlet #5 | 2.00 | 2.00 |
| ***a.*** | | Sheetlet #6 | 2.00 | 2.00 |
| ***b.*** | | Sheetlet #7 | 2.00 | 2.00 |
| ***c.*** | | Sheetlet #8 | 2.00 | 2.00 |

Issued: No. 923, 2/2; No. 923a, 2/3; No. 923b, 2/4; No. 923c, 2/5. No. 923b with gold overprint in margin reading "To commemorate the FIAP Day of HONG KONG 2001 Stamp Exhibition on 4th February, 2001" is a private emission.

See note after No. 940 for unsyncopated stamp.

Greetings — A186

Designs: $1.30, Maple leaves. $1.60, Swans. $2.50, Chicks. $2.60, Cherry blossoms. $3.10, Bamboo. $5, Snow-covered plant.

**2001, Feb. 1** **Photo.**

**Granite Paper**

**Stamps + Labels**

**924-929** A186 Set of 6 5.00 4.00

See note after Nos. 934-937.

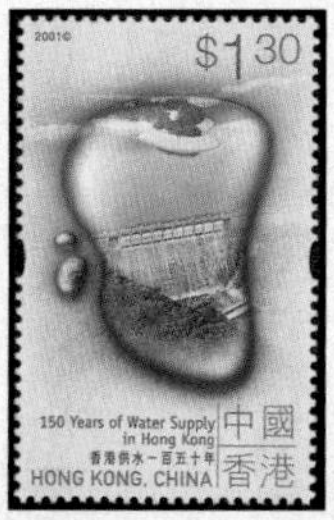

Hong Kong Water Supply, 150th Anniv. — A187

Designs: $1.30, Tai Tam Tuk Reservoir. $2.50, Plover Cove Reservoir. $3.10, Pipelines. $5, Beakers, chemical symbols.

**2001, Mar. 18** **Litho. & Embossed**

**Granite Paper**

| | | | | |
|---|---|---|---|---|
| **930-933** | A187 | Set of 4 | 5.50 | 4.50 |
| *933a* | | Block of 4, #930-933 | 5.50 | 5.50 |

Movie Stars A188

Designs: $1.30, Ng Cho-fan (1911-93) and Pak Yin (1920-87). $2.50, Sun Ma Si-tsang (1916-97) and Tang Bik-wan (1926-91). $3.10, Cheung Wood-yau (1910-85) and Wong Manlei (1913-98). $5, Mak Bing-wing (1915-84) and Fung Wong-nui (1925-92).

**2001, Apr. 8** **Litho.**

**Granite Paper**

| | | | | |
|---|---|---|---|---|
| **934-937** | A188 | Set of 4 | 4.00 | 3.00 |
| *937a* | | Block of 4, #934-937 | 4.00 | 4.00 |

Values are for stamps with surrounding selvage.

On June 12, 2001 Hong Kong sold for $120 limited numbers of a sheet containing 18 examples of the $1.30 stamp, No. 924. The 18 labels to the right of the stamps on this sheet differ from those found on examples of No. 924 sold on the stamp's original date of issue, and the 18 labels to the left of the stamps depict Chinese celebrities.

Dragon Boat Races A189

Dragon boats and: No. 938, $5, Sydney Opera House. No. 939, Hong Kong Convention and Exhibition Center.

**2001, June 25 Litho. *Perf. 14x14½***

**Granite Paper**

| | | | | |
|---|---|---|---|---|
| **938-939** | A189 | Set of 2 | 3.50 | 2.50 |
| *939a* | | Souvenir sheet, #938-939 | 3.50 | 3.50 |

See Australia Nos. 1977-1978.

Emblem of 2008 Summer Olympics, Beijing — A190

**2001, July 14 Photo. *Perf. 13x13¼***

**940** A190 $1.30 multi + label 1.00 1.00

No. 940 printed in sheets of 12 stamp + label pairs with one large central label. See People's Republic of China No. 3119, Macao No. 1067. No. 940 with different label is from People's Republic of China No. 3119a.

On July 21, 2001 Hong Kong sold a booklet containing stamps with a face value of $12.40 for $30. The stamps are the Indigenous Trees type of 1988 with the inscription "Hong Kong, China." The first pane in the booklet contained $1.30 and $2.50 stamps, and those on the second pane contained $3.10 and $5 stamps.

On Aug. 25, 2001 Hong Kong sold a booklet containing stamps with a face value of $30 for $65. The first pane in the booklet contained four stamps with a face value of $1.80 of the Stamp Collecting type of 1992 with the inscription "Hong Kong, China." The second pane contained two $3.10 perf. 13½x13 stamps on granite paper of type A152, and two $3.10 perf. 13¾ syncopated stamps on granite paper of type A172. The third pane contained four $2.60 perf. 14¼ stamps on granite paper of type A162.

Tea Culture — A191

Various tea services and background colors of: $1.30, Lilac. $2.50, Orange brown. $3.10, Bright orange. $5, Green.

***Perf. 14¼x14½ Syncopated***

**2001, Sept. 9** **Litho.**

**944-947** A191 Set of 4 4.00 3.50

Herbs — A192

Designs: $1.30, Centella asiatica. $2.50, Lobelia chinensis. $3.10, Gardenia jasminoides. $5, Scutellaria indica.

***Perf. 14½ Syncopated***

**2001, Oct. 7** **Litho.**

**Granite Paper**

**948-951** A192 Set of 4 4.00 3.50

Children's Stamp Coloring Contest — A193

Designs: $1.30, Bear. $2.50, Penguin. $3.10, Flower. $5, Bee.

***Die Cut Perf. 13¾x13¼ Sync.***

**2001, Nov. 18**

**Granite Paper**

**Self-Adhesive**

| | | | | |
|---|---|---|---|---|
| **952-955** | A193 | Set of 4 | 4.00 | 3.00 |
| *955a* | | Souvenir sheet, #952-955 | 4.00 | 4.00 |

New Year 2002 (Year of the Horse) — A194

Various horses. Denominations: $1.30, $2.50, $3.10, $5.

**2002, Jan. 13 *Perf. 14½ Syncopated***

**Granite Paper**

| | | | | |
|---|---|---|---|---|
| **956-959** | A194 | Set of 4 | 4.00 | 3.50 |
| *959a* | | Souvenir sheet of 1, imperf. | 2.25 | 2.25 |
| *959b* | | Souvenir sheet, #956-959 | 4.50 | 4.50 |

See Nos. 1030c, 1431c, 1479c, 1480c.

Souvenir Sheet

New Year 2002 (Year of the Horse) — A195

No. 960: a, Snake. b, Horse.

**Litho. & Embossed with Foil Application**

**2002, Feb. 9** ***Perf. 13¼***

**960** A195 $50 Sheet of 2, #a-b 45.00 45.00

Works of Art — A196

Details from: $1.30, Lines in Motion, by Chui Tze-hung. $2.50, Volume and Time, by Hon Chi-fun. $3.10, Bright Sun, by Aries Lee. $5, Midsummer, by Irene Chou.

***Perf. 14½ Syncopated***

**2002, Feb. 24** **Litho.**

**Granite Paper**

**961-964** A196 Set of 4 4.00 3.00

**Landmarks Type of 1999**

Designs: $1.40, Hong Kong Railway Museum. $1.80, Hong Kong Stadium. $1.90, Western Market. $2.40, Kwun Yam statue, Repulse Bay. $3, Peak Tower. $13, Hong Kong Cultural Center.

***Perf. 13x13¾ Syncopated***

**2002, Apr. 1** **Photo.**

**Granite Paper**

| | | | | |
|---|---|---|---|---|
| **965** | A172 | $1.80 blue & multi | .45 | .45 |
| **966** | A172 | $1.90 blue & multi | .50 | .50 |
| **967** | A172 | $2.40 blue & multi | .60 | .60 |
| ***a.*** | | Booklet pane of 10 | 6.00 | — |
| | | Complete booklet, #967a | 6.00 | |
| **968** | A172 | $3 blue & multi | .75 | .75 |
| ***a.*** | | Booklet pane of 10 | 7.50 | — |
| | | Complete booklet, #968a | 7.50 | |

**Size: 26x32mm**

***Perf. 13¼ Syncopated***

| | | | | |
|---|---|---|---|---|
| **969** | A172 | $13 blue & multi | 3.50 | 3.50 |
| | | *Nos. 965-969 (5)* | 5.80 | 5.80 |

**Coil Stamps**

**Size: 18x22mm**

***Perf. 14¾x13¼ Syncopated***

| | | | | |
|---|---|---|---|---|
| **970** | A172 | $1.40 blue & multi | .35 | .35 |
| **971** | A172 | $1.80 blue & multi | .45 | .45 |
| **972** | A172 | $2.40 blue & multi | .60 | .60 |
| **973** | A172 | $3 blue & multi | .75 | .75 |
| | | *Nos. 970-973 (4)* | 2.15 | 2.15 |

Cyberindustry in Hong Kong — A197

Designs: $1.40, Innovation. $2.40, Connectivity. $3, Trend. $5, Strength.

***Perf. 13¾ Syncopated***

**2002, Apr. 14 Litho.**

**Granite Paper**

**974-977** A197 Set of 4 4.00 3.50
*977a* Block of 4, #974-977 4.00 4.00

A booklet of two panes, one containing one each of Nos. 974 and 976, and another containing one each of Nos. 975 and 977, sold for $30. Value, $11.

2002 World Cup Soccer Championships, Japan and Korea — A198

No. 978: a, Goalie. b, Crowd and players.

***Perf. 12 Syncopated***

**2002, May 16 Photo.**

**978** Horiz. pair, with central label 1.50 1.50
***a.-b.*** A198 $1.40 Either single .75 .75

No. 978 was printed in sheets of 5 pairs and five different labels.

A souvenir sheet containing Nos. 978a-978b, People's Republic of China No. 3198, and Macao Nos. 1091a-1091b exists.

Corals A199

Designs: $1.40, North Atlantic pink tree, Pacific orange cup, and North Pacific horn corals. $2.40, North Atlantic giant orange tree, and Black corals. $3, Dendronepthea gigantea and Dendronepthea corals. $5, Tubastrea and Echinogorgia corals.

***Perf. 13¾x14 Syncopated***

**2002, May 19 Litho.**

**Granite Paper**

**979-982** A199 Set of 4 4.50 4.00
*982a* Souvenir sheet, #979-982 4.50 4.50

On May 10, 2003, Hong Kong sold a booklet with a face value of $11.80 for $25. The first pane contains Nos. 979-980 perf 13¼x13. The second pane contains Nos. 981-982, perf 13¼x13.

See Canada Nos. 1948-1951.

Beijing — Kowloon Through Trains A200

Train and: $1.40, Hong Kong commercial buildings. $2.40, Wuhan-Changjiang Bridge, Wuchang. $3, Shaolin Monastery Pagodas, Zhengzhou. $5, Temple of Heaven, Beijing.

**2002, June 9** ***Perf. 14¼ Syncopated***

**Granite Paper**

**983-986** A200 Set of 4 4.00 3.50
*986a* Horiz. strip of 4, #983-986 4.00 4.00

Hong Kong Special Administrative Region, 5th Anniv. — A201

Designs: $1.40, White dolphins, corals. $2.40, Students, bauhinia flowers. $3, Flying cranes, Hong Kong International Airport. $5, Flags of Hong Kong and People's Republic of China, fireworks over skyline.

**2002, July 1 Granite Paper**

**987-990** A201 Set of 4 4.00 3.50
*990a* Souvenir sheet, #987-990 4.00 4.00

**Landmarks Type of 1999 with Pink Denomination and Country Name**

Souvenir Sheet

Design: Tsing Ma Bridge.

***Perf. 13¼ Syncopated***

**2002, July 27 Photo.**

**Granite Paper**

**991** A172 $10 pink & multi 4.00 3.50

Philakorea 2002.

**Landmarks Type of 1999 With Olive Green Denomination and Country Name**

Souvenir Sheet

Design: Tsing Ma Bridge.

***Perf. 13¼ Syncopated***

**2002, Aug. 24 Photo.**

**Granite Paper**

**992** A172 $10 ol green & multi 4.00 3.50

Amphilex 2002 Intl. Stamp Exhibition, Amsterdam.

**Landmarks Type of 1999 With Buff Background**

Souvenir Sheet

Design: Tsing Ma Bridge.

**2002, Sept. 7**

**993** A172 $10 blue, buff & multi 4.00 3.50

Rocks A202

Designs: $1.40, Ping Chau (siltstone). $2.40, Port Island (conglomerate). $3, Po Pin Chau (tuff). $5, Lamma Island (granite).

***Perf. 13¼x12¾***

**2002, Sept. 15 Litho.**

**994-997** A202 Set of 4 4.50 4.00
*997a* Souvenir sheet, #994-997 4.50 4.50

Portions of the designs were applied by a thermographic process, producing a shiny, raised effect.

Eastern and Western Cultures A203

Designs: 10c, Radar screen, luopan. 20c, Calculator, abacus. 50c, Incense coil, stained glass window. $1, Chair, Chinese bed. $1.40, Dim sum, loaves of bread. $1.80, Silverware, chopsticks and spoon. $1.90, Canned drinks, tea caddies. $2, Western and Eastern wedding cakes. $2.40, Erhu, violin. $2.50, Letter boxes, internet. $3, Sailboats, dragon boat. $5, Tiled roof, glass wall. $10, Ballet, Chinese opera. $13, Chess, Xiangqi. $20, Christmas decorations, lanterns. $50, Eastern and Western sculptures.

***Perf. 13¼x13 Syncopated***

**2002, Oct. 14 Photo.**

**Granite Paper**

**998** A203 10c multi .25 .25
**999** A203 20c multi .25 .25
**1000** A203 50c multi .25 .25
**1001** A203 $1 multi .25 .25
**1002** A203 $1.40 multi .35 .25
***a.*** Booklet pane of 10 3.50
Complete booklet, #1002a 3.50
**1003** A203 $1.80 multi .45 .25
***a.*** Booklet pane of 10 ('03) 4.75 —
Complete booklet, #1003a 4.75
**1004** A203 $1.90 multi .50 .25
**1005** A203 $2 multi .50 .25
**1006** A203 $2.40 multi .60 .25
***a.*** Booklet pane of 10 6.00
Complete booklet, #1006a 6.00
**1007** A203 $2.50 multi .65 .30
**1008** A203 $3 multi .75 .35
***a.*** Booklet pane of 10 7.50
Complete booklet, #1008a 7.50
**1009** A203 $5 multi 1.25 .40
***a.*** Souvenir sheet, #998-1009 5.75 5.75
***b.*** Booklet pane, #998-1009 5.75
Complete booklet, #1009b 5.75

**Size: 40x24mm**

***Perf. 14¾ Syncopated***

**1010** A203 $10 multi 2.75 .25
**1011** A203 $13 multi 3.50 .75
**1012** A203 $20 multi 6.00 1.00
**1013** A203 $50 multi 15.00 4.00
***a.*** Souvenir sheet #1010-1013 27.50 27.50
*Nos. 998-1013 (16)* 33.30 9.30

**Coil Stamps**

**Size: 22x19mm**

***Perf. 13¼x14¾ Syncopated***

**1014** A203 $1.40 multi .35 .35
**1015** A203 $1.80 multi .45 .45
**1016** A203 $2.40 multi .60 .60
**1017** A203 $3 multi .75 .75
*Nos. 1014-1017 (4)* 2.15 2.15

No. 1003a issued 10/7/04.

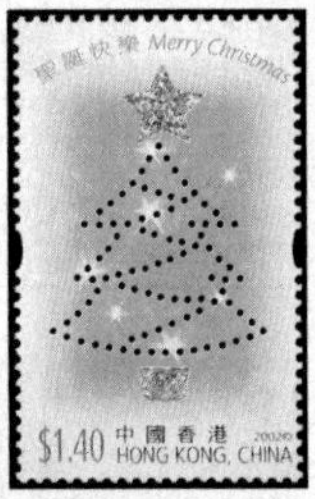


Christmas — A204

Designs: $1.40, Christmas tree. $2.40, Ornament. $3, Snowman. $5, Bell.

**Photo. with Hologram Applied**

***Perf. 13½ Syncopated***

**2002, Nov. 24 Granite Paper**

**1018-1021** A204 Set of 4 4.00 3.50
*1021a* Block or strip of 4, #1018-1021 4.00 4.00

Perforations within the stamp outline the designs.

Hong Kong Disneyland A205

Designs: $1.40, Main Street. $2.40, Fantasyland. $3, Adventureland. $5, Tomorrowland.

***Perf. 13¾ Syncopated***

**2003, Jan. 12 Litho. & Embossed**

**Granite Paper**

**1022-1025** A205 Set of 4 4.00 3.50
*1025a* Souvenir sheet, #1022-1025 4.00 4.00

New Year 2003 (Year of the Ram) — A206

Various rams: $1.40, $2.40, $3, $5.

***Perf. 14¼ Syncopated***

**2003, Jan. 19 Litho.**

**Granite Paper**

**1026-1029** A206 Set of 4 4.00 3.50
*1029a* Souvenir sheet of 1, imperf. 2.25 2.25
*1029b* Souvenir sheet, #1026-1029 4.00 4.00

See Nos. 1030d, 1431d, 1479d, 1480d.

**New Year Types of 2000-03**

**2003, Jan. 19 Litho.** ***Perf. 12¾x13¼***

**Flocked Paper**

**1030** Block of 4 12.00 12.00
***a.*** A177 $10 Like #888 3.00 3.00
***b.*** A184 $10 Like #920 3.00 3.00
***c.*** A194 $10 Like #957 3.00 3.00
***d.*** A206 $10 Like #1029 3.00 3.00

Souvenir Sheet

New Year 2003 (Year of the Ram) — A207

No. 1031: a, Horse. b, Ram.

**Litho. & Embossed with Foil Application**

**2003, Jan. 19** ***Perf. 13¼***

**1031** A207 $50 Sheet of 2, #a-b 36.50 36.50

Traditional Trades and Handicrafts — A208

Designs: $1.40, Letter writing. $1.80, Bird cage making, vert. $2.40, Qipao tailoring. $2.50, Hairdressing, vert. $3, Dough figurine making, vert. $5, Olive selling.

***Perf. 13½x14 Syncopated, 13½ Syncopated (vert. stamps)***

**2003, Mar. 13 Litho.**

**Granite Paper**

**1032-1037** A208 Set of 6 5.25 4.25
*1037a* Souvenir sheet, #1032-1037 5.25 5.25

Souvenir Sheet

Hong Kong 2004 Stamp Expo — A209

**2003, Apr. 8** ***Perf. 13¼ Syncopated***

**Granite Paper**

**1038** A209 $10 multi 4.00 3.50

Souvenir Sheet

Master-of-Nets Garden, Suzhou — A210

**2003, June 27** **Granite Paper**

**1039** A210 $10 multi 4.00 3.50

See No. 1456f.

Miniature Landscapes — A211

Plants: $1.40, Fukien tea. $2.40, Hedge sageretia. $3, Fire-thorn, vert. $5, Chinese hackberry, vert.

***Perf. 13¾x12¾ Syncopated, 12¾x13¾ Syncopated***

**2003, July 17** **Photo.**

**Granite Paper**

**1040-1043** A211 Set of 4 4.00 3.50

Aquarium Fish A212

Various fish: $1.40, $2.40, $3, $5.

**2003, Aug. 7** ***Perf. 14¼ Syncopated***

**Granite Paper**

**With Fish-Shaped Holes in Paper**

**1044-1047** A212 Set of 4 4.00 3.50
*a.* Block of 4, #1044-1047 4.00 4.00

A213

Heartwarming A214

***Perf. 13¾ Syncopated***

**2003, Sept. 10** **Litho.**

**Inscribed "Local Mail Postage"**

**Granite Paper**

**1048** A213 ($1.40) multi .40 .35
**1049** A214 ($1.40) multi .40 .35
*a.* Sheet of 16 + 17 labels ('04) 13.00 13.00

**Inscribed "Air Mail Postage"**

**1050** A213 ($3) multi 1.10 .80
**1051** A214 ($3) multi 1.10 .80
*a.* Sheet, 4 each #1048-1051, + 17 labels 12.00 12.00
*Nos. 1048-1051 (4)* 3.00 2.30

No. 1049a issued 10/7/04. No. 1049a sold for $50 and has a 2004 Olympic Games theme on the labels. A similar sheet issued in 2005 with labels having a Lions Club Convention theme, sold for $108 in conjunction with other items, and was not available separately.

Birds A215

Designs: $1.40, Pied avocet. $2.40, Horned grebe. $3, Black-throated diver. $5, Great crested grebe.

***Perf. 12½ Syncopated***

**2003, Oct. 4** **Litho. & Engr.**

**Granite Paper**

**1052-1055** A215 Set of 4 4.00 3.50
*1055a* Booklet pane, #1052-1055 4.00 —
Complete booklet, 2 #1055a 8.00

See Sweden No. 2469.

Souvenir Sheet

Hong Kong 2004 Stamp Expo — A216

***Perf. 13¼ Syncopated***

**2003, Oct. 14** **Litho.**

**Granite Paper**

**1056** A216 $10 multi 4.00 3.00
*1056a* Sheet, 2 each #1038, 1056, + 2 labels 28.00 28.00

No. 1056a was issued 1/30/04 and sold for $80. Labels could be personalized.

Percussion Instruments — A217

Designs: $1.40, Drum. $2.40, Clappers. $3, Cymbals. $5, Gongs. $13, Chimes.

***Perf. 13½x13¼ Syncopated***

**2003, Nov. 6** **Photo.**

**1057-1060** A217 Set of 4 3.50 3.00

**Souvenir Sheet**

***Perf. 13¾x13¼ Syncopated***

**1061** A217 $13 multi 4.00 3.50

No. 1061 contains one 35x45mm stamp.

Launch of First Manned Chinese Spacecraft — A218

No. 1062: a, Astronaut, Shenzhou spacecraft. b, Rocket lift-off.

**2003, Oct. 16** **Photo.** ***Perf. 13x13¼***

**1062** A218 $1.40 Pair, #a-b 1.75 1.25

A booklet containing No. 1062, People's Republic of China No. 3314 and Macao No. 1128a exists. The booklet sold for a premium over face value.

UNESCO World Heritage Sites in People's Republic of China — A219

Designs: $1.40, Potala Palace, vert. (27x75mm). $1.80, Imperial Palace of the Ming and Qing Dynasties. $2.40, Mausoleum of the First Qin Emperor. $2.50, Mount Huangshan, vert. $3, Old Town of Lijiang, vert. $5, Jiuzhaigou Valley (75x27mm).

***Perf. 13¼ Syncopated***

**2003, Nov. 25** **Litho.**

**Granite Paper**

**1063** A219 $1.40 multi .45 .40
*a.* Perf. 13¼x13¼x13¼x13 Syncopated .45 .40

***Perf. 13x13¼ Syncopated***

**1064** A219 $1.80 multi .55 .50
*a.* Perf. 13x13¼x12½x13¼ Syncopated .55 .50
**1065** A219 $2.40 multi .65 .60
*a.* Perf. 12½x13¼ Syncopated .65 .60

***Perf. 13 Syncopated***

**1066** A219 $2.50 multi .75 .65
*a.* Perf. 13x13x13x13¼ Syncopated .75 .65
*b.* Perf. 13¼x13x13x13 Syncopated .75 .65
*c.* Perf. 13¼x13x13x13¼ Syncopated .75 .65
**1067** A219 $3 multi .90 .80
*a.* Perf. 12½x13x13x13 Syncopated .90 .80

***Perf. 13x12¾ Syncopated***

**1068** A219 $5 multi 1.40 1.25
*a.* Perf. 13x12¾x13 and 13¼x13 Syncopated 1.40 1.25
*b.* Perf. 13 Syncopated 1.40 1.25
*c.* Miniature sheet (see note below) 14.00 14.00
*Nos. 1063-1068 (6)* 4.70 4.20

No. 1068c contains one each of Nos. 1063a, 1064, 1065, 1066a, 1066b, 1066c, 1067a, 1068b and two each of Nos. 1063, 1064a, 1065a, 1067 and 1068a. Perfs for the minor varieties are for the measurement that comprises the longest part of each side, as the sides of some stamps have sections with varying perf measurements. Approximately one half of the bottom row of perfs on No. 1068a is perf. 13 while the other half is perf. 13¼.

Development of Public Housing — A220

Various buildings.

***Perf. 13¼x13 Syncopated***

**2003, Dec. 11** **Photo.**

**Granite Paper**

**1069** A220 $1.40 org & multi .50 .40
*a.* Tete-beche pair 1.00 .80
**1070** A220 $2.40 yel & multi .75 .60
*a.* Tete-beche pair 1.50 1.20
**1071** A220 $3 pur & multi 1.25 .80
*a.* Tete-beche pair 2.50 1.60
**1072** A220 $5 red & multi 2.00 1.25
*a.* Tete-beche pair 4.00 2.50
*Nos. 1069-1072 (4)* 4.50 3.05

New Year 2004 (Year of the Monkey) — A221

Various monkeys: $1.40, $2.40, $3, $5.

***Perf. 13½x13¼ Syncopated***

**2004, Jan. 4** **Litho.**

**Granite Paper**

**1073-1076** A221 Set of 4 3.00 3.00
*1076a* Souvenir sheet of 1, imperf. 1.50 1.50
*1076b* Souvneir sheet, #1073-1076 3.00 3.00

See Nos. 1253a, 1431e, 1479e, 1480e.

Souvenir Sheet

New Year 2004 (Year of the Monkey) — A222

No. 1077: a, Ram. b, Monkey.

**Litho. & Embossed with Foil Application**

**2004, Jan. 4** ***Perf. 13¼***

**1077** A222 $50 Sheet of 2, #a-b 35.00 35.00

Souvenir Sheets

New Year Puddings and Greeting — A223

New Year Puddings With Two Greetings — A224

New Year Parade — A225

Jade — A226

Fire Dragon Dance — A227

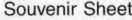

No. 1079: a, Same Chinese text as on No. 1078 when viewed from directly above (top character with long curved line at bottom). b, Text different from that on No. 1078 when viewed from directly above.

**2004 Litho.** ***Perf. 13¼ Syncopated***
**Granite Paper**

**1078** A223 $10 multi 3.00 3.00
**1079** A224 $10 Sheet of 2, #a-b 5.75 5.75
**1080** A225 $10 multi 3.00 3.00
**1081** A226 $10 multi 3.00 3.00
**1082** A227 $10 multi 3.00 3.00
*Nos. 1078-1082 (5)* 17.75 17.75

2004 Hong Kong Stamp Expo. Issued: Nos. 1078-1079, 1/30; No. 1080, 1/31; No. 1081, 2/1; No. 1082, 2/2.

Nos. 1079a and 1079b show the same two Chinese texts, but the texts appear different depending on the angle at which one views the stamps. Under magnification it can be seen that the two Chinese texts are printed differently to achieve this effect.

### Landmarks Type of 1999 With Red Violet Denomination and Country Name

No. 1083: a, Museum of Tea Ware. b, St. John's Cathedral. c, Legislative Council Building. d, Tai Fu Tai. e, Wong Tai Sin Temple. f, Victoria Harbor. g, Hong Kong Railway Museum. h, Tsim Sha Tsui Clock Tower. i, Hong Kong Stadium. j, Western Market. k, Happy Valley Racecourse. l, Kowloon-Canton Railway. m, Repulse Bay. n, Chi Lin Nunnery. o, Peak Tower. p, Buddha at Po Lin Monastery. q, Aw Boon Haw Gardens. r, Tsing Ma Bridge. s, Hong Kong Cultural Center. t, Hong Kong Convention and Exhibition Center. u, Hong Kong Intl. Airport.

***Perf. 13x13¾ Syncopated***
**2004, Feb. 3 Photo.**
**Granite Paper**

**1083** Sheet of 21 7.75 7.75
*a.-u.* A172 $1.40 Any single, red vio & multi (23x27mm) .35 .35

2004 Hong Kong Stamp Expo.

Rugby Sevens A228

Designs: $1.40, Hong Kong Sevens. $2.40, New Zealand Sevens. $3, Hong Kong Stadium. $5, Westpac Stadium, Wellington, New Zealand.

***Perf. 13¼x14¼ Syncopated***
**2004, Feb. 25 Litho.**
**Granite Paper**

**1084-1087** A228 Set of 4 4.00 4.00
*1087a* Block of 4, #1084-1087 4.00 4.00

Children's Games and Activities — A229

Designs: $1.40, Scissors, Paper, Stone. $2.40, Chinese chess. $3, Blowing bubbles. $5, Hopscotch.

**2004, Apr. 7 Granite Paper**

**1088-1091** A229 Set of 4 3.50 3.00
*1091a* Block of 4, #1088-1091 3.50 3.50

**Souvenir Sheet**

Chen Clan Academy — A230

***Perf. 13½x13¼ Syncopated***
**2004, May 6**

**1092** A230 $10 multi 3.00 2.50

See No. 1456g.

Trams in Hong Kong, Cent. — A231

Various trams and tickets: $1.40, Green ticket. $2.40, Brown ticket. $3, Blue ticket. No. 1096, $5, Yellow ticket.

No. 1097, Olive ticket.

**2004, May 27 Granite Paper**

**1093-1096** A231 Set of 4 3.00 2.50
*1096a* Souvenir sheet, #1093-1096 3.00 3.00

**Souvenir Sheet**

**1097** A231 $5 multi 1.25 1.25

People's Liberation Army Forces of Hong Kong — A232

Inscriptions: $1.40, The Powerful and Civilized Military Force. $1.80, Social Services. $2.40, Open Day. $2.50, Army. $3, Navy. $5, Air Force.

***Perf. 13¼x14 Syncopated***
**2004, June 30 Litho.**
**Granite Paper**

**1098** A232 $1.40 multi .35 .35
*a.* Booklet pane of 4 2.00 —
**1099** A232 $1.80 multi .50 .50
*a.* Booklet pane of 4 2.50 —
**1100** A232 $2.40 multi .60 .60
*a.* Booklet pane of 4 3.25 —
**1101** A232 $2.50 multi .65 .65
*a.* Booklet pane of 4 3.50 —
**1102** A232 $3 multi .80 .80
*a.* Booklet pane of 4 4.25 —
**1103** A232 $5 multi 1.25 1.25
*a.* Booklet pane of 4 6.50 —
Complete booklet, #1098a-1103a 22.00
*Nos. 1098-1103 (6)* 4.15 4.15

Complete booklet sold for $85.

Relay Race — A233

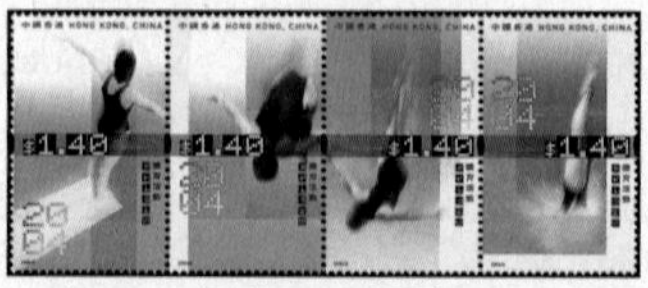
Diving — A234

Volleyball — A235

Cycling — A236

Badminton — A237

No. 1104: a, Runners in blocks. b, Runners. c, Runner taking baton. d, Runner at finish.

No. 1105: a, Diver on board. b, Diver with legs tucked in. c, Diver with arms and legs extended. d, Diver entering water.

No. 1106: a, Player making save. b, Player leaping to get ball. c, Player striking ball above net. d, Player trying to block ball.

No. 1107: a, Cyclists, denomination at left. b, Cyclist at right, denomination at left. c, Cyclists, denomination at right. d, Cyclist with arms extended.

No. 1108: a, Bird above head, racquet at shoulder level. b, Bird at shoulder level, racquet at knee level. c, Bird and racquet above head. d, Player with face covered by arm.

***Perf. 13½x13¼ Syncopated***
**2004, July 20 Granite Paper**

**1104** A233 $1.40 Horiz. strip of 4, #a-d 1.50 1.50
**1105** A234 $1.40 Horiz. strip of 4, #a-d 1.50 1.50
**1106** A235 $1.40 Horiz. strip of 4, #a-d 1.50 1.50
**1107** A236 $1.40 Horiz. strip of 4, #a-d 1.50 1.50
**1108** A237 $1.40 Horiz. strip of 4, #a-d 1.50 1.50
*e.* Miniature sheet, #1104-1108 7.50 7.50

**Souvenir Sheet**

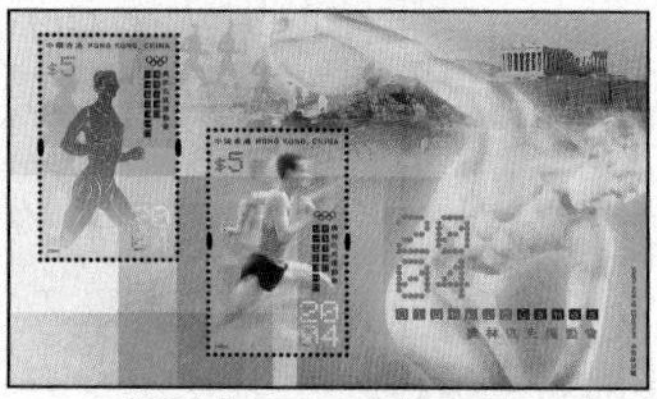
2004 Summer Olympics, Athens — A238

No. 1109: a, Runner without clothes. b, Runner with clothes.

**2004, Aug. 13 Granite Paper**

**1109** A238 $5 Sheet of 2, #a-b 3.00 3.00

Deng Xiaoping (1904-97), Chinese Leader — A239

No. 1110: a, Saluting flags. b, Watching fireworks.

$10, Three photographs.

**2004, Aug. 22** ***Perf. 13x13¼***

**1110** A239 $1.40 Horiz. pair, #a-b .75 .75

**Souvenir Sheet**

**1111** A239 $10 multi 3.50 3.50

Hong Kong Currency — A240

Obverse and reverse of: $1.40, 1863 one mil bronze coin. $2.40, 1866 twenty cent silver coin. $3, 1935 one dollar banknotes. No. 1115, $5, 1997 one thousand dollar gold coin commemorating establishment of Special Administrative Region.

No. 1116, $5, 1993 ten dollar coin.

***Perf. 13¼x14 Syncopated***
**2004, Sept. 2 Granite Paper**

**1112-1115** A240 Set of 4 3.50 3.50
*1115a* Miniature sheet, #1112-1115 3.50 3.50

**Souvenir Sheet**

**1116** A240 $5 multi 1.50 1.50

Pearl River Delta Region Development — A241

Designs: $1.40, Men and bridge. $2.40, Men and crane. $3, Tourist attractions. $5, Men and buildings.

**2004, Oct. 19 Granite Paper**

**1117-1120** A241 Set of 4 3.50 3.50
*1120a* Block of 4, #1117-1120 3.50 3.50

No. 1120a printed in sheets of 4 blocks.

Mushrooms A242

Designs: $1.40, Straw mushrooms. $2.40, Red-orange mushrooms. $3, Violet marasmius. No. 1124, $5, Lingzhi mushrooms.

No. 1125, Hexagon fungi.

***Perf. 13½x13¼ Syncopated***
**2004, Nov. 23 Granite Paper**

**1121-1124** A242 Set of 4 3.50 3.50
*1124a* Souvenir sheet, #1121-1124 3.50 3.50

**Souvenir Sheet**

**1125** A242 $5 multi 1.75 1.75

Letters of the Alphabet — A243

Nos. 1126 and 1127 — Upper half of letters made with common household items: a, Clothespin. b, Scissors. c, Lamp. d, Plastic cap for glue bottle. e, Steaming rack. f, Caliper with ruler. g, Bolt of padlock. h, Bamboo ladder. i, Flashlight. j, Toilet brush. k, Stapler. l, Sock. m, Draftsman's triangle. n, Nail clippers. o, Rubber band. p, Strainer. q, Link from chain. r, Sunglasses. s, Clothes hanger. t, Wooden broom. u, Sandals. v, Compass. w, Corkscrew. x, Faucet. y, Fork. z, Paint roller.

***Perf. 13¼x13 Syncopated***
**2005, Jan. 4 Litho.**
**Granite Paper (#1126)**

**1126** A243 Sheet of 30 (see footnote) 12.00 12.00
*a.-z.* $1.40 Any single .40 .40

**Self-Adhesive**
***Serpentine Die Cut 12½ Syncopated***

**1127** A243 Sheet of 30 (see footnote) 12.00
*a.-z.* $1.40 Any single .40 .40

Each sheet contains one of each letter and an additional example of a, e, i and o stamps.

Covers were prepared in 2006 with se-tenant strips spelling "KUNG," "HEI," "FAT" and "CHOY," which are not found in No. 1126.

New Year 2005 (Year of the Rooster) — A244

Various roosters with background colors of: $1.40, Orange. $2.40, Green. $3, Dark red. $5, Blue.

**2005, Jan. 30** ***Perf. 14¼ Syncopated***
**Granite Paper**

**1128-1131** A244 Set of 4 3.50 3.50
*1128a* Dated "2011," perf. 13½x13¼ syncopated (1431) .40 .40
*1131a* Souvenir sheet of 1, imperf. 1.75 1.75
*1131b* Souvenir sheet, #1128-1131 3.50 3.50

Issued: No. 1128a, 1/22/11. See No. 1253b, 1479f, 1480f.

Souvenir Sheet

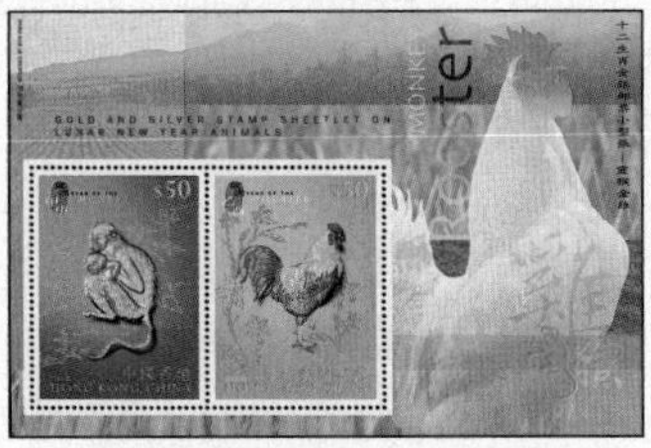

New Year 2005 (Year of the Rooster) — A245

No. 1132: a, Monkey. b, Rooster.

**Litho. & Embossed With Foil Application**

**2005, Jan. 30** ***Perf. 13¼***
**1132** A245 $50 Sheet of 2, #a-b 32.50 32.50

Fairy Tales by Hans Christian Andersen (1805-75) A246

Designs: $1.40, The Ugly Duckling. $2.40, The Little Mermaid. $3, The Little Match Girl. $5, The Emperor's New Clothes.

***Perf. 13¾ Syncopated***
**2005, Mar. 22** **Litho. & Embossed**
**Granite Paper**

**1133-1136** A246 Set of 4 4.00 4.00
*1133a* Souvenir sheet of 4 1.75 1.75
*1134a* Souvenir sheet of 4 3.00 3.00
*1135a* Souvenir sheet of 4 4.00 4.00
*1136a* Souvenir sheet of 4 6.50 6.50

Souvenir Sheet

Hong Kong Skyline, Sydney Opera House — A247

***Perf. 13½ Syncopated***
**2005, Apr. 21** **Litho.**
**Granite Paper**

**1137** A247 $10 multi 3.25 3.25

Pacific Explorer 2005 World Stamp Expo, Sydney.

Goldfish A248

Designs: $1.40, Variegated pearl-scale. $2.40, Red and white swallow-tail. $3, Pale bronze egg-phoenix. No. 1141, $5, Blue wenyu.
No. 1142, $5, Red and white dragon-eye.

***Perf. 13¼x14 Syncopated***
**2005, May 12** **Granite Paper**

**1138-1141** A248 Set of 4 3.50 3.50
*1141a* Souvenir sheet, #1138-1141 3.50 3.50

**Souvenir Sheet**

**1142** A248 $5 multi 2.00 2.00

No. 1142 contains one 45x35mm stamp.

Maritime Expeditions of Zheng He, 600th Anniv. A249

No. 1143 — Ships and: a, Zheng He (1371-1433), explorer. b, Giraffe, ceramics. c, Compass wheel.
$10, Zheng He on ship.

**2005, June 28** ***Perf. 13x13¼***
**1143** Horiz. strip of 3 1.50 1.50
*a.-c.* A249 $1.40 Any single .50 .50

**Souvenir Sheet**
***Perf. 13¼***

**1144** A249 $10 multi 3.00 3.00

No. 1144 contains one 50x30mm stamp.

Creative Industries A250

Designs: $1.40, Circles, squares and triangles (advertising). $2.40, Numerals, letters and symbols (computer and digital industries). $3, Vertical and horizontal lines (broadcasting industries). $5, Curved brushstrokes (arts and crafts).

***Perf. 14x14¼ Syncopated***
**2005, July 21** **Litho.**
**Granite Paper**

**1145-1148** A250 Set of 4 3.25 3.25
*1148a* Block of 4 with selvage, #1145-1148 3.25 3.25
*1148b* Booklet pane, 2 #1148a 6.50 —
Complete booklet, 2 #1148b 13.00

Each block of 4 in the booklet has a different arrangement. Rouletting separates the blocks within each booklet pane.

Great Inventions of Ancient China — A251

Designs: $1.40, Compass. $2.40, Printing. $3, Gunpowder. $5, Papermaking.

***Perf. 13¼x14¼ Syncopated***
**2005, Aug. 18**

**1149-1152** A251 Set of 4 3.50 3.50
*1152a* Miniature sheet, 4 each #1149-1152 14.00 14.00

Opening of Hong Kong Disneyland A252

Designs: $1.40, Mickey and Minnie Mouse. $2.40, Dumbo. $3, Simba and Nala. No. 1156, $5, Pluto.
Nos. 1157, 1158, Mickey Mouse.

***Perf. 13¾x13½ Syncopated***
**2005, Sept. 12** **Litho.**
**Granite Paper (#1153-1157)**

**1153-1156** A252 Set of 4 3.50 3.50
*1156a* Souvenir sheet, #1153-1156 3.50 3.50

**Souvenir Sheets**

**1157** A252 $5 multi 1.50 1.50

**Litho. & Embossed with Foil Application**

**1158** A252 $50 gold & multi 15.00 15.00

Souvenir Sheet

Qiantang Tidal Bore — A253

***Perf. 13¼ Syncopated***
**2005, Sept. 16** **Litho.**
**1159** A253 $10 multi 3.25 3.25

See No. 1456a.

Fishing Villages A254

Desings: $1.40, Tai O, Hong Kong. $2.40, Aldeia da Carrasqueira, Portugal. $3, Tai O, diff. $5, Aldeia da Carrasqueira, diff.

***Perf. 14¼x14 Syncopated***
**2005, Oct. 18**

**1160-1163** A254 Set of 4 3.50 3.50
*1163a* Miniature sheet, 4 each #1160-1163 14.00 14.00

See Portugal Nos. 2767-2768.

Popular Singers — A255

Designs: $1.40, Wong Ka Kui. $1.80, Danny Chan. $2.40, Roman Tam. $3, Leslie Cheung. $5, Anita Mui.

***Perf. 13½x13¼ Syncopated***
**2005, Nov. 8** **Granite Paper**

**1164-1168** A255 Set of 5 4.50 4.50

Because of concerns about the licensing of the images of the singers in foreign countries, the philatelic bureau did not make Nos. 1164-1168 available by mail order to foreign customers. The stamps were freely available to any purchasers over the counter.

New Year 2006 (Year of the Dog) — A256

Designs: $1.40, Golden retriever. $2.40, Pekingese. $3, German shepherd. $5, Beagle.

***Perf. 13½x13¼ Syncopated***
**2006, Jan. 15** **Litho.**
**Granite Paper**

**1169-1172** A256 Set of 4 3.25 3.25
*1172a* Souvenir sheet of #1172, imperf. 2.25 2.25
*1172b* Souvenir sheet, #1169-1172 3.75 3.75

See Nos. 1253c, 1431f. 1479g, 1480g.

Souvenir Sheet

New Year 2006 (Year of the Dog) — A257

No. 1173: a, Rooster. b, Dog.

**Litho. & Embossed with Foil Application**

**2006, Jan. 15** ***Perf. 13½x13¼***
**1173** A257 $50 Sheet of 2, #a-b 35.00 35.00

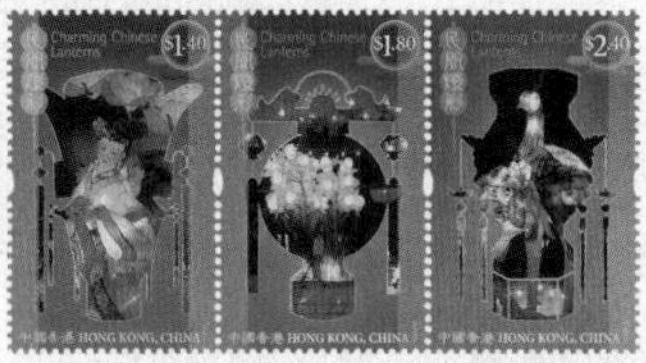

Chinese Lanterns — A258

No. 1174: a, $1.40, Lotus Fairy lantern. $1.80, Narcissus lantern. $2.40, Peacock lantern.
$5, Boys holding Dragon lantern.

***Perf. 12¾x13¼ Syncopated***
**2006, Feb. 12** **Litho.**
**Granite Paper (#1174)**

**1174** A258 Horiz. strip of 3, #a-c 2.50 2.50

**Souvenir Sheet**
***Perf. 13¼ Syncopated***

**1175** A258 $5 multi 2.00 2.00

No. 1175 contains one 35x46mm stamp.

Teddy Bears in Costumes A259

Teddy bears in various costumes.

***Perf. 13¾ Syncopated***
**2006, Mar. 30** **Granite Paper**

**1176** A259 $1.40 multi .35 .35
**1177** A259 $1.80 multi .50 .50
*a.* Booklet pane, #1176-1177 1.60 —
**1178** A259 $2.40 multi .60 .60
**1179** A259 $2.50 multi .65 .65
*a.* Booklet pane, #1178-1179 2.40 —

**1180** A259 $3 multi .80 .80
**1181** A259 $5 multi 1.25 1.25
*a.* Booklet pane, #1180-1181 3.75 —
Complete booklet, #1177a, 1179a, 1181a 7.75
*b.* Souvenir sheet, #1176-1181, + central label 4.25 4.25

Complete booklet sold for $30.

Souvenir Sheet

Gongbei Rock, Mount Taishan — A260

**2006, May 4** ***Perf. 14¼ Syncopated***
**Granite Paper**

**1182** A260 $10 multi 3.00 3.00

See No. 1456i.

Souvenir Sheet

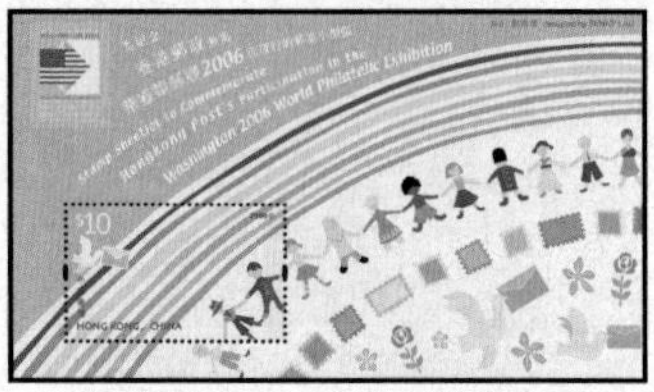

Washington 2006 World Philatelic Exhibition — A261

***Perf. 13¼x12¾ Syncopated***
**2006, May 27** **Granite Paper**

**1183** A261 $10 multi 3.00 3.00

Chinese Idioms A262

Idioms: $1.40, Respect makes successful marriage. $2.40, Reading is always rewarding. $3, Prepare for success. $5, All in the same boat.

***Perf. 13¾ Syncopated***
**2006, June 15** **Granite Paper**

**1184-1187** A262 Set of 4 3.50 3.50
*1187a* Souvenir sheet, #1184-1187 3.50 3.50

Attractions in Hong Kong's Districts — A263

Designs: No. 1188, $1.40, Central Police Station Historical Compound, Peak Tram, International Finance Center, Central and Western District. No. 1189, $1.40, Victoria Park, Island Eastern Corridor, Hong Kong Museum of Coastal Defense, Eastern District. No. 1190, $1.40, Floating restaurant, Murray House, Ocean Park, Southern District. No. 1191, $1.40, Hong Kong Convention and Exhibition Center, Old Wan Chai Post Office, Lovers' Rock, Wan Chai District. No. 1192, $1.40, Hong Kong Cultural Center, Temple Street, Yuen Po Bird Garden, Yau Tsim Mong District. No. 1193, $1.40, Wong Tai Sin Temple, Lion Rock, Chi Lin Nunnery, Wong Tai Sin District. No. 1194, $1.40, Lei Yue Mun Seafood Bazaar, buildings, Child-giving Rocks, Kwun Tong District. No. 1195, $1.40, Computer shopping center, Lingnan Garden, Festival Walk, Sham Shui Po District. No. 1196, $1.40, Kowloon Walled City Park, Wonderful Worlds of Whampoa, Sung Wong Toi, Kowloon City District. No. 1197, $1.40, Seafood Street, Tai Long Wan, Lions Nature Education Center Shell House, Sai Kung District. No. 1198, $1.40, Lantau Link View Point, Kwai Chung Container Terminals, Tsing Ma Bridge, Kwai Tsing District. No. 1199, $1.40, Lookout Tower, Lam Tsuen Wishing Tree, Tai Po Waterfront Park, Tai Po District. No. 1200, $1.40, Fung Ying Seen Koon, Chung Ying Street, Pak Hok Lam, North District. No. 1201, $1.40, Sam Tung Uk Museum, Yuen Yuen Institute, Tai Mo Shan Country Park, Tsuen Wan District. No. 1202, $1.40, Amah Rock, Shing Mun River Promenade, Che Kung Temple, Sha Tin District. No. 1203, $1.40, Hong Kong Gold Coast, Ching Chung Koon, Tsing Shan Monastery, Tuen Mun District. No. 1204, $1.40, Mai Po Nature Reserve, birds over farm, Chinese cakes, Yuen Long District. No. 1205, $1.40, Tian Tan Buddha, Cheung Chau Bun Festival, Tai O, Islands District.

**2006, July 18** ***Perf. 13½ Syncopated***
**Granite Paper**

**1188-1205** A263 Set of 18 7.25 7.25
*1205a* Souvenir sheet, #1188-1205 7.25 7.25

Fireworks A264

Designs: No. 1206, $5, No. 1208a, $50, Fireworks over Hong Kong Harbor. No. 1207, $5, No. 1208b, $50, Fireworks over Prater Ferris Wheel, Vienna, Austria.

**2006, Aug. 22** **Litho.** ***Perf. 14***

**1206-1207** A264 Set of 2 2.60 2.60

**Souvenir Sheet**
**Photo. With Glass Beads Affixed**

**1208** A264 $50 Sheet of 2, #a-b 26.00 26.00
*c.* Sheet, Austria #2060b, Hong Kong #1208a 32.50 32.50

See Austria No. 2060.

No. 1208c sold for €12.40 in Austria and for $120 in Hong Kong, and is identical to Austria No. 2060c.

Intl. Day of Peace — A265

Chinese characters and: $1.40, Flower and "Love." $1.80, Origami crane and "Peace." $2.40, Four-leaf clover and "Hope." $3, Tree and "Caring." $5, Earth and "Harmony."

***Perf. 13½x13¼ Syncopated***
**2006, Sept. 21** **Litho.**
**Granite Paper**

**1209-1213** A265 Set of 5 4.00 4.00
*1213a* Souvenir sheet, #1209-1213 4.00 4.00

Government Vehicles — A266

Designs: $1.40, Correctional Services security bus. $1.80, Customs Department X-ray scanning vehicle. $2.40, Fire Department hydraulic platform pumper truck. $2.50, Government Flying Service Super Puma helicopter. $3, Police Department traffic patrol motorcycle. $5, Immigration Department launch.

***Perf. 13¼x14½ Syncopated***
**2006, Oct. 19** **Litho.**
**Granite Paper**

**1214-1219** A266 Set of 6 5.00 5.00
*1219a* Sheet, 3 each #1214-1219 15.00 15.00

Dr. Sun Yat-sen (1866-1925), Republic of China President — A267

Photographs from: $1.40, 1883. $2.40, 1912. $3, 1916. No. 1223, $5, 1922. No. 1224, $5, 1924 (hands visible).

***Perf. 13¼x13 Syncopated***
**2006, Nov. 12** **Granite Paper**

**1220-1223** A267 Set of 4 4.00 4.00

**Souvenir Sheet**

**1224** A267 $5 multi 2.00 2.00

A booklet containing two panes, one containing Nos. 1220-1221, and one containing Nos. 1222-1223 sold for $25.

Heartwarming A268

***Perf. 13½ Syncopated***
**2006, Nov. 28** **Granite Paper**
**Inscribed "Local Mail Postage"**

**1225** A268 ($1.40) Hearts .35 .35
*a.* Sheet of 8 + 8 labels 3.00 3.00
**1226** A268 ($1.40) Bottles .35 .35
*a.* Sheet of 20 + 21 labels 12.50 12.50

**Inscribed "Air Mail Postage"**

**1227** A268 ($3) Flowers .80 .80
**1228** A268 ($3) Drink glasses .80 .80
*a.* Sheet, 5 each #1225-1228, + 21 labels 11.50 11.50
*b.* Sheet of 20 + 21 labels 27.50 27.50
*Nos. 1225-1228 (4)* 2.30 2.30

Issued: Nos. 1226a, 1228b, 5/2/08; No. 1225a, 2/14/12. Labels on Nos. 1225a, 1226a and 1228b could not be personalized. Nos. 1226a and 1228b sold as a set for $154.

No. 1225a is impregnated with a rose scent.

Birds — A269

Designs: 10c, White-bellied sea eagle. 20c, Collared scops owl. 50c, Scarlet minivet. $1, Common kingfisher. $1.40, Fork-tailed sunbird. $1.80, Roseate tern. $1.90, Black-faced spoonbill. $2, Little egret. $2.40, Greater painted snipe. $2.50, Barn swallow. $3, Red-whiskered bulbul. $5, Long-tailed shrike. $10, White wagtail. $13, Northern shoveler. $20, Common magpie. $50, Dalmatian pelican.

***Perf. 13x13¾ Syncopated***
**2006, Dec. 31** **Photo.**
**Granite Paper**
**Size: 22x26mm**

**1229** A269 10c multi .25 .25
**1230** A269 20c multi .25 .25
**1231** A269 50c multi .25 .25
**1232** A269 $1 multi .25 .25
**1233** A269 $1.40 multi .35 .35
*a.* Booklet pane of 10 3.50 —
Complete booklet, #1233a 3.50
**1234** A269 $1.80 multi .45 .45
*a.* Booklet pane of 10 4.50 —
Complete booklet, #1234a 4.50
**1235** A269 $1.90 multi .50 .50
**1236** A269 $2 multi .55 .55
**1237** A269 $2.40 multi .60 .60
*a.* Booklet pane of 10 6.00 —
Complete booklet, #1237a 6.00
**1238** A269 $2.50 multi .65 .65
**1239** A269 $3 multi .80 .80
*a.* Booklet pane of 10 8.00 —
Complete booklet, #1239a 8.00
**1240** A269 $5 multi 1.40 1.40
*a.* Miniature sheet, #1229-1240 6.25 6.25
*b.* Booklet pane, #1229-1240 6.25 —
Complete booklet, #1240b 6.25

**Size: 25x30mm**
***Perf. 13½x13¼ Syncopated***

**1241** A269 $10 multi 2.60 2.60
*a.* Souvenir sheet of 1 2.60 2.60
**1242** A269 $13 multi 3.50 3.50
**1243** A269 $20 multi 5.25 5.25
**1244** A269 $50 multi 13.00 13.00
*a.* Souvenir sheet, #1241-1244 25.00 25.00
*Nos. 1229-1244 (16)* 30.65 30.65

**Coil Stamps**
**Size: 17x21mm**
***Perf. 14¾x13½ Syncopated***

**1245** A269 $1.40 multi .35 .35
**1246** A269 $1.80 multi .45 .45
**1247** A269 $2.40 multi .60 .60
**1248** A269 $3 multi .80 .80
*Nos. 1245-1248 (4)* 2.20 2.20

Nos. 1241-1244 have microperforations around denominations.

Issued: No. 1241a, 9/21/10.

New Year 2007 (Year of the Pig) — A270

Various pigs with background colors of: $1.40, Brown. $2.40, Orange red. $3, Green. $5, Rose.

**2007, Feb. 4** ***Perf. 13½ Syncopated***
**Granite Paper**

**1249-1252** A270 Set of 4 3.25 3.25
*1249a* Dated "2011," perf. 13½x13¼ syncopated (1431) .35 .35
*1252a* Souvenir sheet of #1252, imperf. 2.00 2.00
*1252b* Souvenir sheet, #1249-1252 3.75 3.75

Issued: No. 1249a, 1/22/11. See Nos. 1253d, 1479h, 1480h.

**New Year Types of 2004-07**

**2007, Feb. 4** **Litho.** ***Perf. 13x13½***
**Flocked Paper**

**1253** Block of 4 10.50 10.50
*a.* A221 $10 Like #1075 2.60 2.60
*b.* A244 $10 Like #1128 2.60 2.60
*c.* A256 $10 Like #1170 2.60 2.60
*d.* A270 $10 Like #1251 2.60 2.60

Souvenir Sheet

New Year 2007 (Year of the Pig) — A271

No. 1254: a, Beagle. b, Pig and piglet.

**Litho. & Embossed With Foil Application**

**2007, Feb. 4** ***Perf. 13¼***

**1254** A271 $50 Sheet of 2, #a-b 26.00 26.00

Scouting, Cent. — A272

Designs: $1.40, Campfire, Lord Robert Baden-Powell. $2.40, Hong Kong Scouting emblem, compass. $3, Backpack, knot. $5, Scouts, tent.

**Litho. With Foil Application**
***Perf. 13¼x14¼ Syncopated***
**2007, Mar. 1**
**Granite Paper**

**1255-1258** A272 Set of 4 3.50 3.50
*1258a* Souvenir sheet, #1255-1258 3.50 3.50

Children's Games and Puzzles A273

Designs: $1.40, Find the difference between the two rabbits. $1.80, Color in the dotted areas. $2.40, Maze. $2.50, Follow lines to hunt for Easter Eggs. $3, Find the ten rabbits. $5, Look for a star.

***Perf. 13¾ Syncopated***

**2007, Mar. 22 — Litho.**

**Granite Paper**

**1259-1264** A273 Set of 6 4.25 4.25
*1264a* Souvenir sheet, #1259-1264 4.25 4.25

A booklet containing three panes, containing Nos. 1259-1260, 1261-1262, and 1263-1264 respectively, sold for $36.

Souvenir Sheet

Stone Forest, Shilin — A274

***Perf. 13¼x14¼ Syncopated***

**2007, May 3 — Granite Paper**

**1265** A274 $10 multi 2.60 2.60

See No. 1456h.

Chinese Martial Arts A275

Designs: $1.40, Southern Lion Dance. $2.40, Nanquan. $3, Northern Lion Dance. $5, Beitui.

**Litho. with Foil Application**

**2007, May 22**

**1266-1269** A275 Set of 4 3.00 3.00
*1269a* Souvenir sheet, #1266-1269 3.00 3.00

Butterflies — A276

Designs: $1.40, Faunis eumeus. $1.80, Prioneris philonome. $2.40, Polyura nepenthes. $3, Tajuria maculata. $5, Acraea issoria.

***Perf. 13½ Syncopated***

**2007, June 14 — Litho.**

**Granite Paper**

**1270-1274** A276 Set of 5 3.50 3.50

A booklet containing two panes, one containing Nos. 1270-1272 and the other containing Nos. 1273-1274, sold for $38.

Return of Hong Kong to China, 10th Anniv. A277

***Perf. 13x12¾ Syncopated***

**2007, July 1 — Photo.**

**1275** A277 $1.40 multi .50 .50

A souvenir sheet containing No. 1275 and People's Republic of China Nos. 3594-3596 sold for $12.95.

A278

Hong Kong Special Administrative Region, 10th Anniv. — A279

Designs: $1.40, Ten children with joined hands. $1.80, Banner on Hong Kong Heritage Museum. $2.40, Vehicles on Tsing Ma Bridge. $2.50, Ten birds over Hong Kong Wetland Park. $3, Two International Finance Center Building and Moon. $5, Fireworks over Hong Kong.

No. 1282: a, "7" over Bank of China Tower, fireworks over Cheung Kong Center. b, Fireworks over smaller buildings. c, Fireworks over smaller buildings, Two International Finance Center Building at right.

***Perf. 13½x14¼ Syncopated***

**2007, July 1 — Litho.**

**Granite Paper**

**1276-1281** A278 Set of 6 4.25 4.25

**Litho. With Foil Application and Hologram**

***Perf. 13½***

**1282** A279 $10 Sheet of 3, #a-c 7.75 7.75

Souvenir Sheet

Bangkok 2007 Asian International Stamp Exhibition — A280

***Perf. 13½x14¼ Syncopated***

**2007, Aug. 3 — Litho.**

**Granite Paper**

**1283** A280 $10 multi 2.60 2.60

Civic Education A281

Designs: $1.40, Human rights. $2.40, Rule of law. $3, Social participation. $5, Corporate citizenship.

**2007, Aug. 23** ***Perf. 13 Syncopated***

**Granite Paper**

**1284-1287** A281 Set of 4 3.00 3.00
*1287a* Miniature sheet, 4 each #1284-1287 12.00 12.00

Declared Monuments — A282

Designs: $1.40, Tin Hau Temple, Causeway Bay. $1.80, Old Wan Chai Post Office. $2.40, Former Central Police Station Compound. $2.50, Former Yamen Building of Kowloon Walled City. $3, Kun Lung Gate Tower, Lung Yeuk Tau. $5, Tang Lung Chau Lighthouse.

**Litho. & Engr.**

**2007, Sept. 20** ***Perf. 14x13¼***

**Granite Paper**

**1288-1293** A282 Set of 6 4.25 4.25
*1293a* Miniature sheet, #1288-1293 4.25 4.25

Christmas — A283

Designs: $1.40, Stocking. $2.40, Gingerbread man-shaped egg tart. $3, Bell decorated with neon lights. $5, Snowman with Chinese vest.

**2007, Oct. 11 Litho.** ***Perf. 13x13½***

**Granite Paper**

**1294-1297** A283 Set of 4 3.00 3.00

Woodwork — A284

Designs: No. 1298, $5, Zitan armchair with dragon design, China, denomination at left. No. 1299, $5, Modern Finnish bowls, denomination at right.

***Perf. 13½x14¼ Syncopated***

**2007, Nov. 2 — Granite Paper**

**1298-1299** A284 Set of 2 2.60 2.60
*1299a* Souvenir sheet, #1298-1299 2.60 2.60

See Finland No. 1298.

Heartwarming A285

Designs: No. 1300, Birds and flowers. No. 1301, Firecrackers. No. 1302, Gifts and balloons. No. 1303, Slippers.

***Perf. 13½ Syncopated***

**2007, Dec. 28 — Litho.**

**Granite Paper**

**Inscribed "Local Mail Postage"**

**1300** A285 ($1.40) multi .35 .35
**1301** A285 ($1.40) multi .35 .35

**Inscribed "Air Mail Postage"**

**1302** A285 ($3) multi .80 .80
**1303** A285 ($3) multi .80 .80
*a.* Sheet, 5 each #1300-1303 + 21 labels 11.50 11.50

New Year 2008 (Year of the Rat) — A286

Various rats with background colors of: $1.40, Blue. $2.40, Green. $3, Orange red. $5, Brown.

***Perf. 13½x13¼ Syncopated***

**2008, Jan. 26 — Litho.**

**Granite Paper**

**1304-1307** A286 Set of 4 3.00 3.00
*1304a* Dated "2011" (1431) .35 .35
*1307a* Souvenir sheet of #1307, imperf. 1.25 1.25
*1307b* Souvenir sheet, #1304-1307 3.00 3.00

Issued: No. 1304a, 1/22/11. See Nos. 1432a, 1479i, 1480i.

Souvenir Sheet

New Year 2008 (Year of the Rat) — A287

No. 1308: a, Pig. b, Rat.

**Litho. & Embossed With Foil Application**

**2008, Jan. 26** ***Perf. 13¼***

**1308** A287 $50 Sheet of 2, #a-b 26.00 26.00

Souvenir Sheet

Huanglong — A288

***Perf. 14¼ Syncopated***

**2008, Feb. 28 — Litho.**

**Granite Paper**

**1309** A288 $10 multi 2.60 2.60

See No. 1456d.

Flowers A289

Designs: $1.40, Chinese hibiscus. $1.80, Tree cotton. $2.40, Allamandas. $2.50, Azaleas. $3, Indian lotus. $5, Morning glories.

***Perf. 13½x13¼ Syncopated***

**2008, Mar. 14 — Granite Paper**

**1310-1315** A289 Set of 6 4.25 4.25
*1315a* Souvenir sheet, #1310-1315 4.25 4.25

Paper Folding Art — A290

Designs: $1.40, Bauhinia blossoms. $1.80, Bear, horiz. $2.40, Lunar New Year decorations. $2.50, Lotus flowers and rainbow, horiz. $3, Koalas, monkey with banana. $5, Christmas party scene, horiz.

***Perf. 14¼x13½, 13½x14¼ Syncopated***

**2008, May 22**

**1316-1321** A290 Set of 6 4.25 4.25
*1321a* Souvenir sheet, #1316-1321 4.25 4.25

Jellyfish — A291

Designs: $1.40, Flower hat jellyfish. $1.80, Octopus jellyfish, horiz. $2.40, Brown sea nettle. $2.50, Moon jellyfish, horiz. $3, Lion's mane jellyfish. $5, Pacific sea nettle.

***Perf. 14¼ Syncopated***

**2008, June 12** **Litho.**

**Granite Paper**

**1322-1327** A291 Set of 6 4.25 4.25
*1327a* Souvenir sheet, #1322-1327 4.25 4.25

Stamps have a glow-in-the dark coating on the jellyfish illustrations. A booklet containing panes of Nos. 1322-1323, 1324-1325, and 1326-1327, sold for $36.

Giant Pandas A292

Designs: $1.40, Ying Ying, Le Le, and hearts. $2.40, Ying Ying and leaves. $3, Le Le and panda heads. $5, Ying Ying, Le Le, and circles.

**2008, July 1** ***Perf. 13¾ Syncopated***

**Granite Paper**

**1328-1331** A292 Set of 4 3.00 3.00
*1331a* Sheet, 2 each # 1328-1331, + 4 labels 6.00 6.00

Hong Kong, Venue for 2008 Summer Olympic Equestrian Events — A293

Desings: $1.40, Horse and rider jumping fence. $2.40, Dressage. $3, Horse and rider jumping over water obstacle. $5, Horse and rider at medal stand.

***Perf. 13¼x14 Syncopated***

**2008, Aug. 9** **Granite Paper**

**1332-1335** A293 Set of 4 3.00 3.00
*1335a* Souvenir sheet, #1332-1335 3.00 3.00

Souvenir Sheet

Praga 2008 World Stamp Exhibition — A294

***Perf. 13¼x14¼ Syncopated***

**2008, Sept. 12** **Litho.**

**Granite Paper**

**1336** A294 $10 multi 2.75 2.75

Big Head Buddha Mask, Hong Kong — A295

Chwibari Mask, Korea — A296

***Perf. 13¼x14 Syncopated***

**2008, Nov. 6** **Granite Paper**

**1337** A295 $5 multi 1.40 1.40
**1338** A296 $5 multi 1.40 1.40
*a.* Souvenir sheet, #1337-1338 3.00 3.00

See South Korea No. 2299.

The Judiciary A297

Designs: $1.40, Statue of Justice. $2.40, Court of Final Appeal. $3, Judicial robes for various courts. $5, Chief Justice's mace.

***Perf. 13¾ Syncopated***

**2008, Nov. 27** **Granite Paper**

**1339-1342** A297 Set of 4 3.75 3.75
*1342a* Souvenir sheet, #1339-1342 3.75 3.75

New Year 2009 (Year of the Ox) — A298

Various oxen with background colors of: $1.40, Purple. $2.40, Brown. $3, Green. $5, Blue.

***Perf. 13½x13¼ Syncopated***

**2009, Jan. 17** **Litho.**

**Granite Paper**

**1343-1346** A298 Set of 4 3.75 3.75
*1346a* Souvenir sheet of #1346, imperf. 1.60 1.60
*1346b* Souvenir sheet, #1343-1346 3.75 3.75

See Nos. 1431g, 1432b, 1479j, 1480j.

Souvenir Sheet

New Year 2009 (Year of the Ox) — A299

No. 1347: a, Rat. b, Ox.

**Litho. & Embossed With Foil Application**

**2009, Jan. 17** ***Perf. 13¼***

**1347** A299 $50 Sheet of 2, #a-b 35.00 35.00

Souvenir Sheet

Mount Tianshan — A300

***Perf. 14¼ Syncopated***

**2009, Feb. 24** **Litho.**

**Granite Paper**

**1348** A300 $10 multi 3.00 3.00

See No. 1456c.

Souvenir Sheet

Peony and Bauhinia Flowers — A301

**2009, Apr. 7** ***Perf. 13¼ Syncopated***

**Granite Paper**

**1349** A301 $5 multi 1.40 1.40

China 2009 World Stamp Exhibition, Luoyang.

Souvenir Sheet

Tangram Figure — A302

**2009, May 14** ***Perf. 13¼***

**Granite Paper**

**1350** A302 $50 multi + 2 labels 13.00 13.00

Hong Kong 2009 Intl. Stamp Exhibition.

Items in Hong Kong Museums — A303

Designs: $1.40, Poem by Wang Duo, Hong Kong Museum of Art. $1.80, Landscape, painting by Wang Yuanqi, Hong Kong Museum of Art. $2.40, Calligraphy by Wang Xizhi, Art Museum of the Chinese University of Hong Kong. $2.50, Bird in Moonlight, painting by Gao Qifeng, Hong Kong Heritage Museum. $3, Flower and Butterfly, fan painting by Ju Lian, Hong Kong Heritage Museum, horiz. (50x30mm). $5, Drawing by Gu Huai, University Museum and Art Gallery of the University of Hong Kong, horiz. (50x30mm).

***Perf. 13½x13¼ Syncopated***

**2009, May 16** **Granite Paper**

**1351-1356** A303 Set of 6 4.25 4.25
*1356a* Souvenir sheet, #1351-1356 4.25 4.25

Heartwarming A304

Designs: No. 1357, Flowers. No. 1358, Lion. No. 1359, Birthday hats. No. 1360, Butterflies and heart.

***Perf. 13½ Syncopated***

**2009, June 25** **Granite Paper**

**Inscribed "Local Mail Postage"**

**1357** A304 ($1.40) multi .35 .35
**1358** A304 ($1.40) multi .35 .35

**Inscribed "Air Mail Postage"**

**1359** A304 ($3) multi .80 .80
**1360** A304 ($3) multi .80 .80
*a.* Sheet of 12, 3 each #1357-1360, + 12 labels 7.00 7.00
*Nos. 1357-1360 (4)* 2.30 2.30

Labels on No. 1360a could not be personalized.

Customs and Excise Service, Cent. A305

Designs: $1.40, Officer with drug-sniffing dog and baggage inspectors of 1960s. $2.40, Mobile x-ray vehicle scanner and Sheng Shui Customs Station, 1935. $3, Patrol boats. $5, Officers raising flag.

***Perf. 13¼x13 Syncopated***

**2009, Sept. 17** **Litho.**

**Granite Paper**

**1361-1364** A305 Set of 4 3.00 3.00
*1364a* Souvenir sheet, #1361-1364 3.00 3.00

A booklet containing two panes, one with Nos. 1361-1362, and the other with Nos. 1363-1364, sold for $36.

A306

People's Republic of China, 60th Anniv. — A307

Designs: $1.40, Cogwheels, Victoria Harbor, Hong Kong and Tiananmen Square, Beijing. $1.80, Flag of People's Republic of China, Forever Blooming Bauhinia statue, Hong Kong. $2.40, Dove, Olympic Stadium, Beijing. $2.50, Shenzhou-7 on launch pad. $3, Doves, Temple of Heaven. $5, Dragon, Great Wall of China.

No. 1371: a, Emblem of People's Republic of China, Tiananmen Square. b, Emblem of Hong Kong, Hong Kong skyline at night.

**2009, Oct. 1** ***Perf. 13¼***

**Granite Paper (A306)**

**1365-1370** A306 Set of 6 4.50 4.50
*1370a* Souvenir sheet, #1365-1370 5.00 5.00

**Souvenir Sheet**

***Perf. 13***

**1371** A307 $5 Sheet of 2, #a-b 4.25 4.25

Soccer A308

Soccer player from: $1.40, Hong Kong. $2.40, Hong Kong, diff. $3, Brazil. $5, Brazil, diff.

***Perf. 13¼x14¼ Syncopated***

**2009, Nov. 5** **Granite Paper**

**1372-1375** A308 Set of 4 3.00 3.00
*1375a* Souvenir sheet, #1372-1375 3.00 3.00

See Brazil No. 3114.

2009 East Asia Games, Hong Kong A309

Designs: No. 1376, $1.40, Judo, rowing and rugby. No. 1377, $1.40, Wushu, track, badminton and shooting. No. 1378, $2.40, Squash, basketball, field hockey and swimming. No. 1379, $2.40, Cycling, weight lifting and tennis. No. 1380, $3, Bowling, windsurfing, soccer and taekwondo. No. 1381, $3, Dancing, table tennis, volleyball and billiards.

**Litho. With Foil Application**

**2009, Dec. 5** ***Perf. 14¼ Syncopated***

**Granite Paper**

**1376-1381** A309 Set of 6 3.50 3.50
*1381a* Souvenir sheet, #1376-1381 3.50 3.50

Stonecutters Bridge — A310

Designs: $1.40, View of bridge tower from water level. $2.40, Aerial view of bridge, horiz. $3, View of bridge from water level, horiz. $5, Aerial view of bridge tower.

***Perf. 14½x14 Syncopated, 14x14½ Syncopated***

**2009, Dec. 17** **Litho.**

**Granite Paper**

**1382-1385** A310 Set of 4 3.25 3.25
*1385a* Souvenir sheet, #1382-1385 3.25 3.25

New Year 2010 (Year of the Tiger) — A311

Various tigers with background colors of: $1.40, Red. $2.40, Green. $3, Blue. $5, Orange.

***Perf. 13½x13¼ Syncopated***

**2010, Feb. 6** **Granite Paper**

**1386-1389** A311 Set of 4 3.00 3.00
*1386a* Dated "2011" (1431) .35 .35
*1389a* Souvenir sheet of #1389, imperf. 1.25 1.25
*1389b* Souvenir sheet, #1386-1389 3.00 3.00

Issued: No. 1386a, 1/22/11. See Nos. 1432c, 1479k, 1480k.

**Souvenir Sheet**

New Year 2010 (Year of the Tiger) — A312

No. 1390: a, Ox. b, Tiger.

**Litho. & Embossed With Foil Application**

**2010, Feb. 6** ***Perf. 13¾***

**1390** A312 $50 Sheet of 2, #a-b 26.00 26.00

**Souvenir Sheet**

Fujian Tulou UNESCO World Heritage Site — A313

***Perf. 13¼ Syncopated***

**2010, Mar. 18** **Litho.**

**Granite Paper**

**1391** A313 $10 multi 3.00 3.00

See No. 1456e.

Expo 2010, Shanghai — A314

Designs: $1.40, Dragon dance. $2.40, Hong Kong on green leaf. $3, Tsing Ma Bridge, Hong Kong. $5, Smart Card chip, head, Hong Kong skyline.

**2010, Apr. 27** ***Perf. 13¼ Syncopated***

**Granite Paper**

**1392-1395** A314 Set of 4 3.50 3.50
*1395a* Souvenir sheet, #1392-1395 3.50 3.50

No. 1395a was printed in sheet containing four souvenir sheets.

**Souvenir Sheet**

London 2010 Intl. Philatelic Exhibition — A315

**2010, May 8** **Litho.** **Granite Paper**

**1396** A315 $10 multi 3.00 3.00

Hong Kong Street Scenes A316

Designs: No. 1397, $1.40, Pottinger Street. No. 1398, $1.40, Nathan Road. No. 1399, $2.40, Hollywood Road. No. 1400, $2.40, Temple Street. No. 1401, $3, Des Voeux Road West. No. 1402, $3, Stanley Market.

***Perf. 13¾ Syncopated***

**2010, June 24** **Granite Paper**

**1397-1402** A316 Set of 6 4.00 4.00
*1402a* Souvenir sheet, #1397-1402 4.00 4.00

Intl. Year of Biodiversity — A317

Designs: $1.40, Macropodus hongkongensis. $2.40, Liuixalus romeri. $3, Sinopora hongkongensis. $5, Fukienogomphus choifongae.

***Perf. 13¼x14¼ Syncopated***

**2010, July 15** **Litho.**

**Granite Paper**

**1403-1406** A317 Set of 4 3.00 3.00
*1406a* Souvenir sheet, #1403-1406 3.00 3.00

Railways in Hong Kong, Cent. — A318

Designs: $1.40, Steam train, Hong Kong Railway Museum. $1.80, Diesel train, clock tower of Kowloon-Canton Railway Terminus. $2.40, Electric train, Hung Hom Terminus. $2.50, Mass Transit Railway train, International Finance Center. $3, Kowloon-Guangzhou through train, Mass Transit Railway Hung Hom Station. $5, Airport Express train, aerial view of Hong Kong International Airport.

$20, Steam train, Hong Kong Railway Museum, diff.

***Perf. 13½x13¼ Syncopated***

**2010, Sept. 28** **Litho.**

**Granite Paper**

**1407-1412** A318 Set of 6 4.50 4.50
*1412a* Souvenir sheet, #1407-1412 4.50 4.50

**Souvenir Sheet**

**Litho. With Three-Dimensional Plastic Affixed**

**1413** A318 $20 multi 5.50 5.50

No. 1413 contains one 37x51mm stamp.

A booklet containing three panes, containing Nos. 1407-1408, 1409-1410, and 1411-1412 respectively, sold for $36.

Winning Entries in Children's Stamp Design Contest — A319

Designs: $1.40, "Harbor of Hong Kong." $2.40, "Beautiful Hong Kong." $3, "Hong Kong is Fun." $5, "City Beat."

***Perf. 13¼x13½ Syncopated***

**2010, Oct. 21** **Litho.**

**Granite Paper**

**1414-1417** A319 Set of 4 3.00 3.00
*1417a* Souvenir sheet, #1414-1417 3.00 3.00

Renovation of Old Neighborhoods — A320

Designs: $1.40, Rehabilitation. $2.40, Revitalization. $3, Preservation. $5, Redevelopment.

***Perf. 13¾ Syncopated***

**2010, Nov. 16** **Granite Paper**

**1418-1421** A320 Set of 4 3.00 3.00
*1421a* Souvenir sheet, #1418-1421 3.00 3.00

Lighthouses A321

Map and: $1.40, Cape D'Aguilar Lighthouse. $1.80, Old Green Island Lighthouse. $2.40, New Green Island Lighthouse. $3, Tang Lung Chau Lighthouse. $5, Waglan Lighthouse.

***Perf. 13½x13¼ Syncopated***

**2010, Dec. 29** **Litho.**

**Granite Paper**

**1422-1426** A321 Set of 5 3.50 3.50
*1426a* Souvenir sheet of 5, #1422-1426 3.50 3.50

New Year 2011 (Year of the Rabbit) — A322

Various rabbits with background color of: $1.40, Green. $2.40, Blue. $3, Brown. $5, Red.

***Perf. 13½x13¼ Syncopated***

**2011, Jan. 22 Granite Paper**

**1427-1430** A322 Set of 4 3.00 3.00
*1430a* Souvenir sheet of #1430, imperf. 1.25 1.25
*1430b* Souvenir sheet of 4, #1427-1430 3.00 3.00

See Nos. 1432d, 1479l, 1480l.

### New Year Types of 2000-11

***Perf. 13½x13¼ Syncopated***

**2011, Jan. 22 Litho.**

**Granite Paper**

**1431** Sheet of 12, #1128a, 1249a, 1304a, 1386a, 1427, 1431a-1431g 4.25 4.25
*a.* A177 $1.40 Dragon .35 .35
*b.* A184 $1.40 Snake .35 .35
*c.* A194 $1.40 Horse .35 .35
*d.* A206 $1.40 Ram (like #1028) .35 .35
*e.* A221 $1.40 Monkey (like #1076) .35 .35
*f.* A256 $1.40 Dog (like #1170) .35 .35
*g.* A298 $1.40 Ox (like #1344) .35 .35

**Flocked Paper**

***Perf. 13½x13¼***

**1432** Block of 4 10.50 10.50
*a.* A286 $10 Rat 2.60 2.60
*b.* A298 $10 Ox 2.60 2.60
*c.* A311 $10 Tiger 2.60 2.60
*d.* A322 $10 Rabbit 2.60 2.60

Souvenir Sheet

New Year 2011 (Year of the Rabbit) — A323

No. 1433: a, Tiger. b, Rabbit.

**Litho. & Embossed With Foil Application**

**2011, Jan. 22 *Perf. 13¾***

**1433** A323 $50 Sheet of 2, #a-b 26.00 26.00

Souvenir Sheet

Powered Flight in Hong Kong, Cent. — A324

No. 1434: a, Drawing of first aircraft. b, Photograph of first flight.

***Perf. 13¼ Syncopated***

**2011, Mar. 18 Litho.**

**Granite Paper**

**1434** A324 $3 Sheet of 2, #a-b 1.60 1.60

A325

Volunteerism — A326

Designs: $1.40, Leaf, child's notebook page. $2.40, Volunteer recruitement web page. $3, E-mail message, children. No. 1438, $5, Written reminder on calendar page.

***Perf. 13½x13¼ Syncopated***

**2011, Mar. 29 Granite Paper**

**1435-1438** A325 Set of 4 3.00 3.00

**Souvenir Sheet**

***Perf.***

**1439** A326 $5 shown 1.25 1.25

Green Living — A327

Growing plant and: $1.40, Water faucet, Earth in water droplet. $2.40, Cloud, tree, Earth. $3, Fluorescent lightbulb, Earth under lampshade. No. 1443, $5, Recycling emblem, recyclable items, Earth.
No. 1444, $5, Growing plant on Earth.

**2011, Apr. 14 *Perf. 13¾ Syncopated***

**Granite Paper**

**1440-1443** A327 Set of 4 3.00 3.00

**Souvenir Sheet**

**1444** A327 $5 multi 1.25 1.25

Hong Kong General Chamber of Commerce, 150th Anniv. A328

Designs: $1.40, Old Hong Kong Club Building. $2.40, Wharf. $3, Handshake, Good Citizen Award Certificate. $5, Chamber of Commerce members in China near train, 1978.

**2011, May 26 Litho.**

**Granite Paper**

**1445-1448** A328 Set of 4 3.00 3.00
*1448a* Souvenir sheet of 4, #1445-1448 3.00 3.00

Chinese Idioms — A329

Idioms: Nos. 1449, 1454a, $1.40, Mutual help in hard times. Nos. 1450, 1454b, $1.80, Water drops wear away rocks. Nos. 1451, 1454c, $2.40, Practice makes perfect. Nos. 1452, 1454d, $3, Save to give. Nos. 1453, 1454e, $5, As deft as a master butcher.

***Perf. 13¼x14¼ Syncopated***

**2011, June 28 Granite Paper**

**Multicolored Designs**

**1449-1453** A329 Set of 5 3.50 3.50

**Stamp Designs With Gray Areas**

**1454** A329 Sheet of 5, #a-e 3.50 3.50

No. 1454 was sold with a sheet of multicolored self-adhesive stickers that could be placed over corresponding gray areas on the souvenir sheet. Value for No. 1454 is for sheet without stickers attached.

Souvenir Sheet

Dunhuang Grottoes — A330

***Perf. 13½x13¼ Syncopated***

**2011, Aug. 2 Granite Paper**

**1455** A330 $10 multi 2.60 2.60

See No. 1456b.

### Chinese Scenery Types of 2003-11

Miniature Sheet

***Perf. 13¼x13½ Syncopated, 13¼ Syncopated (#1456a), 13½x13¼ Syncopated (#1456b, 1456i), 13¼x13 Syncopated (#1456d)***

**2011, Aug. 2 Litho.**

**Granite Paper**

**1456** Sheet of 9 6.00 6.00
*a.* A253 $2.40 Qiantang Bore .65 .65
*b.* A330 $2.40 Dunhuang Grottoes .65 .65
*c.* A300 $2.40 Mount Tianshan .65 .65
*d.* A288 $2.40 Huanglong .65 .65
*e.* A313 $2.40 Fujian Tulou .65 .65
*f.* A210 $2.40 Master-of-Nets Garden .65 .65
*g.* A230 $2.40 Chen Clan Academy .65 .65
*h.* A274 $2.40 Shilin .65 .65
*i.* A260 $2.40 Mount Taishan .65 .65

Souvenir Sheet

Hong Kong Postal Service, 170th Anniv. — A331

**Litho. & Embossed With Foil Application**

***Perf. 13½ Syncopated***

**2011, Aug. 25 Granite Paper**

**1457** A331 $10 multi 2.60 2.60

University of Hong Kong, Cent. — A332

University crest and: $1.40, Main Building, 1910, and golden trowel. $1.80, Main Building, 1912, and University Bazaar poster. $2.40, Union Building, 1919, Main Building, and statue of Dr. Sun Yat-sen. $2.50, Main Building, 1946, and mace. $3, Main Building and West Gate, 1940s, and inkstand. No. 1463, $5, Courtyard and Main Building, 2011, University arms. No. 1464, $5, Letters patent, vert.

***Perf. 13¼x13 Syncopated***

**2011, Sept. 5 Litho.**

**Granite Paper**

**1458-1463** A332 Set of 6 4.25 4.25

**Souvenir Sheet**

***Perf. 13¾x14¼ Syncopated***

**1464** A332 $5 multi 1.40 1.40

A booklet containing two panes, containing Nos. 1458-1460 and 1461-1463, respectively, sold for $45.

Chinese Revolution, Cent. — A333

Designs: $1.40, Monument to the 72 Martyrs of Huanghuagang. $2.40, Wuchang Uprising. $3, Revolution leaders Cai Yuanpei, Zhang Taiyan, Huang Xing and Song Jiaoren. No. 1468, $5, Dr. Sun Yat-sen assuming office of Provisional President.
No. 1469, $5, horiz. — Dr. Sun Yat-sen and: a, Central School. b, Proclamation of the Three Principles of the People.

***Perf. 13½x13¼ Syncopated***

**2011, Oct. 10 Granite Paper**

**1465-1468** A333 Set of 4 3.00 3.00

**Souvenir Sheet**

***Perf. 13¼x13 Syncopated***

**1469** A333 $5 Sheet of 2, #a-b 2.60 2.60

Handicrafts A334

Artisan creating: No. 1470, $5, Dough figurines, Hong Kong. No. 1471, $5, Painted Easter egg, Romania.

***Perf. 13¼ Syncopated***

**2011, Nov. 24 Granite Paper**

**1470-1471** A334 Set of 2 2.60 2.60
*1471a* Souvenir sheet of 2, #1470-1471 2.60 2.60

See Romania Nos. 5311-5312.

Items in Hong Kong Museums — A335

Designs: $1.40, Forehead headdress used in opera, *The Sounds of Battle*. $1.80, Qipao, 1920s-1930s. $2.40, Silver-footed bowl decorated in repousse, horiz. $2.50, Sequined reversible palace costume, horiz. $3, Green glazed barrel for herbal tea, horiz. $5, Traditional baby carrier with head support, horiz.

***Perf. 13¾x14¼ Syncopated, 14¼x13¾ Syncopated***

**2011, Dec. 6 Granite Paper**

**1472-1477** A335 Set of 6 4.25 4.25
*1477a* Souvenir sheet of 6, #1472-1477 4.25 4.25

Souvenir Sheet

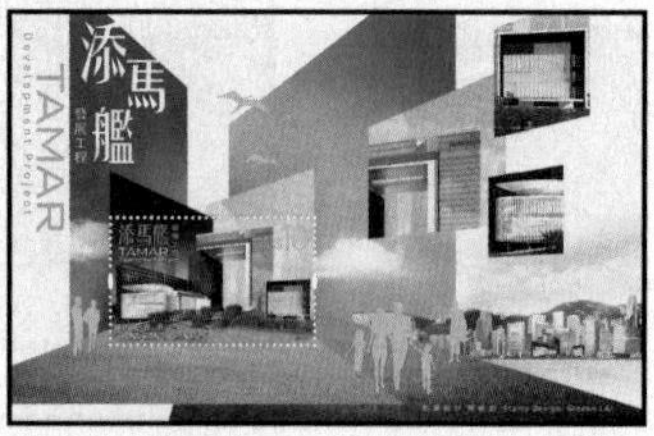


Tamar Development Project — A336

*Perf. 13¼ Syncopated*

**2011, Dec. 15 Litho.**

**Granite Paper**

**1478** A336 $10 multi 2.60 2.60

**New Year Types of 2000-11**

No. 1479: a, Dragon, green background. b, Snake, orange brown background. c, Horse, red background. d, Ram, dull red background. e, Monkey, blue green background. f, Rooster, blue background. g, Dog, green background. h, Pig, dull red background. i, Rat, blue background. j, Ox, red brown background. k, Tiger, blue green background. l, Rabbit, orange brown background.

No. 1480: a, Dragon, blue background. b, Snake, red background. c, Horse, green background. d, Ram, orange brown background. e, Monkey, green background. f, Rooster, orange background. g, Dog, red violet background. h, Pigs, red brown background. i, Rat, brown background. j, Ox, lilac background. k, Tiger, green background. l, Rabbit, dull green background.

*Perf. 13½x13¼ Syncopated*

**2012, Jan. 14 Litho.**

**Granite Paper**

**Animals in Silver and Gold**

| | | | | |
|---|---|---|---|---|
| **1479** | | Sheet of 12 | 5.00 | 5.00 |
| *a.* | A177 | $1.40 multi | .40 | .40 |
| *b.* | A184 | $1.40 multi | .40 | .40 |
| *c.* | A194 | $1.40 multi | .40 | .40 |
| *d.* | A206 | $1.40 multi | .40 | .40 |
| *e.* | A221 | $1.40 multi | .40 | .40 |
| *f.* | A244 | $1.40 multi | .40 | .40 |
| *g.* | A256 | $1.40 multi | .40 | .40 |
| *h.* | A270 | $1.40 multi | .40 | .40 |
| *i.* | A286 | $1.40 multi | .40 | .40 |
| *j.* | A298 | $1.40 multi | .40 | .40 |
| *k.* | A311 | $1.40 multi | .40 | .40 |
| *l.* | A322 | $1.40 multi | .40 | .40 |
| **1480** | | Sheet of 12 | 5.00 | 5.00 |
| *a.* | A177 | $1.40 multi | .40 | .40 |
| *b.* | A184 | $1.40 multi | .40 | .40 |
| *c.* | A194 | $1.40 multi | .40 | .40 |
| *d.* | A206 | $1.40 multi | .40 | .40 |
| *e.* | A221 | $1.40 multi | .40 | .40 |
| *f.* | A244 | $1.40 multi | .40 | .40 |
| *g.* | A256 | $1.40 multi | .40 | .40 |
| *h.* | A270 | $1.40 multi | .40 | .40 |
| *i.* | A286 | $1.40 multi | .40 | .40 |
| *j.* | A298 | $1.40 multi | .40 | .40 |
| *k.* | A311 | $1.40 multi | .40 | .40 |
| *l.* | A322 | $1.40 multi | .40 | .40 |

Souvenir Sheet

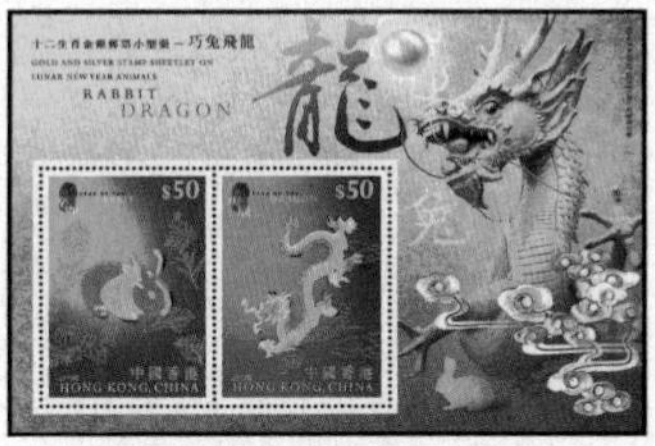

New Year 2012 (Year of the Dragon) — A337

No. 1481: a, Rabbit. b, Dragon.

**Ltho. & Embossed With Foil Application**

**2012, Jan. 14** ***Perf. 14x13¾***

**1481** A337 $50 Sheet of 2, #a-b 26.00 26.00

New Year 2012 (Year of the Dragon) A338

Various dragons with background colors of: $1.40, Orange. $2.40, Red violet. $3, Purple. $5, Green.

$10, Dragon, red background. $50, Dragon, multicolored background.

**Litho. With Foil Application**

**2012, Jan. 14** ***Perf. 13¼ Syncopated***

**Granite Paper**

**1482-1485** A338 Set of 4 3.00 3.00

**Souvenir Sheets**

**1486** A338 $10 multi 2.60 2.60

**Litho.**

**Silk-faced Paper**

**1487** A338 $50 multi 13.00 13.00

Nos. 1487 and 1488 each contain one 45x45mm stamp.

Queen's College, 150th Anniv. A339

**2012, Mar. 27** ***Perf.***

| | | | |
|---|---|---|---|
| **1488** | Sheet of 4 | 10.50 | 10.50 |
| *a.* | A339 $10 Litho., text at top in tan, denomination in black, glitter on shield frame | 2.60 | 2.60 |
| *b.* | A339 $10 Litho., text at top in claret, denomination in tan, lacquer on part of design | 2.60 | 2.60 |
| *c.* | A339 $10 Litho. & embossed, text at top in tan, denomination in black | 2.60 | 2.60 |
| *d.* | A339 $10 Litho & embossed with foil application, denomination and building in gold | 2.60 | 2.60 |

**Souvenir Sheet**

**Litho.**

**1489** A339 $10 Text at top in tan, denomination in black 2.60 2.60

Art A340

Designs: $1.40, Douglas Castle, painting by unknown Chinese artist. $2.40, Crab, sculpture by Cheung Yee. $3, The Racecourse - Amateur Jockeys Close to a Carriage, painting by Edgar Degas. $5, The Horse, sculpture by Raymond Duchamp-Villon.

*Perf. 13 Syncopated*

**2012, May 3 Litho.**

**Granite Paper**

**1490-1493** A340 Set of 4 3.00 3.00

*1493a* Souvenir sheet of 4, #1490-1493 3.00 3.00

See France Nos. 4201-4205.

Festivals — A341

Designs: $1.40, Tin Hau Festival. $2.40, Kwun Yum Festival. $3, Birthday of the Buddha. No. 1497, $5, Tuen Ng Festival.

No. 1498, $5, Mid-autumn Festival.

*Perf. 13¾x14 Syncopated*

**2012, May 22**

**Granite Paper**

**1494-1497** A341 Set of 4 3.00 3.00

**Souvenir Sheet**

**1498** A341 $5 multi 1.40 1.40

Working Dogs — A342

Designs: $1.40, Beagle (quarantine detector dog) and emblem of Agriculture, Fisheries and Conservation Department. $1.80, German shepherd (correctional services dog) and emblem of Correctional Services Department. $2.40, English Springer spaniel (customs detector dog) and emblem of Customs and Excise Department. $2.50, Labrador retriever (fire investigation dog) and emblem of Fire Services Department. $3, Labrador retriever (quarantine detector dog) and emblem of Food and Environmental Hygiene Department. No. 1504, $5, Malinois (police dog) and emblem of Police Force.

No. 1505, Beagle, German shepherd, English Springer spaniel, Labrador retrievers, and Malinois.

*Perf. 13½x14¼ Syncopated*

**2012, June 6**

**Granite Paper**

**1499-1504** A342 Set of 6 4.25 4.25

**Souvenir Sheet**

*Perf. 13¼x13 Syncopated*

**1505** A342 $5 multi 1.40 1.40

No. 1505 contains one 100x40mm stamp. A booklet containing panes of Nos. 1499-1500, 1501-1502, and 1503-1504, respectively, sold for $45.

Souvenir Sheet

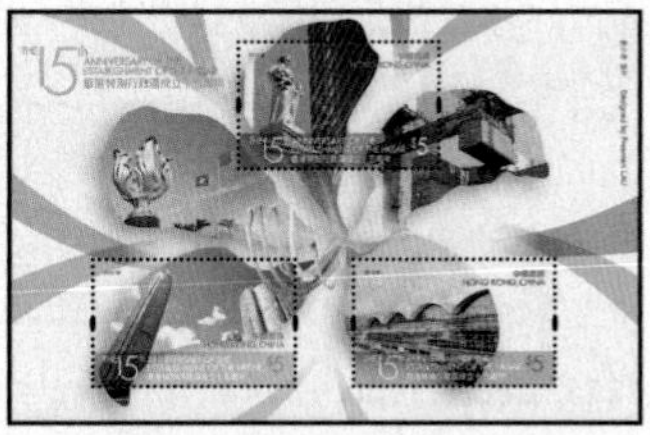

Hong Kong Special Administrative Region, 15th Anniv. — A343

No. 1506 — Various Hong Kong landmarks and panel in: a, Blue. b, Yellow. c, Green.

*Perf. 13½x13 Syncopated*

**2012, June 25**

**Granite Paper**

**1506** A343 $5 Sheet of 3, #a-c 4.00 4.00

On June 19, 2012, Hong Kong issued the stamps pictured above, having franking values of $1.40 and $3 respectively. The stamps were each printed in sheets of 12 + 12 non-personalizable labels depicting various infants. The sheets sold for $40 and $66 respectively. Sheets with other non-personalizable label designs were made available later.

2012 Summer Olympics, London A344

Designs: $1.40, Windsurfing, rowing, "2." $2.40, Badminton, archery, "0." $3, Table tennis, cycling, "1." $5, Swimming, track, "2."

**2012, July 27** ***Perf. 13¾ Syncopated***

**1507-1510** A344 Set of 4 3.00 3.00

*1510a* Souvenir sheet of 4, #1507-1510 3.00 3.00

Delicacies — A345

Designs: $1.40, Egg tart and milk tea. $2.40, Wontons. $3, Roast goose. $5, Crab.

*Perf. 14¼x14 Syncopated*

**2012, Aug. 30 Granite Paper**

**1511-1514** A345 Set of 4 3.00 3.00

*1514a* Souvenir sheet of 4, #1511-1514 3.00 3.00

Souvenir Sheet

Great Wall of China — A346

**Granite Paper**

*Perf. 13¼x14 Syncopated*

**Litho. & Silk-screened**

**2012, Sept. 17**

**1515** A346 $10 multi 2.60 2.60

Signs of the Zodiac — A347

Designs: Nos. 1516, 1528, Capricorn. Nos. 1517, 1529, Aquarius. Nos. 1518, 1530, Pisces. Nos. 1519, 1531, Aries. Nos. 1520, 1532, Taurus. Nos. 1521, 1533, Gemini. Nos. 1522, 1534, Cancer. Nos. 1523, 1535, Leo. Nos. 1524, 1536, Virgo. Nos. 1525, 1537, Libra. Nos. 1526, 1538, Scorpio. Nos. 1527, 1539, Sagittarius.

**Granite Paper (#1516-1527)**

*Perf. 14 Syncopated*

**2012, Nov. 1 Litho.**

| | | | | |
|---|---|---|---|---|
| **1516** | A347 | $1.40 multi | .35 | .35 |
| **1517** | A347 | $1.40 multi | .35 | .35 |
| **1518** | A347 | $1.40 multi | .35 | .35 |
| **1519** | A347 | $1.40 multi | .35 | .35 |
| **1520** | A347 | $1.40 multi | .35 | .35 |
| **1521** | A347 | $1.40 multi | .35 | .35 |
| **1522** | A347 | $1.40 multi | .35 | .35 |
| **1523** | A347 | $1.40 multi | .35 | .35 |
| **1524** | A347 | $1.40 multi | .35 | .35 |
| **1525** | A347 | $1.40 multi | .35 | .35 |
| **1526** | A347 | $1.40 multi | .35 | .35 |
| **1527** | A347 | $1.40 multi | .35 | .35 |
| *a.* | | Souvenir sheet of 12, #1516-1527 | 4.25 | 4.25 |
| | | *Nos. 1516-1527 (12)* | 4.20 | 4.20 |

**Self-Adhesive**

*Die Cut Perf. 14 Syncopated*

| | | | | |
|---|---|---|---|---|
| **1528** | A347 | $1.40 multi | .35 | .35 |
| **1529** | A347 | $1.40 multi | .35 | .35 |
| **1530** | A347 | $1.40 multi | .35 | .35 |
| **1531** | A347 | $1.40 multi | .35 | .35 |
| **1532** | A347 | $1.40 multi | .35 | .35 |
| **1533** | A347 | $1.40 multi | .35 | .35 |
| **1534** | A347 | $1.40 multi | .35 | .35 |
| **1535** | A347 | $1.40 multi | .35 | .35 |
| **1536** | A347 | $1.40 multi | .35 | .35 |
| **1537** | A347 | $1.40 multi | .35 | .35 |
| **1538** | A347 | $1.40 multi | .35 | .35 |
| **1539** | A347 | $1.40 multi | .35 | .35 |
| *a.* | | Vert. coil strip of 12, #1528-1539 | 4.25 | |
| *b.* | | Booklet pane of 12, #1528-1539 | 4.25 | |
| | | *Nos. 1528-1539 (12)* | 4.20 | 4.20 |

A sheet containing Nos. 1516-1527 + 12 non-personalizable labels sold for $40. Sheets containing eight stamps of any of Nos. 1516-1527 + eight non-personalizable labels sold for $30 each.

Insects
A348

Designs: $1.40, Spittle bug. $1.80, Flower mantid. $2.40, Mangrove China-mark moth. $2.25, White dragontail butterfly. $3, Four-spot midget damselfly. $5, Hong Kong bent-winged firefly.

***Perf. 13¼x14 Syncopated***

**2012, Nov. 22 — Granite Paper**

**1540-1545** A348 Set of 6 — 4.25 4.25
*1545a* Souvenir sheet of 6, #1540-1545 — 4.25 4.25

Hong Kong Postage Stamps, 150th Anniv.
A349

Designs: $1.40, Hong Kong #1, quill and inkwell. $1.80, Hong Kong #2, fountain pen. $2.40, Hong Kong #3, ball-point pen. $2.50, Hong Kong #4, typewriter. $3, Hong Kong #5, computer keyboard. $5, Hong Kong #6, quick response code.
$10, Hong Kong #7, bar code, horiz.

**Granite Paper**

**2012, Dec. 8 *Perf. 13¾ Syncopated***

**1546-1551** A349 Set of 6 — 4.25 4.25
*1548a* Booklet pane of 3, #1546-1548 — 2.75 —
*1551a* Booklet pane of 3, #1549-1551 — 5.25 —

**Souvenir Sheet**

***Perf. 13½ Syncopated***

**1552** A349 $10 multi — 2.60 2.60
*a.* Booklet pane of 1 — 5.00 —
Complete booklet, #1548a, 1551a, 1552a — 13.00

No. 1552 contains one 67x24mm stamp. Complete booklet sold for $50.

New Year 2013 (Year of the Snake)
A350

Designs: $1.40, Paper-cutting of snake. $2.40, Painting of snake. $3, Seal carvings depicting snake and Chinese character for snake. $5, Jade carving of snake.
No. 1557: a, Dragon and clouds, green background. b, Snake.
No. 1558, Snake, hexagons with Chinese characters. No. 1559, Snake, no hexagons.

***Perf. 13¼x14 Syncopated***

**2013, Jan. 26 — Litho.**

**Granite Paper**

**1553-1556** A350 Set of 4 — 3.00 3.00

**Litho. With Foil Application (#1557a, 1558), Litho. With Metal Affixed (#1557b)**

***Perf. 13¼ Syncopated***

**1557** A350 $50 Sheet of 2, #a-b — 26.00 26.00

**Souvenir Sheets**

**1558** A350 $10 multi — 2.60 2.60

**Litho.**

**On Silk-faced Paper**

**1559** A350 $50 multi — 13.00 13.00

Nos. 1558 and 1559 each contain one 45x45mm stamp.

## SEMI-POSTAL STAMPS

**Catalogue values for unused stamps in this section are for Never Hinged items.**

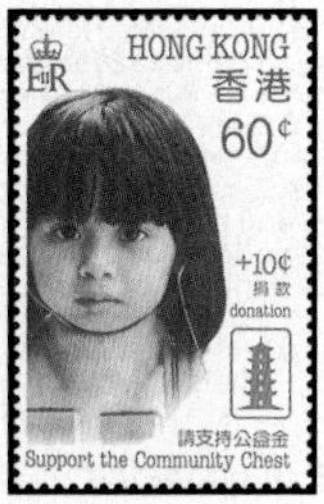


Community Chest of Hong Kong — SP1

**1988, Nov. 30 — Litho. — *Perf. 14½***

**B1** SP1 60c +10c Girl — .60 .35
**B2** SP1 $1.40 +20c Elderly woman — .75 .70
**B3** SP1 $1.80 +30c Blind youth — 1.75 1.00
**B4** SP1 $5 +$1 Mother and child — 4.25 2.75
*Nos. B1-B4 (4)* — 7.35 4.80

Surtax for the social welfare organization.

## POSTAGE DUE STAMPS

Scales Showing Letter Overweight — D1

**1923, Dec. — Typo. — Wmk. 4 — *Perf. 14***

**J1** D1 1c brown — 2.75 .70
*a.* Chalky paper, wmkd. sideways — 1.60 *3.50*
**J2** D1 2c green — 13.00 5.25
**J3** D1 4c red — 37.50 7.50
**J4** D1 6c orange — 35.00 15.00
**J5** D1 10c ultramarine — 30.00 9.00
*Nos. J1-J5 (5)* — 118.25 37.45
Set, never hinged — 300.00

No. J1a issued Mar. 21, 1956.

**1938-47 — *Perf. 14***

**J6** D1 2c gray — 1.40 *10.00*
**J7** D1 4c orange yellow — 2.50 *10.00*
**J8** D1 6c carmine — 10.00 6.00
**J9** D1 8c fawn ('46) — 6.00 *32.50*
**J10** D1 10c violet — 17.50 7.50
**J11** D1 20c black ('46) — 12.50 3.50
**J12** D1 50c blue ('47) — 40.00 16.00
*Nos. J6-J12 (7)* — 89.90 85.50
Set, never hinged — 190.00

Nos. J6-J7 and J10 exist on both ordinary and chalky paper.

**Catalogue values for unused stamps in this section, from this point to the end of the section, are for Never Hinged items.**

**Wmk. 314 Sideways**

**1965-69 — *Perf. 14***

**J13** D1 4c orange yellow — 9.00 *30.00*
**J14** D1 5c orange ver ('69) — 3.75 *5.25*
*a.* 5c carmine, wmk. upright ('67) — 4.00 *5.00*
**J15** D1 10c purple ('67) — 4.75 *6.00*
**J16** D1 20c black — 10.00 4.50
**J17** D1 50c dark blue — 37.50 7.00
*a.* Wmk. upright ('70) — 50.00 11.50
*Nos. J13-J17 (5)* — 65.00 52.75

Size of 5c, 21x18mm.; others, 22x18mm.

**Wmk. 314 Upright**

**1972-74 — *Perf. 13½x14***

**Glazed Ordinary Paper**

**J18** D1 5c red brown ('74) — 3.00 *6.00*

***Perf. 14x14½***

**J19** D1 10c lilac — 7.00 5.00
**J20** D1 20c black — 8.50 7.00
**J21** D1 50c dull blue — 6.00 *11.00*
*Nos. J18-J21 (4)* — 24.50 29.00

**1978 — Wmk. 373**

**J22** D1 10c lilac — 1.00 *5.50*
*f.* Chalk-surfaced paper — 1.00 *2.25*
**J22A** D1 20c black — 1.50 *7.50*
*g.* Chalk-surfaced paper — 1.75 *2.50*
**J22B** D1 50c dull blue — 1.50 *6.00*
*h.* Chalk-surfaced paper — 1.75 *3.00*
**J22C** D1 $1 yellow — 14.00 14.00
*i.* Chalk-surfaced paper — 1.50 *4.25*
*Nos. J22-J22C (4)* — 18.00 33.00

Size of $1, 20½x17mm; others, 22x18mm. Issued: Nos. J22-J22C, 3/19; J22f-J22i, 12/15.

**1986, Jan. 11 — Unwmk.**

**Chalk-surfaced Paper**

**J22D** D1 50c dull blue — 2.25 *5.75*
**J22E** D1 $1 yellow — 3.00 *8.00*

D2

***Perf. 14x15***

**1986, Mar. 25 — Litho. — Unwmk.**

**J23** D2 10c light green — .25 *.50*
**J24** D2 20c dark red brown — .25 *.50*
**J25** D2 50c lilac — .25 .25
**J26** D2 $1 light orange — .25 .25
**J27** D2 $5 grayish blue — 1.00 *1.75*
**J28** D2 $10 rose red — 2.00 *3.50*
*Nos. J23-J28 (6)* — 4.00 *6.75*

D3

***Perf. 14x14¾***

**2004, Sept. 23 — Litho. — Unwmk.**

**J29** D3 10c dark blue — .25 *.50*
**J30** D3 20c blue — .25 *.50*
**J31** D3 50c orange — .30 .25
**J32** D3 $1 pink — .65 *.75*
**J33** D3 $5 olive green — 1.60 *1.75*
**J34** D3 $10 cerise — 3.50 3.50
*Nos. J29-J34 (6)* — 6.55 7.25

## OCCUPATION STAMPS

### Issued under Japanese Occupation

War Factory Girl — A144

Gen. Maresuke Nogi — A84

Admiral Heihachiro Togo — A86

Stamps of Japan, 1942-43 Surcharged in Black

**Wmk. 257**

**1945, Apr. — Typo. — *Perf. 13***

**N1** A144 1½y on 1s org brn — 40.00 35.00
**N2** A84 3y on 2s ver — 14.00 *30.00*
**N3** A86 5y on 5s brn lake — 975.00 175.00
*Nos. N1-N3 (3)* — 1,029. 240.00

No. N1 has eleven characters.

# HORTA

'hor-tə

LOCATION — An administrative district of the Azores, consisting of the islands of Pico, Fayal, Flores and Corvo
GOVT. — A district of the Republic of Portugal
AREA — 305 sq. mi.
POP. — 49,000 (approx.)
CAPITAL — Horta

1000 Reis = 1 Milreis

King Carlos
A1 A2

**Chalk-surfaced Paper**

***Perf. 11½, 12½, 13½***

**1892-93 — Typo. — Unwmk.**

**1** A1 5r yellow — 2.00 1.50
**2** A1 10r reddish violet — 2.00 1.75
**3** A1 15r chocolate — 2.00 2.00
**4** A1 20r lavender — 4.00 3.00
**5** A1 25r dp grn, perf. 11½ — 4.25 1.00
*a.* Perf. 13½ — 5.00 3.75
**6** A1 50r blue — 7.00 3.00
*a.* Perf. 13½ — 9.00 5.25
**7** A1 75r carmine — 6.50 4.00
**8** A1 80r yellow green — 9.00 6.00
**9** A1 100r brn, *yel* ('93) — 35.00 10.00
*a.* Perf. 12½ — 125.00 90.00
**10** A1 150r car, *rose* ('93) — 45.00 32.50
**11** A1 200r dk bl, *bl* ('93) — 50.00 32.50
**12** A1 300r dark blue ('93) — 50.00 35.00
*Nos. 1-12 (12)* — 216.75 132.25

Bisects of No. 1 were used in Aug. 1894. Value, on newsprint, $16.
*The reprints have shiny white gum and clean-cut perforation 13½. The white paper is thinner than that of the originals. Value unused, $12 each.*

**1897-1905 — *Perf. 11½***

**Name and Value in Black Except 500r**

**13** A2 2½r gray — .50 .30
**14** A2 5r orange — .50 .30
**15** A2 10r lt green — .50 .30
**16** A2 15r brown — 4.00 2.50
**17** A2 15r gray grn ('99) — 1.25 .80
**18** A2 20r gray violet — 1.75 .85
**19** A2 25r sea green — 2.25 .45
**20** A2 25r car rose ('99) — .90 .50
**21** A2 50r blue — 3.00 .70
**22** A2 50r ultra ('05) — 15.00 7.00
**23** A2 65r slate blue ('98) — .70 .55
**24** A2 75r rose — 1.90 .95
**25** A2 75r brn, *yel* ('05) — 18.00 10.00
**26** A2 80r violet — 1.25 1.10
**27** A2 100r dk blue, *bl* — 1.75 .95
**28** A2 115r org brn, *pink* ('98) — 4.00 1.50
**29** A2 130r gray brn, *buff* ('98) — 4.00 1.50
**30** A2 150r lt brn, *buff* — 4.00 1.50
**31** A2 180r sl, *pnksh* ('98) — 4.00 1.75
**32** A2 200r red vio, *pale lil* — 5.50 4.00
**33** A2 300r dk blue, *rose* — 9.00 6.75
**34** A2 500r blk & red, *bl* — 12.00 8.50
*Nos. 13-34 (22)* — 95.75 52.75

Stamps of Portugal replaced those of Horta.

## HUNGARY

ˈhəŋ-g‚ə-ˌrē

LOCATION — Central Europe
GOVT. — Republic
AREA — 35,911 sq. mi.
POP. — 10,186,372 (1999 est.)
CAPITAL — Budapest

Prior to World War I, Hungary together with Austria comprised the Austro-Hungarian Empire. The Hungarian post became independent on May 1, 1867. During 1850-1871 stamps listed under Austria were also used in Hungary. Copies showing clear Hungarian cancels sell for substantially more.

100 Krajczár (Kreuzer) = 1 Forint 100 Fillér = 1 Korona (1900) 100 Fillér = 1 Pengö (1926) 100 Fillér = 1 Forint (1946)

**Catalogue values for unused stamps in this country are for Never Hinged items, beginning with Scott 503 in the regular postage section, Scott B92 in the semi-postal section, Scott C35 in the airpost section, Scott CB1 in the airpost semi-postal section, Scott F1 in the registrtation section, Scott J130 in the postage due section, and Scott Q9 in the parcel post section.**

### Watermarks

Wmk. 91 — "ZEITUNGS-MARKEN" in Double-lined Capitals across the Sheet

Wmk. 106 — Multiple Star

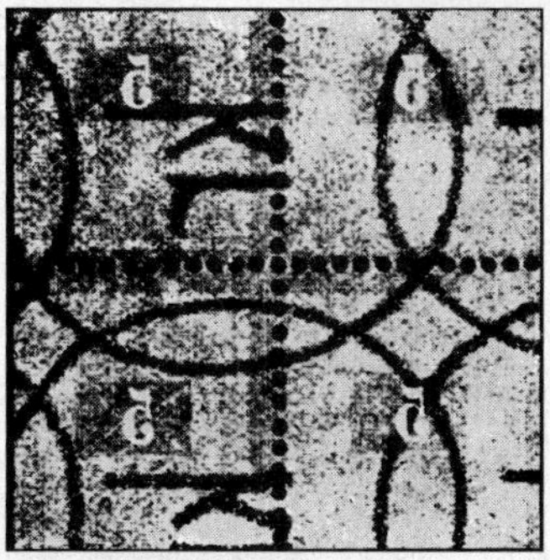

Wmk. 132 — kr in Oval

Wmk. 133 — Four Double Crosses

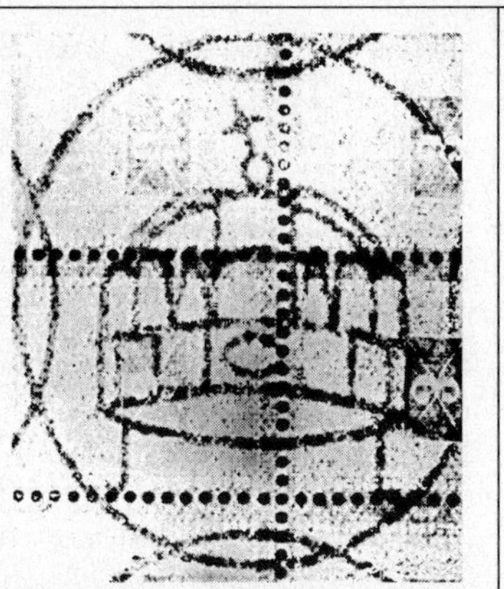

Wmk. 135 — Crown in Oval or Circle, Sideways

Wmk. 136

Wmk. 136a

Wmk. 137 — Double Cross

Wmk. 210 — Double Cross on Pyramid

Wmk. 266 — Double Barred Cross, Wreath and Crown

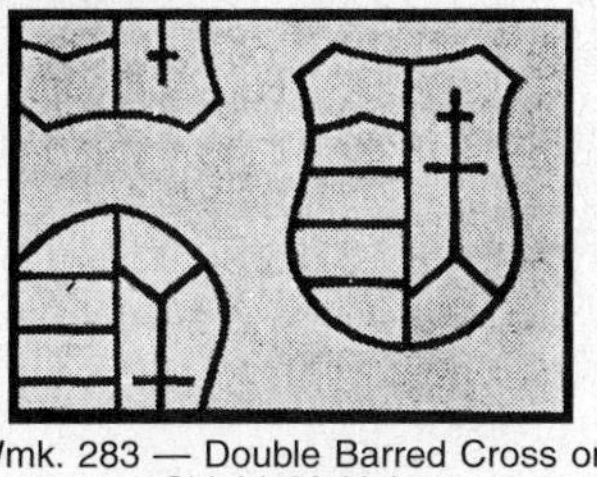

Wmk. 283 — Double Barred Cross on Shield, Multiple

Watermarks 132, 135, 136 and 136a can be found normal, reversed, inverted, or reversed and inverted.

Values for unused stamps are for examples with original gum as defined in the catalogue introduction. Very fine examples of Nos. 1-12 will have perforations touching the framelines on one or two sides due to imperfect perforating methods. Stamps with perfs clear on all four sides are very scarce and will command substantial premiums.

### Issues of the Monarchy

Franz Josef I — A1

**1871 Unwmk. Litho.** ***Perf. 9½***

| | | | | |
|---|---|---|---|---|
| **1** | A1 | 2k orange | 325.00 | 90.00 |
| *a.* | | 2k yellow | 1,200. | 250.00 |
| **2** | A1 | 3k lt green | 1,000. | 550.00 |
| **3** | A1 | 5k rose | 450.00 | 20.00 |
| *a.* | | 5k brick red | 900.00 | 75.00 |
| **4** | A1 | 10k blue | 1,250. | 90.00 |
| *a.* | | 10k pale blue | 1,400. | 150.00 |
| **5** | A1 | 15k yellow brn | 1,250. | 100.00 |
| **6** | A1 | 25k violet | 1,000. | 175.00 |
| *a.* | | 25k bright violet | 1,500. | 300.00 |

The first printing of No. 1, in dark yellow, was not issued because of spots on the King's face. A few stamps were used at Pest in 1873. Value, $2,500.

**1871-72 Engr.**

| | | | | |
|---|---|---|---|---|
| **7** | A1 | 2k orange | 40.00 | 7.50 |
| *a.* | | 2k yellow | 175.00 | 20.00 |
| *b.* | | Bisect on cover | | — |
| **8** | A1 | 3k green | 125.00 | 25.00 |
| *a.* | | 3k blue green | 150.00 | 30.00 |
| **9** | A1 | 5k rose | 110.00 | 1.75 |
| *a.* | | 5k brick red | 200.00 | 8.00 |
| **10** | A1 | 10k deep blue | 300.00 | 10.00 |
| **11** | A1 | 15k brown | 475.00 | 15.00 |
| *a.* | | 15k copper brown | — | 1,500. |
| *b.* | | 15k black brown | 875.00 | 85.00 |
| **12** | A1 | 25k lilac | 200.00 | 40.00 |
| | | *Nos. 7-12 (6)* | 1,250. | 99.25 |

*Reprints are perf. 11½ and watermarked "kr" in oval. Value, set $225.*

Crown of St. Stephen — A2

**1874-76** ***Perf. 13***

| | | | | |
|---|---|---|---|---|
| **13** | A2 | 2k red violet | 30.00 | 2.00 |
| *a.* | | 2k violet | 35.00 | 2.50 |
| **14** | A2 | 3k yellow green | 30.00 | 2.00 |
| *a.* | | 3k blue green | 37.50 | 2.50 |
| **15** | A2 | 5k red | 10.00 | .50 |
| *a.* | | 5k brick red | 45.00 | 1.50 |
| *b.* | | 5k lilac red | 15.00 | .75 |
| *c.* | | 5k rose | 10.00 | .40 |
| **16** | A2 | 10k blue | 35.00 | .75 |
| **17** | A2 | 20k grnsh gray | 700.00 | 9.00 |
| *a.* | | 20k gray | 750.00 | 10.00 |
| | | *Nos. 13-17 (5)* | 805.00 | 14.25 |

***Perf. 11½***

| | | | | |
|---|---|---|---|---|
| *13b* | A2 | 2k red violet | 45.00 | 5.00 |
| *c.* | | 2k violet | — | 6.00 |
| *d.* | | 2k rose lilac | 75.00 | 4.50 |
| *e.* | | 2k gray blue | 60.00 | 3.75 |
| *14b* | A2 | 3k yellow green | 50.00 | 4.00 |
| *c.* | | 3k blue green | 60.00 | 5.00 |
| *15d* | A2 | 5k red | 60.00 | 1.00 |
| *e.* | | 5k rose | 50.00 | .75 |
| *16a* | A2 | 10k blue | 75.00 | 5.00 |
| *17b* | A2 | 20k gray | 700.00 | 45.00 |

***Perf. 13x11½***

| | | | | |
|---|---|---|---|---|
| *13f* | A2 | 2k red violet | 180.00 | 30.00 |
| *g.* | | 2k rose lilac | 200.00 | 30.00 |
| *14d* | A2 | 3k yellow green | 125.00 | 4.50 |
| *15f* | A2 | 5k lilac red | 250.00 | 12.00 |
| *g.* | | 5k rose | 300.00 | 15.00 |
| *16b* | A2 | 10k blue | 250.00 | 6.00 |
| *17c* | A2 | 20k gray | 800.00 | 50.00 |

***Perf. 11½x13***

| | | | | |
|---|---|---|---|---|
| *13h* | A2 | 2k red violet | 60.00 | 5.00 |
| *f.* | | 2k rose lilac | 100.00 | 4.00 |
| *g.* | | 2k gray blue | 75.00 | 3.75 |
| *15h* | A2 | 5k red | 75.00 | 1.00 |
| *17d* | A2 | 20k gray | — | 100.00 |

***Perf. 9½***

| | | | | |
|---|---|---|---|---|
| *14e* | A2 | 3k green | *7,500.* | *2,500.* |

All examples of the 5k perf 9½ are counterfeit.

**1881 Wmk. 132** ***Perf. 11½***

| | | | | |
|---|---|---|---|---|
| **18** | A2 | 2k lilac | 3.50 | .40 |
| *a.* | | 2k violet | 3.50 | .40 |
| *b.* | | 2k gray blue | 4.50 | .50 |
| **19** | A2 | 3k blue green | 3.50 | .40 |
| *a.* | | 3k yellow green | 4.50 | .60 |
| **20** | A2 | 5k rose | 2.50 | .25 |
| **21** | A2 | 10k blue | 6.00 | .40 |
| *a.* | | 10k pale blue | 7.00 | .60 |
| **22** | A2 | 20k gray | 4.50 | .65 |
| *a.* | | 20k greenish gray | 5.00 | .75 |
| | | *Nos. 18-22 (5)* | 20.00 | 2.10 |

***Perf. 13***

| | | | | |
|---|---|---|---|---|
| *18c* | A2 | 2k violet | 150.00 | 20.00 |
| *d.* | | 2k gray blue | 120.00 | 10.00 |
| *19b* | A2 | 3k blue green | 90.00 | 4.00 |
| *c.* | | 3k yellow green | 100.00 | 5.50 |
| *20a* | A2 | 5k rose | 120.00 | 4.00 |
| *21b* | A2 | 10k blue | 75.00 | 5.00 |
| *22b* | A2 | 20k gray | 350.00 | 15.00 |

***Perf. 13x11½***

| | | | | |
|---|---|---|---|---|
| *18e* | A2 | 2k violet | — | 40.00 |
| *19d* | A2 | 3k blue green | 160.00 | 6.00 |
| *e.* | | 3k yellow green | — | 8.00 |
| *20b* | A2 | 5k rose | — | 15.00 |
| *21c* | A2 | 10k blue | — | 8.00 |
| *22c* | A2 | 20k gray | — | 12.50 |

***Perf. 11½x13***

| | | | | |
|---|---|---|---|---|
| *18f* | A2 | 2k violet | 200.00 | 9.00 |
| *g.* | | 2k gray blue | 180.00 | 6.00 |
| *19f* | A2 | 3k blue green | — | 60.00 |
| *g.* | | 3k yellow green | — | 75.00 |
| *20c* | A2 | 5k rose | 150.00 | 1.00 |
| *21d* | A2 | 10k blue | — | 1.75 |
| *22d* | A2 | 20k gray | — | 40.00 |

***Perf. 12x11½***

| | | | | |
|---|---|---|---|---|
| *18h* | A2 | 2k lilac | 1.00 | .25 |
| *i.* | | 2k violet | 15.00 | 1.20 |
| *19h* | A2 | 3k blue green | 1.00 | .25 |
| *20d* | A2 | 5k rose | 2.50 | .25 |
| *21e* | A2 | 10k blue | 3.00 | .25 |
| *22e* | A2 | 20k gray | 300.00 | 7.50 |

Crown of St. Stephen — A3

Design A3 has an overall burelage of dots. Compare with design N3.

**1888-98 Typo. *Perf. 11½, 12x11½***

**Numerals in Black**

| | | | | |
|---|---|---|---|---|
| **22A** | A3 | 1k black, one plate | 1.25 | .30 |
| *c.* | | "1" printed separately | 15.00 | 3.00 |
| **23** | A3 | 2k red violet | 1.50 | .50 |
| *a.* | | Perf. 11½ | 725.00 | 50.00 |
| **24** | A3 | 3k green | 1.75 | .40 |
| *a.* | | Perf. 11½ | 50.00 | 15.00 |
| **25** | A3 | 5k rose | 2.00 | .25 |
| *a.* | | Perf. 11½ | 65.00 | 1.75 |
| **26** | A3 | 8k orange | 6.00 | .60 |
| *a.* | | "8" double | *150.00* | |
| **27** | A3 | 10k blue | 5.00 | 1.25 |
| *a.* | | Perf. 11½ | 450.00 | 325.00 |
| **28** | A3 | 12k brown & green | 12.50 | 1.00 |
| **29** | A3 | 15k claret & blue | 10.00 | .40 |
| **30** | A3 | 20k gray | 7.50 | 2.00 |
| *a.* | | Perf. 11½ | *1,400.* | *600.00* |
| **31** | A3 | 24k brn vio & red | 22.50 | 1.25 |
| **32** | A3 | 30k ol grn & brn | 25.00 | .35 |
| **33** | A3 | 50k red & org | 40.00 | 1.50 |

**Numerals in Red**

| | | | | |
|---|---|---|---|---|
| **34** | A3 | 1fo gray bl & sil | 175.00 | 2.25 |
| *a.* | | Perf. 11½ | 190.00 | 3.50 |
| **35** | A3 | 3fo lilac brn & gold | 25.00 | 12.00 |
| | | *Nos. 22A-35 (14)* | 335.00 | 24.05 |

**1898-99 *Perf. 12x11½***

**Numerals in Black**

**Wmk. 135 (Oval)**

| | | | | |
|---|---|---|---|---|
| **35A** | A3 | 1k black | 1.50 | .50 |
| **36** | A3 | 2k violet | 6.00 | .50 |
| **37** | A3 | 3k green | 4.00 | .60 |
| **38** | A3 | 5k rose | 5.00 | .40 |
| **39** | A3 | 8k orange | 17.50 | 4.00 |
| **40** | A3 | 10k blue | 5.00 | 1.00 |
| **41** | A3 | 12k red brn & grn | 75.00 | 9.00 |
| **42** | A3 | 15k rose & blue | 5.00 | .75 |
| **43** | A3 | 20k gray | 35.00 | 2.00 |
| **44** | A3 | 24k vio brn & red | 6.00 | 4.75 |
| **45** | A3 | 30k ol grn & brn | 40.00 | 1.50 |
| **46** | A3 | 50k dull red & org | 100.00 | 15.00 |
| | | *Nos. 35A-46 (12)* | 300.00 | 40.00 |

***Perf. 11½***

| | | | | |
|---|---|---|---|---|
| *35Ab* | A3 | 1k black | 40.00 | 7.50 |
| *36a* | A3 | 2k violet | 125.00 | 20.00 |
| *37a* | A3 | 3k green | 100.00 | 15.00 |
| *38a* | A3 | 5k rose | 140.00 | 15.00 |
| *39a* | A3 | 8k orange | 250.00 | 120.00 |
| *40a* | A3 | 10k blue | 150.00 | 60.00 |
| *41a* | A3 | 12k red brn & grn | 375.00 | 100.00 |
| *42a* | A3 | 15k rose & blue | 250.00 | 60.00 |
| *43a* | A3 | 20k gray | 375.00 | 75.00 |
| *44a* | A3 | 24k vio brn & red | 450.00 | 200.00 |
| *45a* | A3 | 30k ol grn & brn | 250.00 | 60.00 |
| *46a* | A3 | 50k dull red & org | 500.00 | 250.00 |

**Wmk. 135 (Circle)**

***Perf. 12x11½***

| | | | | |
|---|---|---|---|---|
| *35Ac* | A3 | 1k black | 14.00 | 2.50 |
| *36b* | A3 | 2k violet | 7.50 | 1.50 |
| *37b* | A3 | 3k green | 8.50 | 2.00 |
| *38b* | A3 | 5k rose | 10.00 | 1.00 |
| *39b* | A3 | 8k orange | 50.00 | 25.00 |
| *40b* | A3 | 10k blue | 75.00 | 4.00 |
| *41b* | A3 | 12k red brn & grn | 60.00 | 30.00 |
| *42b* | A3 | 15k rose & blue | 250.00 | 4.00 |
| *43b* | A3 | 20k gray | 5.00 | 6.00 |
| *44b* | A3 | 24k vio brn & red | 1,250. | 45.00 |
| *45b* | A3 | 30k ol grn & brn | 5.00 | 4.00 |
| *46b* | A3 | 50k dull red & org | 15.00 | 35.00 |

***Perf. 11½***

| | | | | |
|---|---|---|---|---|
| *35Ad* | A3 | 1k black | 50.00 | 15.00 |
| *36c* | A3 | 2k violet | 200.00 | 25.00 |
| *37c* | A3 | 3k green | 200.00 | 40.00 |
| *38c* | A3 | 5k rose | 100.00 | 15.00 |
| *39c* | A3 | 8k orange | 80.00 | 12.50 |
| *40c* | A3 | 10k blue | 450.00 | 80.00 |
| *41c* | A3 | 12k red brn & grn | 750.00 | 300.00 |
| *42c* | A3 | 15k rose & blue | 450.00 | 200.00 |
| *43c* | A3 | 20k gray | 1,500. | 350.00 |
| *44c* | A3 | 24k vio brn & red | 2,250. | 600.00 |
| *45c* | A3 | 30k ol grn & brn | 750.00 | 150.00 |
| *46c* | A3 | 50k dull red & org | 500.00 | 400.00 |

In the watermark with circles, a four-pointed star and "VI" appear four times in the sheet in the large spaces between the intersecting circles. The paper with the circular watermark is often yellowish and thinner than that with the oval watermark.

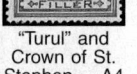

"Turul" and Crown of St. Stephen — A4

Franz Josef I Wearing Hungarian Crown — A5

**1900-04 Wmk. 135 *Perf. 12x11½***

**Numerals in Black**

| | | | | |
|---|---|---|---|---|
| **47** | A4 | 1f gray | .75 | .30 |
| *a.* | | 1f dull lilac | .75 | .30 |
| **48** | A4 | 2f olive yel | 1.00 | .75 |
| **49** | A4 | 3f orange | .75 | .25 |
| **50** | A4 | 4f violet | 1.00 | .25 |
| *a.* | | Booklet pane of 6 | *60.00* | |
| **51** | A4 | 5f emerald | 2.50 | .25 |
| *a.* | | Booklet pane of 6 | *35.00* | |
| **52** | A4 | 6f claret | 1.50 | .60 |
| *a.* | | 6f violet brown | 2.50 | .50 |
| **53** | A4 | 6f bister ('01) | 20.00 | 1.20 |
| **54** | A4 | 6f olive grn ('02) | 7.50 | .50 |
| **55** | A4 | 10f carmine | 4.00 | .25 |
| *a.* | | Booklet pane of 6 | *35.00* | |
| **56** | A4 | 12f violet ('04) | 2.00 | 1.25 |
| **57** | A4 | 20f brown ('01) | 4.00 | .60 |
| **58** | A4 | 25f blue | 5.00 | .60 |
| *a.* | | Booklet pane of 6 | *60.00* | |
| **59** | A4 | 30f orange brn | 24.00 | .25 |
| **60** | A4 | 35f red vio ('01) | 14.00 | 1.00 |
| *a.* | | Booklet pane of 6 | *100.00* | |
| **61** | A4 | 50f lake | 12.00 | 1.00 |
| **62** | A4 | 60f green | 45.00 | .30 |
| **63** | A5 | 1k brown red | 37.50 | .75 |
| **64** | A5 | 2k gray blue ('01) | 600.00 | 22.50 |
| **65** | A5 | 3k sea green | 90.00 | 3.75 |
| **66** | A5 | 5k vio brown ('01) | 125.00 | 40.00 |
| | | *Nos. 47-66 (20)* | 997.50 | 76.35 |

The watermark on Nos. 47 to 66 is always the circular form of Wmk. 135 described in the note following No. 46.

Pairs imperf between of Nos. 47-49, 51 were favor prints made for an influential Budapest collector. Value, $90 each.

For overprints & surcharges see #B35-B52, 2N1-2N3, 6N1-6N6, 6NB127N1-7N6, 7NB1, 10N1.

***Perf. 11½***

| | | | | |
|---|---|---|---|---|
| *47b* | A4 | 1f gray | 350.00 | 80.00 |
| *48a* | A4 | 2f olive yel | 350.00 | 60.00 |
| *49a* | A4 | 3f orange | 100.00 | 20.00 |
| *50b* | A4 | 4f violet | 225.00 | 12.50 |
| *51b* | A4 | 5f emerald | 50.00 | 3.75 |
| *52b* | A4 | 6f claret | — | 60.00 |
| *53a* | A4 | 6f bister ('01) | — | 110.00 |
| *54a* | A4 | 6f olive grn ('02) | — | 300.00 |
| *55b* | A4 | 10f carmine | 400.00 | 25.00 |
| *56a* | A4 | 12f violet ('04) | 250.00 | 80.00 |
| *57a* | A4 | 20f brown ('01) | — | 150.00 |
| *58b* | A4 | 25f blue | — | 75.00 |
| *59a* | A4 | 30f orange brn | — | 125.00 |
| *60b* | A4 | 35f red vio ('01) | — | 275.00 |
| *61a* | A4 | 50f lake | 400.00 | 75.00 |
| *62a* | A4 | 60f green | 600.00 | 150.00 |
| *63a* | A5 | 1k brown red | 175.00 | 15.00 |
| *64a* | A5 | 2k gray blue ('01) | — | 600.00 |
| *65a* | A5 | 3k sea green | — | *4,000.* |
| *66a* | A5 | 5k vio brown ('01) | — | 1,000. |



**1908-13 Wmk. 136 *Perf. 15***

| | | | | |
|---|---|---|---|---|
| **67** | A4 | 1f slate | .30 | .25 |
| **68** | A4 | 2f olive yellow | .25 | .25 |
| **69** | A4 | 3f orange | .30 | .25 |
| **70** | A4 | 5f emerald | .30 | .25 |
| *c.* | | Booklet pane of 6 | *100.00* | |
| **71** | A4 | 6f olive green | .30 | .25 |
| **72** | A4 | 10f carmine | .40 | .25 |
| *c.* | | Booklet pane of 6 | *100.00* | |
| **73** | A4 | 12f violet | .40 | .25 |
| **74** | A4 | 16f gray green ('13) | .50 | .50 |
| **75** | A4 | 20f dark brown | 7.50 | .25 |
| **76** | A4 | 25f blue | 6.25 | .25 |
| **77** | A4 | 30f orange brown | 7.50 | .25 |
| **78** | A4 | 35f red violet | 10.00 | .25 |
| **79** | A4 | 50f lake | 3.00 | .30 |
| **80** | A4 | 60f green | 9.00 | .25 |
| **81** | A5 | 1k brown red | 12.50 | .25 |
| **82** | A5 | 2k gray blue | 90.00 | .40 |
| **83** | A5 | 5k violet brown | 125.00 | 9.00 |
| | | *Nos. 67-83 (17)* | 273.50 | 13.45 |

Nos. 67-73, 75-83 exist imperf. Value, set $1,000.

**1904-05 Wmk. 136a *Perf. 12x11½***

| | | | | |
|---|---|---|---|---|
| *67a* | A4 | 1f slate | 2.50 | *2.50* |
| *68a* | A4 | 2f olive yellow | 5.00 | .30 |
| *69a* | A4 | 3f orange | 2.00 | .40 |
| *70a* | A4 | 5f emerald | 4.00 | .25 |
| *71a* | A4 | 6f olive green | 2.50 | .40 |
| *72a* | A4 | 10f carmine | 7.50 | .25 |
| *73a* | A4 | 12f violet | 4.00 | 3.00 |
| *75a* | A4 | 20f dark brown | 20.00 | 1.00 |
| *76a* | A4 | 25f blue | 40.00 | 1.00 |
| *77a* | A4 | 30f orange brown | 9.00 | .40 |
| *78a* | A4 | 35f red violet | 22.50 | .40 |
| *79a* | A4 | 50f lake | 15.00 | 4.00 |
| *c.* | | 50f magenta | 1.00 | *10.00* |
| *80a* | A4 | 60f green | 250.00 | .40 |
| *81a* | A5 | 1k brown red | 250.00 | .75 |
| *82a* | A5 | 2k gray blue | *900.00* | 50.00 |
| *c.* | | Perf. 11½ | *2,000.* | 150.00 |
| *83a* | A5 | 5k violet brown | 240.00 | 75.00 |
| | | *Nos. 67a-83a (16)* | *1,774.* | 140.05 |

**1906 *Perf. 15***

| | | | | |
|---|---|---|---|---|
| *67b* | A4 | 1f slate | 2.50 | .50 |
| *68b* | A4 | 2f olive yellow | 1.75 | .25 |
| *69b* | A4 | 3f orange | 2.25 | .25 |
| *70b* | A4 | 5f emerald | 2.00 | .25 |
| *71b* | A4 | 6f olive green | 2.00 | .25 |
| *72b* | A4 | 10f carmine | 2.50 | .25 |
| *73b* | A4 | 12f violet | 4.00 | .25 |
| *75b* | A4 | 20f dark brown | 10.00 | .30 |
| *76b* | A4 | 25f blue | 8.00 | .30 |
| *77b* | A4 | 30f orange brown | 10.00 | .25 |
| *78b* | A4 | 35f red violet | 50.00 | .25 |
| *79b* | A4 | 50f lake | 5.00 | 1.00 |
| *80b* | A4 | 60f green | 62.50 | .25 |
| *81b* | A5 | 1k brown red | 60.00 | .60 |
| *82b* | A5 | 2k gray blue | 225.00 | 8.00 |
| | | *Nos. 67b-82b (15)* | 447.50 | 12.95 |

**1913-16 Wmk. 137 Vert. *Perf. 15***

| | | | | |
|---|---|---|---|---|
| **84** | A4 | 1f slate | .25 | .25 |
| **85** | A4 | 2f olive yellow | .25 | .25 |
| **86** | A4 | 3f orange | .25 | .25 |
| **87** | A4 | 5f emerald | .50 | .25 |
| **88** | A4 | 6f olive green | .25 | .25 |
| **89** | A4 | 10f carmine | .25 | .25 |
| **90** | A4 | 12f violet, *yel* | .30 | .25 |
| **91** | A4 | 16f gray green | .35 | .90 |
| **92** | A4 | 20f dark brown | 1.00 | .25 |
| **93** | A4 | 25f ultra | 1.20 | .25 |
| **94** | A4 | 30f orange brown | .90 | .25 |
| **95** | A4 | 35f red violet | .90 | .25 |
| **96** | A4 | 50f lake, *blue* | .30 | .25 |
| *a.* | | Cliché of 35f in plate of 50f | 325.00 | — |
| **97** | A4 | 60f green | 5.75 | 2.00 |
| **98** | A4 | 60f green, *salmon* | .80 | .30 |
| **99** | A4 | 70f red brn, *grn* ('16) | .25 | .25 |
| **100** | A4 | 80f dull violet ('16) | .25 | .25 |
| **101** | A5 | 1k dull red | 2.50 | .25 |
| **102** | A5 | 2k dull blue | 4.25 | .25 |
| **103** | A5 | 5k violet brown | 20.00 | 5.00 |
| | | *Nos. 84-103 (20)* | 40.50 | 12.20 |

Nos. 89-97, 99-103 exist imperf. Value, set $1,200.

For overprints and surcharges see Nos. 2N1-2N3, 6N1-6N6, 6NB12, 7N1-7N6, 7NB1, 10N1.

**Wmk. 137 Horiz.**

| | | | | |
|---|---|---|---|---|
| *84a* | A4 | 1f slate | .75 | .60 |
| *85a* | A4 | 2f olive yellow | 2.00 | .40 |
| *87a* | A4 | 5f emerald | .50 | .25 |
| *88a* | A4 | 6f olive green | 1.00 | .25 |
| *89b* | A4 | 10f carmine | 1.00 | .25 |
| *90a* | A4 | 12f violet, *yellow* | 2.00 | .25 |
| *92a* | A4 | 20f dark brown | 6.25 | .25 |
| *94a* | A4 | 30f orange brown | 50.00 | .25 |
| *95a* | A4 | 35f red violet | 200.00 | .25 |
| *96b* | A4 | 50f lake, *blue* | 15.00 | 6.25 |
| *97a* | A4 | 60f green | 4.25 | 1.75 |
| *98a* | A4 | 60f green, *salmon* | 1.50 | .25 |
| *101a* | A5 | 1k dull red | 16.00 | .25 |
| *102a* | A5 | 2k dull blue | 100.00 | 1.00 |
| | | *Nos. 84a-102a (14)* | 400.25 | 12.25 |

A5a

**1916, July 1 *Perf. 15***

| | | | | |
|---|---|---|---|---|
| **103A** | A5a | 10f violet brown | .25 | .25 |

Although issued as a postal savings stamp, No. 103A was also valid for postage. Used value is for postal usage.

Exists imperf. Value $10.

For overprints and surcharges see Nos. 2N59, 5N23, 6N50, 8N13, 10N42.

Queen Zita — A6

Charles IV — A7

**1916, Dec. 30**

| | | | | |
|---|---|---|---|---|
| **104** | A6 | 10f violet | 1.00 | 1.00 |
| **105** | A7 | 15f red | 1.00 | 1.00 |

Coronation of King Charles IV and Queen Zita on Dec. 30, 1916.

Exist imperf. Value, set $20.

During 1921-24 the two center rows of panes of various stamps then current were punched with three holes forming a triangle. These were sold at post offices. Collectors and dealers who wanted the stamps unpunched would have to purchase them through the philatelic agency at a 10% advance over face value.

Harvesting (White Numerals) — A8

**1916**

| | | | | |
|---|---|---|---|---|
| **106** | A8 | 10f rose | .60 | .25 |
| **107** | A8 | 15f violet | .60 | .25 |

Exist imperf. Value, set $20.

For overprints and surcharges see Nos. B56-B57, 2N4-2N5, 5N1.

Harvesting Wheat — A9

Parliament Building at Budapest — A10

**1916-18 *Perf. 15***

| | | | | |
|---|---|---|---|---|
| **108** | A9 | 2f brown orange | .25 | .25 |
| **109** | A9 | 3f red lilac | .25 | .25 |
| **110** | A9 | 4f slate gray ('18) | .25 | .25 |
| **111** | A9 | 5f green | .25 | .25 |
| **112** | A9 | 6f grnsh blue | .25 | .25 |
| **113** | A9 | 10f rose red | 1.40 | .25 |
| **114** | A9 | 15f violet | .25 | .25 |
| **115** | A9 | 20f gray brown | .25 | .25 |
| **116** | A9 | 25f dull blue | .30 | .25 |
| **117** | A9 | 35f brown | .25 | .25 |
| **118** | A9 | 40f olive green | .25 | .25 |

***Perf. 14***

| | | | | |
|---|---|---|---|---|
| **119** | A10 | 50f red vio & lil | .25 | .25 |
| **120** | A10 | 75f brt bl & pale bl | .25 | .25 |
| **121** | A10 | 80f grn & pale grn | .25 | .25 |

| | | | | |
|---|---|---|---|---|
| **122** | A10 | 1k red brn & claret | .25 | .25 |
| **123** | A10 | 2k ol brn & bister | .25 | .25 |
| **124** | A10 | 3k dk vio & indigo | .60 | .25 |
| **125** | A10 | 5k dk brn & lt brn | .60 | .25 |
| **126** | A10 | 10k vio brn & vio | 1.20 | .25 |
| | | *Nos. 108-126 (19)* | 7.60 | 4.75 |

Nos. 108-126 exist imperf. Value, set $100.

See Nos. 335-377, 388-396. For overprints and surcharges see Nos. 153, 167, C1-C5, J76-J99, 1N1-1N21, 1N26-1N30, 1N33, 1N36-1N39, 2N6-2N27, 2N33-2N38, 2N41, 2N43-2N48, 4N1-4N4, 5N2-5N17, 6N7-6N24, 6N29-6N39, 7N7-7N30, 7N38, 7N41-7N42, 8N1-8N4, 9N1-9N2, 9N4, 10N2-10N16, 10N25-10N29, 10N31, 10N33-10N41, 11N1-11N15, 11N20-24, 11N27, 11N30, 11N32-33.

Charles IV — A11

Queen Zita — A12

**1918** ***Perf. 15***

| | | | | |
|---|---|---|---|---|
| **127** | A11 | 10f scarlet | .25 | .25 |
| **128** | A11 | 15f deep violet | .30 | *.75* |
| **129** | A11 | 20f dark brown | .25 | .25 |
| **130** | A11 | 25f brt blue | .25 | .25 |
| **131** | A12 | 40f olive green | .25 | *.25* |
| **132** | A12 | 50f lilac | .25 | *.25* |
| | | *Nos. 127-132 (6)* | 1.55 | 2.00 |

Exist imperf. Value, set $35.

For overprints see Nos. 168-173, 1N32, 1N34-1N35, 2N28-2N32, 2N39-2N40, 2N42, 2N49-2N51, 5N18-5N22, 6N25-6N28, 6N40-6N43, 7N31-7N37, 7N39-7N40, 8N5, 9N3, 10N17-10N21, 10N30, 10N32, 11N16-19, 11N25-26, 11N28-29, 11N31.

### Issues of the Republic

Hungarian Stamps of 1916-18 Overprinted in Black

**1918-19** **Wmk. 137** ***Perf. 15, 14***

**On Stamps of 1916-18**

| | | | | |
|---|---|---|---|---|
| **153** | A9 | 2f brown orange | .25 | .25 |
| **154** | A9 | 3f red lilac | .25 | .25 |
| **155** | A9 | 4f slate gray | .25 | .25 |
| **156** | A9 | 5f green | .25 | .25 |
| **157** | A9 | 6f grnsh blue | .25 | .25 |
| **158** | A9 | 10f rose red | .25 | .25 |
| **159** | A9 | 20f gray brown | .25 | .25 |
| **162** | A9 | 40f olive green | .25 | .25 |
| **163** | A10 | 1k red brn & claret | .25 | .25 |
| **164** | A10 | 2k ol brn & bis | .25 | .25 |
| **165** | A10 | 3k dk violet & ind | .40 | 1.00 |
| **166** | A10 | 5k dk brn & lt brn | 2.00 | 5.00 |
| **167** | A10 | 10k vio brn & vio | .65 | 1.50 |

**On Stamps of 1918**

| | | | | |
|---|---|---|---|---|
| **168** | A11 | 10f scarlet | .25 | .25 |
| **169** | A11 | 15f deep violet | .25 | .25 |
| **170** | A11 | 20f dark brown | .25 | .25 |
| **171** | A11 | 25f brt blue | .25 | .25 |
| **172** | A12 | 40f olive green | .30 | .60 |
| **173** | A12 | 50f lilac | .25 | .30 |
| | | *Nos. 153-173 (19)* | 7.10 | 11.90 |

Nos. 153-164 exist imperf. Value, set $90.

Nos. 153-162, 168-173 exist with overprint inverted. Value, each $6.

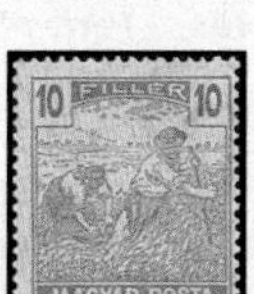
A13

A14

**1919-20** ***Perf. 15***

| | | | | |
|---|---|---|---|---|
| **174** | A13 | 2f brown orange | .25 | .25 |
| **176** | A13 | 4f slate gray | .25 | .25 |
| **177** | A13 | 5f yellow grn | .25 | .25 |
| **178** | A13 | 6f grnsh blue | .25 | .25 |
| **179** | A13 | 10f red | .25 | .25 |
| **180** | A13 | 15f violet | .25 | .25 |
| **181** | A13 | 20f dark brown | .25 | .25 |
| **182** | A13 | 20f green ('20) | .25 | .25 |
| **183** | A13 | 25f dull blue | .25 | .25 |
| **184** | A13 | 40f olive green | .25 | .25 |
| **185** | A13 | 40f rose red ('20) | .25 | .25 |
| **186** | A13 | 45f orange | .25 | .25 |

***Perf. 14***

| | | | | |
|---|---|---|---|---|
| **187** | A14 | 50f brn vio & pale vio | .25 | .25 |
| **188** | A14 | 60f brown & bl ('20) | .25 | .25 |
| **189** | A14 | 95f dk bl & bl | .25 | .25 |
| **190** | A14 | 1k red brn | .25 | .25 |
| **191** | A14 | 1k dk bl & dull bl ('20) | .25 | .25 |
| **192** | A14 | 1.20k dk grn & grn | .25 | .25 |
| **193** | A14 | 1.40k yellow green | .25 | .25 |
| **194** | A14 | 2k ol brn & bis | .25 | .25 |
| **195** | A14 | 3k dk vio & ind | .25 | .25 |
| **196** | A14 | 5k dk brn & brn | .25 | .85 |
| **197** | A14 | 10k vio brn & red vio | .50 | .75 |
| | | *Nos. 174-197 (23)* | 6.00 | 6.85 |

The 3f red lilac, type A13, was never regularly issued without overprint (Nos. 204 and 312). In 1923 a small quantity was sold by the Government at public auction. Value $3.

For overprints see Nos. 203-222, 306-330, 1N40, 2N52-2N58, 6N44-6N49, 8N6-8N12, 10N22-10N24, 11N34-35.

Nos. 174, 177-179, 181-197 exist imperf. Value set $60.

### Issues of the Soviet Republic

Karl Marx — A15

Sándor Petőfi — A16

Ignác Martinovics — A17

György Dózsa — A18

Friedrich Engels — A19

**Wmk. 137 Horiz.**

**1919, June 14** **Litho.** ***Perf. 12½x12***

| | | | | |
|---|---|---|---|---|
| **198** | A15 | 20f rose & brown | .50 | *1.00* |
| **199** | A16 | 45f brn org & dk grn | .50 | *1.00* |
| **200** | A17 | 60f blue gray & brn | 1.50 | *3.00* |
| **201** | A18 | 75f claret & vio brn | 1.50 | *3.00* |
| **202** | A19 | 80f olive db & blk brn | 1.50 | *3.00* |
| | | *Nos. 198-202 (5)* | 5.50 | *11.00* |

Used values are for favor cancels.

Exist imperf. Value, Set $150.

**Wmk. Vertical**

| | | | | |
|---|---|---|---|---|
| *198a* | A15 | 20f | 6.25 | 12.50 |
| *199a* | A16 | 45f | 6.25 | 12.50 |
| *200a* | A17 | 60f | 6.25 | 12.50 |
| *201a* | A18 | 75f | 6.25 | 12.50 |
| *202a* | A19 | 80f | 12.50 | 25.00 |
| | | *Nos. 198a-202a (5)* | 37.50 | |

Nos. 198a-202a were not used postally. Used examples are favor canceled.

Stamps of 1919 Overprinted in Red

**1919, July 21** **Typo.** ***Perf. 15***

| | | | | |
|---|---|---|---|---|
| **203** | A13 | 2f brown orange | .25 | .25 |
| **204** | A13 | 3f red lilac | .25 | .25 |
| **205** | A13 | 4f slate gray | .25 | .25 |
| **206** | A13 | 5f yellow green | .25 | .25 |
| **207** | A13 | 6f grnsh blue | .25 | .25 |
| **208** | A13 | 10f red | .25 | .25 |
| **209** | A13 | 15f violet | .25 | .25 |
| **210** | A13 | 20f dark brown | .25 | .25 |
| **211** | A13 | 25f dull blue | .25 | .25 |
| **212** | A13 | 40f olive green | .25 | .25 |
| **213** | A13 | 45f orange | .25 | .25 |

Overprinted in Red

***Perf. 14***

| | | | | |
|---|---|---|---|---|
| **214** | A14 | 50f brn vio & pale vio | .25 | .30 |
| **215** | A14 | 95f dk blue & blue | .25 | .30 |
| **216** | A14 | 1k red brown | .25 | .30 |
| **217** | A14 | 1.20k dk grn & grn | .25 | .40 |
| **218** | A14 | 1.40k yellow green | .25 | .40 |
| **219** | A14 | 2k ol brn & bister | .40 | 1.25 |
| **220** | A14 | 3k dk vio & ind | .65 | 1.00 |
| **221** | A14 | 5k dk brn & brn | .50 | .80 |
| **222** | A14 | 10k vio brn & red vio | .75 | 1.75 |
| | | *Nos. 203-222 (20)* | 6.30 | 9.25 |

"Magyar Tanacsköztarsasag" on Nos. 198 to 222 means "Hungarian Soviet Republic."

Nos. 203-218, 221-222 exist imperf. Value, set $125.

### Issues of the Kingdom

Stamps of 1919 Overprinted in Black

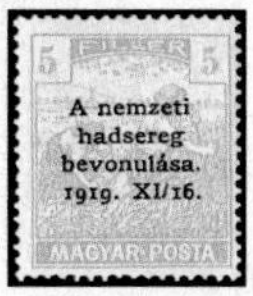


**1919, Nov. 16**

| | | | | |
|---|---|---|---|---|
| **306** | A13 | 5f green | .65 | 1.00 |
| **307** | A13 | 10f rose red | .65 | 1.00 |
| **308** | A13 | 15f violet | .65 | 1.00 |
| **309** | A13 | 20f gray brown | .65 | 1.00 |
| **310** | A13 | 25f dull blue | .65 | 1.00 |
| | | *Nos. 306-310 (5)* | 3.25 | 5.00 |

Issued to commemorate the Romanian evacuation. The overprint reads: "Entry of the National Army-November 16, 1919."

Forged overprints exist.

Nos. 203 to 213 Overprinted in Black

**1920, Jan. 26** ***Perf. 15***

| | | | | |
|---|---|---|---|---|
| **311** | A13 | 2f brown orange | 1.10 | 1.60 |
| **312** | A13 | 3f red lilac | .25 | .30 |
| **313** | A13 | 4f slate gray | 1.10 | 1.60 |
| **314** | A13 | 5f yellow green | .25 | .25 |
| **315** | A13 | 6f blue green | .25 | .40 |
| **316** | A13 | 10f red | .25 | .25 |
| **317** | A13 | 15f violet | .25 | .25 |
| **318** | A13 | 20f dark brown | .25 | .25 |
| **319** | A13 | 25f dull blue | .25 | .30 |
| **320** | A13 | 40f olive green | 1.20 | 2.00 |
| **321** | A13 | 45f orange | 1.20 | 2.00 |

Nos. 214 to 222 Overprinted in Black

***Perf. 14***

| | | | | |
|---|---|---|---|---|
| **322** | A14 | 50f brn vio & pale vio | 1.20 | *2.00* |
| **323** | A14 | 95f dk bl & bl | 1.20 | *2.00* |
| **324** | A14 | 1k red brown | 1.20 | *2.00* |
| **325** | A14 | 1.20k dk grn & grn | 1.20 | *2.50* |
| **326** | A14 | 1.40k yellow green | 1.20 | *2.50* |
| **327** | A14 | 2k ol brn & bis | 7.50 | *14.00* |
| **328** | A14 | 3k dk vio & ind | 7.50 | *14.00* |
| **329** | A14 | 5k dk brn & brn | .25 | *.50* |
| **330** | A14 | 10k vio brn & red vio | 7.50 | 14.00 |
| | | *Nos. 311-330 (20)* | 35.10 | 62.70 |

Counterfeit overprints exist.

**Types of 1916-18 Issue**

Denomination Tablets Without Inner Frame on Nos. 350 to 363

**1920-24** **Wmk. 137** ***Perf. 15***

| | | | | |
|---|---|---|---|---|
| **335** | A9 | 5f brown orange | .25 | .25 |
| **336** | A9 | 10f red violet | .25 | .25 |
| **337** | A9 | 40f rose red | .25 | .25 |
| **338** | A9 | 50f yellow green | .25 | .25 |
| **339** | A9 | 50f blue vio ('22) | .25 | .25 |
| **340** | A9 | 60f black | .25 | .25 |
| **341** | A9 | 1k green ('22) | .25 | .25 |
| **342** | A9 | 1½k brown vio ('22) | .25 | .25 |
| **343** | A9 | 2k grnsh blue ('22) | .25 | .25 |
| **344** | A9 | 2½k dp green ('22) | .25 | .25 |
| **345** | A9 | 3k brown org ('22) | .25 | .25 |
| **346** | A9 | 4k lt red ('22) | .25 | .25 |
| **347** | A9 | 4½k dull violet ('22) | .25 | .25 |
| **348** | A9 | 5k dp brn ('22) | .25 | .25 |
| **349** | A9 | 6k dark blue ('22) | .25 | .25 |
| **350** | A9 | 10k brown ('23) | .25 | .25 |
| **351** | A9 | 15k slate ('23) | .25 | .25 |
| **352** | A9 | 20k red vio ('23) | .25 | .25 |
| **353** | A9 | 25k orange ('23) | .25 | .25 |
| **354** | A9 | 40k gray grn ('23) | .25 | .25 |
| **355** | A9 | 50k dark blue ('23) | .25 | .25 |
| **356** | A9 | 100k claret ('23) | .25 | .25 |
| **357** | A9 | 150k dark green ('23) | .25 | .25 |

| | | | | |
|---|---|---|---|---|
| **358** | A9 | 200k green ('23) | .25 | .25 |
| **359** | A9 | 300k rose red ('24) | .80 | .30 |
| **360** | A9 | 350k violet ('23) | 1.40 | .30 |
| **361** | A9 | 500k dark gray ('24) | 2.50 | .30 |
| **362** | A9 | 600k olive bis ('24) | 2.50 | .30 |
| **363** | A9 | 800k org yel ('24) | 2.50 | .30 |

***Perf. 14***

| | | | | |
|---|---|---|---|---|
| **364** | A10 | 2.50k bl & gray bl | .25 | .25 |
| **365** | A10 | 3.50k gray | .25 | .25 |
| **366** | A10 | 10k brown ('22) | .50 | .25 |
| **367** | A10 | 15k dk gray ('22) | .25 | .25 |
| **368** | A10 | 20k red vio ('22) | .25 | .25 |
| **369** | A10 | 25k orange ('22) | .25 | .25 |
| **370** | A10 | 30k claret ('22) | .25 | .25 |
| **371** | A10 | 40k gray grn ('22) | .25 | .25 |
| **372** | A10 | 50k dp blue ('22) | .25 | .25 |
| **373** | A10 | 100k yel brn ('22) | .25 | .25 |
| **374** | A10 | 400k turq bl ('23) | .75 | .25 |
| **375** | A10 | 500k brt vio ('23) | 1.10 | .25 |
| **376** | A10 | 1000k lilac ('24) | 1.50 | .25 |
| **377** | A10 | 2000k car ('24) | 2.00 | .25 |
| | | *Nos. 335-377 (43)* | 23.80 | 11.00 |

Nos. 372 to 377 have colored numerals.

Nos. 335-338, 340, 350-365, 368, 370, 372-377 exist imperf. Value, set $200.

Madonna and Child — A23

**1921-25** **Typo.** ***Perf. 12***

| | | | | |
|---|---|---|---|---|
| **378** | A23 | 50k dk brn & bl | .25 | .25 |
| **379** | A23 | 100k ol bis & yel brn | .40 | .35 |

**Wmk. 133**

| | | | | |
|---|---|---|---|---|
| **380** | A23 | 200k dk bl & ultra | .40 | .25 |
| **381** | A23 | 500k vio brn & vio | .75 | .40 |
| **382** | A23 | 1000k vio & red vio | 1.00 | .35 |
| **383** | A23 | 2000k grnsh bl & vio | 1.75 | .50 |
| **384** | A23 | 2500k ol brn & buff | 2.00 | .25 |
| **385** | A23 | 3000k brn red & vio | 2.00 | .25 |
| **386** | A23 | 5000k dk grn & yel grn | 2.00 | .25 |
| *a.* | | Center inverted | *15,000.* | *8,000.* |
| **387** | A23 | 10000k gray vio & pale bl | 2.00 | .25 |
| | | *Nos. 378-387 (10)* | 12.55 | 3.10 |

Nos. 380-387 exist imperf. Value, set of 8 $175.

Issue dates: 50k, 100k, Feb. 27, 1921; 2500k, 10,000k, 1925; others, 1923.

**Types of 1916-18**

Denomination Tablets Without Inner Frame on Nos. 388-394

**1924** **Wmk. 133** ***Perf. 15***

| | | | | |
|---|---|---|---|---|
| **388** | A9 | 100k claret | .40 | .25 |
| **389** | A9 | 200k yellow grn | .25 | .25 |
| **390** | A9 | 300k rose red | .30 | .35 |
| **391** | A9 | 400k deep blue | .30 | .35 |
| **392** | A9 | 500k dark gray | .40 | .25 |
| **393** | A9 | 600k olive bister | .45 | .25 |
| *a.* | | "800" in upper right corner | 110.00 | 260.00 |
| **394** | A9 | 800k org yel | .50 | .25 |

***Perf. 14½x14***

| | | | | |
|---|---|---|---|---|
| **395** | A10 | 1000k lilac | 1.50 | .25 |
| **396** | A10 | 2000k carmine | 2.00 | .25 |
| | | *Nos. 388-396 (9)* | 6.10 | 2.45 |

Nos. 395 and 396 have colored numerals.

Exist imperf. Value, set $37.50.

Maurus Jókai (1825-1904), Novelist A24

**1925, Feb. 1** **Unwmk.** ***Perf. 12***

| | | | | |
|---|---|---|---|---|
| **400** | A24 | 1000k dp grn & blk brn | 1.75 | 3.25 |
| **401** | A24 | 2000k lt brn & blk brn | .80 | 1.00 |
| **402** | A24 | 2500k dk bl & blk brn | 1.75 | 3.25 |
| | | *Nos. 400-402 (3)* | 4.30 | 7.50 |

Exist imperf. Value, set $90.

Crown of St. Stephen A25

Matthias Cathedral A26

Palace at Budapest — A27

***Perf. 14x14¼, 15***

**1926-27** **Wmk. 133** **Litho.**

| | | | | |
|---|---|---|---|---|
| **403** | A25 | 1f dk gray | .45 | .25 |
| **404** | A25 | 2f lt blue | .55 | .25 |
| **405** | A25 | 3f orange | .55 | .25 |
| **406** | A25 | 4f violet | .65 | .25 |
| **407** | A25 | 6f lt green | .90 | .25 |
| **408** | A25 | 8f lilac rose | 1.60 | .25 |

**Typo.**

| | | | | |
|---|---|---|---|---|
| **409** | A26 | 10f deep blue | 2.75 | .25 |
| **410** | A26 | 16f dark violet | 2.25 | .25 |
| **411** | A26 | 20f carmine | 2.75 | .25 |
| **412** | A26 | 25f lt brown | 2.75 | .25 |

***Perf. 14¼x14***

| | | | | |
|---|---|---|---|---|
| **413** | A27 | 32f dp vio & brt vio | 4.25 | .25 |
| **414** | A27 | 40f dk blue & blue | 5.00 | .25 |
| | | *Nos. 403-414 (12)* | 24.45 | 3.00 |

See Nos. 428-436. For surcharges see Nos. 450-456, 466-467.

Nos. 403-414, 418-421 exist imperf. Value, set $250.

Madonna and Child — A28

**1926-27** **Engr.** ***Perf. 14***

| | | | | |
|---|---|---|---|---|
| **415** | A28 | 1p violet | 15.00 | .25 |
| **416** | A28 | 2p red | 17.50 | .40 |
| **417** | A28 | 5p blue ('27) | 17.50 | 3.00 |
| | | *Nos. 415-417 (3)* | 50.00 | 3.65 |

Exist imperf. Value, set $400.

Palace at Budapest A29

St. Stephen A30

**1926-27** **Typo.** ***Perf. 14x14¼***

| | | | | |
|---|---|---|---|---|
| **418** | A29 | 30f blue grn ('27) | 4.00 | .25 |
| **419** | A29 | 46f ultra ('27) | 5.25 | .30 |
| **420** | A29 | 50f brown blk ('27) | 6.00 | .25 |
| **421** | A29 | 70f scarlet | 9.75 | .25 |
| | | *Nos. 418-421 (4)* | 25.00 | 1.05 |

For surcharge see No. 480.

**1928-29** **Engr.** ***Perf. 15***

| | | | | |
|---|---|---|---|---|
| **422** | A30 | 8f yellow grn | .65 | .30 |
| **423** | A30 | 8f rose lake ('29) | .65 | .30 |
| **424** | A30 | 16f orange red | .85 | .30 |
| **425** | A30 | 16f violet ('29) | .85 | .30 |
| **426** | A30 | 32f ultra | 2.50 | 4.00 |
| **427** | A30 | 32f bister ('29) | 2.50 | 4.00 |
| | | *Nos. 422-427 (6)* | 8.00 | 9.20 |

890th death anniversary of St. Stephen, the first king of Hungary.

Exist imperf. Value, set $300.

**Types of 1926-27 Issue**

***Perf. 14x14¼, 15***

**1928-30** **Typo.** **Wmk. 210**

| | | | | |
|---|---|---|---|---|
| **428** | A25 | 1f black | .25 | .25 |
| **429** | A25 | 2f blue | .35 | .25 |
| **430** | A25 | 3f orange | .35 | .25 |
| **431** | A25 | 4f violet | .45 | .25 |
| **432** | A25 | 6f blue grn | .60 | .25 |
| **433** | A25 | 8f lilac rose | 1.25 | .25 |
| **434** | A26 | 10f dp blue ('30) | 4.50 | .25 |
| **435** | A26 | 16f violet | 1.50 | .25 |
| **436** | A26 | 20f dull red | 1.25 | .25 |
| | | *Nos. 428-436 (9)* | 10.50 | 2.25 |

On #428-433 the numerals have thicker strokes than on the same values of the 1926-27 issue.

Exist imperf. Value, set $110.

Palace at Budapest — A31

Type A31 resembles A27 but the steamer is nearer the right of the design.

**1928-31** ***Perf. 14¼x14***

| | | | | |
|---|---|---|---|---|
| **437** | A31 | 30f emerald ('31) | 4.00 | .25 |
| **438** | A31 | 32f red violet | 4.00 | .25 |
| **439** | A31 | 40f deep blue | 5.00 | .25 |
| **440** | A31 | 46f apple green | 4.50 | .25 |
| **441** | A31 | 50f ocher ('31) | 4.50 | .25 |
| | | *Nos. 437-441 (5)* | 22.00 | 1.25 |

Exist imperf. Value, set $110.

Admiral Nicholas Horthy — A32

**1930, Mar. 1** **Litho.** ***Perf. 15***

| | | | | |
|---|---|---|---|---|
| **445** | A32 | 8f myrtle green | .75 | .25 |
| **446** | A32 | 16f purple | 1.00 | .25 |
| **447** | A32 | 20f carmine | 6.00 | 1.10 |
| **448** | A32 | 32f olive brown | 4.00 | 1.25 |
| **449** | A32 | 40f dull blue | 7.00 | .50 |
| | | *Nos. 445-449 (5)* | 18.75 | 3.35 |

10th anniv. of the election of Adm. Nicholas Horthy as Regent, Mar. 1, 1920.

Exist imperf. Value, set, $200.

Stamps of 1926-28 Surcharged

**1931, Jan. 1** ***Perf. 14¼, 15***

| | | | | |
|---|---|---|---|---|
| **450** | A25 | 2f on 3f orange | .50 | *.40* |
| **451** | A25 | 6f on 8f magenta | .50 | .25 |
| *a.* | | Perf. 14x14¼ | 30.00 | *30.00* |
| **452** | A26 | 10f on 16f violet | .50 | .25 |

**Wmk. 133**

| | | | | |
|---|---|---|---|---|
| **453** | A25 | 2f on 3f orange | 2.50 | 5.00 |
| *a.* | | Perf. 14x14¼ | 3.00 | *6.00* |
| **454** | A25 | 6f on 8f magenta | 2.00 | 4.00 |
| *a.* | | Perf. 14x14¼ | 50.00 | 100.00 |
| **455** | A26 | 10f on 16f dk vio | 1.75 | 3.50 |
| *a.* | | Perf. 14x14¼ | 2.00 | *4.00* |
| **456** | A26 | 20f on 25f lt brn | 1.25 | 2.50 |
| *a.* | | Perf. 14x14¼ | 1.25 | 2.25 |
| | | *Nos. 450-456 (7)* | 9.00 | 15.90 |

For surcharges see Nos. 466-467.

St. Elizabeth A33

Ministering to Children A34

**Wmk. 210**

**1932, Apr. 21** **Photo.** ***Perf. 15***

| | | | | |
|---|---|---|---|---|
| **458** | A33 | 10f ultra | .75 | .25 |
| **459** | A33 | 20f scarlet | .75 | .25 |

***Perf. 14***

| | | | | |
|---|---|---|---|---|
| **460** | A34 | 32f deep violet | 1.50 | 2.50 |
| **461** | A34 | 40f deep blue | 2.00 | 1.00 |
| | | *Nos. 458-461 (4)* | 5.00 | 4.00 |

700th anniv. of the death of St. Elizabeth of Hungary.

Exist imperf. Value, set $100.

Madonna, Patroness of Hungary — A35

**1932, June 1** ***Perf. 12***

| | | | | |
|---|---|---|---|---|
| **462** | A35 | 1p yellow grn | 30.00 | .25 |
| **463** | A35 | 2p carmine | 30.00 | .40 |
| **464** | A35 | 5p deep blue | 42.50 | 3.00 |
| **465** | A35 | 10p olive bister | 42.50 | 22.50 |
| | | *Nos. 462-465 (4)* | 145.00 | 26.15 |

Exist imperf. Value, set $1,000.

Nos. 451 and 454 Surcharged

**1932, June 14** **Wmk. 210** ***Perf. 15***

| | | | | |
|---|---|---|---|---|
| **466** | A25 | 2f on 6f on 8f mag | .25 | .25 |

**Wmk. 133**

| | | | | |
|---|---|---|---|---|
| **467** | A25 | 2f on 6f on 8f mag | 50.00 | 100.00 |

Imre Madách — A36

Designs: 2f, Janos Arany. 4f, Dr. Ignaz Semmelweis. 6f, Baron Roland Eotvos. 10f, Count Stephen Szechenyi. 16f, Ferenc Deak. 20f, Franz Liszt. 30f, Louis Kossuth. 32f, Stephen Tisza. 40f, Mihaly Munkacsy. 50f, Alexander Csoma. 70f, Farkas Bolyai.

**1932** **Wmk. 210** ***Perf. 15***

| | | | | |
|---|---|---|---|---|
| **468** | A36 | 1f slate violet | .25 | .25 |
| **469** | A36 | 2f orange | .25 | .25 |
| **470** | A36 | 4f ultra | .25 | .25 |
| **471** | A36 | 6f yellow grn | .25 | .25 |
| **472** | A36 | 10f Prus green | .35 | .25 |
| **473** | A36 | 16f dull violet | .35 | .25 |
| **474** | A36 | 20f deep rose | .30 | .25 |
| **475** | A36 | 30f brown | .50 | .25 |
| **476** | A36 | 32f brown vio | .70 | .25 |
| **477** | A36 | 40f dull blue | .85 | .25 |
| **478** | A36 | 50f deep green | 1.10 | .25 |
| **479** | A36 | 70f cerise | 1.50 | .25 |
| | | *Nos. 468-479 (12)* | 6.65 | 3.00 |
| | | Set, never hinged | 11.50 | |

Issued in honor of famous Hungarians.

Exist imperf. Value, set $125.

See Nos. 509-510.

No. 421 Surcharged

**1933, Apr. 15** **Wmk. 133** ***Perf. 14***

| | | | | |
|---|---|---|---|---|
| **480** | A29 | 10f on 70f scarlet | 3.00 | .40 |
| | | Never hinged | 6.00 | |

Leaping Stag and Double Cross — A47

**Wmk. 210**

**1933, July 10** **Photo.** ***Perf. 15***

| | | | | |
|---|---|---|---|---|
| **481** | A47 | 10f dk green | .75 | .80 |
| **482** | A47 | 16f violet brn | 2.00 | *2.50* |
| **483** | A47 | 20f car lake | 1.50 | 1.25 |
| **484** | A47 | 32f yellow | 5.00 | *6.00* |
| **485** | A47 | 40f deep blue | 5.00 | 4.00 |
| | | *Nos. 481-485 (5)* | 14.25 | 14.55 |
| | | Set, never hinged | 27.50 | |

Boy Scout Jamboree at Gödöllö, Hungary, July 20 - Aug. 20, 1933.

Exists imperf. Value, set $150.

Souvenir Sheet

Franz Liszt — A48

**1934, May 6** ***Perf. 15***

| | | | | |
|---|---|---|---|---|
| **486** | A48 | 20f lake | 70.00 | 90.00 |
| | | Never hinged | 140.00 | |

2nd Hungarian Phil. Exhib., Budapest, and Jubilee of the 1st Hungarian Phil. Soc. Sold for 90f, including entrance fee. Size: 64x76mm.
Exists imperf. Value $2,500.

Francis II Rákóczy (1676-1735), Prince of Transylvania A49

**1935, Apr. 8** ***Perf. 12***

| | | | | |
|---|---|---|---|---|
| **487** | A49 | 10f yellow green | .60 | .40 |
| **488** | A49 | 16f brt violet | 3.50 | 3.25 |
| **489** | A49 | 20f dark carmine | 2.00 | 1.20 |
| **490** | A49 | 32f brown lake | 5.00 | 6.00 |
| **491** | A49 | 40f blue | 6.00 | 7.25 |
| | | *Nos. 487-491 (5)* | 17.10 | 18.10 |
| | | Set, never hinged | 32.50 | |

Exists imperf. Value, set $400.

Cardinal Pázmány — A50

Signing the Charter — A51

**1935, Sept. 25**

| | | | | |
|---|---|---|---|---|
| **492** | A50 | 6f dull green | 1.10 | 1.00 |
| **493** | A51 | 10f dark green | .25 | .25 |
| **494** | A50 | 16f slate violet | 1.50 | 1.60 |
| **495** | A50 | 20f magenta | .25 | .40 |
| **496** | A51 | 32f deep claret | 2.50 | 3.25 |
| **497** | A51 | 40f dark blue | 2.00 | 3.25 |
| | | *Nos. 492-497 (6)* | 7.60 | 9.75 |
| | | Set, never hinged | 15.00 | |

Tercentenary of the founding of the University of Budapest by Peter Cardinal Pázmány.
Exists imperf. Value, set $400.

Ancient City and Fortress of Buda — A52

Guardian Angel over Buda — A53

Shield of Buda, Cannon and Massed Flags — A54

First Hungarian Soldier to Enter Buda — A55

**1936, Sept. 2** ***Perf. 11½x12½***

| | | | | |
|---|---|---|---|---|
| **498** | A52 | 10f dark green | .40 | .25 |
| **499** | A53 | 16f deep violet | 2.50 | *3.50* |
| **500** | A54 | 20f car lake | .40 | .25 |
| **501** | A55 | 32f dark brown | 2.50 | *3.25* |
| **502** | A52 | 40f deep blue | 2.50 | *3.25* |
| | | *Nos. 498-502 (5)* | 8.30 | 10.50 |
| | | Set, never hinged | 16.00 | |

250th anniv. of the recapture of Budapest from the Turks.
Exists imperf. Value, set $400.

**Catalogue values for unused stamps in this section, from this point to the end of the section, are for Never Hinged items.**

Budapest International Fair — A56

**1937, Feb. 22** ***Perf. 12***

| | | | | |
|---|---|---|---|---|
| **503** | A56 | 2f deep orange | .25 | .25 |
| **504** | A56 | 6f yellow green | .40 | .25 |
| **505** | A56 | 10f myrtle green | .55 | .25 |
| **506** | A56 | 20f deep cerise | 1.25 | .40 |
| **507** | A56 | 32f dark violet | 2.00 | .55 |
| **508** | A56 | 40f ultra | 1.60 | .80 |
| | | *Nos. 503-508 (6)* | 6.05 | 2.50 |

Exist imperf. Value, set $250.

**Portrait Type of 1932**

5f, Ferenc Kolcsey. 25f, Mihaly Vorosmarty.

**1937, May 5** ***Perf. 15***

| | | | | |
|---|---|---|---|---|
| **509** | A36 | 5f brown orange | .80 | .25 |
| **510** | A36 | 25f olive green | 1.60 | .25 |

Exist imperf. Value, set $400.

Pope Sylvester II, Archbishop Astrik — A59

Designs: 2f, 16f, Stephen the Church builder. 4f, 20f, St. Stephen enthroned. 5f, 25f, Sts. Gerhardt, Emerich, Stephen. 6f, 30f, St. Stephen offering holy crown to Virgin Mary. 10f, same as 1f. 32f, 50f, Portrait of St. Stephen. 40f, Madonna and Child. 70f, Crown of St. Stephen.
See designs A75-A77 for smaller stamps of designs similar Nos. 521-524, but with slanted "MAGYAR KIR POSTA."

**1938, Jan. 1** ***Perf. 12***

| | | | | |
|---|---|---|---|---|
| **511** | A59 | 1f deep violet | .40 | .25 |
| **512** | A59 | 2f olive brown | .40 | .25 |
| **513** | A59 | 4f brt blue | .80 | .25 |
| **514** | A59 | 5f magenta | 1.25 | .25 |
| **515** | A59 | 6f dp yel grn | 1.60 | .25 |
| **516** | A59 | 10f red orange | 1.25 | .25 |
| **517** | A59 | 16f gray violet | 2.00 | .55 |
| **518** | A59 | 20f car lake | 1.25 | .25 |
| **519** | A59 | 25f dark green | 1.60 | .80 |
| **520** | A59 | 30f olive bister | 2.50 | .25 |
| **521** | A59 | 32f dp claret, *buff* | 2.50 | 2.00 |
| **522** | A59 | 40f Prus green | 2.50 | .25 |
| **523** | A59 | 50f rose vio, *grnsh* | 2.75 | .25 |
| **524** | A59 | 70f ol grn, *bluish* | 4.50 | .55 |
| | | *Nos. 511-524 (14)* | 25.30 | 6.40 |

900th anniv. of the death of St. Stephen.
Exists imperf. Value, set $400.
For overprints see Nos. 535-536.

Admiral Horthy — A67

**1938, Jan. 1** ***Perf. 12½x12***

| | | | | |
|---|---|---|---|---|
| **525** | A67 | 1p peacock green | 2.75 | .25 |
| **526** | A67 | 2p brown | 3.25 | .35 |
| **527** | A67 | 5p sapphire blue | 4.00 | 1.90 |
| | | *Nos. 525-527 (3)* | 10.00 | 2.50 |

Exist imperf. Value, set $475.

Souvenir Sheet

St. Stephen — A68

**1938, May 22** **Wmk. 210** ***Perf. 12***

| | | | | |
|---|---|---|---|---|
| **528** | A68 | 20f carmine lake | 32.50 | 25.00 |

3rd Hungarian Phil. Exhib., Budapest. Sheet sold only at exhibition with 1p ticket.
Exists imperf. Value $4,500.

College of Debrecen A69

Three Students — A71

George Marothy — A73

10f, 18th cent. view of College. 20f, 19th cent. view of College. 40f, Stephen Hatvani.

***Perf. 12x12½, 12½x12***

**1938, Sept. 24** **Wmk. 210**

| | | | | |
|---|---|---|---|---|
| **529** | A69 | 6f deep green | .40 | .25 |
| **530** | A69 | 10f brown | .40 | .25 |
| **531** | A71 | 16f brown car | .40 | .30 |
| **532** | A69 | 20f crimson | .40 | .25 |
| **533** | A73 | 32f slate green | 1.10 | .75 |
| **534** | A73 | 40f brt blue | 1.10 | .60 |
| | | *Nos. 529-534 (6)* | 3.80 | 2.40 |

Founding of Debrecen College, 400th anniv.
Exists imperf. Value $300.

**Types of 1938 Overprinted in Blue (#535) or Carmine (#536)**

a

b

**1938** ***Perf. 12***

| | | | | |
|---|---|---|---|---|
| **535** | A59(a) | 20f salmon pink | 2.00 | 1.60 |
| **536** | A59(b) | 70f brn, *grnsh* | 2.00 | 1.60 |
| | *a.* | Overprint omitted | *12,500.* | *7,500.* |

Restoration of the territory ceded by Czechoslovakia.
Exists imperf. Value $135.
Forgeries exist of No. 536a.

Crown of St. Stephen A75

St. Stephen A76

Madonna, Patroness of Hungary A77

Coronation Church, Budapest A78

Reformed Church, Debrecen A79

Cathedral, Esztergom A80

Deak Square Evangelical Church, Budapest — A81

Cathedral of Kassa — A82

**Wmk. 210**

**1939, June 1** **Photo.** ***Perf. 15***

| | | | | |
|---|---|---|---|---|
| **537** | A75 | 1f brown car | .25 | .25 |
| **538** | A75 | 2f Prus green | .25 | .25 |
| **539** | A75 | 4f ocher | .25 | .25 |
| **540** | A75 | 5f brown violet | .25 | .25 |
| **541** | A75 | 6f yellow green | .25 | .25 |
| **542** | A75 | 10f bister brn | .25 | .25 |
| **543** | A75 | 16f rose violet | .25 | .25 |
| **544** | A76 | 20f rose red | .25 | .25 |
| **545** | A77 | 25f blue gray | .25 | .25 |

*Perf. 12*

**546** A78 30f red violet .40 .25
**547** A79 32f brown .25 .25
**548** A80 40f greenish blue .40 .25
**549** A81 50f olive .50 .25
**550** A82 70f henna brown .50 .25
*Nos. 537-550 (14)* 4.30 3.50

See Nos. 521-524, 578-596. For overprints see Nos. 559-560.
Exists imperf. Value, set $250.

Girl Scout Sign and Olive Branch — A83

6f, Scout lily, Hungary's shield, Crown of St. Stephen. 10f, Girls in Scout hat & national headdress. 20f, Dove & Scout emblems.

**1939, July 20 Photo. *Perf. 12***

**551** A83 2f brown orange .50 .35
**552** A83 6f green .50 .35
**553** A83 10f brown .80 .45
**554** A83 20f lilac rose 1.25 .80
*Nos. 551-554 (4)* 3.05 1.95

Girl Scout Jamboree at Gödöllö.
Exists imperf. Value, set $300.

Admiral Horthy at Szeged, 1919 — A87

Admiral Nicholas Horthy A88

Cathedral of Kassa and Angel Ringing "Bell of Liberty" A89

**1940, Mar. 1**

**555** A87 6f green .25 .25
**556** A88 10f ol blk & ol bis .25 .25
**557** A89 20f brt rose brown .80 .55
*Nos. 555-557 (3)* 1.30 1.05

20th anniversary of the election of Admiral Horthy as Regent of Hungary.
Exists imperf. Value, set $100.

Crown of St. Stephen A90

**1940, Sept. 5**

**558** A90 10f dk green & yellow .40 .40

Issued in commemoration of the recovery of northeastern Transylvania from Romania.
Exists imperf. Value $25.

Nos. 542, 544 Overprinted in Red or Black

**1941, Apr. 21 *Perf. 15***

**559** A75 10f bister brn (R) .40 .25
**560** A76 20f rose red (Bk) .40 .25

Return of the Bacska territory from Yugoslavia.
Exist imperf. Value, set $50.

Admiral Nicholas Horthy — A92

**Wmk. 210**

**1941, June 18 Photo. *Perf. 12***

**570** A92 1p dk green & buff .25 .25
**571** A92 2p dk brown & buff .50 .40
**572** A92 5p dk rose vio & buff 2.00 1.00
*Nos. 570-572 (3)* 2.75 1.65

Exist imperf. Value, set $75.
See Nos. 597-599.

Count Stephen Széchenyi A93

Count Széchenyi and Royal Academy of Science A94

Representation of the Narrows of Kazán — A95

Chain Bridge, Budapest A96

Mercury, Train and Boat — A97

**1941, Sept. 21**

**573** A93 10f dk olive grn .25 .25
**574** A94 16f olive brown .25 .25
**575** A95 20f carmine lake .25 .25
**576** A96 32f red orange .65 .25
**577** A97 40f royal blue .65 .25
*Nos. 573-577 (5)* 2.05 1.25

Count Stephen Szechenyi (1791-1860).
Exist imperf. Value, set $250.

**Types of 1939**

***Perf. 12x12½, 12½x12, 15***

**1941-43 Wmk. 266**

**578** A75 1f rose lake ('42) .25 .25
**579** A75 3f dark brown .25 .25
**580** A75 5f violet gray ('42) .25 .25
**581** A75 6f lt green ('42) .25 .25
**582** A75 8f slate grn .25 .25
**583** A75 10f olive brn ('42) .25 .25
**584** A75 12f red orange .25 .25
**585** A76 20f rose red ('42) .25 .25
**586** A76 24f brown violet .25 .25
**587** A78 30f lilac ('42) .25 .25
**588** A82 30f rose red ('43) .25 .25
**589** A80 40f blue green ('42) .25 .25
**590** A79 40f gray black ('43) .25 .25
**591** A81 50f olive grn ('42) .25 .25
**592** A80 50f brt blue ('43) .25 .25
**593** A82 70f copper red ('42) .25 .25
**594** A81 70f gray green ('43) .25 .25
**595** A77 80f brown bister .40 .25
**596** A78 80f bister brn ('43) .25 .25
*Nos. 578-596 (19)* 4.90 4.75

Exist imperf. Value, set $350.

**Horthy Type of 1941**

***Perf. 12x12½***

**1941, Dec. 18 Wmk. 266**

**597** A92 1p dk green & buff .80 .25
**598** A92 2p dk brown & buff .25 .25
**599** A92 5p dk rose vio & buff .55 .25
*Nos. 597-599 (3)* 1.60 .75

Exist imperf. Value, set $60.

Stephen Horthy — A98

**1942, Oct. 15 *Perf. 12***

**600** A98 20f black .40 .40

Death of Stephen Horthy (1904-42), son of Regent Nicholas Horthy, who died in a plane crash.
Exists imperf. Value $40.

Arpád — A99

A109

Portraits: 2f, King Ladislaus I. 3f, Miklós Toldi. 4f, János Hunyadi. 5f, Paul Kinizsi. 6f, Count Miklós Zrinyi. 8f, Francis II Rákóczy. 10f, Count Andrew Hadik. 12f, Arthur Görgei. 18f, 24f, Virgin Mary, Patroness of Hungary.

**1943-45 *Perf. 15***

**601** A99 1f grnsh black .25 .25
**602** A99 2f red orange .25 .25
**603** A99 3f ultra .25 .25
**604** A99 4f brown .25 .25
**605** A99 5f vermilion .25 .25
**606** A99 6f slate blue .25 .25
**607** A99 8f dk ol grn .25 .25
**608** A99 10f brown .25 .25
**609** A99 12f dp blue grn .25 .25
**610** A99 18f dk gray .25 .25
**611** A109 20f chestnut brn .40 .25
**612** A99 24f rose violet .25 .25
**613** A109 30f brt carmine .25 .25
**614** A109 50f blue .25 .25
**615** A109 80f yellow brn .25 .25
**616** A109 1p green .25 .25
**616A** A109 2p brown ('45) .25 .40
**616B** A109 5p dk red violet ('45) .25 .80
*Nos. 601-616B (18)* 4.65 5.20

Exist imperf. Value, set $150.
For overprints and surcharges see Nos. 631-658, 660-661, 664, 666-669, 671-672, 674-677, 679, 680, 682, 685-689, 691-698, 801-803, 805-806, 810-815, F2, Q2-Q3, Q7.

Message to the Shepherds A110

20f, Nativity. 30f, Adoration of the Magi.

**1943, Dec. 1 *Perf. 12x12½***

**617** A110 4f dark green .25 .25
**618** A110 20f dull blue .25 .25
**619** A110 30f brown orange .25 .25
*Nos. 617-619 (3)* .75 .75

Exist imperf. Value, set $150.

St. Margaret — A113

**1944, Jan. 19 *Perf. 15***

**620** A113 30f deep carmine .40 .40

Canonization of St. Margaret of Hungary.
Exists imperf. Value $40.
For surcharges see Nos. 662, 673A.

Kossuth with Family — A114

Lajos Kossuth — A117

Honvéd Drummer A115

Design: 30f, Kossuth orating.

**1944, Mar. 20 *Perf. 12½x12, 12x12½***

**621** A114 4f yellow brown .25 .25
**622** A115 20f dk olive grn .25 .25
**623** A115 30f henna brown .25 .25
**624** A117 50f slate blue .25 .25
*Nos. 621-624 (4)* 1.00 1.00

Louis (Lajos) Kossuth (1802-94).
Exist imperf. Value, set $200.
For surcharges see Nos. B175-B178.

St. Elizabeth — A118

Portraits: 24f, St. Margaret. 30f, Elizabeth Szilágyi. 50f, Dorothy Kanuizsai. 70f, Susanna Lórántffy. 80f, Ilona Zrinyi.

**1944, Aug. 1 *Perf. 15***

**625** A118 20f olive .25 .25
**626** A118 24f rose violet .25 .25
**627** A118 30f copper red .25 .25
**628** A118 50f dark blue .25 .25
**629** A118 70f orange red .25 .25
**630** A118 80f brown car .25 .25
*Nos. 625-630 (6)* 1.50 1.50

Exist imperf. Value, set $120.
For overprints and surcharges see Nos. 659, 663, 665, 670, 673, 678, 681, 683-684, 690, 804, 807-809, F1, F3, Q1, Q4-Q6, Q8.

**Issues of the Republic**

Types of Hungary, 1943 Surcharged in Carmine

**1945, May 1 Wmk. 266**

**Blue Surface-tinted Paper**

**631** A99 10f on 1f grnsh blk 1.50 1.50
**632** A99 20f on 3f ultra 1.50 1.50
**633** A99 30f on 4f brown 1.50 1.50
**634** A99 40f on 6f slate bl 1.50 1.50
**635** A99 50f on 8f dk ol grn 1.50 1.50
**636** A99 1p on 10f brown 1.50 1.50
**637** A99 150f on 12f dp bl grn 1.50 1.50
**638** A99 2p on 18f dk gray 1.50 1.50
**639** A109 3p on 20f chnt brn 1.50 1.50
**640** A99 5p on 24f rose vio 1.50 1.50
**641** A109 6p on 50f blue 1.50 1.50
**642** A109 10p on 80f yel brn 1.50 1.50
**643** A109 20p on 1p green 1.50 1.50

**Yellow Surface-tinted Paper**

**644** A99 10f on 1f grnsh blk 1.50 1.50
**645** A99 20f on 3f ultra 1.50 1.50
**646** A99 30f on 4f brown 1.50 1.50
**647** A99 40f on 6f slate bl 1.50 1.50
**648** A99 50f on 8f dk ol grn 1.50 1.50
**649** A99 1p on 10f brown 1.50 1.50
**650** A99 150f on 12f dp bl grn 1.50 1.50
**651** A99 2p on 18f dk gray 1.50 1.50
**652** A109 3p on 20f chnt brn 1.50 1.50
**653** A99 5p on 24f rose vio 1.50 1.50
**654** A109 6p on 50f blue 1.50 1.50
**655** A109 10p on 80f yel brn 1.50 1.50
**656** A109 20p on 1p green 1.50 1.50
*Nos. 631-656 (26)* 39.00 39.00

Hungary's liberation.

### Types of Hungary, 1943-45, Surcharged in Carmine or Black

**1945 Blue Surface-tinted Paper**

| | | | | |
|---|---|---|---|---|
| **657** | A99 | 10f on 4f brn (C) | .25 | .25 |
| **658** | A99 | 10f on 10f brn (C) | .45 | .45 |
| **659** | A118 | 20f on 20f ol (C) | .25 | .25 |
| **660** | A99 | 28f on 5f ver | .25 | .25 |
| **661** | A109 | 30f on 30f brt car | .25 | .25 |
| **662** | A113 | 30f on 30f dp car | .25 | .25 |
| **663** | A118 | 30f on 30f cop red | .25 | .25 |
| **664** | A99 | 40f on 10f brown | .25 | .25 |
| **665** | A118 | 1p on 70f org red | .25 | .25 |
| **666** | A109 | 1p on 80f yel brn (C) | .25 | .25 |
| **667** | A99 | 2p on 4f brown | .25 | .25 |
| **668** | A109 | 2p on 2p brn (C) | .25 | .25 |
| **669** | A109 | 4p on 30f brt car | .25 | .25 |
| **670** | A118 | 8p on 20f olive | .25 | .25 |
| **671** | A99 | 10p on 2f red org | 8.00 | 8.00 |
| **672** | A109 | 10p on 80f yel brn | .25 | .25 |
| **673** | A118 | 20p on 30f cop red | .25 | .25 |

**Same Surcharge with Thinner Unshaded Numerals of Value**

| | | | | |
|---|---|---|---|---|
| **673A** | A113 | 300p on 30f dp car | .25 | .25 |

**Surcharged as Nos. 657-673 Yellow Surface-tinted Paper**

| | | | | |
|---|---|---|---|---|
| **674** | A99 | 10f on 12f dp bl grn (C) | .25 | .25 |
| **675** | A99 | 20f on 1f grnsh blk (C) | .25 | .25 |
| **676** | A99 | 20f on 18f dk gray (C) | .25 | .25 |
| *a.* | | Double surcharge | | |
| **677** | A99 | 40f on 24f rose vio (C) | .25 | .25 |
| **678** | A118 | 40f on 24f rose vio (C) | .25 | .25 |
| **679** | A109 | 42f on 20f chnt brn (C) | .25 | .25 |
| **680** | A109 | 50f on 50f bl (C) | .25 | .25 |
| **681** | A118 | 50f on 50f dk bl (C) | .25 | .25 |
| **682** | A99 | 60f on 8f dk ol grn (C) | .25 | .25 |
| **683** | A118 | 80f on 24f rose vio | .25 | .25 |
| **684** | A118 | 80f on 80f brn car (C) | .25 | .25 |
| **685** | A109 | 1p on 20f chnt brn | .25 | .25 |
| **686** | A109 | 1p on 1p grn (C) | .25 | .25 |
| **687** | A99 | 150f on 6f sl bl (C) | .90 | .90 |
| **688** | A99 | 1.60p on 12f dp bl grn | .25 | .25 |
| **689** | A99 | 3p on 3f ultra (C) | .25 | .25 |
| **690** | A118 | 3p on 50f dk bl | .25 | .25 |
| **691** | A99 | 5p on 8f dk ol grn | .25 | .25 |
| **692** | A109 | 5p on 5p dk red vio (C) | .25 | .25 |
| **693** | A109 | 6p on 50f blue | .25 | .25 |
| **694** | A109 | 7p on 1p grn | .25 | .25 |
| **695** | A99 | 9p on 1f grnsh blk | .25 | .25 |

**Same Surcharge with Thinner, Unshaded Numerals of Value**

| | | | | |
|---|---|---|---|---|
| **696** | A99 | 40p on 8f dk ol grn | .25 | .25 |
| **697** | A99 | 60p on 18f dk gray | .25 | .25 |
| **698** | A99 | 100p on 12f dp bl grn | .25 | .25 |
| | | *Nos. 657-698 (43)* | 19.35 | 19.35 |

Various shades and errors of overprint exist on Nos. 657-698.

These surface-tinted stamps exist without surcharge, but were not so issued.

Construction A124

Designs: 1.60p, Manufacturing. 2p, Railroading. 3p, Building. 5p, Agriculture. 8p, Communications. 10p, Architecture. 20p, Writing.

**Wmk. 266**

**1945, Sept. 11 Photo. *Perf. 12***

| | | | | |
|---|---|---|---|---|
| **700** | A124 | 40f gray black | 5.50 | 6.50 |
| **701** | A124 | 1.60p olive bis | 5.50 | 6.50 |
| **702** | A124 | 2p slate green | 5.50 | 6.50 |
| **703** | A124 | 3p dark purple | 5.50 | 6.50 |
| **704** | A124 | 5p dark red | 5.50 | 6.50 |
| **705** | A124 | 8p brown | 5.50 | 6.50 |
| **706** | A124 | 10p deep claret | 5.50 | 6.50 |
| **707** | A124 | 20p slate blue | 5.50 | 6.50 |
| | | *Nos. 700-707 (8)* | 44.00 | 52.00 |

World Trade Union Conf., Paris, Sept. 25 to Oct. 10, 1945.

Exist imperf. Value, set $500.

"Reconstruction" — A132

**1945-46**

| | | | | |
|---|---|---|---|---|
| **708** | A132 | 12p brown olive | .25 | .25 |
| **709** | A132 | 20p brt green | .25 | .25 |
| **710** | A132 | 24p orange brn | .25 | .25 |
| **711** | A132 | 30p gray black | .25 | .25 |
| **712** | A132 | 40p olive green | .25 | .25 |
| **713** | A132 | 60p red orange | .25 | .25 |
| **714** | A132 | 100p orange yel | .25 | .25 |
| **715** | A132 | 120p brt ultra | .25 | .25 |
| **716** | A132 | 140p brt red | .55 | .65 |
| **717** | A132 | 200p olive brn | .25 | .25 |
| **718** | A132 | 240p brt blue | .25 | .25 |
| **719** | A132 | 300p dk carmine | .25 | .25 |
| **720** | A132 | 500p dull green | .25 | .25 |
| **721** | A132 | 1000p red violet | .25 | .25 |
| **722** | A132 | 3000p brt red ('46) | .25 | .25 |
| | | *Nos. 708-722 (15)* | 4.05 | 4.15 |

Nos. 708-721 exist tête bêche. Value: $16.

Exist imperf. Value, set $200.

"Liberation" A133

**1946, Feb. 12**

| | | | | |
|---|---|---|---|---|
| **723** | A133 | 3ez p dark red | .25 | .25 |
| **724** | A133 | 15ez p ultra | .25 | .25 |

Exist imperf. Value, set $50.

Postrider — A134

**Photo.; Values Typo.**

**1946 *Perf. 15***

| | | | | |
|---|---|---|---|---|
| **725** | A134 | 4ez p brown org | .25 | .25 |
| **726** | A134 | 10ez p brt red | .25 | .25 |
| **727** | A134 | 15ez p ultra | .25 | .25 |
| **728** | A134 | 20ez p dk brown | .25 | .25 |
| **729** | A134 | 30ez p red violet | .25 | .25 |
| **730** | A134 | 50ez p gray black | .25 | .25 |
| **731** | A134 | 80ez p brt ultra | .25 | .25 |
| **732** | A134 | 100ez p rose car | .25 | .25 |
| **733** | A134 | 160ez p gray green | .25 | .25 |
| **734** | A134 | 200ez p yellow grn | .25 | .25 |
| **735** | A134 | 500ez p red | .25 | .25 |
| **736** | A134 | 640ez p olive bis | .25 | .25 |
| **737** | A134 | 800ez p rose violet | .25 | .25 |
| | | *Nos. 725-737 (13)* | 3.25 | 3.25 |

Exist imperf. Value, set $60.

Abbreviations:
Ez (Ezer) = Thousand
Mil (Milpengo) = Million
Mlrd (Milliard) = Billion
Bil (Billio-pengo) = Trillion

Arms of Hungary — A135

**1946 Wmk. 210**

| | | | | |
|---|---|---|---|---|
| **738** | A135 | 1mil p vermilion | .25 | .25 |
| *a.* | | "1" in center omitted | 600.00 | |
| **739** | A135 | 2mil p ultra | .25 | .25 |
| **740** | A135 | 3mil p brown | .25 | .25 |
| **741** | A135 | 4mil p slate gray | .25 | .25 |
| **742** | A135 | 5mil p rose violet | .25 | .25 |
| **743** | A135 | 10mil p green | .25 | .25 |
| **744** | A135 | 20mil p carmine | .25 | .25 |
| **745** | A135 | 50mil p olive | .25 | .25 |

Arms and Post Horn
A136 A137

| | | | | |
|---|---|---|---|---|
| **746** | A136 | 100mil p henna brn | .25 | .25 |
| **747** | A136 | 200mil p henna brn | .25 | .25 |
| **748** | A136 | 500mil p henna brn | .25 | .25 |
| **749** | A136 | 1000mil p henna brn | .25 | .25 |
| **750** | A136 | 2000mil p henna brn | .25 | .25 |
| **751** | A136 | 3000mil p henna brn | .25 | .25 |
| **752** | A136 | 5000mil p henna brn | .25 | .25 |
| **753** | A136 | 10,000mil p henna brn | .25 | .25 |
| **754** | A136 | 20,000mil p henna brn | .25 | .25 |
| **755** | A136 | 30,000mil p henna brn | .25 | .25 |
| **756** | A136 | 50,000mil p henna brn | .25 | .25 |

**Denomination in Carmine**

| | | | | |
|---|---|---|---|---|
| **757** | A137 | 100mlrd p olive | .25 | .25 |
| **758** | A137 | 200mlrd p olive | .25 | .25 |
| **759** | A137 | 500mlrd p olive | .25 | .25 |

Dove and Letter — A138

**Denomination in Carmine**

| | | | | |
|---|---|---|---|---|
| **760** | A138 | 1bil p grnsh blk | .25 | .25 |
| **761** | A138 | 2bil p grnsh blk | .25 | .25 |
| **763** | A138 | 5bil p grnsh blk | .25 | .25 |
| **764** | A138 | 10bil p grnsh blk | .25 | .25 |
| **765** | A138 | 20bil p grnsh blk | .25 | .25 |
| **766** | A138 | 50bil p grnsh blk | .25 | .25 |
| **767** | A138 | 100bil p grnsh blk | .25 | .25 |
| **768** | A138 | 200bil p grnsh blk | .25 | .25 |
| **769** | A138 | 500bil p grnsh blk | .25 | .25 |
| **770** | A138 | 1000bil p grnsh blk | .25 | .25 |
| **771** | A138 | 10,000bil p grnsh blk | .25 | .25 |
| **772** | A138 | 50,000bil p grnsh blk | .25 | .25 |
| **773** | A138 | 100,000bil p grnsh blk | .25 | .25 |
| **774** | A138 | 500,000bil p grnsh blk | .25 | .25 |

**Denomination in Black**

| | | | | |
|---|---|---|---|---|
| **775** | A137 | 5ez ap green | .25 | .25 |
| **776** | A137 | 10ez ap green | .25 | .25 |
| **777** | A137 | 20ez ap green | .25 | .25 |
| **778** | A137 | 50ez ap green | .25 | .25 |
| **779** | A137 | 80ez ap green | .25 | .25 |
| **780** | A137 | 100ez ap green | .25 | .25 |
| **781** | A137 | 200ez ap green | .25 | .25 |
| **782** | A137 | 500ez ap green | .25 | .25 |
| **783** | A137 | 1mil ap vermilion | .25 | .25 |
| **784** | A137 | 5mil ap vermilion | .25 | .25 |
| | | *Nos. 738-784 (46)* | 11.50 | 11.50 |

Denominations are expressed in "ado" or "tax" pengos.

Nos. 738-784 exist imperf. Value, set $400.

Early Steam Locomotive A139

Designs: 20,000ap, Recent steam locomotive. 30,000ap, Electric locomotive. 40,000ap, Diesel locomotive.

**1946, July 15 Wmk. 266 *Perf. 12***

| | | | | |
|---|---|---|---|---|
| **785** | A139 | 10,000ap vio brn | 2.75 | 3.25 |
| **786** | A139 | 20,000ap dk blue | 2.75 | 3.25 |
| **787** | A139 | 30,000ap dp yel grn | 2.75 | 3.25 |
| **788** | A139 | 40,000ap rose car | 2.75 | 3.25 |
| *b.* | | "40,000 ap" omitted | *3,500.* | |
| | | *Nos. 785-788 (4)* | 11.00 | 13.00 |

Centenary of Hungarian railways.

Exist imperf. Value, set $700.

Industry A143

Agriculture A144

**1946 Wmk. 210 Photo. *Perf. 15***

| | | | | |
|---|---|---|---|---|
| **788A** | A143 | 8f henna brn | .25 | .25 |
| **789** | A143 | 10f henna brn | .30 | .25 |
| **790** | A143 | 12f henna brn | .25 | .25 |
| **791** | A143 | 20f henna brn | .30 | .25 |
| **792** | A143 | 30f henna brn | .40 | .25 |
| **793** | A143 | 40f henna brn | .40 | .25 |
| **794** | A143 | 60f henna brn | .40 | .25 |
| **795** | A144 | 1fo dp yel grn | .75 | .25 |
| **796** | A144 | 1.40fo dp yel grn | .75 | .25 |
| **797** | A144 | 2fo dp yel grn | 1.25 | .25 |
| **798** | A144 | 3fo dp yel grn | 5.50 | .25 |
| **799** | A144 | 5fo dp yel grn | 1.50 | .25 |
| **800** | A144 | 10fo dp yel grn | 3.00 | .35 |
| | | *Nos. 788A-800 (13)* | 15.05 | 3.35 |

For surcharges see Nos. Q9-Q11.

Exist imperf. Value, set $175.

### Stamps and Types of 1943-45 Ovptd. in Carmine or Black to Show Class of Postage for which Valid

a

b

"Any." or "Nyomtatv." = Printed Matter.
"Hl" or "Helyi levél" = Local Letter.
"Hlp." or "Helyi lev.-lap" = Local Postcard.
"Tl." or "Távolsági levél" =Domestic Letter.
"Tlp." or "Távolsági lev.-lap" = Domestic Postcard.

**1946 Wmk. 266**

| | | | | |
|---|---|---|---|---|
| **801** | A99(a) | "Any 1." on 1f (#601;C) | .25 | .25 |
| **802** | A99(a) | "Any 2," on 1f (#601;C) | .25 | .25 |
| **803** | A99(b) | "Nyomtatv. 20gr" on 60f on 8f (#682;Bk + C) | .25 | .25 |
| **804** | A118(a) | "Hl. 1" on 50f (#628;C) | .25 | .25 |
| **805** | A99(a) | "Hl. 2" on 40f on 10f (#664;C + Bk) | .25 | .25 |
| **806** | A99(b) | "Helyi levél" on 10f brn, *bl* (Bk) | .25 | .25 |
| **807** | A118(a) | "Hlp.1" on 8p on 20f (#670;C + Bk) | .25 | .25 |
| **808** | A118(a) | "Hlp.2." on 8p on 20f (#670;C + Bk) | .25 | .25 |
| **809** | A118(b) | "Helyi lev.-lap" on 20f ol, *bl* (C) | .25 | .25 |
| **810** | A99(a) | "Tl.1" on 10f (#608;Bk) | .25 | .25 |
| **811** | A99(a) | "Tl.2." on 10f on 4f (#657;Bk + C) | .25 | .25 |
| **812** | A99(b) | "Tavolsagi level" on 18f (#610;C) | .25 | .25 |
| **813** | A99(a) | "Tlp.1." on 4f (#604;Bk) | .25 | .25 |
| **814** | A99(a) | "Tlp.2." on 4f (#604;Bk) | .25 | .25 |
| **815** | A99(b) | "Tavolsagi lev.-lap" on 4f (#604;Bk) | .25 | .25 |
| | | *Nos. 801-815 (15)* | 3.75 | 3.75 |

Nos. 806, 809 not issued without overprint.

György Dózsa — A145

Designs: 10f, Antal Budai-Nagy. 12f, Tamas Esze. 20f, Ignac Martinovics. 30f, Janos Batsanyi. 40f, Lajos Kossuth. 60f, Mihaly Tancsics. 1fo, Alexander Petőfi. 2fo, Andreas Ady. 4fo, Jozsef Attila.

**1947, Mar. 15 Photo. Wmk. 210**

| | | | | |
|---|---|---|---|---|
| **816** | A145 | 8f rose brown | .25 | .25 |
| **817** | A145 | 10f deep ultra | .35 | .25 |
| **818** | A145 | 12f deep brown | .30 | .25 |
| **819** | A145 | 20f dk yel grn | .40 | .25 |
| **820** | A145 | 30f dk ol bis | .50 | .25 |
| **821** | A145 | 40f brown car | .70 | .25 |
| **822** | A145 | 60f cerise | .70 | .25 |
| **823** | A145 | 1fo dp grnsh bl | .80 | .25 |
| **824** | A145 | 2fo dk violet | 1.75 | .35 |
| **825** | A145 | 4fo grnsh black | 2.75 | .50 |
| | | *Nos. 816-825 (10)* | 8.50 | 2.85 |

Exist imperf. Value, set $175.

Peace and Agriculture A155

Postal Savings Emblem A156

**1947, Sept. 22 *Perf. 12***

| | | | | |
|---|---|---|---|---|
| **826** | A155 | 60f bright red | 1.00 | .25 |
| *a.* | | "60f." omitted | *1,500.* | |

Peace treaty.

Exists imperf. Value, set $120.

**1947, Oct. 31**

60f, Postal Savings Bank, Budapest.

**827** A156 40f rose brown .50 .25
**828** A156 60f brt rose car .50 .25

Savings Day, Oct. 31, 1947.
Exist imperf. Value, set $50.

Hungarian Flag — A157

1848 Printing Press A158

Barred Window and Dove — A159

1848 Shako, Sword and Trumpet A160

"On your feet Hungarian, the Homeland is Calling!" A161

Arms of Hungary — A162

*Perf. 12½x12, 12x12½*

**1948 Wmk. 283 Photo.**

**829** A157 8f dk rose red .30 .25
**830** A158 10f ultra .40 .25
**831** A159 12f copper brn .75 .25
**832** A160 20f deep green 1.50 .25
**833** A161 30f olive brown 1.00 .25
**834** A157 40f dk vio brn 1.25 .25
**835** A161 60f carmine lake 1.50 .25
*a.* Printed on both sides 1,100.
**836** A162 1fo brt ultra 1.50 .25
**837** A162 2fo red brown 2.50 .25
**838** A162 3fo green 5.00 .25
**839** A162 4fo scarlet 7.50 .25
*Nos. 829-839 (11)* 23.20 2.75

Cent. of the beginning of Hungary's war for independence.
No. 834 is inscribed "Kossuth," No. 835 "Petöfi."
Exist imperf. Value, set $300.

Baron Roland Eötvös A163

**1948, July 27**

**840** A163 60f deep red 1.50 .50

Roland Eötvös, physicist, birth cent.
Exists imperf. Value $100.

Hungarian Workers — A164

**1948, Oct. 17 Wmk. 283 *Perf. 12***

**841** A164 30f dk carmine rose 1.00 .50
*a.* Sheet of 4 32.50 32.50

The 17th Trade Union Congress, Budapest, October 1948. No. 841a was sold for 2 forint.
Exist imperf. Value: single $25; sheet of 4 $2,000.

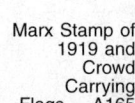

Marx Stamp of 1919 and Crowd Carrying Flags — A165

Petöfi Stamp of 1919 and Flags — A166

**1949, Mar. 19 Flags in Carmine**

**842** A165 40f brown .75 .50
**843** A166 60f olive gray .75 .50

1st Hungarian Soviet Republic, 30th anniv.
Exist imperf. Value, set $50.

Workers of the Five Continents and Flag — A167

**1949, June 29 *Perf. 12x12½***

**Flag in Red**

**844** A167 30f yellow brown 2.75 3.50
**845** A167 40f brown violet 2.75 3.50
**846** A167 60f lilac rose 2.75 3.50
**847** A167 1fo violet blue 2.75 3.50
*Nos. 844-847 (4)* 11.00 14.00

2nd Congress of the World Federation of Trade Unions, Milan, 1949.
Exist imperf. Value, set $125.

Sándor Petöfi — A168

Youth of Three Races — A169

*Perf. 12½x12*

**1949, July 31 Engr. Unwmk.**

**848** A168 40f claret .60 .25
**849** A168 60f dark red .45 .25
**850** A168 1fo deep blue .45 .25
*Nos. 848-850 (3)* 1.50 .75

Cent. of the death of Sándor Petöfi, poet.
Exist imperf. Value, set $30.
See Nos. 867-869.

*Perf. 12½x12*

**1949, Aug. 14 Photo. Wmk. 283**

Designs: 30f, Three fists. 40f, Soldier breaking chain. 60f, Soviet youths carrying flags. 1fo, Young workers displaying books.

**851** A169 20f dk violet brn .50 .50
*a.* 20f blue green 4.00 4.00
**852** A169 30f blue green 1.00 2.00
*a.* 30f violet brown 4.00 4.00
**853** A169 40f olive bister 1.50 2.00
*a.* 40f ultramarine 4.00 4.00
**854** A169 60f rose pink 1.50 1.00
**855** A169 1fo ultra 2.00 1.00
*a.* 1fo olive bister 4.00 4.00
*b.* Souv. sheet of 5, #851a-853a, 854, 855a 32.50 32.50
*Nos. 851-855 (5)* 6.50 6.50

World Festival of Youth and Students, Budapest, Aug. 14-28, 1949.
Exist imperf. Value, set $100. No. 855b imperf, $2,000.

Arms of Hungarian People's Republic A170

**Arms in Bister, Carmine, Blue and Green**

**1949 Wmk. 283**

**856** A170 20f green 1.25 .50
*a.* Unwatermarked 1.75 .80
**857** A170 60f carmine 1.25 .30
*a.* Unwatermarked 1.10 .30
**858** A170 1fo blue 2.50 1.10
*a.* Unwatermarked 1.25 .60
*Nos. 856-858 (3)* 5.00 1.90

Adoption of the Hungarian People's Republic constitution.
Nos. 856-858 exist imperf. Value, set $175. Nos. 856a-858a also exist imperf. Value, set $200.
Nos. 856-858 exist with papermaker's watermark. These sell for the same.

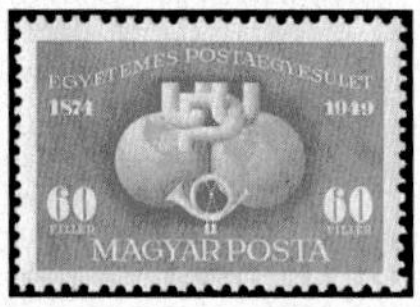

Symbols of the UPU — A171

**1949, Nov. 1 *Perf. 12x12½***

**859** A171 60f rose red .50 .50
*a.* Booklet pane of 6 10.00
**860** A171 1fo blue .50 .50
*a.* Booklet pane of 6 14.00
*Nos. 859-860,C63 (3)* 2.50 2.50

75th anniv. of the UPU.
Nos. 859 and 860 exist imperf. and stamps from 859a and 860a in horiz. pairs, imperf. between. Values: set $15; pairs, imperf between $10.
See No. C63, C81.

Chain Bridge A172

**1949, Nov. 20 Wmk. 283**

**861** A172 40f blue green .50 .30
**862** A172 60f red brown .50 .35
**863** A172 1fo blue .50 .35
*Nos. 861-863,C64-C65 (5)* 5.00 5.00

Cent. of the opening of the Chain Bridge at Budapest to traffic.
Exist imperf. Value, set $12.
For souvenir sheet see No. C66.

Joseph V. Stalin — A173

*Perf. 12½x12*

**1949, Dec. 21 Engr. Unwmk.**

**864** A173 60f dark red 1.00 .25
**865** A173 1fo deep blue 1.00 .30
**866** A173 2fo brown 2.00 .50
*Nos. 864-866 (3)* 4.00 1.05

70th anniv. of the birth of Joseph V. Stalin.
Exist imperf. Value, set $15.

See Nos. 1034-1035.

**Petöfi Type of 1949**

**1950, Feb. 5 *Perf. 12½x12***

**867** A168 40f brown .75 .35
**868** A168 60f dark carmine .40 .25
**869** A168 1fo dark green .40 .25
*Nos. 867-869 (3)* 1.55 .85

Value, set $30.

Philatelic Museum, Budapest A174

*Perf. 12x12½*

**1950, Mar. 12 Photo. Wmk. 283**

**870** A174 60f gray & brown 8.00 8.00

20th anniv. of the establishment of the Hungarian PO Phil. Museum.
Exists imperf. Value $90.
See No. C68.

Coal Mining A175

Designs: 10f, Heavy industry. 12f, Power production. 20f, Textile industry. 30f, "Cultured workers." 40f, Mechanized agriculture. 60f, Village cooperative. 1fo, Train. 1.70fo, "Holiday." 2fo, Defense. 3fo, Shipping. 4fo, Livestock. 5fo, Engineering. 10fo, Sports.

**1950 Wmk. 283**

**871** A175 8f gray .75 .25
**872** A175 10f claret .75 .25
**873** A175 12f orange ver 1.00 .25
**874** A175 20f blue green 1.25 .25
**875** A175 30f rose violet 1.25 .25
**876** A175 40f sepia 1.50 .25
**877** A175 60f red 2.00 .25
**878** A175 1fo gray brn, yel & lil 3.00 .25
**879** A175 1.70fo dk grn & yel 8.50 .25
**880** A175 2fo vio brn & cr 4.00 .25
**881** A175 3fo slate & cream 8.50 .25
**882** A175 4fo blk brn & sal 47.50 1.25
**883** A175 5fo rose vio & yel 22.50 .30
**884** A175 10fo dk brn & yel 47.50 6.00
*Nos. 871-884 (14)* 150.00 10.30
Hinged set 80.00

Issued to publicize Hungary's Five Year Plan.
Exist imperf. Value, set $450.
See Nos. 945-958.

Citizens Welcoming Liberators — A176

**1950, Apr. 4 Unwmk. *Perf. 12***

**885** A176 40f gray black 1.00 .35
**886** A176 60f rose brown 1.00 .25
**887** A176 1fo deep blue 1.00 .25
**888** A176 2fo brown 1.00 .35
*Nos. 885-888 (4)* 4.00 1.20

Fifth anniversary of Hungary's liberation.
Exist imperf. Value, set $50.

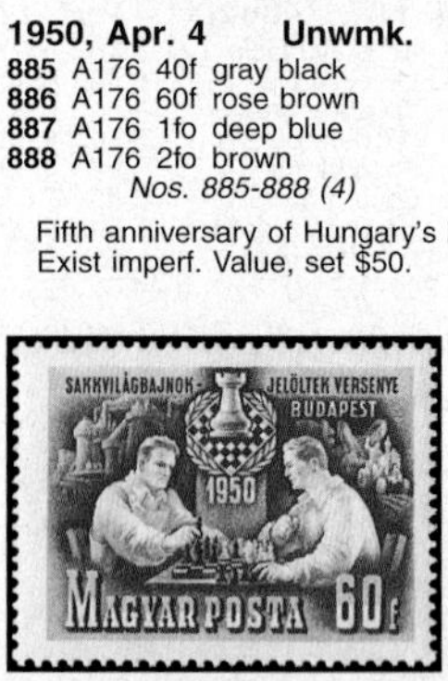

Chess Players A177

Design: 1fo, Iron Workers Union building and chess emblem.

**1950, Apr. 9** **Wmk. 106**

| | | | | |
|---|---|---|---|---|
| **889** | A177 | 60f deep magenta | 2.50 | .50 |
| **890** | A177 | 1fo deep blue | 4.00 | 1.25 |
| | | *Nos. 889-890,C69 (3)* | 12.50 | 3.85 |

World Chess Championship Matches, Budapest.
Exist imperf. Value, set (3) $200.

Workers Symbolizing International Proletariat — A178

Design: 60f, Blast furnace, tractor, workers holding Maypole.

**1950, May 1**

| | | | | |
|---|---|---|---|---|
| **891** | A178 | 40f orange brown | 1.50 | .35 |
| **892** | A178 | 60f rose carmine | 1.50 | .25 |
| **893** | A178 | 1fo deep blue | 2.00 | .50 |
| | | *Nos. 891-893 (3)* | 5.00 | 1.10 |

Issued to publicize Labor Day, May 1, 1950.
Exist imperf. Value, set $75.

Liberty, Cogwheel, Dove and Globes — A179

Design: 60f, Three workers and flag.

**Inscribed: "1950. V. 10.-24."**

**1950, May 10** **Photo.** ***Perf. 12x12½***

| | | | | |
|---|---|---|---|---|
| **894** | A179 | 40f olive green | 1.50 | .35 |
| **895** | A179 | 60f dark carmine | 1.25 | .25 |
| | | *Nos. 894-895,C70 (3)* | 4.35 | 1.25 |

Meeting of the World Federation of Trade Unions, Budapest, May 1950.
Exist imperf. Value, set $70.

Doctor Inspecting Baby's Bath — A180

Children's Day: 30f, Physical Culture. 40f, Education. 60f, Boys' Camp. 1.70fo, Model plane building.

**1950, June 4** **Wmk. 106**

| | | | | |
|---|---|---|---|---|
| **896** | A180 | 20f gray & brn | 1.25 | .60 |
| **897** | A180 | 30f brn & rose lake | .50 | .25 |
| **898** | A180 | 40f indigo & dk grn | .50 | .25 |
| **899** | A180 | 60f SZABAD | 1.25 | .25 |
| *a.* | | UTANPOTLASUNK . . | *950.00* | *750.00* |
| **900** | A180 | 1.70fo dp grn & gray | 1.50 | .30 |
| | | *Nos. 896-900 (5)* | 5.00 | 1.65 |

Exist imperf. Value, set $60.

Youths Marching on Globe — A181

Working Man and Woman — A182

30f, Foundry worker. 60f, Workers on Mt. Gellert. 1.70fo, Worker, peasant & student; flags.

**Inscribed: Budapest 1950. VI. 17-18.**

***Perf. 12x12½, 12½x12***

**1950, June 17**

| | | | | |
|---|---|---|---|---|
| **901** | A181 | 20f dark green | 1.00 | .30 |
| **902** | A181 | 30f deep red org | .30 | .25 |
| **903** | A182 | 40f dark brown | .45 | .25 |
| **904** | A182 | 60f deep claret | 1.00 | .25 |
| **905** | A182 | 1.70fo dark olive grn | 1.25 | .40 |
| | | *Nos. 901-905 (5)* | 4.00 | 1.45 |

Issued to publicize the First Congress of the Working Youth, Budapest, June 17-18, 1950.
Exist imperf. Value, set $60.

Peonies — A183

Designs: 40f, Anemones. 60f, Pheasant's-eye. 1fo, Geraniums. 1.70fo, Bluebells.

**Engraved and Lithographed**
***Perf. 12½x12***

**1950, Aug. 20** **Unwmk.**

| | | | | |
|---|---|---|---|---|
| **906** | A183 | 30f rose brn, rose pink & grn | 1.25 | .30 |
| **907** | A183 | 40f dk green, lil & yel | 1.60 | .30 |
| **908** | A183 | 60f red brn, yel & grn | 2.00 | .30 |
| **909** | A183 | 1fo purple, red & grn | 4.00 | 1.25 |
| **910** | A183 | 1.70fo dk violet & grn | 4.00 | 1.00 |
| | | *Nos. 906-910 (5)* | 12.85 | 3.15 |

Exist imperf. Value, set $60.

Miner — A184

Designs: 60f, High speed lathe. 1fo, Prefabricated building construction.

***Perf. 12x12½***

**1950, Oct. 7** **Photo.** **Wmk. 106**

| | | | | |
|---|---|---|---|---|
| **911** | A184 | 40f brown | 1.00 | .35 |
| **912** | A184 | 60f carmine rose | 1.25 | .25 |
| **913** | A184 | 1fo brt blue | 2.25 | .25 |
| | | *Nos. 911-913 (3)* | 4.50 | .85 |

2nd National Exhibition of Inventions.
Exist imperf. Value, set $35.

Gen. Josef Bem and Battle at Piski A185

***Perf. 12½x12***

**1950, Dec. 10** **Engr.** **Unwmk.**

| | | | | |
|---|---|---|---|---|
| **914** | A185 | 40f dark brown | 1.25 | .50 |
| **915** | A185 | 60f deep carmine | 1.00 | .25 |
| **916** | A185 | 1fo deep blue | 1.50 | .50 |
| | | *Nos. 914-916 (3)* | 3.75 | 1.25 |

Gen. Josef Bem, death centenary.
Exist imperf. Value, set $25.
See No. C80.

Signing Petition A186

Peace Demonstrator Holding Dove — A187

1fo, Mother and Children with soldier.

**Wmk. 106**

**1950, Nov. 23** **Photo.** ***Perf. 12***

| | | | | |
|---|---|---|---|---|
| **917** | A186 | 40f ultra & red brn | 7.50 | 3.00 |
| **918** | A187 | 60f red org & dk grn | 3.50 | 1.00 |
| **919** | A186 | 1fo ol grn & dk brn | 9.00 | 3.50 |
| | | *Nos. 917-919 (3)* | 20.00 | 7.50 |

Exist imperf. Value, set $80.

Women Swimmers A188

Designs: 20f, Vaulting. 1fo, Mountain climbing. 1.70fo, Basketball. 2fo, Motorcycling.

**1950, Dec. 2** ***Perf. 12x12½***

| | | | | |
|---|---|---|---|---|
| **920** | A188 | 10f blue & gray | .30 | .25 |
| **921** | A188 | 20f salmon & dk brn | .30 | .25 |
| **922** | A188 | 1fo olive & grn | .75 | .25 |
| **923** | A188 | 1.70fo ver & brn car | 1.00 | .25 |
| **924** | A188 | 2fo salmon & pur | 1.75 | .30 |
| | | *Nos. 920-924,C82-C86 (10)* | 13.85 | 5.00 |

Exist imperf. Value, set (10) $100.

Canceled to Order
The government stamp agency started about 1950 to sell canceled sets of new issues. Values in the second ("used") column are for these canceled-to-order stamps. Postally used stamps are worth more.
The practice was to end Apr. 1, 1991.

A189

Worker, Peasant, Soldier and Party Flag — A190

60f, Matthias Rakosi & allegory. 1fo, House of Parliament, columns of workers & banner.

**Inscribed: "Budapest * 1951 * Februar 24."**

**1951, Feb. 24** ***Perf. 12½x12, 12x12½***

| | | | | |
|---|---|---|---|---|
| **925** | A189 | 10f yellow green | .70 | .35 |
| **926** | A190 | 30f brown | .80 | .40 |
| **927** | A190 | 60f carmine rose | .80 | .50 |
| **928** | A189 | 1fo blue | 1.00 | .60 |
| | | *Nos. 925-928 (4)* | 3.30 | 1.85 |

2nd Congress of the Hungarian Workers' Party.
Exist imperf. Value, set $40.

Mare and Foal — A191

Designs: 30f, Sow and shoats. 40f, Ram and ewe. 60f, Cow and calf.

**1951, Apr. 5** ***Perf. 12x12½***

| | | | | |
|---|---|---|---|---|
| **929** | A191 | 10f ol bis & rose brn | 1.10 | .25 |
| **930** | A191 | 30f rose brn & ol bis | 1.25 | .55 |
| **931** | A191 | 40f dk green & brn | 1.25 | .55 |
| **932** | A191 | 60f brown org & brn | 1.50 | .35 |
| | | *Nos. 929-932,C87-C90 (8)* | 18.35 | 5.10 |

Issued to encourage increased livestock production.
Exist imperf. Value, set (8) $100.

Flags of Russia and Hungary — A192

Russian Technician Teaching Hungarians A193

**1951, Apr. 4** ***Perf. 12½x12, 12x12½***

| | | | | |
|---|---|---|---|---|
| **933** | A192 | 60f brnsh carmine | 1.25 | .25 |
| **934** | A193 | 1fo dull violet | 1.25 | .50 |

Issued to publicize the "Month of Friendship" between Hungary and Russia, 1951.
Exist imperf. Value, set $30.

Worker Holding Olive Branch and Mallet A194

Workers Carrying Flags — A195

1fo, Workers approaching Place of Heroes.

***Perf. 12x12½, 12½x12***

**1951, May 1** **Photo.** **Wmk. 106**

| | | | | |
|---|---|---|---|---|
| **935** | A194 | 40f brown | .80 | .30 |
| **936** | A195 | 60f scarlet | .60 | .25 |
| **937** | A194 | 1fo blue | 1.10 | .25 |
| | | *Nos. 935-937 (3)* | 2.50 | .80 |

Issued to publicize Labor Day, May 1, 1951.
Exist imperf. Value, set $30.

Leo Frankel — A196

Paris Street Fighting, 1871 — A197

**1951, May 20**
**938** A196 60f dark brown 1.00 .25
**939** A197 1fo blue & red 1.25 .40

80th anniv. of the Commune of Paris.
Exist imperf. Value, set $28.

Children of Various Races — A198

Designs: 40f, Boy and girl at play. 50f, Street car and Girl Pioneer. 60f, Chemistry students. 1.70fo, Pioneer bugler.

**Inscribed: "Nemzetkozi Gyermeknap 1951"**

**1951, June 3** ***Perf. 12½x12***
**940** A198 30f dark brown .60 .25
**941** A198 40f green .60 .25
**942** A198 50f brown red .60 .25
**943** A198 60f plum .85 .35
**944** A198 1.70fo blue 1.10 1.00
*Nos. 940-944 (5)* 3.75 2.10

International Day of Children, 6/3/51.
Exist imperf. Value, set $40.

**5-Year-Plan Type of 1950**

Designs as before.

**1951-52 Wmk. 106** ***Perf. 12x12½***
**945** A175 8f gray .45 .25
**946** A175 10f claret .60 .25
**947** A175 12f orange ver .50 .25
**948** A175 20f blue green .60 .25
**949** A175 30f rose violet .60 .25
**950** A175 40f sepia 1.25 .25
**951** A175 60f red 1.25 .25
**952** A175 1fo gray brn, yel & lil 1.50 .25
**953** A175 1.70fo dk grn & yel 1.50 .25
**954** A175 2fo vio brn & cr 2.25 .25
**955** A175 3fo slate & cream 3.00 .25
**956** A175 4fo blk brn & sal 4.00 .35
**957** A175 5fo rose vio & yel ('52) 5.00 .80
**958** A175 10fo dk brn & yel ('52) 15.00 3.25
*Nos. 945-958 (14)* 37.50 7.15

Maxim Gorky — A199

***Perf. 12½x12***
**1951, June 17 Engr. Unwmk.**
**959** A199 60f copper red .40 .25
**960** A199 1fo deep blue .25 .40
**961** A199 2fo rose violet 1.10 .45
*Nos. 959-961 (3)* 1.75 1.10

15th anniversary of the death of Gorky.
Exist imperf. Value, set $25.

**Budapest Buildings**

Railroad Workshop A200

Building in Lehel Street A201

Suburban Bus Terminal A202

Rakosi House of Culture A203

George Kilian Street School A204

Central Construction Headquarters A205

**Design Size: 22x18mm**

**1951 Wmk. 106 Photo.** ***Perf. 15***
**962** A200 20f green .55 .25
**963** A201 30f red orange .55 .25
**964** A202 40f brown .55 .25
**965** A203 60f red .75 .25
**966** A204 1fo blue 1.00 .25
**967** A205 3fo deep plum 3.00 .25
*Nos. 962-967 (6)* 6.40 1.50

Exist imperf. Value, set $100.
See Nos. 1004-1011, 1048-1056C.

**1958 Design Size: 21x17mm**
*962a* A200 20f green .65 .25
*963a* A201 30f red orange 1.10 .25
*964a* A202 40f brown .95 .25
*965a* A203 60f red 1.40 .25
*966a* A204 1fo blue 1.40 .25
*967a* A205 3fo deep plum 3.00 .25
*Nos. 962a-967a (6)* 8.50 1.50

Tractor Manufacture A206

30f, Fluoroscope examination. 40f, Checking lathework. 60f, Woman tractor operator.

**1951, Aug. 20** ***Perf. 12x12½***
**968** A206 20f black brown .25 .25
**969** A206 30f deep blue .25 .25
**970** A206 40f crimson rose .65 .25
**971** A206 60f brown .80 .25
*Nos. 968-971,C91-C93 (7)* 5.50 2.35

The successful conclusion of the first year under Hungary's 5-year plan.
Exist imperf. Value, set $50.

Soldiers of the People's Army — A207

**1951, Sept. 29**
**972** A207 1fo brown 1.00 .25

Issued to publicize Army Day, Sept. 29, 1951. See No. C94.
Exist imperf. Value (with C94) $30.

Stamp of 1871, Portrait Replaced by Postmark A208

Cornflower A209

***Perf. 12½x12***
**1951, Sept. 12 Engr. Unwmk.**
**973** A208 60f olive green 2.50 .50
*Nos. 973,B207-B208 (3)* 28.50 26.50

80th anniv. of Hungary's 1st postage stamp.
See Nos. C95, CB13-CB14.
Exist imperf. Value, set (3) $60.

**1951, Nov. 4 Engr. & Litho.**
**974** A209 30f shown .75 .25
**975** A209 40f Lily of the Valley 3.00 .75
**976** A209 60f Tulip .75 .25
**977** A209 1fo Poppy 2.00 .25
**978** A209 1.70fo Cowslip 2.00 .30
*Nos. 974-978 (5)* 8.50 1.80

Exist imperf. Value, set $50.

Storming of the Winter Palace A210

Designs: 60f, Lenin speaking to soldiers. 1fo, Lenin and Stalin.

***Perf. 12x12½***
**1951, Nov. 7 Photo. Wmk. 106**
**979** A210 40f gray green 1.00 .50
**980** A210 60f deep blue 1.25 .25
**981** A210 1fo rose lake 1.75 .40
*Nos. 979-981 (3)* 4.00 1.15

34th anniversary of the Russian Revolution.
Exist imperf. Value, set $40.

Marchers Passing Stalin Monument — A211

**1951, Dec. 16 Wmk. 106**
**982** A211 60f henna brown 1.50 .60
**983** A211 1fo deep blue 1.50 .60

Joseph V. Stalin, 72nd birthday.
Exist imperf. Value, set $30.

Grand Theater, Moscow A212

Views of Moscow: 1fo, Lenin Mausoleum. 1.60fo, Kremlin.

**1952, Feb. 20** ***Perf. 12***
**984** A212 60f ol grn & rose brn .65 .25
**985** A212 1fo lil rose & ol brn 1.00 .35
**986** A212 1.60fo red brn & ol 2.00 .65
*Nos. 984-986 (3)* 3.65 1.25

Hungarian-Soviet Friendship Month.
Exist imperf. Value, set $30.

Rakosi and Farmers A213

Matyas Rakosi — A214

Design: 2fo, Rakosi and Workers.

***Perf. 12x12½, 12½x12***
**1952, Mar. 9 Engr. Unwmk.**
**987** A213 60f deep plum .80 .25
**988** A214 1fo dk red brown .90 .25
**989** A213 2fo dp violet blue 1.90 .55
*Nos. 987-989 (3)* 3.60 1.05

60th anniv. of the birth of Matyas Rakosi, communist leader.

Exist imperf. Value, set $35.

Lajos Kossuth and Speech at Debrecen A215

Designs: 30f, Sándor Petőfi. 50f, Gen. Josef Bem. 60f, Mihaly Tancsics. 1fo, Gen. János Damjanich. 1.50fo, Gen. Alexander Nagy.

**1952, Mar. 15** ***Perf. 12x12½***
**990** A215 20f green .25 .25
**991** A215 30f rose violet .25 .25
**992** A215 50f grnsh blk .25 .25
**993** A215 60f brown car .35 .25
**994** A215 1fo blue 1.00 .25
**995** A215 1.50fo redsh brown 1.10 .45
*Nos. 990-995 (6)* 3.20 1.70

Heroes of the 1848 revolution.
Exist imperf. Value, set $32.50.
Nos. 990-995 also exist perf 12. Value, set $300.

**No. B204 Surcharged in Black with Bars Obliterating Inscription and Surtax**

***Perf. 12½x12***
**1952, Apr. 27 Photo. Wmk. 283**
**996** SP121 60f magenta 42.50 42.50

Budapest Philatelic Exhibition. Counterfeits exist.

Girl Drummer Leading Parade A216

Designs: 60f, Workers and soldier. 1fo, Worker, flag-encircled globe and dove.

***Perf. 12x12½***
**1952, May 1 Photo. Wmk. 106**
**997** A216 40f dk grn & dull red 1.50 .50
**998** A216 60f dk red brn & dull red 1.00 .25
**999** A216 1fo sepia & dull red 1.50 .30
*Nos. 997-999 (3)* 4.00 1.05

Issued to publicize Labor Day, May 1, 1952.
Exist imperf. Value, set $60.

Runner — A217

Designs: 40f, Swimmer. 60f, Fencer. 1fo, Woman gymnast.

**1952, May 26** ***Perf. 11***
**1000** A217 30f dark red brown .85 .25
**1001** A217 40f deep green .85 .25
**1002** A217 60f deep lilac rose 1.25 .25
**1003** A217 1fo deep blue 1.40 .50
*Nos. 1000-1003,C107-C108 (6)* 8.95 3.50

Issued to publicize Hungary's participation in the Olympic Games, Helsinki, 1952.
Exist imperf. Value, set (6) $75.

**Building Types of 1951**

Buildings: 8f, School, Stalinvarost. 10f, Szekesfehervar Station. 12f, Building, Ujpest. 50f, Metal works, Inotai. 70f, Grain elevator, Hajdunanas. 80f, Tiszalok dam. 4fo, Miners' union headquarters. 5fo, Workers' apartments, Ujpest.

**Design Size: 22x18mm**

**1952 Wmk. 106 *Perf. 15***

| | | | | |
|---|---|---|---|---|
| **1004** | A202 | 8f green | .45 | .25 |
| **1005** | A200 | 10f purple | .45 | .25 |
| **1006** | A202 | 12f carmine | .45 | .25 |
| **1007** | A202 | 50f gray blue | .65 | .25 |
| **1008** | A202 | 70f yellow brn | 1.25 | .25 |
| **1009** | A200 | 80f maroon | 1.25 | .25 |
| **1010** | A202 | 4fo olive grn | 4.00 | .25 |
| **1011** | A202 | 5fo gray black | 6.00 | .25 |
| | | *Nos. 1004-1011 (8)* | 14.50 | 2.00 |

Exist imperf. Value, set $140.

**1958 Design Size: 21x17mm**

| | | | | |
|---|---|---|---|---|
| *1004a* | A202 | 8f green | .50 | .25 |
| *1005a* | A200 | 10f purple | 2.50 | .25 |
| *1006a* | A202 | 12f carmine | .60 | .25 |
| *1007a* | A202 | 50f gray blue | .90 | .25 |
| *1008a* | A202 | 70f yellow brn | .90 | .25 |
| *1009a* | A200 | 80f maroon | 1.40 | .25 |
| *1010a* | A202 | 4fo olive grn | 4.00 | .25 |
| *1011a* | A202 | 5fo gray black | 5.50 | .25 |
| | | *Nos. 1004a-1011a (8)* | 16.30 | 2.00 |

Approaching Train — A218

Railroad Day: 1fo, Railroad Construction.

**1952, Aug. 10 *Perf. 12x12½***

| | | | | |
|---|---|---|---|---|
| **1012** | A218 | 60f red brown | 1.10 | .35 |
| **1013** | A218 | 1fo deep olive grn | 1.40 | .40 |

Exist imperf. Value, set $30.

Coal Excavator A219

Miners' Day: 1fo, Coal breaker.

**1952, Sept. 7**

| | | | | |
|---|---|---|---|---|
| **1014** | A219 | 60f brown | 1.00 | .25 |
| **1015** | A219 | 1fo dark green | 1.25 | .30 |

Exist imperf. Value, set $25.

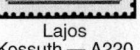

Lajos Kossuth — A220

Janos Hunyadi — A221

Design: 60f, Kossuth statue.

**1952, Sept. 19 *Perf. 12½x12***

| | | | | |
|---|---|---|---|---|
| **1016** | A220 | 40f ol brn, *pink* | .50 | .25 |
| **1017** | A220 | 60f black brn, *bl* | .75 | .25 |
| **1018** | A220 | 1fo purple, *citron* | 1.25 | .25 |
| | | *Nos. 1016-1018 (3)* | 2.50 | .75 |

150th anniv. of the birth of Lajos Kossuth. Exist imperf. Value, set $35.

**1952, Sept. 28 Engr. Unwmk.**

Portraits: 30f, Gyorgy Dozsa. 40f, Miklos Zrinyi. 60f, Ilona Zriuyi. 1fo, Bottyan Vak. 1.50fo, Aurel Stromfeld.

| | | | | |
|---|---|---|---|---|
| **1019** | A221 | 20f purple | .25 | .25 |
| **1020** | A221 | 30f dark green | .25 | .25 |
| **1021** | A221 | 40f indigo | .25 | .25 |
| **1022** | A221 | 60f dk violet brn | .55 | .30 |
| **1023** | A221 | 1fo dk blue grn | .80 | .40 |
| **1024** | A221 | 1.50fo dark brown | 1.90 | 1.00 |
| | | *Nos. 1019-1024 (6)* | 4.00 | 2.45 |

Army Day, Sept. 28, 1952. Exist imperf. Value, set $50.

Lenin and Conference at Smolny Palace A222

Designs: 60f, Stalin and Cavalry Attack. 1fo, Marx, Engels, Lenin and Stalin.

**1952, Nov. 7 Wmk. 106**

**Portraits in Olive Gray**

| | | | | |
|---|---|---|---|---|
| **1025** | A222 | 40f deep claret | 1.75 | .50 |
| **1026** | A222 | 60f gray | 1.25 | .25 |
| **1027** | A222 | 1fo rose red | 2.00 | .35 |
| | | *Nos. 1025-1027 (3)* | 5.00 | 1.10 |

Russian Revolution, 35th anniversary. Exist imperf. Value, set $50.

Peasant Woman Holding Wheat — A223

Peace Meeting A224

***Perf. 12½x12, 12x12½***

**1952, Nov. 22**

| | | | | |
|---|---|---|---|---|
| **1028** | A223 | 40f brn red, *citron* | 1.00 | .30 |
| **1029** | A224 | 1fo brown, *blue* | 1.00 | .45 |

Third Hungarian Peace Congress, 1952. Exist imperf. Value, set $25.

Subway Construction A225

Design: 1fo, Station and map.

**1953, Jan. 19 Photo. *Perf. 12x12½***

| | | | | |
|---|---|---|---|---|
| **1030** | A225 | 60f dk slate green | .75 | .25 |
| **1031** | A225 | 1fo brown red | 1.75 | .35 |

Completion of the Budapest subway extension. Exist imperf. Value, set $25.

Tank and Flag — A226

60f, Map of Central Europe and Soldier.

**1953, Feb. 18**

| | | | | |
|---|---|---|---|---|
| **1032** | A226 | 40f dark car rose | 1.10 | .25 |
| **1033** | A226 | 60f chocolate | 1.10 | .45 |

Battle of Stalingrad, 10th anniversary. Exist imperf. Value, set $25.

Stalin — A227

***Perf. 12x11½***

**1953 Engr. Wmk. 106**

| | | | | |
|---|---|---|---|---|
| **1034** | A227 | 60f pur blk | 1.25 | .50 |

**Souvenir Sheet**

| | | | | |
|---|---|---|---|---|
| **1035** | A227 | 2fo pur blk, Type II | 27.50 | 27.50 |
| *a.* | | Type I | 600.00 | 300.00 |

Death of Joseph Stalin (1879-1953).

Two types of No. 1035. Type I: "MAGYAR POSTA" on solid background. Type II: "MAGYAR POSTA" on background of horiz. lines.

Exist imperf. Values: 60f $20; No. 1035 $150; No. 1035a $450.

Issue dates: No. 1034, Mar. 27; No. 1035, Mar. 9.

Workers' Rest Home, Galyateto A228

Designs: 40f, Home at Mecsek. 50f, Parad Mineral Baths. 60f, Home at Kekes. 70f, Balatonfured Mineral Baths.

**1953, Apr. Photo. *Perf. 12x12½***

| | | | | |
|---|---|---|---|---|
| **1036** | A228 | 30f fawn | .50 | .25 |
| **1037** | A228 | 40f deep blue | .50 | .25 |
| **1038** | A228 | 50f dk olive bis | .50 | .25 |
| **1039** | A228 | 60f dp yellow grn | .50 | .25 |
| **1040** | A228 | 70f scarlet | .50 | .25 |
| | | *Nos. 1036-1040,C121-C122 (7)* | 4.40 | 1.90 |

Exist imperf. Value, set (7) $60.

Young Workers with Red Flags — A229

Karl Marx — A230

**1953, May 1 *Perf. 12½x12***

| | | | | |
|---|---|---|---|---|
| **1041** | A229 | 60f brn & red, *yel* | 1.00 | .25 |

Issued to publicize Labor Day, May 1, 1953. Exist imperf. Value $25.

**1953, May 1 Engr. *Perf. 11½x12***

| | | | | |
|---|---|---|---|---|
| **1042** | A230 | 1fo black, *pink* | *1.50* | .25 |
| *a.* | | Perf 12½x12 | 250.00 | 60.00 |

70th anniv. of the death of Karl Marx. See No. 1898. Exist imperf. Value $30.

Insurgents in the Forest — A231

30f, Drummer & fighters. 40f, Battle scene. 60f, Cavalry attack. 1fo, Francis Rákóczy II.

**1953, June 14 Photo. *Perf. 11***

| | | | | |
|---|---|---|---|---|
| **1043** | A231 | 20f dk ol grn & org red, *grnsh* | .30 | .25 |
| **1044** | A231 | 30f vio brn & red org | 1.00 | .25 |
| **1045** | A231 | 40f gray bl & red org, *pink* | 1.10 | .25 |
| **1046** | A231 | 60f dk ol brn & org, *yel* | 2.25 | .55 |
| **1047** | A231 | 1fo dk red brn & org red, *yel* | 3.00 | .75 |
| | | *Nos. 1043-1047 (5)* | 7.65 | 2.05 |

250th anniv. of the insurrection of 1703. Exist imperf. Value $45.

**Building Types of 1951**

Buildings: 8f, Day Nursery, Ozd. 10f, Medical research institute, Szombathely. 12f, Apartments, Komlo. 20f, Department store, Ujpest. 30f, Brick factory, Maly. 40f, Metropolitan hospital. 50f, Sports building, Stalinvaros. 60f, Post office, Csepel. 70f, Blast furnace, Diosgyor. 1.20fo, Agricultural school, Ajkacsinger Valley. 1.70fo, Iron Works School, Csepel. 2fo, Optical works house of culture.

**Design Size: 22x18mm**

**1953 Wmk. 106 *Perf. 15***

| | | | | |
|---|---|---|---|---|
| **1048** | A204 | 8f olive green | .90 | .25 |
| **1049** | A204 | 10f purple | 1.25 | .25 |
| **1050** | A205 | 12f rose carmine | 1.50 | .25 |
| **1051** | A204 | 20f dark green | .90 | .25 |
| **1052** | A204 | 30f orange | 1.75 | .25 |
| **1053** | A204 | 40f dark brown | 3.00 | .25 |
| **1054** | A205 | 50f blue violet | 3.50 | .25 |
| **1055** | A205 | 60f rose red | 3.25 | .25 |
| **1056** | A204 | 70f yellow brown | 4.00 | .25 |
| **1056A** | A205 | 1.20fo red | 4.00 | .25 |
| **1056B** | A204 | 1.70fo blue | 3.00 | .25 |
| **1056C** | A204 | 2fo green | 7.50 | .25 |
| | | *Nos. 1048-1056C (12)* | 34.55 | 3.00 |

Exist imperf. Value, set $175.

**Design Size: 21x17mm**

**1958**

| | | | | |
|---|---|---|---|---|
| *1048a* | A204 | 8f olive green | 1.50 | .25 |
| *1049a* | A204 | 10f purple | — | .75 |
| *1050a* | A205 | 12f rose carmine | 2.25 | .25 |
| *1051a* | A204 | 20f dark green | 2.25 | .25 |
| *1052a* | A204 | 30f orange | 2.25 | .25 |
| *1053a* | A204 | 40f dark brown | 2.25 | .25 |
| *1054a* | A205 | 50f blue violet | 2.25 | .25 |
| *1055a* | A205 | 60f rose red | 3.25 | .25 |
| *1056a* | A204 | 70f yellow brown | 4.00 | .25 |
| *1056Aa* | A205 | 1.20fo red | 3.50 | .25 |
| *1056Ba* | A204 | 1.70fo blue | 2.25 | .25 |
| *1056Ca* | A204 | 2fo green | 7.50 | .25 |
| | | *Nos. 1048a-1056Ca (12)* | 33.25 | 3.50 |

Exist imperf. Value, set $150.

Bicycling — A232

**1953, Aug. 20 *Perf. 11***

| | | | | |
|---|---|---|---|---|
| **1057** | A232 | 20f shown | .25 | .25 |
| **1058** | A232 | 30f Swimming | .25 | .25 |
| **1059** | A232 | 40f Calisthenics | .25 | .25 |
| **1060** | A232 | 50f Discus | .40 | .25 |
| **1061** | A232 | 60f Wrestling | .50 | .25 |
| | | *Nos. 1057-1061,C123-C127 (10)* | 13.15 | 5.25 |

Opening of the People's Stadium, Budapest. Exist imperf. Value, set (10) $90.

Kazar Costume A233

Provincial Costumes: 30f, Ersekcsanad. 40f, Kalocsa. 60f, Sioagard. 1fo, Sarkoz. 1.70fo, Boldog. 2fo, Orhalom. 2.50fo, Hosszuheteny.

**1953, Sept. 12 Engr. *Perf. 12***

| | | | | |
|---|---|---|---|---|
| **1062** | A233 | 20f blue green | .75 | .50 |
| **1063** | A233 | 30f chocolate | .75 | .50 |
| **1064** | A233 | 40f ultra | 1.25 | .50 |
| **1065** | A233 | 60f red | 1.75 | .50 |
| **1066** | A233 | 1fo grnsh blue | 2.50 | .50 |
| **1067** | A233 | 1.70fo brt green | 3.50 | 1.50 |
| **1068** | A233 | 2fo carmine rose | 6.25 | 1.50 |
| **1069** | A233 | 2.50fo purple | 8.50 | 5.50 |
| | | *Nos. 1062-1069 (8)* | 25.25 | 11.00 |

Exist imperf. Value, set $100.

See No. 1189.

Lenin — A234

Designs: 60f, Lenin and Stalin at meeting. 1fo, Lenin, facing left.

**1954, Jan. 21 Wmk. 106 *Perf. 12***

| | | | | |
|---|---|---|---|---|
| **1073** | A234 | 40f dk blue grn | 1.50 | .75 |
| **1074** | A234 | 60f black brown | 1.50 | .25 |
| **1075** | A234 | 1fo dk car rose | 2.00 | .65 |
| | | *Nos. 1073-1075 (3)* | 5.00 | 1.65 |

30th anniversary, death of Lenin.
Exist imperf. Value, set $50.

Worker Reading A235

Revolutionary and Red Flag — A236

Design: 1fo, Soldier.

***Perf. 12x12½, 12½x12***

**1954, Mar. 21 Photo.**

| | | | | |
|---|---|---|---|---|
| **1076** | A235 | 40f gray blue & red | 3.50 | .50 |
| **1077** | A236 | 60f brown & red | 3.50 | .50 |
| **1078** | A235 | 1fo gray & red | 3.50 | .50 |
| | | *Nos. 1076-1078 (3)* | 10.50 | 1.50 |

35th anniversary of the "First Hungarian Communist Republic."
Exist imperf. Value, set $60.

Blood Test — A237

Designs: 40f, Mother receiving newborn baby. 60f, Medical examination of baby.

**1954, Mar. 8 *Perf. 12***

| | | | | |
|---|---|---|---|---|
| **1079** | A237 | 30f brt blue | .25 | .25 |
| **1080** | A237 | 40f brown bister | .45 | .25 |
| **1081** | A237 | 60f purple | .55 | .25 |
| | | *Nos. 1079-1081,C146-C148 (6)* | 6.05 | 2.90 |

Exist imperf. Value, set $65.

Maypole — A238

Design: 60f, Flag bearer.

**1954, May 1 *Perf. 12½x12***

| | | | | |
|---|---|---|---|---|
| **1082** | A238 | 40f olive | .50 | .25 |
| **1083** | A238 | 60f orange red | .50 | .30 |

Issued to publicize Labor Day, May 1, 1954.
Exist imperf. Value, set $25.

Farm Woman with Fruit A239

**1954, May 24 *Perf. 12***

| | | | | |
|---|---|---|---|---|
| **1084** | A239 | 60f red orange | .80 | .25 |

3rd Congress of the Hungarian Workers Party, Budapest, May 24, 1954.
Exists imperf. Value, set $20.

Natl. Museum, Budapest — A240

Designs: 60f, Arms of People's Republic. 1fo, Dome of Parliament Building.

**1954, Aug. 20 *Perf. 12½x12***

| | | | | |
|---|---|---|---|---|
| **1085** | A240 | 40f brt blue | 1.00 | .35 |
| **1086** | A240 | 60f redsh brown | 1.00 | .25 |
| **1087** | A240 | 1fo dark brown | 1.50 | .25 |
| | | *Nos. 1085-1087 (3)* | 3.50 | .85 |

People's Republic Constitution, 5th anniv.
Exist imperf. Value, set $30.

Peppers A241

Fruit: 50f, Tomatoes. 60f, Grapes. 80f, Apricots. 1fo, Apples. 1.20fo, Plums. 1.50fo, Cherries. 2fo, Peaches.

**1954, Sept. 11 Engr., Litho.**

**Fruit in Natural Colors**

| | | | | |
|---|---|---|---|---|
| **1088** | A241 | 40f gray blue | .50 | .25 |
| **1089** | A241 | 50f plum | .50 | .25 |
| **1090** | A241 | 60f gray blue | .60 | .25 |
| **1091** | A241 | 80f chocolate | 1.40 | .25 |
| **1092** | A241 | 1fo rose violet | 1.75 | .25 |
| **1093** | A241 | 1.20fo dull blue | 1.40 | .25 |
| **1094** | A241 | 1.50fo plum | 2.25 | .75 |
| **1095** | A241 | 2fo gray blue | 1.75 | .40 |
| | | *Nos. 1088-1095 (8)* | 10.15 | 2.65 |

National agricultural fair.
Exist imperf. Value, set $50.

Maurus Jokai — A242

**1954, Oct. 17 Engr.**

| | | | | |
|---|---|---|---|---|
| **1096** | A242 | 60f dk brown olive | 1.00 | .25 |
| **1097** | A242 | 1fo deep claret | 1.50 | .75 |

50th anniv. of the death of Maurus Jokai, writer.
Exist imperf. Value, set $25.
No. 1097 in violet blue is from the souvenir sheet, No. C157.

Janos Apacai Csere A243

Scientists: 10f, Csoma Sandor Korosi. 12f, Anyos Jedlik. 20f, Ignaz Semmelweis. 30f, Janos Irinyi. 40f, Frigyes Koranyi. 50f, Armin Vambery. 60f, Karoly Than. 1fo, Otto Herman. 1.70fo, Tivadar Puskas. 2fo, Endre Hogyes.

**1954, Dec. 5 Photo. *Perf. 12x12½***

| | | | | |
|---|---|---|---|---|
| **1098** | A243 | 8f dk vio brn, *yel* | .25 | .25 |
| **1099** | A243 | 10f brn, car, *pink* | .25 | .25 |
| **1100** | A243 | 12f gray, *bl* | .25 | .25 |
| **1101** | A243 | 20f brn, *yel* | .25 | .25 |
| **1102** | A243 | 30f vio bl, *pink* | .25 | .25 |
| **1103** | A243 | 40f dk grn, *yel* | .25 | .25 |
| **1104** | A243 | 50f red brn, *pale grn* | .25 | .25 |
| **1105** | A243 | 60f blue, *pink* | .25 | .25 |
| **1106** | A243 | 1fo olive | .35 | .25 |
| **1107** | A243 | 1.70fo rose brn, *yel* | .85 | .35 |
| **1108** | A243 | 2fo blue green | 1.50 | .45 |
| | | *Nos. 1098-1108 (11)* | 4.70 | 3.05 |

Exist imperf. Value, set $45.

Readers in Industrial Library — A244

Industry A245

1fo, Agriculture. 2fo, Liberation monument.

**1955, Apr. 4 *Perf. 12½x12, 12x12½***

| | | | | |
|---|---|---|---|---|
| **1109** | A244 | 40f dk car & ol brn | .75 | .35 |
| **1110** | A245 | 60f dk green & red | .75 | .25 |
| **1111** | A245 | 1fo choc & grn | 1.00 | .25 |
| **1112** | A244 | 2fo blue grn & brn | 1.25 | .35 |
| | | *Nos. 1109-1112 (4)* | 3.75 | 1.20 |

10th anniversary of Hungary's liberation.
Exist imperf. Value, set $35.

Date, Flags, Grain Elevator and Tractor A246

**1955, May 1 *Perf. 12x12½***

| | | | | |
|---|---|---|---|---|
| **1113** | A246 | 1fo rose carmine | .80 | .25 |

Labor Day, May 1, 1955.
Exist imperf. Value, set $20.

Government Printing Plant — A247

**1955, May 28 Wmk. 106**

| | | | | |
|---|---|---|---|---|
| **1114** | A247 | 60f gray grn & hn brn | .50 | .25 |

Centenary of the establishment of the government printing plant.
Exist imperf. Value, set $20.

Young Citizens and Hungarian Flag — A248

**1955, June 15 *Perf. 12***

| | | | | |
|---|---|---|---|---|
| **1115** | A248 | 1fo red brown | .65 | .25 |

Issued to publicize the second national congress of the Hungarian Youth Organization.
Exist imperf. Value, set $20.

Truck Farmer A249

10f, Fisherman. 12f, Bricklayer. 20f, Radio assembler. 30f, Woman potter. 40f, Railwayman & train. 50f, Clerk & scales. 60f, Postman emptying mail box. 70f, Cattle & herdsman. 80f, Textile worker. 1fo, Riveter. 1.20fo, Carpenter. 1.40fo, Streetcar conductor. 1.70fo, Herdsman & pigs. 2fo, Welder. 2.60fo, Woman tractor driver. 3fo, Herdsman in national costume & horse. 4fo, Bus driver. 5fo, Lineman. 10fo, Coal miner.

**1955 Wmk. 106 *Perf. 12x12½***

| | | | | |
|---|---|---|---|---|
| **1116** | A249 | 8f chestnut | .25 | .25 |
| **1117** | A249 | 10f Prus green | .25 | .25 |
| **1118** | A249 | 12f red orange | .25 | .25 |
| **1119** | A249 | 20f olive green | .40 | .25 |
| **1120** | A249 | 30f dark red | .35 | .25 |
| **1121** | A249 | 40f brown | .40 | .25 |
| **1122** | A249 | 50f violet bl | .40 | .25 |
| **1123** | A249 | 60f brown red | .50 | .25 |
| **1124** | A249 | 70f olive | .80 | .25 |
| **1125** | A249 | 80f purple | .50 | .25 |
| **1126** | A249 | 1fo blue | 1.00 | .25 |
| **1127** | A249 | 1.20fo olive bis | 1.20 | .25 |
| **1128** | A249 | 1.40fo deep green | 1.00 | .25 |
| **1129** | A249 | 1.70fo purple | 1.00 | .25 |
| **1130** | A249 | 2fo rose brown | 1.00 | .25 |
| **1131** | A249 | 2.60fo vermilion | 1.50 | .25 |
| **1132** | A249 | 3fo green | 2.25 | .25 |
| **1133** | A249 | 4fo peacock blue | 2.00 | .25 |
| **1134** | A249 | 5fo orange brown | 2.00 | .25 |
| **1135** | A249 | 10fo violet | 1.75 | .55 |
| | | *Nos. 1116-1135 (20)* | 18.80 | 5.30 |

Exist imperf. Value, set $120.
For surcharges see Nos. B211-B216.

Postrider Blowing Horn — A250

**1955, June 25 *Perf. 12½x12***

| | | | | |
|---|---|---|---|---|
| **1136** | A250 | 1fo rose violet | .50 | .25 |

Hungarian Postal Museum, 25th anniv.
Exists tete-beche. Value: 2½ times the value of a single.
Exists imperf. Value $25.

Mihaly Csokonai Vitez A251

1fo, Mihaly Vorosmarty. 2fo, Attila József.

**1955, July 28 *Perf. 12***

| | | | | |
|---|---|---|---|---|
| **1137** | A251 | 60f olive black | 1.25 | .30 |
| **1138** | A251 | 1fo dark blue | 1.25 | .40 |
| **1139** | A251 | 2fo rose brown | 1.50 | .65 |
| | | *Nos. 1137-1139 (3)* | 4.00 | 1.35 |

Issued to honor three Hungarian poets.
Exist imperf. Value $35.

Bela Bartok — A252

**1955, Oct. 9**

**1140** A252 60f light brown 1.00 .25
*Nos. 1140,C168-C169 (3)* 6.50 3.50

10th anniversary of the death of Bela Bartok, composer.
Exist imperf. Value, set (3) $30.

Diesel Train A253

Designs: 60f, Bus. 80f, Motorcycle. 1fo, Truck. 1.20fo, Steam locomotive. 1.50fo, Dump truck. 2fo, Freighter.

**1955, Dec. 20** ***Perf. 14½***

**1141** A253 40f grn & vio brn .25 .25
**1142** A253 60f dp grn & ol .25 .25
**1143** A253 80f ol grn & brn .25 .25
**1144** A253 1fo ocher & grn .30 .25
**1145** A253 1.20fo salmon & blk .90 .25
**1146** A253 1.50fo grnsh blk & red brn 1.25 .25
**1147** A253 2fo aqua & brown 2.00 .55
*Nos. 1141-1147 (7)* 5.20 2.05

Exist imperf. Value, set $50.

Puli (Sheepdog) — A254

Puli and Steer A255

Hungarian Pointer — A256

Hungarian Dogs: 60f, Pumi (sheepdog). 1fo, Retriever with fowl. 1.20fo, Kuvasz (sheepdog). 1.50fo, Komondor (sheepdog) and cottage. 2fo, Komondor (head).

***Perf. 11x13 (A254), 12***

**1956, Mar. 17** **Engr. & Litho.**

**1148** A254 40f yel, blk & red .25 .25
**1149** A255 50f blue, bis & blk .25 .25
**1150** A254 60f yel grn, blk & red .25 .25
**1151** A256 80f bluish grn, ocher & blk .25 .30
**1152** A256 1fo turq, ocher & blk .40 .25
**1153** A254 1.20fo salmon, blk & chnt .75 .25
**1154** A255 1.50fo ultra, blk & buff 1.75 .35
**1155** A254 2fo cerise, blk & chnt 2.50 .55
*Nos. 1148-1155 (8)* 6.40 2.45

Exist imperf. Value, set $45.

Pioneer Emblem A257

***Perf. 12x12½***

**1956, June 2** **Photo.** **Wmk. 106**

**1156** A257 1fo red .50 .25
**1157** A257 1fo gray .50 .25

Pioneer movement, 10th anniversary.
Exist imperf. Value, set $27.50.

Janos Hunyadi Statue — A258

**1956, Aug. 12** ***Perf. 12***

**1158** A258 1fo brown, *yelsh* 1.00 .35

500th anniv. of the defeat of the Turks at the battle of Pecs under Janos Hunyadi.
Printed in sheets of 50 with alternate vertical rows inverted and center row of perforation omitted, providing 25 tête bêche pairs, of which 5 are imperf. between. Values for tete-beche pairs: unused $3; used $1.50. Values for tete-beche pairs, imperf between: unused $6; used $250.
Exists imperf. Value $35. Tête bêche pair also exists imperf. Value, $100.

Miner — A259

**1956, Sept. 2**

**1159** A259 1fo dark blue .50 .25

Issued in honor of Miners' Day 1956.
Exists imperf. Value $15.

Kayak Racer A260

Sports: 30f, Horse jumping hurdle. 40f, Fencing. 60f, Women hurdlers. 1fo, Soccer. 1.50fo, Weight lifting. 2fo, Gymnastics. 3fo, Basketball.

**1956, Sept. 25** **Wmk. 106** ***Perf. 11***

**Figures in Brown Olive**

**1160** A260 20f lt blue .25 .25
**1161** A260 30f lt olive grn .25 .25
**1162** A260 40f deep orange .25 .25
**1163** A260 60f bluish grn .25 .25
**1164** A260 1fo vermilion .35 .25
**1165** A260 1.50fo blue violet .65 .25
**1166** A260 2fo emerald .80 .30
**1167** A260 3fo rose lilac 1.40 .40
*Nos. 1160-1167 (8)* 4.20 2.20

16th Olympic Games at Melbourne, Nov. 22-Dec. 8, 1956.
Exist imperf. Value, set $75.

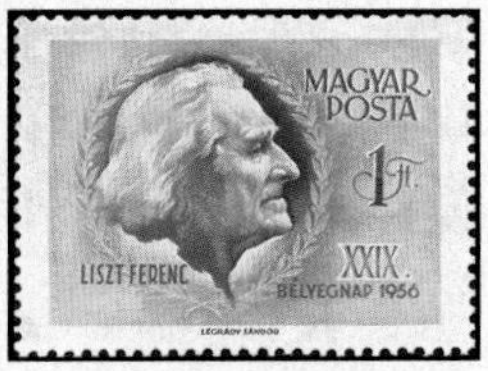


Franz Liszt A261

Portrait: 1fo, Frederic Chopin facing left.

**1956, Oct. 7** **Photo.** ***Perf. 12x12½***

**1168** A261 1fo violet blue 2.00 2.00
**1169** A261 1fo magenta 2.00 2.00
*a.* Pair, #1168-1169 6.00 6.00

29th Day of the Stamp. Sold only at the Philatelic Exhibition together with entrance ticket for 4fo.
Exist imperf. Value, pair $25.

Janos Arany — A262

**1957, Sept. 15** **Wmk. 106** ***Perf. 12***

**1170** A262 2fo bright blue 1.00 .50

75th anniv. of the death of Janos Arany, poet.
Exists imperf. Value $15.

Arms of Hungary A263

**1957, Oct. 1**

**1171** A263 60f brt red .75 .25
**1172** A263 1fo dp yellow grn .75 .25

Exists imperf. Value, set $25.

Trade Union Congress Emblem A264

**1957, Oct. 4**

**1173** A264 1fo dk carmine .50 .25

4th Intl. Trade Union Cong., Leipzig, 10/4-15.
Exists imperf. Value $15.

Dove and Colors of Communist Countries — A265

Design: 1fo, Lenin.

**1957, Nov. 7** **Litho.** ***Perf. 12***

**1174** A265 60f gray, blk & multi .50 .25
*a.* Perf 11 2.50 .25
**1175** A265 1fo ol bis & indigo .50 .35
*a.* Perf 11 2.50 .25

Russian Revolution, 40th anniversary.
Exist imperf. Value, set $25.

Komarom Tumbler Pigeons A266

Pigeons: 40f, Two short-beaked Budapest pigeons. 60f, Giant domestic pigeon. 1fo, Three Szeged pigeons. 2fo, Two Hungarian fantails.

***Perf. 12x12½***

**1957-58** **Photo.** **Wmk. 106**

**1176** A266 30f yel grn, cl & ocher .25 .25
**1177** A266 40f ocher & blk .25 .25
**1178** A266 60f blue & gray .25 .25
**1179** A266 1fo gray & red brn .25 .25
**1180** A266 2fo brt pink & gray .60 .40
*Nos. 1176-1180,C175 (6)* 2.50 1.90

Intl. Pigeon Exhibition, Budapest, 12/14-16.
Exist imperf. Value, set (6) $35.
Issued: 30f, 1/12/58; others, 12/14/57.

Television Station — A267

**1958, Feb. 22** **Engr.** ***Perf. 11***

**1181** A267 2fo rose violet 1.25 .75
*a.* Perf. 12 7.50 7.50

**Souvenir Sheet**

**1182** A267 2fo green 42.50 42.50

Issued to publicize the television industry.
No. 1182 sold for 25fo.
Exist imperf. Values: single $15; souvenir sheet $125.

Mother and Child A268

Designs: 30f, Old man feeding pigeons. 40f, School boys. 60f, "Working ants and fiddling grasshopper." 1fo, Honeycomb and bee. 2fo, Handing over money.

**1958, Mar. 9** **Photo.** ***Perf. 12***

**1183** A268 20f yel grn & ol gray .25 .25
**1184** A268 30f lt olive & mar .25 .25
**1185** A268 40f yel bis & brn .50 .25
**1186** A268 60f rose car & grnsh blk .50 .25
**1187** A268 1fo ol gray & dk brn .75 .25
**1188** A268 2fo org & ol gray 1.25 .35
*Nos. 1183-1188 (6)* 3.50 1.60

Issued to publicize the value of savings and insurance.
Exist imperf. Value, set $40.

**Kazar Costume Type of 1953**

**Souvenir Sheet**

**1958, Apr. 17** **Engr.** ***Perf. 12***

**1189** A233 10fo magenta 27.50 27.50

Issued for the Universal and International Exposition at Brussels.
Exists imperf. Value $60.

Arms of Hungary A269

**1958, May 23** **Litho.** **Wmk. 106**

**Arms in Original Colors**

**1190** A269 60f lt red brn & red .25 .25
**1191** A269 1fo gray grn & grn .50 .25
**1192** A269 2fo gray & dk brn .80 .25
*Nos. 1190-1192 (3)* 1.55 .75

1st anniv. of the law amending the constitution.
Exist imperf. Value, set $20.

Youth Holding Book — A270

**1958, June 14 Photo. *Perf. 12½x12***

| | | | | |
|---|---|---|---|---|
| **1193** | A270 | 1fo brown carmine | .75 | .50 |

5th Hungarian Youth Festival at Keszthely.
Printed with alternating label, inscribed: V. IFJUSAGI TALALKOZO KESZTHELY 1958.
Exists imperf. Value, with label $15.

Post Horn and Town Hall, Prague — A271

**1958, June 30**

| | | | | |
|---|---|---|---|---|
| **1194** | A271 | 60f green | .50 | .25 |
| *a.* | | Pair, #1194, C184 | 1.00 | 1.00 |

Conference of Postal Ministers of Communist Countries at Prague, June 30-July 8.
Exists imperf. Value, $7. In pair with No. C184 imperf, value $15.

Dolomite Flax — A272

Hungarian Thistles — A273

30f, Kitaibelia vitifolia. 60f, Crocuses. 1fo, Hellebore. 2fo, Lilies. 2.50fo, Pinks. 3fo, Dog roses.

***Perf. 11x13, 12½x12 (A273)***

**1958, Aug. 12 Photo. Wmk. 106**

| | | | | |
|---|---|---|---|---|
| **1195** | A272 | 20f red vio & yel | 1.00 | .25 |
| **1196** | A272 | 30f blue, yel & grn | .25 | .25 |
| **1197** | A273 | 40f brown & bis | .25 | .25 |
| **1198** | A273 | 60f bl grn & pink | .30 | .25 |
| **1199** | A273 | 1fo rose car & yel grn | .55 | .25 |
| **1200** | A273 | 2fo grn & yel | .95 | .25 |
| **1201** | A272 | 2.50fo vio bl & pink | 1.10 | .45 |
| **1202** | A272 | 3fo green & pink | 1.90 | .70 |
| *a.* | | Souv. sheet of 4, perf. 12 | 35.00 | *35.00* |
| | | *Nos. 1195-1202 (8)* | 6.30 | 2.65 |

No. 1202a and a similar imperf. sheet were issued for the International Philatelic Congress at Brussels, Sept. 15-17, 1958. They contain the triangular 20f, 30f, 2.50fo and 3fo stamps printed in different colors. Sheets measure 111x111mm. and are printed on unwatermarked, linen-finish paper. Background of stamps, marginal inscriptions and ornaments in green. No. 1202a also exists perf. 11. Value, $45.
Exist imperf. Value, set $35. Value of 1202a imperf, $75.

Paddle, Ball and Olive Branch A274

Designs: 30f, Table tennis player, vert. 40f, Wrestlers, vert. 60f, Wrestlers, horiz. 1fo, Water polo player, vert. 2.50fo, High dive, vert. 3fo, Swimmer.

**1958, Aug. 30 Wmk. 106 *Perf. 12***

| | | | | |
|---|---|---|---|---|
| **1203** | A274 | 20f rose red, *pnksh* | .25 | .25 |
| **1204** | A274 | 30f olive, *grnsh* | .25 | .25 |
| **1205** | A274 | 40f mag, *yel* | .25 | .25 |
| **1206** | A274 | 60f brown, *bluish* | .40 | .25 |
| **1207** | A274 | 1fo ultra, *bluish* | .45 | .25 |
| **1208** | A274 | 2.50fo dk red, *yel* | 1.10 | .30 |
| **1209** | A274 | 3fo grnsh bl, *grnsh* | 1.40 | .50 |
| | | *Nos. 1203-1209 (7)* | 4.10 | 2.05 |

Intl. Wrestling and European Swimming and Table Tennis Championships, held at Budapest.
Exist imperf. Value, set $25.

Red Flag — A275

Design: 2fo, Hand holding newspaper.

**1958, Nov. 21 *Perf. 12½x12***

| | | | | |
|---|---|---|---|---|
| **1210** | A275 | 1fo brown & red | .25 | .25 |
| **1211** | A275 | 2fo dk gray bl & red | .55 | .25 |

40th anniversary of the founding of the Hungarian Communist Party and newspaper.
Exist imperf. Value, set $15.

Satellite, Sputnik and American Rocket A276

Designs: 10f, Eötvös Torsion Balance and Globe. 20f, Deep sea exploration. 30f, Icebergs, penguins and polar light. 40f, Soviet Antarctic camp and map of Pole. 60f, "Rocket" approaching moon. 1fo, Sun and observatory.

**1959, Mar. 14 *Perf. 12x12½***

**Size: 32x21mm**

| | | | | |
|---|---|---|---|---|
| **1212** | A276 | 10f car rose & sepia | .35 | .25 |
| **1213** | A276 | 20f brt blue & gray | .25 | .25 |
| **1214** | A276 | 30f dk slate grn & bis | .40 | .25 |

***Perf. 12***

**Size: 35x26mm**

| | | | | |
|---|---|---|---|---|
| **1215** | A276 | 40f slate bl & lt bl | .25 | .25 |

***Perf. 15***

**Size: 58x21mm**

| | | | | |
|---|---|---|---|---|
| **1216** | A276 | 60f Prus bl & lemon | .45 | .25 |

***Perf. 12***

**Size: 35x26mm**

| | | | | |
|---|---|---|---|---|
| **1217** | A276 | 1fo scarlet & yel | .70 | .30 |
| **1218** | A276 | 5fo brn & red brn | 1.60 | .80 |
| | | *Nos. 1212-1218 (7)* | 4.00 | 2.35 |

Intl. Geophysical Year. See No. 1262.
Exist imperf. Value, set $20.

"Revolution" — A277

**1959, Mar. 21 *Perf. 12½x12***

| | | | | |
|---|---|---|---|---|
| **1219** | A277 | 20f vio brn & red | .25 | .25 |
| **1220** | A277 | 60f blue & red | .25 | .25 |
| **1221** | A277 | 1fo brown & red | .60 | .25 |
| | | *Nos. 1219-1221 (3)* | 1.10 | .75 |

40th anniv. of the proclamation of the Hungarian Soviet Republic.
Exist imperf. Value, set $15.

Rose — A278

**1959, May 1 Photo. *Perf. 11***

| | | | | |
|---|---|---|---|---|
| **1222** | A278 | 60f lilac, dp car & grn | .40 | .25 |
| **1223** | A278 | 1fo lt brn, dl red & grn | .60 | .25 |

Issued for Labor Day, May 1, 1959.
Exist imperf. Value, set $15.

Early Locomotive — A279

Designs: 30f, Diesel coach. 40f, Early semaphore, vert. 60f, Csonka automobile. 1fo, Icarus bus. 2fo, First Lake Balaton steamboat. 2.50fo, Stagecoach.

**1959, May 26 Litho. *Perf. 14½x15***

| | | | | |
|---|---|---|---|---|
| **1224** | A279 | 20f multi | .25 | .25 |
| **1225** | A279 | 30f multi | .25 | .25 |
| **1226** | A279 | 40f multi | .25 | .25 |
| **1227** | A279 | 60f multi | .25 | .25 |
| **1228** | A279 | 1fo multi | .25 | .25 |
| **1229** | A279 | 2fo multi | .25 | .25 |
| **1230** | A279 | 2.50fo multi | 1.25 | .30 |
| | | *Nos. 1224-1230,C201 (8)* | 4.75 | 3.05 |

Transport Museum, Budapest.
Exist imperf. Value, set (8) $25.

***Perf. 10½x11½***

**1959, May 29 Wmk. 106**

| | | | | |
|---|---|---|---|---|
| **1231** | A279 | 2.50fo multi | 2.00 | 2.00 |

Designer's name on No. 1231. Printed in sheets of four with four labels to commemorate the congress of the International Federation for Philately in Hamburg. Value $15.
Exist imperf. Values: paid with label $15; sheetlet $100.

Post Horn and World Map — A280

**1959, June 1 Photo. *Perf. 12***

| | | | | |
|---|---|---|---|---|
| **1232** | A280 | 1fo cerise | .75 | .30 |

Postal Ministers Conference, Berlin.
Printed in sheets of 25 stamps with 25 alternating gray labels showing East Berlin Opera House.
Exists imperf. Value: in pair with label, $15.

Great Cormorant A281

Birds: 20f, Little egret and nest. 30f, Purple heron and nest. 40f, Great egret. 60f, White spoonbill. 1fo, Gray heron. 2fo, Squacco heron and nest. 3fo, Glossy ibis.

**1959, June 14**

| | | | | |
|---|---|---|---|---|
| **1233** | A281 | 10f green & indigo | .25 | .25 |
| **1234** | A281 | 20f gray bl & ol grn | .25 | .25 |
| **1235** | A281 | 30f org, grnsh blk & vio | .25 | .25 |
| **1236** | A281 | 40f dark grn & gray | .25 | .25 |
| **1237** | A281 | 60f dp cl & pale rose | .35 | .25 |
| **1238** | A281 | 1fo dp bl grn & blk | .50 | .25 |
| **1239** | A281 | 2fo dp orange & gray | .85 | .30 |
| **1240** | A281 | 3fo bister & brn lake | 1.50 | .70 |
| | | *Nos. 1233-1240 (8)* | 4.20 | 2.50 |

Exist imperf. Value, set $30.

Warrior, 10th Century — A282

Designs: 20f, Warrior, 15th century. 30f, Soldier, 18th century. 40f, Soldier, 19th century. 60f, Cavalry man, 19th century. 1fo, Fencer, assault. 1.40fo, Fencer on guard. 3fo, Swordsman saluting.

**1959, July 11**

| | | | | |
|---|---|---|---|---|
| **1241** | A282 | 10f gray & blue | .25 | .25 |
| **1242** | A282 | 20f gray & dull yel | .25 | .25 |
| **1243** | A282 | 30f gray & gray vio | .25 | .25 |
| **1244** | A282 | 40f gray & ver | .25 | .25 |
| **1245** | A282 | 60f gray & rose lil | .25 | .25 |
| **1246** | A282 | 1fo ind & lt bl grn | .30 | .25 |
| **1247** | A282 | 1.40fo orange & blk | .60 | .25 |
| **1248** | A282 | 3fo blk & ol grn | .90 | .70 |
| | | *Nos. 1241-1248 (8)* | 3.05 | 2.45 |

24th World Fencing Championships, Budapest.
Exist imperf. Value, set $25.

Sailboat, Lake Balaton — A283

40f, Vintager & lake, horiz. 60f, Bathers. 1.20fo, Fishermen. 2fo, Summer guests & ship.

**1959, July 11 Photo. Wmk. 106**

| | | | | |
|---|---|---|---|---|
| **1249** | A283 | 30f blue, *yel* | .25 | .25 |
| **1250** | A283 | 40f carmine rose | .25 | .25 |
| **1251** | A283 | 60f dp red brown | .25 | .25 |
| **1252** | A283 | 1.20fo violet | .30 | .25 |
| **1253** | A283 | 2fo red org, *yel* | .60 | .50 |
| | | *Nos. 1249-1253,C202-C205 (9)* | 2.90 | 2.55 |

Issued to publicize Lake Balaton and the opening of the Summer University.
Exist imperf. Value, set (9) $25.

Haydn's Monogram A284

Esterhazy Palace A285

Haydn and Schiller Monograms — A286

Design: 1fo, Joseph Haydn and score.

**1959, Sept. 20 Wmk. 106 *Perf. 12***

**1254** A284 40f dp claret & yel .25 .25
**1255** A285 60f Prus bl, gray & yel .75 .75
**1256** A284 1fo dk vio, lt brn & org .65 .25

Designs: 40f, Schiller's monogram. 60f, Pegasus rearing from flames. 1fo, Friedrich von Schiller.

**1257** A284 40f olive grn & org .25 .25
**1258** A285 60f violet bl & lil .40 .25
**1259** A284 1fo dp cl & org brn .80 .25
*Nos. 1254-1259 (6)* 3.10 2.00

**Souvenir Sheet**

***Imperf***

**1260** A286 Sheet of 2 17.50 17.50
*a.* 3fo magenta 3.50 3.50
*b.* 3fo green 3.50 3.50

150th anniv. of the death of Joseph Haydn, Austrian composer, Nos. 1254-1256; 200th anniv. of the birth of Friedrich von Schiller, German poet and dramatist, Nos. 1257-1259; No. 1260 honors both Haydn and Schiller.
Nos. 1254-1260 exist imperf. Value, set $20.

Shepherd — A287

**1959, Sept. 25 Engr. *Perf. 12***

**1261** A287 2fo deep claret 1.50 1.50
*a.* With ticket 2.25 2.25

Day of the Stamp and Natl. Stamp Exhib. Issued in sheets of 8 with alternating ticket. The 4fo sale price marked on the ticket was the admission fee to the Natl. Stamp Exhib.
Exist imperf. Values: single $6; single with ticket $15.

**Type of 1959 Overprinted in Red**

**1959, Sept. 24 Photo. *Perf. 15***

**1262** A276 60f dull bl & lemon .65 .25
*a.* Overprint omitted 3,000.

Landing of Lunik 2 on moon, Sept. 14.
Exists imperf. Value $10.

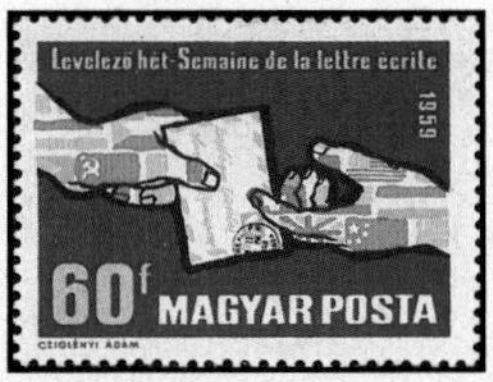

Handing over Letter A288

**1959, Oct. 4 Litho. *Perf. 12***

**1263** A288 60f multicolored .60 .25

Intl. Letter Writing Week, Oct. 4-10.
Exists imperf. Value $12.50.

Szamuely and Lenin — A289

Designs: 40f, Aleksander Pushkin. 60pf, Vladimir V. Mayakovsky. 1fo, Hands holding peace flag.

**1959, Nov. 14 Photo. Wmk. 106**

**1264** A289 20f dk red & bister .25 .25
**1265** A289 40f brn & rose lil, *bluish* .25 .25
**1266** A289 60f dk blue & bis .55 .25
**1267** A289 1fo bl, car, buff, red & grn .55 .30
*Nos. 1264-1267 (4)* 1.60 1.05

Soviet Stamp Exhibition, Budapest.
Exists imperf. Value $20.

European Swallowtail A290

Butterflies: 30f, Arctia hebe, horiz. 40f, Lysandra hylas, horiz. 60f, Apatura ilia.

***Perf. 11½x12, 12x11½***
**1959, Nov. 20**
**Butterflies in Natural Colors**

**1268** A290 20f blk & yel grn .25 .25
**1269** A290 30f lt blue & blk .35 .25
**1270** A290 40f dk gray & org brn .35 .25
**1271** A290 60f dk gray & dl yel .45 .25
*Nos. 1268-1271,C206-C208 (7)* 6.05 2.35

Exist imperf. Value, set (7) $30.

Worker with Banner — A291

Design: 1fo, Congress flag.

**1959, Nov. 30 *Perf. 14½***

**1272** A291 60f brown, grn & red .25 .25
**1273** A291 1fo brn, red, red & grn .25 .25

Issued to commemorate the 7th Congress of the Hungarian Socialist Workers' Party.
Exist imperf. Value, set $15.

Teacher Reading Fairy Tales — A292

Fairy Tales: 30f, Sleeping Beauty. 40f, Matt, the Goose Boy. 60f, The Cricket and the Ant. 1fo, Mashenka and the Three Bears. 2fo, Hansel and Gretel. 2.50fo, Pied Piper. 3fo, Little Red Riding Hood.

**1959, Dec. 15 Litho. *Perf. 11½***
**Designs in Black**

**1274** A292 20f gray & multi .25 .25
**1275** A292 30f brt pink .25 .25
**1276** A292 40f lt blue grn .25 .25
**1277** A292 60f lt blue .45 .25
**1278** A292 1fo yellow .75 .25
**1279** A292 2fo brt yellow grn .75 .25
**1280** A292 2.50fo orange 1.10 .40
**1281** A292 3fo crimson 1.10 .60
*Nos. 1274-1281 (8)* 4.90 2.50

Exist imperf. Value, set $20.

Sumeg Castle — A293

Castles: 20fr, Tata. 30f, Diosgyor. 60f, Saros-Patak. 70f, Nagyvazsony. 1.40fo, Siklos. 1.70fo, Somlo. 3fo, Csesznek, vert. 5fo, Koszeg, vert. 10fo, Sarvar, vert.

**Wmk. 106**
**1960, Feb. 1 Photo. *Perf. 14½***
**Size: 21x17½mm**

**1282** A293 8f purple .25 .25
**1283** A293 20f dk yel grn .25 .25
**1284** A293 30f orange brn .25 .25
**1285** A293 60f rose red .25 .25
**1286** A293 70f emerald .35 .25

***Perf. 12x11½, 11½x12***
**Size: 28x21mm, 21x28mm**

**1287** A293 1.40fo ultra .85 .25
**1288** A293 1.70fo dl vio, "Somlo" 1.00 .25
*b.* "Somlyo" 1.50 .25
**1289** A293 3fo red brown 1.75 .30
**1290** A293 5fo yellow green 2.25 .30
**1291** A293 10fo carmine rose 3.00 .60
*Nos. 1282-1291 (10)* 10.20 2.95

Exist imperf. Value, set $90.

**Tinted Paper**
***Perf. 14½***
**Size: 21x17½mm**

*1282a* A293 8f pur, *bluish* .25 .25
*1283a* A293 20f dk yel grn, *grnsh* .25 .25
*1284a* A293 30f org brn, *yel* .35 .25
*1285a* A293 60f rose red, *pnksh* .25 .25
*1286a* A293 70f emer, *bluish* .65 .25

***Perf. 12x11½***
**Size: 28x21mm**

*1287a* A293 1.40fo ultra, *bluish* .70 .25
*1288a* A293 1.70fo dull vio, *bluish* .90 .25
*Nos. 1282a-1288a (7)* 3.35 1.75

Exist imperf. Value, set $30.
See Nos. 1356-1365, 1644-1646.

Halas Lace — A294

Designs: Various Halas lace patterns.

**Sizes: 20f, 60f, 1fo, 3fo: 27x37mm**
**30f, 40f, 1.50fo, 2fo: 37½x43½mm**

**Wmk. 106**
**1960, Feb. 15 Litho. *Perf. 11½***
**Inscriptions in Orange**

**1292** A294 20f brown black .25 .25
**1293** A294 30f violet .25 .25
**1294** A294 40f Prus blue .40 .25
**1295** A294 60f dark brown .50 .25
**1296** A294 1fo dark green .80 .30
**1297** A294 1.50fo green 1.00 .40
**1298** A294 2fo dark blue 1.75 .60
**1299** A294 3fo dk carmine 3.00 .80
*Nos. 1292-1299 (8)* 7.95 3.10

Exist imperf. Value, set $25.
See Nos. 1570-1577.

**Souvenir Sheet**

**1960, Sept. 3**
**Inscriptions in Orange**

**1300** A294 Sheet of 4 + 4 labels 16.00 16.00
*a.* 3fo brown olive 3.25 3.25
*b.* 3fo bright violet 3.25 3.25
*c.* 3fo emerald 3.25 3.25
*d.* 3fo bright blue 3.25 3.25

Fédération Internationale de Philatélie Congress, Warsaw, Sept. 3-11. No. 1300 contains 4 stamps and 4 alternating labels, printed in colors of adjoining stamps.
Exists imperf. Value $100.

Cross-country Skier — A295

Sports: 40f, Ice hockey player. 60f, Ski jumper. 80f, Woman speed skater. 1fo, Downhill skier. 1.20fo, Woman figure skater.

**1960, Feb. 29 Photo. *Perf. 11½x12***
**Inscriptions and Figures in Bister**

**1301** A295 30f deep blue .25 .25
**1302** A295 40f brt green .25 .25
**1303** A295 60f scarlet .25 .25
**1304** A295 80f purple .25 .25
**1305** A295 1fo brt grnsh blue .60 .25
**1306** A295 1.20fo brown red .70 .45
*Nos. 1301-1306,B217 (7)* 4.05 2.05

8th Olympic Winter Games, Squaw Valley, Calif., Feb. 18-29, 1960.
Exists imperf. Value $20.

Clara Zetkin — A296

Portraits: No. 1308, Kato Haman. No. 1309, Lajos Tüköry. No. 1310, Giuseppe Garibaldi. No. 1311, István Türr. No. 1312, Ottó Herman. No. 1313, Ludwig van Beethoven. No. 1314, Ferenc Mora. No. 1315, Istvan Toth Bucsoki. No. 1316, Donat Banki. No. 1317, Abraham G. Pattantyus. No. 1318, Ignaz Semmelweis. No. 1319, Frédéric Joliot-Curie. No. 1320, Ferenc Erkel. No. 1321, Janos Bolyai. No. 1322, Lenin.

**1960 Photo. *Perf. 10½***

**1307** A296 60f lt red brn .25 .25

**Engr.**

**1308** A296 60f pale purple .25 .25
**1309** A296 60f rose red .25 .25
**1310** A296 60f violet .25 .25
**1311** A296 60f blue green .25 .25
**1312** A296 60f blue .25 .25
**1313** A296 60f gray brown .25 .25
**1314** A296 60f salmon pink .25 .25
**1315** A296 60f gray .25 .25
**1316** A296 60f rose lilac .25 .25
**1317** A296 60f green .25 .25
**1318** A296 60f violet blue .25 .25
**1319** A296 60f brown .25 .25
**1320** A296 60f rose brown .25 .25
**1321** A296 60f grnsh blue .25 .25
**1322** A296 60f dull red .25 .25
*Nos. 1307-1322 (16)* 4.00 4.00

Nos. 1307-1308 commemorate International Women's Day, Mar. 8.
Exists imperf. Value $55.

Flower and Quill — A297

**Wmk. 106**
**1960, Apr. 2 Photo. *Perf. 12***

**1323** 2fo brn, yel & grn 1.25 1.25
*a.* A297 With ticket 1.50 1.50

Issued for the stamp show of the National Federation of Hungarian Philatelists. The olive green 4fo ticket pictures the Federation's headquarters and served as entrance ticket to the show. Printed in sheets of 35 stamps and 35 tickets.
Exists imperf. Value, stamp + ticket, $15.

Soviet Capt. Ostapenko Statue — A298

Designs: 60f, Youth holding flag, horiz.

***Perf. 12½x11½, 11½x12½***

**1960, Apr. 4**

**1324** A298 40f dp carmine & brn .35 .25
**1325** A298 60f red brn, red & grn .65 .25

Hungary's liberation from the Nazis, 15th anniv.
Exist imperf. Value, set $12.50.

Boxers — A299

Sports: 10f, Rowers. 30f, Archer. 40f, Discus thrower. 50f, Girls playing ball. 60f, Javelin thrower. 1fo, Rider. 1.40fo, Wrestlers. 1.70fo, Swordsmen. 3fo, Hungarian Olympic emblem.

**1960, Aug. 21** ***Perf. 11½x12***

**Designs in Ocher and Black**

**1326** A299 10f blue .25 .25
**1327** A299 20f salmon .25 .25
**1328** A299 30f lt violet .25 .25
**1329** A299 40f yellow .25 .25
**1330** A299 50f deep pink .25 .25
**1331** A299 60f gray .25 .25
**1332** A299 1fo pale brn vio .25 .25
**1333** A299 1.40fo lt violet bl .25 .25
**1334** A299 1.70fo ocher .45 .25
**1335** A299 3fo multi 1.00 .50
*Nos. 1326-1335,B218 (11)* 4.70 3.05

17th Olympic Games, Rome, 8/25-9/11.
Exist imperf. Value, set $20.

Souvenir Sheet

Romulus and Remus Statue and Olympic Flame — A300

**1960, Aug. 21**

**1336** A300 10fo multicolored 20.00 20.00

Winter and Summer Olympic Games, 1960.
Exists imperf. Value $40.

Woman of Mezokovesd Writing Letter — A301

***Perf. 11½x12***

**1960, Oct. 15 Photo. Wmk. 106**

**1337** A301 2fo multicolored 1.40 1.40
*a.* With ticket 1.75 1.75

Day of the Stamp and Natl. Stamp Exhib. Issued in sheets of 8 with alternating ticket. The 4fo sale price marked on the ticket was the admission fee to the Natl. Stamp Exhib.
Exists imperf. Value, stamp + ticket, $12.50.

The Turnip, Russian Fairy Tale — A302

Fairy Tales: 30f, Snow White and the Seven Dwarfs. 40f, The Miller, His Son and the Donkey. 60f, Puss in Boots. 80f, The Fox and the Raven. 1fo, The Maple-Wood Pipe. 1.70fo, The Fox and the Stork. 2fo, Momotaro (Japanese).

**1960, Dec. 1** ***Perf. 11½x12***

**1338** A302 20f multi .25 .25
**1339** A302 30f multi .25 .25
**1340** A302 40f multi .25 .25
**1341** A302 60f multi .25 .25
**1342** A302 80f multi .25 .25
**1343** A302 1fo multi .35 .25
**1344** A302 1.70fo multi .65 .35
**1345** A302 2fo multi 1.00 .50
*Nos. 1338-1345 (8)* 3.25 2.35

Exist imperf. Value, set $20.

Brown Bear — A303

Animals: 20f, Kangaroo. 30f, Bison. 60f, Elephants. 80fr, Tiger with cubs. 1fo, Ibex. 1.40fo, Polar bear. 2fo, Zebra and young. 2.60fo, Bison cow with calf. 3fo, Main entrance to Budapest Zoological Gardens. 30f, 60f, 80f, 1.40fo, 2fo, 2.60fo are horizontal.

**1961, Feb. 24** ***Perf. 11½x12***

**1346** A303 20f orange & blk .25 .25
**1347** A303 30f yel grn & blk brn .25 .25
**1348** A303 40f org brn & brn .25 .25
**1349** A303 60f lil rose & gray .25 .25
**1350** A303 80f gray & yel .25 .25
**1351** A303 1fo blue grn & brn .30 .25
**1352** A303 1.40fo grnsh bl, gray & blk .60 .25
**1353** A303 2fo pink & black .50 .25
**1354** A303 2.60fo brt vio & brn 1.00 .40
**1355** A303 3fo multicolored 1.40 .75
*Nos. 1346-1355 (10)* 5.05 3.15

Issued for the Budapest Zoo.
Exist imperf. Value, set $25.

**Castle Type of 1960**

10f, Kisvárda. 12f, Szigliget. 40f, Simon Tornya. 50f, Füzér. 80f, Egervár. 1fo, Vitány. 1.20fo, Sirok. 2fo, Boldogkő. 2.60fo, Hollókő. 4fo, Eger.

**1961, Mar. 3 Photo.** ***Perf. 14½***

**Size: 21x17½mm**

**1356** A293 10f orange brn .25 .25
**1357** A293 12f violet blue .25 .25
**1358** A293 40f brt green .25 .25
**1359** A293 50f brown .25 .25
**1360** A293 80f dull claret .25 .25

***Perf. 12x11½***

**Size: 28x21mm**

**1361** A293 1fo brt blue .25 .25
**1362** A293 1.20fo rose violet .25 .25
**1363** A293 2fo olive bister .40 .25
**1364** A293 2.60fo dull blue .60 .25
**1365** A293 4fo brt violet .75 .25
*Nos. 1356-1365 (10)* 3.50 2.50

Exist imperf. Value, set $65.

Child Chasing Butterfly A304

Ferenc Rozsa, Journalist A305

40f, Man on operating table. 60f, Ambulance & stretcher. 1fo, Traffic light & scooter. 1.70fo, Syringe. 4fo, Emblem of Health Information Service (torch & serpent).

**1961, Mar. 17 Litho.** ***Perf. 10½***

**Cross in Red**

**Size: 18x18mm**

**1366** A304 30f org brn & blk .25 .25
**1367** A304 40f bl grn, bl & sepia .25 .25

**Size: 25x30mm**

**1368** A304 60f multi .25 .25
**1369** A304 1fo multi .25 .25
**1370** A304 1.70fo multi .45 .25
**1371** A304 4fo gray & yel grn 1.25 .50
*Nos. 1366-1371 (6)* 2.70 1.75

Health Information Service.
Exist imperf. Value, set $20.

**Wmk. 106, Unwmk.**

**1961 Photo.** ***Perf. 12***

Portraits: No. 1373, Gyorgy Kilian. No. 1374, Jozsef Rippl-Ronai. No. 1375, Sandor Latinka. No. 1376, Maté Zalka. No. 1377, Jozsef Katona.

**1372** A305 1fo red brown .25 .25
**1373** A305 1fo greenish blue .25 .25
**1374** A305 1fo rose brown .25 .25
**1375** A305 1fo olive bister .25 .25
**1376** A305 1fo olive green .25 .25
**1377** A305 1fo maroon .25 .25
*Nos. 1372-1377 (6)* 1.50 1.50

Press Day (No. 1372); the inauguration of the Gyorgy Kilian Sports Movement (No. 1373); birth cent. of Jozsef Rippl-Ronai, painter (No. 1374); Sandor Latinka, revolutionary leader, 75th death anniv. (No. 1375); Mate Zalka, author and revolutionist (No. 1376); Jozsef Katona, dramatist (No. 1377).
Nos. 1374, 1375, 1377 are unwmkd. Others in this set have wmk. 106.
Exist imperf. Value, set $30.

Yuri A. Gagarin and Vostok 1 A306

Design: 1fo, Launching Vostok 1.

***Perf. 11½x12***

**1961, Apr. 25 Wmk. 106**

**1381** A306 1fo dk bl & bis brn .75 .50
**1382** A306 2fo dp ultra & bis brn 3.25 1.25

1st man in space, Yuri A. Gagarin, 4/12/61.
Exist imperf. Value, set $60.

Roses — A307

Design: 2fo, as 1fo, design reversed.

**1961, Apr. 29** ***Perf. 12½x11½***

**1383** A307 1fo grn & dp car .25 .25
**1384** A307 2fo grn & dp car .80 .25
*a.* Pair, #1383-1384 1.50 .30

Issued for May Day, 1961.
Exist imperf. Value, No. 1384a $20.

"Venus" and Moon A308

Designs: Various Stages of Rocket.

**1961, May 24 Wmk. 106** ***Perf. 14½***

**1385** A308 40f grnsh bl, bis & blk .80 .80
**1386** A308 60f brt bl, bis & blk .80 .80
**1387** A308 80f ultra & blk .80 .80
**1388** A308 2fo violet & yel 1.60 1.60
*Nos. 1385-1388 (4)* 4.00 4.00

Soviet launching of the Venus space probe, Feb. 12, 1961. Exist imperf. Value, set $30. No. 1388 was also printed in sheets of four, perf. and imperf. Size: 130x76mm. Value: perf $16; imperf $200.

Warsaw Mermaid, Letter and Sea, Air and Land Transport — A309

Mermaid and: 60f, Television screen and antenna. 1fo, Radio.

**1961, June 19 Photo.** ***Perf. 13½***

**1389** A309 40f red org & blk .25 .25
**1390** A309 60f lilac & blk .25 .25
**1391** A309 1fo brt blue & blk .60 .25
*Nos. 1389-1391 (3)* 1.10 .75

Conference of Postal Ministers of Communist Countries held at Warsaw.
Exist imperf. Value, set $15.

Flag and Parliament — A310

Designs: 1.70fo, Orchid. 2.60fo, Small tortoise-shell butterfly. 3fo, Goldfinch.

**1961, June 23** ***Perf. 11***

**Background in Silver**

**1392** A310 1fo green, red & blk .40 .35
**1393** A310 1.70fo red & multi .50 .45
**1394** A310 2.60fo purple & multi .75 .75
**1395** A310 3fo blue & multi 1.00 1.00

**1961, Aug. 19**

**Background in Gold**

**1396** A310 1fo green & blk .35 .30
**1397** A310 1.70fo red & multi .50 .40
**1398** A310 2.60fo purple & multi .75 .75
**1399** A310 3fo blue & multi 1.00 1.00
*Nos. 1392-1399 (8)* 5.25 5.00

Issued to publicize the International Stamp Exhibition, Budapest, Sept. 23-Oct. 3, 1961.
Nos. 1392-1399 each printed in sheets of 4.
In gold background issue the top left inscription is changed on 1fo and 3fo.
Exist imperf. Values: set $35; sheetlet set $200.

George Stephenson A311

Winged Wheel, Steering Wheel and Road A312

Design: 2fo, Jenö Landler.

*Perf. 12½x11½*

**1961, July 4 Photo. Wmk. 106**

**1400** A311 60f yellow olive .30 .25
**1401** A312 1fo blue & bister .30 .25
**1402** A311 2fo yellow brown .50 .35
*Nos. 1400-1402 (3)* 1.10 .85

Conference of Transport Ministers of Communist Countries held at Budapest.
Exist imperf. Value, set $20.

Soccer A313

**1961, July 8 Unwmk. *Perf. 14½***

**1403** A313 40f shown .25 .25
**1404** A313 60f Wrestlers .25 .25
**1405** A313 1fo Gymnast .30 .25
*Nos. 1403-1405 (3)* .80 .75

50th anniv. of the Steel Workers Sport Club (VASAS). See No. B219.
Exist imperf. Value, set of 4 (with B219) $20.

Galloping Horses — A314

40f, Hurdle Jump. 60f, Two trotters. 1fo, Three trotters. 1.70fo, Mares & foals. 2fo, Race horse "Baka." 3fo, Race horse "Kincsem."

**1961, July 22**

**1406** A314 30f multi .25 .25
**1407** A314 40f multi .25 .25
**1408** A314 60f multi .35 .25
**1409** A314 1fo multi .35 .25
**1410** A314 1.70fo multi .50 .25
**1411** A314 2fo multi 1.40 .30
**1412** A314 3fo multi 1.60 .65
*Nos. 1406-1412 (7)* 4.70 2.20

Exist imperf. Value, set $25.

Keyboard, Music and Liszt Silhouette A315

Liszt Monument, Budapest A316

Designs: 2fo, Academy of Music, Budapest, and bar of music. 10fo, Franz Liszt.

**1961, Oct. 2 Unwmk. *Perf. 12***

**1413** A315 60f gold & blk .35 .25
**1414** A316 1fo dark gray .60 .25
**1415** A315 2fo dk bl & gray grn .75 .40
*Nos. 1413-1415 (3)* 1.70 .90

**Souvenir Sheet**

**1416** A316 10fo multi 11.00 9.50

150th anniv. of the birth, and the 75th anniv. of the death of Franz Liszt, composer.
Exist imperf. Value: set $20; souvenir sheet $30.

Lenin — A317

**1961, Oct. 22 *Perf. 11½***

**1417** A317 1fo deep brown .40 .25

22nd Congress of the Communist Party of the USSR, Oct. 17-31.
Exist imperf. Value $5.

Monk's Hood — A318

**Wmk. 106**

**1961, Nov. 4 Photo. *Perf. 12***

**1418** A318 20f shown .25 .25
**1419** A318 30f Centaury .25 .25
**1420** A318 40f Blue iris .25 .25
**1421** A318 60f Thorn apple .55 .25
**1422** A318 1fo Purple holly-hock .30 .25
**1423** A318 1.70fo Hop .40 .25
**1424** A318 2fo Poppy .95 .30
**1425** A318 3fo Mullein 1.50 .60
*Nos. 1418-1425 (8)* 4.45 2.40

Exist imperf. Value, set $20.

Nightingale A319

Mihaly Karolyi A320

Birds: 40f, Great titmouse. 60f, Chaffinch, horiz. 1fo, Eurasian jay. 1.20fo, Golden oriole, horiz. 1.50fo, European blackbird, horiz. 2fo, Yellowhammer, 3fo, Lapwing, horiz.

**1961, Dec. 18 Unwmk. *Perf. 12***

**1426** A319 30f multi .25 .25
**1427** A319 40f multi .25 .25
**1428** A319 60f multi .25 .25
**1429** A319 1fo multi .25 .25
**1430** A319 1.20fo multi .25 .25
**1431** A319 1.50fo multi .45 .25
**1432** A319 2fo multi .55 .25
**1433** A319 3fo multi .75 .35
*Nos. 1426-1433 (8)* 3.00 2.10

Exist imperf. Value, set $20.

**1962, Mar. 18**

**1434** A320 1fo black .25 .25

Mihaly Karolyi, (1875-1955), Prime Minister of Hungarian Republic (1918-19).
Exists imperf. Value $4.

**1962, Mar. 29**

Portrait: No. 1435, Ferenc Berkes.

**1435** A320 1fo red brown .25 .25

Fifth Congress of the Hungarian Cooperative Movement, and to honor Ferenc Berkes, revolutionary. See Nos. 1457, 1459.
Exists imperf. Value $4.

Map of Europe, Train Signals and Emblem — A321

**1962, May 2 Photo.**

**1436** A321 1fo blue green .25 .25

14th Intl. Esperanto Cong. of Railway Men.
Exists imperf. Value $2.

Xiphophorus Helleri A322

Tropical Fish: 30f, Macropodus opercularis. 40f, Lebistes reticulatus. 60f, Betta splendens. 80f, Puntius tetrazona. 1fo, Pterophyllum scalare. 1.20fo, Mesogonistius chaetodon. 1.50fo, Aphyosemion australe. 2fo, Hyphessobrycon innesi. 3fo, Symphysodon aequifasciata haraldi.

**1962, May 5 *Perf. 11½x12***

**Fish in Natural Colors, Black Inscriptions**

**1437** A322 20f blue .25 .25
**1438** A322 30f citron .25 .25
**1439** A322 40f lt blue .25 .25
**1440** A322 60f lt yellow grn .25 .25
**1441** A322 80f blue green .30 .25
**1442** A322 1fo brt bl grn .25 .25
**1443** A322 1.20fo blue green .30 .25
**1444** A322 1.50fo grnsh blue .55 .25
*a.* "1962" twice in design 2.00 2.00
**1445** A322 2fo green .70 .25
**1446** A322 3fo gray grn & yel 1.50 1.00
*Nos. 1437-1446 (10)* 4.60 3.25

On No. 1444a, the year date appears both to the left and below the value inscription. On No. 1444, it appears only to the left of the value.
Exists imperf. Value, set $25.

Globe, Soccer Ball and Flags of Colombia and Uruguay — A323

Goalkeeper — A324

Flags of: 40f, USSR and Yugoslavia. 60f, Switzerland and Chile. 1fo, Germany and Italy. 1.70fo, Argentina and Bulgaria. 3fo, Brazil and Mexico.

**Unwmk.**

**1962, May 21 Photo. *Perf. 11***

**Flags in National Colors**

**1447** A323 30f rose & bis .25 .25
**1448** A323 40f pale grn & bis .25 .25
**1449** A323 60f pale lil & bis .25 .25
**1450** A323 1fo blue & bis .75 .25
**1451** A323 1.70fo ocher & bis .55 .25
**1452** A323 3fo pink & blue bis 1.50 .40
*Nos. 1447-1452,B224,C209A (8)* 6.65 2.70

**Souvenir Sheet**

***Perf. 12***

**1453** A324 10fo multicolored 6.50 6.50

World Cup Soccer Championship, Chile, May 30-June 17.
Exist imperf. Value: set (8) $25; souvenir sheet $25.

**Type of 1961 and**

Johann Gutenberg A325

#1456, Miklós Misztófalusi Kis, Hungarian printer (1650-1702). #1457, Jozsef Pach. #1458, András Cházár. #1459, Dr. Ferenc Hutyra. #1460, Gábor Egressy & National Theater.

**1962 Unwmk. Photo. *Perf. 12***

**1455** A325 1fo blue black .25 .25
**1456** A325 1fo red brown .25 .25
**1457** A320 1fo blue .25 .25
**1458** A325 1fo violet .25 .25
**1459** A320 1fo deep blue .30 .25
**1460** A325 1fo rose red .40 .25
*Nos. 1455-1460 (6)* 1.70 1.50

Cent. of Printers' and Papermakers' Union (Nos. 1455-1456). 75th anniv. of founding, by Jozsef Pech, of Hungarian Hydroelectric Service (No. 1457). András Cházár, founder of Hungarian deaf-mute education (No. 1458). Dr. Ferenc Hutyra, founder of Hungarian veterinary medicine (No. 1459). 125th anniv. of National Theater (No. 1460).
Exist imperf. Value, set $20.

Malaria Eradication Emblem — A327

**1962, June 25 *Perf. 15***

**1461** A327 2.50fo lemon & blk .75 .50
*a.* 2.50fo grn & blk, sheet of 4, perf. 11 4.00 3.75

WHO drive to eradicate malaria.
Imperfs exist. Values: single (lemon) $9; single (green) $10; green sheetlet of 4 $50.
Imperf. sheets with control numbers exist.

Sword-into-Plowshare Statue, United Nations, NY — A328

**1962, July 7** *Perf. 12*

| | | | | |
|---|---|---|---|---|
| **1462** | A328 | 1fo brown | .25 | .25 |

World Congress for Peace and Disarmament, Moscow, July 9-14.
Exists imperf. Value $1.25.

Floribunda Rose — A329 Festival Emblem — A330

**1962** *Perf. 12½x11½*

**Various Roses in Natural Colors**

| | | | | |
|---|---|---|---|---|
| **1465** | A329 | 20f orange brn | .25 | .25 |
| **1466** | A329 | 40f slate grn | .35 | .25 |
| **1467** | A329 | 60f violet | .35 | .25 |
| **1468** | A329 | 80f rose red | .50 | .25 |
| **1469** | A329 | 1fo dark green | .70 | .35 |
| **1470** | A329 | 1.20fo orange | .85 | .35 |
| **1471** | A329 | 2fo dk blue grn | 1.75 | .45 |
| **1472** | A330 | 3fo multi | .80 | .35 |
| | | *Nos. 1465-1472 (8)* | 5.55 | 2.50 |

No. 1472 was issued for the 8th World Youth Festival, Helsinki, July 28-Aug. 6.
Exist imperf. Value, set $30.

Weight Lifter — A331

**1962, Sept. 16** *Perf. 12*

| | | | | |
|---|---|---|---|---|
| **1473** | A331 | 1fo copper red | .50 | .25 |

European Weight Lifting Championships.
Exists imperf. Value $3.

Oil Derrick and Primitive Oil Well — A332

*Perf. 12x11½*

**1962, Oct. 8** **Photo.** **Unwmk.**

| | | | | |
|---|---|---|---|---|
| **1474** | A332 | 1fo green | .50 | .25 |

25th anniv. of the Hungarian oil industry.
Exists imperf. Value $1.50.

Racing Motorcyclist — A333

Designs: 30f, Stunt racing. 40f, Uphill race. 60f, Cyclist in curve. 1fo, Start. 1.20fo, Speed racing. 1.70fo, Motorcyclist with sidecar. 2fo, Motor scooter. 3fo, Racing car.

**1962, Dec. 28** *Perf. 11*

| | | | | |
|---|---|---|---|---|
| **1475** | A333 | 20f multi | .25 | .25 |
| **1476** | A333 | 30f multi | .25 | .25 |
| **1477** | A333 | 40f multi | .25 | .25 |
| **1478** | A333 | 60f multi | .25 | .25 |
| **1479** | A333 | 1fo multi | .40 | .25 |
| **1480** | A333 | 1.20fo multi | .45 | .25 |
| **1481** | A333 | 1.70fo multi | .75 | .25 |
| **1482** | A333 | 2fo multi | .85 | .30 |
| **1483** | A333 | 3fo multi | 1.00 | .75 |
| | | *Nos. 1475-1483 (9)* | 4.45 | 2.80 |

Exist imperf. Value, set $20.

Ice Skater — A334

Designs: 20f-3fo, Various figure skating and ice dancing positions. 20f, 3fo horiz. 10fo, Figure skater and flags of participating nations.

*Perf. 12x11½, 11½x12*

**1963, Feb. 5** **Photo.** **Unwmk.**

| | | | | |
|---|---|---|---|---|
| **1484** | A334 | 20f multi | .25 | .25 |
| **1485** | A334 | 40f multi | .25 | .25 |
| **1486** | A334 | 60f multi | .35 | .25 |
| **1487** | A334 | 1fo multi | .45 | .30 |
| **1488** | A334 | 1.40fo multi | .65 | .40 |
| **1489** | A334 | 2fo multi | 1.00 | .45 |
| **1490** | A334 | 3fo multi | 1.60 | .75 |
| | | *Nos. 1484-1490 (7)* | 4.55 | 2.65 |

**Souvenir Sheet**

*Perf. 11½x12*

| | | | | |
|---|---|---|---|---|
| **1491** | A334 | 10fo multi | 6.50 | 6.50 |

European Figure Skating and Ice Dancing Championships, Budapest, Feb. 5-10.
Exist imperf. Value: set $20; souvenir sheet $80.

János Batsányi (1763-1845) — A335

#1493, Helicon Monument. #1494, Actors before Szeged Cathedral. #1495, Leo Weiner, composer. #1496, Ferenc Entz,horticulturist. #1497, Ivan Markovits, inventor of Hungarian shorthand,1863. #1498, Dr. Frigyes Koranyi. #1499, Ferenc Erkel (1810-93), composer. #1500, Geza Gardonyi (1863-1922), writer of Hungarian historical novels for youth. #1501, Pierre de Coubertin, Frenchman, reviver of Olympic Games. #1502, Jozsef Eötvös, author, philosopher, educator. #1503, Budapest Industrial Fair emblem. #1504, Stagecoach and Arc de Triomphe, Paris. #1505, Hungary map and power lines. #1506, Roses.

**1963** **Unwmk.** *Perf. 11*

| | | | | |
|---|---|---|---|---|
| **1492** | A335 | 40f dk car rose | .25 | .25 |
| **1493** | A335 | 40f blue | .25 | .25 |
| **1494** | A335 | 40f violet blue | .25 | .25 |
| **1495** | A335 | 40f olive | .25 | .25 |
| **1496** | A335 | 40f emerald | .25 | .25 |
| **1497** | A335 | 40f dark blue | .25 | .25 |
| **1498** | A335 | 60f dull violet | .25 | .25 |
| **1499** | A335 | 60f bister brn | .25 | .25 |
| **1500** | A335 | 60f gray green | .25 | .25 |
| **1501** | A335 | 60f red brown | .40 | .25 |
| **1502** | A335 | 60f lilac | .25 | .25 |
| **1503** | A335 | 1fo purple | .25 | .25 |
| **1504** | A335 | 1fo rose red | .25 | .25 |
| **1505** | A335 | 1fo gray | .25 | .25 |
| **1506** | A335 | 2fo multi | .50 | .25 |
| | | *Nos. 1492-1506 (15)* | 4.15 | 3.75 |

No. 1493, 10th Youth Festival, Keszthely. No. 1494, Outdoor plays, Szeged. No. 1495, Budapest Music Competition. No. 1496, Cent. of professional horticultural training. No. 1498, 50th anniv. of the death of Prof. Koranyi, pioneer in fight against tuberculosis. No. 1499, Erkel Memorial Festival, Gyula. No. 1501, 10th anniv. of the People's Stadium, Budapest. No. 1502, 150th anniv. of birth of Jozsef Eötvös, organizer of modern public education in Hungary. No. 1504, Paris Postal Conf., 1863. No. 1505, Rural electrification. No. 1506, 5th Natl. Rose Show.
Exist imperf. Value, set $50.

Ship and Chain Bridge, Budapest — A336

Bus and Parliament A337

20f, Trolley. 30f, Sightseeing bus & Natl. Museum. 40f, Bus & trailer. 50f, Railroad tank car. 60f, Trolley bus. 70f, Railroad mail car. 80f, Motorcycle messenger. #1516, Mail plane, vert. #1517, Television transmitter, Miskolc, vert. 1.40fo, Mobile post office. 1.70fo, Diesel locomotive. 2fo, Mobile radio transmitter & stadium. 2.50fo, Tourist bus. 2.60fo, Passenger train. 3fo, P.O. parcel conveyor. 4fo, Television transmitters, Pecs, vert. 5fo, Hydraulic lift truck & mail car. 6fo, Woman teletypist. 8fo, Map of Budapest & automatic dial phone. 10fo, Girl pioneer &woman letter carrier.

**1963-64** **Photo.** *Perf. 11*

| | | | | |
|---|---|---|---|---|
| **1507** | A336 | 10f brt blue | .25 | .25 |
| **1508** | A336 | 20f dp yellow grn | .25 | .25 |
| **1509** | A336 | 30f violet | .25 | .25 |
| **1510** | A336 | 40f orange | .25 | .25 |
| **1511** | A336 | 50f brown | .25 | .25 |
| **1512** | A336 | 60f crimson | .25 | .25 |
| **1513** | A336 | 70f olive gray | .25 | .25 |
| **1514** | A336 | 80f red brn ('64) | .25 | .25 |

*Perf. 12x11½, 11½x12*

| | | | | |
|---|---|---|---|---|
| **1515** | A337 | 1fo rose claret | .25 | .25 |
| **1516** | A337 | 1.20fo orange brn | .80 | .60 |
| **1517** | A337 | 1.20fo dp vio ('64) | .25 | .25 |
| **1518** | A337 | 1.40fo dp yel grn | .25 | .25 |
| **1519** | A337 | 1.70fo maroon | .25 | .25 |
| **1520** | A337 | 2fo grnsh blue | .35 | .25 |
| **1521** | A337 | 2.50fo lilac | 1.20 | .25 |
| **1522** | A337 | 2.60fo olive | 1.25 | .25 |
| **1523** | A337 | 3fo dk blue ('64) | .25 | .25 |
| **1524** | A337 | 4fo blue ('64) | .35 | .25 |
| **1525** | A337 | 5fo ol brn ('64) | .45 | .25 |
| **1526** | A337 | 6fo dk ol bis ('64) | .55 | .25 |
| **1527** | A337 | 8fo red lilac ('64) | .80 | .25 |
| **1528** | A337 | 10fo emerald ('64) | 1.25 | .75 |
| | | *Nos. 1507-1528 (22)* | 10.25 | 6.35 |

Size of 20f, 60f: 20½-21x16¾-17mm.
Minute inscription in lower margin includes year date, number of stamp in set and designer's name (Bokros F. or Legrady S.).
Exist imperf. Value, set $60.
See Nos. 1983-1983B, 2201-2204.

**Size: 21½x16½mm**

**1965-67** **Coil Stamps** *Perf. 14*

| | | | | |
|---|---|---|---|---|
| *1508a* | A336 | 20f deep yellow green | .30 | .25 |
| *1512a* | A336 | 60f crimson ('67) | .50 | .25 |

Black control number on back of every 3rd stamp.

Motorboat — A338

Girl, Steamer and Castle — A339

Design: 60f, Sailboat.

**1963, July 13** *Perf. 11*

| | | | | |
|---|---|---|---|---|
| **1529** | A338 | 20f sl grn, red & blk | .25 | .25 |
| **1530** | A339 | 40f multicolored | .25 | .25 |
| **1531** | A338 | 60f bl, blk, brn & org | .60 | .25 |
| | | *Nos. 1529-1531 (3)* | 1.10 | .75 |

Centenary of the summer resort Siofok.
Exist imperf. Value, set $20.

Child with Towel and Toothbrush A340 Karancsság Woman A341

Designs: 40f, Child with medicines. 60f, Girls of 3 races. 1fo, Girl and heart. 1.40fo, Boys of 3 races. 2fo, Medical examination of child. 3fo, Hands shielding plants.

**1963, July 27** *Perf. 12x11½*

| | | | | |
|---|---|---|---|---|
| **1532** | A340 | 30f multi | .25 | .25 |
| **1533** | A340 | 40f multi | .25 | .25 |
| **1534** | A340 | 60f multi | .25 | .25 |
| **1535** | A340 | 1fo multi | .25 | .25 |
| **1536** | A340 | 1.40fo multi | .35 | .25 |
| **1537** | A340 | 2fo multi | .40 | .25 |
| **1538** | A340 | 3fo multi | 1.20 | .40 |
| | | *Nos. 1532-1538 (7)* | 2.95 | 1.90 |

Centenary of the International Red Cross.
Exist imperf. Value, set $17.50.

**1963, Aug. 18** **Engr.** *Perf. 11½*

Provincial Costumes: 30f, Kapuvár man. 40f, Debrecen woman. 60f, Hortobágy man. 1fo, Csököly woman. 1.70fo, Dunántul man. 2fo, Buják woman. 2.50fo, Alföld man. 3fo, Mezökövesd bride.

| | | | | |
|---|---|---|---|---|
| **1539** | A341 | 20f claret | .25 | .25 |
| **1540** | A341 | 30f green | .25 | .25 |
| **1541** | A341 | 40f brown | .25 | .25 |
| **1542** | A341 | 60f brt blue | .30 | .25 |
| **1543** | A341 | 1fo brown red | .45 | .25 |
| **1544** | A341 | 1.70fo purple | .50 | .35 |
| **1545** | A341 | 2fo dk blue grn | .65 | .35 |
| **1546** | A341 | 2.50fo dk carmine | .75 | .65 |
| **1547** | A341 | 3fo violet blue | 1.60 | .65 |
| | | *Nos. 1539-1547 (9)* | 5.00 | 3.25 |

Popular Art Exhibition in Budapest.
Exist imperf. Value, set $40.

Slalom and 1964 Olympic Emblem — A342

Sports: 60f, Downhill skiing. 70f, Ski jump. 80f, Rifle shooting on skis. 1fo, Figure skating pair. 2fo, Ice hockey. 2.60fo, Speed ice skating. 10fo, Skier and mountains, vert.

**1963-64 Photo. *Perf. 12***

**1964 Olympic Emblem in Black and Red**

| | | | | |
|---|---|---|---|---|
| **1548** | A342 | 40f yel grn & bis | .25 | .25 |
| **1549** | A342 | 60f violet & bis | .25 | .25 |
| **1550** | A342 | 70f ultra & bis | .25 | .25 |
| **1551** | A342 | 80f emerald & bis | .25 | .25 |
| **1552** | A342 | 1fo brn org & bis | .25 | .25 |
| **1553** | A342 | 2fo brt blue & bis | .40 | .25 |
| **1554** | A342 | 2.60fo rose lake & bis | .60 | .40 |
| | | *Nos. 1548-1554,B234 (8)* | 2.95 | 2.20 |

**Souvenir Sheet**

***Perf. 11½x12***

| | | | | |
|---|---|---|---|---|
| **1555** | A342 | 10fo grnsh bl, red & brn ('64) | 5.50 | 5.50 |

9th Winter Olympic Games, Innsbruck, Austria, Jan. 29-Feb. 9, 1964.
Exist imperf. Value: set (8) $20; souvenir sheet $20.

Four-Leaf Clover — A343

Good Luck Symbols: 20f, Calendar and mistletoe, horiz. 30f, Chimneysweep and clover. 60f, Top hat, pig and clover. 1fo, Clown with balloon and clover, horiz. 2fo, Lanterns, mask and clover.

***Perf. 12x11½, 11½x12***

**1963, Dec. 12 Photo. Unwmk.**

**Sizes: 28x22mm (20f, 1fo);**
**22x28mm (40f);**
**28x39mm (30f, 60f, 2fo)**

| | | | | |
|---|---|---|---|---|
| **1556** | A343 | 20f multi | .25 | .25 |
| **1557** | A343 | 30f multi | .25 | .25 |
| **1558** | A343 | 40f multi | .25 | .25 |
| **1559** | A343 | 60f multi | .25 | .25 |
| **1560** | A343 | 1fo multi | .25 | .25 |
| **1561** | A343 | 2fo multi | .45 | .25 |
| | | *Nos. 1556-1561,B235-B236 (8)* | 2.90 | 2.10 |

New Year 1964.
Exist imperf. Value, set $15.
The 20f and 40f issued in booklet panes of 10, perf. and imperf.; sold for 2 times and 1½ times face respectively.

Moon Rocket — A344

U.S. & USSR Spacecraft: 40f, Venus space probe. 60f, Vostok I, horiz. 1fo, Friendship 7. 1.70fo, Vostok III & IV. 2fo, Telstar 1 & 2, horiz. 2.60fo, Mars I. 3fo, Radar, rockets and satellites, horiz.

**1964, Jan. 8 *Perf. 11½x12, 12x11½***

| | | | | |
|---|---|---|---|---|
| **1562** | A344 | 30f grn, yel & brnz | .25 | .25 |
| **1563** | A344 | 40f pur, bl & sil | .25 | .25 |
| **1564** | A344 | 60f bl, blk, yel, sil & red | .25 | .25 |
| **1565** | A344 | 1fo dk brn, red & sil | .35 | .25 |
| **1566** | A344 | 1.70fo vio bl, blk, tan & red | .70 | .25 |
| **1567** | A344 | 2fo sl grn, yel & sil | .70 | .25 |
| **1568** | A344 | 2.60fo dp bl, yel & brnz | .70 | .45 |
| **1569** | A344 | 3fo dp vio, lt bl & sil | 1.00 | .50 |
| | | *Nos. 1562-1569 (8)* | 4.20 | 2.45 |

Achievements in space research.
Exist imperf. Value, set $15.

**Lace Type of 1960**

Various Halas Lace Designs.
Sizes: 20f, 2.60fo: 38x28mm. 30f, 40f, 60f, 1fo, 1.40fo, 2fo: 38x45mm.

**Engr. & Litho.**

**1964, Feb. 28 *Perf. 11½***

| | | | | |
|---|---|---|---|---|
| **1570** | A294 | 20f emerald & blk | .25 | .25 |
| **1571** | A294 | 30f dull yel & blk | .25 | .25 |
| **1572** | A294 | 40f deep rose & blk | .25 | .25 |
| **1573** | A294 | 60f olive & blk | .25 | .25 |
| **1574** | A294 | 1fo red org & blk | .35 | .25 |
| **1575** | A294 | 1.40fo blue & blk | .45 | .25 |
| **1576** | A294 | 2fo bluish grn & blk | .55 | .25 |
| **1577** | A294 | 2.60fo lt vio & blk | .85 | .45 |
| | | *Nos. 1570-1577 (8)* | 3.20 | 2.20 |

Exist imperf. Value, set $35.

**Special Anniversaries-Events Issue**

Imre Madach (1823-64) — A345

Shakespeare A346

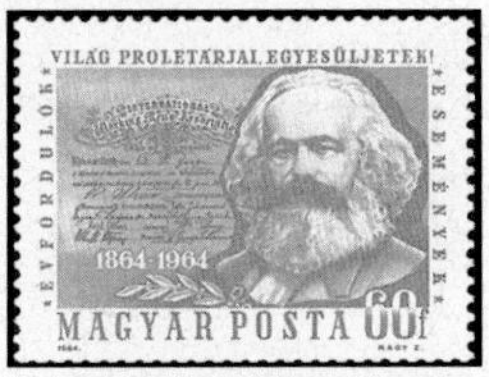


Karl Marx and Membership Card of International Working Men's Association — A347

Michelangelo — A348

Lajos Kossuth and György Dózsa — A349

Budapest Fair Buildings — A350

#1579, Ervin Szabo. #1580, Writer Andras Fay (1786-1864). #1581, Aggtelek Cave scene. #1582, Excavating bauxite. #1584, Equestrian statue, Szekesfehervar. #1585, Bowler. #1586, Waterfall and forest. #1587, Architect Miklos Ybl (1814-91) and Budapest Opera. #1590, Armor, saber, sword & foil. #1592, Galileo Galilei. #1593, Women basketball players. #1595, Two runners breaking tape.

***Perf. 11½x12, 12x11½, 11***

**1964 Photo. Unwmk.**

**Inscribed: "ÉVFORDULÓK-ESEMÉNYEK"**

| | | | | |
|---|---|---|---|---|
| **1578** | A345 | 60f brt purple | .25 | .25 |
| **1579** | A345 | 60f olive | .25 | .25 |
| **1580** | A345 | 60f olive grn | .25 | .25 |
| **1581** | A346 | 60f bluish grn | .25 | .25 |
| **1582** | A346 | 60f Prus blue | .25 | .25 |
| **1583** | A347 | 60f rose red | .25 | .25 |
| **1584** | A348 | 60f slate blue | .25 | .25 |
| **1585** | A345 | 1fo car rose | .25 | .25 |
| *a.* | | With Olympic rings bottom tab | 1.00 | 1.00 |
| **1586** | A346 | 1fo dull blue grn | .25 | .25 |
| **1587** | A348 | 1fo orange brn | .25 | .25 |
| **1588** | A349 | 1fo ultra | .25 | .25 |
| **1589** | A350 | 1fo brt green | .25 | .25 |
| **1590** | A345 | 2fo yellow brn | .25 | .25 |
| **1591** | A346 | 2fo magenta | .35 | .25 |
| **1592** | A346 | 2fo red brown | .25 | .25 |
| **1593** | A346 | 2fo brt blue | .25 | .25 |
| **1594** | A348 | 2fo gray brown | .30 | .25 |
| **1595** | A348 | 2fo brown red | .25 | .25 |
| | | *Nos. 1578-1595 (18)* | 4.65 | 4.50 |

No. 1579, Municipal libraries, 60th anniv., and librarian Szabo (1877-1918). No. 1582, Bauxite mining in Hungary, 30th year. No. 1583, Cent. of 1st Socialist Intl. No. 1584, King Alba Day in Székésfehérvár. No. 1585, 1st European Bowling Championship, Budapest.
No. 1586, Cong. of Natl. Forestry Federation. No. 1588, City of Cegléd, 600th anniv. No. 1589, Opening of 1964 Budapest Intl. Fair. No. 1590, Hungarian Youth Fencing Association, 50th anniv. Nos. 1591-1592, Shakespeare and Galileo, 400th birth anniversaries. No. 1593, 9th European Women's Basketball Championship. No. 1594, Michelangelo's 400th death anniv. No. 1595, 50th anniv. of 1st Hungarian-Swedish athletic meet.
Exists imperf. Value, set $100. No. 1585a imperf value $350.

Eleanor Roosevelt — A351

Design, horiz.: a, d, Portrait at right. b, c, Portrait at left.

**1964, Apr. 27 *Perf. 12½***

| | | | | |
|---|---|---|---|---|
| **1596** | A351 | 2fo gray, black & buff | .30 | .25 |

**Miniature Sheet**

***Perf. 11***

| | | | | |
|---|---|---|---|---|
| **1597** | | Sheet of 4 | 3.00 | 2.75 |
| *a.* | A351 | 2fo dp claret, brn & blk | .65 | .65 |
| *b.* | A351 | 2fo dk bl, brn & blk | .65 | .65 |
| *c.* | A351 | 2fo grn, brn & blk | .65 | .65 |
| *d.* | A351 | 2fo olive, brn & blk | .65 | .65 |

Exist imperf. Value: single $7; souvenir sheet $20.

Fencing — A352

Sport: 40f, Women's gymnastics. 60f, Soccer. 80f, Equestrian. 1fo, Running. 1.40fo, Weight lifting. 1.70fo, Gymnast on rings. 2fo, Hammer throw and javelin. 2.50fo, Boxing.

**1964, June 12 Photo. *Perf. 11***

**Multicolored Design and Inscription**

| | | | | |
|---|---|---|---|---|
| **1598** | A352 | 30f lt ver | .25 | .25 |
| **1599** | A352 | 40f blue | .25 | .25 |
| **1600** | A352 | 60f emerald | .25 | .25 |
| **1601** | A352 | 80f tan | .25 | .25 |
| **1602** | A352 | 1fo yellow | .25 | .25 |
| **1603** | A352 | 1.40fo bis brn | .25 | .25 |
| **1604** | A352 | 1.70fo bluish gray | .30 | .25 |
| **1605** | A352 | 2fo gray grn | .35 | .25 |
| **1606** | A352 | 2.50fo vio gray | .55 | .40 |
| | | *Nos. 1598-1606,B237 (10)* | 3.30 | 3.15 |

18th Olympic Games, Tokyo, Oct. 10-25.
Exist imperf. Value, set (10) $20.

Elberta Peaches A353

Peaches: 40h, Blossoms (J. H. Hale). 60h, Magyar Kajszi. 1fo, Mandula Kajszi. 1.50fo, Borsi Rozsa. 1.70fo, Blossoms (Alexander). 2fo, Champion. 3fo, Mayflower.

**1964, July 24 *Perf. 11½***

| | | | | |
|---|---|---|---|---|
| **1607** | A353 | 40f multi | .25 | .25 |
| **1608** | A353 | 60f multi | .25 | .25 |
| **1609** | A353 | 1fo multi | .25 | .25 |
| **1610** | A353 | 1.50fo multi | .25 | .25 |
| **1611** | A353 | 1.70fo multi | .25 | .25 |
| **1612** | A353 | 2fo multi | .35 | .25 |
| **1613** | A353 | 2.60fo multi | .45 | .30 |
| **1614** | A353 | 3fo multi | .65 | .50 |
| | | *Nos. 1607-1614 (8)* | 2.70 | 2.30 |

National Peach Exhibition, Szeged.
Exist imperf. Value, set $30.

Crossing Street in Safety Zone — A354

60f, "Watch out for Children" (child & ball). 1fo, "Look before Crossing" (mother & child).

**1964, Sept. 27 *Perf. 11***

| | | | | |
|---|---|---|---|---|
| **1615** | A354 | 20f multicolored | .25 | .25 |
| **1616** | A354 | 60f multicolored | .25 | .25 |
| **1617** | A354 | 1fo lilac & multi | .60 | .25 |
| | | *Nos. 1615-1617 (3)* | 1.10 | .75 |

Issued to publicize traffic safety.
Exist imperf. Value, set $20.

Souvenir Sheet

Voskhod 1 and Globe — A355

**1964, Nov. 6 *Perf. 12x11½***

| | | | | |
|---|---|---|---|---|
| **1618** | A355 | 10fo multicolored | 3.75 | 3.50 |

Russian space flight of Vladimir M. Komarov, Boris B. Yegorov and Konstantine Feoktistov.
Exists imperf. Value $32.50.

Arpad Bridge — A356

Danube Bridges, Budapest: 30f, Margaret Bridge. 60f, Chain Bridge. 1fo, Elizabeth Bridge. 1.50fo, Freedom Bridge. 2fo, Petőfi Bridge. 2.50fo, Railroad Bridge.

**1964, Nov. 21 Photo. *Perf. 11x11½***

| | | | | | |
|---|---|---|---|---|---|
| **1619** | A356 | 20f | multi | .25 | .25 |
| **1620** | A356 | 30f | multi | .25 | .25 |
| **1621** | A356 | 60f | multi | .25 | .25 |
| **1622** | A356 | 1fo | multi | .25 | .25 |
| **1623** | A356 | 1.50fo | multi | .30 | .25 |
| **1624** | A356 | 2fo | multi | .50 | .25 |
| **1625** | A356 | 2.50fo | multi | .85 | .40 |
| | | | *Nos. 1619-1625 (7)* | 2.65 | 1.90 |

Opening of the reconstructed Elizabeth Bridge. See No. C250.
Exist imperf. Value, set $30.

Ring-necked Pheasant and Hunting Rifle — A357

Designs: 30f, Wild boar. 40f, Gray partridges. 60f, Varying hare. 80f, Fallow deer. 1fo, Mouflon. 1.70fo, Red deer. 2fo, Great bustard. 2.50fo, Roebuck and roe deer. 3fo, Emblem of National Federation of Hungarian Hunters (antlers).

**1964, Dec. 30 Photo. *Perf. 12x11½***

| | | | | | |
|---|---|---|---|---|---|
| **1626** | A357 | 20f | multi | .25 | .25 |
| **1627** | A357 | 30f | multi | .25 | .25 |
| **1628** | A357 | 40f | multi | .25 | .25 |
| **1629** | A357 | 60f | multi | .25 | .25 |
| **1630** | A357 | 80f | multi | .25 | .25 |
| **1631** | A357 | 1fo | multi | .25 | .25 |
| **1632** | A357 | 1.70fo | multi | .25 | .25 |
| **1633** | A357 | 2fo | multi | .30 | .25 |
| **1634** | A357 | 2.50fo | multi | .50 | .30 |
| **1635** | A357 | 3fo | multi | .75 | .50 |
| | | | *Nos. 1626-1635 (10)* | 3.30 | 2.80 |

Exist imperf. Value, set $30.

### Castle Type of 1960

3fo, Czesznek, vert. 4fo, Eger. 5fo, Koszeg, vert.

**1964 *Perf. 11½x12, 12x11½***
**Size: 21x28mm, 28x21mm**

| | | | | | |
|---|---|---|---|---|---|
| **1644** | A293 | 3fo | red brown | 1.00 | .25 |
| **1645** | A293 | 4fo | brt violet | 1.50 | .25 |
| **1646** | A293 | 5fo | yellow grn | 1.50 | .25 |
| | | | *Nos. 1644-1646 (3)* | 4.00 | .75 |

Equestrian, Gold and Bronze Medals — A358

Medals: 30f, Women's gymnastics, silver & bronze. 50f, Small-bore rifle, gold & bronze. 60f, Water polo, gold. 70f, Shot put, bronze. 80f, Soccer, gold. 1fo, Weight lifting, 1 bronze, 2 silver. 1.20fo, Canoeing, silver. 1.40fo, Hammer throw, silver. 1.50fo, Wrestling, 2 gold. 1.70fo, Javelin, 2 silver. 3fo, Fencing, 4 gold.

**1965, Feb. 20 *Perf. 12***
**Medals in Gold, Silver or Bronze**

| | | | | | |
|---|---|---|---|---|---|
| **1647** | A358 | 20f | lt ol grn & dk brn | .25 | .25 |
| **1648** | A358 | 30f | violet & dk brn | .25 | .25 |
| **1649** | A358 | 50f | olive & dk brn | .25 | .25 |
| **1650** | A358 | 60f | lt bl & red brn | .25 | .25 |
| **1651** | A358 | 70f | lt gray & red brn | .25 | .25 |
| **1652** | A358 | 80f | yel grn & dk brn | .25 | .25 |
| **1653** | A358 | 1fo | lil, vio & red brn | .25 | .25 |
| **1654** | A358 | 1.20fo | lt bl, ultra & red brn | .25 | .25 |
| **1655** | A358 | 1.40fo | gray & red brn | .25 | .25 |
| **1656** | A358 | 1.50fo | tan, lt brn & red brn | .25 | .25 |
| **1657** | A358 | 1.70fo | pink & red brn | .50 | .25 |
| **1658** | A358 | 3fo | grnsh blue & brn | .70 | .55 |
| | | | *Nos. 1647-1658 (12)* | 3.70 | 3.30 |

Victories by the Hungarian team in the 1964 Olympic Games, Tokyo, Oct. 10-25.
Exist imperf. Value, set $20.

Arctic Exploration A359

Designs: 30f, Radar tracking rocket, ionosphere research. 60f, Rocket and earth with reflecting layer diagrams, atmospheric research. 80f, Telescope and map of Milky Way, radio astronomy. 1.50fo, Earth, compass rose and needle, earth magnetism. 1.70fo, Weather balloon and lightning, meteorology. 2fo, Aurora australis and penguins, arctic research. 2.50fo, Satellite, earth and planets, space research. 3fo, IQSY emblem and world map. 10fo, Sun with flares and corona, snow crystals and rain.

***Perf. 11½x12***
**1965, Mar. 25 Photo. Unwmk.**

| | | | | | |
|---|---|---|---|---|---|
| **1659** | A359 | 20f | blue, org & blk | .25 | .25 |
| **1660** | A359 | 30f | gray, blk & emer | .25 | .25 |
| **1661** | A359 | 60f | lilac, blk & yel | .25 | .25 |
| **1662** | A359 | 80f | lt grn, yel & blk | .25 | .25 |
| **1663** | A359 | 1.50fo | lemon, bl & blk | .25 | .25 |
| **1664** | A359 | 1.70fo | blue, pink & blk | .25 | .25 |
| **1665** | A359 | 2fo | ultra, sal & blk | .25 | .25 |
| **1666** | A359 | 2.50fo | org brn, yel & blk | .40 | .25 |
| **1667** | A359 | 3fo | lt bl, cit & blk | .70 | .40 |
| | | | *Nos. 1659-1667 (9)* | 2.85 | 2.40 |

**Souvenir Sheet**

| | | | | | |
|---|---|---|---|---|---|
| **1668** | A359 | 10fo | ultra, org & blk | 2.50 | 2.50 |

Intl. Quiet Sun Year, 1964-65.
Exist imperf. Value: set $15; souvenir sheet $25.

Chrysanthemums A360

30f, Peonies. 50f, Carnations. 60f, Roses. 1.40fo, Lilies. 1.70fo, Anemones. 2fo, Gladioli. 2.50fo, Tulips. 3fo, Mixed flower bouquet.

**1965, Apr. 4**
**Flowers in Natural Colors**

| | | | | | |
|---|---|---|---|---|---|
| **1669** | A360 | 20f | gold & gray | .25 | .25 |
| **1670** | A360 | 30f | gold & gray | .25 | .25 |
| **1671** | A360 | 50f | gold & gray | .25 | .25 |
| **1672** | A360 | 60f | gold & gray | .25 | .25 |
| **1673** | A360 | 1.40fo | gold & gray | .25 | .25 |
| **1674** | A360 | 1.70fo | gold & gray | .25 | .25 |
| **1675** | A360 | 2fo | gold & gray | .25 | .25 |
| **1676** | A360 | 2.50fo | gold & gray | .30 | .25 |
| **1677** | A360 | 3fo | gold & gray | .60 | .50 |
| | | | *Nos. 1669-1677 (9)* | 2.65 | 2.50 |

20th anniversary of liberation from the Nazis.
Exist imperf. Value, set $15.

"Head of a Combatant" by Leonardo da Vinci — A361

***Perf. 11½x12***
**1965, May 4 Photo. Unwmk.**

| | | | | | |
|---|---|---|---|---|---|
| **1678** | A361 | 60f | bister & org brn | .30 | .25 |

Issued to publicize the First International Renaissance Conference, Budapest.
Exists imperf. Value $9.

Nikolayev, Tereshkova and View of Budapest — A362

**1965, May 10 *Perf. 11***

| | | | | | |
|---|---|---|---|---|---|
| **1679** | A362 | 1fo | dull blue & brn | .40 | .25 |

Visit of the Russian astronauts Andrian G. Nikolayev and Valentina Tereshkova (Mr. & Mrs. Nikolayev) to Budapest.
Exists imperf. Value $10.

ITU Emblem, Old and New Communication Equipment A363

**1965, May 17**

| | | | | | |
|---|---|---|---|---|---|
| **1680** | A363 | 60f | violet blue | .25 | .25 |

Cent. of the ITU.
Exists imperf. Value $7.

**Souvenir Sheet**

Austrian WIPA Stamp of 1933 — A363a

**1965, June 4 Photo. *Perf. 11***

| | | | | | |
|---|---|---|---|---|---|
| **1681** | A363a | | Sheet of 2 + 2 labels | 3.50 | 3.50 |
| *a.* | | 2fo | gray & deep ultra | 1.50 | 1.50 |

1965 Vienna Intl. Phil. Exhib. WIPA, 6/4-13.
Exists imperf. Value $30.

Marx and Lenin, Crowds with Flags — A364

**1965, June 15 *Perf. 11½x12***

| | | | | | |
|---|---|---|---|---|---|
| **1682** | A364 | 60f | red, blk & yel | .25 | .25 |

6th Conference of Ministers of Post of Socialist Countries, Peking, June 21-July 15.
Exists imperf. Value $9.

ICY Emblem and Pulley — A365

**1965, June 25**

| | | | | | |
|---|---|---|---|---|---|
| **1683** | A365 | 2fo | dark red | .25 | .25 |
| *a.* | | | Min. sheet of 4, perf. 11 | 2.25 | 2.25 |

Intl. Cooperation Year, 1965. No. 1683a contains rose red, olive, Prussian green and violet stamps.
Exists imperf. Value: single $6; sheetlet of 4 $30.

Musical Clown — A366

Circus Acts: 20f, Equestrians. 40f, Elephant. 50f, Seal balancing ball. 60f, Lions. 1fo, Wildcat jumping through burning hoops. 1.50fo, Black leopards. 2.50fo, Juggler. 3fo, Leopard and dogs. 4fo, Bear on bicycle.

**1965, July 26 Photo. *Perf. 11½x12***

| | | | | | |
|---|---|---|---|---|---|
| **1684** | A366 | 20f | multi | .25 | .25 |
| **1685** | A366 | 30f | multi | .25 | .25 |
| **1686** | A366 | 40f | multi | .25 | .25 |
| **1687** | A366 | 50f | multi | .25 | .25 |
| **1688** | A366 | 60f | multi | .25 | .25 |
| **1689** | A366 | 1fo | multi | .25 | .25 |
| **1690** | A366 | 1.50fo | multi | .25 | .25 |
| **1691** | A366 | 2.50fo | multi | .35 | .25 |
| **1692** | A366 | 3fo | multi | .40 | .25 |
| **1693** | A366 | 4fo | multi | .50 | .40 |
| | | | *Nos. 1684-1693 (10)* | 3.00 | 2.65 |

Exist imperf. Value, set $20.

Dr. Semmelweis A367

**1965, Aug. 20 Photo. Unwmk.**

| | | | | | |
|---|---|---|---|---|---|
| **1694** | A367 | 60f | red brown | .25 | .25 |

Dr. Ignaz Philipp Semmelweis (1818-1865), discoverer of the cause of puerperal fever and introduced antisepsis into obstetrics.
Exists imperf. Value $6.

Runner — A368

Sport: 30f, Swimmer at start. 50f, Woman diver. 60f, Modern dancing. 80f, Tennis. 1.70fo, Fencing. 2fo, Volleyball. 2.50fo, Basketball. 4fo, Water polo. 10fo, People's Stadium, Budapest, horiz.

**1965, Aug. 20 *Perf. 11***
**Size: 38x38mm**

| | | | | | |
|---|---|---|---|---|---|
| **1695** | A368 | 20f | multi | .25 | .25 |
| **1696** | A368 | 30f | blue & red brn | .25 | .25 |
| **1697** | A368 | 50f | bl grn, blk & red brn | .25 | .25 |
| **1698** | A368 | 60f | vio, blk & red brn | .25 | .25 |
| **1699** | A368 | 80f | tan, ol & red brn | .25 | .25 |
| **1700** | A368 | 1.70fo | multi | .25 | .25 |
| **1701** | A368 | 2fo | multi | .30 | .25 |
| **1702** | A368 | 2.50fo | gray, blk & red brn | .45 | .25 |

| | | | | |
|---|---|---|---|---|
| **1703** | A368 | 4fo bl, red brn & blk | .75 | .45 |
| | | *Nos. 1695-1703 (9)* | 3.00 | 2.45 |

**Souvenir Sheet**

***Perf. 12x11½***

| | | | | |
|---|---|---|---|---|
| **1704** | A368 | 10fo bis, red brn & gray | 3.00 | 2.75 |

Intl. College Championships, "Universiade," Budapest. No. 1704 contains one 38x28mm stamp.
Exist imperf. Value: set $25; souvenir sheet $30.

Hemispheres and Warsaw Mermaid — A369

**1965, Oct. 8 Photo. *Perf. 12x11½***

| | | | | |
|---|---|---|---|---|
| **1705** | A369 | 60f brt blue | .35 | .25 |

Sixth Congress of the World Federation of Trade Unions, Warsaw.
Exists imperf. Value $6.

Phyllocactus Hybridus A370

Flowers from Botanical Gardens: 30f, Cattleya Warszewiczii (orchid). 60f, Rebutia calliantha. 70f, Paphiopedilum hybridium. 80f, Opuntia cactus. 1fo, Laelia elegans (orchid). 1.50fo, Christmas cactus. 2fo, Bird-of-paradise flower. 2.50fo, Lithops Weberi. 3fo, Victoria water lily.

**1965, Oct. 11 *Perf. 11½x12***

| | | | | |
|---|---|---|---|---|
| **1706** | A370 | 20f gray & multi | .25 | .25 |
| **1707** | A370 | 30f gray & multi | .25 | .25 |
| **1708** | A370 | 60f gray & multi | .25 | .25 |
| **1709** | A370 | 70f gray & multi | .25 | .25 |
| **1710** | A370 | 80f gray & multi | .25 | .25 |
| **1711** | A370 | 1fo gray & multi | .25 | .25 |
| **1712** | A370 | 1.50fo gray & multi | .25 | .25 |
| **1713** | A370 | 2fo gray & multi | .25 | .25 |
| **1714** | A370 | 2.50fo gray & multi | .40 | .25 |
| **1715** | A370 | 3fo gray & multi | .60 | .35 |
| | | *Nos. 1706-1715 (10)* | 3.00 | 2.60 |

Exist imperf. Value, set $22.

"The Black Stallion" A371

Tales from the Arabian Nights: 30f, Shahriar and Scheherazade. 50f, Sinbad's Fifth Voyage (ship). 60f, Aladdin, or The Wonderful Lamp. 80f, Harun al-Rashid. 1fo, The Flying Carpet. 1.70fo, The Fisherman and the Genie. 2fo, Ali Baba and the Forty Thieves. 3fo, Sinbad's Second Voyage (flying bird).

**1965, Dec. 15 Litho. *Perf. 11½***

| | | | | |
|---|---|---|---|---|
| **1716** | A371 | 20f multi | .25 | .25 |
| **1717** | A371 | 30f multi | .25 | .25 |
| **1718** | A371 | 50f multi | .25 | .25 |
| **1719** | A371 | 60f multi | .25 | .25 |
| **1720** | A371 | 80f multi | .25 | .25 |
| **1721** | A371 | 1fo multi | .25 | .25 |
| **1722** | A371 | 1.70fo multi | .35 | .25 |
| **1723** | A371 | 2fo multi | .45 | .25 |
| **1724** | A371 | 3fo multi | .75 | .45 |
| | | *Nos. 1716-1724 (9)* | 3.05 | 2.45 |

Exist imperf. Value, set $22.50.

Congress Emblem A372

**1965, Dec. 9 Photo. *Perf. 11½x12***

| | | | | |
|---|---|---|---|---|
| **1725** | A372 | 2fo dark blue | .30 | .25 |

Fifth Congress of the International Federation of Resistance Fighters (FIR), Budapest.
Exists imperf. Value $6.

Callimorpha Dominula A373

**1966, Feb. 1 Photo. *Perf. 11½x12***

**Various Butterflies in Natural Colors; Black Inscription**

| | | | | |
|---|---|---|---|---|
| **1726** | A373 | 20f lt aqua | .25 | .25 |
| **1727** | A373 | 60f pale violet | .25 | .25 |
| **1728** | A373 | 70f tan | .25 | .25 |
| **1729** | A373 | 80f lt ultra | .25 | .25 |
| **1730** | A373 | 1fo gray | .25 | .25 |
| **1731** | A373 | 1.50fo emerald | .40 | .25 |
| **1732** | A373 | 2fo dull rose | .30 | .25 |
| **1733** | A373 | 2.50fo bister | .45 | .30 |
| **1734** | A373 | 3fo blue | .70 | .50 |
| | | *Nos. 1726-1734 (9)* | 3.10 | 2.55 |

Exist imperf. Value, set $30.

Lal Bahadur Shastri A374

Designs: 60f, Bela Kun. 2fo, Istvan Széchenyi and Chain Bridge.

**Lithographed; Photogravure (#1736)**

**1966 *Perf. 11½x12, 12x11½***

| | | | | |
|---|---|---|---|---|
| **1735** | A374 | 60f red & black | .25 | .25 |
| **1736** | A374 | 1fo brt violet | .25 | .25 |
| **1737** | A374 | 2fo dull yel, buff & sepia | .25 | .25 |
| | | *Nos. 1735-1737 (3)* | .75 | .75 |

Kun (1886-1939), communist labor leader; Shastri (1904-66), Indian Prime Minister; Count Istvan Széchenyi (1791-1860), statesman.
Exist imperf. Value, set $12.
See Nos. 1764-1765, 1769-1770.

Luna 9 — A375

Design: 3fo, Luna 9 sending signals from moon to earth, horiz.

**1966, Mar. 12 Photo. *Perf. 12***

| | | | | |
|---|---|---|---|---|
| **1738** | A375 | 2fo violet, blk & yel | .45 | .25 |
| **1739** | A375 | 3fo lt ultra, blk & yel | .85 | .60 |

1st soft landing on the moon by the Russian satellite Luna 9, Feb. 3, 1966.
Exist imperf. Value, set $12.

Crocus — A376

Flowers: 30f, Cyclamen. 60f, Ligularia sibirica. 1.40fo, Lilium bulbiferum. 1.50fo, Snake's head. 3fo, Snapdragon and emblem of Hungarian Nature Preservation Society.

**Flowers in Natural Colors**

**1966, Mar. 12 *Perf. 11***

| | | | | |
|---|---|---|---|---|
| **1740** | A376 | 20f brown | .25 | .25 |
| **1741** | A376 | 30f aqua | .25 | .25 |
| **1742** | A376 | 60f rose claret | .25 | .25 |
| **1743** | A376 | 1.40fo gray | .30 | .25 |
| **1744** | A376 | 1.50fo ultra | .45 | .25 |
| **1745** | A376 | 3fo mag & sepia | .65 | .40 |
| | | *Nos. 1740-1745 (6)* | 2.15 | 1.65 |

Exist imperf. Value, set $20.

**Birds in Natural Colors**

Designs: 20f, Barn swallows. 30f, Long-tailed tits. 60f, Red crossbill and pine cone. 1.40fo, Middle spotted woodpecker. 1.50fo, Hoopoe feeding young. 3fo, Forest preserve, lapwing and emblem of National Forest Preservation Society.

**1966, Apr. 16**

| | | | | |
|---|---|---|---|---|
| **1746** | A376 | 20f brt green | .25 | .25 |
| **1747** | A376 | 30f vermilion | .25 | .25 |
| **1748** | A376 | 60f brt green | .40 | .25 |
| **1749** | A376 | 1.40fo vio blue | .90 | .25 |
| **1750** | A376 | 1.50fo blue | 1.00 | .40 |
| **1751** | A376 | 3fo brn, mag & grn | 1.25 | .75 |
| | | *Nos. 1746-1751 (6)* | 4.05 | 2.15 |

Nos. 1740-1751 issued to promote protection of wild flowers and birds.
Exist imperf. Value, set $30.

Locomotive, 1847; Monoplane, 1912; Autobus, 1911; Steamer, 1853, and Budapest Railroad Station, 1846 — A377

Designs: 2fo, Transportation, 1966: electric locomotive V.43; turboprop airliner IL-18; Ikarusz autobus; Diesel passenger ship, and Budapest South Railroad Station.

**1966, Apr. 2 Photo. *Perf. 12***

| | | | | |
|---|---|---|---|---|
| **1752** | A377 | 1fo yel, brn & grn | .25 | .25 |
| **1753** | A377 | 2fo pale grn, bl & brn | .35 | .25 |

Re-opening of the Transport Museum, Budapest.
Exist imperf. Value, set $15.

Bronze Order of Labor — A378

Decorations: 30f, Silver Order of Labor. 50f, Banner Order, third class. 60f, Gold Order of Labor. 70f, Banner Order, second class. 1fo, Red Banner Order of Labor. 1.20fo, Banner Order, first class. 2fo, Order of Merit. 2.50fo, Hero of Socialist Labor. Sizes: 20f, 30f, 60f, 1fo, 2fo, 2.50fo: 19½x38mm. 50f: 21x29mm. 70f, 25x31mm. 1.20fo: 28x38mm.

**1966, Apr. 2 Unwmk. *Perf. 11***

**Decorations in Original Colors**

| | | | | |
|---|---|---|---|---|
| **1754** | A378 | 20f dp ultra | .25 | .25 |
| **1755** | A378 | 30f lt brown | .25 | .25 |
| **1756** | A378 | 50f blue green | .25 | .25 |
| **1757** | A378 | 60f violet | .25 | .25 |
| **1758** | A378 | 70f carmine | .25 | .25 |
| **1759** | A378 | 1fo violet bl | .25 | .25 |
| **1760** | A378 | 1.20fo brt blue | .25 | .25 |
| **1761** | A378 | 2fo olive | .25 | .25 |
| **1762** | A378 | 2.50fo dull blue | .35 | .25 |
| | | *Nos. 1754-1762 (9)* | 2.35 | 2.25 |

Exist imperf. Value, set $15.

**Portrait Type of 1966 and**

Dubna Nuclear Research Institute — A379

WHO Headquarters, Geneva — A380

Designs: No. 1764, Pioneer girl. No. 1765, Tamás Esze (1666-1708), military hero. No. 1767, Old view of Buda and UNESCO emblem. No. 1768, Horse-drawn fire pump and emblem of Sopron Fire Brigade. No. 1769, Miklos Zrinyi (1508-66), hero of Turkish Wars. No. 1770, Sandor Koranyi (1866-1944), physician and scientist.

**1966 Litho. *Perf. 11½x12***

| | | | | |
|---|---|---|---|---|
| **1763** | A379 | 60f blue grn & blk | .25 | .25 |
| **1764** | A374 | 60f multicolored | .25 | .25 |
| **1765** | A374 | 60f brt bl & blk | .25 | .25 |
| **1766** | A380 | 2fo lt ultra & blk | .25 | .25 |
| **1767** | A380 | 2fo lt blue & pur | .25 | .25 |
| **1768** | A380 | 2fo orange & blk | .25 | .25 |
| **1769** | A374 | 2fo ol bis & brn | .25 | .25 |
| **1770** | A374 | 2fo multicolored | .25 | .25 |
| | | *Nos. 1763-1770 (8)* | 2.00 | 2.00 |

No. 1763, 10th anniv. of the United Institute for Nuclear Research, Dubna, USSR; No. 1764, 20th anniv. of Pioneer Movement; No. 1766, Inauguration of the WHO Headquarters, Geneva; No. 1767, 20th anniv. of UNESCO and 72nd session of Executive Council, Budapest, May 30-31; No. 1768, Cent. of Volunteer Fire Brigade.
Exist imperf. Value, set $50.

Hungarian Soccer Player and Soccer Field — A381

Designs (Views of Soccer play): 30f, Montevideo 1930 (Uruguay 4, Argentina 2). 60f, Rome 1934 (Italy 2, Czechoslovakia 1). 1fo, Paris 1938 (Italy 4, Hungary 2). 1.40fo, Rio de Janeiro 1950 (Uruguay 2, Brazil 1). 1.70fo, Bern 1954 (Germany 3, Hungary 2). 2fo, Stockholm 1958 (Brazil 5, Sweden 2). 2.50fo, Santiago 1962 (Brazil 3, Czechoslovakia 1).

**Souvenir Sheet**

**1966, May 16 Photo. *Perf. 11½x12***

| | | | | |
|---|---|---|---|---|
| **1771** | A381 | 10fo multi | 3.25 | 3.00 |

Exists imperf. Value $30.

Jules Rimet, Cup and Soccer Ball — A382

**1966, June 6 *Perf. 12x11½***

| | | | | |
|---|---|---|---|---|
| **1772** | A382 | 20f blue & multi | .25 | .25 |
| **1773** | A382 | 30f orange & multi | .25 | .25 |
| **1774** | A382 | 60f multi | .25 | .25 |
| **1775** | A382 | 1fo multi | .25 | .25 |
| **1776** | A382 | 1.40fo multi | .25 | .25 |
| **1777** | A382 | 1.70fo multi | .25 | .25 |
| **1778** | A382 | 2fo multi | .25 | .25 |
| **1779** | A382 | 2.50fo multi | .60 | .40 |
| | | *Nos. 1772-1779,B258 (9)* | 3.35 | 2.65 |

World Cup Soccer Championship, Wembley, England, July 11-30.
Exist imperf. Value, set (9) $22.75.

European Red Fox — A383

Hunting Trophies: 60f, Wild boar. 70f, Wildcat. 80f, Roebuck. 1.50fo, Red deer. 2.50fo, Fallow deer. 3fo, Mouflon.

**1966, July 4 Photo. *Perf. 11½x12***

**Animals in Natural Colors**

| | | | | |
|---|---|---|---|---|
| **1780** | A383 | 20f gray & lt brn | .25 | .25 |
| **1781** | A383 | 60f buff & gray | .25 | .25 |
| **1782** | A383 | 70f lt bl & gray | .25 | .25 |
| **1783** | A383 | 80f pale grn & yel bis | .25 | .25 |
| **1784** | A383 | 1.50fo pale lem & brn | .35 | .25 |
| **1785** | A383 | 2.50fo gray & brn | .60 | .35 |
| **1786** | A383 | 3fo pale pink & gray | .95 | .50 |
| | | *Nos. 1780-1786 (7)* | 2.90 | 2.10 |

The 80f and 1.50fo were issued with and without alternating labels, which show date and place when trophy was taken; the 2.50fo was issued only with labels, 20f, 60f, 70f and 3fo without labels only.

Nos. 1780-1786 exist imperf. Value, set $25.

Discus Thrower and Matthias Cathedral A384

30f, High jump & Agriculture Museum. 40f, Javelin (women's) & Parliament. 50f, Hammer throw, Mt. Gellert & Liberty Bridge. 60f, Broad jump & view of Buda. 1fo, Shot put & Chain Bridge. 2fo, Pole vault & Stadium. 3fo, Long distance runners & Millenium Monument.

**1966, Aug. 30 Photo. *Perf. 12x11½***

| | | | | |
|---|---|---|---|---|
| **1787** | A384 | 20f grn, brn & org | .25 | .25 |
| **1788** | A384 | 30f multi | .30 | .25 |
| **1789** | A384 | 40f multi | .25 | .25 |
| **1790** | A384 | 50f multi | .25 | .25 |
| **1791** | A384 | 60f multi | .25 | .25 |
| **1792** | A384 | 1fo multi | .25 | .25 |
| **1793** | A384 | 2fo multi | .50 | .25 |
| **1794** | A384 | 3fo multi | .75 | .50 |
| | | *Nos. 1787-1794 (8)* | 2.80 | 2.25 |

8th European Athletic Championships, Budapest, Aug. 30-Sept. 4. See No. C261.
Exist imperf. Value, set $18.

Girl in the Forest by Miklos Barabas A385

Paintings: 1fo, Mrs. Istvan Bitto by Miklos Barabas (1810-98). 1.50fo, Hunyadi's Farewell by Gyula Benczur (1844-1920). 1.70fo, Reading Woman by Gyula Benczur, horiz. 2fo, Woman with Fagots by Mihaly Munkacsi (1844-1900). 2.50fo, Yawning Boy by Mihaly Munkacsi. 3fo, Lady in Violet by Pal Szinyei Merse (1845-1920). 10fo, Picnic in May by Pal Szinyei Merse, horiz.

**1966, Dec. 9 *Perf. 12½***

**Gold Frame**

| | | | | |
|---|---|---|---|---|
| **1795** | A385 | 60f multi | .25 | .25 |
| **1796** | A385 | 1fo multi | .25 | .25 |
| **1797** | A385 | 1.50fo multi | .40 | .25 |
| **1798** | A385 | 1.70fo multi | .40 | .25 |
| **1799** | A385 | 2fo multi | .40 | .25 |
| **1800** | A385 | 2.50fo multi | .45 | .25 |
| **1801** | A385 | 3fo multi | .90 | .80 |
| | | *Nos. 1795-1801 (7)* | 3.05 | 2.30 |

**Souvenir Sheet**

| | | | | |
|---|---|---|---|---|
| **1802** | A385 | 10fo multi | 6.00 | 6.00 |

Issued to honor Hungarian painters. Size of stamp in No. 1802: 56x51mm.
Exist imperf. Value: set $20; souvenir sheet $30.

Vostoks 3 and 4 — A386

Space Craft: 60f, Gemini 6 and 7. 80f, Vostoks 5 and 6. 1fo, Gemini 9 and target rocket. 1.50fo, Alexei Leonov walking in space. 2fo, Edward White walking in space. 2.50fo, Voskhod. 3fo, Gemini 11 docking Agena target.

**1966, Dec. 29 *Perf. 11***

| | | | | |
|---|---|---|---|---|
| **1803** | A386 | 20f multi | .25 | .25 |
| **1804** | A386 | 60f multi | .25 | .25 |
| **1805** | A386 | 80f multi | .25 | .25 |
| **1806** | A386 | 1fo multi | .25 | .25 |
| **1807** | A386 | 1.50fo multi | .30 | .25 |
| **1808** | A386 | 2fo multi | .30 | .25 |
| **1809** | A386 | 2.50fo multi | .50 | .30 |
| **1810** | A386 | 3fo multi | .75 | .50 |
| | | *Nos. 1803-1810 (8)* | 2.85 | 2.30 |

American and Russian twin space flights.

Exist imperf. Value, set $17.

Pal Kitaibel and Kitaibelia Vitifolia — A387

Flowers of the Carpathian Basin: 60f, Dentaria glandulosa. 1fo, Edraianthus tenuifolius. 1.50fo, Althaea pallida. 2fo, Centaurea mollis. 2.50fo, Sternbergia colchiciflora. 3fo, Iris Hungarica.

**1967, Feb. 7 Photo. *Perf. 11½x12***

**Flowers in Natural Colors**

| | | | | |
|---|---|---|---|---|
| **1811** | A387 | 20f rose, blk & gold | .25 | .25 |
| **1812** | A387 | 60f green | .25 | .25 |
| **1813** | A387 | 1fo violet gray | .25 | .25 |
| **1814** | A387 | 1.50fo blue | .25 | .25 |
| **1815** | A387 | 2fo light olive | .25 | .25 |
| **1816** | A387 | 2.50fo gray grn | .45 | .30 |
| **1817** | A387 | 3fo yellow grn | .75 | .50 |
| | | *Nos. 1811-1817 (7)* | 2.45 | 2.05 |

Pal Kitaibel (1757-1817), botanist, chemist and physician.
Exist imperf. Value, set $18.

Militiaman A388

**1967, Feb. 18 Photo. *Perf. 11½x12***

| | | | | |
|---|---|---|---|---|
| **1818** | A388 | 2fo blue gray | .40 | .25 |

Workers' Militia, 10th anniversary.
Exists imperf. Value $3.

Mme. Du Barry and Louis XV, by Gyula Benczur (1844-1920) — A390

Painting: 10fo, Milton dictating "Paradise Lost" to his daughters, by Soma Orlai Petrics.

**Souvenir Sheet**

**1967, May 6 Photo. *Perf. 12½***

| | | | | |
|---|---|---|---|---|
| **1819** | A390 | 10fo multi | 5.00 | 5.00 |

Exists imperf. Value $30.

**1967, June 22 Gold Frame**

Paintings: 60f, Franz Liszt by Mihaly Munkacsi (1844-1900). 1fo, Samuel Lanyi, self-portrait, 1840. 1.50fo, Lady in Fur-lined Jacket by Jozsef Borsos (1821-83). 1.70fo, The Lovers, by Pal Szinyei Merse (1845-1920). 2fo, Portrait of Szidonia Deak, 1861, by Alajos Gyorgyi (1821-63). 2.50fo, National Guardsman, 1848, by Jozsef Borsos.

| | | | | |
|---|---|---|---|---|
| **1820** | A390 | 60f multi | .25 | .25 |
| **1821** | A390 | 1fo multi | .25 | .25 |
| **1822** | A390 | 1.50fo multi | .25 | .25 |
| **1823** | A390 | 1.70fo multi, horiz. | .30 | .25 |
| **1824** | A390 | 2fo multi | .35 | .25 |
| **1825** | A390 | 2.50fo multi | .45 | .25 |
| **1826** | A390 | 3fo multi | .75 | .70 |
| | | *Nos. 1820-1826 (7)* | 2.60 | 2.20 |

Issued to honor Hungarian painters. No. 1819 commemorates AMPHILEX 67 and the F.I.P. Congress, Amsterdam, May 11-21. No. 1819 contains one 56x50mm stamp.
Exist imperf. Value, set $20.
See #1863-1870, 1900-1907, 1940-1947.

Map of Hungary, Tourist Year Emblem, Plane, Train, Car and Ship A391

**1967, May 6 *Perf. 12x11½***

| | | | | |
|---|---|---|---|---|
| **1827** | A391 | 1fo brt blue & blk | .35 | .25 |

International Tourist Year, 1967.
Exists imperf. Value $6.

S.S. Ferencz Deak, Schönbüchel Castle, Austrian Flag — A392

Designs: 60f, Diesel hydrobus, Bratislava Castle and Czechoslovak flag. 1fo, Diesel ship Hunyadi, Buda Castle and Hungarian flag. 1.50fo, Diesel tug Szekszard, Golubac Fortress and Yugoslav flag. 1.70fo, Towboat Miskolc, Vidin Fortress and Bulgarian flag. 2fo, Cargo ship Tihany, Galati shipyard and Romanian flag. 2.50fo, Hydrofoil Siraly I, Izmail Harbor and Russian flag.

**1967, June 1 *Perf. 11½x12***

**Flags in National Colors**

| | | | | |
|---|---|---|---|---|
| **1828** | A392 | 30f lt blue grn | .30 | .25 |
| **1829** | A392 | 60f orange brn | .40 | .30 |
| **1830** | A392 | 1fo grnsh blue | .90 | .30 |
| **1831** | A392 | 1.50fo lt green | 1.75 | .60 |
| **1832** | A392 | 1.70fo blue | 2.75 | .60 |
| **1833** | A392 | 2fo rose lilac | 3.00 | 1.25 |
| **1834** | A392 | 2.50fo lt olive grn | 4.50 | 1.25 |
| | | *Nos. 1828-1834 (7)* | 13.60 | 4.55 |

25th session of the Danube Commission.
Exists imperf. Value, set $250.

Poodle A393

Collie — A394

1fo, Hungarian pointer. 1.40fo, Fox terriers. 2fo, Pumi, Hungarian sheep dog. 3fo, German shepherd. 4fo, Puli, Hungarian sheep dog.

**1967, July 7 Litho. *Perf. 12***

| | | | | |
|---|---|---|---|---|
| **1835** | A393 | 30f multi | .25 | .25 |
| **1836** | A394 | 60f multi | .25 | .25 |
| **1837** | A393 | 1fo multi | .25 | .25 |
| **1838** | A394 | 1.40fo multi | .25 | .25 |
| **1839** | A393 | 2fo multi | .35 | .25 |
| **1840** | A394 | 3fo multi | .60 | .35 |
| **1841** | A393 | 4fo multi | .95 | .60 |
| | | *Nos. 1835-1841 (7)* | 2.90 | 2.20 |

Exist imperf. Value, set $20.

Sterlets A395

Fish: 60f, Pike perch. 1fo, Carp. 1.70fo, European catfish. 2fo, Pike. 2.50fo, Rapfin.

**1967, Aug. 22 Photo. *Perf. 12x11½***

| | | | | |
|---|---|---|---|---|
| **1842** | A395 | 20f multi | .25 | .25 |
| **1843** | A395 | 60f bister & multi | .25 | .25 |
| **1844** | A395 | 1fo multi | .25 | .25 |
| **1845** | A395 | 1.70fo multi | .25 | .25 |
| **1846** | A395 | 2fo green & multi | .30 | .25 |
| **1847** | A395 | 2.50fo gray & multi | .75 | .55 |
| | | *Nos. 1842-1847,B263 (7)* | 2.95 | 2.25 |

14th Cong. of the Intl. Federation of Anglers (C.I.P.S.), Dunaujvaros, Aug. 20-28.
Exist imperf. Value, set $15.

Prince Igor, by Aleksandr Borodin — A396

Opera Scenes: 30f, Freischütz, by Karl Maria von Weber. 40f, The Magic Flute, by Mozart. 60f, Prince Bluebeard's Castle, by Bela Bartok. 80f, Carmen, by Bizet, vert. 1fo, Don Carlos, by Verdi, vert. 1.70fo, Tannhäuser, by Wagner, vert. 3fo. Laszlo Hunyadi, by Ferenc Erkel, vert.

**1967, Sept. 26 Photo. *Perf. 12***

| | | | | |
|---|---|---|---|---|
| **1848** | A396 | 20f multi | .25 | .25 |
| **1849** | A396 | 30f multi | .25 | .25 |
| **1850** | A396 | 40f multi | .25 | .25 |
| **1851** | A396 | 60f multi | .25 | .25 |
| **1852** | A396 | 80f multi | .25 | .25 |
| **1853** | A396 | 1fo multi | .25 | .25 |
| **1854** | A396 | 1.70fo multi | .45 | .30 |
| **1855** | A396 | 3fo multi | 1.00 | .70 |
| | | *Nos. 1848-1855 (8)* | 2.95 | 2.50 |

Exist imperf. Value, set $15.

Teacher, Students and Stone from Pecs University, 14th Century A397

**1967, Oct. 9 Photo. *Perf. 11½x12***

| | | | | |
|---|---|---|---|---|
| **1856** | A397 | 2fo gold & dp grn | .40 | .25 |

600th anniv. of higher education in Hungary; University of Pecs was founded in 1367.
Exists imperf. Value $5.

Eötvös University, and Symbols of Law and Justice — A398

**1967, Oct. 12 *Perf. 12x11½***

| | | | | |
|---|---|---|---|---|
| **1857** | A398 | 2fo slate | .40 | .25 |

300th anniv. of the School of Political Science and Law at the Lorand Eötvös University, Budapest.
Exists imperf. Value $5.

Lenin as Teacher, by Sandor Legrady A399

Paintings by Sandor Legrady: 1fo, Lenin. 3fo, Lenin on board the cruiser Aurora.

**1967, Oct. 31 *Perf. 12½***

| | | | | |
|---|---|---|---|---|
| **1858** | A399 | 60f gold & multi | .25 | .25 |
| **1859** | A399 | 1fo gold & multi | .25 | .25 |
| **1860** | A399 | 3fo gold & multi | .60 | .25 |
| | | *Nos. 1858-1860 (3)* | 1.10 | .75 |

50th anniv. of the Russian October Revolution.
Exist imperf. Value, set $8.

Venera 4 Landing on Venus — A400

**1967, Nov. 6 *Perf. 12***

| | | | | |
|---|---|---|---|---|
| **1861** | A400 | 5fo gold & multi | 1.25 | 1.10 |

Landing of the Russian automatic space station Venera 4 on the planet Venus.
Exists imperf. Value $9.

Souvenir Sheet

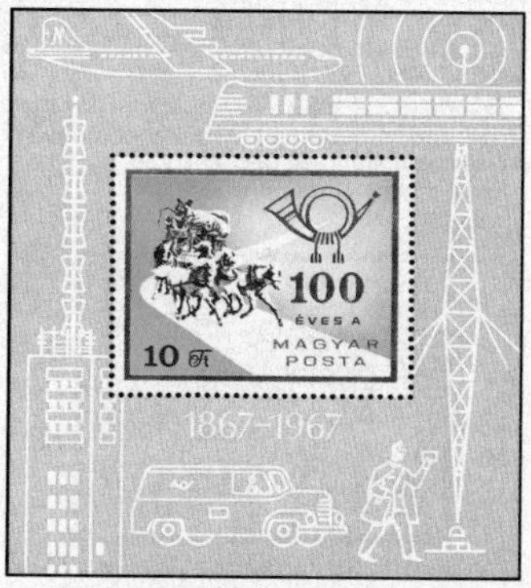


19th Century Mail Coach and Post Horn — A401

**Photogravure; Gold Impressed**

**1967, Nov. 21 *Perf. 12½***

| | | | | |
|---|---|---|---|---|
| **1862** | A401 | 10fo multicolored | 2.50 | 2.50 |

Hungarian Postal Administration, cent.
Exists imperf. Value $35.

**Painting Type of 1967**

Paintings: 60f, Brother and Sister by Adolf Fenyes (1867-1945). 1fo, Wrestling Boys by Oszkar Glatz (1872-1958). 1.50fo, "October" by Karoly Ferenczy (1862-1917). 1.70fo, Women at the River Bank by Istvan Szönyi (1894-1960), horiz. 2fo, Godfather's Breakfast by Istvan Csok (1865-1961). 2.50fo, "Eviction Notice" by Gyula Derkovits (1894-1934). 3fo, Self-portrait by M. T. Czontvary Kosztka (1853-1919). 10fo, The Apple Pickers by Bela Uitz (1887-).

**1967, Dec. 21 Photo. *Perf. 12½***

| | | | | |
|---|---|---|---|---|
| **1863** | A390 | 60f multi | .25 | .25 |
| **1864** | A390 | 1fo multi | .25 | .25 |
| **1865** | A390 | 1.50fo multi | .25 | .25 |
| **1866** | A390 | 1.70fo multi | .25 | .25 |
| **1867** | A390 | 2fo multi | .30 | .25 |
| **1868** | A390 | 2.50fo multi | .40 | .25 |
| **1869** | A390 | 3fo multi | .70 | .45 |
| | | *Nos. 1863-1869 (7)* | 2.40 | 1.95 |

**Miniature Sheet**

| | | | | |
|---|---|---|---|---|
| **1870** | A390 | 10fo multi | 2.75 | 2.50 |

Issued to honor Hungarian painters.
Exists imperf. Value: set $15; souvenir sheet $22.

Biathlon — A402

Sport (Olympic Rings and): 60f, Figure skating, pair. 1fo, Bobsledding. 1.40fo, Slalom. 1.70fo, Women's figure skating. 2fo, Speed skating. 3fo, Ski jump. 10fo, Ice hockey.

**1967, Dec. 30 Photo. *Perf. 12½***

**Souvenir Sheet**

| | | | | |
|---|---|---|---|---|
| **1871** | A402 | 10fo lilac & multi | 2.50 | 2.00 |

Exists imperf. Value $18.

**1968, Jan. 29 *Perf. 11***

| | | | | |
|---|---|---|---|---|
| **1872** | A402 | 30f multi | .25 | .25 |
| **1873** | A402 | 60f multi | .25 | .25 |
| **1874** | A402 | 1fo multi | .25 | .25 |
| **1875** | A402 | 1.40fo rose & multi | .25 | .25 |
| **1876** | A402 | 1.70fo multi | .25 | .25 |
| **1877** | A402 | 2fo multi | .30 | .25 |
| **1878** | A402 | 3fo ol & multi | .80 | .30 |
| | | *Nos. 1872-1878,B264 (8)* | 3.05 | 2.10 |

10th Winter Olympic Games, Grenoble, France, Feb. 6-18. No. 1871 contains one 43x43mm stamp.
Exist imperf. Value, set (8) $15.

Kando Statue, Miskolc, Kando Locomotive and Map of Hungary A403

**1968, Mar. 30 Photo. *Perf. 11½x12***

| | | | | |
|---|---|---|---|---|
| **1879** | A403 | 2fo dark blue | .40 | .25 |

Kalman Kando (1869-1931), engineer, inventor of Kando locomotive.
Exists imperf. Value $4.

Domestic Cat A404

**1968, Mar. 30 *Perf. 11***

| | | | | |
|---|---|---|---|---|
| **1880** | A404 | 20f shown | .25 | .25 |
| **1881** | A404 | 60f Cream Persian | .25 | .25 |
| **1882** | A404 | 1fo Smoky Persian | .25 | .25 |
| **1883** | A404 | 1.20fo Domestic kitten | .25 | .25 |
| **1884** | A404 | 1.50fo White Persian | .30 | .25 |
| **1885** | A404 | 2fo Brown-striped Persian | .30 | .25 |
| **1886** | A404 | 2.50fo Siamese | .60 | .25 |
| **1887** | A404 | 5fo Blue Persian | 1.25 | .55 |
| | | *Nos. 1880-1887 (8)* | 3.45 | 2.30 |

Exist imperf. Value, set $20.

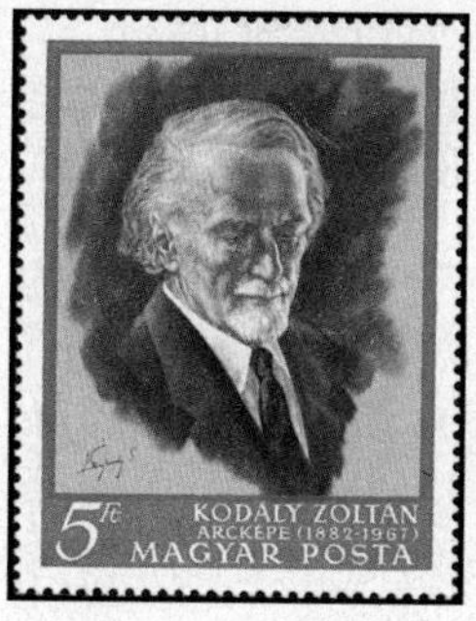


Zoltan Kodaly, by Sandor Légrády A405

**1968, Apr. 17 Photo. *Perf. 12½***

| | | | | |
|---|---|---|---|---|
| **1888** | A405 | 5fo gold & multi | 1.00 | .75 |

Kodaly (1882-1967), composer & musicologist.
Exists imperf. Value $6.

White Storks A406

Birds: 50f, Golden orioles. 60f, Imperial eagle. 1fo, Red-footed falcons. 1.20fo, Scops owl. 1.50fo, Great bustard. 2fo, European bee-eaters. 2.50fo, Graylag goose.

**1968, Apr. 25**

**Birds in Natural Colors**

| | | | | |
|---|---|---|---|---|
| **1889** | A406 | 20f ver & lt ultra | .25 | .25 |
| **1890** | A406 | 50f ver & gray | .25 | .25 |
| **1891** | A406 | 60f ver & lt bl | .25 | .25 |
| **1892** | A406 | 1fo ver & yel grn | .25 | .25 |
| **1893** | A406 | 1.20fo ver & brt grn | .25 | .25 |
| **1894** | A406 | 1.50fo ver & lt vio | .25 | .25 |
| **1895** | A406 | 2fo ver & pale lil | .55 | .30 |
| **1896** | A406 | 2.50fo ver & bl grn | 1.10 | .50 |
| | | *Nos. 1889-1896 (8)* | 3.15 | 2.30 |

International Bird Preservation Congress.
Exists imperf. Value, set $25.

City Hall, Kecskemét — A407

**1968, Apr. 25 *Perf. 12x11½***

| | | | | |
|---|---|---|---|---|
| **1897** | A407 | 2fo brown orange | .30 | .25 |

600th anniversary of Kecskemét.
Exists imperf. Value $4.

**Marx Type of 1953**

**1968, May 5 Engr. *Perf. 12***

| | | | | |
|---|---|---|---|---|
| **1898** | A230 | 1fo claret | .25 | .25 |

Karl Marx (1818-1883).
Exists imperf. Value $5.

Student and Agricultural College — A408

**1968, May 24 Photo. *Perf. 12x11½***

| | | | | |
|---|---|---|---|---|
| **1899** | A408 | 2fo dk olive green | .30 | .25 |

150th anniv. of the founding of the Agricultural College at Mosonmagyaróvár.
Exists imperf. Value $4.

### Painting Type of 1967

Paintings: 40f, Girl with Pitcher, by Goya (1746-1828). 60f, Head of an Apostle, by El Greco (c. 1541-1614). 1fo, Boy with Apple Basket and Dogs, by Pedro Nunez (1639-1700), horiz. 1.50fo, Mary Magdalene, by El Greco. 2.50fo, The Breakfast, by Velazquez (1599-1660), horiz. 4fo, The Virgin from The Holy Family, by El Greco. 5fo, The Knife Grinder, by Goya. 10fo, Portrait of a Girl, by Palma Vecchio (1480-1528).

**1968, May 30** *Perf. 12½*

| | | | | | |
|---|---|---|---|---|---|
| **1900** | A390 | 40f multi | | .25 | .25 |
| **1901** | A390 | 60f multi | | .25 | .25 |
| **1902** | A390 | 1fo multi | | .25 | .25 |
| **1903** | A390 | 1.50fo multi | | .25 | .25 |
| **1904** | A390 | 2.50fo multi | | .50 | .25 |
| **1905** | A390 | 4fo multi | | .70 | .25 |
| **1906** | A390 | 5fo multi | | 1.00 | .35 |
| | | *Nos. 1900-1906 (7)* | | 3.20 | 1.85 |

**Souvenir Sheet**

| | | | | | |
|---|---|---|---|---|---|
| **1907** | A390 | 10fo multi | | 3.25 | 3.00 |

Issued to publicize art treasures in the Budapest Museum of Fine Arts and to publicize an art exhibition.

Exist imperf. Values: set of 7, $15; souvenir sheet $22.50.

Lake Balaton at Badacsony A409

Views on Lake Balaton: 40f like 20f. 60f, Tihanyi Peninsula. 1fo, Sailboats at Almadi. 2fo, Szigliget Bay.

**1968-69** **Litho.** *Perf. 12*

| | | | | | |
|---|---|---|---|---|---|
| **1908** | A409 | 20f multi | | .25 | .25 |
| **1908A** | A409 | 40f multi ('69) | | .25 | .25 |
| *b.* | | Bklt. pane, #1909, 1911, 2 each #1908A, 1910 | | .75 | |
| *c.* | | Bklt. pane, #1909-1911, 3 #1908A | | .75 | |
| *d.* | | Bklt. pane, #1911, 3 #1908A, 2 #1909 | | .75 | |
| **1909** | A409 | 60f multi | | .25 | .25 |
| **1910** | A409 | 1fo multi | | .25 | .25 |
| **1911** | A409 | 2fo multi | | .45 | .25 |
| | | *Nos. 1908-1911 (5)* | | 1.45 | 1.25 |

Exist imperf. Value, set $20.

Locomotive, Type 424 — A410

**1968, July 14** **Photo.** *Perf. 12x11½*

| | | | | |
|---|---|---|---|---|
| **1912** | A410 | 2fo gold, lt bl & slate | .60 | .25 |

Centenary of the Hungarian State Railroad.

Exists imperf. Value $8.

Horses Grazing — A411

Designs: 40f, Horses in storm. 60f, Horse race on the steppe. 80f, Horsedrawn sleigh. 1fo, Four-in-hand and rainbow. 1.40fo, Farm wagon drawn by 7 horses. 2fo, One rider driving five horses. 2.50fo, Campfire on the range. 4fo, Coach with 5 horses.

**1968, July 25** *Perf. 11*

| | | | | |
|---|---|---|---|---|
| **1913** | A411 | 30f multi | .25 | .25 |
| **1914** | A411 | 40f multi | .25 | .25 |
| **1915** | A411 | 60f multi | .25 | .25 |
| **1916** | A411 | 80f multi | .25 | .25 |
| **1917** | A411 | 1fo multi | .25 | .25 |
| **1918** | A411 | 1.40fo multi | .30 | .25 |
| **1919** | A411 | 2fo multi | .30 | .25 |
| **1920** | A411 | 2.50fo multi | .40 | .25 |
| **1921** | A411 | 4fo multi | .75 | .45 |
| | | *Nos. 1913-1921 (9)* | 3.00 | 2.45 |

Horse breeding on the Hungarian steppe (Puszta).

Exist imperf. Value, set $40.

Mihály Tompa (1817-68), Poet — A412

**1968, July 30** **Photo.** *Perf. 12x11½*

| | | | | |
|---|---|---|---|---|
| **1922** | A412 | 60f blue black | .25 | .25 |

Exists imperf. Value $4.

Festival Emblem, Bulgarian and Hungarian National Costumes — A413

**1968, Aug. 3** **Litho.** *Perf. 12*

| | | | | |
|---|---|---|---|---|
| **1923** | A413 | 60f multicolored | .30 | .25 |

Issued to publicize the 9th Youth Festival for Peace and Friendship, Sofia, Bulgaria.

Exists imperf. Value $5.

Souvenir Sheet

Runners and Aztec Calendar Stone — A414

**1968, Aug. 21** **Photo.** *Perf. 12½*

| | | | | |
|---|---|---|---|---|
| **1924** | A414 | 10fo multicolored | 2.50 | 2.25 |

19th Olympic Games, Mexico City, 10/12-27.

Exists imperf. Value $20.

Scientific Society Emblem — A415

*Perf. 12½x11½*

**1968, Dec. 10** **Photo.**

| | | | | |
|---|---|---|---|---|
| **1925** | A415 | 2fo brt blue & blk | .35 | .25 |

Society for the Popularization of Scientific Knowledge.

Exists imperf. Value $4.

Hesperis A416

Garden Flowers: 60f, Pansy. 80f, Zinnias. 1fo, Morning-glory. 1.40fo, Petunia. 1.50fo, Portulaca. 2fo, Michaelmas daisies. 2.50fo, Dahlia.

**1968, Oct. 29** *Perf. 11½x12*

**Flowers in Natural Colors**

| | | | | |
|---|---|---|---|---|
| **1926** | A416 | 20f gray | .25 | .25 |
| **1927** | A416 | 60f lt green | .25 | .25 |
| **1928** | A416 | 80f bluish lilac | .25 | .25 |
| **1929** | A416 | 1fo buff | .25 | .25 |
| **1930** | A416 | 1.40fo lt grnsh bl | .25 | .25 |
| **1931** | A416 | 1.50fo lt blue | .25 | .25 |
| **1932** | A416 | 2fo pale pink | .30 | .25 |
| **1933** | A416 | 2.50fo lt blue | .60 | .40 |
| | | *Nos. 1926-1933 (8)* | 2.40 | 2.15 |

Exist imperf. Value, set $15.

Pioneers Saluting Communist Party — A417

Children's Paintings: 60f, Four pioneers holding banner saluting Communist Party. 1fo, Pioneer camp.

**1968, Nov. 16** **Photo.** *Perf. 12x11½*

| | | | | |
|---|---|---|---|---|
| **1934** | A417 | 40f buff & multi | .25 | .25 |
| **1935** | A417 | 60f buff & multi | .25 | .25 |
| **1936** | A417 | 1fo buff & multi | .30 | .25 |
| | | *Nos. 1934-1936 (3)* | .80 | .75 |

50th anniv. of the Communist Party of Hungary. The designs are from a competition among elementary school children.

Exist imperf. Value, set $15.

Workers, Monument by Z. Olcsai-Kiss — A418

Design: 1fo, "Workers of the World Unite!" poster by N. Por, vert.

*Perf. 11½x12, 12x11½*

**1968, Nov. 24** **Photo.**

| | | | | |
|---|---|---|---|---|
| **1937** | A418 | 1fo gold, red, & blk | .25 | .25 |
| **1938** | A418 | 2fo gold & multi | .25 | .25 |

Communist Party of Hungary, 50th anniv.

Exist imperf. Value, set $15.

Human Rights Flame — A419

**1968, Dec. 10** *Perf. 12½x11½*

| | | | | |
|---|---|---|---|---|
| **1939** | A419 | 1fo dark red brown | .40 | .25 |

International Human Rights Year.

Exists imperf. Value $4.

### Painting Type of 1967

Italian Paintings: 40f, Esterhazy Madonna, by Raphael. 60f, The Annunciation, by Bernardo Strozzi. 1fo, Portrait of a Young Man, by Raphael. 1.50fo, The Three Graces, by Battista Naldini. 2.50fo, Portrait of a Man, by Sebastiano del Piombo. 4fo, The Doge Marcantonio Trevisani, by Titian. 5fo, Venus, Cupid and Jealousy, by Angelo Bronzino. 10fo, Bathsheba Bathing, by Sebastiano Ricci, horiz.

**1968, Dec. 10** **Photo.** *Perf. 12½*

| | | | | |
|---|---|---|---|---|
| **1940** | A390 | 40f multi | .25 | .25 |
| **1941** | A390 | 60f multi | .25 | .25 |
| **1942** | A390 | 1fo multi | .25 | .25 |
| **1943** | A390 | 1.50fo multi | .25 | .25 |
| **1944** | A390 | 2.50fo multi | .30 | .25 |
| **1945** | A390 | 4fo multi | .60 | .25 |
| **1946** | A390 | 5fo multi | .80 | .35 |
| | | *Nos. 1940-1946 (7)* | 2.70 | 1.85 |

**Miniature Sheet**

*Perf. 11*

| | | | | |
|---|---|---|---|---|
| **1947** | A390 | 10fo multi | 2.75 | 2.50 |

Issued to publicize art treasures in the Budapest Museum of Fine Arts. No. 1947 contains one stamp size of stamp: 62x45mm.

Exist imperf. Value: set $18; souvenir sheet $22.

1869 and 1969 Emblems of Athenaeum Press — A420

**1969, Jan. 27** *Perf. 12½x11½*

| | | | | |
|---|---|---|---|---|
| **1948** | A420 | 2fo gold, gray, lt bl & blk | .40 | .25 |

Centenary of Athenaeum Press, Budapest.

Exists imperf. Value $3.50.

Endre Ady (1877-1919), Lyric Poet — A421

**1969, Jan. 27** *Perf. 11½x12*

| | | | | |
|---|---|---|---|---|
| **1949** | A421 | 1fo multicolored | .40 | .25 |

Exists imperf. Value $4.

Olympic Medal and Women's Javelin — A422

Olympic Medal and: 60f, Canadian singles (canoeing). 1fo, Soccer. 1.20fo, Hammer throw. 2fo, Fencing. 3fo, Greco-Roman Wrestling. 4fo, Kayak single. 5fo, Equestrian. 10fo, Head of Mercury by Praxiteles and Olympic torch.

**1969, Mar. 7** **Photo.** *Perf. 12*

| | | | | |
|---|---|---|---|---|
| **1950** | A422 | 40f multi | .25 | .25 |
| **1951** | A422 | 60f multi | .25 | .25 |
| **1952** | A422 | 1fo multi | .25 | .25 |
| **1953** | A422 | 1.20fo multi | .25 | .25 |
| **1954** | A422 | 2fo multi | .25 | .25 |
| **1955** | A422 | 3fo multi | .30 | .25 |
| **1956** | A422 | 4fo multi | .70 | .25 |
| **1957** | A422 | 5fo multi | .75 | .45 |
| | | *Nos. 1950-1957 (8)* | 3.00 | 2.20 |

**Souvenir Sheet**

**Litho.** *Perf. 11½*

| | | | | |
|---|---|---|---|---|
| **1958** | A422 | 10fo multi | 2.75 | 2.75 |

Victories won by the Hungarian team in the 1968 Olympic Games, Mexico City, Oct. 12-

27, 1968. No. 1958 contains one 45x33mm stamp.

Exist imperf. Value: set $20; souvenir sheet $22.

1919 Revolutionary Poster — A423

Revolutionary Posters: 60f, Lenin. 1fo, Man breaking chains. 2fo, Industrial worker looking at family and farm. 3fo, Militia recruiter. 10fo, Shouting revolutionist with red banner, horiz.

**1969, Mar. 21 Photo. *Perf. 11½x12***

**Gold Frame**

| | | | | |
|---|---|---|---|---|
| **1960** | A423 | 40f red & black | .25 | .25 |
| **1961** | A423 | 60f red & black | .25 | .25 |
| **1962** | A423 | 1fo red & black | .25 | .25 |
| **1963** | A423 | 2fo black, gray & red | .25 | .25 |
| **1964** | A423 | 3fo multicolored | .35 | .25 |
| | | *Nos. 1960-1964 (5)* | 1.35 | 1.25 |

**Souvenir Sheet**

***Perf. 12½***

| | | | | |
|---|---|---|---|---|
| **1965** | A423 | 10fo red, gray & blk | 1.50 | 1.50 |

50th anniv. of the proclamation of the Hungarian Soviet Republic.

Exist imperf. Values: set $15; souvenir sheet $15.

The 60f red lilac with 4-line black printing on back was given away by the Hungarian PO. Value $1, mint or canceled.

No. 1965 contains one 51x38½mm stamp.

Jersey Tiger A424

Designs: Various Butterflies and Moths.

**1969, Apr. 15 Litho. *Perf. 12***

| | | | | |
|---|---|---|---|---|
| **1966** | A424 | 40f shown | .25 | .25 |
| **1967** | A424 | 60f Eyed hawk moth | .25 | .25 |
| **1968** | A424 | 80f Painted lady | .25 | .25 |
| **1969** | A424 | 1fo Tiger moth | .25 | .25 |
| **1970** | A424 | 1.20fo Small fire moth | .25 | .25 |
| **1971** | A424 | 2fo Large blue | .35 | .25 |
| **1972** | A424 | 3fo Belted oak egger | .65 | .45 |
| **1973** | A424 | 4fo Peacock | .90 | .50 |
| | | *Nos. 1966-1973 (8)* | 3.15 | 2.45 |

Exist imperf. Value, set $20.

ILO Emblem A426

**1969, May 22 Photo. *Perf. 12x11½***

| | | | | |
|---|---|---|---|---|
| **1974** | A426 | 1fo car lake & lake | .40 | .25 |

50th anniv. of the ILO.

Exist imperf. Value $5.

Black Pigs, by Paul Gauguin A427

French Paintings: 60f, These Women, by Toulouse-Lautrec, horiz. 1fo, Venus in the Clouds, by Simon Vouet. 2fo, Lady with Fan, by Edouard Manet, horiz. 3fo, La Petra Camara (dancer), by Théodore Chassériau. 4fo, The Cowherd, by Constant Troyon, horiz. 5fo, The Wrestlers, by Gustave Courbet. 10fo, Pomona, by Nicolas Fouché.

**1969, May 28 Photo. *Perf. 12½***

| | | | | |
|---|---|---|---|---|
| **1975** | A427 | 40f multicolored | .25 | .25 |
| **1976** | A427 | 60f multicolored | .25 | .25 |
| **1977** | A427 | 1fo multicolored | .25 | .25 |
| **1978** | A427 | 2fo multicolored | .30 | .25 |
| **1979** | A427 | 3fo multicolored | .50 | .25 |
| **1980** | A427 | 4fo multicolored | .70 | .25 |
| **1981** | A427 | 5fo multicolored | 1.00 | .50 |
| | | *Nos. 1975-1981 (7)* | 3.25 | 2.00 |

**Miniature Sheet**

| | | | | |
|---|---|---|---|---|
| **1982** | A427 | 10fo multicolored | 4.00 | 4.00 |

Art treasures in the Budapest Museum of Fine Arts. No. 1982 contains one 40x62mm stamp.

Exist imperf. Value: set $17.50; souvenir sheet $17.50.

Hotel Budapest A428

Budapest Post Office 100 A429

**1969, May Photo. *Perf. 11***

| | | | | |
|---|---|---|---|---|
| **1983** | A428 | 1fo brown | .30 | .25 |

Exists imperf. Value $15.

**Coil Stamps**

**1970, Aug. 3 *Perf. 14***

| | | | | |
|---|---|---|---|---|
| **1983A** | A429 | 40f gray | .40 | .25 |
| *1983B* | A428 | 1fo brown | .50 | .25 |

Black control number on back of every 5th stamp.

Arms and Buildings of Vac A430

Towns of the Danube Bend: 1fo, Szentendre. 1.20fo, Visegrad. 3fo, Esztergom.

**1969, June 9 Litho. *Perf. 12***

| | | | | |
|---|---|---|---|---|
| **1984** | A430 | 40f multi | .25 | .25 |
| *a.* | | Bklt. pane, #1985, 1987, 4 #1984 | 2.75 | |
| *b.* | | Bklt. pane, #1986, 3 #1984, 2 #1985 | 2.75 | |
| **1985** | A430 | 1fo multi | .25 | .25 |
| **1986** | A430 | 1.20fo multi | .25 | .25 |
| **1987** | A430 | 3fo multi | .30 | .25 |
| | | *Nos. 1984-1987 (4)* | 1.05 | 1.00 |

Stamps in booklet panes Nos. 1984a-1984b come in two arrangements.

Exist imperf. Value, set $15.

"PAX" and Men Holding Hands — A431

**1969, June 17 Photo. *Perf. 11½x12***

| | | | | |
|---|---|---|---|---|
| **1988** | A431 | 1fo lt bl, dk bl & gold | .30 | .25 |

20th anniversary of Peace Movement.

Exists imperf. Value $5.

The Scholar, by Rembrandt A432

**1969, Sept. 15 *Perf. 11½x12***

| | | | | |
|---|---|---|---|---|
| **1989** | A432 | 1fo sepia | .50 | .25 |

Issued to publicize the 22nd International Congress of Art Historians, Budapest.

Exists imperf. Value $5.

Fossilized Zelkova Leaves — A433

Designs: 60f, Greenockit calcite sphalerite crystals. 1fo, Fossilized fish, clupea hungarica. 1.20fo, Quartz crystals. 2fo, Ammonite. 3fo, Copper. 4fo, Fossilized turtle, placochelys placodonta. 5fo, Cuprite crystals.

**1969, Sept. 21 Photo.**

| | | | | |
|---|---|---|---|---|
| **1990** | A433 | 40f red, gray & sep | .25 | .25 |
| **1991** | A433 | 60f violet, yel & blk | .25 | .25 |
| **1992** | A433 | 1fo blue, tan & brn | .25 | .25 |
| **1993** | A433 | 1.20fo emer, gray & lil | .25 | .25 |
| **1994** | A433 | 2fo olive, tan & brn | .25 | .25 |
| **1995** | A433 | 3fo orange, brt & dk grn | .30 | .25 |
| **1996** | A433 | 4fo dull blk grn, brn & blk | .55 | .30 |
| **1997** | A433 | 5fo multicolored | .90 | .40 |
| | | *Nos. 1990-1997 (8)* | 3.00 | 2.20 |

Centenary of the Hungarian State Institute of Geology.

Exists imperf. Value, set $18.

Steeplechase — A434

Designs: 60f, Fencing. 1fo, Pistol shooting. 2fo, Swimmers at start. 3fo, Relay race. 5fo, Pentathlon.

**1969, Sept. 15 Photo. *Perf. 12x11½***

| | | | | |
|---|---|---|---|---|
| **1998** | A434 | 40f blue & multi | .25 | .25 |
| **1999** | A434 | 60f multi | .25 | .25 |
| **2000** | A434 | 1fo multi | .25 | .25 |
| **2001** | A434 | 2fo violet & multi | .30 | .25 |
| **2002** | A434 | 3fo lemon & multi | .50 | .30 |
| **2003** | A434 | 5fo bluish grn, gold & dk red | .75 | .50 |
| | | *Nos. 1998-2003 (6)* | 2.30 | 1.80 |

Hungarian Pentathion Championships.

Exists imperf. Value, set $15.

First Hungarian Postal Card — A435

**1969, Oct. 1**

| | | | | |
|---|---|---|---|---|
| **2004** | A435 | 60f ver & ocher | .30 | .25 |

Centenary of the postal card. Hungary and Austria both issued cards in 1869.

Exists imperf. Value $5.

Mahatma Gandhi — A436

**1969, Oct. 1 *Perf. 11½x12***

| | | | | |
|---|---|---|---|---|
| **2005** | A436 | 5fo green & multi | 1.50 | .70 |

Mohandas K. Gandhi (1869-1948), leader in India's fight for independence.

Exists imperf. Value $8.

World Trade Union Emblem A437

**1969, Oct. 17 Photo. *Perf. 12x11½***

| | | | | |
|---|---|---|---|---|
| **2006** | A437 | 2fo fawn & dk blue | .30 | .25 |

Issued to publicize the 7th Congress of the World Federation of Trade Unions.

Exists imperf. Value $5.

Janos Balogh Nagy, Self-portrait A438

**1969, Oct. 17 *Perf. 11½x12***

| | | | | |
|---|---|---|---|---|
| **2007** | A438 | 5fo gold & multi | 1.50 | .80 |

Janos Balogh Nagy (1874-1919), painter.

Exists imperf. Value $7.50.

St. John the Evangelist, by Anthony Van Dyck — A439

Dutch Paintings: 60f, Three Fruit Pickers (by Pieter de Molyn?). 1fo, Boy Lighting Pipe, by Hendrick Terbrugghen. 2fo, The Feast, by Jan Steen. 3fo, Woman Reading Letter, by Pieter de Hooch. 4fo, The Fiddler, by Dirk Hals. 5fo, Portrait of Jan Asselyn, by Frans Hals. 10fo,

Mucius Scaevola before Porsena, by Rubens and Van Dyck.

**1969-70 Photo. *Perf. 12½***

| | | | | |
|---|---|---|---|---|
| **2008** | A439 | 40f multi | .25 | .25 |
| **2009** | A439 | 60f multi | .25 | .25 |
| **2010** | A439 | 1fo multi | .25 | .25 |
| **2011** | A439 | 2fo multi | .25 | .25 |
| **2012** | A439 | 3fo multi | .40 | .25 |
| **2013** | A439 | 4fo multi | .50 | .30 |
| **2014** | A439 | 5fo multi | 1.00 | .50 |
| | | *Nos. 2008-2014 (7)* | 2.90 | 2.05 |

**Miniature Sheet**

| | | | | |
|---|---|---|---|---|
| **2015** | A439 | 10fo multi | 3.25 | 3.25 |

Treasures in the Museum of Fine Arts, Budapest and the Museum in Eger.
Exist imperf. Value: set $15; souvenir sheet $25.
Issued: 40f-5fo, 12/2/69; 10fo, 1/70.

Kiskunfelegyhaza Circling Pigeon — A440

**1969, Dec. 12 Photo. *Perf. 11½x12***

| | | | | |
|---|---|---|---|---|
| **2016** | A440 | 1fo multicolored | .40 | .25 |

Issued to publicize the International Pigeon Show, Budapest, Dec. 1969.
Exists imperf. Value $5.

Subway A441

**1970, Apr. 3 Photo. *Perf. 12***

| | | | | |
|---|---|---|---|---|
| **2017** | A441 | 1fo blk, lt grn & ultra | .40 | .25 |

Opening of new Budapest subway.
Exists imperf. Value $7.50.

Souvenir Sheet

Panoramic View of Budapest 1945 and 1970, and Soviet Cenotaph — A442

**1970, Apr. 3 *Perf. 12x11½***

| | | | | |
|---|---|---|---|---|
| **2018** | A442 | Sheet of 2 | 2.75 | 2.50 |
| *a.* | | 5fo "1945" | 1.00 | 1.00 |
| *b.* | | 5fo "1970" | 1.00 | 1.00 |

25th anniv. of the liberation of Budapest.
Exists imperf. Value $25.

Cloud Formation, Satellite, Earth and Receiving Station — A443

**1970, Apr. 8 Litho. *Perf. 12***

| | | | | |
|---|---|---|---|---|
| **2019** | A443 | 1fo dk bl, yel & blk | .30 | .25 |

Centenary of the Hungarian Meteorological Service.
Exists imperf. Value $5.

Lenin Statue, Budapest — A444

Design: 2fo, Lenin portrait.

**1970, Apr. 22 Photo. *Perf. 11***

| | | | | |
|---|---|---|---|---|
| **2020** | A444 | 1fo gold & multi | .25 | .25 |
| **2021** | A444 | 2fo gold & multi | .25 | .25 |

Lenin (1870-1924), Russian communist leader.
Exist imperf. Value, set $10.

Franz Lehar and "Giuditta" Music — A445

**1970, Apr. 30 Photo. *Perf. 12***

| | | | | |
|---|---|---|---|---|
| **2022** | A445 | 2fo multicolored | .50 | .25 |

Franz Lehar (1870-1948), composer.
Exists imperf. Value $7.50.

Samson and Delilah, by Michele Rocca A446

Paintings: 60f, Joseph Telling Dream, by Giovanni Battista Langetti. 1fo, Clio, by Pierre Mignard. 1.50fo, Venus and Satyr, by Sebastiano Ricci, horiz. 2.50fo, Andromeda, by Francesco Furini. 4fo, Venus, Adonis and Cupid, by Luca Giordano. 5fo, Allegorical Feast, by Corrado Giaquinto. 10fo, Diana and Callisto, by Abraham Janssens, horiz.

**1970, June 2 Photo. *Perf. 12½***

| | | | | |
|---|---|---|---|---|
| **2023** | A446 | 40f gold & multi | .25 | .25 |
| **2024** | A446 | 60f gold & multi | .25 | .25 |
| **2025** | A446 | 1fo gold & multi | .25 | .25 |
| **2026** | A446 | 1.50fo gold & multi | .25 | .25 |
| **2027** | A446 | 2.50fo gold & multi | .30 | .25 |
| **2028** | A446 | 4fo gold & multi | .60 | .30 |
| **2029** | A446 | 5fo gold & multi | .75 | .50 |
| | | *Nos. 2023-2029 (7)* | 2.65 | 2.05 |

**Miniature Sheet**

***Perf. 11***

| | | | | |
|---|---|---|---|---|
| **2030** | A446 | 10fo gold & multi | 3.50 | 3.00 |

No. 2030 contains one 63x46mm horizontal stamp.
Exist imperf. Values: set $15; souvenir sheet $20.

Beethoven Statue, by Janos Pasztor, at Martonvasar A447

**1970, June 27 Litho. *Perf. 12***

| | | | | |
|---|---|---|---|---|
| **2031** | A447 | 1fo plum, gray grn & org yel | .75 | .25 |

Ludwig van Beethoven, composer. The music in the design is from his Sonatina No. 1.
Exists imperf. Value $7.50.

Foundryman A448

**1970, July 28 Litho. *Perf. 12***

| | | | | |
|---|---|---|---|---|
| **2032** | A448 | 1fo multicolored | .40 | .25 |

200th anniversary of the first Hungarian steel foundry at Diosgyor, now the Lenin Metallurgical Works.
Exists imperf. Value $5.

King Stephen I — A449

**1970, Aug. 19 Photo. *Perf. 11½x12***

| | | | | |
|---|---|---|---|---|
| **2033** | A449 | 3fo multicolored | 1.00 | .50 |

Millenary of the birth of Saint Stephen, first King of Hungary.
Exists imperf. Value $5.

Women's Four on Lake Tata and Tata Castle — A450

**1970, Aug. 19 Litho. *Perf. 12***

| | | | | |
|---|---|---|---|---|
| **2034** | A450 | 1fo multicolored | .35 | .25 |

17th European Women's Rowing Championships, Lake Tata.
Exists imperf. Value $5.

Mother Giving Bread to her Children, FAO Emblem — A451

**1970, Sept. 21 Litho. *Perf. 12***

| | | | | |
|---|---|---|---|---|
| **2035** | A451 | 1fo lt blue & multi | .40 | .25 |

7th European Regional Cong. of the UNFAO, Budapest, Sept. 21-25.
Exists imperf. Value $5.

Boxing and Olympic Rings A452

Designs (Olympic Rings and): 60f, Canoeing. 1fo, Fencing. 1.50fo, Water polo. 2fo, Woman gymnast. 2.50fo, Hammer throwing. 3fo, Wrestling. 5fo, Swimming, butterfly stroke.

**1970, Sept. 26 Photo. *Perf. 11***

| | | | | |
|---|---|---|---|---|
| **2036** | A452 | 40f lt violet & multi | .25 | .25 |
| **2037** | A452 | 60f sky blue & multi | .25 | .25 |
| **2038** | A452 | 1fo orange & multi | .25 | .25 |
| **2039** | A452 | 1.50fo multi | .25 | .25 |
| **2040** | A452 | 2fo multi | .25 | .25 |
| **2041** | A452 | 2.50fo multi | .30 | .25 |
| **2042** | A452 | 3fo multi | .40 | .25 |
| **2043** | A452 | 5fo multi | .60 | .40 |
| | | *Nos. 2036-2043 (8)* | 2.55 | 2.15 |

75th anniv. of the Hungarian Olympic Committee. The 5fo also publicizes the 1972 Olympic Games in Munich.
Exist imperf. Value, set $15.

Flame and Family A453

**1970, Sept. 28 Litho. *Perf. 12***

| | | | | |
|---|---|---|---|---|
| **2044** | A453 | 1fo ultra, org & emer | .40 | .25 |

5th Education Congress, Budapest.
Exists imperf. Value $5.

Chalice, by Benedek Suky, 1440 — A454

Hungarian Goldsmiths' Art: 60f, Altar burette, 1500. 1fo, Nadasdy goblet, 16th century. 1.50fo, Coconut goblet, 1600. 2fo, Silver tankard, by Mihaly Toldalaghy, 1623. 2.50fo, Communion cup of Gyorgy Rakoczy I, 1670. 3fo, Tankard, 1690. 4fo, Bell-flower cup, 1710.

**1970, Oct. Photo. *Perf. 12***

| | | | | |
|---|---|---|---|---|
| **2045** | A454 | 40f gold & multi | .25 | .25 |
| **2046** | A454 | 60f gold & multi | .25 | .25 |
| **2047** | A454 | 1fo gold & multi | .25 | .25 |
| **2048** | A454 | 1.50fo gold & multi | .25 | .25 |
| **2049** | A454 | 2fo gold & multi | .25 | .25 |
| **2050** | A454 | 2.50fo gold & multi | .25 | .25 |
| **2051** | A454 | 3fo gold & multi | .40 | .30 |
| **2052** | A454 | 4fo gold & multi | .60 | .40 |
| | | *Nos. 2045-2052 (8)* | 2.50 | 2.20 |

Exist imperf. Value, set $15.

Virgin and Child, by Giampietrino — A455

Paintings from Christian Museum, Esztergom: 60f, "Love" (woman with 3 children), by Gregorio Lazzarini. 1fo, Legend of St. Catherine, by Master of Bat. 1.50fo, Adoration of the Shepherds, by Francesco Fontebasso, horiz. 2.50fo, Adoration of the Kings, by Master of Aranyosmarot. 4fo, Temptation of St. Anthony the Hermit, by Jan de Cock. 5fo, St. Sebastian, by Marco Palmezzano. 10fo, Lady with the Unicorn, by Painter of Lombardy.

**1970, Dec. 7 Photo. *Perf. 12½***

| | | | | | |
|---|---|---|---|---|---|
| **2053** | A455 | 40f | silver & multi | .25 | .25 |
| **2054** | A455 | 60f | silver & multi | .25 | .25 |
| **2055** | A455 | 1fo | silver & multi | .25 | .25 |
| **2056** | A455 | 1.50fo | silver & multi | .25 | .25 |
| **2057** | A455 | 2.50fo | silver & multi | .40 | .25 |
| **2058** | A455 | 4fo | silver & multi | .65 | .30 |
| **2059** | A455 | 5fo | silver & multi | .90 | .40 |
| | | | *Nos. 2053-2059 (7)* | 2.95 | 1.95 |

**Souvenir Sheet**

| | | | | | |
|---|---|---|---|---|---|
| **2060** | A455 | 10fo | silver & multi | 3.00 | 2.75 |

No. 2060 contains one 50½x56mm stamp.
Exist imperf. Values: set $15; souvenir sheet $17.50.

Monument to Hungarian Martyrs, by A. Makrisz — A456

**1970, Dec. 30 Photo. *Perf. 12x11½***

| | | | | | |
|---|---|---|---|---|---|
| **2061** | A456 | 1fo | ultra & sepia | .40 | .25 |

The 25th anniversary of the liberation of the concentration camps at Auschwitz, Mauthausen and Dachau.
Exists imperf. Value $5.

"Souvenir Sheets"
Beginning in 1971, the government stamp agency, as well as a number of other state sanctioned organizations, have created souvenir sheets that do not have postal validity. These are not listed in this catalogue.

Marseillaise, by Francois Rude — A457

**1971, Mar. 18 Litho. *Perf. 12***

| | | | | | |
|---|---|---|---|---|---|
| **2062** | A457 | 3fo | bister & green | .40 | .25 |

Centenary of the Paris Commune.
Exists imperf. Value $5.

Béla Bartók (1881-1945), Composer A458

Design: No. 2064, András L. Achim (1871-1911), peasant leader.

**1971**

| | | | | | |
|---|---|---|---|---|---|
| **2063** | A458 | 1fo | gray & dk car | .55 | .25 |
| **2064** | A458 | 1fo | gray & green | .25 | .25 |

Issued: No. 2063, Mar. 25; No. 2064, Apr. 17.
Exist imperf. Value, set $10.

Györ Castle, 1594 A459

**1971, Mar. 27**

| | | | | | |
|---|---|---|---|---|---|
| **2065** | A459 | 2fo | lt blue & multi | .40 | .25 |

700th anniversary of Györ.
Exists imperf. Value $5.

Bison Hunt — A460

Designs: 60f, Wild boar hunt. 80f, Deer hunt. 1fo, Falconry. 1.20fo, Felled stag and dogs. 2fo, Bustards. 3fo, Net fishing. 4fo, Angling.

**1971, May Photo. *Perf. 12***

| | | | | | |
|---|---|---|---|---|---|
| **2066** | A460 | 40f | ver & multi | .25 | .25 |
| **2067** | A460 | 60f | plum & multi | .25 | .25 |
| **2068** | A460 | 80f | multi | .25 | .25 |
| **2069** | A460 | 1fo | lilac & multi | .25 | .25 |
| **2070** | A460 | 1.20fo | multi | .25 | .25 |
| **2071** | A460 | 2fo | multi | .25 | .25 |
| **2072** | A460 | 3fo | multi | .40 | .30 |
| **2073** | A460 | 4fo | green & multi | .55 | .40 |
| | | | *Nos. 2066-2073 (8)* | 2.45 | 2.20 |

World Hunting Exhibition, Budapest, Aug. 27-30. See No. C313.
Exist imperf. Value, set $20.

Souvenir Sheet

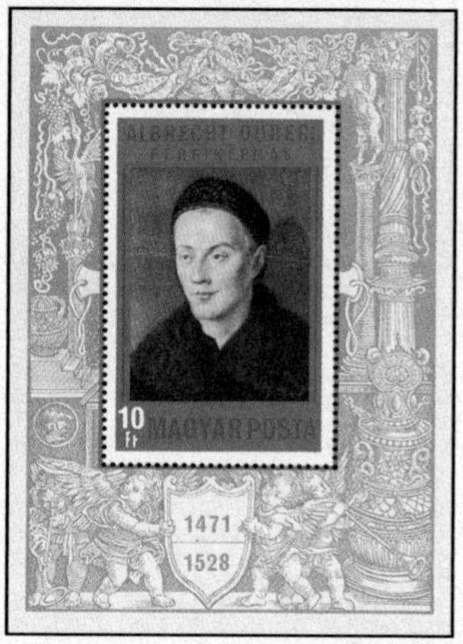

Portrait of a Man, by Dürer — A461

**1971, May 21 *Perf. 12½***

| | | | | | |
|---|---|---|---|---|---|
| **2074** | A461 | 10fo | gold & multi | 2.75 | 2.50 |

Albrecht Dürer (1471-1528), German painter and etcher.
Exists imperf. Value $20.

Carnation and Pioneers' Emblem — A462

**1971, June 2 Photo. *Perf. 12***

| | | | | | |
|---|---|---|---|---|---|
| **2075** | A462 | 1fo | dark red & multi | .40 | .25 |

Hungarian Pioneers' Organization, 25th anniv.
Exists imperf. Value $5.

FIR Emblem, Resistance Fighters — A463

**1971, July 3**

| | | | | | |
|---|---|---|---|---|---|
| **2076** | A463 | 1fo | brown & multi | .40 | .25 |

International Federation of Resistance Fighters (FIR), 20th anniversary.
Exists imperf. Value $5.

Walking in Garden, Tokyo School A464

Japanese Prints from Museum of East Asian Art, Budapest: 60f, Geisha in Boat, by Yeishi (1756-1829). 1fo, Woman with Scroll, by Yeishi. 1.50fo, Courtesans, by Kiyonaga (1752-1815). 2fo, Awabi Fisher Women, by Utamaro (1753-1806). 2.50fo, Seated Courtesan, by Harunobu (1725-1770). 3fo, Peasant Woman Carrying Fagots, by Hokusai (1760-1849). 4fo, Women and Girls Walking, by Yeishi.

**1971, July 9 *Perf. 12½***

| | | | | | |
|---|---|---|---|---|---|
| **2077** | A464 | 40f | gold & multi | .25 | .25 |
| **2078** | A464 | 60f | gold & multi | .25 | .25 |
| **2079** | A464 | 1fo | gold & multi | .25 | .25 |
| **2080** | A464 | 1.50fo | gold & multi | .25 | .25 |
| **2081** | A464 | 2fo | gold & multi | .25 | .25 |
| **2082** | A464 | 2.50fo | gold & multi | .30 | .25 |
| **2083** | A464 | 3fo | gold & multi | .50 | .25 |
| **2084** | A464 | 4fo | gold & multi | .75 | .45 |
| | | | *Nos. 2077-2084 (8)* | 2.80 | 2.20 |

Exist imperf. Value, set $15.

Locomotive, Map of Rail System and Danube — A465

**1971, July 15 Litho. *Perf. 12***

| | | | | | |
|---|---|---|---|---|---|
| **2086** | A465 | 1fo | multi | .40 | .25 |

125th anniversary of first Hungarian railroad between Pest and Vac.
Exists imperf. Value $7.50.

Griffin Holding Ink Balls A466

**1971, Sept. 11 Photo. *Perf. 12x11½***

| | | | | | |
|---|---|---|---|---|---|
| **2087** | A466 | 1fo | multicolored | .75 | .75 |

Centenary of stamp printing in Hungary. Printed se-tenant with 2 labels showing printing presses of 1871 and 1971 and Hungary Nos. P1 and 1171. Value unused, $1.
Exists imperf. Value, strip $12.50.

OIJ Emblem and Printed Page — A467

**1971, Sept. 21 *Perf. 11½x12***

| | | | | | |
|---|---|---|---|---|---|
| **2088** | A467 | 1fo | dk bl, bl & gold | .40 | .25 |

25th anniversary of the International Organization of Journalists (OIJ).
Exists imperf. Value $5.

Josef Jacob Winterl and Barren Strawberry — A468

Plants: 60f, Bromeliaceae. 80f, Titanopsis calcarea. 1fo, Periwinkle. 1.20fo, Gymnocalycium. 2fo, White water lily. 3fo, Iris arenaria. 5fo, Peony.

**1971, Oct. 29 Litho. *Perf. 12***

| | | | | | |
|---|---|---|---|---|---|
| **2089** | A468 | 40f | lt vio & multi | .25 | .25 |
| **2090** | A468 | 60f | gray & multi | .25 | .25 |
| **2091** | A468 | 80f | multi | .25 | .25 |
| **2092** | A468 | 1fo | multi | .25 | .25 |
| **2093** | A468 | 1.20fo | lilac & multi | .25 | .25 |
| **2094** | A468 | 2fo | gray & multi | .30 | .25 |
| **2095** | A468 | 3fo | multi | .50 | .25 |
| **2096** | A468 | 5fo | multi | .75 | .40 |
| | | | *Nos. 2089-2096 (8)* | 2.80 | 2.15 |

Bicentenary of Budapest Botanical Gardens.
Exist imperf. Value, set $17.50.

Galloping — A469

Equestrian Sports: 60f, Trotting. 80f, Horses fording river. 1fo, Jumping. 1.20fo, Start. 2fo, Polo. 3fo, Steeplechase. 5fo, Dressage.

**1971, Nov. 22 Photo. *Perf. 12***

| | | | | |
|---|---|---|---|---|
| **2097** | A469 | 40f blue & multi | .25 | .25 |
| **2098** | A469 | 60f ocher & multi | .25 | .25 |
| **2099** | A469 | 80f olive & multi | .25 | .25 |
| **2100** | A469 | 1fo red & multi | .25 | .25 |
| **2101** | A469 | 1.20fo multi | .25 | .25 |
| **2102** | A469 | 2fo multi | .30 | .25 |
| **2103** | A469 | 3fo violet & multi | .50 | .30 |
| **2104** | A469 | 5fo blue & multi | .75 | .50 |
| | | *Nos. 2097-2104 (8)* | 2.80 | 2.30 |

Exist imperf. Value, set $15.

Beheading of Heathen Chief Koppany A470

Designs: 60f, Samuel Aba pursuing King Peter. 1fo, Basarad's victory over King Charles Robert. 1.50fo, Strife between King Salomon and Prince Geza. 2.50fo, Founding of Obuda Church by King Stephen I and Queen Gisela. 4fo, Reconciliation of King Koloman and his brother Almos. 5fo, Oradea Church built by King Ladislas I. 10fo, Funeral of Prince Emeric and blinding of Vazul.

**1971, Dec. 10 Litho.**

| | | | | |
|---|---|---|---|---|
| **2105** | A470 | 40f buff & multi | .25 | .25 |
| **2106** | A470 | 60f buff & multi | .25 | .25 |
| **2107** | A470 | 1fo buff & multi | .25 | .25 |
| **2108** | A470 | 1.50fo buff & multi | .25 | .25 |
| **2109** | A470 | 2.50fo buff & multi | .25 | .25 |
| **2110** | A470 | 4fo buff & multi | .50 | .30 |
| **2111** | A470 | 5fo buff & multi | .75 | .50 |
| | | *Nos. 2105-2111 (7)* | 2.50 | 2.05 |

**Miniature Sheet**

***Perf. 11½***

**2112** A470 10fo buff & multi 3.00 2.75

History of Hungary, from miniatures from Illuminated Chronicle of King Louis the Great, c. 1370. No. 2112 contains one stamp (size 44½x52mm).

Exist imperf. Value: set $15; souvenir sheet $17.50.

Equality Year Emblem A471

**1971, Dec. 30 Litho. *Perf. 12***

**2113** A471 1fo bister & multi .40 .25

Intl. Year Against Racial Discrimination.

Exists imperf. Value $5.

Ice Hockey and Sapporo '72 Emblem — A472

Sport and Sapporo '72 Emblem: 60f, Men's slalom. 80f, Women's figure skating. 1fo, Ski jump. 1.20fo, Long-distance skiing. 2fo, Men's figure skating. 3fo, Bobsledding. 4fo, Biathlon. 10fo, Buddha.

**1971, Dec. 30 *Perf. 12***

| | | | | |
|---|---|---|---|---|
| **2114** | A472 | 40f black & multi | .25 | .25 |
| **2115** | A472 | 60f black & multi | .25 | .25 |
| **2116** | A472 | 80f black & multi | .25 | .25 |
| **2117** | A472 | 1fo black & multi | .25 | .25 |
| **2118** | A472 | 1.20fo black & multi | .25 | .25 |
| **2119** | A472 | 2fo black & multi | .35 | .25 |
| **2120** | A472 | 3fo black & multi | .50 | .30 |
| **2121** | A472 | 4fo black & multi | .75 | .50 |
| | | *Nos. 2114-2121 (8)* | 2.85 | 2.30 |

**Souvenir Sheet**

***Perf. 11½***

**2122** A472 10fo gold & multi 2.75 2.50

11th Winter Olympic Games, Sapporo, Japan, Feb. 3-13, 1972. No. 2122 contains one 86x48mm stamp.

Exist imperf. Value: set $15; souvenir sheet $20.

Hungarian Locomotive — A473

Locomotives: 60f, Germany. 80f, Italy. 1fo, Soviet Union. 1.20fo, Japan. 2fo, Great Britain. 4fo, Austria. 5fo, France.

**1972, Feb. 23 Photo. *Perf. 12x11½***

| | | | | |
|---|---|---|---|---|
| **2123** | A473 | 40f multi | .25 | .25 |
| **2124** | A473 | 60f ocher & multi | .25 | .25 |
| **2125** | A473 | 80f multi | .25 | .25 |
| **2126** | A473 | 1fo olive & multi | .25 | .25 |
| **2127** | A473 | 1.20fo ultra & multi | .35 | .30 |
| **2128** | A473 | 2fo ver & multi | .25 | .25 |
| **2129** | A473 | 4fo multi | .75 | .25 |
| **2130** | A473 | 5fo multi | 1.25 | .45 |
| | | *Nos. 2123-2130 (8)* | 3.60 | 2.25 |

Exist imperf. Value, set $20.

Janus Pannonius, by Andrea Mantegna A474

**1972, Mar. 27 Litho. *Perf. 12***

**2131** A474 1fo gold & multi .40 .25

Janus Pannonius (Johannes Czezmiczei, 1434-1472), humanist and poet.

Exists imperf. Value $5.

Mariner 9 — A475

Design: No. 2133, Mars 2 and 3 spacecraft.

**1972, Mar. 30 Photo. *Perf. 11½x12***

| | | | | |
|---|---|---|---|---|
| **2132** | A475 | 2fo dk blue & multi | .45 | .45 |
| **2133** | A475 | 2fo multi | .45 | .45 |
| *a.* | | Strip #2132-2133 + label | 1.75 | 1.75 |

Exploration of Mars by Mariner 9 (US), and Mars 2 and 3 (USSR). Issued in sheets containing 4 each of Nos. 2132-2133 and 4 labels inscribed in Hungarian, Russian and English.

Exist imperf. Values: strip $5, sheetlet $25.

13th Century Church Portal — A476

**1972, Apr. 11**

**2134** A476 3fo greenish black .40 .25

Centenary of the Society for the Protection of Historic Monuments.

Exists imperf. Value $7.50.

Hungarian Greyhound — A477

Hounds: 60f, Afghan hound (head). 80f, Irish wolfhound. 1.20fo, Borzoi. 2fo, Running greyhound. 4fo, Whippet. 6fo, Afghan hound.

**1972, Apr. 14 Litho. *Perf. 12***

| | | | | |
|---|---|---|---|---|
| **2135** | A477 | 40f multi | .25 | .25 |
| **2136** | A477 | 60f brown & multi | .25 | .25 |
| **2137** | A477 | 80f multi | .25 | .25 |
| **2138** | A477 | 1.20fo multi | .25 | .25 |
| **2139** | A477 | 2fo multi | .30 | .25 |
| **2140** | A477 | 4fo multi | .70 | .25 |
| **2141** | A477 | 6fo multi | 1.10 | .60 |
| | | *Nos. 2135-2141 (7)* | 3.10 | 2.10 |

Exist imperf. Value, set $25.

József Imre, Emil Grósz, László Blaskovics (Ophthalmologists) — A478

Design: 2fo, Allvar Gullstrand, V. P. Filatov, Jules Gonin, ophthalmologists.

**1972, Apr. 17**

| | | | | |
|---|---|---|---|---|
| **2142** | A478 | 1fo red, brn & blk | .40 | .25 |
| **2143** | A478 | 2fo blue, brn & blk | .95 | .45 |

First European Ophthalmologists' Congress, Budapest.

Exist imperf. Value, set $15.

Girl Reading and UNESCO Emblem A479

Roses — A480

**1972, May 27 Photo. *Perf. 11½x12***

**2144** A479 1fo multicolored .40 .25

International Book Year 1971.

Exists imperf. Value $5.

**1972, June 1**

**2145** A480 1fo multicolored .40 .25

15th Rose Exhibition, Budapest.

Exists imperf. Value $5.

George Dimitrov A481

**1972, June 18 Litho. *Perf. 12***

**2146** A481 3fo black & multi .40 .25

90th anniversary, birth of George Dimitrov (1882-1949), communist leader.

Exists imperf. Value $5.

**Souvenir Sheet**

St. Martin and the Beggar, Stained-glass Window — A482

**1972, June 20 *Perf. 10½***

**2147** A482 10fo multi 2.75 2.50

Belgica 72, International Philatelic Exhibition, Brussels, June 24-July 9.

Exists imperf. Value $20.

Gyorgy Dozsa (1474-1514), Peasant Leader — A483

**1972, June 25 Photo. *Perf. 11½x12***

**2148** A483 1fo red & multi .40 .25

Exists imperf. Value $5.

Olympic Rings, Soccer — A484

Designs (Olympic Rings and): 60f, Water polo. 80f, Javelin, women's. 1fo, Kayak, women's. 1.20fo, Boxing. 2fo, Gymnastics, women's. 5fo, Fencing.

**1972, July 15** *Perf. 11*

| | | | | |
|---|---|---|---|---|
| **2149** | A484 | 40f multi | .25 | .25 |
| **2150** | A484 | 60f multi | .25 | .25 |
| **2151** | A484 | 80f multi | .25 | .25 |
| **2152** | A484 | 1fo lilac & multi | .25 | .25 |
| **2153** | A484 | 1.20fo blue & multi | .25 | .25 |
| **2154** | A484 | 2fo multi | .40 | .25 |
| **2155** | A484 | 5fo green & multi | .75 | .50 |
| | | *Nos. 2149-2155,B299 (8)* | 2.90 | 2.30 |

20th Olympic Games, Munich, Aug. 26-Sept. 11. See No. C325.
Exist imperf. Value, set $17.50.

Prince Geza Selecting Site of Székesfehérvár — A485

Designs: 60f, St. Stephen, first King of Hungary. 80f, Knights (country's defense). 1.20fo, King Stephen dictating to scribe (legal organization). 2fo, Sculptor at work (education). 4fo, Merchants before king (foreign relations). 6fo, View of castle and town of Székesfehérvár, 10th century. 10fo, King Andreas II presenting Golden Bull to noblemen.

**1972, Aug. 20** **Photo.** *Perf. 12*

| | | | | |
|---|---|---|---|---|
| **2156** | A485 | 40f slate & multi | .25 | .25 |
| **2157** | A485 | 60f multi | .25 | .25 |
| **2158** | A485 | 80f lilac & multi | .25 | .25 |
| **2159** | A485 | 1.20fo multi | .25 | .25 |
| **2160** | A485 | 2fo bister & multi | .40 | .25 |
| **2161** | A485 | 4fo blue & multi | .55 | .25 |
| **2162** | A485 | 6fo purple & multi | .75 | .50 |
| | | *Nos. 2156-2162 (7)* | 2.70 | 2.00 |

**Souvenir Sheet**

*Perf. 12½*

| | | | | |
|---|---|---|---|---|
| **2163** | A485 | 10fo black & multi | 3.00 | 3.00 |

Millennium of the town of Székesfehérvár; 750th anniv. of the Golden Bull granting rights to lesser nobility. #2163 contains one 94x45mm stamp.
Exist imperf. Value: set $15; souvenir sheet $15.

Parliament, Budapest A486

Design: 6fo, Session room of Parliament.

**1972, Aug. 20** **Litho.**

| | | | | |
|---|---|---|---|---|
| **2164** | A486 | 5fo dk blue & multi | .60 | .25 |
| **2165** | A486 | 6fo multicolored | .75 | .30 |

Constitution of 1949.
Exist imperf. Value, set $12.50.

Eger, 17th Century View, and Bottle of Bull's Blood — A487

Design: 2fo, Contemporary view of Tokay and bottle of Tokay Aszu.

**1972, Aug. 21** **Litho.** *Perf. 12*

| | | | | |
|---|---|---|---|---|
| **2166** | A487 | 1fo buff & multi | .30 | .25 |
| **2167** | A487 | 2fo green & multi | .65 | .25 |

1st World Wine Exhibition, Budapest, Aug. 1972.
Exist imperf. Value, set $12.50.

Georgikon Emblems, Grain, Potato Flower — A488

**1972, Sept. 3**

| | | | | |
|---|---|---|---|---|
| **2168** | A488 | 1fo multi | .40 | .25 |

175th anniv. of the founding of the Georgikon at Keszthely, the 1st scientific agricultural academy.
Exists imperf. Value $5.

Vase with Bird — A489

Herend Porcelain: 60f, Covered candy dish. 80f, Vase with flowers and butterflies. 1fo, Plate with Mexican landscape. 1.20fo, Covered dish. 2fo, Teapot, cup and saucer. 4fo, Plate with flowers. 5fo, Baroque vase showing Herend factory.

**1972, Sept. 15**

**Sizes: 23x46mm (40f, 80f, 2fo, 5fo); 33x36mm, others**

| | | | | |
|---|---|---|---|---|
| **2169** | A489 | 40f gray & multi | .25 | .25 |
| **2170** | A489 | 60f ocher & multi | .25 | .25 |
| **2171** | A489 | 80f multi | .25 | .25 |
| **2172** | A489 | 1fo multi | .25 | .25 |
| **2173** | A489 | 1.20fo green & multi | .25 | .25 |
| **2174** | A489 | 2fo multi | .30 | .25 |
| **2175** | A489 | 4fo red & multi | .50 | .30 |
| **2176** | A489 | 5fo multi | .70 | .50 |
| | | *Nos. 2169-2176 (8)* | 2.75 | 2.30 |

Herend china factory, founded 1839.
Exist imperf. Value, set $15.

UIC Emblem and M-62 Diesel Locomotive — A490

**1972, Sept. 19** **Photo.** *Perf. 11½x12*

| | | | | |
|---|---|---|---|---|
| **2177** | A490 | 1fo dark red | .40 | .25 |

50th anniversary of International Railroad Union Congress, Budapest, Sept. 19.
Exist imperf. Value $10.

"25" and Graph — A491

**1972, Sept.** *Perf. 11½x12*

| | | | | |
|---|---|---|---|---|
| **2178** | A491 | 1fo yellow & brown | .40 | .25 |

Planned national economy, 25th anniv.
Exists imperf. Value $5.

Budapest, 1972 — A492

#2179, View of Obuda, 1872. #2181, Buda, 1872. #2183, Pest, 1872. #2182, 2184, Budapest, 1972.

**1972, Sept. 26** *Perf. 12x11½*

| | | | | |
|---|---|---|---|---|
| **2179** | A492 | 1fo Prus bl & rose car | .25 | .25 |
| **2180** | A492 | 1fo rose car & Prus bl | .25 | .25 |
| *a.* | | Pair, #2179-2180 | .40 | .25 |
| **2181** | A492 | 2fo ocher & olive | .30 | .25 |
| **2182** | A492 | 2fo olive & ocher | .30 | .25 |
| *a.* | | Pair, #2181-2182 | .75 | .35 |
| **2183** | A492 | 3fo green & lt brn | .40 | .25 |
| **2184** | A492 | 3fo lt brown & grn | .40 | .25 |
| *a.* | | Pair, #2183-2184 | 1.25 | .50 |
| | | *Nos. 2179-2184 (6)* | 1.90 | 1.50 |

Centenary of unification of Obuda, Buda and Pest into Budapest.
Exist imperf. Value, set in pairs $20.

Ear and Congress Emblem A493

**1972, Oct. 3** *Perf. 11½x12*

| | | | | |
|---|---|---|---|---|
| **2185** | A493 | 1fo brown, yel & blk | .40 | .25 |

11th Intl. Audiology Cong., Budapest.
Exists imperf. Value $6.

Flora Martos — A494

Portrait: No. 2187, Miklós Radnóti.

**1972** **Photo.** *Perf. 11½x12*

| | | | | |
|---|---|---|---|---|
| **2186** | A494 | 1fo green & multi | .25 | .25 |
| **2187** | A494 | 1fo brown & multi | .25 | .25 |

Flora Martos (1897-1938), Hungarian Labor Party leader, & Miklós Radnóti (1909-44), poet.
Exist imperf. Value, set $6.
Issued: No. 2186, Nov. 5; No. 2187, Nov. 11.

Muses, by Jozsef Rippl-Ronai A495

Stained-glass Windows, 19th-20th Centuries: 60f, 16th century scribe, by Ferenc Sebesteny. 1fo, Flight into Egypt, by Karoly Lotz and Bertalan Székely. 1.50fo, Prince Arpad's Messenger, by Jenö Percz. 2.50fo, Nativity, by Lili Sztehlo. 4fo, Prince Arpad and Leaders, by Karoly Kernstock. 5fo, King Matthias and Jester, by Jenö Haranghy.

**1972, Nov. 15** *Perf. 12*

| | | | | |
|---|---|---|---|---|
| **2188** | A495 | 40f multi | .25 | .25 |
| **2189** | A495 | 60f multi | .25 | .25 |
| **2190** | A495 | 1fo multi | .25 | .25 |
| **2191** | A495 | 1.50fo multi | .25 | .25 |
| **2192** | A495 | 2.50fo multi | .35 | .25 |
| **2193** | A495 | 4fo multi | .65 | .30 |
| **2194** | A495 | 5fo multi | 1.10 | .50 |
| | | *Nos. 2188-2194 (7)* | 3.10 | 2.05 |

Exist imperf. Value, set $15.

Weaver, Cloth and Cogwheel — A496

**1972, Nov. 27** **Litho.** *Perf. 12*

| | | | | |
|---|---|---|---|---|
| **2195** | A496 | 1fo silver & multi | .40 | .25 |

Opening of Museum of Textile Techniques, Budapest.
Exists imperf. Value $6.

Main Square, Szarvas — A497

Designs: 1fo, Modern buildings, Salgotarjan. 3fo, Tokaj and vineyard. 4fo, Esztergom Cathedral. 7fo, Town Hall, Kaposvar. 20fo, Veszprem.

**1972** **Litho.** *Perf. 11*

| | | | | |
|---|---|---|---|---|
| **2196** | A497 | 40f brown & orange | .25 | .25 |
| **2197** | A497 | 1fo dk & lt blue | .25 | .25 |

Exist imperf. Value, set $15.

Church and City Hall, Tokaj — A498

**1973** *Perf. 12x11½*

| | | | | |
|---|---|---|---|---|
| **2198** | A498 | 3fo dk & lt green | .40 | .25 |
| **2199** | A498 | 4fo red brn & org | .50 | .25 |
| **2200** | A498 | 7fo blue vio & lil | 1.00 | .25 |
| **2200A** | A498 | 20fo multicolored | 2.50 | .40 |
| | | *Nos. 2196-2200A (6)* | 4.90 | 1.65 |

Exist imperf. Value, set $40.
See Nos. 2330-2335.

**Type of 1963-64**

Coil Stamps

Designs as before.

**1972, Nov.** **Photo.** *Perf. 14*

**Size: 21½x17½mm, 17½x21½mm**

| | | | | |
|---|---|---|---|---|
| **2201** | A336 | 2fo blue green | .40 | .25 |
| **2202** | A336 | 3fo dark blue | .55 | .25 |
| **2203** | A336 | 4fo blue, vert. | .75 | .25 |
| **2204** | A336 | 6fo bister | 1.10 | .35 |
| | | *Nos. 2201-2204 (4)* | 2.80 | 1.10 |

Black control number on back of every 5th stamp.

Minute inscription centered in lower margin: "Legrady Sandor."

Arms of Soviet Union — A498a

**1972, Dec. 30 Photo. *Perf. 11½x12***

**2205** A498a 1fo multicolored .40 .25

50th anniversary of Soviet Union.
Exists imperf. Value $10.

Petőfi Speaking at Pilvax Cafe A499

2fo, Portrait. 3fo, Petőfi on horseback, 1848-49.

**1972, Dec. 30 Engr. *Perf. 12***

**2206** A499 1fo rose carmine .25 .25
**2207** A499 2fo violet .35 .25
**2208** A499 3fo Prus green .45 .25
*Nos. 2206-2208 (3)* 1.05 .75

Sesquicentennial of the birth of Sandor Petőfi (1823-49), poet and revolutionary.
Exist imperf. Value, set $15.

Postal Zone Map of Hungary and Letter-carrying Crow — A500

**1973, Jan. 1 Litho. *Perf. 12***

**2209** A500 1fo red & black .40 .25

Introduction of postal code system.
Exists imperf. Value $6.

Imre Madách (1823-64), Poet and Dramatist A501

**1973, Jan. 20 Photo. *Perf. 11½x12***

**2210** A501 1fo multicolored .40 .25

Exists imperf. Value $6.

Busho Mask — A502

Designs: Various Busho masks.

**1973, Feb. 17 Litho. *Perf. 12***

**2211** A502 40f tan & multi .25 .25
**2212** A502 60f dull grn & multi .25 .25
**2213** A502 80f lilac & multi .25 .25
**2214** A502 1.20fo multi .25 .25
**2215** A502 2fo tan & multi .30 .25
**2216** A502 4fo multi .50 .30
**2217** A502 6fo lilac & multi .75 .40
*Nos. 2211-2217 (7)* 2.55 1.95

Busho Walk at Mohacs, ancient ceremony to drive out winter.
Exist imperf. Value, set $15.

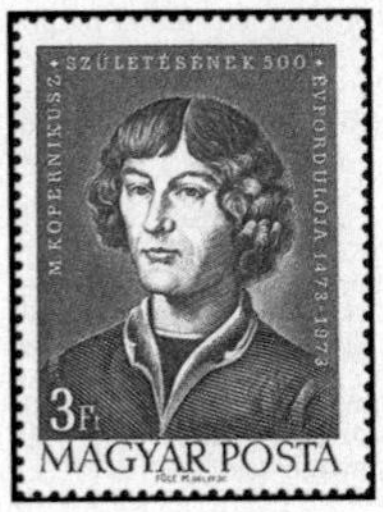


Nicolaus Copernicus A503

**1973, Feb. 19 Engr. *Perf. 12***

**2218** A503 3fo bright ultra .75 .50

Printed with alternating label showing heliocentric system and view of Torun.
Exists imperf. Value $12.50.

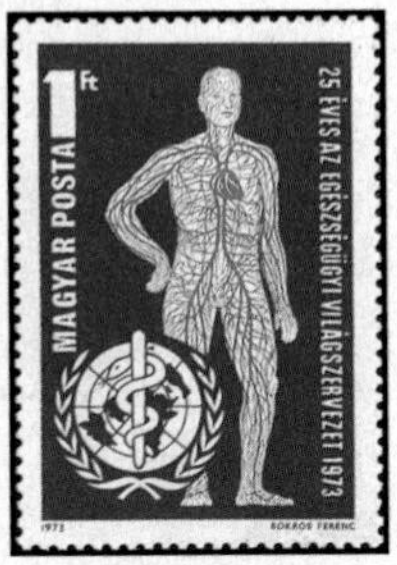


Vascular System and WHO Emblem A504

**1973, Apr. 16 Photo. *Perf. 12***

**2219** A504 1fo sl grn & brn red .40 .25

25th anniv. of WHO.
Exists imperf. Value $6.

Tank, Rocket, Radar, Plane, Ship and Soldier A505

**1973, May 9 Litho. *Perf. 12***

**2220** A505 3fo blue & multi .50 .25

Philatelic Exhibition of Military Stamp Collectors of Warsaw Treaty Member States. No. 2220 was printed with alternating label showing flags of Warsaw Treaty members.
Exists imperf. Value $12.50.

Hungary No. 1396 and IBRA '73 Emblem — A506

**1973, May 11 Litho. *Perf. 12***

**2221** A506 40f shown .25 .25
**2222** A506 60f No. 1397, POLSKA '73 .25 .25
**2223** A506 80f No. 1398, IBRA '73 .25 .25
**2224** A506 1fo No. 1399, POLSKA .25 .25
**2225** A506 1.20fo No. B293a, IBRA .25 .25
**2226** A506 2fo No. B293b, POLSKA .25 .25
**2227** A506 4fo No. B293c, IBRA .50 .30
**2228** A506 5fo No. B293d, POLSKA .75 .40
*Nos. 2221-2228 (8)* 2.75 2.20

Publicity for IBRA '73 International Philatelic Exhibition, Munich, May 11-20; and POLSKA '73, Poznan, Aug. 15-Sept. 2. See No. C345.
Exist imperf. Value, set $17.50.

Typesetting, from "Orbis Pictus," by Comenius A507

3fo, Printer & wooden screw press, woodcut from Hungarian translation of Gospels.

**1973, June 5 Photo. *Perf. 11½x12***

**2229** A507 1fo black & gold .25 .25
**2230** A507 3fo black & gold .40 .25

500th anniv. of book printing in Hungary.
Exist imperf. Value, set $11.

Storm over Hortobagy Puszta, by Csontvary — A508

Paintings: 60f, Mary's Well, Nazareth. 1fo, Carriage Ride by Moonlight in Athens, vert. 1.50fo, Pilgrimage to Cedars of Lebanon, vert. 2.50fo, The Lonely Cedar. 4fo, Waterfall at Jajce. 5fo, Ruins of Greek Theater at Taormina. 10fo, Horseback Riders on Shore.

**1973, June 18 *Perf. 12½***

**2231** A508 40f gold & multi .25 .25
**2232** A508 60f gold & multi .25 .25
**2233** A508 1fo gold & multi .25 .25
**2234** A508 1.50fo gold & multi .25 .25
**2235** A508 2.50fo gold & multi .40 .25
**2236** A508 4fo gold & multi .65 .35
**2237** A508 5fo gold & multi .80 .50
*Nos. 2231-2237 (7)* 2.85 2.10

### Souvenir Sheet

**2238** A508 10fo gold & multi 3.50 3.00

Paintings by Tividar Kosztka Csontvary (1853-1919). No. 2238 contains one stamp (size: 90x43mm).
Exist imperf. Value: set $15; souvenir sheet $20.

Hands Holding Map of Europe — A509

**1973, July 3 Photo. *Perf. 11½x12***

**2239** A509 2.50fo blk & gldn brn 3.00 3.00
*a.* Sheetlet of 4 + 2 labels 10.00 9.00

Conference for European Security and Cooperation. Helsinki, July 1973. No. 2239 was printed in a sheetlet of 4 stamps and 2 blue labels showing conference sites.
Exists imperf. Value, sheetlet $125.

Flowers — A510

**1973, Aug. 4**

**2240** A510 40f Provence roses .25 .25
**2241** A510 60f Cyclamen .25 .25
**2242** A510 80f Lungwort .25 .25
**2243** A510 1.20fo English daisies .25 .25
**2244** A510 2fo Buttercups .30 .25
**2245** A510 4fo Violets .70 .30
**2246** A510 6fo Poppies 1.00 .50
*Nos. 2240-2246 (7)* 3.00 2.05

Exist imperf. Value, set $15.

"Let's be Friends in Traffic" — A511

Designs: 60f, "Not even one drink." 1fo, "Light your bicycle."

**1973, Aug. 18 Photo. *Perf. 12x11½***

**2247** A511 40f green & orange .25 .25
**2248** A511 60f purple & orange .25 .25
**2249** A511 1fo indigo & orange .25 .25
*Nos. 2247-2249 (3)* .75 .75

To publicize traffic rules.
Exist imperf. Value $15.

Adoration of the Kings A512

Paintings: 60f, Angels playing violin and lute. 1fo, Adoration of the Kings. 1.50fo, Annunciation. 2.50fo, Angels playing organ and harp. 4fo, Visitation of Mary. 5fo, Legend of St. Catherine of Alexandria. 10fo, Nativity.

**1973, Nov. 3 Photo. *Perf. 12½***

**2250** A512 40f gold & multi .25 .25
**2251** A512 60f gold & multi .25 .25
**2252** A512 1fo gold & multi .25 .25
**2253** A512 1.50fo gold & multi .25 .25
**2254** A512 2.50fo gold & multi .40 .25
**2255** A512 4fo gold & multi .60 .30
**2256** A512 5fo gold & multi .80 .50
*Nos. 2250-2256 (7)* 2.80 2.05

**Souvenir Sheet**

***Perf. 11***

**2257** A512 10fo gold & multi 3.00 2.75

Paintings by Hungarian anonymous early masters from the Christian Museum at Esztergom. No. 2257 contains one 49x74mm stamp.

Exist imperf. Value: set $15; souvenir sheet $15.

Mihaly Csokonai Vitez — A513

**1973, Nov. 17 Photo.** ***Perf. 11½x12***

**2258** A513 2fo bister & multi .35 .25

Mihaly Csokonai Vitez (1773-1805), poet.

Exists imperf. Value $5.

José Marti and Cuban Flag — A514

**1973, Nov. 30**

**2259** A514 1fo dk brn, red & bl .40 .25

Marti (1853-95), Cuban natl. hero and poet.

Exists imperf. Value $5.

Barnabas Pesti (1920-44), Member of Hungarian Underground Communist Party — A515

**1973, Nov. 30**

**2260** A515 1fo blue, brn & buff .40 .25

Exists imperf. Value $5.

Women's Double Kayak — A516

Designs: 60f, Water polo. 80f, Men's single kayak. 1.20fo, Butterfly stroke. 2fo, Men's fours kayak. 4fo, Men's single canoe. 6fo, Men's double canoe.

**1973, Dec. 29 Litho.** ***Perf. 12x11***

| | | | | | |
|---|---|---|---|---|---|
| **2261** | A516 | 40f | red & multi | .25 | .25 |
| **2262** | A516 | 60f | blue & multi | .25 | .25 |
| **2263** | A516 | 80f | multicolored | .25 | .25 |
| **2264** | A516 | 1.20fo | green & multi | .25 | .25 |
| **2265** | A516 | 2fo | car & multi | .35 | .25 |
| **2266** | A516 | 4fo | violet & multi | .45 | .30 |
| **2267** | A516 | 6fo | multicolored | .50 | .50 |
| | | | *Nos. 2261-2267 (7)* | 2.30 | 2.05 |

Hungarian victories in water sports at Tampere and Belgrade.

Exist imperf. Value, set $17.50.

Souvenir Sheet

Map of Europe — A517

**1974, Jan. 15 Photo.** ***Perf. 12x11½***

**2268** Sheet of 2 + label 8.50 8.00
*a.* A517 5fo multicolored 2.25 2.25

European Peace Conference (Arab-Israeli War), Geneva, Jan. 1974.

Exists imperf. Value $110.

Lenin — A518

**1974, Jan. 21 Photo.** ***Perf. 11½x12***

**2269** A518 2fo gold, dull bl & brn .50 .25

50th anniv. of the death of Lenin (1870-1924).

Exists imperf. Value $6.

Jozsef Boczor, Imre Békés, Tamás Elek — A519

**1974, Feb. 21** ***Perf. 12½***

**2270** A519 3fo brown & multi .40 .25

30th anniversary of the death in France of Hungarian resistance fighters.

Exists imperf. Value $6.

Comecon Building, Moscow and Flags A520

**1974, Feb. 26 Photo.** ***Perf. 12x11½***

**2271** A520 1fo multicolored .40 .25

25th anniversary of the Council of Mutual Economic Assistance.

Exists imperf. Value $7.50.

Bank Emblem, Coins and Banknote A521

**1974, Mar. 1** ***Perf. 11½x12***

**2272** A521 1fo lt green & multi .40 .25

25th anniversary of the State Savings Bank.

Exists imperf. Value $5.

Spacecraft on Way to Mars — A522

Designs: 60f, Mars 2 over Mars. 80f, Mariner 4. 1fo, Mars and Mt. Palomar Observatory. 1.20fo, Soft landing of Mars 3. 5fo, Mariner 9 with Mars satellites Phobos and Deimos.

**1974, Mar. 11 Photo.** ***Perf. 12½***

| | | | | | |
|---|---|---|---|---|---|
| **2273** | A522 | 40f | gold & multi | .25 | .25 |
| **2274** | A522 | 60f | silver & multi | .25 | .25 |
| **2275** | A522 | 80f | gold & multi | .25 | .25 |
| **2276** | A522 | 1fo | silver & multi | .25 | .25 |
| **2277** | A522 | 1.20fo | gold & multi | .25 | .25 |
| **2278** | A522 | 5fo | silver & multi | .75 | .40 |
| | | | *Nos. 2273-2278,C347 (7)* | 2.75 | 2.15 |

Exploration of Mars. See No. C348.

Exist imperf. Value, set (7) $15.

Salvador Allende (1908-73), Pres. of Chile — A523

**1974, Mar. 27 Photo.** ***Perf. 11½x12***

**2279** A523 1fo black & multi .40 .25

Exists imperf. Value $5.

Mona Lisa, by Leonardo da Vinci A524

**1974, Apr. 19** ***Perf. 12½***

**2280** A524 4fo gold & multi 6.25 6.00

Exists imperf. Value $20. Exhibition of the Mona Lisa in Asia.

Printed in sheets of 6 stamps and 6 labels with commemorative inscription. Value, $65.

Exist imperf. Value: single with labels $20; sheetlet $150.

Souvenir Sheet

Issue of 1874 and Flowers — A525

a, Mallow. b, Aster. c, Daisy. d, Columbine.

**1974, May 11 Litho.** ***Perf. 11½***

**2281** A525 Sheet of 4 2.75 2.75
*a.-d.* 2.50fo any single .50 .50

Centenary of the first issue inscribed "Magyar Posta" (Hungarian Post).

Exists imperf. Value, sheet of 4 $20.

Carrier Pigeon, World Map, UPU Emblem — A526

**1974, May 22 Litho.** ***Perf. 12***

| | | | | | |
|---|---|---|---|---|---|
| **2282** | A526 | 40f | shown | .25 | .25 |
| **2283** | A526 | 60f | Mail coach | .25 | .25 |
| **2284** | A526 | 80f | Old mail automobile | .25 | .25 |
| **2285** | A526 | 1.20fo | Balloon post | .35 | .25 |
| **2286** | A526 | 2fo | Mail train | .45 | .25 |
| **2287** | A526 | 4fo | Mail bus | 1.00 | .40 |
| | | | *Nos. 2282-2287,C349 (7)* | 3.80 | 2.55 |

Centenary of the Universal Postal Union.

Exist imperf. Value, set $20.

Dove of Basel, Switzerland No. 3L1, 1845 — A527

**1974, June 7 Photo.** ***Perf. 11½x12***

**2288** A527 3fo gold & multi 1.25 1.25

INTERNABA 1974 Philatelic Exhibition, Basel, June 7-16. No. 2288 issued in sheets of 3 stamps and 3 labels showing Internaba 1974 emblem. Size: 104x125mm.

Exist imperf. Values: single $8; sheet $25.

Chess Players, from 13th Century Manuscript A528

Designs: 60f, Chess players, 15th century English woodcut. 80f, Royal chess party, 15th century Italian chess book. 1.20fo, Chess players, 17th century copper engraving by Selenus. 2fo, Farkas Kempelen's chess playing machine, 1769. 4fo, Hungarian Grand Master Geza Maroczy (1870-1951). 6fo, View of Nice and emblem of 1974 Chess Olympiad.

**1974, June 6 Litho.** ***Perf. 12***

| | | | | | |
|---|---|---|---|---|---|
| **2289** | A528 | 40f | multi | .25 | .25 |
| **2290** | A528 | 60f | multi | .25 | .25 |
| **2291** | A528 | 80f | multi | .25 | .25 |
| **2292** | A528 | 1.20fo | multi | .30 | .25 |
| **2293** | A528 | 2fo | multi | .45 | .25 |
| **2294** | A528 | 4fo | multi | 1.10 | .30 |
| **2295** | A528 | 6fo | multi | 1.75 | .50 |
| | | | *Nos. 2289-2295 (7)* | 4.35 | 2.05 |

50th anniv. of Intl. Chess Federation and 21st Chess Olympiad, Nice, June 6-30.

Exist imperf. Value, set $125.

Souvenir Sheet

Cogwheel Railroad — A529

Designs: a, Passenger train, 1874. b, Freight train, 1874. c, Electric train, 1929-73. d, Twin motor train, 1973.

**1974, June 25 Litho. *Perf. 12***

**2296** A529 Sheet of 4 3.50 3.25
*a.-d.* 2.50fo, any single .50 .50

Cent. of Budapest's cogwheel railroad.
Exist imperf. Value, sheet $30.

Congress Emblem (Globe and Parliament) — A530

**1974, Aug. 18 Photo. *Perf. 12***

**2297** A530 2fo silver, dk & lt bl .40 .25

4th World Congress of Economists, Budapest, Aug. 19-24.
Exists imperf. Value $5.

Bathing Woman, by Károly Lotz A531

Paintings of Nudes: 60f, Awakening, by Károly Brocky. 1fo, Venus and Cupid, by Brocky, horiz. 1.50fo, After the Bath, by Lotz. 2.50fo, Resting Woman, by Istvan Csok, horiz. 4fo, After the Bath, by Bertalan Szekely. 5fo, "Devotion," by Erzsebet Korb. 10fo, Lark, by Pál Szinyei Merse.

**1974, Aug. *Perf. 12½***

**2298** A531 40f gold & multi .25 .25
**2299** A531 60f gold & multi .25 .25
**2300** A531 1fo gold & multi .25 .25
**2301** A531 1.50fo gold & multi .30 .25
**2302** A531 2.50fo gold & multi .35 .25
**2303** A531 4fo gold & multi .70 .25
**2304** A531 5fo gold & multi .90 .40
*Nos. 2298-2304 (7)* 3.00 1.90

**Souvenir Sheet**

***Perf. 11***

**2305** A531 10fo gold & multi 3.25 3.00

No. 2305 contains one stamp (45x70mm).
Exist imperf. Value: set $20; souvenir sheet $20.

Mimi, by Béla Czóbel A532

**1974, Sept. 4**

**2306** A532 1fo multicolored .50 .25

91st birthday of Béla Czóbel, Hungarian painter.
Exists imperf. Value $6.

Intersputnik Tracking Station — A533

High Voltage Line "Peace" and Pipe Line "Friendship" A534

***Perf. 11½x12, 12x11½***

**1974, Sept. 5 Litho.**

**2307** A533 1fo blue & violet .25 .25
**2308** A534 3fo multicolored .60 .25

Technical assistance and cooperation between Hungary and USSR, 25th anniv.
Exist imperf. Value, set $10.

Pablo Neruda — A535

**1974, Sept. 11 Photo. *Perf. 11½x12***

**2309** A535 1fo multicolored .40 .25

Pablo Neruda (Neftali Ricar do Reyes, 1904-1973), Chilean poet.
Exists imperf. Value $5.

Sweden No. 1 and Lion from Royal Palace, Stockholm A536

**1974, Sept. 21 *Perf. 12x11½***

**2310** A536 3fo ultra, yel grn & gold 1.50 1.50

Stockholmia 74 Intl. Philatelic Exhibition, Stockholm, Sept. 21-29. No. 2310 issued in sheets of 3 stamps and 3 labels showing Stockholmia emblem. White margin inscribed "UPU" multiple in white. Size: 126x104mm. Value $6.50.
Exists imperf. Value: single $7.50; sheetlet $22.50.

Tank Battle and Soldier with Anti-tank Grenade — A537

**1974, Sept. 28 Litho. *Perf. 12***

**2311** A537 1fo gold, orange & blk .25 .25
*Nos. 2311,C351-C352 (3)* .95 .75

Army Day.
Exist imperf. Value, set (3) $15.

Segner and Segner Crater on Moon A538

**1974, Oct. 5**

**2312** A538 3fo multicolored .75 .25

270th anniversary of the birth of Janos Andras Segner, naturalist. No. 2312 printed se-tenant with label arranged checkerwise in sheet. Label shows Segner wheel.
Exists imperf. Value, with label $12.50.

Rhyparia Purpurata — A539

Lepidoptera: 60f, Melanargia galathea. 80f, Parnassius Apollo. 1fo, Celerio euphorbia. 1.20fo, Catocala fraxini. 5fo, Apatura iris. 6fo, Palaeochrysophanus hyppothoe.

**1974, Nov. 11 Photo. *Perf. 12½***

**2313** A539 40f multicolored .25 .25
**2314** A539 60f violet & multi .25 .25
**2315** A539 80f multicolored .25 .25
**2316** A539 1fo brown & multi .25 .25
**2317** A539 1.20fo blue & multi .25 .25
**2318** A539 5fo purple & multi .75 .30
**2319** A539 6fo multicolored 1.00 .40
*Nos. 2313-2319 (7)* 3.00 1.95

Exist imperf. Value, set $17.50.

Motherhood A540

**1974, Dec. 24 Litho. *Perf. 12***

**2320** A540 1fo lt blue, blk & yel .40 .25

Exists imperf. Value $5.

Robert Kreutz — A541

**1974, Dec. 24**

**2321** A541 1fo shown .30 .25
**2322** A541 1fo István Pataki .30 .25

30th death anniv. of anti-fascist martyrs Kreutz (1923-44) and Pataki (1914-44).
Exist imperf. Value, set $10.

Puppy A542

Young Animals: 60f, Siamese kittens, horiz. 80f, Rabbit. 1.20fo, Foal, horiz. 2fo, Lamb. 4fo, Calf, horiz. 6fo, Piglet.

**1974, Dec. 30**

**2323** A542 40f lt blue & multi .25 .25
**2324** A542 60f multicolored .25 .25
**2325** A542 80f olive & multi .25 .25
**2326** A542 1.20fo green & multi .25 .25
**2327** A542 2fo brown & multi .30 .25
**2328** A542 4fo orange & multi .70 .30
**2329** A542 6fo violet & multi 1.10 .50
*Nos. 2323-2329 (7)* 3.10 2.05

Exist imperf. Value, set $15.

See Nos. 2403-2409.

**Building Type of 1972**

4fo, Szentendre. 5fo, View of Szolnok across Tisza River. 6fo, Skyscraper, Dunáujváros. 8fo, Church and city hall, Vac. 10fo, City Hall, Kiskunfélegyháza. 50fo, Church (Turkish Mosque), Hunyadi Statue & TV tower, Pecs.

**1974-80 Litho. *Perf. 12x11½***

**2330** A498 4fo red brn & pink .60 .25
**2331** A498 5fo dk blue & ultra .75 .25
**2332** A498 6fo dk brn & org .90 .25
**2333** A498 8fo dk & brt grn 1.25 .25
**2334** A498 10fo brown & yel 1.75 .25
**2335** A498 50fo multi 6.00 1.25
*Nos. 2330-2335 (6)* 11.25 2.50

Exist imperf. Value, set $95.

Issued: 8fo, 12/7; 10fo, 50fo, 12/30; 5fo, 3/8/75; 6fo, 6/10/75; 4fo, 6/20/80.

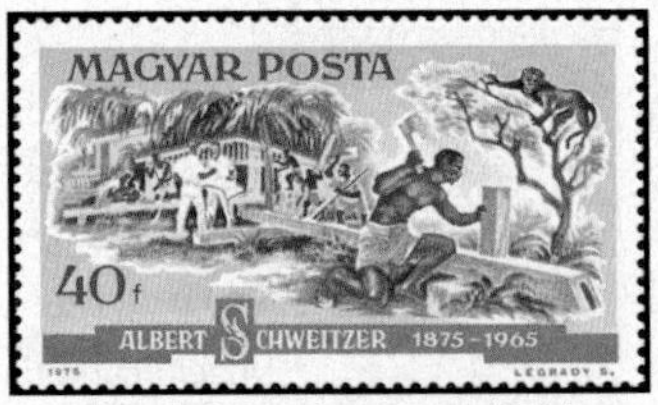


Hospital, Lambarene — A544

60f, Dr. Schweitzer, patient & microscope. 80f, Patient arriving by boat. 1.20fo, Hospital supplies arriving by ship. 2fo, Globe, Red Cross, carrier pigeons. 4fo, Nobel Peace Prize medal. 6fo, Portrait & signature of Dr. Schweitzer, organ pipes & "J. S. Bach."

**1975, Jan. 14 Photo. *Perf. 12***

**2340** A544 40f gold & multi .25 .25
**2341** A544 60f gold & multi .25 .25
**2342** A544 80f gold & multi .25 .25
**2343** A544 1.20fo gold & multi .25 .25
**2344** A544 2fo gold & multi .25 .25
**2345** A544 4fo gold & multi .60 .30
**2346** A544 6fo lil & multi .80 .45
*Nos. 2340-2346 (7)* 2.65 2.00

Dr. Albert Schweitzer (1875-1965), medical missionary and musician, birth centenary.
Exist imperf. Value, set $15.

Farkas Bolyai — A545

**1975, Feb. 7 Litho. *Perf. 11½x12***

**2347** A545 1fo gray & red brown .25 .25

Bolyai (1775-1856), mathematician.
Exists imperf. Value $7.

Mihály Károlyi
A546

**1975, Mar. 4 Litho. *Perf. 12***
**2348** A546 1fo lt blue & brown .40 .25

Birth centenary of Count Mihály Károlyi (1875-1955), prime minister, 1918-1919.
Exists imperf. Value $5.

Woman, IWY Emblem
A547

**1975, Mar. 8 *Perf. 12x11½***
**2349** A547 1fo aqua & black .40 .25

International Women's Year 1975.
Exists imperf. Value $5.

"Let us Build up the Railroads" — A548

Posters: 60f, "Bread starts here." 2fo, "Hungarian Communist Party-a Party of Action." 4fo, "Heavy Industry-secure base of Three-year Plan." 5fo, "Our common interest-a developed socialist society."

**1975, Mar. 17 Photo. *Perf. 11***

| | | | | |
|---|---|---|---|---|
| **2350** | A548 | 40f red & multi | .25 | .25 |
| **2351** | A548 | 60f red & multi | .25 | .25 |
| **2352** | A548 | 2fo red & multi | .25 | .25 |
| **2353** | A548 | 4fo red & multi | .40 | .25 |
| **2354** | A548 | 5fo red & multi | .50 | .30 |
| | | *Nos. 2350-2354 (5)* | 1.65 | 1.30 |

Hungary's liberation from Fascism, 30th anniv.
Exist imperf. Value, set $15.

Arrow, 1915, Pagoda and Mt. Fuji — A549

Antique Cars: 60f, Swift, 1911, Big Ben and Tower of London. 80f, Model T Ford, 1908, Capitol and Statue of Liberty. 1fo, Mercedes, 1901, Towers of Stuttgart. 1.20fo, Panhard Levassor, 1912, Arc de Triomphe and Eiffel Tower. 5fo, Csonka, 1906, Fishermen's Bastion and Chain Bridge. 6fo, Emblems of Hungarian Automobile Club, Alliance Internationale de Tourisme and Federation Internationale de l'Automobile.

**1975, Mar. 27 Litho. *Perf. 12***

| | | | | |
|---|---|---|---|---|
| **2355** | A549 | 40f lt blue & multi | .25 | .25 |
| **2356** | A549 | 60f lt green & multi | .25 | .25 |
| **2357** | A549 | 80f pink & multi | .25 | .25 |
| **2358** | A549 | 1fo lilac & multi | .25 | .25 |
| **2359** | A549 | 1.20fo orange & multi | .25 | .25 |
| **2360** | A549 | 5fo ultra & multi | .65 | .30 |
| **2361** | A549 | 6fo lilac rose & multi | 1.00 | .50 |
| | | *Nos. 2355-2361 (7)* | 2.90 | 2.05 |

Hungarian Automobile Club, 75th anniv.
Exist imperf. Value, set $17.50.

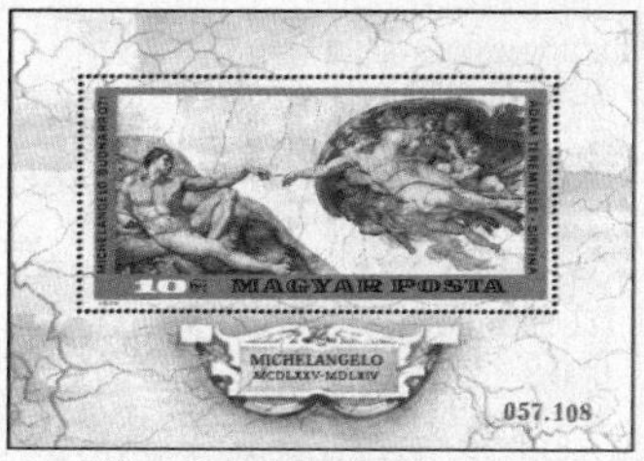


The Creation of Adam, by Michelangelo — A550

**1975, Apr. 23 Photo. *Perf. 12½***
**2362** A550 10fo gold & multi 3.50 3.25

Michelangelo Buonarroti (1475-1564), Italian painter, sculptor and architect.
Exists imperf. Value $22.50.

Academy of Science
A551

Designs: 2fo, Dates "1975 1825." 3fo, Count Istvan Szechenyi.

**1975, May 5 Litho. *Perf. 12***

| | | | | |
|---|---|---|---|---|
| **2363** | A551 | 1fo green & multi | .25 | .25 |
| **2364** | A551 | 2fo green & multi | .30 | .25 |
| **2365** | A551 | 3fo green & multi | .50 | .30 |
| | | *Nos. 2363-2365 (3)* | 1.05 | .80 |

Sesquicentennial of Academy of Science, Budapest, founded by Count Istvan Szechenyi.
Exists imperf. Value, set $15.

Emblem of 1980 Olympics and Proposed Moscow Stadium — A553

**1975, May 8 Photo. *Perf. 11½x12***
**2366** A553 5fo lt blue & multi 1.50 1.25

Socfilex 75 Intl. Philatelic Exhibition, Moscow, 5/8-18. #2366 issued in sheets of 3 stamps and 3 labels showing Socfilex 75 emblem (War Memorial, Berlin-Treptow).
Exists imperf. Value: single with label $12.50; sheetlet $45.

France No. 1100 and Venus of Milo — A554

**1975, June 3 Photo. *Perf. 11½x12***
**2367** A554 5fo lilac & multi 1.50 1.25

ARPHILA 75 International Philatelic Exhibition, Paris, June 6-16. No. 2367 issued in sheets of 3 stamps and 3 labels showing ARPHILA 75 emblem.
Exists imperf. Value: single with label $10; sheetlet $35.

Early Transformer, Kando Locomotive, 1902, Pylon — A555

**1975, June 10 Litho. *Perf. 12***
**2368** A555 1fo multicolored .40 .25

Hungarian Electrotechnical Association, 75th anniversary.
Exists imperf. Value $12.50.

Epée, Saber, Foil and Globe — A556

**1975, July 11**
**2369** A556 1fo multicolored .40 .25

32nd World Fencing Championships, Budapest, July 11-20.
Exists imperf. Value $10.

Souvenir Sheet

Whale Pavilion, Oceanexpo 75 — A557

**1975, July 21 Photo. *Perf. 12½***
**2370** A557 10fo gold & multi 3.00 2.75

Oceanexpo 75, International Exhibition, Okinawa, July 20, 1975-Jan. 1976.
Exists imperf. Value $30.

Dr. Agoston Zimmermann (1875-1963), Veterinarian
A558

**1975, Sept. 4 Litho. *Perf. 12***
**2371** A558 1fo brown & blue .40 .25

Exists imperf. Value $7.50.

Symbolic of 14 Cognate Languages
A559

**1975, Sept. 9**
**2372** A559 1fo gold & multi .40 .25

International Finno-Ugrian Congress.

Exists imperf. Value $6.

Voters — A560

Design: No. 2374, Map of Hungary with electoral districts.

**1975, Oct. 1**

| | | | | |
|---|---|---|---|---|
| **2373** | A560 | 1fo multicolored | .30 | .25 |
| **2374** | A560 | 1fo multicolored | .30 | .25 |

Hungarian Council System, 25th anniv.
Exist imperf. Value, set $11.

Fish and Waves (Ocean Pollution)
A561

Designs: 60f, Skeleton hand reaching for rose in water glass. 80f, Fish gasping for raindrop. 1fo, Carnation wilting in polluted soil. 1.20fo, Bird dying in polluted air. 5fo, Sick human lung and smokestack. 6fo, "Stop Pollution" (raised hand protecting globe from skeleton hand).

**1975, Oct. 16 Litho. *Perf. 11½***

| | | | | |
|---|---|---|---|---|
| **2375** | A561 | 40f multi | .25 | .25 |
| **2376** | A561 | 60f multi | .25 | .25 |
| **2377** | A561 | 80f multi | .25 | .25 |
| **2378** | A561 | 1fo multi | .25 | .25 |
| **2379** | A561 | 1.20fo multi | .25 | .25 |
| **2380** | A561 | 5fo multi | .60 | .30 |
| **2381** | A561 | 6fo multi | .85 | .40 |
| | | *Nos. 2375-2381 (7)* | 2.70 | 1.95 |

Environmental Protection.
Exist imperf. Value, set $15.

Mariska Gárdos (1885-1973)
A562

Portraits: No. 2383, Imre Mezö (1905-56). No. 2384, Imre Tarr (1900-37).

**1975, Nov. 4 Litho. *Perf. 12***

| | | | | |
|---|---|---|---|---|
| **2382** | A562 | 1fo black & red org | .25 | .25 |
| **2383** | A562 | 1fo black & red org | .25 | .25 |
| **2384** | A562 | 1fo black & red org | .25 | .25 |
| | | *Nos. 2382-2384 (3)* | .75 | .75 |

Famous Hungarians, birth anniversaries.
Exist imperf. Value, set $15.

Treble Clef, Organ and Orchestra — A563

**1975, Nov. 14**
**2385** A563 1fo multicolored .40 .25

Franz Liszt Musical Academy, centenary.
Exists imperf. Value $10.

Szigetcsep Icon — A564

Virgin and Child, 18th Century Icons: 60f, Graboc. 1fo, Esztergom. 1.50fo, Vatoped. 2.50fo, Tottos. 4fo, Gyor. 5fo, Kazan.

**1975, Nov. 25 Photo. *Perf. 12½***

**2386** A564 40f gold & multi .25 .25
**2387** A564 60f gold & multi .25 .25
**2388** A564 1fo gold & multi .25 .25
**2389** A564 1.50fo gold & multi .25 .25
**2390** A564 2.50fo gold & multi .35 .25
**2391** A564 4fo gold & multi .70 .30
**2392** A564 5fo gold & multi .90 .60
*Nos. 2386-2392 (7)* 2.95 2.15

Exist imperf. Value, set $15.

Members' Flags, Radar, Mother and Child — A565

**1975, Dec. 15 Litho. *Perf. 12***

**2393** A565 1fo multicolored .40 .25

20th anniversary of the signing of the Warsaw Treaty (Bulgaria, Czechoslovakia, German Democratic Rep., Hungary, Poland, Romania, USSR).
Exists imperf. Value $6.

Ice Hockey, Winter Olympics' Emblem — A566

Designs (Emblem and): 60f, Slalom. 80f, Ski race. 1.20fo, Ski jump. 2fo, Speed skating. 4fo, Cross-country skiing. 6fo, Bobsled. 10fo, Figure skating, pair.

**1975, Dec. 29 Photo. *Perf. 12x11½***

**2394** A566 40f silver & multi .25 .25
**2395** A566 60f silver & multi .25 .25
**2396** A566 80f silver & multi .25 .25
**2397** A566 1.20fo silver & multi .25 .25
**2398** A566 2fo silver & multi .35 .25
**2399** A566 4fo silver & multi .70 .30
**2400** A566 6fo silver & multi .90 .50
*Nos. 2394-2400 (7)* 2.95 2.05

**Souvenir Sheet**

***Perf. 12½***

**2401** A566 10fo silver & multi 3.25 3.00

12th Winter Olympic Games, Innsbruck, Austria, Feb. 4-15, 1976. No. 2401 contains one stamp (59x36mm).
Exist imperf. Value: set $15; souvenir sheet $15.

"P," 5-pengö and 500-pengö Notes — A567

**1976, Jan. 16 Litho. *Perf. 12***

**2402** A567 1fo multicolored .40 .25

Hungarian Bank Note Co., 50th anniversary.
Exists imperf. Value $9.

**Animal Type of 1974**

Young Animals: 40f, Wild boars, horiz. 60f, Squirrels. 80f, Lynx, horiz. 1.20fo, Wolves. 2fo, Foxes, horiz. 4fo, Bears. 6fo, Lions, horiz.

**1976, Jan. 26**

**2403** A542 40f multi .25 .25
**2404** A542 60f blue & multi .25 .25
**2405** A542 80f multi .25 .25
**2406** A542 1.20fo multi .25 .25
**2407** A542 2fo violet & multi .30 .25
**2408** A542 4fo yellow & multi .65 .30
**2409** A542 6fo multi .75 .40
*Nos. 2403-2409 (7)* 2.70 1.95

Exist imperf. Value, set $15.

A.G. Bell, Telephone, Molniya I and Radar — A568

**1976, Mar. 10 Litho. *Perf. 11½x12***

**2410** A568 3fo multicolored .75 .75

Centenary of first telephone call by Alexander Graham Bell, Mar. 10, 1876. Issued in sheets of 4.
Exists imperf. Value: single $4; sheetlet $15.

Battle of Kuruc-Labantz — A569

Paintings: 60f, Meeting of Rakoczi and Tamas Esze, by Endre Veszprem. 1fo, Diet of Onod, by Mor Than. 2fo, Camp of the Kurucs. 3fo, Ilona Zrinyi (Rakoczi's mother), vert. 4fo, Kuruc officers, vert. 5fo, Prince Francis II Rakoczy, by Adam Manyoki, vert. Painters of 40f, 2fo, 3fo, 4fo, are unknown.

**1976, Mar. 27 Photo. *Perf. 12½***

**2411** A569 40f gold & multi .25 .25
**2412** A569 60f gold & multi .25 .25
**2413** A569 1fo gold & multi .30 .25
**2414** A569 2fo gold & multi .60 .25
**2415** A569 3fo gold & multi .85 .25
**2416** A569 4fo gold & multi 1.25 .30
**2417** A569 5fo gold & multi 1.60 .50
*Nos. 2411-2417 (7)* 5.10 2.05

Francis II Rakoczy (1676-1735), leader of Hungarian Protestant insurrection, 300th birth anniversary.
Exist imperf. Value, set $20.

Standard Meter, Hungarian Meter Act — A570

2fo, Istvan Krusper, his vacuum balance, standard kilogram. 3fo, Interferometer & rocket.

**1976, Apr. 5 *Perf. 11½x12***

**2418** A570 1fo multicolored .25 .25
**2419** A570 2fo multicolored .30 .25
**2420** A570 3fo multicolored .50 .30
*Nos. 2418-2420 (3)* 1.05 .80

Introduction of metric system in Hungary, cent.
Exist imperf. Value, set $20.

US No. 1353 and Independence Hall, Philadelphia — A571

**Photogravure and Foil Embossed**

**1976, May 29 *Perf. 11½x12***

**2421** A571 5fo blue & multi 1.40 1.25

Interphil 76 International Philatelic Exhibition, Philadelphia, Pa., May 29-June 6. No. 2421 issued in sheets of 3 stamps and 3 labels showing bells. Size: 115x125mm.
Exists imperf. Value: single with label $8.50; sheetlet $25.

"30" and Various Pioneer Activities — A572

**1976, June 5 Litho. *Perf. 12***

**2422** A572 1fo multicolored .40 .25

Hungarian Pioneers, 30th anniversary.
Exists imperf. Value $5.

Trucks, Safety Devices, Trade Union Emblem — A573

**1976, June *Perf. 12½***

**2423** A573 1fo multicolored .40 .25

Labor safety.
Exists imperf. Value $5.

Intelstat 4, Montreal Olympic Emblem, Canadian Flag — A574

Designs: 60f, Equestrian. 1fo, Butterfly stroke. 2fo, One-man kayak. 3fo, Fencing. 4fo, Javelin. 5fo, Athlete on vaulting horse.

**1976, June 29 Photo. *Perf. 11½x12***

**2424** A574 40f dk blue & multi .25 .25
**2425** A574 60f slate grn & multi .25 .25
**2426** A574 1fo blue & multi .25 .25
**2427** A574 2fo green & multi .35 .25
**2428** A574 3fo brown & multi .45 .25
**2429** A574 4fo bister & multi .60 .30
**2430** A574 5fo maroon & multi .75 .40
*Nos. 2424-2430 (7)* 2.90 1.95

21st Olympic Games, Montreal, Canada, July 17-Aug. 1. See No. C365.
Exist imperf. Value, set $20.

Denmark No. 2 and Mermaid, Copenhagen — A575

**1976, Aug. 19 Photo. *Perf. 11½x12***

**2431** A575 3fo multicolored 1.25 1.25

HAFNIA 76 Intl. Phil. Exhib., Copenhagen, Aug. 20-29. No. 2431 issued in sheets of 3 stamps and 3 labels showing HAFNIA emblem.
Exists imperf. Value: single with label $6; sheetlet $17.50.

**Souvenir Sheet**

Discovery of Body of Lajos II, by Bertalan Székely — A576

**1976, Aug. 27 Photo. *Perf. 12½***

**2432** A576 20fo multicolored 3.00 2.75

450th anniversary of the Battle of Mohacs against the Turks.
Exists imperf. Value $17.50.

Flora, by Titian A577

**1976, Aug. 27**

| | | | | | |
|---|---|---|---|---|---|
| 2433 | A577 | 4fo gold & multi | .75 | .25 |

Titian (1477-1576), Venetian painter.
Exists imperf. Value $9.

Hussar, Herend China — A578

**1976, Sept. 28 Litho. *Perf. 12***

| | | | | |
|---|---|---|---|---|
| 2434 | A578 | 4fo multicolored | .75 | .25 |

Herend China manufacture, sesqui.
Exists imperf. Value $7.50.

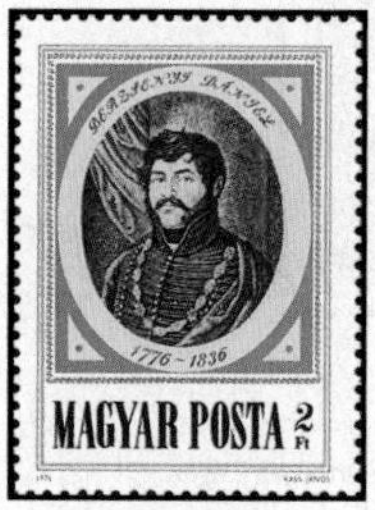


Daniel Berzsenyi (1776-1836), Poet — A579

**1976, Sept. 28**

| | | | | |
|---|---|---|---|---|
| 2435 | A579 | 2fo black, gold & yel | .40 | .25 |

Exists imperf. Value $5.

Pal Gyulai (1826-1909), Poet and Historian A580

**1976, Sept. 28**

| | | | | |
|---|---|---|---|---|
| 2436 | A580 | 2fo orange & black | .40 | .25 |

Exists imperf. Value $5.

Tuscany No. 1 and Emblem — A581

**1976, Oct. 13 Photo. *Perf. 11½x12***

| | | | | |
|---|---|---|---|---|
| 2437 | A581 | 5fo orange & multi | 1.75 | 1.75 |

ITALIA 76 International Philatelic Exhibition, Milan, Oct. 14-24. No. 2437 issued in sheets of 3 stamps and 3 labels showing Italia 76 emblem. Size: 106x127mm.

Exists imperf. Value: single with label $8; sheetlet $25.

Jozsef Madzsar, M.D. — A582

Labor leaders: No. 2439, Ignac Bogar (1876-1933), secretary of printers' union. No. 2440, Rudolf Golub (1901-44), miner.

**1976, Nov. 4 Litho. *Perf. 12***

| | | | | |
|---|---|---|---|---|
| 2438 | A582 | 1fo deep brown & red | .25 | .25 |
| 2439 | A582 | 1fo deep brown & red | .25 | .25 |
| 2440 | A582 | 1fo deep brown & red | .25 | .25 |
| | | *Nos. 2438-2440 (3)* | .75 | .75 |

Exist imperf. Value, set $15.

Science and Culture House, Georgian Dancer, Hungarian and USSR Flags A583

**1976, Nov. 4 *Perf. 12½x12***

| | | | | |
|---|---|---|---|---|
| 2441 | A583 | 1fo multicolored | .40 | .25 |

House of Soviet Science and Culture, Budapest, 2nd anniversary.
Exists imperf. Value $5.

Koranyi Sanitarium and Statue — A584

**1976, Nov. 11 *Perf. 12***

| | | | | |
|---|---|---|---|---|
| 2442 | A584 | 2fo multicolored | .40 | .25 |

Koranyi TB Sanitarium, founded by Dr. Frigyes Koranyi, 75th anniversary.
Exists imperf. Value $5.

Locomotive, 1875, Enese Station — A585

Designs: 60f, Steam engine No. 17, 1885, Rabatamasi Station. 1fo, Railbus, 1925, Fertoszentmiklos Station. 2fo, Express steam engine, Kapuvar Station. 3fo, Engine and trailer, 1926, Gyor Station. 4fo, Eight-wheel express engine, 1934, and Fertoboz Station. 5fo, Raba-Balaton engine, Sopron Station.

**1976, Nov. 26 Litho. *Perf. 12***

| | | | | |
|---|---|---|---|---|
| 2443 | A585 | 40f multicolored | .25 | .25 |
| 2444 | A585 | 60f multicolored | .25 | .25 |
| 2445 | A585 | 1fo multicolored | .25 | .25 |
| 2446 | A585 | 2fo multicolored | .30 | .25 |
| 2447 | A585 | 3fo multicolored | .50 | .25 |
| 2448 | A585 | 4fo multicolored | .70 | .35 |
| 2449 | A585 | 5fo multicolored | .90 | .50 |
| | | *Nos. 2443-2449 (7)* | 3.15 | 2.10 |

Gyor-Sopron Railroad, centenary.
Exist imperf. Value, set $20.

Poplar, Oak, Pine and Map of Hungary A586

**1976, Dec. 14**

| | | | | |
|---|---|---|---|---|
| 2450 | A586 | 1fo multicolored | .40 | .25 |

Millionth hectare of reforestation.
Exists imperf. Value $7.50.

Weight Lifting and Wrestling, Silver Medals — A587

60f, Kayak, men's single & women's double. 1fo, Horse vaulting. 4fo, Women's fencing. 6fo, Javelin. 20fo, Water polo.

**1976, Dec. 14 Photo. *Perf. 11½x12***

| | | | | |
|---|---|---|---|---|
| 2451 | A587 | 40f multicolored | .25 | .25 |
| 2452 | A587 | 60f multicolored | .25 | .25 |
| 2453 | A587 | 1fo multicolored | .25 | .25 |
| 2454 | A587 | 4fo multicolored | .75 | .30 |
| 2455 | A587 | 6fo multicolored | .90 | .50 |
| | | *Nos. 2451-2455 (5)* | 2.40 | 1.55 |

**Souvenir Sheet**

***Perf. 12½x11½***

| | | | | |
|---|---|---|---|---|
| 2456 | A587 | 20fo multicolored | 3.25 | 3.25 |

Hungarian medalists in 21st Olympic Games.
Exist imperf. Value: set $15; souvenir sheet $15.

Spoonbills — A588

Birds: 60f, White storks. 1fo, Purple herons. 2fo, Great bustard. 3fo, Common cranes. 4fo, White wagtails. 5fo, Garganey teals.

**1977, Jan. 3 Litho. *Perf. 12***

| | | | | |
|---|---|---|---|---|
| 2457 | A588 | 40f multicolored | .25 | .25 |
| 2458 | A588 | 60f multicolored | .25 | .25 |
| 2459 | A588 | 1fo multicolored | .25 | .25 |
| 2460 | A588 | 2fo multicolored | .40 | .25 |
| 2461 | A588 | 3fo multicolored | .45 | .30 |
| 2462 | A588 | 4fo multicolored | .90 | .40 |
| 2463 | A588 | 5fo multicolored | 1.10 | .50 |
| | | *Nos. 2457-2463 (7)* | 3.60 | 2.20 |

Birds from Hortobagy National Park.
Exist imperf. Value, set $17.50.

1976 World Champion Imre Abonyi Driving Four-in-hand — A589

Designs: 60f, Omnibus on Boulevard, 1870. 1fo, One-horse cab at Budapest Railroad Station, 1890. 2fo, Mail coach, Buda to Vienna route. 3fo, Covered wagon of Hajduszoboszlo. 4fo, Hungarian coach, by Jeremias Schemel, 1563. 5fo, Post chaise, from a Lübeck wood panel, 1430.

**1977, Jan. 31 Litho. *Perf. 12x11½***

| | | | | |
|---|---|---|---|---|
| 2464 | A589 | 40f multicolored | .25 | .25 |
| 2465 | A589 | 60f multicolored | .25 | .25 |
| 2466 | A589 | 1fo multicolored | .25 | .25 |
| 2467 | A589 | 2fo multicolored | .30 | .25 |
| 2468 | A589 | 3fo multicolored | .30 | .25 |
| 2469 | A589 | 4fo multicolored | .50 | .35 |
| 2470 | A589 | 5fo multicolored | .70 | .45 |
| | | *Nos. 2464-2470 (7)* | 2.55 | 2.05 |

History of the coach.
Exist imperf. Value, set $17.50.

Peacock A590

Birds: 60f, Green peacock. 1fo, Congo peacock. 3fo, Argus pheasant. 4fo, Impeyan pheasant. 6fo, Peacock pheasant.

**1977, Feb. 22 Litho. *Perf. 12***

| | | | | |
|---|---|---|---|---|
| 2471 | A590 | 40f multicolored | .25 | .25 |
| 2472 | A590 | 60f multicolored | .25 | .25 |
| 2473 | A590 | 1fo multicolored | .25 | .25 |
| 2474 | A590 | 3fo multicolored | .40 | .25 |
| 2475 | A590 | 4fo multicolored | .60 | .30 |
| 2476 | A590 | 6fo multicolored | .90 | .50 |
| | | *Nos. 2471-2476 (6)* | 2.65 | 1.80 |

Exist imperf. Value, set $17.50.

Newspaper Front Page, Factories A591

**1977, Mar. 3 Litho. *Perf. 12***

| | | | | |
|---|---|---|---|---|
| 2477 | A591 | 1fo gold, black & ver | .40 | .25 |

Nepszava newspaper, centenary.
Exists imperf. Value $5.

Flowers, by Mihaly Munkacsy A592

Flowers, by Hungarian Painters: 60f, Jakab Bogdany. 1fo, Istvan Csok, horiz. 2fo, Janos Halapy. 3fo, Jozsef Rippl-Ronai, horiz. 4fo, Janos Tornyai. 5fo, Jozsef Koszta.

**1977, Mar. 18 Photo. *Perf. 12½***

| | | | | |
|---|---|---|---|---|
| 2478 | A592 | 40f gold & multi | .25 | .25 |
| 2479 | A592 | 60f gold & multi | .25 | .25 |
| 2480 | A592 | 1fo gold & multi | .25 | .25 |
| 2481 | A592 | 2fo gold & multi | .30 | .25 |
| 2482 | A592 | 3fo gold & multi | .40 | .25 |
| 2483 | A592 | 4fo gold & multi | .55 | .30 |
| 2484 | A592 | 5fo gold & multi | .75 | .50 |
| | | *Nos. 2478-2484 (7)* | 2.75 | 2.05 |

Exist imperf. Value, set $20.

Newton and Double Convex Lens A593

**1977, Mar. 31 Litho. *Perf. 12***

| | | | | |
|---|---|---|---|---|
| **2485** | A593 | 3fo tan & multi | 1.00 | .80 |

Isaac Newton (1643-1727), natural philosopher and mathematician, 250th death anniversary. No. 2485 issued in sheets of 4 stamps and 4 blue and black labels showing illustration from Newton's "Principia Mathematica," and Soviet space rocket.

Exists imperf. Value: single with label $6; sheetlet $25.

Janos Vajda (1827-97), Poet — A594

**1977, May 2 Litho. *Perf. 12***

| | | | | |
|---|---|---|---|---|
| **2486** | A594 | 1fo green, cream & blk | .40 | .25 |

Exists imperf. Value $5.

Netherlands No. 1 and Tulips — A595

**1977, May 23 Photo. *Perf. 11½x12***

| | | | | |
|---|---|---|---|---|
| **2487** | A595 | 3fo multicolored | 1.25 | 1.25 |

AMPHILEX '77, Intl. Stamp Exhib., Amsterdam, May 26-June 5. Issued in sheets of 3 stamps + 3 labels showing Amphilex poster.

Exist imperf. Value: single with label $5; sheetlet $20.

Scene from "Wedding at Nagyrede" A596

**1977, June 14 Litho. *Perf. 12***

| | | | | |
|---|---|---|---|---|
| **2488** | A596 | 3fo multicolored | .50 | .25 |

State Folk Ensemble, 25th anniversary.

Exists imperf. Value $5.

Souvenir Sheet

Bath of Bathsheba, by Rubens — A597

**1977, June 14 Photo. *Perf. 11***

| | | | | |
|---|---|---|---|---|
| **2489** | A597 | 20fo multicolored | 5.00 | 5.00 |

Peter Paul Rubens (1577-1640), Flemish painter.

Exists imperf. Value $45.

Medieval View of Sopron, Fidelity Tower, Arms A598

**1977, June 25 Litho. *Perf. 12x11½***

| | | | | |
|---|---|---|---|---|
| **2490** | A598 | 1fo multicolored | 1.40 | 1.40 |

700th anniv. of Sopron. Printed se-tenant with label showing European Architectural Heritage medal awarded Sopron in 1975.

Exists imperf. Value, single with label $15.

Race Horse Kincsem A599

**1977, July 16 Litho. *Perf. 12***

| | | | | |
|---|---|---|---|---|
| **2491** | A599 | 1fo multicolored | 1.00 | .90 |

Sesquicentennial of horse racing in Hungary. Printed se-tenant with label showing portrait of Count Istvan Szechenyi and vignette from his 1827 book "Rules of Horse Racing in Hungary."

Exists imperf. Value, single with label $15.

German Democratic Republic No. 370 — A600

**1977, Aug. 18 Photo. *Perf. 12x11½***

| | | | | |
|---|---|---|---|---|
| **2492** | A600 | 3fo multicolored | 1.25 | 1.10 |

SOZPHILEX 77 Philatelic Exhibition, Berlin, Aug. 19-28. No. 2492 issued in sheets of 3 stamps and 3 labels showing SOZPHILEX emblem.

Exist imperf. Value: single with label $5; sheetlet $15.

Scythian Iron Bell, 6th Century B.C. — A601

Panel, Crown of Emperor Constantin Monomakhos — A602

Designs: No. 2494, Bronze candlestick in shape of winged woman, 12th-13th centuries. No. 2495, Centaur carrying child, copper aquamanile, 12th century. No. 2496, Gold figure of Christ, from 11th century Crucifix. Designs show art treasures from Hungarian National Museum, founded 1802.

**1977, Sept. 3 Litho. *Perf. 12***

| | | | | |
|---|---|---|---|---|
| **2493** | A601 | 2fo multicolored | .75 | .75 |
| **2494** | A601 | 2fo multicolored | .75 | .75 |
| **2495** | A601 | 2fo multicolored | .75 | .75 |
| **2496** | A601 | 2fo multicolored | .75 | .75 |
| *a.* | | Horiz. strip of 4, #2493-2496 | 3.00 | 3.00 |

**Souvenir Sheet**

| | | | | |
|---|---|---|---|---|
| **2497** | A602 | 10fo multicolored | 3.50 | 3.00 |

50th Stamp Day.

Exist imperf. Value: strip of 4 $15; souvenir sheet $17.50.

Sputnik A603

Spacecraft: 60f, Skylab. 1fo, Soyuz-Salyut 5. 3fo, Luna 24. 4fo, Mars 3. 6fo, Viking.

**1977, Sept. 20**

| | | | | |
|---|---|---|---|---|
| **2498** | A603 | 40f multicolored | .25 | .25 |
| **2499** | A603 | 60f multicolored | .25 | .25 |
| **2500** | A603 | 1fo multicolored | .25 | .25 |
| **2501** | A603 | 3fo multicolored | .40 | .25 |
| **2502** | A603 | 4fo multicolored | .65 | .35 |
| **2503** | A603 | 6fo multicolored | .90 | .45 |
| | | *Nos. 2498-2503 (6)* | 2.70 | 1.80 |

Space explorations, from Sputnik to Viking. See No. C375.

Exist imperf. Value, set $15.

Janos Szanto Kovacs (1852-1908), Agrarian Movement Pioneer A604

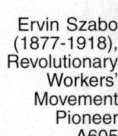

Ervin Szabo (1877-1918), Revolutionary Workers' Movement Pioneer A605

**1977, Nov. 4 Litho. *Perf. 12***

| | | | | |
|---|---|---|---|---|
| **2504** | A604 | 1fo red & black | .30 | .25 |
| **2505** | A605 | 1fo red & black | .30 | .25 |

Exist imperf. Value, set $10.

Monument to Hungarian October Revolutionists, Omsk — A606

**1977, Nov. 4**

| | | | | |
|---|---|---|---|---|
| **2506** | A606 | 1fo black & red | .40 | .25 |

60th anniv. of Russian October Revolution.

Exists imperf. Value $5.

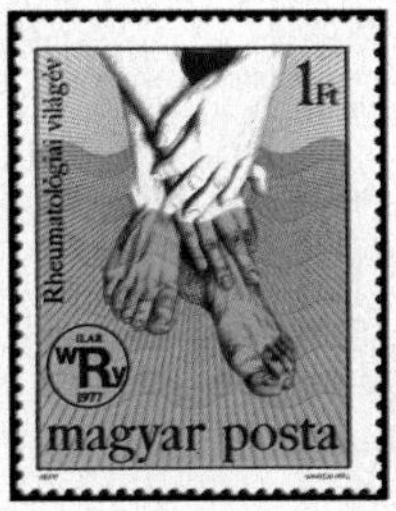


Hands and Feet Bathed in Thermal Spring — A607

**1977, Nov. 1**

| | | | | |
|---|---|---|---|---|
| **2507** | A607 | 1fo multicolored | .40 | .25 |

World Rheumatism Year.

Exists imperf. Value $7.50.

Endre Ady — A608

**1977, Nov. 22 Engr. *Perf. 12***

| | | | | |
|---|---|---|---|---|
| **2508** | A608 | 1fo violet blue | .40 | .35 |

Endre Ady (1877-1919), lyric poet. Issued in sheets of 4.

Exists imperf. Value $5. Sheetlet $25.

Lesser Panda — A609

Designs: 60f, Giant panda. 1fo, Asiatic black bear. 4fo, Polar bear. 6fo, Brown bear.

**1977, Dec. 16 Litho. *Perf. 11½x12***

| | | | | |
|---|---|---|---|---|
| **2509** | A609 | 40f yellow & multi | .25 | .25 |
| **2510** | A609 | 60f yellow & multi | .25 | .25 |
| **2511** | A609 | 1fo yellow & multi | .35 | .25 |

**2512** A609 4fo yellow & multi .75 .30
**2513** A609 6fo yellow & multi 1.00 .50
*Nos. 2509-2513 (5)* 2.60 1.55

Exist imperf. Value $17.50.

Souvenir Sheet

Flags and Ships along Intercontinental Waterway — A610

Flags: a, Austria. b, Bulgaria. c, Czechoslovakia. d, France. e, Luxembourg. f, Yugoslavia. g, Hungary. h, Fed. Rep. of Germany. i, Romania. j, Switzerland. k, USSR.

**1977, Dec. 28 Litho. *Perf. 12***

**2514** A610 Sheet of 11 8.00 7.75
***a.-k.*** 2fo, any single 1.00 1.00

European Intercontinental Waterway: Danube, Main and Rhine.
Exists imperf. Value $125.

Lancer, 17th Century A611

Hussars: 60f, Kuruts, 1710. 1fo, Baranya, 1762. 2fo, Palatine officer, 1809. 4fo, Sandor, 1848. 6fo, Trumpeter, 5th Honved Regiment, 1900.

**1978, Jan. Litho. *Perf. 11½x12***

**2515** A611 40f lilac & multi .25 .25
**2516** A611 60f yel grn & multi .25 .25
**2517** A611 1fo red & multi .25 .25
**2518** A611 2fo dull bl & multi .35 .25
**2519** A611 4fo olive bis & multi .70 .30
**2520** A611 6fo gray & multi 1.10 .50
*Nos. 2515-2520 (6)* 2.90 1.80

Exist imperf. Value, set $15.

School of Arts and Crafts A612

**1978, Mar. 31 Litho. *Perf. 12***

**2521** A612 1fo multicolored .40 .25

School of Arts and Crafts, 200th anniv.
Exists imperf. Value $6.

Soccer Players, Flags of West Germany and Poland — A613

Designs (Various Soccer Scenes and Flags): No. 2523, Hungary and Argentina. No. 2524, France and Italy. No. 2525, Tunisia and Mexico. No. 2526, Sweden and Brazil. No. 2527, Spain and Austria. No. 2528, Peru and Scotland. No. 2529, Iran and Netherlands.

Flags represent first round of contestants. 20fo, Argentina '78 emblem.

**1978, May 25 Litho. *Perf. 12***

**2522** A613 2fo multicolored .25 .25
**2523** A613 2fo multicolored .25 .25
**2524** A613 2fo multicolored .25 .25
**2525** A613 2fo multicolored .25 .25
**2526** A613 2fo multicolored .25 .25
**2527** A613 2fo multicolored .25 .25
**2528** A613 2fo multicolored .55 .30
**2529** A613 2fo multicolored .90 .40
*Nos. 2522-2529 (8)* 2.95 2.20

**Souvenir Sheet**

***Perf. 11½***

**2530** A613 20fo multicolored 3.75 3.75

Argentina '78 11th World Cup Soccer Championships, Argentina, June 2-25.
Exist imperf. Values: set $15; souvenir sheet $17.50.

Vase, Star and Glass Blower's Tube A614

**1978, May 20 Litho. *Perf. 12***

**2531** A614 1fo multicolored .40 .25

Ajka Glass Works, centenary.
Exist imperf. Value $6.

Canada No. 1 and Trillium — A615

**1978, June 2**

**2532** A615 3fo multicolored 1.00 .90

CAPEX '78, Canadian International Philatelic Exhibition, Toronto, Ont., June 9-18. Issued in sheets of 3 stamps and 3 labels showing CAPEX '78 emblem.
Exists imperf. Value: single with label $5; sheetlet $15.

Souvenir Sheets

Leif Ericson and his Ship — A616

Explorers and their ships: #2533b, Columbus. c, Vasco da Gama. d, Magellan. #2534a, Drake. b, Hudson. c, Cook. d, Peary.

**1978, June 10 Litho. *Perf. 12x11½***

**2533** Sheet of 4 3.25 3.00
***a.-d.*** A616 2fo, any single .70 .70
**2534** Sheet of 4 3.25 3.00
***a.-d.*** A616 2fo, any single .70 .70

Exist imperf. Value: set of 2 sheets $75.

Diesel Train, Pioneer's Kerchief — A617

**1978, June 10 *Perf. 12***

**2535** A617 1fo multicolored .40 .25

30th anniversary of Pioneer Railroad.
Exists imperf. Value $7.

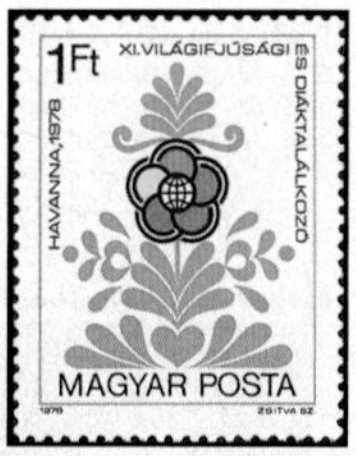


Congress Emblem as Flower — A618

Design: No. 2537, Congress emblem, "Cuba" and map of Cuba.

**1978, June**

**2536** A618 1fo multi .25 .25
**2537** A618 1fo multi .25 .25
***a.*** Pair, #2536-2537 .50 .30

11th World Youth Festival, Havana.
Exist imperf. Value $12.50.

WHO Emblem, Stylized Body and Heart — A619

**1978, Aug. 21 Litho. *Perf. 12***

**2538** A619 1fo multicolored .40 .25

Drive against hypertension.
Exists imperf. Value $7.50.

Clenched Fist, Dove and Olive Branch — A620

**1978, Sept. 1 Litho. *Perf. 12***

**2539** A620 1fo gray, red & black .40 .25

Publication of review "Peace and Socialism," 20th anniversary.
Exists imperf. Value $5.

Train, Telephone, Space Communication — A621

**1978, Sept. 8 Litho. *Perf. 12***

**2540** A621 1fo multicolored .40 .25

20th anniv. of Organization for Communication Cooperation of Socialist Countries.
Exists imperf. Value $5.

"Toshiba" Automatic Letter Sorting Machine — A622

**1978, Sept. 15 Litho. *Perf. 11½x12***

**2541** A622 1fo multicolored .50 .25

Introduction of automatic letter sorting. No. 2541 printed with se-tenant label showing bird holding letter.
Exists imperf. Value: single with label $12.50.

Eros Offering Grapes, Villa Hercules A623

Roman Mosaics Found in Hungary: No. 2543, Tiger (Villa Hercules, Budapest). No. 2544, Bird eating berries (Balacapuszta). No. 2545, Dolphin (Aquincum). 10fo, Hercules aiming at Centaur fleeing with Deianeira (Villa Hercules).

**Photogravure and Engraved**

**1978, Sept. 16 *Perf. 11½***

**2542** A623 2fo multicolored 1.50 1.25
**2543** A623 2fo multicolored 1.50 1.25
**2544** A623 2fo multicolored 1.50 1.25
**2545** A623 2fo multicolored 1.50 1.25
*Nos. 2542-2545 (4)* 6.00 5.00

**Souvenir Sheet**

**2546** A623 10fo multicolored 9.00 8.50

Stamp Day. No. 2546 contains one stamp (52x35mm).
Exist imperf. Value: set $70; souvenir sheet $125.

Count Imre Thököly — A624

**1978, Oct. 1 Photo. *Perf. 12½***

**2547** A624 1fo black & yellow .40 .25

300th anniv. of Hungary's independence movement, led by Imre Thököly (1657-1705).
Exists imperf. Value $5.

Souvenir Sheet

Hungarian Crown Jewels — A625

**1978, Oct. 10**

**2548** A625 20fo gold & multi 6.00 6.00

Return of Crown Jewels from US, 1/6/78.
Exists imperf. Value $30.

"The Red Coach" A626

**1978, Oct. 21 Litho. *Perf. 12***

| | | | | |
|---|---|---|---|---|
| **2549** | A626 | 3fo red & black | .50 | .25 |

Gyula Krudy, 1878-1933, novelist.
Exists imperf. Value $6.

St. Ladislas I Reliquary, Györ Cathedral A627

**1978, Nov. 15 *Perf. 11½x12½***

| | | | | |
|---|---|---|---|---|
| **2550** | A627 | 1fo multicolored | .40 | .25 |

Ladislas I (1040-1095), 900th anniversary of accession to throne of Hungary.
Exists imperf. Value $6.

Miklos Jurisics Statue, Köszeg — A628

**1978, Nov. 15 *Perf. 12***

| | | | | |
|---|---|---|---|---|
| **2551** | A628 | 1fo multicolored | .40 | .25 |

650th anniversary of founding of Köszeg.
Exists imperf. Value $5.

Samu Czaban and Gizella Berzeviczy — A629

**Photogravure and Engraved**

**1978, Nov. 24 *Perf. 11½x12***

| | | | | |
|---|---|---|---|---|
| **2552** | A629 | 1fo brown, buff & red | .50 | .25 |

Samu Czaban (1878-1942) and Gizella Berzeviczy (1878-1954), Communist teachers during Soviet Republic (1918-1919).
Exists imperf. Value $5.

Communist Party Emblem A630

**1978, Nov. 24 Litho. *Perf. 12***

| | | | | |
|---|---|---|---|---|
| **2553** | A630 | 1fo gray, red & blk | .40 | .25 |

Hungarian Communist Party, 60th anniv.
Exists imperf. Value $5.

Woman Cutting Bread A631

Ceramics by Margit Kovacs (1902-1976): 2fo, Woman with pitcher. 3fo, Potter.

**1978, Nov. 30 Litho. *Perf. 11½x12***

| | | | | |
|---|---|---|---|---|
| **2554** | A631 | 1fo multicolored | .25 | .25 |
| **2555** | A631 | 2fo multicolored | .30 | .25 |
| **2556** | A631 | 3fo multicolored | .70 | .60 |
| | | *Nos. 2554-2556 (3)* | 1.25 | 1.10 |

Exist imperf. Value, set $15.

Virgin and Child, by Dürer A632

Dürer Paintings: 60f, Adoration of the Kings, horiz. 1fo, Self-portrait, 1500. 2fo, St. George. 3fo, Nativity, horiz. 4fo, St. Eustatius. 5fo, The Four Apostles. 20fo, Dancing Peasant Couple, 1514 (etching).

**1979, Jan. 8 Photo. *Perf. 12½***

| | | | | |
|---|---|---|---|---|
| **2557** | A632 | 40f gold & multi | .25 | .25 |
| **2558** | A632 | 60f gold & multi | .25 | .25 |
| **2559** | A632 | 1fo gold & multi | .25 | .25 |
| **2560** | A632 | 2fo gold & multi | .30 | .25 |
| **2561** | A632 | 3fo gold & multi | .35 | .25 |
| **2562** | A632 | 4fo gold & multi | .70 | .30 |
| **2563** | A632 | 5fo gold & multi | .80 | .60 |
| | | *Nos. 2557-2563 (7)* | 2.90 | 2.15 |

**Souvenir Sheet**

**Litho.**

| | | | | |
|---|---|---|---|---|
| **2564** | A632 | 20fo buff & brown | 3.50 | 3.25 |

Albrecht Dürer (1471-1528), German painter and engraver.
Exist imperf. Value: set $15; souvenir sheet $35.

Human Rights Flame — A633

**1979, Feb. 8 Litho. *Perf. 11½x12***

| | | | | |
|---|---|---|---|---|
| **2565** | A633 | 1fo dk & lt blue | 1.25 | 1.25 |

Universal Declaration of Human Rights, 30th anniversary. No. 2565 issued in sheets of 12 stamps (3x4) and 4 labels. Alternating horizontal rows inverted.
Exists imperf. Value $10. Strip of 3 $40, Sheetlet $60.

Child at Play — A634

IYC Emblem and: No. 2567, Family. No. 2568, 3 children (international friendship).

**1979, Feb. 26 *Perf. 12***

| | | | | |
|---|---|---|---|---|
| **2566** | A634 | 1fo multicolored | .75 | .75 |
| **2567** | A634 | 1fo multicolored | .75 | .75 |
| **2568** | A634 | 1fo multicolored | 6.50 | 5.50 |
| | | *Nos. 2566-2568 (3)* | 8.00 | 7.00 |

Exist imperf. Value, set $22.50.

Soldiers of the Red Army, by Bela Uitz A635

**1979, Mar. 21 Litho. *Perf. 12***

| | | | | |
|---|---|---|---|---|
| **2569** | A635 | 1fo silver, blk & red | .40 | .25 |

60th anniv. of Hungarian Soviet Republic.
Exists imperf. Value $5.

Calvinist Church, Nyirbator — A636

**1979, Mar. 28 *Perf. 11***

| | | | | |
|---|---|---|---|---|
| **2570** | A636 | 1fo brown & yellow | .40 | .25 |

700th anniv. of Nyirbator. See No. 2601.
Exists imperf. Value $10.

Chessmen, Gold Cup, Flag — A637

**1979, Apr. 12 Litho. *Perf. 12***

| | | | | |
|---|---|---|---|---|
| **2571** | A637 | 3fo multicolored | 1.00 | .50 |

Hungarian victories in 23rd Chess Olympiad, Buenos Aires, 1978.
Exists imperf. Value $15.

Alexander Nevski Cathedral, Sofia, Bulgaria No. 1 — A638

**1979, May 18 Litho. *Perf. 11½x12***

| | | | | |
|---|---|---|---|---|
| **2572** | A638 | 3fo multicolored | .75 | .75 |

Philaserdica '79 Philatelic Exhibition, Sofia, Bulgaria, May 18-27. No. 2572 issued in sheets of 3 stamps and 3 labels showing Philaserdica emblem and arms of Sofia.
Exist imperf. Value: single with label $5.50; sheetlet $17.50.

Stephenson's Rocket, 1829, IVA '79 Emblem — A639

Railroad Development: 60f, Siemens' first electric locomotive, 1879. 1fo, "Pioneer," Chicago & Northwestern Railroad, 1836. 2fo, Orient Express, 1883. 3fo, Trans-Siberian train, 1898. 4fo, Express train on Tokaido line, 1964. 5fo, Transrapid-O5 train, exhibited 1979. 20fo, Map of European railroad network.

**1979, June 8 Litho. *Perf. 12x11½***

| | | | | |
|---|---|---|---|---|
| **2573** | A639 | 40f multi | .25 | .25 |
| **2574** | A639 | 60f multi | .25 | .25 |
| **2575** | A639 | 1fo multi | .25 | .25 |
| **2576** | A639 | 2fo multi | .30 | .25 |
| **2577** | A639 | 3fo multi | .45 | .25 |
| **2578** | A639 | 4fo multi | .60 | .45 |
| **2579** | A639 | 5fo multi | .90 | .50 |
| | | *Nos. 2573-2579 (7)* | 3.00 | 2.20 |

**Souvenir Sheet**

***Perf. 12½x11½***

| | | | | |
|---|---|---|---|---|
| **2580** | A639 | 20fo multi | 4.00 | 3.75 |

Intl. Transportation Exhibition (IVA '79), Hamburg. #2580 contains one 47x32mm stamp.
Exist imperf. Value: set $17.50; souvenir sheet $35.

Natural Gas Pipeline and Compressor A640

2fo, Lenin power station & dam, Dniepropetrovsk & pylon. 3fo, Comecon Building, Moscow, & star symbolizing 10 member states.

**1979, June 26 *Perf. 11½x12***

| | | | | |
|---|---|---|---|---|
| **2581** | A640 | 1fo multi | .25 | .25 |
| **2582** | A640 | 2fo multi | .25 | .25 |
| **2583** | A640 | 3fo multi | .40 | .25 |
| | | *Nos. 2581-2583 (3)* | .90 | .75 |

30th anniversary of the Council of Mutual Economic Assistance, Comecon.
Exist imperf. Value, set $15.

Zsigmond Moricz (1879-1942), Writer, by Jozsef Ripple-Ronai A641

**1979, June 29 *Perf. 12***

| | | | | |
|---|---|---|---|---|
| **2584** | A641 | 1fo multi | .40 | .25 |

Exists imperf. Value $5.

Town Hall, Helsinki, Finnish Flag, Moscow '80 Emblem A642

Designs (Moscow '80 Emblem and): 60f, Colosseum, Rome, Italian flag. 1fo, Asakusa Temple, Tokyo, Japanese flag. 2fo, Mexico City Cathedral, Mexican flag. 3fo, Our Lady's Church, Munich, German flag. 4fo, Skyscrapers, Montreal, Canadian flag. 5fo, Lomonosov University, Misha the bear and Soviet flag.

**1979, July 31** *Perf. 12x11½*

| | | | | |
|---|---|---|---|---|
| **2585** | A642 | 40f multi | .25 | .25 |
| **2586** | A642 | 60f multi | .25 | .25 |
| **2587** | A642 | 1fo multi | .25 | .25 |
| **2588** | A642 | 2fo multi | .25 | .25 |
| **2589** | A642 | 3fo multi | .30 | .25 |
| **2590** | A642 | 4fo multi | .40 | .30 |
| **2591** | A642 | 5fo multi | .70 | .45 |
| | | *Nos. 2585-2591 (7)* | 2.40 | 2.00 |

Pre-Olympic Year.
Exist imperf. Value, set $20.

Boy with Horse and Greyhounds, by Janos Vaszary — A643

Paintings of Horses: 60f, Coach and Five, by Karoly Lotz. 1fo, Boys on Horseback, by Celesztin Pallya. 2fo, Farewell, by Lotz. 3fo, Horse Market, by Pallya. 4fo, Wanderer, by Bela Ivanyi-Grunwald. 5fo, Ready for the Hunt, by Karoly Sterio.

**1979, Aug. 11** **Photo.** *Perf. 12½*

| | | | | |
|---|---|---|---|---|
| **2592** | A643 | 40f multi | .25 | .25 |
| **2593** | A643 | 60f multi | .25 | .25 |
| **2594** | A643 | 1fo multi | .25 | .25 |
| **2595** | A643 | 2fo multi | .25 | .25 |
| **2596** | A643 | 3fo multi | .40 | .25 |
| **2597** | A643 | 4fo multi | .50 | .30 |
| **2598** | A643 | 5fo multi | .75 | .40 |
| | | *Nos. 2592-2598 (7)* | 2.65 | 1.95 |

Exist imperf. Value, set $20.

Sturgeons, Map of Danube, "Calypso" — A644

**1979, Aug. 11**

| | | | | |
|---|---|---|---|---|
| **2599** | A644 | 3fo multi | .50 | .25 |

Environmental protection of rivers and seas.
Exists imperf. Value $6.

Pentathlon A645

**1979, Aug. 12** **Litho.** *Perf. 12*

| | | | | |
|---|---|---|---|---|
| **2600** | A645 | 2fo multi | .50 | .25 |

Pentathlon World Championship, Budapest, Aug. 12-18.
Exists imperf. Value $5.

**Architecture Type of 1979**

Design: Vasvar Public Health Center.

**1979, Aug. 15** **Litho.** *Perf. 11*

| | | | | |
|---|---|---|---|---|
| **2601** | A636 | 40f multi | .40 | .25 |

700th anniversary of Vasvar.
Exists imperf. Value $10.

Denarius of Stephen I, 1000-1038, Reverse A646

Hungarian Coins: 2fo, Copper coin of Bela III, 1172-1196. 3fo, Golden groat of King Louis the Great, 1342-1382. 4fo, Golden forint of Matthias I, 1458-1490. 5fo, Silver gulden of Wladislaw II, 1490-1516.

**Engraved and Photogravure**

**1979, Sept. 3** *Perf. 12x11½*

| | | | | |
|---|---|---|---|---|
| **2602** | A646 | 1fo multi | .25 | .25 |
| **2603** | A646 | 2fo multi | .25 | .25 |
| **2604** | A646 | 3fo multi | .35 | .25 |
| **2605** | A646 | 4fo multi | .50 | .40 |
| **2606** | A646 | 5fo multi | 1.00 | .70 |
| | | *Nos. 2602-2606 (5)* | 2.35 | 1.85 |

9th International Numismatic Congress, Berne, Switzerland.
Exist imperf. Value, set $15.

Souvenir Sheet

Unofficial Stamp, 1848 — A647

**1979, Sept. 15** **Litho.** *Perf. 12*

| | | | | |
|---|---|---|---|---|
| **2607** | A647 | 10fo dk brown, blk & red | 2.75 | 2.50 |

Stamp Day.
Exists imperf. Value $20.

Souvenir Sheet

Gyor-Sopron-Ebenfurt rail service, cent. — A648

Designs: a, Elbel Locomotive. b, Type 424 steam engine. c, "War Locomotive." d, Hydraulic diesel locomotive.

**1979, Oct. 19** **Litho.** *Perf. 12*

| | | | | |
|---|---|---|---|---|
| **2608** | A648 | Sheet of 4 | 3.25 | 3.00 |
| *a.-d.* | | A648 5fo any single | .65 | .65 |

Exists imperf. Value $27.50

Vega-Chess, by Victor Vasarely A649

**1979, Oct. 29**

| | | | | |
|---|---|---|---|---|
| **2609** | A649 | 1fo multi | .40 | .25 |

Exists imperf. Value $15.

International Savings Day — A650

**1979, Oct. 29** **Litho.** *Perf. 12*

| | | | | |
|---|---|---|---|---|
| **2610** | A650 | 1fo multi | .40 | .25 |

Exists imperf. Value $5.

Otter — A651

Wildlife Protection: 60f, Wild cat. 1fo, Pine marten. 2fo, Eurasian badger. 4fo, Polecat. 6fo, Beech marten.

**1979, Nov. 20**

| | | | | |
|---|---|---|---|---|
| **2611** | A651 | 40f multi | .25 | .25 |
| **2612** | A651 | 60f multi | .25 | .25 |
| **2613** | A651 | 1fo multi | .25 | .25 |
| **2614** | A651 | 2fo multi | .30 | .25 |
| **2615** | A651 | 4fo multi | .60 | .25 |
| **2616** | A651 | 6fo multi | .90 | .60 |
| | | *Nos. 2611-2616 (6)* | 2.55 | 1.85 |

Exist imperf. Value, set $15.

Tom Thumb, IYC Emblem A652

IYC Emblem and Fairy Tale Scenes: 60f, The Ugly Duckling. 1fo, The Fisherman and the Goldfish. 2fo, Cinderella. 3fo, Gulliver's Travels. 4fo, The Little Pigs and the Wolf. 5fo, Janos the Knight. 20fo, The Fairy Ilona.

**1979, Dec. 29** **Litho.** *Perf. 12x11½*

| | | | | |
|---|---|---|---|---|
| **2617** | A652 | 40f multi | .25 | .25 |
| **2618** | A652 | 60f multi | .25 | .25 |
| **2619** | A652 | 1fo multi | .25 | .25 |
| **2620** | A652 | 2fo multi | .35 | .25 |
| **2621** | A652 | 3fo multi | .50 | .30 |
| **2622** | A652 | 4fo multi | .70 | .30 |
| **2623** | A652 | 5fo multi | 1.00 | .60 |
| | | *Nos. 2617-2623 (7)* | 3.30 | 2.20 |

**Souvenir Sheet**

| | | | | |
|---|---|---|---|---|
| **2624** | A652 | 20fo multi | 3.75 | 3.50 |

Exist imperf. Value: set $17.50; souvenir sheet $22.50.

Trichodes Apairius and Yarrow — A653

Insects Pollinating Flowers: 60f, Bumblebee and blanketflower. 1fo, Red admiral butterfly and daisy. 2fo, Cetonia aurata and rose. 4fo, Graphosoma lineatum and petroselinum hortense. 6fo, Chlorophorus varius and thistle.

**1980, Jan. 25** **Litho.** *Perf. 12*

| | | | | |
|---|---|---|---|---|
| **2625** | A653 | 40f multi | .25 | .25 |
| **2626** | A653 | 60f multi | .25 | .25 |
| **2627** | A653 | 1fo multi | .25 | .25 |
| **2628** | A653 | 2fo multi | .35 | .25 |
| **2629** | A653 | 4fo multi | .50 | .25 |
| **2630** | A653 | 6fo multi | .75 | .30 |
| | | *Nos. 2625-2630 (6)* | 2.35 | 1.55 |

Exist imperf. Value, set $17.50.

Hanging Gardens of Semiramis, 6th Century B.C., Map showing Babylon — A654

Seven Wonders of the Ancient World (and Map): 60f, Temple of Artemis, Ephesus, 6th century B.C. 1fo, Zeus, by Phidias, Olympia. 2fo, Tomb of Maussolos, Halikarnassos, 3rd century B.C. 3fo, Colossos of Rhodes. 4fo, Pharos Lighthouse, Alexandria, 3rd century B.C. 5fo, Pyramids, 26th-24th centuries B.C.

**1980, Feb. 29** **Litho.** *Perf. 12x11½*

| | | | | |
|---|---|---|---|---|
| **2631** | A654 | 40f multi | .25 | .25 |
| **2632** | A654 | 60f multi | .25 | .25 |
| **2633** | A654 | 1fo multi | .25 | .25 |
| **2634** | A654 | 2fo multi | .30 | .25 |
| **2635** | A654 | 3fo multi | .40 | .25 |
| **2636** | A654 | 4fo multi | .60 | .35 |
| **2637** | A654 | 5fo multi | .85 | .60 |
| | | *Nos. 2631-2637 (7)* | 2.90 | 2.20 |

Exist imperf. Value, set $17.50.

Tihany Benedictine Abbey and Deed — A655

**1980, Mar. 19** **Litho.** *Perf. 12*

| | | | | |
|---|---|---|---|---|
| **2638** | A655 | 1fo multi | .40 | .25 |

Benedictine Abbey, Tihany, 925th anniversary of deed (oldest document in Hungarian).
Exists imperf. Value $5.

Gabor Bethlen, Copperplate Print — A656

**1980, Mar. 19**

| | | | | |
|---|---|---|---|---|
| **2639** | A656 | 1fo multi | .40 | .25 |

Gabor Bethlen (1580-1629), Prince of Transylvania (1613-29) and King of Hungary (1620-29).
Exists imperf. Value $5.

Easter Casket of Garamszentbenedek, 15th Century (Restoration) — A657

**1980, Mar. 19**

| | | | | | |
|---|---|---|---|---|---|
| **2640** | A657 | 1fo | shown | .25 | .25 |
| **2641** | A657 | 2fo | Three Marys | .25 | .25 |
| **2642** | A657 | 3fo | Apostle James | .35 | .35 |
| **2643** | A657 | 4fo | Thaddeus | .55 | .55 |
| **2644** | A657 | 5fo | Andrew | .75 | .55 |
| | | | *Nos. 2640-2644 (5)* | 2.15 | 1.95 |

Exist imperf. Value, set $15.

Liberation from Fascism, 35th Anniversary A658

**1980, Apr. 3 Litho. *Perf. 12***

**2645** A658 1fr multi .40 .25

Exists imperf. Value $5.

Jozsef Attila, Poet and Lyricist — A659

**1980, Apr. 11**

**2646** A659 1fo rose car & olive .40 .25

Exists imperf. Value $5.
See No. 2675.

Hungarian Postal Museum, 50th anniv. — A660

**1980, Apr. 28 *Perf. 11½x12***

**2647** A660 1fo multi 1.90 1.50

Features Hungary No. 386a.
Exists imperf. Value $20.

Two Pence Blue, Mounted Guardsman, London 1980 Emblem — A661

**1980, Apr. 30 *Perf. 11½x12***

**2648** A661 3fo multi 1.00 1.00

London 1980 International Stamp Exhibition, May 6-14. No. 2648 issued in sheets of 3 stamps and 3 labels showing London 1980 emblem and arms of city. Size: 104x125mm.
Exists imperf. Value: single with label $5; sheetlet $15.

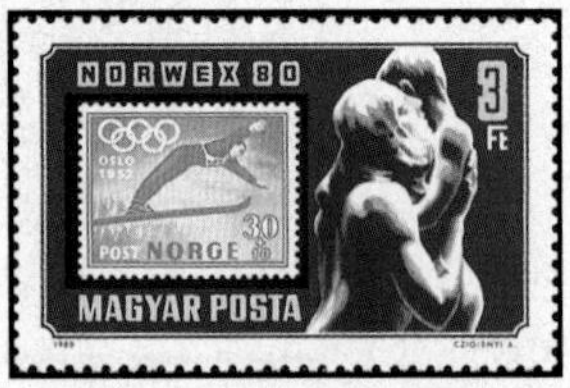


Norway No. B51, Mother with Child, by Gustav Vigeland — A662

**1980, June 9 Litho. *Perf. 11½x12***

**2649** A662 3fo multi 1.00 1.00

NORWEX '80 Stamp Exhibition, Oslo, June 13-22. No. 2649 issued in sheets of 3 stamps and 3 labels showing NORWEX emblem. Size: 108x125mm.
Exists imperf. Value: single with label $5; sheetlet $15.

Margit Kaffka (1880-1918), Writer — A663

**1980, June 9 *Perf. 12***

**2650** A663 1fo blk & pur, *cr* .40 .25

Exists imperf. Value $6.

Zoltan Schönherz (1905-42), Anti-fascist Martyr — A664

**1980, July 25 Litho.**

**2652** A664 1fo multi .40 .25

Exists imperf. Value $5.

Dr. Endre Hogyes and Congress Emblem A665

**1980, July 25**

**2653** A665 1fo multi .40 .25

28th International Congress of Physiological Sciences, Budapest, Dr. Hogyes (1847-1906) first described equilibrium reflex-curve and modified Pasteur's rabies vaccine.
Exists imperf. Value $5.

Decanter, c. 1850 — A666

**1980, Sept. Litho. *Perf. 12***

| | | | | | |
|---|---|---|---|---|---|
| **2654** | A666 | 1fo | shown | .25 | .25 |
| **2655** | A666 | 2fo | Decorated glass | .35 | .35 |
| **2656** | A666 | 3fo | Stem glass | .65 | .65 |
| | | | *Nos. 2654-2656 (3)* | 1.25 | 1.25 |

**Souvenir Sheet**

**2657** A666 10fo Pecs glass 2.50 2.25

53rd Stamp Day.

Exist imperf. Value: set $12.50; souvenir sheet $15.

Bertalan Por, Self-portrait A667

**1980, Nov. 4 Litho. *Perf. 12***

**2658** A667 1fo Artist (1880-1964) .40 .25

Exists imperf. Value $5.

Graylag Goose — A668

**1980, Nov. 11 *Perf. 11½x12***

| | | | | | |
|---|---|---|---|---|---|
| **2659** | A668 | 40f | shown | .25 | .25 |
| **2660** | A668 | 60f | Black-crowned night heron | .25 | .25 |
| **2661** | A668 | 1fo | Shoveler | .25 | .25 |
| **2662** | A668 | 2fo | Chlidonias leucopterus | .30 | .25 |
| **2663** | A668 | 4fo | Great crested grebe | .60 | .30 |
| **2664** | A668 | 6fo | Black-necked stilt | 1.00 | .50 |
| | | | *Nos. 2659-2664 (6)* | 2.65 | 1.80 |

**Souvenir Sheet**

**2665** A668 20fo Great white heron 4.25 4.00

European Nature Protection Year. No. 2665 contains one stamp (37x59mm).

Exist imperf. Value: set $22.50; souvenir sheet $30.

Souvenir Sheet

Dove on Map of Europe — A669

**1980, Nov. 11 *Perf. 12½x11½***

**2666** A669 20fo multi 4.50 4.00

European Security and Cooperation Conference, Madrid.
Exists imperf. Value $30.

Johannes Kepler and Model of his Theory — A670

**1980, Nov. 21 Litho. *Perf. 12***

**2667** A670 1fo multi .50 .25

Johannes Kepler (1571-1630), German astronomer, 350th anniversary of death. No. 2667 printed se-tenant with label showing rocket and satellites orbiting earth.
Exists imperf. Value, single with label $12.50.

Karoly Kisfaludy (1788-1830), Poet and Dramatist A671

**1980, Nov. 21**

**2668** A671 1fo brn red & dull brn .40 .25

Exists imperf. Value $5.

UN Headquarters, New York — A672

UN membership, 25th anniversary.

**Photogravure and Engraved**

**1980, Dec. 12 *Perf. 11½x12***

| | | | | | |
|---|---|---|---|---|---|
| **2669** | A672 | 40f | shown | .25 | .25 |
| **2670** | A672 | 60f | Geneva headquarters | .25 | .25 |
| **2671** | A672 | 1fo | Vienna headquarters | .25 | .25 |
| **2672** | A672 | 2fo | UN & Hungary flags | .30 | .25 |
| **2673** | A672 | 4fo | UN, Hungary arms | .55 | .35 |
| **2674** | A672 | 6fo | World map | .90 | .55 |
| | | | *Nos. 2669-2674 (6)* | 2.50 | 1.90 |

Exist imperf. Value, set $20.

**Attila Type of 1980**

Ferenc Erdei (1910-71), economist & statesman.

**1980, Dec. 23 Litho. *Perf. 12***
**2675** A659 1fo dk green & brown .40 .25

Exists imperf. Value $5.

Bela Szanto — A674

**1981, Jan. 31 Litho. *Perf. 12***
**2676** A674 1fo multi .40 .25

Bela Szanto (1881-1951), labor movement leader.
Exists imperf. Value $5.
See Nos. 2698, 2724, 2767.

Count Lajos Batthyany A675

**1981, Feb. 14**
**2677** A675 1fo multi .40 .25

Count Lajos Batthyany (1806-1849), prime minister, later executed.
Exists imperf. Value $6.

Bela Bartok (1881-1945), Composer A677

Design: b, Cantata Profana illustration.

**1981, Mar. 25 Litho. *Perf. 12½***
**2685** Sheet of 2 2.50 2.50
***a.-b.*** A677 10fo any single 1.25 1.25

Exists imperf. Value $20.

Telephone Exchange System Cent. — A678

**1981, Apr. 29 Litho. *Perf. 12***
**2686** A678 2fo multi .40 .25

Exists imperf. Value $5.

Belling Stag — A679

**1981, Apr. 29**
**2687** A679 2fo multi .40 .25

Exists imperf. Value $5.

Flag of the House of Arpad, 11th Cent. A680

**1981, Apr. 29**
**2688** A680 40f shown .25 .25
**2689** A680 60f Hunyadi family, 15th cent. .25 .25
**2690** A680 1fo Gabor Bethlen, 1600 .25 .25
**2691** A680 2fo Ferenc Rakoczi II, 1716 .25 .25
**2692** A680 4fo Honved, 1848 .60 .25
**2693** A680 6fo Troop flag, 1919 .80 .35
*Nos. 2688-2693 (6)* 2.40 1.60

Exist imperf. Value, set $15.

Red Cross and Ambulance Vehicles A681

Map of Europe and J. Henry Dunant (Red Cross Founder) — A682

**1981, May 4**
**2694** A681 2fo multi .40 .25

**Souvenir Sheet**

***Perf. 12½x11½***

**2695** A682 20fo multi 3.00 3.00

Hungarian Red Cross cent. (2fo); 3rd European Red Cross Conf., Budapest, May 4-7 (20fo).
Exist imperf. Value: single $5; souvenir sheet $22.50.

Souvenir Sheet

1933 WIPA Exhibition Seals — A683

**1981, May 15 *Perf. 12x12½***
**2696** Sheet of 4 2.75 2.75
***a.-d.*** A683 5fo any single .65 .65

WIPA 1981 Phil. Exhib., Vienna, May 22-31.
Exists imperf. Value $20.

Stephenson and his Nonpareil — A684

**1981, June 12 Litho. *Perf. 12***
**2697** A684 2fo multi .40 .25

George Stephenson (1781-1848), British railroad engineer, birth bicentenary.
Exists imperf. Value $6.

**Famous Hungarians Type**

Bela Vago (1881-1939), anti-fascist martyr.

**1981, Aug. 7 Litho. *Perf. 12***
**2698** A674 2fo ocher & brn ol .40 .25

Exists imperf. Value $5.

Alexander Fleming (1881-1955), Discoverer of Penicillin — A686

**1981, Aug. 7**
**2699** A686 2fo multi .40 .25

Exists imperf. Value $7.50.

Bridal Chest A687

Designs: Bridal chests.

**1981, Sept. 12 Litho. *Perf. 12***
**2700** A687 1fo Szentgal, 18th cent. .25 .25
**2701** A687 2fo Hodmezovasarhely, 19th cent. .30 .25

**Souvenir Sheet**

**2702** A687 10fo Bacs County, 17th cent. 1.75 1.75

54th Stamp Day. No. 2702 contains one stamp (44x25mm).
Exist imperf. Values: Nos. 2700-2701 $12.50; No. 2702 $20.

Calvinist College, Papa, 450th Anniv. A688

**1981, Oct. 3 Litho. *Perf. 12***
**2703** A688 2fo multi .40 .25

Exists imperf. Value $5.

World Food Day — A689

**1981, Oct. 16**
**2704** A689 2fo multi .40 .25

Exists imperf. Value $6.

Passenger Ship Rakoczi, 1964, No. 1834 — A690

Sidewheelers and Hungarian stamps.

**1981, Nov. 25 *Perf. 12x11½***
**2705** A690 1fo Franz I, #1828 .25 .25
**2706** A690 1fo Arpad, #1829 .25 .25
**2707** A690 2fo Szechenyi, #1830 .30 .25
**2708** A690 2fo Grof Szechenyi Istvan, #1831 .30 .25
**2709** A690 4fo Sofia, #1832 .65 .30
**2710** A690 6fo Felszabadulas, #1833 .95 .50
**2711** A690 8fo shown 1.25 .65
*Nos. 2705-2711 (7)* 3.95 2.45

**Souvenir Sheet**

***Perf. 13***

**2712** A690 20fo Hydrofoil Solyom, #1830 3.00 3.00

European Danube Commission, 125th anniv.
Exist imperf. Value: set $20; souvenir sheet $25.

Souvenir Sheet

Natl. Costumes — A691

***Perf. 12½x11½***

**1981, Nov. 18 Litho.**
**2713** Sheet of 4 2.00 1.90
***a.*** A691 1fo Slovakian .25 .25
***b.*** A691 2fo German .40 .35
***c.*** A691 3fo Croatian .60 .60
***d.*** A691 4fo Romanian .80 .75

Exists imperf. Value $20.

Christmas 1981 — A692

Sculptures: 1fo, Mary Nursing the Infant Jesus, by Margit Kovacs. 2fo, Madonna of Csurgo.

**1981, Dec. 4 *Perf. 12½x11½***
**2714** A692 1fo multi .25 .25
**2715** A692 2fo multi .40 .25

Exist imperf. Value, set $10.

Pen Pals, by Norman Rockwell A693

Norman Rockwell Illustrations.

**1981, Dec. 29 *Perf. 11½x12***
**2716** A693 1fo shown .25 .25
**2717** A693 2fo Courting Under the Clock at Midnight .25 .25

**2718** A693 2fo Maiden Voyage .25 .25
**2719** A693 4fo Threading the Needle .45 .25
*Nos. 2716-2719,C435-C437 (7)* 3.25 2.65

Exist imperf. Value, set (7) $17.50.

Souvenir Sheet

La Toilette, by Pablo Picasso (1881-1973) — A694

**1981, Dec. 29 Litho.** ***Perf. 11½***
**2720** A694 20fo multicolored 3.50 3.50

Exists imperf. Value $50.

25th Anniv. of Worker's Militia A695

**1982, Jan. 26 Litho.** ***Perf. 12***
**2721** A695 1fo Shooting practice .25 .25
**2722** A695 4fo Members, 3 generations .50 .35

Exist imperf. Value, set $10.

10th World Trade Union Congress — A696

**1982, Feb. 12 Litho.** ***Perf. 12x11½***
**2723** A696 2fo multicolored .40 .25

Exists imperf. Value $5.

**Famous Hungarians Type**

Gyula Alpri (1882-1944), anti-fascist martyr.

**1982, Mar. 24** ***Perf. 12***
**2724** A674 2fo multicolored .40 .25

Exists imperf. Value $5.

Robert Koch — A698

**1982, Mar. 24 Litho.** ***Perf. 12***
**2725** A698 2fo multicolored .40 .25

TB Bacillus centenary.
Exists imperf. Value $6.

1982 World Cup — A699

Designs: Hungary in competition with other World Cup teams.
#2733: a, Barcelona Stadium. b, Madrid Stadium.

**1982, Apr. 16** ***Perf. 11***
**2726** A699 1fo Egypt, 1934 .25 .25
**2727** A699 1fo Italy, 1938 .25 .25
**2728** A699 2fo Germany, 1954 .25 .25
**2729** A699 2fo Mexico, 1958 .25 .25
**2730** A699 4fo England, 1962 .45 .25
**2731** A699 6fo Brazil, 1966 .70 .40
**2732** A699 8fo Argentina, 1978 .90 .55
*Nos. 2726-2732 (7)* 3.05 2.20

**Souvenir Sheet**

**2733** Sheet of 2 3.00 3.00
***a.-b.*** A699 10fo any single 1.40 1.40

No. 2733 contains 44x44mm stamps.
Exist imperf. Value: set $17; souvenir sheet $20.

European Table Tennis Championship, Budapest, Apr. 17-25 — A700

**1982, Apr. 16 Litho.** ***Perf. 11½x12***
**2734** A700 2fo multi .40 .25

Exists imperf. Value $5.

Roses A701

**1982, Apr. 30** ***Perf. 12***
**2735** A701 1fo Pascali .25 .25
**2736** A701 1fo Michele Meilland .25 .25
**2737** A701 2fo Diorama .30 .25
**2738** A701 2fo Wendy Cussons .30 .25
**2739** A701 3fo Blue Moon .40 .25
**2740** A701 3fo Invitation .40 .25
**2741** A701 4fo Tropicana .60 .30
*Nos. 2735-2741 (7)* 2.50 1.80

**Souvenir Sheet**

**2742** A701 10fo Bouquet 2.50 2.50

No. 2742 contains one stamp (34x59mm, perf. 11).
Exist imperf. Value: set $17.50; souvenir sheet $30.

25 Years of Space Travel — A702

**1982, May 18 Photo.** ***Perf. 11½***
**2743** A702 1fo Columbia shuttle, 1981 .25 .25
**2744** A702 1fo Armstrong, Apollo 11, 1969 .25 .25
**2745** A702 2fo A. Leonov, Voskhod 2, 1965 .30 .25
**2746** A702 2fo Yuri Gagarin, Vostok .30 .25
**2747** A702 4fo Laika, Sputnik 2, 1957 .55 .35
**2748** A702 4fo Sputnik I, 1957 .55 .35
**2749** A702 6fo Space researcher K.E. Tsiolkovsky .90 .50
*Nos. 2743-2749 (7)* 3.10 2.20

Exist imperf. Value, set $15.

A703

**1982, May 7 Litho.** ***Perf. 12***
**2750** A703 2fo multi .50 .25

George Dimitrov (1882-1947), 1st prime minister of Bulgaria. SOZPHILEX '82 Stamp Exhib., Sofia, Bulgaria, May. No. 2750 se-tenant with label showing Bulgarian 1300th anniv. emblems.
Exists imperf. Value, with label $12.50.

Diosgyor paper mill, bicent. — A704

**1982, May 27 Litho.** ***Perf. 12x11½***
**2751** A704 2fo multi .40 .25

Exists imperf. Value $5.

First Rubik's Cube World Championship, Budapest, June 5 — A705

**1982, June 4** ***Perf. 11½x12***
**2752** A705 2fo multi .40 .25

Exists imperf. Value $6.

Souvenir Sheet

George Washington, by F. Kemmelmeyer — A706

Washington's 250th Birth Anniv.: a, Michael Kovats de Fabricy (1724-1779), Cavalry Commandant, by Sandor Finta.

**1982, July 2 Litho.** ***Perf. 11***
**2753** A706 Sheet of 2 2.50 2.50
***a.-b.*** 5fo any single .75 .75

Exists imperf. Value $17.50.

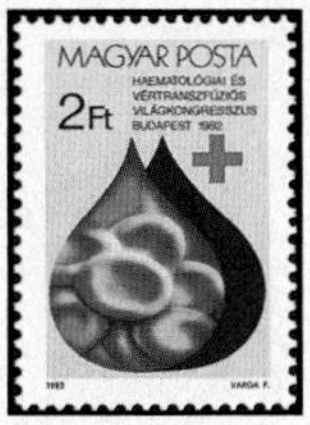


World Hematology Congress, Budapest — A707

**1982, July 30** ***Perf. 12½x11½***
**2754** A707 2fo multi .40 .25

Exists imperf. Value $6.

Zirc Abbey, 800th Anniv. — A708

**1982, Aug. 19** ***Perf. 11½x12***
**2755** A708 2fo multi .40 .25

Exists imperf. Value $5.

KNER Printing Office, Gyoma, Centenary — A709

**1982, Sept. 23 Litho.** ***Perf. 12x11½***
**2756** A709 2fo Emblem .40 .25

Exists imperf. Value $5.

AGROFILA '82 Intl. Agricultural Stamp Exhibition, Godollo — A710

**1982, Sept. 24** ***Perf. 11½x12***
**2757** A710 5fo Map 1.00 .95

Issued in sheets of 3 stamps and 3 labels showing Godollo Agricultural University, emblem. Size: 109x127mm.
Exist imperf. Value: single with label $5; sheetlet $15.

Public Transportation Sesquicentennial — A711

**1982, Oct. 5 Litho.** ***Perf. 12x11½***
**2758** A711 2fo multi .40 .25

Exists imperf. Value $15.

Vuk and a Bird — A712

Scenes from Vuk the Fox Cub, Cartoon by Attila Dargay.

**1982, Nov. 11** *Perf. 12½*

| | | | |
|---|---|---|---|
| **2759** | A712 1fo shown | .25 | .25 |
| **2760** | A712 1fo Dogs | .25 | .25 |
| **2761** | A712 2fo Rooster | .25 | .25 |
| **2762** | A712 2fo Owl | .25 | .25 |
| **2763** | A712 4fo Geese | .50 | .30 |
| **2764** | A712 6fo Frog | .70 | .55 |
| **2765** | A712 8fo Master fox | 1.00 | .70 |
| | *Nos. 2759-2765 (7)* | 3.20 | 2.55 |

Exist imperf. Value, set $17.50.

Engineering Education Bicentenary A713

**1982, Oct. 13** *Perf. 12*

| | | | |
|---|---|---|---|
| **2766** | A713 2fo Budapest Poly-technical Univ. | .40 | .25 |

Exists imperf. Value $5.

**Famous Hungarians Type**

Gyorgy Boloni (1882-1959), writer and journalist.

**1982, Oct. 29**

| | | | |
|---|---|---|---|
| **2767** | A674 2fo multi | .40 | .25 |

Exists imperf. Value $5.

October Revolution, 65th Anniv. — A715

**1982, Nov. 5** **Litho.** *Perf. 11½x12*

| | | | |
|---|---|---|---|
| **2768** | A715 5fo Lenin | .75 | .40 |

Exists imperf. Value $6.

Works of Art in Hungarian Chapel, Vatican — A716

Designs: No. 2769, St. Stephen, first King of Hungary (1001-1038). No. 2770, Pope Sylvester II making donation to St. Stephen. No. 2771, Pope Callixtus III ordering noon victory bell ringing by St. John of Capistrano, 1456. No. 2772, Pope Paul VI showing Cardinal Lekai location of Hungarian Chapel. No. 2773, Pope John Paul II consecrating chapel, 1980. No. 2774, Madonna and Child. Nos. 2769, 2774 sculptures by Imre Varga; others by Amerigo Tot. Nos. 2770-2773, size 37x18mm, in continuous design in block of 4 between Nos. 2769 and 2774.

**1982, Nov. 30** *Perf. 12x11½*

| | | | |
|---|---|---|---|
| **2769** | A716 2fo multi | .40 | .40 |
| **2770** | A716 2fo multi | .40 | .40 |
| **2771** | A716 2fo multi | .40 | .40 |
| **2772** | A716 2fo multi | .40 | .40 |
| **2773** | A716 2fo multi | .40 | .40 |
| **2774** | A716 2fo multi | .40 | .40 |
| *a.* | Block of 6, #2769-2774 | 2.60 | 2.60 |

Exist imperf. Value, block $15.

Souvenir Sheet

Zoltan Kodaly (1882-1967), Composer — A717

**1982, Dec. 16** *Perf. 11½*

| | | | |
|---|---|---|---|
| **2775** | A717 20fo multi | 2.75 | 2.75 |

Exists imperf. Value $17.50.

A718

*Perf. 12½x11½*

**1982, Dec. 16** **Litho.**

| | | | |
|---|---|---|---|
| **2776** | A718 2fo multi | .40 | .25 |

New Year 1983.
Exists imperf. Value $5.

A719

Design: Johann Wolfgang Goethe (1749-1832), German poet, by Heinrich Kolbe.

**1982, Dec. 29** *Perf. 11½x12½*

**Souvenir Sheet**

| | | | |
|---|---|---|---|
| **2777** | A719 20fo multi | 2.75 | 2.75 |

Exists imperf. Value $27.50.

10th Anniv. of Postal Code — A720

**1983, Jan. 24** *Perf. 11½x12*

| | | | |
|---|---|---|---|
| **2778** | A720 2fo multi | .40 | .25 |

Exists imperf. Value $5.

3rd Budapest Spring Festival, Mar. 18-27 A721

**1983, Mar. 18** **Litho.** *Perf. 12x11½*

| | | | |
|---|---|---|---|
| **2779** | A721 2fo Ship of Peace, by Engre Szasz | .40 | .25 |

Exists imperf. Value $5.

Gyula Juhasz (1883-1937), Poet — A722

**1983, Apr. 15** *Perf. 12*

| | | | |
|---|---|---|---|
| **2780** | A722 2fo multi | .40 | .25 |

Exists imperf. Value $5.

City of Szentgotthard, 800th Anniv. — A723

**1983, May 4** **Litho.** *Perf. 11½*

| | | | |
|---|---|---|---|
| **2781** | A723 2fo Monastery, seal, 1489 | .40 | .25 |

Exists imperf. Value $5.

Malomto Lake, Tapolca — A724

**1983, May 17** *Perf. 11½x12*

| | | | |
|---|---|---|---|
| **2782** | A724 5fo multi | .80 | .80 |

TEMBAL '83 Intl. Topical Stamp Exhibition, Basel, May 21-29. Issued in sheets of 3 stamps and 3 labels.
Exists imperf. Value: single with label $4; sheetlet $15.

Souvenir Sheet

5th Interparliamentary Union Conference on European Cooperation, Budapest, May 30-June 5 — A725

**1983, May 30** **Litho.** *Perf. 12½*

| | | | |
|---|---|---|---|
| **2783** | A725 20fo Budapest Parliament | 3.50 | 3.25 |

Exists imperf. Value $20.

Jeno Hamburger (1883-1936) A726

**1983, May 31** *Perf. 12*

| | | | |
|---|---|---|---|
| **2784** | A726 2fo multi | .45 | .25 |

Exists imperf. Value $5.

Lady with Unicorn, by Raphael (1483-1517) A727

Paintings: No. 2786, Joan of Aragon. No. 2787, Granduca Madonna. No. 2788, Madonna and Child with St. John. 4fo, La Muta. 6fo, La Valeta. 8fo, La Fornarina. 20fo, Esterhazy Madonna.

*Perf. 11½x12½*

**1983, June 29** **Litho.**

| | | | |
|---|---|---|---|
| **2785** | A727 1fo multi | .25 | .25 |
| **2786** | A727 1fo multi | .25 | .25 |
| **2787** | A727 2fo multi | .25 | .25 |
| **2788** | A727 2fo multi | .25 | .25 |
| **2789** | A727 4fo multi | .45 | .30 |
| **2790** | A727 6fo multi | .65 | .30 |
| **2791** | A727 8fo multi | .75 | .45 |
| | *Nos. 2785-2791 (7)* | 2.85 | 2.05 |

**Souvenir Sheet**

| | | | |
|---|---|---|---|
| **2792** | A727 20fo multi | 3.00 | 3.00 |

No. 2792 contains one stamp (24x37mm).
Exist imperf. Value: set $17.50; souvenir sheet $17.50.

Simon Bolivar (1783-1830) A728

**1983, July 22** **Litho.** *Perf. 12*

| | | | |
|---|---|---|---|
| **2793** | A728 2fo multi | .40 | .25 |

Exists imperf. Value $5.

Istvan Vagi (1883-1940), Anti-fascist Martyr A729

**1983, July 22** ***Perf. 11½x12½***

**2794** A729 2fo multi .45 .25

Exists imperf. Value $5.

68th World Esperanto Congress, Budapest, July 30-Aug. 6 — A730

**1983, July 29** ***Perf. 12***

**2795** A730 2fo multi .40 .25

Exists imperf. Value $6.

Souvenir Sheet

Martin Luther (1483-1546) — A731

**1983, Aug. 12** ***Perf. 12½***

**2796** A731 20fo multi 2.75 2.50

Exists imperf. Value $20.

Birds — A732

Designs: Protected birds of prey and World Wildlife Fund emblem

**1983, Aug. 18** ***Perf. 11½x12***

**2797** A732 1fo Aquila heliaca .25 .25
**2798** A732 1fo Aquila pomarina .25 .25
**2799** A732 2fo Haliaetus albicilla .75 .25
**2800** A732 2fo Falco vespertinus .75 .25
**2801** A732 4fo Falco cherrug 1.00 .30
**2802** A732 6fo Buteo lagopus 1.25 .35
**2803** A732 8fo Buteo buteo 1.50 .75
*Nos. 2797-2803 (7)* 5.75 2.40

Exist imperf. Value, set $20.

29th Intl. Apicultural Congress, Budapest, Aug. 25-31 — A733

**1983, Aug. 25** ***Perf. 12***

**2804** A733 1fo Bee collecting pollen .40 .25

Exists imperf. Value $6.

Fruit, by Bela Czobel (1883-1976) — A734

**1983, Sept. 15** **Litho.** ***Perf. 12x11½***

**2805** A734 2fo multi .40 .25

Exists imperf. Value $5.

World Communications Year — A735

No. 2806, Telecommunications, Earth Satellite. No. 2807, Intersputnik Earth Station. 2fo, TMM-81 Telephone Service. 3fo, Intelligent Terminal System. 5fo, OCR Optical Reading Instrument. 8fo, Teletext. 20fo, Molniya Communications Satellite.

**1983, Oct. 7** **Litho.** ***Perf. 11½x12***

**2806** A735 1fo multi .25 .25
**2807** A735 1fo multi .25 .25
**2808** A735 2fo multi .25 .25
**2809** A735 3fo multi .40 .25
**2810** A735 5fo multi .70 .40
**2811** A735 8fo multi 1.10 .65
*Nos. 2806-2811 (6)* 2.95 2.05

**Souvenir Sheet**

***Perf. 12x12½***

**2812** A735 20fo multi 3.00 3.00

Exist imperf. Value: set $15; souvenir sheet $15.

34th Intl. Astronautical Federation Congress — A736

**1983, Oct. 10** **Photo.** ***Perf. 12***

**2813** A736 2fo multi .75 .25

Exists imperf. Value $5.

SOZPHILEX 83, Moscow — A737

**1983, Oct. 14** **Litho.** ***Perf. 12***

**2814** A737 2fo Kremlin .50 .50

Issued in sheets of 3 stamps and 3 labels showing emblem. Size: 101x133mm.

Exists imperf. Value: single with label $5; sheetlet $16.

Mihaly Babits (1883-1941), Poet and Translator — A738

**1983, Nov. 25**

**2815** A738 2fo multi .40 .25

Exists imperf. Value $5.

Souvenir Sheet

European Security and Cooperation Conference, Madrid — A739

***Perf. 12½x11½***

**1983, Nov. 10** **Litho.**

**2816** A739 20fo multi 3.75 3.75

Exists imperf. Value $17.50.

1984 Winter Olympics, Sarajevo — A740

Designs: Ice dancers representing the seven phases of a figure cut.

**1983, Dec. 22** **Litho.** ***Perf. 12x12½***

**2817** A740 1fo Emblem upper right .25 .25
**2818** A740 1fo Emblem upper left .25 .25
**2819** A740 2fo Arms extended .25 .25
**2820** A740 2fo Arms bent .25 .25
**2821** A740 4fo Man looking down .55 .30
**2822** A740 4fo Girl looking up .55 .30
**2823** A740 6fo multi .85 .45
*a.* Strip of 7, #2817-2823 3.00 2.00

**Souvenir Sheet**

***Perf. 12½***

**2824** A740 20fo multi 3.00 3.00

No. 2824 contains one 49x39mm stamp.

Exist imperf. Value: strip $20; souvenir sheet $20.

Christmas A741

Designs: 1fo, Madonna with Rose, Kassa, 1500. 2fo, Altar piece, Csikmenasag, 1543.

**1983, Dec. 13** **Litho.** ***Perf. 11½x12***

**2825** A741 1fo multi .25 .25
**2826** A741 2fo multi .50 .25

Exist imperf. Value, set $10.

Resorts and Spas — A742

**1983, Dec. 18**

**2827** A742 1fo Zanka, Lake Balaton .25 .25
**2828** A742 2fo Hajduszoboszlo .30 .25
**2829** A742 5fo Heviz .70 .35
*Nos. 2827-2829 (3)* 1.25 .85

Exist imperf. Value, set $15.

Virgin with Six Saints, by Giovanni Battista Tiepolo — A743

Rest During Flight into Egypt, by Giovanni Domenico Tiepolo — A744

Paintings Stolen and Later Recovered, Museum of Fine Arts, Budapest: b, Esterhazy Madonna, by Raphael. c, Portrait of Giorgione, 16th cent. d, Portrait of a Woman, by Tintoretto. e, Pietro Bempo, by Raphael. f, Portrait of a Man, by Tintoretto.

**1984, Feb. 16** ***Perf. 12½x12***

**2839** Sheet of 7 3.75 3.75
*a.-f.* A743 2fo multi .35
*g.* A744 8fo multi 1.50

Exists imperf. Value $35.

Energy Conservation A745

**1984, Mar. 30** **Litho.** ***Perf. 11½x12***

**2840** A745 1fo multi .40 .25

Exists imperf. Value $5.

Sandor Korosi Csoma (1784-1842), Master of Tibetan Philology A746

**1984, Mar. 30** ***Perf. 11½x12½***

**2841** A746 2fo multi .40 .25

Stamps with silver inscription and with back inscription "Gift of the Hungarian Post" issued to members of Natl. Fed. of Hungarian Philatelists. Value $1.50.

Exists imperf. Value $5.

Miniature Sheet

No. 1900 — A747

Designs: b, No. 1346. c, No. 1259.

**1984, Apr. 20 Litho. *Perf. 12x11½***
**2842** Sheet of 3 + 3 labels 2.75 2.75
***a.-c.*** A747 4fo multi .70

Espana '84; Ausipex '84; Philatelia '84. Exists imperf. Value $20.

Post-Roman Archaeological Discoveries — A748

#2843, Round gold disc hair ornaments, Rakamaz. #2844, Saber belt plates, Szolnok-Strazsahalom and Galgocz. #2845, Silver disc hair ornaments, Sarospatak. #2846, Swords. 4fo, Silver and gold bowl, Ketpo. 6fo, Bone walking stick handles, Hajdudorog and Szabadbattyan. 8fo, Ivory saddle bow, Izsak; bit, stirrups, Muszka.

**1984, May 15 *Perf. 12***
**2843** A748 1fo dk brn & tan .25 .25
**2844** A748 1fo dk brn & tan .25 .25
**2845** A748 2fo dk brn & tan .25 .25
**2846** A748 2fo dk brn & tan .25 .25
**2847** A748 4fo dk brn & tan .50 .25
**2848** A748 6fo dk brn & tan .75 .30
**2849** A748 8fo dk brn & tan 1.00 .40
*Nos. 2843-2849 (7)* 3.25 1.95

Exist imperf. Value, set $15.

View of Cracow — A749

**1984, May 21 Litho. *Perf. 12½x11½***
**2850** A749 2fo multi .25 .25

Permanent Committee of Posts and Telecommunications, 25th Session, Cracow. Exists imperf. Value $5.

Butterflies A750

**1984, June 7 *Perf. 11½x12***
**2851** A750 1fo Epiphille dilecta .25 .25
**2852** A750 1fo Agra sara .25 .25
**2853** A750 2fo Morpho cypris .25 .25
**2854** A750 2fo Ancylusis formossissima .25 .25
**2855** A750 4fo Danaus chrysippus .50 .25
**2856** A750 6fo Catagramma cynosura .75 .30
**2857** A750 8fo Ornithoptera paradisea 1.00 .45
*Nos. 2851-2857 (7)* 3.25 2.00

Exist imperf. Value, set $20.

A751

A752

Archer, by Kisfaludy Strobl (1884-1975).

**1984, July 26 Litho. *Perf. 12½x11½***
**2858** A751 2fo multicolored .30 .25

Exists imperf. Value $5.

**1984, July 26**
**2859** A752 2fo multicolored .25 .25

Akos Hevesi (1884-1937), revolutionary. See Nos. 2884-2885, 2910, 2915, 2962. Exists imperf. Value $5.

Kepes Ujsag Peace Festival A753

Aerobatic Championship A754

**1984, Aug. 3 Litho. *Perf. 12½x11½***
**2860** A753 2fo Map, building .60 .25

Exists imperf. Value $5.

**1984, Aug. 14**
**2861** A754 2fo Plane, map .30 .25

Exists imperf. Value $5.

Horse Team World Championship, Szilvasvarad, Aug. 17-20 — A755

**1984, Aug. 17 *Perf. 12***
**2862** A755 2fo Horse-drawn wagon .30 .25

Exists imperf. Value $5.

Budapest Riverside Hotels — A756

**1984, Sept.**
**2863** A756 1fo Atrium Hyatt .25 .25
**2864** A756 2fo Duna Intercontinental .25 .25
**2865** A756 4fo Forum .50 .25
**2866** A756 4fo Thermal Hotel, Margaret Isld. .50 .25
**2867** A756 5fo Hilton .70 .35
**2868** A756 8fo Gellert 1.00 .50
*Nos. 2863-2868 (6)* 3.20 1.85

**Souvenir Sheet**

**2869** A756 20fo Hilton, diff. 2.75 2.75

Exist imperf. Value: set $15; souvenir sheet $20.

14th Conference of Postal Ministers, Budapest — A757

**1984, Sept. 10 *Perf. 12½x11½***
**2870** A757 2fo Building, post horn .25 .25

Exists imperf. Value $5.

57th Stamp Day A758

**1984, Sept. 21 *Perf. 12***
**2871** A758 1fo Four-handled vase, Zsolnay .25 .25
**2872** A758 2fo Platter, vert. .80 .25

**Souvenir Sheet**

**2872A** A758 10fo #19 on cover 2.50 2.50

No. 2872A contains one stamp (44x27mm, perf. 11).
Exist imperf. Value: set $12.50; souvenir sheet $20.

Edible Mushrooms A759

**Photogravure and Engraved**

**1984, Oct. *Perf. 12x11½***
**2873** A759 1fo Boletus edulis .35 .25
**2874** A759 1fo Marasmius oreades .35 .25
**2875** A759 2fo Morchella esculenta .60 .25
**2876** A759 2fo Agaricus campester .60 .25
**2877** A759 3fo Macrolepiota procera .90 .25
**2878** A759 3fo Cantharellus cibarius .90 .25
**2879** A759 4fo Armillariella mellea 1.25 .30
*Nos. 2873-2879 (7)* 4.95 1.80

Exist imperf. Value, set $15.

Budapest Opera House Centenary — A760

**1984, Sept. 27 *Perf. 12x11½***
**2880** A760 1fo Fresco by Mor Than .25 .25
**2881** A760 2fo Hallway .25 .25
**2882** A760 5fo Auditorium .65 .30
*Nos. 2880-2882 (3)* 1.15 .80

**Souvenir Sheet**

**2883** A760 20fo Building 2.75 2.75

No. 2883 contains one stamp (49x40mm, perf. 12½).
Exist imperf. Value: set $15; souvenir sheet $20.

**Famous Hungarians Type of 1984**

#2884, Bela Balazs, writer (1884-1949); #2885, Kato Haman, labor leader (1884-1936).

**1984, Dec. 3 Litho. *Perf. 12½x11½***
**2884** A752 2fo multi .25 .25
**2885** A752 2fo multi .25 .25

Exist imperf. Value, set $10.

Madonna and Child, Trensceny A763

**1984, Dec. 17 Litho. *Perf. 11½x12***
**2886** A763 1fo multi .30 .30

Exists imperf. Value $5.

Owls — A764

**Photogravure and Engraved**

**1984, Dec. 28 *Perf. 12½x11½***
**2887** A764 1fo Athene Noctua .25 .25
**2888** A764 1fo Tyto alba .25 .25
**2889** A764 2fo Strix aluco .25 .25
**2890** A764 2fo Asio otus .25 .25
**2891** A764 4fo Nyctea scadiaca .45 .30
**2892** A764 6fo Strix uralensis .75 .40
**2893** A764 8fo Bubo bubo .90 .50
*Nos. 2887-2893 (7)* 3.10 2.20

Exist imperf. Value, set $15.

Torah Crown, Buda — A765

19th Cent. Art from Jewish Museum, Budapest.

**1984, Dec. Litho. *Perf. 12***
**2894** A765 1fo shown .25 .25
**2895** A765 1fo Chalice, Moscow .25 .25
**2896** A765 2fo Torah shield, Vienna .25 .25
**2897** A765 2fo Chalice, Warsaw .25 .25
**2898** A765 4fo Container, Augsburg .55 .25
**2899** A765 6fo Candlestick holder, Warsaw .80 .35
**2900** A765 8fo Money box, Pest 1.10 .45
*Nos. 2894-2900 (7)* 3.45 2.05

Exist imperf. Value, set $15.

### Souvenir Sheet

Hungarian Olympic Committee, 90th Anniv. — A766

**1985, Jan. 2 Photo.** ***Perf. 12x12½***

**2901** A766 20fo Long jump 3.00 3.00

Exists imperf. Value $20.

Novi Sad, Yugoslavia — A767

Danube Bridges: No. 2903, Baja. No. 2904, Arpad Bridge, Budapest. No. 2905, Bratislava, Czechoslovakia. 4fo, Reichsbrucke, Vienna. 6fo, Linz, Austria. 8fo, Regensburg, Federal Rep. of Germany. 20fo, Elizabeth Bridge, Budapest, and map.

**1985, Feb. 12 Litho.** ***Perf. 12x11½***

| | | | | | |
|---|---|---|---|---|---|
| **2902** | A767 | 1fo | multi | .25 | .25 |
| **2903** | A767 | 1fo | multi | .25 | .25 |
| **2904** | A767 | 2fo | multi | .25 | .25 |
| **2905** | A767 | 2fo | multi | .25 | .25 |
| **2906** | A767 | 4fo | multi | .50 | .25 |
| **2907** | A767 | 6fo | multi | .75 | .40 |
| **2908** | A767 | 8fo | multi | 1.00 | .45 |
| | *Nos. 2902-2908 (7)* | | | 3.25 | 2.10 |

### Souvenir Sheet

***Perf. 12½***

**2909** A767 20fo multi 3.00 3.00

Exist imperf. Value: set $15; souvenir sheet $20.

### Famous Hungarians Type of 1984

Design: Laszlo Rudas (1885-1950), communist philosopher.

**1985, Feb. 21** ***Perf. 12½x11½***

**2910** A752 2fo gold & brn .25 .25

Exists imperf. Value $5.

Intl. Women's Day, 75th Anniv. A769

**1985, Mar. 5 Photo.** ***Perf. 11½x12½***

**2911** A769 2fo gold & multi .30 .25

Exists imperf. Value $5.

OLYMPHILEX '85, Lausanne A770

**1985, Mar. 14 Litho.** ***Perf. 11½x12***

| | | | | | |
|---|---|---|---|---|---|
| **2912** | A770 | 4fo | No. B81 | .50 | .25 |
| **2913** | A770 | 5fo | No. B82 | .65 | .30 |

Exist imperf. Value, set $10.

### Souvenir Sheet

Liberation of Hungary From German Occupation Forces, 40th Anniv. — A771

Design: Liberty Bridge, Budapest and silhouette of the Liberation Monument on Gellert Hill illuminated by fireworks.

**1985, Mar. 28** ***Perf. 12½***

**2914** A771 20fo multi 2.75 2.75

Exists imperf. Value $20.

### Famous Hungarians Type of 1984

Design: Gyorgy Lukacs (1885-1971) communist philosopher, educator.

**1985, Apr. 12** ***Perf. 12½x11½***

**2915** A752 2fo gold & brn .40 .25

Exists imperf. Value $5.

Totfalusi Bible, 300th Anniv. — A773

**1985, Apr. 25** ***Perf. 12***

**2916** A773 2fo gold & black .40 .25

1st Bible printed in Hungarian by Nicolas Totfalusi Kis (1650-1702), publisher, in 1685. Exists imperf. Value $5.

Lorand Eotvos Univ., 350th Anniv. — A774

Design: Archbishop Peter Pazmany (1570-1637), founder.

**1985, May 14**

**2917** A774 2fo magenta & gray .50 .25

No. 2917 printed se-tenant with label picturing obverse and reverse of university commemorative medal. Exists imperf. Value, with label $5.

26th European Boxing Championships, Budapest — A775

**1985, May 25**

**2918** A775 2fo multi .50 .25

Exists imperf. Value $6.

Intl. Youth Year — A776

**1985, May 29** ***Perf. 11½x12***

| | | | | | |
|---|---|---|---|---|---|
| **2919** | A776 | 1fo | Girl's soccer | .25 | .25 |
| **2920** | A776 | 2fo | Windsurfing | .25 | .25 |
| **2921** | A776 | 2fo | Aerobic exercise | .25 | .25 |
| **2922** | A776 | 4fo | Karate | .45 | .25 |
| **2923** | A776 | 4fo | Go-kart racing | .45 | .25 |
| **2924** | A776 | 5fo | Hang gliding | .65 | .25 |
| **2925** | A776 | 6fo | Skateboarding | .70 | .35 |
| | *Nos. 2919-2925 (7)* | | | 3.00 | 1.85 |

Exist imperf. Value, set $15.

Electro-magnetic High-speed Railway — A777

EXPO '85, Tsukuba, Japan: futuristic technology.

**1985, May 29** ***Perf. 12x11½***

| | | | | | |
|---|---|---|---|---|---|
| **2926** | A777 | 2fo | shown | .30 | .25 |
| **2927** | A777 | 4fo | Fuyo (robot) Theater | .70 | .25 |

Exist imperf. Value, set $12.50.

Audubon Birth Bicentenary A778

Audubon illustrations

**1985, June 19** ***Perf. 12***

| | | | | | |
|---|---|---|---|---|---|
| **2928** | A778 | 2fo | Colaptes cafer | .30 | .25 |
| **2929** | A778 | 2fo | Bombycilla garrulus | .30 | .25 |
| **2930** | A778 | 2fo | Dryocopus pileatus | .30 | .25 |
| **2931** | A778 | 4fo | Icterus galbula | .55 | .30 |
| | *Nos. 2928-2931,C446-C447 (6)* | | | 2.90 | 1.90 |

Exist imperf. Value, set (6) $20.

Mezohegyes Stud Farm, Bicent. — A779

Horses: No. 2932, Nonius-36, 1883, a dark chestnut. No. 2933, Furioso-23, 1889, a light chestnut. No. 2934, Gidrian-1, 1935, a blond breed. No. 2935, Ramses-3, 1960, gray sporting horse. No. 2936, Krozus-1, 1970, chestnut sporting horse.

**1985, June 28**

| | | | | | |
|---|---|---|---|---|---|
| **2932** | A779 | 1fo | multi | .25 | .25 |
| **2933** | A779 | 2fo | multi | .25 | .25 |
| **2934** | A779 | 4fo | multi | .55 | .25 |
| **2935** | A779 | 4fo | multi | .55 | .25 |
| **2936** | A779 | 6fo | multi | .85 | .35 |
| | *Nos. 2932-2936 (5)* | | | 2.45 | 1.35 |

Exist imperf. Value, set $15.

Prevention of Nuclear War — A780

Design: Illustration of a damaged globe and hands, by Imre Varga (b. 1923), 1973 Kossuth prize-winner.

**1985, June 28** ***Perf. 11½x12***

**2937** A780 2fo multi .50 .25

Intl. Physician's Movement for the Prevention of Nuclear War, 5th Congress. Exists imperf. Value $6.

European Music Year — A781

Composers and instruments: 1fo, George Frideric Handel (1685-1759), kettle drum, horn. 2fo, Johann Sebastian Bach (1685-1750), Thomas Church organ. No. 2940, Luigi Cherubini (1760-1842), harp, bass viol, baryton. No. 2941, Frederic Chopin (1810-1849), piano, 1817. 5fo, Gustav Mahler (1860-1911), pardessus de viole, kettle drum, double horn. 6fo, Erkel Ferenc (1810-1893), bass tuba, violin.

**1985, July 10** ***Perf. 11***

| | | | | | |
|---|---|---|---|---|---|
| **2938** | A781 | 1fo | multi | .25 | .25 |
| **2939** | A781 | 2fo | multi | .25 | .25 |
| **2940** | A781 | 4fo | multi | .50 | .25 |
| **2941** | A781 | 4fo | multi | .50 | .25 |
| **2942** | A781 | 5fo | multi | .65 | .25 |
| **2943** | A781 | 6fo | multi | .75 | .30 |
| | *Nos. 2938-2943 (6)* | | | 2.90 | 1.55 |

Exist imperf. Value, set $17.50.

Souvenir Sheet

12th World Youth Festival, Moscow — A782

**1985, July 22** *Perf. 12½*
**2944** A782 20fo Emblem, Red Square 2.75 2.50

Exists imperf. Value $27.50.

Souvenir Sheet

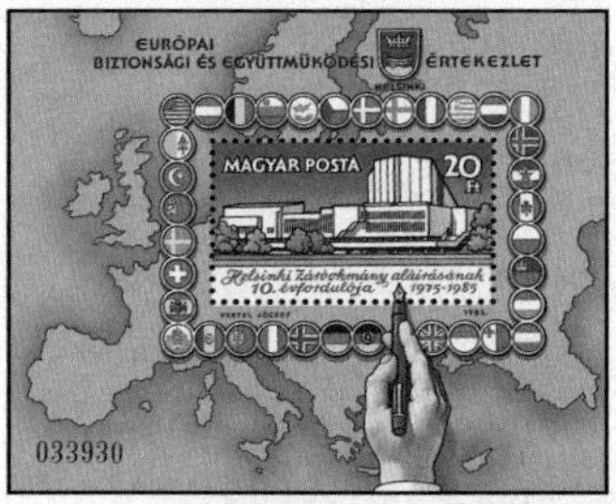


Helsinki Agreement, 10th Anniv. — A783

**1985, Aug. 1** *Perf. 11*
**2945** A783 20fo Finlandia Hall, Helsinki 3.00 3.00

Exists imperf. Value $27.50.

World Tourism Day — A784

*Perf. 12½x11½*
**1985, Sept. 27** **Litho.**
**2946** A784 2fo Key, globe, heart .30 .25

Exists imperf. Value $5.

COMNET '85 — A785

**1985, Oct. 1** *Perf. 11½*
**2947** A785 4fo Computer terminal .60 .30

3rd Computer Sciences Conference, Budapest, Oct. 1-4.

Exists imperf. Value $5.

Souvenir Sheet

Danube River, Budapest Bridges — A786

**1985, Oct. 15** *Perf. 12*
**2948** A786 20fo multi 3.50 3.50

European Security and Cooperation Conference and Cultural Forum, Budapest, Oct. 15-Nov. 25. Exists inscribed "Kuturalis Forum Resztvevoi Tiszteletere" in gold on front and "Gift of the Hungarian Post" on back. Not valid for postage.

Exists imperf. Value $30.

16-17th Century Ceramics — A787

1fo, Faience water jar and dispenser, 1609. 2fo, Tankard, 1670. 10fo, Hexagonal medicine jar, 1774.

**1985, Oct. 18** *Perf. 12½x11½*
**2949** A787 1fo multi .25 .25
**2950** A787 2fo multi .80 .25

**Souvenir Sheet**

**2951** A787 10fo multi 1.75 1.75

EUROPHILEX '85, Oct. 14-31.

Exist imperf. Value: set $10; souvenir sheet $20.

Italy No. 799, view of Rome — A788

**1985, Oct. 21** *Perf. 12x11½*
**2952** A788 5fo multi .90 .90

Italia '85, Rome, Oct. 25-Nov. 3.

Issued in sheets of 3 stamps and 3 labels showing emblem.

Exists imperf. Value: single with label $5.50; sheetlet $17.50.

UN, 40th Anniv. — A789

**1985, Oct. 24** *Perf. 11½x12*
**2953** A789 4fo Dove, globe, emblem .50 .30

Exists imperf. Value $5.

Indigenous Lilies — A790

**Photogravure and Engraved**

**1985, Oct. 28** *Perf. 12x11½*
**2954** A790 1fo Lilium bulbiferum .25 .25
**2955** A790 2fo Lilium martagon .25 .25
**2956** A790 2fo Erythronium dens-canis .25 .25
**2957** A790 4fo Fritillaria meleagris .55 .25
**2958** A790 4fo Lilium tigrinum .55 .25
**2959** A790 5fo Hemerocallis lilio-asphodelus .70 .30
**2960** A790 6fo Bulbocodium vernum .85 .35
*Nos. 2954-2960 (7)* 3.40 1.90

Exists imperf. Value, set $20.

Christmas 1985 — A791

**1985, Nov. 6** **Litho.** *Perf. 13½x13*
**2961** A791 2fo Youths caroling .30 .25

Exists imperf. Value $5.

**Famous Hungarians Type of 1984**

Design: Istvan Ries (1885-1950), Minister of Justice (1949), labor movement.

**1985, Nov. 11** *Perf. 12½x11½*
**2962** A752 2fo gold & ol brn .25 .25

Exists imperf. Value $5.

Motorcycle Centenary — A793

**Photogravure & Engraved**

**1985, Dec. 28** *Perf. 11½x12*
**2963** A793 1fo Fantic Sprinter, 1984 .25 .25
**2964** A793 2fo Suzuki Katana GSX, 1983 .25 .25
**2965** A793 2fo Harley-Davidson Duo-Glide, 1960 .25 .25
**2966** A793 4fo Rudge-Whitworth, 1935 .45 .25
**2967** A793 4fo BMW R47, 1927 .45 .25
**2968** A793 5fo NSU, 1910 .60 .25
**2969** A793 6fo Daimler, 1885 .70 .25
*Nos. 2963-2969 (7)* 2.95 1.75

Exist imperf. Value, set $18.

Bela Kun (1886-1939), Communist Party Founder — A794

*Perf. 12½x11½*
**1986, Feb. 20** **Litho.**
**2970** A794 4fo multi .50 .30

Exist imperf. Value $5.

Souvenir Sheet

US Shuttle Challenger — A795

**1986, Feb. 21** *Perf. 11½*
**2971** A795 20fo multi 3.25 3.25

Memorial to the US astronauts who died when the Challenger exploded during takeoff, Jan. 28.

Exist imperf. Value $20.

Halley's Comet — A796

#2972, US ICE satellite, dinosaurs. #2973, USSR Vega and Bayeaux tapestry detail, 1066, France. #2974, Japanese Suisei and German engraving, 1507. #2975, European Space Agency Giotto and The Three Magi, tapestry by Giotto. #2976, USSR Astron and Apianis constellation, 1531. #2977, US space shuttle and Edmond Halley.

*Perf. 11½x13½*
**1986, Feb. 14** **Litho.**
**2972** A796 2fo multi .25 .25
**2973** A796 2fo multi .25 .25
**2974** A796 2fo multi .25 .25
**2975** A796 4fo multi .45 .25
**2976** A796 4fo multi .45 .25
**2977** A796 6fo multi .80 .35
*Nos. 2972-2977 (6)* 2.45 1.60

Exist imperf. Value, set $17.50.

Seeing-eye Dog, Red Cross A797

Soccer Players in Blue and Red Uniforms A798

*Perf. 12½x11½*
**1986, Mar. 20** **Litho.**
**2978** A797 4fo multi .50 .25

Assistance for the blind.

Exists imperf. Value $12.50.

**1986, Apr. 2** *Perf. 11*

**Color of Uniforms**

**2979** A798 2fo shown .25 .25
**2980** A798 2fo blue & green .25 .25
**2981** A798 4fo red & black .55 .25
**2982** A798 4fo yellow & red .55 .25
**2983** A798 4fo yellow & green .55 .25
**2984** A798 6fo orange & white .75 .30
*Nos. 2979-2984 (6)* 2.90 1.55

### Souvenir Sheet

*Perf. 12½*

**2985** A798 20fo Victors 3.50 3.50

1986 World Cup Soccer Championships, Mexico. No. 2979 contains one stamp (size: 41x32mm). Also exists with added inscription "In honor of the winner . . ." and red control number. Value $90.

Exist imperf. Value: set $17.50; souvenir sheet $17.50.

Buda Castle Cable Railway Station Reopening — A799

**1986, Apr. 30** *Perf. 11½x12*

**2986** A799 2fo org, brn & pale yel .40 .25

Exists imperf. Value $5.

A800

AMERIPEX '86, Chicago, May 22-June 1: a, Yankee doodle rose. b, America rose. c, George Washington, statue by Gyula Bezeredy (1858-1935), Budapest.

**1986, Apr. 30** *Perf. 12½x11½*

### Souvenir Sheet

| | | | |
|---|---|---|---|
| **2987** | Sheet of 3 | 3.25 | 3.00 |
| *a.-b.* | A800 5fo any single | .75 | .75 |
| *c.* | A800 10fo multi | 1.50 | 1.50 |

Size of No. 2987c: 27x74mm.

Exists imperf. Value $25.

A801

**1986, May 6** *Perf. 11½x12*

**2988** A801 4fo Folk dolls .50 .30

Hungary Days in Tokyo.

Exists imperf. Value $5.

Andras Fay (1786-1864), Author, Politician — A802

### Lithographed and Engraved

**1986, May 29** *Perf. 12*

**2989** A802 4fo beige & fawn .65 .30

Printed se-tenant with label picturing First Hungarian Savings Bank Union, founded by Fay.

Exists imperf. Value, with label $12.50.

Automobile, Cent. A803

#2990, 1961 Ferrari Tipo 156, 1985 race car. #2991, 1932 Alfa Romeo Tipo B, 1984 race car. #2992, 1936 Volkswagen, 1986 Porsche 959. #2993, 1902 Renault 14CV, 1985 Renault 5 GT Turbo. #2994, 1899 Fiat 3½, 1985 Fiat Ritmo. 6fo, 1886 Daimler, 1986 Mercedes-Benz 230SE.

**1986, July 24** **Litho.** *Perf. 12*

| | | | | |
|---|---|---|---|---|
| **2990** | A803 2fo multi | .25 | .25 |
| **2991** | A803 2fo multi | .25 | .25 |
| **2992** | A803 2fo multi | .25 | .25 |
| **2993** | A803 4fo multi | .55 | .25 |
| **2994** | A803 4fo multi | .55 | .25 |
| **2995** | A803 6fo multi | .85 | .35 |
| | *Nos. 2990-2995 (6)* | 2.70 | 1.60 |

Exists imperf. Value, set $17.50.

Wasa, 1628, Warship — A804

**1986, Aug. 15** **Litho.** *Perf. 11½x12*

**2996** A804 2fo multi .70 .70

STOCKHOLMIA '86, 8/28-9/7. Printed se-tenant with label (size: 27x34mm) picturing exhibition emblem. Printed in sheets of 3.

Exists imperf. Value: single with label $6; sheetlet $20.

14th Intl. Cancer Congress, Budapest — A805

Design: Moritz Kaposi (1837-1902), Austrian cancer researcher.

**1986, Aug. 21** *Perf. 12½x11½*

**2997** A805 4fo multicolored .50 .30

Exists imperf. Value $9.

Recapture of Buda Castle, by Gyula Benzcur (1844-1920) — A806

**1986, Sept. 2** *Perf. 12*

**2998** A806 4fo multicolored .60 .30

Recapture of Buda from the Turks, 300th anniv.

Exists imperf. Value $6.

Tranquility — A807

Hope — A808

Stamp Day: Paintings by Endre Szasz.

**1986, Sept. 5**

| | | | |
|---|---|---|---|
| **2999** | A807 2fo shown | .40 | .25 |
| **3000** | A807 2fo Confidence | .40 | .25 |

### Souvenir Sheet

*Perf. 11½*

**3001** A808 10fo shown 2.00 2.00

Exist imperf. Value: set $15; souvenir sheet $25.

5th Intl. Conference on Oriental Carpets, Vienna and Budapest A809

**1986, Sept. 17** **Litho.** *Perf. 11*

**3002** A809 4fo Anatolia crivelli, 15th cent. .60 .30

Exists imperf. Value $5.

Franz Liszt, Composer A810

**1986, Oct. 21** **Engr.** *Perf. 12*

**3003** A810 4fo grayish green .50 .30

Exists imperf. Value $5.

Intl. Peace Year — A811

**1986, Oct. 24** **Litho.**

**3004** A811 4fo multicolored .75 .30

No. 3004 printed se-tenant with label.

Exists imperf. Value, with label $20.

### Souvenir Sheet

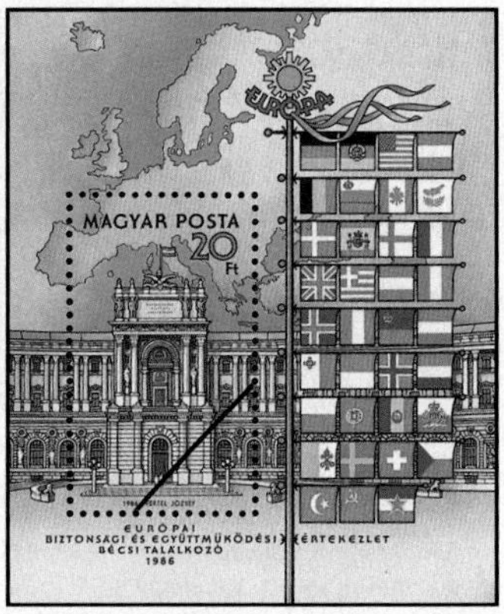


Hofburg Palace, Vienna, and Map — A812

**1986, Nov. 4** *Perf. 11*

**3005** A812 20fo multicolored 3.00 2.75

European Security and Cooperation Conference, Vienna.

Exists imperf. Value $30.

Fruits A813

### Photogravure & Engraved

**1986, Nov. 25** *Perf. 12x11½*

| | | | |
|---|---|---|---|
| **3006** | A813 2fo Sour cherries | .25 | .25 |
| **3007** | A813 2fo Apricots | .25 | .25 |
| **3008** | A813 4fo Peaches | .50 | .25 |
| **3009** | A813 4fo Raspberries | .50 | .25 |
| **3010** | A813 4fo Apples | .50 | .25 |
| **3011** | A813 6fo Grapes | .80 | .35 |
| | *Nos. 3006-3011 (6)* | 2.80 | 1.60 |

Exist imperf. Value, set $17.50.

Natl. Heroes — A814

Designs: No. 3012, Jozseph Pogany (1886-1939), journalist, martyr. No. 3013, Ferenc Munnich (1886-1967), prime minister, 1958-61.

**1986** **Litho.** *Perf. 12½x11½*

| | | | |
|---|---|---|---|
| **3012** | A814 4fo multi | .65 | .30 |
| **3013** | A814 4fo multi | .65 | .30 |

Issued: No. 3012, Nov. 6; No. 3013, Nov. 14.

Exist imperf. Value, set $10.

World Communist Youth Fed., 12th Congress A815

**1986, Nov. 21** *Perf. 12*

**3014** A815 4fo multi .50 .30

Exist imperf. Value $5.

Castles — A816

2fo, Forgach, Szecseny. 3fo, Savoya, Rackeve. 4fo, Batthyany, Kormend. 5fo, Szechenyi, Nagycenk. 6fo, Rudnyanszky, Nagyteteny. 7fo, Esterhazy, Papa. 8fo, Szapary, Buk. 10fo, Festetics, Keszthely. 12fo, Dory Castle, Mihalyi. 20fo, Brunswick, Martonvasar. 30fo, De la Motte, Nosvaj. 40fo, L'Huillier-Coborg, Edeleny. 50fo, Teleki-Degenfeld, Szirak. 70fo, Magochy, Pacin. 100fo, Eszterhazy, Fertod.

***Perf. 12x11½, 11½x12½ (7fo)***

**1986-91** **Litho.**

| | | | | | |
|---|---|---|---|---|---|
| **3015** | A816 | 2fo multi | | .25 | .25 |
| **3016** | A816 | 3fo multi | | .25 | .25 |
| **3017** | A816 | 4fo multi | | .25 | .25 |
| **3018** | A816 | 5fo multi | | .30 | .25 |
| **3019** | A816 | 6fo multi | | .35 | .25 |
| **3020** | A816 | 7fo multi | | .50 | .30 |
| **3021** | A816 | 8fo multi | | .50 | .30 |
| **3022** | A816 | 10fo multi | | .85 | .40 |
| **3023** | A816 | 12fo multi | | .90 | .50 |
| **3024** | A816 | 20fo multi | | 1.75 | .75 |
| **3025** | A816 | 30fo multi | | 2.25 | 1.10 |
| **3026** | A816 | 40fo multi | | 3.00 | 1.60 |
| **3027** | A816 | 50fo multi | | 4.00 | 1.90 |
| **3028** | A816 | 70fo multi | | 5.00 | 2.75 |
| **3029** | A816 | 100fo multi | | 8.00 | 4.00 |
| | | *Nos. 3015-3029 (15)* | | 28.15 | 14.85 |

The 7fo, 12fo are inscribed "Magyarorszag."
Issued: 2fo-6fo, 8fo, 11/28; 10fo, 20fo-30fo, 100fo, 5/28/87; 40fo-70fo, 7/30/87; 7fo, 6/27/91; 12fo, 9/6/91.
Exist imperf. Value, set $175.
For overprint see No. 3320.

Festetics Castle, Keszthely — A816a

**1989-92** **Litho. & Engr.** ***Perf. 12***

**3030** A816a 10fo multi 1.50 .85

**Litho.**

**3031** A816a 15fo multi 1.10 .65

The 15fo is inscribed "Magyarorszag."
Issued: 10fo, Feb. 28; 15fo, Mar. 27, 1992.
No. 3030 exist imperf. Value $110.

Wildlife Conservation A817

**1986, Dec. 15** ***Perf. 12***

| | | | | |
|---|---|---|---|---|
| **3035** | A817 2fo | Felis silvestris | .30 | .25 |
| **3036** | A817 2fo | Lutra lutra | .30 | .25 |
| **3037** | A817 2fo | Mustela erminea | .30 | .25 |
| **3038** | A817 4fo | Sciurus vulgaris | .55 | .30 |
| **3039** | A817 4fo | Erinaceus concolor | .55 | .30 |
| **3040** | A817 6fo | Emys orbicularis | .80 | .40 |
| | | *Nos. 3035-3040 (6)* | 2.80 | 1.75 |

Exist imperf. Value, set $17.50.

Portraits of Hungarian Kings in the Historical Portrait Gallery — A818

King and reign: No. 3041, St. Steven, 997-1038. No. 3042, Geza I, 1074-1077. No. 3043, St. Ladislas, 1077-1095. No. 3044, Bela III, 1172-1196. No. 3045, Bela IV, 1235-1270.

**1986, Dec. 10** ***Perf. 11½x12***

| | | | | |
|---|---|---|---|---|
| **3041** | A818 2fo | multi | .30 | .25 |
| **3042** | A818 2fo | multi | .30 | .25 |
| **3043** | A818 4fo | multi | .60 | .30 |
| **3044** | A818 4fo | multi | .60 | .30 |
| **3045** | A818 6fo | multi | .90 | .45 |
| | | *Nos. 3041-3045 (5)* | 2.70 | 1.55 |

Exist imperf. Value, set $17.50.
See Nos. 3120-3122.

Fungi — A819

**Lithographed and Engraved**

**1986, Dec. 30** ***Perf. 11½***

| | | | | |
|---|---|---|---|---|
| **3046** | A819 2fo | Amanita phalloides | .30 | .25 |
| **3047** | A819 2fo | Inocybe patouillardi | .30 | .25 |
| **3048** | A819 2fo | Amanita muscaria | .30 | .25 |
| **3049** | A819 4fo | Omphalotus olearius | .55 | .30 |
| **3050** | A819 4fo | Amanita pantherina | .55 | .30 |
| **3051** | A819 6fo | Gyromitra esculenta | .80 | .40 |
| | | *Nos. 3046-3051 (6)* | 2.80 | 1.75 |

Exist imperf. Value, set $17.50.

Saltwater Fish — A820

**1987, Jan. 15** **Photo.** ***Perf. 11½***

| | | | | |
|---|---|---|---|---|
| **3052** | A820 2fo | Colisa fasciata | .30 | .25 |
| **3053** | A820 2fo | Pseudotropheus zebra | .30 | .25 |
| **3054** | A820 2fo | Iriatherina werneri | .30 | .25 |
| **3055** | A820 4fo | Aphyosemion multicolor | .55 | .30 |
| **3056** | A820 4fo | Papiliochromis ramirezi | .55 | .30 |
| **3057** | A820 6fo | Hyphessobrycon erythrostigma | .80 | .40 |
| | | *Nos. 3052-3057 (6)* | 2.80 | 1.75 |

Exist imperf. Value, set $20.

Seated Woman, 1918, by Bela Uitz (1887-1972), Painter A821

Abstract, 1960, by Lajos Kassak (1887-1967) A822

**1987, Mar. 6** **Litho.** ***Perf. 12***

**3058** A821 4fo multicolored .50 .30

Exists imperf. Value $5.

**1987, Mar. 20**

**3059** A822 4fo black & red .50 .30

Exists imperf. Value $5.

Medical Pioneers — A823

Designs: 2fo, Hippocrates (460-377 B.C.), Greek physician. No. 3061, Avicenna or Ibn Sina (A.D. 980-1037), Islamic pharmacist, diagnostician. No. 3062, Ambroise Pare (1510-1590), French surgeon. No. 3063, William Harvey (1578-1657), English physician, anatomist. 6fo, Ignaz Semmelweis (1818-1865), Hungarian obstetrician.

**1987, Mar. 31**

| | | | | |
|---|---|---|---|---|
| **3060** | A823 2fo | black & dk red brn | .30 | .25 |
| **3061** | A823 4fo | black & dk grn | .55 | .30 |
| **3062** | A823 4fo | black & steel bl | .55 | .30 |
| **3063** | A823 4fo | black & olive blk | .55 | .30 |
| **3064** | A823 6fo | black & grn blk | .80 | .40 |
| | | *Nos. 3060-3064 (5)* | 2.75 | 1.55 |

Exists imperf. Value, set $17.50.

Neolithic and Copper Age Artifacts — A824

Designs: 2fo, Urn, Hodmezovasarhely. No. 3066, Altar, Szeged. No. 3067, Deity, Szegvar-Tuzkoves. 5fo, Vase, Center.

**1987, Apr. 15** **Litho.** ***Perf. 12***

| | | | | |
|---|---|---|---|---|
| **3065** | A824 2fo | pale bl grn & sep | .25 | .25 |
| **3066** | A824 4fo | buff & sepia | .55 | .30 |
| **3067** | A824 4fo | pale org & sepia | .55 | .30 |
| **3068** | A824 5fo | pale yel grn & sep | .80 | .40 |
| | | *Nos. 3065-3068 (4)* | 2.15 | 1.25 |

Exists imperf. Value, set $17.50.

Souvenir Sheet

Esztergom Cathedral Treasury Reopening — A825

**1987, Apr. 28** ***Perf. 11***

**3069** A825 20fo Calvary of King Matthias 3.50 3.50

No. 3069 margin pictures the Horn Chalice of King Sigismund, Rhineland, 1408 (UL), Crozier of Archbishop Miklos Olah, Hungary, c. 1490 (UR), Monstrance of Imre Eszterhazy, by Gaspar Meichl, Vienna, 1728 (LL), and the Chalice of Matthias, Hungary, c. 1480.
Exists imperf. Value $25.

Hungarian First Aid Assoc., Cent. — A826

**1987, May 5** ***Perf. 11½x12***

**3070** A826 4fo Ambulances, 1887-1987 .50 .30

Exists imperf. Value $5.

Souvenir Sheet

CAPEX '87, Toronto — A827

Stamp exhibitions: b, OLYMPHILEX '87, Rome. c, HAFNIA '87, Copenhagen.

**1987, May 20** **Litho.** ***Perf. 11***

**3071** Sheet of 3 + 3 labels 3.50 2.75
***a.-c.*** A827 5fo any single 1.25 .90

Exists imperf. Value $17.50.

Jozsef Marek (1886-1952), Veterinarian — A828

**1987, May 25** ***Perf. 12x11½***

**3072** A828 4fo multicolored .50 .30

Veterinary education, bicent.
Exists imperf. Value $5.

Teleki's African Expedition, Cent. — A829

**1987, June 10**

**3073** A829 4fo multicolored .50 .30

Samuel Teleki (1845-1916), explorer.
Exists imperf. Value $5.

Woodcut by Abraham von Werdt, 18th Cent. — A830

**Litho. & Engr.**

**1987, June 25** *Perf. 12*

**3074** A830 4fo beige & sepia .50 .30

Hungarian Printing, Paper and Press Workers' Union, 125th anniv.
Exists imperf. Value $5.

Antarctic Research, 75th Anniv. — A831

Helicopter Landing, Mirnij Research Station — A832

Map, explorer and scene: No. 3075, James Cook (1728-1779) and ship. No. 3076, Fabian von Bellingshausen (1778-1852) and seals. No. 3077, Ernest H. Shackleton (1874-1922) and penguins. No. 3078, Roald Amundsen (1872-1928) discovering South Pole, dog team. No. 3079, Robert F. Scott (1868-1912) and ship. No. 3080, Richard E. Byrd (1888-1957) and Floyd Bennett monoplane.

**1987, June 30** **Litho.**

**3075** A831 2fo multi .30 .25
**3076** A831 2fo multi .30 .25
**3077** A831 2fo multi .30 .25
**3078** A831 4fo multi .55 .30
**3079** A831 4fo multi .55 .30
**3080** A831 6fo multi .80 .40
*Nos. 3075-3080 (6)* 2.80 1.75

**Souvenir Sheet**

*Perf. 11½*

**3081** A832 20fo multi 3.00 3.00

Exist imperf. Value: set $20; souvenir sheet $40.

Railway Officers Training Institute, Cent. — A833

**1987, Sept. 4** **Litho.** *Perf. 11½x12*

**3082** A833 4fo blue & black .75 .50

Exists imperf. Value $5.

Stamp Day, 60th Anniv. — A834

Masonry of the medieval Buda Castle: 2fo, Flowers, dolphin. 4fo, Arms of King Matthias. 10fo, "ONDIDIT/GENEROSVM" inscribed on capital.

**Litho. & Engr.**

**1987, Sept. 18** *Perf. 12*

**3083** A834 2fo multi .35 .25
**3084** A834 4fo multi .70 .45

**Souvenir Sheet**

*Perf. 11*

**3085** A834 10fo multi 1.75 1.75

Exist imperf. Value: set $12.50; souvenir sheet $25.

A835

**1987, Sept. 30** **Litho.** *Perf. 12*

**3086** A835 4fo multi .80 .50
*a.* Se-tenant with label .80 .50

No 3086 printed in sheet of 50 and in sheet of 25 plus 25 labels picturing 13th cent. church at Gyongyospata which houses the altar.
Exists imperf. Value $10; with label $30.

A836

Orchids A837

**1987, Oct. 29** **Litho.** *Perf. 11*

**3087** A836 2fo Cypripedium calceolus .35 .25
**3088** A836 2fo Orchis purpurea .35 .25
**3089** A836 4fo Himantoglossum hircinum .60 .50
**3090** A836 4fo Ophrys scolopax cornuta .65 .50
**3091** A836 5fo Cephalanthera rubra .75 .60
**3092** A836 6fo Epipactis atrorubens .80 .75
*Nos. 3087-3092 (6)* 3.50 2.85

**Miniature Sheet**

**3093** A837 20fo shown 3.50 3.25

Exist imperf. Value: set $20; souvenir sheet $35.

1988 Winter Olympics, Calgary — A838

**1987, Nov. 24**

**3094** A838 2fo Speed skating .35 .25
**3095** A838 2fo Cross-country skiing .35 .25
**3096** A838 4fo Biathlon .65 .40
**3097** A838 4fo Ice hockey .65 .40
**3098** A838 4fo 4-Man bobsled .65 .40
**3099** A838 6fo Ski-jumping 1.00 .65
*Nos. 3094-3099 (6)* 3.65 2.35

**Souvenir Sheet**

**3100** A838 20fo Slalom 3.50 3.25

Exist imperf. Value: set $15; souvenir sheet $20.

Souvenir Sheet

U.S.-Soviet Summit, Dec. 7-10 — A839

**1987, Dec. 7** *Perf. 12*

**3101** A839 20fo Shaking hands 3.50 3.25

Meeting of Gen. Secretary Gorbachev and Pres. Reagan to discuss and sign nuclear arms reduction treaty.
Exists imperf. Value $20.

Fairy Tales — A840

Designs: No. 3102, The White Crane, from Japan. No. 3103, The Fox and the Crow, Aesop's Fables. No. 3104, The Tortoise and the Hare, Aesop's Fables. No. 3105, The Ugly Duckling, by Hans Christian Andersen. No. 3106, The Steadfast Tin Soldier, by Andersen.

**1987, Dec. 11**

**3102** A840 2fo multi .40 .25
**3103** A840 2fo multi .40 .25
**3104** A840 4fo multi .75 .50
**3105** A840 4fo multi .75 .50
**3106** A840 6fo multi 1.00 .75
*Nos. 3102-3106 (5)* 3.30 2.25

Exist imperf. Value, set $17.50.

Count Ferdinand von Zeppelin (1838-1917), Designer of Dirigibles — A841

**1988, Jan. 29** **Litho.** *Perf. 12*

**3107** A841 2fo LZ-2, 1905 .40 .25
**3108** A841 4fo LZ-4, 1908 .80 .45
**3109** A841 4fo LZ-10, Schwaben, 1911 .90 .45
**3110** A841 8fo LZ-127, Graf Zeppelin, 1928 1.50 1.00
*Nos. 3107-3110 (4)* 3.60 2.15

Exist imperf. Value, set $17.50.

1988 World Figure Skating Championships, Budapest — A842

Various athletes wearing period costumes.

**1988, Feb. 29** **Photo.** *Perf. 11½*

**3111** A842 2fo Male, 20th cent. .35 .25
**3112** A842 2fo Male, (cap), 19th cent. .35 .25
**3113** A842 4fo Male (hat), 18th cent. .60 .40
**3114** A842 4fo Woman, c. 1930 .60 .40
**3115** A842 5fo Woman (contemporary) .75 .50
**3116** A842 6fo Pair 1.00 .65
*Nos. 3111-3116 (6)* 3.65 2.45

**Souvenir Sheet**

*Perf. 12x11½*

**3117** A842 20fo Death spiral 3.50 3.25

No. 3117 contains one 37x52mm stamp.
Exist imperf. Value: set $17.50; souvenir sheet $20.

Illes Monus (1888-1944), Party Leader — A843

**1988, Mar. 11** **Litho.** *Perf. 11½x12*

**3118** A843 4fo multi .50 .50

Exists imperf. Value $4.
See Nos. 3152, 3160.

Miniature Sheet

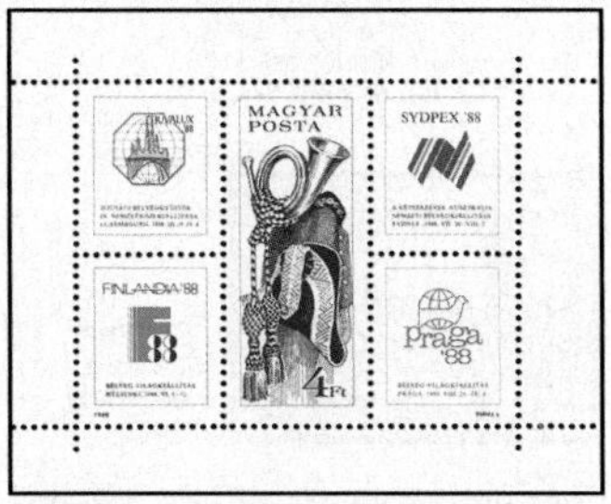


Postmaster's Coat, Hat and Post Horn, 18th Cent. — A844

**1988, Mar. 18** **Litho.** *Perf. 13*

**3119** A844 4fo + 4 labels 1.25 1.25

Intl. stamp exhibitions, 1988. No. 3119 contains 4 labels picturing exhibition emblems: JUVALUX '88, Luxembourg, Mar. 29-Apr. 4 (UL), SYDPEX '88, Sydney, Australia, July 30-Aug.7 (UR), FINLANDIA '88, Helsinki, Finland, June 1-12 (LR), and PRAGA '88, Prague, Czechoslovakia, Aug. 26-Sept. 4 (LL).
Exists imperf. Value $25.

**King Type of 1986**

Portraits of Hungarian kings in the Historical Portrait Gallery. King and reign: 2fo, Charles Robert (1308-1342). 4fo, Louis I (1342-1382). 6fo, Sigismund (1387-1437).

**1988, Mar. 31** *Perf. 11½x12*

**3120** A818 2fo pale grn, sep & red .30 .25
**3121** A818 4fo pale ultra, sep & red .60 .45
**3122** A818 6fo pale vio, sep & red .90 .65
*Nos. 3120-3122 (3)* 1.80 1.35

Exists imperf. Value, set $17.50.

1988 Summer Olympics, Seoul — A845

**1988, Apr. 20** **Litho.** *Perf. 13½x13*

**3123** A845 2fo Rowing .30 .25
**3124** A845 4fo Hurdling .60 .45
**3125** A845 4fo Fencing .60 .45
**3126** A845 6fo Boxing .90 .65
*Nos. 3123-3126 (4)* 2.40 1.80

### Souvenir Sheet

***Perf. 12½***

**3127** A845 20fo Tennis 3.75 3.25

Exist imperf. Value: set $15; souvenir sheet $25.

Computer Animation A846

Design: Graphic from the computer-animated film *Dilemma,* 1972, by graphic artist Janos Kass (b. 1927) and cartoon film director John Halas (b. 1912).

**1988, May 12** ***Perf. 12***

**3128** A846 4fo black, pur & ver .50 .25

Exists imperf. Value $6.

Eurocheck Congress, June 10, Budapest — A847

**1988, June 10** **Litho.** ***Perf. 12***

**3129** A847 4fo multicolored .50 .25

Eurocheck as legal tender, 20th anniv. Exists imperf. Value $6.

*Sovereign of the Seas* — A848

**1988, June 30**

**3130** A848 2fo shown .35 .25
**3131** A848 2fo *Santa Maria* .35 .25
**3132** A848 2fo *Mayflower* .35 .25
**3133** A848 4fo *Jylland* .75 .50
**3134** A848 6fo *St. Jupat* 1.10 .80
*Nos. 3130-3134 (5)* 2.90 2.05

Exist imperf. Value, set $17.50.

Fight Drug Abuse — A849

**1988, July 7** **Litho.** ***Perf. 12***

**3135** A849 4fo multicolored .65 .25

Exists imperf. Value $6.

Ducks A850

**1988, July 29** **Litho.** ***Perf. 13x13½***

**3136** A850 2fo Anas crecca .30 .25
**3137** A850 2fo Bucephala clangula .30 .25
**3138** A850 4fo Anas penelope .65 .45
*a.* Pane of 10 #3136 + 10 #3138 with gutter btwn. 12.00
Complete booklet, #3138a, with text and cover in either English or German 12.00
**3139** A850 4fo Netta rufina .65 .50
**3140** A850 6fo Anas strepera 1.10 .65
*Nos. 3136-3140 (5)* 3.00 2.10

### Souvenir Sheet

***Perf. 12½x11½***

**3141** A850 20fo Anas platyrhynchos 4.75 3.50

No. 3141 contains one 52x37mm stamp.
Exist imperf. Value: set $17.50; souvenir sheet $30.
For surcharges see Nos. 3199-3200.

Antique Toys — A851

**1988, Aug. 12** ***Perf. 12***

**3142** A851 2fo Train .30 .25
**3143** A851 2fo See-saw .30 .25
**3144** A851 4fo +2fo Pecking chickens 1.00 .65
**3145** A851 5fo String-manipulated soldier .85 .55
*Nos. 3142-3145 (4)* 2.45 1.70

Surtax for youth philately programs.
Exist imperf. Value, set $15.

Calvinist College, Debrecen, 450th Anniv. — A852

**1988, Aug. 16** **Litho.** ***Perf. 13½x13***

**3146** A852 4fo multi .40 .25

Exists imperf. Value $5.

58th American Society of Travel Agents World Congress, Oct. 23-29, Budapest A853

**1988, Aug. 30** ***Perf. 12***

**3147** A853 4fo multi .40 .25

Exists imperf. Value $7.50.

P.O. Officials Training School, Cent. — A854

**1988, Sept. 9** **Litho.** ***Perf. 12***

**3148** A854 4fo Badge on collar .40 .25

Exists imperf. Value $6.

Gabor Baross (1848-1892), Minister of Commerce and Communication — A855

Portrait and: 2fo, Postal Savings Bank, Budapest, emblem and postal savings stamp. 4fo, Telephone and telegraph apparatus, registration label and cancellations. 10fo, East Railway Station, Budapest.

**1988, Sept. 16**

**3149** A855 2fo multi .30 .25
**3150** A855 4fo multi .65 .50

### Souvenir Sheet

***Perf. 11½***

**3151** A855 10fo multi 2.25 2.00

No. 3151 contains one 50x29mm stamp.
Exist imperf. Value: set $12.50; souvenir sheet $35.

### Famous Hungarians Type of 1988

Gyula Lengyel (1888-1941), political writer.

**1988, Oct. 7** ***Perf. 11½x12***

**3152** A843 4fo multi .40 .25

Exists imperf. Value $5.

Christmas — A857

***Perf. 12½x11½***

**1988, Nov. 10** **Litho.**

**3153** A857 2fo multi .30 .25

Exists imperf. Value $5.

Nobel Prize Winners — A858

Designs: No. 3154, Richard Adolf Zsigmondy (1865-1929), Germany, chemistry (1925). No. 3155, Robert Barany (1876-1936), Austria, medicine (1914). No. 3156, Georg von Hevesy (1885-1966), Hungary, chemistry (1943). No. 3157, Albert Szent-Gyorgyi (1893-1986), Hungary-US, medicine (1937). No. 3158, Georg von Bekesy (1899-1972), US, medicine (1961). 6fo, Denis Gabor (1900-1979), Great Britain, physics (1971).

### Litho. & Engr.

**1988, Nov. 30** ***Perf. 12***

**3154** A858 2fo red brown .35 .25
**3155** A858 2fo green .35 .25
**3156** A858 2fo deep claret .35 .25
**3157** A858 4fo rose lake .60 .40
**3158** A858 4fo steel blue .60 .40
**3159** A858 6fo sepia .75 .65
*Nos. 3154-3159 (6)* 3.00 2.20

Exist imperf. Value, set $17.

### Famous Hungarians Type of 1988

Arpad Szakasits (1888-1965), party leader.

**1988, Dec. 6** ***Perf. 11½x12***

**3160** A843 4fo multicolored .40 .25

Exists imperf. Value $5.

### Souvenir Sheet

Medals Won by Hungarian Athletes at the 1988 Seoul Olympic Games — A860

**1988, Dec. 19** **Litho.** ***Perf. 12***

**3161** A860 20fo multicolored 3.75 3.50

Exists imperf. Value $20.

Silver and Cast Iron — A861

**1988, Dec. 28** **Litho. & Engr.**

**3162** A861 2fo Teapot, Pest, 1846 .35 .25
**3163** A861 2fo Coffee pot, Buda, 18th cent. .35 .25
**3164** A861 4fo Sugar bowl, Pest, 1822 .65 .45
**3165** A861 5fo Cast iron plate, Romania, 1850 .85 .55
*Nos. 3162-3165 (4)* 2.20 1.50

Exist imperf. Value, set $15.

Postal Savings Bank Inauguration — A862

**1989, Jan. 20** **Litho.** ***Perf. 12x11½***

**3166** A862 5fo royal blue, blk & silver .50 .25

Exists imperf. Value $5.

Kalman Wallisch (1889-1934), Labor Leader — A863

**1989, Feb. 28** **Litho.** ***Perf. 12***

**3167** A863 3fo dk red & brt bl .40 .25

Exists imperf. Value $5.
See No. 3170.

World Indoor Sports Championships, Budapest, Mar. 3-5 — A864

**1989, Mar. 3** *Perf. 13x13½*

**3168** A864 3fo multicolored .40 .25

Exists imperf. Value $5.

Souvenir Sheet

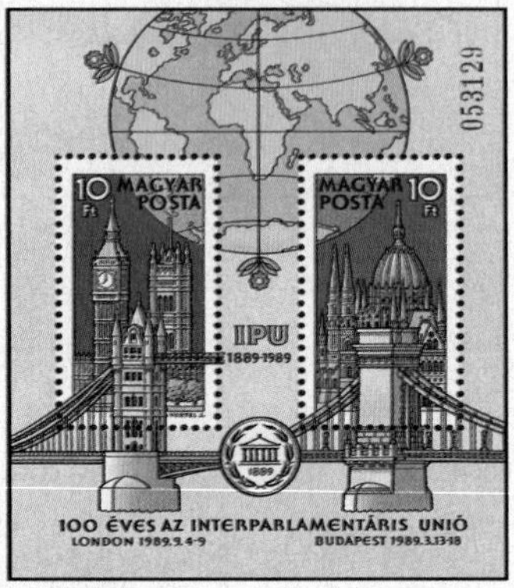


Interparliamentary Union Cent. and 81st Session, Budapest, Mar. 13-18 — A865

a, Parliament, Big Ben & Tower Bridge, London. b, Parliament & Chain Bridge, Budapest.

**1989, Mar. 13** **Litho.** *Perf. 11*

**3169** A865 Sheet of 2 3.75 3.50

***a.-b.*** 10fo any single 1.75 1.60

Exists with red inscriptions and control number. Value $75.

Exists imperf. Value $25.

**Famous Hungarians Type of 1989**

Janos Gyetvai (1889-1967), journalist, diplomat.

**1989, Apr. 7** **Litho.** *Perf. 12*

**3170** A863 3fo dark red & brt grn .40 .25

Exists imperf. Value $5.

Stud Farm at Babolna, 200th Anniv. A867

Horses: a, O Bajan. b, Meneskari Csikos. c, Gazal II.

**1989, May 18** **Litho.** *Perf. 12*

**3171** Strip of 3 1.75 1.10

***a.-c.*** A867 3fo any single .55 .35

Exists imperf. Value, strip $15.

ART '89, May 23-27, Budapest A868

**1989, May 23** *Perf. 12x11½*

**3172** A868 5fo multi .50 .25

Exhibition for disabled artists.

Exists imperf. Value $5.

Flower Arrangements — A869

**1989, May 31** *Perf. 12*

| | | | | |
|---|---|---|---|---|
| **3173** A869 | 2fo | multi, vert. | .35 | .25 |
| **3174** A869 | 3fo | multi, vert. | .40 | .30 |
| **3175** A869 | 3fo | shown | .40 | .30 |
| **3176** A869 | 5fo | multi, diff. | .85 | .50 |
| **3177** A869 | 10fo | multi, vert. | 1.50 | 1.00 |
| | | *Nos. 3173-3177 (5)* | 3.50 | 2.35 |

Exist imperf. Value, set $15.

French Revolution, Bicent. A870

**1989, June 1** *Perf. 12*

**3178** A870 5fo brt blue, blk & red .50 .30

**Souvenir Sheet**

***Perf. 11½***

**3179** A870 20fo like 5fo 3.50 3.25

No. 3179 contains one 50x30mm stamp.

Exist imperf. Value: single $12.50; souvenir sheet $22.50.

Medieval Church of the Csolts Near Veszto — A871

**1989, June 15** **Litho.** *Perf. 12*

**3180** A871 3fo multi .50 .25

Exists imperf. Value $5.

Photography, 150th Anniv. — A872

**1989, June 15**

**3181** A872 5fo multi .50 .25

Exists imperf. Value $5.

Old Mills — A873

Designs: 2fo, Water mill, Turistvandi, 18th cent. 3fo, Horse-driven mill, Szarvas, 1836. 5fo, Windmill, Kiskunhalas, 18th cent. 10fo, Water wheel on the Drava River.

**1989, June 20**

| | | | | |
|---|---|---|---|---|
| **3182** A873 | 2fo | multi | .30 | .25 |
| **3183** A873 | 3fo | multi | .45 | .30 |
| **3184** A873 | 5fo | multi | .75 | .50 |
| **3185** A873 | 10fo | multi | 1.50 | 1.00 |
| | | *Nos. 3182-3185 (4)* | 3.00 | 2.05 |

Exist imperf. Value, set $15.

Souvenir Sheet

1st Moon Landing, 20th Anniv. — A874

**1989, July 12** **Litho.** *Perf. 12½*

**3186** A874 20fo multi 3.75 3.50

Exists imperf. Value $20.

Gliders — A875

**1989, July 20** *Perf. 12*

**3187** A875 3fo Futar .45 .30

**3188** A875 5fo Cimbora .80 .60

17th Intl. Old Timers Rally, Budakeszi Airport, and 60th anniv. of glider flying in Hungary.

Exist imperf. Value, set $15.

Reptiles A876

**1989, July 26** *Perf. 11*

| | | | | |
|---|---|---|---|---|
| **3189** A876 | 2fo | *Lacerta agilis* | .25 | .25 |
| **3190** A876 | 3fo | *Lacerta viridis* | .45 | .25 |
| **3191** A876 | 5fo | *Vipera rakosiensis* | .70 | .40 |
| **3192** A876 | 5fo | *Natrix natrix* | .70 | .40 |
| **3193** A876 | 10fo | *Emys orbicularis* | 1.25 | .75 |
| | | *Nos. 3189-3193 (5)* | 3.35 | 2.05 |

Exist imperf. Value, set $20.

31st Modern Pentathlon World Championships, Aug. 30-Sept. 4, Budapest — A877

**1989, July 31** *Perf. 13½x13*

**3194** A877 5fo multi .50 .25

Exists imperf. Value $5.

Caves — A878

10th World Speleology Congress, Aug. 13-20, Sofia.

**1989, Aug. 14** **Litho.** *Perf. 11*

| | | | | |
|---|---|---|---|---|
| **3195** A878 | 3fo | Baradla | .30 | .25 |
| **3196** A878 | 5fo | Szemlohegy | .55 | .40 |
| **3197** A878 | 10fo | Anna | .90 | .70 |
| **3198** A878 | 12fo | Lake Cave of Tapolca | 1.25 | .80 |
| | | *Nos. 3195-3198 (4)* | 3.00 | 2.15 |

Exist imperf. Value, set $15.

Nos. 3136 and 3138 Surcharged

**1989, Aug. 14** *Perf. 13x13½*

**3199** A850 3fo on 2fo #3136 2.00 1.75

**3200** A850 5fo on 4fo #3138 2.00 1.75

***a.*** Pane of 10 #3199 + pane of 10 #3200 with gutter between 20.00

Complete booklet, #3200a, with text and cover in either English or German 35.00

A879

**1989, Aug. 24** *Perf. 12*

**3201** A879 5fo multi .50 .25

Third World Two-in-Hand Carriage-driving Championships, Balatonfenyves, Aug. 24-27.

Exists imperf. Value $5.

A880

Nurses: 5fo, Zsuzsanna Kossuth (1820-1854) and emblem. 10fo, Florence Nightingale (1820-1910) and medal awarded in her name by the Red Cross.

**1989, Sept. 8** **Litho.** *Perf. 12*

**3202** A880 5fo multi .65 .40

**3203** A880 10fo multi 1.10 .75

Stamp Day. See No. B341.

Exist imperf. Value, set $12.50.

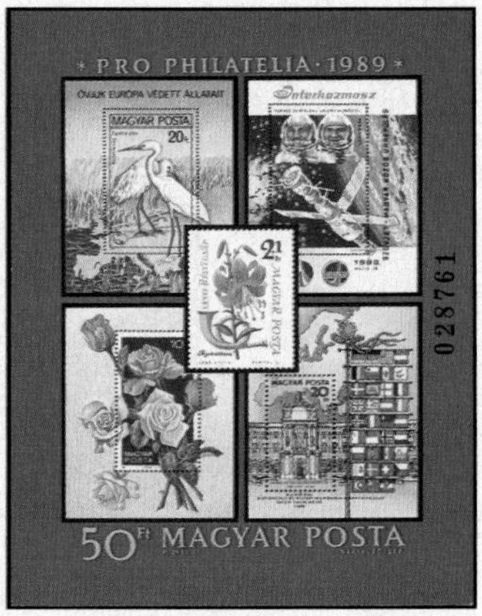


Pro-Philatelia 1989 — A881

**1989, Oct. 10** **Litho.** *Imperf.*

**3204** A881 50fo #2665, C426, 2742, 3005, B233 6.25 5.75

Dismantling of the Electronic Surveillance System (Iron Curtain) on the Hungary-Austria Border — A882

**1989, Oct. 30** ***Perf. 11***
**3205** A882 5fo multi 1.00 .50

Exists imperf. Value $6.

*Conquest of Hungary,* by Mor Than — A883

**1989, Oct. 31**
**3206** A883 5fo multi .60 .25

Arpad, chief who founded the 1st Magyar dynasty of Hungary in 889.
Exists imperf. Value $5.

Christmas — A884

**1989, Nov. 10** **Litho.** ***Perf. 11½x12***
**3207** A884 3fo Flight to Egypt .45 .25

Exists imperf. Value $5.

Jawaharlal Nehru — A885

**Litho. & Engr.**

**1989, Nov. 14** ***Perf. 12***
**3208** A885 3fo buff & rose brn 1.00 .25

Jawaharlal Nehru, 1st prime minister of independent India.
Exists imperf. Value $5.

Modern Art (Paintings) A886

3fo, *Mike,* by Dezso Korniss. 5fo, *Sunrise,* by Lajos Kassak. 10fo, *Grotesque Burial,* by Endre Balint. 12fo, *Memory of Toys,* by Tihamer Gyarmathy.

**1989, Dec. 18** **Litho.** ***Perf. 12***
**3209** A886 3fo multicolored .35 .25
**3210** A886 5fo multicolored .65 .50
**3211** A886 10fo multicolored 1.40 .95
**3212** A886 12fo multicolored 1.60 1.10
*Nos. 3209-3212 (4)* 4.00 2.80

Exist imperf. Value, set $20.

Medical Pioneers — A887

#3213, Galen (129-c.199), Greek physician. #3214, Paracelsus (1493-1541), German alchemist. 4fo, Andreas Vesalius (1514-64), Belgian anatomist. 6fo, Rudolf Virchow (1821-1902), German pathologist. 10fo, Ivan Petrovich Pavlov (1849-1936), Russian physiologist.

**1989, Dec. 29** **Engr.** ***Perf. 12***
**3213** A887 3fo olive gray .40 .25
**3214** A887 3fo brown .40 .25
**3215** A887 4fo black .70 .45
**3216** A887 6fo intense black .85 .55
**3217** A887 10fo brown violet 1.40 .80
*Nos. 3213-3217 (5)* 3.75 2.30

Exist imperf. Value, set $20.

Hungarian Savings Bank, 150th Anniv. — A888

**1990, Jan. 11** **Litho.**
**3218** A888 5fo multicolored .75 .45

Exists imperf. Value $8.

A889

A890

**1990, Jan. 15** ***Perf. 12***
**3219** A889 5fo brown & sepia .75 .45

Singer Sewing Machine, 25th anniv.
Exists imperf. Value $7.

**1990, Jan. 29**

3fo, Telephone, Budapest Exchange. 5fo, Mailbox and main p.o., Budapest, c. 1900.

**3220** A890 3fo multicolored .40 .25
**3221** A890 5fo multicolored .60 .30

**Coil Stamps**

**Size: 17x22mm**

***Perf. 14***

**Photo.**

**3222** A890 3fo shown .40 .25
**3223** A890 5fo multi .60 .30
*Nos. 3220-3223 (4)* 2.00 1.10

Nos. 3220-3221 inscribed "Pj 1989." Nos. 3222-3223 inscribed "1989."
Nos. 3220-3221 exist imperf. Value, set $20.

A891

Designs: Protected bird species.

**1990, Feb. 20** **Litho.** ***Perf. 11½x12***
**3224** A891 3fo *Alcedo atthis* .45 .30
**3225** A891 3fo *Pyrrhula pyrrhula* .45 .30
**3226** A891 3fo *Dendrocopos syriacus* .45 .30
**3227** A891 5fo *Upupa epops* .75 .50
**3228** A891 5fo *Merops apiaster* .75 .50
**3229** A891 10fo *Coracias garrulus* 1.50 1.00
*Nos. 3224-3229 (6)* 4.35 2.90

Exist imperf. Value, set $20.

A892

Flowers of the continents (Africa).

**1990, Mar. 14** **Litho.** ***Perf. 12***
**3230** A892 3fo *Leucadendron* .40 .25
**3231** A892 3fo *Protea compacta* .40 .25
**3232** A892 3fo *Leucadendron spissifolium* .40 .25
**3233** A892 5fo *Protea barbigera* .70 .40
**3234** A892 5fo *Protea lepidocarpodendron* .70 .40
**3235** A892 10fo *Protea cynaroides* 1.25 .85
*Nos. 3230-3235 (6)* 3.85 2.40

**Souvenir Sheet**

***Perf. 12½x12***

**3236** A892 20fo Montage of African flowers 3.75 3.75

No. 3236 contains one 27x38mm stamp.
See Nos. 3278-3283, 3371-3375, 3377-3381, 3451-3455.
Exist imperf. Value: set $20; souvenir sheet $30.

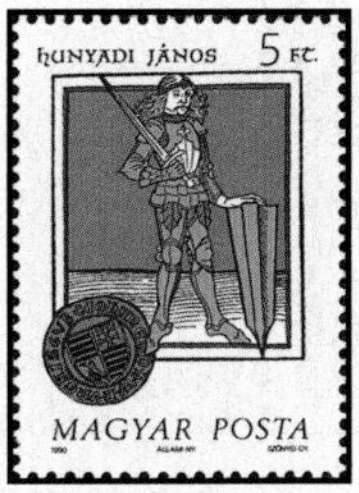


A893

Portraits of Hungarian kings in the Historical Portrait Gallery. King and reign: No. 3237, Janos Hunyadi (c. 1407-1409). No. 3238, Mathias Hunyadi (1443-1490).

**1990, Apr. 6** **Litho.** ***Perf. 11½x12***
**3237** A893 5fo multicolored .70 .40
**3238** A893 5fo multicolored .70 .40
*a.* Pair, #3237-3238 1.40 1.00

Exist imperf. Value, pair $12.50.

Souvenir Sheet

A894

**Litho. & Engr.**

**1990, Apr. 17** ***Perf. 12½x12***
**3239** A894 20fo black & buff 3.75 3.25

Penny Black 150th anniv., Stamp World London '90.
Exists imperf. Value $22.50.

Karoli Bible, 400th Anniv. — A895

**1990, Apr. 24** **Litho.**
**3240** A895 8fo Gaspar Karoli 1.00 .70

No. 3240 printed se-tenant with label picturing Bible frontispiece.
Exists imperf. Value, with label $12.50.

1990 World Cup Soccer Championships, Italy — A896

Various athletes.

**1990, Apr. 27** ***Perf. 11½x12***
**3241** A896 3fo Dribble .30 .25
**3242** A896 5fo Heading the ball .55 .35
**3243** A896 5fo Kick .55 .35
**3244** A896 8fo Goal attempt .80 .55
**3245** A896 8fo Dribble, diff. .80 .55
**3246** A896 10fo Dribble, diff. 1.00 .75
*Nos. 3241-3246 (6)* 4.00 2.80

**Souvenir Sheet**

***Perf. 12½***

**3247** A896 20fo Dribble, diff. 3.50 3.50

No. 3247 contains one 32x42mm stamp.
Exist imperf. Value: set $20; souvenir sheet $20.

Kelemen Mikes (1690-1761), Writer — A897

**1990, May 31** **Litho.** ***Perf. 13½x13***
**3248** A897 8fo black & gold 1.10 .75

Exists imperf. Value $5.

Noemi and Beni Ferenczy, Birth Cent. — A898

Designs: 3fo, Painting by Noemi Ferenczy. 5fo, Sculpture by Beni Ferenczy.

**1990, June 18** **Litho.** ***Perf. 12***
**3249** A898 3fo multicolored .30 .25
**3250** A898 5fo multicolored .50 .30

Exist imperf. Value, set $10.

Ferenc Kazinczy (1759-1831), Hungarian Language Reformer A899

**1990, July 18 Litho. *Perf. 12***

**3251** A899 8fo multicolored .60 .40

Exists imperf. Value $5.

Ferenc Kolcsey (1790-1838), Poet — A900

**1990, Aug. 3**

**3252** A900 8fo multicolored .60 .40

Exists imperf. Value $7.50.

New Coat of Arms A901

**1990, Aug. 17 Litho. *Perf. 13½x13***

**3253** A901 8fo multicolored .60 .40

### Souvenir Sheet

***Perf. 11***

**3254** A901 20fo multicolored 4.00 4.00

No. 3254 contains one 34x50mm stamp.

A souvenir sheet like No. 3254 was released with a hologram as the stamp. The sheet exists with black or red control numbers on the reverse. Values: with black numbers $175; with red numbers $300.

Exist imperf. Value: single $15; souvenir sheet $30.

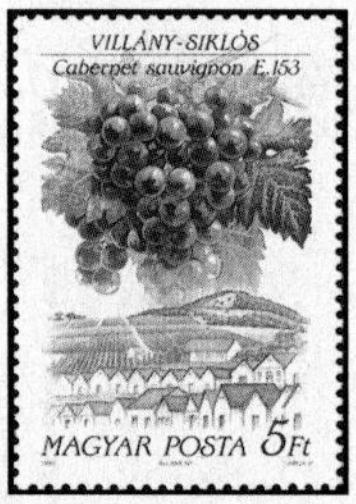


Grapes and Wine Producing Areas — A902

Grapes and Growing Area: 3fo, Cabernet franc, Hajos-Vaskut. 5fo, Cabernet sauvignon, Villany-Siklos. No. 3257, Italian Riesling, Badacsony. No. 3258, Kadarka, Szekszard. No. 3259, Leanyka, Eger. 10fo, Furmint, Tokaj-Hegyalja.

**1990, Aug. 31 *Perf. 13x13½***

**3255** A902 3fo multicolored .25 .25
**3256** A902 5fo multicolored .45 .30
**3257** A902 8fo multicolored .65 .45
**3258** A902 8fo multicolored .65 .45
**3259** A902 8fo multicolored .65 .45
**3260** A902 10fo multicolored .85 .60
*Nos. 3255-3260 (6)* 3.50 2.50

Exist imperf. Value, set $25.

See Nos. 3580-3582, 3656-3657, 3704-3705, 3773-3774, 3832-3833, 3938-3939, 4037-4039.

Paintings by Endre Szasz A903

**1990, Oct. 12 Litho. *Perf. 12***

**3261** A903 8fo Feast .70 .45
**3262** A903 12fo Message 1.10 .65

Stamp Day. See No. B344.
Exist imperf. Value, set $17.50.

Prehistoric Animals A904

**1990, Nov. 16 Litho. *Perf. 12***

**3263** A904 3fo Tarbosaurus .25 .25
**3264** A904 5fo Brontosaurus .40 .25
**3265** A904 5fo Stegosaurus .40 .25
**3266** A904 5fo Dimorphodon .40 .25
**3267** A904 8fo Platybelodon .70 .35
**3268** A904 10fo Mammoth .85 .40
*Nos. 3263-3268 (6)* 3.00 1.75

Exist imperf. Value, set $20.

Intl. Literacy Year — A905

**1990, Nov. 21 *Perf. 13x13½***

**3269** A905 10fo multicolored 1.40 .65

Exist imperf. Value $5.

Budapest Stamp Museum, 60th Anniv. — A906

**1990, Nov. 23 *Perf. 12½***

**3270** A906 5fo brn red & grn .50 .30

Exist imperf. Value $5.

Souvenir Sheet

Thurn & Taxis Postal System, 500th Anniv. — A907

**1990, Nov. 30 Litho. *Perf. 12½x12***

**3271** A907 50fo multicolored *10.00 10.00*

Antique Clocks — A908

**1990, Dec. 14 *Perf. 12***

**3272** A908 3fo Travelling clock, 1576 .25 .25
**3273** A908 5fo Table clock, 1643 .45 .30
**3274** A908 5fo Mantel clock, 1790 .45 .30
**3275** A908 10fo Table clock, 1814 .85 .60
*Nos. 3272-3275 (4)* 2.00 1.45

Exist imperf. Value, set $17.50.

Madonna with Child by Botticelli — A909

**1990, Dec. 14 *Perf. 12½x11½***

**3276** A909 5fo multicolored .50 .25

Exists imperf. Value $5.

Lorand Eotvos (1848-1919) and Torsion Pendulum A910

**1991, Jan. 31 Litho. *Perf. 11***

**3277** A910 12fo multicolored 1.10 .65

Exists imperf. Value $10.

### Flowers of the Continents Type

Flowers of the Americas.

**1991, Feb. 28 Litho. *Perf. 12***

**3278** A892 5fo Mandevilla splendens .35 .25
**3279** A892 7fo Lobelia cardinalis .45 .30
**3280** A892 7fo Cobaea scandens .45 .30
**3281** A892 12fo Steriphoma paradoxa .75 .50
**3282** A892 15fo Beloperone guttata 1.00 .70
*Nos. 3278-3282 (5)* 3.00 2.05

### Souvenir Sheet

***Perf. 11***

**3283** A892 20fo Flowers of the Americas 3.50 1.75

No. 3283 contains one 27x44mm stamp.
Exist imperf. Value: set $20; souvenir sheet $50.

Post Office, Budapest A911

Designs: 7fo, Post Office, Pecs.

***Perf. 11½x12½***

**1991, Mar. 22 Litho.**

**3284** A911 5fo multicolored 5.50 4.00
**3285** A911 7fo multicolored 6.50 4.50
*a.* Pair, #3284-3285 13.00 11.00

Admission to CEPT.
Exist imperf. Value, pair $40.

Europa — A912

**1991, Apr. Litho. *Perf. 12½***

**3286** A912 12fo Ulysses probe *4.00* 2.00
**3287** A912 30fo Cassini-Huygens probe *8.00* 6.00

Exist imperf. Value, set $35.

Budapest Zoological and Botanical Gardens, 125th Anniv. — A913

**1991, May 15 *Perf. 13½x13***

**3288** A913 7fo Gorilla .60 .35
**3289** A913 12fo Rhinoceros .85 .60
**3290** A913 12fo Toucan .85 .60
**3291** A913 12fo Polar bear .85 .60
**3292** A913 20fo Orchid 1.40 1.00
*Nos. 3288-3292 (5)* 4.55 3.15

Exist imperf. Value, set $20.

A914

**1991, May 24 Litho. *Perf. 12***

**3293** A914 12fo multi 1.00 .60

Count Pal Teleki (1879-1941), politician.
Exists imperf. Value $5.

A915

**1991, June 13** ***Perf. 13x13½***

**3294** A915 12fo multicolored 1.00 .60

44th World Fencing Championships, Budapest.
Exists imperf. Value $7.50.

Images of the Virgin and Child in Hungarian Shrines A916

Designs: 7fo, Mariapocs. No. 3296, Mariagyud. No. 3297, Celldomolk. No. 3298, Mariaremete. 20fo, Esztergom.

**1991, June 17** ***Perf. 12½***

**3295** A916 7fo multicolored .55 .35
**3296** A916 12fo multicolored .85 .60
**3297** A916 12fo multicolored .85 .60
**3298** A916 12fo multicolored .85 .60
**3299** A916 20fo multicolored 1.40 1.00
*Nos. 3295-3299 (5)* 4.50 3.15

Compare with design A927.
Exist imperf. Value, set $20.

Souvenir Sheet

Visit of Pope John Paul II, Aug. 16-20, 1991 — A917

**Litho. & Engr.**

**1991, July 15** ***Perf. 12***

**3300** A917 50fo multicolored 4.50 3.50

Exists imperf. Value $25.

Karoly Marko (1791-1860), Painter — A918

**1991, June 17** ***Perf. 12***

**3301** A918 12fo multicolored 1.25 .75

Exists imperf. Value $7.50.

Basketball, Cent. — A919

**1991, June 27** **Litho.** ***Perf. 12***

**3302** A919 10fo multicolored 1.25 .75

Exists imperf. Value $8.

Otto Lilienthal's First Glider Flight, Cent. — A920

Aircraft of aviation pioneers.

**1991, June 27**

**3303** A920 7fo Otto Lilienthal .50 .35
**3304** A920 12fo Wright Brothers .80 .65
**3305** A920 20fo Alberto Santos-Dumont 1.40 1.00
**3306** A920 30fo Aladar Zselyi 2.00 1.50
*Nos. 3303-3306 (4)* 4.70 3.50

Exist imperf. Value, set $20.

3rd Intl. Hungarian Philological Congress A921

**1991, Aug. 12** **Litho.** ***Perf. 13½x13***

**3307** A921 12fo multicolored 1.50 .65

Exists imperf. Value $6.

A922

**1991, Sept. 6** **Engr.** ***Perf. 12***

**3308** A922 12fo dark red .65 .45

Count Istvan Szechenyi (1791-1860), founder of Academy of Sciences.
Exists imperf. Value $6.

A923

Wolfgang Amadeus Mozart (1756-91).

**1991, Sept. 6** **Litho.**

**3309** A923 12fo As child 1.00 .50
**3310** A923 20fo As adult 2.00 .80

**Souvenir Sheet**

**3311** A923 30fo +15fo, in red coat 4.00 2.50

Stamp Day. No. 3311 contains one 30x40mm stamp.
Exist imperf. Value: set $25; souvenir sheet $60.

Telecom '91 — A924

**1991, Sept. 30** **Litho.** ***Perf. 12***

**3312** A924 12fo multicolored .90 .50

6th World Forum and Exposition on Telecommunications, Geneva, Switzerland. Exists imperf. Value $7.50.

A925

**1991, Oct. 30** **Litho.** ***Perf. 13½x13***

**3313** A925 12fo multicolored 1.75 .50

Sovereign Order of the Knights of Malta.
Exists imperf. Value, set $7.50.

A926

Early explorers and Discovery of America, 500th anniv. (in 1992): 7fo, Sebastian Cabot, Labrador Peninsula, Nova Scotia. No. 3315, Amerigo Vespucci, South American region. No. 3316, Hernando Cortez, Mexico. 15fo, Ferdinand Magellan, Straits of Magellan. 20fo, Francisco Pizarro, Peru, Andes Mountain region. 30fo, Christopher Columbus and coat of arms.

**1991, Oct. 30** ***Perf. 12***

**3314** A926 7fo multicolored .50 .25
**3315** A926 12fo multicolored .80 .45
**3316** A926 12fo multicolored .80 .45
**3317** A926 15fo multicolored 1.00 .60
**3318** A926 20fo multicolored 1.40 .75
*Nos. 3314-3318 (5)* 4.50 2.50

**Souvenir Sheet**

**3319** A926 30fo multicolored 2.50 2.00

No. 3319 contains one 26x37mm stamp.
Exist imperf. Value: set $25; souvenir sheet $60.

No. 3023 Overprinted in Brown

**1991, Oct. 22** **Litho.** ***Perf. 12x11½***

**3320** A816 12fo multi 1.25 .45

Anniversary of Hungarian revolution, 1956.

Christmas — A927

Images of the Virgin and Child from: 7fo, Mariapocs. 12fo, Mariaremete.

**1991, Nov. 20** ***Perf. 13½x13***

**3322** A927 7fo multicolored .65 .25
**3323** A927 12fo multicolored 1.10 .45

Nos. 3322-3323 issued in sheets of 20 plus 20 labels.
Exist imperf. Value, set $14.

A928

**1991, Nov. 20** ***Perf. 12***

**3324** A928 12fo multicolored .90 .45

Fight for human rights. Exist imperf. Value $20.

A929

**1991, Dec. 6** ***Perf. 13½x13***

**3325** A929 7fo Cross-country skiing .35 .25
**3326** A929 12fo Slalom skiing .70 .30
**3327** A929 15fo Four-man bob-sled .80 .45
**3328** A929 20fo Ski jump 1.10 .60
**3329** A929 30fo Hockey 1.60 .85
*Nos. 3325-3329 (5)* 4.55 2.45

**Souvenir Sheet**

***Perf. 12½x11½***

**3330** A929 30fo Pairs figure skating 2.50 2.00

1992 Winter Olympics, Albertville.
Exist imperf. Value: set $20; souvenir sheet $20.

Souvenir Sheet

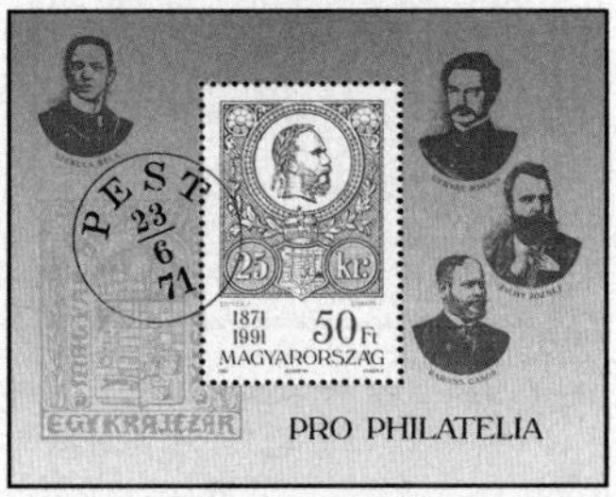

First Hungarian Postage Stamp, 120th Anniv. — A930

**1991, Dec. 20** **Litho.** ***Perf. 12x12½***

**3331** A930 50fo No. 6 4.00 3.00

Piarist Order in Hungary, 350th Anniv. — A931

**1992, Jan. 22** *Perf. 13½x13*

**3332** A931 10fo multicolored .85 .40

World Heritage Village of Holloko A932

**1992, Jan. 22** *Perf. 12*

**3333** A932 15fo multicolored 1.50 .60

1992 Summer Olympics, Barcelona — A933

**1992, Feb. 26** **Litho.** *Perf. 13½x13*

**3334** A933 7fo Swimming .60 .40
**3335** A933 9fo Cycling .80 .50
**3336** A933 10fo Gymnastics 1.40 .60
**3337** A933 15fo Running 2.75 1.40
*Nos. 3334-3337 (4)* 5.55 2.90

Discovery of America, 500th Anniv. — A934

Expo '92, Seville: No. 3338, Map shaped as Indian, Columbus' fleet. No. 3339, Face-shaped map of ocean, sailing ship. No. 3340, Map shaped as European face, ship. No. 3341, Map, square, protractor, compass.

**1992, Mar. 27** **Litho.** *Perf. 12*

**3338** A934 10fo multicolored .90 .35
**3339** A934 10fo multicolored .90 .35
**3340** A934 15fo multicolored .90 .55
**3341** A934 15fo multicolored 1.25 .55
*Nos. 3338-3341 (4)* 3.95 1.80

Jozsef Cardinal Mindszenty (1892-1975), Leader of Hungarian Catholic Church — A935

**1992, Mar. 27** *Perf. 12½x11½*

**3342** A935 15fo red, brn & buff 1.10 .60

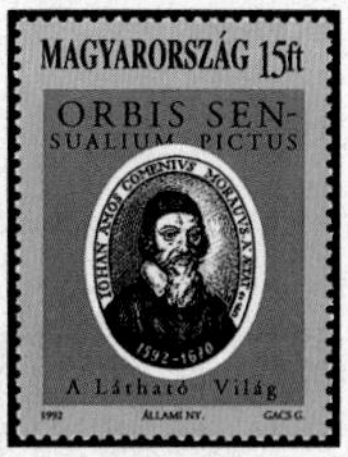


A936

**1992, Mar. 27** *Perf. 13½x13*

**3343** A936 15fo multicolored 1.10 .60

Jan Amos Komensky (Comenius), writer, 400th birth anniv.

A937

**1992, Apr. 14** **Litho.** *Perf. 13½x13*

**3344** A937 15fo Maya Indian sculpture *2.50* 1.00
**3345** A937 40fo Indian sculpture, diff. *7.25* 3.00

Europa. Discovery of America, 500th anniv..

European Gymnastics Championships, Budapest — A938

**1992, May 15** **Litho.** *Perf. 12*

**3346** A938 15fo multicolored 1.10 .60

A939

**1992, June 26** **Litho.** *Perf. 13½x13*

**3347** A939 15fo multicolored 1.00 .50

St. Margaret, 750th Anniv. (in 1991). No. 3347 printed with se-tenant label.

A940

Protected birds.

**1992, June 26** *Perf. 13x13½*

**3348** A940 9fo Falco cherrug .40 .25
**3349** A940 10fo Hieraaetus pennatus .60 .25
**3350** A940 15fo Circaetus gallicus .85 .50
**3351** A940 40fo Milvus milvus 1.60 1.00
*Nos. 3348-3351 (4)* 3.45 2.00

Raoul Wallenberg, Swedish Diplomat, 80th Anniv. of Birth — A941

**1992, July 30** **Litho.** *Perf. 12*

**3352** A941 15fo gray & red 1.50 .45

Theodore von Karman (1881-1963), Physicist and Aeronautical Engineer — A942

Design: 40fo, John von Neumann (1903-1957), mathematician.

**1992, Aug. 3** **Litho.** *Perf. 12x11½*

**3353** A942 15fo multicolored .45 .25
**3354** A942 40fo multicolored 1.90 .70

3rd World Congress of Hungarians A943

**1992, Aug. 3** *Perf. 13½x13*

**3355** A943 15fo multicolored .80 .35

Telecom '92 — A945

**1992, Oct. 6** **Litho.** *Perf. 12½x11½*

**3360** A945 15fo multicolored .80 .35

Stamp Day — A946

**1992, Sept.4** *Perf. 12*

**3361** A946 10fo +5fo Coat of arms, vert. 1.00 .80
**3362** A946 15fo shown 1.00 .40
**3363** A946 15fo +5fo like #3362, inscribed "65. Belyegnap" 1.50 .85
*Nos. 3361-3363 (3)* 3.50 2.05

### Souvenir Sheet

**3364** A946 50fo +20fo Postilion 4.50 3.25

Eurofilex '92 (#3361, 3363-3364). Nos. 3361, 3363 printed with se-tenant label. No. 3364 contains one 40x30mm stamp.

Famous Men — A947

Designs: 10fo, Stephen Bathory (1533-1586), Prince of Transylvania and King of Poland. 15fo, Stephen Bocskay (1557-1606), Prince of Transylvania. 40fo, Gabriel Bethlen (1580-1629), Prince of Transylvania and King of Hungary.

**1992, Oct. 28** **Litho.** *Perf. 12*

**3365** A947 10fo multicolored .40 .25
**3366** A947 15fo multicolored .70 .30
**3367** A947 40fo multicolored 1.25 .85
*Nos. 3365-3367 (3)* 2.35 1.40

Postal Uniforms — A948

Designs: 10fo, Postrider, 1703-1711. 15fo, Letter carrier, 1874.

**1992, Nov. 20** *Perf. 13½x13*

**3368** A948 10fo multicolored .65 .30
**3369** A948 15fo multicolored 1.00 .50

Christmas A949

**Litho. & Engr.**

**1992, Nov. 20** *Perf. 12*

**3370** A949 15fo blue & black 1.00 .50

### Flowers of the Continents Type of 1990

Flowers of Australia: 9fo, Clianthus formosus. 10fo, Leschenaultia biloba. 15fo, Anigosanthos manglesii. 40fo, Comesperma ericinum. 50fo, Bouquet of flowers.

**1992, Nov. 20** **Litho.**

**3371** A892 9fo multicolored .50 .25
**3372** A892 10fo multicolored .55 .40
**3373** A892 15fo multicolored .75 .50
**3374** A892 40fo multicolored 1.75 1.25
*Nos. 3371-3374 (4)* 3.55 2.40

### Souvenir Sheet

*Perf. 12½*

**3375** A892 50fo multicolored 5.00 3.75

No. 3375 contains one 32x41mm stamp.

1992 European Chess Championships A950

**1992, Oct. 28** *Perf. 11*

**3376** A950 15fo multicolored 1.25 .35

### Flowers of the Continents Type of 1990

Flowers of Asia: No. 3377, Dendrobium densiflorum. No. 3378, Arachnis flos-aeris. No. 3379, Lilium speciosum. No. 3380, Meconopsis aculeata. 50fo, Bouquet of flowers.

**1993, Jan. 27 Litho. *Perf. 13½x13***

**3377** A892 10fo multicolored .45 .25
**3378** A892 10fo multicolored .45 .25
**3379** A892 15fo multicolored 1.00 .50
**3380** A892 15fo multicolored 1.00 .50
*Nos. 3377-3380 (4)* 2.90 1.50

**Souvenir Sheet**

***Perf. 12½***

**3381** A892 50fo multicolored 11.00 3.25

No. 3381 contains one 32x41mm stamp.

Scythian Archaeological Artifacts — A951

**1993, Feb. 25 Litho. *Perf. 13x13½***

**3382** A951 10fo Horse standing .50 .25
**3383** A951 17fo Horse lying down 1.00 .25

Hungarian Rowing Association, Cent. — A952

**1993, Feb. 25 Litho. *Perf. 12***

**3384** A952 17fo multicolored .75 .25

Missale Romanum of Matthias Corvinus (Matyas Hunyadi, King of Hungary) — A953

Design: 40fo, Illuminated page.

**1993, Mar. 12 Litho. *Perf. 12***

**3385** A953 15fo multicolored 1.25 .40

**Souvenir Sheet**

**3386** A953 40fo multicolored 7.00 6.00

No. 3386 contains one 60x38mm stamp. See Belgium Nos. 1474, 1476.

Motocross World Championships A954

**1993, May 5 Litho. *Perf. 11½x12***

**3387** A954 17fo multicolored .75 .25

Europa — A955

Buildings designed by Imre Makovecz: 17fo, Roman Catholic Church, Paks. 45fo, Hungarian Pavilion, Expo '92, Seville.

**1993, May 5 *Perf. 13x13½***

**3388** A955 17fo multicolored *1.50* .50
**3389** A955 45fo multicolored *2.75* 1.25

Heliocentric Solar System, Copernicus — A956

**1993, May 5 *Perf. 12***

**3390** A956 17fo multicolored .90 .25

Polska '93. No. 3390 issued in sheets of 8 + 4 labels.

Edible Mushrooms A957

**1993, June 18 Litho. *Perf. 13½x13***

**3391** A957 10fo Ramaria botrytis .40 .25
**3392** A957 17fo Craterellus cornucopioides .70 .25
**3393** A957 45fo Amanita caesarea 2.25 .80
*Nos. 3391-3393 (3)* 3.35 1.30

St. Christopher, by Albrecht Durer — A958

**1993, June 18 *Perf. 12***

**3394** A958 17fo sil, blk & buff .65 .25

Year of the Elderly.

City of Mohacs, 900th Anniv. — A959

**1993, June 18 *Perf. 13½x13***

**3395** A959 17fo buff, mar & red brn .65 .25

Hungarian State Railways, 125th Anniv. A960

**1993, June 18 *Perf. 13x13½***

**3396** A960 17fo lt blue & blue .65 .25

Comedians A961

**1993, July 28 Litho. *Perf. 12***

**3397** A961 17fo Kalman Latabar .75 .25
**3398** A961 30fo Charlie Chaplin 1.25 .65

Butterflies A962

**1993, July 28 *Perf. 13½x13***

**3399** A962 10fo Limenitis populi .30 .25
**3400** A962 17fo Aricia artaxerxes .70 .25
**3401** A962 30fo Plebejides pylaon 1.25 .65
*Nos. 3399-3401 (3)* 2.25 1.15

**Souvenir Sheet**

Helsinki Conference on European Security and Cooperation, 20th Anniv. — A963

**1993, July 28 *Perf. 12***

**3402** A963 50fo multicolored 3.00 3.00

Intl. Solar Energy Society Congress, Budapest — A964

***Perf. 12½x11½***

**1993, Aug. 23 Litho.**

**3403** A964 17fo multicolored .65 .25

No. 3403 printed se-tenant with label.

Writers — A965

Designs: No. 3404, Laszlo Nemeth (1901-75). No. 3405, Dezso Szabo (1879-1945). No. 3406, Antal Szerb (1901-45).

**1993, Aug. 23 *Perf. 12***

**3404** A965 17fo blue .50 .25
**3405** A965 17fo blue .50 .25
**3406** A965 17fo blue .50 .25
*Nos. 3404-3406 (3)* 1.50 .75

School of Agronomy, Pannon Agricultural Univ., 175th Anniv. — A966

**1993, Oct. 22 Litho. *Perf. 12***

**3407** A966 17fo multicolored .60 .30

Ships A967

**1993, Oct. 27 *Perf. 13x13½***

**3408** A967 10fo Steamer with sails .35 .25
**3409** A967 30fo Battleship 1.00 .50
*a.* Pair, #3408-3409 1.60 .70

Prehistoric Man — A968

**1993, Oct. 27 *Perf. 13½x13***

**3410** A968 17fo Skull fragment .75 .30
**3411** A968 30fo Stone tool 1.25 .50

**Souvenir Sheet**

Roman Roads — A969

**1993, Oct. 27 *Perf. 11***

**3412** A969 50fo multicolored 2.75 1.50

Christmas A970

Altarpiece: 10fo, Virgin and Christ Child, Cathedral of Szekesfehervar, by F. A. Hillebrant.

**1993, Nov. 24 *Perf. 13½x13***

**3413** A970 10fo multicolored .50 .25

Sights of Budapest — A971

Designs: 17fo, Szechenyi Chain Bridge. 30fo, Opera House. 45fo, Matthias Church, vert.

**Photo. & Engr.**

**1993, Dec. 16 *Perf. 12***

**3414** A971 17fo lt grn & dk grn 1.10 .55
**3415** A971 30fo lt mag & dk mag 1.75 .65
**3416** A971 45fo lt brn & dk brn 2.75 1.50
*Nos. 3414-3416 (3)* 5.60 2.70

Expo '96.

Josef Antall (1932-93) — A972

**1993** **Litho.** ***Perf. 11***

**3417** A972 19fo multicolored .80 .40
*a.* Souvenir sheet of 1 1.50 1.50

For surcharge, see No. 4167.

ICAO, 50th Anniv. A973

**1994, Jan. 13** ***Perf. 13x13½***

**3418** A973 56fo multicolored 1.90 .95

1994 Winter Olympics, Lillehammer — A974

**1994, Jan. 13** ***Perf. 12***

**3419** A974 12fo Downhill skiing .40 .25
**3420** A974 19fo Ice hockey .70 .30

A975

Easter: 12fo, Golgotha, by Mihaly Munkacsy.

**1994, Feb. 17** **Litho.** ***Perf. 11½x12***

**3421** A975 12fo multicolored .50 .25

A976

Artists: 12fo, Gyula Benczur (1844-1920). 19fo, Mihaly Munkacsy (1844-1900).

**1994, Feb. 17**

**3422** A976 12fo multicolored .40 .25
**3423** A976 19fo multicolored .65 .30

Lajos Kossuth (1802-94) A977

**1994, Feb. 17**

**3424** A977 19fo multicolored .65 .30

Gen. Joseph Bem (1794-1850) A978

**1994, Mar. 10** ***Perf. 12***

**3425** A978 19fo multicolored .75 .30

Otis Tarda — A979

World Wildlife Fund: No. 3426, Female, male with feathers ruffled in mating dance. No. 3427, Nestlings, female on nest. No. 3428, Nestlings, female standing. No. 3429, Three flying.

**1994, Mar. 14**

**3426** A979 10fo multicolored .75 .40
**3427** A979 10fo multicolored .75 .40
**3428** A979 10fo multicolored .75 .40
**3429** A979 10fo multicolored .75 .40
*a.* Block of 4, #3426-3429 3.50 3.00

A980

Europa: 19fo, Sailing steamer Tegetthoff, Franz-Joseph Land, Julius Payer (1842-1915), Austrian explorer. 50fo, Mark Aurel Stein (1862-1943), explorer, archeologist, geographer, Asian scenes.

**1994, Apr. 1** **Litho.** ***Perf. 13x13½***

**3430** A980 19fo multicolored 2.00 .50
**3431** A980 50fo multicolored 3.00 1.25

Austro-Hungarian Arctic Expedition, 120th anniv. (#3430).

A981

#3432, Baron Miklos Josika (1794-1865), Novelist. #3433, Balint Balassi (1551-94), poet.

**1994, May 19** **Litho.** ***Perf. 12***

**3432** A981 19fo gray .65 .30
**3433** A981 19fo rose lake .65 .30

Creation of Magyar Hungary, 1100th Anniv. (in 1996) — A982

Designs: No. 3434, Two soldiers on horseback. No. 3435, Soldier on white horse, others in background with flags. No. 3436, Soldier on black horse, others in background. No. 3437, Man with staff, oxen pulling carts. No. 3438, Oxen pulling royal cart. No. 3439, Man with staff on shoulder, oxen with packs. No. 3440, Minstrels, bard celebrating. No. 3441, Soldiers preparing to sacrifice white horse. No. 3442, Shaman before fire, headsman.

**1994-96**

**3434** A982 19fo multicolored .85 .30
**3435** A982 19fo multicolored .85 .30
**3436** A982 19fo multicolored .85 .30
*a.* Strip of 3, #3434-3436 3.00 3.00
**3437** A982 22fo multicolored .85 .30
**3438** A982 22fo multicolored .85 .30
**3439** A982 22fo multicolored .85 .30
*a.* Strip of 3, #3437-3439 3.00 3.00
**3440** A982 24fo multicolored .85 .30
**3441** A982 24fo multicolored .85 .30
**3442** A982 24fo multicolored .85 .30
*a.* Strip of 3, #3440-3442 3.00 3.00
*Nos. 3434-3442 (9)* 7.65 2.70

**Souvenir Sheet**

**3442B** A982 195fo multicolored 20.00 16.00

Nos. 3436a, 3439a, 3442a are continuous design. No. 3436a sold for 59fo.
Nos. 3435, 3438, 3441 are 60x40mm.
No. 3442B contains one each of Nos. 3436a, 3439a, 3442a.
Issued: Nos. 3434-3436, 5/19/94; Nos. 3437-3439, 2/23/95; Nos. 3440-3442, 2/29/96, No. 3442B, 4/18/96.

Intl. Olympic Committee, Cent. — A985

Designs: 12fo, 1896, 1992 medals. No. 3444, Flag, runners, Olympic flame. No. 3445, Athens Stadium, 1896. 35fo, Pierre de Coubertin (1863-1937), first president.

**1994, June 16** **Litho.** ***Perf. 12½***

**3443** A985 12fo multicolored .45 .25
**3444** A985 19fo multicolored .65 .30
**3445** A985 19fo multicolored .65 .30
**3446** A985 35fo multicolored 1.25 .60
*Nos. 3443-3446 (4)* 3.00 1.45

1994 World Cup Soccer Championships, US — A986

US flag, soccer players and: No. 3447, Elvis Presley. No. 3448, Marilyn Monroe. No. 3449, John Wayne.

**1994, June 16** ***Perf. 12***

**3447** A986 19fo multicolored .65 .30
**3448** A986 19fo multicolored .65 .30
**3449** A986 35fo multicolored 1.25 .60
*Nos. 3447-3449 (3)* 2.55 1.20

Intl. Year of the Family A987

**1994, July 21** **Litho.** ***Perf. 11***

**3450** A987 19fo multicolored .65 .30

### Flowers of the Continents Type of 1990

Flowers of Europe: 12fo, Leucojum aestivum. 19fo, Helianthemum nummularium. 35fo, Eryngium alpinum. 50fo, Thlaspi rotundifolium. 100fo, Bouquet of European flowers.

**1994, Aug. 18** **Litho.** ***Perf. 11½x12***

**3451** A892 12fo multicolored .40 .25
**3452** A892 19fo multicolored .65 .35
**3453** A892 35fo multicolored 1.25 .60
**3454** A892 50fo multicolored 1.60 .85
*Nos. 3451-3454 (4)* 3.90 2.05

**Souvenir Sheet**

***Perf. 12½***

**3455** A892 100fo multicolored 4.00 2.50

No. 3455 contains one 32x41mm stamp.

UPU, 120th Anniv. A988

UPU emblem and: 19fo, Heinrich Von Stephan (1831-97). 35fo, Mihaly Gervay (1819-96).
#3458: a, Von Stephan, vert. b, Gervay, vert.

**1994, Sept. 9** **Litho.** ***Perf. 12***

**3456** A988 19fo multicolored .55 .30
**3457** A988 35fo multicolored 1.00 .50

**Souvenir Sheet of 2**

**3458** A988 50fo +25fo, #a.-b. 4.50 2.25

Stamp Day, 67th anniv.

Folk Designs — A989

Various ornate designs.

**1994-96** **Litho.** ***Perf. 11½x12***

**3459** A989 1fo bl vio & blk .25 .25
**3460** A989 2fo multi .25 .25
**3461** A989 3fo multi .25 .25
**3461A** A989 9fo multi .25 .25
**3462** A989 11fo multi .35 .25
**3463** A989 12fo multi .35 .25
**3463A** A989 13fo grn, red & blk .25 .25
**3464** A989 14fo multi .25 .25
**3465** A989 16fo bl, red & blk .30 .25
**3466** A989 17fo red & blk .30 .25
**3467** A989 19fo multi .50 .25
**3468** A989 22fo multi .35 .25
**3469** A989 24fo multi .40 .25
**3470** A989 32fo multi .95 .50
**3471** A989 35fo multi 1.00 .50
**3472** A989 38fo multi .65 .30
**3473** A989 40fo multi 1.40 .55
**3474** A989 50fo multi 1.75 .70
**3475** A989 75fo multi 1.50 .65
**3476** A989 80fo multi 1.75 .70
**3477** A989 300fo multi 6.25 2.60
**3478** A989 500fo multi 10.00 4.50
*Nos. 3459-3478 (22)* 29.30 14.25

Issued: 11fo, 12fo, 19fo, 32fo, 35fo, 40fo, 50fo, 10/10/94; 1fo, 1/10/95; 2fo, 3fo, 9fo, 14fo, 22fo, 38fo, 4/3/95; 13fo, 16fo, 17fo, 24fo, 75fo, 80fo, 7/1/96.
See #3561, 3615, 3630, 3644-3646, 3649-3650. For surcharge see #3583.

Souvenir Sheet

Summit Meeting of the Conference for European Security & Cooperation — A990

**1994, Sept. 10 Litho. *Perf. 12***

**3479** A990 100fo Budapest 3.50 2.50

Holocaust, 50th Anniv. — A991

**1994, Oct. 20**

**3480** A991 19fo multicolored .80 .30

Buildings in Budapest A992

#3481, Vajdahunyadvar Castle. #3482, Nemzeti Museum. #3483, Muszaki Palace.

**1994, Nov. 17 Engr.**

| | | | | |
|---|---|---|---|---|
| **3481** | A992 19fo violet | .55 | .30 |
| **3482** | A992 19fo green | .55 | .30 |
| **3483** | A992 19fo brown | .55 | .30 |
| | *Nos. 3481-3483 (3)* | 1.65 | .90 |

Christmas — A993

**1994, Nov. 17 Litho.**

**3484** A993 12fo shown .45 .25
**3485** A993 35fo Flight into Egypt 1.40 .60

Hungarian Shipping Co., Cent. — A994

Design: 22fo, Early steamer Francis Joseph I, cargo ship Baross.

**1995, Jan. 24 Litho. *Perf. 13***

**3486** A994 22fo multicolored .65 .30

Easter — A995

**1995, Mar. 7 *Perf. 12***

**3487** A995 14fo black & lilac .45 .25

Hungarian Shipping — A996

Designs: 14fo, Tug-wheeled steamship, map of first navigable section of the Tisza, view of Szeged. 60fo, Pal Vasarhelyi, Tisza survey ship, surveyor.

**1995, Mar. 7 *Perf. 13***

**3488** A996 14fo multicolored .45 .25
**3489** A996 60fo multicolored 2.00 1.00

Natl. Meteorological Service, 125th Anniv. — A997

**1995, Apr. 7 *Perf. 12***

**3490** A997 22fo multicolored .65 .30

FAO, 50th Anniv. — A998

**1995, Apr. 7**

**3491** A998 22fo multicolored .80 .30

European Nature Conservation Year — A999

#3492, Crane, frog, flowers. #3493, Squirrel, insect. #3494, Bird, berries, flowers. #3495, Butterfly, hedgehog, flowers.

**1995, May 9 Litho. *Perf. 13½x13***

| | | | |
|---|---|---|---|
| **3492** A999 14fo multicolored | .55 | .25 |
| **3493** A999 14fo multicolored | .55 | .25 |
| **3494** A999 14fo multicolored | .55 | .25 |
| **3495** A999 14fo multicolored | .55 | .25 |
| *a.* Strip of 4, #3492-3495 | 3.00 | 2.50 |

Peace & Liberty — A1000

**1995, May 9**

**3496** A1000 22fo multicolored *3.50* .40

Europa.

Hungarian Olympic Committee, Cent. — A1001

22fo, Diver, Pierre de Coubertin. 60fo, Javelin. 100fo, Fencing.

**1995, June 12 Litho. *Perf. 12***

| | | | |
|---|---|---|---|
| **3497** A1001 22fo multicolored | .60 | .30 |
| **3498** A1001 60fo multicolored | 1.60 | .80 |
| **3499** A1001 100fo multicolored | 2.75 | 1.40 |
| *Nos. 3497-3499 (3)* | 4.95 | 2.50 |

St. Ladislas I (1040?-1095) A1002

**1995, June 12**

**3500** A1002 22fo multicolored .60 .30

Laszlo Almasy, Sahara Researcher, Birth Cent. — A1003

**1995, Aug. 22 Litho. *Perf. 13x13½***

**3501** A1003 22fo multicolored .75 .30

Odon Lechner, Architect, 150th Birth Anniv. — A1004

Design: 22fo, Museum of Applied Arts, Lechner.

**Litho. & Engr.**

**1995, Aug. 22 *Perf. 12***

**3502** A1004 22fo multicolored .75 .30

Contemporary Paintings A1005

No. 3503, Abstract, by Laszlo Moholy-Nagy (1895-1946). No. 3504, Woman with a violin, by Aurel Bernath (1895-1982).

**1995, Sept. 18 Litho.**

**3503** A1005 22fo multicolored .75 .30
**3504** A1005 22fo multicolored .75 .30

Eotvos College, Cent. — A1006

60fo, Eotvos College, Josef Eotvos (1813-71), statesman, writer, educational leader.

**1995, Sept. 18**

**3505** A1006 60fo red brn, blk 1.60 .80

Stamp Day A1007

Designs: 22fo, Horse-drawn mail chaise. 40fo, Jet, map. 100fo + 30fo, Man, boys looking at stamp album, vert.

**1995, Sept. 29 Litho. *Perf. 13½x13***

**3506** A1007 22fo multicolored .60 .30
**3507** A1007 40fo multicolored 1.10 .55

**Souvenir Sheet**

***Perf. 12x12½***

**3508** A1007 100fo +30fo multi 3.50 2.50

Buildings of Budapest A1008

#3509, Nyugati Palyaudvar. #3510, Vigado.

**1995 Engr. *Perf. 12***

**3509** A1008 22fo dark olive brn 1.00 .30
**3510** A1008 22fo deep claret 1.00 .30

UN, 50th Anniv. A1009

**1995, Oct. 24 Litho. *Perf. 11***

**3511** A1009 60fo multicolored 1.75 .80

Christmas — A1010

Children's designs: 14fo, Spark thrower. 60fo, The Three Magi.

**1995, Nov. 16 *Perf. 12***

**3512** A1010 14fo multicolored .40 .25
**3513** A1010 60fo multicolored 1.60 .80

Nobel Prize Fund Established, Cent. — A1011

**1995, Nov. 16**

**3514** A1011 100fo Medals 3.00 1.40

No. 3514 is printed se-tenant with label.

St. Elizabeth of Hungary Bathing Lepers — A1012

**1995, Nov. 16** ***Perf. 13***

**3515** A1012 22fo multicolored .80 .30

No. 3515 is printed se-tenant with label.

A1013

Archaeological Finds from Karos: a, Gold and silver saber. b, Badge.

**1996, Mar. 14** **Litho.** ***Perf. 13½x13***

**3516** A1013 24fo #a.-b. + 2 labels 2.00 .55

Souvenir Sheet

Pannonhalma, Benedictine Monastery, 1000th Anniv. — A1014

**1996, Mar. 21** **Engr.** ***Perf. 12***

**3517** A1014 100fo deep violet 5.50 3.50

Sheet margin is litho. and multicolored.

1996 Summer Olympics, Atlanta A1015

**1996, Apr. 18** **Litho.** ***Perf. 11½x12***

**3518** A1015 24fo Swimming .55 .30
**3519** A1015 50fo Tennis 1.10 .60
**3520** A1015 75fo Kayak 1.75 .85
*Nos. 3518-3520 (3)* 3.40 1.75

National Productivity A1016

**1996, Apr. 18** **Litho.** ***Perf. 12***

**3521** A1016 24fo multicolored .55 .30

Natl. Writers Assoc., Cent. — A1017

**1996, Apr. 18** ***Perf. 12x11½***

**3522** A1017 50fo multicolored 1.10 .60

Budapest Subway, Cent. — A1018

**1996, May 2** ***Perf. 12***

**3523** A1018 24fo multicolored .80 .30

Famous Women A1019

Europa: 24fo, Queen Gizella. 75fo, Bavarian Princess Elisabeth Wittelsbach.

**1996, May 2** **Litho.** ***Perf. 12***

**3524** A1019 24fo multicolored *1.50* .50
**3525** A1019 75fo multicolored *3.50* 1.25

Pannonhalma, Benedictine Monastery, 1000th Anniv. A1020

Designs: 17fo, Entrance to cathedral. 24fo, Monks in northern wing.

**1996, June 21** **Engr.** ***Perf. 12***

**3526** A1020 17fo red brown .60 .25
**3527** A1020 24fo dark blue .90 .30

See Nos. 3536-3537.

Intl. Anti-Drug Day — A1021

**1996, June 21** **Litho.** ***Perf. 14***

**3528** A1021 24fo multicolored .65 .30

Hungarian Developers of Technolgy — A1022

Inventor, invention: 24fo, Denes Mihaly (1894-1953), Telehor. 50fo, Jozsef Biro Laszlo (1899-1985), mass-produced ball-point pen. 75fo, Zoltan Bay (1900-92), lunar radar set.

**1996, June 21** ***Perf. 12x11½***

**3529** A1022 24fo multicolored .55 .30
**3530** A1022 50fo multicolored 1.10 .60
**3531** A1022 75fo multicolored 1.75 .85
*Nos. 3529-3531 (3)* 3.40 1.75

Hungarian Railways, 150th Anniv. — A1023

Designs: 17fo, 303-Series steam tender locomotive. No. 3533, 325-Series locomotive . No. 3534, "Pest," steam locomotive made by Cokerill and Co.

**1996, July 12** ***Perf. 13½x13***

**3532** A1023 17fo multicolored .55 .25
**3533** A1023 24fo multicolored .70 .30
**3534** A1023 24fo multicolored 1.50 .30
*Nos. 3532-3534 (3)* 2.75 .85

Second European Congress of Mathematicians A1024

**1996, July 12** ***Perf. 12***

**3535** A1024 24fo multicolored .55 .30

**Pannonhalma, Benedictine Monastery, Type of 1996**

Designs: 17fo, Refectory. 24fo, Main library.

**1996, Aug. 12** **Engr.** ***Perf. 12***

**3536** A1020 17fo dark brown .60 .25
**3537** A1020 24fo dark green .90 .25

Nature Expo '96 A1025

**1996, Aug. 12** **Litho.** ***Perf. 12x11½***

**3538** A1025 13fo Egretta alba .25 .25
**3539** A1025 13fo Iris sibirica .25 .25
**3540** A1025 13fo Lynx lynx .25 .25
**3541** A1025 13fo Ropalopus ungaricus 1.20 1.20
*a.* Block of 4, #3538-3541 2.00 2.00

A1026

A1027

**1996, Aug. 12** ***Perf. 12***

**3542** A1026 24fo No. 4 1.00 .25

Hungarian postage stamps, 125th anniv.

Issued in miniature sheets of 6 stamps in two columns of 3 separated by a column of labels. Values, stamp plus label $1.50, miniature sheet $7.50.

**1996, Aug. 21** **Litho.** ***Perf. 11½x12***

Stamp Day, Budapest '96: 17fo, Prince Arpad, people from 14th cent. "Vienna Picture Chronicle," man stirring liquid in pot. 24fo, Prince on horseback, archer.

150fo+50fo, #601, first page from "The Deeds of Hungarians."

**3543** A1027 17fo multicolored .60 .25
**3544** A1027 24fo multicolored .90 .25

**Souvenir Sheet**

***Perf. 12x12½***

**3545** A1027 150fo +50fo multi 5.50 3.00

Steamships on Lake Balaton, 150th Anniv. — A1028

Steamer Kisfaludy.

**1996, Sept. 17** **Litho.** ***Perf. 12***

**3548** A1028 17fo multicolored .60 .25

Hungarian Revolution, 40th Anniv. — A1029

Newspaper clippings and: 13fo, People marching. 16fo, Troops on back of truck. 17fo, Two men with guns. 24fo, Imre Nagy addressing people.

40fo, Nagy Cabinet.

**1996, Oct. 23** **Litho.** ***Perf. 12***

**3549** A1029 13fo multicolored .35 .25
**3550** A1029 16fo multicolored .40 .25
**3551** A1029 17fo multicolored .40 .25
**3552** A1029 24fo multicolored .60 .25
*Nos. 3549-3552 (4)* 1.75 1.00

**Souvenir Sheet**

**3553** A1029 40fo multicolored 4.00 2.25

Souvenir Sheet

1996 Summer Olympic Games, Atlanta — A1030

**1996, Oct. 22**

**3554** A1030 150fo multicolored 4.50 2.25

A1036

**1996, Nov. 14 Litho.** ***Perf. 11½x12***

**3555** A1036 24fo multicolored .40 .20

Miklos Wesselenyi (1796-1850), writer.

A1037

**1996, Nov. 14** ***Perf. 13½x13***

**3556** A1037 24fo multicolored .40 .25

UNICEF, 50th anniv.

Christmas
A1038

Paintings: 17fo, Mary with Infant Jesus and Two Angels, by Matteo di Giovanni. 24fo, Adoration of the Kings, by unknown painter of Salsburg.

**1996, Nov. 14** ***Perf. 12***

**3557** A1038 17fo multicolored .35 .25

**3558** A1038 24fo multicolored .65 .25

Hungarian Literature — A1039

Designs: No. 3559, Scenes from "The Umbrella of St. Peter," Kalman Mikszath (1847-1910). No. 3560, Scenes of men and dogs from "Abel in the Vast Trackless Forest" and "Matthias the Ice-breaker," Aron Tamasi (1897-1966).

**1997, Jan. 16 Litho.** ***Perf. 12x11½***

**3559** A1039 27fo multicolored .50 .25

**3560** A1039 27fo multicolored .50 .25

### Folk Art Type of 1994

**1997, Mar. 26** ***Perf. 11½x12***

**3561** A989 27fo multicolored .65 .25

Coat of Arms of Budapest and Counties — A1040

No. 3562: a, Hajdú-Bihar. b, Baranya. c, Bács-Kiskun. d, Békés. e, Borsod-Abaúj-Zemplén.

No. 3563: a, Fejér. b, Győr-Moson-Sopron. c, Heves. d, Jász-Nagykun-Szolnok. e, Komárom-Esztergom. f, Nógrád.

No. 3564: a, Pest. b, Somogy. c, Toina. d, Vas. e, Veszprém. f, Zala.

No. 3565: a, Budapest. b, Csongrád. c, Szaboics-Szatmár-Bereg.

**1997, Mar. 26** ***Perf. 11½x12***

**3562** A1040 27fo Sheet of 5, #a.-e. + label 5.00 3.25

**3563** A1040 27fo Sheet of 6, #a.-f. 6.25 4.25

**3564** A1040 27fo Sheet of 6, #a.-f. 6.25 4.25

**3564G** A1040 27fo Hajdu-Bihar 5.00 5.00

**Size: 51x33mm**

**3565** A1040 27fo Sheet of 3, #a.-c. 2.25 1.75

No. 3564G is 51x33mm and has the same design as No. 3562a which has a se-tenant label, but lacks the perforations separating these items. Nos. 3262a-3262e, 3563a-3563f, 3564a-3564f, 3565a-3565c were also printed in individual sheets. Value, set of singles (20): mint $11; used $4.

A1041

Youth Stamps — A1042

Designs: 20fo, Scouting emblem, tents, sailboat, waterfall. 27fo+10fo, Knights on horseback from "Toldi," by Janos Arany.

**1997, Apr. 23** ***Perf. 12***

**3566** A1041 20fo multicolored .50 .25

**3567** A1042 27fo +10fo multi 1.25 .35

A1043

**1997, Apr. 23** ***Perf. 13½x13***

**3568** A1043 90fo multicolored 1.60 .80

World Meeting of Custom Directors.

A1044

**1997, Apr. 23 Engr.** ***Perf. 12***

**3569** A1044 80fo deep violet 2.00 .70

St. Adalbert (956-997). See Germany No. 1964, Poland No. 3307, Czech Republic No. 3012, Vatican City No. 1040..

Stories and Legends
A1045

Europa: 27fo, Hunters on horseback shooting bow and arrow at deer. 90fo, Preparing body in sarcophagus of Prince Geza.

**1997, May 5 Litho.** ***Perf. 13x13½***

**3570** A1045 27fo multicolored *1.25* .40

**3571** A1045 90fo multicolored *2.50* .90

African Animals
A1046

16fo, Oryx gazella. #3573, Equus burchelli. #3574, Diceros bicornis. 27fo, Panthera leo. 90fo, Loxodonta africana.

**1997, May 5** ***Perf. 12***

**3572** A1046 16fo multicolored .30 .25

**3573** A1046 20fo multicolored .60 .25

**3574** A1046 20fo multicolored .60 .25

**3575** A1046 27fo multicolored 1.00 .30

*Nos. 3572-3575 (4)* 2.50 1.05

**Souvenir Sheet**

**3576** A1046 90fo multicolored 4.50 3.00

A1047

**1997, June 8 Litho.** ***Perf. 12***

**3577** A1047 90fo multicolored 1.60 .70

Polish Queen Jadwiga (1373-99).

A1048

World Congress on Stress, Budapest: Janos (Hans) Selye (1907-82), founder of theory of stress, face of person under stress.

**1997, July 1**

**3578** A1048 90fo multicolored 1.75 .70

Indigenous Fish
A1049

Designs: a, Gymnocephalus schraetzer. b, Cottus gobio. c, Alburnoides bipunctatus. d, Cobitis taenia.

**1997, June 6 Litho.** ***Perf. 13x13½***

**3579** A1049 20fo Strip of 4, #a.-d. 2.50 1.25

### Grapes and Wine Producing Areas Type of 1990

Grapes and growing area: No. 3580, Nemes kadarka, Great Kiskoros. No. 3581, Teitfürtü ezerjo, Mor. No. 3582, Harslevelu, Gyongyos.

**1997, Aug. 12 Litho.** ***Perf. 13x13½***

**3580** A902 27fo multicolored .50 .25

**3581** A902 27fo multicolored .50 .25

**3582** A902 27fo multicolored 1.00 .25

*Nos. 3580-3582 (3)* 2.00 .75

No. 3469 Surcharged in Red

**1997, July 10 Litho.** ***Perf. 11½x12***

**3583** A989 60fo on 24fo multi 1.00 .45

Christmas
A1050

20fo, Holy family. 27fo, Adoration of the Magi.

**1997, Oct. 31 Litho.** ***Perf. 13x13½***

**3584** A1050 20fo multicolored .40 .25

**3585** A1050 27fo multicolored .60 .25

World Weight Lifting Championships, Thailand
A1051

**1997, Nov. 12** ***Perf. 12***

**3586** A1051 90fo multicolored 1.60 .65

Zsigmond Szechenyi, African Explorer A1052

**1998, Jan. 22 Litho. *Perf. 12***

**3587** A1052 60fo multicolored 1.60 .45

Natl. Anthem by Ferenc Kolcsey, 175th Anniv. A1053

**1998, Jan. 22**

**3588** A1053 75fo multicolored 1.60 .55

1998 Winter Olympic Games, Nagano — A1054

**1998, Jan. 22 *Perf. 13½x13***

**3589** A1054 30fo Downhill skiing .75 .30
**3590** A1054 100fo Snowboarding 1.25 .85

Valentine's Day — A1055

**1998, Feb. 11 *Perf. 11½x12***

**3591** A1055 24fo multi .65 .25

A1056 A1057

**1998, Feb. 11 *Perf. 12***

**3592** A1056 50fo multicolored 1.75 .50

Leo Szilard (1898-1964), physicist.

**1998, Feb. 11 *Perf. 11½x12***

Balint Postas (Post Office Mascot) in front of printed material: 23fo, Holding letter. 24fo, Bowing. 30fo, Standing straight with arms outstretched. 65fo, Flying.

**3593** A1057 23fo multicolored .50 .25
**3594** A1057 24fo multicolored .50 .25
**3595** A1057 30fo multicolored .65 .30
**3596** A1057 65fo multicolored 1.40 .65
*Nos. 3593-3596 (4)* 3.05 1.45

Easter

A1058 A1059

**1998, Mar. 13 Litho. *Perf. 13½x13***

**3597** A1058 24fo Stylized egg .55 .25

***Perf. 11***

**3598** A1059 30fo Christ's resurrection .65 .25

1848-49 Revolution, War of Independence, 150th Anniv. — A1060

23fo, Sandor Petofi (1823-49), poet, handwriting, tricolor. 24fo, Mihaly Tancsics, writer & politician, ink well. 30fo, Lajos Kossuth (1802-94), seal.

**1998, Mar. 13 *Perf. 12***

**3599** A1060 23fo multicolored .40 .25
**3600** A1060 24fo multicolored .50 .25
**3601** A1060 30fo multicolored .60 .25
*Nos. 3599-3601 (3)* 1.50 .75

See Nos. 3640-3643.

Art Nouveau — A1061

Ceramics: 20fo, Vase with relief design of young girl picking flowers, 1899. 24fo, Flower holder with peacock-eyed butterflies, 1901. 30fo, Vase with tulip stems, 1899. 95fo, Round container with legs, 1912.

**1998, Mar. 31 Litho. *Perf. 12***

**3602** A1061 20fo multi, vert. .35 .25
Complete booklet, 10 #3602 3.25
**3603** A1061 24fo multi .40 .25
Complete booklet, 10 #3603 3.75
**3604** A1061 30fo multi, vert. .50 .25
Complete booklet, 10 #3604 4.75
**3605** A1061 95fo multi 1.50 .70
*Nos. 3602-3605 (4)* 2.75 1.45

Postal Regulation, 250th Anniv. — A1062

Designs: 24fo+10fo, Courier of 1748, detail of postal route connecting counties of Zala and Gyor. 30fo+10fo, Mounted courier, blowing post horn, script of regulation.

150fo, Horse-drawn postal coach, detail of postal route.

**1998, Apr. 10**

**3606** A1062 24fo +10fo multi .75 .45
**3607** A1062 30fo +10fo multi 1.25 .60

**Souvenir Sheet**

**3608** A1062 150fo multicolored 5.00 2.50

Stamp Day.

Animals of the Americas A1063

23fo, Bison bison. #3610, Ursus horribilis. #3611, Alligator mississippiensis. 30fo, Leopardus pardalis.

150fo, Loddigesia mirabilis.

**1998, Apr. 30**

**3609** A1063 23fo multicolored .75 .35
**3610** A1063 24fo multicolored .75 .35
**3611** A1063 24fo multicolored .75 .35
**3612** A1063 30fo multicolored 1.00 .45
*Nos. 3609-3612 (4)* 3.25 1.50

**Souvenir Sheet**

**3613** A1063 150fo multicolored 5.00 2.50

Gyorgy Jendrassik, Engineer, Birth Cent. A1064

**1998, May 4 Engr.**

**3614** A1064 100fo dark blue 1.50 .75

**Folk Designs Type of 1994**

**1998, June 5 Litho. *Perf. 11½x12***

**3615** A989 5fo multicolored .40 .25

1998 Canoe-Kayak World Championships, Szeged — A1065

**1998, June 5 *Perf. 12***

**3616** A1065 30fo multicolored .50 .25

1998 World Cup Soccer Championships, France — A1066

Different soccer players.

**1998, June 5**

**3617** A1066 30fo multicolored .45 .25
**3618** A1066 110fo multicolored 1.60 .80
*a.* Pair, 3617-3618 2.10 1.00

1998 European Track & Field Championships, Budapest — A1067

**1998, June 5 *Perf. 12x11***

**3619** A1067 24fo Hurdles .35 .25
**3620** A1067 65fo Pole vault .95 .50
**3621** A1067 80fo Hammer throw 1.25 .60
*Nos. 3619-3621 (3)* 2.55 1.35

Gabor Baross (1848-92), Postal Administrator A1068

**1998, June 5 *Perf. 12***

**3622** A1068 60fo multicolored .90 .45

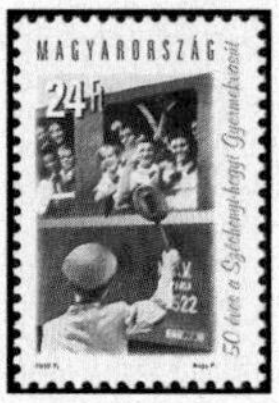


A1069

**1998, July 31 Litho. *Perf. 12***

**3623** A1069 24fo multicolored .60 .25
Complete booklet, 10 #3623 10.00

Széchenyi Hill Children's Railway, 50th anniv.

A1070

**1998, July 31 *Perf. 12x11½***

**3624** A1070 65fo multicolored 1.25 .50

World Congress of Computer Technology, Budapest.

Natl. Holidays — A1071

Europa: 50fo, Sculptures, Festival of the 1956 Revolution, Proclamation of the Republic, 1989, October 23. 60fo, Sheaf of grain, Natl. arms, National Day, August 20.

**1998, Aug. 19 Litho. *Perf. 12***

**3625** A1071 50fo multicolored 1.50 .65
**3626** A1071 60fo multicolored 2.25 .85

A1072

**1998, Aug. 19**

**3627** A1072 100fo multicolored 1.40 .70

World Federation of Hungarians, 60th Anniv.

National Parks A1073

Various flora, fauna, explorer of given region: 24fo, Dr. Miklós Udvardy, Hortobágy Natl. Park. 70fo, Adám Boros, Kiskunság Natl. Park.

**1998, Oct. 6 Litho. *Perf. 12***

**3628** A1073 24fo multicolored .50 .25
**3629** A1073 70fo multicolored 1.25 .50

See Nos. 3654-3655, 3689-3690, 3745-3747, 3689-3690, 4072.

**Folk Designs Type of 1994**

**1998 Litho. *Perf. 11½x12***

**3630** A989 200fo multicolored 5.00 .70

Christmas A1074

Designs: 20fo, Painting, "Visit of the Shepherds," by Agnolo Bronzino (1503-72). 24fo, Artwork, "Mary Upon the Throne with the Infant," by Carlo Crivelli (1430?-94?), vert.

**1998, Oct. 30 *Perf. 12x11½, 11½x12***

**3631** A1074 20fo multicolored .40 .25
Complete booklet, 10 #3631 3.75
**3632** A1074 24fo multicolored .45 .25
Complete booklet, 10 #3632 6.50

See No. 3676.

Easter A1075

**1999, Feb. 11 Litho. *Perf. 12***

**3633** A1075 27fo Decorated eggs .35 .25
**3634** A1075 32fo Shroud of Turin .75 .25

No. 3634 is 38x53mm.

Intl. Year of the Elderly A1076

**1999, Feb. 11 *Perf. 12½x13½***

**3635** A1076 32fo multicolored .75 .25

Sailing Ships A1077

**1999, Feb. 11 *Perf. 12***

**3636** A1077 32fo Novara .40 .25
**3637** A1077 79fo Phoenix 1.00 .50
**3638** A1077 110fo Galley, 15th cent. 1.40 .70
*Nos. 3636-3638 (3)* 2.80 1.45

Souvenir Sheet

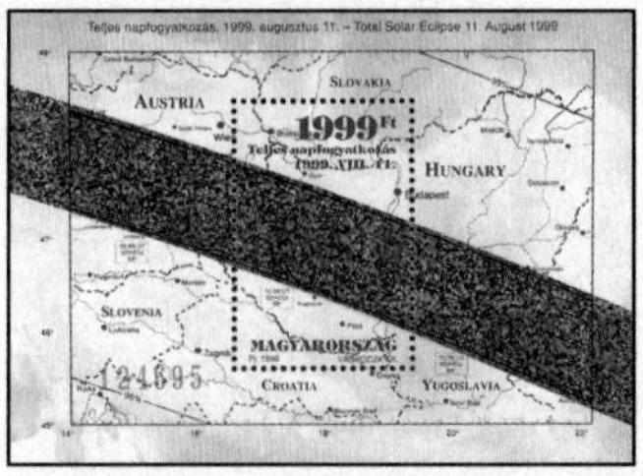


Total Solar Eclipse, Aug. 11 — A1078

**1999, Feb. 11**

**3639** A1078 1999fo multi 22.00 22.00

No. 3639 contains a holographic image. Soaking in water may affect the hologram.

**Revolution of 1848-49 Type of 1998**

24fo, Sword, Artúr Görgey (1818-1916), general. 27fo, Military decoration, Lajos Batthyány (1806-49), premier of 1st Hungarian ministry. 32fo, Military decoration, Jósef Bem (1794-1850), Polish General who joined Hungarian army.
100fo, Battle scene.

**1999, Mar. 12**

**3640** A1060 24fo multicolored .45 .25
**3641** A1060 27fo multicolored .55 .25
**3642** A1060 32fo multicolored .60 .25
*Nos. 3640-3642 (3)* 1.60 .75

**Souvenir Sheet**

**3643** A1060 100fo multicolored 4.00 2.00

No. 3643 contains one 45x28mm stamp.

**Folk Designs Type of 1994**

**1999 Litho. *Perf. 12½***

**3644** A989 24fo multicolored .40 .25
**3645** A989 65fo red & black 1.10 .30
**3646** A989 90fo multicolored 2.00 .55
*Nos. 3644-3646 (3)* 3.50 1.10

Nos. 3644-3646 are inscribed "1999."

Entrance into NATO — A1079

**1999, Mar. 12 Litho. *Perf. 12x11½***

**3647** A1079 110fo multicolored 1.60 .55

Souvenir Sheet

1999 Modern Pentathlon World Championships, Budapest — A1080

**1999, Mar. 24 *Perf. 12½***

**3648** A1080 100fo multicolored 3.50 1.75

**Folk Designs Type of 1994**

Various ornate designs.

**1999, Apr. 19 Litho. *Perf. 11½x12***

**3649** A989 79fo multicolored 1.60 .45
**3650** A989 100fo multicolored 2.40 .60

A1081

**1999, May 3 *Perf. 12***

**3651** A1081 50fo slate & bister .85 .30

Ferenc Pápai Páriz (1649-1716).

A1082

**1999, May 3**

**3652** A1082 100fo multicolored 1.75 .65

Ferencvárosi Torna Sport Club, cent.

World Science Conference A1082a

**1999, May 3 Litho. *Perf. 11½x12½***

**3652A** A1082a 65fo multicolored 2.00 .60

Council of Europe, 50th Anniv. A1083

**1999, May 4 *Perf. 13x13¼***

**3653** A1083 50fo multicolored 2.00 .50

**National Parks Type of 1998**

Europa: 27fo, Aggteleki National Park. 32fo, Bükki National Park.

**1999, May 6 *Perf. 12***

**3654** A1073 27fo multicolored 3.50 1.40
**3655** A1073 32fo multicolored 5.00 3.25

**Grapes and Wine Producing Areas Type of 1990**

Grapes, growing area and: 24fo, Castle ruins, Somló region. 27fo, 17th cent. view of Sopron.

**1999, May 6 Litho. *Perf. 12¼x12½***

**3656** A902 24fo multi, horiz. .70 .25
**3657** A902 27fo multi, horiz. 1.10 .30

Animals of Asia A1085

Designs: 27fo, Tigris regalis. 32fo, Ailuropodus melanoleucus. 52fo, Panthera pardus. 79fo, Pongo pygmaeus.
100fo, Aix galericulata.

**1999, May 6 *Perf. 12***

**3658** A1085 27fo multicolored .50 .25
**3659** A1085 32fo multicolored .65 .30
**3660** A1085 52fo multicolored .95 .40
**3661** A1085 79fo multicolored 1.90 .50
*Nos. 3658-3661 (4)* 4.00 1.45

**Souvenir Sheet**

**3662** A1085 100fo multicolored 6.50 5.00

No. 3662 contains one 50x30mm stamp.

Queen Maria Theresa's Introduction of Mail Coach Service, 250th Anniv. A1086

Stamp Day: 32fo+15fo, Decree by Maria Theresa, coach, street. 52fo+20fo, People entering coach, woman with letters, portion of decree.
150fo, Horse-drawn coach arriving a station.

**1999, May 21 Litho. *Perf. 12½x12¼***

**3663** A1086 32fo +15fo multi .80 .75
**3664** A1086 52fo +20fo multi 1.40 1.00

**Souvenir Sheet**

**3665** A1086 150fo multicolored 4.50 4.00

#3665 contains one 32x42mm stamp.

Red Poppy — A1087

**1999, July 7 Litho. *Perf. 12x11½***

**3666** A1087 27fo shown 1.00 .40
**3667** A1087 32fo Stalkless gentian 1.50 .70

See Nos. 3805-3806.

George Cukor (1899-1983), Film Director — A1088

**1999, July 7 Litho. *Perf. 12***

**3668** A1088 50fo multicolored 1.25 .40

UPU, 125th Anniv. A1089

**1999, Aug. 13 Litho. *Perf. 12***

**3669** A1089 32fo multicolored 1.25 .85

Issued in sheets of 3. Value $4.50.

Frankfurt Book Fair — A1090

**1999, Sept. 9 Litho. *Perf. 12***

**3670** A1090 40fo multicolored 1.75 .25

Antique Furniture A1091

Designs: 10fo, Chair, 17th cent, vert. 20fo, Chair by Károly Lingel, 1915, vert. 50fo, Chair by Pál Esterházy, vert. 70fo, Upholstered chair, vert. 100fo, Couch by Lajos Kozma.

*Perf. 11½x12, 12x11½*

**1999, Oct. 7** **Litho.**

**3671** A1091 10fo bister & dk brn .25 .25
**3672** A1091 20fo green & dk grn .40 .25
**3673** A1091 50fo blue & dk bl .80 .30
**3674** A1091 70fo red & dk red 1.25 .35
**3675** A1091 100fo brown & dk brn 1.75 .50
*Nos. 3671-3675 (5)* 4.45 1.65

Nos. 3671-3673, 3675 exist dated "2001."
See Nos. 3711-3721, 3737-3743, 3790-3791, 3821-3823, 3960-3965, 4134, 4184.

### Bronzino Christmas Painting Type of 1998 and

Magi — A1092

Madonna and Child, Stained Glass by Miksa Róth — A1093

**1999, Oct. 15** *Perf. 12x11½, 11½x12*

**3676** A1074 24fo multi .65 .25
Complete booklet, 10 #3676 10.00
**3677** A1092 27fo multi .85 .25
Complete booklet, 10 #3677 9.50
**3678** A1093 32fo multi 1.00 .25
Complete booklet, 10 #3678 10.00
*Nos. 3676-3678 (3)* 2.50 .75

Jenö Wigner (1902-95), Winner of 1963 Nobel Physics Prize — A1094

**1999, Nov. 3** *Perf. 12*

**3679** A1094 32fo blue 1.00 .30

Souvenir Sheet

Chain Bridge, 150th Anniv. — A1095

**1999, Nov. 3**

**3680** A1095 150fo multi 3.25 2.25

Hungarian Millennium A1096

Designs: 28fo, 30fo, Coronation scepter. 34fo, 40fo, Millennium flag.

**2000** **Litho.** *Perf. 12x11½*

**3681** A1096 28fo multi .80 .25
**3682** A1096 30fo multi .80 .25
**3683** A1096 34fo multi .80 .25
**3684** A1096 40fo multi 1.10 .25
*Nos. 3681-3684 (4)* 3.50 1.00

Coronation of Stephen I, Hungarian conversion to Christianity, 1000th anniv.
Issued: 30fo, 40fo, 1/1; 28fo, 24fo, 2/24.
No. 3681 exists dated 2001.
See No. 3744.

Souvenir Sheet

Famous Hungarians — A1097

No. 3685: a, 30fo, Miklós Misztófalusi Kis (1650-1702), scientist. b, 40fo, Anyos Jedlik (1800-95), physicist. c, 50fo, Jeno Kvassay (1850-1919), engineer. d, 80fo, Jeno Barcsay (1900-88), painter.

**2000, Jan. 11** *Perf. 11½x12*

**3685** A1097 Sheet of 4, #a.-d. 4.00 3.75

Souvenir Sheet

Literary and Theatrical Personalities — A1098

No. 3686: a, Mihály Vörösmarty (1800-55), dramatist. b, Mari Jászai (1850-1926), actress. c, Sándor Márai (1900-89), writer. d, Lujza Blaha (1850-1926), actress. e, Lorinc Szabó (1900-57), writer.

**2000, Feb. 24** *Perf. 12*

**3686** A1098 50fo #a.-e. 4.00 3.50

A1099

Easter — A1100

**2000, Mar. 20**

**3687** A1099 26fo multi .50 .25
**3688** A1100 28fo multi .75 .30

### National Parks Type of 1998

Designs: 29fo, Bluethroat, Siberian iris, ornithologist György Breuer (1887-1955), Ferto-Hanság Park. 34fo, Black stork, fritillary, scientist Pál Kitaibel (1757-1817), Duna-Dráva Park.

**2000, Mar. 20** **Litho.** *Perf. 12*

**3689** A1073 29fo multi .60 .25
Complete booklet, 10 #36892 5.50
**3690** A1073 34fo multi 1.00 .35
Complete booklet, 10 #3690 7.50

Ferihegy Airport, 50th Anniv. — A1101

**2000, May 3** *Perf. 12x11½*

**3691** A1101 136fo multi 2.00 1.00

István Türr (1825-1908) and Canal Boat — A1102

**2000, May 9** *Perf. 12*

**3692** A1102 80fo multi 1.50 .70

Expo 2000, Hanover.

Australian Wildlife — A1103

**2000, May 9**

**3693** A1103 26fo shown .30 .25
**3694** A1103 28fo Opossum .35 .25
**3695** A1103 83fo Koala 1.10 .30
**3696** A1103 90fo Red kangaroo 1.00 .35
*Nos. 3693-3696 (4)* 2.75 1.15

**Souvenir Sheet**

**3697** A1103 110fo Platypus 4.00 2.25

Souvenir Sheet

Millennium — A1104

### Litho., Hologram in Margin

**2000, May 9**

**3698** A1104 2000fo multi 25.00 25.00

Soaking in water may affect the hologram.

### Europa, 2000

Common Design Type and

A1105

**2000, May 9** **Litho.**

**3699** A1105 34fo multi *2.75* .75
**3700** CD17 54fo multi *3.75* 1.75

Stamp Day — A1106

26fo, Queen Gisela in coronation gown. 28fo, King Stephen I in coronation gown.

**2000, May 18**

**3701** A1106 26fo multi .75 .45
**3702** A1106 28fo multi 1.25 .65

Austria No. 4 and Bisect A1107

**2000, May 18**

**3703** A1107 110fo multi 1.75 1.75

WIPA 2000 Philatelic Exhibition, Vienna.

### Grapes and Wine Producing Areas Type of 1990

Grapes and: 29fo, Winery building, Balatonfüred-Csopak region, horiz. 34fo, Storage containers, Aszár-Neszmély region, horiz.

**2000, May 25** *Perf. 13¼x13*

**3704** A902 29fo multi .65 .35
**3705** A902 34fo multi 1.10 .40

Houses of Worship A1108

Designs: No. 3706, 30fo, Abbey Church, Ják. No. 3707, 30fo, Reformed Church, Tákos. No. 3708, 30fo, St. Antal's Church, Eger. No. 3709, 30fo, Deák Evangelical Church, Budapest. 120fo, Dohany Synagogue, Budapest.

**2000** **Litho.** *Perf. 12*

**3706-3710** A1108 Set of 5 3.00 3.00

Issued: 120fo, 9/19; others 6/30. See Israel No. 1416.

### Furniture Type of 1999

Designs: 2fo, Wooden chair, 1838, vert. 3fo, 19th cent. chair, vert. 4fo, Chair by Géza Maróti, 1900, vert. 5fo, Chair by Odon Farago, 1900, vert. 6fo, Chair by Márton Kovács, 1893, vert. 9fo, 18th cent. chair from Dunapataj, vert. 26fo, 1850 chair, vert. 29fo, 19th cent. chair with animal designs, vert. 30fo, Chair by Károly Nagy, 1935, vert. 80fo, 1840-50 chair, vert. 90fo, Chair by Lajos Kozma, 1928, vert.

**2000** *Perf. 11½x12*

**3711-3721** A1091 Set of 11 4.50 2.00

Issued: 2fo, 3fo, 9fo, 26fo, 29fo, 30fo, 6/30; others, 10/9.

Hungarian Aviation, 90th Anniv. A1109

**2000, Aug. 18** *Perf. 12¾x12¼*

**3722** A1109 120fo multi 1.75 1.50

Souvenir Sheets

Hungarian History — A1110

No. 3723: a, King with orb, knights. b, St. Laszlo with sword. c, St. Elizabeth, Mongol invasion. d, King Sigismund, knight on horseback. e, Janos Hunuyadi and Janos Kapisztran.

No. 3724: a, King Matthias. b, Crucifixion scene, Miklos Zrinyi. c, Trumpeter on horseback, battle scenes. d, Gabor Bethlen (in black hat). e, Peer Parmany, university.

**2000, Aug. 18** *Perf. 12*

**3723** Sheet of 5 5.00 3.50
***a.-e.*** A1110 50fo Any single .70 .35
**3724** Sheet of 5 5.00 3.50
***a.-e.*** A1110 50fo Any single .70 .35

See Nos. 3770-3771.

A1111

A1112

Christmas
A1113

**2000, Oct. 16** ***Perf. 12¼x11½***

**3725** A1111 26fo shown .40 .25

***Perf. 13¼x13***

**3726** A1112 28fo shown .65 .25
Booklet, 10 #3726 7.00
**3727** A1112 29fo Christmas tree .65 .25

***Perf. 12***

**3728** A1113 34fo shown .70 .25
Booklet, 10 #3728 8.00
*Nos. 3725-3728 (4)* 2.40 1.00

European Convention on Human Rights, 50th Anniv. — A1114

**2000, Nov. 3** ***Perf. 12½***

**3729** A1114 50fo multicolored .75 .50

2000 Summer Olympics, Sydney
A1115

Sports and total of medals won: 30fo, Shooting, three bronzes. 40fo, Weight lifting, six silvers. 80fo, Men's rings, eight golds. 120fo, Rowing, total count.

**2000, Nov. 22** ***Perf. 12***

**3730-3732** A1115 Set of 3 1.50 1.50

**Souvenir Sheet**

**3733** A1115 120fo multi 3.00 1.75

European Language Year
A1116

**2001, Jan. 15** **Litho.** ***Perf. 13x13¼***

**3734** A1116 100fo multi 1.25 1.25

Souvenir Sheet

Greetings — A1117

No. 3735: a, Bugler on pig. b, Man, woman, flower. c, Baby in cradle. d, Clown. e, Mother and child.

**2001, Feb. 9** ***Perf. 11½x12***

**3735** A1117 36fo Sheet of 5, #a-f 2.50 2.00

World Speed Skating Championships, Budapest — A1118

**2001, Feb. 9** **Litho.** ***Perf. 13***

**3736** A1118 140fo multi 1.75 1.75

**Furniture Type of 1999**

Designs: 1fo, Three-legged stool, by János Vincze, 1910, vert. 7fo, 1853 chair, vert. 8fo, 19th cent. chair, vert. 31fo, Like No. 3717, vert. 40fo, Armchair by Ignác Alpár, 1896, vert. 60fo, Armchair by Ferenc Steindl, 1840, vert. 200fo, Settee by Sebestyén Vogel, 1810.

**2001** ***Perf. 11½x12, 12x11½***

**3737-3743** A1091 Set of 7 4.25 1.50

Issued: 31fo, 3/5; others, 2/9.

**Hungarian Millennium Type of 2000**

**2001, Mar. 5** ***Perf. 12x11½***

**3744** A1096 36fo Millennium flag 1.00 .25

**National Parks Type of 1998**

Designs: 28fo, Balaton. 36fo, Körös-maros. 70fo, Duna-Ipoly.

**2001, Mar. 5** ***Perf. 12***

**3745-3747** A1073 Set of 3 1.75 1.50

Easter
A1119

**2001, Mar. 5** ***Perf. 13***

**3748** A1119 28fo multi .50 .25

Locomotives — A1120

Designs: 31fo, Mk. 48. 36fo, 490. 100fo, 394. 150fo, C50.

**2001, Apr. 13** ***Perf. 13¼x13***

**3749-3752** A1120 Set of 4 3.25 3.25

Esztergom Archbishopric, 1000th Anniv. — A1121

**2001, Apr. 18** ***Perf. 12***

**3753** A1121 124fo multi 1.50 1.25

Organizations — A1122

No. 3754: a, 70fo, Emblems of European and Mediterranean Plant Protection Organization and Intl. Plant Protection Convention. b, 80fo, UN High Commissioner for Refugees, 50th anniv.

**2001, Apr. 18** ***Perf. 13¼x13***

**3754** A1122 Horiz. pair, #a-b 1.75 1.50

Europa
A1123

Designs: 36fo, Open chest with water. 90fo, Split globe with water.

**2001, May 9** ***Perf. 12***

**3755-3756** A1123 Set of 2 *3.25* 1.75

Animals
A1124

Designs: 28fo, Phoca hispida. 36fo, Canis lupus. 70fo, Testudo hermanni. 90fo, Alcedo atthis ispida.
200fo, Cervus elaphus.

**2001, May 9** ***Perf. 12***

**3757-3760** A1124 Set of 4 2.50 2.50

**Souvenir Sheet**

**3761** A1124 200fo multi 3.00 2.25

A1125

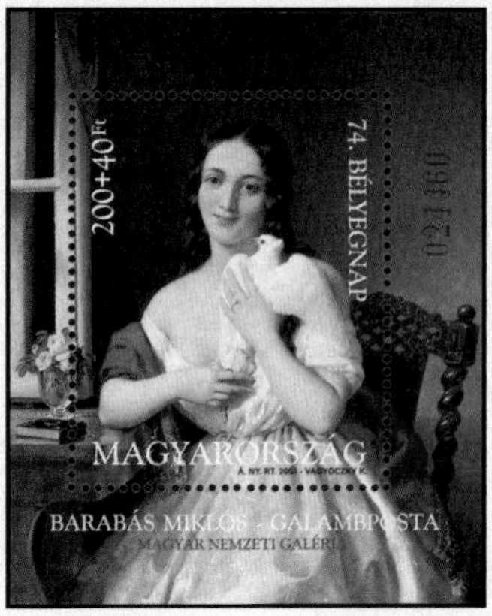


Stamp Day — A1126

Designs: 36fo, #N2. 90fo, #2.
200fo+40fo, Pigeon Post, by Miklos Barabás.

**2001, May 25** ***Perf. 12¼x11½***

**3762-3763** A1125 Set of 2 1.75 1.50
*a.* Sheet, 6 each # 3762-3763 10.50 9.00

**Souvenir Sheet**

***Perf. 12½***

**3764** A1126 200fo +40fo multi 3.50 2.75

European Water Polo Championships
A1127

**2001, June 14** ***Perf. 13½x13***

**3765** A1127 150fo multi 2.00 1.00

Intl. Scouting Conference — A1128

**2001, June 21** ***Perf. 12***

**3766** A1128 150fo multi 2.00 1.00

World Youth Track and Field Championships, Debrecen — A1129

**2001, July 12** **Litho.** ***Perf. 13x13¼***

**3767** A1129 140fo multi 1.50 1.00

Artist's Colony, Gödöllö, Cent. — A1130

Fészek Arts Club, Cent. — A1131

**2001, July 12** ***Perf. 12***
**3768** A1130 100fo multi 1.00 .50
**3769** A1131 150fo blue & blk 1.50 .75

**Hungarian History Type of 2000**
Souvenir Sheets

No. 3770: a, Prince Francis II Rákóczy, swordsman on horseback, Ilona Zrinyi. b, Rider from Royal Horse Guard, Castle at Munkács, Queen Maria Theresa. c, Count Stephen Széchenyi, Chain Bridge. d, Lajos Kossuth, Artúr Görgey with sword on horseback, battle scene. e, Poet János Arany, Parliament building.

No. 3771: a, World War I soldier on horseback, outline map of Hungary and lost parts of empire, Hungarian people. b, Albert Szent-Gyorgi and chemistry equipment. c, Chain Bridge, World War II soldiers, Bishop Vilmos Apor. d, Pictures of 1956 revolution, Polish-Hungarian Solidarity banner. e, Barbed wire, children representing Hungary's future, Hungarian millennium flag.

**2001, Aug. 15**
**3770** Sheet of 5 5.00 2.50
*a.-e.* A1110 50fo Any single 1.00 .35
**3771** Sheet of 5 5.00 2.50
*a.-e.* A1110 50fo Any single 1.00 .35

Souvenir Sheet

Crown of St. Stephen — A1132

**Litho. & Embossed**
**2001, Aug. 15** ***Perf. 13x12¾***
**3772** A1132 2001fo multi 22.00 22.00

**Grapes and Wine Producing Areas Type of 1990**

Grapes and: 60fo, Pannonhalma Abbey, Pannonhalma-Sokoróalja region, horiz. 70fo, Spherical observatory and Red Chapel, Balatonboglár, horiz.

**2001, Aug. 17** **Litho.** ***Perf. 13¼x13***
**3773-3774** A902 Set of 2 1.50 .75

Attempt To Create World's Largest Stamp Mosaic — A1133

**2001, Oct. 9** ***Perf. 12***
**3775** A1133 10fo multi .30 .25

Maria Valeria Bridge Reconstruction — A1134

**2001, Oct. 11** ***Perf. 13¼x13***
**3776** A1134 36fo multi .50 .50

See Slovakia No. 388.

Christmas A1135

**2001, Oct. 16** ***Perf. 12***
**3777** A1135 36fo multi .50 .25

State Printers, 150th Anniv. — A1136

**2001, Nov. 23** **Litho.** ***Perf. 13¼x13***
**3778** A1136 150fo multi 1.75 .75

2002 Winter Olympics, Salt Lake City — A1137

**2002, Feb. 8** **Litho.** ***Perf. 12***
**3779** A1137 160fo multi 2.50 .90

Souvenir Sheet

History of the Bicycle — A1138

No. 3780: a, Large-wheeled bicycle and rider, c. 1880. b, Tricycle, early 1900s. c, Károly Iszer (1860-1929), Budapest Sport Club chairman and bicycle. d, Tandem bicycle.

**2002, Feb. 20** ***Perf. 11½x12¼***
**3780** A1138 40fo Sheet of 4, #a-d 2.50 1.75

Souvenir Sheet

Hungarian — Ottoman Battles of 1552 — A1139

No. 3781: a, 50fo, Siege of Eger Castle (25x30mm). b, 50fo, Battle of Temesvár (25x30mm). c, 100fo+50fo, Battle of Drégely Castle (40x30mm).

**2002, Feb. 20** ***Perf. 12***
**3781** A1139 Sheet of 3, #a-c 4.00 2.75

Easter — A1140

**2002, Mar. 14** ***Perf. 11½x12¼***
**3782** A1140 30fo multi .50 .25

Airplanes Designed by Hungarians — A1141

Designs: 180fo, Libelle, by János adorján, 1910. 190fo, Magyar Lloyd, by Tibor Melczer, 1914.

**2002, Mar. 14** ***Perf. 12½***
**3783-3784** A1141 Set of 2 4.00 2.25

See Nos. 3831-3832, 3968-3969.

Famous Hungarians A1142

Designs: 33fo, Lajos Kossuth (1802-94), leader of Hungarian independence movement. 134fo, János Bolyai (1802-60), mathematician. 150fo, Gyula Illyés (1902-83), writer.

**2002, Mar. 14** ***Perf. 13x13½***
**3785-3787** A1142 Set of 3 4.00 1.75

Souvenir Sheet

Parliament Building, Cent. — A1143

**2002, Mar. 14** ***Perf. 11½x12¼***
**3788** A1143 500fo multi 6.50 5.50

Souvenir Sheet

Opening of National Theater — A1144

**2002, Mar. 14**
**3789** A1144 500fo multi 6.00 5.25

**Furniture Type of 1999**

Designs: 33fo, Chair, 1809, vert. 134fo, Theater armchair, 1900.

**2002, Mar. 28** ***Perf. 11½x12, 12x11½***
**3790-3791** A1091 Set of 2 2.50 1.00

Environmental Protection — A1145

**2002, Mar. 28** ***Perf. 12***
**3792** A1145 158fo multi 1.60 .80

Souvenir Sheet

Founding of Hungarian National Museum and National Széchényi Library, Bicent. — A1146

No. 3793: a, Mihály Apafi psalter, 1686. b, Illuminated letter from Graduale Pars II. c, Standard of the Civil Guard of Pest, 1848. d, Basin for holy water, 12th cent.

**2002, Apr. 29**
**3793** A1146 150fo Sheet of 4, #a-d 7.50 7.50

Halas Lace, Cent. — A1147

Designs: 100fo, Tablecloth with Two Deer, by Mrs. Béla Bazala, 1916. 110fo, Swan Tablecloth, by Erno Stepanek, 1930. 140fo, Jancsi and Iluska, by Antal Tar, 1935.

**Litho. & Embossed**
**2002, May 3** ***Perf. 12***
**3794-3796** A1147 Set of 3 4.00 1.75

Europa A1148

**2002, May 9** **Litho.** ***Perf. 11***
**3797** A1148 62fo multi *1.50* 1.50

2002 World Cup Soccer Championships, Japan and Korea — A1149

**2002, May 9** ***Perf. 13x13½***
**3798** A1149 160fo multi + label 2.00 1.60

Fauna A1150

Designs: 30fo, Felis sylvestris. 38fo, Podarcis taurica. 110fo, Garrulus glandarius. 160fo, Rosalia alpina.
500fo, Acipenser ruthenus.

**2002, May 9** ***Perf. 12***
**3799-3802** A1150 Set of 4 4.00 1.75

**Souvenir Sheet**
**3803** A1150 500fo multi 6.00 5.00

Greetings — A1151

No. 3804: a, Etesd meg! b, Megszülettem! c, Sok boldogságot! d, Ontözd meg! e, Ennyire szeretlek!

***Serpentine Die Cut 12¼x12¾***
**2002, May 29** **Self-Adhesive**
**3804** Booklet pane of 5 2.50
*a.-e.* A1151 38fo Any single .50 .25

**Flower Type of 1999**

Designs: 30fo, Red poppy. 38fo, Stalkless gentian.

**2002, June 24** ***Perf. 12¼x11½***
**3805-3806** A1087 Set of 2 1.00 .35

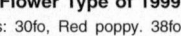

Art — A1152

Designs: 62fo, Kodobálók, by Károly Ferenczy. 188fo, Táncosno, sculpture by Ferenc Megyessy, vert.

***Perf. 12¾x12¼, 12¼x12¾***

**2002, June 24**

**3807-3808** A1152 Set of 2 3.00 1.25

UNESCO World Heritage Sites — A1153

Designs: 100fo, Budapest. 150fo, Hollóko. 180fo, Caves of Aggtelek Karst, horiz.

**2002, June 24** ***Perf. 12***

**3809-3811** A1153 Set of 3 4.50 2.25

See Nos. 3881-3882, 4073.

Kalocsa Archbishopric, 1000th Anniv. — A1154

**2002, Aug. 1 Litho.** ***Perf. 13¼x12½***

**3812** A1154 150fo multi 1.50 .75

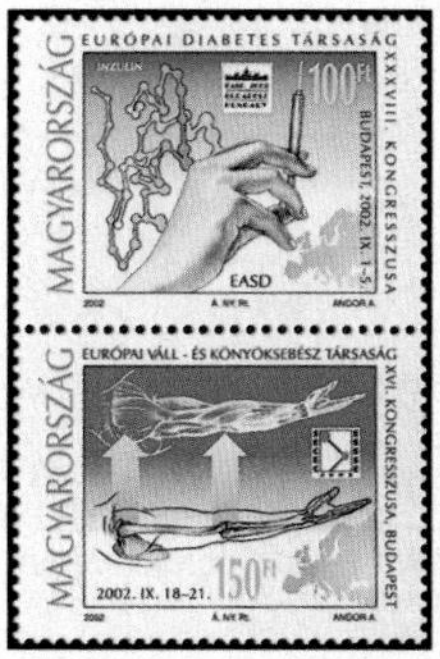


Medical Congresses A1155

No. 3813: a, 100fo, 38th European Diabetes Association Congress. b, 150fo, 16th European Arm and Shoulder Surgeons Congress.

**2002, Aug. 23** ***Perf. 13x13¼***

**3813** A1155 Vert. pair, #a-b 3.00 2.50

Printed in sheets of two pairs. Value $5.50.

Ceramics by Margit Kovács — A1156

No. 3814: a, 33fo, Madonna and Child, 1938. b, 38fo, Mother and Children, 1953. 400fo+200fo, St. George, 1936.

**2002, Oct. 3** ***Perf. 13¼x13***

**3814** A1156 Pair, #a-b 1.00 .35

**Souvenir Sheet**

***Perf. 12¼x11½***

**3815** A1156 400fo +200fo multi 6.00 6.00

Stamp Day. No. 3814 printed in sheets of two pairs. Value $1.75. No. 3815 contains one 25x36mm stamp.

Christmas A1157

Designs: 30fo, Adoration of the Magi. 38fo, Bethlehem.

**Litho. with Foil Application**

**2002, Oct. 30** ***Perf. 12***

**3816-3817** A1157 Set of 2 1.25 .35

See No. 4006.

World Gymnastics Championships, Debrecen — A1158

**2002, Nov. 20 Litho.** ***Perf. 13x13¼***

**3818** A1158 160fo multi 1.60 .80

Hungarian and Turkish Buildings — A1159

Designs: 40fo, Rakoczi House, Tekirdag, Turkey. 110fo, Gazi Kassim Pasha Mosque, Pécs, Hungary.

**2002, Dec. 2 Litho.** ***Perf. 13½x13¼***

**3819-3820** A1159 Set of 2 1.50 .75

See Turkey No. 2844.

**Furniture Type of 1999**

Designs: 32fo, Wooden chair with carved back, 19th cent., vert. 35fo, Armchair, 18th cent., vert. 65fo, Armchair with carved back, 1920, vert.

**2003, Jan. 30** ***Perf. 11½x12¼***

**3821-3823** A1091 Set of 3 1.75 .70

Scientists A1160

Designs: 32fo, John von Neumann (1903-57), mathematician, and computer pioneer. 40fo, Rezsö Soó (1903-80), botanist. 60fo, Károly Zipernowsky (1853-1942), electrical engineer.

**2003, Feb. 12** ***Perf. 13x13¼***

**3824** A1160 32fo multicolored .35 .25
**3825** A1160 40fo multicolored 6.00 6.00
**3826** A1160 60fo multicolored .60 .60
*Nos. 3824-3826 (3)* 6.95 6.85

Souvenir Sheet

Herend Porcelain — A1161

No. 3827: a, Platter with floral design, Frankenthal coffee set. b, Vase with floral design, coffee set. c, Vase with ram's head handles. d, Shell-shaped bowl, pitcher.

**2003, Feb. 12** ***Perf. 12***

**3827** A1161 150fo Sheet of 4, #a-d 6.00 6.00

Defeat of Royal Hungarian Army, 60th Anniv. — A1162

**2003, Feb. 15** ***Perf. 12¼x12½***

**3828** A1162 40fo multi .60 .25

Easter — A1163

**2003, Mar. 14**

**3829** A1163 32fo multi .50 .25

Nemzeti Sport, Cent. — A1164

**2003, Mar. 14** ***Perf. 13x13¼***

**3830** A1164 150fo multi + label 2.00 .75

**Airplanes Type of 2002**

Designs: 142fo, Gerle 13, by Antal Bánhidi, 1933. 160fo, L-2 Róma, by Árpád Lampich, 1925.

**2003, Mar. 20** ***Perf. 12½***

**3831-3832** A1141 Set of 2 3.50 1.50

Hotels — A1165

Designs: 110fo, Rogner Hotel, Héviz. 120fo, Hélia Hotel, Budapest.

**2003, Mar. 20**

**3833-3834** A1165 Set of 2 2.50 1.10

See Nos. 3883-3884.

Souvenir Sheet

Extreme Sports — A1166

No. 3835: a, 100fo, BMX cycling. b, 100fo, Snowboarding. c, 100fo, Parachuting. d, 100fo+50fo, Kayaking.

**2003, Mar. 20** ***Perf. 12***

**3835** A1166 Sheet of 4, #a-d 4.50 4.50

Greetings A1167

No. 3836: a, Church. b, Two flowers. c, One flower. d, Easter eggs. e, Candles in window, Christmas tree.

***Serpentine Die Cut 12¾***

**2003, Mar. 20 Self-Adhesive**

**3836** Booklet pane of 5 2.00
***a.-e.*** A1167 40fo Any single .40 .25

Souvenir Sheet

Space Shuttle Columbia — A1168

**2003, Apr. 9** ***Perf. 12***

**3837** A1168 500fo multi 5.00 2.50

World Ice Hockey Championships, Budapest — A1169

**2003, Apr. 10** ***Perf. 13x13¼***

**3838** A1169 110fo multi + label 1.10 .55

Budapest Sports Arena — A1170

**2003, Apr. 10**

**3839** A1170 120fo multi + label 1.25 .60

Souvenir Sheet

Ratification of European Union Accession Treaty — A1171

**2003, Apr. 14** ***Perf. 12***

**3840** A1171 500fo multi 7.50 7.50

Policeman on Motorcycle and Emergency Phone Number
A1172

**2003, Apr. 24**
**3841** A1172 65fo multi .65 .35

Stamp Day — A1173

Designs: 35fo, Statue of woman with legs crossed. 40fo, Statue of woman with hand on chin.
400fo+100fo, Fountain.

**2003, May 6** ***Perf. 13¼x13***
**3842-3843** A1173 Set of 2 .75 .40

**Souvenir Sheet**
***Perf. 12¾x13***

**3844** A1173 400fo +100fo multi 7.00 5.00

No. 3844 contains one 31x40mm stamp.

Souvenir Sheet

Uprising Against Hapsburgs of Ferenc Rákóczi II, 400th Anniv. — A1174

No. 3845: a, Swords and scabbards. b, Coins. c, Banner, pipes and drums. d, Guns.

**2003, May 6** ***Perf. 12***
**3845** A1174 120fo Sheet of 4, #a-d 6.50 5.50

Europa — A1175

**2003, May 9**
**3846** A1175 65fo multi 1.75 1.75

Fauna
A1176

Designs: 35fo, Mustela eversmanni. 40fo, Calandrella brachydactyla. 100fo, Hyla arborea. 110fo, Misgurnus fossilis.
500fo, Eresus cinnabarinus.

**2003, May 9**
**3847-3850** A1176 Set of 4 4.00 1.75

**Souvenir Sheet**

**3851** A1176 500fo multi 6.00 5.00

**Grapes and Wine Producing Areas Type of 1990**

Grapes and: 60fo, Bükkalja region, horiz. 130fo, Balaton-felvidéki region, horiz.

**2003, June 6** ***Perf. 13¼x12½***
**3852-3853** A902 Set of 2 2.50 1.00

Souvenir Sheet

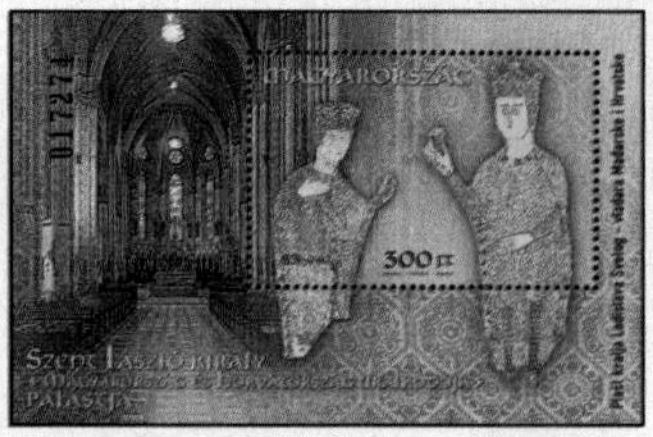

Robe of St. László — A1177

**2003, June 13** ***Perf. 12***
**3854** A1177 300fo multi 4.25 3.00

Art
A1178

Designs: 32fo, Sculpture by Imre Varga, vert. 60fo, Mostar Bridge, by Tivadar Csontváry Kosztka.

***Perf. 12½x13¼, 13¼x12½***
**2003, July 18**
**3855-3856** A1178 Set of 2 1.50 .50

Souvenir Sheet

Sports History — A1179

No. 3857: a, Ferenc Puskás Stadium Budapest, 50th anniv. b, Hungary vs. England soccer match, 50th anniv.

**2003, July 18** ***Perf. 11½x12¼***
**3857** A1179 250fo Sheet of 2, #a-b 5.75 5.00

European Union Membership
A1180

**2003** **Litho.** ***Perf. 12x11½***
**3858** A1180 115fo shown 1.40 .60
**3859** A1180 130fo Clock at 11:35 1.60 .70

Issued: 115fo, 9/16; 130fo, 10/18.
See Nos. 3877-3878.

Nutrition
A1181

**2003, Sept. 16** ***Perf. 12***
**3860** A1181 120fo multi 1.50 .60

European Automobile-free Day — A1182

**2003, Sept. 16**
**3861** A1182 150fo multi 1.50 .75

Reszo Soó (1903-80), Botanist
A1183

**2003, Sept. 23**
**3862** A1183 44fo multi .55 .25

Book Printing — A1184

Designs: No. 3863, 44fo, Hungarian Illuminated Chronicle, 1358. No. 3864, 44fo, Ritual of Zhou, China.

**2003, Sept. 30**
**3863-3864** A1184 Set of 2 1.40 .45

See People's Republic of China Nos. 3309-3310.

Souvenir Sheet

Ferenc Deák (1803-76), Statesman — A1185

**2003, Oct. 18**
**3865** A1185 500fo multi 6.00 5.00

Christmas — A1186

Designs: 35fo, Reindeer. 44fo, Angels, Christmas tree, houses.

**2003, Oct. 31** ***Perf. 11½x12***
**3866-3867** A1186 Set of 2 1.00 .40

Souvenir Sheet

World Science Forum, Budapest — A1187

**2003, Nov. 7** **Litho.** ***Perf. 12***
**3868** A1187 500fo multi 6.00 5.00

**Locomotives Type of 2001**

Designs: 120fo, Muki Diesel locomotive, Kemence Forest Railway. 150fo, Rezét steam locomotive, Gemenc Forest Railway.

**2004, Feb. 4** ***Perf. 13¼x13***
**3869-3870** A1120 Set of 2 3.00 3.00

Famous Men — A1188

Designs: 40fo, Bálint Balassi (1554-94), poet. 44fo, József Bajza (1804-58), poet. 80fo, János András Segner (1704-77), physicist.

**2004, Feb. 4** ***Perf. 13***
**3871-3873** A1188 Set of 3 2.25 .85

Souvenir Sheet

Dogs — A1189

No. 3874: a, 100fo, Puli. b, 100fo, Hungarian greyhound. c, 100fo, Mudi. d, 100fo+50fo, Vizsla.

**2004, Feb. 19** ***Perf. 12***
**3874** A1189 Sheet of 4, #a-d 5.50 4.50

Surtax on No. 3874d for youth philately.

Souvenir Sheet

Festivals — A1190

No. 3875: a, Busójárás Carnival. b, Virágkarnevál (Flower Carnival). c, Borfesztivál (Wine Festival). d, Fesztiválok Karneválok (Festivals and Carnivals).

**2004, Feb. 19**
**3875** A1190 60fo Sheet of 4, #a-d 3.25 2.40

European Ministerial Conference on the Information Society — A1191

No. 3876 — Color of panel and "e:" a, Red violet. b, Dark blue. c, Green. d, Orange.

**2004, Feb. 26** ***Perf. 13¼x13***
**3876** A1191 40fo Block of 4, #a-d 3.00 2.25

**European Union Membership (Clock) Type of 2003**

**2004** ***Perf. 12x11½***
**3877** A1180 100fo Clock at 11:48 1.25 .50
**3878** A1180 190fo Clock at 11:57 2.25 .90

Issued: 100fo, 3/5; 190fo, 4/19.

Tenth World Indoor Track and Field Championships, Budapest
A1192

**2004, Mar. 5** ***Perf. 13x13¼***
**3879** A1192 120fo multi 1.50 .60

Easter — A1193

**2004, Mar. 18** **Litho.**
**3880** A1193 48fo multi .50 .25

### World Heritage Sites Type of 2002

Designs: 150fo, Abbey of Pannonhalma. 170fo, Hortobágy National Park, horiz.

**2004, Mar. 18** ***Perf. 12***
**3881-3882** A1153 Set of 2 3.75 1.60

### Hotels Type of 2003

Designs: 120fo, Bük Thermal and Sports Hotel, Bükfürdo. 150fo, Aqua-Sol Hotel, Hajdúszoboszló.

**2004, Mar. 18**
**3883-3884** A1165 Set of 2 3.25 1.25

Holocaust, 60th Anniv.
A1194

**2004, Apr. 16** ***Perf. 13x13¼***
**3885** A1194 160fo multi 1.90 .75

Souvenir Sheet

Zsolnay Porcelain, 150th Anniv. — A1195

No. 3886: a, Vase with handles. b, Small vase, vessel with horse and rider top. c, Vase. d, Mocha set.

**2004, Apr. 20** **Litho.** ***Perf. 12***
**3886** A1195 160fo Sheet of 4, #a-d 7.00 7.00

Police Boat and Emergency Phone Number
A1196

**2004, Apr. 23** **Litho.** ***Perf. 13x13¼***
**3887** A1196 48fo multi .60 .35

Souvenir Sheet

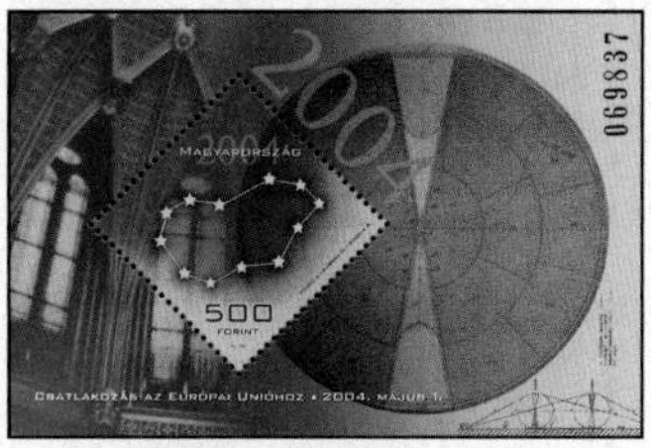


Admission to European Union — A1197

**2004, Apr. 30** ***Perf. 12***
**3888** A1197 500fo multi 5.25 5.25

Expansion of the European Union — A1198

No. 3889: a, 120fo, Stars and flowers. b, 150fo, Stars, map of Europe, flags of nations entering European Union.

**2004, May 1** **Litho.**
**3889** A1198 Horiz. pair, #a-b 3.25 2.75

European Parliament Elections
A1199

**2004, May 7** ***Perf. 12½x13½***
**3890** A1199 150fo multi 1.75 .70

Europa
A1200

**2004, May 7** ***Perf. 12***
**3891** A1200 160fo multi 2.25 1.00

Fauna
A1201

Designs: 48fo, Nannospalax leucodon. 65fo, Panurus biarmicus. 90fo, Ablepharus kitaibelii fitzingeri. 120fo, Huso huso.
500fo, Anthaxia hungarica.

**2004, May 7**
**3892-3895** A1201 Set of 4 4.00 1.50

**Souvenir Sheet**

**3896** A1201 500fo multi 5.25 5.25

Stamp Day — A1202

Designs: 48fo, Walls and Doors, sculpture by Erzsébet Schaár. 65fo, Translucent Red Circle, painting by Tihamér Gyarmathy.
400fo+200fo, The Wasp King, painting by Béla Kondor.

**2004, May 7** **Litho.** ***Perf. 12¼x12¾***
**3897-3898** A1202 Set of 2 2.10 .55

**Souvenir Sheet**

***Perf. 12¾x12¼***

**3899** A1202 400fo +200fo multi 7.25 5.75

No. 3899 contains one 41x31mm stamp.

FIFA (Fédération Internationale de Football Association), Cent. — A1203

**2004, May 21** **Litho.** ***Perf. 13¼x13***
**3900** A1203 100fo multi 1.25 .45

Central European Catholics' Day — A1204

No. 3901: a, Basilica, Mariazell, Austria. b, Statue of Madonna, Mariazell. c, Statue of Madonna and Child, Mariazell. d, Statue of Madonna, Celldömölk, Hungary. e, Framed painting of Madonna and Child, Mariazell. f, Statue of Mary of Kiscell, Obuda Parish, Hungary.

**2004, May 21** **Litho.** ***Perf. 11½x12***
**3901** A1204 100fo Sheet of 6, #a-f 6.50 5.75

Information Technology
A1205

**2004, June 28** ***Perf. 13x13¼***
**3902** A1205 120fo multi 1.25 .60

Theodor Herzl (1860-1904), Zionist Leader
A1206

**2004, July 6** **Litho.** ***Perf. 12***
**3903** A1206 150fo multi 2.25 .75

See Austria No. 1960, Israel No. 1566.

2004 Summer Olympics, Athens — A1207

Designs: 90fo, Canoeing. 130fo, Volleyball. 150fo, Running.

**2004, July 13**
**3904-3906** A1207 Set of 3 3.75 1.75

A1208

A1209

A1210

A1211

A1212

A1213

A1214

Folkloriada Festival — A1215

**2004, Aug. 12**

| | | | |
|---|---|---|---|
| **3907** | Block of 10 + 10 labels | 10.00 | 10.00 |
| *a.* | A1208 65fo dark blue | .75 | .40 |
| *b.* | A1208 65fo orange | .75 | .40 |
| *c.* | A1209 65fo orange brown | .75 | .40 |
| *d.* | A1209 65fo purple | .75 | .40 |
| *e.* | A1210 65fo carmine | .75 | .40 |
| *f.* | A1211 65fo orange brown | .75 | .40 |
| *g.* | A1212 65fo orange brown | .75 | .40 |
| *h.* | A1213 65fo Prussian blue | .75 | .40 |
| *i.* | A1214 65fo green | .75 | .40 |
| *j.* | A1215 65fo orange brown | .75 | .40 |
| *k.* | Sheet, #3907 | 32.00 | 32.00 |

No. 3907k has labels that could be personalized. The personalized sheet sold for 1600fo.

Chess History — A1216

No. 3908 — Beginning of text, square color, piece (if any): a, A sakkjáték, tan, black rook. b, A magyaroknak, brown. c, A magyar történelem, tan, black bishop. d, A magyar sakkirodalom, brown, black king. e, A XVIII. században, tan, black queen. f, Az elso, brown. g, Az 1839-ben, tan, black knight. h, A XIX. század, brown, black rook. i, A magyar sakkfeladványszerok, brown, black pawn. j, Három, a XIX. század, tan, black pawn. k, Maróczy Géza, brown, black pawn. l, Két kiváló, tan, black pawn. m, A levelezási, brown, black bishop. n, A sakkélet, tan, black pawn. o, A férfi országos, brown, black pawn. p, A II. világháború tan után sokáig, black pawn. q, A nol sakkozás, tan. r, 1958-ban már, brown. s, A sakkozók, tan, black knight. t, 1951-ben indult, brown. u, A XX. századnak, tan. v, A II. világháború utá feladvány, brown. w, A XX. században, tan. x, A XX. század elején, brown. y, A világ sakkélетét, brown. z, A két világháború között, tan. aa, A háború után, brown. ab, A férfi sakkolimpián, tan. ac, A nemzetek közti, brown, black pawn. ad, 1957-ben a hollandiai, tan. ae, A noi sakkolimpiákon, brown. af, A XIX. és XX. században, tan. ag, Sakkirodalom nélkül, tan. ah, A XX. század magyar, brown. ai, A széles sakkozó, tan, white bishop. aj, A Magyar Sakkszövetség, brown. ak, Barcza Gedeon, tan, white pawn. al, Szábo László, brown. am, Portisch Lajos, tan. an, Adorján András, brown. ao, Sax Gyula, brown. ap, Ribli Zoltán, tan. aq, Lékó Péter, brown. ar, Almási Zoltán, tan. as, Bilek, István, brown. at, A két világháború közti, tan, white knight. au, Az olimpiákon többször, brown. av, Sok kiváló magyar, tan. aw, Polgár Zsuzsa, tan, white pawn. ax, Polgár Judit, brown, white pawn. ay, Polgár Zsófia, tan, white pawn. az, Lángos Józsa, brown, white pawn. ba, Veroci Zsuzsa, tan. bb, Ivánka Mária, brown, white pawn. bc, Mádl Ildikó, tan, white pawn. bd, Országos bajnoki, brown, white pawn. be, Sakkozásunk a XXI. századot, brown, white rook. bf, A sakkozással, tan, white knight. bg, A magyar sakkozás, brown, white bishop. bh, Minden összefoglaló,tan, white king. bi, A jelen munkában, brown, white queen. bj, Elek Ferenc, tan. bk, Katkó (Regos) Imre, brown. bl, Gróf Pongrácz Arnold, tan, white rook.

**2004, Sept. 24**

| | | | |
|---|---|---|---|
| **3908** | Sheet of 64 | 42.50 | 42.50 |
| *a.-bl.* | A1216 50fo Any single | .60 | .40 |

Souvenir Sheet

Admission to European Union — A1217

No. 3909 — Large stars and time of small clock: a, 11:20. b, 11:35. c, 11:48. d, 11:57.

**2004, Oct. 8** *Perf. 12x11½*

**3909** A1217 100fo Sheet of 4, #a-d 5.50 4.00

Istvan Bocskay (1557-1606), Leader of 1604-06 Rebellion — A1218

**2004, Nov. 11 Litho.** *Perf. 11½x12*

**3910** A1218 120fo multi 1.25 .60

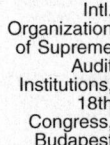

Intl. Organization of Supreme Audit Institutions, 18th Congress, Budapest A1219

**2004, Oct. 11** *Perf. 11¼*

**3911** A1219 150fo multi 1.50 .75

**Christmas Type of 2002 and**

A1220

A1221

A1222

A1223

A1224

A1225

A1226

A1227

A1228

A1229

A1230

A1231

A1232

A1233

A1234

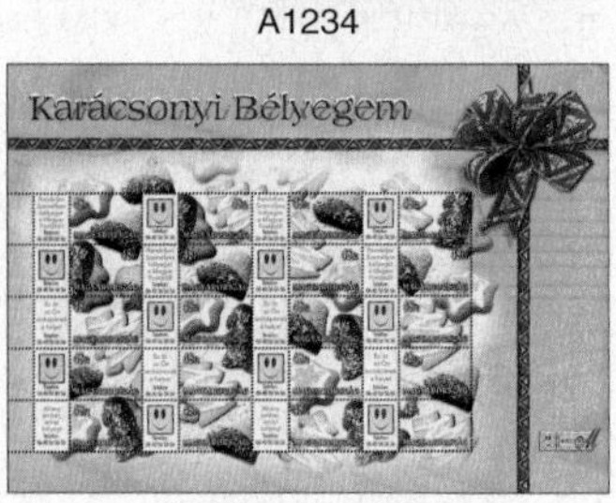

Christmas — A1235

No. 3915: Various Christmas cookies.

**Litho. With Foil Application**

**2004** *Perf. 12*

**3912** A1157 48fo Bethlehem .50 .25

**Litho.**

*Perf. 11¼*

| | | | |
|---|---|---|---|
| **3913** | Sheet of 20 + 20 labels | 30.00 | 16.50 |
| *a.* | A1220 48fo multi + label | 1.25 | .40 |
| *b.* | A1221 48fo multi + label | 1.25 | .40 |
| *c.* | A1222 48fo multi + label | 1.25 | .40 |
| *d.* | A1223 48fo multi + label | 1.25 | .40 |
| *e.* | A1224 48fo multi + label | 1.25 | .40 |
| *f.* | A1225 48fo multi + label | 1.25 | .40 |
| **3914** | Sheet of 20 + 20 labels | 30.00 | 16.50 |
| *a.* | A1226 48fo multi + label | 1.25 | .40 |
| *b.* | A1227 48fo multi + label | 1.25 | .40 |
| *c.* | A1228 48fo multi + label | 1.25 | .40 |
| *d.* | A1229 48fo multi + label | 1.25 | .40 |
| *e.* | A1230 48fo multi + label | 1.25 | .40 |
| *f.* | A1231 48fo multi + label | 1.25 | .40 |
| *g.* | A1232 48fo multi + label | 1.25 | .40 |
| *h.* | A1233 48fo multi + label | 1.25 | .40 |
| *i.* | A1234 48fo multi + label | 1.25 | .40 |
| **3915** | A1235 48fo Sheet of 20, #a-t, + 20 labels | 30.00 | 16.50 |

Issued: No. 3912, 10/28; Nos. 3913-3915, 11/3.

No. 3913 contains 5 #3913b, 3 #3913c, 4 each #3913a, 3913e, 2 each #3913d, 3913f. Background colors on some stamps differ slightly.

No. 3914 contains #3914d, 3914e, 4 each #3914a, 3914b, 2 each #3914c, 3914f, 3914g, 3914h, 3914i.

Nos. 3913-3915 could be personalized, with each sheet selling for 2000fo.

Sándor Korösi Csoma (1784-1842), Philologist and Sir Marc Aurel Stein (1862-1943), Archaeologist A1236

**2004, Nov. 3 Litho.** *Perf. 13x13¼*

**3916** A1236 80fo multi 1.25 .40

Natura 2000 — A1237

**2004, Dec. 3** *Perf. 11½x12*

**3917** A1237 100fo multi 1.10 .55

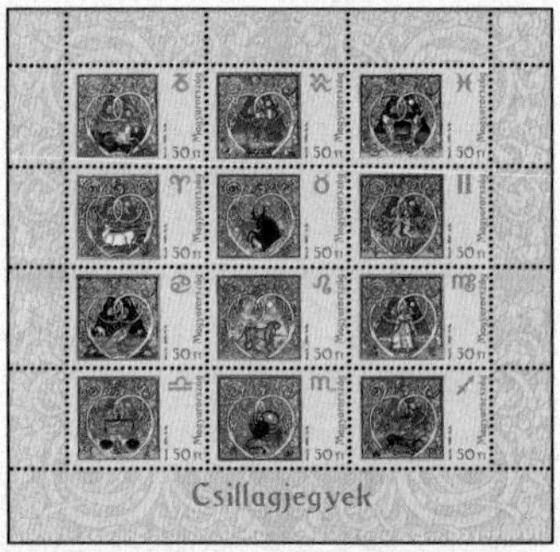

Zodiac — A1238

No. 3918: a, Capricorn (goat). b, Aquarius (water bearer). c, Pisces (fish). d, Aries (ram). e, Taurus (bull). f, Gemini (twins). g, Cancer (crab). h, Leo (lion). i, Virgo (virgin). j, Libra (scales). k, Scorpio (scorpion). l, Sagittarius (archer).

**2005, Jan. 3 Litho.** *Perf. 11¼*

| | | | |
|---|---|---|---|
| **3918** | A1238 50fo Sheet of 12, #a-l | 10.00 | 7.50 |
| *m.* | Sheet of 20 #3918a + 20 labels | 29.00 | — |
| *n.* | Sheet of 20 #3918b + 20 labels | 29.00 | — |
| *o.* | Sheet of 20 #3918c + 20 labels | 29.00 | — |
| *p.* | Sheet of 20 #3918d + 20 labels | 29.00 | — |
| *q.* | Sheet of 20 #3918e + 20 labels | 29.00 | — |
| *r.* | Sheet of 20 #3918f + 20 labels | 29.00 | — |
| *s.* | Sheet of 20 #3918g + 20 labels | 29.00 | — |
| *t.* | Sheet of 20 #3918h + 20 labels | 29.00 | — |
| *u.* | Sheet of 20 #3918i + 20 labels | 29.00 | — |
| *v.* | Sheet of 20 #3918j + 20 labels | 29.00 | — |
| *w.* | Sheet of 20 #3918k + 20 labels | 29.00 | — |
| *x.* | Sheet of 20 #3918l + 20 labels | 29.00 | — |

Nos. 3918m-3918x each sold for 2100fo and had labels that could be personalized.

Rotary International, Cent. — A1239

**2005, Feb. 4** ***Perf. 13¼x13***
**3919** A1239 130fo multi 1.60 .70

Souvenir Sheet

Cats — A1240

No. 3920: a, 100fo, Siamese, silhouette of cat sitting. b, 100fo, Maine Coon cat, silhouette of cat with arched back and thin tail. c, 100fo, Persian, silhouette of cat with large tail. d, 100fo+50fo, Domestic cat, silhouette of cat walking.

**2005, Feb. 4** ***Perf. 12x11½***
**3920** A1240 Sheet of 4, #a-d 4.75 4.75

Easter — A1241

**2005, Feb. 21** ***Perf. 12***
**3921** A1241 50fo multi .55 .25

Intl. Weight Lifting Federation, Cent. A1242

**2005, Mar. 3** ***Perf. 12¼x12½***
**3922** A1242 170fo multi 1.90 .95

Sándor Iharos (1930-96), Runner A1243

**2005, Mar. 10** ***Perf. 13x13¼***
**3923** A1243 90fo multi 1.00 .50

Souvenir Sheet

Opening of Palace of Arts, Budapest — A1244

**2005, Mar. 10** ***Perf. 12***
**3924** A1244 500fo multi 5.50 5.50

World Theater Day — A1245

**2005, Mar. 21** ***Perf. 11¼***
**3925** A1245 50fo multi .80 .25

See No. 4198.

Compass and Map of Hungary — A1246

No. 3926: a, Compass at right, map of western Hungary. b, Compass at left, map of eastern Hungary.

**2005, Apr. 1** **Litho.** ***Perf. 11¼***
**3926** A1246 50fo Pair, #a-b, + 2 labels 2.00 1.10
*c.* Sheet of 20, 10 each #3926a-3926b, + 20 labels 40.00 —

No. 3926c sold for 2100fo. Labels on sheets of 3926 and 3926c could be personalized.

Compare with No. 4054.

Writers A1247

Designs: 90fo, Jeno Rejto (1905-43), novelist, playwright. 140fo, Attila József (1905-37), poet.

**2005, Apr. 11** **Litho.** ***Perf. 13x13¼***
**3927-3928** A1247 Set of 2 2.75 1.25

Police Helicopter and Emergency Phone Number A1248

**2005, Apr. 22** ***Perf. 13x13¼***
**3929** A1248 85fo multi .90 .45

End of World War II, 60th Anniv. A1249

**2005, May 6** ***Perf. 13***
**3930** A1249 150fo multi 1.60 .80

Farm Animals A1250

Designs: 50fo, Hungarian gray bull. 70fo, Hungarian spotted cow. 100fo, Hortobágy Racka sheep. 110fo, Cigája sheep.
500fo, Mangalica pigs.

**2005, May 9** ***Perf. 13x13¼***
**3931-3934** A1250 Set of 4 3.75 1.60

**Souvenir Sheet**

**3935** A1250 500fo multi 6.50 5.00

No. 3935 contains one 41x32mm stamp.

Souvenir Sheet

Europa — A1251

No. 3936 — Plate of Chicken Paprika and Dumplings with: a, Flowers at UR. b, Flowers at UL.

**2005, May 9** ***Perf. 12***
**3936** A1251 160fo Sheet, 2 each #a-b 7.75 6.25

The top and bottom rows of stamps in the sheet are tete-beche.

Souvenir Sheet

Pope John Paul II (1920-2005) — A1252

**2005, May 18**
**3937** A1252 500fo multi 6.00 5.00

**Grapes and Wine Producing Areas Type of 1990**

Designs: 120fo, Pintes grapes, Zala region, horiz. 140fo, Kunleány grapes, Csongrád region, horiz.

**2005, May 25** ***Perf. 13¼x12½***
**3938-3939** A902 Set of 2 3.25 1.40

Church, Ják, and Ornament From Cluny Abbey, France A1253

**2005, May 25** ***Perf. 13x13¼***
**3940** A1253 110fo multi 1.60 .55

Souvenir Sheet

Consecration of St. Stephen's Basilica, Budapest, Cent. — A1254

**2005, May 25** ***Perf. 12¾x13***
**3941** A1254 500fo multi 6.00 5.00

Miniature Sheet

Budapest Tourist Attractions — A1255

No. 3942: a, Hallway and exhibits, Postal Museum. b, #386a and die of vignette, Stamp Museum, horiz. c, Agriculture Museum, Vajdahunyad Castle. d, Ethnographic Museum, horiz. e, Sándor Palace, horiz.

***Perf. 11½x12, 12x11½ (horiz. stamps)***

**2005, May 25**
**3942** A1255 100fo Sheet of 5, #a-e, + 5 labels 6.50 5.00

First Hungarian in Space, 25th Anniv. — A1256

**2005, May 26** ***Perf. 12½***
**3943** A1256 130fo multi 1.25 .65

A1257

Formula I Auto Racing in Hungary, 20th Anniv. (in 2006) A1258

Designs: Nos. 3944, 3947, Hungaroring Race Track. No. 3945, Car No. 12. No. 3946, Driver in red car.

**2005** **Litho.** ***Perf. 11¼***
**3944** A1257 50fo multi + label .50 .25

***Perf. 13x13¼***

**3945** A1258 50fo multi .75 .25
**3946** A1258 90fo multi 1.25 .45

**Souvenir Sheet**

***Perf. 13x12¾***

**3947** A1258 500fo +200fo multi 7.75 7.00

78th Stamp Day (Nos. 3945-3947). Issued: Nos. 3944, 3947, 7/18; Nos. 3945-3946, 6/17. Labels on No. 3944 could be personalized.

Souvenir Sheet

Enameled Pictures on St. Stephen's Crown — A1259

No. 3948: a, 100fo, St. Thomas (20x26mm) . b, 100fo, King Géza I (in square panel with black lettering) (20x26mm). c, 100fo, Byzantine Emperor Michael Ducas (in arched panel with red lettering) (20x26mm). d, 100fo, Byzantine Emperor Constantine (in square panel with red lettering) (20x26mm). e, 100fo, Jesus Christ (in arched panel with no lettering) (20x26mm). f, 500fo, St. Stephen's Crown (30x36mm).

**2005, Aug. 19 Litho.** ***Perf. 12x11½***

**3948** A1259 Sheet of 6, #a-f 11.50 10.50

First Hungarian Mail Vehicle, Cent. A1260

**2005, Sept. 15** ***Perf. 11¼x11***

**3949** A1260 50fo multi .50 .25

Trash Recycling A1261

**2005, Sept. 15** ***Perf. 13x13¼***

**3950** A1261 140fo multi 1.75 .70

World Wrestling Championships, Budapest — A1262

**2005, Sept. 26** ***Perf. 13***

**3951** A1262 150fo multi 1.75 .75

Ferenc Farkas (1905-2000), Composer — A1263

**2005, Sept. 30** ***Perf. 13x13¼***

**3952** A1263 100fo multi 1.75 .50

World Science Forum, Budapest A1264

**2005, Sept. 30**

**3953** A1264 120fo multi 1.75 .60

See No. 4052.

Hungarian University of Craft and Design, 125th Anniv. A1265

**2005, Oct. 19** ***Perf. 12***

**3954** A1265 90fo multi 1.25 .45

The Three Magi — A1266

Christmas A1267

No. 3956: a, Candle. b, Apple. c, Heart-shaped ornament. d, Teddy bear.

**Litho. with Foil Application**

**2005, Oct. 19** ***Perf. 12¾x12¼***

**3955** A1266 50fo blue .75 .25

**Self-Adhesive**

**Litho.**

***Serpentine Die Cut 12¾***

**3956** Booklet pane of 4 3.25

***a.-d.*** A1267 50fo Any single .80 .25

House of the Future A1268

**2005, Dec. 16 Litho.** ***Perf. 12***

**3957** A1268 100fo multi 1.25 .45

Hungarian News Agency, 125th Anniv. — A1269

**2006, Jan. 1 Litho.** ***Perf. 12x11½***

**3958** A1269 90fo multi 1.10 .45

2006 Winter Olympics, Turin A1270

**2006, Feb. 10** ***Perf. 13¼***

**3959** A1270 200fo multi 3.25 1.00

**Furniture Type of 1999**

Designs: 52fo, Like #3790, vert. 75fo, Chair with heart carved in back, 1893, vert. 212fo, Like #3791. 300fo, Settee, 18th cent. 500fo, Rococo settee, c. 1880. 1000fo, Vassily chair, by Marcel Breuer, 1925.

**2006** ***Perf. 11½x12¼***

**3960** A1091 52fo bl & dk bl .50 .25

**3961** A1091 75fo org brn & brn .70 .35

***Perf. 12¼x11½***

**3962** A1091 212fo grn & dk grn 2.00 1.00

***Perf. 12¾x12¼***

**3963** A1091 300fo red & dk red 3.00 1.50

**3964** A1091 500fo bl & dk bl 5.00 2.50

**3965** A1091 1000fo ol & dk ol 10.00 5.00

*Nos. 3960-3965 (6)* 21.20 10.60

Issued: 52fo, 75fo, 212fo, 3/16; others, 5/19.

World Heritage Sites — A1271

Designs: 52fo, Early Christian Necropolis, Pecs. 90fo, Ferto-Neuseidler Lake Cultural Landscape, horiz.

**2006, Mar. 16** ***Perf. 12***

**3966-3967** A1271 Set of 2 1.75 .75

**Airplanes Type of 2002**

Designs: 120fo, Boeing 767-200ER. 140fo, Lockheed Sirius 8A.

**2006, Mar. 16**

**3968-3969** A1141 Set of 2 3.25 1.40

Easter — A1272

**2006, Mar. 22**

**3970** A1272 52fo multi .50 .25

Union of European Football Associations Congress, Budapest A1273

**2006, Mar. 22** ***Perf. 13x13¼***

**3971** A1273 170fo multi 2.25 .85

Sándor Légrády (1906-87), Stamp Designer, and Vignette of Unissued Stamp — A1274

**2006, Mar. 30 Litho.** ***Perf. 12x11½***

**3972** A1274 75fo multi 1.00 .35

Ilona Sasváriné-Paulik (1954-99), Paralymic Athlete — A1275

**2006, Mar. 30** ***Perf. 13x13¼***

**3973** A1275 185fo multi 2.00 .85

László Detre (1906-74), Astronomer — A1276

**2006, Mar. 30** ***Perf. 12***

**3974** A1276 212fo multi 2.75 1.00

Wi-fi Technology A1277

**2006, Mar. 30** ***Perf. 13x13¼***

**3975** A1277 240fo multi 2.50 1.10

Orchid — A1278

Rose — A1279

Lily — A1280

Tulip — A1281

Gerbera Daisy — A1282

Rose — A1283

Rose — A1284

Rose — A1285

Butterfly and Wedding Rings — A1286

Butterfly and Rose — A1287

Daisy and Rubber Duck — A1288

Daisy and Blue Booties — A1289

Daisy and Pink Booties — A1290

Daisy and Rattle — A1291

Rose — A1292

Clematis — A1293

**2006 Litho. *Perf. 11¼***

| | | | |
|---|---|---|---|
| 3976 | Vert. strip of 5 + 5 labels | 12.50 | 12.50 |
| a. | A1278 52fo multi + label | 2.00 | .35 |
| b. | A1279 52fo multi + label | 2.00 | .35 |
| c. | A1280 52fo multi + label | 2.00 | .35 |
| d. | A1281 52fo multi + label | 2.00 | .35 |
| e. | A1282 52fo multi + label | 2.00 | .35 |
| | Sheet, 4 each #3976a-3976e | 45.00 | 45.00 |
| 3977 | Strip of 3 + 3 labels | 2.50 | .50 |
| a. | A1283 52fo multi + label | .75 | .50 |
| b. | A1284 52fo multi + label | .75 | .50 |
| c. | A1285 52fo multi + label | .75 | .50 |
| | Sheet, 7 each #3977a-3977b, 6 #3977c | 20.00 | 20.00 |
| 3978 | Pair + 2 labels | 2.00 | 2.00 |
| a. | A1286 52fo multi + label | 1.00 | .50 |
| b. | A1287 52fo multi + label | 1.00 | .50 |
| | Sheet, 10 each #3978a-3978b | 20.00 | 20.00 |
| 3979 | Block or strip of 4 + 4 labels | 12.00 | 12.00 |
| a. | A1288 52fo multi + label | 2.00 | .50 |
| b. | A1289 52fo multi + label | 2.00 | .50 |
| c. | A1290 52fo multi + label | 2.00 | .50 |
| d. | A1291 52fo multi + label | 2.00 | .50 |
| | Sheet, 3 each #3979b-39779c, 7 each #3977a, 3977d | 55.00 | — |
| 3980 | Pair + 2 labels | 5.00 | 5.00 |
| a. | A1292 90fo multi + label | 2.00 | .50 |
| b. | A1293 90fo multi + label | 2.00 | .50 |
| | Sheet, 10 each #3980a-3980b | 60.00 | — |
| | *Nos. 3976-3980 (5)* | 34.00 | 32.00 |

Issued: Nos. 3976, 3977, 5/4, others, 5/19. Background colors of stamps in full sheets varies. Labels could be personalized for an additional fee.

Compare with Nos. 4092, 4199.

Battle of Belgrade, 550th Anniv. — A1294

**2006, May 9 *Perf. 13½x12½***

3981 A1294 120fo multi 1.75 .65

2006 World Cup Soccer Championships, Germany — A1295

**2006, May 9 *Perf. 13x13¼***

3982 A1295 170fo multi 3.50 .90

Europa — A1296

**2006, May 9 *Perf. 12***

3983 A1296 190fo multi 2.25 1.10

Printed in sheets of 4, with each stamp rotated 90 degrees to create circle of faces. Value $9.50.

Horses A1297

Breeds: 75fo, Shagya Arab. 90fo, Furioso (Mezohegyes halfbreed). 140fo, Gidran. 160fo, Nonius.

No. 3988: a, Huçul. b, Lippizaner. c, Kisbér halfbreed.

**2006, May 9**

3984-3987 A1297 Set of 4 5.50 2.25

**Souvenir Sheet**

3988 A1297 200fo Sheet of 3, #a-c 7.00 3.00

Margin of No. 3988 is embossed.

Composers — A1298

Designs: No. 3989, 90fo, George Enescu (1881-1955), and Romanian flag. No. 3990, 90fo, Béla Bartók (1881-1945) and Hungarian flag.

**2006, June 8 *Perf. 13x13¼***

3989-3990 A1298 Set of 2 2.25 .85

See Romania No. 4838.

Miskolc Intl. Opera Festival A1299

**2006, June 15 *Perf. 13¼x13***

3991 A1299 190fo multi 2.25 .85

Souvenir Sheet

Budapest Museum of Fine Arts, Cent. — A1300

No. 3992: a, Esterházy Madonna, by Raphael. b, Mary Magdalene, by El Greco. c, Equestrian statue, by Leonardo da Vinci, horiz. d, Three Fishing Boats, by Claude Monet, horiz.

**2006, June 23 Litho. *Perf. 12***

3992 A1300 200fo Sheet of 4, #a-d 9.00 4.00

The Four Virtues, Frescoes From Castle Museum, Esztergom — A1301

Iconostasis, Szentendre Cathedral — A1302

No. 3993: a, Bölcsesség and Mértékletesség. b, Allhatatosság and Igazságosság.

**2006, June 23 *Perf. 13¼x13***

3993 A1301 52fo Horiz. pair, #a-b 1.50 .50

**Souvenir Sheet**

***Perf. 12***

3994 A1302 400fo +200fo multi 6.50 5.50

Stamp Day.

Emblem of Border Guard and Falcon A1303

**2006, June 27 *Perf. 12***

3995 A1303 170fo multi 1.75 .80

European Swimming Championships, Budapest — A1304

Designs: 90fo, Synchronized swimmers and diver. 180fo, Swimmers and fish.

**2006, July 27 *Perf. 13x13¼***

3996-3997 A1304 Set of 2 2.75 1.25

Contemporary Art — A1305

Designs: 120fo, Child with Model Aircraft, by László Fehér. 140fo, Circle Dance, sculpture by István Haraszty, vert. 160fo, Aequilibrium, tapestry by Zsuzsa Péreli, vert.

**2006, July 27 *Perf. 13x13¼, 13¼x13***

3998-4000 A1305 Set of 3 4.50 2.00

Hungaroring Race Track, 20th Anniv. — A1306

**2006, Aug. 3 *Perf. 13x13¼***

4001 A1306 75fo multi 1.00 .40

Souvenir Sheet

Budapest Zoo, 140th Anniv. — A1307

**2006, Aug. 9 Litho. *Perf. 12***
**4002** A1307 500fo multi 5.50 2.40

Souvenir Sheet

Consecration of Esztergom Basilica, 150th Anniv. — A1308

**2006, Aug. 18**
**4003** A1308 500fo multi 5.50 2.40

Miniature Sheet

Enamel Paintings on St. Stephen's Crown — A1309

No. 4004: a, St. John (scsiohs inscription at top). b, St. Andrew (scsandreas) c, St. Peter (scspetrvs). d, God. e, St. Paul (scspavlus). f, St. Philip (scsphilipvs). g, St. Jacob (scsiacobvs).

**Litho. (Foil Application on Sheet Margin)**

**2006, Aug. 18 *Perf. 12x11½***
**4004** A1309 100fo Sheet of 7, #a-g 8.00 4.00

Souvenir Sheet

1956 Revolution, 50th Anniv. — A1310

**2006, Oct. 20 Litho. *Perf. 13x12¾***
**4005** A1310 500fo multi 5.50 3.00

No. 4005 has a die cut hole in the middle of the flag.

**Christmas Type of 2002**

**Litho. With Foil Application**

**2006, Oct. 27 *Perf. 12***
**4006** A1157 52fo Adoration of the Magi .60 .25

Souvenir Sheet

1956 Melbourne Summer Olympics, 50th Anniv. — A1311

**2006, Nov. 13 Litho. *Perf. 12***
**4007** A1311 500fo László Papp 5.25 2.60

Hungarian Red Cross, 125th Anniv. A1312

**2006, Nov. 24 *Perf. 12¼x11½***
**4008** A1312 100fo multi 1.10 .55

Launch of Sputnik 1 and Sputnik 2, 50th Anniv. — A1313

**2007, Feb. 6 Litho. *Perf. 12***
**4009** A1313 350fo multi 3.75 1.90

Easter — A1314

**2007, Feb. 9 *Perf. 12¼x12¾***
**4010** A1314 62fo multi .65 .30

Famous Men — A1315

Designs: 107fo, János Ferencsik (1907-84), conductor. 135fo, Count Lajos Batthyány (1807-49), prime minister.

**2007, Feb. 9 *Perf. 12***
**4011-4012** A1315 Set of 2 2.50 1.25

Rural Life — A1316

Designs: 62fo, Man with bottle and woman with glass. 95fo, Girl with flowers and birds. 242fo, Man cooking fish over fire.

**2007, Feb. 9 *Perf. 12¼x11½***
**4013-4015** A1316 Set of 3 4.25 2.10

Customs and Finance Guards, 140th Anniv. A1317

**2007, Mar. 10 *Perf. 12***
**4016** A1317 180fo multi 2.00 1.00

Diets A1318

Designs: 210fo, Prince John Sigismund of Transylvania and Torda Church. 230fo, Prince Ferenc Rákóczi II and Marosvásárhely Castle

**2007, Apr. 10 *Perf. 13¼x12½***
**4017-4018** A1318 Set of 2 5.00 2.50

Diet of Torda, 450th anniv.; Diet of Marosvásárhely, 300th anniv.

Souvenir Sheet

The Boys of Paul Street, Novel by Ferenc Molnár (1878-1952) — A1319

No. 4019: a, 160fo, Molnar. b, 160fo, Posted handbill. c, 160fo+30fo, Boy in red shirt. d, 160fo+30fo, Boy in green shirt.

**2007, Apr. 10 *Perf. 12***
**4019** A1319 Sheet of 4, #a-d 8.00 8.00

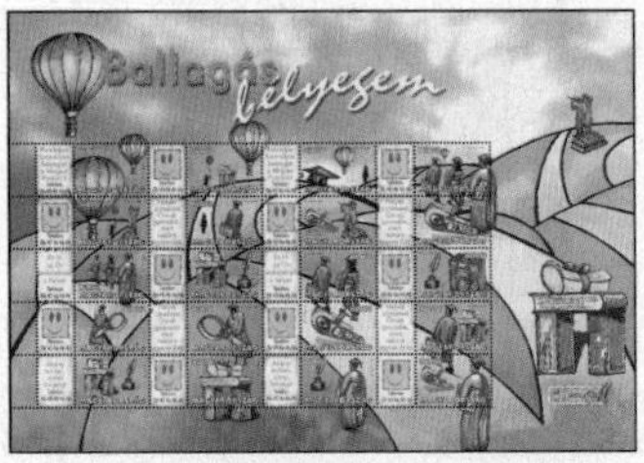

A1320

A1321

A1322

A1323

A1324

A1325

A1326

A1327

A1328

A1329

A1330

A1331

Graduation — A1332

No. 4020: a, Two hot air balloons. b, Graduate pulled by balloon, arch of books, diploma, hot air balloon. c, Graduation cap, hot air balloon, graduate. d, Three graduates, hot air balloon. e, Hot air balloon, graduate pulled by balloon, two graduates standing on books. f, Graduate on path, graduate holding portfolio. g, Diploma, two graduates standing on books. h, Diploma on path, bottom half of graduate at upper right. i, Three graduates on path. j, Arch of books, diploma, inkwell, quill pen, path. k, Two graduates on path. l, Inkwell, quill pen, three books. m, Graduate with magnifying glass, path. n, Graduate with magnifying glass. o, Diploma on path, legs of two graduates, path. p, Graduate carrying portfolio, diploma on arch of books. q, Arch of books, diploma, inkwell, quill pen. r, Arch of books, diploma. s, Inkwell, quill pen, graduate. t, Diploma on path, graduate at right, legs of graduate at top.

**2007, Apr. 16 Litho. *Perf. 11¼***

| | | | |
|---|---|---|---|
| **4020** | A1320 (62fo) Sheet of 20, #a-t, + 20 labels | 20.00 | 14.00 |
| **4021** | Block of 8 + 8 labels | 8.00 | 8.00 |
| *a.* | A1321 (62fo) multi + label | 1.00 | .50 |
| *b.* | A1322 (62fo) multi + label | 1.00 | .50 |
| *c.* | A1323 (62fo) multi + label | 1.00 | .50 |
| *d.* | A1324 (62fo) multi + label | 1.00 | .50 |
| *e.* | A1325 (62fo) multi + label | 1.00 | .50 |
| *f.* | A1326 (62fo) multi + label | 1.00 | .50 |
| *g.* | A1327 (62fo) multi + label | 1.00 | .50 |
| *h.* | A1328 (62fo) multi + label | 1.00 | .50 |
| | Sheet, 3 each #4021a-4021d, 2 each #4021e-4021h, + 20 labels | 20.00 | 20.00 |
| **4022** | Pair + 2 labels | 2.00 | 2.00 |
| *a.* | A1329 (62fo) multi + label | 1.00 | .50 |
| *b.* | A1330 (62fo) multi + label | 1.00 | .50 |
| | Sheet, 10 each #4022a-4022b, + 20 labels | 20.00 | 20.00 |
| **4023** | Pair + 2 labels | 2.10 | 2.10 |
| *a.* | A1331 (95fo) multi + label | 1.00 | .50 |
| *b.* | A1332 (95fo) multi + label | 1.00 | .50 |
| | Sheet, 10 each #4023a-4023b, + 20 labels | 21.00 | 21.00 |

Labels on Nos. 4020-4023 could be personalized for an additional fee.

Stamp Day A1333

Designs: 62fo, St. Elizabeth of Hungary (1207-31) caring for the sick. 95fo, St. Elizabeth caring for poor.

500fo+200fo, St. Emeric (1007-31) praying.

**2007, Apr. 27 Litho. *Perf. 13***

**4024-4025** A1333 Set of 2 1.75 .85

**Souvenir Sheet**

***Perf. 13x12¾***

**4026** A1333 500fo +200fo multi 8.00 8.00

No. 4026 contains one 40x32mm stamp.

Television Broadcasting in Hungary, 50th Anniv. — A1334

**2007, May 9 *Perf. 13x13½***

**4027** A1334 160fo multi 1.75 .85

Souvenir Sheet

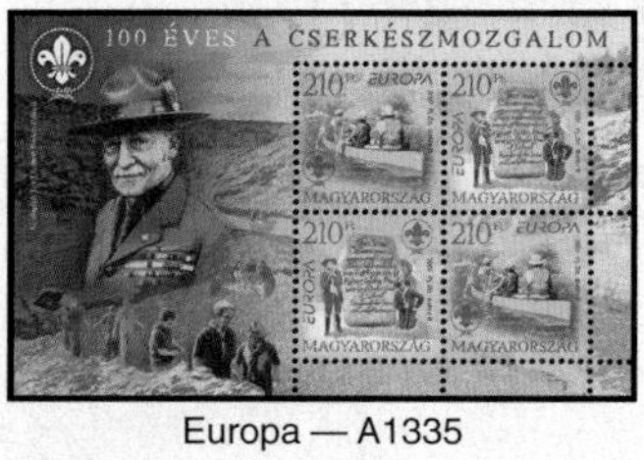

Europa — A1335

No. 4028: a, Scouts in canoe. b, Scouts and Brownsea Island commemorative stone.

**2007, May 9 *Perf. 12***

**4028** A1335 210fo Sheet, 2 each #a-b 9.25 4.50

Scouting, cent.

Dogs A1336

Designs: 62fo, Komondor. 150fo, Transylvanian hound. 180fo, Kuvasz. 240fo, Pumis. 600fo, Hungarian vizsla.

**2007, May 9 *Perf. 13x13½***

**4029-4032** A1336 Set of 4 7.00 3.50

**Souvenir Sheet**

***Perf. 12***

**4033** A1336 600fo multi 6.50 3.25

11th Intl. Cave Rescue Conference, Aggtelek-Jósvafo — A1337

**2007, May 15 Litho. *Perf. 12***

**4034** A1337 200fo multi 2.25 1.10

Academy of Music Building, Budapest, Cent. — A1338

**2007, May 18**

**4035** A1338 250fo multi 2.75 1.40

Souvenir Sheet

National Gallery, 50th Anniv. — A1339

No. 4036: a, The Mystical Betrothal of St. Catherine, c. 1490. b, View of Rome, by Károly Markó the Elder, 1835. c, October, by Károly Ferenczy, 1903. d, Picnic in May, by Pál Szinyei Merse, 1873, horiz.

**2007, May 23 *Perf. 12***

**4036** A1339 150fo Sheet of 4, #a-d 6.50 3.25

**Grapes and Wine Producing Areas Type of 1990**

Designs: 95fo, Cirfandli grapes, Pecs region. 140fo, Ezerfürtü grapes, Etyek-Buda region. 260fo, Zenit grapes, Tolna region.

**2007, May 25 *Perf. 12½x13¼***

**4037-4039** A902 Set of 3 5.50 2.75

Emblem of Border Guard and German Shepherd A1340

**2007, June 27 Litho. *Perf. 12***

**4040** A1340 107fo multi 1.25 .60

**Personalized Stamp Types of 2004-05 Redrawn With "Belföld" Instead of Denomination and**

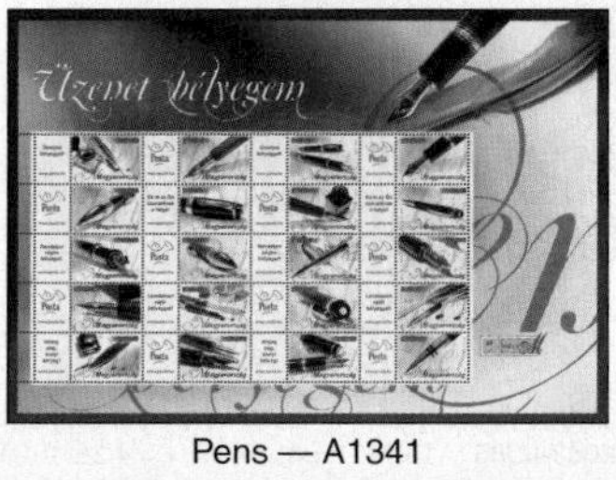

Pens — A1341

A1342

A1343

A1344

A1345

A1346

A1347

A1348

A1349

A1350

Doorknockers A1351

Chain Bridge, Budapest — A1352

Parliament, Budapest — A1353

Buda Castle, Budapest — A1354

Heroes Square, Budapest — A1355

Fisherman's Bastion, Budapest — A1356

No. 4043: a, Quill pen, open inkwell, ink spots, green background. b, Brown fountain pen with point on flourish of "M," brown background. c, Open and closed black and gold fountain pens, green background. d, Black and gold fountain pen with point on flourish of "M," green background. e, Ball-point pen, pen point at LL, pink background. f, Cap of black and gold pen, green background. g, Brown fountain head with flat circular tip on nib, open inkwell, brown background. h, Black and gold pen with pen point at UL, pink background. i, Black and gold fountain pen, pen point at LR, green background. j, Ball-point pen, pen point at LR, pink background. k, Fountain pen and quill, green background. l, Fountain pen, pen point at LR, brown background. m, Brown fountain pen, inkwell, brown background. n, Inkwell, quill, fountain pen, ink spots, green background. o, Plunger and clip of black ball-point pen, pink background. p, Quills, quill pen, ink spots, green background. q, Closed inkwell, pen nib, quill, ink spots, green background. r, Two fountain pens, brown background. s, Black and gold fountain pen and cap, green background. t, Tip of ball-point pen with point on flourish of "M," pink background.

**2007 Litho. *Perf. 11¼***

| | | | |
|---|---|---|---|
| **4041** | Sheet of 20 + 20 labels | 20.00 | 20.00 |
| *a.* | A1220 (62fo) multi + label | 1.00 | .80 |
| *b.* | A1221 (62fo) multi + label | 1.00 | .80 |
| *c.* | A1222 (62fo) multi + label | 1.00 | .80 |
| *d.* | A1223 (62fo) multi + label | 1.00 | .80 |
| *e.* | A1224 (62fo) multi + label | 1.00 | .80 |
| *f.* | A1225 (62fo) multi + label | 1.00 | .80 |
| **4042** | Block or horiz. strip of 4 + 4 labels | 4.00 | 4.00 |
| *a.* | A1288 (62fo) multi + label | 1.00 | .80 |
| *b.* | A1289 (62fo) multi + label | 1.00 | .80 |
| *c.* | A1290 (62fo) multi + label | 1.00 | .80 |

*d.* A1291 (62fo) multi + label 1.00 .80
Sheet of 20, 7 each #4042a, 4042d, 3 each #4042b, 4042c, + 20 labels 20.00 20.00
**4043** A1341 Sheet of 20 + 20 labels 20.00 20.00
*a.-t.* (62fo) Any single + label 1.00 .80
**4044** Block of 10 + 10 labels 10.00 10.00
*a.* A1342 (62fo) multi + label 1.00 .80
*b.* A1343 (62fo) multi + label 1.00 .80
*c.* A1344 (62fo) multi + label 1.00 .80
*d.* A1345 (62fo) multi + label 1.00 .80
*e.* A1346 (62fo) multi + label 1.00 .80
*f.* A1347 (62fo) multi + label 1.00 .80
*g.* A1348 (62fo) multi + label 1.00 .80
*h.* A1349 (62fo) multi + label 1.00 .80
*i.* A1350 (62fo) multi + label 1.00 .80
*j.* A1351 (62fo) multi + label 1.00 .80
Sheet of 20, 2 each #4044a-4044j, + 20 labels 20.00 20.00
**4045** Vert. strip of 5 + 5 labels 5.00 5.00
*a.* A1352 (62fo) multi + label 1.00 .80
*b.* A1353 (62fo) multi + label 1.00 .80
*c.* A1354 (62fo) multi + label 1.00 .80
*d.* A1355 (62fo) multi + label 1.00 .80
*e.* A1356 (62fo) multi + label 1.00 .80
Sheet of 20, 4 each #4045a-4045e, + 20 labels 20.00 20.00
*Nos. 4041-4045 (5)* 59.00 59.00

Issued: No. 4041, 9/27; others, 7/16.

No. 4041 contains 4 each #4041a, 4041e, 2 each #4041d, 4041f, 5 #4041b and 3 #4041c. Background colors on some stamps differ slightly. Labels could be personalized for an additional fee.

Zoltán Kodály (1882-1967), Composer — A1357

**2007, July 16** *Perf. 13x13¼*
**4046** A1357 200fo multi 2.25 1.10

Hungarian University Sports Federation, Cent. — A1358

**2007, July 30** *Perf. 11½x12*
**4047** A1358 360fo multi 4.00 2.00

Dolomite Flax — A1359

Pasque Flower — A1360

**Booklet Stamps**

***Serpentine Die Cut 10¾x10½***

**2007, Aug. 1** **Self-Adhesive**
**4048** A1359 (230fo) multi 2.50 1.25
*a.* Booklet pane of 4 + 4 etiquettes 10.00
**4049** A1360 (260fo) multi 3.00 1.50
*a.* Booklet pane of 4 + 4 etiquettes 12.00

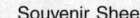

Souvenir Sheet

Enamel Paintings on St. Stephen's Crown — A1361

No. 4050: a, St. Cosmas (light blue robe). b, St. George (holding spear and shield). c, Archangel Michael (holding staff).

**Litho. (Litho. With Foil Application in Sheet Margin)**

**2007, Aug. 17** *Perf. 12x11½*
**4050** A1361 300fo Sheet of 3, #a-c 10.00 5.00

János Selye (1907-82), Stress Researcher — A1362

*Perf. 13¼x12¾*

**2007, Aug. 23** **Litho.**
**4051** A1362 400fo multi 4.50 2.25

Second World Stress Conference, Budapest.

**World Science Forum Type of 2005 Redrawn**

**2007, Sept. 27** *Perf. 13x13¼*
**4052** A1264 230fo multi 2.60 1.25

Christmas — A1363

No. 4053: a, Annunciation. b, Holy Family and Shepherds. c, Adoration of the Magi.

**2007, Oct. 19** *Perf. 12*
**4053** A1363 62fo Horiz. strip of 3, #a-c 2.50 1.25

**Compass and Map Type of 2005 Redrawn With "Belföld" Instead of Denomination**

No. 4054: a, Compass at right, map of western Hungary. b, Compass at left, map of eastern Hungary.

**2008, Feb. 8** **Litho.** *Perf. 11¼*
**4054** A1246 (70fo) Pair, #a-b, + 2 labels 1.60 1.60
Sheet of 18 #4054a, 17 #4054b, + 35 labels 28.00 —

Labels could be personalized.



Easter A1364

**2008, Feb. 27** *Perf. 12*
**4055** A1364 70fo multi .80 .40

King Matthias, 550th Anniv. of Election — A1365

King Matthias, arms and: 70fo, Fountain. 100fo, Castle and horses.
600fo+200fo, King and Queen on throne.

**2008, Mar. 13**
**4056-4057** A1365 Set of 2 2.10 1.10

**Souvenir Sheet**

**4058** A1365 600fo +200fo multi 10.00 10.00

Stamp Day. No. 4058 contains one 40x30mm stamp.

General Károly Knezich (1808-49) A1366

**2008, Mar. 14** *Perf. 13x12½*
**4059** A1366 380fo multi 4.75 2.40

Miniature Sheet

Transportation — A1367

No. 4060: a, 150fo, Automobile. b, 150fo, Ship. c, 150fo+30fo, Train. d, 150fo+30fo, Airplane.

**2008, Mar. 14** *Perf. 12*
**4060** A1367 Sheet of 4, #a-d 8.25 8.25

Romany Dancer and Musicians A1368

German Dancer and Accordion A1369

**2008** *Perf. 13½x13*
**4061** A1368 260fo multi 3.25 1.60
**4062** A1369 275fo multi 3.50 1.75

Hungarian ethnic minorities. Issued: 260fo, 4/8; 275fo, 5/9.

2008 Summer Olympics, Beijing A1370

Designs: 70fo, Water polo. 100fo, Wrestling. 170fo, Fencing.

**2008, Apr. 16** *Perf. 13x13¼*
**4063-4065** A1370 Set of 3 4.25 2.10

Miniature Sheet

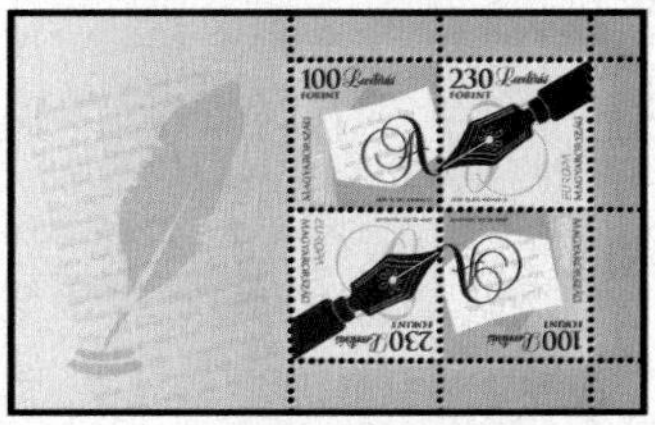

Europa — A1371

No. 4066: a, 100fo, Letter in envelope, capital "A." b, 230fo, Pen nib.

**2008, May 9** *Perf. 12*
**4066** A1371 Sheet, 2 each #a-b 8.25 4.25

Stamps on bottom row are tete-beche in relation to the top row.

Indigenous Animals A1372

Designs: 145fo, Hungarian giant rabbit. 150fo, Hungarian domestic goat. 170fo, Cikta sheep. 310fo, Hungarian donkey.
600fo, Water buffalo.

**2008, May 9**
**4067-4070** A1372 Set of 4 9.50 4.75

**Souvenir Sheet**

**4071** A1372 600fo multi 7.50 3.75

**National Parks Type of 1998**

Design: Orség National Park.

**2008, May 16**
**4072** A1073 220fo multi 3.00 1.50

**UNESCO World Heritage Sites Type of 2002**

Design: Tokaj Wine Region.

**2008, May 16**
**4073** A1153 290fo multi 3.75 1.90

UEFA Euro 2008 Soccer Championships, Austria and Switzerland A1373

**2008, May 16** *Perf. 13½x13*
**4074** A1373 250fo multi 3.25 1.60

Vacation Vouchers, 10th Anniv. A1374

**2008, May 20** *Perf. 12x11½*
**4075** A1374 70fo multi .90 .45

A1375

A1376

A1377

A1378

A1379

Philavillage
A1380

**2008** ***Perf. 12, 13¼x13 (#4077)***

| | | | | |
|---|---|---|---|---|
| **4076** | A1375 | 100fo multi | 1.40 | .70 |
| **4077** | A1376 | 100fo multi | 1.40 | .70 |
| **4078** | A1377 | 100fo multi | 1.40 | .70 |
| **4079** | A1378 | 100fo multi | 1.40 | .70 |
| **4080** | A1379 | 100fo multi | 1.40 | .70 |
| **4081** | A1380 | 100fo multi | 1.40 | .70 |
| | | *Nos. 4076-4081 (6)* | 8.40 | 4.20 |

Issued: Nos. 4076-4077, 6/6; Nos. 4078-4079, 6/20; Nos. 4080-4081, 7/10. Stamps also served as game pieces for Philavillage board game.

A1381

A1382

A1383

A1384

A1385

Philavillage
A1386

**2008** **Litho.** ***Perf. 12***

| | | | | |
|---|---|---|---|---|
| **4082** | A1381 | 100fo multi | 1.25 | .60 |
| **4083** | A1382 | 100fo multi | 1.25 | .60 |

***Perf. 13x13¼, 13¼x13 (#4086)***

| | | | | |
|---|---|---|---|---|
| **4084** | A1383 | 100fo multi | 1.10 | .55 |
| **4085** | A1384 | 100fo multi | 1.10 | .55 |
| **4086** | A1385 | 100fo multi | .95 | .50 |
| **4087** | A1386 | 100fo multi | .95 | .50 |
| | | *Nos. 4082-4087 (6)* | 6.60 | 3.30 |

Issued: Nos. 4082-4083, 9/2; Nos. 4084-4085, 10/9; Nos. 4086-4087, 11/5. Stamps also served as game pieces for Philavillage board game.

Hungarian Illuminated Chronicle, 650th Anniv. — A1387

**Litho. & Embossed With Foil Application**

**2008, June 20** ***Perf. 12***

| | | | | |
|---|---|---|---|---|
| **4088** | A1387 | 400fo multi | 5.50 | 2.75 |

Souvenir Sheet

Debrecen and Veszprém Zoos, 50th Anniv. — A1388

No. 4089: a, Giraffes, cranes, hippopotamus, camel (Debrecen). b, Camel, crane, lion, zebra, rhinoceros, flamingo (Veszprém).

**2008, Aug. 14** **Litho.** ***Perf. 12***

| | | | | |
|---|---|---|---|---|
| **4089** | A1388 | 260fo Sheet of 2, #a-b | 6.50 | 3.25 |

Souvenir Sheet

Enamel Paintings on St. Stephen's Crown — A1389

No. 4090: a, Archangel Gabriel (holding staff). b, St. Demeter (with shield and spear). c, St. Damian (with beard).

**Litho. (Litho. With Foil Application in Sheet Margin)**

**2008, Aug. 19** ***Perf. 12x11½***

| | | | | |
|---|---|---|---|---|
| **4090** | A1389 | 300fo Sheet of 3, #a-c | 11.50 | 5.75 |

Miklós Zrinyi (1508-66), Military Leader
A1390

**2008, Sept. 5** **Litho.** ***Perf. 13x13¼***

| | | | | |
|---|---|---|---|---|
| **4091** | A1390 | 190fo multi | 2.25 | 1.10 |

**Flowers Types of 2006 Redrawn With "Belföld" Instead of Denomination**

**2008, Sept. 2** **Litho.** ***Perf. 11¼***

| | | | |
|---|---|---|---|
| **4092** | Vert. strip of 5 + 5 labels | 4.25 | 4.25 |
| ***a.*** | A1278 (70fo) multi + label | .85 | .85 |
| ***b.*** | A1279 (70fo) multi + label | .85 | .85 |
| ***c.*** | A1280 (70fo) multi + label | .85 | .85 |
| ***d.*** | A1281 (70fo) multi + label | .85 | .85 |
| ***e.*** | A1282 (70fo) multi + label | .85 | .85 |
| | Sheet, 4 each #4092a-4092e, + 20 labels | 17.00 | — |

Background colors of stamps in full sheets varies. Labels could be personalized for an additional fee.

Archangel Gabriel, Sculpture by György Zala (1858-1937)
A1391

**2008, Sept. 25** **Litho.** ***Perf. 13¼x13***

| | | | | |
|---|---|---|---|---|
| **4093** | A1391 | 200fo multi | 2.25 | 1.10 |

Synagogues
A1392

Designs: 200fo, Synagogue, Szeged. 250fo, Synagogue of the Jewish Theological Seminary, Budapest.

**2008, Sept. 25** ***Perf. 12½x13¼***

| | | | | |
|---|---|---|---|---|
| **4094-4095** | A1392 | Set of 2 | 5.00 | 2.50 |

Cat — A1393

Bear — A1394

Rabbit — A1395

Lion — A1396

Giraffe — A1397

**2008, Oct. 9** ***Perf. 11¼***

| | | | |
|---|---|---|---|
| **4096** | Vert. strip of 5 + 5 labels | 3.75 | 3.75 |
| ***a.*** | A1393 (70fo) multi | .75 | .40 |
| ***b.*** | A1394 (70fo) multi | .75 | .40 |
| ***c.*** | A1395 (70fo) multi | .75 | .40 |
| ***d.*** | A1396 (70fo) multi | .75 | .40 |
| ***e.*** | A1397 (70fo) multi | .75 | .40 |
| | Sheet, 4 each #4096a-4096e, + 20 labels | 15.00 | 15.00 |

Labels on No. 4096 could be personalized for an additional fee.

Souvenir Sheet

Ferenc Puskás (1927-2006), Player on 1952 Hungarian Olympic Soccer Team — A1398

**2008, Oct. 28** ***Perf. 12***

| | | | | |
|---|---|---|---|---|
| **4097** | A1398 | 600fo multi | 6.00 | 3.00 |

Christmas
A1399

Art by György Konecsni (1908-70): 70fo, Nativity. 100fo, Adoration of the Magi.

**2008, Oct. 28** ***Perf. 12¼x11½***

| | | | | |
|---|---|---|---|---|
| **4098-4099** | A1399 | Set of 2 | 1.75 | .85 |

Edward Teller (1908-2003), Nuclear Physicist — A1400

**2008, Nov. 3** ***Perf. 13x13¼***
**4100** A1400 250fo multi 2.40 1.25

Ludovika Academy, 200th Anniv. — A1401

**2008, Nov. 5** ***Perf. 13¼x13***
**4101** A1401 300fo multi 3.00 1.50

Crocus — A1402 Scilla — A1403

**2009, Feb. 24 Litho.** ***Perf. 11½x12***
**4102** A1402 (75fo) multi .65 .30
**4103** A1403 (100fo) multi .85 .40

**Self-Adhesive**

***Serpentine Die Cut 10x10¼***
**4104** A1403 (75fo) multi .65 .30
*Nos. 4102-4104 (3)* 2.15 1.00

Easter — A1404

**2009, Feb. 24** ***Perf. 12x12½***
**4105** A1404 75fo multi .65 .30

Franciscan Order, 800th Anniv. — A1405

**2009, Feb. 24** ***Perf. 12***
**4106** A1405 100fo multi .85 .40

1909 Flights of Louis Blériot, Cent. — A1406

No. 4107: a, Flight across English Channel. b, Flight at Kisrákoson, Hungary.

**2009, Mar. 12**
**4107** A1406 105fo Horiz. pair, #a-b, + central label 2.00 1.00

Souvenir Sheet

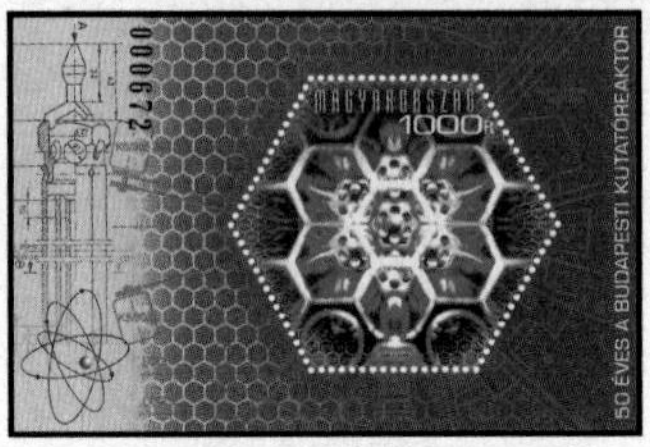


Budapest Research Reactor, 50th Anniv. — A1407

**2009, Mar. 25** ***Perf. 11¼***
**4108** A1407 1000fo multi 9.25 4.50

Preservation of Polar Regions and Glaciers — A1408

Designs: Nos. 4109, 4113, 75fo, Ursus maritimus and walruses. Nos. 4110, 4114, 130fo, Ovibos moschatus. Nos. 4111, 4115, 145fo, Uncia uncia. Nos. 4112, 4116, 275fo, Aptenodytes patagonicus.

No. 4117: a, Ursus maritimus. b, Alopex lagopus.

**2009, Mar. 27 Litho.** ***Perf. 12½x12***
**4109-4112** A1408 Set of 4 5.75 3.00

**Litho. & Silk-screened**

**4113-4116** A1408 Set of 4 5.75 3.00

**Souvenir Sheet**

**4117** A1408 260fo Sheet of 2, #a-b 4.75 2.40

Portions of the designs of Nos. 4113-4117 that were applied by the silk-screen process have a silvery shine when viewed at an angle.

Joseph Haydn (1732-1809), Composer — A1409

**2009, Apr. 2 Litho.** ***Perf. 13x13¼***
**4118** A1409 300fo red & black 2.75 1.40

Locomotives — A1410

Designs: 75fo, Mk48 Diesel locomotive. 100fo, C 50 Diesel locomotive. 125fo, MD 40 Diesel locomotive. 275fo, Morgó steam locomotive.

**2009, Apr. 2** ***Perf. 13¼x13***
**4119-4122** A1410 Set of 4 5.25 2.60

Souvenir Sheet

Ferenc Kazinczy (1759-1831), Writer — A1411

**2009, Apr. 2** ***Perf. 13x12¾***
**4123** A1411 600fo multi 5.50 2.75

Miniature Sheet

Elek Benedek (1859-1929), Fable Writer and Translator — A1412

No. 4124: a, 100fo, Arabian man, chicken and bees. b, 100fo, Three pigs. c, 100fo+50fo, Cat in king's robes. d, 100fo+50fo, Benedek.

**2009, Apr. 2** ***Perf. 12x12½***
**4124** A1412 Sheet of 4, #a-d 4.75 2.40

Miklós Radnóti (1909-44), Poet — A1413

**2009, May 5** ***Perf. 13¼x13***
**4125** A1413 280fo multi 2.60 1.25

Souvenir Sheet

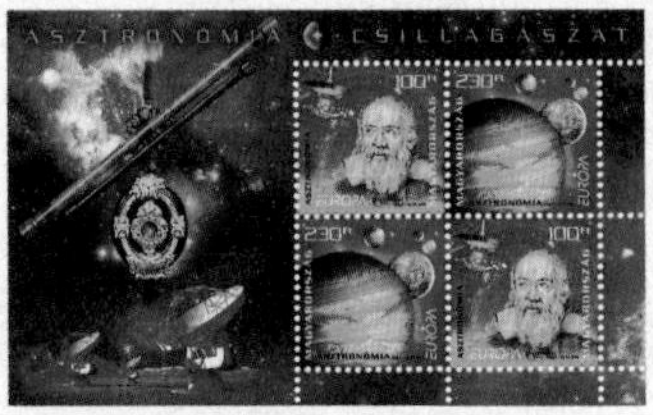

Europa — A1414

No. 4126: a, 100fo, Galileo Galilei and Galileo space probe. b, 230fo, Planets.

**2009, May 8** ***Perf. 12***
**4126** A1414 Sheet, 2 each #a-b 6.25 6.25

Intl. Year of Astronomy.

John Calvin (1509-64), Theologian and Religious Reformer A1415

**2009, May 22** ***Perf. 13¼x13***
**4127** A1415 200fo multi 2.00 1.00

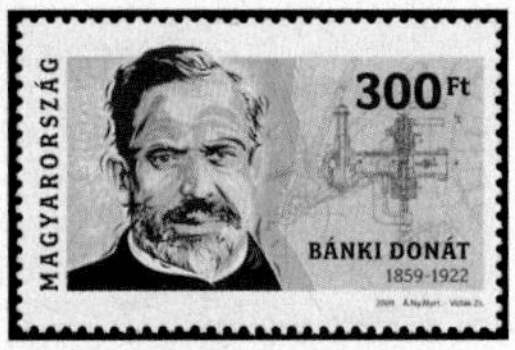


Donát Bánki (1859-1922), Inventor of Carburetor — A1416

**2009, June 5**
**4128** A1416 300fo multi 3.00 1.50

Visegrád, 1000th Anniv. A1417

Designs: 75fo, Column and entableture. 100fo, Solomon Tower, octagonal column, carved head.

600fo+200fo, Summer Palace, fountain, monument, Madonna and Child.

**2009, June 5** ***Perf. 13x13¼***
**4129-4130** A1417 Set of 2 1.75 .85

**Souvenir Sheet**

**4131** A1417 600fo +200fo multi 7.75 4.00

Stamp Day.

Discovery of Statue of Virgin Mary, Máriabesnyo, 250th Anniv. — A1418

**2009, Aug. 14** ***Perf. 13¼x12***
**4132** A1418 200fo multi 2.10 1.10

Bishopric of Pécs, 1000th Anniv. — A1419

**2009, Aug. 19** ***Perf. 12***
**4133** A1419 100fo multi 1.10 .55

**Furniture Type of 1999**

Design like #3791.

**2009, Sept. 4 Litho.** ***Perf. 12¼x11½***
**4134** A1091 230fo blue green 2.40 1.25

Building, Pecs — A1420

Calvary Hill, Pecs — A1421

City Hall, Szechenyi Square, Pecs — A1422

Sts. Peter and Paul Cathedral, Pecs — A1423

Building, Pecs — A1424

Hungarian Academy of Sciences, Sculpture, Pecs — A1425

Synagogue, Pecs — A1426

Sts. Peter and Paul Cathedral, Pecs — A1427

Door Knocker and Handle, Pecs — A1428

Klimó Library, Pecs — A1429

National Theater, Pecs — A1430

Zsolnay Fountain, Pecs — A1431

Roof, Pecs — A1432

Street, Pecs — A1433

Necropolis, Pecs — A1434

Post Office Roof, Pecs — A1435

Mosque, Pecs — A1436

Barbican, Pecs — A1437

Mosque and Minaret, Pecs — A1438

Sculpture, Pecs — A1439

**2009, Sept. 4 Litho. *Perf. 11¼***

| | | | |
|---|---|---|---|
| **4135** | Sheet of 20 + 20 labels | 16.00 | 16.00 |
| *a.* | A1420 (75fo) multi + label | .80 | .80 |
| *b.* | A1421 (75fo) multi + label | .80 | .80 |
| *c.* | A1422 (75fo) multi + label | .80 | .80 |
| *d.* | A1423 (75fo) multi + label | .80 | .80 |
| *e.* | A1424 (75fo) multi + label | .80 | .80 |
| *f.* | A1425 (75fo) multi + label | .80 | .80 |
| *g.* | A1426 (75fo) multi + label | .80 | .80 |
| *h.* | A1427 (75fo) multi + label | .80 | .80 |
| *i.* | A1428 (75fo) multi + label | .80 | .80 |
| *j.* | A1429 (75fo) multi + label | .80 | .80 |
| *k.* | A1430 (75fo) multi + label | .80 | .80 |
| *l.* | A1431 (75fo) multi + label | .80 | .80 |
| *m.* | A1432 (75fo) multi + label | .80 | .80 |
| *n.* | A1433 (75fo) multi + label | .80 | .80 |
| *o.* | A1434 (75fo) multi + label | .80 | .80 |
| *p.* | A1435 (75fo) multi + label | .80 | .80 |
| *q.* | A1436 (75fo) multi + label | .80 | .80 |
| *r.* | A1437 (75fo) multi + label | .80 | .80 |
| *s.* | A1438 (75fo) multi + label | .80 | .80 |
| *t.* | A1439 (75fo) multi + label | .80 | .80 |

Labels could be personalized for an additional fee.

Opening of Border Between Austria and Hungary, 20th Anniv. A1440

**2009, Sept. 10 Litho. *Perf. 12***

**4136** A1440 210fo multi 2.40 1.25

See Austria No. 2219, Germany No. 2548.

Rainbow, by Jòzsef Egry (1883-1951) — A1441

**2009, Sept. 10 *Perf. 13¼x12½***

**4137** A1441 275fo multi 3.00 1.50

Louis Braille (1809-52), Educator of the Blind — A1442

**Litho. & Embossed**

**2009, Oct. 15 *Perf. 13¼x13***

**4138** A1442 200fo multi 2.25 1.10

A1443

Christmas A1444

**2009, Oct. 15 Litho. *Perf. 12***

**4139** A1443 75fo multi .80 .40

***Perf. 12x11½***

**4140** A1444 100fo blue & yel org 1.10 .55

**Miniature Sheet**

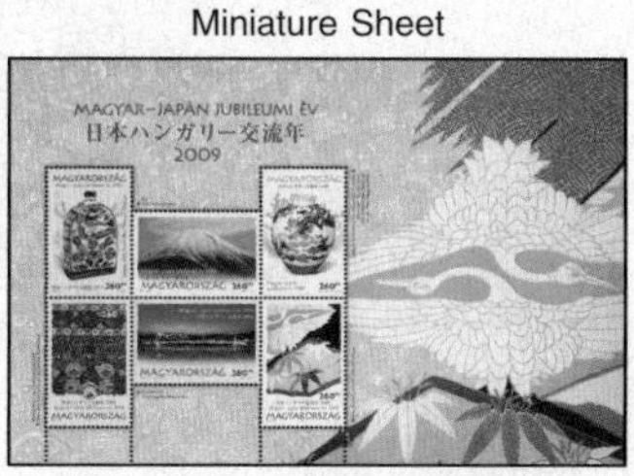

Hungarian-Japanese Jubilee Year — A1445

No. 4141: a, Hungarian flask. b, Mount Fuji, horiz. c, Jar from Japanese tea service. d, Matyo folk embroidery, Hungary. e, Elizabeth Bridge, Hungary, horiz. f, Crane and leaves fabric pattern from Japanese kimono.

**2009, Oct. 16 *Perf. 12***

**4141** A1445 260fo Sheet of 6, #a-f 17.00 8.50

See Japan No. 3167.

Ajka Crystal — A1446

**2009, Oct. 28**

**4142** A1446 300fo multi 3.25 1.60

World Science Forum, Budapest A1447

**2009, Nov. 5 *Perf. 13x13¼***

**4143** A1447 100fo multi 1.10 .55

Filaclub Characters A1448

No. 4144: a, Bogi Fila. b, Levi Fila. c, Pötyi Fila.

**2009, Dec. 4**

**4144** Horiz. strip of 3 .70 .35

*a.-c.* A1448 20fo Any single .25 .25

Promotion of children's philately.

Hassan Jakovali Mosque, Pecs — A1449

Calvary Hill, Pecs — A1450

National Theater, Pecs — A1451

Hungarian Academy of Sciences, Pecs — A1452

Barbican, Pecs — A1453

Synagogue, Pecs — A1454

Statue of St. Francis of Assisi, by György Bársony, Pecs — A1455

Interior of National Theater, Pecs — A1456

Statue of Janus Pannonius, by Sándor Rétfalvi, Pecs — A1457

County Hall, Pecs — A1458

Post Office, Pecs — A1459

St. Peter and Paul Cathedral, Pecs — A1460

St. Peter and Paul Cathedral, Pecs — A1461

Statue of the Holy Trinity, by György Kiss, Pecs — A1462

Mosque of Pasha Gazi Kasim, Pecs — A1463

University Gate, Pecs — A1464

Necropolis, Pecs — A1465

Zsolnay Fountain, Pecs — A1466

Klimó Library, Pecs — A1467

Statue of Tivadar Csontváry Kosztka, Zsolnay Vase, Pecs — A1468

Reformed Church, Pecs — A1469

Tettye Ruins, Pecs — A1470

Lutheran Church, Pecs — A1471

City Hall, Pecs — A1472

Symbol Sculpture, by Victor Vasarely, Pecs — A1473

**2010, Jan. 10** **Litho.** ***Perf. 12***

| | | | |
|---|---|---|---|
| **4145** | Sheet of 25 | 20.00 | 10.00 |
| *a.* | A1449 (75fo) multi | .80 | .40 |
| *b.* | A1450 (75fo) multi | .80 | .40 |
| *c.* | A1451 (75fo) multi | .80 | .40 |
| *d.* | A1452 (75fo) multi | .80 | .40 |
| *e.* | A1453 (75fo) multi | .80 | .40 |
| *f.* | A1454 (75fo) multi | .80 | .40 |
| *g.* | A1455 (75fo) multi | .80 | .40 |
| *h.* | A1456 (75fo) multi | .80 | .40 |
| *i.* | A1457 (75fo) multi | .80 | .40 |
| *j.* | A1458 (75fo) multi | .80 | .40 |
| *k.* | A1459 (75fo) multi | .80 | .40 |
| *l.* | A1460 (75fo) multi | .80 | .40 |
| *m.* | A1461 (75fo) multi | .80 | .40 |
| *n.* | A1462 (75fo) multi | .80 | .40 |
| *o.* | A1463 (75fo) multi | .80 | .40 |
| *p.* | A1464 (75fo) multi | .80 | .40 |
| *q.* | A1465 (75fo) multi | .80 | .40 |
| *r.* | A1466 (75fo) multi | .80 | .40 |
| *s.* | A1467 (75fo) multi | .80 | .40 |
| *t.* | A1468 (75fo) multi | .80 | .40 |
| *u.* | A1469 (75fo) multi | .80 | .40 |
| *v.* | A1470 (75fo) multi | .80 | .40 |
| *w.* | A1471 (75fo) multi | .80 | .40 |
| *x.* | A1472 (75fo) multi | .80 | .40 |
| *y.* | A1473 (75fo) multi | .80 | .40 |

Pecs, 2010 European Cultural Capital.

2010 Winter Olympics, Vancouver A1474

**2010, Feb. 5**
**4146** A1474 260fo multi 2.60 1.40

Izidor Kner (1860-1935), Publisher — A1475

**2010, Feb. 5** ***Perf. 12x13¼***
**4147** A1475 295fo multi 3.00 1.50

Budapest Landmarks A1476

Designs: 295fo, Tympanum of Humanities Building, Loránd Eötvös University, Budapest. 400fo, Elisabeth Tower, Budapest.

**2010, Feb. 19** ***Perf. 12½x12***
**4148-4149** A1476 Set of 2 7.00 3.50

Loránd Eötvös University, 375th anniv., Elisabeth Tower, cent.

Easter A1477

**2010, Mar. 1**
**4150** A1477 80fo multi .85 .40

Republican Guard Regiment, 250th Anniv. A1478

**2010, Mar. 1** ***Perf. 13x13¼***
**4151** A1478 320fo multi 3.25 1.60

**Souvenir Sheet**

Ferenc Erkel (1810-93), Composer — A1479

**2010, Mar. 26** ***Perf. 12***
**4152** A1479 500fo multi 5.25 2.60

Stamp Day — A1480

Sites in Sopron: 80fo, Saint Ursula's Church, Church of the Virgin Mary. 105fo, Sculptur of the Virgin Mary, Gates of Faith, horiz.
500fo+200fo, Statue of the Holy Trinity.

**2010, Mar. 26** ***Perf. 12x12½, 12½x12***
**4153-4154** A1480 Set of 2 1.90 .95

**Souvenir Sheet**

**4155** A1480 500fo +200fo multi 7.25 3.50

Surtax on No. 4155 for Natl. Association of Hungarian Stamp Collectors.

Hungarian Documents on Paper, 700th Anniv. A1481

**2010, Apr. 8** ***Perf. 13x13¼***
**4156** A1481 140fo multi 1.40 .70

*Chronicle of the Ways of the Hungarians*, by Gáspár Heltai (c. 1510-74), Writer — A1482

**2010, Apr. 8** ***Perf. 13¼x13***
**4157** A1482 240fo multi 2.50 1.25

Expo 2010, Shanghai — A1483

Gömböc in various positions with stamps numbered in lower left: Nos. 4158a, 4158ae, 1. Nos. 4158b, 4158af, 2. Nos. 4158c, 4158ag, 3. Nos. 4158d, 4158ah, 2 squared (4). Nos. 4158e, 4158ai, 5. Nos. 4158f, 4158aj, 2*3 (6). Nos. 4158g, 4158ak, 7. Nos. 4158h, 4158al, 2 cubed (8). Nos. 4158i, 4158am, 3 squared (9). Nos. 4158j, 4158an, 2*5 (10). Nos. 4158k, 4158ao, 11. Nos. 4158l, 4158ap, 2 squared * 3 (12). Nos. 4158m, 4158aq, 13. Nos. 4158n, 4158ar, 2*7 (14). Nos. 4158o, 4158as, 3*5 (15). Nos. 4158p, 4158at, 2 to the fourth power (16). Nos. 4158q, 4158au, 17. Nos. 4158r, 4158av, 2*9 (18). Nos. 4158s, 4158aw, 19. Nos. 4158t, 4158ax, 2 squared * 5 (20). Nos. 4158u, 4158ay, 3*7 (21). Nos. 4158v, 4158az, 2*11 (22). Nos. 4158w, 4158ba, 23. Nos. 4158x, 4158bb, 2 cubed * 3 (24). Nos. 4158y, 4158bc, 5 squared (25). Nos. 4158z, 4158bd, 2*13 (26). Nos. 4158aa, 4158be, 3 cubed (27). Nos. 4158ab, 4158bf, 2 squared * 7 (28). Nos. 4158ac, 4158bg, 29. Nos. 4158ad, 4158bh, 2*3*5 (30).

**2010, Apr. 30 Litho. *Perf. 12***

**4158** Sheet of 30 30.00 30.00
***a.-ad.*** A1483 100fo Any single 1.00 .50
***ae.-bh.*** A1483 100fo Any booklet single, perf. 12 horiz. at top 1.00 .50
Complete booklet, #4158ae-4158bh 30.00

Miniature Sheet

The Tragedy of Man, Play by Imre Madách, 150th Anniv. — A1484

No. 4159 — Scenes from play: a, 105fo, Adam and Eve in Garden of Eden (denomination in white). b, 105fo, Men and women in London (denomination in black). c, 105fo+50fo, Men and women in Rome (denomination at bottom in white). d, 105fo+50fo, Woman in Prague (denomination at top in white).

**2010, May 3 *Perf. 13x13¼***

**4159** A1484 Sheet of 4, #a-d 4.75 2.40

Surtax for supporting youth stamp collecting.

2010 World Cup Soccer Championships, South Africa — A1485

**2010, May 7 *Perf. 11***

**4160** A1485 325fo multi 3.00 1.50

Intl. Year of Biodiversity A1486

Designs: 80fo, Spermophilus citellus. 110fo, Phyllomorpha lacinata. 215fo, Parus caeruleus. 350fo, Vipera ursinii rakosiensis. 500fo, Iris aphylla ssp. hungarica.

**2010, May 7 *Perf. 12½x12***

**4161-4164** A1486 Set of 4 7.00 3.50

**Souvenir Sheet**
***Perf. 12***

**4165** A1486 500fo multi 4.75 2.40

Miniature Sheet

Europa — A1487

No. 4166 — Vackor the Bear: a, Holding plant. b, Picking fruit.

**2010, May 7 *Perf. 12***

**4166** A1487 150fo Sheet, 2 each #a-b 5.50 2.75

**No. 3417a Surcharged in Red**

**Method and Perf. As Before**

**2010, June 18**

**4167** A972 200fo on 19fo multi (R) 1.75 .90

Election of Prime Minister József Antall, 20th anniv.

Frédéric Chopin (1810-49), Composer — A1488

**2010, June 18 Litho. *Perf. 12½***

**4168** A1488 240fo multi 2.10 1.10

Self-Portrait of Miklós Barabás (1810-98) A1489

**2010, June 18 *Perf. 12½x13¼***

**4169** A1489 365fo multi 3.25 1.60

World Triathlon Championships, Budapest — A1490

**2010, July 2 Litho. *Perf. 13x13¼***

**4170** A1490 280fo multi 2.50 1.25

European Swimming League Championships, Budapest and Lake Balaton — A1491

**2010, July 2 *Perf. 13¼x13***

**4171** A1491 300fo multi 2.60 1.40

25th Hungarian Formula 1 Grand Prix — A1492

**2010, July 30 *Perf. 12***

**4172** A1492 230fo multi 2.10 1.10

Synagogues A1493

Designs: 110fo, Nagykoros Synagogue. 175fo, New Synagogue, Szolnok.

**2010, Sept. 6 *Perf. 12½x13¼***

**4173-4174** A1493 Set of 2 2.60 1.40

Hungarian Gymnastics Federation, 125th Anniv. — A1494

**2010, Sept. 24 Litho. *Perf. 12x12½***

**4175** A1494 140fo multi 1.40 .70

Christmas A1495

Designs: 80fo, Madonna and Child. 105fo, Angels making music, horiz.

**Litho. With Foil Application**

**2010, Oct. 28 *Perf. 12***

**4176-4177** A1495 Set of 2 1.90 .95

Embroidery — A1496

Designs: 80fo, Termeh embroidery designs, Yazd, Iran. 240fo, Jazgyian embroidery designs, Hungary.

**2010, Nov. 10 Litho. *Perf. 12½x12***

**4178-4179** A1496 Set of 2 3.25 1.60

See Iran No. 3027.

Souvenir Sheet

Rudolf Kárpáti (1920-99), Fencing Gold Medalist at 1960 Summer Olympics — A1497

**2010, Dec. 10 *Perf. 12***

**4180** A1497 500fo multi 4.75 2.40

Sándor Püski (1911-2009), Book Publisher A1498

**2011, Feb. 4 Litho. *Perf. 12x12½***

**4181** A1498 270fo multi 2.75 1.40

Hungarian Presidency of the Council of the European Union — A1499

**2011, Feb. 7 *Perf. 12***

**4182** A1499 90fo multi .90 .45

Visegrád Group, 20th Anniv. — A1500

**2011, Feb. 15**

**4183** A1500 240fo multi 2.40 1.25

See Czech Republic No. 3490, Poland No. 4001, Slovakia No. 611.

**Furniture Type of 1999**

Design like #3738.

**2011, Mar. 1 Litho. *Perf. 11½x12¼***

**4184** A1091 225fo green 2.40 1.25

Hungarian Golgotha, Textile Art by Erzsébet Szekeres A1501

**2011, Mar. 1** ***Perf. 12***
**4185** A1501 90fo multi .95 .45

Easter.

Tourist Attractions A1502

Designs: 160fo, Pauline Piarist Church, Sátoraljaújhely. 220fo, Royal Palace of Gödöllo.

**2011, Mar. 4** ***Perf. 12½x12***
**4186-4187** A1502 Set of 2 4.00 2.00

Vasas Sport Club, Cent. A1503

**2011, Mar. 16**
**4188** A1503 315fo multi 3.50 1.75

Entertainers — A1504

Designs: 250fo, Rodolfo (Rezso Gács) (1911-87), magician. 340fo, Lajos Básti (1911-77), actor. 370fo, Manyi Kiss (1911-71), actress.

**2011, Mar. 28** ***Perf. 12***
**4189-4191** A1504 Set of 3 10.50 5.25

Stamp Day — A1505

Buildings in Balatonfüred: 90fo, Anna Grand Hotel. 115fo, Heart Hospital. 600fo+200fo, Vaszary Villa.

**2011, Apr. 8** ***Perf. 12x12½***
**4192-4193** A1505 Set of 2 2.25 1.10

**Souvenir Sheet**

**4194** A1505 600fo +200fo multi 9.00 9.00

Balatonfüred, 800th anniv. Surtax on No. 4194 is for National Federation of Hungarian Philatelists.

Miniature Sheet

City Park, Budapest — A1506

No. 4195: a, 160fo, Buildings and animals of Budapest Zoo and Botanical Garden. b, 160fo, Vajdahunyad Castle. c, 160fo+50fo, Amusement Park. d, 160fo+50fo, Ice rink.

**2011, Apr. 8** ***Perf. 12***
**4195** A1506 Sheet of 4, #a-d 8.25 8.25

Surtax on Nos. 5195c-4195d for youth philately.

Souvenir Sheet

First Manned Space Flight, 50th Anniv. — A1507

**2011, Apr. 12** ***Perf. 12x12½***
**4196** A1507 600fo multi 6.50 3.25

Souvenir Sheet

Crown of St. Stephen — A1508

**Litho. & Embossed With Foil Application**

**2011, Apr. 25** ***Perf. 13x12¾***
**4197** A1508 2011fo multi 22.00 11.00

Enactment of new Fundamental Law for Hungary. A souvenir sheet with red serial number and affixed glass crystals sold for 5000fo.

**World Theater Day Type of 2005 and Butterfly Types of 2006 Redrawn With "Belföld" Instead of Denomination**

**2011, Apr. 26** **Litho.** ***Perf. 11¼***
**4198** A1245 (90fo) multi + label 1.00 .50
Sheet of 20 + 20 labels 20.00 20.00
**4199** Pair + 2 labels 2.00 2.00
*a.* A1286 (90fo) multi + label 1.00 .50
*b.* A1287 (90fo) multi + label 1.00 .50
Sheet of 20, 10 each #4199a-4199b + 20 labels 20.00 20.00

Labels on Nos. 4198-4199 could be personalized for an extra fee.

Fruit and Blossoms A1509

Designs: 145fo, Apples. 310fo, Pears.

**2011, May 6** ***Perf. 12***
**4200-4201** A1509 Set of 2 5.00 2.50

See Nos. 4238-4239.

Butterflies A1510

Designs: 80fo, Apatura metis. 105fo, Melanargia russiae. 255fo, Arctia caja. 370fo, Proserpinus proserpina.
600fo, Lycaena dispar.

**2011, May 6** ***Perf. 13x13¼***
**4202-4205** A1510 Set of 4 8.75 4.50

**Souvenir Sheet**

***Perf. 13x12¾***

**4206** A1510 600fo multi 6.50 3.25

No. 4206 contains one 40x32mm stamp.

Miniature Sheet

Europa — A1511

No. 4207: a, Orség area forest in summer. b, Forest in Visegrád Mountains in winter.

**2011, May 6** ***Perf. 12***
**4207** A1511 200fo Sheet of 4, 2 each #a-b 8.75 4.50

Intl. Year of Forests.

Paintings A1512

Designs: 195fo, Small Girl with Geranium, by József Koszta (1861-1949). 345fo, Female Profile, Zorka, by József Rippi-Rónai (1861-1927).

**2011, May 18** ***Perf. 13½x13***
**4208-4209** A1512 Set of 2 6.00 3.00

Items in Hungarian Museums A1513

Various items from and building for: 280fo, Rákóczi Museum, Sárospatak. 385fo, Várpalota Museum of Chemistry.

**2011, May 18** ***Perf. 12***
**4210-4211** A1513 Set of 2 7.25 3.75

Pannon Philharmonic Orchestra, Pécs, 200th Anniv. — A1514

**2011, June 2** **Litho.**
**4212** A1514 330fo multi 3.75 1.90

Budapest Spas A1515

Spa and statue at: 240fo, Lukács Spa. 250fo, Gellért Spa.

**2011, July 7** ***Perf. 12½x12***
**4213-4214** A1515 Set of 2 5.25 2.60

István Bibó (1911-79), Politician A1516

**2011, Aug. 5** ***Perf. 12x12½***
**4215** A1516 345fo multi 3.75 1.90

Souvenir Sheet

Franz Liszt (1811-86), Composer — A1517

**2011, Aug. 19** ***Perf. 12¾x13***
**4216** A1517 600fo multi 5.75 3.00

Christmas A1518

Creche scenes and Catholic churches in: 90fo, Nagykarácsony. 115fo, Vörs.

**Litho. With Foil Application**

**2011, Oct. 27** ***Perf. 12***
**4217-4218** A1518 Set of 2 1.90 .95

Bell and Christmas Ornament — A1519

Christmas Ornament and Gift Box — A1520

**2011, Oct. 27** **Litho.** ***Perf. 11¼***
**4219** Pair + 2 labels 1.60 1.60
*a.* A1519 (90fo) multi + label .80 .40
*b.* A1520 (90fo) multi + label .80 .40
Sheet of 20, 10 each #4219a-4219b + 20 labels 16.00 16.00

Labels on Nos. 4219 could be personalized for an extra fee.

World Science Forum, Budapest A1521

**2011, Nov. 3 Litho.** ***Perf. 13x13¼***
**4220** A1521 270fo multi 2.50 1.25

St. Martin of Tours (c. 316-97) A1522

**2011, Nov. 11** ***Perf. 12***
**4221** A1522 160fo multi 1.50 .75

Morning Sunshine, by Károly Ferenczy (1862-1917) A1523

**2012, Feb. 8** ***Perf. 12***
**4222** A1523 420fo multi 4.00 2.00

Greek Orthodox Diocese of Hajdúdorog, Cent. — A1524

**2012, Feb. 17** ***Perf. 13¼x12½***
**4223** A1524 380fo multi 3.50 1.75

Easter — A1525

**2012, Feb. 24** ***Perf. 12¼x12¾***
**4224** A1525 105fo multi .95 .50

University Centenaries — A1526

Buildings at: 180fo, Tivadar Puskás Technical School of Telecommunications, Budapest. 270fo, University of Debrecen, Debrecen.

**2012, Mar. 22** ***Perf. 12½x12***
**4225-4226** A1526 Set of 2 4.00 2.00

Budapest Baths A1527

Designs: 235fo, Király Baths. 260fo, Rudas Baths.

**2012, Mar. 22**
**4227-4228** A1527 Set of 2 4.50 2.25

Performing Artists A1528

Designs: 395fo, Zoltán Várkonyi (1912-79), actor and director. 425fo, Katalin Karády (1910-90), actress and singer.

**2012, Mar. 27**
**4229-4230** A1528 Set of 2 7.25 3.75

Launch of Masat 1, First Hungarian Satellite A1529

**2012, Apr. 12** ***Perf. 13¼x13***
**4231** A1529 310fo multi 3.00 1.50

Souvenir Sheet

Sinking of the Titanic, Cent. — A1530

No. 4232: a, Two aft smokestacks (denomination at UL). b, Two fore smokestacks (denomination at UR).

**Litho. & Embossed**

**2012, Apr. 13** ***Perf. 12***
**4232** A1530 800fo Sheet of 2, #a-b 15.00 7.50

Miniature Sheet

Hungarian Scout Association, Cent. — A1531

No. 4233: a, 105fo, Scouts, emblem of 1933 International Jamboree, Gödöllő. b, 105fo, Scout praying at cross, Scout sign. c, 105fo+50fo, Leaf, Scouts putting up tent. d, 105fo+50fo, Scout trefoil, Scouts bandaging boy's leg.

**2012, Apr. 20 Litho.** ***Perf. 13¼x13***
**4233** A1531 Sheet of 4, #a-d 5.00 5.00

Surtax on Nos. 4233c-4233d for youth philately.

Protected Birds A1532

Designs: 80fo, Aquila heliaca. 140fo, Haliaeetus albicilla. 180fo, Falco vespertinus. 345fo, Falco cherrug.

**2012, May 4** ***Perf. 13x13¼***
**4234-4237** A1532 Set of 4 7.00 3.50

See No. 4246.

**Fruit and Blossoms Type of 2011**

Designs: 185fo, Sour cherries. 230fo, Rose apricots.

**2012, May 9** ***Perf. 12***
**4238-4239** A1509 Set of 2 3.50 1.75

Miniature Sheet

Europa — A1533

No. 4240: a, Peppers and grapes. b. Items in Library of Abbey of Pannohalma.

**2012, May 9** ***Perf. 12½x12***
**4240** A1533 235fo Sheet of 4, 2 each #a-b 8.00 4.00

Raoul Wallenberg (1912-47), Swedish Diplomat Who Saved Jews in World War II — A1534

**2012, May 10** ***Perf. 12***
**4241** A1534 340fo multi 3.00 1.50

"Belföld" — A1535

**2012, May 14** ***Perf. 11***
**4242** A1535 (175fo) green + label 1.50 .75
Sheet of 28+28 labels 42.00 21.00

Labels could be personalized for an additional fee.

Solidarity Between Generations — A1536

**2012, May 17** ***Perf. 12½x12***
**4243** A1536 200fo multi 1.75 .85

Souvenir Sheet

Smokehouses and Pottery — A1537

No. 4244: a, Felsoszönok, Hungary smokehouse at left, pitcher, two lidded jars. b, Filovci, Slovenia smokehouse at right, jug, colander.

**2012, May 25**
**4244** A1537 260fo Sheet of 2, #a-b 4.50 2.25

See Slovenia No. 948.

2012 European Soccer Championships, Poland and Ukraine — A1538

**2012, June 8** ***Perf. 12***
**4245** A1538 270fo multi 2.40 1.25

**Protected Birds Type of 2012**

Souvenir Sheet

**2012, June 15** ***Perf. 12½x12***
**4246** A1532 500fo Buteo buteo 4.25 2.10

Battle of Rozgony, 700th Anniv. — A1539

**2012, June 15** ***Perf. 12x12½***
**4247** A1539 370fo multi 3.25 1.60

2012 Summer Olympics, London — A1540

Designs: 315fo, Swimming. 360fo, Kayaking.

**2012, June 22** ***Perf. 12***
**4248-4249** A1540 Set of 2 5.75 3.00

A1541

Stamp Day — A1542

Designs: 80fo, Kalocsa embroidery. 130fo, Peppers, Paprika Museum, Kaposi. 600fo+200fo, Chalice.

**2012, July 6** ***Perf. 12***

| | | | | |
|---|---|---|---|---|
| **4250-4251** | A1541 | Set of 2 | 1.90 | .95 |

**Souvenir Sheet**

***Perf. 12¾x13***

| | | | | |
|---|---|---|---|---|
| **4252** | A1542 | 600fo +200fo multi | 6.75 | 3.50 |

Surtax on No. 4252 is for National Federation of Hungarian Philatelists.

Miniature Sheet

Famous Men — A1543

No. 4253: a, Istvan Orkény (1912-79), writer. b, Sir Georg Solti (1912-97), conductor. c, Géza Ottlik (1912-90), writer. d, János Szentágothai (1912-94), anatomist.

**2012, July 6** ***Perf. 12x12½***

| | | | | |
|---|---|---|---|---|
| **4253** | A1543 | 105fo Sheet of 4, #a-d | 3.75 | 1.90 |

Synagogues A1544

Synagogue in: 300fo, Baja. 400fo, Kiskunhalas.

**2012, Sept. 4** ***Perf. 12***

| | | | | |
|---|---|---|---|---|
| **4254-4255** | A1544 | Set of 2 | 6.50 | 3.25 |

Sixth World Congress of Finno-Ugric People, Siofók — A1545

**2012, Sept. 5** ***Perf. 12½x12***

| | | | | |
|---|---|---|---|---|
| **4256** | A1545 | 290fo multi | 2.75 | 1.40 |

Miniature Sheet

Parliament Building, 110th Anniv. — A1546

No. 4257: a, Statues, panel in tan at right. b, Speaker's dais and coats of arms, panel in brown at bottom. c, Speaker's chair, panel in gray green at right. d, Decorative arches, panel in gray green at bottom. e, Wall sculpture of horse and rider, panel in tan at bottom. f, Chamber, panel in gray at right. g, Coat of arms, panel in beige at right. h, Chamber, panel in brown at bottom.

**2012, Oct. 8** ***Perf. 13¼***

| | | | | |
|---|---|---|---|---|
| **4257** | A1546 | Sheet of 8 + central label | 14.50 | 7.25 |
| ***a.-h.*** | | 200fo Any single | 1.75 | .90 |

An embossed sheet with a lacquered finish was printed in a limited edition and sold for 3200fo.

Christmas A1547

**Litho. With Foil Application**

**2012, Oct. 26** ***Perf. 12***

| | | | | |
|---|---|---|---|---|
| **4258** | A1547 | 130fo multi | 1.25 | .60 |

No. 4258 was printed in sheets of 4.

Souvenir Sheet

Benedictine Abey, Tihany — A1548

**2012, Oct. 26 Litho.** ***Perf. 12x12½***

| | | | | |
|---|---|---|---|---|
| **4259** | A1548 | 600fo multi | 5.50 | 2.75 |

Souvenir Sheet

Miklos Prison, Kosice, Slovakia — A1549

**2013, Jan. 25** ***Perf. 12***

| | | | | |
|---|---|---|---|---|
| **4260** | A1549 | 600fo multi | 5.50 | 2.75 |

Kosice, 2013 European Capital of Culture.

József Galamb (1881-1955), Mechanical Engineer, and Ford Model Ts — A1550

**2013, Feb. 5**

| | | | | |
|---|---|---|---|---|
| **4261** | A1550 | 145fo multi | 1.40 | .70 |

Dr. Miklós Ujvárosi (1913-81), Botanist A1551

**2013, Feb. 5** ***Perf. 12½x12***

| | | | | |
|---|---|---|---|---|
| **4262** | A1551 | 395fo multi | 3.75 | 1.90 |

## SEMI-POSTAL STAMPS

### Issues of the Monarchy

"Turul" and St. Stephen's Crown — SP1

Franz Josef I Wearing Hungarian Crown — SP2

**Wmk. Double Cross (137)**

**1913, Nov. 20 Typo.** ***Perf. 14***

| | | | | | |
|---|---|---|---|---|---|
| **B1** | SP1 | 1f | slate | .40 | .25 |
| **B2** | SP1 | 2f | olive yellow | .40 | .25 |
| **B3** | SP1 | 3f | orange | .40 | .25 |
| **B4** | SP1 | 5f | emerald | .40 | .25 |
| **B5** | SP1 | 6f | olive green | .40 | .25 |
| **B6** | SP1 | 10f | carmine | .60 | .25 |
| **B7** | SP1 | 12f | violet, *yellow* | .50 | .25 |
| **B8** | SP1 | 16f | gray green | .75 | .25 |
| **B9** | SP1 | 20f | dark brown | 3.00 | .40 |
| **B10** | SP1 | 25f | ultra | 1.75 | .25 |
| **B11** | SP1 | 30f | orange brown | 2.00 | .25 |
| **B12** | SP1 | 35f | red violet | 2.00 | .25 |
| **B13** | SP1 | 50f | lake, *blue* | 3.75 | .60 |
| **B14** | SP1 | 60f | green, *salmon* | 3.75 | .50 |
| **B15** | SP2 | 1k | dull red | 25.00 | 2.00 |
| **B16** | SP2 | 2k | dull blue | 75.00 | 40.00 |
| **B17** | SP2 | 5k | violet brown | 30.00 | 30.00 |
| | | | *Nos. B1-B17 (17)* | 150.10 | 76.25 |

Nos. B1-B17 were sold at an advance of 2f over face value, as indicated by the label at bottom. The surtax was to aid flood victims.

For overprints see Nos. 5NB1-5NB10, 6NB1-6NB11.

Exist imperf. Value, set $1,000.

### Semi-Postal Stamps of 1913 Surcharged in Red, Green or Brown

a

b

**1914**

| | | | | | |
|---|---|---|---|---|---|
| **B18** | SP1(a) | 1f | slate | .25 | .25 |
| **B19** | SP1(a) | 2f | olive yel | .25 | .25 |
| **B20** | SP1(a) | 3f | orange | .25 | .25 |
| **B21** | SP1(a) | 5f | emerald | .25 | .25 |
| **B22** | SP1(a) | 6f | olive green | .25 | .25 |
| **B23** | SP1(a) | 10f | carmine (G) | .35 | .25 |
| **B24** | SP1(a) | 12f | violet, *yel* | .25 | .25 |
| **B25** | SP1(a) | 16f | gray green | .30 | .25 |
| **B26** | SP1(a) | 20f | dark brown | .90 | .25 |
| **B27** | SP1(a) | 25f | ultra | .90 | .25 |
| **B28** | SP1(a) | 30f | orange brn | 1.10 | .25 |
| **B29** | SP1(a) | 35f | red violet | 1.90 | .25 |
| **B30** | SP1(a) | 50f | lake, *bl* | 1.50 | .50 |
| **B31** | SP1(a) | 60f | green, *salmon* | 2.00 | .55 |
| **B32** | SP2(b) | 1k | dull red (Br) | 60.00 | 25.00 |
| **B33** | SP2(b) | 2k | dull blue | 37.50 | 26.00 |
| **B34** | SP2(b) | 5k | violet brn | 30.00 | 21.00 |
| | | | *Nos. B18-B34 (17)* | 137.95 | 76.05 |

Exist imperf. Value, set $800.

### Regular Issue of 1913 Surcharged in Red or Green

c

d

**1915, Jan. 1**

| | | | | | |
|---|---|---|---|---|---|
| **B35** | A4(c) | 1f | slate | .25 | .25 |
| **B36** | A4(c) | 2f | olive yel | .25 | .25 |
| **B37** | A4(c) | 3f | orange | .25 | .25 |
| **B38** | A4(c) | 5f | emerald | .25 | .25 |
| **B39** | A4(c) | 6f | olive grn | .25 | .25 |
| **B40** | A4(c) | 10f | carmine (G) | .25 | .25 |
| **B41** | A4(c) | 12f | violet, *yel* | .25 | .25 |
| **B42** | A4(c) | 16f | gray green | .25 | .25 |
| **B43** | A4(c) | 20f | dark brown | .25 | .25 |
| **B44** | A4(c) | 25f | ultra | .25 | .25 |
| **B45** | A4(c) | 30f | orange brn | .40 | .25 |
| **B46** | A4(c) | 35f | red violet | .45 | .25 |
| **B47** | A4(c) | 50f | lake, *bl* | .65 | .25 |
| ***a.*** | | | On No. 96a | *5,000.* | |
| **B48** | A4(c) | 60f | green, *salmon* | .80 | .30 |
| **B49** | A5(d) | 1k | dull red | 1.10 | 3.00 |
| **B50** | A5(d) | 2k | dull blue | 3.00 | 7.50 |
| **B51** | A5(d) | 5k | violet brown | 9.50 | 17.50 |

### Surcharged as Type "c" but in Smaller Letters

| | | | | |
|---|---|---|---|---|
| **B52** | A4 | 60f green, *salmon* | 2.25 | 1.25 |
| | | *Nos. B35-B52 (18)* | 20.65 | 32.80 |

Nos. B18-B52 were sold at an advance of 2f over face value. The surtax to aid war widows and orphans.

Exist imperf. Value, set $200.

Soldiers Fighting SP3 SP4

Eagle with Sword SP5

Harvesting SP6

**1916-17** ***Perf. 15***

| | | | | |
|---|---|---|---|---|
| **B53** | SP3 | 10f + 2f rose red | .25 | .30 |
| **B54** | SP4 | 15f + 2f dull violet | .25 | .30 |
| **B55** | SP5 | 40f + 2f brn car ('17) | .25 | .40 |
| | | *Nos. B53-B55 (3)* | .75 | 1.00 |

Exist imperf. Value, set $15.

For overprints and surcharge see Nos. B58-B60. 1NB1-1NB3, 2NB1-2NB6, 4NJ1, 5NB11-5NB13, 6NB13-6NB15, 7NB2-7NB3, 9NB1, 10NB1-10NB4, 11NB1-B4.

**1917, Sept. 15**

**Surcharge in Red**

| | | | | |
|---|---|---|---|---|
| **B56** | SP6 | 10f + 1k rose | .60 | *1.00* |
| **B57** | SP6 | 15f + 1k violet | .60 | *1.00* |

Nos. B56 and B57 were issued in connection with the War Exhibition of Archduke Josef.

### Issues of the Republic

Semi-Postal Stamps of 1916-17 Overprinted in Black

**1918**

| | | | | |
|---|---|---|---|---|
| **B58** | SP3 | 10f + 2f rose red | .25 | .25 |
| **B59** | SP4 | 15f + 2f dull violet | .25 | .25 |
| **B60** | SP5 | 40f + 2f brown car | .25 | .25 |
| | | *Nos. B58-B60 (3)* | .75 | .75 |

Nos. B58-B60 exist with inverted overprint.
Exist imperf. Value, set $12.50.

Postally used examples of Nos. B69-B174 sell for more.

### Issues of the Kingdom

Released Prisoner Walking Home — SP7

Prisoners of War — SP8

Homecoming of Soldier — SP9

**Wmk. 137 Vert. or. Horiz.**

**1920, Mar. 10** ***Perf. 12***

| | | | | |
|---|---|---|---|---|
| **B69a** | SP7 | 40f + 1k dull red | 1.75 | 3.50 |
| **B70a** | SP8 | 60f + 2k gray brown | 3.00 | 6.00 |
| **B71** | SP9 | 1k + 5k dk blue | 1.75 | 3.50 |
| | | *Nos. B69a-B71 (3)* | 6.50 | 13.00 |
| | | Set, never hinged | 18.50 | |

The surtax was used to help prisoners of war return home from Siberia.
Exist imperf. Value, set $100.

Statue of Petőfi — SP10

Griffin — SP11

Sándor Petőfi — SP12

Petőfi Dying — SP13

Petőfi Addressing People — SP14

**1923, Jan. 23** ***Perf. 14 (10k, 40k), 12***

| | | | | |
|---|---|---|---|---|
| **B72** | SP10 | 10k slate green | .50 | *1.00* |
| **B73** | SP11 | 15k dull blue | 1.00 | *2.75* |
| **B74** | SP12 | 25k gray brown | .50 | *1.00* |
| **B75** | SP13 | 40k brown violet | 1.50 | 3.00 |
| **B76** | SP14 | 50k violet brown | 1.50 | 3.00 |
| | | *Nos. B72-B76 (5)* | 5.00 | 10.75 |
| | | Set, never hinged | 10.00 | |

Birth centenary of the Hungarian poet Sándor Petőfi. The stamps were on sale at double face value, for a limited time and in restricted quantities, after which the remainders were given to a charitable organization.
Exist imperf. Value, set $100.

Child with Symbols of Peace — SP15

Mother and Infant — SP16

Instruction in Archery — SP17

**Wmk. 133**

**1924, Apr. 8** **Engr.** ***Perf. 12***

| | | | | |
|---|---|---|---|---|
| **B77** | SP15 | 300k dark blue | 1.50 | *4.00* |
| *a.* | | Perf. 11½ | 35.00 | 30.00 |
| **B78** | SP16 | 500k black brown | 1.50 | *4.00* |
| **B79** | SP17 | 1000k black green | 1.50 | *4.00* |
| | | *Nos. B77-B79 (3)* | 4.50 | *12.00* |
| | | Set, never hinged | 12.00 | |

Each stamp has on the back an inscription stating that it was sold at a premium of 100 per cent over the face value.
Exist imperf. Value, set $90.

Parade of Athletes SP18

Skiing — SP19

Skating — SP20

Diving — SP21

Fencing SP22

Scouts Camping — SP23

Soccer SP24

Hurdling — SP25

***Perf. 12, 12½ and Compound***

**1925** **Typo.** **Unwmk.**

| | | | | |
|---|---|---|---|---|
| **B80** | SP18 | 100k bl grn & brn | 2.25 | *2.00* |
| **B81** | SP19 | 200k lt brn & myr grn | 2.90 | *2.50* |
| **B82** | SP20 | 300k dark blue | 3.50 | *3.50* |
| **B83** | SP21 | 400k dp bl & dp grn | 3.80 | *3.50* |
| **B84** | SP22 | 500k purple brown | 7.50 | *10.00* |
| **B85** | SP23 | 1000k red brown | 6.25 | *7.00* |
| **B86** | SP24 | 2000k brown violet | 7.50 | *7.50* |
| **B87** | SP25 | 2500k olive brown | 7.50 | *9.00* |
| | | *Nos. B80-B87 (8)* | 41.20 | *45.00* |
| | | Set, never hinged | 75.00 | |

These stamps were sold at double face value, plus a premium of 10 per cent on orders sent by mail. They did not serve any postal need and were issued solely to raise funds to aid athletic associations. An inscription regarding the 100 per cent premium is printed on the back of each stamp.
Exist imperf. Value, set $450.

St. Emerich SP26

Sts. Stephen and Gisela SP27

St. Ladislaus SP28

Sts. Gerhardt and Emerich SP29

**1930, May 15** **Wmk. 210** ***Perf. 14***

| | | | | |
|---|---|---|---|---|
| **B88** | SP26 | 8f + 2f deep green | .45 | .40 |
| **B89** | SP27 | 16f + 4f brt violet | .65 | *.60* |
| **B90** | SP28 | 20f + 4f deep rose | 1.90 | *2.00* |
| **B91** | SP29 | 32f + 8f ultra | 2.50 | *4.50* |
| | | *Nos. B88-B91 (4)* | 5.50 | *7.50* |
| | | Set, never hinged | 11.00 | |

900th anniv. of the death of St. Emerich, son of Stephen I, king, saint and martyr.
Exist imperf. Value, set $150.

**Catalogue values for unused stamps in this section, from this point to the end of the section, are for Never Hinged items.**

St. Ladislaus — SP30

Holy Sacrament SP31

SP32

**1938 May 16** **Photo.** ***Perf. 12***

| | | | | |
|---|---|---|---|---|
| **B92** | SP30 | 16f + 16f dull slate bl | 3.00 | 3.00 |
| **B93** | SP31 | 20f + 20f dk car | 3.00 | 3.00 |

**Souvenir Sheet**

| | | | | |
|---|---|---|---|---|
| **B94** | SP32 | Sheet of 7 | 50.00 | 32.50 |
| *a.* | | 6f + 6f St. Stephen | 4.00 | 3.00 |
| *b.* | | 10f + 10f St. Emerich | 4.00 | 3.00 |
| *c.* | | 16f + 16f slate blue (B92) | 4.00 | 3.00 |
| *d.* | | 20f + 20f dark carmine (B93) | 4.00 | 3.00 |
| *e.* | | 32f + 32f St. Elizabeth | 4.00 | 3.00 |
| *f.* | | 40f + 40f St. Maurice | 4.00 | 3.00 |
| *g.* | | 50f + 50f St. Margaret | 4.00 | 3.00 |

Printed in sheets measuring 136½x155mm. Nos. B94c and B94d are slightly smaller than B92 and B93.
Eucharistic Cong. in Budapest, May, 1938.
Exist imperf. Value: set $125; souvenir sheet $3,750.

St. Stephen, Victorious Warrior SP33

St. Stephen, Offering Crown SP34

SP35

**1938, Aug. 12** *Perf. 12*

| | | | | |
|---|---|---|---|---|
| **B95** | SP33 | 10f + 10f violet brn | 3.00 | 3.00 |
| **B96** | SP34 | 20f + 20f red org | 3.00 | 3.00 |

**Souvenir Sheet**

| | | | | |
|---|---|---|---|---|
| **B97** | SP35 | Sheet of 7 | 32.50 | 20.00 |
| *a.* | | 6f + 6f St. Stephen the Missionary | 3.25 | 2.00 |
| *b.* | | 10f + 10f violet brown (B95) | 3.25 | 2.00 |
| *c.* | | 16f + 16f Seated Upon Throne | 3.25 | 2.00 |
| *d.* | | 20f + 20f red orange (B96) | 3.25 | 2.00 |
| *e.* | | 32f + 32f Receives Bishops and Monks | 3.25 | 2.00 |
| *f.* | | 40f + 40f St. Gisela, St. Stephen and St. Emerich | 3.25 | 2.00 |
| *g.* | | 50f + 50f St. Stephen on Bier | 3.25 | 2.00 |

Death of St. Stephen, 900th anniversary.

No. B97 is on brownish paper, Nos. B95-B96 on white.

Nos. B95-B97 exist imperf. Values: Nos. B95-B96 $150; No. B97 $4,500.

Statue Symbolizing Recovered Territories SP36

Castle of Munkács SP37

Admiral Horthy Entering Komárom SP38

Cathedral of Kassa SP39

Girl Offering Flowers to Soldier — SP40

**1939, Jan. 16**

| | | | | |
|---|---|---|---|---|
| **B98** | SP36 | 6f + 3f myrtle grn | 1.00 | .65 |
| **B99** | SP37 | 10f + 5f olive grn | .65 | .45 |
| **B100** | SP38 | 20f + 10f dark red | .65 | .45 |
| **B101** | SP39 | 30f + 15f grnsh blue | 1.25 | .80 |
| **B102** | SP40 | 40f + 20f dk bl gray | 1.75 | .80 |
| | | *Nos. B98-B102 (5)* | 5.30 | 3.15 |

The surtax was for the aid of "Hungary for Hungarians" patriotic movement.

Exist imperf. Value, set $175.

Memorial Tablets SP41

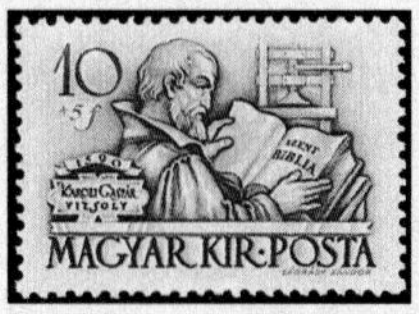

Gáspár Károlyi, Translator of the Bible into Hungarian SP42

Albert Molnár de Szenci, Translator of the Psalms SP43

Prince Gabriel Bethlen — SP44

Susanna Lórántffy — SP45

*Perf. 12x12½, 12½x12*

**1939 Photo. Wmk. 210**

| | | | | |
|---|---|---|---|---|
| **B103** | SP41 | 6f + 3f green | .70 | .70 |
| **B104** | SP42 | 10f + 5f claret | 1.00 | 1.00 |
| **B105** | SP43 | 20f + 10f copper red | 1.00 | 1.00 |
| **B106** | SP44 | 32f + 16f bister | 1.00 | 1.00 |
| **B107** | SP45 | 40f + 20f chalky blue | 1.00 | 1.00 |
| | | *Nos. B103-B107 (5)* | 4.70 | 4.70 |

**Souvenir Sheets**

*Perf. 12*

| | | | | |
|---|---|---|---|---|
| **B108** | SP44 | 32f olive & vio brn | 30.00 | 15.00 |

*Imperf*

| | | | | |
|---|---|---|---|---|
| **B109** | SP44 | 32f bl grn, cop red & gold | 30.00 | 15.00 |

National Protestant Day. The surtax was used to erect an Intl. Protestant Institute.

The souvenir sheets sold for 1.32p each.

Nos. B103-B108 exist imperf. Values: Nos. B103-B107 $350; No. B108 $4,000.

Issue dates: Nos. B103-B107, Oct. 2. Nos. B108-B109, Oct. 27.

Boy Scout Flying Kite — SP47

Allegory of Flight — SP48

Archangel Gabriel from Millennium Monument, Budapest, and Planes — SP49

**1940, Jan. 1** *Perf. 12½x12*

| | | | | |
|---|---|---|---|---|
| **B110** | SP47 | 6f + 6f yellow grn | .75 | 1.00 |
| **B111** | SP48 | 10f + 10f chocolate | .95 | 1.25 |
| **B112** | SP49 | 20f + 20f copper red | 1.40 | 1.25 |
| | | *Nos. B110-B112 (3)* | 3.10 | 3.50 |

The surtax was used for the Horthy National Aviation Fund.

Exist imperf. Value, set $150.

SP50

Souvenir Sheet

**Wmk. 210**

**1940, May 6 Photo.** *Perf. 12*

| | | | | |
|---|---|---|---|---|
| **B113** | SP50 | 20f + 1p dk blue grn | 6.00 | 6.00 |

Exist imperf. Value $4,250.

Soldier Protecting Family from Floods SP51

**1940, May**

| | | | | |
|---|---|---|---|---|
| **B114** | SP51 | 10f + 2f gray brown | .40 | .25 |
| **B115** | SP51 | 20f + 4f orange red | .40 | .25 |
| **B116** | SP51 | 20f + 50f red brown | 1.25 | 1.25 |
| | | *Nos. B114-B116 (3)* | 2.05 | 1.75 |

The surtax on Nos. B113-B116 was used to aid flood victims.

Exist imperf. Value, set $150.

Hunyadi Coat of Arms SP52

King Matthias SP54

Hunyadi Castle SP53

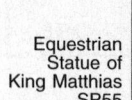

Equestrian Statue of King Matthias SP55

Corvin Codex — SP56

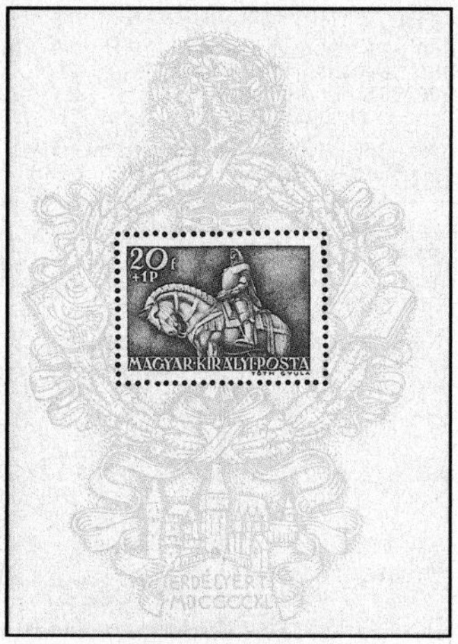

Equestrian Statue of King Matthias — SP57

**1940** *Perf. 12½x12, 12x12½*

| | | | | |
|---|---|---|---|---|
| **B117** | SP52 | 6f + 3f blue grn | .60 | .60 |
| **B118** | SP53 | 10f + 5f gldn brn | .60 | .60 |
| **B119** | SP54 | 16f + 8f dk ol bis | .80 | .80 |
| **B120** | SP55 | 20f + 10f brick red | .80 | .80 |
| **B121** | SP56 | 32f + 16f dk gray | 1.25 | 1.10 |
| | | *Nos. B117-B121 (5)* | 4.05 | 3.90 |

**Souvenir Sheet**

| | | | | |
|---|---|---|---|---|
| **B122** | SP57 | 20f + 1p dk bl grn & pale grn | 6.00 | 6.00 |

King Matthias (1440-1490) at Kolozsvar, Transylvania. The surtax was used for war relief.

Nos. B117-B122 exist imperf. Values: Nos. B117-B121 $220; No. B122 $4,250.

Issued: #B117-B121, July 1. #B122. Nov. 7.

Hungarian Soldier — SP58

20f+50f, Virgin Mary and Szekley, symbolizing the return of transylvania. 32f+50f, Szekley Mother Offering Infant Son to the Fatherland.

**1940, Dec. 2 Photo.** *Perf. 12½x12*

| | | | | |
|---|---|---|---|---|
| **B123** | SP58 | 10f + 50f dk blue grn | .95 | .95 |
| **B124** | SP58 | 20f + 50f brown car | 1.00 | 1.00 |
| **B125** | SP58 | 32f + 50f yellow brn | 1.25 | 1.25 |
| | | *Nos. B123-B125 (3)* | 3.20 | 3.20 |

Occupation of Transylvania. The surtax was for the Pro-Transylvania movement.

Exist imperf. Value, set $200.

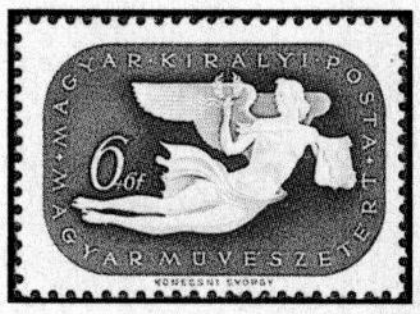

Symbol for Drama SP61

Symbol for Sculpture — SP62

Symbols: 16f+16f, Art. 20f+20f, Literature.

**1940, Dec. 15** *Perf. 12x12½, 12½x12*

| | | | | |
|---|---|---|---|---|
| **B126** | SP61 | 6f + 6f dark green | 1.40 | 1.25 |
| **B127** | SP62 | 10f + 10f olive bis | 1.40 | 1.25 |
| **B128** | SP62 | 16f + 16f dk violet | 1.40 | 1.25 |
| **B129** | SP61 | 20f + 20f fawn | 1.40 | 1.25 |
| | | *Nos. B126-B129 (4)* | 5.60 | 5.00 |

### Souvenir Sheet

**1941, Jan. 5** ***Imperf.***

| | | | |
|---|---|---|---|
| **B130** | Sheet of 4 | 6.00 | 6.00 |
| *a.* | SP61 6f + 6f olive brown | 1.25 | 1.25 |
| *b.* | SP62 10f + 10f henna brown | 1.25 | 1.25 |
| *c.* | SP62 16f + 16f dk blue green | 1.25 | 1.25 |
| *d.* | SP61 20f + 20f rose violet | 1.25 | 1.25 |

Surtax on #B126-B130 was used for the Pension and Assistance Institution for Artists.

Nos. B126-B129 exist imperf. Value, set $70.

Winged Head of Pilot — SP66

Designs: 10f+10f, Boy Scout with model plane. 20f+20f, Glider in flight. 32f+32f, Our Lady of Loreto, patroness of Hungarian pilots.

**1941, Mar. 24** ***Perf. 12x12½***

| | | | | |
|---|---|---|---|---|
| **B131** | SP66 | 6f + 6f grn olive | .55 | .50 |
| **B132** | SP66 | 10f + 10f dp claret | .55 | .50 |
| **B133** | SP66 | 20f + 20f org ver | .65 | .60 |
| **B134** | SP66 | 32f + 32f turq blue | 1.60 | 1.50 |
| | | *Nos. B131-B134 (4)* | 3.35 | 3.10 |

The surtax was used to finance civilian and army pilot training through the Horthy National Aviation Fund.

Exist imperf. Value, set $270.

Infantry SP70

12f+18f, Heavy artillery. 20f+30f, Plane and tanks. 40f+60f, Cavalryman and cyclist.

**1941, Dec. 1** **Photo.** **Wmk. 266**

**Inscribed: "Honvedeink Karacsonyara 1941"**

| | | | | |
|---|---|---|---|---|
| **B135** | SP70 | 8f + 12f dk green | .50 | .50 |
| **B136** | SP70 | 12f + 18f olive grn | .50 | .50 |
| **B137** | SP70 | 20f + 30f slate | .60 | .60 |
| **B138** | SP70 | 40f + 60f red brown | .60 | .60 |
| | | *Nos. B135-B138 (4)* | 2.20 | 2.20 |

The surtax was for the benefit of the Army.

Exist imperf. Value, set $275.

Soldier and Emblem SP74

**1941, Dec. 1**

| | | | | |
|---|---|---|---|---|
| **B139** | SP74 | 20f + 40f dark red | 2.25 | 2.25 |

The surtax was for the soldiers' Christmas.

Exists imperf. Value $70.

Aviator and Plane — SP75

Planes and Ghostly Band of Old Chiefs SP76

Plane and Archer SP77

Aviators and Plane — SP78

**1942, Mar. 15** ***Perf. 12½x12, 12x12½***

| | | | | |
|---|---|---|---|---|
| **B140** | SP75 | 8f + 8f dark green | .80 | .80 |
| **B141** | SP76 | 12f + 12f sapphire | .80 | .80 |
| **B142** | SP77 | 20f + 20f brown | .80 | .80 |
| **B143** | SP78 | 30f + 30f dark red | .80 | .80 |
| | | *Nos. B140-B143 (4)* | 3.20 | 3.20 |

The surtax aided the Horthy National Aviation Fund.

Exist imperf. Value, set $270.

Blood Transfusion — SP79

Designs: 8f+32f, Bandaging wounded soldier. 12f+50f, Radio and carrier pigeons. 20f+1p, Widows and orphans.

**1942, Sept. 1** ***Perf. 12½x12***

| | | | | |
|---|---|---|---|---|
| **B144** | SP79 | 3f + 18f dk ol & red | 1.40 | 1.40 |
| **B145** | SP79 | 8f + 32f dp brn & red | 1.40 | 1.40 |
| **B146** | SP79 | 12f + 50f dp cl & red | 1.40 | 1.40 |
| **B147** | SP79 | 20f + 1p slate bl & red | 1.40 | 1.40 |
| | | *Nos. B144-B147 (4)* | 5.60 | 5.60 |

The surtax aided the Hungarian Red Cross. Sheets of 10. Value, set $85.

Exist imperf. Value, set $300.

Widow of Stephen Horthy — SP83

Red Cross Nurse Aiding Soldier SP84

Magdalene Horthy Mother of Stephen Horthy — SP85

**1942, Dec. 1** ***Perf. 13, Imperf.***

| | | | | |
|---|---|---|---|---|
| **B148** | SP83 | 6f + 1p vio bl & red | 3.00 | 3.00 |
| *a.* | | Sheet of 4 | 27.50 | 27.50 |
| **B149** | SP84 | 8f + 1p dk ol grn & red | 3.00 | 3.00 |
| *a.* | | Sheet of 4 | 27.50 | 27.50 |
| **B150** | SP85 | 20f + 1p dk red brn & red | 3.00 | 3.00 |
| *a.* | | Sheet of 4 | 27.50 | 27.50 |
| | | *Nos. B148-B150 (3)* | 9.00 | 9.00 |

The surtax aided the Hungarian Red Cross.

King Ladislaus I

SP86 SP87

**1942, Dec. 21** **Wmk. 266** ***Perf. 12***

| | | | | |
|---|---|---|---|---|
| **B151** | SP86 | 6f + 6f olive gray | .60 | *1.00* |
| **B152** | SP87 | 8f + 8f green | .60 | *1.00* |
| **B153** | SP86 | 12f + 12f dull violet | .60 | *1.00* |
| **B154** | SP87 | 20f + 20f Prus green | .60 | *1.00* |
| **B155** | SP86 | 24f + 24f brown | .60 | *1.00* |
| **B156** | SP87 | 30f + 30f rose car | .60 | *1.00* |
| | | *Nos. B151-B156 (6)* | 3.60 | 6.00 |

900th anniv. of the birth of St. Ladislaus (1040-95), the 700th anniv. of the beginning of the country's reconstruction by King Béla IV (1206-70) and the 600th anniv. of the accession of King Lajos the Great (1326-82).

The surtax aided war invalids and their families.

Exist imperf. Value, set $350.

Archer on Horseback SP92

Knight with Sword and Shield — SP93

Old Magyar Arms — SP94

Designs: 3f+1f, 4f+1f, Warrior with shield and battle ax. 12f+2f, Knight with lance, 20f+2f, Musketeer. 40f+4f, Hussar. 50f+6f, Artilleryman.

**1943**

| | | | | |
|---|---|---|---|---|
| **B157** | SP92 | 1f + 1f dk gray | .25 | .35 |
| **B158** | SP93 | 3f + 1f dull violet | .50 | *.80* |
| **B159** | SP93 | 4f + 1f lake | .25 | .35 |
| **B160** | SP93 | 8f + 2f green | .25 | .35 |
| **B161** | SP92 | 12f + 2f bister brn | .25 | .35 |
| **B162** | SP93 | 20f + 2f dp claret | .25 | .35 |
| **B163** | SP92 | 40f + 4f gray vio | .25 | .35 |
| **B164** | SP93 | 50f + 6f org brn | .25 | .35 |
| **B165** | SP94 | 70f + 8f slate blue | .40 | .35 |
| | | *Nos. B157-B165 (9)* | 2.65 | 3.60 |

The surtax aided war invalids.

Exist imperf. Value, set $270.

Model Glider — SP101

Gliders — SP102

White-tailed Sea Eagle and Planes — SP103

ME-109E Fighter and Gliders — SP104

**1943, July 17**

| | | | | |
|---|---|---|---|---|
| **B166** | SP101 | 8f + 8f green | .80 | *1.00* |
| **B167** | SP102 | 12f + 12f royal blue | .80 | *1.00* |
| **B168** | SP103 | 20f + 20f chestnut | .80 | *1.00* |
| **B169** | SP104 | 30f + 30f rose car | .80 | *1.00* |
| | | *Nos. B166-B169 (4)* | 3.20 | 4.00 |

The surtax aided the Horthy National Aviation Fund.

Exist imperf. Value, set $270.

Stephen Horthy SP105

**1943, Aug. 16**

| | | | | |
|---|---|---|---|---|
| **B170** | SP105 | 30f + 20f dp rose vio | .55 | .50 |

The surtax aided the Horthy National Aviation Fund.

Exists imperf. Value $70.

Nurse and Soldier SP106

Designs: 30f+30f, Soldier, nurse, mother and child. 50f+50f, Nurse keeping lamp alight. 70f+70f, Wounded soldier and tree shoot.

**1944, Mar. 1** **Cross in Red**

| | | | | |
|---|---|---|---|---|
| **B171** | SP106 | 20f + 20f brown | .50 | .40 |
| **B172** | SP106 | 30f + 30f henna | .50 | .40 |
| **B173** | SP106 | 50f + 50f brown vio | .55 | .40 |
| **B174** | SP106 | 70f + 70f Prus blue | .55 | .40 |
| | | *Nos. B171-B174 (4)* | 2.10 | 1.60 |

The surtax aided the Hungarian Red Cross.

Exist imperf. Value, set $270.

### Issues of the Republic

Types of 1944 Surcharged in Red or Black

a

b

**1945, July 23** **Wmk. 266** ***Perf. 12***

| | | | | |
|---|---|---|---|---|
| **B175** | A115(a) | 3p + 9p on 20f dk ol grn, *yel* | .40 | 1.00 |
| **B176** | A114(b) | 4p + 12p on 4f yel brn, *bl* (Bk) | .40 | 1.00 |
| **B177** | A117(b) | 8p + 24p on 50f sl bl, *yel* | .40 | 1.00 |
| **B178** | A115(a) | 10p + 30p on 30f hn brn, *bl* (Bk) | .40 | 1.00 |
| | | *Nos. B175-B178 (4)* | 1.60 | 4.00 |

The surtax was for the Peoples Universities. "Béke" means "peace".

Imre Sallai and Sandor Fürst
SP110

Designs: 3p+3p, L. Kabok and Illes Monus. 4p+4p, Ferenc Rozsa and Zoltan Schonerz. 6p+6p, Anna Koltai and Mrs. Paul Knurr. 10p+10p, George Sarkozi and Imre Nagy. 15p+15p, Vilmos Tartsay and Jeno Nagy. 20p+20p, Janos Kiss and Andreas Bajcsy-Zsilinszky. 40p+40p, Endre Sagvari and Otto Hoffmann.

**1945, Oct. 6** **Photo.**

**B179** SP110 2p + 2p yel brn 1.75 1.75
**B180** SP110 3p + 3p deep red 1.75 1.75
**B181** SP110 4p + 4p dk pur 1.75 1.75
**B182** SP110 6p + 6p dk yel grn 1.75 1.75
**B183** SP110 10p + 10p dp car 1.75 1.75
**B184** SP110 15p + 15p dk sl grn 1.75 1.75
**B185** SP110 20p + 20p dk brn 1.75 1.75
**B186** SP110 40p + 40p dp bl 1.75 1.75
*Nos. B179-B186 (8)* 14.00 14.00

The surtax was for child welfare.
Exist imperf. Value, set $150.

Andreas Bajcsy-Zsilinszky and Eagle — SP111

**1945, May 27**

**B187** SP111 1p + 1p dk brn vio .90 *.90*

1st anniv. of the death of Andreas Bajcsy-Zsilinszky, hanged by the Nazis for anti-fascist activities.
Exists imperf. Value $135.

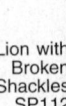

Lion with Broken Shackles
SP112

**1946, May 1**

**B188** SP112 500ez + 500ez p 2.25 2.25
**B189** SP112 1mil p + 1mil p 2.25 2.25
**B190** SP112 1.5mil p + 1.5mil p 2.25 2.25
**B191** SP112 2mil p + 2mil p 2.25 2.25
*Nos. B188-B191 (4)* 9.00 9.00

75th anniv. of Hungary's 1st postage stamp. The surtax was for the benefit of postal employees.
Exist imperf. Value, set $135.

"Agriculture" Holding Wheat — SP113

**1946, Sept. 7** **Photo.**

**B192** SP113 30f + 60f dp yel grn 5.00 *7.00*
**B193** SP113 60f + 1.20fo rose brn 5.00 *7.00*
**B194** SP113 1fo + 2fo dp blue 5.00 *7.00*
*Nos. B192-B194 (3)* 15.00 *21.00*

1st Agricultural Congress and Exhibition.
Exist imperf. Value, set $325.

Physician with Syringe — SP114

Designs: 12f+50f, Physician examining X-ray picture. 20f+50f, Nurse and child. 60f+50f, Prisoner of war starting home.

***Perf. 12½x12***

**1947, May 16** **Wmk. 210**

**B195** SP114 8f + 50f ultra 3.75 *5.00*
**B196** SP114 12f + 50f choc 3.75 *5.00*
**B197** SP114 20f + 50f dk grn 3.75 *5.00*
**B198** SP114 60f + 50f dk red 1.00 1.25
*Nos. B195-B198 (4)* 12.25 *16.25*

The surtax was for charitable purposes.
Exist imperf. Value, set $400.

Franklin D. Roosevelt and Freedom of Speech Allegory
SP115

Pres. F. D. Roosevelt and Allegory: 12f+12f, Freedom of Religion. 20f+20f, Freedom from Want. 30f+30f, Freedom from Fear.

**1947, June 11** **Photo.** ***Perf. 12x12½***

**Portrait in Sepia**

**B198A** SP115 8f + 8f dark red 4.00 *5.25*
**B198B** SP115 12f + 12f deep green 4.00 *5.25*
**B198C** SP115 20f + 20f brown 4.00 *5.25*
**B198D** SP115 30f + 30f blue 4.00 *5.25*
*Nos. B198A-B198D,CB1-CB1C (8)* 33.00 *42.00*

Exist imperf. Value, set $250.
Nos. B198A-B198D and CB1-CB1C were also printed in sheets of 4 of each denomination (size: 117x96mm). Value, set of 8, $700. Exist imperf. Value $900.
A souvenir sheet exists, containing one each of Nos. B198A-B198D with border inscriptions and decorations in brown. Size: 161x122mm. Value $125. Exists imperf. Value $250.

Lenin — SP118

Designs: 60f+60f, Soviet Cenotaph, Budapest. 1fo+1fo, Joseph V. Stalin.

**1947, Oct. 29** **Photo.** **Wmk. 283**

**B199** SP118 40f + 40f ol grn & org brn 4.50 5.50
**B200** SP118 60f + 60f red & sl bl 2.00 2.00
**B201** SP118 1fo + 1fo vio & brn blk 4.50 5.50
*Nos. B199-B201 (3)* 11.00 13.00

The surtax was for the Hungarian-Soviet Cultural Association.
Exist imperf. Value, set $475.

XVI Century Mail Coach
SP119

**1947, Dec. 21** ***Perf. 12x12½***

**B202** SP119 30f (+ 50f) hn brn 9.50 10.00
Sheet of 4 55.00 55.00

Stamp Day. The surtax paid admission to a philatelic exhibition in any of eight Hungarian towns, where the stamps were sold.
No. B202 exists imperf. Values: single $800; sheetlet of 4 $4,000.

Globe and Carrier Pigeon — SP120

Woman Worker — SP121

**1948, Oct. 17** ***Perf. 12½x12***

**B203** SP120 30f (+ 1fo) grnsh bl 5.00 5.00
Sheet of 4 40.00 40.00

5th Natl. Hungarian Stamp Exhib., Budapest. Each stamp sold for 1.30 forint, which included admission to the exhibition.
Exists imperf. Value: single $450; sheetlet $2,250.

**1949, Mar. 8**

**B204** SP121 60f + 60f magenta 2.50 2.50

Intl. Woman's Day, Mar. 8, 1949. The surtax was for the Democratic Alliance of Hungarian Women.
Exists imperf. Value $70.

Aleksander S. Pushkin — SP122

SP123

**1949, June 6** **Photo.**

**B205** SP122 1fo + 1fo car lake 9.00 9.00

**Souvenir Sheet**

***Perf. 12½x12, Imperf***

**B206** SP123 1fo + 1fo red vio & car lake 15.00 15.00

150th anniversary of the birth of Aleksander S. Pushkin. The surtax was for the Hungarian-Russian Culture Society.
No. B205 exists imperf. Value $220.

**IMPERFORATE STAMPS**

Through 1991, most semi-postal stamps were also issued imperforate. Where these items form part of a larger set with regular issues, values for imperfs will be included in that of the sets to which they belong, footnoted in the Regular Issues section. For Nos. B207-B345, values for imperfs will be given only for those items not included in sets with regular issues.

**1st Stamp Type**

***Perf. 12½x12***

**1951, Oct. 6** **Engr.** **Unwmk.**

**B207** A208 1fo + 1fo red 12.00 12.00
**B208** A208 2fo + 2fo blue 14.00 14.00

Exists imperf.

Postwoman Delivering Mail — SP124

**1953, Nov. 1** **Wmk. 106** ***Perf. 12***

**B209** SP124 1fo + 1fo blue grn 4.00 1.25
**B210** SP124 2fo + 2fo rose vio 4.00 1.25

Stamp Day, Nov. 1, 1953.
Exist imperf. Value, set $60.

Stamps of 1955 Surcharged in Red or Lake

**1957, Jan. 31** **Photo.** ***Perf. 12x12½***

**B211** A249 20f + 20f olive grn .25 .25
**B212** A249 30f + 30f dk red (L) .40 .25
*a.* Red (cross) inverted 450.00
**B213** A249 40f + 40f brown .45 .40
**B214** A249 60f + 60f brn red (L) .55 .45
**B215** A249 1fo + 1fo blue 1.20 1.00
**B216** A249 2fo + 2fo rose brn 2.00 1.40
*Nos. B211-B216 (6)* 4.85 3.75

The surtax was for the Hungarian Red Cross.
Exist imperf. Value, set $135.

**Winter Olympic Type of 1960**

Design: Olympic Games emblem.

***Perf. 11½x12***

**1960, Feb. 29** **Wmk. 106**

**B217** A295 2fo + 1fo multi 1.75 .35

Exists imperf.

**Olympic Type of 1960**

Design: 2fo+1fo, Romulus and Remus.

***Perf. 11½x12***

**1960, Aug. 21** **Photo.** **Wmk. 106**

**B218** A299 2fo + 1fo multi 1.25 .30

Exists imperf.

**Sport Club Type of 1961**

Sport: 2fo+1fo, Sailboats.

**1961, July 8** **Unwmk.** ***Perf. 14½***

**B219** A313 2fo + 1fo multi .40 .25

Exists imperf.

St. Margaret's Island and Danube — SP125

Views of Budapest: No. B221, Fishermen's Bastion. No. B222, Coronation Church and Chain Bridge. No. B223, Mount Gellert.

**Unwmk.**

**1961, Sept. 24** **Photo.** ***Perf. 12***

**B220** SP125 2fo + 1fo multi 1.50 1.50
**B221** SP125 2fo + 1fo multi 1.50 1.50
**B222** SP125 2fo + 1fo multi 1.50 1.50
**B223** SP125 2fo + 1fo multi 1.50 1.50
*a.* Horiz. strip of 4, #B220-B223 6.00 6.00

Stamp Day, 1961, and Budapest Intl. Stamp Exhibition.
No. B223a has a continuous design.
Exist imperf. Value, strip $32.
Miniature presentation sheets, perf. and imperf., contain one each of Nos. B220-B223; size: 204x66½mm. Value for both sheets, $2,000.

### Soccer Type of Regular Issue, 1962

Design: Flags of Spain and Czechoslovakia.

**1962, May 21** *Perf. 11*
**Flags in Original Colors**

**B224** A323 4fo + 1fo lt grn & bister 2.00 .75

Exists imperf.

Austrian Stamp of 1850 with Pesth Postmark SP126

Stamps: No. B226, #201. No. B227, #C164. No. B228, #C208.

**Lithographed and Engraved**
**1962, Sept. 22** **Unwmk.** *Perf. 11*
**Design and Inscription in Dark Brown**

**B225** SP126 2fo + 1fo yellow 1.25 1.25
**B226** SP126 2fo + 1fo pale pink 1.25 1.25
**B227** SP126 2fo + 1fo pale blue 1.25 1.25
**B228** SP126 2fo + 1fo pale yel grn 1.25 1.25
*a.* Horiz. strip of 4, #B225-B228 5.00 5.00
*b.* Souv. sheet of 4, #B225-B228 7.50 7.50

35th Stamp Day and 10th anniv. of Mabeosz, the Hungarian Phil. Fed.
Exist imperf. Value: strip $23; souvenir sheet $45.

Emblem, Cup and Soccer Ball — SP127

**1962, Nov. 18** **Photo.** *Perf. 11½x12*

**B229** SP127 2fo + 1fo multi .80 .50

Winning of the "Coupe de l'Europe Centrale" by the Steel Workers Sport Club (VASAS) in the Central European Soccer Championships.
Exists imperf. Value $6.

Stamp Day — SP128

**1963, Oct. 24** *Perf. 11½x12*
**Size: 32x43mm**

**B230** SP128 2fo + 1fo Hyacinth .50 .50
**B231** SP128 2fo + 1fo Narcissus .50 .50
**B232** SP128 2fo + 1fo Chrysanthemum .50 .50
**B233** SP128 2fo + 1fo Tiger lily .50 .50
*a.* Horiz. strip of 4, #B230-B233 3.00 3.00
*b.* Min. sheet of 4, #B230-B233 3.50 3.50

#B233b contains 25x32mm stamps, perf. 11.
Exist imperf. Value: strip $20; miniature sheet $35.

### Winter Olympic Type of 1963

Design: 4fo+1fo, Bobsledding.

**1963, Nov. 11** *Perf. 12*

**B234** A342 4fo + 1fo grnsh bl & bis .70 .30

Exists imperf.

### New Year Type of Regular Issue

Good Luck Symbols: 2.50fo+1.20fo, Horseshoe, mistletoe and clover. 3fo+1.50fo, Pigs, clover and balloon, horiz.

*Perf. 12x11½, 11½x12*
**1963, Dec. 12** **Photo.** **Unwmk.**
**Sizes: 28x39mm (#B235); 28x22mm (#B206)**

**B235** A343 2.50fo + 1.20fo multi .50 .25
**B236** A343 3fo + 1.50fo multi .70 .35

The surtax was for the modernization of the Hungarian Postal and Philatelic Museum.
Exist imperf.

### Olympic Type of Regular Issue

Design: 3fo+1fo, Water polo.

**1964, June 12** *Perf. 11*

**B237** A352 3fo + 1fo multi .60 .75

Exists imperf.

Exhibition Hall — SP129

**1964, July 23** **Photo.**

**B238** SP129 3fo + 1.50fo blk, red org & gray .60 .35

Tennis Exhibition, Budapest Sports Museum.
Exists imperf. Value $8.

Twirling Woman Gymnast SP130

**1964, Sept. 4** *Perf. 11½x12*
**Size: 27x38mm**

**B239** SP130 2fo + 1fo Lilac 1.00 1.00
**B240** SP130 2fo + 1fo Mallards 1.00 1.00
**B241** SP130 2fo + 1fo Gymnast 1.00 1.00
**B242** SP130 2fo + 1fo Rocket & globe 1.00 1.00
*a.* Horiz. strip of 4, #B239-B242 4.00 4.00
*b.* Souv. sheet of 4, #B239-B242 4.00 4.00

37th Stamp Day and Intl. Topical Stamp Exhib., IMEX. No. B242b contains 4 20x28mm stamps, perf. 11.
Exist imperf. Value: strip $17.50; souvenir sheet $32.50.

13th Century Tennis SP131

History of Tennis: 40f+10f, Indoor tennis, 16th century. 60f+10f, Tennis, 18th century. 70f+30f, Tennis court and castle. 80f+40f, Tennis court, Fontainebleau (buildings). 1fo+50f, Tennis, 17th century. 1.50fo+50f, W. C. Wingfield, Wimbledon champion 1877, and Wimbledon Cup. 1.70fo+50f, Davis Cup, 1900. 2fo+1fo, Bela Kehrling (1891-1937), Hungarian champion.

**Lithographed and Engraved**
**1965, June 15** **Unwmk.** *Perf. 12*

**B243** SP131 30f + 10f mar, *dl org* .25 .25
**B244** SP131 40f + 10f blk, *pale lil* .25 .25
**B245** SP131 60f + 10f grn, *ol* .25 .25
**B246** SP131 70f + 30f lil, *brt grn* .25 .25
**B247** SP131 80f + 40f dk bl, *lt vio* .40 .25
**B248** SP131 1fo + 50f grn, *yel* .50 .25
**B249** SP131 1.50fo + 50f sep, *lt ol grn* .50 .25
**B250** SP131 1.70fo + 50f ind, *lt bl* .75 .25
**B251** SP131 2fo + 1fo dk red, *lt grn* .85 .30
*Nos. B243-B251 (9)* 4.00 2.30

Exist imperf. Value, set $20.

Flood Scene SP132

10fo+5fo, Relief commemorating 1838 flood.

**1965, Aug. 14** **Photo.** *Perf. 12x11½*

**B252** SP132 1fo + 50f org brn & bl .30 .30

**Souvenir Sheet**

**B253** SP132 10fo + 5fo gldn brn & buff 2.75 2.75

Surtax for aid to 1965 flood victims.
Exist imperf. Value: No. B252 $6; No. B253 $20.

Geranium Stamp of 1950 (No. 909) SP133

Stamp Day: No. B255, #120. No. B256, #1489. No. B257, #1382.

*Perf. 12x11½*
**1965, Oct. 30** **Photo.** **Unwmk.**
**Stamps in Original Colors**

**B254** SP133 2fo + 1fo gray & dk bl .65 .60
**B255** SP133 2fo + 1fo gray & red .65 .60
**B256** SP133 2fo + 1fo gray & ocher .65 .60
**B257** SP133 2fo + 1fo gray & vio .65 .60
*a.* Horiz. strip of 4, #B254-B257 3.00 3.00
*b.* Souv. sheet of 4, #B254-B257 3.50 3.25

No. B257b contains 32x23mm stamps, perf. 11.
Exist imperf. Value: No. B257a $15; No. B257b $25.

### Soccer Type of Regular Issue

Design: 3fo+1fo, Championship emblem and map of Great Britain showing cities where matches were held.

**1966, June 6** **Photo.** *Perf. 12x11½*

**B258** A382 3fo + 1fo multi 1.00 .50

Exists imperf.

Woman Archer and Danube at Visegrad SP134

Stamp Day: No. B260, Gloria Hungariae grapes and Lake Balaton. No. B261, Red poppies and ruins of Diosgyor Castle. No. B262, Russian space dogs Ugolek and Veterok.

**1966, Sept. 16** **Photo.** *Perf. 12x11½*

**B259** SP134 2fo + 50f multi .60 .60
**B260** SP134 2fo + 50f multi .60 .60
**B261** SP134 2fo + 50f multi .60 .60
**B262** SP134 2fo + 50f multi .60 .60
*a.* Horiz. strip of 4, #B259-B262 2.75 2.75
*b.* Souv. sheet of 4, #B259-B262 2.75 2.75

#B262b contains 4 29x21mm stamps, perf. 11.
Exist imperf. Value: B262a $15; B262b $30.

Anglers, C.I.P.S. Emblem and View of Danube SP135

**1967, Aug. 22** **Photo.** *Perf. 12x11½*

**B263** SP135 3fo + 1fo multi .90 .45

See note after No. 1847.
Exists imperf.

### Olympic Type of Regular Issue

Indoor stadium & Winter Olympics emblem.

**1968, Jan. 29** **Photo.** *Perf. 11*

**B264** A402 4fo + 1fo multi .70 .30

Exists imperf.

Jug, Western Hungary, 1618 SP136

Hungarian Earthenware: No. B266, Tiszafüred vase, 1847. No. B267, Toby jug, 1848. No. B268, Decorative Baja plate, 1870. No. B269a, Jug, Northern Hungary, 1672. No. B269b, Decorative Mezőcsat plate, 1843. No. B269c, Decorative Moragy plate, 1860. No. B269d, Pitcher, Debrecen, 1793.

**1968, Oct. 5** **Litho.** *Perf. 12*

**B265** SP136 1fo + 50f ultra & multi .50 .50
**B266** SP136 1fo + 50f sky bl & multi .50 .50
**B267** SP136 1fo + 50f sepia & multi .50 .50
**B268** SP136 1fo + 50f yel brn & multi .50 .50
*Nos. B265-B268 (4)* 2.00 2.00

**Miniature Sheet**

**B269** Sheet of 4 2.75 2.50
*a.* SP136 2fo + 50f ultra & multi .45 .40
*b.* SP136 2fo + 50f yel brn & multi .45 .40
*c.* SP136 2fo + 50f olive & multi .45 .40
*d.* SP136 2fo + 50f brt rose & multi .45 .40

Issued for 41st Stamp Day. No. B269 contains 4 25x36mm stamps. See Nos. B271-B275.
Exist imperf. Value: Nos. B265-B268 $15; No. B269 $15.

Suspension Bridge, Buda Castle and Arms of Budapest — SP137

**Lithographed and Engraved**
**1969, May 22** *Perf. 12*

**B270** SP137 5fo + 2fo sep, pale yel & gray 1.00 1.00

Budapest 71 Philatelic Exposition.
Exists imperf. Value $7.50.

### Folk Art Type of 1968

Hungarian Wood Carvings: No. B271, Stirrup cup from Okorag, 1880. No. B272, Jar with flower decorations from Felsötiszavidek, 1898. No. B273, Round jug, Somogyharsagy, 1935. No. B274, Two-legged jug, Alföld, 1740. No. B275a, Carved panel (farm couple), Csorna, 1879. No. B275b, Tankard, Okany, 1914. No. B275c, Round jar with soldiers, Sellye, 1899. No. B275d, Square box with 2 women, Lengyeltoti, 1880.

**1969, Sept. 13** **Litho.** *Perf. 12*

**B271** SP136 1fo + 50f rose cl & multi .60 .60
**B272** SP136 1fo + 50f dp bis & multi .60 .60
**B273** SP136 1fo + 50f bl & multi .60 .60

**B274** SP136 1fo + 50f lt bl grn & multi .60 .60
*Nos. B271-B274 (4)* 2.40 2.40

**Miniature Sheet**

**B275** Sheet of 4 2.75 2.50
*a.* SP136 2fo + 50f ultra & multi .50 .45
*b.* SP136 2fo + 50f brn org & multi .50 .45
*c.* SP136 2fo + 50f lt brn & multi .50 .45
*d.* SP136 2fo + 50f bl grn & multi .50 .45

Issued for the 42nd Stamp Day. No. B275 contains 4 stamps (size: 25x36mm).
Exists imperf. Value: B271-B274 $15; B275 $15.

Fishermen's Bastion, Coronation Church and Chain Bridge — SP138

Designs: No. B277, Parliament and Elizabeth Bridge. No. B278, Castle and Margaret Bridge.

**1970, Mar. 7 Litho. *Perf. 12***
**B276** SP138 2fo + 1fo gldn brn & multi .60 .60
**B277** SP138 2fo + 1fo bl & multi .60 .60
**B278** SP138 2fo + 1fo lt vio & multi .60 .60
*Nos. B276-B278 (3)* 1.80 1.80

Budapest 71 Philatelic Exhibition, commemorating the centenary of Hungarian postage stamps.
Exist imperf. Value, set $15.

King Matthias I Corvinus SP139

Initials and Paintings from Bibliotheca Corvina: No. B280, Letter "A." No. B281, Letter "N." No. B282, Letter "O." No. B283a, Ransanus Speaking before King Matthias. No. B283b, Scholar and letter "Q." No. B283c, Portrait of Appianus and letter "C." No. B283d, King David and letter "A."

**1970, Aug. 22 Photo. *Perf. 11½x12***
**B279** SP139 1fo + 50f multi .40 .40
**B280** SP139 1fo + 50f multi .40 .40
**B281** SP139 1fo + 50f multi .40 .40
**B282** SP139 1fo + 50f multi .40 .40
*Nos. B279-B282 (4)* 1.60 1.60

**Miniature Sheet**

**B283** Sheet of 4 2.75 2.50
*a.-d.* SP139 2fo + 50f, any single .50 .45

Issued for the 43rd Stamp Day. No. B283 contains 4 stamps (size: 22½x32mm).
Exist imperf. Value: B279-B282 $15; B283 $20.

View of Buda, 1470 — SP140

#B285, Buda, 1600. #B286, Buda and Pest, about 1638. #B287, Buda and Pest, 1770. #B288a, Buda, 1777. #B288b, Buda, 1850. #B288c, Buda, 1895. #B288d, Budapest, 1970.

**1971, Feb. 26 Litho. *Perf. 12***
**B284** SP140 2fo + 1fo blk & yel .60 .60
**B285** SP140 2fo + 1fo blk & pink .60 .60
**B286** SP140 2fo + 1fo blk & pale grn .60 .60
**B287** SP140 2fo + 1fo blk & pale sal .60 .60
*Nos. B284-B287 (4)* 2.40 2.40

**Souvenir Sheet**

***Perf. 10½***

**B288** Sheet of 4 2.50 2.25
*a.* SP140 2fo + 1fo blk & pale sal .50 .45
*b.* SP140 2fo + 1fo blk & pale grn .50 .45
*c.* SP140 2fo + 1fo blk & lilac .50 .45
*d.* SP140 2fo + 1fo blk & pink .50 .45

Budapest 71 Intl. Stamp Exhib. for the cent. of Hungarian postage stamps, Budapest, Sept. 4-12. No. B288 contains 4 stamps, size: 39½x18mm.
Exist imperf. Value: Nos. B284-B287 $15; No. B288 $15.

Iris and #P1 SP141

Designs: No. B290, Daisy and #199. No. B291, Poppy and #391. No. B292, Rose and #B128. No. B293a, Carnations and #B200. No. B293b, Dahlia and #1068. No. B293c, Tulips and #C196. No. B293d, Anemones and #C251.

**1971, Sept. 4 Photo. *Perf. 12x11½***
**B289** SP141 2fo + 1fo sil & multi .70 .70
**B290** SP141 2fo + 1fo sil & multi .70 .70
**B291** SP141 2fo + 1fo sil & multi .70 .70
**B292** SP141 2fo + 1fo sil & multi .70 .70
*Nos. B289-B292 (4)* 2.80 2.80

**Souvenir Sheet**

***Perf. 11½***

**B293** Sheet of 4 2.75 2.50
*a.-d.* SP141 2fo + 1fo, any single .50 .45

Cent. of 1st Hungarian postage stamps and in connection with Budapest 71 Intl. Stamp Exhib., Sept. 4-12.
Exist imperf. Value: Nos. B289-B292 $16; No. B293 $25.

Miskólcz Postmark, 1818-43 — SP142

Postmarks: No. B295, Szegedin, 1827-48. No. B296, Esztergom, 1848-51. No. B297, Budapest 1971 Exhibition. No. B298a, Paar family signet, 1593. No. B298b, Courier letter, 1708. No. B298c, First well-known Hungarian postmark "V. TOKAI," 1752. No. B298d, Letter, 1705.

**1972, May *Perf. 12x11½***
**B294** SP142 2fo + 1fo blue & blk .70 .70
**B295** SP142 2fo + 1fo yel & blk .70 .70
**B296** SP142 2fo + 1fo yel grn & blk .70 .70
**B297** SP142 2fo + 1fo ver & multi .70 .70
*Nos. B294-B297 (4)* 2.80 2.80

**Souvenir Sheet**

**B298** Sheet of 4 2.50 2.25
*a.* SP142 2fo + 1fo yel grn & multi .50 .45
*b.* SP142 2fo + 1fo brn & multi .50 .45
*c.* SP142 2fo + 1fo ultra & multi .50 .45
*d.* SP142 2fo + 1fo red & multi .50 .45

9th Congress of National Federation of Hungarian Philatelists (Mabeosz). No. B298 contains 4 stamps (size: 32x23mm).
Exist imperf. Value: Nos. B294-B297 $15; No. B298 $17.50.

**Olympic Type of Regular Issue**

Design: Wrestling and Olympic rings.

**1972, July 15 Photo. *Perf. 11***
**B299** A484 3fo + 1fo multi .50 .30

Exists imperf.

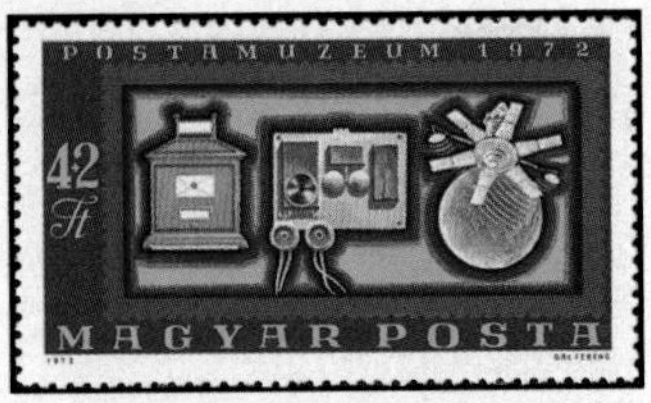


Historic Mail Box, Telephone and Molniya Satellite — SP143

Design: No. B301, Post horn, Tokai postmark, and Nos. 183, 1802, 1809.

**1972, Oct. 27 Litho. *Perf. 12***
**B300** SP143 4fo + 2fo grn & multi .80 .70
**B301** SP143 4fo + 2fo bl & multi .80 .70

Reopening of the Post and Philatelic Museums, Budapest.
Exist imperf. Value, set $15.

Bird on Silver Disk, 10th Century SP144

Treasures from Hungarian Natl. Museum. No. B303, Ring with serpent's head, 11th cent. No. B304, Lovers, belt buckle, 12th cent. No. B305, Flower, belt buckle, 15th cent. No. B306a, Opal pendant, 16th cent. No. B306b, Jeweled belt buckle, 18th cent. No. B306c, Flower pin, 17th cent. No. B306d, Rosette pendant, 17th cent.

**1973, Sept. 22 Litho. *Perf. 12***
**B302** SP144 2fo + 50f brn & multi .65 .65
**B303** SP144 2fo + 50f brt rose lil & multi .65 .65
**B304** SP144 2fo + 50f dk bl & multi .65 .65
**B305** SP144 2fo + 50f grn & multi .65 .65
*Nos. B302-B305 (4)* 2.60 2.60

**Souvenir Sheet**

**B306** Sheet of 4 2.50 2.50
*a.* SP144 2fo + 50f brown & multi .35 .35
*b.* SP144 2fo + 50f car & multi .35 .35
*c.* SP144 2fo + 50f ol grn & multi .35 .35
*d.* SP144 2fo + 50f brt bl & multi .35 .35

46th Stamp Day. No. B306 contains 4 stamps (size: 25x35mm).
Exist imperf. Value: Nos. B302-B305 $15; No. B306 $20.

Gothic Wall Fountain SP145

Visegrad Castle and Bas-reliefs — SP146

Designs: No. B308, Wellhead, Anjou period. No. B309, Twin lion-head wall fountain. B310, Fountain with Hercules riding dolphin. No. B311a, Raven panel. No. B311b, Visegrad Madonna. B311c, Lion panel. No. B311d, Visegrad Castle. Designs show artworks from Visegrad Palace of King Matthias Corvinus I, 15th century.

**1975, Sept. 13 Litho. *Perf. 12***

**Multicolored and:**

**B307** SP145 2fo + 1fo green 1.50 1.50
**B308** SP145 2fo + 1fo ver 1.50 1.50
**B309** SP145 2fo + 1fo blue 1.50 1.50
**B310** SP145 2fo + 1fo lilac 1.50 1.50
*a.* Horizontal strip of 4 6.00 6.00

**Souvenir Sheet**

**B311** SP146 Sheet of 4 7.50 7.50
*a.* 2fo + 1fo 21x32mm 1.40 1.40
*b.* 2fo + 1fo 47x32mm 1.40 1.40
*c.* 2fo + 1fo 21x32mm 1.40 1.40
*d.* 2fo + 1fo 99x32mm 1.40 1.40

European Architectural Heritage Year 1975 and 48th Stamp Day.
Exist imperf. Value: Nos. B307-B310 $125; No. B311 $100.

Knight SP147

Gothic Sculptures, Buda Castle — SP148

Gothic sculptures from Buda Castle.

**1976 Photo. *Perf. 12***
**B312** SP147 2.50 + 1fo shown .60 .60
**B313** SP147 2.50 + 1fo Armor-bearer .60 .60
**B314** SP147 2.50 + 1fo Apostle .60 .60
**B315** SP147 2.50 + 1fo Bishop .60 .60
*a.* Horizontal strip of 4, #B312-B315 2.75 2.75

**Souvenir Sheet**

Designs: a, Man with hat. b, Woman with wimple. c, Man with cloth cap. d, Man with fur hat.

**B316** Sheet of 4 3.00 3.00
*a.-d.* SP148 2.50 + 1fo any single .55 .55

49th Stamp Day.
No. B316 issued in connection with 10th Congress of National Federation of Hungarian Philatelists (Mabeosz).
Exist imperf. Value: Nos. B312-B315 $15; No. B316 $20.
Issued: #B316, May 22; #B312-B315, Sept. 4.

Young Runners SP149

**1977, Apr. 2 Litho. *Perf. 12***
**B317** SP149 3fo + 1.50fo multi .85 .85

Sports promotion among young people.
Exists imperf. Value $5.

Young Man and Woman, Profiles SP150

**1978, Apr. 1** **Litho.** ***Perf. 12***
**B318** SP150 3fo + 1.50fo multi 1.25 1.25

Hungarian Communist Youth Movement, 60th anniversary.
Exists imperf. Value $10.

"Generations," by Gyula Derkovits SP151

**1978, May 6** **Litho.** ***Perf. 12***
**B319** SP151 3fo + 1.50fo multi .90 .90

Szocfilex '78, Szombathely. No. B319 printed in sheets of 3 stamps and 3 labels showing Szocfilex emblem.
Exists imperf. Value: single $5; sheetlet $15.

Girl Reading Book, by Ferenc Kovacs SP152

**1979, Mar. 31** **Litho.** ***Perf. 12***
**B320** SP152 3fo + 1.50fo blk & ultra .45 .45

Surtax was for Junior Stamp Exhibition, Bekescsaba.
Exists imperf. Value $5.

Watch Symbolizing Environmental Protection SP153

**1980, Apr. 3** **Litho.** ***Perf. 12***
**B321** SP153 3fo + 1.50fo multi .70 .70

Surtax was for Junior Stamp Exhibition, Dunaujvaros.
Exists imperf. Value $5.

International Year of the Disabled SP154

Youths and Factory SP155

**1981, May 15** **Litho.** ***Perf. 12***
**B322** SP154 2fo + 1fo multi .45 .45

Exists imperf. Value $6.

**1981, May 29** ***Perf. 12x11½***
**B323** SP155 4fo + 2fo multi .80 .80

Young Communist League, 10th Congress, Budapest, May 29-31.
Exists imperf. Value $7.

European Junior Tennis Cup, July 25-Aug. 1 — SP156

**1982, Apr. 2** **Litho.** ***Perf. 12x11½***
**B324** SP156 4fo + 2fo multi .80 .80

Exists imperf. Value $5.

Souvenir Sheet

SP157

***Perf. 12½x11½***
**1982, June 11** **Litho.**
**B325** SP157 20fo + 10fo multi 4.00 4.00

PHILEXFRANCE '82 Stamp Exhibition, Paris, June 11-21.
Exists imperf. Value $15.

55th Stamp Day — SP158

Budapest Architecture and Statues: No. B326, Fishermen's Bastion, Janos Hunyadi (1403-1456). No. B327, Parliament, Ferenc Rakoczi the Second (1676-1735).

**1982, Sept. 10** **Litho.** ***Perf. 12***
**B326** SP158 4fo + 2fo multi .90 .90
**B327** SP158 4fo + 2fo shown .90 .90

Exist imperf. Value, set $15.

Souvenir Sheet

Parliament, Chain Bridge, Buda Castle, Budapest — SP159

**1982, Sept. 10** ***Perf. 11½***
**B328** SP159 20fo + 10fo multi 3.75 3.75

European Security and Cooperation Conference, 10th anniv.
Exists imperf. Value $24.

21st Junior Stamp Exhibition, Baja, Mar. 31-Apr. 9 — SP160

**1983, Mar. 31** **Litho.** ***Perf. 12x11½***
**B329** SP160 4fo + 2fo multi .90 .90

Surtax was for show.
Exists imperf. Value $6.

56th Natl. Stamp Day SP161

Budapest Architecture (19th Cent. Engravings by): Rudolph Alt, H. Luders (No. B331).

**1983, Sept. 9** **Litho.** ***Perf. 12***
**B330** SP161 4fo + 2fo Old Natl. Theater .90 .90
**B331** SP161 4fo + 2fo Municipal Concert Hall .90 .90

**Souvenir Sheet**

**Lithographed and Engraved**

***Perf. 11***

**B332** SP161 20fo + 10fo Holy Trinity Square 3.75 3.75

No. B332 contains one stamp (28x45mm).
Exist imperf. Value: Nos. B330-B331 $15; No. B332 $20.

SP162

**1984, Apr. 2** **Litho.** ***Perf. 12½x11½***
**B333** SP162 4fo + 2fo Mother & Child .75 .75

Surtax was for children's foundation.
Exists imperf. Value $10.

SP163

Little Red Riding Hood, by the Brothers Grimm.

**1985, Apr. 2** **Litho.** ***Perf. 11½x12***
**B334** SP163 4fo + 2fo multi .75 .75

Jacob (1785-1863) and Wilhelm (1786-1859) Grimm, fabulists and philologists.
Exists imperf. Value $8.

Natl. SOS Children's Village Assoc., 3rd Anniv. SP164

**1985, Dec. 10** **Litho.** ***Perf. 11***
**B335** SP164 4fo + 2fo multi .75 .75

Surtax for natl. SOS Children's Village.
Exists imperf. Value $7.

Natl. Young Pioneers Org., 40th Anniv. SP165

**1986, May 30** ***Perf. 11½x12½***
**B336** SP165 4fo + 2fo multi .75 .60

Exists imperf. Value $6.

Souvenir Sheet

Budapest Natl. Theater — SP166

**Lithographed and Engraved**

**1986, Oct. 10** ***Perf. 11***
**B337** SP166 20fo + 10fo tan, brn & buff 4.00 4.00

Surtax benefited natl. theater construction.
Exists imperf. Value $20.

Natl. Communist Youth League, 30th Anniv. — SP167

**1987, Mar. 20** ***Perf. 13½x13***

**B338** SP167 4fo + 2fo multi .60 .60

Exists imperf. Value $6.

Souvenir Sheet

SOCFILEX '88, Aug. 12-21, Kecskemet — SP168

**1988, Mar. 10** **Litho.** ***Perf. 11½***

**B339** SP168 20fo +10fo multi 4.50 4.50

Surtax for SOCFILEX '88.
Exists imperf. Value $20.

*Sky High Tree,* a Tapestry by Erzsebet Szekeres SP169

**1989, Apr. 12** **Litho.** ***Perf. 12***

**B340** SP169 5fo +2fo multi 1.50 1.50

Surtax to promote youth philately.
Exist imperf. Value, set $7.

Souvenir Sheet

*Battle of Solferino,* by Carlo Bossoli — SP170

**1989, Sept. 8** **Litho.** ***Perf. 10½***

**B341** SP170 20fo +10fo multi 3.75 3.75

Stamp Day.
Exists imperf. Value $35.

Souvenir Sheet

*Martyrs of Arad,* Arad, Romania, 1849 — SP171

**1989, Oct. 6** ***Perf. 11½x12½***

**B342** SP171 20fo +10fo multi 3.75 3.75

Surtax to fund production of another statue.
Exists imperf. Value $20.

Teacher's Training High School, Sarospatak Municipal Arms — SP172

**1990, Mar. 30** **Litho.** ***Perf. 12x11½***

**B343** SP172 8fo +4fo multi 1.75 1.75

28th Youth Stamp Exhib., Sarospatak, Apr. 6-22.
Exists imperf. Value $8.

Souvenir Sheet

Yesterday, by Endre Szasz — SP173

**1990, Oct. 12** **Litho.** ***Perf. 12***

**B344** SP173 20fo +10fo multi 4.50 4.50

Stamp Day. Surtax for National Federation of Hungarian Philatelists.
Exists imperf. Value $30.

Tapestry, Peter and the Wolf, by Gabriella Hajnal — SP174

**1991, Apr. 30** **Litho.** ***Perf. 12***

**B345** SP174 12fo +6fo multi 1.75 1.75

Surtax to promote youth philately.
Exists imperf. Value $8.

Children's Drawings SP175

Designs: 9fo + 4fo, Girl holding flower, vert. 10fo + 4fo, Child standing beneath sun. 15fo + 4fo, Boy wearing crown, vert.

**1992, May 15** **Litho.** ***Perf. 12***

**B346** SP175 9fo +4fo multi 1.10 1.10
**B347** SP175 10fo +4fo multi 1.25 1.25
**B348** SP175 15fo +4fo multi 1.65 1.65
*Nos. B346-B348 (3)* 4.00 4.00

Surtax for children's welfare.

Souvenir Sheet

1992 Summer Olympics, Barcelona — SP176

**1992, Sept. 4** **Litho.** ***Perf. 12***

**B349** SP176 50fo +20fo multi 3.50 3.00

Textile Art, by Erzsebet Szekeres SP177

**1993, Apr. 14** **Litho.** ***Perf. 12***

**B350** SP177 10fo +5fo Outdoor scene .60 .40
**B351** SP177 17fo +8fo Tree of life 1.60 1.00

Stamp Day SP178

Stamp designers, stamps: 10fo + 5fo, Zoltan Nagy (1916-1987), #1062. 17fo + 5fo, Sandor Legrady (1906-1987), #523. 50fo + 20fo, Ferenc Helbing (1870-1959), #465.

**1993, Sept. 10** **Litho.** ***Perf. 12***

**B352** SP178 10fo +5fo multi .75 .30
**B353** SP178 17fo +5fo multi 1.00 .45

**Souvenir Sheet**

**B354** SP178 50fo +20fo multi 3.25 1.75

No. B354 contains one 35x27mm stamp.

The Little Prince, by Antoine de Saint-Exupery SP179

**1994, Apr. 1** **Litho.** ***Perf. 13½x13***

**B355** SP179 19fo +5fo multi 2.00 2.00

Surtax for children's welfare.

Poem, "John the Hero," 150th Anniv. SP180

**1995, Apr. 7** **Litho.** ***Perf. 12***

**B356** SP180 22fo +10fo multi 1.00 .60

Surtax to promote youth philately.

Olympiafila '95, Budapest — SP181

**1995, June 12** **Litho.** ***Perf. 11***

**B357** SP181 22fo +11fo yellow rings 1.10 .50
**B358** SP181 22fo +11fo purple rings 1.10 .50
*a.* Pair, #B357-B358 2.50 1.50

No. B358a also sold in a strip of 3 pairs in a booklet.

World Festival of Puppet Players, Budapest SP182

Laszlo Vitez puppet and ghost puppet.

**1996, June 21** **Litho.** ***Perf. 12***

**B359** SP182 24fo +10fo multi 1.00 .75

Oder River Flood of 1997 SP183

**1997, Sept. 12** **Litho.** ***Perf. 12***

**B360** SP183 27fo +100fo flower in water 2.25 .95

Surtax is for aid to flood victims.

Stamp Day SP184

Early postman using: 27fo + 5fo, Motorized tricycle. 55fo + 5fo, Experimental registered letter-receiving machine, vert.
90fo + 30fo, Postal van.

**1997, Sept. 19**

**B361** SP184 27fo +5fo multi .75 .25
**B362** SP184 55fo +5fo multi 1.50 .45

**Souvenir Sheet**

**B363** SP184 90fo +30fo multi 7.00 3.75

Souvenir Sheet

Revolution of 1848 — SP185

Design: Seven members of movement, newspaper *Nemzeti dal.*

**1998, Mar. 13 Litho. *Perf. 12***
**B364** SP185 150fo +50fo multi 4.50 1.75

Surtax to promote youth philately.

Youth Stamp SP186

**1999, Mar. 12 Litho. *Perf. 12***
**B365** SP186 52fo +25fo multi 1.50 .75

István Fekete (1900-70), Writer — SP187

**2000, Jan. 11 Litho. *Perf. 12***
**B366** SP187 60fo +30fo multi 2.00 2.00

Surtax for youth philately.

Hunphilex 2000 Stamp Exhibition, Budapest SP188

**2000, Jan. 11**
**B367** SP188 200fo +100fo multi 4.00 3.00

Surtax to support stamp exhibition.

Souvenir Sheet

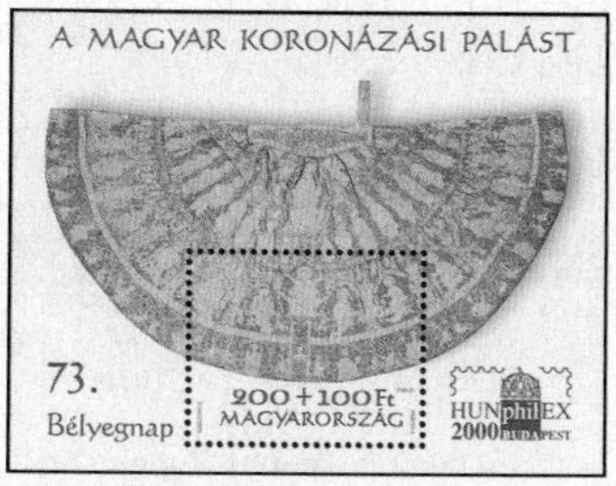

Hunphilex 2000 Stamp Exhibition, Budapest — SP189

**2000, Aug. 18 Litho. *Perf. 12***
**B368** SP189 200fo +100fo Coronation robe 3.75 2.75
*a.* Sheet of 2 9.00 5.75

Star Over Eger, by Geza Gardonyi SP190

**2001, Jan. 15 Litho. *Perf. 13¼x13***
**B369** SP190 60fo +30fo multi 1.75 .50

Surtax for youth philately.

Campaign Against Breast Cancer — SP191

**2005, Sept. 29 Litho. *Perf. 12***
**B370** SP191 90fo +50fo multi 2.50 2.00

Victory in First Grand Prix Race by Ferenc Szisz (1873-1944) — SP192

**2006, May 9 Litho. *Perf. 13x13¼***
**B371** SP192 120fo +50fo multi 2.00 2.00

Smile, by Zita Zagyi SP193

**2008, May 20 Litho. *Perf. 13x13¼***
**B372** SP193 100fo + 50fo multi 1.90 1.90

Design was a winner in a children's art contest. Surtax for Hungarian Ambulance Service.

Togetherness — SP194

**2009, Aug. 31**
**B373** SP194 75fo +50fo multi 1.40 1.40

Surtax for Crisis Foundation.

Hungarian Red Cross — SP195

**2010, Mar. 1 Litho. *Perf. 12¼x12¾***
**B374** SP195 105fo + 55fo multi 1.75 1.75

Surtax for Red Cross.

Interlocking Hands — SP196

**2010, Nov. 24 Litho. *Perf. 13x13¼***
**B375** SP196 (80fo) +100fo multi 1.75 1.75

Surtax for victims of Hungarian Red Sludge disaster of Oct. 4, 2010.

Child and Heart SP197

**2011, Mar. 1 Litho. *Perf. 12½x12***
**B376** SP197 (90fo) +50fo multi 1.50 1.50

Surtax for Intl. Children's Safety Service.

## AIR POST STAMPS

### Issues of the Monarchy

Nos. 120, 123 Surcharged in Red or Blue

**Wmk. 137**

**1918, July 4 Typo. *Perf. 14***
**C1** A10 1k 50f on 75f (R) 25.00 *27.50*
**C2** A10 4k 50f on 2k (Bl) 25.00 *27.50*

Counterfeits exist.
Exist imperf. Value, set $350.

No. 126 Surcharged

**1920, Nov. 7**
**C3** A10 3k on 10k (G) 1.40 *2.25*
**C4** A10 8k on 10k (R) 1.40 *2.25*
**C5** A10 12k on 10k (Bl) 1.40 *2.25*
*Nos. C3-C5 (3)* 4.20 6.75
Set, never hinged 7.50

Icarus — AP3

**1924-25 *Perf. 14***
**C6** AP3 100k red brn & red 1.25 *2.50*
**C7** AP3 500k bl grn & yel grn 1.25 *2.50*
**C8** AP3 1000k bis brn & brn 1.25 *2.50*
**C9** AP3 2000k dk bl & lt bl 1.25 *2.50*

**Wmk. 133**

**C10** AP3 5000k dl vio & brt vio 2.00 *2.50*
**C11** AP3 10000k red & dl vio 2.00 *4.00*
*Nos. C6-C11 (6)* 9.00 16.50
Set, never hinged 20.00

Issue dates: 100k-2000k, Apr. 11, 1924. Others, Apr. 20, 1925.
Exist imperf. Value, set $100.
Forgeries exist.
For surcharges see Nos. J112-J116.

Mythical "Turul" — AP4

"Turul" Carrying Messenger
AP5 AP6

**1927-30 Engr. *Perf. 14***
**C12** AP4 4f orange ('30) .25 *.40*
**C13** AP4 12f deep green .45 *.40*
**C14** AP4 16f red brown .45 *.40*
**C15** AP4 20f carmine .45 *.40*
**C16** AP4 32f brown vio 1.75 1.20
**C17** AP4 40f dp ultra 1.40 .80
**C18** AP5 50f claret 1.40 .80
**C19** AP5 72f olive grn 1.90 1.20
**C20** AP5 80f dp violet 1.90 1.20
**C21** AP5 1p emerald ('30) 2.25 .50
**C22** AP5 2p red ('30) 4.50 3.00
**C23** AP5 5p dk blue ('30) 16.50 *27.50*
*Nos. C12-C23 (12)* 33.20 37.80
Set, never hinged 55.00

Exist imperf. Value, set $250.

**1931, Mar. 27 Overprinted**
**C24** AP6 1p orange (Bk) 40.00 *65.00*
**C25** AP6 2p dull vio (G) 40.00 *65.00*
Set, never hinged 160.00

Exist imperf. Value, set $375.

Monoplane over Danube Valley — AP7

Worker Welcoming Plane, Double Cross and Sun Rays — AP8

Spirit of Flight on Plane Wing AP9

"Flight" Holding Propeller AP10

**Wmk. 210**

**1933, June 20 Photo. *Perf. 15***
**C26** AP7 10f blue green 2.90 .25
**C27** AP7 16f purple 2.00 .25

***Perf. 12½x12***

**C28** AP8 20f carmine 4.50 .25
**C29** AP8 40f blue 4.00 1.25
**C30** AP9 48f gray black 9.50 1.50
**C31** AP9 72f bister brn 20.00 2.75
**C32** AP10 1p yellow grn 25.00 2.50
**C33** AP10 2p violet brn 47.50 17.50
**C34** AP10 5p dk gray 82.50 *140.00*
*Nos. C26-C34 (9)* 197.90 166.25
Set, never hinged 375.00

Exist imperf. Value, set $2,600.

**Catalogue values for unused stamps in this section, from this point to the end of the section, are for Never Hinged items.**

Fokker F VII over Mail Coach AP11

Plane over Parliament AP12

Airplane AP13

**1936, May 8** *Perf. 12x12½*

| | | | | | |
|---|---|---|---|---|---|
| **C35** | AP11 | 10f | brt green | .80 | .40 |
| **C36** | AP11 | 20f | crimson | .80 | .40 |
| **C37** | AP11 | 36f | brown | .90 | .40 |
| **C38** | AP12 | 40f | brt blue | .90 | .40 |
| **C39** | AP12 | 52f | red org | 3.25 | .85 |
| **C40** | AP12 | 60f | brt violet | 20.00 | 2.00 |
| **C41** | AP12 | 80f | dk sl grn | 4.00 | .60 |
| **C42** | AP13 | 1p | dk yel grn | 4.75 | .55 |
| **C43** | AP13 | 2p | brown car | 7.50 | 2.00 |
| **C44** | AP13 | 5p | dark blue | 24.00 | 19.50 |
| | | | *Nos. C35-C44 (10)* | 66.90 | 27.10 |
| | | | Set, hinged | 27.50 | |

Exist imperf. Value, set $675.

### Issues of the Republic

Loyalty Tower, Sopron — AP14

Designs: 20f, Cathedral of Esztergom. 50f, Liberty Bridge, Budapest. 70f, Palace Hotel, Lillafüred. 1fo, Vajdahunyad Castle, Budapest. 1.40fo, Visegrád Fortress on the Danube. 3fo, Lake Balaton. 5fo, Parliament Building, Budapest.

*Perf. 12½x12*

**1947, Mar. 5** **Photo.** **Wmk. 210**

| | | | | | |
|---|---|---|---|---|---|
| **C45** | AP14 | 10f | rose lake | .60 | .25 |
| **C46** | AP14 | 20f | gray green | .50 | .25 |
| **C47** | AP14 | 50f | copper brn | .60 | .25 |
| **C48** | AP14 | 70f | olive grn | .60 | .25 |
| **C49** | AP14 | 1fo | gray blue | .75 | .25 |
| **C50** | AP14 | 1.40fo | brown | 1.75 | .25 |
| **C51** | AP14 | 3fo | green | 2.00 | .25 |
| **C52** | AP14 | 5fo | rose violet | 4.75 | 1.00 |
| | | | *Nos. C45-C52 (8)* | 11.55 | 2.75 |

Exist imperf. Value, set $250.

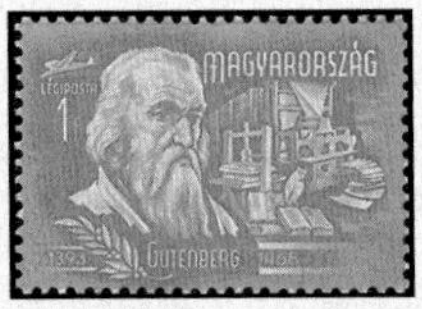


Johannes Gutenberg and Printing Press AP22

Designs: 2f, Columbus. 4f, Robert Fulton. 5f, George Stephenson. 6f, David Schwarz and Ferdinand von Zeppelin. 8f, Thomas A. Edison. 10f, Louis Bleriot. 12f, Roald Amundsen. 30f, Kalman Kando. 40f, Alexander S. Popov.

*Perf. 12x12½*

**1948, May 15** **Wmk. 283**

| | | | | | |
|---|---|---|---|---|---|
| **C53** | AP22 | 1f | orange red | .25 | .25 |
| **C54** | AP22 | 2f | dp magenta | .25 | .25 |
| **C55** | AP22 | 4f | blue | .25 | .25 |
| **C56** | AP22 | 5f | orange brn | .35 | .35 |
| **C57** | AP22 | 6f | green | .35 | .35 |
| **C58** | AP22 | 8f | dp red vio | .35 | .35 |
| **C59** | AP22 | 10f | brown | .50 | .45 |
| **C60** | AP22 | 12f | blue grn | .50 | .45 |
| **C61** | AP22 | 30f | brown rose | 1.75 | 1.50 |
| **C62** | AP22 | 40f | blue violet | 2.25 | 1.75 |
| | | | *Nos. C53-C62 (10)* | 6.80 | 5.95 |

Explorers and inventors.
Exist imperf. Value, set $120.

See Nos. CB3-CB12.

**IMPERFORATE STAMPS**

Through 1991, most air post stamps stamps were also issued imperforate. Where these items form part of a larger set with regular issues, values for imperfs will be included in that of the sets to which they belong, footnoted in the Regular Issues section. For Nos. C63-C452, values for imperfs will be given only for those items not included in sets with regular issues.

### UPU Type

**1949, Nov. 1**

| | | | | | |
|---|---|---|---|---|---|
| **C63** | A171 | 2fo | orange brn | 1.50 | 1.50 |
| *a.* | | | Booklet pane of 6 | 37.50 | |

75th anniv. of the UPU. See No. C81.
Exists imperf.

### Chain Bridge Type and

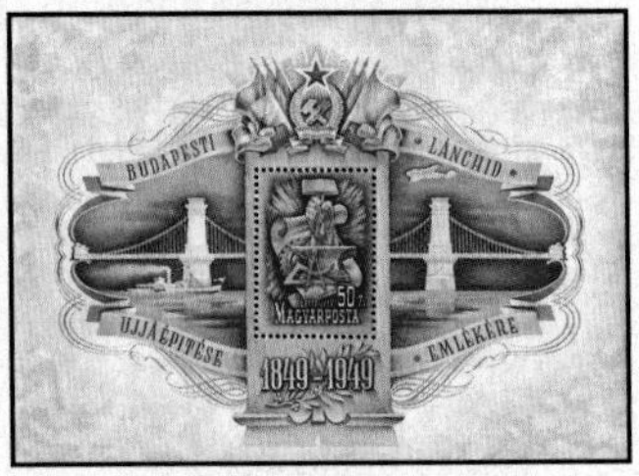


Symbols of Labor — AP25

**1949, Nov. 20**

| | | | | | |
|---|---|---|---|---|---|
| **C64** | A172 | 1.60fo | scarlet | 1.75 | *2.00* |
| **C65** | A172 | 2fo | olive | 1.75 | *2.00* |

**Souvenir Sheet**

***Perf. 12½x12***

| | | | | | |
|---|---|---|---|---|---|
| **C66** | AP25 | 50fo | car lake | 350.00 | 350.00 |

Opening of the Chain Bridge, Budapest, cent.
No. C66 exists imperf. Value $4,000.

Postman and Mail Carrying Vehicles AP26

**1949, Dec. 11** *Perf. 12*

| | | | | | |
|---|---|---|---|---|---|
| **C67** | AP26 | 50f | lilac gray | 6.00 | 6.00 |
| | | | Sheet of 4 | 40.00 | 30.00 |

Stamp Day, 1949.
Exists imperf. Value: single $100; sheet $525.

Plane, Globe, Stamps and Stagecoach — AP27

**1950, Mar. 12** *Perf. 12x12½*

| | | | | | |
|---|---|---|---|---|---|
| **C68** | AP27 | 2fo | red brn & yel | 10.00 | 10.00 |

20th anniv. of the establishment of the Hungarian Post Office Philatelic Museum.
Exists imperf. Value $50.

Chess Emblem, Globe and Plane AP28

**1950, Apr. 9** **Wmk. 106** *Perf. 12*

| | | | | |
|---|---|---|---|---|
| **C69** | AP28 | 1.60fo brown | 6.00 | 2.10 |

World Chess Championship Matches, Budapest.
Exists imperf.

Globes, Parliament Building and Chain Bridge — AP29

**1950, May 16** *Perf. 12x12½*

| | | | | |
|---|---|---|---|---|
| **C70** | AP29 | 1fo red brown | 1.60 | .65 |

Meeting of the World Federation of Trade Unions, Budapest, May 1950.
Exists imperf.

Statue of Liberty and View of Budapest — AP30

Designs: 30f, Crane and apartment house. 70f, Steel mill. 1fo, Stalinyec tractor. 1.60fo, Steamship. 2fo, Reaping-threshing machine. 3fo, Passenger train. 5fo, Matyas Rakosi Steel Mill, Csepel. 10fo, Budaörs Airport.

*Perf. 12½x12*

**1950, Oct. 29** **Engr.** **Unwmk.**

| | | | | | |
|---|---|---|---|---|---|
| **C71** | AP30 | 20f | claret | .65 | .25 |
| **C72** | AP30 | 30f | blue vio | .65 | .25 |
| **C73** | AP30 | 70f | violet brn | .25 | .25 |
| **C74** | AP30 | 1fo | yellow brn | .25 | .25 |
| **C75** | AP30 | 1.60fo | ultra | .70 | .25 |
| **C76** | AP30 | 2fo | red org | .75 | .25 |
| **C77** | AP30 | 3fo | olive blk | 1.00 | .50 |
| **C78** | AP30 | 5fo | gray blue | 2.00 | 1.00 |
| **C79** | AP30 | 10fo | chestnut | 6.25 | 1.75 |
| | | | *Nos. C71-C79 (9)* | 12.50 | 4.75 |

See Nos. C167 and C172.
Exist imperf. Value, set $100.

### Bem Type

**Souvenir Sheet**

**1950, Dec. 10** **Engr.** ***Imperf.***

| | | | | |
|---|---|---|---|---|
| **C80** | A185 | 2fo deep plum | 42.50 | 42.50 |

Stamp Day and Budapest Stamp Exhibition.

### UPU Type of 1949

***Perf. 12x12½, Imperf.***

**1950, July 2** **Photo.** **Wmk. 106**

| | | | | |
|---|---|---|---|---|
| **C81** | A171 | 3fo dk car & dk brn | 40.00 | 40.00 |
| | | Sheet of 4 | 525.00 | 525.00 |

Exists imperf. Value: single $80; sheet of 4 $600.

### Sports Type

Designs: 30f, Volleyball. 40f, Javelin-throwing. 60f, Sports badge. 70f, Soccer. 3fo, Glider meet.

**1950, Dec. 2**

| | | | | | |
|---|---|---|---|---|---|
| **C82** | A188 | 30f | lilac & magenta | .50 | .25 |
| **C83** | A188 | 40f | olive & indigo | .75 | .25 |
| **C84** | A188 | 60f | ol, dk brn & org red | 1.25 | .40 |
| **C85** | A188 | 70f | gray & dk brn | 2.75 | .55 |
| **C86** | A188 | 3fo | buff & dk brn | 4.50 | 2.25 |
| | | | *Nos. C82-C86 (5)* | 9.75 | 3.65 |

Exist imperf.

### Livestock Type

**1951, Apr. 5** **Photo.** *Perf. 12x12½*

| | | | | | |
|---|---|---|---|---|---|
| **C87** | A191 | 20f | Mare & foal | 2.00 | .30 |
| **C88** | A191 | 70f | Sow & shoats | 2.25 | .70 |
| **C89** | A191 | 1fo | Ram & ewe | 3.75 | .90 |
| **C90** | A191 | 1.60fo | Cow & calf | 5.25 | 1.50 |
| | | | *Nos. C87-C90 (4)* | 13.25 | 3.40 |

Exist imperf.

Telegraph Linemen AP34

Designs: 1fo, Workers on vacation. 2fo, Air view of Stalin Bridge.

**1951, Aug. 20**

| | | | | | |
|---|---|---|---|---|---|
| **C91** | AP34 | 70f | henna brown | .85 | .30 |
| **C92** | AP34 | 1fo | blue green | .95 | .35 |
| **C93** | AP34 | 2fo | deep plum | 1.75 | .70 |
| | | | *Nos. C91-C93 (3)* | 3.55 | 1.35 |

Successful conclusion of the 1st year under Hungary's 5-year plan.
Exist imperf.

Tank Column — AP35

**1951, Sept. 29** *Perf. 12½x12*

| | | | | |
|---|---|---|---|---|
| **C94** | AP35 | 60f deep blue | 1.00 | .25 |

Army Day, Sept. 29, 1951.
Exists imperf.

### 1st Stamp Type

**Souvenir Sheet**

**1951, Oct. 6** **Engr.** **Unwmk.**

| | | | | |
|---|---|---|---|---|
| **C95** | A208 | 60f olive green | 75.00 | 65.00 |

Stamp exhibition to commemorate the 80th anniv. of Hungary's 1st postage stamp.
Exists imperf. Value $200.
Twelve hundred copies in rose lilac, perf. and imperf., were presented to exhibitors and members of the arranging committee of the exhibition. Value, each $1,600.

Avocet — AP37

Hungarian Birds: 30f, White stork. 40f, Golden oriole. 50f, Kentish plover. 60f, Black-winged stilt. 70f, Lesser gray shrike. 80f, Great bustard. 1fo, Redfooted falcon. 1.40fo, European bee-eater. 1.60fo, Glossy ibis. 2.50fo, Great white egret.

*Perf. 13x11*

**1952, Mar. 16** **Photo.** **Wmk. 106**

**Birds in Natural Colors**

| | | | | | |
|---|---|---|---|---|---|
| **C96** | AP37 | 20f | emer, *grnsh* | .25 | .25 |
| **C97** | AP37 | 30f | sage grn, *grysh* | .25 | .25 |
| **C98** | AP37 | 40f | brown, *cr* | .35 | .25 |
| **C99** | AP37 | 50f | orange, *cr* | .40 | .25 |
| **C100** | AP37 | 60f | deep carmine | .50 | .25 |
| **C101** | AP37 | 70f | red org, *cr* | .60 | .35 |
| **C102** | AP37 | 80f | olive, *cr* | .80 | .45 |
| **C103** | AP37 | 1fo | dp blue, *bluish* | 1.00 | .55 |
| **C104** | AP37 | 1.40fo | gray, *grysh* | 2.00 | .65 |
| **C105** | AP37 | 1.60fo | org brn, *cr* | 2.50 | .85 |
| **C106** | AP37 | 2.50fo | rose vio, *cr* | 3.50 | 1.25 |
| | | | *Nos. C96-C106 (11)* | 12.15 | 5.35 |

Exist imperf. Value, set $100.

### Olympic Games Type

Designs: 1.70fo, hammer thrower; 2fo, Stadium, Budapest.

**1952, May 26** ***Perf. 11***

| | | | | | |
|---|---|---|---|---|---|
| C107 | A217 | 1.70fo | dp red orange | 2.10 | 1.00 |
| C108 | A217 | 2fo | olive brown | 2.50 | 1.25 |

Issued to publicize Hungary's participation in the Olympic Games, Helsinki, 1952.
Exists imperf.

Leonardo da Vinci — AP39

**1952, June 15** ***Perf. 12½x12***

| | | | | | |
|---|---|---|---|---|---|
| C109 | AP39 | 1.60fo | shown | 1.50 | 1.00 |
| C110 | AP39 | 2fo | Victor Hugo | 1.50 | 1.00 |

Exist imperf. Value, set $35.

AP40

AP41

**1953, Mar. 4** ***Perf. 12x12½***

| | | | | | |
|---|---|---|---|---|---|
| C111 | AP40 | 20f | Red squirrel | .50 | .25 |
| C112 | AP41 | 30f | Hedgehog | .65 | .25 |
| C113 | AP41 | 40f | Hare | .65 | .30 |
| C114 | AP40 | 50f | Beech marten | .80 | .40 |
| C115 | AP41 | 60f | Otter | 1.00 | .45 |
| C116 | AP41 | 70f | Red fox | 1.00 | .50 |
| C117 | AP40 | 80f | Fallow deer | 1.25 | .75 |
| C118 | AP41 | 1fo | Roe deer | 1.60 | 1.00 |
| C119 | AP41 | 1.50fo | Boar | 4.00 | 1.25 |
| C120 | AP40 | 2fo | Red deer | 4.50 | 1.50 |
| | | | *Nos. C111-C120 (10)* | 15.95 | 6.65 |

Exist imperf. Value, set $75.

### Type of Regular Issue

Designs: 1fo, Children at Balaton Lake. 1.50fo, Workers' Home at Lillafured.

**1953, Apr. 19** ***Perf. 12***

| | | | | | |
|---|---|---|---|---|---|
| C121 | A228 | 1fo | brt grnsh blue | .65 | .25 |
| C122 | A228 | 1.50fo | dp red lilac | 1.25 | .40 |

Exist imperf.

### People's Stadium Type

**1953, Aug. 20** ***Perf. 11***

| | | | | | |
|---|---|---|---|---|---|
| C123 | A232 | 80f | Water polo | 1.00 | .25 |
| C124 | A232 | 1fo | Boxing | 2.00 | .25 |
| C125 | A232 | 2fo | Soccer | 2.25 | .80 |
| C126 | A232 | 3fo | Track | 2.50 | .95 |
| C127 | A232 | 5fo | Stadium | 3.75 | 1.75 |
| | | | *Nos. C123-C127 (5)* | 11.50 | 3.40 |

Exist imperf.

### No. C125 Overprinted in Black

**1953, Dec. 3**

| | | | | | |
|---|---|---|---|---|---|
| C128 | A232 | 2fo | green & brown | 22.50 | 20.00 |

Hungary's success in the soccer matches at Wembley, England, Nov. 25, 1953. Counterfeits exist.
Exists imperf. Value $300.

Janos Bihari and Scene from Verbunkos AP44

Portraits: 40f, Ferenc Erkel. 60f, Franz Liszt. 70f, Mihaly Mosonyi. 80f, Karl Goldmark. 1fo, Bela Bartok. 2fo, Zoltan Kodaly.

**1953, Dec. 5** **Photo.** ***Perf. 12***

**Frames and Portraits in Brown**

| | | | | | |
|---|---|---|---|---|---|
| C129 | AP44 | 30f | blue gray | .35 | .25 |
| C130 | AP44 | 40f | orange | .35 | .25 |
| C131 | AP44 | 60f | green | .55 | .25 |
| C132 | AP44 | 70f | red | .45 | .30 |
| C133 | AP44 | 80f | gray blue | .50 | .40 |
| C134 | AP44 | 1fo | olive bis | 1.00 | .60 |
| C135 | AP44 | 2fo | violet | 1.50 | 1.25 |
| | | | *Nos. C129-C135 (7)* | 4.70 | 3.30 |

Hungarian composers.
Exists imperf. Value, set $40.

Carrot Beetle — AP45

May (or June) Beetle AP46

Designs: Various beetles. 60f, Bee.

***Perf. 12½x12, 12x12½***

**1954, Feb. 6** **Wmk. 106**

| | | | | | |
|---|---|---|---|---|---|
| C136 | AP45 | 30f | dp org & dk brn | .50 | .25 |
| C137 | AP46 | 40f | grn & dk brn | .60 | .25 |
| C138 | AP46 | 50f | rose brn & blk | .85 | .30 |
| C139 | AP46 | 60f | vio, dk brn & yel | .85 | .45 |
| C140 | AP45 | 80f | grnsh gray, pur & rose | 1.25 | .70 |
| C141 | AP45 | 1fo | ocher & blk | 1.75 | .80 |
| C142 | AP46 | 1.20fo | dl grn & dk brn | 2.10 | 1.00 |
| C143 | AP46 | 1.50fo | ol brn & dk brn | 3.25 | 1.25 |
| C144 | AP46 | 2fo | hn brn & dk brn | 4.25 | 1.50 |
| C145 | AP45 | 3fo | bl grn & dk brn | 5.50 | 2.00 |
| | | | *Nos. C136-C145 (10)* | 20.90 | 8.50 |

Exists imperf. Value, set $110.

Lunchtime at the Nursery AP47

Designs: 1.50fo, Mother taking child from doctor. 2fo, Nurse and children.

**1954, Mar. 8** ***Perf. 12***

| | | | | | |
|---|---|---|---|---|---|
| C146 | AP47 | 1fo | olive green | 1.00 | .40 |
| C147 | AP47 | 1.50fo | red brown | 1.40 | .50 |
| C148 | AP47 | 2fo | blue green | 2.40 | 1.25 |
| | | | *Nos. C146-C148 (3)* | 4.55 | 2.00 |

Exist imperf.

Model Glider Construction — AP48

Boy Flying Model Glider AP49

Designs: 60f, Gliders. 80f, Pilot leaving plane. 1fo, Parachutists. 1.20fo, Biplane. 1.50fo, Plane over Danube. 2fo, Jet planes.

**1954, June 25** ***Perf. 11***

| | | | | | |
|---|---|---|---|---|---|
| C149 | AP48 | 40f | brn, ol & dk bl gray | .30 | .25 |
| C150 | AP49 | 50f | gray & red brn | .40 | .25 |
| C151 | AP48 | 60f | red brn & dk bl gray | .40 | .25 |
| C152 | AP49 | 80f | violet & sep | .45 | .25 |
| C153 | AP48 | 1fo | brn & dk bl gray | .65 | .25 |
| C154 | AP49 | 1.20fo | olive & sep | 1.00 | .25 |
| C155 | AP48 | 1.50fo | cl & dk bl gray | 1.25 | .50 |
| C156 | AP49 | 2fo | blue & dk brn | 1.90 | .50 |
| | | | *Nos. C149-C156 (8)* | 6.35 | 2.50 |

Exist imperf. Value, set $75.

### Jokai Type

Souvenir Sheet

**1954, Oct. 17** **Engr.** ***Perf. 12½x12***

| | | | | | |
|---|---|---|---|---|---|
| C157 | A242 | 1fo | violet blue | 37.50 | 37.50 |

Stamp Day. Exists imperforate. Value $90.

Children on Sled — AP51

Skaters AP52

50f, Ski racer. 60f, Ice yacht. 80f, Ice hockey. 1fo, Ski jumper. 1.50fo, Downhill ski racer. 2fo, Man and woman exhibition-skating.

**1955** **Photo.** ***Perf. 12***

| | | | | | |
|---|---|---|---|---|---|
| C158 | AP51 | 40f | multi | .55 | .25 |
| C159 | AP52 | 50f | multi | .35 | .25 |
| C160 | AP51 | 60f | multi | .35 | .25 |
| C161 | AP52 | 80f | multi | .45 | .25 |
| C162 | AP51 | 1fo | multi | 1.10 | .30 |
| C163 | AP52 | 1.20fo | multi | 1.10 | .30 |
| C164 | AP51 | 1.50fo | multi | 2.75 | .60 |
| C165 | AP52 | 2fo | multi | 3.25 | .50 |
| | | | *Nos. C158-C165 (8)* | 9.90 | 2.70 |

Exist imperf. Value, set $75.
Issued: 1.20fo, 2fo, Jan. 27; others Feb. 26.

### Government Printing Plant Type

Souvenir Sheet

**1955, May 28** ***Perf. 12x12½***

| | | | | | |
|---|---|---|---|---|---|
| C166 | A247 | 5fo | hn brn & gray grn | 32.50 | 32.50 |

Cent. of the establishment of the government printing plant.
Exists imperf. Value $160.

### No. C78 Printed on Aluminum Foil

***Perf. 12½x12***

**1955, Oct. 5** **Engr.** **Unwmk.**

| | | | | | |
|---|---|---|---|---|---|
| C167 | AP30 | 5fo | gray blue | 15.00 | 12.50 |

Intl. Cong. of the Light Metal Industry and for 20 years of aluminum production in Hungary.
Exists imperf. Value $100.

### Bartok Type

**Wmk. 106**

**1955, Oct. 9** **Photo.** ***Perf. 12***

| | | | | | |
|---|---|---|---|---|---|
| C168 | A252 | 1fo | gray green | 2.00 | 1.25 |
| C169 | A252 | 1fo | violet brn | 3.50 | 2.00 |
| *a.* | | | With ticket | 15.00 | 12.50 |

10th anniv. of the death of Bela Bartok, composer. No. C169a was issued for the Day of the Stamp, Oct. 16, 1955. The 5fo sales price, marked on the attached ticket, was the admission fee to any one of 14 simultaneous stamp shows.
Exist imperf. Value, set with ticket, $135.

"Esperanto" — AP55

Lazarus Ludwig Zamenhof AP56

**1957, June 8**

| | | | | | |
|---|---|---|---|---|---|
| C170 | AP55 | 60f | red brown | .50 | .25 |
| C171 | AP56 | 1fo | dark green | .50 | .30 |

10th anniversary of the death of L. L. Zamenhof, inventor of Esperanto.
Exist imperf. Value $30.

### Type of 1950

Design: 20fo, Budaörs Airport.

***Perf. 12½x12***

**1957, July 18** **Engr.** **Unwmk.**

| | | | | | |
|---|---|---|---|---|---|
| C172 | AP30 | 20fo | dk slate grn | 10.00 | 10.00 |
| | | | Punched 3 holes | 11.00 | 11.00 |

A few days after issuance, stocks of No. C172 were punched with three holes and used on domestic surface mail.
Exist imperf. Value $70.

Courier and Fort Buda
AP57

Design: No. C174, Plane over Budapest.

**Wmk. 106**

**1957, Oct. 13 Photo. *Perf. 12***

**C173** AP57 1fo ol bis & brn, *buff* 1.00 1.00
**C174** AP57 1fo ol bis & dp cl, *buff* 1.00 1.00
*a.* Strip of #C173-C174 + label 2.50 2.50

Stamp Day, Oct. 20th. The triptych sold for 6fo.
Exists imperf. Value, strip $30.

### Type of Regular Pigeon Issue

Design: 3fo, Two carrier pigeons.

**1957, Dec. 14 *Perf. 12x12½***

**C175** A266 3fo red, grn, gray & blk .90 .50

Exists imperf.

Hungarian Pavilion, Brussels — AP58

Designs: 40f, Map, lake and local products. 60f, Parliament. 1fo, Chain Bridge, Budapest. 1.40fo, Arms of Hungary and Belgium. 2fo, Fountain, Brussels, vert. 3fo, City Hall, Brussels vert. 5fo, Exposition emblem.

***Perf. 14½x15***

**1958, Apr. 17 Litho. Wmk. 106**

**C176** AP58 20f red org & red brn .25 .25
**C177** AP58 40f lt blue & brn .25 .25
**C178** AP58 60f crimson & sep .25 .25
**C179** AP58 1fo bis & red brn .25 .25
**C180** AP58 1.40fo dull vio & multi .40 .25
**C181** AP58 2fo gldn brn & dk brn .40 .25
**C182** AP58 3fo bl grn & sep 1.50 .40
**C183** AP58 5fo gray ol, blk, red, bl & yel 1.90 .60
*Nos. C176-C183 (8)* 5.20 2.50

Universal and Intl. Exposition at Brussels.
Exist imperf. Value, set $20.

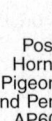

View of Prague and Morse Code
AP59

**1958, June 30 Photo. *Perf. 12x12½***

**C184** AP59 1fo rose brown .35 .25

See No. 1194a for se-tenant pair.
Conference of Postal Ministers of Communist Countries at Prague, June 30-July 8.
Exists imperf.

Post Horn, Pigeon and Pen
AP60

No. C185, Stamp under magnifying glass.

**1958, Oct. 25 Wmk. 106 *Perf. 12***

**C185** AP60 1fo dp car & bis 1.00 1.00
**C186** AP60 1fo yel grn & bis 1.00 1.00
*a.* Strip, #C185-C186 + label 2.50 2.50

Natl. Stamp Exhib., Budapest, 10/25-11/2. #C185 inscribed: "XXXI Belyegnap 1958."
Exist imperf. Value, strip $25.

**1958, Oct. 26**

Designs: 60f, as No. C186. 1fo, Ship, plane, locomotive and pen surrounding letter.

**C187** AP60 60f dp plum & grysh buff .40 .25
**C188** AP60 1fo bl & grysh buff .60 .25

Issued for Letter Writing Week.
Exist imperf. Value, set $18.

Plane over Heroes' Square Budapest — AP61

Design: 5fo, Plane over Tower of Sopron.

***Perf. 12½x12***

**1958, Nov. 3 Engr. Wmk. 106**

**C189** AP61 3fo gray, rose vio & red 1.25 .60
**C190** AP61 5fo gray, dk bl & red 1.50 .90

40th anniv. of Hungarian air post stamps.
Exist imperf. Value, set $20.

### Same Without Commemorative Inscription

Plane over: 20f, Szeged. 30f, Sarospatak. 70f, Gyor. 1fo, Budapest, Opera House. 1.60fo, Veszprém. 2fo, Budapest, Chain Bridge. 3fo, Sopron. 5fo, Heroes' Square, Budapest. 10fo, Budapest, Academy of Science and Parliament. 20fo, Budapest.

**1958, Dec. 31 Engr. Wmk. 106**
**Yellow Paper and Vermilion Inscriptions**

**C191** AP61 20f green .25 .25
**C192** AP61 30f violet .25 .25
**C193** AP61 70f brown vio .25 .25
**C194** AP61 1fo blue .40 .25
**C195** AP61 1.60fo purple .40 .25
**C196** AP61 2fo Prus green .50 .25
**C197** AP61 3fo brown 1.00 .25
**C198** AP61 5fo olive green 1.50 .25
**C199** AP61 10fo dark blue 2.25 .35
**C200** AP61 20fo brown 4.25 .75
*Nos. C191-C200 (10)* 11.05 3.10

Exist imperf. Value, set $60.

### Transport Type of Regular Issue

Design: 3fo, Early plane.

**1959, May Litho. *Perf. 14½x15***

**C201** A279 3fo dl lil, blk, yel & brn 2.00 1.25

Exist imperf.

Tihany — AP62

Designs: 70f, Ship. 1fo, Heviz and water lily. 1.70fo, Sailboat and fisherman statue.

**1959, July 15 Photo. *Perf. 11½x12***

**C202** AP62 20f brt green .25 .25
**C203** AP62 70f brt blue .25 .25
**C204** AP62 1fo ultra & car rose .25 .25
**C205** AP62 1.70fo red brn, *yel* .50 .30
*Nos. C202-C205 (4)* 1.10 .90

Issued to publicize Lake Balaton and the opening of the Summer University.
Exist imperf.

### Moth-Butterfly Type of 1959

Butterflies: 1fo, Lycaena virgaureae. 2fo, Acherontia atropos, horiz. 3fo, Red admiral.

***Perf. 11½x12, 12x11½***

**1959, Nov. 20 Wmk. 106**
**Butterflies in Natural Colors**

**C206** A290 1fo black & lt bl grn .90 .25
**C207** A290 2fo black & lilac 1.50 .35
**C208** A290 3fo dk gray & emer 2.25 .75
*Nos. C206-C208 (3)* 4.65 1.30

Exist imperf.

### Souvenir Sheet

Rockets in Orbit, Gagarin, Titov & Glenn — AP63

***Perf. 11, Imperf.***

**1962, Mar. 29 Unwmk.**

**C209** AP63 10fo multi 12.00 12.00

Cosmonants Yuri A. Gagarin and Gherman Titov, USSR and astronaut John H. Glenn, Jr., US.
Exists imperf. Value $40.

### Soccer Type of 1962

Flags of Hungary and Great Britain.

**1962, May 21 Photo. *Perf. 11***
**Flags in National Colors**

**C209A** A323 2fo greenish bister 1.10 .30

Exists imperf.

Glider and Lilienthal's 1898 Design — AP64

Designs: 30f, Icarus and Aero Club emblem. 60f, Light monoplane and 1912 aerobatic plane. 80f, Airship GZ-1 and Montgolfier balloon. 1fo, IL-18 Malev and Wright 1903 plane. 1.40fo, Stunt plane and Nyesterov's 1913 plane. 2fo, Helicopter and Asboth's 1929 helicopter. 3fo, Supersonic bomber and Zhukovski's turbomotor. 4fo, Space rocket and Tsiolkovsky's rocket.

**1962, July 19 Unwmk. *Perf. 15***

**C210** AP64 30f blue & dull yel .25 .25
**C211** AP64 40f yel grn & ultra .25 .25
**C212** AP64 60f ultra & ver .25 .25
**C213** AP64 80f grnsh bl & sil .25 .25
**C214** AP64 1fo lilac, sil & bl .25 .25
**C215** AP64 1.40fo blue & org .25 .25
**C216** AP64 2fo bluish grn & brn .25 .25
**C217** AP64 3fo vio, sil & bl .50 .25
**C218** AP64 4fo grn, sil & blk .80 .35
*Nos. C210-C218 (9)* 3.05 2.35

Issued to show flight development: "From Icarus to the Space Rocket."
Exist imperf. Value, set $20.

Earth, TV Screens and Rockets — AP65

Design: 2fo, Andrian G. Nikolayev, Pavel R. Popovich and rockets.

**1962, Sept. 4 *Perf. 12***

**C219** AP65 1fo dk bl & org brn .70 .35
**C220** AP65 2fo dk bl & org brn .80 .55
*a* Pair, #C219-C220 1.75 .90

First group space flight of Vostoks 3 and 4, Aug. 11-15, 1962. Printed in alternating horizontal rows.
Exist imperf. Value $16.

John H. Glenn, Jr.
AP66

Astronauts: 40f, Yuri A. Gagarin. 60f, Gherman Titov. 1.40fo, Scott Carpenter. 1.70fo, Andrian G. Nikolayev. 2.60fo, Pavel R. Popovich. 3fo, Walter Schirra.

**1962, Oct. 27 *Perf. 12x11½***
**Portraits in Bister**

**C221** AP66 40f purple .25 .25
**C222** AP66 60f dark green .25 .25
**C223** AP66 1fo dark bl grn .25 .25
**C224** AP66 1.40fo dark brown .25 .25
**C225** AP66 1.70fo deep blue .30 .25
**C226** AP66 2.60fo violet .65 .30
**C227** AP66 3fo red brown 1.10 .45
*Nos. C221-C227 (7)* 3.05 2.00

Issued to honor the first seven astronauts and in connection with the Astronautical Congress in Paris.
Exist imperf. Value, set $15.

Eagle Owl — AP67

Birds: 40f, Osprey. 60f, Marsh harrier. 80f, Booted eagle. 1fo, African fish eagle. 2fo, Lammergeier. 3fo, Golden eagle. 4fo, Kestrel.

**1962, Nov. 18 Litho. *Perf. 11½***
**Birds in Natural Colors**

**C228** AP67 30f yel grn & blk .25 .25
**C229** AP67 40f org yel & blk .25 .25
**C230** AP67 60f bister & blk .25 .25
**C231** AP67 80f lt grn & blk .25 .25
**C232** AP67 1fo ol bis & blk .25 .25
**C233** AP67 2fo bluish grn & blk .35 .25
**C234** AP67 3fo lt vio & blk .65 .30
**C235** AP67 4fo dp org & blk 1.25 .50
*Nos. C228-C235 (8)* 3.50 2.30

Exist imperf. Value, set $25.

Radio Mast and Albania No. 623
AP68

Designs (Communication symbols and rocket stamps of various countries): 30f, Bulgaria #C77, vert. 40f, Czechoslovakia #1108. 50f, Communist China #380. 60f, North Korea. 80f, Poland #875. 1fo, Hungary #1386. 1.20fo, Mongolia #189, vert. 1.40fo, DDR #580. 1.70fo, Romania #1200. 2fo, Russia #2456, vert. 2.60fo, North Viet Nam.

***Perf. 12x11½, 11½x12***

**1963, May 9 Photo. Unwmk.**
**Stamp Reproductions in Original Colors**

**C236** AP68 20f olive green .25 .25
**C237** AP68 30f rose lake .25 .25
**C238** AP68 40f violet .25 .25
**C239** AP68 50f brt blue .25 .25
**C240** AP68 60f orange brn .25 .25
**C241** AP68 80f ultra .25 .25
**C242** AP68 1fo dull red brn .25 .25
**C243** AP68 1.20fo aqua .25 .25
**C244** AP68 1.40fo olive .25 .25
**C245** AP68 1.70fo brown olive .25 .25
**C246** AP68 2fo rose lilac .30 .25
**C247** AP68 2.60fo bluish green .60 .40
*Nos. C236-C247 (12)* 3.40 3.15

5th Conference of Postal Ministers of Communist Countries, Budapest.
Exist imperf. Value, set $20.

Souvenir Sheet

Globe and Spaceships — AP69

***Perf. 11½x12, Imperf.***

**1963, July 13** **Unwmk.**

**C248** AP69 10fo dk & lt blue 8.00 7.00

Space flights of Valeri Bykovski, June 14-19, and Valentina Tereshkova, 1st woman cosmonaut, June 16-19, 1963.

Exists imperf. Value $25.

Souvenir Sheet

Mt. Fuji and Stadium — AP70

**1964, Sept. 22** **Photo.** ***Perf. 11½x12***

**C249** AP70 10fo multi 4.00 3.50

18th Olympic Games, Tokyo, Oct. 10-24.

Exists imperf. Value $20.

**Bridge Type of 1964**

Souvenir Sheet

Design: Elizabeth Bridge.

**1964, Nov. 21** **Photo.** ***Perf. 11***

**C250** A356 10fo silver & dp grn 3.75 3.50

No. C250 contains one 59x20mm stamp.

Exists imperf. Value $100.

Lt. Col. Alexei Leonov in Space — AP71

Design: 2fo, Col. Pavel Belyayev, Lt. Col. Alexei Leonov and Voskhod 2.

**1965, Apr. 17** **Photo.** ***Perf. 11½x12***

**C251** AP71 1fo violet & gray .45 .25

**C252** AP71 2fo rose claret & ocher 1.10 .65

Space flight of Voskhod 2 and of Lt. Col. Alexei Leonov, the first man floating in space.

Exists imperf. Value, set $15.

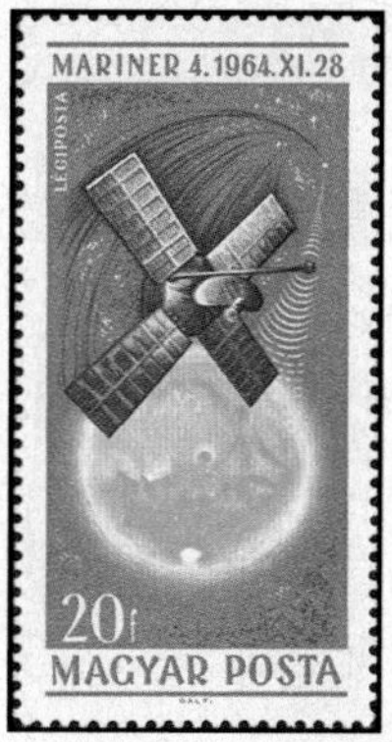


Mariner IV (USA) — AP72

New achievements in space research: 30f, San Marco satellite, Italy. 40f, Molniya satellite, USSR. 60f, Moon rocket, 1965, USSR. 1fo, Shapir rocket, France. 2.50fo, Zond III satellite, USSR. 3fo, Syncom III satellite, US. 10fo, Rocket sending off satellites, horiz.

**1965, Dec. 31** **Photo.** ***Perf. 11***

| | | | | |
|---|---|---|---|---|
| **C253** | AP72 | 20f ultra, blk & org yel | .25 | .25 |
| **C254** | AP72 | 30f brn, vio & yel | .25 | .25 |
| **C255** | AP72 | 40f vio, brn & pink | .25 | .25 |
| **C256** | AP72 | 60f lt pur, blk & org yel | .25 | .25 |
| **C257** | AP72 | 1fo red lil, blk & buff | .30 | .25 |
| **C258** | AP72 | 2.50fo rose cl, blk & gray | .60 | .35 |
| **C259** | AP72 | 3fo bl grn, blk & bis | .75 | .60 |
| | | *Nos. C253-C259 (7)* | 2.65 | 2.20 |

**Souvenir Sheet**

**1965, Dec. 20**

**C260** AP72 10fo brt bl, yel & dk ol 3.50 3.00

Exist imperf. Value: Nos. C253-C259 $20; No. C260 $25.

**Sport Type of Regular Issue**

Souvenir Sheet

10fo, Women hurdlers and Ferihegy airport.

**1966, Sept. 4** **Photo.** ***Perf. 12x11½***

**C261** A384 10fo brt bl, brn & red 3.00 3.00

Exists imperf. Value $20.

Plane over Helsinki — AP73

Plane over Cities Served by Hungarian Airlines: 50f, Athens. 1fo, Beirut. 1.10fo, Frankfort on the Main. 1.20fo, Cairo. 1.50fo, Copenhagen. 2fo, London. 2.50fo, Moscow. 3fo, Paris. 4fo, Prague. 5fo, Rome. 10fo, Damascus. 20fo, Budapest.

**1966-67** **Photo.** ***Perf. 12x11½***

| | | | | |
|---|---|---|---|---|
| **C262** | AP73 | 20f brown org | .25 | .25 |
| **C263** | AP73 | 50f brown | .25 | .25 |
| **C264** | AP73 | 1fo blue | .25 | .25 |
| **C265** | AP73 | 1.10fo black | .25 | .25 |
| **C266** | AP73 | 1.20fo orange | .25 | .25 |
| **C267** | AP73 | 1.50fo blue grn | .25 | .25 |
| **C268** | AP73 | 2fo brt blue | .30 | .25 |
| **C269** | AP73 | 2.50fo brt red | .30 | .25 |
| **C270** | AP73 | 3fo yel grn | .40 | .25 |
| **C271** | AP73 | 4fo brown red | .40 | .25 |
| **C272** | AP73 | 5fo brt pur | .25 | .25 |
| **C273** | AP73 | 10fo violet bl ('67) | .25 | .25 |
| **C274** | AP73 | 20fo gray ol ('67) | .40 | .25 |
| | | *Nos. C262-C274 (13)* | 3.80 | 3.25 |

Exist imperf. Value, set $90.

See No. C276.

Souvenir Sheet

Icarus Falling — AP73a

**1968, May 11** **Photo.** ***Perf. 11***

**C275** AP73a 10fo multicolored 2.75 2.50

In memory of the astronauts Edward H. White, US, Vladimir M. Komarov and Yuri A. Gagarin, USSR.

Exists imperf. Value $20.

**Type of 1966-67 without "Legiposta" Inscription**

Design: 2.60fo, Malev Airlines jet over St. Stephen's Cathedral, Vienna.

**1968, July 4** **Photo.** ***Perf. 12x11½***

**C276** AP73 2.60fo violet .50 .25

50th anniv. of regular airmail service between Budapest and Vienna.

Exists imperf. Value $12.50.

Women Swimmers and Aztec Calendar Stone — AP74

Aztec Calendar Stone, Olympic Rings and: 60f, Soccer. 80f, Wrestling. 1fo, Canoeing. 1.40fo, Gymnast on rings. 3fo, Fencing. 4fo, Javelin.

**1968, Aug. 21** **Photo.** ***Perf. 12***

| | | | | |
|---|---|---|---|---|
| **C277** | AP74 | 20f brt bl & multi | .25 | .25 |
| **C278** | AP74 | 60f green & multi | .25 | .25 |
| **C279** | AP74 | 80f car rose & multi | .25 | .25 |
| **C280** | AP74 | 1fo grnsh bl & multi | .25 | .25 |
| **C281** | AP74 | 1.40fo violet & multi | .25 | .25 |
| **C282** | AP74 | 3fo brt lilac & multi | .65 | .35 |
| **C283** | AP74 | 4fo green & multi | 1.00 | .55 |
| | | *Nos. C277-C283,CB31 (8)* | 3.25 | 2.50 |

Issued to publicize the 19th Olympic Games, Mexico City, Oct. 12-27.

Exist imperf. Value, set (8) $20.

Souvenir Sheet

Apollo 8 Trip Around the Moon — AP75

**1969, Feb.** **Photo.** ***Perf. 12½***

**C284** AP75 10fo multi 2.00 2.00

Man's 1st flight around the moon, Dec. 21-27, 1968.

Exists imperf. Value $20.

Soyuz 4 and 5, and Men in Space — AP76

Design: No. C286, Soyuz 4 and 5.

**1969, Mar. 21** **Photo.** ***Perf. 12x11½***

**C285** AP76 2fo multi .35 .35

**C286** AP76 2fo dk bl, lt bl & red .35 .35

*a.* Strip, # C285-C286 + label .85

First team flights of Russian spacecraft Soyuz 4 and 5, Jan. 16, 1969.

Exist imperf. Value, strip $8.

Journey to the Moon, by Jules Verne — AP77

Designs: 60f, Tsiolkovski's space station. 1fo, Luna 1. 1.50fo, Ranger 7. 2fo, Luna 9 landing on moon. 2.50fo, Apollo 8 in orbit around moon. 3fo, Soyuz 4 and 5 docking in space. 4fo, Lunar landing module landing on moon. 10fo, Apollo 11 astronauts on moon and lunar landing module.

**1969** **Photo.** ***Perf. 12x11½***

| | | | | |
|---|---|---|---|---|
| **C287** | AP77 | 40f multi | .25 | .25 |
| **C288** | AP77 | 60f multi | .25 | .25 |
| **C289** | AP77 | 1fo multi | .25 | .25 |
| **C290** | AP77 | 1.50fo multi | .25 | .25 |
| **C291** | AP77 | 2fo multi | .25 | .25 |
| **C292** | AP77 | 2.50fo multi | .25 | .25 |
| **C293** | AP77 | 3fo multi | .50 | .25 |
| **C294** | AP77 | 4fo multi | .75 | .40 |
| | | *Nos. C287-C294 (8)* | 2.75 | 2.15 |

**Souvenir Sheet**

***Perf. 11***

**C295** AP77 10fo multi 4.00 4.00

Moon landing issue. See note after Algeria No. 427.

No. C295 contains one 74x49mm stamp. Issued: #C287-C294, Nov. 1; #C295, Aug. 15.

Exist imperf. Value: Nos. C287-C294 $15; No. C295 $30.

Daimler, 1886 — AP78

Automobiles: 60f, Peugeot, 1894. 1fo, Benz, 1901. 1.50fo, Cudell mail truck, 1902. 2fo, Rolls Royce, 1908. 2.50fo, Model T Ford, 1908. 3fo, Vermorel, 1912. 4fo, Csonka mail car, 1912.

**1970, Feb. 28** **Photo.** ***Perf. 12***

| | | | | |
|---|---|---|---|---|
| **C296** | AP78 | 40f ocher & multi | .25 | .25 |
| **C297** | AP78 | 60f multi | .25 | .25 |
| **C298** | AP78 | 1fo red & multi | .25 | .25 |
| **C299** | AP78 | 1.50fo bl & multi | .25 | .25 |
| **C300** | AP78 | 2fo multi | .25 | .25 |
| **C301** | AP78 | 2.50fo vio & multi | .30 | .25 |
| **C302** | AP78 | 3fo multi | .40 | .30 |
| **C303** | AP78 | 4fo multi | .70 | .50 |
| | | *Nos. C296-C303 (8)* | 2.65 | 2.30 |

Exist imperf. Value, set $15.

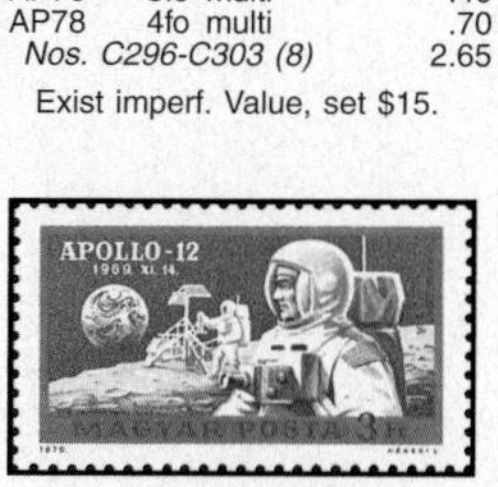


American Astronauts on Moon — AP79

No. C305, Soyuz 6, 7 and 8 in space.

**1970, Mar. 20 Photo.** ***Perf. 11***
**C304** AP79 3fo blue & multi .75 .75
**C305** AP79 3fo car rose & multi .75 .75

Landing of Apollo 12 on the moon, Nov. 14, 1969, and group flight of Russian spacecraft Soyuz 6, 7 & 8, Oct. 11-13, 1969.
Nos. C304-C305 issued in sheets of 4. Size: 112½x78mm.
Exist imperf. Value: set $17.50; sheets of 4 $40.

"Rain at Foot of Fujiyama," by Hokusai, and Pavilion — AP80

3fo, Sun Tower, Peace Bell and globe.

**1970, Apr. 30 Photo.** ***Perf. 12½***
**C306** AP80 2fo multi .75 .75
**C307** AP80 3fo multi .75 .75

Issued to publicize EXPO '70 International Exhibition, Osaka, Japan, Mar. 15-Sept. 13.
Exist imperf. Value, set $10.

Miniature Sheets

Phases of Apollo 13 Moon Flight — AP81

Vignettes of No. C308: Apollo 13 over moon; return to earth; capsule with parachutes; capsule floating, aircraft carrier and helicopter.
Vignettes of No. C309: Soyuz 9 on way to launching pad; launching of Soyuz 9 capsule in orbit; cosmonauts Andrian Nikolayev and Vitaly Sevastyanov.
Vignettes of No. C310: Luna 16 approaching moon; module on moon; landing; nose cone on ground.
Vignettes of No. C311: Lunokhod 1 on moon; trajectories of Luna 17 around earth and moon.

**1970-71 Litho.** ***Perf. 11½***
**C308** AP81 Sheet of 4 2.00 2.00

**Photo.**
**C309** AP81 Sheet of 4 2.00 2.00
**C310** AP81 Sheet of 4 ('71) 2.00 2.00
**C311** AP81 Sheet of 4 ('71) 2.00 2.00

Nos. C308-C311 were valid for postage only as full sheets. Each contains four 2.50fo vignettes.
No. C308 for the aborted moon flight and safe return of Apollo 13, 4/11-17/70.
No. C309 for the 424-hour flight of Soyuz 9, 6/1-9.
No. C310 for Luna 16, the unmanned, automated moon mission, 9/12-24/70.
No. C311 for Luna 17, unmanned, automated moon mission, 11/10-17/70.
Exist imperf. Value, set $70.
Issued: #C308, 6/10; #C309, 9/4; #C310, 1/15; #C311 3/8.

Souvenir Sheet

American Astronauts on Moon — AP82

**1971, Mar. 31** ***Perf. 12½***
**C312** AP82 10fo multi 2.00 2.00

Apollo 14 moon landing, 1/31-2/9/71.
Exists imperf. Value $20.
See Nos. C315, C326-C328.

### Hunting Type of Regular Issue
Souvenir Sheet

Design: 10fo, Red deer group.

**1971, Aug. 27 Photo.** ***Perf. 11***
**C313** A460 10fo multi 3.00 2.50

No. C313 contains one 70x45mm stamp.
Exists imperf. Value $35.

Souvenir Sheet

Astronauts Volkov, Dobrovolsky and Patsayev — AP83

**1971, Oct. 4 Photo.** ***Perf. 12½***
**C314** AP83 10fo multi 2.00 2.00

In memory of the Russian astronauts Vladislav N. Volkov, Lt. Col. Georgi T. Dobrovolsky and Victor I. Patsayev, who died during the Soyuz 11 space mission, June 6-30, 1971.
Exists imperf. Value $15.

### Apollo 14 Type of 1971
Souvenir Sheet

10fo, American Lunar Rover on moon.

**1972, Jan. 20 Photo.** ***Perf. 12½***
**C315** AP82 10fo multi 2.00 2.00

Apollo 15 moon mission, 7/26-8/7/71.
Exists imperf. Value $15.

Soccer and Hungarian Flag — AP84

Various Scenes from Soccer and Natl. Flags of: 60f, Romania. 80f, DDR. 1fo, Great Britain. 1.20fo, Yugoslavia. 2fo, USSR. 4fo, Italy. 5fo, Belgium.

**1972, Apr. 29**
**C316** AP84 40f gold & multi .25 .25
**C317** AP84 60f gold & multi .25 .25
**C318** AP84 80f gold & multi .25 .25
**C319** AP84 1fo gold & multi .25 .25
**C320** AP84 1.20fo gold & multi .25 .25
**C321** AP84 2fo gold & multi .30 .25
**C322** AP84 4fo gold & multi .75 .40
**C323** AP84 5fo gold & multi 1.10 .70
***a.*** Sheet of 8, #C316-C323 3.75 2.75
*Nos. C316-C323 (8)* 3.40 2.60

European Soccer Championships for the Henri Delaunay Cup.
Exist imperf. Value: set $45; sheet $45.
Nos. C316-C321 were later issued individually in sheets of 20 and in partly changed colors.

Souvenir Sheet

Olympic Rings and Globe — AP85

**1972, June 10 Photo.** ***Perf. 12½***
**C324** AP85 10fo multi 4.00 4.00

20th Olympic Games, Munich, 8/26-9/11.
Exists imperf. Value $80.

### Olympic Type of Regular Issue
Souvenir Sheet

Design: Equestrian and Olympic Rings.

**1972, July 15 Photo.** ***Perf. 12½***
**C325** A484 10fo multi 2.50 2.50

20th Olympic Games, Munich, Aug. 26-Sept. 11. #C325 contains one 43x43mm stamp.
Exists imperf. Value $20.

### Apollo 14 Type of 1971
Souvenir Sheets

Design: 10fo, Astronaut in space, Apollo 16 capsule and badge.

**1972, Oct. 10 Photo.** ***Perf. 12½***
**C326** AP82 10fo blue & multi 2.75 2.75

Apollo 16 US moon mission, 4/15-27/72.
Exists imperf. Value $20.

**1973, Jan. 15**

Design: Astronaut exploring moon, vert.

**C327** AP82 10fo blue & multi 3.00 3.00

Apollo 17 US moon mission, Dec. 7-19, 1972. No. C327 contains one vertical stamp.
Exists imperf. Value $20.

**1973, Mar. 12 Photo.** ***Perf. 12½***
**C328** AP82 10fo Venera 8 2.00 2.00

Venera 8 USSR space mission, Mar. 27-July 22, 1972.
Exists imperf. Value $15.

Equestrian (Pentathlon), Olympic Rings and Medal — AP86

Designs (Olympic Rings and Medals): 60f, Weight lifting. 1fo, Canoeing. 1.20fo, Swimming, women's. 1.80fo, Boxing. 4fo, Wrestling. 6fo, Fencing. 10fo, Allegorical figure lighting flame, vert.

**1973, Mar. 31**
**C329** AP86 40f multi .25 .25
**C330** AP86 60f multi .25 .25
**C331** AP86 1fo blue & multi .25 .25
**C332** AP86 1.20fo multi .25 .25
**C333** AP86 1.80fo multi .30 .25
**C334** AP86 4fo multi .65 .30
**C335** AP86 6fo multi 1.00 .50
*Nos. C329-C335 (7)* 2.95 2.05

**Souvenir Sheet**
***Perf. 11***

**C336** AP86 10fo blue & multi 3.75 3.75

Hungarian medalists at 20th Olympic Games. #C336 contains one 44x71mm stamp.
Exist imperf. Value: Nos. C329-C335 $15; No. C336 $60.

Wrens — AP87

**1973, Apr. 16 Litho.** ***Perf. 12***
**C337** AP87 40f shown .25 .25
**C338** AP87 60f Rock thrush .25 .25
**C339** AP87 80f Robins .25 .25
**C340** AP87 1fo Firecrests .25 .25
**C341** AP87 1.20fo Linnets .25 .25
**C342** AP87 2fo Blue titmice .35 .25
**C343** AP87 4fo White-spotted blue throat .60 .25
**C344** AP87 5fo Gray wagtails .75 .35
*Nos. C337-C344 (8)* 2.95 2.10

Exist imperf. Value $20.

### Exhibition Type of Regular Issue
Souvenir Sheet

10fo, Bavaria #1 with mill wheel cancellation; Munich City Hall, TV Tower and Olympic tent.

**1973, May 11 Litho.** ***Perf. 11***
**C345** A506 10fo multi 2.25 2.25

No. C345 contains one 83x45mm stamp.
Exists imperf. Value $20.

Souvenir Sheet

Skylab over Earth — AP88

**1973, Oct. 16 Photo.** ***Perf. 12½***
**C346** AP88 10fo dk bl, lt bl & yel 2.25 2.25

First US manned space station.
Exists imperf. Value $15.

### Space Type of Regular Issue

Designs: 6fo, Mars "canals" and Giovanni V. Schiaparelli. 10fo, Mars 7 spacecraft.

**1974, Mar. 11 Photo.** ***Perf. 12½***
**C347** A522 6fo gold & multi .75 .50

**Souvenir Sheet**
**C348** A522 10fo gold & multi 2.50 2.50

Exist imperf. Value, souvenir sheet $17.50.

### UPU Type of 1974

Designs: a, Mail coach. b, Old mail automobile. c, Jet. d, Apollo 15.

**1974, May 22 Litho.** ***Perf. 12***
**C349** A526 6fo UPU emblem and TU-154 jet 1.25 .90

**Souvenir Sheet**
**C350** Sheet of 4 2.50 2.50
***a.-d.*** A526 2.50fo, any single .40 .40

No. C350 has bister UPU emblem in center where 4 stamps meet.
Exist imperf. Value, souvenir sheet $35.

### Army Day Type of 1974

Designs: 2fo, Ground-to-air missiles, vert. 3fo, Parachutist, helicopter, supersonic jets.

**1974, Sept. 28 Litho.** ***Perf. 12***
**C351** A537 2fo gold, emer & blk .25 .25
**C352** A537 3fo gold, blue & blk .45 .25

Exist imperf.

Carrier Pigeon, Elizabeth Bridge, Mt. Gellert — AP89

**1975, Feb. 7 Litho. *Perf. 12***

**C353** AP89 3fo multi 1.00 1.00

Carrier Pigeons' Olympics, Budapest, Feb. 7-9. No. C353 printed checkerwise with black and violet coupon showing Pigeon Olympics emblem.

Exists imperf. Value $12.

Sputnik 2, Apollo-Soyuz Emblem AP90

Spacecraft and Apollo-Soyuz Emblem: 60f, Mercury-Atlas 5. 80f, Lunokhod I on moon. 1.20fo, Lunar rover, Apollo 15 mission. 2fo, Soyuz take-off, Baikonur. 4fo, Apollo take-off, Cape Kennedy. 6fo, Apollo-Soyuz link-up. 10fo, Apollo, Soyuz, American and Russian flags over earth, horiz.

**1975, July 7 Photo. *Perf. 12x11½***

| | | | | |
|---|---|---|---|---|
| **C354** | AP90 | 40f silver & multi | .25 | .25 |
| **C355** | AP90 | 60f silver & multi | .25 | .25 |
| **C356** | AP90 | 80f silver & multi | .25 | .25 |
| **C357** | AP90 | 1.20fo silver & multi | .25 | .25 |
| **C358** | AP90 | 2fo silver & multi | .25 | .25 |
| **C359** | AP90 | 4fo silver & multi | .45 | .30 |
| **C360** | AP90 | 6fo silver & multi | .75 | .45 |
| | | *Nos. C354-C360 (7)* | 2.45 | 2.00 |

**Souvenir Sheet**

***Perf. 12½***

**C361** AP90 10fo blue & multi 2.50 2.25

Apollo Soyuz space test project (Russo-American cooperation), launching July 15; link-up July 17. No. C361 contains one 59x38mm stamp.

Exist imperf. Value: Nos. C354-C360 $15; No. C361 $22.50.

Souvenir Sheet

Map of Europe and Cogwheels — AP91

**1975, July 30 Litho. *Perf. 12½***

**C362** AP91 10fo multi 4.00 3.25

European Security and Cooperation Conference, Helsinki, July 30-Aug. 1.

Exists imperf. Value $50.

Souvenir Sheet

Hungary Nos. 1585, 1382, 2239, 2280, C81 — AP92

**1975, Sept. 9 Photo. *Perf. 12½***

**C363** AP92 10fo multi 2.75 2.50

30 years of stamps.

Exists imperf. Value $20.

A similar souvenir sheet with blue margin, no denomination and no postal validity was released for the 25th anniversary of Filatelica Hungarica.

Souvenir Sheet

Paintings by Károly Lotz and János Halápi — AP93

**1976, Mar. 19 Photo. *Perf. 12½***

| | | | | |
|---|---|---|---|---|
| **C364** | AP93 | Sheet of 2 | 3.25 | 2.50 |
| *a.* | | 5fo Horses in Storm | 1.00 | 1.00 |
| *b.* | | 5fo Morning at Tihany | 1.00 | 1.00 |

Tourist publicity. #C364a and C364b are imperf. between.

Exists imperf. Value $30.

Souvenir Sheet

Montreal Olympic Stadium — AP94

**1976, June 29 Litho. *Perf. 12½***

**C365** AP94 20fo red, gray & blk 2.75 2.75

21st Olympic Games, Montreal, Canada, July 17-Aug. 1.

Exists imperf. Value $25.

US Mars Mission AP95

60f, Viking in space. 1fo, Viking on Mars. 2fo, Venus, rocket take-off. 3fo, Venera 9 in space. 4fo, Venera 10, separation in space. 5fo, Venera on moon. 20fo, Viking 1 landing on Mars, vert.

**1976, Nov. 11 Photo. *Perf. 11***

| | | | | |
|---|---|---|---|---|
| **C366** | AP95 | 40f silver & multi | .25 | .25 |
| **C367** | AP95 | 60f silver & multi | .25 | .25 |
| **C368** | AP95 | 1fo silver & multi | .25 | .25 |
| **C369** | AP95 | 2fo silver & multi | .25 | .25 |
| **C370** | AP95 | 3fo silver & multi | .35 | .25 |
| **C371** | AP95 | 4fo silver & multi | .55 | .30 |
| **C372** | AP95 | 5fo silver & multi | .75 | .40 |
| | | *Nos. C366-C372 (7)* | 2.65 | 1.95 |

**Souvenir Sheet**

***Perf. 12½***

**C373** AP95 20fo black & multi 3.00 2.75

US-USSR space missions. No. C373 contains one stamp (size: 41x64mm).

Exist imperf. Value: Nos. C366-C372 $15; No. C373 $20.

Hungary No. CB33 — AP96

**1977, Apr. Litho. *Perf. 11½x12***

**C374** AP96 3fo multi 1.50 1.50

European stamp exhibitions. Issued in sheets of 3 stamps and 3 labels. Labels show exhibition emblems respectively: 125th anniversary of Brunswick stamps, Brunswick, May 5-8; Regiofil XII, Lugano, June 17-19; centenary of San Marino Stamps, Riccione, Aug. 27-29.

Exists imperf. Value: single $20; sheetlet $30.

**Space Type 1977**

Souvenir Sheet

Design: 20fo, Viking on Mars.

**1977, Sept. 20 Litho. *Perf. 11½***

**C375** A603 20fo multi 2.75 2.75

Exists imperf. Value $15.

Souvenir Sheet

"EUROPA," Map and Dove — AP97

**1977, Oct. 3 *Perf. 12½***

**C376** AP97 20fo multi 4.50 4.50

European Security Conference, Belgrade, Oct.-Nov.

Exists imperf. Value $25.

TU-154, Malev over Europe AP98

Planes, Airlines, Maps: 1.20fo, DC-8, Swissair, Southeast Asia. 2fo, IL-62, CSA, North Africa. 2.40fo, A 300B Airbus, Lufthansa, Northwest Europe. 4fo, Boeing 747, Pan Am, North America. 5fo, TU-144, Aeroflot, Northern Europe. 10fo, Concorde, Air France, South America. 20fo, IL-86, Aeroflot, Northeast Asia.

**1977, Oct. 26 Litho. *Perf. 11½x12***

**Size: 32x21mm**

| | | | | |
|---|---|---|---|---|
| **C377** | AP98 | 60f orange & blk | .25 | .25 |
| **C378** | AP98 | 1.20fo violet & blk | .35 | .25 |
| **C379** | AP98 | 2fo yellow & blk | .35 | .25 |
| **C380** | AP98 | 2.40fo bl grn & blk | .50 | .25 |
| **C381** | AP98 | 4fo ultra & blk | .50 | .25 |
| **C382** | AP98 | 5fo dp rose & blk | .70 | .25 |
| **C383** | AP98 | 10fo blue & blk | 1.25 | .40 |

***Perf. 12x11½***

**Size: 37½x29mm**

| | | | | |
|---|---|---|---|---|
| **C384** | AP98 | 20fo green & blk | 1.40 | .90 |
| | | *Nos. C377-C384 (8)* | 5.30 | 2.80 |

Exist imperf. Value, set $35.

Montgolfier Brothers and Balloon, 1783 — AP99

Designs: 60f, David Schwarz and airship, 1850. 1fo, Alberto Santos-Dumont and airship flying around Eiffel Tower, 1901. 2fo, Konstantin E. Tsiolkovsky, airship and Kremlin, 1857. 3fo, Roald Amundsen, airship Norge, Polar bears and map, 1872. 4fo, Hugo Eckener, Graf Zeppelin over Mt. Fuji, 1930. 5fo, Count Ferdinand von Zeppelin, Graf Zeppelin over Chicago, 1932. 20fo, Graf Zeppelin over Budapest, 1931.

**1977, Nov. 1 Photo. *Perf. 12x11½***

| | | | | |
|---|---|---|---|---|
| **C385** | AP99 | 40f gold & multi | .25 | .25 |
| **C386** | AP99 | 60f gold & multi | .25 | .25 |
| **C387** | AP99 | 1fo gold & multi | .25 | .25 |
| **C388** | AP99 | 2fo gold & multi | .25 | .25 |
| **C389** | AP99 | 3fo gold & multi | .40 | .25 |
| **C390** | AP99 | 4fo gold & multi | .50 | .30 |
| **C391** | AP99 | 5fo gold & multi | .75 | .50 |
| | | *Nos. C385-C391 (7)* | 2.65 | 2.05 |

**Souvenir Sheet**

***Perf. 12½***

**C392** AP99 20fo silver & multi 2.75 2.50

History of airships. No. C392 contains one 60x36mm stamp.

Exist imperf. Value: Nos. C385-C391 $15; No. C392 $25.

Moon Station — AP100

Science Fiction Paintings by Pal Varga: 60f, Moon settlement. 1fo, Spaceship near Phobos. 2fo, Exploration of asteroids. 3fo, Spaceship in gravitational field of Mars. 4fo, Spaceship and rings of Saturn. 5fo, Spaceship landing on 3rd Jupiter moon.

**1978, Mar. 10 Litho. *Perf. 11***

| | | | | |
|---|---|---|---|---|
| **C393** | AP100 | 40f multi | .25 | .25 |
| **C394** | AP100 | 60f multi | .25 | .25 |
| **C395** | AP100 | 1fo multi | .25 | .25 |
| **C396** | AP100 | 2fo multi | .25 | .25 |
| **C397** | AP100 | 3fo multi | .40 | .25 |
| **C398** | AP100 | 4fo multi | .50 | .30 |
| **C399** | AP100 | 5fo multi | .75 | .40 |
| | | *Nos. C393-C399 (7)* | 2.65 | 1.95 |

Exist imperf. Value, set $15.

Louis Bleriot and La Manche AP101

60f, J. Alcock & R. W. Brown, Vickers Vimy, 1919. 1fo, A. C. Read, Navy Curtiss NC-4, 1919. 2fo, H. Köhl, G. Hünefeld, J. Fitzmaurice, Junkers W33, 1928. 3fo, A. Johnson, J. Mollison, Gipsy Moth, 1930. 4fo, G. Endresz, S. Magyar, Lockheed Sirius, 1931. 5fo, W. Gronau, Dornier WAL, 1932. 20fo, Wilbur & Orville Wright & their plane.

**1978, May 10 Litho. *Perf. 12***

| | | | | |
|---|---|---|---|---|
| **C400** | AP101 | 40f multi | .25 | .25 |
| **C401** | AP101 | 60f multi | .25 | .25 |
| **C402** | AP101 | 1fo multi | .25 | .25 |
| **C403** | AP101 | 2fo multi | .25 | .25 |
| **C404** | AP101 | 3fo multi | .40 | .25 |
| **C405** | AP101 | 4fo multi | .55 | .30 |
| **C406** | AP101 | 5fo multi | .85 | .40 |
| | | *Nos. C400-C406 (7)* | 2.80 | 1.95 |

**Souvenir Sheet**

**C407** AP101 20fo multi 3.00 2.75

75th anniv. of 1st powered flight by Wright brothers. #C407 contains one 75x25mm stamp.

Exist imperf. Value: Nos. C400-C406 $15; No. C407 $25.

Souvenir Sheet

Jules Verne and "Voyage from Earth to Moon" — AP102

**1978, Aug. 21** ***Perf. 12½x11½***

**C408** AP102 20fo multi 3.00 2.75

Jules Verne (1828-1905), French science fiction writer.

Exists imperf. Value $25.

Vladimir Remek Postmarking Mail on Board Salyut 6 — AP103

**1978, Sept. 1** **Photo.** ***Perf. 11½x12***

**C409** AP103 3fo multi 1.50 1.50

PRAGA '78 International Philatelic Exhibition, Prague, Sept. 8-17. Issued in sheets of 3 stamps and 3 labels, showing PRAGA '78 emblem and Golden Tower, Prague. FISA emblems in margin.

Exists imperf. Value: single $4.50; sheetlet $15.

Ski Jump — AP104

Lake Placid '80 Emblem and: 60f, 20fo, Figure skating, diff. 1fo, Downhill skiing. 2fo, Ice hockey. 4fo, Bobsledding. 6fo, Cross-country skiing.

**1979, Dec. 15** **Litho.** ***Perf. 12***

| | | | | | |
|---|---|---|---|---|---|
| **C410** | AP104 | 40f multi | | .25 | .25 |
| **C411** | AP104 | 60f multi | | .25 | .25 |
| **C412** | AP104 | 1fo multi | | .25 | .25 |
| **C413** | AP104 | 2fo multi | | .30 | .25 |
| **C414** | AP104 | 4fo multi | | .60 | .30 |
| **C415** | AP104 | 6fo multi | | 1.00 | .55 |
| | | *Nos. C410-C415 (6)* | | 2.65 | 1.85 |

**Souvenir Sheet**

**C416** AP104 20fo multi 2.75 2.75

13th Winter Olympic Games, Lake Placid, NY, Feb. 12-24, 1980.

Exist imperf. Value: Nos. C410-C415 $20; No. C416 $25.

Soviet and Hungarian Cosmonauts AP105

**1980, May 27** **Litho.** ***Perf. 11½x12***

**C417** AP105 5fo multi .60 .25

Intercosmos cooperative space program.

Exists imperf. Value $20.

Women's Handball, Moscow '80 Emblem, Olympic Rings — AP106

**1980, June 16** **Photo.** ***Perf. 11½x12***

| | | | | | |
|---|---|---|---|---|---|
| **C418** | AP106 | 40f | shown | .25 | .25 |
| **C419** | AP106 | 60f | Double kayak | .25 | .25 |
| **C420** | AP106 | 1fo | Running | .25 | .25 |
| **C421** | AP106 | 2fo | Gymnast | .25 | .25 |
| **C422** | AP106 | 3fo | Equestrian | .40 | .25 |
| **C423** | AP106 | 4fo | Wrestling | .55 | .35 |
| **C424** | AP106 | 5fo | Water polo | .65 | .50 |
| | | | *Nos. C418-C424 (7)* | 2.60 | 2.10 |

**Souvenir Sheet**

**C425** AP106 20fo Torch bearers 3.00 3.00

22nd Summer Olympic Games, Moscow, July 19-Aug. 3.

See No. C427.

Exist imperf. Value: Nos. C418-C424 $20; No. C425 $17.50.

Souvenir Sheet

Cosmonauts Bertalan Farkes and Valery Kubasov, Salyut 6-Soyuz 35 and 36 — AP107

**1980, July 12** **Litho.** ***Perf. 12½***

**C426** AP107 20fo multi 3.25 3.00

Intercosmos cooperative space program (USSR-Hungary).

Exists imperf. Value $25.

**Olympic Type of 1980**

Souvenir Sheet

**1980, Sept. 26** **Litho.** ***Perf. 12½***

**C427** AP106 20fo Greek Frieze and gold medal 3.25 3.00

Olympic Champions.

Exists imperf. Value $20.

Kalman Kittenberger (1881-1958), Zoologist and Explorer — AP108

**1981, Mar. 6** **Photo.** ***Perf. 11½***

| | | | | | |
|---|---|---|---|---|---|
| **C427A** | AP108 | 40f | Cheetah | .25 | .25 |
| **C427B** | AP108 | 60f | Lion | .25 | .25 |
| **C427C** | AP108 | 1fo | Leopard | .25 | .25 |
| **C427D** | AP108 | 2fo | Rhinoceros | .35 | .25 |
| **C427E** | AP108 | 3fo | Antelope | .55 | .25 |
| **C427F** | AP108 | 4fo | African elephant | .65 | .30 |
| **C427G** | AP108 | 5fo | shown | .85 | .40 |
| | | | *Nos. C427A-C427G (7)* | 3.15 | 1.95 |

Exist imperf. Value, set $20.

Graf Zeppelin over Tokyo, First Worldwide Flight, Aug. 7-Sept. 4, 1929 — AP109

Graf Zeppelin Flights (Zeppelin and): 2fo, Icebreaker Malygin, Polar flight, July 24-31, 1931. 3fo, Nine Arch Bridge, Hortobagy, Hungary, Mar. 28-30, 1931. 4fo, Holsten Tor, Lubeck, Baltic Sea, May 12-15, 1931. 5fo, Tower Bridge, England, Aug. 18-20, 1931. 6fo, Federal Palace, Chicago World's Fair, 50th crossing of Atlantic, Oct. 14-Nov. 2, 1933. 7fo, Lucerne, first flight across Switzerland, Sept. 26, 1929.

***Perf. 12½x11½***

**1981, Mar. 16** **Litho.**

| | | | | | |
|---|---|---|---|---|---|
| **C428** | AP109 | 1fo multi | | .25 | .25 |
| **C429** | AP109 | 2fo multi | | .25 | .25 |
| **C430** | AP109 | 3fo multi | | .40 | .25 |
| **C431** | AP109 | 4fo multi | | .55 | .35 |
| **C432** | AP109 | 5fo multi | | .65 | .40 |
| **C433** | AP109 | 6fo multi | | .75 | .55 |
| **C434** | AP109 | 7fo multi | | .85 | .60 |
| | | *Nos. C428-C434 (7)* | | 3.70 | 2.65 |

LURABA '81, First Aviation and Space Philatelic Exhibition, Lucerne, Switzerland, Mar. 20-29. No. C434 se-tenant with label showing exhibition emblem.

Exist imperf. Value, set $15.

**Illustrator Type of 1981**

Designs: Illustrations by A. Lesznai.

**1981, Dec. 29** **Litho.** ***Perf. 11½x12***

| | | | | | |
|---|---|---|---|---|---|
| **C435** | A693 | 4fo | At the End of the Village | .55 | .50 |
| **C436** | A693 | 5fo | Dance | .70 | .55 |
| **C437** | A693 | 6fo | Sunday | .80 | .60 |
| | | | *Nos. C435-C437 (3)* | 2.05 | 1.65 |

Exist imperf.

Manned Flight Bicentenary AP110

Various hot air balloons.

**1983, Apr. 5** **Litho.** ***Perf. 12x11½***

| | | | | | |
|---|---|---|---|---|---|
| **C438** | AP110 | 1fo | 1811 | .25 | .25 |
| **C439** | AP110 | 1fo | 1896 | .25 | .25 |
| **C440** | AP110 | 2fo | 1904 | .25 | .25 |
| **C441** | AP110 | 2fo | 1977 | .25 | .25 |
| **C442** | AP110 | 4fo | 1981 | .50 | .25 |
| **C443** | AP110 | 4fo | 1982 | .50 | .25 |
| **C444** | AP110 | 5fo | 1981 | .70 | .35 |
| | | | *Nos. C438-C444 (7)* | 2.70 | 1.85 |

**Souvenir Sheet**

***Perf. 12½***

**C445** AP110 20fo 1983 2.75 2.75

No. C445 contains one 39x49mm stamp.

Exist imperf. Value: Nos. C438-C444 $15; No. C445 $20.

**Audubon Type of 1985**

**1985, June 19** **Litho.** ***Perf. 12***

| | | | | | |
|---|---|---|---|---|---|
| **C446** | A778 | 4fo | Colaptes auratus | .60 | .35 |
| **C447** | A778 | 6fo | Richmondena cardinalis | .85 | .50 |

Exist imperf.

Aircraft — AP111

**1988, Aug. 31** **Litho.** ***Perf. 11***

| | | | | | |
|---|---|---|---|---|---|
| **C448** | AP111 | 1fo | Lloyd CII | .25 | .25 |
| **C449** | AP111 | 2fo | Brandenburg CI | .30 | .25 |
| **C450** | AP111 | 4fo | UFAG CI | .50 | .35 |
| **C451** | AP111 | 10fo | Gerle 13 | 1.40 | .90 |
| **C452** | AP111 | 12fo | WM 13 | 1.60 | 1.10 |
| | | | *Nos. C448-C452 (5)* | 4.05 | 2.85 |

Exist imperf. Value, set $30.

---

## AIR POST SEMI-POSTAL STAMPS

**Catalogue values for unused stamps in this section are for Never Hinged items.**

**Roosevelt Type of Semipostal Stamps, 1947**

F. D. Roosevelt, Plane and Place: 10f+10f, Casablanca. 20f+20f, Tehran. 50f+50f, Yalta (map). 70f+70f, Hyde Park.

***Perf. 12x12½***

**1947, June 11** **Photo.** **Wmk. 210**

**Portrait in Sepia**

| | | | | |
|---|---|---|---|---|
| **CB1** | SP115 | 10f + 10f red vio | 4.25 | *5.25* |
| **CB1A** | SP115 | 20f + 20f brn ol | 4.25 | *5.25* |
| **CB1B** | SP115 | 50f + 50f vio | 4.25 | *5.25* |
| **CB1C** | SP115 | 70f + 70f blk | 4.25 | *5.25* |
| | | *Nos. CB1-CB1C (4)* | 17.00 | 21.00 |

Exist imperf.

A souvenir sheet contains one each of Nos. CB1-CB1C with border inscriptions and decorations in gray. Size: 161x122mm. Value $125.

Exists imperf. Value $225.

See note below Nos. B198A-B198D.

Souvenir Sheet

Chain Bridge, Budapest — SPAP1

***Perf. 12x12½***

**1948, May 15** **Photo.** **Wmk. 283**

**CB1D** SPAP1 2fo + 18fo brn car 120.00 120.00

Exists imperf. Value $2,500.

Souvenir Sheet

Chain Bridge — SPAP2

**1948, Oct. 16**

**CB2** SPAP2 3fo + 18fo dp grnsh bl 120.00 120.00

Exists imperf. Value $2,500.

**Type of Air Post Stamps of 1948**

Portraits at Right

Writers: 1f, William Shakespeare. 2f, Francois Voltaire. 4f, Johann Wolfgang von Goethe. 5f, Lord Byron. 6f, Victor Hugo. 8f, Edgar Allen Poe. 10f, Sandor Petöfi. 12f, Mark Twain. 30f, Count Leo Tolstoy. 40f, Maxim Gorky.

**1948, Oct. 16** **Photo.**

| | | | | |
|---|---|---|---|---|
| **CB3** | AP22 | 1f dp ultra | .25 | .25 |
| **CB4** | AP22 | 2f rose carmine | .25 | .25 |
| **CB5** | AP22 | 4f dp yellow grn | .25 | .25 |
| **CB6** | AP22 | 5f dp rose lilac | .35 | .35 |

CB7 AP22 6f deep blue .35 .35
CB8 AP22 8f olive brn .35 .35
CB9 AP22 10f red .50 .45
CB10 AP22 12f deep violet .50 .45
CB11 AP22 30f orange brn 1.75 1.50
CB12 AP22 40f sepia 2.25 1.75
*Nos. CB3-CB12 (10)* 6.80 5.95

Sold at a 50 per cent increase over face, half of which aided reconstruction of the Chain Bridge and the other half the hospital for postal employees.
Exist imperf. Value, set $100.

**1st Stamp Type**
Souvenir Sheets
***Perf. 12½x12***

**1951, Sept. 12 Engr. Unwmk.**
CB13 A208 1fo + 1fo red 75.00 75.00
CB14 A208 2fo + 2fo blue 75.00 75.00

Exist imperf. Value, each $175.

Children Inspecting Stamp Album — SPAP3

2fo+2fo, Children at stamp exhibition.

***Perf. 12x12½***

**1952, Oct. 12 Photo. Wmk. 106**
CB15 SPAP3 1fo + 1fo blue 10.00 10.00
CB16 SPAP3 2fo + 2fo brn red 10.00 10.00

Stamp week, Oct. 11-19, 1952.
Exist imperf. Value, set $100.

Globe and Mailbox SPAP4

Designs: 1fo+50f, Mobile post office. 2fo+1fo, Telegraph pole. 3fo+1.50fo, Radio. 5fo+2.50fo, Telephone. 10fo+5fo, Post horn.

**1957, June 20 *Perf. 12x12½, 12***
**Cross in Red**
**Size: 32x21mm**
CB17 SPAP4 60f + 30f bister brn .55 .25
CB18 SPAP4 1fo + 50f lilac .75 .35
CB19 SPAP4 2fo + 1fo org ver 1.00 .45
CB20 SPAP4 3fo + 1.50fo blue 1.50 .70
CB21 SPAP4 5fo + 2.50fo gray 2.25 1.75
**Size: 46x31mm**
CB22 SPAP4 10fo + 5fo pale grn 4.50 4.00
*Nos. CB17-CB22 (6)* 10.55 7.50

The surtax was for the benefit of hospitals for postal and telegraph employees.
Exist imperf. Value, set $70.

Parachute of Fausztusz Verancsics, 1617 SPAP5

History of Hungarian Aviation: No. CB24, Balloon of David Schwarz, 1897. No. CB25, Monoplane of Ernő Horvath, 1911. No. CB26, PKZ-2 helicopter, 1918.

**Engraved and Lithographed**

**1967, May 6 *Perf. 10½***
CB23 SPAP5 2fo + 1fo sep & yel .50 .50
CB24 SPAP5 2fo + 1fo sep & lt bl .50 .50
CB25 SPAP5 2fo + 1fo sep & lt grn .50 .50
CB26 SPAP5 2fo + 1fo sep & pink .50 .50
*a.* Horiz. strip of 4, #CB23-CB26 2.75 2.75
*b.* Souv. sheet of 4, #CB23-CB26 3.00 2.75

"AEROFILA 67" International Airmail Exhibition, Budapest, Sept. 3-10.
Exist imperf. Value: strip $20; souvenir sheet $40.

**1967, Sept. 3**

Aviation, 1967: No. CB27, Parachutist. No. CB28, Helicopter Mi-1. No. CB29, TU-154 jet. No. CB30, Space station Luna 12.

CB27 SPAP5 2fo + 1fo slate & lt grn .50 .50
CB28 SPAP5 2fo + 1fo slate & buff .50 .50
CB29 SPAP5 2fo + 1fo slate & yel .50 .50
CB30 SPAP5 2fo + 1fo slate & pink .50 .50
*a.* Horiz. strip of 4, #CB27-CB30 2.75 2.75
*b.* Souv. sheet of 4, #CB27-CB30 3.75 3.75

Issued to commemorate (in connection with AEROFILA 67) the 7th Congress of FISA (Fédération Internationale des Sociétés Aérophilatéliques) and the 40th Stamp Day.
Exist imperf. Value: strip $20; souvenir sheet $35.

**Olympic Games Airmail Type**

Design: 2fo+1fo, Equestrian.

**1968, Aug. 21 Photo. *Perf. 12***
CB31 AP74 2fo + 1fo multi .35 .35

Exists imperf.

1st Hungarian Airmail Letter, 1918, Plane — SPAP6

Designs: No. CB33, Letter, 1931, and Zeppelin. No. CB34, Balloon post letter, 1967, and balloon. No. CB35, Letter, 1969, and helicopter.
#CB36a, #C1. b, #C7. c, #C305. d, #C312.

**1974, Oct. 19 Litho. *Perf. 12***
CB32 SPAP6 2fo + 1fo multi .95 .95
CB33 SPAP6 2fo + 1fo multi .95 .95
*a.* Pair, #CB32-CB33 2.00 2.00
CB34 SPAP6 2fo + 1fo multi .95 .95
CB35 SPAP6 2fo + 1fo multi .95 .95
*a.* Pair, #CB34-CB35 2.00 2.00
*Nos. CB32-CB35 (4)* 3.80 3.80

**Souvenir Sheet**
CB36 Sheet of 4 3.50 3.50
*a.-d.* SPAP6 2fo+1fo any single .50 .50

AEROPHILA, International Airmail Exhibition, Budapest, Oct. 19-27.
No. CB36 contains 4 35x25mm stamps.
Exist imperf. Value: set of 2 pairs $35; souvenir sheet $30.

## SPECIAL DELIVERY STAMPS

**Issue of the Monarchy**

SD1

**1916 Typo. Wmk. 137 *Perf. 15***
E1 SD1 2f gray green & red .25 .25

Exists imperf. Value $7.50.
For overprints and surcharges see Nos. 1NE1, 2NE1, 4N5, 5NE1, 6NE1, 7NE1, 8NE1, 10NE1, 11NE1, 11NJ7-J8.

**Issues of the Republic**

Special Delivery Stamp of 1916 Overprinted

**1919**
E2 SD1 2f gray green & red .25 *.75*

Exists imperf. Value $12.50.

**General Issue**

SD2

**1919**
E3 SD2 2f gray green & red .25 *.75*

Exists imperf. Value $10.

## REGISTRATION STAMPS

**Catalogue values for unused stamps in this section are for Never Hinged items.**

**Nos. 625, 609 and 626 Overprinted in Carmine**

a

b

"Ajl." or "Ajánlás" = Registered Letter.

**1946 Wmk. 266 *Perf. 15***
F1 A118(a) "Ajl.1." on 20f .25 .25
*a.* "Ajl.1." 50.00
F2 A99(a) "Ajl.2." on 12f .25 .25
F3 A118(b) "Ajánlás" on 24f .25 .25
*Nos. F1-F3 (3)* .75 .75

Hellebore — R1

**2011, May 2 Litho. *Perf. 12¼x12¾***
F4 R1 (315fo) multi 3.50 1.75

## POSTAGE DUE STAMPS

**Issues of the Monarchy**

D1

***Perf. 11½, 11¾x12***

**1903 Typo. Wmk. 135**
J1 D1 1f green & blk .50 .50
J2 D1 2f green & blk 3.00 1.50
J3 D1 5f green & blk 15.00 6.50
J4 D1 6f green & blk 12.00 6.00
J5 D1 10f green & blk 80.00 3.00
J6 D1 12f green & blk 2.50 2.50
J7 D1 20f green & blk 20.00 1.50
J8 D1 50f green & blk 16.00 12.50
J9 D1 100f green & blk 1.00 1.00
*Nos. J1-J9 (9)* 150.00 35.00

See Nos. J10-J26, J28-J43. For overprints and surcharges see Nos. J27, J44-J50, 1NJ1-1NJ5, 2NJ1-2NJ16, 4NJ2-4NJ3, 5NJ1-5NJ8, 6NJ1-6NJ9, 7NJ1-7NJ4, 9NJ1-9NJ3, 10NJ1-10NJ6, 11NJ1-J6.

**1908-09 Wmk. 136 *Perf. 15***
J10 D1 1f green & black .75 .50
J11 D1 2f green & black 1.00 .50
J12 D1 5f green & black 2.50 .75
J13 D1 6f green & black 1.50 .50
J14 D1 10f green & black 1.50 .50
J15 D1 12f green & black 1.25 .50
J16 D1 20f green & black 10.00 .50
*c.* Center inverted 9,000. *9,000.*
J17 D1 50f green & black 1.75 .75
*Nos. J10-J17 (8)* 20.25 4.50

**1905 Wmk. 136a *Perf. 11½x12***
*J12a* D1 5f green & black 175.00 70.00
*J13a* D1 6f green & black 14.00 7.50
*J14a* D1 10f green & black 175.00 5.00
*J15a* D1 12f green & black 25.00 16.00
*J17a* D1 50f green & black 6.00 2.50
J18 D1 100f green & black 5.00

**1906 *Perf. 15***
*J11b* D1 2f green & black 3.50 3.50
*J12b* D1 5f green & black 2.50 2.00
*J13b* D1 6f green & black 2.50 2.00
*J14b* D1 10f green & black 15.00 .60
*J15b* D1 12f green & black .75 .60
*J16b* D1 20f green & black 25.00 .60
*d.* Center inverted *9,000.* *9,000.*
*J17b* D1 50f green & black 1.00 1.00
*Nos. J11b-J17b (7)* 50.25 10.30

**1914 Wmk. 137 Horiz. *Perf. 15***
J19 D1 1f green & black .35 .25
J20 D1 2f green & black .25 .25
J21 D1 5f green & black .40 .40
J22 D1 6f green & black .80 .60
J23 D1 10f green & black .90 .70
J24 D1 12f green & black .40 .25
J25 D1 20f green & black .35 .25
J26 D1 50f green & black .70 .25
*Nos. J19-J26 (8)* 4.15 2.95

**1914 Wmk. 137 Vert.**
*J20a* D1 2f green & black 57.50 57.50
*J21a* D1 5f green & black 4.50 4.50
*J22a* D1 6f green & black 9.00 7.50
*J25a* D1 20f green & black *2,250.* *900.00*
*J26a* D1 50f green & black 2.50 2.50

During 1921-24, a number of Postage Due stamps were punched with three holes prior to sale. See note following No. 105 in the Regular Postage section.

No. J9 Surcharged in Red

**1915 Wmk. 135**
J27 D1 20f on 100f grn & blk .50 2.00
*a.* On No. J18, Wmk. 136a 15.00 *37.50*

**1915-22 Wmk. 137**
J28 D1 1f green & red .25 .25
J29 D1 2f green & red .25 .25
J30 D1 5f green & red .35 .25
J31 D1 6f green & red .25 .25
J32 D1 10f green & red .25 .25
J33 D1 12f green & red .25 .25
J34 D1 15f green & red .35 *.50*
J35 D1 20f green & red .25 .25
J36 D1 30f green & red .25 .25
J37 D1 40f green & red ('20) .25 .25
J38 D1 50f green & red ('20) .25 .25
*a.* Center inverted 60.00
J39 D1 120f green & red ('20) .25 .25
J40 D1 200f green & red ('20) .25 .25
J41 D1 2k green & red ('22) .25 *.90*
J42 D1 5k green & red ('22) .25 .25
J43 D1 50k green & red ('22) .50 .30
*Nos. J28-J43 (16)* 4.45 4.95

**Issues of the Republic**

Postage Due Stamps of 1914-18 Overprinted in Black

**1918-19 On Issue of 1914**
J44 D1 50f green & black 3.00 5.50

**On Stamps and Type of 1915-18**
J45 D1 2f green & red .25 .75
J46 D1 3f green & red .25 .75
*a.* "KOZTARSASAG" omitted *650.00*
J47 D1 10f green & red .25 .75
J48 D1 20f green & red .25 .75
J49 D1 40f green & red .25 .75
*a.* Inverted overprint 60.00 60.00
J50 D1 50f green & red .25 .75
*a.* Center and overprint inverted 75.00 75.00
*Nos. J44-J50 (7)* 4.50 10.00

### Issues of the Kingdom

D3

**1919-20** **Typo.**

| | | | | |
|---|---|---|---|---|
| **J65** | D3 | 2f green & black | .25 | .50 |
| *a.* | | Inverted center | 2,100. | |
| **J66** | D3 | 3f green & black | .25 | .50 |
| **J67** | D3 | 20f green & black | .25 | .50 |
| **J68** | D3 | 40f green & black | .25 | .50 |
| **J69** | D3 | 50f green & black | .25 | .50 |
| | | *Nos. J65-J69 (5)* | 1.25 | 2.50 |

Postage Due Stamps of this type have been overprinted "Magyar Tancskztarsasag" but have not been reported as having been issued without the additional overprint "heads of wheat."

For overprints see Nos. J70-J75.

Additional Overprint in Black

**1920**

| | | | | |
|---|---|---|---|---|
| **J70** | D3 | 2f green & black | .85 | 1.50 |
| **J71** | D3 | 3f green & black | .85 | 1.50 |
| **J72** | D3 | 10f green & black | 1.40 | 2.50 |
| **J73** | D3 | 20f green & black | .85 | 1.50 |
| **J74** | D3 | 40f green & black | .85 | 1.50 |
| **J75** | D3 | 50f green & black | .85 | 1.50 |
| | | *Nos. J70-J75 (6)* | 5.65 | 10.00 |

Postage Issues Surcharged

**1921-25** **Red Surcharge**

| | | | | |
|---|---|---|---|---|
| **J76** | A9 | 100f on 15f violet | .25 | .25 |
| **J77** | A9 | 500f on 15f violet | .25 | .25 |
| **J78** | A9 | 2½k on 10f red vio | .25 | *.25* |
| **J79** | A9 | 3k on 15f violet | .25 | *.25* |
| **J80** | A9 | 6k on 1½k violet | .25 | *1.50* |
| **J81** | A9 | 9k on 40f ol grn | .25 | *.25* |
| **J82** | A9 | 10k on 2½k green | .25 | *1.25* |
| **J83** | A9 | 12k on 60f blk brn | .25 | *.25* |
| **J84** | A9 | 15k on 1½k vio | .25 | *.25* |
| **J85** | A9 | 20k on 2½k grn | .25 | *1.10* |
| **J86** | A9 | 25k on 1½k vio | .25 | *.25* |
| **J87** | A9 | 30k on 1½k vio | .25 | *.25* |
| **J88** | A9 | 40k on 2½k grn | .25 | *1.25* |
| **J89** | A9 | 50k on 1½k vio | .25 | *.25* |
| **J90** | A9 | 100k on 4½k dl vio | .25 | .25 |
| **J91** | A9 | 200k on 4½k dl vio | .25 | .25 |
| **J92** | A9 | 300k on 4½k dl vio | .25 | .25 |
| **J93** | A9 | 500k on 2k grnsh bl | .60 | .25 |
| **J94** | A9 | 500k on 3k org brn | 2.10 | .30 |
| **J95** | A9 | 1000k on 2k grnsh bl | 1.20 | .25 |
| **J96** | A9 | 1000k on 3k org brn | 1.75 | .25 |
| **J97** | A9 | 2000k on 2k grnsh bl | 1.20 | .40 |
| **J98** | A9 | 2000k on 3k org brn | 2.10 | .35 |
| **J99** | A9 | 5000k on 5k brown | .90 | *1.75* |
| | | *Nos. J76-J99 (24)* | 14.10 | 11.90 |

Year of issue: 6k, 15k, 25k, 30k, 50k, 1922. 10k, 20k, 40k, 100k - No. J93, Nos. J95, J97, 1923. 5,000k, 1924. Nos. J94, J96, J98, 1925. Others, 1921.

D6

***Perf. 14x14½, 15***

**1926** **Wmk. 133** **Litho.**

| | | | | |
|---|---|---|---|---|
| **J100** | D6 | 1f rose red | .25 | .25 |
| **J101** | D6 | 2f rose red | .25 | .25 |
| **J102** | D6 | 3f rose red | .30 | .60 |
| **J103** | D6 | 4f rose red | .25 | .25 |
| **J104** | D6 | 5f rose red | 1.75 | *2.50* |
| **J105** | D6 | 8f rose red | .25 | .25 |
| **J106** | D6 | 10f rose red | 1.25 | .25 |
| **J107** | D6 | 16f rose red | .30 | .25 |
| **J108** | D6 | 32f rose red | .50 | .25 |
| **J109** | D6 | 40f rose red | .75 | .25 |
| **J110** | D6 | 50f rose red | .90 | .40 |
| **J111** | D6 | 80f rose red | 1.25 | .65 |
| | | *Nos. J100-J111 (12)* | 8.00 | 6.15 |

Exist imperf. Value, set $100.

See Nos. J117-J123. For surcharges see Nos. J124-J129.

Nos. C7-C11 Surcharged in Red or Green

**1926** **Wmk. 137** ***Perf. 14***

| | | | | |
|---|---|---|---|---|
| **J112** | AP3 | 1f on 500k (R) | .25 | .30 |
| **J113** | AP3 | 2f on 1000k (G) | .25 | .30 |
| **J114** | AP3 | 3f on 2000k (R) | .25 | .30 |

**Wmk. 133**

| | | | | |
|---|---|---|---|---|
| **J115** | AP3 | 5f on 5000k (G) | .65 | *1.50* |
| **J116** | AP3 | 10f on 10000k (G) | .50 | *1.10* |
| | | *Nos. J112-J116 (5)* | 1.90 | *3.50* |

### Type of 1926 Issue

**1928-32** **Wmk. 210** ***Perf. 15***

| | | | | |
|---|---|---|---|---|
| **J117** | D6 | 2f rose red | .25 | .25 |
| **J118** | D6 | 4f rose red ('32) | .25 | .25 |
| **J119** | D6 | 8f rose red | .25 | .25 |
| **J120** | D6 | 10f rose red | .25 | .25 |
| **J121** | D6 | 16f rose red | .35 | .25 |
| **J122** | D6 | 20f rose red | .60 | .25 |
| **J123** | D6 | 40f rose red | .50 | .25 |
| | | *Nos. J117-J123 (7)* | 2.45 | 1.75 |

Exist imperf. Value, set $60.

Postage Due Stamps of 1926 Surcharged in Black

**1931-33** **Wmk. 133**

| | | | | |
|---|---|---|---|---|
| **J124** | D6 | 4f on 5f rose red | .25 | .25 |
| **J125** | D6 | 10f on 16f rose red | 1.50 | *3.75* |
| **J126** | D6 | 10f on 80f rose red ('33) | .30 | .25 |
| **J127** | D6 | 12f on 50f rose red ('33) | .35 | .25 |
| **J128** | D6 | 20f on 32f rose red | .35 | .30 |
| | | *Nos. J124-J128 (5)* | 2.75 | *4.80* |

Surcharged on No. J121

**1931** **Wmk. 210** ***Perf. 15***

| | | | | |
|---|---|---|---|---|
| **J129** | D6 | 10f on 16f rose red | .85 | *1.25* |

**Catalogue values for unused stamps in this section, from this point to the end of the section, are for Never Hinged items.**

Figure of Value — D7

**1934** **Photo.** **Wmk. 210**

| | | | | |
|---|---|---|---|---|
| **J130** | D7 | 2f ultra | .25 | .25 |
| **J131** | D7 | 4f ultra | .25 | .25 |
| **J132** | D7 | 6f ultra | .25 | .25 |
| **J133** | D7 | 8f ultra | .25 | .25 |
| **J134** | D7 | 10f ultra | .25 | .25 |
| **J135** | D7 | 12f ultra | .25 | .25 |
| **J136** | D7 | 16f ultra | .25 | .25 |
| **J137** | D7 | 20f ultra | .40 | .25 |
| **J138** | D7 | 40f ultra | .60 | .25 |
| **J139** | D7 | 80f ultra | 2.00 | .50 |
| | | *Nos. J130-J139 (10)* | 4.75 | 2.75 |

Exist imperf. Value, set $60.

Coat of Arms and Post Horn — D8

**1941**

| | | | | |
|---|---|---|---|---|
| **J140** | D8 | 2f brown red | .25 | .25 |
| **J142** | D8 | 4f brown red | .25 | .25 |
| **J143** | D8 | 6f brown red | .25 | .25 |
| **J144** | D8 | 8f brown red | .25 | .25 |
| **J145** | D8 | 10f brown red | .25 | .25 |
| **J146** | D8 | 12f brown red | .30 | .25 |
| **J147** | D8 | 16f brown red | .40 | .25 |
| **J148** | D8 | 20f brown red | .50 | .25 |
| **J150** | D8 | 40f brown red | .75 | .25 |
| | | *Nos. J140-J150 (9)* | 3.20 | 2.25 |

Exist imperf. Value, set $25.

**1941-44** **Wmk. 266**

| | | | | |
|---|---|---|---|---|
| **J151** | D8 | 2f brown red | .25 | .25 |
| **J152** | D8 | 3f brown red | .25 | .25 |
| **J153** | D8 | 4f brown red | .25 | .25 |
| **J154** | D8 | 6f brown red | .25 | .25 |
| **J155** | D8 | 8f brown red | .25 | .25 |
| **J156** | D8 | 10f brown red | .25 | .25 |
| **J157** | D8 | 12f brown red | .25 | .25 |
| **J158** | D8 | 16f brown red | .25 | .25 |
| **J159** | D8 | 18f brown red ('44) | .25 | .25 |
| **J160** | D8 | 20f brown red | .25 | .25 |
| **J161** | D8 | 24f brown red | .25 | .25 |
| **J162** | D8 | 30f brown red ('44) | .25 | .25 |
| **J163** | D8 | 36f brown red ('44) | .25 | .25 |
| **J164** | D8 | 40f brown red | .25 | .25 |
| **J165** | D8 | 50f brown red | .25 | .25 |
| **J166** | D8 | 60f brown red ('44) | .30 | .25 |
| | | *Nos. J151-J166 (16)* | 4.05 | 4.00 |

Exist imperf. Value, set $30.

For surcharges see Nos. J167-J185.

### Issues of the Republic

Types of Hungary Postage Due Stamps, 1941-44, Surcharged in Carmine

**1945** **Wmk. 266** **Photo.** ***Perf. 15***

**Blue Surface-tinted Paper**

| | | | | |
|---|---|---|---|---|
| **J167** | D8 | 10f on 2f brn red | .25 | .25 |
| **J168** | D8 | 10f on 3f brn red | .25 | .25 |
| **J169** | D8 | 20f on 4f brn red | .25 | .25 |
| **J170** | D8 | 20f on 6f brn red | 9.50 | 9.50 |
| **J171** | D8 | 20f on 8f brn red | .25 | .25 |
| **J172** | D8 | 40f on 12f brn red | .25 | .25 |
| **J173** | D8 | 40f on 16f brn red | .25 | .25 |
| **J174** | D8 | 40f on 18f brn red | .25 | .25 |
| **J175** | D8 | 60f on 24f brn red | .25 | .25 |
| **J176** | D8 | 80f on 30f brn red | .25 | .25 |
| **J177** | D8 | 90f on 36f brn red | .25 | .25 |
| **J178** | D8 | 1p on 10f brn red | .25 | .25 |
| **J179** | D8 | 1p on 40f brn red | .25 | .25 |
| **J180** | D8 | 2p on 20f brn red | .25 | .25 |
| **J181** | D8 | 2p on 50f brn red | .25 | .25 |
| **J182** | D8 | 2p on 60f brn red | .25 | .25 |

**Surcharged in Black, Thicker Type**

| | | | | |
|---|---|---|---|---|
| **J183** | D8 | 10p on 3f brn red | .25 | .25 |
| **J184** | D8 | 12p on 8f brn red | .25 | .25 |
| **J185** | D8 | 20p on 24f brn red | .25 | .25 |
| | | *Nos. J167-J185 (19)* | 14.00 | 14.00 |

D9

**1946-50** **Wmk. 210** ***Perf. 15***

**Numerals in Deep Magenta**

| | | | | |
|---|---|---|---|---|
| **J186** | D9 | 4f magenta | .50 | .25 |
| **J187** | D9 | 10f magenta | 1.25 | .25 |
| **J188** | D9 | 20f magenta | .50 | .25 |
| **J189** | D9 | 30f magenta | .50 | .25 |
| **J190** | D9 | 40f magenta | .75 | .25 |
| **J191** | D9 | 50f mag ('50) | 2.25 | .50 |
| **J192** | D9 | 60f magenta | 1.50 | .25 |
| **J193** | D9 | 1.20fo magenta | 2.25 | .25 |
| **J194** | D9 | 2fo magenta | 3.75 | .30 |
| | | *Nos. J186-J194 (9)* | 13.25 | 2.55 |

**1951** **Wmk. 106**

**Numerals in Deep Magenta**

| | | | | |
|---|---|---|---|---|
| **J194A** | D9 | 4f magenta | .25 | .25 |
| **J194B** | D9 | 10f magenta | .25 | .25 |
| **J194C** | D9 | 20f magenta | 1.25 | .25 |
| *j.* | | "fiellr" | 35.00 | 7.50 |
| **J194D** | D9 | 30f magenta | 1.50 | .25 |
| **J194E** | D9 | 40f magenta | .50 | .25 |
| **J194F** | D9 | 50f magenta | 1.00 | .25 |
| **J194G** | D9 | 60f magenta | .85 | .25 |
| **J194H** | D9 | 1.20fo magenta | 3.50 | .25 |
| **J194I** | D9 | 2fo magenta | 3.00 | .25 |
| | | *Nos. J194A-J194I (9)* | 12.10 | 2.25 |

Nos. J194A-J194I are found in both large format (about 18x22mm) and small (about 17x21mm).

Revenue Stamps with Blue Surcharge — D10

**Paper with Vertical Lines in Green**

**1951** **Unwmk.** **Typo.** ***Perf. 14½x15***

| | | | | |
|---|---|---|---|---|
| **J195** | D10 | 8f dark brown | .25 | .25 |
| **J196** | D10 | 10f dark brown | .25 | .25 |
| **J197** | D10 | 12f dark brown | .40 | .40 |
| | | *Nos. J195-J197 (3)* | .90 | .90 |

D11

**1951** **Wmk. 106** **Photo.** ***Perf. 14½***

| | | | | |
|---|---|---|---|---|
| **J198** | D11 | 4f brown | .25 | .25 |
| **J199** | D11 | 6f brown | .25 | .25 |
| **J200** | D11 | 8f brown | .25 | .25 |
| **J201** | D11 | 10f brown | .25 | .25 |
| **J202** | D11 | 14f brown | .35 | .25 |
| **J203** | D11 | 20f brown | .25 | .25 |
| **J204** | D11 | 30f brown | .25 | .25 |
| **J205** | D11 | 40f brown | .25 | .25 |
| **J206** | D11 | 50f brown | .25 | .25 |
| **J207** | D11 | 60f brown | .30 | .25 |
| **J208** | D11 | 1.20fo brown | .30 | .25 |
| **J209** | D11 | 2fo brown | .50 | .30 |
| | | *Nos. J198-J209 (12)* | 3.45 | 3.05 |

Exist imperf. Value, set $30.

D12

D13

**Photo., Numeral Typo. in Black**

**1953** **Numerals 3mm High**

| | | | | |
|---|---|---|---|---|
| **J210** | D12 | 4f dull green | .25 | .25 |
| **J211** | D12 | 6f dull green | .25 | .25 |
| **J212** | D12 | 8f dull green | .25 | .25 |
| **J213** | D12 | 10f dull green | .25 | .25 |
| **J214** | D12 | 12f dull green | .25 | .25 |
| **J215** | D12 | 14f dull green | .25 | .25 |
| **J216** | D12 | 16f dull green | .25 | .25 |
| **J217** | D12 | 20f dull green | .25 | .25 |
| **J218** | D12 | 24f dull green | .25 | .25 |
| **J219** | D12 | 30f dull green | .25 | .25 |
| **J220** | D12 | 36f dull green | .25 | .25 |
| **J221** | D12 | 40f dull green | .25 | .25 |
| **J222** | D12 | 50f dull green | .25 | .25 |
| **J223** | D12 | 60f dull green | .25 | .25 |
| **J224** | D12 | 70f dull green | .25 | .25 |
| **J225** | D12 | 80f dull green | .30 | .25 |

**Numerals 4½mm High**

| | | | | |
|---|---|---|---|---|
| **J226** | D12 | 1.20fo dull green | .40 | .25 |
| **J227** | D12 | 2fo dull green | .75 | .25 |
| *a.* | | Small "2" (3mm high) | 4.00 | 2.00 |
| | | *Nos. J210-J227 (18)* | 5.20 | 4.50 |

1st Hungarian postage due stamp, 50th anniv.

Exist imperf. Value, set $30.

**Photo., Numeral Typo. in Black on Nos. J228-J243**

**1958** **Wmk. 106** ***Perf. 14½***

**Size: 21x16½mm**

| | | | | |
|---|---|---|---|---|
| **J228** | D13 | 4f red | .25 | .25 |
| **J229** | D13 | 6f red | .25 | .25 |
| **J230** | D13 | 8f red | .25 | .25 |
| **J231** | D13 | 10f red | .25 | .25 |
| **J232** | D13 | 12f red | .25 | .25 |
| **J233** | D13 | 14f red | .25 | .25 |
| **J234** | D13 | 16f red | .25 | .25 |
| **J235** | D13 | 20f red | .25 | .25 |
| **J236** | D13 | 24f red | .25 | .25 |
| **J237** | D13 | 30f red | .25 | .25 |
| **J238** | D13 | 36f red | .25 | .25 |
| **J239** | D13 | 40f red | .25 | .25 |
| **J240** | D13 | 50f red | .25 | .25 |
| **J241** | D13 | 60f red | .25 | .25 |
| **J242** | D13 | 70f red | .25 | .25 |
| **J243** | D13 | 80f red | .25 | .25 |

***Perf. 12***

**Size: 31x21mm**

| | | | | |
|---|---|---|---|---|
| **J244** | D13 | 1.20fo dk red brn | .35 | .25 |
| **J245** | D13 | 2fo dk red brn | .50 | .25 |
| | | *Nos. J228-J245 (18)* | 4.85 | 4.50 |

Exist imperf. Value, set $15.

**Photo., Numeral Typo. in Black on Nos. J246-J261**

**1965-69** **Unwmk.** ***Perf. 11½***

**Size: 21x16½mm**

| | | | | |
|---|---|---|---|---|
| **J246** | D13 | 4f red | .25 | .25 |
| **J247** | D13 | 6f red | .25 | .25 |
| **J248** | D13 | 8f red | .25 | .25 |
| **J249** | D13 | 10f red | .25 | .25 |
| **J250** | D13 | 12f red | .25 | .25 |
| **J251** | D13 | 14f red | .25 | .25 |
| **J252** | D13 | 16f red | .25 | .25 |
| **J253** | D13 | 20f red | .25 | .25 |

J254 D13 24f red .25 .25
J255 D13 30f red .25 .25
J256 D13 36f red .25 .25
J257 D13 40f red .25 .25
J258 D13 50f red .25 .25
J259 D13 60f red .25 .25
J260 D13 70f red .25 .25
J261 D13 80f red .25 .25

***Perf. 11½x12***

**Size: 31x21mm**

J262 D13 1fo dk red brn ('69) .25 .25
J263 D13 1.20fo dk red brn .25 .25
J264 D13 2fo dk red brn .30 .25
J265 D13 4fo dk red brn ('69) .50 .25
*Nos. J246-J265 (20)* 5.30 5.00

Mail Plane and Truck — D14

Designs: 20f, Money order canceling machine. 40f, Scales in self-service P.O. 80f, Automat for registering parcels. 1fo, Keypunch operator. 1.20fo, Mail plane and truck. 2fo, Diesel mail train. 3fo, Mailman on motorcycle with sidecar. 4fo, Rural mail delivery. 8fo, Automatic letter sorting machine. 10fo, Postman riding motorcycle.

**1973-85 Photo. *Perf. 11***

**Size: 21x18mm**

J266 D14 20f brown & ver .25 .25
J267 D14 40f dl bl & ver .25 .25
J268 D14 80f violet & ver .25 .25
J269 D14 1fo ol grn & ver .25 .25

***Perf. 12x11½***

**Size: 28x22mm**

J270 D14 1.20fo green & ver .25 .25
J271 D14 2fo lilac & ver .25 .25
J272 D14 3fo brt blue & ver .25 .25
J273 D14 4fo org brn & ver .35 .25
J274 D14 8fo deep mag & dark red 1.00 .30
J275 D14 10fo green & dark red 1.10 .35
*Nos. J266-J275 (10)* 4.20 2.65

Issued: 20f-4fo, 12/1973; 8fo, 10fo, 12/16/85.

Postal History — D15

Designs: Excerpt from 18th cent. letter, innovations in letter carrying.

**1987, Dec. 10 Litho. *Perf. 12***

J276 D15 1fo Foot messenger, 16th cent. .25 .25
J277 D15 4fo Post rider, 17th cent. .55 .30
J278 D15 6fo Horse-drawn mail coach, 18th cent. .75 .45
J279 D15 8fo Railroad mail car, 19th cent. 1.00 .60
J280 D15 10fo Mail truck, 20th cent. 1.25 .65
J281 D15 20fo Airplane, 20th cent. 2.25 1.25
*Nos. J276-J281 (6)* 6.05 3.50

## OFFICIAL STAMPS

During 1921-24, a number of Official stamps were punched with three holes prior to sale. See note following No. 105 in the Regular Postage section.

O1

**1921-23 Wmk. 137 Typo. *Perf. 15***

O1 O1 10f brn vio & blk .25 .25
O2 O1 20f ol brn & blk .25 .25
a. "HIVATALOS" inverted *10,000.*
O3 O1 60f blk brn & blk .25 .25
O4 O1 100f dl rose & blk .25 .25
O5 O1 250f bl & blk .25 .25
O6 O1 350f gray & blk .25 .25
O7 O1 500f lt brn & blk .25 .25
O8 O1 1000f lil brn & blk .25 .25
O9 O1 5k brn ('23) .25 .25
O10 O1 10k choc ('23) .25 .25
O11 O1 15k gray blk ('23) .25 .25
O12 O1 25k org ('23) .25 .25
O13 O1 50k brn & red ('22) .25 .25
O14 O1 100k bis & red ('22) .25 .25
O15 O1 150k grn & red ('23) .25 .25
O16 O1 300k dl red & red ('23) .25 .25
O17 O1 350k vio & red ('23) .30 .25
O18 O1 500k org & red ('22) .30 .25
O19 O1 600k ol bis & red ('23) .80 .60
O20 O1 1000k bl & red ('22) 1.20 .25
*Nos. O1-O20 (20)* 6.60 5.35

Counterfeits of No. O2a exist.

Stamps of 1921 Surcharged in Red

**1922**

O21 O1 15k on 20f ol brn & blk .25 .25
O22 O1 25k on 60f blk brn & blk .25 .25

Stamps of 1921 Overprinted in Red

**1923**

O23 O1 350k gray & blk .25 .25

**With Additional Surcharge of New Value in Red**

O24 O1 150k on 100f dl rose & blk .30 .25
O25 O1 2000k on 250f bl & blk 1.50 .40
*Nos. O23-O25 (3)* 2.05 .90

**1923-24**

**Paper with Gray Moiré on Face**

O26 O1 500k org & red ('23) 2.10 .25
O27 O1 1000k bl & red ('23) 2.10 .25
O28 O1 3000k vio & red ('24) 2.10 1.25
O29 O1 5000k bl & red ('24) 2.40 1.50
*Nos. O26-O29 (4)* 8.70 3.25

**1924 Wmk. 133**

O30 O1 500k orange & red 1.40 1.00
O31 O1 1000k blue & red 1.40 1.00

## NEWSPAPER STAMPS

### Issues of the Monarchy

St. Stephen's Crown and Post Horn
N1 N2

**Litho. (#P1), Typo. (#P2)**

**1871-72 Unwmk. *Imperf.***

P1 N1 (1k) ver red 50.00 20.00
P2 N2 (1k) rose red ('72) 200.00 60.00
a. (1k) vermilion 10.00 2.00
b. Printed on both sides

*Reprints of No. P2 are watermarked. Value, $450.*

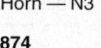

Letter with Crown and Post Horn — N3

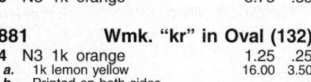

N5

**1874**

P3 N3 1k orange 3.75 .35

**1881 Wmk. "kr" in Oval (132)**

P4 N3 1k orange 1.25 .25
a. 1k lemon yellow 16.00 3.50
b. Printed on both sides

**1898 Wmk. 135**

P5 N3 1k orange 1.25 .25

See watermark note after No. 46.

**1900 Wmk. Crown in Circle (135)**

P6 N5 (2f) red orange .75 .25

**1905 Wmk. Crown (136a)**

P7 N5 (2f) red orange 1.00 .25
a. Wmk. 136 ('08) 1.00 .25

**1914-22 Wmk. Double Cross (137)**

P8 N5 (2f) orange .25 .25
a. Wmk. horiz. 4.50 3.75
P9 N5 (10f) deep blue ('20) .25 .25
P10 N5 (20f) lilac ('22) .25 .25
*Nos. P8-P10 (3)* .75 .75

For overprints and surcharges see Nos. 1NJ6-1NJ10, 1NP1, 2NP1, 5NP1, 6NP1, 8NP1, 10NP1, 11NP1.

## NEWSPAPER TAX STAMPS

### Issues of the Monarchy

NT1

NT2

**Wmk. 91; Unwmk. from 1871**

**1868 Typo. *Imperf.***

PR1 NT1 1k blue 4.00 1.00
a. Pair, one sideways
PR2 NT2 2k brown 20.00 10.00
a. 2k red brown 275.00 47.50

NT3

**1868**

PR2B NT3 1k blue *15,000. 11,000.*

No. PR2B was issued for the Military Border District only. All used stamps are precanceled (newspaper text printed on the stamp). A similar 2k was not issued.

**1889-90 Wmk. "kr" in Oval (132)**

PR3 NT1 1k blue 2.00 .80
PR4 NT2 2k brown 5.50 5.00

**1898 Wmk. Crown in Oval (135)**

PR5 NT1 1k blue 6.00 7.50

These stamps did not pay postage, but represented a fiscal tax collected by the postal authorities on newspapers.

Nos. PR3 and PR5 have a tall "k" in "kr."

## PARCEL POST STAMPS

**Nos. 629, 613, 612, 615, 630, 667 and Type of 1943-45 Overprinted in Black or Carmine**

a

b

"Cs." or "Csomag"=Parcel

**1946 Wmk. 266 *Perf. 15***

Q1 A118 "Cs. 5-1." on 70f .25 .25
Q2 A109 "Cs. 5-1." on 30f 22.50 20.00
Q3 A99 "Cs. 5-2." on 24f .25 .25
Q4 A118 "Cs. 10-1." on 70f .25 .25
Q5 A118 "Cs. 10-1." on 80f 27.50 26.00
Q6 A118 "Cs. 10-2." on 80f .25 .25
Q7 A99 "Csomag 5kg." on 2p on 4f (C+Bk) .25 .25
Q8 A118 "Csomag 10kg." on 30f copper red, *bl* .25 .25
*Nos. Q1-Q8 (8)* 51.50 47.50

No. Q8 was not issued without overprint.

**Catalogue values for unused stamps in this section, from this point to the end of the section, are for Never Hinged items.**

No. 796 Surcharged with New Value in Red or Black

**1954 Wmk. 210**

Q9 A144 1.70fo on 1.40fo 1.40 .25
Q10 A144 2fo on 1.40fo (Bk) 1.60 .30
Q11 A144 3fo on 1.40fo 2.00 .50
*Nos. Q9-Q11 (3)* 5.00 1.05
Set, hinged 1.80

## OCCUPATION STAMPS

### Issued under French Occupation

### ARAD ISSUE

The overprints on this issue have been extensively forged. Even the inexpensive values are difficult to find with genuine overprints. Values are for genuine overprints. Collectors should be aware that stamps sold "as is" are likely to be forgeries, and unexpertized collections should be assumed to consist of mostly forged stamps. Education plus working with knowledgeable dealers is mandatory in this collecting area. More valuable stamps should be expertized.

Stamps of Hungary Overprinted in Red or Blue

**On Issue of 1916-18**

**1919 Wmk. 137 *Perf. 15, 14***

1N1 A9 2f brn org (R) 1.60 1.60
1N2 A9 3f red lil (R) .75 .75
1N3 A9 5f green (R) 20.00 20.00
1N4 A9 6f grnsh bl (R) 1.90 1.90
a. Inverted overprint 30.00 30.00
1N5 A9 10f rose red 4.00 4.00
1N6 A9 15f violet (R) 1.75 1.75
a. Double overprint 50.00 50.00
1N7 A9 20f gray brn (R) 50.00 50.00
1N8 A9 35f brown (R) 65.00 65.00
1N9 A9 40f ol grn (R) 37.50 37.50
1N10 A10 50f red vio & lil 6.00 6.00
1N11 A10 75f brt bl & pale bl 2.00 2.00
1N12 A10 80f grn & pale grn 2.75 2.75
1N13 A10 1k red brn & cl 15.00 15.00
1N14 A10 2k ol brn & bis 3.00 3.00
a. Inverted overprint 50.00 50.00
1N15 A10 3k dk vio & ind 17.50 17.50
1N16 A10 5k dk brn & lt brn 13.50 13.50
1N17 A10 10k vio brn & vio 70.00 70.00
*Nos. 1N1-1N17 (17)* 312.25 312.25

### With Additional Surcharges

a

b

c

d

**1N18** A9 (a) 45f on 2f brn org 8.00 8.00
**1N19** A9 (b) 45f on 2f brn org 8.00 8.00
**1N20** A9 (c) 50f on 3f red lil 8.00 8.00
**1N21** A9 (d) 50f on 3f red lil 8.00 8.00
*Nos. 1N18-1N21 (4)* 32.00 32.00

### Overprinted On Issue of 1918

**1N22** A11 10f scarlet (Bl) 60.00 60.00
**1N23** A11 20f dk brn .90 .90
**1N24** A11 25f brt bl 2.40 2.40
*a.* Inverted overprint 30.00 30.00
**1N25** A12 40f ol grn 3.25 3.25
*Nos. 1N22-1N25 (4)* 66.55 66.55

### Ovptd. On Issue of 1918-19, Overprinted "Koztarsasag"

**1N26** A9 2f brn org 2.00 2.00
*a.* Inverted overprint 50.00 50.00
**1N27** A9 4f slate gray 2.00 2.00
**1N28** A9 5f green .60 .60
**1N29** A9 6f grnsh bl 12.00 12.00
*a.* Inverted overprint 30.00 30.00
**1N30** A9 10f rose red (Bl) 60.00 60.00
**1N31** A9 20f gray brn 15.00 15.00
**1N32** A11 25f brt bl 2.75 2.75
*a.* Inverted overprint 30.00 30.00
**1N33** A9 40f ol grn 2.00 2.00
**1N34** A12 40f ol grn 60.00 60.00
*a.* Inverted overprint 125.00 125.00
**1N35** A12 50f lilac 8.00 8.00
**1N36** A10 1k red brn & cl (Bl) 3.25 3.25
**1N37** A10 3k dk vio & ind (Bl) 15.00 15.00
*Nos. 1N26-1N37 (12)* 182.60 182.60

### No. 1N36 With Additional Surcharge

e

f

**1N38** A10 (e) 10k on 1k 13.50 13.50
**1N39** A10 (f) 10k on 1k 13.50 13.50

### On Issue of 1919 Inscribed "MAGYAR POSTA"

**1N40** A13 5f red (R) 55.00 55.00
**1N41** A13 10f red (Bl) 6.50 6.50

## SEMI-POSTAL STAMPS

Hungarian Semi-Postal Stamps of 1916-17 Overprinted "Occupation francaise" in Blue or Red

**1919 Wmk. 137 *Perf. 15***

**1NB1** SP3 10f + 2f rose red 65.00 65.00
**1NB2** SP4 15f + 2f dl vio (R) 9.50 9.50
**1NB3** SP5 40f + 2f brn car 12.50 12.50
*Nos. 1NB1-1NB3 (3)* 87.00 87.00

## SPECIAL DELIVERY STAMP

Hungarian Special Delivery Stamp of 1916 Overprinted "Occupation francaise"

**1919 Wmk. 137 *Perf. 15***

**1NE1** SD1 2f gray green & red .60 .60

## POSTAGE DUE STAMPS

Hungarian Postage Due Stamps of 1915 Overprinted "Occupation francaise"

**1919 Wmk. 137 *Perf. 15***

**1NJ1** D1 2f green & red 7.50 7.50
**1NJ2** D1 10f green & red 4.00 4.00
**1NJ3** D1 12f green & red 32.50 32.50
**1NJ4** D1 15f green & red 42.50 42.50
**1NJ5** D1 20f green & red 3.00 3.00

Hungarian Newspaper Stamp of 1914 Surcharged

**1NJ6** N5 12f on 2f orange 8.00 8.00
**1NJ7** N5 15f on 2f orange 8.00 8.00
**1NJ8** N5 30f on 2f orange 8.00 8.00
*a.* Double surcharge 50.00 50.00
**1NJ9** N5 50f on 2f orange 8.00 8.00
**1NJ10** N5 100f on 2f orange 8.00 8.00
*Nos. 1NJ1-1NJ10 (10)* 129.50 129.50

## NEWSPAPER STAMP

Hungarian Newspaper Stamp of 1914 Overprinted "Occupation francaise"

**1919 Wmk. 137 *Imperf.***

**1NP1** N5 (2f) orange 1.25 1.25

## ISSUED UNDER ROMANIAN OCCUPATION

## FIRST DEBRECEN ISSUE

The overprints on this issue have been extensively forged. Even the inexpensive values are difficult to find with genuine overprints. The more extensive note before No. 1N1 also applies to Nos. 2N1-2NP16.

Hungarian Stamps of 1913-19 Overprinted in Blue, Red or Black

**1919 Wmk. 137 *Perf. 15, 14½x14***

### On Stamps of 1913

**2N1** A4 2f olive yellow *90.00 90.00*
**2N2** A4 3f orange *125.00 125.00*
**2N3** A4 6f olive grn (R) 50.00 50.00

### On Stamps of 1916

**2N4** A8 10f rose 75.00 75.00
**2N5** A8 15f violet (Bk) 65.00 65.00

### On Stamps of 1916-18

**2N6** A9 2f brown org 1.50 1.50
**2N7** A9 3f red lilac .70 .70
**2N8** A9 5f green 4.75 4.75
**2N9** A9 6f grnsh bl (R) 1.60 1.60
**2N10** A9 15f violet (Bk) .80 .80
*a.* Red overprint 75.00 75.00
**2N11** A9 20f gray brn *125.00 125.00*
**2N12** A9 25f dull bl (Bk) 4.50 4.50
**2N13** A9 35f brown 60.00 60.00
**2N14** A9 40f olive grn 3.75 3.75
**2N15** A10 50f red vio & lil 8.25 8.25
**2N16** A10 75f brt bl & pale bl (Bk) 2.00 2.00
**2N17** A10 80f grn & pale grn (R) 3.50 3.50
**2N18** A10 1k red brn & cl 4.75 4.75
**2N19** A10 2k ol brn & bis (Bk) 1.75 1.75
**2N20** A10 3k dk vio & ind (R) 30.00 30.00
*a.* Blue overprint *65.00 65.00*
*b.* Black overprint *250.00 250.00*
**2N21** A10 5k dk brn & lt brn (Bk) 27.50 27.50
**2N22** A10 10k vio brn & vio *160.00 160.00*

### With New Value Added

**2N23** A9 35f on 3f red lil 2.00 2.00
**2N24** A9 45f on 2f brn org 2.00 2.00
**2N25** A10 3k on 75f brt bl & pale bl (Bk) 4.00 4.00
**2N26** A10 5k on 75f brt bl & pale bl (Bk) 3.75 3.75
**2N27** A10 10k on 80f grn & pale grn (R) 3.50 3.50

### On Stamps of 1918

**2N28** A11 10f scarlet 60.00 60.00
**2N28A** A11 15f violet (R) 75.00 75.00
*b.* Black overprint 125.00 125.00
**2N29** A11 20f dk brown (R) 6.25 6.25
*a.* Black overprint 30.00 30.00
*b.* Blue overprint 75.00 75.00
**2N30** A11 25f brt blue (R) 7.00 7.00
*a.* Black overprint 75.00 75.00
**2N31** A12 40f olive green 3.00 3.00
**2N32** A12 50f lilac 50.00 50.00

### On Stamps of 1918-19, Overprinted "Koztarsasag"

**2N33** A9 2f brn org 3.00 3.00
**2N34** A9 3f red lilac 65.00 65.00
**2N35** A9 4f sl gray (R) 1.75 1.75
**2N36** A9 5f green .65 .65
**2N37** A9 6f grnsh bl (R) 30.00 30.00
**2N38** A9 10f rose red 37.50 37.50
**2N39** A11 10f scarlet 25.00 25.00
**2N40** A11 15f dp vio (Bk) 45.00 45.00
*a.* Red overprint 125.00 125.00
**2N41** A9 20f gray brn 3.25 3.25
**2N42** A11 20f dk brn (Bk) 37.50 37.50
*b.* Red overprint 50.00 50.00
**2N43** A9 40f olive grn 1.75 1.75
**2N44** A10 1k red brn & cl 2.75 2.75
**2N45** A10 2k ol brn & bis (Bk) 60.00 60.00
*a.* Blue overprint 125.00 125.00
**2N46** A10 3k dk vio & ind (R) 9.75 9.75
*a.* Blue overprint 60.00 60.00
*b.* Black overprint *200.00 200.00*
**2N47** A10 5k dk & lt brn (Bk) *225.00 225.00*
**2N48** A10 10k vio brn & vio *500.00 500.00*
**2N49** A11 25f brt bl (R) 3.25 3.25
*a.* Black overprint 25.00 25.00
**2N50** A12 40f olive grn *125.00 125.00*
**2N51** A12 50f lilac 2.25 2.25

### On Stamps of 1919

**2N52** A13 5f green .50 .50
**2N53** A13 6f grnsh bl (Bk) 22.50 22.50
**2N54** A13 10f red .25 .25
**2N55** A13 20f dk brown .25 .25
**2N56** A13 25f dl bl (Bk) 1.25 1.25
**2N56A** A13 40f olive green 125.00 125.00
**2N57** A13 45f orange 15.00 15.00
**2N57A** A14 95f dark blue & blue 125.00 125.00
**2N57B** A14 1.20k dark green & green 125.00 125.00
**2N57C** A14 1.40k yellow green 125.00 125.00

No. 2N58

**2N58** A14 5k dk brn & brn 3,000. 3,000.

#2N58 is handstamped. Counterfeits exist. Expertization is required.

### On No. 103A

**2N59** A5a 10f violet brn (R) 50.00 50.00

### On No. 208

**2N60** A13 10f red 75.00 75.00
*Nos. 2N1-2N57,2N59-2N60 (61)* *2,530. 2,530.*

## SEMI-POSTAL STAMPS

Hungary Nos. B36, B37 Overprinted like Regular Issues in Blue

**1919 Wmk. 137 *Perf. 14***

**2NB1** A4(c) 2f olive yellow 125.00 125.00
**2NB1A** A4(c) 3f orange 125.00 125.00

Same Overprint in Blue or Black on Hungary Nos. B53--B55

**1919 Wmk. 137 *Perf. 15***

**2NB1B** SP3 10f + 2f rose red 4.00 4.00
**2NB2** SP4 15f + 2f dl vio (Bk) 17.00 17.00
**2NB3** SP5 40f + 2f brown car 11.00 11.00
*Nos. 2NB1B-2NB3 (3)* 32.00 32.00

Same Overprint on Hungary Nos. B58-B60 (with "Köztarsasag")

**1919**

**2NB4** SP3 10f + 2f rose red 42.50 42.50
**2NB5** SP4 15f + 2f dl vio (Bk) 75.00 75.00
**2NB6** SP5 40f + 2f brown car 32.50 32.50
*Nos. 2NB4-2NB6 (3)* 150.00 150.00

## SPECIAL DELIVERY STAMP

Hungarian Special Delivery Stamp of 1916 Overprinted like Regular Issues

**1919 Wmk. 137 *Perf. 15***

**2NE1** SD1 2f gray grn & red (Bl) 3.00 3.00

## POSTAGE DUE STAMPS

Hungarian Postage Due Stamps of 1914-19 Overprinted in Black like Regular Issues

**1919 Wmk. 137 *Perf. 15***

### On Stamp of 1914

**2NJ1** D1 50f grn & blk *125.00 125.00*

### On Stamps of 1915

**2NJ2** D1 1f green & red 62.50 62.50
**2NJ3** D1 2f green & red 2.00 2.00
**2NJ4** D1 5f green & red *225.00 225.00*
**2NJ5** D1 6f green & red *125.00 125.00*
**2NJ6** D1 10f green & red .80 .80
**2NJ7** D1 12f green & red *125.00 125.00*
**2NJ8** D1 15f green & red 20.00 20.00
**2NJ9** D1 20f green & red 4.50 4.50
**2NJ10** D1 30f green & red 13.50 13.50

### On Stamps of 1918-19, Overprinted "Koztarsasag"

**2NJ11** D1 2f green & red 25.00 25.00
**2NJ12** D1 3f green & red 30.00 30.00
**2NJ13** D1 10f green & red 30.00 30.00
**2NJ14** D1 20f green & red 30.00 30.00
**2NJ15** D1 40f green & red 30.00 30.00
**2NJ16** D1 50f green & red 30.00 30.00
*Nos. 2NJ1-2NJ16 (16) 878.30 878.30*
*Nos. 2NJ1-2NJ13,2NJ15-2NJ16 (15) 848.30*

## NEWSPAPER STAMP

Hungarian Newspaper Stamp of 1914 Overprinted like Regular Issues

**1919 Wmk. 137 *Imperf.***

**2NP1** N5 (2f) orange (Bl) .55 .55
*a.* Inverted overprint 50.00 50.00
*b.* Double overprint 125.00 125.00

## SECOND DEBRECEN ISSUE

Complete forgeries exist of this issue and are often found in large multiples or even complete sheets. Values are for genuine stamps.

Mythical "Turul" — OS5

Throwing Lariat
OS6

Hungarian Peasant
OS7

**1920 Unwmk. Typo. *Perf. 11½***

| | | | | |
|---|---|---|---|---|
| **3N1** | OS5 | 2f lt brown | 2.25 | 2.25 |
| **3N2** | OS5 | 3f red brown | 2.25 | 2.25 |
| **3N3** | OS5 | 4f gray | 2.25 | 2.25 |
| **3N4** | OS5 | 5f lt green | .50 | .50 |
| **3N5** | OS5 | 6f slate | 2.25 | 2.25 |
| **3N6** | OS5 | 10f scarlet | .50 | .50 |
| **3N7** | OS5 | 15f dk violet | 3.00 | 3.00 |
| **3N8** | OS5 | 20f dk brown | .60 | .60 |
| **3N9** | OS6 | 25f ultra | 1.25 | 1.25 |
| **3N10** | OS6 | 30f buff | .65 | .65 |
| **3N11** | OS6 | 35f claret | 1.25 | 1.25 |
| **3N12** | OS6 | 40f olive grn | .75 | .75 |
| **3N13** | OS6 | 45f salmon | 1.00 | 1.00 |
| **3N14** | OS6 | 50f pale vio | .75 | .75 |
| **3N15** | OS6 | 60f yellow grn | .90 | .90 |
| **3N16** | OS6 | 75f Prus blue | .75 | .75 |
| **3N17** | OS7 | 80f gray grn | .85 | .85 |
| **3N18** | OS7 | 1k brown red | 3.00 | 3.00 |
| **3N19** | OS7 | 2k chocolate | 3.00 | 3.00 |
| **3N20** | OS7 | 3k brown vio | 2.25 | 2.25 |
| **3N21** | OS7 | 5k bister brn | 2.25 | 2.25 |
| **3N22** | OS7 | 10k dull vio | 2.25 | 2.25 |
| | | *Nos. 3N1-3N22 (22)* | 34.50 | 34.50 |

**Thick, Glazed Paper**

| | | | | |
|---|---|---|---|---|
| **3N23** | OS5 | 2f lt brown | 3.00 | 3.00 |
| **3N24** | OS5 | 3f red brown | 3.00 | 3.00 |
| **3N25** | OS5 | 4f gray | 3.00 | 3.00 |
| **3N26** | OS5 | 5f lt green | 3.00 | 3.00 |
| **3N27** | OS5 | 6f slate | 3.00 | 3.00 |
| **3N28** | OS5 | 10f scarlet | .75 | .75 |
| **3N29** | OS5 | 15f dk vio | 3.00 | 3.00 |
| **3N30** | OS5 | 20f dk brown | 1.00 | 1.00 |
| **3N31** | OS7 | 80f gray grn | 1.50 | 1.50 |
| **3N32** | OS7 | 1k brown red | 4.00 | 4.00 |
| **3N33** | OS7 | 1.20k orange | 8.00 | 8.00 |
| **3N34** | OS7 | 2k chocolate | 4.50 | 4.50 |
| | | *Nos. 3N23-3N34 (12)* | 37.75 | 37.75 |

## SEMI-POSTAL STAMPS

Carrying Wounded — SP1

**1920 Unwmk. Typo. *Perf. 11½***

| | | | | |
|---|---|---|---|---|
| **3NB1** | SP1 | 20f green | 1.25 | 1.25 |
| **3NB2** | SP1 | 50f gray brn | 2.25 | 2.25 |
| **3NB3** | SP1 | 1k blue green | 2.25 | 2.25 |
| **3NB4** | SP1 | 2k dk green | 2.25 | 2.25 |

**Colored Paper**

| | | | | |
|---|---|---|---|---|
| **3NB5** | SP1 | 20f green, *bl* | 3.00 | 3.00 |
| **3NB6** | SP1 | 50f brn, *rose* | 3.00 | 3.00 |
| **3NB7** | SP1 | 1k dk grn, *grn* | 3.00 | 3.00 |
| | | *Nos. 3NB1-3NB7 (7)* | 17.00 | 17.00 |

## POSTAGE DUE STAMPS

D1

**1920 Typo. *Perf. 15***

| | | | | |
|---|---|---|---|---|
| **3NJ1** | D1 | 5f blue green | 1.50 | 1.50 |
| **3NJ2** | D1 | 10f blue green | 1.50 | 1.50 |
| **3NJ3** | D1 | 20f blue green | .75 | .75 |
| **3NJ4** | D1 | 30f blue green | .75 | .75 |
| **3NJ5** | D1 | 40f blue green | 1.25 | 1.25 |
| | | *Nos. 3NJ1-3NJ5 (5)* | 5.75 | 5.75 |

## TEMESVAR ISSUE

**Issued under Romanian Occupation**

Forgeries exist of the inverted and color error surcharges.

**Hungary Nos. 108, 155, 109, 111, E1 Surcharged**

**1919 Wmk. 137 *Perf. 15***

| | | | | |
|---|---|---|---|---|
| **4N1** | A9 | 30f on 2f brn org (Bl) | .40 | .40 |
| *a.* | | Red surcharge | 2.00 | 2.00 |
| *b.* | | Inverted surcharge (R) | 25.00 | 25.00 |
| **4N2** | A9 | 1k on 4f sl gray (R) | .30 | .30 |
| **4N3** | A9 | 150f on 3f red lil (Bk) | .25 | .25 |
| **4N4** | A9 | 150f on 5f grn (Bk) | .40 | .40 |
| **4N5** | SD1 | 3k on 2f gray grn & red (Bk) | 2.00 | 2.00 |
| *a.* | | Blue surcharge | .80 | .80 |
| | | *Nos. 4N1-4N5 (5)* | 3.35 | 3.35 |

## POSTAGE DUE STAMPS

D1

D2

**1919 Wmk. 137 *Perf. 15***

| | | | | |
|---|---|---|---|---|
| **4NJ1** | D1 | 40f on 15f + 2f vio (Bk) | .50 | .50 |
| *a.* | | Red surcharge | 2.00 | 2.00 |
| **4NJ2** | D2 | 60f on 2f grn & red (Bk) | 2.50 | 2.50 |
| *a.* | | Red surcharge | 8.00 | 8.00 |
| **4NJ3** | D2 | 60f on 10f grn & red (Bk) | 1.25 | 1.25 |
| *a.* | | Red surcharge | 4.00 | 4.00 |
| | | *Nos. 4NJ1-4NJ3 (3)* | 4.25 | 4.25 |

## FIRST TRANSYLVANIA ISSUE

**Issued under Romanian Occupation**

The scarcer values of this issue have been extensively forged. Genuine common values are more easily found.

**Issued in Kolozsvar (Cluj)**

Hungarian Stamps of 1916-18 Overprinted

**1919 Wmk. 137 *Perf. 15, 14***

**On Stamp of 1916, White Numerals**

| | | | | |
|---|---|---|---|---|
| **5N1** | A8 | 15b violet | 4.75 | 4.75 |

**On Stamps of 1916-18**

| | | | | |
|---|---|---|---|---|
| **5N2** | A9 | 2b brown org | .25 | .25 |
| **5N3** | A9 | 3b red lilac | .25 | .25 |
| **5N4** | A9 | 5b green | .25 | .25 |
| **5N5** | A9 | 6b grnsh blue | .40 | .40 |
| **5N5A** | A9 | 10b rose red | 60.00 | 60.00 |
| **5N6** | A9 | 15b violet | .25 | .25 |
| **5N7** | A9 | 25b dull blue | .25 | .25 |
| **5N8** | A9 | 35b brown | .25 | .25 |
| **5N9** | A9 | 40b olive grn | .50 | .50 |
| **5N10** | A10 | 50b red vio & lil | 1.00 | 1.00 |
| **5N11** | A10 | 75b brt bl & pale bl | .30 | .30 |
| **5N12** | A10 | 80b grn & pale grn | .25 | .25 |
| **5N13** | A10 | 1 l red brn & cl | .25 | .25 |
| **5N14** | A10 | 2 l ol brn & bis | .60 | .60 |
| **5N15** | A10 | 3 l dk vio & ind | 3.50 | 3.50 |
| **5N16** | A10 | 5 l dk brn & lt brn | 2.50 | 2.50 |
| **5N17** | A10 | 10 l vio brn & vio | 3.00 | 3.00 |

**On Stamps of 1918**

| | | | | |
|---|---|---|---|---|
| **5N18** | A11 | 10b scarlet | 40.00 | 40.00 |
| **5N19** | A11 | 15b dp violet | 20.00 | 20.00 |
| **5N20** | A11 | 20b dk brown | .25 | .25 |
| *a.* | | Gold overprint | 75.00 | 75.00 |
| *b.* | | Silver overprint | 75.00 | 75.00 |
| **5N21** | A11 | 25b brt blue | .65 | .65 |
| **5N22** | A12 | 40b olive grn | .30 | .30 |

**On No. 103A**

| | | | | |
|---|---|---|---|---|
| **5N23** | A5a | 10b violet brn | .35 | .35 |
| | | *Nos. 5N1-5N23 (24)* | 140.10 | 140.10 |

## SEMI-POSTAL STAMPS

Hungarian Semi-Postal Stamps of 1913-17 Overprinted like Regular Issues

**On Issue of 1913**

**1919 Wmk. 137 *Perf. 14***

| | | | | |
|---|---|---|---|---|
| **5NB1** | SP1 | 1 l on 1f slate | 27.50 | 27.50 |
| **5NB2** | SP1 | 1 l on 2f ol yel | 70.00 | 70.00 |
| **5NB3** | SP1 | 1 l on 3f org | 37.50 | 37.50 |
| **5NB4** | SP1 | 1 l on 5f emer | 3.25 | 3.25 |
| **5NB5** | SP1 | 1 l on 10f car | 4.50 | 4.50 |
| **5NB6** | SP1 | 1 l on 12f vio, *yel* | 16.00 | 16.00 |
| **5NB7** | SP1 | 1 l on 16f gray grn | 6.25 | 6.25 |
| **5NB8** | SP1 | 1 l on 25f ultra | 60.00 | 60.00 |
| **5NB9** | SP1 | 1 l on 35f red vio | 10.00 | 10.00 |
| **5NB10** | SP2 | 1 l on 1k dl red | 60.00 | 60.00 |

**On Issue of 1916-17**

***Perf. 15***

| | | | | |
|---|---|---|---|---|
| **5NB11** | SP3 | 10b + 2b rose red | .25 | .25 |
| **5NB12** | SP4 | 15b + 2b dull vio | .25 | .25 |
| **5NB13** | SP5 | 40b + 2b brn car | .25 | .25 |
| | | *Nos. 5NB1-5NB13 (13)* | 295.75 | 295.75 |

## SPECIAL DELIVERY STAMP

Hungarian Special Delivery Stamp of 1916 Overprinted like Regular Issues

**1919 Wmk. 137 *Perf. 15***

| | | | | |
|---|---|---|---|---|
| **5NE1** | SD1 | 2b gray grn & red | .30 | .30 |

## POSTAGE DUE STAMPS

Hungarian Postage Due Stamps of 1914-18 Overprinted like Regular Issues

**On Stamp of 1914**

**1919 Wmk. 137 *Perf. 15***

| | | | | |
|---|---|---|---|---|
| **5NJ1** | D1 | 50b green & blk | 13.00 | 13.00 |

**On Stamps of 1915**

| | | | | |
|---|---|---|---|---|
| **5NJ2** | D1 | 1b green & red | *350.00* | *350.00* |
| **5NJ3** | D1 | 2b green & red | .70 | .70 |
| **5NJ4** | D1 | 5b green & red | 60.00 | 60.00 |
| **5NJ5** | D1 | 10b green & red | .45 | .45 |
| **5NJ6** | D1 | 15b green & red | 20.00 | 20.00 |
| **5NJ7** | D1 | 20b green & red | .40 | .40 |
| **5NJ8** | D1 | 30b green & red | 30.00 | 30.00 |
| | | *Nos. 5NJ1-5NJ8 (8)* | *474.55* | *474.55* |

## NEWSPAPER STAMP

Hungarian Newspaper Stamp of 1914 Overprinted like Regular Issues

**1919 Wmk. 137 *Imperf.***

| | | | | |
|---|---|---|---|---|
| **5NP1** | N5 | 2b orange | 3.75 | 3.75 |

## SECOND TRANSYLVANIA ISSUE

The scarcer values of this issue have been extensively forged. Genuine common values are more easily found.

**Issued in Nagyvarad (Oradea)**

Hungarian Stamps of 1916-19 Overprinted

**1919 Wmk. 137 *Perf. 15, 14***

**On Stamps of 1913-16**

| | | | | |
|---|---|---|---|---|
| **6N1** | A4 | 2b olive yel | 7.00 | 7.00 |
| **6N2** | A4 | 3b orange | 13.00 | 13.00 |
| **6N3** | A4 | 6b olive grn | 1.75 | 1.75 |
| **6N4** | A4 | 16b gray grn | 37.50 | 37.50 |
| **6N5** | A4 | 50b lake, *bl* | 1.75 | 1.75 |
| **6N6** | A4 | 70b red brn & grn | 26.00 | 26.00 |

**On Stamp of 1916 (White Numerals)**

| | | | | |
|---|---|---|---|---|
| **6N6A** | A8 | 15b violet | 125.00 | 125.00 |

**On Stamps of 1916-18**

| | | | | |
|---|---|---|---|---|
| **6N7** | A9 | 2b brown org | .25 | .25 |
| **6N8** | A9 | 3b red lilac | .25 | .25 |
| **6N9** | A9 | 5b green | .30 | .30 |
| **6N10** | A9 | 6b grnsh blue | 1.60 | 1.60 |
| **6N11** | A9 | 10b rose red | 2.10 | 2.10 |
| **6N12** | A9 | 15b violet | .25 | .25 |
| **6N13** | A9 | 20b gray brn | 20.00 | 20.00 |
| **6N14** | A9 | 25b dull blue | .30 | .30 |
| **6N15** | A9 | 35b brown | .45 | .45 |
| **6N16** | A9 | 40b olive grn | .30 | .30 |
| **6N17** | A10 | 50b red vio & lil | .60 | .60 |
| **6N18** | A10 | 75b brt bl & pale bl | .25 | .25 |
| **6N19** | A10 | 80b grn & pale grn | .30 | .30 |
| **6N20** | A10 | 1 l red brn & cl | .75 | .75 |
| **6N21** | A10 | 2 l ol brn & bis | .25 | .25 |
| **6N22** | A10 | 3 l dk vio & ind | 6.50 | 6.50 |
| **6N23** | A10 | 5 l dk brn & lt brn | 3.25 | 3.25 |
| **6N24** | A10 | 10 l vio brn & vio | 1.50 | 1.50 |

**On Stamps of 1918**

| | | | | |
|---|---|---|---|---|
| **6N25** | A11 | 10b scarlet | 3.25 | 3.25 |
| **6N26** | A11 | 20b dk brown | .25 | .25 |
| **6N27** | A11 | 25b brt blue | .75 | .75 |
| **6N28** | A12 | 40b olive grn | 1.10 | 1.10 |

**On Stamps of 1918-19, Overprinted "Koztarsasag"**

| | | | | |
|---|---|---|---|---|
| **6N29** | A9 | 2b brown org | 4.00 | 4.00 |
| **6N30** | A9 | 3b red lilac | .25 | .25 |
| **6N31** | A9 | 4b slate gray | .25 | .25 |
| **6N32** | A9 | 5b green | .50 | .50 |
| **6N33** | A9 | 6b grnsh bl | 3.00 | 3.00 |
| **6N34** | A9 | 10b rose red | 17.50 | 17.50 |
| **6N35** | A9 | 20b gray brn | 2.50 | 2.50 |
| **6N36** | A9 | 40b olive grn | .50 | .50 |
| **6N37** | A10 | 1 l red brn & cl | .25 | .25 |
| **6N38** | A10 | 3 l dk vio & ind | .75 | .75 |
| **6N39** | A10 | 5 l dk brn & lt brn | 4.50 | 4.50 |
| **6N40** | A11 | 10b scarlet | *75.00* | *75.00* |
| **6N41** | A11 | 20b dk brown | 4.50 | 4.50 |
| **6N42** | A11 | 25b brt blue | 1.25 | 1.25 |
| **6N43** | A12 | 50b lilac | .25 | .25 |

**On Stamps of 1919**

**Inscribed "MAGYAR POSTA"**

| | | | | |
|---|---|---|---|---|
| **6N44** | A13 | 5b yellow grn | .25 | .25 |
| **6N45** | A13 | 10b red | .25 | .25 |
| **6N46** | A13 | 20b dk brown | .40 | .40 |
| **6N47** | A13 | 25b dull blue | 2.00 | 2.00 |
| **6N48** | A13 | 40b olive grn | .65 | .65 |
| **6N49** | A14 | 5 l dk brn & brn | 6.50 | 6.50 |

**On No. 103A**

| | | | | |
|---|---|---|---|---|
| **6N50** | A5a | 10b violet brn | .85 | .85 |
| | | *Nos. 6N1-6N50 (51)* | *382.45* | *382.45* |

## SEMI-POSTAL STAMPS

Hungarian Semi-Postal Stamps of 1913-17 Overprinted like Regular Issues

**On Stamps of 1913**

**1919 Wmk. 137 *Perf. 14***

| | | | | |
|---|---|---|---|---|
| **6NB1** | SP1 | 1 l on 1f slate | 2.25 | 2.25 |
| **6NB2** | SP1 | 1 l on 2f olive yel | 8.50 | 8.50 |
| **6NB3** | SP1 | 1 l on 3f orange | 2.75 | 2.75 |
| **6NB4** | SP1 | 1 l on 5f emerald | .25 | .25 |
| **6NB5** | SP1 | 1 l on 6f olive grn | 2.25 | 2.25 |
| **6NB6** | SP1 | 1 l on 10f carmine | .30 | .30 |
| **6NB7** | SP1 | 1 l on 12f vio, *yel* | 60.00 | 60.00 |
| **6NB8** | SP1 | 1 l on 16f gray grn | 2.50 | 2.50 |
| **6NB9** | SP1 | 1 l on 20f dk brn | 11.00 | 11.00 |
| **6NB10** | SP1 | 1 l on 25f ultra | 7.50 | 7.50 |
| **6NB11** | SP1 | 1 l on 35f red vio | 7.75 | 7.75 |

**On Stamp of 1915**

**Wmk. 135 *Perf. 11½***

| | | | | |
|---|---|---|---|---|
| **6NB12** | A4 | 5b emerald | 20.00 | 20.00 |

**On Stamps of 1916-17**

**Wmk. 137 — Perf. 15**

| | | | | |
|---|---|---|---|---|
| **6NB13** | SP3 | 10b + 2b rose red | 1.25 | 1.25 |
| **6NB14** | SP4 | 15b + 2b dull vio | .45 | .45 |
| **6NB15** | SP5 | 40b + 2b brown car | .25 | .25 |
| | | *Nos. 6NB1-6NB15 (15)* | 127.00 | 127.00 |

### SPECIAL DELIVERY STAMP

Hungarian Special Delivery Stamp of 1916 Overprinted like Regular Issues

**1919 — Wmk. 137 — Perf. 15**

| | | | | |
|---|---|---|---|---|
| **6NE1** | SD1 | 2b gray grn & red | .40 | .40 |

### POSTAGE DUE STAMPS

**Hungarian Postage Due Stamps of 1915 Overprinted like Regular Issues**

**1919 — Wmk. 137 — Perf. 15**

| | | | | |
|---|---|---|---|---|
| **6NJ1** | D1 | 1b green & red | 30.00 | 30.00 |
| **6NJ2** | D1 | 2b green & red | .25 | .25 |
| **6NJ3** | D1 | 5b green & red | 9.75 | 9.75 |
| **6NJ4** | D1 | 6b green & red | 6.75 | 6.75 |
| **6NJ5** | D1 | 10b green & red | .25 | .25 |
| **6NJ6** | D1 | 12b green & red | 1.50 | 1.50 |
| **6NJ7** | D1 | 15b green & red | 1.50 | 1.50 |
| **6NJ8** | D1 | 20b green & red | .25 | .25 |
| **6NJ9** | D1 | 30b green & red | 1.60 | 1.60 |
| | | *Nos. 6NJ1-6NJ9 (9)* | 51.85 | 51.85 |

**On Hungary No. J27**

***Perf. 11½x12***

**Wmk. 135**

| | | | | |
|---|---|---|---|---|
| **6NJ10** | D1 | 20b on 100b grn & blk | 350.00 | 350.00 |

### NEWSPAPER STAMP

**Hungarian Newspaper Stamp of 1914 Overprinted like Regular Issues**

**1919 — Wmk. 137 — Imperf.**

| | | | | |
|---|---|---|---|---|
| **6NP1** | N5 | 2b orange | .45 | .45 |

### FIRST BARANYA ISSUE

**Issued under Serbian Occupation**

The scarcer values of this issue have been extensively forged. Genuine common values are more easily found.

**Hungarian Stamps of 1913-18 Overprinted in Black or Red**

On A4, A9, A11, A12

On A10

**1919 — Wmk. 137 — Perf. 15**

**On Issue of 1913-16**

| | | | | |
|---|---|---|---|---|
| **7N1** | A4 | 6f olive grn (R) | .90 | .90 |
| **7N2** | A4 | 50f lake, *bl* | .25 | .25 |
| **7N3** | A4 | 60f grn, *salmon* | .75 | .75 |
| **7N4** | A4 | 70f red brn & grn (R) | 2.00 | 2.00 |
| **7N5** | A4 | 70f red brn & grn (Bk) | .25 | .25 |
| **7N6** | A4 | 80f dl vio (R) | 3.25 | 3.25 |

**On Issue of 1916-18**

| | | | | |
|---|---|---|---|---|
| **7N7** | A9 | 2f brown org (Bk) | 4.25 | 4.25 |
| **7N8** | A9 | 2f brown org (R) | .25 | .25 |
| **7N9** | A9 | 3f red lilac (Bk) | .25 | .25 |
| **7N10** | A9 | 3f red lilac (R) | .80 | .80 |
| **7N11** | A9 | 5f green (Bk) | .80 | .80 |
| **7N12** | A9 | 5f green (R) | .25 | .25 |
| **7N13** | A9 | 6f grnsh bl (Bk) | 1.75 | 1.75 |
| **7N14** | A9 | 6f grnsh bl (R) | 2.00 | 2.00 |
| **7N15** | A9 | 15f violet | .35 | .35 |
| **7N16** | A9 | 20f gray brn | 20.00 | 20.00 |
| **7N17** | A9 | 25f dull blue | 3.50 | 3.50 |
| **7N18** | A9 | 35f brown | 5.75 | 5.75 |
| **7N19** | A9 | 40f olive grn | 20.00 | 20.00 |
| **7N20** | A10 | 50f red vio & lil | 2.00 | 2.00 |
| **7N21** | A10 | 75f brt bl & pale bl | .40 | .40 |
| **7N22** | A10 | 80f grn & pale grn | .65 | .65 |
| **7N23** | A10 | 1k red brn & cl | .55 | .55 |
| **7N24** | A10 | 2k ol brn & bis | .65 | .65 |
| **7N25** | A10 | 3k dk vio & ind | .65 | .65 |
| **7N26** | A10 | 5k dk brn & lt brn | 1.25 | 1.25 |
| **7N27** | A10 | 10k vio brn & vio | 4.00 | *4.00* |

| | | | | |
|---|---|---|---|---|
| **7N28** | A9 | 45f on 2f brn org | .35 | .35 |
| **7N29** | A9 | 45f on 5f green | .25 | .25 |
| **7N30** | A9 | 45f on 15f violet | .25 | .25 |

**On Issue of 1918**

| | | | | |
|---|---|---|---|---|
| **7N31** | A11 | 10f scarlet (Bk) | .25 | .25 |
| **7N32** | A11 | 20f dk brn (Bk) | .25 | .25 |
| **7N34** | A11 | 25f dp blue (Bk) | 1.90 | 1.90 |
| **7N35** | A11 | 25f dp blue (R) | 1.10 | 1.10 |
| **7N36** | A12 | 40f olive grn (Bk) | 4.50 | 4.50 |
| **7N37** | A12 | 40f olive grn (R) | 30.00 | 30.00 |

**On Issue of 1918-19 (Koztarsasag)**

| | | | | |
|---|---|---|---|---|
| **7N38** | A9 | 2f brown org (Bk) | 3.50 | 3.50 |
| **7N39** | A12 | 40f ol grn (Bk) | *125.00* | *125.00* |
| **7N40** | A12 | 40f olive grn (R) | 20.00 | 20.00 |

**With New Value Added**

| | | | | |
|---|---|---|---|---|
| **7N41** | A9 | 45f on 2f brn org (Bk) | 2.00 | 2.00 |
| **7N42** | A9 | 45f on 2f brn org (R) | .45 | .45 |

The overprints were set in groups of 25. In each group two stamps have the figures "1" of "1919" with serifs.

### SEMI-POSTAL STAMPS

**Hungarian Semi-Postal Stamps Overprinted Regular Issue First Type On Stamp of 1915**

**1919 — Wmk. 137 — Perf. 15**

| | | | | |
|---|---|---|---|---|
| **7NB1** | A4 | 50f + 2f lake, *bl* | 16.00 | 16.00 |

**On Stamps of 1916**

| | | | | |
|---|---|---|---|---|
| **7NB2** | SP3 | 10f + 2f rose red | .30 | .30 |
| **7NB3** | SP4 | 15f + 2f dull vio | .40 | .40 |
| | | *Nos. 7NB1-7NB3 (3)* | 16.70 | 16.70 |

### SPECIAL DELIVERY STAMP

SD1

**1919 — Wmk. 137 — Perf. 15**

| | | | | |
|---|---|---|---|---|
| **7NE1** | SD1 | 105f on 2f gray grn & red | 1.25 | 1.25 |

### POSTAGE DUE STAMPS

Overprinted or Surcharged on Hungary Nos. J29, J32, J35

**1919 — Wmk. 137 — Perf. 15**

| | | | | |
|---|---|---|---|---|
| **7NJ1** | D1 | 2f green & red | 3.75 | 3.75 |
| **7NJ2** | D1 | 10f green & red | 1.25 | 1.25 |
| **7NJ3** | D1 | 20f green & red | 1.60 | 1.60 |

**With New Value Added**

| | | | | |
|---|---|---|---|---|
| **7NJ4** | D1 | 40f on 2f grn & red | 1.50 | 1.50 |
| | | *Nos. 7NJ1-7NJ4 (4)* | 8.10 | 8.10 |

### SECOND BARANYA ISSUE

The scarcer values of this issue have been extensively forged. Genuine common values are more easily found.

Hungarian Stamps of 1916-19 Surcharged in Black and Red

**1919 — On Stamps of 1916-18**

| | | | | |
|---|---|---|---|---|
| **8N1** | A9 | 20f on 2f brn org | 4.25 | 4.25 |
| **8N2** | A9 | 50f on 5f green | 2.00 | 2.00 |
| **8N3** | A9 | 150f on 15f violet | 2.00 | 2.00 |
| **8N4** | A10 | 200f on 75f brt bl & pale bl | .75 | .75 |

**On Stamp of 1918-19, Overprinted "Koztarsasag"**

| | | | | |
|---|---|---|---|---|
| **8N5** | A11 | 150f on 15f dp vio | .50 | .50 |

**On Stamps of 1919**

| | | | | |
|---|---|---|---|---|
| **8N6** | A13 | 20f on 2f brn org | .35 | .35 |
| **8N7** | A13 | 30f on 6f grnsh bl | .70 | .70 |
| **8N8** | A13 | 50f on 5f yel grn | .25 | .25 |
| **8N9** | A13 | 100f on 25f dull bl | .25 | .25 |
| **8N10** | A13 | 100f on 40f ol grn | .25 | .25 |
| **8N11** | A13 | 100f on 45f orange | 1.10 | 1.10 |
| **8N12** | A13 | 150f on 20f dk brn | 1.40 | 1.40 |

**On No. 103A**

| | | | | |
|---|---|---|---|---|
| **8N13** | A5a | 10f on 10f vio brn | .75 | .75 |
| | | *Nos. 8N1-8N13 (13)* | 14.55 | 14.55 |

### SPECIAL DELIVERY STAMP

**Hungarian Special Delivery Stamp of 1916 Surcharged like Regular Issues**

**1919 — Wmk. 137 — Perf. 15**

| | | | | |
|---|---|---|---|---|
| **8NE1** | SD1 | 10f on 2f gray grn & red | .65 | .65 |

### NEWSPAPER STAMP

**Hungarian Newspaper Stamp of 1914 Surcharged like Regular Issues**

**1919 — Wmk. 137 — Imperf.**

| | | | | |
|---|---|---|---|---|
| **8NP1** | N5 | 10f on 2f orange | .80 | .80 |

### TEMESVAR ISSUES

**Issued under Serbian Occupation**

Forgeries exist of the inverted and color error surcharges.

**Hungarian Stamps of 1916-18 Surcharged in Black, Blue or Brown**

a

b

**1919**

| | | | | |
|---|---|---|---|---|
| **9N1** | A9(a) | 10f on 2f brn org (Bl) | .25 | .25 |
| *a.* | | Black surcharge | 15.00 | 15.00 |
| **9N2** | A9(b) | 30f on 2f brn org | .25 | .25 |
| *a.* | | Inverted surcharge | 75.00 | 75.00 |
| **9N3** | A11(b) | 50f on 20f dk brn (Bl) | .25 | .25 |
| *a.* | | Inverted surcharge | | |
| **9N4** | A9(b) | 1k 50f on 15f vio | .30 | .30 |
| *a.* | | Brown surcharge | .75 | .75 |
| *b.* | | Double surcharge (Bk) | 50.00 | 50.00 |
| | | *Nos. 9N1-9N4 (4)* | 1.05 | 1.05 |

### SEMI-POSTAL STAMP

Hungarian Semi-Postal Stamp of 1916 Surcharged in Blue

**1919 — Wmk. 137 — Perf. 15**

| | | | | |
|---|---|---|---|---|
| **9NB1** | SP3 | 45f on 10f + 2f rose red | .25 | .25 |

### POSTAGE DUE STAMPS

Hungarian Postage Due Stamps of 1915 Surcharged

**1919 — Wmk. 137 — Perf. 15**

| | | | | |
|---|---|---|---|---|
| **9NJ1** | D1 | 40f on 2f grn & red | .80 | .80 |
| **9NJ2** | D1 | 60f on 2f grn & red | .80 | .80 |
| **9NJ3** | D1 | 100f on 2f grn & red | .80 | .80 |
| | | *Nos. 9NJ1-9NJ3 (3)* | 2.40 | 2.40 |

### BANAT, BACSKA ISSUE

**Issued under Serbian Occupation**

Postal authorities at Temesvar applied these overprints. The stamps were available for postage, but were chiefly used to pay postal employees' salaries.

The overprints on this issue have been extensively forged. Even the inexpensive values are difficult to find with genuine overprints. The more extensive note before 1N1 also applies to Nos. 10N1-10NP1.

**Hungarian Stamps of 1913-19 Overprinted in Black or Red**

a

b

**1919**

**Type "a" on Stamp of 1913**

| | | | | |
|---|---|---|---|---|
| **10N1** | A4 | 50f lake, *blue* | 4.00 | 4.00 |

**Type "a" on Stamps of 1916-18**

| | | | | |
|---|---|---|---|---|
| **10N2** | A9 | 2f brown org | 4.00 | 4.00 |
| **10N3** | A9 | 3f red lilac | 4.00 | 4.00 |
| **10N4** | A9 | 5f green | 4.00 | 4.00 |
| **10N5** | A9 | 6f grnsh blue | 4.00 | 4.00 |
| **10N6** | A9 | 15f violet | 4.00 | 4.00 |
| **10N7** | A9 | 35f brown | 35.00 | 35.00 |

**Type "b"**

| | | | | |
|---|---|---|---|---|
| **10N8** | A10 | 50f red vio & lil (R) | 30.00 | 30.00 |
| **10N9** | A10 | 75f brt bl & pale bl | 4.00 | 4.00 |
| **10N10** | A10 | 80f grn & pale grn | 4.00 | 4.00 |
| *a.* | | Red overprint | 37.50 | 37.50 |
| **10N11** | A10 | 1k red brn & cl | 4.00 | 4.00 |
| **10N12** | A10 | 2k ol brn & bis | 4.00 | 4.00 |
| *a.* | | Red overprint | 37.50 | 37.50 |
| **10N14** | A10 | 3k dk vio & ind | 65.00 | 65.00 |
| **10N15** | A10 | 5k dk brn & lt brn | 4.00 | 4.00 |
| **10N16** | A10 | 10k vio brn & vio | 4.00 | 4.00 |

**Type "a" on Stamps of 1918**

| | | | | |
|---|---|---|---|---|
| **10N17** | A11 | 10f scarlet | 4.00 | 4.00 |
| **10N18** | A11 | 20f dk brown | 4.00 | 4.00 |
| **10N19** | A11 | 25f brt blue | 4.00 | 4.00 |
| **10N20** | A12 | 40f olive grn | 4.00 | 4.00 |
| **10N21** | A12 | 50f lilac | 4.00 | 4.00 |

**Type "a" on Stamps of 1919 Inscribed "Magyar Posta"**

| | | | | |
|---|---|---|---|---|
| **10N22** | A13 | 10f red | *30.00* | *30.00* |
| **10N23** | A13 | 20f dk brown | *30.00* | *30.00* |
| **10N24** | A13 | 25f dull blue | *37.50* | *37.50* |

**Type "a" on Stamps of 1918-19 Overprinted "Koztarsasag"**

| | | | | |
|---|---|---|---|---|
| **10N25** | A9 | 4f slate gray | 3.50 | 3.50 |
| **10N26** | A9 | 4f sl gray (R) | 42.50 | 42.50 |
| **10N27** | A9 | 5f green | 4.00 | 4.00 |
| **10N28** | A9 | 6f grnsh blue | 4.00 | 4.00 |
| **10N29** | A9 | 10f rose red | 30.00 | 30.00 |
| **10N30** | A11 | 15f dp violet | 30.00 | 30.00 |
| **10N31** | A9 | 20f gray brn | 30.00 | 30.00 |
| **10N32** | A11 | 25f brt blue | 30.00 | 30.00 |
| **10N33** | A9 | 40f olive grn | 3.50 | 3.50 |
| **10N34** | A9 | 40f ol grn (R) | 32.50 | 32.50 |

### Type "b"

10N35 A10 1k red brn & cl 4.00 4.00
10N36 A10 2k ol brn & bis 30.00 30.00
10N37 A10 3k dk vio & ind 30.00 30.00
10N38 A10 5k dk brn & lt brn 30.00 30.00
10N39 A10 10k vio brn & vio 30.00 30.00

### Type "a" on Temesvár Issue

10N40 A9 10f on 2f brn org (Bl & Bk) 4.00 4.00
10N41 A9 1k50f on 15f vio 4.00 4.00

10N42 A5a 50f on 10f vio brn 4.00 4.00
*a.* Red overprint 75.00 75.00
*Nos. 10N1-10N42 (41)* *641.50 641.50*

## SEMI-POSTAL STAMPS

### Semi-Postal Stamps of 1916-17 Overprinted Type "a" in Black

**1919**

10NB1 SP3 10f + 2f rose red 4.00 4.00
10NB2 SP4 15f + 2f dull vio 4.00 4.00
10NB3 SP5 40f + 2f brn car 4.00 4.00

### Same Overprint on Temesvar Issue

10NB4 SP3 45f on 10f + 2f rose red (Bl & Bk) 4.00 4.00
*Nos. 10NB1-10NB4 (4)* 16.00 16.00

## SPECIAL DELIVERY STAMP

Hungary No. E1 Surcharged in Black

**1919**

10NE1 SD1 30f on 2f gray grn & red 4.00 4.00
*a.* Red overprint 75.00 75.00

## POSTAGE DUE STAMPS

### Postage Due Stamps of 1914-15 Overprinted Type "a" in Black

**1919**

10NJ1 D1 2f green & red 4.00 4.00
10NJ2 D1 10f green & red 4.00 4.00
10NJ3 D1 15f green & red 32.50 32.50
10NJ4 D1 20f green & red 4.00 4.00
10NJ5 D1 30f green & red 30.00 30.00
10NJ6 D1 50f green & blk 30.00 30.00
*Nos. 10NJ1-10NJ6 (6)* 104.50 104.50

## NEWSPAPER STAMP

### Stamp of 1914 Overprinted Type "a" in Black

**1919**

10NP1 N5 (2f) orange 4.00 4.00

## SZEGED ISSUE

The "Hungarian National Government, Szeged, 1919," as the overprint reads, was an anti-Bolshevist government which opposed the Soviet Republic then in control at Budapest.

The overprints on this issue have been extensively forged. Even the inexpensive stamps are difficult to find with genuine overprints. The more extensive note before No. 1N1 also applies to Szeged Nos. 11N1-11NP1.

Hungary Stamps of 1916-19 Overprinted in Green, Red and Blue

### On Stamps of 1916-18

**1919** *Perf. 15, 14*

11N1 A9 2f brn org (G) 2.25 2.25
11N2 A9 3f red lilac (G) .75 .75
11N3 A9 5f green 2.75 2.75
11N4 A9 6f grnsh blue 32.50 32.50
11N5 A9 15f violet 3.50 3.50
11N6 A10 50f red vio & lil 19.00 19.00
11N7 A10 75f brt bl & pale bl 4.25 4.25
11N8 A10 80f grn & pale grn 18.00 18.00
11N9 A10 1k red brn & cl (G) 2.25 2.25
11N10 A10 2k ol brn & bis 4.75 4.75
11N11 A10 3k dk vio & ind 7.25 7.25
11N12 A10 5k dk brn & lt brn 60.00 60.00
11N13 A10 10k vio brn & vio 60.00 60.00

### With New Value Added

11N14 A9 45f on 3f red lil (R & G) .80 .80
11N15 A10 10k on 1k red brn & cl (Bl & G) 8.00 8.00

### On Stamps of 1918

11N16 A11 10f scarlet (G) 2.50 2.50
11N17 A11 20f dk brown .60 .60
11N18 A11 25f brt blue 22.50 22.50
11N19 A12 40f olive grn 11.00 11.00

### On Stamps of 1918-19 Overprinted "Koztarsasag"

11N20 A9 3f red lil (G) 42.50 42.50
11N21 A9 4f slate gray 11.00 11.00
11N22 A9 5f green 25.00 25.00
11N23 A9 6f grnsh blue 15.00 15.00
11N24 A9 10f rose red (G) 32.50 32.50
11N25 A11 10f scarlet) 30.00 30.00
11N26 A11 15f dp violet 10.00 10.00
11N27 A9 20f gray brown 50.00 50.00
11N28 A11 20f dk brown 65.00 65.00
11N29 A11 25f brt blue 20.00 20.00
11N30 A9 40f olive 2.25 2.25
11N31 A12 50f lilac 1.75 1.75
11N32 A10 3k dk vio & ind 37.50 37.50

### With New Value Added

11N33 A9 20f on 2f brn org (R & G) .80 .80

### On Stamps of 1919 Inscribed "Magyar Posta"

11N34 A13 20f dk brown 60.00 60.00
11N35 A13 25f dull blue 1.75 1.75
*Nos. 11N1-11N35 (35)* 667.70 667.70

## SEMI-POSTAL STAMPS

### Szeged Overprint on Semi-Postal Stamps of 1916-17 in Green or Red

**1919**

11NB1 SP3 10f + 2f rose red (G) .85 .85
11NB2 SP4 15f + 2f dl vio (R) 3.75 3.75
11NB3 SP5 40f + 2f brn car (G) 10.00 10.00

### With Additional Overprint "Koztarsasag"

11NB4 SP5 40f + 2f brn car (Bk & G) 15.00 15.00
*Nos. 11NB1-11NB4 (4)* 29.60 29.60

## SPECIAL DELIVERY STAMP

### Szeged Overprint on Special Delivery Stamp of 1916 in Red

**1919**

11NE1 SD1 2f gray grn & red 11.00 11.00

## POSTAGE DUE STAMPS

### Szeged Overprint on Stamps of 1915-18 in Red

**1919**

11NJ1 D1 2f green & red 3.00 3.00
11NJ2 D1 6f green & red 9.75 9.75
11NJ3 D1 10f green & red 3.75 3.75
11NJ4 D1 12f green & red 4.75 4.75
11NJ5 D1 20f green & red 6.00 6.00
11NJ6 D1 30f green & red 9.00 9.00

### Red Surcharge

11NJ7 SD1 50f on 2f gray grn & red 2.75 2.75
11NJ8 SD1 100f on 2f gray grn & red 2.75 2.75
*Nos. 11NJ1-11NJ8 (8)* 41.75 41.75

## NEWSPAPER STAMP

### Szeged Overprint on Stamp of 1914 in Green

**1919** **Wmk. 137** *Imperf.*

11NP1 N5 (2f) orange .85 .85

# ICELAND

'is-lənd

LOCATION — Island in the North Atlantic Ocean, east of Greenland
GOVT. — Republic
AREA — 39,758 sq. mi.
POP. — 272,069 (1997)
CAPITAL — Reykjavik

Iceland became a republic on June 17, 1944. Formerly this country was united with Denmark under the government of King Christian X who, as a ruling sovereign of both countries, was assigned the dual title of king of each. Although the two countries were temporarily united in certain affairs beyond the king's person, both were acknowledged as sovereign states.

96 Skillings = 1 Rigsdaler
100 Aurar (singular "Eyrir") = 1 Krona (1876)

**Catalogue values for unused stamps in this country are for Never Hinged items, beginning with Scott 246 in the regular postage section, Scott B7 in the semi-postal section and Scott C21 in the air post section.**

### Watermarks

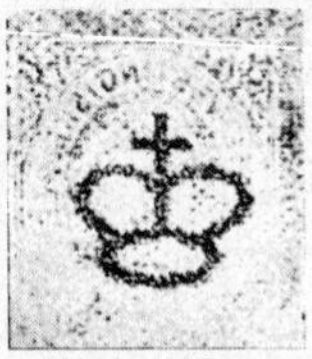

Wmk. 112 — Crown

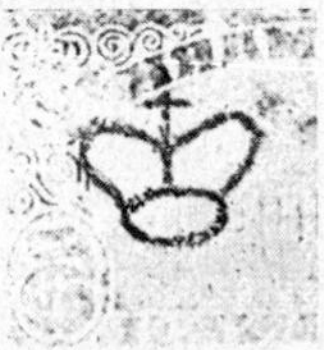

Wmk. 113 — Crown

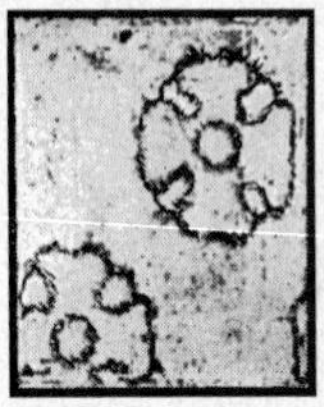

Wmk. 47 — Multiple Rosette

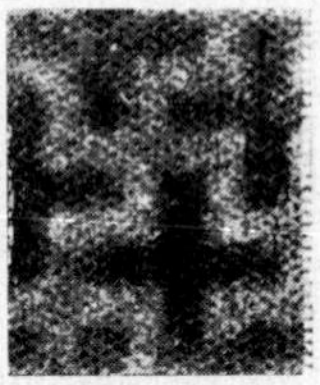

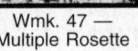

Wmk. 114 — Multiple Crosses

Wmk. 409 — State Shield

Wmk. 410 — State Arms

Values for unused stamps are for examples with original gum as defined in the catalogue introduction. Very fine examples of Nos. 1-33A and O1-O12 will have centering with perforations clear of the framelines but with design noticeably off center, and Nos. 1-7 and O1-O3 additionally will have some irregular or shorter perforations. Well centered stamps are quite scarce and will command higher prices.

A1

*Perf. 14x13½*

**1873 Typo. Wmk. 112**

| | | | | |
|---|---|---|---|---|
| 1 | A1 | 2s ultra | 1,300. | *3,000.* |
| *a.* | | Imperf. | 850. | |
| 2 | A1 | 4s dark carmine | 225. | *1,250.* |
| *a.* | | Imperf. | 850. | — |
| 3 | A1 | 8s brown | 425. | *1,500.* |
| *a.* | | Imperf. | 450. | |
| 4 | A1 | 16s yellow | 2,000. | *3,000.* |
| *a.* | | Imperf. | 550. | |

*Perf. 12½*

| | | | | |
|---|---|---|---|---|
| 5 | A1 | 3s gray | 650. | *2,000.* |
| *a.* | | Imperf. | 1,000. | |
| 6 | A1 | 4s carmine | 1,900. | *2,900.* |
| 7 | A1 | 16s yellow | 175. | *850.* |

False and favor cancellations are often found on Nos. 1-7. Values are considerably less than those shown.

A2

**1876**

| | | | | |
|---|---|---|---|---|
| 8 | A2 | 5a blue | 475.00 | *1,000.* |

*Perf. 14x13½*

| | | | | |
|---|---|---|---|---|
| 9 | A2 | 5a blue | 600.00 | *1,200.* |
| *a.* | | Imperf. | 2,450. | |
| 10 | A2 | 6a gray | 200.00 | 40.00 |
| 11 | A2 | 10a carmine | 300.00 | 10.00 |
| *a.* | | Imperf. | 850.00 | *1,000.* |
| 12 | A2 | 16a brown | 175.00 | 67.50 |
| 13 | A2 | 20a dark violet | 45.00 | *675.00* |
| 14 | A2 | 40a green | 140.00 | *300.00* |

Fake and favor cancellations are often found on No. 13, and value is considerably less than that shown.

Small "3" — A3

Large "3" — A3a

**1882-98**

| | | | | |
|---|---|---|---|---|
| 15 | A3 | 3a orange | 82.50 | 35.00 |
| 16 | A2 | 5a green | 75.00 | 18.00 |
| 17 | A2 | 20a blue | 425.00 | 67.50 |
| *a.* | | 20a ultramarine | 1,000. | 375.00 |
| 18 | A2 | 40a red violet | 75.00 | 57.50 |
| *a.* | | Perf. 13 ('98) | *6,750.* | |
| 19 | A2 | 50a bl & car ('92) | 120.00 | *140.00* |
| 20 | A2 | 100a brn & vio ('92) | 110.00 | *175.00* |
| | | *Nos. 15-20 (6)* | 887.50 | 493.00 |

See note after No. 68.

**1896-1901** ***Perf. 13***

| | | | | |
|---|---|---|---|---|
| 21 | A3 | 3a orange ('97) | 145.00 | 15.00 |
| 22 | A3a | 3a yellow ('01) | 11.00 | *30.00* |
| 23 | A2 | 4a rose & gray ('99) | 24.00 | *27.50* |
| 24 | A2 | 5a green | 5.25 | 3.75 |
| 25 | A2 | 6a gray ('97) | 22.50 | *24.00* |
| 26 | A2 | 10a carmine ('97) | 18.00 | 3.75 |
| 27 | A2 | 16a brown | 97.50 | *140.00* |
| 28 | A2 | 20a dull blue ('98) | 62.50 | 50.00 |
| *a.* | | 20a dull ultramarine | 675.00 | 57.50 |
| 29 | A2 | 25a yel brown & blue ('00) | 30.00 | *42.50* |
| 30 | A2 | 50a bl & car ('98) | 600.00 | *900.00* |

See note after No. 68.
For surcharges see Nos. 31-33A, 45-68.

### Black and Red Surcharge

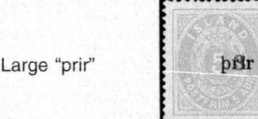

Large "prir"

**1897** ***Perf. 13***

| | | | | |
|---|---|---|---|---|
| 31 | A2 | 3a on 5a green | 900. | 750. |
| *a.* | | Perf. 14x13½ | 26,500. | *4,750.* |
| *b.* | | Inverted surcharge | 1,500. | 1,250. |
| *c.* | | As "a," inverted surcharge | | *7,500.* |

Large "prir" is 6.1mm to 6.3mm wide by 3.5mm tall.

Small "prir"

| | | | | |
|---|---|---|---|---|
| 32 | A2 | 3a on 5a green | 900. | 750. |
| *a.* | | Inverted surcharge | 1,650. | 1,350. |
| *b.* | | Perf. 14x13½ | *13,500.* | *3,000.* |
| *c.* | | In vert. pair with #31 | 2,250. | 2,000. |
| *d.* | | As "b," in vert. pair with #31a | | — |

All 5 known unused examples of #32b lack gum.

Small "prir" is 5.5mm to 5.6mm wide by 3.1mm tall.

### Black Surcharge

Large "prir"

| | | | | |
|---|---|---|---|---|
| 33 | A2 | 3a on 5a green | 1,450. | 1,050. |
| *b.* | | Inverted surcharge | 1,950. | 1,650. |

Large "prir" is 6.1mm to 6.3mm wide by 3.5mm tall.

Small "prir"

| | | | | |
|---|---|---|---|---|
| 33A | A2 | 3a on 5a green | 1,100. | 750. |
| *c.* | | Inverted surcharge | 1,800. | 1,500. |

Excellent counterfeits are known.

Small "prir" is 5.5mm to 5.6mm wide by 3.1mm tall.

King Christian IX — A4

**1902-04 Wmk. 113** ***Perf. 13***

| | | | | |
|---|---|---|---|---|
| 34 | A4 | 3a orange | 7.00 | 4.50 |
| 35 | A4 | 4a gray & rose | 4.50 | 1.60 |
| 36 | A4 | 5a yel green | 40.00 | 1.40 |
| 37 | A4 | 6a gray brown | 24.00 | 13.00 |
| 38 | A4 | 10a car rose | 7.00 | 1.40 |
| 39 | A4 | 16a chocolate | 10.00 | *13.00* |
| 40 | A4 | 20a deep blue | 3.50 | *5.50* |
| *a.* | | Inscribed "PJONUSTA" | 75.00 | *110.00* |
| 41 | A4 | 25a brn & grn | 5.00 | *8.25* |
| 42 | A4 | 40a violet | 5.50 | *7.75* |
| 43 | A4 | 50a gray & bl blk | 7.00 | *29.00* |
| 44 | A4 | 1k sl bl & yel brn | 8.25 | *13.00* |
| 44A | A4 | 2k olive brn & brt blue ('04) | 32.50 | *87.50* |
| 44B | A4 | 5k org brn & slate blue ('04) | 175.00 | *275.00* |
| | | *Nos. 34-44B (13)* | 329.25 | *460.90* |

For surcharge see No. 142.

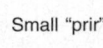

Stamps of 1882-1901 Overprinted

**1902-03 Wmk. 112** ***Perf. 13***

### Red Overprint

| | | | | |
|---|---|---|---|---|
| 45 | A2 | 5a green | 1.75 | *13.50* |
| *a.* | | Inverted overprint | 100.00 | *140.00* |
| *b.* | | "I" before Gildi omitted | 225.00 | |
| *c.* | | '03-'03 | 990.00 | |
| *d.* | | 02'-'03 | 850.00 | |
| *e.* | | Pair, one without overprint | 225.00 | |
| 46 | A2 | 6a gray | 1.50 | *13.50* |
| *a.* | | Double overprint | 175.00 | |
| *b.* | | Inverted overprint | 100.00 | |
| *c.* | | '03-'03 | 675.00 | |
| *d.* | | 02'-'03 | 675.00 | |
| *e.* | | Pair, one with invtd. ovpt. | 525.00 | |
| *f.* | | Pair, one without overprint | 300.00 | |
| *g.* | | As "f", inverted | 525.00 | |
| 47 | A2 | 20a dull blue | 1.50 | *16.50* |
| *a.* | | Inverted overprint | 100.00 | *135.00* |
| *b.* | | "I" before Gildi omitted | 225.00 | |
| *c.* | | 02'-'03 | 900.00 | |
| 48 | A2 | 25a yel brn & bl | 1.50 | *24.00* |
| *a.* | | Inverted overprint | 97.50 | *110.00* |
| *b.* | | '03-'03 | 600.00 | |
| *c.* | | 02'-'03 | 600.00 | |
| *d.* | | Double overprint | 225.00 | |

### Black Overprint

| | | | | |
|---|---|---|---|---|
| 49 | A3 | 3a orange | 300.00 | *675.00* |
| *b.* | | Inverted overprint | 375.00 | 850.00 |
| *c.* | | "I" before Gildi omitted | 850.00 | |
| *d.* | | '03-'03 | 850.00 | |
| *e.* | | 02'-'03 | 850.00 | |
| 50 | A3a | 3a yellow | 1.75 | *3.25* |
| *a.* | | Double overprint | 525.00 | |
| *b.* | | Inverted overprint | 110.00 | *135.00* |
| *c.* | | "I" before Gildi omitted | 850.00 | |
| *d.* | | 02'-'03 | 975.00 | |
| 51 | A2 | 4a rose & gray | 52.50 | *75.00* |
| *a.* | | Double overprint | 525.00 | |
| *b.* | | Inverted overprint | 150.00 | |
| *c.* | | Dbl. ovpt., one invtd. | 525.00 | |
| *d.* | | "I" before Gildi omitted | 375.00 | |
| *e.* | | '03-'03 | 675.00 | |
| *f.* | | 02'-'03 | 675.00 | |
| *g.* | | Pair, one with invtd. ovpt. | 525.00 | |
| 52 | A2 | 5a green | 450.00 | *1,200.* |
| *a.* | | Inverted overprint | 525.00 | |
| *b.* | | Pair, one without overprint | 675.00 | |
| *c.* | | As "b", inverted | 825.00 | |
| 53 | A2 | 6a gray | 990.00 | *1,500.* |
| *a.* | | Inverted overprint | 1,050. | |
| *b.* | | Pair, one without overprint | 1,050. | |
| *c.* | | Double overprint | 1,150. | |
| 54 | A2 | 10a carmine | 1.75 | *16.50* |
| *a.* | | Inverted overprint | 100.00 | 140.00 |
| *b.* | | Pair, one without overprint | 275.00 | |
| 55 | A2 | 16a brown | 35.00 | *52.50* |
| *a.* | | Inverted overprint | 225.00 | |
| *b.* | | "I" before Gildi omitted | 375.00 | |
| *c.* | | '03-'03 | 900.00 | |
| *d.* | | 02'-'03 | 850.00 | |
| 56 | A2 | 20a dull blue | *14,500.* | |
| *a.* | | Inverted overprint | *13,000.* | |
| 57 | A2 | 25 yel brn & bl | *13,700.* | |
| *a.* | | Inverted overprint | *14,500.* | |
| 58 | A2 | 40a red vio | 1.50 | *52.50* |
| *a.* | | Inverted overprint | 120.00 | |
| 59 | A2 | 50a bl & car | 4.50 | *90.00* |
| *a.* | | Double overprint | 335.00 | |
| *b.* | | 02'-'03 | 1,100. | |
| *c.* | | '03-'03 | 1,100. | |

### *Perf. 14x13½*
### Red Overprint

| | | | | |
|---|---|---|---|---|
| 60 | A2 | 5a green | 2,750. | — |
| a. | | '03-'03 | — | |
| b. | | 02'-'03 | 45,500. | |
| 61 | A2 | 6a gray | 2,750. | — |
| a. | | 02'-'03 | 45,000. | |
| 62 | A2 | 20a blue | 7,500. | — |
| b. | | 02'-'03 | 15,000. | |

### Black Overprint

| | | | | |
|---|---|---|---|---|
| 63 | A3 | 3a orange | 1,800. | 2,750. |
| a. | | Inverted overprint | 2,300. | |
| b. | | 02'-'03 | 2,750. | |
| c. | | '03-'03 | 3,000. | |
| 64 | A2 | 10a carmine | 13,000. | — |
| 65 | A2 | 16a brown | 2,000. | 2,300. |
| a. | | Inverted overprint | 2,400. | |
| b. | | 02'-'03 | 3,000. | |
| d. | | '03-'03 | 22,000. | |
| 65C | A2 | 20a dull blue | 12,000. | — |
| a. | | Inverted overprint | 15,500. | |
| 66 | A2 | 40a red vio | 27.50 | 135.00 |
| a. | | Inverted overprint | 450.00 | — |
| b. | | '03-'03 | 675.00 | |
| c. | | 02'-'03 | 675.00 | |
| 67 | A2 | 50a bl & car | 67.50 | 175.00 |
| a. | | Inverted overprint | 450.00 | |
| b. | | '03-'03 | 600.00 | |
| c. | | 02'-'03 | 600.00 | |
| d. | | As "c," inverted | — | |
| 68 | A2 | 100a brn & vio | 75.00 | 110.00 |
| a. | | Inverted overprint | 275.00 | |
| b. | | 02'-'03 | 750.00 | |
| c. | | '03-'03 | 900.00 | |

"I GILDI" means "valid."

*In 1904 Nos. 20, 22-30, 45-59 (except 49, 52, 53, 56 and 57) and No. 68 were reprinted for the Postal Union. The reprints are perforated 13 and have watermark type 113. Value $120 each. Without overprint, $250 each.*

Kings Christian IX and Frederik VIII — A5

### Typo., Center Engr.
**1907-08 Wmk. 113 *Perf. 13***

| | | | | |
|---|---|---|---|---|
| 71 | A5 | 1e yel grn & red | 2.00 | 1.40 |
| 72 | A5 | 3a yel brn & ocher | 4.75 | 1.75 |
| 73 | A5 | 4a gray & red | 2.60 | 2.10 |
| 74 | A5 | 5a green | 95.00 | 1.40 |
| 75 | A5 | 6a gray & gray brn | 60.00 | 4.00 |
| 76 | A5 | 10a scarlet | 165.00 | 1.60 |
| 77 | A5 | 15a red & green | 8.50 | 1.50 |
| 78 | A5 | 16a brown | 9.75 | 47.50 |
| 79 | A5 | 20a blue | 9.00 | 6.75 |
| 80 | A5 | 25a bis brn & grn | 7.25 | 14.00 |
| 81 | A5 | 40a claret & vio | 7.00 | 17.00 |
| 82 | A5 | 50a gray & vio | 8.00 | 17.00 |
| 83 | A5 | 1k blue & brn | 32.50 | 77.50 |
| 84 | A5 | 2k dk brn & dk grn | 42.50 | 90.00 |
| 85 | A5 | 5k brn & slate | 225.00 | 425.00 |
| | | *Nos. 71-85 (15)* | 678.85 | 708.50 |

See Nos. 99-107.

For surcharges and overprints see Nos. 130-138, 143, C2, O69.

Jon Sigurdsson A6

Frederik VIII A7

**1911 Typo. and Embossed**

| | | | | |
|---|---|---|---|---|
| 86 | A6 | 1e olive green | 3.00 | 2.75 |
| 87 | A6 | 3a light brown | 5.75 | 17.50 |
| 88 | A6 | 4a ultramarine | 2.25 | 2.25 |
| 89 | A6 | 6a gray | 14.50 | 30.00 |
| 90 | A6 | 15a violet | 17.50 | 2.25 |
| 91 | A6 | 25a orange | 32.50 | 57.50 |
| | | *Nos. 86-91 (6)* | 75.50 | 112.25 |

Sigurdsson (1811-79), statesman and author.

For surcharge see No. 149.

**1912, Feb. 17**

| | | | | |
|---|---|---|---|---|
| 92 | A7 | 5a green | 37.50 | 14.00 |
| 93 | A7 | 10a red | 37.50 | 14.00 |
| 94 | A7 | 20a pale blue | 52.50 | 20.00 |
| 95 | A7 | 50a claret | 10.50 | 40.00 |
| 96 | A7 | 1k yellow | 32.50 | 80.00 |
| 97 | A7 | 2k rose | 30.00 | 80.00 |
| 98 | A7 | 5k brown | 175.00 | 250.00 |
| | | *Nos. 92-98 (7)* | 375.50 | 498.00 |

For surcharges and overprints see Nos. 140-141, O50-O51.

### Type of 1907-08
### Typo., Center Engr.
**1915-18 Wmk. 114 *Perf. 14x14½***

| | | | | |
|---|---|---|---|---|
| 99 | A5 | 1e yel grn & red | 9.50 | 20.00 |
| 100 | A5 | 3a bister brn | 4.75 | 3.25 |
| 101 | A5 | 4a gray & red | 4.75 | 10.50 |
| 102 | A5 | 5a green | 110.00 | 1.50 |
| 103 | A5 | 6a gray & gray brn | 22.50 | 150.00 |
| 104 | A5 | 10a scarlet | 4.25 | 1.40 |
| 107 | A5 | 20a blue | 275.00 | 26.00 |
| | | *Nos. 99-107 (7)* | 430.75 | 212.65 |

Revenue cancellations consisting of "TOLLUR" boxed in frame are found on stamps used to pay the tax on parcel post packages entering Iceland.

Christian X — A8

**1920-22 Typo.**

| | | | | |
|---|---|---|---|---|
| 108 | A8 | 1e yel grn & red | 1.00 | 1.25 |
| 109 | A8 | 3a bister brn | 9.00 | 18.50 |
| 110 | A8 | 4a gray & red | 5.25 | 2.75 |
| 111 | A8 | 5a green | 2.50 | 2.25 |
| 112 | A8 | 5a ol green ('22) | 5.25 | 1.75 |
| 113 | A8 | 6a dark gray | 15.00 | 9.50 |
| 114 | A8 | 8a dark brown | 9.00 | 2.50 |
| 115 | A8 | 10a red | 2.75 | 12.50 |
| 116 | A8 | 10a green ('21) | 3.75 | 2.00 |
| 117 | A8 | 15a violet | 45.00 | 1.60 |
| 118 | A8 | 20a deep blue | 3.00 | 19.00 |
| 119 | A8 | 20a choc ('22) | 65.00 | 1.75 |
| 120 | A8 | 25a brown & grn | 19.00 | 2.00 |
| 121 | A8 | 25a red ('21) | 19.00 | 62.50 |
| | | Revenue cancellation | | 4.25 |
| 122 | A8 | 30a red & green | 57.50 | 3.75 |
| | | Revenue cancellation | | 8.75 |
| 123 | A8 | 40a claret | 50.00 | 3.25 |
| | | Revenue cancellation | | 9.50 |
| 124 | A8 | 40a dk bl ('21) | 87.50 | 15.00 |
| | | Revenue cancellation | | 11.00 |
| 125 | A8 | 50a dk gray & cl | 240.00 | 14.00 |
| | | Revenue cancellation | | 13.50 |
| 126 | A8 | 1k dp bl & dk brn | 110.00 | 2.00 |
| | | Revenue cancellation | | 1.75 |
| 127 | A8 | 2k ol brn & myr green | 300.00 | 37.50 |
| | | Revenue cancellation | | 3.50 |
| 128 | A8 | 5k brn & ind | 62.50 | 20.00 |
| | | Revenue cancellation | | 3.50 |
| | | *Nos. 108-128 (21)* | 1,112. | 235.35 |

See Nos. 176-187, 202.

For surcharges and overprints see Nos.139, 150, C1, C9-C14, O52, O70-O71.

A9

A10

A11

**1921-25 Wmk. 113 *Perf. 13***

| | | | | |
|---|---|---|---|---|
| 130 | A9 | 5a on 16a brown | 5.25 | 34.00 |
| 131 | A11 | 5a on 16a brown | 3.00 | 9.75 |
| 132 | A10 | 20a on 25a brn & green | 11.00 | 10.00 |
| a. | | Double surcharge | 600.00 | |
| 133 | A11 | 20a on 25a bis brn & green | 6.50 | 9.25 |
| 134 | A9 | 20a on 40a violet | 11.00 | 25.00 |
| 135 | A11 | 20a on 40a cl & vio | 18.00 | 27.50 |
| 137 | A9 | 30a on 50a gray & bl blk ('25) | 45.00 | 40.00 |
| | | Revenue cancellation | | 22.50 |
| 138 | A9 | 50a on 5k org brn & sl bl ('25) | 82.50 | 62.50 |
| | | Revenue cancellation | | 35.00 |
| | | *Nos. 130-138 (8)* | 182.25 | 218.00 |

No. 111 Surcharged

**1922 Wmk. 114 *Perf. 14x14½***

| | | | | |
|---|---|---|---|---|
| 139 | A8 | 10a on 5a green | 10.00 | 4.00 |

Nos. 95-96, 44A, 85 Surcharged

**1924-30 Wmk. 113 *Perf. 13***

| | | | | |
|---|---|---|---|---|
| 140 | A7 | 10k on 50a ('25) | 375.00 | 575.00 |
| | | Revenue cancellation | | 45.00 |
| 141 | A7 | 10k on 1k | 500.00 | 850.00 |
| | | Revenue cancellation | | 90.00 |
| 142 | A4 | 10k on 2k ('29) | 100.00 | 40.00 |
| | | Revenue cancellation | | 13.50 |
| 143 | A5 | 10k on 5k ('30) | 600.00 | 750.00 |
| | | Revenue cancellation | | 45.00 |

Landing the Mail — A12

Designs: 7a, 50a, Landing the mail. 10a, 35a, View of Reykjavik. 20a, Museum building.

### *Perf. 14x15*
**1925, Sept. 12 Typo. Wmk. 114**

| | | | | |
|---|---|---|---|---|
| 144 | A12 | 7a yel green | 52.50 | 10.00 |
| 145 | A12 | 10a dp bl & brn | 52.50 | 1.00 |
| 146 | A12 | 20a vermilion | 52.50 | 1.00 |
| 147 | A12 | 35a deep blue | 90.00 | 12.00 |
| 148 | A12 | 50a yel grn & brn | 90.00 | 2.25 |
| | | *Nos. 144-148 (5)* | 337.50 | 26.25 |

No. 91 Surcharged

**1925 Wmk. 113 *Perf. 13***

| | | | | |
|---|---|---|---|---|
| 149 | A6 | 2k on 25a orange | 180.00 | 190.00 |
| | | Revenue cancellation | | 22.50 |

No. 124 Surcharged in Red

**1926**

| | | | | |
|---|---|---|---|---|
| 150 | A8 | 1k on 40a dark blue | 200.00 | 45.00 |
| | | Revenue cancellation | | 30.00 |

Parliament Building A15

Designs: 5a, Viking ship in storm. 7a, Parliament meeting place, 1690. 10a, Viking funeral. 15a, Vikings naming land. 20a, The dash for Thing. 25a, Gathering wood. 30a, Thingvalla Lake. 35a, Iceland woman in national costume. 40a, Iceland flag. 50a, First Althing, 930 A.D. 1k, Map of Iceland. 2k, Winter-bound home. 5k, Woman spinning. 10k, Viking Sacrifice to Thor.

### *Perf. 12½x12*
**1930, Jan. 1 Litho. Unwmk.**

| | | | | |
|---|---|---|---|---|
| 152 | A15 | 3a dull vio & gray vio | 4.75 | 12.00 |
| 153 | A15 | 5a dk bl & sl grn | 4.75 | 12.00 |
| 154 | A15 | 7a grn & gray grn | 4.75 | 12.00 |
| 155 | A15 | 10a dk vio & lilac | 11.50 | 25.00 |
| 156 | A15 | 15a dp ultra & bl gray | 3.50 | 13.50 |
| 157 | A15 | 20a rose red & sal | 55.00 | 110.00 |
| a. | | Double impression | 400.00 | |
| 158 | A15 | 25a dk brn & lt brown | 9.25 | 17.50 |
| 159 | A15 | 30a dk grn & sl grn | 7.75 | 17.00 |
| 160 | A15 | 35a ultra & bl gray | 8.50 | 16.50 |
| 161 | A15 | 40a dk ultra, red & slate grn | 7.50 | 17.00 |
| 162 | A15 | 50a red brn & cinnamon | 75.00 | 195.00 |
| 163 | A15 | 1k ol grn & gray green | 75.00 | 195.00 |
| 164 | A15 | 2k turq bl & gray green | 105.00 | 240.00 |
| 165 | A15 | 5k org & yellow | 60.00 | 190.00 |
| 166 | A15 | 10k mag & dl rose | 60.00 | 190.00 |
| | | *Nos. 152-166 (15)* | 492.25 | 1,262. |

Millenary of the "Althing," the Icelandic Parliament, oldest in the world.

Imperfs were privately printed.

For overprints see Nos. O53-O67.

Gullfoss (Golden Falls) — A30

**1931-32 Unwmk. Engr. *Perf. 14***

| | | | | |
|---|---|---|---|---|
| 170 | A30 | 5a gray | 17.50 | 1.10 |
| 171 | A30 | 20a red | 15.00 | .25 |
| 172 | A30 | 35a ultramarine | 30.00 | 16.00 |
| | | Revenue cancellation | | 2.25 |
| 173 | A30 | 60a red lil ('32) | 18.00 | 1.25 |
| 174 | A30 | 65a red brn ('32) | 3.00 | 1.25 |
| 175 | A30 | 75a grnsh bl ('32) | 120.00 | 40.00 |
| | | Revenue cancellation | | 6.00 |
| | | *Nos. 170-175 (6)* | 203.50 | 59.85 |

Issued: 5a-35a, Dec. 15; 60a-75a, May 30.

### Type of 1920 Christian X Issue Redrawn
### *Perf. 14x14½*
**1931-33 Typo. Wmk. 114**

| | | | | |
|---|---|---|---|---|
| 176 | A8 | 1e yel grn & red | 1.00 | 1.75 |
| 177 | A8 | 3a bister brown | 16.00 | 16.50 |
| | | Revenue cancellation | | 8.00 |
| 178 | A8 | 4a gray & red | 2.50 | 2.50 |
| 179 | A8 | 6a dark gray | 2.00 | 4.25 |
| 180 | A8 | 7a yel grn ('33) | .65 | 1.75 |
| 181 | A8 | 10a chocolate | 175.00 | 1.10 |
| 182 | A8 | 25a brn & green | 19.00 | 4.25 |
| | | Revenue cancellation | | 4.50 |
| 183 | A8 | 30a red & green | 30.00 | 6.50 |
| | | Revenue cancellation | | 11.00 |
| 184 | A8 | 40a claret | 300.00 | 24.00 |
| | | Revenue cancellation | | 15.00 |
| 185 | A8 | 1k dk bl & lt brn | 47.50 | 8.00 |
| | | Revenue cancellation | | 4.50 |
| 186 | A8 | 2k choc & dk grn | 300.00 | 90.00 |
| | | Revenue cancellation | | 11.00 |
| 187 | A8 | 10k yel grn & blk | 350.00 | 225.00 |
| | | Revenue cancellation | | 22.50 |
| | | *Nos. 176-187 (12)* | 1,243. | 385.60 |

On the redrawn stamps the horizontal lines of the portrait and the oval are closer together than on the 1920 stamps and are crossed by many fine vertical lines.

See No. 202.

Dynjandi Falls — A31

Mount Hekla — A32

**Perf. 12½**

**1935, June 28 Engr. Unwmk.**

| | | | |
|---|---|---|---|
| **193** | A31 10a blue | 30.00 | .25 |
| | Never hinged | 100.00 | |
| **194** | A32 1k greenish gray | 52.50 | .25 |
| | Never hinged | 170.00 | |

Matthias Jochumsson — A33

**1935, Nov. 11**

| | | | |
|---|---|---|---|
| **195** | A33 3a gray green | .75 | *4.50* |
| **196** | A33 5a gray | 15.00 | 1.50 |
| **197** | A33 7a yel green | 22.50 | 2.50 |
| **198** | A33 35a blue | .65 | *1.50* |
| | *Nos. 195-198 (4)* | 38.90 | *10.00* |
| | Set, never hinged | 130.00 | |

Birth cent. of Matthias Jochumsson, poet.
For surcharges see Nos. 212, 236.

King Christian X — A34

**1937, May 14 Perf. 13x12½**

| | | | |
|---|---|---|---|
| **199** | A34 10a green | 2.50 | *27.50* |
| **200** | A34 30a brown | 2.50 | *12.00* |
| **201** | A34 40a claret | 2.50 | *12.00* |
| | *Nos. 199-201 (3)* | 7.50 | *51.50* |
| | Set, never hinged | 15.00 | |

Reign of Christian X, 25th anniv.

### Christian X Type of 1931-33

**1937 Unwmk. Typo. Perf. 11½**

| | | | |
|---|---|---|---|
| **202** | A8 1e yel grn & red | 1.00 | *2.25* |
| | Never hinged | 3.75 | |

Geyser

A35 A36

**1938-47 Engr. Perf. 14**

| | | | |
|---|---|---|---|
| **203** | A35 15a dp rose vio | 7.00 | *13.00* |
| *a.* | Imperf., pair | *900.00* | |
| | Never hinged | 1,050. | |
| **204** | A35 20a rose red | 27.50 | .30 |
| **205** | A35 35a ultra | .85 | *1.10* |
| **206** | A36 40a dk brn ('39) | 17.00 | *32.50* |
| **207** | A36 45a brt ultra ('40) | 1.00 | *1.10* |
| **208** | A36 50a dk slate grn | 26.00 | 1.10 |
| **208A** | A35 60a brt ultra ('43) | 7.00 | 1.25 |
| *c.* | Perf. 11½ ('47) | 3.75 | *15.00* |
| | Never hinged (#208Ac) | 9.00 | |
| **208B** | A36 1k indigo ('45) | 2.50 | .50 |
| *d.* | Perf. 11½ ('47) | 3.75 | *15.00* |
| | Never hinged (#208Bd) | 9.00 | |
| | *Nos. 203-208B (8)* | 88.85 | *50.85* |
| | Set, never hinged | 190.00 | |

University of Iceland A37

**1938, Dec. 1 Perf. 13½**

| | | | |
|---|---|---|---|
| **209** | A37 25a dark grn | 8.50 | *18.00* |
| **210** | A37 30a brown | 8.50 | *18.00* |
| **211** | A37 40a brt red vio | 8.50 | *18.00* |
| | *Nos. 209-211 (3)* | 25.50 | *54.00* |
| | Set, never hinged | 40.00 | |

20th anniversary of independence.

### No. 198 Surcharged with New Value

**1939, Mar. 17 Perf. 12½**

| | | | |
|---|---|---|---|
| **212** | A33 5a on 35a blue | 1.00 | *1.75* |
| | Never hinged | 2.00 | |
| *a.* | Double surcharge | *325.00* | |
| | Never hinged | 675.00 | |

Trylon and Perisphere A38

Leif Ericsson's Ship and Route to America A39

Statue of Thorfinn Karlsefni — A40

**1939 Engr. Perf. 14**

| | | | |
|---|---|---|---|
| **213** | A38 20a crimson | 4.00 | *7.75* |
| **214** | A39 35a bright ultra | 4.50 | *9.75* |
| **215** | A40 45a bright green | 4.75 | *13.00* |
| **216** | A40 2k dark gray | 62.50 | *160.00* |
| | *Nos. 213-216 (4)* | 75.75 | *190.50* |
| | Set, never hinged | 140.00 | |

New York World's Fair.
For overprints see Nos. 232-235.

Codfish — A41

Herring — A42

Flag of Iceland — A43

**1939-45 Engr. Perf. 14, 14x13½**

| | | | |
|---|---|---|---|
| **217** | A41 1e Prussian blue | .55 | *5.00* |
| *a.* | Perf. 14x13½ | 2.00 | *5.50* |
| **218** | A42 3a dark violet | .55 | *1.25* |
| *a.* | Perf. 14x13½ | 2.75 | *10.00* |
| **219** | A41 5a dark brown | .55 | .50 |
| *c.* | Perf. 14x13½ | 2.75 | 1.40 |
| **220** | A42 7a dark green | 7.00 | *12.00* |
| **221** | A42 10a green ('40) | 45.00 | 1.75 |
| *b.* | Perf. 14x13½ | 77.50 | 4.50 |
| | Never hinged | 210.00 | |
| **222** | A42 10a slate gray ('45) | .40 | .25 |
| **223** | A42 12a dk grn ('43) | .50 | 1.00 |
| **224** | A41 25a brt red ('40) | 32.50 | .70 |
| *b.* | Perf. 14x13½ | 65.00 | 3.00 |
| | Never hinged (#224b) | 210.00 | |
| **225** | A41 25a hn brn ('45) | .45 | .45 |
| **226** | A42 35a carmine ('43) | .60 | .75 |
| **227** | A41 50a dk bl grn ('43) | .80 | .40 |

**Typo.**

| | | | |
|---|---|---|---|
| **228** | A43 10a car & ultra | 2.50 | 1.60 |
| | *Nos. 217-228 (12)* | 91.40 | *25.65* |
| | Set, never hinged | 240.00 | |

Statue of Thorfinn Karlsefni — A44

**1939-45 Engr. Perf. 14**

| | | | |
|---|---|---|---|
| **229** | A44 2k dark gray | 3.50 | .50 |
| **230** | A44 5k dk brn ('43) | 27.50 | .65 |
| **231** | A44 10k brn yel ('45) | 15.00 | 2.10 |
| | *Nos. 229-231 (3)* | 46.00 | 3.25 |
| | Set, never hinged | 200.00 | |

**1947 Perf. 11½**

| | | | |
|---|---|---|---|
| *229a* | A44 2k | 9.25 | 1.90 |
| *230a* | A44 5k | 35.00 | 2.50 |
| *231a* | A44 10k | 15.00 | *55.00* |
| | *Nos. 229a-231a (3)* | 59.25 | *59.40* |
| | Set, never hinged | 200.00 | |

### New York World's Fair Issue of 1939 Overprinted "1940" in Black

**1940, May 11 Perf. 14**

| | | | |
|---|---|---|---|
| **232** | A38 20a crimson | 10.00 | *32.50* |
| **233** | A39 35a bright ultra | 10.00 | *32.50* |
| **234** | A40 45a bright green | 10.00 | *32.50* |
| **235** | A40 2k dark gray | 125.00 | *500.00* |
| | *Nos. 232-235 (4)* | 155.00 | *597.50* |
| | Set, never hinged | 300.00 | |

### No. 195 Surcharged in Red

**1941, Mar. 6 Perf. 12½**

| | | | |
|---|---|---|---|
| **236** | A33 25a on 3a gray green | 1.20 | *1.75* |
| | Never hinged | 2.00 | |

Statue of Snorri Sturluson A45

Jon Sigurdsson A46

**1941, Nov. 17 Engr. Perf. 14**

| | | | |
|---|---|---|---|
| **237** | A45 25a rose red | 1.50 | *2.75* |
| **238** | A45 50a deep ultra | 2.10 | *6.25* |
| **239** | A45 1k dk olive grn | 2.10 | *6.25* |
| | *Nos. 237-239 (3)* | 5.70 | 15.25 |
| | Set, never hinged | 10.00 | |

Snorri Sturluson, writer and historian, 700th death anniv.

### Republic

**1944, June 17 Perf. 14x13½**

| | | | |
|---|---|---|---|
| **240** | A46 10a gray black | .45 | *1.00* |
| **241** | A46 25a dk red brn | .55 | *1.00* |
| **242** | A46 50a slate grn | .55 | *1.00* |
| **243** | A46 1k blue black | .95 | *1.00* |
| **244** | A46 5k henna | 3.00 | *13.00* |
| **245** | A46 10k golden brn | 47.50 | *110.00* |
| | *Nos. 240-245 (6)* | 53.00 | *127.00* |
| | Set, never hinged | 110.00 | |

Founding of Republic of Iceland, June 17, 1944.

**Catalogue values for unused stamps in this section, from this point to the end of the section, are for Never Hinged items.**

A47

A48

Eruption of Hekla Volcano: 35a, 60a, Close view of Hekla.

**Unwmk.**

**1948, Dec. 3 Engr. Perf. 14**

| | | | |
|---|---|---|---|
| **246** | A47 12a dark vio brn | .25 | *.65* |
| **247** | A48 25a green | 2.00 | .25 |
| **248** | A47 35a carmine rose | .55 | .40 |
| **249** | A47 50a brown | 2.75 | .25 |
| **250** | A47 60a bright ultra | 9.75 | 5.50 |
| **251** | A48 1k orange brown | 14.00 | .25 |
| **252** | A48 10k violet black | 70.00 | .55 |
| | *Nos. 246-252 (7)* | 99.30 | 7.85 |
| | Set, hinged | 47.50 | |

For surcharge see No. 283.

Pack Train and UPU Monument, Bern — A49

UPU, 75th Anniv.: 35a, Reykjavik. 60a, Map. 2k, Thingvellir Road.

**1949, Oct. 9**

| | | | |
|---|---|---|---|
| **253** | A49 25a dark green | .40 | *.65* |
| **254** | A49 35a deep carmine | .40 | *.65* |
| **255** | A49 60a blue | .65 | *1.40* |
| **256** | A49 2k orange red | 1.60 | 1.50 |
| | *Nos. 253-256 (4)* | 3.05 | *4.20* |

Trawler — A50

Jon Arason — A51

Designs: 20a, 75a, 1k, Tractor plowing. 60a, 5k, Flock of sheep. 5a, 90a, 2k, Vestmannaeyjar harbor.

**1950-54 Perf. 13**

| | | | |
|---|---|---|---|
| **257** | A50 5a dk brn ('54) | .25 | .25 |
| **258** | A50 10a gray | .50 | .50 |
| **259** | A50 20a brown | .50 | .50 |
| **260** | A50 25a car ('54) | .25 | .25 |
| **261** | A50 60a green | 20.00 | *25.00* |
| **262** | A50 75a red org ('52) | .55 | .25 |
| **263** | A50 90a carmine | .65 | .55 |
| **264** | A50 1k chocolate | 7.50 | .25 |
| **265** | A50 1.25k red vio ('52) | 25.00 | .45 |
| **266** | A50 1.50k deep ultra | 18.00 | .70 |
| **267** | A50 2k purple | 37.50 | .35 |
| **268** | A50 5k dark grn | 52.50 | 1.50 |
| | *Nos. 257-268 (12)* | 163.20 | 30.55 |
| | Set, hinged | 57.50 | |

For surcharges see Nos. B12-B13.

**1950, Nov. 7 Perf. 14**

| | | | |
|---|---|---|---|
| **269** | A51 1.80k carmine | 4.50 | *5.25* |
| **270** | A51 3.30k green | 3.00 | *4.50* |

Bishop Jon Arason, 400th anniv. of death.

Mail Delivery, 1776 — A52

Design: 3k, Airmail, 1951.

**1951, May 13**

| | | | |
|---|---|---|---|
| **271** | A52 2k deep ultra | 3.75 | 3.75 |
| **272** | A52 3k dark purple | 5.25 | 5.25 |

175th anniv. of Iceland's postal service.

Parliament Building — A53

**1952, Apr. 1 Perf. 13x12½**

| | | | |
|---|---|---|---|
| **273** | A53 25k gray black | 240.00 | 22.50 |
| | Hinged | 100.00 | |

Sveinn Björnsson A54

Reykjabok A55

**1952, Sept. 1** *Perf. 13½*

| | | | | |
|---|---|---|---|---|
| **274** | A54 | 1.25k deep blue | 3.75 | .25 |
| **275** | A54 | 2.20k deep green | .85 | *5.25* |
| **276** | A54 | 5k indigo | 13.00 | 1.90 |
| **277** | A54 | 10k brown red | 55.00 | 32.50 |
| | | *Nos. 274-277 (4)* | 72.60 | 39.90 |

Sveinn Björnsson, 1st President of Iceland.

**1953, Oct. 1** *Perf. 13½x13*

Designs: 70a, Lettering manuscript. 1k, Corner of 15th century manuscript, "Stjorn." 1.75k, Reykjabok. 10k, Corner from law manuscript.

| | | | | |
|---|---|---|---|---|
| **278** | A55 | 10a black | .25 | .25 |
| **279** | A55 | 70a green | .30 | .30 |
| **280** | A55 | 1k carmine | .40 | .25 |
| **281** | A55 | 1.75k blue | 37.50 | 1.90 |
| **282** | A55 | 10k orange brn | 17.00 | 1.50 |
| | | *Nos. 278-282 (5)* | 55.45 | 4.20 |

No. 248 Surcharged With New Value and Bars in Black

**1954, Mar. 31** *Perf. 14*

| | | | | |
|---|---|---|---|---|
| **283** | A47 | 5a on 35a car rose | .35 | .35 |
| *a.* | | Bars omitted | 90.00 | |
| *b.* | | Inverted surcharge | 250.00 | |

Hannes Hafstein A56

Icelandic Wrestling A57

Portraits: 2.45k, in oval. 5k, fullface.

**1954, June 1** **Engr.** *Perf. 13*

| | | | | |
|---|---|---|---|---|
| **284** | A56 | 1.25k deep blue | 5.75 | .70 |
| **285** | A56 | 2.45k dark green | 29.00 | *35.00* |
| **286** | A56 | 5k carmine | 32.50 | 3.25 |
| | | *Nos. 284-286 (3)* | 67.25 | *38.95* |

Appointment of the first native minister to Denmark, 50th anniv.

**1955, Aug. 9** **Unwmk.** *Perf. 14*

| | | | | |
|---|---|---|---|---|
| **287** | A57 | 75a shown | .75 | .25 |
| **288** | A57 | 1.25k Diving | 1.60 | .30 |

See Nos. 300-301.

Skoga Falls — A58

Ellidaar Power Plant — A59

Waterfalls: 60a, Goda. 2kr, Detti. 5kr, Gull. Electric Power Plants: 1.50kr, Sogs. 2.45kr, Andakilsar. 3kr, Laxar.

***Perf. 11½, 13½x14 (A59)***

**1956, Apr. 4** **Unwmk.**

| | | | | |
|---|---|---|---|---|
| **289** | A58 | 15a vio blue | .25 | .25 |
| **290** | A59 | 50a dull green | .30 | .25 |
| **291** | A59 | 60a brown | 4.25 | *5.25* |
| **292** | A59 | 1.50k violet | 37.50 | .25 |
| **293** | A59 | 2k sepia | 2.25 | .65 |
| **294** | A59 | 2.45k gray black | 8.50 | *12.00* |
| **295** | A59 | 3k dark blue | 7.00 | 1.25 |
| **296** | A58 | 5k dark green | 16.00 | 2.25 |
| | | *Nos. 289-296 (8)* | 76.05 | 22.15 |

Telegraph-Telephone Emblem and Map — A60

**1956, Sept. 29** **Engr.** *Perf. 13*

| | | | | |
|---|---|---|---|---|
| **297** | A60 | 2.30k ultramarine | .35 | *1.10* |

Telegraph and Telephone service in Iceland, 50th anniv.

**Northern Countries Issue**

Whooper Swans — A60a

**1956, Oct. 30** *Perf. 12½*

| | | | | |
|---|---|---|---|---|
| **298** | A60a | 1.50k rose red | .70 | *1.25* |
| **299** | A60a | 1.75k ultra | 10.50 | *12.50* |

To emphasize the bonds among Denmark, Finland, Iceland, Norway and Sweden.

**Sports Type of 1955**

1.50k, Icelandic wrestling. 1.75k, Diving.

**1957, Apr. 1** **Engr.** *Perf. 14*

| | | | | |
|---|---|---|---|---|
| **300** | A57 | 1.50k carmine | 1.75 | .25 |
| **301** | A57 | 1.75k ultramarine | .90 | .25 |

**Type of 1952 Air Post Stamps, Plane Omitted**

Glaciers: 2k, Snaefellsjokull. 3k, Eiriksjokull. 10k, Oraefajokull.

**1957, May 8** *Perf. 13½x14*

| | | | | |
|---|---|---|---|---|
| **302** | AP16 | 2k green | 5.25 | .30 |
| **303** | AP16 | 3k dark blue | 5.75 | .30 |
| **304** | AP16 | 10k reddish brn | 7.75 | .45 |
| | | *Nos. 302-304 (3)* | 18.75 | 1.05 |

Bessastadir, President's Residence A61

**1957, Aug. 1** **Engr.** **Unwmk.**

| | | | | |
|---|---|---|---|---|
| **305** | A61 | 25k gray blk | 30.00 | 5.25 |

Evergreen and Volcanoes A62

Jonas Hallgrimsson A63

**1957, Sept. 4** *Perf. 13½x13*

| | | | | |
|---|---|---|---|---|
| **306** | A62 | 35a shown | .25 | .25 |
| **307** | A62 | 70a Birch | .25 | .25 |

Issued to publicize a reforestation program.

**1957, Nov 16**

| | | | | |
|---|---|---|---|---|
| **308** | A63 | 5k grn & blk | 2.25 | .65 |

150th birth anniv. of Jonas Hallgrimsson, poet.

Willow Herb — A64

Icelandic Pony — A65

**1958, July 8** **Litho.** **Unwmk.**

| | | | | |
|---|---|---|---|---|
| **309** | A64 | 1k shown | .25 | .50 |
| **310** | A64 | 2.50k Wild pansy | .50 | .50 |

**1958, Sept. 27** **Engr.**

| | | | | |
|---|---|---|---|---|
| **311** | A65 | 10a gray black | .25 | .25 |
| **312** | A65 | 2.25k brown | .70 | .35 |

See No. 324.

Flag — A66

Old Icelandic Government Building — A67

***Perf. 13½x14***

**1958, Dec. 1** **Litho.** **Unwmk.**

**Size: 17½x21mm**

| | | | | |
|---|---|---|---|---|
| **313** | A66 | 3.50k brt ultra & red | 3.00 | .90 |

**Size: 23x26½mm**

| | | | | |
|---|---|---|---|---|
| **314** | A66 | 50k brt ultra & red | 9.00 | 9.00 |

40th anniversary of Icelandic flag.

**1958, Dec. 9** **Photo.** *Perf. 11½*

| | | | | |
|---|---|---|---|---|
| **315** | A67 | 2k deep green | .55 | .25 |
| **316** | A67 | 4k deep brown | .75 | .40 |

See Nos. 333-334.

Jon Thorkelsson Teaching — A68

**1959, May 5** **Engr.** *Perf. 13½*

| | | | | |
|---|---|---|---|---|
| **317** | A68 | 2k green | .60 | *.55* |
| **318** | A68 | 3k dull purple | .65 | *.75* |

Death bicentenary of Jon Thorkelsson, headmaster of Skaholt.

Sockeye Salmon A69

Eider Ducks — A70

Design: 25k, Gyrfalcon.

**1959-60** **Engr.** *Perf. 14*

| | | | | |
|---|---|---|---|---|
| **319** | A69 | 25a dark blue | .25 | .25 |
| **320** | A70 | 90a chestnut & blk | .30 | .25 |
| **321** | A70 | 2k olive grn & blk | .65 | .25 |
| **322** | A69 | 5k gray green | 11.00 | 1.10 |

**Litho.** *Perf. 11½*

| | | | | |
|---|---|---|---|---|
| **323** | A70 | 25k dl pur, gray & yel | 17.50 | 14.00 |
| | | *Nos. 319-323 (5)* | 29.70 | *15.85* |

Issued: 25k, Mar. 1, 1960; others, Nov. 25.

Pony Type of 1958

**1960, Apr. 7** **Engr.** *Perf. 13½x13*

| | | | | |
|---|---|---|---|---|
| **324** | A65 | 1k dark carmine | .75 | .50 |

"The Outlaw" by Einar Jonsson A71

Wild Geranium A72

**1960, Apr. 7** *Perf. 14*

| | | | | |
|---|---|---|---|---|
| **325** | A71 | 2.50k reddish brn | .30 | .30 |
| **326** | A71 | 4.50k ultramarine | 1.00 | 1.00 |

World Refugee Year, 7/1/59-6/30/60.

Common Design Types pictured following the introduction.

**Europa Issue, 1960**

Common Design Type

**1960, Sept. 18** **Photo.** *Perf. 11½*

**Size: 32½x22mm**

| | | | | |
|---|---|---|---|---|
| **327** | CD3 | 3k grn & lt grn | *.50* | *.50* |
| **328** | CD3 | 5.50k dk bl & lt bl | *.80* | *.80* |

**1960-62 Photo. *Perf. 11½***

Flowers: 50a, Bellflower. 2.50k, Dandelion. 3.50k, Buttercup.

329 A72 50a gray grn, grn & violet ('62) .25 .25
330 A72 1.20k sep, vio & grn .25 .25
331 A72 2.50k brn, yel & grn .25 .25
332 A72 3.50k dl bl, yel & green ('62) .65 .25
*Nos. 329-332 (4)* 1.40 1.00

See Nos. 363-366, 393-394.

**Building Type of 1958**

**1961, Apr. 11 Unwmk. *Perf. 11½***

333 A67 1.50k deep blue .30 .25
334 A67 3k dark carmine .30 .25

Jon Sigurdsson A73

Reykjavik A74

**Typographed and Embossed**

**1961, June 17 *Perf. 12½x14***

335 A73 50a crimson .25 .25
336 A73 3k dark blue 1.75 1.25
337 A73 5k deep plum .60 .55
*Nos. 335-337 (3)* 2.60 2.05

Jon Sigurdsson (1811-1879), statesman and scholar.

**1961, Aug. 18 Photo. *Perf. 11½***

338 A74 2.50k blue & grn .75 .30
339 A74 4.50k lilac & vio bl 1.25 .50

Municipal charter of Reykjavik, 175th anniv.

**Europa Issue, 1961**

Common Design Type

**1961, Sept. 18 Size: 32x22½mm**

340 CD4 5.50k multicolored *.45 .45*
341 CD4 6k multicolored *.45 .45*

Benedikt Sveinsson — A75

University of Iceland — A76

Design: 1.40k, Björn M. Olsen.

**1961, Oct. 6 Photo. *Perf. 11½***

342 A75 1k red brown .25 .25
343 A75 1.40k ultramarine .25 .25
344 A76 10k green 1.50 .60
  *a.* Souv. sheet of 3, #342-344, imperf. 1.00 *1.60*
*Nos. 342-344 (3)* 2.00 1.10

50th anniv. of the University of Iceland; Benedikt Sveinsson (1827-1899), statesman; and Björn M. Olsen (1850-1919), first rector.

Production Institute — A77

New Buildings: 4k, Fishing Research Institute. 6k, Farm Bureau.

**1962, July 6 Unwmk. *Perf. 11½***

345 A77 2.50k ultramarine .40 .25
346 A77 4k dull green .55 .25
347 A77 6k brown .65 .30
*Nos. 345-347 (3)* 1.60 .80

**Europa Issue, 1962**

Common Design Type

**1962, Sept. 17 *Perf. 11½***

**Size: 32½x22½mm**

348 CD5 5.50k yel, lt grn & brn *.25 .25*
349 CD5 6.50k lt grn, grn & brn *.60 .60*

Map Showing Submarine Telephone Cable — A78

**1962, Nov. 20 Granite Paper**

350 A78 5k multicolored 1.25 .65
351 A78 7k grn, lt bl & red .75 .50

Inauguration of the submarine telephone cable from Newfoundland, via Greenland and Iceland to Scotland.

Sigurdur Gudmundsson, Self-portrait A79

Herring Boat A80

5.50k, Knight slaying dragon, Romanesque door from Valthjofsstad Church, ca. 1200 A.D.

**1963, Feb. 20 Photo. *Perf. 11½***

352 A79 4k bis brn & choc .75 .50
353 A79 5.50k gray ol & brn .60 .50

National Museum of Iceland, cent., and its first curator, Sigurdur Gudmundsson.

**1963, Mar. 21**

354 A80 5k multicolored 1.00 .30
355 A80 7.50k multicolored .25 .25

FAO "Freedom from Hunger" campaign.

View of Akureyri A81

**1963, July 2 Unwmk. *Perf. 11½***

356 A81 3k gray green .25 *.50*

**Europa Issue, 1963**

Common Design Type

**1963, Sept. 16 Size: 32½x23mm**

357 CD6 6k org brn & yel *.75 .75*
358 CD6 7k blue & yellow *.75 .75*

M.S. Gullfoss A82

**1964, Jan. 17 Photo. *Perf. 11½***

359 A82 10k ultra, blk & gray 3.00 2.25
  *a.* Accent on 2nd "E" omitted 45.00 *60.00*

Iceland Steamship Company, 50th anniv.

Scout Emblem and "Be Prepared" A83

Icelandic Coat of Arms A84

**1964, Apr. 24**

360 A83 3.50k multicolored .75 .50
361 A83 4.50k multicolored .75 .50

Issued to honor the Boy Scouts.

**1964, June 17 *Perf. 11½***

362 A84 25k multicolored 3.50 2.75

20th anniversary, Republic of Iceland.

**Flower Type of 1960-62**

Flowers: 50a, Eight-petal dryas. 1k, Crowfoot (Ranunculus glacialis). 1.50k, Buck bean. 2k, Clover (trifolium repens).

**Flowers in Natural Colors**

**1964, July 15**

363 A72 50a vio bl & lt vio bl .30 .25
364 A72 1k gray & dk gray .30 .25
365 A72 1.50k brn & pale brn .30 .25
366 A72 2k ol & pale olive .30 .25
*Nos. 363-366 (4)* 1.20 1.00

**Europa Issue, 1964**

Common Design Type

**1964, Sept. 14 Photo. *Perf. 11½***

**Granite Paper**

**Size: 22½x33mm**

367 CD7 4.50k golden brn, yel & Prus grn *.75 .65*
368 CD7 9k bl, yel & dk brn *1.25 1.00*

Jumper — A85

**1964, Oct. 20 Unwmk. *Perf. 11½***

369 A85 10k lt grn & blk 1.50 1.20

18th Olympic Games, Tokyo, Oct. 10-25.

ITU Emblem A86

**1965, May 17 Photo. *Perf. 11½***

370 A86 4.50k green 1.20 .60
371 A86 7.50k bright ultra .25 .25

ITU, centenary.

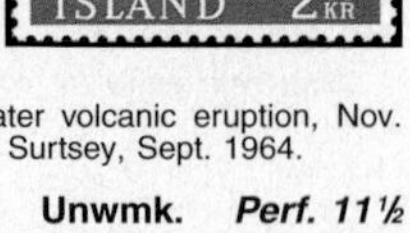

Surtsey Island, April 1964 — A87

1.50k, Underwater volcanic eruption, Nov. 1963, vert. 3.50k, Surtsey, Sept. 1964.

**1965, June 23 Unwmk. *Perf. 11½***

372 A87 1.50k bl, bis & blk .85 .85
373 A87 2k multicolored .85 .85
374 A87 3.50k bl, blk & red 1.00 .85
*Nos. 372-374 (3)* 2.70 2.55

Emergence of a new volcanic island off the southern coast of Iceland.

**Europa Issue, 1965**

Common Design Type

**1965, Sept. 27 Photo. *Perf. 11½***

**Size: 33x22½mm**

375 CD8 5k tan, brn & brt grn *1.50 1.00*
376 CD8 8k brt grn, brn & yel green *1.00 .75*

Einar Benediktsson A88

**Engr. & Litho.**

**1965, Nov. 16 *Perf. 14***

377 A88 10k brt blue & brn 4.50 *5.00*

Einar Benediktsson, poet (1864-1940).

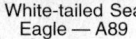

White-tailed Sea Eagle — A89

National Costume — A90

**1965-66 Photo. *Perf. 11½***

378 A89 50k multicolored 15.00 15.00
379 A90 100k multicolored 12.00 11.00

Issued: #378, 4/26/66; #379, 12/3/65.

West Iceland — A91

**1966, Aug. 4 Photo. *Perf. 11½***

380 A91 2.50k shown .35 .35
381 A91 4k North Iceland .65 .35
382 A91 5k East Iceland 1.10 .35
383 A91 6.50k South Iceland .85 .35
*Nos. 380-383 (4)* 2.95 1.40

**Europa Issue, 1966**

Common Design Type

**1966, Sept. 26 Photo. *Perf. 11½***

**Size: 22½x33mm**

384 CD9 7k grnsh bl, lt bl & red *2.50 1.90*
385 CD9 8k brn, buff & red *2.50 1.90*

Literary Society Emblem A92

**1966, Nov. 18 Engr. *Perf. 11½***

386 A92 4k ultramarine .35 .30
387 A92 10k vermilion 1.00 .60

Icelandic Literary Society, 150th anniv.

Common Loon — A93

**1967, Mar. 16 Photo. *Perf. 11½***

388 A93 20k multicolored 7.50 7.50

**Europa Issue, 1967**

Common Design Type

**1967, May 2 Photo. *Perf. 11½***

**Size: 22½x33mm**

389 CD10 7k yel, brn & dk bl *1.50 1.00*
390 CD10 8k emer, gray & dk bl *1.50 1.00*

Old and New Maps of Iceland and North America
A94

**1967, June 8 Photo. *Perf. 11½***
**391** A94 10k blk, tan & lt bl .35 .30

EXPO '67 Intl. Exhibition, Montreal, Apr. 28-Oct. 27, 1967. The old map, drawn about 1590 by Sigurdur Stefansson, is at the Royal Library, Copenhagen.

Symbols of Trade, Fishing, Husbandry and Industry
A95

**1967, Sept. 14 Photo. *Perf. 11½***
**392** A95 5k dk bl, yel & emerald .35 .25

Icelandic Chamber of Commerce, 50th anniv.

### Flower Type of 1960-62

Flowers: 50a, Saxifraga oppositifolia. 2.50k, Orchis maculata.

**1968, Jan. 17 Photo. *Perf. 11½***
**Flowers in Natural Colors**
**393** A72 50a green & dk brn .25 .25
**394** A72 2.50k dk brn, yel & grn .35 .35

### Europa Issue, 1968

Common Design Type

**1968, Apr. 29 Photo. *Perf. 11½***
**Size: 33½x23mm**
**395** CD11 9.50k dl yel, car rose & blk *1.75 1.50*
**396** CD11 10k brt yel grn, blk & org *1.25 1.00*

Right-hand Driving — A96

**1968, May 21 Photo. *Perf. 11½***
**397** A96 4k yellow & brn .35 .25
**398** A96 5k lt reddish brn .35 .25

Introduction of right-hand driving in Iceland, May 26, 1968.

Fridrik Fridriksson, by Sigurjón Olafsson — A97

**1968, Sept. 5 Photo. *Perf. 11½***
**399** A97 10k sky bl & dk gray .60 *.55*

Rev. Fridrik Fridriksson (1868-1961), founder of the YMCA in Reykjavik and writer.

Reading Room, National Library
A98

Prime Minister Jon Magnusson (1859-1926)
A99

**1968, Oct. 30 Photo. *Perf. 11½***
**Granite Paper**
**400** A98 5k yellow & brn .25 .25
**401** A98 20k lt bl & dp ultra 1.50 1.50

Natl. Library, Reykjavik, sesquicentennial.

**1968, Dec. 12 Granite Paper**
**402** A99 4k carmine lake .35 .25
**403** A99 50k dark brown 4.50 *4.25*

50th anniversary of independence.

### Nordic Cooperation Issue

Five Ancient Ships — A99a

**1969, Feb. 28 Engr. *Perf. 12½***
**404** A99a 6.50k vermilion .75 .60
**405** A99a 10k bright blue .90 .75

50th anniv. of the Nordic Society and centenary of postal cooperation among the northern countries. The design is taken from a coin found at the site of Birka, an ancient Swedish town. See also Denmark Nos. 454-455, Finland No. 481, Norway Nos. 523-524, and Sweden Nos. 808-810.

### Europa Issue, 1969

Common Design Type

**1969, Apr. 28 Photo. *Perf. 11½***
**Size: 32½x23mm**
**406** CD12 13k pink & multi *3.75 2.00*
**407** CD12 14.50k yel & multi *.45 .40*

Flag of Iceland and Rising Sun — A100

**1969, June 17 Photo. *Perf. 11½***
**408** A100 25k gray, gold, vio bl & red 1.20 .75
**409** A100 100k lt bl, gold, vio bl & red 7.50 7.50

25th anniversary, Republic of Iceland.

Boeing 727
A101

Design: 12k, Rolls Royce 400.

**1969, Sept. 3 Photo. *Perf. 11½***
**410** A101 9.50k dk bl & sky bl .75 .75
**411** A101 12k dk bl & ultra .75 .75

50th anniversary of Icelandic aviation.

Snaefellsjökull Mountain
A102

**1970, Jan. 6 Photo. *Perf. 11½***
**412** A102 1k shown .25 .25
**413** A102 4k Laxfoss .35 .35
**414** A102 5k Hattver, vert. .40 .35
**415** A102 20k Fjardargill, vert. 2.00 .75
*Nos. 412-415 (4)* 3.00 1.70

First Meeting of Icelandic Supreme Court
A103

**1970, Feb. 16 Photo. *Perf. 11½***
**416** A103 6.50k multicolored .30 .25

Icelandic Supreme Court, 50th anniv.

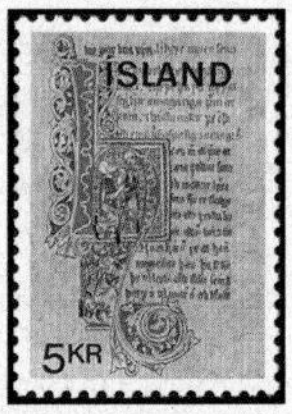


Column from "Skarosbók," 1363 (Law Book) — A104

Icelandic Manuscripts: 15k, Preface to "Flateyjarbók" (History of Norwegian Kings), 1387-1394. 30k, Initial from "Flateyjarbók" showing Harald Fairhair cutting fetters of Dofri.

**1970, Mar. 20 Photo. *Perf. 11½***
**417** A104 5k multicolored .25 .25
**418** A104 15k multicolored .65 .65
**419** A104 30k multicolored 1.25 1.25
*Nos. 417-419 (3)* 2.15 2.15

### Europa Issue, 1970

Common Design Type

**1970, May 4 Photo. *Perf. 11½***
**Size: 32x22mm**
**420** CD13 9k brn & yellow *2.50 1.50*
**421** CD13 25k brt grn & bister *3.50 2.50*

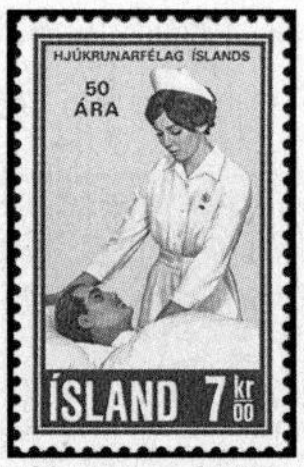


Nurse — A105

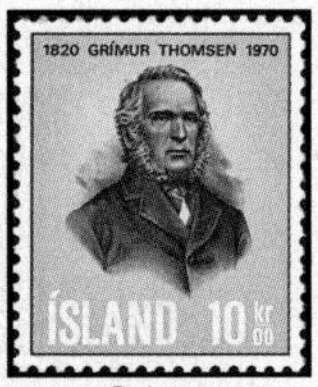


Grimur Thomsen — A106

The Rest, by Thorarinn B. Thorlaksson
A107

**1970, June 19 Photo. *Perf. 11½***
**422** A105 7k ultra & lt bl .35 .25
**423** A106 10k ind & lt grnsh bl .35 *.45*
**424** A107 50k gold & multi 2.00 1.50
*Nos. 422-424 (3)* 2.70 2.20

50th anniv. (in 1969) of the Icelandic Nursing Association (No. 422); 150th birth anniv. of Grimur Thomsen (1820-1896), poet (No. 423); Intl. Arts Festival, Reykjavik, June 1970 (No. 424).

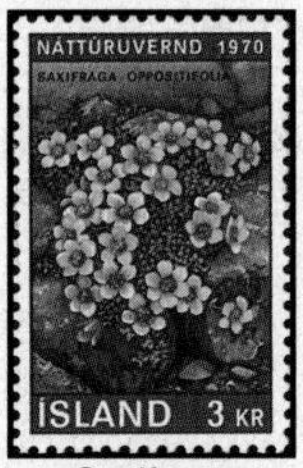


Saxifraga Oppositifolia
A108

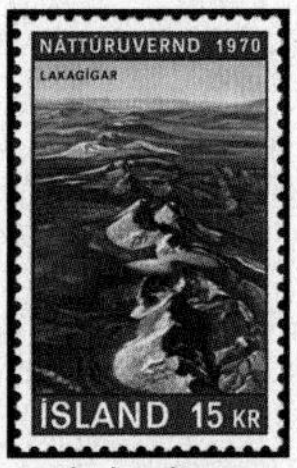


Lakagigar
A109

**1970, Aug. 25 Photo. *Perf. 11½***
**425** A108 3k multicolored .30 .30
**426** A109 15k multicolored .90 .80

European Nature Conservation Year.

UN Emblem and Map of Iceland
A110

**1970, Oct. 23 Photo. *Perf. 11½***
**427** A110 12k multicolored .55 *.65*

25th anniversary of United Nations.

"Flight," by Asgrimur Jonsson
A111

**1971, Mar. 26 Photo. *Perf. 11½***
**428** A111 10k multicolored .90 .90

Joint northern campaign for the benefit of refugees.

### Europa Issue, 1971

Common Design Type

**1971, May 3 Photo. *Perf. 11½***
**Size: 33x22mm**
**429** CD14 7k rose cl, yel & blk *2.25 1.75*
**430** CD14 15k ultra, yel & blk *2.75 2.00*

Postal Checking Service Emblem
A112

**1971, June 22 Photo. *Perf. 11½***
**431** A112 5k vio bl & lt blue .25 .25
**432** A112 7k dk grn & yel grn .30 .25

Introduction of Postal Checking Service, Apr. 30, 1971.

Tryggvi Gunnarsson
A113

Haddock Freezing Plant
A114

Design: 30k, Patriotic Society emblem.

**1971, Aug. 19 Photo. *Perf. 11½***
**433** A113 30k lt bl & vio blk 1.50 1.00
**434** A113 100k gray & vio blk 6.50 6.50

Icelandic Patriotic Society, cent.; Tryggvi Gunnarsson (1835-1917), founder and president.

**1971, Nov. 18**

Fish Industry: 7k, Cod fishing. 20k, Shrimp canning plant.

**435** A114 5k multicolored .25 .25
**436** A114 7k multicolored .25 .25
**437** A114 20k green & multi .55 .55
*Nos. 435-437 (3)* 1.05 1.05

Herdubreid Mountain — A115

**Engr. & Litho.**

**1972, Mar. 9 *Perf. 14***
**438** A115 250k blue & multi .70 .30

### Europa Issue 1972
Common Design Type

**1972, May 2 Photo. *Perf. 11½***
**Size: 22x32mm**

**439** CD15 9k lt vio & multi *1.00 .90*
**440** CD15 13k yel grn & multi *1.90 1.75*

"United Municipalities" — A116

**1972, June 14 Photo. *Perf. 11½***
**441** A116 16k multicolored .25 .25

Legislation for local government, cent.

Chessboard, World Map, Rook — A117

**1972, July 2 Litho. *Perf. 13***
**442** A117 15k lt ol & multi .45 .35

World Chess Championship, Reykjavik, July-Sept. 1972.

Hothouse Tomatoes A118

Designs: 12k, Steam valve and natural steam. 40k, Hothouse roses.

**1972, Aug. 23 Photo. *Perf. 11½***
**443** A118 8k Prus bl & multi .25 .25
**444** A118 12k green & multi .25 .25
**445** A118 40k dk pur & multi .90 .90
*Nos. 443-445 (3)* 1.40 1.40

Hothouse gardening in Iceland, using natural steam and hot springs.

Iceland and the Continental Shelf — A119

**1972, Sept. 27 Litho. *Perf. 13***
**446** A119 9k blue & multi .25 .25

To publicize Iceland's offshore fishing rights.

### Europa Issue 1973
Common Design Type

**1973, Apr. 30 Photo. *Perf. 11½***
**Size: 32½x22mm**

**447** CD16 13k vio & multi *6.00 3.25*
**448** CD16 25k olive & multi *1.00 .80*

Iceland No. 1 and Messenger — A120

Designs (First Issue of Iceland and): 15k, No. 5 and pony train. 20k, No. 2 and mailboat "Esja." 40k, No. 3 and mail truck. 80k, No. 4 and Beech-18 mail plane.

**Litho. & Engr.**

**1973, May 23 *Perf. 13x13½***
**449** A120 10k dl bl, blk & ultra .30 .30
**450** A120 15k grn, blk & gray .25 .25
**451** A120 20k maroon, blk & car .25 .25
**452** A120 40k vio, blk & brn .25 .25
**453** A120 80k olive, blk & yel 1.25 1.00
*Nos. 449-453 (5)* 2.30 2.05

Centenary of Iceland's first postage stamps.

### Nordic Cooperation Issue

Nordic House, Reykjavik A120a

**1973, June 26 Engr. *Perf. 12½***
**454** A120a 9k multicolored .35 .25
**455** A120a 10k multicolored 1.10 1.10

A century of postal cooperation among Denmark, Finland, Iceland, Norway and Sweden, and in connection with the Nordic Postal Conference, Reykjavik.

Ásgeir Ásgeirsson, (1894-1972),President of Iceland 1952-1968 — A121

***Perf. 13x13½***
**1973, Aug. 1 Wmk. 409 Engr.**
**456** A121 13k carmine .25 .25
**457** A121 15k blue .25 *.25*

Islandia 73 Emblem A122

20k, Islandia 73 emblem; diff. arrangement.

**1973, Aug. 31 Photo. *Perf. 11½***
**458** A122 17k gray & multi .45 .45
**459** A122 20k brn, ocher & yel .35 .35

Islandia 73 Philatelic Exhibition, Reykjavik, Aug. 31-Sept. 9.

Man and WMO Emblem A123

The Settlement, Tapestry by Vigdis Kristjansdottir A124

**1973, Nov. 14 Photo. *Perf. 12½***
**460** A123 50k silver & multi .80 .65

Intl. meteorological cooperation, cent.

**1974 Photo. *Perf. 11½***

Designs: 13k, Establishment of Althing, painting by Johannes Johannesson, horiz. 15k, Gudbrandur Thorlakkson, Bishop ofHolar 1571-1627. 17k, Age of Sturlungar (Fighting Vikings), drawing by Thorvaldur Skulason. 20k, Stained glass window honoring Hallgrimur Petursson (1614-74), hymn writer. 25k, Illumination from Book of Flatey, 14th century. 30k, Conversion to Christianity (altarpiece, Skalholt), mosaic by Nina Tryggvadottir. 40k, Wood carving (family and plants), 18th century. 60k, Curing the Catch, cement bas-relief. 70k, Age of Writing (Saemundur Riding Seal), sculpture by Asmundur Sveinsson. 100k, Virgin and Child with Angels, embroidered antependium, Stafafell Church, 14th century, horiz.

**461** A124 10k multicolored .25 .25
**462** A124 13k multicolored .25 .25
**463** A124 15k multicolored .25 .25
**464** A124 17k multicolored .35 .25
**465** A124 20k multicolored .35 .25
**466** A124 25k multicolored .25 .25
**467** A124 30k multicolored .85 .70
**468** A124 40k multicolored 1.15 .90
**469** A124 60k multicolored 1.15 1.15
**470** A124 70k multicolored 1.15 1.15
**471** A124 100k multicolored 1.50 .75
*Nos. 461-471 (11)* 7.50 6.15

1100th anniv. of settlement of Iceland.
Issued: 10k, 13k, 30k, 70k, 3/12; 17k, 25k, 100k, 6/11; 15k, 20k, 40k, 60k, 7/16.

Horseback Rider, Wood, 17th Century — A125

Europa: 20k, "Through the Sound Barrier," contemporary bronze by Asmundur Sveinsson.

**1974, Apr. 29 Photo. *Perf. 11½***
**472** A125 13k brn red & multi *.45 .40*
**473** A125 20k gray & multi *1.00 1.00*

Clerk Selling Stamps, UPU Emblem A126

Design: 20k, Mailman delivering mail.

**1974, Oct. 9 Photo. *Perf. 11½***
**474** A126 17k ocher & multi .35 .35
**475** A126 20k olive & multi .35 .35

Centenary of Universal Postal Union.

Volcanic Eruption, Heimaey, Jan. 23, 1973 — A127

Design: 25k, Volcanic eruption, night view.

**1975, Jan. 23 Photo. *Perf. 11½***
**476** A127 20k multicolored .45 .45
**477** A127 25k multicolored .35 .35

### Europa Issue 1975

Bird, by Thorvaldur Skulason A128

Sun Queen, by Johannes S. Kjarval — A129

**1975, May 12 Photo. *Perf. 11½***
**478** A128 18k multicolored *.40 .40*
**479** A129 23k gold & multi *1.10 1.00*

Stephan G. Stephansson A130

**1975, Aug. 1 Engr. *Perf. 13***
**480** A130 27k green & brn .55 .35

Stephan G. Stephansson (1853-1927), Icelandic poet and settler in North America; centenary of Icelandic emigration to North America.

Petursson, by Hjalti Thorsteinsson A131

Einar Jonsson, Self-portrait A132

23k, Arni Magnusson, by Hjalti Thorsteinsson. 30k, Jon Eiriksson, sculpture by Olafur Olafsson.

**1975, Sept. 18 Engr. *Perf. 13***
**481** A131 18k slate green & indigo .25 .25
**482** A131 23k Prussian blue .25 .25
**483** A131 30k deep magenta .25 .25
**484** A132 50k indigo .50 .25
*Nos. 481-484 (4)* 1.25 1.00

Famous Icelanders: Hallgrimur Petursson (1614-1674), minister and religious poet; Arni Magnusson (1663-1730), historian, registrar and manuscript collector; Jon Eiriksson (1728-1787), professor of law and cabinet member; Einar Jonsson (1874-1954), sculptor, painter and writer.

Red Cross A133

**1975, Oct. 15 Photo. *Perf. 11½x12***
**485** A133 23k multicolored .45 .25

Icelandic Red Cross, 50th anniversary.

Abstract Painting, by Nina Tryggvadottir A134

**1975, Oct. 15 *Perf. 12x12½***
**486** A134 100k multicolored 1.40 .65

International Women's Year 1975.

Thorvaldsen Statue, by Thorvaldsen
A135

Saplings Growing in Bare Landscape
A136

**1975, Nov. 19 Photo. *Perf. 11½***
**487** A135 27k lt vio & multi .60 .45

Centenary of Thorvaldsen Society, a charity honoring Bertel Thorvaldsen (1768-1844), sculptor.

**1975, Nov. 19 *Perf. 12x11½***
**488** A136 35k multicolored .60 .45

Reforestation.

Lang Glacier, by Asgrimur Jonsson
A137

**1976, Mar. 18 Photo. *Perf. 11½***
**489** A137 150k gold & multi 1.75 1.50

Asgrimur Jonsson (1876-1958), painter.

Wooden Bowl — A138

Europa: 45k, Spinning wheel, vert.

**1976, May 3 Photo. *Perf. 11½***
**490** A138 35k ver & multi *1.40 1.00*
**491** A138 45k blue & multi *1.40 1.40*

No. 9 with First Day Cancel — A139

Decree Establishing Postal Service — A140

**1976, Sept. 22 Photo. *Perf. 11½***
**Granite Paper**
**492** A139 30k bis, blk & gray bl .35 .25

Centenary of aurar stamps.

**1976, Sept. 22 Engr. *Perf. 13***

45k, Conclusion of Decree with signatures.

**493** A140 35k dark brown .45 .35
**494** A140 45k dark blue .45 .35

Iceland's Postal Service, bicentenary.

Federation Emblem, People — A141

**1976, Dec. 2 Photo. *Perf. 12½***
**Granite Paper**
**495** A141 100k multicolored 1.25 .75

Icelandic Federation of Labor, 60th anniv.

Five Water Lilies — A142

Ofaerufoss, Eldgja — A143

**Photo. & Engr.**

**1977, Feb. 2 *Perf. 12½***
**496** A142 35k brt grn & multi .90 .65
**497** A142 45k ultra & multi .90 .65

Nordic countries cooperation for protection of the environment and 25th Session of Nordic Council, Helsinki, Feb. 19.

**1977, May 2 Photo. *Perf. 12***

Europa: 85k, Kirkjufell Mountain, seen from Grundarfjord.

**498** A143 45k multicolored *3.00 1.00*
**499** A143 85k multicolored *2.00 .45*

Harlequin Duck — A144

**1977, June 14 Photo. *Perf. 11½***
**500** A144 40k multicolored .55 .35

Wetlands conservation, European campaign.

Society Emblem — A145

**1977, June 14**
**501** A145 60k vio bl & ultra .75 .65

Federation of Icelandic Cooperative Societies, 75th anniversary.

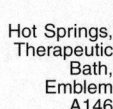

Hot Springs, Therapeutic Bath, Emblem
A146

**1977, Nov. 16 Photo. *Perf. 11½***
**502** A146 90k multicolored .65 .55

World Rheumatism Year.

Stone Marker — A147

**1977, Dec. 12 Engr. *Perf. 11½***
**503** A147 45k dark blue .90 .65

Touring Club of Iceland, 50th anniversary.

Thorvaldur Thoroddsen, (1855-1921), Geologist, Scientist and Writer — A148

Design: 60k, Briet Bjarnhedinsdottir (1856-1940), Founder of Icelandic Women's Association and Reykjavik city councillor.

**1977, Dec. 12 Engr. *Perf. 11½***
**504** A148 50k brn & slate grn .25 .25
**505** A148 60k grn & vio brn .70 .60

Bailiff's Residence, Videy Island, 1752 — A149

Europa: 120k, Husavik Church, 1906.

**1978, May 2 Photo. *Perf. 11½***
**506** A149 80k multicolored *2.25 .75*
**507** A149 120k multi, vert. *3.00 1.00*

Alexander Johannesson, Junkers Planes — A150

100k, Fokker Friendship plane over mountains.

**1978, June 21 Photo. *Perf. 12½***
**508** A150 60k multicolored .55 .30
**509** A150 100k multicolored .55 .40

50th anniv. of domestic flights in Iceland.

Skeioara River Bridge
A151

**1978, Aug. 17 Photo. *Perf. 11½***
**510** A151 70k multicolored .30 .30

Lava Near Mt. Hekla, by Jon Stefansson — A152

**1978, Nov. 16 Photo. *Perf. 12***
**511** A152 1000k multicolored 5.00 4.25

Jon Stefansson (1881-1962), Icelandic painter.

Ship to Shore Rescue
A153

**1978, Dec. 1 Engr. *Perf. 13***
**512** A153 60k black .30 .30

National Life Saving Assoc., 50th anniv.

Halldor Hermannsson (1878-1958), Historian, Librarian — A154

**1978, Dec. 1**
**513** A154 150k indigo .60 .50

Lighthouse
A155

Telephone, c. 1900
A156

**1978, Dec. 1 Photo. *Perf. 11½***
**514** A155 90k multicolored .60 .50

Centenary of Icelandic lighthouses.

**1979, Apr. 30 Photo. *Perf. 11½***

Europa: 190k, Post horn and satchel.

**515** A156 110k multicolored *1.75 .75*
**516** A156 190k multicolored *3.25 1.00*

Jon Sigurdsson and Ingibjorg Einarsdottir
A157

**1979, Nov. 1 Engr. *Perf. 13x12½***
**517** A157 150k black .60 .60

Jon Sigurdsson (1811-1879), Icelandic statesman and leader in independence movement.

Excerpt from Olafs Saga Helga — A158

**1979, Nov. 1 Photo. *Perf. 11½***
**518** A158 200k multicolored .80 .55

Snorri Sturluson (1178-1241), Icelandic historian and writer.

Children with Flowers ICY Emblem
A159

**1979, Nov. 12**
**519** A159 140k multicolored .80 .55

International Year of the Child.

A160

A161

Icelandic Arms, before 1904 and 1904-1919.

**1979, Nov. 12**
**520** A160 500k multicolored 1.50 1.00

Home rule, 75th anniversary.

**1979 Engr. *Perf. 13***

Designs: 80k, Ingibjorg H. Bjarnason (1867-1941). 100k, Bjarni Thorsteinsson (1861-1938), composer. 120k, Petur Gudjohnsen (1812-77), organist. 130k, Sveinbjorn Sveinbjornson (1847-1927), composer. 170k, Torfhildur Holm (1845-1918), poet.

**521** A161 80k rose violet .25 .25
**522** A161 100k black .25 .25
**523** A161 120k rose carmine .25 .25
**524** A161 130k sepia .45 .45
**525** A161 170k carmine rose .55 .40
*Nos. 521-525 (5)* 1.75 1.60

Issued: 80k, 170k, Aug. 3; others, Dec. 12.

Canis Familiaris — A162

Design: 90k, Alopex lagopus.

**1980, Jan. 24**
**526** A162 10k black .25 .25
**527** A162 90k sepia .25 .25

See Nos. 534-536, 543-545, 552, 553, 556-558, 610-612.

Jon Sveinsson Nonni (1857-1944), Writer — A163

Europa: 250k, Gunnar Gunnarsson (1889-1975), writer.

**1980, Apr. 28 Photo. *Perf. 11½***
**Granite Paper**
**528** A163 140k dl rose & blk *1.00* .50
**529** A163 250k tan & blk *1.25* .75

Mountain Ash Branch and Berries — A164

**1980, July 8 Photo. *Perf. 12½***
**530** A164 120k multicolored .35 .35

Year of the Tree.

Laugardalur Sports Complex, Reykjavik A165

**1980, July 8 Engr. *Perf. 13x12½***
**531** A165 300k slate green .70 .55

1980 Olympic Games.

Carved and Painted Cabinet Door, 18th Cent. — A166

Nordic Cooperation: 180k, Embroidered cushion, 19th cent.

**1980, Sept. 9 Photo. *Perf. 11½***
**Granite Paper**
**532** A166 150k multicolored .65 .50
**533** A166 180k multicolored .75 .60

**Animal Type of 1980**

**1980, Oct. 16 Engr. *Perf. 13***

Designs: 160k, Sebastes marinus. 170k, Fratercula arctica. 190k, Phoca vitulina.

**534** A162 160k rose violet .90 .25
**535** A162 170k black 1.00 .60
**536** A162 190k dark brown .25 .35
*Nos. 534-536 (3)* 2.15 1.20

Radio Receiver, 1930 — A168

**1980, Nov. 20 Photo. *Perf. 12½***
**Granite Paper**
**537** A168 400k multicolored 1.10 .50

State Broadcasting Service, 50th anniv.

University Hospital, 50th Anniversary A169

**1980, Nov. 20 *Perf. 11½***
**538** A169 200k multicolored .45 .45

A170

Design: 170a, Magnus Stephensen (1762-1833), Chief Justice. 190a, Finnur Magnusson (1781-1847), Privy Archives keeper.

**1981, Feb. 24 Engr. *Perf. 13***
**539** A170 170a bright ultra .25 .35
**540** A170 190a olive green .25 .35

**Europa Issue 1981**

Europa — A171

**1981, May 4 Photo. *Perf. 11½***
**Granite Paper**
**541** A171 180a Luftur the Sorcerer *1.50 1.00*
**542** A171 220a Sea witch *1.50 1.00*

**Animal Type of 1980**

**1981, Aug. 20 Engr. *Perf. 13***

Designs: 50a, Troglodytes troglodytes. 100a, Pluvialis apricaria. 200a, Corvus corax.

**543** A162 50a brown .25 .25
**544** A162 100a blue .25 .25
**545** A162 200a black .25 .25
*Nos. 543-545 (3)* .75 .75

Intl. Year of the Disabled — A173

**1981, Sept. 29 Photo. *Perf. 11½***
**546** A173 200a multicolored .30 .25

Skyggnir Earth Satellite Station, First Anniv. — A174

**1981, Sept. 29 Photo. *Perf. 11½***
**547** A174 500a multicolored 1.25 .70

Hauling the Line, by Gunnlaugur Scheving (1904-1972) A175

**1981, Oct. 21 Photo. *Perf. 11½***
**548** A175 5000a multi 6.00 3.75

Christian Missionary Work in Iceland Millennium A176

**1981, Nov. 24 Engr. *Perf. 13***
**549** A176 200a dark violet .55 .55

Christmas A177

**1981, Nov. 24 Photo. *Perf. 12½***
**Granite Paper**
**550** A177 200a Leaf bread *.75* .65
**551** A177 250a Leaf bread, diff. *.75* .55

**Animal Type of 1980**

**1982, Mar. 23 Engr. *Perf. 13***

Designs: 20a, Buccinum undatum, vert. 600a, Chlamys islandica.

**552** A162 20a copper brn .25 .25
**553** A162 600a vio brown 1.00 .50

**Europa Issue 1982**

First Norse Settlement, 874 — A179

**1982, May 3 Photo. *Perf. 11½***
**Granite Paper**
**554** A179 350a shown *7.50* 1.25
**555** A179 450a Discovery of North America, 1000 *7.50* 1.25

**Animal Type of 1980**

Designs: 300a, Ovis aries, vert. 400a, Bos taurus, vert. 500a, Felis catus, vert.

**1982, June 3 Engr. *Perf. 13***
**556** A162 300a brown .90 .50
**557** A162 400a lake .65 .35
**558** A162 500a gray .25 .25
*Nos. 556-558 (3)* 1.80 1.10

Kaupfelag Thingeyinga Cooperative Society Centenary — A181

**1982, June 3**
**559** A181 1000a black & red 1.10 .65

Man Riding Iceland Pony — A182

**1982, July 1 Photo. *Perf. 11½***
**Granite Paper**
**560** A182 700a multicolored .80 .35

Centenary of School of Agriculture, Holar A183

**1982, July 1 Granite Paper**
**561** A183 1500a multi 1.25 1.10

Mount Herdubreid, by Isleifur Konradsson (1889-1972) A184

**1982, Sept. 8 Photo. *Perf. 11½***
**Granite Paper**
**562** A184 800a multicolored .75 .65

UN World Assembly on Aging, 7/26-8/6.

Borbjorg Sveinsdottir (1828-1903) — A185

**1982, Sept. 8 Engr. *Perf. 13***
**563** A185 900a red brown .70 .55

Borbjorg Sveinsdottir (1828-1903), midwife and Univ. founder.

Souvenir Sheet

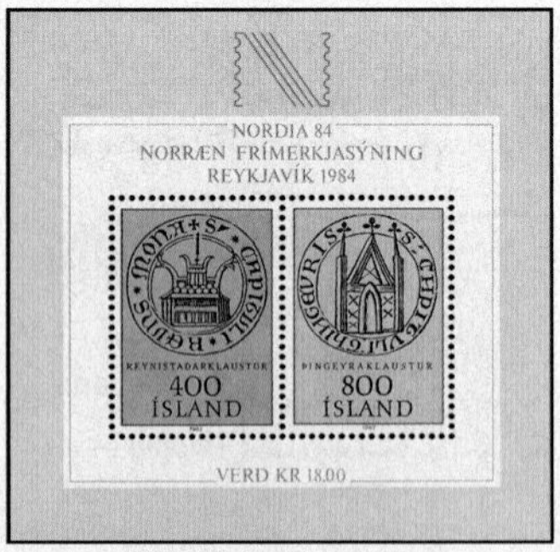


NORDIA '84 — A186

**Photo. & Engr.**

**1982, Oct. 7** *Perf. 13½*
**564** Sheet of 2 7.00 7.00
*a.* A186 400a Reynistaour Monastery seal 3.50 3.50
*b.* A186 800a Bingeyrar 3.50 3.50

NORDIA '84 Intl. Stamp Exhibition, Reykjavik, July 3-8, 1984. Sold for 18k.
See No. 581.

Christmas
A187

Score from The Night was Such a Splendid One.

**1982, Nov. 16 Photo.** *Perf. 11½*
**Granite Paper**
**565** A187 3k Birds .90 .55
**566** A187 3.50k Bells 1.00 .55

Caltha Palustris — A188

**1983, Feb. 10 Photo.**
**Granite Paper**
**567** A188 7.50k shown .50 .50
**568** A188 8k Lychnis alpina .80 .50
**569** A188 10k Potentilla palustris 1.25 .50
**570** A188 20k Myosotis scorpioides 2.25 .75
*Nos. 567-570 (4)* 4.80 2.25

See #586-587, 593-594, 602-605, 663-664.

Nordic Cooperation
A189

**1983, Mar. 24 Granite Paper**
**571** A189 4.50k Mt. Sulur .90 .75
**572** A189 5k Urrida Falls .90 .75

**Europa Issue, 1983**

Thermal Energy Projects — A190

**1983, May 5 Granite Paper**
**573** A190 5k shown *4.50 2.00*
**574** A190 5.50k multi, diff. *25.00 2.50*

Fishing Industry
A191

**1983, June 8 Engr.** *Perf. 13x12½*
**575** A191 11k Fishing boats .30 .30
**576** A191 13k Fishermen 1.40 .80

Bicentenary of Skaftareldar Volcanic Eruption
A192

**1983, June 8 Photo.** *Perf. 11½*
**Granite Paper**
**577** A192 15k Volcano, by Finnur Jonsson .85 .75

Skiing — A193

**1983, Sept. 8 Photo.** *Perf. 11½*
**578** A193 12k shown .85 .65
**579** A193 14k Running 1.00 .75

World Communications Year — A194

**1983, Sept. 8** *Perf. 12½*
**580** A194 30k multi 2.75 1.40

**NORDIA '84 Type of 1982**
Souvenir Sheet

Bishops' Seals: 8k, Magnus Eyjolfsson of Skalholt, 1477-90. 12k, Ogmundur Palsson of Skalhot, 1521-40.

**Photo. & Engr.**

**1983, Oct. 6** *Perf. 13½*
**581** Sheet of 2 8.25 8.25
*a.* A186 8k violet blue & black 4.00 4.00
*b.* A186 12k pale green & black 4.00 4.00

Sold for 30k.

Christmas
A195

Pres. Kristjan Eldjarn (1916-82)
A196

**1983, Nov. 10 Photo.** *Perf. 11½*
**Granite Paper**
**582** A195 6k Virgin and Child .90 .55
**583** A195 6.50k Angel .90 .55

*Perf. 14x13½*

**1983, Dec. 6 Engr. Wmk. 410**
**584** A196 6.50k brn carmine .90 .80
**585** A196 7k dark blue .35 .25

**Flower Type of 1983**

**1984, Mar. 1 Photo.** *Perf. 11½*
**Granite Paper**
**586** A188 6k Rosa pimpinellifolia .90 .55
**587** A188 25k Potentilla anserium 1.25 .55

Europa 1959-84
A197

**1984, May 3**
**588** A197 6.50k grnsh bl & blk *2.75* .75
**589** A197 7.50k rose & black *1.50* .75

Souvenir Sheet

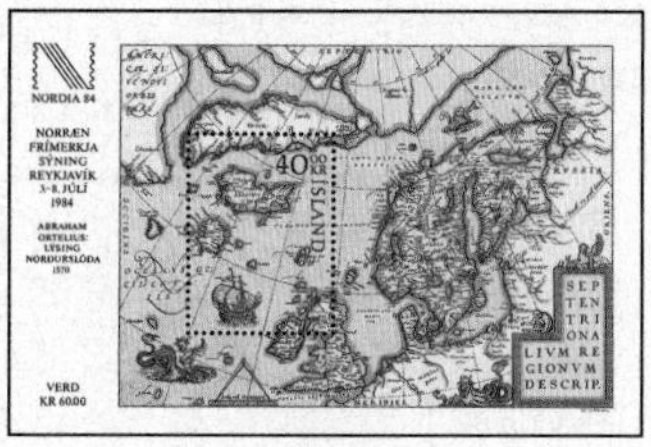


A198

Design: Abraham Ortelius' map of Northern Europe, 1570.

**Photo. & Engr.**

**1984, June 6** *Perf. 14x13½*
**590** A198 40k multi 18.00 18.00

NORDIA '84 Intl. Stamp Exhibition, Reykjavik, July 3-8. Sold for 60k.

A199

**1984, June 17 Photo.** *Perf. 11½*
**Granite Paper**
**591** A199 50k Flags 6.50 4.00

40th Anniv. of Republic.

Good Templars Headquarters, Akureyri — A200

**1984, July 18 Engr.** *Perf. 13*
**592** A200 10k green .70 .50

Order of the Good Templars, centenary in Iceland, temperance org.

**Flower Type of 1983**

**1984, Sept. 11 Photo.** *Perf. 11½*
**Granite Paper**
**593** A188 6.50k Loiseleuria procumbens .55 .30
**594** A188 7.50k Arctostaphylos uva-ursi .55 .30

Christmas
A201

Gudbrand's Bible, 400th Anniv.
A202

**1984, Nov. 29 Photo.**
**595** A201 600a Madonna and Child .65 .30
**596** A201 650a Angel, Christmas rose .65 .45

**1984, Nov. 29 Engr.** *Perf. 12½x13*
**597** A202 6.50k Text .55 .30
**598** A202 7.50k Illustration .35 *.45*

First Icelandic Bible.

Confederation of Employers, 50th Anniv.
A203

Bjorn Bjarnarson (1853-1918)
A204

**1984, Nov. 9 Photo.** *Perf. 12x12½*
**Granite Paper**
**599** A203 30k Building blocks 1.75 1.75

**1984, Nov. 9 Photo.** *Perf. 11½*
**Granite Paper**
**600** A204 12k shown .65 .65
**601** A204 40k New gallery building, horiz. 2.25 1.75

Natl. Gallery centenary.

**Flower Type of 1983**

**1985, Mar. 20 Photo.** *Perf. 11½*
**Granite Paper**
**602** A188 8k Rubus saxatilis .75 .35
**603** A188 9k Veronica fruticans .75 .35
**604** A188 16k Lathyrus japonicus 2.50 .65
**605** A188 17k Draba alpina .70 .60
*Nos. 602-605 (4)* 4.70 1.95

Music Year Emblem, Woman Playing the Langspil — A205

Europa: 7.50k, Man playing the Icelandic violin.

**1985, May 3 Photo.** *Perf. 11½*
**Granite Paper**
**606** A205 6.50k multicolored *3.50* .75
**607** A205 7.50k multicolored *3.50* .95

Natl. Horticulture Soc., Cent. — A206

Intl. Youth Year — A207

**1985, June 20 Photo.** *Perf. 12*
**608** A206 20k Sorbus intermedia 1.10 .70

**1985, June 20 Photo.** *Perf. 11½*
**609** A207 25k Icelandic girl 1.25 .95

**Animal Type of 1980**

Designs: 700a, Todarodes sagittatus. 800a, Hyas araneus. 900a, Tealia felina.

**1985, Sept. 10 Engr.** *Perf. 13*
**610** A162 700a brn carmine .25 *.30*
**611** A162 800a dk brown .90 .25
**612** A162 900a carmine 1.40 .45
*Nos. 610-612 (3)* 2.55 1.00

Hannes Stephensen (1799-1856), Cleric, Politician, Translator — A209

Famous men: 30k, Jon Gudmudsson (1807-1875), editor, politician.

**1985, Sept. 10** **Engr.**

**613** A209 13k dp magenta .65 .55
**614** A209 30k deep violet 1.50 .75

Yearning to Fly, by Johannes S. Kjarval (1885-1972), Reykjavik Natl. Museum A210

**1985, Oct. 15** **Photo.** ***Perf. 12x11½***

**615** A210 100k multi 6.00 5.25

A211

Abstract ice crystal paintings, by Snorri Sveinn Fridriksson (b. 1934).

**1985, Nov. 14** **Photo.** ***Perf. 11½***

**616** A211 8k Crucifix .60 .35
**617** A211 9k Pine Trees .60 .35

Christmas.

Birds — A212

**1986, Mar. 19** **Photo.** ***Perf. 11½***
**Granite Paper**

**618** A212 6k Motacilla alba .25 .25
**619** A212 10k Anas acuta 1.50 .65
**620** A212 12k Falco columbarius 1.00 .65
**621** A212 15k Alca torda .70 .45
*Nos. 618-621 (4)* 3.45 2.00

See Nos. 642-645, 665-666, 671-672, 686-687, 721, 725.

**Europa Issue 1986**

Natl. Parks — A213

**1986, May 5**

**622** A213 10k Skaftafell *13.50 1.10*
**623** A213 12k Jokulsargljufur *5.00 1.40*

Nordic Cooperation Issue A214

Sister towns.

**1986, May 27** ***Perf. 11½***

**624** A214 10k Stykkisholmur 1.10 .75
**625** A214 12k Seydisfjordur 1.10 .75

Natl. Bank, Cent. A215

**1986, July 1** **Engr.** ***Perf. 14***

**626** A215 13k Headquarters, Reykjavik 1.10 .80
**627** A215 250k Banknote reverse, 1928 11.00 10.00

Reykjavik Bicent. A216

**1986, Aug. 18** **Engr.** ***Perf. 13½x14***

**628** A216 10k City seal, 1815 .85 .40
**629** A216 12k View from bank, illustration, 1856 .85 .40
**630** A216 13k Laugardalur hot water brook .85 .75
**631** A216 40k City Theater 2.25 1.75
*Nos. 628-631 (4)* 4.80 3.30

Introduction of the Telephone in Iceland, 80th Anniv. — A217

**1986, Sept. 29** **Photo.** ***Perf. 11½***
**Granite Paper**

**632** A217 10k Morse receiver, 1906 .55 .40
**633** A217 20k Handset, microchip, 1986 1.25 .70

Souvenir Sheet

Hvita River Crossing, Loa, 1836, by Auguste Mayer — A218

**Photo. & Engr.**

**1986, Oct. 9** ***Perf. 14***

**634** A218 20k bluish black 6.25 6.25

Stamp Day. Sold for 30k to benefit philatelic organizations. See Nos. 646, 667.

Christmas — A219

Paintings by Bjoerg Thorsteinsdottir: 10k, Christmas at Peace. 12k, Christmas Night.

**1986, Nov. 13** **Photo.** ***Perf. 12***

**635** A219 10k multicolored 1.00 .30
**636** A219 12k multicolored .45 .30

Olafsvik Trading Station, 300th Anniv. A220

**1987, Mar. 26** **Engr.** ***Perf. 14x13½***

**637** A220 50k Merchantman Svanur, 1777 2.50 1.25

Keflavik Intl. Airport Terminal Inauguration — A221

**1987, Apr. 14** **Photo.** ***Perf. 12x11½***

**638** A221 100k multi 4.50 1.75

**Europa Issue 1987**

Stained Glass Windows by Leifur Breidfjoerd, Fossvogur Cemetery Chapel A222

**1987, May 4** **Photo.** ***Perf. 12x11½***

**639** A222 12k Christ carrying the cross *2.00 .75*
**640** A222 15k Soldiers, peace dove *2.00 .80*

Rasmus Christian Rask (1787-1832), Danish Linguist — A223

**1987, June 10** **Engr.** ***Perf. 13½***

**641** A223 20k black .90 .80

Preservation of the Icelandic language.

**Bird Type of 1986**

**1987, Sept. 16** **Photo.** ***Perf. 11½***
**Granite Paper**

**642** A212 13k Asio flammeus 1.00 .50
**643** A212 40k Turdus iliacus 1.90 .70
**644** A212 70k Haematopus ostralegus 2.75 1.10
**645** A212 90k Anas platyrhynchos 4.50 1.50
*Nos. 642-645 (4)* 10.15 3.80

**Stamp Day Type of 1986**
Souvenir Sheet

**1987, Oct. 9** **Engr.** ***Perf. 13½x14***

Trading Station of Djupivogur in 1836, by Auguste Mayer.

**646** A218 30k black 5.50 5.50

Stamp Day. Sold for 45k to benefit the Stamp and Postal History Fund.

Dental Protection — A226

**1987, Oct. 9** **Photo.** ***Perf. 11½x12***
**Granite Paper**

**647** A226 12k multi .45 .30

Eagle — A227

Guardian Spirits of the North, East, South and West.

***Perf. 13 on 3 sides***

**1987, Oct. 9** **Engr.**
**Booklet Stamps**

**648** A227 13k shown .75 .50
**649** A227 13k Dragon .75 .50
**650** A227 13k Bull .75 .50
**651** A227 13k Giant .75 .50
*a.* Block of 4, #648-651 3.00 3.00
*b.* Bklt. pane of 12, 3 #651a 9.00 —

Legend of Heimskringla, the story of the Norse kings. Haraldur Gormsson, king of Denmark, deterred from invading Iceland after hearing of the guardian spirits.

See Nos. 656-659, 677, 688-695.

Christmas — A228

**1987, Oct. 21** **Photo.** ***Perf. 11½x12***

**652** A228 13k Fir branch .65 .25
**653** A228 17k Candle flame .65 .45

Steinn Steinarr (1908-1958) A229

Poets: 21k, David Stefansson (1895-1964).

**1988, Feb. 25** **Photo.** ***Perf. 12***

**654** A229 16k multi .75 .35
**655** A229 21k multi .90 .65

**Guardian Spirit Type of 1987**
***Perf. 13 on 3 sides***

**1988, May 2** **Engr.**
**Booklet Stamps**

**656** A227 16k Eagle .80 .55
**657** A227 16k Dragon .80 .55
**658** A227 16k Bull .80 .55
**659** A227 16k Giant .80 .55
*a.* Block of 4, #656-659 3.25 3.25
*b.* Bklt. pane of 12, 3 #659a 9.75 —

**Europa Issue, 1988**

Modern Communication — A230

**1988, May 2** **Photo.** ***Perf. 12x11½***

**660** A230 16k Data transmission system *1.25 .60*
**661** A230 21k Facsimile machine *5.00 2.00*

1988 Summer Olympics, Seoul A231

**1988, June 9** **Photo.** ***Perf. 12***
**Granite Paper**

**662** A231 18k Handball .80 .70

**Flower Type of 1983**

**1988, June 9** ***Perf. 11½***
**Granite Paper**

**663** A188 10k Vicia cracca .55 .30
**664** A188 50k Thymus praecox 3.00 .65

**Bird Type of 1986**

**1988, Sept. 21** **Photo.** ***Perf. 11½***
**Granite Paper**

**665** A212 5k Limosa limosa .50 .25
**666** A212 30k Clangula hyemalis 1.75 .65

**Stamp Day Type of 1986**
Souvenir Sheet

Nupsstadur Farm, Fljotshverfi, 1836, by Auguste Mayer.

**1988, Oct. 9 Engr. *Perf. 14***
**667** A218 40k black 5.25 5.25

Stamp Day. Sold for 60k to benefit the Stamp and Postal History Fund.

WHO, 40th Anniv. — A234

**1988, Nov. 3 Photo. *Perf. 11½x12***
**Granite Paper**
**668** A234 19k multicolored .80 .40

Christmas A235

**1988, Nov. 3 *Perf. 11½***
**Granite Paper**
**669** A235 19k Fisherman at sea 1.00 .30
**670** A235 24k Ship, buoy 1.25 1.25

**Bird Type of 1986**

**1989, Feb. 2 Photo.**
**671** A212 19k Phalaropus lobatus 1.25 .40
**672** A212 100k Plectrophenax nivalis 5.25 1.60

Women's Folk Costumes — A236

**1989, Apr. 20 Photo. *Perf. 11½x12***
**Granite Paper**
**673** A236 21k Peysufot 1.75 .40
**674** A236 26k Upphlutur 1.75 .65

Nordic cooperation.

Europa 1989 A237

Children's games.

**1989, May 30 Photo. *Perf. 11½***
**Granite Paper**
**675** A237 21k Sailing toy boats *6.25 1.25*
**676** A237 26k Hoop, stick pony *6.25 1.25*

**Guardian Spirit Type of 1987**

**1989, June 27 Engr. *Perf. 13***
**677** A227 500k Dragon 19.00 8.50

Landscapes A238

**1989, Sept. 20 Photo. *Perf. 11½***
**Granite Paper**
**678** A238 35k Mt. Skeggi, Arnarfjord 1.40 .55
**679** A238 45k Thermal spring, Namaskard 1.75 .55

See Nos. 713-714, 728, 737.

Agricultural College at Hvanneyri, Cent. A239

**1989, Sept. 20 Engr. *Perf. 14***
**680** A239 50k multi 1.75 1.25

Souvenir Sheet

NORDIA '91 — A240

Detail of *A Chart and Description of Northern Routes and Wonders to Be Found in the Nordic Countries,* 1539, by Olaus Magnus (1490-1557).

**1989, Oct. 9 *Perf. 12½***
**681** A240 Sheet of 3 11.00 11.00
*a.-c.* 30k any single 3.50 3.50

Stamp Day. Sold for 130k to benefit the exhibition.
See Nos. 715, 740.

Natural History Soc., Cent. A241

Flowers or fish and: 21k, Stefan Stefansson (1863-1921), botanist and founder. 26k, Bjarni Saemundsson (1867-1940), chairman.

**1989, Nov. 9 Photo. *Perf. 11½***
**Granite Paper**
**682** A241 21k multi .85 .85
**683** A241 26k multi 1.00 .75

Christmas — A242

Paintings like stained-glass windows by Johannes Johannesson (b. 1921): 21k, Madonna and Child. 26k, Three Wise Men.

**1989, Nov. 9**
**Granite Paper**
**684** A242 21k multi 1.00 .35
**685** A242 26k multi 1.00 1.10

**Bird Type of 1986**

**1990, Feb. 15**
**Granite Paper**
**686** A212 21k *Anas penelope* 1.60 .70
**687** A212 80k *Anser brachyrhynchus* 4.00 1.60

**Guardian Spirit Type of 1987**
***Perf. 13 on 3 Sides***

**1990, Feb. 15 Engr.**
**688** A227 5k Eagle .25 .25
**689** A227 5k Dragon .25 .25
**690** A227 5k Bull .25 .25
**691** A227 5k Giant .25 .25
*a.* Block of 4, #688-691 1.00 1.00
**692** A227 21k Eagle .75 .75
**693** A227 21k Dragon .75 .75
**694** A227 21k Bull .75 .75
**695** A227 21k Giant .75 .75
*a.* Block of 4, #692-695 3.00 3.00
*b.* Block of 8, #688-695 5.25 5.25
*c.* Bklt. pane, 2 each #691a, 695a 9.00 9.00

Famous Women — A243

No. 696, Gudrun Larusdottir (1880-1938), author and politician, by Halldor Petursson. No. 697, Ragnhildur Petursdottir (1880-1961), educator, by Asgrimur Jonsson.

**1990, Mar. 22 Litho. *Perf. 13½x14***
**696** A243 21k multicolored .90 .75
**697** A243 21k multicolored .90 .75

Europa 1990 A244

Old and new post offices in Reykjavik and letter scales.

**1990, May 7 Photo. *Perf. 12x11½***
**Granite Paper**
**698** A244 21k 1915 *5.00 .90*
**699** A244 40k 1989 *5.00 2.00*

Sports — A245

**1990-94 Litho. *Perf. 13x14½***
**700** A245 21k Archery .90 .45
**701** A245 21k Soccer .90 .45
**706** A245 26k Golf .90 .65
**707** A245 26k Icelandic wrestling .90 .65

***Perf. 13½x14½***
**Photo.**
**708** A245 30k Volleyball 1.10 .60
**709** A245 30k Skiing 1.10 .60
**710** A245 30k Running 1.10 .60
**711** A245 30k Team handball 1.10 .60

**Litho.**
***Perf. 14x14½***
**711A** A245 30k Swimming 1.00 .45
**711B** A245 30k Weight lifting 1.00 .45
*Nos. 700-711B (10)* 10.00 5.50

Issued: #700-701, 6/28; #706-707, 8/14/91; #708-709, 2/20/92; #710-711, 3/10/93; #711A-711B, 2/25/94.

European Tourism Year — A246

**1990, Sept. 6 Litho. *Perf. 13½***
**712** A246 30k multicolored 1.10 .70

**Landscape Type of 1989**

**1990, Sept. 6 Photo. *Perf.***
**713** A238 25k Hvitserkur 1.00 .65
**714** A238 200k Lomagnupur 6.25 2.25

**NORDIA '91 Map Type of 1989**
Souvenir Sheet

Detail of 1539 Map by Olaus Magnus: a, Dania. b, Gothia. c, Gotlandia.

***Perf. 12x12½***

**1990, Oct. 9 Lith & Engr.**
**715** A240 Sheet of 3 12.50 12.50
*a.-c.* 40k any single 4.00 4.00

Stamp Day. Sold for 170k to benefit the exhibition.

Christmas A247

**1990, Nov. 8 *Perf. 13½x13***
**716** A247 25k shown 1.25 .45
**717** A247 30k Carolers 1.25 .55

**Bird Type of 1986**

**1991, Feb. 7 Photo. *Perf. 11½***
**Granite Paper**
**721** A212 25k Podiceps auritus 1.25 .45
**722** A212 100k Sula bassana 6.50 1.00

**Landscape Type of 1989**

**1991, Mar. 7 Photo. *Perf. 11½***
**Granite Paper**
**728** A238 10k Vestrahorn .55 .30
**737** A238 300k Kverkfjoll 11.00 2.75

Europa A248

**1991, Apr. 29 Litho. *Perf. 14***
**738** A248 26k Weather map *11.00 1.00*
**739** A248 47k Solar panels *5.50 2.00*

**NORDIA '91 Map Type of 1989**
Souvenir Sheet

Detail of 1539 Map by Olaus Magnus: a, Iceland's west coast. b, Islandia. c, Mare Glacial.

**Litho. & Engr.**

**1991, May 23 *Perf. 12½***
**740** A240 Sheet of 3 15.00 15.00
*a.-c.* 50k any single 4.75 4.75

Sold for 215k to benefit the exhibition.

Jokulsarlon Lagoon A249

Design: 31k, Strokkur hot spring.

**1991, May 23 Litho. *Perf. 15x14***
**741** A249 26k multicolored 1.00 .45
**742** A249 31k multicolored 1.00 .55

Ragnar Jonsson (1904-1984), Patron of the Arts — A250

70k, Pall Isolfsson (1893-1974), musician, vert.

**1991, Aug. 14 Litho. *Perf. 14***
**743** A250 60k multicolored 2.00 1.00
**744** A250 70k multicolored 2.50 1.25

Ships A251

Designs: a, Soloven, schooner, 1840. b, Arcturus, steamer with sails, 1858. c, Gullfoss, steamer, 1915. d, Esja II, diesel ship, 1939.

**1991, Oct. 9 Litho. *Perf. 14***
**745** Block or strip of 4 20.00 20.00
*a.-d.* A251 30k any single 3.50 1.75
*e.* A251 Bklt. pane, 2 #745 25.00

Issued in sheet of 8. No. 745e is distinguished from sheet of 8 by rouletted selvage at left.
See Nos. 803-806.

College of Navigation, Reykjavik, Cent. A252

**1991, Oct. 9 *Perf. 13½***
**746** A252 50k multicolored 1.75 1.25

Christmas — A253

Paintings by Eirikur Smith (b. 1925): 30k, Christmas star. 35k, Star over winter landscape.

**1991, Nov. 7 Litho. *Perf. 13½***
**747** A253 30k multicolored 1.10 .50
**748** A253 35k multicolored 1.10 1.50

Europa A254

Map and: No. 749, Viking longboat of Leif Eriksson. No. 750, Sailing ship of Columbus.

**1992, Apr. 6 Litho. *Perf. 13½x14***
**749** A254 55k multicolored *5.00 2.25*
**750** A254 55k multicolored *5.00 2.25*

**Souvenir Sheet**

**751** A254 Sheet of 2, #749-750 *13.50 8.00*

First landing in the Americas by Leif Erikson (#749). Discovery of America by Christopher Columbus, 500th anniv. (#750).
Stamps on #751 printed in continuous design. #749-751 have borders.

Export Trade and Commerce A255

Designs: 35k, Fishing boat, fish.

**1992, June 16 Litho. *Perf. 13½***
**752** A255 30k multicolored 2.25 .75
**753** A255 35k multicolored 2.25 .75

Bridges A256

**1992, Oct. 9 Litho. *Perf. 13½***
**754** A256 5k Fnjoska, 1908 .25 .25
**755** A256 250k Olfusa, 1891 9.50 5.50

See Nos. 766-767.

Mail Trucks A257

#756, Mail transport car RE 231, 1933. #757, Ford bus, 1946. #758, Ford TT, 1920-26. #759, Citroen snowmobile, 1929.

**1992, Oct. 9 *Perf. 14***
**756** A257 30k multicolored 2.40 .90
**757** A257 30k multicolored 2.40 .90
**758** A257 30k multicolored 2.40 .90
**759** A257 30k multicolored 2.40 .90
*a.* Block or strip of 4, #756-759 9.75 9.75
*b.* Bklt. pane, 2 ea #756-759 30.00

Issued in sheets of 8. No. 759b has rouletted selvage at left.
See Nos. 820-823.

Christmas — A258

Paintings by Bragi Asgeirsson.

**1992, Nov. 9 Litho. *Perf. 13½x13***
**760** A258 30k shown 1.50 .35
**761** A258 35k Sun over mountains 1.50 .65

Falco Rusticolus — A259

**1992, Dec. 3 Photo. *Perf. 11½***
**Granite Paper**
**762** A259 5k Adult, two young 2.30 .55
**763** A259 10k Adult feeding 2.90 .90
**764** A259 20k Adult, head up 2.90 1.00
**765** A259 35k Adult 2.90 1.60
*Nos. 762-765 (4)* 11.00 4.05

**Bridges Type of 1992**

**1993, Mar. 10 Litho. *Perf. 13½x13***
**766** A256 90k Hvita, 1928 2.75 1.60
**767** A256 150k Jokulsa a Fjollum, 1947 5.00 2.25

Nordica '93 — A260

Designs: 30k, The Blue Lagoon therapeutic bathing area, hot water plant, Svartsengi. 35k, Perlan hot water storage tanks, restaurant.

**1993, Apr. 26 Litho. *Perf. 13½x13***
**768** A260 30k multicolored 1.25 .65
**769** A260 35k multicolored 1.60 1.25

Sculptures — A261

Europa: 35k, Sailing, by Jon Gunnar Arnason. 55k, Hatching of the Jet, by Magnus Tomasson.

**1993, Apr. 26 *Perf. 13x13½***
**770** A261 35k multicolored *2.00 1.25*
**771** A261 55k multicolored *3.25 2.50*

**Souvenir Sheet**

Italian Group Flight, 60th Anniv. — A262

**1993, Oct. 9 Litho. *Perf. 13½***
**772** A262 Sheet of 3, #a.-c. 8.00 8.00
*a.* 10k #C12 .65 .65
*b.* 50k #C13 2.50 2.50
*c.* 100k #C14 4.50 4.50

No. 772 sold for 200k.

Seaplanes — A263

**1993, Oct. 9 *Perf. 14***
**773** A263 30k Junkers F-13 (D463) 2.50 1.00
**774** A263 30k Waco YKS-7 (TF-ORN) 2.50 1.00
**775** A263 30k Grumman G-21A/JRF-5 (RVK) 2.50 1.00
**776** A263 30k PBY-5 Catalina (TF-ISP) 2.50 1.00
*a.* Block or strip of 4, #773-776 10.00 10.00
*b.* Bklt. pane, 2 ea #773-776 22.50

No. 776b is distinguished from sheet of 8 by rouletted selvage at left.
Issued in sheet of 8.
See Nos. 838-841.

Christmas A264

**1993, Nov. 8 Litho. *Perf. 12½***
**777** A264 30k Adoration of the Magi 1.25 .45
**778** A264 35k Virgin and Child 1.25 1.25

Intl. Year of the Family A265

**1994, Feb. 25 Litho. *Perf. 13½x13***
**779** A265 40k multicolored 1.25 1.25

Voyages of St. Brendan (484-577) A266

Europa: 35k, St. Brendan, Irish monks sailing past volcano. 55k, St. Brendan on island with sheep, monks in boat.

**1994, Apr. 18 Litho. *Perf. 14½x14***
**780** A266 35k multicolored *2.50 1.10*
Booklet, 10 #780 *25.00*
**781** A266 55k multicolored *2.75 1.40*
Booklet, 10 #781 *27.50*
*a.* Miniature sheet of 2, #780-781 *5.75 4.25*

See Ireland Nos. 923-924; Faroe Islands Nos. 264-265.

Icelandic Art and Culture A267

**1994, May 25 Litho. *Perf. 13½x13***
**782** A267 30k Music 1.00 .40
**783** A267 30k Crafts 1.00 .70
**784** A267 30k Film making 1.00 .70
**785** A267 30k Ballet, modern dance 1.00 .70
**786** A267 30k Theatre 1.00 .70
*Nos. 782-786 (5)* 5.00 3.20

Independence, 50th anniv.

Gisli Sveinsson (1880-1959), Politician — A268

**1994, June 14 *Perf. 14***
**787** A268 30k multicolored 1.10 1.00

Proclamation of new constitution, 50th anniv.

**Souvenir Sheet**

Republic of Iceland, 50th Anniv. — A269

Presidents of Iceland: a, Sveinn Bjornsson (1881-1952). b, Asgeir Asgeirsson (1894-1972). c, Kristjan Eldjarn (1916-82). d, Vigdis Finnbogadottir (b. 1930).

**1994, June 17 Photo. *Perf. 11½***
**Granite Paper**
**788** A269 Sheet of 4, #a.-d. 7.00 7.00
*a.-d.* 50k any single 1.75 1.75

**Souvenir Sheet**

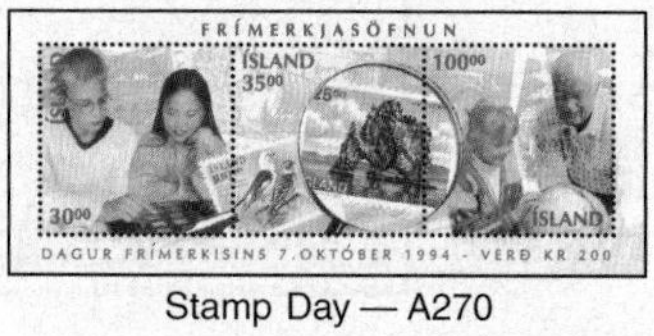

Stamp Day — A270

Designs: a, Boy, girl with stamp album. b, Nos. 672, 713, portions of other Icelandic stamps. c, Girl, elderly man looking at globe.

**1994, Oct. 7 Litho. *Perf. 13½***
**789** A270 Sheet of 3 9.50 9.50
*a.* 30k multicolored 2.50 2.50
*b.* 35k multicolored 2.50 2.50
*c.* 100k multicolored 4.00 3.50

No. 789 sold for 200k for the benefit of the Stamp and Postal History Fund.

Christmas A271

**1994, Nov. 9 Litho. *Perf. 14½***

**790** A271 30k Woman, stars 1.00 .30
**791** A271 35k Man, stars 1.25 .70

ICAO, 50th Anniv. A272

**1994, Nov. 9 *Perf. 13½x14***

**792** A272 100k multicolored 3.50 2.25

A273

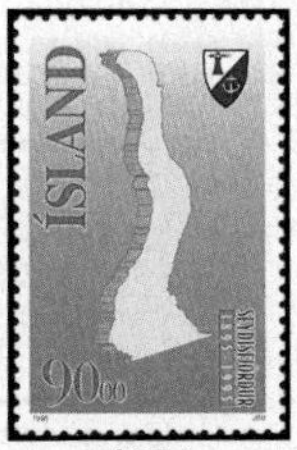

A274

**1995, Mar. 14 Litho. *Perf. 13***

**793** A273 35k multicolored 1.25 .80

Salvation Army in Iceland, cent.

**1995, Mar. 14**

**794** A274 90k multicolored 4.50 2.00

Town of Seydisfjordur, cent.

1995 Men's Team Handball World Championships, Iceland — A275

Federation emblem, handball and: No. 795, Geyser, landscape. No. 796, Silhouette of building, landscape. No. 797, Volcano, lake. No. 798, Inlet, sunlight on water.

**1995, Mar. 14 Litho. *Perf. 14***

**795** A275 35k multicolored 1.75 1.10
**796** A275 35k multicolored 1.75 1.10
**797** A275 35k multicolored 1.75 1.10
**798** A275 35k multicolored 1.75 1.10
*a.* Block or strip of 4, #795-798 7.25 7.00
*b.* Booklet pane, 2 #798a 17.50
Complete booklet, #798b 17.50

Nos. 795-798 issued in sheets of 8 containing 2 each. No. 798b is separated from booklet by rouletted selvage at left, and sold for 480k in the complete booklet.

Norden 1995 — A276

Designs: 30k, Turf farmhouses, church. 35k, Volcano, Fjallsjokull glacier.

**1995, May 5 Litho. *Perf. 13½x13***

**799** A276 30k multicolored 1.00 .55
Booklet, 10 #799 10.00
**800** A276 35k multicolored 1.40 .90

Spell-Broken, by Einar Jonsson (1874-1954) — A277

**1995, May 5 *Perf. 13x13½***

**801** A277 35k brown & multi *1.10 1.00*
Booklet, 10 #801 *12.60*
**802** A277 55k blue & multi *2.00 1.75*
Booklet, 10 #802 *20.00*

Europa.

**Ship Type of 1991**

**1995, June 30 Litho. *Perf. 14***

**803** A251 30k SS Laura 1.20 .90
**804** A251 30k MS Dronning Alexandrine 1.20 .90
**805** A251 30k MS Laxfoss 1.20 .90
**806** A251 30k MS Godafoss III 1.20 .90
*a.* Block or strip of 4, #803-806 5.00 4.50
*b.* Bklt. pane, 2 ea #803-806 10.00
Prestige booklet, #806b 16.00

No. 806b is distinguished from sheet of 8 by rouletted selvage at left.
Issued in sheets of 8.
Prestige booklet sold for 400k.

Luxembourg-Reykjavik, Iceland Air Route, 40th Anniv. — A278

**1995, Sept. 18 Litho. *Perf. 13½***

**807** A278 35k multicolored 1.75 1.25

See Luxembourg No. 936.

Birds A279

**1995, Sept. 18 *Perf. 13½***

**808** A279 25k Acanthis flammea .80 .65
**809** A279 250k Gallinago gallinago 8.50 6.00

Souvenir Sheet

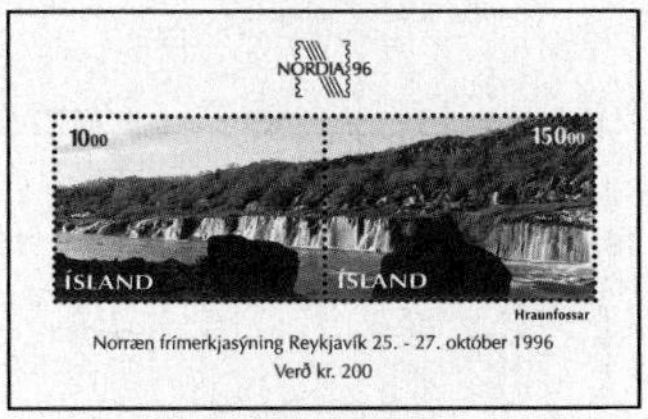

Nordia '96, Reykjavik — A280

Design: Hraunfossar Waterfalls, Hvita River.

**1995, Oct. 9 *Perf. 13½x14***

**810** A280 Sheet of 2, #a.-b. 11.00 11.00
*a.* 10k multicolored 3.25 3.25
*b.* 150k multicolored 7.00 7.00

See No. 830.

Christmas A281

**1995, Nov. 8 Litho. *Perf. 13½***

**811** A281 30k Snowman, woman 1.00 .75
**812** A281 35k Three trees 1.10 .90

UN, 50th Anniv. — A282

**1995, Nov. 8 *Perf. 13x13½***

**813** A282 100k multicolored 3.25 2.50

Water Birds A283

Designs: 20k, Phalacrocorax carbo. 40k, Bucephala islandica.

**1996, Feb. 7 Litho. *Perf. 13½***

**814** A283 20k multicolored .95 .55
**815** A283 40k multicolored 2.00 1.00

See Nos. 834-835.

Paintings A284

100k, Seamen in a Boat, by Gunnlaugur Scheving (1904-72). 200k, At the Washing Springs, by Kristín Jónsdóttir (1888-1959).

**1996, Feb. 7**

**816** A284 100k multicolored 4.25 3.75
**817** A284 200k multicolored 5.25 4.25

Famous Women A285

Europa: 35k, Halldóra Bjarnadóttir (1873-1981), educator. 55k, Olafía Jóhannsdóttir (1863-1924), representative of women's rights, temperance affairs.

**1996, Apr. 18 Litho. *Perf. 14½***

**818** A285 35k multicolored *1.25 1.00*
Booklet, 10 #818 *12.50*
**819** A285 55k multicolored *1.45 1.25*
Booklet, 10 #819 *14.50*

**Postal Vehicle Type of 1992**

Designs: No. 820, 1931 Buick. No. 821, 1933 Studebaker, Reykjavik Municipal Bus Service. No. 822, 1937 Ford, Iceland Motor Coach Service. No. 823, 1946 REO, Post and Telecommunications.

**1996, May 13 Litho. *Perf. 14***

**820** A257 35k multicolored 1.25 .85
**821** A257 35k multicolored 1.25 .85
**822** A257 35k multicolored 1.25 .85
**823** A257 35k multicolored 1.25 .85
*a.* Block or strip of 4, #820-823 5.00 5.00
*b.* Bklt. pane, 2 ea #820-823 10.00 10.00
Souvenir booklet, #823b 12.00

No. 823a issued in sheets of 8 stamps. No. 823b has rouletted selvage at left.

1996 Summer Olympic Games, Atlanta A286

**1996, June 25 Litho. *Perf. 12½***

**824** A286 5k Running .25 .25
**825** A286 25k Javelin .75 .40
**826** A286 45k Long jump 1.40 1.10
**827** A286 65k Shot put 2.10 1.50
*Nos. 824-827 (4)* 4.50 3.25

Order of the Sisters of St. Joseph in Iceland, Cent. — A287

**1996, Sept. 17 Litho. *Perf. 14½x13***

**828** A287 65k multicolored 2.00 2.00

Reykjavik School, 150th Anniv. A288

**1996, Sept. 17 *Perf. 12½x13***

**829** A288 150k multicolored 4.75 3.75

**Nordia '96 Type of 1995**

Design: Godafoss Waterfalls, Skjalfandafljot River.

**1996, Oct. 9 Litho. *Perf. 13½x14***

**830** A280 Sheet of 3, #a.-c. 11.50 11.50
*a.* 45k multicolored 3.75 3.75
*b.* 65k multicolored 3.75 3.75
*c.* 90k multicolored 3.75 3.75

Reykjavik Cathedral, Bicent. — A289

**1996, Nov. 5 *Perf. 14***

**831** A289 45k multicolored 1.80 1.10

Christmas — A290

Artifacts from Natl. Museum of Iceland: 35k, Figurine of Madonna and Child carved from walrus tusk. 45k, Pax showing Nativity.

**1996, Nov. 5 *Perf. 13½***

**832** A290 35k multicolored 1.25 .75
*a.* Booklet pane of 10 12.50
Booklet, #832a 13.00
**833** A290 45k multicolored 1.50 1.25

**Bird Type of 1996**

10k, Mergus serrator. 500k, Anas crecca.

**1997, Apr. 2 Litho. *Perf. 13½***

**834** A283 10k multicolored .35 .25
**835** A283 500k multicolored 15.00 13.50

Paintings A291

150k, Song of Iceland, by Svavar Guthnason. 200k, The Harbor, by Thorvaldur Skúlason.

**1997, Mar. 6 Litho. *Perf. 14***

**836** A291 150k multicolored 5.25 4.50
**837** A291 200k multicolored 6.50 5.25

### Airplane Type of 1993

#838, De Havilland DH-89A (TF-ISM). #839, Stinson SR 8B Reliant (TF-RVB). #840, Douglas DC-3 (TF-ISH). #841, De Havilland DHC-6 Twin Otter (TF-REG).

**1997, Apr. 15 Litho. *Perf. 14***

**838** A263 35k multicolored 1.45 .90
**839** A263 35k multicolored 1.45 .90
**840** A263 35k multicolored 1.45 .90
**841** A263 35k multicolored 1.45 .90
*a.* Block or strip of 4, #838-841 6.00 6.00
*b.* Booklet pane, 2 each #838-841 12.00
Booklet, #841b 12.00

Issued in sheet of 8.
No. 841b has rouletted selvage at left.

European Games A292

**1997, May 13 Litho. *Perf. 14½***

**842** A292 35k Hurdles 1.10 .90
**843** A292 45k Sailing 1.40 1.10

Europa A293

Stories and legends by Asgrimur Jonsson: 45k, Couple on galloping horse. 65k, Old woman reaching for children.

**1997, May 13 *Perf. 13½***

**844** A293 45k multicolored *2.00 1.50*
Complete booklet of 10 *20.00*
**845** A293 65k multicolored *2.50 1.75*
Complete booklet of 10 *25.00*

Union of Graphic Workers, Cent. — A294

**1997, Sept. 3 Litho. *Perf. 13½***

**846** A294 90k multicolored 2.75 2.75

Reykjavik Theater, Cent. — A295

**1997, Sept. 3 *Perf. 13½x14***

**847** A295 100k multicolored 3.00 2.75

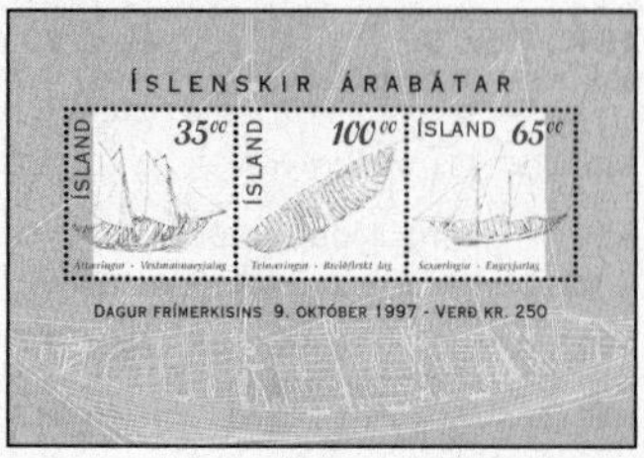


Stamp Day — A296

Icelandic row boats: a, Gideon, eight-oared lugger, 1836. b, Breidafjördur double-ended transport, 1904. c, Engey, six-oared craft, 1912.

**1997, Oct. 9 Litho. *Perf. 15***

**848** A296 Sheet of 3 11.00 11.00
*a.* 35k multicolored 2.40 2.40
*b.* 100k multicolored 4.50 4.50
*c.* 65k multicolored 3.50 3.50

Christmas A297

**1997, Nov. 5 Litho. *Perf. 13½x13***

**849** A297 35k Magi 1.00 .70
*a.* Booklet pane of 10 10.00
Booklet, #849a 10.00
**850** A297 45k Nativity 1.40 .90

Rural Postman A298

**Litho. & Engr.**

**1997, Nov. 5 *Perf. 13½***

**851** A298 50k multicolored 1.50 1.25

1998 Winter Olympic Games, Nagano A299

**1998, Jan. 22 Litho. *Perf. 13½***

**852** A299 35k Downhill skier 1.00 1.00
**853** A299 45k Cross country skier 1.40 1.25

Nordic Stamps A300

**1998, Mar. 5 Litho. *Perf. 13½x13***

**854** A300 35k Sailboats 1.00 1.00
**855** A300 45k Power boats 1.40 1.00

Fish — A301

**1998, Apr. 16**

**856** A301 5k Cyclopterus lumpus .25 .25
**857** A301 10k Gadus morhua .30 .25
**858** A301 60k Raja batis 1.75 1.40
**859** A301 300k Anarhicus lupus 8.75 7.50
*a.* Min. sheet of 4, #856-859 11.00 11.00
*Nos. 856-859 (4)* 11.05 9.40

Intl. Year of the Ocean (#859a).
See Nos. 871-872, 915-916, 928-929.

National Holidays and Festivals A302

Independence Day, June 17th: 45k, Children standing at attention, flag. 65k, Monument, parade.

**1998, May 12 Litho. *Perf. 14½***

**860** A302 45k multicolored *1.60 1.00*
Complete booklet, 10 #860 *16.00*
**861** A302 65k multicolored *2.10 1.50*
Complete booklet, 10 #861 *21.00*

Europa.

Minerals — A303

**1998, Sept. 3 Litho. *Perf. 13½***

**862** A303 35k Stilbite 1.20 .90
**863** A303 45k Scolecite 1.40 1.10

See Nos. 885-886.

Leprosy Hospital, Laugarnes A304

**1998, Sept. 3 *Perf. 13½x14***

**864** A304 70k multicolored 2.00 1.60

First Icelandic Postage Stamp, 125th Anniv. — A305

**1998, Oct. 9 Litho. *Perf. 13½***

**865** A305 35k multicolored 1.20 .80

Agricultural Tools — A306

**1998, Oct. 9 *Perf. 15***

**866** A306 Sheet of 3 7.50 7.50
*a.* 35k Turf scythe 1.75 1.75
*b.* 65k Hay mower 2.50 2.50
*c.* 100k Manure mincer 3.25 3.25

Stamp Day.

Christmas, Children's Drawings — A307

35k, Black cat, homes, mountains. 45k, Angels, Christmas tree, moon and stars.

**1998, Nov. 5 Litho. *Perf. 13x13½***

**867** A307 35k multicolored 1.10 .90
*a.* Booklet pane of 10 11.00
Complete booklet, #867a 11.00
**868** A307 45k multicolored 1.25 1.10

Universal Declaration of Human Rights, 50th Anniv. — A308

**1998, Nov. 5 *Perf. 14½***

**869** A308 50k multicolored 1.50 1.50

Jón Leifs (1899-1968), Composer — A309

**1999, Jan. 22 Litho. *Perf. 14½***

**870** A309 35k multicolored 2.40 1.60

### Fish Type of 1998

35k, Pleuronectez platessa. 55k, Clupea harengus.

**1999, Jan. 22 *Perf. 14½x15***

**871** A301 35k multicolored 1.25 .90
**872** A301 55k multicolored 1.60 1.60

Marine Mammals — A311

Designs: 35k, Orcinus orca. 45k, Physeter macrocephalus. 65k, Balaenoptera musculus. 85k, Phocoena phocoena.

**1999, Mar. 4 Litho. *Perf. 14½***

**873** A311 35k multicolored 1.00 .90
**874** A311 45k multicolored 1.25 1.10
**875** A311 65k multicolored 1.90 1.90
**876** A311 85k multicolored 2.40 2.40
*a.* Sheet of 4, #873-876 6.50 6.50
*Nos. 873-876 (4)* 6.55 6.30

See Nos. 911-914, 945-948. For surcharge see No. 944.

Locomotive A312

***Perf. 13 on 2 or 3 Sides***

**1999, Apr. 15 Booklet Stamps**

**877** A312 25k green & multi 7.00 7.00
**878** A312 50k brown & multi 2.50 2.50
*a.* Booklet pane, 1 #877, 3 #878 14.50
Complete booklet, #878a 14.50
**879** A312 75k Ship 3.50 3.50
*a.* Booklet pane of 4 14.00
Complete booklet, #879a 14.00
*Nos. 877-879 (3)* 13.00 13.00

See Nos. 908-909.

Council of Europe, 50th Anniv. A313

**1999, Apr.15 *Perf. 13x13½***

**880** A313 35k multicolored 1.20 .90

Mushrooms A314

35k, Suillus grevillei. 75k, Agaricus campestris.

**1999, May 20 Litho. *Perf. 14½***

**881** A314 35k multicolored 1.10 1.10
**882** A314 75k multicolored 2.25 2.25

See Nos. 898-899, 957-958, 1021-1022, 1087-1088.

National Parks — A315

**1999, May 20** *Perf. 13¼*

**883** A315 50k Skutustadagigar *2.00 1.50*
*a.* Booklet pane of 10 *20.00*
Complete booklet, #883a *21.00*
**884** A315 75k Vid Arnarstapa *2.50 2.00*
*a.* Booklet pane of 10 *25.00*
Complete booklet, #884a *26.00*

Europa.

### Minerals Type of 1998

**1999, Sept. 9 Litho.** *Perf. 14¾*

**885** A303 40k Calcite 1.25 1.25
**886** A303 50k Heulandite 1.75 1.75

Nature Conservation A316

**1999, Sept. 9 Litho.** *Perf. 14¼*

**887** A316 35k "Hreinar" 1.40 1.40
**888** A316 35k "Markviss" 1.40 1.40
**889** A316 35k "Hreint" 1.40 1.40
**890** A316 35k "Endurheimt" 1.40 1.40
**891** A316 35k "Eflum" 1.40 1.40
*a.* Strip of 5, #887-891 7.00 7.00

Reykjavik, European Cultural City for 2000 A317

35k, Facescape, by Erro. 50k, Book, violin, palette, masks, camera, computer.

**1999, Oct. 7 Litho.** *Perf. 13¼*

**892** A317 35k multi 1.35 1.50
**893** A317 50k multi 1.75 2.00

Souvenir Sheet

View of Skagafhordur, by Carl Emil Baagoe — A318

**1999, Oct. 7** *Perf. 13¼x13*

**894** A318 200k olive & black 8.50 8.50

Stamp Day. #894 sold for 250k.

Children's Art — A319

**1999, Nov. 4 Litho.** *Perf. 13*

**895** A319 35k multi 1.00 1.00

Christmas — A320

No. 896, Elf: a, With walking stick. b, Jumping over rock. c, Waving. d, Licking spoon. e, With hand in cauldron. f, With cup. g, At door. h, With ladle and barrel. i, With sausages. j, At window.

No. 897, Elf: a, Looking up. b, With ham. c, With candles.

**1999, Nov. 4**

**896** Strip of 10 15.00 15.00
*a.-j.* A320 35k any single 1.50 1.50
*k.* Booklet pane, #896a-896j 15.00
Complete booklet, #896k 15.00
**897** Strip of 3 5.25 5.25
*a.-c.* A320 50k any single 1.75 1.75

See Nos. 924-926.

Nos. 896a-896k and 897a-897c were also released in a sheet of 15 undenominated labels made available as a gift to buyers of the stamps..

### Mushroom Type of 1999

Designs: 40k, Cantharellus cibarius. 50k, Coprinus comatus.

**2000, Feb. 4 Litho.** *Perf. 13*

**898** A314 40k multi 1.25 1.25
*a.* Booklet pane of 10 12.50
Complete booklet, #898a 12.50
**899** A314 50k multi 1.75 1.75

A321

Christianity in Iceland, 1000th Anniv. — A322

**2000, Feb. 4** *Perf. 13¼x13¾*

**900** A321 40k multi 1.25 1.25

### Souvenir Sheet

*Perf. 13¼x13*

**901** A322 40k multi 1.25 1.25

See Vatican City #1151.

Discovery of Vinland, 1000th Anniv. A323

Designs: 40k, Viking with shield, globe. 50k, Viking ship sailing. 75k, Viking ship at shore. 90k, Viking without shield, globe.

**Litho. & Engr.**

**2000, Mar. 16** *Perf. 12½x13*

**902** A323 40k multi 1.40 1.40
**903** A323 50k multi 1.60 1.60
**904** A323 75k multi 2.25 2.25
**905** A323 90k multi 2.75 2.75
*a.* Souvenir sheet, #902-905 8.00 8.00
*Nos. 902-905 (4)* 8.00 8.00

Millennium A324

Designs: 40k, Head, quill pen. 50k, Man, genealogical chart, circuit board.

**2000, Apr. 27 Litho.** *Perf. 13x13¼*

**906** A324 40k multi 1.25 1.25
**907** A324 50k multi 1.50 1.50

### Locomotive Type of 1999

*Perf. 13 on 2 or 3 sides*

**2000, Apr. 27 Litho.**

**Booklet Stamps**

**908** A312 50k Steam roller 1.50 1.50
*a.* Booklet pane of 4 6.00
Booklet, #908a 6.00
**909** A312 75k Fire pumper 2.25 2.25
*a.* Booklet pane of 4 9.00
Booklet, #909a 9.00

### Europa, 2000

Common Design Type

**2000, May 18 Litho.** *Perf. 13¼x13*

**910** CD17 50k multi *2.00 2.00*
*a.* Booklet pane of 10 *20.00*
Booklet, #910a *21.00*

### Marine Mammals Type of 1999

Designs: 5k, Hyperoodon ampullatus. 40k, Lagenorhynchus acutus. 50k, Megaptera novaeangliae. 75k, Balaenoptera acutorostrata.

**2000, May 18** *Perf. 14½*

**911** A311 5k multi .25 .25
**912** A311 40k multi 1.10 1.10
**913** A311 50k multi 1.40 1.40
**914** A311 75k multi 2.00 2.00
*Nos. 911-914 (4)* 4.75 4.75

### Fish Type of 1998

Designs: 10k, Melanogrammus aeglefinus. 250k, Mallotus villosus.

**2000, Sept. 14 Litho.** *Perf. 13*

**915-916** A301 Set of 2 9.00 9.00

Flowers — A325

Designs: 40k, Viola x wittrockiana. 50k, Petunia x hybrida.

**2000, Sept. 14** *Perf. 13*

**917-918** A325 Set of 2 3.25 2.50

See Nos. 931-932, 968-969, 982-983, 1005-1006.

Butterflies A326

Designs: 40k, Chloroclysta citrata. 50k, Cerapteryx graminis.

**2000, Oct. 9** *Perf. 14x14½*

**919-920** A326 Set of 2 3.50 2.50

Souvenir Sheet

Stamp Day — A327

**Litho. & Engr.**

**2000, Oct. 9** *Perf. 13¼*

**921** A327 200k multi 9.00 9.00

No. 921 sold for 250k.

Ancient Architecture — A328

Various buildings. Denominations: 45k, 75k.

**2000, Nov. 9 Litho.** *Perf. 14*

**922-923** A328 Set of 2 4.75 3.50

### Christmas Type of 1999

Designs: 40k, Elf grasping walking stick. 50k, Female elf carrying bag.

**2000, Nov. 9** *Perf. 13*

**924** A320 40k multi 1.25 1.00
*a.* Perf. 12¾x13¼ 1.50 1.00
*b.* Booklet pane, 4 #924a 6.00
*c.* Booklet pane, 6 #924a 9.00
Booklet, #924b, 924c 15.00
**925** A320 50k multi 1.50 1.25

### Souvenir Sheet

**926** Sheet of 2 2.75 2.25
*a.* A320 40k As #924, 25x38mm 1.25 .95
*b.* A320 50k As #925, 25x38mm 1.50 1.25

Coast Guard, 75th Anniv. A329

**2001, Jan. 18 Litho.** *Perf. 13*

**927** A329 (40k) multi 1.50 1.50
*a.* Booklet pane of 10 15.00
Booklet, #927a 15.00

### Fish Type of 1998

Designs: 55k, Reinhardtius hippoglossoides. 80k, Pollachius virens.

**2001, Jan. 18**

**928-929** A301 Set of 2 4.00 4.00

UN High Commissioner for Refugees, 50th Anniv. — A330

**2001, Mar. 8** *Perf. 13¼x13*

**930** A330 50k multi 1.50 1.25

### Flower Type of 2000

Designs: 55k, Calendula officinalis. 65k, Dorotheanthus bellidiformis.

**2001, Mar. 8** *Perf. 13*

**931-932** A325 Set of 2 3.75 3.25

Icelandic Sheepdog A331

Dog's coat: 40k, Brown. 80k, Black.

**2001, Apr. 18** *Perf. 14¼*

**933-934** A331 Set of 2 4.00 3.25

Airplanes A332

Designs: 55k: TF-OGN (biplane). 80k, Klemm TF-SUX (monoplane).

*Perf. 13½x12¾ on 2 or 3 Sides*

**2001, Apr. 18 Booklet Stamps**

**935** A332 55k multi 1.60 1.40
*a.* Booklet pane of 4 6.50
Booklet, #935a 6.50
**936** A332 80k multi 2.50 2.25
*a.* Booklet pane of 4 10.00
Booklet, #936a 10.00

Europa A333

Designs: 55k, Head, waterfall. 80k, Hand, wave.

**2001, May 17** ***Perf. 13***

**937** A333 55k multi *1.60 1.50*
*a.* Booklet pane of 10 *16.00*
Booklet, #937a *17.00*
**938** A333 80k multi *2.40 2.00*
*a.* Booklet pane of 10 *24.00*
Booklet, #938a *26.00*

Horses A334

Designs: 40k, Fet. 50k, Tölt. 55k, Brokk. 60k, Skeidh. 80k, Stökk.

**2001, May 17** ***Perf. 13x13¼***

**939-943** A334 Set of 5 8.75 8.75

**No. 873 Surcharged in Red**

**2001, July 10 Litho.** ***Perf. 14½***

**944** A311 (53k) on 35k multi 1.75 1.75

**Marine Mammals Type of 1999**

Designs: 5k, Lagenorhynchus albirostris. 40k, Balaenoptera physalus. 80k, Balaenoptera borealis. 100k, Globicephala melas.

**2001, Sept. 6 Litho.** ***Perf. 14½***

**945** A311 5k multi .30 .30
**946** A311 40k multi 1.25 1.25
**947** A311 80k multi 2.50 2.50
**948** A311 100k multi 3.25 3.25
*Nos. 945-948 (4)* 7.30 7.30

Islands A335

Designs: 40k, Grimsey. 55k, Papey.

**2001, Oct. 9 Litho.** ***Perf. 13¼x13***

**949-950** A335 Set of 2 3.00 2.50

See Nos. 975-976, 1001-1002, 1033-1034, 1158-1159.

Souvenir Sheet

Esja Mountain — A336

**2001, Oct. 9** ***Perf. 13¼***

**951** A336 250k multi 9.00 9.00

Stamp Day.

Birds — A337

Designs: 42k, Oenanthe oenanthe. 250k, Charadrius hiaticula.

**2001, Nov. 8** ***Perf. 13¼x13***

**952-953** A337 Set of 2 10.00 10.00

Christmas A338

Churches: (42k), Brautarholt. 55k, Vidhmyri.

**2001, Nov. 8**

**954** A338 (42k) multi 1.25 1.25
*a.* Booklet pane of 6 7.50 —
Booklet, #954a, 4 #954 12.50
**955** A338 55k multi 1.60 1.40

First Motorboat in Iceland, Cent. A339

**2002, Jan. 17 Litho.** ***Perf. 13x13½***

**956** A339 60k multi 1.90 1.90

**Mushroom Type of 1999**

Designs: (40k), Leccinum scabrum. 85k, Hydnum repandum.

**2002, Jan. 17** ***Perf. 13¼x12¾***

**957-958** A314 Set of 2 3.75 3.75
Booklet, 10 #957 12.50

No. 957 is inscribed "Bref 20g."

Intl. Year of Mountains A340

**2002, Mar. 7 Litho.** ***Perf. 13***

**959** A340 (42k) multi 1.50 1.50

Halldór Laxness (1902-98), 1955 Nobel Literature Laureate A341

**2002, Mar. 7 Litho.** ***Perf. 13x13¼***

**960** A341 100k multi 3.50 3.50
*a.* Souvenir sheet of 1 3.75 3.75

Examples of No. 960a with Nobel Prize medal in margin printed in gold foil and embossed sold for 1700k. Value, $125.

Lighthouses — A342

*Perf. 12¾x13¼ on 2 or 3 Sides*

**2002, Apr. 18 Booklet Stamps**

**961** A342 60k Grótta 1.75 1.60
*a.* Booklet pane of 4 7.00 —
Complete booklet, #961a 7.00
**962** A342 85k Kögur 2.50 2.25
*a.* Booklet pane of 4 10.00 —
Complete booklet, #962a 10.00

Fyssa, by Rúrí — A343

Spenna, by Hafsteinn Austmann A344

**2002, Apr. 18 Litho.** ***Perf. 14½x14¾***

**963** A343 (42k) multi 1.25 1.10
**964** A344 60k multi 1.75 1.50

Nordic Council, 50th anniv. (No. 963).

Sesselja Sigmundsdóttir (1902-74), Advocate for Mentally Handicapped A345

**2002, May 9**

**965** A345 45k multi 1.40 1.10

Europa A346

Designs: 60k, Acrobats, juggling clown. 85k, Head on stick, lion jumping through ring of fire.

**2002, May 9** ***Perf. 13***

**966** A346 60k multi *1.75 1.25*
*a.* Booklet pane of 10 *17.50*
Booklet, #966a *19.00*
**967** A346 85k multi *2.50 1.50*
*a.* Booklet pane of 10 *25.00*
Booklet, #967a *26.00*

**Flowers Type of 2000**

Designs: 10k, Lobelia erinus. 200k, Centaurea cyanus.

**2002, Sept. 5 Litho.** ***Perf. 14¾x14½***

**968-969** A325 Set of 2 7.50 7.50

Fish of Lake Thingvallavatn — A347

Designs: (45k), Salvelinus alpinus (Murta). (55k), Salmo trutta, vert. 60k, Salvelinus alpinus (Sílableikja). 90k, Salvelinus alpinus (Kuthungableikja). 200k, Salvelinus alpinus (Dvergbleikja).

***Perf. 13¼x12¾, 12¾x13¼ (#971)***

**2002, Sept. 5**

**970** A347 (45k) multi 1.50 1.50
*a.* Perf. 13¼x12½x13¼x13 1.50 1.50
**971** A347 (55k) multi 2.50 2.50
*a.* Perf 13¼x12½:13x13¼x13:12½ 2.50 2.50
**972** A347 60k multi 2.00 2.00
*a.* Perf. 13¼x13 2.00 2.00
**973** A347 90k multi 2.75 2.75
*a.* Perf. 13¼x13 2.75 2.75
**974** A347 200k multi 6.00 6.00
*a.* Perf. 13¼x13 6.00 6.00
*b.* Booklet pane, #970a-974a 27.50
Complete booklet, #974b 27.50
*Nos. 970-974 (5)* 14.75 14.75

Nos. 970-974 were issued both in sheet format, perf 13¼x12¾ or 12¾x13¼ (#971), and in booklet pane format (#970a-974a), with small differences in the gauge of the stamps' perforations.

**Islands Type of 2001**

Designs: 45k, Vigur. 55k, Flatey.

**2002, Oct. 9** ***Perf. 14***

**975-976** A335 Set of 2 3.00 2.75

Souvenir Sheet

Sudurgata, Reykjavik — A348

**2002, Oct. 9** ***Perf. 14½x14¾***

**977** A348 250k multi 9.00 9.00

Stamp Day.

Birds A349

Christmas A350

Designs: 50k, Tringa totanus. 85k, Phalaropus fulicarius.

**2002, Nov. 7** ***Perf. 13¼x13***

**978-979** A349 Set of 2 4.50 4.50

See Nos. 997-998, 1029-1030, 1059-1060.

**2002, Nov. 7** ***Perf. 13***

Designs: 45k, Gifts and ornaments. 60k, Gifts.

**980** A350 45k multi 1.40 1.40
*a.* Booklet pane of 10 14.00
Booklet, #980a 14.00
**981** A350 60k multi 1.90 1.75

**Flower Type of 2000**

Designs: 45k, Phlox drummondii. 60k, Gazania x hybrida.

**2003, Jan. 16** ***Perf. 13***

**982** A325 45k multi 1.40 1.40
*a.* Booklet pane of 10 14.00
Booklet, #982a 14.00
**983** A325 60k multi 1.90 1.75

Icelandic Police Force, Bicent. — A351

Designs: 45k, Police officers, 2003. 55k, Policeman, 1803.

**2003, Jan. 16**

**984-985** A351 Set of 2 3.25 3.25

Icelandic Cattle A352

Designs: 45k, Bull. 85k, Cow.

**2003, Mar. 13 Litho.** ***Perf. 13x13¼***

**986-987** A352 Set of 2 4.25 4.25

Souvenir Sheet

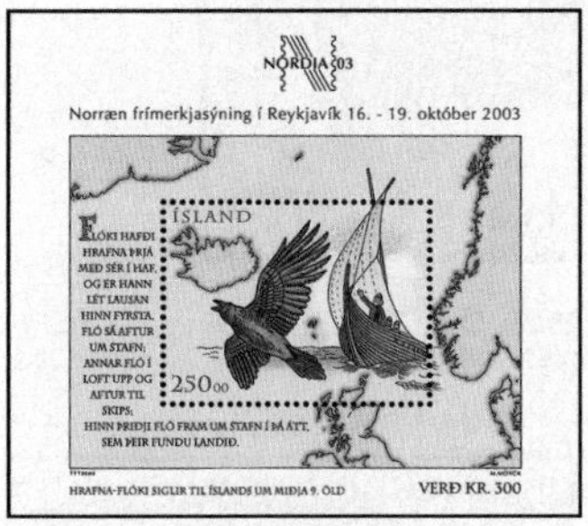


Nordia 2003 Philatelic Exhibition, Reykjavik — A353

**Litho. & Engr.**

**2003, Mar. 13** *Perf. 14*
**988** A353 250k multi 9.00 9.00

No. 988 sold for 300k.

Free Church, Reykjavik, Cent. — A354

**2003, Apr. 23** **Litho.** *Perf. 13*
**989** A354 200k multi 7.00 7.00

Ferries A355

No. 990: a, Saefari. b, Saevar.
No. 991: a, Herjólfur. b, Baldur.

***Perf. 13 on 2 or 3 Sides***

**2003, Apr. 23** **Booklet Stamps**

**990** Pair 2.75 2.75
*a.-b.* A355 45k Either single 1.35 1.35
*c.* Booklet pane, 2 #990 5.50 —
Complete booklet, #990c 5.50
**991** Pair 3.75 3.75
*a.-b.* A355 60k Either single 1.75 1.75
*c.* Booklet pane, 2 #991 7.50 —
Complete booklet, #991c 7.50

Icelandic Chickens — A356

**2003, May 22** *Perf. 13¼*
**992** A356 45k multi 1.50 1.50

Europa — A357

Poster art.

**2003, May 22** *Perf. 13½*
**993** A357 60k red & multi 1.75 *1.25*
*a.* Booklet pane of 10, perf. 13½ on 3 sides 17.50 —
Complete booklet, #993a 19.00
**994** A357 85k red & multi 2.50 *1.75*
*a.* Booklet pane of 10, perf. 13½ on 3 sides 25.00 —
Complete booklet, #994a 26.00

Friendship A358

**2003, Sept. 4** *Perf. 14¼x14½*
**995** A358 45k multi 1.40 1.40

First Census, 300th Anniv. — A359

**2003, Sept. 4** *Perf. 13*
**996** A359 60k multi 2.10 2.10

**Bird Type of 2002**

Designs: 70k, Anthus pratensis. 250k, Numenius phaeopus.

**2003, Sept. 4** *Perf. 13¼x13*
**997-998** A349 Set of 2 10.00 10.00

Rangifer Tarandus A360

**2003, Oct. 9** **Litho.** *Perf. 13*
**999** A360 45k multi 1.50 1.50

Souvenir Sheet

Quonset Hut — A361

**2003, Oct. 9**
**1000** A361 250k multi 8.25 8.25

Stamp Day.

**Islands Type of 2001**

Designs: 85k, Heimaey. 200k, Hrísey.

**2003, Nov. 6** *Perf. 13¼x13*
**1001-1002** A335 Set of 2 9.50 9.50

Christmas — A362

Designs: 45k, Girl placing ornament on Christmas tree. 60k, Boy lighting candle.

**2003, Nov. 6** *Perf. 14¼*
**1003-1004** A362 Set of 2 3.25 3.25
*a.* Booklet pane of 10, #1003 14.00
Booklet, #1003a 14.00

**Flowers Type of 2000**

Designs: 50k, Tagetes patula. 55k, Begonia x tuberhybrida.

**2004, Jan. 15** **Litho.** *Perf. 13*
**1005-1006** A325 Set of 2 3.50 3.50

Hannes Hafstein (1861-1922), Politician, Poet — A363

**2004, Jan. 15** *Perf. 13¼x13½*
**1007** A363 150k multi 5.00 5.00
*a.* Souvenir sheet of 1 5.00 5.00

Icelandic home rule, cent.

Trawler "Coot," Cent. A364

**2004, Mar. 11** **Litho.** *Perf. 13¼*
**1008** A364 50k multi 1.50 1.50

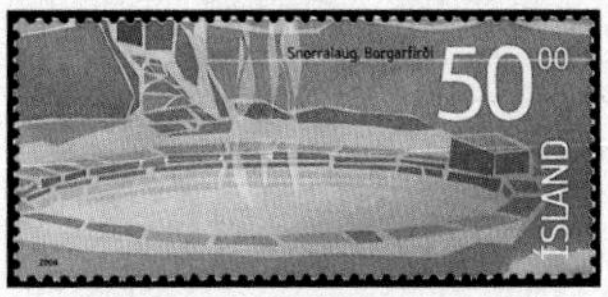


Geothermal Energy — A365

Designs: 50k, Snorralaug hot water pool. 55k, Valve on geodesic dome, steam cloud, vert. (29x47mm). 60k, Steam pipes. 90k, Turbine. 250k, Map of Iceland showing geothermal zones, vert. (29x47mm).

***Perf. 13x13¼, 13¼ (55k, 250k)***

**2004, Mar. 11**
**1009** A365 50k multi 1.50 1.50
*a.* Perf. 13¼ *4.00* *4.00*
**1010** A365 55k multi 1.75 1.75
**1011** A365 60k multi 2.00 2.00
*a.* Perf. 13¼ *5.00* *5.00*
**1012** A365 90k multi 2.75 2.75
*a.* Perf. 13¼ *7.00* *7.00*
**1013** A365 250k multi 7.50 7.50
*a.* Booklet pane, #1009a, 1010, 1011a, 1012a, 1013 25.00 —
Complete booklet, #1013a 25.00
*Nos. 1009-1013 (5)* 15.50 15.50

Complete booklet sold for 750k.

Nos. 1009a, 1011a and 1012a only come from the booklet pane No. 1013a.

Souvenir Sheet

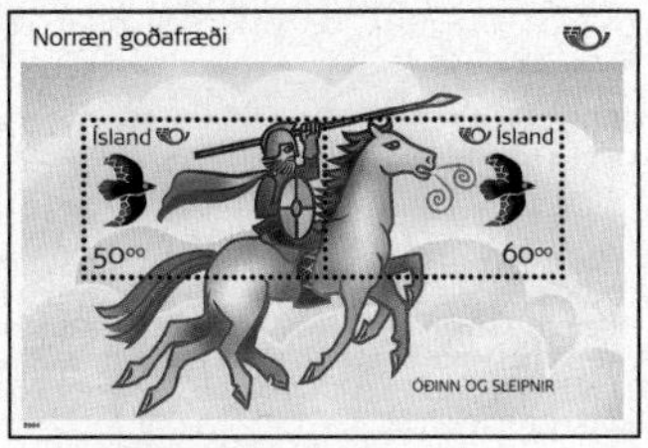


Norse Mythology — A366

No. 1014: a, God Odin and bird. b, Odin's horse, Sleipnir, and bird.

**2004, Mar. 26** *Perf. 13*
**1014** A366 Sheet of 2 4.25 4.25
*a.* 50k multi 2.00 2.00
*b.* 60k multi 2.25 2.25

Automobiles A367

No. 1015: a, 1956 Ford Fairlane Victoria. b, 1954 Pobeta.

No. 1016: a, 1955 Chevrolet Bel Air. b, 1952 Volkswagen.

***Perf. 13 on 2 or 3 Sides***

**2004, Apr. 15** **Booklet Stamps**

**1015** Pair 6.50 6.50
*a.-b.* A367 60k Either single 3.25 3.25
*c.* Booklet pane, 2 #1015 13.00 —
Complete booklet, #1015c 13.00
**1016** Pair 9.50 9.50
*a.-b.* A367 85k Either single 4.75 4.75
*c.* Booklet pane, 2 #1016 19.00 —
Complete booklet, #1016c 19.00

Herring Industry, Cent. — A368

**2004, May 19** *Perf. 13¼*
**1017** A368 65k multi 2.00 2.00

Hringurin Women's Society, Cent. A369

**2004, May 19** *Perf. 13x13¼*
**1018** A369 100k violet blue 3.25 3.25

Europa A370

**2004, May 19** *Perf. 13*
**1019** A370 65k Cyclists *2.00* *2.00*
*a.* Booklet pane of 10 *20.00* —
Complete booklet, #1019a *20.00*
**1020** A370 90k Cars in snow *2.75* *2.75*
*a.* Booklet pane of 10 *27.50* —
Complete booklet, #1020a *27.50*

**Mushrooms Type of 1999**

Designs: 50k, Amanita vaginata. 60k, Camarophyllus pratensis.

**2004, Sept. 2** **Litho.** *Perf. 13*
**1021-1022** A314 Set of 2 3.50 3.50

Reykdal Power Station, Cent. — A371

**2004, Sept. 2** *Perf. 13¼*
**1023** A371 50k multi 1.50 1.50

First Automobile in Iceland, Cent. A372

**2004, Sept. 2**
**1024** A372 100k multi 3.25 3.25

French Hospital, Fáskrúthsfirthi, Cent. — A373

**Litho. & Engr.**

**2004, Oct. 8** ***Perf. 13¾***

**1025** A373 60k multi 1.90 1.90

Souvenir Sheet

Brúarhlöth — A374

**2004, Oct. 8** **Litho.** ***Perf. 13***

**1026** A374 250k multi 8.00 8.00

Stamp Day.

Insects A375

Designs: 50k, Nebria gyllenhali. 70k, Bombus lucorum.

**2004, Oct. 8**

**1027-1028** A375 Set of 2 3.75 3.75

See Nos. 1043-1044, 1089-1090, 1121-1122, 1161-1161.

**Bird Type of 2002**

Designs: 55k, Calidris maritima. 75k, Calidris alpina.

**2004, Nov. 4** **Litho.** ***Perf. 13¼x13***

**1029-1030** A349 Set of 2 4.00 4.00

Christmas — A376

Designs: 45k, Ptarmigan in snow. 65k, Reindeer in snow.

**2004, Nov. 4**

**1031-1032** A376 Set of 2 3.50 3.50

*1031a* Booklet pane of 10 #1031 14.00 —

Complete booklet, #1031a 14.00

**Islands Type of 2001**

Designs: 5k, Vithey. 90k, Flatey.

**2005, Jan. 13** **Litho.** ***Perf. 14***

**1033-1034** A335 Set of 2 3.25 3.25

Organized Forestation, Cent. A377

**2005, Jan. 13**

**1035** A377 45k multi 1.50 1.50

See No. 1155.

Souvenir Sheet

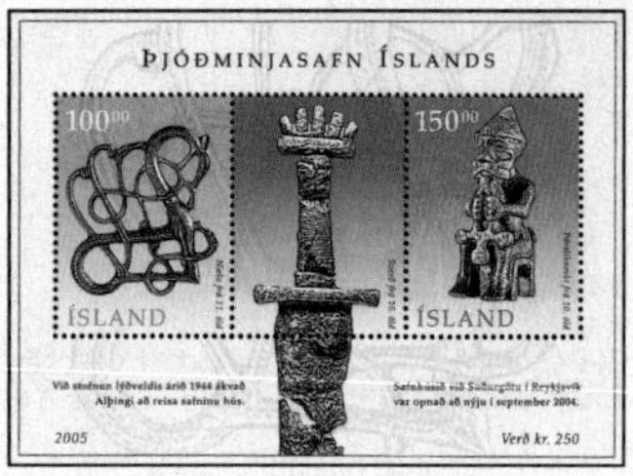

National Museum Artifacts — A378

No. 1036: a, Brooch, 11th cent. b, Statue of Thor, 10th cent.

**Litho. & Embossed**

**2005, Jan. 13** ***Perf. 13½x13***

**1036** A378 Sheet of 2 + central label 8.50 8.50

*a.* 100k multi 3.50 3.50

*b.* 150k multi 5.00 5.00

Mice A379

Designs: 45k, Apodemus sylvaticus. 125k, Mus musculus.

***Perf. 13½x12¾***

**2005, Mar. 10** **Litho.**

**1037-1038** A379 Set of 2 5.75 5.75

Flowers — A380

Designs: No. 1039, 50k, Roses. No. 1040, 50k, African daisies. No. 1041, 50k, Red calla lilies. 70k, Tulip.

**2005, Mar. 10** ***Perf. 13¼***

**1039-1042** A380 Set of 4 7.50 7.50

*1042a* Booklet pane, 2 each #1039-1042 15.00 —

Nos. 1039-1042 each printed in sheets of 10, with each stamp in the sheet having a different background swirl pattern. Stamps of the same kind in the booklet pane have the same swirl pattern, which is the same as one found on the sheet.

**Insects Type of 2004**

Designs: 50k, Araneus diadematus (spider). 70k, Musca domestica.

**2005, Apr. 14** ***Perf. 13¼x13***

**1043-1044** A375 Set of 2 4.00 4.00

Fishing Boats A381

No. 1045: a, Vörthur ThH4. b, Karl VE47. No. 1046: a, Saedís IS67. b, Guthbjörg NK74.

***Perf. 13 on 2 or 3 Sides***

**2005, Apr. 14**

**Booklet Stamps**

**1045** Pair 4.50 4.50

*a.-b.* A381 70k Either single 2.25 2.25

*c.* Booklet pane, 2 #1045 9.00 —

Complete booklet, #1045c 9.00

**1046** Pair 6.00 6.00

*a.-b.* A381 95k Either single 3.00 3.00

*c.* Booklet pane, 2 #1045 12.00 —

Complete booklet, #1045c 12.00

Bridges, Cent. A382

Designs: 50k, Sogith Bridge. 95k, Lagarfljót Bridge. 165k, Jökulsá Bridge.

**2005, May 26** **Litho.** ***Perf. 13¼x13½***

**1047-1049** A382 Set of 3 10.00 10.00

Europa A383

Fork, knife and: 70k, Fish dish, gutted fish, waterfall. 90k, Meat dish, hanging meat, flowers.

**2005, May 26** ***Perf. 13½***

**1050** A383 70k multi *2.10 2.10*

*a.* Booklet pane of 10 *21.00*

Complete booklet, #1050a *21.00*

**1051** A383 90k multi *2.75 2.75*

*a.* Booklet pane of 10 *27.50*

Complete booklet, #1050a *27.50*

Salmon Fishermen and Fishing Flies — A384

Designs; 50k, Fisherman on Laxáí Kjós River, Raud Frances fly. 60k, Fishermen in boat on Laxá i Athaldal River, Laxá Bla fly, vert.

***Perf. 13¾x13½, 13½x13¾***

**2005, Sept. 1** **Litho.**

**1052-1053** A384 Set of 2 3.75 3.75

Berries — A385

Designs: 65k, Vaccinium uliginosum. 90k, Fragaria vesca.

**2005, Sept. 1** ***Perf. 14***

**1054** A385 65k multi 2.10 2.10

*a.* Tete-beche pair 4.25 4.25

**1055** A385 90k multi 3.00 3.00

*a.* Tete-beche pair 6.00 6.00

See Nos. 1082-1083, 1116-1117.

Motorcycles — A386

**2005, Oct. 7** ***Perf. 13¼x13½***

**1056** A386 50k multi 1.75 1.75

First motorcycle in Iceland, cent.

Commercial College of Iceland, Cent. A387

**2005, Oct. 7** ***Perf. 13½x14¼***

**1057** A387 70k multi 2.25 2.25

Souvenir Sheet

Aerial View of Reykjavik Rooftops — A388

**2005, Oct. 7** ***Perf. 13¼***

**1058** A388 200k multi 6.50 6.50

Stamp Day.

**Birds Type of 2002**

Designs: 60k, Anser anser. 105k, Sturnus vulgaris.

**2005, Nov. 3** ***Perf. 14***

**1059-1060** A349 Set of 2 5.50 5.50

Christmas — A389

**2005, Nov. 3** ***Perf. 13½***

**1061** A389 50k Apple 1.75 1.75

*a.* White border at top or bottom, perf. 13½ on 2 or 3 sides 1.75 1.75

*b.* Booklet pane of 10 #1061a 17.50 —

Complete booklet, #1061b 17.50

**1062** A389 70k Christmas tree 2.40 2.40

No. 1061 is impregnated with an apple and cinnamon scent; No. 1062 with a pine scent.

National Flower Dryas Octopetala — A390

**2006, Feb. 2** **Litho.** ***Perf. 13¾***

**1063** A390 50k multi 1.60 1.60

Rock and Roll Music, 50th Anniv. — A391

**2006, Feb. 2**

**1064** A391 60k multi 1.90 1.90

Arrival in Iceland of Refugees of Hungarian Uprising, 50th Anniv. A392

**2006, Feb. 2** ***Perf. 13½x13¾***

**1065** A392 70k multi 2.25 2.25

Souvenir Sheet

Europa Stamps, 50th Anniv. — A393

No. 1066: a, #407. b, #395.

**2006, Feb. 2** ***Perf. 14¼x14***
**1066** A393 150k Sheet of 2, #a-b *9.50 9.50*

Motion Pictures in Iceland, Cent. — A394

Designs: 50k, Early theater, projector and program. 95k, Projector reel, actor and actress. 160k, Actor in mask, clapboard, bag of popcorn, cameraman on location.

***Perf. 13¾x13½***

**2006, Mar. 29** **Litho.**
**1067-1069** A394 Set of 3 8.50 8.50

Souvenir Sheet

Mythical Beings of Nordic Folklore — A395

**2006, Mar. 29** ***Perf. 13¼x13***
**1070** A395 95k multi 3.25 3.25

General Purpose Vehicles A396

No. 1071: a, 1951 Land Rover. b, 1946 Willys.
No. 1072: a, 1965 Austin Gypsy. b, 1955 GAZ-69.

***Perf. 13 on 2 or 3 Sides***

**2006, Mar. 29** **Booklet Stamps**

| | | |
|---|---|---|
| **1071** | Pair | 4.00 4.00 |
| *a.-b.* | A396 70k Either single | 2.00 2.00 |
| *c.* | Booklet pane, 2 #1071 | 8.00 — |
| | Complete booklet, #1071c | 8.00 |
| **1072** | Pair | 5.00 5.00 |
| *a.-b.* | A396 90k Either single | 2.50 2.50 |
| *c.* | Booklet pane, 2 #1072 | 10.00 — |
| | Complete booklet, #1072c | 10.00 |

A397

Europa A398

**2006, May 18** ***Perf. 13¼x13¾***
**1073** A397 75k blk & red 2.40 2.40

***Perf. 13¾x13¼***

**1074** A398 95k blue & blk 3.25 3.25

**Booklet Stamps**
**Self-Adhesive**

***Serpentine Die Cut 11¾x12¼***

| | | |
|---|---|---|
| **1075** | A397 75k blk & red | 2.40 2.40 |
| *a.* | Booklet pane of 10 | 24.00 |

***Serpentine Die Cut 12¼x11¾***

| | | |
|---|---|---|
| **1076** | A398 95k blue & blk | 3.25 3.25 |
| *a.* | Booklet pane of 10 | 32.50 |

Waterfalls — A399

Designs: 55k, Faxi. 65k, Oxaráfoss, vert. (29x47mm). 75k, Glymur, vert. (29x47mm). 95k, Hjálparfoss. 220k, Skeifárfoss.

**2006, May 18** ***Perf. 13¼***

| | | |
|---|---|---|
| **1077-1081** | A399 Set of 5 | 14.50 14.50 |
| *1081a* | Booklet pane, #1077-1081, perf. 13½ | 21.00 — |
| | Complete booklet, #1081a | 21.00 |

Booklet containing No. 1081a sold for 750k.

**Berries Type of 2005**

Designs: 75k, Empetrum nigrum. 130k, Rubus saxatilis.

**2006, Sept. 21** ***Perf. 13¼x13¾***

| | | |
|---|---|---|
| **1082** | A385 75k multi | 2.25 2.25 |
| *a.* | Tete-beche pair | 5.00 5.00 |
| **1083** | A385 130k multi | 3.75 3.75 |
| *a.* | Tete-beche pair | 8.00 8.00 |

Iceland's First Olympic Medal, 50th Anniv. — A400

**Litho. & Embossed**

**2006, Sept. 21** ***Perf. 13¼***
**1084** A400 55k multi 1.75 1.75

First Telephone Service in Iceland, Cent. — A401

**2006, Sept. 21** **Litho.** ***Perf. 14***
**1085** A401 65k multi 2.25 2.25

Souvenir Sheet

Icelandic Wrestling Tournament, Cent. — A402

**Litho. & Embossed**

**2006, Sept. 21** ***Perf. 13¼x14***
**1086** A402 200k multi 7.00 7.00

Stamp Day.

**Mushrooms Type of 1999**

Designs: 70k, Xerocomus subtomentosus. 95k, Kuehneromyces mutabilis.

**2006, Nov. 2** **Litho.** ***Perf. 13¾x13¼***
**1087-1088** A314 Set of 2 5.00 5.00

**Insects Type of 2004**

Designs: 65k, Dolichovespula norwegica. 110k, Coccinella undecimpunctata.

**2006, Nov. 2** **Litho.** ***Perf. 13¾x14¼***
**1089-1090** A375 Set of 2 5.25 5.25

Christmas — A403

Designs: Nos. 1091, 1093, Angel, denomination at LL. 75k, Heart. No. 1094, Angel, denomination at LR.

**2006, Nov. 2** ***Perf. 13½x13¾***

| | | |
|---|---|---|
| **1091** | A403 55k multi | 1.60 1.60 |
| **1092** | A403 75k multi | 2.25 2.25 |

**Self-Adhesive**
**Booklet Stamps**

***Serpentine Die Cut 9½x9¾***

| | | |
|---|---|---|
| **1093** | A403 55k multi | 1.75 1.75 |
| **1094** | A403 55k multi | 1.75 1.75 |
| *a.* | Booklet pane, 5 each #1093-1094 | 20.00 — |
| | *Nos. 1091-1094 (4)* | 7.35 7.35 |

Women's Rights in Iceland, Cent. — A404

***Perf. 13½x13¼***

**2007, Feb. 15** **Litho.**
**1095** A404 60k multi .95 .95

Fishing Trawler Jón Forseti, Cent. A405

**2007, Feb. 15** ***Perf. 13¾x13½***
**1096** A405 65k multi 1.00 1.00

Geothermal Energy A406

**2007, Feb. 15** ***Perf. 14***
**1097** A406 75k multi 1.20 1.20

West Nordic Council, 10th anniv.

Souvenir Sheet

Intl. Polar Year — A407

**2007, Feb. 15** ***Perf. 14x13½***

| | | |
|---|---|---|
| **1098** | A407 Sheet of 2 | 2.75 2.75 |
| *a.* | 75k Volcano | 1.20 1.20 |
| *b.* | 95k Ice cap mapping equipment | 1.50 1.50 |

Youth Organization of Iceland, Cent. — A408

**2007, Apr. 20** ***Perf. 14***
**1099** A408 70k multi 1.10 1.10

National Archives, 125th Anniv. — A409

**2007, Apr. 20** ***Perf. 12½***

| | | |
|---|---|---|
| **1100** | A409 80k multi | 1.25 1.25 |
| *a.* | Tete-beche pair, with tabs | 3.00 3.00 |

Organized Forestry in Iceland, Cent. — A410

Various tree branches with frame color of: 10k, Olive green. 60k, Rose carmine.

**2007, Apr. 20** ***Perf. 14***

| | | |
|---|---|---|
| **1101-1102** | A410 Set of 2 | 2.25 2.25 |
| *1101a* | Perf. 13½x14 | .25 .25 |
| *1102a* | Perf. 13½x14 | 1.50 1.50 |

Issued: 1101a, 1102a, 11/6/08.

Cargo Boats A411

No. 1103: a, Hamrafell. b, Tröllafoss.
No. 1104: a, Langjökull. b, Akranes.

***Perf. 13 on 2 or 3 Sides***

**2007, Apr. 20** **Booklet Stamps**

| | | |
|---|---|---|
| **1103** | Pair | 2.50 2.50 |
| *a.-b.* | A411 80k Either single | 1.25 1.25 |
| *c.* | Booklet pane, 2 #1103 | 5.00 — |
| | Complete booklet, #1103c | 5.00 |
| **1104** | Pair | 3.50 3.50 |
| *a.-b.* | A411 105k Either single | 1.75 1.75 |
| *c.* | Booklet pane, 2 #1104 | 7.00 — |
| | Complete booklet, #1104c | 7.00 |

Glaciers
A412

Designs: 5k, Breithamerkurjökull. 60k, Eystri Hagafellsjökull and Langjökull, vert. 80k, Mulajökull and Hofsjökull. 110k, Snaefellsjökull. 300k, Hvannadalshnúkur and Oraefajökull (70x30mm).

**2007, May 24** *Perf. 14x13¼*

**1105-1109** A412 Set of 5 9.00 9.00
*1109a* Booklet pane, #1105-1109 12.50 —
Complete booklet, #1109a 12.50

No. 1109a sold for 750k.

Europa — A413

Designs: 80k, Scouting fleur-de-lis. 105k, Scouting clover emblem.

**2007, May 24** *Perf. 13¼*

**1110** A413 80k multi 1.25 1.25
**1111** A413 105k multi 1.75 1.75

**Booklet Stamps**
**Self-Adhesive**
***Die Cut***

**1112** A413 80k multi 1.25 1.25
*a.* Booklet pane of 10 12.50 12.50
**1113** A413 105k multi 1.75 1.75
*a.* Booklet pane of 10 17.50
*Nos. 1110-1113 (4)* 6.00 6.00

Scouting, cent.

Soil Conservation Service, Cent. — A414

***Perf. 13¾x14¼***

**2007, May 24** **Photo.**

**1114** A414 (60k) multi 1.00 1.00

**Self-Adhesive**
***Serpentine Die Cut 12***

**1115** A414 (60k) multi 1.00 1.00

No. 1114 was printed in a sheet of 10, No. 1115 was printed in a folded sheet of 50.

**Berries Type of 2005**

Designs: 120k, Vaccinium myrtillus. 145k, Cornus suecica.

**2007, Sept. 20** **Litho.** *Perf. 14*

**1116** A385 120k multi 2.00 2.00
*a.* Tete-beche pair 4.25 4.25
**1117** A385 145k multi 2.25 2.25
*a.* Tete-beche pair 4.75 4.75

New Bible Translation — A415

**Litho. With Foil Application**

**2007, Sept. 20** *Perf. 13½*

**1118** A415 60k multi 1.00 1.00

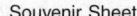

Souvenir Sheet

Royal Visit, Cent. — A416

**Litho. & Engr.**

**2007, Sept. 20** *Perf. 13x13¼*

**1119** A416 250k multi 4.00 4.00

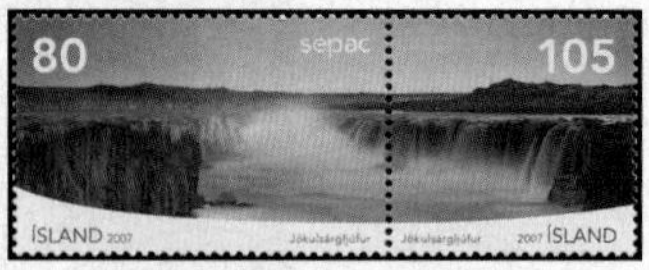


Jökulsá Canyon and Selfoss Waterfall — A417

No. 1120: a, Jökulsá Canyon (45x29mm). b, Selfoss Waterfall (30x29mm)

**2007, Oct. 1** **Litho.** *Perf. 13¼x13¾*

**1120** A417 Horiz. pair 3.25 3.25
*a.* 80k multi 1.25 1.25
*b.* 105k multi 1.75 1.75

**Insects Type of 2004**

Designs: 70k, Prionocera turcica. 190k, Euceraphis punctipennis.

**2007, Nov. 8** **Litho.** *Perf. 14*

**1121-1122** A375 Set of 2 4.25 4.25

Jónas Hallgrímsson (1807-45), Poet — A418

**2007, Nov. 8** **Engr.** *Perf. 12¾x13*

**1123** A418 65k brown 1.00 1.00

Kleppur Psychiatric Hospital, Cent. — A419

**2007, Nov. 8** **Litho.** *Perf. 13¼*

**1124** A419 80k multi 1.25 1.25

Christmas
A420

Various cut patterns in Icelandic leaf bread: 60k, 80k.

**2007, Nov. 8** ***Serpentine Die Cut***
**Self-Adhesive**

**1125** A420 60k red & multi .95 .95
*a.* Booklet pane of 10 9.50
**1126** A420 80k grn & multi 1.25 1.25

Teachers' College of Iceland, Cent. — A421

**2008, Feb. 14** **Litho.** *Perf. 14x13¼*

**1127** A421 85k multi 1.30 1.30

Kisses — A422

Lines from poem by Erla Thorsteindottir and people kissing with photograph colors in: No. 1128, 65k, Blue. No. 1129, 65k, Sepia. 75k, Green. 85k, Red violet.

**2008, Feb. 14**

**1128-1131** A422 Set of 4 4.50 4.50

Agricultural Tools — A423

No. 1132: a, Ferguson tractor. b, International Harvester TD6 bulldozer.

No. 1133: a, Horse-drawn plow. b, Lanz turfkiller.

**2008, Mar. 27** **Litho.** *Perf. 13¼*

**Booklet Stamps**

**1132** Pair 2.60 2.60
*a.-b.* A423 85k Either single 1.30 1.30
*c.* Booklet pane, 2 #1132 5.25
Complete booklet, #1132c 5.25
**1133** Pair 3.50 3.50
*a.-b.* A423 110k Either single 1.75 1.75
*c.* Booklet pane, 2 #1133 7.00
Complete booklet, #1133c 7.00

Embroidery — A424

Designs: 65k, Refilsaumur. 85k, Augnsaumur. 110k, Krosssaumur.

**2008, Mar. 27** *Perf. 14*

**1134-1136** A424 Set of 3 4.00 4.00

Souvenir Sheet

Snaefellsnes — A425

**2008, Mar. 27** *Perf. 14x13¼*

**1137** A425 120k multi 1.90 1.90

Personalized Stamp — A426

***Serpentine Die Cut 10 Syncopated***

**2008, May 8** **Self-Adhesive** **Litho.**

**1138** A426 (75k) multi 1.20 1.20

The vignette of the stamp shown above is the generic image for the issue, which was available at face value. Other images with the stamp frame shown are personalized stamps which sold for 3120k for a sheet of 24 stamps.

Geothermal Space Heating, Cent. — A427

**2008, May 8** *Perf. 14x13½*

**1139** A427 75k multi 1.20 1.20

Hafnarfjördhur, Cent. — A428

**2008, May 8** *Perf. 13x12½*

**1140** A428 80k multi 1.25 1.25

Icelandic Industrial Design
A429

Designs: 65k, Proprio Foot prosthetic foot. 120k, Marel OptiCut volumetric portioning and meat cutting machine. 155k, Wish fly fishing reel. 200k, Gavia submarine.

**2008, May 8** *Perf. 12½x13*

**1141-1144** A429 Set of 4 8.50 8.50
*1141a* Tete beche pair 2.25 2.25
*1142a* Tete beche pair 4.00 4.00
*1143a* Tete beche pair 5.00 5.00

Europa — A430

Letter folded into: 85k, Boat. 110k, Airplane.

**2008, May 8** *Perf. 14*

**1145** A430 85k multi 1.30 1.30
**1146** A430 110k multi 1.75 1.75

### Booklet Stamps
### Self-Adhesive
*Serpentine Die Cut 9½x10*

**1147** A430 85k multi 1.30 1.30
*a.* Booklet pane of 10 13.00
**1148** A430 110k multi 1.75 1.75
*a.* Booklet pane of 10 17.50

Knight and Final Position of 1958 Chess Match Between Fridhrik Olafsson and Bobby Fischer — A431

**2008, Sept. 18 Litho. *Perf. 13¼***
**1149** A431 80k multi 1.25 1.25

First Cod War, 50th Anniv. A432

**2008, Sept. 18 *Perf. 13¼x13***
**1150** A432 90k multi 1.40 1.40

Aegagropila Linnaei — A433

**2008, Sept. 18 *Perf. 13¼x13¾***
**1151** A433 140k multi 2.25 2.25

Souvenir Sheet

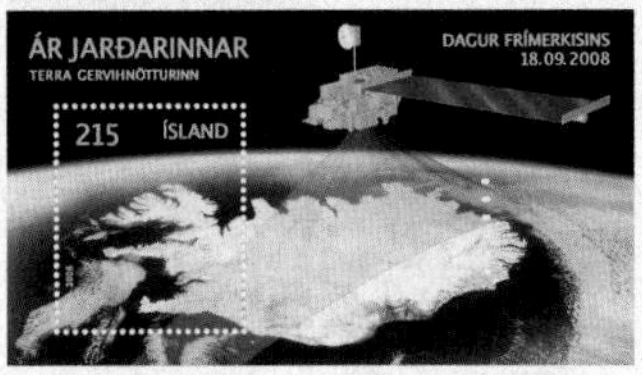


Intl. Year of Planet Earth — A434

**2008, Sept. 18**
**1152** A434 215k multi 3.50 3.50

Stamp Day.

Peace Tower, Videy — A435

**2008, Oct. 9 Litho. *Perf. 13¼***
**1153** A435 120k multi + label 1.90 1.90

Parts of the design were printed with a glow-in-the-dark ink.

### Forestry Type of 2005 Redrawn and

Forestry in Vaglaskógur, Cent. — A436

**2008, Nov. 6 Litho. *Perf. 13½x14***
**1154** A436 400k multi 6.25 6.25
**1155** Booklet pane of 4, #1101a, 1102a, 1154, 1155a 13.50 13.50
*a.* A377 45k multi, denomination as "45" only *3.00 3.00*
Complete booklet, #1155 14.00 14.00

No. 1155 sold for 800k.

Christmas A437

Winning designs in children's stamp art contest: 70k, Christmas goblin Stiff-legs, by Heidhar Jökull Hafsteinsson. 90k, Christmas Cat, by Konrádh Kárason Thormar.

*Serpentine Die Cut 12½*
**2008, Nov. 6**
### Self-Adhesive
**1156** A437 70k multi 1.10 1.10
*a.* Booket pane of 10 11.00
**1157** A437 90k multi 1.40 1.40

Vertical pairs in booklet pane are tete-beche.

### Islands Type of 2001

Designs: 75k, Hjörsey. 90k, Málmey.

**2009, Jan. 29 Litho. *Perf. 14***
**1158-1159** A335 Set of 2 2.60 2.60

### Insects Type of 2004

Designs: 80k, Psychodidae. 120k, Gnaphosidae (spider).

**2009, Jan. 29**
**1160-1161** A375 Set of 2 3.25 3.25

Souvenir Sheet

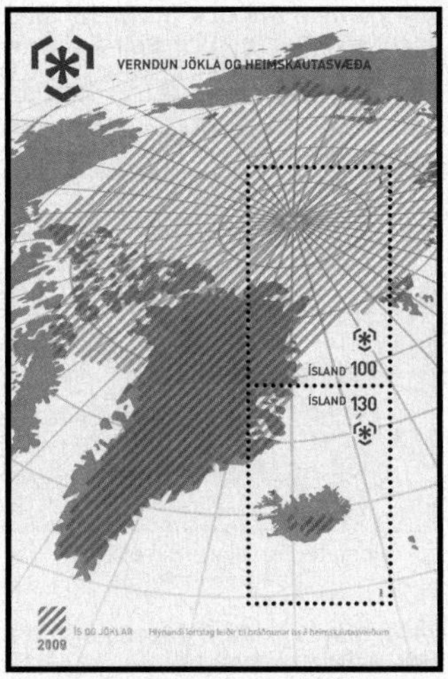


Intl. Polar Year — A438

No. 1162 — Map of ice cover of: a, 100k, North Pole, Northern Greenland. b, 130k, Iceland, Eastern Greenland.

### Litho. & Photo.
**2009, Jan. 29 *Perf. 13x13½***
**1162** A438 Sheet of 2, #a-b 3.75 3.75

Parts of the design were printed with a thermographic ink that disappeared when warmed.

Civil Aviation in Iceland, 90th Anniv. A439

No. 1163: a, Avro 504K. b, Waco ZKS-7.
No. 1164: a, Boeing 757. b, Fokker 50.

***Perf. 14¼ Horiz.***
**2009, Mar. 19 Litho.**
### Booklet Stamps
**1163** Vert. pair 3.00 3.00
*a.-b.* A439 90k Either single 1.50 1.50
*c.* Booklet pane, 2 #1163 6.00 —
Complete booklet, #1163c 6.00
**1164** Vert. pair 4.25 4.25
*a.-b.* A439 120k Either single 2.10 2.10
*c.* Booklet pane, 2 #1164 8.50 —
Complete booklet, #1164c 8.50

Miniature Sheet

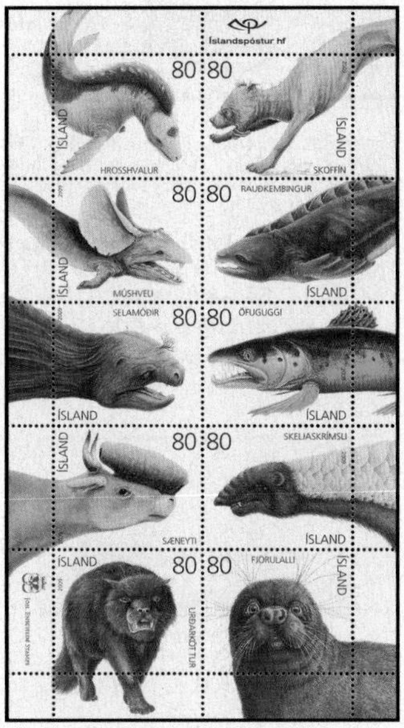


Legendary Creatures from Folktales — A440

No. 1165: a, Hrosshvalur. b, Skoffín. c, Múshveli. d, Raudhkembingur. e, Selamódhir. f, Ofuguggi. g, Saeneyti. h, Skeljaskrímsli. i, Urdharköt tur. j, Fjörulalli.

**2009, Mar. 19 *Perf. 13¼***
**1165** A440 80k Sheet of 10, #a-j 12.50 12.50

Reykjavik Water Works, Cent. — A441

**2009, May 7 Litho. *Perf. 12½***
**1166** A441 10k multi .25 .25

Iceland Youth Organization National Tournaments, Cent. — A442

**2009, May 7 *Perf. 13¼***
**1167** A442 105k multi 1.60 1.60

Skrúdhur Garden, Cent. — A443

**2009, May 7 *Perf. 12½***
**1168** A443 140k multi 2.25 2.25

Europa — A444

Designs: 105k, Sun and shadows at different times. 140k, Observatory.

**2009, May 7 *Perf. 13¼***
**1169** A444 105k multi 1.75 1.75
**1170** A444 140k multi 2.25 2.25

### Booklet Stamps
### Self-Adhesive
*Serpentine Die Cut 9¾x10*
**1171** A444 105k multi 1.75 1.75
*a.* Booklet pane of 10 17.50
**1172** A444 140k multi 2.25 2.25
*a.* Booklet pane of 10 22.50

Intl. Year of Astronomy.

Souvenir Sheet

Nordia 2009 Philatelic Exhibition, Hafnarfjördhur — A445

**2009, May 7 *Perf. 13***
**1173** A445 190k multi 3.00 3.00

Icelandic Sheep A446

Shepherds and sheep in: 95k, Open pasture. 160k, Pen, vert.

***Perf. 12½x13, 13x12½***
**2009, Sept. 16**
**1174-1175** A446 Set of 2 4.00 4.00

Skaftafell, Vatnajökull National Park — A447

No. 1176 — Denomination at: a, UL (45x30mm). b, UR (30x30mm).

**2009, Sept. 16 *Perf. 13½x14***
**1176** A447 120k Horiz. pair, #a-b 3.75 3.75

Souvenir Sheet

National Center for Cultural Heritage, Cent. — A448

**2009, Sept. 16 *Perf. 13***
**1177** A448 150k multi 2.40 2.40

Stamp Day.

Birds — A449

Designs: 110k, Uria lomvia. 130k, Larus hyperboreus.

**2009, Nov. 5** ***Perf. 13x13¼***
**1178-1179** A449 Set of 2 3.75 3.75

Thingvellir Church, 150th Anniv. — A450

**2009, Nov. 5**
**1180** A450 190k multi 3.00 3.00

Christmas A451

Stained-glass windows: (70k), The Sermon on the Mount, by Gudmundur Einarsson. 120k, Holy Mother of God, by Finnur Jónsson.

**2009, Nov. 5** ***Die Cut Perf. 13½***
**Self-Adhesive**
**1181** A451 (70k) multi 1.10 1.10
*a.* Booklet pane of 10 11.00
**1182** A451 120k multi 1.90 1.90

Seals A452

Designs: 5k, Phoca vitulina. 220k, Phoca groenlandica.

**2010, Jan. 28 Litho.** ***Perf. 13¼x13¾***
**1183-1184** A452 Set of 2 3.50 3.50

Home Furnishings — A453

Designs: 75k, Hanger tree, designed by Katrín Ólina Pétursdóttir and Michael Young. 140k, Tango chair, designed by Sigurdhur Gústafsson. 155k, MGO 180 dining room table, designed by Gudhrún M. Olafsdóttir and Oddgeir Thórdharson, horiz. 165k, Dimon sofa, designed by Erla Sólveig Oskarsdóttir.

***Perf. 13¼x12½, 12½x13¼***
**2010, Jan. 28**
**1185-1188** A453 Set of 4 8.50 8.50
*1185a* Tete-beche pair 2.40 2.40
*1186a* Tete-beche pair 4.50 4.50
*1187a* Tete-beche pair 5.00 5.00
*1188a* Tete-beche pair 5.25 5.25

Wood and Bone Carvings A454

Designs: 10k, Door of Valthjófsstadhir. Nos. 1190, 1192, (75k), Judge's drinking horn. 200k, Play in Leaves, sculpture by Sigrídhur Jóna Kristjánsdóttir.

**2010, Mar. 18** ***Perf. 14x13¼, 13¼x14***
**1189-1191** A454 Set of 3 5.00 5.00

**Self-Adhesive**
***Serpentine Die Cut 12***
**Size: 32x27mm**
**1192** A454 (75k) multi 1.25 1.25

Fishing Trawlers — A455

No. 1193: a, Bjarni Riddari GK 1. b, Ingólfur Arnarson RE 201.
No. 1194: a, Sólborg IS 260. b, Hardhbakur EA 3.

**2010, Mar. 18** ***Perf. 14 Horiz.***
**Booklet Stamps**
**1193** Vert. pair 2.50 2.50
*a.-b.* A455 75k Either single 1.25 1.25
*c.* Booklet pane, 2 #1193 5.00 —
Complete booklet, #1193c 5.00
**1194** Vert. pair 5.25 5.25
*a.-b.* A455 165k Either single 2.60 2.60
*c.* Booklet pane, 2 #1194 10.50 —
Complete booklet, #1194c 10.50

Souvenir Sheet

Life by the Sea — A456

No. 1195: a, Man rolling herring barrel. b, Women filling herring barrels, fish.

**2010, Mar. 18** ***Perf. 13¼x14***
**1195** A456 75k Sheet of 2, #a-b 2.50 2.50

Europa A457

Illustrations from children's books: 165k, The Fate of the Gods, by Ingunn Asdísardóttir and Kristin Ragna Gunnarsdóttir. 220k, Good Evening, by Aslaug Jónsdóttir.

**2010, May 6 Litho.** ***Perf. 13¾x14***
**1196** A457 165k multi 2.60 2.60
**1197** A457 220k multi 3.50 3.50

**Booklet Stamps**
**Self-Adhesive**
***Die Cut Perf. 13¼***
**1198** A457 165k multi 2.60 2.60
*a.* Booklet pane of 10 26.00
**1199** A457 220k multi 3.50 3.50
*a.* Booklet pane of 10 35.00

Garden Parks — A458

Designs: 90k, Jónsgardhur, Isafjödhur. 130k, Hellisgerdhi, Hafnarfjödhur. 285k, Skalla-grímsgardhur, Borgarnes, horiz.

***Perf. 13¼x13¾, 13¾x13¼***
**2010, May 6**
**1200-1202** A458 Set of 3 7.75 7.75

A460

Personalized Stamps — A461

***Serpentine Die Cut 10 Syncopated***
**2010, May 6** **Self-Adhesive**
**1203** A460 (165k) silver & blue 2.60 2.60
**1204** A461 (220k) bronze & brn 3.50 3.50

The vignettes shown above of Nos. 1203-1204 are generic images. The vignette portion of the stamp could be personalized.

Souvenir Sheet

Iceland Pavilion, Expo 2010, Shanghai — A462

**2010, May 6** ***Perf. 13x12½x12¾x13***
**1205** A462 130k multi 2.00 2.00

A463

A464

2010 Eruption of Eyjafjallajökull Volcano — A465

**Litho. & Silk-screened**
**2010, July 22** ***Perf. 13¼***
**1206** A463 (75k) multi 1.25 1.25
**1207** A464 (165k) multi 2.75 2.75
**1208** A465 (220k) multi 3.75 3.75
*Nos. 1206-1208 (3)* 7.75 7.75

Volcanic ash from the eruption was added to the ink used on the silk-screened parts of Nos. 1206-1208.

Vífilsstadhir Sanatorium, Cent. — A466

***Perf. 13½x13¼***
**2010, Sept. 16** **Litho.**
**1209** A466 (90k) multi 1.50 1.50

2010 Youth Olympics, Singapore A467

**2010, Sept. 16** ***Perf. 13x12½***
**1210** A467 165k multi 2.50 2.50

Gas Lighting In Reykjavik, 150th Anniv. — A468

**2010, Sept. 16** ***Perf. 13***
**1211** A468 450k multi 7.00 7.00

Souvenir Sheet

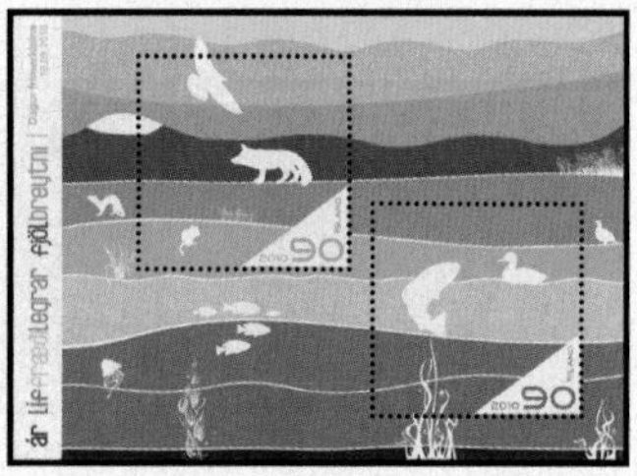


Intl. Year of Biodiversity — A469

No. 1212: a, Hawk, wolf, rodent. b, Fish, duck.

**2010, Sept. 16** ***Perf. 13¼***
**1212** A469 90k Sheet of 2, #a-b 3.00 3.00

Visir Newspaper, Cent. — A470

**2010, Nov. 4 Litho.** ***Perf. 13***
**1213** A470 140k drab & blk 2.25 2.25

Foss, by Isleifur Konrádhsson — A471

Skeggjadhur Madhur og Blómaflúr, by Sölvi Helgason A472

Breidhfirskur Víkingur, by Sigurlaug Jónasdóttir A473

Fiskar, by Karl Einarsson Dunganon A474

**2010, Nov. 4**
**1214** A471 (75k) multi 1.25 1.25
**1215** A472 (90k) multi 1.40 1.40
**1216** A473 (165k) multi 2.60 2.60
**1217** A474 (220k) multi 3.50 3.50
*Nos. 1214-1217 (4)* 8.75 8.75

A booklet containing single stamps of Nos. 1214-1217 in mounts sold for 1,550k.

Wreath and Dove — A475

Wreath and Two Doves — A476

**2010, Nov. 4** ***Die Cut Perf. 13¾***
**Self-Adhesive**
**1218** A475 (75k) multi 1.25 1.25
*a.* Booklet pane of 10 12.50
**1219** A476 (165k) multi 2.60 2.60

Halichoerus Grypus — A477

Phoca Hispida A478

**2011, Jan. 27 Litho.** ***Perf. 13¼x13¾***
**1220** A477 (90k) multi 1.40 1.40
**1221** A478 (220k) multi 3.50 3.50

Branta Leucopsis A479

Melanitta Nigra A480

Anser Albifrons A481

Anas Strepera A482

**2011, Jan. 27**
**1222** A479 (75k) multi 1.25 1.25
**1223** A480 (75k) multi 1.25 1.25
**1224** A481 (165k) multi 2.50 2.50
**1225** A482 (165k) multi 2.50 2.50
*Nos. 1222-1225 (4)* 8.50 8.50

Worldwide Fund for Nature (WWF).

Motor Sports A483

No. 1226 — Inscriptions: a, Mótokross. b, Rally.
No. 1227 — Inscriptions: a, Torfaera. b, Kvartmíla.

**2011, Mar. 17 Litho.** ***Perf. 14 Horiz.***
**Booklet Stamps**
**1226** Vert. pair 2.50 2.50
*a.-b.* A483 (75k) Either single 1.25 1.25
*c.* Booklet pane, 2 #1226 5.00 —
Complete booklet, #1226c 5.00 —
**1227** Vert. pair 5.00 5.00
*a.-b.* A483 (165k) Either single 2.50 2.50
*c.* Booklet pane, 2 #1227 10.00 —
Complete booklet, #1227c 10.00 —

Langanes Lighthouse A484

Stokknes Lighthouse A485

***Die Cut Perf. 13¼ at Bottom***
**2011, Mar. 17 Self-Adhesive**
**1228** A484 (75k) multi 1.25 1.25
***Die Cut Perf. 13¼ at Right***
**1229** A485 (165k) multi 2.50 2.50

Tree Rings and Table A486

Leaf and Curved Arrows A487

**Litho. With Foil Application**
**2011, Mar. 17** ***Perf. 13¾x14***
**1230** A486 (165k) multi 2.50 2.50
**1231** A487 (220k) multi 3.50 3.50
**Booklet Stamps**
**Self-Adhesive**
***Die Cut Perf. 13¼***
**1232** A486 (165k) multi 2.60 2.60
*a.* Booklet pane of 10 26.00
**1233** A487 (220k) multi 3.50 3.50
*a.* Booklet pane of 10 35.00

Europa, Intl. Year of Forests.

University of Iceland, Cent. — A488

**2011, May 4 Litho.** ***Perf. 12½x13***
**1234** A488 (75k) multi 1.25 1.25

Melavöllur Stadium, Reykjavik, Cent. A489

**2011, May 4** ***Perf. 13¼***
**1235** A489 (130k) multi 2.00 2.00

Austurvöllur Park, Reykjavik — A490

Parliament Park, Reykjavik — A491

**2011, May 4** ***Perf. 13¼x12½***
**1236** A490 (90k) multi 1.40 1.40
**1237** A491 (285k) multi 4.50 4.50

Miniature Sheet

Opening of Harpa Reykjavik Concert Hall and Conference Center — A492

No. 1238 — Portions of building facade in colors of: a, Black and blue green. b, Black and gray with country name on white area. c, Black and gray with country name on gray area. d, Black and pink. e, Black and yellow green. Stamps are polygonal and various sizes.

**2011, May 4 Litho. & Engr.** ***Die Cut***
**Self-Adhesive**
**1238** A492 Sheet of 5 6.25
*a.-e.* (75k) Any single 1.25 1.25

Pres. Jón Sigurdhsson (1811-79) A493

Sigurdhsson as: Nos. 1239, 1241a, Young man. No. 1240, Old man.

**2011, June 17 Litho. *Perf. 13***

**1239** A493 (75k) multi 1.25 1.25
**1240** A493 1000k multi, year date 2 ¼mm wide 15.50 15.50
*a.* Year date 2 ½mm wide 15.50 15.50

**Souvenir Sheet**

**1241** Sheet of 2, #1240a, 1241a 17.50 17.50
*a.* A493 100k multi 1.60 1.60

Wetlands Conservation A494

**2011, Sept. 15 *Perf. 13¼***

**1242** A494 (90k) multi 1.40 1.40

Amnesty International, 50th Anniv. — A495

**2011, Sept. 15 *Perf. 13½x14***

**1243** A495 (285k) yellow & black 4.50 4.50

Snaefell Glacier National Park — A496

No. 1244: a, Mountain (45x29mm). b, Mountain, diff. (30x29mm).

**2011, Sept. 15 *Perf. 13¼x13¾***

**1244** A496 Horiz. pair 5.25 5.25
*a.-b.* (165k) Either single 2.60 2.60

**Souvenir Sheet**

Fishing Boat at Húsavik — A497

**2011, Sept. 15 *Perf. 13x13¼***

**1245** A497 (165k) multi 2.60 2.60

See Malta No. 1438.

**Souvenir Sheet**

Saga of Burnt Niall — A498

No. 1246: a, Flying horseman carrying torch. b, Burning of Niall and family. c, Swordsman raising sword, dead swordsman.

**2011, Sept. 15 *Perf. 12½***

**1246** A498 Sheet of 3 5.25 5.25
*a.-c.* (110k) Any single 1.75 1.75

Sólarlag vidh Tjörnina, by Thórarinn B. Thorláksson — A499

Botnssúlur, by Asgrímur Jónsson A500

Utreidharfólk, by Jón Stefánsson — A501

Fornar Slódhir, by Jóhannes Kjarval A502

**2011, Nov. 3 Litho. *Perf. 13x13¼***

**1247** A499 (90k) multi 1.40 1.40
**1248** A500 (110k) multi 1.75 1.75
**1249** A501 (165k) multi 2.60 2.60
**1250** A502 (220k) multi 3.50 3.50
*Nos. 1247-1250 (4)* 9.25 9.25

A503

Christmas A504

***Die Cut Perf. 13¾x13½***

**2011, Nov. 3 Litho. & Embossed**

**Self-Adhesive**

**1251** A503 (90k) multi 1.40 1.40
*a.* Booklet pane of 10 14.00
**1252** A504 (165k) multi 2.60 2.60

National Olympic and Sports Association, Cent. — A505

**2012, Jan. 26 Litho. *Perf. 13¼x13¾***

**1253** A505 (97k) multi 1.40 1.40

Landmannalaugar — A506

Lake Hnausapollur A507

**2012, Jan. 26 *Perf. 13¾***

**1254** A506 (175k) multi 2.75 2.75
**1255** A507 (230k) multi 3.75 3.75

Silver Chalice, 15th Cent. — A508

Silver Headdress, by Sigurdhar Gudhmundsson — A509

Silver Bowl, by Pétur Tryggvi Hjálmarsson A510

Silver Chalice, 15th Cent. — A511

**2012, Jan. 26 *Perf. 13¼x14, 14x13¼***

**1256** A508 (97k) multi 1.60 1.60
**1257** A509 (175k) multi 2.75 2.75
**1258** A510 (230k) multi 3.75 3.75
*Nos. 1256-1258 (3)* 8.10 8.10

**Self-Adhesive**

***Serpentine Die Cut 12***

**1259** A511 (97k) multi 1.60 1.60

Shoes and Socks Designed by Hugrün Dögg Arnadóttir and Magni Thorsteinsson — A512

Dress Designed by Steinunn Sigurdardottir — A513

Wool Sweater Designed by Bergthora Gudnadottir — A514

Coat Designed by 66 Degrees North — A515

**2012, Mar. 22 *Perf. 12½x13***

**1260** A512 (97k) multi 1.60 1.60
**1261** A513 (110k) multi 1.75 1.75
**1262** A514 (175k) multi 2.75 2.75
**1263** A515 (230k) multi 3.75 3.75
*Nos. 1260-1263 (4)* 9.85 9.85

Waterfall A516

Aluminum A517

Geothermal Energy A518

Tomatoes A519

**Booklet Stamps**

***Serpentine Die Cut 13¼***

**2012, Mar. 22 Self-Adhesive**

**1264** A516 (75k) multi 1.25 1.25
**1265** A517 (75k) multi 1.25 1.25
*a.* Booklet pane of 4, 2 each #1264-1265 5.00
**1266** A518 (175k) multi 2.75 2.75
**1267** A519 (175k) multi 2.75 2.75
*a.* Booklet pane of 4, 2 each #1266-1267 11.00
*Nos. 1264-1267 (4)* 8.00 8.00

Green energy.

**Souvenir Sheet**

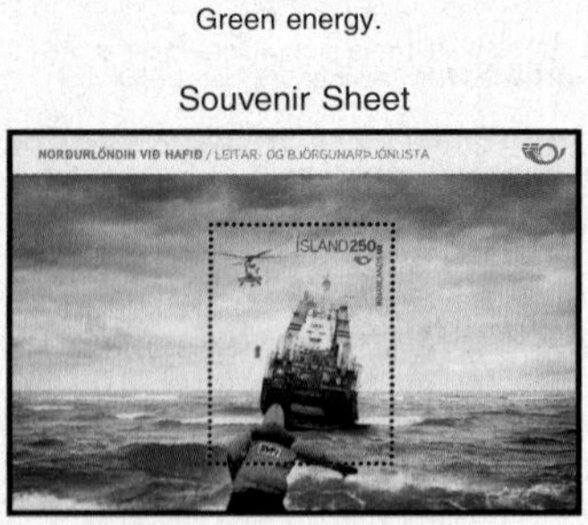


Sea Rescue — A520

**2012, Mar. 22 *Perf. 14¼x14¾***

**1268** A520 (155k) multi 2.50 2.50

Akureyri, 150th Anniv. A521

**2012, May 3** ***Perf. 14x13½***

**1269** A521 (75k) multi 1.25 1.25
*a.* With period after "08" 1.25 1.25

No. 1269 is missing period after "08". Issued: No. 1269a, 7/2.

Scouting in Iceland, Cent. A522

**2012, May 3** ***Perf. 13¾***

**1270** A522 (75k) multi 1.25 1.25

2012 Summer Olympics, London A523

**2012, May 3** ***Perf. 14x13½***

**1271** A523 (580k) multi 9.50 9.50

Akureyri Park, Akureyri — A524

Hallargardhur Park, Reykjavik — A525

**2012, May 3** ***Perf. 13¼***

**1272** A524 (225k) multi 3.75 3.75
**1273** A525 (300k) multi 5.00 5.00

Geyser — A526

Aurora Borealis — A527

**2012, May 3** ***Serpentine Die Cut 18***

**Self-Adhesive**

**1274** A526 (175k) multi 3.00 3.00
**1275** A527 (230k) multi 3.75 3.75

**Booklet Stamps**

***Serpentine Die Cut 18 on 3 Sides***

**1276** A526 (175k) multi 3.00 3.00
*a.* Booklet pane of 10 30.00
**1277** A527 (230k) multi 3.75 3.75
*a.* Booklet pane of 10 37.50

Europa.

**No. 1150 Surcharged**

**Method and Perf. As Before**

**2012, July 2**

**1278** A432 (103k) on 90k #1150 1.60 1.60

Russula Xerampelina A528

**2012, July 2 Litho.** ***Perf. 13¼x12¾***

**1279** A528 (103k) multi 1.60 1.60

Cystophora Cristata — A529

Odobenus Rosmarus — A530

**2012, Sept. 13** ***Perf. 13¼x13¾***

**1280** A529 (475k) multi 7.75 7.75
**1281** A530 (480k) multi 8.00 8.00

Engey Lighthouse A531

Kálfshamar Lighthouse A532

***Die Cut Perf. 13¼ at Bottom***

**2012, Sept. 13** **Self-Adhesive**

**1282** A531 (103k) multi 1.75 1.75

***Die Cut Perf. 13¼ at Right***

**1283** A532 (175k) multi 3.00 3.00

Souvenir Sheet

Archaeological Excavations at Skridhuklaustur — A533

**2012, Sept. 13** ***Perf. 14x13¼***

**1284** A533 (565k) multi 9.25 9.25

Consecration of Skridhuklaustur Church, 500th anniv.

Boletus Edulis A534

**2012, Nov. 1** ***Perf. 13¼x12¾***

**1285** A534 (103k) multi 1.60 1.60

Dapri Prinsinn, by Gudhmundur Thorsteinsson — A535

Uppstilling, by Kristín Jónsdóttir A536

Frá Vestmannaeyjum, by Júlíana Sveinsdóttir — A537

Módhurást, Sculpture by Nína Saemundsson A538

**2012, Nov. 1** ***Perf. 14x13¼***

**1286** A535 (120k) multi 1.90 1.90
**1287** A536 (125k) multi 2.00 2.00
**1288** A537 (175k) multi 2.75 2.75

***Perf. 13¼x14***

**1289** A538 (230k) multi 3.75 3.75
*Nos. 1286-1289 (4)* 10.40 10.40

A539

Christmas A540

**Self-Adhesive**

**Litho. With Foil Application**

**2012, Nov. 1** ***Die Cut Perf. 13½***

**1290** A539 (120k) multi 1.90 1.90
*a.* Booklet pane of 10 19.00
**1291** A540 (175k) multi 2.75 2.75

Intl. Year of Water Cooperation A541

**2013, Jan. 24 Litho.** ***Perf. 13¾x13½***

**1292** A541 (103k) multi 1.60 1.60

Aldeyjarfoss A542

Hafursey A543

**2013, Jan. 24** ***Perf. 13¾***

**1293** A542 (175k) multi 2.75 2.75
**1294** A543 (230k) multi 3.75 3.75

National Museum, 150th Anniv. — A544

**Self-Adhesive**

**2013, Jan. 24** ***Perf. 13½***

**1295** A544 (125k) rose & blue 2.00 2.00

---

**SEMI-POSTAL STAMPS**

Shipwreck and Rescue by Breeches Buoy SP1

Children Gathering Rock Plants SP2

Old Fisherman at Shore SP3

**Unwmk.**

**1933, Apr. 28 Engr.** ***Perf. 14***

**B1** SP1 10a + 10a red brown 2.25 *7.50*
**B2** SP2 20a + 20a org red 2.25 *7.50*
**B3** SP1 35a + 25a ultra 2.25 *7.50*
**B4** SP3 50a + 25a blue grn 2.25 *7.50*
*Nos. B1-B4 (4)* 9.00 *30.00*
Set, never hinged 18.00

Receipts from the surtax were devoted to a special fund for use in various charitable works especially those indicated on the stamps: "Slysavarnir" (Rescue work), "Barnahaeli" (Asylum for scrofulous children), "Ellhaeli" (Asylum for the Aged).

Souvenir Sheets

King Christian X — SP4

**1937, May 15 Typo.**

**B5** SP4 Sheet of 3 55.00 *375.00*
Never hinged 105.00
*a.* 15a violet 12.00 *67.50*
*b.* 25a red 12.00 *67.50*
*c.* 50a blue 12.00 *67.50*

Reign of Christian X, 25th anniv. Sheet sold for 2kr.

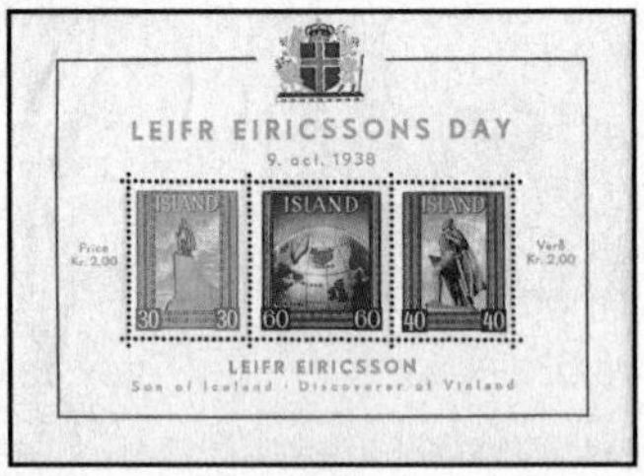


SP5

Designs: 30a, 40a, Ericsson statue, Reykjavik. 60a, Iceland's position on globe.

**1938, Oct. 9 Photo.** ***Perf. 12***

**B6** SP5 Sheet of 3 6.00 *32.50*
Never hinged 10.00
*a.* 30a scarlet 1.40 *13.00*
*b.* 40a purple 1.40 *13.00*
*c.* 60a deep green 1.40 *13.00*

Leif Ericsson Day, Oct. 9, 1938.

**Catalogue values for unused stamps in this section, from this point to the end of the section, are for Never Hinged items.**

Ill Child — SP6

Red Cross Nurse and Patient — SP7

Nurse Covering Patient — SP8

Elderly Couple — SP9

Rescue at Sea — SP10

**Unwmk.**

**1949, June 8 Engr.** ***Perf. 14***

**B7** SP6 10a + 10a olive grn .80 *1.50*
**B8** SP7 35a + 15a carmine 1.10 *1.50*
**B9** SP8 50a + 25a choc 1.10 *1.50*
**B10** SP9 60a + 25a brt ultra 1.10 *1.50*
**B11** SP10 75a + 25a slate gray 1.10 *1.50*
*Nos. B7-B11 (5)* 5.20 *7.50*

The surtax was for charitable purposes.

Nos. 262 and 265 Surcharged in Black

**1953, Feb. 12 Unwmk.** ***Perf. 13***

**B12** A50 75a + 25a red org 1.75 *6.75*
**B13** A50 1.25k + 25a red vio 3.00 *6.75*

The surtax was for flood relief in the Netherlands.

St. Thorlacus — SP11

Cathedral at Skalholt SP12

1.75k+1.25k, Bishop Jon Thorkelsson Vidalin.

**1956, Jan. 23** ***Perf. 11½***

**B14** SP11 75a + 25a car .25 *.30*
**B15** SP12 1.25k + 75a dk brn .25 *.65*
**B16** SP11 1.75k + 1.25k black 2.00 *2.00*
*Nos. B14-B16 (3)* 2.50 *2.95*

Bishopric of Skalholt, 900th anniv.
The surtax was for the rebuilding of Skalholt, former cultural center of Iceland.

Ambulance SP13

**1963, Nov. 15 Photo. Unwmk.**

**B17** SP13 3k + 50a multi .60 *1.75*
**B18** SP13 3.50k + 50a multi .60 *1.75*

Centenary of International Red Cross.

Rock Ptarmigan in Summer SP14

Design: #B20, Rock ptarmigan in winter.

**1965, Jan. 27 Photo.** ***Perf. 12½***

**Granite Paper**

**B19** SP14 3.50k + 50a multi 1.10 *3.00*
**B20** SP14 4.50k + 50a multi 1.10 *3.00*

Ringed Plover's Nest — SP15

Design: 5k+50a, Rock ptarmigan's nest.

**1967, Nov. 22 Photo.** ***Perf. 11½***

**B21** SP15 4k + 50a multi 1.00 *2.25*
**B22** SP15 5k + 50a multi 1.00 *2.25*

Arctic Terns — SP16

**1972, Nov. 22 Litho.** ***Perf. 13***

**B23** SP16 7k + 1k multi .75 *1.50*
**B24** SP16 9k + 1k multi .75 *1.50*

---

**AIR POST STAMPS**

No. 115 Overprinted

***Perf. 14x14½***

**1928, May 31 Wmk. 114**

**C1** A8 10a red 1.10 *15.00*
Never hinged 2.25

Same Overprint on No. 82

**1929, June 29 Wmk. 113** ***Perf. 13***

**C2** A5 50a gray & violet 75.00 *145.00*
Never hinged 230.00

Gyrfalcon AP1

***Perf. 12½x12***

**1930, Jan. 1 Litho. Unwmk.**

**C3** AP1 10a dp ultra & gray blue 30.00 *90.00*
Never hinged 60.00

Imperfs were privately printed.
For overprint see No. CO1.

Snaefellsjokull, Extinct Volcano — AP2

Parliament Millenary: 20a, Fishing boat. 35a, Iceland pony. 50a, Gullfoss (Golden Falls). 1k, Ingolfour Arnarson Statue.

**Wmk. 47**

**1930, June 1 Typo.** ***Perf. 14***

**C4** AP2 15a org brn & dl bl 37.50 *72.50*
**C5** AP2 20a bis brn & sl bl 37.50 *72.50*
**C6** AP2 35a olive grn & brn 72.50 *145.00*
**C7** AP2 50a dp grn & dp bl 72.50 *145.00*
**C8** AP2 1k olive grn & dk red 72.50 *145.00*
*Nos. C4-C8 (5)* 292.50 *580.00*
Set, never hinged 600.00

Regular Issue of 1920 Overprinted

***Perf. 14x14½***

**1931, May 25 Wmk. 114**

**C9** A8 30a red & green 50.00 *175.00*
**C10** A8 1k dp bl & dk brn 17.50 *175.00*
**C11** A8 2k ol brn & myr grn 75.00 *175.00*
*Nos. C9-C11 (3)* 142.50 *525.00*
Set, never hinged 335.00

Nos. 185, 128 and 187 Overprinted in Red

**1933, June 16**

**C12** A8 1k dk bl & lt brn 235. *850.*
Never hinged 525.
**C13** A8 5k brn & indigo 775. *2,000.*
Never hinged 1,800.
**C14** A8 10k yel grn & blk 1,650. *3,750.*
Never hinged 4,000.

Excellent counterfeit overprints exist.
Visit of the Italian Flying Armada en route from Rome to Chicago; also for the payment of the charges on postal matter sent from Iceland to the US via the Italian seaplanes.

Plane over Thingvalla Lake — AP7

10a-20a, Plane over Thingvalla Lake. 25a-50a, Plane and Aurora Borealis. 1k-2k, Map of Iceland.

***Perf. 12½x14***

**1934, Sept. 1 Engr. Unwmk.**

**C15** AP7 10a blue 2.30 *4.00*
**C16** AP7 20a emerald 5.00 *9.00*
*a.* Perf. 14 37.50 27.00
Never hinged 135.00
**C17** AP7 25a dark violet, perf. 14 13.00 *20.00*
Revenue cancellation 50.00
*a.* Perf. 12½x14 37.50 *45.00*
Never hinged 135.00
**C18** AP7 50a red vio, perf. 14 4.00 *9.00*
**C19** AP7 1k dark brown 22.50 *40.00*
Revenue cancellation 30.00
**C20** AP7 2k red orange 11.50 *15.00*
*Nos. C15-C20 (6)* 58.30 *97.00*
Set, never hinged 165.00

**Catalogue values for unused stamps in this section, from this point to the end of the section, are for Never Hinged items.**

Thingvellir, Old Site of the Parliament AP10

Isafjörthur AP11

Eyjafjörthur AP12

Mt. Strandatindur AP13

Mt. Thyrill AP14

Aerial View of Reykjavik AP15

**1947, Aug. 18** — *Perf. 14*

**C21** AP10 15a red orange 1.20 *1.90*
**C22** AP11 30a gray black 1.20 *1.90*
**C23** AP12 75a brown red 1.20 *1.50*
**C24** AP13 1k indigo 1.20 *1.50*
**C25** AP14 2k chocolate 2.10 *3.00*
**C26** AP15 3k dark green 2.10 *3.00*
*Nos. C21-C26 (6)* 9.00 *12.80*

Snaefellsjokull AP16

Views: 2.50k, Eiriksjokull. 3.30k, Oraefajokull.

**1952, May 2 Unwmk.** — *Perf. 13½x14*

**C27** AP16 1.80k slate blue 21.00 16.00
**C28** AP16 2.50k green 37.50 1.40
**C29** AP16 3.30k deep ultra 8.50 10.50
*Nos. C27-C29 (3)* 67.00 *27.90*

See Nos. 302-304.

Vickers Viscount and Plane of 1919 AP17

4.05k, Skymaster and plane of 1919.

**1959, Sept. 3 Engr.** — *Perf. 13½*

**C30** AP17 3.50k steel blue 1.20 1.10
**C31** AP17 4.05k green 1.10 1.50

40th anniv. of air transportation in Iceland.

## AIR POST OFFICIAL STAMPS

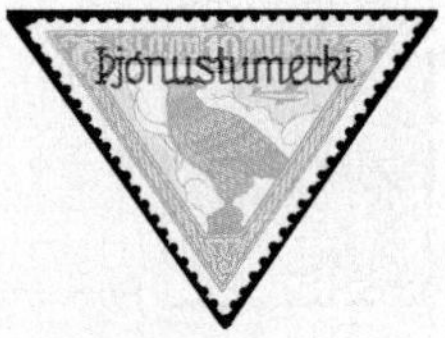


No. C3 Overprinted In Red

**1930, Jan. 1 Unwmk.** — *Perf. 12½x12*

**CO1** AP1 10a dp ultra & gray blue 30.00 *170.00*

Imperfs were privately printed.

## OFFICIAL STAMPS

For Nos. O1-O12, see note on condition before No. 1.

O1

O2

*Perf. 14x13½*

**1873 Typo. Wmk. 112**

**O1** O1 4s green *10,500.* *12,000.*
*a.* Imperf. 150.
**O2** O1 8s red lilac 750. *900.*
*a.* Imperf. 750.

*Perf. 12½*

**O3** O1 4s green 120. *525.*

The imperforate varieties lack gum.

No. O1 values are for stamps with perfs just touching the design on at least one side.

Fake and favor cancellations are often found on Nos. O1-O37. Values are considerably less than those shown.

**1876-95** — *Perf. 14x13½*

**O4** O2 3a yellow 55.00 *82.50*
**O5** O2 5a brown 13.00 *22.50*
*a.* Imperf. 450.00
**O6** O2 10a blue 95.00 21.00
*a.* 10a ultramarine 600.00 85.00
**O7** O2 16a carmine 35.00 *70.00*
**O8** O2 20a yellow green 35.00 *62.50*
**O9** O2 50a rose lilac ('95) 110.00 *115.00*
*Nos. O4-O9 (6)* 343.00 *373.50*

**1898-1902** — *Perf. 13*

**O10** O2 3a yellow 18.00 *47.50*
**O11** O2 4a gray ('01) 47.50 *60.00*
**O12** O2 10a ultra ('02) 87.50 *150.00*
*Nos. O10-O12 (3)* 153.00 *257.50*

A 5a brown and 20a yellow green, both perf. 13 with Wmk. 112, exist. They were not regularly issued.

See note after No. O30.

For overprints see Nos. O20-O30.

O3

**1902 Wmk. 113** — *Perf. 13*

**O13** O3 3a buff & black 6.25 3.75
**O14** O3 4a dp grn & blk 6.25 3.25
**O15** O3 5a org brn & blk 5.00 *5.50*
**O16** O3 10a ultra & black 5.50 *5.50*
**O17** O3 16a carmine & blk 5.00 *20.00*
**O18** O3 20a green & blk 25.00 10.00
**O19** O3 50a violet & blk 10.00 *15.00*
*Nos. O13-O19 (7)* 63.00 *63.00*

Stamps of 1876-1901 Overprinted in Black

**1902-03 Wmk. 112** — *Perf. 13*

**O20** O2 3a yellow 1.50 *3.25*
*a.* "I" before Gildi omitted 210.00
*b.* Inverted overprint 52.50 *82.50*
*c.* As "a," invtd. 250.00
*d.* Pair, one with invtd. ovpt. 225.00
*e.* '03-'03 600.00
*f.* 02'-'03 600.00
**O21** O2 4a gray 1.50 *3.25*
*a.* "I" before Gildi omitted 210.00
*b.* Inverted overprint 75.00 *97.50*
*e.* '03-'03 675.00
*f.* 02'-'03 675.00
*g.* Pair, one without ovpt. 275.00
*h.* Pair, one with invtd. ovpt. *125.00*
*i.* "L" only of "I GILDI" inverted *15,000.*
**O22** O2 5a brown 1.25 *3.25*
**O23** O2 10a ultramarine 1.25 *3.25*
*a.* "I" before Gildi omitted 325.00
*b.* Inverted overprint 67.50 *97.50*
*c.* '03-'03 525.00
*d.* 02'-'03 525.00
*e.* "L" only of "I GILDI" 60.00
*f.* As "e," inverted 525.00
*g.* "IL" only of "I GILDI" 275.00
**O24** O2 20a yel green 1.20 *30.00*
*Nos. O20-O24 (5)* 6.70 *43.00*

*Perf. 14x13½*

**O25** O2 3a yellow 400.00 *1,800.*
*a.* "02'-'03" 700.00
*b.* '03-'03 700.00
**O26** O2 5a brown 11.00 *210.00*
*a.* Inverted overprint 115.00
*b.* '03-'03 525.00
*c.* 02'-'03 525.00
*d.* "L" only of "I GILDI" inverted *15,000.*
**O27** O2 10a blue 550.00 *990.00*
*a.* "I" before Gildi omitted *30,000.*
*b.* Inverted overprint 825.00 *1,150.*
*c.* '03-'03 1,200.
*d.* 02'-'03 1,200.
**O28** O2 16a carmine 22.50 *90.00*
*a.* "I" before Gildi omitted 825.00
*b.* Double overprint 150.00
*c.* Dbl. ovpt., one inverted 525.00
*d.* Inverted overprint 240.00 *325.00*
*e.* '03-'03 900.00
*f.* '02-'03 900.00
**O29** O2 20a yel green 37.50 *120.00*
*a.* Inverted overprint 225.00 *240.00*
*b.* '03-'03 600.00
*c.* 02'-'03 600.00
**O30** O2 50a red lilac 7.50 *75.00*
*a.* "I" before Gildi omitted 60.00 135.00
*b.* Inverted overprint 225.00
*Nos. O25-O30 (6)* 1,028. *3,285.*

*Nos. O10-O12, O20-O24, O28 and O30 were reprinted in 1904. They have the watermark of 1902 (type 113) and are perf. 13. Value $70 each. Without overprint $90 each.*

Christian IX, Frederik VIII — O4

Christian X — O5

**Engraved Center**

**1907-08 Wmk. 113** — *Perf. 13*

**O31** O4 3a yellow & gray 9.50 *11.00*
**O32** O4 4a green & gray 5.00 *11.50*
**O33** O4 5a brn org & gray 15.00 5.50
**O34** O4 10a deep bl & gray 3.25 *4.25*
**O35** O4 15a lt blue & gray 6.50 *11.50*
**O36** O4 16a carmine & gray 6.50 *40.00*
**O37** O4 20a yel grn & gray 19.00 7.50
**O38** O4 50a violet & gray 10.00 *14.00*
*Nos. O31-O38 (8)* 74.75 *105.25*

**1918 Wmk. 114** — *Perf. 14x14½*

**O39** O4 15a lt bl & gray 18.00 *45.00*

**1920-30** — **Typo.**

**O40** O5 3a yellow & gray 7.00 *4.75*
**O41** O5 4a dp grn & gray 1.75 *4.50*
**O42** O5 5a orange & gray 1.75 1.50
**O43** O5 10a dk bl & gray 22.50 1.75
**O44** O5 15a lt blue & gray 1.10 *1.50*
**O45** O5 20a yel grn & gray 70.00 5.50
**O46** O5 50a violet & gray 65.00 2.75
**O47** O5 1k car & gray 65.00 2.75
**O48** O5 2k bl & blk ('30) 11.00 *25.00*
**O49** O5 5k brn & blk ('30) 57.50 *70.00*
*Nos. O40-O49 (10)* 302.60 120.00

See No. O68.

Nos. 97 and 98 Overprinted

**1922, May Wmk. 113** — *Perf. 13*

**O50** A7 2k rose, larger letters, no period 37.50 *75.00*
*a.* Smaller letters, with period 120.00 75.00
**O51** A7 5k brown 300.00 *335.00*

No. 115 Surcharged

**1923 Wmk. 114** — *Perf. 14x14½*

**O52** A8 20a on 10a red 37.50 3.00

**Parliament Millenary Issue**

#152-166 Overprinted in Red or Blue

**1930, Jan. 1 Unwmk.** — *Perf. 12½x12*

**O53** A15 3a (R) 18.00 *52.50*
**O54** A15 5a (R) 18.00 *52.50*
**O55** A15 7a (R) 18.00 *52.50*
**O56** A15 10a (Bl) 18.00 *52.50*
**O57** A15 15a (R) 18.00 *52.50*
**O58** A15 20a (Bl) 18.00 *52.50*
**O59** A15 25a (Bl) 18.00 *52.50*
**O60** A15 30a (R) 18.00 *52.50*
**O61** A15 35a (R) 18.00 *52.50*
**O62** A15 40a (Bl) 18.00 *52.50*
**O63** A15 50a (Bl) 170.00 *440.00*
**O64** A15 1k (R) 170.00 *440.00*
**O65** A15 2k (R) 225.00 *470.00*
**O66** A15 5k (Bl) 225.00 *470.00*
**O67** A15 10k (Bl) 170.00 *440.00*
*Nos. O53-O67 (15)* 1,140. *2,785.*

**Type of 1920 Issue Redrawn**

**1931 Wmk. 114** — **Typo.**

**O68** O5 20a yel grn & gray 52.50 3.75

For differences in redrawing see note after No. 187.

No. 82 Overprinted in Black

**Overprint 15mm long**

**1936, Dec. 7 Wmk. 113** — *Perf. 13*

**O69** A5 50a gray & vio 30.00 *37.50*

**Same Overprint on Nos. 180 and 115**

*Perf. 14x14½*

**Wmk. 114**

**O70** A8 7a yellow green 3.75 *32.50*
**O71** A8 10a red 15.00 2.75
*Nos. O69-O71 (3)* 48.75 *72.75*

# IFNI

'if-nē

LOCATION — An enclave in southern Morocco on the Atlantic coast
GOVT. — Spanish possession
AREA — 580 sq. mi.
POP. — 51,517 (est. 1964)
CAPITAL — Sidi Ifni

Ifni was ceded to Spain by Morocco in 1860, but the Spanish did not occupy it until 1934. Sidi Ifni was also the administrative capital for Spanish West Africa. Spain turned Ifni back to Morocco June 30, 1969.

100 Centimos = 1 Peseta

**Catalogue values for unused stamps in this country are for Never Hinged items, beginning with Scott 28 in the regular postage section, Scott B1 in the semi-postal section, and Scott C38 in the airpost section.**

Stamps of Spain, 1936-40, Overprinted in Red or Blue

**1941-42 Unwmk. *Imperf.***

| | | | | |
|---|---|---|---|---|
| 1 | A159 | 1c green | 8.50 | 6.00 |

***Perf. 10 to 11***

| | | | | |
|---|---|---|---|---|
| 2 | A160 | 2c org brn (Bl) | 8.50 | 6.00 |
| 3 | A161 | 5c gray brown | 1.25 | 1.10 |
| 5 | A161 | 10c dk car (Bl) | 5.00 | 2.25 |
| *a.* | | Red overprint | 17.50 | 8.25 |
| 6 | A161 | 15c lt green | 1.25 | 1.10 |
| 7 | A166 | 20c brt violet | 1.25 | 1.10 |
| 8 | A166 | 25c deep claret | 1.25 | 1.10 |
| 9 | A166 | 30c blue | 1.25 | 1.10 |
| 10 | A166 | 40c Prus green | 1.75 | 1.10 |
| 11 | A166 | 50c indigo | 9.25 | 2.00 |
| 12 | A166 | 70c blue | 9.25 | 5.00 |
| 13 | A166 | 1p gray black | 9.25 | 5.00 |
| 14 | A166 | 2p dull brown | 125.00 | 120.00 |
| 15 | A166 | 4p dl rose (Bl) | 550.00 | 210.00 |
| 16 | A166 | 10p light brn | 1,300. | 600.00 |
| | | *Nos. 1-16 (15)* | 2,032. | 962.85 |
| | | Set, never hinged | 3,000. | |

Counterfeit overprints exist.

Nomads — A1

Alcazaba Fortress — A3

Designs: 2c, 20c, 45c, 3p, Marksman.

**1943 Litho. *Perf. 12½***

| | | | | |
|---|---|---|---|---|
| 17 | A1 | 1c brn & lil rose | .30 | .25 |
| 18 | A1 | 2c yel grn & sl lil | .30 | .25 |
| 19 | A3 | 5c magenta & vio | .30 | .25 |
| 20 | A1 | 15c sl grn & grn | .30 | .25 |
| 21 | A1 | 20c vio & red brn | .30 | .25 |
| 22 | A1 | 40c rose vio & vio | .35 | .30 |
| 23 | A1 | 45c brn vio & red | .40 | .35 |
| 24 | A3 | 75c indigo & bl | .40 | .35 |
| 25 | A1 | 1p red & brown | 2.25 | 1.75 |
| 26 | A1 | 3p bl vio & sl grn | 4.00 | 2.75 |
| 27 | A3 | 10p blk brn & blk | 40.00 | 27.50 |
| | | *Nos. 17-27,E1 (12)* | 51.15 | 35.85 |
| | | Set, never hinged | 90.00 | |

Nos. 17-27 exist imperf. Value, set $150.

**Catalogue values for unused stamps in this section, from this point to the end of the section, are for Never Hinged items.**

**1947, Feb. *Perf. 10***

| | | | | |
|---|---|---|---|---|
| 28 | A1 | 50c Nomad family | 18.00 | .80 |

No. 28 exists imperf. Value, $50.

Stamps of Spain, 1939-48, Overprinted in Carmine

**1948, Aug. 2 *Perf. 9½x10½, 11, 13***

| | | | | |
|---|---|---|---|---|
| 29 | A161 | 5c gray brown (#664) | 4.50 | .75 |
| 30 | A194 | 15c gray green | 5.00 | .75 |
| 31 | A167 | 90c dark green (#714a) | 20.00 | 4.25 |
| 32 | A166 | 1p gray black | .70 | .30 |
| | | *Nos. 29-32 (4)* | 30.20 | 6.05 |

See Nos. 36 and 45.

**Spain Nos. 769 and 770 Overprinted in Violet Blue or Carmine**

**1949, Oct. 9 *Perf. 12½x13***

| | | | | |
|---|---|---|---|---|
| 33 | A202 | 50c red brown (VB) | 2.50 | 1.25 |
| 34 | A202 | 75c violet blue (C) | 2.50 | 1.25 |
| | | *Nos. 33-34,C40 (3)* | 8.00 | 4.00 |

75th anniv. of the UPU.

Stamps of Spain, 1938-48, Overprinted in Blue or Carmine like Nos. 29-32

***Perf. 13, 13½, 12½x13, 9½x10½***

**1949 Unwmk.**

| | | | | |
|---|---|---|---|---|
| 35 | A160 | 2c orange brn (Bl) | .30 | .25 |
| 36 | A161 | 5c gray brown (#664a) | .30 | .25 |
| 37 | A161 | 10c dk carmine (Bl) | .30 | .25 |
| 38 | A161 | 15c dk green (II) | .30 | .25 |
| 39 | A166 | 25c brown violet | .30 | .25 |
| 40 | A166 | 30c blue | .40 | .25 |
| 41 | A195 | 40c red brown | .40 | .25 |
| 42 | A195 | 45c car rose (Bl) | .70 | .30 |
| 43 | A166 | 50c indigo | .75 | .30 |
| 44 | A195 | 75c dk vio bl | .85 | .45 |
| 45 | A167 | 90c dark green (#714) | .95 | .60 |
| 47 | A167 | 1.35p purple | 5.00 | 4.50 |
| 48 | A166 | 2p dl brn | 4.75 | 2.75 |
| 49 | A166 | 4p dl rose (Bl) | 17.50 | 8.00 |
| 50 | A166 | 10p lt brn | 42.50 | 24.00 |
| | | *Nos. 35-50 (15)* | 75.30 | 42.65 |

Gen. Francisco Franco and Desert Scene A4

***Perf. 12½x13***

**1951, July 18 Photo. Unwmk.**

| | | | | |
|---|---|---|---|---|
| 51 | A4 | 50c dp org | .45 | .25 |
| 52 | A4 | 1p chocolate | 3.00 | 1.25 |
| 53 | A4 | 5p bl grn | 32.50 | 12.00 |
| | | *Nos. 51-53 (3)* | 35.95 | 13.50 |

Visit of Gen. Francisco Franco, 1950.

View of Granada and Globe — A5

**1952, Dec. 10 *Perf. 13x12½***

| | | | | |
|---|---|---|---|---|
| 54 | A5 | 5c red org | .35 | .25 |
| 55 | A5 | 35c dk ol grn | .40 | .25 |
| 56 | A5 | 60c brown | .40 | .30 |
| | | *Nos. 54-56 (3)* | 1.15 | .80 |

400th anniversary of the death of Leo Africanus (c. 1485-c. 1554), Arab traveler and scholar, author of "Descrittione dell' Africa."

Musician A6

Design: 60c, Two musicians.

**1953, June 1 *Perf. 12½x13***

| | | | | |
|---|---|---|---|---|
| 57 | A6 | 15c olive gray | .30 | .25 |
| 58 | A6 | 60c brown | .35 | .30 |
| | | *Nos. 57-58,B13-B14 (4)* | 1.30 | 1.10 |

Issued to promote child welfare.

Fish and Branched Sponges A7

15c, Fish and jellyfish.

**1953, Nov. 23**

| | | | | |
|---|---|---|---|---|
| 59 | A7 | 15c dark green | .30 | .25 |
| 60 | A7 | 60c brown | .45 | .30 |
| | | *Nos. 59-60,B15-B16 (4)* | 1.40 | 1.10 |

Colonial Stamp Day, Nov. 23, 1953.

Sea Gull — A8

Cactus — A9

25c, 60c, 2p, 5p, Salsola vermiculata.

**1954, Apr. 22 *Perf. 12½x13, 13x12½***

| | | | | |
|---|---|---|---|---|
| 61 | A8 | 5c red org | .25 | .25 |
| 62 | A9 | 10c olive | .25 | .25 |
| 63 | A9 | 25c brn car | .25 | .25 |
| 64 | A8 | 35c olive gray | .25 | .25 |
| 65 | A9 | 40c rose lilac | .25 | .25 |
| 66 | A9 | 60c dk brn | .25 | .25 |
| 67 | A8 | 1p brown | 7.25 | .70 |
| 68 | A9 | 1.25p car rose | .30 | .25 |
| 69 | A9 | 2p darp blue | .35 | .25 |
| 70 | A9 | 4.50p olive grn | .45 | .40 |
| 71 | A9 | 5p olive blk | 37.50 | 10.50 |
| | | *Nos. 61-71 (11)* | 47.35 | 13.60 |

Mother and Child
A10 A11

**1954, June 1 *Perf. 13x12½***

| | | | | |
|---|---|---|---|---|
| 72 | A10 | 15c dk gray grn | .30 | .25 |
| 73 | A11 | 60c dk brn | .35 | .30 |
| | | *Nos. 72-73,B17-B18 (4)* | 1.30 | 1.10 |

Lobster A12

Design: 60c, Hammerhead shark.

**1954, Nov. 23 *Perf. 12½x13***

| | | | | |
|---|---|---|---|---|
| 74 | A12 | 15c olive green | .35 | .25 |
| 75 | A12 | 60c rose brown | .45 | .35 |
| | | *Nos. 74-75,B19-B20 (4)* | 1.45 | 1.15 |

Issued to publicize Colonial Stamp Day.

Farmer Plowing and Statue of "Justice" A13

**1955, June 1 Photo. Unwmk.**

| | | | | |
|---|---|---|---|---|
| 76 | A13 | 50c gray olive | .35 | .30 |
| | | *Nos. 76,B21-B22 (3)* | 1.00 | .85 |

Squirrel A14

**1955, Nov. 23**

| | | | | |
|---|---|---|---|---|
| 77 | A14 | 70c yellow green | .35 | .30 |
| | | *Nos. 77,B23-B24 (3)* | 1.00 | .85 |

Issued to publicize Colonial Stamp Day.

Senecio Antheuphorbium A15

Design: 50c, Limoniastrum Ifniensis.

**1956, June 1 *Perf. 13x12½***

| | | | | |
|---|---|---|---|---|
| 78 | A15 | 20c bluish green | .35 | .25 |
| 79 | A15 | 50c brown | .40 | .35 |
| | | *Nos. 78-79,B25-B26 (4)* | 1.40 | 1.15 |

Arms of Sidi Ifni and Shepherd A16

**1956, Nov. 23 *Perf. 12½x13***

| | | | | |
|---|---|---|---|---|
| 80 | A16 | 70c light green | .35 | .25 |

Issued for Colonial Stamp Day.

Rock Doves — A17

**1957, June 1 Photo. *Perf. 13x12½***

| | | | | |
|---|---|---|---|---|
| 81 | A17 | 70c yel grn & brn | .40 | .35 |
| | | *Nos. 81,B29-B30 (3)* | 1.05 | .90 |

See No. 86.

Jackal A18

Design: 70c, Jackal's head, vert.

*Perf. 12½x13, 13x12½*

**1957, Nov. 23**

| | | | | |
|---|---|---|---|---|
| **82** | A18 | 20c emerald & lt grn | .35 | .25 |
| **83** | A18 | 70c green & brown | .45 | .35 |
| | | *Nos. 82-83,B31-B32 (4)* | 1.45 | 1.15 |

Issued for the Day of the Stamp, 1957.
See Nos. 87, B41.

Basketball Players — A19

Design: 70c, Cyclists.

**1958, June 1** *Perf. 13x12½*

| | | | | |
|---|---|---|---|---|
| **84** | A19 | 20c bluish green | .30 | .25 |
| **85** | A19 | 70c olive green | .45 | .35 |
| | | *Nos. 84-85,B36-B37 (4)* | 1.40 | 1.15 |

**Types of 1957 inscribed "Pro-Infancia 1959"**

Designs: 20c, Goat. 70c, Ewe and lamb.

**1959, June 1** *Perf. 13x12½, 12½x13*

| | | | | |
|---|---|---|---|---|
| **86** | A17 | 20c dull green | .30 | .25 |
| **87** | A18 | 70c yellow green | .40 | .35 |
| | | *Nos. 86-87,B41-B42 (4)* | 1.35 | 1.15 |

Issued to promote child welfare.

Red-legged Partridges — A20

**1960, June 10** *Perf. 13x12½*

| | | | | |
|---|---|---|---|---|
| **88** | A20 | 35c shown | .30 | .25 |
| **89** | A20 | 80c Camels | .40 | .35 |
| | | *Nos. 88-89,B46-B47 (4)* | 1.35 | 1.15 |

White Stork A21

Birds: 50c, 1.50p, 5p, European goldfinches. 75c, 2p, 10p, Skylarks, vert.

**1960** **Unwmk.** *Perf. 12½x13*

| | | | | |
|---|---|---|---|---|
| **90** | A21 | 25c violet | .25 | .25 |
| **91** | A21 | 50c olive black | .25 | .25 |
| **92** | A21 | 75c dull purple | .30 | .25 |
| **93** | A21 | 1p orange ver | .40 | .25 |
| **94** | A21 | 1.50p brt grnsh bl | .45 | .30 |
| **95** | A21 | 2p red lilac | .50 | .35 |
| **96** | A21 | 3p dark blue | .85 | .40 |
| **97** | A21 | 5p red brown | 1.40 | .65 |
| **98** | A21 | 10p olive | 5.25 | 1.75 |
| | | *Nos. 90-98 (9)* | 9.65 | 4.45 |

Map of Ifni — A22

General Franco A23

Design: 70c, Government palace.

*Perf. 13x12½, 12½x13*

**1961, Oct. 1** **Photo.**

| | | | | |
|---|---|---|---|---|
| **99** | A22 | 25c gray violet | .25 | .25 |
| **100** | A23 | 50c olive brown | .30 | .25 |
| **101** | A23 | 70c brt green | .35 | .30 |
| **102** | A23 | 1p red orange | .40 | .35 |
| | | *Nos. 99-102 (4)* | 1.30 | 1.15 |

25th anniv. of the nomination of Gen. Francisco Franco as Head of State.

Admiral Jofre Tenoria — A24

Mailman — A25

Design: 50c, Cesareo Fernandez-Duro (1830-1908), writer.

**1962, July 10** *Perf. 13x12½*

| | | | | |
|---|---|---|---|---|
| **103** | A24 | 25c dull violet | .25 | .25 |
| **104** | A24 | 50c deep blue grn | .30 | .25 |
| **105** | A24 | 1p orange brown | .35 | .35 |
| | | *Nos. 103-105 (3)* | .90 | .85 |

**1962, Nov. 23** **Unwmk.**

Stamp Day: 35c, Hands, letter and winged wheel.

| | | | | |
|---|---|---|---|---|
| **106** | A25 | 15c dark blue | .25 | .25 |
| **107** | A25 | 35c lilac rose | .35 | .30 |
| **108** | A25 | 1p rose brown | .40 | .35 |
| | | *Nos. 106-108 (3)* | 1.00 | .90 |

Golden Tower, Seville A26

Butterflies A27

**1963, Jan. 29** **Photo.**

| | | | | |
|---|---|---|---|---|
| **109** | A26 | 50c green | .30 | .25 |
| **110** | A26 | 1p brown orange | .40 | .35 |

Issued for flood relief in Seville.

**1963, July 6** *Perf. 13x12½*

Design: 50c, Butterfly and flower.

| | | | | |
|---|---|---|---|---|
| **111** | A27 | 25c deep blue | .30 | .25 |
| **112** | A27 | 50c light green | .35 | .30 |
| **113** | A27 | 1p carmine rose | .45 | .40 |
| | | *Nos. 111-113 (3)* | 1.10 | .95 |

Issued for child welfare.

Child with Flowers and Arms A28

**1963, July 12** *Perf. 12½x13*

| | | | | |
|---|---|---|---|---|
| **114** | A28 | 50c gray olive | .30 | .25 |
| **115** | A28 | 1p reddish brown | .40 | .35 |

Issued for Barcelona flood relief.

Beetle (Steraspis Speciosa) A29

Mountain Gazelle A30

Stamp Day: 50c, Grasshopper.

**1964, Mar. 6** *Perf. 13x12½*

| | | | | |
|---|---|---|---|---|
| **116** | A29 | 25c violet blue | .25 | .25 |
| **117** | A29 | 50c olive green | .35 | .30 |
| **118** | A29 | 1p red brown | .45 | .30 |
| | | *Nos. 116-118 (3)* | 1.05 | .85 |

**1964, June 1** **Photo.**

Design: 50c, Head of roebuck.

| | | | | |
|---|---|---|---|---|
| **119** | A30 | 25c brt violet | .25 | .25 |
| **120** | A30 | 50c slate blk | .35 | .25 |
| **121** | A30 | 1p orange red | .40 | .35 |
| | | *Nos. 119-121 (3)* | 1.00 | .85 |

Issued for child welfare.

Bicycle Race A31

Stamp Day: 1p, Motorcycle race.

**1964, Nov. 23** *Perf. 12½x13*

| | | | | |
|---|---|---|---|---|
| **122** | A31 | 50c brown | .30 | .25 |
| **123** | A31 | 1p orange ver | .35 | .30 |
| **124** | A31 | 1.50p Prus green | .40 | .35 |
| | | *Nos. 122-124 (3)* | 1.05 | .90 |

Man — A32

Two Boys in School — A33

Cable Cars, Sidi Ifni — A34

*Perf. 13x12½, 12½x13*

**1965, Mar. 1** **Photo.** **Unwmk.**

| | | | | |
|---|---|---|---|---|
| **125** | A32 | 50c dark green | .30 | .25 |
| **126** | A33 | 1p orange ver | .35 | .30 |
| **127** | A34 | 1.50p dark blue | .40 | .35 |
| | | *Nos. 125-127 (3)* | 1.05 | .90 |

25 years of peace after the Spanish Civil War.

Eugaster Fernandezi A35

Insect: 1p, Halter halteratus.

**1965, June 1** **Photo.** **Unwmk.**

| | | | | |
|---|---|---|---|---|
| **128** | A35 | 50c purple | .30 | .25 |
| **129** | A35 | 1p rose red | .35 | .30 |
| **130** | A35 | 1.50p violet blue | .40 | .35 |
| | | *Nos. 128-130 (3)* | 1.05 | .90 |

Issued for child welfare.

Eagle — A36

Arms of Sidi Ifni — A37

*Perf. 13x12½, 12½x13*

**1965, Nov. 23** **Photo.**

| | | | | |
|---|---|---|---|---|
| **131** | A36 | 50c dk red brown | .25 | .25 |
| **132** | A37 | 1p orange ver | .35 | .30 |
| **133** | A36 | 1.50p grnsh blue | .40 | .35 |
| | | *Nos. 131-133 (3)* | 1.00 | .90 |

Issued for Stamp Day 1965.

Jetliner over Sidi Ifni — A38

Design: 2.50p, Two 1934 biplanes, horiz.

*Perf. 13x12½, 12½x13*

**1966, June 1** **Photo.** **Unwmk.**

| | | | | |
|---|---|---|---|---|
| **134** | A38 | 1p orange brn | .30 | .30 |
| **135** | A38 | 1.50p brt blue | .50 | .40 |
| **136** | A38 | 2.50p dull violet | 2.25 | 2.00 |
| | | *Nos. 134-136 (3)* | 3.05 | 2.70 |

Issued for child welfare.

Syntomis Alicia — A39

40c, 4p, Danais chrysippus (butterfly).

**1966, Nov. 23** **Photo.** *Perf. 13*

| | | | | |
|---|---|---|---|---|
| **137** | A39 | 10c green & red | .40 | .25 |
| **138** | A39 | 40c dk brn & gldn brn | .45 | .30 |
| **139** | A39 | 1.50p violet & yel | .55 | .35 |
| **140** | A39 | 4p dk pur & brt bl | .65 | .40 |
| | | *Nos. 137-140 (4)* | 2.05 | 1.30 |

Issued for Stamp Day, 1966.

Coconut Palms — A40

Designs: 40c, 4p, Cactus.

**1967, June 1** **Photo.** *Perf. 13*

| | | | | |
|---|---|---|---|---|
| **141** | A40 | 10c dp grn & brn | .25 | .25 |
| **142** | A40 | 40c Prus grn & ocher | .25 | .25 |
| **143** | A40 | 1.50p bl grn & sepia | .35 | .30 |
| **144** | A40 | 4p sepia & ocher | .45 | .35 |
| | | *Nos. 141-144 (4)* | 1.30 | 1.15 |

Issued for child welfare.

Sidi Ifni Harbor A41

**1967, Sept. 28 Photo.** ***Perf. 12½x13***
**145** A41 1.50p grn & red brn .35 .25

Modernization of harbor installations.

Needlefish (Skipper) — A42

Fish: 1.50p, John Dory, vert. 3.50p, Gurnard (Trigla lucerna).

**1967, Nov. 23 Photo.** ***Perf. 13***
**146** A42 1p blue & green .30 .25
**147** A42 1.50p vio blk & yel .35 .25
**148** A42 3.50p brt bl & scar .45 .35
*Nos. 146-148 (3)* 1.10 .85

Issued for Stamp Day 1967.

### Zodiac Issue

Pisces — A43

Signs of the Zodiac: 1.50p, Capricorn. 2.50p, Sagittarius.

**1968, Apr. 25 Photo.** ***Perf. 13***
**149** A43 1p brt mag, *lt yel* .30 .25
**150** A43 1.50p brown, *pink* .35 .30
**151** A43 2.50p dk vio, *yel* .45 .35
*Nos. 149-151 (3)* 1.10 .90

Issued for child welfare.

Mailing a Letter A44

Designs: 1.50p, Carrier pigeon carrying letter. 2.50p, Stamp under magnifying glass.

**1968, Nov. 23 Photo.** ***Perf. 12½x13***
**152** A44 1p org yel & sl grn .25 .25
**153** A44 1.50p brt bl & vio blk .35 .30
**154** A44 2.50p emer & vio blk .45 .35
*Nos. 152-154 (3)* 1.05 .90

Issued for Stamp Day.

---

## SEMI-POSTAL STAMPS

**Catalogue values for unused stamps in this section are for Never Hinged items.**

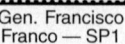

Gen. Francisco Franco — SP1

Fennec — SP2

***Perf. 13x12½***
**1950, Oct. 19 Unwmk.**
**B1** SP1 50c + 10c sepia .70 .55
**B2** SP1 1p + 25c blue 18.00 7.00
**B3** SP1 6.50p + 1.65p dl grn 7.50 3.25
*Nos. B1-B3 (3)* 26.20 10.80

The surtax was for child welfare.

**1951, Nov. 30**
**B4** SP2 5c + 5c brown .30 .25
**B5** SP2 10c + 5c red org .35 .25
**B6** SP2 60c + 15c olive brn .55 .30
*Nos. B4-B6 (3)* 1.20 .80

Colonial Stamp Day, Nov. 23, 1951.

Mother and Child — SP3

**1952, June 1**
**B7** SP3 5c + 5c brn .30 .25
**B8** SP3 50c + 10c brn blk .40 .30
**B9** SP3 2p + 30c dp bl 2.25 .85
*Nos. B7-B9 (3)* 2.95 1.40

The surtax was for child welfare.

Common Shag — SP4

**1952, Nov. 23**
**B10** SP4 5c + 5c brn .30 .25
**B11** SP4 10c + 5c brn car .30 .25
**B12** SP4 60c + 15c dk grn .50 .35
*Nos. B10-B12 (3)* 1.10 .85

Colonial Stamp Day, Nov. 23, 1952.

### Musician Type of Regular Issue

**1953, June 1** ***Perf. 12½x13***
**B13** A6 5c + 5c as No. 57 .30 .25
**B14** A6 10c + 5c as No. 58 .35 .30

The surtax was for child welfare.

### Fish Type of Regular Issue

**1953, Nov. 23**
**B15** A7 5c + 5c as No. 59 .30 .25
**B16** A7 10c + 5c as No. 60 .35 .30

Colonial Stamp Day, Nov. 23, 1953.

### Type of Regular Issue

**1954, June 1** ***Perf. 13x12½***
**B17** A10 5c + 5c org .30 .25
**B18** A11 10c + 5c rose vio .35 .30

The surtax was for child welfare.

### Type of Regular Issue

**1954, Nov. 23** ***Perf. 12½x13***
**B19** A12 5c + 5c as No. 74 .30 .25
**B20** A12 10c + 5c as No. 75 .35 .30

"Dama de Elche" Protecting Caravan SP5

**1955, June 1 Photo. Unwmk.**
**B21** A13 10c + 5c rose lilac .30 .25
**B22** SP5 25c + 10c violet .35 .30

The surtax was to help Ifni people.

### Squirrel Type of Regular Issue

Design: 15c+5c, Squirrel holding nut.

**1955, Nov. 23**
**B23** A14 5c + 5c red brown .30 .25
**B24** A14 15c + 5c olive bister .35 .30

### Type of Regular Issue

**1956, June 1** ***Perf. 13x12½***
**B25** A15 5c + 5c as No. 78 .30 .25
**B26** A15 15c + 5c as No. 79 .35 .30

The tax was for child welfare.

Dorcas Gazelles and Arms of Spain — SP6

Design: 15c+5c, Arms of Sidi Ifni, boat and woman with drum.

**1956, Nov. 23**
**B27** SP6 5c + 5c dark brown .30 .25
**B28** SP6 15c + 5c golden brn .35 .30

Issued for Colonial Stamp Day.

### Dove Type of Regular Issue

**1957, June 1 Photo.** ***Perf. 13x12½***
**B29** A17 5c + 5c as No. 81 .30 .25
**B30** A17 15c + 5c Stock doves .35 .30

The surtax was for child welfare.

### Type of Regular Issue

***Perf. 12½x13, 13x12½***
**1957, Nov. 23 Photo. Unwmk.**
**B31** A18 10c + 5c as No. 82 .30 .25
**B32** A18 15c + 5c as No. 83 .35 .30

Swallows and Arms of Valencia and Sidi Ifni — SP7

**1958, Mar. 6** ***Perf. 12½x13***
**B33** SP7 10c + 5c org brn .30 .25
**B34** SP7 15c + 10c bister .35 .25
**B35** SP7 50c + 10c brn olive .40 .30
*Nos. B33-B35 (3)* 1.05 .80

The surtax was to aid the victims of the Valencia flood, Oct. 1957.

### Sport Type of Regular Issue, 1958

**1958, June 1 Photo.** ***Perf. 13x12½***
**B36** A19 10c + 5c as No. 84 .30 .25
**B37** A19 15c + 5c as No. 85 .35 .30

The surtax was for child welfare.

Guitarfish — SP8

Sailboats SP9

Stamp Day: 10c+5c, Spotted dogfish.

***Perf. 13x12½, 12½x13***
**1958, Nov. 23**
**B38** SP9 10c + 5c brn red .30 .25
**B39** SP8 25c + 10c dull vio .35 .25
**B40** SP9 50c + 10c olive .40 .30
*Nos. B38-B40 (3)* 1.05 .80

### Type of 1957 and

Donkey and Man — SP10

Design: 10c+5c, Ewe and lamb.

***Perf. 12½x13, 13x12½***
**1959, June 1 Photo. Unwmk.**
**B41** A18 10c + 5c lt red brn .30 .25
**B42** SP10 15c + 5c golden brn .35 .30

The surtax was for child welfare.

Soccer — SP11

Designs: 20c+5c, Soccer players. 50c+20c, Javelin thrower.

**1959, Nov. 23** ***Perf. 13x12½***
**B43** SP11 10c + 5c fawn .30 .25
**B44** SP11 20c + 5c slate green .35 .30
**B45** SP11 50c + 20c olive gray .40 .35
*Nos. B43-B45 (3)* 1.05 .90

Issued for the day of the Stamp, 1959.
See Nos. B52-B54.

### Type of Regular Issue, 1960

**1960, June 10** ***Perf. 13x12½***
**B46** A20 10c + 5c as No. 89 .30 .25
**B47** A20 15c + 5c Wild boars .35 .30

The surtax was for child welfare.

Santa Maria del Mar — SP12

Stamp Day: 20c+5c, 50c+20c, New school building, horiz.

***Perf. 13x12½, 12½x13***
**1960, Dec. 29 Photo.**
**B48** SP12 10c + 5c org brn .30 .25
**B49** SP12 20c + 5c dk sl grn .30 .25
**B50** SP12 30c + 10c red brn .35 .30
**B51** SP12 50c + 20c sepia .35 .30
*Nos. B48-B51 (4)* 1.30 1.10

### Type of 1959 inscribed: "Pro-Infancia 1961"

Designs: 10c+5c, 80c+20c, Pole vaulting, horiz. 25c+10c, Soccer player.

***Perf. 12½x13, 13x12½***
**1961, June 21 Unwmk.**
**B52** SP11 10c + 5c rose brn .30 .25
**B53** SP11 25c + 10c gray vio .35 .25
**B54** SP11 80c + 20c dk green .40 .30
*Nos. B52-B54 (3)* 1.05 .80

The surtax was for child welfare.

Camel Rider and Truck SP13

Stamp Day: 25c+10c, 1p+10c, Ship in Sidi Ifni harbor.

**1961, Nov. 23** *Perf. 12½x13*

| | | | | |
|---|---|---|---|---|
| **B55** | SP13 | 10c + 5c rose brn | .30 | .25 |
| **B56** | SP13 | 25c + 10c dk pur | .30 | .25 |
| **B57** | SP13 | 30c + 10c dk red brn | .35 | .30 |
| **B58** | SP13 | 1p + 10c red org | .35 | .35 |
| | | *Nos. B55-B58 (4)* | 1.30 | 1.15 |

## AIR POST STAMPS

Stamps formerly listed as Nos. C1-C29 were privately overprinted. These include 1936 stamps of Spain overprinted "VIA AEREA" and plane, and 1939 stamps of Spain, type AP30, overprinted "IFNI" or "Territorio de Ifni."

Oasis
AP1

The Sanctuary
AP2

**1943 Unwmk. Litho.** *Perf. 12½*

| | | | | |
|---|---|---|---|---|
| **C30** | AP2 | 5c cer & vio brn | .35 | .25 |
| **C31** | AP1 | 25c yel grn & ol grn | .35 | .25 |
| **C32** | AP2 | 50c ind & turq grn | .45 | .35 |
| **C33** | AP1 | 1p pur & grnsh bl | .50 | .35 |
| **C34** | AP2 | 1.40p gray grn & bl | .55 | .35 |
| **C35** | AP1 | 2p mag & org brn | 1.50 | 1.25 |
| **C36** | AP2 | 5p brn & pur | 2.25 | 1.75 |
| **C37** | AP1 | 6p brt bl & gray grn | 35.00 | 30.00 |
| | | *Nos. C30-C37 (8)* | 40.95 | 34.55 |
| | | Set, never hinged | 80.00 | |

Nos. C30-C37 exist imperforate. Value, set $115.

**Catalogue values for unused stamps in this section, from this point to the end of the section, are for Never Hinged items.**

**Type of Spain, 1939-47, Overprinted in Carmine**

**1947, Nov. 29**

| | | | | |
|---|---|---|---|---|
| **C38** | AP30 | 5c dull yellow | 2.75 | .85 |
| **C39** | AP30 | 10c dk bl green | 2.75 | .85 |

Spain No. C126 Overprinted in Carmine like Nos. 33-34

**1949, Oct. 9** *Perf. 12½x13*

| | | | | |
|---|---|---|---|---|
| **C40** | A202 | 4p dk olive grn | 3.00 | 1.50 |

75th anniv. of the UPU.

Spain, Nos. C110 and C112 to C116, Overprinted in Blue or Carmine like Nos. 29-32

**1949** *Perf. 10*

| | | | | |
|---|---|---|---|---|
| **C41** | AP30 | 25c redsh brn (Bl) | .65 | .25 |
| **C42** | AP30 | 50c brown | .75 | .25 |
| **C43** | AP30 | 1p chalky blue | .85 | .25 |
| **C44** | AP30 | 2p lt gray grn | 5.00 | .85 |
| **C45** | AP30 | 4p gray blue | 13.00 | 4.50 |
| **C46** | AP30 | 10p brt purple | 17.50 | 8.75 |
| | | *Nos. C41-C46 (6)* | 37.75 | 14.85 |

Lope Sancho de Valenzuela and Sheik — AP3

Woman Holding Dove — AP4

**1950, Nov. 23 Photo.** *Perf. 13x12½*

| | | | | |
|---|---|---|---|---|
| **C47** | AP3 | 5p brown black | 3.25 | .85 |

Stamp Day, Nov. 23, 1950.

**1951, Apr. 22 Engr.** *Perf. 10*

| | | | | |
|---|---|---|---|---|
| **C48** | AP4 | 5p red | 24.00 | 8.25 |

500th anniversary of the birth of Queen Isabella I of Spain.

The majority of this issue are poorly centered. Values are for very fine examples.

Ferdinand the Catholic — AP5

*Perf. 13x12½*

**1952, July 18 Photo. Unwmk.**

| | | | | |
|---|---|---|---|---|
| **C49** | AP5 | 5p brown | 32.00 | 8.25 |

500th anniv. of the birth of Ferdinand the Catholic of Spain.

Plane and Mountain Gazelle — AP6

**1953, Apr. 1**

| | | | | |
|---|---|---|---|---|
| **C50** | AP6 | 60c light grn | .40 | .30 |
| **C51** | AP6 | 1.20p brn car | .45 | .30 |
| **C52** | AP6 | 1.60p lt brown | .50 | .35 |
| **C53** | AP6 | 2p deep blue | 3.50 | .50 |
| **C54** | AP6 | 4p grnsh blk | 2.00 | .65 |
| **C55** | AP6 | 10p brt red vio | 11.00 | 2.00 |
| | | *Nos. C50-C55 (6)* | 17.85 | 4.10 |

## SPECIAL DELIVERY STAMPS

**Inscribed: "URGENTE"**

**1943** *Perf. 12½*

| | | | | |
|---|---|---|---|---|
| **E1** | A3 | 25c slate green & car | 2.25 | 1.60 |

Spain, No. E20, Overprinted in Blue like Nos. 29-32

**1949 Unwmk.** *Perf. 10*

| | | | | |
|---|---|---|---|---|
| **E2** | SD10 | 25c carmine | .35 | .25 |

# INDIA

'in-dē-ə

LOCATION — Southern, central Asia
GOVT. — Republic
AREA — 1,266,732 sq. mi.
POP. — 1,000,848,550 (1999 est.)
CAPITAL — New Delhi

On August 15, 1947, India was divided into two self-governing dominions: Pakistan and India. India became a republic in 1950.

The stamps of pre-partition India fall into three groups:

1) Issues inscribed simply "East India" (to 1881) and "India" (from 1882), for use mainly in British India proper, but available and valid throughout the country;

2) Issues as above and overprinted with one of the names of the six "Convention" states (Chamba, Faridkot, Gwalior, Jind, Nabha and Patiala) which had a postal convention with British India, for use in these states.

3) Issues of the feudatory states, over which the British India government exercised little internal control, valid for use only within the states issuing them.

12 Pies = 1 Anna
16 Annas = 1 Rupee
100 Naye Paise = 1 Rupee (1957)
100 Paise = 1 Rupee (1964)

**Catalogue values for unused stamps in this country are for Never Hinged items, beginning with Scott 168 in the regular postage section, Scott C7 in the air post section, Scott M44 in the military section, Scott O113 in the official section, Scott RA1 in the postal tax section, Scott 51 in Hyderabad regular issues, Scott O54 in Hyderabad officials, Scott 49 in Jaipur regular issues, Scott O30 in Jaipur officials, Scott 39 in Soruth regular issues and Scott O19 in Soruth official**

**All of the values are for Never Hinged for all of the items in the sections for the International Commission in Indo-China, Jasdan, Rajasthan, and Travancore-Cochin.**

**Watermarks**

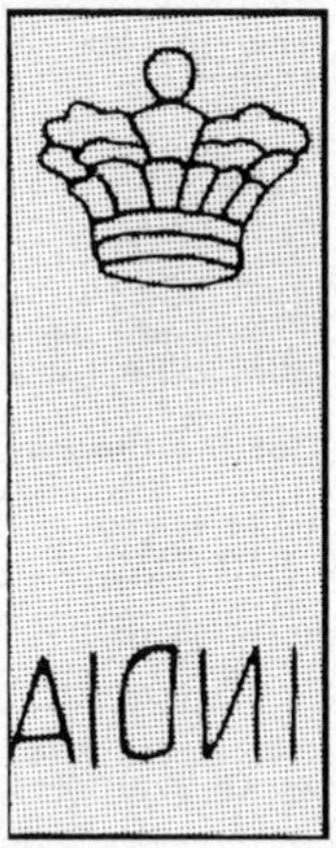

Wmk. 36 — Crown and INDIA

Wmk. 37 — Coat of Arms in Sheet. (Reduced illustration. Watermark covers a large section of the sheet.)

Wmk. 38 — Elephant's Head

Wmk. 39 — Star

Wmk. 40

Wmk. 41 — Small Umbrella

Wmk. 42 — Urdu Characters

Wmk. 43 — Shell

Wmk. 196 — Multiple Stars

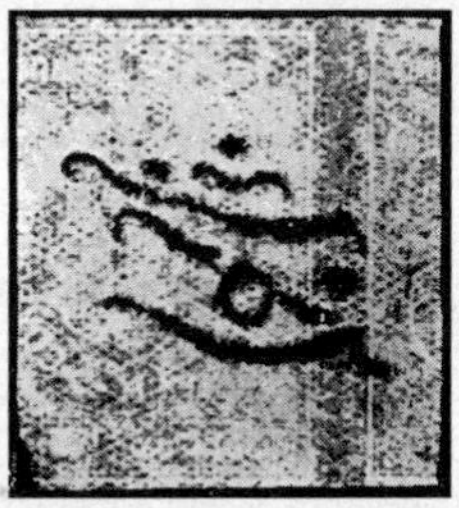

Wmk. 211 — Urdu Characters

Wmk. 294 — Letters and Ornaments in Sheet (size reduced)

Wmk. 324 — Asoka Pillar, Multiple

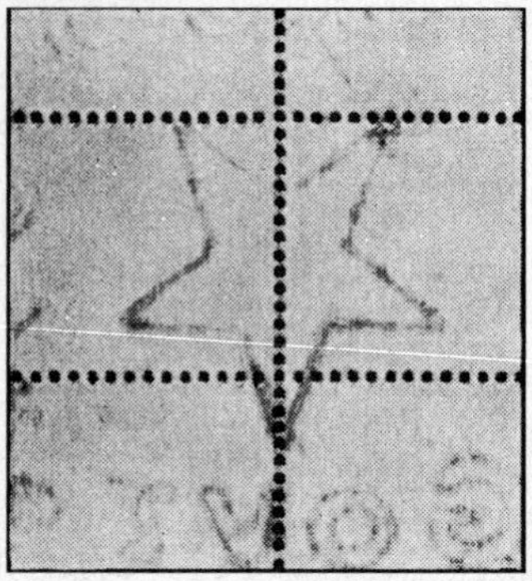

Wmk. 360 — Star and GOVT INDIA

## SCINDE DISTRICT POST

A1

**1852, July 1 Embossed *Imperf.***

**A1** A1 ½a *white* 10,000. 1,600.
**A2** A1 ½a blue 40,000. 7,250.
**A3** A1 ½a *red* 105,000. 17,500.

Obsolete October, 1854.

Nos. A1-A3 were issued without gum. No. A3 is embossed on red wafer. It is usually found with cracks and these examples are worth somewhat less than the values given, depending on the degree of cracking.

## GENERAL ISSUES

Unused stamps of India are valued with original gum as defined in the catalogue introduction except for Nos. 1-7 which are valued without gum.

### East India Company

A1

A2

A3

A4

A5

Queen Victoria

**Litho.; Typo. (#5)**

**1854 Wmk. 37 *Imperf.***

**1** A1 ½a red 1,200.
**2** A2 ½a blue 85.00 30.00
*a.* ½a deep blue 95.00 35.00
*b.* Printed on both sides *11,000.*
**4** A3 1a red 100.00 47.50
*a.* 1a scarlet 175.00 52.50
**5** A4 2a green 120.00 32.50
*a.* Half used as 1a on cover *200,000.*
**6** A5 4a red & blue 4,500. 500.00
*a.* 4a deep red & blue 4,500. 575.00
Cut to shape 42.50
*c.* Head inverted *225,000.*
As "c," cut to shape *165,000.*
*e.* Double impression of head *6,250.*

No. 1 was not placed in use.

Nos. 2, 4, 5 and 6 are known with unofficial perforation.

There are 3 dies of No. 2, and 2 dies of No. 4, showing slight differences.

There are 4 dies of the head and 2 dies of the frame of No. 6.

No. 5 is known with the watermark having the words "One Anna" in place of the lions and shield, with Urdu and Bengali characters. Values: $625 unused; $450 used.

Beware of forgeries.

A6

**1855**

**7** A6 1a red 1,300. 175.00

No. 7 was printed from a lithographic transfer made from the original die retouched. The lines of the bust at the lower left are nearly straight and meet in a point.

Beware of forgeries.

Nos. 9-35 are normally found with very heavy cancellations, and values are for stamps so canceled. Lightly canceled stamps are seldom seen. The same holds true for Nos. O1-O26.

Diadem includes Maltese Crosses — A7

**1855-64 Unwmk. Typo. *Perf. 14***
**Blue Glazed Paper**

**9** A7 4a black 725.00 22.50
*a.* Imperf., pair *5,500.* *5,500.*
*b.* Half used as 2a on cover *12,000.*
**10** A7 8a rose 650.00 19.00
*a.* Imperf., pair 3,000. —
*b.* Half used as 4a on cover *80,000.*

See #11-18, 20, 22-25, 31. For overprints see #O1-O5, O7-O9, O16-O19, O22-O24.

**1855-64 White Paper**

**11** A7 ½a blue 95.00 4.50
*a.* Imperf., pair 475.00 *1,750.*
**12** A7 1a brown 80.00 3.00
*a.* Imperf., pair 800.00 *2,200.*
*b.* Vert. pair, imperf between
*c.* Half used as ½a on cover *85,000.*
**13** A7 2a dull rose 750.00 37.50
*a.* Imperf., pair 2,500. 2,000.
**14** A7 2a yellow green 725.00 825.00
*a.* Imperf., pair 2,000.
**15** A7 2a buff 450.00 37.50
*a.* 2a orange 700.00 45.00
*b.* Imperf., pair 1,750. 3,250.
**16** A7 4a black 450.00 10.00
*a.* Imperf., pair 2,750. 2,750.
*b.* Diagonal half used as 2a on cover *35,000.*
**17** A7 4a green ('64) 1,750. 45.00
**18** A7 8a rose 600.00 27.50
*a.* Half used as 4a on cover *80,000.*

No. 14 was not regularly issued. See note after No. 25.

**Many stamps of types A7-A90 are overprinted "Service" or "On H. M. S." For these, see listings of Official stamps.**

### Crown Colony

Queen Victoria — A8

**1860-64 Unwmk. *Perf. 14***

**19** A8 8p lilac 55.00 6.00
*a.* Diagonal half used as 4p on cover *85,000.*
*b.* Imperf., pair 4,000. *5,000.*
**19C** A8 8p lilac, *bluish* 275.00 100.00

See #21. For overprint see #O6 and footnote after #O4.

**1865-67 Wmk. 38**

**20** A7 ½a blue 19.00 1.25
*a.* Imperf., pair 1,600.
**21** A8 8p lilac 10.00 *12.00*
**22** A7 1a brown 9.00 1.50
**23** A7 2a brownish orange 27.50 2.00
*a.* 2a yellow 175.00 7.00
*b.* Imperf., pair 4,250.
**24** A7 4a green 575.00 27.50
**25** A7 8a rose 2,000. 85.00

No. 21 was variously surcharged locally, "NINE" or "NINE PIE," to indicate that it was being sold for 9 pies (the soldier's letter rate had been raised from 8 to 9 pies). These surcharges were made without government authorization.

Stamps of types A7 and A9 overprinted with crown and surcharged with new values were for use in Straits Settlements.

A9

A10

Diadem: Rows of pearls & diamonds — A11

FOUR ANNAS

Type I — Slanting line at corner of mouth extends downward only. Shading about mouth and chin. Pointed chin.

Type II — Line at corner of mouth extends both up and down. Upper lip and chin are defined by a colored line. Rounded chin.

**1866-68**

**26** A9 4a green, type I 95.00 4.25
**26B** A9 4a blue grn, type II 30.00 3.50
**27** A10 6a8p slate 70.00 27.50
*a.* Imperf., pair 3,000.
**28** A11 8a rose ('68) 45.00 7.00
*Nos. 26-28 (4)* 240.00 42.25

Type A11 is a redrawing of type A7. Type A7 has Maltese crosses in the diadem, while type A11 has shaded lozenges.

For overprints see #O10, O20-O21, O25-O26.

For designs A9-A85 overprinted CHAMBA, FARIDKOT, GWALIOR, JIND (JHIND, JEEND), NABHA, PATIALA (PUTTIALLA), see the various Convention States.

A12

SIX ANNAS
Type I — "POSTAGE" 3½mm high
Type II — "POSTAGE" 2½mm high

Blue Glazed Paper
Green Overprint
***Perf. 14 Vert.***

**1866, June 28 Wmk. 36**

**29** A12 6a violet, type I 1,000. 140.00
*a.* Inverted overprint *14,000.*
**30** A12 6a violet, type II 1,850. 175.00

Nos. 29 and 30 were made from revenue stamps with the labels at top and bottom cut off. Most and sometimes all of the watermark was removed with the labels.

These stamps are often found with cracked surface or scuffs. Such examples sell for somewhat less.

A13

A14

A15

A16

**1873-76 Wmk. 38 *Perf. 14***

**31** A7 ½a blue, redrawn 7.50 1.00
**32** A13 9p lilac ('74) 19.00 19.00
**33** A14 6a bister ('76) 8.50 2.50
**34** A15 12a red brown ('76) 12.00 *27.50*
**35** A16 1r slate ('74) 65.00 30.00
*Nos. 31-35 (5)* 112.00 80.00

In the redrawn ½ anna the lines of the mouth are more deeply cut, making the lips appear fuller and more open, and the nostril is defined by a curved line.

Victorian and Edwardian stamps overprinted "Postal Service" and new denominations were customs fee due stamps, not postage stamps.

### Empire

A17 A18

A19 A20

A21 A22

A23 A24

A25 A26

A27

**1882-87** **Wmk. 39**

**36** A17 ½a green 4.50 .25
*a.* Double impression 750.00 *1,000.*
**37** A18 9p rose 1.10 *2.25*
**38** A19 1a maroon 5.25 .35
*a.* 1a violet brown 5.25 .35
**39** A20 1a6p bister brown 1.10 *1.40*
**40** A21 2a ultra 4.00 .35
*a.* Double impression 1,050. *1,400.*
**41** A22 3a brown org 9.50 1.75
*a.* 3a orange 14.00 6.25
**42** A23 4a olive green 15.00 1.60
**43** A24 4a6p green 30.00 5.50
**44** A25 8a red violet 27.50 2.25
*a.* 8a rose lilac 25.00 2.25
**45** A26 12a violet, *red* 8.00 3.50
**46** A27 1r gray 27.50 6.00
*Nos. 36-46 (11)* 133.45 25.20

A 6a die essay was prepared, but no stamps were printed.

A postal counterfeit exists of No. 46. Examples are scarce.

No. 40a used value is for copy with postal cancellation.

See Nos. 56-58. For surcharges see Nos. 47, 53 and British East Africa No. 59. For overprints see Nos. M2-M4, M6-M9, Gwalior Nos. O1-O5.

Beginning with the 1882-87 issue, higher denomination stamps exist used for telegrams. The telegraph cancellation has concentric circles. These sell for 10-15% of the postally used values.

No. 43 Surcharged

**1891, Jan. 1**

**47** A24 2½a on 4a6p green 4.00 .65

A28 A29

**1892**

**48** A28 2a6p green 3.25 .45
**49** A29 1r aniline car & grn 17.50 2.25

See No. 59. For overprints see Nos. M5, M10 and Gwalior No. O6.

Queen Victoria
A30 A31

**1895, Sept. 1**

**50** A30 2r brown & rose 42.50 12.50
**51** A30 3r green & brown 37.50 11.00
**52** A30 5r violet & ultra 47.50 30.00
*Nos. 50-52 (3)* 127.50 53.50

Used high values such as Nos. 50-52, 71-76, 95-98, 124-125, as well as similar high value official issues are for postally used examples. Stamps bearing telegraph or revenue cancellations sell for much lower prices. Most telegraph cancellations on issues of Edward VII and George V can be recognized by the appearance of "T," "TEL" or "GTO" or if they contain the concentric circles of a target.

No. 36 Surcharged

**1898**

**53** A17 ¼a on ½a green .25 *.55*
*a.* Double surcharge 250.00
*b.* Double impression of stamp 260.00

For #61, 81 with this overprint see #77, 105.

**1899**

**54** A31 3p carmine rose .45 .25

For overprint see No. M1, Gwalior No. O11.

**1900**

**55** A31 3p gray .80 *1.40*
**56** A17 ½a light green 1.75 .50
**57** A19 1a carmine rose 2.50 .25
**58** A21 2a violet 4.50 2.50
**59** A28 2a6p ultramarine 3.75 4.25
*Nos. 55-59 (5)* 13.30 8.90

For overprints see Nos. M11, Gwalior O7-O10.

Edward VII — A32 A33

A34 A35

A36 A37

A38 A39

A40 A41

A42 A43

**1902-09**

**60** A32 3p gray 1.10 .25
**61** A33 ½a green 1.75 .25
*a.* Booklet pane of 6 ('04) 32.50
**62** A34 1a carmine rose 1.60 .25
*a.* Booklet pane of 6 ('04) 92.50
**63** A35 2a violet 4.25 .45
**64** A36 2a6p ultra 5.00 .65
**65** A37 3a brown org 5.00 .65
**66** A38 4a olive green 3.25 .65
**67** A39 6a bister 12.50 4.75
**68** A40 8a red violet 8.75 1.10
**69** A41 12a violet, *red* 9.50 2.25
**70** A42 1r car rose & grn 6.75 .75
**71** A43 2r brown & rose 47.50 4.50
**72** A43 3r green & brn ('04) 30.00 20.00
**73** A43 5r violet & ultra ('04) 72.50 40.00
**74** A43 10r carmine rose & green ('09) 125.00 30.00
**75** A43 15r olive gray & ultra ('09) 175.00 45.00
**76** A43 25r ultra & org brown 925.00 925.00
Telegraph cancel 300.00
*Nos. 60-75 (16)* 509.45 151.50

For overprints and surcharge see #M12-M20, O33, O37-O44, O47-O51, O67-O69, O73, Gwalior O12-O18.

No. 61 Surcharged Like No. 53

**1905**

**77** A33 ¼a on ½a green .60 .25
*a.* Inverted surcharge 925.00

A44 A45

**1906**

**78** A44 ½a green 3.25 .25
*a.* Booklet pane of 4 17.50
**79** A45 1a carmine rose 1.90 .25
*a.* Booklet pane of 4 25.00

For overprints see #O45-O46, Gwalior Nos. O19-O20.

A46 A47

A48 A49

A50 A51

A52 A53

A54 A55

George V — A56

**1911-23** **Wmk. 39**

**80** A46 3p gray 1.50 .25
*a.* Booklet pane of 4 25.00
**81** A47 ½a green 2.25 .25
*a.* Double impression 175.00
*b.* Booklet pane of 4 21.00
**82** A48 1a carmine rose 2.75 .25
*a.* Printed on both sides
*b.* Booklet pane of 4 35.00
**83** A48 1a dk brown ('22) .85 .25
*a.* Booklet pane of 4 42.50
**84** A49 2a dull violet 3.50 .40
*a.* Booklet pane of 4 42.50
**85** A50 2a6p ultramarine 2.90 *3.25*
**86** A51 3a brown org 4.25 .25
**87** A51 3a ultra ('23) 13.00 .65
**88** A52 4a olive green 8.00 .55
**89** A53 6a yel bister 4.25 1.50
**90** A53 6a bister ('15) 4.25 1.10
**91** A54 8a red violet 6.25 1.25
**92** A55 12a claret 6.50 2.40
**93** A56 1r grn & red brn 19.00 1.75
**94** A56 2r brn & car rose 22.50 1.90
**95** A56 5r vio & ultra 55.00 7.00
**96** A56 10r car rose & grn 82.50 13.00
**97** A56 15r ol grn & ultra 115.00 26.00
**98** A56 25r ultra & brn org 190.00 37.50
*Nos. 80-98 (19)* 544.25 99.50

See #106-108, 110-111, 113-125. For surcharges and overprints see #104-105, M23-M25, M27, M29-M37, M39-M43, O52-O66, O70-O71, O74, O78-O81, O85, O87-O92, Gwalior O28-O29.

Nos. 93-98 also were used to pay for radio licenses, and stamps so used include "WIRELESS" in the cancel. Used values so canceled are worth 10-15% of the values shown, which are for postally used examples.

A57

**1913-26**
**99** A57 2a6p ultramarine 2.90 .25
**100** A57 2a6p brown org ('26) 6.00 6.00

See #112. For overprints see #M28, M38.

"One and Half" — A58

"One and a Half" — A59

**1919**
**101** A58 1½a chocolate 3.75 .45
*a.* Booklet pane of 4 35.00

For overprint and surcharge see Nos. M26, O75.

**1921-26**
**102** A59 1½a chocolate 3.50 *4.75*
**103** A59 1½a rose ('26) 3.25 .35

See No. 109. For surcharge see #O76.

Type of 1911-26 Surcharged

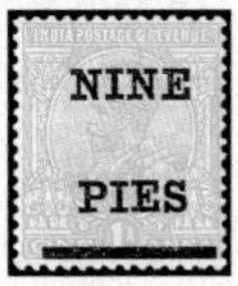


**1921**
**104** A48 9p on 1a rose .90 .35
*a.* Surcharged "NINE-NINE" 80.00 *150.00*
*b.* Surcharged "PIES-PIES" 80.00 *150.00*
*c.* Double surcharge 175.00 *210.00*
*e.* Booklet pane of 4 27.50

Forgeries exist of Nos. 104a-104c.

No. 81 Surcharged Like No. 53

**1922**
**105** A47 ¼a on ½a green .60 .40
*a.* Inverted surcharge 10.00
*b.* Pair, one without surcharge 240.00

### Types of 1911-26 Issues

**1926-36** **Wmk. 196**
**106** A46 3p slate .35 .25
**107** A47 ½a green 1.40 .25
**108** A48 1a dark brown .55 .25
*a.* Tete beche pair 1.50 *11.00*
*b.* Booklet pane of 4 16.00
**109** A59 1½a car rose ('29) 3.50 .25
**110** A49 2a dull violet 2.00 .25
*a.* Booklet pane of 4 32.50
**111** A49 2a ver ('34) 4.00 .55
*a.* Small die ('36) 5.00 .35
**112** A57 2a6p buff 2.50 .25
**113** A51 3a ultramarine 11.50 1.25
**114** A51 3a blue ('30) 10.00 .25
**115** A51 3a car rose ('32) 9.75 .25
**116** A52 4a olive green 1.60 .25
**117** A53 6a bister ('35) 9.50 2.00
**118** A54 8a red violet 4.25 .25
**119** A55 12a claret 5.25 .35
**120** A56 1r green & brown 5.50 .50
**121** A56 2r brn org & car rose 15.00 .85
**122** A56 5r dk vio & ultra 30.00 1.40
**123** A56 10r carmine & grn 62.50 3.50
**124** A56 15r ol grn & ultra 28.00 32.50
**125** A56 25r blue & ocher 115.00 40.00
*Nos. 106-125 (20)* 322.15 85.40

No. 111 measures 19x22½mm, while the small die, No. 111a, measures 18½x22mm.
For overprints see Gwalior #O30-O39, O44-O45.

A60

A61

**1926-32** **Typo.**
**126** A60 2a dull violet .55 .25
*a.* Tete beche pair 10.00 37.50
*b.* 2a rose violet .45 .25
*c.* Booklet pane of 4 19.00
**127** A60 2a vermilion ('32) 11.00 7.00
**128** A61 4a olive green 6.25 .25
*Nos. 126-128 (3)* 17.80 7.50

For overprints see #O82-O83, O86, Gwalior O33-O34.

Fortress of Purana Qila — A62

George V Flanked by Dominion Columns A67

½a, War Memorial Arch. 1a, Council Building. 2a, Viceroy's House. 3a, Parliament Building.

**Wmk. 196 Sideways**

**1931, Feb. 9** **Litho.** ***Perf. 13½x14***
**129** A62 ¼a brown & ol grn 3.00 4.50
**130** A62 ½a green & violet 1.75 .60
**131** A62 1a choc & red vio 1.75 .30
**132** A62 2a blue & green 2.25 1.50
**133** A62 3a car & choc 5.25 3.00
**134** A67 1r violet & green 13.50 *30.00*
*Nos. 129-134 (6)* 27.50 39.90
Set, never hinged 66.00

Change of the seat of Government from Calcutta to New Delhi.

A68

A69

A70

**Wmk. 196**

**1932, Apr. 22** **Litho.** ***Perf. 14***
**135** A68 9p dark green 1.90 .25
**136** A69 1a3p violet .95 .25
**137** A70 3a6p deep blue 4.75 .25
*Nos. 135-137 (3)* 7.60 .75

No. 135 exists both litho. and typo.
For overprints see Nos. O94, O96, O104 and Gwalior #O41 and O43.

A71

A72

**1934** **Typo.**
**138** A71 ½a green 5.75 .25
**139** A72 1a dark brown 4.00 .25

For overprints see Nos. O93, O95 and Gwalior #O40 and O42.

### Silver Jubilee Issue

Gateway of India, Bombay A73

Designs: 9p, Victoria Memorial, Calcutta. 1a, Rameswaram Temple, Madras. 1¼a, Jain Temple, Calcutta. 2½a, Taj Mahal, Agra. 3½a, Golden Temple, Amritsar. 8a, Pagoda, Mandalay.

**Wmk. 196 Sideways**

**1935** **Litho.** ***Perf. 13½x14***
**142** A73 ½a lt green & black 1.50 .55
**143** A73 9p dull green & blk 1.50 .55
**144** A73 1a brown & black 2.25 .55
**145** A73 1¼a violet & black 1.00 .55
**146** A73 2½a brown org & blk 3.25 1.10
**147** A73 3½a blue & black 6.50 2.50
**148** A73 8a rose lilac & blk 7.25 6.00
*Nos. 142-148 (7)* 23.25 11.80
Set, never hinged 32.00

25th anniv. of the reign of George V.

King George VI
A80 A82

Dak Runner A81

Mail transport: 2a6p, Dak bullock cart. 3a, Dak tonga. 3a6p, Dak camel. 4a, Mail train. 6a, Mail steamer. 8a, Mail truck. 12a, 14a, Mail plane.

***Perf. 13½x14 or 14x13½***

**1937-40** **Typo.** **Wmk. 196**
**150** A80 3p slate .40 .25
**151** A80 ½a brown 1.10 .25
**152** A80 9p green 3.00 .30
**153** A80 1a carmine .35 .25
*a.* Tete beche pair 3.50 2.10
*b.* Booklet pane of 4 5.25
**154** A81 2a scarlet 2.10 .35
**155** A81 2a6p purple .65 .30
**156** A81 3a yellow green 3.75 .35
**157** A81 3a6p ultramarine 2.50 .60
**158** A81 4a dark brown 10.00 .30
**159** A81 6a peacock blue 10.00 .95
**160** A81 8a blue violet 6.00 .60
**161** A81 12a car lake 13.00 1.25
**161A** A81 14a rose vio ('40) 15.00 1.50
**162** A82 1r brown & slate .90 .25
**163** A82 2r dk brn & dk violet 3.25 .40
**164** A82 5r dp ultra & dk green 14.00 .70
**165** A82 10r rose car & dk violet 14.00 1.10
**166** A82 15r dk green & dk brown 70.00 *90.00*
**167** A82 25r dk vio & blue violet 100.00 24.00
*Nos. 150-167 (19)* 270.00 *123.70*
Set, never hinged 580.00

The King's portrait is larger on No. 161A than on other stamps of type A81.
For overprints see Nos. O97-O103, Gwalior Nos. O48-O51.

**Catalogue values for unused stamps in this section, from this point to the end of the section, are for Never Hinged items.**

A83

A84

A85

***Perf. 13½x14***

**1941-43** **Typo.** **Wmk. 196**
**168** A83 3p slate ('42) 1.00 .25
**169** A83 ½a rose vio ('42) 3.50 .25
**170** A83 9p light green 3.50 .25
**171** A83 1a car rose ('43) 3.50 .25
**172** A84 1a3p bister 3.50 .25
**172A** A84 1½a dark pur ('42) 4.00 .25
**173** A84 2a scarlet 5.00 .25
**174** A84 3a violet 10.00 .25
**175** A84 3½a ultramarine 3.50 .65
**176** A85 4a chocolate 2.50 .25
**177** A85 6a peacock blue 11.50 .25
**178** A85 8a blue violet 5.00 .65
**179** A85 12a carmine lake 10.50 1.10
*Nos. 168-179 (13)* 67.00 4.90

Early printings of the 1½a and 3a were lithographed.
For surcharge see No. 199.

For stamps with this overprint, or a smaller type, see Oman (Muscat).

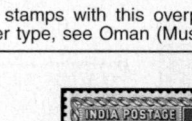

Symbols of Victory A86

**1946, Jan. 2** **Litho.** ***Perf. 13***
**195** A86 9p green .80 1.10
**196** A86 1½a dull purple .45 .40
**197** A86 3½a ultramarine 1.00 1.00
**198** A86 12a brown lake 2.50 1.10
*Nos. 195-198 (4)* 4.75 3.60

Victory of the Allied Nations in WWII.

No. 172 Surcharged With New Value and Bars

**1946, Aug. 8** ***Perf. 13½x14***
**199** A84 3p on 1a3p bister .35 .25

### Dominion of India

Asoka Pillar — A87

National Flag A88

Four-Motor Plane A89

***Perf. 14x13½, 13½x14***

**1947** **Litho.** **Wmk. 196**
**200** A87 1½a greenish gray 1.50 .45
**201** A88 3½a multicolored 4.50 *4.75*
**202** A89 12a ultramarine 6.00 *4.75*
*Nos. 200-202 (3)* 12.00 9.95

Elevation to dominion status, Aug. 15, 1947.

Mahatma Gandhi — A90

Design: 10r, Gandhi profile.

*Perf. 11½*

**1948, Aug. 15 Unwmk. Photo.**

**Size: 22x32½mm**

**203** A90 1½a brown 8.25 1.25
**204** A90 3½a violet 18.00 5.00
**205** A90 12a dark gray green 21.00 3.00

**Size: 22x37mm**

**206** A90 10r rose brn & brn 260.00 95.00
*Nos. 203-206 (4)* 307.25 104.25

Mohandas K. Gandhi, 1869-1948.
For overprints see #O112A-O112D.

Ajanta Panel — A91

Konarak Horse — A92

Bodhisattva A93

Tomb of Muhammad Adil Shah, Bijapur A95

Sanchi Stupa A94

Victory Tower, Chittorgarh A96

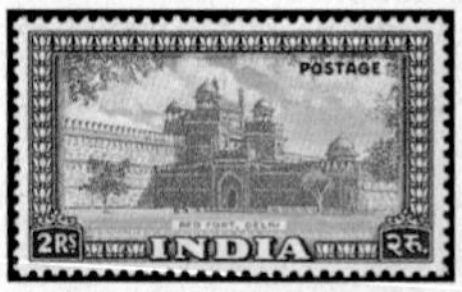


Red Fort, Delhi A97

Satrunjaya Temple, Palitana A98

9p, Trimurti. 2a, Nataraja. 3½a, Bodh Gaya Temple. 4a, Bhuvanesvara. 8a, Kandarya Mahadeva Temple. 12a, Golden Temple, Amritsar. 5r, Taj Mahal. 10r, Qutb Minar.

*Perf. 13½x14, 14x13½*

**1949, Aug. 15 Typo. Wmk. 196**

**207** A91 3p gray violet .30 .25
**208** A92 6p red brown .35 .25
**209** A93 9p green .60 .25
**210** A93 1a turquoise .85 .25
**211** A93 2a carmine 1.25 .25
**212** A94 3a red orange 3.00 .25
**213** A94 3½a ultramarine 2.50 5.00
**214** A94 4a brown lake 6.00 .35
**215** A95 6a purple 2.75 .90
**216** A95 8a blue green 2.25 .25
**217** A95 12a blue 3.00 .35

**Litho.**

**218** A96 1r dk green & pur 22.50 .25
**219** A97 2r pur & rose red 20.00 .50
**220** A97 5r brn car & dk grn 45.00 2.00
**221** A96 10r dp bl & brn car 80.00 12.00

*Perf. 13½x13*

**222** A98 15r dp car & dk brn 32.50 *35.00*
*Nos. 207-222 (16)* 222.85 58.10

See #231, 235-236. For overprints see #M44-M46, M48-M55 and Intl. Commission in Indo-china issues for Cambodia, #1, 3-5, Laos #1, 3-5 and Vietnam #1, 3-5.

Symbols of UPU and Asoka Pillar — A99

**1949, Oct. Litho. *Perf. 13½x13***

**223** A99 9p dull green 2.75 1.75
**224** A99 2a carmine rose 2.75 1.75
**225** A99 3½a ultramarine 6.00 3.00
**226** A99 12a red brown 24.00 4.00
*Nos. 223-226 (4)* 35.50 10.50

75th anniv. of the formation of the UPU.

**Republic of India**

Rejoicing Crowds A100

Designs: 3½a, Quill pen, vert. 4a, Plow and wheat. 12a, Charkha and cloth.

*Perf. 13½x13*

**1950, Jan. 26 Wmk. 196**

**227** A100 2a carmine 2.75 .75
**228** A100 3½a ultramarine 4.00 *6.25*
**229** A100 4a purple 4.00 1.50
**230** A100 12a claret 15.00 4.75
*Nos. 227-230 (4)* 25.75 13.25

**Type of 1949 Redrawn**

Bodhisattva — A101

**1950, July 15 Typo. *Perf. 13½x14***

**231** A101 1a turquoise 4.00 .30

For overprints see No. M47, Intl. Commission in Indo-china issues for Cambodia, No. 2, Laos, No. 2, and Vietnam, No. 2.

Extinct Stegodon Ganesa A102

**1951, Jan. 13 *Perf. 13***

**232** A102 2a deep carmine & black 6.00 1.25

Geological Survey of India, cent.

Torch and Map — A103

**1951, Mar. 4 Typo.**

**233** A103 2a red vio & red org 3.50 .90
**234** A103 12a dark brown & ultra 14.00 2.25

First Asian Games, New Delhi.

**Temple Type of 1949**

2½a, Bodh Gaya Temple. 4a, Bhuvanesvara.

*Perf. 13½x14*

**1951, Apr. 30 Wmk. 196**

**235** A94 2½a brown lake 6.00 3.50
**236** A94 4a ultramarine 12.00 .40

Kabir — A104

1a, Tulsidas, poet & saint. 2a, Meera, Rajput princess. 4a, Surdas, blind poet and saint. 4½a, Ghalib, Urdu poet. 12a, Rabindranath Tagore.

**1952, Oct. 1 Photo. *Perf. 14x13½***

**237** A104 9p emerald 2.25 .75
**238** A104 1a crimson 2.25 .30
**239** A104 2a red orange 8.75 .30
**240** A104 4a ultramarine 13.50 1.00
**241** A104 4½a red violet 2.75 1.75
**242** A104 12a brown 19.00 1.50
*Nos. 237-242 (6)* 48.50 5.60

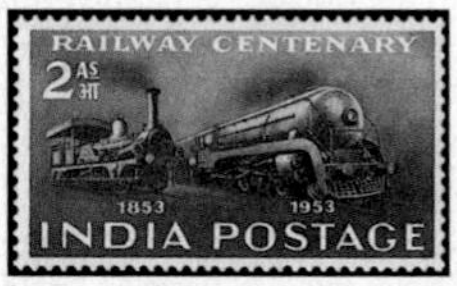


First Locomotive and Streamliner A105

**1953, Apr. 16 *Perf. 14½x14***

**243** A105 2a black 3.00 .50

Centenary of India's railroads.

Mt. Everest A106

**1953, Oct. 2**

**244** A106 2a violet 4.50 .35
**245** A106 14a brown 12.50 1.50

Conquest of Mt. Everest, May 29, 1953.

Telegraph Poles of 1851 and 1951 A107

**1953, Nov. 1**

**246** A107 2a blue green 2.00 .35
**247** A107 12a blue 18.00 .85

Centenary of the telegraph in India.

Mail Transport, 1854 A108

Designs: 2a and 14a, Pigeon and plane. 4a, Mail transport, 1954.

**1954, Oct. 1**

**248** A108 1a rose lilac .55 .30
**249** A108 2a rose pink 1.25 .30
**250** A108 4a yellow brown 11.50 1.25
**251** A108 14a blue 7.00 .40
*Nos. 248-251 (4)* 20.30 2.25

Centenary of India's postage stamps.

UN Emblem and Lotus Blossom A109

**1954, Oct. 24**

**252** A109 2a Prussian green 2.00 .45

United Nations Day.

Forest Research Institute, Dehra Dun A110

**1954, Dec. 11**

**253** A110 2a ultramarine 2.50 .30

4th World Forestry Cong., Dehra Dun.

Tractor A111

Charkha Operator A112

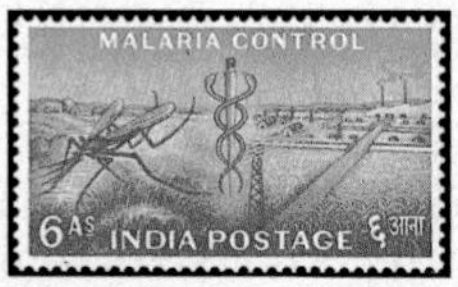


Symbols of Malaria Control A113

Designs: 6p, Power looms. 9p, Bullock irrigation pump. 1a, Damodar Valley dam. 3a, Naga woman at hand loom. 4a, Bullock team. 8a, Chittaranjan Locomotive Works. 10a, Plane over Marine Drive, Bombay. 12a, Hindustan aircraft factory. 14a, Plane over Kashmir valley. 1r, Telephone factory worker. 1r2a, Plane over Cape Comorin. 1r8a, Plane over Kanchenjunga Mountains. 2r, Rare earth factory. 5r, Sindri fertilizer factory. 10r, Steel mill.

*Perf. 14x14½, 14½x14*

**1955, Jan. 26 Photo.**

**254** A111 3p rose lilac .40 .25
**255** A111 6p deep violet .40 .25
**256** A111 9p orange brown .55 .25
**257** A111 1a dp blue green .55 .25
**258** A112 2a blue .40 .25
**259** A112 3a blue green .60 .25
**260** A111 4a rose red .60 .25
**261** A113 6a yellow brown 1.75 .25
**262** A111 8a deep blue 8.75 .25
**263** A113 10a aquamarine 4.50 2.75
**264** A111 12a violet blue 4.00 .25
**265** A113 14a emerald 6.50 .40
**266** A111 1r greenish black 5.00 .25
**267** A113 1r2a gray 2.75 *5.75*
**268** A113 1r8a claret 10.00 6.00
**269** A111 2r carmine rose 5.25 .25
**270** A111 5r brown 17.00 .40
**271** A111 10r orange 18.00 3.75
*Nos. 254-271 (18)* 87.00 22.05

See Nos. 316-319.

Bodhi Tree — A114

Ornament and Bodhi Tree A115

**1956, May 24 Wmk. 196 *Perf. 13***

**272** A114 2a brown 1.75 .30
**273** A115 14a brick red 12.00 4.00

2500th anniv. of the birth of Buddha.

Bal Gangadhar Tilak — A116

Map of India — A117

**1956, July 23 Wmk. 196 Photo.**

**274** A116 2a orange brown .55 .55

Birth cent. of Bal Gangadhar Tilak, independence leader.

**1957-58** ***Perf. 14x14½***

**275** A117 1np blue green .25 .25
**276** A117 2np light brown .25 .25
**277** A117 3np brown .25 .25
**278** A117 5np emerald 4.00 .25
**279** A117 6np gray .60 .25
**280** A117 8np brt green ('58) 6.50 .50
**281** A117 10np dark green 4.50 .25
**282** A117 13np brt carmine 1.10 .25
**283** A117 15np violet ('58) 4.00 .25
**284** A117 20np bright blue 1.25 .25
**285** A117 25np ultramarine .95 .25
**286** A117 50np orange 3.50 .25
**287** A117 75np plum 2.00 .25
**288** A117 90np red lilac ('58) 6.00 2.50
*Nos. 275-288 (14)* 35.15 6.00

Denominations of the 8np, 15np and 90np are inscribed nP.
See #302-315. For overprints see #M60 and Intl. Commission in Indo-China issues for Cambodia, #6-10, Laos, #6-10, and Vietnam, #6-10.

Laxmibai, Rani of Jhansi A118

Banyan Sapling, Arch and Flames — A119

***Perf. 14½x14, 13***

**1957, Aug. 15 Wmk. 196**

**289** A118 15np brown .50 .50
**290** A119 90np bright red violet 9.50 1.40

Centenary of the struggle for independence (Indian Mutiny).

Henri Dunant A120

**1957, Oct. 28** ***Perf. 13½x13***

**291** A120 15np car rose & black .40 .40

19th Intl. Red Cross Conf., New Delhi.

Boy Eating Banana A121

Bankura Horse — A122

Children's Day: 15np, Girl writing on tablet.

**1957, Nov. 14** ***Perf. 13½***

**292** A121 8np rose lilac .35 .35
**293** A121 15np aquamarine .35 .35
**294** A122 90np lt orange brown 1.25 .35
*Nos. 292-294 (3)* 1.95 1.05

Madras University A123

University Centenaries: No. 296, Calcutta. No. 297, Bombay, vert.

**1957, Dec. 31 Photo.**

**Size: 29½x25mm**

**295** A123 10np light brown 1.50 *.50*
**296** A123 10np gray .75 *.50*

**Size: 21½x38mm**

**297** A123 10np violet .75 *.50*
*Nos. 295-297 (3)* 3.00 1.50

J. N. Tata and Steel Works, Jamshedpur — A124

**1958, Mar. 1** ***Perf. 14½x14***

**298** A124 15np red orange .40 .40

50th anniv. of Indian steel industry.

Dr. Dhondo Keshav Karve — A125

**1958, Apr. 18** ***Perf. 14x13½***

**299** A125 15np orange brown .40 .40

Cent. of the birth of Karve, educator and pioneer of women's education.

Wapiti and Hunter Planes A126

**1958, Apr. 30** ***Perf. 14½x14***

**300** A126 15np bright blue 2.50 .35
**301** A126 90np ultramarine 2.75 2.50

25th anniv. of the Indian Air Force.

**Map Type of 1957-58 and Industrial Type of 1955**

1r, Telephone factory worker. 2r, Rare earth factory. 5r, Sindri fertilizer factory. 10r, Steel mill.

***Perf. 14x14½***

**1958-63 Photo. Wmk. 324**

**302** A117 1np blue grn ('60) 1.40 .25
*a.* Imperf., pair 240.00
**303** A117 2np light brown .25 .25
**304** A117 3np brown .25 .25
**305** A117 5np emerald .25 .25
**306** A117 6np gray ('63) .25 *4.00*
**307** A117 8np bright green .25 .25
**308** A117 10np dark green .25 .25
**309** A117 13np bright car ('63) 1.40 *4.75*
**310** A117 15np violet ('59) .80 .25
**311** A117 20np bright blue .50 .25
**312** A117 25np ultramarine .50 .25
**313** A117 50np orange ('59) .50 .25
**314** A117 75np plum ('59) .90 .25
**315** A117 90np red lilac ('60) 8.00 .25
**316** A111 1r dk grn ('59) 5.75 .25
**317** A111 2r lilac rose ('59) 8.00 .25
**318** A111 5r brown ('59) 14.00 .25
**319** A111 10r orange ('59) 32.50 5.50
*Nos. 302-319 (18)* 75.75 18.00

For overprints see Nos. M56-M59, M61, Intl. Commission in Indo-china issues for Cambodia, No. 12, Laos, Nos. 12-16, and Vietnam Nos. 11-16.

Bipin Chandra Pal — A128

**1958, Nov. 7** ***Perf. 13½***

**320** A128 15np dull green .50 .50

Birth cent. of Pal, early leader of India's freedom movement.

**1958, Nov. 30**

Portrait: Sir Jagadis Chandra Bose.

**321** A128 15np brt greenish blue .50 .50

Bose, physicist, plant physiologist, birth cent.

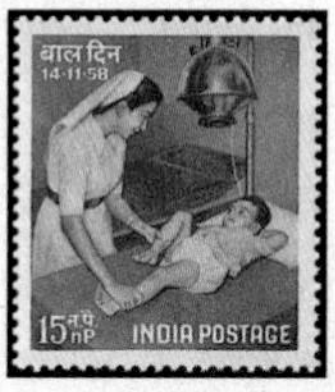


Nurse and Child — A129

**1958, Nov. 14 Wmk. 324**

**322** A129 15np violet .50 .50

Children's Day, Nov. 14.

Exhibition Gate A130

**1958, Dec. 30** ***Perf. 14½x14***

**323** A130 15np claret .50 .50

India 1958 Exhibition at Kampur.

Sir Jamsetjee Jejeebhoy — A131

**1959, Apr. 13** ***Perf. 13½***

**324** A131 15np brown .50 .50

Cent. of the death of Jejeebhoy, philosopher and philanthropist.

"Triumph of Labor," by D. P. Roy Chowdhary A132

**1959, June 15** ***Perf. 14½x14***

**325** A132 15np dull green .50 .50

40th anniv. of the ILO.

Children Arriving at Institution — A133

***Perf. 14x14½***

**1959, Nov. 14 Photo. Wmk. 324**

**326** A133 15np dull green .50 .50
*a.* Imperf., pair *1,200.*

Children's Day, Nov. 14.

Farmer Plowing with Bullocks A134

**1959, Dec. 30** ***Perf. 13***

**327** A134 15np gray .50 .40

World Agriculture Fair, New Delhi.

Thiruvalluvar Holding Stylus and Palmyra Leaf — A135

**1960, Feb. 15** ***Perf. 14***

**328** A135 15np rose lilac .50 .50

Honoring the ancient and saintly Tamil poet, Thiruvalluvar.

Scene from Meghduta — A136

Scene from Sakuntala A137

**1960, June 22** ***Perf. 13***

**329** A136 15np gray 1.00 .40
**330** A137 1.03r brown & bister 3.50 2.50

Honoring Kalidasa, 5th cent. poet and dramatist.
For surcharge see No. 371.

Subramania Bharati — A138

**1960, Sept. 11 Photo.** ***Perf. 14x13½***

**331** A138 15np bright blue .50 .50

Honoring the poet and statesman Subramania Bharati (1882-1921).

Dr. M. Visvesvaraya A139

**1960, Sept. 15** ***Perf. 13x13½***

**332** A139 15np car rose & brown .50 .50

Birth cent. of Visvesvaraya, engineer and statesman.

Children Playing and Studying A140

**1960, Nov. 14** ***Perf. 13½x13***

**333** A140 15np green .50 .50

Children's Day, Nov. 14.

Children and UN Emblem A141

**1960, Dec. 11** **Wmk. 324**

**334** A141 15np olive gray & org brn .50 .50

UNICEF Day.

Tyagaraja, Indian Musician — A142

**1961, Jan. 6** **Photo.** ***Perf. 14***

**335** A142 15np bright blue .50 .50

114th anniv. of Tyagaraja's death.

First Airmail Postmark — A143

Boeing 707 Jetliner — A144

Design: 1r, Humber-Sommer biplane.

***Perf. 14, 13x13½***

**1961, Feb. 18** **Wmk. 324**

**336** A143 5np olive bister 2.25 .40
**337** A144 15np gray & green 2.25 .40
**338** A144 1r gray & claret 7.00 3.00
*Nos. 336-338 (3)* 11.50 3.80

50th anniv. of the world's 1st airmail. The flight was from Allahabad to Naini, Feb. 18, 1911.

Chatrapati Sivaji Maharaj (1627-1680) A145

**1961, Apr. 17** ***Perf. 13x13½***

**339** A145 15np gray green & brown 1.40 .65

Leader of the Maharattas in the fight against the Moguls.

Motilal Nehru — A146

**1961, May 6** ***Perf. 14x13½***

**340** A146 15np orange & ol gray .50 .40

Cent. of the birth of Motilal Nehru, leader in India's fight for freedom.

Rabindranath Tagore — A147

**1961, May 7** ***Perf. 13***

**341** A147 15np blue grn & org 1.40 .60

Cent. of the birth of Tagore, poet.

Radio Masts and All India Radio Emblem A148

**1961, June 8** **Photo.** **Wmk. 324**

**342** A148 15np ultramarine .50 .50

25th anniv. of All India Radio.

Prafulla Chandra Ray — A149

**1961, Aug. 2** ***Perf. 14x13½***

**343** A149 15np gray .50 .50

Cent. of the birth of Ray, scientist.

Vishnu Narayan Bhatkhande A150

**1961, Sept. 1** ***Perf. 13***

**344** A150 15np olive gray .50 .50

Bhatkhande (1860-1936), musician.

Boy Making Pottery — A151

**1961, Nov. 14** ***Perf. 13½***

**345** A151 15np brown .50 .50

Children's Day, Nov. 14.

Gate at Fair — A152

**1961, Nov. 14** ***Perf. 14x14½***

**346** A152 15np blue & carmine .50 .50

Indian Industries Fair at New Delhi.

Forest and Himalayas — A153

**1961, Nov. 21** ***Perf. 13***

**347** A153 15np brown & green .80 .45

Cent. of the introduction of scientific forestry in India.

Yaksha, God of Fertility — A154

Kalibangan Seal — A155

**1961, Dec. 14** **Photo.** ***Perf. 14***

**348** A154 15np orange brown .50 .40
**349** A155 90np orange brn & olive 4.50 .40

Cent. of the Archaeological Survey of India.

Madan Mohan Malaviya — A156

**1961, Dec. 25** ***Perf. 14x13½***

**350** A156 15np slate .50 .50

Cent. of the birth of Malaviya, Pres. of the Indian Natl. Cong. and Vice Chancellor of Benares University.

Nunmati Refinery, Gauhati — A157

**1962, Jan. 1** **Photo.** ***Perf. 13***

**351** A157 15np blue .70 .40

1st Indian oil refinery at Gauhati.

Bhikaiji Cama — A158

**1962, Jan. 26** ***Perf. 14***

**352** A158 15np rose lilac .50 .50

Cent. of the birth of Madame Cama, a leader in India's fight for independence.

Village Council, Banyan Tree, Parliament and Map — A159

**1962, Jan. 26** ***Perf. 13***

**353** A159 15np red lilac .50 .50

Panchayati Raj, the system of government by village council.

Dayananda Sarasvati — A160

**1962, Mar. 4** ***Perf. 14***

**354** A160 15np brown orange .50 .50

135th anniv. of the birth of Sarasvati, reformer of the Vedic religion and founder of the Arya Samaj educational institutions.

Ganesh Shankar Vidyarthi — A161

**1962, Mar. 25**

**355** A161 15np reddish brown .50 .50

Vidyarthi (1890-1931), reformer of community life.

Malaria Eradication Emblem — A162

**1962, Apr. 7** ***Perf. 13***

**356** A162 15np dk car rose & yel .50 .50

WHO drive to eradicate malaria.

Dr. Rajendra Prasad — A163

**1962, May 13** ***Perf. 13***

**357** A163 15np bright red lilac .50 .40

Prasad, President of India (1950-62).

High Court, Calcutta A164

**1962 Photo.** ***Perf. 13½x14***

**358** A164 15np green .90 .35
**359** A164 15np Madras .90 .35
**360** A164 15np Bombay .90 .35
*Nos. 358-360 (3)* 2.70 1.05

Indian High Courts, cent. Issued: No. 358, July 1; No. 359, Aug. 8; No. 360, Aug. 14.

Ramabai Ranade — A165

**1962, Aug. 15** ***Perf. 14***

**361** A165 15np brown orange .50 .50

Ramabai Ranade (1862-1924), woman social reformer.

Indian Rhinoceros A166

10np, Gaur. No. 363, Lesser panda, vert. 30np, Elephant, vert. 50np, Tiger. 1r, Lion.

**1962-63 Wmk. 324** ***Perf. 14***

**Size: 30x26mm**

**361A** A166 10np yel org & blk ('63) 1.25 *1.75*
**362** A166 15np Prus blue & brn .75 .30

***Perf. 13x13½, 13½x13***

**Size: 25x36mm, 36x25mm**

**363** A166 15np green & red brown ('63) 2.50 .70
**364** A166 30np bister & slate ('63) 5.75 1.25
**365** A166 50np dp grn, ocher & brown ('63) 4.50 .90
**366** A166 1r brt bl & pale brown ('63) 4.25 .65
*Nos. 361A-366 (6)* 19.00 5.55

Child Reaching for Flag A167

**1962, Nov. 14** ***Perf. 13***

**367** A167 15np lt bluish grn & ver .50 .50

Children's Day.

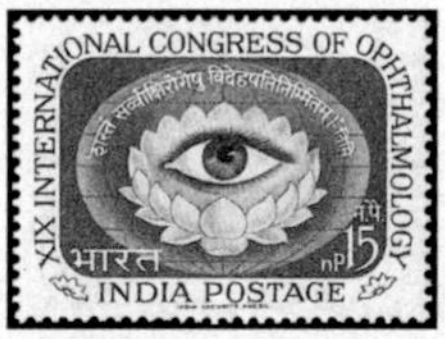


Eye within Lotus Blossom A168

**1962, Dec. 3** **Photo.**

**368** A168 15np olive gray .50 .40

16th Intl. Cong. of Ophthalmology, New Delhi, Dec. 1962.

Srinivasa Ramanujan A169

**1962, Dec. 22** ***Perf. 13½x14***

**369** A169 15np olive gray .80 .55

75th anniv. of the birth of Ramanujan (1887-1920), mathematician.

Swami Vivekananda — A170

**1963, Jan. 17** ***Perf. 14x14½***

**370** A170 15np olive & orange brn .50 .50

Cent. of the birth of Vivekananda (1863-1902), philosopher.

No. 330 Surcharged with New Value and Two Bars

**1963, Feb. 2** ***Perf. 13***

**371** A137 1r on 1.03r brown & bis 1.50 .45

Hands Reaching for "FAO" Emblem — A171

**1963, Mar. 21** **Photo.**

**372** A171 15np chalky blue 2.50 .70

UNFAO Freedom from Hunger campaign.

Henri Dunant and Centenary Emblem — A172

**1963, May 8** ***Perf. 13***

**373** A172 15np gray & red 4.50 .60

Centenary of the International Red Cross.

Field Artillery and Helicopter A173

Design: 1r, Soldier guarding frontier and plane dropping supplies.

**1963, Aug. 15** ***Perf. 13½x14***

**374** A173 15np dull green 1.00 .30
**375** A173 1r red brown 1.60 1.25

Honoring the Armed Forces and the 16th anniv. of independence.

Dadabhoy Naoroji — A174

**1963, Sept. 4** ***Perf. 13***

**376** A174 15np gray green .50 .50

Honoring Dadabhoy Naoroji (1825-1917), mathematician and statesman.

Annie Besant — A175

**1963, Oct. 1 Photo.** ***Perf. 14***

**377** A175 15np blue green .50 .50

Besant (1847-1933), an English woman devoted to the cause of India's freedom, theosophist and writer. Stamp gives birth date as 1837.

School Lunch — A176

**1963, Nov. 14 Wmk. 324** ***Perf. 14***

**378** A176 15np olive bister .50 .50

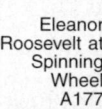

Children's Day.

Eleanor Roosevelt at Spinning Wheel A177

**1963, Dec. 10** ***Perf. 13***

**379** A177 15np rose violet .50 .50

Honoring Eleanor Roosevelt on the 15th anniv. of the Universal Declaration of Human Rights.

Gopabandhu Das (1877-1928) A178

**1964, Jan. 4** ***Perf. 13***

**380** A178 15np dull purple .50 .50

Gopabandhu Das, social reformer.

Lakshmi, Goddess of Wealth — A179

**1964, Jan. 4** **Photo.**

**381** A179 15np dull violet blue .50 .50

26th Intl. Cong. of Orientalists, New Delhi, Jan. 4-14.

Purandaradasa Holding Veena and Chipala — A180

**1964, Jan. 14**

**382** A180 15np golden brown .50 .50

400th anniv. of the death of Purandaradasa (1484-1564), musician.

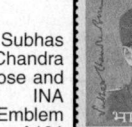

Subhas Chandra Bose and INA Emblem A181

Design: 55np, Bose addressing troops.

**1964, Jan. 23** ***Perf. 13***

**383** A181 15np olive .85 .45
**384** A181 55np red & black .85 .85

67th anniv. of the birth of Bose, organizer of the Indian Natl. Army.

Sarojini Naidu (1879-1949) A182

Kasturba Gandhi A183

**1964, Feb. 13** ***Perf. 14x13½***

**385** A182 15np dull lilac & slate grn .50 .50

Mrs. Sarojini Naidu, poet, politician, governor of United Provinces.

**1964, Feb. 22** **Photo.** **Wmk. 324**

**386** A183 15np brown orange .50 .50

20th anniv. of the death of Kasturba Gandhi (1869-1944), wife of Mahatma Gandhi.

Dr. Waldemar M. Haffkine (1860-1930) A184

**1964, Mar. 16** ***Perf. 13***

**387** A184 15np violet brown, *buff* .50 .50

Haffkine, bacteriologist, who as director of Haffkine Institute introduced inoculations against cholera and plague.

Jawaharlal Nehru (1889-1964) and People A185

**1964, June 12** **Unwmk.** ***Perf. 13***

**388** A185 15p grayish blue .50 .50

Prime Minister Jawaharlal Nehru.

Asutosh Mookerjee and High Court, Calcutta A186

**1964, June 29** **Wmk. 324**

**389** A186 15p olive green & brn .50 .50

Cent. of the birth of Asutosh Mookerjee (1864-1924), educator, lawyer and judge.

Sri Aurobindo Ghose (1872-1950), Writer and Philosopher A187

**1964, Aug. 15** **Photo.**

**390** A187 15p violet brown .50 .50

Raja Rammohun Roy — A188

**1964, Sept. 27** ***Perf. 13***

**391** A188 15p reddish brown .50 .50

Roy (1772-1833), Hindu religious reformer.

Globe, Lotus, and Calipers — A189

**1964, Nov. 9** **Unwmk.** **Photo.**

**392** A189 15p carmine rose .50 .50

6th gen. assembly of the Intl. Organization for Standardization.

Nehru Medal and Rose — A190

**1964, Nov. 14** ***Perf. 13½***

**393** A190 15p blue gray .50 .50

Children's Day. For overprints, see Nos. M62, Intl. Commission in Indo-china issues for Laos and Vietnam, No. 1.

St. Thomas Statue, Ortona, Italy — A191

Globe and Pickax — A192

**1964, Dec. 2** **Unwmk.** ***Perf. 13½***

**394** A191 15p rose violet .50 .50

Visit of Pope Paul VI, Nov. 30-Dec. 2.

**1964, Dec. 14** **Wmk. 324**

**395** A192 15p bright green .65 .65

22nd Intl. Geological Cong., New Delhi.

Jamsetji N. Tata A193

**1965, Jan. 7** **Unwmk.** ***Perf. 13***

**396** A193 15p dk brown & orange .50 .25

125th anniv. of the birth of Tata (1839-1904), founder of India's steel industry.

Lala Lajpatrai (1865-1928), a Leader in India's Fight for Independence A194

**1965, Jan. 28** **Photo.** ***Perf. 13***

**397** A194 15p brown .50 .50

ICC Emblem and Globe A195

**1965, Feb. 8** **Litho.**

**398** A195 15p dull green & car .50 .50

20th cong. of the Intl. Chamber of Commerce, New Delhi.

Freighter Jalausha at Visakhapatnam — A196

***Perf. 14½x14***

**1965, Apr. 5** **Photo.** **Wmk. 324**

**399** A196 15p ultramarine .70 .70

National Maritime Day.

Death Centenary of Abraham Lincoln — A197

**1965, Apr. 15** ***Perf. 13***

**400** A197 15p yellow & dk brown .60 .60

ITU Emblem, Old and New Communication Equipment — A198

**1965, May 17** **Photo.** ***Perf. 14½x14***

**401** A198 15p rose violet 2.00 .75

Cent. of the ITU.

Torch and Rose — A199

**1965, May 27** **Wmk. 324** ***Perf. 13***

**402** A199 15p carmine & blue .40 .40

1st anniv. of the death of Jawaharlal Nehru.

ICY Emblem A200

**1965, June 26** **Photo.** **Unwmk.**

**403** A200 15p bister & dk green 2.25 1.25

International Cooperation Year.

Indians Raising Flag on Everest — A201

**1965, Aug. 15** **Unwmk.** ***Perf. 13***

**404** A201 15p plum .75 .60

Success of the Indian Mt. Everest Expedition, May 20, 1965.

Elephant from Konarak Temple, Orissa A202

Tea Picking A203

Woman Writing Letter, Chandella Carving, 11th Century — A204

Trombay Atomic Center A205

Designs: 2p, Vase (bidri ware). 3p, Brass lamp. 4p, Coffee berries. 5p, Family (family planning). 8p, Axis deer (chital). 10p, Electric locomotive, 1961. 20p, Gnat plane. 30p, Male and female figurines. 40p, General Post Office, Calcutta, 1868. 50p, Mangoes. 60p, Somnath Temple. 70p, Stone chariot, Hampi, Mysore. 2r, Dal Lake, Kashmir. 5r, Bhakra Dam, Punjab.

***Perf. 14½x14, 14x14½***

**1965-68** **Photo.** **Wmk. 324**

| | | | | | |
|---|---|---|---|---|---|
| **405** | A202 | 2p | redsh brown ('67) | .25 | *.55* |
| **406** | A202 | 3p | olive bis ('67) | .40 | *2.40* |
| **407** | A203 | 4p | orange brn ('68) | .25 | *2.10* |
| **408** | A202 | 5p | cerise ('67) | .25 | .25 |
| **409** | A202 | 6p | gray ('66) | .25 | *3.25* |
| **410** | A202 | 8p | red brown ('67) | .40 | *4.00* |
| **411** | A203 | 10p | brt blue ('66) | .60 | .25 |
| **412** | A203 | 15p | dk yel green | 3.50 | .25 |
| **413** | A203 | 20p | plum ('67) | 8.00 | .25 |
| **414** | A202 | 30p | brown ('67) | .25 | .25 |
| **415** | A203 | 40p | brown vio ('68) | .25 | .25 |
| **416** | A202 | 50p | green ('67) | .35 | .25 |
| **417** | A202 | 60p | dark gray ('67) | .45 | .25 |
| **418** | A203 | 70p | violet ('67) | .95 | .25 |
| **419** | A204 | 1r | deep claret & red brown ('66) | .95 | .25 |
| **420** | A205 | 2r | vio & brt bl ('67) | 3.25 | .25 |
| **421** | A205 | 5r | brn & vio ('67) | 3.50 | 1.60 |
| **422** | A205 | 10r | green & gray | 24.00 | 1.10 |
| | | | *Nos. 405-422 (18)* | 47.85 | 17.75 |

See Nos. 623, 666-670, 678, 680, 684-685. For overprints see Nos. RA1-RA2, Intl. Commission in Indo-china issues for Laos and Vietnam, Nos. 2-9.

**1975-76 Wmk. 360** ***Perf. 14½x14***

**422A** A202 2p redsh brown 1.50 *2.25*
**423** A202 5p cerise 1.75 .25

**Unwmk.**

**423A** A202 5p cerise ('76) 1.50 .25

A206

**1965, Sept. 10 Unwmk.** ***Perf. 13***

**424** A206 15p dark green & brown .50 .50

Govind Ballabh Pant (1887-1961), Home Minister of India.

A207

**1965, Oct. 31** ***Perf. 14***

**425** A207 15p gray .50 .50

Vallabhbhai Patel (1875-1950), Deputy Prime Minister of India.

Chittaranjan Das (1870-1925) A208

Vidyapati, 15th Cent. Poet A209

**1965, Nov. 5 Photo.** ***Perf. 13***

**426** A208 15p brown .50 .50

Das, freedom fighter, pres. of Indian Natl. Cong., mayor of Calcutta.

**1965, Nov. 17** ***Perf. 14x14½***

**427** A209 15p brown .50 .50

Tomb of Akbar the Great, Sikandra A210

**1966, Jan. 24** ***Perf. 14***

**428** A210 15p dark gray .50 .50

Pacific Area Travel Assoc. Conf., New Delhi.

Soldier, Planes and Warships A211

**1966, Jan. 26**

**429** A211 15p bright violet 2.00 .65

Honoring the Indian armed forces.

Lal Bahadur Shastri A212

Kambar A213

**1966, Jan. 26** ***Perf. 13***

**430** A212 15p gray 1.00 .60

Prime Minister Shastri (1904-66).

**1966, Apr. 9** ***Perf. 14x14½***

**431** A213 15p green .50 .50

Kambar, 9th century Tamil poet.

B. R. Ambedkar A214

Kunwar Singh A215

**1966, Apr. 14 Unwmk.** ***Perf. 14***

**432** A214 15p violet brown .50 .50

10th anniv. of the death of Dr. Bhimrao R. Ambedkar (1891-1956), lawyer and leader in social reform.

**1966, Apr. 23** **Photo.**

**433** A215 15p orange brown .50 .50

Kunwar Singh (1777-1858), hero of 1857 War of Independence (1857 Mutiny).

Gopal Krishna Gokhale A216

**1966, May 9 Unwmk.** ***Perf. 13***

**434** A216 15p violet brown & yel .50 .50

Cent. of the birth of Gokhale (1866-1915), professor of history and political economy and leader of the opposition party.

A. M. P. Dvivedi (1864-1938) A217

**1966, May 15** ***Perf. 14***

**435** A217 15p olive gray .50 .50

Acharya Mahavir Prasad Dvivedi, Hindi writer.

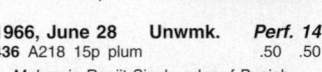

Ranjit Singh (1780-1839) — A218

**1966, June 28 Unwmk.** ***Perf. 14***

**436** A218 15p plum .50 .50

Maharaja Ranjit Singh, ruler of Punjab.

Homi Bhabha and Atomic Reactor A219

**1966, Aug. 4** ***Perf. 14½x14***

**437** A219 15p brown violet 1.00 1.00

Dr. Homi Bhabha (1909-1966), scientist.

Rama Tirtha A220

**1966, Nov. 11 Unwmk.** ***Perf. 13***

**438** A220 15p greenish blue .50 .50

60th anniv. of the death of Swami Rama Tirtha (1873-1906).

A221

**1966, Nov. 11 Photo.** ***Perf. 13½***

**439** A221 15p dark violet blue .50 .50

Abdul Kalam Azad (1888-1958), president of the All-India Congress.

A222

**1966, Nov. 14** ***Perf. 13***

**440** A222 15p Child and dove 1.10 .70

Children's Day.

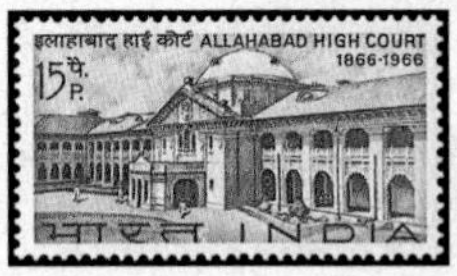


Allahabad High Court, Cent. A223

**1966, Nov. 25** ***Perf. 14½x14***

**441** A223 15p violet brown .50 .50

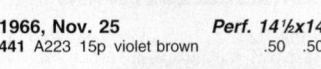

Family A224

**1966, Dec. 12** ***Perf. 13½x13***

**442** A224 15p brown .50 .50

Intl. Conf. for Marriage Guidance, New Delhi, and Family Planning Week.

Hockey A225

**1966, Dec. 31 Unwmk.** ***Perf. 13***

**443** A225 15p bright blue 1.50 1.50

Victory of the Indian hockey team at the 5th Asian Games, Bangkok, Dec. 19.

Grain Harvest A226

**1967, Jan. 11** ***Perf. 13½***

**444** A226 15p yellow green .75 .90

1st anniv. of the death of Prime Minister Lal Bahadur Shastri, who advocated self-sufficiency in food production.

Voters — A227

**1967, Jan. 13** **Photo.**

**445** A227 15p light red brown .50 .50

General elections, Feb. 1967.

Guru Dwara Shrine, Patna — A228

**1967, Jan. 17** ***Perf. 14***

**446** A228 15p violet .70 .70

300th anniv. of the birth of Gobind Singh (1666-1708), religious leader.

Taj Mahal A229

**1967, Mar. 19** ***Perf. 14½x14***

**447** A229 15p brown & orange .60 .60

International Tourist Year.

Nandalal Bose and Garuda — A230

**1967, Apr. 16** ***Perf. 13½***

**448** A230 15p brown .50 .50

Nandalal Bose (1882-1966), painter.

Survey of India Emblem A231

**1967, May 1 Unwmk. *Perf. 13***
**449** A231 15p lilac .90 .80

Bicentenary of Survey of India.

Basaveswara, 12th Cent. Statesman and Philosopher, at Work — A232

**1967, May 11 *Perf. 13½x14***
**450** A232 15p deep orange .50 .50

Narsinha Mehta — A233

Maharana Pratap — A234

**1967, May 30 *Perf. 13½***
**451** A233 15p gray brown .50 .50

Narsina Mehta, 15th cent. musician.

**1967, June 11 *Perf. 14x14½***
**452** A234 15p reddish brown .50 .50

Pratap (1540-1597), Mewar ruler.

Narayana Guru A235

Dr. Sarvepalli Radhakrishnan A236

**1967, Aug. 21 Photo. *Perf. 14***
**453** A235 15p brown .60 .60

Narayana Guru (1855-1928), religious reformer.

**1967, Sept. 5 Unwmk. *Perf. 13***
**454** A236 15p dull claret .80 .40

Radhakrishnan, Pres. of India 1962-67.

Martyrs' Memorial, Patna A237

**1967, Oct. 1 Photo. *Perf. 14½x14***
**455** A237 15p dark carmine .50 .50

25th anniv. of the "Quit India" revolt led by Gandhi.

Map Showing Indo-European Telegraph A238

**1967, Nov. 9 Photo. *Perf. 13½***
**456** A238 15p blue & black 1.00 .80

Cent. of the laying of the Indo-European telegraph line.

Wrestlers A239

**1967, Nov. 12**
**457** A239 15p ocher & plum .80 .55

World Wrestling Championships, New Delhi, Nov. 1967.

Nehru and Naga Tribesmen — A240

Rashbehari Basu — A241

**1967, Dec. 4 Photo. *Perf. 13***
**458** A240 15p ultramarine .50 .50

**1967, Dec. 26 *Perf. 13½***
**459** A241 15p dull purple .50 .50

Basu (1886-1945), Bengali leader.

Bugle, Scout Emblem and Scout Sign A242

**1967, Dec. 27 *Perf. 14½x14***
**460** A242 15p orange brown 1.50 .60

Boy Scout Movement, 60th anniv.

People Encircling the Globe and Human Rights Flame A243

**1968, Jan. 1 *Perf. 13***
**461** A243 15p dark green .80 .75

Intl. Human Rights Year.

Conference Emblem and Gopuram Temple — A244

**1968, Jan. 3 Photo. Unwmk.**
**462** A244 15p purple .80 .55

2nd Intl. Conf. on Tamil Studies, Madras.

UN Emblem, Plane and Ship A245

**1968, Feb. 1 *Perf. 14½x14***
**463** A245 15p greenish blue 1.00 .55

UN Conference on Trade and Development, New Delhi, Feb. 1968.

Symbolic Bow and Quill Pen — A246

**1968, Feb. 20 *Perf. 13½x14***
**464** A246 15p ocher & sepia .50 .50

Cent. of the newspaper Amrit Bazar Patrika, Calcutta.

Maxim Gorky (1868-1936), Russian Writer — A247

**1968, Mar. 28 Photo. *Perf. 14***
**465** A247 15p brown violet .50 .50

Exhibition Emblem — A248

**1968, Mar. 31 *Perf. 13***
**466** A248 15p dark blue & org .60 .30

First Triennial Exhibition, New Delhi.

Symbolic Mail Box — A249

**1968, July 1 Unwmk. *Perf. 13***
**467** A249 20p vermilion & blue .60 .45

Opening of 100,000th Indian post office.

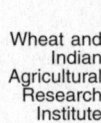

Wheat and Indian Agricultural Research Institute A250

**1968, July 15 Photo. *Perf. 13***
**468** A250 20p brt grn & brn org .60 .35

India's 1968 bumper wheat crop.

Gaganendranath Tagore (1867-1938), Self-portrait A251

**1968, Sept. 17 Unwmk. *Perf. 13***
**469** A251 20p ocher & deep clar .80 .55

Lakshminath Bezbaruah (1868-1938), Writer — A252

**1968, Oct. 5 Photo. *Perf. 13½***
**470** A252 20p sepia .50 .40

19th Olympic Games, Mexico City A253

**1968, Oct. 12 *Perf. 14½x14***
**471** A253 20p blue gray & red brn .40 .40
**472** A253 1r olive gray & dk brn .85 .40

Bhagat Singh (1907-1931), Revolutionary — A254

**1968, Oct. 19 Photo. *Perf. 13½x13***
**473** A254 20p orange brown .80 .80

Bose Reading Proclamation A255

Sister Nivedita A256

**1968, Oct. 21 *Perf. 14x14½***
**474** A255 20p dark blue .60 .60

25th anniv. of the establishment of the Azad Hind (Free India) government by Subhas Chandra Bose (1897-1945), independence leader.

**1968, Oct. 27**
**475** A256 20p blue green .60 .50

Sister Nivedita (Margaret Noble, 1867-1911), Irish-born friend of India.

Marie Curie and Patient Receiving Radiation A257

**1968, Nov. 6 *Perf. 14½x14***
**476** A257 20p purple 2.50 .70

Marie Sklodowska Curie (1867-1934), discoverer of radium and polonium.

World Map — A258

**1968, Dec. 1** ***Perf. 13***

**477** A258 20p blue .60 .45

21st Intl. Geographical Congress.

Interior of Cochin Synagogue A259

***Perf. 13x13½***

**1968, Dec. 15 Photo. Unwmk.**

**478** A259 20p vio bl & car rose 1.75 .75

400th anniv. of Cochin Synagogue.

Frigate Nilgiri A260

**1968, Dec. 15** ***Perf. 13½x13***

**479** A260 20p dull violet blue 2.75 .60

Navy Day. The Nilgiri, launched Oct. 23, 1968, was the 1st Indian warship.

Redbilled Blue Magpie A261

Birds: 50p, Brown-fronted pied woodpecker. 1r, Slaty-headed scimitar babbler, vert. 2r, Yellow-backed sunbirds.

**1968, Dec. 31** ***Perf. 14½x14, 14x14½***

| | | | |
|---|---|---|---|
| **480** A261 | 20p pink & multi | 1.10 | .70 |
| **481** A261 | 50p multicolored | 1.50 | 1.75 |
| **482** A261 | 1r multicolored | 2.60 | 1.40 |
| **483** A261 | 2r multicolored | 2.25 | 2.00 |
| *Nos. 480-483 (4)* | | 7.45 | 5.85 |

Chatterjee (1838-94) A262

Dr. Bhagavan Das A263

**1969, Jan. 1** ***Perf. 13½***

**484** A262 20p ultramarine .50 .50

Bankim Chandra Chatterjee, writer.

**1969, Jan. 12 Photo.** ***Perf. 13½***

**485** A263 20p red brown .50 .50

Das (1869-1958), philosopher.

Martin Luther King, Jr. (1929-1968), American Civil Rights Leader — A264

**1969, Jan. 25**

**486** A264 20p olive gray .90 .35

Mirza Ghalib A265

**1969, Feb. 17** ***Perf. 14½x14***

**487** A265 20p dk gray & salmon .50 .50

Mirza Ghalib (Asad Ullah Beg Khan 1797-1869), poet who modernized the Urdu language.

Osmania University, Hyderabad, 50th Avviv. A266

**1969, Mar. 15 Photo.** ***Perf. 14½x14***

**488** A266 20p green .50 .50

Rafi Ahmed Kidwai A267

**1969, Apr. 1** ***Perf. 13***

**489** A267 20p grayish blue 1.75 .60

Minister of communications and food, introduced around-the-clock airmail service.

ILO Emblems A268

**1969, Apr. 11** ***Perf. 14½x14***

**490** A268 20p orange brown .50 .50

50th anniv. of the ILO.

Memorial Monument and Hands Strewing Flowers — A269

**1969, Apr. 13** ***Perf. 13½***

**491** A269 20p rose carmine .50 .50

50th anniv. of Jallianwala Bagh, Amritsar, massacre.

Nageswara Rao (1867-1938), Journalist and Congressman A270

**1969, May 1 Photo.** ***Perf. 13½x14***

**492** A270 20p brown .50 .50

Ardaseer Cursetjee Wadia and Ships A271

**1969, May 27 Photo.** ***Perf. 14½x14***

**493** A271 20p blue green .80 .75

Wadia (1808-1877), shipbuilder.

Serampore College, 150th Anniv. — A272

**1969, June 7 Photo.** ***Perf. 13½***

**494** A272 20p violet brown .50 .50

Dr. Zakir Husain (1897-1969), President of India 1967-1969 A273

**1969, June 11** ***Perf. 13***

**495** A273 20p olive gray .50 .50

Laxmanrao Kirloskar and Plow A274

**1969, June 20**

**496** A274 20p gray .50 .50

Kirloskar (1869-1956), industrialist and social reformer, introduced the iron plow to India.

Mahatma Gandhi (1869-1948) A275

Gandhi on the Dandi March A276

20p, Gandhi and his wife Kasturba, horiz. 5r, Gandhi with spinning wheel, horiz.

**1969, Oct. 2 Photo. Unwmk.**

**Size: 29x25mm**

***Perf. 13½***

**497** A275 20p sepia .80 .80

**Size: 28x38mm**

***Perf. 13***

**498** A275 75p ol gray, sal & brn 1.90 .30

**Size: 20x38mm**

***Perf. 14x14½***

**499** A276 1r bright blue 1.90 1.60

**Size: 35½x25½mm**

***Perf. 13***

**500** A275 5r orange & sepia 6.50 5.50

*Nos. 497-500 (4)* 11.10 8.20

Freighter and IMCO Emblem A277

**1969, Oct. 14** ***Perf. 13***

**501** A277 20p ultramarine 2.75 .70

10th anniv. of the Intergovernmental Maritime Consultative Organization.

Globe and Parliament, New Delhi A278

**1969, Oct. 30 Photo.** ***Perf. 14½x14***

**502** A278 20p bright blue .50 .50

57th Interparliamentary Conf., New Delhi.

Astronaut on Moon — A279

Nanak Mausoleum, Talwandi, Punjab — A280

**1969, Nov. 19** ***Perf. 14x14½***

**503** A279 20p olive brown 1.00 .60

See note after US No. C76.

**1969, Nov. 23 Photo.** ***Perf. 13½***

**504** A280 20p gray violet .50 .50

500th anniv. of the birth of the Guru Nanak, Sikh leader.

Tiger and Globe A281

**1969, Nov. 24** ***Perf. 14½x14***

**505** A281 20p olive grn & red brn .90 .65

Intl. Union for the Conservation of Nature and Natural Resources.

T. L. Vaswani A282

Thakkar Bapa A283

**1969, Nov. 25** ***Perf. 14x14½***

**506** A282 20p dark gray .50 .50

T. L. Vaswani (1879-1966), writer and orator.

**1969, Nov. 29** ***Perf. 13½***

**507** A283 20p dark brown .50 .50

Thakkar Bapa (1869-1951), statesman who worked to help the untouchables.

Globe and Telecommunications Symbols — A284

**1970, Jan. 21** ***Perf. 13***
**508** A284 20p Prussian blue .50 .25

12th Plenary Assembly of the Intl. Radio Consultative Committee.

C. N. Annadurai (1909-1969), Journalist — A285

**1970, Feb. 2**
**509** A285 20p dk blue & magenta .50 .50

Munshi Newal Kishore and Printing Plant — A286

**1970, Feb. 19** **Photo.** ***Perf. 13x13½***
**510** A286 20p dark carmine .50 .50

Kishore (1836-1895), publisher.

Cent. of Nalanda College A287

**1970, Mar. 27** **Photo.** ***Perf. 14½x14***
**511** A287 20p light red brown .80 .45

Swami Shraddhanand (1856-1926), Patriot — A288

**1970, Mar. 30** ***Perf. 13½***
**512** A288 20p orange brown 1.00 .50

Lenin A289

**1970, Apr. 22** **Photo.** ***Perf. 13***
**513** A289 20p multicolored .60 .30

UPU Headquarters, Bern — A290

**1970, May 20**
**514** A290 20p black & green .50 .50

New UPU Headquarters in Bern.

Sher Shah Suri — A291

**1970, May 22** **Photo.** ***Perf. 13***
**515** A291 20p blue green .50 .50

Suri, 15th cent. ruler of Delhi and postal service reformer.

Vir D. Savarkar and Prison at Port Blair, Andamans A292

**1970, May 28**
**516** A292 20p orange brown .80 .80

V. D. Savarkar (1883-1966), patriot.

"UN" and UN Emblem — A293

**1970, June 26** **Photo.** ***Perf. 13***
**517** A293 20p blue .60 .35

25th anniv. of the UN.

Harvest, Crane, Factory and Emblem A294

**1970, Aug. 18** ***Perf. 14½x14***
**518** A294 20p violet .50 .40

Asian Productivity Year.

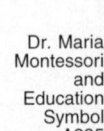

Dr. Maria Montessori and Education Symbol A295

**1970, Aug. 31** ***Perf. 13½x13***
**519** A295 20p dull claret .60 .50

Intl. Education Year and Maria Montessori (1870-1952), Italian educator and physician.

Jatindra Nath Mukherjee A296

**1970, Sept. 9** ***Perf. 14½x14***
**520** A296 20p dark red brown 1.75 .60

Mukherjee (1879-1915), revolutionary leader.

Srinivasa Sastri (1869-1946) A297

**1970, Sept. 22** **Photo.** ***Perf. 13***
**521** A297 20p dk brown & ocher .60 .50

V. S. Srinivasa Sastri, statesman.

Iswar Chandra Vidyasagar A298

**1970, Sept. 26**
**522** A298 20p rose lilac & brown .60 .60

Vidyasagar (1820-91), educator and writer.

Maharishi Valmiki (born c. 1400 B.C.), Poet A299

**1970, Oct. 14** **Photo.** ***Perf. 13***
**523** A299 20p plum .60 .40

Calcutta Harbor A300

**1970, Oct. 17**
**524** A300 20p blue 2.25 1.00

Cent. of Calcutta Port Commissioners.

Jamia Millia Islamia University, 50th Anniv. A301

**1970, Oct. 29** ***Perf. 14½x14***
**525** A301 20p yellow green .90 .90

Jamnalal Bajaj (1889-1942), Patriot — A302

**1970, Nov. 4** **Wmk. 324** ***Perf. 13***
**526** A302 20p sepia .50 .40

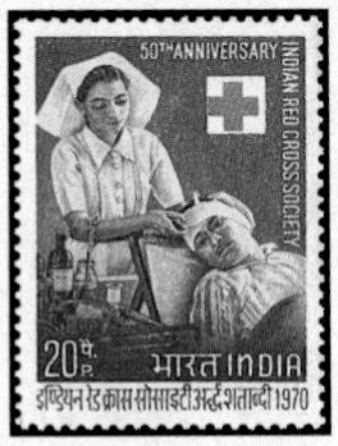


Nurse and Patient — A303

**1970, Nov. 5**
**527** A303 20p Prus. blue & red .90 .65

50th anniv. of the Indian Red Cross Soc.

Sant Namdeo (1270-1350), Holy Man — A304

**1970, Nov. 9** **Photo.**
**528** A304 20p orange .50 .50

Ludwig van Beethoven A305

**1970, Dec. 16** **Unwmk.** ***Perf. 13***
**529** A305 20p dk brn & org 3.00 .90

Children with Stamp Album A306

Design: 1r, Hands holding magnifying glass over Gandhi stamp.

**1970, Dec. 23** **Photo.** ***Perf. 13***
**530** A306 20p dull green & lt brn .75 .35
**531** A306 1r ocher & brown 5.00 1.25

INPEX 1970, Indian Natl. Phil. Exhib., New Delhi, Dec. 23, 1970-Jan. 6, 1971.

Girl Guide and Sign — A307

**1970, Dec. 27**
**532** A307 20p dark brown violet .80 .40

Girl Guides, 60th anniv.

Hands Shielding Flame — A308

**1971, Jan. 11**
**533** A308 20p bis brn & dp clar .50 .40

Centenary of Indian Life Insurance.

Kashi Vidyapith, 50th Anniv.
A309

**1971, Feb. 10** ***Perf. 14½x14***
**534** A309 20p black brown .50 .40

Kashi Vidyapith University, Benares.

Charles Freer Andrews (1871-1940), British Publicist, Friend of Gandhi — A310

**1971, Feb. 12** ***Perf. 13x13½***
**535** A310 20p orange brown .60 .45

Ravidas, 15th Cent. Poet and Holy Man
A311

**1971, Feb.** ***Perf. 13***
**536** A311 20p rose carmine 1.10 .60

Acharya Narendra Deo (1889-1956), Educator, Patriot, Statesman
A312

**1971, Feb. 18** **Photo.** ***Perf. 13***
**537** A312 20p olive bister .50 .50

Cent. of Indian Census
A313

**1971, Mar. 10**
**538** A313 20p ultra & sepia .50 .40

Ramana Maharshi (1879-1950), Holy Man — A314

**1971, Apr. 14** **Photo.** ***Perf. 13½x14***
**539** A314 20p ol gray & orange .60 .50

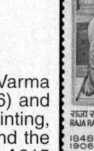

Raja Ravi Varma (1848-1906) and His Painting, Damayanti and the Swan — A315

**1971, Apr. 29** ***Perf. 13x13½***
**540** A315 20p deep yellow green .80 .65

Dadasaheb Phalke, Movie Camera
A316

**1971, Apr. 30** ***Perf. 13½x13***
**541** A316 20p violet brown 1.25 .60

Dadasaheb Phalke (1870-1944), motion picture pioneer.

Abhisarika, by Abanindranath Tagore
A317

Swami Virjanand
A318

**1971, Aug. 7** **Unwmk.** ***Perf. 14x14½***
**542** A317 20p dark brn & ocher .60 .50

Tagore (1871-1951), painter.

**1971, Sept. 14** ***Perf. 14x13½***
**543** A318 20p orange brown .60 .50

Virjanand (1778-1868), scholar and sage.

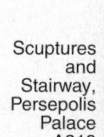

Scuptures and Stairway, Persepolis Palace
A319

**1971, Oct. 12** ***Perf. 13***
**544** A319 20p sepia 1.25 .70

2500th anniv. of the founding of the Persian empire by Cyrus the Great.

World Thrift Day
A320

**1971, Oct. 31** ***Perf. 14½x14***
**545** A320 20p dark violet blue .50 .40

Bodhisatva Padampani, from Ajanta Cave — A321

Girls at Work, by Geeta Gupta — A322

**1971, Nov. 4** ***Perf. 13***
**546** A321 20p brown 2.50 .90

25th anniv. of UNESCO.

**1971, Nov. 14** ***Perf. 14x14½***
**547** A322 20p salmon pink .50 .50

Chidren's Day.

C. V. Raman
A323

**1971, Nov. 21** ***Perf. 13***
**548** A323 20p brown & dp org 1.00 .55

Sir Chandrasekhara Venkata Raman (1888-1970), physicist, Nobel Prize winner.

Rabindranath Tagore, Visva-Bharati Building — A324

**1971, Dec. 24** ***Perf. 14½x14***
**549** A324 20p blk brn & org brn 1.00 .80

50th anniv. of Visva-Bharati, center for Eastern cultural studies.

Indian Cricket Victories
A325

**1971, Dec. 24**
**550** A325 20p green 3.50 1.10

Intelsat 3 over Map of Eastern Hemisphere
A326

**1972, Feb. 26** **Photo.** ***Perf. 13½***
**551** A326 20p dark purple .50 .40

Arvi Satellite Earth Station.

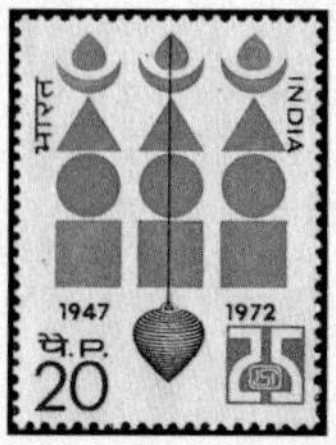


Plumb Line and Symbols — A327

**1972, May 29** **Photo.** ***Perf. 13***
**552** A327 20p bluish gray & black .50 .50

Indian Standards Institution (ISI), 25th anniv.

Signal Panel and Route Diagram — A328

**1972, June 30**
**553** A328 20p black & multi 2.50 1.25

Intl. Railroad Union (UIC), 50th anniv.

Hockey, Olympic Rings
A329

20th Olympic Games, Munich, Aug. 26-Sept. 11: 1.45r, "1972," Olympic rings, symbols for running, wrestling, shooting and hockey.

**1972, Aug. 10** **Photo.** ***Perf. 13***
**554** A329 20p dull violet 3.50 .35
**555** A329 1.45r bl grn & dk red 4.00 3.00

Marchers with Flag, Parliament
A330

**1972, Aug. 15**
**556** A330 20p blue & multi 1.00 .60

25th anniv. of Independence.

Armed Forces' Emblems — A331

**1972, Aug. 15**
**557** A331 20p blue & multi .75 .55

Honoring India's defense forces.

Symbol of Aurobindo and Sun — A332

**1972, Aug. 15** ***Perf. 14x13½***
**558** A332 20p yellow & blue .50 .50

Sri Aurobindo Ghose (1872-1950).

V.O. Chidambaram Pillai and Ship — A333

*Perf. 13½x13*

**1972, Sept. 5** **Unwmk.**
**559** A333 20p bl & dk red brn 1.25 .65

V.O. Chidambaram Pillai (1872-1936), founder of steamship company, trade union leader, resistance fighter.

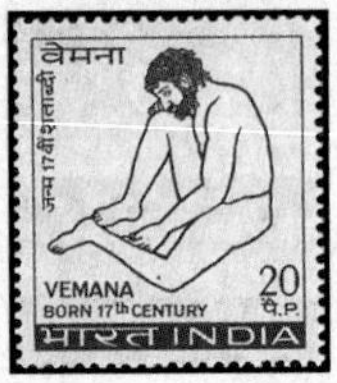


Vemana, 17th-18th Cent. Poet — A334

**1972, Oct. 16** **Wmk. 324** ***Perf. 14***
**560** A334 20p black .50 .50

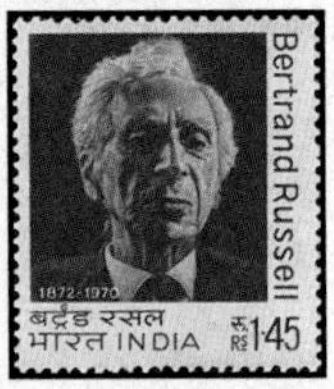


Bertrand Russell — A335

**1972, Oct. 16** **Unwmk.**
**561** A335 1.45r black 5.25 4.00

British philosopher and pacifist (1872-1970).

Bhai Vir Singh — A336

**1972, Oct. 16** ***Perf. 13½***
**562** A336 20p dull purple .90 .45

Bhai Vir Singh (1872-1957), poet and scholar.

T. Prakasam — A337

**1972, Oct. 16**
**563** A337 20p yellow brown .50 .40

T. Prakasam (1872-1957), national leader and lawyer.

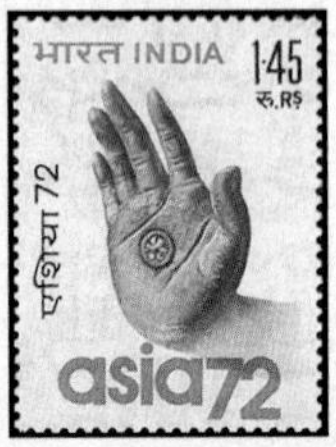


Hand of Buddha, 9th Century Sculpture — A338

20p, Stylized Hand of Buddha as Fair emblem.

**1972, Nov. 3** **Wmk. 324** ***Perf. 13***
**564** A338 20p orange & black .40 .40
**565** A338 1.45r orange, blk & ind 1.00 *2.40*

3rd Asian Intl. Trade Fair, ASIA 72, New Delhi.

Vikram Ambalal Sarabhai, Rohini Rocket and Dove A339

**1972, Dec. 30** **Unwmk.**
**566** A339 20p slate grn & brn .60 .60

1st anniv. of the death of Dr. Vikram Ambalal Sarabhai (1919-1971), chairman of Natl. Committee for Space Research.

Flag of USSR and Spasski Tower A340

**1972, Dec. 30** ***Perf. 13***
**567** A340 20p red & yellow .60 .60

50th anniv. of the Soviet Union.

INDIPEX 73 Emblem — A341

**1973, Jan. 8** **Photo.** ***Perf. 13***
**568** A341 1.45r black, pink & gold .80 *1.40*

Intl. Phil. Exhib., New Delhi, 11/14-23/73. See Nos. 597-599.

Wheel of Asoka, Naga (Serpent) — A342

India Gate, Gnat Planes, India's Colors A343

**1973, Jan. 26** ***Perf. 13***
**569** A342 20p orange & multi .35 .35
***Perf. 14½x14***
**570** A343 1.45r violet & multi 2.00 2.00

Republic Day, 25th year of Independence.

Ramakrishna Paramahamsa (1836-86) — A344

**1973, Feb. 18** **Photo.** ***Perf. 13***
**571** A344 20p yellow brown .60 .50

Hindu spiritual leader; Ramakrishna Mission founded by his followers.

Army Postal Service Corps Emblem — A345

**1973, Mar. 1**
**572** A345 20p violet blue & red .60 .60

1st anniv. of establishment of Army Postal Service Corps.

Flower, Flag, Map — A346

**1973, Apr. 10** **Unwmk.** ***Perf. 13***
**573** A346 20p blue & multi .60 .60

1st anniv. of Bangladesh independence.

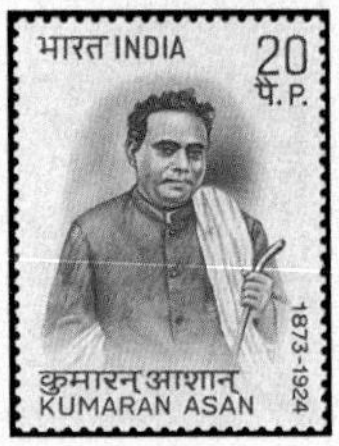


Kumaran Asan — A347

**1973, Apr. 12**
**574** A347 20p brown .50 .50

Kumaran Asan (1873-1924), Kerala social reformer and writer.

Flame and Flag of India — A348

**1973, Apr. 13**
**575** A348 20p deep blue & multi .50 .50

In honor of the martyrs of the massacre of Jallianwala Bagh, Apr. 13, 1919.

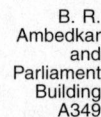

B. R. Ambedkar and Parliament Building A349

**1973, Apr. 14** ***Perf. 14½x14***
**576** A349 20p olive & plum .50 .50

Bhimrao R. Ambedkar (1891-1956), lawyer, reformer of Hindu law and one of the writers of India's Constitution.

Radha-Kishangarh, by Nihal Chand, 1778 — A350

Indian Miniatures: 50p, Dancing Couple, late 17th century. 1r, Lovers on a Camel, by Nasir-ud-Din, c. 1605. 2r, Chained Elephant, by Zain-al-Abidin, 16th century.

**1973, May 5** **Photo.** ***Perf. 13½x13***
**577** A350 20p gold & multi .55 *.60*
**578** A350 50p lilac & multi 1.25 *2.25*
**579** A350 1r ocher & multi 1.60 *1.75*
**580** A350 2r gold & multi 2.25 *3.75*
*Nos. 577-580 (4)* 5.65 8.35

Himalayas A351

**1973, May 15** ***Perf. 13½x13***
**581** A351 20p blue .80 .65

15th anniv. of Indian Mountaineering Foundation.

Air India Jet — A352

**1973, June 8** **Photo.** ***Perf. 13***
**582** A352 1.45r multicolored 5.50 5.50

Air India, 25 years of intl. service.

Stone Cross on St. Thomas's Mount, Madras — A353

**1973, July 3**
**583** A353 20p gray ol & blue gray .50 .50

1900th anniv. of the death of St. Thomas.

Michael Madhusudan Dutt — A354

**1973, July 21** **Photo.** ***Perf. 13***
**584** A354 20p ocher & olive 1.00 .80

Dutt (1824-1873), writer and poet.

Vishnu Dingambar Paluskar (1872-1931), Musician — A355

**1973, July 21**
**585** A355 30p red brown 1.75 1.75

Dr. Armauer G. Hansen, Microscope, Petri Dish with Bacilli A356

**1973, July 21**
**586** A356 50p deep brown 2.00 2.00

Cent. of the discovery by Hansen of the Hansen bacillus, the cause of leprosy.

Nicolaus Copernicus, Heliocentric System A357

**1973, July 21**
**587** A357 1r vio blue & red brown 2.00 2.00

500th anniv. of the birth of Nicolaus Copernicus (1473-1543), Polish astronomer.

Allan Octavian Hume (1829-1912) A358

**1973, July 31**
**588** A358 20p gray .50 .50

Hume, British civil servant and friend of India, on the 25th anniv. of independence.

Nehru and Gandhi A359

**1973, Aug. 15 Photo. *Perf. 13***
**589** A359 20p blue vio & red brown .50 .50

25th anniv. of India's independence.

Romesh Chunder Dutt — A360

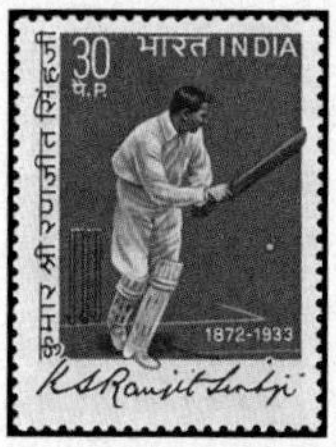

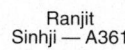

Ranjit Sinhji — A361

Vithalbhai Patel (1873-1933), National Leader — A362

**1973, Sept. 27 Photo. *Perf. 13***
**590** A360 20p brown .50 .50
**591** A361 30p dark green 5.50 5.50
**592** A362 50p brown .50 .50
*Nos. 590-592 (3)* 6.50 6.50

Birth anniv.: Dutt (1848-1909), economist and pres. of Natl. Cong. in 1890; Sinhji, Maharaja of Nawanagar (1872-1933), cricketer.

President's Body Guard — A363

**1973, Sept. 30**
**593** A363 20p multicolored 2.00 1.50

Bicentenary of President's Body Guard.

INTERPOL Emblem — A364

**1973, Oct. 9 Photo. *Perf. 13***
**594** A364 20p brown .70 .70

50th anniv. of Intl. Criminal Police Org.

Syed Ahmad Khan, Aligarh University A365

**1973, Oct. 17**
**595** A365 20p olive gray .50 *1.00*

Khan (1817-1898), founder of Aligarh Muslim Univ.

Child's Drawing A366

**1973, Nov. 14 Photo. *Perf. 13***
**596** A366 20p multicolored .50 .50

Children's Day.

Elephant with Howdah, and No. 200 — A367

**1973, Nov. 14**
**597** A367 20p Emblem .30 .30
**598** A367 1r shown 1.25 1.25
**599** A367 2r Peacock, vert. 1.50 1.50
*a.* Souvenir sheet of 4 9.00 9.00
*Nos. 597-599 (3)* 3.05 3.05

Intl. Phil. Exhib., INDIPEX 73, New Delhi, Nov. 14-23. No. 599a contains 4 imperf. stamps similar to Nos. 568, 597-599. The imperf. stamps from No. 599a were not valid individually.

NCC Emblem — A368

**1973, Nov. 25**
**600** A368 20p multicolored .50 .40

National Cadet Corps, 25th anniv.

Rajagopalachari A369

**1973, Dec. 25**
**601** A369 20p gray olive .50 .50

Chakravarti Rajagopalachari (1878-1972), statesman, governor general (1948-50).

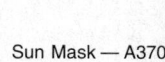

Sun Mask — A370

Narasimha Mask — A371

Designs: Masks.

**1974, Apr. 15 Photo. *Perf. 13***
**602** A370 20p shown .40 .40
**603** A370 50p Moon .60 .50
**604** A371 1r shown .95 .80
**605** A371 2r Ravana, horiz. 1.25 1.50
*a.* Souvenir sheet of 4, #602-605 4.00 4.00
*Nos. 602-605 (4)* 3.20 3.20

300th Anniv. of the Coronation of Chatrapati Sivaji Maharaj (1627-1680), Military Leader of the Maharattas and Enlightened Ruler — A372

**1974, June 2 Photo. *Perf. 13***
**606** A372 25p gold & multi 1.00 .90

Maithili Sharan Gupta — A373

Utkal Gourab Madhusudan Das — A374

Kandukuri Veeresalingam A375

Tipu Sultan — A376

No. 608, Jainarain Vyas. 1r, Max Mueller.

**1974 Photo. *Perf. 13***
**607** A373 25p red brown .30 .35
**608** A373 25p brown .30 .35
**609** A374 25p olive gray .30 .35
**610** A375 25p red brown .40 .45
**611** A376 50p violet brown .85 1.10
**612** A376 1r brown .95 1.10
*Nos. 607-612 (6)* 3.10 3.70

Gupta (1886-1964), poet and patriot; Vyas (1899-1963), writer and member of parliament; Das (1848-1934), writer and patriot. Veeresalingam (1848-1919), reformer; Sultan (1750-99), military leader and reformer; Mueller (1823-1900), German scholar of Sanskrit and Indian culture.

Issued: #607-609, 7/3; #610-612, 7/15.

Kamala Nehru — A377

**1974, Aug 1 Photo. *Perf. 14½x14***

**613** A377 25p multicolored 1.00 1.00

Kamala Nehru (1899-1936), champion of India's freedom, mother of Indira Gandhi.

WPY Emblem — A378

**1974, Aug. 14 Unwmk. *Perf. 13½***

**614** A378 25p buff & plum .50 .40

V. V. Giri — A379

**1974, Aug. 24 *Perf. 13x13½***

**615** A379 25p green & multi .50 .50

Vaharagiri Venkata Giri, pres. of India, 1969-74.

**Type of 1965-68 and**

Tiger — A380

Veena A381

Design: 25p, Axis deer (chital).

**1974 Wmk. 324 *Perf. 14½x14***

| | | | | |
|---|---|---|---|---|
| **622** | A380 | 15p dk brn (white "15") | 4.50 | .75 |
| **623** | A202 | 25p brown | 1.25 | 1.00 |
| **624** | A381 | 1r black & brown | 3.25 | .25 |
| | | *Nos. 622-624 (3)* | 9.00 | 2.00 |

Issue dates: 25p, Aug. 20; 15p, 1r, Oct. 1.

See Nos. 671-682.

Madhubani Folk Design, UPU Emblem A384

Designs: 25p, UPU emblem. 2r, Arrows circling globe, UPU emblem, vert.

**1974, Oct. 3 Unwmk. *Perf. 13***

| | | | | |
|---|---|---|---|---|
| **634** | A384 | 25p brt blue & gray | .85 | .30 |
| **635** | A384 | 1r olive & multi | 1.25 | .85 |
| **636** | A384 | 2r ocher & multi | 2.00 | 1.90 |
| *a.* | | Souvenir sheet of 3, #634-636 | 10.00 | 10.00 |
| | | *Nos. 634-636 (3)* | 4.10 | 3.05 |

Cent. of UPU.

A385

**1974, Oct. 9 Photo. *Perf. 13½***

| | | | |
|---|---|---|---|
| **637** | 25p Flute player | .60 | .50 |
| **638** | 25p Vidyadhara with garland | .60 | .50 |
| *a.* | A385 Pair, #637-638 | 2.00 | 2.00 |

Cent. of Mathura Museum.

Nicholas Konstantin Roerich, by Henry Dropsy A387

**1974, Oct. 9 *Perf. 13***

**639** A387 1r dark gray & yellow .80 .80

Roerich (1874-1947), Russian painter and sponsor of Roerich Peace Pact.

Pavapuri Temple, Bihar A388

**1974, Nov. 13 Photo. *Perf. 13***

**640** A388 25p slate .60 .25

2500th anniv. of attainment of Nirvana by Bhagwan Mahavira, leader and preacher of Jainism.

Dancers and Musician (Child's Drawing) A389

**1974, Nov. 14 *Perf. 14½x14***

**641** A389 25p multicolored .60 .55

UNICEF in India.

Cat (Child's Drawing) — A390

**1974, Nov. 14 *Perf. 13***

**642** A390 25p multicolored 1.00 .50

Children's Day.

Territorial Army Emblem — A391

**1974, Nov. 16 *Perf. 13***

**643** A391 25p green, yel & black .80 .60

Territorial Army, 25th anniv.

Cows, from Handpainted Rajasthan Cloth — A392

**1974, Dec. 2 *Perf. 14***

**644** A392 25p ocher & maroon .60 .35

19th Intl. Dairy Cong., New Delhi, Dec. 2-6.

Symbol of Retardates and Child A393

**1974, Dec. 8 Photo. *Perf. 13½x13***

**645** A393 25p black & vermilion .75 .65

Help the Retardates!

Guglielmo Marconi — A394

**1974, Dec. 12 *Perf. 13x13½***

**646** A394 2r slate 4.00 3.00

Marconi (1874-1937), Italian electrical engineer and inventor.

St. Francis Xavier's Tomb and Statue A395

**1974, Dec. 24 *Perf. 13½x13***

**647** A395 25p multicolored .50 .50

Showing of the body of St. Francis Xavier, Apostle to the Indies.

Saraswati, Goddess of Language and Learning, Inscription in Hindi — A396

**1975, Jan. 10 Photo. *Perf. 14x14½***

**648** A396 25p dark red & gray .50 .50

World Hindi Convention, Nagpur, Jan. 10-14. See No. 654.

Parliament House A397

**1975, Jan. 26 *Perf. 13***

**649** A397 25p black, blue & silver 1.00 .95

Republic of India, 25th anniv.

Table Tennis Paddle and Ball — A398

**1975, Feb. 6 *Perf. 13½x13***

**650** A398 25p black, red & olive 1.50 .55

33rd World Table Tennis Championship, Calcutta.

Woman's Hands Releasing Doves A399

**1975, Feb. 16**

**651** A399 25p yellow & multi .90 .55

International Women's Year.

Bicentenary of Army Ordnance Corps — A400

**1975, Apr. 8 Photo. *Perf. 13x13½***

**652** A400 25p black & vermilion 1.75 1.10

Flame A401

**1975, Apr. 11 *Perf. 13½x13***

**653** A401 25p orange & black .60 .50

Cent. of the founding of Arya Samaj, a movement dedicated to enlightenment and progress and to a revival of Vedic Law and Aryan culture.

**Saraswati Type of 1975**

25p, Saraswati and inscription in Telugu.

**1975, Apr. 12 *Perf. 14x14½***

**654** A396 25p dp green & dk gray .80 .45

World Telugu Conf., Hyderabad, Apr. 12-18.

Aryabhata Satellite A402

**1975, Apr. 20 *Perf. 13½x13***

**655** A402 25p multicolored .90 .85

Launching of 1st Indian satellite, Apr. 19, 1975.

Bluewinged Pitta A403

Birds: 50p, Black-headed oriole. 1r, Western tragopan, vert. 2r, Himalayan monal pheasant, vert.

**1975, Apr. 28** ***Perf. 13½x13, 13x13½***

**656** A403 25p multicolored .95 .30
**657** A403 50p multicolored 2.25 2.25
**658** A403 1r multicolored 3.25 3.25
**659** A403 2r multicolored 4.50 4.50
*Nos. 656-659 (4)* 10.95 10.30

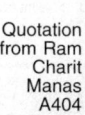

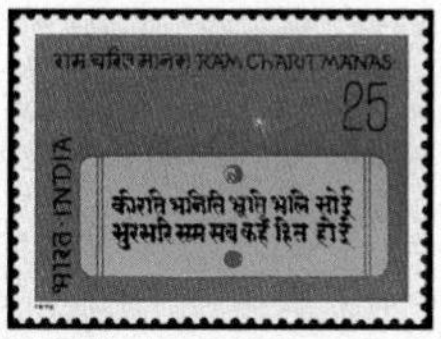

Quotation from Ram Charit Manas A404

**1975, May 24** **Photo.** ***Perf. 13½x13***

**660** A404 25p red, orange & black 1.00 .25

Ram Charit Manas, Hindi poem by Goswami Tulsidas (1532-1623).

Women and YWCA Emblem — A405

**1975, June 20** **Photo.** ***Perf. 13x13½***

**661** A405 25p gray & multi .60 .50

YWCA of India, cent.

Creation of Adam, by Michelangelo — A406

Design: Nos. 664-665, Creation of sun, moon and stars, by Michelangelo.

**1975, June 28** ***Perf. 14x13½***

**662** 50p multicolored .65 .50
**663** 50p multicolored 1.25 1.00
*a.* A406 Pair #662-663 2.75 2.75
**664** 50p multicolored 1.25 1.00
**665** 50p multicolored 1.25 1.00
*b.* A406 Pair #664-665 2.75 2.75

Michelangelo Buonarroti (1475-1564), Italian sculptor, painter and architect.

**Types of 1965-1974 Without Currency Designation and**

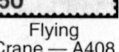

Flying Crane — A408

Jawaharlal Nehru — A409

Mahatma Gandhi — A410

Himalayas A411

Designs: 2p, Bidri vase. 5p, Family. 10p, Electric locomotive. 15p, Tiger. 20p, Wooden toy horse. 30p, Male and female figurines. No. 680, Somnath Temple. 1r, Veena. 5r, Bhakra Dam, Punjab. 10r, Trombay Atomic Center.

**Three types of 25p Nehru:**
Type I: Size at top, 25mm. Character before NEHRU has 2 lower points.
Type II: Smaller portrait. Size at top, 23mm. Character has 3 points.
Type III: Portrait as in type I. Size at top, 25½mm. Character has 3 points.

***Perf. 14½x14, 14x14½, 14 (#674-676), 13 (#681)***
**Wmk. 324; 360 (# 666A, 667, 668, 670)**

**1975-88** **Photo.**

**666** A202 2(p) redsh brn, wmk. 324 ('76) 1.25 *2.25*
**666A** A202 2(p) redsh brn, wmk. 360 ('76) 1.25 *2.25*
**667** A202 2(p) redsh brn, wmk. 360, litho. ('79) 1.25 *2.25*
**668** A202 5(p) cerise ('76) .75 .25
**669** A203 10(p) brt blue ('76) .75 .25
**670** A203 10(p) brt blue ('79) 4.00 .60
**671** A380 15(p) dk brn (brown "15") 2.00 .25
**672** A408 20(p) green .40 .25
**673** A409 25(p) vio, I ('76) 10.00 .75
**674** A409 25(p) vio, II ('76) 6.50 .75
**675** A409 25(p) vio, III ('76) 5.00 .75
**676** A410 25(p) red brn ('76) (23x29mm) 1.25 .30
**677** A410 25(p) red brn ('78) (17x20mm) 8.00 2.25
**678** A202 30(p) brown ('79) 4.00 .50
**679** A408 50(p) violet blue 6.50 .30
**680** A202 60(p) dk gray ('76) 2.00 1.00
**681** A410 60(p) black ('88) 1.10 .25
**682** A381 1(r) brown & blk 4.25 .25
**683** A411 2(r) violet & brn 17.00 .50
**684** A205 5(r) brn & vio ('76) 2.50 .90
**685** A205 10(r) dl grn & sl ('76) 2.25 1.10
*Nos. 666-685 (21)* 82.00 17.95

No. 667 has a background of fine horizontal lines.
See #841-842, 844-845, 846A-846B, 916.
Size of No. 681, 17x20mm.

Irrigation Commission Emblem — A412

**Unwmk.**

**1975, July 28** **Photo.** ***Perf. 14***

**686** A412 25p multicolored .65 .30

9th Intl. Cong. on Irrigation and Drainage, Moscow, and 25th anniv. of the Intl. Commission on Irrigation and Drainage.

"Educational Television" A413

**1975, Aug. 1** ***Perf. 13x13½***

**687** A413 25p multicolored .65 .45

Inauguration of the Satellite Instructional Television Experiment (SITE).

Arunagirinathar A414

**1975, Aug. 14** **Photo.** ***Perf. 13½***

**688** A414 50p rose lilac 1.75 1.25

600th birth anniv. of Arunagirinathar, Advaita philosopher, saint and author of Tiruppugazh, a collection of songs.

A415

**1975, Aug. 26** **Photo.** ***Perf. 13½***

**689** A415 25p rose & black .80 .55

Namibia Day. See note after UN No. 241.

A416

**1975, Sept. 4**

**690** A416 25p slate green .50 .50

Mir Anees (1803-1874), Urdu poet.

Chhatri at Maheshwar A417

**1975, Sept. 4** ***Perf. 13x13½***

**691** A417 25p red brown .50 .50

Queen Ahilyabai Holkar (1725-1795); building shown was place of last rites.

Bharata Natyam Dance — A418

Designs: Indian traditional dances.

**1975, Oct. 20** **Photo.** ***Perf. 13x13½***

**692** A418 25p shown .95 .65
**693** A418 50p Orissi 1.40 .70
**694** A418 75p Kathak 1.90 .90
**695** A418 1r Kathakali 2.25 1.10
**696** A418 1.50r Kuchipudi 2.75 1.60
**697** A418 2r Manipuri 2.75 1.60
*Nos. 692-697 (6)* 12.00 6.55

Krishna Menon — A419

Ameer Khusrau — A420

Poem by Bahadur Shah Zafar A421

Design: No. 699, Sardar Vallabhbhai Patel.

**1975** ***Perf. 13x13½, 13½x13***

**698** A419 25p olive 1.40 .70
**699** A419 25p slate .50 .50
**700** A420 50p yellow & brown 1.60 .80
**701** A421 1r black, brn & buff 2.00 1.00
*Nos. 698-701 (4)* 5.50 3.00

Men of India: V. K. Krishna Menon (1896-1974), founder of India League and member of Parliament; Patel (1875-1950), statesman who unified India, birth cent.; Khusrau (1253-1325), poet; Zafar (1775-1862), last Mogul emperor and poet.
Issue dates: #699, Oct. 31; others Oct. 24.

Parliament Annex, New Delhi A422

**1975, Oct. 28** ***Perf. 14½x14***

**702** A422 2r gray olive 3.25 2.00

21st Commonwealth Parliamentary Conf., New Delhi, Oct. 28-Nov. 4.

Karmavir Nabin Chandra Bardoloi (1875-1936), Writer and Gandhi Associate — A423

**1975, Nov. 3** **Photo.** ***Perf. 13***

**703** A423 25p reddish brown .50 .35

Cow, Child's Painting A424

**1975, Nov. 14**

**704** A424 25p multicolored 1.00 .55

Children's Day.

Security Press Building A425

**1975, Dec. 13 Photo. *Perf. 13***
**705** A425 25p multicolored .70 .35

India Security Press, 50th anniv.

Gurdwara Sisganj, Chandni Chawk — A426

**1975, Dec. 16**
**706** A426 25p multicolored .80 .50

300th anniv. of martyrdom of Tegh Bahadur (1621-75), 9th Sikh Guru; building shown was place of beheading.

Theosophical Society Emblem — A427

**1975, Dec. 20**
**707** A427 25p multicolored .70 .35

Centenary of Theosophical Society.

Meteorological Instruments A428

**1975, Dec. 24 Photo. *Perf. 13***
**708** A428 25p blue vio, blk & grn 1.00 .55

Indian Meteorological Dept., cent.

Early Mail Cart A429

Indian Bishop Mark, 1775 — A430

**1975, Dec. 25**
**709** A429 25p brown & black 1.00 .40
**710** A430 2r reddish brn & blk 3.25 1.75

INPEX 75, Indian Natl. Phil. Exhib., Calcutta, Dec. 25-31.

Lalit Narayan Mishra — A431

**1976, Jan. 3**
**711** A431 25p sepia .60 .30

Mishra (1923-75), Minister of Railroads.

Tiger — A432

**1976, Jan. 24**
**712** A432 25p multicolored 1.75 .90

Jim Corbett (1875-1955), conservationist.

Painted Storks A433

**1976, Feb. 10 Photo. *Perf. 13***
**713** A433 25p sky blue & multi 1.75 .85

Keoladeo Ghana, Bharatpur Water Bird Sanctuary.

Tank A434

**1976, Mar. 4 Photo. *Perf. 13***
**714** A434 25p multicolored 2.25 .55

16th Light Cavalry, senior regiment of Armoured Corps, bicentenary.

Alexander Graham Bell — A435

**1976, Mar. 10 Photo. *Perf. 13x13½***
**715** A435 25p yellow & black 1.40 .90

Cent. of 1st telephone call by Bell, Mar. 10, 1876.

Muthuswami Dikshitar — A436

**1976, Mar. 18 *Perf. 14x13½***
**716** A436 25p dull violet 1.00 .55

Dikshitar (1775-1835), musician, composer.

Eye and Red Cross A437

**1976, Apr. 7 *Perf. 13½x13***
**717** A437 25p dark brown & red 1.40 .55

World Health Day: "Foresight prevents blindness."

"Industries" A438

***Perf. 13x13½***
**1976, Apr. 30 Unwmk.**
**718** A438 25p multicolored .40 .25

Industrial development and progress.

1 F/I type, Ajmer, 1895 A439

Locomotives: 25p, WDM 2 Diesel Locomotive, 1963. 1r, 1 WP./1, 4-6-2 Pacific type, 1963. 2r, 1 GIP No. 1, 1853.

**1976, May 15 *Perf. 15x14***
**719** A439 25p multicolored 1.10 .25
**720** A439 50p multicolored 1.75 .80
**721** A439 1r multicolored 4.00 1.90
**722** A439 2r multicolored 4.75 2.10
*Nos. 719-722 (4)* 11.60 5.05

Kumaraswamy Kamaraj (1903-1975), Independence Fighter — A440

**1976, July 15 Photo. *Perf. 13x13½***
**723** A440 25p sepia .50 .50

Target, Olympic Rings — A441

Hockey — A442

**1976, July 17 *Perf. 14***
**724** A441 25p dk blue & carmine .40 .30
**725** A441 1r "Team handball" 1.60 .80
**726** A442 1.50r black & brt purple 2.75 1.60
**727** A441 2.80r "Running" 2.75 2.75
*Nos. 724-727 (4)* 7.50 5.45

21st Olympic Games, Montreal, Canada, July 17-Aug. 1.

Subhadra Kumari Chauhan — A443

**1976, Aug. 6 Photo. *Perf. 13x13½***
**728** A443 25p grayish blue .50 .50

Chauhan (1904-1948), Hindi poetess and member of Legislative Assembly.

Param Vir Chakra Medal — A444

**1976, Aug. 15**
**729** A444 25p yellow & multi .50 .50

Medal of Honor awarded for bravery to military men.

Women's University, Bombay A445

**1976, Sept. 3 Photo. *Perf. 13½x14***
**730** A445 25p violet .50 .30

Indian Women's Univ., 60th anniv.

Bharatendu Harishchandra A446

**1976, Sept. 9 *Perf. 13***
**731** A446 25p black brown .50 .50

Harishchandra (1850-1885), writer, "Father of Modern Hindi."

Sarat Chandra Chatterji — A447

**1976, Sept. 15 Unwmk.**
**732** A447 25p dull purple .50 .50

Chatterji (1876-1938), writer.

Family Planning — A448

**1976, Sept. 22 Photo.** ***Perf. 14x14½***

**733** A448 25p multicolored .50 .50

Maharaja Agrasen, Coin and Brick Wall A449

**1976, Sept. 24** ***Perf. 13½x13***

**734** A449 25p red brown .50 .50

Maharaja Agrasen, legendary ruler of Agra.

India Blood Donation Day — A450

**1976, Oct. 1** ***Perf. 13x13½***

**735** A450 25p bister, car & black 1.25 .70

Wildlife Protection A451

**1976, Oct. 1** ***Perf. 14x14½, 14½x14***

| | | | | |
|---|---|---|---|---|
| **736** A451 | 25p | Swamp deer | .70 | .35 |
| **737** A451 | 50p | Lion | 1.90 | .95 |
| **738** A451 | 1r | Leopard, horiz. | 2.75 | 1.25 |
| **739** A451 | 2r | Caracal, horiz. | 3.00 | 1.50 |
| | | *Nos. 736-739 (4)* | 8.35 | 4.05 |

Suryakant Tripathi "Nirala" (1896-1961), Hindi poet — A452

**1976, Oct. 15** ***Perf. 13***

**740** A452 25p dark violet .50 .50

Children's Day — A453

**1976, Nov. 14 Unwmk.** ***Perf. 14***

**741** A453 25p Mongoose and Woman .60 .30

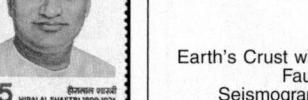

Hiralal Shastri — A454

**1976, Nov. 24** ***Perf. 13***

**742** A454 25p red brown .50 .50

Hiralal Shastri (1899-1974), social worker and political leader.

Hari Singh Gour — A455

**1976, Nov. 26**

**743** A455 25p plum .50 .50

Hari Singh Gour (1870-1949), University administrator, member Indian Legislative and Constituent Assemblies.

Airbus A456

**1976, Dec. 1** ***Perf. 14½x14***

**744** A456 2r multicolored 4.00 2.10

Inauguration of Indian Airlines Airbus.

Hybrid Coconut Palm — A457

**1976, Dec. 27 Photo.** ***Perf. 13x13½***

**745** A457 25p multicolored .50 .40

75th anniv. of coconut research in India.

Vande Mataram, First Stanza A458

**1976, Dec. 30** ***Perf. 13***

**746** A458 25p multicolored .50 .40

Vande Mataram, national song of India, music by Bankim Chandra Chatterjee, 1896, words by Rabindranath Tagore, 1911.

Film and Globe A459

**1977, Jan. 3**

**747** A459 2r multicolored 2.50 1.25

6th Intl. Film Festival, New Delhi, Jan. 3-16.

Earth's Crust with Fault, Seismograph A460

**1977, Jan. 10**

**748** A460 2r dull purple 1.75 1.40

6th World Conference on Earthquake Engineering, New Delhi, Jan. 10-14.

Tarun Ram Phookun — A461

**1977, Jan. 22 Photo.** ***Perf. 13x13½***

**749** A461 25p sepia .50 .50

Phookun (1877-1939), lawyer, Assam political leader.

Paramahansa Yogananda A462

**1977, Mar. 7 Photo.** ***Perf. 13½***

**750** A462 25p deep orange 1.50 .80

Yogananda (1893-1952), religious leader, founder of Self-realization Society in America.

Red Cross Conference Emblem — A463

**1977, Mar. 9**

**751** A463 2r multicolored 3.50 2.00

1st Asian Regional Red Cross Conference, New Delhi, Mar. 9-16.

Fakhruddin Ali Ahmed (1905-77) — A464

**1977, Mar. 22 Photo.** ***Perf. 13½x13***

**752** A464 25p multicolored .60 .40

Ahmed, Pres. of India, 1974-77.

Asian-Oceanic Postal Union Emblem — A465

**1977, Apr, 1** ***Perf. 13***

**753** A465 2r silver & multi 1.50 1.25

Asian-Oceanic Postal Union, 15th anniv.

"Loyalty" and Morarjee A466

**1977, Apr. 2** ***Perf. 13½x13***

**754** A466 25p blue 1.25 .70

Narottam Morarjee (1877-1929), founder of Scindia Steam Ship Navigation Co.

Makhanlal Chaturvedi A467

**1977, Apr. 4** ***Perf. 13***

**755** A467 25p orange brown .50 .50

Chaturvedi (1889-1968), Hindi writer.

Mahaprabhu Vallabhacharya A468

**1977, Apr. 14**

**756** A468 1r olive brown .50 .50

Vallabhacharya (1479-1531), philosopher.

Federation Emblem A469

**1977, Apr. 23** ***Perf. 13½x13***

**757** A469 25p ocher & purple .50 .50

Federation of Indian Chambers of Commerce, 50th anniv.

Protection of Environment A470

**1977, June 5 Photo.** ***Perf. 13***

**758** A470 2r multicolored .80 .55

Council of States Chamber A471

**1977, June 21**

**759** A471 25p multicolored .50 .50

Council of States, Rajya Sabha (Parliament), 25th anniv.

Lotus A472

50p and 1r are vert.

**1977, July 1** ***Perf. 15x14, 14x15***

**760** A472 25p shown .50 .30
**761** A472 50p Rhododendron .85 .50
**762** A472 1r Kadamba 1.10 .75
**763** A472 2r Gloriosa lily 1.90 1.10
*Nos. 760-763 (4)* 4.35 2.65

Berliner Gramaphone — A473

**1977, July 20** ***Perf. 13½x13***

**764** A473 2r black & brown 1.50 .90

Centenary of the phonograph.

Ananda Kentish Coomaraswamy (1877-1947) and Dancing Shiva — A474

**1977, Aug. 22 Photo.** ***Perf. 13x13½***

**765** A474 25p multicolored .60 .30

Coomaraswamy, art historian and critic.

Ganga Ram (1851-1927) and Hospital, New Delhi — A475

**1977, Sept. 4** ***Perf. 14½x14***

**766** A475 25p rose carmine .50 .35

Ram, social reformer and philanthropist.

Dr. Samuel Hahnemann and Cinchona — A476

**1977, Oct. 6 Photo.** ***Perf. 13***

**767** A476 2r black & green 5.50 2.75

32nd Intl. Homeopathic Cong., New Delhi.

19th Century Postman — A477

Lion and Palm Tree, East India Co. Essay — A478

**1977, Oct. 12** ***Perf. 13***

**768** A477 25p multicolored 1.00 .50

***Perf. 13½***

**769** A478 2r mag & gray, *buff* 2.75 1.75

INPEX '77 Phil. Exhib., Bangalore, 10/12-16.

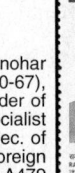

Ram Manohar Lohia (1910-67), Founder of Congress Socialist Party, Sec. of Foreign Dept. — A479

**1977, Oct. 12** ***Perf. 13x13½***

**770** A479 25p red brown 1.25 1.10

Red Scinde Dawks, 1852 A480

Design: 3r, Foreign mail arriving at Ballard Pier, Bombay, 1927.

**1977, Oct. 19** ***Perf. 13½x13***

**771** A480 1r orange & multi 2.00 1.10
**772** A480 3r orange & multi 4.00 2.10

ASIANA 77, First Asian International Philatelic Exhibition, Bangalore, Oct. 19-23.

Statue of Rani Channamma — A481

**1977, Oct. 23**

**773** A481 25p gray green 2.25 1.10

Rani Channamma of Kittue (1778-1829), who fought against British rule.

Mother and Child, Khajuraho Sculpture — A482

**1977, Oct. 23** ***Perf. 13x13½***

**774** A482 2r gray & sepia 3.50 2.25

15th Intl. Pediatrics Congress.

Sun and National Colors — A483

**1977, Nov. 8 Photo.** ***Perf. 13***

**775** A483 25p multicolored .60 .35

Union Public Service Commission, founded 1926.

Stylized Grain — A484

**1977, Nov. 13**

**776** A484 25p green .60 .30

AGRIEXPO '77, Intl. Agriculture Exhib.

Cats A485

1r, Friends. Designs are from children's drawings.

**1977, Nov. 14**

**777** A485 25p multicolored .95 .45
**778** A485 1r multicolored 3.00 2.25

Children's Day.

Jotirao Phooley — A486

**1977, Nov. 28** **Wmk. 324**

**779** A486 25p gray olive .50 .40

Phooley (1827-1890), social reformer.

Senapati Bapat — A487

**1977, Nov. 28**

**780** A487 25p brown orange .50 .40

Senapati Bapat (Pandurang Mahadev Bapat, 1880-1967), scholar and fighter for India's independence.

Diagram of Population Growth — A488

***Perf. 13x13½***

**1977, Dec. 13** **Unwmk.**

**781** A488 2r carmine & blue grn .80 .55

41st Session of Intl. Statistical Institute, New Delhi, Dec. 5-15.

Kamta Prasad (1875-1947) and Hindi Grammar A489

**1977, Dec. 25** **Wmk. 324** ***Perf. 14***

**782** A489 25p sepia .50 .50

Prasad, compiler of Hindi Grammar.

Spasski Tower, Russian Flag — A490

**1977, Dec. 30** **Unwmk.** ***Perf. 13***

**783** A490 1r multicolored .80 .55

60th anniv. of Russian October revolution.

Climber Crossing Crevasse — A491

Indian Flag near Summit A492

***Perf. 13½x13, 13x13½***

**1978, Jan. 15** **Photo.**

**784** A491 25p multicolored .30 .30
**785** A492 1r multicolored .70 .55

Conquest of Kanchenjunga (Himalayas), by Indian team under Col. N. Kumar, May 31, 1977.

Tourists in Shikara on Dal Lake A493

**1978, Jan. 23** ***Perf. 13x13½***

**786** A493 1r multicolored 3.00 1.75

27th Pacific Area Travel Assoc. Conf., New Delhi, Jan. 23-26.

Children in Library, Fair Emblem A494

**1978, Feb. 11** **Photo.** ***Perf. 13***
**787** A494 1r rose brown & indigo .65 .40

3rd World Book Fair, New Delhi, Feb. 1978.

Mother of Pondicherry A495

**1978, Feb. 21**
**788** A495 25p dark & light brown .50 .40

Mother of the Sri Aurobindo Ashram, Pondicherry (Mira Richard, 1878-1973, born in Paris).

Wheat, Globe and Genetic Helix — A496

**1978, Feb. 23**
**789** A496 25p yellow & blue green .50 .40

5th Intl. Wheat Genetics Symposium.

Nanalal Dalpatram Kavi — A497

**Wmk. 324**

**1978, Mar. 16** **Photo.** ***Perf. 13***
**790** A497 25p rose brown .50 .40

Kavi (1877-1946), Gujarati poet.

Surjya Sen (1894-1934), Patriot — A498

**1978, Mar. 22**
**791** A498 25p ver, black & brown .50 .40

Two Vaishnavas (Vishnu Worshippers) by Jaminy Roy — A499

Modern Indian Paintings: 50p, The Mosque, by Sailoz Mookherjea. 1r, Woman's Head, by Rabindranath Tagore. 2r, Hill Women, by Amrita Sher Gil.

***Perf. 13½x14***

**1978, Mar. 23** **Unwmk.**

| | | |
|---|---|---|
| **792** A499 25p black & multi | .30 | .30 |
| **793** A499 50p black & multi | .60 | .60 |
| **794** A499 1r black & multi | 1.10 | 1.10 |
| **795** A499 2r black & multi | 1.25 | 1.25 |
| *Nos. 792-795 (4)* | 3.25 | 3.25 |

Rubens, Self-portrait A500

**1978, Apr. 4** **Photo.** ***Perf. 13½x13***
**796** A500 2r multicolored 4.00 2.40

"The Little Tramp," Charlie Chaplin — A501

**1978, Apr. 16** ***Perf. 13***
**797** A501 25p gold & indigo 2.75 1.25

Deendayal Upadhyaya (1916-68) — A502

**1978, May 5** **Photo.** ***Perf. 13***
**798** A502 25p multicolored .50 .40

Upadhyaya, social and political reformer.

Syama Prasad Mookerjee (1901-1953) A503

**1978, July 6** **Photo.** ***Perf. 13***
**799** A503 25p gray olive .50 .35

Dr. Mookerjee, educator, member of 1st natl. government.

"Airavat," 19th Century Wood Carving — A504

Kushan Gold Coin, 1st Century A505

Designs: 50p, Wish-fulfilling tree, 2nd century B.C. 2r, Dagger and knife.

**1978, July 27**

| | | |
|---|---|---|
| **800** A504 25p multicolored | .60 | .60 |
| **801** A504 50p multicolored | .80 | .80 |
| **802** A505 1r multicolored | 1.10 | 1.10 |
| **803** A505 2r multicolored | 1.40 | 1.40 |
| *Nos. 800-803 (4)* | 3.90 | 3.90 |

Treasures from Indian museums.

Krishna and Arjuna on Battlefield, Quotation A506

**1978, Aug. 25** **Unwmk.** ***Perf. 13***
**804** A506 25p orange red & gold .50 .40

Bhagavad Gita, part of Mahabharata Epic, the Divine Song of the Lord.

Bethune College for Women, Calcutta A507

**1978, Sept. 4**
**805** A507 25p green & brown .50 .40

E. V. Ramasami A508

**1978, Sept. 17**
**806** A508 25p black .50 .40

E. V. Ramasami (1879-1973), founder of Self-respect Movement, fighting caste system and social injustice.

Uday Shankar — A509

**1978, Sept. 26**
**807** A509 25p buff & violet brown .50 .40

Uday Shankar (1900-77), dancer.

Leo Tolstoi — A510

**1978, Oct. 2**
**808** A510 1r multicolored .75 .40

Tolstoi, novelist and philosopher.

Vallathol Narayana Menon — A511

**1978, Oct. 15** **Photo.** ***Perf. 13***
**809** A511 25p multicolored .50 .50

Menon (1878-1958), poet.

"Two Friends" A512

**1978, Nov. 14** **Photo.** ***Perf. 13***
**810** A512 25p multicolored .50 .40

Children's Day.

Worker at Lathe — A513

**1978, Nov. 17** ***Perf. 13½***
**811** A513 25p green .50 .40

Small Industries Fair.

Skinner's Horse Soldiers — A514

**1978, Nov. 25** ***Perf. 13***
**812** A514 25p multicolored 1.25 .80

175th anniv. of Skinner's Horse Regiment.

Chakravarti Rajagopalachari A515

**1978, Dec. 10** **Photo.** ***Perf. 13***
**813** A515 25p maroon .50 .40

Chakravarti Rajagopalachari (1878-1972), first post-independence Governor General.

A516

**1978, Dec. 10**
**814** A516 25p olive green .50 .40

Mohammad Ali Jauhar (1878-1931), writer and patriot.

A517

**1978, Dec. 23** ***Perf. 13x14***
**815** A517 1r ocher & purple 1.25 .40

Wright Brothers, Flyer, 75th anniv. of 1st powered flight.

Ravenshaw College, Orissa, Centenary
A518

**1978, Dec. 24** ***Perf. 14***
**816** A518 25p green & maroon .50 .40

Franz Schubert (1797-1828), Austrian Composer — A519

**1978, Dec. 25** ***Perf. 13***
**817** A519 1r multicolored 1.75 .90

Punjab Regiment, Uniforms and Crest
A520

**1979, Feb. 20** **Photo.** **Unwmk.**
**818** A520 25p multicolored 2.00 1.00

Oldest Indian infantry unit.

Bhai Parmanand (1876-1947)
A521

**1979, Feb. 24**
**819** A521 25p violet blue .50 .40

Parmanand, writer and educator.

Gandhi and Child — A522

Design: 1r, IYC emblem.

**1979, Mar. 5** **Photo.** ***Perf. 13***
**820** A522 25p dk brown & red .50 .30
**821** A522 1r dp org & dk brn .75 .60

Albert Einstein (1879-1955), Theoretical Physicist — A523

**1979, Mar. 14**
**822** A523 1r black 1.25 .65

Rajarshi Shahu Chhatrapati (1874-1922), Ruler of Kolhapur — A524

**1979, May 1** **Photo.** ***Perf. 13x13½***
**823** A524 25p dull purple .50 .40

Lotus, India '80 Emblem
A525

**1979, July 2** **Photo.** ***Perf. 13***
**824** A525 30p deep orange & green .50 .40

India '80 Phil. Exhib., New Delhi, Jan. 25-Feb. 3, 1980.

Postal Cards, 1879 and 1979 — A526

**1979, July 2**
**825** A526 50p multicolored .50 .40

Raja Mahendra Pratap (1886-1979), Patriot — A527

**1979, Aug. 15** **Photo.** ***Perf. 13***
**826** A527 30p olive gray .50 .40

Jatindra Nath Das (1904-1929)
A528

**1979, Sept. 13**
**827** A528 30p dark brown .50 .40

Das, political martyr.

Early and Modern Light Bulbs — A529

**1979, Oct. 21** **Photo.** ***Perf. 13***
**828** A529 1r rose magenta .80 .65

Centenary of invention of electric light.

Buddhist Text
A530

**1979, Oct. 23** ***Perf. 14½x14***
**829** A530 30p brown & bister .50 .40

National Archives.

Hirakud Dam
A531

***Perf. 13½x13***
**1979, Oct. 29** **Wmk. 324**
**830** A531 30p brown red & dull grn .50 .40

13th Congress (Golden Jubilee) of the Intl. Commission on Large Dams, New Delhi, 10/29-11/2.

Boy and Alphabet Book
A532

**1979, Nov. 10** **Photo.** ***Perf. 14½x14***
**831** A532 30p multicolored .50 .40

Intl. Children's Book Fair, New Delhi, 11/10-19.

Fair Emblem — A533

**1979, Nov. 10** ***Perf. 13***
**832** A533 1r black & orange .50 .40

India Intl. Trade Fair, New Delhi, 11/10-12/9.

Dove, Agency Emblem
A534

**1979, Dec. 4** ***Perf. 13½x13***
**833** A534 1r multicolored .60 .45

23rd Intl. Atomic Energy Agency Conf., New Delhi, Dec. 4-10.

Hindustan Pushpak Plane, Rohini-1 Glider
A535

**1979, Dec. 10** ***Perf. 13½x13***
**834** A535 30p multicolored 2.25 1.40

Gurdwara Baoli Shrine, Goindwal — A536

**1979, Dec. 21** ***Perf. 13x13½***
**835** A536 30p multicolored .50 .40

Guru Amardas (1469-1574), Sikh spiritual leader.

**Types of 1975-79 and**

Adult Education — A536a

Fish — A536b

Agriculture Technology — A536c

Child Nutrition — A536d

Chick and Eggs — A536e

Farm, Wheat, Tractor — A536f

Women in Rice Field — A537

Family Planning — A537a

Hybrid Cotton — A537b

Weaver — A537c

Rubber Tapping — A537d

Designs: Nos. 841, 844, 846A, Jawaharlal Nehru. Nos. 842, 845, 846B, Mahatma Gandhi.

***Perf. 14x14½, 14½x14, 13 (#840B)***

**1979-85 Photo. Wmk. 324**

| | | | | | |
|---|---|---|---|---|---|
| **836** | A536a | 2p | violet | .80 | .65 |
| **837** | A536b | 5p | blue | .80 | .65 |
| **838** | A536c | 15p | blue grn ('80) | .80 | .65 |
| **839** | A536d | 20p | henna brn ('81) | .80 | .65 |
| **840** | A536e | 25p | brown | .80 | .65 |
| **840B** | A536f | 25p | brt green ('85) | .80 | .65 |
| **841** | A409 | 30p | violet ('80) | 3.00 | .80 |
| **842** | A410 | 30p | red brown ('80) | 2.00 | .80 |
| **843** | A537 | 30p | yel green | .80 | .65 |
| **844** | A409 | 35p | violet ('80) | 2.00 | .80 |
| **845** | A410 | 35p | red brown ('80) | 1.40 | .80 |
| **846** | A537a | 35p | cerise ('80) | .80 | .65 |
| **846A** | A409 | 50p | violet ('83) | .80 | .65 |
| **846B** | A410 | 50p | red brown ('83) | 2.00 | .80 |
| **847** | A537b | 1r | brown ('80) | .80 | .65 |
| **848** | A537c | 2r | rose violet ('80) | 1.25 | .65 |
| **849** | A537d | 5r | multi ('80) | 1.75 | .80 |
| | | | *Nos. 836-849 (17)* | 21.40 | 11.95 |

Size: #841-842, 844-845, 846A-846B, 17x20mm.

See Nos. 895-900A, 903-917.

**1979-83** ***Perf. 13***

| | | | | | |
|---|---|---|---|---|---|
| *837a* | A537 | 5p | | .25 | .25 |
| *837b* | A537 | 5p | Litho. ('82) | .60 | .30 |
| *838a* | A537a | 15p | | .25 | .25 |
| *839a* | A537a | 20p | | .40 | .25 |
| *840a* | A537 | 25p | brown | .40 | .25 |
| *843a* | A537 | 30p | | .60 | .25 |
| *844a* | A409 | 35p | | .90 | .30 |
| *845a* | A410 | 35p | | .30 | .25 |
| *846c* | A537a | 35p | | .60 | .25 |
| *846d* | A409 | 50p | | .60 | .25 |
| *846e* | A410 | 50p | | .25 | .25 |

***Perf. 12½x13***

| | | | | | |
|---|---|---|---|---|---|
| *847a* | A537a | 1r | | .25 | .25 |

***Perf. 13x13½, 13½x13***

| | | | | | |
|---|---|---|---|---|---|
| *848a* | A537a | 2r ('83) | | .25 | .25 |
| *849a* | A537a | 5r ('83) | | .50 | .35 |
| | | | *Nos. 837a-849a (14)* | 6.15 | 3.70 |

People Holding Hands, UN Emblem — A538

**1980, Jan. 21 Photo. *Perf. 13***

**851** A538 1r multicolored .50 .40

UN Industrial Development Org. (INIDO), 3rd Gen. Conf., New Delhi, Jan. 21-Feb. 8.

Field Post Office, Cancels — A539

Money Order Centenary — A540

2-Anna Copper Coins, 1774 — A541

Rowland Hill, Birthplace, Kidderminster A542

**Wmk. 360, Unwmkd. (1r)**

**1980, Jan. 25**

| | | | | | |
|---|---|---|---|---|---|
| **852** | A539 | 30p | gray olive | .55 | .40 |
| **853** | A540 | 50p | brown & citron | .85 | .85 |
| **854** | A541 | 1r | bronze | 1.10 | 1.00 |
| **855** | A542 | 2r | dark gray | 1.10 | 1.00 |
| | | | *Nos. 852-855 (4)* | 3.60 | 3.25 |

INDIA '80 Intl. Stamp Exhib., New Delhi, Jan. 25-Feb. 3.

India Institution of Engineers, 60th Anniversary

***Perf. 13x13½***

**1980, Feb. 17 Unwmk.**

**856** A543 30p dark blue & gold .50 .40

Uniforms, 1780 and 1980, Arms and Ribbon — A544

**1980, Feb. 26**

**857** A544 30p multicolored 1.60 1.00

Madras Sappers bicentennial.

2nd Intl. Apiculture Conf., New Delhi A545

**1980, Feb. 29 *Perf. 13½***

**858** A545 1r multicolored 1.60 1.00

A546

**1980, Feb. 29 Wmk. 360**

**859** A546 30p bright blue .60 .40

4th World Book Fair, New Delhi.

A547

**1980, Mar. 18 *Perf. 13x13½***

**860** A547 30p blue gray .50 .35

Welthy Fisher (b. 1879), educator, Literacy House, Lucknow.

Darul Uloom Islamic School, Deoband A548

**1980, Mar. 21 *Perf. 13½***

**861** A548 30p gray green .50 .40

Keshub Chunder Sen — A549

***Perf. 13x13½***

**1980, Apr. 15 Photo. Wmk. 360**

**862** A549 30p brown .50 .40

Sen (1838-84), scholar, writer, journalist.

Sivaji, Raigad Fort — A550

**1980, Apr. 21 Unwmk.**

**863** A550 30p multicolored .50 .40

Sivaji (1627-80), Indian patriot.

Narayan Malhar Joshi — A551

***Perf. 13x13½***

**1980, June 5 Wmk. 360**

**864** A551 30p lilac rose .80 .50

Joshi (1879-1955), trade union pioneer.

Ulloor S. Parameswara Iyer — A552

**1980, June 6**

**865** A552 30p dull purple .80 .50

Iyer (1877-1949), poet and scholar.

Syed Mohammad Zamin Ali — A553

**1980, June 25**

**866** A553 30p dk yellow green .50 .40

Ali (1880-1955), linguist and educator.

Helen Keller (1880-1968) — A554

**1980, June 27**

**867** A554 30p orange & black 1.25 .75

Keller, blind and deaf writer and lecturer.

High Jump, Olympic Rings A555

**1980, July 19 Photo. *Perf. 13½x14***

| | | | | | |
|---|---|---|---|---|---|
| **868** | A555 | 1r | shown | .70 | .25 |
| **869** | A555 | 2.80r | Equestrian | 1.75 | 1.50 |

22nd Summer Olympic Games, Moscow, July 19-Aug. 3.

Prem Chand (1880-1936) A556

**1980, July 31** *Perf. 13*
**870** A556 30p red brown .50 .40

Pen name of Nawab Rai, writer.

Mother Teresa, Nobel Peace Prize Medallion A557

*Perf. 13½x13*
**1980, Aug. 27 Photo. Wmk. 360**
**871** A557 30p violet, *grayish* 2.50 1.25

Mother Teresa, founder of Missionaries of Charity, 70th birthday.

Earl Mountbatten of Burma — A558

**1980, Aug. 28** *Perf. 13x13½*
**872** A558 2.80r multicolored 4.00 2.00

Mountbatten (1900-79), 1st governor gen. of India.

Asian Table Tennis Championship A559

**1980, Sept. Photo.** *Perf. 13x13½*
**873** A559 30p magenta .80 .55

Scottish Church College, Calcutta, Sesquicentennial — A560

**1980, Sept. 27 Photo.** *Perf. 13½*
**874** A560 35p dull purple .50 .40

Rajah Annamalai Chettiar (1881-1948), Banker, Founder of Annamalai University — A561

**1980, Sept. 30 Unwmk.** *Perf. 14x15*
**875** A561 35p dull purple .50 .40

Gandhi A562

**1980, Oct. 2** *Perf. 15x14*
**876** 35p Gandhi on Dandi March .60 .50
**877** 35p Gandhi Defying Salt Law .60 .50
*a.* A562 Pair, #876-877 2.40 2.40

Jayaprakash Narayan (1902-79), Writer — A564

**1980, Oct. 8 Wmk. 360** *Perf. 14x15*
**878** A564 35p red brown .80 .55

Intl. Symposium on Bustards, Jaipur — A565

**1980, Nov. 1 Photo.** *Perf. 13*
**879** A565 2.30r Great Indian bustards 2.25 1.75

Hegira (Pilgrimage Year) A566

**1980, Nov. 3** *Perf. 13x13½*
**880** A566 35p multicolored .50 .50

Children's Day — A567

*Perf. 13½x13*
**1980, Nov. 14 Unwmk.**
**881** A567 35p multicolored 1.50 .90

Dhyan Chand — A568

Miner, Molten Gold — A569

**1980, Dec. 3 Wmk. 360** *Perf. 14x15*
**882** A568 35p dark rose brown 1.50 1.00

Chand (1906-1979), field hockey player.

*Perf. 13x13½*
**1980, Dec. 20 Unwmk.**
**883** A569 1r multicolored 2.75 .70

Kolar gold fields centenary.

Mukhtar Ahmad Ansari (1880-1936), Surgeon — A570

*Perf. 14x15*
**1980, Dec. 25 Wmk. 360**
**884** A570 35p olive gray .60 .30

Government Mint, Bombay, Sesquicentennial — A571

*Perf. 13½x13*
**1980, Dec. 27 Unwmk.**
**885** A571 35p multicolored .40 .25

Regional Bridal Outfits — A572

Mazharul Haque (1866-1930), Patriot — A573

**1980, Dec. 30** *Perf. 13x13½*
**886** A572 1r Kashmir .75 .50
**887** A572 1r Bengal .75 .50
**888** A572 1r Rajasthan .75 .50
**889** A572 1r Tamilnadu .75 .50
*Nos. 886-889 (4)* 3.00 2.00

**1981, Jan. 2 Wmk. 360** *Perf. 14x15*
**890** A573 35p violet .50 .40

St. Stephen's College Centenary — A574

**1981, Feb. 1 Photo.** *Perf. 14x14½*
**891** A574 35p dull red .50 .40

Gommateshwara Statue, Shravanabelgola A575

**1981, Feb. 9 Unwmk.**
**892** A575 1r multicolored .50 .40

Ganesh V. Mavalankar (1888-1956) A576

**1981, Feb. 27**
**893** A576 35p light red brown .50 .40

Mavalankar, 1st speaker of parliament.

Fruit and Nuts — A576a

Trees on Hillside — A576b

Windmill — A576c

Designs: 2.25r, Cashew. 2.80r, Apples. 3.25r, Oranges.

*Perf. 14½x14*
**1981-86 Photo. Wmk. 324**
**895** A576a 2.25r multi .75 .50
*a.* Perf. 14x14½ .30 .25
*b.* Perf. 13 .25 .25
**896** A576a 2.80r multi 1.00 .60
*a.* Perf. 14x14½ .40 .25
**897** A576a 3.25r multi ('83) .60 .45
*a.* Perf. 13½x13 ('85) .30 .25
*b.* Perf. 13 .30 .25
**900** A576b 10r multi ('84) .75 .40
*b.* Perf. 13x13½ 1.25 .60

*Perf. 13½x13*
**900A** A576c 50r multi ('86) 2.00 1.25
*Nos. 895-900A (5)* 5.10 3.20

Homage to Martyrs — A577

**1981, Mar. 23 Unwmk.** *Perf. 14x15*
**901** A577 35p multicolored .50 .40

Heinrich von Stephan and UPU Emblem A578

**1981, Apr. 8** *Perf. 15x14*
**902** A578 1r red brown & brt blue .50 .40

**Types of 1975-79 and**

Telecommunications — A578a

Natural Gas — A578b

Irrigation — A578c

Dairy Industry — A578d

Design: 1r, Mahatma Gandhi.

***Perf. 14x14½, 14½x14, 13 (40p, 75p), 13x13½ (20r)***

**Wmk. 324, 360 (2p, 5p, 15p)**

**1981-90 Photo.**

**Size: 20x17mm, 17x20mm (1r)**

**903** A536a 2p violet .25 .25
**904** A536b 5p blue .25 .25
**905** A578c 10p green .25 .25
*a.* Perf. 13 .25 .25
**906** A536c 15p blue green .25 .25
**912** A578a 40p dull red .25 .25
**914** A578d 50p dark blue .25 .25
*a.* Perf. 13 .25 .25
**915** A537a 75p vermilion .25 .25
**916** A410 1r orange brown .25 .25

**Size: 32x19mm**

**917** A578b 20r sepia & dark blue 1.00 .60
*Nos. 903-917 (9)* 3.00 2.60

Issued: 10p, 50p, 1/25/82; 40p, 10/15/88; 20r, 11/30/88; 75p, 1990; 1r, 1/30/91; others, 3/25/81.

Intl. Year of the Disabled A579

***Perf. 14½x14***

**1981, Apr. 20 Photo. Unwmk.**

**919** A579 1r blue & black .60 .40

Tribesman — A580

**1981, May 30** ***Perf. 14x14½***

**920** A580 1r Khiamngan Naga .70 .50
**921** A580 1r Toda .70 .50
**922** A580 1r Bhil .70 .50
**923** A580 1r Dandami Maria .70 .50
*Nos. 920-923 (4)* 2.80 2.00

World Environment Day — A581

**1981, June 15**

**924** A581 1r multicolored .50 .40

Nilmoni Phukan (1880-1978), Writer — A582

**1981, June 22**

**925** A582 35p red brown .50 .40

Sanjay Gandhi (1946-1980), Politician — A583

**1981, June 23** ***Perf. 13x13½***

**926** A583 35p multicolored .75 .60

SLV-3 Take-off — A584

**1981, July 18 Photo.** ***Perf. 14x15***

**927** A584 1r multicolored .60 .40

Launching of India's 1st satellite, 1st anniv.

Mascot, Field Hockey A585

**1981, July 28** ***Perf. 13½x13***

**928** A585 1r shown 1.60 .75
**929** A585 1r Emblem 1.60 .75

9th Asian Games, New Delhi, 1982.

Flame of the Forest — A586

Designs: Flowering trees.

**1981, Sept. 1 Photo.** ***Perf. 13***

**930** A586 35p shown 1.00 .35
**931** A586 50p Crateva .60 .45
**932** A586 1r Golden shower 1.40 .75
**933** A586 2r Bauhinia 2.00 1.50
*Nos. 930-933 (4)* 5.00 3.05

World Food Day — A587

**1981, Oct. 16 Photo.** ***Perf. 14x14½***

**934** A587 1r multicolored .60 .45

Cyrestis Achates — A588

**1981, Oct. 20** ***Perf. 13***

**935** A588 35p Stichophthalma camadeva, horiz. 1.50 .50
**936** A588 50p Cethosia biblis, horiz. 2.50 1.50
**937** A588 1r shown 3.25 1.00
**938** A588 2r Treinopalpus imperialis 4.00 4.00
*Nos. 935-938 (4)* 11.25 7.00

Bellary Raghava (1880-1946), Actor — A589

**1981, Oct. 31** ***Perf. 14½x14***

**939** A589 35p olive gray 1.10 .60

40th Anniv. of Mahar Regiment — A590

Children's Day — A591

**1981, Nov. 9** ***Perf. 13***

**940** A590 35p multicolored 1.75 .60

**1981, Nov. 14** ***Perf. 14x14½***

**941** A591 35p multicolored 1.10 .45

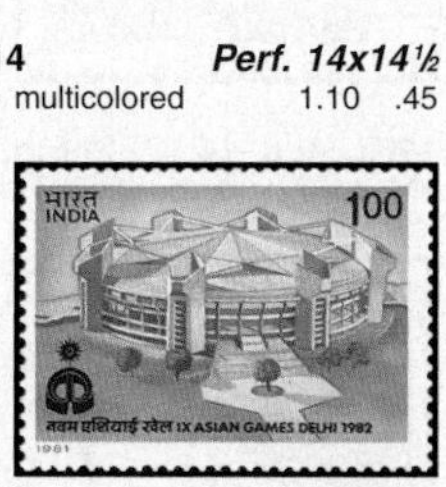


Rajghat Stadium A591a

**1981** ***Perf. 13½x13***

**942** A591a 1r shown 2.40 .45
**943** A591a 1r Nehru Stadium .35 .25

Asian games. Issued: #942, 11/19; #943, 12/30.

Kashi Prasad Jayaswal (1881-1937), Historian — A592

**1981, Nov. 27** ***Perf. 14x14½***

**944** A592 35p chalky blue .80 .35

Intl. Palestinian Solidarity Day A593

**1981, Nov. 29** ***Perf. 14½x14***

**945** A593 1r multicolored 3.50 .70

Naval Ship Taragiri A594

**1981, Dec. 4**

**946** A594 35p multicolored 4.00 2.25

Henry Heras (1888-1955), Historian — A595

**1981, Dec. 14 Photo.** ***Perf. 14½x14***

**947** A595 35p rose violet .60 .35

Indian Ocean Commonwealth Submarine Telephone Cable — A596

**1981, Dec. 24** ***Perf. 13½***

**948** A596 1r multicolored 3.00 .55

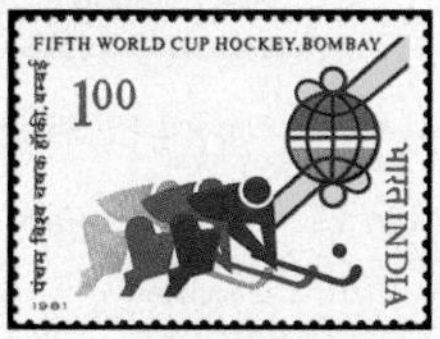


5th World Field Hockey Championship, Bombay — A597

**1981, Dec. 29** ***Perf. 13½x13***

**949** A597 1r multicolored 2.00 .60

Telephone Service Centenary — A598

*Perf. 13x13½*

**1982, Jan. 28** **Unwmk.**

**950** A598 2r multicolored .75 .50

12th Intl. Soil Science Congress, New Delhi, Feb. 8-16 — A599

**1982, Feb. 8** ***Perf. 13½x13***

**951** A599 1r multicolored .40 .25

Sir Jamsetjee Jejeebhoy School of Art, Bombay — A600

**1981, Mar. 2** **Photo.** ***Perf. 14x14½***

**952** A600 35p multicolored .40 .30

Three Musicians, by Pablo Picasso (1881-1973) — A601

**1982, Mar. 15** **Photo.** ***Perf. 14***

**953** A601 2.85r multicolored 2.50 1.00

Deer, 5th Cent. Bas Relief — A602

Radio Telescope, Ooty — A603

Festival of India, England: No. 955, Krishna, 9th cent. bronze sculpture.

**1982, Mar. 23** ***Perf. 14x15***

**954** A602 2r multicolored .60 .60
**955** A602 3.05r multicolored .40 .40

***Perf. 13***

**956** A603 3.05r multicolored .60 .35
*Nos. 954-956 (3)* 1.60 1.35

TB Bacillus Centenary — A604

**1982, Mar. 24** ***Perf. 13***

**957** A604 35p rose violet 3.00 1.60

Durgabai Deshmukh (1909-1981), Social Worker — A605

**1982, May 9** **Photo.** ***Perf. 14½x14***

**958** A605 35p blue .80 .35

Himalayan Flowers — A606

**1982, May 29** ***Perf. 14x14½***

**959** A606 35p Blue poppies 1.00 .60
**960** A606 1r Showy inula 2.50 .60
**961** A606 2r Cobra lily 3.00 2.50
**962** A606 2.85r Brahma kamal 3.50 4.25
*Nos. 959-962 (4)* 10.00 7.95

Ariana Passenger Payload Experimental (APPLE) Satellite, First Anniv. — A607

**1982, June 19** ***Perf. 13½x13***

**963** A607 2r multicolored 1.00 .65

Bidhan Chandra Roy (1882-1962), Physician and Politician — A608

**1982, July 1** ***Perf. 14½x14***

**964** A608 50p orange brown 1.40 .95

Sagar Samrat Drilling Rig — A609

**1982, Aug. 14** **Photo.** ***Perf. 13***

**985** A609 1r multicolored 2.50 1.25

Bindu (Cosmic Spirit), by Raza — A610

Kashmir Stag — A611

Paintings; 3.05r, Between the Spider and the Lamp, 1956, by M.F. Husain.

**1982, Sept. 17** ***Perf. 14x14½***

**986** A610 2r multicolored .75 .55
**987** A610 3.05r multicolored 1.00 1.00

**1982, Oct. 1** ***Perf. 13x13½***

**988** A611 2.85r multicolored 4.00 3.25

50th Anniv. of Indian Air Force — A612

**1982, Oct. 8** ***Perf. 13½x13***

**989** A612 1r Wapiti, MiG 25 8.00 2.00

50th Anniv. of Civil Aviation — A613

**1982, Oct. 15**

**990** A613 3.25r J.R.D. Tata and his Puss Moth, 1932 7.00 3.00

Police Memorial Day — A614

**1982, Oct. 21**

**991** A614 50p Beat patrol .90 .55

Post Office Savings Bank Centenary — A615

**1982, Oct. 23**

**992** A615 50p brown .50 .40

9th Asian Games — A616

**1982** ***Perf. 13½x14***

**993** A616 1r Wrestling, by Janaki, 17th cent. 1.25 .70
**993A** A616 1r Archery 2.75 .60

Issued: #993, Oct. 30; #993A, Nov. 6.

India-USSR Troposcatter Communications Link — A617

**1982, Nov. 2** ***Perf. 13½x13***

**994** A617 3.05r multicolored .70 .50

Children's Day — A618

**1982, Nov. 14** ***Perf. 14x15***

**995** A618 50p multicolored .60 .40

9th Asian Games — A619

**1982** ***Perf. 13***

**996** A619 50p Cycling .25 .25
**997** A619 2r Yachting .40 .30
**998** A619 2r Javelin .45 .40
**999** A619 2.85r Rowing .65 .45
**1000** A619 2.85r Discus 2.00 .45
**1001** A619 3.25r Soccer 2.50 .65
*Nos. 996-1001 (6)* 6.25 2.50

Issued: #997, 999, Nov. 25; others Nov. 19.

50th Anniv. of Indian Military Academy, Dehradun — A620

**1982, Dec. 10** ***Perf. 13½x13***

**1002** A620 50p multicolored .70 .50

Purushottamdas Tandon (1882-1962), Politician — A621

**1982, Dec. 15** ***Perf. 13***

**1003** A621 50p bister .50 .40

Darjeeling Himalayan Railway Centenary — A622

**1982, Dec. 18** ***Perf. 13½x13***

**1004** A622 2.85r multicolored 8.00 7.50

Indian Railway Car — A623

Nos. 2 and 201 — A624

**1982, Dec. 30 Photo.** ***Perf. 13, 14***
**1005** A623 50p multicolored 1.90 1.10
**1006** A624 2r multicolored 3.00 3.00

INPEX '82 Stamp Exhibition.

First Anniv. of Antarctic Expedition A625

**1983, Jan. 9 Photo.** ***Perf. 13½x13***
**1007** A625 1r multicolored 6.00 3.50

Pres. Franklin D. Roosevelt (1882-1945) — A626

**1983, Jan. 30** ***Perf. 13***
**1008** A626 3.25r brown .90 .75

Siberian Cranes — A627

**1983, Feb. 7** ***Perf. 13x13½***
**1009** A627 2.85r multicolored 4.25 3.25

180th Anniv. of Jat Regiment A628

**1983, Feb. 16** ***Perf. 13½x13***
**1010** A628 50p Soldiers, emblem 2.75 2.10

7th Non-aligned Summit Conference A629

**1983, Mar. 7**
**1011** A629 1r Emblem .35 .35
**1012** A629 2r Jawaharlal Nehru .45 .45

Commonwealth Day — A630

**1983, Mar. 14** ***Perf. 13***
**1013** A630 1r Shore Temple, Mahabalipuram .25 .30
**1014** A630 2r Mountains, Gomukh .45 .45

86th Session of Intl. Olympic Committee, New Delhi, Mar. 21-28 A631

**1983, Mar. 25 Litho.** ***Perf. 13½x13***
**1015** A631 1r Acropolis .60 .40

A632

A633

St. Francis of Assisi (1182-1226), by Giovanni Collina.

**1983, Apr. 4 Photo.** ***Perf. 13***
**1016** A632 1r brown 1.10 .55

**1983, May 5 Photo.** ***Perf. 13x12½***
**1017** A633 1r brown .70 .50

Karl Marx (1818-1883).

Charles Darwin (1809-1882) — A634

**1983, May 18** ***Perf. 12½x13***
**1018** A634 2r multicolored 4.25 2.50

50th Anniv. of Kanha Natl. Park A635

**1983, May 30** ***Perf. 13½x13***
**1019** A635 1r Barasinga stag 3.50 1.25

World Communications Year — A636

**1983, July 18 Photo.** ***Perf. 13***
**1020** A636 1r multicolored .60 .30

Simon Bolivar (1783-1830) — A637

**1983, July 24**
**1021** A637 2r multicolored 3.00 2.50

Quit India Resolution, Aug. 8, 1942 — A638

Meera Behn (Madeleine Slade). Disciple of Gandhi, d. 1982 — A639

Design: No. 1024, Mahadev Desai (1892-1942).

**1983, Aug. 9 Photo.** ***Perf. 14***
**1022** A638 50p shown 1.40 1.10

***Perf. 13½x13***
**1023** A639 50p shown 1.40 1.10
**1024** A639 50p org, green & brn 1.40 1.10
*a.* Pair, #1023-1024 2.75 2.75

See Nos. 1033, 1035, 1042, 1052-1057, 1077, 1093-1094, 1103, 1107, 1109, 1122, 1137-1139, 1144, 1147-1149, 1163, 1167, 1198, 1202-1205, 1229-1231, 1238, 1243, 1257, 1268-1271, 1277.

Ram Nath Chopra (1882-1973), Pharma- cologist — A640

**1983, Aug. 17** ***Perf. 13***
**1025** A640 50p brown .80 .65

Indian Mountaineering Foundation, 25th Anniv. — A641

**1983, Aug. 27** ***Perf. 13½***
**1026** A641 2r Nanda Devi, Himalayas 3.25 2.25

Bombay Natural History Soc. — A642

**1983, Sept. 15** ***Perf. 13x13½***
**1027** A642 1r multicolored 5.00 1.60

Rock Garden, Chandigarh A643

**1983, Sept. 23** ***Perf. 13x13½***
**1028** A643 1r multicolored 2.50 1.25

Wildlife A644

**1983, Oct. 1** ***Perf. 13½x13***
**1029** A644 1r Golden langur 2.75 .75
**1030** A644 2r Lion-tailed macaque 4.25 3.75

World Tourism, 5th General Assembly — A645

**1983, Oct. 3 Photo.** ***Perf. 14***
**1031** A645 2r Ghats of Varanasi 1.00 .50

Krishna Kanta Handique, Linguist, Sanskritist, Educator and Scholar — A646

**1983, Oct. 7 Litho.** ***Perf. 13***
**1032** A646 50p deep gray violet .50 .35

**Famous Indians Type of 1983**

Design: Hemu Kalani, revolutionary patriot.

**1983, Oct. 18 Photo.** ***Perf. 13½x13***
**1033** A639 50p org, grn & red brn .50 .50

Children's Day — A648

Painting: Festival, by Kashyap Premswala

**1983, Nov. 14 Photo.** ***Perf. 13***
**1034** A648 50p multicolored .60 .45

**Famous Indians Type of 1983**

Design: Acharya Vinoba Bhave (1895-1982), freedom fighter.

**1983, Nov. 15 Photo.** ***Perf. 13½x13***
**1035** A639 50p org, grn & dull brn .50 .50

Manned Flight Bicent. — A650

**1983, Nov. 21 Photo. *Perf. 13***

**1036** A650 1r 1st Indian Balloon 1.25 .55
**1037** A650 2r Montgolfier Balloon 1.75 1.10

Project Tiger — A651

**1983, Nov. 22 Photo. *Perf. 13***

**1038** A651 2r multicolored 5.00 4.25

Commonwealth Heads of Government Meeting, New Delhi — A652

Design: 2r, Goanese Couple, 19th century.

**1983, Nov. 23 Photo. *Perf. 13***

**1039** A652 1r lt brnsh blue & multi .50 .40
**1040** A652 2r pink & multi 1.00 .50

Pratiksha — A653

**1983, Dec. 5 Photo. *Perf. 13***

**1041** A653 1r multi .40 .30

Nanda Lal Bose (1882-1966), artist.

**Famous Indians Type of 1983**

Design: Surendranath Banerjee, journalist.

**1983, Dec. 28 Photo. *Perf. 13½x13***

**1042** A639 50p org, green & olive .50 .50

7th Light Cavalry Bicent. A655

Deccan Horse Regiment, 194th Anniv. A656

**1984, Jan. 7**

**1043** A655 1r Soldier, banner 4.75 2.25

**1984, Jan. 9 *Perf. 13x13½***

**1044** A656 1r multicolored 4.50 2.00

Asiatic Society Bicentenary — A657

Design: Society building, Calcutta; founder William Jones.

**1984, Jan. 15 *Perf. 13***

**1045** A657 1r brt green & dp lilac .50 .35

Postal Life Insurance Centenary — A658

**1984, Feb. 1 Photo. *Perf. 13x13½***

**1046** A658 1r Emblem .50 .35

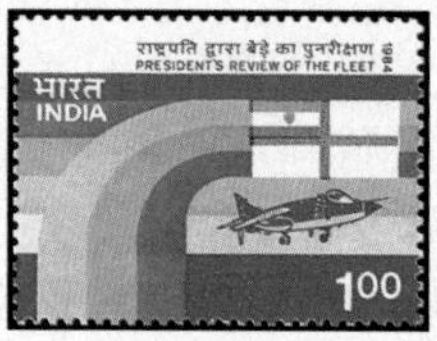

Presidential Review of Naval Fleet A659

**1984, Feb. 3 *Perf. 13½x13***

**1047** A659 1r Jet 2.50 1.50
**1048** A659 1r Aircraft carrier 2.50 1.50
**1049** A659 1r Submarine 2.50 1.50
**1050** A659 1r Missile destroyer 2.50 1.50
*a.* Block of 4, #1047-1050 14.00 14.00

12th Intl. Leprosy Congress, New Delhi A660

**1984, Feb. 10 *Perf. 13x13½***

**1051** A660 1r Globe, emblem .80 .60

**Famous Indians Type of 1983**

#1052, Vasudeo Balvant Phadke (d. 1884), freedom fighter. #1053, Baba Kanshi Ram. #1054, Begum Hazrat Mahal. #1055, Mangal Pandey. #1056, Nana Sahib. #1057, Tatya Tope.

**1984 *Perf. 13½x13***

**1052** A639 50p org, grn & dk ol .55 .55
**1053** A639 50p org, grn & brn .55 .55
**1054** A639 50p org, grn, red org & gray 1.25 .80
**1055** A639 50p org, grn, brn & gray 1.25 .80
**1056** A639 50p org, grn, vio & gray 1.25 .80
**1057** A639 50p org, grn, dk ol & gray 1.25 .80
*Nos. 1052-1057 (6)* 6.10 4.30

Issue dates: No. 1052, Feb. 23. No. 1053, Apr. 23. Nos. 1054-1057, May 10.

Indian-Russian Space Cooperation — A662

**1984, Apr. 3 Photo. *Perf. 14***

**1058** A662 3r Spacecraft 1.25 .85

G. D. Birla (1894-1983), Industrialist — A663

Birla, Birla Institute of Technology, Pilani.

**1984, June 11**

**1060** A663 50p sepia .80 .45

1984 Summer Olympics — A664

***Perf. 13x12½, 12½x13***

**1984, July 28 Photo.**

**1061** A664 50p Basketball 1.25 .65
**1062** A664 1r High jump 1.00 .35
**1063** A664 2r Gymnastics, horiz. 1.40 .95
**1064** A664 2.50r Weight lifting, horiz. 1.60 1.50
*Nos. 1061-1064 (4)* 5.25 3.45

Vellore Fort — A665

**1984, Aug. 3 *Perf. 13½x13, 13x13½***

**1065** A665 50p Gwalior, horiz. .85 .55
**1066** A665 1r shown 1.25 .40
**1067** A665 1.50r Simhagad 2.25 1.90
**1068** A665 2r Jodhpur, horiz. 2.60 2.50
*Nos. 1065-1068 (4)* 6.95 5.35

B.V. Paradkar, Editor — A665a

**1984, Sept. 14 Photo. *Perf. 13x13½***

**1068A** A665a 50p sepia .80 .55

Dr. D.N. Wadia (1883-1969), Geologist — A665b

**1984, Oct. 23 *Perf. 13***

**1068B** A665b 1r multicolored 2.00 .40

Indira Gandhi — A666

**1984, Nov. 19 Photo. *Perf. 15x14***

**1069** A666 50p multicolored 3.00 3.00

Children's Day — A667

**1984, Nov. 14 Photo. *Perf. 13***

**1070** A667 50p Birds in trees 1.10 .70

12th World Mining Congress — A668

**1984, Nov. 20 Photo. *Perf. 13***

**1071** A668 1r Congress emblem 1.90 .45

Dr. Rajendra Prasad (1884-1963), 1st, Pres. — A669

**1984, Dec. 3 Photo. *Perf. 13***

**1072** A669 50p multicolored 1.25 .90

Roses — A670

**1984, Dec. 23 Litho. *Perf. 13***

**1073** A670 1.50r Mrinalini 3.25 2.25
**1074** A670 2r Sugandha 3.50 2.50

Fergusson College Centenary A671

**1985, Jan. 2 Photo. *Perf. 13x13½***

**1076** A671 100p multicolored 1.00 .50

### Famous Indians Type of 1983

Design: Narhar Vishnu Gadgil (1896-1966), freedom fighter.

**1985, Jan. 10 Photo.** ***Perf. 13½x13***
**1077** A639 50p org, grn & brn 6.00 4.00

Artillery Regiment, 50th Anniv. A673

**1985, Jan. 15** ***Perf. 13½x13***
**1078** A673 1r Gunner, howitzer 5.50 2.25

Indira Gandhi (1917-1984) — A674

**1985, Jan. 31** ***Perf. 14***
**1079** A674 2r Addressing UN General Assembly 5.25 4.25

See Nos. 1098-1099.

Minicoy Lighthouse Cent. — A675

**1985, Feb. 2** ***Perf. 13***
**1080** A675 1r multicolored 6.75 1.60

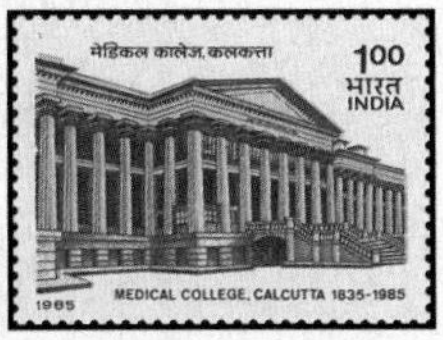

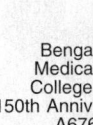

Bengal Medical College, 150th Anniv. A676

**1985, Feb. 20** ***Perf. 13½x13***
**1081** A676 1r multicolored 4.00 .95

Madras Medical College, 150th Anniv. A677

**1985, Mar. 8** ***Perf. 13½x13***
**1082** A677 1r multicolored 4.00 .95

Assam Rifles, North-East Sentinels, 150th Anniv. A679

**1985, Mar. 29**
**1084** A679 1r multicolored 6.00 2.50

Potato Research, 50th Anniv. — A680

Baba Jassa Singh Ahluwalia, 1718-1783, Sikh Leader — A681

**1985, Apr. 1** ***Perf. 13***
**1085** A680 50p brown & pale brown 2.00 1.60

**1985, Apr. 4**
**1086** A681 50p rose violet 2.00 1.60

St. Xavier's College, 125th Anniv. A682

**1985, Apr. 12**
**1087** A682 1r multicolored 2.25 .80

White-winged Wood Duck — A683

**1985, May 18** ***Perf. 14***
**1088** A683 2r multicolored 9.00 5.50

Bougainvillea A684

**1985, June 5** ***Perf. 13***
**1089** A684 50p multicolored 2.00 1.75
**1090** A684 1r multicolored 2.50 1.50

Statue of Didarganj Yakshi, Indian Deity — A685

Yaudheya Tribal Republic Copper Coin, c. 200 B.C. — A686

**1985**
**1091** A685 1r multicolored 4.00 2.10
**1092** A686 2r multicolored 2.25 .50

Festival of India, festival in France and the US for cultural exchange.

Issue dates: 1r, June 7. 2r, June 13.

### Famous Indians Type of 1983

Designs: No. 1093, Jairamdas Doulatram (1891-1979), journalist and politician. No. 1094, Nellie (1909-1973) & Jatindra Mohan (d. 1933) Sengupta, political activists, horiz.

**1985** ***Perf. 13½x13***
**1093** A639 50p org, grn & dl red brn .75 .50

***Perf. 13x13½***
**1094** A639 50p org, green & fawn .75 .50

Issued: #1093, July 21; #1094, July 22.

Swami Haridas (1478-1573), Philosopher A689

**1985, Sept. 19 Photo.** ***Perf. 13½x13***
**1095** A689 1r multicolored 2.50 1.50

Border Roads Org., 25th Anniv. — A690

**1985, Oct. 10** ***Perf. 13x14***
**1096** A690 2r multicolored 2.75 2.75

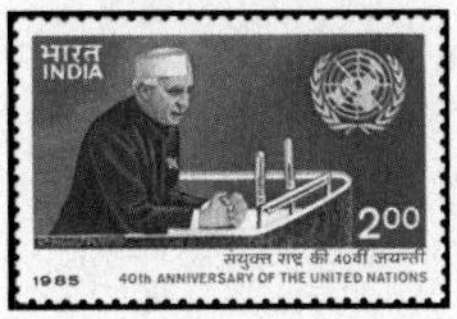


Prime Minister Nehru at Podium A691

**1985, Oct. 24** ***Perf. 13x13½***
**1097** A691 2r multicolored 1.50 1.10

UN, 40th anniv.

### Indira Gandhi Memorial Type of 1985

**1985** ***Perf. 14***
**1098** A674 2r Gandhi addressing crowd 3.50 3.50
**1099** A674 3r Portrait 3.50 3.50

Issue dates: 2r, Oct. 31. 3r, Nov. 19.

Children's Day — A692

**1985, Nov. 14** ***Perf. 13½x13***
**1100** A692 50p multicolored 1.40 .80

Halley's Comet — A693

**1985, Nov. 19** ***Perf. 13x13½***
**1101** A693 1r multicolored 2.50 1.60

Intl. Astronomical Union, 19th General Assembly, New Delhi, Nov. 19-28.

St. Stephen's Hospital, Delhi, Cent. A694

**1985, Nov. 25** ***Perf. 13***
**1102** A694 1r multicolored 1.25 .55

### Famous Indians Type of 1983

Design: Kakasaheb Kalelkar (1885-1981), author.

**1985, Dec. 2** ***Perf. 13½x13***
**1103** A639 50p org, grn & ol brn .75 .50

Map of South Asia A696

Flags of India, Pakistan, Bangladesh, Nepal, Bhutan, Sri Lanka and the Maldive Islands — A697

**1985, Dec. 8** ***Perf. 13½x13, 14***
**1104** A696 1r multicolored 2.50 .50
**1105** A697 3r multicolored 4.00 3.50

South Asian Regional Cooperation, SARC.

Shyama Shastri (1762-1827), Composer — A698

**1985, Dec. 21** ***Perf. 13½x13***
**1106** A698 1r multicolored 3.50 1.60

### Famous Indians Type of 1983

Master Tara Singh (1885-1967), Sikh leader.

**1985, Dec. 23** ***Perf. 13½x13***
**1107** A639 50p org, green & blue .75 .50

Intl. Youth Year A700

**1985, Dec. 24**
**1108** A700 2r multicolored 3.50 2.25

### Famous Indians Type of 1983

Design: Ravishankar Maharaj (1884-1984), freedom fighter, politician.

**1985, Dec. 24** ***Perf. 13½x13***
**1109** A639 50p org, green & slate .75 .50

Handel and Bach — A702

**1985, Dec. 27** *Perf. 13x13½*
1110 A702 5r multicolored 6.50 4.75

Congress Presidents, 1924-1985
A703

**1985, Dec. 28** *Perf. 14*
1111 Block of 4 13.00 13.00
*a.-d.* A703 1r any single 2.50 2.25

Indian Natl. Congress, cent. Withdrawn on day of issue for a period of two weeks.

Naval Dockyard, Bombay, 250th Anniv.
A704

**1986, Jan. 11 Photo.** *Perf. 13½*
1112 A704 2.50r multicolored 6.00 4.50

INPEX '86, Jaipur, Feb. 14-19
A705

Designs: 50p, Hawa Mahal Palace, Jaipur No. 3. 2r, Khar Desert mobile post office.

**1986, Feb. 14** *Perf. 13½x13*
1113 A705 50p multicolored 2.00 .90
1114 A705 2r multicolored 3.00 2.10

Vikrant Aircraft Carrier, 25th Anniv. — A706

**1986, Feb. 16** *Perf. 13x13½*
1115 A706 2r multicolored 9.00 8.00

Inaugural Airmail Flight, 75th Anniv.
A707

**1986, Feb. 18** *Perf. 13½x13, 13x13½*
1116 A707 50p Biplane 3.25 2.10

**Size: 41x28mm**

1117 A707 3r Jet 7.25 5.50

Sixth Triennale of the Arts, Lalit Kala Academy
A708

Sri Chaitanya Mahaprabhu
A709

**1986, Feb. 22** *Perf. 13x13½*
1118 A708 1r multicolored 2.00 1.50

**1986, Mar. 3** *Perf. 13*
1119 A709 2r multicolored 3.75 3.25

Mayo College, Ajmer, 111th Anniv.
A710

**1986, Apr. 12** *Perf. 13½x13*
1120 A710 1r multicolored 2.25 1.10

1986 World Cup Soccer Championships, Mexico — A711

**1986, May 31 Photo.** *Perf. 13*
1121 A711 5r multicolored 6.25 4.25

**Famous Indians Type of 1983**

Bhim Sen Sachar (1894-1978), freedom fighter.

**1986, Aug. 14 Photo.** *Perf. 13½x13*
1122 A639 50p org, green & sepia 2.00 1.00

Swami Sivananda (1887-1963), Religious Author — A713

**1986, Sept. 8 Photo.** *Perf. 13½x13*
1123 A713 2r multicolored 4.00 3.00

10th Asian Games — A714

**1986, Sept. 16** *Perf. 13x13½*
1124 A714 1.50r Women's volleyball 3.75 2.50
1125 A714 3r Hurdling 4.00 3.50

Madras Post Office, Bicent.
A715

**1986, Oct. 9 Photo.** *Perf. 13x13½*
1126 A715 5r black & brown orange 6.50 4.50

1st Battalion of Parachutists Regiment, 225th Anniv. — A716

**1986, Oct. 17**
1127 A716 3r multicolored 7.00 4.50

Indian Police Force, 125th Anniv. — A717

Uniforms, 1861-1986. No. 1129a has a continuous design.

**1986, Oct. 21** *Perf. 13½*
1128 A717 1.50r multicolored 5.00 5.00
1129 A717 2r multicolored 5.00 5.00
*a.* Pair, #1129, 1128 12.00 12.00

Intl. Peace Year
A718

**1986, Oct. 24**
1130 A718 5r sage grn, blue & rose 4.50 2.75

Children's Day — A719

**1986, Nov. 14 Photo.** *Perf. 13x13½*
1131 A719 50p multicolored 3.25 2.10

UN, 40th Anniv.
A720

**1986, Dec. 11** *Perf. 13½x13*
1132 A720 50p Growth monitoring 2.75 2.25
1133 A720 5r Immunization 5.50 5.00

Child Survival Campaign.

Miyan Tansen, 17th Cent. Dhrupad Singer, Playing the Surbahar — A721

**1986, Dec. 12**
1134 A721 1r multicolored 2.75 1.00

Corbett Natl. Park, 50th Anniv.
A722

**1986, Dec. 15**
1135 A722 1r Elephant 5.00 1.75
1136 A722 2r Gavial 6.00 5.25

**Famous Indians Type of 1983**

Designs: No. 1137, Alluri Seetarama Raju (b. 1897), freedom fighter. No. 1138, Sagarmal Gopa (b. 1900), freedom fighter. No. 1139, Veer Surendra Sai (b. 1809), freedom fighter.

**1986, Dec.** *Perf. 13½x13*
1137 A639 50p red, green & sepia 2.00 1.00
1138 A639 50p red, green & sl blue 2.00 1.00
1139 A639 50p red, green & dp red brn 2.00 1.00
*Nos. 1137-1139 (3)* 6.00 3.00

Issued: #1137, 26th; #1138, 29th; #1139, 30th.

St. Martha's Hospital, Bangalore, Cent.
A724

**1986, Dec. 30** *Perf. 13½*
1140 A724 1r multicolored 3.00 2.25

Yacht Trishna
A725

**1987, Jan. 10**
1141 A725 6.50r multicolored 6.25 4.25

1st Indian Army circumnavigation of the world, Sept. 28, 1985 to 1987.

Africa Fund — A726

**1987, Jan. 25 Photo.** *Perf. 14x14½*
1142 A726 6.50r black 6.50 4.50

ICC 29th Congress, New Delhi — A727

**1987, Feb. 11** *Perf. 13½*
1143 A727 5r multicolored 4.50 3.00

**Famous Indians Type of 1983**

Design: Hakim Ajmal Khan (1864-1927), physician, politician.

**1987, Feb. 13** *Perf. 13½x13*
1144 A639 60p org, grn & brn 2.75 .30

A729

Family Planning A730

**1987, Feb. 27** ***Perf. 13, 13x13½***

**1145** A729 35p dark red .40 .25
**1146** A730 60p green & dark red 1.00 .25

**Famous Indians Type of 1983**

Designs: No. 1147, Lala Har Dayal (1884-1939). No. 1148, Manabendra Nath Roy (1887-1954). No. 1149, T. Ramaswamy Chowdary (1887-1943).

**1987** **Photo.** ***Perf. 13½x13***

**1147** A639 60p org, green & purple .50 .25
**1148** A639 60p org, green & red brn .50 .25
**1149** A639 60p org, grn & brt blue .50 .25
*Nos. 1147-1149 (3)* 1.50 .75

Issued: #1147, 3/18; #1148, 3/21; #1149, 4/25.

SER Emblem, Blast Furnaces — A732

Steam Locomotive No. 691 — A733

Electric Train Crossing Bridge — A734

**1987, Mar. 28** ***Perf. 13x13½, 13½x13***

**1150** A732 1r shown .25 .25
**1151** A733 1.50r shown .65 .35
**1152** A734 2r shown 1.10 .45
**1153** A733 4r Steam locomotive, c. 1890 1.50 .75
*Nos. 1150-1153 (4)* 3.50 1.80

Southeastern Railway, cent.

Kalia Bhomora Bridge, Assam A735

**1987, Apr. 14** ***Perf. 13½***

**1154** A735 2r multicolored .60 .30

Madras Christian College, 150th Anniv. A736

**1987, Apr. 16** ***Perf. 13x13½***

**1155** A736 1.50r black & rose lake .50 .40

A737

A738

**1987, May 1** ***Perf. 13½***

**1156** A737 1r dull brown .60 .30

Shree Shree Ma Anandamayee (1896-1982), spiritualist.

**1987, May 8** ***Perf. 14***

**1157** A738 2r multicolored .70 .35

Rabindranath Tagore (1861-1941), 1913 Nobel Laureate for literature.

A739

**1987, May 10** ***Perf. 13½***

**1158** A739 1r multicolored 1.00 .50

Garhwal Rifles and Garhwal Scouts, cent.

A740

**1987, May 11**

**1159** A740 60p black brn & buff 1.10 .90

J. Krishnamurti (1895-1986), mystic.

7th Battalion, Mechanised Infantry Regiment, Cent. A741

**1987, June 3** ***Perf. 13½x13***

**1160** A741 1r multicolored .90 .45

INDIA '89, New Delhi, Jan. 20-29, 1989 A742

**1987, June 15**

**1161** A742 50p Swan emblem .25 .25
*a.* Bklt. pane of 4+inscribed margin ('89) .50
**1162** A742 5r Hall of Nations, New Delhi 1.25 .45
*a.* Souv. sheet of 2, #1161-1162 3.50 3.50
*b.* Bklt. pane of 4+inscribed margin ('89) 6.00 6.00

Inscribed 1986. No. 1162a sold for 8r.

**Famous Indians Type of 1983**

Kailas Nath Katju (1887-1968), Chief Minister.

**1987, June 17** ***Perf. 13½x13***

**1163** A639 60p org, grn & yel brn .35 .25

Sadyah-Snata, Sanghol Sculpture, c. 2000 B.C. A744

**1987, July 3**

**1164** A744 6.50r multicolored 1.45 .55

Festival of India in the USSR, July 3, 1987-88.

Natl. Independence, 40th Anniv. — A745

**1987, Aug. 15** **Photo.** ***Perf. 13x13½***

**1165** A745 60p orange, brt blue & dk green .50 .40

Sant Harchand Singh Longowal (1932-1985), Social Reformer — A746

**1987, Aug. 20** ***Perf. 13½***

**1166** A746 1r multicolored 1.10 .40

**Famous Indians Type of 1983**

Design: S. Satyamurti (1887-1943), political reformer, martyr.

**1987, Aug. 22** ***Perf. 13½x13***

**1167** A639 60p org, green & brn .50 .25

Guru Ghasidas (1756-1837), Founder of the Saman Sect — A748

**1987, Sept. 1**

**1168** A748 60p henna brown .50 .40

Sri Sri Thakur Anukul Chandra (1888-1969), Physician, Guru — A749

**1987, Sept. 2** ***Perf. 13½***

**1169** A749 1r multicolored .60 .60

University of Allahabad, Cent. A750

**1987, Sept. 23** ***Perf. 13½x13***

**1170** A750 2r multicolored .50 .30

Phoolwalon Ki Sair — A751

**1987, Oct. 1** ***Perf. 13x13½***

**1171** A751 2r Pankha (embroidered apron) .50 .30

Festival of thanksgiving for fulfilled prayers.

Maharaja Chhatrasal A752

**1987, Oct. 2** ***Perf. 14***

**1172** A752 60p henna brown .50 .35

Chhatrasal (1649-1731), military commander during the war against the Moguls.

Intl. Year of Shelter for the Homeless A753

**1987, Oct. 5** ***Perf. 13½x13***

**1173** A753 5r multicolored .80 .40

Asia Regional Conference of Rotary Intl. — A754

**1987, Oct. 14**

**1174** A754 60p shown .25 .25
**1175** A754 6.50r Polio immunization 1.10 .50

Service to the Blind, Cent. A755

**1987, Oct. 15**

**1176** A755 1r shown .30 .30
**1177** A755 2r Eye donation .50 .35

World White Cane Day.

INDIA '89 — A756

Designs: 60p, The Iron Pillar, Quwwat-ul-Islam Mosque courtyard, 5th cent., Delhi.

1.50r, The India Gate, New Delhi, war memorial by Luytens, 1921. 5r, The Dewan-E-Khas, Hall of Private Audience, Red Fort, Delhi, c. 1648. 6.50r, Purana Qila, Old Fort, Delhi, c. 1540.

**1987, Oct. 17**

| | | | |
|---|---|---|---|
| **1178** | A756 60p multicolored | .25 | .25 |
| *a.* | Bklt. pane of 4 + inscribed margin ('89) | .80 | |
| **1179** | A756 1.50r multicolored | .50 | .25 |
| *a.* | Bklt. pane of 4 + inscribed margin ('89) | 2.10 | |
| **1180** | A756 5r multicolored | 1.25 | .45 |
| *a.* | Bklt. pane of 4 + inscribed margin ('89) | 5.25 | |
| **1181** | A756 6.50r multicolored | 2.00 | .60 |
| *a.* | Souv. sheet of 4, #1178-1811 | 4.00 | 4.00 |
| *b.* | Bklt. pane of 4 + inscribed margin ('89) | 7.75 | |
| | *Nos. 1178-1181 (4)* | 4.00 | 1.55 |

No. 1181a sold for 15r.

Tyagmurti Goswami Ganeshdutt (1889-1959), Educator, Social Activist — A757

**1987, Nov. 2** *Perf. 13½*

**1182** A757 60p terra cotta .50 .40

Children's Day — A758

**1987, Nov. 14**

**1183** A758 60p multicolored .50 .30

Trees A759

**1987, Nov. 19 Photo.** *Perf. 13½*

| | | | |
|---|---|---|---|
| **1184** | A759 60p Chinar, vert. | .35 | .30 |
| **1185** | A759 1.50r Pipal | .40 | .30 |
| **1186** | A759 5r Sal, vert. | 1.10 | .65 |
| **1187** | A759 6.50r Banyan | 1.50 | .90 |
| | *Nos. 1184-1187 (4)* | 3.35 | 2.15 |

Festival of the USSR in India — A760

Votive coin based on The Worker and the Peasant Woman, by Soviet sculptor Mukhina.

**1987, Nov. 21** *Perf. 14*

**1188** A760 5r multicolored .80 .50

White Tiger — A761

**1987, Nov. 29 Photo.** *Perf. 13½*

| | | | |
|---|---|---|---|
| **1189** | A761 1r shown | .75 | .25 |
| **1190** | A761 5r Snow leopard, horiz. | 2.25 | .90 |

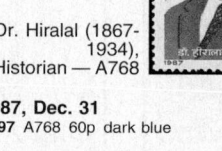

Rameshwari Nehru (1886-1966), Human Rights and World Peace Activist — A762

**1987, Dec. 10**

**1191** A762 60p red brown .50 .40

Execution of Veer Narayan Singh (1795-1857), Sikh Uprising Leader — A763

**1987, Dec. 10**

**1192** A763 60p .50 .40

Father Kuriakose Elias Chavara (1806-1871), Theologian Beatified by Pope John Paul II Feb. 8, 1986 — A764

**1987, Dec. 20**

**1193** A764 60p dark brown olive .50 .40

Dr. Rajah Sir M.A. Muthiah Chettiar (1905-1984), Politician, Pro-chancellor of Annamalai University — A765

**1987, Dec. 21** *Perf. 13*

**1194** A765 60p chalky blue black .50 .40

Sri Harmandir Sahib (Gold Temple), Amritsar, 400th Anniv. — A766

**1987, Dec. 26** *Perf. 13½*

**1195** A766 60p multicolored 1.00 .70

Rukmini Devi (1904-1986), Dancer, Choreographer — A767

**1987, Dec. 27**

**1196** A767 60p dark red .60 .35

Dr. Hiralal (1867-1934), Historian — A768

**1987, Dec. 31**

**1197** A768 60p dark blue .50 .40

**Famous Indians Type of 1983**

Design: Pandit Hriday Nath Kunzru (1887-1978), human rights activist, statesman.

**1987, Dec. 31** *Perf. 13½x13*

**1198** A639 60p org, grn & red brn .35 .25

75th Session of the Indian Science Congress Assoc. A770

**1988, Jan. 1**

**1199** A770 4r multicolored .90 .55

Solar Energy A771

13th Asia Pacific Dental Congress, New Delhi, Jan. 28-Feb.2 A772

**Wmk. 324**

**1988, Jan. 1 Photo.** *Perf. 13*

**1200** A771 5r dp orange & sepia .80 .40

**1988, Jan. 28 Unwmk.** *Perf. 13*

**1201** A772 4r multicolored .75 .50

**Famous Indians Type of 1983**

Designs: No. 1202, Mohan Lal Sukhadia (1916-1982). No. 1203, Dr. S.K. Sinha (1887-1961). No. 1204, Chandra Shekhar Azad (1906-1931). No. 1205, Govind Ballabh Pant (1887-1961).

**1988** *Perf. 13½x13*

| | | | |
|---|---|---|---|
| **1202** | A639 60p org, grn & bluish blk | .75 | .60 |
| **1203** | A639 60p org, grn & org brn | .75 | .60 |
| **1204** | A639 60p org, grn & rose red | .75 | .60 |
| **1205** | A639 60p org, grn & purple | .75 | .60 |
| | *Nos. 1202-1205 (4)* | 3.00 | 2.40 |

Issue dates: Nos. 1202, Feb. 2; No. 1203, Feb. 4; No. 1204, Feb. 27; No. 1205, Mar. 7.

U. Tirot Sing (1800-1833), Patriot — A774

**1988, Feb. 3**

**1206** A774 60p dull brown .50 .40

Kumaon Regiment 4th Battalion, Bicent. — A775

**1988, Feb. 19** *Perf. 14*

**1207** A775 1r Uniforms of 1788, 1947, 1988 .60 .30

Balgandharva (1888-1967), Musician — A776

**1988, Feb. 22** *Perf. 13x13½*

**1208** A776 60p brown .50 .40

Mechanised Infantry Regiment A777

**1988, Feb. 24** *Perf. 13½x13*

**1209** A777 1r multicolored .90 .45

A778

**1988, Feb. 26** *Perf. 13*

**1210** A778 60p bluish black .50 .40

Sir B.N. Rau (1887-1953), constitutional advisor.

A779

**1988, Mar. 14 Photo.** *Perf. 13x13½*

**1211** A779 1r bright rose .50 .40

Mohindra College, Patiala, founded in 1875 by Maharaja Mohinder Singh, is now part of Punjabi University.

Dr. D.V. Gundappa (1887-1975), Journalist, and Gikhala Institute of Public Affairs — A780

**1988, Mar. 17** *Perf. 13½x13*

**1212** A780 60p slate blue .50 .40

Woman Warrior Riding into Battle — A781

**1988, Mar. 20** ***Perf. 13x13½***
**1213** A781 60p bright rose .50 .40

Rani Avantibai (d. 1858), heroine of the 1857 independence war.

Malayala Manorama Newspaper, Cent. — A782

**1988, Mar. 23**
**1214** A782 1r blue & black .50 .40

Malayala Manorama, published in Kottayam, is the largest circulated daily newspaper in India.

Maharshi Dadhichi, Vedic Period Saint Purported to Have Introduced Fire to Man — A783

**1988, Mar. 26**
**1215** A783 60p deep orange .50 .40

Mohammad Iqbal (1877-1938), Poet — A784

**1988, Apr. 21**
**1216** A784 60p carmine & gold .50 .40

Samarth Ramdas (1608-1682), Philosopher A785

**1988, May 1** ***Perf. 13***
**1217** A785 60p dk yellow green .50 .40

Swati Tirunal Rama Varma (1813-1846), Carnatic Composer — A786

**1988, May 2** ***Perf. 13x13½***
**1218** A786 60p brt violet .50 .40

1st War of Independence, the "Indian Mutiny of 1857" — A787

Painting: Rani Laxmi Bai transformed from a queen into a warrior fighting for justice, by M.F. Husain.

**1988, May 9 Photo.** ***Perf. 13x13½***
**1219** A787 60p multicolored .50 .40

Bhaurao Patil (b. 1887), Educator A788

**1988, May 9** ***Perf. 13½x13***
**1220** A788 60p red brown .50 .40

Himalayan Peaks A789

**1988, May 19**

| | | | | | |
|---|---|---|---|---|---|
| **1221** | A789 | 1.50r | Broad Peak | 1.40 | .30 |
| **1222** | A789 | 4r | Godwin Austin | 1.60 | .40 |
| **1223** | A789 | 5r | Kanchenjunga | 1.60 | .55 |
| **1224** | A789 | 6.50r | Nandadevi | 1.60 | .70 |
| | | | *Nos. 1221-1224 (4)* | 6.20 | 1.95 |

Care for the Elderly — A790

**1988, May 24** ***Perf. 13x13½***
**1225** A790 60p multicolored .50 .40

Victoria Terminal, Bombay, Cent. A791

**1988, May 30** ***Perf. 13½x13***
**1226** A791 1r multicolored .80 .30

Lawrence School, Lovedale, 130th Anniv. A792

**1988, May 31** ***Perf. 13***
**1227** A792 1r dk green & red brown .70 .40

World Environment Day — A793

**1988, June 5** ***Perf. 14***
**1228** A793 60p Khejri tree .50 .40

### Famous Indians Type of 1983

#1229, Dr. Anugrah Narain Singh (1887-1957), statesman. #1230, Kuladhor Chaliha (1886-1963), political and social reformer. #1231, Shivprasad Gupta (1883-1944), freedom fighter.

**1988** ***Perf. 13½x13***

| | | | | | |
|---|---|---|---|---|---|
| **1229** | A639 | 60p | org, grn & rose vio | .65 | .40 |
| **1230** | A639 | 60p | org, grn & gray blk | .65 | .40 |
| **1231** | A639 | 60p | org, grn & dk vio | .65 | .40 |
| | | | *Nos. 1229-1231 (3)* | 1.95 | 1.20 |

Issued: #1229, 6/18; #1230, 6/19; #1231, 6/28.

Rani Durgawati (d. 1564), Ruler of Gondwana — A795

**1988, June 24**
**1232** A795 60p red .50 .40

A796

**1988, July 28 Photo.** ***Perf. 13x13½***
**1233** A796 60p red brown .50 .40

Acharya Shanti Dev (687-765), Sanskrit and Pali scholar.

A797

**1988, Aug. 4**
**1234** A797 60p blue violet .50 .40

Yashwant Singh Parmar (1906-1981), administrator of Himachal Pradesh State.

Painting by M.F. Husain — A798

**1988, Aug. 16 Photo.** ***Perf. 13x13½***

| | | | | |
|---|---|---|---|---|
| **1235** | | 60p India at upper left | .60 | .60 |
| **1236** | | 60p India at lower left | .60 | .60 |
| | *a.* | A798 Pair, #1235-1236 | 2.00 | 2.00 |

Natl. Independence 40th anniv.

Durgadas Rathore (1638-1718), Guardian of King Ajit Singh — A799

**1988, Aug. 26** **Litho.**
**1237** A799 60p dark red brown .50 .40

### Famous Indians Type of 1983

Design: Sarat Chandra Bose (1889-1950), politician, lawyer, publisher.

**1988, Sept. 6 Photo.** ***Perf. 13½x13***
**1238** A639 60p org, grn & dk blue grn .50 .40

Gopinath Kaviraj (1887-1976), Scholar — A801

**1988, Sept. 7** ***Perf. 13x13½***
**1239** A801 60p brown olive .50 .40

Hindi Language Day, Sept. 14 A802

Indian Olympic Assoc. Emblem A803

Glory of Sport, Independence 40th Anniv. — A804

**1988, Sept. 14 Photo.** ***Perf. 13x13½***
**1240** A802 60p ver & dk olive green .50 .40

*Perf. 13½x13, 13x13½*

**1988, Sept. 17**
**1241** A803 60p deep claret .80 .45
**1242** A804 5r multicolored 3.25 1.60

**Famous Indians Type of 1983**

Baba Kharak (1867-1963), nationalist.

**1988, Oct. 6** *Perf. 13½x13*
**1243** A639 60p org, green & org brn .50 .40

Jerdon's Courser — A806

**1988, Oct. 7** *Perf. 13½*
**1244** A806 1r multicolored 4.00 .65

The Times of India, Newspaper, 150th Anniv. — A807

**1988, Nov. 3** *Perf. 13½x14*
**1245** A807 1.50r black & gold .50 .35

INDIA '89 — A808

*Perf. 13½x13*

**1988, Oct. 9** **Unwmk.** **Photo.**
**1246** A808 4r Bangalore P.O. .75 .30
*a.* Bklt. pane of 6+inscribed margin ('89) 4.50
**1247** A808 5r Bombay P.O. 1.50 .35
*a.* Bklt. pane of 6+inscribed margin ('89) 9.00

Portrait of Azad by K.K. Hebbar — A809

**1988, Nov. 11**
**1248** A809 60p multicolored .50 .40

Maulana Abul Kalam Azad (1888-1958), minister of education, natl. resources and scientific research.

Jawaharlal Nehru — A810

*Perf. 13x13½, 13½x13 (1r)*

**1988, Nov. 14**
**1249** A810 60p dk gray, dk orange & dk grn .65 .35
**1250** A810 1r Portrait, vert. .75 .35

Birsa, Munda Leader A811

**1988, Nov. 15** *Perf. 13½x13*
**1251** A811 60p brown .50 .40

Bhakra Dam, 25th Anniv. — A812

**1988, Dec. 15** *Perf. 14*
**1252** A812 60p carmine rose .70 .70

INDIA '89 — A813

60p, Dead-letter cancellations, 1886. 6.50r, Traveling p.o. cancellation, 1864-69.

**1988, Dec. 20** *Perf. 13½x13*
**1253** A813 60p multicolored .75 .40
*a.* Bklt. pane of 6+inscribed margin ('89) 5.00
**1254** A813 6.50r multicolored 2.50 1.40
*a.* Bklt. pane of 6+inscribed margin ('89) 15.00

K.M. Munshi (1887-1971), Environmentalist, Statesmen — A814

**1988, Dec. 30**
**1255** A814 60p dark olive green .50 .40

Mannathu Padmanabhan (1878-1970), Social Reformer — A815

**1989, Jan. 2** *Perf. 13½x13*
**1256** A815 60p dull brown .50 .40

**Famous Indians Type of 1983**

Hare Krushna Mahtab (1899-1987), author.

**1989, Jan. 2** *Perf. 13½x13*
**1257** A639 60p orange, grn & black .60 .40

Lok Sabha Secretariat, 60th Anniv. A817

**1989, Jan. 10** *Perf. 13½x13*
**1258** A817 60p dark olive green .50 .40

State Museum, Lucknow, 125th Anniv. — A818

**1989, Jan. 11** *Perf. 14*
**1259** A818 60p Goddess Durga, lion .50 .40

INDIA '89 — A819

**1989, Jan. 20** *Perf. 13½x13*
**1260** A819 60p Youth collecting .25 .25
*a.* Bklt. pane of 6 + inscribed margin .60
**1261** A819 1.50r Postal coach & p.o., 1842 .40 .25
*a.* Bklt. pane of 6 + inscribed margin 2.40
**1262** A819 5r Travancore #2 1.00 .40
*a.* Bklt. pane of 6 + inscribed margin 6.00
**1263** A819 6.50r Philatelic journal mastheads 1.50 .50
*a.* Bklt. pane of 6 + inscribed margin 9.00
*Nos. 1260-1263 (4)* 3.15 1.40

St. John Bosco (1815-1888), Educator — A820

**1989, Jan. 31** *Perf. 13*
**1264** A820 60p carmine rose .50 .40

3rd Cavalry, 148th Anniv. A821

**1989, Feb. 8** *Perf. 13½x13*
**1265** A821 60p multicolored .80 .55

Dargah Sharif Ajmer A822

**1989, Feb. 13** **Litho.** *Perf. 13½x13*
**1266** A822 1r multicolored .50 .40

President's Review of the Naval Fleet — A823

**1989, Feb. 15** *Perf. 14*
**1267** A823 6.50r multicolored 3.00 1.90

**Famous Indians Type of 1983**

#1268, Sheikh Mohammad Abdullah. #1269, Balasaheb Gangadhar Kher (1888-1957), politician. #1270, Saifuddin Kitchlew (1888-1963), lawyer, diplomat. #1271, Rajkumari Amrit Kaur (d. 1964), minister of health and welfare.

**1988-89** **Photo.** *Perf. 13½x13*
**1268** A639 60p org, grn & lil rose .50 .40
**1269** A639 60p org, grn & dk vio .50 .40
**1270** A639 60p org, grn & blk brn .50 .40
**1271** A639 60p org, grn & grnsh blk .50 .40
*Nos. 1268-1271 (4)* 2.00 1.60

Issue dates: No. 1268, Dec. 5; No. 1269, Mar. 8, 1989; Nos. 1270-1271, Apr. 13, 1989.

Freedom Fighters — A825

#1272, Baldev Ramji Mirdha (1889-1956). #1273, Rao Gopal Singh (1899-1939).

**1989** *Perf. 13x13½*
**1272** A825 60p slate .50 .40
**1273** A825 60p dark olive .50 .40

Issue dates: #1272, Jan. 17; #1273, Mar. 30.

Freedom Fighters A826

Designs: No. 1274, Shaheed Laxman Nayak (1899-1943), protest leader. No. 1275, Bishu Ram Medhi (1888-1981), politician.

**1989** *Perf. 13½x13*
**1274** A826 60p org, sage grn & brn .25 .25

**Size: 24x37mm**

**1275** A826 60p org, sage grn & dp yel grn .35 .25

Issued: #1274, Mar. 29; #1275, Apr. 24.
See #1292, 1299-1300, 1317, 1429, 1487.

Sydenham College, Bombay A827

**1989, Apr. 19** *Perf. 13½*
**1276** A827 60p black .50 .40

**Famous Indians Type of 1983**

Design: Asaf Ali (1888-1953), patriot.

**1989, May 11** **Photo.** *Perf. 13½x13*
**1277** A639 60p org, green & sepia .25 .25

N.S. Hardikar (1889-1975), Freedom Fighter — A829

**1989, May 13** ***Perf. 13x13½***
**1278** A829 60p chestnut brown .50 .40

Sankaracharya (b. 788), Philosopher — A830

**1989, May 17** ***Perf. 14x13½***
**1279** A830 60p multicolored .50 .40

Punjab University, Chandigarh A831

**1989, May 19** ***Perf. 13½x13***
**1280** A831 1r blue green & brn .50 .40

Film Industry, 75th Anniv. — A832

**1989, May 30 Photo.** ***Perf. 14***
**1281** A832 60p dk olive bis & blk .60 .45

Kirloskar Corporation, Cent. A833

**1989, June 20 Photo.** ***Perf. 13½x13***
**1282** A833 1r multicolored .50 .40

DAV Education Movement, Cent. A834

**1989, June 27 Photo.** ***Perf. 13½x13***
**1283** A834 1r multicolored .50 .40

Dakshin Gangotri Post Office in the Antarctic, 1988 A835

**1989, July 11** ***Perf. 14***
**1284** A835 1r multicolored 2.00 .50

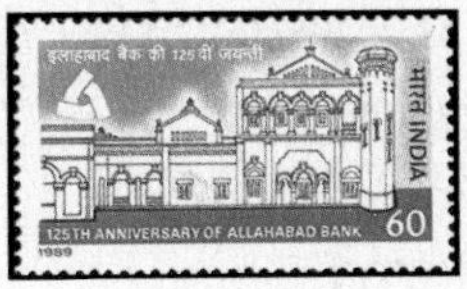


Allahabad Bank, 125th Anniv. A836

**1989, July 19**
**1285** A836 60p multicolored .50 .40

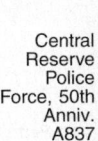

Central Reserve Police Force, 50th Anniv. A837

**1989, July 27** ***Perf. 13½x13***
**1286** A837 60p golden brown 2.00 .80

Military Farms, Cent. A838

**1989, Aug. 18**
**1287** A838 1r multicolored 1.20 4.50

Kemal Ataturk (1881-1938), 1st President of Turkey — A839

**1989, Aug. 30** ***Perf. 13x13½***
**1288** A839 5r multicolored 1.90 .80

Sarvepalli Radhakrishnan, President of India, 1962-67 — A840

**1989, Sept. 11 Photo.** ***Perf. 13x13½***
**1289** A840 60p black .50 .40

P. Subbarayan (1889-1962), Lawyer, Political Reformer — A841

**1989, Sept. 30** ***Perf. 13x13½***
**1290** A841 60p brown orange .50 .40

Mohun Bagan Soccer Team, Cent. A842

**1989, Sept. 23 Photo.** ***Perf. 13½x13***
**1291** A842 1r multicolored 1.90 1.00

### Freedom Fighter Type of 1989

Shyamji Krishna Varma (1857-1930).

**1989, Oct. 4 Photo.** ***Perf. 13½x13***
**1292** A826 60p org, sage grn & dk red brn .50 .40

Sayaji Rao Gaekwad III (1863-1939), Maharaja of the Former State of Baroda — A843

**1989, Oct. 6** ***Perf. 13x13½***
**1293** A843 60p black .50 .40

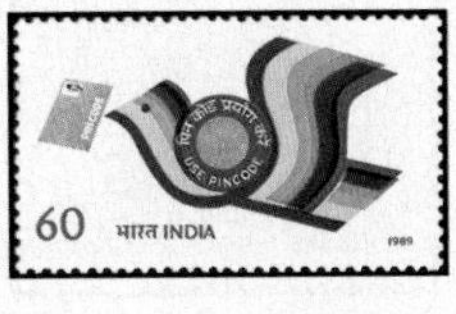


Use Pin Code A844

**1989, Oct. 14** ***Perf. 14***
**1294** A844 60p multicolored .65 .25

Namakkal Kavignar (1888-1972), Poet Laureate — A845

**1989, Oct. 19 Photo.** ***Perf. 13x13½***
**1295** A845 60p black .50 .40

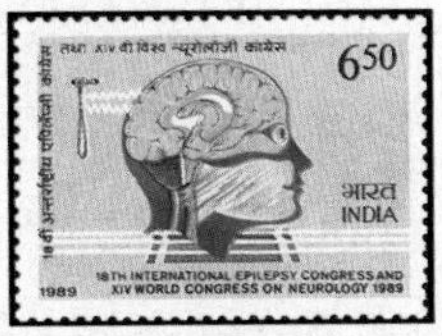


18th Intl. Epilepsy Congress and 14th World Neurology Congress, New Delhi A846

**1989, Oct. 21** ***Perf. 13½x13***
**1296** A846 6.50r multicolored 3.50 1.10

Ramabai and Sharada Sadan School A847

**1989, Oct. 26**
**1297** A847 60p brown .50 .30

Pandita Ramabai (1858-1920), women's rights activist, founder of mission to help destitute women and children.

Pigeon Post A848

**1989, Nov. 3**
**1298** A848 1r brown orange .90 .35

### Freedom Fighter Type of 1989

#1299, Acharya Narendra Deo (1889-1956), democratic socialist movement founder. #1300, Acharya Kripalani (1888-1982), politician.

**1989** ***Perf. 13½x13***
**1299** A826 60p org, sage grn & brn .50 .40
**1300** A826 60p org, sage grn & dp gray .50 .40

Issue dates: #1299, Nov. 6; #1300, Nov. 11.

Jawaharlal Nehru, Birth Cent. — A849

**1989, Nov. 14** ***Perf. 14x15***
**1301** A849 1r buff, dk red brn & sepia 1.00 .30

8th Asian Track and Field Meet, Nov. 14-19, New Delhi — A850

**1989, Nov. 19** ***Perf. 14x14½***
**1302** A850 1r black, org & dp grn .80 .45

A851

**1989, Nov. 20** ***Perf. 13x13½***
**1303** A851 60p deep brown .60 .45

Gurunath Bewoor (b. 1888), 1st Indian appointed postmaster general.

A852

**1989, Dec. 8 Photo.** ***Perf. 13x13½***
**1304** A852 60p black .60 .45

Balkrishna Sharma Navin (1897-1960), litterateur, politician.

Bombay Art Soc., Cent. A853

**1989, Dec. 15** ***Perf. 13½x13***
**1305** A853 1r multicolored .60 .45

Likh Florican — A854

**1989, Dec. 20** ***Perf. 13x13½***

**1306** A854 2r multicolored 2.50 .95

Digboi Oil Field, 1889 — A855

**1989, Dec. 29** ***Perf. 14***

**1307** A855 60p dark red brown .80 .45

Discovery of oil, Digboi, Assam, cent.

M.G. Ramachandran (1917-1987), Actor, Chief Minister — A856

**1990, Jan. 17** ***Perf. 13x13½***

**1308** A856 60p dark red brown .80 .30

Extracting Silt from Sukhna Lake, Chandigarh A857

**1990, Jan. 29** ***Perf. 13½x13***

**1309** A857 1r multicolored .60 .45

Sukhna Shramda, society for the preservation of Sukhna Lake.

Presentation of Colors by Pres. Venkataraman to the Bombay Sappers (Corps of Engineers), Feb. 21 — A858

***Perf. 15x14x14***

**1990, Feb. 21** **Photo.**

**1310** A858 60p multicolored 1.50 1.25

Asian Development Bank — A859

**1990, May 2** **Photo.** ***Perf. 14***

**1311** A859 2r Seashell 1.10 .45

Great Britain No. 1, Simulated Cancel of India, Envelope A860

**1990, May 6** ***Perf. 13x13½***

**1312** A860 6r multicolored 2.00 .75

Penny Black, 150th anniv.

Residence and Portrait A861

**1990, May 17** **Photo.** ***Perf. 13½x13***

**1313** A861 2r red brown & green .60 .40

Ho Chi Minh (1890-1969), Vietnamese Communist Party leader.

A862 A863

**1990, May 29**

**1314** A862 1r orange brown .50 .45

Prime Minister Chaudhary Charan Singh (1902-1987).

**1990, July 30** **Photo.** ***Perf. 13x13½***

**1315** A863 2r multicolored .80 .55

Indian peace keeping force in Sri Lanka.

Indian Council of Agricultural Research — A864

**1990, July 31** ***Perf. 14***

**1316** A864 2r multicolored .60 .40

**Freedom Fighter Type of 1989**

Design: Khudiram Bose (1889-1908), vert.

**1990, Aug. 11** **Photo.** ***Perf. 13x13½***

**Size: 26x35mm**

**1317** A826 1r orange, grn & red brn .60 .45

Russian Child's Drawing of India — A865

6.50r, Indian child's drawing of Red Square.

**1990, Aug. 16** **Photo.** ***Perf. 14***

**1318** A865 1r multicolored 2.40 1.60

**1319** A865 6.50r multicolored 2.40 1.60

*a.* Pair, #1318-1319 5.50 5.50

See Russia Nos. 5925-5926.

A866

**1990, Aug. 24** ***Perf. 13***

**1320** A866 1r lt red brown .60 .45

K. Kelappan (1889-1971), social revolutionary.

A867

**1990, Sept. 5** ***Perf. 13x13½***

**1321** A867 1r multicolored .75 .50

Care for young girls.

Intl. Literacy Year A868

**1990, Sept. 8** ***Perf. 13½x13***

**1322** A868 1r blue, brn & tan .75 .50

A869

**1990, Sept. 10** ***Perf. 13x14***

**1323** A869 4r blue grn & red 2.00 1.60

Safe drinking water.

A870

**1990, Sept. 28** **Photo.** ***Perf. 13x13½***

**1324** A870 60p rose lake .75 .50

Sunder Lal Sharma (1881-1940), social reformer.

11th Asian Games, Beijing — A871

**1990, Sept. 29**

**1325** A871 1r Kabbadi .65 .35

**1326** A871 4r Sprinting 1.90 1.75

**1327** A871 4r Cycling 1.90 1.75

**1328** A871 6.50r Archery 2.50 2.25

*Nos. 1325-1328 (4)* 6.95 6.10

A.K. Gopalan (1904-1977), Political and Social Reformer — A872

**1990, Oct. 1**

**1329** A872 1r red brown .75 .50

5th Gurkha Rifles, 3rd and 5th Battalions — A873

**1990, Oct. 1**

**1330** A873 2r yel brown & dk vio 2.25 1.75

Suryamall Mishran (1815-1868), Poet — A874

**1990, Oct. 19**

**1331** A874 2r brown & yel brown .80 .60

Children's Day — A875

***Perf. 13½x13***

**1990, Nov. 14** **Photo.** **Unwmk.**

**1332** A875 1r multicolored .90 .60

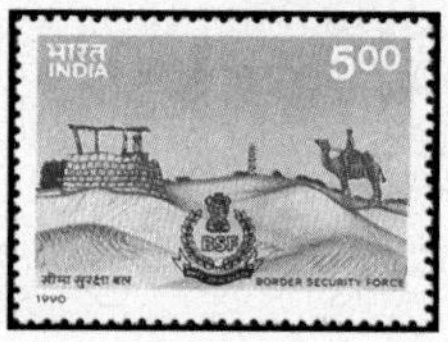


Border Security Force, 25th Anniv. A876

**1990, Nov. 30**

**1333** A876 5r multicolored 2.50 1.60

Greetings — A877

4r, Two elephants carrying riders, horiz.

*Perf. 13x13½, 13½x13*

**1990, Dec. 17** **Photo.**

| | | | | |
|---|---|---|---|---|
| **1334** | A877 | 1r multicolored | .35 | .30 |
| **1335** | A877 | 4r multicolored | 1.00 | .50 |

Cities of India A878

**1990, Dec. 24** **Photo.** ***Perf. 13½x13***

| | | | | |
|---|---|---|---|---|
| **1336** | A878 | 4r Bikaner | .80 | .65 |
| **1337** | A878 | 5r Hyderabad | 1.25 | .95 |
| **1338** | A878 | 6.50r Cuttack | 1.75 | 1.25 |
| | | *Nos. 1336-1338 (3)* | 3.80 | 2.85 |

Bhakta Kanakadas (1488-1578), Mystic — A879

**1990, Dec. 26** ***Perf. 14***

| | | | | |
|---|---|---|---|---|
| **1339** | A879 | 1r red orange | .90 | .45 |

Dnyaneshwari, 700th Anniv. — A880

**1990, Dec. 31** ***Perf. 13½x13***

| | | | | |
|---|---|---|---|---|
| **1340** | A880 | 2r org red, red brown & blk | .60 | .40 |

Calcutta, 300th Anniv. — A881

Designs: 1r, Shaheed Minar. 6r, Sailing ships on Ganges River.

**Unwmk.**

**1990, Dec. 28** **Photo.** ***Perf. 14***

| | | | | |
|---|---|---|---|---|
| **1341** | A881 | 1r multicolored | .50 | .30 |

**Size: 44x35mm**

| | | | | |
|---|---|---|---|---|
| **1342** | A881 | 6r multicolored | 2.00 | 1.50 |

Pandit Mohan Malaviya, Banaras Hindu University A882

**1991, Jan. 20** ***Perf. 13½x13***

| | | | | |
|---|---|---|---|---|
| **1343** | A882 | 1r dk carmine rose | .60 | .35 |

Banaras Hindu University, 75th Anniv.

Intl. Conference on Traffic Safety A883

**1991, Jan. 30** ***Perf. 13½x13***

| | | | | |
|---|---|---|---|---|
| **1344** | A883 | 6.50r blue, red & blk | 1.25 | .80 |

7th Art Triennial — A884

**1991, Feb. 12** **Photo.** ***Perf. 13x13½***

| | | | | |
|---|---|---|---|---|
| **1345** | A884 | 6.50r multicolored | 1.00 | .60 |

Jagannath Sunkersett A885

**1991, Feb. 15**

| | | | | |
|---|---|---|---|---|
| **1346** | A885 | 2r ultra & henna brn | .80 | .50 |

Jagannath Sunkersett (1803-1865), educator, reformer.

Tata Memorial Center, 50th Anniv. A886

**1991, Feb. 28** ***Perf. 13½x13***

| | | | | |
|---|---|---|---|---|
| **1347** | A886 | 2r brown & buff | .60 | .35 |

River Dolphin A887

**1991, Mar. 4**

| | | | | |
|---|---|---|---|---|
| **1348** | A887 | 4r shown | 2.25 | 1.75 |
| **1349** | A887 | 6.50r Sea cow | 3.00 | 2.40 |

Fight Against Drugs — A888

**1991, Mar. 5** ***Perf. 13x13½***

| | | | | |
|---|---|---|---|---|
| **1350** | A888 | 5r dp violet & red | 2.50 | 1.90 |

World Peace — A889

**1991, Mar. 7** **Photo.** ***Perf. 13x13½***

| | | | | |
|---|---|---|---|---|
| **1351** | A889 | 6.50r black & tan | 1.25 | .75 |

Indian Remote Sensing Satellite 1A — A890

**1991, Mar. 18** ***Perf. 14***

| | | | | |
|---|---|---|---|---|
| **1352** | A890 | 6.50r blue, red brn & blk | 1.00 | .60 |

Babu Jagjivan Ram (1908-1976), Politician — A891

**1991, Apr. 5** **Photo.** ***Perf. 13½***

| | | | | |
|---|---|---|---|---|
| **1353** | A891 | 1r yellow & brown | .60 | .50 |

Dr. B.R. Ambedkar (1891-1956), Social Reformer — A892

**1991, Apr. 14** ***Perf. 13½x13***

| | | | | |
|---|---|---|---|---|
| **1354** | A892 | 1r red brown & blue | .60 | .35 |

Tribal Dances A893

**1991, Apr. 30** **Photo.** ***Perf. 13½x13***

| | | | | |
|---|---|---|---|---|
| **1355** | A893 | 2.50r Valar | .70 | .50 |
| **1356** | A893 | 4r Kayang | .90 | .60 |
| **1357** | A893 | 5r Hozagiri | 1.20 | .70 |
| **1358** | A893 | 6.50r Velakali | 1.40 | .85 |
| | | *Nos. 1355-1358 (4)* | 4.20 | 2.65 |

Ariyakudi Ramanuja Iyengar (1890-1967), Musician — A894

**1991, May 18**

| | | | | |
|---|---|---|---|---|
| **1359** | A894 | 2r green & red brown | 1.00 | .60 |

Karpoori Thakur (1924-1988), Politician — A895

**1991, May 30** ***Perf. 13x13½***

| | | | | |
|---|---|---|---|---|
| **1360** | A895 | 1r red brown | .60 | .50 |

Antarctic Treaty, 30th Anniv. A896

**1991, June 23** **Photo.** ***Perf. 13½x13***

| | | | | |
|---|---|---|---|---|
| **1361** | A896 | 5r Penguins | 3.00 | 2.10 |
| **1362** | A896 | 6.50r Map, penguins | 3.00 | 2.10 |
| *a.* | | Pair, #1361-1362 | 6.50 | 6.50 |

No. 1362a printed in continuous design.

New Delhi, 60th Anniv. A897

Views of New Delhi architecture.

**1991, June 25**

| | | | | |
|---|---|---|---|---|
| **1363** | A897 | 5r multicolored | 3.00 | 1.60 |
| **1364** | A897 | 6.50r multicolored | 3.00 | 1.60 |
| *a.* | | Pair, #1363-1364 | 6.00 | 6.00 |

No. 1364a printed in continuous design.

Sri Ram Sharma Acharya (1911-1990), Social Reformer — A898

**1991, June 27**

| | | | | |
|---|---|---|---|---|
| **1365** | A898 | 1r red & blue green | .60 | .50 |

K. Shankar Pillai (1902-1989), Cartoonist — A899

**1991, July 31** **Photo.** ***Perf. 13½x13***

| | | | | |
|---|---|---|---|---|
| **1366** | A899 | 4r shown | 1.45 | 1.25 |

***Perf. 13x13½***

| | | | | |
|---|---|---|---|---|
| **1367** | A899 | 6.50r The Big Show, vert. | 2.00 | 1.90 |

Sriprakash (1890-1971), Politician — A900

**1991, Aug. 3** *Perf. 13½x13*
**1368** A900 2r yellow brown .60 .40

Gopinath Bardoloi (1890-1950), Politician — A901

**1991, Aug. 5** *Perf. 13x13½*
**1369** A901 1r violet .60 .50

Rajiv Gandhi (1944-1991), Prime Minister — A902

**1991, Aug. 20** *Perf. 13*
**1370** A902 1r multicolored 1.50 1.00

Jain Muni Mishrimalji (1891-1984), Philospher — A903

**1991, Aug. 24 Photo.** *Perf. 13½*
**1371** A903 1r brown .60 .35

Mahadevi Verma (1907-1987), Writer and Poet — A904

No. 1373: Jayshankar Prasad (1890-1937), poet and dramatist.

**1991, Sept. 16**
**1372** A904 2r black & blue *10.00* .50
**1373** A904 2r black & blue *10.00* .50
*a.* Pair, #1372-1373 *40.00* *27.50*

37th Commonwealth Parliamentary Conference — A905

**1991, Sept. 27 Photo.** *Perf. 13½x13*
**1374** A905 6.50r dk blue & brown .80 .60

Greetings — A906

**1991, Sept. 30** *Perf. 13x13½*
**1375** A906 1r Frog .25 .25
**1376** A906 6.50r Bird .90 .45
*a.* Pair, #1375-1376 1.10 1.00

Orchids — A907

**1991, Oct. 12**
**1377** A907 1r Cymbidium aloifolium .40 .30
**1378** A907 2.50r Paphiopedilum venustum .75 .40
**1379** A907 3r Aerides crispum 1.00 .50
**1380** A907 4r Cymbidium bicolour 1.50 .60
**1381** A907 5r Vanda spathulata 1.75 .85
**1382** A907 6.50r Cymbidium devonianum 2.25 1.25
*Nos. 1377-1382 (6)* 7.65 3.90

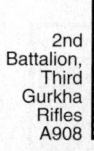

2nd Battalion, Third Gurkha Rifles A908

**1991, Oct. 18** *Perf. 13½x13*
**1383** A908 4r multicolored 2.75 2.00

Kamaladevi Chattopadhyaya (1903-1988), Founder of All-India Handicrafts Board — A909

**1991, Oct. 29** *Perf. 13x13½*
**1384** A909 1r Horsemen .70 .30
**1385** A909 6.50r Puppet 1.90 1.10

Chithira Tirunal Bala Rama Varma (1912-1991), Maharaja of Travancore — A910

**1991, Nov. 7 Photo.** *Perf. 13½x13*
**1386** A910 2r violet 1.00 .90

Children's Day — A911

**1991, Nov. 14** *Perf. 13x13½*
**1387** A911 1r multicolored 1.00 .50

18th Cavalry, Sesquicentennial (in 1992) — A912

**1991, Nov. 14** *Perf. 13½x13*
**1388** A912 6.50r multicolored 3.50 2.50

India Tourism Year A913

**1991, Nov. 15**
**1389** A913 6.50r multicolored 1.25 .95

Intl. Conference on Youth Tourism — A914

**1991, Nov. 18 Photo.** *Perf. 13x13½*
**1390** A914 6.50r multicolored 1.50 1.25

Wolfgang Amadeus Mozart, Death Bicent. — A915

**1991, Dec. 5**
**1391** A915 6.50r multicolored 2.50 1.90

SAARC Year of Shelter A916

**1991, Dec. 7** *Perf. 13½x13*
**1392** A916 4r lake & bister 1.00 .75

Run for Your Heart A917

**1991, Dec. 11**
**1393** A917 1r black, red & gray .60 .50

Siddhartha With An Injured Bird — A918

**1991, Dec. 28** *Perf. 13x13½*
**1394** A918 2r multicolored .60 .40

Asit Kumar Haldar (1890-1964), Painter

Yoga Exercises A919

**1991, Dec. 30 Photo.** *Perf. 13½x13*
**1395** A919 2r Bhujangasana .35 .30
**1396** A919 5r Dhanurasana .80 .35
**1397** A919 6.50r Ustrasana 1.10 .50
**1398** A919 10r Utthita trikonasana 1.90 .75
*Nos. 1395-1398 (4)* 4.15 1.90

Intl. Assoc. for Bridge and Structural Engineering A920

#1399, Hooghly River Bridge, Madurai Temple. #1400, Sanchi Stupa gates, Hall of Nations.

**1992, Mar. 1 Photo.** *Perf. 13½x13*
**1399** A920 2r sal, brn & blue *10.00* *.85*
**1400** A920 2r sal, brn & blue *10.00* *.85*
*a.* Pair, #1399-1400 *35.00* *25.00*

Fifth Intl. Conference on Goats — A921

**1992, Mar. 2** *Perf. 13x13½*
**1401** A921 6r dk blue & brown 3.75 2.75

Natl. Council of YMCAs, Cent. (in 1991) — A922

**1992, Feb. 21**
**1402** A922 1r blue & vermilion .60 .40

National Archives A923

**1992, Apr. 20 Photo. *Perf. 13½x13***
**1403** A923 6r multicolored .80 .55

Krushna Chandra Gajapathi — A924

Vijay Singh Pathik, Writer — A925

**1992, Apr. 29 *Perf. 13x13½***
**1404** A924 1r violet .60 .40
**1405** A925 1r red brown .60 .40

Adventure Sports A926

**1992, Apr. 29 *Perf. 13½x13***
**1406** A926 2r Hang gliding .45 .40
**1407** A926 4r Wind surfing 1.25 .65
**1408** A926 5r River rafting 1.75 1.10
**1409** A926 11r Skiing 2.25 1.75
*Nos. 1406-1409 (4)* 5.70 3.90

Henry Gidney (1873-1942), Physician and Politician — A927

**1992, May 9 *Perf. 13½x13***
**1410** A927 1r blue & black .90 .55

Telecommunication Training Center, Jabalpur, 50th Anniv. — A928

**1992, May 30**
**1411** A928 1r lemon .60 .50

Sardar Udham Singh (1899-1940), freedom fighter. — A929

**1992, July 31 *Perf. 13x13½***
**1412** A929 1r black & brown .60 .50

1992 Summer Olympics, Barcelona. A930

**1992, Aug. 8**
**1413** A930 1r Discus .45 .25
**1414** A930 6r Gymnastics 1.25 .85
**1415** A930 8r Field hockey 3.00 1.90
**1416** A930 11r Boxing 3.00 2.25
*Nos. 1413-1416 (4)* 7.70 5.25

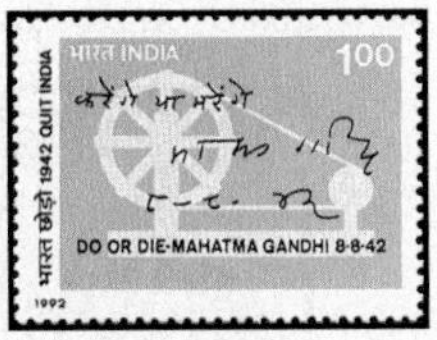


Quit India Movement, 50th Anniv. A931

Designs: 1r, Spinning wheel, inscription. 2r, Mahatma Gandhi, inscription.

**1992, Aug. 9 *Perf. 13½x13***
**1417** A931 1r pink, blk & pale pink 1.75 .65
**1418** A931 2r gray, black & claret 2.75 3.00

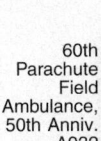

60th Parachute Field Ambulance, 50th Anniv. A932

**1992, Aug. 10**
**1419** A932 1r multicolored 2.25 .90

Indian Air Force, 60th Anniv. A933

**1992, Oct. 8 Photo. *Perf. 13½x13***
**1420** A933 1r shown *10.00 .85*
**1421** A933 10r Biplane, jet fighter *10.00 1.50*
*a.* Pair, #1420-1421 *35.00 25.00*

Phad Painting of Dev Narayan A934

**1992, Sept. 2 Photo. *Perf. 13½x14***
**1422** A934 5r multicolored 1.00 .95

Sisters of Jesus and Mary, 150th Anniv. — A935

**1992, Nov. 13 Photo. *Perf. 13x13½***
**1423** A935 1r gray & blue .60 .35

Children's Day A936

**1992, Nov. 14 *Perf. 13½x13***
**1424** A936 1r multicolored .60 .35

Shri Yogiji Maharaj, Religious Leader, Birth Cent. — A937

**1992, Dec. 2 Photo. *Perf. 13x13½***
**1425** A937 1r blue 2.25 1.50

Army Service Corps 1760-1992 A938

**1992, Dec. 8 Photo. *Perf. 13½x13***
**1426** A938 1r multicolored 3.00 .80

Stephen Smith (1891-1951), Rocket Mail Pioneer — A939

**1992, Dec. 19 Photo. *Perf. 13½x13***
**1427** A939 11r multicolored 1.75 1.10

State of Haryana, 25th Anniv. A940

**1992, Dec. 20**
**1428** A940 2r green & orange .60 .60

**Freedom Fighter Type of 1989**

Design: Madan Lal Dhingra, vert.

**1992, Dec. 28 *Perf. 13x13½***
**1429** A826 1r org, grn & brn .60 .35

Dr. Shri Shiyali Ramamrita Ranganathan (1892-1972), Writer and Librarian — A941

**1992, Aug. 30 Photo. *Perf. 13½x13***
**1430** A941 1r blue 2.00 .65

Hanuman Prasad Poddar — A942

**1992, Sept. 19 Photo. *Perf. 13x13½***
**1431** A942 1r green .60 .30

Pandit Ravishankar Shukla — A943

**1992, Dec. 31**
**1432** A943 1r rose lake .60 .30

Birds — A944

2r, Pandion haliaetus. 6r, Falco peregrinus. 8r, Gypaetus barbatus. 11r, Aquila chrysaetos.

**1992, Dec. 30**
**1433** A944 2r multicolored 1.25 .85
**1434** A944 6r multicolored 1.75 1.25
**1435** A944 8r multicolored 1.90 1.40
**1436** A944 11r multicolored 2.10 1.90
*Nos. 1433-1436 (4)* 7.00 5.40

William Carey, Baptist Missionary to India, Bicent. of Appointment A945

**1993, Jan. 9 Photo. *Perf. 13½x13***
**1437** A945 6r multicolored 2.00 1.10

Fakir Mohan Senapati, Writer — A946

**1993, Jan. 14** ***Perf. 13x13½***
**1438** A946 1r orange brown .75 .40

Council of Scientific and Industrial Research, 50th Anniv. — A947

**1993, Feb. 28** ***Perf. 13½x13***
**1439** A947 1r violet brown .90 .45

Squadron No. 1, Indian Air Force, 60th Anniv. A948

**1993, Apr. 1**
**1440** A948 1r shown 1.25 .35
**1441** A948 1r Paratroopers, planes, artillery 1.25 .35

Parachute Field Regiment 9, 50th anniv. (#1441).

Rahul Sankrityayan (1893-1963), Politician — A949

**1993, Apr. 9**
**1442** A949 1r multicolored .75 .35

Mountain Locomotives A950

**1993, Apr. 16** ***Perf. 13½x13***
**1443** A950 1r Neral Matheran 1.00 .30
**1444** A950 6r DHR (Darjeeling) 2.00 1.00
**1445** A950 8r Nilgiri Mountain Railway 2.25 1.25
**1446** A950 11r Kalka-Simla 3.25 1.60
*Nos. 1443-1446 (4)* 8.50 4.15

89th Inter-Parliamentary Union Conference, New Delhi — A951

**1993, Apr. 11 Photo.** ***Perf. 13x13½***
**1447** A951 1r indigo .75 .35

Meerut College, Cent. (in 1992) — A952

**1993, Apr. 25** ***Perf. 14***
**1448** A952 1r indigo & red brown .75 .60

P.C. Mahalanobis (b. 1893), Statistician — A953

**1993, June 29** ***Perf. 13x13½***
**1449** A953 1r olive yellow .60 .35

Dadabhai Naoroji's Election to House of Commons, Cent. — A957

**1993, Aug. 26 Photo.** ***Perf. 14***
**1453** A957 6r blue & red brown 1.00 .70

A958

**1993, Sept. 11** ***Perf. 13x13½***
**1454** A958 2r gray, red brn & org 1.00 .55

Swami Vivekananda, Chicago address, cent.

A959

Trees: 1r, Lagerstroemia speciosa. 6r, Cochlospermum religiosum. 8r, Erythrina variegata. 11r, Thespesia populnea.

**1993, Oct. 9 Photo.** ***Perf. 13x13½***
**1455** A959 1r multicolored .40 .30
**1456** A959 6r multicolored 1.00 .30
**1457** A959 8r multicolored 1.50 .65
**1458** A959 11r multicolored 2.25 .90
*Nos. 1455-1458 (4)* 5.15 2.15

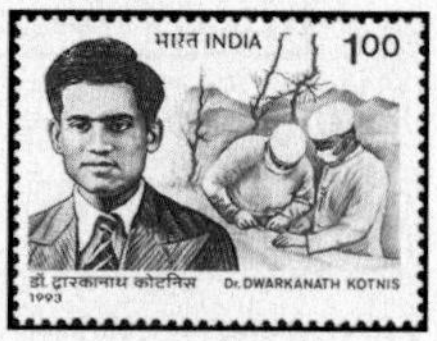


Dr. Dwarkanath Kotnis A960

**1993, Dec. 9 Photo.** ***Perf. 13½x13***
**1459** A960 1r black & gray .80 .40

A961

**1993, Nov. 14** ***Perf. 14***
**1460** A961 1r multicolored .60 .35

Children's Day.

A962

**1993, Nov. 8** ***Perf. 13x13½***
**1461** A962 2r multicolored .60 .35

College of Military Engineering, Pune, 50th anniv.

A963

Design: Dr. Dwarm Venkataswamy Naidu.

**1993, Nov. 8**
**1462** A963 1r orange brown .60 .35

A964

**1993, July 31**
**1463** A964 2r multicolored .60 .35

Bombay Municipal Corporation Building, cent.

India Tea A965

**1993, Dec. 11** ***Perf. 13***
**1464** A965 6r green & red 1.10 .75

Papal Seminary, Pune, Cent. A966

**1993, Dec. 16** ***Perf. 13½x13***
**1465** A966 6r multicolored 1.25 .85

Natl. Integration A967

**1993, Aug. 19**
**1466** A967 1r orange & green .60 .30

Khan Abdul Ghaffar Khan A968

**1993, Aug. 9**
**1467** A968 1r multicolored .60 .30

Heart Care Festival A969

**1993, Dec. 9**
**1468** A969 6.50r multicolored 1.40 .75

Inpex '93 — A970

**1993**
**1469** A970 1r shown .40 .40
**1470** A970 2r Boats, beach 1.00 .40

Issued: 1r, Dec. 25; 2r, Dec. 27.

Meghnad Saha (1893-1956), Astrophysicist A971

**1993, Dec. 23 Photo.** ***Perf. 13x13½***
**1471** A971 1r dark blue .75 .45

Dinanath Mageshkar, Musician A972

**1993, Dec. 29** ***Perf. 13½x13***
**1472** A972 1r orange brown .60 .30

Nargis Dutt, Actress and Social Worker — A973

**1993, Dec. 30** ***Perf. 13***
**1473** A973 1r orange brown .60 .30

Indian Natl. Army, 50th Anniv. A974

1r, Netaji Subhash Bose inspecting soldiers.

**1993, Dec. 31** *Perf. 13½x13*
**1474** A974 1r multicolored .80 .50

Satyendra Nath Bose (1894-1974), Mathematician and Physicist — A975

**1994, Jan. 1**
**1475** A975 1r dark rose brown .80 .45

Satyajit Ray (1921-92) A976

6r, Scene from film, Pather Panchali.

**1994, Jan. 11** *Perf. 13*
**1476** A976 6r multicolored 2.40 1.60
**1477** A976 11r multicolored 2.75 1.60
*a.* Pair, #1476-1477 5.25 5.25

No. 1476 is 68x30mm. No. 1477a is a continuous design.

Dr. Sampurnanand — A977

**1994, Jan. 10 Photo.** *Perf. 13½x13*
**1478** A977 1r multicolored .60 .60

Dr. Shanti Swarup Bhatnagar A978

**1994, Feb. 21**
**1479** A978 1r dark blue .70 .70

Eighth Triennale A979

**1994, Mar. 14**
**1480** A979 6r multicolored 1.00 .50

Prajapita Brahma (1876-1969), Religious Leader — A980

**1994, Mar. 7 Photo.** *Perf. 13½x13*
**1481** A980 1r multicolored .70 .70

Sanchi Stupa A981

**Wmk. 324**

**1994, Apr. 4 Photo.** *Perf. 13*
**1482** A981 5r blue green & brn .60 .40

ILO, 75th Anniv. A982

**1994, May 1 Unwmk.** *Perf. 13½x13*
**1483** A982 6r multicolored 1.00 .70

United Planters Assoc. of Southern India, Cent. — A983

**1994, Mar. 26 Photo.** *Perf. 13x13½*
**1484** A983 2r multicolored .70 .50

Rani Rashmoni (1793-1861), Philanthropist — A984

**1994, Apr. 9** *Perf. 13½x13*
**1485** A984 1r brown .70 .55

Jallianwala Bagh Martyrdom, 75th Anniv. A985

**1994, Apr. 13**
**1486** A985 1r red & black .70 .70

**Freedom Fighter Type of 1989**

1r, Chandra Singh Garhwali (1891-1979).

**1994, Apr. 23**
**1487** A826 1r org, sage grn & grn .70 .70

IPTA — A986

**1994, May 25** *Perf. 13*
**1488** A986 2r multi .70 .40

Small Families — A987

1r, Family of 3 in front of house.

**1994** *Perf. 13x12½*
**1489** A987 75p red brn & brn .30 .30
**1490** A987 1r green & rose .30 .30

4th Battalion Madras Regiment, Bicent. — A988

**1994, Aug. 12**
**1491** A988 6.50r multicolored 1.25 .85

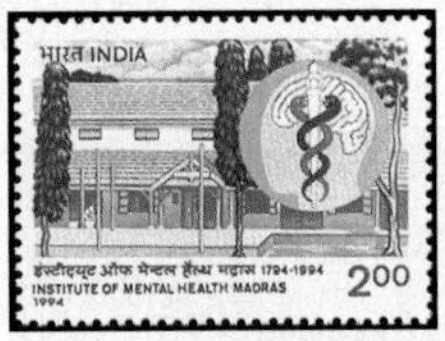

Institute of Mental Health, Madras, Bicent. A989

**1994, Sept. 23 Photo.** *Perf. 13½x13*
**1492** A989 2r multicolored .70 .40

Mahatma Gandhi (1869-1948) A990

Design: 11r, Flag colors, Gandhi walking and at spinning wheel.

**1994, Oct. 2** *Perf. 13*
**1493** A990 6r multicolored 2.25 1.50
**1494** A990 11r multicolored 3.00 2.50
*a.* Pair, #1493-1494 5.50 5.50

No. 1494 is 68x30mm.

16th Intl. Cancer Congress — A991

**1994, Oct. 30 Photo.** *Perf. 13½*
**1495** A991 6r multicolored 1.25 .70

World Conference on Human Resource Development — A992

**1994, Nov. 8** *Perf. 13½x13*
**1496** A992 6r multicolored 1.00 .65

Intl. Year of the Family — A993

**1994, Nov. 20** *Perf. 13x12½*
**1497** A993 2r multicolored .60 .35

Children's Day A994

**1994, Nov. 14** *Perf. 13½x13*
**1498** A994 1r multicolored .60 .50

J.R.D. Tata (1904-93) — A995

**1994, Nov. 29** *Perf. 14*
**1499** A995 2r multicolored .60 .40

Calcutta School for the Blind, Cent. A996

**1994 Nov. 30** *Perf. 13½x13*
**1500** A996 2r brown & carmine .60 .35

Endangered Waterbirds — A996A

Designs: 1r, Andaman teal. 6r, Eastern white stork. 8r, Black-necked crane. 11r, Pink-headed duck.

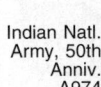

**1994, Nov. 23** *Perf. 13*

| | | | | |
|---|---|---|---|---|
| **1501** | A996A | 1r multicolored | 12.50 | 3.75 |
| **1502** | A996A | 6r multicolored | 19.00 | 7.50 |
| **1503** | A996A | 8r multicolored | 19.00 | 8.00 |
| **1504** | A996A | 11r multicolored | 20.00 | 11.00 |
| *a.* | | Block of 4, #1501-1504 | 75.00 | 75.00 |

This set was withdrawn shortly after issue, when it was discovered that it was printed with water soluble ink.

Begum Akhtar A996B

**1994, Dec 2** *Perf. 13x13½*

**1504B** A996B 2r multicolored 15.00 10.00

No. 1504B was withdrawn shortly after issue, when it was discovered that it was printed with water soluble ink.

Remount Veterinary Corps, 215th Anniv. — A998

**1994, Dec. 14 Photo.** *Perf. 13x13½*

**1505** A998 6r multicolored 2.25 1.60

College of Engineering, Guindy, Madras, Bicent. — A999

**1994, Dec. 19** *Perf. 14*

**1506** A999 2r multicolored .60 .35

Baroda Museum, Vadodara — A1000

Designs: 6r, Ancient artifact. 11r, Ancient artifact, man standing on pedestal.

**1994, Dec. 20** *Perf. 14x13½*

| | | | | |
|---|---|---|---|---|
| **1507** | | 6r black & bister | 4.50 | 2.25 |
| **1508** | | 11r black & bister | 4.50 | 2.25 |
| *a.* | A1000 | Pair, #1507-1508 | 9.50 | 9.50 |

Khuda Bakhsh Oriental Public Library A1001

**1994, Nov. 21 Photo.** *Perf. 14*

**1509** A1001 6r multicolored 6.50 1.60

A1002

**1995, Jan. 9 Photo.** *Perf. 13x13½*

**1510** A1002 1r Chhoturam 1.25 .30

A1003

**1995, Jan. 7**

**1511** A1003 6r multicolored .80 .55

India Natl. Science Academy, 30th Anniv.

St. Xavier's College, Bombay, 125th Anniv. A1005

**1994, Dec. 4 Photo.** *Perf. 13½*

**1513** A1005 2r multicolored .35 .25

General Post Office, Bombay, Bicent. — A1006

**1994, Dec. 28 Litho.** *Perf. 13½*

**1514** A1006 6r multicolored 8.00 3.00

Motion Pictures, Cent. A1007

Designs: 6r, Colored film, world map. 11r, Early camera, black & white film.

**1995, Jan. 11 Litho.** *Perf. 13*

| | | | | |
|---|---|---|---|---|
| **1515** | A1007 | 6r multicolored | 1.60 | 1.60 |
| **1516** | A1007 | 11r multicolored | 2.50 | 2.50 |
| *a.* | | Pair, #1515-1516 | 4.25 | 4.25 |

Oil Conservation A1008

Rafi Ahmed Kidwai A1009

**1995, Feb. 18 Photo.** *Perf. 13*

**1517** A1008 1r red brown & black .25 .25

**1995, Feb. 18**

**1518** A1009 1r red brown .60 .60

K. L. Saigal A1010

**1995, Apr. 4 Photo.** *Perf. 13½x13*

**1519** A1010 5r black & brown 1.75 1.00

A1011

**1995, Jan. 5 Photo.** *Perf. 13*

**1520** A1011 2r King Rajaraja Chola 5.50 1.10

8th Intl. Conference of Tamil Studies.

A1012

**1995, Jan. 12 Photo.** *Perf. 13½x13*

**1521** A1012 2r multicolored .60 .40

SAARC Youth Year.

A1013

**1995, Jan. 15**

**1522** A1013 2r multicolored 5.75 1.10

Prithvi Theater, 50th anniv.

A1014

Field Marshall K.M. Cariappa (1900-93).

**1995, Jan. 15**

**1523** A1014 2r multicolored .55 .45

A1015

**1995, Jan. 18**

**1524** A1015 2r multicolored .60 .40

Tex-Styles India '95, National Textile Fair, Bombay.

A1017

UN, 50th Anniv.: 6r, Planting seedling, mother and child, child reading.

**1995, June 6 Photo.** *Perf. 13*

| | | | | |
|---|---|---|---|---|
| **1526** | A1017 | 1r multicolored | .25 | .25 |
| **1527** | A1017 | 6r multicolored | .65 | .45 |

R.S. Ruikar — A1018

**1995, May 1 Photo.** *Perf. 13½*

**1528** A1018 1r brown violet .60 .60

Bharti Bhavan Library, Allahabad A1019

**1995, Aug. 30** *Perf. 14*

**1529** A1019 6r multicolored .75 .60

Asian Pacific Postal Training Center, Bangkok, 25th Anniv. A1020

**1995, Sept. 4 Litho.** *Perf. 13½x13*

**1530** A1020 10r multicolored 1.75 1.25

Headquarters Delhi Area — A1021

**1995, Sept. 26 Photo.** *Perf. 13*

**1531** A1021 2r multicolored .75 .55

Louis Pasteur (1822-95) A1022

**1995, Sept. 28**

**1532** A1022 5r pale yel & black 3.00 1.50

La Martiniere College, Lucknow, 150th Anniv. A1023

**1995, Oct. 1**
**1533** A1023 2r multicolored .60 .40

Mahatma Gandhi (1869-1948) — A1024

**1995, Oct. 2**
**1534** 1r As young man .85 .40
**1535** 2r As older man .85 .40
*a.* A1024 Pair, #1534-1535 1.75 1.75
*b.* Souvenir sheet, #1535a 3.00 3.00

See South Africa Nos. 918-919.

FAO, 50th Anniv. A1025

**1995, Oct. 16** *Perf. 13½*
**1536** A1025 5r multicolored 1.40 1.00

A1026

**1995, Oct. 30** *Perf. 13*
**1537** A1026 1r carmine .60 .50

P.M. Thevar (1908-63), politician.

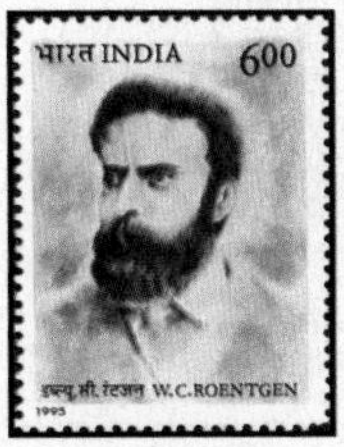


A1027

**1995, Nov. 8 Photo.** *Perf. 13x13½*
**1538** A1027 6r multicolored 2.50 1.90

Wilhelm Roentgen (1845-1923), discovery of the X-Ray, cent.

JAT Regiment, Bicent. A1028

**1995, Nov. 20** *Perf. 13*
**1539** A1028 5r multicolored 2.25 1.75

Radio Communication, Cent. — A1029

**1995, May 17 Litho.** *Perf. 13½x13*
**1540** A1029 5r multicolored 1.75 1.75

Dehli Development Authority — A1030

**1995, May 23**
**1541** A1030 2r multicolored .60 .60

Children's Day — A1031

**1995, Nov. 14 Photo.** *Perf. 13x13½*
**1542** A1031 1r multicolored .60 .50

Rajputana Rifles, 175th Anniv. A1032

**1995, Nov. 28** *Perf. 13½*
**1543** A1032 5r multicolored 2.75 1.75

Communal Harmony — A1033

**1995, Nov. 19 Photo.** *Perf. 13*
**1544** A1033 2r multicolored 2.50 1.40

Sant Tukdoji Maharaj, Patriot, Social Worker A1034

**1995, Dec. 10**
**1545** A1034 1r brown .70 .55

Dated 1993.

A1035

A1036

Design: Yellapragada Subbarow (1895-1948), biochemist.

**1995, Dec. 19**
**1546** A1035 1r yellow brown .70 .55

**1995, Dec. 25**

Giani Zail Singh (1916-94), Pres. of India.

**1547** A1036 1r multicolored .70 .55

Dome Barelvi's Mausoleum, Dargah — A1037

**1995, Dec. 31** **Litho.**
**1548** A1037 1r multicolored .70 .55

Ala Hazrat Barelvi (1856-1921), poet.

Cricket Players — A1038

**1996, Mar. 13 Photo.** *Perf. 14*
**1549** A1038 2r Deodhar 1.00 .75
**1550** A1038 2r Vijay Merchant 1.00 .75
**1551** A1038 2r Vinoo Mankad 1.00 .75
**1552** A1038 2r C.K. Nayudu 1.00 .75
*Nos. 1549-1552 (4)* 4.00 3.00

Dated 1995.

Homi Bhabha and Tata Institute of Fundamental Research — A1039

**1996, Feb. 9 Photo.** *Perf. 13*
**1553** A1039 2r multicolored .80 .50

Kasturba Trust — A1040

**1996, Feb. 22**
**1554** A1040 1r multicolored .60 .35

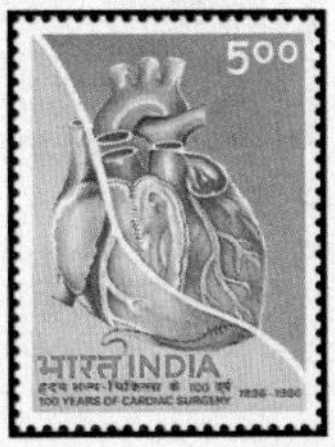


Cardiac Surgery, Cent. — A1041

**1996, Feb. 25** **Litho.**
**1555** A1041 5r multicolored 2.75 1.25

Miniature Paintings A1042

#1556, Two women picking berries from trees. #1557, Woman, man embracing. #1558, Women looking upward, men, animals. #1559, Ceremony, black clouds.

**1996, Mar. 13** *Perf. 13½*
**1556** A1042 5r multicolored 2.00 1.00
**1557** A1042 5r multicolored 2.00 1.00
**1558** A1042 5r multicolored 2.00 1.00
**1559** A1042 5r multicolored 2.00 1.00
*Nos. 1556-1559 (4)* 8.00 4.00

Pt. Kunjilal Dubey — A1043

**1996, Mar. 18 Photo.** *Perf. 13*
**1560** A1043 1r brown .60 .50

Himalayan Wildlife A1044

#1561, Saussurea simpsoniana. #1562, Capra falconeri. #1563, Ithaginis cruentus. #1564, Meconopsis horridula.

**1996, May 10** **Litho.**
**1561** A1044 5r multicolored 2.25 1.75
**1562** A1044 5r multicolored 2.25 1.75
**1563** A1044 5r multicolored 2.25 1.75
**1564** A1044 5r multicolored 2.25 1.75
*a.* Souv. sheet of 4, #1561-1564 9.00 9.00
*Nos. 1561-1564 (4)* 9.00 7.00

No. 1564a sold for 30r. Stamps in No. 1564a do not have "1996."

Morarji Desai — A1045

**1996, Apr. 10 Photo.** *Perf. 13x13½*
**1565** A1045 1r carmine .60 .35

SKCG College A1047

**1996, May 25** **Photo.**
**1567** A1047 1r lt brn & dk brn .80 .65

Muhammad Ismail Sahib — A1048

**1996, June 5** *Perf. 13x13½*

**1568** A1048 1r claret .80 .80

1996 Summer Olympic Games, Atlanta — A1049

**1996, June 25**

**1569** A1049 5r Olympic stadium .90 .55
**1570** A1049 5r Torch .90 .55

A1050

**1996, July 19** *Perf. 13x13½*

**1571** A1050 1r blue & black .65 .65

Sister Alphonsa (1910-46).

A1051

**1996, Aug. 2** **Litho.** *Perf. 14*

**1572** A1051 5r multicolored 2.25 1.40

VSNL, 125th anniv.

A1052

A1053

1r, Chembai Vaidyanatha Bhagavathar. 2r, Ahilyabai Holkar.

**1996** **Photo.** *Perf. 13x13½*

**1573** A1052 1r dk bl grn & brn .80 .55
**1574** A1052 2r rose brn & lt brn .80 .65

Issued: 1r, 8/28; 2r, 8/25.

**1996, Aug. 4** **Photo.** *Perf. 13*

**1575** A1053 1r Sir Pherozsha Mehta .80 .80

Poultry Production A1054

**1996, Sept. 2**

**1576** A1054 5r Gallus gallus 4.00 3.00

Rani Gaidinliu — A1055

**1996, Sept. 12**

**1577** A1055 1r dark blue green .80 .80

Barrister Nath Pai — A1056

**1996, Sept. 25**

**1578** A1056 1r blue .80 .80

Indepex '97 World Philatelic Exhibition A1057

**1996, Oct. 5** **Litho.** *Perf. 13x13½*

**1579** A1057 2r lake & bister .80 .50

Children's Day A1058

**1996, Nov. 14** **Photo.** *Perf. 13½x13*

**1580** A1058 8r multicolored 2.00 1.25

South Asian Assoc. for Regional Cooperation (SAARC), 10th Anniv. A1059

**1996, Dec. 8** *Perf. 13*

**1581** A1059 11r multicolored 2.40 1.60

Abai Konunbaev (1845-1904), Poet — A1060

**1996, Dec. 9** *Perf. 13x13½*

**1582** A1060 5r red brown & lake 2.40 1.60

Dated 1995.

2nd Intl. Crop Science Congress A1061

**1996, Nov. 17** *Perf. 13*

**1583** A1061 2r multicolored 1.10 .70

Sikh Regiment, 150th Anniv. A1062

**1996, Oct. 19**

**1584** A1062 5r multicolored 2.40 1.50

Natl. Rail Museum, 25th Anniv. — A1063

**1996, Oct. 7** **Litho.** *Perf. 13½*

**1585** A1063 5r multicolored 3.75 2.10

Jananayak Debeswar Sarmah (1896-1993), Politician — A1064

**1996, Oct. 10**

**1586** A1064 2r lt brn & red brn .80 .50

Dr. Salim Ali, Birth Cent. — A1065

**1996, Nov. 12** **Photo.** *Perf. 13*

**1587** 8r Dr. Salim Ali 3.75 2.50
**1588** 11r Water fowl 3.75 2.50
*a.* A1065 Pair, #1587-1588 9.00 9.00

Second Battalion, The Grenadiers, Bicent. A1066

**1996, Dec. 4** *Perf. 14*

**1589** A1066 5r multicolored 2.40 1.25

Vijay Divas A1067

**1996, Dec. 16**

**1590** A1067 2r multicolored .35 .25

Vivekananda Rock Memorial, Kanyakumari — A1068

**1996, Dec. 26** **Litho.** *Perf. 13*

**1591** A1068 5r multicolored 3.25 1.90

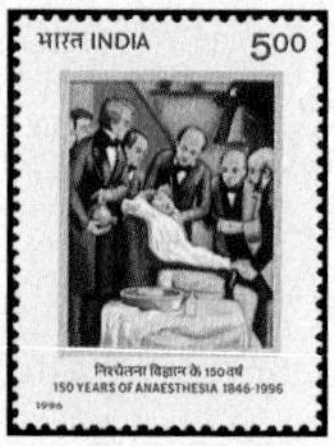


Use of Anesthesia, 150th Anniv. — A1069

**1996, Dec. 27** *Perf. 13*

**1592** A1069 5r multicolored 2.40 1.40

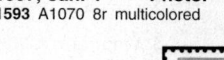

University of Roorkee, 150th Anniv. A1070

**1997, Jan. 1** **Photo.** *Perf. 13*

**1593** A1070 8r multicolored 1.50 1.10

Vrindavan Lal Verma, Writer — A1071

**1997, Jan. 9** **Photo.** *Perf. 13x13½*

**1594** A1071 2r red .80 .50

Army Postal Service Corps. (APS), 25th Anniv. A1072

**1997, Jan. 22** *Perf. 13½x13*
**1595** A1072 5r multicolored 2.75 1.90

Jose Marti (1853-95), Cuban Revolutionary A1073

**1997, Jan. 28** *Perf. 13x13½*
**1596** A1073 11r multicolored 2.25 1.00

Inter-Parliamentary Specialized Conference, New Dehli — A1074

**1997, Feb. 15** **Photo.** *Perf. 13*
**1597** A1074 5r multicolored .80 .40

A1075

**1997, Mar. 4** **Photo.** *Perf. 13*
**1598** A1075 1r lt brn & dk brn .80 .50

Shyam Lal Gupt (b. 1896), composer of song on natl. flag.

A1076

**1997, Mar. 8** *Perf. 13x13½*
**1599** 5r Parijat Tree 1.25 .75
**1600** 6r Branch, flower 1.25 .75
*a.* A1076 Pair, #1599-1600 2.50 2.50

Rashtriya Indian Military College, Dehra Dun, 75th Anniv. A1077

**1997, Mar. 13** *Perf. 13½*
**1601** A1077 2r multicolored 1.60 .60

Netaji Subhas Chandra Bose (1897-1945), Nationalist Leader — A1078

**1997, Jan. 23** *Perf. 13*
**1602** A1078 1r dk brn & lt brn .80 .45

A1079

**1997, Feb. 25** **Photo.** *Perf. 13x13½*
**1603** A1079 8r St. Andrews Church 1.60 .95

Morarji Desai, Prime Minister, 1977-79 — A1080

**1997, Feb. 28** **Photo.** *Perf. 13*
**1604** A1080 1r brown & buff .80 .45

Saint Dnyaneshwar (1274-95), Poet — A1081

**1997, Mar. 5** **Photo.** *Perf. 13*
**1605** A1081 5r multicolored 1.10 .65

Ram Manohar Lohia (1910-67), Politician — A1082

**1997, Mar. 23** **Litho.** *Perf. 13x13½*
**1606** A1082 1r multicolored .75 .40

CENTIPEX '97 — A1083

Philatelic Society of India, Cent.: No. 1608, #1, Front cover of "The Philatelic Journal of India," 1897.

**1997, Mar. 27**
**1607** 2r multicolored 1.25 1.00
**1608** 2r multicolored 1.25 1.00
*a.* Pair, #1607-1608 2.50 2.50

Jnanpith Award Winners — A1084

K.V. Puttappa, D.R. Bendre, Prof. V.K. Gokak, Dr. Masti V. Iyengar, writers.

**1997, Mar. 28** **Photo.** *Perf. 13*
**1609** A1084 2r multi .80 .50

Madhu Limaye (1922-95), Politician — A1085

**1997, May 1**
**1610** A1085 2r green .80 .50

A1086

**1997, June 24** **Photo.** *Perf. 13x13½*
**1611** A1086 2r Pandit Omkarnath Thakar 1.10 .65

A1087

**1997, Aug. 6** **Photo.** *Perf. 13*
**1612** A1087 2r brown 1.75 1.25

Thirumathi Rukmini Lakshmipathi (1892-1951), reformer.

Independence, 50th Anniv. — A1088

Officers from Indian Natl. Army, Shah Nawaz Khan, G.S. Dhillon, P.K. Sahgal.

**1997, Aug. 15**
**1613** A1088 2r multicolored .40 .25

Newspaper Swantantra Bharat, 50th Anniv. A1089

**1997, Aug. 15** *Perf. 13½x13*
**1614** A1089 2r multicolored .60 .40

A1090

**1997, Aug. 20** *Perf. 13*
**1615** A1090 2r black & gray 1.75 .75

Sir Ronald Ross (1857-1932), physician, medical researcher.

A1091

**1997, Sept. 6**
**1616** A1091 5r red brown 1.75 1.00

Swami Bhaktivedanta (b. 1896), humanitarian.

A1092

**1997, Sept. 14**
**1617** A1092 2r black & gray .60 .40

Swami Brahmanand (1894-1984), social reformer.

A1093

**1997, Aug. 8**
**1618** A1093 2r Sri Basaveswara .60 .40

Maratha Parachute Regiment, Bicent. A1094

**1997, Sept. 7** *Perf. 13½x13*
**1619** A1094 2r multicolored .90 .45

Hazari Prasad Dwivedi — A1095

**1997, Dec. 13** **Photo.** *Perf. 13x13½*
**1620** A1095 2r gray brown .60 .40

Firaq Gorakhpuri
A1096

**1997, Aug. 28**
**1621** A1096 2r brown .60 .40

Fossil Plants — A1097

No. 1622, Birbalsahnia divyadarshanii. No. 1623, Glossopteris. 6r, Pentoxylon. 10r, Williamsonia sewardiana.

**1997, Sept. 11**
**1622** A1097 2r multicolored .50 .35
**1623** A1097 2r multicolored .50 .35
**1624** A1097 6r multicolored 1.50 .90
**1625** A1097 10r multicolored 2.25 1.50
*Nos. 1622-1625 (4)* 4.75 3.10

Sir William Jones, 250th Birth Anniv. — A1098

**1997, Sept. 28**
**1626** A1098 4r multicolored .70 .35

Lawrence School, Sanawar, 150th Anniv. A1099

**1997, Oct. 4** ***Perf. 13½x13***
**1627** A1099 2r multicolored .90 .55

Indepex '97 A1100

**1997, June 6 Photo.** ***Perf. 13½x13***
**1628** A1100 2r Nalanda .50 .40
**1629** A1100 6r Bodhgaya .80 .50
**1630** A1100 10r Vaishali 1.25 .80
**1631** A1100 11r Kushinagar 1.60 .80
*a.* Block of 4, #1628-1631 4.50 4.50

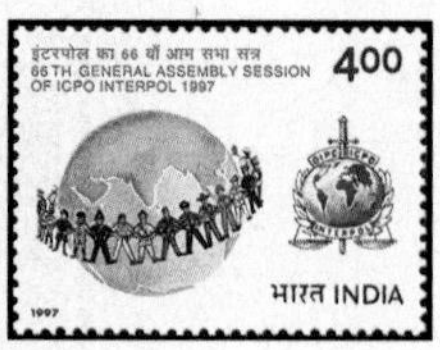

66th General Assembly Session of Interpol, 1997 A1101

**1997, Oct. 15** ***Perf. 13½***
**1632** A1101 4r multicolored 1.25 .80

V.K. Krishna Menon — A1102

**1997, Oct. 6** ***Perf. 13***
**1633** A1102 2r brown carmine .75 .75

Indepex '97 World Philatelic Exhibition A1103

Rural Indian women.

**1997, Oct. 15 Photo.** ***Perf. 13x13½***
**1634** A1103 2r Arunachal Pradesh .50 .30
**1635** A1103 6r Gujarat .95 .50
**1636** A1103 10r Ladakh 1.25 .70
**1637** A1103 11r Kerala 1.50 .95
*a.* Block of 4, #1634-1637 4.50 4.50

Scindia School, Cent. — A1104

Designs: No. 1638, Outdoor class. No. 1639, Founder, school building, aerial view.

**1997, Oct. 20** ***Perf. 14***
**1638** 5r multicolored .70 .35
**1639** 5r multicolored .70 .35
*a.* A1104 Pair, #1638-1639 1.40 1.40

Medicinal Plants A1105

2r, Ocimum sanctum. 5r, Curcuma longa. 10r, Rauvolfia serpentina. 11r, Aloe barbadensis.

**1997, Oct. 28**
**1640** A1105 2r multicolored .60 .35
**1641** A1105 5r multicolored 1.25 .60
**1642** A1105 10r multicolored 1.60 1.10
**1643** A1105 11r multicolored 1.90 1.10
*a.* Block of 4, #1640-1643 5.50 4.50

A1106

**1997, July 2 Litho.** ***Perf. 13x13½***
**1644** A1106 2r brown & sepia .60 .40

Ram Sewak Yadav (1926-74), politician, social reformer.

A1107

**1997, July 11**
**1645** A1107 2r multicolored .60 .40

Sibnath Banerjee (1897-1982), politician, union leader.

Indepex '97 A1110

Indian beaches: 2r, Gopalpur on Sea, Orissa. 6r, Kovalam Beach, Thiruvananthapuram. 10r, Anjuna Beach, Goa. 11r, Bogmalo Beach, Goa.

**1997, Aug. 11 Photo.** ***Perf. 13½x13***
**1648** A1110 2r multicolored .60 .30
**1649** A1110 6r multicolored .90 .55
**1650** A1110 10r multicolored 1.60 .80
**1651** A1110 11r multicolored 2.25 1.00
*Nos. 1648-1651 (4)* 5.35 2.65

Sant Kavi Sunderdas (1596-1689) A1111

**1997, Nov. 8 Photo.** ***Perf. 13x13½***
**1652** A1111 2r lt brn & dk brn 1.00 .50

Kotamaraju Rama Rao — A1112

**1997, Nov. 9**
**1653** A1112 2r dk brn & yel brn 1.40 .70

Children's Day A1113

**1997, Nov. 14** ***Perf. 13½x13***
**1654** A1113 2r Nehru with child .70 .40

A1114

**1997, Nov. 23 Photo.** ***Perf. 13***
**1655** A1114 4r multicolored 1.75 1.10

World Convention on Reverence for All Life.

A1115

**1997, Dec. 15 Photo.** ***Perf. 13x13½***
**1656** A1115 2r dk brn & lt brn .60 .40

Sardar Vallabhbhai Patel (1875-1950), politician.

Indepex '97 A1116

Designs: 2r, Post Office Heritage Building. 6r, Indian River Mail. 10r, Cancellations, Jal Cooper. 11r, Mail ship, SS Hindosthan.

**1997, Dec, 15 Photo.** ***Perf. 13½x13***
**1657** A1116 2r multicolored .60 .50
**1657A** A1116 6r multicolored 1.25 .55
**1657B** A1116 10r multicolored 1.60 1.10
**1657C** A1116 11r multicolored 2.25 1.25
*d.* Block of 4, #1657-1657C 5.75 4.75

Souvenir Sheet

Mother Teresa (1910-97) — A1117

**1997, Dec. 15 Litho.** ***Perf. 13x13½***
**1658** A1117 45r multicolored 6.00 6.00

Indian Armed Forces, 50th Anniv. A1118

**1997, Dec. 16 Photo.** ***Perf. 13½x13***
**1659** A1118 2r multicolored .80 .40

Dr. B. Pattabhi Sitaramayya (1880-1959), Author, Politician — A1119

**1997, Dec. 17** ***Perf. 13x13½***
**1660** A1119 2r dk brn & lt brn .85 .55

Fr. Jerome D'Souza (1897-1977) A1120

**1997, Dec. 18** ***Perf. 13½x13***
**1661** A1120 2r red brown .60 .40

Ashfaquallah Khan and Ram Prasad Bismil, Revolutionaries
A1121

**1997, Dec. 19** *Perf. 13*
**1662** A1121 2r dk brn & brn .60 .40

Cellular Jail Natl. Memorial, Port Blair
A1122

**1997, Dec. 30**
**1663** A1122 2r multicolored .60 .40

A1123

**1998, Jan. 2**
**1664** A1123 2r red brown .40 .25

Nanak Singh (1897-1971), novelist.

A1124

**1998, Jan. 9**
**1665** A1124 2r plum .40 .25

Nahar Singh, minor leader of Great Mutiny.

Rotary Intl., 1998 Council on Legislation, New Delhi
A1125

**1998, Jan. 12** *Perf. 13½X13*
**1666** A1125 8r multicolored 1.25 1.00

A1126

A1127

#1667, Maharana Pratap (1540-97), ruler, warrior. #1668, Vishnu S. Khandekar (b. 1898), writer.

**1998, Jan. 19** *Perf. 13x13½*
**1667** A1126 2r violet brown .80 .50
**1668** A1127 2r rose red & dull red .80 .50

A1128

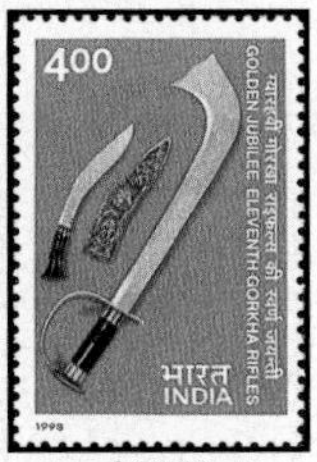


A1129

**1998, Jan. 25**
**1669** A1128 10r multicolored 2.25 1.50

Bharat Paryatan Diwas (India Tourism Day).

**1998, Jan. 2** *Perf. 13½x13*
**1670** A1129 4r multicolored 3.00 1.75

11th Gurkha Rifles, 50th anniv.

A1130

Mahatma Gandhi, 50th Anniv. of Death: 2r, Peasants' welfare. 6r, Social upliftment. 10r, Salt Satyagraha. 11r, Communal harmony.

**1998, Jan. 30** **Photo.** *Perf. 14*
**1671** A1130 2r multicolored .60 .45
**1672** A1130 6r multicolored .90 .75
**1673** A1130 10r multicolored 1.10 1.10
**1674** A1130 11r multicolored 1.75 1.25
*a.* Block of 4, #1671-1674 4.75 4.25

A1131

**1998, Mar. 8** **Photo.** *Perf. 13x13½*
**1675** A1131 6r multicolored 1.00 .60

Universal Declaration of Human Rights, 50th anniv.

Savitribai Phule (1831-97), Educator, Women's Reformer
A1132

**1998, Mar. 10** *Perf. 13½x13*
**1676** A1132 2r dk brn & lt brn .80 .50

Jagdish Chandra Jain
A1133

**1998, Jan. 28** **Photo.** *Perf. 13x13½*
**1677** A1133 2r red brown .80 .50

Syed Ahmad Khan (1817-98), Writer — A1134

**1998, Mar. 27**
**1678** A1134 2r brn & olive brn .80 .50

Sardar A. Vedaratnam
A1135

**1998, Feb. 25**
**1679** A1135 2r violet black .80 .50

Global Environment Facility First Assembly Meeting — A1136

**1998, Apr. 1** *Perf. 13*
**1680** A1136 11r multicolored 1.45 1.10

A1137

**1998, Apr. 16** **Photo.** *Perf. 14*
**1681** A1137 6r carmine 1.10 .70

Defense Services Staff College.

A1138

Design: Pres. Zakir Husain (1897-1969).

**1998, May 3** **Photo.** *Perf. 13*
**1682** A1138 2r sepia .60 .40

A1139

A1140

Jnanpith Literary Award winners, year: Shri Bishnu Dey (1909-82), 1971; Shri Tarashankar Bandopadhyay (1898-1971), 1966; Smt. Ashapurna Devi (1909-95), 1976.

**1998, June 5**
**1683** A1139 2r olive brown .60 .40

**1998, June 8** **Photo.** *Perf. 13*

Designs: 5r, Parliament Clock Tower, London. 6r, Airplane, mascot, Gateway of India, Bombay.

**1684** A1140 5r multicolored .75 .40

**Size: 56x35mm**

**1685** A1140 6r multicolored 1.00 .50
*a.* Pair, #1684-1685 1.75 1.75

Air India's 1st intl. flight, 50th anniv.

A1141

Design: Salem C. Vijiaraghavachariar (1852-1944), freedom fighter.

**1998, June 18**
**1686** A1141 2r red brown .60 .35

A1142

**1998, May 1**
**1687** A1142 2r N.G. Goray .60 .35

Sri Ramana Maharshi
A1143

**1998, Apr. 14**
**1688** A1143 2r violet black .60 .40

Konkan Railway — A1143a

**1998, May 1** **Photo.** *Perf. 13*
**1689** A1143a 8r multicolored 2.00 .95

A1144

Mohammed Abdurahiman Shahib.

**1998, May 15**
**1690** A1144 2r red brown .60 .40

A1145

**1998, May 21** **Photo.** ***Perf. 14***
**1691** A1145 2r brown & sepia .60 .40

Lokanayak Omeo Kumar Das, freedom fighter.

Revolutionaries — A1146

Design: Satyendra Chandra Bardhan, Vakkom Abdul Khader, Fouja Singh.

**1998, May 25** ***Perf. 13***
**1692** A1146 2r brn & red brn .60 .40

Natl. Savings Organization, 50th Anniv. — A1147

Design: 6r, Hand dropping coin into bank.

**1998, June 30**
**1693** A1147 5r multicolored .80 .30
**1694** A1147 6r multicolored 1.00 .50
*a.* Pair, #1693-1694 1.90 1.25

Bhagwan Gopinathji, Spiritual Leader, Birth Cent. — A1148

**1998, July 3** ***Perf. 13½***
**1695** A1148 3r brown & sepia .60 .40

Ardeshir (1868-1926) & Pirojsha (1882-1972) Godrej, Environmentalists — A1149

**1998, July 11** ***Perf. 13***
**1696** A1149 3r green .60 .40

Aruna Asaf Ali, Revolutionay A1150

**1998, July 16**
**1697** A1150 3r brown .60 .40

Vidyasagar College, 125th Anniv. A1151

**1998, July 29**
**1698** A1151 2r dark gray .60 .30

Shivpujan Sahai (1893-1963), Writer — A1152

**1998, Aug. 9** **Photo.** ***Perf. 13***
**1699** A1152 2r brown .60 .30

Homage to Martyrs A1153

Designs: 3r, Minaret, silhouettes of soldiers standing in fort, flag of India. 8r, Symbols of industrial, scientific and technological developments.

**1998, Aug. 15** ***Perf. 14***
**1700** A1153 3r multicolored .50 .30
**1701** A1153 8r multicolored 1.10 .55
*a.* Pair, #1700-1701 1.60 1.40

Gostha Behari Paul (1896-1976), Soccer Player — A1154

**1998, Aug. 20** ***Perf. 13***
**1702** A1154 3r sepia .60 .40

Youth Hostels Assoc. of India, 50th Anniv. — A1155

**1998, Aug. 23** ***Perf. 14***
**1703** A1155 5r multicolored .80 .45

Brigade of the Guards, Fourth Battalion, Bicent. A1156

**1998, Sept. 15** **Photo.** ***Perf. 13½***
**1704** A1156 6r multicolored 1.10 .55

Bhai Kanhaiyaji A1157

**1998, Sept. 18** ***Perf. 13***
**1705** A1157 2r red .60 .30

20th Intl. Congress of Radiology A1158

**1998, Sept. 18** ***Perf. 13½x13***
**1706** A1158 8r multicolored 1.40 .90

28th IBBY Congress A1159

**1998, Sept. 20** ***Perf. 13***
**1707** A1159 11r multicolored 1.40 .85

Dr. Tristao Braganza Cunha — A1160

**1998, Sept. 26**
**1708** A1160 3r dark brown .60 .40

Jananeta Hijam Irawat Singh — A1161

**1998, Sept. 30**
**1709** A1161 3r brown .60 .40

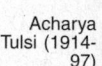

Acharya Tulsi (1914-97) A1162

**1998, Oct. 20** **Photo.** ***Perf. 13½x13***
**1710** A1162 3r brown & orange .60 .40

Indian Women in Aviation A1163

Pulse Polio Immunization A1164

**1998, Oct. 15** ***Perf. 13***
**1711** A1163 8r blue 1.40 .85

**1998, Sept. 21**
**1712** A1164 3r maroon .25 .25

2nd Battalion of the Rajput Regiment (Kalichindi), Bicent. — A1165

**1998, Nov. 30**
**1713** A1165 3r multicolored .60 .30

David Sassoon Library & Reading Room, Mumbai — A1166

**1998, Nov. 30**
**1714** A1166 3r lt blue & dk blue .60 .40

Army Postal Service Center, Kamptee, 50th Anniv. A1167

**1998, Dec. 2**
**1715** A1167 3r multicolored 1.45 .55

Connemara Public Library, Chennai A1168

**1998, Dec. 5** ***Perf. 13½x13***
**1716** A1168 3r bister & brown .80 .40

A1169

**1998, Dec. 10 Litho. *Perf. 13½***
**1717** A1169 3r multicolored 1.45 .60

Indian Pharmaceutical Cong. Assoc., 50th anniv.

A1170

Design: Baba Raghv Das (1896-1958), reformer, freedom fighter.

**1998, Dec. 12 Photo. *Perf. 13***
**1718** A1170 2r deep gray violet .60 .30

Indra Lal Roy (1898-1918), World War I Pilot — A1171

**1998, Dec. 19**
**1719** A1171 3r multicolored 1.45 .40

Sant Gadge Baba (1876-1956), Religious Philosopher — A1172

**1998, Dec. 20**
**1720** A1172 3r multicolored .60 .40

Traditional Musical Instruments A1173

Designs: 2r, Rudra veena (stringed instrument). 6r, Flute (wind insrument). 8r, Pakhawaj (percussion instrument). 10r, Sarod (stringed instrument).

**1998, Dec. 29**

| | | | | | |
|---|---|---|---|---|---|
| **1721** | A1173 | 2r multicolored | | .35 | .25 |
| **1722** | A1173 | 6r multicolored | | .85 | .55 |
| **1723** | A1173 | 8r multicolored | | 1.10 | .70 |
| **1724** | A1173 | 10r multicolored | | 1.50 | .90 |
| | | *Nos. 1721-1724 (4)* | | 3.80 | 2.40 |

Children's Day A1174

**1998, Nov. 14 Photo. *Perf. 13½***
**1725** A1174 3r multicolored .60 .40

INS Delhi A1175

**1998, Nov. 15**
**1726** A1175 3r multicolored 1.45 .60

President's Bodyguard A1176

**1998, Nov. 16**
**1727** A1176 3r multicolored 1.45 .60

Shells A1177

Designs: No. 1728, Cypraea staphylaea. No. 1729, Cassis cornuta. No. 1730, Chicoreus brunneus. 11r, Lambis lambis.

**1998, Dec. 30**

| | | | | |
|---|---|---|---|---|
| **1728** | A1177 | 3r multicolored | .65 | .80 |
| **1729** | A1177 | 3r multicolored | .90 | .80 |
| **1730** | A1177 | 3r multicolored | 1.60 | .80 |
| **1731** | A1177 | 11r multicolored | 2.25 | 1.60 |
| | | *Nos. 1728-1731 (4)* | 5.40 | 4.00 |

Indian Police Service, 50th Anniv. A1178

**1999, Jan. 13 Litho. *Perf. 13½x13¼***
**1732** A1178 3r multicolored 2.00 .55

Defense Research & Development Organization — A1179

**1999, Jan. 26 Photo. *Perf. 13***
**1733** A1179 10r multicolored 2.00 1.00

Newpapers in Assam, 150th Anniv. — A1180

**1999, Jan. 29 *Perf. 13x13½***
**1734** A1180 3r multicolored 1.00 .70

Sanskrit College, Calcutta, 175th Anniv. A1181

**1999, Feb. 25 *Perf. 13½x13***
**1735** A1181 3r brown & yellow 1.00 .45

National Defense Academy, 50th Anniv. A1182

***Perf. 13½x13¼***
**1999, Feb. 19 Litho.**
**1736** A1182 3r multicolored 1.75 .70

Hindu College, Delhi, Cent. A1183

**1999, Feb. 17 Photo. *Perf. 13½x13***
**1737** A1183 3r blue .60 .40

Biju Patnaik (1916-97), Politician A1184

**1999, Mar. 5**
**1738** A1184 3r multicolored 1.00 .50

A1185

A1186

**1999, Mar. 12 *Perf. 13***
**1739** A1185 15r multicolored 1.75 1.00

Press Trust of India, 50th anniv.

**1999, Mar. 6**
**1740** A1186 15r multicolored 1.75 1.00

Temple Complex of Khajuraho, 1000th anniv.

Dr. K.B. Hedgewar (1889-1940) A1187

**1999, Mar. 18**
**1741** A1187 3r multicolored .60 .40

Bethune Collegiate School, 150th Anniv. A1188

**1999 Photo. *Perf. 13***
**1742** A1188 3r green .70 .50

Creation of the Khalsa, 300th Anniv. A1189

**1999, Apr. 14**
**1743** A1189 3r multicolored 1.75 .55

Maritime Heritage A1190

**1999, Apr. 5 Litho. *Perf. 13½x13¼***

| | | | | |
|---|---|---|---|---|
| **1744** | A1190 | 3r Boat from 2200 B.C. | .70 | .50 |
| **1745** | A1190 | 3r Ship from 1700 | .70 | .50 |

Technology Day A1191

**1999, May 11 Litho. *Perf. 13½x13¼***
**1746** A1191 3r multicolored .70 .50

Mumbai Port Trust, 125th Anniv. A1192

**1999, June 26 Photo. *Perf. 12¾x13***
**1747** A1192 3r blue gray .70 .50

A1193

A1194

**1999, June 30 Photo. *Perf. 13x12¾***
**1748** A1193 3r multicolored .60 .40

Mizoram Accord.

**1999, July 4 Photo. *Perf. 13¼***
**1749** A1194 3r multicolored .60 .40

Gulzari Lal Nanda (b. 1899), interim Prime Minister.

Jijabai, Mother of Shivaji — A1195

**1999, July 7 Photo. *Perf. 14x13½***
**1750** A1195 3r claret .60 .40

P. S. Kumaraswamy Raja — A1196

**1999, July 8 Photo. *Perf. 13¼***
**1751** A1196 3r sky blue & brown .60 .40

Balai Chand Mukhopadhyay (1879-1979), Writer — A1197

**1999, July 19 Photo. *Perf. 13¼***
**1752** A1197 3r slate blue .60 .40

Sindh River Festival A1198

***Perf. 13½x13¼***
**1999, July 28 Photo.**
**1753** A1198 3r multicolored .60 .40

Geneva Conventions, 50th Anniv. — A1199

**1999, Aug. 12 Photo. *Perf. 13¾***
**1754** A1199 15r black & red 2.25 1.60

Freedom Fighters A1200

#1755, Swami Ramanand Teerth. #1756, Vishwambhar Dayalu Tripathi. #1757, Swami Keshawanand. #1758, Sardar Ajit Singh.

***Perf. 13½x13¼***
**1999, Aug. 15 Photo.**
**1755** A1200 3r multicolored .55 .40
**1756** A1200 3r multicolored .55 .40
**1757** A1200 3r multicolored .55 .40
**1758** A1200 3r multicolored .55 .40
*Nos. 1755-1758 (4)* 2.20 1.60

Kalki Krishnamurthy (1899-1954), Novelist — A1201

**1999, Sept. 9 Photo. *Perf. 13¾***
**1759** A1201 3r black .60 .50

Qazi Nazrul Islam (1899-1976), Poet — A1202

Rambriksh Benipuri, Writer A1203

Ramdhari Sinha "Dinkar," Poet A1204

Jhaverchand Kalidas Meghani (b. 1896), Poet — A1205

**1999, Sept. 14 Photo. *Perf. 13x13¼***
**1760** A1202 3r multicolored .60 .50
***Perf. 13¼***
**1761** A1203 3r multicolored .60 .50
***Perf. 13¼x13***
**1762** A1204 3r multicolored .60 .50
**1763** A1205 3r multicolored .60 .50
*Nos. 1760-1763 (4)* 2.40 2.00

Arati Gupta, First Asian Woman to Swim Across English Channel A1206

**1999, Sept. 29 Photo. *Perf. 13x13¼***
**1764** A1206 3r multi .60 .50

Worldwide Fund for Nature A1207

Asiatic lion: No. 1765, Male atop female. No. 1766, Two lions. No. 1767, Three lions. 15r, Two lions, diff.

**1999, Oct. 4 *Perf. 13¼x13***
**1765** A1207 3r multi 2.00 .60
**1766** A1207 3r multi 2.00 .60
**1767** A1207 3r multi 2.00 .60
**1768** A1207 15r multi 3.50 1.75
*Nos. 1765-1768 (4)* 9.50 3.55

UPU, 125th Anniv. A1208

#1769, Muria ritual object. #1770, Mask for Chhau dance. #1771, Rathva wall painting. 15r, Angami ornament.

**1999, Oct. 9 *Perf. 13¼x13, 13x13¼***
**1769** A1208 3r multi .70 .35
**1770** A1208 3r multi .70 .35
**1771** A1208 3r multi, vert. .70 .35
**1772** A1208 15r multi, vert. 2.25 1.40
*Nos. 1769-1772 (4)* 4.35 2.45

Dr. T. M. A. Pai (1898-1979) — A1209

Chhaganlal K. Parekh (1894-1968) — A1209a

A. B. Walawalkar, Draftsman for Konkar Railway — A1209b

A. D. Shroff — A1209c

**1999, Oct. 9 *Perf. 13x13¼***
**1773** A1209 3r yel & brn .60 .60
***Perf. 12¾x13¼***
**1774** A1209a 3r org brn & ind .60 .60
***Perf. 13¼***
**1775** A1209b 3r lilac & maroon .60 .60
**1776** A1209c 3r bister & olive .60 .60
*Nos. 1773-1776 (4)* 2.40 2.40

Veerapandia Kattabomman (1760-99), Freedom Fighter — A1210

**1999, Oct. 16 Photo. *Perf. 13x13¼***
**1777** A1210 3r olive green .60 .50

Musicians A1211

#1778, Ustad Allauddin Khan Saheb (1870-1972), sarod player. #1779, Musiri Subramania Iyer (1899-1975), music teacher.

**1999, Oct. 19 Photo. *Perf. 13¾***
**1778** A1211 3r multicolored .75 .60
**1779** A1211 3r multicolored .75 .60

A1212

***Perf. 13¼x13½***
**1999, Oct. 27 Photo.**
**1780** A1212 3r violet brown .70 .50

Brigadier Rajinder Singh (1899-1947).

A1213

**1999, Nov. 14 Photo. *Perf. 14***
**1781** A1213 3r multi .60 .40

Children's Day.

Sri Sathya Sai Water Supply Project A1214

***Perf. 12¾x13¼***
**1999, Nov. 23 Photo.**
**1782** A1214 3r multi .90 .50

Supreme Court, 50th Anniv. A1215

***Perf. 12¾x13¼***
**1999, Nov. 26 Photo.**
**1783** A1215 3r multi .60 .50

Dr. Punjabrao Deshmukh, Agriculture Minister A1215a

A. Vaidyanatha Iyer (d. 1955), Advocate of Untouchables — A1216

P. Kakkan, Politician A1217

Indulal Kanaiyalal Yagnik, Politician
A1218

**1999, Dec. 9** *Perf. 13¼*

| | | | | |
|---|---|---|---|---|
| **1784** | A1215a | 3r brown & grn | .35 | .25 |
| **1785** | A1216 | 3r orange brown | .35 | .25 |
| **1786** | A1217 | 3r green & brn | .35 | .25 |
| **1787** | A1218 | 3r tan & black | .35 | .25 |
| | | *Nos. 1784-1787 (4)* | 1.40 | 1.00 |

Thermal Power, Cent.
A1219

**1999, Dec. 14 Photo.** *Perf. 13¼x13*

| | | | | |
|---|---|---|---|---|
| **1788** | A1219 | 3r bister & brn | .60 | .50 |

Hindustan Times Newspaper, 75th Anniv.
A1220

**1999, Dec. 16 Photo.** *Perf. 13¼*

| | | | | |
|---|---|---|---|---|
| **1789** | A1220 | 15r multi | 2.25 | 1.60 |

Family Planning Assoc. of India, 50th Anniv. — A1221

**1999, Dec. 18** *Perf. 14x13¾*

| | | | | |
|---|---|---|---|---|
| **1790** | A1221 | 3r multi | .60 | .50 |

Birth of Jesus Christ, 2000th Anniv. — A1222

**1999, Dec. 25**

| | | | | |
|---|---|---|---|---|
| **1791** | A1222 | 3r multi | 1.00 | .80 |

Tabo Monastery
A1223

**1999, Dec. 31** *Perf. 12¾x13¼*

| | | | | |
|---|---|---|---|---|
| **1792** | A1223 | 5r shown | .90 | .90 |
| **1793** | A1223 | 10r People | 1.00 | 1.00 |
| *a.* | | Pair, #1792-1793 | 2.00 | 2.00 |

First Sunrise of the Millennium
A1224

**2000, Jan. 1** *Perf. 13¼x13*

| | | | | |
|---|---|---|---|---|
| **1794** | A1224 | 3r multi | 2.00 | 2.00 |

Agni II Missile
A1225

**2000, Jan. 1 Litho.** *Perf. 13x13¼*

| | | | | |
|---|---|---|---|---|
| **1795** | A1225 | 3r multi | .95 | .95 |

Mahatma Gandhi — A1226

**2000, Jan. 27** *Perf. 14x13¾*

| | | | | |
|---|---|---|---|---|
| **1796** | A1226 | 3r red & black | .60 | .60 |

Republic of India, 50th anniv.

Gallantry Award Winners
A1227

Designs: No. 1797, Karam Singh, regimental crest. No. 1798, Abdul Hamid, jeep-mounted artillery gun. No. 1799, Albert Ekka, grenades, knife. No. 1800, N. J. S. Sekhon, airplane. No. 1801, M. N. Mulla, ship.

**2000, Jan. 27** *Perf. 13¼x13*

| | | | | |
|---|---|---|---|---|
| **1797** | A1227 | 3r multi | .60 | .60 |
| **1798** | A1227 | 3r multi | .60 | .60 |
| **1799** | A1227 | 3r multi | .60 | .60 |
| **1800** | A1227 | 3r multi | .60 | .60 |
| **1801** | A1227 | 3r multi | .60 | .60 |
| *a.* | | Strip of 5, #1797-1801 | 2.50 | 2.50 |

Republic of India, 50th anniv.

Millepex 2000
A1228

Endangered reptiles: No. 1802, Batagur terrapin. No. 1803, Olive ridley turtle.

**2000, Jan. 29** *Perf. 13¼*

| | | | | |
|---|---|---|---|---|
| **1802** | A1228 | 3r multi | .50 | .40 |
| **1803** | A1228 | 3r multi | .50 | .40 |
| *a.* | | Pair, #1802-1803 | 2.00 | 1.75 |

Famous Men — A1229

Designs: No. 1804, Balwantrai Mehta. No. 1805, Arun Kumar Chanda. No. 1806, Dr. Harekrushna Mahatab, politician.

**2000, Feb. 17 Litho.** *Perf. 13x13¼*

| | | | | |
|---|---|---|---|---|
| **1804** | A1229 | 3r multi | .60 | .60 |
| **1805** | A1229 | 3r multi | .60 | .60 |
| **1806** | A1229 | 3r multi | .60 | .60 |
| | | *Nos. 1804-1806 (3)* | 1.80 | 1.80 |

Patna Medical College, 75th Anniv.
A1230

**2000, Feb. 26** *Perf. 13¼x13*

| | | | | |
|---|---|---|---|---|
| **1807** | A1230 | 3r multi | .60 | .60 |

Dr. Burgula Ramakrishna Rao, Politician — A1231

**2000, Mar. 13** *Perf. 13x13¾*

| | | | | |
|---|---|---|---|---|
| **1808** | A1231 | 3r brn & ocher | .60 | .60 |

Potti Sriramulu (1901-52), Advocate of Untouchables — A1232

**2000, Mar. 16** *Perf. 13¼x13*

| | | | | |
|---|---|---|---|---|
| **1809** | A1232 | 3r red | .60 | .60 |

Basawon Sinha (1909-89), Socialist Party Leader — A1233

**2000, Mar. 23** *Perf. 13x13¼*

| | | | | |
|---|---|---|---|---|
| **1810** | A1233 | 3r multi | .60 | .60 |

Indepex Asiana 2000 — A1234

**2000, Mar. 31** *Perf. 13x13¼*

| | | | | |
|---|---|---|---|---|
| **1811** | A1234 | 3r Siroi lily | .55 | .55 |
| **1812** | A1234 | 3r Wild guava | .55 | .55 |
| **1813** | A1234 | 3r Sangai deer | .55 | .55 |
| **1814** | A1234 | 15r Slow loris | 2.00 | 2.00 |
| *a.* | | Souvenir sheet, #1811-1814 | 4.50 | 4.50 |
| | | *Nos. 1811-1814 (4)* | 3.65 | 3.65 |

See Nos. 1831-1834.

Arya Samaj, 125th Anniv. — A1235

*Perf. 13x13¼*

**2000, Apr. 5 Litho. Unwmk.**

| | | | | |
|---|---|---|---|---|
| **1815** | A1235 | 3r multi | 1.45 | 1.45 |

Indigenous Cattle Breeds
A1236

*Perf. 13¼x13*

**2000, Apr. 25 Litho. Unwmk.**

| | | | | |
|---|---|---|---|---|
| **1816** | A1236 | 3r Gir | .60 | .50 |
| **1817** | A1236 | 3r Kangayam | .60 | .50 |
| **1818** | A1236 | 3r Kankrej | .60 | .50 |
| **1819** | A1236 | 15r Hallikar | 2.25 | 1.60 |
| | | *Nos. 1816-1819 (4)* | 4.05 | 3.10 |

Blackbuck
A1237

Patel
A1237a

Smooth Indian Otter — A1238

Leopard Cat — A1239

Tiger
A1240

Amaltaas — A1241

50p, Nilgiri tahr. 1r, Saras crane. 2r, Sardar Vallabhbhai Patel (1875-1950), Politician. 15r, Butterfly. 50r, Paradise flycatcher.

*Perf. 12¾x13, 13x12¾*

**2000 Photo. Wmk. 324**

| | | | | |
|---|---|---|---|---|
| **1820** | A1237 | 25p olive brn | .30 | .30 |
| **1821** | A1237 | 50p yel brn | .30 | .30 |
| **1822** | A1237 | 1r blue | .30 | .30 |
| **1823** | A1237a | 2r black | .30 | .30 |
| **1824** | A1238 | 3r gray vio | .30 | .30 |
| **1825** | A1239 | 5r multi | .30 | .30 |
| **1826** | A1240 | 10r multi | .70 | .70 |
| **1827** | A1240 | 15r multi | 1.00 | 1.00 |
| **1828** | A1241 | 20r multi | 1.50 | 1.50 |
| **1829** | A1241 | 50r multi | 4.00 | 4.00 |
| | | *Nos. 1820-1829 (10)* | 9.00 | 9.00 |

Issued: 25p, 50p, 1r, 3r, 7/20; 2r, 10/31; 5r, 10r, 4/30; 15r, 20r, 11/20; 50r, 10/30.

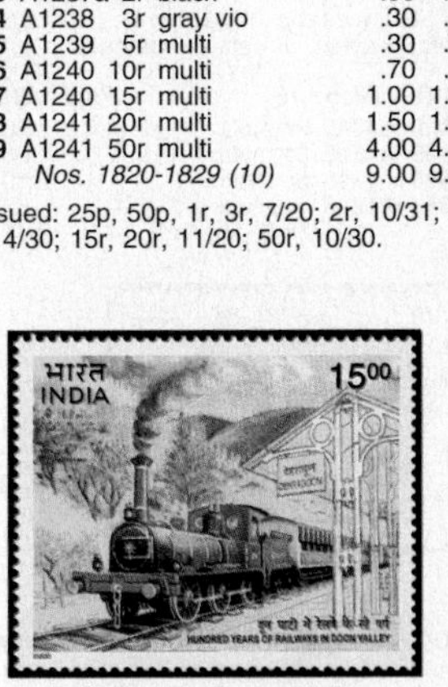

Railways in Doon Valley, Cent. — A1244

*Perf. 13¼*

**2000, May 6 Litho. Unwmk.**

| | | | | |
|---|---|---|---|---|
| **1830** | A1244 | 15r multi | 3.00 | 3.00 |

### Indepex Asiana Type of 2000

Birds: #1831, Rosy pastor. #1832, Garganey teal. #1833, Forest wagtail. #1834, White stork.

**2000, May 24** *Perf. 13¼x13*

**1831** A1234 3r multi, horiz. 1.10 1.10
**1832** A1234 3r multi, horiz. 1.10 1.10
**1833** A1234 3r multi, horiz. 1.10 1.10
**1834** A1234 3r multi, horiz. 1.10 1.10
*a.* Block of strip of 4, #1831-1834 4.50 4.50
*b.* Souvenir sheet, #1831-1834 6.00 6.00

Dr. Nandamuri Taraka Rama Rao (1923-96), Actor, Politician A1245

**2000, May 28**

**1835** A1245 3r multi .60 .60

Swami Sahajanand Saraswati (1889-1950), Freedom Fighter — A1246

**2000, June 26** *Perf. 13x13¼*

**1836** A1246 3r multi .80 .80

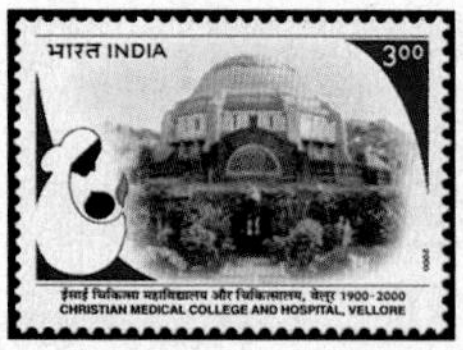

Christian Medical College and Hospital, Vellore, Cent. A1247

**2000, Aug. 12** *Perf. 13¼x13*

**1837** A1247 3r multi .80 .80

Social and Political Leaders — A1248

Designs: No. 1838, Radha Gobinda Baruah (1900-75), newspaper publisher. No. 1839, Vijaya Lakshmi Pandit (1900-90), President of UN General Assembly. No. 1840, Jaglal Choudhary (1895-1975), politician. No. 1841, R. Srinivasan (1859-1945), advocate of untouchables, newspaper founder.

**2000, Aug. 15** *Perf. 13x13¼*

**1838** A1248 3r multi .60 .60
**1839** A1248 3r multi .60 .60
**1840** A1248 3r multi .60 .60
**1841** A1248 3r multi .60 .60
*Nos. 1838-1841 (4)* 2.40 2.40

Kodaikanal Intl. School, Cent. A1249

*Perf. 13¼x13*

**2000, Aug. 26** **Litho.** **Unwmk.**

**1842** A1249 15r multi 2.25 2.25

2000 Summer Olympics, Sydney A1250

Designs: 3r, Discus. 6r, Tennis. 10r, Field hockey. 15r, Weight lifting.

**2000, Sept. 17** *Perf. 13x13¼*

**1843-1846** A1250 Set of 4 5.50 5.50

India in Space A1251

#1847, Oceansat 1. #1848, Insat 3B in orbit. No. 1849, vert.: a, Astronaut on planet, spacecraft. b, Earth, spacecraft.

*Perf. 13¼x13, 13x13¼*

**2000, Sept. 29**

**1847-1848** A1251 3r Set of 2 1.50 1.50
**1849** Pair 1.50 1.50
*a.-b.* A1251 3r Any single 1.00 1.00

Madhubani-Mithila Painting — A1252

#1850, 3 figures. #1851, 2 figures and bird. #1852, 2 figures and cow, vert.

No. 1853, vert.: a, Red fish, palanquin. b, Yellow fish, elephant.

**2000, Oct. 15** *Perf. 13¼*

**1850-1852** A1252 3r Set of 3 1.25 1.25
**1853** Pair 2.10 2.10
*a.* A1252 5r multi .55 .55
*b.* A1252 10r multi 1.40 1.40

Raj Kumar Shukla (b. 1875), Farmer — A1253

**2000, Oct. 16** **Litho.** *Perf. 13x13¼*

**1854** A1253 3r multi *16.00 16.00*

Pres. Shanker Dayal Sharma (1918-99) A1254

**2000, Oct. 29** **Litho.**

**1855** A1254 3r multicolored .80 .80

Children's Day — A1255

**2000, Nov. 14**

**1856** A1255 3r multicolored .80 .80

Maharaja Bijli Pasi A1256

**2000, Nov. 16** *Perf. 13¼x13*

**1857** A1256 3r multicolored .90 .90

Gems and Jewelry — A1257

#1858, 3r, Ancient India. #1859, 3r, Sarpech. #1860, 3r, Taxila. #1861, 3r, Navratna. #1862, 3r, Temple. #1863, 3r, Bridal.

**2000, Dec. 7** *Perf. 13¼*

**1858-1863** A1257 Set of 6 6.50 6.50
*a.* Block of 6, #1858-1863 7.50 7.50
*b.* Souvenir sheet, #1858, 1860-1861, 1863 8.00 8.00

Issued: No. 1863b, 12/11. No. 1863b sold fo 15r.

Warship of Adm. Mohammed Kunjali Marakkar — A1258

**2000, Dec. 17** *Perf. 13¼x13*

**1864** A1258 3r multi 1.45 1.45

Ustad Hafiz Ali Khan (1888-1972), Musician — A1259

**2000, Dec. 28**

**1865** A1259 3r multi 1.00 1.00

Famous Men A1260

#1866, Gen. Zorawar Singh (1786-1841). #1867, Rajarshi Bhagyachandra (1740-98), King of Manipur, vert. #1868, Samrat Prithviraj Chauhan (1162-92), ruler of Delhi, vert. #1869, Raja Bhamashah (c. 1542-98), military leader, vert.

**2000, Dec. 31** *Perf. 13¼x13, 13x13¼*

**1866-1869** A1260 3r Set of 4 2.40 2.40

St. Aloysius College Chapel Paintings, Cent. A1261

*Perf. 13¼*

**2001, Jan. 12** **Litho.** **Unwmk.**

**1870** A1261 15r multi 2.40 2.40

Subhas Chandra Bose A1262

Dr. B. R. Ambedkar A1263

*Perf. 12¾x13*

**2001** **Photo.** **Wmk. 324**

**1871** A1262 1r brown .25 .25
**1872** A1263 3r blue green .25 .25

Issued: 1r, 1/23; 3r, 4/14.

Famous Men — A1264

Designs: No. 1873, 3r, Sane Guruji (1899-1950), social reformer. No. 1874, 3r, N. G. Ranga (1900-95), politician. No. 1875, 3r, E. M. S. Namboodiripad (1909-98), Marxist leader. No. 1876, 3r, Giani Gurmukh Singh Musafir (1899-1976), politician.

*Perf. 13x13¼*

**2001, Jan.** **Litho.** **Unwmk.**

**1873-1876** A1264 Set of 4 2.40 2.40

Issued: No. 1873, 1/25; others, 1/27.

Famous Men — A1265

Designs: No. 1877, 3r, Sheel Bhadra Yajee (1906-96), freedom figher. No. 1878, 3r, Jubba Sahni (1906-44), revolt leader. No. 1879, 3r, Yogendra (1896-1966) and Baikunth (1907-34) Shukla, freedom fighters.

**2001, Jan.**

**1877-1879** A1265 Set of 3 1.75 1.75

Issued: No. 1877, 1/28; others, 1/29.

Western Railways Building, Mumbai, Cent. (in 1999) A1266

**2001, Feb. 6** ***Perf. 13¼x13***
**1880** A1266 15r multi 3.75 3.75

Dated 1999.

2001 Census — A1267

**2001, Feb. 10** ***Perf. 13x13¼***
**1881** A1267 3r multi .95 .95

President's International Fleet Review — A1268

Designs: No. 1882, 3r, Pal. No. 1883, 3r, Galbat. No. 1884, 3r, Tarangini. 15r, Emblem.

**2001, Feb. 18** ***Perf. 13¼x13***
**1882-1885** A1268 Set of 4 3.00 3.00

Geological Survey of India, 150th Anniv. A1269

**2001, Mar. 4**
**1886** A1269 3r multi .95 .95

4th Battalion of Maratha Light Infantry, Bicent. — A1270

**2001, Mar. 6** ***Perf. 13x13¼***
**1887** A1270 3r multi 1.75 1.75

Bhagwan Mahavira, 2600th Anniv. of Birth — A1271

**2001, Apr. 6**
**1888** A1271 3r multi 1.25 1.25

First Manned Space Flight, 40th Anniv. A1272

**2001, Apr. 12** ***Perf. 13¼x13***
**1889** A1272 15r multi 3.25 3.25

Frederic Chopin (1810-49), Composer A1273

**2001, May 4**
**1890** A1273 15r multi 3.25 3.25

Suraj Narain Singh (1908-73), Politician A1274

**2001, May 31** ***Perf. 13x13¼***
**1891** A1274 3r multi .80 .80

B. P. Mandal (1918-82), Politician — A1275

**2001, June 1**
**1892** A1275 3r multi .80 .80

Samanta Chandra Sekhar (1835-1904), Astronomer A1276

**2001, June 11**
**1893** A1276 3r multi .80 .80

Sant Ravidas, 15th Cent Religious Leader — A1277

**2001, June 24**
**1894** A1277 3r multi .80 .80

Famous Men — A1278

Designs: No. 1895, 4r, Krishna Nath Sarmah (1887-1947), social reformer. No. 1896, 4r, C. Sankaran Nair (1857-1934), President of Indian National Congress. No. 1897, 4r, Syama Prasad Mookerjee (1901-53), politician. No. 1898, 4r, U Kiang Nongbah (d. 1862), soldier.

**2001, July 6 Litho.** ***Perf. 13x13¼***
**1895-1898** A1278 Set of 4 2.40 2.40

Chandragupta Maurya, Emperor, 3rd Cent. B.C. — A1279

**2001, July 21 Litho.** ***Perf. 13¼***
**1899** A1279 4r multi .80 .80

Jhalkari Bai — A1280

**2001, July 22 Litho.** ***Perf. 13x13¼***
**1900** A1280 4r multi .80 .80

Corals A1281

Designs: No. 1901, 4r, Acropora digitifera. No. 1902, 4r, Fungia horrida. 15r, Montipora acquituberculata. 45r, Acropora formosa.

**2001, Aug. 2** ***Perf. 13¼***
**1901-1904** A1281 Set of 4 5.50 5.50

Dwarka Prasad Mishra (1901-88), Politician — A1282

**2001, Aug. 5** ***Perf. 13x13¼***
**1905** A1282 4r multi .80 .80

Chaudhary Brahm Parkash (1918-93), Government Minister — A1283

**2001, Aug. 11**
**1906** A1283 4r multi .80 .80

Ballia Revolution of August 1942 — A1284

**2001, Aug. 19**
**1907** A1284 4r multi .80 .80

Jagdev Prasad (1922-74), Socialist Politician — A1285

**2001, Sept. 5**
**1908** A1285 4r multi .80 .80

Rani Avantibai (d. 1858), Queen of Ramgarh — A1286

**2001, Sept. 19**
**1909** A1286 4r multi .80 .80

Painted Stork — A1287

***Perf. 12¾x13***
**2001, Sept. 20 Photo. Wmk. 324**
**1910** A1287 4r bister brown 1.45 1.45

Rao Tula Ram (1825-63), Chieftain — A1288

***Perf. 13x13¼***
**2001, Sept. 23 Litho. Unwmk.**
**1911** A1288 4r multi .80 .80

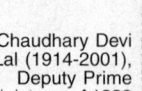

Chaudhary Devi Lal (1914-2001), Deputy Prime Minister — A1289

**2001, Sept. 25**
**1912** A1289 4r multi .80 .80

Satis Chandra Samanta (1900-83), Politician — A1290

**2001, Sept. 29**
**1913** A1290 4r multi .80 .80

Sivaji Ganesan (1928-2001), Actor — A1291

**2001, Oct. 1**
**1914** A1291 4r multi .80 .80

Mahatma Gandhi, Man of the Millennium — A1292

No. 1915: a, Gandhi and followers, birds. b, Gandhi.

Type A Syncopation (1st stamp #1915): On the two longer sides, an oval hole equal in width to 3 holes is located in the center, with an equal number of normal round holes to either side.

***Perf. 13x13¼ Syncopated Type A***

**2001, Oct. 2**
**1915** A1292 4r Horiz. pair, #a-b 2.50 2.50

Literary and Performing Arts Personalities A1293

Designs: No. 1916, 4r, Lachhu Maharaj (1901-78), choreographer. No. 1917, 4r, Master Mitrasen (1895-1946), playwright, theater founder. No. 1918, 4r, Bharathidasan (1891-1964), Tamil poet.

**2001, Oct. 9** ***Perf. 13¼x13***
**1916-1918** A1293 Set of 3 2.00 2.00

Jayaprakash Narayan (1902-79), Socialist Politician A1294

**2001, Oct. 11**
**1919** A1294 4r multi .95 .95

Panchatantra Fables — A1295

No. 1920 — The Monkey and the Crocodile, 4r: a, Monkey in tree. b, Monkey on crocodile's back.

No. 1921 — The Lion and the Rabbit, 4r: a, Lion and rabbit. b, Lion and rabbit on bridge.

No. 1922 — The Crows and the Snake, 4r: a, Crows with necklace. b, Villagers pursuing snake.

No. 1923 — The Tortoise and the Geese, 4r: a, Tortoise in pond. b, Tortoise flying with geese.

Sizes: Nos. 1920a-1923a, 58x39mm; Nos. 1920b-1923b, 29x39mm.

**2001, Oct. 17** ***Perf. 13x13¼***
**Horiz. Pairs, #a-b**
**1920-1923** A1295 Set of 4 6.00 6.00

Global Iodine Deficiency Disorders Day — A1296

**2001, Oct. 21**
**1924** A1296 4r multi 1.25 1.25

Thangal Kunju Musaliar (1897-1966), Industrialist A1297

**2001, Oct. 26**
**1925** A1297 4r multi .90 .90

Children's Day — A1298

**2001, Nov. 14 Litho.** ***Perf. 13x13¼***
**1926** A1298 4r multi .80 .80

Dr. V. Shantaram (1901-90), Movie Producer A1299

***Perf. 13¼x13 Syncopated***

**2001, Nov. 17**
**1927** A1299 4r multi .80 .80

Sobha Singh (1901-86), Artist — A1300

**2001, Nov. 29 Litho.** ***Perf. 13x13¼***
**1928** A1300 4r multi 1.25 1.25

Sun Temple, Konark — A1301

No. 1929: a, 4r, Carved wheel. b, 15r, Sun Temple.

***Perf. 13¼x13 Syncopated***

**2001, Dec. 1**
**1929** A1301 Horiz. pair, #a-b 3.50 3.50

Intl. Volunteers Year A1302

**2001, Dec. 5 Litho.** ***Perf. 13¼x13***
**1930** A1302 4r multi .80 .80

Raj Kapoor (1924-88), Film Actor, Director and Producer A1303

***Perf. 13¼x13 Syncopated***

**2001, Dec. 14** **Litho.**
**1931** A1303 4r multi 1.25 1.25

Greetings — A1304

Flowers and: 3r, Fireworks. 4r, Butterflies.

***Perf. 13x13¼ Syncopated***

**2001, Dec. 18** **Litho.**
**1932-1933** A1304 Set of 2 2.00 2.00

Digboi Refinery, Cent. A1305

**2001, Dec. 18** ***Perf. 13¼x13***
**1934** A1305 4r multi 1.25 1.25

Vijaye Raje Scindia (1919-2001), Politician — A1306

***Perf. 13x13¼ Syncopated***

**2001, Dec. 20**
**1935** A1306 4r multi .80 .80

Temples A1307

Designs: No. 1936, 4r, Kedarnath. No. 1937, 4r, Tryambakeshwar. No. 1938, 4r, Aundha Nagnath. 15r, Rameswaram.

**2001, Dec. 22** ***Perf. 13¼x13***
**1936-1939** A1307 Set of 4 3.75 3.75

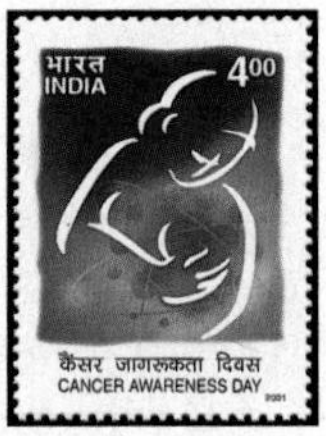


Cancer Awareness Day — A1308

**2001, Nov. 7** ***Perf. 13x13¼***
**1940** A1308 4r multi .80 .80

Maharaja Ranjit Singh (1780-1839), Founder of Sikh Kingdom of the Punjab — A1309

**2001, Nov. 9**
**1941** A1309 4r multi 1.25 1.25

Directorate General of Mine Safety, Cent. — A1310

***Perf. 13x13¼ Syncopated***

**2002, Jan. 7** **Litho.**
**1942** A1310 4r multi 1.00 1.00

May 2001 Ascent of Mt. Everest by Indian Army Mountaineers A1311

**2002, Jan. 15** ***Perf. 13x13¼***
**1943** A1311 4r multi 1.50 1.50

Bauddha Mahotsav Festival A1312

Designs: No. 1944, 4r, Dhamek Stupa, Sarnath. No. 1945, 4r, Gridhakuta Hills, Rajgir. 8r, Mahaparinirvana Temple, Kushinagar. 15r, Mahabodhi Temple, Bodhgaya.

***Perf. 13¼x13 Syncopated***

**2002, Jan. 21**
**1944-1947** A1312 Set of 4 4.50 4.50

Book Year
A1313

**2002, Jan. 28** ***Perf. 13¼x13***
**1948** A1313 4r multi 1.00 1.00

Swami Ramanand
A1314

**2002, Feb. 4** ***Perf. 13x13¼***
**1949** A1314 4r multi 1.00 1.00

Indian Munitions Factories, 50th Anniv.
A1315

***Perf. 13¼ Syncopated***
**2002, Mar. 18** **Litho.**
**1950** A1315 4r multi 1.00 1.00

Sido and Kanhu Murmu, 1855-57 Revolt Leaders
A1316

**2002, Apr. 6** ***Perf. 13¼***
**1951** A1316 4r multi 1.00 1.00

Indian Railways, 150th Anniv. — A1317

**2002, Apr. 16** ***Perf. 13¼x13***
**1952** A1317 15r multi 4.25 4.25
*a.* Souvenir sheet of 1 4.25 4.25

India — Japan Diplomatic Relations, 50th Anniv. — A1318

No. 1953: a, Kathakali actor, India. b, Kabuki actor, Japan.

**2002, Apr. 26** **Litho.** ***Perf. 13x13¼***
**1953** A1318 15r Horiz. pair, #a-b 6.00 6.00
*c.* Souvenir sheet, #1953a-1953b 5.00 5.00

Parliament, 50th Anniv.
A1319

**Litho. & Embossed**
**2002, May 13** ***Perf. 13¼***
**1954** A1319 4r gold 1.00 1.00

Prabodhankar Thackeray (1885-1973), Writer — A1320

***Perf. 13x13¼ Syncopated***
**2002, May 19** **Litho.**
**1955** A1320 4r black 1.00 1.00

Cotton College, Guwahati
A1321

**2002, May 26** **Photo.** ***Perf. 13¼x13***
**1956** A1321 4r grn & claret .80 .80

P. L. Deshpande (1919-2000), Actor — A1322

**2002, June 16** **Litho.** ***Perf. 13¼***
**1957** A1322 4r multi .80 .80

Brajlal Biyani (1896-1968), Politician and Writer — A1323

***Perf. 13x13¼ Syncopated***
**2002, June 22**
**1958** A1323 4r multi .80 .80

Writers — A1324

Designs: No. 1959, 5r, Babu Gulabrai (1888-1963). No. 1960, 5r, Pandit Suryanarayan Vyas (1902-76).

**2002, June 22**
**1959-1960** A1324 Set of 2 1.60 1.60

Sree Thakur Satyananda (1902-69), Writer — A1325

**2002, July 23** **Litho.** ***Perf. 13x13¼***
**1961** A1325 5r multi .80 .80

Anna Bhau Sathe (1920-69), Writer — A1326

***Perf. 13x13¼ Syncopated***
**2002, Aug. 1** **Litho.**
**1962** A1326 4r gray & black .80 .80

Anand Rishiji Maharaj (1900-92), Humanitarian
A1327

**2002, Aug. 9** ***Perf. 13¼***
**1963** A1327 4r multi .80 .80

Vithalrao Vikhe Patil (1901-80), Initiator of Cooperatives
A1328

***Perf. 13x13¼ Syncopated***
**2002, Aug. 10**
**1964** A1328 4r multi .80 .80

Sant Tukaram (1608-50), Poet — A1329

**2002, Aug. 10**
**1965** A1329 4r multi 1.00 1.00

Bhaurao Krishnaroao Gaikwad (1902-71), Politician — A1330

**2002, Aug. 26**
**1966** A1330 4r multi .80 .80

Social Reformers
A1331

Designs: No. 1967, 5r, Ayyan Kali (1863-1941), advocate of rights for untouchables. No. 1968, 5r, Chandraprabha Saikiani (1901-72), women's rights advocate. No. 1969, 5r, Gora (1902-75), advocate of atheism.

***Perf. 13¼x13 Syncopated***
**2002, Sept. 12**
**1967-1969** A1331 Set of 3 2.50 2.50

Ananda Nilayam Vimanam
A1332

**2002, Oct. 11** ***Perf. 13¼x13***
**1970** A1332 15r multi 3.25 3.25

Kanika Bandopadhyay (1924-2000), Singer — A1333

**2002, Oct. 12** **Photo.** ***Perf. 13x13¼***
**1971** A1333 5r multi 1.00 1.00

Arya Vaidya Sala Health Organization, Cent. — A1334

***Perf. 13¼x13 Syncopated***
**2002, Oct. 12** **Litho.**
**1972** A1334 5r multi 1.00 1.00

Bhagwan Baba (1896-1965), Religious Leader — A1335

***Perf. 13x13¼ Syncopated***
**2002, Oct. 15**
**1973** A1335 5r multi .90 .90

Bihar Chamber of Commerce, 75th Anniv. (in 2001) — A1336

**2002, Oct. 28**
**1974** A1336 4r multi 1.10 1.10

UN Climate Change Convention
A1337

Mangroves: No. 1975, 5r, Rhizophora mucronata. No. 1976, 5r, Nypa fruticans. No. 1977, 5r, Bruguiera gymnorrhiza. 15r, Sonneratia alba.

***Perf. 13¼x13 Syncopated***

**2002, Oct. 30**

**1975-1978** A1337 Set of 4 4.00 4.00
*1978a* Souvenir sheet, #1975-1978 5.00 5.00

Rose — A1338

***Perf. 12¾x13***

**2002, Aug. 16 Photo. Wmk. 324**

**1979** A1338 2r multi .25 .25

Swami Pranavananda (1896-1941), Religious Leader — A1339

***Perf. 12¾x13¼***

**2002, Nov. 3 Litho. Unwmk.**

**1980** A1339 5r multi 1.50 1.50

Nagpur, 300th Anniv. — A1340

**2002, Nov. 11** ***Perf. 13x13¼***

**1981** A1340 5r multi 1.40 1.40

Children's Day A1341

**2002, Nov. 14** ***Perf. 12¾x13¼***

**1982** A1341 5r multi 1.40 1.40

Crafts — A1342

No. 1983: a, Cane and bamboo containers. b, Thewa. c, Patan's Patola. d, Dhokra.

**2002, Nov. 15** ***Perf. 13¼***

**1983** A1342 5r Block of 4, #a-d 3.00 3.00
***e.*** Souvenir sheet of 1 #1983 5.25 5.25

Santidev Ghose (1910-99), Dancer and Musician A1343

**2002, Dec. 1**

**1984** A1343 5r multi 1.40 1.40

Formation of Tamralipta Jatiya Sarkar (National Government of Tamluk), 60th Anniv. — A1344

No. 1985: a, Ajoy Kumar Mukherjee (1901-86). b, Matangini Hazra (d. 1942).

**2002, Dec. 17** ***Perf. 13¼x13***

**1985** A1344 5r Horiz. pair, #a-b 2.25 2.25

Anglo-Bengali Inter College, Allahabad — A1345

***Perf. 13¼x13 Syncopated***

**2002, Dec. 23**

**1986** A1345 5r multi .80 .80

Gurukula Kangri Vishwavidyalaya, Hardwar — A1346

***Perf. 13x13¼ Syncopated***

**2002, Dec. 24**

**1987** A1346 5r multi 1.00 1.00

Dhirubhai H. Ambani (1932-2002), Industrialist A1347

**2002, Dec. 28** ***Perf. 13¼***

**1988** A1347 5r multi 1.25 1.25

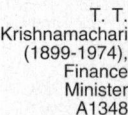

T. T. Krishnamachari (1899-1974), Finance Minister A1348

**2002, Dec. 31**

**1989** A1348 5r multi 1.25 1.25

Forts in Andhra Pradesh — A1349

Designs: No. 1990, 5r, Goloconda Fort. No. 1991, 5r, Palace, Chandragiri Fort.

**2002, Dec. 31** ***Perf. 13¼x13***

**1990-1991** A1349 Set of 2 1.60 1.60

Aircraft A1350

Designs: No. 1992, 5r, HT-2 airplane. No. 1993, 5r, Marut airplane. No. 1994, 5r, LCA airplane. 15r, Dhruv helicopter.

**2003, Feb. 5** ***Perf. 13¼***

**1992-1995** A1350 Set of 4 5.00 5.00
*1995a* Souvenir sheet, #1992-1995 5.25 5.25

Ghantasala (1922-74), Singer — A1351

**2003, Feb. 11**

**1996** A1351 5r multi .80 .80

S. L. Kirloskar (1903-94), Industrialist A1352

**2003, Feb. 26**

**1997** A1352 5r multi .80 .80

Kusumagraj (V. V. Shirwadkar) (1912-99), Poet A1353

**2003, Mar. 14**

**1998** A1353 5r multi .80 .80

Sant Eknath (1533-99) — A1354

**2003, Mar. 23**

**1999** A1354 5r multi .80 .80

Frank Anthony (b. 1908), Philantropist A1355

**2003, Mar. 28** ***Perf. 13x13¼***

**2000** A1355 5r multi .80 .80

Kakaji Maharaj (1918-86), Yogi — A1356

**2003, Mar. 30** ***Perf. 13¼***

**2001** A1356 5r multi .80 .80

Medicinal Plants — A1357

No. 2002: a, Commiphora wightii. b, Bacopa monnieri. c, Withania somnifera. d, Emblica officinalis.

**2003, Apr. 7 Litho.** ***Perf. 13x13¼***

**2002** A1357 5r Block of 4, #a-d 3.50 3.50
***e.*** Souvenir sheet, #2002a-2002d 4.50 4.50

Durga Das (1900-74), Journalist — A1358

**2003, May 2 Photo.** ***Perf. 13x13¼***

**2003** A1358 5r multi .80 .80

Singers — A1359

Designs: No. 2004, 5r, Kishore Kumar (1929-87). No. 2005, 5r, Mukesh (1923-76). No. 2006, 5r, Mohammed Rafi (1924-80). No. 2007, 5r, Hemant Kumar (1920-89).

***Perf. 13x13¼ Syncopated***

**2003, May 15 Litho.**

**2004-2007** A1359 Set of 4 3.25 3.25
*2007a* Souvenir sheet, #2004-2007 4.50 4.50

Ascent of Mt. Everest, 50th Anniv. — A1360

Muktabai (1279-99), Poet Saint — A1361

**2003, May 29** ***Perf. 13x13¼***

**2008** A1360 15r multi 2.50 2.50
***a.*** Souvenir sheet of 1 4.50 4.50

**2003, May 30** ***Perf. 13¼x12½***

**2009** A1361 5r multi .80 .80

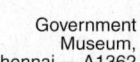

Government Museum, Chennai — A1362

Designs: No. 2010, 5r, Sculpted medallion, Amravati, c. 150. No. 2011, 5r, Natesa, 12th cent. bronze sculpture. 15r, Museum Theater (58x28mm).

**2003, June 19** ***Perf. 13x13¼***
**2010-2012** A1362 Set of 3 3.25 3.25
*2012a* Souvenir sheet, #2010-2012 *4.75 4.75*

V. K. Rajwade (1863-1926), Historian — A1363

**2003, June 23** **Photo.**
**2013** A1363 5r multi 1.25 1.25

Bade Ghulam Ali Khan (1902-68), Singer — A1364

**2003, June 30** **Litho.**
**2014** A1364 5r multi 1.25 1.25

Temples — A1365

Designs: No.2015, Vishal Badri Temple, Badrinath. No.2016, Mallikarjunaswamy Temple, Srisailam. No.2017, Tripureswari Temple, Udaipur. No.2018, Jagannath Temple, Puri.

**2003, Sept. 15** **Photo.** ***Perf. 13¼x13***
**2015** A1365 5r multicolored .85 .85
**2016** A1365 5r multicolored .85 .85
**2017** A1365 5r multicolored .85 .85
**2018** A1365 5r multicolored .85 .85
***a.*** Horiz. strip of 4, #2015-2018 3.50 3.50

Janardan Swami — A1366

**2003, Sept. 24** **Photo.** ***Perf. 13x13¼***
**2019** A1366 5r brown .80 .80

Intl. Autism Conference, Delhi A1367

**2003, Sept. 30** **Litho.** ***Perf. 13¼x13***
**2020** A1367 5r multi 1.25 1.25

Waterfalls A1368

Designs: No. 2021, 5r, Kempty Falls, No. 2022, 5r, Athirapalli Falls. No. 2023, 5r, Kakolat Falls. 15r, Jog Falls.

**2003, Oct. 3** **Litho.** ***Perf. 13x13¼***
**2021-2024** A1368 Set of 4 4.50 4.50
*2024a* Souvenir sheet, #2021-2024 6.00 6.00

Jnanpith Award Winners for Literature A1369

No. 2025: a, G. Sankara Kurup (1901-78), poet. b, S. K. Pottekkatt (1913-82), novelist. c, Thakazhi Sivasankara Pillai (1912-99), novelist.

**2003, Oct. 9** **Photo.** ***Perf. 13¼x13***
**2025** Horiz. strip of 3 7.50 7.50
***a.-c.*** A1369 5r Any single 1.00 1.00

Kota Shivarama Karanth (1902-97), Writer and Educator A1370

**2003, Oct. 10** ***Perf. 13x13¼***
**2026** A1370 5r multi .80 .80

Narendra Mohan (1934-2002), Journalist A1371

**2003, Oct. 14** **Litho.** ***Perf. 13¼***
**2027** A1371 5r brown .80 .80

Govindrao Pansare (1913-46), Martyr A1372

**2003, Oct. 21** **Photo.** ***Perf. 13¾x14***
**2028** A1372 5r multi .80 .80

Greetings — A1373

No. 2029: a, Birds. b, Fish and starfish. c, Squirrels. d, Butterflies and flowers.

**2003, Oct. 30** **Litho.** ***Perf. 13¼x13***
**2029** Horiz. strip of 4 4.50 4.50
***a.-b.*** A1373 4r Either single .95 .95
***c.-d.*** A1373 5r Either single 1.25 1.25

First Telegraph Line in India, 150th Anniv. A1374

**2003, Nov. 1** ***Perf. 13¼***
**2030** A1374 5r multi 1.45 1.45

Bengal Sappers, Bicent. A1375

**2003, Nov. 7** **Photo.** ***Perf. 13¼x13***
**2031** A1375 5r multi 1.45 1.45

Kalka-Shimla Railway, Cent. — A1376

**2003, Nov. 9** **Litho.**
**2032** A1376 5r multi 1.50 1.50

Snakes A1377

Designs: No. 2033, 5r, Python. No. 2034, 5r, Bamboo pit viper. No. 2035, 5r, King cobra. No. 2036, 5r, Gliding snake.

**2003, Nov. 12**
**2033-2036** A1377 Set of 4 3.50 3.50
*2036a* Souvenir sheet, #2033-2036 6.00 6.00

Children's Day A1378

**2003, Nov. 14**
**2037** A1378 5r multi 1.00 1.00

2nd Guards Batttalion (1st Grenadiers Battalion), 225th Anniv. — A1379

**2003, Nov. 22** **Photo.** ***Perf. 13***
**2038** A1379 5r multi 1.45 1.45

Harivansh Rai Bachchan (1907-2003), Poet — A1380

**2003, Nov. 27** **Litho.** ***Perf. 13x13¼***
**2039** A1380 5r sepia & blk .80 .80

French and Indian Artisan's Work — A1381

No. 2040: a, Illumination depicting rooster, France, 15th cent. b, Jewelry design, India, 19th cent.

**2003, Nov. 29**
**2040** A1381 22r Horiz. pair, #a-b 5.75 5.75
***c.*** Souvenir sheet, #2040 10.00 10.00

See France Nos. 2986-2987.

Yashpal (1903-76), Writer A1382

**2003, Dec. 3** **Photo.** ***Perf. 13¼***
**2041** A1382 5r multi .80 .80

India — South Korea Diplomatic Relations, 30th Anniv. — A1383

No. 2042: a, Cheomsongdae Astronomical Observatory, Gyeongju, Korea. b, Jantar Mantar, Jaipur, India.

**2003, Dec. 10** **Litho.**
**2042** A1383 15r Pair, #a-b 4.50 4.50

See South Korea No. 2136.

A privately-produced booklet containing two strips of No. 2046 exists.

Rajya Sabha, 200th Session — A1384

**2003, Dec. 11**
**2043** A1384 5r multi .80 .80

Mukut Behari Lal Bhargava (b. 1903), Politician A1385

**2003, Dec. 18** **Photo.**
**2044** A1385 5r multi .80 .80

Swami Swaroopanandji (1903-74), Religious Leader — A1386

**2003, Dec. 20 Litho. *Perf. 13¼x13***

| | | | |
|---|---|---|---|
| **2045** A1386 5r multi | | .80 | .80 |

Sangeet Natak Akademi, 50th Anniv. A1387

No. 2046: a, Musicians. b, Actors. c, Dancers.

**2003, Dec. 22**

| | | | |
|---|---|---|---|
| **2046** | Strip of 3, #a-c | 4.75 | 4.75 |
| *a.-c.* | A1387 5r Any single | 1.10 | 1.10 |
| *d.* | Souvenir sheet, #2046 | 5.00 | 5.00 |

Folk Musicians A1388

Designs: No. 2047, 5r, Allah Jilai Bai (1902-92). No. 2048, 5r, Lalan Fakir (1774-1890).

**2003, Dec. 29**

| | | | |
|---|---|---|---|
| **2047-2048** A1388 | Set of 2 | 2.00 | 2.00 |

Siddavanahalli Nijalingappa (1902-2000), Politician A1389

**2003, Dec. 31 *Perf. 13x13¼***

| | | | |
|---|---|---|---|
| **2049** A1389 5r multi | | 1.00 | 1.00 |

Major Somnath Sharma (1923-47), Military Hero — A1390

***Perf. 13¼x12¾***

**2003, Dec. 31 Photo.**

| | | | |
|---|---|---|---|
| **2050** A1390 5r multi | | .80 | .80 |

Chintaman D. Deshmukh (1896-1982), Finance Minister — A1391

**2004, Jan. 14 Litho. *Perf. 13¼x13***

| | | | |
|---|---|---|---|
| **2051** A1391 5r multi | | .80 | .80 |

Nani A. Palkhivala (1920-2002), Jurist — A1392

**2004, Jan. 16**

| | | | |
|---|---|---|---|
| **2052** A1392 5r multi | | .80 | .80 |

A privately-produced booklet containing six examples of No. 2052 exists.

Dr. Bhalchandra D. Garware, Businessman — A1393

**2004, Feb. 6**

| | | | |
|---|---|---|---|
| **2053** A1393 5r multi | | .80 | .80 |

Annamacharya, Mystic Saint — A1394

**2004, Mar. 18 Photo. *Perf. 13¾***

| | | | |
|---|---|---|---|
| **2054** A1394 5r multi | | .80 | .80 |

9th Battalion of Madras Regiment (Travancore), 300th Anniv. — A1395

**2004, Apr. 1 Litho. *Perf. 13¼x13***

| | | | |
|---|---|---|---|
| **2055** A1395 5r multi | | 1.50 | 1.50 |

V. Lakshminarayana, Violinist — A1396

**2004, Apr. 14 Photo.**

| | | | |
|---|---|---|---|
| **2056** A1396 5r multi | | 1.50 | 1.50 |

Indian Institute of Social Welfare and Business Management, 51st Anniv. — A1397

**2004, Apr. 25 Litho. *Perf. 13x13¼***

| | | | |
|---|---|---|---|
| **2057** A1397 5r multi | | 1.00 | 1.00 |

Baji Rao Peshwa, General, Statesman A1398

**2004, Apr. 25 Photo.**

| | | | |
|---|---|---|---|
| **2058** A1398 5r multi | | 1.00 | 1.00 |

Circumnavigation of I.N.S. Tarangini — A1399

**2004, Apr. 25 Litho. *Perf. 13¼x13***

| | | | |
|---|---|---|---|
| **2059** A1399 5r multi | | 1.00 | 1.00 |
| *a.* | Souvenir sheet of 1 | 19.00 | 19.00 |

Siddhar Swamigal (1904-64), Spiritual Leader — A1400

**2004, May 15 *Perf. 13x13¼***

| | | | |
|---|---|---|---|
| **2060** A1400 5r multi | | .80 | .80 |

Indra Chandra Shastri (1912-86), Philosopher A1401

**2004, May 27 Photo.**

| | | | |
|---|---|---|---|
| **2061** A1401 5r black & green | | .80 | .80 |

Woodstock School, Mussoorie, 150th Anniv. A1402

**2004, June 2 Litho. *Perf. 12½x13¼***

| | | | |
|---|---|---|---|
| **2062** A1402 5r multi | | .80 | .80 |

Jyotiprasad Agarwalla (1903-51), Musician, Cinematographer A1403

**2004, June 17 Photo. *Perf. 13x13¼***

| | | | |
|---|---|---|---|
| **2063** A1403 5r multi | | 1.00 | 1.00 |

P. N. Panicker (1909-95), Educator A1404

**2004, June 19**

| | | | |
|---|---|---|---|
| **2064** A1404 5r multi | | .80 | .80 |

Great Trigonometrical Survey — A1405

Designs: No. 2065, 5r, Nain Singh (c. 1826-1882), Himalayan explorer. No. 2066, 5r, Radhanath Sikdar (1813-70), Surveyor who calculated height of Mt. Everest. No. 2067, 5r, Stylized map of India, triangles (38x28mm).

**2004, June 27 Litho. *Perf. 13¼***

| | | | |
|---|---|---|---|
| **2065-2067** A1405 | Set of 3 | 2.50 | 2.50 |
| *2067a* | Souvenir sheet, #2065-2067 | 8.00 | 8.00 |

A privately-produced booklet containing six examples of No. 2067 exists.

Aacharya Bhikshu, Founder of Jain Swetamber Terapanth Sect — A1406

**2004, June 30 Photo.**

| | | | |
|---|---|---|---|
| **2068** A1406 5r multi | | .75 | .75 |

2004 Summer Olympics, Athens — A1407

No. 2069: a, 5r, Wrestling. b, 5r, Women's long jump. c, 15r, Shooting. d, 15r, Field hockey.

***Perf. 13¾x14¼***

**2004, Aug. 13 Photo.**

| | | | |
|---|---|---|---|
| **2069** A1407 | Block of 4, #a-d | 3.00 | 3.00 |

Poets — A1408

No. 2070: a, Kabir (1440-1518), Indian poet. b, Hafiz Shirazi (c. 1325-c. 1389), Persian poet.

**2004, Aug. 16** ***Perf. 13¼***
**2070** A1408 15r Horiz. pair, #a-b 2.00 2.00

See Iran No. 2894.

Murasoli Maran (1934-2003), Politician, Film Maker, Journalist — A1409

**2004, Aug. 17** ***Perf. 12½x13¼***
**2071** A1409 5r multi 1.00 1.00

Prime Minister Rajiv Gandhi (1944-91) and Windmills — A1410

**2004, Aug. 20** **Litho.** ***Perf. 13¼***
**2072** A1410 5r multi 1.00 1.00

Rajiv Gandhi Renewable Energy Day.

S. S. Vasan (1904-69), Film Producer, Magazine Publisher A1411

**2004, Aug. 28** **Photo.** ***Perf. 13x13¼***
**2073** A1411 5r multi 1.00 1.00

Panini (c. 520 B.C.-c. 460 B.C.), Grammarian — A1412

**2004, Aug. 30** ***Perf. 13¼x13***
**2074** A1412 5r multi .75 .75

K. Subrahmanyam (1904-71), Film Director and Producer — A1413

**2004, Sept. 10**
**2075** A1413 5r multi .80 .80

M. C. Chagla (1900-81), Judge, Diplomat A1414

**2004, Oct. 1**
**2076** A1414 5r multi .75 .75

Tirupur Kumaran (1904-32), Martyred Protester — A1415

**2004, Oct. 4** ***Perf. 13x13¼***
**2077** A1415 5r multi .50 .50

India Post, 150th Anniv. — A1416

No. 2078: a, Boat, #2, coach, train on bridge. b, Train on bridge, airplane, man with spear, frame of #C1. c, Mail box, building, #201. d, Computer, emblems for postal consumer services.

**2004, Oct. 4** ***Perf. 14¼x13¾***
**2078** Horiz. strip of 4 2.00 2.00
*a.-d.* A1416 5r Any single .30 .30
*e.* Souvenir sheet, #2078, perf. 13¼ 10.00 10.00

Ashoka Chakra Winners — A1417

No. 2079: a, Neerja Bhanot (1963-86), airline purser killed in hijacking. b, Randhir Prasad Verma (1952-91), slain policeman.

**2004, Oct. 8** ***Perf. 13¼x13***
**2079** A1417 5r Horiz. pair, #a-b 1.00 1.00

Guru Dutt (1925-64), Film Actor, Director A1418

**2004, Oct. 10**
**2080** A1418 5r multi 1.00 1.00

Indian Soldiers in UN Peacekeeping Forces — A1419

**2004, Oct. 24** ***Perf. 13¼***
**2081** A1419 5r multi .80 .80
*a.* Souvenir sheet of 1 12.00 12.00

Periya (1748-1801) and Chinna (1753-1801) Marudhu, Rulers of Sivaganga, Rebellion Leaders A1420

**2004, Oct. 24** ***Perf. 13¾x14***
**2082** A1420 5r multi .80 .80

A privately-produced booklet containing six examples of No. 2082 exists.

Greetings — A1421

No. 2083: a, Kites. b, Dolls.

**2004, Oct. 25** ***Perf. 13½x13***
**2083** A1421 4r Horiz. pair, #a-b 1.10 1.10

Dr. Svetoslav Roerich (1904-93), Painter A1422

**2004, Oct. 27** ***Perf. 13¼x13***
**2084** A1422 5r multi .80 .80

Tenneti Viswanatham (1895-1979), Politician — A1423

**2004, Nov. 10** **Photo.** ***Perf. 13x13¼***
**2085** A1423 5r multi .80 .80

Children's Day — A1424

**2004, Nov. 14**
**2086** A1424 5r multi .75 .75

Walchand Hirachand (1882-1953), Industrialist A1425

**2004, Nov. 23** ***Perf. 13¾***
**2087** A1425 5r multi .75 .75

Dula Bhaya Kag (1903-77), Poet — A1426

**2004, Nov. 25** ***Perf. 13x13¼***
**2088** A1426 5r multi .75 .75

Aga Khan Award for Architecture — A1427

No. 2089: a, Khas Mahal (blue panel). b, Agra Fort (orange panel).

**2004, Nov. 28** ***Perf. 14x13¾***
**2089** Horiz. pair 2.50 2.50
*a.-b.* A1427 15r Either single .95 .95
*c.* Souvenir sheet, #2089a, 2089b, perf. 13¼ 15.00 15.00

Bhagat Puran Singh (1904-92), Founder of Home for Poor — A1428

**2004, Dec. 10** **Litho.** ***Perf. 13x13¼***
**2090** A1428 5r multi .75 .75

Women's Insurrections of 1904 and 1939 — A1429

**2004, Dec. 12** **Photo.** ***Perf. 13¼x13***
**2091** A1429 5r multi .75 .75

Energy Conservation Day — A1430

**2004, Dec. 14**
**2092** A1430 5r multi .75 .75

Completion of Taj Mahal, 350th Anniv. — A1431

**2004, Dec. 16** ***Perf. 14x13¾***
**2093** A1431 15r multi 1.25 1.25
*a.* Souvenir sheet of 1, perf. 13¼ 13.00 13.00

A privately produced booklet containing 3 #2093 exists.

Sahitya Academy, 50th Anniv. A1432

**2004, Dec. 21** ***Perf. 13¼x13***
**2094** A1432 5r multi .75 .75

Bhaskara Sethupathy (1868-1903), Ramanathapuram Ruler — A1433

**2004, Dec. 27** ***Perf. 13x13¼***
**2095** A1433 5r multi .75 .75

Dogs A1434

No. 2096: a, Himalayan sheepdog. b, Rampur hound. c, Mudhol hound. d, Rajapalayam.

**2005, Jan. 9** ***Perf. 13¼***
**2096** Horiz. strip of 4 4.00 4.00
***a.-c.*** A1434 5r Any single .40 .40
***d.*** A1434 15r multi .90 .90

Padampat Singhania (1905-79), Industrialist A1435

**2005, Feb. 3**
**2097** A1435 5r multi .75 .75

Rotary International, Cent. — A1436

**2005, Feb. 23** ***Perf. 13¼x13***
**2098** A1436 5r multi .90 .90

Vice-President Krishan Kant (1927-2002) — A1437

**2005, Feb. 27** **Photo.** ***Perf. 13¼***
**2099** A1437 5r multi .75 .75

Madhavrao Scindia (1945-2001), Government Minister — A1438

**2005, Mar. 10**
**2100** A1438 5r multi .75 .75

Flora and Fauna — A1439

No. 2101: a, Clouded leopard. b, Dillenia indica. c, Mishmi takin. d, Pitcher plant.

**2005, Mar. 24** **Photo.** ***Perf. 13¼***
**2101** A1439 5r Block of 4, #a-d 2.00 2.00
***e.*** Souvenir sheet, #2101 11.00 11.00

Intl. Year of Physics A1440

***Perf. 12¾x13***
**2005, Mar. 31** **Wmk. 324**
**2102** A1440 5r multi 1.00 1.00

Salt March to Dandi, 75th Anniv. — A1441

Mohandas Gandhi and: a, Marchers. b, Newspaper. c, Map of march. d, Text by Gandhi.

***Perf. 13¼***
**2005, Apr. 5** **Photo.** **Unwmk.**
**2103** A1441 5r Block of 4, #a-d 2.00 2.00
***e.*** Souvenir sheet, #2103 10.00 10.00

15th Punjab (Patiala) Battalion, 300th Anniv. A1442

**2005, Apr. 13**
**2104** A1442 5r multi .75 .75

Bandung Conference, 50th Anniv. — A1443

**2005, Apr. 18**
**2105** A1443 15r multi 1.25 1.25

Narayan Meghaji Lokhande (1848-1897), Labor Activist A1444

**2005, May 3** ***Perf. 13¾***
**2106** A1444 5r multi .75 .75

Cooperative Movement in India, Cent. — A1445

**2005, May 8** ***Perf. 13¼***
**2107** A1445 5r multi .75 .75

World Environment Day — A1446

**2005, June 5**
**2108** A1446 5r multi 1.25 1.25

Guru Granth Sahib A1447

**2005, June 16** **Photo.** ***Perf. 14x13¾***
**2109** A1447 10r multi *45.00* —
***a.*** Souvenir sheet of 1 *90.00* —

Because of a lack of an agreement with Indian postal officials and Sikh religious representatives, local post offices were alerted that the issuance of Nos. 2109 and 2109a was to be postponed and the stamps were not to be placed on sale on June 16. Examples were sold at several locations that apparently did not receive the message.

Abdul Qaiyum Ansari (1905-73), Nationalist Leader A1448

**2005, July 1** **Photo.** ***Perf. 13¼***
**2110** A1448 5r brown .75 .75

Dheeran Chinnamalai (1765-1805), Freedom Fighter — A1449

**2005, July 31**
**2111** A1449 5r multi .75 .75

State Bank of India, Bicent. — A1450

**2005, Aug. 31**
**2112** A1450 15r multi 1.25 1.25

Intl. Day of Peace — A1451

**2005, Sept. 21** **Photo.** ***Perf. 13x13¼***
**2113** A1451 5r multi .75 .75

A. M. M. Murugappa Chettiar (1902-65), Industrialist A1452

**2005, Oct. 1**
**2114** A1452 5r multi .75 .75

Pratap Singh Kairon (1901-65), Government Minister — A1453

**2005, Oct. 1** ***Perf. 13¼x13***
**2115** A1453 5r multi .75 .75

Dr. T. S. Soundram (1904-84), Founder of Gandhigram Development Program — A1454

**2005, Oct. 2**
**2116** A1454 5r multi .90 .90

Mailboxes
A1455

No. 2117: a, Victorian era box, horse-drawn carriage. b, Man inserting letter into Penfold box. c, Two cylindrical boxes. d, Two square letter boxes.

**2005, Oct. 18** ***Perf. 13x13¼***

| | | | |
|---|---|---|---|
| **2117** | Horiz. strip of 4 | 3.50 | 3.50 |
| ***a.-d.*** | A1415 5r Any single | .75 | .30 |
| ***e.*** | Souvenir sheet, #2117a-2117d, perf. 13¾ | *15.00* | *15.00* |

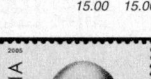

V. Kalyanasundarnar (1883-1953), Union Leader — A1456

**2005, Oct. 21** ***Perf. 13¼***
**2118** A1456 5r multi .75 .75

Ayothidhasa Pandithar (1845-1914), Social Reformer
A1457

**2005, Oct. 21**
**2119** A1457 5r multi .75 .75

Kavimani Desiga Vinayagam Pillai (1876-1954), Poet — A1458

**2005, Oct. 21** ***Perf. 13¼x13***
**2120** A1458 5r multi .75 .75

Prabodh Chandra (1911-86), Writer — A1459

**2005, Oct. 24** ***Perf. 13x13¼***
**2121** A1459 5r multi .75 .75

Children's Day — A1460

**2005, Nov. 14**
**2122** A1460 5r multi .75 .75

Children's Film Society, 50th Anniv.
A1461

**2005, Nov. 14** ***Perf. 13¾***
**2123** A1461 5r multi 1.00 1.00

Progress, Harmony and Development Chamber of Commerce and Industry, Cent. — A1462

**2005, Nov. 16**
**2124** A1462 5r multi .75 .75

World Summit on the Information Society, Tunis
A1463

**2005, Nov. 17** **Photo.** ***Perf. 13¼x13***
**2125** A1463 5r multi .75 .75

Calcutta Police Commissionerate, 150th Anniv. — A1464

**2005, Nov. 19** ***Perf. 13¾***
**2126** A1464 5r multi .40 .40

Newborn Health — A1465

**2005, Nov. 24** ***Perf. 13¼***
**2127** A1465 5r blue .40 .40

Jawaharlal Darda, Politician
A1466

**2005, Dec. 2**
**2128** A1466 5r multi .25 .25

Navy Ships Delhi, Kora and Udaygiri — A1467

**2005, Dec. 4** ***Perf. 13***
**2129** A1467 5r multi .60 .60

M. S. Subbulakshmi (1916-2004), Singer — A1468

**2005, Dec. 18** ***Perf. 13¼x13***
**2130** A1468 5r multi .40 .40

Integral Coach Factory, 50th Anniv. — A1469

**2005, Dec. 19** ***Perf. 13¾***
**2131** A1469 5r multi .70 .70

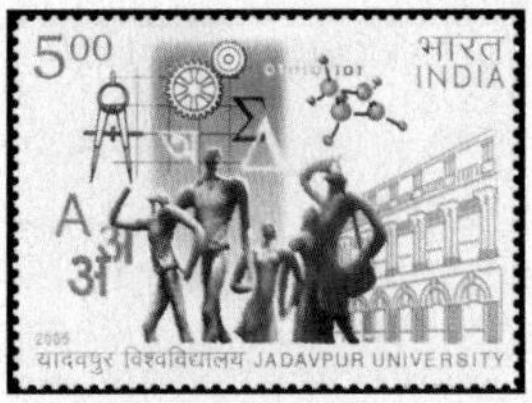


Jadavpur University, 50th Anniv. — A1470

**2005, Dec. 21**
**2132** A1470 5r multi .40 .40

16th Air Force Squadron, 55th Anniv. — A1471

**2005, Dec. 27** ***Perf. 14x13¾***
**2133** A1471 5r multi .40 .40

De Facto Transfer of Pondicherry, 50th Anniv. (in 2006) — A1472

**2005, Dec. 30** ***Perf. 13¼x13***
**2134** A1472 5r multi .35 .35

Pongal Festival
A1473

**2006, Jan. 12** ***Perf. 13¾***
**2135** A1473 5r multi .70 .70

A. V. Meiyappan (1907-79), Film Producer and Director
A1474

**2006, Jan. 22** ***Perf. 13¼***
**2136** A1474 5r multi .70 .70

N. M. R. Subbaraman, Politician, Cent. of Birth — A1475

**2006, Jan. 29** **Photo.**
**2137** A1475 5r multi .35 .35

Dated 2005.

Third Battalion of the Sikh Regiment, 150th Anniv.
A1476

**2006, Feb. 1** ***Perf. 13¼x13***
**2138** A1476 5r multi .50 .50

President's Fleet Review, Visakhapatnam — A1477

No. 2139: a, Aircraft carrier and jet. b, Helicopter and two ships. c, Airplane and two ships. d, Two submarines.

**2006, Feb. 12** ***Perf. 13¾x13***
**2139** A1477 5r Block of 4, #a-d 2.50 2.50

Thirumuruga Kirubananda Variyar (1906-93), Tamil Magazine Publisher
A1478

Devaneya Pavanar (1902-81), Tamil Writer — A1479

Dr. U. V. Swaminatha Iyer (1855-1942), Tamil Literature Researcher
A1480

Tamilavel Umamaheswarar, Editor of Tamil Literary Magazine
A1481

**2006, Feb. 18** ***Perf. 13¼***

**2140** A1478 5r red brown .35 .35
**2141** A1479 5r blue .35 .35
**2142** A1480 5r brown .35 .35
**2143** A1481 5r black .35 .35
*Nos. 2140-2143 (4)* 1.40 1.40

St. Bede's College, Shimla, 102nd Anniv. — A1482

**2006, Feb. 24** ***Perf. 13x13¼***

**2144** A1482 5r multi .35 .35

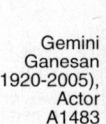

Gemini Ganesan (1920-2005), Actor
A1483

**2006, Feb. 25** ***Perf. 13¼x13***

**2145** A1483 5r black .70 .70

Salesians of Don Bosco in India, Cent. — A1484

**2006, Feb. 27** ***Perf. 13x13¼***

**2146** A1484 5r brown .40 .40

M. Singaravelar (1860-1946), Communist Politician
A1485

**2006, Mar. 2**

**2147** A1485 5r multi .35 .35

World Consumer Rights Day
A1486

**2006, Mar. 15** ***Perf. 13¼x13***

**2148** A1486 5r multi .40 .40

Indian Agricultural Research Institute, Delhi, Cent.
A1487

**2006, Mar. 30**

**2149** A1487 5r multi .40 .40

62nd Cavalry Armored Regiment, 50th Anniv.
A1488

**2006, Apr. 1**

**2150** A1488 5r multi .40 .40

Folk Dances — A1489

No. 2151 — Folk dances from: a, India. b, Cyprus.

**2006, Apr. 12** ***Perf. 13x13¾***

**2151** A1489 15r Horiz. pair, #a-b 2.75 2.75
*c.* Souvenir sheet, #2151, perf. 13¾x13¼ *8.50 8.50*

See Cyprus No. 1052.

Calcutta Girls' High School, 150th Anniv.
A1490

**2006, Apr. 21** ***Perf. 13¾x13***

**2152** A1490 5r multi .40 .40

Pannalal Barupal (1913-83), Politician
A1491

**2006, Apr. 28** ***Perf. 13x13¼***

**2153** A1491 5r multi .35 .35

Kurinji Flower
A1492

**2006, Apr. 29** ***Perf. 13x13¾***

**2154** A1492 15r multi 2.00 2.00
*a.* Souvenir sheet of 1 *9.00 9.00*

Rainwater Harvesting
A1493

**2006, June 5** ***Perf. 13¼x13***

**2155** A1493 5r multi .70 .70

Sri Pratap College, Srinigar, Cent. — A1494

**2006, June 15** ***Perf. 13***

**2156** A1494 5r multi .40 .40

Indraprastha Girls' School, New Delhi, 102nd Anniv. — A1495

**2006, July 8** ***Perf. 13¾x13***

**2157** A1495 5r multi .40 .40

Voorhees College, Vellore, 111th Anniv.
A1496

**2006, July 10** ***Perf. 13¼***

**2158** A1496 5r multi .35 .35

Vellore Mutiny, Bicent. — A1497

**2006, July 10** **Litho.** ***Perf. 13¼***

**2159** A1497 5r multi .70 .70

High Court of Jammu and Kashmir — A1498

***Perf. 13¾x13¼***

**2006, July 29** **Photo.**

**2160** A1498 5r multi .40 .40

Pankaj Kumar Mullick (1904-78), Composer
A1499

**2006, Aug. 4** ***Perf. 13¼x13***

**2161** A1499 5r multi .50 .50

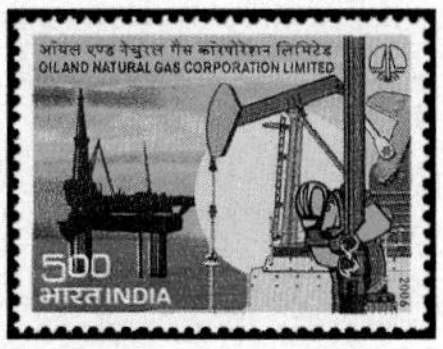


Oil and Natural Gas Corporation, Limited
A1500

**2006, Aug. 14**

**2162** A1500 5r multi .60 .60

M. P. Sivagnanam, Tamil Politician, Cent. of Birth — A1501

**2006, Aug. 15** **Litho.** ***Perf. 13¼***

**2163** A1501 5r multi .35 .35

University of Madras
A1502

**2006, Sept. 4** **Photo.**

**2164** A1502 5r multi .40 .40

L. V. Prasad (1908-94), Film Actor and Director
A1503

**2006, Sept. 5**

**2165** A1503 5r multi .65 .65

Indian Merchants Chamber — A1504

**2006, Sept. 7** ***Perf. 13x13¼***

**2166** A1504 5r multi .40 .40

Horse Sculptures — A1505

No. 2167: a, Horse and rider. b, Horse only.

**2006, Sept. 11** ***Perf. 13¼x13¾***

**2167** A1505 15r Horiz. pair, #a-b 2.75 2.75
*c.* Souvenir sheet, #2167 *8.50 8.50*

See Mongolia No. 2621.

Birds
A1506

No. 2168: a, Greater adjutant stork. b, Nilgiri laughing thrush. c, Manipur bush-quail. d, Lesser florican.

**2006, Oct. 5** ***Perf. 13***

**2168** Vert. strip of 4 1.75 1.75
*a.-d.* A1506 5r Any single .40 .40
*e.* Souvenir sheet, #2168a-2168d *7.00 7.00*

Madhya Pradesh Chamber of Commerce and Industry, Cent.
A1507

**2006, Oct. 12 Photo.** ***Perf. 13¼***

**2169** A1507 5r multi .40 .40

Bishwanath Roy (1906-84), Politician
A1508

**2007, Oct. 31 Litho.** ***Perf. 13¼x13***

**2170** A1508 5r multi .40 .40

G. Varadaraj, Industrialist (1936-90)
A1509

**2006, Nov. 1**

**2171** A1509 5r multi .40 .40

Lakes — A1510

No. 2172: a, Roop Kund. b, Chandra Tal, vert. c, Tsomo Riri. d, Sela. e, Tsangu.

**2006, Nov. 6 Photo.** ***Perf. 13***

**2172** A1510 5r Block of 5, #a-e 3.00 3.00

Lala Deen Dayal (1844-1905), Photographer
A1511

**2006, Nov. 11**

**2173** A1511 5r multi .40 .40

Children's Day — A1512

No. 2174 — Various children's drawings: a, Denomination at LL. b, Denomination at UL.

**2006, Nov. 14 Litho.** ***Perf. 13***

**2174** A1512 5r Horiz. pair, #a-b .60 .60

The Tribune, 125th Anniv.
A1513

**2006, Nov. 24 Photo.** ***Perf. 14***

**2175** A1513 5r multi .40 .40

World AIDS Day — A1514

**2006, Dec. 1** ***Perf. 13x13¼***

**2176** A1514 5r multi .70 .70

Bartholomaeus Ziegenbalg (1682-1719), First Lutheran Missionary to India — A1515

**2006, Dec. 8** ***Perf. 13¼***

**2177** A1515 5r multi .40 .40

Army Field Post Offices, 150th Anniv. — A1516

No. 2178: a, Soldier, cancel, ship, map of Bushire-Bombay route. b, Soldier writing letter, camel. c, Soldier reading letter, sign. d, Soldier reading letter, helicopter.

**2006, Dec. 10 Litho.** ***Perf. 13x13¼***

**2178** Horiz. strip of 4 1.60 1.60
*a.-d.* A1516 5r Any single .40 .40

Sandalwood Carving
A1517

**2006, Dec. 18 Photo.** ***Perf. 13¼x13***

**2179** A1517 15r multi 2.00 2.00
*a.* Souvenir sheet of 1, perf. 13 *8.50 8.50*

Stamps are impregnated with a sandalwood scent.

Stop Child Labor — A1518

No. 2180: a, Girl on tightrope. b, Boy with hoe. c, Boy pouring tea. d, Boy with large basket.

**2006, Dec. 28** ***Perf. 13¼x13***

**2180** A1518 5r Block of 4, #a-d 1.40 1.40

Bimal Roy (1909-66), Film Director
A1519

**2007, Jan. 8 Litho.** ***Perf. 13***

**2181** A1519 5r multi .40 .40

Tamil Nadu Cricket Association, 70th Anniv. — A1520

**2007, Jan. 26** ***Perf. 13x13¼***

**2182** A1520 5r multi .40 .40

Rose Varieties — A1521

No. 2183: a, 5r, Bhim. b, 5r, Neelam. c, 15r, Delhi Princess. d, 15r, Jawahar.

**2007, Feb. 7 Photo.** ***Perf. 13x13¼***

**2183** A1521 Block of 4, #a-d 1.90 1.90
*e.* Souvenir sheet, #2183 *5.00 5.00*

Stamps are impregnated with a rose scent.

Manoharbhai Patel (1906-70), Politician
A1522

**2007, Feb. 9**

**2184** A1522 5r multi .40 .40

Fairs — A1523

Designs: No. 2185, 5r, Sonepur Fair. No. 2186, 5r, Pushkar Fair. No. 2187, 5r, Goa Carnival. No. 2188, 5r, Baul Mela.

**2007, Feb. 27** **Litho.**

**2185-2188** A1523 Set of 4 1.60 1.60
*2188a* Souvenir sheet, #2185-2188 *3.00 3.00*

Women's Day — A1524

No. 2189: a, Two women. b, Woman, three birds. c, Two women and birds. d, Woman and birds.

**2007, Mar. 8 Photo.** ***Perf. 13x13¼***

**2189** Horiz. strip of 4 1.90 1.90
*a.-b.* A1524 5r Either single .25 .25
*c.-d.* A1524 15r Either single .70 .70
*e.* Souvenir sheet, #2189 *3.50 3.50*

Raj Narain (1917-86), Politician
A1525

**2007, Mar. 23 Litho.** ***Perf. 13¼***

**2190** A1525 5r multi .40 .40

Mehboob Khan (1907-64), Film Producer and Director — A1526

**2007, Mar. 30**

**2191** A1526 5r multi .40 .40

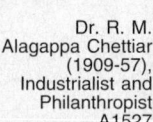

Dr. R. M. Alagappa Chettiar (1909-57), Industrialist and Philanthropist
A1527

**2007, Apr. 6 Photo. *Perf. 13x13¼***

**2192** A1527 5r multi .40 .40

A1528

A1529

A1530

A1531

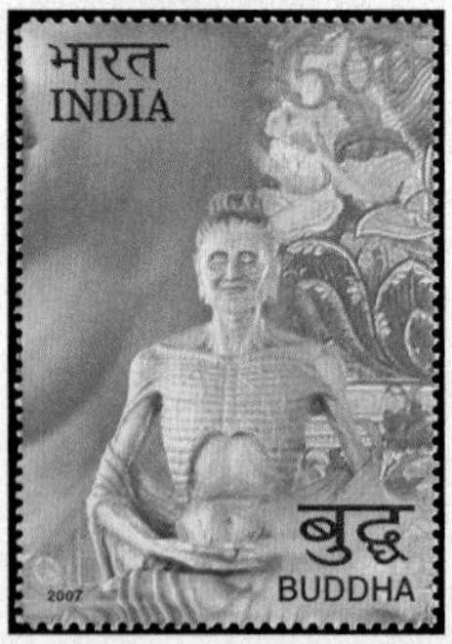


A1532

Mahaparinirvana of Buddha, 2550th Anniv. — A1533

**2007, May 2 *Perf. 13¼***

**2193** A1528 5r multi .30 .30
**2194** A1529 5r multi .30 .30
**2195** A1530 5r multi .30 .30
**2196** A1531 5r multi .30 .30
**2197** A1532 5r multi .30 .30
**2198** A1533 5r multi .30 .30
*a.* Miniature sheet, #2193-2198 3.50 3.50
*Nos. 2193-2198 (6)* 1.80 1.80

Natl. Parks — A1534

No. 2199: a, Bandhavgarh Natl. Park. b, Bandipur Natl. Park. c, Kaziranga Natl. Park. d, Mudumalai Natl. Park. e, Periyar Natl. Park.

**2007, May 31**

**2199** Vert. strip of 5 2.00 2.00
*a.-e.* A1534 5r Any single .40 .40

First War of Independence, 150th Anniv. — A1535

**2007, Aug. 9 *Perf. 13¼x13***

**2200** A1535 Vert. pair 1.50 1.50
*a.* 5r Battle of Lucknow .40 .40
*b.* 15r Battle of Kanpur 1.10 1.10
*c.* Souvenir sheet, #2200a-2200b 2.50 2.50

Saint Vallalar (1823-74)
A1536

Maraimalai Adigal (1876-1950), Tamil Scholar
A1537

V. G. Suryanarayana Sastriar (1870-1903), Tamil Writer — A1538

**2007, Aug. 18 Litho. *Perf. 13x13¼***

**2201** A1536 5r multi .35 .35
**2202** A1537 5r multi .35 .35
**2203** A1538 5r multi .35 .35
*Nos. 2201-2203 (3)* 1.05 1.05

Bridges
A1539

No. 2204: a, Howrah Bridge. b, Mahatma Gandhi Bridge. c, Pamban Bridge. d, Vidyasagar Bridge.

**2007, Aug. 17 Photo.**

**2204** Vert. strip or block of 4 2.00 2.00
*a.-d.* A1539 5r Any single .50 .50
*e.* Souvenir sheet, #2204a-2204d 2.50 2.50

J. P. Naik (1907-81), Education Reformer — A1540

**2007, Sept. 5 Litho. *Perf. 13¼x13***

**2205** A1540 5r multi .40 .40

53rd Commonwealth Parliamentary Conference, New Delhi — A1541

**2007, Sept. 23 Litho. *Perf. 13¼***

**2206** A1541 15r multi 1.00 1.00

Sachin Deb Burman (1906-75), Composer
A1542

**2007, Oct. 1 *Perf. 13¼x13***

**2207** A1542 15r multi 1.00 1.00

Satyagraha (Non-Violent Resistance), Cent.
A1543

No. 2208 — Mohandas Gandhi and: a, Train. b, House, newspaper article. c, Crowd, building. d, People marching.

**2007, Oct. 2 Photo. *Perf. 13¼x13***

**2208** Horiz. strip of 4 1.60 1.60
*a.-d.* A1543 5r Any single .40 .40
*e.* Souvenir sheet, #2208a-2208d 3.00 3.00

Indian Air Force, 75th Anniv.
A1544

Designs: No. 2209, 5r, DHRUV helicopter. No. 2210, 5r, Westland Wapiti biplane. No. 2211, 5r, AWACS airplane (84x32mm). 15r, IL-78 (84x32mm).

**2007, Oct. 8 Litho. *Perf. 13¼x13***

**2209-2212** A1544 Set of 4 1.60 1.60
*2212a* Souvenir sheet, #2209-2212 4.00 4.00

Fourth Military World Games, Hyderabad
A1545

No. 2213: a, Parachutist. b, Soccer player. c, Swimmer.

**2007, Oct. 14 *Perf. 13¼x13***

**2213** Vert. strip of 3 .80 .80
*a.-c.* A1545 5r Any single .25 .25
*d.* Souvenir sheet, #2213, perf. 13 3.50 3.50

Maharashtra Police Academy — A1546

**2007, Nov. 3 Photo. *Perf. 13¼***

**2214** A1546 5r multi .50 .50

Children's Day
A1547

Children's art: No. 2215, 5r, Children and stars. No. 2216, 5r, Fishermen and canoes at night.

**2007, Nov. 14 Litho. *Perf. 13¼x13***

**2215-2216** A1547 Set of 2 .80 .80
*2216a* Souvenir sheet, #2215-2216 2.00 2.00

Renewable Energy — A1548

Designs: No. 2217, 5r, Solar energy. No. 2218, 5r, Wind energy. No. 2219, 5r, Small hydroelectric power, vert. No. 2220, 5r, Biomass energy, vert.

**2007, Nov. 22 Photo. *Perf. 13***

**2217-2220** A1548 Set of 4 1.60 1.60
*2220a* Souvenir sheet, #2217-2220, perf. 13¾x13¼, 13¼x13¾ 3.50 3.50
*2220b* Miniature sheet, 6 each #2217-2218, 3 each #2219-2220 5.25 5.25

First Battalion of the Fourth Gorkha Rifles, 150th Anniv. A1549

**2007, Nov. 27 Litho. *Perf. 13¼***
**2221** A1549 5r multi .60 .60

Intl. Day of Disabled Persons — A1550

**Photo. & Embossed**
**2007, Dec. 3 *Perf. 13***
**2222** A1550 5r multi .60 .60

Daly College, Indore, 125th Anniv. — A1551

**2007, Dec. 8 Litho. *Perf. 13¼***
**2223** A1551 5r multi .40 .40

Wilson College, Bombay, 175th Anniv. — A1552

**2007, Dec. 11 Photo. *Perf. 13***
**2224** A1552 5r multi .40 .40

Greetings A1553

No. 2225: a, Sun, wheat, path. b, Fish, lotus flower. c, Bird. d, Man, flower, butterfly, deer. e, Flowers, stars and text, "Happy New Year," (58x29mm).

**2007, Dec. 15 Photo. *Perf. 13***
**2225** Horiz. strip of 5 1.50 1.50
*a.-e.* A1553 5r Any single .30 .30

S. B. Chavan (1920-2004), Politician — A1554

**2007, Dec. 17 Litho. *Perf. 13¼x13***
**2226** A1554 5r multi .50 .50

Snows Basilica, 425th Anniv. — A1555

**2007, Dec. 25 *Perf. 13***
**2227** A1555 5r multi .50 .50

Water Year — A1556

**2007, Dec. 28**
**2228** A1556 5r multi .40 .40

Ritwik Ghatak (1925-76), Film Director A1557

**2007, Dec. 31 Photo. *Perf. 13¼x13***
**2229** A1557 5r brown & black .40 .40

Butterflies Of Andaman and Nicobar Islands — A1558

No. 2230: a, Male Papilio mayo. b, Female Papilio mayo. c, Female Pachliopta rhodifer. d, Male Pachliopta rhodifer.

**2008, Jan. 2 *Perf. 13***
**2230** A1558 5r Block of 4, #a-d 1.60 1.60
*e.* Souvenir sheet, #2230 3.00 3.00

Dr. Benjamin Peary Pal (1906-89), Rose Breeder and Plant Scientist A1559

**2008, Jan. 5 Litho.**
**2231** A1559 5r multi .40 .40

Dr. Dhananjaya Ramachandra Gadgil (1901-71), Economist A1560

**2008, Feb. 8 Photo.**
**2232** A1560 5r multi .40 .40

Damodaram Sanjeevaiah (1921-72), Politician — A1561

**2008, Feb. 14 Litho.**
**2233** A1561 5r multi .40 .40

Maharshi Bulusu Sambamurthy (1886-1958), Lawyer — A1562

**2008, Mar. 4**
**2234** A1562 5r multi .40 .40

Madhubala (1933-1969), Film Actress — A1563

**2008, Mar. 18 Photo. *Perf. 13***
**2235** A1563 5r multi .40 .40
*a.* Souvenir sheet of 1, perf. 13x13¾ 1.75 1.75

Asrar Ul Haq (Majaaz) (1909-55), Urdu Poet A1564

**2008, Mar. 28 Litho. *Perf. 13***
**2236** A1564 5r multi .40 .40

Civil Service A1565

**Photo. & Embossed**
**2008, Apr. 21**
**2237** A1565 5r multi .40 .40

Tata Steel, Cent. — A1566

**2008, Apr. 22 Litho.**
**2238** A1566 5r multi .40 .40

Jasmine Flowers — A1567

**2008, Apr. 26 Photo.**
**2239** A1567 5r shown .40 .40
**2240** A1567 15r Flowers, horiz. 1.00 1.00
*a.* Souvenir sheet, #2239-2240 3.00 3.00

Nos. 2239-2240, 2240a are impregnated with a jasmine scent.

Aga Khan Foundation, 30th Anniv. — A1568

No. 2241: a, 5r, Heritage restoration (46x39mm). b, 15r, Social commitment (70x39mm).

**2008, May 17 Photo. *Perf. 13***
**2241** A1568 Horiz. pair, #a-b 1.10 1.10
*c.* Souvenir sheet, #2241a-2241b 3.00 3.00

Shri Shirdi Sai Baba (1835-1918), Hindu Saint — A1569

**2008, May 20**
**2242** A1569 5r multi .40 .40

Rajesh Pilot (1945-2008), Politician A1570

**2008, June 12 Litho. *Perf. 13***
**2243** A1570 5r multi .40 .40

Henning Holck-Larsen (1907-2003), Engineer and Industrialist A1571

**2008, June 12 Litho. *Perf. 13¼x13***
**2244** A1571 5r multi .40 .40

Madhav Institute of Technology, Gwalior, 50th Anniv. — A1572

**2008, June 30 Litho. *Perf. 13¼***
**2245** A1572 5r multi .40 .40

Temples — A1573

No. 2246: a, Maha Bodhi Temple, India. b, White Horse Temple, China.

**2008, July 11 Photo. *Perf. 13***
**2246** A1573 15r Horiz. pair, #a-b 1.75 1.75
*c.* Souvenir sheet, #2246 4.00 4.00

See People's Republic of China Nos. 3678-3679.

Punjab Regiment 14th Battalion, 250th Anniv. — A1574

**2008, July 21 Litho. *Perf. 13¼***
**2247** A1574 5r multi .40 .40

Damodar Dharmananda Kosambi (1907-66), Mathematician — A1575

**2008, July 31**
**2248** A1575 5r multi .40 .40

Aldabra Giant Tortoise A1576

Tortoise facing: 5r, Left. 15r, Forward.

**2008, Aug. 2 Photo. *Perf. 13***
**2249-2250** A1576 Set of 2 1.40 1.40

2008 Summer Olympics, Beijing — A1577

No. 2251 — 2008 Summer Olympics emblem and: a, 5r, Olympic torch and mascot. b, 5r, Boxing. c, 15r, Shooting. d, 15r, Archery.

**2008, Aug. 8**
**2251** A1577 Block of 4, #a-d 2.50 2.50
*e.* Souvenir sheet, #2251a-2251d 3.50 3.50

Indian Coast Guard, 30th Anniv. — A1578

No. 2252: a, Airplane. b, Helicopter. c, Hovercraft (large wave at LL). d, Patrol boat (large wave at LR).

**2008, Aug. 12 Litho. *Perf. 13¼***
**2252** A1578 5r Block of 4, #a-d 1.60 1.60
*e.* Souvenir sheet, #2252a-2252d 3.00 3.00

Ustad Bismillah Khan (1916-2006), Musician — A1579

**2008, Aug. 21**
**2253** A1579 5r multi .40 .40

Sir Pitti Theagarayar (1853-1925) — A1580

Dr. Taravat Mahadevan Nair (1868-1919) A1581

Dr. C. Natesan (1869-1937) A1582

**2008, Sept. 17 *Perf. 13x13¼***
**2254** A1580 5r multi .40 .40

***Perf. 13¾ Syncopated***

**2255** A1581 5r multi .40 .40
**2256** A1582 5r multi .40 .40
*Nos. 2254-2256 (3)* 1.20 1.20

Founders of South Indian Welfare Association.

Festivals — A1583

Designs: No. 2257, 5r, Dussehra Festival, Calcutta (Kolkata). No. 2258, 5r, Dussehra Festival, Mysore. No. 2259, 5r, Deepavali Festival, vert.

**2008, Oct. 7 Photo. *Perf. 13***
**2257-2259** A1583 Set of 3 1.25 1.25
*2259a* Souvenir sheet, #2257-2259 *3.00 3.00*

3rd Commonwealth Youth Games, Pune — A1584

No. 2260: a, Tiger mascot. b, Wrestling. c, Badminton. d, Hurdling.

**2008, Oct. 12 *Perf. 13x13¼***
**2260** Horiz. strip of 4 1.20 1.20
*a.-d.* A1584 5r Any single .30 .30
*e.* Souvenir sheet, #2260a-2260d *3.00 3.00*

Indian Post Office A1585

***Perf. 13¾ Syncopated***

**2008, Oct. 13 Litho.**
**2261** A1585 5r multi .40 .40

Philately Day. A souvenir sheet of one sold for 15r.

Food Safety and Quality Year — A1586

**2008, Oct. 16**
**2262** A1586 5r multi .40 .40

19th Commonwealth Games, Delhi — A1587

**2008, Oct. 18 Photo. *Perf. 13¼x13***
**2263** A1587 5r multi .40 .40

A souvenir sheet of one sold for 15r.

A1588

A1589

Children's Day — A1590

**2008, Nov. 14 Litho. *Perf. 13¼***
**2264** A1588 5r multi .25 .25
**2265** A1589 5r multi .25 .25
**2266** A1590 5r multi .25 .25
*a.* Souvenir sheet of 3, #2264-2266 2.75 2.75
*Nos. 2264-2266 (3)* .75 .75

Bomireddi N. Reddi (1908-77), Film Director A1591

**2008, Nov. 16**
**2267** A1591 5r multi .40 .40

Canonization of Saint Alphonsa (1910-46) A1592

**2008, Nov. 16 Photo. *Perf. 13x13¼***
**2268** A1592 5r multi .40 .40

A souvenir sheet of one sold for 15r.

Standard Chartered Bank, 150th Anniv. A1593

**2008, Nov. 17** **Litho.** ***Perf. 13¼***
**2269** A1593 5r multi .40 .40

Gas Authority of India Limited, 25th Anniv. A1594

**2008, Nov. 19** ***Perf. 13***
**2270** A1594 5r multi .40 .40

Joachim (1907-79) and Violet (1908-69) Alva, Politicians A1595

***Perf. 13¾ Syncopated***

**2008, Nov. 20**
**2271** A1595 5r multi .40 .40

Sardar Vallabhbhai Patel Natl. Police Academy, Hyderabad A1596

Building and: 5r, Police cadets training and marching. 20r, Statue, policeman with sword.

**2008, Nov. 27**
**2272-2273** A1596 Set of 2 1.25 1.25
*2273a* Souvenir sheet, #2272-2273 *3.50 3.50*

St. Joseph's Boys' High School, Bangalore, 150th Anniv. A1597

**2008, Nov. 28**
**2274** A1597 5r multi .40 .40

Buddhadeva Bose (1908-74), Writer — A1598

**2008, Nov. 30** ***Perf. 13***
**2275** A1598 5r multi .40 .40

Prime Minister Jawaharlal Nehru (1889-1964) A1599

E.V. Ramasami (1879-1973), Politician A1600

Mahatma Gandhi (1869-1948) A1601

Dr. Bhimrao R. Ambedkar (1891-1956), Politician A1602

Satyajit Ray (1921-92), Film Director A1603

Homi Jahangir Bhabha (1909-66), Nuclear Physicist A1604

Prime Minister Indira Gandhi (1917-84) A1605

Prime Minister Rajiv Gandhi (1944-91) A1606

C.V. Raman (1888-1970), 1930 Nobel Physics Laureate A1607

J. R. D. Tata (1904-93), Industrialist A1608

Mother Teresa (1910-97), 1979 Nobel Peace Laureate A1609

Rukmini Devi Arundale (1904-86), Dancer A1610

***Perf. 12¾x13¼***

**2008-09** **Photo.** **Wmk. 324**

| | | | | | |
|---|---|---|---|---|---|
| **2276** | A1599 | 25p | rose lil & blk | .25 | .25 |
| **2277** | A1600 | 50p | blue | .25 | .25 |
| **2278** | A1601 | 1r | olive brown | .25 | .25 |
| **2279** | A1602 | 2r | rose lilac | .25 | .25 |
| **2280** | A1603 | 3r | vio brown | .25 | .25 |
| **2281** | A1604 | 4r | brt blue | .25 | .25 |
| **2282** | A1605 | 5r | gray grn & blk | .25 | .25 |
| **2283** | A1606 | 5r | brown | .25 | .25 |
| **2284** | A1607 | 10r | multi | .45 | .45 |
| **2285** | A1608 | 15r | purple | .60 | .60 |
| **2286** | A1609 | 20r | multi | .80 | .80 |
| **2287** | A1610 | 50r | multi | 2.10 | 2.10 |
| | | | *Nos. 2276-2287 (12)* | 5.95 | 5.95 |

Issued: 25p, Nos. 2282, 2283, 12/1; 1r, 2r, 3r, 4r, 15r, 20r, 3/1/09; 50p, 10r, 5/11/09. 50r, 5/11/09.

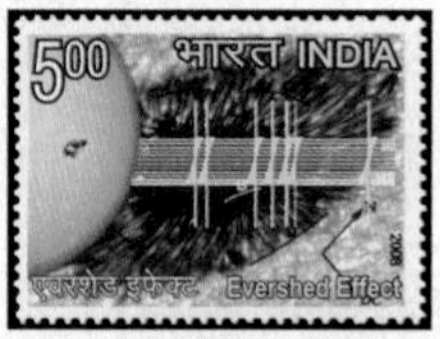

Discovery of Evershed Effect at Kodaikanal Solar Observatory, Cent. — A1611

***Perf. 13¾ Syncopated***

**2008, Dec. 2** **Litho.** **Unwmk.**
**2288** A1611 5r multi .40 .40

Map, Handshake, Indian Ship and Helicopter A1612

**2008, Dec. 4**
**2289** A1612 5r multi .40 .40

Navy Day.

Dr. Laxmi Mall Singhvi (1931-2007), Jurist — A1613

**2008, Dec. 8**
**2290** A1613 5r multi .40 .40

Christmas — A1614

No. 2291: a, 5r, Lambs. b, 20r, Madonna and Child.

**2008, Dec. 8** **Photo.** ***Perf. 13***
**2291** A1614 Horiz. pair, #a-b 1.10 1.10

Universal Declaration of Human Rights, 60th Anniv. A1615

**2008, Dec. 10**
**2292** A1615 5r multi .40 .40

Indian Institute of Science, Bangalore, Cent. — A1616

No. 2293: a, 5r, Building. b, 20r, Building and scientists.

**2008, Dec. 14**
**2293** A1616 Horiz. pair, #a-b 1.40 1.40
*c.* Souvenir sheet, #2293a-2293b *3.50 3.50*

Swami Ranganathananda (1908-2005), Hindu Monk — A1617

***Perf. 13¾ Syncopated***

**2008, Dec. 15** **Litho.**
**2294** A1617 5r multi .40 .40

Field Marshal S. H. F. J. Manekshaw (1914-2008) A1618

**2008, Dec. 16** **Photo.** ***Perf. 13x13¼***
**2295** A1618 5r multi .40 .40

Thazhuvia V. Ramasubbaiyer (1908-84), Founder of Dinamalar Newspaper A1619

***Perf. 13¾ Syncopated***

**2008, Dec. 21** **Litho.**
**2296** A1619 5r multi .40 .40

Brahmos Cruise Missile, 10th Anniv. — A1620

Designs: 5r, Missile in flight, airplane. 20r, Missiles, airplane, ship, launch vehicle, horiz.

**2008, Dec. 22** **Photo.** ***Perf. 13***
**2297-2298** A1620 Set of 2 1.40 1.40
*2298a* Souvenir sheet, #2297-2298 *3.50 3.50*

Udumalai Narayana Kavi (1899-1981), Lyricist — A1621

**2008, Dec. 31** ***Perf. 13x13¼***
**2299** A1621 5r multi .40 .40

Thillaiyadi Valliammai (1898-1914), Freedom Fighter — A1622

**2008, Dec. 31** ***Perf. 13***
**2300** A1622 5r multi .40 .40

Sheik Thambi Pavalar (1874-1950), Freedom Fighter — A1623

**2008, Dec. 31**
**2301** A1623 5r multi .40 .40

A. T. Paneerselvam, Politician A1624

**2008, Dec. 31** ***Perf. 13x13¼***
**2302** A1624 5r multi .40 .40

M. Bhakthavatsalam (1897-1987), Politician A1625

**2008, Dec. 31** ***Perf. 13***
**2303** A1625 5r multi .40 .40

Velu Nachchiyar, Tamil Queen A1626

**2008, Dec. 31** **Litho.**
**2304** A1626 5r multi .40 .40

Louis Braille (1809-52), Educator of the Blind — A1627

**Photo. & Embossed**
**2009, Jan. 4** ***Perf. 13¼x13***
**2305** A1627 5r multi .50 .50

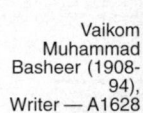

Vaikom Muhammad Basheer (1908-94), Writer — A1628

**2009, Jan. 21** **Litho.** ***Perf. 13***
**2306** A1628 5r multi .25 .25

St. Paul's Church, Madras A1629

**2009, Jan. 25** ***Perf. 13¾ Syncopated***
**2307** A1629 5r multi .25 .25

Preservation of Heritage Monuments — A1630

No. 2308: a, Jaisalmer Fort, Jaisalmer. b, Mongyu Monastery, Laddakh. c, St. Anne Church, Goa. d, Qila Mubarak, Patiala.

**2009, Jan. 28** **Photo.** ***Perf. 13***
**2308** A1630 5r Block of 4, #a-d 1.25 1.25
*e.* Souvenir sheet, #2308a-2308d *2.75 2.75*

Bishnu Prasad Rabha (1909-69), Writer, Singer A1631

***Perf. 13¾ Syncopated***
**2009, Jan. 31** **Litho.**
**2309** A1631 5r multi .25 .25

Steel Authority of India, 50th Anniv. — A1632

**2009, Mar. 3** **Photo.** ***Perf. 13***
**2310** A1632 5r multi .25 .25

Natl. Girl Child Day — A1633

**2009, Feb. 5**
**2311** A1633 5r multi .25 .25

Santaji Jagnade Maharaj (1624-88), Marathi Saint — A1634

***Perf. 13¾ Syncopated***
**2009, Feb. 9** **Litho.**
**2312** A1634 5r multi .25 .25

Mahi Kavi Magh, 8th Cent. Poet — A1635

**2009, Feb. 9** **Photo.** ***Perf. 13***
**2313** A1635 5r multi .25 .25

Postal Life Insurance, 125th Anniv. — A1636

***Perf. 13¾ Syncopated***
**2009, Feb. 11** **Litho.**
**2314** A1636 5r multi .25 .25

Vallabh Suri (1870-1954), Jain Religious Leader — A1637

**2009, Feb. 21**
**2315** A1637 5r multi .25 .25

Harakh Chand Nahata (1936-99), Film Financer A1638

**2009, Feb. 28**
**2316** A1638 5r multi .25 .25

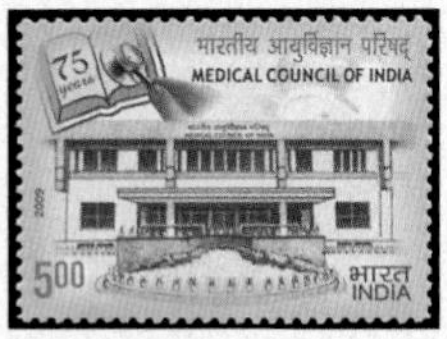


Medical Council of India, 75th Anniv. A1639

**2009, Mar. 1** **Photo.** ***Perf. 13***
**2317** A1639 5r multi .25 .25

Pterospermum Acerifolium Tree and Flower — A1640

**2009, Mar. 6** **Litho.**
**2318** A1640 5r multi .25 .25

Baburao Puleshwar Shedmake, 19th Cent. Freedom Fighter A1641

**2009, Mar. 12**
**2319** A1641 5r multi .25 .25

Dr. Krishna Kumar Birla (1918-2008), Industrialist — A1642

**2009, Mar. 13**
**2320** A1642 5r multi .25 .25

Spices — A1643

No. 2321: a, Black pepper. b, Cinnamon. c, Cardamom d, Cloves. e, Turmeric, coriander and chili peppers.

**2009, Apr. 29** **Photo.**
**2321** Strip of 5 1.60 1.60
*a.-d.* A1643 5r Any single .25 .25
*e.* A1643 20r multi .80 .80
*f.* Souvenir sheet of 5, #2321a-2321e *4.75 4.75*

R. Sankar (1909-72), Politician A1644

*Perf. 13¾ Syncopated*

**2009, Apr. 30** **Litho.**

**2322** A1644 5r multi .25 .25

Lifeline Express Hospital Train — A1645

**2009, May 12** ***Perf. 13***

**2323** A1645 5r multi .25 .25

Madras Regiment, 250th Anniv. — A1646

*Perf. 13¾ Syncopated*

**2009, May 28** **Litho.** **Unwmk.**

**2324** A1646 5r multi .25 .25

Rev. J.J.M. Nichols Roy (1883-1959), Politician — A1647

**2009, June 12** **Photo.** ***Perf. 13***

**2325** A1647 5r multi .25 .25

Sacred Heart Church, Pudducherry, Cent. — A1648

*Perf. 13¾ Syncopated*

**2009, June 19**

**2326** A1648 5r multi .25 .25

Raza Library, Rampur A1649

Ram, Laxman and Jatayu From Valmiki Ramayana, by Sumer Chand — A1650

Madonna Holding Book — A1651

Illustrated Page from Diwan-i-Hafiz of Akbar's Collection A1652

**2009, June 19** **Litho.**

**2327** A1649 5r multi .25 .25
**2328** A1650 5r multi .25 .25
**2329** A1651 5r multi .25 .25
**2330** A1652 5r multi .25 .25
*a.* Souvenir sheet, #2327-2330 *3.00 3.00*
*Nos. 2327-2330 (4)* 1.00 1.00

Indian Oil Corporation, 50th Anniv. — A1653

**2009, June 30** ***Perf. 13***

**2331** A1653 5r multi .25 .25

Lal Bahadur Shastri Natl. Academy of Administration, Mussoorie, 50th Anniv. — A1654

**2009, July 4** **Photo.**

**2332** A1654 5r multi .25 .25

Ramcharan Agarwal (1919-77), Politician A1655

*Perf. 13¾ Syncopated*

**2009, July 25** **Litho.**

**2333** A1655 5r multi .25 .25

A1656

A1657

A1658

A1659

A1660

A1661

A1662

A1663

A1664

A1665

Scenes from Geetagovinda, Poem by Jayadeva — A1666

**2009, July 27** **Photo.** ***Perf. 13***

**2334** Horiz. strip of 11 2.75 2.75
*a.* A1656 5r multi .25 .25
*b.* A1657 5r multi .25 .25
*c.* A1658 5r multi .25 .25
*d.* A1659 5r multi .25 .25
*e.* A1660 5r multi .25 .25
*f.* A1661 5r multi .25 .25
*g.* A1662 5r multi .25 .25
*h.* A1663 5r multi .25 .25
*i.* A1664 5r multi .25 .25
*j.* A1665 5r multi .25 .25
*k.* A1666 5r multi .25 .25
*l.* Souvenir sheet, #2334a-2334k *5.00 5.00*

St. Joseph's College, Bangalore A1667

*Perf. 13¾ Syncopated*

**2009, Aug. 1** **Litho.**

**2335** A1667 5r multi .25 .25

Maharishi Patanjali, Compiler of Yoga Sutras — A1668

**2009, Aug. 4** ***Perf. 13***

**2336** A1668 5r multi .25 .25

Pingali Venkaiah (1876-1963), Designer of Indian Flag — A1669

**2009, Aug. 12** **Photo.** ***Perf. 13¼x13***

**2337** A1669 5r multi .25 .25

Railway Stations — A1670

Designs: No. 2338, 5r, Howrah Station, Calcutta. No. 2339, 5r, Chennai Central Station. No. 2340, 5r, Mumbai CST (Chhatrapati Shivaji Terminus). No. 2341, 5r, Old Delhi Station.

**2009, Aug. 16** **Litho.** ***Perf. 13***

**2338-2341** A1670 Set of 4 1.25 1.25
*2341a* Souvenir sheet, #2338-2341 *3.25 3.25*

Uttam Kumar (1926-80), Actor — A1671

***Perf. 13¾ Syncopated***

**2009, Sept. 3** **Litho.**
**2342** A1671 5r multi .25 .25

Sacred Heart Matriculation Higher Secondary School, Chennai — A1672

**2009, Sept. 9** **Photo.** ***Perf. 13***
**2343** A1672 5r multi .25 .25

Holy Cross Church, Mapranam A1673

***Perf. 13¾ Syncopated***

**2009, Sept. 14** **Litho.**
**2344** A1673 5r multi .25 .25

Dushyant Kumar (1933-75), Writer A1674

**2009, Sept. 27** ***Perf. 13¼x13***
**2345** A1674 5r multi .25 .25

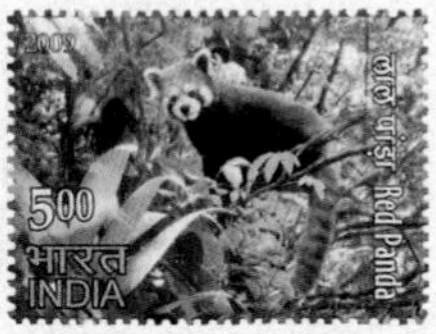


Mammals A1675

Designs: No. 2346, 5r, Red panda. No. 2347, 5r, Marbled cat, vert. No. 2348, 5r, Barbe's leaf monkey, vert.

***Perf. 13¾ Syncopated***

**2009, Oct. 1** **Litho.**
**2346-2348** A1675 Set of 3 1.00 1.00
*2348a* Souvenir sheet, #2346-2348 *2.50 2.50*

Mahatma Gandhi — A1676

**Wmk. 324**

**2009, Oct. 2** **Photo.** ***Perf. 13¼***
**2349** A1676 25r multi 1.10 1.10

Bishop Cotton School, Shimla — A1677

**Unwmk.**

**2009, Oct. 6** **Litho.** ***Perf. 13***
**2350** A1677 5r multi .25 .25

R.K. Narayan (1906-2001), Writer — A1678

***Perf. 13¼***

**2009, Oct. 10** **Litho.** **Unwmk.**
**2351** A1678 5r multi .25 .25

Dineshnandini Dalmia (1928-2007), Writer — A1679

***Perf. 13¾ Syncopated***

**2009, Oct. 11** **Litho.**
**2352** A1679 5r multi .25 .25

India Post Airplane A1680

**2009, Oct. 12** **Litho.** ***Perf. 13¼x13***
**2353** A1680 5r multi .25 .25

Temples — A1681

Designs: No. 2354, 5r, Dilwara Temple. No. 2355, 5r, Ranakpur Temple.

**2009, Oct. 14** ***Perf. 13***
**2354-2355** A1681 Set of 2 .60 .60

Gulab Singh (1792-1857), First Maharaja of Jammu and Kashmir — A1682

***Perf. 13¾ Syncopated***

**2009, Oct. 21** **Litho.**
**2356** A1682 5r multi .25 .25

Major General Dewan Misri Chand (1907-70), Pilot — A1683

**2009, Oct. 22**
**2357** A1683 5r multi .25 .25

Canonization of Jeanne Jugan — A1684

No. 2358: a, 5r, Little Sisters of the Poor Home for the Aged, Bangalore (40x32mm). b, 20r, St. Jeanne Jugan (1792-1879), Founder of Little Sisters of the Poor (29x32mm).

**2009, Oct. 29** ***Perf. 13***
**2358** A1684 Horiz. pair, #a-b 1.10 1.10

Dr. Rajkumar (1929-2006), Actor — A1685

**2009, Nov. 1**
**2359** A1685 5r multi .25 .25

Dr. Mahendra Lal Sircar (1833-1904), Founder of Indian Association for the Cultivation of Science — A1686

**2009, Nov. 2** ***Perf. 13¾***
**2360** A1686 5r multi .25 .25

Apollo Hospitals A1687

**2009, Nov. 2**
**2361** A1687 5r multi .25 .25

Danmal Mathur, Scouting Leader — A1688

**2009, Nov. 7** **Photo.** ***Perf. 13x13¼***
**2362** A1688 5r multi .25 .25

Virchand Raghavji Gandhi (1864-1901), Representative of Jains at 1893 World Parliament of Religions — A1689

**2009, Nov. 8** **Litho.** ***Perf. 13***
**2363** A1689 5r multi .25 .25

Horse Breeds A1690

Designs: No. 2364, 5r, Kathiawari. No. 2365, 5r, Marwari. No. 2366, 5r, Zanskari. No. 2367, 5r, Manipuri.

**2009, Nov. 9** ***Perf. 13¾ Syncopated***
**2364-2367** A1690 Set of 4 .90 .90
*2367a* Souvenir sheet, #2364-2367 *2.50 2.50*

Rajabhau Khobragade (1925-84), Politician — A1691

**2009, Nov. 11**
**2368** A1691 5r multi .25 .25

Gaurishankar Dalmia (1910-88), Magazine Publisher A1692

**2009, Nov. 12** ***Perf. 13¼***
**2369** A1692 5r multi .25 .25

British Commonwealth, 60th Anniv. — A1693

**2009, Nov. 13** ***Perf. 13***
**2370** A1693 5r multi .25 .25

Children's Day A1694

Designs: No. 2371, 5r, Deer at pond. No. 2372, 5r, Tiger.

**2009, Nov. 14** ***Perf. 13¼***
**2371-2372** A1694 Set of 2 .45 .45

Silent Valley National Park — A1695

**2009, Nov. 15** *Perf. 13*
**2373** A1695 5r multi .25 .25
*a.* Souvenir sheet of 1 *1.40 1.40*

Marine Life — A1696

No. 2374: a, 5r, Gangetic dolphin. b, 20r, Butanding.

**2009, Nov. 16**
**2374** A1696 Horiz. pair, #a-b 1.10 1.10
*c.* Souvenir sheet, #2374a-2374b *3.00 3.00*

See Philippines Nos. 3246-3247.

Ganpatrao Govindrao Jadhav (1908-87), Newspaper Publisher A1697

**2009, Nov. 18** *Perf. 13¼*
**2375** A1697 5r multi .25 .25

Tamil Nadu Police, 150th Anniv. — A1698

**2009, Nov. 30** *Perf. 13*
**2376** A1698 5r multi .25 .25

A1699

A1700

A1701

Greetings A1702

**2009, Dec. 1**
**2377** A1699 5r multi .25 .25
**2378** A1700 5r multi .25 .25
**2379** A1701 5r brown .25 .25
**2380** A1702 5r multi .25 .25
*a.* Souvenir sheet, #2377-2380 *2.50 2.50*
*Nos. 2377-2380 (4)* 1.00 1.00

Convent of Jesus and Mary, Ambala Cantonment, Cent. — A1703

**2009, Dec. 2**
**2381** A1703 5r multi .25 .25

Second Lancers (Gardiner's Horse) Regiment A1704

**2009, Dec. 2** *Perf. 13¼*
**2382** A1704 5r multi .25 .25

Traditional Textiles A1705

Designs: No. 2383, 5r, Kalamkari. No. 2384, 5r, Apa Tani weaves. No. 2385, 5r, Kanchipuram silk. No. 2386, 5r, Banaras silk.

**2009, Dec. 10** *Perf. 13*
**2383-2386** A1705 Set of 4 .90 .90
*2386a* Souvenir sheet, #2383-2386 *2.50 2.50*

Henry Louis Vivian Derozio (1809-31), Poet — A1706

**2009, Dec. 15** *Perf. 13x13¼*
**2387** A1706 5r multi .25 .25

Lal Pratap Singh, Prince of Kalakankar A1707

*Perf. 13¾ Syncopated*
**2009, Dec. 17**
**2388** A1707 5r multi .25 .25

Preservation of Polar Regions and Glaciers — A1708

Designs: No. 2389, 5r, Penguins. No. 2390, 5r, Polar bear.

**2009, Dec. 19** *Perf. 13*
**2389-2390** A1708 Set of 2 .45 .45
*2390a* Souvenir sheet, #2389-2390 *1.75 1.75*

Indian Mathematical Society, Cent. — A1709

**2009, Dec. 27** *Perf. 13¼*
**2391** A1709 5r multi .25 .25

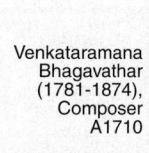

Venkataramana Bhagavathar (1781-1874), Composer A1710

**2009, Dec. 27** *Perf. 13¾*
**2392** A1710 5r multi .25 .25

Maharaja Surajmal (1707-63), Ruler of Bharatpur A1711

*Perf. 13¾ Syncopated*
**2009, Dec. 29**
**2393** A1711 5r multi .25 .25

20th Conference of Speakers and Presiding Officers of the Commonwealth, New Delhi — A1712

**2010, Jan. 5** *Perf. 13¼*
**2394** A1712 5r multi .25 .25

Reserve Bank of India, 75th Anniv. — A1713

**2010, Jan. 16** *Perf. 13*
**2395** A1713 5r multi .40 .40

Election Commission of India, 60th Anniv. — A1714

**2010, Jan. 25** **Litho.**
**2396** A1714 5r multi .25 .25

Bible Society of India, Bicent. — A1715

**2010, Feb. 21** **Photo.** *Perf. 13x13¼*
**2397** A1715 5r multi .25 .25

P. C. Sorcar (1913-71), Magician A1716

**2010, Feb. 23** **Litho.**
**2398** A1716 5r multi .25 .25

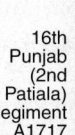

16th Punjab (2nd Patiala) Regiment A1717

**2009, Mar. 19** **Photo.** *Perf. 13¼x13*
**2399** A1717 5r multi .25 .25

Muthuramalinga Sethupathi (1760-1809), King of Ramanathapuram A1718

**2010, Mar. 30** *Perf. 13x13¼*
**2400** A1718 5r multi .25 .25

Special Protection Group — A1719

**2010, Mar. 30** **Litho.** *Perf. 13*
**2401** A1719 5r multi .25 .25

Vallal Pachaiyappa (1754-94), Philantropist — A1720

**2010, Mar. 31 Photo.** ***Perf. 13¼x13***

**2402** A1720 5r multi .25 .25

Signs of the Zodiac A1721

Designs: No. 2403, 5r, Aries. No. 2404, 5r, Taurus. No. 2405, 5r, Gemini. No. 2406, 5r, Cancer, vert. No. 2407, 5r, Leo, vert. No. 2408, 5r, Virgo, vert. No. 2409, 5r, Libra. No. 2410, 5r, Scorpio. No. 2411, 5r, Sagittarius. No. 2412, 5r, Capricorn, vert. No. 2413, 5r, Aquarius, vert. No. 2414, 5r, Pisces, vert.

***Perf. 13¼x13, 13x13¼***

**2010, Apr. 14 Litho.**

**2403-2414** A1721 Set of 12 2.75 2.75

*2414a* Souvenir sheet, #2403-2414, perf. 13 *5.00 5.00*

Chandra Shekhar (1927-2007), Prime Minister — A1722

**2010, Apr. 17 Photo.** ***Perf. 13x13¼***

**2415** A1722 5r multi .25 .25

Kanwar Ram Sahib (1885-1939), Religious Leader — A1723

**2010, Apr. 26 Litho.**

**2416** A1723 5r multi .25 .25

Velu Thampi (1765-1809), Prime Minister of Travancore A1724

**2010, May 6** ***Perf. 13x13¼***

**2417** A1724 5r multi .25 .25

Robert Caldwell (1814-91), Bishop and Linguist — A1725

**2010, May 7 Photo.**

**2418** A1725 5r multi .25 .25

Dr. Guduru Venkata Chalam (1909-67), Agricultural Scientist — A1726

**2010, May 8 Litho.**

**2419** A1726 5r multi .25 .25

Indian Post Offices — A1727

Post offices in: No. 2420, 5r, Lucknow. No. 2421, 5r, Cooch Behar. No. 2422, 5r, Nagpur. No. 2423, 5r, Udagamandalam. No. 2424, 5r, Delhi. No. 2425, 5r, Shimla.

**2010, May 13 Litho.** ***Perf. 13***

**2420-2425** A1727 Set of 6 1.40 1.40

*2425a* Souvenir sheet, #2420-2425 *2.50 2.50*

Indipex 2011 World Philatelic Exhibition, New Delhi.

C. V. Raman Pillai (1858-1922), Writer — A1728

**2010, May 19 Photo.** ***Perf. 13x13¼***

**2426** A1728 5r multi .25 .25

Intl. Year of Biodiversity A1729

Designs: 5r, Owl, sunflower, people in rice paddy. 20r, Birds, crab, water lilies.

***Perf. 13¾ Syncopated***

**2010, June 5 Litho.**

**2427-2428** A1729 Set of 2 1.10 1.10

*2428a* Souvenir sheet, #2427-2428 *3.00 3.00*

Deshbandhu Gupta (1905-51), Politician and Journalist — A1730

**2010, June 14**

**2429** A1730 5r multi .25 .25

2010 Commonwealth Games, Delhi — A1731

Map and: 5r, Tiger mascot holding torch. 20r, Hand holding torch, mascot running with torch.

**2010. June 25 Photo.** ***Perf. 13***

**2430-2431** A1731 Set of 2 1.10 1.10

*2431a* Souvenir sheet, #2430-2431 *3.00 3.00*

Kumaraguruparar Swamigal (1625-88), Poet — A1732

***Perf. 13¾ Syncopated***

**2010, June 27 Litho.**

**2432** A1732 5r multi .25 .25

World Classical Tamil Conference, Kovai — A1733

**2010, June 27 Photo.** ***Perf. 13x13¼***

**2433** A1733 5r multi .25 .25

Indian Naval Air Squadron 300, 50th Anniv. — A1734

***Perf. 13¾ Syncopated***

**2010, July 7 Litho.**

**2434** A1734 5r multi .25 .25

Birds A1735

Designs: No. 2435, 5r, Pigeons. No. 2436, 5r, Sparrows.

**2010, July 9 Litho.** ***Perf. 13***

**2435-2436** A1735 Set of 2 .45 .45

*2436a* Souvenir sheet of 2, #2435-2436 *2.00 2.00*

Rath Yatra Festival, Puri A1736

**2010, July 12 Photo.** ***Perf. 13***

**2437** A1736 5r multi .25 .25

Stadia for 2010 Commonwealth Games, Delhi — A1737

Designs: No. 2438, 5r, Jawaharlal Nehru Stadium. No. 2439, 5r, Talkatora Stadium.

**2010, Aug. 1 Litho.** ***Perf. 13***

**2438-2439** A1737 Set of 2 .45 .45

*2439a* Souvenir sheet, #2438-2439 *2.00 2.00*

Syed Mohammed Ali Shihab Thangal (1936-2009), Politician — A1738

***Perf. 13¾ Syncopated***

**2010, Aug. 2 Litho.**

**2440** A1738 5r multi .25 .25

Vethathiri (1911-2006), Founder of World Community Service Center — A1739

**2010, Aug. 14**

**2441** A1739 5r multi .25 .25

P. Jeevanandham (1907-63), Tamil Communist Leader — A1740

***Perf. 13¾ Syncopated***

**2010, Aug. 21 Litho.**

**2442** A1740 5r multi .25 .25

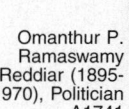

Omanthur P. Ramaswamy Reddiar (1895-1970), Politician A1741

**2010, Aug. 25**
**2443** A1741 5r multi .25 .25

G. K. Moopanar (1931-2001), Politician and Philanthropist A1742

**2010, Aug. 30 Photo. *Perf. 13x13¼***
**2444** A1742 5r multi .25 .25

Dr. Y. S. Rajasekhara Reddy (1949-2009), Politician A1743

**2010, Sept. 2 Litho. *Perf. 13¾x14***
**2445** A1743 5r multi .25 .25

Brihadeeswarar Temple, Thanjavur — A1744

***Perf. 13¾ Syncopated***
**2010, Sept. 26**
**2446** A1744 5r multi .25 .25

Sports of 2010 Commonwealth Games, Delhi — A1745

Designs: No. 2447, 5r, Badminton. No. 2448, 5r, Archery. No. 2449, 5r, Field hockey. No. 2450, 5r, Track.

**2010, Oct. 3 *Perf. 13¾ Syncopated***
**2447-2450** A1745 Set of 4 .90 .90
*2450a* Souvenir sheet, #2447-2450 *3.50 3.50*

Feudatory States Stamps A1746

Designs: No. 2451, 5r, Indore #2, type A6, vignette of #1. No. 2452, 5r, Sirmoor #22, 2, 13. No. 2453, 5r, Bamra type A2, revenue stamp. No. 2454, 5r, Cochin #15, type A4.

**2010, Oct. 6 *Perf. 13¼x13***
**2451-2454** A1746 Set of 4 .90 .90
*2454a* Souvenir sheet, #2451-2454, perf. 13 *3.50 3.50*

Indipex 2011 World Philatelic Exhibition, New Delhi (No. 2454a).

Doon School, Dehradun, 75th Anniv. A1747

**2010, Oct. 22 *Perf. 13¾ Syncopated***
**2455** A1747 5r multi .25 .25

Sant Shadaram Sahib (1708-93), Religious Leader — A1748

**2010, Oct. 25 *Perf. 13x13¼***
**2456** A1748 5r multi .25 .25

Cathedral and John Connon School, Mumbai, 150th Anniv. A1749

**2010, Oct. 27 *Perf. 13¼x13***
**2457** A1749 5r multi .25 .25

Kranti Trivedi (1930-2009), Writer — A1750

**2010, Oct. 29 *Perf. 13x13¼***
**2458** A1750 5r multi .25 .25

K. A. P. Viswanatham (1899-1994), Medical Writer — A1751

**2010, Nov. 10 *Perf. 13¼x13***
**2459** A1751 5r multi .25 .25

Children's Day — A1752

Designs: No. 2460, 5r, Dolls depicting women carrying baskets on heads. No. 2461, 5r, Kite. No. 2462, 5r, Tops. No. 2463, 5r, Dolls depicting women in native costumes (28x38mm).

***Perf. 13¼, 13x13¼ (#2463)***
**2010, Nov. 14**
**2460-2463** A1752 Set of 4 .90 .90
*2463a* Souvenir sheet, #2460-2463, perf. 13 *3.00 3.00*

Lakshmipat Singhania (1910-76), Industrialist A1753

***Perf. 13¾ Syncopated***
**2010, Nov. 15**
**2464** A1753 5r multi .25 .25

Comptroller and Auditor General of India, 150th Anniv. — A1754

**2010, Nov. 16 Photo. *Perf. 13x13¼***
**2465** A1754 5r multi .25 .25

Chidambaram Subramanian (1910-2000), Statesman — A1755

***Perf. 13¾ Syncopated***
**2010, Nov. 28 Litho.**
**2466** A1755 5r multi .25 .25

Kamlapat Singhania (1884-1937), Industrialist A1756

**2010, Dec. 1**
**2467** A1756 5r multi .25 .25

Performing Artists — A1757

Designs: No. 2468, 5r, Thanjavur Balasaraswathi (1918-84), dancer. No. 2469, 5r, T. N. Rajarathinam Pillai (1898-1956), musician. No. 2470, 5r, Veenai Dhanammai (1867-1938), musician, horiz.

**2010, Dec. 3**
**2468-2470** A1757 Set of 3 .70 .70

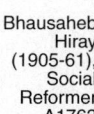

Sri Sri Borda (1911-94), Philosopher A1758

**2010, Dec. 6 Photo. *Perf. 13x13¼***
**2471** A1758 5r multi .25 .25

Prafulla Chandra Chaki (1888-1908), Assassin of British Colonialists A1759

**2010, Dec. 11**
**2472** A1759 5r multi .25 .25

Dances A1760

Designs: 5r, Jarabe Tapatío (Mexican Hat dance), Mexico. 20r, Kalbelia dance, India.

**2010, Dec. 15 Litho. *Perf. 13***
**2473-2474** A1760 Set of 2 1.10 1.10
*2474a* Souvenir sheet of 2, #2473-2474, perf. 13¼ syncopated *3.00 3.00*

See Mexico No. 2726.

Crafts Museum, New Delhi A1761

Designs: No. 2475, 5r, Tiger. No. 2476, 5r, Figurines of two men and dog.

**2010, Dec. 21 Litho. *Perf. 13***
**2475-2476** A1761 Set of 2 .45 .45
*2476a* Souvenir sheet of 2, #2475-2476 *1.75 1.75*

Yashwantrao Balwantrao Chavan (1913-84), Politician A1762

**2010, Dec. 22 Photo. *Perf. 13x13¼***
**2477** A1762 5r multi .25 .25

Bhausaheb Hiray (1905-61), Social Reformer A1763

**2010, Dec. 22 Litho. *Perf. 13¼x13***
**2478** A1763 5r multi .25 .25

Central Bank of India, Cent. A1764

***Perf. 13¾ Syncopated***
**2010, Dec. 23**
**2479** A1764 5r multi .25 .25

Bhai Jeevan Singh (1649-1705), Sikh Warrior — A1765

**2010, Dec. 23** ***Perf. 13x13¼***
**2480** A1765 5r multi .25 .25

A1766

No. 2481: a, National Council of Education Building (39x29mm). b, Dr. Triguna Sen (1905-98), educator.

**2010, Dec. 24** ***Perf. 13¼***
**2481** A1766 5r Horiz. pair, #a-b .45 .45

Immanuel Sekaranar (1924-57), Social Reformer A1767

**2010, Dec. 31** ***Perf. 13¾***
**2482** A1767 5r multi .25 .25

National Academy of Art, New Delhi — A1768

***Perf. 13¼ Syncopated***
**2010, Dec. 31**
**2483** A1768 5r multi .25 .25

Doot Magazine, Cent. A1769

**2011, Jan. 15** ***Perf. 13¼x13***
**2484** A1769 5r multi .25 .25

Krishnadevaraya (d. 1529), Vijayanagara Emperor — A1770

**2011, Jan. 27** ***Perf. 13¼ Syncopated***
**2485** A1770 5r multi .25 .25
*a.* Souvenir sheet of 1 1.40 1.40

Chaudhary Ranbir Singh (1914-2009), Politician — A1771

**2011, Feb. 1** ***Perf. 13¾ Syncopated***
**2486** A1771 5r multi .25 .25

Mary Ward (1585-1645), Nun and Educational Buildings — A1772

**2011, Feb. 2** ***Perf. 13¼ Syncopated***
**2487** A1772 5r multi .25 .25

Loreto Institutions founded by Ward, 400th anniv.

Army Corps of Signals, Cent. A1773

**2011, Feb. 4** ***Perf. 13***
**2488** A1773 5r multi .25 .25

V. Subbiah (1911-93), Communist Leader — A1774

**2011, Feb. 7** ***Perf. 13¾ Syncopated***
**2489** A1774 5r multi .25 .25

2011 Census A1775

**2011, Feb. 8** **Litho.**
**2490** A1775 5r multi .25 .25

V. Venkatasubba Reddiar (d. 1981), Politician — A1776

***Perf. 13¾ Syncopated***
**2011, Feb. 11**
**2491** A1776 5r multi .25 .25

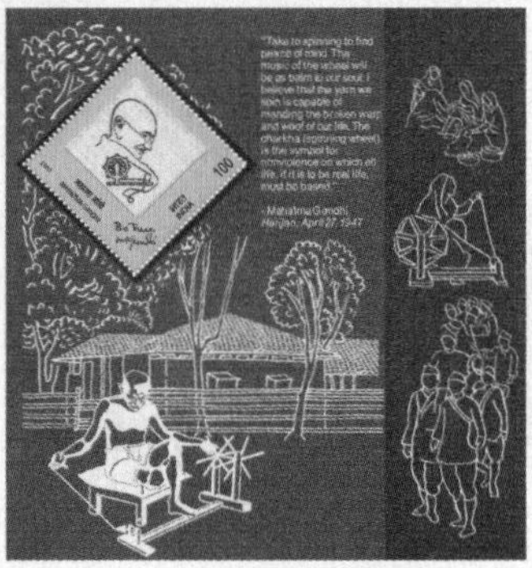

The souvenir sheet above was issued in limited quantities and sold for well above the face value of the stamp.

First Airmail Flight, Cent. A1777

Designs: No. 2492, 5r, Henri Pequet (1888-1974), pilot for first airmail flight, his airplane, newspaper clipping. No. 2493, 5r, Covers and cancels. No. 2494, 5r, Map of first flight, fort, vert. (32x58mm). No. 2495, 5r, Airplane, cancel, boat, vert. (32x58mm).

***Perf. 13¼x13, 13 (#2494-2495)***
**2011, Feb. 12**
**2492-2495** A1777 Set of 4 .90 .90
*2495a* Souvenir sheet of 4, #2492-2495 *2.60 2.60*

Taj Mahal — A1778

Aries — A1779

Taurus — A1780

Gemini — A1781

Cancer — A1782

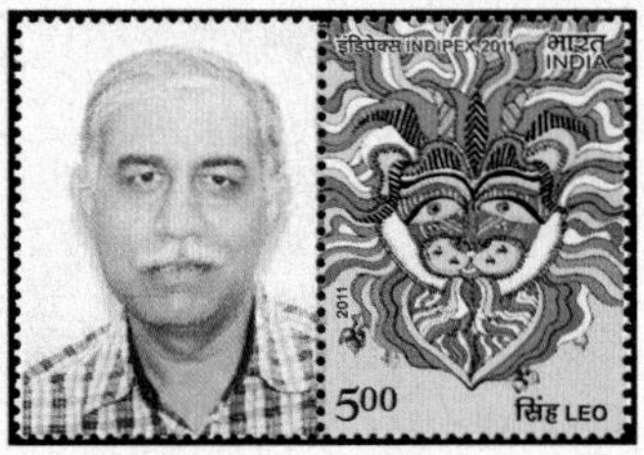

Leo — A1783

Virgo — A1784

Libra — A1785

Scorpio — A1786

Sagittarius — A1787

Capricorn — A1788

Aquarius — A1789

Pisces — A1790

Trains — A1791

Aircraft — A1792

Fables — A1793

Wildlife — A1794

No. 2509: a, 1WP/1, 1963. b, 2 WDM 2, 1963. c, 1 GIP NO 1, 1853. d, 1 F/1, 1895.

No. 2510: a, LCA-Tejas airplane. b, Dhruv helicopter with red paint at top of fuselage. c, Dhruv helicopter with camouflage paint. d, HT-2 airplane.

No. 2511: a, The Lion and the Rabbit. b, The Monkey and the Crocodile. c, The Crows and the Snake. d, The Tortoise and the Geese.

No. 2512: a, Indian lion. b, Indian elephant. c, Tiger. d, Rhinoceros.

**2011, Feb. 12** ***Perf. 13***

**2496** A1778 5r multi + label .55 .55
**2497** A1779 5r multi + label .55 .55
**2498** A1780 5r multi + label .55 .55
**2499** A1781 5r multi + label .55 .55
**2500** A1782 5r multi + label .55 .55
**2501** A1783 5r multi + label .55 .55
**2502** A1784 5r multi + label .55 .55
**2503** A1785 5r multi + label .55 .55
**2504** A1786 5r multi + label .55 .55
**2505** A1787 5r multi + label .55 .55
**2506** A1788 5r multi + label .55 .55
**2507** A1789 5r multi + label .55 .55
**2508** A1790 5r multi + label .55 .55
**2509** A1791 5r Block of 4, #a-d, + 4 labels 2.25 2.25
**2510** A1792 5r Block of 4, #a-d, + 4 labels 2.25 2.25
**2511** A1793 5r Block of 4, #a-d, + 4 labels 2.25 2.25
**2512** A1794 5r Block of 4, #a-d, + 4 labels 2.25 2.25
*Nos. 2496-2512 (17)* 16.15 16.15

Indipex 2011, New Delhi. Nos. 2496-2508 were each printed in sheets of 12 + 12 labels. Nos. 2509-2512 were each printed in sheets containing 3 blocks of 4 + 12 labels. Each sheet sold for 150r and labels could be personalized. Compare types A1779-A1790 with type A1727, type A1791 with type A439, and type A1793 with type A1295.

Film Actresses A1795

Designs: No. 2513, 5r, Devika Rani (1908-94). No. 2514, 5r, Nutan (1936-91). No. 2515, 5r, Kanan Devi (1916-92). No. 2516, 5r, Savithri (1935-81). No. 2517, 5r, Meena Kumari (1932-72). No. 2518, 5r, Leela Naidu (1940-2009).

**2011, Feb. 13** ***Perf. 13¼x13***

**2513-2518** A1795 Set of 6 1.40 1.40
*2518a* Souvenir sheet of 6, #2513-2518 *3.50 3.50*

La Martiniere Schools, 175th Anniv. A1796

**2011, Mar. 1** ***Perf. 13¾ Syncopated***

**2519** A1796 5r multi .25 .25

Subhadra Joshi (1919-2003), Politician — A1797

**2011, Mar. 23** ***Perf. 13¼x13***

**2520** A1797 5r multi .25 .25

Chitralekha Magazine, 61st Anniv. — A1798

**2011, Apr. 20** ***Perf. 13¾ Syncopated***

**2521** A1798 5r multi .25 .25

Umrao Kunwar Ji Archana (1922-2009), Hospital Founder — A1799

**2011, Apr. 30**

**2522** A1799 5r multi .25 .25

Rabindranath Tagore (1861-1941), Poet — A1800

Designs: No. 2523, 5r, Tagore writing. No. 2524, 5r, Tagore, flower.

**2011, May 7** ***Perf. 13***

**2523-2524** A1800 Set of 2 .45 .45
*2524a* Souvenir sheet of 2, #2523-2524 *1.75 1.75*

Second Africa-India Forum Summit, Addis Ababa, Ethiopia — A1801

Designs: 5r, Asian elephants. 25r, African elephants.

**2011, May 25** ***Perf. 13¼x13***

**2525-2526** A1801 Set of 2 1.40 1.40
*2526a* Souvenir sheet of 2, #2525-2526 *3.50 3.50*

Dr. Daulat Singh Kothari (1906-93), Physicist A1802

**2011, July 6** ***Perf. 13¾ Syncopated***

**2527** A1802 5r multi .25 .25

United Theological College, Bangalore, 101st Anniv. — A1803

***Perf. 13¼x13 Syncopated***

**2011, July 8**

**2528** A1803 5r multi .25 .25

Vitthal Sakharam Page (1910-90), Politician A1804

**2011, July 21** ***Perf. 13¼x13***

**2529** A1804 5r multi .25 .25

Kasu Brahmananda Reddy (1909-94), Politician A1805

**2011, July 28** ***Perf. 13¾ Syncopated***

**2530** A1805 5r multi .25 .25

K. M. Mathew (1917-2010), Journalist A1806

**2011, Aug. 1** **Litho.**

**2531** A1806 5r multi .25 .25

Rashtrapati Bhavan (Presidential Palace), New Delhi — A1807

Designs: No. 2532, 5r, Elephant statues. No. 2533, 5r, Flag over central dome. No. 2534, 5r, Latticed stone screen. No. 2535, 5r, Rashtrapati Bhavan, horiz. (87x35mm).

**2011, Aug. 5** ***Perf. 13x13¼***

**2532-2535** A1807 Set of 4 .90 .90
*2535a* Souvenir sheet of 4, #2532-2535, perf. 13 *2.75 2.75*

Pandit K. Santanam (1885-1949), Life Insurance Company Founder — A1808

**2011, Aug. 25** **Photo.** ***Perf. 13¼x13***

**2536** A1808 5r multi .25 .25

Dr. Madhav Srihari Aney (1880-1968), Politician A1809

**2011, Aug. 29** **Litho.** ***Perf. 13x13¼***

**2537** A1809 5r multi .25 .25

Surendranath Jauhar (1903-86), Founder of Youth and National Integration Camps — A1810

**2011, Sept. 2** ***Perf. 13***

**2538** A1810 5r multi .25 .25

Dev Narayan, Rajasthan Folk Deity — A1811

Tejaji Maharaj, Rajasthan Folk Deity — A1812

**2011, Sept. 7** ***Perf. 13¾ Syncopated***

**2539** A1811 5r multi .25 .25
**2540** A1812 5r multi .25 .25

Tripuraneni Gopichand (1910-62), Writer — A1813

**2011, Sept. 8** **Litho.**

**2541** A1813 5r multi .25 .25

Jaimalji Maharaj (1708-96), Religious Leader — A1814

**2011, Sept. 25 Litho.** ***Perf. 13x13¼***

**2542** A1814 5r multi .25 .25

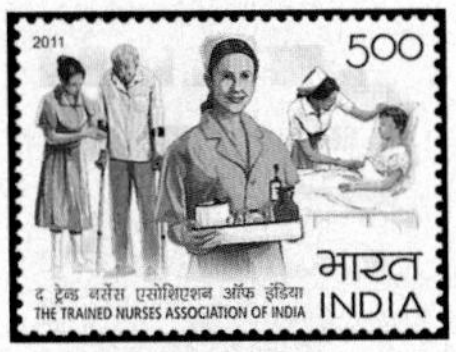


Trained Nurses Association of India, 103rd Anniv. A1815

***Perf. 13¾ Syncopated***

**2011, Sept. 30**

**2543** A1815 5r multi .25 .25

Chitrapur Math (Community Temple) — A1816

**2011, Oct. 9**

**2544** A1816 5r multi .25 .25

Punjab Regiment — A1817

***Perf. 13¼ &13¾ Syncopated x13¼***

**2011, Oct. 12**

**2545** A1817 5r multi .25 .25

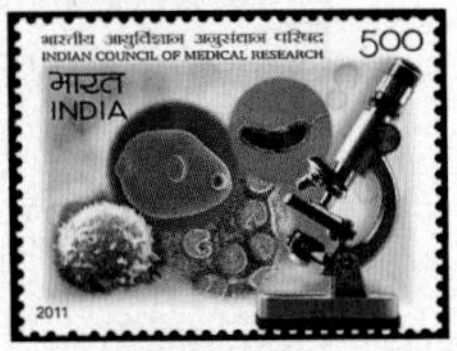


Indian Council of Medical Research, Cent. A1818

**2011, Nov. 8** ***Perf. 13¾ Syncopated***

**2546** A1818 5r multi .25 .25

Children's Day — A1819

Designs: 5r, Tiger. 20r, Tiger, diff.

**2011, Nov. 14 Photo.** ***Perf. 13x13¼***

**2547-2548** A1819 Set of 2 1.00 1.00

*2548a* Souvenir sheet of 2, #2547-2548 *3.25 3.25*

Grand Masonic Lodge of India, New Delhi, 50th Anniv. — A1820

**2011, Nov. 25 Litho.** ***Perf. 13x13¼***

**2549** A1820 5r multi .25 .25

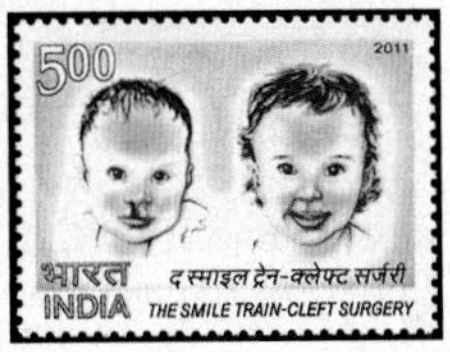


Cleft Palate Surgery of Smile Train Charity A1821

**2011, Dec. 6** ***Perf. 13¼x13***

**2550** A1821 5r multi .25 .25

Kavi Pradeep (1915-98), Songwriter A1822

**2011, Dec. 14 Photo.** ***Perf. 13x13¼***

**2551** A1822 5r multi .25 .25

President's Fleet Review, Mumbai — A1823

Designs: No. 2552, 5r, Submarine. No. 2553, 5r, Warship. No. 2554, 5r, President's yacht. No. 2555, 5r, Airplane.

***Perf. 13¼ & 13¾ Syncopated x13¼***

**2011, Dec. 19 Litho.**

**2552-2555** A1823 Set of 4 .75 .75

Liberation of Goa, 50th Anniv. A1824

**2011, Dec. 19** ***Perf. 13¼x13***

**2556** A1824 5r multi .25 .25

Archaeological Survey of India, 150th Anniv. — A1825

Designs: 5r, Zoomorphic figurines. 20r, Archaeological artifacts.

***Perf. 13¾ Syncopated***

**2011, Dec. 20**

**2557-2558** A1825 Set of 2 .95 .95

*2558a* Souvenir sheet of 2, #2557-2558 *3.25 3.25*

Chhatrapati Shahuji Maharaj Medical University (King George's Medical College), Lucknow, Cent. — A1826

**2011, Dec. 23** ***Perf. 13***

**2559** A1826 5r multi .25 .25

Srinivasa Ramanujan (1887-1920), Mathematician — A1827

***Perf. 13¾ Syncopated***

**2011, Dec. 26**

**2560** A1827 5r multi .25 .25

Mahan Mohan Malaviya (1861-1946), President of Indian National Congress A1828

**2011, Dec. 27** ***Perf. 13x13¼***

**2561** A1828 5r multi .25 .25

Puran Chandra Gupta (1912-86), Newspaper Publisher A1829

**2012, Jan. 2 Photo.** ***Perf. 13¼x13***

**2562** A1829 5r multi .25 .25

Bhai Jagta Ji, 19th Century Sikh Saint — A1830

**2012, Jan. 15** ***Perf. 13x13¼***

**2563** A1830 5r multi .25 .25

Shyam Narayan Singh (1901-68), Politician A1831

**2012, Jan. 24**

**2564** A1831 5r multi .25 .25

Dedication of India International Center, New Delhi, 50th Anniv. — A1832

**2012, Feb. 9 Litho.** ***Perf. 13***

**2565** A1832 5r multi .25 .25

Employees' State Insurance Corporation A1833

***Perf. 13¾ Syncopated***

**2012, Feb. 24**

**2566** A1833 5r multi .25 .25

Vasantdada Patil (1917-89), Politician A1834

**2012, Mar. 1**

**2567** A1834 5r multi .25 .25

Shyama Charan Shukla (1925-2007), Politician A1835

**2012, Mar. 9 Photo.** ***Perf. 13x13¼***

**2568** A1835 5r multi .25 .25

Civil Aviation in India, Cent. A1836

Designs: No. 2569, 5r, Helicopter in flight above terminal, airplane on ground. No. 2570, 5r, Terminal, airplanes on ground and in flight, air traffic controllers. No. 2571, 5r, Control tower, airplanes on ground and in flight, members of runway crew. 20r, Early airplane.

**2012, Mar. 14** ***Perf. 13***

**2569-2572** A1836 Set of 4 1.40 1.40

*2572a* Souvenir sheet of 4, #2569-2572 *4.25 4.25*

Isabella Thoburn College, Lucknow, 125th Anniv. (in 2011) A1837

***Perf. 13¾ Syncopated***

**2012, Apr. 12 Litho.**

**2573** A1837 5r multi .25 .25

Godiji Temple, Mumbai, 200th Anniv. — A1838

**2012, Apr. 17 Photo.** ***Perf. 13x13¼***
**2574** A1838 5r multi .25 .25

Pres. Ramaswamy Venkataraman (1910-2009) A1839

**2012, Apr. 18**
**2575** A1839 5r multi .25 .25

Karpoor Chandra Kulish (1926-2006), Founder of Rajasthan Patrika Newspaper — A1840

***Perf. 13¾ Syncopated***

**2012, May 16 Litho.**
**2576** A1840 5r multi .25 .25

M. B. Kadadi (1909-92), Founder of Sangameshwar College, Solapur — A1841

**2012, May 17**
**2577** A1841 5r multi .25 .25

800th Urs of Moinuddin Chishti, Dargah Sharif, Ajmer A1842

Designs: 5r, Muslims seated. 20r, Dargah.

**2012, May 27**
**2578-2579** A1842 Set of 2 .90 .90
*2579a* Souvenir sheet of 2, #2578-2579 *3.50 3.50*

Warli Painting A1843

Shekhawati Painting — A1844

***Perf. 13¼ Syncopated***

**2012, June 20**
**2580** A1843 5r red brown .25 .25
**2581** A1844 20r multi .75 .75
*a.* Sheet of 16, 8 each #2580-2581 *16.00 16.00*

2012, Summer Olympics, London — A1845

Designs: No. 2582, 5r, Rowing. No. 2583, 5r, Sailboarding. No. 2584, 20r, Volleyball. No. 2585, 20r, Badminton.

**2012, July 25** ***Perf. 13¼x13***
**2582-2585** A1845 Set of 4 1.90 1.90
*2585a* Souvenir sheet of 4, #2582-2585, perf. 13 *5.25 5.25*

Customs Act, 50th Anniv. — A1846

**2012, July 26 Photo.** ***Perf. 13x13¼***
**2586** A1846 5r multi .25 .25

Durga Prasad Chaudhary, Newspaper Publisher — A1847

***Perf. 13¾ Syncopated***

**2012, July 31 Litho.**
**2587** A1847 5r multi .25 .25

Armed Forces Medical College, Pune, 50th Anniv. — A1848

**2012, Aug. 4** ***Perf. 13¼***
**2588** A1848 5r multi .25 .25

Husain Ahmad Madani (1879-1957), Islamic Scholar — A1849

**2012, Aug. 29** ***Perf. 13x13¼***
**2589** A1849 5r multi .25 .25

Motilal Nehru (1861-1931), President of Indian National Congress A1850

**2012, Sept. 25 Photo.**
**2590** A1850 5r multi .25 .25

Indo-Tibetan Border Police Force, 50th Anniv. A1851

**2012, Oct. 1 Litho.** ***Perf. 13¼x13***
**2591** A1851 5r multi .25 .25

AWACS (Airborne Warning and Control System) Airplane A1852

**2012, Oct. 8**
**2592** A1852 5r multi .25 .25

Souvenir Sheet

India Nos. 6c and 200 — A1853

**2012, Oct. 12** ***Perf. 13***
**2593** A1853 20r multi .75 .75

Philately Day.

Fauna — A1854

Designs: No. 2594, 5r, Nicobar megapode. No. 2595, 5r, Hoolock gibbon. No. 2596, 5r, Venated gliding frog. 25r, Bugun liocichla.

**2012, Oct. 16** ***Perf. 13¾***
**2594-2597** A1854 Set of 4 1.50 1.50
*2597a* Souvenir sheet of 4, #2594-2597 *4.75 4.75*

T.S. Narayanawami (1911-68), Industrialist A1858

**2012, Nov. 11 Litho.** ***Perf. 13x13¼***
**2604** A1858 5r multi .25 .25

Children's Day A1859

***Perf. 13¾ Syncopated***

**2012, Nov. 14**
**2605** A1859 5r multi .25 .25

Scinde Horse Cavalry Regiment A1860

**2012, Nov. 16** ***Perf. 13¼x13***
**2606** A1860 5r multi .25 .25

Ramgopal Maheshwari (1911-99), Newspaper Publisher A1861

**2012, Nov. 20** ***Perf. 13¼***
**2607** A1861 5r multi .25 .25

Consumer Protection Act of 1986 A1862

***Perf. 13¾ Syncopated***

**2012, Nov. 29**
**2608** A1862 5r multi .25 .25

---

## AIR POST STAMPS

De Havilland Hercules over Lake AP1

**Wmk. 196 Sideways**

**1929-30 Typo.** ***Perf. 14***

| | | | | |
|---|---|---|---|---|
| **C1** | AP1 | 2a dull green | 1.00 | .50 |
| **C2** | AP1 | 3a deep blue | 1.40 | .90 |
| **C3** | AP1 | 4a gray olive | 4.00 | 1.90 |
| *a.* | | 4a olive green ('30) | 5.00 | 1.90 |
| **C4** | AP1 | 6a bister | 5.00 | 1.10 |
| **C5** | AP1 | 8a red violet | 5.75 | 5.75 |
| **C6** | AP1 | 12a brown red | 17.50 | 17.50 |
| | | *Nos. C1-C6 (6)* | 34.65 | 27.65 |

**Catalogue values for unused stamps in this section, from this point to the end of the section, are for Never Hinged items.**

**Dominion of India**

Lockheed Constellation — AP2

***Perf. 13½x14***

**1948, May 29 Litho. Wmk. 196**
**C7** AP2 12a ultra & slate blk 3.25 3.25

Bombay-London flight of June 8, 1948.

### Republic of India

The Spirit of '76, by Archibald M. Willard — AP3

**1976, May 29** ***Perf. 13x13½***

| | | | | |
|---|---|---|---|---|
| **C8** | AP3 | 2.80r multicolored | 2.00 | 2.00 |

American Bicentennial.

INDIA '80 Emblem, De Havilland Puss Moth AP4

**1979, Oct. 15 Photo.** ***Perf. 14½x14***

| | | | | |
|---|---|---|---|---|
| **C9** | AP4 | 30p shown | .60 | .30 |
| **C10** | AP4 | 50p Chetak helicopter | .75 | .50 |
| **C11** | AP4 | 1r Boeing 737 | .95 | .90 |
| **C12** | AP4 | 2r Boeing 747 | 1.25 | 1.10 |
| | | *Nos. C9-C12 (4)* | 3.55 | 2.80 |

INDIA '80 Intl. Stamp Exhib., New Delhi, Jan. 25-Feb. 3, 1980.

## MILITARY STAMPS

### China Expeditionary Force

Regular Issues of India, 1882-99, Overprinted

**1900 Wmk. 39** ***Perf. 14***

| | | | | |
|---|---|---|---|---|
| **M1** | A31 | 3p carmine rose | .70 | *2.10* |
| **M2** | A17 | ½a dark green | 1.25 | .45 |
| **M3** | A19 | 1a maroon | 7.00 | 2.50 |
| **M4** | A21 | 2a ultra | 5.25 | *15.00* |
| **M5** | A28 | 2a6p green | 4.75 | *21.00* |
| **M6** | A22 | 3a orange | 4.75 | *27.50* |
| **M7** | A23 | 4a olive green | 4.75 | *13.00* |
| **M8** | A25 | 8a red violet | 4.75 | *30.00* |
| **M9** | A26 | 12a violet, *red* | 30.00 | *30.00* |
| **M10** | A29 | 1r car rose & grn | 37.50 | *37.50* |
| *a.* | | Double overprint | | |
| | | *Nos. M1-M10 (10)* | 100.70 | *179.05* |

The 1a6p of this set was overprinted, but not issued. Value $250.

Overprinted on 1900 Issue of India

**1904, Feb. 27**

| | | | | |
|---|---|---|---|---|
| **M11** | A19 | 1a carmine rose | 55.00 | 15.00 |

Overprinted on 1902-09 Issue of India

**1904**

| | | | | |
|---|---|---|---|---|
| **M12** | A32 | 3p gray | 8.00 | *10.00* |
| **M13** | A34 | 1a carmine rose | 12.00 | 1.10 |
| **M14** | A35 | 2a violet | 22.50 | 3.75 |
| **M15** | A36 | 2a6p ultra | 5.25 | *8.00* |
| **M16** | A37 | 3a brown org | 5.75 | *6.50* |
| **M17** | A38 | 4a olive green | 13.50 | *19.00* |
| **M18** | A40 | 8a red violet | 13.00 | *12.00* |
| **M19** | A41 | 12a violet, *red* | 18.00 | *30.00* |
| **M20** | A42 | 1r car rose & grn | 20.00 | *45.00* |
| | | *Nos. M12-M20 (9)* | 118.00 | *135.35* |

Overprinted on 1906 Issue of India

**1909**

| | | | | |
|---|---|---|---|---|
| **M21** | A44 | ½a green | 1.50 | 1.00 |
| **M22** | A45 | 1a carmine rose | 1.50 | .40 |

Overprinted on 1911-19 Issues of India

**1913-21**

| | | | | |
|---|---|---|---|---|
| **M23** | A46 | 3p gray | 8.00 | *35.00* |
| **M24** | A47 | ½a green | 6.25 | *7.50* |
| **M25** | A48 | 1a carmine rose | 7.25 | 4.75 |
| **M26** | A58 | 1½a chocolate | 40.00 | *95.00* |
| **M27** | A49 | 2a violet | 27.50 | *80.00* |
| **M28** | A57 | 2a6p ultra | 20.00 | *30.00* |
| **M29** | A51 | 3a brown org | 40.00 | *240.00* |
| **M30** | A52 | 4a olive green | 37.50 | *210.00* |
| **M31** | A54 | 8a red violet | 40.00 | *400.00* |
| **M32** | A55 | 12a claret | 37.50 | *140.00* |
| **M33** | A56 | 1r grn & red brn | 110.00 | *375.00* |
| | | *Nos. M23-M33 (11)* | 374.00 | *1,617.* |

Issue dates: No. M23, 1913; others, 1921.

### Indian Expeditionary Force

Regular Issues of India, 1911-13, Overprinted

**1914 Wmk. 39** ***Perf. 14***

| | | | | |
|---|---|---|---|---|
| **M34** | A46 | 3p gray | .30 | .55 |
| *a.* | | Double overprint | 70.00 | 55.00 |
| **M35** | A47 | ½a green | .80 | .55 |
| *a.* | | Double overprint | 175.00 | *300.00* |
| **M36** | A48 | 1a carmine rose | 2.10 | .55 |
| **M37** | A49 | 2a violet | 2.10 | .55 |
| **M38** | A57 | 2a6p ultra | 2.50 | 4.00 |
| **M39** | A51 | 3a brown org | 1.75 | 2.75 |
| **M40** | A52 | 4a olive green | 1.75 | 2.75 |
| **M41** | A54 | 8a red violet | 2.10 | 4.25 |
| **M42** | A55 | 12a claret | 3.75 | 10.50 |
| **M43** | A56 | 1r grn & red brn | 4.50 | 7.25 |
| | | *Nos. M34-M43 (10)* | 21.65 | 33.70 |

**Catalogue values for unused stamps in this section, from this point to the end of the section, are for Never Hinged items.**

### Korea Custodial Unit

Regular Issues of India Overprinted in Black

***Perf. 13½x14, 14x13½***

**1953** **Wmk. 196**

| | | | | |
|---|---|---|---|---|
| **M44** | A91 | 3p gray violet | .35 | *5.50* |
| **M45** | A92 | 6p red brown | .35 | *5.50* |
| **M46** | A91 | 9p green | .35 | *4.50* |
| **M47** | A101 | 1a turquoise | .50 | *4.50* |
| **M48** | A93 | 2a carmine | .80 | *4.50* |
| **M49** | A94 | 2½a brown lake | 1.50 | *4.75* |
| **M50** | A94 | 3a red orange | 1.75 | *5.50* |
| **M51** | A94 | 4a ultra | 2.10 | *4.75* |
| **M52** | A95 | 6a purple | 8.00 | *9.00* |
| **M53** | A95 | 8a blue green | 5.75 | *11.00* |
| **M54** | A95 | 12a blue | 7.75 | *17.00* |
| **M55** | A96 | 1r dk grn & pur | 12.50 | *17.00* |
| | | *Nos. M44-M55 (12)* | 41.70 | *93.50* |

Hindi overprint reads "Indian Custodial Unit, Korea."

### Indian UN Force in Congo

Nos. 302-303, 305, 307, 282 and 313 Overprinted: "U.N. FORCE (INDIA) CONGO"

**Wmk. 324, 196 (13np)**

**1962, Jan. 15 Photo.** ***Perf. 14x14½***

| | | | | |
|---|---|---|---|---|
| **M56** | A117 | 1np blue green | .90 | .90 |
| **M57** | A117 | 2np light brown | .90 | .90 |
| **M58** | A117 | 5np emerald | .90 | .90 |
| **M59** | A117 | 8np bright green | .90 | .90 |
| **M60** | A117 | 13np brt carmine | 1.50 | 1.50 |
| **M61** | A117 | 50np orange | 2.75 | 2.75 |
| | | *Nos. M56-M61 (6)* | 7.85 | 7.85 |

### Indian UN Force in Gaza

No. 393 Overprinted in Carmine

**1965, Jan. 15 Unwmk.** ***Perf. 13½***

| | | | | |
|---|---|---|---|---|
| **M62** | A190 | 15p blue gray | 4.00 | *8.00* |

Overprint letters stand for "United Nations Emergency Force."

### INTERNATIONAL COMMISSION IN INDO-CHINA

**Catalogue values for all unused stamps in this section are for Never Hinged items.**

### Cambodia

India Nos. 207, 231, 211, 216 and 217 Overprinted in Black

***Perf. 13½x14***

**1954, Dec. 1** **Wmk. 196**

| | | | | |
|---|---|---|---|---|
| **1** | A91 | 3p gray violet | .50 | .50 |
| **2** | A101 | 1a turquoise | .60 | .60 |
| **3** | A93 | 2a carmine | 1.00 | *1.00* |
| **4** | A95 | 8a blue green | 4.00 | *4.25* |
| **5** | A95 | 12a blue | 5.50 | *6.25* |
| | | *Nos. 1-5 (5)* | 11.60 | *12.60* |

The overprint reads "International Commission Cambodia." Top line is 18mm on Nos. 4-5; 15½mm on Nos. 1-3, 6-12.

Same Overprint on India Nos. 276, 279, 282, 286 and 287

**1957, Apr. 1** ***Perf. 14x14½***

| | | | | |
|---|---|---|---|---|
| **6** | A117 | 2np light brown | .40 | .40 |
| **7** | A117 | 6np gray | .40 | .40 |
| **8** | A117 | 13np bright carmine | 1.00 | .70 |
| **9** | A117 | 50np orange | 4.75 | 2.50 |
| **10** | A117 | 75np plum | 5.25 | 4.75 |
| | | *Nos. 6-10 (5)* | 11.80 | 8.75 |

Same Overprint on India No. 303

**1962** **Wmk. 324**

| | | | | |
|---|---|---|---|---|
| **12** | A117 | 2np light brown | .65 | .65 |

### Laos

India Nos. 207, 231, 211, 216 and 217 Overprinted in Black

***Perf. 13½x14***

**1954, Dec. 1** **Wmk. 196**

| | | | | |
|---|---|---|---|---|
| **1** | A91 | 3p gray violet | .50 | .50 |
| **2** | A101 | 1a turquoise | .60 | .60 |
| **3** | A93 | 2a carmine | 1.00 | 1.00 |
| **4** | A95 | 8a blue green | 4.00 | *4.25* |
| **5** | A95 | 12a blue | 5.50 | *6.25* |
| | | *Nos. 1-5 (5)* | 11.60 | *12.60* |

The overprint reads "International Commission Laos." Top line is 18mm on Nos. 4-5; 15½mm on Nos. 1-3, 6-16.

Same Overprint on India Nos. 276, 279, 282, 286 and 287

**1957, Apr. 1** ***Perf. 14x14½***

| | | | | |
|---|---|---|---|---|
| **6** | A117 | 2np light brown | .40 | .40 |
| **7** | A117 | 6np gray | .40 | .40 |
| **8** | A117 | 13np brt carmine | 1.00 | .70 |
| **9** | A117 | 50np orange | 4.75 | 2.50 |
| **10** | A117 | 75np plum | 5.25 | 4.75 |
| | | *Nos. 6-10 (5)* | 11.80 | 8.75 |

Same Overprint on India Nos. 303-305, 313-314

**1962-65** **Wmk. 324**

| | | | | |
|---|---|---|---|---|
| **12** | A117 | 2np light brown | 2.50 | *3.00* |
| **13** | A117 | 3np brown ('63) | .60 | .60 |
| **14** | A117 | 5np emerald ('63) | .60 | .60 |
| **15** | A117 | 50np orange ('65) | 2.00 | *2.25* |
| **16** | A117 | 75np plum ('65) | 4.25 | *4.75* |
| | | *Nos. 12-16 (5)* | 9.95 | *11.20* |

### Laos and Viet Nam

No. 393 Overprinted in Carmine

**1965, Jan. 15 Unwmk.** ***Perf. 13½***

| | | | | |
|---|---|---|---|---|
| **1** | A190 | 15p blue gray | 4.00 | 4.00 |

Overprint letters stand for "International Control Commission."

Nos. 406-408, 411-412, 417 and 419-420 Overprinted in Carmine

***Perf. 14½x14, 14x14½***

**1968, Oct. 2 Photo.** **Wmk. 324**

| | | | | |
|---|---|---|---|---|
| **2** | A202 | 2p reddish brown | .50 | .50 |
| **3** | A202 | 3p olive bister | .50 | .50 |
| **4** | A202 | 5p cerise | .50 | .50 |
| **5** | A203 | 10p bright blue | 2.50 | 2.50 |
| **6** | A203 | 15p green | 1.00 | 1.00 |
| **7** | A202 | 60p dark gray | 1.10 | 1.10 |
| **8** | A204 | 1r dp cl & red brn | 1.75 | *2.25* |
| **9** | A205 | 2r violet & brt blue | 4.00 | *5.50* |
| | | *Nos. 2-9 (8)* | 11.85 | *13.85* |

The arrangement of the lines of the overprint varies on each denomination.

### Viet Nam

India Nos. 207, 231, 211, 216 and 217 Overprinted in Black

***Perf. 13½x14***

**1954, Dec. 1** **Wmk. 196**

| | | | | |
|---|---|---|---|---|
| **1** | A91 | 3p gray violet | .50 | .50 |
| **2** | A101 | 1a turquoise | .60 | .60 |
| **3** | A93 | 2a carmine | 1.00 | 1.00 |
| **4** | A95 | 8a blue green | 4.00 | *4.25* |
| **5** | A95 | 12a blue | 5.50 | *6.25* |
| | | *Nos. 1-5 (5)* | 11.60 | *12.60* |

The overprint reads "International Commission Viet Nam." Top line of overprint is 18mm on Nos. 4-5; 15½mm on Nos. 1-3, 6-16.

Same Overprint on India Nos. 276, 279, 282, 286 and 287

**1957, Apr. 1** ***Perf. 14x14½***

| | | | | |
|---|---|---|---|---|
| **6** | A117 | 2np light brown | .40 | .40 |
| **7** | A117 | 6np gray | .40 | .40 |
| **8** | A117 | 13np bright carmine | 1.00 | .70 |
| **9** | A117 | 50np orange | 4.75 | 2.10 |
| **10** | A117 | 75np plum | 5.25 | 4.75 |
| | | *Nos. 6-10 (5)* | 11.80 | 8.35 |

Same Overprint on India Nos. 302-305, 313-314

**1961-65** **Wmk. 324**

| | | | | |
|---|---|---|---|---|
| **11** | A117 | 1np blue green | 1.40 | *1.40* |
| **12** | A117 | 2np light brown ('62) | 2.75 | 2.75 |
| **13** | A117 | 3np brown ('63) | 1.00 | 1.00 |
| **14** | A117 | 5np emerald ('63) | .65 | .80 |
| **15** | A117 | 50np orange ('65) | 2.25 | *2.75* |
| **16** | A117 | 75np plum ('65) | 4.25 | *4.75* |
| | | *Nos. 11-16 (6)* | 12.30 | *13.45* |

## OFFICIAL STAMPS

Nos. O1-O26 are normally found with very heavy cancellations, and values are for stamps so canceled. Lightly canceled stamps are seldom seen.

Nos. 11-12, 18, 20-22, 23a, 24, 26 Overprinted in Black

**1866, Aug. 1 Unwmk. *Perf. 14***

**O1** A7 ½a blue 1,100. 140.00
*a.* Inverted overprint
**O3** A7 1a brown 140.00
**O4** A7 8a rose 22.50 50.00

The 8p lilac unwatermarked (No. 19) with "Service" overprint was not officially issued.

**Wmk. 38**

**O5** A7 ½a blue 300.00 12.50
*a.* Inverted overprint
*b.* Without period 210.00
**O6** A8 8p lilac 20.00 *52.50*
**O7** A7 1a brown 300.00 15.00
*a.* Inverted overprint
**O8** A7 2a yellow 300.00 85.00
*a.* Imperf.
*b.* Inverted overprint
**O9** A7 4a green 200.00 80.00
*a.* Inverted overprint
**O10** A9 4a green (I) 1,000. 250.00

*Reprints were made of #O5, O7, O10 (type II).*

**Revenue Stamps Surcharged or Overprinted**

Queen Victoria — O1

**Blue Glazed Paper**
**Black Surcharge**

**1866 Wmk. 36 *Perf. 14 Vertically***

**O11** O1 2a violet 350.00 250.00

The note after No. 30 will apply here also.
No. O11 is often found with cracked surface or scuffs. Such examples sell for somewhat less.
*Reprints of No. O11 are surcharged in either black or green, and have the word "SERVICE" 16½x2½mm, instead of 16½x2¾mm and "TWO ANNAS" 18x3mm, instead of 20x3¼mm.*

O2

O3

O4

**1866 Green Overprint**

**O12** O2 2a violet 1,000. 325.
**O13** O3 4a violet *4,500. 1,250.*
**O14** O4 8a violet *5,000. 5,000.*

The note after No. 30 will apply here also.
These stamps are often found with cracked surface or scuffs. Such examples sell for somewhat less.
*Reprints of No. O12 have the overprint in sans-serif letters 2¼mm high, instead of Roman letters 2½mm high. On the reprints of No. O13 "SERVICE" measures 16½x2¼mm, instead of 20¼x3mm and "POSTAGE" 18x2¼mm, instead of 22x3mm.*
*On No. O14 "SERVICE" is 20½mm long, instead of 20mm and "POSTAGE" is 23mm long, instead of 22mm. All three overprints are in a darker green than on the original stamps.*

O5

**Green Overprint**

**1866 Wmk. 40 *Perf. 15½x15***
**Lilac Paper**

**O15** O5 ½a violet 425.00 85.00
*a.* Double overprint 3,000.

Nos. 20, 31, 22-23, 23a, 26, 28 Overprinted in Black

**1866-73 Wmk. 38 *Perf. 14***

**O16** A7 ½a blue 30.00 .35
**O17** A7 ½a bl, re-engraved 140.00 67.50
*a.* Double overprint
**O18** A7 1a brown 32.50 .40
**O19** A7 2a orange 4.50 2.00
*a.* 2a yellow 20.00 2.25
**O20** A9 4a green (I) 2.75 1.50
**O21** A11 8a rose 3.00 1.50
*Nos. O16-O21 (6)* 212.75 73.25

The 6a8p with this overprint was not issued. Value $25.

Nos. 31, 22-23, 26, 28 Overprinted in Black

**1874-82**

**O22** A7 ½a blue, re-engraved 8.00 .25
*a.* Blue overprint 350.00 45.00
**O23** A7 1a brown 12.50 .25
*a.* Blue overprint 550.00 120.00
**O24** A7 2a orange 40.00 17.50
**O25** A9 4a green (I) 12.50 2.75
**O26** A11 8a rose 4.25 4.00
*Nos. O22-O26 (5)* 77.25 24.75

**Same Overprint on Nos. 36, 38, 40, 42, 44, 49**

**1883-97 Wmk. 39**

**O27** A17 ½a green .40 .25
*a.* Pair, one without overprint
*b.* Double overprint 1,150.
**O28** A19 1a maroon .75 .25
*a.* Inverted overprint 350.00 475.00
*b.* Double overprint 1,150.
*c.* 1a violet brown 2.25 .35
**O29** A21 2a ultramarine 4.50 .50
**O30** A23 4a olive green 15.00 .40
**O31** A25 8a red violet 7.00 .40
**O32** A29 1r car rose & grn 11.00 .40
*Nos. O27-O32 (6)* 38.65 2.20

**Same Overprint on No. 54**

**1899**

**O33** A31 3p carmine rose .25 .25

**Same Overprint on Nos. 56-58**

**1900**

**O34** A17 ½a light green 1.25 .30
**O35** A19 1a carmine rose 2.50 .25
*a.* Double overprint 1,350.
*b.* Inverted overprint 1,400.
**O36** A21 2a violet 27.50 .50
*Nos. O34-O36 (3)* 31.25 1.05

**Same Overprint on Nos. 60-63, 66-68, 70**

**1902-09**

**O37** A32 3p gray .85 .25
**O38** A33 ½a green 1.00 .25
**O39** A34 1a carmine rose .85 .25
**O40** A35 2a violet *2.50* .25
**O41** A38 4a olive green *4.25* .25
**O42** A39 6a bister *2.25* .25
**O43** A40 8a red lilac *5.25* .50
**O44** A42 1r car rose & green ('05) *4.50* .25
*Nos. O37-O44 (8)* *21.45* 2.25

**Same Overprint on Nos. 78-79**

**1906-07**

**O45** A44 ½a green 1.00 .25
**O46** A45 1a carmine rose 1.75 .25
*a.* Pair, one without overprint
*b.* Overprint on back —

**Same Overprint on Nos. 71, 73-76**

**1909**

**O47** A43 2r brown & rose *6.50* .90
**O48** A43 5r violet & ultra *11.00* 1.00
**O49** A43 10r car rose & grn *21.00* 8.50
*a.* 10r red & green 52.50 6.00
**O50** A43 15r ol gray & ultra 52.50 30.00
**O51** A43 25r ultra & org brn 130.00 50.00
*Nos. O47-O51 (5)* 221.00 90.40

For surcharges see Nos. O67-O69.

Nos. 80-84, 88, 90-91 Overprinted in Black

**1912-22**

**O52** A46 3p gray .25 .25
**O53** A47 ½a green .25 .25
*a.* Double overprint 110.00
**O54** A48 1a carmine rose .75 .25
*a.* Double overprint 950.00
**O55** A48 1a dark brown ('22) 1.00 .25
*a.* Imperf., pair 75.00
**O56** A49 2a violet .50 .25
**O57** A52 4a olive green .75 .25
**O58** A53 6a bister 1.25 *1.75*
**O59** A54 8a red violet 1.75 .75

Nos. 93-98 Overprinted in Black

**O60** A56 1r green & red brn 2.00 .80
**O61** A56 2r yel brn & car rose 2.50 *3.50*
**O62** A56 5r violet & ultra 10.50 *13.50*
**O63** A56 10r car rose & grn 35.00 32.50
**O64** A56 15r ol grn & ultra 80.00 *95.00*
**O65** A56 25r ultra & brn org 180.00 150.00
*Nos. O52-O65 (14)* 316.50 299.30

For surcharge see No. O69b.

O6

**1921 Black Surcharge**

**O66** O6 9p on 1a rose .75 .60

For overprint see Gwalior No. O28.

Nos. O49-O51 Surcharged

**1925**

**O67** A43 1r on 15r ol gray & ultra 4.00 3.00
**O68** A43 1r on 25r ultra & org brn 20.00 *60.00*
**O69** A43 2r on 10r red & grn 3.50 3.50
*a.* 2r on 10r car rose & green 210.00 55.00
*b.* Surcharge on #O63 (error) 800.00

Nos. O64-O65 Surcharged

**O70** A56 1r on 15r ol grn & ultra 19.00 *65.00*
*a.* Inverted surcharge
**O71** A56 1r on 25r ultra & brn org 5.00 *9.00*
*a.* Inverted surcharge 600.00
*Nos. O67-O71 (5)* 51.50 *140.50*

O7

**1926 Black Surcharge**

**O73** O7 1a on 6a bister .40 .40

Nos. 83, 101, 102, 99 Surcharged

**O74** A48 1a on 1a dk brn (error) 180.00 180.00
**O75** A58 1a on 1½a choc .25 .25
**O76** A59 1a on 1½a choc 1.75 *4.00*
*b.* Double surcharge 30.00
**O77** A57 1a on 2a6p ultra .50 .50
*Nos. O73-O77 (5)* 182.90 185.15

Nos. O74, O75 and O76 have short bars over the numerals in the upper corners.

Nos. 106-108, 111, 126-127, 112, 116, 128, 118-119 Overprinted — a

**1926-35 Wmk. 196**

**O78** A46 3p slate ('29) .25 .25
**O79** A47 ½a green ('31) 5.00 .40
**O80** A48 1a dark brown .25 .25
*a.* Overprint as on No. O55 100.00 4.75
**O81** A49 2a vermilion ('35) 1.00 1.00
*a.* Small die .85 .25
**O82** A60 2a dull violet .25 .25
**O83** A60 2a vermilion ('32) .90 2.00
**O84** A57 2a6p buff ('32) .25 .25
**O85** A52 4a olive green ('35) 1.00 .25
**O86** A61 4a olive green .35 .25
**O87** A53 6a bister('35) 18.00 9.00
**O88** A54 8a red violet .50 .25
**O89** A55 12a claret .50 *1.75*

Nos. 120-121, 123 Overprinted

**O90** A56 1r green & brn ('30) 2.25 .90
**O91** A56 2r brn org & car rose ('30) 6.00 6.00
**O92** A56 10r car & green ('31) 70.00 50.00
*Nos. O78-O92 (15)* 106.50 72.80

**#138, 135, 139, 136 Overprinted Type "a"**

**1932-35**

**O93** A71 ½a green ('35) .60 .25
**O94** A68 9p dark green .25 .25
**O95** A72 1a dark brown ('35) 1.90 .25
**O96** A69 1a3p violet .25 .25
*Nos. O93-O96 (4)* 3.00 1.00

**Nos. 151-153, 162-165 Overprinted Type "a"**

**1937-39 *Perf. 13½x14***

**O97** A80 ½a brown ('38) 22.50 .45
**O98** A80 9p green 25.00 .60
**O99** A80 1a carmine 4.75 .35

### Type "b" Overprint

**O100** A82 1r brown & slate ('38) .70 .55
**O101** A82 2r dk brown & dk vio ('38) 1.90 *3.25*
**O102** A82 5r dp ultra & dk green ('38) 3.25 *7.50*
**O103** A82 10r rose car & dark violet ('39) 19.00 6.75
*Nos. O97-O103 (7)* 77.10 19.45

No. 136 Surcharged in Black

**1939, May Wmk. 196 *Perf. 14***
**O104** A69 1a on 1a3p violet *17.00* 3.00

King George VI — O8

**1939-43 Typo. *Perf. 13½x14***
**O105** O8 3p slate .40 .40
**O106** O8 ½a brown 8.00 .40
**O106A** O8 ½a dk rose vio ('43) .40 .40
**O107** O8 9p green .40 .40
**O108** O8 1a car rose .40 .40
**O108A** O8 1a3p bister ('41) *7.00* *1.25*
**O108B** O8 1½a dull pur ('43) .40 .40
**O109** O8 2a scarlet .40 .40
**O110** O8 2½a purple .40 .40
**O111** O8 4a dark brown .40 .40
**O112** O8 8a blue violet .60 .40
*Nos. O105-O112 (11)* *18.80* *5.25*

For overprints see Gwalior Nos. O52-O61. Stamps overprinted "Postal Service" or "I. P. N." were not used as postage stamps.

**Catalogue values for unused stamps in this section, from this point to the end of the section, are for Never Hinged items.**

Nos. 203-206 (Gandhi Issue) Overprinted Type "a"

***Perf. 11½***
**1948, Aug. Unwmk. Photo.**
**O112A** A90 1½a brown *65.00* *45.00*
**O112B** A90 3½a violet *1,300.* *750.00*
**O112C** A90 12a dk gray green *4,000.* *2,500.*
**O112D** A90 10r rose brn & brown *25,000.*

Overprint forgeries exist.

Capital of Asoka Pillar
O9 O10

***Perf. 13½x14***
**1950 Wmk. 196 Typo.**
**O113** O9 3p violet blue .40 .40
**O114** O9 6p chocolate .40 .40
**O115** O9 9p green .65 .40
**O116** O9 1a turquoise .95 .40
**O117** O9 2a red .40 .40
**O118** O9 3a vermilion 4.75 2.75
**O119** O9 4a brown car 7.00 .40
**O120** O9 6a purple 5.75 .40
**O121** O9 8a orange brn 2.75 .40

**Litho.**
***Perf. 14x13½***
**O122** O10 1r dark purple 3.75 .40
**O123** O10 2r brown red 1.50 .40
**O124** O10 5r dark green 2.75 2.25
**O125** O10 10r red brown 8.50 *22.50*
*Nos. O113-O125 (13)* 39.55 *31.50*

Issue dates: 1r-10r, Jan. 2, others, July 1.

**1951, Oct. 1 Typo.**
**O126** O9 4a violet blue .25 .25

### Type of 1950 Redrawn, Denomination in Naye Paise

**Typo. or Litho.**
**1957-58 *Perf. 13½x14***
**O127** O9 1np slate blue .55 .55
**O128** O9 2np blue violet .55 .55
**O129** O9 3np chocolate .55 .55
**O130** O9 5np yellow green .55 .55
**O131** O9 6np turquoise .55 .55
**O132** O9 13np red .55 .55
**O133** O9 15np dk purple ('58) .55 .55
**O134** O9 20np vermilion .55 .55
**O135** O9 25np violet blue .55 .55
**O136** O9 50np reddish brown 1.00 .55
*Nos. O127-O136 (10)* 5.95 5.50

Issue dates: 15np, June; others, Apr. 1.

### Redrawn Type of 1957-58

**Typo. or Litho.**
**1958-71 Wmk. 324 *Perf. 13½x14***
**O137** O9 1np slate blue ('59) .30 .30
**O138** O9 2np blue violet ('59) .30 .30
**O139** O9 3np chocolate .30 .30
**O140** O9 5np yel green .30 .30
**O141** O9 6np turquoise ('59) .30 .30
**O142** O9 10np dk green ('63) .30 .30
**O142A** O9 13np red ('63) .30 .30
**O143** O9 15np dk purple .30 .30
**O144** O9 20np ver ('59) .30 .30
**O145** O9 25np vio blue ('59) .30 .30
**O146** O9 50np redsh brown ('59) .30 .30

**Litho.**
***Perf. 14***
**O147** O10 1r rose vio ('59) .30 .30
**O148** O10 2r rose red ('60) .50 .30
*a.* Watermark sideways ('69) .50 *.60*
**O149** O10 5r green ('59) 1.00 1.40
*a.* Watermark sideways ('69) .90 .30
**O150** O10 10r rose lake ('59) 1.50 1.10
*a.* Watermark sideways ('71) 3.75 3.75
*Nos. O137-O150 (15)* 6.60 6.40

Capital of Asoka Pillar
O11 O12

***Perf. 14½x14***
**1967-76 Photo. Wmk. 360**
**Without Gum**
**O151** O11 2p violet black .85 .85
**O152** O11 3p dk red brown .85 .85
**O153** O11 5p bright green .85 .85
**O154** O11 6p Prussian blue 3.25 3.25
**O155** O11 10p slate green .85 .85
**O156** O11 15p purple .85 .85
**O157** O11 20p orange ver .85 .85
**O158** O11 25p deep car ('76) 26.00 11.00
**O159** O11 30p violet blue .85 .85
**O160** O11 50p red brown .85 .85
*Nos. O151-O160 (10)* 36.05 21.05

No. O153 Overprinted

**1971, Nov. 15 Wmk. 360**
**Without Gum**
**O161** O11 5p green .40 .40

**No. O153 Overprinted "Refugee / Relief"**
**O162** O11 5p green 1.00 1.00

No. O162 was used in Maharashtra state.

**1971, Dec. 1(?) Without Gum**
**O163** O12 5p green .25 .25

Nos. O161-O163 were obligatory on all official mail as a postal tax to benefit refugees from East Pakistan. The tax was paid out of the various governmental departments' budgets.

### Type of 1968

**1967-74 Wmk. 324 *Perf. 14½x14***
**O164** O11 2p violet .80 *1.00*
**O165** O11 5p brt green ('74) .80 .25
**O166** O11 10p slate green ('74) 1.25 .25
**O167** O11 15p purple ('73) 1.60 .40
**O168** O11 20p dp orange ('74) 5.25 5.00
**O169** O11 30p ultramarine 3.50 1.00
**O170** O11 50p red brown ('73) 2.75 2.00
**O171** O11 1r dull purple .55 .25
*Nos. O164-O171 (8)* 16.50 10.15

O13 O14

**Without Currency Designation**

***Perf. 14½x14***
**1976-80 Litho. Wmk. 360**
**Without Gum**
**O172** O13 2p violet black .35 .35
**O173** O13 5p bright green .35 .35
**O174** O13 10p slate green .35 .35
**O175** O13 15p purple .35 .35
**O176** O13 20p brown orange .35 .35
**O177** O13 25p carmine rose .80 .80
**O178** O13 30p blue ('79) 2.50 2.50
**O179** O13 35p violet ('80) .75 .35
**O180** O13 50p red brown 3.50 1.75
**O181** O13 1r dull purple ('80) 4.00 .90

**Wmk. 324**
**O182** O13 1r dull purple .90 .90

***Perf. 14x13½***
**O183** O14 2r salmon rose 3.50 3.50
**O184** O14 5r deep green 3.50 3.50
**O185** O14 10r red brown 1.25 1.25
*Nos. O172-O185 (14)* 22.45 17.20

O15

***Perf. 15x14***
**1981, Feb. Litho. Wmk. 360**
**Without Gum**
**O186** O15 2r orange vermilion 1.00 .60
**O187** O15 5r dark green 3.00 1.40
**O188** O15 10r dark red brown 6.00 3.00
*Nos. O186-O188 (3)* 10.00 5.00

**Unwmk.**
**1981, Dec. 10 Litho. *Imperf.***
**Cream Paper**
**O189** O13 5p bright green .90 *1.25*
**O190** O13 10p slate green 1.00 *1.25*
**O191** O13 15p purple 1.00 *1.25*
**O192** O13 20p brown orange 1.00 *1.25*
**O193** O13 25p carmine rose 2.25 *2.75*
**O194** O13 35p violet 1.25 .90
**O195** O13 50p brown 2.25 2.25
**O196** O13 1r dull purple 2.50 2.25
**O197** O15 2r salmon rose 2.50 *5.25*
**O198** O15 5r deep green 2.75 *7.25*
**O199** O15 10r red brown 3.75 *9.75*
*Nos. O189-O199 (11)* 21.15 35.40

***Perf. 12½x13***
**1982, Nov. 22 Photo. Wmk. 360**
**Without Gum**
**O200** O13 5p bright green .80 *1.10*
**O201** O13 10p slate green 1.00 *1.25*
**O202** O13 15p purple 1.10 *1.25*
**O203** O13 20p fawn 1.25 1.25
**O204** O13 25p car rose 1.60 *2.50*
**O205** O13 30p dark blue 1.60 *2.50*
**O206** O13 35p violet 1.60 .70
**O207** O13 50p light brown 2.50 2.50
**O208** O13 1r dull purple 2.50 2.50
**O209** O15 2r salmon rose 2.75 3.75
**O210** O15 5r deep green 3.25 6.50
**O211** O15 10r red brown 4.00 9.00
*Nos. O200-O211 (12)* 23.95 34.80

***Perf. 12½x13***
**1984-99 Photo. Wmk. 324**
**Without Gum**
**O212** O13 5p green .25 .25
**O213** O13 10p dark green .25 .25
**O214** O13 15p rose lake .25 .25
**O215** O13 20p fawn .25 .25
**O216** O13 25p deep carmine .25 .25
**O217** O13 30p blue .25 .25
**O218** O13 35p purple .25 .25
**O219** O13 40p violet .25 .25
**O220** O13 50p brown .25 .25
**O221** O13 60p brown .25 .25
**O222** O15 1r violet brown .25 .25
**O223** O15 2r orange ver .40 .25
**O223A** O15 3r orange .25 .25
**O224** O15 5r gray green 1.00 .50
**O225** O15 10r red brown 2.00 1.00
*Nos. O213-O225 (14)* 6.15 4.50

Issued: 25p, 1986. 60p, 4/15/88; 40p, 10/15/88; 3r, 3/22/99; others, 4/16/84.

This is an expanding set. Numbers may change again.

## POSTAL TAX STAMPS

**Catalogue values for unused stamps in this section are for Never Hinged items.**

No. 408 Overprinted

***Perf. 14½x14***
**1971, Nov. 15 Photo. Wmk. 324**
**RA1** A202 5p cerise .25 .25

**No. 408 Overprinted "Refugee/Relief"**
**RA2** A202 5p cerise .25 .25

No. RA2 was used in Maharashtra. In order to make the obligatory tax stamps available immediately throughout India postmasters were authorized to overprint locally No. 408. This resulted in a great variety of mostly handstamped overprints of various types and sizes.

Refugees — PT1

***Perf. 14x14½***
**1971, Dec. 1 Photo. Wmk. 324**
**RA3** PT1 5p cerise .25 .25

Nos. RA1-RA3 were obligatory on all mail. The tax was for refugees from East Pakistan. See Nos. O161-O163.

# INDIA - CONVENTION STATES

**CONVENTION STATES OF THE BRITISH EMPIRE IN INDIA**

**Stamps of British India overprinted for use in the States of Chamba, Faridkot, Gwalior, Jhind, Nabha and Patiala.**

**These stamps had franking power throughout all British India.**

### Forgeries

Numerous forgeries exist of the high valued Convention States stamps, unused and used. Most cancelled examples of those stamps whose value used is far greater than unused bear favor or counterfeit cancels. Such stamps are worth far less than the values below, which are for postally used examples. More valuable Indian States stamps should be expertized.

## CHAMBA

'chəm-bə

LOCATION — A State of India located in the north Punjab, south of Kashmir.
AREA — 3,127 sq. mi.
POP. — 168,908 (1941)
CAPITAL — Chamba

The varieties with small letters in the overprint are not listed as the letters are merely broken and not from another font of type.

Indian Stamps Overprinted in Black

**1887-95 Wmk. 39 *Perf. 14***
1 A17 ½a green 1.50 *1.75*
a. "CHMABA" *600.00* *950.00*
c. Double overprint 950.00
2 A19 1a violet brown 3.75 *3.75*
a. "CHMABA" *700.00* 950.00
3 A20 1a6p bis brown ('95) 4.50 *21.00*
4 A21 2a ultramarine 2.00 *3.25*
a. "CHMABA" *2,750.* *4,000.*
5 A28 2a6p green ('95) 52.50 *150.00*
6 A22 3a brn org 4.50 *9.00*
a. 3a orange 16.00 *35.00*
b. Inverted overprint
c. "CHMABA" *7,500.* *11,000.*
7 A23 4a olive green 8.25 *14.00*
a. "CHMABA" *2,400.* *4,000.*
8 A25 8a red violet 13.50 *18.00*
a. "CHMABA" 6,000. *6,250.*
9 A26 12a vio, *red* ('90) 10.50 *24.00*
a. "CHMABA" 12,500.
b. 1st "T" of "STATE" invtd. 12,500.
10 A27 1r gray 72.50 *225.00*
a. "CHMABA" 21,000.
11 A29 1r car rose & grn ('95) 14.00 *25.00*
12 A30 2r brown & rose ('95) 150.00 *600.00*
13 A30 3r grn & brown ('95) 175.00 *525.00*
14 A30 5r vio & bl ('95) 190.00 *825.00*

**Wmk. 38**
15 A14 6a bister ('90) 8.25 *32.50*
*Nos. 1-15 (15)* 710.75 *2,477.*

**1900 Wmk. 39**
15B A31 3p carmine rose .90 *1.40*

**1902-04**
16 A31 3p gray ('04) .90 *3.25*
a. Inverted overprint 120.00
17 A17 ½a light green 1.00 *2.50*
18 A19 1a carmine rose 1.00 .60
19 A21 2a violet ('03) 16.00 *52.50*
*Nos. 16-19 (4)* 18.90 *58.85*

**1903-05**
20 A32 3p gray .35 *2.40*
21 A33 ½a green 1.20 .90
22 A34 1a carmine rose 2.40 1.40
23 A35 2a violet 2.75 *5.25*
24 A37 3a brown org ('05) 7.00 *9.00*
25 A38 4a olive green ('04) 10.50 *32.50*
26 A39 6a bister ('05) 6.50 *35.00*
27 A40 8a red violet ('04) 9.00 *35.00*
28 A41 12a violet, *red* 12.00 *47.50*
29 A42 1r car rose & grn ('05) 11.00 *35.00*
*Nos. 20-29 (10)* 62.70 *203.95*

**1907**
30 A44 ½a green 3.75 *6.00*
31 A45 1a carmine rose 3.75 *6.00*

**1913-24**
32 A46 3p gray .60 *1.90*
33 A47 ½a green 1.50 *1.90*
34 A48 1a carmine rose 15.00 *17.50*
35 A48 1a dark brown ('22) 5.25 *8.25*
36 A49 2a violet 6.00 *17.50*
37 A51 3a brown orange 7.00 *13.00*
38 A51 3a ultra ('24) 6.25 *35.00*
39 A52 4a olive green 6.00 *8.25*
40 A53 6a bister 6.50 *11.00*
41 A54 8a red violet 9.00 *24.00*
42 A55 12a claret 8.25 *19.00*
43 A56 1r green & red brown 27.50 *47.50*
*Nos. 32-43 (12)* 98.85 *204.80*

India No. 104 Overprinted

**1921**
44 A48 9p on 1a rose 1.50 *27.50*

India Stamps of 1913-26 Overprinted

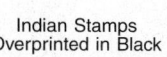

**1922-27**
45 A58 1½a chocolate 40.00 *190.00*
46 A59 1½a chocolate 3.75 *9.50*
47 A59 1½a rose 1.40 *35.00*
48 A57 2a6p ultramarine .90 *6.50*
49 A57 2a6p brown orange 4.00 *35.00*
*Nos. 45-49 (5)* 50.05 *276.00*

India Stamps of 1926 Overprinted

**1927-28 Wmk. 196**
50 A46 3p slate .30 *2.50*
51 A47 ½a green .45 *3.75*
52 A48 1a dark brown 2.50 2.25
53 A60 2a dull violet 3.25 6.00
54 A51 3a ultramarine 1.90 *32.50*
55 A61 4a olive green 1.90 *10.00*
57 A54 8a red violet 2.40 *17.50*
58 A55 12a claret 2.40 *24.00*

Overprinted

59 A56 1r green & brown 17.50 *45.00*
*Nos. 50-55,57-59 (9)* 32.60 *143.50*

India Stamps of 1926-35 Overprinted

**1932-37**
60 A71 ½a green 1.60 *16.00*
61 A68 9p dark green 7.50 *32.50*
62 A72 1a dark brown 2.50 2.25
63 A69 1a3p violet 2.10 *9.50*
64 A59 1½a carmine rose 9.50 *11.00*
65 A49 2a vermilion 1.90 *37.50*
a. Small die 175.00 *210.00*
66 A57 2a6p buff 5.00 *30.00*
67 A51 3a carmine rose 3.25 *17.50*
68 A52 4a olive green ('36) 8.25 *25.00*
69 A53 6a bister ('37) 45.00 *250.00*
*Nos. 60-69 (10)* 86.60 *431.25*

Same Overprint on India Stamps of 1937

**1938 Wmk. 196 *Perf. 13½x14***
70 A80 3p slate 14.00 *32.50*
71 A80 ½a brown 2.00 21.00
72 A80 9p green 12.50 *57.50*
73 A80 1a carmine 2.50 *5.50*

74 A81 2a scarlet 10.00 *24.00*
75 A81 2a6p purple 11.00 *47.50*
76 A81 3a yellow green 11.50 *42.50*
77 A81 3a6p ultra 11.50 *45.00*
78 A81 4a dark brown 30.00 *45.00*
79 A81 6a peacock blue 32.50 *100.00*
80 A81 8a blue violet 30.00 *97.50*
81 A81 12a carmine lake 22.50 *97.50*

Overprinted

82 A82 1r brown & slate 45.00 *110.00*
83 A82 2r dk brn & dk vio 75.00 *525.00*
84 A82 5r dp ultra & dk green 120.00 *700.00*
85 A82 10r rose car & dk vio 190.00 *1,100.*
86 A82 15r dk grn & dk brown 200.00 *1,500.*
87 A82 25r dk vio & bl vio 290.00 *1,600.*
*Nos. 70-87 (18)* 1,110. *6,150.*
Set, never hinged 1,300.

India Nos. 151 and 153 Overprinted

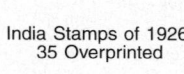

**1942**
87B A80 ½a brown 62.50 *67.50*
Never hinged 75.00
88 A80 1a carmine 95.00 *90.00*
Never hinged 110.00

Same Ovpt. on India Stamps of 1941-42

**1942-44**
89 A83 3p slate 1.50 *8.25*
90 A83 ½a rose violet ('43) 1.00 *9.50*
91 A83 9p lt green ('43) 1.40 *30.00*
92 A83 1a car rose ('43) 2.50 *8.25*
93 A84 1½a dk purple ('44) 3.00 *21.00*
94 A84 2a scarlet ('43) 11.00 *24.00*
95 A84 3a violet ('43) 26.00 *72.50*
96 A84 3½a ultra ('43) 14.00 *67.50*
97 A85 4a chocolate ('43) 19.00 75.00
98 A85 6a pck blue ('43) 21.00 *62.50*
99 A85 8a blue violet ('43) 22.50 *75.00*
100 A85 12a car lake ('43) 30.00 *97.50*
*Nos. 89-100 (12)* 152.90 *551.00*
Set, never hinged 200.00

India Nos. 162-167 Overprinted

**1943 Wmk. 196 *Perf. 13½x14***
101 A82 1r brown & slate 26.00 *97.50*
102 A82 2r dk brown & dk vio 30.00 *400.00*
103 A82 5r dp ultra & dk grn 55.00 *450.00*
104 A82 10r rose car & dk vio 85.00 *700.00*
105 A82 15r dk grn & dk brn 190.00 *1,250.*
106 A82 25r dk vio & bl vio 175.00 *1,250.*
*Nos. 101-106 (6)* 561.00 *4,147.*
Set, never hinged 850.00

India No. 161A Ovptd.

**1947**
107 A81 14a rose violet 17.50 4.50

### OFFICIAL STAMPS

Indian Stamps Overprinted in Black

**1887-98 Wmk. 39 *Perf. 14***
O1 A17 ½a green .90 .25
a. "CHMABA" 375.00 375.00
c. "SERV CE"
O2 A19 1a violet brown 3.00 2.25
a. "CHMABA" 600.00 600.00
c. "SERV CE" *5,250.*
d. "SERVICE" double *3,000.* *1,600.*
O3 A21 2a ultra 3.75 3.00
a. "CHMABA" *1,500.* *3,250.*
O4 A22 3a brown orange 3.00 *19.00*
a. 3a orange — —
b. "CHMABA" *4,500.* *5,250.*
O5 A23 4a olive green 4.50 *12.00*
a. "CHMABA" *1,600.* *3,250.*
c. "SERV CE" 6,000.
O6 A25 8a red violet 4.50 *4.50*
a. "CHMABA" *12,000.* *12,000.*
O7 A26 12a vio, *red* ('90) 12.50 *72.50*
a. "CHMABA" *11,000.*
b. 1st "T" of "STATE" invtd. *10,000.*
O8 A27 1r gray ('90) 19.00 *225.00*
a. "CHMABA" *7,500.*
O9 A29 1r car rose & grn ('98) 9.00 *62.50*

**Wmk. 38**
O10 A14 6a bister 6.25 *22.50*
*Nos. O1-O10 (10)* 66.40 423.50

**1902-04 Wmk. 39**
O11 A31 3p gray ('04) .75 *1.20*
O12 A17 ½a light green 1.50 *6.00*
O13 A19 1a carmine rose 1.90 .90
O14 A21 2a violet ('03) 14.50 *52.50*
*Nos. O11-O14 (4)* 18.65 *60.60*

**1903-05**
O15 A32 3p gray .40 .25
O16 A33 ½a green .30 .25
O17 A34 1a carmine rose 1.50 .45
O18 A35 2a violet 1.50 *2.25*
O19 A38 4a olive green ('05) 4.25 *30.00*
O20 A40 8a red violet ('05) 10.00 *30.00*
O21 A42 1r car rose & grn ('05) 2.00 *21.00*
*Nos. O15-O21 (7)* 19.95 *84.20*

**1907**
O22 A44 ½a green .85 *1.10*
a. Inverted overprint *6,750.* *8,250.*
O23 A45 1a carmine rose 4.75 *3.75*

**1913**
O24 A49 2a violet 22.50
O25 A52 4a olive green 20.00

India No. 63 Overprinted

O26 A35 2a violet 60.00

No. O26 was never placed in use.

**India Stamps of 1911-29 Overprinted**

a

b

**1913-25**
O27 A46 (a) 3p gray .30 *.60*
O28 A47 (a) ½a green .30 *.90*
O29 A48 (a) 1a carmine rose .30 .25
O30 A48 (a) 1a dk brown ('25) 6.50 1.00
O31 A49 (a) 2a violet ('14) 1.60 *22.50*
O32 A52 (a) 4a olive green 1.60 *30.00*
O33 A54 (a) 8a red violet 2.50 *30.00*
O34 A56 (b) 1r grn & red brn 8.25 *47.50*
*Nos. O27-O34 (8)* 21.35 132.75

India No. O66 Overprinted

**1921**
O35 O6 9p on 1a rose .25 *12.50*

India Stamps of 1926-35 Overprinted

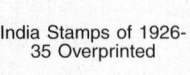

**1927-39** **Wmk. 196**
O36 A46 3p slate .65 .60
O37 A47 ½a green .40 .25
O38 A68 9p dark green ('32) 5.00 *16.00*
O39 A48 1a dark brown .25 .25
O40 A69 1a3p violet ('32) 7.50 1.50
O41 A60 2a dull violet 3.25 *.90*
O42 A61 4a olive green 1.90 4.00
O43 A54 8a red violet 10.00 *16.00*
O44 A55 12a claret 6.50 *37.50*

Overprinted

O45 A56 1r green & brown 19.00 *72.50*
O45A A56 2r brn org & car rose ('39) 30.00 *375.00*
O45B A56 5r dk vio & ultra ('39) 52.50 *450.00*
O45C A56 10r car & grn ('39) 82.50 *450.00*
*Nos. O36-O45C (13)* 219.45 1,424.

India Stamps of 1926-35 Overprinted

**1935-36**
O46 A71 ½a green 7.00 *.75*
O47 A72 1a dark brown 6.75 .65
O48 A49 2a vermilion 7.00 1.90
a. Small die 9.50 *30.00*
O49 A52 4a olive grn ('36) 10.00 9.50
*Nos. O46-O49 (4)* 30.75 *12.80*

Same Overprint on India Stamps of 1937

**1938** ***Perf. 13½x14***
O50 A80 9p green 30.00 *100.00*
Never hinged 37.50
O51 A80 1a carmine 37.50 9.00
Never hinged 45.00

India Stamps of 1937 Overprinted

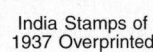

**1940-41**
O51A A82 1r brn & sl ('41) 300.00 *1,100.*
O52 A82 2r dk brn & dk vio 52.50 *600.00*
O53 A82 5r dp ultra & dk grn 75.00 *650.00*
O54 A82 10r rose car & dk vio 105.00 *1,200.*
Set, never hinged 625.00

India Official Stamps of 1939-43 Overprinted

**1941-46** **Wmk. 196**
O55 O8 3p slate ('44) .85 *1.90*
O56 O8 ½a brown 37.50 5.50
O57 O8 ½a dk rose vio ('44) .85 *5.50*
O58 O8 9p green 8.75 *17.50*
O59 O8 1a carmine rose 1.25 *4.50*
O60 O8 1a3p bister ('46) 105.00 32.50
O61 O8 1½a dull pur ('46) 9.50 *12.50*
O62 O8 2a scarlet ('44) 9.50 *12.50*
O63 O8 2½a purple ('44) 5.50 *35.00*
O64 O8 4a dark brown ('44) 9.50 *27.50*
O65 O8 8a blue vio ('41) 21.00 *100.00*
*Nos. O55-O65 (11)* 209.20 *254.90*
Set, never hinged 250.00

India Nos. 162-165 Overprinted

**1944**
O66 A82 1r brown & slate 27.50 *325.00*
O67 A82 2r dk brn & dk vio 42.50 *450.00*
O68 A82 5r dp ultra & dk grn 80.00 *650.00*
O69 A82 10r rose car & dk vio 95.00 *1,100.*
*Nos. O66-O69 (4)* 245.00 *2,525.*
Set, never hinged 295.00

## FARIDKOT

fe-ˈrēd-ˌkōt

LOCATION — A State of India lying northeast of Nabha in the central Punjab.
AREA — 638 sq. mi.
POP. — 164,364
CAPITAL — Faridkot

Previous stamp issues are listed under Feudatory States. Stamps of Faridkot were superseded by those of India in 1901.

The varieties with small letters in the overprint are not listed as the letters are merely broken and not from another font.

India Stamps Overprinted in Black

**1887-93** **Wmk. 39** ***Perf. 14***
4 A17 ½a green 3.75 2.50
a. "ARIDKOT"
b. "FAR DKOT" — *2,500.*
5 A19 1a violet brown 2.25 *3.75*
6 A21 2a ultramarine 4.75 *10.50*
7 A22 3a orange 5.50 *9.00*
8 A23 4a olive green 12.50 *27.50*
a. "ARIDKOT" 2,100.
9 A25 8a red violet 22.50 *67.50*
a. "ARIDKOT" 4,500.
10 A27 1r gray 67.50 *550.00*
a. "ARIDKOT" *5,250.*
11 A29 1r car rose & grn ('93) 60.00 *175.00*

**Wmk. 38**

12 A14 6a bister 3.00 *27.50*
a. "ARIDKOT" 2,750.
*Nos. 4-12 (9)* 181.75 *873.25*

**1900** **Wmk. Star. (39)**
13 A31 3p car rose 2.25 *67.50*
14 A26 12a violet, *red* 67.50 *625.00*

### OFFICIAL STAMPS

India Stamps Overprinted in Black

**1886** **Wmk. 39** ***Perf. 14***
O1 A17 ½a green .90 *1.10*
a. "SERV CE" 3,750.
b. "FAR DKOT" 3,500.
c. "ESRVICE" 3,500.
O2 A19 1a violet brown 1.50 *3.00*
a. "SERV CE" 5,500.
O3 A21 2a ultramarine 3.00 *16.00*
a. "SERV CE" 5,500.
O4 A22 3a orange 6.00 *57.50*
O5 A23 4a olive green 7.00 *45.00*
a. "SERV CE" 4,750.
O6 A25 8a red lilac 15.00 *45.00*
a. "SERV CE" 4,500.
O7 A27 1r gray 82.50 *400.00*

**Wmk. 38**

O8 A14 6a bister 37.50 *42.50*
a. "ARIDKOT" 2,100.
b. "SERVIC" 4,500.
*Nos. O1-O8 (8)* 153.40 *610.10*

**1896** **Wmk. 39**
O9 A29 1r car rose & green 140.00 *1,000.*

Obsolete March 31, 1901.

## GWALIOR

ˈgwäl-ē-ˌo̦ə̦r

LOCATION — One of the Central Provinces of India
AREA — 26,008 sq. mi.
POP. — 4,006,159 (1941)
CAPITAL — Lashkar

The varieties with small letters in the overprint are not listed as the letters are merely broken and not from another font.

India Stamps Overprinted in Black

Lines Spaced 16-17mm

**1885** **Wmk. 39** ***Perf. 14***
1 A17 ½a green 90.00
2 A19 1a violet brown 97.50
3 A20 1a6p bister brown 125.00
4 A21 2a ultramarine 100.00
5 A25 8a red lilac 110.00
6 A27 1r gray 110.00

**Wmk. 38**

7 A9 4a green 140.00
8 A14 6a bister 140.00
*Nos. 1-8 (8)* 912.50

The Hindi overprint measures 13½-14x2mm and 15-15½x2½mm.

The two sizes are found in the same sheet in the proportion of one of the smaller to three of the larger.

The ½a, 1a, 2a, also exist with lines 13mm apart and the short Hindi overprint.

*Reprints of the ½a and 1a have the 13mm spacing, the short Hindi overprint and usually carry the overprint "Specimen."*

India Stamps Overprinted

**Red Overprint**

**1885** **Wmk. 39**
9 A17 ½a green 1.90 .25
10 A21 2a ultramarine 35.00 *27.50*
11 A27 1r gray 12.50 *37.50*

**Wmk. 38**

12 A9 4a green 42.50 24.00
*Nos. 9-12 (4)* 91.90 89.25

*Nos. 9-12 have been reprinted. They have the short Hindi overprint. Most stamps bear the word "Reprint." Those without it cannot be distinguished from the originals.*

**Black Overprint**

**1885-91** **Wmk. 39**
13 A17 ½a green .75 .25
a. "GWALICR" 125.00 *150.00*
b. Double overprint 1,400.
14 A18 9p rose 47.50 *82.50*
15 A19 1a violet brown 3.00 .25
16 A20 1a6p bister brown 3.25 2.00
17 A21 2a ultramarine 4.00 .25
18 A22 3a orange 7.00 .25
19 A23 4a olive green 8.50 2.00
20 A25 8a red violet 9.00 2.00
21 A26 12a violet, *red* 5.00 1.00
22 A27 1r gray 6.50 5.25

**Wmk. 38**

23 A14 6a bister 7.50 18.00
*Nos. 13-23 (11)* 102.00 *113.75*

The Hindi overprint measures 13½-14x2mm and 15-15½x2½mm as in the preceding issue.

**1896** **Wmk. 39**
24 A28 2a6p green 14.00 *30.00*
a. "GWALICR" 1,000.
25 A29 1r car rose & grn 12.00 8.50
a. "GWALICR" 1,350 *2,400.*
26 A30 2r bis brn & rose 8.25 4.50
27 A30 3r green & brown 11.00 5.25
28 A30 5r violet & blue 21.00 9.50
*Nos. 24-28 (5)* 66.25 57.75

The Hindi inscription varies from 13 to 15½mm long.

**1899**
29 A31 3p carmine rose .75 .25
a. Inverted overprint 1,650. 825.00

**1901-04**
30 A31 3p gray ('04) 11.00 *90.00*
31 A17 ½a light green 2.10 *2.40*
32 A19 1a carmine rose 1.90 .50
33 A21 2a violet 4.00 8.25
34 A28 2a6p ultra ('03) 2.25 9.50
*Nos. 30-34 (5)* 21.25 *110.65*

**1903-08**
35 A32 3p gray 2.10 .25
36 A33 ½a green 2.25 .45
37 A34 1a carmine rose .30 .25
38 A35 2a violet 3.00 1.50
39 A36 2a6p ultra ('05) 37.50 *120.00*
40 A37 3a brown org ('04) 3.00 .50
41 A38 4a olive green 3.75 .60
42 A39 6a bister ('06) 9.00 2.10
43 A40 8a red violet 7.50 2.40
44 A41 12a vio, *red* ('05) 4.50 *30.00*
45 A42 1r car rose & grn ('05) 4.50 2.50
46 A43 2r brown & rose 13.50 *16.50*
47 A43 3r grn & brn ('08) 42.50 *75.00*
48 A43 5r vio & bl ('08) 27.50 *40.00*
*Nos. 35-48 (14)* 160.90 *292.05*

There are two settings of the overprint on Nos. 35, 37-46. In the first (1903), "GWALIOR" is 14mm long and lines are spaced 1¾mm. In the second (1908), "GWALIOR" is 13mm long and lines are 2¾mm apart. No. 36 exists only with first overprint, Nos. 47-48 only with second.

**1907**
49 A44 ½a green .30 *1.00*
50 A45 1a carmine rose 2.25 .25

No. 49 exists with both settings of overprint. See note below No. 48.

**1912-23**

**51** A46 3p gray .30 .25
**52** A47 ½a green .30 .25
*a.* Inverted overprint 600.00
**53** A48 1a car rose .35 .25
*a.* Double overprint 37.50
**54** A48 1a dk brown ('23) 1.60 .25
**55** A49 2a violet 1.20 .25
**56** A51 3a brown orange 1.00 .25
**57** A52 4a olive grn ('13) .90 .90
**58** A53 6a bister 1.90 2.10
**59** A54 8a red vio ('13) 3.25 1.20
**60** A55 12a claret ('14) 2.10 *6.00*
**61** A56 1r green & red brn 13.50 .65
**62** A56 2r brn & car rose 7.50 6.50
**63** A56 5r violet & ultra 35.00 9.50
*Nos. 51-63 (13)* 68.90 28.35

India No. 104 Overprinted

**1921**

**64** A48 9p on 1a rose 1.00 *.75*
*a.* Inverted overprint —

India Stamps of 1911-26 Overprinted

**Hindi Overprint 15mm Long**

**1923-27**

**66** A59 1½a choc ('25) 3.25 .75
**67** A59 1½a rose ('27) .30 .25
*a.* Inverted overprint — —
**68** A57 2a6p ultra ('25) 3.25 2.50
**69** A57 2a6p brown org ('27) .50 *.75*
**70** A51 3a ultra ('24) 3.75 .90
*Nos. 66-70 (5)* 11.05 5.15

Similar Ovpt. on India Stamps of 1926-35

**Hindi Overprint 13½mm Long**

**1928-32** **Wmk. 196**

**71** A46 3p slate ('32) 1.25 .25
**72** A47 ½a green ('30) 1.90 .25
**73** A48 1a dark brown 1.10 .25
**74** A60 2a dull violet .70 .45
**75** A51 3a ultramarine 1.25 .60
**76** A61 4a olive green 1.60 1.50
**77** A54 8a red violet 1.60 1.60
**78** A55 12a claret 2.75 *5.25*

Overprinted

**79** A56 1r green & brown 3.75 *6.00*
**80** A56 2r brn org & car rose 6.75 6.50
**81** A56 5r dk vio & ultra ('29) 24.00 *37.50*
**82** A56 10r car & grn ('30) 82.50 62.50
**83** A56 15r olive green & ultra ('30) 130.00 100.00
**84** A56 25r bl & ocher ('30) 275.00 250.00
*Nos. 71-84 (14)* 534.15 472.65

India Stamps of 1932-35 Overprinted in Black

**Hindi Overprint 13½mm Long**

**1933-36**

**85** A71 ½a green ('36) .65 .25
**86** A68 9p dk green ('33) 3.75 .45
**87** A72 1a dk brown ('36) .30 .25
**88** A69 1a3p violet ('36) .65 .25
**89** A49 2a vermilion ('36) 3.75 5.25
*Nos. 85-89 (5)* 9.10 6.45

Same Ovpt. on India Stamps of 1937

**1938-40** ***Perf. 13½x14***

**90** A80 3p slate ('40) 10.00 .25
**91** A80 ½a brown 11.00 .25
**92** A80 9p green ('40) 60.00 6.00
**93** A80 1a carmine 10.00 .25
**94** A81 3a yel green ('39) 35.00 7.50
**95** A81 4a dark brown 55.00 5.25
**96** A81 6a pck blue ('39) 5.00 *16.50*
*Nos. 90-96 (7)* 186.00 36.00
Set, never hinged 225.00

Same Overprinted on India Stamps of 1941-43

**1942-49**

**100** A83 3p slate ('44) .55 .25
**101** A83 ½a rose vio ('46) 1.25 .25
**102** A83 9p light green .55 .25
**103** A83 1a car rose ('44) 1.25 .25
**104** A84 1½a dk purple ('44) 8.75 .25
**105** A84 2a scarlet ('44) 1.90 .25
**106** A84 3a violet ('44) 20.00 2.50
**108** A85 4a choc ('44) 4.00 .25
**109** A85 6a pck blue ('48) 17.50 *40.00*
**110** A85 8a blue violet 4.75 *4.00*
**111** A85 12a carmine lake 7.00 *35.00*

India Nos. 162-167 Overprinted

***Perf. 13½x14***

**112** A82 1r brn & sl ('45) 15.00 2.50
**113** A82 2r dk brn & dk vio ('49) 62.50 14.00
**114** A82 5r dp ultra & dk grn ('49) 40.00 60.00
**115** A82 10r rose car & dk vio ('49) 40.00 *62.50*
**116** A82 15r dk grn & dk brn ('48) 110.00 *250.00*
**117** A82 25r dk vio & blue vio ('48) 110.00 *190.00*
*Nos. 100-106,108-117 (17)* 445.00 662.25
Set, never hinged 525.00

India Stamps of 1941-43 Overprinted

**1949**

**118** A83 3p slate 2.50 .75
**119** A83 ½a rose violet 2.50 .75
**120** A83 1a carmine rose 2.25 .90
**121** A84 2a scarlet 32.50 3.25
**122** A84 3a violet 80.00 45.00
**123** A85 4a chocolate 9.25 5.00
**124** A85 6a pck blue 67.50 *97.50*
**125** A85 8a blue violet 140.00 82.50
**126** A85 12a carmine lake 525.00 225.00
*Nos. 118-126 (9)* 861.50 460.65
Set, never hinged 1,050.

**OFFICIAL STAMPS**

India Stamps Overprinted in Black

**1895** **Wmk. 39** ***Perf. 14***

**O1** A17 ½a green .75 .25
*a.* Double overprint 1,400.
**O2** A19 1a maroon 18.00 2.10
**O3** A21 2a ultramarine 5.00 .60
**O4** A23 4a olive green 5.25 2.25
**O5** A25 8a red violet 6.50 5.00
**O6** A29 1r car rose & grn 12.50 4.50
*Nos. O1-O6 (6)* 48.00 14.70

Nos. O1 to O6 inclusive are known with the last two characters of the lower word transposed.

**1901-04**

**O7** A31 3p gray ('04) 3.75 *5.25*
**O8** A17 ½a light green 1.10 .25
**O9** A19 1a carmine rose 9.00 .25
**O10** A21 2a violet ('03) 2.50 2.25
*Nos. O7-O10 (4)* 16.35 8.00

**1902**

**O11** A31 3p carmine rose 1.90 .35

**1903-05**

**O12** A32 3p gray .90 .25
**O13** A33 ½a green 4.00 .25
**O14** A34 1a carmine rose 1.40 .25
**O15** A35 2a violet 2.25 .45
**O16** A38 4a olive grn ('05) 22.50 2.50
**O17** A40 8a red violet 9.50 1.00
**O18** A42 1r car rose & grn ('05) 3.50 3.00
*Nos. O12-O18 (7)* 44.05 7.70

**1907**

**O19** A44 ½a green 2.50 .25
**O20** A45 1a carmine rose 10.00 .25

Two spacings of the overprint lines, 10mm and 8mm, are found on Nos. O12-O20.

**1913**

**O21** A46 3p gray .35 .25
**O22** A47 ½a green .30 .25
**O23** A48 1a carmine rose .45 .25
*a.* Double overprint 97.50
**O24** A49 2a violet 2.25 .25
**O25** A52 4a olive green .90 *2.25*
**O26** A54 8a red violet 1.90 1.50
**O27** A56 1r grn & red brn 40.00 35.00
*Nos. O21-O27 (7)* 46.15 39.75

India No. O66 Overprinted

**1921**

**O28** O6 9p on 1a rose .25 *.45*

India No. 83 Overprinted

**1923**

**O29** A48 1a dark brown 5.50 .25

Similar Ovpt. on India Stamps of 1926-35

**1927-35** **Wmk. 196**

**O30** A46 3p slate .30 .25
**O31** A47 ½a green .30 .25
**O32** A48 1a dark brown .30 .25
**O33** A60 2a dull violet .30 .25
**O34** A61 4a olive green 1.00 .45
**O35** A54 8a red violet .90 *1.60*

Overprinted

**O36** A56 1r green & brown 1.50 *2.50*
**O37** A56 2r brn org & car rose ('35) 29.00 *30.00*
**O38** A56 5r dk vio & ultra ('32) 35.00 *250.00*
**O39** A56 10r car & grn ('32) 240.00 *650.00*
*Nos. O30-O39 (10)* 308.60 *935.55*

India Stamps of 1926-35 Overprinted

**1933-37** ***Perf. 13½x14, 14***

**O40** A71 ½a green ('36) .35 .25
**O41** A68 9p dk green ('35) .30 .25
**O42** A72 1a dk brown ('36) .30 .25
**O43** A69 1a3p violet ('33) .75 .25
**O44** A49 2a ver ('36) .30 *.60*
*a.* Small die ('36) 3.75 1.90
**O45** A52 4a olive green ('37) .90 *1.10*
*Nos. O40-O45 (6)* 2.90 2.70

For surcharge see No. O62.

Same Overprint on India Stamps

**1938** ***Perf. 13½x14***

**O46** A80 ½a brown 8.00 .45
Never hinged 9.50
**O47** A80 1a carmine 2.00 .25
Never hinged 2.25

India Nos. 162-165 Overprinted

**1945-48** **Wmk. 196** ***Perf. 13½x14***

**O48** A82 1r brown & slate 12.50 *32.50*
**O49** A82 2r dk brn & dk vio 22.50 *140.00*
**O50** A82 5r dp ultra & dk grn ('46) 37.50 *825.00*
**O51** A82 10r rose car & dk vio ('48) 100.00 *1,650.*
*Nos. O48-O51 (4)* 172.50 *2,647.*
Set, never hinged 200.00

India Official Stamps of 1939-43 Overprinted

**1940-44** **Wmk. 196** ***Perf. 13½x14***

**O52** O8 3p slate .65 .25
**O53** O8 ½a brown 5.50 .35
**O54** O8 ½a dk rose vio ('43) .75 .25
**O55** O8 9p green ('43) .85 *1.00*
**O56** O8 1a car rose ('41) 2.75 .25
**O57** O8 1a3p bister ('42) 55.00 2.50
**O58** O8 1½a dull purple ('43) 1.50 .45
**O59** O8 2a scarlet ('41) 1.50 .45
**O60** O8 4a dark brown ('44) 1.50 *5.00*
**O61** O8 8a blue vio ('44) 6.00 *14.00*
*Nos. O52-O61 (10)* 76.00 24.50
Set, never hinged 95.00

Gwalior No. O43 with Additional Surcharge in Black

**1942**

**O62** A69 1a on 1a3p violet 30.00 4.50
Never hinged 37.50

## JIND

'jind

(Jhind)

LOCATION — A State of India in the north Punjab.
AREA — 1,299 sq. mi.
POP. — 361,812 (1941)
CAPITAL — Sangrur

Previous stamp issues are listed under Feudatory States.

The varieties with small letters are not listed as the letters are merely broken and not from another font.

India Stamps Overprinted in Black

**1885** **Wmk. 39** ***Perf. 14***

**33** A17 ½a green 7.00 *8.25*
*a.* Overprint reading down 140.00 *160.00*
**34** A19 1a violet brown 62.50 *90.00*
*a.* Overprint reading down 1,400. *1,500.*
**35** A21 2a ultra 29.00 *32.50*
*a.* Overprint reading down 1,000. *1,200.*
**36** A25 8a red lilac 625.00
*a.* Overprint reading down *18,000.*
**37** A27 1r gray 700.00
*a.* Overprint reading down *21,000.*

**Wmk. 38**

**38** A9 4a green 97.50 *140.00*
*Nos. 33-38 (6)* 1,521. *270.75*

On the reprints of Nos. 33 to 38 "Jhind" measures 8mm instead of 9mm and "State" 9mm instead of 9½mm.

Examples of "inverted overprints" exist of the ½a, 1a and 2a with the lines much less curved. These are thought to come from a trial printing.

India Stamps Overprinted in Red or Black

**1885** **Wmk. 39**
39 A17 ½a green (R) 210.00
40 A19 1a violet brown 210.00
41 A21 2a ultra (R) 210.00
42 A25 8a red lilac 290.00
43 A27 1r gray (R) 290.00

**Wmk. 38**
44 A9 4a green (R) 290.00
*Nos. 39-44 (6)* 1,500.

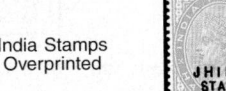

India Stamps Overprinted

**1886** **Wmk. 39** **Red Overprint**
45 A17 ½a green 52.50
a. "JEIND" 1,800.
46 A21 2a ultramarine 57.50
a. "JEIND" 1,800.
47 A27 1r gray 90.00
a. "JEIND" 2,750.

**Wmk. 38**
48 A9 4a green 90.00
*Nos. 45-48 (4)* 290.00

Nos. 46, 47 and 48 were not placed in use.

**1886-98** **Wmk. 39** **Black Overprint**
49 A17 ½a green ('88) 1.20 .25
a. Inverted overprint 300.00
50 A19 1a violet brown 3.75 .25
a. "JEIND" 750.00
51 A20 1a6p bister brn ('97) 3.75 *5.50*
52 A21 2a ultra 3.75 .60
53 A22 3a orange 5.00 1.00
54 A23 4a olive green 6.00 3.25
55 A25 8a red violet 12.50 *30.00*
a. "JEIND" 2,400.
56 A26 12a vio, *red* ('97) 10.00 *37.50*
57 A27 1r gray ('91) 17.50 *82.50*
58 A29 1r car rose & green ('98) 16.50 *90.00*
59 A30 2r brn & rose ('97) 525.00 *1,500.*
60 A30 3r grn & brn ('97) 750.00 *1,350.*
61 A30 5r vio & bl ('97) 750.00 *1,250.*

**Wmk. 38**
62 A14 6a bister 6.50 *21.00*
*Nos. 49-62 (14)* 2,111. *4,371.*

**1900** **Wmk. 39**
63 A31 3p carmine rose 1.60 *2.50*

**1902-04**
64 A31 3p gray ('04) .60 *6.00*
65 A17 ½a light green 7.00 *10.00*
66 A19 1a carmine rose 1.90 *10.00*
*Nos. 64-66 (3)* 9.50 *26.00*

**1903-09**
67 A32 3p gray .35 .25
68 A33 ½a green 2.50 *2.50*
69 A34 1a car rose ('09) 2.75 2.40
70 A35 2a violet ('06) 4.25 3.25
70A A36 2a6p ultra ('09) .85 *10.00*
71 A37 3a brown orange 3.25 .60
a. Double overprint 175.00 *325.00*
72 A38 4a olive green 11.50 *14.00*
73 A39 6a bister ('05) 9.25 *32.50*
74 A40 8a red violet 4.00 *32.50*
75 A41 12a vio, *red* ('05) 4.25 *17.50*
76 A42 1r car rose & grn ('05) 4.75 *32.50*
*Nos. 67-76 (11)* 47.70 *148.00*

**1907**
77 A44 ½a green .60 .25
78 A45 1a carmine rose 2.25 1.00

**1913**
80 A46 3p gray .30 3.50
81 A47 ½a green .30 1.10
82 A48 1a carmine rose .30 .65
83 A49 2a violet .30 6.25
84 A51 3a brown orange 2.25 *21.00*
85 A53 6a bister 12.50 *42.50*
*Nos. 80-85 (6)* 15.95 *75.00*

India Stamps of 1911-26 Overprinted

**1913-14**
88 A46 3p gray 1.50 .25
89 A47 ½a green 3.75 .25
90 A48 1a carmine rose 2.40 .25
91 A49 2a violet 6.50 1.90
92 A51 3a brown orange .75 *6.00*
93 A52 4a olive green 3.00 *14.00*
94 A53 6a bister 6.00 *24.00*
95 A54 8a red violet 8.25 *24.00*
96 A55 12a claret 7.50 *30.00*
97 A56 1r grn & red brn 17.50 *35.00*
*Nos. 88-97 (10)* 57.15 *135.65*

India No. 104 Overprinted

**1921**
98 A48 9p on 1a rose 1.90 *22.50*

India Stamps of 1913-19 Overprinted

**1922**
99 A58 1½a chocolate 5.00 *9.00*
100 A57 2a6p ultramarine .75 *7.00*

Same Overprint on India Stamps of 1911-26

**1924**
101 A48 1a dark brown 9.00 4.50
102 A59 1½a chocolate .75 *2.25*

Same Overprint on India No. 87

**1925**
103 A51 3a ultramarine 3.00 *7.50*

Same Overprint on India Stamps of 1911-26

**1927**
104 A59 1½a rose .30 *2.25*
105 A57 2a6p brown orange 1.90 12.00
106 A56 2r yel brn & car rose 9.50 *225.00*
107 A56 5r violet & ultra 67.50 *450.00*
*Nos. 104-107 (4)* 79.20 *689.25*

India Stamps of 1926-35 Overprinted

**1927-32** **Wmk. 196**
108 A46 3p slate .30 .25
109 A47 ½a green .30 *.50*
110 A68 9p dark green ('32) 2.75 .60
111 A48 1a dark brown .30 .25
112 A69 1a3p violet ('32) .35 *.45*
113 A59 1½a carmine rose .75 *5.50*
114 A60 2a dull violet 4.25 .60
115 A57 2a6p buff 2.00 *16.00*
116 A51 3a ultramarine 8.00 *27.50*
117 A61 4a olive green 2.00 *5.25*
118 A54 8a red violet 7.50 3.25
119 A55 12a claret 12.00 *32.50*

Indian Stamps of 1911-23 Overprinted

120 A56 1r green & brown 6.50 *9.00*
121 A56 2r buff & car rose 55.00 *225.00*
122 A56 5r dk vio & ultra 16.00 *62.50*
123 A56 10r car rose & grn 19.00 *27.50*
124 A56 15r ol grn & blue 120.00 *1,050.*
125 A56 25r blue & ocher 190.00 *1,250.*
*Nos. 108-125 (18)* 447.00 *2,716.*

India Stamps of 1926-35 Overprinted

**1934-37**
126 A71 ½a green .45 .35
127 A72 1a dark brown 2.50 .45
128 A49 2a vermilion 4.75 .90
129 A51 3a carmine rose 4.25 .60
130 A70 3a6p deep blue ('37) 3.25 *30.00*
131 A52 4a olive green 4.25 2.25
132 A53 6a bister ('37) .85 *32.50*
*Nos. 126-132 (7)* 20.30 *67.05*

Same Overprint on India Stamps of 1937

**1937-38** **Wmk. 196** ***Perf. 13½x14***
133 A80 3p slate ('38) 11.00 3.75
134 A80 ½a brown ('38) .80 *7.50*
135 A80 9p green .80 *6.00*
136 A80 1a carmine .80 .90
137 A81 2a scarlet ('38) 1.75 *27.50*
138 A81 2a6p purple ('38) 1.40 *35.00*
139 A81 3a yel grn ('38) 6.75 *30.00*
140 A81 3a6p ultra ('38) 4.25 *35.00*
141 A81 4a dk brown ('38) 10.00 *27.50*
142 A81 6a pck blue ('38) 6.50 *42.50*
143 A81 8a blue vio ('38) 5.25 *35.00*
144 A81 12a car lake ('38) 3.00 *45.00*

Indian Stamps of 1937-40 Overprinted

**1938**
145 A82 1r brown & slate 13.00 *62.50*
146 A82 2r dk brn & dk violet 16.00 *190.00*
147 A82 5r dp ultra & dk green 25.00 *125.00*
148 A82 10r rose car & dk violet 50.00 *120.00*
149 A82 15r dk grn & dk brown 110.00 *1,200.*
150 A82 25r dk vio & bl vio 575.00 *1,400.*
*Nos. 133-150 (18)* 841.30 *3,393.*
Set, never hinged 1,200.

India Stamps of 1937 Overprinted

**1942-43** **Wmk. 196** ***Perf. 13½x14***
155 A80 3p slate 17.50 *32.50*
156 A80 ½a brown 1.25 *3.75*
157 A80 9p green 16.00 *30.00*
158 A80 1a carmine 1.25 *9.00*
159 A82 1r brn & slate 11.00 *40.00*
160 A82 2r dk brn & dk violet 22.50 *52.50*
161 A82 5r dp ultra & dk green 50.00 *140.00*
162 A82 10r rose car & dk vio ('43) 75.00 *140.00*
163 A82 15r dk grn & dk brn ('43) 160.00 *250.00*
164 A82 25r dk vio & bl vio 75.00 *525.00*
*Nos. 155-164 (10)* 429.50 *1,222.*
Set, never hinged 510.00

Same Overprint on India Stamps of 1941-43
165 A83 3p slate .60 *2.10*
166 A83 ½a rose vio ('43) .60 *3.25*
167 A83 9p light green .95 *6.50*
168 A83 1a car rose ('43) 1.25 *2.25*
169 A84 1a3p bister ('43) 1.25 *7.50*
170 A84 1½a dark purple 10.00 7.50
171 A84 2a scarlet 2.25 *7.50*
172 A84 3a violet ('43) 30.00 9.00
173 A84 3½a ultramarine 11.00 *17.50*
174 A85 4a chocolate 7.50 *9.00*
175 A85 6a peacock blue 8.00 *25.00*
176 A85 8a blue violet 5.25 *22.50*
177 A85 12a carmine lake 17.50 *27.50*
*Nos. 165-177 (13)* 96.15 *147.10*
Set, never hinged 115.00

## OFFICIAL STAMPS

India Stamps Overprinted in Black

**1885** **Wmk. 39** ***Perf. 14***
O1 A17 ½a green 3.00 .60
a. "JHIND STATE" reading down 150.00 90.00
O2 A19 1a violet brown 1.00 .25
a. "JHIND STATE" reading down 17.50 11.00
O3 A21 2a ultra 60.00 *72.50*
a. "JHIND STATE" reading down *1,500.* *1,750.*
*Nos. O1-O3 (3)* 64.00 73.35

*The reprints may be distinguished by the same measurements as the reprints of the corresponding regular issue.*

India Stamps Overprinted in Red or Black

**1885**
O4 A17 ½a green (R) 150.00
O5 A19 1a violet brown 125.00
O6 A21 2a ultra (R) 140.00
*Nos. O4-O6 (3)* 415.00

India Stamps Overprinted

**1886** **Red Overprint**
O7 A17 ½a green 42.50
a. "JEIND" *1,050.*
b. "ERVICE" 6,000.
O8 A21 2a ultramarine 47.50
a. "JEIND" *1,750.*
b. "ERVICE" 3,750.

No. O8 was not placed in use.

**1886-96** **Black Overprint**
O9 A17 ½a green ('88) 2.50 .25
O10 A19 1a violet brown 16.00 2.25
a. "JEIND" *750.00*
b. "ERVICE"
O11 A21 2a ultramarine 4.25 1.50
O12 A23 4a olive green 4.50 3.00
O13 A25 8a red violet 7.00 *12.50*
O14 A29 1r car rose & grn ('96) 8.00 *75.00*
*Nos. O9-O14 (6)* 42.25 *94.50*

**1902**
O15 A17 ½a light green 3.75 .45

**1903-06**
O16 A32 3p gray .85 .25
O17 A33 ½a green 4.50 .25
a. "HIND" 4,500. 450.00
O18 A34 1a carmine rose 3.75 .25
a. "HIND" 5,250. 400.00
O19 A35 2a violet 2.50 .25
O20 A38 4a olive green 2.10 .65
O21 A40 8a red violet 7.50 2.25
O22 A42 1r car rose & grn ('06) 3.25 3.25
*Nos. O16-O22 (7)* 24.45 7.15

**1907**
O23 A44 ½a green 1.50 .25
O24 A45 1a carmine rose 2.50 .25

**Indian Stamps of 1911-26 Overprinted**

a

b

**1914-27**

| | | | | |
|---|---|---|---|---|
| O25 | A46(a) | 3p gray | .30 | .25 |
| O26 | A47(a) | ½a green | .40 | .25 |
| O27 | A48(a) | 1a car rose | 1.00 | .25 |
| O28 | A49(a) | 2a violet | .35 | .45 |
| O29 | A52(a) | 4a olive green | 1.90 | .25 |
| O30 | A54(a) | 8a red violet | 1.00 | 1.50 |
| O31 | A56(b) | 1r grn & red brn | 3.75 | 2.50 |
| O32 | A56(b) | 2r yel brn & car rose ('27) | 27.50 | 100.00 |
| O33 | A56(b) | 5r vio & ultra ('27) | 35.00 | 375.00 |
| | | *Nos. O25-O33 (9)* | 71.20 | 480.45 |

India Nos. 83 and 89 Overprinted Type "a"

**1924-27**

| | | | | |
|---|---|---|---|---|
| O34 | A48 | 1a dark brown | .90 | .25 |
| O35 | A53 | 6a bister ('27) | 2.50 | 3.25 |

India Stamps of 1926-35 Overprinted — c

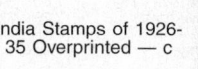

**1927-32**

| | | | | |
|---|---|---|---|---|
| O36 | A46 | 3p slate | .25 | .25 |
| O37 | A47 | ½a green | .25 | 1.50 |
| O38 | A68 | 9p dark green ('32) | .90 | .25 |
| O39 | A48 | 1a dark brown | .25 | .25 |
| O40 | A69 | 1a3p violet ('32) | .60 | .25 |
| O41 | A60 | 2a dull violet | .35 | .25 |
| O42 | A61 | 4a olive green | .50 | .35 |
| O43 | A54 | 8a red violet | .90 | 2.50 |
| O44 | A55 | 12a claret | 3.25 | 27.50 |

Indian Stamps of 1911-23 Overprinted — d

| | | | | |
|---|---|---|---|---|
| O45 | A56 | 1r green & brown | 7.50 | 8.25 |
| O46 | A56 | 2r buff & car rose | 75.00 | 62.50 |
| O47 | A56 | 5r dk vio & ultra | 19.00 | 400.00 |
| O48 | A56 | 10r car rose & grn | 57.50 | 225.00 |
| | | *Nos. O36-O48 (13)* | 166.25 | 728.85 |

India Stamps of 1926-35 Overprinted Type "c"

**1934-37**

| | | | | |
|---|---|---|---|---|
| O49 | A71 | ½a green | .30 | .25 |
| O50 | A72 | 1a dark brown | .30 | .25 |
| O51 | A49 | 2a vermilion | .45 | .25 |
| O52 | A57 | 2a6p buff ('37) | 1.90 | 30.00 |
| O53 | A52 | 4a olive green | 9.00 | .45 |
| O54 | A53 | 6a bister ('37) | 5.50 | 25.00 |
| | | *Nos. O49-O54 (6)* | 17.45 | 56.20 |

India Nos. 151-153 Overprinted Type "c"

**1937-42** ***Perf. 13½x14***

| | | | | |
|---|---|---|---|---|
| O55 | A80 | ½a brown ('42) | 67.50 | .45 |
| O56 | A80 | 9p green | 2.50 | 24.00 |
| O57 | A80 | 1a carmine | 1.90 | .45 |

India Nos. 162-165 Overprinted Type "d"

| | | | | |
|---|---|---|---|---|
| O58 | A82 | 1r brn & sl ('40) | 45.00 | 67.50 |
| O59 | A82 | 2r dk brn & dk vio ('40) | 47.50 | 375.00 |
| O60 | A82 | 5r dp ultra & dk grn ('40) | 100.00 | 600.00 |
| O61 | A82 | 10r rose car & dk vio ('40) | 450.00 | 1,500. |
| | | *Nos. O55-O61 (7)* | 714.40 | 2,567. |
| | | Set, never hinged | 875.00 | |

India Official Stamps of 1939-43 Overprinted

**1940-43**

| | | | | |
|---|---|---|---|---|
| O62 | O8 | 3p slate | .65 | 3.00 |
| O63 | O8 | ½a brown | 2.10 | 1.90 |
| O64 | O8 | ½a dk rose vio ('43) | .65 | .45 |
| O65 | O8 | 9p green | 3.25 | 19.00 |
| O66 | O8 | 1a car rose | 3.75 | .25 |
| O67 | O8 | 1½a dull pur ('43) | 9.25 | 2.40 |
| O68 | O8 | 2a scarlet | 8.50 | .45 |
| O69 | O8 | 2½a purple | 5.25 | 14.00 |
| O70 | O8 | 4a dark brown | 9.50 | 7.00 |
| O71 | O8 | 8a blue violet | 9.50 | 12.00 |

India Nos. 162-165 Overprinted

**1942** **Wmk. 196** ***Perf. 13½x14***

| | | | | |
|---|---|---|---|---|
| O72 | A82 | 1r brown & slate | 19.00 | 82.50 |
| O73 | A82 | 2r dk brn & dk violet | 45.00 | 250.00 |
| O74 | A82 | 5r dp ultra & dk green | 75.00 | 625.00 |
| O75 | A82 | 10r rose car & dk violet | 150.00 | 825.00 |
| | | *Nos. O62-O75 (14)* | 341.40 | 1,842. |
| | | Set, never hinged | 500.00 | |

## NABHA

'näb-hə

LOCATION — A State of India in the eastern and southeastern Punjab
AREA — 966 sq. mi.
POP. — 340,044 (1941)
CAPITAL — Nabha

The varieties with small letters in the overprint are not listed as the letters are merely broken and not from another font.

Indian Stamps Overprinted in Black

**1885** **Wmk. 39** ***Perf. 14***

| | | | | |
|---|---|---|---|---|
| 1 | A17 | ½a green | 6.25 | 9.00 |
| 2 | A19 | 1a violet brown | 82.50 | 290.00 |
| 3 | A21 | 2a ultramarine | 37.50 | 97.50 |
| 4 | A25 | 8a red lilac | 475.00 | |
| 5 | A27 | 1r gray | 550.00 | |

**Wmk. 38**

| | | | | |
|---|---|---|---|---|
| 6 | A9 | 4a green | 125.00 | 375.00 |

*On the reprints "Nabha" and "State" each measure 9½mm. On the originals they measure 11 and 10mm respectively.*

Indian Stamps Overprinted

**1885** **Wmk. 39** **Red Overprint**

| | | | | |
|---|---|---|---|---|
| 7 | A17 | ½a green | 1.90 | 1.50 |
| 8 | A21 | 2a ultramarine | 3.75 | 3.25 |
| 9 | A27 | 1r gray | 190.00 | 450.00 |

**Wmk. 38**

| | | | | |
|---|---|---|---|---|
| 10 | A9 | 4a green | 67.50 | 325.00 |

**1885-97** **Wmk. 39** **Black Overprint**

| | | | | |
|---|---|---|---|---|
| 11 | A17 | ½a green | .90 | .25 |
| 12 | A18 | 9p rose ('92) | .30 | 5.25 |
| 13 | A19 | 1a violet brown | 4.50 | 1.50 |
| 14 | A20 | 1a6p bister brn | 2.50 | 6.00 |
| *a.* | | "ABHA" | 450.00 | |
| 15 | A21 | 2a ultramarine | 4.50 | 3.00 |
| 16 | A22 | 3a orange | 16.00 | 32.50 |
| 17 | A23 | 4a olive green | 9.00 | 5.00 |
| 18 | A25 | 8a red lilac | 6.00 | 5.25 |
| 19 | A26 | 12a vio, *red* ('89) | 7.00 | 8.25 |
| 20 | A27 | 1r gray | 22.50 | 90.00 |
| 21 | A29 | 1r car rose & grn ('93) | 21.00 | 10.50 |
| *a.* | | "N BHA" | | — |
| 22 | A30 | 2r brn & rose ('97) | 210.00 | 450.00 |
| 23 | A30 | 3r grn & brn ('97) | 210.00 | 550.00 |
| 24 | A30 | 5r vio & blk ('97) | 225.00 | 825.00 |

**Wmk. 38**

| | | | | |
|---|---|---|---|---|
| 25 | A14 | 6a bister ('89) | 5.50 | 6.50 |
| | | *Nos. 11-25 (15)* | 744.70 | 1,999. |

*Nos. 7, 8, 9, 10, 13, and 18 have been reprinted. They usually bear the overprint "Specimen."*

**1900** **Wmk. 39**

| | | | | |
|---|---|---|---|---|
| 26 | A31 | 3p carmine rose | .45 | .25 |

**1903-09**

| | | | | |
|---|---|---|---|---|
| 27 | A32 | 3p gray | .95 | .25 |
| 28 | A33 | ½a green | 1.40 | 1.00 |
| *a.* | | "NABH" | 1,650. | |
| 29 | A34 | 1a car rose | 2.10 | 2.25 |
| 30 | A35 | 2a violet | 3.25 | 5.25 |
| 30A | A36 | 2a6p ultra | 24.50 | 130.00 |
| 31 | A37 | 3a brown orange | 2.00 | .60 |
| 32 | A38 | 4a olive green | 6.00 | 2.50 |
| 33 | A39 | 6a bister | 5.00 | 30.00 |
| 34 | A40 | 8a red violet | 13.00 | 40.00 |
| 35 | A41 | 12a violet, *red* | 5.50 | 40.00 |
| 36 | A42 | 1r car rose & grn | 12.00 | 27.50 |
| | | *Nos. 27-36 (11)* | 75.70 | 279.35 |

**1907**

| | | | | |
|---|---|---|---|---|
| 37 | A44 | ½a green | 2.25 | 1.90 |
| 38 | A45 | 1a carmine rose | 2.25 | 1.00 |

**1913**

| | | | | |
|---|---|---|---|---|
| 40 | A46 | 3p gray | .75 | .75 |
| 41 | A47 | ½a green | .75 | .45 |
| 42 | A48 | 1a carmine rose | 1.60 | .25 |
| 43 | A49 | 2a violet | 1.50 | 1.50 |
| 44 | A51 | 3a brown orange | .75 | .45 |
| 45 | A52 | 4a olive green | 1.00 | 3.00 |
| 46 | A53 | 6a bister | 1.90 | 9.50 |
| 47 | A54 | 8a red violet | 9.50 | 9.00 |
| 48 | A55 | 12a claret | 4.50 | 35.00 |
| 49 | A56 | 1r green & red brn | 15.00 | 11.00 |
| | | *Nos. 40-49 (10)* | 37.25 | 70.90 |

**1924**

| | | | | |
|---|---|---|---|---|
| 50 | A48 | 1a dark brown | 10.00 | 6.00 |

India Stamps of 1926-35 Overprinted

**1927-32** **Wmk. 196**

| | | | | |
|---|---|---|---|---|
| 51 | A46 | 3p slate ('32) | 2.50 | .25 |
| 52 | A47 | ½a green | 1.50 | .45 |
| 53 | A48 | 1a dark brown | 2.25 | .25 |
| 54 | A60 | 2a dull violet ('32) | 3.75 | .50 |
| 55 | A57 | 2a6p buff ('32) | 1.75 | 14.00 |
| 56 | A51 | 3a blue ('30) | 4.50 | 2.10 |
| 57 | A61 | 4a olive green ('32) | 6.75 | 3.75 |

Indian Stamps of 1937-40 Overprinted

| | | | | |
|---|---|---|---|---|
| 58 | A56 | 2r brown org & car rose ('32) | 47.50 | 210.00 |
| 59 | A56 | 5r dk violet & ultra ('32) | 110.00 | 600.00 |
| | | *Nos. 51-59 (9)* | 180.50 | 831.30 |

India Stamps of 1926-35 Overprinted

**1936-37**

| | | | | |
|---|---|---|---|---|
| 63 | A71 | ½a green | .75 | .60 |
| 64 | A68 | 9p dark green ('37) | 3.00 | 1.60 |
| 65 | A72 | 1a dark brown | .75 | .45 |
| 66 | A69 | 1a3p violet ('37) | 3.50 | 11.00 |
| 67 | A51 | 3a car rose ('37) | 5.00 | 25.00 |
| 68 | A52 | 4a olive green ('37) | 7.50 | 7.50 |
| | | *Nos. 63-68 (6)* | 20.50 | 46.15 |
| | | Set, never hinged | 25.00 | |

Same Overprint in Black on 1937 Stamps of India

**1938-39** ***Perf. 13½x14***

| | | | | |
|---|---|---|---|---|
| 69 | A80 | 3p slate | 9.50 | 2.25 |
| 70 | A80 | ½a brown | 7.50 | 2.50 |
| 71 | A80 | 9p green | 21.00 | 7.50 |
| 72 | A80 | 1a carmine | 3.25 | 1.50 |
| 73 | A81 | 2a scarlet | 1.25 | 12.00 |
| 74 | A81 | 2a6p purple | 1.25 | 17.50 |
| 75 | A81 | 3a yel green | 1.50 | 9.00 |
| 76 | A81 | 3a6p ultramarine | 1.75 | 37.50 |
| 77 | A81 | 4a dark brown | 8.00 | 10.50 |
| 78 | A81 | 6a peacock blue | 3.50 | 40.00 |
| 79 | A81 | 8a blue violet | 2.25 | 37.50 |
| 80 | A81 | 12a car lake | 3.00 | 37.50 |

Overprinted

| | | | | |
|---|---|---|---|---|
| 81 | A82 | 1r brown & slate | 13.00 | 52.50 |
| 82 | A82 | 2r dk brn & dk vio | 32.50 | 175.00 |
| 83 | A82 | 5r dp ultra & dk green | 42.50 | 300.00 |
| 84 | A82 | 10r rose car & dk vio ('39) | 65.00 | 600.00 |
| 85 | A82 | 15r dk grn & dk brn ('39) | 200.00 | 1,250. |
| 86 | A82 | 25r dk vio & blue vio ('39) | 150.00 | 1,250. |
| | | *Nos. 69-86 (18)* | 566.75 | 3,842. |
| | | Set, never hinged | 1,200. | |

India Stamps of 1937 Overprinted in Black

**1942** ***Perf. 13½x14***

| | | | | |
|---|---|---|---|---|
| 87 | A80 | 3p slate | 50.00 | 9.00 |
| 88 | A80 | ½a brown | 100.00 | 10.50 |
| 89 | A80 | 9p green | 14.00 | 24.00 |
| 90 | A80 | 1a carmine | 15.00 | 6.50 |
| | | *Nos. 87-90 (4)* | 179.00 | 50.00 |
| | | Set, never hinged | 210.00 | |

Same on India Nos. 168-179

**1942-46** **Wmk. 196**

| | | | | |
|---|---|---|---|---|
| 100 | A83 | 3p slate | 1.25 | 1.25 |
| 101 | A83 | ½a rose vio ('43) | 3.25 | 2.50 |
| 102 | A83 | 9p lt green ('43) | 2.50 | 2.50 |
| 103 | A83 | 1a car rose ('46) | 1.10 | 6.50 |
| 104 | A84 | 1a3p bister ('44) | 1.10 | 5.50 |
| 105 | A84 | 1½a dark pur ('43) | 2.50 | 4.50 |
| 106 | A84 | 2a scarlet ('44) | 1.20 | 6.50 |
| 107 | A84 | 3a violet ('44) | 7.00 | 7.00 |
| 108 | A84 | 3½a ultramarine | 18.00 | 100.00 |
| 109 | A85 | 4a choc ('43) | 1.90 | 1.50 |
| 110 | A85 | 6a pck blue ('44) | 15.00 | 82.50 |
| 111 | A85 | 8a blue vio ('44) | 13.50 | 62.50 |
| 112 | A85 | 12a car lake ('44) | 12.00 | 100.00 |
| | | *Nos. 100-112 (13)* | 80.30 | 382.75 |
| | | Set, never hinged | 110.00 | |

### OFFICIAL STAMPS

Indian Stamps Overprinted in Black

**1885** **Wmk. 39** ***Perf. 14***

| | | | | |
|---|---|---|---|---|
| O1 | A17 | ½a green | 7.50 | 2.25 |
| O2 | A19 | 1a violet brown | 1.00 | .30 |
| O3 | A21 | 2a ultra | 125.00 | 250.00 |
| | | *Nos. O1-O3 (3)* | 133.50 | 252.55 |

*The reprints have the same measurements as the reprints of the regular issue of the same date.*

Indian Stamps Overprinted

**1885** **Red Overprint**

| | | | | |
|---|---|---|---|---|
| O4 | A17 | ½a green | 11.00 | 8.25 |
| O5 | A21 | 2a ultramarine | 2.40 | .80 |

**1885-97 Black Overprint**

O6 A17 ½a green .60 .25
 a. Period after "SERVICE" 190.00 3.25
O7 A19 1a violet brown 3.00 .35
 a. "NABHA STATE" double 2,750. *375.00*
 b. Period after "SERVICE" 13.50 1.10
O8 A21 2a ultra 5.00 2.50
O9 A22 3a orange 37.50 *140.00*
O10 A23 4a olive green 5.25 2.25
O11 A25 8a red vio ('89) 4.00 2.25
O12 A26 12a vio, *red* ('89) 9.50 *32.50*
O13 A27 1r gray ('89) 62.50 *525.00*
O14 A29 1r car rose & grn ('97) 24.00 *35.00*

**Wmk. 38**

O15 A14 6a bister ('89) 32.50 *52.50*
 *Nos. O6-O15 (10)* 183.85 *792.60*

*Nos. O4, O5, and O7 have been reprinted. They usually bear the overprint "Specimen."*

**1903-06 Wmk. 39**

O16 A32 3p gray ('06) 3.75 25.00
O17 A33 ½a green 1.20 .50
O18 A34 1a carmine rose 1.20 .25
O19 A35 2a violet 5.00 2.10
O20 A38 4a olive green 2.40 .75
O21 A40 8a red violet 2.50 2.25
O22 A42 1r car rose & grn 2.50 *3.75*
 *Nos. O16-O22 (7)* 18.55 34.60

**1907**

O23 A44 ½a green 2.50 .75
O24 A45 1a carmine rose 1.00 .40

**1913**

O25 A52 4a olive green 17.50 *100.00*
O26 A56 1r grn & red brn 92.50 *750.00*

**Indian Stamps of 1911-26 Overprinted**

a

b

**1913**

O27 A46(a) 3p gray 1.40 *15.00*
O28 A47(a) ½a green .85 .25
O29 A48(a) 1a carmine rose .75 .25
O30 A49(a) 2a violet 1.60 .25
O31 A52(a) 4a olive green 1.25 .90
O32 A54(a) 8a red violet 2.10 *3.00*
O33 A56(b) 1r grn & red brn 8.50 6.50
 *Nos. O27-O33 (7)* 16.45 *26.15*

India Stamps of 1926-35 Overprinted

***Perf. 13½x14, 14***

**1932-45 Wmk. 196**

O34 A46 3p slate .30 .25
O35 A72 1a dark brown ('35) .30 .25
O36 A52 4a olive green ('45) 35.00 3.75
O37 A54 8a red violet ('37) 1.50 *4.00*
 *Nos. O34-O37 (4)* 37.10 8.25

Same Overprint in Black on India Stamps of 1937

**1938**

O38 A80 9p green 6.00 6.00
 Never hinged 7.00
O39 A80 1a carmine 22.50 1.60
 Never hinged 27.50

Official Stamps of India 1939-43 Overprinted in Black

**1942-44 *Perf. 13½x14***

O40 O8 3p slate 1.25 *3.00*
O41 O8 ½a brown ('43) 1.20 .45
O42 O8 ½a dk rose vio ('44) 4.75 2.25
O43 O8 9p green ('43) 1.25 .45
O44 O8 1a car rose ('43) .65 .25
O45 O8 1½a dull purple ('43) .70 .60
O46 O8 2a scarlet ('43) 2.25 2.25
O47 O8 4a dark brown ('43) 3.50 *5.25*
O48 O8 8a blue violet ('43) 6.75 *30.00*

India Nos. 162-164 Overprinted in Black

O49 A82 1r brown & slate 9.00 *62.50*
O50 A82 2r dk brn & dk vio 32.50 *275.00*
O51 A82 5r dp ultra & dk green 175.00 *825.00*
 *Nos. O40-O51 (12)* 238.80 *1,207.*
 Set, never hinged 300.00

## PATIALA

ˌpət-ē-ˈäl-ə

LOCATION — A State of India in the central Punjab
AREA — 5,942 sq. mi.
POP. — 1,936,259 (1941)
CAPITAL — Patiala

The varieties with small letters in the overprint are not listed as the letters are merely broken and not from another font.

Indian Stamps Overprinted in Red

**1884 Wmk. 39 *Perf. 14***

1 A17 ½a green 6.00 *7.00*
 a. Double ovpt., one horiz. 4,750. 1,200.
2 A19 1a violet brown 75.00 *110.00*
 a. Double overprint
 b. Double ovpt., one in black 1,050.
 c. Pair, one as "b," one without overprint
3 A21 2a ultra 19.00 *24.00*
4 A25 8a red lilac 650.00 *1,600.*
 a. Double ovpt., one in black 190.00 *650.00*
 c. Overprint reversed
 d. Pair like "a," one with overprint reversed
5 A27 1r gray 225.00 *950.00*

**Wmk. 38**

6 A9 4a green 140.00 150.00
 *Nos. 1-6 (6)* 1,115. *2,841.*

Indian Stamps Overprinted in Red

**1885 Wmk. 39**

7 A17 ½a green 3.25 .45
 a. "AUTTIALLA" 24.00 *52.50*
 c. "STATE" only
8 A21 2a ultra 9.00 2.50
 a. "AUTTIALLA" 62.50
9 A27 1r gray 24.00 *125.00*
 a. "AUTTIALLA" 650.00

**Wmk. 38**

10 A9 4a green 6.00 *6.25*
 a. Double overprint, one in black 375.00
 b. Pair, one as "a," one with black overprint

**Same, Overprinted in Black**

**Wmk. 39**

11 A19 1a violet brown .90 .45
 a. "AUTTIALLA" 100.00
 c. Double overprint, one in red 17.50 *140.00*
 d. Pair, one as "c," one without overprint
12 A25 8a red lilac 35.00 *82.50*
 a. "AUTTIALLA" 550.00
 *Nos. 7-12 (6)* 78.15 *217.15*

*Nos. 7-12 have been reprinted. Most of them bear the word "Reprint." The few stamps that escaped the overprint cannot be distinguished from the originals.*

*The error "AUTTIALLA" has been reprinted in entire sheets, in red on the ½, 2, 4a and 1r and in black on the ½, 1, 2, 4, 8a and 1r. "STATE" is 7¾mm long, instead of 8½mm. Most stamps are overprinted "Reprint."*

Same, Overprinted in Black

**1891-96**

13 A17 ½a green .75 .25
14 A18 9p rose 1.50 3.25
15 A19 1a violet brown 2.10 .45
 a. "STATE" only 300.00 *625.00*
16 A20 1a6p bister brown 2.10 *3.00*
17 A21 2a ultra 3.25 1.50
18 A22 3a orange 3.75 1.10
19 A23 4a olive grn ('96) 3.75 1.10
 a. "STATE" only 750.00 375.00
20 A25 8a red violet ('96) 5.50 *24.00*
21 A26 12a violet, *red* 3.75 *24.00*
22 A29 1r car rose & grn ('96) 6.50 *82.50*
23 A30 2r brn & rose ('95) 210.00 *1,250.*
24 A30 3r grn & brn ('95) 290.00 *1,350.*
25 A30 5r vio & bl ('95) 325.00 *1,400.*

**Wmk. 38**

26 A14 6a bister 3.75 *22.50*
 *Nos. 13-26 (14)* 861.70 4,163.

**1899 Wmk. 39**

27 A31 3p carmine rose .45 .25
 a. Pair, one without overprint 6,000.

**1902**

28 A17 ½a light green 1.50 .90
29 A19 1a carmine rose 3.75 2.50

**1903-06**

31 A32 3p gray .50 .25
32 A33 ½a green 1.40 .25
33 A34 1a carmine rose 1.75 .25
 a. Pair, one without overprint *1,500.*
34 A35 2a violet 2.00 1.00
35 A37 3a brown orange 2.00 .50
36 A38 4a olive green ('06) 3.50 2.25
37 A39 6a bister ('05) 4.25 *15.00*
38 A40 8a red violet ('06) 4.75 4.50
39 A41 12a vio, *red* ('06) 9.25 *40.00*
40 A42 1r car rose & grn ('05) 5.50 *9.00*
 *Nos. 31-40 (10)* 34.90 *73.00*

**1908**

41 A44 ½a green .60 .35
42 A45 1a carmine rose 2.50 1.50

**1912-14**

43 A46 3p gray .35 .25
44 A47 ½a green .85 .25
45 A48 1a carmine rose 2.00 .25
46 A49 2a violet 1.90 2.25
47 A51 3a brown orange 3.25 2.50
48 A52 4a olive green 4.50 5.25
49 A53 6a bister 2.50 *6.50*
50 A54 8a red violet 3.75 3.75
51 A55 12a claret 4.75 *15.00*
52 A56 1r green & red brn 12.00 *22.50*
 *Nos. 43-52 (10)* 35.85 *58.50*

**1922-26**

53 A48 1a dk brown ('23) 3.50 .75
54 A58 1½a chocolate .35 *.85*
55 A51 3a ultra ('26) 4.25 *14.00*
56 A56 2r yel brn & car rose ('26) 18.00 *225.00*
57 A56 5r vio & ultra ('26) 45.00 *300.00*
 *Nos. 53-57 (5)* 71.10 *540.60*

India Stamps of 1926-35 Overprinted

**1928-34 Wmk. 196**

60 A46 3p slate 2.50 .25
61 A47 ½a green .35 .25
62 A68 9p dark green 2.75 1.50
63 A48 1a dark brown .95 .35
64 A69 1a3p violet 3.75 .25
65 A60 2a dull violet 2.10 .60
66 A57 2a6p buff 6.00 4.00
67 A51 3a blue 3.75 4.00
68 A61 4a olive green 6.50 3.00
69 A54 8a red violet 10.50 6.00

Indian Stamps of 1911-23 Overprinted

70 A56 1r green & brown 9.00 *15.00*
71 A56 2r buff & car rose 13.50 *82.50*
 *Nos. 60-71 (12)* 61.65 117.70

India Stamps of 1926-35 Overprinted Like Nos. 60-69

**1935-37 *Perf. 14***

75 A71 ½a green ('37) 1.00 .45
76 A72 1a dk brown ('36) 1.40 .25
77 A49 2a ver ('36) .50 *2.25*
78 A51 3a car rose ('37) 7.00 *8.00*
79 A52 4a olive green 2.25 3.50
 *Nos. 75-79 (5)* 12.15 *14.45*
 Set, never hinged 29.00

Same Overprint in Black on Stamps of India, 1937

**1937-38 *Perf. 13½x14***

80 A80 3p slate ('38) 21.00 .50
81 A80 ½a brown ('38) 8.50 .75
82 A80 9p green 5.25 1.50
83 A80 1a carmine 3.00 .25
84 A81 2a scarlet ('38) 1.60 *14.00*
85 A81 2a6p purple ('38) 6.00 *30.00*
86 A81 3a yel green ('38) 6.50 *13.50*
87 A81 3a6p ultra ('38) 6.75 *37.50*
88 A81 4a dark brown ('38) 24.00 25.00
89 A81 6a pck blue ('38) 25.00 *90.00*
90 A81 8a blue violet ('38) 27.50 *62.50*
91 A81 12a car lake ('38) 25.00 *105.00*

Overprinted Like Nos. 70-71

**1938**

92 A82 1r brown & slate 30.00 *62.50*
93 A82 2r dk brn & dk vio 30.00 *160.00*
94 A82 5r dp ultra & dk green 40.00 *375.00*
95 A82 10r rose car & dk vio 52.50 *600.00*
96 A82 15r dk grn & dk brn 130.00 *950.00*
97 A82 25r dk vio & bl vio 150.00 *950.00*
 *Nos. 80-97 (18)* 592.60 *3,478.*
 Set, never hinged 850.00

India Nos. 150-153 Overprinted in Black

**1942-43 *Perf. 13½x14***

98 A80 3p slate 11.50 4.00
99 A80 ½a brown ('43) 6.75 3.25
100 A80 9p green ('43) 320.00 12.00
101 A80 1a carmine 25.00 3.75
 *Nos. 98-101 (4)* 363.25 23.00
 Set, never hinged 515.00

India Stamps of 1941-43 with same Overprint in Black

**1942-47 *Perf. 13½x14***

102 A83 3p slate 4.25 .25
103 A83 ½a rose violet ('43) 4.25 .25
104 A83 9p lt green ('43) 1.60 .25
 a. Pair, one without overprint *4,750.*
105 A83 1a car rose ('46) 1.10 .25
106 A84 1a3p bister ('43) 1.75 *5.25*
107 A84 1½a dk purple ('43) 13.50 5.50
108 A84 2a scarlet ('46) 9.50 .75
109 A84 3a violet ('46) 8.50 3.75
110 A84 3½a ultra ('46) 20.00 *57.50*
111 A85 4a choc ('46) 9.25 6.50
112 A85 6a pck blue ('46) 3.50 *45.00*
113 A85 8a blue vio ('46) 3.25 *22.50*
114 A85 12a car lake ('45) 30.00 *125.00*

No. 102 India No. 162 Overprinted in Black

**115** A82 1r brown & slate ('47) 16.00 *120.00*
*Nos. 102-115 (14)* 126.45 *392.75*
Set, never hinged 170.00

---

## OFFICIAL STAMPS

Indian Stamps Overprinted in Black and Red

**1884** **Wmk. 39** ***Perf. 14***

**O1** A17 ½a green 27.50 .60
**O2** A19 1a vio brown 1.50 .25
*a.* "SERVICE" double 3,000. 950.00
*b.* "SERVICE" inverted 2,500.
*c.* "PUTTIALLA STATE" dbl. 175.00
*d.* "PUTTIALLA STATE" invtd. 3,000. 400.00
**O3** A21 2a ultra *7,500.* 175.00

### Overprinted in Red or Black

a

b

**1885-90**

**O4** A17(a) ½a green (R & Bk) 2.25 .35
*a.* "AUTTIALLA" 80.00 25.00
*d.* "SERVICE" double 1,050.
**O5** A17(b) ½a green (Bk) 2.25 .25
**O6** A19(a) 1a vio brn (Bk) 2.25 .25
*a.* "AUTTILLA" 1,050. 72.50
*c.* "SERVICE" dble., one invtd. 900.00
*d.* "SERVICE" double 3,000.
**O7** A21(b) 2a ultra (R) 1.10 .60
*c.* "SERVICE" dbl., one invtd. 45.00 *290.00*
*Nos. O4-O7 (4)* 7.85 1.45

*There are reprints of Nos. O4, O6 and O7. That of No. O4 has "SERVICE" overprinted in red in large letters and that of No. O6 has the same overprint in black. The originals have the word in small black letters. The reprints of No. O7, except those overprinted "Reprint," cannot be distinguished from the originals. These three reprints also exist with the error "AUTTIALLA."*

Same, Overprinted in Black

**1891-1900**

**O8** A17 ½a green ('95) .75 .25
*b.* "SERVICE" inverted 90.00
**O9** A19 1a vio brown ('00) 9.00 .25
*a.* "SERVICE" inverted 90.00
**O10** A21 2a ultramarine 5.00 3.25
*a.* "SERVICE" inverted 90.00 *300.00*
**O11** A22 3a orange 3.75 5.00
**O12** A23 4a olive green 3.00 .45
**O13** A25 8a red violet 5.25 2.50
**O14** A26 12a violet, *red* 3.50 .80
**O15** A27 1r gray 3.75 1.00

**Wmk. 38**

**O16** A14 6a bister 2.40 .50
*Nos. O8-O16 (9)* 36.40 14.00

**1902** **Wmk. 39**

**O17** A19 1a carmine rose 1.40 .25

**1903**

**O18** A29 1r car rose & green 9.00 15.00

**1903-09**

**O19** A32 3p gray .60 .25
**O20** A33 ½a green 1.50 .25
**O21** A34 1a carmine rose .90 .25
**O22** A35 2a violet 1.20 .25
**O23** A37 3a brown orange 6.00 5.25
**O24** A38 4a olive green ('05) 4.00 .25
**O25** A40 8a red violet 2.50 1.10
**O26** A42 1r car rose & grn ('06) 3.00 1.20
*Nos. O19-O26 (8)* 19.70 8.80

**1907**

**O27** A44 ½a green .75 .25
**O28** A45 1a carmine rose .90 .25

### India Stamps of 1911-26 Overprinted

a

b

**1913-26**

**O29** A46(a) 3p gray .30 .25
**O30** A47(a) ½a green .25 .25
**O31** A48(a) 1a car rose .25 .25
**O32** A49(a) 2a violet 1.20 1.10
**O33** A52(a) 4a olive green .75 .50
**O34** A54(a) 8a red violet .80 *1.00*
**O35** A56(b) 1r grn & red brn 1.75 2.10
**O36** A56(b) 2r yel brn & car rose ('26) 24.00 *75.00*
**O37** A56(b) 5r vio & ultra ('26) 15.00 *35.00*
*Nos. O29-O37 (9)* 44.30 *115.45*

Same Overprint on India Nos. 83 and 89

**1925-26**

**O38** A48(a) 1a dark brown 9.50 1.50
**O39** A53(a) 6a bister ('26) 2.10 *3.75*

India Stamps of 1926-35 Overprinted

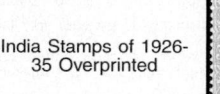

**1927-36** **Wmk. 196**

**O40** A46 3p slate .25 .25
**O41** A47 ½a green 1.25 .80
**O42** A48 1a dark brown .25 .25
**O43** A69 1a3p violet .60 .25
**O44** A60 2a dull violet .25 *.45*
**O45** A60 2a vermilion .45 .50
**O46** A57 2a6p buff 3.75 .50
**O47** A61 4a olive green .75 .45
**O48** A54 8a red violet 1.60 1.00

Indian Stamps of 1911-23 Overprinted

**O49** A56 1r green & brown 6.50 5.00
**O50** A56 2r brn org & car rose ('36) 20.00 *62.50*
*Nos. O40-O50 (11)* 35.65 *71.95*

India Stamps of 1926-34 Overprinted

**1935-36**

**O51** A71 ½a green ('36) .25 .25
**O52** A72 1a dark brown ('36) .45 .45
**O53** A49 2a vermilion .30 *.45*
*a.* Small die 21.00 7.50
**O54** A52 4a olive green ('36) 3.50 2.50
*Nos. O51-O54 (4)* 4.50 *3.65*
Set, never hinged 5.00

Same Overprint on India #151-153

**1938-39** ***Perf. 13½x14***

**O55** A80 ½a brown ('39) .95 .30
**O56** A80 9p green ('39) 16.00 *95.00*
**O57** A80 1a carmine .95 .60
*Nos. O55-O57 (3)* 17.90 *95.90*
Set, never hinged 22.00

India No. 136 Surcharged in Black

**1939** ***Perf. 14***

**O58** A69 1a on 1a3p violet 15.00 5.25
Never hinged 18.00

"SERVICE" measures 9¼mm.

No. 64 Surcharged in Black

**1940**

**O59** A69 1a on 1a3p violet 12.50 5.00
Never hinged 15.00

"SERVICE" measures 8½mm.

India Nos. 162-164 Overprinted

***Perf. 13½x14***

**O60** A82 1r brown & slate 1.25 *10.50*
**O61** A82 2r dk brn & dk vio 7.50 7.50
**O62** A82 5r dp ultra & dk grn 21.00 95.00
Set, never hinged 36.00

India Official Stamps of 1939-43 Overprinted

**1940-45**

**O63** O8 3p slate ('41) 1.90 .25
**O64** O8 ½a brown 5.25 .25
**O65** O8 ½a dk rose vio ('43) 1.10 .25
**O66** O8 9p green 1.10 .75
**O67** O8 1a carmine rose 3.50 .25
**O68** O8 1a3p bister ('41) 1.25 .35
**O69** O8 1½a dull purple ('45) 6.75 1.90
**O70** O8 2a scarlet ('41) 11.00 .50
**O71** O8 2½a purple ('41) 4.00 1.50
**O72** O8 4a dk brown ('45) 1.90 *3.75*
**O73** O8 8a blue violet ('45) 5.25 *9.00*

India Nos. 162-164 Overprinted in Black

**O74** A82 1r brn & slate ('43) 5.25 *16.00*
**O75** A82 2r dk brn & dk vio ('45) 13.50 *95.00*
**O76** A82 5r dp ultra & dk grn ('45) 22.00 *125.00*
*Nos. O63-O76 (14)* 83.75 *254.75*
Set, never hinged 145.00

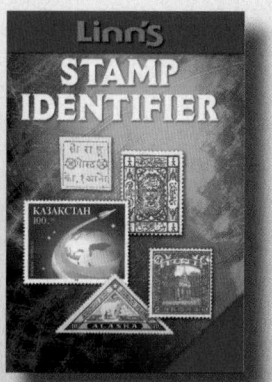

# INDIA - FEUDATORY STATES

## FEUDATORY STATES

**These stamps had franking power solely in the states in which they were issued, except for Cochin and Travancore which had a reciprocal postal agreement.**

## ALWAR

'əl-wər

LOCATION — A Feudatory State of India, lying southwest of Delhi in the Jaipur Residency.
AREA — 3,158 sq. mi.
POP. — 749,751.
CAPITAL — Alwar

Katar (Indian Dagger) — A1

**1877 Unwmk. Litho.** ***Rouletted***

**1** A1 ¼a ultramarine 7.00 1.60
*a.* ¼a blue 7.00 1.60
**2** A1 1a brown 5.25 1.90
*a.* 1a yellow brown 16.00 8.25
*b.* 1a red brown 5.00 2.25

**Redrawn**

**1899-1901** ***Pin-perf. 12***

**3** A1 ¼a sl blue, wide margins 12.50 4.50
*a.* Horiz. pair, imperf. between 600.00 *750.00*
*b.* Vert. pair, imperf. between 1,200. *1,250.*
**4** A1 ¼a yel grn, narrow margins ('01) 11.00 4.00
*a.* Horiz. pair, imperf. between 950.00
*b.* Imperf, pair 950.00
*c.* ¼a emer, wide margins ('99) 600.00
*d.* ¼a emer, narrow margins 5.25 4.75
*e.* As "d," imperf, pair 550.00
*f.* As "d," vert. pair, imperf horiz. 500.00
*g.* As "d," horiz. pair, imperf vert. 450.00 *525.00*
*h.* As "d," vert. pair, imperf horiz. 450.00 *525.00*

Nos. 3 and 4b are printed farther apart in the sheet.

On Nos. 3 and 4, the shading of the left border line is missing.

Nos. 1 to 4 occasionally show portions of the papermaker's watermark, W. T. & Co.

Alwar stamps became obsolete in 1902.

## BAMRA

'bäm-rə

LOCATION — A Feudatory State in the Eastern States, Orissa States Agency, Bengal.
AREA — 1,988 sq. mi.
POP. — 151,259
CAPITAL — Deogarh

Stamps of Bamra were issued without gum.

A1

A2

**1888 Unwmk. Typeset** ***Imperf.***

**1** A1 ¼a black, *yellow* 700.00
*a.* "g" inverted *7,000.*
**2** A1 ½a black, *rose* 125.00
*a.* "g" inverted *2,400.*
**3** A1 1a black, *blue* 100.00
*a.* "g" inverted *2,100.*
**4** A1 2a black, *green* 140.00 *550.00*
*a.* "postge" *2,400.*
**5** A1 4a black, *yellow* 120.00 *550.00*
*a.* "postge" *2,250.*
**6** A1 8a black, *rose* 72.50
*a.* "postge" *1,900.*
*Nos. 1-6 (6)* 1,257.

All values may be found with the scroll inverted, and with the long end of the scroll pointing to the right or left.

On No. 5 the last character on the 3rd line is a vertical line. On No. 1 it is not vertical.

On No. 2 the last character on the 3rd line looks like a backwards "R" with a bent leg. On No. 6 it looks like an apostrophe.

*Nos. 1 and 2 have been reprinted in blocks of 8 and Nos. 1-6 in blocks of 20. In the reprints the 4th character of the native inscription often has the curved upper line broken at the left, but in many instances comparison with photographic reproductions of the original settings is the only certain test.*

**1890**

**7** A2 ¼a black, *rose lilac* 7.00 *9.00*
*a.* "Quatrer" 32.50 *57.50*
*b.* "e" of "Postage" inverted 32.50 *57.50*
*c.* "Eeudatory" 32.50 *57.50*
**8** A2 ½a black, *green* 5.25 5.25
*a.* "Eeudatory" 90.00 *110.00*
*b.* "postage" with small "p" 5.25 5.25
**9** A2 1a black, *yellow* 6.50 5.00
*a.* "Eeudatory" 195.00 *225.00*
*b.* "postage" with small "p" 6.50 5.00
*c.* "annas" 300.00 *325.00*
**10** A2 2a black, *rose lilac* 30.00 *57.50*
*a.* "Eeudatory" 275.00 *550.00*
**11** A2 4a black, *bright rose* 9.50 *12.50*
*a.* "Eeudatory" 6,750.
**12** A2 8a black, *rose lilac* 40.00 *100.00*
*a.* "BAMBA" 375.00 *550.00*
*b.* "Foudatory" & "Postage" 375.00 *550.00*
*c.* "postage" with small "p" 40.00 *100.00*
**13** A2 1r black, *rose lilac* 100.00 *160.00*
*a.* "BAMBA" 650.00 *825.00*
*b.* "Eeudatory" 825.00 *1,050.*
*c.* "postage" with small "p" 100.00 160.00
*Nos. 7-13 (7)* 198.25 *349.25*

**1893**

**14** A2 ¼a black, *rose* 3.00 *4.50*
*a.* "postage" with small "p" 3.00 *4.50*
**15** A2 ¼a black, *magenta* 3.00 *4.00*
*a.* "postage" with small "p" 3.00 *4.00*
*d.* "AMRA" of "BAMRA" inverted 100.00 100.00
*e.* "M" and 2nd "A" of "BAMRA" inverted 140.00 140.00
*f.* First "a" of "anna" inverted 72.50 82.50
**16** A2 2a black, *rose* 21.00 12.00
*a.* "postage" with small "p" 21.00 12.00
**17** A2 4a black, *rose* 16.00 12.00
*a.* "postage" with small "p" 16.00 12.00
*b.* "BAMBA" 1,600. *1,800.*
**18** A2 8a black, *rose* 42.50 29.00
*a.* "postage" with small "p" 42.50 29.00
**19** A2 1r black, *rose* 35.00 35.00
*a.* "postage" with small "p" 35.00 35.00
*Nos. 14-19 (6)* 120.50 96.50

The central ornament varies in size and may be found in various positions.

Bamra stamps became obsolete Dec. 31, 1894.

## BARWANI

bər-'wän-ē

LOCATION — A Feudatory State of Central India, in the Malwa Agency.
AREA — 1,178 sq. mi.
POP. — 141,110
CAPITAL — Barwani

The stamps of Barwani were all typographed and normally issued in booklets containing panes of four. Exceptions are noted (Nos. 14-15, 20-25). The majority were completely perforated, but some of the earlier printings were perforated only between the stamps, leaving one or two sides imperf. Nos. 1-25 were issued without gum. Many shades exist.

Rana Ranjit Singh
A1 A2

**1921, April (?) Unwmk.** ***Pin-Perf 7***
**Toned Medium Wove Paper**
**Clear Impression**

**1** A1 ¼a dull Prus green 225.00 *625.00*
**2** A1 ½a dull blue 500.00 *950.00*

**1921** ***Coarse Perf. 7 x Imperf.***
**White Thin Wove Paper**
**Blurred Impression**

**3** A1 ¼a dull green 37.50 *190.00*
**4** A1 ½a pale blue 25.00 *275.00*

**1921 Toned Laid Paper** ***Imperf.***

**5** A1 ¼a light green 30.00 *125.00*
**6** A1 ½a light green 8.25
*a.* Perf. 11, top or bottom only 7.00

**1921** ***Coarse Perf. 7, 7 x Imperf.***
**Thick Wove Paper**
**Very Blurred Impression**

**7** A1 ¼a dull blue 25.00
**8** A1 ½a dull green 22.50

In 1927 #7-8 were printed on thin hard paper.

**1922** ***Perf. 7 x Imperf.***
**Thick Glazed Paper**

**9** A1 ¼a dull ultra 160.00

***Rough Perf. 11 x Imperf.***

**10** A2 1a vermilion 3.75 *30.00*
**11** A2 2a violet 3.25 *37.50*
*a.* Double impression *450.00*
*Nos. 9-11 (3)* 167.00 67.50

Shades of No. 11 include purple. No. 11 was also printed on thick dark toned paper.

**1923-26 Wove, Laid Paper** ***Perf.***

**12** A1 ¼a grayish ultra, perf. 8½ 2.40 *72.50*
**13** A1 ¼a black, perf. 7 x imperf. 110.00 *550.00*
**14** A1 ¼a dull rose, perf. 11½-12 3.75 *21.00*
**15** A1 ¼a dk bl, perf. 11 ('26) 2.25 *16.00*
**16** A1 ½a grn, perf. 11 x imperf. 1.90 *30.00*
*Nos. 12-16 (5)* 120.30 *689.50*

No. 12 was also printed on pale gray thin toned paper.

No. 14 was printed on horizontally laid paper in horizontal sheets of 12 containing three panes of 4.

No. 15 was printed on vertically laid paper in horizontal sheets of 8.

Rana Ranjit Singh — A3

**1927-28 Thin Wove Paper** ***Perf. 7***

**17** A3 4a dull orange 140.00 *675.00*

No. 17 was also printed in light brown on thick paper, pin-perf. 6, and in orange brown on thick paper, rough perf. 7.

**1928** ***Coarse Perf. 7***
**Thick Glazed Paper**

**18** A1 ¼a bright blue 16.00
**19** A1 ½a bright yel green 37.50

**1928, Nov.** ***Rough Perf. 10½***

**20** A1 ¼a deep ultra 9.50
*a.* Tête bêche pair 19.00
**21** A1 ½a yellow green 7.00
*a.* Tête bêche pair 14.00

**1929-31** ***Perf. 11***

**22** A1 ¼a blue 3.25 *21.00*
*a.* ¼a ultramarine 3.00 *21.00*
**23** A1 ½a emerald green 4.00 *24.00*
**24** A2 1a car pink ('31) 24.00 *67.50*
**25** A3 4a salmon 120.00 *325.00*
*Nos. 22-25 (4)* 151.25 437.50

Nos. 20-25 were printed in sheets of 8 (4x2).

No. 22 had five printings in various shades (bright to deep blue) in horizontal or vertical format.

No. 23 also printed in dark myrtle green.

Rana Devi Singh
A4 A5

**1932-48 Glazed Paper** ***Perf. 11, 12***

**26** A4 ¼a dark gray 3.75 *35.00*
**27** A4 ½a blue green 6.00 *35.00*
**28** A4 1a brown 6.00 *32.50*
*a.* 1a chocolate, perf. 8½ ('48) 21.00 75.00
**29** A4 2a deep red violet 5.50 *62.50*
*a.* Perf. 12x11
*b.* 2a red lilac 12.50
**30** A4 4a olive green 9.00 *62.50*
*Nos. 26-30 (5)* 30.25 *227.50*

**Types of 1921-27**

**1934-48** ***Perf. 11***

**31** A1 ¼a slate gray 6.00 *47.50*
**32** A1 ½a green 6.50 *60.00*
**33** A2 1a dark brown 16.00 *29.00*
*a.* 1a brown, perf. 8½ ('48) 15.00 *75.00*
**34** A2 2a brt purple ('38) 125.00 *490.00*
**35** A2 2a rose car ('46) 35.00 *190.00*
**36** A3 4a olive green 20.00 *67.50*
*Nos. 31-36 (6)* 208.50 884.00

In the nine printings of Nos. 26-36, several plate settings spaced the cliches from 2 to 9mm apart. Hence the stamps come in different overall sizes. Not all values were in each printing. Values are for the commonest varieties.

No. 36 was also printed in pale sage green.

**1938**

**37** A5 1a dark brown 50.00 *110.00*
*a.* Booklet pane of 4 —

Stamps of type A5 in red are revenues.

Barwani stamps became obsolete July 1, 1948.

## BHOPAL

bō-'päl

LOCATION — A Feudatory State of Central India, in the Bhopal Agency.
AREA — 6,924 sq. mi.
POP. — 995,745
CAPITAL — Bhopal

Inscription in Urdu in an octagon embossed on Nos. 1-83, in a circle embossed on Nos. 84-90. On designs A1-A3, A7, A11-A12, A14-A15, A19-A21 the embossing makes up the central part of the design.

The embossing may be found inverted or sideways.

Expect irregular perfs on the perforated stamps, Nos. 19-77, due to a combination of imperfect perforating methods and the fragility of the papers.

Nos. 1-90 issued without gum.

A1

A2

**Double Lined Frame**

**1876 Unwmk. Litho.** ***Imperf.***

**1** A1 ¼a black 950.00 700.00
*a.* "EGAM" 2,750. 2,400.
*b.* "BFGAM" 2,750. 2,400.
*c.* "BEGAN" 1,500. 1,250.
**2** A1 ½a red 30.00 *72.50*
*a.* "EGAM" 110.00 *250.00*
*b.* "BFGAM" 110.00 *250.00*
*c.* "BEGAN" 72.50 *160.00*

**1877 Single Lined Frame**

**3** A2 ¼a black *9,000.*
**4** A2 ½a red 52.50 *110.00*
*a.* "NWAB" 250.00 *490.00*

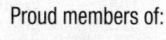

A3

A4

**1878**

| | | | | |
|---|---|---|---|---|
| 5 | A3 | ¼a black | 12.00 | *24.00* |
| a. | | "J" diagonal, plate II | 13.50 | *27.50* |

All stamps of type A3 are lettered "EEGAM" for "BEGAM."

**1878**

| | | | | |
|---|---|---|---|---|
| 6 | A4 | ½a pale red | 10.50 | *24.00* |
| a. | | ½a brown red | 42.50 | 67.50 |
| b. | | "NWAB" | 35.00 | |
| c. | | "JAHN" | 57.50 | |
| d. | | "EECAM" | 57.50 | |

A5

A6

**1879-80**

| | | | | |
|---|---|---|---|---|
| 7 | A5 | ¼a green | 21.00 | *40.00* |
| 8 | A5 | ½a red | 27.50 | *35.00* |

***Perf.***

| | | | | |
|---|---|---|---|---|
| 9 | A5 | ¼a green | 16.00 | *27.50* |
| 10 | A5 | ½a red | 160.00 | |
| | | *Nos. 7-10 (4)* | 224.50 | *102.50* |

Nos. 7 and 9 have the value in parenthesis; Nos. 8 and 10 are without parenthesis.

**1881** ***Imperf.***

| | | | | |
|---|---|---|---|---|
| 11 | A6 | ¼a green | 13.50 | |
| a. | | "NAWA" | 42.50 | |
| b. | | "CHAH" | 120.00 | |

***Perf.***

| | | | | |
|---|---|---|---|---|
| 12 | A6 | ¼a green | 18.00 | |
| a. | | "NAWA" | 67.50 | |
| b. | | "CHAH" | 160.00 | |

A7

**1881-89** ***Imperf.***

| | | | | |
|---|---|---|---|---|
| 13 | A7 | ¼a black | 9.00 | *35.00* |
| a. | | "NWAB" | 22.50 | |
| 14 | A7 | ½a red | 7.50 | *25.00* |
| a. | | "NWAB" | 18.00 | |
| 15 | A7 | 1a brown | 6.50 | *29.00* |
| a. | | "NWAB" | 14.00 | |
| 16 | A7 | 2a blue | 5.00 | *29.00* |
| a. | | "NWAB" | 9.50 | |
| 17 | A7 | 4a yellow | 30.00 | *100.00* |
| a. | | "NWAB" | 82.50 | |
| | | *Nos. 13-17 (5)* | 58.00 | *218.00* |

A8

A9

**1884** ***Perf.***

| | | | | |
|---|---|---|---|---|
| 19 | A8 | ¼a green | 225.00 | *275.00* |
| a. | | "JAN" | 225.00 | *275.00* |
| b. | | "BEGM" | 450.00 | *625.00* |
| c. | | "NWAB" | 950.00 | |
| d. | | "SHAHAN" | 950.00 | |
| f. | | "JAHA" | 450.00 | |
| 20 | A9 | ¼a green | 8.25 | *27.50* |

On type A9 there is a dash at the left of "JA" of "JAHAN" instead of a character like a comma as on types A5 and A6.

Imitations of No. 19 were printed about 1904 in black on wove paper and in red on laid paper, both imperf. and pin-perf.

A10

**1884 Laid Paper** ***Imperf.***

| | | | | |
|---|---|---|---|---|
| 21 | A10 | ¼a blue green | 240.00 | *275.00* |
| a. | | "NWAB" | 675.00 | |
| b. | | "NAWAJANAN" | 675.00 | |
| c. | | "SAH" | 675.00 | |
| 22 | A10 | ½a black | 3.25 | *3.75* |
| a. | | "NWAB" | 15.00 | *18.00* |
| b. | | "NAWAJANAN" | 15.00 | *18.00* |
| c. | | "SAH" | 15.00 | *18.00* |

***Perf.***

| | | | | |
|---|---|---|---|---|
| 23 | A10 | ¼a blue green | 1.50 | *6.00* |
| a. | | "NWAB" | 6.00 | |
| b. | | "NAWAJANAN" | 6.00 | |
| c. | | "SAH" | 6.00 | |
| 24 | A10 | ½a black | 1.40 | *5.00* |
| a. | | "NWAB" | 5.50 | *12.50* |
| b. | | "NAWAJANAN" | 5.50 | *12.50* |
| c. | | "SAH" | 5.50 | *12.50* |
| | | *Nos. 21-24 (4)* | 246.15 | 289.75 |

**Type Redrawn**

**1886 Wove Paper** ***Imperf.***

| | | | | |
|---|---|---|---|---|
| 25 | A10 | ¼a grayish green | .80 | *5.00* |
| a. | | ¼a green | .80 | *5.00* |
| b. | | "NWAB" | 4.50 | *13.50* |
| c. | | "NAWA" | 3.00 | *10.50* |
| d. | | "NAWAA" | 4.50 | *13.50* |
| e. | | "NAWABABEGAAM" | 4.50 | *13.50* |
| f. | | "NWABA" | 4.50 | *13.50* |
| 26 | A10 | ½a red | 1.00 | *2.50* |
| a. | | "SAH" | 6.00 | *9.50* |
| b. | | "NAWABA" | 4.50 | *7.50* |

***Perf.***

| | | | | |
|---|---|---|---|---|
| 27 | A10 | ¼a green | 3.75 | *6.00* |
| a. | | "NWAB" | 20.00 | |
| b. | | "NAWA" | 12.00 | |
| c. | | "NAWAA" | 20.00 | |
| d. | | "NAWABABEGAAM" | 20.00 | |
| e. | | "NWABA" | 20.00 | |
| 28 | A10 | ½a red | 1.20 | *3.00* |
| a. | | "SAH" | 9.00 | |
| b. | | "NAWABA" | 12.00 | |
| | | *Nos. 25-28 (4)* | 6.75 | 16.50 |

On Nos. 25-28 the inscriptions are closer to the value than on Nos. 21-24.

A11

A12

**1886** ***Imperf.***

| | | | | |
|---|---|---|---|---|
| 29 | A11 | ½a red | 4.00 | *15.00* |
| a. | | "BEGAM" | 18.00 | *47.50* |
| b. | | "NWAB" | 18.00 | |

**Laid Paper**

| | | | | |
|---|---|---|---|---|
| 30 | A12 | 4a yellow | 18.00 | *57.50* |
| a. | | "EEGAM" | 24.00 | |
| b. | | Wove paper | 1,500. | |
| c. | | As "a," wove paper | *1,900.* | |

***Perf.***

| | | | | |
|---|---|---|---|---|
| 31 | A12 | 4a yellow | 6.50 | *30.00* |
| a. | | "EEGAM" | 9.50 | *42.50* |
| | | *Nos. 29-31 (3)* | 28.50 | |

A13

A14

**1889 Wove Paper** ***Imperf.***

| | | | | |
|---|---|---|---|---|
| 32 | A13 | ¼a green | 1.50 | *3.00* |
| a. | | "SAH" | 6.50 | *10.50* |
| b. | | "NAWA" | 6.50 | *10.50* |
| 33 | A14 | ¼a black | 3.25 | 8.25 |
| a. | | "EEGAN" | 27.50 | *47.50* |

***Perf.***

| | | | | |
|---|---|---|---|---|
| 34 | A13 | ¼a green | 3.00 | *4.00* |
| a. | | "SAH" | 11.00 | *13.50* |
| b. | | "NAWA" | 11.00 | *13.50* |
| c. | | Vert. pair, imperf between | 325.00 | |
| 35 | A14 | ¼a black | 2.50 | *8.25* |
| a. | | "EEGAN" | 22.50 | *47.50* |
| b. | | Horiz. pair, imperf. between | 400.00 | |
| | | *Nos. 32-35 (4)* | 10.25 | 23.50 |

Type A13 has smaller letters in the upper corners than Type A10.

A15

A16

**1890** ***Imperf.***

| | | | | |
|---|---|---|---|---|
| 36 | A15 | ¼a black | 3.25 | *3.00* |
| 37 | A15 | 1a brown | 3.25 | *7.00* |
| a. | | "EEGAM" | 21.00 | *40.00* |
| b. | | "BBGAM" | 21.00 | *40.00* |
| 38 | A7 | 2a greenish blue | 3.00 | *3.25* |
| a. | | "BBEGAM" | 12.50 | *21.00* |
| b. | | "NAWAH" | 12.50 | *21.00* |
| 39 | A7 | 4a yellow | 3.75 | *5.50* |
| 40 | A16 | 8a blue | 100.00 | *180.00* |
| a. | | "HAH" | 110.00 | *190.00* |
| b. | | "JABAN" | 120.00 | |
| | | *Nos. 36-40 (5)* | 113.25 | 198.75 |

An imperf. imitation of Nos. 36 and 41 was printed about 1904 in black on wove paper.

***Perf.***

| | | | | |
|---|---|---|---|---|
| 41 | A15 | ¼a black | 4.50 | *6.25* |
| a. | | Pair, imperf. between | 500.00 | |
| 42 | A15 | 1a brown | 6.50 | *11.00* |
| a. | | "EECAM" | 37.50 | *52.50* |
| b. | | "BBGAM" | 37.50 | *52.50* |
| 43 | A7 | 2a greenish blue | 3.75 | *5.50* |
| a. | | "BBEGAM" | 14.00 | *27.50* |
| b. | | "NAWAH" | 14.00 | *27.50* |
| 44 | A7 | 4a yellow | 4.50 | *12.00* |
| 45 | A16 | 8a blue | 100.00 | *180.00* |
| a. | | "HAH" | 110.00 | |
| b. | | "JABAN" | 120.00 | |
| | | *Nos. 41-45 (5)* | 119.25 | 214.75 |

Nos. 40 and 45 have a frame line around each stamp.

***Imperf***

| | | | | |
|---|---|---|---|---|
| 46 | A12 | ½a red (BECAM) | 3.00 | *5.50* |
| 47 | A13 | ½a red (NWAB) | 3.00 | 2.25 |
| a. | | Inverted "N" | | |
| b. | | "SAH" | 9.00 | |

***Perf.***

| | | | | |
|---|---|---|---|---|
| 48 | A12 | ½a red (BECAM) | 2.50 | 7.00 |
| a. | | Without embossing | | |
| 49 | A13 | ½a red (NWAB) | 1.20 | 3.00 |
| a. | | Inverted "N" | | |
| b. | | "SAH" | 7.50 | |
| | | *Nos. 46-49 (4)* | 9.70 | 17.75 |

**1891-93 Laid Paper** ***Imperf.***

| | | | | |
|---|---|---|---|---|
| 50 | A16 | 8a deep green | 110.00 | *225.00* |
| a. | | "HAH" | 125.00 | |
| b. | | "JABAN" | 140.00 | |

***Perf.***

| | | | | |
|---|---|---|---|---|
| 51 | A16 | 8a deep green | 110.00 | *225.00* |
| a. | | "HAH" | 125.00 | |
| b. | | "JABAN" | 140.00 | |

For overprint, see No. 83.

**1894 Redrawn** ***Imperf.***

| | | | | |
|---|---|---|---|---|
| 53 | A10 | ¼a green | 2.25 | *2.50* |
| a. | | "NAWAH" | 11.00 | *12.00* |
| 54 | A11 | ½a brick red | 3.25 | 3.25 |
| 55 | A16 | 8a blue black | 32.50 | 32.50 |
| a. | | Laid paper | 300.00 | *450.00* |

***Perf.***

| | | | | |
|---|---|---|---|---|
| 56 | A10 | ¼a green | 4.50 | 3.25 |
| a. | | "NAWAH" | 19.00 | 16.00 |
| 57 | A11 | ½a brick red | 1.20 | *3.00* |
| 58 | A16 | 8a blue black | 45.00 | *60.00* |
| | | *Nos. 53-58 (6)* | 88.70 | 104.50 |

The ¼a redrawn has letters in corners larger; value in very small characters.

The 8a redrawn has no frame to each stamp but a frame to the sheet.

**1898** ***Imperf.***

| | | | | |
|---|---|---|---|---|
| 60 | A16 | 8a black | 62.50 | *82.50* |
| b. | | "E" of "BEGAM" inverted | 140.00 | 150.00 |

A17

A18

A19

A20

A21

**1895 Laid Paper**

| | | | | |
|---|---|---|---|---|
| 61 | A17 | ¼a green | 2.25 | 2.50 |
| 62 | A18 | ¼a red | 10.50 | 5.00 |
| 63 | A19 | ¼a black | 5.25 | 4.50 |
| a. | | "A" inserted in "NAW B" | 12.50 | 10.00 |
| 64 | A20 | ½a black | 2.25 | *2.50* |
| 65 | A21 | ½a red | 3.25 | 3.25 |

***Perf.***

| | | | | |
|---|---|---|---|---|
| 66 | A17 | ¼a green | 4.50 | 3.25 |
| 67 | A18 | ¼a red | | 1,250. |
| | | *Nos. 61-67 (7)* | 28.00 | 1,271. |

On No. 63a, the second "A" in "NAWAB" has been inserted by hand and varies somewhat in size.

Imperf. imitations of No. 65 were printed about 1904 in deep red on laid paper and in black on wove paper.

Stamps of types A16 and A19-A21 with a circular embossed seal and perforated, were prepared but not issued.

A22

A23

**1898** ***Imperf.***

| | | | | |
|---|---|---|---|---|
| 72 | A22 | ¼a black | .75 | .75 |
| a. | | "SHAN" | 5.00 | 5.00 |
| 73 | A22 | ¼a green | 1.10 | *1.20* |
| a. | | "SHAN" | 5.25 | 5.25 |
| 74 | A23 | ¼a black | 2.10 | 2.10 |
| | | *Nos. 72-74 (3)* | 3.95 | 4.05 |

**1899**

| | | | | |
|---|---|---|---|---|
| 75 | A13 | ½a black ("NWAB") | 6.50 | *9.50* |
| b. | | "NWASBAHJAHNJ" | 32.50 | *42.50* |
| d. | | "SBAH" | 15.00 | *22.50* |
| e. | | "SBAN" | 32.50 | *42.50* |
| f. | | "NWIB" | 32.50 | *42.50* |
| g. | | "BEIAM" | 32.50 | *42.50* |

A24

Coat of Arms — A25

**1902**

| | | | | |
|---|---|---|---|---|
| 76 | A24 | ¼a red | 5.50 | *9.00* |
| 77 | A24 | ½a black | 6.00 | *10.00* |
| a. | | Printed on both sides | 1,100. | |
| 78 | A24 | 1a brown | 10.00 | *25.00* |
| 79 | A24 | 2a blue | 12.50 | *22.50* |
| 80 | A24 | 4a orange | 110.00 | *160.00* |
| 81 | A24 | 8a violet | 150.00 | *290.00* |
| 82 | A24 | 1r rose | 400.00 | *600.00* |
| | | *Nos. 76-82 (7)* | 694.00 | *1,116.* |

No. 50 Overprinted in Red

**1903**

**83** A16 8a deep green 210.00 225.00
*a.* Inverted overprint 550.00 *600.00*

There are two types of the overprint which is the Arabic S, initial of the Begum.

**Inscription in Circle Embossed on Each Stamp**

**1903** **Wove Paper**

**84** A24 ¼a red 2.25 *7.50*
**85** A24 ½a black 1.90 *7.50*
**86** A24 1a brown 4.50 *11.00*
**87** A24 2a blue 10.00 *37.50*
**88** A24 4a orange 27.50 *75.00*
**89** A24 8a violet 82.50 *190.00*
**90** A24 1r rose 125.00 *290.00*
*Nos. 84-90 (7)* 253.65 *618.50*

**Laid Paper**

*84a* A24 ¼a red 1.50 *12.00*
*85a* A24 ½a black 1.50 *12.50*
*86a* A24 1a brown 10.00
*87a* A24 2a blue 250.00 *325.00*
*88a* A24 4a orange 500.00 500.00
*89a* A24 8a violet 2,400.
*90a* A24 1r rose 1,900.
*Nos. 84a-90a (7)* 5,063. *849.50*

*The embossing in a circle, which was first used in 1903, has been applied to many early stamps and impressions from redrawn plates of early issues. So far as is now known, these should be classed as reprints.*

**1908** **Engr.** ***Perf. 13½***

**99** A25 1a yellow green 5.50 *6.75*
*a.* Printed on both sides 180.00

---

**OFFICIAL STAMPS**

O1

Overprinted

**Size: 20½x25mm**

**1908** **Unwmk.** **Engr.** ***Perf. 13½***

**O1** O1 ½a yellow green 3.25 .25
*a.* Pair, one without ovpt. 950.00
*b.* Inverted overprint 275.00 225.00
*c.* Double ovpt., one invtd. 160.00
**O2** O1 1a carmine 6.25 .60
*a.* Inverted overprint 180.00 150.00
**O3** O1 2a blue 36.00 .25
**O4** O1 4a red brown 21.00 .80
*Nos. O1-O4 (4)* 66.50 1.90

Overprinted

**O5** O1 ½a yellow green 11.00 1.90
**O6** O1 1a carmine 14.00 1.40
**O7** O1 2a blue 6.00 .90
*a.* Inverted overprint 37.50
**O8** O1 4a red brown 120.00 2.25
*a.* Inverted overprint 30.00 *100.00*
*Nos. O5-O8 (4)* 151.00 6.45

The difference in the two overprints is in the shape of the letters, most noticeable in the "R."

**Type of 1908 Issue**

Overprinted

**Size: 25½x30½mm**

**1930-31** **Litho.** ***Perf. 14***

**O9** O1 ½a gray green ('31) 18.00 2.50
**O10** O1 1a carmine 16.00 .25
**O11** O1 2a blue 14.00 .65
**O12** O1 4a brown 15.00 1.40
*Nos. O9-O12 (4)* 63.00 4.80

½a, 2a, 4a are inscribed "POSTAGE" on the left side; 1a "POSTAGE AND REVENUE."

**Similar to Type O1**
**Size: 21x25mm**
"POSTAGE" at left
"BHOPAL STATE" at right

**1932-33** ***Perf. 11½, 13, 13½, 14***

**O13** O1 ¼a orange yellow 3.75 .75
*a.* Pair, one without overprint 180.00
*b.* Perf. 13½ 16.00 .45
*c.* Perf. 14 18.00 .45

**"BHOPAL GOVT." at right**
***Perf. 13½***

**O14** O1 ½a yellow green 11.00 .25
*a.* Perf 14 ('34) 24.00 .60
**O15** O1 1a brown red 16.00 .25
**O16** O1 2a blue 16.00 .65
**O17** O1 4a brown 16.00 1.50
*a.* Perf 14 ('34) 24.00 16.00
*Nos. O13-O17 (5)* 62.75 3.40

**No. O14, O16-O17 Surcharged in Red, Violet, Black or Blue**

a

b

c

**1935-36** ***Perf. 13½***

**O18** O1(a) ¼a on ½a (R) 47.50 21.00
*a.* Inverted surcharge 300.00 125.00
**O19** O1(b) 3p on ½a (R) 5.50 5.25
**O20** O1(a) ¼a on 2a (R) 42.50 30.00
*a.* Inverted surcharge 300.00 110.00
**O21** O1(b) 3p on 2a (R) 6.75 6.75
*a.* Inverted surcharge 120.00 60.00
**O22** O1(a) ¼a on 4a (R) 1,500. 500.00
**O23** O1(a) ¼a on 4a (Bk) ('36) 120.00 40.00
**O24** O1(b) 3p on 4a (R) 210.00 100.00
**O25** O1(b) 3p on 4a (Bk) ('36) 3.75 *5.00*
**O26** O1(c) 1a on ½a (V) 7.50 2.25
*a.* Inverted surcharge 100.00 67.50
**O27** O1(c) 1a on 2a (R) 3.25 3.00
*a.* Inverted surcharge 140.00 140.00
**O28** O1(c) 1a on 2a (Bk) ('36) 1.00 *3.75*
**O29** O1(c) 1a on 4a (Bl) 10.50 *7.50*
*Nos. O18-O29 (12)* 1,958. 724.50

Nos. O18-O25 are arranged in composite sheets of 100. The 2 top horizontal rows of each value are surcharged "a" and the next 5 rows as "b." The next 3 rows as "b" but in a narrower setting.

Various errors of spelling or inverted letters are found on Nos. O18-O29.

Arms of Bhopal — O2

**1935** **Litho.**

**O30** O2 1a3p claret & blue 5.25 2.25

Inscribed: "Bhopal State Postage"
Ovptd. "SERVICE" 11mm long

**1937** ***Perf. 12***

**O31** O2 1a6p dk claret & blue 3.75 1.50
*a.* Overprint omitted 275.00 210.00
*b.* Double overprint, one inverted 750.00 750.00
*c.* Blue printing double 250.00
*d.* Imperf, pair 275.00
*e.* Pair, imperf between 300.00 *325.00*

See Nos. O42, O45.

Arms of Bhopal — O3

**Brown or Black Overprint**

**1936-38** **Typo.**

**O32** O3 ¼a orange (Br) 1.40 .90
*a.* Inverted overprint 525.00 400.00
*b.* Vert. pair, imperf between 250.00
*c.* Horiz. pair, imperf between 450.00
*d.* Black overprint 12.50 1.10
*e.* As "d," inverted ovpt. 600.00
*f.* As "d," double ovpt. 450.00
**O32B** O3 ¼a yellow (Br) ('38) 5.25 2.25
**O33** O3 1a carmine 1.90 .25
*a.* Horiz. pair, imperf vert. 250.00
*b.* Vert. pair, imperf between 490.00
*c.* Horiz. pair, imperf between 200.00 *225.00*
*d.* Block of 4, imperf between 625.00 625.00
*Nos. O32-O33 (3)* 8.55 3.40

Moti Mahal O4

**Overprinted in Black**

**1936** ***Perf. 11½***

**O34** O4 ½a green & chocolate .85 *1.20*
*a.* Double impression of stamp 150.00 22.50
*b.* Double overprint 350.00 250.00
*c.* Vert. pair, imperf between 325.00
*d.* Horiz. pair, imperf between 325.00

Moti Masjid — O5

4a, Taj Mahal and Be-Nazir Palaces.

**Overprinted in Black**

**1937** ***Perf. 11½***

**O35** O5 2a dk blue & brown 2.50 1.40
*a.* Inverted overprint 375.00 *550.00*
*b.* Vert. pair, imperf between 525.00
*c.* Horiz. pair, imperf between 375.00
**O36** O5 4a bister brn & blue 4.50 .75
*a.* Double overprint 240.00
*b.* Center double 600.00
*c.* Horiz. pair, imperf between 1,000.
*d.* Overprint omitted 490.00

**Types of 1937**

Overprinted "SERVICE" in Black or Brown

Designs: 4a, Taj Mahal. 8a, Ahmadabad Palace. 1r, Rait-Ghat.

**1938-44**

**O37** O4 ½a dp green & brown .90 .60
**O38** O5 2a violet & dp grn 15.00 .45
**O39** O5 4a red brn & brt bl 4.25 .80
*a.* Frame double 450.00
**O40** O5 8a red vio & blue 7.00 3.25
*a.* "SERAICE" 550.00 *825.00*
*b.* Overprint omitted 250.00
*c.* Double overprint 240.00
*d.* Vert. pair, imperf between 625.00
*e.* "1" for "I" in "SERVICE" 550.00 *825.00*
**O41** O5 1r bl & red vio (Br) 27.50 12.50
*a.* Black overprint ('44) 21.00 6.50
*b.* "SREVICE" 160.00 *375.00*
*c.* Overprint omitted 1,100.
*d.* Vert. pair, imperf horiz. 2,250.
*Nos. O37-O41 (5)* 54.65 17.60

#O39 measures 36½x22½mm, #O40 39x24mm, #O41 45½x27¾mm.

**Type of 1935**

**1939** ***Perf. 12***

**O42** O2 1a6p dark claret 7.50 2.50
*a.* Overprint omitted 625.00
*b.* Double overprint 625.00
*c.* Double overprint, one inverted 625.00
*d.* Pair, imperf between 250.00 *325.00*

Tiger — O6

Design: 1a, Deer.

**1940** **Typo.** ***Perf. 11½***

**O43** O6 ¼a ultramarine 6.00 2.50
**O44** O6 1a red violet 35.00 4.50

**Type of 1935**

Inscribed: "Bhopal State Postage"

**1941**

**O45** O2 1a3p emerald 2.50 3.25
*a.* Pair, imperf between 550.00 *700.00*

Moti Palace — O7

Coat of Arms — O8

2a, Moti Mosque. 4a, Be-Nazir Palaces.

***Perf. 11½, 12***

**1944-46** **Unwmk.** **Typo.**

**O46** O8 3p ultramarine 1.25 1.25
**O47** O7 ½a light green 1.10 *1.50*
**O48** O8 9p orange brn ('46) 12.00 5.00
*a.* Imperf., pair 290.00
**O49** O8 1a brt red vio ('45) 6.25 2.60
**O50** O8 1½a deep plum 1.90 1.90
**O51** O7 2a red violet ('45) 13.50 6.00
**O52** O8 3a yellow ('46) 16.00 *21.00*
*a.* Imperf., pair 290.00
**O53** O7 4a brown ('45) 8.75 3.25
**O54** O8 6a brt rose ('46) 24.00 *75.00*
*a.* Imperf., pair 400.00
*Nos. O46-O54 (9)* 84.75 *117.50*

For surcharges see Nos. O58-O59.

**1946-47** **Unwmk.** ***Perf. 11½***

**O55** O8 1a violet 11.00 4.75
**O56** O7 2a violet ('47) 13.50 22.50
**O57** O8 3a deep orange 125.00 *160.00*
*a.* Imperf., pair — 275.00
*Nos. O55-O57 (3)* 149.50 187.25

No. O50 Surcharged "2 As." and Bars

**1949** ***Perf. 12***

**O58** O8 2a on 1½a dp plum 3.00 *11.00*
*c.* Imperf., pair 300.00 *450.00*

Same Surcharged "2 As." and Rosettes

**1949** ***Imperf.***

**O59** O8 2a on 1½a dp plum 1,250. 1,500.
*a.* Perf 12 1,350. *1,600.*

Three or more types of "2" in surcharge. Bhopal stamps became obsolete in 1950.

## BHOR

ˈbō̤ə̤r

LOCATION — A Feudatory State in the Kolhapur Residency and Deccan States Agency.
AREA — 910 sq. mi.
POP. — 141,546
CAPITAL — Bhor

A1

A2

**Handstamped**

**1879 Unwmk. *Imperf.***
**Without Gum**

| | | | | |
|---|---|---|---|---|
| **1** | A1 | ½a carmine | 5.50 | *7.50* |
| **2** | A2 | 1a carmine | 8.25 | *12.00* |

Pant Sachiv Shankarrao — A3

**1901 Without Gum Typo.**

| | | | | |
|---|---|---|---|---|
| **3** | A3 | ½a red | 24.00 | *60.00* |

## BIJAWAR

bi-ˈjä-wər

LOCATION — A Feudatory State in the Bundelkhand Agency of Central India.
AREA — 973 sq. mi.
POP. — 115,852
CAPITAL — Bijawar

Maharaja Sir Sawant Singh — A1

**1935-36 Typo. Unwmk. *Perf. 10½***

| | | | | |
|---|---|---|---|---|
| **1** | A1 | 3p brown | 11.00 | 8.25 |
| *a.* | | Imperf., pair | 13.50 | |
| *b.* | | Rouletted 7 ('36) | 9.00 | *9.00* |
| **2** | A1 | 6p carmine | 9.50 | 8.25 |
| *a.* | | Rouletted 7 ('36) | 12.00 | *32.50* |
| **3** | A1 | 9p purple | 12.50 | 7.50 |
| *a.* | | Rouletted 7 ('36) | 9.00 | *160.00* |
| **4** | A1 | 1a dark blue | 14.00 | 8.25 |
| *a.* | | Rouletted 7 ('36) | 15.00 | *180.00* |
| **5** | A1 | 2a slate green | 13.50 | 7.50 |
| *a.* | | Rouletted 7 ('36) | 19.00 | *190.00* |

Maharaja Sir Sawant Singh — A2

**1937 *Perf. 9***

| | | | | |
|---|---|---|---|---|
| **6** | A2 | 4a red orange | 22.50 | *120.00* |
| **7** | A2 | 6a yellow | 22.50 | *120.00* |
| **8** | A2 | 8a emerald | 24.00 | *160.00* |
| **9** | A2 | 12a turquoise blue | 24.00 | *160.00* |
| **10** | A2 | 1r purple | 62.50 | *250.00* |
| *a.* | | "1Rs" instead of "1R" | 75.00 | *500.00* |
| | | *Nos. 1-10 (10)* | 216.00 | *849.75* |

Bijawar stamps became obsolete in 1939.

## BUNDI

ˈbün-dē

LOCATION — A Feudatory State in the Rajputana Agency of India.
AREA — 2,220 sq. mi.
POP. — 216,722
CAPITAL — Bundi

Katar (Indian Dagger) — A1

**Laid Paper**
**Without Gum**
**Gutters between Stamps**

**1894 Unwmk. Litho. *Imperf.***

| | | | | |
|---|---|---|---|---|
| **1** | A1 | ½a slate | 19,000. | *3,250.* |

**Redrawn; Blade Does Not Touch Oval**
**No Gutters between Stamps**
**Wove Paper**

| | | | | |
|---|---|---|---|---|
| **1A** | A1 | ½a slate | 67.50 | *72.50* |
| *b.* | | Value above, name below | 400.00 | *525.00* |
| *c.* | | Top right ornament omitted | 3,750. | *4,000.* |

On No. 1A, the dagger is thinner and its point does not touch the oval inner frame.

A2

**Without Gum**

**1896 Laid Paper**

| | | | | |
|---|---|---|---|---|
| **2** | A2 | ½a slate | 9.00 | 14.00 |

A3

**1897-98 Without Gum**

| | | | | |
|---|---|---|---|---|
| **3** | A3 | 1a red | 18.00 | *27.50* |
| **4** | A3 | 2a yellow green | 21.00 | *40.00* |
| **5** | A3 | 4a yellow green | 100.00 | *140.00* |
| **6** | A3 | 8a red | 160.00 | *450.00* |
| **7** | A3 | 1r yellow, *blue* | 500.00 | *825.00* |
| | | *Nos. 3-7 (5)* | 799.00 | *1,482.* |

A4

A5

**Redrawn; Blade Wider and Diamond-shaped**

**1898-1900 Without Gum**

| | | | | |
|---|---|---|---|---|
| **8** | A3 | ½a slate | 7.00 | 7.00 |
| **9** | A3 | 1a red | 5.50 | 5.50 |
| **10** | A3 | 2a emerald | 19.00 | 25.00 |
| *a.* | | 1st 2 characters of value omitted | 3,000. | 3,000. |
| **11** | A3 | 4a yel grn | 42.50 | *100.00* |
| **12** | A4 | 8a red | 21.00 | *27.50* |
| **13** | A5 | 1r yellow, *blue* | 47.50 | *82.50* |
| *a.* | | Wove paper | 24.00 | *40.00* |
| | | *Nos. 8-13 (6)* | 142.50 | *247.50* |

On Nos. 9-10, the blade is wider and nearly diamond-shaped.

**Point of Dagger to Left**

| | | | | |
|---|---|---|---|---|
| **14** | A3 | 4a green | 5.00 | 5.00 |

Maharao Rajah with Symbols of Spiritual and Temporal Power — A6

***Rouletted 11 to 13 in Color***

**1915 Typo. Without Gum**
**"Bundi" in 3 Characters (word at top right)**

| | | | | |
|---|---|---|---|---|
| **15** | A6 | ¼a blue | 2.90 | *6.25* |
| *a.* | | Laid paper | 6.75 | *35.00* |
| **16** | A6 | ½a black | 4.00 | *9.00* |
| **17** | A6 | 1a vermilion | 5.50 | *18.00* |
| *a.* | | Laid paper | 15.00 | *45.00* |
| **18** | A6 | 2a emerald | 11.00 | *35.00* |
| **19** | A6 | 2½a yellow | 11.00 | *40.00* |
| **20** | A6 | 3a brown | 12.50 | *67.50* |
| **21** | A6 | 4a yel green | 5.25 | *62.50* |
| **23** | A6 | 6a ultramarine | 21.00 | *160.00* |
| *a.* | | 6a deep blue | 11.00 | *180.00* |
| **24** | A6 | 8a orange | 11.00 | *160.00* |
| **25** | A6 | 10a olive | 24.00 | *150.00* |
| **26** | A6 | 12a dark green | 19.00 | *140.00* |
| **27** | A6 | 1r violet | 40.00 | *250.00* |
| **28** | A6 | 2r car brn & blk | 125.00 | *325.00* |
| **29** | A6 | 3r blue & brown | 200.00 | *450.00* |
| **30** | A6 | 4r pale grn & red brown | 400.00 | *550.00* |
| **31** | A6 | 5r ver & pale grn | 400.00 | *550.00* |
| | | *Nos. 15-31 (16)* | 1,292. | *2,973.* |

Minor differences in lettering in top and bottom panels may be divided into 8 types, but not all values come in each type. In one subtype the top appears as one word. Nos. 30-31 have an ornamental frame around the design.

For overprints see Nos. O1-O39.

**1941 *Perf. 11***
**"Bundi" in 4 Characters (word at top right)**

| | | | | |
|---|---|---|---|---|
| **32** | A6 | ¼a light blue | 2.25 | 62.50 |
| **33** | A6 | ½a black | 40.00 | 47.50 |
| **34** | A6 | 1a carmine | 15.00 | *75.00* |
| **35** | A6 | 2a yellow green | 20.00 | 110.00 |
| | | *Nos. 32-35 (4)* | 77.25 | 295.00 |

The 4-character spelling of "Bundi" is found also on stamps rouletted in color: on ½a and 4a in small characters, and on ¼a, ½a, 1a, 4a, 4r and 5r in large characters like those on Nos. 32-35.

For overprints see Nos. O41-O48.

Arms of Bundi — A7

**1941-45 Typo. *Perf. 11***

| | | | | |
|---|---|---|---|---|
| **36** | A7 | 3p bright ultra | 3.50 | *7.50* |
| **37** | A7 | 6p indigo | 5.25 | *12.50* |
| **38** | A7 | 1a red orange | 8.00 | *15.00* |
| **39** | A7 | 2a fawn | 10.50 | *27.50* |
| *a.* | | 2a brown ('45) | 19.00 | *30.00* |
| **40** | A7 | 4a brt yel green | 19.00 | *82.50* |
| **41** | A7 | 8a dull green | 25.00 | *300.00* |
| **42** | A7 | 1r royal blue | 52.50 | *450.00* |
| | | *Nos. 36-42 (7)* | 123.75 | *895.00* |

The 1st printing of Nos. 36-42 was gummed. All later printings were without gum. **Values are for stamps without gum.**

For overprints see Nos. O49-O55.

A8

Maj. Maharao Rajah Bahadur Singh — A9

View of Bundi — A10

**1947 *Perf. 11***

| | | | | |
|---|---|---|---|---|
| **43** | A8 | ¼a deep green | 2.75 | *57.50* |
| **44** | A8 | ½a purple | 2.50 | *47.50* |
| **45** | A8 | 1a yellow green | 2.50 | *47.50* |
| **46** | A9 | 2a red | 2.40 | *97.50* |
| **47** | A9 | 4a deep orange | 2.75 | *140.00* |
| **48** | A10 | 8a violet blue | 3.75 | |
| **49** | A10 | 1r chocolate | 19.00 | |
| | | *Nos. 43-49 (7)* | 35.65 | |

For overprints see Rajasthan Nos. 1-14.

### OFFICIAL STAMPS

Regular Issue of 1915 Handstamped in Black, Red or Green

a

***Rouletted 11 to 13 in Color***

**1918 Unwmk. Without Gum**

| | | | |
|---|---|---|---|
| **O1** | A6 | ¼a dark blue | 1.90 |
| **O2** | A6 | ½a black | 1.10 |
| **O3** | A6 | 1a vermilion | 1.90 |
| **O4** | A6 | 2a emerald | 9.50 |
| **O5** | A6 | 2½a yellow | 6.00 |
| **O6** | A6 | 3a brown | 5.50 |
| **O7** | A6 | 4a yel green | 18.00 |
| **O8** | A6 | 6a blue | 22.50 |
| **O9** | A6 | 8a orange | 22.50 |
| **O10** | A6 | 10a olive green | 75.00 |
| **O11** | A6 | 12a dark green | 75.00 |
| **O12** | A6 | 1r violet | 90.00 |
| **O13** | A6 | 2r car brn & blk | 600.00 |
| **O14** | A6 | 3r blue & brown | 525.00 |
| **O15** | A6 | 4r pale grn & red brn | 450.00 |
| **O16** | A6 | 5r ver & pale grn | 490.00 |
| | | *Nos. O1-O16 (16)* | 2,393. |

All values come with black handstamp and most exist in red. The overprint is found in various positions, double, inverted, etc.

Several denominations exist in two or more types. See notes following Nos. 31 and 35.

**Regular Issue of 1915 Handstamped in Black, Red or Green**

b

**1919 Without Gum**

| | | | |
|---|---|---|---|
| **O17** | A6 | ¼a dark blue | 2.60 |
| **O18** | A6 | ½a black | 4.50 |
| **O19** | A6 | 1a vermilion | 16.00 |
| **O20** | A6 | 2a emerald | 29.00 |
| **O21** | A6 | 2½a yellow | 30.00 |
| **O22** | A6 | 3a brown | 35.00 |
| **O23** | A6 | 4a yel green | 120.00 |
| **O24** | A6 | 6a blue | 45.00 |
| **O25** | A6 | 8a orange | 52.50 |
| **O26** | A6 | 10a olive green | 140.00 |
| **O27** | A6 | 12a dark green | 120.00 |
| **O28** | A6 | 1r violet | 82.50 |
| **O29** | A6 | 2r car brn & blk | 275.00 |
| **O30** | A6 | 3r blue & brown | 325.00 |
| **O31** | A6 | 4r pale grn & red brn | 450.00 |
| **O32** | A6 | 5r ver & pale grn | 490.00 |
| | | *Nos. O17-O32 (16)* | 2,217. |

Note following No. O16 applies to this issue.

**Regular Issue of 1915 Handstamped in Carmine or Black**

c

**1919** ***Rouletted in Color***
**Without Gum**

| | | | | |
|---|---|---|---|---|
| **O33** | A6 | ¼a blue | 11.00 | |
| **O34** | A6 | ½a black | 18.00 | |
| **O35** | A6 | 1a vermilion | 35.00 | |
| **O36** | A6 | 2a yel green | 140.00 | |
| **O37** | A6 | 8a orange | 450.00 | |
| **O38** | A6 | 10a olive | 700.00 | |
| **O39** | A6 | 12a dark green | 900.00 | |
| | | *Nos. O33-O39 (7)* | 2,254. | |

Nos. 33 and 35 Handstamped Type "a" in Black or Carmine

**1941** ***Perf. 11***

| | | | | |
|---|---|---|---|---|
| **O41** | A6 | ½a black | 24.00 | |
| **O42** | A6 | 2a yellow green | 825.00 | |

Nos. 32 and 35 Handstamped Type "b" in Black or Carmine

| | | | | |
|---|---|---|---|---|
| **O43** | A6 | ¼a light blue | 90.00 | |
| **O44** | A6 | 2a yellow green | 210.00 | |

Nos. 32-35 Handstamped Type "c" in Black or Carmine

**1941**

| | | | | |
|---|---|---|---|---|
| **O45** | A6 | ¼a light blue | 190.00 | |
| **O46** | A6 | ½a black | 375.00 | |
| **O47** | A6 | 1a carmine | 700.00 | |
| **O48** | A6 | 2a yellow green | 625.00 | |
| | | *Nos. O45-O48 (4)* | 1,890. | |

Nos. 36 to 42 Overprinted in Black or Carmine

**1941** ***Perf. 11***

| | | | | |
|---|---|---|---|---|
| **O49** | A7 | 3p brt ultra (C) | 7.50 | *24.00* |
| **O50** | A7 | 6p indigo (C) | 20.00 | *24.00* |
| **O51** | A7 | 1a red orange | 19.00 | *16.00* |
| **O52** | A7 | 2a fawn | 20.00 | *19.00* |
| **O53** | A7 | 4a brt yel green | 72.50 | *160.00* |
| **O54** | A7 | 8a dull green | 225.00 | *950.00* |
| **O55** | A7 | 1r royal blue (C) | 310.00 | *950.00* |
| | | *Nos. O49-O55 (7)* | 674.00 | *2,143.* |

## BUSSAHIR

ˈbus-ə-ˌhi̦ə̦r

(Bashahr)

LOCATION — A Feudatory State in the Punjab Hill States Agency
AREA — 3,439 sq. mi.
POP. — 100,192
CAPITAL — Bashahr

Tiger

A1 A2

A3

A4

A5

A6

A7

A8

Overprinted "R S" in Violet, Rose, or Blue Green (BG)

**Laid Paper**

**1895** **Unwmk.** **Litho.** ***Imperf.***

| | | | | |
|---|---|---|---|---|
| **1** | A1 | ¼a pink (V) | 3,750. | |
| **2** | A2 | ½a slate (R) | 750.00 | *1,000.* |
| **3** | A3 | 1a red (V) | 300.00 | |
| **4** | A4 | 2a yellow (V,R) | 110.00 | *300.00* |
| **5** | A5 | 4a violet (V,R) | 190.00 | |
| **6** | A6 | 8a brown (V,BG) | 210.00 | *375.00* |
| *a.* | | Without overprint | 400.00 | |
| **7** | A7 | 12a green (R) | 450.00 | |
| **8** | A8 | 1r ultra (R) | 190.00 | |
| | | *Nos. 1-8 (8)* | 5,950. | |

***Perf. 7 to 14***

| | | | | |
|---|---|---|---|---|
| **9** | A1 | ¼a pink (V,BG) | 100.00 | *150.00* |
| **10** | A2 | ½a slate (R) | 35.00 | *210.00* |
| **11** | A3 | 1a red (V) | 35.00 | *140.00* |
| *a.* | | Pin-perf. | 275.00 | *300.00* |
| **12** | A4 | 2a yel (V,R,BG) | 47.50 | *140.00* |
| *a.* | | Pin-perf. (V,R) | 100.00 | *240.00* |
| **13** | A5 | 4a vio (V,R,BG) | 37.50 | *140.00* |
| *a.* | | Pin-perf. (R) | 450.00 | |
| **14** | A6 | 8a brown (V,BG) | 35.00 | *160.00* |
| **15** | A7 | 12a green (V,R) | 120.00 | *200.00* |
| *a.* | | Pin-perf. (R) | 650.00 | *825.00* |
| *b.* | | Without overprint | 325.00 | |
| **16** | A8 | 1r ultra (V,R) | 65.00 | *180.00* |
| *a.* | | Pin-perf. (R) | 700.00 | |
| | | *Nos. 9-16 (8)* | 475.00 | *1,320.* |

"R. S." are the initials of Tika Raghunath Singh, son of the Raja.

**Overprinted "R S" Like Nos. 1-16**

A9

A10

A11

A12

A13

A14

**Wove Paper**

**1896** **Engr.** ***Pin-perf.***

| | | | | |
|---|---|---|---|---|
| **17** | A9 | ¼a dk gray vio (R) | — | 1,500. |
| **18** | A10 | ½a blue gray (R) | 1,200. | 450.00 |

**1900** **Litho.** ***Imperf.***

| | | | | |
|---|---|---|---|---|
| **19** | A9 | ¼a red (V,BG) | 7.50 | *16.00* |
| **20** | A9 | ¼a violet (V,R) | 12.50 | |
| **21** | A10 | ½a blue (V,R) | 15.00 | *40.00* |
| **22** | A11 | 1a olive (R) | 27.50 | *65.00* |
| **23** | A11 | 1a red (V,BG) | 7.00 | *24.00* |
| **24** | A12 | 2a yellow (V) | 75.00 | |
| *a.* | | 2a ocher (R) | 75.00 | |
| **25** | A13 | 2a yellow (V) | 90.00 | |
| **26** | A14 | 4a brn vio (V,R,BG) | 82.50 | *180.00* |
| | | *Nos. 19-26 (8)* | 317.00 | |

***Pin-perf.***

| | | | | |
|---|---|---|---|---|
| **27** | A9 | ¼a red (V,BG) | 6.25 | *16.00* |
| **28** | A9 | ¼a violet (R) | 30.00 | 27.50 |
| **29** | A10 | ½a blue (V,R) | 90.00 | 140.00 |
| **30** | A11 | 1a olive (V,R) | 40.00 | |
| **31** | A11 | 1a red (V) | — | 300.00 |
| **32** | A11 | 1a vermilion (BG) | 11.00 | *22.50* |
| **33** | A12 | 2a yellow (BG) | 1,250. | *1,300.* |
| **34** | A13 | 2a yellow (V,R) | 75.00 | *120.00* |
| *a.* | | 2a ocher (V) | 100.00 | |
| **35** | A14 | 4a brn vio (V,R,BG) | 120.00 | |
| | | *Nos. 27-35 (9)* | 1,622. | |

Obsolete March 31, 1901.

Stamps overprinted with the monogram above (RNS) or with the monogram "PS" were never issued for postal purposes. They are either reprints or remainders to which this overprint has been applied. Many other varieties have appeared since the stamps became obsolete. It is probable that all or nearly all of them are reprints.

## CHARKHARI

chər-ˈkär-ē

LOCATION — A Feudatory State in the Bundelkhand Agency in Central India.
AREA — 880 sq. mi.
POP. — 120,351
CAPITAL — Maharajnagar

A1

**Thin White or Blue Wove Paper**

**1894** **Unwmk.** **Typo.** ***Imperf.***
**Value in the Plural**
**Without Gum**

| | | | | |
|---|---|---|---|---|
| **1** | A1 | 1a green | 2,750. | *3,750.* |
| **2** | A1 | 2a green | 3,250. | |
| **3** | A1 | 4a green | 2,100. | |

**Value in the Singular**

**1897** **Without Gum**

| | | | | |
|---|---|---|---|---|
| **3A** | A1 | ¼a rose | 1,800. | 1,100. |
| **4** | A1 | ¼a purple | 5.50 | 5.50 |
| **5** | A1 | ½a purple | 3.75 | *4.50* |
| **6** | A1 | 1a green | 6.50 | *9.50* |
| **7** | A1 | 2a green | 11.00 | *12.50* |
| **8** | A1 | 4a green | 17.50 | *27.50* |
| | | *Nos. 4-8 (5)* | 44.25 | *59.50* |

In a later printing, the numerals of Nos. 4-8 are smaller or of different shape.

Proofs are known on paper of various colors.

A2

A3

**Size: 19½x23mm**

**1909** **Litho.** ***Perf. 11***

| | | | | |
|---|---|---|---|---|
| **9** | A2 | 1p red brown | 7.00 | *57.50* |
| **10** | A2 | 1p pale blue | .90 | .65 |
| **11** | A2 | ½a scarlet | 1.50 | *1.90* |
| **12** | A2 | 1a light green | 3.75 | 2.40 |
| **13** | A2 | 2a ultra | 4.50 | *5.25* |
| **14** | A2 | 4a deep green | 6.25 | *8.25* |
| **15** | A2 | 8a brick red | 11.00 | *30.00* |
| **16** | A2 | 1r red brown | 19.00 | *62.50* |
| | | *Nos. 9-16 (8)* | 53.90 | *168.45* |

See #22-27, 39-43. For surcharges see #37-38A.

**1912-17** **Handstamped** ***Imperf.***
**Without Gum**

| | | | | |
|---|---|---|---|---|
| **21** | A3 | 1p violet ('17) | 10.50 | 7.50 |
| *c.* | | Double frameline | 1,050. | 125.00 |

The 1p black, type A3, is a proof.

A3a

**Wove Paper**

**1922** **Handstamped** ***Imperf.***
**Without Gum**

| | | | | |
|---|---|---|---|---|
| **21A** | A3a | 1a violet | 120.00 | *125.00* |
| *b.* | | Perf. 11, laid paper | 110.00 | *210.00* |

**Type of 1909 Issue Redrawn**
**Size: 20x23½mm**

**1930-40** **Without Gum** **Typo.**

| | | | | |
|---|---|---|---|---|
| **22** | A2 | 1p dark blue | .90 | *21.00* |
| **23** | A2 | ½a olive green | 3.75 | *21.00* |
| **23A** | A2 | ½a cop brown ('40) | 9.00 | *37.50* |
| **24** | A2 | 1a light green | 3.75 | *24.00* |
| **25** | A2 | 1a chocolate | 19.00 | *40.00* |
| **25A** | A2 | 1a dull red ('40) | 190.00 | 100.00 |
| **26** | A2 | 2a light blue | 1.90 | *25.00* |
| *a.* | | Tête bêche pair | 14.00 | |
| **27** | A2 | 4a carmine | 4.50 | *30.00* |
| *a.* | | Tête bêche pair | 21.00 | |
| | | *Nos. 22-27 (8)* | 232.80 | *298.50* |

Guesthouse of Raja at Charkhari Reservoir — A4

Imlia Palace — A5

Industrial School — A6

View of City — A7

Maharajnagar Fort, Charkhari City — A8

Guesthouse A9

Palace Gate — A10

Temples at Rampur — A11

Govordhan Temple — A12

**1931** ***Perf. 11, 11½, 12***

| | | | | |
|---|---|---|---|---|
| 28 | A4 | ½a dull green | 3.25 | .25 |
| 29 | A5 | 1a black brown | 2.40 | .25 |
| 30 | A6 | 2a purple | 2.50 | .25 |
| 31 | A7 | 4a olive green | 2.25 | .25 |
| 32 | A8 | 8a magenta | 3.00 | .25 |
| 33 | A9 | 1r rose & green | 4.00 | .30 |
| 34 | A10 | 2r brown & red | 6.00 | .35 |
| 35 | A11 | 3r bl grn & choc | 22.50 | .60 |
| 36 | A12 | 5r violet & blue | 14.00 | .75 |
| | | *Nos. 28-36 (9)* | 59.90 | 3.25 |

Size range of A4-A12: 30-31x19½-24mm.
Many errors of perforation and printing exist.
Used values are for canceled to order stamps.

Nos. 15-16 Surcharged in Black

**1940** ***Perf. 11***

| | | | | |
|---|---|---|---|---|
| 37 | A2 | ½a on 8a brick red | 52.50 | *200.00* |
| *a.* | | Surcharge inverted | 450.00 | 600.00 |
| *b.* | | "1" of "½" inverted | 400.00 | |
| 38 | A2 | 1a on 1r red brown | 175.00 | *625.00* |
| *b.* | | Surcharge inverted | 490.00 | |
| 38A | A2 | "1 ANNA" on 1r red brown | 400.00 | *450.00* |

### Type of 1930

**1943** **Unwmk.** **Typo.** ***Imperf.***
**Size: 20x23½mm**

| | | | | |
|---|---|---|---|---|
| 39 | A2 | 1p violet | 32.50 | *240.00* |
| *a.* | | Tête bêche pair | 82.50 | |
| 40 | A2 | 1p apple green | 90.00 | *325.00* |
| 41 | A2 | ½a orange red | 30.00 | *62.50* |
| 42 | A2 | ½a black | 90.00 | *290.00* |
| 43 | A2 | 2a grayish green | 140.00 | *290.00* |
| *a.* | | Tête bêche pair | 180.00 | |
| | | *Nos. 39-43 (5)* | 382.50 | *1,207.* |

## COCHIN

kō-'chin

LOCATION — A Feudatory State in the Madras States Agency in Southern India.
AREA — 1,480 sq. mi.
POP. — 1,422,875 (1941)
CAPITAL — Ernakulam

See the United State of Travancore and Cochin.

6 Puttans = 5 Annas
12 Pies = 1 Anna
16 Annas = 1 Rupee

A1

A1a

### State Seal

**1892** **Unwmk.** **Typo.** ***Perf. 12***

| | | | | |
|---|---|---|---|---|
| 1 | A1 | ½p yellow | 3.75 | 4.50 |
| *a.* | | Imperf., pair | — | |
| *b.* | | Laid paper | 700.00 | 200.00 |
| 2 | A1 | 1p red violet | 4.50 | 4.00 |
| *a.* | | 1p purple (error) | 175.00 | 125.00 |
| 3 | A1 | 2p purple | 3.00 | *3.25* |
| *a.* | | Imperf. | | |
| | | *Nos. 1-3 (3)* | 11.25 | 11.75 |

Nos. 1 to 3 sometimes have watermark large umbrella in the sheet.

### Wmk. Coat of Arms and Inscription in Sheet

**1896**

| | | | | |
|---|---|---|---|---|
| 4 | A1a | 1p violet | 140.00 | *140.00* |

**Wmk. 43**

| | | | | |
|---|---|---|---|---|
| 4A | A1a | 1p violet | 27.50 | *47.50* |

Originally intended for revenue use, Nos. 4-4A were later authorized for postal use. Beware of fraudulently removed fiscal markings.

**1894** **Wmk. 41** **Thin Paper**

| | | | | |
|---|---|---|---|---|
| 5 | A1 | ½p orange | 3.75 | 2.25 |
| *a.* | | Imperf., pair | | |
| 6 | A1 | 1p magenta | 10.50 | 10.50 |
| 7 | A1 | 2p purple | 6.25 | *6.75* |
| *a.* | | Imperf., pair | — | — |
| | | *Nos. 5-7 (3)* | 20.50 | 19.50 |

A2

A3

A4

A5

**1898** **Thin Paper**

| | | | | |
|---|---|---|---|---|
| 8 | A2 | 3p ultra | 2.10 | 1.60 |
| *a.* | | Double impression | 950.00 | |
| 9 | A3 | ½p gray green | 2.50 | 2.25 |
| *a.* | | Pair, one sideways | | 3,750. |
| 10 | A4 | 1p rose | 5.50 | 2.50 |
| *a.* | | Laid paper | | 2,400. |
| *b.* | | Tete beche pair | 5,250. | 3,250. |
| *c.* | | As "a," tete beche pair | | *12,000.* |
| 11 | A5 | 2p purple | 5.00 | 3.25 |
| | | *Nos. 8-11 (4)* | 15.10 | 9.60 |

**1903** **Thick Paper**

| | | | | |
|---|---|---|---|---|
| 12 | A2 | 3p ultra | 1.80 | .25 |
| *d.* | | Double impression | | 450.00 |
| 12A | A3 | ½p gray green | 1.90 | .60 |
| *e.* | | Double impression | | 450.00 |
| *f.* | | Pair, one sideways | 1,250. | 1,250. |
| 12B | A4 | 1p rose | 2.50 | .25 |
| *g.* | | Tete beche pair | | 5,250. |
| 12C | A5 | 2p purple | 3.75 | .75 |
| *h.* | | Double impression | 1,250. | 450.00 |
| | | *Nos. 12-12C (4)* | 9.95 | 1.85 |

Beware of fake overprint surcharge varieties, such as double, inverted, etc. This applies also to early official varieties. Such varieties require expertization.

Type of 1898 Surcharged

**1909**

| | | | | |
|---|---|---|---|---|
| 13 | A2 | 2p on 3p red violet | .25 | *.75* |
| *a.* | | Inverted surcharge | 150.00 | 150.00 |
| *b.* | | Pair, stamps tete beche | 250.00 | *290.00* |
| *c.* | | Pair, stamps & surch. tete beche | 300.00 | *375.00* |

The surcharge is also known in a thin "2" measuring 5½x7mm, with curving foot. Values: unused $1,200; used $600.

Sri Rama Varma I — A6

**1911-13** **Engr.** ***Perf. 14***

| | | | | |
|---|---|---|---|---|
| 14 | A6 | 2p brown | .45 | .25 |
| *a.* | | Imperf., pair | | |
| 15 | A6 | 3p blue | 2.25 | .25 |
| *a.* | | Perf. 14x12½ | 40.00 | 3.00 |
| 16 | A6 | 4p yel green | 2.50 | .25 |
| 17 | A6 | 9p car rose | 2.10 | .25 |
| 18 | A6 | 1a orange buff | 4.50 | .25 |
| 19 | A6 | 1½a lilac | 11.00 | .65 |
| 20 | A6 | 2a gray | 11.00 | .60 |
| 21 | A6 | 3a vermilion | 57.50 | 57.50 |
| | | *Nos. 14-21 (8)* | 91.30 | 60.00 |

For surcharge and overprints see Nos. 34, O2-O9, O23-O24, O27.

Sri Rama Varma II
A7 A8

**1918-23** **Engr.** ***Perf. 14***

| | | | | |
|---|---|---|---|---|
| 23 | A7 | 2p brown | 12.00 | .25 |
| 24 | A7 | 4p green | 1.50 | .25 |
| 25 | A7 | 6p red brown ('22) | 3.75 | .25 |
| 26 | A7 | 8p black brown ('23) | 2.50 | .25 |
| 27 | A7 | 9p carmine rose | 30.00 | .50 |
| 28 | A7 | 10p deep blue | 9.00 | .25 |
| 29 | A8 | 1a brown orange | 27.50 | 4.50 |
| 30 | A7 | 1½a red violet ('21) | 5.50 | .30 |
| 31 | A7 | 2a gray | 6.25 | .25 |
| 32 | A7 | 2¼a yel green ('22) | 10.50 | 4.75 |
| 33 | A7 | 3a vermilion | 17.50 | .50 |
| | | *Nos. 23-33 (11)* | 126.00 | 12.05 |

The 2p and 1a are found in two types, the difference lying in the first of the three characters directly above the maharaja's head.
For surcharges and overprints see Nos. 36-40, 52-53, O10-O22, O25-O26, O28-O36, O71A.

No. 15 Surcharged

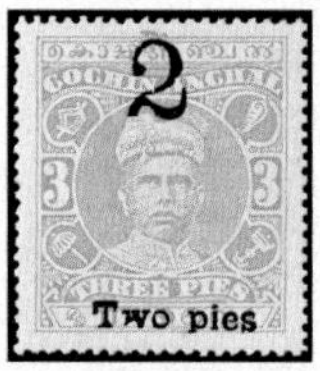


Type I — Numeral 8mm high. Curved foot. Top begins with a ball. (As illustrated.)
Type II — Numeral 9mm high. Curved foot. Top begins with a curved line.
Type III — Numeral 6mm high. Straight foot. "Two pies" 15mm wide.
Type IV — "2" as in type III. Capital "P" in "Pies." "Two Pies" 13mm wide.
Type V — Heavy gothic numeral. Capital "P" in "Pies."

**1922-29**

| | | | | |
|---|---|---|---|---|
| 34 | A6 | 2p on 3p blue (Type I) | .60 | .45 |
| *a.* | | Type II | 5.00 | 1.50 |
| *b.* | | Type III | 10.50 | .50 |
| *c.* | | Type IV | 16.00 | 16.00 |
| *d.* | | Type V | 110.00 | *200.00* |
| *e.* | | Double surcharge, I | 500.00 | 500.00 |
| *f.* | | Double surcharge II | 1,100. | |

Types II and III exist with a capital "P" in "Pies." It occurs once in each sheet of the second and third settings. There are four settings.
Type V is the first stamp, fourth row, of the fourth setting.

No. 32 Surcharged

**1928**

| | | | | |
|---|---|---|---|---|
| 36 | A7 | 1a on 2¼a yel green | 9.00 | *18.00* |
| *a.* | | Double surcharge | | |

Nos. 24, 26 and 28 Surcharged in Black

**1932-33**

| | | | | |
|---|---|---|---|---|
| 38 | A7 | 3p on 4p green | 1.90 | *2.10* |
| 39 | A7 | 3p on 8p black brown | 3.25 | *4.00* |
| 40 | A7 | 9p on 10p deep blue | 2.25 | *5.00* |
| | | *Nos. 38-40 (3)* | 7.40 | 11.10 |

Sri Rama Varma III
A9 A10

**1933-38** **Engr.** ***Perf. 13x13½***

| | | | | |
|---|---|---|---|---|
| 41 | A9 | 2p brown ('36) | 1.25 | .75 |
| 42 | A9 | 4p green | .90 | .25 |
| 43 | A9 | 6p red brown | 1.00 | .25 |
| 44 | A10 | 1a brown org ('34) | 1.25 | .30 |
| 45 | A9 | 1a8p rose red | 4.50 | *9.50* |
| 46 | A9 | 2a gray black ('38) | 9.00 | 2.40 |
| 47 | A9 | 2¼a yellow green | 2.50 | .45 |
| 48 | A9 | 3a red org ('38) | 8.25 | 2.40 |
| 49 | A9 | 3a4p violet | 2.50 | 2.10 |
| 50 | A9 | 6a8p black brown | 2.50 | 22.50 |
| 51 | A9 | 10a deep blue | 4.50 | 25.00 |
| | | *Nos. 41-51 (11)* | 38.15 | 65.90 |

See Nos. 55-58. For overprints and surcharges see Nos. 54, 59-62, 73A-74, 76-77, 89, O37-O57, O70-O71, O72-O77A, O89.

Nos. 26 and 28 Surcharged in Red

**1934** ***Perf. 13½***

| | | | | |
|---|---|---|---|---|
| 52 | A7 | 6p on 8p black brown | 1.10 | .90 |
| 53 | A7 | 6p on 10p dark blue | 2.50 | *3.00* |

No. 44 Overprinted in Black — a

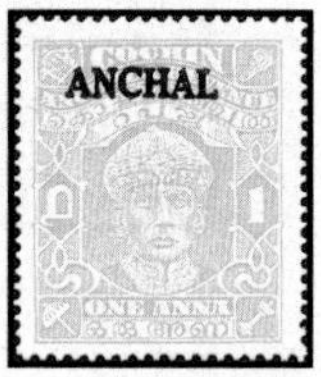


**1939** **Engr.**

| | | | | |
|---|---|---|---|---|
| 54 | A10 | 1a brown orange | 6.25 | 2.50 |

### Types of 1933-38

**1938-41** **Litho.** ***Perf. 11, 13***

| | | | | |
|---|---|---|---|---|
| 55 | A9 | 2p dull brown | 1.25 | .60 |
| 56 | A9 | 4p dull green ('41) | 1.25 | .50 |
| 57 | A9 | 6p red brown | 4.50 | .25 |
| *c.* | | Perf. 13 | | *4,750.* |
| 57A | A10 | 1a brown orange | 95.00 | *140.00* |
| 58 | A10 | 2¼a yellow green | 7.50 | .35 |
| | | *Nos. 55-58 (5)* | 109.50 | *141.70* |

Type of 1934 Overprinted in Black Type "a" or — b

**1941-42** *Perf. 11 (#59), 13 (#60)*

59 A10(a) 1a brown orange 425.00 2.50
a. Perf. 13 525.00
60 A10(b) 1a brown org ('42) 16.00 .90
a. Perf. 11 1.00 2.50

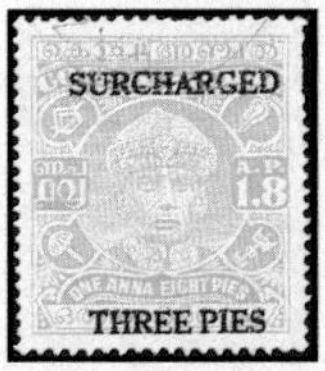


No. 45 Surcharged in Black — c

**1943-44 Engr.** *Perf. 13x13½*

61 A9 3p on 1a8p rose red ('44) 4.25 *30.00*
62 A9 1a3p on 1a8p rose red 1.25 .75

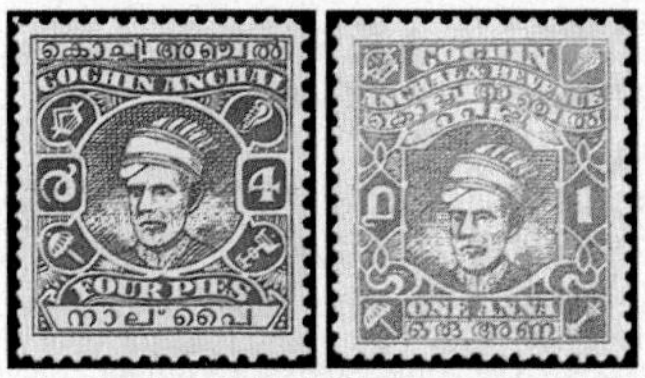

Maharaja Sri Kerala Varma
A11 A12

**1943 Litho. Wmk. 294** *Perf. 11, 13*

63 A11 2p dull gray brn, wmk. 41 4.25 *6.75*
a. Wmk. 294 37.50 5.50
64 A11 4p gray green 4.50 8.25
a. Wmk. 41 1,100. 550.00
65 A11 6p red brown 4.75 .25
66 A11 9p ultramarine 55.00 1.90
67 A12 1a brown orange 29.00 80.00
a. Wmk. 41 120.00 *175.00*
68 A11 2¼a lt ol green 32.50 3.75
*Nos. 63-68 (6)* 130.00 100.90

For surcharges and overprints see Nos. 69-73, 75, 78, 78B, O58-O69.

No. 64 Surcharged Type "c"

69 A11 3p on 4p gray green 8.75 .25
a. Wmk. 41 110.00 35.00

Nos. 64, 64a and 65 Surcharged in Black — d

**1944-48** **Wmk. 294**

70 A11 2p on 6p red brown .95 *6.00*
71 A11 3p on 4p gray green 8.75 .25
72 A11 3p on 6p red brown 1.00 .25
73 A11 4p on 6p red brown 6.25 *18.00*
*Nos. 70-73 (4)* 16.95 24.50

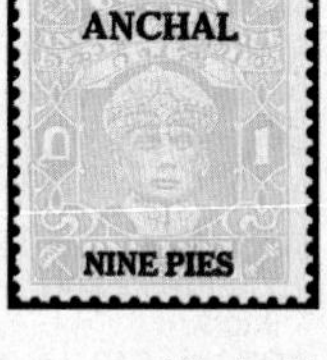


Nos. 57A, 67a Surcharged in Black

**1944 Litho. Wmk. 41**

73A A10 6p on 1a brown org *300.00* 225.00
74 A10 9p on 1a brown org 450.00 60.00
75 A12 9p on 1a brown org 8.00 5.50
*Nos. 73A-75 (3)* *758.00* 290.50

No. 56 Surcharged Type "c" in Black

76 A9 3p on 4p dull green 8.75 6.00

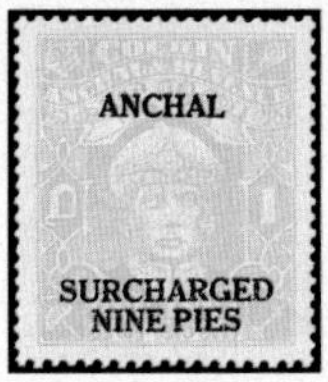


Nos. 57A, 67a Surcharged in Black

**1944**

77 A10 9p on 1a brown orange 30.00 12.00
78 A12 9p on 1a brown orange 9.50 3.25

No. 67a Surcharged Type "c"

**1944 Wmk. 41**

78B A12 1a3p on 1a brn org 7,750.

Maharaja Ravi Varma
A13 A15

**1944-46 Wmk. 294** *Perf. 13*

79 A13 9p ultra ('46) 20.00 27.50
a. Perf. 11 20.00 6.00
80 A13 1a3p magenta 10.00 12.50
81 A13 1a9p ultra ('46) 12.00 24.00
*Nos. 79-81 (3)* 42.00 64.00

For overprints and surcharges see Nos. O78-O80, Travancore 12, 14, O10.

**1946-50 Litho.** *Perf. 13*

82 A15 2p dull brown 3.25 .25
a. Perf. 11 10.00 .90
b. Perf. 11x13 450.00 210.00
83 A15 3p carmine rose .60 .45
83A A15 4p gray green ('50) *3,100.* 120.00
84 A15 6p red brown ('47) 30.00 9.50
a. Perf. 11 210.00 8.25
85 A15 9p ultramarine 1.90 .25
86 A15 1a dp orange ('47) 11.00 *47.50*
a. Perf. 11 625.00
87 A15 2a gray ('47) 150.00 12.50
a. Perf. 11 190.00 10.00
88 A15 3a vermilion 100.00 2.25
*Nos. 82-83,84-88 (7)* 296.75 72.70

For surcharges and overprints see Nos. 98-99, O81-O88, Travancore 8, 13, 15-15A, O11.

No. 45 Surcharged Type "d"

*Perf. 13x13½*

**1947-48 Wmk. 41 Engr.**

89 A9 6p on 1a8p rose red 4.25 30.00

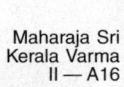

Maharaja Sri Kerala Varma II — A16

Die I

Die II

Two dies on 2p: Die I, back of headdress almost touches value tablet; Die II, back of headdress farther away from value tablet.

Die I

Die II

Two dies on 3a4p: Die I, white frame line around head is continuous, and two white lines beneath value inscriptions at bottom; Die II, white frame line around head broken by value tablets at the sides, and single white line beneath value inscriptions at bottom. Die II comes from the first two stamps of the bottom row of the sheet.

**1948-49 Wmk. 294** *Perf. 11*

90 A16 2p olive brown 2.25 .25
a. Die II 190.00 3.25
91 A16 3p car ('49) 1.90 .25
92 A16 4p gray green 21.00 5.25
a. Horiz. pair, imperf. vert. 350.00 *500.00*
93 A16 6p red brown 22.50 .35
94 A16 9p ultra ('49) 3.00 .75
95 A16 2a black 80.00 3.75
96 A16 3a ver ('49) 87.50 1.50
97 A16 3a4p violet ('49) 87.50 525.00
a. Die II 275.00
*Nos. 90-97 (8)* 305.65 537.10

For overprints see Nos. O90-O97, Travancore 9-11, O8-O9.

No. 86 Surcharged Type "d" in Black

**1949**

98 A15 6p on 1a dp orange 80.00 *225.00*
99 A15 9p on 1a dp orange 120.00 *225.00*

Dutch Palace A17

Design: 2a, Chinese fishing net.

**1949 Unwmk.** *Perf. 11*

100 A17 2a gray 6.25 *12.50*
a. Imperf. vert., horiz. pair 600.00
101 A17 2¼a gray green 3.50 *14.00*
a. Imperf. vert., horiz. pair 600.00 600.00

See Travancore-Cochin for succeeding issues.

## OFFICIAL STAMPS

See note above No. 13.

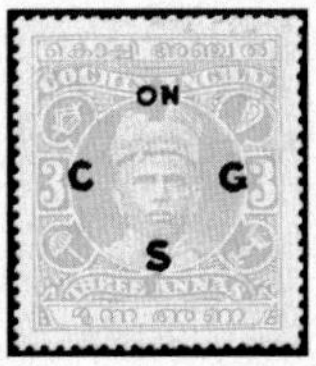


Stamps and Type of 1911-14 Overprinted — h

**1913-14 Wmk. 41 Engr.** *Perf. 14*

O2 A6 4p yel green 13.50 .25
a. Inverted overprint — 450.00
O3 A6 9p car rose 160.00 .25
O4 A6 1½a red violet 72.50 .25
a. Double overprint — 1,000.
O5 A6 2a gray 19.00 .25
O6 A6 3a vermilion 82.50 .65
O7 A6 6a violet 90.00 3.00
O8 A6 12a blue 60.00 10.00
O9 A6 1½r deep green 52.50 *110.00*
*Nos. O2-O9 (8)* 550.00 124.65

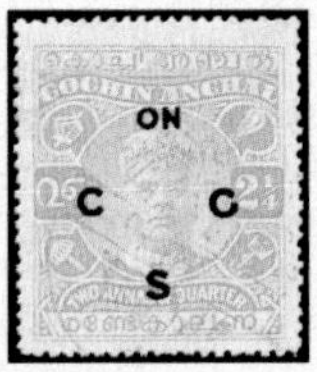


Stamps and Type of 1918-23 Overprinted — i

**1918-34**

O10 A7 4p green 6.00 .25
a. Double overprint — 750.00
O11 A7 6p red brn ('22) 18.00 .25
a. Double overprint — 650.00
O12 A7 8p blk brn ('26) 16.00 .25
O13 A7 9p carmine rose 97.50 .25
O14 A7 10p dp blue ('23) 21.00 .25
O16 A7 1½a red vio ('21) 8.25 .25
a. Double overprint 1,000.
O17 A7 2a gray 62.50 .45
O18 A7 2¼a yel grn ('22) 19.00 .25
b. Double overprint 625.00
O19 A7 3a ver ('22) 27.50 .35
a. Double overprint 650.00
O20 A7 6a violet ('22) 57.50 .75
O21 A7 12a blue ('29) 25.00 7.50
O22 A7 1½r dk green ('34) 37.50 *175.00*
*Nos. O10-O22 (12)* *395.75* *185.80*

On Nos. O2-O22, width of overprint varies from 14¾mm to 16½mm.

No. 15 Overprinted in Red — j

**1921**

O23 A6 3p blue 175.00 .25
a. Overprint in black *1,750.*

Nos. O3 and O13 Surcharged with New Values

**1923-29**

O24 A6 8p on 9p car rose 525.00 2.50
O25 A7 8p on 9p car rose 100.00 .25
a. Double surcharge 400.00
O26 A7 10p on 9p car rose ('25) 120.00 1.50
a. Double surcharge 450.00
O27 A6 10p on 9p car rose ('29) 1,750. 27.50
*Nos. O24-O27 (4)* 2,495. 31.75

Regular Issue of 1918-23 Overprinted — k

**1933-34**

O28 A7 4p green 32.50 2.50
O29 A7 6p red brown ('34) 21.00 .25
O30 A7 8p black brown 10.00 .25
O31 A7 10p deep blue 9.00 .25
O32 A7 2a gray ('34) 60.00 .35
O33 A7 3a vermilion 12.50 .30
O34 A7 6a dk violet ('34) 150.00 4.50
*Nos. O28-O34 (7)* 295.00 8.40

Same with Additional Surcharge on Type of Regular Issue of 1918-23 in Red

O35 A7 6p on 8p black brown 3.75 .25
O36 A7 6p on 10p dk blue ('34) 6.00 .25

Regular Issue of 1933 Overprinted Type "k" in Black as in 1933-34

**1933-35** *Perf. 13x13½*

O37 A9 4p green 6.25 .25
O38 A9 6p red brown 5.50 .25
O39 A10 1a brown orange 24.00 .25
O40 A9 1a8p rose red 2.25 .45
O41 A9 2a gray 27.50 .25
O42 A9 2¼a yellow green 9.00 .25
O43 A9 3a vermilion 67.50 .25
O44 A9 3a4p violet 2.25 .25
O45 A9 6a8p black brown 2.25 .30
O46 A9 10a deep blue 2.25 1.50
*Nos. O37-O46 (10)* 148.75 4.00

Regular Stamps of 1934-38 Overprinted in Black — m

**1939-41** *Perf. 11, 13x13½*

O47 A10 1a brown orange 50.00 .90
O48 A9 2a gray black 27.50 3.00
O49 A9 3a red orange 13.50 3.75
*Nos. O47-O49 (3)* 91.00 7.65

Similar Overprint on Types of 1933-36

*Perf. 11, 13x13½*

**1939-41 Litho. Wmk. 294**

O50 A9 4p dull green ('41) 92.50 24.00

**Wmk. 41**

O51 A9 6p red brown ('41) 14.00 6.50
a. Wmk. 294 25.00 1.50
O52 A10 1a brown orange 1.25 .25
a. Wmk. 294 2.25 *6.50*
O53 A9 3a orange ('40) 3.75 2.50
b. Wmk. 294 24.00 11.00
*Nos. O50-O53 (4)* 111.50 33.25

Similar Overprint in Narrow Serifed Capitals on No. 57

**Wmk. 41** ***Perf. 11***

**O53A** A9 6p red brown 1,050. 600.00

Type of 1933-36 Overprinted in Black — o

***Perf. 10½, 11, 13x13½***

**O54** A9 4p dull green ('41) 35.00 4.00
**O55** A9 6p red brown ('41) 32.50 .60
**O56** A9 2a gray black 25.00 1.50
*Nos. O54-O56 (3)* 92.50 6.10

Type of 1934 Overprinted in Black — p

**1941** ***Perf. 11***

**O57** A10 1a brown orange 375.00 3.75

Stamps and Types of 1944 Overprinted in Black — q

***Perf. 11, 13x13½***

**1944-48** **Wmk. 294**

**O58** A11 4p gray green 50.00 10.00
*a.* Perf. 11 175.00 8.25
**O59** A11 6p red brown 3.50 .25
**O60** A11 2a gray black 8.75 1.50
**O61** A11 2¼a dull yel green 5.25 1.60
*a.* Additional ovpt. on back 160.00
**O62** A11 3a red orange 12.50 2.50
*Nos. O58-O62 (5)* 80.00 15.85

Same Overprint with Additional Surcharge

**O63** A11 3p on 4p gray green 4.25 .25
*a.* Additional overprint on back 210.00
**O64** A12 3p on 1a brown org 32.50 11.00
**O65** A11 9p on 6p red brown 16.00 5.25
**O66** A12 1a3p on 1a brown org 16.00 4.00
*Nos. O63-O66 (4)* 68.75 20.50

Same Overprint in Black on Types of 1944 Surcharged Type "c"

**O67** A11 3p on 4p gray green 6.25 .60
**O68** A11 9p on 6p red brown 5.50 .60
**O69** A12 1a3p on 1a brown org 4.50 .25
*Nos. O67-O69 (3)* 16.25 1.45

Nos. O52 and O16 Surcharged Type "d"

**1944 Wmk. 41** ***Perf. 11, 13x13½, 14***

**O70** A10 3p on 1a brown org 2.75 *5.00*
**O71** A10 9p on 1a brown org 325.00 82.50

**Engr.**

**O71A** A7 9p on 1⅛a red vio 800.00 40.00

No. O52 Surcharged Type "c"

**O72** A10 1a3p on 1a brn org 375.00 150.00

No. 76 Overprinted in Black

***Perf. 13***

**O72A** A9 3p on 4p dull green 210.00 90.00

No. 45 Overprinted Type "k" and Surcharged Type "d"

**1944-48** **Wmk. 41** ***Perf. 13x13½***

**O73** A9 9p on 1a8p rose red 160.00 50.00
**O74** A9 1a9p on 1a8p rose red 3.50 *4.00*

No. 45 Overprinted Type "k" and Surcharged Type "c"

**O75** A9 3p on 1a8p rose red 7.00 4.50
**O76** A9 1a9p on 1a8p rose red 1.90 .60

Type of 1939-41 Overprinted in Black

**1946** **Wmk. 294** ***Perf. 11***

**O77** A9 2a gray 92.50 1.20
**O77A** A9 2¼a yellow green 2,000. 10.00

Same Overprint in Black on #79-81

**1946** **Litho.** ***Perf. 13***

**O78** A13 9p ultramarine 3.75 .25
**O79** A13 1a3p magenta 2.00 .25
*a.* Double overprint 25.00 18.00
**O80** A13 1a9p ultramarine .50 *1.50*
*Nos. O78-O80 (3)* 6.25 2.00

Types and Stamps of 1946-48 Overprinted Type "h"

**1946-48**

**O81** A15 3p car rose 1.50 .25
**O82** A15 4p gray green 37.50 10.00
**O83** A15 6p red brown 17.50 2.50
**O84** A15 9p ultra .95 .25
**O85** A15 1a3p magenta 5.00 2.10
**O86** A15 1a9p ultra 6.00 .60
**O87** A15 2a gray black 19.00 4.50
**O88** A15 2¼a olive green 29.00 7.50
*Nos. O81-O88 (8)* 116.45 27.70

No. 56 Overprinted Type "q" and Surcharged Type "d"

**1947 Wmk. 41 Engr.** ***Perf. 13x13½***

**O89** A9 3p on 4p dull green 32.50 11.00

Stamps and Type of 1948-49 Overprinted Type "o"

**1948-49 Wmk. 294 Litho.** ***Perf. 11***

**O90** A16 3p carmine ('49) 1.50 .25
**O91** A16 4p gray green 1.90 .60
**O92** A16 6p red brown 3.50 .45
**O93** A16 9p ultramarine 4.00 .25
**O94** A16 2a black ('49) 3.50 .25
**O95** A16 2¼a lt ol green ('49) 4.00 *9.50*
**O96** A16 3a vermilion ('49) 1.40 *1.50*
**O97** A16 3a4p deep pur ('49) 55.00 *67.50*
*Nos. O90-O97 (8)* 74.80 80.30

See Travancore-Cochin for succeeding issues.

## DHAR

'där

LOCATION — A Feudatory State in the Malwa Agency in Central India.
AREA — 1,800 sq. mi.
POP. — 243,521
CAPITAL — Dhar

A1

Arms of Dhar — A2

The stamps of type A1 have an oval control mark handstamped in black.

**Unwmk.**
**1897-1900 Typeset** ***Imperf.***
**Without Gum**

**1** A1 ½p black, *red* 4.50 *5.00*
*a.* Characters for "pice" transposed 100.00
*b.* Four characters in first word 4.00 *6.00*
*c.* Without control mark 500.00
**2** A1 ¼a black, *org red* ('00) 5.50 *7.50*
*a.* Without control mark 375.00
**3** A1 ½a black, *lil rose* 6.75 *8.25*
**4** A1 1a black, *bl grn* 12.50 *25.00*
**5** A1 2a black, *yel* ('00) 42.50 *75.00*
*Nos. 1-5 (5)* 71.75 *120.75*

**1898-1900 Typo.** ***Perf. 11½***

**6** A2 ½a red 7.00 *9.50*
**7** A2 ½a rose ('00) 6.25 *9.00*
*a.* Imperf., pair 60.00
**8** A2 1a maroon 6.25 *12.00*
**9** A2 1a violet ('00) 6.25 *22.50*
**10** A2 1a claret ('00) 6.25 *12.00*
**11** A2 2a dark green ('00) 11.00 *37.50*
*Nos. 6-11 (6)* 43.00 *102.50*

Obsolete Mar. 31, 1901.

## DUNGARPUR

LOCATION — A princely state in Rajasthan, in northwestern India.
AREA — 1,447 sq. mi.
POP. — 100,103 (1901)
CAPITAL — Dungarpur

Arms of Dungarpur — A1

**1933-1947 Unwmk. Litho.** ***Perf. 11***

**1** A1 ¼a bister yellow 2,000. 400.00
*a.* ¼a lemon yellow ('34) 2,500. 500.00
**2** A1 ¼a salmon ('35) 5,000. 1,000.
*a.* ¼a red brown ('36) 3,750. 750.00
*b.* ¼a orange red ('38) 6,250. 1,250.
**3** A1 1a pale turquoise blue 1,500. 300.00
*a.* 1a turquoise blue 2,000. 400.00
**4** A1 1a3p deep red violet ('35) 3,000. 600.00
**5** A1 2a deep dull green ('47) 3,750. 750.00
**6** A1 4a dull rose red 6,250. 1,250.
*a.* 4a rose red ('34) 7,000. 1,400.

A2

A3

A4

A5

A6

A7

A8

A9

A10

Maharawal Lakshman Singh

**1934-38** **Typo.** ***Perf. 12***

**7** A2 ¼a org buff ('36) 1,750. 200.00
**8** A3 ½a vermilion, Die I 500.00 125.00
**9** A4 1a blue
*a.* Perf 11½ ('38) 750.00 125.00
**10** A5 4a gray brown 2,000. 650.00

There are three dies of the ½ anna: Die I measures 21x25½mm, and width of turban is 7½mm; Die II measures 20x20½mm; Die III measures 21x25½mm, and width of turban is 6½mm. There are 4 distinct cliches of Die III, printed in a block of 4, differing in the space between the top of the turban and the frame: Pos. 1 = 2mm; Pos. 2 = 2.5mm; Pos. 3 = 1mm; Pos. 4 = 1.5mm.

**1940-41** ***Perf. 11, 11½ (#15)***

**11** A2 ¼a dull org('41) 1,500. 150.00
**12** A3 ½a carmine, Die I 500.00 150.00
**13** A4 1a blue 500.00 100.00
**14** A6 2a bright green 2,500. 900.00
**15** A5 4a gray brown 1,800. 450.00

**1943** ***Pin-Perf 11½***

**16** A6 2a bright green 2,500. 900.00

**1943-44** ***Perf. 10½***

**17** A2 ¼a dull org('44) 1,500. 150.00
**18** A3 ½a vermilion, Die I ('44) 600.00 175.00
**19** A7 ½a vermilion, Die II ('44) 600.00 175.00
*a.* Horiz. pair, #18 + #19 1,300. 450.
*b.* Vert. pair, imperf between 5,000.
**20** A4 1a blue ('44) 500.00 100.00
**21** A8 1a3p mauve 2,000. 450.00
**22** A5 4a pale brown ('44) 2,400. 650.00

**1945** ***Perf. 10***

**23** A2 ¼a orange 2,000. 150.00
**24** A9 ½a vermilion, Die III ('44) 800.00 100.00
**25** A4 1a blue 500.00 100.00
**26** A8 1a3p bright mauve 2,000. 450.00
**27** A10 1½a deep violet 2,000. 450.00
**28** A5 4a brown 1,600. 400.00

The stamps of Dungarpur became obsolete in Sept. 1949.

## DUTTIA

'dət-ē-ə

(Datia)

LOCATION — A Feudatory State in the Bundelkhand Agency in Central India.
AREA — 912 sq. mi.
POP. — 158,834
CAPITAL — Datia

Ganesh, Elephant-headed God
A1 A2

All Duttia stamps have a circular control mark, about 23mm in diameter, handstamped in blue or black. All were issued without gum.

**1893 Typeset Unwmk. *Imperf.***

1 A1 ¼a black, *org red* 6,250.
2 A1 ½a blk, *grysh grn* 24,000.
3 A2 1a black, *red* 4,750. *7,500.*
4 A1 2a black, *yellow* 5,250.
5 A1 4a black, *rose* 1,900.

**Type A2 with Frameline around God, Rosettes in Lower Corners**

**1896 (?)**

5A A2 ½ black, *green* *15,000.*
5C A2 2a dk blue, *lemon* *3,750.*

A 1a in this revised type has been reported.

**1897**

6 A2 ½a black, *green* 100.00 *675.00*
7 A2 1a black 150.00 *525.00*
 *a.* Laid paper 32.50
8 A2 2a black, *yellow* 42.50 *500.00*
9 A2 4a black, *rose* 40.00 *325.00*
 *Nos. 6-9 (4)* 332.50 *2,025.*

A3

A4

10 A3 ½a black, *green* 150.00 *825.00*
11 A3 1a black 290.00
12 A3 2a black, *yellow* 175.00 *825.00*
13 A3 4a black, *rose* 175.00 *825.00*
 *Nos. 10-13 (4)* 790.00 2,475.

**1899-1900**

**Rouletted in Colored Lines on 2 or 3 Sides**

14 A4 ¼a red (shades) 5.00 *32.50*
 *b.* Tete beche pair *4,900.*
15 A4 ½a black, *green* 4.00 *30.00*
16 A4 1a black 4.50 *30.00*
17 A4 2a black, *yellow* 5.25 *35.00*
18 A4 4a black, *rose red* 5.00 *32.50*
 *a.* Tete beche pair
 *Nos. 14-18 (5)* 23.75 160.00

**1904 *Imperf.***

22 A4 ¼a carmine 5.50 *47.50*
23 A4 ½a black, *green* 27.50
24 A4 1a black 21.00 *75.00*
 *Nos. 22-24 (3)* 54.00 122.50

**1911 *Perf. 13½***

25 A4 ¼a carmine 9.50 *75.00*

**1916 *Imperf.***

26 A4 ¼a dull blue 8.25 *40.00*
27 A4 ½a green 8.25 *40.00*
28 A4 1a violet 10.00 *42.50*
 *a.* Tete beche pair 35.00
29 A4 2a brown 22.50 *52.50*
29A A4 4a brick red 110.00
 *Nos. 26-29A (5)* 159.00 175.00

**1918**

31 A4 ½a ultramarine 5.25 *27.50*
32 A4 1a rose 5.25 *27.50*
33 A4 2a violet 11.00 *40.00*

***Perf. 12***

34 A4 ¼a black 7.50 *37.50*
 *Nos. 31-34 (4)* 29.00 *132.50*

**1920 *Rouletted***

35 A4 ¼a blue 4.00 *21.00*
36 A4 ½a rose 5.25 *24.00*

***Perf. 7***

37 A4 ½a dull red 24.00 *62.50*
 *Nos. 35-37 (3)* 33.25 *107.50*

Duttia stamps became obsolete in 1921.

## FARIDKOT

fe-ˈrēd-ˌkōt

LOCATION — A Feudatory State in the Punjab Agency of India.
AREA — 638 sq. mi.
POP. — 164,364
CAPITAL — Faridkot

4 Folus or Paisas = 1 Anna

A1

A2

A3

**Handstamped**

**1879-86 Unwmk. *Imperf.***

**Without Gum**

1 A1 1f ultramarine 4.00 *6.00*
 *a.* Laid paper 21.00 *24.00*
 *b.* Tete beche pair 400.00
2 A2 1p ultramarine 7.50 *16.00*
 *a.* Laid paper 125.00 *150.00*
3 A3 1p ultramarine 2.25
 *a.* Tete beche pair 340.00
 *Nos. 1-3 (3)* 13.75 22.00

Several other varieties exist, but it is believed that only the stamps listed here were issued for postal use. They became obsolete Dec. 31, 1886. See Faridkot under Convention States for issues of 1887-1900.

## HYDERABAD (DECCAN)

ˈhīd-ə-ˌrə-ˌbad

LOCATION — Central India
AREA — 82,313 sq. mi.
POP. — 16,338,534 (1941)
CAPITAL — Hyderabad

This independent princely state was occupied and annexed by India in 1948.

**Catalogue values for unused stamps in this State are for Never Hinged items, beginning with Scott 51 in the regular postage section, and Scott O54 in the officials section.**

Expect irregular perfs on the Nos. 1-14 and O1-O20 due to the nature of the paper.

A1

A2

**1869-71 Engr. Unwmk. *Perf. 11½***

1 A1 ½a brown ('71) 6.00 *6.50*
2 A2 1a olive green 27.50 11.00
 *a.* Imperf. horiz., pair 900.00 175.00
3 A1 2a green ('71) 90.00 72.50
 *Nos. 1-3 (3)* 123.50 90.00

For overprints see Nos. O1-O3, O11-O13.
*The reprints are perforated 12½.*

A3

**Wove Paper**

**1871-1909 *Perf. 12½***

4 A3 ½a orange brown 4.00 .25
 *a.* ½a red brown 4.00 .25
 *b.* ½a magenta (error) 75.00 12.00
 *c.* Perf. 11½ 27.50 *30.00*
 *d.* ½a rose 4.00 .30
 *e.* ½a bright vermilion 4.00 .25
5 A3 1a dark brown 1.90 .25
 *a.* Imperf., pair 550.00
 *b.* Horiz. pair, imperf. vert. 1,350.
 *c.* Vert. pair, imperf. horiz. 1,350.
 *d.* Perf. 11½ 180.00 *200.00*
6 A3 1a black ('09) 3.50 .25
7 A3 2a green 5.50 .25
 *a.* 2a olive green ('09) 5.50 .50
 *b.* Perf. 11½ 1,900.
8 A3 3a yellow brown 4.50 2.25
 *a.* Perf. 11½ 60.00 *82.50*
9 A3 4a slate 11.00 5.25
 *a.* Imperf. horiz., pair 1,350. 1,350.
 *b.* Perf. 11½ 225.00 225.00
10 A3 4a deep green 8.25 5.00
 *a.* 4a olive green 9.00 3.75
11 A3 8a bister brown 5.25 *6.50*
 *a.* Perf. 11½
12 A3 12a blue 7.00 *12.00*
 *a.* Perf. 11½ 500.00
 *b.* 12a slate green 7.50 7.50
 *Nos. 4-12 (9)* 50.90 32.00

For overprints see Nos. 13, O4-O10, O14-O20, O25-O26.

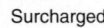

Surcharged

**1900**

13 A3 ¼a on ½a brt ver .75 *1.25*
 *a.* Inverted surcharge 57.50 35.00

A4

**1900, Sept. 20**

14 A4 ¼a blue 8.25 5.25

Seal of the Nizam
A5 A6

**Engraved by A. G. Wyon**

**1905 Wmk. 42**

17 A5 ¼a blue 3.75 .90
18 A5 ½a red 6.00 .35
19 A5 ½a orange 9.00 .50
 *Nos. 17-19 (3)* 18.75 1.75

For overprints see Nos. O21-O23.

***Perf. 11, 11½, 12½, 13½ and Compound***

**1908-11**

20 A5 ¼a gray 1.50 .25
21 A5 ½a green 7.00 .25
22 A5 1a carmine 5.25 .25
23 A5 2a lilac 2.40 .25
24 A5 3a brn orange ('09) 4.00 1.50
25 A5 4a olive green ('09) 4.50 1.90
26 A5 8a violet ('11) 1.90 1.20
27 A5 12a blue green ('11) 10.50 6.00
 *Nos. 20-27 (8)* 37.05 11.60

For overprints see Nos. O24, O27-O38.

**Engr. by Bradbury, Wilkinson & Co.**

**1912**

28 A5 ¼a brown violet 1.20 .25
29 A5 ½a deep green 2.50 .25
 *a.* Imperf., pair 550.00

The frame of type A5 differs slightly in each denomination.
Nos. 20-21 measure 19½x20½mm.
Nos. 28-29 measure 20x21½mm.

For overprints see Nos 37, O39-O40, O44.

**1915-16**

30 A6 ½a green 1.50 .25
31 A6 1a carmine rose 3.75 .25
32 A6 1a red 2.50 .25
 *Nos. 30-32 (3)* 7.75 .75

Unless used, imperf. stamps of types A5 and A6 are from plate proof sheets.
See #58. For overprints see #38, O41-O43, O45.

A7

**1927 Wmk. 211 *Perf. 13½***

36 A7 1r yellow 13.50 *18.00*

**Stamps of 1912-16 Surcharged in Red**

(4 pies)

(8 pies)

**1930**

37 A5 4p on ¼a brown violet .45 .25
 *a.* Perf. 11 675.00
 *b.* Double surcharge 350.00
38 A6 8p on ½a green .60 .25
 *a.* Perf. 11 400.00 210.00

For overprints see Nos. O44-O45.

Seal of Nizam — A8

Char Minar — A9

High Court of Justice
A10

Reservoir for City of Hyderabad
A11

Bidar College — A13

Entrance to Ajanta Caves
A12

Victory Tower at Daulatabad
A14

**Wmk. 211**

**1931-48 Engr. *Perf. 13½***

**39** A8 4p black .45 .25
*a.* Laid paper ('47) 3.75 *8.25*
**39B** A8 6p car lake ('48) 15.00 12.50
**40** A8 8p green .75 .25
*a.* 8p yel grn, laid paper ('47) 4.50 *6.75*
*b.* Imperf., pair 90.00 *180.00*
**41** A9 1a dark brown .75 .25
**42** A10 2a dark violet 4.50 .25
*a.* Imperf., pair 195.00 *400.00*
**43** A11 4a ultramarine 2.40 1.00
*a.* Imperf., pair 210.00 *500.00*
**44** A12 8a deep orange 10.50 6.00
**45** A13 12a scarlet 11.00 *18.00*
**46** A14 1r yellow 7.50 7.00
*Nos. 39-46 (9)* 52.85 45.50

On No. 39B, "POSTAGE" has been moved to ribbon at bottom of design.

Nos. 39a and 40a are printed from worn plates. The background of the design is unshaded.

See #59. For overprints see #O46-O53, O56.

Unani General Hospital A15

Osmania General Hospital A16

Osmania University A17

Osmania Jubilee Hall — A18

***Perf. 13½x14***

**1937, Feb. 13 Litho. Unwmk.**

**47** A15 4p violet & black .75 *3.25*
**48** A16 8p brown & black 1.25 *3.25*
**49** A17 1a dull orange & gray 1.75 *2.10*
**50** A18 2a dull green & gray 2.25 *6.75*
*Nos. 47-50 (4)* 6.00 *15.35*

The Nizam's Silver Jubilee.

**Catalogue values for unused stamps in this section, from this point to the end of the section, are for Never Hinged items.**

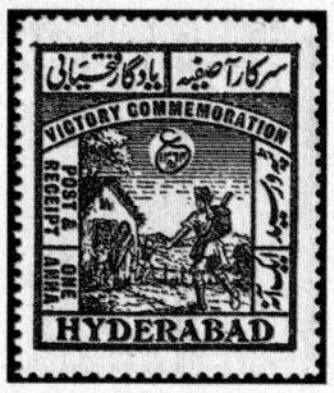


Returning Soldier — A19

**1946 Typo. *Perf. 13½***

**51** A19 1a dark blue .25 .25

**Wmk. 211**

**52** A19 1a blue .25 .25

**Wmk. Nizam's Seal in Sheet**

**Laid Paper**

**53** A19 1a dark blue 1.00 *1.20*
*Nos. 51-53 (3)* 1.50 1.70

Victory of the Allied Nations in WW II.

Town Hall, Hyderabad A20

**1947, Feb. 17 Litho. Wove Paper**

**54** A20 1a black 2.00 *2.90*

Inauguration of the Reformed Legislature, Feb. 17th, 1947.

Power House, Hyderabad A21

Designs: 3a, Kaktyai Arch, Warangal Fort. 6a, Golkunda Fort.

***Perf. 13½x14***

**1947-49 Typo. Wmk. 211**

**55** A21 1a4p dark green 1.50 *3.25*
**56** A21 3a blue 2.50 *6.50*
**57** A21 6a olive brown 5.50 *27.50*
*a.* 6a red brown ('49) 25.00 *47.50*
*b.* Imperf., pair 190.00
*Nos. 55-57 (3)* 9.50 37.25

**Seal Type of 1915**

**1947 Engr. *Perf. 13½***

**58** A6 ½a rose lake 3.75 1.10

For overprint see No. O54.

**Seal Type of 1931**

**1949 Litho.**

**59** A8 2p brown 3.00 3.50

For overprint see No. O55.

**OFFICIAL STAMPS**

Regular Issues of 1869-71 Overprinted

**1873 Unwmk. *Perf. 11½, 12½***

**Red Overprint**

**O1** A1 ½a brown 195.00 125.00
**O2** A2 1a olive green 35.00 35.00
**O3** A1 2a green 72.50 57.50
**O4** A3 ½a red brown 27.50 9.00
**O5** A3 1a dark brown 195.00 125.00
**O6** A3 2a green 72.50 57.50
**O7** A3 3a yel brown 250.00 250.00
**O8** A3 4a slate 120.00 72.50
**O9** A3 8a bister 125.00 *225.00*
**O10** A3 12a blue 195.00 *240.00*

**Black Overprint**

**O11** A1 ½a brown 52.50
**O12** A2 1a olive green 4.50 3.75
**O13** A1 2a green 7.50 *9.00*
**O14** A3 ½a red brown 16.00 5.25
**O15** A3 1a dark brown — 52.50
**O16** A3 2a green 7.50 *9.00*
**O17** A3 3a yel brown 62.50 52.50
**O18** A3 4a slate 32.50 30.00
**O19** A3 8a bister 75.00 62.50
**O20** A3 12a blue 90.00 *120.00*

*The above official stamps became obsolete in August, 1878. Since that date the "Official" overprint has been applied to the reprints and probably to original stamps. Two new varieties of the overprint have also appeared, both on the reprints and on the current stamps. These are overprinted in various colors, positions and combinations.*

Same Ovpt. On Regular Issues of 1905-11

**1908 Wmk. 42**

**O21** A5 ½a green 30.00 .25
**O22** A5 1a carmine 97.50 .25
**O23** A5 2a lilac 97.50 .25
*Nos. O21-O23 (3)* 225.00 .75

***Perf. 11, 11½, 12½, 13½ and Compound***

**1909-11**

**O24** A5 ½a red 210.00 .25
**O25** A3 1a black 140.00 .75
**O26** A3 2a olive green 150.00 1.50
**O27** A5 3a brown orange 11.00 5.00
**O28** A5 4a olive green ('11) 45.00 1.90
**O29** A5 8a violet ('11) 19.00 5.25
**O30** A5 12a blue green ('11) 15.00 5.00
*Nos. O24-O30 (7)* 590.00 19.65

Regular Issue of 1908-11 Overprinted

**1911-12**

**O31** A5 ¼a gray 6.75 1.10
**O32** A5 ½a green 5.25 .25
**O33** A5 1a carmine 3.00 .25
**O34** A5 2a lilac 2.50 1.90
**O35** A5 3a brown orange 27.50 1.10
**O36** A5 4a olive green 7.00 .25
**O37** A5 8a violet 11.00 .30
**O38** A5 12a blue green 36.00 3.75
*Nos. O31-O38 (8)* 99.00 8.90

Same Overprint on Regular Issue of 1912

**1912**

**O39** A5 ¼a brown violet 5.50 .25
*a.* ¼a gray violet 5.50 .25
**O40** A5 ½a deep green 5.25 .25

Same Ovpt. On Regular Issue of 1915-16

**1917**

**O41** A6 ½a green 5.25 .25
**O42** A6 1a carmine rose 7.00 .25
**O43** A6 1a red 4.00 .25
*Nos. O41-O43 (3)* 16.25 .75

Same Overprint on Nos. 37 and 38

**1930**

**O44** A5 4p on ¼a brown violet 3.25 .25
**O45** A6 8p on ½a green 2.25 .25

Same Overprint on Regular Issue of 1931

**1934-47 Wmk. 211 *Perf. 13½***

**O46** A8 4p black 4.00 .25
*a.* Laid paper ('47) 7.50
*b.* Imperf., pair 120.00
**O47** A8 8p green 1.90 .25
*a.* 8p yel grn, laid paper ('47) 10.00 7.50
*b.* Inverted overprint 240.00
**O48** A9 1a dark brown 3.00 .25
**O49** A10 2a dark violet 11.00 .25
**O50** A11 4a ultramarine 6.00 .35
**O51** A12 8a deep orange 21.00 .90
**O52** A13 12a scarlet 19.00 2.50
**O53** A14 1r yellow 30.00 3.75
*Nos. O46-O53 (8)* 95.90 8.50

**Catalogue values for unused stamps in this section, from this point to the end of the section, are for Never Hinged items.**

Same Overprint on Nos. 58-59, 39B

**1947-50 *Perf. 13½***

**O54** A6 ½a rose lake 9.00 *10.50*
**O55** A8 2p brown ('49) 9.00 *15.00*
**O56** A8 6p car lake ('50) 11.00 *35.00*
*Nos. O54-O56 (3)* 29.00 *60.50*

## IDAR

'ē-dər

LOCATION — A Feudatory State in the Western India States Agency.
AREA — 1,669 sq. mi.
POP. — 262,660
CAPITAL — Himmatnagar

Stamps of Idar are in booklet panes of four. All stamps have one or two straight edges.

Maharaja Shri Himatsinhji
A1 A2

**1939 Unwmk. Typo. *Perf. 11***

**1** A1 ½a light green 21.00 *37.50*

**1941 Same Redrawn**

**2** A1 ½a green 17.50 *40.00*

The panels containing denomination and name of state are shaded.

**1944 Unwmk. *Perf. 12***

**3** A2 ½a green 4.00 *110.00*
**4** A2 1a purple 4.00 *100.00*
*a.* Imperf., pair 250.00
**5** A2 2a blue 4.50 *150.00*
**6** A2 4a red 4.75 *160.00*
*Nos. 3-6 (4)* 17.25

## INDORE

in-'dō̦ə̦r

(Holkar)

LOCATION — A Feudatory State in the Indore Agency in Central India.
AREA — 9,902 sq. mi.
POP. — 1,513,966
CAPITAL — Indore

Maharaja Tukoji Rao II — A1

A2

**1886 Unwmk. Litho. *Perf. 15***

**1** A1 ½a lilac 5.50 3.25

**1889 Handstamped *Imperf.***

**3** A2 ¼a black, *rose* 5.25 *5.50*

No. 3 exists in two types.

*The originals of this stamp are printed in water color. The reprints are in oil color and on paper of a deeper shade of rose.*

Maharaja Shivaji Rao — A3

**1889-92 Engr. *Perf. 15***

**4** A3 ¼a orange 2.25 1.20
**5** A3 ½a brown violet 3.75 .25
**6** A3 1a green 4.50 1.90
**7** A3 2a vermilion 10.50 3.00
*Nos. 4-7 (4)* 21.00 6.35

For overprint see No. 14.

Maharaja Tukoji Rao III
A4 A5

**1904-08** *Perf. 13½, 14*

8 A4 ¼a orange .90 .25
9 A5 ½a lake ('08) 13.50 .25
*a.* Imperf., pair 35.00
10 A5 1a green ('07) 3.75 .25
*a.* Imperf., pair 175.00
11 A5 2a brown ('05) 22.50 1.50
*a.* Imperf., pair 120.00
12 A5 3a violet 35.00 10.50
13 A5 4a ultramarine 7.50 2.10
*Nos. 8-13 (6)* 83.15 14.85

For overprints see Nos. O1-O7.

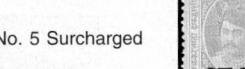

No. 5 Surcharged

**1905** *Perf. 15*

14 A3 ¼a on ½a brown violet 9.00 *30.00*

Maharaja Yeshwant Rao II
A6 A7

**1928-38** **Engr.** *Perf. 13½*

15 A6 ¼a orange .90 .30
16 A6 ½a claret 3.25 .25
17 A6 1a green 4.00 .25
18 A6 1¼a green ('33) 6.00 1.25
19 A6 2a dark brown 19.00 3.25
20 A6 2a Prus blue ('36) 19.00 3.25
*a.* Imperf, pair 37.50 *275.00*
21 A6 3a dull violet 3.00 *14.00*
22 A6 3½a dull violet ('34) 10.50 *15.00*
*a.* Imperf, pair 100.00 *650.00*
23 A6 4a ultramarine 10.50 7.50
24 A6 4a bister ('38) 52.50 2.50
*a.* Imperf, pair 45.00 *500.00*
25 A6 8a gray 9.50 6.50
26 A6 8a red orange ('38) 40.00 35.00
27 A6 12a rose red ('34) 7.50 *15.00*

*Perf. 14*

28 A7 1r lt blue & black 12.50 *22.50*
29 A7 2r car lake & black 82.50 *90.00*
30 A7 5r org brn & black 140.00 140.00
*Nos. 15-30 (16)* 420.65 *356.55*

Imperforates of types A6 and A7 were used with official sanction at Indore City during a stamp shortage in 1938. They were from sheets placed by the printers (Perkins, Bacon) on top of packets of 100 perforated sheets as identification.

Stamps of 1929-33 Surcharged in Black

**1940** *Perf. 13, 14*

31 A7 ¼a on 5r org brn & blk 19.00 2.50
*a.* Dbl. surch., black over green 700.00
32 A7 ½a on 2r car lake & blk 32.50 5.00
33 A6 1a on 1¼a green 32.50 1.20
*a.* Inverted surcharge 110.00
*Nos. 31-33 (3)* 84.00 8.70

Stamps with green surcharge only are proofs.

A8

**1941-47** **Typo.** *Perf. 11*

34 A8 ¼a orange 2.50 .25
35 A8 ½a rose lilac 4.75 .25
36 A8 1a dk olive green 12.50 .25
37 A8 1¼a yellow green 20.00 20.00
*a.* Imperf., pair 275.00
38 A8 2a turquoise blue 14.00 1.75
39 A8 4a bister ('47) 20.00 20.00

**Size: 23x28¼mm**

40 A8 2r car lake & blk ('47) 16.00 *250.00*
41 A8 5r brn org & blk 15.00 *325.00*
*Nos. 34-41 (8)* 104.75 *617.50*

**OFFICIAL STAMPS**

Stamps and Type of 1904-08 Overprinted

**1904-06** *Perf. 13½, 14*

O1 A5 ½a lake 1.10 *1.90*
*a.* Inverted overprint 35.00 *62.50*
*b.* Double overprint 35.00
*c.* Imperf., pair 110.00
O2 A5 1a green .25 .25
O3 A5 2a brown ('05) .45 .45
O4 A5 3a violet ('06) 2.50 *5.50*
*a.* Imperf., pair 425.00
O5 A5 4a ultra ('05) 7.50 2.25
*Nos. O1-O5 (5)* 11.80 10.35

Same Overprint on No. 8

**1907**

O6 A4 ¼a orange 1.10 *1.90*

No. 9 Overprinted

O7 A5 ½a lake .25 1.75

#O1, O7 differ mainly in the shape of the "R."

## JAIPUR

'jī-ˌpu̇ə̇r

LOCATION — A Feudatory State in the Jaipur Residency of India.
AREA — 15,610 sq. mi.
POP. — 3,040,876
CAPITAL — Jaipur

**Catalogue values for unused stamps in this State are for Never Hinged items, beginning with Scott 49 in the regular postage section, and Scott O30 in the officials section.**

A1

A1a

Chariot of Surya, Sun God

*Pin-perf. 14x14½*

**1904** **Typo.** **Unwmk.**

1 A1 ½a ultramarine 290.00 275.00
*a.* ½a pale blue 210.00 *275.00*
*b.* ½a gray blue 3,250. 300.00
*c.* As "b," imperf. 525.00 *900.00*
1D A1a ½a blue 5.00 *10.00*
*e.* ½a ultramarine 5.50 *10.00*
*f.* Imperf. 5.50 *10.00*
2 A1 1a dull red 8.25 *21.00*
*a.* 1a chestnut 8.25 *21.00*
3 A1 2a pale green 8.25 *21.00*
*a.* 2a emerald 9.00
*Nos. 1-3 (4)* 311.50 *327.00*

No. 1 has 36 varieties (on 2 plates), differing in minor details. Nos. 1b and 1c are from plate II. No. 1D has 24 varieties (one plate).

Chariot of Surya — A2

*Perf. 12½x12 and 13½*

**1904-06** **Engr.**

4 A2 ¼a olive green ('06) 1.25 *1.60*
5 A2 ½a deep blue 2.75 .75
6 A2 1a carmine 3.75 *6.75*
7 A2 2a dark green 5.25 2.25
8 A2 4a red brown 11.00 3.25
9 A2 8a violet 6.00 4.00
10 A2 1r yellow 35.00 24.00
*Nos. 4-10 (7)* 65.00 42.60

For overprints see Nos. 21-22.

A3

A4

**1911** **Typo.** *Imperf.*

**Without Gum**

11 A3 ¼a yellow green 3.75 *5.00*
*a.* ¼a olive green 3.75 *5.00*
*b.* "¼" inverted 9.00
12 A3 ¼a olive yellow .45 *1.50*
*b.* ¼a blue (error) —
13 A3 ½a ultramarine .45 *1.50*
*a.* ½a dull blue 4.00 4.00
*b.* "½" for "½" 7.00
14 A3 1a carmine .75 *1.50*
15 A3 2a deep green 3.00 *9.50*
*a.* 2a gray green 4.00 *8.25*
*Nos. 11-15 (5)* 8.40 *19.00*

There are six types for each value and several settings of the ¼a and ½a in the 1911 issue.

**Wmk. "Dorling & Co., London" in Sheet**

**1913-18** *Perf. 11*

16 A4 ¼a olive bister 1.00 *2.25*
*a.* Vert. pair, imperf. between 300.00 300.00
*b.* Horiz. pair, imperf. between — 240.00
17 A4 ½a ultramarine 2.25 1.90
18 A4 1a carmine ('18) 8.25 8.25
*a.* 1a scarlet 6.00 5.50
*b.* Vert. pair, imperf. btwn. 1,250. 1,250.
*c.* Vert. pair, imperf. horiz. 1,250.
19 A4 2a green ('18) 6.00 7.50
20 A4 4a red brown 10.50 *15.00*
*Nos. 16-20 (5)* 28.00 *34.90*

For overprints see Nos. O1-O6, O9-O10.

Stamps of 1904-06 Surcharged

**1926** **Unwmk.** **Engr.** *Perf. 13½*

21 A2 3a on 8a violet 3.00 *5.25*
*a.* Inverted surcharge 275.00 210.00
22 A2 3a on 1r yellow 4.00 *9.50*
*a.* Inverted surcharge 825.00 275.00

**Wmk. "Overland Bank" in Sheet**

**1928** **Typo.** *Perf. 12*

*17a* A4 ½a ultramarine 4.75 *6.00*
*18d* A4 1a rose red 40.00 25.00
*18e* A4 1a scarlet 62.50 17.50
*19a* A4 2a green 140.00 45.00
*20a* A4 4a pale brown
23 A4 1r red orange 600.00 *825.00*

**Durbar Commemorative Issue**

Chariot of Surya, Sun God — A5

Maharaja Man Singh II — A6

Elephant with Standard — A7

Sowar in Armor — A8

Blue Peafowl — A9

Royal Bullock Carriage — A10

Royal Elephant Carriage — A11

Albert Museum — A12

Sireh-Deorhi Gate — A13

Chandra Palace — A14

Amber Palace — A15

Rajas Jai Singh II and Man Singh II — A16

*Perf. 13½x14, 14, 14x13½*

**1931, Mar. 14 Typo. Unwmk.**

| | | | | |
|---|---|---|---|---|
| **24** | A5 | ¼a red brown & blk | 4.50 | 4.00 |
| **25** | A6 | ½a dull vio & blk | .75 | .30 |
| **26** | A7 | 1a blue & black | 13.50 | *14.00* |
| **27** | A8 | 2a ocher & black | 13.50 | *14.00* |
| **28** | A9 | 2½a rose & black | 47.50 | *90.00* |
| **29** | A10 | 3a dk green & blk | 27.50 | *67.50* |
| **30** | A11 | 4a dull grn & blk | 27.50 | *82.50* |
| **31** | A12 | 6a dk blue & blk | 9.00 | *82.50* |
| **32** | A13 | 8a brown & black | 30.00 | *140.00* |
| **33** | A14 | 1r olive & black | 60.00 | *500.00* |
| **34** | A15 | 2r lt green & blk | 62.50 | *550.00* |
| **35** | A16 | 5r violet & black | 82.50 | *600.00* |
| | | *Nos. 24-35 (12)* | 378.75 | *2,144.* |

Investiture of the Maharaja Man Singh II with full ruling powers.

Eighteen sets of this issue were overprinted in red "INVESTITURE—MARCH 14, 1931" for presentation to distinguished personages.

For surcharges see Nos. 47, 48, 58. For overprints see Nos. O12-O16, Rajasthan 16.

**Man Singh II Type of 1931 and**

Raja Man Singh II — A18

**1932-46** ***Perf. 14***

| | | | | |
|---|---|---|---|---|
| **36** | A6 | ¼a red brn & blk | .75 | .75 |
| **36A** | A6 | ¾a brn orange & black ('43) | 12.00 | 6.25 |
| **37** | A18 | 1a blue & black | 5.00 | 2.50 |
| **37A** | A6 | 1a blue & black | 14.00 | 6.75 |
| **38** | A18 | 2a ocher & black | 6.75 | 4.00 |
| **38A** | A6 | 2a ocher & blk ('45) | 19.00 | 7.50 |
| **39** | A6 | 2½a dk car & blk | 6.75 | 5.00 |
| **40** | A6 | 3a green & black | 6.00 | 1.00 |
| **41** | A18 | 4a gray grn & blk | 6.75 | *17.50* |
| **41A** | A6 | 4a gray green & blk ('45) | 72.50 | 2.40 |
| **42** | A6 | 6a blue & black | 9.00 | *45.00* |
| **43** | A18 | 8a choc & black | 9.00 | *22.50* |
| **43A** | A6 | 8a choc & blk ('45) | 42.50 | *190.00* |
| **44** | A18 | 1r bis & gray blk | 40.00 | *175.00* |
| **44A** | A6 | 1r bis & gray blk ('46) | 30.00 | *240.00* |
| **45** | A18 | 2r yel grn & blk | 140.00 | *700.00* |
| | | *Nos. 36-45 (16)* | 420.00 | *1,426.* |

For overprints see Nos. O17-O30, Rajasthan Nos. 15, 17-25.

Stamps of 1931-32 Surcharged in Red or Black

**1936** ***Perf. 14x13½, 13½x14***

| | | | | |
|---|---|---|---|---|
| **46** | A18 | 1r on 2r yel grn & blk (R) | 15.00 | *160.00* |
| **47** | A16 | 1r on 5r violet & blk | 15.00 | *125.00* |

No. 25 Surcharged in Red

**1938** ***Perf. 14x13½***

| | | | | |
|---|---|---|---|---|
| **48** | A6 | ¼aon ½a dull vio & blk | 17.50 | *25.00* |

**Catalogue values for unused stamps in this section, from this point to the end of the section, are for Never Hinged items.**

Amber Palace A19

Designs: ¼a, Palace gate. ¾a, Map of Jaipur. 1a, Observatory. 2a, Palace of the Winds. 3a, Arms of the Raja. 4a, Gate of Amber Fort. 8a, Chariot of the Sun. 1r, Raja Man Singh II.

**1947-48 Unwmk. Engr.** ***Perf. 14***

| | | | | |
|---|---|---|---|---|
| **49** | A19 | ¼a dk green & red brn ('48) | 2.25 | *7.50* |
| **50** | A19 | ½a blue vio & dp grn | .75 | *6.75* |
| **51** | A19 | ¾a dk car & blk ('48) | 2.25 | *9.00* |
| **52** | A19 | 1a dp ultra & choc | 1.50 | *7.00* |
| **53** | A19 | 2a car & blue vio | 1.50 | *7.50* |
| **54** | A19 | 3a dk gray & grn ('48) | 2.50 | *9.50* |
| **55** | A19 | 4a choc & dp ultra | 1.50 | *7.50* |
| **56** | A19 | 8a dk brown & red | 1.50 | *9.00* |
| **57** | A19 | 1r dk red vio & bl grn ('48) | 4.00 | *67.50* |
| | | *Nos. 49-57 (9)* | 17.75 | *131.25* |

25th anniv. of the enthronement of Raja Man Singh II.

No. 25 Surcharged in Carmine with New Value and Bars

**1947**

| | | | | |
|---|---|---|---|---|
| **58** | A6 | 3p on ½a | 25.00 | 40.00 |
| *a.* | | "3 PIE" | 75.00 | *160.00* |
| *b.* | | Inverted surcharge | 72.50 | 62.50 |
| *c.* | | Double surch., one inverted | 110.00 | 82.50 |
| *d.* | | As "a," inverted surcharge | 375.00 | 325.00 |

For overprint see No. O31.

**OFFICIAL STAMPS**

Regular Issue of 1913-22 Overprinted in Black or Red

**1929 Unwmk.** ***Perf. 12½x12, 11***

| | | | | |
|---|---|---|---|---|
| **O1** | A4 | ¼a olive green | 3.75 | *4.00* |
| **O2** | A4 | ½a ultramarine | 1.90 | .30 |
| *a.* | | Inverted overprint | | 675.00 |
| **O3** | A4 | ½a ultra (R) | 4.00 | .45 |
| **O4** | A4 | 1a red | 2.25 | .45 |
| **O5** | A4 | 2a green | 2.25 | .60 |
| **O6** | A4 | 4a red brown | 3.00 | 2.50 |
| **O7** | A4 | 8a purple (R) | 25.00 | *82.50* |
| **O8** | A4 | 1r red orange | 57.50 | *550.00* |
| | | *Nos. O1-O8 (8)* | 99.65 | *640.80* |

The 8a and 1r not issued without overprint.

For overprint see No. O11.

Regular Issue of 1913-22 Overprinted in Black or Red — b

**1931** ***Perf. 11, 12½x12***

| | | | | |
|---|---|---|---|---|
| **O9** | A4 | ½a ultra | 575.00 | .25 |
| **O10** | A4 | ½a ultra (R) | 300.00 | .25 |
| **O10A** | A4 | 8a purple | 675.00 | 300.00 |
| **O10B** | A4 | 1r red orange | 700.00 | 400.00 |
| | | *Nos. O9-O10B (4)* | 2,250. | 700.50 |

No. O5 Surcharged

**1932**

| | | | | |
|---|---|---|---|---|
| **O11** | A4 | ½a on 2a green | 225.00 | 3.00 |

Regular Issue of 1931 Overprinted in Red

**1931-37** ***Perf. 13½x14, 14***

| | | | | |
|---|---|---|---|---|
| **O12** | A6 | ¼a red brn & blk ('36) | .60 | .25 |
| **O13** | A6 | ½a dull vio & blk | .45 | .25 |
| **O14** | A7 | 1a blue & black | 400.00 | 4.50 |
| **O15** | A8 | 2a ocher & blk ('36) | 6.75 | *8.25* |
| **O16** | A11 | 4a dl grn & blk ('37) | 72.50 | 60.00 |

For overprint see No. O32.

Same on Regular Issue of 1932 in Red

**1932-37** ***Perf. 14***

| | | | | |
|---|---|---|---|---|
| **O17** | A18 | 1a blue & black | 6.75 | .30 |
| **O18** | A18 | 2a ocher & black | 8.25 | .30 |
| **O19** | A18 | 4a gray grn & blk ('37) | *550.00* | *16.00* |
| **O20** | A18 | 8a choc & black | 17.50 | 1.60 |
| **O21** | A18 | 1r bister & gray blk | 45.00 | 40.00 |
| | | *Nos. O17-O21 (5)* | *627.50* | *58.20* |

No. 36 Overprinted Type "b" in Black

**1939** ***Perf. 14***

| | | | | |
|---|---|---|---|---|
| **O22** | A6 | ¼a red brown & blk | 140.00 | 110.00 |

Nos. 36A, 38A, 39, 41A, 43A, 44A and Type of 1931 Overprinted in Carmine

**1941-46 Unwmk.** ***Perf. 13½, 14***

| | | | | |
|---|---|---|---|---|
| **O23** | A6 | ¾a brn org & blk ('43) | 2.25 | .75 |
| **O24** | A6 | 1a blue & blk ('41) | 6.75 | .45 |
| **O25** | A6 | 2a ocher & black | 6.00 | 5.00 |
| **O26** | A6 | 2½a dk car & blk ('46) | 16.00 | *160.00* |
| **O27** | A6 | 4a gray grn & blk ('46) | 9.00 | *11.00* |
| **O28** | A6 | 8a choc & black | 6.00 | 12.50 |
| **O29** | A6 | 1r bis & gray blk | *60.00* | |
| | | *Nos. O23-O28 (6)* | 46.00 | *189.70* |

**Catalogue values for unused stamps in this section, from this point to the end of the section, are for Never Hinged items.**

No. O24 Surcharged with New Value and Bars in Carmine

**1947** ***Perf. 13½***

| | | | | |
|---|---|---|---|---|
| **O30** | A6 | 9p on 1a blue & blk | 5.50 | 5.50 |

**No. 58 Overprinted in Red "SERVICE"**

***Perf. 14***

| | | | | |
|---|---|---|---|---|
| **O31** | A6 | 3p on ½a | 9.00 | *21.00* |
| *a.* | | Inverted surcharge | — | 2,250. |
| *b.* | | Double surch., one inverted | 72.50 | 72.50 |
| *c.* | | "3 PIE" | 400.00 | *450.00* |

No. O13 Surcharged "Three-quarter Anna" in Devanagari, similar to surcharge on No. 48, and Bars in Carmine

**1949** ***Perf. 14x13½***

| | | | | |
|---|---|---|---|---|
| **O32** | A6 | ¾a on ½a dl vio & blk | 27.50 | *30.00* |

For later issues see Rajasthan.

## JAMMU AND KASHMIR

'jəm-ˌü and 'kash-ˌmi(ə)r

LOCATION — A Feudatory State in the Kashmir Residency in the extreme north of India.

AREA — 82,258 sq. mi.

POP. — 4,021,616 (1941)

CAPITAL — Srinagar

All stamps of Jammu and Kashmir were issued without gum.

½ Anna — A1

1 Anna — A2

4 Annas (¼ Rupee) — A3

**Native Grayish Laid Paper**

**Handstamped**

**1866-67 Unwmk.** ***Imperf.***

**Printed in Water Colors**

| | | | | |
|---|---|---|---|---|
| **1** | A1 | ½a gray black | 375.00 | 150.00 |
| | | Cut to shape | 75.00 | 30.00 |
| **2** | A2 | 1a dull blue | 900.00 | 180.00 |
| *a.* | | 1a ultramarine | 900.00 | 180.00 |
| *b.* | | 1a royal blue | — | 750.00 |
| | | Cut to shape | — | 150.00 |
| **3** | A2 | 1a gray black | 2,400. | 2,100. |
| | | Cut to shape | 475.00 | 425.00 |
| **4** | A3 | 4a dull blue | *4,500.* | *4,500.* |
| *a.* | | 4a ultramarine | *4,500.* | *4,500.* |
| *b.* | | 4a indigo | *4,500.* | *4,500.* |
| | | Cut to shape | 900.00 | 900.00 |
| **5** | A3 | 4a gray black | 3,000. | |
| | | Cut to shape | 1,600. | — |
| | | *Nos. 1-5 (5)* | 11,175. | 6,930. |

It has now been proved by the leading authorities on Indian stamps that all stamps of ½ anna and 1 anna printed from the so-called Die A are forgeries and that no such die was ever in use.

See Nos. 24-59.

**JAMMU**

A part of the Feudatory State of Jammu & Kashmir, both being ruled by the same sovereign.

½ Anna — A4

1 Anna — A5

Printed in blocks of four, three types of the ½a and one of the 1a.

**Native Grayish Laid Paper**

**Printed in Water Colors**

**1867-77 Unwmk.** ***Imperf.***

| | | | | |
|---|---|---|---|---|
| **6** | A4 | ½a black | 1,800. | 625.00 |
| **7** | A4 | ½a indigo | 625.00 | 490.00 |
| *a.* | | ½a deep ultramarine | 490.00 | 290.00 |
| *b.* | | ½a deep violet blue | 325.00 | 160.00 |
| **8** | A4 | ½a red | 12.50 | 6.75 |
| *a.* | | ½a orange red | 375.00 | 120.00 |
| *b.* | | ½a orange | 195.00 | *225.00* |
| **9** | A5 | 1a black | 3,750. | 2,600. |
| **10** | A5 | 1a indigo | 1,350 | 625.00 |
| *a.* | | 1a deep ultramarine | 1,200. | 625.00 |
| *b.* | | 1a deep violet blue | 1,200. | 625.00 |
| **11** | A5 | 1a red | 30.00 | 19.00 |
| *a.* | | 1a orange red | 1,250. | 525.00 |
| *b.* | | 1a orange | 4,750. | 2,750. |

**1876**

| | | | | |
|---|---|---|---|---|
| **12** | A4 | ½a emerald | 3,750. | 1,900. |
| **13** | A4 | ½a bright blue | 2,400. | 550.00 |
| **14** | A5 | 1a emerald | 5,250. | 3,000. |
| **15** | A5 | 1a bright blue | 700.00 | *750.00* |

**Native Grayish Laid Paper**

**1877 Printed in Oil Colors**

| | | | | |
|---|---|---|---|---|
| **16** | A4 | ½a red | 18.00 | 13.50 |
| *a.* | | ½a brown red | — | 67.50 |
| **17** | A4 | ½a black | | 1,800. |
| **18** | A5 | 1a red | 57.50 | 40.00 |
| *a.* | | 1a brown red | — | 225.00 |
| **19** | A5 | 1a black | *3,750.* | *2,750.* |

*The formerly listed ½a dark blue, ½a dark green, 1a dark blue and 1a dark green are believed to be reprints.*

**European White Laid Paper**

| | | | | |
|---|---|---|---|---|
| 20 | A4 | ½a red | — | *1,600.* |
| *a.* | | Thin laid bâtonné paper | | *2,750.* |
| 21 | A5 | 1a red | — | |
| *a.* | | Thin laid bâtonné paper | *6,750.* | |

**European White Wove Paper**

| | | | | |
|---|---|---|---|---|
| 22 | A4 | ½a red | | *675.00* |
| 23 | A5 | 1a red | | |

### RE-ISSUES
### For Jammu Only

Native Grayish Laid Paper

**Printed in Water Colors**

**1869-76** ***Imperf.***

| | | | | |
|---|---|---|---|---|
| 24 | A1 | ½a deep black | *500.00* | |
| 25 | A1 | ½a bright blue | 550.00 | *675.00* |
| 26 | A1 | ½a orange red | 1,000. | 1,100. |
| *a.* | | ½a orange to salmon | 400.00 | |
| *b.* | | ½a red | 150.00 | 525.00 |
| 27 | A1 | ½a emerald | 175.00 | *450.00* |
| 28 | A1 | ½a yellow | 1,100. | *1,400.* |
| 29 | A2 | 1a deep black | 500.00 | |
| 30 | A2 | 1a bright blue | 195.00 | *550.00* |
| 31 | A2 | 1a orange red | 1,000. | *1,100.* |
| *b.* | | 1a red | 300.00 | *500.00* |
| 32 | A2 | 1a emerald | 195.00 | 450.00 |
| 33 | A2 | 1a yellow | 1,400. | |
| 34 | A3 | 4a deep black | 450.00 | — |
| 35 | A3 | 4a bright blue | 325.00 | |
| *a.* | | 4a indigo | — | — |
| 36 | A3 | 4a orange red | 325.00 | *425.00* |
| *a.* | | 4a orange | | — |
| *b.* | | 4a red | 325.00 | *425.00* |
| 37 | A3 | 4a emerald | 450.00 | *1,000.* |
| 38 | A3 | 4a yellow | 900.00 | |

**Native Grayish Laid Paper**

**1877** **Printed in Oil Colors**

| | | | | |
|---|---|---|---|---|
| 39 | A1 | ½a red | 52.50 | *90.00* |
| 40 | A1 | ½a black | 57.50 | *97.50* |
| 41 | A1 | ½a slate blue | 240.00 | *400.00* |
| 42 | A1 | ½a sage green | 210.00 | |
| 43 | A2 | 1a red | 72.50 | *290.00* |
| 45 | A2 | 1a slate blue | 57.50 | *450.00* |
| 46 | A2 | 1a sage green | 225.00 | |
| 47 | A3 | 4a red | 475.00 | *825.00* |
| 50 | A3 | 4a sage green | 225.00 | |

**European White Laid Paper**

| | | | | |
|---|---|---|---|---|
| 51 | A1 | ½a red | | 1,800. |
| 52 | A1 | ½a black | 47.50 | *97.50* |
| 53 | A1 | ½a slate blue | 82.50 | *450.00* |
| 54 | A1 | ½a yellow | *240.00* | |
| 56 | A2 | 1a slate blue | 90.00 | *600.00* |
| 57 | A3 | 4a red | 650.00 | *750.00* |
| 58 | A3 | 4a sage green | *2,250.* | |

**European Brownish Wove Paper**

| | | | | |
|---|---|---|---|---|
| 59 | A1 | ½a red | | *1,400.* |

It is probable that the issues of 1876, 1877 and the re-issues of the circular stamps were made to supply the demands of philatelists more than for postal needs. They were, however, available for postage.

There exist also reprints, printed in a variety of colors, on native and European thin wove paper. Collectors are warned against official imitations, which are very numerous. They are printed on several kinds of paper and in a great variety of colors.

A5a

**Handstamped in Oil Color**

**1877, Nov.**

| | | | | |
|---|---|---|---|---|
| 60 | A5a | (½a) red | | *1,900.* |

This provisional, made with a canceling device, was used only in Nov. 1877, at Jammu city.

## KASHMIR

A part of the Feudatory State of Jammu & Kashmir, both being ruled by the same sovereign.

½ Anna — A6

**Printed in Water Colors**

Native Grayish Laid Paper

Printed from a Single Die

**1866** **Unwmk.** ***Imperf.***

| | | | | |
|---|---|---|---|---|
| 62 | A6 | ½a black | *5,250.* | 675.00 |

¼ Anna — A7

½ Anna — A8

1 Anna A9

2 Annas A10

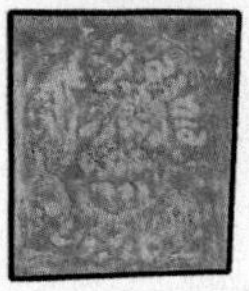

4 Annas — A11

8 Annas — A12

The ¼a, 1a and 2a are printed in strips of five varieties, the ½a in sheets of twenty varieties and the 4a and 8a from single dies.

**1866-70**

| | | | | |
|---|---|---|---|---|
| 63 | A7 | ¼a black | 6.75 | *7.00* |
| 64 | A8 | ½a black | *2,250.* | *300.00* |
| 65 | A8 | ½a ultra | 7.50 | 2.50 |
| *a.* | | ½a blue | 13.50 | 6.75 |
| 66 | A9 | 1a black | 4,000. | 750.00 |
| 67 | A9 | 1a red orange | 22.50 | 17.50 |
| 68 | A9 | 1a Venetian red | 27.50 | 19.00 |
| 69 | A9 | 1a orange brown | 22.50 | 17.50 |
| 70 | A9 | 1a ultra | *6,500.* | *2,500.* |
| 71 | A10 | 2a olive yellow | 30.00 | *32.50* |
| 72 | A11 | 4a emerald | 75.00 | 72.50 |
| 73 | A12 | 8a red | 75.00 | 72.50 |

*All the stamps printed in oil colors are reprints.*

*As in Jammu, official imitations are numerous and are found in many colors and on various papers.*

## JAMMU & KASHMIR

¼ Anna — A13

½ Anna — A14

1 Anna — A15

2 Annas — A16

4 Annas — A17

8 Annas — A18

**Laid Paper**

**Printed in Oil Colors**

**1878** ***Rough Perf. 10-14***

| | | | | |
|---|---|---|---|---|
| 74 | A13 | ¼a red | — | — |
| 75 | A14 | ½a red | 21.00 | *25.00* |
| *a.* | | Wove paper | | *500.00* |
| 76 | A14 | ½a slate blue | 110.00 | 110.00 |
| 77 | A15 | 1a red | 1,900. | |
| 78 | A15 | 1a bright violet | — | — |

**1878-80** ***Imperf.***

| | | | | |
|---|---|---|---|---|
| 79 | A13 | ¼a red | 35.00 | 30.00 |
| 80 | A14 | ½a red | 15.00 | *16.00* |
| 81 | A14 | ½a slate | 27.50 | 24.00 |
| 82 | A15 | 1a red | 14.00 | 17.50 |
| 83 | A15 | 1a violet | 40.00 | 42.50 |
| *a.* | | 1a dull purple | 67.50 | 62.50 |
| 84 | A16 | 2a red | 140.00 | 140.00 |
| 85 | A16 | 2a bright violet | 60.00 | 57.50 |
| 86 | A16 | 2a dull ultra | *175.00* | 175.00 |
| 87 | A17 | 4a red | 340.00 | 290.00 |

**Thick Wove Paper**

| | | | | |
|---|---|---|---|---|
| 88 | A14 | ½a red | 47.50 | *90.00* |
| 89 | A15 | 1a red | 75.00 | 37.50 |
| 90 | A16 | 2a red | 32.50 | 40.00 |

**1879-80** **Thin Toned Wove Paper**

| | | | | |
|---|---|---|---|---|
| 91 | A13 | ¼a red | 5.50 | *6.75* |
| 92 | A14 | ½a red | 1.50 | 1.50 |
| 93 | A15 | 1a red | 3.75 | *5.25* |
| 94 | A16 | 2a red | 5.00 | *7.00* |
| 95 | A17 | 4a red | 16.00 | 16.00 |
| 96 | A18 | 8a red | 17.50 | 20.00 |
| | | *Nos. 91-96 (6)* | 49.25 | 56.50 |

*Thin Laid Bâtonné Paper* **Printed in Water Color**

**1880**

| | | | | |
|---|---|---|---|---|
| 97 | A13 | ¼a ultramarine | 1,350. | 900.00 |

**Thin Toned Wove Paper**

**1881** **Printed in Oil Colors**

| | | | | |
|---|---|---|---|---|
| 98 | A13 | ¼a orange | 17.50 | *24.00* |
| 99 | A14 | ½a orange | 35.00 | 25.00 |
| 100 | A15 | 1a orange | 37.50 | 21.00 |
| 101 | A16 | 2a orange | 27.50 | 21.00 |
| 102 | A17 | 4a orange | 67.50 | *82.50* |
| 103 | A18 | 8a orange | 110.00 | *120.00* |
| | | *Nos. 98-103 (6)* | 295.00 | 293.50 |

⅛ Anna — A19

**Thin White or Yellowish Wove Paper**

**1883-94**

| | | | | |
|---|---|---|---|---|
| 104 | A19 | ⅛a yellow brown | 2.25 | *3.00* |
| *a.* | | ⅛a yellow | 2.25 | *3.00* |
| 105 | A13 | ¼a brown | 1.90 | 1.50 |
| *a.* | | Double impression | 1,800. | |
| 106 | A14 | ½a red | 1.90 | 1.25 |
| *a.* | | ½a rose | 2.40 | 1.50 |
| 106B | A19 | ½a bright blue | 82.50 | |
| *c.* | | ½a dull blue | 12.00 | |
| 107 | A15 | 1a bronze green | 1.50 | 1.50 |
| 108 | A15 | 1a yel green | 1.50 | 1.50 |
| 109 | A15 | 1a blue green | 3.00 | |
| 110 | A15 | 1a bister | — | |
| 111 | A17 | 4a green | 6.50 | 6.00 |
| 112 | A17 | 4a olive green | 6.00 | *7.00* |
| 113 | A18 | 8a deep blue | 19.00 | *22.50* |
| 114 | A18 | 8a dark ultra | 18.00 | *21.00* |
| 115 | A18 | 8a gray violet | 15.00 | *32.50* |

**Printed in Water Color**

| | | | | |
|---|---|---|---|---|
| 116 | A18 | 8a gray blue | 225.00 | 225.00 |

**Printed in Oil Colors**

**Yellow Pelure Paper**

| | | | | |
|---|---|---|---|---|
| 117 | A16 | 2a red | 4.00 | 1.90 |

**Yellow Green Pelure Paper**

| | | | | |
|---|---|---|---|---|
| 118 | A16 | 2a red | 5.50 | *6.00* |

**Deep Green Pelure Paper**

| | | | | |
|---|---|---|---|---|
| 119 | A16 | 2a red | 27.50 | 27.50 |

**Coarse Green Pelure Paper**

| | | | | |
|---|---|---|---|---|
| 120 | A16 | 2a red | 4.00 | 1.90 |
| | | *Nos. 104-120 (18)* | 425.05 | 360.05 |

**Thin Creamy Laid Paper**

**1886-94**

| | | | | |
|---|---|---|---|---|
| 121 | A19 | ⅛a yellow | 90.00 | *100.00* |
| 122 | A13 | ¼a brown | 13.50 | *10.00* |
| 123 | A14 | ½a vermilion | 15.00 | 9.50 |
| 124 | A14 | ½a rose red | | 110.00 |
| 125 | A15 | 1a green | 150.00 | 150.00 |
| 126 | A17 | 4a green | — | — |

**Printed in Water Color**

| | | | | |
|---|---|---|---|---|
| 127 | A18 | 8a gray blue | 160.00 | 150.00 |
| | | *Nos. 121-127 (7)* | 428.50 | 529.50 |

Impressions of types A13 to A19 in colors other than the issued stamps are proofs. Forgeries to defraud the post exist, and some are common.

1/4 Anna

Stamps of the above type, printed in red or black, were never placed in use.

### OFFICIAL STAMPS

Same Types as Regular Issues

White Laid Paper

**1878** **Unwmk.** ***Rough Perf. 10-14***

| | | | | |
|---|---|---|---|---|
| O1 | A14 | ½a black | | *3,000.* |

***Imperf***

| | | | | |
|---|---|---|---|---|
| O3 | A14 | ½a black | 150.00 | 140.00 |
| O4 | A15 | 1a black | 100.00 | 100.00 |
| O5 | A16 | 2a black | 82.50 | *90.00* |
| | | *Nos. O3-O5 (3)* | 332.50 | 330.00 |

**Thin White or Yellowish Wove Paper**

**1880**

| | | | | |
|---|---|---|---|---|
| O6 | A13 | ¼a black | 2.50 | *3.00* |
| O7 | A14 | ½a black | .25 | *1.10* |
| O8 | A15 | 1a black | 3.00 | *1.50* |
| O9 | A16 | 2a black | .45 | *.65* |
| O10 | A17 | 4a black | 1.90 | *2.50* |
| O11 | A18 | 8a black | 3.75 | 1.60 |
| | | *Nos. O6-O11 (6)* | 11.85 | 10.35 |

**Thin Creamy Laid Paper**

**1890-91**

| | | | | |
|---|---|---|---|---|
| O12 | A13 | ¼a black | 12.50 | *13.50* |
| O13 | A14 | ½a black | 7.00 | *7.00* |
| O14 | A15 | 1a black | 4.00 | *5.25* |
| O15 | A16 | 2a black | 22.50 | |
| O16 | A17 | 4a black | 82.50 | *97.50* |
| O17 | A18 | 8a black | 42.50 | *75.00* |
| | | *Nos. O12-O17 (6)* | 171.00 | |

Obsolete October 31, 1894.

## JASDAN

LOCATION — A Feudatory State in the Kathiawar Agency in Western India.

AREA — 296 sq. mi.

POP. — 34,056 (1931)

CAPITAL — Jasdan

In 1948 Jasdan was incorporated in the United State of Saurashtra (see Soruth).

**Catalogue values for all unused stamps in this state are for Never Hinged items.**

Sun — A1

***Perf. 8½ to 10½***

**1942** **Unwmk.** **Typo.**

| | | | | |
|---|---|---|---|---|
| 1 | A1 | 1a green | 30.00 | 240.00 |

Issued in booklet panes of 4 and 8.

The 1a carmine is a revenue stamp.

Jasdan's stamp became obsolete Feb. 15, 1948.

## JHALAWAR

'jäl-ə-ˌwär

LOCATION — A Feudatory State in the Rajputana Agency of India.

AREA — 813 sq. mi.

POP. — 107,890

CAPITAL — Jhalrapatan

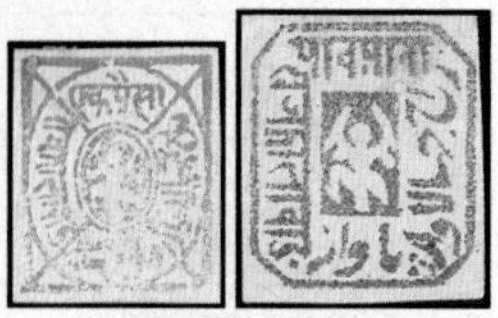

Apsaras, Hindu Nymph
A1 A2

**Laid Paper**

**1887-90 Unwmk. *Imperf.***
**Without Gum**

| | | | | |
|---|---|---|---|---|
| 1 | A1 | 1p yellow green | 7.00 | *22.50* |
| 2 | A2 | ¼a green | 1.90 | *3.75* |

Obsolete October 31, 1900.

## JIND

'jind

(Jhind)

LOCATION — A State of India in the north Punjab.
AREA — 1,299 sq. mi.
POP. — 361,812 (1941)
CAPITAL — Sangrur

A1

A2

A3

A4

A5

**1874 Unwmk. Litho. *Imperf.***
**Without Gum**
**Thin White Wove Paper**

| | | | | |
|---|---|---|---|---|
| 1 | A1 | ½a blue | 10.00 | 6.25 |
| 2 | A2 | 1a lilac | 10.00 | 9.50 |
| 3 | A3 | 2a yellow | 1.50 | 6.75 |
| 4 | A4 | 4a green | 37.50 | 9.00 |
| 5 | A5 | 8a dark violet | 340.00 | 140.00 |
| | | *Nos. 1-5 (5)* | 399.00 | 171.50 |

**Thick Blue Laid Paper**

**1875 Without Gum**

| | | | | |
|---|---|---|---|---|
| 6 | A1 | ½a blue | 1.50 | *7.00* |
| 7 | A2 | 1a red violet | 4.00 | *16.00* |
| 8 | A3 | 2a brown orange | 6.50 | *22.50* |
| 9 | A4 | 4a green | 5.50 | *22.50* |
| 10 | A5 | 8a purple | 13.50 | *32.50* |
| | | *Nos. 6-10 (5)* | 31.00 | *100.50* |

Nos. 3 and 6 were perforated 12 in 1885 for use as fiscal stamps.

A6

A7

A8

A9

A10

A11

**1882-84 Without Gum *Imperf.***
**Thin Yellowish Wove Paper**

| | | | | |
|---|---|---|---|---|
| 12 | A6 | ¼a buff | .45 | *2.25* |
| *a.* | | Double impression | 75.00 | |
| 13 | A7 | ½a yellow | 3.75 | 2.50 |
| 14 | A8 | 1a brown | 2.50 | *5.00* |
| 15 | A9 | 2a blue | 3.00 | *13.50* |
| 16 | A10 | 4a green | 2.25 | 1.50 |
| 17 | A11 | 8a red | 9.50 | 6.75 |
| | | *Nos. 12-17 (6)* | 21.45 | *31.50* |

***Perf. 12***

| | | | | |
|---|---|---|---|---|
| 18 | A6 | ¼a buff | 1.50 | *4.00* |
| 19 | A7 | ½a yellow | 240.00 | 240.00 |
| 20 | A8 | 1a brown | 3.75 | *8.25* |
| 21 | A9 | 2a blue | 5.50 | *15.00* |
| 22 | A10 | 4a green | 7.50 | 16.00 |
| 23 | A11 | 8a red | 18.00 | |
| *a.* | | Thick white paper | 15.00 | |
| | | *Nos. 18-23 (6)* | 276.25 | *283.25* |

**Laid Paper**

***Imperf***

| | | | | |
|---|---|---|---|---|
| 24 | A6 | ¼a buff | 1.90 | |
| 25 | A7 | ½a yellow | 1.90 | |
| 26 | A8 | 1a brown | 1.90 | *3.75* |
| 27 | A9 | 2a blue | 27.50 | *30.00* |
| 28 | A11 | 8a red | 3.75 | *16.00* |
| | | *Nos. 24-28 (5)* | 36.95 | *49.75* |

***Perf. 12***

| | | | | |
|---|---|---|---|---|
| 29 | A6 | ¼a buff | 12.50 | |
| 30 | A7 | ½a yellow | 190.00 | 40.00 |
| 31 | A8 | 1a brown | 2.25 | |
| 32 | A11 | 8a red | 3.75 | *15.00* |
| | | *Nos. 29-32 (4)* | 208.50 | 55.00 |

As postage stamps these issues became obsolete in July, 1885, but some possibly remained in use as revenue stamps.

For later issues see Jind under Convention States.

## KISHANGARH

'kish-ən-ˌgär

LOCATION — A Feudatory State in the Jaipur Residency of India.
AREA — 858 sq. mi.
POP. — 85,744
CAPITAL — Kishangarh

Kishangarh was incorporated in Rajasthan in 1947-49.

Stamps were issued without gum except Nos. 27-35.

Coat of Arms — A1

**1899-1900 Unwmk. Typo. *Imperf.***
**Soft Porous Paper**

| | | | | |
|---|---|---|---|---|
| 1 | A1 | 1a green | 32.50 | *90.00* |
| 2 | A1 | 1a blue ('00) | *600.00* | |

***Pin-perf***

| | | | | |
|---|---|---|---|---|
| 3 | A1 | 1a green | 110.00 | |

A2

A3

Coat of Arms — A4

Maharaja Sardul Singh — A5

A6

A7

Coat of Arms—A9
A8

**Thin Wove Paper**

**1899-1900 Handstamped *Imperf.***

| | | | | |
|---|---|---|---|---|
| 4 | A2 | ¼a rose pink | 1.90 | *4.00* |
| *a.* | | ¼a carmine | 12.50 | |
| 5 | A2 | ¼a green | 825.00 | 1,200. |
| 6 | A3 | ½a light blue | 1.90 | *2.50* |
| 7 | A3 | ½a green | 57.50 | *62.50* |
| 8 | A3 | ½a carmine | 3,750. | *1,900.* |
| 9 | A3 | ½a violet | 240.00 | *490.00* |
| 10 | A4 | 1a gray violet | 1.60 | 1.50 |
| *a.* | | 1a gray | 7.50 | 7.50 |
| 11 | A4 | 1a rose | 110.00 | *300.00* |
| 11A | A5 | 2a orange | 7.50 | 6.75 |
| 12 | A6 | 4a chocolate | 9.00 | *15.00* |
| *a.* | | Laid paper | 125.00 | 125.00 |
| 13 | A7 | 1r dull green | 35.00 | *52.50* |
| 13A | A7 | 1r light brown | 30.00 | *37.50* |
| 14 | A8 | 2r brown red | 125.00 | *190.00* |
| *a.* | | Laid paper | 100.00 | |
| 15 | A9 | 5r violet | 120.00 | 150.00 |
| *a.* | | Laid paper | 120.00 | |

***Pin-perf***

| | | | | |
|---|---|---|---|---|
| 16 | A2 | ¼a magenta | 7.50 | *10.00* |
| *a.* | | ¼a rose | .35 | *.60* |
| 17 | A2 | ¼a green | *400.00* | *700.00* |
| *a.* | | Imperf. vertically, pair | 1,900. | |
| 18 | A3 | ½a blue | 1.50 | *.75* |
| *a.* | | ½a dark blue | 3.75 | *5.00* |
| 19 | A3 | ½a green | 27.50 | *40.00* |
| *a.* | | Imperf. vert., pair | 275.00 | |
| 20 | A4 | 1a gray violet | 1.10 | *1.50* |
| *a.* | | 1a gray | 8.25 | 5.25 |
| *b.* | | 1a red lilac | 2.25 | 3.00 |
| *d.* | | As "b," laid paper | 62.50 | 19.00 |
| 20E | A4 | 1a rose | 125.00 | *375.00* |
| 21 | A5 | 2a orange | 6.00 | *7.50* |
| 21B | A6 | 4a pale red brown | 5.25 | *9.00* |
| *c.* | | 4a chocolate | 3.50 | *9.00* |
| 22 | A7 | 1r dull green | 16.00 | *22.50* |
| *b.* | | Laid paper | 140.00 | |
| 23 | A8 | 2r brown red | 52.50 | 82.50 |
| *b.* | | Laid paper | 67.50 | |
| 24 | A9 | 5r red violet | 52.50 | 82.50 |
| *d.* | | Laid paper | 110.00 | |

Nos. 4-24 exist tête bêche and sell for a slight premium.

For overprints see #O1-O11, Rajasthan #26-28, 30-32.

A9a

A9b

**1901 Soft Porous Paper Typo.**

| | | | | |
|---|---|---|---|---|
| 24A | A9a | ½a rose | 12.00 | 9.00 |
| 24B | A9b | 1a dull violet | 72.50 | 40.00 |

For overprint see No. O12.

A10

A11

**1903 Stout Hard Paper *Imperf.***

| | | | | |
|---|---|---|---|---|
| 25 | A10 | ½a pink | 20.00 | 5.25 |
| *a.* | | Printed on both sides | | *2,100.* |

**1904 Thin Wove Paper *Pin-perf.***

| | | | | |
|---|---|---|---|---|
| 25B | A11 | 8a gray | 7.50 | *11.00* |
| *c.* | | tête bêche pair | 40.00 | |

For overprints see #O13, O33, Rajasthan #29.

A11a

Maharaja Sardul Singh — A12

| | | | | |
|---|---|---|---|---|
| 25D | A11a | 1r green | 27.50 | 27.50 |

For overprint see No. O13A.

**1903 Stout Hard Paper *Imperf.***

| | | | | |
|---|---|---|---|---|
| 26 | A12 | 2a yellow | 4.50 | 9.00 |

For overprints see Nos. O14, O34.

Maharaja Madan Singh
A13 A14

**1904-05 Engr. *Perf. 12½, 13½***

| | | | | |
|---|---|---|---|---|
| 27 | A13 | ¼a carmine | .65 | *1.10* |
| 28 | A13 | ½a chestnut | 1.90 | .45 |
| 29 | A13 | 1a deep blue | 3.75 | *4.00* |
| 30 | A13 | 2a orange | 22.50 | 10.00 |
| 31 | A13 | 4a dark brown | 22.50 | *25.00* |
| 32 | A13 | 8a purple ('05) | 19.00 | *37.50* |
| 33 | A13 | 1r dark green | 42.50 | *67.50* |
| 34 | A13 | 2r lemon yellow | 42.50 | *250.00* |
| 35 | A13 | 5r purple brown | 35.00 | *300.00* |
| | | *Nos. 27-35 (9)* | 190.30 | *695.55* |

For overprints see Nos. O15-O22, O35-O38, Rajasthan Nos. 33-39.

**Thin Wove Paper**

**1913 Typo. *Rouletted 9½***

| | | | | |
|---|---|---|---|---|
| 37 | A14 | 2 "ANNA" violet | 8.25 | *13.50* |
| *a.* | | tête bêche pair | 18.00 | *60.00* |

See #40-50. For overprint see Rajasthan #43.

Maharaja Madan Singh
A15 A16

**Thick, Chalk-surfaced Paper**

**1913 *Rouletted 6½, 12***

| | | | | |
|---|---|---|---|---|
| 38 | A15 | ¼a pale blue | .45 | *1.40* |
| *a.* | | "Kishangahr" | 7.50 | *10.00* |
| *b.* | | Imperf., pair | 11.00 | |
| 39 | A16 | 2a purple | 12.50 | *27.50* |
| *a.* | | "Kishangahr" | 75.00 | *140.00* |

For overprint see No. O23.

**1913-16** *Rouletted 12, 14½*

| | | | | |
|---|---|---|---|---|
| 40 | A14 | ¼a pale blue | .30 | *.65* |
| 41 | A14 | ½a green ('15) | .30 | *1.50* |
| *a.* | | Printed on both sides | 350.00 | |
| 42 | A14 | 1a carmine | 1.90 | 3.75 |
| 43 | A14 | 2 "ANNAS" purple | 9.00 | *12.00* |
| 44 | A14 | 4a ultramarine | 9.00 | *12.00* |
| 45 | A14 | 8a brown | 10.00 | *60.00* |
| 46 | A14 | 1r rose lilac | 24.00 | *190.00* |
| 47 | A14 | 2r dark green | 150.00 | *525.00* |
| 48 | A14 | 5r brown | 60.00 | *675.00* |
| | | *Nos. 40-48 (9)* | 264.50 | *1,479.* |

On Nos. 40-48 the halftone screen covers the entire design.

Nos. 41-48 have ornaments on both sides of value in top panel.

For overprints see Nos. O24-O30, O39-O43, Rajasthan Nos. 40-42, 44-48.

### Type of 1913-16 Redrawn

**1918** *Rouletted*

| | | | | |
|---|---|---|---|---|
| 50 | A14 | 1a rose red | 2.25 | *8.25* |

The redrawn stamp is 24¾mm wide instead of 26mm. There is a white oval around the portrait with only traces of the red line. There is less shading outside the wreath.

For overprint see No. O44.

Maharaja Jagjanarajan Singh
A17 A18

**Thick Glazed Paper**

**1928-29** *Pin-perf. 14½ to 16*

| | | | | |
|---|---|---|---|---|
| 52 | A17 | ¼a light blue | 1.90 | *3.00* |
| 53 | A17 | ½a lt yellow green | 6.00 | 3.50 |
| *a.* | | Imperf., pair | 180.00 | 180.00 |
| 54 | A18 | 1a carmine rose | 1.10 | *2.25* |
| 55 | A18 | 2a red violet | 5.00 | *12.50* |
| 56 | A17 | 4a yellow brown | 2.50 | 2.50 |
| 57 | A17 | 8a purple | 8.25 | *42.50* |
| 58 | A17 | 1r green | 30.00 | *95.00* |
| 59 | A17 | 2r lemon | 42.50 | *340.00* |
| 60 | A17 | 5r red brown | 67.50 | *400.00* |
| *a.* | | Imperf., pair | 190.00 | |
| | | *Nos. 52-60 (9)* | 164.75 | *901.25* |

**1945-47**

**Thick Soft Unglazed Paper**

| | | | | |
|---|---|---|---|---|
| 52a | A17 | ¼a gray blue | 6.25 | *19.00* |
| *b.* | | ¼a greenish blue ('47) | 4.00 | *15.00* |
| 53b | A17 | ½a deep green | 2.25 | *4.00* |
| 54a | A18 | 1a dull carmine | 12.50 | 6.50 |
| 55a | A18 | 2a deep red violet | 16.00 | *19.00* |
| *b.* | | 2a violet brown, imperf. | 125.00 | 30.00 |
| 56a | A17 | 4a brown | 35.00 | *30.00* |
| 57a | A17 | 8a violet | 60.00 | *240.00* |
| 58a | A17 | 1r deep green | 75.00 | *250.00* |
| 59a | A17 | 2r lemon | — | |
| 60b | A17 | 5r red brown | 875.00 | *1,100.* |

For overprints see Rajasthan Nos. 49-58.

For later issues see Rajasthan.

## OFFICIAL STAMPS

Used values are for CTO stamps.

Regular Issues of 1899-1916 Handstamped in Black

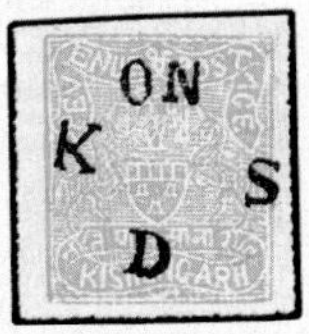


### On Issue of 1899-1900

**1918** **Unwmk.** *Imperf.*

| | | | | |
|---|---|---|---|---|
| O1 | A2 | ¼a carmine | | 12.00 |
| O2 | A4 | 1a gray violet | 82.50 | 8.25 |
| O3 | A6 | 4a chocolate | — | 190.00 |

*Pin-perf*

| | | | | |
|---|---|---|---|---|
| O4 | A2 | ¼a carmine | 3.25 | .90 |
| O4A | A2 | ¼a green | — | 175.00 |
| O4B | A3 | ½a blue | 640.00 | 67.50 |
| O6 | A4 | 1a gray violet | 67.50 | 2.25 |
| O7 | A5 | 2a orange | — | 225.00 |
| O8 | A6 | 4a chocolate | 100.00 | 24.00 |
| O9 | A7 | 1r dull green | 250.00 | 180.00 |
| O10 | A8 | 2r brown red | — | 1,400. |
| O11 | A9 | 5r red violet | — | 3,000. |

See tete beche note after No. 24.

### On Issue of 1901

| | | | | |
|---|---|---|---|---|
| O12 | A9b | 1a dull violet | 75.00 | 2.25 |

### On Issue of 1904

| | | | | |
|---|---|---|---|---|
| O13 | A11 | 8a gray | 140.00 | 35.00 |
| O13A | A11a | 1r green | | *1,350.* |

*Imperf.*

| | | | | |
|---|---|---|---|---|
| O14 | A12 | 2a yellow | 125.00 | 7.50 |

### On Issue of 1904-05

*Perf. 12½, 13*

| | | | | |
|---|---|---|---|---|
| O15 | A13 | ¼a carmine | | *450.00* |
| O16 | A13 | ½a chestnut | 1.50 | .50 |
| O17 | A13 | 1a deep blue | 16.00 | 6.00 |
| O18 | A13 | 2a orange | — | 1,500. |
| O19 | A13 | 4a dark brown | 90.00 | 27.50 |
| O20 | A13 | 8a purple | 600.00 | 375.00 |
| O21 | A13 | 1r dark green | 1,200. | 1,100. |
| O22 | A13 | 5r purple brn | | |

### On Issue of 1913

*Rouletted*

| | | | | |
|---|---|---|---|---|
| O23 | A15 | ¼a pale blue | 11.00 | |

### On Issue of 1913-16

| | | | | |
|---|---|---|---|---|
| O24 | A14 | ¼a pale blue | .90 | .75 |
| O25 | A14 | ½a green | 1.50 | 1.10 |
| O26 | A14 | 1a carmine | 24.00 | 13.50 |
| O27 | A14 | 2a purple | 12.50 | 6.00 |
| O28 | A14 | 4a ultra | 42.50 | 22.50 |
| O29 | A14 | 8a brown | 190.00 | 67.50 |
| O30 | A14 | 1r rose lilac | 525.00 | 500.00 |
| O31 | A14 | 2r dark green | | |
| O32 | A14 | 5r brown | 2,750. | |

### Red Handstamp

### On Issue of 1904

*Pin-perf*

| | | | | |
|---|---|---|---|---|
| O33 | A11 | 8a gray | — | 450.00 |

*Imperf*

| | | | | |
|---|---|---|---|---|
| O34 | A12 | 2a yellow | 675.00 | 400.00 |

### On Issue of 1904-05

*Perf. 12½, 13*

| | | | | |
|---|---|---|---|---|
| O35 | A13 | 1a deep blue | 35.00 | 10.00 |
| O36 | A13 | 4a dark brown | 140.00 | 62.50 |
| O37 | A13 | 8a purple | — | *400.00* |
| O38 | A13 | 1r dark green | — | *1,000.* |

### On Issue of 1913-16

*Rouletted*

| | | | | |
|---|---|---|---|---|
| O39 | A14 | ¼a pale blue | 3.00 | 2.50 |
| O40 | A14 | ½a green | 6.50 | 2.40 |
| O41 | A14 | 2a purple | 210.00 | 100.00 |
| O42 | A14 | 4a ultra | — | 52.50 |
| O43 | A14 | 8a brown | — | 140.00 |

### On Issue of 1918

**Redrawn**

| | | | | |
|---|---|---|---|---|
| O44 | A14 | 1a rose red | | |

The overprint on Nos. O1 to O44 is handstamped and, as usual with that style of overprint, is found inverted, double, etc. In this instance there is evidence that many of the varieties were deliberately made.

## KOTAH

LOCATION — A Feudatory State in the Rajputana Agency of India.
AREA — 5714 sq. mi.
POP. — 526,827 (1880)
CAPITAL — Kotah City

All Kotah stamps are only known on cover, including the uncanceled stamps. Values are for covers bearing a single stamp.

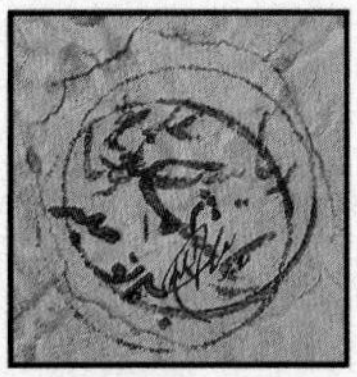

A1

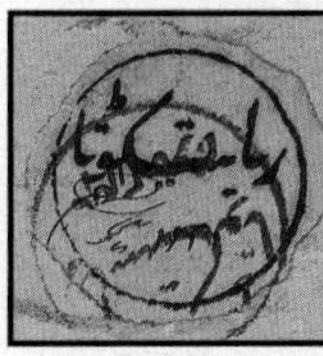

A2

A3

**Handstamped**

**1883** **Unwmk.** *Imperf.*

**Wove Paper**

| | | | | |
|---|---|---|---|---|
| 1 | A1 | 2p green, *yellow* | *20,000.* | *8,500.* |
| *a.* | | Double impression | | — |
| 2 | A2 | 2p black, *yellow* | | *20,000.* |
| 3 | A3 | 2p indigo, *pink* | | *20,000.* |

A4

**1886** **Wove Paper**

| | | | | |
|---|---|---|---|---|
| 4 | A4 | 1p green, *yellow* | | — |

The stamps of Kotah became obsolete in 1886.

## LAS BELA

ləs 'bāl-ə

LOCATION — A Feudatory State in the Baluchistan District.
AREA — 7,132 sq. mi.
POP. — 63,008
CAPITAL — Bela

A1

A2

**1897-98** **Unwmk.** **Typo.** *Perf. 12*

| | | | | |
|---|---|---|---|---|
| 1 | A1 | ½a black, *white* | 45.00 | 25.00 |
| 2 | A1 | ½a black, *gray* | 25.00 | 16.00 |
| 3 | A1 | ½a black, *blue* ('98) | 30.00 | 16.00 |
| | | *Nos. 1-3 (3)* | 100.00 | 57.00 |

**1901**

| | | | | |
|---|---|---|---|---|
| 4 | A2 | 1a black, *red orange* | 35.00 | *40.00* |

**1904** *Pin-perf*

| | | | | |
|---|---|---|---|---|
| 5 | A1 | ½a black, *lt blue* | 24.00 | 13.50 |

**Granite Paper**

| | | | | |
|---|---|---|---|---|
| 6 | A1 | ½a black, *greenish gray* | 24.00 | 13.50 |

Las Bela stamps became obsolete in Mar. 1907.

## MORVI

'mor-vē

LOCATION — A Feudatory State in the Kathiawar Agency, Western India.
AREA — 822 sq. mi.
POP. — 113,023
CAPITAL — Morvi

In 1948 Morvi was incorporated in the United State of Saurashtra (see Soruth).

Sir Lakhdhirji Waghji The Thakur Sahib of Morvi — A1

**1931** **Unwmk.** **Typo.** *Perf. 12*

**Size: 21½x26½mm**

| | | | | |
|---|---|---|---|---|
| 1 | A1 | 3p red | 4.50 | *22.50* |
| *a.* | | 3p deep blue (error) | 6.50 | *35.00* |
| 2 | A1 | ½a deep blue | 40.00 | 67.50 |
| 3 | A1 | 1a red brown | 5.00 | *25.00* |
| 4 | A1 | 2a yellow brown | 6.00 | *60.00* |
| | | *Nos. 1-4 (4)* | 55.50 | *175.00* |

Nos. 1-4 and 1a were printed in two blocks of four, with stamps 5½mm apart, and perforated on four sides. Nos. 1 and 2 were also printed in blocks of four, with stamps 10mm apart, and perforated on two or three sides.

A2

A3

**1932** **Size: 21x25½mm** *Perf. 11*

| | | | | |
|---|---|---|---|---|
| 5 | A2 | 3p rose | 7.50 | *21.00* |
| 6 | A2 | 6p gray green | 12.00 | *25.00* |
| 7 | A2 | 6p emerald | 9.50 | *21.00* |
| 8 | A2 | 1a ultramarine | 6.50 | *21.00* |
| 9 | A2 | 2a violet | 16.00 | *60.00* |
| | | *Nos. 5-9 (5)* | 51.50 | *148.00* |

**1934-48** *Perf. 14, Rough Perf. 11*

| | | | | |
|---|---|---|---|---|
| 10 | A3 | 3p carmine rose | 3.75 | *5.25* |
| *a.* | | 3p red | 2.50 | *6.50* |
| 11 | A3 | 6p emerald | 2.50 | *10.00* |
| *a.* | | 6p green | 10.00 | *25.00* |
| 12 | A3 | 1a red brown | 2.75 | *21.00* |
| *a.* | | 1a brown | 15.00 | *25.00* |
| 13 | A3 | 2a violet | 3.75 | *30.00* |
| | | *Nos. 10-13 (4)* | 12.75 | *66.25* |

The 1934 London printing of Nos. 10-13 is perf. 14; the later Morvi Press printing is rough perf. 11.

Morvi stamps became obsolete Feb. 15, 1948.

## NANDGAON

'nän͵d͵-gaun

LOCATION — A Feudatory State in the Chhattisgarh States Agency in Central India.
AREA — 871 sq. mi.
POP. — 182,380
CAPITAL — Rajnandgaon

A1

**White Paper**

**1892, Feb.** **Unwmk.** **Typo.** *Imperf.*

**Without Gum**

| | | | | |
|---|---|---|---|---|
| 1 | A1 | ½a blue | 10.00 | *275.00* |
| 2 | A1 | 2a rose | 40.00 | *825.00* |

Some authorities claim that No. 2 was a revenue stamp.

For overprints see Nos. O1-O2.

A2

**1893** **Without Gum**

| | | | | |
|---|---|---|---|---|
| 4 | A2 | ½a green | 19.00 | *140.00* |
| 5 | A2 | 2a rose | 19.00 | *140.00* |

For overprint see No. O5.

### Same Redrawn

**1894 — Without Gum**

| | | | | |
|---|---|---|---|---|
| 6 | A2 | ½a yellow green | 37.50 | *140.00* |
| 7 | A2 | 1a rose | 82.50 | *175.00* |
| *a.* | | Laid paper | 375.00 | |

The redrawn stamps have smaller value characters and wavy lines between the stamps.

For overprints see Nos. O3-O4.

---

### OFFICIAL STAMPS

Regular Issues Handstamped in Violet

**1893-94 — Unwmk. — *Imperf.***
**Without Gum**

| | | | | |
|---|---|---|---|---|
| O1 | A1 | ½a blue | *550.00* | |
| O2 | A1 | 2a red | *1,350.* | |
| O3 | A2 | ½a yellow green | 9.50 | 17.50 |
| O4 | A2 | 1a rose | 16.00 | *37.50* |
| *a.* | | Laid paper | 16.00 | *125.00* |
| O5 | A2 | 2a rose | 3.00 | 3.00 |

Some authorities believe that this handstamp was used as a control mark, rather than to indicate a stamp for official mail.

*The 1 anna has been reprinted in brown and in blue.*

Nandgaon stamps became obsolete in July, 1895.

---

## NOWANUGGUR

ˌnau-ə-ˈnəg-ər

## (Navanagar)

LOCATION — A Feudatory State in the Kathiawar Agency, Western India.
AREA — 3,791 sq. mi.
POP. — 402,192
CAPITAL — Navanagar

Stamps of Nowanuggur were superseded by those of India.

6 Dokra = 1 Anna
16 Annas = 1 Rupee

Kandjar (Indian Dagger) — A1

**1877 — Unwmk. — Typo. — *Imperf.***
**Without Gum**
**Laid Paper**

| | | | | |
|---|---|---|---|---|
| 1 | A1 | 1d dull blue | 1.00 | *37.50* |
| *a.* | | 1d ultramarine | 1.00 | *37.50* |
| *b.* | | Tete beche pair | 1,900. | |

***Perf. 12½***

| | | | | |
|---|---|---|---|---|
| 2 | A1 | 1d slate | 120.00 | 175.00 |
| *a.* | | Tete beche pair | 2,400. | |

No. 2 on wove paper is of private origin.

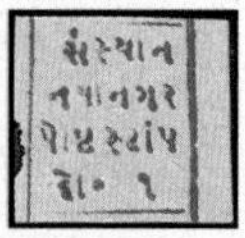

A2

**1877-88 — Without Gum — *Imperf.***
**Wove Paper**

| | | | | |
|---|---|---|---|---|
| 3 | A2 | 1d black, *red violet* | 5.25 | *16.00* |
| *a.* | | 1d black, *rose* | 5.25 | |
| *b.* | | Characters at beginning of 3rd line read "4102" instead of "418" | | |
| 4 | A2 | 2d black, *green* | 8.25 | *21.00* |
| *a.* | | 2d black, *blue green* | 12.50 | |
| *b.* | | "4102" instead of "418" | | |
| 5 | A2 | 3d black, *yellow* | 9.00 | *30.00* |
| *a.* | | 3d black, *orange yellow* | 19.00 | |
| *b.* | | "4102" instead of "418" | | |
| *c.* | | Laid paper | 160.00 | |
| *d.* | | 2d black, *yellow* (error in sheet of 3d) | 600.00 | |
| | | *Nos. 3-5 (3)* | 22.50 | *67.00* |

Nos. 3-5 range in width from 14 to 19mm.

Seal of the State — A3

**1893 — Thick Paper — *Imperf.***
**Without Gum**

| | | | | |
|---|---|---|---|---|
| 6 | A3 | 1d black | 450.00 | |

***Perf. 12***

| | | | | |
|---|---|---|---|---|
| 7 | A3 | 1d black | 6.50 | |
| 8 | A3 | 3d orange | 7.50 | |

***Imperf***
**Thin Paper**

| | | | | |
|---|---|---|---|---|
| 9 | A3 | 1d black | 350.00 | |
| 10 | A3 | 2d dark green | 450.00 | |
| 11 | A3 | 3d orange | 400.00 | |
| | | *Nos. 9-11 (3)* | 1,200. | |

***Perf. 12***

| | | | | |
|---|---|---|---|---|
| 12 | A3 | 1d black | 2.50 | *9.00* |
| 13 | A3 | 2d green | 3.40 | *12.00* |
| 14 | A3 | 3d orange | 3.40 | *17.50* |
| *a.* | | Imperf. vert., pair | | |
| | | *Nos. 12-14 (3)* | 9.30 | 38.50 |

Obsolete at end of 1895.

---

## ORCHHA

ˈor-chə

## (Orcha)

LOCATION — A Feudatory State in the Bundelkhand Agency in Central India.
AREA — 2,080 sq. mi.
POP. — 314,661
CAPITAL — Tikamgarh

Seal of Orchha — A1

**1913-17 — Unwmk. — Litho. — *Imperf.***
**Without Gum**

| | | | | |
|---|---|---|---|---|
| 1 | A1 | ¼a ultra ('15) | 3.00 | *7.50* |
| 2 | A1 | ½a emerald ('14) | .85 | *9.50* |
| *a.* | | Background of arms unshaded | 52.50 | *150.00* |
| 3 | A1 | 1a carmine ('14) | 3.75 | *10.00* |
| *a.* | | Background of arms unshaded | 30.00 | *275.00* |
| 4 | A1 | 2a brown ('17) | 6.75 | *35.00* |
| 5 | A1 | 4a orange ('14) | 12.00 | *57.50* |
| | | *Nos. 1-5 (5)* | 26.35 | *119.50* |

Essays similar to Nos. 2-5 are in different colors.

A2

Maharaja Singh Dev — A3

**1939-40 — *Perf. 13½, 13½x14***

| | | | | |
|---|---|---|---|---|
| 6 | A2 | ¼a chocolate | 5.00 | *12.00* |
| 7 | A2 | ½a yellow green | 4.50 | *100.00* |
| 8 | A2 | ¾a ultramarine | 7.00 | *150.00* |
| 9 | A2 | 1a rose red | 4.50 | *30.00* |
| 10 | A2 | 1¼a deep blue | 5.50 | *150.00* |
| 11 | A2 | 1½a lilac | 6.00 | *190.00* |
| 12 | A2 | 2a vermilion | 4.50 | *120.00* |
| 13 | A2 | 2½a turq green | 7.50 | *340.00* |
| 14 | A2 | 3a dull violet | 8.00 | *180.00* |
| 15 | A2 | 4a blue gray | 9.00 | *42.50* |
| 16 | A2 | 8a rose lilac | 15.00 | *340.00* |
| 17 | A3 | 1r sage green | 26.00 | *750.00* |
| 18 | A3 | 2r lt violet ('40) | 60.00 | *1,000.* |
| 19 | A3 | 5r yel org ('40) | 200.00 | *2,750.* |
| 20 | A3 | 10r blue | 700.00 | *4,500.* |
| | | *Nos. 6-20 (15)* | 1,062. | *10,654.* |

## POONCH

ˈpünch

LOCATION — A Feudatory State in the Kashmir Residency in India.
AREA — 1,627 sq. mi.
POP. — 287,000 (estimated)
CAPITAL — Poonch

Poonch was feudatory to Jammu and Kashmir. Cancellations of Jammu and Kashmir are found on Poonch stamps, which became obsolete in 1894. The stamps are all printed in watercolor and handstamped from single dies. They may be found on various papers, including wove, laid, wove batonne, laid batonne and ribbed, in various colors and tones. Nearly all Poonch stamps exist tete beche and impressed sideways. Issued without gum.

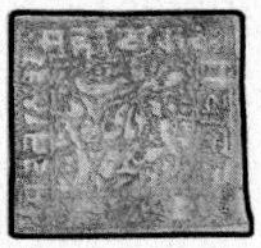

A1

**White Paper**
**Handstamped**
**1876 — Unwmk. — *Imperf.***
**Size: 22x21mm**

| | | | | |
|---|---|---|---|---|
| 1 | A1 | 6p red | 18,000. | 240. |

**1877 — Size: 19x17mm**

| | | | | |
|---|---|---|---|---|
| 1A | A1 | ½a red | 22,500. | *7,500.* |

**1879 — Size: 21x19mm**

| | | | | |
|---|---|---|---|---|
| 1B | A1 | ½a red | — | 7,500. |

A2

A3

A4

A5

A6

**1880-88 — White Paper**

| | | | | |
|---|---|---|---|---|
| 2 | A2 | 1p red ('84) | 40.00 | 40.00 |
| 3 | A3 | ½a red | 4.00 | *5.25* |
| 4 | A4 | 1a red | 6.75 | |
| 5 | A5 | 2a red | 16.00 | *19.00* |
| 6 | A6 | 4a red | 25.00 | |

**Yellow Paper**

| | | | | |
|---|---|---|---|---|
| 7 | A2 | 1p red | 5.50 | 5.50 |
| 8 | A3 | ½a red | 9.50 | 9.50 |
| 9 | A4 | 1a red | 82.50 | |
| 10 | A5 | 2a red | 15.00 | *17.50* |
| 11 | A6 | 4a red | 7.50 | 7.50 |

**Blue Paper**

| | | | | |
|---|---|---|---|---|
| 12 | A2 | 1p red | 4.00 | 3.75 |
| 13 | A4 | 1a red | 600.00 | *625.00* |

**Orange Paper**

| | | | | |
|---|---|---|---|---|
| 14 | A2 | 1p red | 5.50 | 5.50 |
| 15 | A3 | ½a red | 42.50 | |
| 16 | A5 | 2a red | 150.00 | |
| 17 | A6 | 4a red | 37.50 | |

**Green Paper**

| | | | | |
|---|---|---|---|---|
| 18 | A3 | ½a red | 67.50 | |
| 19 | A4 | 1a red | 5.00 | *7.50* |
| 20 | A5 | 2a red | 67.50 | |
| 21 | A6 | 4a red | 100.00 | |

**Lavender Paper**

| | | | | |
|---|---|---|---|---|
| 22 | A2 | 1p red | 75.00 | *82.50* |
| 23 | A4 | 1a red | 125.00 | *160.00* |
| 24 | A5 | 2a red | 5.00 | *5.50* |

---

### OFFICIAL STAMPS

White Paper

**Handstamped**
**1888 — Unwmk. — *Imperf.***

| | | | | |
|---|---|---|---|---|
| O1 | A2 | 1p black | 4.00 | *4.50* |
| O2 | A3 | ½a black | 4.50 | *6.00* |
| O3 | A4 | 1a black | 4.00 | *4.50* |
| O4 | A5 | 2a black | 7.50 | 7.50 |
| O5 | A6 | 4a black | 12.00 | *16.00* |
| | | *Nos. O1-O5 (5)* | 32.00 | *38.50* |

**1890 — Yellowish Paper**

| | | | | |
|---|---|---|---|---|
| O6 | A2 | 1p black | 3.75 | |
| O7 | A3 | ½a black | 4.50 | *5.25* |
| O8 | A4 | 1a black | 22.50 | 21.00 |
| O9 | A5 | 2a black | 9.50 | 9.50 |
| O10 | A6 | 4a black | 15.00 | |
| | | *Nos. O6-O10 (5)* | 55.25 | 35.75 |

Obsolete since 1894.

---

## RAJASTHAN

ˈrä-jə-ˌstän

## (Greater Rajasthan Union)

AREA — 128,424 sq. miles
POP. — 13,085,000

The Rajasthan Union was formed in 1947-49 by 14 Indian States, including the stamp-issuing States of Bundi, Dungarpur, Jaipur and Kishangarh.

**Catalogue values for all unused stamps in this state are for Never Hinged items.**

Bundi Nos. 43 to 49 Overprinted — a

**1948 — Unwmk. — *Perf. 11***
**Handstamped in Black**

| | | | | |
|---|---|---|---|---|
| 1 | A8 | ¼a dp grn | 8.25 | *50.00* |
| *a.* | | Pair, one without overprint | 550.00 | |
| 2 | A8 | ½a purple | 8.25 | *50.00* |
| *a.* | | Pair, one without overprint | 600.00 | |
| 3 | A8 | 1a yel green | 7.00 | *42.50* |
| 4 | A9 | 2a red | 21.00 | *125.00* |
| 5 | A9 | 4a dp orange | 72.50 | *450.00* |
| 6 | A10 | 8a vio blue | 13.50 | *80.00* |
| | | *Nos. 1-6 (6)* | 130.50 | *797.50* |

**Handstamped in Violet**

| | | | | |
|---|---|---|---|---|
| *1b* | A8 | ¼a dp grn | 9.00 | *55.00* |
| *2b* | A8 | ½a purple | 9.00 | *55.00* |
| *c.* | | Pair, one without overprint | 550.00 | |
| *3a* | A8 | 1a yel green | 24.00 | *140.00* |
| *b.* | | Pair, one without overprint | 550.00 | |
| *4a* | A9 | 2a red | 47.50 | *275.00* |
| *5a* | A9 | 4a dp orange | 47.50 | *275.00* |
| *6a* | A10 | 8a vio blue | 14.00 | *80.00* |
| 7 | A10 | 1r chocolate | 400.00 | 2,400. |
| | | *Nos. 1b-7 (7)* | 551.00 | *3,280.* |

**Handstamped in Blue**

| | | | | |
|---|---|---|---|---|
| *1c* | A8 | ¼a dp grn | 52.50 | *300.00* |
| *2d* | A8 | ½a purple | 72.50 | *450.00* |
| *3c* | A8 | 1a yel green | 67.50 | *400.00* |
| *5b* | A9 | 4a dp orange | 190.00 | *1,100.* |
| *6b* | A10 | 8a vio blue | 120.00 | *725.00* |
| 7a | A10 | 1r chocolate | 140.00 | 825.00 |
| | | *Nos. 1c-7a (6)* | 642.50 | *3,800.* |

**Typo. in Black**

| | | | | |
|---|---|---|---|---|
| 11 | A9 | 2a red | 15.00 | *100.00* |
| a. | | Inverted overprint | 450.00 | |
| 12 | A9 | 4a deep orange | 6.00 | *100.00* |
| a. | | Double overprint | 400.00 | |
| 13 | A10 | 8a violet blue | 27.50 | |
| a. | | Inverted overprint | 950.00 | |
| b. | | Double overprint | 600.00 | |
| 14 | A10 | 1r chocolate | 11.00 | |
| | | *Nos. 11-14 (4)* | 59.50 | |

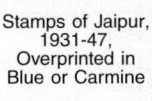

Stamps of Jaipur, 1931-47, Overprinted in Blue or Carmine

**1949 Center in Black *Perf. 14***

| | | | | |
|---|---|---|---|---|
| 15 | A6 | ¼a red brown (Bl) | 12.00 | *32.50* |
| 16 | A6 | ½a dull violet | 9.50 | *35.00* |
| 17 | A6 | ¾a brown org (Bl) | 15.00 | *40.00* |
| 18 | A6 | 1a blue | 11.00 | *72.50* |
| 19 | A6 | 2a ocher | 12.50 | *100.00* |
| 20 | A6 | 2½a rose (Bl) | 13.50 | *45.00* |
| 21 | A6 | 3a green | 16.00 | *110.00* |
| 22 | A6 | 4a gray green | 14.00 | *125.00* |
| 23 | A6 | 6a blue | 14.00 | *180.00* |
| 24 | A6 | 8a chocolate | 24.00 | *250.00* |
| 25 | A6 | 1r bister | 35.00 | *375.00* |
| | | *Nos. 15-25 (11)* | 176.50 | *1,365.* |

Kishangarh Stamps and Types of 1899-1904 Handstamped Type "a" in Rose

**1949 *Pin-perf., Rouletted***

| | | | | |
|---|---|---|---|---|
| 26 | A3 | ½a blue (#18) | 900.00 | |
| 27 | A4 | 1a dull lilac (#20) | 21.00 | *62.50* |
| 28 | A6 | 4a pale red brown (#21B) | 125.00 | *160.00* |
| 29 | A11 | 8a gray (#25B) | 160.00 | *275.00* |
| 30 | A7 | 1r dull green (#22) | 450.00 | *500.00* |
| 31 | A8 | 2r brown red (#23) | 550.00 | |
| 32 | A9 | 5r red violet (#24) | 525.00 | 525.00 |
| | | *Nos. 26-32 (7)* | 2,731. | |

Kishangarh Nos. 28, 31-36 Handstamped Type "a" in Rose or Green

**1949 Engr. *Perf. 13½, 12½***

| | | | | |
|---|---|---|---|---|
| 33 | A13 | ½a chestnut (R) | | 300.00 |
| 34 | A13 | 4a dark brown (G) | 375.00 | |
| 35 | A13 | 4a dark brown (R) | 20.00 | |
| 36 | A13 | 8a purple (R) | 16.00 | |
| 37 | A13 | 1r dark green (R) | 21.00 | |
| 38 | A13 | 2r lemon yellow (R) | 27.50 | |
| 39 | A13 | 5r purple brown (R) | 47.50 | |
| | | *Nos. 33-39 (7)* | 507.00 | |

Kishangarh Nos. 40-42, 37, 43, 46-48 Handstamped Type "a" in Rose

**1949 Typo. *Rouletted***

| | | | | |
|---|---|---|---|---|
| 40 | A14 | ¼a pale blue | 8.00 | 8.00 |
| 41 | A14 | ½a green | 675.00 | 375.00 |
| 42 | A14 | 1a carmine | — | 450.00 |
| 43 | A14 | 2 "anna" violet | 825.00 | |
| 44 | A14 | 2 "annas" purple | 4.50 | 12.50 |
| 45 | A14 | 8a brown | 7.50 | |
| 46 | A14 | 1r rose lilac | 15.00 | |
| 47 | A14 | 2r dark green | 15.00 | |
| 48 | A14 | 5r brown | 675.00 | |
| | | *Nos. 40-48 (9)* | 2,225. | |

Kishangarh Stamps and Types of 1928-29 Handstamped Type "a" in Rose

**1949 *Pin-perf***

| | | | | |
|---|---|---|---|---|
| 49 | A17 | ¼a greenish blue | 75.00 | 75.00 |
| 50 | A17 | ½a yel green | 60.00 | 60.00 |
| 51 | A18 | 1a car rose | 110.00 | 110.00 |
| 52 | A18 | 2a red violet | 325.00 | 325.00 |
| 53 | A17 | 4a yel brown | 4.00 | *12.50* |
| 54 | A17 | 8a purple | 21.00 | *90.00* |
| 55 | A17 | 1r deep green | 10.00 | |
| 56 | A17 | 2r lemon | 140.00 | |
| 57 | A17 | 5r red brown | 75.00 | |
| | | *Nos. 49-57 (9)* | 820.00 | |

Type of Kishangarh 1928-29, Handstamped Type "a" in Rose

**1949 *Pin-perf***

| | | | | |
|---|---|---|---|---|
| 58 | A18 | 1a dark violet blue | | 140.00 |

No. 58 exists imperf.

Rajasthan stamps became obsolete Apr. 1, 1950.

## RAJPEEPLA

räj-ˈpē-plə

(Rajpipla)

LOCATION — A Feudatory State near Bombay in the Gujarat States Agency in India.

AREA — 1,517 sq. mi.

POP. — 206,086

CAPITAL — Nandod

4 Paisas = 1 Anna

Kandjar (Indian Daggers) — A1

A2

A3

**1880 Unwmk. Litho. *Perf. 11, 12½***
**Without Gum**

| | | | | |
|---|---|---|---|---|
| 1 | A1 | 1pa ultramarine | 5.25 | *57.50* |
| 2 | A2 | 2a green | 45.00 | *160.00* |
| a. | | Horiz. pair, imperf. btwn. | 900.00 | 900.00 |
| 3 | A3 | 4a red | 24.00 | *100.00* |
| | | *Nos. 1-3 (3)* | 74.25 | *317.50* |

The stamps of Rajpeepla have been obsolete since 1886.

## SIRMOOR

sir-ˈmu̦ə̦r

(Sirmur)

LOCATION — A Feudatory State in the Punjab District of India.

AREA — 1,046 sq. mi.

POP. — 148,568

CAPITAL — Nahan

A1

Raja Sir Shamsher Prakash — A2

**1879 Unwmk. *Perf. 11½***
**Wove Paper**

| | | | | |
|---|---|---|---|---|
| 1 | A1 | 1p green | 24.00 | *500.00* |
| a. | | Imperf., pair | | |

**Laid Paper**

| | | | | |
|---|---|---|---|---|
| 2 | A1 | 1p blue | 6.75 | *250.00* |
| a. | | Imperf., pair | | |

**1885-88 Litho. *Perf. 14 and 14½.***

| | | | | |
|---|---|---|---|---|
| 3 | A2 | 3p brown | 1.00 | .60 |
| 4 | A2 | 3p orange | 2.50 | .45 |
| 5 | A2 | 6p green | 6.50 | 6.00 |
| 6 | A2 | 1a blue | 4.00 | *5.50* |
| 7 | A2 | 2a carmine | 6.25 | *21.00* |
| | | *Nos. 3-7 (5)* | 20.25 | *33.55* |

There are several printings, dies and minor variations of this issue.

For overprints see Nos. O1-O16.

A3

Elephant — A4

**1893 *Perf. 11½***

| | | | | |
|---|---|---|---|---|
| 9 | A3 | 1p yellow green | 1.60 | 1.60 |
| a. | | 1pa dark blue green | 1.10 | 1.10 |
| 10 | A3 | 1p ultramarine | 1.90 | 1.20 |
| b. | | Imperf., pair | 110.00 | |

Nos. 9 and 10 are re-issues, which were available for postage.

The printed perforation, which is a part of the design, is in addition to the regular perforation.

**1895-99 Engr. *Perf. 14***

| | | | | |
|---|---|---|---|---|
| 11 | A4 | 3p orange | 5.45 | .45 |
| 12 | A4 | 6p green | 1.10 | .45 |
| a. | | Vert. pair, imperf between | 15,000. | |
| 13 | A4 | 1a dull blue | 6.50 | 5.25 |
| 14 | A4 | 2a dull red | 5.25 | 2.25 |
| 15 | A4 | 3a yellow green | 35.00 | *67.50* |
| 16 | A4 | 4a dark green | 24.00 | *35.00* |
| 17 | A4 | 8a deep blue | 27.50 | *42.50* |
| 18 | A4 | 1r vermilion | 57.50 | *110.00* |
| | | *Nos. 11-18 (8)* | 162.30 | *263.40* |

No. 12a is unique.

Sir Surendar Bikram Prakash — A5

**1899**

| | | | | |
|---|---|---|---|---|
| 19 | A5 | 3a yellow green | 6.25 | *32.50* |
| 20 | A5 | 4a dark green | 8.25 | *35.00* |
| 21 | A5 | 8a blue | 11.00 | *30.00* |
| 22 | A5 | 1r vermilion | 18.00 | *75.00* |
| | | *Nos. 19-22 (4)* | 43.50 | *172.50* |

### OFFICIAL STAMPS

Regular Stamps Overprinted in Black

**1890-91 Unwmk. *Perf. 14, 14½***

| | | | | |
|---|---|---|---|---|
| O1 | A2 | 3p orange | 4.50 | *52.50* |
| O2 | A2 | 6p green | 2.25 | 2.25 |
| a. | | Double overprint | 275.00 | |
| b. | | Double ovpt., one in red | 1,250. | |
| O3 | A2 | 1a blue | 600.00 | *700.00* |
| O4 | A2 | 2a carmine | 27.50 | *100.00* |
| | | *Nos. O1-O4 (4)* | 634.25 | |

**1890-92 Red Overprint**

| | | | | |
|---|---|---|---|---|
| O5 | A2 | 6p green | 42.50 | 3.50 |
| O6 | A2 | 1a blue | 37.50 | *47.50* |

| | | | | |
|---|---|---|---|---|
| O7 | A2 | 6p green | 8.25 | .75 |
| b. | | Inverted overprint | 210.00 | 150.00 |
| O8 | A2 | 1a blue | 27.50 | 6.25 |
| a. | | Inverted overprint | 500.00 | 300.00 |
| b. | | Double overprint | 500.00 | |

**1892 Black Overprint**

| | | | | |
|---|---|---|---|---|
| O9 | A2 | 3p orange | .90 | .75 |
| a. | | Inverted overprint | 375.00 | |
| O10 | A2 | 6p green | 12.00 | 3.25 |
| O11 | A2 | 1a blue | 18.00 | 1.50 |
| a. | | Double overprint | 600.00 | |
| O12 | A2 | 2a carmine | 10.00 | 10.00 |
| a. | | Inverted overprint | 1,350. | 1,350. |
| | | *Nos. O9-O12 (4)* | 40.90 | 15.50 |

**Black Overprint**

| | | | | |
|---|---|---|---|---|
| O13 | A2 | 3p orange | 19.00 | 1.90 |
| a. | | Inverted overprint | | |
| b. | | Double overprint | | 1,000. |
| O14 | A2 | 6p green | 8.25 | .90 |
| O15 | A2 | 1a blue | 11.00 | 1.90 |
| O16 | A2 | 2a carmine | 25.00 | 21.00 |
| | | *Nos. O13-O16 (4)* | 63.25 | 25.70 |

There are several settings of some of these overprints, differing in the sizes and shapes of the letters, the presence or absence of the periods, etc.

The overprints on Nos. O1-O16 are press printed. In addition, nine varieties of handstamped overprints were applied in 1894-96. Most of the handstamps are very similar to the press printed overprints.

Obsolete Mar. 31, 1901.

## SORUTH

(Sorath)

(Junagarh)

(Saurashtra)

LOCATION — A Feudatory State near Bombay in the Western India States Agency in India.

AREA — 3,337 sq. mi.

POP. — 670,719

CAPITAL — Junagarh

The United State of Saurashtra (area 31,885 sq. mi.; population 2,900,000) was formed in 1948 by 217 States, including the stamp-issuing States of Jasdan, Morvi, Nowanuggur and Wadhwan.

Nos. 1-27 were issued without gum.

**Catalogue values for unused stamps in this State are for Never Hinged items, beginning with Scott 39 in the regular postage section, and Scott O19 in the officials section.**

**Junagarh**

A1

A2

**Handstamped in Watercolor**
**1864 Unwmk. *Imperf.***
**Laid Paper**

| | | | | |
|---|---|---|---|---|
| 1 | A1 | (1a) black, *bluish* | 950.00 | 125.00 |
| a. | | Wove paper | | 275.00 |
| 1B | A1 | (1a) black, *gray* | 950.00 | 125.00 |

**Wove Paper**

| | | | | |
|---|---|---|---|---|
| 2 | A1 | (1a) black, *cream* | | 1,500. |

**1868 Typo. *Imperf.***
**Wove Paper**

| | | | | |
|---|---|---|---|---|
| 3 | A2 | 1a black, *yellowish* | | 37,500. |
| 4 | A2 | 1a red, *green* | | 16,000. |
| 5 | A2 | 1a red, *blue* | | 12,500. |
| 6 | A2 | 1a black, *pink* | 825.00 | 110.00 |
| 7 | A2 | 2a black, *yellow* | | 16,000. |

**Laid Paper**

| | | | | |
|---|---|---|---|---|
| 8 | A2 | 1a black, *blue* | 140.00 | 13.50 |
| a. | | Left character, 3rd line, omitted | | |
| 9 | A2 | 1a red | 32.50 | 37.50 |
| a. | | Left character, 3rd line, omitted | | |
| 10 | A2 | 4a black | 400.00 | *675.00* |
| a. | | Left character, 3rd line, omitted | | |

A 1a black on white laid paper exists in type A2. Value, used $9,500.

*In 1890 official imitations of 1a and 4a stamps, type A2, were printed in sheets of 16 and 4. Original sheets have 20 stamps. Four of these imitations are perf. 12, six are imperf.*

A3

A4

**1877-86 Laid Paper *Imperf.***

| | | | | |
|---|---|---|---|---|
| 11 | A3 | 1a green | 1.50 | .75 |
| a. | | Printed on both sides | 750.00 | *825.00* |

| | | | | |
|---|---|---|---|---|
| 12 | A4 | 4a vermilion | 4.00 | 2.50 |
| *a.* | | Printed on both sides | 950.00 | |
| 13 | A4 | 4a scarlet, *bluish* | 5.50 | 5.00 |
| | | *Nos. 11-13 (3)* | 11.00 | 8.25 |

***Perf. 12***

| | | | | |
|---|---|---|---|---|
| 14 | A3 | 1a green | .60 | .25 |
| *a.* | | 1a blue (error) | 900.00 | 900.00 |
| *c.* | | Wove paper | 5.25 | 2.25 |
| *d.* | | Imperf., pair | 120.00 | 160.00 |
| *e.* | | As "a," wove paper | — | 900.00 |
| *f.* | | As "c," vert. pair, imperf horiz. | 240.00 | |
| 15 | A3 | 1a green, *bluish* | 5.25 | *6.75* |
| *a.* | | Vert. pair, imperf horiz. | | 525.00 |
| *b.* | | Horiz. pair, imperf vert. | 210.00 | — |
| 16 | A4 | 4a red | 4.00 | 1.90 |
| *a.* | | 4a carmine | 6.50 | 5.25 |
| *c.* | | Wove paper | 7.50 | 18.00 |
| *d.* | | As "c," imperf., pair | 340.00 | 450.00 |
| 17 | A4 | 4a scarlet, *bluish* | 16.00 | *25.00* |
| | | *Nos. 14-17 (4)* | 25.85 | *33.90* |

**Nos. 14d and 16c Surcharged**

**1913-14** ***Perf. 12***

| | | | | |
|---|---|---|---|---|
| 18 | A3 | 3p on 1a green | .25 | .45 |
| *a.* | | Laid paper | 110.00 | 45.00 |
| *b.* | | Inverted surcharge | 52.50 | 30.00 |
| *c.* | | Imperf., pair | 52.50 | |
| 19 | A4 | 1a on 4a red | 3.75 | 10.00 |
| *a.* | | Laid paper | 11.00 | *82.50* |
| *b.* | | Imperf., pair | 950.00 | |
| *c.* | | Double surcharge | 1,000. | |

A5

A6

**1914** ***Perf. 12***

| | | | | |
|---|---|---|---|---|
| 20 | A5 | 3p green | 2.10 | .50 |
| *a.* | | Imperf., pair | 12.50 | *40.00* |
| 21 | A6 | 1a rose carmine | 2.25 | *3.25* |
| *a.* | | Imperf., pair | 30.00 | 140.00 |
| *b.* | | Laid paper | 375.00 | 160.00 |

Nawab Mahabat Khan III
A7 A8

**1923-29** **Wove Paper** ***Perf. 12***

| | | | | |
|---|---|---|---|---|
| 22 | A7 | 3p violet | .50 | .65 |
| *a.* | | Imperf, pair | 450.00 | |
| *b.* | | Laid paper ('29) | 7.50 | 6.50 |
| *c.* | | As "b," imperf, pair ('29) | 5.25 | *52.50* |
| *d.* | | As "b," horiz. pair, imperf btwn. | 4.50 | *37.50* |
| 23 | A8 | 1a red | 4.50 | *14.00* |
| *b.* | | Laid paper | 4.50 | 14.00 |

Single examples of Nos. 23 and 23b cannot usually be distinguished.

Surcharged with New Value

| | | | | |
|---|---|---|---|---|
| 27 | A8 | 3p on 1a red | 7.50 | 10.00 |

Two types of surcharge.

Junagarh City and The Girnar
A9

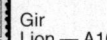

Gir Lion — A10

Nawab Mahabat Khan III — A11

Kathi Horse
A12

**1929** ***Perf. 14***

| | | | | |
|---|---|---|---|---|
| 30 | A9 | 3p dk green & blk | 1.50 | .25 |
| 31 | A10 | ½a dk blue & blk | 9.00 | .25 |
| 32 | A11 | 1a claret & blk | 7.50 | 1.50 |
| 33 | A12 | 2a org buff & blk | 19.00 | 3.00 |
| 34 | A9 | 3a car rose & blk | 9.00 | *19.00* |
| 35 | A10 | 4a dull vio & blk | 19.00 | *42.50* |
| 36 | A12 | 8a apple grn & blk | 25.00 | *35.00* |
| 37 | A11 | 1r dull blue & blk | 21.00 | *45.00* |
| | | *Nos. 30-37 (8)* | 111.00 | *146.50* |

For surcharges see Nos. 40-42, O20-O25. For overprints see Nos. O1-O14.

**Type of 1929**

Inscribed "Postage and Revenue"

**1937**

| | | | | |
|---|---|---|---|---|
| 38 | A11 | 1a claret & black | 15.00 | 1.50 |

For overprint see No. O15.

**Catalogue values for unused stamps in this section, from this point to the end of the section, are for Never Hinged items.**

**United State of Saurashtra**

A13

Bhavnagar Court Fee Stamp Overprinted in Black "U.S.S. Revenue & Postage Saurashtra"

**1949** **Unwmk.** **Typo.** ***Perf. 11***

| | | | | |
|---|---|---|---|---|
| 39 | A13 | 1a deep claret | 16.00 | 15.00 |
| *a.* | | "POSTAGE" omitted | 525.00 | 375.00 |
| *b.* | | Double overprint | 525.00 | *600.00* |

Nos. 30, 31 Surcharged in Black or Carmine "POSTAGE & REVENUE ONE ANNA"

**1949-50** ***Perf. 14***

| | | | | |
|---|---|---|---|---|
| 40 | A9 | 1a on 3p dk grn & blk (bl) ('50) | 60.00 | *82.50* |
| *a.* | | "OSTAGE" | 750.00 | *900.00* |
| 41 | A10 | 1a on ½a dk bl & blk (C) | 14.00 | 7.50 |
| *a.* | | Double surcharge | | 825.00 |

For overprint see No. O19.

No. 33 Surcharged in Green "Postage & Revenue ONE ANNA"

**1949**

| | | | | |
|---|---|---|---|---|
| 42 | A12 | 1a on 2a org buff & blk | 24.00 | *40.00* |
| *a.* | | "EVENUE" omitted | | 1,100. |

For overprint see No. O26.

**OFFICIAL STAMPS**

Regular Issue of 1929 Overprinted in Red

a

**1929** **Unwmk.** ***Perf. 14***

| | | | | |
|---|---|---|---|---|
| O1 | A9 | 3p dk green & black | 2.50 | .25 |
| O2 | A10 | ½a dk blue & black | 6.00 | .25 |
| O3 | A11 | 1a claret & black | 6.00 | .25 |
| O4 | A12 | 2a org buff & black | 3.75 | .90 |
| O5 | A9 | 3a car rose & black | 1.10 | .75 |
| O6 | A10 | 4a dull violet & blk | 6.25 | .65 |
| O7 | A12 | 8a apple green & blk | 5.50 | 4.50 |
| O8 | A11 | 1r dull blue & blk | 5.50 | *35.00* |
| | | *Nos. O1-O8 (8)* | 36.60 | 42.55 |

For surcharges see Nos. O20-O24.

**Regular Issue of 1929 Overprinted in Red**

b

**1933-49**

| | | | | |
|---|---|---|---|---|
| O9 | A9 | 3p dk grn & black ('49) | 375.00 | 25.00 |
| O10 | A10 | ½a dk bl & black ('49) | 900.00 | 22.50 |
| O11 | A9 | 3a car rose & blk | 32.50 | 27.50 |
| O12 | A10 | 4a dull vio & blk | 42.50 | 24.00 |
| O13 | A12 | 8a apple grn & blk | 47.50 | 27.50 |
| O14 | A11 | 1r dull blue & blk | 52.50 | 140.00 |

The 3p is also known with ms. "SARKARI" overprint in carmine.

For surcharge see No. O25.

No. 38 Overprinted Type "a" in Red

**1938**

| | | | | |
|---|---|---|---|---|
| O15 | A11 | 1a claret & black | 21.00 | 2.25 |

**Catalogue values for unused stamps in this section, from this point to the end of the section, are for Never Hinged items.**

**United State of Saurashtra**

No. 41 with Manuscript "Service" in Carmine

**1949**

| | | | | |
|---|---|---|---|---|
| O19 | A10 | 1a on ½a dk bl & blk (C) | | 225.00 |

Used value for No. O19 is for an example used on piece, cancelled at Gadhda or Una between June and December, 1949.

No. 42 is also known with carmine ms. "Service" overprint in English or Gujarati.

Nos. O4-O8 and O14 Surcharged "ONE ANNA" in Blue or Black

**1949**

**Surcharge 2¼mm high**

| | | | | |
|---|---|---|---|---|
| O20 | A12 | 1a on 2a (Bl) | 21,000. | 40.00 |
| O21 | A9 | 1a on 3a | 5,250. | 100.00 |
| O22 | A10 | 1a on 4a | 600.00 | 100.00 |
| O23 | A12 | 1a on 8a | 525.00 | 72.50 |

**Surcharge 4mm High, Handstamped**

| | | | | |
|---|---|---|---|---|
| O24 | A11 | 1a on 1r (#O8) | 3,250. | 72.50 |
| O25 | A11 | 1a on 1r (#O14) | 1,350. | 75.00 |
| | | *Nos. O20-O25 (6)* | 31,975. | 460.00 |

No. 42 Overprinted Type "b" in Carmine

**1949** **Unwmk.** ***Perf. 14***

| | | | | |
|---|---|---|---|---|
| O26 | A12 | 1a on 2a | 125.00 | 35.00 |

## TONK

LOCATION — A Feudatory State in the Rajputana Agency of India.
AREA — 2509 sq. mi.
POP. — 307,528 (1900)
CAPITAL — Nimbahera

Three examples of Tonk No. 1 are known. All are on covers dated 1906.

A1

**Handstamped with black octagonal control seal**

**1906** **Unwmk.** **Litho.** ***Imperf.***

**Wove Paper**

| | | | | |
|---|---|---|---|---|
| 1 | A1 | ¼a yellow brown | | — |

The stamps of Tonk became obsolete in 1907.

## TRAVANCORE

ˈtrav-ən-ˌkō̜ə̜r

LOCATION — A Feudatory State in the Madras States Agency, on the extreme southwest coast of India.
AREA — 7,662 sq. mi.
POP. — 6,070,018 (1941)
CAPITAL — Trivandrum

16 Cash = 1 Chuckram
2 Chuckrams = 1 Anna

Conch Shell (State Seal)
A1 A2

**1888** **Unwmk.** **Typo.** ***Perf. 12***

**Laid Paper**

| | | | | |
|---|---|---|---|---|
| 1 | A1 | 1ch ultramarine | 6.50 | 6.50 |
| 2 | A1 | 2ch orange red | 8.50 | *16.00* |
| 3 | A1 | 4ch green | 25.00 | 25.00 |
| | | *Nos. 1-3 (3)* | 40.00 | 47.50 |

The frame and details of the central medallion differ slightly on each denomination of type A1.

Laid paper printings of Nos. 1-3, 5-7 in completely different colors are essays.

**1889-99** **Wmk. 43** **Wove Paper**

| | | | | |
|---|---|---|---|---|
| 4 | A1 | ½ch violet | .90 | .35 |
| *a.* | | Vertical pair, imperf. between | 450.00 | 450.00 |
| 5 | A1 | 1ch ultramarine | 2.25 | .25 |
| *a.* | | Vertical pair, imperf. between | | 675.00 |
| 6 | A1 | 2ch scarlet | 4.50 | .25 |
| *a.* | | Horiz. pair, imperf. between | 550.00 | 550.00 |
| *b.* | | Vertical pair, imperf. between | 250.00 | |
| 7 | A1 | 4ch dark green | 5.00 | 1.00 |
| | | *Nos. 4-7 (4)* | 12.65 | 1.85 |

Shades exist for each denomination.

For surcharges see #10-11. For type surcharged see #20. For overprints see #O1-O2, O4, O6, O18, O24-O25, O27B, O32-O33, O42.

**1901-32**

| | | | | |
|---|---|---|---|---|
| 8 | A2 | ¾ch black | 4.50 | 2.10 |
| 9 | A2 | ¾ch brt violet ('32) | .50 | .25 |
| *a.* | | Horizontal pair, imperf. between | | |

For overprints see Nos. O26-O27, O44, O52.

No. 4 Surcharged

**1906**

| | | | | |
|---|---|---|---|---|
| 10 | A1 | ¼ch on ½ch violet | 1.10 | .45 |
| *a.* | | Inverted surcharge | 90.00 | 52.50 |
| 11 | A1 | ⅜ch on ½ch violet | .60 | .50 |
| *a.* | | Pair, one without surcharge | | — |
| *b.* | | Inverted surcharge | | 75.00 |
| *c.* | | Double surcharge | | |

A3

A4

**1908-11**

| | | | | |
|---|---|---|---|---|
| 12 | A3 | 4ca rose | .45 | .25 |
| 13 | A1 | 6ca red brown ('10) | .45 | .25 |
| *a.* | | Printed on both sides | 75.00 | |
| 14 | A4 | 3ch purple ('11) | 4.00 | .30 |
| | | *Nos. 12-14 (3)* | 4.90 | .80 |

For surcharge & overprints see #19, O3, O5, O8, O13, O15, O20, O22, O30-O31, O53.

A5

A6

**1916**

| | | | | |
|---|---|---|---|---|
| 15 | A5 | 7ch red violet | 3.50 | .75 |
| 16 | A6 | 14ch orange | 4.00 | 3.75 |

For overprints see Nos. O11-O12, O34-O35.

A7

A8

**1920-33**

| | | | | |
|---|---|---|---|---|
| 17 | A7 | 1 ¼ch claret | .80 | .80 |
| 18 | A7 | 1 ½ch light red ('33) | 4.00 | .25 |

For surcharges see Nos. 27-28. For overprints see Nos. O7, O17, O28-O29, O38, O56.

No. 12 and Type of 1888 Surcharged

**1921**

| | | | | |
|---|---|---|---|---|
| 19 | A3 | 1ca on 4ca rose | .25 | .25 |
| *a.* | | Inverted surcharge | 37.50 | 16.00 |
| 20 | A1 | 5ca on 1ch dull bl (R) | 1.50 | .25 |
| *a.* | | Inverted surcharge | 19.00 | 12.50 |
| *b.* | | Double surcharge | 100.00 | 67.50 |

**1921-32**

| | | | | |
|---|---|---|---|---|
| 21 | A8 | 5ca bister | 1.20 | .25 |
| 22 | A8 | 5ca brown ('32) | 4.00 | .25 |
| 23 | A8 | 10ca rose | .60 | .25 |
| | | *Nos. 21-23 (3)* | 5.80 | .75 |

For surcharges & overprints see #29-30, O9-O10, O14, O16, O19, O21, O23, O36-O37.

Sri Padmanabha Shrine at Trivandrum A9

State Chariot — A10

Maharaja Sir Bala Rama Varma — A11

**1931, Nov. 6**

| | | | | |
|---|---|---|---|---|
| 24 | A9 | 6ca emerald & black | 2.40 | 2.40 |
| 25 | A10 | 10ca ultra & black | 1.90 | 1.00 |
| 26 | A11 | 3ch violet & black | 4.00 | 4.50 |
| | | *Nos. 24-26 (3)* | 8.30 | 7.90 |

Investiture of Sir Bala Rama Varma with full ruling powers.

No. 17 Surcharged

**1932, Jan. 14**

| | | | | |
|---|---|---|---|---|
| 27 | A7 | 1ca on 1 ¼ch claret | .25 | *.75* |
| *a.* | | Inverted surcharge | 6.50 | *10.00* |
| *b.* | | Double surcharge | 47.50 | 47.50 |
| 28 | A7 | 2ca on 1 ¼ch claret | .25 | .25 |
| *a.* | | Inverted surcharge | 6.50 | *10.00* |
| *b.* | | Double surcharge | 42.50 | |
| *c.* | | Pair, one without surcharge | 180.00 | 190.00 |

Type of 1932 and No. 23 Surcharged like Nos. 19-20

**1932, Mar. 5**

| | | | | |
|---|---|---|---|---|
| 29 | A8 | 1ca on 5ca vio brown | .25 | .25 |
| *a.* | | Inverted surcharge | 11.00 | *15.00* |
| *b.* | | Double surcharge | | |
| *c.* | | Pair, one without surcharge | 180.00 | |
| 30 | A8 | 2ca on 10ca rose | .25 | .25 |
| *a.* | | Inverted surcharge | 7.50 | *12.00* |
| *b.* | | Double surcharge | 32.50 | *35.00* |

Untouchables Entering Temple and Maharaja — A12

Designs: Different temples and frames.

***Perf. 11½, 12½***

**1937, Mar. 29** **Litho.**

| | | | | |
|---|---|---|---|---|
| 32 | A12 | 6ca carmine | 3.75 | 1.90 |
| 33 | A12 | 12ca ultramarine | 5.25 | .60 |
| 34 | A12 | 1 ½ch light green | 2.25 | *3.00* |
| 35 | A12 | 3ch purple | 6.50 | 3.50 |
| | | *Nos. 32-35 (4)* | 17.75 | 9.00 |

Temple Entry Bill.

Lake Ashtamudi A13

A14

A15

Sir Bala Rama Varma — A16

Sri Padmanabha Shrine — A17

View of Cape Comerin A18

Pachipara Reservoir A19

***Perf. 11, 12, 12½ or Compound***

**1939, May 9** **Litho.**

| | | | | |
|---|---|---|---|---|
| 36 | A13 | 1ch yellow green | 8.25 | .25 |
| 37 | A14 | 1 ½ch carmine | 5.25 | *6.75* |
| *a.* | | Perf. 13½ | 27.50 | *100.00* |
| 38 | A15 | 2ch orange | 10.00 | 3.50 |
| 39 | A16 | 3ch chocolate | 9.50 | .25 |
| 40 | A17 | 4ch henna brown | 12.50 | .60 |
| 41 | A18 | 7ch light blue | 16.00 | *30.00* |
| 42 | A19 | 14ch turq green | 10.00 | *100.00* |
| | | *Nos. 36-42 (7)* | 71.50 | 141.35 |

27th birthday of Maharaja Sir Bala Rama Varma.

For surcharges and overprints see Nos. 45, O45-O51, Travancore-Cochin 3-7, O3-O7.

Maharaja Sir Bala Rama Varma and Aruvikara Falls A20

Maharaja and Marthanda Varma Bridge, Alwaye A21

**1941, Oct. 20** **Typo.**

| | | | | |
|---|---|---|---|---|
| 43 | A20 | 6ca violet black | 11.00 | .25 |
| 44 | A21 | ¾ch dull brown | 12.50 | .30 |

29th birthday of the Maharaja, Oct. 20, 1941.

For overprints & surcharges see #46-47, 49, O54-O55, Travancore-Cochin 1, O1.

Stamps and Types of 1939-41 Surcharged in Black

***Perf. 11, 12½***

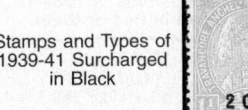

**1943, Sept. 17** **Wmk. 43**

| | | | | |
|---|---|---|---|---|
| 45 | A14 | 2ca on 1 ½ch carmine | 2.25 | 1.90 |
| 46 | A21 | 4ca on ¾ch dull brown | 6.00 | .45 |
| 47 | A20 | 8ca on 6ca red | 7.00 | .25 |
| | | *Nos. 45-47 (3)* | 15.25 | 2.60 |

For overprints see Nos. O57-O59.

Maharaja Sir Bala Rama Varma — A22

**1946, Oct. 24** **Typo.** ***Perf. 11, 12***

| | | | | |
|---|---|---|---|---|
| 48 | A22 | 8ca rose red | 1.90 | *3.00* |

For overprint see No. O60. For surcharges see Travancore-Cochin Nos. 2, O2.

No. O54 Overprinted "SPECIAL" Vertically in Orange

**1946** ***Perf. 12½***

| | | | | |
|---|---|---|---|---|
| 49 | A20 | 6ca violet black | 9.50 | 4.50 |

---

## OFFICIAL STAMPS

Nos. O1-O60 were issued without gum.

Regular Issues of 1889-1911 Overprinted in Red or Black

***Perf. 12, 12½***

**1911, Aug. 16** **Wmk. 43**

| | | | | |
|---|---|---|---|---|
| O1 | A1 | 1ch indigo (R) | 1.10 | .25 |
| *a.* | | Inverted overprint | 10.00 | 6.50 |
| *b.* | | "nO" for "On" | 120.00 | 120.00 |
| *c.* | | Double overprint | 100.00 | 75.00 |
| O2 | A1 | 2ch scarlet | .50 | .25 |
| *a.* | | Inverted overprint | 12.00 | 12.00 |
| O3 | A4 | 3ch purple | .50 | .25 |
| *a.* | | Inverted overprint | 15.00 | 15.00 |
| *b.* | | Double overprint | 120.00 | 100.00 |
| O4 | A1 | 4ch dark green | .80 | .25 |
| *a.* | | Inverted overprint | 82.50 | 19.00 |
| *b.* | | Double overprint | 190.00 | 140.00 |
| | | *Nos. O1-O4 (4)* | 2.90 | 1.00 |

Same Ovpt. on Regular Issues of 1889-1920

**1918-20**

| | | | | |
|---|---|---|---|---|
| O5 | A3 | 4ca rose | .25 | .25 |
| *a.* | | Imperf., pair | 450.00 | 450.00 |
| *b.* | | Inverted overprint | | 120.00 |
| *c.* | | Double overprint | 180.00 | 140.00 |
| O6 | A1 | ½ch violet (R) | 3.75 | .35 |
| *a.* | | Inverted overprint | 19.00 | 5.25 |
| O7 | A7 | 1 ¼ch claret | .60 | .25 |
| *a.* | | Inverted overprint | 14.00 | 12.00 |
| *b.* | | Double overprint | 67.50 | |
| | | *Nos. O5-O7 (3)* | 4.60 | .85 |

Same Ovpt. on Regular Issues of 1909-21

**1921**

| | | | | |
|---|---|---|---|---|
| O8 | A1 | 6ca red brown | .45 | .25 |
| *a.* | | Inverted overprint | 200.00 | 180.00 |
| O9 | A8 | 10ca rose | 1.00 | .25 |
| *a.* | | Inverted overprint | | 27.50 |
| *b.* | | Double overprint | 140.00 | 110.00 |

Same Overprint on Regular Issue of 1921

**1922**

| | | | | |
|---|---|---|---|---|
| O10 | A8 | 5ca bister | 1.40 | .25 |
| *a.* | | Inverted overprint | 21.00 | 13.50 |

For surcharge see No. O39B.

Same Overprint on Regular Issue of 1916

**1925**

| | | | | |
|---|---|---|---|---|
| O11 | A5 | 7ch plum | 2.50 | .45 |
| O12 | A6 | 14ch orange | 3.25 | .60 |

Same Overprint in Blue on Regular Issues of 1889-1921

| | | | | |
|---|---|---|---|---|
| O13 | A3 | 4ca rose | 80.00 | *1.00* |
| O14 | A8 | 5ca bister | .90 | .25 |
| O15 | A1 | 6ca red brown | 19.00 | 2.50 |
| O16 | A8 | 10ca rose | 120.00 | 32.50 |
| O17 | A7 | 1 ¼ch claret | | — 120.00 |
| O18 | A1 | 4ch dark green | | — 100.00 |

Some authorities question the authenticity of No. O14.

**1930** **Black Overprint**

| | | | | |
|---|---|---|---|---|
| O19 | A8 | 5ca brown | .35 | *.90* |

Regular Issues of 1889-1932 Overprinted in Black or Red

**1930-34**

| | | | | |
|---|---|---|---|---|
| O20 | A3 | 4ca rose | 18.00 | *60.00* |
| O21 | A8 | 5ca brown | 35.00 | 14.00 |
| *a.* | | Inverted overprint | 100.00 | 100.00 |
| O22 | A1 | 6ca org brown | .25 | .25 |
| O23 | A8 | 10ca rose | 6.50 | 4.50 |
| O24 | A1 | ½ch violet ('34) | .75 | .25 |
| O25 | A1 | ½ch purple (R) | .25 | .25 |

| | | | | |
|---|---|---|---|---|
| O26 | A2 | ¾ch black (R) ('32) | .60 | .45 |
| O27 | A2 | ¾ch brt vio ('33) | .45 | .25 |
| O27B | A1 | 1ch gray blue (R) ('33) | 1.50 | .35 |
| O28 | A7 | 1¼ch claret | 2.10 | *2.40* |
| O29 | A7 | 1½ch dull red ('32) | .60 | .25 |
| O30 | A4 | 3ch purple ('33) | 1.90 | .90 |
| O31 | A4 | 3ch purple (R) | 1.20 | .25 |
| O32 | A1 | 4ch deep green (R) | 2.25 | .25 |
| O33 | A1 | 4ch deep green | 2.75 | 1.40 |
| O34 | A5 | 7ch maroon | 1.90 | .45 |
| O35 | A6 | 14ch orange ('31) | 2.50 | .60 |
| | | *Nos. O20-O35 (17)* | 78.50 | 86.80 |

The overprint on Nos. O22, O26 and O28 is smaller than the illustration. There are two sizes of the overprint on No. O27.

For surcharges see Nos. O39, O40-O41.

Type of 1921-32 and No. 17 Surcharged and Overprinted

**1932**

| | | | | |
|---|---|---|---|---|
| O36 | A8 | 6ca on 5ca dk brown | .25 | *.45* |
| O36A | A8 | 6ca on 5ca bister | 2.50 | *3.00* |
| O37 | A8 | 12ca on 10a rose | .25 | .25 |
| a. | | New value inverted | 9.00 | *11.00* |
| O38 | A7 | 1ch8ca on 1¼ch cl | .50 | .30 |
| | | *Nos. O36-O38 (4)* | 3.50 | *4.00* |

Nos. O21, O10, O23 and O28 Surcharged in Black

| | | | | |
|---|---|---|---|---|
| O39 | A8 | 6ca on 5ca dk brown | .30 | .45 |
| a. | | New value inverted | 16.00 | *19.00* |
| O39B | A8 | 6ca on 5ca bis | .60 | .25 |
| O40 | A8 | 12ca on 10ca rose | 3.00 | 2.25 |
| a. | | New value inverted | 10.00 | 10.00 |
| b. | | "On S S" inverted | 24.00 | 27.50 |
| c. | | Ovpt. & surch. inverted | 60.00 | *62.50* |
| O41 | A7 | 1ch8ca on 1¼ch cl | 4.50 | 1.90 |
| a. | | New value inverted | | 150.00 |
| | | *Nos. O39-O41 (4)* | 8.40 | 4.85 |

Regular Issue of 1889-94 Overprinted

**1933**

O42 A1 ½ch violet 1.75 1.25

Regular Issue of 1901 Overprinted in Red

**1933**

O44 A2 ¾ch black .50 .25

**Regular Issue of 1939 Overprinted in Black**

a 

**1939** ***Perf. 11, 12, 12½***

| | | | | |
|---|---|---|---|---|
| O45 | A13 | 1ch yellow green | 10.00 | .50 |
| a. | | Inverted overprint | 15.00 | 15.00 |
| b. | | Double overprint | 15.00 | 15.00 |
| O46 | A14 | 1½ch carmine | 11.00 | 1.90 |
| a. | | "SESVICE" | | 250.00 |
| O47 | A15 | 2ch orange | 11.00 | 11.00 |
| a. | | "SESVICE" | 190.00 | *210.00* |
| O48 | A16 | 3ch chocolate | 9.50 | .30 |
| a. | | "SESVICE" | 150.00 | 30.00 |
| O49 | A17 | 4ch henna brown | 22.50 | 7.50 |
| O50 | A18 | 7ch light blue | 24.00 | 5.50 |
| O51 | A19 | 14ch turq green | 30.00 | 8.25 |
| | | *Nos. O45-O51 (7)* | 118.00 | 34.95 |

27th birthday of Maharaja Sir Bala Rama Varma.

No. 9 Overprinted — b

**1939** **Wmk. 43** ***Perf. 12.***

O52 A2 ¾ch violet 27.50 .30

No. 13 Overprinted Type "b"

**1941**

O53 A1 6ca red brown 1.20 .45

Nos. 43-44 Overprinted Type "a"

**1941** ***Perf. 12½***

| | | | | |
|---|---|---|---|---|
| O54 | A20 | 6ca violet black | .90 | .75 |
| O55 | A21 | ¾ch dull brown | 9.50 | .25 |

29th birthday of the Maharaja, Oct. 20, 1941.

For overprint see No. 49.

No. 18 Overprinted Type "b"

**1945** ***Perf. 12***

O56 A7 1½ch light red 21.00 12.00

Nos. 45-48 Overprinted Type "a"

**1945-49** ***Perf. 11, 12***

| | | | | |
|---|---|---|---|---|
| O57 | A14 | 2ca on 1½ch car | .90 | *1.50* |
| O58 | A21 | 4ca on ¾ch dull brn | 6.00 | .60 |
| O59 | A20 | 8ca on 6ca red | 5.25 | .45 |
| O60 | A22 | 8ca rose red ('49) | 3.75 | 1.25 |
| a. | | Double impression of stamp | 47.50 | |
| | | *Nos. O57-O60 (4)* | 15.90 | 3.80 |

Travancore stamps became obsolete June 30, 1949.

## TRAVANCORE-COCHIN

ˈtrav-ən-ˌkō̜ə̜r kō-ˈchin

LOCATION — Southern India
AREA — 9,155 sq. mi.
POP. — 7,492,000

The United State of Travancore-Cochin was established July 1, 1949.

**Catalogue values for all unused stamps in this state are for Never Hinged items.**

**Travancore Stamps of 1939-47 Surcharged in Red or Black**

a 

***Perf. 11, 12, 12½***

**1949, July 1** **Wmk. 43**

| | | | | |
|---|---|---|---|---|
| 1 | A20 | 2p on 6ca vio blk (R) | .75 | .30 |
| 2 | A22 | 4p on 8ca rose red | 2.25 | .45 |
| 3 | A13 | ½a on 1ch yel grn | 5.25 | .45 |
| a. | | Inverted surcharge | 7.50 | |
| b. | | "NANA" | 300.00 | 180.00 |
| 4 | A15 | 1a on 2ch orange | 1.10 | .45 |
| 5 | A17 | 2a on 4ch hn brn | 5.00 | .80 |
| a. | | Inverted surcharge | — | 450.00 |
| 6 | A18 | 3a on 7ch lt blue | 9.00 | 5.50 |
| 7 | A19 | 6a on 14ch turq grn | 27.50 | *45.00* |
| | | *Nos. 1-7 (7)* | 50.85 | 52.95 |

For overprints see Nos. O1-O7, O12-O17. For types overprinted see Nos. O18-O23.

Cochin Nos. 80, 91 and Types of 1944-46 Surcharged in Black or Carmine — b

**1949-50** **Wmk. 294** ***Perf. 11, 13***

| | | | | |
|---|---|---|---|---|
| 8 | A15 | 3p on 9p ultra | 18.00 | *35.00* |
| 9 | A16 | 3p on 9p ultra | 4.00 | 3.00 |
| 10 | A16 | 3p on 9p ultra (C) | 8.25 | *4.00* |
| 11 | A16 | 6p on 9p ultra (C) | 2.50 | .60 |
| 12 | A13 | 6p on 1a3p mag ('50) | 8.25 | *6.75* |
| 13 | A15 | 6p on 1a3p magenta | 24.00 | *22.50* |
| 14 | A13 | 1a on 1a9p ultra (C) | 3.50 | *2.10* |
| 15 | A15 | 1a on 1a9p ultra (C) | 5.25 | 3.50 |
| | | *Nos. 8-15 (8)* | 73.75 | 77.45 |

The surcharge exists with line of Hindi characters varying from 16½ to 23mm wide.

For overprints see Nos. O10-O11, O24.

Cochin No. 86 Overprinted

**1949**

15A A15 1a deep orange 9.00 *100.00*

Conch Shell — A23

View of River — A24

**Wmk. 196**

**1950, Oct.** **Litho.** ***Perf. 14***

| | | | | |
|---|---|---|---|---|
| 16 | A23 | 2p rose red | 4.50 | *5.00* |
| 17 | A24 | 4p ultramarine | 5.50 | *24.00* |

Cochin No. 86 and Type of 1948-50 Overprinted in Black

**1950, Apr. 1** **Wmk. 294** ***Perf. 13, 11***

18 A15 1a deep orange 11.00 *100.00*

No. 18 Surcharged in Black

| | | | | |
|---|---|---|---|---|
| 20 | A15 | 6p on 1a deep orange | 6.75 | *82.50* |
| 21 | A15 | 9p on 1a deep orange | 6.50 | *72.50* |

### OFFICIAL STAMPS

Travancore Stamps of 1939-46 Surcharged Type "a" in Red or Black and Overprinted

c 

**1949** **Wmk. 43** ***Perf. 11, 12, 12½***

| | | | | |
|---|---|---|---|---|
| O1 | A20 | 2p on 6ca vio blk (R) | .90 | .70 |
| O2 | A22 | 4p on 8ca rose red | 5.50 | .50 |
| O3 | A13 | ½a on 1ch yel grn | 1.50 | .35 |
| O4 | A15 | 1a on 2ch orange | 24.00 | 11.00 |
| O5 | A17 | 2a on 4ch hn brn | 3.50 | .90 |
| O6 | A18 | 3a on 7ch lt blue | 5.50 | 1.50 |
| O7 | A19 | 6a on 14ch turq grn | 24.00 | 16.00 |
| | | *Nos. O1-O7 (7)* | 64.90 | 30.95 |

Cochin Nos. O90-O91 Surcharged Type "b" in Black

**1950** **Wmk. 294** ***Perf. 11***

| | | | | |
|---|---|---|---|---|
| O8 | A16 | 6p on 3p carmine | 1.90 | 1.10 |
| a. | | Double surcharge | — | 525.00 |
| O9 | A16 | 9p on 4p gray grn | 1.60 | *1.60* |

No. O9 exists with Hindi characters varying from 18 to 22mm wide.

Travancore-Cochin Nos. 14-15 Overprinted "ON C G S"
***Perf. 13***

| | | | | |
|---|---|---|---|---|
| O10 | A13 | 1a on 1a9p ultra | .90 | 1.00 |
| O11 | A15 | 1a on 1a9p ultra | 35.00 | 25.00 |

Nos. 2-7 Overprinted in Black — d

**1949-51** **Wmk. 43** ***Perf. 11, 12½***

| | | | | |
|---|---|---|---|---|
| O12 | A22 | 4p on 8ca rose red | .75 | .30 |
| O13 | A13 | ½a on 1ch yel green | 1.50 | .30 |
| a. | | "AANA" | 260.00 | 85.00 |
| O14 | A15 | 1a on 2ch orange | .60 | .30 |
| O15 | A17 | 2a on 4ch hn brn | 2.25 | 1.60 |
| O16 | A18 | 3a on 7ch lt blue | 2.25 | 1.60 |
| O17 | A19 | 6a on 14ch turq grn | 2.25 | *6.50* |
| | | *Nos. O12-O17 (6)* | 9.60 | 10.60 |

Types of 1949 Overprinted Type "d"

**1951** **Wmk. 294**

| | | | | |
|---|---|---|---|---|
| O18 | A13 | ½a on 1ch yel green | .60 | .60 |
| O19 | A15 | 1a on 2ch orange | .75 | .60 |

Type of 1949 Overprinted Type "c"
**Unwmk.**

O20 A22 4p on 8ca rose red 1.40 1.10

No. O20 is not from an unwatermarked part of sheet with wmk. 294 but is printed on paper entirely without watermark.

Nos. 1, 3 and 5 Overprinted Type "c"
**Wmk. 294**

| | | | | |
|---|---|---|---|---|
| O21 | A13 | ½a on 1ch yel green | 1.10 | .50 |
| O22 | A20 | 2p on 6ca violet black | .25 | *1.00* |
| O23 | A17 | 2a on 4ch henna brn | 1.10 | .75 |
| | | *Nos. O21-O23 (3)* | 2.45 | 2.25 |

No. 9 Overprinted in Black

**1951**

O24 A16 3p on 9p ultra .90 *1.20*

## WADHWAN

wə-ˈdwän

LOCATION — A Feudatory State in Kathiawar Agency, Western India.
AREA — 242 sq. mi.
POP. — 44,259
CAPITAL — Wadhwan

Coat of Arms — A1

**1888 Litho. Unwmk.** ***Pin-perf.***

**Thin Paper**

| | | | | |
|---|---|---|---|---|
| 1 | A1 | ½p black | 160.00 | |

***Perf. 12½***

| | | | | |
|---|---|---|---|---|
| 2 | A1 | ½p black | 30.00 | *100.00* |

**1889** ***Perf. 12 and 12½***

**Thick Paper**

| | | | | |
|---|---|---|---|---|
| 3 | A1 | ½p black | 12.50 | *14.00* |
| | | *Nos. 1-3 (3)* | 202.50 | |

# INDO-CHINA

ˌin-ˌdō-ˈchī-nə

LOCATION — French possessions on the Cambodian Peninsula in southeastern Asia, bordering on the South China Sea and the Gulf of Siam
GOVT. — French Colony and Protectorate
AREA — 280,849 sq. mi.
POP. — 27,030,000 (estimated 1949)
CAPITAL — Hanoi

In 1949, Indo-China was divided into Cambodia, Laos and Viet Nam each issuing its own stamps.

100 Centimes = 1 Franc
100 Cents = 1 Piaster (1918)

### Stamps of French Colonies Surcharged in Black or Red

a

b

**1889 Unwmk. *Perf. 14x13½***

| | | | | |
|---|---|---|---|---|
| 1 | A9(a) | 5c on 35c dp vio, *org* | 14.00 | *12.00* |
| *a.* | | Date in smaller type | 240.00 | 225.00 |
| 2 | A9(b) | 5c on 35c dp vio, *org* (R) | 100.00 | 95.00 |
| *a.* | | Date in smaller type | 200.00 | 200.00 |
| *b.* | | Inverted surcharge, #2 | 1,900. | 1,900. |
| *c.* | | Inverted surcharge, #2a | 2,600. | 2,600. |

Issue dates: No. 1, Jan. 8; No. 2, Jan. 10.
"R" is the Colonial Governor, P. Richaud, "D" is the Saigon P.M. General P. Demars.

For other overprints on designs A3-A27a see various issues of French Offices in China.

Navigation & Commerce — A3

### Name of Colony in Blue or Carmine

**1892-1900 Typo. *Perf. 14x13½***

| | | | | |
|---|---|---|---|---|
| 3 | A3 | 1c blk, *lil bl* | 1.25 | 1.25 |
| 4 | A3 | 2c brn, *buff* | 1.60 | 1.60 |
| 5 | A3 | 4c claret, *lav* | 1.60 | 1.60 |
| 6 | A3 | 5c grn, *grnsh* | 2.40 | 2.40 |
| 7 | A3 | 5c yel grn ('00) | 2.00 | 1.25 |
| 8 | A3 | 10c blk, *lavender* | 7.50 | 2.00 |
| 9 | A3 | 10c red ('00) | 3.50 | 2.00 |
| 10 | A3 | 15c blue, quadrille paper | 37.50 | 2.00 |
| 11 | A3 | 15c gray ('00) | 9.00 | 2.40 |
| 12 | A3 | 20c red, *grn* | 10.00 | 7.00 |
| 13 | A3 | 25c blk, *rose* | 19.00 | 3.75 |
| *a.* | | "INDO-CHINE" omitted | *7,200.* | *7,200.* |
| 14 | A3 | 25c blue ('00) | 22.00 | 5.00 |
| 15 | A3 | 30c brn, *bis* | 26.00 | 7.50 |
| 16 | A3 | 40c red, *straw* | 26.00 | 13.50 |
| 17 | A3 | 50c car, *rose* | 42.00 | 16.00 |
| 18 | A3 | 50c brn, *az* ('00) | 29.00 | 9.50 |
| 19 | A3 | 75c dp vio, *org* | 23.00 | 17.00 |
| *a.* | | "INDO-CHINE" inverted | *7,200.* | *7,200.* |
| 20 | A3 | 1fr brnz grn, *straw* | 55.00 | 36.00 |
| *a.* | | "INDO-CHINE" double | 1,100. | 1,300. |
| 21 | A3 | 5fr red lil, *lav* ('96) | 140.00 | 110.00 |
| | | *Nos. 3-21 (19)* | 458.35 | 241.75 |

Perf. 13½x14 stamps are counterfeits.
For surcharges and overprints see Nos. 22-23, Q2-Q4.

Nos. 11 and 14 Surcharged in Black

**1903**

| | | | | |
|---|---|---|---|---|
| 22 | A3 | 5c on 15c gray | 2.00 | 1.25 |
| 23 | A3 | 15c on 25c blue | 2.50 | 1.60 |

Issue dates: No. 22, Dec. 4; No. 23, Aug. 8.

France — A4

**1904-06**

| | | | | |
|---|---|---|---|---|
| 24 | A4 | 1c olive grn | .80 | .80 |
| 25 | A4 | 2c vio brn, *buff* | 1.25 | .80 |
| 26 | A4 | 4c claret, *bluish* | .80 | .80 |
| 27 | A4 | 5c deep green | 1.25 | .50 |
| 28 | A4 | 10c carmine | 1.60 | .75 |
| 29 | A4 | 15c org brn, *bl* | 1.60 | 1.00 |
| 30 | A4 | 20c red, *grn* | 3.50 | 1.60 |
| 31 | A4 | 25c deep blue | 14.00 | 1.60 |
| 32 | A4 | 30c pale brn | 6.00 | 3.00 |
| 33 | A4 | 35c blk, *yel* ('06) | 22.00 | 3.25 |
| 34 | A4 | 40c blk, *bluish* | 5.50 | 1.60 |
| 35 | A4 | 50c bister brn | 10.50 | 3.00 |
| 36 | A4 | 75c red, *org* | 45.00 | 29.00 |
| 37 | A4 | 1fr pale grn | 21.50 | 8.25 |
| 38 | A4 | 2fr brn, *org* | 52.50 | 40.00 |
| 39 | A4 | 5fr dp vio, *lil* | 220.00 | 180.00 |
| 40 | A4 | 10fr org brn, *grn* | 220.00 | 180.00 |
| | | *Nos. 24-40 (17)* | 627.80 | 455.95 |

For surcharges see Nos. 59-64.

Annamite Girl — A5

Cambodian Girl — A6

Cambodian Woman — A7

Annamite Women — A8

Hmong Woman — A9

Laotian Woman — A10

Cambodian Woman — A11

**1907 *Perf. 14x13½***

| | | | | |
|---|---|---|---|---|
| 41 | A5 | 1c ol brn & blk | .40 | .40 |
| 42 | A5 | 2c yel brn & blk | .40 | .40 |
| 43 | A5 | 4c blue & blk | 1.25 | 1.25 |
| 44 | A5 | 5c grn & blk | 1.60 | .80 |
| 45 | A5 | 10c red & blk | 1.60 | .55 |
| 46 | A5 | 15c vio & blk | 1.40 | 1.25 |
| 47 | A6 | 20c vio & blk | 3.00 | 1.60 |
| 48 | A6 | 25c bl & blk | 7.25 | 1.25 |
| 49 | A6 | 30c brn & blk | 12.00 | 6.50 |
| 50 | A6 | 35c ol grn & blk | 2.75 | 2.25 |
| 51 | A6 | 40c yel brn & blk | 4.50 | 2.00 |
| 52 | A6 | 45c org & blk | 10.50 | 6.50 |
| 53 | A6 | 50c car & blk | 15.00 | 5.75 |
| | | ***Perf. 13½x14*** | | |
| 54 | A7 | 75c ver & blk | 12.00 | 7.75 |
| 55 | A8 | 1fr car & blk | 55.00 | 20.00 |
| 56 | A9 | 2fr grn & blk | 17.00 | 16.00 |
| 57 | A10 | 5fr blue & blk | 42.50 | *47.50* |
| 58 | A11 | 10fr pur & blk | 92.50 | *95.00* |
| | | *Nos. 41-58 (18)* | 280.65 | 216.75 |

For surcharges see Nos. 65-93, B1-B7.

### Stamps of 1904-06 Surcharged in Black or Carmine

**1912, Nov. *Perf. 14x13½***

| | | | | |
|---|---|---|---|---|
| 59 | A4 | 5c on 4c cl, *bluish* | 6.00 | 6.00 |
| 60 | A4 | 5c on 15c org brn, *bl* (C) | 1.25 | 1.25 |
| 61 | A4 | 5c on 30c pale brn | 1.60 | 1.60 |
| 62 | A4 | 10c on 40c blk, *bluish* (C) | 1.60 | 1.60 |
| 63 | A4 | 10c on 50c bis brn (C) | 2.00 | 2.00 |
| 64 | A4 | 10c on 75c red, *org* | 5.25 | 5.25 |
| | | *Nos. 59-64 (6)* | 17.70 | 17.70 |

Two spacings between the surcharged numerals are found on Nos. 59-64.

Nos. 41-58 Surcharged in Cents or Piasters in Black, Red or Blue

**1919, Jan.**

| | | | | |
|---|---|---|---|---|
| 65 | A5 | 2/5c on 1c | .80 | .55 |
| 66 | A5 | 4/5c on 2c | 1.25 | .90 |
| 67 | A5 | 1 3/5c on 4c (R) | 2.00 | .80 |
| 68 | A5 | 2c on 5c | 1.60 | .30 |
| *a.* | | Inverted surcharge | 135.00 | |
| 69 | A5 | 4c on 10c (Bl) | 1.60 | .55 |
| *a.* | | Closed "4" | 9.00 | 3.25 |
| *b.* | | Double surcharge | 130.00 | |
| 70 | A5 | 6c on 15c | 6.50 | 1.25 |
| *a.* | | Inverted surcharge | 130.00 | |
| 71 | A6 | 8c on 20c | 5.25 | 1.90 |
| 72 | A6 | 10c on 25c | 5.00 | 1.00 |
| 73 | A6 | 12c on 30c | 6.75 | 1.10 |
| 74 | A6 | 14c on 35c | 3.25 | .75 |
| *a.* | | Closed "4" | 12.00 | 5.75 |
| 75 | A6 | 16c on 40c | 6.50 | 2.00 |
| 76 | A6 | 18c on 45c | 8.00 | 2.75 |
| 77 | A6 | 20c on 50c (Bl) | 12.00 | 1.25 |
| 78 | A7 | 30c on 75c (Bl) | 16.00 | 2.75 |
| 79 | A8 | 40c on 1fr (Bl) | 24.00 | 2.75 |
| 80 | A9 | 80c on 2fr (R) | 27.50 | 8.50 |
| *a.* | | Double surcharge | 350.00 | 275.00 |
| 81 | A10 | 2pi on 5fr (R) | 110.00 | 110.00 |
| 82 | A11 | 4pi on 10fr (R) | 150.00 | 150.00 |
| | | *Nos. 65-82 (18)* | 388.00 | 289.10 |

### Types of 1907 Issue Surcharged with New Values in Black or Red

Nos. 88-92

No. 93

**1922**

| | | | |
|---|---|---|---|
| 88 | A5 | 1c on 5c ocher & blk | 1.60 |
| 89 | A5 | 2c on 10c gray grn & blk | 2.40 |
| 90 | A6 | 6c on 30c lt red & blk | 2.75 |
| 91 | A6 | 10c on 50c lt bl & blk | 2.75 |
| 92 | A6 | 11c on 55c vio & blk, *bluish* | 2.90 |
| 93 | A6 | 12c on 60c lt bl & blk, *pnksh* (R) | 2.75 |
| | | *Nos. 88-93 (6)* | 15.15 |

Nos. 88-93 were sold officially in Paris but were never placed in use in the colony.

Nos. 88-93 exist without surcharge but were not regularly issued in that condition. Value, Nos. 88-89, each $190; Nos. 90-91, each $140; Nos. 92-93, each $100.

A12

A13

Two types of "CENTS" for the 4c, 5c, 10c-12c values: Type 1, thin font (April 1922); type 2, thicker font (Oct. 1922 and later printings). All other denominations are type 2. For more detailed listings, see the *Scott Classic Specialized Catalogue of Stamps and Covers.*

### "CENTS" below Numerals

**1922-23 *Perf. 14x13½***

| | | | | |
|---|---|---|---|---|
| 94 | A12 | 1/10c blk & sal ('23) | .25 | .25 |
| *a.* | | Double impression of frame | | |
| 95 | A12 | 1/5c blue & blk | .25 | .25 |
| 96 | A12 | 2/5c ol brn & blk | .25 | .25 |
| *a.* | | Head and value doubled | 260.00 | 260.00 |
| 97 | A12 | 4/5c rose & blk, *lav* | .40 | .35 |
| 98 | A12 | 1c yel brn & blk | .25 | .25 |
| 99 | A12 | 2c gray grn & blk | .75 | .55 |
| 100 | A12 | 3c vio & blk | .35 | .35 |
| 101 | A12 | 4c org & blk, type 2 | .35 | .35 |
| *b.* | | Head and value doubled | 175.00 | 175.00 |
| 102 | A12 | 5c car & blk, type 2 | .35 | .35 |
| *b.* | | Head and value doubled | 290.00 | 290.00 |
| 103 | A13 | 6c dl red & blk | .50 | .30 |
| 104 | A13 | 7c grn & blk | .75 | .65 |
| 105 | A13 | 8c blk, *lav* | 2.00 | 1.25 |
| 106 | A13 | 9c ocher & blk, *grnsh* | 1.50 | .90 |
| 107 | A13 | 10c bl & blk, type 2 | .80 | .75 |
| 108 | A13 | 11c vio & blk, type 2 | .75 | .75 |
| 109 | A13 | 12c brn & blk, type 2 | .55 | .55 |
| *b.* | | Head and value double (11c+12c) | 450.00 | 450.00 |
| 110 | A13 | 15c org & blk | 1.00 | .80 |
| 111 | A13 | 20c bl & blk, *straw* | 1.60 | .80 |
| 112 | A13 | 40c ver & blk, *bluish* | 2.75 | 1.40 |
| 113 | A13 | 1pi bl grn & blk, *grnsh* | 5.00 | 5.25 |
| 114 | A13 | 2pi vio brn & blk, *pnksh* | 13.00 | 13.00 |
| | | *Nos. 94-114 (21)* | 33.40 | 29.35 |

For overprints see Nos. O17-O32.

Plowing near Tower of Confucius A14

Ha Long Bay A15

Angkor Wat, Cambodia A16

Carving Wood A17

That Luang Temple, Laos A18

Founding of Saigon A19

**1927, Sept. 26**

| | | | | |
|---|---|---|---|---|
| 115 | A14 | 1/10c lt olive grn | .25 | .25 |
| 116 | A14 | 1/5c yellow | .25 | .25 |
| 117 | A14 | 2/5c light blue | .25 | .25 |
| 118 | A14 | 4/5c dp brn | .55 | .55 |
| 119 | A14 | 1c orange | .65 | .30 |
| 120 | A14 | 2c blue grn | 1.10 | .50 |
| 121 | A14 | 3c indigo | .70 | .30 |
| 122 | A14 | 4c lil rose | 1.60 | 1.25 |
| 123 | A14 | 5c dp vio | .80 | .30 |
| *a.* | | Booklet pane of 10 | *200.00* | |
| 124 | A15 | 6c deep red | 2.10 | .80 |
| *a.* | | Booklet pane of 10 | *200.00* | |
| 125 | A15 | 7c lt brn | 1.50 | .80 |
| 126 | A15 | 8c gray green | 2.10 | 1.00 |
| 127 | A15 | 9c red vio | 1.50 | 1.00 |
| 128 | A15 | 10c light blue | 2.00 | 1.25 |
| 129 | A15 | 11c orange | 2.00 | 1.25 |

| | | | | |
|---|---|---|---|---|
| **130** | A15 | 12c myrtle grn | 1.50 | 1.00 |
| **131** | A16 | 15c dl rose & ol brn | 7.50 | 7.50 |
| **132** | A16 | 20c vio & slate | 4.00 | 2.40 |
| **133** | A17 | 25c org brn & lil rose | 8.00 | 6.50 |
| **134** | A17 | 30c dp bl & ol gray | 5.00 | 4.00 |
| **135** | A18 | 40c ver & lt bl | 7.50 | 3.25 |
| **136** | A18 | 50c lt grn & slate | 10.00 | 3.25 |
| **137** | A19 | 1pi dk bl, blk & yel | 22.00 | 9.50 |
| *a.* | | Yellow omitted | 275.00 | |
| **138** | A19 | 2pi red, dp bl & org | 27.50 | 16.50 |
| | | *Nos. 115-138 (24)* | 110.35 | 63.95 |

Common Design Types pictured following the introduction.

### Colonial Exposition Issue

Common Design Types Surcharged

No. 140

No. 141

No. 142

**1931, Apr. 13 Engr. *Perf. 12½***

**Name of Country in Black**

| | | | | |
|---|---|---|---|---|
| **140** | CD71 | 4c on 50c violet | 3.25 | 3.25 |
| **141** | CD72 | 6c on 90c red org | 3.25 | 3.25 |
| **142** | CD73 | 10c on 1.50fr dl bl | 4.00 | 4.00 |
| | | *Nos. 140-142 (3)* | 10.50 | 10.50 |
| | | Set, never hinged | 17.50 | |

Junk — A20

Tower at Ruins of Angkor Thom — A21

Planting Rice — A22

Apsaras, Celestial Dancer A23

**1931-41 Photo. *Perf. 13½x13***

| | | | | |
|---|---|---|---|---|
| **143** | A20 | 1/10c Prus blue | .25 | .25 |
| **144** | A20 | 1/5c lake | .25 | .25 |
| **145** | A20 | 2/5c org red | .25 | .25 |
| **146** | A20 | 1/2c red brn | .25 | .25 |
| **147** | A20 | 4/5c dk vio | .25 | .25 |
| **148** | A20 | 1c blk brn | .25 | .25 |
| **149** | A20 | 2c dk grn | .25 | .25 |
| **150** | A21 | 3c dp brn | .25 | .25 |
| **151** | A21 | 3c dk grn ('34) | 5.75 | 1.60 |
| **152** | A21 | 4c dk bl | 1.25 | .50 |
| **153** | A21 | 4c dk grn ('38) | .80 | .55 |
| **153A** | A21 | 4c yel org ('40) | .40 | .40 |
| **154** | A21 | 5c dp vio | .30 | .30 |
| **154A** | A21 | 5c dp grn ('41) | .40 | .40 |
| **155** | A21 | 6c org red | .25 | .25 |
| *a.* | | Bklt. pane 5 + 1 label | 100.00 | |
| **156** | A21 | 7c blk ('38) | .30 | .30 |
| **157** | A21 | 8c rose lake ('38) | .40 | .40 |
| **157A** | A21 | 9c blk, *yel* ('41) | .75 | .75 |
| **158** | A22 | 10c dark blue | .65 | .50 |
| **158A** | A22 | 10c ultra, *pink* ('41) | .55 | .55 |
| **159** | A22 | 15c dk brn | 5.75 | 1.40 |
| **160** | A22 | 15c dk bl ('33) | .25 | .25 |
| **161** | A22 | 18c blue ('38) | .75 | .50 |
| **162** | A22 | 20c rose | .30 | .25 |
| **163** | A22 | 21c olive grn | .30 | .30 |
| **164** | A22 | 22c dk grn ('38) | .55 | .55 |
| **165** | A22 | 25c dp vio | 3.25 | 1.60 |
| **165A** | A22 | 25c dk bl ('41) | .55 | .55 |
| **166** | A22 | 30c org brn ('32) | .50 | .30 |

***Perf. 13½***

| | | | | |
|---|---|---|---|---|
| **167** | A23 | 50c dk brn | .75 | .25 |
| **168** | A23 | 60c dl vio ('32) | .90 | .65 |
| **168A** | A23 | 70c lt bl ('41) | .55 | .55 |
| **169** | A23 | 1pi yel grn | .90 | .65 |
| **170** | A23 | 2pi red | 1.10 | .75 |
| | | *Nos. 143-170 (34)* | 30.20 | 17.05 |

Nos. 166, 167, 169 and 170 were issued without the letters "RF" in 1943, by the Vichy Government.

For surcharge & overprints see #214A, O1-O16.

Emperor Bao-Dai A24

King Sisowath Monivong A25

### For Use in Annam

**1936, Nov. 20 Engr. *Perf. 13***

| | | | | |
|---|---|---|---|---|
| **171** | A24 | 1c brown | 1.00 | 1.00 |
| **172** | A24 | 2c green | 1.00 | 1.00 |
| **173** | A24 | 4c violet | 1.00 | 1.00 |
| **174** | A24 | 5c red brn | 1.50 | 1.50 |
| **175** | A24 | 10c lil rose | 2.00 | 2.00 |
| **176** | A24 | 15c ultra | 2.75 | 2.75 |
| **177** | A24 | 20c scarlet | 2.75 | 2.75 |
| **178** | A24 | 30c plum | 3.50 | 3.50 |
| **179** | A24 | 50c slate grn | 3.50 | 3.50 |
| **180** | A24 | 1pi rose vio | 4.50 | 4.50 |
| **181** | A24 | 2pi black | 5.25 | 5.25 |
| | | *Nos. 171-181 (11)* | 28.75 | 28.75 |

### For Use in Cambodia

| | | | | |
|---|---|---|---|---|
| **182** | A25 | 1c brown | 1.00 | 1.00 |
| **183** | A25 | 2c green | 1.00 | 1.00 |
| **184** | A25 | 4c violet | 1.10 | 1.10 |
| **185** | A25 | 5c red brn | 1.10 | 1.10 |
| **186** | A25 | 10c lil rose | 2.40 | 2.40 |
| **187** | A25 | 15c ultra | 3.25 | 3.25 |
| **188** | A25 | 20c scarlet | 2.75 | 2.75 |
| **189** | A25 | 30c plum | 3.25 | 3.25 |
| **190** | A25 | 50c slate grn | 3.25 | 3.25 |
| **191** | A25 | 1pi rose vio | 4.00 | 4.00 |
| **192** | A25 | 2pi black | 5.25 | 5.25 |
| | | *Nos. 182-192 (11)* | 28.35 | 28.35 |

### Paris International Exposition Issue

Common Design Types

**1937, Apr. 15**

| | | | | |
|---|---|---|---|---|
| **193** | CD74 | 2c dp vio | 1.60 | 1.60 |
| **194** | CD75 | 3c dk grn | 1.10 | 1.10 |
| **195** | CD76 | 4c car rose | 1.10 | 1.10 |
| **196** | CD77 | 6c dk brn | 1.10 | 1.10 |
| **197** | CD78 | 9c red | 1.10 | 1.10 |
| **198** | CD79 | 15c ultra | 1.25 | 1.25 |
| | | *Nos. 193-198 (6)* | 7.25 | 7.25 |
| | | Set, never hinged | 11.50 | |

### Colonial Arts Exhibition Issue

Souvenir Sheet

Common Design Type

**1937, Apr. 15 *Imperf.***

| | | | | |
|---|---|---|---|---|
| **199** | CD79 | 30c dull violet | 9.00 | *12.00* |
| | | Never hinged | 14.50 | |

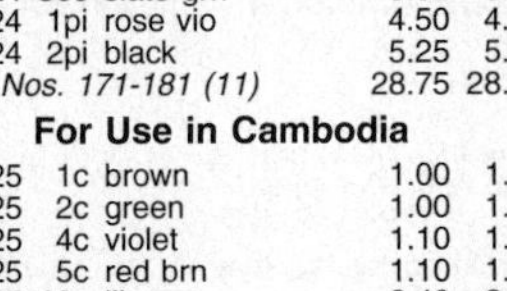

Governor-General Paul Doumer — A26

**1938, June 8 Photo. *Perf. 13½x13***

| | | | | |
|---|---|---|---|---|
| **200** | A26 | 5c rose car | 1.00 | .65 |
| **201** | A26 | 6c brown | 1.10 | 1.10 |
| **202** | A26 | 18c brt bl | 1.10 | 1.10 |
| | | *Nos. 200-202,C18 (4)* | 3.95 | 3.10 |
| | | Set, never hinged | 6.00 | |

Trans-Indo-Chinese Railway, 35th anniv.

### New York World's Fair Issue

Common Design Type

**1939, May 10 Engr. *Perf. 12½x12***

| | | | | |
|---|---|---|---|---|
| **203** | CD82 | 13c car lake | .80 | .80 |
| | | Never hinged | 1.40 | |
| **204** | CD82 | 23c ultra | 1.25 | 1.25 |
| | | Never hinged | 2.25 | |

Mot Cot Pagoda, Hanoi — A27

**1939, June 12 *Perf. 13***

| | | | | |
|---|---|---|---|---|
| **205** | A27 | 6c blk brn | 1.10 | 1.10 |
| **206** | A27 | 9c vermilion | 1.10 | 1.10 |
| **207** | A27 | 23c ultra | 1.10 | 1.10 |
| **208** | A27 | 39c rose vio | 1.50 | 1.50 |
| | | *Nos. 205-208 (4)* | 4.80 | 4.80 |
| | | Set, never hinged | 7.25 | |

Golden Gate International Exposition.

Angkor Wat and Marshal Pétain A27a

**1941 Engr. *Perf. 12½x12***

| | | | | |
|---|---|---|---|---|
| **209** | A27a | 10c dk car | .80 | |
| **209A** | A27a | 25c blue | .80 | |

Nos. 209-209A were issued by the Vichy government in France, but were not placed on sale in Indo-China.

For overprints, see Nos. 262-263. For surcharges, see B21A-B21B.

**Gum**

#210-261 issued without gum.

### Imperfs

Many issues between Nos. 209-263, B19A-B26 and C1-C28, plus some postage dues and official stamps, exist imperf.

King Norodom Sihanouk of Cambodia A28

Harnessed Elephant on Parade A29

***Pin-perf. 12½***

**1941, Oct. 15 Unwmk. Litho.**

| | | | | |
|---|---|---|---|---|
| **210** | A28 | 1c red org | 1.60 | 1.60 |
| **211** | A28 | 6c violet | 3.25 | 3.25 |
| **212** | A28 | 25c dp ultra | 21.00 | 21.00 |
| | | *Nos. 210-212 (3)* | 25.85 | 25.85 |

Coronation of Norodom Sihanouk, King of Cambodia, October, 1941.

**1942, Mar. 29**

| | | | | |
|---|---|---|---|---|
| **213** | A29 | 3c reddish brown | 2.00 | 1.60 |
| **214** | A29 | 6c crimson | 2.00 | 1.60 |

Fête of Nam-Giao in Annam.

No. 165 Surcharged in Black

**1942 *Perf. 13***

| | | | | |
|---|---|---|---|---|
| **214A** | A22 | 10c on 25c dp vio | .50 | .30 |

View of Saigon Fair — A30

**1942, Dec. 20 *Perf. 13½***

| | | | | |
|---|---|---|---|---|
| **215** | A30 | 6c carmine rose | .80 | .80 |

Saigon Fair of 1942.

Nam-Phuong, Empress of Annam — A31

Marshal Pétain — A32

**1942, Sept. 1 *Pin-perf. 11½***

| | | | | |
|---|---|---|---|---|
| **216** | A31 | 6c carmine rose | 1.25 | .80 |

***Perf. 11½, 12, 13½ and Compound***

**1942-44**

| | | | | |
|---|---|---|---|---|
| **217** | A32 | 1c blk brn | .35 | .35 |
| **218** | A32 | 3c olive brn ('43) | .35 | .35 |
| **219** | A32 | 6c rose red | .55 | .55 |
| **220** | A32 | 10c dull grn ('43) | 1.20 | 1.20 |
| **221** | A32 | 40c dk blue ('43) | 1.60 | 1.60 |
| **222** | A32 | 40c slate bl ('44) | .80 | *1.25* |
| | | *Nos. 217-222 (6)* | 4.85 | 5.30 |

Values are for the lowest-valued perforation varieties.

Bao-Dai, Emperor of Annam A33

Norodom Sihanouk, King of Cambodia A34

**1942 *Perf. 13½***

| | | | | |
|---|---|---|---|---|
| **223** | A33 | 1/2c brown | 1.25 | *1.60* |
| **224** | A33 | 6c carmine rose | 1.25 | 1.25 |

Issue dates: 1/2c, Nov. 1; 6c, Sept. 1.

**1943 *Perf. 12***

| | | | | |
|---|---|---|---|---|
| **225** | A34 | 1c brown | 1.25 | .80 |
| *a.* | | Perf. 13¾ | 8.00 | 8.00 |
| **226** | A34 | 6c red | 1.00 | .55 |
| *a.* | | Perf. 13¾ | 8.00 | 8.00 |

Issue dates: 1c, Mar. 10; 6c, May 10.

### Types of 1931-32 Without "RF"

**1943 Photo. *Perf. 13½x13***

| | | | | |
|---|---|---|---|---|
| **226A** | A22 | 30c orange brown | 1.60 | |
| **226B** | A23 | 50c dark brown | 1.60 | |
| **226C** | A23 | 1pi yellow green | 2.75 | |
| **226D** | A23 | 2pi red | 3.50 | |
| | | *Nos. 226A-226D (4)* | 9.45 | |

Nos. 226A-226D were issued by the Vichy government in France, but were not placed on sale in Indo-China.

Sisavang-Vong, King of Laos — A35

Family, Country and Labor — A36

**1943** ***Perf. 12***

**227** A35 1c bister brown .80 *1.25*
*a.* Perf. 13¾ 10.00 10.00
**228** A35 6c carmine rose 1.25 .65
*a.* Perf. 11½x12 32.50 32.50
*b.* Perf. 13¾ 32.50 32.50

Issue dates: 1c, Mar. 10; 6c, June 1.

**1943, Nov. 5** ***Perf. 12***

**229** A36 6c carmine rose .65 .50
*a.* Perf. 11½ .80 .80

National revolution, 3rd anniversary.

Admiral Rigault de Genouilly A37

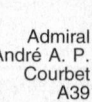

François Chasseloup-Laubat A38

Admiral André A. P. Courbet A39

**1943** ***Perf. 11½, 12, 12x11½***

**230** A37 6c carmine rose .50 *1.40*
**231** A38 6c carmine rose .50 .35
**232** A39 6c carmine rose 1.40 .25
*Nos. 230-232 (3)* 2.40 2.00

Issued: #230, 232, Sept. 1; #231, Oct. 5.
A 5c dull brown, type A37, was not regularly issued without the Viet Nam overprint. Value, $10.
A 3c light brown, type A39, was prepared but not issued. Value, $10.

Pigneau de Behaine, Bishop of Adran — A40

Alexandre Yersin — A41

**1943, June 10** ***Perf. 12***

**233** A40 20c dull red 1.50 *1.75*

**1943-45** ***Perf. 12x11½***

**234** A41 6c carmine rose 1.50 1.50
**235** A41 15c vio brn ('44) .55 .55
**236** A41 1pi yel grn ('45) .75 .75
*Nos. 234-236 (3)* 2.80 2.80

Issued to honor Dr. Alexandre Yersin (1863-1943), the Swiss bacteriologist who introduced rubber culture into Indo-China.
Issued: 6c, 10/5; 15c, 12/10; 1pi, 1/10.

Lt. M. J. François Garnier A42

**1943, Sept.** ***Perf. 12***

**237** A42 1c dull olive bister .90 *1.25*

A 15c brown violet was prepared but not issued. Value, $16.

Alexandre de Rhodes A43

**1943-45** ***Pin-perf., Perf. 12***

**238** A43 15c dk vio brn ('45) .40 .40
**239** A43 30c org brn .80 .80
*a.* 30c yellow brown, perf. 13½ .80 .80

Nos. 239, 239a carry the monogram "EF."
Issue dates: 15c, Mar. 10; 30c, June 15.

Athlete Giving Olympic Salute A44

**1944, July 10** ***Perf. 12***

**241** A44 10c dk vio brn & yel 2.40 2.40
**242** A44 50c dl red 2.75 2.75

Adm. Pierre de La Grandière A45

**1943-45**

**243** A45 1c dull brn .25 *1.25*
**244** A45 5c dark brn ('45) .30 .30

The upper left corner of No. 244 contains the denomination "5c" instead of "EF" monogram.
Issue dates: 1c, Aug.; 5c, Jan. 10.

Auguste Pavie A46

**1944** ***Perf. 12***

**245** A46 4c org yel .50 .30
**246** A46 10c dl grn .30 *.65*

Issue dates: 4c, Feb. 10; 10c, Jan. 5.
A 20c dark red, type A46, was not regularly issued without the Viet Nam overprint. Value without overprint, $10.

Governor-General Pierre Pasquier — A47

**1944**

**247** A47 5c brn vio .65 .65
**248** A47 10c dl grn .30 *1.25*

Issue dates: 5c, Nov. 1; 10c, Sept.

Joost Van Vollenhoven — A48

**1944, Oct. 10**

**249** A48 1c olive brown .35 .35
**250** A48 10c green .75 .90

Governor-General J. M. A. de Lanessan — A49

**1944**

**251** A49 1c dl gray brn .65 .50
**252** A49 15c dl rose vio 1.90 1.60

Issued: 1c, Dec. 10; 15c, Oct. 16.

Governor-General Paul Doumer — A50

**1944**

**253** A50 2c red vio .30 .30
**254** A50 4c lt brn .30 .30
**255** A50 10c yel grn .30 .30
*Nos. 253-255 (3)* .90 .90

Issue dates: 2c, May 15; 4c, June 15; 10c, Jan. 5.

Admiral Charner — A51

Doudart de Lagrée — A52

**1944**

**256** A51 10c green .50 *1.40*
**257** A51 20c brn red .65 *1.40*
**258** A51 1pi pale yel grn 1.00 1.00
*Nos. 256-258 (3)* 2.15 3.80

Issue dates: 10c, 20c, Aug. 10; 1pi, July.

**1944-45**

**259** A52 1c dl gray brn ('45) .25 .25
**260** A52 15c dl rose vio .50 .55
**261** A52 40c brt bl .65 1.00
*Nos. 259-261 (3)* 1.40 1.80

Issue dates: 1c, Jan. 10; 15c, 40c, Nov.

Nos. 209-209A Overprinted in Black

**1946** **Unwmk.** ***Perf. 12½x12***

**262** A27a 10c dk car 1.10 *1.60*
**263** A27a 25c blue 2.75 *3.25*

## SEMI-POSTAL STAMPS

No. 45 Surcharged

***Perf. 14x13½***

**1914, Oct. 28** **Unwmk.**

**B1** A5 10c +5c red & blk 1.60 1.60

Nos. 44-46 Surcharged

**1915-17**

**B2** A5 5c + 5c grn & blk ('17) 1.60 1.60
*a.* Double surcharge 210.00 210.00
**B3** A5 10c + 5c red & blk 2.40 2.00
**B4** A5 15c + 5c vio & blk ('17) 2.40 2.00
*a.* Triple surcharge 190.00
*b.* Quadruple surcharge 190.00
*Nos. B2-B4 (3)* 6.40 5.60

Nos. B2-B4 Surcharged with New Values in Blue or Black

**1918-19**

**B5** A5 4c on 5c + 5c (Bl) 4.00 4.00
*a.* Closed "4" 220.00
**B6** A5 6c on 10c + 5c 3.75 *4.00*
**B7** A5 8c on 15c + 5c ('19) 13.00 13.00
*a.* Double surcharge 220.00
*Nos. B5-B7 (3)* 20.75 21.00

France Nos. B5-B10 Surcharged

**1919 (?)**

**B8** SP5 10c on 15c + 10c 1.60 1.60
*a.* "10 CENTS" double 525.00 525.00
**B9** SP5 16c on 25c + 15c 4.00 4.00
**B10** SP6 24c on 35c + 25c 6.50 6.50
*a.* Double surcharge 800.00 800.00
*b.* CENTS" double 875.00
**B11** SP7 40c on 50c + 50c 12.50 12.50
**B12** SP8 80c on 1fr + 1fr 27.50 27.50
**B13** SP8 4pi on 5fr + 5fr 220.00 220.00
*a.* PIASTRES" double 6,000. 5,400.
*Nos. B8-B13 (6)* 272.10 272.10

**Curie Issue**
Common Design Type
Inscription and Date in Upper Margin

**1938, Oct. 24** **Engr.** ***Perf. 13***

**B14** CD80 18c + 5c brt ultra 11.00 11.00

**French Revolution Issue**
Common Design Type
**Name and Value Typo. in Black**

**1939, July 5** **Photo.**

**B15** CD83 6c + 2c green 12.00 12.00
**B16** CD83 7c + 3c brown 12.00 12.00
**B17** CD83 9c + 4c red org 12.00 12.00
**B18** CD83 13c + 10c rose pink 12.00 12.00
**B19** CD83 23c + 20c blue 12.00 12.00
*Nos. B15-B19 (5)* 60.00 60.00
Set, never hinged 112.50

**Common Design Type and**

Tonkinese Sharpshooter SP1

Legionary SP2

**1941 Photo. *Perf. 13½***
**B19A** SP1 10c + 10c red 1.60
**B19B** CD86 15c + 30c maroon 1.60
**B19C** SP2 25c + 10c blue 1.60
*Nos. B19A-B19C (3)* 4.80

Nos. B19A-B19C were issued by the Vichy government in France, but were not placed on sale in Indo-China.

Portal and Flags, City University, Hanoi — SP3

Coat of Arms and Sword — SP4

***Perf. 11½***

**1942, June 1 Unwmk. Litho.**
**B20** SP3 6c + 2c car rose 1.25 1.25
*a.* Perf. 13¾ 120.00
**B21** SP3 15c + 5c brn vio 1.25 1.25

Nos. 209-209A Srchd. in Black or Red

**1944 Engr. *Perf. 12½x12***
**B21A** 5c + 15c on 25c blue (R) .95
**B21B** + 25c on 10c dk car 1.00

Colonial Development Fund.
Nos. B21A-B21B were issued by the Vichy government in France, but were not placed on sale in Indo-China.

No. B20 Surcharged in Black

**1944, June 10**
**B22** SP3 10c + 2c on 6c + 2c 1.25 1.25

**1942, Aug. 1 *Perf. 12***
**B23** SP4 6c + 2c red & blue .80 .80
**B24** SP4 15c + 5c vio blk, red & bl .80 .80

#B23 Surcharged in Black Like #B22
**1944, Mar. 15**
**B25** SP4 10c + 2c on 6c + 2c .80 .80

Aviator Do-Huu-Vi SP5

**1943, Aug. 1**
**B26** SP5 6c + 2c car rose .65 1.60

#B26 Surcharged in Black Like #B22
**1944, Feb. 10**
**B27** SP5 10c + 2c on 6c + 2c .80 .80

Surcharge arranged to fit size of stamp.

Aviator Roland Garros — SP6

**1943, Nov. 15**
**B28** SP6 6c + 2c rose car .80 .80

#B28 Surcharged in Black Like #B22
**1944, Feb. 10**
**B29** SP6 10c + 2c on 6c + 2c .80 .80

Cathedral of Orléans SP7

**1944, Dec. 20**
**B30** SP7 15c + 60c brn vio 1.60 1.60
**B31** SP7 40c + 1.10pi blue 1.60 2.75

Type of France, 1945, Surcharged in Black

**1945 Unwmk. Engr. *Perf. 13***
**B32** A152 50c + 50c on 2fr green .65 .65
**B33** A152 1pi + 1pi on 2fr hn brn .65 .65
**B34** A152 2pi + 2pi on 2fr Prus grn 1.00 1.00
*Nos. B32-B34 (3)* 2.30 2.30

## AIR POST STAMPS

Airplane AP1

**1933-41 Unwmk. Photo. *Perf. 13½***
**C1** AP1 1c ol brn .25 .25
**C2** AP1 2c dk grn .30 .25
**C3** AP1 5c yel grn .30 .25
**C4** AP1 10c red brn .65 .30
**C5** AP1 11c rose car ('38) .80 .30
**C6** AP1 15c dp bl .70 .25
**C6A** AP1 16c brt pink ('41) .35 .35
**C7** AP1 20c grnsh gray .50 .50
**C8** AP1 30c org brn .30 .25
**C9** AP1 36c car rose 1.90 .35
**C10** AP1 37c ol grn ('38) .80 .30
**C10A** AP1 39c dk ol grn ('41) .35 .35
**C11** AP1 60c dk vio 1.90 .35
**C12** AP1 66c olive grn .55 .25
**C13** AP1 67c brt bl ('38) 1.20 1.00
**C13A** AP1 69c brt ultra ('41) .65 .65
**C14** AP1 1pi black .70 .25
**C15** AP1 2pi yel org 1.00 .35
**C16** AP1 5pi purple 1.90 .50
**C17** AP1 10pi deep red 3.75 .90
*Nos. C1-C17 (20)* 18.85 7.95

See Nos. C27-C28.
Issue dates: 11c, 37c, June 8; 67c, Oct. 5; 16c, 39c, 69c, Feb. 5; others, June 1, 1933.
See Nos. C18A-C18O, C27-C28.

**Trans-Indo-Chinese Railway Type**
**1938, June 8**
**C18** A26 37c red orange .75 .25

**Type of 1933-38 Without "RF"**
**1942-44 *Perf. 13½***
**C18A** AP1 5c yellow green .25
**C18B** AP1 10c red brown .25
**C18C** AP1 11c rose carmine .30
**C18D** AP1 15c deep blue .40
**C18E** AP1 20c greenish gray .40
**C18F** AP1 36c carmine rose .40
**C18G** AP1 37c olive green .70
**C18H** AP1 60c dark violet .70
**C18I** AP1 66c brown olive .70
**C18J** AP1 67c bright blue .80
**C18K** AP1 69c br ultramarine .90
**C18L** AP1 1pi black 1.30
**C18M** AP1 2pi yellow orange 1.30
**C18N** AP1 5pi purple 1.75
**C18O** AP1 10pi deep red 3.50
*Nos. C18A-C18O (15)* 13.65

Nos. C18A-C18O were issued by the Vichy government in France, but were not placed on sale in Indo-China.

**Victory Issue**
Common Design Type
***Perf. 12½***
**1946, May 8 Unwmk. Engr.**
**C19** CD92 80c red org 1.00 .55

**Chad to Rhine Issue**
Common Design Types
**1946, June 6**
**C20** CD93 50c yel grn .90 .90
**C21** CD94 1pi violet .90 .90
**C22** CD95 1.50pi carmine 1.10 1.10
**C23** CD96 2pi vio brn 1.10 1.10
**C24** CD97 2.50pi dp bl 1.10 1.10
**C25** CD98 5pi org red 1.30 1.30
*Nos. C20-C25 (6)* 6.40 6.40

**UPU Issue**
Common Design Type
**1949, July 4 *Perf. 13***
**C26** CD99 3pi dp bl, dk vio, grn & red 4.75 4.00

**Plane Type of 1933-41**
**1949, June 13 Photo. *Perf. 13½***
**C27** AP1 20pi dk bl grn 11.50 6.50
**C28** AP1 30pi brown 13.00 6.50

## AIR POST SEMI-POSTAL STAMP

**French Revolution Issue**
Common Design Type
**Unwmk.**
**1939, July 5 Photo. *Perf. 13***
**Name and Value Typo. in Orange**
**CB1** CD83 39c + 40c brn blk 25.00 25.00

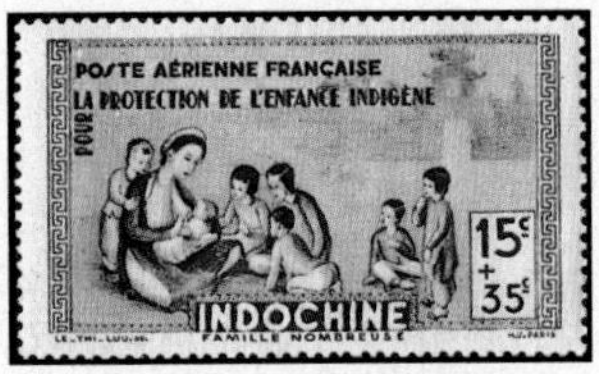


Poor Family — SPAP1

Orphans SPAP2

Caring for Children — SPAP3

***Perf. 13½x12½, 13 (#CB4)***
**Photo, Engr. (#CB4)**
**1942, June 22**
**CB2** SPAP1 15c + 35c green 1.00
**CB3** SPAP2 20c + 60c brown 1.00
**CB4** SPAP3 30c + 90c car red 1.05
*Nos. CB2-CB4 (3)* 3.05

Native children's welfare fund.
Nos. CB2-CB4 were issued by the Vichy government in France, but were not placed on sale in Indo-China.

**Colonial Education Fund**
Common Design Type
***Perf. 12½x13½***
**1942, June 22 Engr.**
**CB5** CD86a 12c + 18c blue & red 1.10

No. CB5 was issued by the Vichy government in France, but was not placed on sale in Indo-China.

## POSTAGE DUE STAMPS

French Colonies No. J21 Surcharged

**1904, June 26 Unwmk. *Imperf.***
**J1** D1 5c on 60c brn, *buff* 14.50 14.50

French Colonies Nos. J10-J11 Surcharged in Carmine
**1905, July 22**
**J2** D1 5c on 40c black 32.00 16.00
**J3** D1 10c on 60c black 32.00 20.00
**J4** D1 30c on 60c black 32.00 20.00
*Nos. J2-J4 (3)* 96.00 56.00

Dragon from Steps of Angkor Wat
D1 D2

**1908 Typo. *Perf. 14x13½***
**J5** D1 2c black 1.30 1.00
**J6** D1 4c dp bl 1.30 1.00
**J7** D1 5c bl grn 1.60 1.10
**J8** D1 10c carmine 2.90 1.10
**J9** D1 15c violet 3.50 2.50
**J10** D1 20c chocolate 1.75 1.40
**J11** D1 30c ol grn 1.75 1.40
**J12** D1 40c claret 8.25 6.50
**J13** D1 50c grnsh bl 7.00 1.60
**J14** D1 60c orange 11.00 9.50
**J15** D1 1fr gray 24.00 18.50
**J16** D1 2fr yel brn 24.00 18.50
**J17** D1 5fr red 40.00 37.50
*Nos. J5-J17 (13)* 128.35 101.60

Surcharged in Cents or Piasters

**1919**
**J18** D1 ⅕c on 2c blk 1.60 1.25
**J19** D1 1⅗c on 4c dp bl 1.60 1.25
**J20** D1 2c on 5c bl grn 2.90 1.60
**J21** D1 4c on 10c car 4.00 1.25
**J22** D1 6c on 15c vio 9.00 2.75
**J23** D1 8c on 20c choc 6.50 2.40
**J24** D1 12c on 30c ol grn 9.25 2.40
**J25** D1 16c on 40c cl 9.25 2.00
**J26** D1 20c on 50c grnsh bl 12.00 6.50
**J27** D1 24c on 60c org 3.25 2.00
*a.* Closed "4" 20.00 16.00
**J28** D1 40c on 1fr gray 5.25 1.60
*a.* Closed "4" 20.00 16.00
**J29** D1 80c on 2fr yel brn 40.00 19.00
**J30** D1 2pi on 5fr red 57.50 40.00
*a.* Double surcharge 220.00 175.00
*b.* Triple surcharge 220.00 175.00
*Nos. J18-J30 (13)* 162.10 84.00

**"CENTS" below Numerals**
**1922, Oct.**
**J31** D2 ⅖c black .25 .25
**J32** D2 ⅘c red .30 .30
**J33** D2 1c buff .50 .40
**J34** D2 2c gray grn .65 .50
**J35** D2 3c violet .75 .75
**J36** D2 4c orange .75 .40
*a.* "4 CENTS" omitted 675.00
*b.* "4 CENTS" double 105.00 105.00
**J37** D2 6c ol grn 1.60 .65
**J38** D2 8c blk, *lav* 1.25 .65
**J39** D2 10c dp bl 2.00 .65
**J40** D2 12c ocher, *grnsh* 1.60 1.10
**J41** D2 20c dp bl, *straw* 2.00 .90
**J42** D2 40c red, *bluish* 2.00 1.10
**J43** D2 1pi brn vio, *pnksh* 6.50 3.50
*Nos. J31-J43 (13)* 20.15 11.15

Pagoda of Mot Cot, Hanoi — D3

Dragon of Annam — D4

***Perf. 14x13½, 13½x14***

**1927, Sept. 26**

| | | | | |
|---|---|---|---|---|
| **J44** | D3 | ⅖c vio brn & org | .25 | .25 |
| **J45** | D3 | ⅘c vio & blk | .25 | .25 |
| **J46** | D3 | 1c brn red & sl | .90 | .90 |
| **J47** | D3 | 2c grn & brn ol | 1.00 | 1.00 |
| **J48** | D3 | 3c red brn & bl | 1.60 | 1.60 |
| **J49** | D3 | 4c ind & brn | 1.60 | 1.60 |
| **J50** | D3 | 6c dp red & ver | 2.00 | 1.60 |
| **J51** | D3 | 8c ol brn & vio | 1.60 | 1.25 |
| **J52** | D4 | 10c dp bl | 2.40 | 1.25 |
| **J53** | D4 | 12c olive | 5.25 | 4.50 |
| **J54** | D4 | 20c rose | 3.50 | 2.00 |
| **J55** | D4 | 40c bl grn | 3.50 | 3.25 |
| **J56** | D4 | 1pi red org | 17.50 | 17.50 |
| | | *Nos. J44-J56 (13)* | 41.35 | 36.95 |

Surcharged in Black or Blue — D5

**1931-41** ***Perf. 13***

| | | | | |
|---|---|---|---|---|
| **J57** | D5 | ⅕c red, *org* ('38) | .25 | .25 |
| **J58** | D5 | ⅖c red, *org* | .25 | .25 |
| **J59** | D5 | ⅘c red, *org* | .25 | .25 |
| **J60** | D5 | 1c red, *org* | .25 | .25 |
| **J61** | D5 | 2c red, *org* | .25 | .25 |
| **J62** | D5 | 2.5c red, *org* ('40) | .25 | .25 |
| **J63** | D5 | 3c red, *org* ('38) | .40 | .25 |
| **J64** | D5 | 4c red, *org* | .30 | .30 |
| **J65** | D5 | 5c red, *org* ('38) | .40 | .30 |
| **J66** | D5 | 6c red, *org* | .30 | .30 |
| **J67** | D5 | 10c red, *org* | .30 | .30 |
| **J68** | D5 | 12c red, *org* | .50 | .30 |
| **J69** | D5 | 14c red, *org* ('38) | .50 | .30 |
| **J70** | D5 | 18c red, *org* ('41) | .50 | .50 |
| **J71** | D5 | 20c red, *org* | .50 | .50 |
| **J72** | D5 | 50c red, *org* | .75 | .50 |
| **J72A** | D5 | 1pi red, *org* | 9.50 | 8.50 |
| **J73** | D5 | 1pi red, *org* (Bl) | 2.25 | 1.25 |
| | | *Nos. J57-J73 (18)* | 17.70 | 14.80 |

D6

D7

***Perf. 12, 13½ and Compound***

**1943-44** **Litho.** **Unwmk.**

| | | | | |
|---|---|---|---|---|
| **J74** | D6 | 1c red, *org* | .25 | .25 |
| **J75** | D6 | 2c red, *org* | .25 | .25 |
| **J76** | D6 | 3c red, *org* | .30 | .30 |
| **J77** | D6 | 4c red, *org* | .30 | .30 |
| **J78** | D6 | 6c red, *org* | .40 | .40 |
| **J79** | D6 | 10c red, *org* | .40 | .40 |
| **J80** | D7 | 12c blue, *pnksh* | .50 | .50 |
| **J81** | D7 | 20c blue, *pnksh* | .50 | .50 |
| **J82** | D7 | 30c blue, *pnksh* | .50 | .50 |
| | | *Nos. J74-J82 (9)* | 3.40 | 3.40 |

Issued: 2c, 3c, 7/15/43; 6c-30c, 8/43; 1c, 4c, 6/10/44.

## OFFICIAL STAMPS

Regular Issues of 1931-32 Overprinted in Blue or Red

***Perf. 13, 13½***

**1933, Feb. 27** **Unwmk.**

| | | | | |
|---|---|---|---|---|
| **O1** | A20 | 1c black brown (Bl) | .80 | .75 |
| **O2** | A20 | 2c dark green (Bl) | .90 | .50 |

Regular Issues of 1931-32 Overprinted in Blue or Red

| | | | | |
|---|---|---|---|---|
| **O3** | A21 | 3c deep brown (Bl) | 1.25 | .65 |
| *a.* | | Inverted overprint | 150.00 | |
| **O4** | A21 | 4c dark blue (R) | 1.50 | .90 |
| *a.* | | Inverted overprint | 150.00 | |
| **O5** | A21 | 5c deep violet (Bl) | 2.40 | .90 |
| **O6** | A21 | 6c orange red (Bl) | 2.40 | 1.25 |

Regular Issues of 1931-32 Overprinted in Blue or Red

| | | | | |
|---|---|---|---|---|
| **O7** | A22 | 10c dk blue (R) | 1.25 | .90 |
| **O8** | A22 | 15c dk brown (Bl) | 2.75 | 1.60 |
| **O9** | A22 | 20c rose (Bl) | 3.25 | .75 |
| **O10** | A22 | 21c olive grn (Bl) | 2.75 | 1.50 |
| **O11** | A22 | 25c dp violet (Bl) | 1.60 | .50 |
| **O12** | A22 | 30c orange brn (Bl) | 3.25 | .80 |

Regular Issues of 1931-32 Overprinted in Blue or Red

| | | | | |
|---|---|---|---|---|
| **O13** | A23 | 50c dark brown (Bl) | 11.50 | 3.50 |
| **O14** | A23 | 60c dull violet (Bl) | 2.75 | 2.40 |
| **O15** | A23 | 1pi yellow green (Bl) | 28.00 | 10.50 |
| **O16** | A23 | 2pi red (Bl) | 10.00 | 9.00 |
| | | *Nos. O1-O16 (16)* | 76.35 | 36.40 |

Type of Regular Issue, 1922-23 Overprinted diagonally in Black or Red "SERVICE"

**1934, Oct. 4** ***Perf. 14x13***

| | | | | |
|---|---|---|---|---|
| **O17** | A13 | 1c olive green | 1.00 | .75 |
| **O18** | A13 | 2c brown orange | 1.00 | .75 |
| **O19** | A13 | 3c yellow green | 1.25 | .65 |
| **O20** | A13 | 4c cerise | 2.25 | 1.30 |
| **O21** | A13 | 5c yellow | 1.25 | .75 |
| **O22** | A13 | 6c orange red | 5.25 | 5.00 |
| **O23** | A13 | 10c gray grn (R) | 3.00 | 2.25 |
| **O24** | A13 | 15c ultra | 2.10 | 1.50 |
| **O25** | A13 | 20c gray black (R) | 1.80 | 1.50 |
| **O26** | A13 | 21c light violet | 10.00 | 8.25 |
| **O27** | A13 | 25c rose lake | 11.50 | 10.00 |
| **O28** | A13 | 30c lilac gray | 1.50 | 1.30 |
| **O29** | A13 | 50c brt violet | 7.50 | 6.25 |
| **O30** | A13 | 60c gray | 14.00 | 10.50 |
| **O31** | A13 | 1pi blue (R) | 27.50 | 23.00 |
| **O32** | A13 | 2pi deep red | 45.00 | 32.50 |
| | | *Nos. O17-O32 (16)* | 135.90 | 106.25 |

The value tablet has colorless numeral and letters on solid background.

## PARCEL POST STAMPS

French Colonies No. 50 Overprinted

**1891** **Unwmk.** ***Perf. 14x13½***

| | | | | |
|---|---|---|---|---|
| **Q1** | A9 | 10c black, *lavender* | 24.00 | 10.50 |

The overprint on No. Q1 was also handstamped in shiny ink. Value unused, $750.

Indo-China No. 8 Overprinted

**1898**

| | | | | |
|---|---|---|---|---|
| **Q2** | A3 | 10c black, *lavender* | 28.00 | 28.00 |

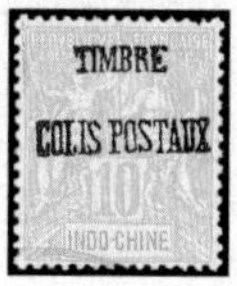


Nos. 8 and 9 Overprinted

**1902**

| | | | | |
|---|---|---|---|---|
| **Q3** | A3 | 10c black, *lavender* | 52.50 | 32.50 |
| *a.* | | Inverted overprint | 110.00 | 48.00 |
| **Q4** | A3 | 10c red | 52.50 | 24.00 |
| *a.* | | Inverted overprint | 80.00 | 48.00 |
| *b.* | | Double overprint | 80.00 | 48.00 |

# INDONESIA

ˌin-də-ˈnē-zhə

LOCATION — In the East Indies
GOVT. — Republic
AREA — 741,101 sq. mi.
POP. — 195,280,000 (1995 est.)
CAPITAL — Jakarta

Formerly Netherlands Indies, Indonesia achieved independence late in 1949 as the United States of Indonesia and became the Republic of Indonesia August 15, 1950. See Netherlands Indies for earlier issues.

100 Sen = 1 Rupiah

**Catalogue values for all unused stamps in this country are for Never Hinged items.**

### Watermarks

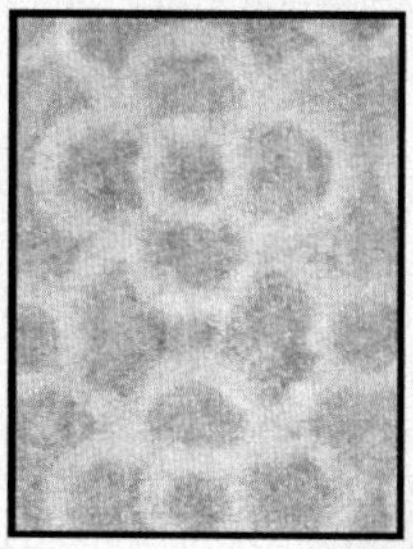

Wmk. 404

Wmk. 228

## REVOLUTIONARY ISSUES

Following the surrender of Japan to the Allies in 1945, Indonesian nationalists declared independence and formed the Republic of Indonesia. On Sept. 27, the Djawan PTT (now PT Pos Indonesia) was established and assumed reponsibility for the postal system. Within days, civil war had broken out between the nationalists and the returning Dutch, who sought to reestablish control over their East Indies colony. During the hostilities, which continued until Dec. 1949, a Dutch blockade of the rebel strongholds in Java and Sumatra made regular communications between the two islands impossible, and the Djawan PTT was forced to organize separate postal services, using locally produced stamps, on Java and Sumatra.

## JAVA ISSUES

Netherlands Indies Nos. 168, 200, 201 Ovptd. in Black or Red (R)

**1945, Nov.** ***Perf. 11½***

| | | | | |
|---|---|---|---|---|
| **1L1** | A17 | 1c lilac gray (R) | 2.25 | *2.75* |
| **1L2** | A17 | 2c plum | 4.50 | *6.25* |
| **1L3** | A17 | 3½c dark gray (R) | 60.00 | 60.00 |
| | | *Nos. 1L1-1L3 (3)* | 66.75 | 69.00 |

Forgeries of Nos. 1L1-1L3 exist.

Netherlands Indies Nos. 228-231 Ovptd. in Black or Red (R)

**1945, Nov.** ***Perf. 12½***

| | | | | |
|---|---|---|---|---|
| **1L4** | A23 | 2½c rose violet | 1.75 | *2.75* |
| **1L5** | A24 | 3c green (R) | 1.75 | *2.75* |
| **1L6** | A25 | 4c olive green (R) | 1.90 | *3.00* |
| **1L7** | A26 | 5c blue (R) | 75.00 | 65.00 |
| | | *Nos. 1L4-1L7 (4)* | 80.40 | 73.50 |

Forgeries of Nos. 1L4-1L7 exist.

Netherlands Indies Nos. N2, N3 Ovptd. in Black or Red (R)

**1945, Nov.** ***Perf. 12½***

| | | | | |
|---|---|---|---|---|
| **1L8** | OS2 | 3½s carmine | 350.00 | 325.00 |
| **1L9** | OS3 | 5s green (R) | 22.50 | 20.00 |

Forgeries of Nos. 1L8-1L9 exist.

Netherlands Indies Nos. N5-N11 Ovptd. in Black or Red (R)

**1945, Nov.** ***Perf. 12½***

| | | | | |
|---|---|---|---|---|
| **1L10** | OS5 | 3½s rose red | 40.00 | 40.00 |
| **1L11** | OS6 | 5s yel green (R) | .65 | *1.40* |
| **1L12** | OS7 | 10s dk blue (R) | .65 | *1.40* |
| *a.* | | Perf 12 | 1.75 | 2.25 |
| **1L13** | OS8 | 20s gray olive (R) | .65 | *1.40* |
| **1L14** | OS9 | 40s rose lilac (R) | .70 | *1.40* |
| **1L15** | OS10 | 60s red orange | .90 | *1.20* |
| **1L16** | OS11 | 80s fawn | 20.00 | 20.00 |
| | | *Nos. 1L10-1L16 (7)* | 63.55 | *66.80* |

Forgeries of Nos. 1L10-1L16 exist.

Netherlands Indies Nos. 200, 201, 228-230, N38 Overprinted in Red or Brown (Br)

***Perf. 12½, 12x12½ (#A18, A19)***

**1945, Nov.**

| | | | | |
|---|---|---|---|---|
| **1L17** | A17 | 1s lilac gray | 2.25 | *2.90* |
| **1L18** | A17 | 1s lilac gray (Br) | 10.00 | *12.00* |
| **1L19** | OS21 | 2s carmine | 1.40 | 2.25 |
| **1L20** | A23 | 2½s rose violet | 20.00 | 20.00 |
| **1L21** | A24 | 3s green | 3.50 | 3.50 |
| **1L22** | A25 | 4s olive green | 3.50 | *3.50* |
| | | *Nos. 1L17-1L22 (6)* | 40.65 | *44.15* |

Forgeries of Nos. 1L17-1L22 exist.

A large number of proofs, both perf and imperf, in original and in different colors, exist for Nos. 1L23-1L50. All are scarce.

Bull — A1

Bull & Flag — A2

***Perf. 11½***

**1945, Dec. 1 Typo. Unwmk.**
**With Gum**

**1L23** A1 10s chocolate 7.00 7.00
*a.* Imperf 95.00 *150.00*
**1L24** A2 20s choc & carmine red 6.50 6.50

Issued to celebrate the first half-year of Indonesian independence.

Nos. 1L25-1L49 were issued without gum.

Road & Mountains — A3

Sentry — A4

Boat in Storm — A5

Wayang Puppet — A6

Kris & Flag — A7

Temple — A8

**1946-47** ***Various perfs***

**1L25** A3 5s pale gray blue .75 *.95*
**1L26** A4 20s lt red brown .75 *.95*
**1L27** A5 30s carmine red .80 *1.00*
**1L28** A6 50s deep blue 17.50 16.00
**1L29** A7 60s deep rose 6.50 *300.00*
**1L30** A8 80s dp red vio ('47) 65.00 *600.00*
*Nos. 1L25-1L30 (6)* 91.30 *918.90*

Issued: 5s, 20s, 6/1/46. 30s, 50s, 7/1/46. 60s, 9/1/46. 80s, 7/1/47.

Buffalo Breaking Chains — A9

Bandung, March 1946 — A10

Bombing of Soerabaya, Nov. 1945 — A11

Anti-aircraft Crew — A12

Quai at Tandjong Priok — A13

Pilot — A14

Ambarawa A15

Wonokroma Dam, Soerabaya A16

Meeting, Jakarta — A17

Mounted Soldier — A18

**1946-47** ***Various perfs***

**1L31** A9 3s dull carmine .35 *1.75*
*a.* Imperf .25 .25
**1L32** A10 5s gray blue .60 *.95*
*a.* Imperf .35 .50
**1L33** A11 10s blue black 11.50 6.25
*a.* Imperf 11.50 11.50
**1L34** A11 15s dark purple .95 *1.25*
*a.* Imperf .95 .95
**1L35** A12 30s green 2.40 *5.75*
*a.* Imperf 1.75 2.40
**1L36** A13 40s dk blue vio .95 *2.40*
*a.* Imperf 1.00 1.00
**1L37** A9 50s violet black 1.75 *2.90*
*a.* Imperf 1.20 1.20
**1L38** A10 60s dp red vio 3.50 *4.50*
*a.* Imperf 1.75 1.75
**1L39** A14 80s br rose red 1.20 *7.00*
*a.* Imperf *150.00*
**1L40** A15 100s dull brn red 1.75 *3.50*
*a.* Imperf 1.20 1.20
**1L41** A16 200s dull lilac 2.90 *3.50*
*a.* Imperf 1.50 2.40
**1L42** A17 500s car red 14.00 *24.00*
*a.* Imperf 9.00 9.00
**1L43** A18 1000s lt blue green 14.00 *30.00*
*a.* Imperf 7.00 7.00
*Nos. 1L31-1L43 (13)* 55.85 *93.75*

First anniv. of independence.

Issued: 3s, 10s-200s, 8/17/46. 5s, 500s, 1000s, 2/1/47.

Worker & Ship — A19

**1948, Aug. 17** ***Imperf.***

**1L44** A19 50s dull blue 3.50 *4.50*
*a.* Perf 11 11.50
**1L45** A19 100s dull scarlet 4.00 *5.00*
*a.* Perf 11 11.50

Nos. 1L44 and 1L45 were printed on paper with papermaker's watermark. Nos. 1L44a and 1L45a were printed on unwatermarked paper.

Flag Over Waves — A20

**1949, July 20** ***Imperf.***

**1L46** A20 100s car rose 5.25 *6.75*
*a.* Perf 11 175.00 290.00
**1L47** A20 150s car rose 7.50 *17.00*
*a.* Perf 11 47.50 180.00

Return of the Indonesian government to Jakarta.

Nos. 1L46-1L47 were printed on paper bearing papermaker's watermark "MADE IN U.S.A." once in each sheet, and a few stamps within each sheet bear portions of the watermark.

Nos. 1L46a, 1L47a overprinted in Black

**1949, Dec. 27** ***Perf. 11***

**1L48** A20 100s car rose 17.00
**1L49** A20 150s car rose 19.00

Return of the Indonesian government to Jakarta.

## POSTAGE DUE STAMPS

Netherlands Indies Nos. J29, J32a Overprinted — No. AJ1

**1948** ***Perf. 12½***

**1LJ1** D5 25s on 7½c salmon 24.00 *35.00*
**1LJ2** D5 25s on 15c salmon 12.50 *30.00*

## MILITARY STAMP

M1

**1949, Aug. Without Gum** ***Imperf.***

**1LM1** M1 15r ultramarine *6,750. 5,250.*

No. 1LM1 was issued for provisional use at Surakarta, a Dutch stronghold in central Java, occupied by Indonesian forces in August, 1949.

## SUMATRA ISSUES

**Netherlands Indies Nos. 231, 201 Overprinted in Black**

**1946**

**2L1** A26 15s on 5c blue .75 *1.00*
**2L2** A17 40s on 2c plum .40 *1.00*

Netherlands Indies Nos. 168//201 Overprinted

Overprint Bar is 5mm's thick.

**1946**

**2L3** A17 20s on 3½c dk gray 24.00 24.00
**2L4** A17 30s on 1c lilac gray 12.00 12.00
**2L5** A17 40s on 2c plum 1.00 1.50
**2L6** A17 60s on 2½c bister 175.00 175.00
**2L7** A17 80s on 3c yel grn 12.50 12.50
*Nos. 2L3-2L7 (5)* 224.50 225.00

Netherlands Indies Nos. 234, 236 Overprinted

**1946**

**2L8** A28 50s on 17½c orange 90.00 90.00
**2L9** A28 1r on 10c red orange 15.00 15.00

Some examples of Nos. 2L8 and 2L9 bear handstamps previously applied by local authorities during and after the Japanese occupation. Such multiply-overprinted stamps command prices that may be more or less than the values shown, which are for examples without other overprints.

Nos. 2L10-2L84 were issued without gum.

Farmer & Oxen in Rice Paddy — A23

Sentry & Flag — A24

Airplane over City — A25

**1946, May 17** ***Perf. 11½x10***

**2L10** A23 5s (+25s) yel grn 1.00 2.25
**2L11** A24 15s (+35s) deep red 2.00 4.75
**2L12** A25 40s (+60s) orange 1.00 2.25
*Nos. 2L10-2L12 (3)* 4.00 9.25

Nos. 2L10-2L12 were sold at a premium over face value, not indicated on the stamps themselves, to benefit the Freedom Fund ("Fonds Kemerdekkan").

Pres. Soekarno — A26

**1946, June 1** *Perf. 10¾*

**2L13** A26 40s (+60s) red 1.50 3.00
**2L14** A26 40s (+60s) deep red 12.00 12.00

Nos. 2L13-2L14 were sold at a premium over face value, not indicated on the stamps themselves, to benefit the Freedom Fund ("Fonds Kemerdekkan").

**As Nos. 2L10-2L12, in different colors on thicker paper**

**1946, Aug. 17** *Perf. 11½x10*

**2L15** A23 5s (+25s) turquoise .75 *2.40*
**2L16** A24 15s (+35s) purple .75 *2.40*
**2L17** A25 40s (+60s) deep red 6.25 *7.00*
**2L18** A25 40s (+60s) bister 13.00 *32.50*
*Nos. 2L15-2L18 (4)* 20.75 *44.30*

Nos. 2L15-2L18 were sold at a premium over face value, not indicated on the stamps themselves, to benefit the Freedom Fund ("Fonds Kemerdekkan").

Nos. 2L15-2L17, One- or two-bar Overprint

**1946** *Perf. 11½x10¾*

**2L19** A23 5s turquoise 100.00 *175.00*
**2L20** A24 15s purple 100.00 *175.00*
**2L21** A25 40s deep red 100.00 87.50
*Nos. 2L19-2L21 (3)* 300.00 437.50

Farmer & Oxen in Rice Paddy — A26a

Sentry & Flag — A26b

Airplane over City — A26c

**First Issue**

**1946-47** *Perf. 11¾x10½*

**2L22** A26a 2s red .75 *4.00*
**2L23** A26a 3s green 1.20 *7.00*
**2L24** A26a 5s turquoise .40 *7.00*
**2L25** A26b 15s purple .40 *2.40*
**2L26** A26c 40s brown .50 *25.00*
*Nos. 2L22-2L26 (5)* 3.25 45.40

**Second Issue**

**2L27** A26a 2s chocolate 4.00 *5.50*
**2L28** A26a 3s orange 4.75 *4.50*
**2L29** A26b 15s green 4.75 *5.00*
**2L30** A26c 40s blue 24.00 *40.00*
*Nos. 2L27-2L30 (4)* 37.50 55.00

Japanese Occupation of Sumatra Revenue Stamps Overprinted — A27

**1947, May 12** ***Various Rough Perfs***

**2L31** A27 50s light red 30.00 *50.00*
**2L32** A27 1f light red 30.00 *40.00*
**2L33** A27 2f light red 25.00 *50.00*
**2L34** A27 2.50f light red 22.50 *30.00*
*Nos. 2L31-2L34 (4)* 107.50 170.00

No. 2L13 Surcharged

**1947, May 12**

**2L35** A26 50s on 40s red 7.75 7.75
**2L36** A26 1f on 40s red 14.50 14.50
**2L37** A26 1.50f on 40s red 9.00 9.00
**2L38** A26 2.50f on 40s red 1.20 3.75
**2L39** A26 3.50f on 40s red 1.75 4.00
**2L40** A26 5f on 40s red 1.20 3.75
*Nos. 2L35-2L40 (6)* 35.40 42.75

Nos. 2L24, 2L26 Srchd., with Small Ornament covering Original Value

**1947**

**2L41** A26a 50s on 5s turq 9.50 9.50
**2L42** A26a 1f on 5s turq 8.25 8.25
**2L43** A26a 1.50f on 5s turq 9.75 9.75
**2L44** A26c 1r on 40s purple .85 4.50
**2L45** A26a 2r on 5s turq 1.00 4.50
*Nos. 2L41-2L45 (5)* 29.35 36.50

The tail of the surcharged "5" ends in a ball on No. 2L41. Compare with No. 2L65.

Types A26a-A26b Srchd., in Black or Red (R), with Large Ornament covering Original Value

**1947**

**2L46** A26b 1s on 15s violet (R) .80 *3.00*
**2L47** A26a 5s on 3s slate blue (R) .75 *3.00*
**2L48** A26b 10s on 15s orange .85 *3.00*
**2L49** A26a 50s on 3s br red 25.00 *35.00*
*Nos. 2L46-2L49 (4)* 27.40 44.00

Nos. 2L48 and 2L49 were not issued without ovpt.

No. 2L15 Surcharged

**1947**

**2L50** A25 30s on 40s dp red 1.00 *2.50*
**2L51** A25 50s on 40s dp red 17.50 *25.00*
**2L52** A25 1f on 40s dp red 3.50 2.50
**2L53** A25 1.50f on 40s dp red 5.00 *8.50*
**2L54** A25 2.50f on 40s dp red .75 *2.50*
*Nos. 2L50-2L54 (5)* 27.75 41.00

Nos. 2L23-2L26, Srchd. in Black or Red, New Value 2.8mm High

**1948**

**2L55** A26a .50f on 5s turq *900.00 850.00*
**2L56** A26b .50f on 15s purple *900.00 850.00*
**2L57** A26a 1f on 5s turq 175.00 175.00
**2L58** A26b 1f on 15s purple 350.00 350.00
**2L59** A26c 1f on 40s brown 575.00
**2L60** A26a 2.50f on 5s turq *900.00 850.00*
**2L61** A26b 2.50f on 15s purple 575.00 475.00
**2L62** A26b 5f on 15s purple *900.00 900.00*
**2L63** A26c 5f on 40s brown 400.00 400.00
**2L64** A26a 50s on 5s turq *1,000. 1,000.*
**2L65** A26b 50s on 15s purple 400.00 *450.00*
*Nos. 2L55-2L65 (11)* 7,075. 6,300.

The tail of the surcharged "5" is plain on No. 2L64. Compare with No. 2L41.

**New Currency**
Values 3.2mm High

**1949**

**2L66** A26a 2.50r on 3s green 25.00 *30.00*
*a.* Red overprint 25.00 30.00
**2L67** A26b 5r on 15s purple 10.00 30.00
*a.* Red overprint 10.00 30.00
**2L68** A26a 10r on 3s green 110.00 110.00
*a.* Red overprint 110.00 110.00
*Nos. 2L66-2L68 (3)* 145.00 170.00

Emergency provisional issue for Aceh Province.

Nos. 2L22, 2L23, 2L25, 2L26 Srchd. in Black or Red, New Value 4.5mm High

**1949**

**2L69** A26a 2r on 3s green 42.50 *80.00*
*a.* Red overprint 42.50 *80.00*
**2L70** A26a 2.50r on 3s green 24.00 *60.00*
*a.* Red overprint 24.00 *60.00*
**2L71** A26b 5r on 15s purple 10.00 *16.00*
*a.* Red overprint 10.00 *16.00*
**2L72** A26a 10r on 3s green 18.00 *40.00*
*a.* Red overprint 18.00 *40.00*
**2L73** A26a 20r on 2s red 300.00 *600.00*
*a.* Red overprint 350.00 *600.00*
**2L74** A26b 50r on 15s purple 400.00 *575.00*
*a.* Red overprint 400.00 *575.00*
**2L75** A26b 100r on 15s purple 150.00 150.00
*a.* Red overprint 150.00 150.00
**2L76** A26c 200r on 40s brown 175.00 175.00
*a.* Red overprint 175.00 175.00
*Nos. 2L69-2L76 (8)* 1,119. 1,696.

Nos. 2L22, 2L25, 2L26 Srchd. in Black, New Value 7.2mm High

**1949**

**2L77** A26b 10s on 15s purple 18.00 18.00
**2L78** A26b 20s on 15s purple 18.00 18.00
**2L79** A26b 30s on 15s purple 18.00 8.50
**2L80** A26a 1r on 2s red 60.00 *125.00*
**2L81** A26b 1.50f on 15s purple *500.00*
**2L82** A26b 2.50f on 15s purple 22.50 *50.00*
**2L83** A26c 5r on 40s brown 290.00 210.00
*Nos. 2L77-2L83 (7)* 426.50 929.50

Nos. 1L46-1L47 Surcharged

**1949**

**2L84** A20 15r on 100s car rose 25.00 *60.00*
**2L85** A20 15r on 150s car rose 27.50 *70.00*

---

**AIR POST STAMPS**

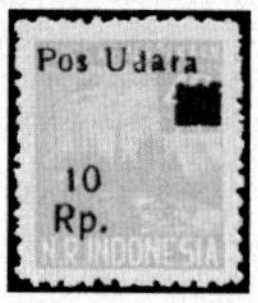

Nos. 66, 75 Overprinted

**1947**

**2LC1** A26 10r on 40s br red 3.00 *4.50*
**2LC2** A26 20r on 5s turq 1.80 *4.50*

---

**REPUBLIC OF INDONESIA**

Nos. 1-119, C1-C61, CE1-CE4, CO1-CO16, E1-E1G, J1-J39 and O1-O24 were authorized by the Indonesia PTT and were produced in Vienna and Philadelphia. Because most were printed by the Austrian State Printing Office (Staatsdruckerei), they are usually described as the "Vienna" issues. The first issue was released in Dec. 1948, but supplies did not reach republican-held areas of Java and Sumatra until mid-Jan., 1949. Through 1949, small supplies of these issues were sent to some 20 post offices in Java and Sumatra, where they were used both for local mail and for mail to foreign destinations, which was carried through the Dutch blockade by overseas (largely Indian) air carriers.

Following independence, the Vienna issues continued to be valid for postage for several years. While most covers on the market are philatelic in nature, commercial covers dated 1949-53 exist.

The Vienna issues were produced and heavily marketed by a U.S. stamp dealer. Proofs, deluxe sheetlets of one, and various overprints exist for these issues, as well as several unissued sets.

Values for the Vienna Issues are for mint never hinged stamps. Hinged examples are generally offered at 50-75% of these values. Used stamps are scarce, though generally not rare, and pricing information on values for used stamps is not presently available.

---

Map, Indonesian Archipelago A28

Farmer — A29

Red Cross Airplane A30

Balinese Dancer — A31

Military Officer, Flag of Republic A32

Designs: 1s, Map of Indonesian Archipelago. 2s, Republican sentry and Toba Lake, Sumatra. 2½, Military review, Gen. Soedirmari. 3s, Farmer working field with pitchfork. 3½s, Sultan Sjahrir and Thomas Jefferson. 4s, Buffalo Canyon, Sumatra. 5s, Policemen on motorcycles, Sastroamidjojo. 7½s, Red Cross nurse with wounded soldier. 10s, Dr. Maramis, Minister of Finance, and Alexander Hamilton. 15s, Construction of Great Postal Road, Java. 17½s, Hadji Agoes

Salim, philosopher, and Benjamin Franklin. 20s, Red Cross Boeing aircraft. 30s, Djanger dancer, Bali. 35s, Planting rice. 40s, Vice Pres. Mohammed Hatta and Abraham Lincoln. 50s, Mountain, Sumatra. 60s, Rice fields, Java. 80s, Boy holding pineapple. 1r, Pres. Soekarno and George Washington. 2r, Mosque, Medan, Sumatra. 2½r, Fish ponds, Tjipanas. 5r, Officer presenting flag. 10r, Vice Pres. Hatta. 25r, Pres. Soekarno.

***Perf. 14x13¾, 13¼x14 (#6), 13½x14¼ (#12, 14-16, 19, 20), 14¼x13½ (#13, 17, 17, 21), 12½ (#22-24)***

**Photo, Engr. (#22-24)**

**1948, Dec. 15 — Unwmk.**

| | | | | | |
|---|---|---|---|---|---|
| 1 | A28 | 1s | dk turq grn & brn | .45 | — |
| 2 | A28 | 2s | dp brn & dp blue | .25 | — |
| 3 | A28 | 2½s | dk brn & org red | .35 | — |
| 4 | A29 | 3s | dk lil & dp red brn | .25 | — |
| 5 | A28 | 3½s | dk bl vio & br grn | .25 | — |
| 6 | A29 | 4s | dk bl vio & dp ol grn | .30 | — |
| 7 | A28 | 5s | turq & dull blue | .25 | — |
| 8 | A28 | 7½s | dp brn & dk lil | .35 | — |
| 9 | A28 | 10s | dp blue & brn rose | .50 | — |
| 10 | A28 | 15s | brown & dk grn | .60 | — |
| 11 | A28 | 17½s | ultra & org brn | .30 | — |
| 12 | A30 | 20s | Prus grn & dp bis brn | .45 | — |
| 13 | A31 | 30s | dk brn & dull vio | .30 | — |
| 14 | A30 | 35s | dk lilac & brn | .30 | — |
| 15 | A30 | 40s | dk brn & blue | .30 | — |
| 16 | A30 | 50s | dk brn & turq | .30 | — |
| 17 | A31 | 60s | dk brn & lt red brn | .50 | — |
| 18 | A31 | 80s | dk lilac & slate | .45 | — |
| 19 | A30 | 1r | br blue & pur brn | .35 | — |
| 20 | A30 | 2r | dk brn & dk grn | .55 | — |
| 21 | A31 | 2½r | dk lilac & blue | .65 | — |
| 22 | A32 | 5r | yel brn & black | 3.50 | — |
| 23 | A32 | 10r | emerald & black | 5.00 | — |
| 24 | A32 | 25r | rose red & blk | 7.00 | — |
| | | | *Nos. 1-24 (24)* | 23.50 | |

See Nos. C1-C13.
For overprints, see Nos. 70-90, O1-O6.

A33

Designs: 10s, 25s, Map, ships. 15s, 60s, Dockworkers loading ship, vert. 1r, Ships.

**1949, Aug. 17 — Photo. — *Perf. 12½***

| | | | | | |
|---|---|---|---|---|---|
| 25 | A33 | 10s | gray & green | .80 | — |
| 26 | A33 | 15s | gray & maroon | .80 | — |
| 27 | A33 | 25s | gray & blue | .80 | — |
| 28 | A33 | 60s | maroon & gray | 3.00 | — |
| 29 | A33 | 1r | org & dull blue | 8.00 | — |
| | | | *Nos. 25-29 (5)* | 13.40 | |

Failure of Dutch blockade.
See Nos. C14-C18.

Sentry — A34

Soekarno Decorating Soldier — A35

Planting Rice — A36

Boy Holding Pineapple — A37

Military Officer, Flag of Republic A38

Designs: 1s, Republican sentry and Toba Lake, Sumatra. 2s, Soekarno decorating soldier. 2½s, Woman weaving batik. 3s, Metalcraft worker. 3½s, Construction of Great Postal Road, Java. 4s, Farmer working field with pitchfork. 5s, Javanese Wajang Wong dancer. 7½s, Planting rice on the sawah. 10s, Red Cross nurse with wounded soldier. 15s, Buffalo Canyon, Sumatra. 17½s, Plowing with oxen. 20s, Planting rice. 30s, Mountain, Sumatra. 35s, Boy holding pineapple. 40s, Fish ponds, Tjipanas. 50s, Djanger dancer, Bali. 60s, Javanese Serimpi court dancer. 80s, Mosque, Medan, Sumatra. 1r, Overcoming illiteracy. 2r, Idol. 2½r, Map of Indonesian Archipelago. 5r, Officer presenting flag. 10r, Vice Pres. Mohammed Hatta. 25r, Pres. Soekarno.

Country name inscription has been changed from "Repoeblik" to "Republik," to make spelling more American and less Dutch. This spelling change also officially changed Pres. Soekarno's name to Sukarno.

***Perf. 14x13¾, 13¾x14 (#31-33, 35, 36, 39), 13½x14¼ (#41, 42, 47, 50), 14¼x13½ (#43-46), 12½ (#51-53)***

**Photo, Engr. (#51-53)**

**1949, Aug. 17**

| | | | | | |
|---|---|---|---|---|---|
| 30 | A34 | 1s | dp brn & dp blue | .30 | — |
| 31 | A35 | 2s | dk red vio & dp grn | .40 | — |
| 32 | A35 | 2½s | dk brn & br scarlet | .35 | — |
| 33 | A35 | 3s | dp turq & org ver | .45 | — |
| 34 | A34 | 3½s | dp brn & dp grn | .40 | — |
| 35 | A35 | 4s | turq & dull blue | .50 | — |
| 36 | A35 | 5s | dull vio & dk yel brn | .35 | — |
| 37 | A34 | 7½s | dp brn & dk lil | .40 | — |
| 38 | A34 | 10s | dk brn & dp vio | .50 | — |
| 39 | A35 | 15s | dk vio & dp dull grn | .65 | — |
| 40 | A34 | 17½s | dk brn & red org | .55 | — |
| 41 | A36 | 20s | dull vio & dp brn | .25 | — |
| 42 | A36 | 30s | dp brn & dk blue vio | .45 | — |
| 43 | A37 | 35s | sl vio & blue | .25 | — |
| 44 | A37 | 40s | dull vio & dk yel brn | .45 | — |
| 45 | A37 | 50s | dk brn & Prus grn | .40 | — |
| 46 | A37 | 60s | br blue & dk yel brn | .55 | — |
| 47 | A36 | 80s | dull vio & dull bl | .50 | — |
| 48 | A36 | 1r | dp blue & dp choc | .50 | — |
| 49 | A37 | 2r | dp brn & org ver | .30 | — |
| 50 | A36 | 2½r | dp brn & br blue | 1.00 | — |
| 51 | A38 | 5r | red vio & black | 6.50 | — |
| 52 | A38 | 10r | green & black | 4.25 | — |
| 53 | A38 | 25r | orange & black | 6.50 | — |
| | | | *Nos. 30-53 (24)* | 26.75 | |

For overprints, see Nos. 91-111, O7-O12.

A39

A40

Designs: 10s, 25s, Map, ships. 15s, 60s, Dockworkers loading ship, vert. 1r, Ships.

**1948, Dec. 15 — Photo. — *Perf. 14½***

| | | | | | |
|---|---|---|---|---|---|
| 54 | A39 | 10s | gray & red | 1.25 | — |
| 55 | A39 | 15s | gray & dp blue | 1.25 | — |
| 56 | A39 | 25s | gray & red brn | 1.10 | — |
| 57 | A39 | 60s | gray & maroon | 2.00 | — |
| 58 | A39 | 1r | gray & maroon | 4.50 | — |
| | | | *Nos. 54-58 (5)* | 10.10 | |

**Souvenir Sheets**

| | | | | |
|---|---|---|---|---|
| 59 | A40 | 10s, 15s, 25s, 60s | 50.00 | — |
| *a.* | | Imperf | 325.00 | — |
| 60 | A40 | 30s, 50s, 1r, 2½r | 25.00 | — |
| *a.* | | Imperf | 150.00 | — |
| *b.* | | A39 2½r gray & maroon | — | — |
| *c.* | | As "b," imperf | — | — |
| 61 | A40 | 1r, 4½r | 40.00 | — |
| *a.* | | Imperf | 50.00 | — |
| *b.* | | A39 4½r maroon | — | — |
| *c.* | | As "b," imperf | — | — |

Failure of Dutch blockade, second issue.

The stamps contained in No. 60 and the 4½r stamp contained in No. 61 are air post stamps and are inscribed "POS UDARA."

See Nos. C32-C36.
For overprints, see Nos. 112-119.

Map, UPU Emblem & *Banteng* (Nationalist Symbol) — A41

**Wmk. 404**

**1949, Dec. 1 — Photo. — *Perf. 14***

| | | | | | |
|---|---|---|---|---|---|
| 62 | A41 | 10s | multicolored | .55 | — |
| *a.* | | | Imperf | .60 | — |
| 63 | A41 | 20s | multicolored | .55 | — |
| *a.* | | | Imperf | .60 | — |
| 64 | A41 | 50s | multicolored | .60 | — |
| *a.* | | | Imperf | .70 | — |
| 65 | A41 | 1r | multicolored | .60 | — |
| *a.* | | | Imperf | .75 | — |
| *b.* | | | Souvenir Sheet of 4, #62-65 | 22.50 | — |
| *c.* | | | As "b," imperf | 25.00 | — |
| | | | *Nos. 62-65 (4)* | 2.30 | |

**Unwatermarked**

| | | | | | |
|---|---|---|---|---|---|
| 66 | A41 | 10s | multicolored | .45 | — |
| *a.* | | | Imperf | .45 | — |
| 67 | A41 | 20s | multicolored | .45 | — |
| *a.* | | | Imperf | .45 | — |
| 68 | A41 | 50s | multicolored | .45 | — |
| *a.* | | | Imperf | .45 | — |
| 69 | A41 | 1r | multicolored | .45 | — |
| *a.* | | | Imperf | .45 | — |
| | | | *Nos. 66-69 (4)* | 1.80 | |

Nos. 64, 65, 68 and 69 are air post stamps and are inscribed "POS UDARA."

Souvenir sheets of 4, as No. 65c, without watermark, are proofs.

Most varieties of Nos. 1-69 exist overprinted "RIS," "RIS Merdeka" and "RIS Djakarta." These were not issued in Indonesia.

**Liberation of Jakarta**

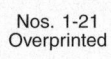

Nos. 1-21 Overprinted

**1949, Dec. 7**

| | | | | | |
|---|---|---|---|---|---|
| 70 | A28 | 1s | dk turq grn & brn | .25 | — |
| 71 | A28 | 2s | dp brn & dp blue | .90 | — |
| 72 | A28 | 2½s | dk brn & org red | .25 | — |
| 73 | A29 | 3s | dk lil & dp red brn | .45 | — |
| 74 | A28 | 3½s | dk bl vio & br grn | .25 | — |
| 75 | A29 | 4s | dk bl vio & dp ol grn | .55 | — |
| 76 | A28 | 5s | turq & dull blue | .25 | — |
| 77 | A28 | 7½s | dp brn & dk lil | .45 | — |
| 78 | A28 | 10s | dp blue & brn rose | .25 | — |
| 79 | A28 | 15s | brown & dk grn | 1.25 | — |
| 80 | A28 | 17½s | ultra & org brn | 2.00 | — |
| 81 | A30 | 20s | Prus grn & dp bis brn | 1.00 | — |
| 82 | A31 | 30s | dk brn & dull vio | 3.50 | — |
| 83 | A30 | 35s | dk lilac & brn | 5.75 | — |
| 84 | A30 | 40s | dk brn & blue | .85 | — |
| 85 | A30 | 50s | dk brn & turq | 4.50 | — |
| 86 | A31 | 60s | dk brn & lt red brn | 6.75 | — |
| 87 | A31 | 80s | dk lilac & slate | 1.75 | — |
| 88 | A30 | 1r | br blue & pur brn | 3.50 | — |
| 89 | A30 | 2r | dk brn & dk grn | 1.00 | — |
| 90 | A31 | 2½r | dk lilac & blue | 7.50 | — |
| | | | *Nos. 70-90 (21)* | 42.95 | |

Nos. 30-50 overprinted

| | | | | | |
|---|---|---|---|---|---|
| 91 | A34 | 1s | dp brn & dp blue | .25 | — |
| 92 | A35 | 2s | dk red vio & dp grn | 1.25 | — |
| 93 | A35 | 2½s | dk brn & br scarlet | .25 | — |
| 94 | A35 | 3s | dp turq & org ver | .25 | — |
| 95 | A34 | 3½s | dp brn & dp grn | .25 | — |
| 96 | A35 | 4s | turq & dull blue | .25 | — |
| 97 | A35 | 5s | dull vio & dk yel brn | .50 | — |
| 98 | A34 | 7½s | dp brn & dk lil | .60 | — |
| 99 | A34 | 10s | dk brn & dp vio | .75 | — |
| 100 | A35 | 15s | dk vio & dp dull grn | 1.25 | — |
| 101 | A34 | 17½s | dk brn & red org | 1.25 | — |
| 102 | A36 | 20s | dull vio & dp brn | 3.25 | — |
| 103 | A36 | 30s | dp brn & dk blue vio | 2.75 | — |
| 104 | A37 | 35s | sl vio & blue | 2.75 | — |
| 105 | A37 | 40s | dull vio & dk yel brn | 2.75 | — |
| 106 | A37 | 50s | dk brn & Prus grn | 5.00 | — |
| 107 | A37 | 60s | br blue & dk yel brn | 5.00 | — |
| 108 | A36 | 80s | dull vio & dull bl | 5.00 | — |
| 109 | A36 | 1r | dp blue & dp choc | 2.75 | — |
| 110 | A37 | 2r | dp brn & org ver | 2.75 | — |
| 111 | A36 | 2½r | dp brn & br blue | 6.00 | — |
| | | | *Nos. 91-111 (21)* | 44.85 | |

**Nos. 54-61 overprinted**

| | | | | | |
|---|---|---|---|---|---|
| 112 | A39 | 10s | gray & red | .40 | — |
| 113 | A39 | 15s | gray & dp blue | .40 | — |
| 114 | A39 | 25s | gray & red brn | 1.40 | — |
| 115 | A39 | 60s | gray & maroon | 1.40 | — |
| 116 | A39 | 1r | gray & maroon | 2.75 | — |
| | | | *Nos. 112-116 (5)* | 6.35 | |

**Souvenir Sheets**

| | | | | |
|---|---|---|---|---|
| 117 | A40 | 10s, 15s, 25s, 60s | 650.00 | — |
| *a.* | | Imperf | 1,750. | — |
| 118 | A40 | 30s, 50s, 1r, 2½r | 50.00 | — |
| *a.* | | Imperf | 100.00 | — |
| *b.* | | A39 2½r gray & maroon | — | — |
| *c.* | | As "b," imperf | — | — |

| | | | | |
|---|---|---|---|---|
| 119 | A40 | 1r, 4½r | 35.00 | — |
| a. | | Imperf | 50.00 | — |
| b. | A39 | 4½r maroon | — | — |
| c. | | As "b," imperf | — | — |

The stamps contained in No. 118 and the 4½r stamp contained in No. 119 are air post stamps and are inscribed "POS UDARA."

### United States of Indonesia

Mountain, Palms and Flag of Republic — A49

*Perf. 12½x12*

**1950, Jan. 17 Photo. Unwmk.**

**Size: 20½x26mm**

| | | | | |
|---|---|---|---|---|
| 333 | A49 | 15s red | 1.40 | .30 |

Exists imperf, without gum. Value $70.

**1950, June** *Perf. 11½*

**Size: 18x23mm**

| | | | | |
|---|---|---|---|---|
| 334 | A49 | 15s red | 6.25 | 2.00 |

Exists imperf, without gum. Value $50.

Netherlands Indies Nos. 307-315 Overprinted in Black

**1950** *Perf. 11½, 12½*

| | | | | |
|---|---|---|---|---|
| 335 | A42 | 1s gray | 1.00 | .80 |
| 336 | A42 | 2s claret | 1.40 | 3.50 |
| a. | | Perf 11½ | 1.75 | 2.25 |
| 337 | A42 | 2½s olive brown | 1.00 | .80 |
| a. | | Perf 12½ | 1.40 | .70 |
| 338 | A42 | 3s rose pink | 1.00 | .65 |
| a. | | Perf 12½ | 1.00 | .55 |
| 339 | A42 | 4s green | 1.00 | .80 |
| a. | | Perf 12½ | 1.75 | 1.00 |
| 340 | A42 | 5s blue | 1.00 | .80 |
| 341 | A42 | 7½s dark green | 1.00 | .80 |
| 342 | A42 | 10s violet | 1.00 | .75 |
| a. | | Perf 12½ | 1.75 | 1.75 |
| 343 | A42 | 12½s bright red | 1.25 | .80 |

Netherlands Indies Nos. 317-330 Overprinted in Black

*Perf. 11½, 12½*

| | | | | |
|---|---|---|---|---|
| 345 | A43 | 20s gray black | 30.00 | 35.00 |
| 346 | A43 | 25s ultra | 1.00 | .80 |
| a. | | Perf 12½ | 1.75 | .80 |
| 347 | A44 | 30s bright red | 10.00 | 22.50 |
| a. | | Perf 12½ | 52.50 | 72.50 |
| 348 | A44 | 40s gray green | 1.00 | .50 |
| a. | | Perf 12½ | 1.00 | .50 |
| 349 | A44 | 45s claret | 2.10 | 1.25 |
| 350 | A45 | 50s orange brown | 1.75 | 1.10 |
| 351 | A45 | 60s brown | 8.75 | 13.50 |
| a. | | Perf 12½ | — | 37.50 |
| 352 | A45 | 80s scarlet | 4.00 | 1.25 |
| a. | | Perf 12½ | 3.75 | 1.25 |

Perf. 11½, 20s, 45s, 50s. Others, both perfs.

**Overprint 12mm High**

*Perf. 12½*

| | | | | |
|---|---|---|---|---|
| 353 | A46 | 1r purple | 2.75 | .75 |
| 354 | A46 | 2r olive green | 450.00 | 160.00 |
| 355 | A46 | 3r red violet | 150.00 | 72.50 |
| 356 | A46 | 5r dark brown | 65.00 | 24.00 |
| 357 | A46 | 10r gray | 110.00 | 45.00 |
| 358 | A46 | 25r orange brown | 30.00 | 17.50 |
| | | *Nos. 335-358 (23)* | 876.00 | 405.35 |
| | | Set, hinged | 325.00 | |

For overprints see Riau Archipelago #17-22.

### Republic of Indonesia

Arms of the Republic A50

Doves in Flight A51

*Perf. 12½x12*

**1950, Aug. 17 Photo. Unwmk.**

| | | | | |
|---|---|---|---|---|
| 359 | A50 | 15s red | 2.00 | .50 |
| 360 | A50 | 25s dull green | 3.00 | 2.00 |
| 361 | A50 | 1r sepia | 10.00 | 2.50 |
| | | *Nos. 359-361 (3)* | 15.00 | 5.00 |

5th anniv. of Indonesia's proclamation of independence.

**1951, Oct. 24 Engr.** *Perf. 12*

| | | | | |
|---|---|---|---|---|
| 362 | A51 | 7½s blue green | 5.00 | 1.00 |
| 363 | A51 | 10s violet | 1.25 | .45 |
| 364 | A51 | 20s red | 2.50 | 1.00 |
| 365 | A51 | 30s carmine rose | 3.25 | 1.25 |
| 366 | A51 | 35s ultra | 3.25 | 1.25 |
| 367 | A51 | 1r sepia | 27.50 | 4.00 |
| | | *Nos. 362-367 (6)* | 42.75 | 8.95 |

6th anniv. of the UN and the 1st anniv. of the Republic of Indonesia as a member.

A52

Post Office — A53

Mythological Hero — A54

Pres. Sukarno — A55

**1951-53 Photo.** *Perf. 12½*

| | | | | |
|---|---|---|---|---|
| 368 | A52 | 1s gray | .45 | .90 |
| 369 | A52 | 2s plum | .45 | .80 |
| 370 | A52 | 2½s brown | 6.50 | .50 |
| 371 | A52 | 5s car rose | .45 | .25 |
| 372 | A52 | 7½s green | .45 | .50 |
| 373 | A52 | 10s blue | 1.25 | .25 |
| a. | | Perf 11½ | 8.75 | 8.75 |
| 374 | A52 | 15s purple | .90 | .40 |
| 375 | A52 | 20s rose red | .50 | .40 |
| 376 | A52 | 25s deep green | .50 | .25 |
| 377 | A53 | 30s red orange | .25 | .25 |
| 378 | A53 | 35s purple | .80 | .25 |
| 379 | A53 | 40s dull green | .25 | .25 |
| 380 | A53 | 45s deep claret | .25 | .40 |
| 381 | A53 | 50s brown | 5.75 | .25 |
| 382 | A54 | 60s dark brown | .25 | .25 |
| 383 | A54 | 70s gray | .25 | .25 |
| 384 | A54 | 75s ultra | .25 | .25 |
| 385 | A54 | 80s claret | .25 | .25 |
| 386 | A54 | 90s gray green | .25 | .25 |
| | | *Nos. 368-386 (19)* | 20.00 | 6.90 |

*Perf. 12½x12*

| | | | | |
|---|---|---|---|---|
| 387 | A55 | 1r purple | .30 | .25 |
| 388 | A55 | 1.25r dp orange | 2.10 | .25 |
| 389 | A55 | 1.50r brown | .30 | .25 |
| 390 | A55 | 2r green | .30 | .25 |
| 391 | A55 | 2.50r rose brown | .30 | .25 |
| 392 | A55 | 3r blue | .30 | .25 |
| 392A | A55 | 4r apple green | .30 | .25 |
| 393 | A55 | 5r brown | .30 | .25 |
| 394 | A55 | 6r rose lilac | .30 | .25 |
| 395 | A55 | 10r slate | .30 | .25 |
| 396 | A55 | 15r yellow | .30 | .25 |
| 397 | A55 | 20r sepia | .30 | .25 |
| 398 | A55 | 25r scarlet | .80 | .25 |
| 399 | A55 | 40r yellow green | 1.00 | 2.75 |
| 400 | A55 | 50r violet | 1.40 | .75 |
| | | *Nos. 387-400 (15)* | 8.60 | 6.75 |

Nos. 368-376, 387, 390, 392, 393, 395, 398 were issued in 1951; Nos. 377-386, 388-389, 391, 392A, 394, 396-397, 399-400 in 1953.

Values are for the later Djakarta printings which have thicker numerals and a darker over-all impression. Earlier printings by Joh. Enschede and Sons, Haarlem, Netherlands, sell for more.

For surcharge see No. B68. For overprints see Riau Archipelago Nos. 1-16, 32-40.

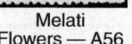

Melati Flowers — A56

Crowd Releasing Doves — A57

**1953, Dec. 22** *Perf. 12½*

| | | | | |
|---|---|---|---|---|
| 401 | A56 | 50s blue green | 12.00 | .70 |

25th anniv. of the formation of the Indonesian Women's Congress.

**1955, Apr. 18** *Perf. 13x12½*

| | | | | |
|---|---|---|---|---|
| 402 | A57 | 15s gray | .75 | .75 |
| 403 | A57 | 35s brown | .90 | .75 |
| 404 | A57 | 50s deep magenta | 2.40 | .75 |
| 405 | A57 | 75s blue green | 1.50 | .75 |
| | | *Nos. 402-405 (4)* | 5.55 | 3.00 |

Asian-African Conf., Bandung, April 18-24.

Proclamation of Independence A58

**1955, Aug. 17 Photo.** *Perf. 12½*

| | | | | |
|---|---|---|---|---|
| 406 | A58 | 15s green | .75 | 1.00 |
| 407 | A58 | 35s ultra | 1.25 | 1.00 |
| 408 | A58 | 50s brown | 8.00 | .90 |
| 409 | A58 | 75s magenta | 1.25 | .60 |
| | | *Nos. 406-409 (4)* | 11.25 | 3.50 |

Ten years of independence.

Voters — A59

**1955, Sept. 29** *Perf. 12*

**Without gum**

| | | | | |
|---|---|---|---|---|
| 410 | A59 | 15s rose violet | .60 | .60 |
| 411 | A59 | 35s green | .60 | .80 |
| 412 | A59 | 50s carmine rose | 2.10 | 1.00 |
| 413 | A59 | 75s lt ultra | .85 | .45 |
| | | *Nos. 410-413 (4)* | 4.15 | 2.85 |

First free elections in Indonesia.

Mas Soeharto Postmaster General A60

Helmet, Wreath and Monument A61

**1955, Sept. 27** *Perf. 12½*

| | | | | |
|---|---|---|---|---|
| 414 | A60 | 15s brown | 1.25 | .35 |
| 415 | A60 | 35s dark carmine | 1.25 | .35 |
| 416 | A60 | 50s ultra | 5.50 | 4.00 |
| 417 | A60 | 75s dull green | 1.25 | .35 |
| | | *Nos. 414-417 (4)* | 9.25 | 5.05 |

Issued to mark 10 years of Indonesia's Postal, Telegraph and Telephone system.

**1955, Nov. 10**

| | | | | |
|---|---|---|---|---|
| 418 | A61 | 25s bluish green | 1.25 | .60 |
| 419 | A61 | 50s ultra | 1.50 | .70 |
| 420 | A61 | 1r dk car rose | 11.00 | .40 |
| | | *Nos. 418-420 (3)* | 13.75 | 1.70 |

Issued in honor of the soldiers killed in the war of liberation from the Netherlands.

Torch, Book and Map A62

Lesser Malay Chevrotain A63

**1956, May 26 Photo.**

| | | | | |
|---|---|---|---|---|
| 421 | A62 | 25s ultra | 1.40 | .50 |
| 422 | A62 | 50s carmine rose | 7.00 | 1.25 |
| 423 | A62 | 1r dark green | 2.00 | 1.25 |
| | | *Nos. 421-423 (3)* | 10.40 | 3.00 |

Asia-Africa Student Conf., Bandung, May, 1956.

**1956 Unwmk.** *Perf. 12½x13½*

Animals: 5s, 10s, Lesser Malay chevrotain. 20s, 25s, Otter. 35s, Malayan pangolin. 50s, Banteng. 75s, Asiatic two-horned rhinoceros.

| | | | | |
|---|---|---|---|---|
| 424 | A63 | 5s deep ultra | .25 | .25 |
| 425 | A63 | 10s yellow brown | .25 | .25 |
| 426 | A63 | 15s rose violet | .40 | .25 |
| 427 | A63 | 20s dull green | .40 | .25 |
| 428 | A63 | 25s deep claret | .40 | .25 |
| 429 | A63 | 35s brt violet blue | .40 | .25 |
| 430 | A63 | 50s brown | .75 | .25 |
| 431 | A63 | 75s dark brown | .40 | .25 |
| | | *Nos. 424-431 (8)* | 3.25 | 2.00 |

See Nos. 450-456. For overprints see Riau Archipelago Nos. 23-31.

Dancing Girl and Gate — A64

Telegraph Key — A65

**1956, Oct. 7** *Perf. 12½x12*

| | | | | |
|---|---|---|---|---|
| 432 | A64 | 15s slate green | 1.25 | .65 |
| 433 | A64 | 35s brown violet | 1.25 | .65 |
| 434 | A64 | 50s blue black | 2.50 | 2.00 |
| 435 | A64 | 75s deep claret | 3.00 | 1.00 |
| | | *Nos. 432-435 (4)* | 8.00 | 4.30 |

Founding of the city of Jogjakarta, 200th anniv.

**1957, May 10 Unwmk.**

| | | | | |
|---|---|---|---|---|
| 436 | A65 | 10s lt crimson | 2.40 | .60 |
| 437 | A65 | 15s brt blue | .55 | .45 |
| 438 | A65 | 25s gray | .50 | .25 |
| 439 | A65 | 50s brown red | .65 | .30 |
| 440 | A65 | 75s lt blue green | .80 | .25 |
| | | *Nos. 436-440 (5)* | 4.90 | 1.85 |

Indonesian telegraph system centenary.

Thrift Symbolism A66

Douglas DC-3 A67

Design: 15s, 1r, People and hands holding wreath of rice and cotton.

**1957, July 12 Photo.** *Perf. 12½*

| | | | | |
|---|---|---|---|---|
| 441 | A66 | 10s blue | .50 | .45 |
| 442 | A66 | 15s rose carmine | .65 | .45 |
| 443 | A66 | 50s green | 1.25 | .95 |
| 444 | A66 | 1r brt violet | 1.25 | .50 |
| | | *Nos. 441-444 (4)* | 3.65 | 2.35 |

Cooperation Day, July 12.

**1958, Apr. 9** *Perf. 12½x12*

Aircraft: 15s, Helicopter. 30s, Miles Magister. 50s, Two-motor plane of Indonesian Airways. 75s, De Havilland Vampire.

| | | | | |
|---|---|---|---|---|
| 445 | A67 | 10s reddish brown | .45 | .25 |
| 446 | A67 | 15s blue | .45 | .25 |
| 447 | A67 | 35s orange | .45 | .25 |

| | | | | |
|---|---|---|---|---|
| **448** | A67 | 50s bright green | .45 | .40 |
| **449** | A67 | 75s gray | .45 | .55 |
| | | *Nos. 445-449 (5)* | 2.25 | 1.70 |

Issued for National Aviation Day, April 9.

### Animal Type of 1956

Animals: 30s, Otter. 40s, 45s, Malayan pangolin. 60s, 70s, Banteng. 80s, 90s, Asiatic two-horned rhinoceros.

**1958 Photo. *Perf. 12½x13½***

| | | | | |
|---|---|---|---|---|
| **450** | A63 | 30s orange | .25 | .25 |
| **451** | A63 | 40s brt yellow grn | .30 | .25 |
| **452** | A63 | 45s rose lilac | 1.40 | .25 |
| **453** | A63 | 60s dark blue | .45 | .25 |
| **454** | A63 | 70s orange ver | 2.00 | .30 |
| **455** | A63 | 80s red | .60 | .25 |
| **456** | A63 | 90s yellow green | .60 | .25 |
| | | *Nos. 450-456 (7)* | 5.60 | 1.80 |

Thomas Cup A68

**1958, Aug. 15 *Perf. 13½x13***

| | | | | |
|---|---|---|---|---|
| **457** | A68 | 25s rose carmine | .25 | .25 |
| **458** | A68 | 50s orange | .25 | .25 |
| **459** | A68 | 1r brown | .30 | .25 |
| | | *Nos. 457-459 (3)* | .80 | .75 |

Indonesia's victory in the 1958 Thomas Cup World Badminton Championship.

Satellite Circling Globe — A69

**1958, Oct. 15 Litho. *Perf. 12½x12***

| | | | | |
|---|---|---|---|---|
| **460** | A69 | 10s dk grn, pink & lt bl | 1.10 | .60 |
| **461** | A69 | 15s vio, gray & pale bluish grn | .30 | .25 |
| **462** | A69 | 35s brown, blue & pink | .30 | .25 |
| **463** | A69 | 50s bl, redsh brn & gray | .30 | .25 |
| **464** | A69 | 75s black, vio & buff | .30 | .25 |
| | | *Nos. 460-464 (5)* | 2.30 | 1.60 |

International Geophysical Year, 1957-58.

Bicyclist and Map A70

**1958, Nov. 15 Photo. *Perf. 13½x13***

| | | | | |
|---|---|---|---|---|
| **465** | A70 | 25s bright blue | .45 | .30 |
| **466** | A70 | 50s brown carmine | .80 | .30 |
| **467** | A70 | 1r gray | .45 | .30 |
| | | *Nos. 465-467 (3)* | 1.70 | .90 |

Bicycle Tour of Java, Aug. 15-30.

Man Looking into Light A71

Wild Boar (Babirusa) A72

Designs: 15s, Hands and flame. 35s, Woman holding candle. 50s, Family hailing torch. 75s, Torch and "10."

**1958, Dec. 10 *Perf. 12½x12***

| | | | | |
|---|---|---|---|---|
| **468** | A71 | 10s gray brown | .25 | .25 |
| **469** | A71 | 15s dull red brn | .25 | .25 |
| **470** | A71 | 35s ultra | .25 | .25 |
| **471** | A71 | 50s pale brown | .25 | .25 |
| **472** | A71 | 75s lt blue grn | .30 | .25 |
| | | *Nos. 468-472 (5)* | 1.30 | 1.25 |

10th anniv. of the signing of the Universal Declaration of Human Rights.

**1959, June 1 Photo. *Perf. 12***

Animals: 15s, Anoa (smallest buffalo). 20s, Orangutan. 50s, Javan rhinoceros. 75s, Komodo dragon (lizard). 1r, Malayan tapir.

| | | | | |
|---|---|---|---|---|
| **473** | A72 | 10s olive bis & sepia | .25 | .25 |
| **474** | A72 | 15s org brn & sepia | .25 | .25 |
| **475** | A72 | 20s lt ol grn & sepia | .30 | .30 |
| **476** | A72 | 50s bister brn & sepia | .60 | .45 |
| **477** | A72 | 75s dp rose & sepia | .80 | .25 |
| **478** | A72 | 1r blue grn & blk | 1.00 | .25 |
| | | *Nos. 473-478 (6)* | 3.20 | 1.75 |

Issued to publicize wildlife preservation.

A73

**1959, Aug. 17 Litho. *Perf. 12***

| | | | | |
|---|---|---|---|---|
| **479** | A73 | 20s blue & red | .25 | .25 |
| **480** | A73 | 50s rose red & blk | .25 | .25 |
| **481** | A73 | 75s brown & red | .25 | .25 |
| **482** | A73 | 1.50r lt green & blk | .40 | .40 |
| | | *Nos. 479-482 (4)* | 1.15 | 1.15 |

Introduction of the constitution of 1945 embodying "guided democracy."

Factories — A74

Designs: 20s, 75s, Cogwheel and train. 1.15r, Means of transportation.

**1959, Oct. 26 Photo. *Perf. 12***

| | | | | |
|---|---|---|---|---|
| **483** | A74 | 15s brt green & blk | .25 | .25 |
| **484** | A74 | 20s dull org & blk | .25 | .25 |
| **485** | A74 | 50s red & black | .25 | .25 |
| **486** | A74 | 75s brt grnsh bl & blk | .25 | .25 |
| **487** | A74 | 1.15r magenta & blk | .25 | .25 |
| | | *Nos. 483-487 (5)* | 1.25 | 1.25 |

11th Colombo Plan Conference, Jakarta.

Mother & Child, WRY Emblem — A75

15s, 75s, Destroyed town & fleeing family. 20s, 1.15r, World Refugee Year emblem.

**1960, Apr. 7 Unwmk. *Perf. 12½x12***

| | | | | |
|---|---|---|---|---|
| **488** | A75 | 10s claret & blk | .25 | .25 |
| **489** | A75 | 15s bister & blk | .25 | .25 |
| **490** | A75 | 20s org brn & blk | .25 | .25 |
| **491** | A75 | 50s green & blk | .25 | .25 |
| **492** | A75 | 75s dk blue & blk | .25 | .25 |
| **493** | A75 | 1.15r scarlet & blk | .25 | *1.10* |
| | | *Nos. 488-493 (6)* | 1.50 | 2.35 |

World Refugee Year, 7/1/59-6/3/60.

Tea Plantation — A76

5s, Oil palms. 10s, Sugar cane and railroad. 15s, Coffee. 20s, Tobacco. 50s, Coconut palms. 75s, Rubber plantation. 1.15r, Rice.

**1960 *Perf. 12x12½***

| | | | | |
|---|---|---|---|---|
| **494** | A76 | 5s gray | .25 | .25 |
| **495** | A76 | 10s red brown | .25 | .25 |
| **496** | A76 | 15s plum | .25 | .25 |
| **497** | A76 | 20s ocher | .25 | .25 |
| **498** | A76 | 25s brt blue grn | .25 | .25 |
| **499** | A76 | 50s deep blue | .25 | .25 |
| **500** | A76 | 75s scarlet | .25 | .25 |
| **501** | A76 | 1.15r plum | .25 | .25 |
| | | *Nos. 494-501 (8)* | 2.00 | 2.00 |

For surcharges see Nos. B132-B134.

Anopheles Mosquito — A77

**1960, Nov. 12 Photo. *Perf. 12x12½***

| | | | | |
|---|---|---|---|---|
| **502** | A77 | 25s carmine rose | .25 | .25 |
| **503** | A77 | 50s orange brown | .25 | .25 |
| **504** | A77 | 75s brt green | .25 | .25 |
| **505** | A77 | 3r orange | .30 | .30 |
| | | *Nos. 502-505 (4)* | 1.05 | 1.05 |

World Health Day, Nov. 12, 1960, and to promote malaria control.

Pres. Sukarno with Hoe — A78

**1961, Feb. 15 *Perf. 12½x12***

| | | | | |
|---|---|---|---|---|
| **506** | A78 | 75s gray | .70 | .25 |

Planned National Development.

Dayak Dancer of Borneo A79

Designs: 10s, Ambonese boat. 15s, Tangkubanperahu crater. 20s, Bull races. 50s, Toradja houses. 75s, Balinese temple. 1r, Lake Toba. 1.50r, Balinese dancer and musicians. 2r, Buffalo hole, view. 3r, Borobudur Temple, Java.

**1961 *Perf. 13½x13***

| | | | | |
|---|---|---|---|---|
| **507** | A79 | 10s rose lilac | .65 | .50 |
| **508** | A79 | 15s gray | .65 | .50 |
| **509** | A79 | 20s orange | .65 | .50 |
| **510** | A79 | 25s orange ver | .65 | .50 |
| **511** | A79 | 50s carmine rose | .65 | .50 |
| **512** | A79 | 75s red brown | .65 | .50 |
| **513** | A79 | 1r brt green | 1.25 | .50 |
| **514** | A79 | 1.50r bister brn | 1.25 | .50 |
| **515** | A79 | 2r grnsh blue | 1.60 | .50 |
| **516** | A79 | 3r gray | 1.75 | .50 |
| | | Set of 4 souvenir sheets | 24.00 | 22.50 |
| | | *Nos. 507-516 (10)* | 9.75 | 5.00 |

Issued for tourist publicity.

The four souvenir sheets among them contain one each of Nos. 507-516 imperf., with two or three stamps to a sheet and English marginal inscriptions: "Visit Indonesia" and "Visit the Orient Year." Size: 139x105mm or 105x139mm.

Sports Hall and Thomas Cup A80

***Perf. 13½x12½***

**1961, June 1 Photo.**

| | | | | |
|---|---|---|---|---|
| **517** | A80 | 75s pale violet & blue | .25 | .25 |
| **518** | A80 | 1r citron & dk grn | .25 | .25 |
| **519** | A80 | 3r salmon pink & dk bl | .30 | .25 |
| | | *Nos. 517-519 (3)* | .80 | .75 |

1961 Thomas Cup World Badminton Championship.

New Buildings and Workers A81

**1961, July 6 Unwmk.**

| | | | | |
|---|---|---|---|---|
| **520** | A81 | 75s violet & grnsh bl | .25 | .25 |
| **521** | A81 | 1.50r emerald & buff | .25 | .25 |
| **522** | A81 | 3r dk red & salmon | .40 | .25 |
| | | *Nos. 520-522 (3)* | .90 | .75 |

16th anniversary of independence.

Sultan Hasanuddin — A82

Portraits: 20s, Abdul Muis. 30s, Surjopranoto. 40s, Tengku Tjhik Di Tiro. 50s, Teuku Umar. 60s, K. H. Samanhudi. 75s, Captain Pattimura. 1r, Raden Adjeng Kartini. 1.25r, K. H. Achmad Dahlan. 1.50r, Tuanku Imam Bondjol. 2r, Si Singamangaradja XII. 2.50r, Mohammad Husni Thamrin. 3r, Ki Hadjar Dewantoro. 4r, Djenderal Sudirman. 4.50r, Dr. G. S. S. J. Ratulangie. 5r, Pangeran Diponegoro. 6r, Dr. Setyabudi. 7.50r, H. O. S. Tjokroaminoto. 10r, K. H. Agus Salim. 15r, Dr. Soetomo.

***Perf. 13½x12½***

**1961-62 Unwmk. Photo.**

**Black Inscriptions; Portraits in Sepia**

| | | | | |
|---|---|---|---|---|
| **523** | A82 | 20s olive | .25 | .30 |
| **524** | A82 | 25s gray olive | .25 | .30 |
| **525** | A82 | 30s brt lilac | .25 | .30 |
| **526** | A82 | 40s brown orange | .50 | .30 |
| **527** | A82 | 50s bluish green | .50 | .30 |
| **528** | A82 | 60s green ('62) | .25 | .30 |
| **529** | A82 | 75s lt red brown | .50 | .30 |
| **530** | A82 | 1r lt blue | .85 | .30 |
| **531** | A82 | 1.25r lt ol grn ('62) | .55 | .30 |
| **532** | A82 | 1.50r emerald | .85 | .30 |
| **533** | A82 | 2r org red ('62) | .55 | .30 |
| **534** | A82 | 2.50r rose claret | .85 | .30 |
| **535** | A82 | 3r gray blue | .70 | .30 |
| **536** | A82 | 4r olive green | .90 | .30 |
| **537** | A82 | 4.50r red lilac ('62) | .55 | .30 |
| **538** | A82 | 5r brick red | 1.10 | .30 |
| **539** | A82 | 6r bister ('62) | .55 | .30 |
| **540** | A82 | 7.50r violet bl ('62) | .80 | .30 |
| **541** | A82 | 10r green ('62) | 1.25 | .30 |
| **542** | A82 | 15r dp org ('62) | 1.10 | .30 |
| | | *Nos. 523-542 (20)* | 13.10 | 6.00 |

National heroes. The 25s, 75s, 1.50r, 5r issued on 8/17, Independence Day; 40s, 50s, 4r on 10/5, Army Day; 20s, 30s, 1r, 2.50r, 3r on 11/10, Republic Day; 60s, 2r, 7.50r, 15r on 10/5/62; 1.25r, 4.50r, 6r, 10r on 11/10/62.

Symbols of Census A83

**1961, Sept. 15 *Perf. 13½x12½***

| | | | | |
|---|---|---|---|---|
| **543** | A83 | 75s rose violet | .60 | .25 |

First census in Indonesia.

Djataju — A84

Scenes from Ramayana Ballet: 40s, Hanuman. 1r, Dasamuka. 1.50r, Kidang Kentiana. 3r, Dewi Sinta. 5r, Rama.

***Perf. 12x12½***

**1962, Jan. 15 Unwmk.**

| | | | | |
|---|---|---|---|---|
| **544** | A84 | 30s ocher & red brn | .40 | .45 |
| **545** | A84 | 40s rose lilac & vio | .40 | .45 |
| **546** | A84 | 1r green & claret | .65 | .45 |
| **547** | A84 | 1.50r sal pink & dk grn | .75 | .45 |
| **548** | A84 | 3r pale grn & dp bl | 2.00 | .45 |
| **549** | A84 | 5r brn org & dk brn | 1.75 | .45 |
| | | *Nos. 544-549 (6)* | 5.95 | 2.70 |

Asian Games Emblem — A85

Main Stadium — A86

Designs: 10s, Basketball. 15s, Main Stadium, Jakarta. 20s, Weight lifter. 25s, Hotel Indonesia. 30s, Cloverleaf intersection. 40s, Discus thrower. 50s, Woman diver. 60s, Soccer. 70s, Press House. 75s, Boxers. 1r, Volleyball. 1.25r, 2r, 3r, 5r, Asian Games emblem. 1.50r, Badminton. 1.75r, Wrestlers. 2.50r, Woman rifle shooter. 4.50r, Hockey. 6r, Water polo. 7.50r, Tennis. 10r, Table tennis. 15r, Bicyclist. 20r, Welcome Monument.

**1962 Photo. *Perf. 12½***

| | | | | |
|---|---|---|---|---|
| **550** | A85 | 10s green & yel | .25 | .25 |
| **551** | A86 | 15s grnsh blk & bis | .25 | .25 |
| **552** | A85 | 20s red lil & lt grn | .30 | .25 |
| **553** | A86 | 25s car & lt grn | .25 | .25 |
| **554** | A86 | 30s bl grn & yel | .35 | .25 |
| **555** | A85 | 40s ultra & pale bl | .35 | .25 |
| **556** | A85 | 50s choc & gray | .35 | .30 |
| **557** | A85 | 60s lil rose & vio gray | .35 | .30 |
| **558** | A85 | 70s dk brn & rose | .35 | .30 |
| **559** | A85 | 75s choc & org | .35 | .25 |
| **560** | A85 | 1r purple & lt bl | .35 | .30 |
| **561** | A85 | 1.25r dk bl & rose car | .35 | .40 |
| **562** | A85 | 1.50r red org & lil | 1.25 | .40 |
| **563** | A85 | 1.75r dk car & rose | .80 | .40 |
| **564** | A85 | 2r brn & yel grn | .55 | .40 |
| **565** | A85 | 2.50r dp bl & lt grn | .70 | .40 |
| **566** | A85 | 3r black & dk red | .70 | .40 |
| **567** | A85 | 4.50r dk grn & red | .70 | .40 |
| **568** | A85 | 5r gray grn & lem | .70 | .40 |
| **569** | A85 | 6r brn red & dp yel | .75 | .40 |
| **570** | A85 | 7.50r red brn & sal | .75 | .25 |
| **571** | A85 | 10r dk blue & blue | 1.00 | .55 |
| **572** | A85 | 15r dl vio & pale vio | 1.25 | 1.10 |
| **573** | A85 | 20r dk grn & ol bis | 2.40 | 1.25 |
| | | *Nos. 550-573 (24)* | 15.40 | 9.70 |

4th Asian Games, Jakarta.

Malaria Eradication Emblem — A87

**1962, Apr. 7 *Perf. 12½x12***

| | | | | |
|---|---|---|---|---|
| **574** | A87 | 40s dull bl & vio bl | .25 | .25 |
| **575** | A87 | 1.50r yel org & brn | .25 | .25 |
| **576** | A87 | 3r green & indigo | .25 | .25 |
| **577** | A87 | 6r lilac & blk | .25 | .25 |
| | | *Nos. 574-577 (4)* | 1.00 | 1.00 |

WHO drive to eradicate malaria. The 1.50r and 6r have Indonesian inscription on top.

Atom Diagram — A88

**1962, Sept. 24 Photo. *Perf. 12x12½***

| | | | | |
|---|---|---|---|---|
| **578** | A88 | 1.50r dk blue & yel | .25 | .25 |
| **579** | A88 | 4.50r brick red & yel | .25 | .30 |
| **580** | A88 | 6r green & yel | .40 | .30 |
| | | *Nos. 578-580 (3)* | .90 | .85 |

Development through science.

Pacific Travel Association Emblem — A89

1.50r, Prambanan Temple and Mount Merapi. 6r, Balinese Meru (Buildings), Pura Taman Ajun.

**1963, Mar. 14 Unwmk.**

| | | | | |
|---|---|---|---|---|
| **581** | A89 | 1r grn & indigo | .25 | .25 |
| **582** | A89 | 1.50r olive & indigo | .25 | .25 |
| **583** | A89 | 3r ocher & indigo | .40 | .25 |
| **584** | A89 | 6r dp org & indigo | .40 | .25 |
| | | *Nos. 581-584 (4)* | 1.30 | 1.00 |

12th conf. of the Pacific Area Travel Assoc., Bandung.

Mechanized Plow — A90

1r, 3r, Hand holding rice stalks, vert.

**1963, Mar. 21 *Perf. 12½x12, 12x12½***

| | | | | |
|---|---|---|---|---|
| **585** | A90 | 1r blue & yel | .25 | .25 |
| **586** | A90 | 1.50r brt grn & indigo | .25 | .25 |
| **587** | A90 | 3r rose car & org | .25 | .25 |
| **588** | A90 | 6r orange & blk | .25 | .25 |
| | | *Nos. 585-588 (4)* | 1.00 | 1.00 |

FAO "Freedom from Hunger" campaign. English inscription on 3r and 6r.

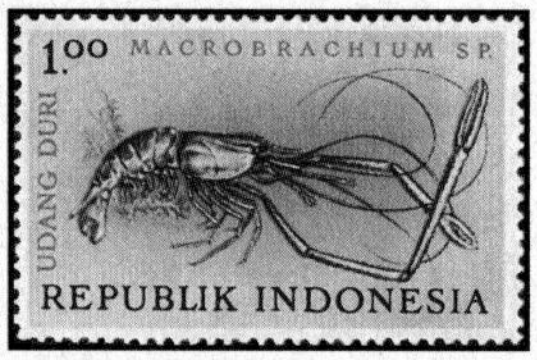


Long-Armed Lobster — A91

Fish: 1.50r, Little tuna. 3r, River roman. 6r, Chinese pompano.

**1963, Apr. 6 *Perf. 12½x12***

| | | | | |
|---|---|---|---|---|
| **589** | A91 | 1r ver, blk & yel | .45 | .25 |
| **590** | A91 | 1.50r ultra, blk & yel | .45 | .25 |
| **591** | A91 | 3r Prus bl, bis & car | .95 | .40 |
| **592** | A91 | 6r ol grn, blk & ocher | .95 | .65 |
| | | *Nos. 589-592 (4)* | 2.80 | 1.55 |

Pen and Conference Emblem — A92

Designs: 1.50r, Pen, Emblem and map of Africa and Southeast Asia. 3r, Globe, pen and broken chain, vert. 6r, Globe, hand holding pen and broken chain, vert.

***Perf. 12½x12, 12x12½***

**1963, Apr. 24 Photo. Unwmk.**

| | | | | |
|---|---|---|---|---|
| **593** | A92 | 1r lt bl & dp org | .25 | .25 |
| **594** | A92 | 1.50r pale vio & mar | .25 | .25 |
| **595** | A92 | 3r olive, bl & blk | .40 | .25 |
| **596** | A92 | 6r brick red & blk | .55 | .25 |
| | | *Nos. 593-596 (4)* | 1.45 | 1.00 |

Asian-African Journalists' Conference.

"Indonesia's Flag from Sabang to Merauke" — A93

4.50r, Parachutist landing in New Guinea. 6r, Bird of paradise & map of New Guinea.

**1963, May 1 *Perf. 12½x12***

| | | | | |
|---|---|---|---|---|
| **597** | A93 | 1.50r org brn, blk & red | .25 | .25 |
| **598** | A93 | 4.50r multicolored | .25 | .25 |
| **599** | A93 | 6r multicolored | .95 | .65 |
| | | *Nos. 597-599 (3)* | 1.45 | 1.15 |

Issued to mark the acquisition of Netherlands New Guinea (West Irian).

Centenary Emblem — A94

Design: 1.50r, 6r, Red Cross.

**1963, May 8 *Perf. 12***

| | | | | |
|---|---|---|---|---|
| **600** | A94 | 1r brt grn & red | .25 | .25 |
| **601** | A94 | 1.50r lt bl & red | .25 | .25 |
| **602** | A94 | 3r gray & red | .25 | .25 |
| **603** | A94 | 6r yel bis & red | .25 | .25 |
| | | *Nos. 600-603 (4)* | 1.00 | 1.00 |

Centenary of the International Red Cross.

Bank of Indonesia, Djalan A95

Daneswara, God of Prosperity A96

**1963, July 5 Photo. *Perf. 12***

| | | | | |
|---|---|---|---|---|
| **604** | A95 | 1.75r lt bl & pur | .25 | .25 |
| **605** | A96 | 4r citron & sl grn | .25 | .25 |
| **606** | A95 | 6r lt green & brn | .25 | .25 |
| **607** | A96 | 12r org & dk red brn | .25 | .25 |
| | | *Nos. 604-607 (4)* | 1.00 | 1.00 |

Issued for National Banking Day.

Standard Bearers — A97

Designs: 1.75r, "Pendet" dance. 4r, GANEFO building, Senajan, Jakarta. 6r, Archery. 10r, Badminton. 12r, Javelin. 25r, Sailing. 50r, Torch.

**1963, Nov. 10 Unwmk. *Perf. 12½***

| | | | | |
|---|---|---|---|---|
| **608** | A97 | 1.25r gray vio & dk brn | .25 | .25 |
| **609** | A97 | 1.75r org & ol grn | .25 | .25 |
| **610** | A97 | 4r emer & dk brn | .25 | .25 |
| **611** | A97 | 6r rose brn & blk | .25 | .25 |
| **612** | A97 | 10r lt ol grn & dk brn | .25 | .25 |
| **613** | A97 | 12r rose car & grnsh blk | .30 | .25 |
| **614** | A97 | 25r blue & dk blue | .40 | .40 |
| **615** | A97 | 50r red & black | .45 | .45 |
| | | *Nos. 608-615 (8)* | 2.40 | 2.35 |

1st Games of the New Emerging Forces, GANEFO, Jakarta, Nov. 10-22.

Pres. Sukarno — A98

**1964 Photo. *Perf. 12½x12***

| | | | | |
|---|---|---|---|---|
| **616** | A98 | 6r brown & dk bl | .25 | .25 |
| **617** | A98 | 12r bister & plum | .25 | .25 |
| **618** | A98 | 20r blue & org | .25 | .25 |
| **619** | A98 | 30r red org & bl | .25 | .25 |
| **620** | A98 | 40r green & brn | .25 | .25 |
| **621** | A98 | 50r red & dp grn | .25 | .25 |
| **622** | A98 | 75r vio & red org | .25 | .25 |
| **623** | A98 | 100r sil & red brn | .25 | .25 |
| **624** | A98 | 250r dk blue & sil | .25 | .25 |
| **625** | A98 | 500r red & gold | .30 | .30 |
| | | *Nos. 616-625 (10)* | 2.55 | 2.55 |

See Nos. B165-B179. For surcharges see Nos. 661, 663-667.

Trailer Truck — A99

Designs: 1r, Oxcart. 1.75r, Freighter. 2r, Lockheed Electra plane. 2.50r, Buginese sailboat, vert. 4r, Mailman with bicycle. 5r, Dakota plane. 7.50r, Teletype operator. 10r, Diesel train. 15r, Passenger ship. 25r, Convair Coronado Plane. 35r, Telephone switchboard operator.

**1964 *Perf. 12x12½, 12½x12***

| | | | | |
|---|---|---|---|---|
| **626** | A99 | 1r dull claret | .25 | .25 |
| **627** | A99 | 1.25r red brown | .25 | .25 |
| **628** | A99 | 1.75r Prus blue | .25 | .25 |
| **629** | A99 | 2r red orange | .25 | .25 |
| **630** | A99 | 2.50r brt blue | .25 | .25 |
| **631** | A99 | 4r bluish grn | .25 | .25 |
| **632** | A99 | 5r olive bister | .25 | .25 |
| **633** | A99 | 7.50r brt green | .25 | .25 |
| **634** | A99 | 10r orange | .25 | .25 |
| **635** | A99 | 15r dark blue | .25 | .25 |
| **636** | A99 | 25r violet blue | .30 | .25 |
| **637** | A99 | 35r red brown | .30 | .25 |
| | | *Nos. 626-637 (12)* | 3.10 | 3.00 |

For surcharges see Nos. 659-660, 662.

Ramses II — A100

Design: 6r, 18r, Kiosk of Trajan, Philae.

**1964, Mar. 8 *Perf. 12½x12***

| | | | | |
|---|---|---|---|---|
| **638** | A100 | 4r ol bis & ol grn | .30 | .25 |
| **639** | A100 | 6r grnsh bl & ol grn | .30 | .25 |
| **640** | A100 | 12r rose & ol grn | .35 | .25 |
| **641** | A100 | 18r emer & ol grn | .45 | .25 |
| | | *Nos. 638-641 (4)* | 1.40 | 1.00 |

UNESCO world campaign to save historic monuments in Nubia.

Stamps of Netherlands Indies and Indonesia — A101

**1964, Apr. 1 *Perf. 12½***

| | | | | |
|---|---|---|---|---|
| **642** | A101 | 10r gold, dk bl & red org | 1.00 | .40 |

Centenary of postage stamps in Indonesia.

Indonesian Pavilion — A102

**1964, May 16** ***Perf. 12½x12***
**643** A102 25r sil, blk, red & dk bl .45 .45
**644** A102 50r gold, Prus bl, red & grn 1.25 .45

New York World's Fair, 1964-65.

Thomas Cup — A103

**1964, Aug. 15** ***Perf. 12½x13½***
**645** A103 25r brt grn, gold & red .25 .30
**646** A103 50r ultra, gold & red .30 .30
**647** A103 75r purple, gold & red .80 *.95*
*Nos. 645-647 (3)* 1.35 1.55

Thomas Cup Badminton World Championship, 1964.

Cruisers and Map of West Irian — A104

30r, Submarine. 40r, Torpedo boat.

***Perf. 12½x12***
**1964, Oct. 5** **Photo.** **Unwmk.**
**648** A104 20r yellow & brn .30 .25
**649** A104 30r rose & blk .40 .25
**650** A104 40r brt grn & ultra .70 *.95*
*Nos. 648-650 (3)* 1.40 1.45

Issued to honor the Indonesian Navy.

Map of Africa and Asia and Mosque — A105

15r, 50r, Mosque and clasped hands.

**1965, Mar. 6** **Photo.** ***Perf. 12½***
**651** A105 10r lt blue & pur .30 .25
**652** A105 15r org & red brn .30 .25
**653** A105 25r brt grn & brn .45 .25
**654** A105 50r brn red & blk .45 *.70*
*Nos. 651-654 (4)* 1.50 1.45

Afro-Asian Islamic Conf., Bandung, Mar. 1965.

Hand Holding Scroll — A106

Design: 25r, 75r, Conference emblem (globe, cotton and grain).

**1965, Apr. 18** **Unwmk.** ***Perf. 12½***
**655** A106 15r silver & dp car .25 .25
**656** A106 25r aqua, gold & red .25 .25
**657** A106 50r gold & dp ultra .40 .25
**658** A106 75r pale vio, gold & red .55 *.80*
*Nos. 655-658 (4)* 1.45 1.55

10th anniv. of the First Afro-Asian Conf.

Nos. 618-623 and Nos. 634-636 Surcharged in Orange or Black

**1965, Dec.** ***Perf. 12x12½, 12½x12***
**659** A99 10s on 10r (B) .25 .25
**660** A99 15s on 15r .25 .25
**661** A98 20s on 20r .25 .25
**662** A99 25s on 25r (B) .25 .25
**663** A98 30s on 30r .25 .25
**664** A98 40s on 40r .25 .25
**665** A98 50s on 50r .25 .25
**666** A98 75s on 75r .25 *2.00*
**667** A98 100s on 100r .30 .25
*Nos. 659-667 (9)* 2.30 4.00

The surcharge on Nos. 659-660 and No. 662 is in two lines and larger.

Pres. Sukarno — A107

**1966-67** **Photo.** ***Perf. 12½x12***
**668** A107 1s sep & Prus grn .25 .25
**669** A107 3s sep & lt ol grn .25 .25
**670** A107 5s sep & dp car .25 .25
**671** A107 8s sep & Prus grn .25 .25
**672** A107 10s sep & vio bl .25 .25
**673** A107 15s sep & blk .25 .25
**674** A107 20s sep & dp grn .25 .25
**675** A107 25s sep & dk red brn .25 .25
**676** A107 30s sep & dp bl .25 .25
**677** A107 40s sep & red brn .25 .25
**678** A107 50s sep & brt vio .25 .25
**679** A107 80s sep & org .25 .25
**680** A107 1r sep & emer .25 .25
**681** A107 1.25r sep & dk gray ol .25 .25
**682** A107 1.50r sep & emer .25 .25
**683** A107 2r sep & mag .25 .25
**684** A107 2.50r sep & gray .25 .25
**685** A107 5r sep & ocher .25 .30
**686** A107 10r sep & ol grn .25 .25
**686A** A107 12r grn & org ('67) .30 .25
**686B** A107 25r grn & brt pur ('67) .25 .30
*Nos. 668-686B (21)* 5.30 5.35

The 12r is inscribed "1967" instead of "1966."

Dockyard Workers — A108

Gen. Ahmad Yani — A109

Designs: 40s, Lighthouse. 50s, Fishermen. 1r, Maritime emblem (wheel and eagle). 1.50r, Sailboat. 2r, Loading dock. 2.50r, Diver emerging from water. 3r, Liner at pier.

**1966** **Photo.** ***Perf. 12x12½***
**687** A108 20s lt ultra & grn .25 .25
**688** A108 40s pink & dk bl .25 .25
**689** A108 50s green & brn .25 .25
**690** A108 1r salmon, bl & yel .25 .25
**691** A108 1.50r dull lil & dl grn .25 .25
**692** A108 2r gray & dp org .25 .25
**693** A108 2.50r rose lil & dk red .25 .25
**694** A108 3r brt green & blk .25 .25
*a.* Souvenir sheet 10.50 *13.50*
*Nos. 687-694 (8)* 2.00 2.00

Maritime Day. Issued: #687-690, Sept. 23; #691-694, Oct. 23.

No. 694a contains one imperf. stamp similar to No. 694.

**1966, Nov. 10** **Deep Blue Frame**

Heroes of the Revolution: #696, Lt. Gen. R. Suprapto. #697, Lt. General Harjono. #698, Lt. Gen. S. Parman. #699, Maj. Gen. D. I. Pandjaitan. #700, Maj. Gen. Sutojo Siswomihardjo. #701, Brig. General Katamso. #702, Colonel Soegijono. #703, Capt. Pierre Andreas Tendean. #704, Adj. Insp. Karel Satsuit Tubun.

**695** A109 5r org brn .30 .30
**696** A109 5r brt grn .30 .30
**697** A109 5r gray brn .30 .30
**698** A109 5r olive .30 .30
**699** A109 5r gray .30 .30
**700** A109 5r brt purple .30 .30
**701** A109 5r red lilac .30 .30
**702** A109 5r slate green .30 .30
**703** A109 5r dull rose lil .30 .30
**704** A109 5r orange .30 .30
*Nos. 695-704 (10)* 3.00 3.00

Issued to honor military men killed during the Communist uprising, October, 1965.

Tjlempung, Java — A110

Musical Instruments and Maps: 1r, Sasando, Timor. 1.25r, Foi doa, Flores. 1.50r, Kultjapi, Sumatra. 2r, Arababu, Sangihe and Talaud Islands. 2.50r, Drums, West New Guinea. 3r, Katjapi, Celebes. 4r, Hape, Borneo. 5r, Gangsa, Bali. 6r, Serunai, Sumatra. 8r, Rebab, Java. 10r, Trompet, West New Guinea. 12r, Totobuang, Moluccas. 15r, Drums, Nias. 20r, Kulintang, Celebes. 25r, Keledi, Borneo.

**1967** **Unwmk.** **Photo.** ***Perf. 12½x12***
**705** A110 50s red & gray .40 .40
**706** A110 1r brn & dp org .40 .40
**707** A110 1.25r mar & ultra .40 .40
**708** A110 1.50r grn & lt vio .40 .40
**709** A110 2r vio bl & yel bis .40 .40
**710** A110 2.50r ol grn & dl red .40 .40
**711** A110 3r brt grn & dl cl .40 .40
**712** A110 4r vio bl & org .65 .40
**713** A110 5r dull red & bl .65 .40
**714** A110 6r blk & brt pink .45 .45
**715** A110 8r red brn & brt grn .45 .45
**716** A110 10r lilac & red .45 .40
**717** A110 12r ol grn & lil .70 .65
**718** A110 15r vio & lt ol grn .65 .40
**719** A110 20r gray & sepia .65 .40
**720** A110 25r black & green .90 .40
*Nos. 705-720 (16)* 8.35 6.75

Issued: 1.25r, 10r, 12r, 15r, 20r, 25r, Mar. 1; others Feb. 1.

For surcharges see Nos. J118-J137.

Aviator and MiG-21 — A111

Aviation Day: 4r, Traffic control tower and 990A Convair jetliner. 5r, Hercules transport plane.

**1967, Apr. 9** ***Perf. 12½***
**721** A111 2.50r multicolored .50 .30
**722** A111 4r multicolored .50 .30
**723** A111 5r multicolored .80 .30
*Nos. 721-723 (3)* 1.80 .90

Thomas Cup with Victory Dates — A112

Design: 12r, Thomas Cup and globe.

**1967, May 31** ***Perf. 12x12½***
**724** A112 5r multicolored .25 .25
**725** A112 12r multicolored .50 .25

Issued to commemorate the Thomas Cup Badminton World Championship of 1967.

Balinese Girl in Front of Temple Gate — A113

**1967, July 1** **Photo.** ***Perf. 12½***
**726** A113 12r multicolored 1.25 1.00
*a.* Souv. sheet of 1, imperf. 4.50 5.50

Intl. Tourist Year, 1967. See No. 739.

Heroes of the Revolution Monument, Lubang Buaja — A114

Designs: 5r, Full view of monument, horiz. 7.50r, Shrine at monument.

*Perf. 12x12½, 12½x12*

**1967, Aug. 17** **Photo.**

**727** A114 2.50r pale grn & dk brn .25 .25
**728** A114 5r brt rose lil & pale brn .50 .30
**729** A114 7.50r pink & Prus grn .50 .30
*Nos. 727-729 (3)* 1.25 .85

Issued to publicize the "Heroes of the Revolution" Monument in Lubang Buaja.

Forest Fire, by Raden Saleh A115

50r, Fight to Death, by Raden Saleh.

**1967, Oct. 30** **Photo.** ***Perf. 12½***

**730** A115 25r org & gray grn .30 .50
*a.* Souvenir sheet of 1 5.50 7.00
**731** A115 50r vio brn & org .60 .45

Indonesian painter Raden Saleh (1813-80).

Human Rights Flame — A116

**1968, Jan. 1** **Photo.** ***Perf. 12½***

**732** A116 5r grn, lt vio bl & red .30 .25
**733** A116 12r grn, ol bis & red .35 .25

International Human Rights Year 1968.

Armed Forces College Emblem — A117

**1968, Jan. 29** **Litho.** ***Perf. 12½***

**734** A117 10r lt blue, yel & brn .55 .30

Integration of the Armed Forces College.

WHO Emblem and "20" — A118

20th anniv. of WHO: 20r, WHO emblem.

**1968, Apr. 7** **Photo.** ***Perf. 12½***

**735** A118 2r dp yel, pale yel & dk brn .30 .30
**736** A118 20r emerald & blk .40 .30

Trains of 1867 and 1967 and Railroad's Emblem — A119

**1968, May 15** **Photo.** ***Perf. 12½x12***

**737** A119 20r multicolored .70 .30
**738** A119 30r multicolored 1.00 1.00

Indonesian railroad centenary (in 1967).

**Tourist Type of 1967**

Tourist Publicity: 30r, Butterfly dancer from West Java.

**1968, July 1** ***Perf. 12½***

**739** A113 30r gray & multi 1.40 1.60
*a.* Souv. sheet of 1 + label 5.50 7.50

Bosscha Observatory and Andromeda Nebula — A120

30r, Observatory, globe and sky, vert.

**1968, Sept. 20** **Photo.** ***Perf. 12½x12***

**740** A120 15r ultra & yellow .50 .30
**741** A120 30r violet & orange .75 .30

Bosscha Observatory, 40th anniversary.

Weight Lifting — A121

Designs: 7.50r+7.50r, Sailing, horiz. 12r, Basketball. 30r, Dove, Olympic flame and emblem, horiz.

**1968, Oct. 12** ***Perf. 12½***

**742** A121 5r ocher, blk & grn .25 .25
**743** A121 Pair .55 .55
*a.* 7.50r Left half .25 .25
*b.* 7.50r Right half .25 .25
*c.* Souvenir sheet 5.50 8.00
**744** A121 12r blue & multi .30 .40
**745** A121 30r blue grn & multi .80 .25
*Nos. 742-745 (4)* 1.90 1.45

19th Olympic Games, Mexico City, Oct. 12-27. No. 743 is perforated vertically in the center, dividing it into two separate stamps, each inscribed "Republic Indonesia" and "7.50r." There is no gutter along the center perforation; and the design is continous over the two stamps.

No. 743c contains one No. 743 with track design surrounding the stamps.

Eugenia Aquea Burm. f. — A122

Fruits: 15r, Papaya. 30r, Durian, vert.

*Perf. 12½x12, 12x12½*

**1968, Dec. 20** **Photo.**

**746** A122 7.50r multicolored .40 .35
**747** A122 15r multicolored .55 .45
*a.* Souvenir sheet of 1 4.25 6.00
**748** A122 30r multicolored .85 .85
*a.* Souvenir sheet of 1 4.25 6.00
*Nos. 746-748 (3)* 1.80 1.65

Issued for the 11th Social Day.

Globe, ILO and UN Emblems A123

Designs: 7.50r, 25r, ILO and UN emblems.

**1969, Feb. 1** **Photo.** ***Perf. 12½***

**749** A123 5r yel grn & scar .25 .25
**750** A123 7.50r org & dk grn .25 .25
**751** A123 15r lilac & org .25 .25
**752** A123 25r bl grn & dull red .40 .25
*Nos. 749-752 (4)* 1.15 1.00

50th anniv. of the ILO.

R. Dewi Sartika A124

Red Crosses A125

#754, Tjoet Nja Din. #755, Tjoet Nja Meuthia. #756, General Gatot Subroto. #757, Sutan Sjahrir. #758, Dr. F. L. Tobing. #753-755 show portraits of women.

**1969, Mar. 1** **Photo.** ***Perf. 12½x12***

**753** A124 15r green & pur .30 .25
**754** A124 15r red lilac & grn .30 .25
**755** A124 15r dk blue & ver .30 .25
**756** A124 15r lilac & dk blue .30 .25
**757** A124 15r lemon & red .30 .25
**758** A124 15r pale brn & blue .30 .25
*Nos. 753-758 (6)* 1.80 1.50

Heroes of Indonesian independence.

**1969, May 5** **Photo.** ***Perf. 12***

20r, Red Cross surrounded by arms.

**759** A125 15r green & dp red .45 .25
**760** A125 20r org yel & red .50 .40

50th anniversary of the League of Red Cross Societies.

"Family Planning Leads to National Development and Prosperity" — A126

Design: 10r, Family, birds and factories.

**1969, June 2** **Photo.** ***Perf. 12½***

**761** A126 10r blue grn & org .30 .25
**762** A126 20r gray & magenta .50 .30

Planned Parenthood Conference of Southeast Asia and Oceania, Bandung, June 1-7.

Map of Bali and Mask A127

Designs: 15r, Map of Bali and woman carrying basket with offerings on head. 30r, Map of Bali and cremation ceremony.

**1969, July 1** **Litho.** ***Perf. 12½x12***

**763** A127 12r gray & multi .55 .55
**764** A127 15r lilac & multi 1.00 1.00
**765** A127 30r multicolored 1.00 .65
*a.* Souvenir sheet of 1 4.75 6.00
*Nos. 763-765 (3)* 2.55 2.20

Issued for tourist publicity.

Agriculture A128

Designs: 5r, Religious coexistence (roofs of mosques and churches). 10r, Social welfare (house and family). 12r, Import-export (cargo and ship). 15r, Clothing industry (cloth and spindles). 20r, Education (school children). 25r, Research (laboratory). 30r, Health care (people and syringe). 40r, Fishing (fish and net). 50r, Statistics (charts).

**1969** **Photo.** ***Perf. 12x12½***

**766** A128 5r yel grn & bl .25 .25
**767** A128 7.50r rose brn & yel .25 .25
**768** A128 10r slate & red .30 .25
**769** A128 12r blue & dp org 1.40 .65
**770** A128 15r slate grn & org .50 .25
**771** A128 20r purple & yel .50 .25
**772** A128 25r orange & blk .50 .25
**773** A128 30r car rose & gray .60 .25
**774** A128 40r green & org .80 .25
**775** A128 50r sepia & org .90 .25
*Nos. 766-775 (10)* 6.00 2.90

Five-year Development Plan.

See No. 968a.

Radar, Djatiluhur Station — A129

30r, Communications satellite and earth.

**1969, Sept. 29** ***Perf. 12½***

**776** A129 15r multicolored .45 .25
**777** A129 30r multicolored .70 .55

Vickers Vimy and Borobudur Temple A130

100r, Vickers Vimy and map of Indonesia.

**1969, Nov. 1** ***Perf. 13½x12½***

**778** A130 75r dp org & dull pur .60 .60
**779** A130 100r yellow & green .80 .60

50th anniv. of the 1st flight from England to Australia (via Java).

EXPO '70, Indonesian Pavilion — A131

Designs: 15r, Garuda, symbol of Indonesian EXPO '70 committee. 30r, like 5r.

**1970, Feb. 15** **Photo.** ***Perf. 12x12½***

**780** A131 5r brown, yel & grn .50 .30
**781** A131 15r dk bl, yel grn & red .80 .40
**782** A131 30r red, yel & dk bl 1.40 .65
*Nos. 780-782 (3)* 2.70 1.35

Issued to publicize EXPO '70 International Exposition, Osaka, Japan, Mar. 15-Sept. 13.

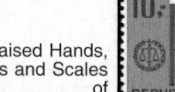

Upraised Hands, Bars and Scales of Justice — A132

**1970, Mar. 15** **Photo.** ***Perf. 12½***

**783** A132 10r red orange & pur .65 .40
**784** A132 15r brt green & pur .80 .40

Rule of law and justice in Indonesia.

UPU Monument, Bern — A133

Design: 30r, UPU Headquarters, Bern.

**1970, May 20** **Photo.** ***Perf. 12x12½***

**785** A133 15r emer & copper red .75 .40
**786** A133 30r ocher & blue 1.25 .95

Inauguration of the new UPU Headquarters in Bern, Switzerland.

Dancers — A134

**1970, July 1** **Photo.** ***Perf. 12***

**787** A134 20r Timor dancers 1.00 .60
**788** A134 45r Bali dancers 2.25 .95
*a.* Souvenir sheet of 1 7.75 10.00

Tourist publicity. No. 788a sold for 60r.

Asian Productivity Year — A135

Independence Proclamation Monument — A136

**1970, Aug. 1** **Photo.** ***Perf. 12***

**789** A135 5r emerald, org & red .45 .25
**790** A135 30r violet, org & red 1.25 .75

**1970, Aug. 17**

**791** A136 40r lt ultra & magenta 13.50 6.00

The 25th anniversary of independence.

Post and Telecommunications Emblems — A137

Postal Worker and Telephone Dial — A138

***Perf. 12x12½, 12½x12***

**1970, Sept. 27** **Photo.**

**792** A137 10r green, ocher & yel 4.75 1.00
**793** A138 25r pink, blk & yel 8.00 .80

25th anniversary of the postal service.

UN Emblem A139

Education Year and UNESCO Emblems A140

**1970, Oct. 10** **Photo.** ***Perf. 12½***

**794** A139 40r pur, red & yel grn 13.50 6.00

25th anniversary of the United Nations.

**1970, Nov. 16** **Photo.** ***Perf. 12½***

Design: 50r, similar to 25r, but without oval background.

**795** A140 25r yel, dk red & brn 10.50 3.75
**796** A140 50r lt blue, blk & red 15.00 6.00

International Education Year.

Batik Worker — A141

50r, Woman with bamboo musical instrument (angklung). 75r, Menangkabau house & family in traditional costumes.

**1971, May 26** **Litho.** ***Perf. 12½***

**797** A141 20r multi 3.00 1.50
**798** A141 50r multi, vert. 5.00 4.00
*a.* Souvenir sheet of 1 50.00 *65.00*
**799** A141 75r multi 9.50 6.00
*Nos. 797-799 (3)* 17.50 11.50

"Visit ASEAN lands." No. 798a sold for 70r.

Fatahillah Park, Djakarta — A142

30f, City Hall. 65r, Lenong Theater performance. 80r, Ismail Marzuki Cultural Center.

**1971, June 19** **Photo.** ***Perf. 12½***

**800** A142 15r yel grn, brn & bl 2.75 1.25
**801** A142 65r org brn, dk brn & lt grn 5.50 4.75
**802** A142 80r olive, bl & mag 9.50 4.00
*Nos. 800-802 (3)* 17.75 10.00

**Souvenir Sheet**

**803** A142 30r bl, yel & lil rose 25.00 27.50

444th anniv. of Djakarta. #803 sold for 60r.

Rama and Sita — A143

Design: 100r, Rama with bow.

**1971, Aug. 31**

**804** A143 30r yellow, grn & blk 2.40 .95
**805** A143 100r blue, red & blk 4.50 2.00

International Ramayana Festival.

Carrier Pigeon and Conference Emblem — A144

**1971, Sept. 20**

**806** A144 50r ocher & dp brown 1.90 1.10

5th Asian Regional Postal Conference.

Globes and UPU Monument, Berne — A145

**1971, Oct. 4** **Photo.** ***Perf. 13½x13***

**807** A145 40r blue & dull vio 2.00 1.10

Universal Postal Union Day.

Boy Writing, UNICEF Emblem — A146

40r, Boy with sheaf of rice, emblem.

**1971, Dec. 11** ***Perf. 12½***

**808** A146 20r orange & multi 2.50 .65
**809** A146 40r blue & multi 4.00 1.25

25th anniv. UNICEF.

Lined Tang A147

Fish: 30r, Moorish goddess. 40r, Imperial angelfish.

**1971, Dec. 27** **Litho.** ***Perf. 12½***

**810** A147 15r lilac & multi 4.75 1.40
**811** A147 30r dull grn & multi 11.00 3.50
**812** A147 40r blue & multi 13.00 5.25
*Nos. 810-812 (3)* 28.75 10.15

See #834-836, 859-861, 926-928, 959-961.

UN Emblem A148

Radio Tower A149

Design: 100r, Road and dam.

**1972, Mar. 28** **Photo.** ***Perf. 12½***

**813** A148 40r lt grnsh bl & bl 3.00 1.10
**814** A149 75r dk car, yel & grnsh bl 3.50 1.10
**815** A148 100r green, yel & blk 6.00 2.40
*Nos. 813-815 (3)* 12.50 4.60

UN Economic Commission for Asia and the Far East (ECAFE), 25th anniv.

"Your Heart is your Health" — A150

Woman Weaver, Factories — A151

**1972, Apr. 7**

**816** A150 50r multicolored 2.00 .85

World Health Day.

**1972, Apr. 22**

**817** A151 35r orange, yel & pur 2.00 .85

Textile Technology Institute, 50th anniv.

Book Readers A152

**1972, May 15** ***Perf. 13½x12½***

**818** A152 75r blue & multi 3.00 1.40

International Book Year 1972.

Weather Satellite — A153

**1972, July 20** **Photo.** ***Perf. 12½***

**819** A153 35r shown 2.50 .70
**820** A153 50r Astronaut on moon 3.50 3.50
**821** A153 60r Indonesian rocket Kartika 1 6.00 1.25
*Nos. 819-821 (3)* 12.00 5.45

Space achievements.

Hotel Indonesia — A154

**1972, Aug. 5**

**822** A154 50r grn, lt bl & car 2.60 1.25

Hotel Indonesia, 10th anniversary.

Silat (Self Defense) A155

Family, Houses of Worship A156

Olympic Emblems and: 35r, Running. 50r, Diving. 75r, Badminton. 100r, Olympic Stadium.

**1972, Aug. 26** **Photo.**

**823** A155 20r lt blue & multi 1.50 .25
**824** A155 35r multicolored 1.50 .40
**825** A155 50r yel grn & multi 2.75 .70
**826** A155 75r multicolored 3.00 1.75
**827** A155 100r multicolored 4.75 2.75
*Nos. 823-827 (5)* 13.50 5.85

20th Olympic Games, Munich, 8/26-9/11.

**1972, Sept. 27** ***Perf. 12½x13½***

Family planning: 75r, Healthy family. 80r, Working family (national prosperity).

**828** A156 30r lemon & multi 1.75 .70
**829** A156 75r lilac & multi 3.25 2.50
**830** A156 80r multicolored 5.50 3.25
*Nos. 828-830 (3)* 10.50 6.45

Moluccas Dancer — A157

60r, Man, woman and Toradja house, Celebes. 100fr, West Irian house, horiz.

***Perf. 12½x13½, 13½x12½***

**1972, Oct. 28** **Photo.**

**831** A157 30r olive pink & brn 1.90 .70
**832** A157 60r multicolored 4.25 3.00
**833** A157 100r lt bl, brn & dl yel 6.25 3.00
*Nos. 831-833 (3)* 12.40 6.70

**Fish Type of 1971**

Fish: 30r, Butterflyfish. 50r, Regal angelfish. 100r, Spotted triggerfish.

**1972, Dec. 4 Litho. *Perf. 12½***

**834** A147 30r blue & multi 6.00 2.00
**835** A147 50r blue & multi 10.50 2.75
**836** A147 100r blue & multi 13.50 5.00
*Nos. 834-836 (3)* 30.00 9.75

Thomas Cup, Shuttlecock — A158

Thomas Cup, Shuttlecock and: 75r, National monument & Istora Sports Hall. 80r, Indonesian flag & badminton player.

**1973, Jan. 2 Litho. *Perf. 12½***

**837** A158 30r emerald & brt bl 1.00 .30
**838** A158 75r dull grn & dk car 2.00 .55
**839** A158 80r gold & red 2.75 1.10
*Nos. 837-839 (3)* 5.75 1.95

Thomas Cup Badminton World Championship 1973.

WMO Emblem, Anemometer, Wayang Figure — A159

***Perf. 13½x12½***

**1973, Feb. 15 Litho.**

**840** A159 80r blue, grn & claret 2.00 .85

Cent. of intl. meteorological cooperation.

"Health Begins at Home" — A160

**1973, Apr. 7 Photo. *Perf. 12½***

**841** A160 80r dk grn, org & ultra 2.00 .85

25th anniv. of WHO.

Ceremonial Mask, Java — A161

**1973, June 1 Photo. *Perf. 12½***

**842** A161 30r shown 4.50 1.00
**843** A161 60r Mask, Kalimantan 8.00 4.00
**844** A161 100r Mask, Bali 12.50 2.00
*Nos. 842-844 (3)* 25.00 7.00

Tourist publicity.

Hand Putting Coin into Bank — A162

30r, Symbolic coin bank and hand, horiz.

**1973, July 2 Photo. *Perf. 12½***

**845** A162 25r yellow, lt brn & blk 1.10 .55
**846** A162 30r green, yel & gold 1.60 .55

National savings movement.

Chess — A163

INTERPOL Emblem and Policemen — A164

8th National Sports Week: 60r, Karate. 75r, Hurdling, horiz.

**1973, Aug. 4 Photo. *Perf. 12½***

**847** A163 30r red, yellow & blk 2.00 1.25
**848** A163 60r black, ocher & lt grn 2.50 1.25
**849** A163 75r black, lt bl & rose 4.00 1.00
*Nos. 847-849 (3)* 8.50 3.50

**1973, Sept. 3**

Design: 50r, INTERPOL emblem and guard statue from Sewu Prambanan Temple, vert.

**850** A164 30r yellow, grn & blk 1.40 .40
**851** A164 50r yellow, brn & blk 2.00 .70

50th anniv. of Intl. Police Organization.

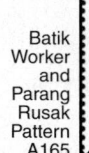

Batik Worker and Parang Rusak Pattern A165

Batik designs: 80r, Man and Pagi Sore pattern. 100r, Man and Merak Ngigel pattern.

**1973, Oct. 9 Photo. *Perf. 12½***

**852** A165 60r multicolored 2.75 2.00
**853** A165 80r multicolored 4.75 2.25
**854** A165 100r multicolored 8.00 4.00
*Nos. 852-854 (3)* 15.50 8.25

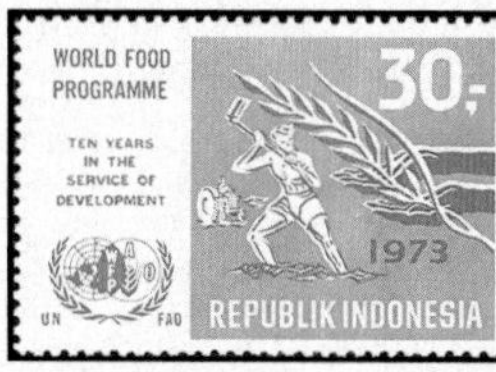


Farmer, Grain, UN and FAO Emblems — A166

**1973, Oct. 24 Photo. *Perf. 12½***

**855** A166 30r lilac & multi 2.50 .70

World Food Program, 10th anniversary.

Houses of Worship — A167

Family planning: 30r, Classroom. 60r, Family and home.

**1973, Nov. 10**

**856** A167 20r dk bl, lt bl & ver .90 .45
**857** A167 30r ocher, blk & yel 1.40 .70
**858** A167 60r lt grn, yel & blk 3.75 .60
*Nos. 856-858 (3)* 6.05 1.75

### Fish Type of 1971

Fish: 40r, Acanthurus leucosternon. 65r, Chaetodon trifasciatus. 100r, Pomacanthus annularis.

**1973, Dec. 10 Litho. *Perf. 12½***

**859** A147 40r multicolored 3.00 1.10
**860** A147 65r multicolored 7.75 2.00
**861** A147 100r multicolored 11.00 3.25
*Nos. 859-861 (3)* 21.75 6.35

Adm. Sudarso and Battle of Arafuru — A168

**1974, Jan. 15**

**862** A168 40r brt blue & multi 2.50 .85

12th Navy Day.

Bengkulu Costume A169

Designs: Regional Costumes.

**1974, Mar. 28 Litho. *Perf. 12½***

**863** A169 5r shown 14.00 1.10
**864** A169 7.50r Kalimantan, Timor 8.00 1.10
**865** A169 10r Kalimantan, Tengah 4.75 .80
**866** A169 15r Jambi 1.25 .80
**867** A169 20r Sulawesi, Tenggara 1.25 .80
**868** A169 25r Nusatenggara, Timor 1.40 .80
**869** A169 27.50r Maluku 1.40 *2.50*
**870** A169 30r Lampung 1.40 *1.50*
**871** A169 35r Sumatra, Barat 1.40 .80
**872** A169 40r Aceh 1.40 .80
**873** A169 45r Nusatenggara, Barat 3.50 .80
**874** A169 50r Riouw 2.75 2.00
**875** A169 55r Kalimantan, Barat 2.75 .80
**876** A169 60r Sulawesi, Utara 2.75 .80
**877** A169 65r Sulawesi, Tengah 2.75 .80
**878** A169 70r Sumatra, Selatan 2.75 .80
**879** A169 75r Java, Barat 2.75 .80
**880** A169 80r Sumatra, Utara 2.75 .80
**881** A169 90r Yogyakarta 2.75 *5.00*
**882** A169 95r Kalimantan, Selatan 2.75 .80
**883** A169 100r Java, Timor 2.75 1.60
**884** A169 120r Irian, Java 7.00 1.10
**885** A169 130r Java, Tengah 7.00 .80
**886** A169 135r Sulawesi, Selatan 6.25 .80
**887** A169 150r Bali 6.25 .80
**888** A169 160r Djakarta 6.25 1.60
*Nos. 863-888 (26)* 100.00 31.10

Baladewa A170

Designs (Figures from Shadow Plays): 80r, Kresna. 100r, Bima.

**1974, June 1 Photo. *Perf. 12½***

**889** A170 40r lt violet & multi 3.25 1.40
**890** A170 80r salmon & multi 5.75 2.75
**891** A170 100r rose 7.00 2.75
*Nos. 889-891 (3)* 16.00 6.90

Pres. Suharto — A171

**1974-76 Photo. *Perf. 12½***

**Portrait in Dark Brown**

**901** A171 40r lt green & blk .80 .25
**903** A171 50r ultra & blk 1.90 .25
**906** A171 65r brt pink & blk 1.10 .65
**908** A171 75r yellow & blk 1.90 .25
**912** A171 100r buff & blk 1.90 .25
**913** A171 150r citron & blk 2.75 .30
**914** A171 200r green & blue 5.25 .40
**915** A171 300r brn org & car 3.00 .55
**916** A171 400r green & yellow 6.00 .75
**917** A171 500r lilac & car 8.00 1.00
*Nos. 901-917 (10)* 32.60 4.65

#914-917 have wavy lines in background.
Issued: #901-913, 8/17/74; #914-917, 8/17/76.

Family and WPY Emblem — A172

**1974, Aug. 19**

**918** A172 65r ultra, gray & ocher 1.60 .55

World Population Year 1974.

"Welfare" A173

"Development" A174

"Religion" A175

**1974, Sept. 9**

**919** A173 25r green & multi .80 .45
**920** A174 40r yellow grn & multi 1.60 .45
**921** A175 65r dk vio brn & multi 2.40 .45
*Nos. 919-921 (3)* 4.80 1.35

Family planning.

Mailmen with Bicycles, UPU Emblem — A176

UPU cent.: 40r, Horse-drawn mail cart. 65r, Mailman on horseback. 100r, Sailing ship, 18th century.

**1974, Oct. 9**

**922** A176 20r dk green & multi 2.50 .45
**923** A176 40r dull blue & multi 2.50 .70
**924** A176 65r black brn & yel 2.50 .70
**925** A176 100r maroon & multi 2.50 1.90
*Nos. 922-925 (4)* 10.00 3.75

### Fish Type of 1971

Fish: 40fr, Zebrasoma veliferum. 80r, Euxiphipops navarchus. 100r, Synchiropus splendidus.

**1974, Oct. 30 Photo. *Perf. 12½***

**926** A147 40r blue & multi 4.00 .45
**927** A147 80r blue & multi 6.00 1.90
**928** A147 100r blue & multi 6.00 2.40
*Nos. 926-928 (3)* 16.00 4.75

Drill Team Searching for Oil — A177

Designs (Pertamina Emblem and): 75r, Oil refinery. 95r, Pertamina telecommunications and computer center. 100r, Gasoline truck and station. 120r, Plane over storage tanks. 130r, Pipes and tanker. 150r, Petro-chemical storage tanks. 200r, Off-shore drilling platform. 95r, 100r, 120r, 130r, vertical.

**1974, Dec. 10 *Perf. 13½***

**929** A177 40r black & multi .55 .45
**930** A177 75r black & multi .55 .45
**931** A177 95r black & multi .70 .45
**932** A177 100r black & multi .70 .45
**933** A177 120r black & multi .85 .45
**934** A177 130r black & multi .90 .45
**935** A177 150r black & multi 1.10 .45
**936** A177 200r black & multi 1.50 .45
*Nos. 929-936 (8)* 6.85 3.60

Pertamina State Oil Enterprise, 17th anniv.

Spittoon, Sumatra A178

Artistic Metalware: 75r, Condiment dish, Sumatra. 100r, Condiment dish, Kalimantan.

**1975, Feb. 24 Photo. *Perf. 12½***

**937** A178 50r red & black 1.90 1.40
**938** A178 75r green & black 2.25 1.40
**939** A178 100r brt blue & multi 3.75 1.40
*Nos. 937-939 (3)* 7.90 4.20

Blood Donors' Emblem A179

Globe, Standard Meter and Kilogram A180

**1975, Apr. 7**

**940** A179 40r yellow, red & grn 1.40 .70

"Give blood, save lives."

**1975, May 20**

**941** A180 65r blue, red & yel 2.50 .70

Cent. of Intl. Meter Convention, Paris, 1875.

Farmer, Teacher, Mother, Policewoman and Nurse — A181

IWY Emblem — A182

**1975, June 26 Photo. *Perf. 12½***

**942** A181 40r multicolored 1.50 .70
**943** A182 100r multicolored 2.25 .70

International Women's Year 1975.

Dendrobium Pakarena A183

Orchids: 70r, Aeridachnis bogor. 85r, Vanda genta.

**1975, July 21**

**944** A183 40r multicolored 4.00 1.25
**945** A183 70r multicolored 6.00 2.40
**946** A183 85r multicolored 10.00 3.50
*Nos. 944-946 (3)* 20.00 7.15

See Nos. 1010-1012, 1036-1038.

Stupas and Damaged Temple — A184

Designs (UNESCO Emblem and): 40r, Buddha statues, stupas and damaged wall. 65r, Stupas and damaged wall, horiz. 100r, Buddha statue and stupas, horiz.

**1975, Aug. 10 *Perf. 12½***

**947** A184 25r yellow, brn & org 2.60 .80
**948** A184 40r black, grn & yel 4.25 1.00
**949** A184 65r lemon, cl & grn 8.50 4.25
**950** A184 100r bister, brn & sl bl 12.50 4.25
*Nos. 947-950 (4)* 27.85 10.30

UNESCO campaign to save Borobudur Temple, Java.

Banjarmasin Battle — A185

Battle Scenes: 40r, Batua, 9/8/46. 75r, Margarana, 11/20/46. 100r, Palembang, 1/1/47.

**1975, Aug. 17**

**951** A185 25r yellow & blk .65 .45
**952** A185 40r org ver & red .95 .45
**953** A185 75r vermilion & blk 1.75 1.25
**954** A185 100r orange & blk 2.75 .90
*Nos. 951-954 (4)* 6.10 3.05

Indonesian independence, 30th anniversary.

"Education" A186

Heroes' Monument, Surabaya A187

Family plannings: 25r, "Religion." 40r, "Prosperity."

**1975, Oct. 20 Photo. *Perf. 12½***

**955** A186 20r blue, salmon & blk 1.00 .25
**956** A186 25r emerald, sal & blk 1.25 .40
**957** A186 40r dp org, blue & blk 1.50 .55
*Nos. 955-957 (3)* 3.75 1.20

**1975, Nov. 10**

**958** A187 100r maroon & green 3.00 .60

War of independence, 30th anniversary.

**Fish Type of 1971**

Fish: 40r, Coris angulata. 75r, Chaetodon ephippium. 150r, Platax pinnatus, vert.

**1975, Dec. 15 Litho. *Perf. 12½***

**959** A147 40r multicolored 2.25 .45
**960** A147 75r multicolored 4.25 1.40
**961** A147 150r multicolored 8.50 2.75
*Nos. 959-961 (3)* 15.00 4.60

Thomas Cup — A188

40r, Uber Cup. 100r, Thomas & Uber Cups.

**1976, Jan. 31 Photo. *Perf. 12½***

**962** A188 20r blue & multi .75 .35
**963** A188 40r multicolored 1.00 .60
**964** A188 100r green & multi 2.50 .60
*Nos. 962-964 (3)* 4.25 1.55

Indonesia, Badminton World Champions.

Refugees on Truck and New Village — A189

Designs: 50r, Neglected and restored village streets. 100r, Derelict and rebuilt houses.

**1976, Feb. 28 Photo. *Perf. 12½***

**965** A189 30r yellow & multi .80 .25
**966** A189 50r blue & multi 1.25 .45
**967** A189 100r ocher & multi 2.25 .50
*Nos. 965-967 (3)* 4.30 1.20

World Human Settlements Day.

Telephones, 1876 and 1976 — A190

**1976, Mar. 10 Photo. *Perf. 12½***

**968** A190 100r yel, org & brn 1.60 .55
*a.* Bklt. pane of 8, 4 #968, 4 #775 + 2 labels ('78) 7.75

Centenary of first telephone call by Alexander Graham Bell, Mar. 10, 1876. Stamps from #968a have straight edges.

Eye and WHO Emblem — A191

Design: 40r, Blind man, eye and World Health Organization emblem.

**1976, Apr. 7 Photo. *Perf. 12½***

**969** A191 20r yel, lt grn & blk .75 .35
**970** A191 40r yel, blue & blk .95 .50

Foresight prevents blindness.

Montreal Stadium — A192

**1976, May 17**

**971** A192 100r ultra 1.60 .65

21st Olympic Games, Montreal, Canada, July 17-Aug. 1.

Lake Tondano, Celebes — A193

Tourist publicity: 40r, Lake Kelimutu, Flores. 75r, Lake Maninjau, Sumatra.

**1976, June 1**

**972** A193 35r lt green & blk .90 .45
**973** A193 40r gray, rose & lt grn 1.10 .45
**974** A193 75r blue & sl grn 2.00 .55
*a.* Bklt. pane of 8 (7 #974, #998, 2 labels) ('78) 7.75
*Nos. 972-974 (3)* 4.00 1.45

Stamps from #974a have straight edges.

Radar Station — A194

Designs: 50r, Master control radar station. 100r, Apalata satellite.

**1976, July 8 Photo. *Perf. 12½***

**975** A194 20r multicolored .65 .40
**976** A194 50r green & blk 1.25 .40
**977** A194 100r multicolored 2.25 .75
*a.* Bklt. pane of 9 (4 #977, 5 #987, label) ('78) 13.50
*Nos. 975-977 (3)* 4.15 1.55

Inauguration of domestic satellite system. Stamps from #977a have straight edges.

Arachnis Flos-aeris — A195

Orchids: 40r, Vanda putri serang. 100r, Coelogyne pandurata.

**1976, Sept. 7**

**978** A195 25r multicolored 1.60 1.10
*a.* Souvenir sheet of 1 *57.50 72.50*
**979** A195 40r multicolored 2.00 1.10
**980** A195 100r multicolored 6.00 2.40
*Nos. 978-980 (3)* 9.60 4.60

Tree and Mountain — A196

**1976, Oct. 4**

**981** A196 20r green, blue & brn 1.10 .40

16th National Reforestation Week.

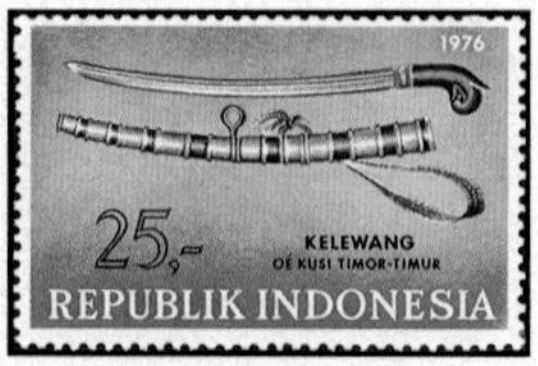


Dagger and Sheath from Timor — A197

Historic Daggers and Sheaths: 40r, from Borneo. 100r, from Aceh.

**1976, Nov. 1** *Perf. 12½*

**982** A197 25r multicolored 1.25 .45
**983** A197 40r multicolored 2.00 .85
*a.* Souvenir sheet of 1, imperf 22.50 22.50
**984** A197 100r green & multi 4.00 2.25
*Nos. 982-984 (3)* 7.25 3.55

No. 983a exists perf. Value $15.

Open Book A198

Children Reading A199

**1976, Dec. 8** **Photo.** *Perf. 12½*

**985** A198 20r multicolored .80 .30
**986** A199 40r multicolored 1.50 .45

Better books for children.

UNICEF Emblem A200

Ballot Box A201

**1976, Dec. 11**

**987** A200 40r multicolored 1.75 .50

UNICEF, 30th anniv.

See No. 977a.

**1977, Jan. 5** **Photo.** *Perf. 12½*

1977 elections: 75r, Ballot box, grain and factory. 100r, Coat of arms.

**988** A201 40r multicolored 2.25 .30
**989** A201 75r multicolored 2.50 .45
**990** A201 100r multicolored 4.00 1.40
*Nos. 988-990 (3)* 8.75 2.15

Camp and Flags Scout Emblems, A202

Designs: 30r, Tent, emblems and trees. 40r, Boy and Girl Scout flags and emblems.

**1977, Feb. 28**

**991** A202 25r multicolored 1.60 .55
**992** A202 30r multicolored 1.75 .55
**993** A202 40r multicolored 2.00 1.25
*Nos. 991-993 (3)* 5.35 2.35

11th National Scout Jamboree.

Letter with "AOPU" — A203

Anniversary Emblem, Djakarta Arms — A204

Design: 100r, Stylized bird and letter.

**1977, Apr. 1** **Photo.** *Perf. 12½*

**994** A203 65r multicolored 1.00 .40
**995** A203 100r multicolored 1.50 .55

Asian-Oceanic Postal Union, 15th convention.

**1977, May 23** **Photo.** *Perf. 12½*

Designs: Anniversary emblem and arms of Djakarta in different arrangements.

**996** A204 20r orange & blue .75 .45
**997** A204 40r emerald & blue 1.00 .50
**998** A204 100r slate & blue 2.00 .85
*a.* Souvenir sheet of 1 10.00 10.00
*Nos. 996-998 (3)* 3.75 1.80

450th anniversary of Djakarta. No. 998a also issued imperf. Value $27.50.

Rose — A205

Various Sports Emblems — A206

**1977, May 26** **Photo.** *Perf. 12½*

**999** A205 100r shown 2.00 .60
*a.* Souvenir sheet 12.00 12.00
**1000** A205 100r Envelope 2.00 .60
*a.* Souvenir sheet of 4 12.00 12.00
*b.* Pair, Nos. 999-1000 4.00 3.00

Amphilex 77 Phil. Exhib., Amsterdam, May 26-June 5. No. 999a contains one stamp similar to No. 999 with blue background. No. 1000a contains 2 each of Nos. 999-1000.

Nos. 999a, 1000a exist imperf. Values: No. 999a, $27.50; No. 1000a, $32.50.

See No. 1013a.

**1977, June 22**

9th Natl. Sports Week: 50r, 100r, Different sports emblems.

**1001** A206 40r silver & multi 2.25 1.75
**1002** A206 50r silver & multi 3.25 1.75
**1003** A206 100r gold & multi 8.00 4.00
*Nos. 1001-1003 (3)* 13.50 7.50

Contest Trophy A207

Emblem A208

**1977, July 20**

**1004** A207 40r green & multi 2.00 .55
**1005** A208 100r yellow & multi 3.75 1.00

10th Natl. Koran Reading Contest, 7/20-27.

Map of ASEAN Countries, Satellite — A209

35r, Map of ASEAN countries. 50r, Flags of founding members: Indonesia, Malaysia, Philippines, Singapore & Thailand; ship, plane & train.

**1977, Aug. 8**

**1006** A209 25r multicolored 1.50 .25
**1007** A209 35r multicolored 1.90 .70
**1008** A209 50r multicolored 2.50 .85
*Nos. 1006-1008 (3)* 5.90 1.80

Association of South East Asian Nations (ASEAN), 10th anniversary.

Uniform, Jakarta Regiment A210

**1977, Aug. 19**

**1009** A210 25r green, gold & brn .75 .30

Indonesia-Pakistan Economic and Cultural Organization, 1968-1977.

**Orchid Type of 1975**

Orchids: 25r, Taeniophyllum. 40r, Phalaenopsis violacea. 100r, Dendrobium spectabile.

**1977, Oct. 28** **Photo.** *Perf. 12½*

**1010** A183 25r orange & multi 1.75 .85
**1011** A183 40r blue & multi 2.75 1.75
**1012** A183 100r yel grn & multi 5.75 2.75
*a.* Souvenir sheet of 1, imperf 12.00 12.00
*Nos. 1010-1012 (3)* 10.25 5.35

No. 1012a contains one stamp similar to No. 1012 with blue background. No. 1012a exists perf. Value $14.

Child and Mosquito A211

**1977, Nov. 7** *Perf. 12½*

**1013** A211 40r brt grn, red & blk .75 .35
*a.* Bklt. pane of 9+label (4 #999, 5 #1013) ('78) 7.75

Natl. Health campaign to eradicate malaria. Stamps from #1013a have straight edges. Issue date: No. 1013a, Sept. 27, 1978.

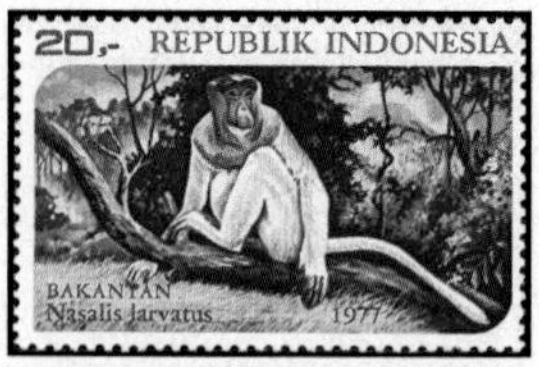


Proboscis Monkey — A212

Designs: 40r, Indian elephant. 100r, Tiger.

**1977, Dec. 22**

**1014** A212 20r multicolored 1.60 .70
**1015** A212 40r multicolored 2.25 1.25
**1016** A212 100r multicolored 6.00 3.00
*a.* Souvenir sheet of 1 10.00 10.00
*Nos. 1014-1016 (3)* 9.85 4.95

Wildlife protection. No. 1016a exists imperf. Value $13.

Conference Emblem A213

Mother and Child A214

**1978, Mar. 27** **Photo.** *Perf. 12½*

**1017** A213 100r lt blue & ultra 1.50 .65

United Nations Conference on Technical Cooperation among Developing Countries.

**1978, Apr. 7** **Photo.** *Perf. 12½*

75r, Mother and child, symbolic design.

**1018** A214 40r lt green & blue .90 .35
**1019** A214 75r orange red & brn 1.40 .65

Promotion of breast feeding.

Dome of The Rock, Jerusalem — A215

**1978, May 15** **Photo.** *Perf. 12½*

**1020** A215 100r multicolored 2.75 .60

Palestinian fighters and their families.

Argentina '78 Emblem A216

Head and "Blood Circulation" A217

**1978, June 1**

**1021** A216 40r multicolored .70 .30
**1022** A216 100r multicolored 1.50 .70

11th World Cup Soccer Championships, Argentina, June 1-25.

**1978, June 17** **Photo.** *Perf. 12½*

**1023** A217 100r black, blue & red 1.25 .55

World Health Day and drive against hypertension.

Leather Puppets — A218

Art from Wayang Museum, Djakarta: 75r, Wooden puppets. 100r, Actors with puppet masks.

**1978, July 22** **Litho.** *Perf. 12½*

**1024** A218 40r multicolored 2.40 .70
**1025** A218 75r multicolored 3.50 1.40
**1026** A218 100r multicolored 5.25 2.40
*Nos. 1024-1026 (3)* 11.15 4.50

Congress Emblem A219

IAAY Emblem A220

**1978, Aug. 1**
**1027** A219 100r slate 1.25 .45

27th Congress of World Confederation of Organizations of Teachers (WCOTP), Djakarta, June 26-Aug. 2.

**1978, Aug. 16 Photo. *Perf. 12½***
**1028** A220 100r org & dk blue 1.50 .45

International Anti-Apartheid Year.

Congress Emblem A221

Youth Pledge Emblem A222

Design: 100r, People and trees.

**1978, Oct. 16 Photo. *Perf. 12½***
**1029** A221 40r emerald & blue .60 .35
**1030** A221 100r emerald & blk 1.10 .75

8th World Forestry Congress, Djakarta.

**1978, Oct. 28**
**1031** A222 40r dk brown & red .85 .50
**1032** A222 100r salmon, brn & red 1.40 .75

50th anniv. of Youth Pledge. See #1044b.

Wildlife Protection — A223

**1978, Nov. 1**
**1033** A223 40r Porcupine ant-eater 1.60 .50
**1034** A223 75r Deer 2.75 1.40
*a.* Souv. sheet of 5, #1034, 4 #1035 + label 14.00 14.00
**1035** A223 100r Clouded tiger 4.50 1.60
*a.* Souvenir sheet of 1 4.75 4.75
*Nos. 1033-1035 (3)* 8.85 3.50

Stamps in No. 1034a are in changed colors. Souvenir sheets inscribed for Essen 2nd Intl. Stamp Fair.

**Orchid Type of 1975**

Orchids: 40r, Phalaenopsis sri rejeki. 75r, Dendrobium macrophilium. 100r, Cymbidium fynlaysonianum.

**1978, Dec. 22 Photo. *Perf. 12½***
**1036** A183 40r multicolored 1.50 .50
**1037** A183 75r multicolored 2.25 .85
**1038** A183 100r multicolored 3.75 1.10
*a.* Souvenir sheet of 1 5.50 6.75
*Nos. 1036-1038 (3)* 7.50 2.45

Douglas DC-3, 1949, over Volcano — A224

Designs: 75r, Douglas DC-9 over village. 100r, Douglas DC-10 over temple.

**1979, Jan. 26 Photo. *Perf. 12½***
**1039** A224 40r multicolored 1.00 .40
**1040** A224 75r multicolored 1.25 .40
**1041** A224 100r multicolored 2.10 1.10
*Nos. 1039-1041 (3)* 4.35 1.90

Garuda Indonesian Airways, 30th anniv.

A225

40r, Thomas Cup and badminton player.

**1979, Feb. 24 Photo. *Perf. 12½***
**1042** A225 40r Thomas Cup& player .50 .55
**1043** A225 100r Player hitting ball 1.10 .85
**1044** A225 100r Player facing left 1.40 .85
*a.* Pair, #1043-1044 2.50
*b.* Blkt. pane, 3 each #1032, 1043-1044 + label 8.00
*Nos. 1042-1044 (3)* 3.00 2.25

11th Thomas Cup, Djakarta, May 24-June 2. #1044a forms a continuous design. Stamps from #1044b have straight edges.

Paphiopedilum Lowii — A227

Orchids: 100r, 300r, Vanda limbata. 125r, Phalaenopsis gigantea. 250r, as 60r.

**1979, Mar. 22 Photo. *Perf. 12½***
**1045** A227 60r multi 1.40 .40
**1046** A227 100r multi 2.00 .60
**1047** A227 125r multi 2.75 1.00
*a.* Souvenir sheet of 1 7.50 7.50
*b.* Souv. sheet of 2 (250r, 300r) 10.00 10.00
*Nos. 1045-1047 (3)* 6.15 2.00

No. 1047b, issued for Asian Phil. Exhib., Dortmund, West Germany, May 24-27. Sold for 650r.

Family and Houses — A228

Third Five-year Plan: 60r, Pylon and fields. 100r, School and clinic. 125r, Factories and trucks. 150r, Motorized mail delivery.

**1979-82**
**1047C** A228 12.50r Plane ('80) .50 .25
**1047D** A228 17.50r Bridge ('82) .60 .25
**1048** A228 35r green & olive .25 .25
**1049** A228 60r blue & olive .35 .25
**1050** A228 100r blue & dk brn .60 .25
**1051** A228 125r red brn & ol .85 .25
**1052** A228 150r carmine & yel .90 .45
*Nos. 1047C-1052 (7)* 4.05 1.95

See No. 1058a.

R. A. Kartini and Girls' School A229

**1979, Apr. 21 Photo. *Perf. 12½***
**1053** A229 100r Kartini 1.00 .40
**1054** A229 100r School 1.00 .40
*a.* Pair, #1053-1054 2.00 2.00

Mrs. R. A. Kartini, educator, birth centenary.

Bureau of Education, UNESCO Emblems — A231

**1979, May 25 Photo. *Perf. 12½***
**1055** A231 150r multicolored 1.75 .45

50th anniversary of the statutes of the International Bureau of Education.

Self Defense A232

Cooperation Emblem A233

Designs: 125r, Games' emblem. 150r, Senayan Main Stadium.

**1979, June 21 Photo. *Perf. 12½***
**1056** A232 60r multicolored .60 .30
**1057** A232 125r multicolored 1.10 .45
**1058** A232 150r multicolored 1.50 .70
*a.* Bklt. pane of 6+4 labels (#1052, 5 #1058) 7.75
*Nos. 1056-1058 (3)* 3.20 1.45

10th So. East Asia Games, Djakarta, Sept. 21-30.
Stamps from #1058a have straight edges.
Issue date: No. 1058a, Sept. 27.

**1979, July 12 Photo. *Perf. 12½***
**1059** A233 150r multicolored 1.25 .40

32nd Indonesian Cooperative Day.

A234

Designs: 60r, IYC and natl. IYC emblems. 150r, IYC emblem.

**1979, Aug. 4 Photo. *Perf. 12½***
**1060** A234 60r emerald & blk .55 .25
**1061** A234 150r blue & blk 1.00 .45

International Year of the Child.

A235

**1979, Sept. 20 Photo. *Perf. 12½***
**1062** A235 150r TELECOM 79 1.25 .55

3rd World Telecommunications Exhibition, Geneva, Sept. 20-26.

Fight Drug Abuse — A236

**1979, Oct. 17 Photo. *Perf. 12½***
**1063** A236 150r deep rose & blk 1.25 .55

Dolphin — A237

Wildlife Protection: 125r, Freshwater dolphin. 150r, Leatherback turtle.

**1979, Nov. 24 Photo. *Perf. 12½***
**1064** A237 60r multi 1.50 .75
**1065** A237 125r multi 3.00 .85
**1066** A237 150r multi 5.50 1.25
*Nos. 1064-1066 (3)* 10.00 2.85

**Souvenir Sheet**

**1066A** A237 200r like #1066 8.00 8.00

Ship Made of Cloves — A238

Spice Race, Jakarta-Amsterdam (Sailing Ships): 60r, Penisi, vert. 150r, Madurese boat, vert.

**1980, Mar. 12 Photo. *Perf. 12½***
**1067** A238 60r bright blue .50 .25
**1068** A238 125r red brown 1.00 .45
**1069** A238 150r red lilac 1.50 .45
*Nos. 1067-1069 (3)* 3.00 1.15

**1980 Souvenir Sheets**
**1069A** A238 300r like #1068 5.50 2.10
**1069B** A238 500r like #1067 7.50 2.75

Issue dates: 300r, Mar. 12. 500r, May 6. 500r for London 1980 Intl. Stamp Exhib.

Rubber Raft in Rapids A239

***Perf. 13½x13, 13x13½***
**1980, Mar. 21 Photo.**
**1070** A239 60r shown .40 .25
**1071** A239 125r Mountain climbing, vert. 1.10 .55
**1072** A239 150r Hang gliding, vert. 1.50 .85
*Nos. 1070-1072 (3)* 3.00 1.65

**Souvenir Sheet**

**1072A** A239 300r like #1070 5.00 5.00

A240

A241

**1980, Apr. 15 *Perf. 12½***
**1073** A240 150r multicolored 1.25 .45

Anti-smoking Campaign.

**1980, Apr. 21 Photo. *Perf. 12½***
**1074** A241 125r Flowers In vase 1.10 .45
**1075** A241 150r Bouquet 1.60 .70

2nd Flower Festival, Jakarta, Apr. 19-21. See No. 1080a-1080b.

A242

A243

Conference building.

**1980, Apr. 24** *Perf. 13x13½*
**1076** A242 150r gold & lil rose 1.40 .45

**Souvenir Sheet**

**1076A** A242 300r multicolored 4.00 5.25

1st Asian-African Conf., 25th anniv.

**1980, May 2** *Perf. 12½*

Designs: 60r, Male figure. 125r, Elephant stone. 150r, Taman Bali Stone Sarcophagus, 2000 B.C.

**1077** A243 60r multicolored .65 .30
**1078** A243 125r multicolored 1.25 .55
**1079** A243 150r multicolored 1.75 .70
*Nos. 1077-1079 (3)* 3.65 1.55

**Flower and Sculpture Types of 1980**

Souvenir Sheet

**1980 Photo.** *Perf. 12½*
**1080** Sheet of 8 18.00 18.00
*a.* A241 100r like #1074 1.10 1.10
*b.* A241 100r like #1075 1.10 1.10
*c.* A243 200r like #1077 2.00 2.00
*d.* A243 200r like #1079 2.00 2.00

London 1980 Intl. Stamp Exhib., May 6-14. No. 1080 contains 2 stamps of each design (4x2).

Draftsman in Wheelchair A244

Discus Thrower A245

**1980, May 18 Photo.** *Perf. 12½*
**1081** A244 100r multicolored 1.00 .30

Disabled Veterans Corp, 30th anniversary.

**1980, May 18**
**1082** A245 75r dp orange & sep 1.10 .30

Olympics for the Disabled, Arnhem, Netherlands, June 21-July 5.

Pres. Suharto — A246

A246a

A246b

*Perf. 13½x12½, 12½*

**1980-83 Photo.**
**1083** A246 12.50r lt grn & grn .50 .25
**1084** A246 50r lt grn & bl .50 .30
**1084A** A246 55r red rose & red lil .50 .25
**1085** A246 75r lem & gldn brn .75 .25
**1086** A246 100r brt pink & bl 1.25 .40
*a.* Bklt pane of 8 + 2 labels (6 #1086, 2 #1088, Inscribed 1981) 8.00
**1087** A246a 110r dull org & dp red lil .50 .25
**1088** A246 200r dull org & brn 1.25 1.25
**1088A** A246a 250r dull org & brn 2.25 .50
**1089** A246a 275r lt ap grn & dk grn 1.25 .25
**1090** A246 300r rose lil & gold 3.25 .60
**1091** A246 400r multicolored 3.50 .80

**Engr.**

*Perf. 12½x13*

**1092** A246b 500r dk red brown 3.75 1.00
*Nos. 1083-1092 (12)* 19.25 6.10

Issued: 12.50r, 50r, 75r, 100r, 200r, 6/8; 300r, 400r, 8/8/81; 250r, 9/82; 500r, 3/11/83; 55r, 7/83; 110r, 275r, 9/27/83.

See Nos. 1257-1261, 1265, 1268. For surcharge see No. 1527.

Map of Indonesia, People — A247

**1980, July 17** *Perf. 12½*
**1093** A247 75r blue & pink .45 .25
**1094** A247 200r blue & dull yel 1.50 .40

1980 population census.

Ship Laying Cable — A248

**1980, Aug. 8 Photo.** *Perf. 12½*
**1095** A248 75r multicolored .45 .25
**1096** A248 200r multicolored 1.50 .45

Singapore-Indonesia submarine cable opening.

50s Stamp of 1946 — A249

100r, 15s Battle of Surabaya stamp, 1946, horiz. 200r, 15s Independence Fund stamp, 1946.

**1980, Aug. 17**
**1097** A249 75r dk brn & dp org .60 .40
**1098** A249 100r gold & purple 1.25 .50
**1099** A249 200r multicolored 1.90 .80
*Nos. 1097-1099 (3)* 3.75 1.70

Independence, 35th anniversary.

Asian Oceanic Postal Training School — A250

OPEC Anniv. Emblem — A251

**1980, Sept. 10 Photo.** *Perf. 12½*
**1100** A250 200r multicolored 1.60 .40

**1980, Sept. 14**
**1101** A251 200r multicolored 1.60 .40

Organization of Petroleum Exporting Countries, 20th anniversary.

Armed Forces, 35th Anniversary — A252

**1980, Oct. 5 Photo.** *Perf. 13½x13*
**1102** A252 75r shown .80 .50
**1103** A252 200r Service men and emblem 1.40 .75

Vulturine Parrot — A253

Designs: Parrots.

**1980, Nov. 25 Photo.** *Perf. 13x12½*
**1104** A253 75r shown 1.90 .70
**1105** A253 100r Yellow-backed lory 3.00 1.40
**1106** A253 200r Red lory 6.00 2.00
*Nos. 1104-1106 (3)* 10.90 4.10

**Souvenir Sheet**

*Perf. 12½*

**1106A** Sheet of 3 25.00 25.00
*b.* A253 250r like #1105 4.50 4.50
*c.* A253 350r like #1104 7.00 7.00
*d.* A253 400r like #1106 8.00 8.00

One Day Beauty Orchid — A254

Designs: Orchids.

**1980, Dec. 10** *Perf. 13x13½*
**1107** A254 75r shown 1.25 .35
**1108** A254 100r Dendrobium discolor 2.25 1.00
**1109** A254 200r Dendrobium lasianthera 4.00 .85
*Nos. 1107-1109 (3)* 7.50 2.20

**Souvenir Sheet**

**1980** *Perf. 13x13½*
**1110** Sheet of 2 19.00 15.00
*a.* A254 250r like #1109 8.00 5.00
*b.* A254 350r like #1108 10.50 7.00

Heinrich von Stephan (1831-1897), UPU Founder — A255

**1981, Jan. 7** *Perf. 13½x12½*
**1111** A255 200r brt bl & dk bl 1.60 .80

6th Asian Pacific Scout Jamboree A256

**1981** *Perf. 13½x12½, 12½x13½*
**1112** A256 75r Emblems .65 .50
**1113** A256 100r Scouts, vert. 1.00 .50
**1114** A256 200r Emblems, diff. 1.60 .90
*Nos. 1112-1114 (3)* 3.25 1.90

**Souvenir Sheet**

**1115** A256 150r like #1113 5.50 .60

Issued: #1112-1114, 2/22; #1115, 8/14.

4th Asian-Oceanian Postal Union Congress A257

Blood Donor Campaign A258

**1981, Mar. 18** *Perf. 12½*
**1116** A257 200r multicolored 1.90 .40

**1981, Apr. 22**
**1117** A258 75r Girl holding blood drop .50 .25
**1118** A258 100r Hands holding blood drop .90 .40
**1119** A258 200r Hands, blood, diff. 1.60 .70
*Nos. 1117-1119 (3)* 3.00 1.35

Intl. Family Planning Conference — A259

**1981, Apr. 26**
**1120** A259 200r multicolored 1.50 .60

Natl. Education Day — A260

Traditional Bali Paintings: Nos. 1121-1122, Song of Sritanjung. No. 1123, Birth of the Eagle.

**1981, May 2**
**1121** 100r multicolored 1.10 .25
**1122** 200r multicolored 2.10 .40
*a.* A260 Pair #1121-1122 3.20 .60

**Souvenir Sheet**

**1123** Sheet of 2 12.00 12.00
*a.* A260 400r multicolored 3.50 3.50
*b.* A261 600r multicolored 6.00 6.00

No. 1123 has margin showing WIPA '81 emblem. No. 1123 exists with marginal inscription "Indonesien grusst WIPA." Value, $17.50.

A262

A263

**1981, May 9**
**1124** A262 200r multicolored 1.75 .45

ASEAN Building Jakarta, opening.

**1981, May 22**
**1125** A263 200r multicolored 3.00 .45

Uber Cup '81 Badminton Championship, Tokyo.

World Environment Day — A264

Bas-reliefs, Candhi Merut Buddhist Temple, Central Java: 75r, Tree of Life. 200r, Reclining Buddha.

**1981, June 5**
**1126** A264 75r multicolored .65 .25
**1127** A264 200r multicolored 1.50 .40

12th Koran Reading Competition, June 7-14 — A265

**1981, June 7** ***Perf. 13½x12½***
**1128** A265 200r multicolored 1.25 .45

Intl. Year of the Disabled A266

**1981, July 31** ***Perf. 12½***
**1129** A266 75r Blind man .60 .25
**1130** A266 200r Speech, hearing disabilities 1.40 .45

Soekarno-Hatta Independence Monument, Jakarta — A267

**1981, Aug. 17**
**1131** A267 200r multicolored 1.75 .40

Natl. Sports Week, Sept. 19-30 — A268

World Food Day — A268a

**1981, Sept. 19**
**1132** A268 75r Skydiving .50 .25
**1133** A268 100r Skin diving, horiz. .90 .70
**1134** A268 200r Equestrian 1.60 .55
*Nos. 1132-1134 (3)* 3.00 1.50

The horse on No. 1134 is brown black, See Nos. 1374-1375 for souvenir sheets containing No. 1134 in different colors.

**1981, Oct. 16**
**1135** A268a 200r multicolored 3.00 .70

Provincial Arms — A269

Natl. Arms A270

**1981-83**
**1136** A269 100r Aceh 2.00 .75
**1137** A269 100r Bali 2.00 .75
**1138** A269 100r Bengkulu 2.00 .75
**1139** A269 100r Jakarta 2.50 1.50
**1140** A269 100r West Irian 5.00 .85
**1141** A269 100r West Java 2.00 .65
**1142** A269 100r Jambi 2.00 .65
**1143** A269 100r Central Java 2.00 .65
**1144** A269 100r East Java 2.00 .65
**1145** A269 100r South Kalimantan 2.00 .65
**1146** A269 100r East Kalimantan 2.00 .65
**1147** A269 100r West Kalimantan 2.00 .65
**1148** A269 100r Lampung 2.00 .65
**1149** A269 100r Central Kalimantan 2.00 .65
**1150** A269 100r Moluccas 2.00 .65
**1151** A269 100r West Nusa Tenggara 2.00 .65
**1152** A269 100r East Nusa Tenggara 2.00 .65
**1153** A269 100r Southeast Sulawesi 2.00 .65
**1154** A269 100r Central Sulawesi 2.00 .65
**1155** A269 100r West Sumatra 2.00 .65
**1156** A269 100r North Sulawesi 2.00 .65
**1157** A269 100r North Sumatra 2.00 .65
**1158** A269 100r South Sumatra 2.00 .65
**1159** A269 100r Riau 2.00 .65
**1160** A269 100r South Sulawesi 2.00 .65
**1161** A269 100r Yogyakarta 2.00 .65
**1161A** A269 100r Timor 1.00 .60
**1162** A270 250r shown 5.75 1.75
*Nos. 1136-1162 (28)* 62.25 20.60

Issued: Nos. 1136-1140, 1981; Nos. 1141-1161, 1162, 1982; No. 1161A, 1983.

Pink-crested Cockatoo — A271

**1981, Dec. 10**
**1163** A271 75r shown 2.50 .80
**1164** A271 100r Sulphur-crested cockatoo 3.25 .80
**1165** A271 200r King cockatoo 6.75 2.75
*Nos. 1163-1165 (3)* 12.50 4.35

**Souvenir Sheet**

**1166** Sheet of 2 21.00 21.00
*a.* A271 150r like #1164 4.75 4.75
*b.* A271 350r like #1165 15.00 15.00

Bumiputra Mutual Life Insurance Co., 70th Anniv. — A272

**1982, Feb. 12**
**1167** A272 75r Family .50 .25
**1168** A272 100r Family, diff. .85 .40
**1169** A272 200r Hands holding symbols 1.40 .65
*Nos. 1167-1169 (3)* 2.75 1.30

Search and Rescue Institute, 10th Anniv. — A273

General Election — A274

**1982, Feb. 28** ***Perf. 12½x13½***
**1170** A273 250r multicolored 1.90 .50

**1982, Mar. 1** ***Perf. 12½***
**1171** A274 75r Ballot, houses .50 .25
**1172** A274 100r Farm .85 .30
**1173** A274 200r Arms 1.40 .70
*Nos. 1171-1173 (3)* 2.75 1.25

2nd UN Conference on Exploration and Peaceful Uses of Outer Space, Vienna, Aug. 9-21 — A275

**1982, Apr. 19** ***Perf. 13x13½***
**1174** A275 150r Couple 1.10 .40
**1175** A275 250r Emblem 2.50 .65

12th Thomas Badminton Cup, London, May — A276

**1982, May 19**
**1176** A276 250r multicolored 2.00 .50
*a.* Souvenir sheet of 2 8.00

No. 1176a also exists overprinted "INDONESIE SALUE PHILEXFRANCE" in red or black. Value, each $60.

1982 World Cup — A277

**1982, June 14**
**1177** A277 250r multi 2.50 .50
*a.* Souvenir sheet of 2 10.00
*b.-c.* Souvenir sheets of 2, each *150.00* 80.00

No. 1177b overprinted "ITALIA WORLD CHAMPION" in black; No. 1177c overprinted same in red. Fake overprints exist.

60th Anniv. of Taman Siswa Educational System — A278

**1982, July 3**
**1178** A278 250r multicolored 1.25 .50

15th Anniv. of Assoc. of South East Asian Nations (ASEAN) — A279

**1982, Aug. 8** **Photo.** ***Perf. 12½***
**1179** A279 150r Members' flags 2.50 .45

Balinese Starling A280

Red Birds of Paradise A281

**1982, Oct. 11** **Photo.** ***Perf. 13x13½***
**1180** A280 100r shown 2.50 .40
**1181** A280 250r King birds of paradise 4.75 .55

**Souvenir Sheet**

**1181A** A280 500r like 100r 15.00 15.00

3rd World Natl. Park Cong., Denpasar Bali.

**1982, Dec. 20** ***Perf. 12½x13½***
**1182** A281 100r Lawe's six-wired parotia 2.75 .40
**1183** A281 150r Twelve-wired birds of paradise 4.50 .80
**1184** A281 250r shown 6.25 1.25
*Nos. 1182-1184 (3)* 13.50 2.45

**Souvenir Sheet**
***Perf. 12½x13½***

**1184A** Sheet of 2 25.00 25.00
*b.* A281 200r like 100r 7.75 7.75
*c.* A281 300r like 250r 12.50 12.50

Scouting Year A282

**1983, Feb. 22** **Photo.** ***Perf. 13½x13***
**1185** A282 250r multi 2.25 .50

Restoration of Borobudur Temple — A283

**1983, Feb. 23** ***Perf. 12½***
**1186** A283 100r Scaffolding, crane, vert. 1.75 .45
**1187** A283 150r Buddha statue, stupas, vert. 2.75 .45
**1188** A283 250r Statue, temple 6.00 2.75
*Nos. 1186-1188 (3)* 10.50 3.65

**Souvenir Sheet**

**1189** A283 500r Temple 19.00 19.00

Gas Plant — A284

World Communications Year — A285

**1983, May 16 Photo. *Perf. 12½***
1190 A284 275r multi 1.75 .40

7th Intl. Liquefied Natural Gas Conference and Exhibition, Jakarta, May 16-19.

**1983, May 17 *Perf. 12½x13½***
1191 A285 75r Dove, ships .55 .25
1192 A285 110r Satellite .70 .25
1193 A285 175r Dish antenna, jet 1.10 .40
1194 A285 275r Airmail envelope, globe 1.40 .65
*Nos. 1191-1194 (4)* 3.75 1.55

See Nos. 1215-1216.

13th Natl. Koran Reading Competition, Padang, May 23-31 — A286

**1983, May 23 *Perf. 13½x13***
1195 A286 275r multi 1.75 .55

Total Solar Eclipse, June 11 — A287

**1983, June 11 *Perf. 12½***
1196 A287 110r Map, eclipse 1.10 .25
1197 A287 275r Map 2.25 .40

**Souvenir Sheet**
1198 A287 500r like 275r 17.00 17.00

Launch of Palapa B Satellite — A288

Agricultural Census — A289

**1983, June 18 *Perf. 12½x13½***
1199 A288 275r multi 1.75 .55

**1983, July 1 Photo. *Perf. 12½***
1200 A289 110r Produce .80 .25
1201 A289 275r Farmer 1.60 .25

15th Anniv. of Indonesia-Pakistan Economic and Cultural Cooperation Org. — A290

Weavings.

**1983, Aug. 19**
1202 A290 275r Indonesian, Lombok 2.00 .85
1203 A290 275r Pakistani, Baluchistan 2.00 .85

Krakatoa Eruption Centenary A291

**1983, Aug. 26**
1204 A291 110r Volcano 1.00 .30
1205 A291 275r Map 2.00 .45

CN-235, Light Air Transport — A292

**1983, Sept. 10 Photo. *Perf. 12½***
1206 A292 275r multi 1.60 .55

Tropical Fish — A293

**1983, Oct. 17 Photo. *Perf. 12½***
1207 A293 110r Puntius tetrazona 2.50 .65
1208 A293 175r Rasbora einthoveni 3.50 .65
1209 A293 275r Toxotes jaculator 7.00 2.00
*Nos. 1207-1209 (3)* 13.00 3.30

Canderawasih Birds — A294

**1983, Nov. 30 Photo. *Perf. 12½***
1210 A294 110r Diphyllodes respublica 1.60 .25
1211 A294 175r Epimachus fastuosus 2.25 .25
1212 A294 275r Drepanornis albertisi 4.25 .25
1213 A294 500r as #1212 6.75 .40
*a.* Souvenir sheet of 1 24.00 24.00
*Nos. 1210-1213 (4)* 14.85 1.15

Inalienable Rights of the Palestinian People A295

**1983, Dec. 20 *Perf. 13½x13***
1214 A295 275r multi 1.75 .30

**WCY Type of 1983**
**Souvenir Sheets**

**1983 Photo. *Perf. 12½x13½***
1215 A285 400r like No. 1192 11.00 8.00
1216 A285 500r like No. 1194 11.00 7.00

Telecom '83 exhib., Geneva, Oct. 26-Nov. 1 (400r). Philatelic Museum opening, Jakarta (500r). Issued: 400r, Oct. 26; 500r, Sept. 29.

Fight Against Polio — A296

4th Five-Year Development Plan — A297

**1984, Feb. 17 Photo. *Perf. 12½***
1217 A296 110r Emblem .65 .25
1218 A296 275r Stylized person 1.50 .30

**1984, Apr. 1 Photo. *Perf. 12½***
1219 A297 55r Fertilizer industry .25 .25
1220 A297 75r Aviation .35 .25
1221 A297 110r Shipping .50 .25
1222 A297 275r Communications 1.25 .60
*Nos. 1219-1222 (4)* 2.35 1.35

Forestry Resources A298

**1984, May 17 Photo. *Perf. 12½***
1223 A298 75r Forest, paper mill .65 .25
1224 A298 110r Seedling 1.10 .25
1225 A298 175r Tree cutting 1.50 .40
1226 A298 275r Logs 2.75 .55
*a.* Souv. sheet of 2, #1225-1226 20.00 12.00
*Nos. 1223-1226 (4)* 6.00 1.45

17th Annual Meeting of ASEAN Foreign Ministers — A299

**1984, July 9 Photo. *Perf. 12½***
1227 A299 275r Flags 2.75 .55

1984 Summer Olympics A300

**1984, July 28 Photo. *Perf. 12½***
1228 A300 75r Pole vault .75 .25
1229 A300 110r Archery .75 .25
1230 A300 175r Boxing 1.25 .25
1231 A300 250r Shooting 2.25 .45
1232 A300 275r Weight lifting 2.50 .45
1233 A300 325r Swimming 2.50 .30
*Nos. 1228-1233 (6)* 10.00 1.95

Horse Dancers, Central Java — A301

Processions.

**1984, Aug. 17 *Perf. 12½x13½***
1234 A301 75r shown .75 .25
1235 A301 110r Reyog Ponorogo, East Java 1.25 .25
1236 A301 275r Lion Dance, West Java 2.50 .60
1237 A301 325r Barong of Bali 3.50 .60
*Nos. 1234-1237 (4)* 8.00 1.70

Natl. Sports Day A302

**1984, Sept. 9 Photo. *Perf. 13½x13***
1238 A302 110r Thomas Cup victory .75 .30
1239 A302 275r Gymnastics 2.00 .45

Postcode System Inauguration A303

**1984, Sept. 27 Photo. *Perf. 12½***
1240 A303 110r multi .55 .30
1241 A303 275r multi 1.25 .70

Birds of Irian Jaya — A304

Oath of the Youth — A305

**1984, Oct. 15 *Perf. 12½x13½***
1242 A304 75r Chlamydera lauterbachi 1.60 .25
1243 A304 110r Sericulus aureus 2.50 .25
1244 A304 275r Astrapia nigra 6.00 .25
1245 A304 325r Lophorhina superba 6.50 .30
*a.* Souv. sheet of 2, #1242, 1245 29.00 29.00
*Nos. 1242-1245 (4)* 16.60 1.05

No. 1245a for PHILAKOREA '84.

**1984, Oct. 28 *Perf. 12½***
1246 A305 275r Emblem 1.60 .70

ICAO, 40th Anniversary — A306

**1984, Dec. 7 Photo. *Perf. 13½x12½***
1247 A306 275r Airplane, Emblem 2.25 .70

Indonesia Netherlands Marine Exped., 1984-85 — A307

75th Intl. Women's Day — A308

Survey ship Snellius II and: 50r, Marine geological and geophysical exploration. 100r, Mapping ocean currents. 275r, Studying marine flora and fauna.

**1985, Feb. 27 Photo. *Perf. 13x13½***

**1248** A307 50r multi .50 .25
**1249** A307 100r multi 1.00 .25
**1250** A307 275r multi 3.00 .40
*Nos. 1248-1250 (3)* 4.50 .90

**1985, Mar. 8**

**1251** A308 100r Emblem 2.25 .65
**1252** A308 275r Silhouettes, emblem 5.75 2.50

Five Year Plan A309

**1985, Apr. 1 *Perf. 13½x13***

**1254** A309 75r Mecca pilgrimage program .40 .25
**1255** A309 140r Compulsory education .75 .45
**1256** A309 350r Cement industry, Padang works 1.90 1.00
*Nos. 1254-1256 (3)* 3.05 1.70

**Suharto Type of 1980-83 and**

A310

A310a

A310b

A310c

***Perf. 13½x12½, 12½ (A310, A310a, A310b, A310c)***

**1983-93 Photo.**

**1257** A246 10r pale grn & dk grn 1.60 .25
**1258** A246 25r pale org & dk cop red .45 .25
**1259** A246 50r beige & dk brn .45 .25
**1260** A246 55r sal rose & rose .45 .25
**1261** A246 100r lt blue green & ultra .45 .25
**1262** A310 140r rose & dp brn .85 .25
**1263** A310c 150r yel grn & multi .75 .25
**1264** A310b 200r pink, bl & red .75 .25
**1265** A246 300r lt dull grn, bl grn & gold 2.00 .25
**1266** A310c 300r multicolored 1.75 .25
**1267** A310 350r red & brt lil 2.40 .35
**1268** A246 400r blue grn, int blue & gold 2.50 .30
**1268A** A310b 700r pale grn, rose lil & grn 2.75 .35
**1268B** A310c 700r red & multi 4.00 1.10
**1269** A310a 1000r multi 6.50 .75
*Nos. 1257-1269 (15)* 27.65 5.35

Issued: 10r, 25r, 3/11; 140r, 350r, 4/10/85; 50r, 100r, #1265, 12/24/86; 55r, 400r, 12/87; 200r, 12/89; 700r, 3/90; 1000r, 8/17/88; 150r, #1266, 1268B, 8/17/93.

For surcharge see No. 1527.

Asia-Africa Conference, 30th Anniv. — A311

**1985, Apr. 24 *Perf. 12½***

**1270** A311 350r Emblem, inscription 2.50 .45

Intl. Youth Year — A312

UN Decade for Women — A313

**1985, July 12 *Perf. 12½x13½***

**1271** A312 75r Three youths, globe 1.00 .25
**1272** A312 140r Youths supporting globe 2.00 .25

**1985, July 26**

**1273** A313 55r Profiles of women, emblem .55 .25
**1274** A313 140r Globe, emblem 1.25 .25

Indonesian Trade Fair — A314

**1985, Aug. 1**

**1275** A314 140r Hydro-electric plant 1.00 .25
**1276** A314 350r Farmer, industrial plant 2.50 .40

Republic of Indonesia, 40th anniv.

11th Natl. Sports Week, Jakarta, Sept. 9-20 A315

***Perf. 13½x12½, 12½x13½***

**1985, Sept. 9 Photo.**

**1277** A315 55r Sky diving .40 .25
**1278** A315 100r Combat sports .75 .25
**1279** A315 140r High jump 1.00 .25
**1280** A315 350r Wind surfing, vert. 2.50 .45
*Nos. 1277-1280 (4)* 4.65 1.20

Org. of Petroleum Exporting Countries, OPEC, 25th Anniv. — A316

**1985, Sept. 14 *Perf. 12½***

**1281** A316 140r multi 1.50 .30

Natl. Oil Industry, Cent. A317

**1985, Oct. 8 *Perf. 13½x13***

**1282** A317 140r Oil tankers .80 .30
**1283** A317 250r Refinery 1.40 .45
**1284** A317 350r Offshore oil rig 2.00 .90
*Nos. 1282-1284 (3)* 4.20 1.65

UN, 40th Anniv. — A318

Design: 140r, Doves, 40, emblem. 300r, Bombs transformed into plants.

**1985, Oct. 24 *Perf. 12½***

**1285** A318 140r multicolored .85 .25
**1286** A318 300r multicolored 1.60 .45

Wildlife A318a

**1985, Dec. 27 Photo. *Perf. 14½x13***

**1286A** A318a 75r Rhinoceros sondaicus 1.25 .30
**1286B** A318a 150r Anoa depressicornis 2.50 .45
**1286C** A318a 300r Varanus komodoensis 5.00 .70
*Nos. 1286A-1286C (3)* 8.75 1.45

1986 Industrial Census — A319

**1986, Feb. 8 Photo. *Perf. 12½***

**1287** A319 Pair 1.75 1.25
*a.* 175r Census emblem .85 .30
*b.* 175r Symbols of industry .85 .30

UN Child Survival Campaign A320

**1986, Mar. 15 Photo. *Perf. 12½***

**1288** A320 75r Breastfeeding .80 .25
**1289** A320 140r Immunization 1.40 .30

UNICEF, 40th anniv.

4th 5-year Development Plan — A321

14th Thomas Cup, 13th Uber Cup, Jakarta — A322

**1986, Apr. 1 Photo. *Perf. 12½***

**1290** A321 140r Construction .30 .30
**1291** A321 500r Agriculture 1.25 .40

**1986, Apr. 22**

**1292** A322 55r Cup, racket .90 .25
**1293** A322 150r Cups, horiz. 2.00 .25

EXPO '86, Vancouver — A323

**1986, May 2 *Perf. 12½x14½***

**1294** A323 75r Pinisi junk .65 .25
**1295** A323 150r Kentongan, satellite 1.25 .30
**1296** A323 300r Pavilion emblem 2.25 .40
*Nos. 1294-1296 (3)* 4.15 .95

Natl. Scout Jamboree, JAMNAS '86, Cibubur Jakarta East A324

***Perf. 13½x12½, 12½x13½***

**1986, June 21 Photo.**

**1297** A324 100r Saluting flag 1.25 .25
**1298** A324 140r Cookout 1.75 .30
**1299** A324 210r Map-reading, vert. 2.50 .40
*Nos. 1297-1299 (3)* 5.50 .95

Air Show '86, Jakarta, June 22-July 1 A325

**1986, June 23 *Perf. 13½x12½***

**1300** A325 350r multi 2.25 .40

Folk Dances — A326

**1986, July 30 Photo. *Perf. 12½***

**1301** A326 140r Legong Kraton 1.25 .25
**1302** A326 350r Barong 3.25 .45
**1303** A326 500r Kecak 4.50 .60
*Nos. 1301-1303 (3)* 9.00 1.30

19th Congress of Intl. Society of Sugar Cane Technologists, Jakarta — A327

**1986, Aug. 5 *Perf. 12½x13½***

**1304** A327 150r Planting 1.00 .25
**1305** A327 300r Sugar 1.75 .40

Sea-Me-We Submarine Cable Inauguration — A328

**1986, Sept. 8** *Perf. 12½*

**1306** A328 140r shown .75 .25
**1307** A328 350r Map, diff. 2.25 .45

Southeast Asia, Middle East, Western Europe Submarine Cable.

Intl. Peace Year — A329

1987 General Election — A330

**1986, Dec. 17 Photo.** *Perf. 12½*

**1308** A329 350r shown 1.25 .30
**1309** A329 500r Dove circling Earth 2.50 .35

**1987, Jan. 19**

75r, Tourism, party emblems, industry. 350r, Emblems, natl. eagle, ballot box.

**1310** A330 75r multi .35 .25
**1311** A330 140r multi .70 .25
**1312** A330 350r multi 1.60 .40
*Nos. 1310-1312 (3)* 2.65 .90

A331

A332

**1987, Mar. 21 Photo.** *Perf. 12½*

**1313** A331 350r Satellite, horiz. 1.00 .40
**1314** A331 500r shown 2.25 .35

Launch of Palapa B-2P, Cape Canaveral.

**1987, Apr. 1**

**1315** A332 140r Boy carving figurines, horiz. .40 .25
**1316** A332 350r shown 1.00 .35

4th 5-Year Development Plan.

Folk Costumes — A333

**1987, May 25** *Perf. 13x13½*

**1317** A333 140r Kalimantan Timur 4.25 .40
**1318** A333 350r Daerah Aceh 10.00 4.75
**1319** A333 400r Timor Timur 11.50 1.10
*Nos. 1317-1319 (3)* 25.75 6.25

See Nos. 1358-1363, 1412-1417, 1448-1453, 1464-1469.

14th Southeast Asia Games, Jakarata, Sept. 9-20 A334

Anniv. Emblems A335

**1987, June 10** *Perf. 12½*

**1320** A334 140r Weight lifting .70 .25
**1321** A334 250r Swimming 1.40 .30
**1322** A334 350r Running 1.90 .45
*Nos. 1320-1322 (3)* 4.00 1.00

**1987, June 20**

**1323** A335 75r multi, horiz. 1.50 .25
**1324** A335 100r shown 2.00 .25

City of Jakarta, 460th anniv.; Jakarta Fair, 20th anniv.

Children's Day — A336

ASEAN Headquarters, Jakarta — A337

**1987, July 23**

**1325** A336 100r Education, horiz. .60 .25
**1326** A336 250r Universal immunization 1.40 .25

**1987, Aug. 8**

**1327** A337 350r multi 1.75 .45

ASEAN, 20th anniv.

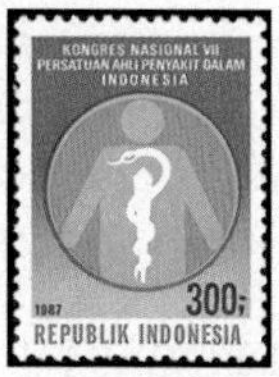


Assoc. of Physicians Specializing in Internal Diseases, 30th Anniv. — A338

**1987, Aug. 23** **Photo.**

**1328** A338 300r Stylized man, caduceus 1.40 .25

Sand Craters, Mt. Bromo, Timur A339

**1987, Oct. 20** *Perf. 13½x12½*

**1329** A339 140r shown .75 .25
**1330** A339 350r Bratan (Bedugul) Lake, Bali 2.50 .65
**1331** A339 500r Sea gardens, Bunaken Is. 3.50 .45
*Nos. 1329-1331 (3)* 6.75 1.35

Tourism. See Nos. 1367-1370A, 1408-1410, 1420-1422.

Role of Women in the Fight for Independence A340

**1987, Nov. 10** *Perf. 12½*

**1332** A340 75r Veteran .65 .25
**1333** A340 100r Soldiers, barbed wire (Laskar Wanita) .85 .25

Fish — A341

**1987, Dec. 30**

**1334** A341 150r Osphronemus goramy 1.50 .65
**1335** A341 200r Cyprinus carpio 2.00 .30
**1336** A341 500r Clarias batrachus 5.00 .55
*Nos. 1334-1336 (3)* 8.50 1.50

Natl. Veteran's League, 31st Anniv. — A342

**1988, Jan. 2**

**1337** A342 250r blue grn & org 1.25 .25

Occupational Health and Safety for Greater Efficiency and Productivity — A343

**1988, Jan. 12** *Perf. 13½x12½*

**1338** A343 350r Worker using safety equipment 1.75 .45

See No. 1419.

Natl. Craft Council, 8th Anniv. — A344

Crafts: 120r, Carved wood snake and frog. 350r, Cane rocking chair. 500r, Ornate carved bamboo containers and fan.

**1988, Mar. 3 Photo.** *Perf. 12½*

**1339** A344 120r ultra & dark brn .65 .25
**1340** A344 350r lt blue & dark brn 1.60 .45
**1341** A344 500r yel grn & dark brn 2.25 .40
*Nos. 1339-1341 (3)* 4.50 1.10

Pelita IV (Five-Year Development Plan) — A345

**1988, Apr. 1**

**1342** A345 140r Oil rig, refinery .30 .25
**1343** A345 400r Crayfish, trawler .95 .30

World Expo '88, Brisbane, Australia A346

Intl. Red Cross and Red Crescent Organizations, 125th Annivs. A347

Designs: 200r, Two children, Borobudur Temple in silhouette. 300r, Boy wearing armor and headdress. 350r, Girl, boy and a Tongkonan house, Toraja, South Sulawesi.

**1988, Apr. 30 Photo.** *Perf. 12½*

**1344** A346 200r multi .90 .25
**1345** A346 300r multi 1.40 .25
**1346** A346 350r multi 1.90 .35
*a.* Souv. sheet of 3, #1344-1346 15.00 12.00
*Nos. 1344-1346 (3)* 4.20 .85

No. 1346a exists imperf. Value: $40 unused, $30 used.

**1988, May 8**

**1347** A347 350r black & red 1.60 .30

Orchids — A348

**1988, May 17** *Perf. 13x13½*

**1348** A348 400r Dendrobium none 2.00 .45
**1349** A348 500r Dendrobium abang 2.50 .35

1988 Summer Olympics, Seoul — A349

Intl. Council of Women, Cent. — A350

**1988, June 15 Photo.** *Perf. 12½*

**1350** A349 75r Running .50 .25
**1351** A349 100r Weight lifting .55 .25
**1352** A349 200r Archery 1.10 .25
**1353** A349 300r Table tennis 1.60 .25
**1354** A349 400r Swimming 2.25 .30
*a.* Souv. sheet of 3 + label, #1351-1352, 1354, imperf 22.50 16.00
**1355** A349 500r Tennis 2.75 .35
*a.* Souv. sheet of 3 + label, #1350, 1353, 1355, imperf 22.50 16.00
*Nos. 1350-1355 (6)* 8.75 1.65

Sheets exist perf. Value, each $30.

**1988, June 26**

**1356** A350 140r brt blue & blk 1.00 .25

7th Natl. Farmers' Week — A351

**1988, July 9**

**1357** A351 350r lake & bister 1.75 .55

**Folk Costumes Type of 1987**

Traditional wedding attire from: 55r, West Sumatra. 75p, Jambi. 100r, Bengkulu. 120r, Lampung. 200r, Moluccas. 250r, East Nusa.

**1988, July 15** *Perf. 12½x14½*

**1358** A333 55r multicolored .55 .25

*Perf. 12½x13½*

**1359** A333 75r multicolored .80 .25
**1360** A333 100r multicolored 1.00 .25
**1361** A333 120r multicolored 1.25 .25

*Perf. 12½x14½*

**1362** A333 200r multicolored 1.90 .25
**1363** A333 250r multicolored 2.50 1.00
*Nos. 1358-1363 (6)* 8.00 2.25

A352

A353

**1988, Sept. 29 Photo.** *Perf. 12½*

**1364** A352 500r multicolored 2.00 .30

13th Congress of the Non-Aligned News Agencies Pool, Jakarta, Sept. 29-Oct. 1.

**1988, Oct. 9**

**1365** A353 140r multi 1.10 .25

Intl. Letter Writing Week.

Transportion and Communications Decade for Asia and the Pacific (1985-1995) A354

**1988, Oct. 24**
**1366** A354 350r blk & lt blue 2.25 .55

### Tourism Type of 1987

Architecture: 250r, Al Mashun Mosque, Medan. 300r, Pagaruyung Palace, Batusangkar. 500r, 1000r, Keong Emas Taman Theater, Jakarta.

**1988-89 Photo.** ***Perf. 13½x13***
**1367** A339 250r multi 1.25 .40
**1368** A339 300r multi 1.50 .30
**1369** A339 500r multi 2.50 .35
*Nos. 1367-1369 (3)* 5.25 1.05

### Souvenir Sheets
***Imperf***

**1370** A339 1000r multi 15.00 10.00

***Perf. 14½x13***

**1370A** Sheet of 2 21.00 15.00
*b.* A339 1500r like No. 1367 *7.25* 1.60
*c.* A339 2500r like No. 1368 *11.50* 2.75

No. 1370 exists perf 14½x12½. Value $10.
Issue dates: No. 1370A, Nov. 1989; others, Nov. 25, 1988. World Stamp Expo '89, Washington, DC.

Butterflies A356 — Flora A357

**1988, Dec. 20** ***Perf. 12½x13½***
**1371** A356 400r *Papilio gigon* 2.25 .45
**1372** A356 500r *Graphium androcles* 3.00 .65

### Souvenir Sheet
***Imperf***

**1373** A356 1000r like 500r 12.00 8.00

No. 1373 exists perf. 12½x14½. Value $26.

### Equestrian Type of 1981
Souvenir Sheets

**1988** ***Imperf.***
**1374** Sheet of 4 12.50 5.00
*a.* A268 200r blk, dark red & grn .50 .25
**1375** Sheet of 1 + label, dk bl, dark red & deep org *12.50* 5.00

FILACEPT '88, The Hague, Oct. 18-23, 1988. Nos. 1374-1375 exist perf. 12½. Value, each $18.

**1989, Jan. 7 Photo.** ***Perf. 13½x13***
**1376** A357 200r *Rafflesia* .90 .40
**1377** A357 1000r *Amorphophallus titanum* 4.50 .70

### Souvenir Sheet
***Perf. 13½x14½***

**1378** A357 1000r like No. 1377, value in blk 35.00 27.50

Garuda Indonesia Airlines, 40th Anniv. — A358

**1989, Jan. 26** ***Perf. 12½***
**1379** A358 350r bl grn & brt bl 2.00 .65

World Wildlife Fund — A359

Orangutans, *Pongo pygmaeus.*

**1989, Mar. 6 Photo.** ***Perf. 12½***
**1380** A359 75r Adult and young 4.00 .85
**1381** A359 100r Adult hanging in tree 4.00 .45
*a.* Souv. sheet of 2, #1380-1381 72.50 72.50
**1382** A359 140r Adult, young in tree 4.00 .55
**1383** A359 500r Adult's head 11.00 3.00
*a.* Souv. sheet of 2, #1382-1383 72.50 72.50
*Nos. 1380-1383 (4)* 23.00 4.85

Use of Postage Stamps in Indonesia, 125th Anniv. — A360

**1989, Apr. 1**
**1384** A360 1000r grn, rose lilac & deep blue 2.75 .40

5th Five-year Development Plan — A361

Industries.

**1989, Apr. 1**
**1385** A361 55r Fertilizer .25 .25
**1386** A361 150r Cilegon Iron and Steel Mill .35 .25
**1387** A361 350r Petroleum .90 .25
*Nos. 1385-1387 (3)* 1.50 .75

See Nos. 1427-1428, 1461-1462, 1488-1489, 1530-1532.

Natl. Education Day — A362

Ki Hadjar Dewantara (b. 1889), founder of Taman Siswa school and: 140r, Graduate. 300r, Pencil, globe and books.

**1989, May 2**
**1388** A362 140r ver, lake & brt rose lil .60 .25
**1389** A362 300r vio & pale grn 1.40 .30

Terbuka University (140r) and freedom from illiteracy (300r).

Asia-Pacific Telecommunity, 10th Anniv. — A363

Sudirman Cup, Flag — A364

**1989, July 1 Photo.** ***Perf. 12½***
**1390** A363 350r green & vio 1.60 .85

**1989, July 3**
**1391** A364 100r scar, gold & dark red brn 1.90 .25

Sudirman Cup world badminton mixed team championships, Jakarta, May 24-28.

Natl. Children's Day — A365

CIRDAP, 10th Anniv. — A366

**1989, July 23**
**1392** A365 100r Literacy .60 .25
**1393** A365 250r Physical fitness 1.40 .30

**1989, July 29**
**1394** A366 140r blue & dark red brn 1.10 .25

Center on Integrated Rural Development for Asia and the Pacific.

A367 — A368

Paleoanthropological Discoveries in Indonesia: Fossils of *Homo erectus* and *Homo sapiens* men.

**1989, Aug. 31**
**1395** A367 100r Sangiran 17 .90 .25
**1396** A367 150r Perning 1 1.25 .25
**1397** A367 200r Sangiran 10 1.75 .40
**1398** A367 250r Wajak 1 2.10 .30
**1399** A367 300r Sambungmacan 3.00 .45
**1400** A367 350r Ngandong 7 3.00 .30
*Nos. 1395-1400 (6)* 12.00 1.95

Nos. 1398-1400 vert.

**1989, Sept. 4**
**1401** A368 350r deep blue & yel grn 1.50 .35

Interparliamentary Union, Cent.

12th Natl. Sports Week — A369

**1989, Sept. 18**
**1402** A369 75r Tae kwando .45 .25
**1403** A369 100r Tennis .55 .25
**1404** A369 140r Judo .80 .25
**1405** A369 350r Volleyball 2.00 .70
**1406** A369 500r Boxing 2.75 .35
**1407** A369 1000r Archery 5.00 .70
*Nos. 1402-1407 (6)* 11.55 2.50

### Tourism Type of 1987

Structures in Miniature Park: 120r, Taman Burung. 350r, Natl. Philatelic Museum. 500r, Istana Anak-Anak, vert.

***Perf. 13½x12½, 12½x13½***

**1989, Oct. 9**
**1408** A339 120r multicolored .65 .25
**1409** A339 350r multicolored 1.75 .60
**1410** A339 500r multicolored 2.50 .50
*Nos. 1408-1410 (3)* 4.90 1.35

Film Festival — A370

**1989, Nov. 11 Photo.** ***Perf. 12½***
**1411** A370 150r yel bister & blk 1.50 .25

### Folk Costumes Type of 1987

Traditional wedding attire from: 50r, North Sumatra. 75r, South Sumatra. 100r, Jakarta. 140r, North Sulawesi. 350r, Mid Sulawesi. 500r, South Sulawesi. 1500r, North Sulawesi.

**1989, Dec. 11** ***Perf. 13x13½***
**1412** A333 50r multicolored .30 .25
**1413** A333 75r multicolored .40 .25
**1414** A333 100r multicolored .50 .25
**1415** A333 140r multicolored .70 .25
**1416** A333 350r multicolored 2.25 .90
**1417** A333 500r multicolored 3.00 .50
*Nos. 1412-1417 (6)* 7.15 2.40

### Souvenir Sheet
***Imperf***

**1418** A333 1500r multicolored 10.50 8.00

No. 1418 exists perf. 12½x13½. Value $13.

### Health and Safety Type of 1988

**1990, Jan. 12** ***Perf. 13x12½***
**Size: 29x21mm**
**1419** A343 200r Lineman, power lines 1.25 .25

### Tourism Type of 1987

Architecture: 200r, Fort Marlborough, Bengkulu. 400r, 1000r, National Museum, Jakarta. 500r, 1500r, Mosque of Baiturrahman, Banda Aceh.

**1990, Feb. 1** ***Perf. 13½x13***
**1420** A339 200r multicolored .75 .25
**1421** A339 400r multicolored 1.60 .25
**1422** A339 500r multicolored 2.00 .30
*Nos. 1420-1422 (3)* 4.35 .80

### Souvenir Sheet

**1423** Sheet of 2 12.00 8.00
*a.* A339 1000r multicolored 4.75 .50
*b.* A339 1500r multicolored 7.25 .75

Flora A371

**1990, Mar. 1**
**1424** A371 75r Mammilaria fragilis .25 .25
**1425** A371 1000r Gmelina elliptica 3.00 1.00

### Souvenir Sheet

**1426** A371 1500r like #1425 15.00 9.50

### 5th Five-year Development Plan Type of 1989

**1990, Apr. 1** ***Perf. 12½***
**1427** A361 200r Road construction .35 .25
**1428** A361 1000r Lighthouse, ship 1.90 1.10

Visit Indonesia Year, 1991 A372

***Perf. 13½x12½, 12½x13½***

**1990, May 1**
**1429** A372 100r shown .35 .25
**1430** A372 500r Steps, ruin 1.90 .40

### Souvenir Sheet
***Perf. 14½x12½***

**1430A** A372 5000r like #1429 21.00 14.00

No. 1430A, Stamp World London '90.

A373

A374

**1990, May 18** *Perf. 12½*

**1431** A373 1000r gray grn & brn org 2.25 .90

Disabled Veterans Corps, 40th anniv.

**1990, June 8** *Perf. 12½*

**1432** A374 75r shown .45 .25
**1433** A374 150r multi, diff. .90 .25
**1434** A374 400r multi, diff. 2.25 .40
*Nos. 1432-1434 (3)* 3.60 .90

**Souvenir Sheet**

**1435** A374 1500r multi 12.00 8.50

World Cup Soccer Championships, Italy.

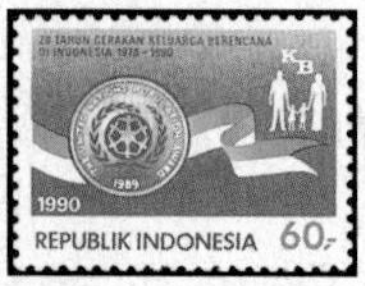


Family Planning in Indonesia, 20th Anniv. — A375

**1990, June 29**

**1436** A375 60r brown & red .85 .25

Natl. Census — A376

**1990, July 1**

**1437** A376 90r yel grn & dk grn 1.10 .25

Natl. Children's Day — A377

**1990, July 23**

**1438** A377 500r multicolored 1.60 .40

Souvenir Sheet

Traditional Lampung Wedding Costumes — A378

*Perf. 12½x14½*

**1990, June 10** **Photo.**

**1439** A378 2000r multicolored 9.50 6.00

Natl. Philatelic Exhibition, Stamp World London '90 and New Zealand '90.

Independence, 45th Anniv. — A379

**1990, Aug. 17** *Perf. 12½x13½*

**1440** A379 200r Soldier raising flag .70 .25
**1441** A379 500r Skyscraper, highway 1.60 .45

**Souvenir Sheet**

**1442** A379 1000r like #1441 9.50 6.00

Indonesia-Pakistan Economic & Cultural Cooperation Organization — A380

Designs: 400r, Woman dancing in traditional costume, vert.

*Perf. 13½x12½, 12½x13½*

**1990, Aug. 19** **Litho.**

**1443** A380 75r multicolored .55 .25
**1444** A380 400r multicolored 1.75 .55

Asian Pacific Postal Training Center, 20th Anniv. — A381

**1990, Sept. 10** **Photo.** *Perf. 12½*

**1445** A381 500r vio bl, bl & ultra 1.40 .45

A382

**1990, Sept. 14**

**1446** A382 200r gray, blk & org 1.25 .25

Organization of Petroleum Exporting Countries (OPEC), 30th anniv.

A383

**1990, Oct. 24**

**1447** A383 1000r multicolored 2.75 .85

Environmental Protection Laws, 40th anniv.

**Folk Costumes Type of 1987**

Traditional wedding attire from: 75r, West Java. 100r, Central Java. 150r, Yogyakarta. 200r, East Java. 400r, Bali. 500r, West Nusa Tenggara.

**1990, Nov. 1** *Perf. 13x13½*

**1448** A333 75r multicolored .35 .25
**1449** A333 100r multicolored .45 .25
**1450** A333 150r multicolored .70 .25
**1451** A333 200r multicolored .90 .25
**1452** A333 400r multicolored 1.75 .40
**1453** A333 500r multicolored 2.10 .55
*Nos. 1448-1453 (6)* 6.25 1.95

A385

Visit Indonesia Year 1991: Women in traditional costumes.

**1991, Jan. 1** **Photo.** *Perf. 12½x13½*

**1454** A385 200r multicolored .60 .25
**1455** A385 500r multicolored 1.75 .60
**1456** A385 1000r multicolored 3.00 .45
*Nos. 1454-1456 (3)* 5.35 1.30

**Souvenir Sheet**

**1456A** A385 1500r As No. 1454 17.00 12.00

A386

**1991, Feb. 4** *Perf. 12½*

**1457** A386 200r yel, grn & bl grn 1.40 .25

16th natl. Koran reading competition, Jogjakarta.

Palace of Sultan Ternate, the Moluccas A387

Design: 1000r, 2500r, Bari House, Palembang, South Sumatra.

**1991, Mar. 1** *Perf. 13½x12½*

**1458** A387 500r multicolored 1.10 .30
**1459** A387 1000r multicolored 2.25 .55

**Souvenir Sheet**

**1460** A387 2500r multicolored 9.50 6.00

**5th Five Year Development Plan Type of 1989**

**1991, Apr. 1** *Perf. 12½*

**1461** A361 75r Steel mill, vert. .35 .25
**1462** A361 200r Computers .80 .25

Danger of Smoking — A388

**1991, May 31** **Photo.** *Perf. 12½*

**1463** A388 90r multicolored 1.40 .25

**Folk Costumes Type of 1987**

Traditional wedding attire from: 100r, West Kalimantan. 200r, Mid Kalimantan. 300r, South Kalimantan. 400r, Southeast Sulawesi. 500r, Riau. 1000r, Irian Jaya.

**1991, June 15** *Perf. 13x13½*

**1464** A333 100r multicolored .30 .25
**1465** A333 200r multicolored .60 .25
**1466** A333 300r multicolored .90 .25
**1467** A333 400r multicolored 1.40 .25
**1468** A333 500r multicolored 1.75 .30
**1469** A333 1000r multicolored 3.25 .65
*Nos. 1464-1469 (6)* 8.20 1.95

Natl. Scouting Jamboree, Cibubur A389

Monument A390

**1991, June 15** *Perf. 12½*

**1470** A389 200r multicolored 1.50 .25

**1991, July 6**

**1471** A390 200r multicolored 1.50 .25

Natl. Farmers' Week — A391

Indonesian Chemical Society, 4th Natl. Congress — A392

**1991, July 15**

**1472** A391 500r brt bl, yel & grn 1.90 .25

**1991, July 28**

**1473** A392 400r grn, ver & dull grn 1.90 .25

Chemindo '91.

A393

A394

**1991, Aug. 24** **Photo.** *Perf. 12½*

**1474** A393 300r blk, red & gray 1.75 .35

5th Junior Men's and 4th Women's Asian Weightlifting Championships.

**1991, Aug. 30**

**1475** A394 500r lilac & sky blue 1.90 .45

World Cup Parachuting Championships.

A395

A396

**1991, Sept. 17**

**1476** A395 200r multicolored 1.60 .25

Indonesian Red Cross, 46th aAnniv.

**1991, Oct. 6**

**1477** A396 300r yellow & blue 1.60 .35

Intl. Amateur Radio Union, 8th regional conf., Bandung.

Istiqlal (Independence) Festival, Jakarta — A397

**1991, Oct. 15**

**1478** A397 200r gray, blk & ver 1.60 .25

Intl. Conference on the Great Apes — A398

Pongo pygmaeus: 200r, Sitting in tree. 500r, Walking. 1000r, 2500r, Sitting on ground.

**1991, Dec. 18** *Perf. 12½x13½*

**1479** A398 200r multicolored .75 .25
**1480** A398 500r multicolored 1.75 .55
**1481** A398 1000r multicolored 3.50 1.00
*Nos. 1479-1481 (3)* 6.00 1.80

**Souvenir Sheet**

**1481A** A398 2500r multicolored 11.00 8.00

Intl. Convention on Quality Control Circles, Bali — A399

**1991, Oct. 22** *Perf. 12½*

**1482** A399 500r multicolored 2.00 .50

Automation of the Post Office — A400

200r, P.O. 500r, Mail sorting equipment.

**1992, Jan. 9** **Photo.** *Perf. 13½x13*

**1483** A400 200r multicolored .40 .25
**1484** A400 500r multicolored .95 .30

National Elections A401

**1992, Feb. 10** *Perf. 12½*

**1485** A401 75r shown .25 .25
**1486** A401 100r Ballot boxes, globe .25 .25
**1487** A401 500r Hands dropping ballots in ballot boxes 1.25 .35
*Nos. 1485-1487 (3)* 1.75 .85

**5th Five-year Development Plan Type of 1989**

**1992, Apr. 1** **Photo.** *Perf. 12½*

**1488** A361 150r Construction worker .30 .25
**1489** A361 300r Aviation technology .65 .25

Visit Asia Year, 1992 A402

**1992, Mar. 1** *Perf. 13½x13*

**1490** A402 300r Lembah Baliem, Irian Jaya .75 .25
**1491** A402 500r Tanah Lot, Bali 1.25 .40
**1492** A402 1000r Lombah Anai, Sumatra Barat 2.75 .60
*Nos. 1490-1492 (3)* 4.75 1.25

**Souvenir Sheet**

**1493** A402 3000r like #1491 10.00 8.00

Birds — A403

**1992, July 1** **Photo.** *Perf. 12½x13½*

**1494** A403 100r Garrulax leucolophus .25 .25
**1495** A403 200r Dinopium javanense .50 .25
**1496** A403 400r Buceros rhinoceros 1.00 .45
**1497** A403 500r Alisterus amboinensis 1.50 .55
*Nos. 1494-1497 (4)* 3.25 1.50

**Souvenir Sheet**

**1498** A403 3000r like #1494 11.00 8.00

Children's Day — A404

75r, Street scene. 100r, Children with balloons. 200r, Boating scene. 500r, Girl feeding bird.

**1992, July 23** *Perf. 12½*

**1499** A404 75r multicolored .25 .25
**1500** A404 100r multicolored .30 .25
**1501** A404 200r multicolored .65 .25
**1502** A404 500r multicolored 1.50 .75
*Nos. 1499-1502 (4)* 2.70 1.50

1992 Summer Olympics, Barcelona — A405

Designs: No. 1508a, 2000r, like #1504. b, 3000r, like #1507.

**1992, June 1** *Perf. 12½x13½*

**1503** A405 75r Weight lifting .25 .25
**1504** A405 200r Badminton .40 .25
**1505** A405 300r Symbols of events .65 .25
**1506** A405 500r Women's tennis 1.10 .35
**1507** A405 1000r Archery 2.10 .65
*Nos. 1503-1507 (5)* 4.50 1.75

**Souvenir Sheet**

**1508** A405 Sheet of 2, #a.-b. 13.00 9.00

ASEAN, 25th Anniv. A406

**1992, Aug. 8** *Perf. 13½x12½*

**1509** A406 200r shown .55 .25
**1510** A406 500r Flags, map 1.25 .40
**1511** A406 1000r Flags on poles 2.50 .65
*Nos. 1509-1511 (3)* 4.30 1.30

Flowers A407

Designs: 200r, Phalaenopsis ambilis. 500r, Rafflesia arnoldii. 1000r, 2000r, Jasminum sambae.

*Perf. 13½x12½*

**1992, Jan. 20** **Photo.**

**1512** A407 200r multicolored .50 .25
**1513** A407 500r multicolored 1.25 .40
**1514** A407 1000r multicolored 2.25 .65
*Nos. 1512-1514 (3)* 4.00 1.30

**Souvenir Sheet**

*Perf. 13½x13*

**1515** A407 2000r multicolored 10.00 8.00

A408

*Perf. 12½x13½*

**1992, Sept. 6** **Photo.**

**1516** A408 200r shown .55 .25
**1517** A408 500r Flags, emblem 1.25 .45

10th Non-Aligned Summit, Jakarta.

A409

**1992, Nov. 29** **Photo.** *Perf. 12½*

**1518** A409 200r green & blue 1.10 .25

Intl. Planned Parenthood Federation, 40th anniv.

A410

A411

*Perf. 12½x13½*

**1992, Aug. 16** **Photo.**

**1519** A410 200r Globe, satellite .45 .25
**1520** A410 500r Palapa satellite 1.10 .40
**1521** A410 1000r Old, new telephones 2.10 .65
*Nos. 1519-1521 (3)* 3.65 1.30

Satellite Communications in Indonesia, 16th anniv.

**1992, Oct. 1** *Perf. 12½x13½*

Traditional Dances: 200r, 3000r, Tari Ngremo, Timor. 500r, Tari Gending Sriwijaya, Sumatra.

**1522** A411 200r multicolored .65 .25
**1523** A411 500r multicolored 1.40 1.40

**Souvenir Sheet**

**1524** A411 3000r like #1522 9.00 6.00

No. 1523 was withdrawn from sale on 10/5.

See Nos. 1564-1567, 1596-1600, 1628-1632, 1688-1692, 1747-1751, 1815-1820.

Antara News Agency, 55th Anniv. — A412

**1992, Dec. 13** **Photo.** *Perf. 12½*

**1525** A412 500r blue & black 1.40 .25

Natl. Afforestation Campaign — A413

*Perf. 13½x12½*

**1992, Dec. 24** **Photo.**

**1526** A413 500r multicolored 1.40 .30

No. 1260 Surcharged

**1993, Feb. 1** **Photo.** *Perf. 13½x12½*

**1527** A246 50r on 55r #1260 .75 .25

1993 General Session of the People's Consultative Assembly — A414

**1993, Mar. 1** **Photo.** *Perf. 13½x12½*

**1528** A414 300r Building exterior .50 .25
**1529** A414 700r Building interior 1.25 .55

**5th Five Year Development Plan Type of 1989**

300r, Soldier's silhouettes over city. 700r, Immunizing children. 1000r, Runners.

**1993, Apr. 1** *Perf. 12½*

**1530** A361 300r multicolored .40 .30
**1531** A361 700r multicolored .85 .75
**1532** A361 1000r multicolored 1.25 1.00
*Nos. 1530-1532 (3)* 2.50 2.05

Ornithoptera Goliath — A415

**1993, Apr. 20** **Photo.** *Perf. 12½*

**1533** A415 1000r multicolored 2.25 .95

For overprint see No. 1540.

Surabaja, 700th Anniv. A416

Designs: 300r, Siege of Yamato Hotel. 700r, World Habitat Award, Surabaya skyline. 1000r, Candi Bajang Ratu, natl. monument.

*Perf. 13½x12½*

**1993, May 29** **Photo.**

**1534** A416 300r multicolored .50 .40
**1535** A416 700r multicolored 1.10 .80
**1536** A416 1000r multicolored 1.75 1.25
*Nos. 1534-1536 (3)* 3.35 2.45

For overprints see Nos. 1538-1539, 1541.

Nos. 1533-1536 Ovptd. in Red

and

Indopex '93 — A417

**1993** ***Perfs. as Before***

**1538** A416 300r on #1534 .50 .25
**1539** A416 700r on #1535 1.40 .40
**1540** A415 1000r on #1533 2.25 .80
**1541** A416 1000r on #1536 2.00 .60
*Nos. 1538-1541 (4)* 6.15 2.05

**Souvenir Sheet**

***Perf. 13½x12½***

**1542** A417 3500r multicolored 6.00 4.50

Location of overprint varies. Issued: No. 1540, Apr. 20; others, May 29.

Environmental Protection — A418

Flowers: Nos. 1543a, 1545a, Jasminum sambac. No. 1543b, Phalaenopsis amabilis. No. 1543c, Rafflesia arnoldi.
Wildlife: Nos. 1544a, 1545b, Varanus komodoensis. No. 1544b, Scleropages formasus. No. 1544c, Spizaetus bartelsi.

***Perf. 12½x13½***

**1993, June 5** **Photo.**

**1543** A418 300r Tripytych, #a.-c. 2.50 .85
**1544** A418 700r Tripytych, #a.-c. 5.75 1.90

**Souvenir Sheet of 2**

**1545** A418 1500r #a.-b. 8.25 5.00

1st World Community Development Camp — A419

Designs: 300r, Boy scouts working on road. 700r, Pres. Suharto shaking hands with scout.

***Perf. 13½x12½***

**1993, July 27** **Photo.**

**1546** A419 300r multicolored .50 .25
**1547** A419 700r multicolored 1.25 .45

Papilio Blumei — A420

Armed Forces Day — A421

***Perf. 12½x13½***

**1993, Aug. 24** **Photo.**

**1548** A420 700r multicolored 1.50 .60

**Souvenir Sheets**

**1549** A420 3000r multicolored 8.00 6.00
**1550** A420 3000r multicolored 8.00 6.00

Inscription at top of No. 1549 is like that on No. 1548. No. 1550 contains a stamp inscribed "1993," a se-tenant label and Bangkok '93 Philatelic Exhibition inscription in sheet margin.

**1993, Oct. 5** ***Perf. 12½***

**1551** A421 300r Soedirman .55 .25
**1552** A421 300r Oerip Soemohardjo .55 .25
*a.* Pair, #1551-1552 1.10 .45

Tourism — A422

13th Natl. Sports Week — A423

300r, 3000r, Waterfall. 700r, Cave formations. 1000r, Dormant volcanic crater, horiz.

***Perf. 12½x13½, 13½x12½***

**1993, Oct. 4**

**1553** A422 300r multicolored .45 .40
**1554** A422 700r multicolored .95 .85
**1555** A422 1000r multicolored 1.60 1.25
*Nos. 1553-1555 (3)* 3.00 2.50

**Souvenir Sheet**

**1556** A422 3000r multicolored 5.50 4.00

**1993, Sept. 9** ***Perf. 12½x13½***

**1557** A423 150r Swimming .25 .25
**1558** A423 300r Cycling .50 .30
**1559** A423 700r Mascot 1.10 .70
**1560** A423 1000r High jump 1.60 1.00
*Nos. 1557-1560 (4)* 3.45 2.25

**Souvenir Sheet**

**1561** A423 3500r like No. 1560 7.00 4.50

Flora and Fauna — A424

Designs: a, Michelia champaca. b, Cananga odorata. c, Copsychus pyrropygus. d, Gracula religiosa robusta.

**1993, Nov. 5** **Photo.** ***Perf. 12½x13½***

**1562** A424 300r Block of 4, #a.-d. 5.00 3.50

Migratory Farm Workers — A425

**1993, Dec. 4** ***Perf. 12½***

**1563** A425 700r Field workers 1.00 .70

**Traditional Dance Type of 1992**

Dance and region: 300r, Gending Sriwijaya, South Sumatra. 700r, Tempayan, West Kalimantan. 1000r, 3500r, Tifa, Irian Jaya.

**1993, Dec. 22** ***Perf. 12½x13½***

**1564** A411 300r multicolored .75 .25
**1565** A411 700r multicolored 1.40 .40
**1566** A411 1000r multicolored 2.00 .55
*Nos. 1564-1566 (3)* 4.15 1.20

**Souvenir Sheet**

**1567** A411 3500r multicolored 6.00 4.50

Intl. Year of the Family A426

**1994, Mar. 1** **Photo.** ***Perf. 13½x12½***

**1568** A426 300r multicolored .75 .25

Indonesian Postage Stamps, 130th Anniv. — A427

Design: 700r, Netherlands Indies #B7, #N7, Indonesia #B214.

**1994, Apr. 1** ***Perf. 12½***

**1569** A427 700r multicolored 1.25 .55

**Souvenir Sheet**

***Imperf***

**1569A** A427 3500r like #1569 7.00 4.00

PHILAKOREA '94 (#1569A).

6th Five Year Development Plan — A428

Buddhist dieties and: 100r, Professional women. 700r, Education. 2000r, Medical care for children.

**1994, Apr. 1** ***Perf. 12½***

**1570** A428 100r multicolored .30 .25
**1571** A428 700r multicolored 1.25 .70
**1572** A428 2000r multicolored 4.00 2.00
*Nos. 1570-1572 (3)* 5.55 2.95

Tropical Fish A429

Designs: 300r, Telmatherina ladigesi. 700r, 3500r, Melanotaenia boesemani.

**1994, Apr. 20** **Photo.** ***Perf. 13***

**1573** A429 300r multicolored .80 .25
**1574** A429 700r multicolored 1.60 .70

**Souvenir Sheet**

**1575** A429 3500r multicolored 7.00 4.00

No. 1575 has continuous design.

Intl. Federation of Red Cross & Red Crescent Societies, 75th Anniv. — A429a

**1994, May 5** ***Perf. 12½x13***

**1575A** A429a 300r multicolored .90 .25

Second Asian and Pacific Ministerial Conference on Women, Jakarta — A430

**1994, June 13** ***Perf. 13½x12½***

**1576** A430 700r multicolored 1.40 .45

A431

1994 World Cup Soccer Championships, US: 150r, Player dribbling ball, vert. 300r, Mascot chasing ball, vert. 700r, 1994 Tournament emblem. 1000r, Ball in net. 3500r, Soccer ball in net.

**1994, June 17** ***Perf. 12½x13½***

**1577** A431 150r multicolored .25 .25
**1578** A431 300r multicolored .60 .25

***Perf. 13½x12½***

**1579** A431 700r multicolored 1.40 .50
**1580** A431 1000r multicolored 1.90 .65
*Nos. 1577-1580 (4)* 4.15 1.65

**Souvenir Sheet**

**1581** A431 3500r multicolored 6.50 4.00

Thomas & Uber Cups — A432

Designs: a, Uber Cup. b, Thomas Cup.

**1994, June 22** ***Perf. 12½***

**1582** A432 300r Pair, #a.-b. 1.25 .55

**Souvenir Sheet of 2**

**1583** A432 1750r #a.-b. 6.00 3.50

A433

A434

***Perf. 12½x13½***

**1994, July 27** **Photo.**

**1584** A433 700r multicolored 1.25 .50

Human Rights Day.

***Perf. 13]x13½***

**1994, Aug. 19** **Photo.**

**1585** A434 300r Brown pottery vase .75 .25
**1586** A434 700r Blue & white vase 1.75 .65

Indonesia-Pakistan Econiomic & Cultural Cooperation Organization.
See Pakistan Nos. 822-823.

Bogoriense Zoological Museum, Cent. — A435

700r, Skeleton of Javan rhinoceros. 1000r, 3500r, Skeleton of blue whale.

**1994, Aug. 20** ***Perf. 13½x13***

**1587** A435 700r multicolored 1.50 .55

**Size: 80x22mm**

**1588** A435 1000r multicolored 3.00 1.20

**Souvenir Sheet**

***Perf. 13x13½***

**1588A** A435 3500r multicolored 7.50 4.75

12th Asian Games, Hiroshima 1994 A436

**1994, Oct. 2 Litho. *Perf. 13½x13***
**1589** A436 300r Mascots .70 .25
**1590** A436 700r Hurdlers 1.50 .70

Bakosurtanal, 25th Anniv. — A437

**1994, Oct. 17 Litho. *Perf. 13½x13***
**1591** A437 700r multicolored 1.50 .50

Flora & Fauna — A438

Designs: a, Morus macroura. b, Oncosperma tigillaria. c, Eucalyptus urophylla. d, Phalaenopsis amabilis. e, Pometia pinnata. f, Argusianus argus. g, Loriculus pusillus. h, Philemon buceroides. i, Alisterus amboinensis. j, Seleucidis melanoleuca.
3500r, Philemon buceroides, diff.

**1994, Nov. 5 Photo. *Perf. 12½x13½***
**1592** A438 150r Block or strip of 10, #a.-j. 10.00 5.00

**Souvenir Sheet**

**1593** A438 3500r multicolored 8.00 4.00
*a.* With added inscription in blue 12.00

Inscription in sheet margin of No. 1593a contains emblem and "PRIMERA '95." Issued: No. 1593a, 8/21/95.
See Nos. 1622, 1680-1682, 1737-1738, 1812-1814.

Asian-Pacific Economic Cooperation Summit (APEC '94) — A439

Design: 700r, Presidential retreat, Bogor.

**1994, Nov. 15 *Perf. 13½X13***
**1594** A439 700r multicolored 1.50 .50

For overprint see No. 1616A.

ICAO, 50th Anniv. A440

**1994, Dec. 7**
**1595** A440 700r multicolored 1.75 .50

**Traditional Dance Type of 1992**

Dance, region: 150r, Mengaup, Jambi. 300r, Mask, West Java. 700r, Anging Mamiri, South Sulawesi. 1000r, Pisok, North Sulawesi. 2000r, Bidu, East Nusa Tenggara. 3500r, Mask dance, West Java.

**1994, Dec. 27 *Perf. 12½x13½***
**1596** A411 150r multicolored .25 .25
**1597** A411 300r multicolored .60 .25
**1598** A411 700r multicolored 1.40 .50
**1599** A411 1000r multicolored 1.90 .70
**1600** A411 2000r multicolored 4.00 1.50
*a.* Bklt. pane, 2 ea #1596-1600 19.00
Complete booklet, #1600a 19.00
*Nos. 1596-1600 (5)* 8.15 3.20

**Souvenir Sheet**

**1601** A411 3500r multicolored 7.00 5.75

World Tourism Organization, 20th Anniv. — A441

Designs: 300r, Yogyakarta Palace. 700r, Floating market. 1000r, Pasola Sumba ritual.

**1995, Jan. 2 *Perf. 13½x12½***
**1602** A441 300r multicolored .50 .25
**1603** A441 700r multicolored 1.25 .65
**1604** A441 1000r multicolored 1.40 .85
*Nos. 1602-1604 (3)* 3.15 1.75

Indonesian Children, First Lady & Pres. Suharto A442

***Perf. 13½x12½***
**1995, Mar. 11 Photo.**
**1605** A442 700r multicolored 1.50 .65

6th Five Year Development Plan — A443

Designs: 300r, Letter from King of Klungkung, 18th-19th cent. 700r, Carrier pigeon mascot of natl. letter writing campaign.

**1995, Apr. 1 Photo. *Perf. 12½***
**1606** A443 300r multicolored .60 .25
**1607** A443 700r multicolored 1.40 .70

4th Intl. Bamboo Conference — A444

Designs: 300r, Schizostachyum brachycladum. 700r, Dendrocalamus asper.

***Perf. 12½x13½***
**1995, June 19 Photo.**
**1608** A444 300r multicolored .60 .25
**1609** A444 700r multicolored 1.40 .70

First Flight of N250 Turboprop Commuter Airplane A445

**1995, Aug. 10 *Perf. 13½x12½***
**1610** A445 700r multicolored 1.40 .65

Independence, 50th Anniv. — A446

**1995, Aug. 17**
**1611** A446 300r Anniv. emblem .55 .25
**1612** A446 700r Boy, natl. flag 1.50 .70

**Souvenir Sheet**

**1612A** A446 2500r like No. 1612 6.00 4.00

JAKARTA '95, 8th Asian Intl. Philatelic Exhibition A447

Scenes in Jakarta: 300r, Kota Intan Drawbridge. 700r, Fatahillah Historical Museum.

**1995, Aug. 19**
**1613** A447 300r multicolored .60 .25
**1614** A447 700r multicolored 1.40 .70

No. 1613 exists in 7 souvenir sheets of 1, each with different color margins. Sold at the 2nd International Stamp Exhibition in Jakarta. Value, set of 7 sheets $125.

Sail Indonesia '95 A448

**1995, Aug. 19**
**1615** A448 700r multicolored 1.25 .60

**Souvenir Sheet**

**1616** A448 2500r multicolored 6.50 4.00

**No. 1594 Overprinted "PRIMERA '95" in Blue**

**1995, Aug. 21 Photo. *Perf. 13½x13***
**1616A** A439 700r on #1594 3.00 3.00

Istiqlal (Independence) Festival II 1995, Jakarta — A449

**1995, Sept. 23 *Perf. 12½x13½***
**1617** A449 700r multicolored 1.25 .60

Takeover of Post, Telegraph, & Telephone Headquarters, 50th Anniv. — A450

**1995, Sept. 27 *Perf. 13½x12½***
**1618** A450 700r multicolored 1.25 .60

FAO, 50th Anniv. — A451

UN, 50th Anniv. — A452

**1995, Oct. 16 *Perf. 12½x13½***
**1619** A451 700r multicolored 1.25 .60

**1995, Oct. 24 *Perf. 12½***

UN emblem, "50," and: 300r, Flags of nations. 700r, Rainbow over earth.

**1620** A452 300r multicolored .60 .25
**1621** A452 700r multicolored 1.40 .70

**Flora and Fauna Type of 1994**

Designs: a, Cyrtostachys renda. b, Panthera tigris sumatrae. c, Bouea macrophylla. d, Rhinoceros sondaicus. e, Santalum album. f, Varanus komodoensis. g, Diospyros celebica. h, Macrocephalon maleo. i, Nephleium ramboutan-ake. j, Polyplectron schleiermacheri.
2500r, Panthera tigris sumatrae.

**1995, Nov. 5 Photo. *Perf. 12½x13½***
**1622** A438 150r Block of 10, #a.-j. 7.50 3.25

**Souvenir Sheet**

**1623** A438 2500r multicolored 13.00 8.00

1995 Aga Khan Award for Architecture — A453

Designs: 300r, Masjid Agung, Kraton Yogyakarta. 700r, Kraton Surakarta.

**1995, Nov. 23 *Perf. 13½x13***
**1624** A453 300r multicolored .60 .25
**1625** A453 700r multicolored 1.40 .70

Sir Rowland Hill (1795-1879) — A454

300r, Hill, letter carriers on motorcycles. 700r, Hill, Indonesian postal service logo.

**1995, Dec. 3 *Perf. 13½x12½***
**1626** A454 300r multicolored .60 .25
**1627** A454 700r multicolored 1.40 .70

**Traditional Dance Type of 1992**

Dance and region: 150r, Nguri, West Nusa Tenggara. 300r, Muli Betanggai, Lampung. 700r, Mutiara, Maluku. 1000r, Gantar, East Kalimantan. 2500r, Tari Nguri, Nusa Tenggara Barrat.

**1995, Dec. 27 *Perf. 12½x13½***
**1628** A411 150r multicolored .25 .25
**1629** A411 300r multicolored .60 .25
**1630** A411 700r multicolored 1.40 .60
**1631** A411 1000r multicolored 1.90 .80
*Nos. 1628-1631 (4)* 4.15 1.90

**Souvenir Sheet**

**1632** A411 2500r multicolored *4.50* 3.00

1996 Economic Census — A455

Design: 300r, Economic sectors, vert.

**1996, Jan. 2 *Perf. 12½***
**1633** A455 300r multicolored .60 .25
**1634** A455 700r multicolored 1.40 .70

Greetings Stamps — A456

Various flowers.

**1996, Feb. 1 Photo. *Perf. 12½***
**1635** A456 150r multicolored .25 .25
**1636** A456 300r multicolored .50 .25
**1637** A456 700r multicolored 1.25 .55
*Nos. 1635-1637 (3)* 2.00 1.05

See Nos. 1657-1659.

PWI Journalists' Assoc., 50th Anniv. — A457

Designs: 300r, RM Soemanang Soeriowinoto. 700r, Djamaluddin Adinegoro.

**1996, Feb. 9**

**1638** A457 300r multicolored .45 .25
**1639** A457 700r multicolored 1.25 .55

Australian Spotted Cuscus — A458

Design: Nos. 1640, 1642a, shown. Nos. 1641, 1642b, Indonesian bear cuscus.

**1996, Mar.22 Photo. *Perf. 13x13½***

**1640** A458 300r multicolored .60 .40
**1641** A458 300r multicolored .60 .40
*a.* Pair, Nos. 1640-1641 1.25 1.25
*b.* Sheet of 5 #1641a *35.00* *17.50*

**Souvenir Sheet**

**1642** A458 1250r Sheet of 2, #a.-b. *4.50* 2.50
*c.* #1642 with added inscription, ovpt. *10.00* 2.75

Indonesia '96 (#1641b).

No. 1642c has black CHINA '96 exhibition emblem in upper right corner. The bottom sheet margin contains gold overprint: "CHINA '96 - 9th Asian International Philatelic Exhibition" in both Chinese and English.

No. 1641b exists folded and affixed to a booklet cover. Value, $15.

See Australia Nos. 1489-1490.

A459

Launching of Palapa C Satellite — A460

**1996, Jan. 31 *Perf. 13***

**1643** A459 300r multicolored .65 .25

***Perf. 12½***

**1644** A460 700r multicolored 1.60 .60

Indonesia '96, World Junior Philatelic Exhibition A461

Designs: 300r, No. 1647a, Building. 700r, No. 1647b, Decorated sun umbrellas.

**1996, Mar. 21 *Perf. 13½x13***

**1645** A461 300r multicolored .45 .25
**1646** A461 700r multicolored 1.25 .55

**Souvenir Sheet of 2**

**1647** A461 1250r #a.-b. *6.50* 3.25

No. 1647 exists imperf with different color margins. A souvenir sheet containing No. 1645-1646 and progressive color proofs of No. 1646 exists.

Education Day A462

Children's drawings: 150r, Teachers, students with outstretched arms. 300r, Children carrying books to school. 700r, Classroom instruction.

**1996, May 2 Photo. *Perf. 13½x13***

**1648** A462 150r multicolored .25 .25
**1649** A462 300r multicolored .50 .50
**1650** A462 700r multicolored 1.40 1.00
*Nos. 1648-1650 (3)* 2.15 1.75

Natl. Youth Kirab A463

**1996, June 8**

**1651** A463 300r shown .60 .25
**1652** A463 700r Holding flag, emblem 1.40 .70

1996 Summer Olympics, Atlanta A464

**1996, May 15**

**1653** A464 300r Archery .50 .30
**1654** A464 700r Weight lifting 1.25 .60
**1655** A464 1000r Badminton 1.60 1.00
*Nos. 1653-1655 (3)* 3.35 1.90

**Souvenir Sheet**

**1656** A464 2500r like #1653 4.50 2.50

No. 1656 is a continuous design.

**Greetings Type of 1996**

**1996, Apr. 15 Photo. *Perf. 12½***

**1657** A456 150r Roses .25 .25
**1658** A456 300r Orchids .50 .25
**1659** A456 700r Chrysanthemums 1.40 .55
*Nos. 1657-1659 (3)* 2.15 1.05

Maritime and Aviation Year — A465

300r, N-2130 aircraft, control tower at Soekarno-Hatta Airport. 700r, Inter-island passenger ship.

**1996, June 22**

**1660** A465 300r multicolored .50 .25
**1661** A465 700r multicolored 1.25 .90

1996 Natl. Scout Jamboree A466

Designs: a, Climbing rope. b, Sliding down rope. c, Girls at bottom of ropes. d, Girls assembling wood and rope ladder. e, Riding unicycle, eagle emblem, boys building scaffolding. f, Girls building scaffolding, campground. g, Two boys with project. h, Woman seated at control center.

No. 1662I, like #1662a-1662d. No. 1662J, like #1662e-1662h.

**1996, June 26**

**1662** A466 150r Block of 8, #a.-h. 3.75 1.75

**Souvenir Sheets**

**1662I** A466 1250d multicolored 4.25 2.25
**1662J** A466 1250d multicolored 4.25 2.25

Istanbul '96 (#1662I-1662J). Nos. 1662I-1662J each contain one 64x48mm stamp.

Nos. 1662a-1662d, 1663e-1662h are continuous designs.

Bank BNI, 50th Anniv. A467

**1996, July 5**

**1663** A467 300r shown .45 .25
**1664** A467 700r Sailing ship 1.25 .55

UNICEF, 50th Anniv. A468

**1996, July 23 *Perf. 13½x13***

**1665** A468 300r Child reading .45 .30
**1666** A468 700r Two children 1.10 .60
**1667** A468 1000r Three children 1.50 .90
*Nos. 1665-1667 (3)* 3.05 1.80

Ibu Tien Suharto (1923-96) First Lady — A469

**1996, Aug. 5 *Perf. 12½x13½***

**1668** A469 700r multicolored 1.25 .55

**Souvenir Sheet**

**1669** A469 2500r like #1668 4.00 2.00

No. 1669 is a continuous design.

14th Natl. Sports Week, Jakarta A470

***Perf. 13½x12½***

**1996, Sept. 2 Photo.**

**1670** A470 300r Softball .50 .30
**1671** A470 700r Field hockey 1.25 .60
**1672** A470 1000r Basketball 1.60 .90
*Nos. 1670-1672 (3)* 3.35 1.80

World Wildlife Fund A471

Rhinoceros sondaicus: a, #1674a, Adult. b, Adult with young. Dicerorhinus sumatrensis: c, Up close. d, #1674b, Adult.

**1996, Oct. 2 Photo. *Perf. 13½x13***

**1673** A471 300r Block of 4, #a.-d. 2.75 1.75
*e.* Souvenir sheet, 2 #1673 7.25 4.00
*f.* As "e," ovptd. in sheet margin 5.75 3.75

Overprint in margin of No. 1673f reads: "Bursa Filateli SEA Games XIX / Jakarta, 11-19 Oktober 1997" in gold.

**Souvenir Sheet**

**1674** A471 1500r Sheet of 2, #a.-b. 6.75 4.00

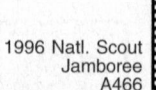

Greetings Stamps — A472

Bouquets of various flowers.

**1996, Oct. 15 Photo. *Perf. 12½***

**Background Colors**

**1675** A472 150r yellow & blue .25 .25
**1676** A472 300r yellow & green .50 .25
**1677** A472 700r pink & blue 1.25 .55
*Nos. 1675-1677 (3)* 2.00 1.05

Financial Day, 50th Anniv. A473

**1996, Oct. 30 *Perf. 13½x12½***

**1678** A473 700r multicolored 2.00 .55

**Flora & Fauna Type of 1994**

Fauna: No. 1680: a, Aceros cassidix. b, Orcaella brevirostris. c, Oriolus chinensis. d, Helarctos malayanus. e, Leucopsar rothschildi.

Flora: f, Borassus flabellifer. g, Coelogyne pandurata. h, Michelia alba. i, Amorphophallus titanum. j, Dysoxylum densiflorium.

No. 1681, Like #1680e. No. 1682, Like #1680g.

**1996, Nov. 5 Litho. *Perf. 12½x13½***

**1680** A438 300r Block or strip of 10, #a.-j. 6.50 3.25
*a.-j.* Any single .65 .30

**Souvenir Sheets**

**1681** A438 1250r multicolored 3.75 2.00
**1682** A438 1250r multicolored 3.75 2.00

Souvenir Sheet

Aceros Cassidix — A474

***Perf. 12½x13½***

**1996, Dec. 14 Photo.**

**1683** A474 2000r multicolored *22.50* *22.50*

ASEANPEX '96.

Scenes from Timor A475

Designs: 300r, Deep sea diving. 700r, Sailing ships entering harbor, 18th cent.

**1996-97 *Perf. 13½x12½***

**1684** A475 300r multicolored .60 .30
**1685** A475 700r multicolored 1.75 .60

**Souvenir Sheet**

**1685A** A475 2000d like #1685 5.50 2.75

Hong Kong '97 (#1685A).

Issued: #1686-1687, 12/18/96; #1685A, 2/12/97.

Foster Parents A476

150r, Children at playground, vert. 300r, Children, adult's hand holding picture of girl.

***Perf. 12½x13½, 13½x12½***

**1996, Dec. 20**

**1686** A476 150r multicolored .30 .25
**1687** A476 300r multicolored .60 .25

### Traditional Dance Type of 1992

Dance, region: 150r, Tari Baksa Kembang, Kalimantan Selatan. 300r, 2000r, Tari Ngarojeng, Jakarta. 700r, Tari Rampai, Aceh. 1000r, Tari Boituka, Timor.

**1996, Dec. 27** ***Perf. 12½x13½***

**1688** A411 150r multicolored .50 .25
**1689** A411 300r multicolored .50 .25
**1690** A411 700r multicolored 1.10 .55
**1691** A411 1000r multicolored 1.75 .80
*Nos. 1688-1691 (4)* 3.85 1.85

**Souvenir Sheet**

**1692** A411 2000r multicolored 4.00 2.00

Telecommunications Year — A477

Designs: 300r, Satellite dish, men at computers, map. 700r, Telephone keypad, woman using telephone, satellite in earth orbit.

**1997, Jan. 1** ***Perf. 13½x12½***

**1693** A477 300r multicolored .50 .25
**1694** A477 700r multicolored 1.40 .70

Greetings Stamps — A478

Designs: No. 1695, Heart, ribbon. No. 1696, Children, "Happy Birthday."

**1997, Jan. 15** ***Perf. 12½***

**1695** A478 600r multicolored .95 .45
**1696** A478 600r multicolored .95 .45

1997 General Election A479

Ballot box and: 300r, Means of transportion. 700r, Indonesian Archipelago, House of Representatives Building. 1000r, Map, symbols of development.

**1997, Feb. 3** ***Perf. 13½x13***

**1697** A479 300r multicolored .45 .30
**1698** A479 700r multicolored 1.40 .60
**1699** A479 1000r multicolored 1.75 .90
*Nos. 1697-1699 (3)* 3.60 1.80

Birth of Indonesia's 200-millionth Citizen — A480

***Perf. 13½x12½***

**1997, Mar. 24** **Litho.**

**1700** A480 700r Pres. Suharto, baby 1.25 .55

A481

A482

Indonesian Philatelists Assoc., 75th Anniv.: 300r, Youth examining stamps, #1672. 700r, Magnifying glass, #1660, #1592h, #1580.

**1997, Mar. 29** ***Perf. 12½x13½***

**1701** A481 300r multicolored .60 .30
**1702** A481 700r multicolored 1.50 .75

**1997, Apr. 30** **Litho.** ***Perf. 13x13½***

Indonesian Artists: 300r, Wage Rudolf Soepratman (1903-38), composer, violinist. 700r, Usmar Ismail (1921-71), film pioneer, director. 1000r, Affandi (1907-90), painter.

**1703** A482 300r multicolored .50 .30
**1704** A482 700r multicolored 1.25 .60
**1705** A482 1000r multicolored 1.75 .90
*b.* Sheet, 3 each #1703-1705 + label 15.00 7.00
*Nos. 1703-1705 (3)* 3.50 1.80

**Souvenir Sheet**

**1705A** A482 2000r like #1705 3.00 1.50

Indonesia 2000 A483

Gemstones: 300r, Picture jasper. 700r, Chrysocolla. 1000r, Geode. 2000r, Banded agate.

**1997, May 20** **Litho.** ***Perf. 13½x13***

**1706** A483 300r multicolored .55 .30
**1707** A483 700r multicolored 1.40 .60
**1708** A483 1000r multicolored 2.00 .90
*a.* Sheet, 3 each, #1706-1708 + label 10.00 4.75
*b.* As "a," control No. in margin *17.50 8.75*
*Nos. 1706-1708 (3)* 3.95 1.80

**Souvenir Sheet**

**1709** A483 2000r multicolored 3.00 .85
*a.* Control No. in margin *4.75 2.50*

Nos. 1708b, 1709a promote INDONESIA 2000, Jakarta, Aug. 15-21, 2000. Nos. 1708a-1709 and 1708b-1709a were issued in presentation packs with certificate of authenticity.

See Nos. 1764-1767A, 1848-1851, 1851A, 1888-1891.

A484

**1997, May 31** **Photo.** ***Perf. 12½***

**1710** A484 1000r multicolored 1.75 .80

World Day to Stop Smoking.

World Environment Day — A485

Various marine life of the coral reefs.

**1997, June 5** **Litho.** ***Perf. 13x13½***

**1711** A485 150r multicolored .45 .25
**1712** A485 300r multicolored .55 .25
**1713** A485 700r multicolored 1.25 .55
*Nos. 1711-1713 (3)* 2.25 1.05

**Souvenir Sheet**

**1714** A485 2000r multicolored 5.50 2.50

ASEAN, 30th Anniv. A486

300r, Hands reaching out to each other. 700r, Rice stalks arranged to form number 30, globe.

**1997, Aug. 8** **Litho.** ***Perf. 13½x13***

**1715** A486 300r multicolored .45 .25
**1716** A486 700r multicolored 1.25 .60

19th Southeast Asia Games, Jakarta — A487

#1717, Logo, "Hanoman" mascot. #1718, Runner carrying torch, flags of participating nations, logo. #1719, Runner, track, discus thrower. #1720, Hurdler, runners.

**1997, Sept. 9** **Litho.** ***Perf. 12½***

**1717** A487 300r multicolored .45 .25
**1718** A487 300r multicolored .45 .25
*a.* Pair, #1717-1718 .90 .50
**1719** A487 700r multicolored 1.25 .50
**1720** A487 700r multicolored 1.25 .50
*a.* Pair, #1719-1720 2.50 1.00
*b.* Bklt. pane, 2 ea #1717-1720 7.00
Complete booklet, 1 #1720b 7.00
*Nos. 1717-1720 (4)* 3.40 1.50

Transportation — A488

**1997, Sept. 17**

**1721** A488 300r Buses, ox cart .45 .25
**1722** A488 300r Trains .45 .25
*a.* Pair, #1721-1722 .90 .50
**1723** A488 700r Ships 1.25 .50
**1724** A488 700r Airplanes 1.25 .50
*a.* Pair, #1723-1724 2.50 1.00
*Nos. 1721-1724 (4)* 3.40 1.50

Souvenir Sheet

Oriolus Chinensis — A489

**1997, May 29** ***Perf. 12½x13½***

**1725** A489 2000r multicolored 6.50 3.25

PACIFIC 97.

Nusantara Royal Palace Festival A490

Royal carriages: 300r, Singa Baraong wooden carriage, 1549, with carving of mythical animal. 700r, Paksi Naga Liman carriage, phoenix-like bird.

**1997, July 1** **Litho.** ***Perf. 13½x12½***

**1726** A490 300r multicolored .45 .25
**1727** A490 700r multicolored 1.25 .50

18th Natl. Koran Reading Contest — A491

Designs: 300r, Decorated roof peaks, windows. 700r, Al-Ikhsaniah Mosque.

**1997, July 9** ***Perf. 12½***

**1728** A491 300r multicolored .45 .25
**1729** A491 700r multicolored 1.25 .50

Indonesian Membership in UPU, 50th Anniv. — A492

Emblem of UPU and: 300r, Mas Soeharto. 700r, Heinrich von Stephan.

**1997, Sept. 27** **Litho.** ***Perf. 13½x13***

**1730** A492 300r multicolored .45 .25
**1731** A492 700r multicolored 1.25 .50

1997-98 General Session of People's Consultative Assembly — A493

**1997, Oct. 1** ***Perf. 12½***

**1732** A493 700r multicolored 1.10 .50

Indonesian Armed Forces Day A494

Designs: a, ABRI Village Program. b, Jalesveva Jayamahe Monument. c, Blue Falcon Flight Demonstration Team. d, Police Fast Reaction Unit.

**1997, Oct. 5** ***Perf. 13½x12½***

**1733** A494 300r Block of 4, #a.-d. 2.00 1.00

### Flora and Fauna Type of 1994

Fauna: No. 1737: a, Chitala lopis. b, Haliastur indus. c, Rhinoplax vigil. d, Cervus timorensis. e, Bubalus depressicornis.

Flora: f, Lansium domesticum. g, Salacca zalacca. h, Shorea stenoptera. i, Diospyros macrophylla. j, Diplocaulobium utile.

#1738: a, Shorea stenoptera. b, Haliastur indus.

**1997, Nov. 5** ***Perf. 12½x13½***

**1737** A438 300r Block of 10 5.00 2.50
*a.-j.* Any single .50 .25

**Souvenir Sheet**

**1738** A438 1250r Sheet of 2, #a.-b. 4.00 2.00

A495

Indonesian Cooperatives Day — A496

Designs: No. 1739, Cooperatives Monument, Tasikmalaya. No. 1740, Cooperatives Monument, Jakarta. No. 1741, Adult taking child's hand. No. 1742, Globe, movement towards globalization. No. 1743, Dr. Mohammad Hatta, Pres. Suharto.

**1997, July 12 Litho. *Perf. 12½x13½***

**1739** A495 150r multicolored .40 .25
**1740** A495 150r multicolored .40 .25
*a.* Pair, #1739-1740 .80 .40
**1741** A495 300r multicolored .50 .25
**1742** A495 300r multicolored .50 .25
*a.* Pair, #1741-1742 1.00 .50

***Perf. 12½***

**1743** A496 700r multicolored 1.40 .60
*Nos. 1739-1743 (5)* 3.20 1.60

ASCOPE '97 (Asian Council on Petroleum) A497

a, LNG tanker. b, Petroleum trucks. c, Drilling rig, pumping wells. d, Refinery.

**1997, Nov. 24 *Perf. 13½x12½***

**1744** A497 300r Block of 4, #a.-d. 1.75 .90

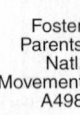

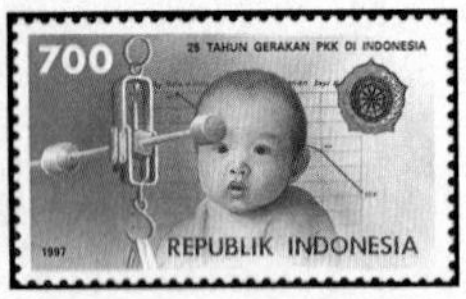


Foster Parents Natl. Movement A498

**1997, Dec. 20 Photo.**

**1745** A498 700r multicolored .80 .40

Family Welfare Movement, 25th Anniv. A499

**1997, Dec. 27 Litho.**

**1746** A499 700r multicolored .80 .45

### Traditional Dance Type of 1992

Dance, region: 150r, Mopuputi Cengke (clove picking), Central Sulawesi. 300r, Mandau Talawang Nyai Balau, Central Kalimantan. 600r, 2000r, Gambyong, Central Java. 700r, Cawan (bowl,) North Sumatra. 1000r, Legong Keraton, Bali.

**1997, Dec. 27**

**1747** A411 150r multicolored .35 .25
**1748** A411 300r multicolored .35 .25
**1749** A411 600r multicolored .70 .40
**1750** A411 700r multicolored .85 .45
**1751** A411 1000r multicolored 1.25 .60
*Nos. 1747-1751 (5)* 3.50 1.95

**Souvenir Sheet**

***Perf. 12½x13½***

**1752** A411 2000r multicolored 3.25 1.60

No. 1752 is a continuous design.

Souvenir Sheet

Sulawesi Selatan — A500

**1997, Oct. 11 Litho. *Perf. 13½x12½***

**1753** A500 2000r multicolored 3.50 1.75

Makasser '97 National Philatelic Exhibition.

Year of Art and Culture 1998 — A501

Designs: 300r, Erau Festival, East Kalimantan. 700r, Tabot Festival, Bengkulu.

**1998, Jan. 1 Litho. *Perf. 12½***

**1754** A501 300r multicolored .35 .25
**1755** A501 700r multicolored .90 .25

Indonesian Folktales A502

Folktale, region — No. 1759; a-e, Malin Kundang, West Sumatra. f-j: Sangkuriang, West Java. k-o, Roro Jonggrang, Central Java. p-t: Tengger, East Java. Each horizontal strip of 5 has continuous design.

2500r, Kasodo Ceremony, Tenegger, East Java.

**1998, Feb. 2 *Perf. 13½x12½***

**1759** Sheet of 20 7.50 4.00
*a.-t.* A502 300r Any single .35 .25

**Souvenir Sheet**

**1760** A502 2500r like #1759e 2.75 1.50

See Nos. 1828-1829, 1886-1887, 1929-1930.

Presidential Palaces — A503

Designs: a, Jakarta. b, Bogor. c, Cipanas. d, Yogyakarta. e, Tampak Siring.

**1998, Apr. 1**

**1761** A503 300r Strip of 5, #a.-e. 1.25 .65

World Health Organization, 50th Anniv. — A504

Designs: 300r, Pregnant woman, man, vert. 700r, Woman holding baby.

**1998, Apr. 7 Litho. *Perf. 12½***

**1762** A504 300r multicolored .30 .25
**1763** A504 700r multicolored .75 .40

### Indonesia 2000 Type of 1997

Gemstones: 300r, Chrysopal. 700r, Tektite. 1000r, Amethyst. #1767, Petrified wood. #1767A, opal.

**1998, May 20 *Perf. 13½x12½***

**1764** A483 300r multicolored .40 .25
**1765** A483 700r multicolored .40 .25
**1766** A483 1000r multicolored .40 .30
*a.* Sheet, 3 each #1764-1766 + label *5.00* *2.50*
*Nos. 1764-1766 (3)* 1.20 .80

**Souvenir Sheets**

**1767** A483 2500r multicolored 2.00 1.00

***Perf. 13½x14***

**1767A** A483 2500r multicolored 6.00 3.50
*b.* Sheet, 2 each, #1764-1766, 1 each #1767, 1767A 18.00 16.00

Nos. 1767A, 1767Ab were issued in presentation packs with control numbers printed in margin and certificate of authenticity.

No. 1767A sold for 10,000r. No. 1767Ab sold for 25,000r.

1998 World Cup Soccer Championships, France — A505

Young boys playing soccer in Indonesia: 300r, Outside school, boy on bicycle. 700r, In neighborhood lot. 1000r, 2500r, In rural area.

**1998, June 1**

**1768** A505 300r multicolored .30 .25
**1769** A505 700r multicolored .70 .35
**1770** A505 1000r multicolored 1.00 .45
*Nos. 1768-1770 (3)* 2.00 1.05

**Souvenir Sheet**

**1771** A505 2500r multicolored 2.50 2.50

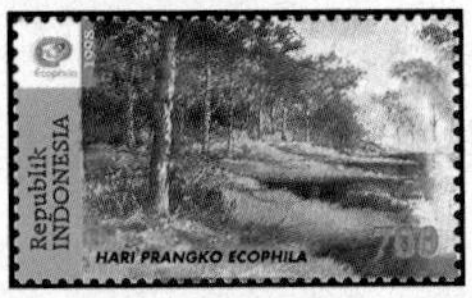


World Environment Day — A506

Trees along river bank, denomination at: No. 1772, lower right. No. 1773, lower left.

**1998, June 5**

**1772** A506 700r multicolored .70 .35
**1773** A506 700r multicolored .70 .35
*a.* Pair, #1772-1773 1.40 .70

Souvenir Sheet

Juvalux '98, World Philatelic Exhibition, Luxembourg — A507

**1998, June 18 *Perf. 12½x13½***

**1774** A507 5000r Felis viverrina 6.00 3.00

World Day to Fight Drug Abuse and Illicit Drug Trafficking — A508

Cartoons depicting how to say no to drugs.

**1998, June 26**

**1775** A508 700r red & multi .70 .35
**1776** A508 700r yellow & multi .70 .35
*a.* Pair, #1775-1776 1.40 .70
*b.* Tete beche pair, #1775-1776 1.40 .70

Tourism — A509

Temples, shrines in Bali: Nos. 1777, 1779, Pura Besakih. No. 1778, Pura Taman Ayun.

**1998, July 1 *Perf. 12½***

**1777** A509 700r multicolored .70 .35
**1778** A509 700r shown .70 .35
*a.* Pair, #1777-1778 1.40 .70

**Souvenir Sheet**

***Perf. 13½x13***

**1779** A509 2500r multicolored 3.75 1.75

No. 1777 is 64x24mm. No. 1779 contains one 41x25mm stamp.

Souvenir Sheet

Panthera Tigris — A510

**1998, July 23 Litho. *Perf. 13½x12½***

**1780** A510 5000r multicolored 4.00 2.00

Singpex '98.

Trains A511

Train going right: a, Cattle, freight cars. b, Freight, box cars. c, Passenger cars. d, Passenger car, tender. e, Locomotive 850.

Train going left: f, Locomotive D52. g, Coal tender. h, Car with 2 doors. i, Dining car with large windows. j, Car with two windows.

2500r, Locomotive.

**1998, Aug. 10**

**1781** A511 300r Block of 10, #a.-j. 4.50 2.25

**Souvenir Sheet**

**1782** A511 2500r multicolored 2.25 1.10

No. 1781 issued in sheets of 20 stamps consisting of two tete-beche blocks of 10. No. 1782 contains one 41x25mm stamp.

Pres. H.B.J. Habibie — A512

**1998, Aug. 17** *Perf. 12½x13½*

**1783** A512 300r pink & multi .45 .25
**1784** A512 700r blue & multi .45 .25
**1785** A512 4500r green & multi 2.25 1.10
**1786** A512 5000r yellow & multi 2.50 1.25
*Nos. 1783-1786 (4)* 5.65 2.85

13th Asian Games A513

**1998, Sept. 9** *Perf. 13½x12½*

**1787** A513 300r Fencing .40 .25
**1788** A513 700r Taekwondo .40 .25
**1789** A513 4000r Wushu 2.00 .85
*a.* Sovenir sheet, #1787-1789 3.00 1.50
*Nos. 1787-1789 (3)* 2.80 1.35

Intl. Year of the Ocean A514

*Perf. 13½x12½*

**1998, Sept. 26** **Litho.**

**1790** A514 700r multicolored 1.10 .25

Souvenir Sheets

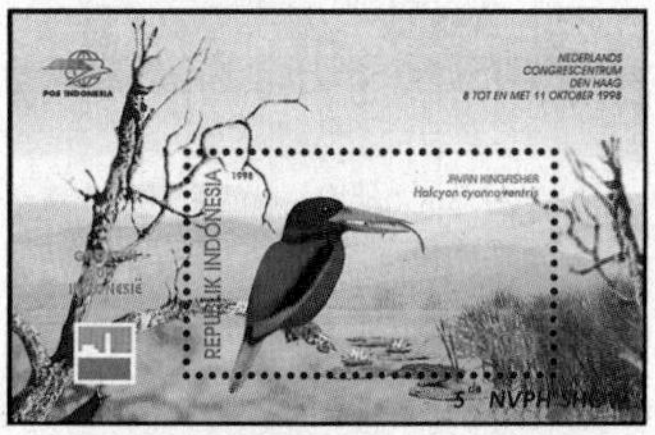

5th NVPH (Netherlands Philatelic Congress) Exhibition, The Hague — A514a

Birds: 5000r, Halcyon cyannoventris. 35,000r, Vannelus macropterus, vert.

**1998, Oct. 8** **Litho.** *Perf. 13½x12½*

**1790A** A514a 5000r multi 4.00 4.00
**1790B** A514a 35,000r multi 15.00 15.00

A515

A516

**1998, Oct. 9** *Perf. 12½x13½*

**1791** A515 700r #922 .60 .25
**1792** A515 700r #414 .60 .25
*a.* Pair, #1791-1792 1.25 .30

World Stamp Day.

**Litho. (#1793-1799, 1805)**

**1998** *Perf. 12½*

Ducks and Geese: 250r, #1805, Aythya australis. 500r, Anas superciliosa. 700r, Anas gibberifrons. 1000r, Nettapus coromandelianus. 1500r, Nettapus pulchelus. 2500r, Dendrocygna javanica. 3500r, Dendrocygna arcuata. 4000r, Anseranas semipalmata. #1801, Dendrocygna guttata. 10,000r, Anas waigiuensis. 15,000r, Tadorna radjah. 20,000r, Cairina scutulata.

**1793** A516 250r multi .50 .25
**1794** A516 500r multi .50 .25
**1795** A516 700r multi .50 .25
**1796** A516 1000r multi .60 .30
**1797** A516 1500r multi .90 .40
**1798** A516 2500r multi 1.50 .65
**1799** A516 3500r multi 1.90 .85

**Litho. With Hologram**

*Perf. 13½x12½*

**Size: 42x25mm**

**1800** A516 4000r horiz. 1.50 .90
**1801** A516 5000r horiz. 2.00 1.25
**1802** A516 10,000r horiz. 4.00 2.25
**1803** A516 15,000r horiz. 6.25 3.25
**1804** A516 20,000r horiz. 7.50 4.25
*a.* Sheet of 5, #1800-1804, + 4 labels 25.00 12.50
*Nos. 1793-1804 (12)* 27.65 14.85

**Souvenir Sheet**

*Perf. 12½*

**1805** A516 5000r lt blue sky 3.25 3.25

Soaking in water may affect the hologram on #1800-1804.

Issued: #1793-1799, 1805, 12/1; others 10/19.

See Nos. 1918-1919.

Souvenir Sheet

Italia '98 — A516a

**1998, Oct. 23** *Perf. 12½x13½*

**1805A** A516a 5000r Jakarta Cathedral 3.25 3.25

National Flag — A517

Mountains and: #1806, Flagpole at right. #1807, Flagpole at left.

**1998, Oct. 28** **Litho.** *Perf. 12½x13½*

**1806** A517 700r multicolored .60 .25
**1807** A517 700r multicolored .60 .25
*a.* Pair, #1806-1807 1.25 .40

Reform Movement A518

No. 1809, Dove, national flag. No. 1810, Students, Parliament Building.

**1998, Oct. 28** *Perf. 13½x12½*

**1808** A518 700r shown .60 .25
**1809** A518 700r multicolored .60 .25
*a.* Pair, #1808-1809 1.25 .40

**Size: 83x25mm**

**1810** A518 1000r multicolored .65 .30

**Flora and Fauna Type of 1994**

Flora — #1812: a, Stelechocarpus burahol. b, Polianthes tuberosa. c, Mirabilis jalapa. d, Mangifera casturi. e, Ficus minahassae.

Fauna — f, Geopelia striata. g, Gallus varius. h, Elephas maximus. i, Nasalis larvatus. j, Tarsius spectrum.

No. 1813, like #1812b. No. 1814, like #1812i.

**1998, Nov. 5** *Perf. 12½x13½*

**1812** A438 500r Block of 10 4.00 2.00
*a.-j.* Any single .40 .25

**Souvenir Sheets**

**1813** A438 2500r multicolored 2.00 2.00
**1814** A438 2500r multicolored 2.00 2.00

**Traditional Dance Type of 1992**

Dance, region: 300r, Oreng-oreng Gae, Southeast Sulawesi. 500r, Tribute dance, Bengkulu. 700r, Fan dance, Riau. 1000r, Srimpi, Yogyakarta. 2000r, 5000r, Tribute dance, West Sumatra.

**1998, Dec. 27**

**1815** A411 300r multicolored .45 .25
**1816** A411 500r multicolored .45 .25
**1817** A411 700r multicolored .45 .25
**1818** A411 1000r multicolored .55 .25
**1819** A411 2000r multicolored 1.25 .40
*Nos. 1815-1819 (5)* 3.15 1.40

**Souvenir Sheet**

**1820** A411 5000r multicolored 3.00 1.40

Creation and Engineering Year — A519

Designs: 500r, Hydroelectric turbine, power lines. 700r, Plumbing fixture, water pipes.

**1999, Jan. 1** **Litho.** *Perf. 12½*

**1821** A519 500r multicolored .40 .25
**1822** A519 700r multicolored .50 .25

7th Far East & South Pacific Games for Disabled A520

Garuda Indonesia Airways, 50th Anniv. A521

**1999, Jan. 10** *Perf. 12½x13½*

**1823** A520 500r Throwing shotput .40 .25
**1824** A520 500r Medals, wheelchair .40 .25
*a.* Pair, #1823-1824 .80 .25

**1999, Jan. 26** *Perf. 13x13½*

**1825** A521 500r Logo .50 .25
**1826** A521 700r Aircraft maintenance .50 .25
**1827** A521 2000r Pilot, attendant 1.10 .50
*Nos. 1825-1827 (3)* 2.10 1.00

**Indonesian Folktales Type of 1998**

Folktale, region — #1828: a-e, Danau Toba, North Sumatra. f-j, Banjarmasin, South Kalimantan. k-o, Buleleng, Bali. p-t, Woiram, Irian Jaya.

5000r, like #1828e.

**1999, Feb. 15** *Perf. 13½x12½*

**1828** Sheet of 20 8.00 4.00
*a.-e.* A502 500r Strip of 5 2.00 1.00
*f.-j.* A502 500r Strip of 5 2.00 1.00
*k.-o.* A502 500r Strip of 5 2.00 1.00
*p.-t.* A502 500r Strip of 5 2.00 1.00

**Souvenir Sheet**

**1829** A502 5000r multicolored 3.00 1.50

Nos. 1829 is a continuous design.

Souvenir Sheet

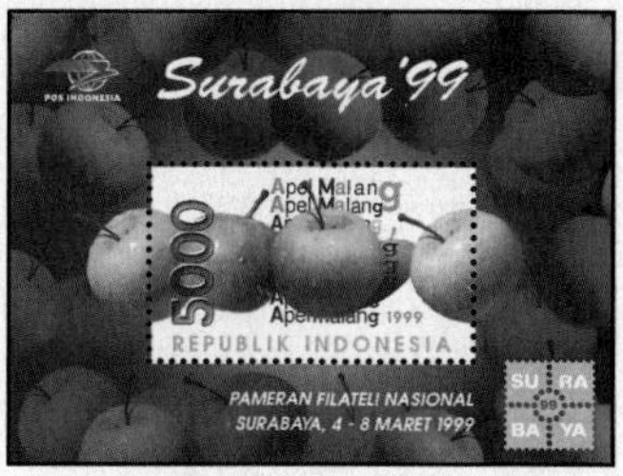


Surabaya '99, Natl. Philatelic Exhibition — A522

**1999, Mar. 4** **Litho.** *Perf. 13½x12½*

**1830** A522 5000r Apples 3.50 1.75
*a.* Ovptd. in sheet margin 6.00 3.00

No. 1830a Overprinted in Gold in Sheet Margin with "APPI SHOW '99 / SURABAYA, 10-18 JULI 1999" and Emblem. Issued, 7/10.

Souvenir Sheet

Australia '99, World Stamp Expo — A523

**1999, Mar. 19** *Perf. 12½x13½*

**1831** A523 5000r Tarsius spectrum 3.50 3.50
*a.* Ovptd. in sheet margin 6.00 6.00

No. 1831a Overprinted in Gold in Sheet Margin with "The 13th / Thaipex / China / Stamp Exhibition / Bangkok '99 / 4 -15. 8. 99" and Emblem. Issued, 8/15.

Mushrooms — A524

No. 1832: a, Mutinus bambusinus. b, Ascosparassis heinricherii. c, Mycena sp.

No. 1833: a, Microporus xanthopus. b, Gloeophyllum imponens. c, Termitomyces eurrhizus.

No. 1834: a, Aseroe rubra. b, Calostoma orirubra. c, Boedijnopeziza insititia.

5000r, Termitomyces eurrhizus.

**1999, Apr. 1** *Perf. 12½*

**1832** A524 500r Triptych, #a.-c. 1.40 .70
**1833** A524 700r Triptych, #a.-c. 1.90 .90
**1834** A524 1000r Triptych, #a.-c. 2.50 1.25
*d.* Souvenir sheet, #1832-1834 6.00 3.00

**Souvenir Sheet**

**1835** A524 5000r multicolored 3.50 1.75

**Booklet Stamps**
**Size:32x24mm**

**1836** A524 500r Like #1832a .80 .25
**1837** A524 500r Like #1832b .80 .25
**1838** A524 500r Like #1832c .80 .25
*a.* Booklet pane, 3 each #1836-1838, + label 7.50
Complete booklet, #1838a 7.50
*Nos. 1836-1838 (3)* 2.40 .75

No. 1835 contains one 25x41mm stamp. Numbers have been reserved for additional values in this set.

Public Health Care Insurance A525

**1999, Apr. 7** ***Perf. 13½x12½***
**1845** A525 700r multicolored .70 .25

Souvenir Sheet

IBRA '99, Intl. Philatelic Exhibition, Nuremberg — A526

**1999, Apr. 27** ***Perf. 12½x13½***
**1846** A526 5000r Dendrobium abang betawi 3.50 3.50

Y2K Millennium Bug — A527

Designs: a, "Bug." b, Circuit, android.

**1999, May 2** ***Perf. 13½x12½***
**1847** A527 500r Pair, #a.-b. 1.10 .25

**Indonesia 2000 Type of 1997**

**1999, May 20 Litho.** ***Perf. 13½x12¾***
**1848** A483 500r Chrysoprase .40 .25
**1849** A483 1000r Smoky quartz .60 .30
**1850** A483 2000r Opal blue 1.25 .65
*a.* Sheet, 3 ea #1848-1850 + label 9.50 9.50
*Nos. 1848-1850 (3)* 2.25 1.20

**Souvenir Sheet**

**1851** A483 4000r Silicified coral 7.50 7.50
**1851A** A483 4000r Javan jade 15.00 15.00
*b.* Sheet, #1851-1851A, 2 ea # 1849-1850, 4 #1848 25.00 25.00

Nos. 1851A, 1851Ab were issued in presentation packs with certificate of authenticity. Control numbers and silver overpint "1 Tahun/ Lagi / 1 Year / to Go" printed in margin. No. 1851A sold for 10,000r; No. 1851Ab for 30,000r.

Environmental Care — A528

Winning designs of 1999 Ecophila Stamp Design Contest: 500r, Girl wrapped in blanket, people walking through water. 1000r, 3000r, Boy swimming with duck, plant, cherry. 2000r, Elderly woman drinking water from pitcher, outdoor scene.

**1999, June 5**
**1852** A528 500r multicolored .40 .25
**1853** A528 1000r multicolored .60 .45
**1854** A528 2000r multicolored 1.25 .80
*Nos. 1852-1854 (3)* 2.25 1.50

**Souvenir Sheet**

**1855** A528 3000r multicolored 2.50 1.10

1999 General Election — A529

Designs: a, "48," Banner, people standing in line to vote. b, People waiting turn to enter election booth, map.

**1999, June 4**
**1856** A529 1000r Pair, #a.-b. 1.60 .75

Souvenir Sheet

PhilexFrance '99 — A530

**1999, July 2 Litho.** ***Perf. 12¾x13½***
**1858** A530 5000r multi 4.00 4.00

Red Cross / Red Crescent Millennium Year Campaign — A531

**Photo. & Litho.**

**1999, Aug. 12** ***Perf. 12½***
**1859** A531 1000r multicolored .80 .40

National Heroes — A532

No. 1860: a, Dr. W. Z. Johannes (1895-1924). b, Martha Christina Tijahahu (1800-18), freedom fighter. c, Frans Kaisiepo (1921-79), politician. d, Maria Walanda Maramis (1872-1924), educator.

**Litho. & Engr.**

**1999, Aug. 17** ***Perf. 12½***
**1860** Strip of 4 1.75 .80
*a.-d.* A532 500r any single .40 .25
*e.* Booklet pane of 4, #1860a 2.00
*f.* Booklet pane of 4, #1860b 2.00
*g.* Booklet pane of 4, #1860c 2.00
*h.* Booklet pane of 4, #1860d 2.00
Complete bklt., #1860e-1860h 8.00

Complete booklet sold for 10,000r.

Souvenir Sheet

China 1999 World Philatelic Exhibition — A533

***Perf. 13½x12¾***
**1999, Aug. 21** **Litho.**
**1861** A533 5000r multi 5.00 2.50

Gadjah Mada University, 50th Anniv. — A534

**1999, Sept. 19** ***Perf. 12½***
**1862** A534 500r shown .50 .25
**1863** A534 1000r Building, diff. .60 .30

Intl. Year of Older Persons A535

**1999, Oct. 1** ***Perf. 13½x12¾***
**1864** A535 500r multi .60 .30

UPU, 125th Anniv. — A536

**1999, Oct. 9** ***Perf. 12½***
**1865** A536 500r Postman on horse .40 .25
**1866** A536 500r Postman on motorcycle .40 .25
*a.* Pair, #1865-1866 + label .80 .25
**1866B** Pair + 2 labels *6.00 3.00*
*c.* A536 1000r Like #1865, 30x32mm *3.00 1.50*
*d.* A536 1000r Like #1866, 30x32mm *3.00 1.50*

No. 1866B issued in sheets of 5 pairs. As the labels could be personalized, sheets were available only through special orders with Indonesia Post and sold for 20,000r.

Batik Designs — A537

**1999, Oct. 1**
**1867** A537 500r Cirebon .45 .25
**1868** A537 500r Madura .45 .25
**1869** A537 500r Jambi .45 .25
**1870** A537 500r Yogyakarta .45 .25
*Nos. 1867-1870 (4)* 1.80 1.00

Domesticated Animals — A538

**1999, Nov. 5** ***Perf. 13½x12¾***
**1871** A538 500r Dogs .60 .25
**1872** A538 500r Chickens .60 .25
*a.* Pair, #1871-1872 1.25 .40
**1873** A538 500r Cat .60 .25
**1874** A538 500r Rabbits .60 .25
*a.* Pair, #1873-1874 1.25 .40
**1875** A538 1000r Pigeon .80 .40
**1876** A538 1000r Geese .80 .40
*a.* Pair, #1875-1876 1.60 .80
*b.* Sheet of 6, #1871-1876 5.00 2.50
*Nos. 1871-1876 (6)* 4.00 1.80

**Souvenir Sheet**

**1877** A538 4000r Like #1874 3.75 1.75

Millennium — A539

Designs: No. 1878, 1000r, No. 1880, 20,000r, 1999 agenda book. No. 1879, 1000r, No. 1881, 20,000r, Clock, child.

**Litho. & Photo.**

**1999-2000** ***Perf. 13½x12¾***
**1878-1879** A539 Set of 2 1.00 .50
*a.* Sheet of 20 + 20 labels 22.50 22.50

**Souvenir Sheets**

**1880-1881** A539 Set of 2 20.00 8.00

Labels on No. 1879a could be personalized. The sheet sold for 38,000r.

Issued: Nos. 1878, 1880, 12/31/99; Nos. 1879, 1879a, 1881, 1/1/00.

Visit Indonesia Decade — A540

Designs: 500r, Satellite, fish. 1000r, Hydroponic agriculture.

**2000, Jan. 1** ***Perf. 12¾x13½***
**1882-1883** A540 Set of 2 1.40 .65

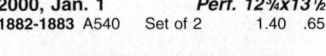

University of Indonesia, 50th Anniv. — A541

Designs: 500r, Salemba campus. 1000r, University building, Depok.

**2000, Feb. 2** ***Perf. 12½***
**1884-1885** A541 Set of 2 1.40 .65

**Indonesian Folktales Type of 1998**

Folktale, region — #1886: a-e, Tapak Tuan, Aceh. f-j, Batu Ballah, West Kalimantan. k-o, Sawerigading, South Sulawesi. p-t, 7 Putri kahyangan, Moluccas.
5000r, Like #1886e

**2000, Feb. 5** *Perf. 13½x12¾*

| | | | | |
|---|---|---|---|---|
| **1886** | | Sheet of 20 | 10.00 | 5.00 |
| *a.-e.* | | 500r Strip of 5 | 2.50 | 1.25 |
| *f.-j.* | | 500r Strip of 5 | 2.50 | 1.25 |
| *k.-o.* | | 500r Strip of 5 | 2.50 | 1.25 |
| *p.-t.* | | 500r Strip of 5 | 2.50 | 1.25 |

**Souvenir Sheet**

| | | | | |
|---|---|---|---|---|
| **1887** | A502 | 5000r multi | 4.00 | 2.00 |

**Indonesia 2000 Type of 1997**

Designs: 500r, Prehnite. 1000r, Chalcedony. 2000r, Volcanic obsidian.

**2000, Mar. 1**

| | | | | |
|---|---|---|---|---|
| **1888-1890** | A483 | Set of 3 | 3.00 | 1.50 |
| *1890a* | | Souvenir sheet, 3 each #1888-1890 + label | 7.00 | 3.50 |

**Souvenir Sheet**

| | | | | |
|---|---|---|---|---|
| **1891** | A483 | 5000r Jasperized limestone | 4.00 | 2.00 |
| *a.* | | Sheet, #1891, 14 #1888, 2 #1889, 3 #1890 + 20 labels | 20.00 | — |

No. 1891a sold for 41,000r with labels personalized.

Comic Strip Characters — A542

Designs: No. 1892, 500r, I Brewok, by Gungun. No. 1893, 500r, Pak Tuntung, by Basuki. No. 1894, Pak Bei, by Masdi Sunardi. No. 1895, 500r, Mang Ohle, by Didin D. Basuni. No. 1896, 500r, Panji Koming, by Dwi Koendoro.

*Perf. 12¾x13½*

**2000, Mar. 13** **Photo.**

| | | | | |
|---|---|---|---|---|
| **1892-1896** | A542 | Set of 5 | 2.25 | 1.10 |
| *1896a* | | Souvenir sheet, 3 each #1892-1896 + label | 7.50 | 3.50 |

World Meteorological Organization, 50th Anniv. — A543

**Litho. & Photo.**

**2000, Mar. 23** *Perf. 12½*

| | | | | |
|---|---|---|---|---|
| **1897** | A543 | 500r multi | 1.00 | .50 |

Souvenir Sheet

Bangkok 2000 Stamp Exhibition — A544

**2000, Mar. 23** *Perf. 13½x12¾*

| | | | | |
|---|---|---|---|---|
| **1898** | A544 | 5000r multi | 5.00 | 2.25 |

15th Natl. Sports Week A545

Designs: 500r, Cycling. 1000r, Canoeing. 2000r, High jump.

**2000, Apr. 1**

| | | | | |
|---|---|---|---|---|
| **1899-1901** | A545 | Set of 3 | 3.50 | 1.60 |

Souvenir Sheet

The Stamp Show 2000, London — A546

**2000, May 22**

| | | | | |
|---|---|---|---|---|
| **1902** | A546 | 5000r multi | 5.00 | 2.50 |

Environmental Care — A547

Designs; 500r, Birds in nest. 1000r, Monkeys. 2000r, Fish.

**2000, June 5**

| | | | | |
|---|---|---|---|---|
| **1903-1905** | A547 | Set of 3 | 3.50 | 1.75 |

**Souvenir Sheet**

| | | | | |
|---|---|---|---|---|
| **1906** | A547 | 4000r Like #1904 | 4.00 | 2.00 |

2000 Summer Olympics, Sydney — A548

No. 1907, 500r: a, Boxing. b, Judo.
No. 1908, 1000r: a, Badminton. b, Weight lifting.
No. 1909, 2000r: a, Swimming. b, Running.

**2000, July 1**

**Pairs, #a-b**

| | | | | |
|---|---|---|---|---|
| **1907-1909** | A548 | Set of 3 | 6.00 | 3.00 |

**Souvenir Sheet**

| | | | | |
|---|---|---|---|---|
| **1910** | A548 | 5000r Like #1908b | 5.00 | 2.25 |

Worldwide Fund for Nature (WWF) — A549

Komodo dragon: No. 1911, 500r, No. 1915a, 2500r, With tongue extended. No. 1912, 500r, On log. No. 1913, 500r, Pair walking. No. 1914, 500r, No. 1915b, 2500r, Pair fighting.

**2000, Aug. 13**

| | | | | |
|---|---|---|---|---|
| **1911-1914** | A549 | Set of 4 | 3.00 | 2.00 |
| *a.* | | Souvenir sheet, 2 each #1911-1914 | 10.00 | 7.50 |

**Souvenir Sheet**

| | | | | |
|---|---|---|---|---|
| **1915** | A549 | 2500r Sheet of 2, #a-b | 6.50 | 4.00 |

Souvenir Sheet

Olymphilex 2000 Stamp Exhibition — A550

**2000, Sept. 15** *Perf. 12¾x13½*

| | | | | |
|---|---|---|---|---|
| **1916** | A550 | 5000r multi | 4.50 | 2.25 |

A551

No. 1917: a, Pres. Abdurrahman Wahid. b, Vice Pres. Megawati Soekarnoputri

**Photo. & Engr.**

**2000, Sept. 27** *Perf. 12½*

| | | | | |
|---|---|---|---|---|
| **1917** | A551 | 1000r Pair, #a-b | 2.00 | 1.00 |

**Ducks and Geese Type of 1998**

**2000, Sept. 27** **Photo.** *Perf. 12½*

| | | | | |
|---|---|---|---|---|
| **1918** | A516 | 800r Like #1798 | 1.25 | 1.00 |
| **1919** | A516 | 900r Like #1793 | 1.25 | 1.00 |

Traditional Costumes A552

Provinces and regions: a, Aceh. b, Jambi. c, Banten. d, Yogyakarta. e, Central Kalimantan (Kalimantan Tengah). f, Southeast Sulawesi (Sulawesi Tenggara). g, East Nusa Tenggara (Nusa Tenggara Timur). h, North Sumatra (Sumatera Utara). i, Bengkulu. j, Jakarta. k, East Java (Jawa Timur). l, East Kalimantan (Kalimantan Timur). m, South Sulawesi (Sulawesi Selatan). n, Maluku. o, West Sumatra (Sumatera Barat). p, South Sumatra (Sumatera Selatan). q, West Java (Jawa Barat). r, West Kalimantan (Kalimantan Barat). s, North Sulawesi (Sulawesi Utara). t, Bali. u, North Maluku (Maluku Utara). v, Riau. w, Lampung. x, Central Java (Jawa Tengah). y, South Kalimantan (Kalimantan Selatan). z, Central Sulawesi (Sulawesi Tengah). aa, West Nusa Tenggara (Nusa Tenggara Barat). ab, Irian Jaya.

**Litho. & Photo.**

**2000, Oct. 28** *Perf. 12½*

| | | | | |
|---|---|---|---|---|
| **1920** | | Sheet of 28 + 7 labels | 25.00 | 15.00 |
| *a.-ab.* | | A552 900r Any single | .70 | .50 |

Artists and Entertainers — A553

No. 1921, horiz.: a, Bing Slamet (1927-74), singer, comedian. b, S. Sudjojono (1913-86), painter. c, I Ketut Maria (1897-1968), dancer. d, Chairil Anwar (1922-49), poet. e, Ibu Sud (1908-93), musician.

**2000, Nov. 1** *Perf. 13½x12¾*

| | | | | |
|---|---|---|---|---|
| **1921** | | Horiz. strip of 5 | 4.00 | 2.00 |
| *a.-e.* | | A553 900r Any single | .80 | .40 |

**Souvenir Sheet**

| | | | | |
|---|---|---|---|---|
| **1922** | A553 | 4000r Chairil Anwar | 4.00 | 2.00 |

Indonesia Post in the 21st Century — A554

Designs: 800r, Philately, vert. 900r, Business communications. 1000r, Business financial services, vert. 4000r, Business logistics, vert.

**Litho. & Photo.**

**2000, Dec. 20** *Perf. 12½*

| | | | | |
|---|---|---|---|---|
| **1923** | A554 | 800r multi | .60 | .30 |
| **1924** | A554 | 900r multi | .60 | .40 |
| **1925** | A554 | 1000r multi | 1.00 | .50 |
| **1926** | A554 | 4000r multi | 3.50 | 1.75 |
| | | *Nos. 1923-1926 (4)* | 5.70 | 2.95 |

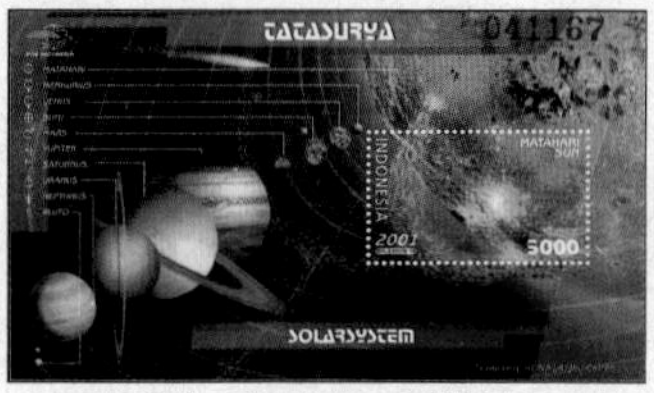


Solar System — A555

No. 1927: a, Sun. b, Mercury. c, Venus. d, Earth. e, Mars. f, Jupiter. g, Saturn. h, Uranus. i, Neptune. j, Pluto.

**2001, Jan. 1** **Litho.** *Perf. 13½x12¾*

| | | | | |
|---|---|---|---|---|
| **1927** | | Block of 10 + 5 labels | 7.50 | |
| *a.-j.* | | A555 900r Any single | .75 | .30 |
| *k.* | | Sheet of 10 + 5 labels | 10.00 | |
| *l.* | | Sheet of 20 + 20 labels | 25.00 | 25.00 |

**Souvenir Sheet**

| | | | | |
|---|---|---|---|---|
| **1928** | A555 | 5000r Sun | 4.00 | 2.00 |

Labels on No. 1927l could be personalized. The sheet sold for 36,000r.

**Indonesian Folktales Type of 1998**

Folktale, region — No. 1929: a-e, Batang Tuaka, Riau. f-j, Si Pitung, Jakarta. k-o, Terusan Nusa, Central Kalimantan. p-t, Ile Mauraja, East Nusa Tenggara.
5000r, Like No. 1929h.

**Litho. & Photo.**

**2001, Feb. 2** *Perf. 13½x12¾*

| | | | | |
|---|---|---|---|---|
| **1929** | | Sheet of 20 | 16.00 | 8.00 |
| *a.-e.* | | A502 900r Strip of 5 | 4.00 | 2.00 |
| *f.-j.* | | A502 900r Strip of 5 | 4.00 | 2.00 |
| *k.-o.* | | A502 900r Strip of 5 | 4.00 | 2.00 |

*p.-t.* A502 900r Strip of 5 4.00 2.00

### Souvenir Sheet

**1930** A502 5000r multi 2.75 1.25

Masks — A556

No. 1931, 500r — Arsa Wijaya, Bali: a, Denomination at L. b, Denomination at R.
No. 1932, 800r — Asmat, Irian Jaya: a, Denomination at L. b, Denomination at R.
No. 1933, 800r — Cirebon, West Java: a, Denomination at L. b, Denomination at R.
No. 1934, 900r — Hudoq, East Kalimantan: a, Denomination at L. b, Denomination at R.
No. 1935, 900r — Wayang Wong, Yogyakarta: a, Denomination at L. b, Denomination at R.
5000r, Like No. 1934b.

**2001, Mar. 2** ***Perf. 12¾x13½***

### Pairs, #a-b

**1931-1935** A556 Set of 5 6.00 2.25
*c.* Sheet, #1931-1935 +2 labels 6.00

### Souvenir Sheet

**1936** A556 5000r multi 4.00 2.00
*a.* Ovptd. in margin in silver 6.00 3.00

Issued: No. 1936a, 10/16/01. No. 1936 overprinted with "HAFNIA '01 / World Philatelic Exhibition / Copenhagen / 16-21 October 2001," show emblem and new price of 7500r.

Traditional Communication Instruments — A557

No. 1937: a, Beduk. b, Bendé. c, Kentongan. d, Nafiri.

**2001, Mar. 10** ***Perf. 12½***

**1937** Vert. strip of 4 3.00 1.50
*a.-d.* A557 900r Any single .75 .35
*e.* Sheet, 2 each #1937a-1937d 8.00 4.00

Greetings — A558

Various flowers. Denominations: 800, 900, 1000, 1500, 2000, 4000, 5000, 10000r

### Litho. & Typo.

**2001, Apr. 21** ***Perf. 12½***

**1938-1945** A558 Set of 8 17.50 8.75

A558a

Greetings — A558b

***Perf. 13½x12¾***

**2001, Apr. 21** **Litho. & Typo.**

**1945A** A558a 900r multi + label 4.00 4.00

***Perf. 12½***

**1945B** A558b 900r multi + label 4.00 4.00

No. 1945A was issued in sheets of 20 + 20 labels that could be personalized. The sheet sold for 36,000r. No. 1945B was issued in sheets of 10 + 10 labels that could be personalized. The sheet sold for 20,000r.

Environmental Care — A559

Children and: 800r, Fish. 900r, 5000r, Deer. 1000r, Sea turtle.

### Litho. & Photo.

**2001, June 5** ***Perf. 13½x12¾***

**1946** A559 800r multi 1.25 .40
*a.* Tete-beche pair 2.50 2.50
**1947** A559 900r multi 1.25 .40
*a.* Tete-beche pair 2.50 2.50
**1948** A559 1000r multi 1.25 .40
*a.* Tete-beche pair 2.50 2.50
*Nos. 1946-1948 (3)* 3.75 1.20

### Souvenir Sheet

**1949** A559 3000r multi 4.00 3.00

No. 1949 exists imperf. Value $5.

Pres. Sukarno (1901-70) — A560

Various portraits: 500, 800, 900, 1000r. 5000r, Sukarno at microphone.

**2001, June 6** ***Perf. 12½***

**1950-1953** A560 Set of 4 2.50 1.25
*a.* Sheet, 2 each #1950-1953 6.50 3.25

### Souvenir Sheet

***Perf. 13½x12¾***

**1954** A560 5000r multi 4.00 2.00

No. 1954 contains one 41x25mm stamp

National Police — A561

Police and: a, Children. b, Helicopter.

**2001, July 1** **Photo.** ***Perf. 13½x12¾***

**1955** A561 1000r Horiz. pair, #a-b 2.50 1.10

National Scouting Jamboree — A562

Scouts: a, Raising flag. b, Pitching tent.

**2001, July 3**

**1956** A562 1000r Horiz. pair, #a-b 3.00 1.25

Children's Games A563

Designs: 800r, Kaki Siapa. 900r, Egrang Bambu. 1000r, Dakon. 2000r, Kuda Pelepah Pisang.

### Litho. & Photo.

**2001, July 23** ***Perf. 13½x12¾***

**1957-1960** A564 Set of 4 3.75 1.75
*a.* Sheet, 2 each #1957-1960 9.00 4.50

### Souvenir Sheet

Phila Nippon '01, Japan — A564

**2001, Aug. 1** **Photo.**

**1961** A564 10,000r multi 8.00 4.00

Dr. R. Soeharso Orthopedic Hospital, Surakarta, 50th Anniv. A565

### Litho. & Photo.

**2001, Aug. 28** ***Perf. 13½x12¾***

**1962** A565 1000r multi 1.25 .40

Traditional Transportation — A566

Designs: No. 1963, 1000r, Rowboat. No. 1964, 1000r, Trishaw. No. 1965, Horse-drawn carriage.

**2001, Sept. 17**

**1963-1965** A566 Set of 3 3.50 1.00
*a.* Sheet, 3 each #1963-1965 +label 9.00 9.00

Post Offices A567

Buildings in: 800r, Makassar. 900r, Bandung. 1000r, Balikpapan. 2000r, Padang.

**2001, Sept. 27**

**1966-1969** A567 Set of 4 3.50 1.60

Gemstones — A568

Designs: 800r, Rose quartz. 900r, Brecciated jasper. 1000r, Malachite.
5000r, Diamond.

**2001, Oct. 1**

**1970-1972** A568 Set of 3 2.50 1.10
*a.* Sheet, 3 each #1970-1972 + label 10.00 6.75

### Souvenir Sheet

**1973** A568 5000r multi 4.00 2.00

Year of Dialogue Among Civilizations — A569

**2001, Oct. 9** **Litho.** ***Perf. 12¾x13½***

**1974** A569 1000r multi 1.60 .40

Beetles — A570

Designs: 800r, Agestrata dehaan. 900r, Mormolyce phyllodes. No. 1977, 1000r, Batocera rosenbergi. No. 1978, 1000r, Chrysochroa buqueti. 2000r, 5000r, Chalcosoma caucasus.

**2001, Nov. 5** **Litho. & Photo.**

**1975-1979** A570 Set of 5 4.50 2.25
*a.* Booklet pane, #1975-1979 + label 6.00 —
Booklet, 2 #1979a 12.00

### Souvenir Sheet

**1980** A570 5000r multi 4.00 2.00

Folktales — A571

No. 1981, 1000r — Pulau Kembara, South Sumatra: a, Four people, lanterns. b, Two men, woman, boat. c, Man and woman standing in boat. d, Man and woman in water. e, Boat, snake, fish.
No. 1982, 1000r — Nyi Koro Kidul, Yogyakarta: a, Woman at tight pointing. b, Woman at foreground with hand at mouth. c, Two men with hats at right. d, Woman in sea. e, Sea and island.
No. 1983, 1000r — Aji Tatin, East Kalimantan: a, Bird in tree, woman, man with hand outstretched. b, Woman, bird boat. c, Sinking boat. d, Woman and tree. e, Bird in tree.
No. 1984, 1000r — Danau Tondano, North Sulawesi: a, Woman with long hair in foreground. b, Man holding spear. c, Man at left with arm to head. d, Man and woman embracing. e, Sea and island.
5000r, Like No. 1981e.
Illustration reduced.

### Litho. & Photo.

**2002, Feb. 2** ***Perf. 13½x12¾***

### Blocks of 5, #a-e

**1981-1984** A571 Set of 4 8.00 4.00

### Souvenir Sheet

**1985** A571 5000r multi 4.00 2.00

Nos. 1981-1984 are printed in sheets of four blocks of five. Stamp "e" is always adjacent to the LL stamp in the block of the remaining four stamps, and is found tete beche to both stamps "a" and "e" from adjacent blocks of five.

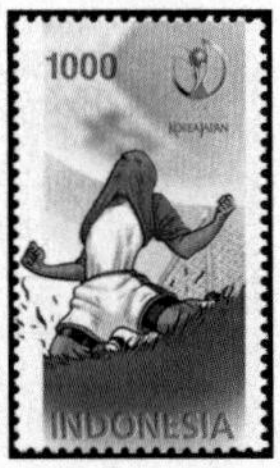


2002 World Cup Soccer Championships, Japan and Korea — A572

Celebrations: 1000r, Player lifting shirt over face. 1500r, Four players with fists raised, horiz. 2000r, 5000r, Player with arms outstretched.

***Perf. 12¾x13½, 13½x12¾***

**2002, Apr. 1** **Litho. & Photo.**

**1986-1988** A572 Set of 3 3.75 1.60

### Souvenir Sheet

**1989** A572 5000r multi 4.00 2.00

Indonesian Cancer Foundation, 25th Anniv. — A573

**2002, Apr. 17** ***Perf. 12¾x13½***
**1990** A573 1000r multi 1.50 .60
*a.* Tete-beche pair 4.50 2.25

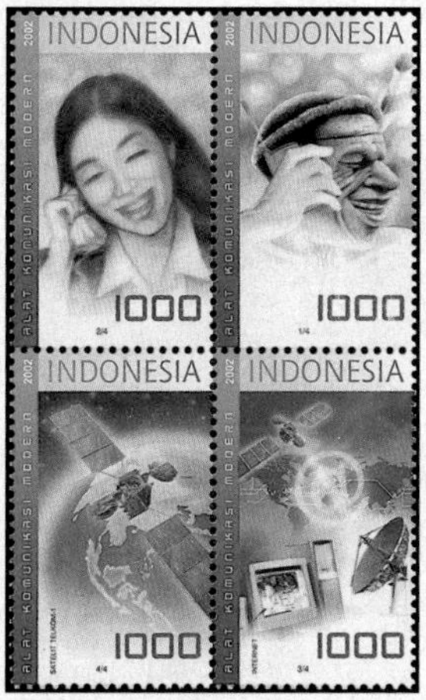

Telecommunications — A574

No. 1991: a, Woman using telephone (2/4). b, Man using cellular phone (1/4). c, Satellite above Earth (4/4). d, Satellite, world map, computer, satellite dish (3/4).

**2002, May 17**
**1991** A574 1000r Block of 4, #a-d 3.50 1.75
*e.* Sheet, 2 each #1991a-1991d 7.00 3.50
*f.* Booklet pane, 4 #1991a 3.50
*g.* Booklet pane, 4 #1991b 3.50
*h.* Booklet pane, 4 #1991c 3.50
*i.* Booklet pane, 4 #1991d 3.50
Booklet, #1991f-1991i 14.00

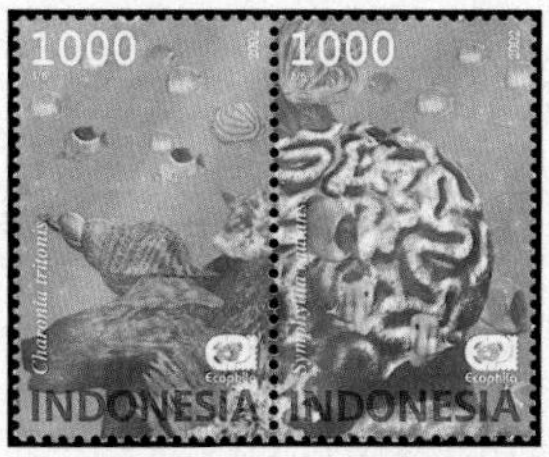

Marine Life — A575

No. 1992, 1000r: a, Charonia tritonis. b, Symphyllia radians.
No. 1993, 1500r: a, Cromileptes altivelis. b, Acanthaster planci.
No. 1994, 2000r, horiz.: a, Paracanthurus hepatus. b, Tridacna gigas.
5000r, Acanthaster planci.

**2002, June 5**
**Horiz. Pairs, #a-b**
**1992-1994** A575 Set of 3 7.00 3.50
*c.* Sheet, #1992, 1993, 1994a, 1994b 7.00 3.50
**Souvenir Sheet**
**1995** A575 5000r multi 4.00 2.00

Aceh Province — A576

Designs: 1500r, Student, Aceh dance, map of Aceh. 3500r, Masjid Raya Banda Aceh, map of Indonesia.

**2002, June 15** ***Perf. 12½***
**1996-1997** A576 Set of 2 4.00 2.00

Natl. Family Day A577

***Perf. 13½x12¾***
**2002, June 29** **Litho. & Typo.**
**1998** A577 1000r multi 1.50 .60

33rd Intl. Physics Olympiad, Bali — A578

No. 1999: a, Eclipse (1/2). b, Spectrum colors and Balinese symbols (2/2).

**2002, July 14** ***Perf. 12¾x13½***
**1999** A578 1000r Horiz. pair, #a-b 2.00 1.00

Kites A579

No. 2000: a, Popotengan (bird-shaped) (1/5). b, Barong (dragon head) (2/5). c, Fighting (3/5). d, Bebean (4/5). e, Modern (box and wing) (5/5).
5000r, Popotengan.

**Litho. & Photo.**
**2002, July 15** ***Perf. 13½x12¾***
**2000** Horiz. strip of 5 4.00 2.00
*a.-e.* A579 1000r Any single .80 .30
**Souvenir Sheet**
**2001** A579 5000r multi 4.00 2.00

Fruit — A580

Designs: 300r, Morinda citrifolia. 500r, Mangifera indica. 1500r, Averrhoa carambola. 3000r, Durio zibethinus.

**2002, Aug. 1 Photo.** ***Perf. 13½x12¾***
**2002** A580 300r multi .60 .25
**2003** A580 500r multi .60 .30
**2004** A580 1500r multi 1.60 .80
**2005** A580 3000r multi 2.40 1.10
*Nos. 2002-2005 (4)* 5.20 2.45

Souvenir Sheet

Philakorea 2002 World Stamp Exhibition, Seoul — A581

**2002, Aug. 2 Litho.** ***Perf. 12¾x13½***
**2006** A581 7000r multi 5.00 2.50

Mohammad Hatta (1902-80), Prime Minister — A582

No. 2007, 1000r: a, Denomination at left. b, Denomination at right.
No. 2008, 1500r: a, Denomination at left. b, Denomination at right.
5000r, Hatta standing.

**Litho. & Photo.**
**2002, Aug. 12** ***Perf. 12½***
**Pairs, #a-b**
**2007-2008** A582 Set of 2 4.00 2.00
*c.* Sheet, 2 each #2007-2008 + 2 labels 9.00 4.50
**Souvenir Sheet**
***Perf. 12¾x13½***
**2009** A582 5000r multi 4.00 2.25

No. 2009 contains one 25x41mm stamp.

President and Vice-President — A583

No. 2010, 1500r: a, Pres. Megawati Soekarnoputri. b, Vice-president Hamzah Haz.

**Photo. with Foil Application**
**2002, Aug. 17** ***Perf. 12½***
**2010** A583 Horiz. pair, #a-b, + central label 4.50 4.50

Souvenir Sheet

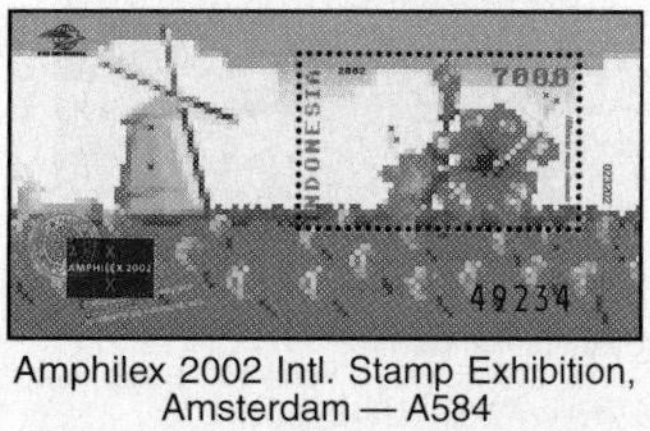

Amphilex 2002 Intl. Stamp Exhibition, Amsterdam — A584

***Perf. 13½x12¾***
**2002, Aug. 30** **Photo.**
**2011** A584 7000r multi 7.00 3.50

Souvenir Sheet

Panfila 2002 Philatelic Exhibition, Yogyakarta — A585

**2002, Sept. 19** ***Perf. 12¾x13½***
**2012** A585 6000r multi 5.00 2.50

Paintings — A586

No. 2013, 1000r: a, Seko, Guerrilla Vanguard, by S. Sudjojono. b, Cat, by Popo Iskandar.
No. 2014, 1500r, vert.: a, Catching Lice, by Hendra Gunawan. b, Gatut Kaca with Prigiwa and Prigiwati, by R. Basuki Abdullah.

**Litho. & Photo.**
**2002, Sept. 27** ***Perf. 12½***
**Pairs, #a-b**
**2013-2014** A586 Set of 2 5.00 2.50
*c.* Sheet, 2 each #2013-2014 9.00 4.50

Souvenir Sheet

España 2002 Youth Philatelic Exhibition, Salamanca — A587

**2002, Oct. 4 Photo.** ***Perf. 13½x12¾***
**2015** A587 7000r multi 5.00 2.50

Flora and Fauna A588

No. 2016, 1000r: a, Trimeresurus hageni. b, Rafflesia micropylora.
No. 2017, 1500r: a, Panthera pardus. b, Terminalia catappa.
No. 2018, 2000r: a, Papilionanthe hookeriana. b, Varanus salvator.
3500r, Panthera pardus.

**Litho. & Photo.**

**2002, Nov. 5** ***Perf. 12¾x13½***

**Horiz. Pairs, #a-b**

**2016-2018** A588 Set of 3 7.00 3.50

**Souvenir Sheet**

**2019** A588 3500r multi 4.00 2.00

No. 2019 exists imperf. Value $5.

Antara, Indonesian News Agency — A589

**Litho. & Typo.**

**2002, Dec. 13** ***Perf. 12½***

**2020** A589 1500r multi 2.00 1.00

Happy Birthday — A590

No. 2021: a, Food platter. b, Birthday cake.

**2003** **Photo.** ***Perf. 12½***

**2021** Strip of 2 stamps and 2 alternating labels 3.50 1.75
*a.-b.* A590 1500r Any single 1.75 .85
*c.* Sheet of 5 #2021 15.00 15.00

No. 2021 was printed in sheets containing 10 strips with labels that could be personalized. The sheet sold for 45,000r. The labels on No. 2021c could also be personalized, and that sheet sold for 30,000r.

Folklore — A591

No. 2022 — Scenes from Danau Ranau, Lampung (#a.-e.), Kongga Owose, Southeast Sulawesi (#f.-j.), Putri Gading Cempaka, Bengkulu (#k.-o.), Putri Mandalika Nyale, West Nusa Tenggara (#p.-t.) and stamp numbers: a, 01/20. b, 02/20. c, 03/20. d, 04/20. e, 05/20. f, 06/20. g, 07/20. h, 08/20. i, 09/20. j, 10/20. k, 11/20. l, 12/20. m, 13/20. n, 14/20. o, 15/20. p, 16/20. q, 17/20. r, 18/20. s, 19/20. t, 20/20.
5000r, Like #2022e.

**Litho. & Photo.**

**2003, Feb. 2** ***Perf. 13½x12¾***

**2022** A591 1500r Sheet of 20, #a-t 15.00 7.00

**Souvenir Sheet**

**2023** A591 5000r multi 3.00 2.00

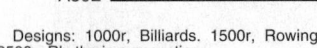

22nd South East Asia Games, Hanoi, Viet Nam
A592

Designs: 1000r, Billiards. 1500r, Rowing. 2500r, Rhythmic gymnastics.

**Litho. & Photo.**

**2003, May 12** ***Perf. 14***

**2024-2026** A592 Set of 3 4.00 2.00

Values are for stamps with surrounding selvage.

Volcanoes — A593

Designs: 500r, Kerinci. No. 2028, 1000r, Krakatoa. No. 2029, 1000r, Merapi. No. 2030, 1000r, Tambora. 2000r, Ruang.

**2003, June 5** ***Perf. 12½***

**2027-2031** A593 Set of 5 4.00 2.00
*2031a* Sheet, 2 each #2027-2031 + 2 labels 9.00 4.50

Astronomy — A594

No. 2032: a, Andromeda Galaxy (1/5). b, Earth and Mars (2/5). c, Moon (3/5).
No. 2033: a, External view of observatory (4/5). b, Zeiss telescope (5/5).
5000r, Like No. 2033a.

**2003, June 7** ***Perf. 12½***

**2032** Strip of 3 2.00 1.00
*a.-c.* A594 1000r Any single .65 .40
**2033** Pair 2.00 1.00
*a.-b.* A594 1500r Either single 1.00 .40
*c.* Sheet, 2 each #2032a-2032c, 2033a-2033b 7.00 3.50

**Souvenir Sheet**

***Perf. 13½x12¾***

**2034** A594 5000r multi 4.00 2.50

Stamps in No. 2033c are tete-beche. No. 2034 contains one 41x25mm stamp.

Bank Indonesia, 50th Anniv. — A595

Designs: 1000r, Tower and flowers. 1500r, People at graduation ceremony, books.

***Perf. 13½x13¼ Syncopated***

**2003, July 1**

**2035-2036** A595 Set of 2 3.00 1.50

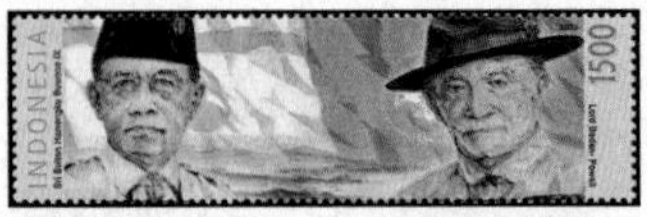


Sri Sultan Hamengku Buwono IX and Lord Robert Baden-Powell — A596

***Perf. 13½x12¾***

**2003, Aug. 14** **Photo.**

**2037** A596 1500r multi 3.00 1.50

Independence Day Games — A597

No. 2038, 1000r: a, Panjat Pinang (1/4). b, Pukul Bantal (2/4).
No. 2039, 1500r, horiz.: a, Balap Kelom (3/4). b, Balap Karung (4/4).

***Perf. 12¾x13½, 13½x12¾***

**2003, Aug. 17** **Litho. & Photo.**

**Pairs, #a-b**

**2038-2039** A597 Set of 2 3.50 1.75
*2039c* Sheet, 2 each #2038a-2038b, 2039a-2039b 8.00 3.75

Souvenir Sheet

Paintings of Srihadi Soedarsono — A598

No. 2040: a, Pendet, Dinamika Remaja. b, Borobudur-Purnama dalam Keheningan.

**2003** ***Perf. 13½ Syncopated***

**2040** A598 3000r Sheet of 2, #a-b 6.00 6.00
*c.* Sheet with margin design in cyan only 6.00 6.00
*d.* As "c," with magenta added to margin design 6.00 6.00
*e.* As "d," with yellow added to margin design 6.00 6.00
*f.* As "e," with black added to margin design, but lacking artist's face and signature 6.00 6.00
*g.* Sheet, 2 each #2040a-2040b 11.00 11.00

Emmitan-Philex 2003, Surabaya (#2040, 2040c, 2040d, 2040e, 2040f), 10th ASEAN Postal Business Meeting (#2040g).
Issued: No. 2040, 9/4; No. 2040c, 8/29; No. 2040d, 8/30; No. 2040e, 8/31; No. 2040f, 9/1; No. 2040g, 9/3. No. 2040 exists imperf, issued 9/2. Value, $6.

Tourism — A599

No. 2041, 1000r: a, Jou Uci Sabea, North Maluku (1/4). b, Mome'ati, Gorontalo (2/4).
No. 2042, 1500r: a, Muang Jong, Bangka Belitung (3/4). b, Seba Baduy, Banten (4/4).
5000r, Like No. 2042a.

**2003, Sept. 27** ***Perf. 12½***

**Vert. Pairs, #a-b**

**2041-2042** A599 Set of 2 3.00 1.50

**Souvenir Sheet**

**2043** A599 5000r multi 5.00 2.50

Souvenir Sheet

Bangkok 2003 World Philatelic Exhibition — A600

**2003, Oct. 4** ***Perf. 13½x12¾***

**2044** A600 8000r multi 3.00 1.75

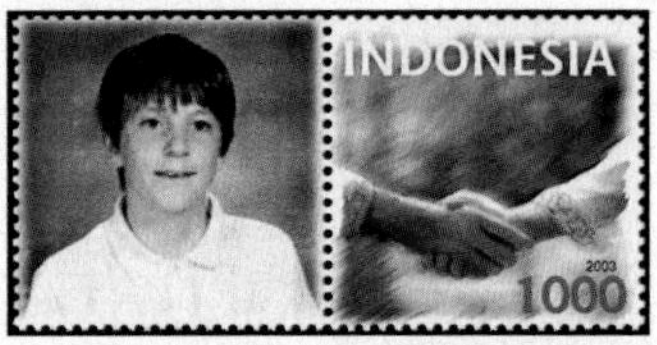


Handshake — A601

Fish and Water Lily — A602

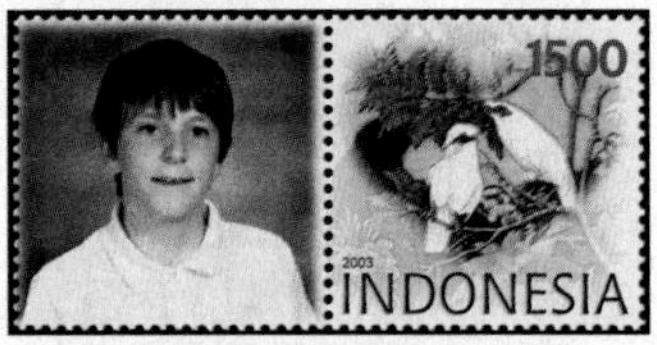


Birds — A603

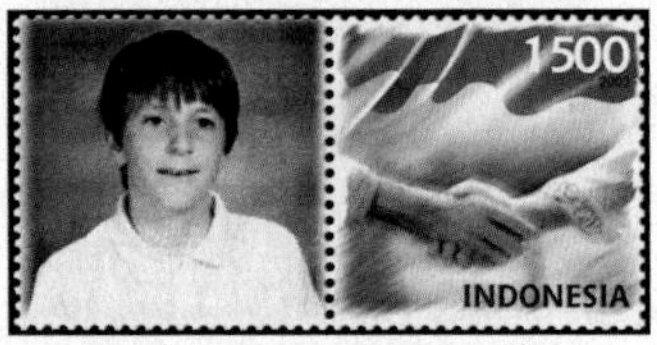


Handshake and Flag — A604

Flower — A605

**2003, Oct. 27** **Litho.** ***Perf. 12½***

**2045** A601 1000r multi + label 1.50 1.50
**2046** A602 1500r multi + label 1.75 1.75
**2047** A603 1500r multi + label 1.75 1.75
**2048** A604 1500r multi + label 1.75 1.75
**2049** A605 1500r multi + label 1.75 1.75
*Nos. 2045-2049 (5)* 8.50 8.50

Nos. 2045-2049 were each issued in sheets of 20 stamps + 20 labels that could be personalized. Sheets of No. 2045 sold for 35,000r, while sheets of Nos. 2046-2049 each sold for 45,000r.

Indonesian Youth Pledge, 75th Anniv. — A606

**2003, Oct. 28** **Litho.** ***Perf. 12¾x13¼***

**2050** A606 1500r Nos. 1031-1032, 1246 2.00 1.00

Flowers and Insects — A607

No. 2051: a, Paphiopedilum mastersianum (9/12). b, Platylomia flavida (8/12). c, Osmoxylon palmatum (7/12). d, Apis dorsata (12/12). e, Freycinetia pseudoinsignis (11/12). f, Sia ferox (10/12). g, Aularches miliaris (3/12). h,

Butea monosperma (2/12). i, Orthetrum testaceum (1/12). j, Anaphalis javanica (6/12). k, Hierodula vitrea (5/12). l, Saraca declinata (4/12).

No. 2052: a, Like #2051j. b, Like #2051i.

**Litho. & Photo.**

**2003, Nov. 5** *Perf. 12½*

**2051** A607 1500r Block of 12, #a-l 15.00 7.50
*m.* Booklet pane, #2051a, 2051c, 2051e, 2051h, 2051j, 2051l 7.50 —
*n.* Booklet pane, #2051b, 2051d, 2051f, 2051g, 2051i, 2051k 7.50 —
Complete booklet, #2051m, 2051n 15.00

**Souvenir Sheet**

**2052** A607 3000r Sheet of 2, #a-b, + label 4.50 2.25

Famous Men A608

No. 2053: a, Prof. Roosseno (1908-96) (3/4). b, Prof. Sutami (1928-80) (4/4). c, Nurtanio Pringgoadisuryo (1923-66) (1/4). d, Martinus Putuhena (1901-82) (2/4).

**Litho. & Engr.**

**2003, Nov. 10** *Perf. 13¼x13*

**2053** Strip of 4 4.50 2.25
*a.-d.* A608 2000r Any single 1.10 .55

Flowers — A609

No. 2054: a, Styrax benzoin (1/30). b, Kopsia fruticosa (2/30). c, Impatiens tujuhensis (3/30). d, Hoya diversifolia (4/30). e, Etlingera elatior (5/30). f, Dillenia suffruticosa (6/30). g, Papilionanthe hookerianum (7/30). h, Medinilla speciosa (8/30). i, Costus speciosus (9/30). j, Melastoma sylvaticum (10/30). k, Nelumbo nucifera (11/30). l, Begonia robusta (12/30). m, Anaphalis longifolia (13/30). n, Pisonia grandis (14/30). o, Ixora javanica (15/30). p, Plumeria acuminata (16/30). q, Cassia fistula (17/30). r, Calotropis gigantea (18/30). s, Dimorphorchis lowii (19/30). t, Aeschynanthus radicans (20/30). u, Sonneratia caseolaris (21/30). v, Rhododendron orbiculatum (22/30). w, Passiflora edulis (23/30). x, Pterospermum celebicum (24/30). y, Quisqualis indica (25/30). z, Spathiphyllum commutatum (26/30). aa, Lilium longiflorum (27/30). ab, Clitoria ternatea (28/30). ac, Pecteilis susannae (29/30). ad, Grammatophyllum speciosum (30/30).

**Litho. & Photo.**

**2004, Jan. 5** *Perf. 12½*

**2054** Sheet of 30 22.50 11.00
*a.-ad.* A609 1500r Any single .75 .30

Folktales — A610

No. 2055 — Scenes from Putri Selaras Pinang Masak, Jambi (#a.-e.), Tanjung Lesung, Banten (#f.-j.), Patung Palindo, Central Sulawesi (#k.-o.), Danau Tolire, North Maluku (#p.-t.) and stamp number: a, 01/20. b, 02/20. c, 03/20. d, 04/20. e, 05/20. f, 06/20. g, 07/20. h, 08/20. i, 09/20. j, 10/20. k, 11/20. l, 12/20. m, 13/20. n, 14/20. o, 15/20. p, 16/20. q, 17/20. r, 18/20. s, 19/20. t, 20/20.

6000r, Like # 2055j.

**Litho. & Photo.**

**2004, Feb. 20** *Perf. 13½x12¾*

**2055** A610 1500r Sheet of 20, #a-t 15.00 7.00

**Souvenir Sheet**

**2056** A610 6000r multi 4.50 2.50

Museums — A611

No. 2057: a, Sri Baduga Museum, Bandung (3/4). b, Bahari Museum, Jakarta (1/4). c, Telecommunications Museum, Jakarta (4/4). d, Geology Museum, Bandung (2/4).

**2004, Feb. 29** *Perf. 13¼x12¾*

**2057** Vert. strip of 4 3.50 1.75
*a.-d.* A611 1500r Any single .85 .40

General Elections — A612

No. 2058: a, Man and woman pointing at people holding flags (1/2). b, Man and woman casting ballots (2/2).

**2004, Apr. 5 Litho.** *Perf. 12¾x13¼*

**2058** A612 1500r Horiz. pair, #a-b 2.25 1.10

Famous Women — A613

No. 2059: a, Gedong Bagoes Oka (1921-2002), social worker, religious leader (2/4). b, Ani Idrus (1918-99), journalist (1/4). c, Nyonya Meneer (1895-1978), founder of herbal medicine factory (3/4). d, Sandiah (Ibu Kasur) (1926-2002), composer of children's songs, television personality (4/4).

*Perf. 13¼x13½ Syncopated*

**2004, Apr. 21** **Litho. & Engr.**

**2059** Horiz. strip of 4 5.00 2.50
*a.-d.* A613 2500r Any single 1.25 .60

2004 Summer Olympics, Athens A614

No. 2060: a, Swimming (1/3). b, Women's high jump (2/3). c, Hurdling (3/3).

**Litho. & Photo.**

**2004, May 5** *Perf. 14*

**2060** Horiz. strip of 3 4.50 2.25
*a.-c.* A614 2500r Any single 1.50 .75

Environmental Protection — A615

Designs: Nos. 2061a, 2062a, Bird, killer whale (1/2). Nos. 2061b, 2062b, Shark, turtle (2/2).

**2004, June 5** *Perf. 13¼x12¾*

**2061** A615 1500r Vert. pair, #a-b 2.25 1.10

**Souvenir Sheet**

**2062** A615 2500r Sheet of 2, #a-b 4.50 2.50

Indonesian Cuisine — A616

No. 2063: a, Gajebo, West Sumatra (1/4). b, Sambal Udang Terung Pipit, West Kalimantan (3/4). c, Kare Rajungan, East Java (2/4). d, Tinotuan, North Sulawesi (4/4).

**2004, July 6 Litho.** *Perf. 13¼x12¾*

**2063** A616 1500r Block of 4, #a-d 4.00 2.00

Presidential Limousines — A617

No. 2064: a, 1939 Buick with REP-1 license plate (1/2). b, 1942 DeSoto with REP-2 license plate (2/2).

**2004, Aug. 17**

**2064** A617 2500r Vert. pair, #a-b 4.00 2.00
*c.* Souvenir sheet #2064a-2064b 4.00 2.00

16th National Games — A618

No. 2065: a, Volleyball (1/2). b, Sepak takraw (2/2).

**Litho. & Photo.**

**2004, Sept. 2** *Perf. 14*

**2065** A618 1500r Pair, #a-b 3.00 1.50

**Flowers and Insects Type of 2003**

No. 2066: a, Gryllotalpa hirsuta (4/6). b, Alstonia scholaris (5/6). c, Scolopendra subspinipes (6/6). d, Cinnamomun sintok (3/6). e, Heterometrus cyaneus (2/6). f, Parkia roxburghii (1/6).

No. 2067: a, Like #2066e. b, Like #2066f.

**2004, Nov. 5** *Perf. 12½*

**2066** A607 1500r Block of 6, #a-f 6.00 3.25

**Souvenir Sheet**

**2067** A607 3000r Sheet of 2, #a-b, + label 5.00 2.50

National Teacher's Day — A619

No. 2068: a, Teacher, students with microscope and book (1/2). b, Teacher students with pen and book (2/2).

**2004, Nov. 25** *Perf. 12¾x13¼*

**2068** A619 1500r Horiz. pair, #a-b 3.00 1.50

Souvenir Sheet

National Philatelic Exhibition, Surabaya — A620

No. 2069 — Paintings by Sunaryo: a, Setagen Rhythm. b, Sebelum Pentas. c, Bercinta.

**2004, Dec. 16 Litho.** *Perf. 12½*

**2069** A620 5000r Sheet of 3, #a-c 8.00 3.50
*d.* Souvenir sheet of 1, #2069a 3.00 2.00
*e.* Souvenir sheet of 1, #2069b 3.00 2.00
*f.* Souvenir sheet of 1, #2069c 3.00 2.00
*g.* Souvenir sheet of 1, #2069a, imperf. 3.00 2.00
*h.* Souvenir sheet of 1, #2069b, imperf. 3.00 2.00
*i.* Souvenir sheet of 1, #2069c, imperf. 3.00 2.00

Folktales — A621

No. 2070 — Scenes from Lahilote, Gorontalo (#a.-e.), Kolam Putri, Riau Islands (#f.-j.), Batu Balai, Bangka Belitung (#k.-o.), Bulan & Sagu di Ibuanari, Papua (#p.-t.) and stamp number: a, 1/20. b, 2/20. c, 3/20. d, 4/20. e, 5/20. f, 6/20. g, 7/20. h, 8/20. i, 9/20. j, 10/20. k, 11/20. l, 12/20. m, 13/20. n, 14/20. o, 15/20. p, 16/20. q, 17/20. r, 18/20. s, 19/20. t, 20/20.

6000r, Like #2070j.

**2005, Feb. 2 Litho.** *Perf. 13½x12¾*

**2070** A621 1500r Sheet of 20, #a-t 14.00 7.00

**Souvenir Sheet**

**2071** A621 6000r multi 4.00 2.00

Asian-African Summit, 50th Anniv. — A622

No. 2072: a, Dove and "50." b, Dove, world map and people.

***Perf. 13½x13¼ Syncopated***

**2005, Apr. 18 Litho. & Photo.**

**2072** Horiz. pair + central label 3.00 1.50
*a.-b.* A622 2500r Either single 1.50 .75
*c.* Souvenir sheet, #2072b 1.50 .75

Mangrove Forest Protection — A623

No. 2073 — Mangroves and: a, Bird. b, Fish.

**2005, June 5 Litho. *Perf. 12¾x13¼***

**2073** A623 1500r Horiz. pair, #a-b 2.00 1.00
*c.* Souvenir sheet, #2073 2.00 1.00

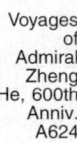

Voyages of Admiral Zheng He, 600th Anniv. A624

**Litho. & Photo.**

**2005, June 28 *Perf. 13½x12¾***

**2074** A624 2500r multi 2.00 1.00
*a.* Souvenir sheet of 1 3.00 1.00

Traditional Food A625

No. 2075: a, Sayur Tauco (North Sumatra) (1/4). b, Soto Banjar (South Kalimantan) (3/4). c, Nasi Timbel (West Java) (2/4). d, Langga Roko (South Sulawesi) (4/4).

**2005, July 6 Litho.**

**2075** Vert. strip of 4 2.75 1.40
*a.-d.* A625 1500r Any single .70 .30

Energy Conservation A626

Designs: 1500r, Bus, electric plug (1/3). 2000r, Electric plugs and outlet (2/3). 2500r, Automobile (3/3).

**2005, Aug. 17 *Perf. 12½***

**2076-2078** A626 Set of 3 2.75 1.40

Indonesian Leaders A627

Designs: Nos. 2079a, 2080a, Pres. Susilo Banbang Yudhoyono. Nos. 2079b, 2080b, Vice-president Muhammad Jusuf Kalla.

**2005, Aug. 17 Litho.**

**2079** Horiz. pair with central label 1.50 .75
*a.-b.* A627 1500r Either single .75 .25

**Litho. With Foil Application**

**2080** Horiz. pair with central label 3.00 1.50
*a.-b.* A627 2500r Either single 1.50 .75
*c.* Souvenir sheet, #2080a, 2080b 3.00 1.50

Borobudur Ship Expedition — A628

No. 2081: a, Ship, head of Buddha (2/2). b, Carving of ship (1/2).

**2005, Sept. 17**

**2081** A628 1500r Pair, #a-b 3.00 1.50
*c.* As "a," with "2/2" removed 2.00 1.00
*d.* As "b," with "1/2" removed 2.00 1.00
*e.* Souvenir sheet, #2081c, 2081d + central label 4.00 2.00

**Souvenir Sheet**

National Philatelic Exhibition, Cilegon — A629

No. 2082 — Paintings by Sudjana Kerton: a, Nyawer. b, Makan Siang. c, Wayang Golek. d, Tanah Air Indonesia.

**2005, Sept. 23 *Perf. 12½***

**2082** A629 Sheet of 4 8.00 4.00
*a.-c.* 5000r Any single 2.00 1.00
*d.* 8000r multi 3.00 1.50
*e.* Souvenir sheet, #2082a, imperf. 1.75 .85
*f.* Souvenir sheet, #2082b, imperf. 1.75 .85
*g.* Souvenir sheet, #2082c, imperf. 1.75 .85
*h.* Souvenir sheet, #2082d, imperf. 3.00 1.50

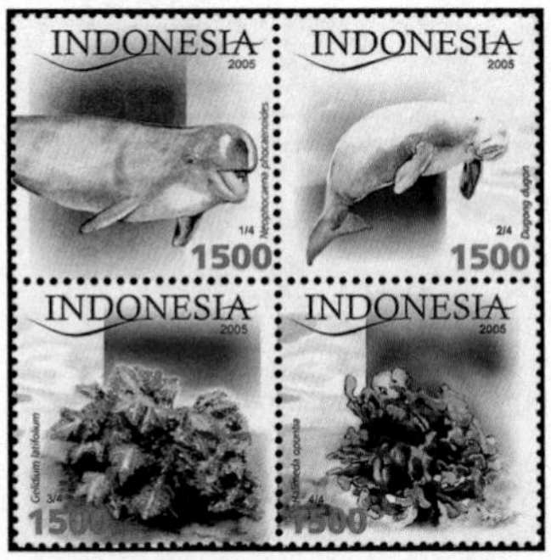


Sea Mammals and Plants — A630

No. 2083: a, Neophocaena phocaenoides (1/4). b, Dugong dugon (2/4). c, Gelidium latifolium (3/4). d, Halimeda opuntia (4/4).

**2005, Nov. 5 *Perf. 12½***

**2083** A630 1500r Block of 4, #a-d 3.00 1.50
*e.* As "a," with "1/4" removed 2.00 1.00
*f.* As "b," with "3/4" removed 2.00 1.00
*g.* Souvenir sheet, #2083e, 2083f + central label 2.00 1.00

Folktales — A631

No. 2084: a, Bawang Merah & Bawang Putih (1/4). b, Keong Emas (2/4). c, Si Kancil (3/4). d, Timun Emas (4/4).

**2006, Feb. 6 Litho. *Perf. 12¾x13½***

**2084** Block or strip of 4 3.25 1.60
*a.-d.* A631 1500r Any single .80 .40
*e.* Souvenir sheet, #2084a-2084d, imperf. 5.00 2.50

**Miniature Sheets**

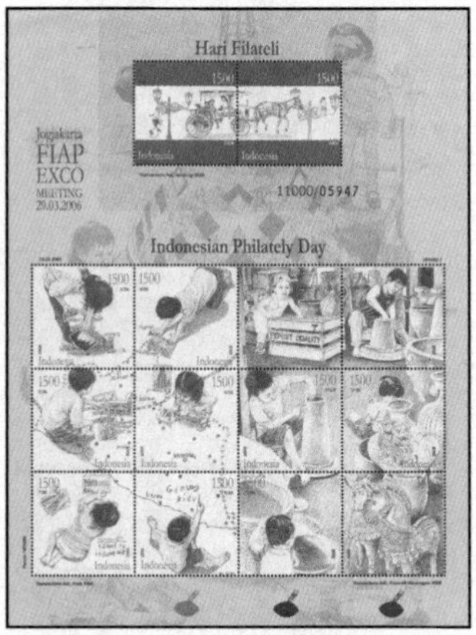


Philately Day — A632

No. 2085, 1500r — Illustrations in brown: a, Family in coach (1/28). b, Horse pulling coach (2/28). c, Girl, standing, with three photographs (3/28). d, Boy with one photograph (4/28). e, Boy with three photographs (5/28). f, Girl, wearing sandals, holding photograph (6/28). g, Barefoot girl touching photograph (7/28). h, Boy drawing map (8/28). i, Boy and crate (9/28). j, Boy at potter's wheel, finished pottery (10/28). k, Boy at potter's wheel (11/28). l, Girl pointing (12/28). m, Boy touching pottery (13/28). n, Caparisoned pottery horses (14/28).

No. 2086, 1500r — Illustrations in color: a, Like #2085a (15/28). b, Like #2085b (16/28). c, Like #2085c (17/28). d, Like #2085d (18/28). e, Like #2085e (19/28). f, Like #2085f (20/28). g, Like #2085g (21/28). h, Like #2085h (22/28). i, Like #2085i (23/28). j, Like #2085j (24/28). k, Like #2085k (25/28). l, Like #2085l (26/28). m, Like #2085m (27/28). n, Like #2085n (28/28).

**2006, Mar. 29 Litho. *Perf. 14***

**Sheets of 14, #a-n**

**2085-2086** A632 Set of 2 16.00 8.25

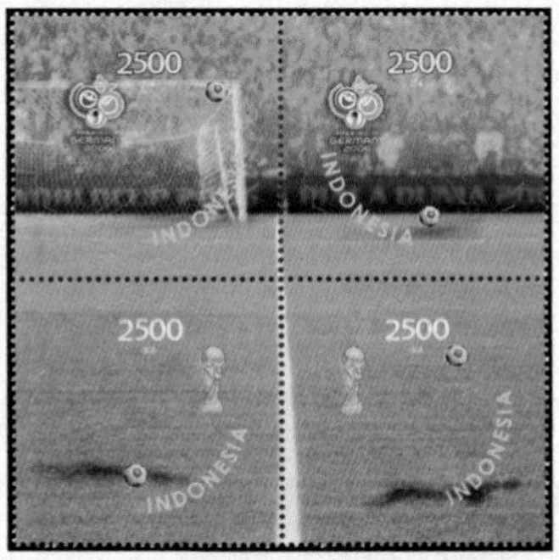


2006 World Cup Soccer Championships, Germany — A633

No. 2087: a, World Cup emblem, goal, soccer ball (1/4). b, World Cup emblem, soccer ball (2/4). c, World Cup trophy at right, soccer ball at bottom (3/4). d, World Cup trophy at left, soccer ball at right (4/4).

***Die Cut, With Perf. 14 Selvage Between Stamps***

**2006, May 6**

**Self-Adhesive**

**2087** A633 2500r Block of 4, #a-d 5.50 2.75
*e.* Booklet pane, #2087a-2087d, die cut, imperf. selvage between stamps 6.00 —
Complete booklet, #2087e 7.00

Individual stamps have various die cut soccer players in center. Values are for unused stamps with surrounding selvage. Used stamps may or may not have the die cut soccer players.

Environmental Care — A634

No. 2088: a, Village, flowers, butterfly (1/2). b, Girl (2/2).

**2006, June 5 Litho. *Perf. 13¼x12¾***

**2088** A634 1500r Pair, #a-b 2.00 .90
*c.* Souvenir sheet, #2088a-2088b 2.00 .90

Local Foods A635

No. 2089: a, Pempek (South Sumatra, 1/4). b, Gudeg (Yogyakarta, 2/4). c, Ayam Betutu (Bali, 3/4). d, Aunu Senebre (Papua, 4/4).

**2006, July 6**

**2089** Block or strip of 4 2.50 1.25
*a.-d.* A635 1500r Any single .60 .30

National Scout Jamboree — A636

No. 2090: a, Kak Mashudi and scouts around campfire (1/2). b, Jigsaw puzzle of scouts (2/2).

**Litho. & Photo.**

**2006, July 16 *Perf. 12½***

**2090** A636 1500r Pair, #a-b 2.00 1.00

Sultans A637

No. 2091d Overprinted in Red Foil

No. 2091: a, Sultan Ma'moen Al Rasyid Perkasa Alamsyah Sultan Deli IX (1873-1924) (1/4). b, Sultan Agung Sultan Mataram III (1613-45) (2/4). c, Sultan Adji Mohamad Parikesit Sultan Kutai Kertanegara XX (1920-60) (3/4). d, Sultan Hasanuddin Sultan Gowa XVI (1653-69) (4/4).

**Litho., Litho. with Foil Application (#2091e)**

***Perf. 13½ Syncopated***

**2006, Aug. 17**

**2091** Block or strip of 4 3.00 1.50
*a.-d.* A637 1500r Any single .75 .35
*e.* As "d," overprinted in red foil 3.00 1.50
*f.* Block or strip of 4, #2091a-2091c, 2091e 8.00 4.00

Puppets — A638

No. 2092: a, Indonesian puppet (1/2). b, Slovakian marionette (2/2).

**Litho. & Photo.**

**2006, Sept. 27** ***Perf. 13x13¼***

**2092** A638 2500r Horiz. pair, #a-b 2.00 1.00
*c.* Souvenir sheet, #2092 2.00 1.00

See Slovakia Nos. 506-507.

Miniature Sheet

Eid ul-Fitr — A639

No. 2093: a, Man sitting with crossed legs in prayer (1/8). b, Drummer (5/8). c, Older woman hugging young woman (2/8). d, Woman and man with hands in prayer (6/8). e, Mosque (3/8). f, People getting on bus (7/8). g, Geometric design (4/8). h, People and horse cart (8/8).

Nos. 2093lj-2093lq: As Nos. 2039a-2093h, but with Prisma emblem in lower corner of stamp and persoanlized photo above arc.

**2006, Oct. 3** **Litho.** ***Perf. 12½***

**2093** A639 1500r Sheet of 8, #a-h 4.00 2.00
**2093I** A639 1500r Sheet of 8, #j-q 5.25 5.25

No. 2093l sold for 20,000r.

Flora and Fauna — A640

No. 2094: a, Licuala arbuscula (3/4). b, Livistona mamberamoensis (4/4). c, Melipotes carolae (1/4). d, Amblyornis flavifrons (2/4).

**2006, Nov. 5** ***Perf. 12½***

**2094** A640 1500r Block of 4, #a-d 3.00 1.50
*e.* As "a," with "3/4" removed 2.00 1.00
*f.* As "d," with "2/4" removed 2.00 1.00
*g.* Souvenir sheet, #2094e-2094f + label 4.00 2.00

Souvenir Sheet

Bandung '06 Natl. Philatelic Exhibition — A641

No. 2095: a, Panthera pardus (1/2). b, Bouea macrophylla (2/2).

***Perf. 13½x12¾***

**2006, Nov. 30** **Litho.**

**2095** A641 2500r Sheet of 2, #a-b 4.00 2.00
*c.* Like #2095, with margin illustration in blue and black 2.00 1.00
*d.* Like #2095, with margin illustration in red and black 2.00 1.00
*e.* Like #2095, with margin illustration in yellow and black 2.00 1.00
*f.* Like #2095, with margin illustration in black 2.00 1.00

On No. 2095, the code number at lower left of sheet ends with "5," that of Nos. 2095c-2095f end in "1" to "4" respectively. Margin illustrations show progressive color printing.

Containers — A642

No. 2096: a, Container from Bali (2/2). b, Lidded basket from East Kalimantan (1/2).

**2006, Dec. 23** ***Perf. 13½x12¾***

**2096** A642 1500r Horiz. pair, #a-b 1.50 .75

New Year 2007 (Year of the Pig) A643

No. 2097: a, Chinese zodiac animals and lanterns (1/2). b, Chinese zodiac animals, people and temple (2/2).

No. 2098: a, Rat (1/13). b, Ox (2/13). c, Tiger (3/13). d, Rabbit (4/13). e, Dragon (5/13). f, Snake (6/13). g, Horse (7/13). h, Goat (8/13). i, Monkey (9/13). j, Rooster (10/13). k, Dog (11/13). l, Pig (12/13). m, Like #2097b (96x64mm, 13/13)

No. 2099, Like #2097b.

**Litho., Litho. With Foil Application (#2098m, 2099)**

**2007, Feb. 1** ***Perf. 12½***

**2097** Pair 1.10 .70
*a.-b.* A643 1500r Either single .55 .30
**2098** Sheet of 13 10.00 10.00
*a.-l.* A643 2000r Any single .60 .30
*m.* A643 6000r multi 2.00 1.00

**Souvenir Sheet**

**2099** A643 6000r multi 2.00 1.00

Dances — A644

No. 2100: a, Lion dance (1/2). b, Dragon dance (2/2).

***Perf. 13¼x13½ Syncopated***

**2007, Apr. 13** **Litho.**

**2100** A644 2500r Pair, #a-b 1.60 .80
*c.* Souvenir sheet, #2100a-2100b 2.50 1.25

See People's Republic of China Nos. 3581-3582.

Reading and Writing A645

No. 2101: a, Boy writing in book, mother reading (2/2). b, Boy looking at girl writing in book (1/2).

**2007, May 2** **Litho.** ***Perf. 13½x12¾***

**2101** A645 1500r Pair, #a-b 1.10 .55

A646

Environmental Care — A647

Nos. 2102, 2104: a, Iceberg, top of polar bear's head (1/4). b, Crying polar bear (2/4).

No. 2103: a, Forest fire (3/4). b, Burnt forest (4/4).

**2007, June 5**

**2102** A646 1500r Vert. pair, #a-b 1.10 .55
**2103** A647 1500r Vert. pair, #a-b 1.10 .55

**Souvenir Sheet**

**2104** A646 2500r Sheet of 2, #a-b 1.75 .85

Nos. 2102 and 2103 were each printed in sheets containing 10 pairs with the bottom stamp in the pair tete-beche with the same stamp.

Campaign Against Drug Abuse — A648

No. 2105: a, Guitarist, Indonesian inscription (1/2). b, Basketball player, English inscription (2/2).

**2007, June 26** ***Perf. 12¾x13½***

**2105** A648 1500r Pair, #a-b 1.75 .85

Traditional Foods — A649

No. 2106: a, Roti Cane and Kari Kambing (Aceh, 1/4). b, Gecok (West Nusa Tenggara, 3/4). c, Soto Kudus (Central Java, 2/4). d, Ikan Air Garam (Maluku, 4/4).

**2007, July 6** ***Perf. 13½x12¾***

**2106** Strip of 4 2.50 1.25
*a.-d.* A649 1500r Any single .60 .30

A650

A651

A652

Greetings With Hands — A653

**2007, June 3** **Litho.** ***Perf. 12½***

**2107** A650 1500r multi + label 2.00 2.00
**2108** A651 1500r multi + label 2.00 2.00
*a.* Pair, #2107-2108, + 2 labels 4.00 4.00
**2109** A652 1500r multi + label 2.00 2.00
**2110** A653 1500r multi + label 2.00 2.00
*a.* Pair, #2109-2110, + 2 labels 4.00 4.00
*Nos. 2107-2110 (4)* 8.00 8.00

Nos. 2107-2108 and 2109-2110 were each printed in sheets of 20 stamps + 20 labels, containing ten of each stamp. Sheets sold for 45,000r. Labels could be personalized. A sheet of 20 No. 2107 + 20 non-personalizable labels, issued in 2008, also sold for 45,000r.

Fireworks — A654

Guitar and G Clef A655

Paint Brushes — A656

Film and Reel A657

***Perf. 12½x12½x12½x4***

**2007, July 21 Litho.**

| | | | | |
|---|---|---|---|---|
| **2111** | A654 | 1500r multi + label | 2.00 | 2.00 |
| **2112** | A655 | 1500r multi + label | 2.00 | 2.00 |
| **2113** | A656 | 1500r multi + label | 2.00 | 2.00 |
| **2114** | A657 | 1500r multi + label | 2.00 | 2.00 |
| | | *Nos. 2111-2114 (4)* | 8.00 | 8.00 |

Nos. 2111-2114 were each printed in sheets of 8 stamps + 8 labels that sold for 15,000r face. No. 2111 also was printed in four different sheets of 12 stamps + 12 labels that each sold for 30,000r. Labels could not be personalized.

Scouting, Cent. — A658

No. 2115, 2500r: a, Centenary emblem, full color background (1/4). b, Scout, full color (2/4).

No. 2116, 1500r: a, Centenary emblem, blue background (3/4). b, Scout in blue (4/4).

**2007, Aug. 1** ***Perf. 13½ Syncopated***

| | | | | |
|---|---|---|---|---|
| **2115** | A658 | Horiz. pair, #a-b | 2.25 | 1.10 |

**Booklet Stamps**

| | | | | |
|---|---|---|---|---|
| **2116** | A658 | Horiz. pair, #a-b | 1.10 | .55 |
| *c.* | | Booklet pane, 5 #2116 | 5.50 | — |
| | | Complete booklet, #2116c | 5.50 | |

Nepenthes Mirabilis — A659

Nepenthes Ampuliaria — A660

**2007, Aug. 3** ***Perf. 13½x12¾***

| | | | | |
|---|---|---|---|---|
| **2117** | A659 | 1500r multi | .60 | .30 |

***Perf. 12¾x13½***

| | | | | |
|---|---|---|---|---|
| **2118** | A660 | 1500r multi | .60 | .30 |

**Souvenir Sheet**

***Perf. 13½x12¾***

| | | | | |
|---|---|---|---|---|
| **2119** | | Sheet of 2 | 2.50 | 1.25 |
| *a.* | | A659 2500r multi | 1.25 | .60 |
| *b.* | | A660 2500r multi | 1.25 | .60 |

Bangkok 2007 Intl. Stamp Exhibition.

Association of South East Asian Nations (ASEAN), 40th Anniv. A661

Designs: 1500r, Fatahillah Museum, Jakarta.

No. 2121: a, Secretariat Building, Bandar Seri Begawan, Brunei (1/10). b, National Museum of Cambodia (2/10). c, Fatahillah Museum, Jakarta (3/10). d, Typical house, Laos (4/10). e, Malayan Railway Headquarters Building, Kuala Lumpur, Malaysia (5/10). f, Yangon Post Office, Myanmar (6/10). g, Malacañang Palace, Philippines (7/10). h, National Museum of Singapore (8/10). i, Vimanmek Mansion, Bangkok, Thailand (9/10). j, Presidential Palace, Hanoi, Viet Nam (10/10).

**2007, Aug. 8** ***Perf. 13½ Syncopated***

| | | | | |
|---|---|---|---|---|
| **2120** | A661 | 1500r multi | 1.00 | .50 |
| **2121** | | Sheet of 10 | 9.00 | 4.50 |
| *a.-j.* | | A661 2500r Any single | .90 | .45 |

See Brunei No. 607, Burma No. 370, Cambodia No. 2339, Laos Nos. 1717-1718, Malaysia No. 1170, Philippines Nos. 3103-3105, Singapore No. 1265, Thailand No. 2315, and Viet Nam Nos. 3302-3311.

Lighthouses — A662

No. 2122: a, Semarang Lighthouse (1/2). b, Cikoneng Lighthouse (2/2).

**2007, Aug. 17** ***Perf. 12¾x13½***

| | | | | |
|---|---|---|---|---|
| **2122** | A662 | 1500r Horiz. pair, #a-b | 1.25 | .60 |

Padjadjaran University, 50th Anniv. — A663

No. 2123: a, Tiger and ram (1/4). b, Men and dancers (2/4). c, Building (3/4). d, Symbols and globe (4/4).

**2007, Sept. 5** ***Perf. 13½x12¾***

| | | | | |
|---|---|---|---|---|
| **2123** | | Horiz. strip of 4 + central label | 4.00 | 2.00 |
| *a.-d.* | | A663 1500r Any single | 1.00 | .50 |

Butterflies — A664

No. 2124: a, Delias kristianiae (1/4). b, Ornithoptera aesacus (2/4). c, Ornithoptera croesus (3/4). d, Troides hypolitus (4/4).

No. 2125: a, Like #2124a. b, Like #2124c.

**2007, Nov. 5** ***Perf. 12½***

| | | | | |
|---|---|---|---|---|
| **2124** | | Block of 4 | 2.25 | 1.10 |
| *a.-d.* | | A664 1500r Any single | .35 | .30 |

**Souvenir Sheet**

| | | | | |
|---|---|---|---|---|
| **2125** | | Sheet of 2 + central label | 2.00 | 1.00 |
| *a.-b.* | | A664 2500r Either single | 1.00 | .50 |

**No. 2125 Surcharged in Gold**

**2007, Nov. 21 Litho.** ***Perf. 12½***

| | | | | |
|---|---|---|---|---|
| **2126** | | Sheet of 2 + central label | 6.00 | 3.00 |
| *a.-b.* | | A664 5000r on 2500r Either single | 3.00 | 1.50 |

No. 2126 also is overprinted in gold in margin and label with emblem and text for Bandungfilex 2007 and Jakarta 2008 Intl. Stamp Exhibition.

24th South East Asian Games, Nakhon Ratchasima, Thailand — A665

No. 2127: a, Bowling (1/4). b, Indoor soccer (2/4). c, Kempo (3/4). d, Hammer throw (4/4).

**2007, Dec. 6** ***Perf. 14***

| | | | | |
|---|---|---|---|---|
| **2127** | | Horiz. strip of 4 | 4.00 | 2.00 |
| *a.-d.* | | A665 2500r Any single | 1.00 | .50 |

Djuanda Declaration, 50th Anniv. — A666

No. 2128: a, Map of Indonesia, children (1/3). b, Prime Minister Djuanda Kartawidjaja, eagle, and procession (2/3). c, Djuanda Kartawidjaja and map of Indonesia (3/3).

**2007, Dec. 13** ***Perf. 13½x12¾***

| | | | | |
|---|---|---|---|---|
| **2128** | | Vert. strip of 3 | 2.50 | 1.25 |
| *a.-c.* | | A666 1500r Any single | .80 | .40 |

Miniature Sheet

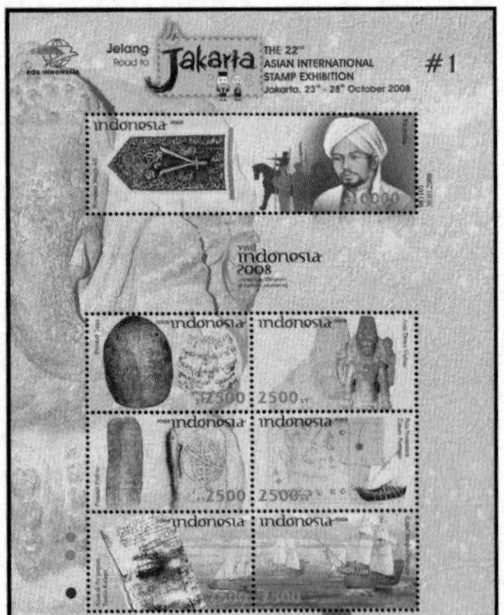


Jakarta 2008 Intl. Stamp Exhibition — A667

No. 2129: a, Prasasti Tugu (2/7). b, Arca Dewa Visnu (statue of Vishnu) (3/7). c, Prasasti Padrao (4/7). d, Peta Nusantara Zaman Portugis (5/7). e, Naskah Perjanjian Sunda Kelapa (6/7). f, Kapal Bangsa Portugis (7/7). g, Bendera Singa Ali and Fatahillah (1/7). Nos. 2129a-2129f are 41x25mm; No. 2129g, 83x25mm.

**2008, Jan. 20 Litho.** ***Perf. 13½x12¾***

| | | | | |
|---|---|---|---|---|
| **2129** | A667 | Sheet of 7 | 5.50 | 2.75 |
| *a.-f.* | | 2500r Any single | .55 | .25 |
| *g.* | | 10,000r multi | 2.10 | 1.10 |

A668 

New Year 2008 (Year of the Rat) — A669

No. 2130: a, Rat facing right (1/3). b, Rat facing left (2/3). c, Rat on hind legs (3/3).

**2008, Jan. 26** ***Perf. 13½x12¾***

| | | | | |
|---|---|---|---|---|
| **2130** | | Vert. strip of 3 + label | 1.60 | .80 |
| *a.-c.* | | A668 2000r Any single | .50 | .25 |

**Souvenir Sheet**

***Perf. 12½***

| | | | | |
|---|---|---|---|---|
| **2131** | A669 | 5000r black & gray | 2.25 | 1.10 |

Souvenir Sheet

Flora and Fauna — A670

No. 2132: a, Casuarius casuarius (1/2). b, Crinum asiaticum (2/2).

**2008, Mar. 7** ***Perf. 12¾x13½***

| | | | | |
|---|---|---|---|---|
| **2132** | A670 | 5000r Sheet of 2, #a-b | 3.00 | 1.50 |

Jakarta 2008 Intl. Stamp Exhibition, Taipei 2008 Intl. Stamp Exhibition, Stamp Passion '08 Stamp Exhibition, Netherlands.

2008 Summer Olympics, Beijing — A671

No. 2133: a, Sailboarding (1/4). b, Soccer (2/4). c, Badminton (3/4). d, Weight lifting (4/4).

**2008, Mar. 18** ***Perf. 14***

| | | | | |
|---|---|---|---|---|
| **2133** | A671 | 2500r Block of 4, #a-d | 3.00 | 1.50 |

Miniature Sheet

Jakarta 2008 Intl. Stamp Exhibition — A672

No. 2134: a, Istana Pemerintahan Batavia (2/7). b, Gedung Keuangan (3/7). c, Penyerangan Batavia oleh Sultan Agung, denomination at LR (4/7). d, Penyerangan Batavia oleh Sultan Agung, denomination at LL (5/7). e, Perubahan Batavia Menjadi Jakarta (6/7). f, Penyerahan Kekuasaan Indonesia (7/7). g, Penangkapan Pangeran Jayawikarta oleh Pasukan Banten (1/7). Nos. 2134a-2134f are 41x25mm; No. 2134g, 83x25mm.

*Perf. 13½x12¾*

**2008, Mar. 29** **Litho.**
**2134** A672 Sheet of 7 5.50 2.75
*a.-f.* 2500r Any single .55 .25
*g.* 10,000r multi 2.10 1.10

Diplomatic Relations Between Indonesia and Japan, 50th Anniv. — A673

No. 2135, 2500r: a, Kelimutu Volcano, Indonesia (1/10). b, Mt. Fuji, Japan (2/10).
No. 2136, 2500r: a, Borobudur, Indonesia (3/10). b, Toji Temple, Japan (4/10).
No. 2137, 2500r: a, Rafflesia arnoldi (5/10). b, Cherry blossoms (6/10).
No. 2138, 2500r: a, Angklung (7/10). b, Gaku biwa (8/10).
No. 2139, 2500r, horiz: a, Scleropages formosus (9/10). b, Nishiki-goi (10/10).

**2008, Apr. 15** ***Perf. 12½***
**Horiz. Pairs, #a-b**
**2135-2139** A673 Set of 5 6.50 3.25
*2139c* Miniature sheet, #2135-2139 6.50 3.25

Nos. 2135-2139 were each printed in sheets of 4 pairs. See Japan No. 3018.

Special Needs Education A674

No. 2140: a, Boy in wheelchair waving flags (1/3). b, Man in racing wheelchair (2/3). c, Handicapped children playing anklungs (3/3).

**Litho. & Embossed**
**2008, May 2** ***Perf. 13½x12¾***
**2140** Strip of 3 1.60 .80
*a.-c.* A674 1500r Any single .50 .25

National Awakening, Cent. — A675

No. 2141: a, People with fists raised, flag. b, Flag, people, satellite.

**2008, May 20 Litho.** ***Perf. 12¾x13½***
**2141** A675 1500r Horiz. pair, #a-b .80 .40

Environmental Care — A676

Nos. 2142 and 2143: a, Cyclists, motor vehicles (1/2). b, Seedling, forest (2/2). Stamps from No. 2143 lack stamp numbers.

**2008, June 5** ***Perf. 13½x12¾***
**2142** A676 1500r Pair, #a-b .80 .40

**Souvenir Sheet**

**2143** A676 2500r Sheet of 2, #a-b 1.25 1.25

Miniature Sheet

Jakarta 2008 Intl. Stamp Exhibition — A677

No. 2144: a, Jakarta Philatelic Center (Kantor Filateli Jakarta) (2/7). b, National Museum (3/7). c, Dunia Fantasi (4/7). d, Taman Mini Indonesia (5/7). e, Wisana Seni and Budaya (6/7). f, Wisata Bihari (7/7). g, Warna Warni Jakarta (1/7). Nos. 2144a-2144f are 41x25mm; No. 2144g, 83x25mm.

**2008, June 22** ***Perf. 13½x12¾***
**2144** A677 Sheet of 7 5.50 2.75
*a.-f.* 2500r Any single .55 .25
*g.* 10,000r multi 2.10 1.10

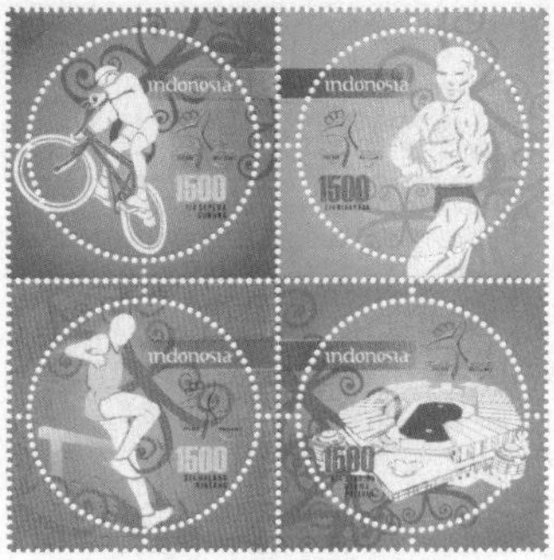


17th National Games — A678

No. 2145: a, Mountain biking (1/4). b, Bodybuilding (2/4). c, Steeplechase (3/4). d, Palaran Main Stadium, Samarinda (4/4).

**2008, July 5** ***Perf. 14***
**2145** A678 1500r Block of 4, #a-d 2.00 1.00

**Traditional Foods Type of 2007**

No. 2146: a, Nasi Lemak (Riau, 1/4). b, Sate Bandeng (Banten, 2/4). c, Ayem Cincane (East Kalimantan, 3/4). d, Kaledo (Central Sulawesi, 4/4).

**2008, July 6** ***Perf. 13½x12¾***
**2146** Block of 4 1.60 .80
*a.-d.* A649 1500r Any single .40 .25

Printed in sheets containing four of each stamp + four labels.

Provincial Arms and Architecture — A679

Arms of: Nos. 2147, 1500r, 2158a, 2500r, Bali (1/33). Nos. 2148, 1500r, 2158b, 2500r, Gorontalo (2/33). Nos. 2149, 1500r, 2158c, 2500r, Jawa Barat (West Java) (3/33). Nos. 2150, 1500r, 2158d, 2500r, Jawa Tengah (Central Java) (4/33). Nos. 2151, 1500r, 2158e, 2500r, Kalimantan Barat (West Kalimantan) (5/33). Nos. 2152, 1500r, 2158f, 2500r, Maluku (Moluccas) (6/33). Nos. 2153, 1500r, 2158g, 2500r, Aceh (7/33). Nos. 2154, 1500r, 2158h, 2500r, Papua (8/33). Nos. 2155, 1500r, 2158i, 2500r, Riau (9/33). Nos. 2156, 1500r, 2158j, 2500r, Sulawesi Barat (West Sulawesi) (10/33). Nos. 2157, 1500r, 2158k, 2500r, Sumatera Barat (West Sumatra) (11/33).

**2008, Aug. 17** ***Perf. 12½***
**2147-2157** A679 Set of 11 5.50 2.75
**2158** Sheet of 11 + label 7.50 4.00
*a.-k.* A679 2500r Any single .65 .30

Nos. 2147-2157 each were printed in sheets of 10.
See Nos. 2200-2211, 2253-2264.

Great Post Road of Java A680

No. 2159: a, Lighthouse, map of western part of road (1/4). b, Building, map of central part of road (2/4). c, Lighthouse, map of eastern part of road (3/4). d, Letter from Governor General Herman Daendels (4/4).
10,000r, Map of entire road.

**2008, Sept. 27** ***Perf. 13½x12¾***
**2159** Horiz. strip of 4 3.00 1.50
*a.-d.* A680 2500r Any single .75 .35

**Souvenir Sheet**

**2160** A680 10,000r multi 3.50 1.75

No. 2160 contains one 125x25mm stamp.

Souvenir Sheets

A681

A682

A683

A684

A685

Jakarta 2008 Intl. Stamp Exhibition — A686

**2008** ***Perf. 13½x12¾***
**2161** A681 5000r multi 1.40 .70
**2162** A682 5000r multi 1.40 .70
**2163** A683 5000r multi 1.40 .70
**2164** A684 5000r multi 1.40 .70

**2165** A685 5000r multi 1.40 .70
**2166** A686 5000r multi 1.40 .70
*Nos. 2161-2166 (6)* 8.40 4.20

Issued: No. 2161, 10/23; No. 2162, 10/24; No. 2163, 10/25; No. 2164, 10/26; No. 2165, 10/27; No. 2166, 10/28.

Miniature Sheet

Friendship Between Indonesia and Turkey — A687

No. 2167: a, Blue Mosque, Turkey (1/10). b, Istiqlal Mosque, Indonesia (2/10). c, Bosporus Bridge, Turkey (3/10). d, Barelang Bridge, Indonesia (4/10). e, Whirling dervishes (5/10). f, Saman dance (6/10). g, Turkish tulip (7/10). h, Flame of Irian (8/10). i, Turkish Van cat (9/10). j, Flat-headed cat (10/10).

**2008, Oct. 24** ***Perf. 13½ Syncopated***
**2167** A687 2500r Sheet of 10, #a-j 7.50 3.75

See Turkey No. 3142.

Miniature Sheet

Flora and Fauna of the Provinces — A688

No. 2168: a, Leucopsar rothschildi, Dysoxylum densiflorum, Bali (1/11). b, Liza dussumieri, Vitex cofassus, Gorontalo (2/11). c, Panthera pardus, Bouea macrophylla, Jawa Barat (West Java) (3/11). d, Oriolus chinensis, Michelia alba, Jawa Tengah (Central Java) (4/11). e, Rhinoplax vigil, Shorea stenoptera, Kalimantan Barat (West Kalimantan) (5/11). f, Alisterus amboinensis, Dendrobium phalaenopsis, Maluku (Moluccas) (6/11). g, Copsychus pyrropygus, Michelia champaca, Aceh (7/11). h, Seleucidis melanoleuca, Pometia pinnata, Papua (8/11). i, Loriculus galgulus, Oncosperma tigillarium, Riau (9/11). j, Aramidopsis plateni, Elmerrillia ovalis, Sulawesi Barat (West Sulawesi) (10/11). k, Argusianus argus, Morus macroura, Sumatera Barat (West Sumatra) (11/11).

**2008, Nov. 5** ***Perf. 13½x12¾***
**2168** A688 2500r Sheet of 11, #a-k, + label 8.00 4.00

See Nos. 2217, 2249-2252.

Cut Nyak Dhien (1848-1908), Leader of Aceh Resistance to Dutch Rule — A689

No. 2169: a, House (1/2). b, Cut Nyak Dhien (2/2).

**2008, Nov. 5**
**2169** A689 1500r Horiz. pair, #a-b 1.00 .50

Islands A690

No. 2170: a, Damar Island (1/4). b, Sebatik Island (2/4). c, Batubawaikang Island (3/4). d, Bras Island (4/4).

**2008, Dec. 3**
**2170** Block or strip of 4 2.00 1.00
*a.-d.* A690 1500r multi .50 .25
*e.* Miniature sheet, 4 each #2170a-2170d 8.00 4.00

New Year 2009 (Year of the Ox) A691

Designs: Nos. 2171, 2174a, 2000r, Head of ox (1/3). Nos. 2172, 2174b, 2000r, Ox looking left (2/3). Nos. 2173, 2174c, 2000r, Ox in water (3/3).
10,000r, Ox, diff.

**2009, Jan. 10** **Litho.**
**2171-2173** A691 Set of 3 1.75 .85

**Litho. & Embossed With Foil Application (Chinese Character in Gold)**

**2174** A691 2000r Vert. strip of 3, #a-c 2.00 1.00

**Souvenir Sheet**

**2175** A691 10,000r multi 2.75 1.40

Nos. 2171-2173 were printed in a sheet of 24 stamps containing 8 of each stamp. No. 2174 was printed in a sheet containing 2 strips.

Bandung Institute of Technology, 50th Anniv. — A692

No. 2176: a, Building, colored triangles (1/4). b, Emblems, crowd of dignitaries (2/4). c, "89 Tahun," text (3/4). d, Emblem dated "1920" (4/4).

**2009, Mar. 2** **Litho.**
**2176** Horiz. strip of 4 + central label 1.75 .85
*a.-d.* A692 1500r Any single .45 .25

A693

A694

A695

General Elections — A696

**2009, Mar. 5** ***Perf. 13x13¼***
**2177** Strip of 4 1.60 .80
*a.* A693 1500r multi .40 .25
*b.* A694 1500r multi .40 .25
*c.* A695 1500r multi .40 .25
*d.* A696 1500r multi .40 .25

Souvenir Sheet

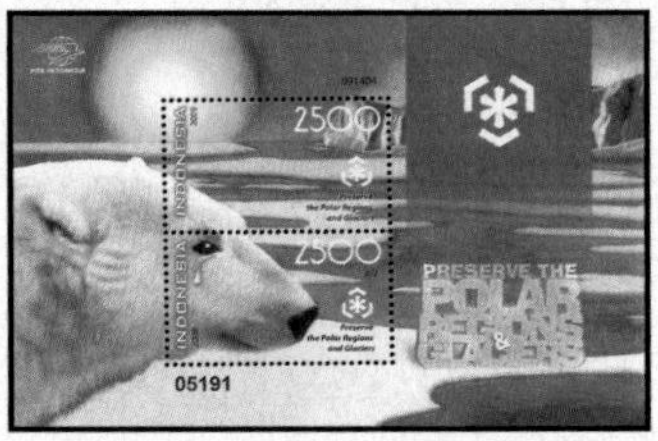


Preservation of Polar Regions and Glaciers — A697

No. 2178 — Snowflake emblem and: a, Iceberg, top of polar bear's head. b, Crying polar bear.

**2009, Mar. 18** ***Perf. 13½x12¾***
**2178** A697 2500r Sheet of 2, #a-b 2.00 1.00

Compare with No. 2104.

Souvenir Sheet

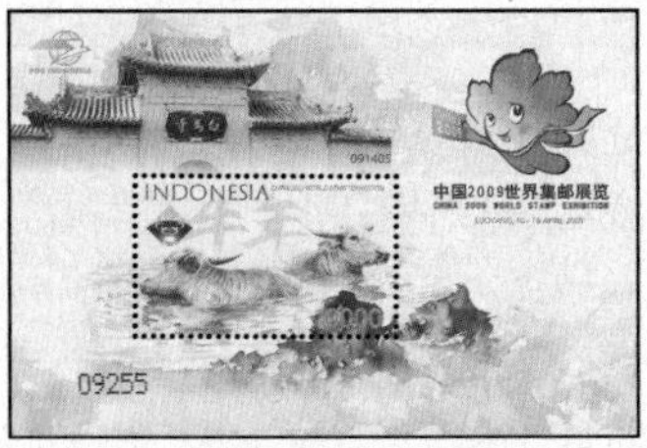


China 2009 World Stamp Exhibition, Luoyang — A698

**2009, Apr. 10**
**2179** A698 10,000r multi 2.75 1.40

Intl. Year of Astronomy A699

Nos. 2180 and 2181: a, Galileo's telescope (1/3). b, Intl. Year of Astronomy emblem (2/3). c, Galileo Galilei (1564-1642) (3/3).

**2009, May 2** **Litho.** ***Perf. 13x13¼***
**2180** Horiz. strip of 3 2.50 1.25
*a.-c.* A699 2500r Any single .80 .25

**Souvenir Sheet**

**Litho. With Hologram**

**2181** Sheet of 3 5.00 2.50
*a.-c.* A699 5000r Any single 1.60 .80

World Ocean Conference, Manado — A700

No. 2182: a, Blue-ringed angelfish (1/4). b, Anemone shrimp and sea anemone (2/4). c, Goldback anthias (3/4). d, Coral reef (4/4).
5000r, Sea turtle.

**2009, May 11** ***Perf. 13½x12¾***
**2182** A700 2500r Block or strip of 4, #a-d 3.00 1.50

**Souvenir Sheet**

**2183** A700 5000r multi 1.75 .85

World Environment Day — A701

No. 2184: a, Boy holding plant, parched earth (3/3). b, Factories, people in bubble (2/3). c, Smokestacks, tree, boy near forest (1/3).
5000r, Like 2184c.

**2009, June 5**
**2184** Strip of 3 1.50 .75
*a.-c.* A701 1500r Any single .50 .25

**Souvenir Sheet**

**2185** A701 5000r multi 1.50 .75

Opening of Suramadu Bridge — A702

No. 2186: a, City, statue, end of bridge (1/3). b, Bridge towers (2/3). c, End of bridge, boat, farmer with oxen (3/3).
10,000r, Entire bridge, city, sculpture, boat, farmer with oxen.

**2009, June 10**
**2186** Horiz. strip of 3 1.50 .75
*a.-c.* A702 1500r Any single .50 .25

**Souvenir Sheet**

**2187** A702 10,000r multi 3.00 1.50

No. 2187 contains one 126x25mm stamp.

Traditional Foods A703

No. 2188: a, Ihutilinanga (Gorontalo, 1/6). b, Gulai Balak (Lampung, 2/6). c, Sate Tambulinas (Southeast Sulawesi, 3/6). d, Sambal Goreng Papai (Central Kalimantan, 4/6). e, Nasi Uduk (Jakarta, 5/6). f, Ikan Bobara Kuah Asam (West Papua, 6/6).

**2009, July 6**
**2188** Block of 6 3.00 1.50
*a.-f.* A703 1500r Any single .50 .25

BirdLife International — A704

No. 2189, 2500r: a, Ciconia stormi, with first "0" in denomination below bird (6/6). b, Aceros corrugatus, with first "0" in denomination touching central line of leaf (1/6).

No. 2190, 2500r, horiz.: a, Harpactes kasumba, with "A" of "Indonesia" barely touching bird's tail (41x25mm, 2/6). b, Actenoides concretus, with entire center of "D" in "Indonesia" over tree branch (41x25mm, 3/6).

No. 2191, 2500r, horiz.: a, Cairina scutulata, with farthest extent of white water ripple line running through "5" in denomination (41x25mm, 4/6). b, Argusianus argus, with white water ripple line touching "2" and "5" in denomination (41x25mm, 5/6).

No. 2192, 2500r: a, Like #2189a, with first "0" in denomination touching bird. b, Like #2189b, with first "0" in denomination above central line of leaf. c, Like #2190a, with "A" of "Indonesia" half on bird's tail, and without "2/6." d, Like #2190b, with center of "D" of "Indonesia" partly on tree branch. e, Like #2191a, with farthest extent of white water ripple line to left of "5" in denomination. f, Like #2191b, with white water ripple line below "2" and "5" in denomination.

**2009, July 15** ***Perf. 13½x12¾***

**Horiz. Pairs, #a-b**

**"Burung" in Blue**

**2189-2191** A704 Set of 3 5.00 2.50

**Souvenir Sheet**

**"Burung" in Black**

**2192** A704 2500r Sheet of 6, #a-f 5.00 2.50

For overprint see No. 2212.

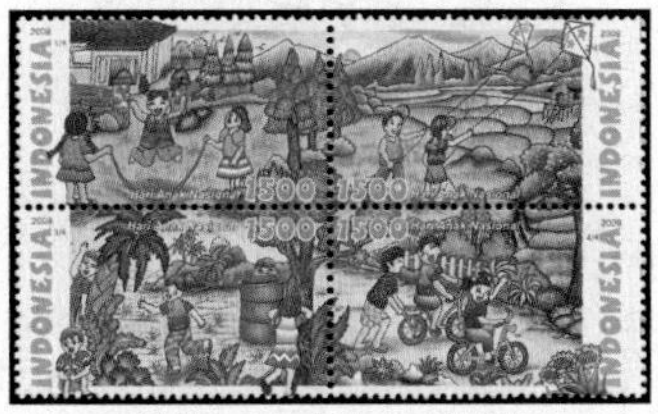


Children's Day — A705

No. 2193 — Children: a, Jumping rope (1/4). b, Flying kites (2/4). c, Playing hide-and-seek (3/4). d, Riding bicycles (4/4).

**2009, July 23**

**2193** A705 1500r Block of 4, #a-d 2.00 1.50

Souvenir Sheet

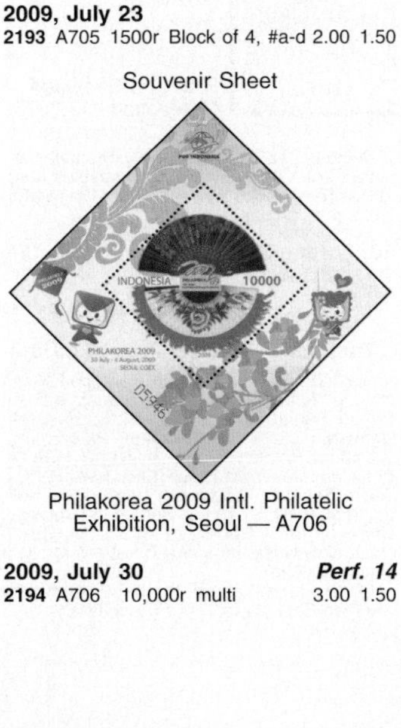


Philakorea 2009 Intl. Philatelic Exhibition, Seoul — A706

**2009, July 30** ***Perf. 14***

**2194** A706 10,000r multi 3.00 1.50

A707

A708

A709

A710

Personalizable Stamps — A711

**2009 Litho. *Perf. 12½x4x12½x12½***

**2195** A707 1500r multi + label 2.00 2.00
**2196** A708 1500r multi + label 2.00 2.00
**2197** A709 1500r multi + label 2.00 2.00
**2198** A710 1500r multi + label 2.00 2.00
**2199** A711 1500r multi + label 2.00 2.00
*Nos. 2195-2199 (5)* 10.00 10.00

Nos. 2195-2199 each were printed in sheets of 8 stamps + 8 labels that could be personalized. Each sheet sold for 20,000r.

**Provincial Arms Type of 2008**

Arms of: Nos. 2200, 1500r, 2211a, 2500r, Banten (12/33). Nos. 2201, 1500r, 2211b, 2500r, Jawa Timur (East Java) (13/33). Nos. 2202, 1500r, 2211c, 2500r, Kalimantan Tengah (Central Kalimantan) (14/33). Nos. 2203, 1500r, 2211d, 2500r, Kalimantan Timur (East Kalimantan) (15/33). Nos. 2204, 1500r, 2211e, 2500r, Kepulauan Riau (Riau Archipelago) (16/33). Nos. 2205, 1500r, 2211f, 2500r, Lampung (17/33). Nos. 2206, 1500r, 2211g, 2500r, Nusa Tenggara Timur (East Nusa Tenggara) (18/33). Nos. 2207, 1500r, 2211h, 2500r, Papua Barat (West Papua) (19/33). Nos. 2208, 1500r, 2211i, 2500r, Sulawesi Tengah (Central Sulawesi) (20/33). Nos. 2209, 1500r, 2211j, 2500r, Sulawesi Tenggara (Southeast Sulawesi) (21/33). Nos. 2210, 1500r, 2211k, 2500r, Sumatera Selatan (South Sumatra) (22/33).

**2009, Aug. 17 Litho. *Perf. 12½***

**2200-2210** A679 Set of 11 5.50 2.75
**2211** Sheet of 11 + label 8.00 4.00
*a.-k.* A679 2500r Any single .75 .35

**No. 2192 Overprinted in Gold With JIPEX 2009 Emblem**

**Methods and Perfs As Before**

**2009, Oct. 28**

**2212** A704 2500r Sheet of 6, #a-f 5.50 2.25

Tourist Sites in Indonesia and Singapore — A712

Designs: 1500r, Sentosa, Singapore (4/4). 2500r, Taman Mini Indonesia Indah (Beautiful Indonesia Miniature Park), Indonesia (3/4). 4000r, Merlion, Singapore (2/4). 7500r, Singaraja Statue, Indonesia (1/4).

**2009, Oct. 28 Litho. *Perf. 13½x12¾***

**2213-2216** A712 Set of 4 5.50 2.75
*2216a* Miniature sheet, 2 each #2213-2216 10.00 5.00

See Singapore Nos. 1402-1405.

**Flora and Fauna of the Provinces Type of 2008**

Miniature Sheet

No. 2217: a, Rhinoceros sondaicus, Vatica bantenensis, Banten (1/11). b, Gallus varius x Gallus gallus, Polyanthes tuberosa, Jawa Timur (East Java) (2/11). c, Polyplectron schleirmacheri, Nephelium ramboutan-ake, Kalimantan Tengah (Central Kalimantan) (3/11). d, Orcaella brevirostris, Coelogyne pandurata, Kalimantan Timur (East Kalimantan) (4/11). e, Lutjanus sanguineus, Piper betle, Kepulauan Riau (Riau Archipelago) (5/11). f, Elephas maximus sumatranus, Magnolia candolili, Lampung (6/11). g, Varanus komodoensis, Santalum album, Nusa Tenggara Timur (East Nusa Tenggara) (7/11). h, Paradisaea rubra, Pandanus conoideus, Papua Barat (West Papua) (8/11). i, Macrocephalon maleo, Diospyros celebica, Sulawesi Tengah (Central Sulawesi) (9/11). j, Bubalus depressicornis, Diplocaulobium utile, Sulawesi Tenggara (Southeast Sulawesi) (10/11). k, Notopterus chitala, Lansium domesticum, Sumatera Selatan (South Sumatra) (11/11).

**2009, Nov. 5**

**2217** A688 2500r Sheet of 11, #a-k, + label 9.00 4.50

Buildings in Indonesia and Iran — A713

Designs: 1500r, Soltanieh Dome, Iran (2/2). 3000r, Al-Markaz Mosque, Indonesia (1/2).

**2009, Dec. 18** ***Perf. 13x13¼***

**2218** A713 1500r multi .70 .35
**2219** A713 3000r multi 1.40 .70
*a.* Miniature sheet of 12, 6 each #2218-2219 9.00 4.50

See Iran No. 3013.

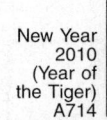

New Year 2010 (Year of the Tiger) A714

Tiger: No. 2220, 1500r, Head (1/3). No. 2221, 1500r, Walking (2/3). No. 2222, 1500r, Running (3/3).
5000r, Tiger, sky.

**2010, Feb. 6 Litho. *Perf. 13½x12¾***

**2220-2222** A714 Set of 3 1.00 .50
*2222a* Souvenir sheet of 6, 2 each #2220-2222 2.00 1.00

**Souvenir Sheet**

**2223** A714 5000r multi 1.10 .55

UNESCO Intangible Cultural Heritage A720

Designs: 1000r, Batik in Campuran design (4/6). 1500r, Hanoman puppet, vert. (3/6). 2000r, Arjuna puppet, vert. (1/6). 2500r, Kresna puppet, vert. (2/6). 3000r, Kris, vert. (6/6). No. 2234, 5000r, Batik in Kembangan design (5/6).
No. 2235, 5000r, Hanoman puppet, diff., vert. No. 2236, 5000r, Kris, diff., vert.

***Perf. 13½x12¾, 12¾x13½***

**2010, Mar. 29 Litho.**

**2229-2234** A720 Set of 6 3.50 1.75

**Souvenir Sheets**

**2235-2236** A720 Set of 2 2.25 1.10

Nos. 2235-2236 exist imperforate.

2010 World Cup Soccer Championships, South Africa — A721

No. 2237: a, Soccer player (1/4). b, Mascot (2/4). c, Emblem (3/4). d, Goalie making save (4/4).

**2010, May 1** ***Perf. 12¾x13½***

**2237** A721 1500r Block or horiz. strip of 4, #a-d 1.40 .70
*e.* Booklet pane of 4, #2237a-2237d 1.40 —
Complete booklet, #2237e 1.40

A722

Environmental Care — A723

Designs: No. 2238, Hands holding seedling (3/3).
No. 2239: a, Bird, sheep, palm tree, child (1/3). b, Earth and hands (2/3).
5000r, Like #2238.

***Perf. 12¾x13½, 13½x12¾***

**2010, June 5**

**2238** A722 1500r multi .35 .25

**2239** A723 1500r Vert. pair, #a-b .65 .30

**Souvenir Sheet**

**2240** A722 5000r multi 1.10 .55

Muhammadiyah Islamic Organization, Cent. — A724

No. 2241: a, Building (1/3). b, Kyai Haji Ahmad Dahlan (1868-1923), founder (2/3). c, Student, graduate, building (3/3).

**2010, July 3** *Perf. 12½*

**2241** Strip of 3 1.10 .55
*a.-c.* A724 1500r Any single .35 .25
*d.* Souvenir sheet of 6, 2 each #2241a-2241c 2.25 1.10

Traditional Foods A725

No. 2242: a, Sup Lobster Kelapa Muda, West Sulawesi (1/7). b, Gulai Iga Kemba'ang, Bengkulu (2/7). c, Ayam Cincane, East Kalimantan (3/7). d, Sate Udang Pentuk Asam Manis, Jambi (4/7). e, Lempah Kuning, Bangka Belitung (5/7). f, Asam Padeh Baung, Riau (6/7). g, Lapis Palaro, North Moluccas (7/7).

**2010, July 6** *Perf. 13½x12¾*

**2242** Block of 7 + label 2.50 1.25
*a.-g.* A725 1500r Any single .35 .25

Elected Leaders A726

No. 2243 — Flag and: a, Pres. Susilo Bambang Yudhoyono (1/2). b, Vice-president Boediono (2/2).

**2010, Aug. 17** *Perf. 14*

**2243** Pair 1.10 .55
*a.-b.* A726 2500r Either single .55 .25
*c.* Souvenir sheet of 2, #2243a-2243b 1.10 .55

2010 Youth Olympic Games, Singapore — A727

No. 2244 — Badminton player with denomination at: a, LR. b, LL.

**2010, July 15 Litho.** *Perf. 13½x12¾*

**2244** A727 1500r Pair, #a-b .70 .35

Bandung, 200th Anniv. — A728

No. 2245: a, Soccer player. b, R. Dewi Sartika (1884-1947), advocate for women's education.

No. 2246: a, Pasupati Bridge. b, City street. 5000r, Pasupati Bridge.

**2010, Sept. 25** *Perf. 12¾x13½*

**2245** A728 1000r Pair, #a-b .45 .25
**2246** A728 1500r Pair, #a-b .70 .35

**Souvenir Sheet**

**2247** A728 5000r multi 1.25 .60

Worldwide Fund for Nature (WWF) — A729

No. 2248 — Sea turtles: a, Lepidochelys olivacea (1/4). b, Chelonia mydas (2/4). c, Dermochelys coriacea (3/4). d, Eretmochelys imbricata (4/4).

**2010, Oct. 24** *Perf. 13½x12¾*

**2248** Strip or block of 4 3.25 2.75
*a.-d.* A729 1500r Any single .75 .25

**Flora and Fauna of the Provinces Type of 2008**

No. 2249: a, Haliastur indus, Salacca zalacca, Jakarta (5/11). b, Geopelia striata, Stelechocarpus burahol, Yogyakarta (6/11).

No. 2250: a, Gracula religiosa robusta, Cananga odorata, Sumatera Utara (North Sumatra) (1/11). b, Panthera tigris sumatrae, Cyrtostachys renda, Jambi (2/11). c, Helarctos malayanus, Amorphophallus titanum, Bengkulu (3/11). d, Tarsius bancanus saltator, Palaquium rostratum, Bangka Belitung (4/11).

2000r, Cervus timorensis, Diospyros macrophylla, Nusa Tenggara Barat (West Nusa Tenggara) (11/11).

No. 2252: a, Nasalis larvatus, Mangifera casturi, Kalimantan Selatan (South Kalimantan) (7/11). b, Aceros cassadix, Borassus flabellifer, Sulawesi Selatan (South Sulawesi) (8/11). c, Tarsius spectrum, Ficus minahassae, Sulawesi Utara (North Sulawesi) (9/11). d, Semioptera wallacii, Syzygium aromaticum, Maluku Utara (North Moluccas) (10/11).

**2010, Nov. 5** **Litho.**

**2249** A688 1000r Pair, #a-b .45 .25
**2250** A688 1500r Strip or block of 4, #a-d 1.40 .70
**2251** A688 2000r multi .45 .25
**2252** A688 2500r Strip or block of 4, #a-d 2.25 1.10
*e.* Souvenir sheet, #2249a-2249b, 2250a-2250d, 2251, 2252a-2252d, + label 4.75 2.25
*Nos. 2249-2252 (4)* 4.55 2.20

**Provincial Arms Type of 2008**

Arms of: No. 2253, 1500r, Sumatera Utara (North Sumatra) (23/33). No. 2254, 1500r, Jambi (24/33). No. 2255, 1500r, Bengkulu (25/35). No. 2256, 1500r, Kepulauan Bangka Belitung (26/33). No. 2257, 1500r, DKI Jakarta (27/33). No. 2258, 1500r, Yogyakarta (28/33). No. 2259, 1500r, Kalimantan Selatan (South Kalimantan) (29/33). No. 2260, 1500r, Sulawesi Selatan (South Sulawesi) (30/33). No. 2261, 1500r, Sulawesi Utara (North Sulawesi) (31/33). No. 2262, 1500r, Maluku Utara (North Maluku) (32/33). No. 2263, 1500r, Nusa Tenggara Barat (West Nusa Tenggara) (33/33).

No. 2264, Like #2257.

**2010, Dec. 13** **Litho.** *Perf. 12½*

**2253-2263** A679 Set of 11 3.75 1.90
*2263a* Sheet of 11, #2253-2263, + label 3.75 1.90

**Souvenir Sheet**

**2264** A679 5000r multi 1.10 .55

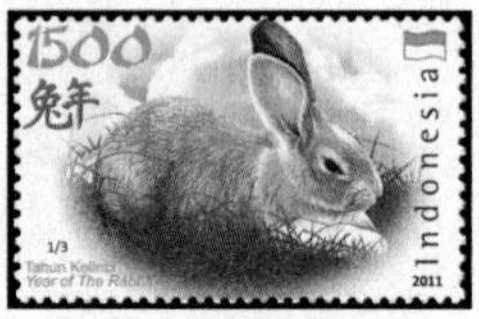


New Year 2011 (Year of the Rabbit) A730

Indonesian flag and: 1500r, Brown rabbit (1/3). 3000r, Gray rabbit (2/3). 4000r, Gray and brown rabbits (3/3).

5000r, Head of brown rabbit.

**2011, Jan. 25 Litho.** *Perf. 13½x12¾*

**2265-2267** A730 Set of 3 1.90 .95
*2267a* Sheet of 6, 2 each #2265-2267, + 2 labels 3.80 1.90

**Souvenir Sheet**

**Litho. with Foil Application**

**2268** A730 5000r multi 1.10 .55

Traditional Rituals — A731

No. 2269: a, Grebeg Syawal ritual, Yogyakarta (1/4). b, Ngaben ritual, Bali (2/4). c, Pasola ritual, Sumba, East Nusa Tenggara (3/4). d, Tiwah ritual, Dayak, Central Kalimantan (4/4).

*Perf. 13½x12¾*

**2011, Feb. 24** **Litho.**

**2269** A731 1500r Block or horiz. strip of 4, #a-d 1.40 .70

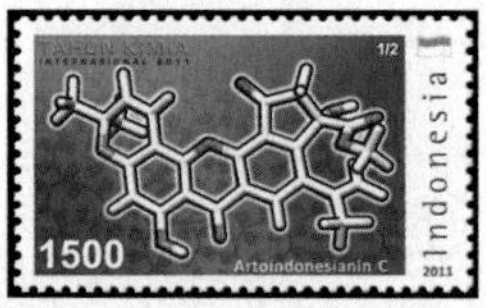


Intl. Year of Chemistry — A732

Designs: 1500r, Molecular model of Artoindonesianin C. 2500r, International Year of Chemistry emblem, vert.

*Perf. 13½x12¾, 12¾x13½*

**2011, Mar. 1**

**2270-2271** A732 Set of 2 .95 .45

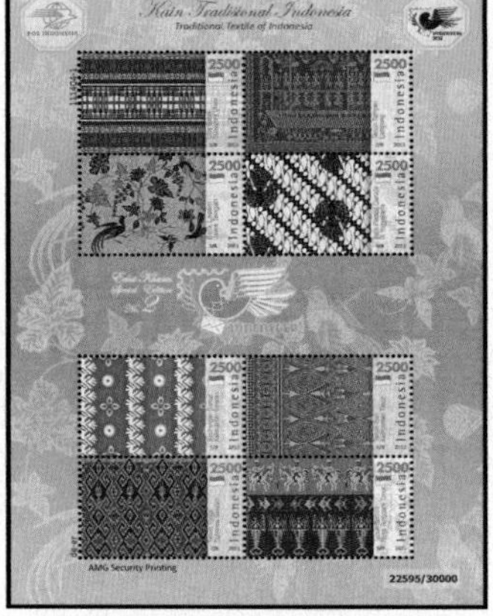


Traditional Textiles — A733

No. 2272: a, Ulos Batak, Sulawesi Utara (North Sulawesi) (1/8). b, Tenun Tampan, Lampung (2/8). c, Batik Lasem, Jawa Tengah (Central Java) (3/8). d, Batik Parang Garuda, Yogyakarta (4/8). e, Sasirangan Banjar, Kalimantan Selatan (South Kalimantan) (5/8). f, Tenun Iban, Kalimantan Timur (East Kalimantan) (6/8). g, Tenun Toraja, Sulawesi Selatan (South Sulawesi) (7/8). h, Tenun Sumba, Nusa Tenggara Timur (East Nusa Tenggara) (8/8).

5000r, Woman weaving fabric.

**2011, Mar. 30** *Perf. 13½x12¾*

**2272** A733 2500r Sheet of 8, #a-h 4.75 2.40
*i.* As #2272, with Indonesia 2012 emblem overprinted in sheet margin in metallic red 4.75 2.40

**Souvenir Sheet**

**2273** A733 5000r multi 1.25 .60
*a.* As #2273, with Indonesia 2012 emblem overprinted in sheet margin in metallic red 1.25 .60

See Nos. 2281-2282, 2292-2293, 2307-2308.

Nos. 2272i and 2273a exist imperforate.

Spacecraft — A734

No. 2274: a, Rocket on launch pad (1/2). b, TUBSAT (2/2).

**2011, Apr. 12** *Perf. 12¾x13½*

**2274** A734 2500r Pair, #a-b 1.25 .60

Internet Safety — A735

No. 2275 — Child in helmet and: a, Plug in outlet in globe (1/2). b, Children using laptop computer (2/2).

**2011, Apr. 21** *Perf. 13½x12¾*

**2275** A735 2500r Horiz. pair, #a-b 1.25 .60

No. 2275 was printed in sheets containing eight pairs and four labels.

Environmental Care — A736

No. 2276: a, Pine cone on branch (1/2). b, Squirrel on pine tree (2/2).

**2011, June 5** **Litho.**

**2276** A736 2500r Vert. pair, #a-b 1.25 .60
*c.* Souvenir sheet, #2276a-2276b 1.25 .60

Fish and Seaweed Production — A737

Designs: 1500r, Fish and vegetables on plate (3/4). 2000r, Fish and vegetables (2/4). 3000r, Man processing seaweed (4/4). 5000r, Fisherman and fish (1/4).

**2011, June 22** *Perf. 12½*

**2277-2280** A737 Set of 4 2.75 1.40
*2280a* Souvenir sheet of 4, #2277-2280 2.75 1.40

**Traditional Textiles Type of 2011**

No. 2281: a, Tenun Aceh Nanggroe, Aceh (1/8). b, Tenun Pandai Sikek, Sumatara Barat (West Sumatra) (2/8). c, Batik Basurek, Bengkulu (3/8). d, Songket Palembang, Sumatera Selatan (South Sumatra) (4/8). e, Batik Madura, Jawa Timur (East Java) (5/8). f, Tenun Sambas, Kalimantan Barat (West Kalimantan) (6/8). g, Tenun Bentenan, Sulawesi Utara (North Sulawesi) (7/8). h, Batik Masambo, Nusa Tenggara Barat (West Nusa Tenggara) (8/8).

5000r, Man behind team of oxen with Karapan Sabi, Jawa Timur (East Java).

**2011, July 6** *Perf. 13½x12¾*

**2281** A733 2500r Sheet of 8, #a-h 4.75 2.40
*i.* Like #2281, with gold design in sheet margin 4.75 2.40

**Souvenir Sheet**

**2282** A733 5000r multi 1.25 .60

Nos. 2281i, 2282 exist imperf.

Souvenir Sheet

PhilaNippon '11 World Stamp Exhibition, Yokohama, Japan — A738

**2011, July 28**

**2283** A738 10,000r multi 2.40 1.25

Friendship Between Malaysia and Indonesia A739

No. 2284: a, Proclamation Monument, Indonesia (1/8). b, 1945 Indonesia 5-sen banknote (2/8). c, Indonesia #1LM1 (3/8). d, Gallus varius (4/8).

No. 2285: a, National Monument, Malaysia (5/8). b, 1959 Malaya and North Borneo $1 banknote (6/8). c, Malaya #84 (7/8). d, Gallus gallus (8/8).

**2011, Aug. 8** *Perf. 13¼x13*

**2284** Vert strip of 4 2.40 1.25
*a.-d.* A739 2500r Any single .60 .30
**2285** Vert strip of 4 2.40 1.25
*a.-d.* A739 2500r Any single .60 .30
*e.* Sheet of 8, #2284a-2284d, 2285a-2285d 4.80 2.50

See Malaysia No. 1360.

Scouting In Indonesia, 50th Anniv. — A740

Designs: No. 2286, 2500r, Dove, Scout holding Scouting flag (1/3). No. 2287, 2500r, Four Scouts, Scouting and Indonesian flag (2/3). No. 2288, 2500r, Scout leaders teaching Scouts (3/3).
5000r, Like No. 2286.

**2011, Apr. 14** *Perf. 13½x12¾*

**2286-2288** A740 Set of 3 1.75 .90

**Souvenir Sheet**

**2289** A740 5000r multi 1.25 .60

Landmarks — A741

No. 2290: a, Lawang Sewu Building, Semarang (2/5). b, Equator Monument, Pontianak (3/5). c, Garuda Wisnu Kencana Cultural Park, Denpasar (4/5). d, Fort Rotterdam, Makassar (5/5). e, Ampera Bridge, Palembang (1/5).

**2011, Sept. 27** *Perf. 13½x12¾*

**2290** Strip of 5 3.00 1.50
*a.-e.* A741 2500r Any single .60 .30

Famous Men — A742

No. 2291: a, Dr. Mohammed Natsir (1908-93), Prime minister. b, Sutomo (1920-81), politician.

**2011, Aug. 17** *Perf. 13x13¼*

**2291** A742 2500r Horiz. pair, #a-b 1.10 .55

**Traditional Textiles Type of 2011**

No. 2292: a, Songket Malayu, Riau (1/8). b, Songket Mentok, Bangka Belitung (2/8). c, Batik Mega Mendung, Jawa Barat (West Java) (3/8). d, Tenun Sora Langi, Sulawesi Barat (West Sulawesi) (4/8). e, Tenun Tolaki, Sulawesi Tenggara (Southeast Sulawesi) (5/8). f, Tenun Tanimbar, Maluku (6/8). g, Batik Papua, Papua (7/8). h, Batik Papua Barat, Papua Barat (West Papua) (8/8).
5000r, Masked dancer, Tari Topeng, Jawa Barat (West Java).

**2011, Oct. 2 Litho.** *Perf. 13½x12¾*

**2292** A733 2500r Sheet of 8, #a-h 4.50 2.25

**Souvenir Sheet**

**2293** A733 5000r multi 1.10 .55

Operation Trikora, 50th Anniv. A743

Designs: No. 2294, 2500r, Trikora Monument, ships, map of West Papua, helicopter (1/4). No. 2295, 2500r, Soldiers and armored personnel carrier (2/4). No. 2296, 2500r, Navy ships, soldiers in water (3/4). No. 2297, 2500r, Soldiers and jet fighter (4/4).

**2011, Oct. 5** *Perf. 13½x12¾*

**2294-2297** A743 Set of 4 2.25 1.10
*2297a* Souvenir sheet of 8, 2 each #2294-2297 + 2 labels 4.50 2.25

Indonesian Historical Links With South Africa A744

No. 2298: a, Sheikh Yusuf (1626-99), establisher of Islam in South Africa (1/10). b, Balla Lampoa Museum, Sulawesi Selantan (South Sulawesi) (2/10). c, Alat Musik Tifa, Papua (3/10). d, Topi Tilangga, Nusa Tenggara Timur, and Kelom Geulis, Jawa Barat (West Java) (4/10). e, Tari Pakarena, Sulawesi Selatan (South Sulawesi) (5/10).

**2011, Oct. 15** *Perf. 13¼x13*

**2298** A744 2500r Vert. strip of 5, #a-e 3.00 1.50

See South Africa No. 1469.

2011 South East Asian Games, Jakarta and Palembang — A745

No. 2299: a, Mascot and tower in Jakarta (1/6). b, Mascot and towers in Palembang (2/6). c, Mascot playing soccer (5/6). d, Mascot in pencak silat outfit (6/6). e, Mascot playing table tennis (3/6). f, Mascot playing badminton (4/6).

**2011, Oct. 18** *Perf. 12¾x13½*

**2299** A745 2500r Block of 6, #a-f 3.50 1.75

Flora and Fauna — A746

Nos. 2300 and 2301: a, Leptophryne cruentata. b, Nymphoides indica.

**2011, Nov. 5** *Perf. 13½x12¾*

**2300** A746 2500r Horiz. pair, #a-b 1.10 .55
*c.* Vert. tete-beche pair 1.10 .55

**Souvenir Sheet**

**2301** A746 5000r Sheet of 2, #a-b 2.25 1.10

No. 2301 has a curved die-cut slit that encompasses the stamps and text in the sheet margin.

China 2011 International Stamp Exhibition, Wuxi, People's Republic of China — A747

**2011** **Litho.**

**2302** A747 10,000r multi 2.25 1.10

New Year 2012 (Year of the Dragon) A748

No. 2303 — Various dragons: a, Green and multicolored (1/3). b, Red brown and multicolored (2/3). c, Indigo and multicolored (3/3).
5000r, Dragon, diff.

**2012, Jan. 15** *Perf. 13½x12¾*

**2303** Strip of 3 1.75 .85
*a.-c.* A748 2500r Any single .55 .25
*d.* Souvenir sheet of 6, 2 each #2303a-2303c, + 2 labels 3.50 1.75

**Souvenir Sheet**

**2304** A748 5000r multi 1.10 .55

National Sports Week — A749

No. 2305 — Mascot: a, Parachuting (1/6). b, Shooting (2/6). c, On gymnastic rings (3/6). d, Playing sepak takraw (4/6). e, Sailboarding (5/6). f, Canoeing (6/6).

**2012, Feb. 22**

**2305** A749 2500r Block of 6, #a-f 3.50 1.75

Asian-Pacific Postal Union, 50th Anniv. — A750

**2012, Apr. 1**

**2306** A750 5000r multi 1.10 .55

**Traditional Textiles Type of 2011**

No. 2307: a, Batik Bongbong, Riau Kepulauan (25/33). b, Batik Angso Duo, Jambi (26/33). c, Tenun Baduy, Banten (27/33). d, Tenun Gringsing, Bali (28/33). e, Kain Benang Bintik, Kalimantan Tengah (Central Kalimantan) (29/33). f, Tenun Donggala, Sulawesi Tengah (Central Sulawesi) (30/33). g, Kain Kerawang, Gorontalo (31/33). h, Batik Ternate, Maluku Utara (North Moluccas) (32/33). i, As "a," numbered 1/8. j, As "b," numbered 2/8. k, As "c," numbered 3/8. l, As "d," numbered 4/8. m, As "e," numbered 5/8. n, As "f," numbered 6/8. o, As "g," numbered 7/8. p, As "h," numbered 8/8.
5000r, Tari Barong, Bali.

**2012, Apr. 21**

**2307** A733 2500r Block of 8, #a-h 4.50 2.25
*i.-p.* Any single .55 .25
*q.* Souvenir sheet of 8, #2307i-2307p 4.50 2.25

**Souvenir Sheet**

**2308** A733 5000r multi 1.10 .55

No. 2307 was printed in a sheet containing three blocks of eight stamps. No. 2308 is dated 2011.

Environmental Care — A751

No. 2309: a, Gasoline pump nozzle (1/2). b, Rhinoceros, Earth in drop of gasoline (2/2).
5000r, Gasoline pump nozzle, rhinoceros, Earth in drop of gasoline, vert.

**2012, June 5** *Perf. 13½x12¾*

**2309** A751 2000r Vert. pair, #a-b .85 .40

**Souvenir Sheet**

**2310** A751 5000r multi 1.10 .55

No. 2310 contains one 42x51mm stamp.

Traditional Foods A752

No. 2311: a, Daging Sei and Jagung Bose, Nusa Tenggara Timur (1/2). b, Gulai Asam Pedas, Kepulauan Riau (2/2).

**2012, July 6** **Litho.**

**2311** A752 2500r Pair, #a-b 1.10 .55

No. 2311 was printed in sheets containing 10 pairs and a central label.

Endangered Birds — A753

No. 2312: a, Otus siaoensis (1/4). b, Nisaetus floris (2/4). c, Aethopyga duyvenbodei (3/4). d, Habroptila wallacii (4/4).

**2012, July 15** *Perf. 14*

**2312** A753 2500r Block of 4, #a-d 2.10 1.10
*e.* Souvenir sheet of 4, #2312a-2312d 2.10 1.10

Scouting in Indonesia, Cent. — A763

No. 2324 — Scouts at flag ceremony with denomination at: a, Left (1/2). b, Right (2/2).

*Perf. 13½x12¾*

**2012, Aug. 14** **Litho.**

**2324** A763 2500r Horiz. pair, #a-b 1.10 .55
*c.* Souvenir sheet of 2, #2324a-2324b 1.10 .55

Television Broadcasting in Indonesia, 50th Anniv. — A764

No. 2325: a, Black-and-white television (1/2). b, High-definition color television (2/2).

**2012, Aug. 24**

**2325** A764 2500r Pair, #a-b 1.10 .55

People at Building Site — A765

Various People A766

People Holding Hands — A767

*Perf. 12¾x13½, 13½x12¾ (A766)*

**2012, Oct. 1**

**2326** Strip of 3 1.60 .80
*a.* A765 2500r multi (1/3) .50 .25
*b.* A766 2500r multi (2/3) .50 .25
*c.* A767 2500r multi (3/3) .50 .25

Houses of Worship A768

No. 2327: a, Masjid Agung, Palembang (3/5). b, Pura, Besakih (4/5). c, Wihara Dharma Bhakti, Jakarta (5/5). d, Gereja Blenduk, Semarang (1/5). e, Gereja Puhsarang, Kediri (2/5).

**2012, Oct. 27** *Perf. 13½x12¾*

**2327** Strip of 5 2.60 1.25
*a.-e.* A768 2500r Any single .50 .25

Flora and Fauna — A769

Nos. 2328 and 2329: a, Spilocuscus rufoniger (1/2). b, Kandelia candel (2/2). Stamps on No. 2329 lack "1/2" and "2/2."

**2012, Nov. 5** *Perf. 12¾x13½*

**2328** A769 2500r Pair, #a-b 1.10 .55

**Souvenir Sheet**

**2329** A769 5000r Sheet of 2, #a-b 2.10 1.10

---

## SEMI-POSTAL STAMPS

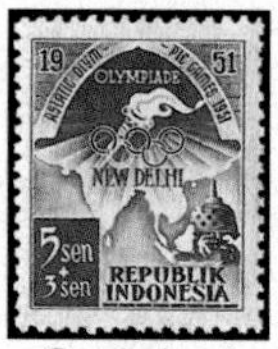

Symbols of Olympic Games SP43

Wings and Flame SP44

*Perf. 12½x12*

**1951, Jan. 2** **Photo.** **Unwmk.**

**B58** SP43 5s + 3s gray grn .25 .25
**B59** SP43 10s + 5s dk vio bl .25 .25
**B60** SP43 20s + 5s org red .25 .25
**B61** SP43 30s + 10s dk brn .65 .25
**B62** SP43 35s + 10s ultra 3.00 2.10
*Nos. B58-B62 (5)* 4.40 3.10

Issued to publicize the Asiatic Olympic Games of 1951 at New Delhi, India.

**1951, Oct. 15**

**B63** SP44 5s + 3s olive green .30 .30
**B64** SP44 10s + 5s dull blue .30 .30
**B65** SP44 20s + 5s red .35 .30
**B66** SP44 30s + 10s brown .45 .30
**B67** SP44 35s + 10s ultra .80 *1.10*
*Nos. B63-B67 (5)* 2.20 2.30

2nd Natl. Games, Djakarta, 10/21-28/51.

No. 378 Surcharged in Black

**1953, May 8** *Perf. 12½*

**B68** A53 35s + 10s purple .40 .25

The surcharge reads "Natural Disaster." Surtax was for emergency relief following volcanic eruption and floods.

Merapi Erupting SP45

Young Musicians SP46

**1954, Apr. 15** **Litho.** *Perf. 12½x12*

**B69** SP45 15s + 10s bl grn 1.25 *1.75*
**B70** SP45 35s + 15s pur 1.25 *1.40*
**B71** SP45 50s + 25s red 1.25 *1.40*
**B72** SP45 75s + 25s vio bl 1.25 *1.40*
**B73** SP45 1r + 25s car 1.25 *1.40*
**B74** SP45 2r + 50s blk brn 3.25 *1.40*
**B75** SP45 3r + 1r gray grn 12.00 8.75
**B76** SP45 5r + 2.50r org brn 14.00 12.00
*Nos. B69-B76 (8)* 35.50 29.50

The surtax was for victims of the Merapi volcano eruption.

**1954, Dec. 22** **Photo.** *Perf. 12½*

15s+10s, Parasol dance. 35s+15s, Girls playing dakon. 50s+15s, Boy on stilts. 75s+25s, Bamboo flute players. 1r+25s, Javanese dancer.

**B77** SP46 10s + 10s dk pur .25 *.70*
**B78** SP46 15s + 10s dk grn .25 *.80*
**B79** SP46 35s + 15s car rose .25 *.80*
**B80** SP46 50s + 15s rose brn .45 *.80*
**B81** SP46 75s + 25s ultra .40 *3.00*
**B82** SP46 1r + 25s red org .70 *5.00*
*Nos. B77-B82 (6)* 2.30 *11.10*

The surtax was for child welfare.

Scout Emblem SP47

Scout Signaling SP48

Designs: 50s+25s, Campfire. 75s+25s, Scout feeding fawn. 1r+50s, Scout saluting.

**1955, June 27** **Unwmk.** *Perf. 12½*

**B83** SP47 15s + 10s bl grn .40 *.50*
**B84** SP48 35s + 15s ultra .40 *.50*
**B85** SP48 50s + 25s scar .40 *.50*
**B86** SP48 75s + 25s brn .40 *.50*
**B87** SP48 1r + 50s vio .40 *.50*
*Nos. B83-B87 (5)* 2.00 *2.50*

First National Boy Scout Jamboree.

Blind Weaver SP49

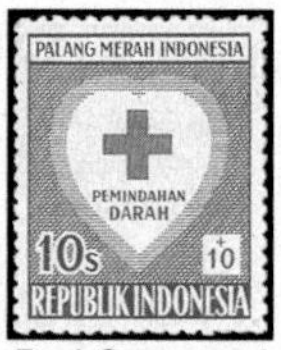

Red Cross and Heart SP50

35s+15s, Basket weaver. 50s+25s, Boy studying map. 75s+50s, Woman reading Braille.

**1956, Jan. 4**

**B88** SP49 15s + 10s dp grn .25 .70
**B89** SP49 35s + 15s yel brn .30 .70
**B90** SP49 50s + 25s rose car 2.25 1.50
**B91** SP49 75s + 50s ultra 1.25 .70
*Nos. B88-B91 (4)* 4.05 3.60

The surtax was for the benefit of the blind.

**1956, July 26** **Litho.**

Designs: 35s+15s, 50s+15s, Transfusion bottle. 75s+25s, 1r+25s, Outstretched hands.

**Cross in Red**

**B92** SP50 10s + 10s ultra .25 .25
**B93** SP50 15s + 10s carmine .25 .25
**B94** SP50 35s + 15s lt brn .25 .25
**B95** SP50 50s + 15s bl grn .45 .25
**B96** SP50 75s + 25s orange .45 .30
**B97** SP50 1r + 25s brt pur .45 .45
*Nos. B92-B97 (6)* 2.10 1.75

Surtax for the Indonesian Red Cross.

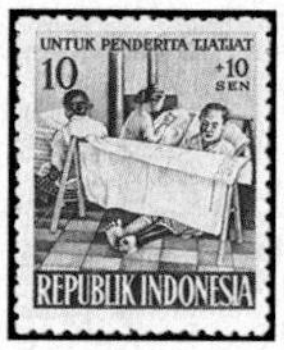

Invalids Doing Batik Work — SP51

Designs: 15s+10s, Amputee painting. 35s+15s, Lathe operator. 50s+15s, Crippled child learning to walk. 75s+25s, Treating amputee. 1r+25s, Painting with artificial hand.

**1957, Mar. 26** **Photo.** *Perf. 12½*

**B98** SP51 10s + 10s dp blue .25 .25
**B99** SP51 15s + 10s brown .30 .25
**B100** SP51 35s + 15s red .30 .25
**B101** SP51 50s + 15s dp vio .30 .30
**B102** SP51 75s + 25s green .45 .40
**B103** SP51 1r + 25s dk car rose .45 *.65*
*Nos. B98-B103 (6)* 2.05 2.10

The surtax was for rehabilitation of invalids.

Kembodja Flower
SP52

Designs: 15s+10s, Michelia. 35s+15s, Sunflower. 50s+15s, Jasmine. 75s+50s, Orchid.

**1957, Dec. 23** ***Perf. 13½x12½***
**Flowers in Natural Colors**

**B104** SP52 10s + 10s blue 2.00 1.25
**B105** SP52 15s + 10s dp yel grn 1.40 1.25
**B106** SP52 35s + 15s dk red brn .70 *.95*
**B107** SP52 50s + 15s ol & dk brn .50 *.80*
**B108** SP52 75s + 60s rose brn .55 *.80*
*Nos. B104-B108 (5)* 5.15 5.05

Children
SP53

Indonesian Scout Emblem
SP54

15s+10s, 50s+25s, 1r+50s, Girl and boy.

**1958, July 1** **Photo.** ***Perf. 12½x12***

**B109** SP53 10s + 10s blue .25 .25
**B110** SP53 15s + 10s rose brn .25 .25
**B111** SP53 35s + 15s gray green .25 .25
**B112** SP53 50s + 25s gray olive .25 .25
**B113** SP53 75s + 50s brn car .25 .25
**B114** SP53 1r + 50s brown .25 .25
*Nos. B109-B114 (6)* 1.50 1.50

The surtax was for orphans.

**1959, July 17** **Photo.** **Unwmk.**

Design: 15s + 10s, 50s + 25s, 1r + 50s, Scout emblem and compass.

**Emblem in Red**

**B115** SP54 10s + 5s bister .25 .25
**B116** SP54 15s + 10s bluish grn .25 .25
**B117** SP54 20s + 10s lilac gray .25 *.30*
**B118** SP54 50s + 25s olive .30 *.50*
**B119** SP54 75s + 35s yel brn .30 *.50*
**B120** SP54 1r + 50s dark gray .30 *.50*
*Nos. B115-B120 (6)* 1.65 2.30

10th World Scout Jamboree, Makiling National Park near Manila, July 17-26.

Palm-leaf Ribs, Gong and 5 Rings
SP55

Young Couple Holding Sharpened Bamboo Weapon
SP56

Design: 20s+10s, 75s+35s, Bamboo musical instrument and 5-ring emblem.

**1960, Feb. 14** ***Perf. 12½x12***

**B121** SP55 15s + 5s bis & dk brn .25 .30
**B122** SP55 20s + 10s grn & blk .25 .30
**B123** SP55 50s + 25s bl & pur .25 .30
**B124** SP55 75s + 35s ol & dk grn .25 .30
**B125** SP56 1.15r + 50s car & blk .35 .30
*Nos. B121-B125 (5)* 1.35 1.50

All-Indonesian Youth Cong., Bandung, 2/14-21/60.

Social Emblem — SP57

Designs: 15s+15s, Rice, lotus and cotton. 20s+20s, Lotus blossom and tree. 50s+25s, Girl and boy. 75s+25s, Watering of plant in man's hand. 3r+50s, Woman nursing infant.

***Perf. 12½x12***
**1960, Dec. 20** **Photo.** **Unwmk.**
**Inscribed: "Hari Sosial Ke III"**

**B126** SP57 10s + 10s ocher & blk .25 .25
**B127** SP57 15s + 15s dp cl & blk .25 .25
**B128** SP57 20s + 20s bl & blk .25 .25
**B129** SP57 50s + 25s bis brn & blk .25 .30
**B130** SP57 75s + 25s emer & blk .25 .30
**B131** SP57 3r + 50s red & blk .30 .30
*Nos. B126-B131 (6)* 1.55 1.65

3rd Social Day, Dec. 20.

Type of 1960 Surcharged: "BENTJANA ALAM 1961"

**1961, Feb. 17** ***Perf. 12x12½***

**B132** A76 15s + 10s plum .25 .25
**B133** A76 20s + 15s ocher .25 .25
**B134** A76 75s + 25s scarlet .25 .25
*Nos. B132-B134 (3)* .75 .75

The surtax was for flood relief.

Pineapple — SP58

4th Social Day: 75s+25s, Mangosteen. 3r+1r, Rambutan.

**1961, Dec. 20** ***Perf. 12½x13½***

**B135** SP58 20s + 10s bl, yel & red .40 .50
**B136** SP58 75s + 25s gray, grn & dp claret .65 .50
**B137** SP58 3r + 1r grn, yel & red 1.25 1.40
*Nos. B135-B137 (3)* 2.30 2.40

Istiqlal Mosque, Djakarta — SP59

40s+20s, 3r+1r, Different view of mosque.

**1962, Feb. 22** ***Perf. 12½x12***

**B138** SP59 30s + 20s Prus grn & yel .25 .30
**B139** SP59 40s + 20s dk red & yel .25 .30
**B140** SP59 1.50r + 50s brn & yel .50 .30
**B141** SP59 3r + 1r grn & yel .55 .30
*Nos. B138-B141 (4)* 1.55 1.20

Issued for the benefit of the new Istiqlal Mosque.

National Monument, Djakarta — SP60

1.50r+50s, 6r+1.50r, Aerial view of monument.

**1962, May 20** **Photo.** ***Perf. 12x12½***

**B142** SP60 1r + 50s org brn & blk .25 .25
**B143** SP60 1.50r + 50s ol grn & ultra .25 .25
**B144** SP60 3r + 1r lil rose & dk grn .30 .25
**B145** SP60 6r + 1.50r vio bl & red .45 .25
*Nos. B142-B145 (4)* 1.25 1.00

Vanda Tricolor
SP61

Orchids: 1.50r+50s, Phalaenopsis amabilis, vert. 3r+1r, Dendrobium phalaenopsis, vert. 6r+1.50r, Paphiopedilum praestans.

***Perf. 13½x12½, 12½x13½***
**1962, Dec. 20** **Unwmk.**
**Orchids in Natural Colors**

**B146** SP61 1r + 50s ultra & yel .40 .25
**B147** SP61 1.50r + 50s grnsh bl & ver .40 .25
**B148** SP61 3r + 1r dp bl & ocher .40 .25
**B149** SP61 6r + 1.50r org & dl vio .40 .25
*Nos. B146-B149 (4)* 1.60 1.00

Issued for the 5th Social Day.

West Irian Monument, Djakarta — SP62

**1963, Feb. 15** ***Perf. 12½x13½***

**B150** SP62 1r + 50s rose red & blk .25 .25
**B151** SP62 1.50r + 50s mag & dk brn .25 .25
**B152** SP62 3r + 1r bl & dk brn .25 .25
**B153** SP62 6r + 1.50r grn & brn .25 .25
*Nos. B150-B153 (4)* 1.00 1.00

The surtax was for the construction of the West Irian Monument in Djakarta.

Erupting Volcano
SP63

**1963, June 29** **Photo.** ***Perf. 13½x13***

**B154** SP63 4r + 2r rose red .25 .25
**B155** SP63 6r + 3r grnsh bl .25 .25

The surtax was for victims of national natural disasters.

Papilio Blumei, Celebes — SP64

Butterflies: 4r+1r, Charaxes dehaani, Java. 6r+1.50r, Graphium, West Irian. 12r+3r, Troides amphrysus, Sumatra.

**1963, Dec. 20** ***Perf. 12x12½***

**B156** SP64 1.75r + 50s multi .35 .25
**B157** SP64 4r + 1r multi .35 .25
**B158** SP64 6r + 1.50r multi .35 .25
**B159** SP64 12r + 3r multi .70 .40
*Nos. B156-B159 (4)* 1.75 1.15

Issued for the 6th Social Day.

Malaysian Fantails — SP65

Birds: 6r+1.50r, Zebra doves. 12r+3r, Black drongos. 20r+5r, Black-naped orioles. 30r+7.50r, Javanese sparrows.

***Perf. 12½x13½***
**1965, Jan. 25** **Photo.** **Unwmk.**

**B160** SP65 4r + 1r dl yel, lil & blk .50 .25
**B161** SP65 6r + 1.50 grn, blk & pink .50 .25
**B162** SP65 12r + 3r ol & blk .50 .30
**B163** SP65 20r + 5r gray, yel & red .50 .40
**B164** SP65 30r + 7.50r car rose, sl bl & blk .75 .40
*Nos. B160-B164 (5)* 2.75 1.60

Issued for the 7th Social Day.

Type of Regular Issue, 1964, Inscribed Vertically "Conefo"

**1965** ***Perf. 12½x12***

**B165** A98 1r + 1r org red & brn .25 .25
**B166** A98 1.25r + 1.25r org red & brn .25 .25
**B167** A98 1.75r + 1.75r org, red & brn blk .25 .25
**B168** A98 2r + 2r org red & sl grn .25 .25
**B169** A98 2.50r + 2.50r org red & red brn .25 .25
**B170** A98 4r + 3.50r org red & dp bl .25 .25
**B171** A98 6r + 4r org red & emer .25 .25
**B172** A98 10r + 5r org red & yel grn .25 .25
**B173** A98 12r + 5.50r org red & org .25 .25
**B174** A98 15r + 7.50r org red & bl grn .25 .25
**B175** A98 20r + 10r org red & dk gray .25 .25
**B176** A98 25r + 10r org red & pur .25 .25
**B177** A98 40r + 15r ver & plum .25 .25
**B178** A98 50r + 15r org red & dp vio .25 .25
**B179** A98 100r + 25r org red & dk ol gray .25 .25
*Nos. B165-B179 (15)* 3.75 3.75

Conference of New Emerging Forces.

Makara Mask and Magic Rays — SP66

**1965, July 17** ***Perf. 12***

**B180** SP66 20r + 10r red & dk bl .35 .25
**B181** SP66 30r + 15r bl & dk red .35 .25

Issued to publicize the fight against cancer.

Family and Produce
SP67

State Principles: 20r+10r, Humanitarianism; clasped hands, globe, flags and chain. 25r+10r, Nationalism; map of Indonesia and tree. 40r+15r, Democracy; conference and bull's head. 50r+15r, Belief in God; houses of worship and star.

**1965, Aug. 17 Photo. *Perf. 12½***

| | | | |
|---|---|---|---|
| **B182** SP67 | 10r + 5r fawn, yel & blk | .40 | .25 |
| **B183** SP67 | 20r + 10r dp yel, red & blk | .30 | .25 |
| **B184** SP67 | 25r + 10r rose red, red, grn & blk | .30 | .25 |
| **B185** SP67 | 40r + 15r bl, red & blk | .45 | .25 |
| **B186** SP67 | 50r + 15r lil, yel & blk | .45 | .25 |
| | *Nos. B182-B186 (5)* | 1.90 | 1.25 |

Samudra Beach Hotel and Pres. Sukarno — SP68

Designs: 25r+10r, 80r+20r, Ambarrukmo Palace Hotel and Pres. Sukarno.

**1965, Dec. 1 Photo. *Perf. 12½***

| | | | |
|---|---|---|---|
| **B187** SP68 | 10r + 5r dk bl & lt bl grn | .25 | .30 |
| **B188** SP68 | 25r + 10r vio blk & yel grn | .30 | .30 |
| **B189** SP68 | 40r + 15r dk brn & vio bl | .40 | .40 |
| **B190** SP68 | 80r + 20r dk pur & org | .60 | .40 |
| | *Nos. B187-B190 (4)* | 1.55 | 1.40 |

Issued for tourist publicity.

Gloriosa — SP69

40r+15r, Magaguabush. 80r+20r, Balsam. 100r+25r, Crape myrtle.

**1965, Dec. 20 Photo. *Perf. 12***

**Flowers in Natural Colors**

| | | | |
|---|---|---|---|
| **B191** SP69 | 30r + 10r deep blue | .70 | .95 |
| **B192** SP69 | 40r + 15r deep blue | .70 | .95 |
| **B193** SP69 | 80r + 20r deep blue | .70 | .95 |
| **B194** SP69 | 100r + 25r deep blue | .70 | .95 |
| | *Nos. B191-B194 (4)* | 2.80 | 3.80 |

**Dated "1966"**

10s+5s, Senna. 20s+5s, Crested barleria. 30s+10s, Scarlet ixora. 40s+10s, Rose of China (hibiscus).

**1966, Feb. 10**

**Flowers in Natural Colors**

| | | | |
|---|---|---|---|
| **B195** SP69 | 10s + 5s Prus bl | .55 | .95 |
| **B196** SP69 | 20s + 5s grn | .55 | .95 |
| **B197** SP69 | 30s + 10s grn | .55 | .95 |
| **B198** SP69 | 40s + 10s Prus bl | .55 | .95 |
| | *Nos. B195-B198 (4)* | 2.20 | 3.80 |

Nos. B191-B198 issued for the 8th Social Day, Dec. 20, 1965. An imperf. souvenir sheet contains one No. B198. Size: 58x78mm. Value, $7.

Type of 1965 Inscribed: "BENTJANA ALAM / NASIONAL 1966"

15s+5s, Gloriosa. 25s+5s, Magaguabush. 30s+10s, Balsam. 80s+20s, Crape myrtle.

**1966, May 2**

**Flowers in Natural Colors**

| | | | |
|---|---|---|---|
| **B199** SP69 | 15s + 5s blue | .40 | .65 |
| **B200** SP69 | 25s + 5s dk bl | .40 | .65 |
| **B201** SP69 | 30s + 10s dk bl | .45 | .65 |
| **B202** SP69 | 80s + 20s lt bl | 1.00 | .65 |
| | *Nos. B199-B202 (4)* | 2.25 | 2.60 |

The surtax was for victims of national natural disasters.

Reticulated Python — SP70

Reptiles: 3r+50s, Bloodsucker. 4r+75s. Saltwater crocodile. 6r+1r, Hawksbill turtle (incorrectly inscribed *chelonia mydas,* "green turtle").

**1966, Dec. 20 Photo. *Perf. 12½x12***

| | | | |
|---|---|---|---|
| **B203** SP70 | 2r + 25s multi | .30 | .30 |
| **B204** SP70 | 3r + 50s multi | .30 | .30 |
| **B205** SP70 | 4r + 75s multi | .55 | .30 |
| **B206** SP70 | 6r + 1r multi | .65 | .30 |
| | *Nos. B203-B206 (4)* | 1.80 | 1.20 |

Flooded Village SP71

Buddha & Stupa, Borobudur Temple SP72

2.50r+25s, Landslide. 4r+40s, Fire destroying village. 5r+50s, Erupting volcano.

**1967, Dec. 20 Photo. *Perf. 12½***

| | | | |
|---|---|---|---|
| **B207** SP71 | 1.25r + 10s dl vio bl & yel | .30 | .40 |
| **B208** SP71 | 2.50r + 25s dl vio bl & yel | .30 | .40 |
| **B209** SP71 | 4r + 40s dp org & blk | .30 | .40 |
| **B210** SP71 | 5r + 50s dp org & blk | .50 | .40 |
| *a.* | Souv. sheet of 2, #B209-B210 | *30.00* | *45.00* |
| | *Nos. B207-B210 (4)* | 1.40 | 1.60 |

Surtax for victims of natl. natural disasters.

**1968, Mar. 1 Photo. *Perf. 12½***

Designs: No. B211, Musicians. No. B212, Sudhana and Princess Manohara. No. B213, Procession with elephant and horses.

| | | | |
|---|---|---|---|
| **B211** SP72 | 2.50r + 25s brt grn & gray ol | .55 | .30 |
| **B212** SP72 | 2.50r + 25s brt grn & gray ol | .55 | .30 |
| **B213** SP72 | 2.50r + 25s brt grn & gray ol | .55 | .30 |
| *a.* | Souv. sheet of 3, #B211-B213 | *30.00* | *40.00* |
| *b.* | Strip of 3, #B211-B213 | 1.75 | 1.75 |
| **B214** SP72 | 7.50r + 75s org & gray ol | .55 | .30 |
| | *Nos. B211-B214 (4)* | 2.20 | 1.20 |

The surtax was to help save Borobudur Temple in Central Java, c. 800 A.D.

No. B213b has continuous design showing a frieze from Borobudur.

Scout with Pickax — SP73

Designs: 10r+1r, Bugler. 30r+3r, Scouts singing around campfire, horiz.

**1968, June 1 Photo. *Perf. 12½***

**Size: 28½x44½mm**

| | | | |
|---|---|---|---|
| **B215** SP73 | 5r + 50 dp org & brn | .50 | .50 |
| **B216** SP73 | 10r + 1r brn & gray ol | .60 | .75 |

**Size: 68x28½mm**

| | | | |
|---|---|---|---|
| **B217** SP73 | 30r + 3r ol gray & grn | 1.00 | .65 |
| | *Nos. B215-B217 (3)* | 2.10 | 1.90 |

Surtax for Wirakarya Scout Camp.

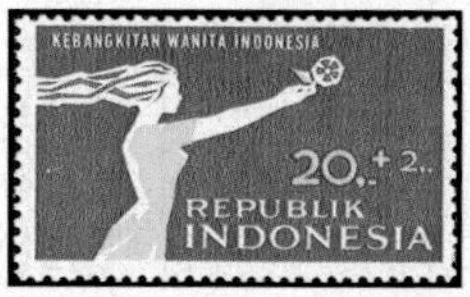


Woman with Flower SP74

**1969, Apr. 21 *Perf. 13½x12½***

| | | | |
|---|---|---|---|
| **B218** SP74 | 20r + 2r emer, red & yel | .75 | .40 |

Emancipation of Indonesian women.

Noble Voluta — SP75

Sea shells: 7.50r+50s, Common hairy triton. 10r+1r, Spider conch. 15r+1.50r, Murex ternispina.

**1969, Dec. 20 Photo. *Perf. 12½***

| | | | |
|---|---|---|---|
| **B219** SP75 | 5r + 50s multi | .40 | .55 |
| **B220** SP75 | 7.50r + 50s multi | .45 | .55 |
| **B221** SP75 | 10r + 1r multi | .75 | .80 |
| **B222** SP75 | 15r + 1.50r multi | .65 | .80 |
| | *Nos. B219-B222 (4)* | 2.25 | 2.70 |

Issued for the 12th Social Day, Dec. 20.

Chrysocoris Javanus SP76

Insects: 15r+1.50r, Dragonfly. 20r+2r, Carpenter bee.

**1970, Dec. 21 Photo. *Perf. 12½***

| | | | |
|---|---|---|---|
| **B223** SP76 | 7.50r + 50c multi | *6.00* | *1.60* |
| **B224** SP76 | 15r + 1.50r multi | *15.00* | *8.00* |
| **B225** SP76 | 20r + 2r multi | *19.00* | *5.50* |
| | *Nos. B223-B225 (3)* | *40.00* | *15.10* |

The 13th Social Day, Dec. 20.

Fight Against Cancer — SP77

Patient receiving radiation treatment, Jakarta Hospital.

**1983, July 1 Photo. *Perf. 12½***

| | | | |
|---|---|---|---|
| **B226** SP77 | 55r + 20r multi | .80 | .50 |
| **B227** SP77 | 75r + 25r multi | 1.40 | .50 |

Children's Day SP78

Children's Drawings. Surtax was for Children's Palace building fund.

**1984, June 17 Photo. *Perf. 13½x13***

| | | | |
|---|---|---|---|
| **B228** SP78 | 75r + 25r multi | .95 | .25 |
| **B229** SP78 | 110r + 25r multi | 1.25 | .25 |
| **B230** SP78 | 175r + 25r multi | 1.75 | .40 |
| **B231** SP78 | 275r + 25r multi | 3.00 | .50 |
| *a.* | Souv. sheet of 2, #B230-B231 | *30.00* | *30.00* |
| *b.* | Souv. sheet of 4 + 2 labels | *25.00* | *25.00* |
| | *Nos. B228-B231 (4)* | 6.95 | 1.40 |

AUSIPEX '84. No. B231b for FILACENTO '84, Netherlands, Sept. 6-9.

SP79

SP80

**1987, May 12 Photo. *Perf. 12½***

| | | | |
|---|---|---|---|
| **B232** SP79 | 350r +25r dark ultra & yel | 2.25 | .60 |

Yayasan Cancer Medical Assoc., 10th anniv.

**1991, June 1 Photo. *Perf. 12½***

| | | | |
|---|---|---|---|
| **B233** SP80 | 200r +25r multi | 1.25 | .30 |

Natl. Fed. for Welfare of Mentally Handicapped, 24th anniv.

Yayasan Cancer Medical Assoc., 15th Anniv. — SP81

**1992, May 12 Photo. *Perf. 12½***

| | | | |
|---|---|---|---|
| **B234** SP81 | 200r +25r brown & mag | .50 | .25 |
| **B235** SP81 | 500r +50r blue & mag | 1.00 | .35 |

Natl. Kidney Foundation — SP82

***Perf. 13½x12½***

**1994, Apr. 30 Photo.**

| | | | |
|---|---|---|---|
| **B236** SP82 | 300r +30r multi | 1.00 | .30 |

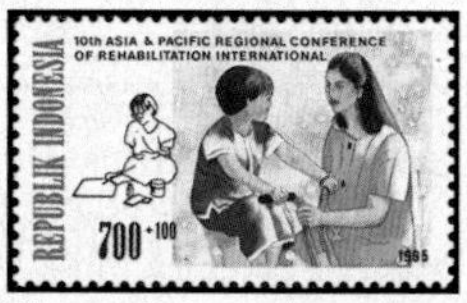


Rehibilitation Intl., 10th Asia & Pacific Regional Conference — SP83

Design: 700r+100r, Painting, Mother's Love, by disabled artist Patricia Saerang.

***Perf. 13½x12½***

**1995, Sept. 12 Photo.**

| | | | |
|---|---|---|---|
| **B238** SP83 | 700r +100r multi | 1.60 | .85 |

March 1, 1949, Day of Total Attack SP84

Designs: No. B239, Natl. flag, tanks, map. No. B240, Soldiers fighting, soldiers standing at attention, natl. flag.

**1996, Mar. 1 Photo. *Perf. 13½x12½***

| | | | |
|---|---|---|---|
| **B239** SP84 | 700r +100r multi | 1.60 | .80 |
| **B240** SP84 | 700r +100r multi | 1.60 | .80 |
| *a.* | Pair, #B239-B240 | 3.25 | 1.60 |

World AIDS Day SP85

**1997, Dec. 1 Photo. *Perf. 13½x12½***

**B241** SP85 700r +100r multi 1.25 .65

PETA (Pembela Tanah Air) Volunteer Army — SP86

***Perf. 12½x13½***

**1998, Nov. 10 Litho.**

**B242** SP86 700r Statue, museum .80 .25

National Disaster Fund — SP87

**2005, May 20 Litho. *Perf. 12½***

**B243** SP87 1500r +300r multi + label 1.25 1.25

Surtax for victims of Dec. 26, 2004 tsunami.

---

## AIR POST STAMPS

Airplane, Marshal Surydarma AP1

Airplane Over Buffalo Canyon AP2

Designs: 10s, Airplane, Air Chief Marshal Suryadi Surydarma. 20s, Sentry and aircraft, Lake Toba, Sumatra. 30s, Pilots. 40c, Indian Red Cross plane, Sumatra. 50s, Red Cross plane. 75s, Airplane over Buffalo Canyon. 1r, Crew studying flight plan. 1½r, Aircraft over Tjipanas Fish Ponds, Java. 4½r, DC-3 over rice fields. 7½r, DC-4 over Indonesian Archipelago.

Nos. C10, C12 and C13 are overprinted ("POS UDARA" and Airplane) on Nos. 22-24.

***Perf. 14½, 12½ (#C10, C12, C13)***

**1948, Dec. 15 Photo.**

**C1** AP1 10s dk lilac & brn .35 —
**C2** AP1 20s Pruss grn & org red .40 —
**C3** AP1 30s dp blue & dull lil .45 —
**C4** AP1 40s red brn & blue emerald .25 —
**C5** AP1 50s dp vio & dull bl .25 —
**C6** AP2 75s dp brn & org brn .75 —
**C7** AP2 1r dp choc & purple brown .90 —
**C8** AP2 1½r dk viol & dp yel brown 2.25 —
**C9** AP2 4½r Pruss grn & dull purple 2.25 —
**C10** A32 5r yel brn & black 7.50 —
**C11** AP1 7½r brn & slate vio 3.75 —
**C12** A32 10r emerald & black 9.00 —
**C13** A32 25r rose red & black 12.00 —
*Nos. C1-C13 (13)* 40.10

AP3

Designs: 30s, 1r, Map, ships. 50s, Harbor scene, vert. 2½r, 4½r, Ships.

**1949, Aug. 17 Photo. *Perf. 12½***

**C14** AP3 30s blue & orange 1.75 —
**C15** AP3 50s green & orange 3.00 —
**C16** AP3 1r brn & green 1.90 —
**C17** AP3 2½r blk & dull grn 6.00 —
**C18** AP3 4½r blue & rose red 15.00 —
*Nos. C14-C18 (5)* 27.65

Failure of Dutch blockade.

Airplane, Indonesian Archipelago — AP4

Hot Spring, Java — AP5

Designs: 10s, DC-4 over Indonesian Archipelago. 20s, Aircraft mechanics working on plane. 30s, Servicing plane on runway. 40c, Pilots. 50s, Briefing pilots. 75s, Sentry and aircraft, Lake Toba, Sumatra. 1r, Plane, mountain in Sumatra. 1½r, DC-3 over rice fields. 4½r, Airplane over Buffalo Canyon. 7½r, Aircraft over Tjipanas Fish Ponds, Java.

Nos. C28, C30 and C31 are overprinted ("POS UDARA" and Airplane) on Nos. 51-53.

***Perf. 14½, 12½ (#C10, C12, C13)***

**1949, Aug. 17 Photo.**

**C19** AP4 10s pur & lt blue .50 —
**C20** AP5 20s brn & sl blue 1.00 —
**C21** AP4 30s red brn & bl grn 2.00 —
**C22** AP4 40s dk brn & pur 1.50 —
**C23** AP4 50s dp bl grn & red brn 2.25 —
**C24** AP4 75s bl grn & brn .95 —
**C25** AP4 1r pur & dk grn 1.25 —
**C26** AP4 1½r blk bl & org 3.00 —
**C27** AP5 4½r pur & chestnut 3.50 —
**C28** A38 5r red vio & black 3.50 —
**C29** AP5 7½r dk grn & vio brn 3.50 —
**C30** A38 10r grn & black 6.00 —
**C31** A38 25r red & black 14.00 —
*Nos. C19-C31 (13)* 42.95

AP6

Designs: 50s, Map, airplanes, horiz. 30s, 1r, Harbor scene. 2½r, Airplane on runway, horiz. 4½r, Airplane landing, horiz.

**1949 Photo. *Perf. 14½***

**C32** AP6 30s multicolored 1.75 —
**C33** AP6 50s multicolored 2.00 —
**C34** AP6 1r multicolored 1.25 —
**C35** A39 2½r multicolored 2.00 —
**C36** A39 4½r multicolored 3.50 —
*Nos. C32-C36 (5)* 10.50

**Liberation of Jakarta**

Nos. C1-C9, C11 Overprinted

**1949, Dec. 7**

**C37** AP1 10s dk lilac & brn .25 —
**C38** AP1 20s Pruss grn & org red .25 —
**C39** AP1 30s dp blue & dull lil .25 —
**C40** AP1 40s red brn & blue emerald 12.00 —
**C41** AP1 50s dp vio & dull bl .55 —
**C42** AP2 75s dp brn & org brn .55 —
**C43** AP2 1r dp choc & purple brown 1.25 —
**C44** AP2 1½r dk viol & dp yel brown 1.40 —
**C45** AP2 4½r Pruss grn & dull purple 2.00 —
**C46** AP1 7½r brn & slate vio 12.50 —
*Nos. C37-C46 (10)* 31.00

Nos. C19-C27, C29 Overprinted

**C47** AP4 10s pur & lt blue .25 —
**C48** AP5 20s brn & sl blue 1.25 —
**C49** AP4 30s red brn & bl grn .30 —
**C50** AP4 40s dk brn & pur 1.10 —
**C51** AP4 50s dp bl grn & red brn .30 —
**C52** AP4 75s bl grn & brn .30 —
**C53** AP4 1r pur & dk grn 1.50 —
**C54** AP4 1½r blk bl & org 2.00 —
**C55** AP5 4½r pur & chestnut 2.50 —
**C56** AP5 7½r dk grn & vio brn 2.75 —
*Nos. C47-C56 (10)* 12.25

Nos. C32-C36 Overprinted

**C57** AP6 30s multicolored 5.00 —
**C58** AP6 50s multicolored 3.00 —
**C59** AP6 1r multicolored 3.00 —
**C60** A39 2½r multicolored 4.50 —
**C61** A39 4½r multicolored 6.50 —
*Nos. C57-C61 (5)* 22.00

---

## AIR POST SPECIAL DELIVERY STAMPS

Aircraft Over Beach APSD1

***Perf. 14½***

**1948, Dec. 15 Photo. Unwmk.**

**CE1** APSD1 40s dk brn & blue emerald 1.00 —

Type APSD1, inscribed "REPUBLIK"

**1948, Dec. 15 *Perf. 13½x14***

**CE2** APSD1 40s brn & blue emer .75 —

No. CE1, Overprinted "Merdeka Djojakarta 6 Djuli 1949"

**1949, Dec. 7**

**CE3** APSD1 40s brn & blue emer .75 —

**No. CE2 Overprinted**

**1949, Dec. 7**

**CE4** APSD1 40s brn & blue emer 7.00 —

---

## AIR POST OFFICIAL STAMPS

**Nos. C1, C3, C5, C7 Overprinted**

**1948, Dec. 15**

**CO1** AP1 10s dk lilac & brown 1.25 —
**CO2** AP1 30s dp blue & dull lil 2.00 —
**CO3** AP1 50s dp vio & dull blue 2.25 —
**CO4** AP2 1r dp choc & purle brown 5.00 —
*Nos. CO1-CO4 (4)* 10.50

**Nos. C19//C25 Overprinted**

**1949, Aug. 17**

**CO5** AP4 10s pur & lt blue 3.50 —
**CO6** AP4 30s red brn & bl grn 2.00 —
**CO7** AP4 50s dp bl grn & red brn 4.50 —
**CO8** AP4 1r pur & dk grn 3.25 —
*Nos. CO5-CO8 (4)* 13.25

**Nos. CO1-CO4 Overprinted**

**1949, Dec. 7**

**CO9** AP1 10s dk lilac & brown 2.50 —
**CO10** AP1 30s dp blue & dull lil 5.00 —
**CO11** AP1 50s dp vio & dull bl 2.50 —
**CO12** AP2 1r dp choc & purle brown 2.00 —
*Nos. CO9-CO12 (4)* 12.00

**Nos. CO5-CO8 Overprinted**

**1949, Dec. 7**

| | | | | |
|---|---|---|---|---|
| **CO13** | AP4 | 10s pur & lt blue | 2.00 | — |
| **CO14** | AP4 | 30s red brn & bl grn | 6.00 | — |
| **CO15** | AP4 | 50s dp bl grn & red brn | 1.25 | — |
| **CO16** | AP4 | 1r pur & dk grn | 3.50 | — |
| | | *Nos. CO13-CO16 (4)* | 12.75 | |

### SPECIAL DELIVERY STAMPS

Train & Minangkabau House — SD1

***Perf. 13½x14¼***

**1948, Dec. 15 Unwmk. Photo.**

| | | | | |
|---|---|---|---|---|
| **E1** | SD1 | 10s dp bluish grn & chestnut | .25 | — |
| **E1A** | SD1 | 15s ches & steel bl | .45 | — |

Type SD1, Inscribed "REPUBLIK"

**1949, Aug. 17**

| | | | | |
|---|---|---|---|---|
| **E1B** | SD1 | 10s red brn & dp blue | .50 | — |
| **E1C** | SD1 | 15s turq & dk yel brn | .35 | — |

Nos. E1-E1A Overprinted

**1949, Dec. 7**

| | | | | |
|---|---|---|---|---|
| **E1D** | SD1 | 10s dp bluish grn & chestnut | .30 | — |
| **E1E** | SD1 | 15s ches & steel bl | .75 | — |

Nos. E1B-E1C Overprinted "Merdeka Djojakarta 6 Djuli 1949"

**1949, Dec. 7**

| | | | | |
|---|---|---|---|---|
| **E1F** | SD1 | 10s red brn & dp blue | .30 | — |
| **E1G** | SD1 | 15s urq & dk yel brn | .60 | — |

Garuda SD2

***Perf. 13½x12½***

**1967 Unwmk. Photo.**

| | | | | |
|---|---|---|---|---|
| **E1H** | SD2 | 10r lt ultra & dl pur | .50 | .25 |
| **E2** | SD2 | 15r org & dl pur | 1.10 | .50 |

**1968 Inscribed "1968"**

| | | | | |
|---|---|---|---|---|
| **E3** | SD2 | 10r lt ultra & dl pur | .60 | .25 |
| **E4** | SD2 | 15r org & dl pur | .80 | .30 |
| **E5** | SD2 | 20r yel & dl pur | .90 | .30 |
| **E6** | SD2 | 30r brt grn & dl pur | 1.25 | .60 |
| **E7** | SD2 | 40r lil & dl pur | 1.75 | .30 |
| | | *Nos. E3-E7 (5)* | 5.30 | 1.75 |

**Same Inscribed "1969"**

**1969**

| | | | | |
|---|---|---|---|---|
| **E8** | SD2 | 20r yel & dl pur | .50 | .25 |
| **E9** | SD2 | 30r brt grn & dl pur | .75 | .25 |
| **E10** | SD2 | 40r lil & dl pur | .85 | .25 |
| | | *Nos. E8-E10 (3)* | 2.10 | .75 |

### POSTAGE DUE STAMPS

D1

***Perf. 13¾x14, 14½ (#J8-J13)***

**1948 Unwmk.**

| | | | | |
|---|---|---|---|---|
| **J1** | D1 | 1s blue & brn | .30 | — |
| **J2** | D1 | 2½s dk brn & dk pur | .45 | — |
| **J3** | D1 | 3½s pur & lt grn | .25 | — |
| **J4** | D1 | 5s dk grn & brn | .40 | — |
| **J5** | D1 | 7½s dk brn & dk grn | .50 | — |
| **J6** | D1 | 10s dk pur & brn | .45 | — |
| **J7** | D1 | 20s brn & org yel | 1.25 | — |
| **J8** | D1 | 25s dk pur & dk brn | 1.50 | — |
| **J9** | D1 | 30s blue & car red | 1.25 | — |
| **J10** | D1 | 40s blue & org yel | 1.50 | — |
| **J11** | D1 | 50s lt brn & pur | 2.00 | — |
| **J12** | D1 | 75s dk bl & dk grn | 3.50 | — |
| **J13** | D1 | 1r brn & green | 4.00 | — |
| | | *Nos. J1-J13 (13)* | 17.35 | |

**As Type D1, inscribed "REPUBLIK"**

***Perf. 13¾x14, 14½ (#J8-J13)***

**1949, Aug. 17 Unwmk.**

| | | | | |
|---|---|---|---|---|
| **J14** | D1 | 1s dk blue & brn | 35.00 | — |
| **J15** | D1 | 2½s dk brn & pur | 35.00 | — |
| **J16** | D1 | 3½s pur & grn | 35.00 | — |
| **J17** | D1 | 5s dk grn & brn | 35.00 | — |
| **J18** | D1 | 7½s dk brn & dk grn | 35.00 | — |
| **J19** | D1 | 10s pur & brn | 35.00 | — |
| **J20** | D1 | 20s dk brn & yel | 35.00 | — |
| **J21** | D1 | 25s vio & dk pur | 35.00 | — |
| **J22** | D1 | 30s blue & red | 35.00 | — |
| **J23** | D1 | 40s blue & yel | 35.00 | — |
| **J24** | D1 | 50s brn & pur | 35.00 | — |
| **J25** | D1 | 75s dk bl & dk grn | 35.00 | — |
| **J26** | D1 | 1r dk brn & green | 35.00 | — |
| | | *Nos. J14-J26 (13)* | 455.00 | |

Nos. J1-J13 Overprinted

**1949, Dec. 7**

| | | | | |
|---|---|---|---|---|
| **J27** | D1 | 1s blue & brn | 1.25 | — |
| **J28** | D1 | 2½s dk brn & dk pur | .65 | — |
| **J29** | D1 | 3½s pur & lt grn | .75 | — |
| **J30** | D1 | 5s dk grn & brn | .75 | — |
| **J31** | D1 | 7½s dk brn & dk grn | 1.25 | — |
| **J32** | D1 | 10s dk pur & brn | .35 | — |
| **J33** | D1 | 20s brn & org yel | 9.00 | — |
| **J34** | D1 | 25s dk pur & dk brn | 4.50 | — |
| **J35** | D1 | 30s blue & car red | 12.50 | — |
| **J36** | D1 | 40s blue & org yel | 15.00 | — |
| **J37** | D1 | 50s lt brn & pur | 7.50 | — |
| **J38** | D1 | 75s dk bl & dk grn | 22.50 | — |
| **J39** | D1 | 1r brn & green | 15.00 | — |
| | | *Nos. J27-J39 (13)* | 91.00 | |

Netherlands Indies Nos. J57 to J59 Surcharged in Black

**1950 Wmk. 228 *Perf. 14½x14***

| | | | | |
|---|---|---|---|---|
| **J60** | D7 | 2½s on 50c yellow | 1.50 | .50 |
| **J61** | D7 | 5s on 100c apple grn | 3.50 | 1.25 |
| **J62** | D7 | 10s on 75c aqua | 8.00 | 1.75 |
| | | *Nos. J60-J62 (3)* | 13.00 | 3.50 |

D8

**Wmk. 228**

**1951-52 Litho. *Perf. 12½***

| | | | | |
|---|---|---|---|---|
| **J63** | D8 | 2½s vermilion | .25 | .50 |
| **J64** | D8 | 5s vermilion | .25 | .25 |
| **J65** | D8 | 10s vermilion | .25 | .25 |
| **J66** | D8 | 20s blue ('52) | .25 | .25 |
| **J67** | D8 | 25s olive bister ('52) | .85 | .50 |
| **J68** | D8 | 50s vermilion | 9.00 | 2.00 |
| **J69** | D8 | 1r citron | 3.00 | 3.00 |
| | | *Nos. J63-J69 (7)* | 13.85 | 6.75 |

**1953-55 Unwmk.**

| | | | | |
|---|---|---|---|---|
| **J70** | D8 | 15s lt magenta ('55) | 1.00 | .25 |
| **J71** | D8 | 30s red brown | 1.25 | .30 |
| **J72** | D8 | 40s green | 1.25 | .30 |
| | | *Nos. J70-J72 (3)* | 3.50 | .85 |

**1958-61 *Perf. 13½x12½***

| | | | | |
|---|---|---|---|---|
| **J73** | D8 | 10s orange | .30 | .55 |
| **J74** | D8 | 15s orange ('59) | .30 | .55 |
| **J74A** | D8 | 20s orange ('61) | 1.00 | .55 |
| **J75** | D8 | 25s orange | .30 | .55 |
| **J76** | D8 | 30s orange ('60) | .30 | .55 |
| **J77** | D8 | 50s orange | 3.00 | .55 |
| **J78** | D8 | 100s orange ('60) | 1.50 | .55 |
| | | *Nos. J73-J78 (7)* | 6.70 | 3.85 |

**1962-65 *Perf. 13½x12½***

| | | | | |
|---|---|---|---|---|
| **J79** | D8 | 50s light bluish green | .25 | .25 |
| **J80** | D8 | 100s bister | .25 | .25 |
| **J81** | D8 | 250s blue | .25 | .25 |
| **J82** | D8 | 500s dull yellow | .25 | .25 |
| **J83** | D8 | 750s pale lilac | .25 | .25 |
| **J84** | D8 | 1000s salmon | .50 | .25 |
| **J85** | D8 | 50r red ('65) | .25 | .25 |
| **J86** | D8 | 100r maroon ('65) | .45 | .25 |
| | | *Nos. J79-J86 (8)* | 2.45 | 2.00 |

"1966" — D9

**1966-67 Unwmk. Photo.**

| | | | | |
|---|---|---|---|---|
| **J91** | D9 | 5s dl grn & dl yel | .35 | .25 |
| **J92** | D9 | 10s red & lt bl | .35 | .25 |
| **J93** | D9 | 20s dk bl & pink | .35 | .25 |
| **J94** | D9 | 30s brn & rose | .35 | .25 |
| **J95** | D9 | 40s plum & bis | .35 | .25 |
| **J96** | D9 | 50s ol grn & pale lil | .35 | .25 |
| **J97** | D9 | 100s dk red & yel grn | .60 | .25 |
| **J98** | D9 | 200s brt grn & pink ('67) | .45 | .25 |
| **J99** | D9 | 500s yel & lt bl ('67) | .60 | .25 |
| **J100** | D9 | 1000s rose lil & yel ('67) | 1.00 | .30 |
| | | *Nos. J91-J100 (10)* | 4.75 | 2.55 |

**1967 Dated "1967"**

| | | | | |
|---|---|---|---|---|
| **J101** | D9 | 50s ol grn & pale lil | .30 | .40 |
| **J102** | D9 | 100s dk red & yel grn | .40 | .40 |
| **J103** | D9 | 200s brt grn & pink | .50 | .40 |
| **J104** | D9 | 500s yel & lt bl | .25 | .40 |
| **J105** | D9 | 1000s rose lil & yel | 1.40 | .40 |
| **J106** | D9 | 15r org & gray | 1.40 | .60 |
| **J107** | D9 | 25r lil & citron | 2.25 | 1.00 |
| | | *Nos. J101-J107 (7)* | 6.50 | 3.60 |

**Similar stamps inscribed "Bajar" or "Bayar", year date and "Sumbangan Ongkos Tjetak" or ". . . Cetak" are revenues.**

**Inscribed "BAYAR PORTO"**

**1973 Dated "1973"**

| | | | | |
|---|---|---|---|---|
| **J108** | D9 | 25r lilac & citron | 2.00 | .30 |

**Inscribed "BAYAR PORTO"**

**1974 Dated "1974"**

| | | | | |
|---|---|---|---|---|
| **J109** | D9 | 65r olive grn & bister | 1.90 | 1.00 |
| **J110** | D9 | 125r lil & pale pink | 8.00 | 4.00 |

**Dated "1975"**

**Inscribed "BAYAR PORTO"**

**1975 Photo. *Perf. 13½x12½***

| | | | | |
|---|---|---|---|---|
| **J111** | D9 | 25r lilac & citron | 2.25 | 1.00 |

"1976" — D10

**1976**

| | | | | |
|---|---|---|---|---|
| **J112** | D10 | 125r lil & pale pur | 3.75 | 1.25 |

**1977 Dated "1977"**

| | | | | |
|---|---|---|---|---|
| **J113** | D10 | 100r dp vio & pale pink | .75 | .50 |
| **J114** | D10 | 200r brt bl & lt lil | 1.00 | .85 |
| **J115** | D10 | 300r choc & lt sal | 1.50 | 1.25 |
| **J116** | D10 | 400r brt grn & tan | 2.25 | 2.00 |
| **J117** | D10 | 500r red & tan | 2.75 | 2.50 |
| | | *Nos. J113-J117 (5)* | 8.25 | 7.10 |

See Nos. J138, J139, J142.

Nos. 706, 709, 712-713, 716, 718 Surcharged in Red

**1978 Photo. *Perf. 12½x12***

| | | | | |
|---|---|---|---|---|
| **J118** | A110 | 25r on 1r | .30 | .30 |
| **J119** | A110 | 50r on 2r | .55 | .55 |
| **J120** | A110 | 100r on 4r | 1.75 | 1.75 |
| **J121** | A110 | 200r on 5r | 3.25 | 3.25 |
| **J122** | A110 | 300r on 10r | 4.25 | 4.25 |
| **J123** | A110 | 400r on 15r | 6.00 | 6.00 |
| | | *Nos. J118-J123 (6)* | 16.10 | 16.10 |

**Surcharged in Black**

| | | | | |
|---|---|---|---|---|
| **J124** | A110 | 25r on 1r | .30 | .30 |
| **J125** | A110 | 50r on 2r | .60 | .60 |
| **J126** | A110 | 100r on 4r | 1.75 | 1.75 |
| **J127** | A110 | 200r on 5r | 4.25 | 4.25 |
| **J128** | A110 | 300r on 10r | 5.25 | 5.25 |
| **J129** | A110 | 400r on 15r | 7.00 | 7.00 |
| | | *Nos. J124-J129 (6)* | 19.15 | 19.15 |

Nos. 710, 717 Surcharged

**1978 Photo. *Perf. 12½x12***

| | | | | |
|---|---|---|---|---|
| **J130** | A110 | 40r on 2.50r | 1.10 | 1.10 |
| **J131** | A110 | 40r on 12r | 1.10 | 1.10 |
| **J132** | A110 | 65r on 2.50r | 1.50 | 1.50 |
| **J133** | A110 | 65r on 12r | 1.50 | 1.50 |
| **J134** | A110 | 125r on 2.50r | 3.00 | 3.00 |
| **J135** | A110 | 125r on 12r | 3.00 | 3.00 |
| **J136** | A110 | 150r on 2.50r | 4.00 | 4.00 |
| **J137** | A110 | 150r on 12r | 2.50 | 2.50 |
| | | *Nos. J130-J137 (8)* | 17.70 | 17.70 |

**Type of 1976 Dated "1979"**

**1979 *Perf. 13½x12½***

| | | | | |
|---|---|---|---|---|
| **J138** | D10 | 25r lilac & citron | 1.00 | .25 |

**Type of 1976 and**

D11

***Perf. 13½x12½, 13½x13 (#J144-J148, J150-J153), 14½x13 (#J154-J156A)***

**1980-90 Photo. Dated "1980"**

| | | | | |
|---|---|---|---|---|
| **J139** | D10 | 25r dk lil & beige | .25 | .25 |
| **J140** | D11 | 50r multi | .60 | .50 |
| **J141** | D11 | 75r rose lake & rose | 1.00 | .90 |
| **J142** | D10 | 125r rose lil & lt pink | 1.50 | 1.00 |
| | | *Nos. J139-J142 (4)* | 3.35 | 2.65 |

**Dated "1981"**

| | | | | |
|---|---|---|---|---|
| **J144** | D11 | 25r brt vio & pale yel grn | .30 | .30 |
| **J145** | D11 | 50r sl grn & lt vio | .60 | .60 |
| **J146** | D11 | 75r rose vio & pink | 1.10 | 1.10 |
| **J147** | D11 | 125r pur & yel grn | 1.75 | 1.75 |
| | | *Nos. J144-J147 (4)* | 3.75 | 3.75 |

**Dated "1982"**

| | | | | |
|---|---|---|---|---|
| **J148** | D11 | 125r dp rose lil & pink | 4.00 | .50 |

**Dated "1983"**

| | | | | |
|---|---|---|---|---|
| **J149** | D11 | 125r dp rose & lil pink | .60 | .40 |
| **J150** | D11 | 200r dp vio & lt bl | 1.25 | .55 |
| **J151** | D11 | 300r dk grn & cit | 1.50 | .80 |
| **J152** | D11 | 400r ol grn & brn ol | 2.00 | 1.00 |
| **J153** | D11 | 500r sepia & beige | 2.50 | 1.25 |
| | | *Nos. J149-J153 (5)* | 7.85 | 4.00 |

**Dated "1984"**

| | | | | |
|---|---|---|---|---|
| **J154** | D11 | 25r brt vio & pale yel grn | 1.25 | .35 |
| **J155** | D11 | 50r sl grn & lt vio | 1.25 | .90 |
| **J156** | D11 | 125r rose lil & lt pink | 3.50 | .35 |
| **J156A** | D11 | 500r sepia & beige | 15.00 | 2.50 |
| | | *Nos. J154-J156A (4)* | 21.00 | 4.10 |

**Dated "1988"**

| | | | | | |
|---|---|---|---|---|---|
| **J157** | D11 | 1000r | dp vio & gray | 1.40 | .75 |
| **J158** | D11 | 2000r | red & dp rose lil | 2.75 | 1.25 |
| **J159** | D11 | 3000r | brn & dl org | 4.50 | 2.00 |
| **J160** | D11 | 5000r | grn & bl grn | 8.75 | 2.50 |
| | | | *Nos. J157-J160 (4)* | 17.40 | 6.50 |

**Dated "1990"**

| | | | | | |
|---|---|---|---|---|---|
| **J161** | D11 | 2000r | emer & brt yel | 4.75 | 2.50 |
| **J162** | D11 | 3000r | dk bl grn & rose lil | 7.00 | 3.50 |
| **J163** | D11 | 4000r | brn vio & brt yel grn | 12.50 | 6.50 |
| | | | *Nos. J161-J163 (3)* | 24.25 | 12.50 |

## OFFICIAL STAMPS

Nos. 2//16 Overprinted

**1948, Dec. 15**

| | | | | | |
|---|---|---|---|---|---|
| **O1** | A28 | 2s | dp brn & dp blue | .25 | — |
| **O2** | A28 | 5s | turq & dull blue | .50 | — |
| **O3** | A28 | 10s | dp blue & brn rose | .45 | — |
| **O4** | A28 | 15s | brown & dk grn | .25 | — |
| **O5** | A31 | 30s | dk brn & dull vio | 1.50 | — |
| **O6** | A30 | 50s | dk brn & turq | .60 | — |
| | | | *Nos. O1-O6 (6)* | 3.55 | |

Nos. 31//45 Overprinted

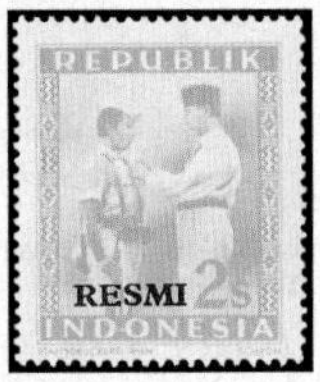


**1949, Aug. 17**

| | | | | | |
|---|---|---|---|---|---|
| **O7** | A35 | 2s | dk red vio & dp grn | .30 | — |
| **O8** | A35 | 5s | dk yel brn & dull vio | .30 | — |
| **O9** | A34 | 10s | dk brn & dp vio | 1.00 | — |
| **O10** | A35 | 15s | dk vio & dp dull grn | 1.50 | — |
| **O11** | A36 | 30s | dp brn & dk blue vio | .75 | — |
| **O12** | A37 | 50s | dk brn & Prus grn | 2.00 | — |
| | | | *Nos. O7-O12 (6)* | 5.85 | |

Nos. O1-O6 Overprinted

**1948, Dec. 15**

| | | | | | |
|---|---|---|---|---|---|
| **O13** | A28 | 2s | dp brn & dp blue | .75 | — |
| **O14** | A28 | 5s | turq & dull blue | 1.60 | — |
| **O15** | A28 | 10s | dp blue & brn rose | 1.60 | — |
| **O16** | A28 | 15s | brown & dk grn | 1.60 | — |
| **O17** | A31 | 30s | dk brn & dull vio | 3.00 | — |
| **O18** | A30 | 50s | dk brn & turq | 3.00 | — |
| | | | *Nos. O13-O18 (6)* | 11.55 | |

Nos. O7-O12 Overprinted

**1948, Dec. 15**

| | | | | | |
|---|---|---|---|---|---|
| **O19** | A35 | 2s | dk red vio & dp grn | 1.00 | — |
| **O20** | A35 | 5s | dk yel brn & dull vio | .45 | — |
| **O21** | A34 | 10s | dk brn & dp vio | .45 | — |
| **O22** | A35 | 15s | dk vio & dp dull grn | 1.00 | — |
| **O23** | A36 | 30s | dp brn & dk blue vio | 2.50 | — |
| **O24** | A37 | 50s | dk brn & Pruss grn | 3.00 | — |
| | | | *Nos. O19-O24 (6)* | 8.40 | |

## RIAU ARCHIPELAGO

(Riouw Archipelago)
100 Sen = 1 Rupiah
(1 rupiah = 1 Malayan dollar)

**Indonesia Nos. 371-386 Overprinted in Black**

a

b

**Overprint "a"**

| **1954** | | **Unwmk.** | | | ***Perf. 12½*** |
|---|---|---|---|---|---|
| **1** | A52 | 5s | car rose | 67.50 | 57.50 |
| **2** | A52 | 7½s | green | 1.50 | 1.50 |
| **3** | A52 | 10s | blue | 80.00 | 80.00 |
| **4** | A52 | 15s | purple | 3.00 | 3.00 |
| **5** | A52 | 20s | rose red | 3.00 | 3.00 |
| **6** | A52 | 25s | dp green | 150.00 | 42.50 |

**Overprint "b"**

| | | | | | |
|---|---|---|---|---|---|
| **7** | A53 | 30s | red orange | 6.00 | 6.00 |
| **8** | A53 | 35s | purple | 1.50 | 1.50 |
| **9** | A53 | 40s | dull green | 1.50 | 1.50 |
| **10** | A53 | 45s | dp claret | 1.50 | 1.50 |
| **11** | A53 | 50s | brown | 525.00 | 100.00 |
| **12** | A54 | 60s | dk brown | 1.50 | 1.50 |
| **13** | A54 | 70s | gray | 2.75 | 2.75 |
| **14** | A54 | 75s | ultra | 12.00 | 3.25 |
| **15** | A54 | 80s | claret | 2.40 | 3.50 |
| **16** | A54 | 90s | gray green | 2.40 | 3.50 |

Netherlands Indies Nos. 325-330 Overprinted Type "a" in Black

| | | | | | |
|---|---|---|---|---|---|
| **17** | A46 | 1r | purple | 15.00 | 5.25 |
| **18** | A46 | 2r | olive grn | 3.25 | 6.00 |
| **19** | A46 | 3r | red violet | 5.25 | 6.00 |
| **20** | A46 | 5r | dk brown | 5.25 | 6.00 |
| **21** | A46 | 10r | gray | 6.75 | 10.00 |
| **22** | A46 | 25r | orange brn | 6.75 | 10.00 |
| | | | *Nos. 1-22 (22)* | 903.80 | 355.75 |

Mint values are for stamps with somewhat tropicalized gum (stained brown and cracked). Stamps with clean, clear gum sell for about twice as much.

Indonesia Nos. 424-428, 450 and 430 Overprinted Type "b" or

| **1957-64** | | **Photo.** | | | ***Perf. 12½x13½*** |
|---|---|---|---|---|---|
| **23** | A63(b) | 5s | dp ultra | .90 | .90 |
| **24** | A63 | 10s | yellow brn | 13.00 | 10.00 |
| **25** | A63(b) | 10s | yellow brn | .90 | .90 |
| **26** | A63(b) | 15s | rose vio ('64) | .90 | *.90* |
| **27** | A63(b) | 20s | dull grn ('60) | .90 | .90 |
| **27A** | A63 | 25s | dp claret | *40.00* | *40.00* |
| **28** | A63(b) | 25s | dp claret | .90 | .90 |
| **29** | A63(b) | 30s | orange | .90 | .90 |
| **30** | A63 | 50s | brown | 13.00 | 10.00 |
| **31** | A63(b) | 50s | brown | .90 | .90 |

The "b" overprint measures 12mm in this set.

Sukarno Type of Indonesia Overprinted Type "a"

| **1960** | | | | | ***Perf. 12½x12*** |
|---|---|---|---|---|---|
| **32** | A55 | 1.25r | dp orange | 4.50 | 6.75 |
| **33** | A55 | 1.50r | brown | 4.50 | 6.75 |
| **34** | A55 | 2.50r | rose brown | 6.75 | 10.00 |
| **35** | A55 | 4r | apple green | 1.25 | *.50* |
| **36** | A55 | 6r | rose lilac | 1.25 | *.50* |
| **37** | A55 | 15r | yellow | 1.25 | *.50* |
| **38** | A55 | 20r | sepia | 1.25 | .50 |
| **39** | A55 | 40r | yellow grn | 1.25 | *.50* |
| **40** | A55 | 50r | violet | 2.40 | *.50* |
| | | | *Nos. 23-40 (19)* | 96.70 | 92.80 |

Nos. 26, 35-37, 39-40 are valued CTO with Bandung cancels. Postally used sell for much more.

## WEST IRIAN

ˈwest ˌir-ē-ˈän

(Irian Barat)
(West New Guinea)

LOCATION — Western half of New Guinea, southwest Pacific Ocean
GOVT. — Province of Indonesia
AREA — 162,927 sq. mi.
POP. — 923,440 (1973)
CAPITAL — Djajapura (formerly Hollandia)

The former Netherlands New Guinea became a territory under the administration of the United Nations Temporary Executive Authority on Oct. 1, 1962.

The territory came under Indonesian administration on May 1, 1963.

100 Sen = 1 Rupiah
(1 rupiah = 1 former Netherlands New Guinea gulden)

**Catalogue values for all unused stamps in this country are for Never Hinged items.**

Netherlands New Guinea Stamps of 1950-60 Overprinted

**Type 2 Overprint**

***Perf. 12½x12, 12½x13½***

| **1962-63** | | **Photo.** | | | **Unwmk.** |
|---|---|---|---|---|---|
| **1a** | A4 | 1c | vermilion & yel | .25 | .25 |
| **2a** | A1 | 2c | deep orange | .25 | .25 |
| **3a** | A4 | 5c | choc & yel | .25 | .25 |
| **4a** | A5 | 7c | org red, bl & brn vio | .25 | .25 |
| **5a** | A4 | 10c | aqua & red brn | .25 | .25 |
| **6a** | A5 | 12c | grn, bl & brn vio | .25 | .25 |
| **7a** | A4 | 15c | dp yel & red brn | .50 | .25 |
| **8a** | A5 | 17c | brn vio & bl | .60 | .35 |
| **9a** | A4 | 20c | lt bl grn & red brn | .60 | .35 |
| **10a** | A6 | 25c | red | .35 | .30 |
| **11a** | A6 | 30c | deep blue | .80 | .35 |
| **12a** | A6 | 40c | deep orange | .80 | .35 |
| **13a** | A6 | 45c | dark olive | 1.40 | .75 |
| **14a** | A6 | 55c | slate blue | 1.25 | .55 |
| **15a** | A6 | 80c | dl gray vio | 8.00 | *10.00* |
| **16a** | A6 | 85c | dk vio brn | 4.00 | *5.00* |
| **17a** | A6 | 1g | plum | 3.50 | 1.90 |

**Engr.**

| | | | | | |
|---|---|---|---|---|---|
| **18a** | A3 | 2g | reddish brn | 15.00 | *20.00* |
| **19a** | A3 | 5g | green | 7.50 | *6.00* |
| | | | *Nos. 1a-19a (19)* | 45.80 | 47.65 |

The overprint exists in four types:

1) Size 17½mm. Applied locally and sold in 1962 in West New Guinea. Top of "N" is slightly lower than the "U," and the base of the "T" is straight, or nearly so. This set sells for about $20 more than Nos. 1a-19a.

2) Size 17½mm. Applied in the Netherlands and sold in 1963 by the UN in New York. Top of the "N" is slightly higher than the "U," and the base of the "T" is concave. This is the set listed above.

3) Size 14mm. Exists on eight values. Set value, $200.

4) Size 19mm. Exists on 1c and 10c. Set value, $160.

Types 3 and 4 were applied in West New Guinea and it is doubtful whether they were regularly issued.

See the *Scott U.S. Specialized Catalogue* for complete listings and values of the UNTEA overprints.

Indonesia Nos. 454, 456, 494-501, 387, 390, 392 and 393 Surcharged or Overprinted: "IRIAN BARAT"

***Perf. 12½x13½***

| **1963, May 1** | | **Photo.** | | | **Unwmk.** |
|---|---|---|---|---|---|
| **20** | A63 | 1s | on 70s org ver | .25 | .25 |
| **21** | A63 | 2s | on 90s yel grn | .25 | .25 |

***Perf. 12x12½***

| | | | | | |
|---|---|---|---|---|---|
| **22** | A76 | 5s | gray | .25 | .25 |
| **23** | A76 | 6s | on 20s ocher | .25 | .25 |
| **24** | A76 | 7s | on 50s dp bl | .25 | .25 |
| **25** | A76 | 10s | red brn | .25 | .25 |
| **26** | A76 | 15s | plum | .25 | .25 |
| **27** | A76 | 25s | brt bl grn | .25 | .25 |
| **28** | A76 | 30s | on 75s scar | .25 | *.25* |
| **29** | A76 | 40s | on 1.15r plum | .25 | *.30* |

***Perf. 12½x12***

| | | | | | |
|---|---|---|---|---|---|
| **30** | A55 | 1r | purple | .45 | *.55* |
| **31** | A55 | 2r | green | .80 | *.90* |
| **32** | A55 | 3r | dk bl | 1.40 | *1.50* |
| **33** | A55 | 5r | brown | 2.25 | *3.00* |
| | | | *Nos. 20-33 (14)* | 7.40 | 8.50 |

"Indonesia's Flag from Sabang to Merauke" — A1

20s, 50s, Parachutist landing in New Guinea. 60s, 75s, Bird of paradise and map of New Guinea.

**1963, May 1**

| | | | | | |
|---|---|---|---|---|---|
| **34** | A1 | 12s | org brn, blk & red | .25 | *.30* |
| **35** | A1 | 17s | org brn, blk & red | .25 | *.40* |
| **36** | A1 | 20s | multi | .30 | *.60* |
| **37** | A1 | 50s | multi | .30 | *1.00* |
| **38** | A1 | 60s | multi | .70 | *1.10* |
| **39** | A1 | 75s | multi | .90 | *2.00* |
| | | | *Nos. 34-39 (6)* | 2.70 | *5.40* |

Liberation of West New Guinea.

Maniltoa Gemmipara — A2

15s, Dendrobium lancifolium (orchid). 30s, Gardenia gjellerupii. 40s, Maniltoa flower. 50s, Phalanger. 75s, Cassowary. 1r, Kangaroo. 3r, Crowned pigeons.

| **1968, Aug. 17** | | **Photo.** | | | ***Perf. 12½x12*** |
|---|---|---|---|---|---|
| **40** | A2 | 5s | dl grn & vio blk | .60 | *.85* |
| **41** | A2 | 15s | emer & dk pur | .90 | *1.75* |
| **42** | A2 | 30s | org & dp grn | 2.00 | *2.75* |
| **43** | A2 | 40s | lemon & brt pur | 2.10 | *3.00* |
| **44** | A2 | 50s | rose car & blk | 2.75 | *3.75* |
| **45** | A2 | 75s | dl bl & blk | 3.00 | *5.25* |
| **46** | A2 | 1r | brn org & blk | 5.00 | *8.00* |
| **47** | A2 | 3r | apple grn & blk | 7.75 | *10.50* |
| | | | *Nos. 40-47 (8)* | 24.10 | *35.85* |

Man, Map of Indonesia and Torches — A3

**1968, Aug. 17**

| | | | | | |
|---|---|---|---|---|---|
| **48** | A3 | 10s | ultra & gold | 4.00 | 2.75 |
| **49** | A3 | 25s | crimson & gold | 6.25 | 3.50 |

Issued to publicize the pledge of the people of West Irian to remain unified and integrated with the Republic of Indonesia.

Carving, Mother and Child — A4

Black-capped Lory — A5

West Irian Wood Carvings: 6s, Shield with 3 human figures. 7s, Child atop filigree carving. 10s, Drum. 25s, Seated man. 30s, Drum (3-tiered base). 50s, Carved bamboo. 75s, Man-shaped ornament. 1r, Shield. 2r, Seated man (hands raised).

| **1970** | | **Photo.** | | | ***Perf. 12½x12*** |
|---|---|---|---|---|---|
| **50** | A4 | 5s | multi | .40 | *.55* |
| **51** | A4 | 6s | multi | .40 | *.55* |
| **52** | A4 | 7s | multi | .55 | *1.50* |
| **53** | A4 | 10s | multi | .55 | *1.50* |
| **54** | A4 | 25s | multi | .55 | *.55* |
| **55** | A4 | 30s | multi | .65 | *.80* |
| **56** | A4 | 50s | multi | .70 | *.80* |
| **57** | A4 | 75s | multi | .80 | *.95* |
| **58** | A4 | 1r | multi | .90 | *1.25* |
| **59** | A4 | 2r | multi | 1.25 | *1.40* |
| | | | *Nos. 50-59 (10)* | 6.75 | *9.85* |

Issued: #50-54, 4/30; #55-59, 4/15.

**1970, Oct. 26 Photo. *Perf. 12x12½***

| | | | | |
|---|---|---|---|---|
| 60 | A5 | 5r shown | 2.50 | *6.00* |
| 61 | A5 | 10r Bird of paradise | 2.25 | *7.50* |

## POSTAGE DUE STAMPS

Type of Indonesia Overprinted: "IRIAN BARAT"

***Perf. 13½x12½***

**1963, May 1 Litho. Unwmk.**

| | | | | |
|---|---|---|---|---|
| J1 | D8 | 1s light brown | .25 | *.50* |
| J2 | D8 | 5s light gray olive | .30 | *.55* |
| J3 | D8 | 10s light blue | .30 | *.55* |
| J4 | D8 | 25s gray | .30 | *1.00* |
| J5 | D8 | 40s salmon | .50 | *1.60* |
| J6 | D8 | 100s bister | 1.10 | *3.75* |
| | | *Nos. J1-J6 (6)* | 2.75 | 7.95 |

Type of Indonesia Dated "1968" and Overprinted: "IRIAN BARAT"

**1968 Photo. *Perf. 13½x12½***

| | | | | |
|---|---|---|---|---|
| J7 | D9 | 1s blue & lt grn | .25 | *.60* |
| J8 | D9 | 5s grn & pink | .25 | *.70* |
| J9 | D9 | 10s red & gray | .30 | *.70* |
| J10 | D9 | 25s grn & yel | .30 | *1.10* |
| J11 | D9 | 40s vio brn & pale grn | .65 | *1.75* |
| J12 | D9 | 100s org & bister | 1.25 | *4.75* |
| | | *Nos. J7-J12 (6)* | 3.00 | 9.60 |

# INHAMBANE

ˌin-yəm-ˈban-ə

LOCATION — East Africa
GOVT. — A district of Mozambique, former Portuguese colony
AREA — 21,000 sq. mi. (approx.)
POP. — 248,000 (approx.)
CAPITAL — Inhambane

1000 Reis = 1 Milreis
100 Centavos = 1 Escudo (1913)

Stamps of Mozambique Overprinted

**On 1886 Issue**

**1895, July 1 Unwmk. *Perf. 12½***

**Without Gum**

| | | | | |
|---|---|---|---|---|
| 1 | A2 | 5r black | 37.50 | 30.00 |
| 2 | A2 | 10r green | 50.00 | 25.00 |
| a. | | Perf. 13½ | 80.00 | 75.00 |
| 3 | A2 | 20r rose | 60.00 | 30.00 |
| 4 | A2 | 25r lilac | *600.00* | *250.00* |
| 5 | A2 | 40r chocolate | 60.00 | 40.00 |
| 6 | A2 | 50r blue | 60.00 | 32.50 |
| a. | | Perf. 13½ | 50.00 | 50.00 |
| 7 | A2 | 100r yellow brown | *800.00* | *400.00* |
| 8 | A2 | 200r gray violet | 75.00 | 40.00 |
| 9 | A2 | 300r orange | 75.00 | 40.00 |
| | | *Nos. 1-9 (9)* | *1,817.* | 887.50 |

**On 1894 Issue**

***Perf. 11½***

| | | | | |
|---|---|---|---|---|
| 10 | A3 | 50r lt blue | 42.50 | 35.00 |
| a. | | Perf. 12½ | 55.00 | 42.50 |
| 11 | A3 | 75r rose | 55.00 | 40.00 |
| 12 | A3 | 80r yellow green | 45.00 | 37.50 |
| 13 | A3 | 100r brown, *buff* | 150.00 | 60.00 |
| 14 | A3 | 150r carmine, *rose* | 50.00 | 45.00 |
| | | *Nos. 10-14 (5)* | 342.50 | 217.50 |

700th anniv. of the birth of St. Anthony of Padua.

The status of Nos. 4 and 7 is questionable. No. 3 is always discolored.

Forged overprints exist. Genuine overprints are 21mm high.

King Carlos — A1

**1903, Jan. 1 Typo. *Perf. 11½***

**Name and Value in Black except 500r**

| | | | | |
|---|---|---|---|---|
| 15 | A1 | 2½r gray | .30 | .30 |
| 16 | A1 | 5r orange | .30 | .30 |
| 17 | A1 | 10r lt green | .60 | .40 |
| 18 | A1 | 15r gray green | 1.00 | .75 |
| 19 | A1 | 20r gray violet | .85 | .55 |
| 20 | A1 | 25r carmine | .70 | .55 |
| 21 | A1 | 50r brown | 1.75 | 1.25 |
| 22 | A1 | 65r dull blue | 20.00 | 15.00 |
| 23 | A1 | 75r lilac | 2.00 | 1.40 |
| 24 | A1 | 100r dk blue, *blue* | 2.75 | 1.25 |
| 25 | A1 | 115r org brn, *pink* | 5.00 | 5.00 |
| 26 | A1 | 130r brown, *straw* | 5.00 | 5.00 |
| 27 | A1 | 200r red vio, *pink* | 5.00 | 4.25 |
| 28 | A1 | 400r dull bl, *straw* | 8.25 | 7.50 |
| 29 | A1 | 500r blk & red, *bl* | 18.00 | 12.00 |
| 30 | A1 | 700r gray blk, *straw* | 20.00 | 13.00 |
| | | *Nos. 15-30 (16)* | 91.50 | 68.50 |

For surcharge & overprints see #31-47, 88-101.

No. 22 Surcharged in Black

**1905**

| | | | | |
|---|---|---|---|---|
| 31 | A1 | 50r on 65r dull blue | 3.00 | 2.00 |

Nos. 15-21, 23-30 Overprinted in Carmine or Green

**1911**

| | | | | |
|---|---|---|---|---|
| 32 | A1 | 2½r gray | .25 | .25 |
| 33 | A1 | 5r orange | .25 | .25 |
| 34 | A1 | 10r lt green | .25 | .25 |
| 35 | A1 | 15r gray green | .30 | .30 |
| 36 | A1 | 20r gray violet | .30 | .30 |
| 37 | A1 | 25r carmine (G) | .70 | .50 |
| 38 | A1 | 50r brown | .50 | .50 |
| 39 | A1 | 75r lilac | .50 | .50 |
| 40 | A1 | 100r dk blue, *bl* | .50 | .50 |
| 41 | A1 | 115r org brn, *pink* | 1.00 | .95 |
| 42 | A1 | 130r brown, *straw* | 1.00 | .95 |
| 43 | A1 | 200r red vio, *pink* | 1.00 | .95 |
| 44 | A1 | 400r dull bl, *straw* | 1.25 | 1.00 |
| 45 | A1 | 500r blk & red, *bl* | 1.50 | 1.00 |
| 46 | A1 | 700r gray blk, *straw* | 1.75 | 1.50 |
| | | *Nos. 32-46 (15)* | 11.05 | 9.70 |

No. 31 Overprinted in Red

**1914**

| | | | | |
|---|---|---|---|---|
| 47 | A1 | 50r on 65r dull blue | 1.75 | 1.25 |
| a. | | "Republica" inverted | 25.00 | 25.00 |

**Vasco da Gama Issue of Various Portuguese Colonies**

Common Design Types CD20-CD27 Surcharged

**1913 On Stamps of Macao**

| | | | | |
|---|---|---|---|---|
| 48 | CD20 | ¼c on ½a bl grn | 1.25 | 1.25 |
| 49 | CD21 | ½c on 1a red | 1.25 | 1.25 |
| 50 | CD22 | 1c on 2a red vio | 1.25 | 1.25 |
| a. | | Inverted surcharge | 35.00 | 35.00 |
| 51 | CD23 | 2½c on 4a yel grn | 1.25 | 1.25 |
| 52 | CD24 | 5c on 8a dk bl | 1.25 | 1.25 |
| 53 | CD25 | 7½c on 12a vio brn | 2.25 | 2.25 |
| 54 | CD26 | 10c on 16a bis brn | 1.75 | 1.75 |
| 55 | CD27 | 15c on 24a bis | 1.75 | 1.75 |
| | | *Nos. 48-55 (8)* | 12.00 | 12.00 |

**On Stamps of Portuguese Africa**

| | | | | |
|---|---|---|---|---|
| 56 | CD20 | ¼c on 2½r bl grn | 1.00 | 1.00 |
| 57 | CD21 | ½c on 5r red | 1.00 | 1.00 |
| 58 | CD22 | 1c on 10r red vio | 1.00 | 1.00 |
| 59 | CD23 | 2½c on 25r yel grn | 1.00 | 1.00 |
| 60 | CD24 | 5c on 50r dk bl | 1.00 | 1.00 |
| 61 | CD25 | 7½c on 75r vio brn | 2.00 | 2.00 |
| 62 | CD26 | 10c on 100r bis brn | 1.50 | 1.50 |
| 63 | CD27 | 15c on 150r bis | 1.50 | 1.50 |
| | | *Nos. 56-63 (8)* | 10.00 | 10.00 |

**On Stamps of Timor**

| | | | | |
|---|---|---|---|---|
| 64 | CD20 | ¼c on ½a bl grn | 1.25 | 1.25 |
| a. | | Inverted surcharge | 35.00 | 35.00 |
| 65 | CD21 | ½c on 1a red | 1.25 | 1.25 |
| 66 | CD22 | 1c on 2a red vio | 1.25 | 1.25 |
| 67 | CD23 | 2½c on 4a yel grn | 1.25 | 1.25 |
| 68 | CD24 | 5c on 8a dk bl | 1.25 | 1.25 |
| 69 | CD25 | 7½c on 12a vio brn | 2.50 | 2.50 |
| 70 | CD26 | 10c on 16a bis brn | 1.75 | 1.75 |
| 71 | CD27 | 15c on 24a bis | 1.75 | 1.75 |
| | | *Nos. 64-71 (8)* | 12.25 | 12.25 |
| | | *Nos. 48-71 (24)* | 34.25 | 34.25 |

Ceres — A2

**1914 Typo. *Perf. 15x14***

**Name and Value in Black**

| | | | | |
|---|---|---|---|---|
| 72 | A2 | ¼c olive brown | .50 | .50 |
| 73 | A2 | ½c black | .50 | .50 |
| a. | | Imperf. | | |
| 74 | A2 | 1c blue green | .50 | .50 |
| 75 | A2 | 1½c lilac brown | .50 | .50 |
| 76 | A2 | 2c carmine | .50 | .50 |
| 77 | A2 | 2½c lt violet | .35 | .35 |
| 78 | A2 | 5c deep blue | .80 | .80 |
| 79 | A2 | 7½c yellow brown | 1.25 | 1.25 |
| 80 | A2 | 8c slate | 1.25 | 1.25 |
| 81 | A2 | 10c orange brown | 1.10 | 1.10 |
| 82 | A2 | 15c plum | 2.00 | 1.60 |
| 83 | A2 | 20c yellow green | 2.00 | 1.60 |
| 84 | A2 | 30c brown, *grn* | 3.00 | 2.50 |
| 85 | A2 | 40c brown, *pink* | 3.00 | 3.00 |
| 86 | A2 | 50c orange, *sal* | 5.00 | 5.00 |
| 87 | A2 | 1e green, *blue* | 6.00 | 6.00 |
| | | *Nos. 72-87 (16)* | 28.25 | 26.95 |

No. 31 Overprinted in Carmine

**1915 *Perf. 11½***

| | | | | |
|---|---|---|---|---|
| 88 | A1 | 50c on 65r dull blue | 9.00 | 6.00 |

Nos. 15-21, 23-30 Overprinted Locally

**1917**

| | | | | |
|---|---|---|---|---|
| 89 | A1 | 2½r gray | 25.00 | 25.00 |
| 90 | A1 | 5r orange | 25.00 | 25.00 |
| 91 | A1 | 15r gray green | 3.00 | 2.50 |
| 92 | A1 | 20r gray violet | 3.00 | 2.00 |
| 93 | A1 | 50r brown | 2.50 | 2.00 |
| 94 | A1 | 75r lilac | 2.50 | 2.00 |
| 95 | A1 | 100r blue, *blue* | 3.00 | 2.50 |
| 96 | A1 | 115r org brn, *pink* | 3.00 | 2.50 |
| 97 | A1 | 130r brn, *straw* | 3.00 | 2.50 |
| 98 | A1 | 200r red vio, *pink* | 3.00 | 2.50 |
| 99 | A1 | 400r dull bl, *straw* | 6.00 | 3.00 |
| 100 | A1 | 500r blk & red, *bl* | 7.00 | 3.00 |
| 101 | A1 | 700r gray blk, *straw* | 14.00 | 8.00 |
| | | *Nos. 89-101 (13)* | 100.00 | 82.50 |

The stamps of Inhambane have been superseded by those of Mozambique.

# ININI

ˌē-ni-ˈnē

LOCATION — In northeastern South America, adjoining French Guiana
GOVT. — Territory of French Guiana
AREA — 30,301 sq. mi.
POP. — 5,024 (1946)
CAPITAL — St. Elie

Inini was separated from French Guiana in 1930 and reunited with it in when the colony became an integral part of the Republic, acquiring the same status as the departments of Metropolitan France, under a law effective Jan. 1, 1947.

100 Centimes = 1 Franc

Used values are for canceled-to-order stamps.

**Stamps of French Guiana, 1929-40, Overprinted in Black, Red or Blue**

Nos. 1-9

Nos. 10-26

Nos. 27-40

**1932-40 Unwmk. *Perf. 13½x14***

| | | | | |
|---|---|---|---|---|
| 1 | A16 | 1c gray lil & grnsh bl | .40 | *.55* |
| 2 | A16 | 2c dk red & bl grn | .40 | *.55* |
| 3 | A16 | 3c gray lil & grnsh bl ('40) | .55 | *.70* |
| 4 | A16 | 4c ol brn & red vio ('38) | .55 | *.80* |
| 5 | A16 | 5c Prus bl & red org | .55 | *.80* |
| 6 | A16 | 10c magenta & brn | .40 | *.55* |
| 7 | A16 | 15c yel brn & red org | .40 | *.55* |
| 8 | A16 | 20c dk bl & ol grn | .40 | *.55* |
| 9 | A16 | 25c dk red & dk brn | .90 | *1.25* |

***Perf. 14x13½***

| | | | | |
|---|---|---|---|---|
| 10 | A17 | 30c dl grn & lt grn | 2.40 | *2.40* |
| 11 | A17 | 30c grn & brn ('40) | .55 | *.90* |
| 12 | A17 | 35c Prus grn & ol ('38) | 1.10 | *1.40* |
| 13 | A17 | 40c org brn & ol gray | .80 | *1.20* |
| 14 | A17 | 45c ol grn & lt grn ('40) | 1.40 | *1.50* |
| 15 | A17 | 50c dk bl & ol gray | .70 | *1.05* |
| 16 | A17 | 55c vio bl & car ('38) | 5.25 | *6.50* |
| 17 | A17 | 60c sal & grn ('40) | .70 | *1.05* |
| 18 | A17 | 65c sal & grn ('38) | 2.10 | *2.25* |
| 19 | A17 | 70c ind & sl bl ('40) | 1.00 | *1.10* |
| 20 | A17 | 75c ind & sl bl (Bl) | 4.25 | *3.50* |
| 21 | A17 | 80c blk & vio bl (R) ('38) | 1.25 | *1.25* |
| 22 | A17 | 90c dk red & ver | 3.50 | *2.25* |
| 23 | A17 | 90c red vio & brn ('39) | 1.75 | *1.40* |
| 24 | A17 | 1fr lt vio & brn | 22.50 | *24.00* |
| 25 | A17 | 1fr car & lt red ('38) | 2.75 | *1.75* |
| 26 | A17 | 1fr blk & vio bl ('40) | 1.00 | *1.40* |
| 27 | A18 | 1.25fr blk brn & bl grn ('33) | 2.25 | *1.60* |
| 28 | A18 | 1.25fr rose & lt red ('39) | 1.40 | *1.40* |
| 29 | A18 | 1.40fr ol brn & red vio ('40) | 1.25 | *1.40* |
| 30 | A18 | 1.50fr dk bl & lt bl | 1.05 | *1.50* |
| 31 | A18 | 1.60fr ol brn & bl grn ('40) | 1.00 | *1.40* |
| 32 | A18 | 1.75fr brn, red & blk brn ('33) | 30.00 | 27.50 |
| 33 | A18 | 1.75fr vio bl ('38) | 1.75 | *2.40* |
| 34 | A18 | 2fr dk grn & rose red | 1.25 | *1.75* |
| 35 | A18 | 2.25fr vio bl ('39) | 1.10 | *1.40* |
| 36 | A18 | 2.50fr cop red & brn ('40) | 1.00 | *1.40* |
| 37 | A18 | 3fr brn red & red vio | 1.50 | *1.75* |
| 38 | A18 | 5fr dl vio & yel grn | 1.25 | *1.75* |

**39** A18 10fr ol gray & dp ultra (R) 1.75 *2.10*
**40** A18 20fr indigo & ver 1.75 *2.10*
*Nos. 1-40 (40)* 105.85 *110.65*

Without "RF," see Nos. 46-49.

Common Design Types pictured following the introduction.

**Colonial Arts Exhibition Issue**
Souvenir Sheet
Common Design Type

**1937** ***Imperf.***
**41** CD75 3fr red brown 19.00 *22.50*

**New York World's Fair Issue**
Common Design Type

**1939, May 10 Engr.** ***Perf. 12½x12***
**42** CD82 1.25fr car lake 3.75 *4.50*
**43** CD82 2.25fr ultra 3.75 *4.50*

**French Guiana Nos. 170A-170B Overprinted in Green or Red**

**1941 Engr.** ***Perf. 12½x12***
**44** A21a 1fr deep lilac 1.00
**45** A21a 2.50fr blue (R) 1.00

Nos. 44-45 were issued by the Vichy government in France, but were not placed on sale in Inini.

For surcharges, see Nos. B9-B10.

Types of 1932-40 Without "RF"
**Methods and Perfs as Before**

**1942**
**46** A16 20c dk bl & ol grn 2.00
**47** A17 1fr black & ultra 2.00
**48** A18 10fr ol gr & dp ultra (R) 2.50
**49** A18 20fr indigo & ver 4.00
*Nos. 46-49 (4)* 10.50

Nos. 46-49 were issued by the Vichy government in France, but were not placed on sale in Inini.

**SEMI-POSTAL STAMPS**

French Revolution Common Design Type
**Photo.; Name & Value Typo. in Black**

**1939, July 5 Unwmk.** ***Perf. 13***
**B1** CD83 45c + 25c green 14.50 *17.50*
**B2** CD83 70c + 30c brown 14.50 *17.50*
**B3** CD83 90c + 35c red org 14.50 *17.50*
**B4** CD83 1.25fr + 1fr rose pink 14.50 *17.50*
**B5** CD83 2.25fr + 2fr blue 14.50 *17.50*
*Nos. B1-B5 (5)* 72.50 87.50

**"Defense" Common Design Type and French Guiana Nos. B9 and B11 Ovptd. in Blue or Red**

**1941 Photo.** ***Perf. 13½***
**B6** SP1 1fr + 1fr red (B) 1.75
**B7** CD86 1.50fr + 3fr maroon 1.75
**B8** SP2 2.50fr + 1fr blue (R) 1.75
*Nos. B6-B8 (3)* 5.25

Nos. B6-B8 were issued by the Vichy government in France, but were not placed on sale in Inini.

Nos. 44-45 Srchd. in Black or Red

**1944 Engr.** ***Perf. 12½x12***
**B9** 50c + 1.50fr on 2.50fr deep blue (R) 1.25
**B10** + 2.50fr on 1fr dp lilac 1.25

Colonial Development Fund.

Nos. B9-B10 were issued by the Vichy government in France, but were not placed on sale in Inini.

**AIR POST SEMI-POSTAL STAMPS**

Nurse with Mother & Child — SPAP1

**Unwmk.**

**1942, June 22 Engr.** ***Perf. 13***
**CB1** SPAP1 1.50fr + 50c green 1.25
**CB2** SPAP1 2fr + 6fr brn & red 1.25

Native children's welfare fund.

Nos. CB1-CB2 were issued by the Vichy government in France, but were not placed on sale in Inini.

**Colonial Education Fund**
Common Design Type

**1942, June 22**
**CB3** CD86a 1.20fr + 1.80fr blue & red 1.25

No. CB3 was issued by the Vichy government in France, but was not placed on sale in Inini.

**POSTAGE DUE STAMPS**

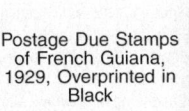

Postage Due Stamps of French Guiana, 1929, Overprinted in Black

**1932, Apr. 7 Unwmk.** ***Perf. 13½x14***
**J1** D3 5c indigo & Prus bl .25 *.40*
**J2** D3 10c bis brn & Prus grn .65 *1.00*
**J3** D3 20c grn & rose red .65 *1.00*
**J4** D3 30c ol brn & rose red .65 *1.00*
**J5** D3 50c vio & ol brn 1.00 *1.50*
**J6** D3 60c brn red & ol brn 1.10 *1.50*

Overprinted in Black or Red

**J7** D4 1fr dp bl & org brn 1.75 *1.75*
**J8** D4 2fr brn red & bluish grn 2.50 *2.50*
**J9** D4 3fr vio & blk (R) 10.00 *11.00*
**J10** D4 3fr vio & blk 4.25 *5.00*
*Nos. J1-J10 (10)* 22.80 *26.65*

# IONIAN ISLANDS

ī-ˈō-nē-ən ˈī-ləndz

LOCATION — Seven Islands, of which six-Corfu, Paxos, Lefkas (Santa Maura), Cephalonia, Ithaca and Zante-are in the Ionian Sea west of Greece, and a seventh-Cerigo (Kithyra)-is in the Mediterranean south of Greece
GOVT. — Integral part of Kingdom of Greece
AREA — 752 sq. miles
POP. — 231,510 (1938)

These islands were acquired by Great Britain in 1815 but in 1864 were ceded to Greece on request of the inhabitants.

In 1941 the islands were occupied by Italian forces. The Italians withdrew in 1943 and German forces continued the occupation, using current Greek stamps without overprinting, except for Zante.

For stamps of the Italian occupation of Corfu, see Corfu.

10 Oboli = 1 Penny
12 Pence = 1 Shilling
100 Lepta = 1 Drachma
100 Centesimi = 1 Lira

**Watermarks**

Wmk. 138 — "2"

Wmk. 139 — "1"

**ISSUES OF THE BRITISH PROTECTORATE**

Queen Victoria — A1

**1859 Unwmk. Engr.** ***Imperf.***
**1** A1 (½p) orange 130.00 *700.00*

**Wmk. 138**
**2** A1 (1p) blue 32.50 *275.00*

**Wmk. 139**
**3** A1 (2p) lake 26.00 *275.00*
*Nos. 1-3 (3)* 188.50 *1,250.*

Forged cancellations are plentiful.

**ISSUED UNDER ITALIAN OCCUPATION**

Values of stamps overprinted by letterpress in pairs are for unsevered pairs. Single stamps, unused, sell for one third the price of a pair; used, one half the price of a pair.

Handstamped overprints were also applied to pairs, with "isola" instead of "isole."

**Issue for Cephalonia and Ithaca**
Stamps of Greece, 1937-38, Overprinted in Pairs Vertically, Reading Down, or Horizontally (H) in Black

***Perf. 12½x12, 13½x12, 12x13½***
**1941 Wmk. 252, Unwmk.**
**N1** A69 5 l brn red & bl 55.00 *55.00*
**N2** A70 10 l bl & red brn (#413) (H) 55.00 *55.00*
*a.* On No. 397 400.00 *400.00*
**N3** A71 20 l blk & grn (H) 55.00 *55.00*
*a.* Overprint inverted 275.00 225.00
**N4** A72 40 l green & blk 55.00 *55.00*
**N5** A73 50 l brown & blk 55.00 *55.00*
**N6** A74 80 l ind & yel brn (H) 95.00 95.00
*a.* Overprint inverted 350.00 275.00
**N7** A67 1d green (H) 260.00 200.00
**N8** A84 1.50d green (H) 200.00 130.00
*a.* Overprint inverted 325.00 240.00
**N9** A75 2d ultra 55.00 55.00
**N10** A76 5d red 200.00 90.00
**N11** A77 6d olive brown 200.00 90.00
**N12** A78 7d dark brown 200.00 90.00
**N13** A67 8d dp blue (H) 225.00 130.00
**N14** A79 10d red brn 200.00 90.00
**N15** A80 15d green 275.00 145.00
**N16** A81 25d dk blue (H) 300.00 200.00
*a.* Overprint inverted 650.00 525.00
**N17** A84 30d org brn (H) 1,400. 950.00
*a.* Overprint inverted 2,100. 1,050.
*Nos. N1-N17 (17)* 3,885. 2,540.

A variety with wrong font "C" in "Cephalonia" is found in several positions in each sheet of all denominations except those overprinted on single stamps. It sells for about three times the price of a normal pair.

Several other minor spelling errors in the overprint occur on several denominations in one of the printings.

Forgeries exist of many of the higher valued stamps and minor varieties of Nos. N1-N17, NC1-NC11 and NRA1-NRA5.

**Overprint Reading Up**

*N1a* A69 5 l 55.00 *55.00*
*N4a* A72 40 l 55.00 *55.00*
*N5a* A73 50 l 55.00 *55.00*
*N9a* A75 2d 72.50 65.00
*N10a* A76 5d 200.00 87.50
*N11a* A77 6d 200.00 87.50
*N12a* A78 7d 200.00 87.50
*N14a* A79 10d 200.00 95.00
*N15a* A80 15d 275.00 145.00
*Nos. N1a-N15a (9)* 1,312. 732.50

**General Issue**

Stamps of Italy, 1929, Overprinted in Red or Black

**1941 Wmk. 140** ***Perf. 14***
**N18** A90 5c olive brn (R) .80 *2.75*
**N19** A92 10c dk brown (R) .80 *2.75*
**N20** A91 20c rose red .80 *2.75*
**N21** A94 25c deep green .80 *2.75*
**N22** A95 30c olive brn (R) .80 *2.75*
*a.* "SOLE" for "ISOLE" 72.50
**N23** A95 50c purple (R) .80 *2.75*
**N24** A94 75c rose red .80 *2.75*
**N25** A94 1.25 l dp blue (R) .80 *2.75*
*Nos. N18-N25 (8)* 6.40 *22.00*

The stamps overprinted "Isole Jonie" were issued for all the Ionian Islands except Cerigo which used regular postage stamps of Greece.

### ISSUED UNDER GERMAN OCCUPATION

#### Zante Issue

Nos. N21 and N23 with Additional Handstamped Ovpt. in Black

**1943 Wmk. 140 *Perf. 14***

| | | | |
|---|---|---|---|
| **N26** | A94 25c deep green | 25.00 | *45.00* |
| *a.* | Carmine overprint | 35.00 | *75.00* |
| **N27** | A95 50c purple | 25.00 | *45.00* |
| *a.* | Carmine overprint | 35.00 | *75.00* |

No. N19 with this overprint is a proof. Value, black $70; carmine $375.

Nos. N26-N27 were in use 8 days, then were succeeded by stamps of Greece.

Forgeries of Nos. N26-N27, NC13 and their cancellations are plentiful.

---

Greek stamps with Italian overprints for the islands of Cerigo (Kithyra), Paxos and Lefkas (Santa Maura) are fraudulent.

---

### OCCUPATION AIR POST STAMPS

#### Issued under Italian Occupation

#### Issue for Cephalonia and Ithaca

Stamps of Greece Overprinted in Pairs Vertically, Reading Down, or Horizontally (H) in Black Like Nos. N1-N17

***Perf. 13x12½, 12½x13***

**1941 Unwmk.**

**On Greece Nos. C22, C23, C25 and C27 to C30**

**Grayish Paper**

| | | | |
|---|---|---|---|
| **NC1** | AP16 1d dp red | 145.00 | *130.00* |
| **NC1A** | AP17 2d dl bl | 80.00 | *65.00* |
| **NC2** | AP19 7d bl vio (H) | 160.00 | *190.00* |
| *a.* | Overprint inverted | 350.00 | 175.00 |
| **NC3** | AP21 25d rose (H) | 650.00 | 475.00 |
| *a.* | Overprint inverted | 1,050. | 525.00 |
| **NC4** | AP22 30d dk grn | 800.00 | 550.00 |
| *a.* | Overprint reading up | 800.00 | 550.00 |
| *b.* | Horizontal overprint on single stamp | — | — |
| *c.* | As "b," inverted | — | |
| **NC5** | AP23 50d vio (H) | 4,500. | 3,500. |
| *a.* | Overprint inverted | 6,500. | 4,000. |
| **NC6** | AP24 100d brown | 2,250. | 1,900. |
| *a.* | Overprint reading up | 2,250. | 1,900. |

No. NC1A is known only with overprint reading up.

**On Greece Nos. C31-C34**

**Reengraved; White Paper**

| | | | |
|---|---|---|---|
| **NC7** | AP16 1d red | 145.00 | *130.00* |
| **NC8** | AP17 2d gray bl | 120.00 | *110.00* |
| *a.* | Overprint reading up | 120.00 | 110.00 |
| *b.* | Horiz. ovpt. on pair | *2,400.* | *1,900.* |
| *c.* | Horizontal overprint on single stamp | | |
| **NC9** | AP18 5d vio (H) | 130.00 | 105.00 |
| *a.* | Overprint inverted | 1,100. | 500.00 |
| *b.* | Vert. ovpt. on single stamp, up or down | 1,100. | 525.00 |
| **NC10** | AP19 7d dp ultra (H) | 325.00 | 250.00 |
| *a.* | Overprint inverted | 1,050. | 450.00 |

**Overprinted Horizontally on No. C36**

***Rouletted 13½***

| | | | |
|---|---|---|---|
| **NC11** | D3 50 l vio brn | 2,400. | 1,900. |
| *a.* | Pair, one without ovpt. | | — |
| *b.* | On No. C36a | | — |

See footnote following No. N17.

#### General Issue

Italy No. C13 Overprinted in Red Like Nos. N18-N25

**1941 Wmk. 140 *Perf. 14***

| | | | |
|---|---|---|---|
| **NC12** | AP3 50c olive brown | .80 | *3.25* |
| *a.* | "SOLE" for "ISOLE" | 65.00 | |

Used in all the Ionian Islands except Cerigo which used air post stamps of Greece.

No. NC12 with additional overprint "BOLLO" is a revenue stamp.

**Issued under German Occupation**

**ZANTE ISSUE**

No. NC12 with Additional Handstamped Overprint in Black Like Nos. N26-N27

**1943 Wmk. 140 *Perf. 14***

| | | | |
|---|---|---|---|
| **NC13** | AP3 50c olive brown | 27.50 | *55.00* |
| *a.* | "SOLE" for "ISOLE" | *450.00* | |
| *b.* | Carmine overprint | 150.00 | *300.00* |

See note after No. N27.

---

### OCCUPATION POSTAGE DUE STAMPS

#### General Issue

Postage Due Stamps of Italy, 1934, Overprinted in Black Like Nos. N18-N25

**1941 Wmk. 140 *Perf. 14***

| | | | |
|---|---|---|---|
| **NJ1** | D6 10c blue | 3.25 | *6.50* |
| **NJ2** | D6 20c rose red | 3.25 | *6.50* |
| **NJ3** | D6 30c red orange | 3.25 | *6.50* |
| **NJ4** | D7 1 l red orange | 3.25 | *6.50* |
| | *Nos. NJ1-NJ4 (4)* | 13.00 | *26.00* |

See footnote after No. N25.

---

### OCCUPATION POSTAL TAX STAMPS

#### Issued under Italian Occupation

#### Issue for Cephalonia and Ithaca

Greece No. RA56 with Additional Overprint on Horizontal Pair in Black Like Nos. N1-N17

***Serrate Roulette 13½***

**1941 Unwmk.**

| | | | |
|---|---|---|---|
| **NRA1** | D3 10 l car (Bl+Bk) | 32.50 | *40.00* |
| *a.* | Blue overprint double | 105.00 | 105.00 |
| *b.* | Inverted overprint | 300.00 | 300.00 |

**Same Overprint Reading Down on Vertical Pairs of Nos. RA61-RA63**

***Perf. 13½x12***

| | | | |
|---|---|---|---|
| **NRA2** | PT7 10 l brt rose, *pale rose* | 35.00 | 35.00 |
| *a.* | Overprint on horiz. pair | 120.00 | 75.00 |
| *b.* | Horizontal overprint on single stamp | *1,100.* | |
| *c.* | Overprint reading up | 35.00 | 35.00 |
| **NRA3** | PT7 50 l gray grn, *pale grn* | 32.50 | 24.00 |
| *a.* | Overprint reading up | 32.50 | 24.00 |
| *b.* | Ovpt. on horiz. pair | — | — |
| *c.* | Horizontal overprint on single stamp | — | — |
| **NRA4** | PT7 1d dl bl, *lt bl* | 90.00 | 72.50 |
| *a.* | Overprint reading up | 105.00 | 95.00 |

**Same Overprint Reading Down on Vertical Pair of No. RA65**

| | | | |
|---|---|---|---|
| **NRA5** | PT7 50 l gray grn, *pale grn* | 875.00 | 875.00 |
| *a.* | Overprint reading up | 875.00 | 875.00 |

Nos. NRA5 and NRA5a were not placed in use on any compulsory day.

See footnote following No. N17.

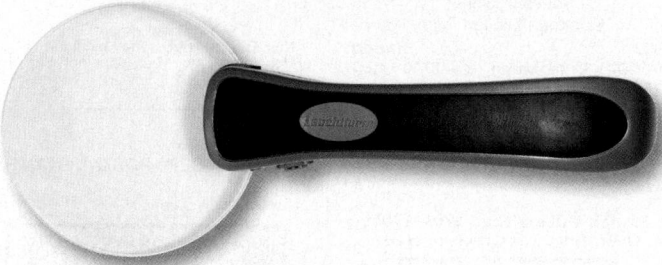

# IRAN

i-'rän

## (Persia)

LOCATION — Western Asia, bordering on the Persian Gulf and the Gulf of Oman
GOVT. — Islamic republic
AREA — 636,000 sq. mi.
POP. — 65,179,752 (1999 est.)
CAPITAL — Tehran

20 Shahis (or Chahis) = 1 Kran
10 Krans = 1 Toman
100 Centimes = 1 Franc = 1 Kran (1881)
100 Dinars = 1 Rial (1933)
100 Rials = 1 Pahlavi
100 Rials = 1 Toman

**Catalogue values for unused stamps in this country are for Never Hinged items, beginning with Scott 1054 in the regular postage section, Scott B36 in the semi-postal section, Scott C83 in the airpost section, Scott O72 in the officials section, Scott Q36 in the parcel post section, and Scott RA4 in the postal tax section.**

Values of early stamps vary according to condition. Quotations for Nos. 1-20, 33-40 are for fine copies. Very fine to superb specimens sell at much higher prices, and inferior or poor copies sell at reduced prices, depending on the condition of the individual specimen.

Cracked gum on unused stamps does not detract from the value.

Beware of forgeries and/or reprints of most Iran stamps between the years 1870-1925. Scott values are for genuine stamps. Collectors should be aware that forgeries of many issues outnumber genuine examples by factors of 10 or 20 to one. Failing specialized knowledge on the part of the collector, these stamps should be examined or authenticated by acknowledged experts before purchase.

### Watermarks

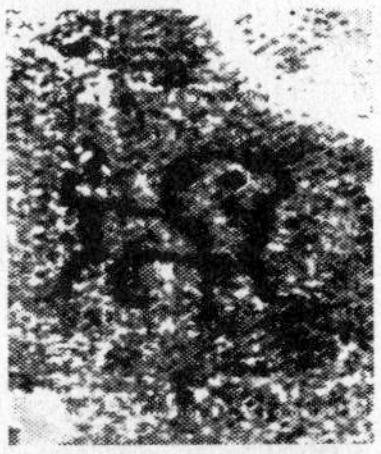

Wmk. 161 — Lion

Wmk. 306 — Arms of Iran

Wmk. 316 — Persian Inscription

Wmk. 349 — Persian Inscription and Crown in Circle

Illustration of Wmk. 349 shown sideways. Circles in Wmk. 349 are 95mm apart.

Wmk. 353 — Persian Inscription and Coat of Arms in Circle

Wmk. 381 — "Islamic Republic of Iran" in Persian (Partial Illustration)

Many issues have handstamped surcharges. As usual with such surcharges there are numerous inverted, double and similar varieties.

Coat of Arms
A1 A2

Design A2 has value numeral below lion.

**1870 Unwmk. Typo. *Imperf.***

| | | |
|---|---|---|
| **1** | A1 1s dull violet | 275.00 |
| **2** | A1 2s green | 225.00 |
| **3** | A1 4s greenish blue | 175.00 |
| **4** | A1 8s red | 175.00 |
| | *Nos. 1-4 (4)* | 850.00 |

Values for used examples of Nos. 1-4 are omitted, since this issue was only pen canceled. After 1875, postmarked remainders were sold to collectors. Values same as unused.

Printed in blocks of 4. Many shades exist. Forgeries exist.

### Printed on Both Sides

| | | |
|---|---|---|
| *1a* | A1 1s | 10,000. |
| *2a* | A1 2s | 5,000. |
| *3a* | A1 4s | 2,000. |
| *4a* | A1 8s | 5,000. |

### *Vertically Rouletted 10½ on 1 or 2 Sides*

**1875 Thick Wove Paper**

| | | | |
|---|---|---|---|
| **11** | A2 1s black | 200.00 | 75.00 |
| *a.* | Imperf. | *2,000.* | *5,000.* |
| **12** | A2 2s blue | 175.00 | 75.00 |
| *a.* | Tête bêche pair | *30,000.* | |
| *b.* | Imperf. | — | — |
| **13** | A2 4s vermilion | 300.00 | 100.00 |
| *a.* | Imperf. | — | — |
| *b.* | 4s bright red, thin paper, imperf. | 525.00 | *525.00* |
| **14** | A2 8s yellow green | 200.00 | 75.00 |
| *b.* | Tête bêche pair | *12,500.* | *7,500.* |
| *c.* | Imperf. | *400.00* | *400.00* |
| | *Nos. 11-14 (4)* | 875.00 | 325.00 |

Four varieties of each.

Nos. 11-14 were printed in horizontal strips of 4 with 3-10mm spacing between stamps. The strips were then cut very close all around (generally touching or cutting the outer frame-lines). Then they were hand-rouletted between the stamps. Values are for stamps with rouletting on both sides and margins clear at top and bottom. Stamps showing the rouletting on only one side sell for considerably less.

Nos. 11 to 14 also exist pin-perforated and percé en scie.

No. 13b has spacing of 2-3mm.

See Nos. 15-20, 33-40.

### Medium to Thin White or Grayish Paper

**1876 *Imperf.***

| | | | |
|---|---|---|---|
| **14A** | A2 1s black | 275.00 | *375.00* |
| **15** | A2 1s gray black | 45.00 | *100.00* |
| *a.* | Printed on both sides | *1,500.* | |
| *b.* | Laid paper | 1,000. | 1,500. |
| **16** | A2 2s gray blue | 550.00 | *700.00* |
| *a.* | Printed on both sides | *3,000.* | |
| **17** | A2 2s black | 650.00 | |
| *a.* | Tête bêche pair | *5,750.* | |
| **18** | A2 4s vermilion | 325.00 | 100.00 |
| *a.* | Printed on both sides | 1,500. | 600.00 |
| **19** | A2 1k rose | 1,000. | 100.00 |
| *a.* | Printed on both sides | | 1,200. |
| *b.* | Laid paper | *3,500.* | 400.00 |
| *c.* | 1k yellow (error) | *20,000.* | 5,500. |
| *d.* | Tête bêche pair | | *100,000.* |
| **20** | A2 4k yellow | 3,000. | 200.00 |
| *a.* | Printed on both sides | | *2,000.* |
| *b.* | Laid paper | *3,000.* | 275.00 |
| *c.* | Tête bêche pair | | *20,000.* |

Nos. 15-16, 18-20 were printed in blocks of 4, and Nos. 14A and 17 in vertical strips of 4, with spacing of 2mm or less.

Nos. 14A and 17 are on medium to thick grayish wove paper. Forgeries exist.

*Official reprints of the 1s and 4s are on thick coarse white paper without gum. Value, each $350.*

### Unofficial Reprints

*1875 and 1876 issues.*

*The reprints of the 1s and 1k stamps are readily told; the pearls of the circle are heavier, the borders of the circles containing the Persian numeral of value are wider and the figure "1" below the lion is always Roman.*

*The reprints of the 2s have the outer line of the frame at the left and at the bottom broken and on some specimens entirely missing.*

*A distinguishing mark by which to tell the 4s and 4k stamps is the frame, the outer line of which is of the same thickness as the inner line, while on the originals the inner line is very thin and the outer line thick; another feature of most of the reprints is a gash in the lower part of the circle below the figure "4."*

*In the reprints of the 8s stamps the small scroll nearest to the circles with Persian numerals at the bottom of the stamp touches the frame below it; the inner and outer lines of the frame are of equal thickness, while in the originals the outer line is much heavier than the inner one.*

*All reprints are found canceled to order.*

Nasser-eddin Shah Qajar — A3

### *Perf. 10½, 11, 12, 13, and Compounds*

**1876 Litho.**

| | | | |
|---|---|---|---|
| **27** | A3 1s lilac & blk | 30.00 | 6.00 |
| **28** | A3 2s green & blk | 35.00 | 7.50 |
| **29** | A3 5s rose & blk | 30.00 | 4.00 |
| **30** | A3 10s blue & blk | 45.00 | 8.00 |
| | *Nos. 27-30 (4)* | 140.00 | 25.50 |

Bisects of the 5s and 1s, the latter used with 2s stamps, were used to make up the 2½ shahis postcard rate. Bisects of the 10s were used in the absence of 5s stamps to make up the letter rate.

The 10s was bisected and surcharged "5 Shahi" or "5 Shahy" for local use in Azerbaijan province and Khoy in 1877.

"Imperfs" of the 5s are envelope cutouts.

Forgeries and official reprints exist.

Very fine examples will have perforations cutting the background net on one side. Genuine stamps withs perfs clear of net on all four sides are very scarce.

**1878 Typo. *Imperf.***

| | | | | |
|---|---|---|---|---|
| 33 | A2 | 1k car rose | 600.00 | 110.00 |
| 34 | A2 | 1k red, *yellow* | *3,750.* | 140.00 |
| *a.* | | Tête bêche pair | | *10,000.* |
| 35 | A2 | 4k ultramarine | 325.00 | 110.00 |
| *a.* | | Printed on both sides | | *5,000.* |
| 36 | A2 | 5k violet | 1,000. | 250.00 |
| 37 | A2 | 5k gold | *6,000.* | 500.00 |
| 38 | A2 | 5k red bronze | *17,500.* | 2,000. |
| 39 | A2 | 5k vio bronze | *40,000.* | 3,000. |
| 40 | A2 | 1t bronze, *bl* | *70,000.* | *7,500.* |

Four varieties of each except for 4k which has 3.

Nos. 33 and 34 are printed from redrawn clichés. They have wide colorless circles around the corner numerals.

Nasser-eddin Shah Qajar — A6

***Perf. 10½, 12, 13, and Compounds***

**1879 Litho.**

| | | | | |
|---|---|---|---|---|
| 41 | A6 | 1k brown & blk | 450.00 | 7.00 |
| *a.* | | Pair, imperf between | | — |
| *b.* | | Inverted center | | *5,000.* |
| 42 | A6 | 5k blue & blk | 400.00 | 5.00 |
| *a.* | | Imperf., pair | 3,000. | *600.00* |
| *b.* | | Inverted center | | 2,500. |
| *c.* | | Inverted center, imperf | | 2,500. |

**1880**

| | | | | |
|---|---|---|---|---|
| 43 | A6 | 1s red & black | 50.00 | 15.00 |
| *b.* | | Pair, imperf between | *4,500.* | |
| 44 | A6 | 2s yellow & blk | 85.00 | 10.00 |
| *a.* | | Imperf., pair | | 2,500. |
| 45 | A6 | 5s green & blk | 350.00 | 2.00 |
| 46 | A6 | 10s violet & blk | 700.00 | 30.00 |
| | | *Nos. 43-46 (4)* | 1,185. | 57.00 |

Forgeries and official reprints exist.

*The 2, 5 and 10sh of this issue and the 1 and 5kr of the 1879 issue have been reprinted from a new die which resembles the 5 shahi envelope. The aigrette is shorter than on the original stamps and touches the circle above it.*

**Imperf., Pair**

| | | | | |
|---|---|---|---|---|
| *43a* | A6 | 1s | 1,500. | |
| *44a* | A6 | 2s | | *2,000.* |
| *46a* | A6 | 10s | — | 600.00 |

Sun — A7

**1881 Litho. *Perf. 12, 13, 12x13***

| | | | | |
|---|---|---|---|---|
| 47 | A7 | 5c dull violet | 50.00 | 25.00 |
| 48 | A7 | 10c rose | 50.00 | 25.00 |
| 49 | A7 | 25c green | 6,750. | 100.00 |
| | | *Nos. 47-49 (3)* | 6,850. | 150.00 |

**1882 Engr., Border Litho.**

| | | | | |
|---|---|---|---|---|
| 50 | A7 | 5c blue vio & vio | 50.00 | 60.00 |
| 51 | A7 | 10c dp pink & rose | 50.00 | 60.00 |
| 52 | A7 | 25c deep grn & grn | 1,400. | 40.00 |
| | | *Nos. 50-52 (3)* | 1,500. | 160.00 |

Very fine examples of Nos. 50-52 will have perforations cutting the outer colored border but clear of the inner framelines.

Counterfeits of Nos. 50-52, 53, 53a are plentiful and have been used to create forgeries of Nos. 66, 66a, 70 and 70a. They usually have a strong, complete inner frameline at right. On genuine stamps that line is weak or missing.

A8

Type I

Type II (error)

Shah Nasr-ed-Din
A9 A10

A11

Type I: Three dots at right end of scroll.
Type II: Two dots at right end of scroll.

**1882-84 Engr.**

| | | | | |
|---|---|---|---|---|
| 53 | A8 | 5s green, type I | 50.00 | 1.50 |
| *a.* | | 5s green, type II | 100.00 | 10.00 |
| 54 | A9 | 10s buff, org & blk | 85.00 | 10.00 |
| 55 | A10 | 50c buff, org & blk | 700.00 | 80.00 |
| 56 | A10 | 50c gray & blk ('84) | 150.00 | 70.00 |
| 57 | A10 | 1fr blue & black | 150.00 | 20.00 |
| 58 | A10 | 5fr rose red & blk | 140.00 | 20.00 |
| 59 | A11 | 10fr buff, red & blk | 150.00 | 30.00 |
| | | *Nos. 53-59 (7)* | 1,425. | 231.50 |

Crude forgeries of Nos. 58-59 exist. Halves of the 10s, 50c and 1fr surcharged with Farsi characters in red or black are frauds. The 50c and 1fr surcharged with a large "5" surrounded by rays are also frauds.

No. 59 used is valued for c-t-o.

For overprints and surcharges see #66-72.

Very fine examples of Nos. 53-59 will have perforations cutting the outer colored border but clear of the inner framelines.

A12

A13

***Perf. 12-12½, 13***

**1885, March-May Litho.**

| | | | | |
|---|---|---|---|---|
| 59A | A12 | 5c blue | 1,200. | 50.00 |
| *a.* | | 5c violet blue | 1,200. | 75.00 |
| *b.* | | 5c ultramarine | 1,200. | 75.00 |
| *c.* | | 5c dp reddish lilac | 2,000. | 300.00 |
| *d.* | | As "a," imperf | 6,000. | |

No. 59A was issued because of an urgent need for 5c stamps, pending the arrival of No. 62 in July. No. 59A has 88 sunrays instead of the 124 sunrays on the typographed stamp, No. 62.

**1885-86 Typo.**

| | | | | |
|---|---|---|---|---|
| 60 | A12 | 1c green | 25.00 | 2.00 |
| 61 | A12 | 2c rose | 25.00 | 2.00 |
| 62 | A12 | 5c dull blue | 200.00 | 1.00 |
| 63 | A13 | 10c brown | 40.00 | 2.00 |
| 64 | A13 | 1k slate | 100.00 | 3.00 |
| 65 | A13 | 5k dull vio ('86) | 800.00 | 40.00 |
| | | *Nos. 60-65 (6)* | 1,190. | 50.00 |

**Nos. 53, 54, 56 and 58 Surcharged in Black**

a

b

c

d

e

f

**1885**

| | | | | |
|---|---|---|---|---|
| 66 | (a) | 6c on 5s grn, type I | 150.00 | 30.00 |
| *a.* | | 6c on 5s green, type II | *275.00* | *100.00* |
| 67 | (b) | 12c on 50c gray & blk | 150.00 | 30.00 |
| 68 | (c) | 18c on 10s buff, org & black | 150.00 | 30.00 |
| 69 | (d) | 1t on 5fr rose red & black | 150.00 | 50.00 |
| | | *Nos. 66-69 (4)* | 600.00 | 140.00 |

**1887**

| | | | | |
|---|---|---|---|---|
| 70 | (e) | 3c on 5s grn, type I | 150.00 | 30.00 |
| *a.* | | 3c on 5s green, type II | *275.00* | *100.00* |
| 71 | (a) | 6c on 10s buff, org & blk | 150.00 | 30.00 |
| 72 | (f) | 8c on 50c gray & blk | 150.00 | 30.00 |
| | | *Nos. 70-72 (3)* | 450.00 | 90.00 |

The word "OFFICIEL" indicated that the surcharged stamps were officially authorized.

Surcharges on the same basic stamps of values other than those listed are believed to be bogus.

Counterfeits of Nos. 66-72 abound.

Very fine examples of Nos. 66-72 will have perforations cutting the outer colored border but clear of the inner framelines.

Beware of forgeries and/or reprints of most Iran stamps between the years 1870-1925. Scott values are for genuine stamps. Collectors should be aware that forgeries of many issues outnumber genuine examples by factors of 10 or 20 to one. Failing specialized knowledge on the part of the collector, these stamps should be examined or authenticated by acknowledged experts before purchase.

A14

A15

**1889 Typo. *Perf. 11, 13½, 11x13½***

| | | | | |
|---|---|---|---|---|
| 73 | A14 | 1c pale rose | 2.50 | .75 |
| 74 | A14 | 2c pale blue | 2.50 | .75 |
| 75 | A14 | 5c lilac | 1.50 | .50 |
| 76 | A14 | 7c brown | 7.50 | 1.50 |
| 77 | A15 | 10c black | 2.50 | .75 |
| 78 | A15 | 1k red orange | 4.50 | .75 |
| 79 | A15 | 2k rose | 40.00 | 6.00 |
| 80 | A15 | 5k green | 25.00 | 6.00 |
| | | *Nos. 73-80 (8)* | 86.00 | 17.00 |

All values exist imperforate.

Canceled to order stamps of No. 76 abound.

For surcharges see Nos. 622-625.

Nos. 73-80 with average centering, faded colors and/or toned paper sell for much less.

A16

A17

**1891 *Perf. 10½, 11½***

| | | | | |
|---|---|---|---|---|
| 81 | A16 | 1c black | 2.50 | 1.00 |
| 82 | A16 | 2c brown | 2.50 | 1.00 |
| 83 | A16 | 5c deep blue | 2.50 | .25 |
| 84 | A16 | 7c gray | 350.00 | 12.00 |
| 85 | A16 | 10c rose | 2.50 | .50 |
| 86 | A16 | 14c orange | 2.50 | 1.50 |
| 87 | A17 | 1k green | 30.00 | 2.00 |
| 88 | A17 | 2k orange | 700.00 | 25.00 |
| 89 | A17 | 5k ocher yellow | 8.00 | *30.00* |
| | | *Nos. 81-89 (9)* | 1,100. | 73.25 |

For surcharges see Nos. 626-629.

A18

Nasser-eddin Shah Qajar — A19

**1894 *Perf. 12½***

| | | | | |
|---|---|---|---|---|
| 90 | A18 | 1c lilac | 1.00 | .25 |
| 91 | A18 | 2c blue green | 1.00 | .25 |
| 92 | A18 | 5c ultramarine | 1.00 | .25 |
| 93 | A18 | 8c brown | 1.00 | .25 |

***Perf. 11½x11***

| | | | | |
|---|---|---|---|---|
| 94 | A19 | 10c orange | 1.25 | .75 |
| 95 | A19 | 16c rose | 25.00 | *75.00* |
| 96 | A19 | 1k red & yellow | 3.00 | .75 |
| 97 | A19 | 2k brn org & pale bl | 4.00 | 1.00 |
| 98 | A19 | 5k violet & silver | 10.00 | 1.50 |
| 99 | A19 | 10k red & gold | 20.00 | 10.00 |
| 100 | A19 | 50k green & gold | 50.00 | 15.00 |
| | | *Nos. 90-100 (11)* | 117.25 | 105.00 |

Canceled to order stamps sell for one-third of listed values.

*Reprints exist. They are hard to distinguish from the originals. Value, set $15.*

See Nos. 104-112, 136-144. For overprints see Nos. 120-128, 152-167, 173-181. For surcharges see Nos. 101-103, 168, 206, 211.

**Nos. 93, 98 With Violet or Magenta Surcharge**

a

b

**1897 *Perf. 12½, 11½x11***

| | | | | |
|---|---|---|---|---|
| 101 | A18(a) | 5c on 8c brown (V) | 30.00 | 5.00 |
| *a.* | | Inverted surcharge | *150.00* | *25.00* |
| 102 | A19(b) | 1k on 5k vio & sil (V) | 40.00 | 20.00 |
| 103 | A19(b) | 2k on 5k vio & sil (M) | 60.00 | 35.00 |
| | | *Nos. 101-103 (3)* | 130.00 | 60.00 |

Forgeries exist.

**Lion Type of 1894 and**

Mozaffar-eddin Shah Qajar — A22

**1898 Typo. *Perf. 12½***

| | | | | |
|---|---|---|---|---|
| 104 | A18 | 1c gray | 5.00 | .35 |
| 105 | A18 | 2c pale brown | 5.00 | .35 |
| 106 | A18 | 3c dull violet | 10.00 | 3.00 |
| 107 | A18 | 4c vermilion | 10.00 | 3.00 |
| 108 | A18 | 5c yellow | 5.00 | .25 |
| 109 | A18 | 8c orange | 20.00 | 7.00 |
| 110 | A18 | 10c light blue | 5.00 | .50 |
| 111 | A18 | 12c rose | 15.00 | 1.00 |
| 112 | A18 | 16c green | 20.00 | 7.00 |
| 113 | A22 | 1k ultramarine | 10.00 | 1.00 |
| 114 | A22 | 2k pink | 10.00 | 2.00 |
| 115 | A22 | 3k yellow | 10.00 | 3.00 |
| 116 | A22 | 4k gray | 10.00 | 5.00 |
| 117 | A22 | 5k emerald | 10.00 | 6.00 |
| 118 | A22 | 10k orange | 40.00 | 15.00 |
| 119 | A22 | 50k bright vio | 60.00 | 25.00 |
| | | *Nos. 104-119 (16)* | 245.00 | 79.45 |

*Unauthorized reprints of Nos. 104-119 were made from original clichés. Paper shows a vertical mesh. These abound unused and canceled to order. Value set, unused, hinged, $20.*

See Nos. 145-151. For overprints see Nos. 129-135, 182-188. For surcharges see Nos. 169, 171, 207, 209, 215.

Reprints have been used to make counterfeits of Nos. 120-135, 152-167.

### Stamps of 1898 Handstamped in Violet

a

b

c

d

e

f

g

h

**1899**

| | | | | |
|---|---|---|---|---|
| **120** | (a) | 1c gray | 5.00 | 5.00 |
| **121** | (b) | 2c pale brown | 5.00 | *8.00* |
| **122** | (b) | 3c dull violet | 12.00 | *15.00* |
| **123** | (c) | 4c vermilion | 18.00 | *30.00* |
| **124** | (c) | 5c yellow | 10.00 | 3.00 |
| **125** | (d) | 8c orange | 15.00 | *40.00* |
| **126** | (d) | 10c light blue | 6.50 | *10.00* |
| *a.* | | Type "b" handstamp | *500.00* | *500.00* |
| **127** | (d) | 12c rose | 15.00 | 8.00 |
| **128** | (d) | 16c green | 25.00 | *30.00* |
| **129** | (e) | 1k ultramarine | 25.00 | 10.00 |
| **130** | (f) | 2k pink | 30.00 | 25.00 |
| **131** | (f) | 3k yellow | 80.00 | *250.00* |
| **132** | (g) | 4k gray | 100.00 | *250.00* |
| **133** | (g) | 5k emerald | 30.00 | *40.00* |
| **134** | (h) | 10k orange | 60.00 | 60.00 |
| **135** | (h) | 50k brt violet | 120.00 | *150.00* |
| | | *Nos. 120-135 (16)* | 556.50 | 934.00 |

The handstamped control marks on Nos. 120-135 exist sideways, inverted and double. Counterfeits are plentiful.

### Types of 1894-98

**1899** **Typo.** ***Perf. 12½***

| | | | | |
|---|---|---|---|---|
| **136** | A18 | 1c gray, *green* | 7.50 | .75 |
| **137** | A18 | 2c brown, *green* | 7.50 | .75 |
| **138** | A18 | 3c violet, *green* | 20.00 | 5.00 |
| **139** | A18 | 4c red, *green* | 12.00 | 5.00 |
| **140** | A18 | 5c yellow, *green* | 5.00 | .30 |
| **141** | A18 | 8c orange, *green* | 15.00 | 5.00 |
| **142** | A18 | 10c pale blue, *grn* | 5.00 | .50 |
| **143** | A18 | 12c lake, *green* | 15.00 | 1.25 |
| **144** | A18 | 16c green, *green* | 25.00 | 5.00 |
| **145** | A22 | 1k red | 30.00 | 1.25 |
| **146** | A22 | 2k deep green | 35.00 | 8.50 |
| **147** | A22 | 3k lilac brown | 35.00 | 17.00 |
| **148** | A22 | 4k orange red | 35.00 | 17.00 |
| **149** | A22 | 5k gray brown | 40.00 | 17.00 |
| **150** | A22 | 10k deep blue | 400.00 | 100.00 |
| **151** | A22 | 50k brown | 75.00 | 30.00 |
| | | *Nos. 136-151 (16)* | 762.00 | 214.30 |

Canceled to order stamps abound.

*Unauthorized reprints of Nos. 136-151 were made from original clichés. Paper is chalky and has white gum. The design can be seen through the back of the reprints. Value unused, hinged, set, $30.*

For surcharges and overprints see Nos. 171, 173-188, 206-207, 209, 211, 215.

### Nos. 104-111 Handstamped in Violet

(Struck once on every two stamps.)

**1900**

| | | | | |
|---|---|---|---|---|
| **152** | A18 | 1c gray | 50.00 | 20.00 |
| **153** | A18 | 2c pale brown | 60.00 | 25.00 |
| **154** | A18 | 3c dull violet | 100.00 | 50.00 |
| **155** | A18 | 4c vermilion | 100.00 | 50.00 |
| **156** | A18 | 5c yellow | 25.00 | 10.00 |
| **158** | A18 | 10c light blue | *2,000.* | *2,000.* |
| **159** | A18 | 12c rose | 100.00 | 50.00 |
| | | *Nos. 152-159 (7)* | 2,435. | 2,205. |

Values are for single authenticated stamps. Pairs sell for much more.

This control mark, in genuine state, was not applied to the 8c orange (Nos. 109, 125).

### Same Overprint Handstamped on Nos. 120-127 in Violet

(Struck once on each block of 4.)

| | | | | |
|---|---|---|---|---|
| **160** | A18 | 1c gray | 100.00 | 50.00 |
| **163** | A18 | 4c vermilion | 300.00 | 140.00 |
| **164** | A18 | 5c yellow | 50.00 | 20.00 |
| **166** | A18 | 10c light blue | 1,000. | 500.00 |
| *a.* | | Type "b" handstamp | 400.00 | 200.00 |
| **167** | A18 | 12c rose | 150.00 | 50.00 |
| | | *Nos. 160-167 (5)* | 550.00 | 760.00 |

Values are for single authenticated stamps. Blocks are rare and worth much more.

Counterfeits exist of Nos. 152-167.

No. 93 Surcharged in Violet

**1900**

| | | | | |
|---|---|---|---|---|
| **168** | A18 | 5c on 8c brown | 50.00 | 2.50 |
| *a.* | | Inverted surcharge | *250.00* | *25.00* |

No. 145 Surcharged in Violet

**1901**

| | | | | |
|---|---|---|---|---|
| **169** | A22 | 12c on 1k red | 100.00 | 100.00 |
| *a.* | | Blue surcharge | 125.00 | 125.00 |

Counterfeits exist.

Some specialists state that No. 169 with black surcharge was made for collectors.

A23

**1902** **Violet Surcharge**

| | | | | |
|---|---|---|---|---|
| **171** | A23 | 5k on 50k brown | 200.00 | 80.00 |
| *a.* | | Blue surcharge | 200.00 | 90.00 |

Counterfeits exist. See No. 207.

Nos. 136-151 Overprinted in Black

**1902**

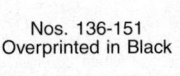

| | | | | |
|---|---|---|---|---|
| **173** | A18 | 1c gray, *green* | 50.00 | 20.00 |
| **174** | A18 | 2c brown, *green* | 50.00 | 20.00 |
| **175** | A18 | 3c violet, *green* | 150.00 | 100.00 |
| **176** | A18 | 4c red, *green* | 200.00 | *200.00* |
| **177** | A18 | 5c yellow, *green* | 20.00 | 5.00 |
| **178** | A18 | 8c orange, *green* | 200.00 | *200.00* |
| **179** | A18 | 10c pale blue, *grn* | 50.00 | 15.00 |
| **180** | A18 | 12c lake, *green* | 125.00 | 50.00 |
| **181** | A18 | 16c green, *green* | 300.00 | 200.00 |
| **182** | A22 | 1k red | 100.00 | 45.00 |
| **183** | A22 | 2k deep green | 250.00 | 100.00 |
| **188** | A22 | 50k brown | 400.00 | 125.00 |

### Overprinted on No. 168

| | | | | |
|---|---|---|---|---|
| **206** | A18 | 5c on 8c brown | 200.00 | 100.00 |

### Overprinted on Nos. 171 and 171a

| | | | | |
|---|---|---|---|---|
| **207** | A23 | 5k on 50k brown | 200.00 | 100.00 |
| *a.* | | On #171a | 250.00 | 100.00 |

### Overprinted on Nos. 169 and 169a

| | | | | |
|---|---|---|---|---|
| **209** | A22 | 12c on 1k red | 100.00 | 50.00 |
| *a.* | | On #169a | 100.00 | 50.00 |

Counterfeits of the overprint of Nos. 173-183, 188, 206-207, 209 are plentiful. Practically all examples with overprint sideways, inverted, double and double with one inverted are frauds.

Nos. 142 Surcharged in Violet

**1902**

| | | | | |
|---|---|---|---|---|
| **211** | A18 | 5c on 10c pale bl, *grn* | 60.00 | 20.00 |

Surcharges in different colors were made for collectors.

Initials of Victor Castaigne, Postmaster of Meshed — A24

**1902** **Typo.** ***Imperf.***

| | | | | |
|---|---|---|---|---|
| **222** | A24 | 1c black | 1,500. | *450.00* |
| *a.* | | Inverted frame | | — |
| *b.* | | Inverted center | — | *3,000.* |
| **223** | A24 | 2c black | 1,250. | *450.00* |
| *a.* | | Inverted frame | | — |
| *b.* | | "2" in right upper corner | *3,000.* | *1,750.* |
| *c.* | | Frame printed on both sides | | — |
| **224** | A24 | 3c black | 3,250. | *1,750.* |
| **225** | A24 | 5c violet | 750.00 | *200.00* |
| *a.* | | "5" in right upper corner | | — |
| *b.* | | Frame printed on both sides | *2,250.* | *1,000.* |
| *c.* | | Inverted center | | — |
| **226** | A24 | 5c black | 900.00 | *350.00* |
| *a.* | | Persian "5" in lower left corner | | — |
| *b.* | | Inverted center | | — |
| **227** | A24 | 12c dull blue | 4,000. | *1,500.* |
| *a.* | | Inverted frame | | — |
| *b.* | | Inverted center | | — |
| **228** | A24 | 1k rose | 30,000. | *3,500.* |

Used values for Nos. 222-228 canceled to order are about ⅓ to ½ the values shown, which are for postally used stamps.

The design of No. 228 differs slightly from the illustration.

Nos. 222-228 were printed in three operations. Inverted centers have frames and numerals upright. Inverted frames have centers and numerals upright.

### *Pin-perforated*

| | | | | |
|---|---|---|---|---|
| **234** | A24 | 12c dull blue | 4,000. | *1,500.* |

The post office at Meshed having exhausted its stock of stamps, the postmaster issued the above series provisionally. The center of the design is the seal of the postmaster who also wrote his initials upon the upper part, using violet ink for the 1k and red ink for the others.

Unauthorized reprints, including pinperforated examples of Nos. 222-226, and forgeries exist.

Expert knowledge or certificates of authenticity are required.

A25

TWO TYPES:

Type I — "CHAHI" or "KRANS" are in capital letters.

Type II — Only "C" of "Chahi" or "K" of "Krans" is a capital.

The 3c and 5c sometimes have a tall narrow figure in the upper left corner. The 5c is also found with the cross at the upper left broken or missing. These varieties are known with many of the overprints.

Stamps of Design A25 have a faint fancy background in the color of the stamp. All issued stamps have handstamped controls as listed.

### Type I
### Handstamp Overprinted in Black

**1902** **Typeset** ***Imperf.***

| | | | | |
|---|---|---|---|---|
| **235** | A25 | 1c gray & buff | *300.00* | 150.00 |
| **236** | A25 | 2c brown & buff | *400.00* | 150.00 |
| **237** | A25 | 3c green & buff | *400.00* | 150.00 |
| **238** | A25 | 5c red & buff | *300.00* | 100.00 |
| **239** | A25 | 12c ultra & buff | *500.00* | 150.00 |
| | | *Nos. 235-239 (5)* | *1,900.* | 700.00 |

Counterfeits abound. Type II stamps with this overprint are forgeries.

The 3c with violet overprint is believed not to have been regularly issued.

Handstamp Overprinted in Rose

**1902** **Type I**

| | | | | |
|---|---|---|---|---|
| **247** | A25 | 1c gray & buff | 25.00 | 2.00 |
| **248** | A25 | 2c brown & buff | 25.00 | 2.00 |
| **249** | A25 | 3c dp grn & buff | 25.00 | 2.00 |
| **250** | A25 | 5c red & buff | 25.00 | .75 |
| **251** | A25 | 10c ol yel & buff | 50.00 | 3.00 |
| **252** | A25 | 12c ultra & buff | 75.00 | 5.00 |
| **253** | A25 | 1k violet & bl | 60.00 | 6.00 |
| **254** | A25 | 2k ol grn & bl | 100.00 | 12.50 |
| **256** | A25 | 10k dk bl & bl | 150.00 | 30.00 |
| **257** | A25 | 50k red & blue | 1,500. | 800.00 |
| | | *Nos. 247-257 (10)* | 2,035. | 863.25 |

A 5k exists but its status is doubtful. Value *$500.*

Nos. 247-257 and the 12c on brown paper and on blue paper with blue quadrille lines are known without overprint but are not believed to have been regularly issued in this condition.

The 1c to 10k, A25 type I, with violet overprint are believed not to have been regularly issued. Five denominations also exist with overprint in blue, black or green.

### Type II

| | | | | |
|---|---|---|---|---|
| **280** | A25 | 1c gray & yellow | 250.00 | 200.00 |
| **281** | A25 | 2c brown & yel | 200.00 | 200.00 |
| **282** | A25 | 3c dk grn & yel | *2,000.* | *750.00* |
| *a.* | | "Persans" | — | — |
| **283** | A25 | 5c red & yellow | 50.00 | *15.00* |
| **284** | A25 | 10c ol yel & yel | 100.00 | 15.00 |
| **285** | A25 | 12c blue & yel | 150.00 | 25.00 |
| **290** | A25 | 50k org red & bl | 1,250. | 600.00 |

The 3c, inscribed "Persans," is not believed to have been regularly issued.

The same overprint in violet was applied to nine denominations of the Type II stamps, but these, too, are believed not to have been regularly issued. The overprint also exists in blue, black and green.

Reprints, counterfeits, counterfeit overprints, with or without cancellations, are plentiful for Nos. 247-257, 280-290.

Five stamps of type A25, type II, in high denominations (10, 20, 25, 50 and 100 tomans), with "Postes 1319" lion overprint in blue, were used only on money orders, not for postage. They are usually numbered on the back in red, blue or black.

> Beware of forgeries and/or reprints of most Iran stamps between the years 1870-1925. Scott values are for genuine stamps. Collectors should be aware that forgeries of many issues outnumber genuine examples by factors of 10 or 20 to one. Failing specialized knowledge on the part of the collector, these stamps should be examined or authenticated by acknowledged experts before purchase.

Handstamp Surcharged in Black

**1902** **Type I**

| | | | | |
|---|---|---|---|---|
| **308** | A25 | 5k on 5k ocher & bl | *200.00* | *50.00* |

Counterfeits of No. 308 abound.

This surcharge in rose, violet, blue or green is considered bogus.

This surcharge on 50k orange red and blue, and on 5k ocher and blue, type II, is considered bogus.

Handstamp Overprinted Diagonally in Black

**1902** **Type I**

| | | | | |
|---|---|---|---|---|
| **315** | A25 | 2c brown & buff | 200.00 | 100.00 |
| *a.* | | Rose overprint | *500.00* | *500.00* |

**Type II**

| | | | | |
|---|---|---|---|---|
| **316** | A25 | 2c brown & yel | — | — |
| *a.* | | Rose overprint | — | — |

"P. L." stands for "Poste Locale."

Counterfeits of Nos. 315-316 exist.

Some specialists believe that Type II stamps were not used officially for this overprint.

Handstamp Overprinted in Black or Rose

**1902** **Type II**

| | | | | |
|---|---|---|---|---|
| **317** | A25 | 2c brn & yellow | 200.00 | 100.00 |
| **318** | A25 | 2c brown & yel (R) | *500.00* | *500.00* |

Counterfeits of Nos. 317-318 exist.

Overprinted in Blue

**1903** **Type I**

| | | | | |
|---|---|---|---|---|
| **321** | A25 | 1k violet & blue | 125.00 | 125.00 |

**Type II**

| | | | | |
|---|---|---|---|---|
| **336** | A25 | 1c gray & yellow | 60.00 | 60.00 |
| **337** | A25 | 2c brown & yellow | 60.00 | 60.00 |
| **338** | A25 | 5c red & yellow | 40.00 | 40.00 |
| **339** | A25 | 10c olive yel & yel | 75.00 | 75.00 |
| **340** | A25 | 12c blue & yellow | 90.00 | 90.00 |
| | | *Nos. 321-340 (6)* | 450.00 | 450.00 |

A 3c Type I exists but was not regularly issued. Value $250.

The overprint also exists in violet and black, but it is doubtful whether such items were regularly issued.

Forgeries of Nos. 321, 336-340 abound. Genuine unused examples are seldom found.

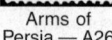

Arms of Persia — A26

Mozaffar-eddin Shah Qajar — A27

**1902 (Dec.)-1904** **Typo.** ***Perf. 12½***

| | | | | |
|---|---|---|---|---|
| **351** | A26 | 1c violet | 2.00 | .25 |
| **352** | A26 | 2c gray | 2.00 | .25 |
| **353** | A26 | 3c green | 2.00 | .25 |
| **354** | A26 | 5c rose | 2.00 | .25 |
| **355** | A26 | 10c yellow brn | 3.00 | 1.50 |
| **356** | A26 | 12c blue | 4.00 | .50 |

**Engr.**

***Perf. 11½x11***

| | | | | |
|---|---|---|---|---|
| **357** | A27 | 1k violet | 15.00 | .50 |
| **358** | A27 | 2k ultramarine | 25.00 | 1.25 |
| **359** | A27 | 5k orange brn | 40.00 | 2.00 |
| **360** | A27 | 10k rose red | 50.00 | 4.00 |
| **361** | A27 | 20k orange ('04) | 40.00 | 5.00 |
| **362** | A27 | 30k green ('04) | 70.00 | 12.50 |
| **363** | A27 | 50k green | 500.00 | 100.00 |
| | | *Nos. 351-363 (13)* | 755.00 | 128.25 |

Nos. 351-363 used are valued canceled to order.

No. 355 exists with blue diagonal surcharge "1 CHAHI"; its status is questioned.

A government decree in November, 1903, required that all picture postcards be censored by the Central Post Office, which would apply a control mark on each card to show that the 2c tax for this service had been paid. No. 352 was overprinted "Controle" in several styles, for this purpose. Value: unused $100; used, from $25.

See Nos. 428-433. For surcharges and overprints see #364-420, 446-447, 464-469, O8-O28, P1.

No. 353 Surcharged in Violet or Blue

**1903**

| | | | | |
|---|---|---|---|---|
| **364** | A26 | 1c on 3c green (V) | 50.00 | 20.00 |
| **365** | A26 | 2c on 3c green (Bl) | 50.00 | 20.00 |

A 2c surcharge on No. 354 exists, but its status is dubious.

No. 360 Surcharged in Blue

| | | | | |
|---|---|---|---|---|
| **366** | A27 | 12c on 10k rose red | 75.00 | 40.00 |
| *a.* | | Black surcharge | 150.00 | 70.00 |
| *b.* | | Violet surcharge | 150.00 | 70.00 |
| | | *Nos. 364-366 (3)* | 175.00 | 80.00 |

Nos. 366, 366a and 366b used are valued canceled to order.

No. 363 Surcharged in Blue or Black

**1903**

| | | | | |
|---|---|---|---|---|
| **368** | A27 | 2t on 50k grn (Bl) | 200.00 | 60.00 |
| *a.* | | Rose surcharge | 225.00 | 100.00 |
| *b.* | | Black surcharge | 225.00 | 100.00 |
| **370** | A27 | 3t on 50k grn (Bk) | 200.00 | 60.00 |
| *a.* | | Violet surcharge | 225.00 | 60.00 |
| *b.* | | Rose surcharge | 250.00 | 125.00 |

No. 363 Surcharged in Blue or Black

**1904**

| | | | | |
|---|---|---|---|---|
| **372** | A27 | 2t on 50k grn (Bl) | 200.00 | 60.00 |
| **375** | A27 | 3t on 50k grn (Bk) | 200.00 | 60.00 |

The 2t on 50k also exists with surcharge in rose, violet, black and magenta; the 3t on 50k in rose, violet and blue. Values about the same unused; about 50 percent higher used.

No. 352 Overprinted in Violet

**1904** ***Perf. 12½***

| | | | | |
|---|---|---|---|---|
| **393** | A26 | 2c gray | 85.00 | 25.00 |
| *a.* | | Black overprint | 100.00 | 30.00 |
| *b.* | | Rose overprint | 90.00 | 25.00 |

This overprint also exists in blue, violet blue, maroon and gray, but these were not regularly issued.

**Stamps of 1903 Surcharged in Black**

a

b

c

**1904**

| | | | | |
|---|---|---|---|---|
| **400** | A26(a) | 3c on 5c rose | 40.00 | .75 |
| **401** | A26(b) | 6c on 10c brown | 50.00 | .75 |
| **402** | A27(c) | 9c on 1k violet | 50.00 | 3.50 |
| | | *Nos. 400-402 (3)* | 140.00 | 5.00 |

**Stamps of 1903 Surcharged in Black, Magenta or Violet**

**1905-06**

| | | | | |
|---|---|---|---|---|
| **404** | A26 | 1c on 3c green ('06) | 50.00 | 20.00 |
| **405** | A27 | 1c on 1k violet | 35.00 | 15.00 |
| **406** | A27 | 2c on 5k orange brn | 40.00 | 25.00 |
| **407** | A26 | 1c on 3c grn (M) ('06) | 15.00 | 5.00 |
| **408** | A27 | 1c on 1k violet (M) | 20.00 | 10.00 |
| **409** | A27 | 2c on 5k org brn (V) | 30.00 | 15.00 |
| | | *Nos. 404-409 (6)* | 190.00 | 90.00 |

Nos. 355 and 358 Surcharged in Violet

**1906**

| | | | | |
|---|---|---|---|---|
| **419** | A26 | 1c on 10c brown | *150.00* | — |
| **420** | A27 | 2c on 2k ultra | *250.00* | — |

Forgeries of Nos. 419-420 are common. Forgeries of No. 420, especially, are hard to distinguish since the original handstamp was used. Genuine used stamps may, in some cases, be identified by the cancellation.

A28

**Typeset; "Provisoire" Overprint Handstamped in Black**

**1906** ***Imperf.***

| | | | | |
|---|---|---|---|---|
| **422** | A28 | 1c violet | 17.50 | 1.00 |
| *a.* | | Irregular pin perf. or perf. 10½ | 50.00 | 17.50 |
| **423** | A28 | 2c gray | 60.00 | 10.00 |
| **424** | A28 | 3c green | 17.50 | 1.00 |
| **425** | A28 | 6c red | 17.50 | .75 |
| **426** | A28 | 10c brown | 70.00 | *90.00* |
| **427** | A28 | 13c blue | 50.00 | 10.00 |
| | | *Nos. 422-427 (6)* | 232.50 | 112.75 |

Stamps of type A28 have a faint background pattern of tiny squares within squares, an ornamental frame and open rectangles for the value corners.

The 3c and 6c also exist perforated.

Nos. 422-427 are known without overprint but were probably not issued in that condition. Nearly all values are known with overprint inverted and double.

Forgeries are plentiful.

**Lion Type of 1903 and**

Mohammed-Ali Shah Qajar

A29 A30

**1907-09** **Typo.** ***Perf. 12½***

| | | | | |
|---|---|---|---|---|
| **428** | A26 | 1c vio, *blue* | 5.00 | .25 |
| **429** | A26 | 2c gray, *blue* | 5.00 | .25 |
| **430** | A26 | 3c green, *blue* | 5.00 | .25 |
| **431** | A26 | 6c rose, *blue* | 5.00 | .25 |
| **432** | A26 | 9c org, *blue* | 5.00 | .30 |
| **433** | A26 | 10c brown, *blue* | 6.00 | 1.00 |

**Engr.**

***Perf. 11, 11½***

| | | | | |
|---|---|---|---|---|
| **434** | A29 | 13c dark blue | 5.00 | 2.00 |
| **435** | A29 | 1k red | 7.00 | 1.50 |
| **436** | A29 | 26c red brown | 7.00 | 2.00 |
| **437** | A29 | 2k deep grn | 20.00 | 1.50 |
| **438** | A29 | 3k pale blue | 20.00 | 1.00 |
| **439** | A29 | 4k brt yellow | 400.00 | 10.00 |
| **440** | A29 | 4k bister | 20.00 | 3.00 |
| **441** | A29 | 5k dark brown | 20.00 | 3.00 |
| **442** | A29 | 10k pink | 25.00 | 3.00 |
| **443** | A29 | 20k gray black | 25.00 | 10.00 |
| **444** | A29 | 30k dark violet | 25.00 | 15.00 |
| **445** | A30 | 50k gold, ver & black ('09) | 125.00 | 25.00 |
| | | *Nos. 428-445 (18)* | 730.00 | 79.30 |

Frame of No. 445 lithographed. Nos. 434-444 were issued in 1908.

Remainders canceled to order abound. Used values for Nos. 437-445 are for c-t-os.

Nos. 428-429 Overprinted in Black

**1909** ***Perf. 12½***

| | | | | |
|---|---|---|---|---|
| **446** | A26 | 1c violet, *blue* | 90.00 | 40.00 |
| **447** | A26 | 2c gray, *blue* | 80.00 | 30.00 |

Counterfeits of Nos. 446-447 exist.

Coat of Arms — A31

**1909** **Typo.** ***Perf. 12½x12***

| | | | | |
|---|---|---|---|---|
| **448** | A31 | 1c org & maroon | *.50* | .35 |
| **449** | A31 | 2c vio & maroon | *.50* | .35 |
| **450** | A31 | 3c yel grn & mar | *.50* | .35 |
| **451** | A31 | 6c red & maroon | *.50* | .25 |
| **452** | A31 | 9c gray & maroon | *.50* | .35 |
| **453** | A31 | 10c red vio & mar | *.50* | .35 |
| **454** | A31 | 13c dk blue & mar | *.50* | *2.00* |
| **455** | A31 | 1k sil, vio & bis brown | *1.00* | *2.00* |
| **456** | A31 | 26c dk grn & mar | *1.00* | *3.00* |
| **457** | A31 | 2k sil, dk grn & bis brown | *1.00* | *2.00* |
| **458** | A31 | 3k sil, gray & bis brown | *1.00* | *3.50* |
| **459** | A31 | 4k sil, by & bis brn | *1.00* | *3.50* |
| **460** | A31 | 5k gold, brn & bis brown | *2.50* | *3.50* |
| **461** | A31 | 10k gold, org & bis brown | *5.00* | *10.00* |
| **462** | A31 | 20k gold, ol grn & bister brn | *7.00* | 20.00 |
| **463** | A31 | 30k gold, car & bis brown | *12.00* | *20.00* |
| | | *Nos. 448-463 (16)* | 35.00 | 71.50 |

Unauthorized reprints of Nos. 448-463 abound. Originals have clean, bright colors, centers stand out clearly, and paper is much thinner. Nos. 460-463 originals have gleaming gold margins; reprint margins appear as blackish yellow. Centers of reprints of Nos. 448-454, 456 are brown.

Values above are for unused reprints and for authenticated used stamps. Original unused stamps sell for much higher prices.

For surcharges & overprints see #516-519, 541-549. 582-585, 588-594, 597, 601-606, 707-722, C1-C16, O31-O40.

In 1909 two sets of 16 stamps were prepared for the coronation of Ahmad Shad Qajar. The first set with lion and sun high values and gold borders was for postal use, while the second set with city gate high values and silver borders was inscribed "SERVICE". While neither set was placed in use, both were sold to collectors at a later date.

**Nos. 428-444, Imperf., Surcharged in Red or Black**

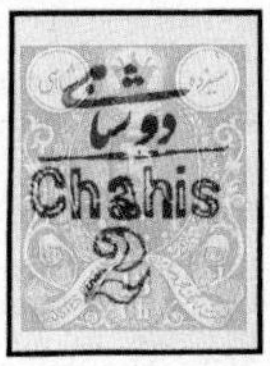


**1910 Blue Paper *Imperf.***

| | | | | |
|---|---|---|---|---|
| **464** | A26 | 1c on 1c violet | 200.00 | 140.00 |
| **465** | A26 | 1c on 2c gray | 200.00 | 140.00 |
| **466** | A26 | 1c on 3c green | 200.00 | 140.00 |
| **467** | A26 | 1c on 6c rose (Bk) | 200.00 | 140.00 |
| **468** | A26 | 1c on 9c orange | 200.00 | 140.00 |
| **469** | A26 | 1c on 10c brown | 200.00 | 140.00 |

**White Paper**

| | | | | |
|---|---|---|---|---|
| **470** | A29 | 2c on 13c dp bl | 200.00 | 140.00 |
| **471** | A29 | 2c on 26c red brown (Bk) | 200.00 | 140.00 |
| **472** | A29 | 2c on 1k red (Bk) | 200.00 | 140.00 |
| **473** | A29 | 2c on 2k dp grn | 200.00 | 140.00 |
| **474** | A29 | 2c on 3k pale bl | 200.00 | 140.00 |
| **475** | A29 | 2c on 4k brt yel | 200.00 | 140.00 |
| **476** | A29 | 2c on 4k bister | 200.00 | 140.00 |
| **477** | A29 | 2c on 5k dk brn | 200.00 | 140.00 |
| **478** | A29 | 2c on 10k pink (Bk) | 200.00 | 140.00 |
| **479** | A29 | 2c on 20k gray blk | 200.00 | 140.00 |
| **480** | A29 | 2c on 30k dk vio | 200.00 | 140.00 |
| | | *Nos. 464-480 (17)* | 3,400. | 2,380. |

Nos. 464-480 were prepared for use on newspapers, but nearly the entire printing was sold to stamp dealers. The issue is generally considered speculative. Counterfeit surcharges exist on trimmed stamps.

Used values are for c-t-o.

Ahmad Shah Qajar — A32

***Perf. 11½, 11½x11, 11½x12***
**Engr. center, Typo. frame**

**1911-13**

| | | | | |
|---|---|---|---|---|
| **481** | A32 | 1c green & org | *.50* | .25 |
| **482** | A32 | 2c red & sepia | *.50* | .25 |
| **483** | A32 | 3c gray brn & grn | *.50* | .25 |
| *a.* | | 3c bister brown & green | *.50* | *1.00* |
| **484** | A32 | 5c brn & car ('13) | *.50* | *.75* |
| **485** | A32 | 6c gray & car | *.50* | .25 |
| **486** | A32 | 6c grn & red brown ('13) | *.50* | .25 |
| **487** | A32 | 9c yel brn & vio | *.75* | .25 |
| **488** | A32 | 10c red & org brn | *.75* | .25 |
| **489** | A32 | 12c grn & ultra ('13) | *.50* | .50 |
| **490** | A32 | 13c violet & ultra | *1.00* | *2.00* |
| **491** | A32 | 1k ultra & car | *1.00* | .50 |
| **492** | A32 | 24c vio & grn ('13) | *1.00* | 1.00 |
| **493** | A32 | 26c ultra & green | *1.00* | *5.00* |
| **494** | A32 | 2k grn & red vio | *2.00* | 1.00 |
| **495** | A32 | 3k violet & blk | *2.00* | 1.50 |
| **496** | A32 | 4k ultramarine & gray ('13) | *2.00* | *20.00* |
| **497** | A32 | 5k red & ultra | *3.00* | 2.00 |
| **498** | A32 | 10k ol bis & cl | *5.00* | *3.00* |
| **499** | A32 | 20k vio brn & bis | *6.00* | *4.00* |
| **500** | A32 | 30k red & green | *7.00* | *5.00* |
| | | *Nos. 481-500 (20)* | *36.00* | *48.00* |

Values for Nos. 481-500 unused are for reprints, which cannot be distinguished from the late printings of the stamps. These are perf 11½ (11½x12 for the 4k) with the distance between the inner lines of the inscription tablets at top and bottom of the portrait being 19mm. Unused stamps with other perfs or a shorter vignette sell for much higher prices.

The reprints include inverted centers for some denominations. Values, each $30-$50.

For surcharges and overprints see Nos. 501-515, 520-540, 586-587, 595, 598, 600, 607-609, 630-634, 646-666.

Stamps of 1911 Overprinted in Black

**1911**

| | | | | |
|---|---|---|---|---|
| **501** | A32 | 1c grn & orange | 45.00 | 6.00 |
| **502** | A32 | 2c red & sepia | 45.00 | 6.00 |
| **503** | A32 | 3c gray brn & grn | 45.00 | 6.00 |
| **504** | A32 | 6c gray & carmine | 45.00 | 6.00 |
| **505** | A32 | 9c yel brn & vio | 45.00 | 6.00 |
| **506** | A32 | 10c red & org brn | 75.00 | 6.00 |
| **507** | A32 | 13c vio & ultra | 100.00 | 8.00 |
| **508** | A32 | 1k ultra & car | 150.00 | 10.00 |
| **509** | A32 | 26c ultra & green | 150.00 | 12.00 |
| **510** | A32 | 2k grn & red vio | 200.00 | 15.00 |
| **511** | A32 | 3k vio & black | 250.00 | 15.00 |
| **512** | A32 | 5k red & ultra | 300.00 | 20.00 |
| **513** | A32 | 10k ol bis & claret | 1,250. | 40.00 |
| **514** | A32 | 20k vio brn & bis | 1,000. | 50.00 |
| **515** | A32 | 30k red & green | 1,000. | 50.00 |
| | | *Nos. 501-515 (15)* | 4,700. | 256.00 |

The "Officiel" overprint does not signify that the stamps were intended for use on official correspondence but that they were issued by authority. It was applied to the stocks in Tabriz and all post offices in the Tabriz region after a large quantity of stamps had been stolen during the Russian occupation of Tabriz.

The "Officiel" overprint has been counterfeited.

Stamps of 1909-11 Overprinted in Black

**1911, Oct. On #449-451, 454**

| | | | | |
|---|---|---|---|---|
| **516** | A31 | 2c vio & maroon | 300.00 | 150.00 |
| **517** | A31 | 3c yel grn & mar | 300.00 | 150.00 |
| **518** | A31 | 6c red & maroon | 300.00 | 150.00 |
| **519** | A31 | 13c dk blue & mar | 300.00 | 150.00 |

**On #482-483, 485, 490**

| | | | | |
|---|---|---|---|---|
| **520** | A32 | 2c red & sepia | 400.00 | 200.00 |
| **521** | A32 | 3c gray brn & grn | 400.00 | 200.00 |
| **522** | A32 | 6c gray & car | 400.00 | 200.00 |
| **523** | A32 | 13c violet & ultra | 400.00 | 200.00 |

Stamps were sold at a 10% discount to stagecoach station keepers on the Tehran-Recht route. To prevent speculation, these stamps were overprinted "Stagecoach Stations" in French and Farsi.

Forgeries exist, usually overprinted on reprints of the 1909 issue and used examples of the 1911 issue. Values are for authenticated stamps.

In 1912 this overprint, reading 'Sultan Mohammad Ali Shah Kajar,' was handstamped on outgoing mail in the Persian Kurdistan region occupied by the forces of the former Shah Mohammad Ali. It was applied after the stamps were on cover and is found on 8 of the Shah Ahmed stamps of 1911 (1c, 2c, 3c, 6c, 9c, 13c, 1k and 26c). Some specialists add the 10c. Forgeries are abundant.

**Nos. 490 and 493 Surcharged**

a

b

**1914**

| | | | | |
|---|---|---|---|---|
| **535** | A32(a) | 1c on 13c | 25.00 | 2.00 |
| **536** | A32(b) | 3c on 26c | 25.00 | 4.00 |

In 1914 a set of 19 stamps was prepared as a coronation issue. The 10 lower values each carry a different portrait; the 9 higher values show buildings and scenes. The same set printed with black centers was overprinted in red "SERVICE." The stamps were never placed in use, but were sold to stamp dealers in 1923.

**Nos. 484 and 489 Surcharged in Black or Violet**

c

d

**1915**

| | | | | |
|---|---|---|---|---|
| **537** | A32(c) | 1c on 5c | 20.00 | 2.00 |
| **538** | A32(c) | 2c on 5c (V) | 20.00 | 2.00 |
| **539** | A32(c) | 2c on 5c | 200.00 | 40.00 |
| **540** | A32(d) | 6c on 12c | 30.00 | 2.00 |
| | | *Nos. 537-540 (4)* | 270.00 | 46.00 |

**Nos. 455, 454 Surcharged**

e

f

**1915 *Perf. 12½x12***

| | | | | |
|---|---|---|---|---|
| **541** | A31(e) | 5c on 1k multi | 60.00 | 5.00 |
| **542** | A31(f) | 12c on 13c multi | 90.00 | 7.00 |

Counterfeit surcharges on reprints abound.

Nos. 448-453, 455 Overprinted

**1915**

| | | | | |
|---|---|---|---|---|
| **543** | A31 | 1c org & maroon | 70.00 | 5.00 |
| **544** | A31 | 2c vio & maroon | 50.00 | 5.00 |
| **545** | A31 | 3c grn & maroon | 60.00 | 5.00 |
| **546** | A31 | 6c red & maroon | 60.00 | 5.00 |
| **547** | A31 | 9c gray & maroon | 100.00 | 7.00 |
| **548** | A31 | 10c red vio & mar | 150.00 | 10.00 |
| **549** | A31 | 1k sil, vio & bis brn | 250.00 | 10.00 |
| | | *Nos. 543-549 (7)* | 740.00 | 47.00 |

This overprint ("1333") also exists on the 2k, 10k, 20k and 30k, but they were not issued.

Counterfeit overprints, usually on reprints, abound.

Beware of forgeries and/or reprints of most Iran stamps between the years 1870-1925. Scott values are for genuine stamps. Collectors should be aware that forgeries of many issues outnumber genuine examples by factors of 10 or 20 to one. Failing specialized knowledge on the part of the collector, these stamps should be examined or authenticated by acknowledged experts before purchase.

Imperial Crown — A33

King Darius, Farohar overhead — A34

Ruins of Persepolis — A35

***Perf. 11½ or Compound 11x11½***
**Engr., Typo.**

**1915, Mar. Wmk. 161**

| | | | | |
|---|---|---|---|---|
| **560** | A33 | 1c car & indigo | .25 | *2.00* |
| **561** | A33 | 2c bl & carmine | .25 | *2.00* |
| **562** | A33 | 3c dark green | .25 | *2.00* |
| *a.* | | Inverted center | — | |
| **564** | A33 | 5c red | .25 | *2.50* |
| **565** | A33 | 6c olive grn & car | .25 | *2.00* |
| *a.* | | Inverted center | — | |
| **566** | A33 | 9c yel brn & vio | .25 | *2.00* |
| **567** | A33 | 10c bl grn & yel brn | .25 | *2.00* |
| **568** | A33 | 12c ultramarine | .25 | *2.00* |
| **569** | A34 | 1k sil, yel brn & gray | .65 | *5.00* |
| **570** | A33 | 24c yel brn & dk brn | .25 | *5.00* |
| **571** | A34 | 2k silver, bl & rose | .65 | *5.00* |
| **572** | A34 | 3k sil, vio & brn | .65 | *5.00* |
| **573** | A34 | 5k sil, brn & green | .65 | *7.00* |
| **574** | A35 | 1t gold, pur & blk | .65 | *10.00* |
| **575** | A35 | 2t gold, grn & brn | 1.00 | *10.00* |
| **576** | A35 | 3t gold, cl & red brn | 1.00 | *10.00* |
| **577** | A35 | 5t gold, blue & ind | 1.00 | *10.00* |
| | | *Nos. 560-577 (17)* | 8.50 | *83.50* |

Coronation of Shah Ahmed.

Nos. 560-568, 570 are engraved. Nos. 569, 571-573 are engraved except for silver margins. Nos. 574-577 have centers engraved, frames typographed.

The 3c and 6c with inverted centers are considered genuine errors. Unauthorized reprints exist of these varieties and of other denominations with inverted centers. **Values unused for Nos. 560-577 are for reprints.**

For surcharges and overprints see Nos. 610-616, 635-646, O41-O57, Q19-Q35.

Nos. 455, 461-463 Overprinted

**1915 Unwmk. Typo. *Perf. 12½x12***

| | | | | |
|---|---|---|---|---|
| **582** | A31 | 1k sil, vio & bis brn | *2.00* | *20.00* |
| **583** | A31 | 10k multicolored | *5.00* | *30.00* |
| **584** | A31 | 20k multicolored | *10.00* | *100.00* |
| **585** | A31 | 30k multicolored | *12.00* | *60.00* |
| | | *Nos. 582-585 (4)* | *29.00* | *210.00* |

Genuine unused examples are rare. Most unused stamps offered in the marketplace are reprints, and the unused values above are for reprints. Used values for authenticated stamps.

Forgeries abound of Nos. 582-585.

No. 491 Surcharged

**1917** ***Perf. 11½***

**586** A32 12c on 1k multi *3,000. 3,500.*
**587** A32 24c on 1k multi *1,500. 1,750.*

Issued during the Turkish occupation of Kermanshah. Forgeries exist.

Values for unused stamps are for reprints. Unused examples of the original stamps are rare, and most stamps offered in the marketplace are reprints.

No. 448 Overprinted "1335" in Persian Numerals

**1917** ***Perf. 12½x12***

**588** A31 1c org & maroon *350.00* 250.00

Overprint on No. 588 is similar to date in "k" and "l" surcharges. Forgeries exist.

**Nos. 449, 452-453, 456 Surcharged**

k

l

**1917**

**589** A31(k) 1c on 2c 30.00 3.00
**590** A31(k) 1c on 9c 40.00 4.00
**591** A31(k) 1c on 10c 30.00 3.00
**592** A31(l) 3c on 9c 50.00 4.00
**593** A31(l) 3c on 10c 40.00 3.00
**594** A31(l) 3c on 26c 40.00 5.00

**Same Surcharge on No. 488**

**595** A32(k) 1c on 10c 75.00 1.50
**596** A32(l) 3c on 10c 75.00 1.50

**Nos. 454 & 491 Surcharged Type "e"**

**597** A31 5c on 13c 50.00 5.00
**598** A32 5c on 1k 45.00 2.00

Counterfeit surcharges on "canceled" reprints of Nos. 449, 452-454, 456 abound.

No. 489 Surcharged

**600** A32 6c on 12c grn & ultra 125.00 15.00

No. 457 Overprinted

**1918**

**601** A31 2k multi 125.00 20.00

**Nos. 459-460 Surcharged**

**1918**

**602** A31 24c on 4k multi 75.00 15.00
**603** A31 10k on 5k multi 125.00 20.00

The surcharges of Nos. 602-603 have been counterfeited.

Nos. 457-463 Overprinted

**1918**

**603A** A31 2k multicolored *3.00 65.00*
**604** A31 3k multicolored *3.00 15.00*
**604A** A31 4k multicolored *5.00 150.00*
**604B** A31 5k multicolored *5.00 75.00*
**605** A31 10k multicolored *8.00 50.00*
**605A** A31 20k multicolored *20.00 200.00*
**606** A31 30k multicolored *15.00 100.00*
*Nos. 603A-606 (7)* *59.00 655.00*

Genuine unused examples are rare. Most unused stamps offered in the marketplace are reprints, and the unused values above are for reprints. Used values for for authenticated stamps.

Forgeries abound of Nos. 603A-606.

**Nos. 489, 488 and 491 Surcharged**

m

n

**607** A32(m) 3c on 12c 75.00 1.50
**608** A32(n) 6c on 10c 100.00 1.50
**609** A32(m) 6c on 1k 75.00 1.50
*Nos. 607-609 (3)* 250.00 4.50

Genuine unused examples are rare. Most unused stamps offered in the marketplace are reprints, and the unused values above are for reprints.

Nos. 571-577 Overprinted in Black or Red

**1918** **Wmk. 161**

**610** A34 2k sil, blue & rose 10.00 10.00
**611** A34 3k sil, vio & brn (R) 10.00 10.00
**612** A34 5k sil, brn & grn (R) 10.00 10.00
**613** A35 1t gold, pur & black (R) 15.00 15.00
**614** A35 2t gold, grn & brn 15.00 15.00
**615** A35 3t gold, cl & red brn 15.00 15.00
**616** A35 5t gold, bl & ind (R) 15.00 20.00
*Nos. 610-616 (7)* 90.00 95.00

The overprint commemorates the end of World War I. Counterfeits of this overprint are plentiful.

A36

**Color Litho., Black Typo.**

**1919** **Unwmk.** ***Perf. 11½***

**617** A36 1c yel & black 20.00 1.00
**618** A36 3c green & black 20.00 1.00
**619** A36 5c rose & black 55.00 3.00
**620** A36 6c vio & black 35.00 1.00
**621** A36 12c blue & black 125.00 10.00
*Nos. 617-621 (5)* 255.00 16.00

Nos. 617-621 exist imperf., in colors other than the originals, with centers inverted and double impressions. Some specialists call them fraudulent, others call them reprints.

This issue has been extensively counterfeited, and most examples in the marketplace are forgeries.

Counterfeits having double line over "POSTES" abound.

Nos. 75, 85-86 Surcharged in Various Colors

**1919** ***Perf. 10½, 11, 11½, 13½***

**622** A14 2k on 5c lilac (Bk) 7.50 7.50
**623** A14 3k on 5c lilac (Br) 7.50 7.50
**624** A14 4k on 5c lilac (G) 7.50 7.50
**625** A14 5k on 5c lilac (V) 7.50 7.50
**626** A16 10k on 10c rose (Bl) 20.00 20.00
**627** A16 20k on 10c rose (G) 20.00 20.00
**628** A16 30k on 10c rose (Br) 20.00 20.00
**629** A16 50k on 14c org (V) 20.00 20.00
*Nos. 622-629 (8)* 110.00 110.00

Nos. 622-629 exist with inverted and double surcharge. Some specialists consider these fraudulent.

Nos. 486, 489 Handstamp Surcharged

**1921** ***Perf. 11½, 11½x11***

**630** A32 10c on 6c 75.00 15.00
**631** A32 1k on 12c 75.00 15.00

Counterfeits exist.

No. 489 Surcharged

**632** A32 6c on 12c 400.00 20.00

**Nos. 486, 489 Surcharged in Violet**

**1921**

**633** A32 10c on 6c 150.00 50.00
*a.* Surcharge handstamped in black 350.00 350.00
**634** A32 1k on 12c 150.00 50.00
*a.* Surcharge handstamped in black 350.00 350.00

Counterfeits exist.

Coronation Issue of 1915 Overprinted

**1921, May** **Wmk. 161** ***Perf. 11, 11½***

**635** A33 3c dark grn 15.00
*a.* Center and overprint inverted —
**636** A33 5c red 15.00
**637** A33 6c olive grn & car 15.00
**638** A33 10c bl grn & yel brn 15.00
**639** A33 12c ultramarine 15.00
**640** A34 1k sil, yel brn & gray 20.00
**641** A34 2k sil, blue & rose 20.00
**642** A34 5k sil, brn & green 20.00
**643** A35 2t gold, grn & brn 25.00
**644** A35 3t gold, cl & red brn 30.00
**645** A35 5t gold, blue & ind 30.00
*Nos. 635-645 (11)* 220.00

Counterfeits of this Feb. 21, 1921, overprint are plentiful. Inverted overprints exist on all values; some specialists consider them fraudulent.

Stamps of 1911-13 Overprinted

**1922** **Unwmk.** ***Perf. 11½, 11½x11***

**646** A32 1c grn & orange 10.00 .25
*a.* Inverted overprint 200.00
**647** A32 2c red & sepia 10.00 .25
**648** A32 3c brn & green *15.00* .25
*a.* 3c bister brown & green 10.00 .25
**649** A32 5c brown & car 100.00 35.00
**650** A32 6c grn & red brn 10.00 .25
**651** A32 9c yel brn & vio 10.00 .25
**652** A32 10c red & org brn 15.00 .25
*a.* Double ovpt., one inverted *400.00*
**653** A32 12c green & ultra 25.00 .50
*a.* Double overprint *400.00*
**654** A32 1k ultra & car 30.00 1.00
**655** A32 24c vio & green 25.00 1.00
**656** A32 2k grn & red vio 85.00 1.00
**657** A32 3k vio & black 90.00 1.50
**658** A32 4k ultra & gray 225.00 45.00
**659** A32 5k red & ultra 150.00 2.00
**660** A32 10k ol bis & cl *750.00* 5.00
**661** A32 20k vio brn & bis *850.00* 7.00
**662** A32 30k red & green *900.00* 10.00
*Nos. 646-662 (17)* *3,300.* 110.50

The status of inverted overprints on 5c and 12c is dubious. Unlisted inverts on other denominations are generally considered fraudulent. Counterfeits of this overprint exist.

Nos. 653, 655 Surcharged

**1922**

**663** A32 3c on 12c 75.00 1.00
**664** A32 6c on 24c 110.00 2.00

**Nos. 661-662 Surcharged**

**1923**

**665** A32 10c on 20k 120.00 10.00
**666** A32 1k on 30k 145.00 15.00

Ahmed Shah Qajar — A37

***Perf. 11½, 11x11½, 11½x11***

**1924-25** **Engr.**

**667** A37 1c orange 2.50 .25
**668** A37 2c magenta 2.50 .25
*a.* Imperf. btwn., pair *2,000.*
**669** A37 3c orange brown 2.50 .25
**670** A37 6c black brown 2.50 .25
**671** A37 9c dark green 2.00 5.00
**672** A37 10c dark violet 2.00 .30
**673** A37 12c red 2.00 .30
**674** A37 1k dark blue 2.00 .35

| | | | | |
|---|---|---|---|---|
| **675** | A37 | 2k indigo & red | 2.00 | 5.00 |
| *a.* | | Center inverted | 35,000. | *5,500.* |
| **676** | A37 | 3k dk vio & red brown | 17.00 | 2.00 |
| **677** | A37 | 5k red & brown | 20.00 | *30.00* |
| **678** | A37 | 10k choc & lilac | 25.00 | 25.00 |
| **679** | A37 | 20k dk grn & brn | 30.00 | 30.00 |
| **680** | A37 | 30k org & blk brn | 40.00 | 40.00 |
| | | *Nos. 667-680 (14)* | 152.00 | 138.95 |

For overprints see Nos. 703-706.

A38

SIX CHAHIS

Type I

Type II

**Dated 1924**

**Color Litho., Black Typo.**

**1924** ***Perf. 11***

| | | | | |
|---|---|---|---|---|
| **681** | A38 | 1c yel brn & blk | 20.00 | 1.00 |
| **682** | A38 | 2c gray & blk | 20.00 | 1.00 |
| **683** | A38 | 3c dp rose & blk | 20.00 | 1.00 |
| **684** | A38 | 6c orange & blk (I) | 30.00 | 1.50 |
| *a.* | | 6c orange & blk (II) | 35.00 | 2.00 |
| | | *Nos. 681-684 (4)* | 90.00 | 4.50 |

The 1c was surcharged "Chahis" by error. Later the "s" was blocked out in black.

Counterfeits having double line over "POSTES" are plentiful.

**1925** **Dated 1925**

| | | | | |
|---|---|---|---|---|
| **686** | A38 | 2c yel grn & blk | 10.00 | 1.00 |
| **687** | A38 | 3c red & blk | 10.00 | 1.00 |
| **689** | A38 | 6c chalky bl & blk | 10.00 | 1.00 |
| **690** | A38 | 9c lt brn & blk | 30.00 | 2.00 |
| **691** | A38 | 10c gray & blk | 75.00 | 5.00 |
| **694** | A38 | 1k emer & blk | 65.00 | 10.00 |
| **695** | A38 | 2k lilac & blk | 175.00 | 40.00 |
| | | *Nos. 686-695 (7)* | 375.00 | 60.00 |

Counterfeits having double line over "POSTES" are plentiful.

A39

**Gold Overprint on Treasury Department Stamps**

**1925**

| | | | | |
|---|---|---|---|---|
| **697** | A39 | 1c red | 10.00 | 6.00 |
| **698** | A39 | 2c yellow | 10.00 | 6.00 |
| **699** | A39 | 3c yellow green | 10.00 | 6.00 |
| **700** | A39 | 5c dark gray | 45.00 | 30.00 |
| **701** | A39 | 10c deep orange | 25.00 | 10.00 |
| **702** | A39 | 1k ultramarine | 25.00 | 15.00 |
| | | *Nos. 697-702 (6)* | 125.00 | 73.00 |

Deposition of Ahmad Shah Qajar and establishment of provisional government of Reza Shah Pahlavi.

#697-702 have same center (Persian lion in sunburst) with 6 different frames. Overprint reads: "Post / Provisional Government / of Pahlavi / 9th Abanmah / 1304 / 1925."

Nos. 667-670 Overprinted

**1926** ***Perf. 11½, 11x11½, 11½x11***

| | | | | |
|---|---|---|---|---|
| **703** | A37 | 1c orange | 5.00 | 3.00 |
| **704** | A37 | 2c magenta | 5.00 | 5.00 |
| **705** | A37 | 3c orange brown | 5.00 | 3.00 |
| **706** | A37 | 6c black brown | 100.00 | 85.00 |
| | | *Nos. 703-706 (4)* | 115.00 | 96.00 |

Overprinted to commemorate the Pahlavi dynasty, dated 16 December 1925. Counterfeits exist.

Nos. 448-463 Overprinted

**1926** ***Perf. 11½, 12½x12***

| | | | | |
|---|---|---|---|---|
| **707** | A31 | 1c org & maroon | 15.00 | .25 |
| *a.* | | Inverted overprint | 1,600. | |
| **708** | A31 | 2c vio & maroon | 15.00 | .25 |
| **709** | A31 | 3c yel grn & mar | 15.00 | .25 |
| *a.* | | Inverted overprint | 1,250. | |
| **710** | A31 | 6c red & maroon | 15.00 | .25 |
| **711** | A31 | 9c gray & maroon | 15.00 | .25 |
| **712** | A31 | 10c red vio & mar | 20.00 | .35 |
| **713** | A31 | 13c dk bl & mar | 25.00 | .35 |
| **714** | A31 | 1k multi | 50.00 | .35 |
| **715** | A31 | 26c dk grn & mar | 25.00 | .35 |
| **716** | A31 | 2k multi | 55.00 | 1.00 |
| **717** | A31 | 3k multi | 140.00 | 2.00 |
| **718** | A31 | 4k sil, bl & bis brn | 500.00 | 35.00 |
| **719** | A31 | 5k multi | 200.00 | 10.00 |
| **720** | A31 | 10k multi | 650.00 | 15.00 |
| **721** | A31 | 20k multi | 750.00 | 15.00 |
| **722** | A31 | 30k multi | 750.00 | 20.00 |
| | | *Nos. 707-722 (16)* | 3,240. | 100.65 |

Overprinted to commemorate the Pahlavi government in 1926.

Values for Nos. 707-722 are for stamps perf. 11½, on thick paper. Stamps perf. 12½x12 on thin paper are worth substantially more.

Forgeries exist perf. 12½x12, with either machine overprints or handstamps. Most of these fakes can be identified by the absence of the top serif of the "1" in "1926."

A40

Reza Shah Pahlavi — A41

**1926-29** **Typo.** ***Perf. 11***

| | | | | |
|---|---|---|---|---|
| **723** | A40 | 1c yellow green | 6.00 | .25 |
| **724** | A40 | 2c gray violet | 6.00 | .25 |
| **725** | A40 | 3c emerald | 6.00 | .25 |
| **727** | A40 | 6c magenta | 6.00 | .25 |
| **728** | A40 | 9c rose | 12.00 | .50 |
| **729** | A40 | 10c bister brown | 30.00 | 5.00 |
| **730** | A40 | 12c deep orange | 30.00 | 3.00 |
| **731** | A40 | 15c pale ultra | 35.00 | 2.00 |
| **733** | A41 | 1k dull bl ('27) | 60.00 | 15.00 |
| **734** | A41 | 2k brt vio ('29) | 180.00 | 75.00 |
| | | *Nos. 723-734 (10)* | 371.00 | 101.50 |

**1928** **Redrawn**

| | | | | |
|---|---|---|---|---|
| **740** | A40 | 1c yellow green | 30.00 | .25 |
| **741** | A40 | 2c gray violet | 30.00 | .25 |
| **742** | A40 | 3c emerald | 30.00 | .25 |
| **743** | A40 | 6c rose | 30.00 | .50 |
| | | *Nos. 740-743 (4)* | 120.00 | 1.25 |

On the redrawn stamps much of the shading of the face, throat, collar, etc., has been removed.

The letters of "Postes Persanes" and those in the circle at upper right are smaller. The redrawn stamps measure 20¼x25¾mm instead of 19¾x25¼mm.

A42

Reza Shah Pahlavi — A43

***Perf. 11½, 12, 12½, Compound***

**1929** **Photo.**

| | | | | |
|---|---|---|---|---|
| **744** | A42 | 1c yel grn & cer | 3.50 | .25 |
| **745** | A42 | 2c scar & brt blue | 3.50 | .25 |
| **746** | A42 | 3c mag & myr grn | 3.50 | .25 |
| **747** | A42 | 6c yel brn & ol grn | 3.50 | .25 |
| **748** | A42 | 9c Prus bl & ver | 5.00 | .25 |
| **749** | A42 | 10c bl grn & choc | 6.00 | .25 |
| **750** | A42 | 12c gray blk & pur | 8.00 | .30 |
| **751** | A42 | 15c citron & ultra | 10.00 | .30 |
| **752** | A42 | 1k dull bl & blk | 15.00 | .50 |
| **753** | A42 | 24c ol grn & red brn | 12.00 | .50 |
| | | **Engr.** | | |
| | | ***Perf. 11½*** | | |
| **754** | A42 | 2k brn org & dk vio | 125.00 | 3.00 |
| **755** | A42 | 3k dark grn & dp rose | 150.00 | 5.00 |
| **756** | A42 | 5k red brn & dp green | 75.00 | 5.00 |
| **757** | A42 | 1t ultra & dp rose | 75.00 | 10.00 |
| **758** | A42 | 2t carmine & blk | 100.00 | 20.00 |
| | | **Engr. and Typo.** | | |
| **759** | A43 | 3t gold & dp vio | 175.00 | 35.00 |
| | | *Nos. 744-759 (16)* | 770.00 | 81.10 |

For overprints see Nos. 810-817.

Reza Shah Pahlavi — A44

**1931-32** **Litho.** ***Perf. 11***

| | | | | |
|---|---|---|---|---|
| **760** | A44 | 1c ol brn & ultra | 6.00 | .25 |
| **761** | A44 | 2c red brn & blk | 6.00 | .25 |
| **762** | A44 | 3c lilac rose & ol | 6.00 | .25 |
| **763** | A44 | 6c red org & vio | 6.00 | .25 |
| **764** | A44 | 9c ultra & red org | 12.00 | .40 |
| **765** | A44 | 10c ver & gray | 30.00 | 1.00 |
| **766** | A44 | 11c bl & dull red | 37.50 | 35.00 |
| **767** | A44 | 12c turq blue & lil rose | 45.00 | .70 |
| **768** | A44 | 16c black & red | 50.00 | 1.75 |
| **769** | A44 | 1k car & turq bl | 85.00 | 1.75 |
| **770** | A44 | 27c dk gray & dl bl | 90.00 | 1.75 |
| | | *Nos. 760-770 (11)* | 373.50 | 43.35 |

For overprints see Nos. 818-826.

A45

Reza Shah Pahlavi — A46

**1933-34**

| | | | | |
|---|---|---|---|---|
| **771** | A45 | 5d olive brown | 3.00 | .25 |
| **772** | A45 | 10d blue | 3.00 | .25 |
| **773** | A45 | 15d gray | 3.00 | .25 |
| **774** | A45 | 30d emerald | 3.00 | .25 |
| **775** | A45 | 45d turq blue | 3.00 | .50 |
| **776** | A45 | 50d magenta | 4.00 | .50 |
| **777** | A45 | 60d green | 5.00 | .50 |
| **778** | A45 | 75d brown | 8.00 | 1.50 |
| **779** | A45 | 90d red | 10.00 | 2.50 |
| **780** | A46 | 1r dk rose & blk | 25.00 | 2.00 |
| **781** | A46 | 1.20r gray blk & rose | 30.00 | 2.00 |
| **782** | A46 | 1.50 citron & bl | 35.00 | 2.00 |
| **783** | A46 | 2r lt bl & choc | 45.00 | 2.00 |
| **784** | A46 | 3r mag & green | 60.00 | 4.00 |
| **785** | A46 | 5r dk brn & red org | 225.00 | 50.00 |
| | | *Nos. 771-785 (15)* | 462.00 | 68.50 |

For overprints see Nos. 795-809.

"Justice" A47

"Education" A49

Ruins of Persepolis A48

Tehran Airport A50

Sanatorium at Sakhtessar — A51

Cement Factory, Chah-Abdul-Azim — A52

Gunboat "Palang" A53

Railway Bridge over Karun River A54

Post Office and Customs Building, Tehran A55

**1935, Feb. 21** **Photo.** ***Perf. 12½***

| | | | | |
|---|---|---|---|---|
| **786** | A47 | 5d red brn & grn | 1.00 | .75 |
| **787** | A48 | 10d red org & gray black | 1.00 | .75 |
| **788** | A49 | 15d mag & Prus bl | 1.50 | .75 |
| **789** | A50 | 30d black & green | 1.50 | .75 |
| **790** | A51 | 45d ol grn & red brn | 2.00 | .75 |
| **791** | A52 | 75d grn & dark brn | 6.00 | 1.25 |
| **792** | A53 | 90d blue & car rose | 20.00 | 5.00 |
| **793** | A54 | 1r red brn & pur | 60.00 | 30.00 |
| **794** | A55 | 1½r violet & ultra | 25.00 | 10.00 |
| | | *Nos. 786-794 (9)* | 118.00 | 50.00 |

Reign of Riza Shah Pahlavi, 10th anniv.

Stamps of 1933-34 Overprinted in Black

**1935** ***Perf. 11***

| | | | | |
|---|---|---|---|---|
| **795** | A45 | 5d olive brown | 3.00 | .50 |
| **796** | A45 | 10d blue | 3.00 | .50 |
| **797** | A45 | 15d gray | 3.00 | .50 |
| **798** | A45 | 30d emerald | 3.00 | .50 |
| **799** | A45 | 45d turq blue | 10.00 | 3.00 |
| **800** | A45 | 50d magenta | 6.00 | .50 |
| **801** | A45 | 60d green | 6.00 | .50 |
| **802** | A45 | 75d brown | 10.00 | 10.00 |
| **803** | A45 | 90d red | 35.00 | 40.00 |
| **804** | A46 | 1r dk rose & blk | 100.00 | *200.00* |
| **805** | A46 | 1.20r gray black & rose | 15.00 | 2.00 |
| **806** | A46 | 1.50r citron & bl | 15.00 | 2.00 |
| **807** | A46 | 2r lt bl & choc | 40.00 | 2.00 |
| **808** | A46 | 3r mag & green | 75.00 | 10.00 |
| **809** | A46 | 5r dk brn & red org | 300.00 | *500.00* |
| | | *Nos. 795-809 (15)* | 624.00 | 772.00 |

Same Overprint on Stamps of 1929

**1935** ***Perf. 12, 12x12½***

| | | | | |
|---|---|---|---|---|
| **810** | A42 | 1c yel green & cer | 500.00 | *600.00* |
| **811** | A42 | 2c scar & brt blue | 300.00 | *400.00* |
| **812** | A42 | 3c mag & myr grn | 200.00 | *200.00* |
| **813** | A42 | 6c yel brn & ol grn | 140.00 | *150.00* |
| **814** | A42 | 9c Prus bl & ver | 85.00 | *100.00* |

***Perf. 11½***

| | | | | |
|---|---|---|---|---|
| **815** | A42 | 1t ultra & dp rose | 50.00 | *75.00* |
| **816** | A42 | 2t carmine & blk | 50.00 | 40.00 |
| **817** | A43 | 3t gold & dp vio | 70.00 | 50.00 |
| | | *Nos. 810-817 (8)* | 1,395. | 1,615. |

No. 817 is overprinted vertically.
Forged overprints exist.

Same Ovpt. on Stamps of 1931-32

**1935** ***Perf. 11***

| | | | | |
|---|---|---|---|---|
| **818** | A44 | 1c ol brn & ultra | 400.00 | 400.00 |
| **819** | A44 | 2c red brn & blk | 150.00 | 150.00 |
| **820** | A44 | 3c lilac rose & ol | 100.00 | 125.00 |
| **821** | A44 | 6c red org & vio | 200.00 | 200.00 |
| **822** | A44 | 9c ultra & red org | 200.00 | *225.00* |
| **823** | A44 | 11c blue & dull red | 12.50 | 3.50 |
| **824** | A44 | 12c turq bl & lil rose | 600.00 | *900.00* |
| **825** | A44 | 16c black & red | 15.00 | 5.00 |
| **826** | A44 | 27c dk gray & dull bl | 19.00 | 5.00 |
| | | *Nos. 818-826 (9)* | 1,696. | 2,013. |

Forged overprints exist.

Reza Shah Pahlavi — A56

**1935** **Photo.** ***Perf. 11***

**Size: 19x27mm**

| | | | | |
|---|---|---|---|---|
| **827** | A56 | 5d violet | 2.00 | .25 |
| **828** | A56 | 10d lilac rose | 2.00 | .25 |
| **829** | A56 | 15d turquoise bl | 2.00 | .25 |
| **830** | A56 | 30d emerald | 2.00 | .25 |
| **831** | A56 | 45d orange | 2.00 | .25 |
| **832** | A56 | 50d dull lt brn | 2.75 | .30 |
| **833** | A56 | 60d ultramarine | 10.00 | .65 |
| **834** | A56 | 75d red orange | 10.00 | .75 |
| **835** | A56 | 90d rose | 12.50 | .75 |

**Size: 21½x31mm**

| | | | | |
|---|---|---|---|---|
| **836** | A56 | 1r dull lilac | 25.00 | .50 |
| **837** | A56 | 1.50r blue | 40.00 | 2.00 |
| **838** | A56 | 2r dk olive grn | 40.00 | .75 |
| **839** | A56 | 3r dark brown | 45.00 | 2.00 |
| **840** | A56 | 5r slate black | 250.00 | 15.00 |
| | | *Nos. 827-840 (14)* | 445.25 | 23.95 |

Reza Shah Pahlavi
A57 A58

**1936-37** **Litho.** ***Perf. 11***

**Size: 20x27mm**

| | | | | |
|---|---|---|---|---|
| **841** | A57 | 5d bright vio | 2.00 | .25 |
| **842** | A57 | 10d magenta | 2.00 | .25 |
| **843** | A57 | 15d bright ultra | 2.00 | .25 |
| **844** | A57 | 30d yellow green | 2.00 | .25 |
| **845** | A57 | 45d vermilion | 3.00 | .25 |
| **846** | A57 | 50d black brn ('37) | 3.00 | .25 |
| **847** | A57 | 60d brown orange | 3.00 | .25 |
| **848** | A57 | 75d rose lake | 3.00 | .25 |
| **849** | A57 | 90d rose red | 5.00 | .35 |

**Size: 23x31mm**

| | | | | |
|---|---|---|---|---|
| **850** | A57 | 1r turq green | 15.00 | .25 |
| **851** | A57 | 1.50r deep blue | 15.00 | .35 |
| **852** | A57 | 2r bright blue | 20.00 | .35 |
| **853** | A57 | 3r violet brown | 25.00 | .80 |
| **854** | A57 | 5r slate green | 40.00 | 1.25 |
| **855** | A57 | 10r dark brown & ultra ('37) | 225.00 | 25.00 |
| | | *Nos. 841-855 (15)* | 365.00 | 30.35 |

**1938-39** **Size: 20x27mm** ***Perf. 11***

| | | | | |
|---|---|---|---|---|
| **856** | A58 | 5d light violet | 2.00 | .25 |
| **857** | A58 | 10d magenta | 2.00 | .25 |
| **858** | A58 | 15d violet blue | 2.00 | .25 |
| **859** | A58 | 30d bright green | 2.00 | .25 |
| **860** | A58 | 45d vermilion | 3.00 | .25 |
| **861** | A58 | 50d black brown | 3.00 | .25 |
| **862** | A58 | 60d brown orange | 3.00 | .25 |
| **863** | A58 | 75d rose lake | 3.00 | .25 |
| **864** | A58 | 90d rose red ('39) | 5.00 | .25 |

**Size: 22½x30mm**

| | | | | |
|---|---|---|---|---|
| **865** | A58 | 1r turq green | 10.00 | .25 |
| **866** | A58 | 1.50r deep blue | 15.00 | .30 |
| **867** | A58 | 2r lt blue ('39) | 20.00 | .30 |
| **868** | A58 | 3r violet brown | 30.00 | .70 |
| **869** | A58 | 5r gray grn ('39) | 50.00 | 1.25 |
| **870** | A58 | 10r dark brown & ultra ('39) | 175.00 | 10.00 |
| | | *Nos. 856-870 (15)* | 325.00 | 15.05 |

Reza Shah Pahlavi — A58a

**1939, Mar. 15** ***Perf. 13***

| | | | | |
|---|---|---|---|---|
| **870A** | A58a | 5d gray blue | 3.00 | 3.00 |
| **870B** | A58a | 10d brown | 3.00 | 3.00 |
| **870C** | A58a | 30d green | 3.00 | 3.00 |
| **870D** | A58a | 60d dark brown | 3.00 | 3.00 |
| **870E** | A58a | 90d red | 5.00 | 5.00 |
| **870F** | A58a | 1.50r blue | 15.00 | 10.00 |
| **870G** | A58a | 5r lilac | 35.00 | 30.00 |
| **870H** | A58a | 10r carmine | 50.00 | 50.00 |
| | | *Nos. 870A-870H (8)* | 117.00 | 107.00 |

60th birthday of Riza Shah Pahlavi. Printed in sheets of 4, perf. 13 and imperf. The 1r violet and 2r orange were not available to the public. Value, perf. 13 unused $35 each, imperf, 35% more. Value of sheets (including 1r and 2r), perf. 13 $1,100, imperf. $1,500.

Crown Prince and Princess Fawziya A59

**1939, Apr. 25** **Photo.** ***Perf. 11½***

| | | | | |
|---|---|---|---|---|
| **871** | A59 | 5d red brown | .50 | .50 |
| **872** | A59 | 10d bright violet | .50 | .50 |
| **873** | A59 | 30d emerald | 1.50 | .50 |
| **874** | A59 | 90d red | 12.00 | 2.00 |
| **875** | A59 | 1.50r bright blue | 20.00 | 4.00 |
| | | *Nos. 871-875 (5)* | 34.50 | 7.50 |

Wedding of Crown Prince Mohammad Reza Pahlavi to Princess Fawziya of Egypt.

Bridge over Karun River A60

Veresk Bridge, North Iran — A61

Granary, Ahwaz A62

Train and Bridge A63

Museum, Side View
A64 A67

Ministry of Justice A65

School Building A66

Mohammad Reza Shah Pahlavi
A68 A69

**1942-46** **Unwmk.** **Litho.** ***Perf. 11***

| | | | | |
|---|---|---|---|---|
| **876** | A60 | 5d violet | 3.00 | .25 |
| **877** | A60 | 5d red org ('44) | 1.00 | .25 |
| **878** | A61 | 10d magenta | 3.00 | .25 |
| **879** | A61 | 10d pck grn ('44) | 1.00 | .25 |
| **880** | A62 | 20d lt red violet | 4.00 | .25 |
| **881** | A62 | 20d mag ('44) | 2.00 | .25 |
| **882** | A63 | 25d rose carmine | 30.00 | 5.00 |
| **883** | A63 | 25d violet ('44) | 7.50 | .50 |
| **884** | A64 | 35d emerald | 2.00 | .30 |
| **885** | A65 | 50d ultramarine | 3.50 | .30 |
| **886** | A65 | 50d emerald ('44) | 2.00 | .25 |
| **887** | A66 | 70d dull vio brn | 2.00 | .35 |
| **888** | A67 | 75d rose lake | 15.00 | .35 |
| **889** | A67 | 75d rose car ('46) | 15.00 | .35 |
| **890** | A68 | 1r carmine | 15.00 | .25 |
| **891** | A68 | 1r maroon ('45) | 15.00 | .25 |
| **892** | A68 | 1.50r red | 15.00 | .25 |
| **893** | A68 | 2r light blue | 35.00 | .25 |
| **894** | A68 | 2r sage grn ('44) | 35.00 | .30 |
| **895** | A68 | 2.50r dark blue | 20.00 | .30 |
| **896** | A68 | 3r peacock grn | 100.00 | 1.00 |
| **897** | A68 | 3r brt vio ('44) | 45.00 | .35 |
| **898** | A68 | 5r sage green | 250.00 | 10.00 |
| **899** | A68 | 5r lt blue ('44) | 35.00 | .50 |
| **900** | A69 | 10r brn org & blk | 60.00 | 3.00 |
| **901** | A69 | 10r dk org brn & black ('44) | 35.00 | 1.00 |
| **902** | A69 | 20r choc & vio | 800.00 | 50.00 |
| **903** | A69 | 20r orange & black ('44) | 130.00 | 4.00 |
| **904** | A69 | 30r gray blk & emerald | *1,250.* | 50.00 |
| **905** | A69 | 30r emer & black ('44) | 50.00 | 5.00 |
| **906** | A69 | 50r dl bl & brn red | 250.00 | 25.00 |
| **907** | A69 | 50r brt vio & black ('45) | 75.00 | 10.00 |
| **908** | A69 | 100r rose red & blk ('45) | 500.00 | 50.00 |
| **909** | A69 | 200r bl & blk ('45) | 400.00 | 50.00 |
| | | *Nos. 876-909 (34)* | 4,206. | 270.35 |

Sixteen denominations of this issue were handstamped at Tabriz in 1945-46 in Persian characters: "Azerbaijan National Government, Dec. 12, 1945." A rebel group did this overprinting while the Russian army held that area.

Flag of Iran A70

Designs: 50d, Docks at Bandar Shapur. 1.50r, Motor convoy. 2.50r, Gorge and railway viaduct. 5r, Map and Mohammad Reza Shah Pahlavi.

**Inscribed: "En souvenir des efforts de l'Iran pour la Victoire"**

**Engr. & Litho.**

**1949, Apr. 28** ***Perf. 12½***

| | | | | |
|---|---|---|---|---|
| **910** | A70 | 25d multicolored | 5.00 | 3.00 |

**Engr.**

| | | | | |
|---|---|---|---|---|
| **911** | A70 | 50d purple | 5.00 | 3.00 |
| *a.* | | Imperf. | *400.00* | |
| **912** | A70 | 1.50r carmine rose | 12.50 | 3.00 |
| **913** | A70 | 2.50r deep blue | 17.50 | 4.00 |
| *a.* | | Imperf. | *500.00* | |
| **914** | A70 | 5r green | 45.00 | 5.00 |
| *a.* | | Imperf. | *750.00* | |
| | | *Nos. 910-914 (5)* | 85.00 | 18.00 |

Iran's contribution toward the victory of the Allied Nations in World War II.

Bank Melli Building, Tehran A71

Post and Customs House, Tehran A72

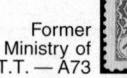

Former Ministry of P.T.T. — A73

Mohammad Reza Shah Pahlavi — A74

Shah and: 5d, Ramsar Hotel, Caspian Sea. 10d, Bridge over Zaindeh River. 25d, Old Royal Palace, Isfahan. 50d, Chaharbagh Madrassa, Isfahan. 75d, Railway Station. 1r, Ministry of Justice, Tehran. 1.50r, Shah Mosque, Tehran. 2.50r, Parliament, Tehran. 3r, Great Gate, Isfahan. 5r, Building, Isfahan.

**1949-50 Unwmk. Litho. *Perf. 10½***

| | | | | |
|---|---|---|---|---|
| **915** | A71 | 5d rose & dk grn | 1.50 | .25 |
| **916** | A71 | 10d ultra & brown | 1.50 | .25 |
| **917** | A71 | 20d vio & ultra | 1.50 | .25 |
| **918** | A71 | 25d blk brn & dp blue | 1.50 | .25 |
| **919** | A71 | 50d grn & ultra | 1.50 | .25 |
| **920** | A71 | 75d dk brn & red | 2.50 | .25 |
| **921** | A72 | 1r vio & green | 2.50 | .25 |
| **922** | A72 | 1.50r dk grn & ver | 3.00 | .25 |
| **923** | A72 | 2r dp car & blk brn | 6.00 | .25 |
| **924** | A72 | 2.50r chlky bl & bl | 6.00 | .25 |
| **925** | A72 | 3r vio bl & red orange | 6.00 | .25 |
| **926** | A72 | 5r dp car & vio | 10.00 | .25 |
| **927** | A73 | 10r car & blue green ('50) | 35.00 | .50 |
| *a.* | | Inverted center | 2,750. | |
| **928** | A73 | 20r brown black & red ('50) | 350.00 | 20.00 |
| **929** | A74 | 30r choc & deep blue ('50) | 100.00 | 15.00 |
| **930** | A74 | 50r red & deep blue ('50) | 100.00 | 15.00 |
| | | *Nos. 915-930 (16)* | 628.50 | 53.50 |

Globes and Pigeons A75

Symbols of UPU — A76

**1950, Mar. 16 Photo.**

| | | | | |
|---|---|---|---|---|
| **931** | A75 | 50d brn carmine | 30.00 | 25.00 |
| **932** | A76 | 2.50r deep blue | 35.00 | 32.50 |

UPU, 75th anniv. (in 1949).

Riza Shah Pahlavi and his Tomb — A77

**1950, May 8**

| | | | | |
|---|---|---|---|---|
| **933** | A77 | 50d brown | 18.00 | 10.00 |
| **934** | A77 | 2r sepia | 30.00 | 15.00 |

Re-burial of Riza Shah Pahlavi, May 12, 1950.

Mohammad Reza Shah Pahlavi, 31st Birthday — A78

Various portraits.

**1950, Oct. 26 Engr. *Perf. 12½***
**Center in Black**

| | | | | |
|---|---|---|---|---|
| **935** | A78 | 25d carmine | 10.00 | 2.00 |
| **936** | A78 | 50d orange | 10.00 | 2.00 |
| **937** | A78 | 75d brown | 30.00 | 12.00 |
| **938** | A78 | 1r green | 25.00 | 10.00 |
| **939** | A78 | 2.50r deep blue | 25.00 | 10.00 |
| **940** | A78 | 5r brown lake | 40.00 | 10.00 |
| | | *Nos. 935-940 (6)* | 140.00 | 46.00 |

Shah and Queen Soraya A79

A80

**1951, Feb. 12 Litho. *Perf. 10½***

| | | | | |
|---|---|---|---|---|
| **941** | A79 | 5d rose violet | 2.50 | 1.00 |
| **942** | A79 | 25d orange red | 3.50 | 1.00 |
| **943** | A79 | 50d emerald | 6.00 | 2.00 |
| **944** | A80 | 1r brown | 10.00 | 2.00 |
| **945** | A80 | 1.50r carmine | 15.00 | 2.00 |
| **946** | A80 | 2.50r blue | 25.00 | 2.50 |
| | | *Nos. 941-946 (6)* | 62.00 | 10.50 |

Wedding of Mohammad Reza Shah Pahlavi to Soraya Esfandiari.

Farabi — A81

**1951, Feb. 20**

| | | | | |
|---|---|---|---|---|
| **947** | A81 | 50d red | 12.50 | 1.50 |
| **948** | A81 | 2.50r blue | 17.50 | 2.50 |

Death millenary of Farabi, Persian philosopher.

Mohammad Reza Shah Pahlavi
A82 A83

**1951-52 Unwmk. Photo. *Perf. 10½***

| | | | | |
|---|---|---|---|---|
| **950** | A82 | 5d brown orange | .50 | .25 |
| **951** | A82 | 10d violet | .50 | .25 |
| **952** | A82 | 20d choc ('52) | 1.50 | .35 |
| **953** | A82 | 25d blue ('52) | 1.50 | .25 |
| **954** | A82 | 50d green | 1.50 | .25 |
| **955** | A82 | 75d rose | 1.50 | .30 |
| **956** | A83 | 1r gray green | 1.50 | .25 |
| **957** | A83 | 1.50r cerise | 1.50 | .45 |
| **958** | A83 | 2r chocolate | 5.00 | .25 |
| **959** | A83 | 2.50r deep blue | 5.00 | .25 |
| **960** | A83 | 3r red orange | 6.00 | .25 |
| **961** | A83 | 5r dark green | 12.00 | .25 |
| **962** | A83 | 10r olive ('52) | 35.00 | .50 |
| **963** | A83 | 20r org brn ('52) | 20.00 | 3.00 |
| **964** | A83 | 30r vio bl ('52) | 15.00 | 2.00 |
| **965** | A83 | 50r blk brn ('52) | 45.00 | 7.50 |
| | | *Nos. 950-965 (16)* | 153.00 | 16.35 |

See Nos. 975-977.

Oil Well and Mosque — A84

Oil Well, Mosque and Monument A85

**1953, Feb. 20 Litho.**

| | | | | |
|---|---|---|---|---|
| **966** | A84 | 50d green & yel | 2.00 | .50 |
| **967** | A85 | 1r lil rose & yel | 2.00 | .50 |
| **968** | A84 | 2.50r blue & yellow | 3.00 | 1.00 |
| **969** | A85 | 5r blk brn & yel | 6.00 | 2.50 |
| | | *Nos. 966-969 (4)* | 13.00 | 4.50 |

Discovery of oil at Qum.

Abadan Oil Refinery A86

Super Fractionators — A87

Designs: 1r, Storage tanks. 5r, Pipe lines. 10r, Abadan refinery.

**1953, Mar. 20 Photo.**

| | | | | |
|---|---|---|---|---|
| **970** | A86 | 50d blue green | 2.00 | .50 |
| **971** | A86 | 1r rose | 3.00 | .50 |
| **972** | A87 | 2.50r bright ultra | 4.00 | 1.50 |
| **973** | A86 | 5r red orange | 6.00 | 1.50 |
| **974** | A86 | 10r dark violet | 12.00 | 2.00 |
| | | *Nos. 970-974 (5)* | 27.00 | 6.00 |

Nationalization of oil industry, 2nd anniv.

**Shah Types of 1951-52**

**1953-54 Photo. *Perf. 10½***

| | | | | |
|---|---|---|---|---|
| **975** | A82 | 50d dark gray grn | 20.00 | .35 |
| **976** | A83 | 1r dk blue green | 2.50 | .25 |
| **977** | A83 | 1.50r cerise ('54) | 2.50 | .25 |
| | | *Nos. 975-977 (3)* | 25.00 | .85 |

The background has been highlighted on the 1r and 1.50r.

Gymnast — A88

Archery A89

Designs: 3r, Climbing Mt. Demavend. 5r, Ancient polo. 10r, Lion hunting.

**1953, Oct. 26**

| | | | | |
|---|---|---|---|---|
| **978** | A88 | 1r deep green | 5.00 | 3.00 |
| **979** | A89 | 2.50fr brt grnsh bl | 17.50 | 5.00 |
| **980** | A89 | 3r gray | 22.50 | 6.00 |
| **981** | A88 | 5r bister | 20.00 | 12.00 |
| **982** | A88 | 10r rose lilac | 65.00 | 20.00 |
| | | *Nos. 978-982 (5)* | 130.00 | 46.00 |

Mother with Children and UN Emblem A90

**1953, Oct. 24**

| | | | | |
|---|---|---|---|---|
| **983** | A90 | 1r bl grn & dk grn | 2.00 | .30 |
| **984** | A90 | 2.50r lt bl & indigo | 3.00 | .70 |

United Nations Day, Oct. 24.

Herring A91

Refrigeration Compressor — A92

Processing Equipment, National Fisheries — A93

Designs: 2.50r, Sardines. 10r, Sturgeon.

**1954, Jan. 31**

| | | | | |
|---|---|---|---|---|
| **985** | A91 | 1r multi | 5.00 | 3.00 |
| **986** | A91 | 2.50r multi | 35.00 | 15.00 |
| **987** | A92 | 3r vermilion | 15.00 | 7.00 |
| **988** | A93 | 5r deep bl grn | 15.00 | 10.00 |
| **989** | A91 | 10r multi | 55.00 | 25.00 |
| | | *Nos. 985-989 (5)* | 125.00 | 60.00 |

Nationalization of fishing industry.

Broken Shackles — A94

3r, Torch flag. 5r, Citizen holding flag of Iran.

**1954, Aug. 19 Litho.**

| | | | | |
|---|---|---|---|---|
| **990** | A94 | 2r multicolored | 7.00 | 3.00 |
| **991** | A94 | 3r multicolored | 12.00 | 5.00 |
| **992** | A94 | 5r multicolored | 16.00 | 7.00 |
| | | *Nos. 990-992 (3)* | 35.00 | 15.00 |

Return of the royalist government, 1st anniv.

Mother Feeding Baby — A95

**1954, Oct. 24** **Photo.**

| | | | | |
|---|---|---|---|---|
| **993** | A95 | 2r red lil & org | 2.50 | .75 |
| **994** | A95 | 3r vio bl & org | 3.50 | 1.25 |

Issued to honor the United Nations.

Woodsman Felling Tree — A96

Designs: 2.50r, Laborer carrying firewood. 5r, Worker operating saw. 10r, Wooden galley.

**1954, Dec. 11**

| | | | | |
|---|---|---|---|---|
| **995** | A96 | 1r brn & grnsh black | 30.00 | 20.00 |
| **996** | A96 | 2.50r grnsh blk & bl | 35.00 | 30.00 |
| **997** | A96 | 5r lil & dk brn | 60.00 | 40.00 |
| **998** | A96 | 10r bl & claret | 80.00 | 50.00 |
| | | *Nos. 995-998 (4)* | 205.00 | 140.00 |

4th World Forestry Congress, Dehra Dun, India, 1954.

Mohammad Reza Shah Pahlavi
A97 A98

**1954-55** **Unwmk.**

| | | | | |
|---|---|---|---|---|
| **999** | A97 | 5d yellow brn | 1.00 | .25 |
| **1000** | A97 | 10d violet | 1.00 | .25 |
| **1001** | A97 | 25d scarlet | 1.00 | .25 |
| **1002** | A97 | 50d black brn | 1.00 | .25 |
| **1003** | A98 | 1r blue green | 1.00 | .25 |
| **1004** | A98 | 1.50r cerise | 1.00 | .25 |
| **1005** | A98 | 2r ocher | 2.50 | .25 |
| **1006** | A98 | 2.50r blue | 3.00 | .25 |
| **1007** | A98 | 3r olive | 7.50 | .25 |
| **1008** | A98 | 5r dk sl grn | 7.50 | 1.50 |
| **1009** | A98 | 10r lilac rose | 25.00 | 1.50 |
| **1010** | A98 | 20r indigo | 40.00 | 8.00 |
| **1011** | A98 | 30r dp yel brn | 175.00 | 12.50 |
| **1012** | A98 | 50r dp orange | 40.00 | 15.00 |
| **1013** | A98 | 100r light vio | 400.00 | 75.00 |
| **1014** | A98 | 200r yellow | 150.00 | 35.00 |
| | | *Nos. 999-1014 (16)* | 856.50 | 150.75 |

See Nos. 1023-1036.

Regional Costume — A99

Regional Costumes: 1r, 2r, Men's costumes. 2.50r, 3r, 5r, Women's costumes.

**1955, June 26** **Photo.** ***Perf. 11***

| | | | | |
|---|---|---|---|---|
| **1015** | A99 | 1r bluish gray & multi | 10.00 | 3.00 |
| **1016** | A99 | 2r dl rose & multi | 10.00 | 4.00 |
| **1017** | A99 | 2.50r buff & multi | 30.00 | 5.00 |
| **1018** | A99 | 3r rose lil & multi | 15.00 | 6.00 |
| **1019** | A99 | 5r gray brn & multi | 30.00 | 10.00 |
| | | *Nos. 1015-1019 (5)* | 95.00 | 28.00 |

Parliament Gate — A100

Designs: 3r, Statue of Liberty, vert. 5r, Old Gate of Parliament.

**1955, Aug. 6** **Wmk. 306** ***Perf. 11***

| | | | | |
|---|---|---|---|---|
| **1020** | A100 | 2r red vio & grn | 5.00 | 2.00 |
| **1021** | A100 | 3r dk bl & aqua | 12.00 | 3.00 |
| **1022** | A100 | 5r Prus grn & red org | 15.00 | 7.00 |
| | | *Nos. 1020-1022 (3)* | 32.00 | 12.00 |

50th anniversary of constitution.

**Shah Types of 1954-55**

**1955-56** **Wmk. 306** ***Perf. 11***

| | | | | |
|---|---|---|---|---|
| **1023** | A97 | 5d violet ('56) | 5.00 | 1.50 |
| **1024** | A97 | 10d carmine ('56) | 1.00 | .25 |
| **1025** | A97 | 25d brown | 1.00 | .25 |
| **1026** | A97 | 50d dk carmine | 1.00 | .25 |
| **1027** | A98 | 1r dark bl grn | 1.00 | .25 |
| **1028** | A98 | 1.50r red brn ('56) | 50.00 | 3.00 |
| **1029** | A98 | 2r ol grn ('56) | 25.00 | .25 |
| **1030** | A98 | 2.50r blue ('56) | 5.00 | .30 |
| **1031** | A98 | 3r bister | 7.00 | .25 |
| **1032** | A98 | 5r red lilac | 10.00 | .25 |
| **1033** | A98 | 10r brt grnsh bl | 12.00 | .35 |
| **1034** | A98 | 20r slate green | 30.00 | 4.00 |
| **1035** | A98 | 30r red org ('56) | 150.00 | 25.00 |
| **1036** | A98 | 50r red brn ('56) | 125.00 | 30.00 |
| | | *Nos. 1023-1036 (14)* | 423.00 | 65.90 |

UN Emblem and Globes A101

**1955, Oct. 24** ***Perf. 11x12½***

| | | | | |
|---|---|---|---|---|
| **1039** | A101 | 1r dp car & org | 1.50 | .75 |
| **1040** | A101 | 2.50r dk bl & grnsh blue | 2.00 | 1.50 |

UN, 10th anniv.Nations, Oct. 24, 1955.

Wrestlers A102

**1955, Oct. 26** **Wmk. 306** ***Perf. 11***

| | | | | |
|---|---|---|---|---|
| **1041** | A102 | 2.50r multi | 15.00 | 7.50 |

Victory in intl. wrestling competitions.

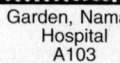

Garden, Namazi Hospital A103

*Immortal Guardsman* A105

Nemazi Hospital, Shiraz A104

5r, Gate of the Koran. 10r, Ha'fez of Shiraz.

**1956, Mar. 21** ***Perf. 11x12½***

| | | | | |
|---|---|---|---|---|
| **1042** | A103 | 50d multi | 5.00 | 2.00 |
| **1043** | A104 | 1r multi | 6.00 | 2.50 |
| **1044** | A105 | 2.50r multi | 9.00 | 7.00 |
| **1045** | A104 | 5r multi | 15.00 | 6.00 |
| **1046** | A105 | 10r multi | 25.00 | 10.00 |
| | | *Nos. 1042-1046 (5)* | 60.00 | 27.50 |

Opening of Namazi Hospital, Shiraz.

Arms of Iran and Olympic Rings — A106

**1956, May 15** **Wmk. 306**

| | | | | |
|---|---|---|---|---|
| **1047** | A106 | 5r rose lilac | 40.00 | 30.00 |

National Olympic Committee, 10th anniv.

Tomb at Maragheh A107

2.50r, Astrolabe. 5r, Nasr-ud-Din of Tus.

**1956, May 26** **Photo.** ***Perf. 11x12½***

| | | | | |
|---|---|---|---|---|
| **1048** | A107 | 1r orange | 5.00 | 2.50 |
| **1049** | A107 | 2.50r deep ultra | 7.50 | 3.50 |
| **1050** | A107 | 5r sepia & pur | 12.50 | 4.00 |
| | | *Nos. 1048-1050 (3)* | 25.00 | 10.00 |

700th death anniv. of Nasr-up-Din of Tus, mathematician and astronomer.

WHO Emblem — A108

***Perf. 11x12½***

**1956, Sept. 19** **Wmk. 306**

| | | | | |
|---|---|---|---|---|
| **1051** | A108 | 6r cerise | 4.00 | 1.50 |

6th Regional Congress of the WHO.

Scout Bugler and Camp A109

5r, Scout badge and Shah in scout uniform.

**1956, Aug. 5** ***Perf. 12½x11***

| | | | | |
|---|---|---|---|---|
| **1052** | A109 | 2.50r ultra & blue | 15.00 | 9.00 |
| **1053** | A109 | 5r lil & red lil | 20.00 | 12.00 |

National Boy Scout Jamboree.

**Catalogue values for unused stamps in this section, from this point to the end of the section, are for Never Hinged items.**

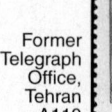

Former Telegraph Office, Tehran A110

6r, Telegraph lines & ancient monument.

**1956, Oct. 26**

| | | | | |
|---|---|---|---|---|
| **1054** | A110 | 2.50r brt bl & grn, *bluish* | 12.00 | 5.00 |
| **1055** | A110 | 6r rose car & lil | 13.00 | 7.50 |

Centenary of Persian telegraph system.

UN Emblem and People of the World A111

Design: 2.50r, UN Emblem and scales.

**1956, Oct. 24**

| | | | | |
|---|---|---|---|---|
| **1056** | A111 | 1r bluish green | 1.50 | .40 |
| **1057** | A111 | 2.50r blue & green | 3.00 | .60 |

United Nations Day, Oct. 24.

Shah and Pres. Iskander Mirza of Pakistan A112

**1956, Oct. 31**

| | | | | |
|---|---|---|---|---|
| **1058** | A112 | 1r multicolored | 10.00 | 2.50 |

Visit of Pres. General Iskander Mirza of Pakistan to Tehran, Oct. 31-Nov. 10.

Mohammad Reza Shah Pahlavi
A113 A114

***Perf. 13½x11***

**1956-57** **Wmk. 306** **Photo.**

| | | | | |
|---|---|---|---|---|
| **1058A** | A113 | 5d brt car & red | .50 | *1.00* |
| **1058B** | A113 | 10d vio bl & dl vio | .50 | *1.00* |
| **1059** | A113 | 25d dk brn & brn | .75 | .35 |
| **1059A** | A113 | 50d brn & ol brn | .75 | .25 |
| ***b.*** | | Inverted center | *3,750.* | |
| **1060** | A113 | 1r brn & brt grn | .75 | .25 |
| **1061** | A113 | 1.50r brt lil & brown | 1.00 | .25 |
| **1062** | A113 | 2r red vio & red | 1.00 | .25 |
| **1063** | A113 | 2.50r ultra & blue | 1.50 | .25 |
| **1064** | A113 | 3r brn & dk ol bis | 1.50 | .25 |
| **1065** | A113 | 5r ver & mar | 2.00 | .25 |
| **1066** | A114 | 6r dk vio & brn lil | 7.00 | .25 |
| **1067** | A114 | 10r lt blue & grn | 15.00 | .25 |
| **1068** | A114 | 20r green & blue | 30.00 | 3.00 |
| **1069** | A114 | 30r rose red & org | 35.00 | 5.00 |
| **1070** | A114 | 50r dk grn & ol grn | 35.00 | 5.00 |
| **1071** | A114 | 100r lilac & cer | 350.00 | 27.50 |
| **1072** | A114 | 200r dp plum & vio bl | 210.00 | 15.00 |
| | | *Nos. 1058A-1072 (17)* | 692.25 | 60.10 |

Issued: 1.50r, 2r, 3r, 5r, 6r, 1956; others, 1957.

See Nos. 1082-1098.

Lord Baden-Powell A115

**1957, Feb. 22** *Perf. 12½*

| | | | | |
|---|---|---|---|---|
| **1073** | A115 | 10r dk grn & brn | 12.50 | 7.00 |

Birth cent. of Robert Baden-Powell, founder of the Boy Scout movement.

Railroad Tracks — A116

Train and Map A117

Design: 10r, Train and mosque.

**1957, May 2** *Perf. 11x12½, 12½x11*

| | | | | |
|---|---|---|---|---|
| **1074** | A116 | 2.50r grnsh blk, bl & ocher | 15.00 | 2.00 |
| **1075** | A117 | 5r multi | 20.00 | 7.00 |
| **1076** | A116 | 10r blk, yel & bl | 35.00 | 11.00 |
| | | *Nos. 1074-1076 (3)* | 70.00 | 20.00 |

Opening of the Tehran Meshed-Railway.

Pres. Giovanni Gronchi of Italy and Shah — A118

Design: 6r, Ruins of Persepolis and Colosseum in Rome and flags.

**Wmk. 316**

**1957, Sept. 7** **Photo.** *Perf. 11*

| | | | | |
|---|---|---|---|---|
| **1077** | A118 | 2r slate bl, grn & red | 5.00 | 2.00 |
| **1078** | A118 | 6r slate bl, grn & red | 10.00 | 3.00 |

Visit of Pres. Giovanni Gronchi of Italy to Iran, Sept. 7.

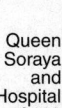

Queen Soraya and Hospital A119

**1957, Sept. 29** **Wmk. 316** *Perf. 11*

| | | | | |
|---|---|---|---|---|
| **1079** | A119 | 2r lt bl & grn | 10.00 | 3.00 |

Sixth Medical Congress, Ramsar.

Globes Showing Location of Iran — A120

**1957, Oct. 22** **Litho.** *Perf. 12½x11*

| | | | | |
|---|---|---|---|---|
| **1080** | A120 | 10r blk, lt bl, yel & red | 10.00 | 3.00 |

Intl. Cartographic Conference, Tehran.

Shah and King Faisal II — A121

**1957, Oct. 18** **Photo.**

| | | | | |
|---|---|---|---|---|
| **1081** | A121 | 2r slate bl, grn & red | 10.00 | 3.00 |

Visit of King Faisal of Iraq, Oct. 19.

**Shah Types of 1956-57**

**1957-58** **Wmk. 316** *Perf. 11*

| | | | | |
|---|---|---|---|---|
| **1082** | A114 | 5d violet & pur | .50 | *2.00* |
| **1083** | A114 | 10d claret & rose car | .50 | *2.00* |
| **1084** | A114 | 25d rose car & brick red | .50 | .35 |
| **1085** | A114 | 50d grn & olive grn | .60 | .25 |
| **1086** | A114 | 1r dark green | .90 | .25 |
| **1087** | A114 | 1.50r claret & red lil | 1.00 | .25 |
| **1088** | A114 | 2r bl & grnsh blue | 2.00 | .25 |
| **1089** | A114 | 2.50r dk bl & blue | 2.00 | .25 |
| **1090** | A114 | 3r rose car & ver | 2.00 | .25 |
| **1091** | A114 | 5r violet blue | 2.00 | .25 |
| **1092** | A113 | 6r bright blue | 3.00 | .25 |
| **1093** | A113 | 10r deep green | 6.00 | .30 |
| **1094** | A113 | 20r grn & olive grn | 30.00 | .45 |
| **1095** | A113 | 30r vio bl & dk brn | 35.00 | 10.00 |
| **1096** | A113 | 50r dk brn & lt brn | 40.00 | 12.00 |
| **1097** | A113 | 100r rose lil & car rose | 150.00 | 30.00 |
| **1098** | A113 | 200r vio & yel brn | 125.00 | 35.00 |
| | | *Nos. 1082-1098 (17)* | 401.00 | 94.10 |

Issued: 1.50r, 2r, 3r, 1957; others, 1958.

Weight Lifter — A122

**1957, Nov. 8** *Perf. 11x14½*

| | | | | |
|---|---|---|---|---|
| **1099** | A122 | 10r bl, grn & red | 10.00 | 4.00 |

Iran's victories in weight lifting.

Modern and Old Houses, Radio Transmitter A123

**1958, Feb. 22** **Litho.**

| | | | | |
|---|---|---|---|---|
| **1100** | A123 | 10r brn, ocher & bl | 10.00 | 4.00 |

30th anniversary of radio in Iran.

Oil Derrick and Symbolic Flame — A124

**Wmk. 316**

**1958, Mar. 10** **Photo.** *Perf. 11*

| | | | | |
|---|---|---|---|---|
| **1101** | A124 | 2r gray & multi | 10.00 | 2.00 |
| **1102** | A124 | 10r multicolored | 15.00 | 3.00 |

Drilling of Iran's 1st oil well, 50th anniv.

Train on Viaduct — A125

Design: 8r, Train and map.

**1958, Apr. 24** **Wmk. 306** *Perf. 11*

| | | | | |
|---|---|---|---|---|
| **1103** | A125 | 6r dull purple | 25.00 | 7.50 |
| **1104** | A125 | 8r green | 35.00 | 12.50 |

Opening of Tehran-Tabriz railway line.

Exposition Emblem A126

**1958, Apr. 17** *Perf. 12½x11*

| | | | | |
|---|---|---|---|---|
| **1105** | A126 | 2.50r bl & light bl | 1.25 | .30 |
| **1106** | A126 | 6r car & salmon | 2.25 | .50 |

World's Fair, Brussels, Apr. 17-Oct. 19.

Mohammad Reza Shah Pahlavi — A127

UN Emblem and Map of Iran — A128

**1958-59** **Wmk. 316** **Photo.** *Perf. 11*

| | | | | |
|---|---|---|---|---|
| **1107** | A127 | 5d blue violet | .75 | .25 |
| **1108** | A127 | 10d lt vermilion | .75 | .25 |
| **1109** | A127 | 25d crimson | .75 | .25 |
| **1110** | A127 | 50d brt blue | .75 | .25 |
| **1111** | A127 | 1r dark green | 1.50 | .25 |
| **1113** | A127 | 2r dark brown | 10.00 | .25 |
| **1115** | A127 | 3r dk red brown | 17.50 | .25 |
| **1117** | A127 | 6r bright blue | 8.00 | .45 |
| **1118** | A127 | 8r magenta | 8.00 | .35 |
| **1120** | A127 | 14r blue violet | 15.00 | 1.75 |
| **1121** | A127 | 20r green | 25.00 | .45 |
| *a.* | | Wmk. 306 | 30.00 | 15.00 |
| **1122** | A127 | 30r brt car rose | 20.00 | 3.00 |
| **1123** | A127 | 50r rose violet | 60.00 | 10.00 |
| **1124** | A127 | 100r red orange | 30.00 | 6.00 |
| **1125** | A127 | 200r slate green | 75.00 | 12.00 |
| | | *Nos. 1107-1125 (15)* | 273.00 | 35.75 |

See Nos. 1138-1151, 1173-1179.

**1958, Oct. 24**

| | | | | |
|---|---|---|---|---|
| **1126** | A128 | 6r bright blue | 1.50 | 1.00 |
| **1127** | A128 | 10r dk violet & grn | 2.50 | 1.25 |

Issued for United Nations Day, Oct. 24.

Globe and Hands A129

**1958, Dec. 10**

| | | | | |
|---|---|---|---|---|
| **1128** | A129 | 6r dk red brn & brn | 1.50 | .50 |
| **1129** | A129 | 8r dk grn & gray grn | 2.50 | .75 |

Universal Declaration of Human Rights, 10th anniv.

Rudaki — A130

Design: 5r, Rudaki, different pose. 10r, Same design as No. 1130.

**1958, Dec. 24** **Photo.** **Wmk. 306**

| | | | | |
|---|---|---|---|---|
| **1130** | A130 | 2.50r bluish black | 10.00 | 2.00 |
| **1131** | A130 | 5r violet | 15.00 | 3.00 |
| **1132** | A130 | 10r dark brown | 25.00 | 4.00 |
| | | *Nos. 1130-1132 (3)* | 50.00 | 9.00 |

1100th birth anniv. of Rudaki, blind Persian poet.

Flag — A130a

Design: 1r & 6r, Red Lion & Sun flag (Iranian Red Cross Organization).

*Perf. 14½x11*

**1959, May 8** **Wmk. 316**

| | | | | |
|---|---|---|---|---|
| **1132A** | A130a | 1r multicolored | 3.00 | 1.00 |
| **1132B** | A130a | 6r multicolored | 5.00 | 1.50 |

Centenary of the Red Cross.

Wrestlers, Flag and Globe — A131

**1959** **Litho.** *Perf. 11x12½*

| | | | | |
|---|---|---|---|---|
| **1133** | A131 | 6r multicolored | 25.00 | 10.00 |

World Wrestling Championships, Tehran.

Globe, UN Building and Hand Holding Torch of Freedom A132

**1959, Oct. 24** **Photo.** *Perf. 11*

| | | | | |
|---|---|---|---|---|
| **1134** | A132 | 6r gray brn, red & bister | 2.00 | .60 |

Issued for United Nations Day, Oct. 24.

Shah and Pres. Ayub Khan of Pakistan — A133

**1959, Nov. 9 Litho. *Perf. 11x16***

| | | | | |
|---|---|---|---|---|
| **1135** | A133 | 6r multicolored | 10.00 | 3.00 |

Visit of Pres. Khan to Iran.

ILO Emblem — A134

**1959, Nov. 12 *Perf. 16***

| | | | | |
|---|---|---|---|---|
| **1136** | A134 | 1r blue | 1.50 | .40 |
| **1137** | A134 | 5r brown | 2.00 | .60 |

ILO, 40th anniversary.

**Shah Type of 1958-59**

**1959-63 Wmk. 316 Photo. *Perf. 11***

| | | | | |
|---|---|---|---|---|
| **1138** | A127 | 5d red brn ('60) | .50 | .30 |
| **1139** | A127 | 10d Prus grn ('60) | .50 | .30 |
| *a.* | | 10d Prussian blue ('63) | .75 | .50 |
| **1140** | A127 | 25d orange | 1.50 | .25 |
| *a.* | | Perf. 12x11½ | 75.00 | 20.00 |
| **1141** | A127 | 50d scarlet | 1.50 | .25 |
| **1142** | A127 | 1r deep violet | 1.50 | .25 |
| **1142A** | A127 | 2r brown | 10.00 | .25 |
| **1143** | A127 | 3r olive | 4.00 | .25 |
| **1143A** | A127 | 6r cobalt blue | 7.50 | .25 |
| **1144** | A127 | 8r brown olive | 2.00 | .25 |
| **1145** | A127 | 10r ol blk ('60) | 2.00 | .25 |
| **1146** | A127 | 14r yel green | 2.50 | .25 |
| *a.* | | 14r emerald green | 4.00 | .50 |
| **1147** | A127 | 20r sl grn ('60) | 7.00 | .35 |
| **1148** | A127 | 30r choc ('60) | 10.00 | 2.00 |
| **1149** | A127 | 50r dp blue ('60) | 10.00 | 2.00 |
| **1150** | A127 | 100r green ('60) | 135.00 | 12.50 |
| **1151** | A127 | 200r cer ('60) | 250.00 | 17.50 |
| | | *Nos. 1138-1151 (16)* | 445.50 | 37.20 |

See Pakistan 274-276, Turkey 1813-1815.

Pahlavi Foundation Bridge, Karun River — A135

Design: 5r, Bridge, different view.

**1960, Feb. 29 Litho. *Perf. 16x11***

| | | | | |
|---|---|---|---|---|
| **1152** | A135 | 1r dk brn & brt bl | 2.00 | .25 |
| **1153** | A135 | 5r blue & emerald | 3.00 | .70 |

Opening of Pahlavi Foundation Bridge at Khorramshahr on the Karun River.

Uprooted Oak Emblem A136

Design: 6r, Arched frame.

**1960, Apr. 7 *Perf. 11***

| | | | | |
|---|---|---|---|---|
| **1154** | A136 | 1r brt ultra | .70 | .30 |
| **1155** | A136 | 6r gray olive | .80 | .35 |

World Refugee Year, 7/1/59-6/30/60.

Mosquito — A137

Man with Spray Gun — A138

Design: 3r, Mosquito on water.

**1960, Apr. 7 Wmk. 316**

| | | | | |
|---|---|---|---|---|
| **1156** | A137 | 1r blk & red, *yel* | 2.00 | 1.00 |
| **1157** | A138 | 2r lt bl, ultra & blk | 3.00 | 1.00 |
| **1158** | A137 | 3r blk & red, *yel grn* | 5.00 | 1.50 |
| | | *Nos. 1156-1158 (3)* | 10.00 | 3.50 |

Issued to publicize malaria control.

Polo Player — A139

Design: 6r, Persian archer.

**1960, June 9 Litho. Wmk. 316**

| | | | | |
|---|---|---|---|---|
| **1159** | A139 | 1r deep claret | 3.00 | .50 |
| **1160** | A139 | 6r dk blue & lt blue | 5.00 | 1.00 |

17th Olympic Games, Rome, 8/25-9/11.

Shah and King Hussein of Jordan — A140

**1960, July 6 *Perf. 11***

| | | | | |
|---|---|---|---|---|
| **1161** | A140 | 6r multicolored | 10.00 | 3.00 |

Visit of King Hussein of Jordan to Tehran.

Iranian Scout Emblem in Flower — A141

Tents and Pillars of Persepolis A142

**1960, July 18**

| | | | | |
|---|---|---|---|---|
| **1162** | A141 | 1r green | 1.00 | .50 |
| **1163** | A142 | 6r brn, brt bl & buff | 2.00 | .75 |

3rd National Boy Scout Jamboree.

Shah and Queen Farah — A143

**1960, Sept. 9 Litho. *Perf. 11***

| | | | | |
|---|---|---|---|---|
| **1164** | A143 | 1r green | 5.00 | 1.50 |
| **1165** | A143 | 5r blue | 10.00 | 2.00 |

Marriage of Shah Mohammad Reza Shah Pahlavi and Farah Diba.

UN Emblem and Globe — A144

**1960, Oct. 24 Wmk. 316**

| | | | | |
|---|---|---|---|---|
| **1166** | A144 | 6r bl, blk & lt brn | 2.00 | .50 |

15th anniversary of the United Nations.

Shah and Queen Elizabeth II A145

**1961, Mar. 2 Litho. *Perf. 11***

| | | | | |
|---|---|---|---|---|
| **1167** | A145 | 1r lt red brown | 3.00 | .45 |
| **1168** | A145 | 6r bright ultra | 5.00 | .90 |

Visit of Queen Elizabeth II to Tehran, Feb. 1961.

Girl Playing Arganoon — A146

Safiaddin Amavi — A147

**1961, Apr. 10 Wmk. 316 *Perf. 11***

| | | | | |
|---|---|---|---|---|
| **1169** | A146 | 1r dk brown & buff | 2.00 | .50 |
| **1170** | A147 | 6r greenish gray | 3.00 | .75 |

International Congress of Music, Tehran.

**Shah Type of 1958-59 Redrawn**

**1961-62 Litho. *Perf. 11***

| | | | | |
|---|---|---|---|---|
| **1173** | A127 | 25d orange | 3.50 | .50 |
| **1174** | A127 | 50d scarlet | 3.50 | .40 |
| **1175** | A127 | 1r deep violet | 6.00 | .25 |
| **1176** | A127 | 2r chocolate | 7.00 | .25 |
| **1177** | A127 | 3r olive brown | 10.00 | .50 |
| **1178** | A127 | 6r brt blue ('62) | 50.00 | 3.50 |
| **1179** | A127 | 8r brown ol ('62) | 20.00 | 2.25 |
| | | *Nos. 1173-1179 (7)* | 100.00 | 7.65 |

On Nos. 1173-1179 (lithographed), a single white line separates the lower panel from the shah's portrait. On Nos. 1107-1125, 1138-1151 (photogravure), two lines, one in color and one in white, separate panel from portrait. Other minor differences exist.

Shah and Queen Farah Holding Crown Prince — A148

**1961, June 2 Litho.**

| | | | | |
|---|---|---|---|---|
| **1186** | A148 | 1r bright pink | 5.00 | 2.50 |
| **1187** | A148 | 6r light blue | 10.00 | 5.00 |

Birth of Crown Prince Reza Kourosh Pahlavi, Oct. 31, 1960.

Swallows and UN Emblem — A149

**1961, Oct. 24 *Perf. 11***

| | | | | |
|---|---|---|---|---|
| **1188** | A149 | 2r blue & car rose | 1.50 | .25 |
| **1189** | A149 | 6r blue & violet | 2.00 | .35 |

Issued for United Nations Day, Oct. 24.

Planting Tree — A150

**1962, Jan. 11**

| | | | | |
|---|---|---|---|---|
| **1190** | A150 | 2r ol grn, citron & dk bl | 1.50 | .25 |
| **1191** | A150 | 6r ultra, grn & pale bl | 2.00 | .35 |

Tree Planting Day.

Worker and Symbols of Labor and Agriculture A151

**1962, Mar. 15 Litho.**

| | | | | |
|---|---|---|---|---|
| **1192** | A151 | 2r bl grn, brn & blk | 1.50 | .25 |
| **1193** | A151 | 6r lt ultra, brn & blk | 2.00 | .35 |

Issued for Workers' Day.

Map, Family and Cogwheel
A152

**1962, Mar. 20** *Perf. 11*
**1194** A152 2r black, yel & lil 2.00 .30
**1195** A152 6r black, bl & ultra 2.50 .65

Social Insurance Week.

Sugar Refinery, Khuzistan — A153

**1962, Apr. 14** **Wmk. 316**
**1196** A153 2r dk & lt blue & grn 2.00 .35
**1197** A153 6r ultra, buff & blue 2.50 .65

Opening of sugar refinery in Khuzistan.

Karaj Dam — A154

**1962, May 15**
**1198** A154 2r dk brn & gray grn 1.50 .25
**1199** A154 6r vio bl & lt blue 2.00 .50

Inauguration of Karaj Dam, renamed Amir Kabir Dam.

Sefid Rud Dam
A155

**1962, May 19** **Litho.**
**1200** A155 2r dk grn, lt bl & buff 2.00 .35
**1201** A155 6r red brn, sl grn & lt blue 2.50 .65

Inauguration of Sefid Rud Dam.

"UNESCO" and UN Emblem — A156

**1962, June 2** **Wmk. 316** *Perf. 11*
**1202** A156 2r black, emer & red 1.50 .30
**1203** A156 6r blue, emer & red 2.50 .50

15th anniv. of UNESCO.

Malaria Eradication Emblem and Sprayer
A157

2r, Emblem & arrow piercing mosquito, horiz. 10r, Emblem & globe, horiz. Sizes: 2r, 10r, 40x25mm; 6r, 29½x34½mm.

**1962, June 20**
**1204** A157 2r black & bluish grn 2.00 .35
**1205** A157 6r pink & vio blue 2.50 .50
**1206** A157 10r lt blue & ultra 3.00 .75
*Nos. 1204-1206 (3)* 7.50 1.60

WHO drive to eradicate malaria.

Oil Field and UN Emblem
A158

**1962, Sept. 1** **Photo.**
**1207** A158 6r grnsh blue & brn 3.00 .50
**1208** A158 14r gray & sepia 5.00 1.50

2nd Petroleum Symposium of ECAFE (UN Economic Commission for Asia and the Far East).

Mohammad Reza Shah Pahlavi — A159

Palace of Darius, Persepolis
A160

*Perf. 11, 10½x11, 11x10½*

**1962** **Photo.** **Wmk. 316**
**1209** A159 5d green 1.00 .25
**1210** A159 10d chestnut 1.00 .50
**1211** A159 25d dark blue 1.00 .35
**1212** A159 50d Prus green 1.00 .25
**1213** A159 1r orange 3.00 .25
**1214** A159 2r violet blue 2.00 .25
**1215** A159 5r dark brown 3.00 .25
**1216** A160 6r blue 12.00 2.50
**1217** A160 8r yellow grn 5.00 1.00
**1218** A160 10r grnsh blue 8.00 .50
**1219** A160 11r slate green 4.50 .65
**1220** A160 14r purple 10.00 .65
**1221** A160 20r red brown 11.00 1.50
**1222** A160 50r vermilion 15.00 1.50
*Nos. 1209-1222 (14)* 77.50 10.40

See Nos. 1331-1344.
No. 1219 perf. 10½x11 is valued unused $9. Otherwise, all perf. varieties have the same values.

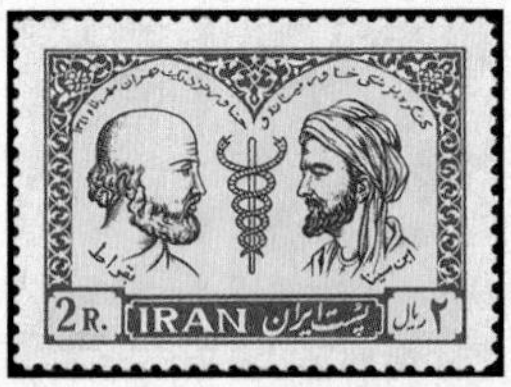


Hippocrates and Avicenna — A161

**1962, Oct. 7** **Litho.**
**1226** A161 2r brown, buff & ultra 3.00 .35
**1227** A161 6r grn, pale grn & ultra 3.50 .60

Near and Middle East Medical Congress.

Hands Laying Bricks
A162

Design: 6r, Houses and UN emblem, vert.

**1962, Oct. 24**
**1228** A162 6r dk blue & ultra 3.00 .35
**1229** A162 14r dk blue & emer 3.50 .60

Issued for United Nations Day, Oct. 24.

Crown Prince Receiving Flowers — A163

**1962, Oct. 31**
**1230** A163 6r blue gray 6.00 1.00
**1231** A163 14r dull green 12.00 1.90

Children's Day, Oct. 31; 2nd birthday of Crown Prince Riza.

Map of Iran and Persian Gulf — A164

**1962, Dec. 12** **Wmk. 316** *Perf. 11*
**1232** A164 6r dk & lt bl, vio bl & rose 3.00 .35
**1233** A164 14r dk & lt bl, pink & rose 3.50 .60

The Persian Gulf Seminar.

Hilton Hotel, Tehran — A165

**1963, Jan. 21** **Photo.**
**1234** A165 6r deep blue 4.00 .45
**1235** A165 14r dark red brown 6.00 .60

Opening of the Royal Tehran Hilton Hotel.

Mohammad Riza Shah Dam
A166

**1963, Mar. 14** **Litho.**
**Center Multicolored**
**1236** A166 6r violet blue 4.00 .40
**1237** A166 14r dark brown 7.00 .75

Mohammad Riza Shah Dam inauguration (later Dez Dam).

Worker with Pickax — A167

**1963, Mar. 15**
**1238** A167 2r cream & black 1.50 .25
**1239** A167 6r lt blue & blk 2.50 .30

Issued for Labor Day.

Stylized Bird over Globe — A168

Designs: 6r, Stylized globe and "FAO." 14r, Globe in space and wheat emblem.

**1963, Mar. 21** *Perf. 11*
**1240** A168 2r ultra, lt bl & bis 2.00 .25
**1241** A168 6r lt ultra, ocher & blk 3.00 .30
**1242** A168 14r slate bl & ocher 4.00 .85
*Nos. 1240-1242 (3)* 9.00 1.40

FAO "Freedom from Hunger" campaign.

Shah and List of Bills — A169

**1963, Mar. 21** **Wmk. 316**
**1243** A169 6r green & lt blue 7.00 2.00
**1244** A169 14r green & dull yel 10.00 3.00

Signing of six socioeconomic bills by Shah, 1st anniv.

Shah and King of Denmark — A170

**1963, May 3** **Litho.** *Perf. 11*
**1245** A170 6r indigo & dk ultra 5.00 .55
**1246** A170 14r dk brn & red brn 7.00 1.00

Visit of King Frederik IX of Denmark.

Flags, Shah Mosque, Isfahan, and Taj Mahal, Agra
A171

**1963, May 19**
**1247** A171 6r blue, yel grn & red 5.00 .55
**1248** A171 14r multicolored 7.00 1.00

Visit of Dr. Sarvepalli Radhakrishnan, president of India.

Chahnaz Dam — A172

**1963, June 8 Wmk. 316 *Perf. 11***

**1249** A172 6r ultra, bl & grn 3.50 .45
**1250** A172 14r dk grn, bl & buff 5.00 .75

Inauguration of Chahnaz Dam (later Hamadan Dam).

Cent. Emblem with Red Lion and Sun — A173

**1963, June 10**

**1251** A173 6r blue, gray & red 5.00 .65
**1252** A173 14r buff, gray & red 7.00 .90

Centenary of International Red Cross.

Shah and Queen Juliana A174

***Perf. 11x10½***

**1963, Oct. 3 Wmk. 349**

**1253** A174 6r ultra & blue 5.00 .50
**1254** A174 14r sl grn & dull grn 7.00 .75

Visit of Queen Juliana of the Netherlands.

Literacy Corps Emblem and Soldier Teaching Village Class — A175

**1963, Oct. 15 Litho. *Perf. 10½***

**1255** A175 6r multicolored 7.00 1.00
**1256** A175 14r multicolored 8.00 1.00

Issued to publicize the Literacy Corps.

Gen. Charles de Gaulle and View of Persepolis — A176

**1963, Oct. 16**

**1257** A176 6r ultra & blue 5.00 1.00
**1258** A176 14r brn & pale brn 7.00 1.00

Visit of General de Gaulle of France.

Fertilizer Plant, Oil Company Emblem and Map — A177

Design: 14r, Factory and Iranian Oil Company emblem, horiz.

***Perf. 10½x11, 11x10½***

**1963, Oct. 18 Wmk. 316**

**1259** A177 6r black, yel & red 6.00 .50
**1260** A177 14r black, bl & yel 8.00 1.50

Opening of Shiraz Chemical Factory.

Pres. Heinrich Lübke of Germany and Mosque in Tehran A178

**1963, Oct. 23 Wmk. 349 *Perf. 10½***

**1261** A178 6r ultra & dk blue 5.00 .65
**1262** A178 14r gray & brown 7.00 1.60

Visit of Pres. Lubke of Germany.

UN Emblem and Iranian Flag A179

**1963, Oct. 24**

**1263** A179 8r multicolored 5.00 .50

Issued for United Nations Day.

UN Emblem and Jets A180

**1963, Oct. 24**

**1264** A180 6r multicolored 6.00 1.00

Iranian jet fighters with UN Force in the Congo.

Crown Prince Rzza — A181

**1963, Oct. 31**

**1265** A181 2r brown 3.00 .25
**1266** A181 6r blue 6.00 .50

Children's Day; Crown Prince Riza's 3rd birthday.

Pres. Brezhnev of USSR — A182

**1963, Nov. 16 Wmk. 349 *Perf. 10½***

**1267** A182 6r dk brn, yel & bl 5.00 .35
**1268** A182 11r dk brn, yel & red 8.00 .75

Visit of Pres. Leonid I. Brezhnev.

Atatürk's Mausoleum, Ankara — A183

**1963, Nov. 28 Litho.**

**1269** A183 4r shown 4.50 .30
**1270** A183 5r Kemal Ataturk 5.50 .30

25th death anniv. of Kemal Atatürk, president of Turkey.

Scales and Globe — A184

**1963, Dec. 10**

**1271** A184 6r brt yel grn, blk & ultra 3.00 .35
**1272** A184 14r org brn, blk & buff 5.00 .45

Universal Declaration of Human Rights, 15th anniv.

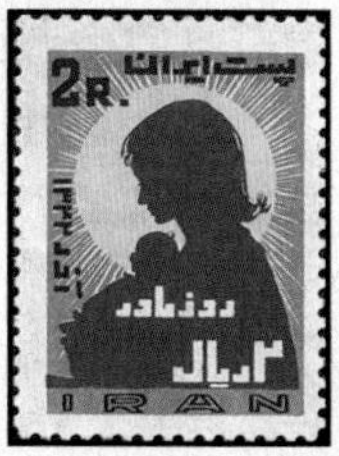

Mother and Child — A185

**1963, Dec. 16**

**1273** A185 2r multicolored 3.00 .25
**1274** A185 4r multicolored 5.00 .50

Issued for Mother's Day.

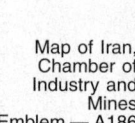

Map of Iran, Chamber of Industry and Mines Emblem — A186

**1963, Dec. 17 Litho.**

**1275** A186 8r bl grn, buff & dk bl 5.00 .40

Chamber of Industry and Mines.

Factories and Hand Holding Bill — A187

Designs: 4r, Factories and bills on scale. 6r, Man on globe carrying torch of education. 8r, Tractor, map and yardstick. 10r, Forest. 12r, Gate of Parliament and heads of man and woman.

**1964, Jan. 26 Wmk. 349 *Perf. 10½***

**1276** A187 2r multicolored 4.00 .75
**1277** A187 4r brown & gray 5.00 .75
**1278** A187 6r multicolored 6.00 .75
**1279** A187 8r multicolored 7.00 1.00
**1280** A187 10r multicolored 8.00 1.25
**1281** A187 12r red org & brn 10.00 1.50
*Nos. 1276-1281 (6)* 40.00 6.00

2nd anniv. of six socioeconomic bills: 2r, Shareholding for factory workers. 4r, Sale of shares in government factories. 6r, Creation of Army of Education. 8r, Land reforms. 10r, Nationalization of forests. 12r, Reforms in parliamentary elections.

"ECAFE" and UN Emblem A188

**1964, Mar. 2 Wmk. 349**

**1282** A188 14r brt green & blk 4.00 .45

20th session of ECAFE (Economic Commission for Asia and the Far East), Mar. 2-17.

Flowering Branch — A189

**1964, Mar. 5 *Perf. 10½***

**1283** A189 50d emerald, blk & org .60 .25
**1284** A189 1r brt blue, blk & org .90 .25

Novrooz, Iranian New Year, Mar. 21.

Anemometer A190

**1964, Mar. 23 Litho.**

**1285** A190 6r brt blue & vio bl 3.50 .25

4th World Meteorological Day.

Mosque and Arches, Isfahan — A191

11r, Griffon & winged bull, Persepolis.

**1964, Apr. 7 *Perf. 10½***

**1286** A191 6r lilac, grn & blk 4.00 .40
**1287** A191 11r orange, brn & blk 6.00 .55

Issued for tourist publicity.

Rudaki and Harp — A192

**1964, May 16 Photo. Wmk. 349**

**1288** A192 6r blue 3.50 .45
**1289** A192 8r red brown 6.00 .55

Opening of an institute for the blind. The inscription translates: "Wisdom is better than eye and sight."

Sculpture, Persepolis
A193

Designs: 4r, Achaemenian horse-drawn mail cart, map of Iran, horiz. 6r, Vessel with sculptured animals. 10r, Head of King Shapur, sculpture.

**1964, June 5 Wmk. 349 Litho.**

**1290** A193 2r gray & blue 6.00 1.75
**1291** A193 4r vio bl, lt bl & bl 10.00 2.00
**1292** A193 6r brown & yellow 12.00 2.50
**1293** A193 10r yel & ol grn 15.00 3.50
*Nos. 1290-1293 (4)* 43.00 9.75

Opening of the "7000 Years of Persian Art" exhibition in Washington, D.C.

Shah and Emperor Haile Selassie
A194

**1964, Sept. 14 Wmk. 349 *Perf. 10½***

**1294** A194 6r ultra & lt blue 5.00 .60

Visit of Emperor Haile Selassie of Ethiopia.

Tooth and Dentists' Assoc. Emblem
A195

"2 I.D.A."
A196

**1964, Sept. 14 Litho.**

**1295** A195 2r blue, red & dk blue 3.00 .30
**1296** A196 4r ultra, bl & pale brn 4.00 .35

Iranian Dentists' Association, 2nd congress.

Research Institute, Microscope, Wheat and Locust — A197

Beetle under Magnifying Glass — A198

**1964, Sept. 23 Wmk. 349 *Perf. 10½***

**1297** A197 2r red, orange & brn 5.00 .40
**1298** A198 6r blue, brn & indigo 6.00 .60

Fight against plant diseases and damages.

Mithras (Mehr) on Ancient Seal — A199

**1964, Oct. 8 Litho.**

**Size: 26x34mm**

**1299** A199 8r org & brn org 4.00 1.00

Mehragan celebration. See No. 1406.

Eleanor Roosevelt (1884-1962)
A200

**1964, Oct. 11**

**1300** A200 10r vio bl & rose vio 6.00 .75

Clasped Hands and UN Emblem — A201

Symbolic Airplane and UN Emblem — A202

**1964, Oct. 24 Wmk. 349 *Perf. 10½***

**1301** A201 6r ultra, yel, red & blk 3.00 .30
**1302** A202 14r org, ultra & red 4.00 .50

Issued for United Nations Day.

Persian Gymnast — A203

Polo Player
A204

**1964, Oct. 26**

**1303** A203 4r tan, sep & Prus bl 3.00 .35
**1304** A204 6r red & black 4.00 .40

18th Olympic Games, Tokyo, Oct. 10-25.

Crown Prince Riza — A205

**1964, Oct. 31 Litho.**

**1305** A205 1r dull green & brn 2.00 .30
**1306** A205 2r deep rose & ultra 3.50 .50
**1307** A205 6r ultra & red 5.00 .65
*Nos. 1305-1307 (3)* 10.50 1.45

Children's Day; Crown Prince Riza's 4th birthday.

UN Emblem, Flame and Smokestack — A206

**1964, Nov. 16 Wmk. 349 *Perf. 10½***

**1308** A206 6r black, lt bl & car 2.00 .35
**1309** A206 8r black, emer & car 3.50 .40

Petro-Chemical Conference and Gas Seminar, Nov.-Dec. 1964.

Shah and King Baudouin — A207

**1964, Nov. 17**

**1310** A207 6r black, org & yel 2.00 .35
**1311** A207 8r black, org & emer 4.00 .75

Visit of King Baudouin of Belgium.

Rhazes
A208

**1964, Dec. 27 Wmk. 349 *Perf. 10½***

**1312** A208 2r multicolored 3.00 .35
**1313** A208 6r multicolored 5.00 .60

1100th birth anniv. of Rhazes (abu-Bakr Mohammad Zakariya Razi), Persian physician.

Shah and King Olav V
A209

**1965, Jan. 7 Litho.**

**1314** A209 2r dk brown & lilac 3.00 .35
**1315** A209 4r brown & green 4.00 .75

Visit of King Olav V of Norway.

Map of Iran and Six-pointed Star — A210

**1965, Jan. 26 Wmk. 349 *Perf. 10½***

**1316** A210 2r black, brt bl & org 2.50 .25

Shah's six socioeconomic bills, 3rd anniv.

Woman and UN Emblem — A211

Green Wheat and Tulip — A212

**1965, Mar. 1 Wmk. 349 *Perf. 10½***

**1317** A211 6r black & blue 1.50 .25
**1318** A211 8r ultra & red 2.50 .25

18th session of the UN commission on the status of women.

**1965, Mar. 6**

**1319** A212 50d multicolored .50 .25
**1320** A212 1r multicolored .70 .25

Novrooz, Iranian New Year, Mar. 21.

Pres. Habib Bourguiba and Minarets of Tunis Mosque — A213

**1965, Mar. 14 Litho. *Perf. 10½***

**1321** A213 4r multicolored 2.25 .35

Visit of Pres. Habib Bourguiba of Tunisia.

Map of Iran and Trade Mark of Iranian Oil Co.
A214

**1965, Mar. 20 Litho.**

**1322** A214 6r multicolored 3.50 .25
**1323** A214 14r multicolored 4.50 .55

Oil industry nationalization, 14th anniv.

ITU Emblem, Old and New Communication Equipment — A215

**1965, May 17 Wmk. 349 *Perf. 10½***

**1324** A215 14r dp car rose & gray 2.00 .60

ITU, centenary.

ICY Emblem A216

**1965, June 22 Litho. *Perf. 10½***

**1325** A216 10r sl grn & gray bl 3.00 .60

International Cooperation Year, 1965.

Iran Airways Emblem A217

**1965, July 17 Wmk. 349 *Perf. 10½***

**1326** A217 14r multicolored 3.50 .75

Tenth anniversary of Iran Airways.

Hands Holding Book A218

Map and Flags of Turkey, Iran and Pakistan A219

**1965, July 21 Litho.**

**1327** A218 2r dk brn, org brn & buff 1.50 .25

**1328** A219 4r multicolored 2.00 .25

Signing of the Regional Cooperation for Development Pact by Turkey, Iran and Pakistan, 1st anniv.

See Pakistan 217-218, Turkey 1648-1649.

Iranian Scout Emblem and Ornament A220

**1965, July 23**

**1329** A220 2r multicolored 2.00 .25
*a.* Vert. pair, imperf. horiz. 75.00

Middle East Rover Moot (senior Boy Scout assembly).

Majlis Gate A221

**1965, Aug. 5 Wmk. 349 *Perf. 10½***

**1330** A221 2r lilac rose & brn 1.00 .25

60th anniversary of Iranian constitution.

### Types of Regular Issue, 1962

**Wmk. 349**

**1964-65 Photo. *Perf. 10½***

| | | | | |
|---|---|---|---|---|
| **1331** | A159 | 5d dk sl grn ('65) | .35 | .30 |
| *a.* | | Wmk. 353 | .35 | .30 |
| **1332** | A159 | 10d chestnut | .35 | .30 |
| **1333** | A159 | 25d dk blue ('65) | .50 | .25 |
| **1334** | A159 | 50d Prus green | .75 | .25 |
| **1335** | A159 | 1r orange | .75 | .25 |
| **1336** | A159 | 2r violet blue | .50 | .25 |
| **1337** | A159 | 5r dark brown | 3.00 | .50 |
| **1338** | A160 | 6r blue ('65) | 11.00 | 1.00 |
| **1339** | A160 | 8r yel grn ('65) | 3.50 | .25 |
| **1340** | A160 | 10r grnsh bl ('65) | 3.00 | .25 |
| **1341** | A160 | 11r sl grn ('65) | 10.00 | 1.50 |
| **1342** | A160 | 14r purple ('65) | 7.00 | 1.40 |
| **1343** | A160 | 20r red brn ('65) | 6.00 | 2.00 |
| **1344** | A160 | 50r org ver ('65) | 7.50 | 2.00 |
| | | *Nos. 1331-1344 (14)* | 54.20 | 10.50 |

***Perf. 11x10½***

| | | | | |
|---|---|---|---|---|
| *1331b* | A159 | 5d Wmk. 353 | 4.00 | 1.00 |
| *1332a* | A159 | 10d | .55 | .50 |
| *1333a* | A159 | 25d | .80 | .25 |
| *1334a* | A159 | 50d | 3.00 | 2.00 |
| *1335a* | A159 | 1r | 3.00 | 2.00 |
| *1337a* | A159 | 5r | 6.00 | .50 |
| | | *Nos. 1331b-1337a (6)* | 17.35 | 6.25 |

Dental Congress Emblem — A222

**1965, Sept. 7 Litho. *Perf. 10½***

**1345** A222 6r gray, ultra, & car 1.00 .25

Iranian Dentists' Association, 3rd congress.

Classroom and Literacy Corps Emblem A223

Alphabets on Globe — A224

Designs: 6r, UNESCO emblem and open book (diamond shape). 8r, UNESCO emblem and inscription, horiz. 14r, Mohammad Reza Shah Pahlavi and inscription in six languages.

**1965, Sept. 8**

**1346** A223 2r multi .60 .25

**1347** A224 5r multi .75 .30

**Size: 30x30mm**

**1348** A223 6r multi 1.25 .40

**Size: 35x23mm**

**1349** A223 8r dk bl, car emer & buff 1.50 .45

**Size: 34x46mm**

**1350** A223 14r cit, dk bl & brn 3.00 .75
*Nos. 1346-1350 (5)* 7.10 2.15

World Congress Against Illiteracy, Tehran, Sept. 8-19.

Mohammad Reza Pahlavi — A225

**1965, Sept. 16 Litho. *Perf. 10½***

**1351** A225 1r crim, rose red & gray 2.00 .50

**1352** A225 2r dk red, rose red & yel 3.00 .75

Reign of Shah, 25th year. (in 1966).

Emblem of Persian Medical Society A226

**1965, Sept. 21 Wmk. 349**

**1353** A226 5r ultra, dp ultra & gold .75 .25

14th Medical Congress, Ramsar.

Pres. Jonas of Austria A227

**1965, Sept. 30**

**1354** A227 6r bl, brt bl & gray 2.00 .25

Visit of President Franz Jonas of Austria.

Mithras (Mehr) on Ancient Seal — A228

**1965, Oct. 8 Litho. Wmk. 353**

**1355** A228 4r brt grn, gold, brn & blk 2.50 .25

Mehragan celebration during month of Mehr, Sept. 23-Oct. 22. Persian inscription of watermark vertical on No. 1355.

UN Emblem — A229

**1965, Oct. 24 Wmk. 353 *Perf. 10½***

**1356** A229 5r bl, grn & rose car 1.00 .25

20th anniversary of the United Nations.

Symbolic Arches A230

**1965, Oct. 26**

**1357** A230 3r vio bl, blk, yel & red 1.00 .25

Exhibition of Iranian Commodities.

Crown Prince Reza A231

**1965, Oct. 31**

**1358** A231 2r brown & yellow 1.50 .45

Children's Day; Crown Prince Reza's 5th birthday.

Weight Lifters — A232

**1965, Nov. 1**

**1359** A232 10r brt bl, vio & brt pink 1.25 .25

World Weight Lifting Championships, Tehran.

Open Book A233

**1965, Dec. 1 Wmk. 353 *Perf. 10½***

**1360** A233 8r bl, brt pink & blk 1.00 .25

Issued for Book Week.

Shah and King Faisal A234

**1965, Dec. 8 Litho.**

**1361** A234 4r olive bister & brn 3.50 .50

Visit of King Faisal of Saudi Arabia.

Scales and Olive Branch A235

**1965, Dec. 12**

**1362** A235 14r multicolored .90 .25

Human Rights Day (Dec. 10).

Tractor, "Land Reform" A236

Symbols of Reform Bills: 2r, Trees, nationalization of forests. 3r, Factory and gear wheel, sale of shares in government factories. 4r, Wheels, shareholding for factory workers. 5r, Parliament gate, women's suffrage. 6r, Children before blackboard, Army of Education. 7r, Caduceus, Army of Hygiene. 8r, Scales, creation of rural courts. 9r, Two girders, creation of Army of Progress.

**1966, Jan. 26 Wmk. 353 *Perf. 10½***

**1363** A236 1r orange & brown .40 .25
**1364** A236 2r dl grn & green .50 .25
**1365** A236 3r silver & gray .60 .40
**1366** A236 4r light & dk vio .70 .50
**1367** A236 5r rose & brown .90 .55
**1368** A236 6r olive & brown 1.25 .65
**1369** A236 7r bl & vio blue 1.50 .75
**1370** A236 8r ultra & dp ultra 1.75 .85
**1371** A236 9r brn org & dk brn 2.00 .90
*Nos. 1363-1371 (9)* 9.60 5.10

Parliamentary approval of the Shah's reform plan.

Shah — A237

Ruins of Persepolis A238

**1966-71 Wmk. 353 Photo. *Perf. 10½***

**1372** A237 5d green .30 .25
**1373** A237 10d chestnut .30 .25
**1374** A237 25d dark blue .30 .25
**1375** A237 50d Prussian green .50 .25
*a.* 50d blue green ('71) .50 .30
**1376** A237 1r orange .50 .25
**1377** A237 2r violet .50 .25
**1377A** A237 4r cl brn ('68) 6.00 1.00
**1378** A237 5r dark brn 1.00 .25
**1379** A238 6r deep blue 1.50 .25
**1380** A238 8r yellow grn 1.50 .25
*a.* 8r dull green ('71) 1.00 .25
**1381** A238 10r Prus bl 1.50 .25
**1382** A238 11r slate grn 1.50 .25
**1383** A238 14r purple 2.00 .25
**1384** A238 20r brown 17.00 .50
**1385** A238 50r cop red 7.50 1.50
**1386** A238 100r brt blue 17.00 2.50
**1387** A238 200r chnt brn 12.50 4.50
*Nos. 1372-1387 (17)* 71.40 13.00

Set, except 4r, issued Feb. 22, 1966.

Student Nurse Taking Oath A239

Narcissus A240

**1966, Feb. 24 Litho.**

**1388** A239 5r brt pink & mag 2.00 .50
**1389** A239 5r lt bl & brt bl 2.00 .50
*a.* Se-tenant pair, #1388-1389 5.00 3.00

Nurses' Day. Nos. 1388-1389 printed in sheets of 50 arranged checkerwise.

**1966, Mar. 7**

**1390** A240 50d ultra, yel & emer .60 .25
**1391** A240 1r lilac, yel & emer .75 .30

Novrooz, Iranian New Year, Mar. 21.

Oil Derricks in Persian Gulf — A241

**1966, Mar. 20 *Perf. 10½***

**1392** A241 14r blk, brt bl & brt rose lil 2.50 .50

Formation of six offshore oil companies.

Radio Tower — A242

2r, Radar, horiz. 6r, Emblem & waves. 8r, Compass rose & waves. 10r, Tower & waves.

**1966, Apr. 27 Litho. Wmk. 349**

**1393** A242 2r dark grn .40 .35
**1394** A242 4r ultra & dp org .50 .35
**1395** A242 6r gray ol & plum .60 .40
**1396** A242 8r brt bl & dk bl .65 .50
**1397** A242 10r brn & bister .80 .55
*Nos. 1393-1397 (5)* 2.95 2.15

Inauguration of the radio telecommunication system of the Central Treaty Organization of the Middle East (CENTO).

WHO Headquarters, Geneva — A243

**1966, May 3 Wmk. 353**

**1398** A243 10r brt bl, yel & blk .90 .30

Opening of the WHO Headquarters, Geneva.

World Map — A244

**1966, May 14 Litho.**

**1399** A244 6r bl & multi .70 .30
**1400** A244 8r multicolored .85 .30

Intl. Council of Women, 18th Conf., Tehran, May 1966.

Globe, Map of Iran and Ruins of Persepolis — A245

**1966, Sept. 5 Wmk. 353 *Perf. 10½***

**1401** A245 14r multicolored 1.40 .50

International Iranology Congress, Tehran.

Emblem of Iranian Medical Society A246

**1966, Sept. 21**

**1402** A246 4r ultra, grnsh bl & bis .75 .30

15th Medical Congress, held at Ramsar.

Gate of Parliament, Mt. Demavend and Congress Emblem — A247

8r, Senate building, Mt. Demavend & emblem.

**1966, Oct. 2 Wmk. 353 *Perf. 10½***

**1403** A247 6r brick red, ultra & dk grn .65 .30
**1404** A247 8r lt lil, ultra & dk grn .85 .30

55th Interparliamentary Union Conf., Tehran.

Visit of President Cevdet Sunay of Turkey — A248

**1966, Oct. 2 Litho.**

**1405** A248 6r vio & dk brn .75 .25

**Mithras Type of 1964**

**1966, Oct. 8 Size: 30x40mm**

**1406** A199 6r olive bister & brn .75 .30

Mehragan celebration.

Farmers — A249

**1966, Oct. 13**

**1407** A249 5r olive bister & brn 3.00 1.00

Establishment of rural courts of justice.

UN Emblem — A250

**1966, Oct. 24 Wmk. 353 *Perf. 10½***

**1408** A250 6r brn org & blk .60 .30

21st anniversary of United Nations.

Crown Prince Reza — A251

**1966, Oct. 31 Litho.**

**1409** A251 1r ultramarine 1.25 .75
**1410** A251 2r violet 1.75 .75
*a.* Pair, #1409-1410 3.50 2.50

Children's Day; Crown Prince Reza's 6th birthday.

Symbolic Woman's Face — A252

**1966, Nov. 6**

**1411** A252 5r gold, blk & ultra .60 .25

Founding of the Iranian Women's Org.

Film Strip and Song Bird A253

**1966, Nov. 6**

**1412** A253 4r blk, red lil & vio .75 .25

First Iranian children's film festival.

"Census Count" — A254

**1966, Nov. 11**

**1413** A254 6r dk brn & gray .60 .25

National census.

Book Cover — A255

**1966, Nov. 15**

**1414** A255 8r tan, brn & ultra .60 .25

Issued to publicize Book Week.

Reza Shah Pahlavi
A256

Design: 2r, Reza Shah Pahlavi without kepi.

**1966, Nov. 16** **Litho.**

| | | | | |
|---|---|---|---|---|
| 1415 | A256 | 1r slate blue | 3.25 | 1.00 |
| 1416 | A256 | 1r brown | 3.25 | 1.00 |
| *a.* | | Pair, #1415-1416 | 7.75 | 3.00 |
| 1417 | A256 | 2r gray green | 3.50 | 1.00 |
| 1418 | A256 | 2r violet blue | 3.50 | 1.00 |
| *a.* | | Pair, #1417-1418 | 8.00 | 3.00 |
| | | *Nos. 1415-1418 (4)* | 13.50 | 4.00 |

Reza Shah Pahlavi (1877-1944), founder of modern Iran.

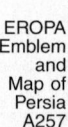

EROPA Emblem and Map of Persia
A257

**1966, Dec. 4** **Wmk. 353** ***Perf. 10½***

| | | | | |
|---|---|---|---|---|
| 1419 | A257 | 8r dk brn & emerald | 1.10 | .25 |

4th General Assembly of the Org. of Public Administrators, EROPA.

Shah Giving Deeds to Farmers
A258

**1967, Jan. 9** **Wmk. 353** ***Perf. 10½***

| | | | | |
|---|---|---|---|---|
| 1420 | A258 | 6r ol bis, yel & brn | 2.25 | .25 |

Approval of land reform laws, 5th anniv.

Shah and 9-Star Crescent — A259

Design: 2r, Torch and 9-star crescent.

**1967, Jan. 26** **Wmk. 353** **Litho.**

| | | | | |
|---|---|---|---|---|
| 1421 | A259 | 2r multicolored | 2.00 | .50 |
| 1422 | A259 | 6r multicolored | 2.75 | .50 |

5th anniv. of Shah's reforms, the "White Revolution."

Ancient Sculpture of Bull — A260

Designs: 5r, Sculptured mythical animals. 8r, Pillar from Persepolis.

**1967, Feb. 25** **Wmk. 353** ***Perf. 10½***

| | | | | |
|---|---|---|---|---|
| 1423 | A260 | 3r dk brn & ocher | 1.25 | .35 |
| 1424 | A260 | 5r Prus grn, brn & ocher | 1.50 | .45 |
| 1425 | A260 | 8r vio, blk & sil | 2.00 | .65 |
| | | *Nos. 1423-1425 (3)* | 4.75 | 1.45 |

Issued to publicize Museum Week.

Planting Tree — A261

**1967, Mar. 6**

| | | | | |
|---|---|---|---|---|
| 1426 | A261 | 8r brn org & grn | .60 | .25 |

Tree Planting Day.

Goldfish — A262

**1967, Mar. 11** **Size: 26x20mm**

| | | | | |
|---|---|---|---|---|
| 1427 | A262 | 1r shown | .40 | .25 |

**Size: 35x27mm**

| | | | | |
|---|---|---|---|---|
| 1428 | A262 | 8r Swallows | 1.50 | .30 |

Issued for Novrooz, Iranian New Year.

Microscope, Animals and Emblem — A263

**1967, Mar. 11** ***Perf. 10½***

| | | | | |
|---|---|---|---|---|
| 1429 | A263 | 5r blk, gray & mag | .60 | .25 |

Second Iranian Veterinary Congress.

Pres. Arif of Iraq, Mosque — A264

**1967, Mar. 14** **Litho.** **Wmk. 353**

| | | | | |
|---|---|---|---|---|
| 1430 | A264 | 6r brt bl & grn | .60 | .30 |

Visit of Pres. Abdul Salam Mohammad Arif.

Fireworks
A265

**1967, Mar. 17**

| | | | | |
|---|---|---|---|---|
| 1431 | A265 | 5r vio bl & multi | 3.00 | .50 |

Issued for United Nations Stamp Day.

Map of Iran and Oil Company Emblem — A266

**1967, Mar. 20**

| | | | | |
|---|---|---|---|---|
| 1432 | A266 | 6r multicolored | 2.10 | .45 |

Nationalization of Iranian Oil Industry.

Fencers
A267

**1967, Mar. 23**

| | | | | |
|---|---|---|---|---|
| 1433 | A267 | 5r vio & bister | 1.50 | .60 |

Intl. Youth Fencing Championships, Tehran.

Shah and King of Thailand
A268

**1967, Apr. 23** **Wmk. 353** ***Perf. 10½***

| | | | | |
|---|---|---|---|---|
| 1434 | A268 | 6r brn org & dk brn | 1.90 | .45 |

Visit of King Bhumibol Adulyadej.

Old and Young Couples
A269

**1967, Apr. 24** **Litho.**

| | | | | |
|---|---|---|---|---|
| 1435 | A269 | 5r ol bis & vio bl | .60 | .25 |

15th anniversary of Social Insurance.

Skier and Iranian Olympic Emblem
A270

Designs: 6r, Assyrian soldiers, Olympic rings and tablet inscribed "I.O.C." 8r, Wrestlers and Iranian Olympic emblem.

**1967, May 5**

| | | | | |
|---|---|---|---|---|
| 1436 | A270 | 3r brown & black | .90 | .25 |
| 1437 | A270 | 6r multicolored | 1.10 | .45 |
| 1438 | A270 | 8r ultra & brown | 1.40 | .75 |
| | | *Nos. 1436-1438 (3)* | 3.40 | 1.45 |

65th Intl. Olympic Cong., Tehran, May 2-11.

Lions International — A271

**1967, May 11** **Size: 41½x30½mm**

| | | | | |
|---|---|---|---|---|
| 1439 | A271 | 3r shown | 1.00 | .50 |

**Size: 36x42mm**

| | | | | |
|---|---|---|---|---|
| 1440 | A271 | 7r Emblem, vert. | 1.50 | .75 |

50th anniversary of Lions International.

Visit of Pres. Chivu Stoica of Romania — A272

**1967, May 13**

| | | | | |
|---|---|---|---|---|
| 1441 | A272 | 6r orange & dk bl | .60 | .25 |

International Tourist Year Emblem — A273

**1967, June 6** **Wmk. 353** ***Perf. 10½***

| | | | | |
|---|---|---|---|---|
| 1442 | A273 | 3r brick red & ultra | .60 | .25 |

Iranian Pavilion and Ornament
A274

**1967, June 7** **Litho.**

| | | | | |
|---|---|---|---|---|
| 1443 | A274 | 4r dk brn, red & gold | .60 | .25 |
| 1444 | A274 | 10r red, dk brn & gold | 1.00 | .30 |

EXPO '67, Montreal, Apr. 28-Oct. 27.

Stamp of 1870, No. 1
A275

**1967, July 23** **Wmk. 353** ***Perf. 10½***

| | | | | |
|---|---|---|---|---|
| 1445 | A275 | 6r multri | .60 | .30 |
| 1446 | A275 | 8r multi | .90 | .30 |

Centenary of first Persian postage stamp.

World Map and School Children — A276

**1967, Sept. 8** **Litho.** **Wmk. 353**

| | | | | |
|---|---|---|---|---|
| 1447 | A276 | 3r ultra & brt & brt bl | .50 | .25 |
| 1448 | A276 | 5r brown & yellow | .75 | .35 |

World campaign against illiteracy.

Globe and Oriental Musician — A277

**1967, Sept. 10** ***Perf. 10½***

**1449** A277 14r brn org & dk brn .90 .50

Intl. Conf. on Music Education in Oriental Countries, Sept. 1967.

Child's Hand Holding Adult's — A278

**1967, Sept. 14 Litho. Wmk. 353**

**1450** A278 8r dk brn & yel 7.50 3.00

Introduction of Children's Villages in Iran. (Modelled after Austrian SOS Villages for homeless children).

Winged Wild Goat — A279

**1967, Sept. 19**

**1451** A279 8r dk brn & lemon .85 .25

Festival of Arts, Persepolis.

UN Emblem A280

**1967, Oct. 17**

**1452** A280 6r olive bister & vio bl .40 .25

Issued for United Nations Day.

Shah and Empress Farah — A281

**1967, Oct. 26 Wmk. 353** ***Perf. 10½***

**Various Frames**

**1453** A281 2r sil, bl & brn 1.25 .40
**1454** A281 10r sil, bl & vio 1.50 .60
**1455** A281 14r lt bl, bl, gold & vio 3.00 1.50
*Nos. 1453-1455 (3)* 5.75 2.50

Coronation of Shah Mohammad Reza Pahlavi and Empress Farah, Oct. 26, 1967.

Nos. 1453-1455 exist in imperf between pairs, with top sheet margin, and in imperf between blocks of 4, ungummed. Fake imperf between pairs, lacking the top sheet margin, have been manufactured by fraudulently perforating imperf-between blocks.

**1967, Oct. 31 Litho.**

Design: Crown Prince Reza.

**1456** A281 2r silver & violet 1.00 .35
**1457** A281 8r sil & red brown 1.50 .45

Children's Day; Crown Prince Reza's 7th birthday.

Visit of Pres. Georgi Traikov of Bulgaria — A283

**1967, Nov. 20**

**1458** A283 10r lilac & dk brn .50 .25

Persian Boy Scout Emblem A284

**1967, Dec. 3 Wmk. 353** ***Perf. 10½***

**1459** A284 8r olive & red brn 1.75 .50

Cooperation Week of the Iranian Boy Scouts, Dec. 5-12.

Hands Holding Chain Link A285

**1967, Dec. 6 Litho.**

**1460** A285 6r multicolored .60 .25

Issued to publicize Cooperation Year.

Visit of Sheik Sabah of Kuwait — A286

**1968, Jan. 10 Wmk. 353** ***Perf. 10½***

**1461** A286 10r lt bl & slate grn .70 .25

List of Shah's 12 Reform Laws 4 — A287

**1968, Jan. 27 Litho. Wmk. 353**

**1462** A287 2r sl grn, brn & sal .35 .30
**1463** A287 8r vio, dk grn & lt grn 1.75 .35
**1464** A287 14r brn, pink & lt lil 2.25 .50
*Nos. 1462-1464 (3)* 4.35 1.15

"White Revolution of King and People."

Almond Blossoms A288

Haji Firooz (New Year Singer) A289

Design: 2r, Tulips.

**1968, Mar. 12 Wmk. 353** ***Perf. 10½***

**1465** A288 1r multi .50 .25
**1466** A288 2r bluish gray & multi .50 .25
**1467** A288 2r brt rose lil & multi .50 .25
**1468** A289 6r multi 1.50 .45
*Nos. 1465-1468 (4)* 3.00 1.20

Issued for Novrooz, Iranian New Year.

Oil Worker and Derrick A290

**1968, Mar. 20 Litho.**

**1469** A290 14r grn, blk & org yel 1.75 .50

Oil industry nationalization, 17th anniv.

WHO Emblem A291

**1968, Apr. 7 Wmk. 353** ***Perf. 10½***

**1470** A291 14r brn, bl & org .90 .30

WHO, 20th anniversary.

Marlik Chariot, Ancient Sculpture A292

**1968, Apr. 13**

**1471** A292 8r blue, brn & buff .60 .25

Fifth World Congress of Persian Archaeology and Art, Tehran.

Shah and King Hassan II A293

**1968, Apr. 16**

**1472** A293 6r bright vio & buff 1.25 .25

Visit of King Hassan II of Morocco.

Human Rights Flame — A294

Design: 14r, Frameline inscription reads, "International Conference on Human Rights Tehran 1968"; "Iran" at left.

**1968, May 5 Wmk. 353** ***Perf. 10½***

**1473** A294 8r red & dk grn .50 .25
**1474** A294 14r vio bl & bl 1.00 .30

Intl. Human Rights Year. The 8r commemorates the Iranian Human Rights Committee; the 14r, the Intl. Conference on Human Rights, Tehran, 1968.

Soccer Player — A295

**1968, May 10 Litho.**

**1475** A295 8r multicolored .50 .30
**1476** A295 10r multicolored .85 .30

Asian Soccer Cup Finals, Tehran.

Tehran Oil Refinery A296

**1968, May 21 Wmk. 353** ***Perf. 10½***

**1477** A296 14r brt bl & multi 1.50 .35

Opening of the Tehran Oil Refinery.

Queen Farah as Girl Guide — A297

**1968, June 24 Litho.** ***Perf. 10½***

**1478** A297 4r brt rose lil & bl green 2.25 .75
**1479** A297 6r car & brn 2.75 1.00

Great Camp of Iranian Girl Guides.

A set of 2 stamps (8r, 14r) were prepared for the International Tennis Congress, Tehran. The stamps were not released when the congress was cancelled.

Anopheles Mosquito, Congress Emblem — A298

**1968, Sept. 7 Wmk. 353 *Perf. 10½***

**1480** A298 6r brt pur & blk .75 .35
**1481** A298 14r dk grn & mag 1.25 .40

8th Intl. Congress on Tropical Medicine and Malaria, Tehran, Sept. 7-15.

Winged Figure with Banner, and Globe — A299

**1968, Sept. 8 Litho.**

**1482** A299 6r lt vio, bis & bl .60 .25
**1483** A299 14r dl yel, sl grn & brn .90 .30

World campaign against illiteracy.

Oramental Horse and Flower — A300

**1968, Sept. 11**

**1484** A300 14r sl grn, org & yel grn 1.00 .25

2nd Festival of Arts, Shiraz-Persepolis.

INTERPOL Emblem and Globe — A301

**1968, Oct. 6 Wmk. 353 *Perf. 10½***

**1485** A301 10r dk brn & bl .90 .25

37th General Assembly of the Intl. Police Org. (INTERPOL) in Tehran.

Police Emblem on Iran Map in Flag Colors — A302

**1968, Oct. 7 Litho.**

**1486** A302 14r multicolored 1.40 .30

Issued for Police Day.

Peace Dove and UN Emblem — A303

**1968, Oct. 24**

**1487** A303 14r bl & vio bl 1.25 .25

Issued for United Nations Day.

Empress Farah — A304

Designs: 8r, Mohammad Reza Shah Pahlavi. 10fr, Shah, Empress and Crown Prince.

**1968, Oct. 26**

**1488** A304 6r multi 7.50 3.75
**1489** A304 8r multi 8.50 5.50
**1490** A304 10r multi 11.00 6.75
*Nos. 1488-1490 (3)* 27.00 16.00

Coronation of Mohammad Reza Shah Pahlavi and Empress Farah, 1st anniv.

Shah's Crown and Bull's Head Capital — A305

UNICEF Emblem and Child's Drawing — A306

**1968, Oct. 30**

**1491** A305 14r ultra, gold, sil & red .85 .25

Festival of Arts and Culture.

**1968, Oct. 31 Litho.**

Children's Drawings and UNICEF Emblem: 3r, Boat on lake, house and trees, horiz. 5r, Flowers, horiz.

**1492** A306 2r dk brn & multi .35 .25
**1493** A306 3r dk grn & multi .50 .30
**1494** A306 5r multicolored .70 .40
*Nos. 1492-1494 (3)* 1.55 .95

Issued for Children's Day.

Labor Union Emblem A307

Factory and Insurance Company Emblem A308

Designs: 8r, Members of Army of Hygiene, and Insurance Company emblem. 10r, Map of Persia, Insurance Company emblem, car, train, ship and plane.

**1968, Nov. 6 Wmk. 353 *Perf. 10½***

**1495** A307 4r sil & vio bl .50 .35
**1496** A308 5r multicolored .65 .35
**1497** A308 8r ultra, gray & yel .85 .35
**1498** A308 10r multicolored .95 .40
*Nos. 1495-1498 (4)* 2.95 1.45

Issued to publicize Insurance Day.

Human Rights Flame, Man and Woman — A309

**1968, Dec. 10 Litho. *Perf. 10½***

**1499** A309 8r lt bl, vio bl & car .65 .25

International Human Rights Year.

Symbols of Shah's Reform Plan — A310

Design: Each stamp shows symbols of 3 of the Shah's reforms. No. 1503a shows the 12 symbols in a circle with a medallion in the center picturing 3 heads and a torch.

**1969, Jan. 26 Wmk. 353 *Perf. 10½***

**1500** 2r ocher, grn & lil 1.75 .50
**1501** 4r lil, ocher & grn 2.00 .60
**1502** 6r lil, ocher & grn 2.25 .75
**1503** 8r lil, ocher & grn 3.00 1.10
*a.* A310 Block of 4, #1500-1503 10.00 4.50
*Nos. 1500-1503 (4)* 9.00 2.95

Declaration of the Shah's Reform Plan.

Shah and Crowd A311

**1969, Feb. 1 Litho.**

**1504** A311 6r red, bl & brn 2.50 .35

10,000th day of the reign of the Shah.

European Goldfinch A312

2r, Ring-necked pheasant. 8r, Roses.

**1969, Mar. 6 Wmk. 353 *Perf. 10½***

**1505** A312 1r multicolored .35 .25
**1506** A312 2r multicolored .50 .25
**1507** A312 8r multicolored 1.25 .25
*Nos. 1505-1507 (3)* 2.10 .75

Issued for Novrooz, Iranian New Year.

"Woman Lawyer" Holding Scales of Justice — A313

**1969, Apr. 8 Litho. *Perf. 10½***

**1508** A313 6r blk & brt bl .60 .25

15th General Assembly of Women Lawyers, Tehran, Apr. 8-14.

Workers, ILO and UN Emblems — A314

**1969, Apr. 30 Wmk. 353 *Perf. 10½***

**1509** A314 10r bl & vio bl .75 .25

ILO, 50th anniversary.

Freestyle Wrestlers and Aryamehr Cup — A315

**1969, May 6 Litho.**

**1510** A315 10r lilac & multi 2.50 .75

Intl. Freestyle Wrestling Championships, 3rd round.

Birds and Flower A316

**1969, June 10 Wmk. 353 *Perf. 10½***

**1511** A316 10r vio bl & multi .85 .25

Issued to publicize Handicrafts Day.

Boy Scout Symbols A317

**1969, July 9 Wmk. 353 *Perf. 10½***

**1512** A317 6r lt bl & multi 1.40 .30

Philia 1969, an outdoor training course for Boy Scout patrol leaders.

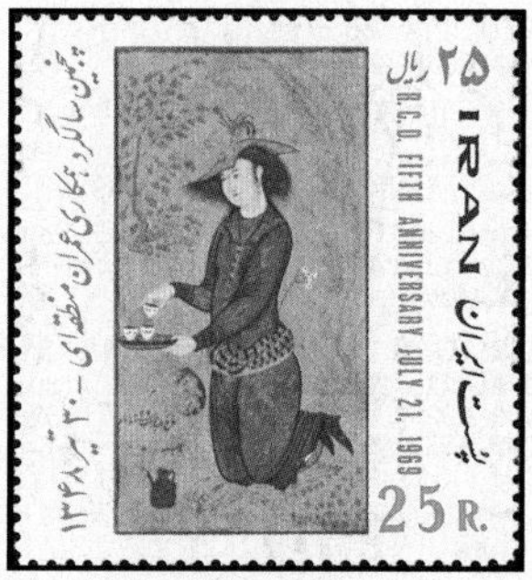


Lady Serving Wine, Safavi Miniature, Iran — A318

#1514, Lady on Balcony, Mogul miniature, Pakistan. #1515, Sultan Suleiman Receiving Sheik Abdul Latif, 16th cent. miniature, Turkey.

**1969, July 21 Litho.**

**1513** A318 25r multi 3.00 1.00
**1514** A318 25r multi 3.00 1.00
**1515** A318 25r multi 3.00 1.00
*Nos. 1513-1515 (3)* 9.00 3.00

Signing of the Regional Cooperation for Development Pact by Turkey, Iran and Pakistan, 5th anniv.

Neil A. Armstrong and Col. Edwin E. Aldrin on Moon — A319

**1969, July 26**

**1516** A319 24r bister, bl & brn 9.00 3.50

See note after Algeria No. 427.

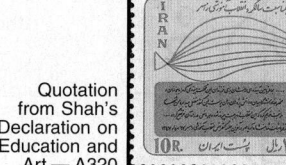

Quotation from Shah's Declaration on Education and Art — A320

**1969, Aug. 6 Wmk. 353 *Perf. 10½***

**1517** A320 10r car, cream & emer .85 .25

Anniv. of educational and art reforms.

Offshore Oil Rig in Persian Gulf — A321

**1969, Sept. 1 Litho.**

**1518** A321 8r multicolored 1.50 .35

Marine drillings by the Iran-Italia Oil Co., 10th anniv.

Dancers Forming Flower — A322

**1969, Sept. 6 Wmk. 353 *Perf. 10½***

**1519** A322 6r multicolored .50 .25
**1520** A322 8r multicolored .75 .25

3rd Festival of Arts, Shiraz and Persepolis, Aug. 30-Sept. 9.

Crossed-out Fingerprint, Moon and Rocket — A323

**1969, Sept. 8 Litho.**

**1521** A323 4r multicolored .50 .25

World campaign against illiteracy.

Persepolis, Simulated Stamp with UPU Emblem, and Shah — A324

**1969, Sept. 28**

**1522** A324 10r lt bl & multi 3.50 1.00
**1523** A324 14r multicolored 4.00 1.50

16th Congress of the UPU, Tokyo.

Fair Emblem — A325

14r, like 8r, inscribed "ASIA 69." 20r, Fair emblem, world map and "ASIA 69," horiz.

**1969, Oct. 5 Wmk. 353 *Perf. 10½***

**1524** A325 8r rose & multi .65 .30
**1525** A325 14r blue & multi .75 .30
**1526** A325 20r tan & multi 1.40 .40
*Nos. 1524-1526 (3)* 2.80 1.00

2nd Asian Trade Fair, Tehran.

Justice — A326

**1969, Oct. 13 Litho.**

**1527** A326 8r bl grn & dk brn .70 .25

Rural Courts of Justice Day.

UN Emblem A327

**1969, Oct. 24**

**1528** A327 2r lt bl & dp bl .50 .25

25th anniversary of the United Nations.

Emblem and Column Capital, Persepolis — A328

**1969, Oct. 28**

**1529** A328 2r deep blue & multi .70 .25

2nd Festival of Arts and Culture. See Nos. 1577, 1681, 1735.

Child's Drawing and UNICEF Emblem A329

Children's Drawings and UNICEF Emblem: 1r, Boy and birds, vert. 5r, Dinner.

**1969, Oct. 31 Wmk. 353 *Perf. 10½***

**Size: 28x40mm, 40x28mm**

**1530** A329 1r lt blue & multi .35 .25
**1531** A329 2r lt grn & multi .45 .25
**1532** A329 5r lt lil & multi .75 .25
*Nos. 1530-1532 (3)* 1.55 .75

Children's Week. See Nos. 1578-1580.

Globe Emblem A330

**1969, Nov. 6**

**1533** A330 8r dk brn & bl .65 .25

Meeting of the Natl. Society of Parents and Educators, Tehran.

Satellite Communications Station — A331

**1969, Nov. 19 Litho.**

**1534** A331 6r blk brn & bis 1.10 .30

1st Iranian Satellite Communications Earth Station, Hamadan.

Mahatma Gandhi (1869-1948) A332

**1969, Dec. 29 Wmk. 353 *Perf. 10½***

**1535** A332 14r gray & dk rose brn 9.00 3.00

Globe, Flags and Emblems A333

Design: 6r, Globe and Red Cross, Red Lion and Sun, and Red Crescent Emblems.

**1969, Dec. 31**

**1536** A333 2r red & multi 1.10 .35
**1537** A333 6r red & multi 1.60 .45

League of Red Cross Societies, 50th anniv.

Symbols of Reform Laws and Shah A334

**1970, Jan. 26 Litho. Wmk. 353**

**1538** A334 1r bister & multi 1.40 .40
**1539** A334 2r multicolored 1.60 .60

Declaration of the Shah's Reform Plan.

Pansies A335

New Year's Table A336

**1970, Mar. 6 Wmk. 353 *Perf. 10½***

| | | | | |
|---|---|---|---|---|
| **1540** | A335 | 1r multicolored | .40 | .25 |
| **1541** | A336 | 8r multicolored | 2.10 | .30 |

Issued for the Iranian New Year.

Chemical Plant, Kharg Island, and Iranian Oil Company Emblem — A337

Designs (Iranian Oil Company Emblem and): 2r, Shah's portrait and quotation. 4r, Laying of gas pipe line and tractor. 8r, Tankers at pier of Kharg Island, vert. 10r, Tehran refinery.

**1970, Mar. 20 Wmk. 353 *Perf. 10½***

| | | | | |
|---|---|---|---|---|
| **1542** | A337 | 2r gray & multi | 1.60 | .50 |
| **1543** | A337 | 4r multicolored | 1.90 | .75 |
| **1544** | A337 | 6r lt bl & multi | 2.10 | .95 |
| **1545** | A337 | 8r multicolored | 2.60 | 1.00 |
| **1546** | A337 | 10r multicolored | 3.25 | 1.25 |
| | | *Nos. 1542-1546 (5)* | 11.45 | 4.45 |

Nationalization of the oil industry, 20th anniv.

EXPO '70 Emblem — A338

**1970, Mar. 27 Litho.**

| | | | | |
|---|---|---|---|---|
| **1547** | A338 | 4r brt rose lil & vio bl | .50 | .25 |
| **1548** | A338 | 10r lt bl & pur | .85 | .25 |

EXPO '70, Osaka, Japan, Mar. 15-Sept. 13.

Radar, Satellite and Congress Emblem — A339

**1970, Apr. 20 Wmk. 353 *Perf. 10½***

| | | | | |
|---|---|---|---|---|
| **1549** | A339 | 14r multicolored | 1.40 | .35 |

Asia-Australia Telecommunications Congress, Tehran.

UPU Headquarters, Bern — A340

**1970, May 10**

| | | | | |
|---|---|---|---|---|
| **1550** | A340 | 2r gray, brn & lil rose | .60 | .25 |
| **1551** | A340 | 4r lil, brn & lil rose | .85 | .25 |

Inauguration of the new UPU Headquarters, Bern.

Asia Productivity Year Emblem — A341

**1970, May 19 Wmk. 353 *Perf. 10½***

| | | | | |
|---|---|---|---|---|
| **1552** | A341 | 8r gray & multi | .65 | .25 |

Asian Productivity Year, 1970.

Bird Bringing Baby A342

**1970, June 15 Litho.**

| | | | | |
|---|---|---|---|---|
| **1553** | A342 | 8r brn & dk blue | .75 | .25 |

Iranian School for Midwives, 50th anniv.

Tomb of Cyrus the Great, Meshed-Morghab in Fars — A343

Designs: 8r, Pillars of Apadana Palace, Persepolis, vert. 10r, Bas-relief from a Mede tomb, Iraq. 14r, Achaemenian officers, bas-relief, Persepolis.

**1970, June 21 Photo. *Perf. 13***

| | | | | |
|---|---|---|---|---|
| **1554** | A343 | 6r gray, red & vio | 2.00 | .25 |
| **1555** | A343 | 8r pale rose, blk & bl grn | 2.25 | .50 |
| **1556** | A343 | 10r yel, red & brn | 2.50 | .65 |
| **1557** | A343 | 14r bl, blk & red brn | 2.75 | 1.00 |
| | | *Nos. 1554-1557 (4)* | 9.50 | 2.40 |

2500th anniversary of the founding of the Persian Empire by Cyrus the Great.

See #1561-1571, 1589-1596, 1605-1612.

Seeyo-Se-Pol Bridge, Isfahan — A344

#1559, Saiful Malook Lake, Pakistan, vert. #1560, View of Fethiye, Turkey, vert.

**Wmk. 353**

**1970, July 21 Litho. *Perf. 10½***

| | | | | |
|---|---|---|---|---|
| **1558** | A344 | 2r multicolored | 1.10 | .30 |
| **1559** | A344 | 2r multicolored | 1.10 | .30 |
| **1560** | A344 | 2r multicolored | 1.10 | .30 |
| | | *Nos. 1558-1560 (3)* | 3.30 | .90 |

Signing of the Regional Cooperation for Development Pact by Iran, Turkey and Pakistan, 6th anniv.

See Pakistan 290-292, Turkey 1857-1859.

Queen Buran, Dirhem Coin A345

Wine Goblet with Lion's Head — A346

Designs: No. 1562, Achaemenian eagle amulet. No. 1563, Mithridates I, dirhem coin. No. 1564, Sassanidae art (arch, coin, jugs). No. 1566, Shapur I, dirhem coin. No. 1567, Achaemenian courier. No. 1568, Winged deer. No. 1569, Ardashir I, dirhem coin. No. 1570, Seal of Darius I (chariot, palms, lion). 14r, Achaemenian tapestry.

**1970 Wmk. 353 Photo. *Perf. 13***

| | | | | |
|---|---|---|---|---|
| **1561** | A345 | 1r gold & multi | 1.50 | .50 |
| **1562** | A346 | 2r gold & multi | 1.60 | .40 |
| **1563** | A345 | 2r gold & multi | 1.75 | .50 |
| **1564** | A346 | 2r lilac & multi | 2.00 | .50 |
| **1565** | A346 | 6r lilac & multi | 1.90 | .40 |
| **1566** | A345 | 6r lilac & multi | 2.50 | .60 |
| **1567** | A345 | 6r lilac & multi | 2.50 | .60 |
| **1568** | A346 | 8r lilac & multi | 2.50 | .50 |
| **1569** | A345 | 8r lilac & multi | 2.50 | .75 |
| **1570** | A345 | 8r lilac & multi | 2.50 | .75 |
| **1571** | A345 | 14r lt bl & multi | 3.00 | 1.10 |
| | | *Nos. 1561-1571 (11)* | 24.25 | 6.60 |

2500th anniversary of the founding of the Persian Empire by Cyrus the Great.

Issued: 1r, #1563, 1566, 1569, 8/22; #1562, 1565, 1568, 14r, 8/6; others, 9/22.

Candle and Globe — A347

**1970, Sept. 8 Litho. *Perf. 10½***

| | | | | |
|---|---|---|---|---|
| **1572** | A347 | 1r lt bl & multi | .30 | .25 |
| **1573** | A347 | 2r pale sal & multi | .40 | .25 |

Issued to publicize World Literacy Day.

Persian Decoration A348

**1970, Sept. 14**

| | | | | |
|---|---|---|---|---|
| **1574** | A348 | 6r multi | .50 | .25 |

Isfahan Intl. Cong. of Architects, Sept. 1970.

Emblem — A349

**1970, Sept. 28 *Perf. 10½***

| | | | | |
|---|---|---|---|---|
| **1575** | A349 | 2r lt bl & pur | .40 | .25 |

Congress of Election Committees of Persian States and Tehran.

UN Emblem, Dove and Scales — A350

**1970, Oct. 24 Litho. Wmk. 353**

| | | | | |
|---|---|---|---|---|
| **1576** | A350 | 2r lt bl, mag & dk bl | .40 | .25 |

Issued for United Nations Day.

**Festival Type of 1969**

**1970, Oct. 28 *Perf. 10½***

| | | | | |
|---|---|---|---|---|
| **1577** | A328 | 2r org & multi | .50 | .25 |

3rd Festival of Arts and Culture.

**UNICEF Type of 1969**

Children's Drawings and UNICEF Emblem: 50d, Herdsman and goats. 1r, Family picnic. 2r, Mosque.

**1970, Oct. 31 Size: 43½x31mm**

| | | | | |
|---|---|---|---|---|
| **1578** | A329 | 50d black & multi | .30 | .25 |
| **1579** | A329 | 1r black & multi | .35 | .25 |
| **1580** | A329 | 2r black & multi | .50 | .25 |
| | | *Nos. 1578-1580 (3)* | 1.15 | .75 |

Issued for Children's Week.

Mohammad Reza Shah Pahlavi A351

**1971, Jan. 26 Wmk. 353 *Perf. 10½***

| | | | | |
|---|---|---|---|---|
| **1581** | A351 | 2r lt bl & multi | 3.50 | 1.00 |

Publicizing the "White Revolution of King and People" and the 12 reform laws.

Sheldrake — A352

2r, Ruddy shelduck. 8r, Flamingo, vert.

**1971, Jan. 30 Litho.**

| | | | | |
|---|---|---|---|---|
| **1582** | A352 | 1r multicolored | 1.75 | .50 |
| **1583** | A352 | 2r multicolored | 2.00 | .75 |
| **1584** | A352 | 8r multicolored | 3.25 | 1.00 |
| | | *Nos. 1582-1584 (3)* | 7.00 | 2.25 |

Intl. Wetland and Waterfowl Conf., Ramsar.

Reza Shah Pahlavi — A353

**1971, Feb. 22 Wmk. 353 *Perf. 10½***

| | | | | |
|---|---|---|---|---|
| **1585** | A353 | 6r multicolored | 6.50 | 2.75 |

50th anniversary of the Pahlavi dynasty's accession to power.

Rooster
A354

2r, Barn swallow and nest. 6r, Hoopoe.

**1971, Mar. 6 Photo. *Perf. 13½x13***

| | | | | |
|---|---|---|---|---|
| **1586** | A354 | 1r multicolored | 1.40 | .45 |
| **1587** | A354 | 2r multicolored | 1.90 | .75 |
| **1588** | A354 | 6r multicolored | 3.25 | 1.00 |
| | | *Nos. 1586-1588 (3)* | 6.55 | 2.20 |

Novrooz, Iranian New Year.

Religious School, Chaharbagh, Ispahan
A358

#1600, Mosque of Selim, Edirne, Turkey. #1601, Badshahi Mosque, Lahore, Pakistan, horiz.

**1971, July 21 Litho. *Perf. 10½***

| | | | | |
|---|---|---|---|---|
| **1599** | A358 | 2r multicolored | .55 | .25 |
| **1600** | A358 | 2r multicolored | .55 | .25 |
| **1601** | A358 | 2r multicolored | .55 | .25 |
| | | *Nos. 1599-1601 (3)* | 1.65 | .75 |

7th anniversary of Regional Cooperation among Iran, Pakistan and Turkey.

See Pakistan 305-307, Turkey 1886-1888.

Shapur II Hunting — A355

Bull's Head, Persepolis
A356

1r, Harpist, mosaic. #1591, Investiture of Ardashir I, bas-relief. 5r Winged lion ornament. 6r, Persian archer, bas-relief. 8r, Royal audience, bas-relief. 10r, Bronze head of Parthian prince.

**1971 Litho. *Perf. 10½***

| | | | | |
|---|---|---|---|---|
| **1589** | A356 | 1r multicolored | 1.60 | .45 |
| **1590** | A355 | 2r blk & brn org | 2.00 | .45 |
| **1591** | A355 | 2r lil, gldn brn & blk | 2.00 | .45 |
| **1592** | A356 | 4r pur & multi | 2.00 | .45 |
| **1593** | A356 | 5r multicolored | 2.25 | .55 |
| **1594** | A356 | 6r multicolored | 2.25 | .55 |
| **1595** | A356 | 8r lt bl & multi | 3.00 | .80 |
| **1596** | A356 | 10r dp bis, blk & slate | 3.00 | .90 |
| | | *Nos. 1589-1596 (8)* | 18.10 | 4.60 |

2500th anniversary of the founding of the Persian Empire by Cyrus the Great.

Issued: 4r, 5r, 6r, 8r, 5/15; others, 6/15.

Prisoners Leaving Jail — A357

**1971, May 20 Litho. Wmk. 353**

| | | | | |
|---|---|---|---|---|
| **1597** | A357 | 6r multicolored | 2.00 | .25 |
| **1598** | A357 | 8r multicolored | 3.25 | .25 |

Rehabilitation of Prisoners Week.

"Fifth Festival of Arts" — A359

**1971, Aug. 26 Litho. & Typo.**

| | | | | |
|---|---|---|---|---|
| **1602** | A359 | 2r lt & dk grn, red & gold | .90 | .30 |

5th Festival of Arts, Shiraz-Persepolis.

"Fight Against Illiteracy" — A360

**1971, Sept. 8 Litho.**

| | | | | |
|---|---|---|---|---|
| **1603** | A360 | 2r grn & multi | .65 | .30 |

International Literacy Day, Sept. 8.

Kings Abdullah and Hussein II of Jordan
A361

**1971, Sept. 11**

| | | | | |
|---|---|---|---|---|
| **1604** | A361 | 2r yel grn, blk & red | .75 | .35 |

Hashemite Kingdom of Jordan, 50th anniv.

Shahyad Aryamehr Monument — A362

Designs: 1r, Aryamehr steel mill, near Isfahan. 3r, Senate Building, Tehran. 11r, Shah Abbas Kabir Dam, Zayandeh River.

**1971, Sept. 22**

| | | | | |
|---|---|---|---|---|
| **1605** | A362 | 1r blue & multi | 1.75 | .50 |
| **1606** | A362 | 2r multicolored | 2.00 | .50 |
| **1607** | A362 | 3r brt pink & multi | 2.00 | .50 |
| **1608** | A362 | 11r org & multi | 2.75 | 1.00 |
| | | *Nos. 1605-1608 (4)* | 8.50 | 2.50 |

2500th anniversary of the founding of the Persian empire by Cyrus the Great.

Mohammad Reza Shah Pahlavi — A363

Designs: 2r, Riza Shah Pahlavi. 5r, Stone tablet with proclamation of Cyrus the Great, horiz. 10r, Crown of present empire (erroneously inscribed *Le* Couronne).

**1971, Oct. 12**

| | | | | |
|---|---|---|---|---|
| **1609** | A363 | 1r gold & multi | 4.50 | 2.50 |
| **1610** | A363 | 2r gold & multi | 4.50 | 2.50 |
| **1611** | A363 | 5r gold & multi | 5.50 | 3.00 |
| **1612** | A363 | 10r gold & multi | 6.50 | 3.00 |
| | | *Nos. 1609-1612 (4)* | 21.00 | 11.00 |

2500th anniversary of the founding of the Persian empire by Cyrus the Great.

Ghatour Railroad Bridge — A364

**1971, Oct. 7**

| | | | | |
|---|---|---|---|---|
| **1613** | A364 | 2r multicolored | 2.25 | .85 |

Iran-Turkey railroad.

Racial Equality Emblem
A365

**1971, Oct. 24**

| | | | | |
|---|---|---|---|---|
| **1614** | A365 | 2r lt blue & multi | .25 | .25 |

Intl. Year Against Racial Discrimination.

Mohammad Riza Pahlavi — A366

***Perf. 13½x13***

**1971, Oct. 26 Photo. Wmk. 353**

**Size: 20½x28mm**

| | | | | |
|---|---|---|---|---|
| **1615** | A366 | 5d lilac | .25 | .25 |
| **1616** | A366 | 10d henna brown | .25 | .25 |
| **1617** | A366 | 50d brt bl grn | .25 | .25 |
| **1618** | A366 | 1r dp yel grn | .30 | .25 |
| **1619** | A366 | 2r brown | .30 | .25 |

**Size: 27x36½mm**

| | | | | |
|---|---|---|---|---|
| **1620** | A366 | 6r slate green | 1.10 | .25 |
| **1621** | A366 | 8r violet blue | 1.60 | 1.10 |
| **1622** | A366 | 10r red lilac | 1.40 | .30 |
| **1623** | A366 | 11r blue green | 5.00 | 1.10 |
| **1624** | A366 | 14r brt blue | 8.50 | .50 |
| **1625** | A366 | 20r car rose | 8.00 | .65 |
| **1626** | A366 | 50r yellow bis | 6.75 | 1.25 |
| | | *Nos. 1615-1626 (12)* | 33.70 | 6.40 |

See Nos. 1650-1661B, 1768-1772.

Child's Drawing and Emblem — A367

Designs: No. 1631, Ruins of Persepolis, vert. No. 1632, Warrior, mosaic, vert.

**1971, Oct. 31 Litho. *Perf. 10½***

| | | | | |
|---|---|---|---|---|
| **1630** | A367 | 2r multicolored | .50 | .25 |
| **1631** | A367 | 2r multicolored | .50 | .25 |
| **1632** | A367 | 2r multicolored | .50 | .25 |
| | | *Nos. 1630-1632 (3)* | 1.50 | .75 |

Children's Week.

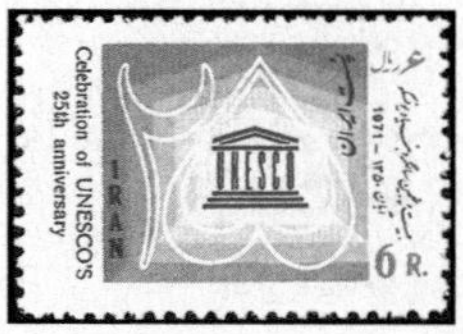


UNESCO Emblem and "25"
A368

**1971, Nov. 4**

| | | | | |
|---|---|---|---|---|
| **1633** | A368 | 6r ultra & rose claret | .60 | .25 |

25th anniversary of UNESCO.

Domestic Animals and Emblem
A369

**1971, Nov. 22**

| | | | | |
|---|---|---|---|---|
| **1634** | A369 | 2r gray, blk & car | .50 | .30 |

4th Iranian Veterinarians' Congress.

ILO Emblem, Cog Wheels and Globe
A370

**1971, Dec. 4**

| | | | | |
|---|---|---|---|---|
| **1635** | A370 | 2r black, org & bl | .50 | .25 |

7th ILO Conference for the Asian Region.

UNICEF Emblem, Bird Feeding Young
A371

**1971, Dec. 16 *Perf. 13x13½***

| | | | | |
|---|---|---|---|---|
| **1636** | A371 | 2r lt bl, mag & blk | .60 | .30 |

25th anniversary of UNICEF.

Mohammad Reza Shah Pahlavi
A372

**1972, Jan. 26 Wmk. 353 *Perf. 10½***

**1637** A372 2r lt green & multi 4.50 2.25
*a.* 20r Souvenir sheet 16.00 11.50

"White Revolution of King and People" and the 12 reform laws. No. 1637a contains one stamp with simulated perforations.

Pintailed Sandgrouse — A373

#1639, Rock ptarmigan. 2r, Yellow-billed waxbill and red-cheeked cordon-bleu.

**1972, Mar. 6 Litho. *Perf. 13x13½***

**1638** A373 1r lt green & multi 1.10 .50
**1639** A373 1r lt blue & multi 1.10 .50
**1640** A373 2r yellow & multi 2.25 .60
*Nos. 1638-1640 (3)* 4.45 1.60

Iranian New Year.

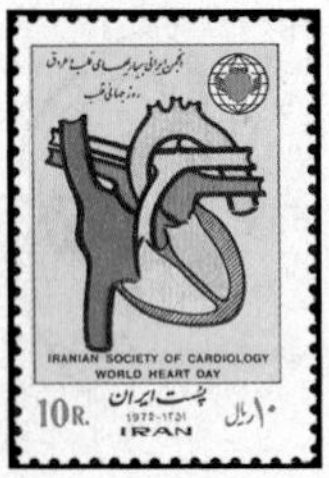


"Your Heart is your Health" — A374

**1972, Apr. 4 *Perf. 10½***

**1641** A374 10r lemon & multi 2.00 .30

World Health Day; Iranian Society of Cardiology.

Film Strip and Winged Antelope
A375

8r, Film strips and winged antelope.

**1972, Apr. 16 Litho. & Engr.**

**1642** A375 6r ultra & gold 1.00 .30
**1643** A375 8r yellow & multi 1.75 .35

Tehran International Film Festival.

Rose and Bud — A376

**1972, May 5 Litho.**

**1644** A376 1r shown .40 .30
**1645** A376 2r Yellow roses .70 .35
**1646** A376 5r Red rose .85 .40
*Nos. 1644-1646 (3)* 1.95 1.05

See Nos. 1711-1713.

Persian Woman, by Behzad
A377

Paintings: No. 1648, Fisherman, by Cevat Dereli (Turkey). No. 1649, Young Man, by Abdur Rehman Chughtai (Pakistan).

**1972, July 21 Wmk. 353**

**1647** A377 5r gray & multi 1.40 .30
**1648** A377 5r gray & multi 1.40 .30
**1649** A377 5r gray & multi 1.40 .30
*Nos. 1647-1649 (3)* 4.20 .90

Regional Cooperation for Development Pact among Iran, Turkey and Pakistan, 8th anniv. See Pakistan 322-324, Turkey 1912-1914.

### Shah Type of 1971

**1972-73 Photo. *Perf. 13½x13***

**Bister Frame & Crown**

**Size: 20½x28mm**

**1650** A366 5d lilac .25 .25
**1651** A366 10d henna brown .25 .25
**1652** A366 50d brt blue grn .25 .25
**1653** A366 1r dp yel grn .30 .25
*a.* Brn frame & crown ('73) *.55* .25
**1654** A366 2r brown .50 .25

**Size: 27x36½mm**

**1655** A366 6r slate grn .75 .25
**1656** A366 8r violet blue .75 .25
**1657** A366 10r red lilac 1.00 .25
**1658** A366 11r blue green 1.40 .80
**1659** A366 14r dull blue 5.50 .60
**1660** A366 20r car rose 8.50 .50
**1661** A366 50r grnsh blue 3.75 1.00
**1661A** A366 100r violet ('73) 5.00 2.00
**1661B** A366 200r slate ('73) 11.00 3.50
*Nos. 1650-1661B (14)* 39.20 10.40

Festival Emblem
A378

**1972, Aug. 31 Litho. *Perf. 10½***

**1662** A378 6r emerald, red & blk 1.10 .25
**1663** A378 8r brt mag, blk & grn 1.60 .25

6th Festival of Arts, Shiraz-Persepolis, Aug. 31-Sept. 8.

Pens and Emblem
A379

**1972, Sept. 8**

**1664** A379 1r lt blue & multi .25 .25
**1665** A379 2r yellow & multi .40 .25

World Literacy Day, Sept. 8.

"10" and Emblems
A380

**1972, Sept. 18**

**1666** A380 1r lilac & multi .25 .25
**1667** A380 2r dull yel & multi .45 .25

10th Congress of Iranian Dentists' Assoc., Sept. 18-22.

Asian Broadcasting Union Emblem — A381

**1972, Oct. 1**

**1668** A381 6r lt green & multi .75 .25
**1669** A381 8r gray & multi 1.50 .25

9th General Assembly of Asian Broadcasting Union, Tehran, Oct. 1972.

No. 450 on Cover — A382

**1972, Oct. 9**

**1670** A382 10r lt blue & multi 2.25 .25

International Stamp Day.

Chess and Olympic Rings — A383

Olympic Rings and: 2r, Hunter. 3r, Archer. 5r, Equestrians. 6r, Polo. 8r, Wrestling.

**1972, Oct. 17**

**1671** A383 1r brown & multi 3.00 1.50
**1672** A383 2r blue & multi 2.50 .50
**1673** A383 3r lilac & multi 2.50 .50
**1674** A383 5r bl grn & multi 3.00 .75
**1675** A383 6r red & multi 4.00 .75
**1676** A383 8r yel grn & multi 6.00 1.00
*a.* Souv. sheet of 6, #1671-1676, imperf. 25.00 15.00
*Nos. 1671-1676 (6)* 21.00 5.00

20th Olympic Games, Munich, 8/26-9/11.

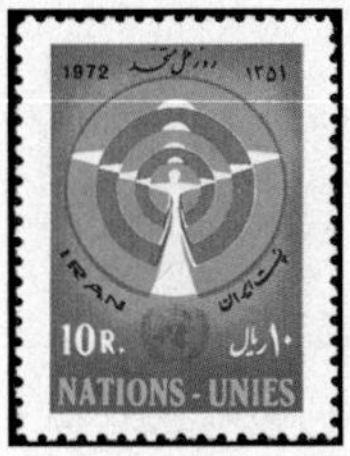


Communications Symbol, UN Emblem — A384

**1972, Oct. 24**

**1677** A384 10r multicolored 2.00 .25

United Nations Day.

Children and Flowers — A385

Children's Drawings and Emblem: No. 1679, Puppet show. 6r, Boys cutting wood, horiz.

**1972, Oct. 31 Litho. Wmk. 353**

**1678** A385 2r gray & multi .35 .25
**1679** A385 2r bister & multi .70 .25
**1680** A385 6r pink & multi 1.40 .25
*Nos. 1678-1680 (3)* 2.45 .75

Children's Week.

### Festival Type of 1969

Design: 10r, Crown, emblems and column capital, Persepolis.

**1972, Nov. 11**

**1681** A328 10r dp blue & multi 6.00 1.00

10th anniv. of White Revolution; Festival of Culture and Art.

Family Planning Emblem
A386

**1972, Dec. 5**

**1682** A386 1r blue & multi .30 .25
**1683** A386 2r brt pink & multi .40 .25

To promote family planning.

Iranian Scout Organization, 20th anniv. — A387

**1972, Dec. 9**

**1684** A387 2r multicolored .50 .25

Ancient Seal
A388

Designs: Various ancient seals.

**1973, Jan. 5** *Perf. 10½*

| | | | | |
|---|---|---|---|---|
| **1685** | A388 | 1r blue, red & brn | .60 | .25 |
| **1686** | A388 | 1r yellow & multi | .60 | .25 |
| **1687** | A388 | 1r pink & multi | .60 | .25 |
| **1688** | A388 | 2r lt brick red & multi | .60 | .25 |
| **1689** | A388 | 2r dull org & multi | .60 | .25 |
| **1690** | A388 | 2r olive & multi | .60 | .25 |
| | | *Nos. 1685-1690 (6)* | 3.60 | 1.50 |

Development of writing.

Books and Book Year Emblem A389

Design: 6r, Illuminated page, 10th century, from Shahnameh, by Firdousi.

**1973, Jan. 10**

| | | | | |
|---|---|---|---|---|
| **1691** | A389 | 2r black & multi | .75 | .25 |
| **1692** | A389 | 6r yellow & multi | 1.10 | .25 |

International Book Year.

"12 Improvements by the King" — A390

Designs: 2r, 10r, 12 circles symbolizing 12 improvements. 6r, like 1r.

**1973, Jan. 26** **Litho.**

**Size: 29x43mm**

| | | | | |
|---|---|---|---|---|
| **1693** | A390 | 1r gold, ultra, red & yel | .30 | .25 |
| **1694** | A390 | 2r sil, plum, ol & yel | .35 | .25 |

**Size: 65x84mm**

| | | | | |
|---|---|---|---|---|
| **1695** | A390 | 6r gold, ultra, red & yel | 2.50 | 1.50 |
| | | *Nos. 1693-1695 (3)* | 3.15 | 2.00 |

**Souvenir Sheet**

***Imperf***

| | | | | |
|---|---|---|---|---|
| **1696** | A390 | 10r sil, plum, ol & yel | 4.25 | 2.50 |

Introduction of the King's socioeconomic reforms, 10th anniv.

Blue Surgeonfish A391

Fish: No. 1698, Gilthead. No. 1699, Banded sergeant major. No. 1700, Porkfish. No. 1701, Black-spot snapper.

**1973, Mar. 6** **Wmk. 353** *Perf. 10½*

| | | | | |
|---|---|---|---|---|
| **1697** | A391 | 1r multicolored | .75 | .30 |
| **1698** | A391 | 1r multicolored | .75 | .30 |
| **1699** | A391 | 2r multicolored | 1.25 | .45 |
| **1700** | A391 | 2r multicolored | 1.25 | .45 |
| **1701** | A391 | 2r multicolored | 1.25 | .45 |
| | | *Nos. 1697-1701 (5)* | 5.25 | 1.95 |

Iranian New Year.

WHO Emblem A392

**1973, Apr. 7** **Litho.** **Wmk. 353**

| | | | | |
|---|---|---|---|---|
| **1702** | A392 | 10r brn, grn & red | 1.25 | .25 |

25th anniversary of the WHO.

Soccer — A393

Tracks and Globe — A394

**1973, Apr. 13**

| | | | | |
|---|---|---|---|---|
| **1703** | A393 | 14r orange & multi | 1.40 | .25 |

15th Asian Youth Football (soccer) Tournament.

**1973, May 10** **Wmk. 353** *Perf. 10½*

| | | | | |
|---|---|---|---|---|
| **1704** | A394 | 10r dk grn, lil & vio bl | 2.00 | .60 |

13th International Railroad Conference.

Clay Tablet with Aryan Script — A395

Designs: Clay tablets with various scripts.

**1973, June 5** *Perf. 10½*

| | | | | |
|---|---|---|---|---|
| **1705** | A395 | 1r shown | .50 | .25 |
| **1706** | A395 | 1r Kharoshthi | .50 | .25 |
| **1707** | A395 | 1r Achaemenian | .50 | .25 |
| **1708** | A395 | 2r Parthian (Mianeh) | .90 | .25 |
| **1709** | A395 | 2r Parthian (Arsacide) | .90 | .25 |
| **1710** | A395 | 2r Gachtak (Dabireh) | .90 | .25 |
| | | *Nos. 1705-1710 (6)* | 4.20 | 1.50 |

Development of writing.

**Flower Type of 1972**

**1973, June 20**

| | | | | |
|---|---|---|---|---|
| **1711** | A376 | 1r Orchid | .25 | .25 |
| **1712** | A376 | 2r Hyacinth | .55 | .25 |
| **1713** | A376 | 6r Columbine | 1.25 | .25 |
| | | *Nos. 1711-1713 (3)* | 2.05 | .75 |

Regional Cooperation for Development Pact Among Iran, Turkey and Pakistan, 9th Anniv. — A396

Designs: No. 1714, Head from mausoleum of King Antiochus I (69-34 B.C.), Turkey. No. 1715, Statue, Shahdad Kerman, Persia, 4000 B.C. No. 1716, Street, Mohenjo-Daro, Pakistan.

**1973, July 21**

| | | | | |
|---|---|---|---|---|
| **1714** | A396 | 2r brown & multi | .35 | .25 |
| **1715** | A396 | 2r green & multi | .35 | .25 |
| **1716** | A396 | 2r blue & multi | .35 | .25 |
| *a.* | | Strip of 3, #1714-1716 | 1.25 | .75 |

See Pakistan 343-345, Turkey 1941-1943.

Shah, Oil Pump, Refinery and Tanker A397

**1973, Aug. 4**

| | | | | |
|---|---|---|---|---|
| **1717** | A397 | 5r blue & black | 2.50 | .75 |

Nationalization of oil industry.

Soldiers and Rising Sun — A398

**1973, Aug. 19** **Litho.** **Wmk. 353**

| | | | | |
|---|---|---|---|---|
| **1718** | A398 | 2r ultra & multi | .45 | .25 |

20th anniversary of return of monarchy.

Gymnasts and Globe — A399

**1973, Aug. 23** *Perf. 10½*

| | | | | |
|---|---|---|---|---|
| **1719** | A399 | 2r olive & multi | .30 | .25 |
| **1720** | A399 | 2r violet bl & multi | .30 | .25 |

7th Intl. Congress of Physical Education and Sports for Girls and Women, Tehran, Aug. 19-25.

Shahyad Monument (later Azadi Monument), Rainbow and WMO Emblem — A400

**1973, Sept. 4**

| | | | | |
|---|---|---|---|---|
| **1721** | A400 | 5r multicolored | .75 | .25 |

Intl. meteorological cooperation, centenary.

Festival Emblem — A401

**1973, Aug. 31**

| | | | | |
|---|---|---|---|---|
| **1722** | A401 | 1r silver & multi | .30 | .25 |
| **1723** | A401 | 5r gold & multi | .50 | .25 |

7th Festival of Arts, Shiraz-Persepolis.

Wrestlers A402

**1973, Sept. 6** **Litho.** **Wmk. 353**

| | | | | |
|---|---|---|---|---|
| **1724** | A402 | 6r lt green & multi | 1.50 | .50 |

World Wrestling Championships, Tehran, Sept. 6-14.

"Literacy as Light" — A403

**1973, Sept. 8**

| | | | | |
|---|---|---|---|---|
| **1725** | A403 | 2r multicolored | .30 | .25 |

World Literacy Day, Sept. 8.

Audio-Visual Equipment A404

**1973, Sept. 11**

| | | | | |
|---|---|---|---|---|
| **1726** | A404 | 10r yellow & multi | 1.00 | .35 |

Tehran Intl. Audio-Visual Exhib., Sept. 11-24.

Warrior Taming Winged Bull A405

**1973, Sept. 16**

| | | | | |
|---|---|---|---|---|
| **1727** | A405 | 8r blue gray & multi | .75 | .25 |

Intl. Council of Military Sports, 25th anniv.

Abu Rayhan Biruni (973-1048), Philosopher and Mathematician A406

**1973, Sept. 16**

| | | | | |
|---|---|---|---|---|
| **1728** | A406 | 10r brown & black | 1.50 | .50 |

Soccer Cup — A407

**1973, Oct. 2 Wmk. 353 *Perf. 10½***

**1729** A407 2r lilac, blk & buff .35 .25

Soccer Games for the Crown Prince's Cup.

INTERPOL Emblem — A408

**1973, Oct. 7**

**1730** A408 2r multicolored .35 .25

50th anniversary of INTERPOL.

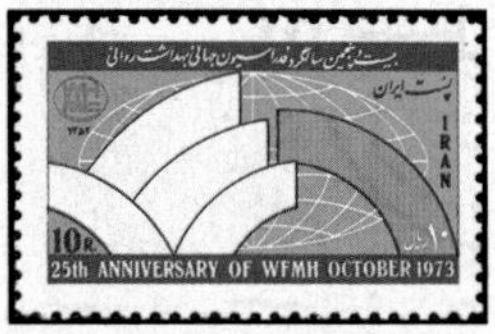

Symbolic Arches and Globe A409

**1973, Oct. 8**

**1731** A409 10r orange & multi .55 .25

World Federation for Mental Health, 25th anniv.

UPU Emblem, Letter, Post Horn — A410

**1973, Oct. 9**

**1732** A410 6r blue & orange .50 .25

World Post Day, Oct. 9.

Honeycomb A411

**1973, Oct. 24**

**1733** A411 2r lt brown & multi .30 .25
**1734** A411 2r gray olive & multi .30 .25

UN Volunteer Program, 5th anniv.

### Festival Type of 1969

2r, Crown & column capital, Persepolis.

**1973, Oct. 26**

**1735** A328 2r yellow & multi .40 .25

Festival of Culture and Art.

Turkish Bosporus Bridge, Flag A412

8r, Kemal Ataturk & Reza Shah Pahlavi.

**1973, Oct. 29 Litho. *Perf. 10½***

**1736** A412 2r multicolored .75 .25
**1737** A412 8r multicolored 1.25 .25

50th anniversary of the Turkish Republic.

Mother and Child, Emblem — A413

Children's Drawings and Emblem: No. 1739, Wagon, horiz. No. 1740, House and garden with birds.

**1973, Oct. 31**

**1738** A413 2r multicolored .30 .25
**1739** A413 2r multicolored .30 .25
**1740** A413 2r multicolored .30 .25
*Nos. 1738-1740 (3)* .90 .75

Children's Week.

Cow, Wheat and FAO Emblem A414

**1973, Nov. 4**

**1741** A414 10r multicolored 1.00 .25

10th anniversary of World Food Program.

Proclamation of Cyrus the Great; Red Cross, Lion and Crescent Emblems A415

**1973, Nov. 8**

**1742** A415 6r lt blue & multi .75 .25

22nd Intl. Red Cross Conf., Tehran, 1972.

"Film Festival" — A416

**1973, Nov. 26 Wmk. 353 *Perf. 10½***

**1743** A416 2r black & multi .35 .25

2nd International Tehran Film Festival.

Globe and Travelers — A417

**1973, Nov. 26 Litho.**

**1744** A417 10r orange & multi .60 .25

12th annual Congress of Intl. Assoc. of Tour Managers.

Human Rights Flame A418

**1973, Dec. 10**

**1745** A418 8r lt blue & multi .75 .25

Universal Declaration of Human Rights, 25th anniv.

Score and Emblem — A419

Design: No. 1747, Score and emblem, diff.

**1973, Dec. 21**

**1746** A419 10r yel grn, red & blk .75 .25
**1747** A419 10r lt bl, ultra & red .75 .25

Dedicated to the art of music.

Forestry, Printing, Education — A420

Designs (Symbols of Reforms): No. 1749, Land reform, sales of shares, women's suffrage. No. 1750, Army of progress, irrigation, women's education. No. 1751, Hygiene, rural courts, housing.

**1974, Jan. 26 Litho. *Perf. 10½***

**1748** 1r lt blue & multi .25 .25
**1749** 1r lt blue & multi .25 .25
**1750** 2r lt blue & multi .25 .25
**1751** 2r lt blue & multi .25 .25
*a.* A420 Block of 4, #1748-1751 2.25 1.50

***Imperf***

**Size: 76½x102mm**

**1752** A420 20r multicolored 5.00 3.00

"White Revolution of King and People" and 12 reform laws.

Pir Amooz Ketabaty Script — A421

Various Scripts: No. 1754, Mo Eghely Ketabaty. No. 1755, Din Dabireh, Avesta script. No. 1756, Pir Amooz, Naskh style. No. 1757, Pir Amooz, decorative style. No. 1758, Decorative and architectural style.

**1974, Feb. 14 Wmk. 353 *Perf. 10½***

**1753** A421 1r silver, ocher & multi .75 .30
**1754** A421 1r gold, gray & multi .75 .30
**1755** A421 1r silver, yel & multi .75 .30
**1756** A421 2r gold, gray & multi .75 .30
**1757** A421 2r gold, slate & multi .75 .30
**1758** A421 2r gold, claret & multi .75 .30
*Nos. 1753-1758 (6)* 4.50 1.80

Development of writing.

Fowl, Syringe and Emblem A422

**1974, Feb. 23**

**1759** A422 6r red brown & multi .60 .25

5th Iranian Veterinary Congress.

Monarch Butterfly A423

Designs: Various butterflies.

**1974, Mar. 6 Litho. *Perf. 10½***

**1760** A423 1r rose lilac & multi 1.00 .35
**1761** A423 1r brt rose & multi 1.00 .35
**1762** A423 2r lt blue & multi 1.50 .45
**1763** A423 2r green & multi 1.50 .45
**1764** A423 2r bister & multi 1.50 .45
*Nos. 1760-1764 (5)* 6.50 2.05

Novrooz, Iranian New Year.

Jalaludin Mevlana (1207-1273), Poet — A424

**1974, Mar. 12 *Perf. 13***

**1765** A424 2r pale violet & multi .50 .25

### Shah Type of 1971

**1974 Photo. *Perf. 13½x13***

**Size: 20½x28mm**

**1768** A366 50d orange & bl .45 .25
**1769** A366 1r emerald & bl .50 .25
**1770** A366 2r red & blue .80 .25

**Size: 27x36½mm**

**1771** A366 10r lt green & bl 7.00 .25
**1772** A366 20r lilac & bl 4.25 .25
*Nos. 1768-1772 (5)* 13.00 1.25

Palace of the Forty Columns, Hippocrates, Avicenna — A425

**1974, Apr. 11 Litho. *Perf. 10½***
**1773** A425 10r multicolored .75 .25

9th Medical Congress of the Near and Middle East, Isfahan.

Onager — A426

**1974, Apr. 13**
**1774** A426 1r shown .50 .25
**1775** A426 2r Great bustard .75 .25
**1776** A426 6r Fawn and deer 1.50 .35
**1777** A426 8r Caucasian black grouse 2.25 .40
*a.* Strip of 4, #1774-1777 6.00 3.00
*Nos. 1774-1777 (4)* 5.00 1.25

Intl. Council for Game and Wildlife Preservation.

Athlete and Games Emblem — A427

**1974, Apr. 30**
**1778** A427 1r shown .55 .25
**1779** A427 1r Table tennis .55 .25
**1780** A427 2r Boxing 1.00 .25
**1781** A427 2r Hurdles 1.00 .25
**1782** A427 6r Weight lifting 1.60 .25
**1783** A427 8r Basketball 2.50 .25
*Nos. 1778-1783 (6)* 7.20 1.50

7th Asian Games, Tehran; first issue.

Lion of Venice — A428

Painting: 8r, Audience with the Doge of Venice.

**1974, May 5**
**1784** A428 6r multicolored .55 .25
**1785** A428 8r multicolored 1.00 .35

Safeguarding Venice.

Links and Grain — A429

**1974, May 13 Litho. *Perf. 10½***
**1786** A429 2r multicolored .30 .25

Cooperation Day.

Military Plane, 1924 A430

**1974, June 1**
**1787** A430 10r shown 2.00 .40
**1788** A430 10r Jet, 1974 2.00 .40

50th anniversary of Iranian Air Force.

Swimmer and Games Emblem A431

**1974, July 1 Wmk. 353 *Perf. 10½***
**1789** A431 1r shown .65 .25
**1790** A431 1r Tennis, men's doubles .65 .25
**1791** A431 2r Wrestling .80 .25
**1792** A431 2r Hockey .80 .25
**1793** A431 4r Volleyball 1.25 .40
**1794** A431 10r Tennis, women's singles 2.50 .50
*Nos. 1789-1794 (6)* 6.65 1.90

7th Asian Games, Tehran; second issue.

Bicyclists and Games Emblem A432

**1974, Aug. 1**
**1795** A432 2r shown .90 .25
**1796** A432 2r Soccer .90 .25
**1797** A432 2r Fencing .90 .25
**1798** A432 2r Small-bore rifle shooting .90 .25
*Nos. 1795-1798 (4)* 3.60 1.00

7th Asian Games, Tehran; third issue.

Ghaskai Costume — A433

Regional Costumes: No. 1800, Kurdistan, Kermanshah District. No. 1801, Kurdistan, Sanandaj District. No. 1802, Mazandaran. No. 1803, Bakhtiari. No. 1804, Torkaman.

**1974, July 6**
**1799** A433 2r lt ultra & multi 1.40 .75
**1800** A433 2r buff & multi 1.40 .75
**1801** A433 2r green & multi 1.40 .75
**1802** A433 2r lt blue & multi 1.40 .75
**1803** A433 2r gray & multi 1.40 .75
**1804** A433 2r dull grn & multi 1.40 .75
*a.* Block of 6, #1799-1804 8.50 4.50

Gold Winged Lion Cup — A434

**1974, July 13**
**1805** A434 2r dull green & multi .30 .25

Iranian Soccer Cup.

Tabriz Rug, Late 16th Century — A435

Designs: No. 1807, Anatolian rug, 15th century. No. 1808, Kashan rug, Lahore.

**1974, July 21**
**1806** A435 2r brown & multi .45 .25
**1807** A435 2r blue & multi .45 .25
**1808** A435 2r red & multi .45 .25
*a.* Strip of 3, #1806-1808 1.40 .30

Regional Cooperation for Development Pact among Iran, Turkey and Pakistan, 10th anniv. See Pakistan 365-367, Turkey 1979-1981

King Carrying Vases, Bas-relief — A436

**1974, Aug. 15 Litho. *Perf. 10½***
**1809** A436 2r black & multi .30 .25

8th Iranian Arts Festival, Shiraz-Persepolis.

Aryamehr Stadium, Tehran — A437

#1811, Games' emblem and inscription. #1812, Aerial view of games' site.

**1974**
**1810** A437 6r multicolored 1.00 .25

**Souvenir Sheets**

**1811** A437 10r multicolored *3.00 1.50*
**1812** A437 10r multicolored *3.00 1.50*

7th Asian Games, Tehran; fourth and fifth issues. Nos. 1811-1812 contain one imperf 51x38mm stamp each.
Issued: #1811-1812, 9/1; #1810, 9/16.

"Welfare" — A438

"Education" A439

**1974, Sept. 11**
**1813** A438 2r orange & multi .30 .25
**1814** A439 2r blue & multi .30 .25

Welfare and free education.

Map of Hasanlu, 1000-800 B.C. — A440

**1974, Sept. 24**
**1815** A440 8r multicolored .70 .25

2nd Intl. Congress of Architecture, Shiraz-Persepolis, Sept. 1974.

Achaemenian Mail Cart and UPU Emblem — A441

Design: 14r, UPU emblem and letters.

**1974, Oct. 9 Wmk. 353 *Perf. 10½***
**1816** A441 6r orange, grn & blk 1.00 .40
**1817** A441 14r multicolored 1.50 .50

Centenary of Universal Postal Union.

Road Through Farahabad Park — A442

**1974, Oct. 16**
**1818** A442 1r shown .30 .25
**1819** A442 2r Recreation Bldg. .35 .25

Inauguration of Farahabad Park, Tehran.

Farahnaz Dam and Mohammad Reza Shah Pahlavi — A443

Designs: 5d, Kharg Island petro-chemical plant. 10d, Ghatour Railroad Bridge. 1r, Tehran oil refinery. 2r, Satellite communication station, Hamadan, and Mt. Alvand. 6r, Aryamehr steel mill, Isfahan. 8r, University of

Tabriz. 10r, Shah Abbas Kabir Dam. 14r, Rudagi (later Vahdat) Music Hall. 20r, Shayad Monument. 50r, Aryamehr Stadium.

**1974-75 Photo. *Perf. 13x13½***

**Size: 28x21mm**

**Frame & Shah in Brown**

| | | | | |
|---|---|---|---|---|
| **1820** | A443 | 5d slate green | .30 | .25 |
| **1821** | A443 | 10d orange | .30 | .25 |
| **1822** | A443 | 50d blue green | .30 | .25 |
| **1823** | A443 | 1r ultra | .30 | .25 |
| **1824** | A443 | 2r deep lilac | .30 | .25 |

**Size: 36x26½mm**

**Frame & Shah in Dark Blue**

| | | | | |
|---|---|---|---|---|
| **1825** | A443 | 6r brown | .50 | .30 |
| **1826** | A443 | 8r grnsh blue | .50 | .40 |
| **1827** | A443 | 10r deep lilac | .80 | .30 |
| *a.* | | Value in Farsi omitted | *30.00* | 30.00 |
| **1828** | A443 | 14r deep green | 17.00 | .60 |
| **1829** | A443 | 20r magenta | 3.50 | .50 |
| **1830** | A443 | 50r violet | 4.50 | 1.40 |
| | | *Nos. 1820-1830 (11)* | 28.30 | 4.75 |

Issued: 50d, 1r, 2r, 10/16/74; 14r, 11/1974; others 3/6/75.

See Nos. 1831-1841. For overprints see Nos. 2008, 2010.

**1975-77 Size: 28x21mm**

**Frame & Shah in Green**

| | | | | |
|---|---|---|---|---|
| **1831** | A443 | 5d orange ('77) | .30 | .25 |
| **1832** | A443 | 10d rose mag ('77) | .30 | .25 |
| **1833** | A443 | 50d lilac | .30 | .25 |
| **1834** | A443 | 1r dark blue | .30 | .25 |
| **1835** | A443 | 2r brown | .30 | .25 |

**Size: 36x26½mm**

**Frame & Shah in Brown**

| | | | | |
|---|---|---|---|---|
| **1836** | A443 | 6r vio bl ('76) | .40 | .35 |
| **1837** | A443 | 8r deep org ('77) | 2.00 | .30 |
| **1838** | A443 | 10r dp yel grn ('76) | 1.75 | .25 |
| **1839** | A443 | 14r lilac | 8.00 | .25 |
| **1840** | A443 | 20r brt green ('76) | 3.50 | .40 |
| **1841** | A443 | 50r dp blue ('76) | 3.00 | .90 |
| | | *Nos. 1831-1841 (11)* | 20.15 | 3.70 |

Festival Emblem, Crown and Column Capital, Persepolis — A444

**1974, Oct. 26 Litho. *Perf. 10½***

| | | | | |
|---|---|---|---|---|
| **1842** | A444 | 2r multicolored | .40 | .25 |

Festival of Culture and Art.

Destroyer "Palang" and Flag — A445

**1974, Nov. 5**

| | | | | |
|---|---|---|---|---|
| **1843** | A445 | 10r multicolored | 1.50 | .35 |

Navy Day.

Girl at Spinning Wheel A446

Designs: Children's drawings.

**1974, Nov. 7 *Perf. 10½***

| | | | | |
|---|---|---|---|---|
| **1844** | A446 | 2r shown | .35 | .25 |
| **1845** | A446 | 2r Scarecrow, vert. | .35 | .25 |
| **1846** | A446 | 2r Picnic | .35 | .25 |
| | | *Nos. 1844-1846 (3)* | 1.05 | .75 |

Children's Week.

Winged Ibex — A447

**1974, Nov. 25 Litho. Wmk. 353**

| | | | | |
|---|---|---|---|---|
| **1847** | A447 | 2r vio, org & blk | .35 | .25 |

Third Tehran International Film Festival.

WPY Emblem A448

**1974, Dec. 1**

| | | | | |
|---|---|---|---|---|
| **1848** | A448 | 8r orange & multi | .60 | .25 |

World Population Year.

Gold Bee A449

Design: 8r, Gold crown, gift of French people to Empress Farah. Bee pin was gift of the Italian people.

**1974, Dec. 20**

| | | | | |
|---|---|---|---|---|
| **1849** | A449 | 6r multicolored | .70 | .30 |
| **1850** | A449 | 8r multicolored | .90 | .35 |

15th wedding anniv. of Shah and Empress Farah.

Angel with Banner — A450

**1975, Jan. 7 Litho. *Perf. 10½***

| | | | | |
|---|---|---|---|---|
| **1851** | A450 | 2r org & vio bl | .30 | .25 |

International Women's Year.

Symbols of Agriculture, Industry and the Arts — A451

**1975, Jan. 26 Wmk. 353**

| | | | | |
|---|---|---|---|---|
| **1852** | A451 | 2r multicolored | .30 | .25 |

"White Revolution of King and People."

Tourism Year 75 Emblem — A452

**1975, Feb. 17**

| | | | | |
|---|---|---|---|---|
| **1853** | A452 | 6r multicolored | .30 | .25 |

South Asia Tourism Year.

"Farabi" in Shape of Musical Instrument or Alembic — A453

**1975, Mar. 1**

| | | | | |
|---|---|---|---|---|
| **1854** | A453 | 2r brn red & multi | .30 | .25 |

Abu-Nasr al-Farabi (870?-950), physician, musician and philosopher, 1100th birth anniversary.

Ornament, Rug Pattern — A454

**1975, Mar. 6**

| | | | | |
|---|---|---|---|---|
| **1855** | A454 | 1r shown | .25 | .25 |
| **1856** | A454 | 1r Blossoms and cypress trees | .25 | .25 |
| **1857** | A454 | 1r Shah Abbasi flower | .25 | .25 |
| *a.* | | Strip of 3, #1855-1857 | 1.00 | .60 |

Novrooz, Iranian New Year. Nos. 1855-1857 printed in sheets of 45 stamps + 5 labels.

Nasser Khosrov, Poet, Birth Millenary — A455

**1975, Mar. 11**

| | | | | |
|---|---|---|---|---|
| **1858** | A455 | 2r blk, gold & red | .30 | .25 |

Formula — A456

**1975, May 5 Litho. *Perf. 10½***

| | | | | |
|---|---|---|---|---|
| **1859** | A456 | 2r buff & multi | .40 | .25 |

5th Biennial Symposium of Iranian Biochemical Society.

Charioteer, Bas-relief, Persepolis — A457

Design: 2r, Heads of Persian warriors, bas-relief from Persepolis, vert.

**1975, May 5**

| | | | | |
|---|---|---|---|---|
| **1860** | A457 | 2r lt brn & multi | 2.00 | .75 |
| **1861** | A457 | 10r blue & multi | 4.00 | 1.25 |

Rotary International, 70th anniversary.

Signal Fire, Persian Castle A458

Design: 8r, Communications satellite.

**1975, May 17**

| | | | | |
|---|---|---|---|---|
| **1862** | A458 | 6r multicolored | .75 | .45 |
| **1863** | A458 | 8r lil & multi | .85 | .55 |

7th World Telecommunications Day.

Cooperation Day — A459

**1975, May 13**

| | | | | |
|---|---|---|---|---|
| **1864** | A459 | 2r multicolored | .30 | .25 |

Jet, Shayad Monument, Statue of Liberty — A460

**1975, May 29 Litho. Wmk. 353**

| | | | | |
|---|---|---|---|---|
| **1865** | A460 | 10r org & multi | 1.00 | .50 |

Iran Air's 1st flight to New York, May 1975.

Emblem — A461

**1975, June 5**

| | | | | |
|---|---|---|---|---|
| **1866** | A461 | 6r blue & multi | .45 | .25 |

World Environment Day.

Dam
A462

**1975, June 10**
**1867** A462 10r multicolored .70 .25

9th Intl. Congress on Irrigation & Drainage.

Resurgence Party
Emblem — A463

**1975, July 1 Wmk. 353 *Perf. 10½***
**1868** A463 2r multicolored .30 .25

Organization of Resurgence Party.

Girl Scout
Symbols
A464

**1975, July 16**
**1869** A464 2r multicolored .50 .25

2nd Natl Girl Scout Camp, Tehran, July 1976.

Festival of
Tus — A465

**1975, July 17**
**1870** A465 2r gray, lil & vio .30 .25

Festival of Tus in honor of Firdausi (940-1020), Persian poet born near Tus in Khorasan.

Ceramic
Plate,
Iran
A466

#1872, Camel leather vase, Pakistan, vert.
#1873, Porcelain vase, Turkey, vert.

**1975, July 21**
**1871** A466 2r bister & multi .35 .25
**1872** A466 2r bister & multi .35 .25
**1873** A466 2r bister & multi .35 .25
*Nos. 1871-1873 (3)* 1.05 .75

Regional Cooperation for Development Pact among Iran, Pakistan and Turkey.
See Pakistan 383-385, Turkey 2006-2008.

Majlis
Gate
A467

**1975, Aug. 5 Litho. *Perf. 10½***
**1874** A467 10r multi .75 .25

Iranian Constitution, 70th anniversary.

Column with
Stylized
Branches — A468

**1975, Aug. 21 Litho. Wmk. 353**
**1875** A468 8r red & multi .60 .25

9th Iranian Arts Festival, Shiraz-Persepolis.

Flags over
Globe — A469

**1975, Sept. 8**
**1876** A469 2r vio bl & multi .30 .25

Intl. Literacy Symposium, Persepolis.

Stylized
Globe — A470

**1975, Sept. 13**
**1877** A470 2r vio & multi .30 .25

3rd Tehran International Trade Fair.

World Map and Envelope — A471

**1975, Oct. 9 Litho. *Perf. 10½***
**1878** A471 14r ultra & multi 1.00 .25

World Post Day, Oct. 9.

Crown, Column
Capital,
Persepolis — A472

**1975, Oct. 26 Litho. Wmk. 353**
**1879** A472 2r ultra & multi .35 .25

Festival of Culture and Art. See No. 1954.

Face and
Film — A473

**1975, Nov. 2**
**1880** A473 6r multicolored .65 .25

Tehran Intl. Festival of Children's Films.

"Mother's
Face" — A474

Girl — A475

Design: No. 1882, 2r, "Our House," horiz. All designs after children's drawings.

**1975, Nov. 5**
**1881** A474 2r multicolored .35 .25
**1882** A475 2r multicolored .35 .25
**1883** A475 2r multicolored .35 .25
*Nos. 1881-1883 (3)* 1.05 .75

Children's Week.

"Film" — A476

**1975, Dec. 4 Wmk. 353 *Perf. 10½***
**1884** A476 8r multicolored .60 .25

4th Tehran International Film Festival.

Symbols of
Reforms — A477

People — A478

**1976, Jan. 26 Litho. *Perf. 10½***
**1885** A477 2r shown .35 .25
**1886** A478 2r shown .35 .25
**1887** A477 2r Five reform symbols .35 .25
*Nos. 1885-1887 (3)* 1.05 .75

"White Revolution of King and People."

Motorcycle
Policeman
A479

Police Helicopter — A480

**1976, Feb. 16**
**1888** A479 2r multicolored 1.25 .75
**1889** A480 6r multicolored 2.00 1.00

Highway Police Day.

Soccer
Cup — A481

**1976, Feb. 24 Litho. Wmk. 353**
**1890** A481 2r org & multi .30 .25

3rd Intl. Youth Soccer Cup, Shiraz and Ahvaz.

Candlestick
A482

Designs: No. 1892, Incense burner. No. 1893, Rose water container.

**1976, Mar. 6**

**1891** A482 1r olive & multi .30 .25
**1892** A482 1r claret & multi .30 .25
**1893** A482 1r Prus bl & multi .30 .25
*a.* Strip of 3, #1891-1893 1.00 .60

Novrooz, Iranian New Year.

Telephones, 1876 and 1976 — A483

**1976, Mar. 10**

**1894** A483 10r multicolored .75 .25

Centenary of first telephone call by Alexander Graham Bell, Mar. 10, 1876.

Eye Within Square — A484

**1976, Apr. 29** **Litho.** ***Perf. 10½***

**1895** A484 6r blk & multi 2.00 .25
*a.* Perf. 12½ 9.50 7.50

World Health Day: "Foresight prevents blindness."

Nurse with Infant
A485

Young Man Holding Old Man's Hand — A486

**1976, May 10**

**1896** A485 2r shown .50 .25
**1897** A485 2r Engineering apprentices .50 .25
**1898** A486 2r shown .50 .25
*Nos. 1896-1898 (3)* 1.50 .75

Royal Org. of Social Services, 30th anniv.

Map of Iran, Men Linking Hands — A487

Waves and Ear Phones — A488

**1976, May 13** **Wmk. 353**

**1899** A487 2r yel & multi .30 .25

Iranian Cooperatives, 10th anniversary.

**1976, May 17**

**1900** A488 14r gray & multi .75 .25

World Telecommunications Day.

Emblem, Woman with Flag, Man with Gun — A489

**1976, June 6**

**1901** A489 2r bister & multi .35 .25

To publicize the power of stability.

Map of Iran, Columns of Persepolis, Nasser Khosrow — A490

**1976, July 6** **Litho.** ***Perf. 10½***

**1902** A490 6r yel & multi .50 .25

Tourist publicity.

Reza Shah Pahlavi — A491

6r, Mohammad Ali Jinnah. 8r, Kemal Ataturk.

**1976, July 21** **Litho.** **Wmk. 353**

**1903** A491 2r gray & multi .50 .25
**1904** A491 6r gray & multi .60 .25
**1905** A491 8r gray & multi .75 .25
*Nos. 1903-1905 (3)* 1.85 .75

Regional Cooperation for Development Pact among Iran, Turkey and Pakistan, 12th anniversary.

See Pakistan 412-414, Turkey 2041-2043.

Torch, Montreal and Iranian Olympic Emblems
A492

**1976, Aug. 1**

**1906** A492 14r multicolored 1.00 .25

21st Olympic Games, Montreal, Canada, July 17-Aug. 1.

Reza Shah Pahlavi in Coronation Robe — A493

Designs: 2r, Reza Shah and Mohammad Reza Shah Pahlavi, horiz. 14r, 20r, Mohammad Reza Shah Pahlavi in coronation robe and crown.

**1976, Aug. 19** **Wmk. 353** ***Perf. 10½***

**1907** A493 2r lilac & multi 1.00 .50
**1908** A493 6r blue & multi 2.00 .75
**1909** A493 14r grn & multi 3.00 1.00
*Nos. 1907-1909 (3)* 6.00 2.25

**Souvenir Sheet**

**1976, Oct. 8** ***Imperf.***

**1910** A493 20r multi 10.00 6.00

50th anniv. of Pahlavi dynasty; 35th anniv. of reign of Mohammad Reza Shah Pahlavi. No. 1910 contains one stamp 43x62mm.

Festival Emblem — A494

**1976, Aug. 29** **Litho.** ***Perf. 10½***

**1911** A494 10r multicolored .65 .25

10th Iranian Arts Festival, Shiraz-Persepolis.

Iranian Scout Emblem — A495

**1976, Oct. 2** **Litho.** ***Perf. 10½***

**1912** A495 2r lt bl & multi .30 .25

10th Asia Pacific Conference, Tehran 1976.

Cancer Radiation Treatment — A496

**1976, Oct. 6**

**1913** A496 2r black & multi .30 .25

Fight against cancer.

Target, Police Woman Receiving Decoration
A497

**1976, Oct. 7**

**1914** A497 2r lt bl & multi .30 .25

Police Day.

UPU Emblem, No. 1907 on Cover
A498

**1976, Oct. 9**

**1915** A498 10r multicolored 1.00 .25

International Post Day.

Crown Prince Riza with Cup — A499

**1976, Oct. 10**

**1916** A499 6r multicolored .50 .25

Natl. Soc. of Village Culture Houses, anniv.

Riza Shah and Mohammad Reza Shah Pahlavi, Railroad
A500

**1976, Oct. 15**

**1917** A500 8r black & multi 4.00 1.50

Railroad Day.

Emblem & Column Capital, Persepolis — A501

Census Emblem — A502

**1976, Oct. 26**

**1918** A501 14r blue & multi 1.00 .30

Festival of Culture and Art.

**1976, Oct. 30**

**1919** A502 2r gray & multi .30 .25

Natl. Population & Housing Census, 1976.

Flowers and Birds — A503

Mohammad Ali Jinnah — A504

Designs: No. 1921, Flowers and bird. No. 1922, Flowers and butterfly. Designs are from covers of children's books.

**1976, Oct. 31** ***Perf. 10½***

| | | | | |
|---|---|---|---|---|
| **1920** | A503 | 2r multicolored | .35 | .25 |
| **1921** | A503 | 2r multicolored | .35 | .25 |
| **1922** | A503 | 2r multicolored | .35 | .25 |
| | | *Nos. 1920-1922 (3)* | 1.05 | .75 |

Children's Week.

**1976, Dec. 25 Litho. Wmk. 353**

| | | | | |
|---|---|---|---|---|
| **1923** | A504 | 10r multicolored | .60 | .25 |

Jinnah (1876-1948), 1st Governor General of Pakistan.

Development and Agriculture Corps — A505

17-Point Reform Law: 5d, Land reform. 10d, Nationalization of forests. 50d, Sale of shares of state-owned industries. 1r, Profit sharing for factory workers. 2r, Parliament Gate, Woman suffrage. 3r, Education Corps formation. 5r, Health Corps. 8r, Establishment of village courts. 10r, Nationalization of water resources. 12r, Reconstruction program, urban and rural. 14r, Administrative and educational reorganization. 20r, Sale of factory shares. 30r, Commodity pricing. 50r, Free education. 100r, Child care. 200r, Care of the aged (social security).

**1977, Jan. 26 Photo.** ***Perf. 13x13½***

**Frame and Shah's Head in Gold**

**Size: 28x21mm**

| | | | | |
|---|---|---|---|---|
| **1924** | A505 | 5d rose & green | .25 | .25 |
| **1925** | A505 | 10d lt grn & brn | .25 | .25 |
| **1926** | A505 | 50d yel & vio bl | .25 | .25 |
| **1927** | A505 | 1r lil & vio bl | .25 | .25 |
| **1928** | A505 | 2r org & green | .25 | .25 |
| **1929** | A505 | 3r lt bl & red | .40 | .25 |
| **1930** | A505 | 5r bl grn & mag | .40 | .25 |

**Size: 37x27mm**

| | | | | |
|---|---|---|---|---|
| **1931** | A505 | 6r brn, mar & black | .55 | .25 |
| **1932** | A505 | 8r ultra, mar & blk | .55 | .25 |
| **1933** | A505 | 10r lt grn, bl & black | 1.50 | .25 |
| **1934** | A505 | 12r vio, mar & black | 1.10 | .25 |
| **1935** | A505 | 14r org, red & blk | 1.60 | .75 |
| **1936** | A505 | 20r gray, ocher & black | 3.25 | .50 |
| **1937** | A505 | 30r bl, grn & blk | 3.25 | .65 |
| **1938** | A505 | 50r yel, brn & blk | 5.50 | .60 |
| **1939** | A505 | 100r multi | 5.00 | 1.25 |
| **1940** | A505 | 200r multi | 11.00 | 2.50 |
| | | *Nos. 1924-1940 (17)* | 35.35 | 9.00 |

"White Revolution of King and People" reform laws.

Man in Guilan Costume — A506

Electronic Tree — A507

2r, Woman in Guilan costume (Northern Iran).

**1977, Mar. 6 Wmk. 353** ***Perf. 13***

| | | | | |
|---|---|---|---|---|
| **1941** | A506 | 1r multicolored | .30 | .25 |
| **1942** | A506 | 2r multicolored | .35 | .25 |

Novrooz, Iranian New Year.

**1977, May 17 Photo.** ***Perf. 13***

| | | | | |
|---|---|---|---|---|
| **1943** | A507 | 20r multicolored | 1.25 | .35 |

World Telecommunications Day.

Reza Shah Dam A508

**1977, May 31** ***Perf. 13x13½***

| | | | | |
|---|---|---|---|---|
| **1944** | A508 | 5r multicolored | .40 | .25 |

Inauguration of Reza Shah Dam.

Olympic Rings A509

**1977, June 23 Litho.** ***Perf. 10½***

| | | | | |
|---|---|---|---|---|
| **1945** | A509 | 14r multicolored | .90 | .25 |

Olympic Day.

Terra-cotta Jug, Iran A510

#1947, Terra-cotta bullock cart, Pakistan. #1948, Terra-cotta pot with human face, Turkey.

***Perf. 13x13½***

**1977, July 21 Photo. Wmk. 353**

| | | | | |
|---|---|---|---|---|
| **1946** | A510 | 5r violet & multi | .40 | .25 |
| **1947** | A510 | 5r emer & multi | .40 | .25 |
| **1948** | A510 | 5r green & multi | .40 | .25 |
| | | *Nos. 1946-1948 (3)* | 1.20 | .75 |

Regional Cooperation for Development Pact among Iran, Turkey and Pakistan, 13th anniv. See Pakistan 431-433, Turkey 2053-2055.

Flowers with Scout Emblems, Map of Asia — A511

**1977, Aug. 5 Litho.** ***Perf. 13***

| | | | | |
|---|---|---|---|---|
| **1949** | A511 | 10r multicolored | 1.00 | .25 |

2nd Asia-Pacific Jamboree, Nishapur.

Map of Eastern Hemisphere with Iran — A512

Tree of Learning, Symbolic Letters — A513

**1977, Sept. 20 Photo. Wmk. 353**

| | | | | |
|---|---|---|---|---|
| **1950** | A512 | 3r multicolored | .35 | .25 |

9th Asian Electronics Conference, Tehran.

**1977, Oct. 8 Wmk. 353** ***Perf. 13***

| | | | | |
|---|---|---|---|---|
| **1951** | A513 | 10r multicolored | .60 | .25 |

Honoring the teachers.

Globe, Envelope, UPU Emblem A514

**1977, Oct. 9 Photo.**

| | | | | |
|---|---|---|---|---|
| **1952** | A514 | 14r multicolored | 1.00 | .25 |

Iran's admission to the UPU, cent.

Folk Art — A515

**1977, Oct. 16**

| | | | | |
|---|---|---|---|---|
| **1953** | A515 | 5r multicolored | .40 | .25 |

Festival of Folk Art.

**Festival Type of 1975**

Design: 20r, similar to 1975 issue, but with small crown within star.

**1977, Oct. 26** ***Perf. 10½***

| | | | | |
|---|---|---|---|---|
| **1954** | A472 | 20r bis, grn, car & blk | 1.25 | .25 |

Festival of Culture and Art.

Joust — A516

Emblem — A517

#1956, Rapunzel. #1957, Little princess with attendants.

**1977, Oct. 31 Photo.**

| | | | | |
|---|---|---|---|---|
| **1955** | A516 | 3r multicolored | .30 | .25 |
| **1956** | A516 | 3r multicolored | .30 | .25 |
| **1957** | A516 | 3r multicolored | .30 | .25 |
| *a.* | | Strip of 3, #1955-1957 | 1.25 | .60 |

Children's Week.

**1977, Nov. 7 Wmk. 353** ***Perf. 13***

| | | | | |
|---|---|---|---|---|
| **1958** | A517 | 5r multicolored | .40 | .25 |

First Regional Seminar on the Education and Welfare of the Deaf.

Mohammad Iqbal A518

African Sculpture A519

**1977, Nov. 9 Litho.** ***Perf. 10½***

| | | | | |
|---|---|---|---|---|
| **1959** | A518 | 5r multicolored | .45 | .25 |

Iqbal (1877-1938) of Pakistan, poet and philosopher.

**1977, Dec. 14**

| | | | | |
|---|---|---|---|---|
| **1960** | A519 | 20r multicolored | 3.25 | .55 |

African art.

Shah Mosque, Isfahan — A520

Designs: 1r, Ruins, Persepolis. 2r, Khajou Bridge, Isfahan. 5r, Imam Riza Shrine, Meshed. 9r, Warrior frieze, Persepolis. 10r, Djameh Mosque, Isfahan. 20r, King on throne, bas-relief. 25r, Sheik Lotfollah Mosque. 30r, Ruins, Persepolis, diff. view. 50r, Ali Ghapou Palace, Isfahan. 100r, Bas-relief, Tagh Bastan. 200r, Horseman and prisoners, bas-relief, Naqsh Rostam.

**1977-78 Photo.** ***Perf. 13x13½***

**"Iran" and Head in Gold**

**Size: 28x21mm**

| | | | | |
|---|---|---|---|---|
| **1961** | A520 | 1r deep brn | .30 | .25 |
| **1962** | A520 | 2r emerald | .30 | .25 |
| **1963** | A520 | 3r magenta | .50 | .25 |
| **1964** | A520 | 5r Prus blue | .70 | .25 |

**Size: 36x27mm**

| | | | | |
|---|---|---|---|---|
| **1965** | A520 | 9r sepia ('78) | 1.75 | .75 |
| **1966** | A520 | 10r brt bl ('78) | 5.75 | .85 |
| **1967** | A520 | 20r rose | 1.75 | .55 |
| **1968** | A520 | 25r ultra ('78) | 25.00 | 9.75 |
| **1969** | A520 | 30r magenta | 2.75 | .55 |
| **1970** | A520 | 50r deep yel grn ('78) | 4.50 | 3.50 |
| **1971** | A520 | 100r dk bl ('78) | 14.00 | 9.75 |
| **1972** | A520 | 200r vio bl ('78) | 19.00 | 19.00 |
| | | *Nos. 1961-1972 (12)* | 76.30 | 45.70 |

For overprints see Nos. 2009, 2011-2018.

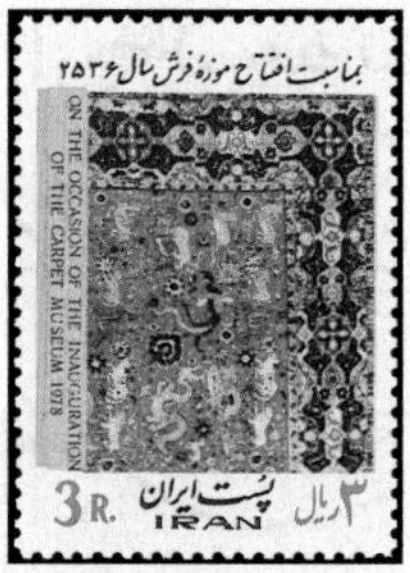

Persian Rug — A521

Designs: Persian rugs.

**1978, Feb. 11 Litho.** ***Perf. 10½***

| | | | | |
|---|---|---|---|---|
| **1973** | A521 | 3r sil & multi | .35 | .25 |
| **1974** | A521 | 5r sil & multi | .45 | .25 |
| **1975** | A521 | 10r sil & multi | .75 | .35 |
| | | *Nos. 1973-1975 (3)* | 1.55 | .85 |

Opening of Carpet Museum.

Mazanderan Man — A522

Design: 5r, Mazanderan woman.

**1978, Mar. 6** *Perf. 13*

| | | | | |
|---|---|---|---|---|
| **1976** | A522 | 3r yel & multi | .35 | .25 |
| **1977** | A522 | 5r lt bl & multi | .55 | .25 |

Novrooz, Iranian New Year.

Mohammad Reza Shah Pahlavi — A523

**1978, Jan. 26**

| | | | | |
|---|---|---|---|---|
| **1978** | A523 | 20r multicolored | 4.00 | 1.25 |

Shah's White Revolution, 15th anniv.

Reza Shah Pahlavi and Crown Prince Inspecting Girls' School — A524

Designs (Reza Shah Pahlavi and Crown Prince Mohammad Reza Shah Pahlavi): 5r, Inauguration of Trans-Iranian railroad. 10r, At stairs of Palace, Persepolis. 14r, Shah handing Crown Prince (later Shah) officer's diploma at Tehran Officers' Academy.

**1978, Mar. 15**

| | | | | |
|---|---|---|---|---|
| **1979** | A524 | 3r multicolored | .50 | .25 |
| **1980** | A524 | 5r multicolored | .75 | .35 |
| **1981** | A524 | 10r multicolored | 1.25 | .40 |
| **1982** | A524 | 14r multicolored | 1.75 | .70 |
| | | *Nos. 1979-1982 (4)* | 4.25 | 1.70 |

Reza Shah Pahlavi (1877-1944), founder of Pahlavi dynasty.

Communications Satellite over Map of Iran — A525

**1978, Apr. 19** **Litho.** *Perf. 10½*

| | | | | |
|---|---|---|---|---|
| **1983** | A525 | 20r multicolored | 1.25 | .30 |

ITU, 7th meeting, Tehran; 10th anniv. of Iran's membership.

Antenna, ITU Emblem A526

**1978, May 17** **Litho.** *Perf. 10½*

| | | | | |
|---|---|---|---|---|
| **1984** | A526 | 15r multicolored | .90 | .30 |

10th World Telecommunications Day.

Welfare Legion Emblem — A527

**1978, June 13** **Photo.** *Perf. 13x13½*

| | | | | |
|---|---|---|---|---|
| **1985** | A527 | 10r multicolored | .60 | .30 |

Universal Welfare Legion, 10th anniversary.

Pink Roses, Iran — A528

Designs: 10r, Yellow rose, Turkey. 15r, Red roses, Pakistan.

*Perf. 13½x13*

**1978, July 21** **Wmk. 353**

| | | | | |
|---|---|---|---|---|
| **1986** | A528 | 5r multicolored | .60 | .25 |
| **1987** | A528 | 10r multicolored | .90 | .25 |
| **1988** | A528 | 15r multicolored | 1.00 | .40 |
| | | *Nos. 1986-1988 (3)* | 2.50 | .90 |

Regional Cooperation for Development Pact among Iran, Turkey and Pakistan, 14th anniversary.

See Pakistan 449-451, Turkey 2094-2096.

Rhazes, Pharmaceutical Tools — A529

**1978, Aug. 26** **Wmk. 353** *Perf. 13*

| | | | | |
|---|---|---|---|---|
| **1989** | A529 | 5r multicolored | .60 | .25 |

Pharmacists' Day. Rhazes (850-923), chief physician of Great Hospital in Baghdad.

Girl Scouts, Aryamehr Arch A530

**1978, Sept. 2** *Perf. 10½*

| | | | | |
|---|---|---|---|---|
| **1990** | A530 | 5r multicolored | 1.00 | .35 |

23rd World Girl Scouts Conference, Tehran, Sept. 1978.

Reza Shah Pahlavi A531

Design: 5r, Mohammad Reza Shah Pahlavi.

**1978, Sept. 11** **Litho.** *Perf. 10½*

| | | | | |
|---|---|---|---|---|
| **1991** | A531 | 3r multicolored | 1.50 | .40 |
| **1992** | A531 | 5r multicolored | 1.75 | .50 |

Bank Melli Iran, 50th anniversary.

Girl and Bird A532

**1978, Oct. 31** **Photo.** *Perf. 13*

| | | | | |
|---|---|---|---|---|
| **1993** | A532 | 3r multicolored | .75 | .30 |

Children's Week.

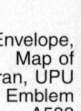

Envelope, Map of Iran, UPU Emblem A533

**1978, Nov. 22** *Perf. 13x13½*

| | | | | |
|---|---|---|---|---|
| **1994** | A533 | 14r gold & multi | 1.50 | .40 |

World Post Day, Oct. 22.

Communications Symbols and Classroom — A534

**1978, Nov. 22** *Perf. 10½*

| | | | | |
|---|---|---|---|---|
| **1995** | A534 | 10r multicolored | 1.25 | .40 |

Faculty of Communications, 50th anniv.

Human Rights Flame A535

**1978, Dec. 17** **Photo.** *Perf. 13*

| | | | | |
|---|---|---|---|---|
| **1996** | A535 | 20r bl, blk & gold | 3.50 | .50 |

Universal Declaration of Human Rights, 30th anniv.

Kurdistani Man — A536

Design: 5r, Kurdistani woman.

**1979, Mar. 17**

| | | | | |
|---|---|---|---|---|
| **1997** | A536 | 3r multicolored | .90 | .25 |
| **1998** | A536 | 5r multicolored | 1.25 | .25 |

Rose — A537

**1979, Mar. 17**

| | | | | |
|---|---|---|---|---|
| **1999** | A537 | 2r multicolored | .25 | .25 |

Novrooz, Iranian New Year.

See No. 2310i.

## Islamic Republic

Demonstrators — A538

Islamic revolution: 3r, Demonstrators. 5r, Hands holding rose, gun and torch breaking through newspaper. 20r, Hands breaking prison bars, and dove, vert.

**1979, Apr. 20** *Perf. 10½*

| | | | | |
|---|---|---|---|---|
| **2000** | A538 | 3r multicolored | 2.00 | .35 |
| **2001** | A538 | 5r multicolored | 1.40 | .35 |
| **2002** | A538 | 10r multicolored | 1.40 | .65 |
| **2003** | A538 | 20r multicolored | 3.00 | .75 |
| | | *Nos. 2000-2003 (4)* | 7.80 | 2.10 |

### Nos. 1837-1838, 1966, 1970 and Type A520 Overprinted

Designs: 15r, Warriors on horseback, bas-relief, Naqsh-Rostam. 19r, Chehel Sotoon Palace, Isfahan.

**1979** **Wmk. 353** *Perf. 13x13½*

| | | | | |
|---|---|---|---|---|
| **2008** | A443 | 8r org & brown | *3.00* | 1.00 |
| **2009** | A520 | 9r gold & dp brn | 1.50 | 1.50 |
| **2010** | A443 | 10r dp yel grn | *50.00* | 10.00 |
| **2011** | A520 | 10r gold & brt bl | 1.75 | 1.00 |
| **2012** | A520 | 15r gold & red lil | 1.75 | 1.00 |
| **2013** | A520 | 19r gold & slate grn | 1.75 | 1.00 |
| **2016** | A520 | 50r gold & dp yel grn | 5.00 | 2.00 |
| **2017** | A520 | 100r gold & vio bl | 10.00 | 4.00 |
| **2018** | A520 | 200r gold & vio bl | 12.50 | 8.50 |
| | | *Nos. 2008-2018 (9)* | *87.25* | 30.00 |

Overprint means Islamic revolution. Forgeries of No. 2010 exist.

Symbolic Tulip — A539

**1979, June 5** **Photo.** *Perf. 13*

| | | | | |
|---|---|---|---|---|
| **2019** | A539 | 5r multicolored | 1.50 | .40 |

Potters, by Kamalel Molk A540

No. 2021, at the Well, by Allah Baksh, Pakistan. No. 2022, Threshing, by Namik Ismail, Turkey.

**1979, July 21** **Litho.** *Perf. 10½*

| | | | | |
|---|---|---|---|---|
| **2020** | A540 | 5r multicolored | 3.75 | .35 |
| **2021** | A540 | 5r multicolored | 2.75 | .35 |
| **2022** | A540 | 5r multicolored | 2.75 | .35 |
| | | *Nos. 2020-2022 (3)* | 9.25 | 1.05 |

Regional Cooperation for Development Pact among Iran, Turkey and Pakistan, 15th anniv.

See Pakistan 486-488, turkey 2112-2114.

"TELECOM 79" — A541

**1979, Sept. 20** *Perf. 10½*

| | | | | |
|---|---|---|---|---|
| **2023** | A541 | 20r multicolored | *15.00* | .30 |

3rd World Telecommunications Exhibition, Geneva, Sept. 20-26.

Greeting the Sunrise — A542

Persian Rug Design — A543

Children's Drawings and IYC Emblem: 2r, Tulip over wounded man. 2r, Children with banners.

**1979, Sept. 23**

**2024** A542 2r multicolored 3.00 .50
**2025** A542 3r multicolored 3.00 .50
**2026** A542 5r multicolored 4.00 .50
*Nos. 2024-2026 (3)* 10.00 1.50

International Year of the Child.

**1979-80 Photo. *Perf. 13½x13***

**2027** A543 50d brn & pale sal .25 .25
**2028** A543 1r dark & lt bl .25 .25
**2029** A543 2r red & yellow .25 .25
**2030** A543 3r dk bl & lt lil .25 .25
**2031** A543 5r slate grn & lt grn .25 .25
**2032** A543 10r blk & salmon pink ('80) .30 .25
**2033** A543 20r brn & gray ('80) .55 .25

**Size: 27x37½mm**

**2034** A543 50r dp violet & gray ('80) 1.40 .50
**2035** A543 100r blk & slate grn ('80) 5.00 1.40
**2036** A543 200r dk bl & cr ('80) 5.50 2.75
*Nos. 2027-2036 (10)* 14.00 6.40

Globe in Envelope — A544

**1979, Oct. 9 Litho. *Perf. 10½***

**2041** A544 10r multicolored *3.00* .40

World Post Day.

Ghyath-al-din Kashani, Astrolabe A545

**1979, Dec. 5 Litho. *Perf. 10½***

**2042** A545 5r ocher & blk *1.50* .40

Kashani, mathematician, 550th death anniv.

Ka'aba, Flame and Mosque A546

Hegira (Pilgrimage Year): 5r, Koran open over globe, vert. 10r, Salman Farsi (follower of Mohammad), map of Iran.

**1980, Jan. 19**

**2043** A546 3r multicolored .25 .25
**2044** A546 5r multicolored .25 .25
**2045** A546 10r multicolored .55 .25
*Nos. 2043-2045 (3)* 1.05 .75

Reissued in May-June, 1980, with shiny gum and watermark position changed.

People, Map and Flag of Iran — A547

Islamic Revolution, 1st Anniversary: 3r, Blood dripping on broken sword. 5r, Window open on sun of Islam, people.

**1980, Feb. 11**

**2046** A547 1r multicolored .25 .25
**2047** A547 3r multicolored .35 .25
**2048** A547 5r multicolored .65 .30
*Nos. 2046-2048 (3)* 1.25 .80

For similar stamps measuring 24x36mm see Nos. 2310a, 2310b, 2310d.

Dehkhoda, Dictionary Editor, Birth Cent. — A548

**1980, Feb. 26**

**2049** A548 10r multicolored .30 .25

East Azerbaijani Woman A549

Mohammad Mossadegh A550

Novrooz (Iranian New Year): 5r, East Azerbaijani man.

**1980, Mar. 5**

**2050** A549 3r multicolored .25 .25
**2051** A549 5r multicolored .25 .25

**1980, Mar. 19 Photo. *Perf. 13x13½***

**2052** A550 20r multi .60 .25

Oil industry nationalization, 29th anniv.; Mohammad Mossadegh, prime minister who initiated nationalization.

Professor Morteza Motahhari, 1st Death Anniversary — A551

**1980, May 1 Litho. *Perf. 10½***

**2053** A551 10r black & red .50 .25

World Telecommunications Day — A552

**1980, May 17 Photo. *Perf. 13x13½***

**2054** A552 20r multicolored .50 .25

Interior of Mosque A553

**1980, June 11 Litho. *Perf. 10½***

**2055** A553 50d shown .25 .25
**2056** A553 1r Demonstration .25 .25
**2057** A553 3r Avicenna, al-Biruni, Farabi .40 .25
**2058** A553 5r Hegira emblem .30 .25
*Nos. 2055-2058 (4)* 1.20 1.00

Hegira, 1400th anniv.

Ali Sharyati, Educator A554

**1980, June 15 Photo. *Perf. 13x13½***

**2059** A554 5r multicolored .30 .25

Holy Ka'aba and Hand Waving Banner — A555

**1980, June 28**

**2060** A555 5r multicolored .30 .25

Hazrat Mehdi, 12th Imam's birth anniv.

A556

OPEC Emblem — A557

**1980, Sept. 10 *Perf. 13½x13***

**2061** A556 5r multicolored .30 .25

Ayatollah Seyed Mahmood Talegani, death anniv. Compare with design A829.

**1980, Sept. 15**

**2062** A557 5r shown .30 .25
**2063** A557 10r Men holding OPEC emblem .60 .25

20th anniversary of OPEC.

"Let Us Liberate Jerusalem" A558

Tulip and Fayziyye Seminary, Qum A559

**1980, Oct. 9 *Perf. 13x13½***

**2064** A558 5r multicolored .25 .25
**2065** A558 20r multicolored .85 .25

**1981, Feb. 11 *Perf. 13***

**2066** A559 3r shown .25 .25
**2067** A559 5r Blood spilling on tulip .25 .25
**2068** A559 20r Tulip, Republic emblem .50 .25
*Nos. 2066-2068 (3)* 1.00 .75

Islamic Revolution, 2nd anniversary.

See Nos. 2310c, 2310e, 2310j, watermark 381 (3r, unserifed "R" in denomination. 5r, bright yellow background; 20r, light blue background behind flower.)

Lorestani Man — A560

Telecommunications Day — A561

Novrooz (Iranian New Year): 10r, Lorestani woman.

**1981, Mar. 11**

**2069** A560 5r multicolored .25 .25
**2070** A560 10r multicolored .30 .25

***Perf. 13½x13***

**1981, May 17 Photo. Wmk. 353**

**2071** A561 5r dk grn & org .25 .25

Ayatollah Kashani Birth Centenary — A562

***Perf. 13x13½***

**1981, July 21 Wmk. 381**

**2072** A562 15r dk grn & dl pur .40 .25

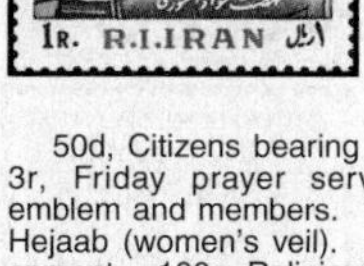

Adult Education A563

50d, Citizens bearing arms. 2r, Irrigation. 3r, Friday prayer service. 5r, Paasdaar emblem and members. 10r, Koran text. 20r, Hejaab (women's veil). 50r, Industrial development. 100r, Religious ceremony, Mecca. 200r, Mosque interior. 5r, 10r, 200r vert.

***Perf. 13x13½, 13½x13 (5r, 10r, 200r)***

**1981, Aug.**

**2073** A563 50d blk & dp bister .25 .25
**2074** A563 1r dl pur & grn .25 .25
**2075** A563 2r brn & grnsh bl .25 .25

**Size: 38x28mm, 28x38mm**

| | | | | |
|---|---|---|---|---|
| **2076** | A563 | 3r brt yel grn & black | .25 | .25 |
| **2077** | A563 | 5r dk bl & brn org | .25 | .25 |
| **2078** | A563 | 10r dk bl & grnsh blue | .25 | .25 |
| **2079** | A563 | 20r red & black | .60 | .25 |
| **2080** | A563 | 50r lilac & black | 1.40 | .30 |
| **2081** | A563 | 100r org brn & blk | 3.00 | .60 |
| **2082** | A563 | 200r blk & bl grn | 5.75 | 1.25 |
| | | *Nos. 2073-2082 (10)* | 12.25 | 3.90 |

Islamic Iranian Army A564

**1981, Sept. 21 Photo. *Perf. 13***
**2087** A564 5r multicolored .65 .30

World Post Day and 12th UPU Day — A565

***Perf. 13x13½***
**1981, Oct. 9 Wmk. 381**
**2088** A565 20r black & blue .85 .45

Millennium of Nahjul Balaghah (Sacred Book) A566

**1981, Oct. 17 *Perf. 13***
**2089** A566 25r multicolored .60 .25

Martyrs' Memorial — A567

**1981, Nov. 9 Photo. *Perf. 13***

| | | | | |
|---|---|---|---|---|
| **2090** | A567 | 3r June 28, 1981 victims | .25 | .25 |
| **2091** | A567 | 5r Pres. Rajai, Prime Minister Bahonar | .25 | .25 |
| **2092** | A567 | 10r Gen. Chamran | .25 | .25 |
| | | *Nos. 2090-2092 (3)* | .75 | .75 |

Ayatollah M. H. Tabatabaee, Scholar — A568

**1981, Dec. 25 Photo. *Perf. 13***
**2093** A568 5r multicolored .25 .25

Literacy Campaign A569

**1982, Jan. 20 Photo. *Perf. 13x13½***
**2094** A569 5r blue & gold .25 .25

Islamic Revolution, 3rd Anniv. — A570

**1982, Feb. 11 Wmk. 381 *Perf. 13***

| | | | | |
|---|---|---|---|---|
| **2095** | A570 | 5r Map | .25 | .25 |
| **2096** | A570 | 10r Tulip | .25 | .25 |
| **2097** | A570 | 20r Globe | .50 | .25 |
| *a.* | | Strip of 3, #2095-2097 | .90 | .40 |

See Nos. 2310f, 2310g, 2310k (5r, orange background, Arabian "5" 6mm above black panel. 10r, dark green background, gray dove with thick black lines around it. 20r, pink background, bright blue globe, faint latitude and longitude lines.)

Unity Week — A571

**1982, Feb. 20 Photo. *Perf. 13***
**2098** A571 25r multicolored 1.00 .25

Koran Verse Relative to Christ A572

**1982, Mar. 11 Photo. Wmk. 381**
**2099** A572 20r multicolored .50 .25

Khuzestan Man — A573

**1982, Mar. 13**

| | | | | |
|---|---|---|---|---|
| **2100** | A573 | 3r shown | .25 | .25 |
| **2101** | A573 | 5r Khuzestan woman | .25 | .25 |
| *a.* | | Pair, #2100-2101 | .25 | .25 |

Novrooz (New Year).

3rd Anniv. of Islamic Revolution A574

**1982, Apr. 1**
**2102** A574 30r multicolored .90 .25

Seyed Mohammad Bagher Sadr — A575

**1982, Apr. 8 Photo. *Perf. 13½x13***
**2103** A575 50r multicolored 1.00 .40

Martyrs of Altar (Ayatollahs Madani and Dastgeyb) — A576

**1982, Apr. 21 *Perf. 13***
**2104** A576 50r multicolored 1.00 .40

A577

A578

**1982, May 1 Photo. *Perf. 13½x13***
**2105** A577 100r multi 2.25 .80

Intl. Workers' Solidarity Day.

**1982, May 17 *Perf. 13x13½***
**2106** A578 100r multi 2.25 .80

14th World Telecommunications Day.

Mab'as Day (Mohammad's Appointment as Prophet) — A579

**1982, May 21 *Perf. 13½x13***
**2107** A579 32r multicolored .90 .30

1963 Islamic Rising, 19th Anniv. — A580

**1982, June 5 Wmk. 381 *Perf. 13***
**2108** A580 28r multicolored .60 .30

Lt. Islambuli, Assassin of Anwar Sadat — A581

1st Death Anniv. of Ayatollah Beheshti — A582

**1982, June 17**
**2109** A581 2r multicolored .40 .25

**1982, June 28**

| | | | | |
|---|---|---|---|---|
| **2110** | A582 | 10r multicolored | .40 | .25 |
| *a.* | | Missing dot in Arabic numeral | 1.00 | 1.00 |

Iran-Iraq War A583

**1982, July 7 *Perf. 13x13½***
**2111** A583 5r multicolored .25 .25

Universal Jerusalem Day A584

**1982, July 15 *Perf. 13***
**2112** A584 1r Dome of the Rock .25 .25

Pilgrimage to Mecca — A585

**1982, Sept. 28**
**2113** A585 10r multicolored .30 .25

13th World UPU Day — A586

**1982, Oct. 9 *Perf. 13½x13***
**2114** A586 30r multicolored .75 .25

4th Anniv. of Islamic Revolution — A587

**1983, Feb. 11 Photo. *Perf. 13***
**2115** A587 30r multicolored .75 .25

See No. 2310n for stamp with orange or orange red crowd and thick sharp lettering in black panels.

4th Anniv. of Islamic Republic — A588

**1983, Apr. 1 Photo. *Perf. 13***
**2116** A588 10r multicolored .30 .25

Teachers' Day — A589

World Communications Year — A590

***Perf. 13½x13***

**1983, May 1 Wmk. 381**
**2117** A589 5r multicolored .25 .25

**1983, May 17**
**2118** A590 20r multicolored .60 .25

First Session of Islamic Consultative Assembly — A591

**1983, May 28 *Perf. 13***
**2119** A591 5r multicolored .25 .25

20th Anniv. of Islamic Movement — A592

**1983, June 5 Photo. *Perf. 13***
**2120** A592 10r multicolored .30 .25

Iraqi MiG Bombing Now Rooz Oil Well A593

**1983, June 11 *Perf. 13x13½***
**2121** A593 5r multicolored .50 .25

Ecology week.

Ayatollah Mohammad Sadooghi — A594

**1983, July 2 Photo. *Perf. 13½***
**2122** A594 20r blk & dl red .60 .25

Universal Day of Jerusalem — A595

**1983, July 8**
**2123** A595 5r Dome of the Rock .25 .25

Government Week — A596

**1983, Aug. 30 Wmk. 381 *Perf. 13***
**2124** A596 3r multicolored .25 .25

Death of Pres. Rajai and Prime Minister Bahonar, 2nd anniv.

Iran-Iraq War, 3rd Anniv. — A597

**1983, Sept. 28 Photo. *Perf. 13***
**2125** A597 5r rose red & blk .25 .25

Ayatollah Ashrafi Esphahani, Martyr of Altar — A598

Mirza Kuchik Khan — A599

**1983, Oct. 15 Photo. *Perf. 13***
**2126** A598 5r multicolored .25 .25

**1983-84 Photo. *Perf. 13***

Religious and Political Figures: 1r, Sheikh Mohammad Khiabani. 3r, Seyd Majtaba Navab Safavi. 5r, Seyd Jamal-ed-Din Assadabadi. 10r, Seyd Hassan Modaress. 20r, Sheikh Fazel Assad Nouri. 30r, Mirza Mohammad Hossein Naiyni. 50r, Sheikh Mohammad Hossein Kashef. 100r, Seyd Hassan Shirazi. 200r, Mirza Reza Kermani.

| | | | | |
|---|---|---|---|---|
| **2128** | A599 | 1r black & pink | .25 | .25 |
| **2129** | A599 | 2r org & black | .25 | .25 |
| **2130** | A599 | 3r brt bl & blk | .25 | .25 |
| **2131** | A599 | 5r rose red & blk | .25 | .25 |
| **2132** | A599 | 10r yel grn & blk | .30 | .25 |
| **2133** | A599 | 20r lilac & blk | .60 | .25 |
| **2134** | A599 | 30r gldn brn & blk | .90 | .30 |
| **2135** | A599 | 50r blk & lt bl | 1.50 | .50 |
| **2136** | A599 | 100r blk & org | 3.00 | 1.00 |
| **2137** | A599 | 200r blk & bluish grn | 6.00 | 2.00 |
| | | *Nos. 2128-2137 (10)* | 13.30 | 5.30 |

Issue dates: 1r, 50r-200r, Feb. 1984. Others, Oct. 23, 1983.

UPU Day A600

**1983, Oct. 9 Photo. Wmk. 381**
**2138** A600 10r multi .25 .25

Takeover of the US Embassy, 4th Anniv. — A601

**1983, Nov. 4 Photo. *Perf. 13***
**2139** A601 28r multicolored .50 .50

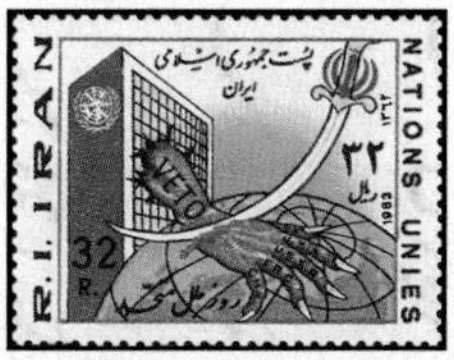


UN Day A602

**1983, Oct. 24 *Perf. 13½***
**2140** A602 32r multicolored .90 .25

Protest of veto by US, Russia, People's Rep. of China, France and Great Britain.

Intl. Medical Seminar, Tehran — A603

**1983, Nov. 20**
**2141** A603 3r Avicenna .25 .25

People's Forces Preparation Day — A604

**1983, Nov. 26 *Perf. 13***
**2142** A604 20r multicolored .60 .25

Conference on Crimes of Iraqi Pres. Saddam Hussein — A605

**1983, Nov. 28 *Perf. 13½x13***
**2143** A605 5r multicolored .25 .25

Mohammad Mofatteh — A606

**1983, Dec. 18 Photo. *Perf. 13***
**2144** A606 10r multicolored .30 .25

Birth Anniversary of the Prophet Mohammad A607

**1983, Dec. 22 Photo. *Perf. 13***
**2145** A607 5r multicolored .45 .25

Approximately 700,000 examples of No. 2145 were issued before a spelling error was discovered, and the remainder of the issue was then withdrawn from sale.

5th Anniv. of Islamic Revolution — A608

**1984, Feb. 11 Photo. *Perf. 13x13½***
**2146** A608 10r multicolored .75 .25

See No. 2310h for stamp with splotchy colors in blue background and denomination, flag colors and darker, thicker black lines around tulips. Background and denominations on No. 2146 have a screened appearance.

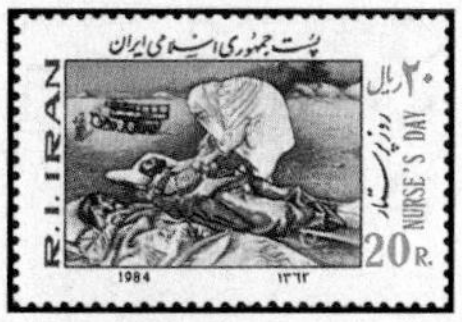


Nurses' Day A609

**1984, Feb. 24 *Perf. 13***
**2147** A609 20r Attending wounded soldiers .45 .25

Invalids' Day — A610

Local Flowers — A611

**1984, Feb. 29**
**2148** A610 5r Man in wheelchair .25 .25

**1984, Mar. 10 *Perf. 13½x13***

| | | | | |
|---|---|---|---|---|
| **2149** | A611 | 3r Lotus gebelia | .25 | .25 |
| **2150** | A611 | 5r Tulipa chrysantha | .25 | .25 |
| **2151** | A611 | 10r Glycyrhiza glabra | .25 | .25 |
| **2152** | A611 | 20r Matthiola alyssifolia | .45 | .25 |

Novrooz (New Year).

Islamic Republic, 5th Anniv. — A612

**1984, Apr. 1 Photo. *Perf. 13***
**2153** A612 5r Flag, globe, map .25 .25

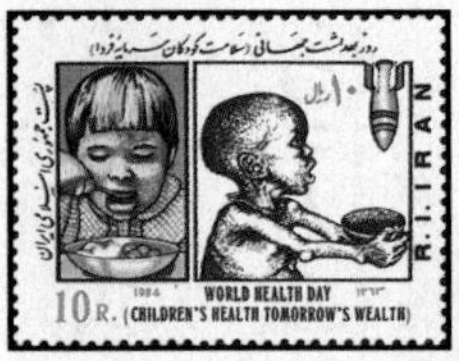


World Health Day A613

**1984, Apr. 7**
**2154** A613 10r Children .30 .25

Sheik Ragheb Harb, Lebanese Religious Leader — A614

**1984, Apr. 18**
**2155** A614 5r multicolored .25 .25

World Red Cross Day — A615

**1984, May 8 Photo.** ***Perf. 13½x13***
**2156** A615 5r multicolored .25 .25

16th World Telecommunications Day — A616

**1984, May 17**
**2157** A616 20r multicolored .45 .25

Martyrdom of Seyyed Ghotb — A617

**1984, May 28** ***Perf. 13***
**2158** A617 10r multicolored .30 .25

Struggle Against Discrimination — A618

**1984, Mar. 21 Photo.** ***Perf. 13***
**2159** A618 5r Malcolm X 2.50 .25

Conquest of Mecca Anniv. A619

**1984, June 20**
**2160** A619 5r Holy Ka'aba, idol destruction .25 .25

Universal Day of Jerusalem A620

Id Al-fitr Feast A621

**1984, June 29**
**2161** A620 5r Map, Koran .25 .25
**2162** A621 10r Moon, praying crowd, mosque .25 .25
*a.* Pair, #2161-2162 .40 .25

Tchogha Zanbil Excavation, Susa — A622

Cultural Heritage Preservation: b, Emamzadeh Hossein Shrine, Kazvin. c, Emam Mosque, Isfahan. d, Ark Fortress, Tabriz. e, Mausoleum of Daniel Nabi, Susa.

**1984, Aug. 20** ***Perf. 13½***
**2163** Strip of 5 .75 .25
*a.-e.* A622 5r, any single .25 .25

"Eid Ul-Adha" A623

***Perf. 13x13½***
**1984, Sept. 6 Photo. Wmk. 381**
**2164** A623 10r Holy Ka'aba .30 .25

Feast of Sacrifices (end of pilgrimage to Mecca).

10th Tehran Intl. Trade Fair — A624

Iraq-Iran War, 4th Anniv. — A625

**1984, Sept. 11**
**2165** A624 10r multicolored .30 .25

**1984, Sept. 22 Photo.** ***Perf. 13x13½***
**2166** A625 5r Flower, bullets .25 .25

UPU Day A626

**1984, Oct. 9** ***Perf. 13½***
**2167** A626 20r Dove, UPU emblems .50 .25

Haj Seyyed Mostafa Khomeini Memorial A627

**1984, Oct. 23**
**2168** A627 5r multicolored .25 .25

Ghazi Tabatabaie Memorial — A628

**1984, Nov. 1** ***Perf. 13x13½***
**2169** A628 5r Portrait .25 .25

Intl. Saadi Congress A629

**1984, Nov. 25** ***Perf. 13½***
**2170** A629 10r Portrait, mausoleum, emblem .50 .25

Saadi (c. 1213-1292), Persian poet.

Mohammad's Birthday, Unity Week — A630

**1984, Dec. 6 Photo.** ***Perf. 13x13½***
**2171** A630 5r Koran, mosque .25 .25

Islamic Revolution, 6th Anniv. — A631

Arbor Day — A632

**1985, Feb. 11** ***Perf. 13x13½***
**2172** A631 40r multicolored .90 .40

See No. 2310o for stamp with bright pink denomination and dove tail.

**1985, Mar. 6** ***Perf. 13***
**2173** A632 3r Sapling, deciduous trees .25 .25
**2174** A632 5r Maturing trees .25 .25
*a.* Pair, #2173-2174 .30 .25

Local Flowers — A633

**1985, Mar. 9** ***Perf. 13½x13***
**2175** A633 5r Fritillaria imperialis .25 .25
**2176** A633 5r Ranunculus ficarioides .25 .25
**2177** A633 5r Crocus sativus .25 .25
**2178** A633 5r Primula heterochroma stapf .25 .25
*a.* Block of 4, #2175-2178 .50 .30

Novrooz (New Year).

Women's Day — A634

Republic of Iran, 6th Anniv. — A635

**1985, Mar. 13** ***Perf. 13x13½***
**2179** A634 10r Procession of women .30 .25

Birth anniv. of Mohammad's daughter, Fatima.

**1985, Apr. 1**
**2180** A635 20r Tulip, ballot box .45 .25

Mab'as Festival A636

**1985, Apr. 18**
**2181** A636 10r Holy Koran .30 .25

Religious festival celebrating the recognition of Mohammad as the true prophet.

Day of the Oppressed A637

World Telecommunications Day A638

**1985, May 6**
**2182** A637 5r Koran, flag, globe .25 .25

Birthday of the 12th Imam.

**1985, May 17** ***Perf. 13½x13***
**2183** A638 20r ITU emblem .45 .25

Liberation of Khorramshahr, 1st Anniv. — A639

**1985, May 24**
**2184** A639 5r Soldier, bridge .25 .25

Fist, Theological Seminary, Qum — A640

**1985, June 5** ***Perf. 13x13½***
**2185** A640 10r multicolored .50 .25

1963 Uprising, 22nd Anniv.

World Handicrafts Day A641

**1985, June 10** ***Perf. 13½***
**2186** A641 20r Plates, flasks .45 .25

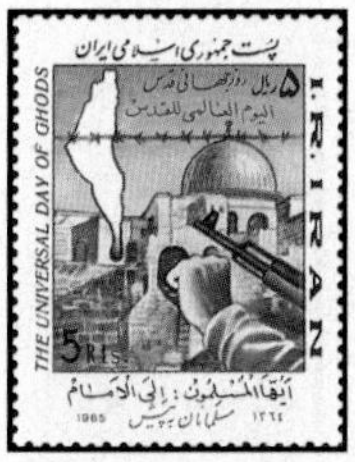

Day of Jerusalem A642

**1985, June 14**
**2187** A642 5r multicolored .25 .25

Id Al-fitr Feast — A643

Founding of the Islamic Propagation Org. — A644

**1985, June 20** ***Perf. 13x13½***
**2188** A643 5r multicolored .25 .25

**1985, June 22**
**2189** A644 5r tan & emerald .25 .25

Ayatollah Sheikh Abdolhossein Amini — A645

**1985, July 3** **Photo.** ***Perf. 13***
**2190** A645 5r multicolored .25 .25

Pilgrimage to Mecca — A646

**1985, July 20** **Photo.** ***Perf. 13½***
**2191** A646 10r multicolored .30 .25

Cultural Heritage Preservation — A647

Ceramic plates from Nishabur: a, Swords. b, Farsi script. c, Peacock. d, Four leaves.

**1985, Aug. 20**
**2192** Block of 4 .60 .25
***a.-d.*** A647 5r, any single .25 .25

Goharshad Mosque Uprising, 50th Anniv. — A648

**1985, Aug. 21** ***Perf. 13x13½***
**2193** A648 10r multicolored .25 .25

Week of Government A649

Bleeding Tulips A650

Designs: a, Industry and communications. b, Industry and agriculture. c, Health care, red crescent. d, Education.

**1985, Aug. 30** **Photo.** ***Perf. 13x13½***
**2194** Block of 4 .60 .25
***a.-d.*** A649 5r, any single .25 .25

**1985, Sept. 8**
**2195** A650 10r multicolored .30 .25

17th Shahrivar, Bloody Friday memorial.

OPEC, 25th Anniv. — A651

Design: No. 2196b, OPEC emblem and 25.

**1985, Sept. 14** ***Perf. 13½***
**2196** Pair .50 .25
***a.-b.*** A651 5r, any single .25 .25

Iran-Iraq War, 5th Anniv. — A652

Designs: a, Dead militiaman. b, Mosque and Ashura in Persian. c, Rockets descending on doves. d, Palm grove, rifle shot exploding rocket.

**1985, Sept. 22**
**2197** Block of 4 .60 .25
***a.-d.*** A652 5r any single .25 .25

Ashura mourning.

Ash-Sharif Ar-Radi — A653

**1985, Sept. 26** **Photo.** ***Perf. 13x13½***
**2198** A653 20r brt bl, lt bl & gold .60 .25

Ash-Sharif Ar-Radi, writer, death millennium.

UPU Day A654

**1985, Oct. 9** ***Perf. 13½***
**2199** A654 20r multicolored .60 .25

World Standards Day A655

**1985, Oct. 14**
**2200** A655 20r Natl. Standards Office emblem .60 .25

Agricultural Training and Development Year — A656

**1985, Oct. 19** ***Perf. 13x13½***
**2201** A656 5r Hand, wheat .25 .25

Takeover of US Embassy, 6th Anniv. — A657

**1985, Nov. 4** ***Perf. 13***
**2202** A657 40r multicolored .60 .40

Moslem Unity Week A658

High Council of the Cultural Revolution A659

**1985, Nov. 25** ***Perf. 13x13½***
**2203** A658 10r Holy Ka'aba .30 .25

Birth of prophet Mohammad, 1015th anniv.

**1985, Dec. 10**
**2204** A659 5r Roses .25 .25

Intl. Youth Year — A660

Designs: a, Education. b, Defense. c, Construction. d, Sports.

**1985, Dec. 18** **Photo.** ***Perf. 13x13½***
**2205** Block of 4 .60 .25
***a.-d.*** A660 5r, any single .25 .25

Ezzeddin al-Qassam, 50th Death Anniv. — A661

**1985, Dec. 20** ***Perf. 13½***
**2206** A661 20r sil, sep & hn brn .60 .25

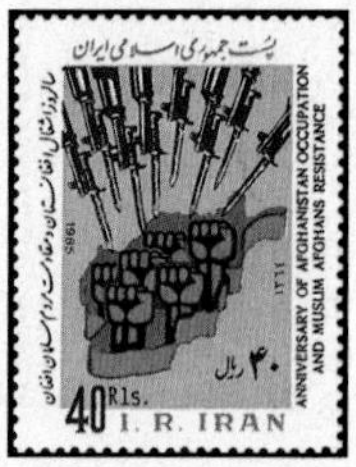

Map, Fists, Bayonets A662

**1985, Dec. 25** **Wmk. 381**
**2207** A662 40r multi 1.25 .40

Occupation of Afghanistan and Moslem resistance, 6th anniv.

Mirza Taqi Khan Amir Kabir (d. 1851) — A663

**1986, Jan. 8 Litho. *Perf. 13***
2208 A663 5r multicolored 1.25 .25

Students Destroying Statue of the Shah, Tulips — A664

**1986, Feb. 11 Photo. *Perf. 13½***
2209 A664 20r multicolored .60 .25

Iranian Revolution, 7th anniv.
See No. 2310l for 24x36mm stamp with yellow Arabic script.

Sulayman Khater, 40th Death Anniv. — A665

**1986, Feb. 15 *Perf. 13***
2210 A665 10r multicolored .30 .25

Women's Day — A666

**1986, Mar. 3 *Perf. 13½***
2211 A666 10r multicolored .30 .25

Birth anniv. of Mohammad's daughter, Fatima.

Flowers — A667

a, Papaver orientale. b, Anemone coronaria. c, Papaver bracteatum. d, Anemone biflora.

**1986, Mar. 11 Photo. *Perf. 13½***
2212 Block of 4 .60 .25
*a.* A667 5r any single .25 .25

Novrooz (New Year).

2000th Day of Sacred Defense A668

Intl. Day Against Racial Discrimination A669

**1986, Mar. 14 Photo. *Perf. 13x13½***
2213 A668 5r scarlet & grn .25 .25

**1986, Mar. 21**
2214 A669 5r multicolored .25 .25

Islamic Republic of Iran, 7th Anniv. — A670

**1986, Apr. 1 *Perf. 13***
2215 A670 10r Flag, map .30 .25

Mab'as Festival A671

**1986, Apr. 7**
2216 A671 40r multicolored .60 .25

Army Day — A672

**1986, Apr. 18 *Perf. 13½***
2217 A672 5r multicolored .25 .25

Day of the Oppressed — A673

**1986, Apr. 25 *Perf. 13x13½***
2218 A673 10r blk, gold & dk red .25 .25

Helicopter Crash — A674

Teacher's Day — A675

**1986, Apr. 25 Wmk. 381**
2219 A674 40r multicolored 1.25 .40

US air landing at Tabass Air Base, 6th anniv.

**1986, May 2 Photo. *Perf. 13x13½***
2220 A675 5r multicolored .25 .25

World Telecommunications Day — A676

**1986, May 17 *Perf. 13½x13***
2221 A676 20r blk, sil & ultra .60 .25

Universal Day of the Child — A677

**1986, June 1 *Perf. 13***
2222 A677 15r Child's war drawing .45 .25
2223 A677 15r Hosein Fahmide, Iran-Iraq war hero .45 .25
*a.* Pair, #2222-2223 .90 .30

1963 Uprising, 23rd Anniv. — A678

**1986, June 5 *Perf. 13x13½***
2224 A678 10r Qum Theological Seminary .30 .25

Day of Jerusalem — A679

**1986, June 6**
2225 A679 10r multicolored .30 .25

Id Al-Fitr Feast A680

**1986, June 9 *Perf. 13***
2226 A680 10r Moslems praying .75 .25

World Handicrafts Day A681

a, Baluchi cross-hatched rug. b, Craftsman. c, Qalamkar flower rug. d, Copper repousse vase.

**1986, June 10 *Perf. 13½***
2227 Block of 4 1.25 .40
*a.-d.* A681 10r, any single .30 .25

Intl. Day for Solidarity with Black So. Africans — A682

**1986, June 26**
2228 A682 10r multicolored .30 .25

Ayatollah Beheshti — A683

**1986, June 28 *Perf. 13x13½***
2229 A683 10r multicolored .30 .25

Death of Beheshti and Islamic Party workers, Tehran headquarters bombing, 5th anniv.

Ayatollah Mohammad Taqi Shirazi, Map of Iraq — A684

**1986, June 30 Photo. Wmk. 381**
2230 A684 20r multicolored .60 .25

Iraqi Moslem uprising against the British.

Shrine of Imam Reza — A685

**1986, July 19 *Perf. 13½***
2231 A685 10r multicolored .30 .25

Eid Ul-Adha, Feast of Sacrifice — A686

**1986, Aug. 17** ***Perf. 13x13½***

**2232** A686 10r multicolored .30 .25

Cultural Heritage Preservation — A687

Designs: No. 2233, Bam Fortress. No. 2234, Kabud (Blue) Mosque, Tabriz. No. 2235, Mausoleum of Sohel Ben Ali at Astenah, Arak. No. 2236, Soltanieh Mosque, Zendjan Province.

**1986, Aug. 20**

| | | | | | |
|---|---|---|---|---|---|
| **2233** | A687 | 5r Hilltop | | .25 | .25 |
| **2234** | A687 | 5r shown | | .25 | .25 |
| **2235** | A687 | 5r Intact roof | | .25 | .25 |
| **2236** | A687 | 5r Damaged roof | | .25 | .25 |
| | | *Nos. 2233-2236 (4)* | | 1.00 | 1.00 |

Eid Ul-Ghadir Feast — A688

**1986, Aug. 25**

**2237** A688 20r multicolored .60 .25

Population and Housing Census — A689

**1986, Sept. 9** ***Perf. 13½x13***

**2238** A689 20r multicolored .40 .25

Iran-Iraq War, 6th Year — A690

**1986, Sept. 22** ***Perf. 13***

| | | | | |
|---|---|---|---|---|
| **2239** | A690 | 10r Battleship Paykan | .30 | .25 |
| **2240** | A690 | 10r Susangerd | .30 | .25 |
| **2241** | A690 | 10r Khorramshahr | .30 | .25 |
| **2242** | A690 | 10r Howeizeh | .30 | .25 |
| **2243** | A690 | 10r Siege of Abadan | .30 | .25 |
| | | *Nos. 2239-2243 (5)* | 1.50 | 1.25 |

10th Asian Games, Seoul A691

**1986, Oct. 2** **Photo.** **Wmk. 381**

| | | | | |
|---|---|---|---|---|
| **2244** | A691 | 15r Wrestling | .40 | .25 |
| **2245** | A691 | 15r Rifle shooting | .40 | .25 |

World Post Day A692

**1986, Oct. 9**

**2246** A692 20r multicolored .60 .25

UNESCO, 40th Anniv. — A693

**1986, Nov. 4** **Photo.** ***Perf. 13x13½***

**2247** A693 45r blk, sky bl & brt rose 1.25 .45

Ayatollah Tabatabaie (d. 1981) — A694

**1986, Nov. 15** **Photo.** ***Perf. 13½x13***

**2248** A694 10r multicolored .30 .25

Unity Week — A695

**1986, Nov. 20**

**2249** A695 10r multicolored .30 .25

Birth anniv. of Mohammad.

People's Militia — A696

**1986, Nov. 26** ***Perf. 13***

**2250** A696 5r multicolored .25 .25

Mobilization of the Oppressed Week.

Afghan Resistance Movement, 7th Anniv. — A697

**1986, Dec. 27**

**2251** A697 40r multicolored 1.25 .40

Nurses' Day — A698

**1987, Jan. 12** **Photo.** ***Perf. 13***

**2252** A698 20r multicolored .60 .25

Hazrat Zainab birth anniv.

Fifth Islamic Theology Conference, Tehran — A699

**Wmk. 381**

**1987, Jan. 29** **Photo.** ***Perf. 13***

**2253** A699 20r multicolored .60 .25

Islamic Revolution, 8th Anniv. — A700

**1987, Feb. 11**

**2254** A700 20r multicolored .60 .25

See No. 2310m for 24x36mm stamp.

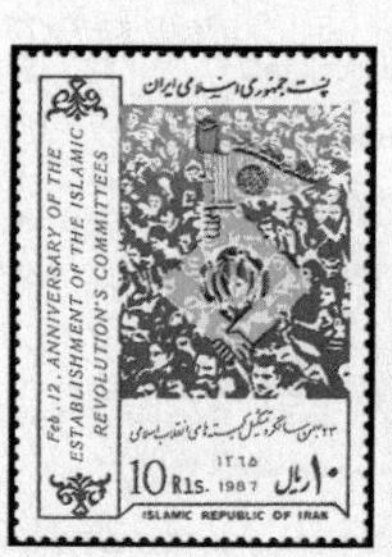


Islamic Revolutionary Committees, 8th Anniv. — A701

**1987, Feb. 12**

**2255** A701 10r brt bl, scar & yel .30 .25

Women's Day — A702

**1987, Feb. 19**

**2256** A702 10r multicolored .30 .25

Birthday of Fatima, daughter of Mohammad.

Iran Air, 25th Anniv. A703

**1987, Feb. 24**

**2257** A703 30r multicolored .90 .30

Ayatollah Mirza Mohammad Hossein Naeini, 50th Death Anniv. — A704

**1987, Mar. 6** **Photo.** ***Perf. 13***

**2258** A704 10r multicolored .30 .25

New Year — A705

Flowers: a, Iris persica. b, Rosa damascena. c, Iris paradoxa. d, Tulipa clusiana.

**1987, Mar. 11** ***Perf. 13½x13***

| | | | |
|---|---|---|---|
| **2259** | Block of 4 | 2.00 | .50 |
| ***a.-d.*** | A705 5r, any single | .50 | .25 |

See Nos. 2313, 2361, 2411, 2443.

Mab'as Festival A706

**1987, Mar. 28** ***Perf. 13***

**2260** A706 45r gold, dk grn & grn 1.40 .45

Universal Day of the Oppressed
A707

**1987, Apr. 14**
**2261** A707 20r multicolored .60 .25

Savior Mahdi's birthday.

Memorial to Lebanese Hizbollah Martyrs — A708

**1987, Apr. 5**
**2262** A708 10r grn, gray & brt car .30 .25

Revolutionary Guards Day — A709

**1987, Apr. 2**
**2263** A709 5r multi .25 .25

Imam Hossein's birthday.

8th Anniv. of Islamic Republic
A710

**1987, Apr. 1**
**2264** A710 20r multicolored .60 .25

World Health Day — A711

Child survival through immunization: 3r, Intravenous. 5r, Oral.

**1987, Apr. 7** ***Perf. 13x13½***
**2265** A711 3r multicolored .25 .25
**2266** A711 5r multicolored .30 .25
*a.* Pair, #2265-2266 .50 .25

Int'l. Labor Day — A712

**1987, May 1** **Photo.** ***Perf. 13***
**2267** A712 5r multicolored .25 .25

Teachers' Day — A713

**1987, May 2** **Wmk. 381**
**2268** A713 5r Ayatollah Mottahari .25 .25

A714

**1987, May 17** ***Perf. 13½x13***
**2269** A714 20r multicolored .70 .25

World Telecommunications Day.

A715

**1987, May 18** ***Perf. 13***
**2270** A715 20r Sassanian silver gilt vase .60 .25
**2271** A715 20r Bisque pot, Rey, 12th cent. .60 .25

Intl. Museum Day.

Universal Day of Jerusalem — A716

**1987, May 22** ***Perf. 13½x13***
**2272** A716 20r multicolored .60 .25

World Crafts Day
A717

a, Blown glass tea service. b, Stained glass window. c, Ceramic plate. d, Potter.

**1987, June 10** ***Perf. 13x13½***
**2273** Block of 4 .75 .25
*a.-d.* A717 5r any single .25 .25

1963 Uprising, 24th Anniv. — A718

**1987, June 5** **Photo.** ***Perf. 13½***
**2274** A718 20r multicolored .60 .25

Tax Reform Week — A719

**1987, July 10** ***Perf. 13***
**2275** A719 10r black, sil & gold .30 .25

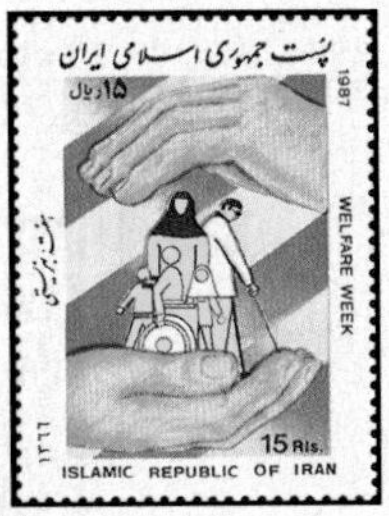


Welfare Week — A720

**1987, July 17**
**2276** A720 15r multicolored .45 .25

Eid Ul-adha, Feast of Sacrifice — A721

**1987, Aug. 6**
**2277** A721 12r sil, blk & Prus grn .45 .25

Eid Ul-Ghadir Festival
A722

**1987, Aug. 14**
**2278** A722 18r black, green & gold .55 .25

Banking Week — A723

**1987, Aug. 17** ***Perf. 13½x13***
**2279** A723 15r red brn, gold & pale grnsh bl .45 .25

1st Cultural and Artistic Congress of Iranian Calligraphers
A724

**1987, Aug. 21** **Photo.** ***Perf. 13x13½***
**2280** A724 20r multicolored .60 .25

Memorial to Iranian Pilgrims Killed in Mecca — A725

**1987, Aug. 26** **Wmk. 381** ***Perf. 13***
**2281** A725 8r multicolored .30 .25

Assoc. of Iranian Dentists, 25th Anniv. — A726

**1987, Aug. 27** **Photo.** ***Perf. 13½x13***
**2282** A726 10r multicolored .30 .25

Intl. Peace Day — A727

**1987, Sept. 1** ***Perf. 13***
**2283** A727 20r gold & lt ultra .60 .25

Iran-Iraq War, 7th Anniv. — A728

Police Day — A729

**1987, Sept. 22** ***Perf. 13½x13***
**2284** A728 25r shown .75 .25
**2285** A728 25r Soldier, battle scene .75 .25
*a.* Pair, #2284-2285

**1987, Sept. 28**
**2286** A729 10r multicolored .30 .25

Intl. Social Security Week, Oct. 4-10 — A730

**1987, Oct. 4** **Wmk. 381**
**2287** A730 15r blk, gold & brt blue .45 .25

World Post Day — A731

UPU emblem and: No. 2288, M. Ghandi, minister of the Post and Telecommunications Bureau. No. 2289, Globe, dove.

**1987, Oct. 9** ***Perf. 13x13½***
**2288** A731 15r multicolored .45 .25
**2289** A731 15r multicolored .45 .25

Importation Prohibited
Importation of stamps was prohibited effective Oct. 29, 1987.

A732

**Wmk. 381**
**1987, Nov. 4** **Photo.** ***Perf. 13***
**2290** A732 40r multicolored 1.25 .25

Takeover of US Embassy, 8th anniv.

A733

**1987, Nov. 5**
**2291** A733 20r multicolored .90 .25

1st Intl. Tehran Book Fair.

Mohammad's Birthday, Unity Week — A734

**1987, Nov. 10**
**2292** A734 25r multicolored .60 .25

Ayatollah Modarres Martyrdom, 50th Anniv. — A735

**1987, Dec. 1**
**2293** A735 10r brn & bister .40 .25

Agricultural Training and Extension Week — A736

**1987, Dec. 6**
**2294** A736 10r multicolored .50 .25

Afghan Resistance, 8th Anniv. — A737

**1987, Dec. 27**
**2295** A737 40r multicolored 1.25 .40

Main Mosques A738

**1987-92** ***Perf. 13x13½, 13½x13***
**Silver Background**

| | | | | |
|---|---|---|---|---|
| **2295A** | A738 | 1r Shoushtar | .50 | .25 |
| **2296** | A738 | 2r Ouroumieh | .50 | .25 |
| **2296A** | A738 | 3r Kerman | .50 | .25 |
| **2297** | A738 | 5r Kazvin | .50 | .30 |
| **2298** | A738 | 10r Varamin | .50 | .30 |
| *a.* | | Unwatermarked ('91) | 3.00 | 2.00 |
| **2299** | A738 | 20r Saveh | .75 | .75 |
| *a.* | | Unwatermarked ('91) | 2.00 | 1.25 |
| **2300** | A738 | 30r Natanz, vert. | 1.50 | 1.40 |
| **2301** | A738 | 40r Shiraz | 2.00 | 1.75 |
| *a.* | | Unwatermarked ('92) | 10.00 | 5.00 |
| **2302** | A738 | 50r Isfahan, vert. | 1.50 | 1.25 |
| *a.* | | Unwatermarked ('91) | 3.00 | 2.00 |
| **2303** | A738 | 100r Hamadan | 2.00 | 2.00 |
| *a.* | | Unwatermarked ('91) | 5.00 | 3.00 |
| **2304** | A738 | 200r Dezfoul, vert. | 4.00 | 3.50 |
| *a.* | | Unwatermarked ('91) | 15.00 | 5.00 |
| **2305** | A738 | 500r Yazd, vert. | 13.00 | 10.00 |
| *a.* | | Unwatermarked ('91) | 20.00 | 15.00 |
| | | *Nos. 2295A-2305 (12)* | 27.25 | 22.00 |
| | | Nos. 2298a-2305a (7) | 18.00 | 18.00 |

Issued: 10r, 12/1; 5r, 12/30; 500r, 1/10/88; 20r, 1/14/88; 2r, 1/24/88; 50r, 1/24/89; 100r, 10/21/89; 200r, 10/28/89; 30r, 40r, 3/17/90; 1r, 3r, 3/92.

For surcharges see #2750-2751.

Watermarks on this issue can be difficult to discern. The paper of the unwatermarked stamps show fluoresence under long wave ultraviolet light.

Qum Uprising, 10th Anniversary — A739

**1988, Jan. 9** ***Perf. 13***
**2306** A739 20r multicolored .50 .25

Bombing of Schools by Iraq — A740

**1988, Feb. 1** ***Perf. 13x13½***
**2307** A740 10r multicolored .80 .25

Gholamreza Takhti, World Wrestling Champion — A741

**1988, Feb. 4** ***Perf. 13½***
**2308** A741 15r multicolored .50 .50

Women's Day — A742

**1988, Feb. 9** ***Perf. 13***
**2309** A742 20r multicolored .40 .25

Birth anniv. of Mohammad's daughter, Fatima.

**Types of 1979-88 and**
Souvenir Sheet

Islamic Revolution, 9th Anniv. — A743

**1988, Feb. 11** **Wmk. 381** ***Perf. 13***
**2310** Sheet of 16 7.00
*a.* A547 1r like #2046
*b.* A547 3r like #2047
*c.* A559 3r like #2066
*d.* A547 5r like #2048
*e.* A559 5r like #2067
*f.* A570 5r like #2095
*g.* A570 10r like #2096
*h.* A608 10r like #2146
*i.* A537 18r like #1999
*j.* A559 20r like #2068
*k.* A570 20r like #2097
*l.* A664 20r like #2209
*m.* A700 20r like #2254
*n.* A587 30r like #2115
*o.* A631 40r like #2172
*p.* A743 40r shown

Nos. 2310a, 2310b, 2310d, 2310l, 2310m are smaller than the original issues. See original issues for distinguishing features on other stamps.

Exists imperf. Value $14.

Tabriz Uprising, 10th Anniv. — A744

**1988, Feb. 18** ***Perf. 13***
**2311** A744 25r multicolored .50 .40

Arbor Day — A745

**1988, Mar. 5**
**2312** A745 15r multicolored .70 .25

**New Year Festival Type of 1987**

Flowers: a, Anthemis hyalina. b, Malva silvestria. c, Viola odorata. d, Echium amaenum.

**1988, Mar. 10** ***Perf. 13½x13***
**2313** Block of 4
*a.-d.* A705 10r any single 2.00 2.00

Islamic Republic, 9th Anniv. — A746

**1988, Apr. 1** ***Perf. 13***
**2314** A746 20r multicolored .40 .25

Universal Day of the Oppressed A747

**1988, Apr. 3**
**2314A** A747 20r multicolored .30 .25

Savior Mahdi's Birthday.

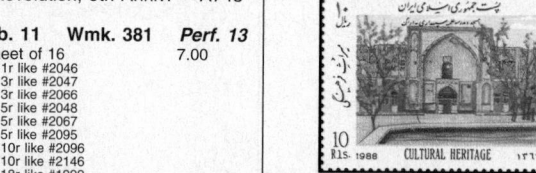

Cultural Heritage — A748

**1988, Apr. 18**

**2315** A748 10r Mosque .50 .40
**2316** A748 10r Courtyard .50 .40
*a.* Pair, #2315-2316 1.50 1.00
**2317** A748 10r Minarets, vert. .50 .40
**2318** A748 10r Corridor, vert. .50 .40
*a.* Pair, #2317-2318 1.50 1.00

Chemical Bombardment of Halabja, Iraq — A749

**1988, Apr. 26**

**2319** A749 20r multicolored .90 .40

A750

A750a

Palestinian Uprising A750b

**1988, May 13**

**2320** Strip of 5 2.50 1.75
*a.* A750 10r multi
*b.* A750a 10r multi
*c.* A750b 10r multi
*d.* A750b 10r multi, diff.
*e.* A750b 10r Rock in hand, rioters

World Telecommunications Day — A751

**1988, May 17** *Perf. 13x13½*

**2321** A751 20r green & blue .80 .30

Intl. Museum Day — A752

Designs: a, Ceramic vase, 1982. b, Bastan Museum, entranceway. c, Tabriz silk rug, 14th cent. d, Gold ring, 7th cent. B.C.

**1988, May 18** *Perf. 13*

**2322** Block of 4 1.50 1.50
*a.-d.* A752 10r any single .30 .25

Mining Day — A753

**1988, May 22** **Photo.** **Wmk. 381**

**2323** A753 20r multicolored 1.25 .50

Intl. Day of the Child — A754

**1988, June 1**

**2324** A754 10r multicolored .50 .30

June 5th Uprising, 25th Anniv. — A755

**1988, June 5**

**2325** A755 10r multicolored .40 .40

World Crafts Day A756

**1988, June 10** *Perf. 13x13½*

**2326** A756 10r Straw basket .30 .25
**2327** A756 10r Weaver .30 .25
*a.* Pair, #2326-2327 .80 .60
**2328** A756 10r Tapestry, vert. .30 .25
**2329** A756 10r Miniature, vert. .30 .25
*a.* Pair, #2328-2329 .80 .60

Child Health Campaign A757

**1988, July 6** *Perf. 13*

**2330** A757 20r blk, blue & green .40 .25

Tax Reform Week — A758

**1988, July 10**

**2331** A758 20r multicolored .40 .25

A759

**1988, July 15** *Perf. 13½x13*

**2332** A759 20r Allameh Balkhi .40 .25

A760

**1988, July 21** *Perf. 13*

**2333** A760 10r Holy Ka'aba, dove, stars .25 .25
**2334** A760 10r shown .25 .25

Massacre of Muslim Pilgrims at Mecca.

Nos. 2333-2334 were printed together in one sheet, with alternating placement.

Destruction of Iranian Airliner — A761

**1988, Aug. 11**

**2335** A761 45r multicolored 1.25 1.00

A762

**1988, Aug. 13**

**2336** A762 20r Seyyed Ali Andarzgou .50 .25

A763

**1988, Sept. 1** *Perf. 13½x13*

**2337** A763 20r multicolored .50 .25

Islamic Banking Week.

Divine Day of 17 Shahrivar, 10th Anniv. — A764

**1988, Sept. 8**

**2338** A764 25r multicolored .70 .25

1988 Summer Olympics, Seoul — A765

Designs: a, Weightlifting. b, Pommel horse. c, Judo. d, Soccer. e, Wrestling.

**1988, Sept. 10**

**2339** Strip of 5 2.00 1.50
*a.-e.* A765 10r any single .35 .25

A766

A767

**1988, Sept. 17** *Perf. 13½x13*

**2340** A766 30r blk, grn & yel .60 .25

Agricultural census.

**1988, Sept. 22** *Perf. 13x13½*

**2341** A767 20r multicolored .50 .25

Iran-Iraq War, 8th anniv.

World Post Day A768

**1988, Oct. 9** ***Perf. 13***
**2342** A768 20r blk, ultra & grn .80 .30

Parents and Teachers Cooperation Week — A769

**1988, Oct. 16**
**2343** A769 20r multicolored .70 .25

Mohammad's Birthday, Unity Week — A770

**1988, Oct. 29**
**2344** A770 10r multicolored .50 .30

A771

**1988, Nov. 4**
**2345** A771 45r multicolored 1.10 .50

Takeover of US embassy, 9th anniv.

A772

**1988, Nov. 6** ***Perf. 13½x13***
**2346** A772 10r multicolored .80 .30

Insurance Day.

Intl. Congress on the Writings of Hafiz — A773

**1988, Nov. 19** ***Perf. 13x13½***
**2347** A773 20r blue, gold & pink .50 .30

Agricultural Training and Extension Week — A774

**1988, Dec. 6** ***Perf. 13***
**2348** A774 15r multicolored .60 .30

Scientists, Artists and Writers A775

**1988, Dec. 18** ***Perf. 13x13½***
**2349** A775 10r Parvin E'Tessami .35 .35
**2350** A775 10r Jalal Al-Ahmad .35 .35
**2351** A775 10r Muhammad Mo'in .35 .35
*a.* Pair, #2350-2351 .80 .35
**2352** A775 10r Qaem Maqam Farahani .35 .35
**2353** A775 10r Kamal Al-Molk .35 .35
*a.* Pair, #2352-2353 .80 .75

See Nos. 2398-2402.

Afghan Resistance, 9th Anniv. — A776

**1988, Dec. 27** ***Perf. 13***
**2354** A776 40r multicolored .45 .40

Transportation and Communication Decade — A777

***Perf. 13x13½***
**1989, Jan. 16** **Wmk. 381**
**2355** A777 20r Satellite, envelopes, microwave dish .70 .70
**2356** A777 20r Cargo planes .70 .70
*a.* Pair, #2355-2356 1.90 1.75
**2357** A777 20r Train, trucks .70 .70
**2358** A777 20r Ships .70 .70
*a.* Pair, #2357-2358 1.90 1.75

Prophethood of Mohammad A778

**1989, Mar. 6** ***Perf. 13***
**2359** A778 20r multicolored .50 .40

Mab'as festival.

Arbor Day — A779

**1989, Mar. 6**
**2360** A779 20r multicolored .70 .40

### New Year Festival Type of 1987

Flowers: a, Cephalanthera kurdica. b, Dactylorhiza romana. c, Comperia comperiana. d, Orchis mascula.

**1989, Mar. 11** ***Perf. 13½x13***
**2361** Block of 4 1.25 1.25
*a.-d.* A705 10r any single .25 .25

A780

**1989, Mar. 23**
**2362** A780 20r shown .60 .60
**2363** A780 30r Meteorological devices, ship .60 .60
*a.* Pair, #2362-2363 1.50 1.25

World Meteorology Day.

A781

**1989, Apr. 1** ***Perf. 13***
**2364** A781 20r multicolored .40 .40

Islamic Republic, 10th anniv.

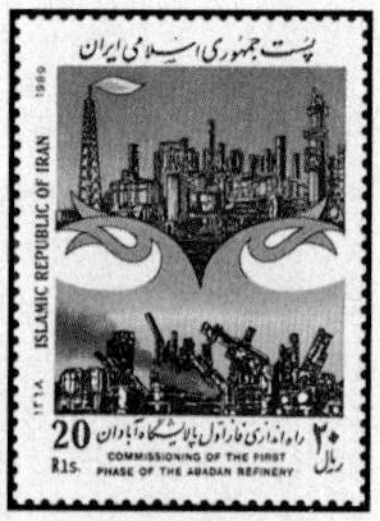


Reconstruction of Abadan Refinery A782

**1989, Apr. 1**
**2365** A782 20r multicolored .70 .30

Ayatollah Morteza Motahhari, 10th Death Anniv. — A783

**1989, May 2**
**2366** A783 20r multi .40 .30

Teachers' Day.

A784

**1989, May 5**
**2367** A784 30r multicolored .75 .30

Universal Day of Jerusalem.

A785

**1989, May 17** ***Perf. 13½x13***
**2368** A785 20r multicolored .70 .30

World Telecommunications Day.

A786

Intl. Museum Day: Gurgan pottery, 6th cent.

**1989, May 18** ***Perf. 13x13½***
**2369** A786 20r Jar .50 .50
**2370** A786 20r Bottle .50 .50
*a.* Pair, #2369-2370 1.25 1.10

A787

**1989, June 4** ***Perf. 13***
**2371** A787 20r multicolored .40 .25

Nomads' Day.

World Crafts Day A788

**1989, July 5** ***Perf. 13x13½***
**2372** A788 20r Engraver .40 .40
**2373** A788 20r Copper vase .40 .40
*a.* Pair, #2372-2373 1.10 1.00
**2374** A788 20r Copper plate, vert. .40 .40
**2375** A788 20r Copper wall hanging, vert. .40 .40
*a.* Pair, #2374-2375 1.10 1.00

Ayatollah Khomeini (1900-89) A789

**1989, July 6** *Perf. 13*
**2376** A789 20r multicolored .50 .30

Pasteur and Avicenna A790

**1989, July 7**
**2377** A790 30r multicolored .70 .70
**2378** A790 50r multicolored 1.00 1.00
*a.* Pair, #2377-2378 1.75 1.75

PHILEXFRANCE.

Asia-Pacific Telecommunity, 10th Anniv. — A791

**1989, July 25**
**2379** A791 30r blk, org brn & bl .80 .40

Mehdi Araghi, 10th Death Anniv. — A792

**1989, Aug. 30**
**2380** A792 20r brn org & org brn .40 .25

M.H. Shahryar, Poet — A793

**1989, Sept. 17**
**2381** A793 20r multicolored .50 .25

Iran-Iraq War, 9th Anniv. — A794

**1989, Sept. 22**
**2382** A794 20r UN Security Council res. 598 .60 .60

Ayatollah Khomeini — A795

Designs: 1r, Khomeini's birthplace, flower. 2r, Portrait as youth. 3r, Giving speech. 5r, Map, rifles, exile. 10r, Khomeini returns to Iran, Feb. 1, 1979. 20r, Khomeini seated before microphone. 30r, Khomeini with grandson.40r, Other mullahs. 50r, Khomeini gesturing with hands. 70r, On balcony before crowd. 100r, Slogan. 200r, Empty lectern. 500r, Mausoleum. 1000r, Sun rays.

**1989-92 Litho. Unwmk.** *Perf. 13½*
**2382A** A795 1r green & multi .25 .25
**2382B** A795 2r green & multi .25 .25
**2383** A795 3r green & multi .25 .25
**2384** A795 5r brt vio & multi .25 .25
**2385** A795 10r brt bl & multi .35 .25
**2386** A795 20r blue & multi .30 .25
**2387** A795 30r pink & multi .35 .25
**2388** A795 40r red & multi .35 .30
**2389** A795 50r gray & multi .40 .30
**2390** A795 70r brt grn & multi .55 .35
**2391** A795 100r ultra & multi .75 .45
**2392** A795 200r red brn & multi 1.50 .75
**2393** A795 500r black & multi 3.50 1.75
**2393A** A795 1000r multi 7.50 3.50
*Nos. 2382A-2393A (14)* 16.55 9.15

Issued: 1r, 1/3/91; 3r, 3/16/90; 5r, 12/13; 10r, 10/22; 20r, 30r, 50r, 9/23/90; 40r, 2/9/90; 100, 200r, 9/26/90; 70r, 500r, 6/4/91; 2r, 1000r, 3/16/92.

World Post Day A796

**Wmk. 381**
**1989, Oct. 9 Photo.** *Perf. 13*
**2394** A796 20r multicolored .85 .50

Mohammad's Birthday, Unity Week — A797

**1989, Oct. 18**
**2395** A797 10r multi .80 .50

Takeover of US Embassy, 10th Anniv. — A798

**1989, Nov. 4** *Perf. 13½x13*
**2396** A798 40r multicolored .40 .30

Bassij of the Oppressed (Militia), 10th Anniv. — A799

**1989, Nov. 27** *Perf. 13*
**2397** A799 10r multicolored .40 .30

### Scientists, Artists and Writers Type of 1988

**1989, Dec. 18** *Perf. 13x13½*
**2398** A775 10r Mehdi Elahi Ghomshei .30 .30
**2399** A775 10r Dr. Abdulazim Gharib .30 .30
**2400** A775 10r Seyyed Hossein Mirkhani .30 .30
*a.* Pair, #2399-2400 .80 .75
**2401** A775 10r Ayatollah Seyyed Hossein Boroujerdi .30 .30
**2402** A775 10r Ayatollah Sheikh Abdulkarim Haeri .30 .30
*a.* Pair, #2401-2402 .80 .75

Intl. Literacy Year — A800

**Wmk. 381**
**1990, Jan. 1 Photo.** *Perf. 13½*
**2403** A800 20r multicolored .70 .40

Cultural Heritage A801

Designs: No. 2404, Drinking vessel, 1980. No. 2405, Footed vase, 1979.

**1990, Jan. 21** *Perf. 13*
**2404** A801 20r blk & deep org .50 .30
**2405** A801 20r blk & yel grn .50 .30
*a.* Pair, #2404-2405 1.25 1.00

New Identification Card System — A802

**1990, Feb. 9**
**2406** A802 10r multicolored .25 .25

Islamic Revolution, 11th Anniv. — A803

**1990, Feb. 11**
**2407** A803 50r multicolored 1.00 .40

Intl. Koran Recitation Competition A804

**1990, Feb. 23**
**2408** A804 10r blk, bl & grn .70 .40

A805

**1990, Mar. 2** *Perf. 13½x13*
**2409** A805 10r multicolored .70 .40

Invalids of Islamic Revolution.

A806

**1990, Mar. 6** *Perf. 13*
**2410** A806 20r multicolored .40 .30

Arbor Day.

### New Year Festival Type of 1987

Flowers: a, Coronilla varia. b, Astragalus cornu-caprae. c, Astragalus obtusifolius. d, Astragalus straussii.

**1990, Mar. 11** *Perf. 13½x13*
**2411** Block of 4 1.00 .80
*a.-d.* A705 10r any single .25 .25

Islamic Republic, 11th Anniv. — A807

**1990, Apr. 1** *Perf. 13*

**2412** A807 30r multicolored .70 .60

World Health Day — A808

**1990, Apr. 7**

**2413** A808 40r multicolored .90 .50

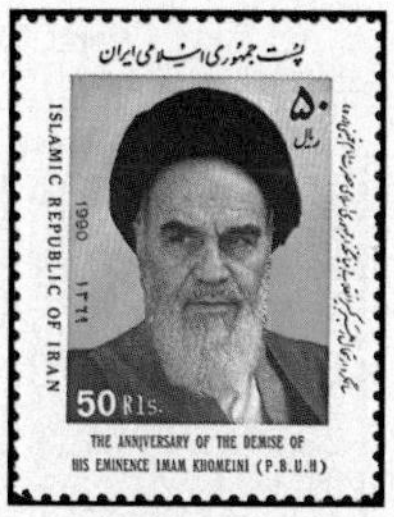


A809

**1990, June 4 Unwmk.** *Perf. 11x10½*

**2414** A809 50r multicolored .70 .50

Ayatollah Khomeini, 1st death anniv.

A810

**1990, Dec. 15 Litho.** *Perf. 10½*

**2415** A810 100r multicolored 2.00 .60

Jerusalem Day.

A811

**1990, Oct. 20** *Perf. 13*

**2416** A811 20r Turkoman jewelry .40 .40

**2417** A811 50r Gilded steel bird 1.00 1.00

*a.* Pair, #2416-2417 1.90 1.75

World Crafts Day.

A812

**1990, Nov. 17** *Perf. 10½*

**2418** A812 20r multicolored .60 .30

Intl. Day of the Child.

Aid to Earthquake Victims — A813

**1990, Nov. 19** *Perf. 13x13½*

**2419** A813 100r multicolored .45 .30

Return and Tribute to Former Prisoners of Iran-Iraq War — A814

**1990, Nov. 21** *Perf. 13*

**2420** A814 250r multicolored 3.00 .50

Ferdowsi Intl. Congress — A815

**1990, Dec. 22 Litho.** *Imperf.*

**Size: 60x75mm**

**2421** A815 100r Portrait 3.50 *4.00*

**2422** A815 100r Statue 3.50 *4.00*

**2423** A815 100r Monument 3.50 *4.00*

**2424** A815 100r Slogan, diamond cartouche 3.50 *4.00*

**2425** A815 100r Rectangular slogan 3.50 *4.00*

**2426** A815 100r Slogan, diff. 3.50 *4.00*

**2427** A815 200r Two riders embracing 5.50 *6.00*

**2428** A815 200r Archer, birds 5.50 *6.00*

**2429** A815 200r Six men 5.50 *6.00*

**2430** A815 200r White elephant 5.50 *6.00*

**2431** A815 200r Warrior, genie, horse 5.50 *6.00*

**2432** A815 200r Hunting scene 5.50 *6.00*

**2433** A815 200r Riding through fire 5.50 *6.00*

**2434** A815 200r Four slogan tablets 5.50 *6.00*

**2435** A815 200r Man with feet shackled 5.50 *6.00*

**2436** A815 200r Palace scene 5.50 *6.00*

*Nos. 2421-2436 (16)* 76.00 *84.00*

Conference on epic poem "Book of Kings" by Ferdowsi.

In 1991 some imperf between blocks of 4 were released. Value, set $250.

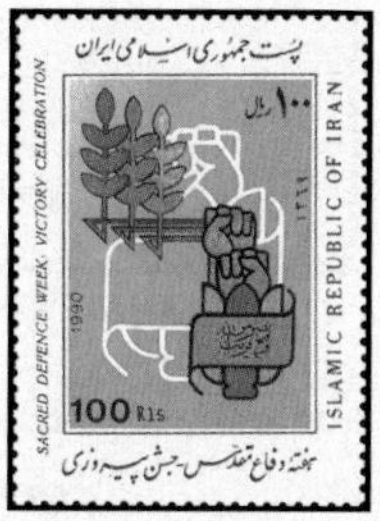


"Victory Over Iraq" — A816

**1991, Feb. 25** *Perf. 13*

**2437** A816 100r multicolored 1.25 .50

Intl. Museum Day — A817

Designs: No. 2438, Gold jug with Kufric inscription, 10th cent. A.D. No. 2439, Silver-inlaid brass basin, 14th cent. A.D.

**1991, Feb. 25**

**2438** A817 50r multicolored 1.10 .50

**2439** A817 50r multicolored 1.10 .50

*a.* Pair, #2438-2439 2.25 1.50

A818

**1991, Mar. 12** *Perf. 10½*

**2440** A818 50r multicolored 1.00 .50

World Telecommunications Day.

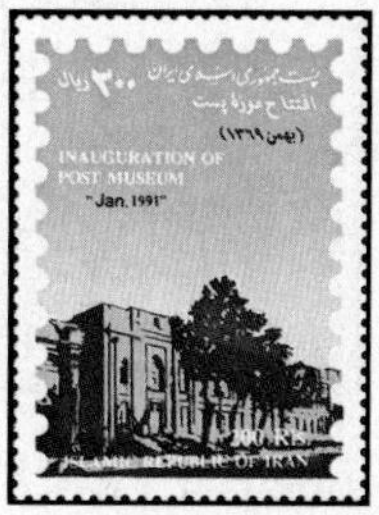


A819

**1991, Feb. 25** *Perf. 13*

**2441** A819 200r org brn & blk 3.00 2.00

Opening of Postal Museum.

Islamic Revolution, 12th Anniv. — A820

**1991, Feb. 11 Photo.** *Perf. 13*

**2442** A820 100r multicolored 2.50 1.00

**New Year Festival Type of 1987**

Designs: No. 2443a, Iris spuria. b, Iris lycotis. c, Iris demawendica. d, Iris meda.

**1991, Mar. 11** *Perf. 13½x13*

**2443** A705 20r Block of 4, #a.-d. 2.00 1.50

Saleh Hosseini, 10th Death Anniv. — A821

**1991, Mar. 19** *Perf. 13½x13*

**2444** A821 30r red & black .90 .50

Mab'as Festival A822

**1991, Mar. 19** *Perf. 13x13½*

**2445** A822 100r multicolored 1.50 .50

Universal Day of the Oppressed A823

**1991, Mar. 25** *Perf. 13*

**2446** A823 50r multicolored 1.00 .50

Savior Mahdi's Birthday.

Revolutionaries, 25th Death Anniv. — A824

**1990, June 16**
**2447** A824 50r maroon & red org .80 .50

Dated 1990.

Islamic Republic, 12th Anniv. — A825

**Unwmk.**

**1991, Apr. 1 Photo. *Perf. 13***
**2448** A825 20r blk, slate, grn & red .60 .50

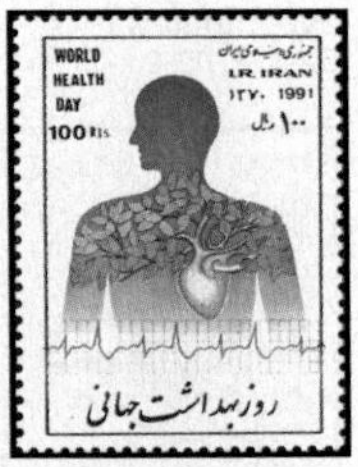

World Health Day — A826

**1991, Apr. 7 *Perf. 13½x13***
**2449** A826 100r multicolored 1.50 .50

Day of Jerusalem A827

**1991, Apr. 12 *Perf. 13***
**2450** A827 100r bl, blk & brn 1.60 .75

A828

A829

**1991, Apr. 12 Litho. *Perf. 10½***
**2451** A828 50r multicolored .80 .50

Women's Day. Birth anniv. of Mohammad's daughter, Fatima.

***Perf. 13½x13***

**1991, Apr. 28 Photo. Unwmk.**
**2452** A829 200r bl grn & blk 4.00 .50

Ayatollah Borujerdi, 30th death anniv.

Teachers' Day — A830

**1991, May 2 *Perf. 13x13½***
**2453** A830 50r multicolored 1.10 .50

Decade for Natural Disaster Reduction A831

**1991, May 11 Litho. *Perf. 10½***
**2454** A831 100r multicolored 1.75 .50

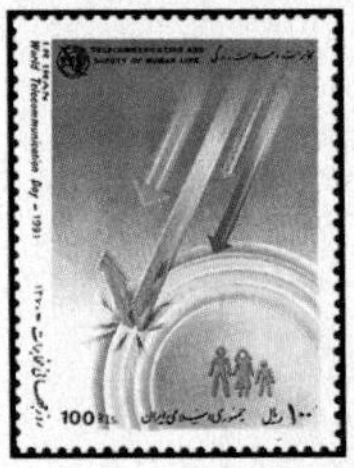

World Telecommunications Day — A832

***Perf. 13½x13***

**1991, May 17 Photo. Unwmk.**
**2455** A832 100r multicolored 1.50 .50

Intl. Museum Day — A833

Ewers, Kashan, 13th cent.: 20r, With spout. 40r, Baluster.

**1991, May 18 *Perf. 13***
**2456** A833 20r multicolored .50 .50
**2457** A833 40r multicolored 1.00 .50
*a.* Pair, #2456-2457 2.00 1.10

Flags — A834

**1991, May 24 *Perf. 13x13½***
**2458** A834 30r multicolored .85 .50

Liberation of Khorramshahr, 7th anniv.

Abol-Hassan Ali-ebne-Mosa Reza, Birth Anniv. — A835

Views of shrine, Meshed.

**1991, May 26 *Perf. 13***
**2459** 10r Mausoleum .25 .25
**2460** 30r Gravestone .75 .50
*a.* A835 Pair, #2459-2460 1.25 1.10

First Intl. Conf. on Seismology and Earthquake Engineering A836

**1991, May 27 *Perf. 13½x13***
**2461** A836 100r multicolored 2.00 .50

World Child Day — A837

**1991, June 1 Photo. *Perf. 13½***
**2462** A837 50r multicolored 1.00 .50

Holy Shrine at Karbola, Iraq Destroyed by Invasion — A838

**Unwmk.**

**1991, June 3 Photo. *Perf. 13***
**2463** A838 70r multicolored 1.10 .50

Ayatollah Khomeini, 2nd Death Anniv. — A839

**1991, June 4**
**2464** A839 100r multicolored 2.50 .75

World Handicrafts Day — A840

Designs: No. 2465, Engraved brass wares. No. 2466, Gilded samovar set.

**1991, June 10 *Perf. 13½x13***
**2465** A840 40r multicolored 1.00 .50
**2466** A840 40r multicolored 1.00 .50
*a.* Pair #2465-2466 2.50 1.25

Intl. Congress on Poet Nezami — A841

**1991, June 22 *Perf. 13***
**2467** A841 50r multicolored 1.10 .50

A842

**1991, July 15 Photo. *Perf. 13***
**2468** A842 50r multicolored .80 .50

Ali Ibn Abi Talib, 1330th death anniv.

A843

**Unwmk.**

**1991, July 29 Photo. *Perf. 13***
**2469** A843 50r multicolored 1.00 .50

Blood Transfusion Week.

Return of Prisoners of War, First Anniv. — A844

**1991, Aug. 27 *Perf. 13x13½***
**2470** A844 100r multicolored 1.75 .50

Ayatollah Marashi, Death Anniv. — A845

**1991, Aug. 29** *Perf. 13½x13*
**2471** A845 30r multicolored 1.25 .50

Ayatollah-ol-Ozma Seyyed Abdol-Hossein Lary, Revolutionary — A846

Design includes 1909 stamp issued by Lary.

**1991, Sept. 9** *Perf. 13x13½*
**2472** A846 30r multicolored .70 .50

Start of Iran-Iraq War, 11th Anniv. — A847

**1991, Sept. 22** *Perf. 13½x13*
**2473** A847 20r multicolored .50 .50

Mosque, Kaaba, Unity Week — A848

**1991, Sept. 22** *Perf. 13*
**2474** A848 30r multicolored .70 .50

World Tourism Day A849

**1991, Sept. 27** **Photo.** *Perf. 13½*
**2475** A849 200r multicolored 4.50 1.00

Dr. Mohammad Gharib, Pediatrician A849a

**1991, Sept. 29** **Photo.** *Perf. 13*
**2475A** A849a 100r bl & blk 1.50 .50

Official first day covers are dated 1/19/1991.

World Post Day A850

**Unwmk.**

**1991, Oct. 9** **Photo.** *Perf. 13*
**2476** A850 70r #2071 on cover 1.00 .50

Khaju-ye Kermani Intl. Congress — A851

**1991, Oct. 15**
**2477** A851 30r multicolored 1.00 .50

A852

**1991, Oct. 16**
**2478** A852 80r multicolored .90 .50

World Food Day.

A853

**1991, Oct. 19** *Perf. 13½x13*
**2479** A853 40r bl vio & gold .70 .50

Intl. Conference Supporting Palestinians.

Illustrators of Children's Books, 1st Asian Biennial A854

**1991, Oct. 25** *Perf. 13*
**2480** A854 100r Hoopoe 1.75 .50

"Children" misspelled.

World Standards Day — A855

**1991, Oct. 14** *Perf. 13½*
**2481** A855 100r multicolored 2.00 .50

1st Seminar on Adolescent and Children's Literature A856

**1991, Nov. 3** *Perf. 13*
**2482** A856 20r multicolored .70 .50

Roshid Intl. Educational Film Festival A857

**1991, Nov. 6**
**2483** A857 50r multicolored 1.20 .75

7th Ministerial Meeting of the Group of 77 — A858

**1991, Nov. 16**
**2484** A858 30r vio & bl grn .70 .50

Bassij of the Oppressed (Militia), 12th Anniv. — A859

**1991, Nov. 25**
**2485** A859 30r multicolored .65 .50

Ayatollah Aref Hosseini — A860

**1991, Dec. 18** *Perf. 13½*
**2486** A860 50r multicolored 1.10 .50

Sadek Ghanji A861

**1991, Dec. 20**
**2487** A861 50r multicolored 1.10 .50

Agricultural Training and Extension Week — A862

**1991, Dec. 22** *Perf. 13*
**2488** A862 70r multicolored 1.25 .50

World Telecommunications Day — A863

#2489: a, 20r, Telegraph key. b, 20r, Phone lines. c, 20r, Early telephones. d, 40r, Satellite dishes. e, 40r, Telecommunications satellite.

**1992, May 17** **Photo.** *Perf. 13*
**2489** A863 Strip of 5, #a.-e. 3.50 1.50

New Year — A863a

Flora of Iran: Nos. 2490a, 2490d, 20r. Nos. 2490b, 2490c, 40r.

**1992, Apr. 18** *Perf. 13½x13*
**2490** A863a Block of 4, #a.-d. 3.00 1.50

Mosque of Jerusalem A864

**1992, Mar. 27** *Perf. 13x13½*
**2491** A864 200r multicolored 2.50 1.25

Day of Jerusalem and honoring A. Mousavi, the Shiva leader of Lebanon, with Sheikh Ragheb Harb in background.

Reunification of Yemen — A865

**1992, May 22** *Perf. 13½x13*

**2492** A865 50r multicolored .90 .50

World Child Day A866

**1992, June 1** *Perf. 13x13½*

**2493** A866 50r multicolored .90 .50

Intl. Conference of Surveying and Mapping A867

**1992, May 25** *Perf. 13*

**2494** A867 40r multicolored .70 .50

21st FAO Regional Conference A868

**1992, May 17** *Perf. 13x13½*

**2495** A868 40r blk, bl & grn .50 .35

South and West Asia Postal Union — A869

Mosques: No. 2496, Imam's Mosque, Isfahan. No. 2497, Lahore Mosque, Pakistan. No. 2498, St. Sophia Mosque, Turkey.

**1992, Mar. 27** *Perf. 13½x13*

**2496** A869 50r multicolored .90 .50
**2497** A869 50r multicolored .90 .50
**2498** A869 50r multicolored .90 .50

Economic Cooperation Organization Summit — A870

Design: 20r, Flags, emblem, vert.

**1992** *Perf. 13½x13, 13x13½*

**2499** A870 20r multicolored .75 .50
**2500** A870 200r multicolored 4.50 1.00

Issued: 20r, Apr. 25; 200r, Feb. 17.

Natural Resources A871

**1992, Apr. 15 Litho.** *Perf. 13½x13*

**2501** A871 100r multicolored 2.00 1.00

Islamic Republic, 13th Anniv. — A872

**1992, Apr. 1** *Perf. 13½x13*

**2502** A872 50r multicolored .70 .50

Establishment of Postal Airline — A873

**1992, Apr. 1** *Perf. 13x13½*

**2503** A873 60r multicolored 1.25 .50

Islamic Revolution, 13th Anniv. — A874

**Unwmk.**

**1992, Feb. 11 Photo.** *Perf. 13*

**2504** 30r multicolored 1.00 .50
**2505** 50r multicolored 1.25 .50
*a.* A874 Pair, #2504-2505 2.50 1.25

A875

**1992, Mar. 23 Photo.** *Perf. 13½x13*

**2506** A875 100r multicolored 1.10 .50

World Meteorological Day.

A876

Famous Men: No. 2507, Mohammad Bagher Madjlessi. No. 2508, Hadi Sabzevari, wearing turban. No. 2509, Omman Samani, wearing fez. No. 2510, Chapter of praise from Koran (Arabic script), by Ostad Mir Emad.

**1991-92** *Perf. 13x13½*

**2507** A876 50r shown .70 .50
**2508** A876 50r brown & multi .70 .50
**2509** A876 50r multicolored .70 .50
**2510** A876 50r multicolored .70 .50

Issued: #2510, 12/18/91; others, 5/17/92. First day covers of #2507-2509 may be dated 12/18/91.

Intl. Museum Day A877

#2511, Gray ceramic ware, 1st millennium B.C. #2512, Painted ceramic bowl.

**1992, May 18**

**2511** A877 40r multicolored .90 .50
**2512** A877 40r multicolored .90 .50

Ayatollah Khomeini, 3rd Anniv. of Death — A878

**1992, June 4** *Perf. 13*

**2513** A878 100r multicolored 1.40 .50

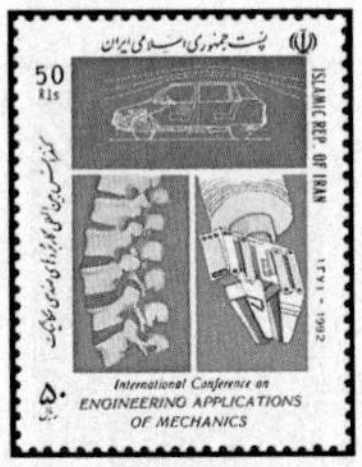

Intl. Conference on Engineering Applications of Mechanics A879

**1992, June 9** *Perf. 13½x13*

**2514** A879 50r multicolored .80 .50

A880

**1992, June 13** *Perf. 13x13½*

**2515** A880 20r multicolored .60 .40

In memory of clergy-lady Amini.

Sixth Conference of Nonaligned News Agencies — A881

**1992, June 15**

**2516** A881 100r multicolored 1.10 .50

A882

**1992, June 23** *Perf. 13x13½*

**2517** A882 100r grn, blk & gold 1.25 .50

Meeting of Ministers of Industry and Technology.

A883

**1992, June 26** *Perf. 13½x13*

**2518** A883 100r multicolored 1.75 .60

World Anti-narcotics Day.

Holy Ka'aba — A884

Prayer Calligraphy A885

Designs: No. 2520, Ayatollah Khomeini in prayer. No. 2521, Khomeini holding prayer beads. No. 2522, Khomeini unwrapping turban. Nos. 2523-2524, Islamic prayers.

**1992 Photo.** *Perf. 13½x13*

**2519** A884 50r multicolored .70 .50
**2520** A884 50r multicolored .70 .50
**2521** A884 50r multicolored .70 .50
**2522** A884 50r multicolored .70 .50

*Perf. 13x13½*

**2523** A885 50r dk green & lt green .70 .50
**2524** A885 50r dk blue & lt blue .70 .50

Issue dates: July 27, Aug. 24.

Iran Shipping Line, 25th Anniv. A886

**1992, Aug. 24 Photo.** *Perf. 13x13½*

**2525** A886 200r multicolored 2.00 1.00

A887

**1992, Sept. 15** ***Perf. 13½x13***
**2526** A887 40r multicolored .60 .45

Mohammad's Birthday, Unity Week.

A888

Iranian Defense Forces: 20r, Soldiers on patrol. 40r, Soldier seated at water's edge, horiz.

***Perf. 13½x13, 13x13½***

**1992, Sept. 22**
**2527** A888 20r multicolored .50 .40
**2528** A888 40r multicolored .50 .40

Intl. Congress on the History of Islamic Medicine — A889

**1992, Sept. 23** **Litho.** ***Perf. 13***
**2529** A889 20r Avicenna, child .60 .50
**2530** A889 40r Physician's instruments .90 .50
*a.* Pair, #2529-2530 1.75 1.10

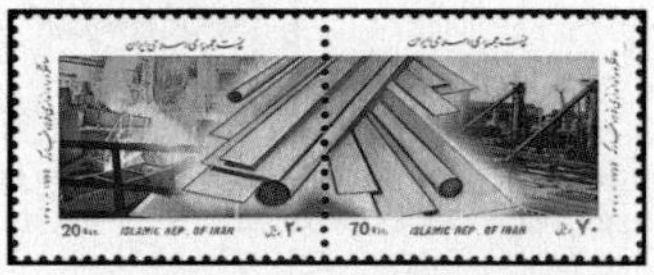

Mobarake Steel Plant — A890

**1992, Sept. 26** **Photo.** ***Perf. 13x13½***
**2531** 20r Inside plant .40 .50
**2532** 70r Outside plant .70 .50
*a.* A890 Pair, #2531-2532 1.40 1.25

Intl. Tourism Day A891

**1992, Sept. 27** ***Perf. 13x13½***
**2533** A891 20r Mazandaran .45 .35
**2534** A891 20r Isfahan .45 .35
**2535** A891 30r Bushehr (Bushire) .65 .50
**2536** A891 30r Hormozgan .65 .50

Intl. Trade Fair — A892

**1992, Oct. 2** ***Perf. 13½x13***
**2537** A892 200r multicolored 2.25 1.00

World Post Day A893

**1992, Oct. 9** ***Perf. 13x13½***
**2538** A893 30r Early post office .80 .50

World Food Day A894

**1992, Oct. 16** ***Perf. 13***
**2539** A894 100r blk, bl & yel 1.10 .50

Intl. Youth Photo Festival — A895

**1992, Nov. 1** **Photo.** ***Perf. 13½x13***
**2540** A895 40r multicolored 1.00 .50

A896

a, Seizure of US embassy, 12th anniv. b, Student's day (Eagles flying over dead doves). c, Khomeini's exile (Eagles, dove).

**1992, Nov. 4** ***Perf. 13***
**2541** A896 100r Strip of 3, #a.-c. 4.50 1.50

Fighting in Bosnia and Herzegovina A897

**1992, Nov. 4** ***Perf. 13½x13***
**2542** A897 40r multicolored .90 .50

Islamic Development Bank — A898

**1992, Nov. 10** **Litho.** ***Perf. 13½x13***
**2543** A898 20r multicolored .50 .40

Iran-Azerbaijan Telecommunications — A899

**1992, Nov. 21** **Photo.** ***Perf. 13x13½***
**2544** A899 40r multicolored .90 .50

Azad (Open) University, 10th Anniv. — A900

**1992, Nov. 23** ***Perf. 13½x13***
**2545** A900 200r dark grn & emer 1.75 .50

Week of the Basij (Militia) A901

**1992, Nov. 26** ***Perf. 13x13½***
**2546** A901 40r multicolored .60 .50

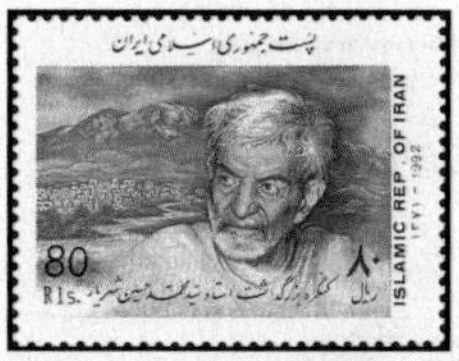


Seyed Mohammad Hosseyn Shahrian, Poet — A902

**1992, Dec. 1**
**2547** A902 80r multicolored .70 .50

Women's Day — A903

**1992, Dec. 15**
**2548** A903 70r multicolored .70 .50

Birth anniv. of Fatima.

Famous Iranians — A904

Scientists and writers: No. 2551a, Ayatollah Mirza Abolhassan Shar'rani (in turban). b, Prof. Mahmoud Hessabi, U=o formula. c, Mohiyt Tabatabaiy, books on shelves. d, Mehrdad Avesta, calligraphy.

**1992, Dec. 18**
**2549** A904 20r Block of 4, #a.-d. 2.00 1.00

Natl. Iranian Oil Drilling Co. A905

**1992, Dec. 22**
**2550** A905 100r shown 1.50 .50
**2551** A905 100r Ocean drilling platform 1.50 .50

A906

A907

**1992, Dec. 28** ***Perf. 13½x13***
**2552** A906 80r multicolored .70 .50

Promotion of literacy.

**1993-95** **Photo.** ***Perf. 13½x13***
**2553** A907 20r Narcissus
**2554** A907 30r Iris
**2555** A907 35r Tulips
**2556** A907 40r Tuberose
**2557** A907 50r White jasmine
**2558** A907 60r Guelder rose
**2559** A907 70r Pansies
**2560** A907 75r Snapdragons
**2561** A907 100r Lily
**2562** A907 120r Petunia
**2563** A907 150r Hyacinth
**2564** A907 200r Damascus rose
**2565** A907 500r Morning glory
**2566** A907 1000r Corn rose
*Nos. 2553-2566 (14)* 15.00 8.00

The 60r exists with inverted flowers. Value $9.

Issued: 20r, 1/12/93; 40r, 2/22/93; 100r, 4/21/93; 200r, 4/29/93; 500r, 6/27/93; 1000r, 7/19/93; 30r, 60r, 10/93; 50r, 8/93; 120r, 5/94; 35r, 75r, 3/95; 70r, 150r, 5/95.

For surcharges see Nos. 2759-2760, 2792-2794.

Prophethood of Mohammad — A908

**1993, Jan. 21** **Photo.** ***Perf. 13x13½***
**2567** A908 200r multicolored 1.75 .50

Mab'as Festival.

Day of the Disabled — A909

Designs: 40r, Player wearing medal, team members with hands raised.

**1993, Jan. 27**

**2568** 20r multicolored .50 .50
**2569** 40r multicolored .50 .50
*a.* A909 Pair, #2568-2569 1.25 1.10

Cultural Heritage Preservation A910

**1993, Jan. 31** ***Perf. 13½x13***

**2570** A910 40r Mosque, exterior 1.00 .50
**2571** A910 40r Mosque, interior 1.00 .50
*a.* Pair, #2570-2571 2.50 1.75

Planning Day — A911

**1993, Jan. 31** ***Perf. 13***

**2572** A911 100r multicolored 2.00 .50

Universal Day of the Oppressed A912

**1993, Feb. 8** **Litho.** ***Perf. 13***

**2573** A912 60r multicolored .80 .50

Savior Mahdi's Birthday.

Islamic Revolution, 14th Anniv. A913

a, Iranian flag. b, Flag, soldiers. c, Soldiers, shellbursts. d, Oil derricks, storage tanks, people harvesting. e, Crowd, car, Ayatollah Khomeini.

**1993, Feb. 11** **Photo.** ***Perf. 13x13½***

**2574** A913 20r Strip of 5, #a.-e. 5.00 3.00

A914

1st Islamic Women's Games: a, Volleyball. b, Basketball. c, Medal. d, Swimming. e, Running.

**1993, Feb. 13** ***Perf. 13***

**2575** A914 40r Strip of 5, #a.-e. 6.00 3.00

A915

**1993, Feb. 16** ***Perf. 13½***

**2576** A915 40r Morteza Ansari .80 .50

Arbor Day A916

**1993, Mar. 6**

**2577** A916 70r multicolored 1.10 .50

New Year A917

a, 20r, Butterfly, tulip. b, 20r, Butterfly, lily. c, 40r, Butterfly, flowers. d, 40r, Butterfly, 3 roses.

**1993, Mar. 11** ***Perf. 13½x13***

**2578** A917 Block of 4, #a.-d. 5.00 2.00

World Jerusalem Day — A918

**1993, Mar. 14** ***Perf. 13½x13***

**2579** A918 20r multicolored .90 .50

End of Ramadan A919

**1993, Mar. 26** ***Perf. 13½x13***

**2580** A919 100r multicolored 3.00 1.00

Islamic Republic, 14th Anniv. A920

**1993, Apr. 1** ***Perf. 13x13½***

**2581** A920 40r Natl. anthem .90 .50

Intl. Congress on the Millennium of Sheik Mofeed — A921

**1993, Apr. 17** ***Perf. 13***

**2582** A921 80r multicolored 1.10 .50

A922

**1993, Apr. 21** ***Perf. 13½x13***

**2583** A922 100r multicolored 1.10 .50

13th Conference of Asian and Pacific Labor Ministers.

A924

**1993, May 17** ***Perf. 13½x13***

**2585** A924 50r multicolored 1.20 .50

Intl. Congress for Advancement of Science and Technology in Islamic World.

A925

**1993, May 1**

**2586** A925 40r multicolored 1.00 .50

Intl. Museum Day.

A928

**1993, June 1** **Photo.** ***Perf. 13½x13***

**2589** A928 50r multicolored 1.00 .50

Intl. Child Day.

Ayatollah Khomeini, 4th Death Anniv. — A929

**1993, June 4** ***Perf. 13***

**2590** A929 20r multicolored .70 .50

World Crafts Day A930

**1993, June 10** ***Perf. 13½x13***

**2591** A930 70r multicolored 1.50 .60

World Population Day — A931

**1993, July 11** ***Perf. 13***

**2592** A931 30r multicolored .90 .50

1st Cultural-Athletic Olympiad of Iran University Students — A932

Various sports.

**1993, July 22** ***Perf. 13x13½***

**Background Colors**

**2593** A932 20r blue 1.00 .35
**2594** A932 40r henna brown 2.50 .75
**2595** A932 40r ocher 2.50 .75

Intl. Festival of Films for Children and Young Adults, Isfahan — A935

**1993, Sept. 11 Photo. *Perf. 13***

**2598** A935 60r multicolored 1.25 .50

World Post Day — A937

**1993, Oct. 9 Photo. *Perf. 13***

**2600** A937 60r multicolored 1.25 .50

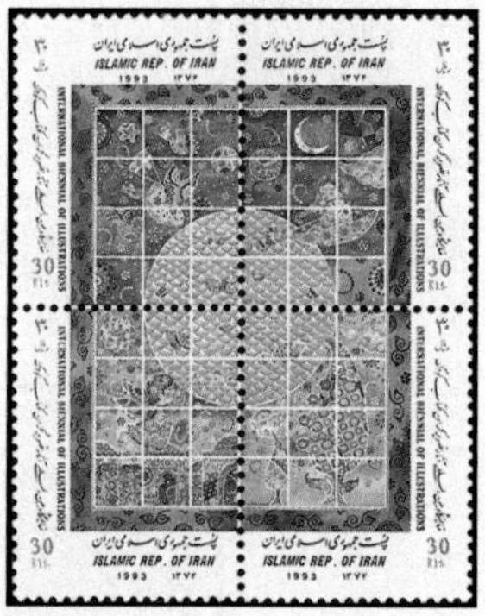


A939

World of water with fish and: a, Birds. b, Girl. c, Angel with trumpet. d, Trees.

**1993, Nov. 5 Photo. *Perf. 13½x13***

**2602** A939 30r Block of 4, #a.-d. 3.50 2.00

Illustrators of Children's Books, Intl. Biennial.

A940

**1993, Nov. 16 Photo. *Perf. 13***

**2603** A940 30r multicolored .80 .50

Khaje Nassireddin Tussy, scientist and astronomer.

Week of the Bassij (Militia) A941

Designs: No. 2604, Woman tying bandana around militiman's head. No. 2605, Militiaman facing line of tanks.

**1993, Dec. 1 *Perf. 13x13½***

**2604** A941 50r multicolored 1.00 .50

**2605** A941 50r multicolored 1.00 .50

Death of Grand Ayatollah Mohammad Reza Golpaigani A942

**1993, Dec. 20 *Perf. 13***

**2606** A942 300r multicolored 4.00 2.00

Support for Bosnia and Herzegovina A943

#2607, Children playing hopscotch. #2608, Soldier, minaret. #2609, Woman, mosque.

**1993, Dec. 27**

**2607** A943 40r multicolored 1.00 .50

**2608** A943 40r multicolored 1.00 .50

**2609** A943 40r multicolored 1.00 .50

*a.* Strip of 3, #2607-2609 4.00 2.00

Day of Invalids — A944

**1994, Jan. 18**

**2610** A944 80r multicolored .90 .50

Agriculture Week — A945

**1994, Jan. 23**

**2611** A945 60r multicolored .80 .50

Conf. on Islamic Law — A946

**1994, Feb. 20**

**2612** A946 60r multicolored 1.00 .50

Islamic Revolution, 15th Anniv. — A947

Designs: a, Town, farm, telephone lines. b, Flag, Ayatollah Khomeini, revolutionaries. c, Fisherman, bridge. d, Women working.

**1994, Feb. 11**

**2613** A947 40r Block of 4, #a.-d. 3.50 2.25

Youth Welfare A948

**1994, Mar. 1**

**2614** A948 30r multicolored .90 .50

A949

**1994, Mar. 28 Photo. *Perf. 13½x13***

**2615** A949 30r multicolored .90 .50

25th Iranian Mathematics Conference, Shareef Industrial University.

A950

**1994, Mar. 11 *Perf. 13***

**2616** A950 50r multicolored .90 .50

World Jerusalem Day.

A951

**1994, Mar. 16 *Perf. 13x13½, 13½x13***

**2617** A951 40r Partridges, horiz. 3.50 1.25

**2618** A951 40r Heron 3.50 1.25

**2619** A951 40r Bustard 3.50 1.25

**2620** A951 40r Pheasants, horiz. 3.50 1.25

New year.

Islamic Republic, 15th Anniv. — A952

**1994, Apr. 1 Photo. *Perf. 13***

**2621** A952 40r multicolored .90 .50

A953

**1994, Apr. 7**

**2622** A953 100r multicolored 1.50 .50

Intl. congress of Dentist's Assoc. and World Health Day.

Re-els Ali Delvary, 80th Anniv. of Death A954

**1994, Apr. 9 *Perf. 13x13½***

**2623** A954 50r multicolored 1.00 .50

Intl. Year of the Family — A955

**1994, May 10 Photo. *Perf. 13½x13***

**2624** A955 50r multicolored .75 .50

World Telecommunications Day — A956

**1994, May 17 *Perf. 13x13½***

**2625** A956 50r multicolored 6.50 2.00

A957

**1994, May 18 *Perf. 13***

**2626** A957 40r Marlik gold cup .90 .50

World Museum Day.

A958

Cultural Preservation: 40r, Enameled pot with Kufic inscription, 13th cent.

**1994, May 21**

**2627** A958 40r multicolored .80 .25

Ayatollah Khomeini, 5th Death Anniv. — A959

**1994, June 4**

**2628** A959 30r multicolored .50 .25

Ayatollah Motahari, 15th Anniv. of Death — A961

**1994, June 10**

**2630** A961 30r multicolored .60 .25

World Crafts Day — A962

**1994, June 10 Photo. *Perf. 13***

**2631** A962 60r Weaver 2.50 1.00

**2632** A962 60r Glass pitcher 2.50 1.00

Islamic University Students' Solidarity Games — A963

**1994, July 18**

**2633** A963 60r multicolored .90 .40

Mohammad's Birthday, Unity Week — A964

**1994, Aug. 26**

**2634** A964 30r multicolored .80 .40

Seyed Mortaza Avini, Sacred Defense Week A965

**1994, Sept. 22** ***Perf. 13x13½***

**2635** A965 70r multicolored .80 .50

World Post Day A966

**1994, Oct. 9**

**2636** A966 50r multicolored .75 .50

Women's Day — A967

**1994, Nov. 24** ***Perf. 13***

**2637** A967 70r multicolored .90 .50

Birth anniv. of Fatima.

A968

**1994, Nov. 26**

**2638** A968 30r multicolored .45 .25

Week of the Bassij (Militia).

Book Week — A969

**1994, Dec. 10**

**2639** A969 40r multicolored .60 .50

Support for Moslems of Bosnia & Herzegovina A970

**1994, Dec. 27**

**2640** A970 80r Moslem family 1.25 .50

**2641** A970 80r Map, arms, homes 1.25 .50

Grand Ayatollah Araky — A971

**1995, Jan. 5**

**2642** A971 100r multicolored 1.25 .50

Universal Day of the Oppressed A972

**1995, Jan. 17**

**2643** A972 50r multicolored .75 .50

Savior Mahdi's birthday.

Major General Mehdi Zin-el-Din A973

Major General Mehdi Bakeri — A974

Major General Hasan Bagheri A975

Martyred commanders: #2647, Major General Hosein Kherazi.

**1995, Feb. 2**

**2644** A973 50r multicolored .55 .25

**2645** A974 50r multicolored .55 .25

**2646** A975 50r multicolored .55 .25

**2647** A975 50r multi, diff. .55 .25

A976

**1995, Feb. 11**

**2648** A976 100r multicolored 1.50 .50

Islamic Revolution, 16th anniv.

A977

**1995, Feb. 24**

**2649** A977 100r multicolored 2.25 .75

World Jerusalem Day.

Arbor Day — A978

**1995, Mar. 6**

**2650** A978 50r multicolored .70

New Year — A979

**1995, Mar. 16** ***Perf. 13½x13***

**2651** A979 50r shown 1.50 .55

**2652** A979 50r Pansies 1.50 .55

**2653** A979 50r Hyacinths 1.50 .55

**2654** A979 50r Tulips, fish bowl 1.50 .55

Opening of Bafq-Bandar Abbas Railway Line — A980

**1995, Mar. 17**

**2655** A980 100r multicolored 1.75 1.00

Islamic Republic of Iran, 16th Anniv. — A981

**1995, Apr. 1** **Photo.** ***Perf. 13***
**2656** A981 100r multicolored 1.10 .50

Second Press Fesitval A982

**1995, Apr. 26**
**2657** A982 100r multicolored .90 .50

Ayatollah Ahmad Khomeini A983

**1995, Apr. 27**
**2658** A983 50r multicolored .70 .50

Day of Invalids — A984

**1995, June 1**
**2659** A984 80r Arabic script .80 .50

Ayatollah Ali Vaziri — A985

**1995, May 4**
**2660** A985 100r multicolored .80 .50

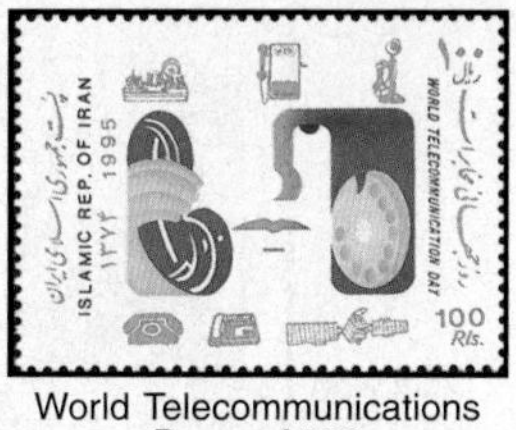

World Telecommunications Day — A986

**1995, May 17**
**2661** A986 100r multicolored 1.10 .50

Ayatollah Khomeini, 6th Death Anniv. — A987

**1995, June 4**
**2662** A987 100r multicolored 1.25 .50

UN, 50th Anniv. — A988

a, Infant, hand holding vaccination (WHO). b, Child laughing (UNICEF). c, Shafts of grain, world map (FAO). d, Woman reading (UNESCO).

**1995, June 10** ***Perf. 13x13½***
**2663** A988 100r Block of 4, #a.-d. 3.50 2.25

Iqbal Ashtiany, Writer — A989

**1995, Aug. 14** ***Perf. 13***
**2664** A989 100r multicolored 1.10 .50

Government Week — A990

**1995, Aug. 28** ***Perf. 13x13½***
**2665** A990 100r Workers, dam 1.10 .50

Construction of the Karun dam and hydo-electric power station.

Sacred Defense Week — A991

**1995, Sept. 22** ***Perf. 13***
**2666** A991 100r Gun, Koran 1.25 .50

World Post Day — A992

**1995, Oct. 9** ***Perf. 13½x13***
**2667** A992 100r Globe, envelopes 1.25 .50

M.J. Tondgooyan, Oil Minister A993

**1995, Dec. 20** ***Perf. 13***
**2668** A993 100r multicolored 1.10 .50

Prophet Mohammad A994

**1995, Dec. 20**
**2669** A994 100r Arabic calligraphy 1.25 .50

Fathi Shaghaghi, Islamic Jihad Secretary General A995

**1995, Dec. 31**
**2670** A995 100r multicolored 1.25 .50

Islamic Revolution, 17th Anniv. — A996

**1996, Feb. 11**
**2671** A996 100r multicolored 1.40 .60

World Jerusalem Day — A997

**1996, Feb. 17**
**2672** A997 100r Dome of the Rock 1.25 .60

Birds A998

**1996, Mar. 15**
**2673** A998 100r shown 2.00 .75
**2674** A998 100r Crested head 2.00 .75
**2675** A998 100r blue & multi 2.00 .75
**2676** A998 100r yel, grn & multi 2.00 .75

New year.

Air Force Maj. Gen. Abbas Babai — A999

Major Ali Akbar Shiroody A1000

Maj. Gen. Mahammed Ebrahim Hemmat A1001

Maj. Gen. Mohammad Broujerdi A1002

**1996, Mar. 18**

| | | | | | |
|---|---|---|---|---|---|
| **2677** | A999 | 100r multicolored | | 2.25 | 1.00 |
| **2678** | A1000 | 100r multicolored | | 2.25 | 1.00 |
| **2679** | A1001 | 100r multicolored | | 2.25 | 1.00 |
| **2680** | A1002 | 100r multicolored | | 2.25 | 1.00 |

See Nos. 2700-2707 for similar stamps dated 1997.

Islamic Republic of Iran, 17th Anniv. — A1003

**1996, Mar. 31 Photo. *Perf. 13***

**2681** A1003 200r multicolored 2.25 1.00

Intl. Book Fair, Tehran A1004

**1996, May 8**

**2682** A1004 85r multicolored 1.25 .50

For surcharge see No. 2759A.

Mashhad-Sarakhs-Tajan Intl. Railway — A1005

**1996, May 13**

**2683** A1005 200r multicolored 2.00 1.00

Turkmenistan intl. railway link,

Prisoners of War — A1006

**1996, May 29**

**2684** A1006 200r multicolored 2.25 1.00

Captives and Missing Day.

Ayatollah Khomeini, 7th Death Anniv. — A1007

**1996, June 3**

**2685** A1007 200r multicolored 2.00 1.00

World Crafts Day — A1008

**1996, June 24 Photo. *Perf. 13***

**2686** A1008 200r multicolored 2.00 1.00

Third PTT Ministerial Conference, Tehran A1009

**1996, July 8**

**2687** A1009 200f multicolored 1.60 .50

Prophet Mohammad's Birthday, Unity Week — A1010

Designs: a, Zouqeblateyne Mosque. b, Tomb of Imam Hossein (red flag on top of dome). c, Mohammad's Mosque (dome without flag). d, Tomb of Imam Riza (green flag on top of dome). e, Qaba Mosque (four minarets).

**1996, Aug. 3**

**2688** A1010 200r Strip of 5, #a.-e. 12.50 3.00

Government Week — A1011

Flag colors and: a, Tehran Subway. b, Iron works, Isfahan. c, Merchant fleet. d, Oil refinery, Bandar-e-Imam (clouds in sky). e, Satellite dish, Boumehen.

**1996, Aug. 23**

**2689** A1011 200r Strip of 5, #a.-e. 13.00 3.50

Ayatollah Moqddas Ardebily A1012

**1996, Sept. 12 Photo. *Perf. 13***

**2690** A1012 200r multicolored 1.60 .75

Sacred Defense Week — A1013

**1996, Sept. 21**

**2691** A1013 200r multicolored 1.60 .60

World Standards Day — A1014

**1996, Oct. 13**

**2692** A1014 200r multicolored 1.60 .50

World Food Day — A1015

**1996, Oct. 16**

**2693** A1015 200r multicolored 1.60 .60

Natl. Census A1016

**1996, Oct. 22**

**2694** A1016 200r multicolored 1.50 .65

2nd World University Wrestling Championships, Tehran — A1017

**1996, Dec. 10**

**2695** A1017 500r multicolored 5.00 2.00

Islamic Revolution, 18th Anniv. — A1018

a, Ayatollah Khomeini holding man to his chest. b, Martyrs. c, Khomeini waving. d, Khomeini, leaders, airplane. e, Soldiers wearing helmets.

**1997, Feb. 10**

**2696** A1018 200r Strip of 5, #a.-e. 16.00 7.50

Arbor Day — A1019

**1997, Mar. 5**

**2697** A1019 200r multicolored 2.00 .80

Islamic Republic, 18th Anniv. — A1020

**1997, Apr. 1**

**2698** A1020 200r multicolored 1.60 .60

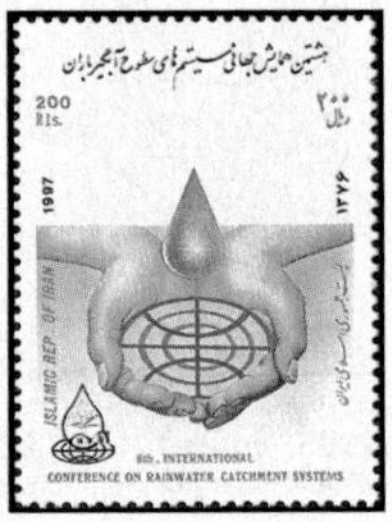


8th Intl. Conference on Rainwater Catchment Systems A1021

**1997, Apr. 21**

**2699** A1021 200r multicolored 1.50 .60

Sheikh Fazlollah Mahallati A1022

Brig. Gen. Abbas Karimi A1023

Brig. Gen. Alireza Movahed Danesh A1024

Sheikh Abdollah Mishmi A1025

Brig. Gen. Naser Kazemi A1026

Gen. Mohammad Reza Vasture A1027

Maj. Gen. Yousef Kolahdooz A1028

Brig. Gen. Yadollah Kalhor A1029

**1997, May 4**

| | | | | | |
|---|---|---|---|---|---|
| **2700** | A1022 | 100r | multicolored | 1.25 | .50 |
| **2701** | A1023 | 100r | multicolored | 1.25 | .50 |
| **2702** | A1024 | 100r | multicolored | 1.25 | .50 |
| **2703** | A1025 | 100r | multicolored | 1.25 | .50 |
| **2704** | A1026 | 100r | multicolored | 1.25 | .50 |
| **2705** | A1027 | 100r | multicolored | 1.25 | .50 |
| **2706** | A1028 | 100r | multicolored | 1.25 | .50 |
| **2707** | A1029 | 100r | multicolored | 1.25 | .50 |

Martyred commanders. See Nos. 2677-2680 for similar stamps.

Post, Telecommunications — A1030

**1997, May 22**

| | | | | | |
|---|---|---|---|---|---|
| **2708** | A1030 | 200r | multicolored | 1.75 | .50 |

Ayatollah Khomeini, 8th Death Anniv. — A1031

**1997, June 4**

| | | | | | |
|---|---|---|---|---|---|
| **2709** | A1031 | 200r | multicolored | 1.60 | .50 |

Montreal Protocol on Substances that Deplete Ozone Layer, 10th Anniv. — A1032

**1997, Sept. 16 Photo. *Perf. 13***

| | | | | | |
|---|---|---|---|---|---|
| **2710** | A1032 | 200r | multicolored | 1.50 | .50 |

Tehran Subway — A1033

Designs: 50r, Grain elevator. 65r, Medals, Students' Science Olympiad. 70r, Mobarake Steel Plant. 100r, Telecommunications. 130r, Port facilities. 150r, Bandar Abbas Oil Refinery. 200r, Rajai Dam. 350r, Rajai power station. 400r, Front of Foreign Affairs office. 500r, Child receiving oral polio vaccine. 650r, Printing house for Koran. 1000r, Imam Khomeini Intl. Airport. 2000r, Prayer place and tomb of Ayatollah Khomeini, Teheran.

**1997 Photo. *Perf. 13½x13***

| | | | | | |
|---|---|---|---|---|---|
| **2711** | A1033 | 40r | multicolored | | |
| **2712** | A1033 | 50r | multicolored | | |
| **2713** | A1033 | 65r | multicolored | | |
| **2714** | A1033 | 70r | multicolored | | |
| **2715** | A1033 | 100r | multicolored | | |
| **2716** | A1033 | 130r | multicolored | | |
| **2717** | A1033 | 150r | multicolored | | |
| **2718** | A1033 | 200r | multicolored | | |
| **2719** | A1033 | 350r | multicolored | | |
| **2720** | A1033 | 400r | multicolored | | |
| **2721** | A1033 | 500r | multicolored | | |
| **2722** | A1033 | 650r | multicolored | | |
| **2723** | A1033 | 1000r | multicolored | | |
| **2724** | A1033 | 2000r | multicolored | | |
| | *Nos. 2711-2724 (14)* | | | 30.00 | 18.50 |

Issued: 2000r, 10/22; others, Sept.

Sacred Defense Week — A1034

**1997, Sept. 28 Photo. *Perf. 13***

| | | | | | |
|---|---|---|---|---|---|
| **2725** | A1034 | 200r | multicolored | 1.50 | .50 |

Poets — A1035

#2726, Maitre Eqbal Lahouri. #2727, Molana Djalaleddin Mohammad Molavi.

**1997, Oct. 15**

| | | | | | |
|---|---|---|---|---|---|
| **2726** | A1035 | 200r | green & multi | 1.50 | .50 |
| **2727** | A1035 | 200r | salmon & multi | 1.50 | .50 |

Compare with Pakistan 870-871.

World Post Day — A1036

**1997, Oct. 15**

| | | | | | |
|---|---|---|---|---|---|
| **2728** | A1036 | 200r | multicolored | 1.50 | .50 |

Naim Frasheri (1846-1900), Albanian Moslem Poet — A1037

**1997, Nov. 5**

| | | | | | |
|---|---|---|---|---|---|
| **2729** | A1037 | 200r | multicolored | 1.50 | .50 |

Eighth Islamic Summit A1038

Various ornate designs, Islamic texts: a, Seven ornaments. b, Ornament at bottom. c, Ornament at right. d, Ornament at upper left. e, Ornament above crescent.

**1997, Dec. 9**

| | | | | | |
|---|---|---|---|---|---|
| **2730** | A1038 | 300r | Strip of 5, #a.-e. | 20.00 | 7.50 |

2nd Islamic Countries Women's Sports Games, Tehran A1039

**1997, Dec. 12**

| | | | | | |
|---|---|---|---|---|---|
| **2731** | A1039 | 200r | multicolored | 1.50 | .50 |

Islamic Revolution, 19th Anniv. A1040

a, Natl. flags. b, Harvesting grain, factory. c, Soldiers carrying flags. d, Crowd cheering, picture of Ayatollah Khomeini. e, Ayatollah Khomeini.

**1998, Feb. 11**

| | | | | | |
|---|---|---|---|---|---|
| **2732** | A1040 | 200r | Strip of 5, #a.-e. | 12.50 | 5.00 |

World Jerusalem Day — A1041

**1998, Feb. 17**

| | | | | | |
|---|---|---|---|---|---|
| **2733** | A1041 | 250r | multicolored | 3.00 | 1.25 |

New Year — A1042

**1998, Mar. 5**

| | | | | | |
|---|---|---|---|---|---|
| **2734** | A1042 | 200r | Still life | 1.60 | .60 |

Arbor Day A1043

**1998, Mar. 11**

| | | | | | |
|---|---|---|---|---|---|
| **2735** | A1043 | 200r | multicolored | 1.60 | .90 |

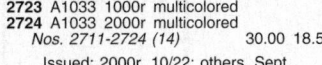

Islamic Republic, 19th Anniv. — A1044

**1998, Apr. 1** **Photo.** ***Perf. 13***
**2736** A1044 250r multicolored 4.00 1.50

A1045

**1998, May 17** ***Perf. 13½x13***
**2737** A1045 200r multicolored 2.25 1.00

World Telecommunications Day.

A1046

**1998, May 23** **Photo.** ***Perf. 13***
**2738** A1046 200r multicolored 2.25 1.00

Election day.

**War Martyrs**

A1047

A1048

A1049

A1050

**1998, May 24** **Photo.** ***Perf. 13***
**2739** A1047 100r multicolored 2.50 .90
**2740** A1048 100r multicolored 2.50 .90
**2741** A1049 100r multicolored 2.50 .90
**2742** A1050 100r multicolored 2.50 .90

Shahriyar, Poet — A1051

**1998, May 27**
**2743** A1051 200r multicolored 2.25 1.00

Ayatollah Khomeini, 9th Death Anniv. — A1052

**1998, June 4** ***Perf. 13***
**2744** A1052 200r multicolored 2.50 1.25

2nd Congress of the South West Asia Postal Union, Tehran A1053

**1998, June 8**
**2745** A1053 250r multicolored 1.75 1.00

1998 World Cup Soccer Championships, France — A1054

**1998, June 10**
**2746** A1054 500r multicolored 3.50 1.00

A1055

**1998, June 10**
**2747** A1055 200r multicolored 2.25 1.25

World Handicrafts Day.

A1056

**1998, Sept. 4**
**2748** A1056 250r Union Day 2.50 1.50

1000th Friday of Public Prayer A1057

**1998, Oct. 30** **Litho.** ***Perf. 13***
**2749** A1057 250r multicolored 2.50 1.50

Nos. 2295A & 2296A Surcharged in Black or Green

**1998, Nov. 11** ***Perf. 13x13½***
**2750** A738 200r on 1r Shoustar 5.50 3.00
**2751** A738 200r on 3r Kerman (G) 5.50 3.00

Intl. Year of the Ocean A1058

**1998, Nov. 14** ***Perf. 13***
**2752** A1058 250r multicolored 3.00 1.75

Sacred Defense Week — A1059

**1998, Nov. 23**
**2753** A1059 250r multicolored 2.50 1.00

World Post Day A1060

**1998, Dec. 2**
**2754** A1060 200r multicolored 2.00 .75

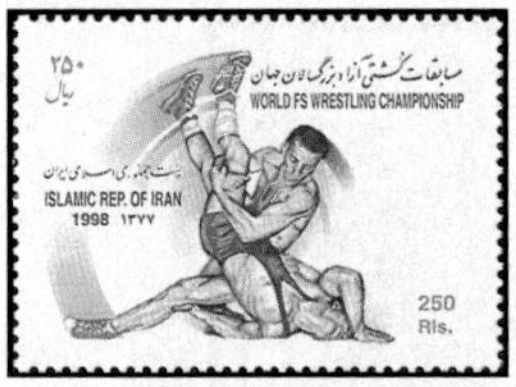


1998 World Wrestling Championships, Tehran — A1061

**1998, Dec. 8**
**2755** A1061 250r multicolored 5.00 2.75

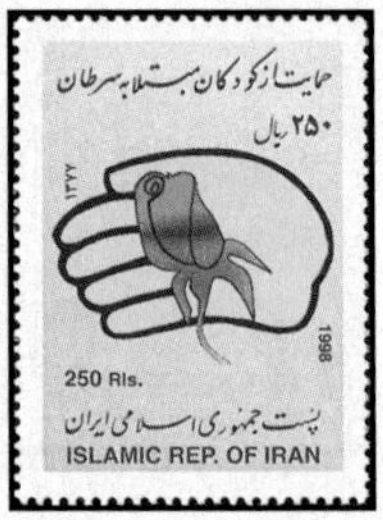


Children and Cancer A1062

**1998, Dec. 13**
**2756** A1062 250r multicolored 2.00 .75

Cultural Development A1063

**1998, Dec. 16** **Photo.** ***Perf. 13***
**2757** A1063 250r multicolored 2.25 1.00

Islamic Revolution, 20th Anniv. — A1064

**1999, Feb. 11** **Photo.** ***Perf. 13***
**2758** A1064 250r multicolored 2.00 .75

**Nos. 2554, 2682, 2555 Surcharged in Black or Red**

#2759, 2760

#2759A

**1999, Feb. Photo. *Perf. 13, 13½x13***

**2759** A907 200r on 35r (#2555) *15.00* —
**2759A** A1004 250r on 85r (R, #2682) *35.00* —
**2760** A907 900r on 30r (#2554) *25.00* —

Establishment of Islamic Republic, 20th Anniv. — A1065

**1999, Apr. 1 Photo. *Perf. 13***

**2761** A1065 250r multicolored 2.00 1.00

Ghadir Khom Religious Feast — A1066

**1999, Apr. 5 Photo. *Perf. 13***

**2762** A1066 250r multicolored 2.00 1.00

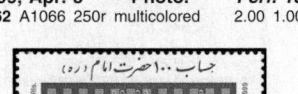

Ayatollah Khomieni's Charity Account — A1067

**1999, Apr. 10 Photo. *Perf. 13***

**2763** A1067 250r Houses 2.25 1.00
**2764** A1067 250r Village, palm trees 2.25 1.00

Army Day A1068

**1999, Apr. 18**

**2765** A1068 250r multicolored 2.50 1.25

Mullah Sadra — A1069

**1999, May 22**

**2766** A1069 250r multicolored 2.00 1.00

Ayatollah Khomeini, 10th Anniv. of Death — A1070

**1999, May 25**

**2767** A1070 250r multicolored 4.00 2.00

Islamic Parliament, 20th Anniv. — A1071

**1999, May 28 Photo. *Perf. 13***

**2768** A1071 250r multicolored 2.00 1.00

Islamic Inter-parliamentary Conference — A1072

**1999, June 15 Photo. *Perf. 13***

**2769** A1072 250r multicolored 2.00 1.25

Unity Week A1073

**1999, July 1 Photo. *Perf. 13***

**2770** A1073 250r multicolored 2.00 1.25

Handicrafts Day — A1074

**1999, July 25 Photo. *Perf. 13***

**2771** A1074 250r multicolored 3.00 1.25

Total Solar Eclipse, Aug. 11 — A1075

Designs: a, Moon over right portion of sun. b, Baily's beads at top. c, Totality. d, Baily's beads at right. e, Moon over left portion of sun.

**1999, Feb. 11 Photo. *Perf. 13***

**2772** A1075 250r Strip of 5, #a.-e. *25.00 20.00*

Birds — A1076

**1999-2002 Photo. *Perf. 13x13½***

**2776** A1076 100r Hoopoe .50
**2778** A1076 150r Kingfisher .50
**2779** A1076 200r Robin .50
**2780** A1076 250r Lark .50
**2781** A1076 300r Red-backed shrike .50
**2782** A1076 350r Eurasian roller .50
**2782A** A1076 400r Blue tit .50
**2783** A1076 500r Eurasian bee-eater .50
**2784** A1076 1000r Redwing 1.00
**2785** A1076 2000r Twite 1.00
**2786** A1076 3000r White throat 1.00
**2786A** A1076 4500r Turtle dove 1.00

Numbers have been reserved for additional values in this set.

Issued: 150r, 8/6; 250r, 8/4; 100r, 6/17/00; 300r, 5/31/00; 500r, 8/30/00; 1000r, 10/30/00; 2000r, 1/13/01; 3000r, 1/23/01. 200r, 4/24/02; 400r, 5/18/02; 4500r, 7/16/02; 350r, 4/17/01.

UPU, 125th Anniv. A1077

**1999, Oct. 2 Photo. *Perf. 13***

**2787** A1077 250r multicolored 2.25 1.00

Children's Day — A1078

a, Iranian girl. b, Latin American boy. c, Eskimo boy. d, African girl. e, Russian boy. f, French girl. g, Chinese girl. h, Asian Indian girl. i, American Indian girl. j, Arabian boy.

**1999, Oct. 8**

**2788** A1078 150r Strip of 10, #a.-j. *20.00 15.00*

Order of stamps in strip varies.

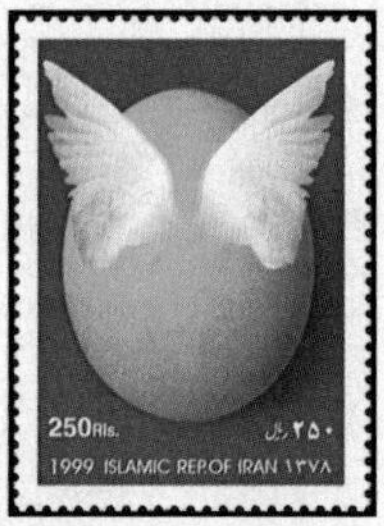


Intl. Exhibition of Children's Book Illustrators A1079

Background colors: a, Blue. b, Yellow. c, Red. d, Green.

**1999, Nov. 15**

**2789** A1079 250r Block of 4, #a.-d. *17.50 10.00*

Ayatollah Mohammad Taghi Jafari — A1080

**1999, Nov. 16**

**2790** A1080 250r multicolored 2.00 1.00

Islamic Revolution, 21st Anniv. — A1081

**2000, Feb. 11 Photo. *Perf. 13***

**2791** A1081 300r multi 2.25 1.25

### Nos. 2558, 2560, 2562 Surcharged Like No. 2759

### Methods and Perfs. as Before

**2000, Feb.**

**2792** A907 250r on 60r 5.00 3.25
**2793** A907 250r on 75r 5.00 3.25
**2794** A907 250r on 120r 5.00 3.25

The 60r stamp with the inverted flowers footnoted after No. 2566 is known with the 250r surcharge. Value $35.

New Year — A1082

**2000, Mar. 13 Photo. *Perf. 13***

**2795** A1082 300r multi 2.75 1.50

Science & Technology University, 70th Anniv. — A1083

**2000, July 9** **Photo.** ***Perf. 13***
**2796** A1083 300r multi *8.00 5.00*

Dated 1999.

Dr. Mohammad Mofatteh (1928-79), Martyr — A1084

**2000, July 22**
**2797** A1084 300r multi 2.00

A1085

A1086

A1087

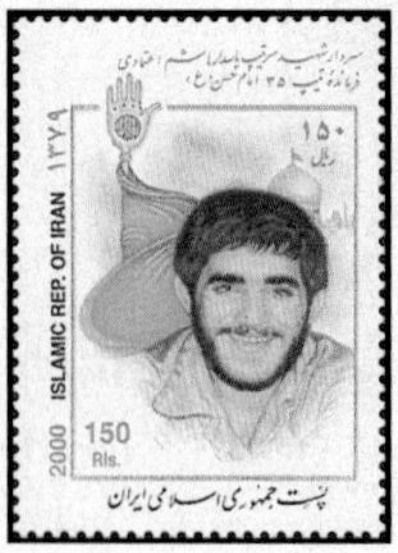


A1088

A1089

A1090

A1091

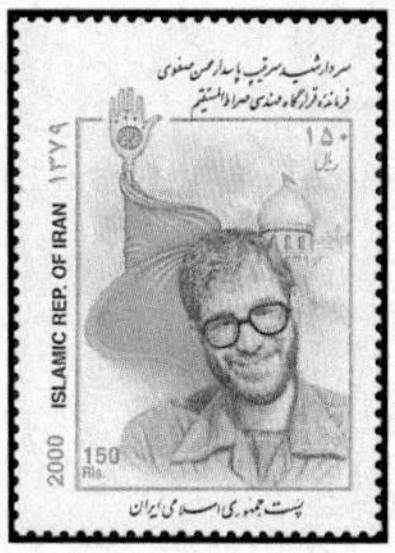


Martyrs A1092

**2000**

| | | | | |
|---|---|---|---|---|
| **2798** | A1085 | 150r multi | 2.00 | .50 |
| **2799** | A1086 | 150r multi | 2.00 | .50 |
| **2800** | A1087 | 150r multi | 2.00 | .50 |
| **2801** | A1088 | 150r multi | 2.00 | .50 |
| **2802** | A1089 | 150r multi | 1.25 | .50 |
| **2803** | A1090 | 150r multi | 1.25 | .50 |
| **2804** | A1091 | 150r multi | 1.25 | .50 |
| **2805** | A1092 | 150r multi | 1.25 | .50 |
| | *Nos. 2798-2805 (8)* | | 13.00 | 4.00 |

Issued: Nos. 2798-2801, 8/6/00; Nos. 2802-2805, 7/30/01.

National Archives Day — A1093

**2000, May 5** **Photo.** ***Perf. 13***
**2806** A1093 300r multi 2.25 1.50

University Jihad Movement A1094

**2000, Aug. 6**
**2807** A1094 300r multi 2.00 1.25

8th Asia-Pacific Postal Union Congress, Tehran — A1095

**2000, Sept. 12**
**2808** A1095 300r multi 2.00 1.25

World Space Week A1096

Satellite and: No. 2809, 500r, Dish at R. No. 2810, 500r, Dish at L.

**2000, Oct. 4**
**2809-2810** A1096 Set of 2 6.00 4.00

World Breastfeeding Week A1097

**2000, Oct.**
**2811** A1097 300r multi 2.00 1.25

Ghadir Khom Festival A1098

**2001, Mar. 14**
**2812** A1098 500r multi 2.25 1.25

Year of H. H. Ali — A1099

**2001, Mar. 14**
**2813** A1099 500r multi 2.25 1.00

New Year — A1100

Birds: No. 2814, 300r, shown. No. 2815, 300r, Bird, diff., vert.

**2001, Mar. 18** ***Perf. 13x13½, 13½x13***
**2814-2815** A1100 Set of 2 6.50 3.00

Palestinian Intifada — A1100a

**2001, Apr. 24** **Photo.** ***Perf. 13***
**2815A** A1100a 350r multi *7.00 5.00*

Belgica 2001 Intl Stamp Exhibition, Brussels — A1101

Designs: No. 2816, 350r, Chaffinch (shown). No. 2817, 350r, Waxwing. No. 2818, 350r, National Garden, vert.

**2001, June 9** ***Perf. 13***
**2816-2818** A1101 Set of 3 *12.00 8.00*

Phila Nippon '01, Japan A1102

Emblem and: No. 2819, 250r, Mount Fuji, Japan. No. 2820, 250r, Mount Damavand, Iran.

**2001, Aug. 1** **Photo.** ***Perf. 13***
**2819-2820** A1102 Set of 2 4.00 2.50

World Tourism Day — A1103

**2001, Sept. 22**
**2821** A1103 500r multi 2.00 1.25

Police Week — A1104

No. 2822: a, Helicopters, parachutists, police cars, motorcycle police. b, Parachutists, officer saluting flag, motorcycle police, naval patrol.

**2001, Sept. 29** ***Perf. 13x13½***
**2822** A1104 250r Horiz. pair, #a-b 2.75 2.00

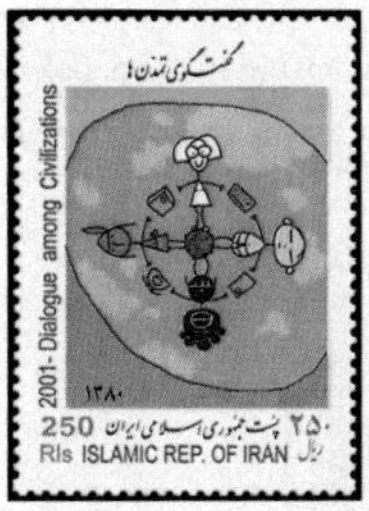


Year of Dialogue Among Civilizations A1105

Designs: No. 2823, 250r, Shown. No. 2824, 250r, Cubist and Oriental art, horiz.

**2001, Oct. 9** ***Perf. 13***
**2823-2824** A1105 Set of 2 4.50 2.50

Third Moslem Women's Games, Tehran — A1106

**2001, Oct. 24**
**2825** A1106 250r multi 2.00 1.25

Spring of the Holy Koran — A1107

**2001, Nov. 26**
**2826** A1107 500r multi 2.50 1.50

Honeybee — A1108

**2001, Dec. 3**
**2827** A1108 500r multi 2.75 1.75

UN High Commissioner for Refugees, 50th Anniv. — A1109

**2001, Dec. 10**
**2828** A1109 500r multi 2.00 1.00

Transportation Day — A1110

No. 2829: a, Truck on road. b, Truck on bridge, truck on road, gate.

**2001, Dec. 17** ***Perf. 13x13½***
**2829** A1110 350r Horiz. pair, #a-b 5.00 3.00

Navy Day A1111

No. 2830, 500r: a, Ship heading right. b, Ship heading left.
No. 2831, 500r: a, Helicopter, hovercraft. b, Submarine.

**2001, Nov. 28** **Photo.** ***Perf. 13***
**Vert. Pairs, #a-b**
**2830-2831** A1111 Set of 2 8.50 8.50

Tehran Subway A1112

No. 2832: a, Train headed right. b, Train headed left.

**2001, Dec. 13**
**2832** A1112 500r Vert. pair, #a-b 4.00 3.00

Iranian-made Automobiles — A1113

Designs: No. 2833, 500r, shown. No. 2834, 500r, Automobile, vert.

**2002, Jan. 15**
**2833-2834** A1113 Set of 2 4.00 2.50

Arbor Day — A1114

**2002, Mar. 6**
**2835** A1114 500r multi 1.75 1.25

A1115

New Year's Day — A1116

No. 2836: a, Bird with yellow breast. b, Parrot.
No. 2837: a, Stork facing left. b, Hoopoe facing right.

**2002, Mar. 16**
**2836** A1115 500r Horiz. pair, #a-b 3.75 3.00
**2837** A1116 500r Horiz. pair, #a-b 3.75 3.00

Imam Hossein — A1117

**2002, July 8** **Photo.** ***Imperf.***
**2838** A1117 400r multi 1.50 1.50

Butterflies — A1118

No. 2839: a, Danaus sita. b, Polygonia c-album. c, Precis orithya. d, Vanessa cardui. e, Papilio maacki.

**2002, July 29** ***Perf. 13***
**2839** Horiz. strip of 5 6.50 6.50
***a.-e.*** A1118 400r Any single 1.10 .90

A1119

PhilaKorea 2002 World Stamp Exhibition, Seoul — A1120

No. 2840 — Flowers: a, Hyoscyamus muticus. b, Frittillaria. c, Calotropis procera. d, Ranuculus.
No. 2841 — Horse breeds: a, Caspian. b, Kurd. c, Turkoman. d, Arab.

**2002, Aug. 2**
**2840** A1119 400r Block of 4, #a-d, + 2 labels 6.00 6.00
**2841** A1120 400r Block of 4, #a-d, + 2 labels 6.00 6.00

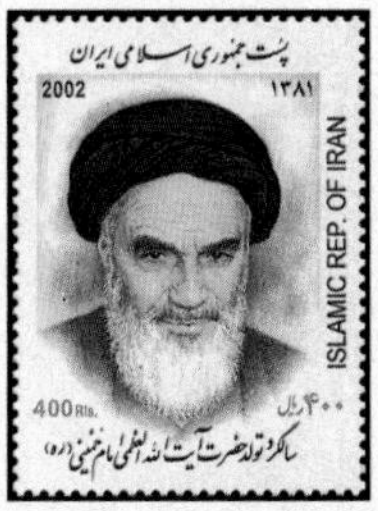


Ayatollah Khomeini (1900-89) A1121

**2002, Aug. 20**
**2842** A1121 400r multi 2.00 1.00

Jerusalem Day — A1122

**2002, Nov. 29**
**2843** A1122 400r multi 2.00 1.00

Iran — Brazil Diplomatic Relations, Cent. — A1123

No. 2844: a, Iranian ceramics. b, Brazilian ceramics.

**2002, Dec. 15**
**2844** Horiz. pair + label 5.00 5.00
*a.-b.* A1123 400r Either single 2.00 1.00

See Brazil Nos. 2868-2869.

2nd Biennial of Contemporary Painting of the Islamic World — A1124

**2002, Dec. 25**
**2845** A1124 400r multi 2.00 1.00

Esco Production Line, 30th Anniv. — A1125

**2003, Jan. 13** ***Perf. 13x13½***
**2846** A1125 400r multi 2.50 1.50

Air Force Day A1126

Various aircraft: 300r, 400r, 500r, 600r, 700r.

**2003, Feb. 8 Photo.** ***Perf. 13***
**2847-2851** A1126 Set of 5 7.50 7.50

New Year 2003 A1127

Mammals: No. 2852, 1000r, Goitered gazelle without horns. No. 2853, 1000r, Goitered gazelle with horns. No. 2854, 1000r, Red deer. No. 2855, 1000r, Urial.

**2003, Mar. 15**
**2852-2855** A1127 Set of 4 9.00 9.00

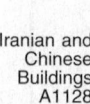

Iranian and Chinese Buildings A1128

No. 2856: a, Mosque, Isfahan. b, Bell Tower, Xian, People's Republic of China.

**2003, Apr. 15** ***Perf. 13x13½***
**2856** Horiz. pair + label 6.00 6.00
*a.-b.* A1128 400r Either single 1.50 1.25

See China (People's Republic) Nos. 3271-3272.

Book, Children and Family — A1129

**2003, May 4 Photo.** ***Perf. 13***
**2857** A1129 500r multi 1.75 1.25

Butterflies A1130

**2003-05 Photo.** ***Perf. 13x13½***
**2858** A1130 100r Zygaena sp. .25 —
**2859** A1130 200r Issoria lathonia .40 —
**2859A** A1130 250r Utethesia pulchella .50 —
**2860** A1130 300r Argynnis paphia .60 —
*a.* Longer "Rls." + label ('04) 1.50 —
**2862** A1130 500r Polygonia egea 1.00 —
**2863** A1130 600r Papilio machaon 1.25 —
*a.* Longer "Rls." + label ('04) 2.50 —
**2864** A1130 650r Colias aurorina ('04) 1.25 —
**2866** A1130 1000r Inachis io ('04) 1.40 —
**2867** A1130 2000r Papilio demoleus ('04) 4.00 —
**2867A** A1130 2100r Papilio domoleus ('05) 2.25 —
**2868** A1130 3000r Euphydryas aurinia ('04) 3.75 —
**2868A** A1130 4400r Danaus melanippus 4.25 —
**2869** A1130 5500r Colias aurorina 5.50 —

Issued: 100r, 7/14; 200r, 5/12; 300r, 5/14; 500r, 8/25; 600r, 6/10; 250r, 12/17; 1000r, 1/6/04; Nos. 2860a, 2863a, 1/21/04; 1000r, 2/22/04; 3000r, 3/10/04, 650r, 2004. 2100r, 4/18/05; 4400r, 3/15/05; 5500r, 4/13/05.

The period in "Rls." is under the second zero on Nos. 2860a and 2863a. It is under the first zero on Nos. 2860 and 2863. Examples of No. 2860a exist with and without perforations separating the stamp from the label.

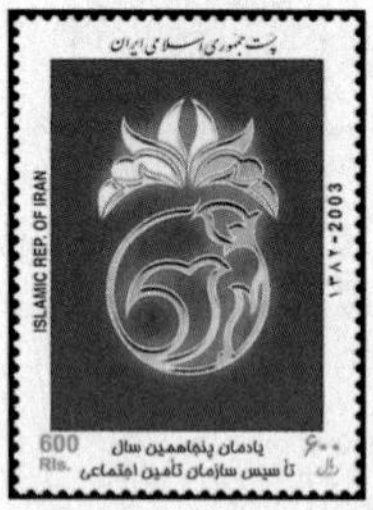

Social Security Organization, 50th Anniv. — A1131

**2003, Aug. 16 Photo.** ***Perf. 13***
**2870** A1131 600r multi 1.75 1.00

Government Martyrs — A1132

**2003, Aug. 24**
**2871** A1132 600r multi + label 2.00 2.00

Government Week — A1133

**2003, Aug. 25**
**2872** A1133 600r multi 1.50 1.00

Caspian Sea Fauna A1134

No. 2873: a, Caspian seal. b, Beluga.

**2003, Sept. 9**
**2873** Horiz. pair + label 7.50 7.50
*a.-b.* A1134 600r Either single 1.50 1.50
*c.* Souvenir sheet, 2 each #2873a-2873b 9.50 9.50

See Russia No. 6795.

World Post Day A1135

No. 2874: a, Computer, UPU emblem, satellite. b, Post office loading dock, mail box, airplanes. c, Postal clerk at desk, truck. d, Post rider, ruins and statues.

**2003, Oct. 9**
**2874** Horiz. strip of 4 8.00 8.00
*a.-d.* A1135 600r Any single 1.00 .75

Shared Functions of the Police and Post Office — A1136

**2003, Oct. 5 Photo.** ***Perf. 13***
**2875** A1136 500r multi 1.00 .75

Worldwide Fund for Nature (WWF) — A1137

No. 2876 — Cheetah: a, Cub. b, Two adults lying in grass. c, Two adults standing. d, Head of adult.

**2003, Nov. 18**
**2876** A1137 500r Block of 4, #a-d 4.75 4.75

Eid ul-Fitr A1138

**2003, Nov. 26**
**2877** A1138 600r multi 1.75 1.25

Miniature Sheet

Bam Earthquake, Dec. 26, 2003 — A1139

No. 2878: a, Landmarks in Bam before earthquake. b, Earthquake devastation. c, Doctors treating injured people. d, Rescue personnel, map of world.

**2004, Feb. 4**
**2878** A1139 500r Sheet of 4, #a-d 3.25 3.25

Islamic Revolution, 25th Anniv. A1140

**2004, Feb. 11**
**2879** A1140 600r multi 1.00 1.00

Hossein Rezazadeh, Weightlifter — A1141

**2004, Feb. 15**
**2880** A1141 1200r multi 2.00 2.00

Dated 2003.

ISO 9001-2000 Certification A1142

**2004, Feb. 29**
**2881** A1142 600r multi 1.00 1.00

Freshwater Fish — A1143

Designs: Nos. 2882, 2888a, 100r, Carassius auratus. Nos. 2883, 2888b, 200r, Carassius auratus, diff. Nos. 2884, 2888c, 300r, Poecilia reticlate. Nos. 2885, 2888d, 400r, Betta splendens. Nos. 2886, 2888e, 500r, Carassius auratus, diff. Nos. 2887, 2888f, 600r, Carassius auratus, diff.

**2004, Mar. 6**

**Stamps With White Frames**

**2882-2887** A1143 Set of 6 4.00 4.00

**Miniature Sheet**

**Stamps Without White Frames**

**2888** A1143 Sheet of 6, #a-f 5.00 5.00

FIFA (Fédération Internationale de Football Association), Cent. — A1144

**2004, May 21** ***Perf. 13***

**2889** A1144 600r multi 1.00 1.00

Miniature Sheet

Saltwater Fish — A1145

No. 2890: a, 250r, Balistoides conspicillum. b, 350r, Acanthurus glaucopareius. c, 450r, Pterois volitans. d, 550r, Zebrasoma veliferum. e, 650r, Pygoplites diacanthus. f, 750r, Pseudobalistes fuscus.

**2004, May 22** ***Perf. 13***

**2890** A1145 Sheet of 6, #a-f 4.25 4.25

España 2004 Intl. Philatelic Exhibition, Riccione Philatelic Exhibition.

Reporter's Day — A1147

**2004, Aug. 7**

**2892** A1147 650r multi .80 .80

2004 Summer Olympics, Athens — A1148

No. 2893: a, Taekwondo. b, Weight lifting. c, Wrestling. d, Judo.

**2004, Aug. 12**

**2893** A1148 650r Block of 4, #a-d 3.50 3.50

Poets — A1149

No. 2894: a, Kabir (1440-1518), Indian poet. b, Hafiz Shirazi (c. 1325-c. 1389), Persian poet.

**2004, Aug. 16** ***Perf. 13***

**2894** A1149 600r Horiz. pair, #a-b 1.50 1.50

See India No. 2070.

International Avicenna Congress — A1150

No. 2895: a, Memorial. b, Avicenna (980-1037), scientist, philosopher.

**2004, Aug. 22**

**2895** A1150 650r Horiz. pair, #a-b 1.60 1.60

Miniature Sheet

Primates — A1151

No. 2896: a, Chacma baboons. b, Chimpanzee. c, Chimpanzees. d, Mandrill.

**2004, Aug. 28**

**2896** A1151 500r Sheet of 4, #a-d 5.00 5.00

World Stamp Championship 2004, Singapore.

Miniature Sheet

Cats — A1152

No. 2897: a, Gray cat, no tail visible. b, Gray cat, tail at right. c, Brown and white cat. d, White cat. e, Gray cat on rock. f, Gray cat, tail at left.

**2004, Aug. 31**

**2897** A1152 500r Sheet of 6, #a-f 6.00 6.00

12th Paralympic Games, Athens A1153

**2004, Sept. 17**

**2898** A1153 650r multi .80 .50

Iran - Iraq War, 24th Anniv. A1154

**2004, Sept. 21**

**2899** A1154 650r multi .80 .50

Tehran University, 70th Anniv. A1155

**2004, Oct. 22**

**2900** A1155 650r multi .80 .50

Poets — A1156

No. 2901: a, Dr. Jalal-eddin Ashtiani (wearing turban). b, Mahmoud Farschian (with hand on chin). c, Dr. Jafar Shahidi (looking right). d, Dr. Hosain Mirshamsi (looking left).

**2004, Nov. 9** **Photo.** ***Perf. 13***

**2901** A1156 500r Block of 4, #a-d 2.50 2.00

Mountains — A1157

No. 2902: a, Damavand Mountain, Iran. b, Bolivar Peak, Venezuela.

**2004, Nov. 28** **Photo.** ***Perf. 13***

**2902** A1157 650r Horiz. pair, #a-b 1.50 1.00

First Intl. Biennale of Islamic Poster Art — A1158

No. 2903: a, Hand. b, Dove in nest. c, Slingshot. d, Crescent.

**2004, Nov. 29**

**2903** A1158 500r Block of 4, #a-d 2.50 2.00

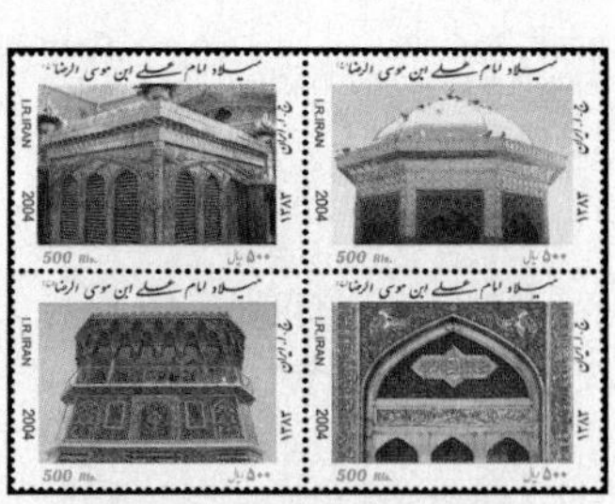


Imam Reza's Birthday — A1159

No. 2904: a, Corner of mosque. b, Dome. c, Facade. d, Archway.

**2004, Dec. 24** **Photo.** ***Perf. 13x13¼***

**2904** A1159 500r Block of 4, #a-d 2.50 2.00

Ali Daei, Soccer Player A1160

**2005, Feb. 2** **Photo.** ***Perf. 13***

**2905** A1160 650r multi .75 .50

Iran Film Museum — A1161

No. 2906: a, Scene from *Where is the Friend's Home?* b, Scene from *The Children of Heaven*. c, Museum building. d, Scene from *The Cow*.

**2005, Feb. 10**

**2906** A1161 500r Block of 4, #a-d 2.00 1.00

Airplanes — A1162

No. 2907: a, AN-140. b, IR-140.

**2005, Mar. 6** ***Perf. 13x13½***

**2907** Horiz. pair with central label 2.00 1.00

***a.-b.*** A1162 850r Either single

See Ukraine No. 568.

Souvenir Sheet

Expo 2005, Aichi, Japan — A1163

No. 2908: a, Persepolis. b, Yazd air ventilation towers. c, Iranian flag, typical Iranian desert architecture. d, Clay tablet with inscriptions.

**2005, Mar. 24** ***Perf. 13***

**2908** A1163 650r Sheet of 4, #a-d 2.50 2.00

Tehran University of Medical Sciences, 70th Anniv. — A1164

**2005, May 2**

**2909** A1164 650r multi .75 .50

Police Week — A1165

**2005, Oct. 29**

**2910** A1165 650r multi .75 .50

Mevlana Jalal ad-Din ar-Rumi (1207-73), Islamic Philosopher A1166

**2005, Dec. 3**

**2911** A1166 650r multi 1.50 1.00

See Afghanistan Nos. 1449-1451, Syria No. 1574, Turkey No. 2971.

Gardens — A1167

No. 2912: a, Gardens of Royal Palace of La Granja de San Ildefonso, Segovia, Spain. b, Bagh-e-Shahzadeh, Kerman, Iran.

**2005, Dec. 17**

**2912** A1167 650r Horiz. pair, #a-b 1.50 1.00

See Spain No. 3374.

Self-Sufficiency in Wheat Production A1168

**2006, Jan. 4**

**2913** A1168 650r multi .75 .50

Souvenir Sheet

Maps of the Persian Gulf — A1169

No. 2914: a, German map, 16th cent. b, Egyptian Ministry of Culture map, 1966. c, Saudi Arabian map, 1952. d, Map by Scoteri Motthaei, 18th cent.

**2006, June 7**

**2914** A1169 650r Sheet of 4, #a-d 5.00 2.50

2006 World Cup Soccer Championships, Germany — A1170

**2006, June 10**

**2915** A1170 650r multi .90 .50

Abbas Shafi — A1171

Alama Mohammed Reza Hakimi A1172

Mohamed Hossein Gandji A1173

Alama Mohammed Hassan Amoli — A1174

**2006, Sept. 18** **Litho.** ***Perf. 13***

**2916** Block of 4 1.00 .75

***a.*** A1171 650r multi 1.00 .75

***b.*** A1172 650r multi 1.00 .75

***c.*** A1173 650r multi 1.00 .75

***d.*** A1174 650r multi 1.00 .75

Dated 2005.

Third Meeting of Economic Cooperation Organization Postal Authorities, Tehran — A1175

**2006, Sept. 20**

**2917** A1175 650r multi 2.00 1.00

See Kazakhstan No. 526, Pakistan No. 1101 and Turkey No. 3041.

Basij, 27th Anniv. A1176

**2006, Nov. 26**

**2918** A1176 650r multi 2.00 1.00

Souvenir Sheet

Isfahan, 2006 Islamic Cultural Capital — A1177

No. 2919: a, Chehel Sotun Palace. b, Emam Mosque. c, Aliqapu Palace. d, Khajo Bridge.

**2006, Dec. 30**

**2919** A1177 650r Sheet of 4, #a-d 5.00 2.50

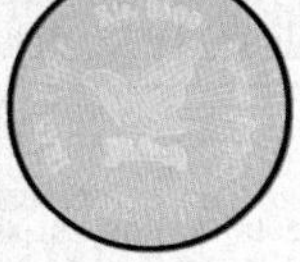

A1177a A1177b

Iran Post Emblem

**Hologram on Foil**

**2006, Dec.** **Self-Adhesive** ***Die Cut***

**2919E** A1177a 4400r silver *3.50 3.50*

**2919F** A1177b 5500r silver *4.50 4.50*

Martyrs — A1178

No. 2920: a, Man and flags. b, Ten men.

**2007, Jan. 7**

**2920** A1178 650r Horiz. pair, #a-b 2.00 1.00

Dated 2006.

Souvenir Sheet

Iranian Constitution, Cent. — A1179

No. 2921: a, Man, gate. b, Parliament. c, Three men, gate. d, Two men, gate.

**2006, May 8** **Litho.** ***Perf. 13***
**2921** A1179 650r Sheet of 4, #a-d 5.00 3.00

Souvenir Sheet

Seventh General Assembly of Association of Asian Parliaments for Peace, Tehran — A1180

No. 2922: a, Emblem of Association of Asian Parliaments for Peace. b, Dove, colors of Iranian flag. c, Gate and flags. d, Emblem of Islamic Consultative Assembly.

**2006, Nov. 14**
**2922** A1180 650r Sheet of 4, #a-d 5.00 2.50

Peaceful Nuclear Energy — A1181

**2007, Feb. 11**
**2923** A1181 650r multi 2.00 1.00

Iranian-built Engine A1182

**2007, Feb. 26**
**2924** A1182 650r multi 1.50 .60

Shrine of Fatima, Qom — A1183

**2007, Mar. 18**
**2925** A1183 650r multi 1.50 .50

New Year — A1184

No. 2926: a, Flowers, man with drum. b, Trumpeters, fishbowl, Koran, apples, grass.

**2007, Mar. 19**
**2926** A1184 650r Horiz. pair, #a-b 2.00 1.00

Map of Persian Gulf — A1185

**2007** **Litho.** ***Perf. 13x13½***

**Side Panel Color**

| | | | | |
|---|---|---|---|---|
| **2927** | A1185 | 200r brown | 1.00 | .50 |
| **2928** | A1185 | 300r yellow | 1.00 | .50 |
| *a.* | | Taller Arabic "Rls." + label | — | — |
| **2929** | A1185 | 650r orange | 1.00 | .50 |
| *a.* | | Wider "650" + label | — | — |
| **2930** | A1185 | 2100r blue | 4.00 | 2.00 |
| **2931** | A1185 | 4400r blue | 8.00 | 3.00 |

Issued: 200r, 9/9; 300r, 5/23; 4400r, 7/25. 650r, 10/30; 2100r, 11/24; No. 2929a, 1/27/09.
See Nos. 2943-2945, 2956-2960.

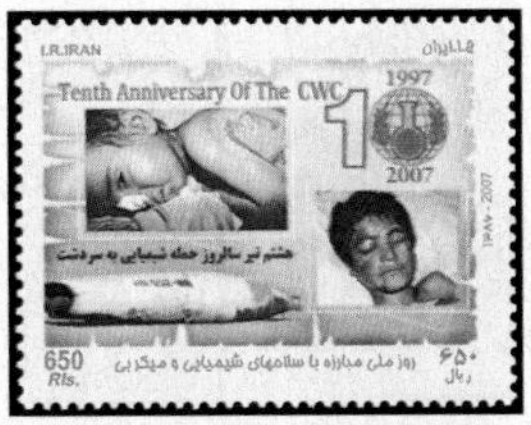


Chemical Weapons Convention, 10th Anniv. — A1186

**2007, June 29** ***Perf. 13***
**2932** A1186 650r multi 1.50 .50

38th Intl. Physics Olympiad, Isfahan — A1187

**2007, July 3**
**2933** A1187 650r multi 1.50 .50

K. K. Sarughy A1188

**2007, Aug. 22**
**2934** A1188 650r multi 1.50 .50

Imam Moussa Sadr, Shiite Leader Who Disappeared in 1978 — A1189

**2007, Aug. 31**
**2935** A1189 650r multi 1.50 .50

Worldwide Fund for Nature (WWF) — A1190

No. 2936 — Grus leucogranus: a, Pair, one with head raised, other with head lowered. b, Pair, facing each other. c, Pair, both standing on one leg. d, Running with wings extended.

**2007, Sept. 9**
**2936** A1190 650r Block of 4, #a-d 4.00 2.50

Miniature Sheet

Great Messenger Year — A1191

No. 2937 — Arabic text and: a, Arch. b, Arabic text in diamond. c, Roman Colosseum. d, Pyramids.

**2007, Jan. 6** **Litho.** ***Perf. 13***
**2937** A1191 650r Sheet of 4, #a-d 5.00 2.50

Communications and Public Relations Day — A1192

**2007, May 17**
**2938** A1192 650r multi 1.50 .50

Miniature Sheet

Return of Prisoners of War — A1193

No. 2939 — Flowers and: a, Geese. b, Iranian man, hand symbol. c, Prisoners of war on bus. d, People on motorcycles greeting prisoners of war.

**2007, Aug. 17**
**2939** A1193 650r Sheet of 4, #a-d 5.00 2.50

Jamkaran Mosque A1194

**2007, Aug. 29**
**2940** A1194 650r multi 1.50 .50

World Post Day — A1195

**2007, Sept. 10**
**2941** A1195 650r multi 2.00 1.00

Mevlana Jalal ad-Din ar-Rumi (1207-73), Islamic Philosopher A1196

**2007, Oct. 28**
**2942** A1196 650r multi 2.00 1.00

### Map of Persian Gulf Type of 2007

**2008** *Perf. 13x13½*

**Side Panel Color**

**2943** A1185 1000r green 2.00 1.00
**2944** A1185 2000r lilac 4.00 2.00
**2945** A1185 5500r red 10.00 4.00

Issued: 1000r, 1/16; 2000r, 2/5; 5500r, 1/5.

Information Technology Infrastructure Development
A1197

**2008, Jan. 16** *Perf. 13*
**2946** A1197 650r multi 2.00 .75

Navvab Safavi (1924-55), Founder of Islamic Fedayeen
A1198

**2008, Jan. 17**
**2947** A1198 650r multi 1.50 .75

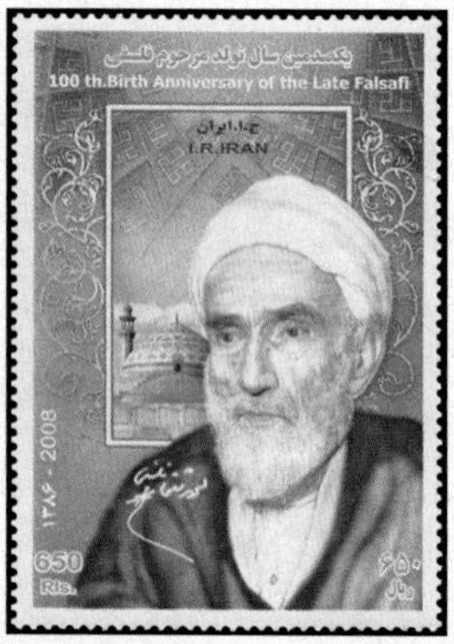

Falsafi, Preacher, 100th Anniv. of Birth — A1199

**2008, Feb. 27**
**2948** A1199 650r multi 1.50 .75

Death of Emad Moghnie, Hezbollah Leader — A1200

**2008, Mar. 10**
**2949** A1200 650r multi 2.00 1.00

New Year
A1201

**2008, Mar. 15**
**2950** A1201 650r multi 1.50 .75

Abdulazim Shrine — A1202

**2008, Apr. 11** *Perf. 13x13½*
**2951** A1202 650r multi 1.50 .75

Children and Youth Water Festival
A1203

**2008, Apr. 21** *Perf. 13*
**2952** A1203 650r multi 1.50 .75

Islamic City Councils, 10th Anniv.
A1204

**2008, Apr. 28**
**2953** A1204 650r multi 1.50 .75

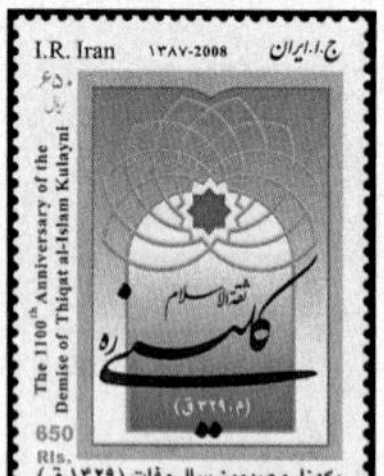

Thiqat al-Islam Kulayni, Islamic Legal Scholar, 1100th Anniv. of Death — A1205

**2008, May 8**
**2954** A1205 650r multi 1.50 .75

Buildings in Morocco and Iran — A1206

No. 2955: a, Kasbah, Oudayas, Morocco. b, Falak-Ol-Aflak Castle, Iran.

**2008, May 12** **Litho.** *Perf. 13*
**2955** A1206 650r Horiz. pair, #a-b, + label 2.50 1.50

See Morocco No. 1061.

### Map of Persian Gulf Type of 2007

**2008-09** **Litho.** *Perf. 13x13½*

**Side Panel Color**

**2956** A1185 100r blue .50 .50
**2957** A1185 250r pale orange .50 .50
**2958** A1185 400r red .50 .50
**2959** A1185 500r dark green .50 .50
**2960** A1185 3000r pink — —
*Nos. 2956-2960 (5)* 2.00 2.00

Issued: 100r, 9/8; 250r, 10/20; 400r, 9/13; 500r, 5/28; 3000r, 2/15/09.

Handicrafts Day — A1207

No. 2961: a, Engraved copper cup. b, Mina vase.

**2008, June 10** **Litho.** *Perf. 13*
**2961** A1207 650r Horiz. pair, #a-b 2.50 1.50

Miniature Sheet

Trenchless Trench Makers — A1207a

No. 2962 — Men and: a, Construction equipment with extendable arm. b, Bulldozer under roof. c, Utility vehicle. d, Ship on truck's flat-bed trailer.

**2008, June 16** **Litho.** *Perf. 13*
**2962** A1207a 650r Sheet of 4, #a-d .60 .60

Javid-al-Asar Haj Ahmed Motevasselian, Diplomat
A1208

**2008, July 3**
**2963** A1208 650r multi 1.50 .75

Mountains in Kyrgyzstan and Iran — A1209

No. 2964: a, Khan-Tengri, Kyrgyzstan. b, Sabalan Peak, Iran.

**2008, Aug. 15**
**2964** A1209 650r Horiz. pair, #a-b, + central label 2.50 1.50

See Kyrgyzstan No. 313.

Ancient Jewelry From Iran and Kazakhstan — A1210

No. 2965: a, Gold medal depicting lions, 7th cent. B.C., Iran. b, Buckle depicting snow leopard and mountains, 4th-5th cent. B.C., Kazakhstan.

**2008, Sept. 7**
**2965** A1210 650r Horiz. pair, #a-b 2.50 1.50

See Kazakhstan No. 578.

Iran Post Corporation, 20th Anniv. — A1211

**2008, Oct. 8** *Perf. 13x13½*
**2966** A1211 1200r multi 2.00 1.00

Consumer Rights Day — A1212

**2008, Feb. 28** *Perf. 13*
**2967** A1212 650r multi

Ayatollah Sheikh Hashem Ghazvini
A1213

**2008, May 5**
**2968** A1213 650r multi

Bank Melli Iran, 80th Anniv.
A1214

**2008, Sept. 10**
**2969** A1214 650r multi

World Jerusalem Day — A1215

**2008, Sept. 26**
**2970** A1215 650r multi

Statue of Sheikh Abulhassan Kharaghani A1216

**2008, Nov. 6**
**2971** A1216 650r multi

Commander M. R. Pourkian and Tank — A1217

**2008, Nov. 13**
**2972** A1217 650r multi

28-Year Achievements of Security Services A1218

**2008, Nov. 19**
**2973** A1218 650r multi

Zabol Burnt City Archaeological Site — A1219

**2008, Dec. 21**
**2974** A1219 650r multi

National Day of Exports A1220

**2008, Oct. 21** ***Perf. 13***
**2975** A1220 650r multi

Musical Instruments — A1221

No. 2976: a, Gijak of Badahshon. b, Khorasan local dotaar.

**2008, Dec. 15**
**2976** A1221 650r Horiz. pair, #a-b

See Tajikistan No. 340.

Support for Gaza Palestinians — A1222

**2009, Jan. 27**
**2977** A1222 1200r multi

Ayatollah Khomeini (1900-89) — A1223

**2009, Feb. 10**
**2978** A1223 650r multi

Islamic Revolution, 30th anniv.

Abbas, Karimi, Reza Cheraghi, and Mohammad Hemat — A1224

**2009, Mar. 3**
**2979** A1224 650r multi

Safir Omid, First Iranian Satellite — A1225

No. 2980: a, Iranian flag, rocket on launch pad, emblem. b, Satellite, Earth.

**2009, Mar. 7**
**2980** A1225 1300r Horiz. pair, #a-b

10th Economic Cooperation Organization Summit, Tehran — A1226

**2009, Mar. 11**
**2981** A1226 1300r multi

See Azerbaijan 895, compare with Pakistan 1111.

New Year 2009 A1227

**2009, Mar. 25**
**2982** A1227 1300r multi

Nurse's Day — A1228

**2009, Apr. 28**
**2983** A1228 1300r multi

Fish — A1229

Designs: 100r, Chaetodon mesoleucos. 200r, Holacanthus ciliaris. 250r, Euxiphipops xanthomelapon. 300r, Pomacanthus maculosus. 350r, Pomacanthus annularis. 400r, Chaetodon rafflesi. 500r, Centropyge bicolor. 1000r, Chaetodontoplus septentrionalis. 2000r, Chaetodon larvatus. 3000r, Chaetodon auriga. 3100r, Chaetodon semilarvatus. 4000r, Pomacanthus chrysurus. 5000r, Pomacanthus navarchus. 6400r, Paracanthurus hepatus. 7500r, Premnas biaculeatus.

**2009-11 Litho.** ***Perf. 13x13½***
**Size: 32x25mm**

| | | | | |
|---|---|---|---|---|
| **2984** | A1229 | 100r multi | .25 | .25 |
| **2985** | A1229 | 200r multi | .25 | .25 |
| **2986** | A1229 | 250r multi | .25 | .25 |
| **2987** | A1229 | 300r multi | .25 | .25 |
| **2988** | A1229 | 350r multi | .25 | .25 |
| **2989** | A1229 | 400r multi | .25 | .25 |
| **2990** | A1229 | 500r multi | .25 | .25 |
| **2993** | A1229 | 1000r multi | .25 | .25 |
| **2994** | A1229 | 2000r multi | .40 | .40 |
| **2994A** | A1229 | 3000r multi | .60 | .60 |
| **2995** | A1229 | 3100r multi | .65 | .65 |
| **2996** | A1229 | 4000r multi | .80 | .80 |
| **2997** | A1229 | 5000r multi | 1.00 | 1.00 |
| **2998** | A1229 | 6400r multi | 1.40 | 1.40 |
| **2999** | A1229 | 7500r multi | 1.50 | 1.50 |
| | *Nos. 2984-2999 (12)* | | 6.95 | 6.95 |

Issued: 100r, 9/25/10; 200r, 10/26; 250r, 4/7/10; 300r, 4/12/10; 350r, 2/26/11. 400r, 12/27/10. 500r, 12/21; 1000r, 6/22; 2000r, 8/1/10; 3000r, 5/8/11; 3100r, 1/19/10; 4000r, 7/18/10; 5000r, 6/15/10; 6400r, 11/10; 7500r, 10/12.

See Nos. 3055A-3055I.

Epic of Presence A1230

**2009, June 12 Litho.** ***Perf. 13***
**3000** A1230 1300r multi .30 .30

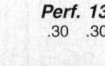

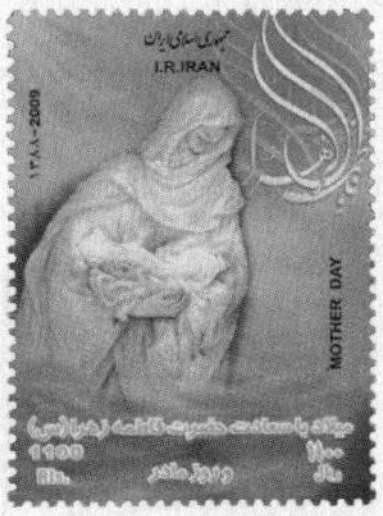


Mother's Day — A1231

**2009, June 14**
**3001** A1231 1100r multi .25 .25

Birds — A1232

No. 3002: a, White-tailed eagle. b, Osprey.

**2009, June 24**
**3002** A1232 2000r Horiz. pair, #a-b .80 .80

See Portugal Nos. 3155-3156.

Left Part of Stamp

Center Part of Stamp

Birds (Right Part of Stamp) — A1233

**2009, July 11** *Perf. 13x13½*
**3003** A1233 1500r multi .30 .30

The illustration of No. 3003 is shown above broken into the three sections shown on the stamp. See Cuba No. 4835.

Marwa El-Sherbini (1977-2009), Woman Murdered in German Courtroom A1234

**2009, July 19** *Perf. 13*
**3004** A1234 1300r multi .30 .30

Islamic Human Rights and Human Dignity Day A1235

**2009, Aug. 5**
**3005** A1235 1200r multi .25 .25

Rural Information and Communication Technologies in Iran — A1236

**2009, Aug. 11**
**3006** A1236 1000r multi .25 .25

Miniature Sheet

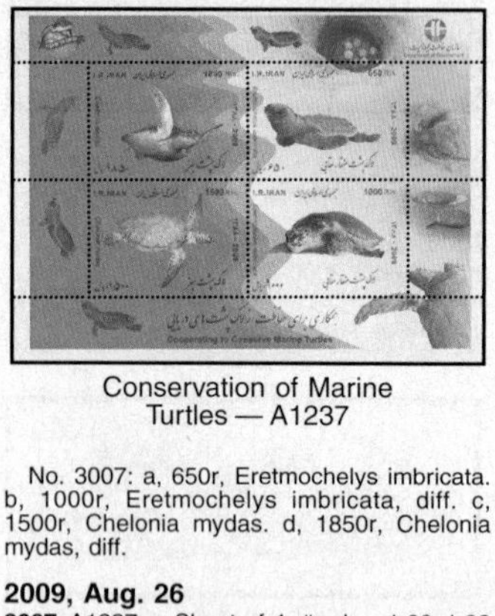

Conservation of Marine Turtles — A1237

No. 3007: a, 650r, Eretmochelys imbricata. b, 1000r, Eretmochelys imbricata, diff. c, 1500r, Chelonia mydas. d, 1850r, Chelonia mydas, diff.

**2009, Aug. 26**
**3007** A1237 Sheet of 4, #a-d 1.00 1.00

A1238

No. 3008: a, World Post Day. b, World Child Day.

**2009, Oct. 9**
**3008** A1238 1200r Horiz. pair, #a-b .50 .50

17th Book Week — A1239

**2009, Nov. 14**
**3009** A1239 1200r multi .25 .25

Rob'e Rashidi University Endowment Document — A1240

**2009, Dec. 1** **Litho.**
**3010** A1240 1200r multi .25 .25

Ghadir Khom Festival — A1240a

**2009, Dec. 6** **Litho.** *Perf. 13¾x14¼*
**3010A** A1240a 1200r multi .25 .25

Universal Declaration of Human Rights, 60th Anniv. — A1241

**2009, Dec. 13** *Perf. 13*
**3011** A1241 1200r multi .25 .25

Ayatollah Mohammad Mofatteh (1928-79) A1242

**2009, Dec. 18** *Perf. 13¾x14¼*
**3012** A1242 1200r multi .25 .25

Buildings in Indonesia and Iran — A1243

No. 3013: a, Soltanieh Dome, Iran. b, Al-Markaz Mosque, Indonesia.

**2009, Dec. 23** *Perf. 13*
**3013** A1243 2000r Horiz. pair, #a-b, + central label .80 .80

See Indonesia Nos. 2218-2219.

Intl. Year of Astronomy — A1244

No. 3014: a, 1000r, Artificial plan of Maragheh Observatory. b, 1200r, Al-Tafhim, by Abu Ryehan Biruni. c, 1300r, Armillary sphere. d, 1500r, Taqi al-Din and astronomers, 16th cent.

**2010, Feb. 24** *Perf. 13¾x14¼*
**3014** A1244 Block of 4, #a-d 1.00 1.00

Mullah Sadra (c. 1571-1641) A1245

**2010, May 18**
**3015** A1245 1300r multi .25 .25

Khaje Abdullah Ansari (1006-88), Religious Commentator — A1246

**2010, July 25** *Perf. 13¾*
**3016** A1246 2000r multi .40 .40

See Afghanistan No. , Tajikistan No. 366.

Destroyer Jamaran — A1247

**2010, Sept. 1** *Perf. 14¼x13¾*
**3017** A1247 2000r multi .40 .40

Martyred Engineers of the Sacred Defense A1248

**2010, Oct. 20** *Perf. 13¾x14¼*
**3018** A1248 2000r multi .40 .40

Shah-e-Cheragh Holy Shrine, Shiraz — A1249

No, 3019: a, 1200r, Mosque dome and minaret. b, 1300r, Shrine.

**2010, Nov. 14** *Perf. 13¾*
**3019** A1249 Horiz. pair, #a-b .50 .50

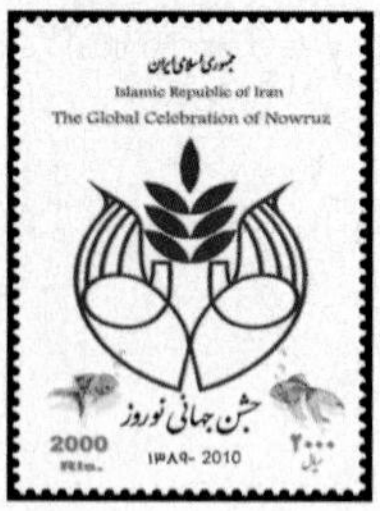


A1250

New Year — A1251

No. 3021: a, Flowers and ribbon. b, Candle and Iranian inscription. c, Goldfish in bowl and apples. d, Koran on bookstand and oranges.

***Perf. 13¾x14¼***

**2010, Mar. 27** **Litho.**

**3020** A1250 2000r multi .40 .40

***Perf. 14¼x13¾***

**3021** A1251 1250r Sheet of 4, #a-d 1.00 1.00

Nature Day — A1252

No. 3022 — Trees in: a, Spring. b, Summer. c, Autumn. d, Winter.

**2010, Apr. 2** ***Perf. 13¾x14¼***

**3022** Horiz. strip of 4 1.00 1.00
*a.* A1252 1100r pink & multi .25 .25
*b.* A1252 1200r green & multi .25 .25
*c.* A1252 1300r orange & multi .25 .25
*d.* A1252 1400r blue & multi .30 .30

Towers in Pakistan and Iran — A1253

No. 3023: a, Minar-e-Pakistan, Lahore. b, Milad Tower, Tehran.

**2010, July 28**

**3023** A1253 2000r Horiz. pair, #a-b, + flanking label .80 .80

See Pakistan No. 1149.

Miniature Sheet

Products of Iranian Military Industries — A1254

No. 3024: a, 1000r, Sedjil missile. b, 1500r, Saegheh airplane. c, 2000r, Mersad radar system. d, 2500r, Ghadir submarine.

**2010, Aug. 22** ***Perf. 14¼x13¾***

**3024** A1254 Sheet of 4, #a-d 1.40 1.40

Martyrs of Holy Defense A1255

**2010, Sept. 27** ***Perf. 13¾x14¼***

**3025** A1255 2000r multi .40 .40

Miniature Sheet

World Post Day — A1256

No. 3026: a, 1000r, Airplane and S.P.S. emblem. b, 1100r, Financial Post emblem. c, 1300r, Mail truck and EMS emblem. d, 1400r, Shopping cart and "@" symbol. e, 1500r, Iran Post e-mail emblem. f, 1700r, Mailman on motorcycle. g, 2000r, UPU emblem, map of Iran.

**2010, Oct. 9** ***Perf. 14¼***

**3026** A1256 Sheet of 7, #a-g 2.00 2.00

Embroidery — A1257

No. 3027: a, Jazygian embroidery designs, Hungary. b, Termeh embroidery designs, Yazd, Iran.

**2010, Nov. 10** ***Perf. 14¼x13¾***

**3027** A1257 2000r Horiz. pair, #a-b .80 .80

See Hungary Nos. 4178-4179.

18th Book Week — A1258

**2010, Nov. 14** ***Perf. 13¾x14¼***

**3028** A1258 2000r multi .40 .40

Sheikh Abbas Qummi (1877-1940), Historian A1259

**2010, Dec. 2**

**3029** A1259 2000r multi .40 .40

A1259a

A1259b

Personalized Stamps — A1259c

No. 3029E: f, 300r, Rainbow, denomination on green and blue stripes. g, 700r, Rainbos, denomination on orange, yellow and green stripes. h, 900r, Rainbow and tree, denomination on tree and grass. i, 1200r, Clouds, butterfly and city, denomination on city.

**2010-11** **Litho.** ***Perf. 13¾x14¼***

**Denomination on One Line Country Name at Center**

**3029A** A1259a 300r multi + label — —
**3029B** A1259a 650r multi + label — —
**3029C** A1259a 1000r multi + label — —

**Country Name at Left Above Denomination on Two Lines**

**3029D** A1259b 650r multi + label — —

**Souvenir Sheet Country Name Not Shown in English**

***Perf. 14¼x13¾ on 3 Sides***

**3029E** A1259c Sheet of 4, #f-i + 4 labels — —

Issued: No. 3029A, 2010, others, 2011. Labels on Nos. 3029A-3029E are separated from the stamps by a line of simulated perforations. Other labels exist for No. 3029A. Other labels may exist for Nos. 3029B-3029E.

Space — A1259d

No. 3029J — Inscriptions: a, Space Technology Day. b, Kavoshgar 2. c, Tolou National Satellite. d, Mesbah 2 National Satellite. e, Satellite Ground Stations.

**2010, Dec. 6** **Litho.** ***Perf. 13¾x14¼***

**3029J** Horiz. strip of 5 1.40 1.40
*k.-l.* A1259d 1200r Either single .25 .25
*m.* A1259d 1400r multi .25 .25
*n.* A1259d 1600r multi .30 .30
*o.* A1259d 1800r multi .35 .35

Bank Maskan Mehr Housing Project, 73rd Anniv. — A1260

**2011, Jan. 15**

**3030** A1260 2000r multi .40 .40

Electronic Communication Between People and Government A1261

**2011, Jan. 17**

**3031** A1261 2000r multi .40 .40

Islamic Revolution, 32nd Anniv. — A1262

No. 3032 — Ayatollah Khomeini and: a, Red flowers at LR. b, Candle at UL. c, White flowers and three candles at top. d, Birds and white flowers.

**2011, Feb. 11**

**3032** Horiz. strip of 4 .80 .80
*a.-d.* A1262 1000r Any single .25 .25

Convergence of Montheistic Religions — A1263

**2011, Feb. 15** ***Perf. 14¼x13¾***

**3033** A1263 2000r multi .40 .40

Ayatollah Mahmoud Taleghani (1911-79) A1264

**2011, Mar. 5** ***Perf. 13¾x14¼***

**3034** A1264 2500r multi .50 .50

Miniature Sheet

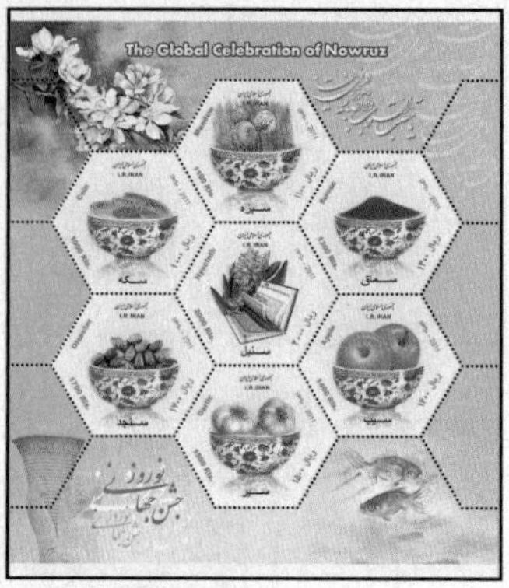


New Year — A1265

No. 3035: a, 1000r, Bowl of coins. b, 1100r, Grass and painted eggs in bowl. c, 1300r, Bowl of sumac. d, 1400r, Apples in bowl. e, 1500r, Garlic bulbs in bowl. f, 1700r, Oleaster in bowl. g, 2000r, Hyacinth and Koran.

**2011, Mar. 26** ***Perf. 14¼***

**3035** A1265 Sheet of 7, #a-g 2.00 2.00

Bridges A1266

Designs: 10,000r, Jahanara Bridge. 14,800r, Khajoo Bridge. 20,000r, Veresk Bridge. 20,700r, Javadieh Bridge.

| **2011** | **Litho.** | ***Perf. 14*** | |
|---|---|---|---|
| **3036** A1266 10,000r multi | | 1.90 | 1.90 |
| **3037** A1266 14,800r multi | | 2.75 | 2.75 |
| **3038** A1266 20,000r multi | | 3.50 | 3.50 |
| **3039** A1266 20,700r multi | | 4.00 | 4.00 |
| *Nos. 3036-3039 (4)* | | 12.15 | 12.15 |

Issued: 10,000r, 6/15; 14,800r, 7/20; 20,000r, 5/22; 20,700r, 7/6.

World Crafts Day — A1267

No. 3040: a, Vase. b, Lidded container.

**2011, June 10** ***Perf. 13¾x14¼***

**3040** A1267 2000r Horiz. pair, #a-b .70 .70

Ayatollah Muhammad Fazel Lankarani (1931-2007) A1268

**2011, June 15**

**3041** A1268 2000r multi .40 .40

Souvenir Sheet

Green Pheasants — A1269

**2011, July 26** ***Perf. 14¼x13¾***

**3042** A1269 5000r multi .95 .95

PhilaNippon '11 Intl. Philatelic Exhibition, Yokohama, Japan.

Souvenir Sheet

Iranian Men's Volleyball Team, Champions of 16th Asian Tournament — A1269a

**2011, Sept. 29** ***Perf. 14***

**3042A** A1269a 3400r multi .65 .65

National Veterinary Day — A1270

**2011, Oct. 6** ***Perf. 14¼x13¾***

**3043** A1270 2200r multi .45 .45

2011 Population and Housing Census A1271

**2011, Oct. 23** ***Perf. 13¾x14¼***

**3044** A1271 2200r multi .40 .40

Shams Tabrizi (1185-c.1248), Teacher of Poet Mevlana A1272

**2011, Oct. 30**

**3045** A1272 2200r multi .40 .40

Souvenir Sheet

Buildings in Belarus and Iran — A1273

No. 3046: a, Mir Castle, Mir, Belarus. b, Karimkhani Citadel, Shiraz, Iran.

***Perf. 14¼x13¾***

**2011, Sept. 28** **Litho.**

**3046** A1273 2200r Sheet of 2, #a-b .85 .85

See Belarus No. 783.

World Post Day — A1274

**2011, Oct. 9** ***Perf. 13¾***

**3047** A1274 2000r multi .40 .40

19th Book Week — A1275

**2011, Nov. 13** ***Perf. 13¾x14¼***

**3048** A1275 2200r multi .40 .40

Souvenir Sheet

Revival Week — A1276

**2011, Nov. 27** ***Perf. 14¼x13¾***

**3049** A1276 2200r multi .40 .40

Worldwide Fund for Nature (WWF) — A1277

Designs: Nos. 3050, 3054a, 600r, Long-eared owl. Nos. 3051, 3054b, 1100r, Spotted owlet. Nos. 3052, 3054c, 1600r, Pallid scops owl. Nos. 3053, 3054d, 2200r, Brown fish owl.

**2011, Dec. 14** **Litho.**

**Stamps With White Frames**

**3050-3053** A1277 Set of 4 1.00 1.00

**Souvenir Sheet**

**Stamps Without White Frame**

**3054** A1277 Sheet of 4, #a-d 1.00 1.00

Islamic Awakening A1278

**2011, Dec. 22** ***Perf. 13¾x14¼***

**3055** A1278 2200r multi .40 .40

**Fish Type of 2009-11**

Designs as before.

**2011** **Litho.** ***Perf. 14***

**Size: 30x23mm**

| | | | | |
|---|---|---|---|---|
| **3055A** | A1229 | 300r multi | — | — |
| **3055B** | A1229 | 400r multi | — | — |
| **3055C** | A1229 | 500r multi | — | — |
| **3055D** | A1229 | 1000r multi | — | — |
| **3055E** | A1229 | 2000r multi | — | — |
| **3055F** | A1229 | 4000r multi | — | — |
| **3055G** | A1229 | 5000r multi | — | — |
| **3055H** | A1229 | 6400r multi | — | — |
| **3055I** | A1229 | 7500r multi | — | — |

Islamic and Iranian Culture and Civilization — A1279

**2012, Feb. 1** ***Perf. 14¼x13¾***

**3056** A1279 2200r multi .40 .40

Souvenir Sheet

Islamic Revolution, 33rd Anniv. — A1280

No. 3057: a, Toppled statue of Shah of Iran, flames. b, Ayatollah Khomeini, tulips.

**2012, Feb. 11** ***Perf. 13¾x14¼***

**3057** A1280 2200r Sheet of 2, #a-b .80 .80

New Year 2012 — A1281

No. 3058 — Flowers and: a, Pen, goldfish in bowl. b, Apples, oil lamp.

**2012, Mar. 26** ***Perf. 14¼x13¾***

**3058** A1281 2200r Horiz. pair, #a-b .80 .80

A souvenir sheet containing Nos. 3058a-3058b was printed in limited quantities.

Grand Ayatollah Mohammed Taghi Bahjat (1913-2009) A1282

**2012, May 17** ***Perf. 13¾x14¼***

| | | | | | |
|---|---|---|---|---|---|
| **3059** | A1282 | 2200r multi | | .35 | .35 |

A1283

Bridges A1284

Designs: 200r, Broken Bridge. 1000r, Khosro Abad Bridge. 5000r, Martyr Kalantari Bridge. 9000r, Mardogh Bridge. 20,000r, Veresk Bridge.

***Perf. 14 (A1283), 13x13½ (A1284)***

**2012-13**

| | | | | |
|---|---|---|---|---|
| **3060** | A1283 | 200r multi | .25 | .25 |
| **3061** | A1284 | 1000r multi | .25 | .25 |
| **3063** | A1284 | 5000r multi | .85 | .85 |
| **3065** | A1283 | 9000r multi | 1.60 | 1.60 |
| **3066** | A1283 | 20,000r multi | 3.25 | 3.25 |
| | | *Nos. 3060-3066 (5)* | 6.20 | 6.20 |

Issued: 200r, Dec. 2012; 1000r, 5000r, Jan. 2013; 9000r, 2/9. 20,000r, 2012.

Islamic Republic of Iran Day — A1285

**2012, Mar. 30** **Litho.** ***Perf. 13¾x14***

| | | | | |
|---|---|---|---|---|
| **3067** | A1285 | 2200r multi | .40 | .40 |

25th Tehran Intl. Book Fair — A1286

**2012, May 5**

| | | | | |
|---|---|---|---|---|
| **3068** | A1286 | 2200r multi | .35 | .35 |

Souvenir Sheet

Dedication and Sacrifice — A1288

No. 3070: a, Mohammad Hussein Fahmideh (1967-80), war hero. b, Riz Ali Khajavi, farmer who prevented 1962 train crash.

**2012, Dec. 11** ***Perf. 14 Syncopated***

| | | | | |
|---|---|---|---|---|
| **3070** | A1288 | 2200r Sheet of 2, #a-b | .75 | .75 |

Miniature Sheet

World Crafts Day — A1289

No. 3071 — Various textile crafts with: a, Green panel, denomination at LL. b, Green panel, denomination at LR. c, Red panel, denomination at UL. d, Red panel, denomination at UR.

***Perf. 14x13¾ Syncopated***

**2012, Dec. 11**

| | | | | |
|---|---|---|---|---|
| **3071** | A1289 | 2000r Sheet of 4, #a-d | 1.40 | 1.40 |

A1290

Personalized Stamps — A1291

**2012** ***Perf. 13¾x14***

| | | | | |
|---|---|---|---|---|
| **3072** | A1290 | 2200r multi + label | .35 | .35 |

***Perf. 13¾***

| | | | | |
|---|---|---|---|---|
| **3073** | A1291 | 2500r multi + label | .40 | .40 |

Labels on Nos. 3072-3073 are separated from the stamps by a line of simulated perforations. Another label exists for No. 3073. Other labels may exist for No. 3072.

## SEMI-POSTAL STAMPS

Lion and Bull, Persepolis SP1

Persian Soldier, Persepolis — SP2

Palace of Darius the Great — SP3

Tomb of Cyrus the Great, Pasargadae SP4

King Darius on his Throne — SP5

***Perf. 13x13½, 13½x13***

**1948, Jan. 30** **Engr.** **Unwmk.**

| | | | | |
|---|---|---|---|---|
| **B1** | SP1 | 50d + 25d emer | 2.00 | 2.00 |
| **B2** | SP2 | 1r + 50d red | 2.00 | 2.00 |
| **B3** | SP3 | 2½r + 1¼r blue | 2.00 | 2.00 |
| **B4** | SP4 | 5r + 2½r pur | 3.00 | 3.00 |
| **B5** | SP5 | 10r + 5r vio brn | 3.00 | 3.00 |
| | | *Nos. B1-B5 (5)* | 12.00 | 12.00 |

The surtax was for reconstruction of the tomb of Avicenna (980-1037), Persian physician and philosopher, at Hamadan.

Ardashir II — SP6

Shapur I and Valerian SP7

Designs: 1r+50d, King Narses, Naqsh-i-Rustam. 5r+2½r, Taq-i-Kisra, Ctesiphon. 10r+5r, Ardashir I and Ahura Mazda.

**1949, June 11**

| | | | | |
|---|---|---|---|---|
| **B6** | SP6 | 50d + 25d green | 1.75 | 2.00 |
| **B7** | SP6 | 1r + 50d ver | 1.75 | 2.00 |
| **B8** | SP7 | 2½r + 1½r blue | 1.75 | 2.00 |
| **B9** | SP7 | 5r + 2½r magenta | 3.00 | 3.25 |
| **B10** | SP7 | 10r + 5r grnsh gray | 3.00 | 3.25 |
| | | *Nos. B6-B10 (5)* | 11.25 | 12.50 |

The surtax was for reconstruction of Avicenna's tomb at Hamadan.

Gunbad-i-Ali — SP8

Alaviyan, Hamadan SP9

Seldjukide Coin — SP10

Designs: 1r+½r, Masjid-i-Jami, Isfahan. 5r+2½r, Masjid-i-Jami, Ardistan.

**1949, Dec. 22**

| | | | | |
|---|---|---|---|---|
| **B11** | SP8 | 50d + 25d bl grn | 1.50 | 1.50 |
| **B12** | SP8 | 1r + ½r dk brn | 1.50 | 1.50 |
| **B13** | SP9 | 2½r + 1¼r blue | 1.50 | 1.50 |
| **B14** | SP9 | 5r + 2½r red | 2.50 | 2.50 |
| **B15** | SP10 | 10r + 5r olive gray | 2.75 | 3.00 |
| | | *Nos. B11-B15 (5)* | 9.75 | 10.00 |

The surtax was for reconstruction of Avicenna's tomb at Hamadan.

Koran, Crescent and Flag — SP11

**1950, Oct. 2** **Litho.** ***Perf. 11***

| | | | | |
|---|---|---|---|---|
| **B16** | SP11 | 1.50r + 1r multi | 32.50 | 20.00 |

Economic Conference of the Islamic States.

Tomb of Baba Afzal at Kashan SP12

Gorgan Vase — SP13

Designs: 2½r+1¼r, Tower of Ghazan. 5r+2½r, Masjid-i Gawhar. 10r+5r, Mihrab of the Mosque at Rezaieh.

***Perf. 13x13½, 13½x13***

**1950, Aug. 23** **Engr.**

| | | | | |
|---|---|---|---|---|
| **B17** | SP12 | 50d + 25d dk grn | 1.50 | *1.50* |
| **B18** | SP13 | 1r + ½r blue | 1.50 | *1.50* |
| **B19** | SP13 | 2½r + 1¼r choc | 1.50 | *1.50* |
| **B20** | SP12 | 5r + 2½r red | 2.50 | *2.50* |
| **B21** | SP12 | 10r + 5r gray | 2.75 | *3.00* |
| | | *Nos. B17-B21 (5)* | 9.75 | 10.00 |

The surtax was for reconstruction of Avicenna's tomb at Hamadan.

Mohammad Reza Shah Pahlavi and Map — SP14

Monument to Fallen Liberators of Azerbaijan SP15

Designs: 1r+50d, Marching troops. 1.50r+75d, Running advance with flag. 2.50r+1.25r, Mohammad Reza ShahPahlavi. 3r+1.50r, Parade of victors.

**1950, Dec. 12** **Litho.**

| | | | | |
|---|---|---|---|---|
| **B22** | SP14 | 10d + 5d blk brn | 10.00 | 5.00 |
| **B23** | SP15 | 50d + 25d blk brn | 12.00 | 5.00 |
| **B24** | SP15 | 1r + 50d brown lake | 18.00 | 7.00 |
| **B25** | SP14 | 1.50r + 75d org ver | 20.00 | 10.00 |
| **B26** | SP14 | 2.50r + 1.25r blue | 25.00 | 17.50 |
| **B27** | SP15 | 3r + 1.50r ultra | 27.50 | 16.00 |
| | | *Nos. B22-B27 (6)* | 112.50 | 60.50 |

Liberation of Azerbaijan Province from communists, 4th anniv.

The surtax was for families of Persian soldiers who died in the struggle.

Koran Gate at Shiraz SP16

Saadi — SP17

Design: 50d+50d, Tomb of Saadi, Shiraz.

***Perf. 11x10½, 10½x11***

**1952, Apr. 30** **Photo.** **Unwmk.**

| | | | | |
|---|---|---|---|---|
| **B28** | SP16 | 25d + 25d dl bl grn | 3.75 | 2.50 |
| **B29** | SP16 | 50d + 50d brn ol | 4.25 | 2.50 |
| **B30** | SP17 | 1.50r + 50d vio bl | 25.00 | 7.50 |
| | | *Nos. B28-B30 (3)* | 33.00 | 12.50 |

770th birthday of Saadi, Persian poet. The surtax was to help complete Saadi's tomb at Shiraz.

Three stamps of same denominations and colors, with values enclosed in tablets, were prepared but not officially issued.

View of Hamadan SP18

Avicenna — SP19

Designs: 2½r+1¼r, Gonbad Qabus (tower of tomb). 5r+2½r, Old tomb of Avicenna. 10r+5r, New tomb.

***Perf. 13x13½, 13½x13***

**1954, Apr. 21** **Engr.** **Unwmk.**

| | | | | |
|---|---|---|---|---|
| **B31** | SP18 | 50d + 25d dp grn | 1.50 | 1.50 |
| **B32** | SP19 | 1r + ½r vio brn | 1.50 | 1.50 |
| **B33** | SP19 | 2½r + 1¼r blue | 1.50 | 1.50 |
| **B34** | SP18 | 5r + 2½r ver | 2.50 | 2.50 |
| **B35** | SP18 | 10r + 5r ol gray | 3.50 | 3.50 |
| | | *Nos. B31-B35 (5)* | 10.50 | 10.50 |

The surtax was for reconstruction of Avicenna's tomb at Hamadan.

**Catalogue values for unused stamps in this section, from this point to the end of the section, are for Never Hinged items.**

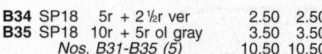

Mother with Children and Ruins — SP20

**Wmk. 316**

**1963, Feb. 4** **Litho.** ***Perf. 10½***

| | | | | |
|---|---|---|---|---|
| **B36** | SP20 | 14r + 6r dk bl grn & lt brn | 3.00 | 1.00 |

The surtax was for the benefit of survivors of the Kazvin earthquake.

For overprints see Nos. C86-C88.

---

## AIR POST STAMPS

Type of 1909 Overprinted

**1927** **Unwmk.** **Typo.** ***Perf. 11½***

| | | | | |
|---|---|---|---|---|
| **C1** | A31 | 1c org & maroon | 3.50 | 1.50 |
| **C2** | A31 | 2c vio & maroon | 3.50 | 1.50 |
| **C3** | A31 | 3c grn & maroon | 3.50 | 1.50 |
| **C4** | A31 | 6c red & maroon | 3.50 | 1.50 |
| **C5** | A31 | 9c gray & maroon | 5.00 | 2.00 |
| **C6** | A31 | 10c red vio & mar | 7.00 | 2.50 |
| **C7** | A31 | 13c dk bl & mar | 8.00 | 3.00 |
| **C8** | A31 | 1k sil, vio & bis brown | 8.00 | 3.00 |
| **C9** | A31 | 26c dk grn & mar | 8.00 | 4.00 |
| **C10** | A31 | 2k sil, dk grn & bis brown | 15.00 | 5.00 |
| **C11** | A31 | 3k sil, gray & bis brown | 25.00 | 7.50 |
| **C12** | A31 | 4k sil, bl & bis brown | 45.00 | 17.50 |
| **C13** | A31 | 5k gold, brn & bis brown | 45.00 | 15.00 |
| **C14** | A31 | 10k gold, org & bis brown | 275.00 | 300.00 |
| **C15** | A31 | 20k gold, ol grn & bis brn | 275.00 | 300.00 |
| **C16** | A31 | 30k gold, car & bis brown | 275.00 | 300.00 |
| | | *Nos. C1-C16 (16)* | 1,005. | 965.50 |

Counterfeit overprints are plentiful. They are found on Nos. 448-463, perf. 12½x12 instead of 11½.

Exist without overprint. Value, set $4,000.

AP1

AP2

AP3

AP4

AP5

**Airplane, Value and "Poste aérièn" Surcharged on Revenue Stamps**

**1928** ***Perf. 11***

| | | | | |
|---|---|---|---|---|
| **C17** | AP1 | 3k yellow brn | 125.00 | 40.00 |
| **C18** | AP2 | 5k dark brown | 30.00 | 15.00 |
| **C19** | AP3 | 1t gray vio | 30.00 | 15.00 |
| **C20** | AP4 | 2t olive bister | 30.00 | 15.00 |
| **C21** | AP5 | 3t deep green | 45.00 | 25.00 |
| | | *Nos. C17-C21 (5)* | 260.00 | 110.00 |

AP6

AP7

**1928-29** **"Poste aerienne"**

| | | | | |
|---|---|---|---|---|
| **C22** | AP6 | 1c emerald | 2.50 | .50 |
| *a.* | | 1c yellow green | 2.50 | .50 |
| *b.* | | Double overprint | 35.00 | |
| **C23** | AP6 | 2c light blue | 2.50 | .25 |
| **C24** | AP6 | 3c bright rose | 2.50 | .25 |
| **C25** | AP6 | 5c olive brn | 1.25 | .25 |
| *a.* | | "5" omitted | 1,250. | *1,500.* |
| *b.* | | Horiz. pair, imperf. btwn. | *300.00* | |
| **C26** | AP6 | 10c dark green | 2.00 | .25 |
| *a.* | | "10" omitted | 40.00 | |
| *b.* | | "1" inverted | 75.00 | |
| **C27** | AP7 | 1k dull vio | 3.00 | 1.00 |
| *a.* | | "1" inverted | 100.00 | |
| **C28** | AP7 | 2k orange | 10.00 | 3.50 |
| *a.* | | "S" for "s" in "Krs" | 150.00 | *175.00* |
| | | *Nos. C22-C28 (7)* | 23.75 | 6.00 |

Counterfeits exist.

Revenue Stamps Similar to Nos. C17 to C21, Overprinted like Nos. C22 to C28: "Poste aerienne"

**1929**

| | | | | |
|---|---|---|---|---|
| **C29** | AP1 | 3k yellow brn | 100.00 | 25.00 |
| **C30** | AP2 | 5k dark brn | 20.00 | 10.00 |
| **C31** | AP3 | 10k violet | 25.00 | 15.00 |
| **C32** | AP4 | 20k olive grn | 30.00 | 15.00 |
| **C33** | AP5 | 30k deep grn | 40.00 | 20.00 |
| | | *Nos. C29-C33 (5)* | 215.00 | 85.00 |

Reza Shah Pahlavi and Eagle — AP8

**1930, July 6** **Photo.** ***Perf. 12½x11½***

| | | | | |
|---|---|---|---|---|
| **C34** | AP8 | 1c ol bis & brt bl | .85 | .50 |
| **C35** | AP8 | 2c blue & gray blk | .85 | .50 |
| **C36** | AP8 | 3c ol grn & dk vio | .85 | .50 |
| **C37** | AP8 | 4c dk vio & pck bl | .85 | .50 |
| **C38** | AP8 | 5c lt grn & mag | .85 | .50 |
| **C39** | AP8 | 6c mag & bl grn | .85 | .50 |
| **C40** | AP8 | 8c dk gray & dp violet | .85 | .50 |
| **C41** | AP8 | 10c dp ultra & ver | .85 | .50 |
| **C42** | AP8 | 12c slate & org | .85 | .50 |
| **C43** | AP8 | 15c org brn & ol green | .85 | .50 |
| **C44** | AP8 | 1k Prus bl & scar | 7.50 | 3.50 |
| | | **Engr.** | | |
| **C45** | AP8 | 2k black & ultra | 8.50 | 5.00 |
| **C46** | AP8 | 3k dk brn & gray green | 15.00 | 6.00 |
| **C47** | AP8 | 5k dp red & gray black | 10.00 | 5.00 |
| **C48** | AP8 | 1t orange & vio | 35.00 | 12.00 |
| **C49** | AP8 | 2t dk grn & red brown | 40.00 | 40.00 |
| **C50** | AP8 | 3t brn vio & sl bl | 225.00 | 85.00 |
| | | *Nos. C34-C50 (17)* | 349.50 | 161.50 |

**Nos. C34-C50 Overprinted in Black**

**1935** **Photo.**

| | | | | |
|---|---|---|---|---|
| **C51** | AP8 | 1c ol bis & brt bl | .50 | .50 |
| **C52** | AP8 | 2c blue & gray blk | .50 | .50 |
| **C53** | AP8 | 3c ol grn & dk vio | .50 | .50 |
| **C54** | AP8 | 4c dk vio & pck bl | .50 | .50 |
| **C55** | AP8 | 5c lt grn & mag | .50 | .50 |
| **C56** | AP8 | 6c mag & bl grn | .50 | .50 |
| **C57** | AP8 | 8c dk gray & dp violet | .50 | .50 |
| **C58** | AP8 | 10c dp ultra & ver | .50 | .50 |
| **C59** | AP8 | 12c slate & org | .50 | .50 |
| **C60** | AP8 | 15c org brn & ol green | .50 | .50 |
| **C61** | AP8 | 1k Prus bl & scar | 45.00 | *65.00* |
| | | **Engr.** | | |
| **C62** | AP8 | 2k blk & ultra | 35.00 | *55.00* |
| **C63** | AP8 | 3k dk brn & gray green | 25.00 | 15.00 |
| **C64** | AP8 | 5k dp red & gray black | 10.00 | 10.00 |
| **C65** | AP8 | 1t orange & vio | 225.00 | 175.00 |
| **C66** | AP8 | 2t dk grn & red brown | 45.00 | 30.00 |
| **C67** | AP8 | 3t brn vio & sl bl | 75.00 | 40.00 |
| | | *Nos. C51-C67 (17)* | 465.00 | 395.00 |

Plane Over Mt. Demavend AP9

Plane above Mosque AP10

**Unwmk.**

**1953, Jan. 21** **Photo.** ***Perf. 11***

| | | | | |
|---|---|---|---|---|
| **C68** | AP9 | 50d bl green | 1.50 | .25 |
| **C69** | AP10 | 1r car rose | 1.50 | .25 |
| **C70** | AP10 | 2r dark blue | 1.50 | .25 |
| **C71** | AP10 | 3r dark brn | 1.50 | .25 |
| **C72** | AP10 | 5r purple | 3.50 | .25 |
| **C73** | AP10 | 10r org ver | 4.00 | .30 |
| **C74** | AP10 | 20r vio blue | 5.00 | .50 |
| **C75** | AP10 | 30r olive | 10.00 | 7.00 |
| **C76** | AP10 | 50r brown | 20.00 | 4.00 |
| **C77** | AP10 | 100r black brn | 70.00 | 15.00 |
| **C78** | AP10 | 200r dk bl grn | 50.00 | 20.00 |
| | | *Nos. C68-C78 (11)* | 168.50 | 48.05 |

AP11

Golden Dome Mosque and Oil Well AP12

**1953, May 4 Litho. *Perf. 10½***

**Mosque in Deep Yellow**

| | | | | |
|---|---|---|---|---|
| **C79** | AP11 | 3r violet | 15.00 | 10.00 |
| **C80** | AP12 | 5r chocolate | 20.00 | 15.00 |
| **C81** | AP11 | 10r bl green | 55.00 | 30.00 |
| **C82** | AP12 | 20r red vio | 110.00 | 50.00 |
| | | *Nos. C79-C82 (4)* | 200.00 | 105.00 |

Discovery of oil at Qum.

**Catalogue values for unused stamps in this section, from this point to the end of the section, are for Never Hinged items.**

Globe and UN Emblem AP13

***Perf. 10½x12½***

**1957, Oct. 24 Photo. Wmk. 316**

| | | | | |
|---|---|---|---|---|
| **C83** | AP13 | 10r brt red lil & rose | 3.00 | .90 |
| **C84** | AP13 | 20r dl vio & rose vio | 6.00 | 1.25 |

United Nations Day, Oct. 24, 1957.

UNESCO Emblem AP14

**Wmk. 353**

**1966, June 20 Litho. *Perf. 10½***

| | | | | |
|---|---|---|---|---|
| **C85** | AP14 | 14r multi | 1.10 | .30 |

20th anniversary of UNESCO.

**No. B36 Surcharged in Maroon, Brown or Red**

**1969, Dec. 4 Wmk. 316 *Perf. 10½***

| | | | | |
|---|---|---|---|---|
| **C86** | SP20 | 4r on 14r + 6r (M) | 3.00 | .95 |
| **C87** | SP20 | 10r on 14r + 6r (B) | 3.25 | .95 |
| **C88** | SP20 | 14r on 14r + 6r (R) | 3.50 | .95 |
| | | *Nos. C86-C88 (3)* | 9.75 | 2.85 |

1st England-Australia flight, via Iran, made by Capt. Ross Smith and Lt. Keith Smith, 50th anniv.

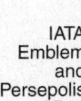

IATA Emblem and Persepolis AP15

***Perf. 13x13½***

**1970, Oct. 27 Photo. Wmk. 353**

| | | | | |
|---|---|---|---|---|
| **C89** | AP15 | 14r multi | 6.50 | .80 |

26th meeting of the Intl. Air Transport Assoc. (IATA), Tehran.

"UIT" AP16

**1972, May 17 Litho. *Perf. 10½***

| | | | | |
|---|---|---|---|---|
| **C90** | AP16 | 14r multicolored | 3.25 | .75 |

4th World Telecommunications Day.

Shah and Jet AP17

**1974, June 1 Photo. *Perf. 13***

| | | | | |
|---|---|---|---|---|
| **C91** | AP17 | 4r org & black | .75 | .25 |
| **C92** | AP17 | 10r blue & black | 2.00 | .25 |
| **C93** | AP17 | 12r dull yel & blk | 2.00 | .40 |
| **C94** | AP17 | 14r lt green & blk | 2.25 | .40 |
| **C95** | AP17 | 20r red lilac & blk | 3.00 | .65 |
| **C96** | AP17 | 50r dull bl & blk | 7.50 | 1.60 |
| | | *Nos. C91-C96 (6)* | 17.50 | 3.55 |

Crown Prince at Controls of Light Aircraft — AP18

**1974, Oct. 31 Litho. *Perf. 10½***

| | | | | |
|---|---|---|---|---|
| **C97** | AP18 | 14r gold & multi | 1.75 | .65 |

Crown Prince Reza's 14th birthday.

**Importation Prohibited**

Importation of stamps was prohibited effective Oct. 29, 1987.

Islamic Revolution, 10th Anniv. — AP19

**1989, Feb. 11 *Perf. 13x13½***

| | | | | |
|---|---|---|---|---|
| **C98** | AP19 | 40r red vio, blk & gold | .75 | .50 |
| **C99** | AP19 | 50r bl vio, blk & gold | .75 | .50 |
| *a.* | | Pair, #C98-C99 | 1.75 | 1.50 |

Ayatollah Khomeini — AP20

**1989, July 11 *Perf. 13***

| | | | | |
|---|---|---|---|---|
| **C100** | AP20 | 70r multicolored | 1.00 | .50 |

## OFFICIAL STAMPS

Four bicolored stamps of this design (1s, 2s, 5s, 10s), with centers embossed, exist, but were never issued or used in Iran. Value $40. They are known imperforate and in many trial colors.

Shah Muzaffar-ed-Din O1

**No. 145 Surcharged in Black**

**1902 *Perf. 12½***

| | | | | |
|---|---|---|---|---|
| **O5** | O1 | 5c on 1k red | 30.00 | 30.00 |
| **O6** | O1 | 10c on 1k red | 30.00 | 30.00 |
| **O7** | O1 | 12c on 1k red | 40.00 | 40.00 |
| | | *Nos. O5-O7 (3)* | 100.00 | 100.00 |

Nos. 351-363 Overprinted in Black

**1903-06**

| | | | | |
|---|---|---|---|---|
| **O8** | A26 | 1c violet | 5.00 | .75 |
| **O9** | A26 | 2c gray | 5.00 | .75 |
| **O10** | A26 | 3c green | 5.00 | .75 |
| **O11** | A26 | 5c rose | 5.00 | .75 |
| **O12** | A26 | 10c yel brown | 8.00 | .75 |
| **O13** | A26 | 12c blue | 12.00 | .75 |
| | | ***Perf. 11½x11*** | | |
| **O14** | A27 | 1k violet | 14.00 | 7.50 |
| **O15** | A27 | 2k ultra | 25.00 | 12.50 |
| *a.* | | Violet overprint | 75.00 | |
| **O16** | A27 | 5k org brown | 40.00 | 20.00 |
| **O17** | A27 | 10k rose red | 50.00 | 19.00 |
| *a.* | | Violet overprint | | 75.00 |
| **O18** | A27 | 20k orange ('06) | 200.00 | 40.00 |
| **O19** | A27 | 30k green ('06) | 250.00 | 90.00 |
| **O20** | A27 | 50k green | 250.00 | 125.00 |
| | | *Nos. O8-O20 (13)* | 869.00 | 318.50 |

**Overprinted on Nos. 368, 370a**

| | | | | |
|---|---|---|---|---|
| **O21** | A27 | 2t on 50k grn (Bl) | 175.00 | 75.00 |
| **O22** | A27 | 3t on 50k grn (V) | 175.00 | 75.00 |

Overprinted on Nos. 372, 375, New Value Surcharged in Blue or Black

**1905**

| | | | | |
|---|---|---|---|---|
| **O23** | A27 | 2t on 50k grn (Bl) | 200.00 | 75.00 |
| **O28** | A27 | 3t on 50k grn (Bk) | 200.00 | 75.00 |

The 2t on 50k also exists with surcharge in black and magenta; the 3t on 50k in violet and magenta. Values about the same.

Regular Issue of 1909 Overprinted

There is a space between the word "Service" and the Persian characters.

**1911 *Perf. 12½x12***

| | | | | |
|---|---|---|---|---|
| **O31** | A31 | 1c org & maroon | 15.00 | 7.50 |
| **O32** | A31 | 2c vio & maroon | 15.00 | 7.50 |
| **O33** | A31 | 3c yel grn & mar | 15.00 | 7.50 |
| **O34** | A31 | 6c red & maroon | 15.00 | 7.50 |
| **O35** | A31 | 9c gray & maroon | 25.00 | 13.00 |
| **O36** | A31 | 10c multicolored | 30.00 | 13.00 |
| **O38** | A31 | 1k multicolored | 60.00 | 45.00 |
| **O40** | A31 | 2k multicolored | 150.00 | 90.00 |
| | | *Nos. O31-O40 (8)* | 325.00 | 191.00 |

The 13c, 26c and 3k to 30k denominations were not regularly issued with this overprint.

Dangerous counterfeits exist, usually on reprints.

Regular Issue of 1915 Overprinted

**1915 Wmk. 161 *Perf. 11, 11½***

| | | | | |
|---|---|---|---|---|
| **O41** | A33 | 1c car & indigo | 2.50 | *4.00* |
| **O42** | A33 | 2c bl & carmine | 2.50 | *4.00* |
| **O43** | A33 | 3c dark green | 2.50 | *4.00* |
| **O44** | A33 | 5c red | 2.50 | *4.00* |
| **O45** | A33 | 6c ol grn & car | 2.50 | *4.00* |
| **O46** | A33 | 9c yel brn & vio | 2.50 | *4.00* |
| **O47** | A33 | 10c multicolored | 2.50 | *4.50* |
| **O48** | A33 | 12c ultramarine | 3.00 | *5.00* |
| **O49** | A34 | 1k multicolored | 7.00 | *10.00* |
| **O50** | A33 | 24c multicolored | 3.50 | *10.00* |
| **O51** | A34 | 2k sil, bl & rose | 7.00 | *15.00* |
| **O52** | A34 | 3k sil, vio & brn | 7.00 | *15.00* |
| **O53** | A34 | 5k multicolored | 7.50 | *15.00* |
| **O54** | A35 | 1t gold, pur & blk | 10.00 | *20.00* |
| **O55** | A35 | 2t gold, grn & brn | 10.00 | *27.50* |
| **O56** | A35 | 3t multicolored | 12.50 | *27.50* |
| **O57** | A35 | 5t gold, bl & ind | 15.00 | *30.00* |
| | | *Nos. O41-O57 (17)* | 100.00 | *203.50* |

Coronation of Shah Ahmed.

*Reprints have dull rather than shiny overprint.* **Value, set, $17.50.**

Coat of Arms — O2

**1941 Unwmk. Litho. *Perf. 11***

**For Internal Postage**

| | | | | |
|---|---|---|---|---|
| **O58** | O2 | 5d violet | 5.00 | .25 |
| **O59** | O2 | 10d magenta | 5.00 | .25 |
| **O60** | O2 | 25d carmine | 5.00 | .25 |
| **O61** | O2 | 50d brown black | 5.00 | .25 |
| **O62** | O2 | 75d claret | 10.00 | .45 |
| | | **Size: 22½x30mm** | | |
| **O63** | O2 | 1r peacock grn | 15.00 | .45 |
| **O64** | O2 | 1½r deep blue | 20.00 | 1.50 |
| **O65** | O2 | 2r light blue | 25.00 | 1.50 |
| **O66** | O2 | 3r vio brown | 32.50 | 1.50 |
| **O67** | O2 | 5r gray green | 50.00 | 2.00 |
| **O68** | O2 | 10r dk brn & bl | 400.00 | 5.00 |
| **O69** | O2 | 20r chlky bl & brt pink | 500.00 | 40.00 |
| **O70** | O2 | 30r vio & brt grn | 800.00 | 150.00 |
| **O71** | O2 | 50r turq grn & dk brown | 1,500. | 350.00 |
| | | *Nos. O58-O71 (14)* | 3,372. | 553.40 |

**Catalogue values for unused stamps in this section, from this point to the end of the section, are for Never Hinged items.**

Coat of Arms — O3

***Perf. 13½x13***

**1974, Feb. 25 Photo. Wmk. 353**

**Size: 20x28mm**

| | | | | |
|---|---|---|---|---|
| **O72** | O3 | 5d vio & lilac | .30 | .25 |
| **O73** | O3 | 10d mag & grnsh bl | .30 | .25 |
| **O74** | O3 | 50d org & lt green | .30 | .25 |
| **O75** | O3 | 1r green & gold | .40 | .25 |
| **O76** | O3 | 2r emerald & org | .70 | .25 |
| | | ***Perf. 13*** | | |
| | | **Size: 23x37mm** | | |
| **O77** | O3 | 6r slate grn & org | .75 | .25 |
| **O78** | O3 | 8r ultra & yellow | 1.00 | .25 |
| **O79** | O3 | 10r dk bl & lilac | 4.25 | .25 |
| **O80** | O3 | 11r pur & light bl | 1.75 | .25 |
| **O81** | O3 | 14r red & lt ultra | 1.75 | .60 |
| **O82** | O3 | 20r vio blue & org | 3.50 | .50 |
| **O83** | O3 | 50r dk brn & brt grn | 9.00 | 1.75 |
| | | *Nos. O72-O83 (12)* | 24.00 | 5.10 |

**1977-79 Wmk. 353 *Perf. 13½x13***

**Size: 20x28mm**

| | | | | |
|---|---|---|---|---|
| **O87** | O3 | 1r black & lt grn | .35 | .25 |
| **O88** | O3 | 2r brown & gray | .40 | .25 |
| **O89** | O3 | 3r ultra & orange | .50 | .25 |
| **O90** | O3 | 5r green & rose | .65 | .25 |

***Perf. 13***

**Size: 23x37mm**

| | | | | |
|---|---|---|---|---|
| **O91** | O3 | 6r dk bl & lt bl ('78) | .75 | .45 |
| **O92** | O3 | 8r red & bl grn ('78) | .80 | .50 |
| **O93** | O3 | 10r dk grn & yel grn | .80 | .25 |
| **O94** | O3 | 11r dk blue & brt yellow ('79) | 1.75 | .50 |
| **O95** | O3 | 14r dl grn & gray | 1.75 | .50 |
| **O96** | O3 | 15r bl & rose lil ('78) | 3.25 | 1.00 |
| **O97** | O3 | 20r purple & yel | 3.25 | .40 |
| **O98** | O3 | 30r brn & ocher ('78) | 3.75 | 1.25 |
| **O99** | O3 | 50r blk & gold ('78) | 10.00 | 1.25 |
| | | *Nos. O87-O99 (13)* | 28.00 | 7.10 |

## NEWSPAPER STAMP

No. 429 Overprinted

**1909 Typo. Unwmk. *Perf. 12½***

| | | | | |
|---|---|---|---|---|
| **P1** | A26 | 2c gray, *blue* | 60.00 | 30.00 |

## PARCEL POST STAMPS

Regular issues of 1907-08 (types A26, A29) with the handstamp above in blue, black or green are of questionable status as issued stamps. The handstamp probably is a cancellation.

No. 436 Overprinted in Black

**1909 Engr. *Perf. 11½***

| | | | | |
|---|---|---|---|---|
| **Q18** | A29 | 26c red brown | 20.00 | 15.00 |

The overprint is printed.

Regular Issue of 1915 Overprinted in Black

**1915 Wmk. 161 *Perf. 11, 11½***

| | | | | |
|---|---|---|---|---|
| **Q19** | A33 | 1c car & indigo | *2.50* | *2.50* |
| **Q20** | A33 | 2c bl & carmine | *2.50* | *2.50* |
| **Q21** | A33 | 3c dark green | *2.50* | *2.50* |
| **Q22** | A33 | 5c red | *2.50* | *2.50* |
| **Q23** | A33 | 6c ol green & car | *2.50* | *2.50* |
| **Q24** | A33 | 9c yel brn & vio | *2.50* | *2.50* |
| **Q25** | A33 | 10c bl grn & yel brn | *2.50* | *2.50* |
| **Q26** | A33 | 12c ultramarine | *3.00* | *3.00* |
| **Q27** | A34 | 1k multicolored | *7.00* | *7.00* |
| **Q28** | A33 | 24c multicolored | *3.50* | *3.50* |
| **Q29** | A34 | 2k multicolored | *7.00* | *7.00* |
| **Q30** | A34 | 3k multicolored | *7.00* | *7.00* |
| **Q31** | A34 | 5k multicolored | *7.50* | *7.50* |
| **Q32** | A35 | 1t multicolored | *10.00* | *10.00* |
| **Q33** | A35 | 2t gold, grn & brn | *10.00* | *10.00* |
| **Q34** | A35 | 3t multicolored | *12.50* | *12.50* |
| **Q35** | A35 | 5t multicolored | *15.00* | *15.00* |
| | | *Nos. Q19-Q35 (17)* | 100.00 | *100.00* |

Coronation of Shah Ahmed.

*Reprints have dull rather than shiny overprint.* **Value, set, $16.**

**Catalogue values for unused stamps in this section, from this point to the end of the section, are for Never Hinged items.**

Post Horn — PP1

Black frame and "IRAN" (reversed) are printed on back of Nos. Q36-Q65, to show through when stamp is attached to parcel.

**1958 Wmk. 306 Typo. *Perf. 12½***

| | | | | |
|---|---|---|---|---|
| **Q36** | PP1 | 50d olive bis | .75 | .25 |
| **Q37** | PP1 | 1r carmine | 1.00 | .25 |
| **Q38** | PP1 | 2r blue | 1.00 | .25 |
| *a.* | | Imperf., pair | 100.00 | |
| **Q39** | PP1 | 3r green | 1.00 | .25 |
| **Q40** | PP1 | 5r purple | 1.00 | .25 |
| **Q41** | PP1 | 10r orange brn | 3.75 | .25 |
| **Q42** | PP1 | 20r dp orange | 10.00 | .35 |
| **Q43** | PP1 | 30r lilac | 12.50 | 1.60 |
| **Q44** | PP1 | 50r dk carmine | 19.00 | 2.50 |
| **Q45** | PP1 | 100r yellow | 40.00 | 5.00 |
| **Q46** | PP1 | 200r light grn | 60.00 | 9.00 |
| | | *Nos. Q36-Q46 (11)* | 150.00 | 19.95 |

**1961-66 Wmk. 316**

| | | | | |
|---|---|---|---|---|
| **Q51** | PP1 | 5r purple ('66) | 12.50 | 5.00 |
| **Q52** | PP1 | 10r org brn ('62) | 12.50 | 5.00 |
| **Q53** | PP1 | 20r orange | 17.50 | 7.00 |
| **Q54** | PP1 | 30r red lil ('63) | 17.50 | 8.00 |
| **Q55** | PP1 | 50r dk car ('63) | 25.00 | 10.00 |
| **Q56** | PP1 | 100r yellow ('64) | 65.00 | 30.00 |
| **Q57** | PP1 | 200r emer ('64) | 80.00 | 30.00 |
| | | *Nos. Q51-Q57 (7)* | 230.00 | 95.00 |

**1967-74 Wmk. 353 Shiny Gum**

| | | | | |
|---|---|---|---|---|
| **Q58** | PP1 | 2r blue ('74) | 5.00 | — |
| **Q59** | PP1 | 5r dk pur ('69) | 5.00 | — |
| **Q60** | PP1 | 10r orange brn | 5.00 | — |
| **Q61** | PP1 | 20r orange ('69) | 10.00 | — |
| **Q62** | PP1 | 30r red lilac | 12.00 | — |
| **Q63** | PP1 | 50r red brn ('68) | 15.00 | — |
| **Q64** | PP1 | 100r yellow | 50.00 | — |
| **Q65** | PP1 | 200r emerald ('69) | 80.00 | — |
| | | *Nos. Q58-Q65 (8)* | 182.00 | |

**1977 Wmk. 353 White Dry Gum**

| | | | | |
|---|---|---|---|---|
| *Q58a* | PP1 | 2r blue | 1.00 | .25 |
| *Q59a* | PP1 | 5r dk pur | 1.00 | .25 |
| *Q60a* | PP1 | 10r orange brn | 1.00 | .25 |
| *Q61a* | PP1 | 20r orange | 1.50 | .25 |
| *Q62a* | PP1 | 30r pink | 2.00 | .25 |
| *Q63a* | PP1 | 50r red brn | 2.50 | .50 |
| *Q64a* | PP1 | 100r yellow | 3.50 | 1.00 |
| *Q65a* | PP1 | 200r emerald | 6.00 | 3.00 |
| | | *Nos. Q58a-Q65a (8)* | 18.50 | 5.75 |

**Without Black Frame and IRAN on Back**

***Perf. 13½x13, 10½ (#100r)***

**1981 Typo. Wmk. 353**

| | | | | |
|---|---|---|---|---|
| **Q67** | PP1 | 50r orange brown | 25.00 | 25.00 |
| **Q68** | PP1 | 100r yellow | 125.00 | 100.00 |
| *a.* | | 100r dull orange | | |
| **Q69** | PP1 | 200r green | *25.00* | 25.00 |

Nos. Q67, Q69 printed from new dies. Numerals are larger and higher in the value tablet on No. Q67. Numerals read down from upper left to lower right in value tablet on No. Q69.

## POSTAL TAX STAMPS

Iranian Red Cross Lion and Sun Emblem PT1

**1950 Unwmk. Litho. *Perf. 11***

| | | | | |
|---|---|---|---|---|
| **RA1** | PT1 | 50d grn & car rose | 10.00 | .90 |
| **RA2** | PT1 | 2r vio & lil rose | 4.00 | 1.50 |

**1955 Wmk. 306**

| | | | | |
|---|---|---|---|---|
| **RA3** | PT1 | 50d emer & car rose | *75.00* | 5.00 |

**Catalogue values for unused stamps in this section, from this point to the end of the section, are for Never Hinged items.**

**1957-58 Wmk. 316**

| | | | | |
|---|---|---|---|---|
| **RA4** | PT1 | 50d emer & rose lil | 4.00 | .90 |
| **RA5** | PT1 | 2r vio & car rose ('58) | 2.50 | 1.00 |

**1965 Wmk. 349 *Perf. 10½***

| | | | | |
|---|---|---|---|---|
| **RA6** | PT1 | 50d emer & car rose | 2.00 | .50 |
| **RA7** | PT1 | 2r vio & lil rose | 2.50 | .65 |

**1965-66 Wmk. 353**

| | | | | |
|---|---|---|---|---|
| **RA8** | PT1 | 50d emer & car rose (I) | 1.00 | .25 |
| *a.* | | Type II | 3.00 | .25 |
| **RA9** | PT1 | 2r vio & car rose ('66) | 3.00 | .35 |

No. RA8 was printed in two types: I. Without diagonal line before Persian "50." II. With line.

**1976, Sept.-78 Photo. *Perf. 13x13½***

| | | | | |
|---|---|---|---|---|
| **RA10** | PT1 | 50d emerald & red | 2.50 | .30 |
| **RA11** | PT1 | 2r slate & red ('78) | 2.50 | 2.50 |

Nos. RA10-RA11 are redrawn and have vertical watermark.

Nos. RA1-RA11 were obligatory on all mail. 50d stamps were for registered mail, 2r stamps for parcel post. The tax was for hospitals.

The 2.25r and 2.50r of type PT1 were used only on telegrams.

# IRAQ

i-räk

LOCATION — In western Asia, bounded on the north by Syria and Turkey, on the east by Iran, on the south by Saudi Arabia and Kuwait, and on the west by Jordan
GOVT. — Republic
AREA — 167,925 sq. mi.
POP. — 22,427,150 (1999 est.)
CAPITAL — Baghdad

Iraq, formerly Mesopotamia, a province of Turkey, was mandated to Great Britain in 1920. The mandate was terminated in 1932. For earlier issues, see Mesopotamia.

16 Annas = 1 Rupee
1000 Fils = 1 Dinar (1932)

**Catalogue values for unused stamps in this country are for Never Hinged items, beginning with Scott 79 in the regular postage section, Scott C1 in the air post section, Scott CO1 in the air post official section, Scott O90 in the officials section, Scott RA1 in the postal tax section, and Scott RAC1 in the air post postal tax section.**

### Issues under British Mandate

Sunni Mosque — A1

Gufas on the Tigris — A2

Assyrian Winged Bull — A4

Ctesiphon Arch — A5

Motif of Assyrian Origin — A3

Colors of the Dulaim Camel Corps — A6

Golden Shiah Mosque of Kadhimain — A7

Conventionalized Date Palm or "Tree of Life" — A8

**1923-25 Engr. Wmk. 4 *Perf. 12***

| | | | | | |
|---|---|---|---|---|---|
| 1 | A1 | ½a olive grn | 1.00 | .25 |
| 2 | A2 | 1a brown | 1.75 | .25 |
| 3 | A3 | 1½a car lake | .95 | .25 |
| 4 | A4 | 2a brown org | .95 | .25 |
| 5 | A5 | 3a dp blue | 2.00 | .25 |
| 6 | A6 | 4a dull vio | 3.50 | .35 |
| 7 | A7 | 6a blue grn | 2.75 | .35 |
| 8 | A6 | 8a olive bis | 4.00 | .75 |
| 9 | A8 | 1r grn & brn | 6.00 | .90 |
| 10 | A1 | 2r black | 21.00 | 8.50 |
| 11 | A1 | 2r bister ('25) | 57.50 | 4.00 |
| 12 | A6 | 5r orange | 52.50 | 17.50 |
| 13 | A7 | 10r carmine | 67.50 | 25.00 |
| | | *Nos. 1-13 (13)* | 221.40 | 58.60 |

For overprints see Nos. O1-O24, O42, O47, O51-O53.

King Faisal I — A9

**1927**

| | | | | |
|---|---|---|---|---|
| 14 | A9 | 1r red brown | 13.50 | 2.00 |

See No. 27. For overprint and surcharges see Nos. 43, O25, O54.

King Faisal I
A10 A11

**1931**

| | | | | |
|---|---|---|---|---|
| 15 | A10 | ½a green | 1.00 | .30 |
| 16 | A10 | 1a chestnut | 1.00 | .30 |
| 17 | A10 | 1½a carmine | 1.50 | .45 |
| 18 | A10 | 2a orange | 1.25 | .25 |
| 19 | A10 | 3a light blue | 1.50 | .25 |
| 20 | A10 | 4a pur brown | 2.00 | *1.75* |
| 21 | A10 | 6a Prus blue | 2.50 | .80 |
| 22 | A10 | 8a dark green | 3.00 | 2.00 |
| 23 | A11 | 1r dark brown | 5.50 | 1.75 |
| 24 | A11 | 2r yel brown | 7.75 | 5.00 |
| 25 | A11 | 5r dp orange | 27.50 | *35.00* |
| 26 | A11 | 10r red | 82.50 | *85.00* |
| 27 | A9 | 25r violet | 700.00 | *800.00* |
| | | *Nos. 15-27 (13)* | 837.00 | *932.85* |

See Nos. 44-60. For overprints see Nos. O26-O41, O43-O46, O48-O50, O54-O71.

### Issues of the Kingdom

Nos. 6, 15-27 Surcharged in "Fils" or "Dinars" in Red, Black or Green

a

b

c

d

**1932, Apr. 1**

| | | | | |
|---|---|---|---|---|
| 28 | A10(a) | 2f on ½a (R) | .50 | .25 |
| 29 | A10(a) | 3f on ½a | .50 | .25 |
| *a.* | | Double surcharge | *160.00* | |
| *b.* | | Inverted surcharge | *160.00* | |
| 30 | A10(a) | 4f on 1a (G) | 1.75 | .35 |
| 31 | A10(a) | 5f on 1a | .65 | .25 |
| *a.* | | Double surcharge | 275.00 | |
| *b.* | | Inverted Arabic "5" | *35.00* | *40.00* |
| 32 | A10(a) | 8f on 1½a | .75 | .50 |
| *a.* | | Inverted surcharge | *160.00* | |
| 33 | A10(a) | 10f on 2a | .80 | .25 |
| 34 | A10(a) | 15f on 3a | 1.75 | 1.50 |
| 35 | A10(a) | 20f on 4a | 2.75 | 1.50 |
| 36 | A6(b) | 25f on 4a | 4.50 | 3.75 |
| *a.* | | "Flis" for "Fils" | *350.00* | *425.00* |
| *b.* | | Inverted Arabic "5" | *425.00* | *550.00* |
| 37 | A10(a) | 30f on 6a | 3.25 | .75 |
| 38 | A10(a) | 40f on 8a | 4.25 | 2.75 |
| 39 | A11(c) | 75f on 1r | 4.00 | 2.75 |
| 40 | A11(c) | 100f on 2r | 10.00 | 4.75 |
| 41 | A11(c) | 200f on 5r | 22.50 | *24.00* |
| 42 | A11(d) | ½d on 10r | 125.00 | 95.00 |
| *a.* | | Bar in "½" omitted | *800.00* | *925.00* |
| 43 | A9(d) | 1d on 25r | 250.00 | 200.00 |
| | | *Nos. 28-43 (16)* | 432.95 | *338.60* |

King Faisal I
A12 A13

A14

### Values in "Fils" and "Dinars"

**1932, May 9 Engr.**

| | | | | |
|---|---|---|---|---|
| 44 | A12 | 2f ultra | .50 | .25 |
| 45 | A12 | 3f green | .50 | .25 |
| 46 | A12 | 4f vio brown | .50 | .25 |
| 47 | A12 | 5f gray green | .60 | .25 |
| 48 | A12 | 8f deep red | .80 | .25 |
| 49 | A12 | 10f yellow | 1.00 | .25 |
| 50 | A12 | 15f deep blue | 1.50 | .25 |
| 51 | A12 | 20f orange | 1.75 | .55 |
| 52 | A12 | 25f rose lilac | 1.75 | .55 |
| 53 | A12 | 30f olive grn | 3.00 | .25 |
| 54 | A12 | 40f dark violet | 2.25 | 1.00 |
| 55 | A13 | 50f deep brown | 2.25 | .30 |
| 56 | A13 | 75f lt ultra | 3.75 | 2.00 |
| 57 | A13 | 100f deep green | 5.50 | 1.25 |
| 58 | A13 | 200f dark red | 25.00 | 7.00 |
| 59 | A14 | ½d gray blue | 90.00 | 40.00 |
| 60 | A14 | 1d claret | 175.00 | *100.00* |
| | | *Nos. 44-60 (17)* | 315.65 | 154.65 |

For overprints see Nos. O55-O71.

A15

A16

King Ghazi — A17

**1934-38 Unwmk.**

| | | | | |
|---|---|---|---|---|
| 61 | A15 | 1f purple ('38) | .75 | .25 |
| 62 | A15 | 2f ultra | .45 | .25 |
| 63 | A15 | 3f green | .45 | .25 |
| 64 | A15 | 4f pur brown | .45 | .25 |
| 65 | A15 | 5f gray green | .45 | .25 |
| 66 | A15 | 8f deep red | .75 | .25 |
| 67 | A15 | 10f yellow | .95 | .25 |
| 68 | A15 | 15f deep blue | .95 | .25 |
| 69 | A15 | 20f orange | .95 | .25 |
| 70 | A15 | 25f brown vio | 1.75 | .35 |
| 71 | A15 | 30f olive grn | 1.50 | .25 |
| 72 | A15 | 40f dark vio | 1.75 | .25 |
| 73 | A16 | 50f deep brown | 3.50 | .25 |
| 74 | A16 | 75f ultra | 4.00 | .40 |
| 75 | A16 | 100f deep green | 5.00 | .50 |
| 76 | A16 | 200f dark red | 7.50 | 3.00 |
| 77 | A17 | ½d gray blue | 27.50 | 20.00 |
| 78 | A17 | 1d claret | 85.00 | 30.00 |
| | | *Nos. 61-78 (18)* | 143.65 | 57.25 |

For overprints see Nos. 226, O72-O89.

**Catalogue values for unused stamps in this section, from this point to the end of the section, are for Never Hinged items.**

Sitt Zubaidah Mosque — A18

Mausoleum of King Faisal I — A19

Lion of Babylon — A20

Malwiye of Samarra (Spiral Tower) — A21

Oil Wells — A22

Mosque of the Golden Dome, Samarra — A23

***Perf. 14, 13½, 12½, 12x13½, 13½x12, 14x13½***

**1941-42 Engr.**

| | | | | |
|---|---|---|---|---|
| 79 | A18 | 1f dark violet ('42) | .40 | .25 |
| 80 | A18 | 2f chocolate ('42) | .40 | .25 |
| 81 | A19 | 3f brt green ('42) | .40 | .25 |
| 82 | A19 | 4f purple ('42) | .40 | .25 |
| 83 | A19 | 5f dk car rose ('42) | .40 | .25 |
| 84 | A20 | 8f carmine | .70 | .25 |
| 85 | A20 | 8f ocher ('42) | .55 | .25 |
| 86 | A20 | 10f ocher | 16.00 | 3.25 |
| 87 | A20 | 10f carmine ('42) | 1.25 | .25 |
| 88 | A20 | 15f dull blue | 2.10 | .25 |
| 89 | A20 | 15f black ('42) | 2.50 | .25 |
| 90 | A20 | 20f black | 4.25 | .60 |
| 91 | A20 | 20f dull blue ('42) | 1.00 | .25 |
| 92 | A21 | 25f dark violet | .45 | .30 |
| 93 | A21 | 30f deep orange | .45 | .30 |
| 94 | A21 | 40f brn orange | 1.75 | .50 |
| 95 | A21 | 40f chestnut ('42) | 1.75 | .45 |
| 96 | A21 | 50f ultra | 3.00 | .60 |
| 97 | A21 | 75f rose violet | 2.50 | .60 |
| 98 | A22 | 100f olive green ('42) | 3.00 | 1.00 |
| 99 | A22 | 200f dp orange ('42) | 10.00 | 1.00 |
| 100 | A23 | ½d lt bl, perf. 12x13½ ('42) | 40.00 | 6.50 |
| *a.* | | Perf. 14 | 50.00 | 9.00 |
| 101 | A23 | 1d grnsh bl ('42) | 65.00 | 14.00 |
| | | *Nos. 79-101 (23)* | 158.25 | 31.85 |

Nos. 92-95 measure 17¾x21½mm, Nos. 96-97 measure 21x24mm.

For overprints see #O90-O114, O165, RA5.

King Faisal II
A24 A25

**Photo.; Frame Litho.**

**1942 *Perf. 13 x 13½***

| | | | | |
|---|---|---|---|---|
| 102 | A24 | 1f violet & brown | .50 | .50 |
| 103 | A24 | 2f dk blue & brown | .50 | .50 |
| 104 | A24 | 3f lt green & brown | .50 | .50 |
| 105 | A24 | 4f dull brown & brn | .50 | .50 |
| 106 | A24 | 5f sage green & brn | .50 | .50 |
| 107 | A24 | 6f red orange & brn | .50 | .50 |

| | | | | |
|---|---|---|---|---|
| **108** | A24 | 10f dl rose red & lt brn | .50 | .50 |
| **109** | A24 | 12f yel green & brown | .50 | .50 |
| | | *Nos. 102-109 (8)* | 4.00 | 4.00 |

For overprints see Nos. O115-O122.

***Perf. 11½x12***

**1948, Jan. 15 Engr. Unwmk.**

**Size: 17¾x20½mm**

| | | | | |
|---|---|---|---|---|
| **110** | A25 | 1f slate | .60 | .25 |
| **111** | A25 | 2f sepia | .35 | .25 |
| **112** | A25 | 3f emerald | .35 | .25 |
| **113** | A25 | 4f purple | .35 | .25 |
| **114** | A25 | 5f rose lake | .35 | .25 |
| **115** | A25 | 6f plum | 2.00 | .25 |
| **116** | A25 | 8f ocher | 4.50 | .75 |
| **117** | A25 | 10f rose red | .45 | .25 |
| **118** | A25 | 12f dark olive | .45 | .25 |
| **119** | A25 | 15f black | 8.00 | 2.00 |
| **120** | A25 | 20f blue | 1.00 | .25 |
| **121** | A25 | 25f rose violet | 1.10 | .25 |
| **122** | A25 | 30f red orange | 1.10 | .25 |
| **123** | A25 | 40f orange brn | 2.25 | .75 |

***Perf. 12x11½***

**Size: 22x27½mm**

| | | | | |
|---|---|---|---|---|
| **124** | A25 | 60f deep blue | 1.50 | .70 |
| **125** | A25 | 75f lilac rose | 1.50 | .70 |
| **126** | A25 | 100f olive green | 7.00 | 1.50 |
| **127** | A25 | 200f deep orange | 5.75 | 1.50 |
| **128** | A25 | ½d blue | 15.00 | 5.00 |
| **129** | A25 | 1d green | 50.00 | 17.50 |
| | | *Nos. 110-129 (20)* | 103.60 | 33.15 |

Sheets of 6 exist, perforated and imperforate, containing Nos. 112, 117, 120 and 125-127, with arms and Arabic inscription in blue green in upper and lower margins. Value perf or imperf, unused $100 each, used $160 each.

See Nos. 133-138. For overprints see Nos. 188-194, O123-O142, O166-O177, O257, O258, O272-O282, RA1-RA4, RA6.

Post Rider and King Ghazi — A26

Designs: 40f, Equestrian statue & Faisal I. 50f, UPU symbols & Faisal II.

**1949, Nov. 1** ***Perf. 13x13½***

| | | | | |
|---|---|---|---|---|
| **130** | A26 | 20f blue | 2.50 | 2.00 |
| **131** | A26 | 40f red orange | 3.50 | 2.00 |
| **132** | A26 | 50f purple | 10.00 | 7.00 |
| | | *Nos. 130-132 (3)* | 16.00 | 11.00 |

75th anniv. of the UPU.

**Type of 1948**

**1950-51 Unwmk.** ***Perf. 11½x12***

**Size: 17¾x20½mm**

| | | | | |
|---|---|---|---|---|
| **133** | A25 | 3f rose lake | 8.00 | 2.00 |
| **134** | A25 | 5f emerald | 8.50 | 4.00 |
| **135** | A25 | 14f dk olive ('50) | 2.10 | .75 |
| **136** | A25 | 16f rose red | 2.00 | .75 |
| **137** | A25 | 28f blue | 2.10 | .45 |

***Perf. 12x11½***

**Size: 22x27½mm**

| | | | | |
|---|---|---|---|---|
| **138** | A25 | 50f deep blue ('50) | 6.50 | 1.50 |
| | | *Nos. 133-138 (6)* | 29.20 | 9.45 |

For overprints see Nos. 160, O143-O148, O258, O273, O275-O276.

King Faisal II
A27 A28

**1953, May 2 Engr.** ***Perf. 12***

| | | | | |
|---|---|---|---|---|
| **139** | A27 | 3f deep rose car | 1.25 | 1.25 |
| **140** | A27 | 14f olive | 2.50 | 1.25 |
| **141** | A27 | 28f blue | 7.00 | 1.75 |
| *b.* | | Souv. sheet of 3, #139-141 | 110.00 | *200.00* |
| | | *Nos. 139-141 (3)* | 10.75 | 4.25 |

Coronation of King Faisal II, May 2, 1953.

**1954-57** ***Perf. 11½x12***

**Size: 18x20½mm**

| | | | | |
|---|---|---|---|---|
| **141A** | A28 | 1f blue ('56) | .65 | .25 |
| **142** | A28 | 2f chocolate | .25 | .25 |
| **143** | A28 | 3f rose lake | .25 | .25 |
| **144** | A28 | 4f violet | .25 | .25 |
| **145** | A28 | 5f emerald | .30 | .25 |
| **146** | A28 | 6f plum | .30 | .25 |
| **147** | A28 | 8f ocher | .30 | .25 |
| **148** | A28 | 10f blue | .30 | .25 |
| **149** | A28 | 15f black | 1.75 | 1.25 |
| **149A** | A28 | 16f brt rose ('57) | 2.75 | 2.25 |
| **150** | A28 | 20f olive | 1.25 | .30 |
| **151** | A28 | 25f rose vio ('55) | 1.25 | .25 |
| **152** | A28 | 30f ver ('55) | 1.25 | .25 |
| **153** | A28 | 40f orange brn | 1.50 | .45 |

**Size: 22x27½mm**

| | | | | |
|---|---|---|---|---|
| **154** | A28 | 50f blue | 2.00 | .70 |
| **155** | A28 | 75f pink | 3.00 | .75 |
| **156** | A28 | 100f olive green | 6.00 | .80 |
| **157** | A28 | 200f orange | 10.00 | 1.75 |
| | | *Nos. 141A-157 (18)* | 33.35 | 10.75 |

For overprints see Nos. 158-159, 195-209, 674, 676, 678, O148A-O161A, O178-O191, O259-O260, O263, O266, O268, O270, O283-O291.

No. 143, 148 and 137 Overprinted in Black

**1955, Apr. 6** ***Perf. 11½x12***

| | | | | |
|---|---|---|---|---|
| **158** | A28 | 3f rose lake | 1.10 | .45 |
| **159** | A28 | 10f blue | 1.25 | .45 |
| **160** | A25 | 28f blue | 2.10 | 1.00 |
| | | *Nos. 158-160 (3)* | 4.45 | 1.90 |

Abrogation of Anglo-Iraq treaty of 1930.

King Faisal II — A29

**1955, Nov. 26** ***Perf. 13½x13***

| | | | | |
|---|---|---|---|---|
| **161** | A29 | 3f rose lake | .90 | .40 |
| **162** | A29 | 10f light ultra | 1.60 | .60 |
| **163** | A29 | 28f blue | 2.25 | 1.50 |
| | | *Nos. 161-163 (3)* | 4.75 | 2.50 |

6th Arab Engineers' Conf., Baghdad, 1955.
For surcharge see No. 227.

Faisal II and Globe — A30

**1956, Mar. 3** ***Perf. 13x13½***

| | | | | |
|---|---|---|---|---|
| **164** | A30 | 3f rose lake | 1.25 | .60 |
| **165** | A30 | 10f light ultra | 1.60 | .60 |
| **166** | A30 | 28f blue | 2.25 | 1.25 |
| | | *Nos. 164-166 (3)* | 5.10 | 2.45 |

Arab Postal Conf., Baghdad, Mar. 3.
For overprint see #173. For surcharge see #251.

Mechanical Loom A31

Designs: 3f, Dam. 5f, Modern city development. 10f, Pipeline. 40f, Tigris Bridge.

**1957, Apr. 8 Photo.** ***Perf. 11½***

**Granite Paper**

| | | | | |
|---|---|---|---|---|
| **167** | A31 | 1f Prus bl & org yel | .50 | .25 |
| **168** | A31 | 3f multicolored | .50 | .25 |
| **169** | A31 | 5f multicolored | .60 | .25 |
| **170** | A31 | 10f lt bl, ocher & red | 1.00 | .25 |
| **171** | A31 | 40f lt bl, blk & ocher | 2.00 | .70 |
| | | *Nos. 167-171 (5)* | 4.60 | 1.70 |

Development Week, 1957. See #185-187.

Fair Emblem — A32

**1957, June 1 Unwmk.**

**Granite Paper**

| | | | | |
|---|---|---|---|---|
| **172** | A32 | 10f brown & buff | 1.00 | 1.00 |

Agricultural and Industrial Exhibition, Baghdad, June 1.

No. 166 Overprinted in Red

**1957, Nov. 14** ***Perf. 13x13½***

| | | | | |
|---|---|---|---|---|
| **173** | A30 | 28f blue | 5.00 | 2.25 |
| *a.* | | Double overprint | 250.00 | *275.00* |

Iraqi Red Crescent Soc., 25th anniv.

King Faisal II — A33

***Perf. 11½x12***

**1957-58 Unwmk. Engr.**

| | | | | |
|---|---|---|---|---|
| **174** | A33 | 1f blue | .40 | .40 |
| **175** | A33 | 2f chocolate | .40 | .40 |
| **176** | A33 | 3f dark car ('57) | .40 | .40 |
| **177** | A33 | 4f dull violet | .40 | .40 |
| **177A** | A33 | 5f emerald | 1.00 | 1.00 |
| **178** | A33 | 6f plum | 1.00 | 1.00 |
| **179** | A33 | 8f ocher | 2.00 | 1.25 |
| **180** | A33 | 10f blue | 2.00 | 1.25 |
| | | *Nos. 174-180 (8)* | 7.60 | *6.10* |

Higher denominations exist without Republic overprint. They were probably not regularly issued.

See note below No. 225.

For overprints see Nos. 210-225, 675, O162-O164, O192-O199, O269, O292-O294. For types overprinted see #677, 679, O261, O264, O267, O271, O295.

Tanks — A34

King Faisal II — A35

Army Day, Jan. 6: 10f, Marching soldiers. 20f, Artillery and planes.

**1958, Jan. 6** ***Perf. 13x13½***

| | | | | |
|---|---|---|---|---|
| **181** | A34 | 8f green & black | 1.00 | .85 |
| **182** | A34 | 10f brown & black | 1.25 | 1.10 |
| **183** | A34 | 20f blue & red brown | 1.25 | 1.10 |
| **184** | A35 | 30f car & purple | 2.00 | 1.50 |
| | | *Nos. 181-184 (4)* | 5.50 | 4.55 |

**Type of 1957**

3f, Sugar beet, bag & refining machinery, vert. 5f, Farm. 10f, Dervendi Khan dam.

**1958, Apr. 26 Photo.** ***Perf. 11½***

**Granite Paper**

| | | | | |
|---|---|---|---|---|
| **185** | A31 | 3f gray vio, grn & lt gray | .60 | .35 |
| **186** | A31 | 5f multicolored | .90 | .55 |
| **187** | A31 | 10f multicolored | 2.25 | 1.10 |
| | | *Nos. 185-187 (3)* | 3.75 | 2.00 |

Development Week, 1958.

**Republic**

Stamps of 1948-51 Overprinted

***Perf. 11½x12, 12x11½***

**1958 Engr. Unwmk.**

**Size: 17¾x20½mm**

| | | | | |
|---|---|---|---|---|
| **188** | A25 | 12f dark olive | .80 | .25 |
| **189** | A25 | 14f olive | 1.00 | .25 |
| **190** | A25 | 16f rose red | 15.00 | 4.50 |
| **191** | A25 | 28f blue | 1.25 | .65 |

**Size: 22x27½mm**

| | | | | |
|---|---|---|---|---|
| **192** | A25 | 60f deep blue | 4.00 | .75 |
| **193** | A25 | ½d blue | 25.00 | 6.00 |
| **194** | A25 | 1d green | 50.00 | 22.00 |
| | | *Nos. 188-194 (7)* | 97.05 | 34.40 |

Other denominations of type A25 exist with this overprint, but these were probably not regularly issued.

Same Overprint on Stamps of 1954-57

**Size: 18x20½mm**

| | | | | |
|---|---|---|---|---|
| **195** | A28 | 1f blue | .85 | .30 |
| **196** | A28 | 2f chocolate | .85 | .30 |
| **196A** | A28 | 4f violet | .85 | .30 |
| **196B** | A28 | 5f emerald | .85 | .30 |
| **197** | A28 | 6f plum | .85 | .30 |
| **198** | A28 | 8f ocher | .85 | .30 |
| **199** | A28 | 10f blue | 1.00 | .30 |
| **200** | A28 | 15f black | 1.25 | .30 |
| **201** | A28 | 16f bright rose | 3.25 | .50 |
| **202** | A28 | 20f olive | 1.50 | .65 |
| **203** | A28 | 25f rose violet | 1.00 | .65 |
| **204** | A28 | 30f vermilion | 1.75 | .35 |
| **205** | A28 | 40f orange brn | 1.75 | .35 |

**Size: 22½x27½mm**

| | | | | |
|---|---|---|---|---|
| **206** | A28 | 50f blue | 8.00 | 4.00 |
| **207** | A28 | 75f pink | 6.50 | 1.50 |
| **208** | A28 | 100f olive green | 7.00 | 4.00 |
| **209** | A28 | 200f orange | 20.00 | 7.50 |
| | | *Nos. 195-209 (17)* | 58.10 | 21.90 |

The lines of this overprint are found transposed on Nos. 195, 196 and 199.

Same Overprint on Stamps and Type of 1957-58

**Size: 18x20mm**

| | | | | |
|---|---|---|---|---|
| **210** | A33 | 1f blue | 3.50 | .75 |
| **211** | A33 | 2f chocolate | .75 | .30 |
| **212** | A33 | 3f dark carmine | .75 | .30 |
| **213** | A33 | 4f dull violet | .80 | .30 |
| **214** | A33 | 5f emerald | .75 | .30 |
| **215** | A33 | 6f plum | .75 | .30 |
| **216** | A33 | 8f ocher | .75 | .50 |
| **217** | A33 | 10f blue | .75 | .30 |
| **218** | A33 | 20f olive | .75 | .30 |
| **219** | A33 | 25f rose violet | 1.60 | .80 |
| **220** | A33 | 30f vermilion | 1.75 | .30 |
| **221** | A33 | 40f orange brn | 4.50 | 1.60 |

**Size: 22x27½mm**

| | | | | |
|---|---|---|---|---|
| **222** | A33 | 50f rose violet | 3.50 | .75 |
| **223** | A33 | 75f olive | 3.50 | 1.50 |
| **224** | A33 | 100f orange | 4.50 | 1.50 |
| **225** | A33 | 200f blue | 12.50 | 2.50 |
| | | *Nos. 210-225 (16)* | 41.40 | 12.30 |

#218-225 were not issued without overprint.

The lines of this overprint are found transposed on Nos. 210 and 214.

Many errors of overprint exist of #188-226.

For overprint see No. O198.

**Same Overprint on No. 78**

***Perf. 12***

| | | | | |
|---|---|---|---|---|
| **226** | A17 | 1d claret | 37.50 | 35.00 |

No. 163 Surcharged in Red

**1958, Nov. 26** ***Perf. 13x13½***

| | | | | |
|---|---|---|---|---|
| **227** | A29 | 10f on 28f blue | 2.00 | 1.00 |

Arab Lawyers' Conf., Baghdad, Nov. 26.

Soldier and Flag A36

**1959, Jan. 6 Photo. *Perf. 11½***

| | | | | |
|---|---|---|---|---|
| 228 | A36 | 3f bright blue | .40 | .25 |
| 229 | A36 | 10f olive green | .75 | .35 |
| 230 | A36 | 40f purple | 1.40 | .70 |
| | | *Nos. 228-230 (3)* | 2.55 | 1.30 |

Issued for Army Day, Jan. 6.

Orange Tree — A37

Emblem of Republic — A38

**1959, Mar. 21 Unwmk. *Perf. 11½***

| | | | | |
|---|---|---|---|---|
| 231 | A37 | 10f green, dk grn & org | .90 | .25 |

Issued for Arbor Day.

**1959-60 Litho. & Photo. *Perf. 11½***
**Granite Paper**
**Emblem in Gold, Red and Blue; Blue Inscriptions**

| | | | | |
|---|---|---|---|---|
| 232 | A38 | 1f gray | .25 | .25 |
| 233 | A38 | 2f salmon | .25 | .25 |
| 234 | A38 | 3f pale violet | .25 | .25 |
| 235 | A38 | 4f bright yel | .25 | .25 |
| 236 | A38 | 5f light blue | .25 | .25 |
| 237 | A38 | 10f bright pink | .25 | .25 |
| 238 | A38 | 15f light green | .75 | .25 |
| 239 | A38 | 20f bister brn | .75 | .25 |
| 240 | A38 | 30f light gray | .75 | .25 |
| 241 | A38 | 40f orange yel | 1.40 | .35 |
| 242 | A38 | 50f yel green | 5.50 | .90 |
| 243 | A38 | 75f pale grn ('60) | 2.25 | .45 |
| 244 | A38 | 100f orange ('60) | 4.00 | .90 |
| 245 | A38 | 200f lilac ('60) | 6.50 | 1.00 |
| 246 | A38 | 500f bister ('60) | 10.00 | 3.50 |
| 247 | A38 | 1d brt grn ('60) | 22.00 | 9.00 |
| | | *Nos. 232-247 (16)* | 55.40 | 18.35 |

See Nos. 305A-305B. For overprints see Nos. 252, 293-295, O200-O221.

Worker and Buildings — A39

Victorious Fighters A40

***Perf. 12½x13, 13x12½***

**1959, July 14 Photo.**

| | | | | |
|---|---|---|---|---|
| 248 | A39 | 10f ocher & blue | .60 | .55 |
| 249 | A40 | 30f ocher & emerald | 1.10 | .70 |

1st anniv. of the Revolution of July 14 (1958), which overthrew the kingdom.

Harvest — A41

**1959, July 14 *Perf. 11½***

| | | | | |
|---|---|---|---|---|
| 250 | A41 | 10f lt grn & dk grn | .65 | .25 |

No. 166 Surcharged in Dark Red

**1959, June 1 Engr. *Perf. 13x13½***

| | | | | |
|---|---|---|---|---|
| 251 | A30 | 10f on 28f blue | 1.75 | .75 |

Issued for Children's Day, 1959.

No. 237 Overprinted

**Litho. and Photo.**

**1959, Oct. 23 *Perf. 11½***

| | | | | |
|---|---|---|---|---|
| 252 | A38 | 10f multicolored | 1.10 | .55 |

Health and Sanitation Week.

Abdul Karim Kassem and Army Band — A42

Abdul Karim Kassem and: 16f, Field maneuvers, horiz. 30f, Antiaircraft. 40f, Troops at attention, flag and bugler. 60f, Fighters and flag, horiz.

**1960, Jan. 6 Photo. *Perf. 11½***

| | | | | |
|---|---|---|---|---|
| 253 | A42 | 10f blue, grn & mar | .80 | .55 |
| 254 | A42 | 16f brt blue & red | 1.25 | .70 |
| 255 | A42 | 30f ol grn, yel & brn | 1.25 | .70 |
| 256 | A42 | 40f deep vio & buff | 1.90 | .90 |
| 257 | A42 | 60f dk brown & buff | 2.50 | 1.00 |
| | | *Nos. 253-257 (5)* | 7.70 | 3.85 |

Issued for Army Day, Jan. 6.

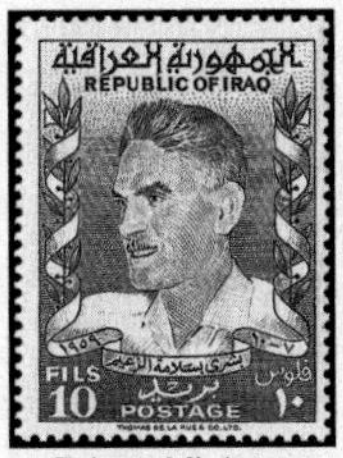


Prime Minister Abdul Karim Kassem — A43

Maroof el Rasafi — A44

**1960, Feb. 1 Engr. *Perf. 12½***

| | | | | |
|---|---|---|---|---|
| 258 | A43 | 10f lilac | .90 | .45 |
| 259 | A43 | 30f emerald | 1.50 | .65 |

Issued to honor Prime Minister Kassem on his recovery from an assassination attempt.

**1960, May 10 Photo. *Perf. 13½x13***

| | | | | |
|---|---|---|---|---|
| 260 | A44 | 10f maroon & blk | 4.00 | 1.40 |
| *a.* | | Inverted overprint | 150.00 | 150.00 |
| *b.* | | Without overprint ('66) | 11.00 | 11.00 |

No. 260b was released for postal use in 1966.

Symbol of the Army — A45

Unknown Soldier's Tomb and Kassem with Freedom Torch — A46

**1960, July 14 *Perf. 11½***

| | | | | |
|---|---|---|---|---|
| 261 | A45 | 6f ol grn, red & gold | .90 | .55 |
| 262 | A46 | 10f green, blue & red | .95 | .55 |
| 263 | A46 | 16f vio, blue & red | 1.00 | .80 |
| 264 | A45 | 18f ultra, red & gold | 1.00 | .80 |
| 265 | A45 | 30f brown, red & gold | 1.50 | 1.00 |
| 266 | A46 | 60f dk brn, bl & red | 2.50 | 1.50 |
| | | *Nos. 261-266 (6)* | 7.85 | 5.20 |

2nd anniv. of the July 14, 1958 revolution.

Gen. Kassem and Marching Troops — A47

Gen. Kassem and Arch — A48

**1961, Jan. 6 *Perf. 11½***
**Granite Paper**

| | | | | |
|---|---|---|---|---|
| 267 | A47 | 3f gray ol, emer, yel & gold | .65 | .25 |
| 268 | A47 | 6f pur, emer, yel & gold | .70 | .25 |
| 269 | A47 | 10f sl, emer, yel & gold | .85 | .25 |
| 270 | A48 | 20f bl grn, blk & buff | 1.25 | .25 |
| 271 | A48 | 30f bis brn, blk & buff | 1.50 | .35 |
| 272 | A48 | 40f ultra, black & buff | 1.75 | .65 |
| | | *Nos. 267-272 (6)* | 6.70 | 2.00 |

Issued for Army Day, Jan. 6.

Gen. Kassem and Children A49

**1961, June 1 Photo. Unwmk.**
**Granite Paper**

| | | | | |
|---|---|---|---|---|
| 273 | A49 | 3f yellow & brown | .80 | .45 |
| 274 | A49 | 6f blue & brown | 1.10 | .45 |
| 275 | A49 | 10f pink & brown | 1.50 | .45 |
| 276 | A49 | 30f yellow & brown | 1.75 | .45 |
| 277 | A49 | 50f lt grn & brown | 2.75 | .70 |
| | | *Nos. 273-277 (5)* | 7.90 | 2.50 |

Issued for World Children's Day.

Gen. Kassem and Flag — A50

5f, 30f, 40f, Gen. Kassem saluting and flags.

**1961, July 14 *Perf. 11½***
**Granite Paper**

| | | | | |
|---|---|---|---|---|
| 278 | A50 | 1f multicolored | .50 | .25 |
| 279 | A50 | 3f multicolored | .50 | .25 |
| 280 | A50 | 5f multicolored | .50 | .25 |
| 281 | A50 | 6f multicolored | .50 | .25 |
| 282 | A50 | 10f multicolored | .50 | .25 |
| 283 | A50 | 30f multicolored | .75 | .55 |
| 284 | A50 | 40f multicolored | 1.00 | .55 |
| 285 | A50 | 50f multicolored | 1.75 | 1.00 |
| 286 | A50 | 100f multicolored | 4.50 | 1.75 |
| | | *Nos. 278-286 (9)* | 10.50 | 5.10 |

3rd anniv. of the July 14, 1958 revolution.

Gen. Kassem and Flag — A51

Gen. Kassem and Symbol of the Army A52

***Perf. 11½***

**1962, Jan. 6 Unwmk. Photo.**
**Granite Paper**

| | | | | |
|---|---|---|---|---|
| 287 | A51 | 1f multicolored | .65 | .25 |
| 288 | A51 | 3f multicolored | .65 | .25 |
| 289 | A51 | 6f multicolored | .75 | .25 |
| 290 | A52 | 10f blk, lilac & gold | 1.25 | .25 |
| 291 | A52 | 30f black, org & gold | 1.50 | .30 |
| 292 | A52 | 50f blk, pale grn & gold | 2.25 | .50 |
| | | *Nos. 287-292 (6)* | 7.05 | 1.80 |

Issued for Army Day, Jan. 6.

Nos. 234, 237 and 240 Overprinted

**Litho. & Photo.**

**1962, May 29 *Perf. 11½***

| | | | | |
|---|---|---|---|---|
| 293 | A38 | 3f multicolored | .50 | .25 |
| 294 | A38 | 10f multicolored | .50 | .25 |
| 295 | A38 | 30f multicolored | 1.25 | .35 |
| | | *Nos. 293-295 (3)* | 2.25 | .85 |

Fifth Islamic Congress.

Hands Across Map of Arabia and North Africa — A53

**1962, July 14 Photo.**

| | | | | |
|---|---|---|---|---|
| 296 | A53 | 1f brn, org, grn & gold | .65 | .25 |
| 297 | A53 | 3f brn, yel grn, grn & gold | .65 | .25 |
| 298 | A53 | 6f blk, lt brn, grn & gold | .75 | .25 |
| 299 | A53 | 10f brn, lil, grn & gold | 1.00 | .25 |
| 300 | A53 | 30f brn, rose, grn & gold | 1.25 | .30 |
| 301 | A53 | 50f brn, gray, grn & gold | 2.00 | .45 |
| | | *Nos. 296-301 (6)* | 6.30 | 1.75 |

Revolution of July 14, 1958, 4th anniv.

al-Kindi — A54

Emblem of Republic — A54a

Designs: 3f, Horsemen with standards and trumpets. 10f, Old map of Baghdad and Tigris. 40f, Gen. Kassem, modern building and flag.

*Perf. 14x13½*

| 1962, Dec. 1 | Litho. | Unwmk. | |
|---|---|---|---|
| **302** A54 | 3f multicolored | .65 | .25 |
| **303** A54 | 6f multicolored | .65 | .25 |
| **304** A54 | 10f multicolored | .75 | .35 |
| **305** A54 | 40f multicolored | 2.00 | 1.00 |
| | *Nos. 302-305 (4)* | 4.05 | 1.85 |

9th century Arab philosopher al-Kindi; millenary of the Round City of Baghdad.

| 1962, Dec. 20 | *Perf. 13½x14* | | |
|---|---|---|---|
| **305A** A54a | 14f brt green & blk | 2.25 | .50 |
| **305B** A54a | 35f ver & black | 2.75 | .75 |

Nos. 305A-305B were originally sold affixed to air letter sheets, obliterating the portrait of King Faisal II. They were issued in sheets for general use in 1966.

For overprints see Nos. RA15-RA16.

Tanks on Parade and Gen. Kassem — A55

Malaria Eradication Emblem — A56

| 1963, Jan. 6 | Photo. | *Perf. 11½* | |
|---|---|---|---|
| **306** A55 | 3f black & yellow | .60 | .25 |
| **307** A55 | 5f brown & plum | .65 | .25 |
| **308** A55 | 6f blk & lt green | .75 | .25 |
| **309** A55 | 10f blk & lt blue | .80 | .25 |
| **310** A55 | 10f black & pink | .85 | .25 |
| **311** A55 | 20f black & ultra | 1.00 | .25 |
| **312** A55 | 40f blk & rose lilac | 1.25 | .25 |
| **313** A55 | 50f brn & brt ultra | 1.75 | .40 |
| | *Nos. 306-313 (8)* | 7.65 | 2.15 |

Issued for Army Day, Jan. 6.

| 1962, Dec. 31 | *Perf. 14* | | |
|---|---|---|---|

**Republic Emblem in Red, Blue & Gold**

| | | | |
|---|---|---|---|
| **314** A56 | 3f yel grn, blk & dk grn | .50 | .25 |
| **315** A56 | 10f org, blk & dark blue | .75 | .25 |
| **316** A56 | 40f lilac, black & blue | 1.00 | .30 |
| | *Nos. 314-316 (3)* | 2.25 | .80 |

WHO drive to eradicate malaria.

Gufas on the Tigris — A57

Designs: 2f, 500f, Spiral tower, Samarra. 4f, 15f, Ram's head harp, Ur. 5f, 75f, Map and Republic emblem. 10f, 50f, Lion of Babylon. 20f, 40f, Baghdad University. 30f, 200f, Kadhimain mosque. 100f, 1d, Winged bull, Khorsabad.

**Engr.; Engr. and Photo. (bicolored)**

| 1963, Feb. 16 | Unwmk. | *Perf. 12x11* | |
|---|---|---|---|
| **317** A57 | 1f green | .65 | .25 |
| **318** A57 | 2f purple | .65 | .25 |
| **319** A57 | 3f black | .65 | .25 |
| **320** A57 | 4f black & yel | .65 | .25 |
| **321** A57 | 5f lilac & lt grn | .70 | .25 |
| **322** A57 | 10f rose red | 1.00 | .25 |
| **323** A57 | 15f brn & buff | 1.50 | .25 |
| **324** A57 | 20f violet blue | 1.60 | .25 |
| **325** A57 | 30f orange | 1.00 | .35 |
| **326** A57 | 40f brt green | 1.75 | .25 |
| **327** A57 | 50f dark brown | 7.50 | .65 |
| **328** A57 | 75f blk & lt grn | 3.75 | .45 |
| **329** A57 | 100f brt lilac | 4.00 | .25 |
| **330** A57 | 200f brown | 7.50 | .55 |
| **331** A57 | 500f blue | 10.00 | 2.25 |
| **332** A57 | 1d deep claret | 13.50 | 4.50 |
| | *Nos. 317-332 (16)* | 56.40 | 11.25 |

For overprints see Nos. O314-O317, RA7-RA12.

Shepherd and Sheep A58

10f, Man holding sheaf. 20f, Date palm grove.

| 1963, Mar. 21 | Litho. | *Perf. 13½x14* | |
|---|---|---|---|
| **333** A58 | 3f emerald & gray | .40 | .25 |
| **334** A58 | 10f dp brn & lil rose | .65 | .25 |
| **335** A58 | 20f dk bl & red brn | 1.10 | .35 |
| *a.* | Souv. sheet of 3, #333-335 | 7.00 | |
| | *Nos. 333-335 (3)* | 2.15 | .85 |

FAO "Freedom from Hunger" campaign. No. 335a sold for 50f.

No. 335a was overprinted in 1970 in black to commemorate the UN 25th anniv. Denominations on the 3 stamps were obliterated, leaving "Price 50 Fils" in the margin. Value $7.50.

Cent. Emblem — A59

Rifle, Helmet and Flag — A60

Design: 30f, Iraqi Red Crescent Society Headquarters, horiz.

*Perf. 11x11½, 11½x11*

| 1963, Dec. 30 | | Photo. | |
|---|---|---|---|
| **336** A59 | 3f violet & red | .40 | .30 |
| **337** A59 | 10f gray & red | .60 | .30 |
| **338** A59 | 30f blue & red | 1.25 | .65 |
| | *Nos. 336-338 (3)* | 2.25 | 1.25 |

Centenary of International Red Cross.

| 1964, Jan. 6 | Unwmk. | *Perf. 11½* | |
|---|---|---|---|

**Granite Paper**

| | | | |
|---|---|---|---|
| **339** A60 | 3f brn, blue & emer | .40 | .30 |
| **340** A60 | 10f brn, pink & emer | .60 | .30 |
| **341** A60 | 30f brown, yel & emer | 1.25 | .70 |
| | *Nos. 339-341 (3)* | 2.25 | 1.30 |

Issued for Army Day, Jan. 6.

Flag and Soldiers Storming Ministry of Defense A61

| 1964, Feb. 8 | *Perf. 11½* | | |
|---|---|---|---|

**Granite Paper**

| | | | |
|---|---|---|---|
| **342** A61 | 10f pur, red, grn & blk | .65 | .30 |
| **343** A61 | 30f red brn, red, grn & blk | 1.10 | .65 |
| *a.* | Souv. sheet of 2, imperf | 6.25 | 2.75 |
| *b.* | Souv. sheet of 2 (4th anniv.) ('67) | 7.25 | 2.75 |

Revolution of Ramadan 14, 1st anniv. #343a contains stamps similar to #342-343 in changed colors (10f olive, red, green & black; 30f ultra, red, green & black). Sold for 50f.

No. 343b consists of various block-outs and overprints on No. 343a. It commemorates the 4th anniv. of the Revolution of Ramadan 14. Sold for 70f. Issued Feb. 8, 1967.

Hammurabi and a God from Stele in Louvre — A62

Design: 10f, UN emblem and scales.

| 1964, June 10 | Litho. | *Perf. 13½* | |
|---|---|---|---|
| **344** A62 | 6f lilac & pale grn | .60 | .50 |
| **345** A62 | 10f org & vio blue | 1.10 | .50 |
| **346** A62 | 30f blue & pale grn | 1.80 | .75 |
| | *Nos. 344-346 (3)* | 3.50 | 1.75 |

15th anniv. (in 1963) of the Universal Declaration of Human Rights.

"Industrialization of Iraq" — A63

Soldier Planting New Flag — A64

| 1964, July 14 | *Perf. 11* | | |
|---|---|---|---|
| **347** A63 | 3f gray, org & black | .40 | .30 |
| **348** A64 | 10f rose red, blk & emer | .40 | .30 |
| **349** A64 | 20f rose red, blk & emer | .60 | .30 |
| **350** A63 | 30f gray, org & black | 1.25 | .60 |
| | *Nos. 347-350 (4)* | 2.65 | 1.50 |

6th anniv. of the July 14, 1958 revolution.

Star and Fighters A65

| 1964, Nov. 18 | Photo. | *Perf. 11½* | |
|---|---|---|---|
| **351** A65 | 5f sepia & orange | .40 | .30 |
| **352** A65 | 10f lt bl & orange | 1.25 | .30 |
| **353** A65 | 50f vio & red orange | 1.25 | .60 |
| | *Nos. 351-353 (3)* | 2.90 | 1.20 |

Revolution of Nov. 18, 1963, 1st anniv.

Musician with Lute — A66

*Perf. 13x13½*

| 1964, Nov. 28 | Litho. | Unwmk. | |
|---|---|---|---|
| **354** A66 | 3f bister & multi | 1.00 | .30 |
| **355** A66 | 10f dl grn & multi | 1.00 | .30 |
| **356** A66 | 30f dl rose & multi | 1.50 | .90 |
| | *Nos. 354-356 (3)* | 3.50 | 1.50 |

International Arab Music Conference.

Map of Arab Countries and Emblem A67

| 1964, Dec. 13 | *Perf. 12½x14* | | |
|---|---|---|---|
| **357** A67 | 10f lt grn & rose lilac | 1.00 | .30 |

9th Arab Engineers' Conference, Baghdad.

Arab Postal Union Emblem — A67a

Soldier, Flag and Rising Sun — A68

| 1964, Dec. 21 | Photo. | *Perf. 11* | |
|---|---|---|---|
| **358** A67a | 3f sal pink & blue | .40 | .25 |
| **359** A67a | 10f brt red lil & brn | .50 | .25 |
| **360** A67a | 30f orange & blue | 1.40 | .50 |
| | *Nos. 358-360 (3)* | 2.30 | 1.00 |

10th anniv. of Permanent Office of APU

For overprint see No. 707.

*Perf. 14x12½*

| 1965, Jan. 6 | Litho. | Unwmk. | |
|---|---|---|---|
| **361** A68 | 5f dull green & multi | .40 | .25 |
| **362** A68 | 15f henna brn & multi | .40 | .30 |
| **363** A68 | 30f black brn & multi | 1.40 | .65 |
| | *Nos. 361-363 (3)* | 2.20 | 1.20 |

Issued for Army Day, Jan. 6.

An imperf. souvenir sheet carries a revised No. 363 with "30 FILS" omitted, and a portrait of Pres. Abdul Salam Arif. Violet inscriptions including "PRICE 60 FILS." Value $10.

Symbols of Agriculture and Industry A69

| 1965, Jan. 8 | *Perf. 12½x14* | | |
|---|---|---|---|
| **364** A69 | 10f ultra, brn & blk | .60 | .30 |

Arab Labor Ministers' Conference.

Tanker A70

| 1965, Jan. 30 | *Perf. 14* | | |
|---|---|---|---|
| **365** A70 | 10f multicolored | 1.00 | .45 |

Inauguration (in 1962) of the deep sea terminal for oil tankers.

Soldier with Flag and Rifle — A71

Tree Week — A72

| 1965, Feb. 8 | Litho. | *Perf. 13½* | |
|---|---|---|---|
| **366** A71 | 10f multicolored | .75 | .25 |

Revolution of Ramadan 14, 2nd anniv.

| 1965, Mar. 6 | Unwmk. | *Perf. 13* | |
|---|---|---|---|
| **367** A72 | 6f multicolored | .40 | .30 |
| **368** A72 | 20f multicolored | 1.25 | .30 |

Federation Emblem — A73

Dagger in Map of Palestine — A74

**1965, Mar. 24 Unwmk. *Perf. 14***

| | | | |
|---|---|---|---|
| **369** A73 | 3f lt bl, vio bl & gold | .40 | .30 |
| **370** A73 | 10f gray, black & gold | .40 | .30 |
| **371** A73 | 30f rose, car & gold | 1.00 | .75 |
| | *Nos. 369-371 (3)* | 1.80 | 1.35 |

Arab Federation of Insurance.

**1965, Apr. 9 Litho. *Perf. 14x12½***

| | | | |
|---|---|---|---|
| **372** A74 | 10f gray & black | 3.50 | .35 |
| **373** A74 | 20f lt brn & dk blue | 6.50 | .55 |

Deir Yassin massacre, Apr. 9, 1948.
See Jordan No. 499 and Kuwait Nos. 281-282.

Smallpox Attacking People — A75

**1965, Apr. 30 Litho. *Perf. 14***

| | | | |
|---|---|---|---|
| **374** A75 | 3f multicolored | .60 | .30 |
| **375** A75 | 10f multicolored | .75 | .30 |
| **376** A75 | 20f multicolored | 1.75 | .80 |
| | *Nos. 374-376 (3)* | 3.10 | 1.40 |

WHO's fight against smallpox. Exist imperf. Value $6.25.

ITU Emblem, Old and New Telecommunication Equipment — A76

**1965, May 17 *Perf. 14, Imperf.***

| | | | |
|---|---|---|---|
| **377** A76 | 10f multicolored | .75 | .25 |
| **378** A76 | 20f multicolored | 2.00 | .55 |
| *a.* | Souv. sheet of 2, #377-378 | 20.00 | 15.00 |

ITU, centenary. No. 378a sold for 40f and exists imperf. Value same.

Map of Arab Countries and Banner — A77

**1965, May 26 Litho. *Perf. 14x12½***

| | | | |
|---|---|---|---|
| **379** A77 | 10f multicolored | .50 | .25 |

Anniversary of the treaty with the UAR.

Library Aflame and Lamp A78

**1965, June Photo. *Perf. 11***

| | | | |
|---|---|---|---|
| **380** A78 | 5f black, grn & red | .50 | .30 |
| **381** A78 | 10f blk, green & red | .75 | .30 |

Burning of the Library of Algiers, 6/7/62.

Revolutionist with Club, Cannon, Sun and Flames — A79

**1965, June 30 Litho. *Perf. 13***

| | | | |
|---|---|---|---|
| **382** A79 | 5f multicolored | .40 | .25 |
| **383** A79 | 10f multicolored | .45 | .25 |

45th anniversary, Revolution of 1920.

Mosque — A80

**1965, July 12 Photo. *Perf. 12***

| | | | |
|---|---|---|---|
| **384** A80 | 10f multicolored | 1.25 | .60 |

Prophet Mohammed's birthday. A souvenir sheet contains one imperf. stamp similar to No. 384. Sold for 50f. Value $8.

Factories and Grain — A81

**1965, July 14 Litho. *Perf. 13***

| | | | |
|---|---|---|---|
| **385** A81 | 10f multicolored | .55 | .55 |

7th anniv. of the July 14, 1958 Revolution.

Arab Fair Emblem — A82

**1965, Oct. 22 Unwmk. *Perf. 13***

| | | | |
|---|---|---|---|
| **386** A82 | 10f multicolored | .55 | .25 |

Second Arab Fair, Baghdad.

Pres. Abdul Salam Mohammed Arif — A83

**1965, Nov. 18 Photo. *Perf. 11½***
**Granite Paper**

| | | | |
|---|---|---|---|
| **387** A83 | 5f org, buff & dk blue | .65 | .25 |
| **388** A83 | 10f lt ultra, gray & dk brn | .90 | .25 |
| **389** A83 | 50f lil, pale pink & sl blk | 2.50 | .90 |
| | *Nos. 387-389 (3)* | 4.05 | 1.40 |

Revolution of Nov. 18, 1963, 2nd anniv.

Census Chart and Adding Machine — A84

**1965, Nov. 29 Litho. *Perf. 13***

| | | | |
|---|---|---|---|
| **390** A84 | 3f gray & plum | .50 | .25 |
| **391** A84 | 5f brown red & brn | .60 | .25 |
| **392** A84 | 15f olive bis & dl bl | 1.50 | .60 |
| | *Nos. 390-392 (3)* | 2.60 | 1.10 |

Issued to publicize the 1965 census.

Date Palms — A85

**1965, Dec. 27 Litho. *Perf. 13½x14***

| | | | |
|---|---|---|---|
| **393** A85 | 3f olive bis & multi | .40 | .25 |
| **394** A85 | 10f car rose & multi | .90 | .25 |
| **395** A85 | 15f blue & multi | 2.40 | .90 |
| | *Nos. 393-395 (3)* | 3.70 | 1.40 |

2nd FAO Intl. Dates Conference, Baghdad, Dec. 1965.
For surcharges see Nos. 694-695.

Soldiers' Monument A86

**1966, Jan. 6 Photo. *Perf. 12***

| | | | |
|---|---|---|---|
| **396** A86 | 2f car rose & multi | .45 | .25 |
| **397** A86 | 5f multicolored | .45 | .25 |
| **398** A86 | 40f yel grn & multi | 1.75 | .75 |
| | *Nos. 396-398 (3)* | 2.65 | 1.25 |

Issued for Army Day.

Eagle and Flag of Iraq — A87

***Perf. 12½***
**1966, Feb. 8 Photo. Unwmk.**

| | | | |
|---|---|---|---|
| **399** A87 | 5f dl bl & multi | .40 | .25 |
| **400** A87 | 10f orange & multi | .75 | .25 |

3rd anniv. of the Revolution of Ramadan 14, which overthrew the Kassem government.

Arab League Emblem — A88

**1966, Mar. 22 *Perf. 11x11½***

| | | | |
|---|---|---|---|
| **401** A88 | 5f org, brn & brt grn | .50 | .25 |
| **402** A88 | 15f ol, rose lil & ultra | .50 | .25 |

Arab Publicity Week.

Soccer Players — A89

5f, Player and goal post. 15f, As 2f. 50f, Legs of player, ball and emblem, horiz.

**1966, Apr. 1 *Perf. 12***

| | | | |
|---|---|---|---|
| **403** A89 | 2f multicolored | .75 | .25 |
| **404** A89 | 5f multicolored | .50 | .25 |
| **405** A89 | 15f multicolored | 1.50 | .45 |
| | *Nos. 403-405 (3)* | 2.75 | .95 |

**Miniature Sheet**
***Imperf***

| | | | |
|---|---|---|---|
| **406** A89 | 50f vio & multi | 7.50 | *10.50* |

3rd Arab Soccer Cup, Baghdad, Apr. 1-10.
For overprint, see No. O296.

Steam Shovel Within Cogwheel A90

**1966, May 1 Litho. *Perf. 13½***

| | | | |
|---|---|---|---|
| **407** A90 | 15f multicolored | .40 | .25 |
| **408** A90 | 25f red, blk, & sil | .50 | .25 |

Issued for Labor Day, May 1, 1966.

Queen Nefertari — A91

Facade of Abu Simbel A92

***Perf. 12½x13, 13½***
**1966, May 20 Litho.**

| | | | |
|---|---|---|---|
| **409** A91 | 5f olive, yel & blk | .40 | .25 |
| **410** A91 | 15f blue, yel & brn | .40 | .25 |
| **411** A92 | 40f bis brn, red & blk | 2.00 | 1.50 |
| | *Nos. 409-411 (3)* | 2.80 | 2.00 |

UNESCO world campaign to save historic monuments in Nubia.

President Arif and Flag — A93

**1966, July 14 Photo. *Perf. 11½***

**412** A93 5f multicolored .40 .25
**413** A93 15f multicolored .50 .25
**414** A93 50f multicolored 1.75 1.00
*Nos. 412-414 (3)* 2.65 1.50

8th anniv. of the July 14, 1958 revolution.

A94

**1966, July 22 Litho. *Perf. 12***
**Multicolored Vignette**

**415** A94 5f lt olive green .40 .25
**416** A94 15f lt greenish blue .40 .25
**417** A94 30f lt yellow green 1.00 .75
*Nos. 415-417 (3)* 1.80 1.25

Mohammed's 1,396th birthday.

Iraqi Museum, Baghdad A95

Designs: 50f, Golden headdress, Ur. 80f, Carved Sumerian head, vert.

**1966, Nov. 9 Litho. *Perf. 14***

**418** A95 15f multicolored .50 .25
**419** A95 50f lt bl, blk, gold & pink 1.50 .80
**420** A95 80f crim, blk, bl & gold 3.25 1.00
*Nos. 418-420 (3)* 5.25 2.05

Opening of New Iraqi Museum, Baghdad.

UNESCO Emblem — A96

**1966, Dec. *Perf. 13½***

**421** A96 5f blue, black & tan .40 .25
**422** A96 15f brt org brn, blk & gray .40 .30

20th anniv. of UNESCO.

Iraqi Citizens — A97

**1966, Nov. 18 *Perf. 13½x13***

**423** A97 15f multicolored .60 .50
**424** A97 25f multicolored 1.10 1.10

3rd anniv. of the Revolution of 11/18/63.

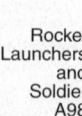

Rocket Launchers and Soldier A98

**1967, Jan. 6 Photo. *Perf. 11½***

**425** A98 15f citron, dk brn & dp bis .45 .25
**426** A98 20f brt lil, dk brn & dp bis .60 .25

Issued for Army Day, Jan. 6.

Oil Derrick, Pipeline, Emblem — A99

15f, 50f, Refinery and emblem, horiz.

**1967, Mar. 6 Litho. *Perf. 14***

**427** A99 5f ol grn, pale yel & blk .40 .25
**428** A99 15f multicolored .40 .25
**429** A99 40f vio, yel & blk .80 .70
**430** A99 50f multicolored 1.75 1.00
*Nos. 427-430 (4)* 3.35 2.20

6th Arab Petroleum Cong., Baghdad, Mar. 1967.

New Year's Emblem and Spider's Web A100

**1967, Apr. 11 Litho. *Perf. 13½***

**431** A100 5f multicolored .40 .25
**432** A100 15f multicolored .40 .25

Issued for the Hajeer Year (New Year).

Worker Holding Cogwheel and Map of Arab Countries — A101

**1967, May 1 *Perf. 12½x13***

**433** A101 10f gray & multi .40 .25
**434** A101 15f lt ultra & multi .40 .25

Issued for Labor Day.

A102

**1967, June 20 Litho. *Perf. 14***

**435** A102 5f multicolored .40 .25
**436** A102 15f blue & multi .50 .25

Mohammed's 1,397th birthday.

Flag, Hands with Clubs — A103

**1967, July 7 *Perf. 13x13½***

**437** A103 5f multicolored .40 .25
**438** A103 15f multicolored .50 .25

47th anniversary of Revolution of 1920.

Um Qasr Harbor A104

10f, 15f, Freighter loading in Um Qasr harbor.

**1967, July 14 Litho. *Perf. 14x13½***

**439** A104 5f multicolored .40 .25
**440** A104 10f multicolored .60 .30
**441** A104 15f multicolored 1.10 .30
**442** A104 40f multicolored 2.00 1.00
*Nos. 439-442 (4)* 4.10 1.85

9th anniv. of the July 14, 1958 revolution and the inauguration of the port of Um Qasr.

Iraqi Man — A105

President Arif — A106

Iraqi Costumes: 5f, 15f, 25f, Women's costumes. 10f, 20f, 30f, Men's costumes.

**1967, Nov. 10 Litho. *Perf. 13***

**443** A105 2f pale brn & multi .40 .25
**444** A105 5f ver & multi .40 .25
**445** A105 10f multicolored .70 .25
**446** A105 15f ultra & multi .95 .50
**447** A105 20f lilac & multi 1.25 .50
**448** A105 25f lemon & multi 1.25 .60
**449** A105 30f fawn & multi 1.50 .60
*Nos. 443-449,C19-C21 (10)* 17.95 6.85

For overprints see Nos. 597-599, O228-O231, RA17.

***Perf. 11x11½, 11½x11***

**1967, Nov. 18**

15f, Pres. Arif and map of Iraq, horiz.

**450** A106 5f bl, vio blk & yel .40 .25
**451** A106 15f rose & multi .75 .40

4th anniversary of Nov. 18th revolution.

Ziggurat of Ur — A107

Designs: 5f, Gate with Nimrod statues. 10f, Gate, Babylon. 15f, Minaret of Mosul, vert. 25f, Arch and ruins of Ctesiphon.

**1967, Dec. 1 Litho. *Perf. 13***

**452** A107 2f orange & multi .40 .25
**453** A107 5f lilac & multi .40 .25
**454** A107 10f orange & multi .40 .25
**455** A107 15f rose red & multi .60 .25
**456** A107 25f vio bl & multi .80 .25
*Nos. 452-456,C22-C26 (10)* 58.85 24.35

International Tourist Year.

For overprints see Nos. 593, 680, O225-O227, O308, RA18.

Iraqi Girl Scout Emblem and Sign — A108

5f, Girl Scouts at campfire & Girl Scout emblem. 10f, Boy Scout emblem & Boy Scout sign. 15f, Boy Scouts pitching tent & Boy Scout sign.

**1967, Dec. 15**

**457** A108 2f orange & multi 1.40 .40
**458** A108 5f blue & multi 1.60 .40
**459** A108 10f green & multi 1.75 .65
**460** A108 15f blue & multi 1.75 .80
*a.* Souv. sheet of 4 12.00 9.00
*Nos. 457-460 (4)* 6.50 2.25

Issued to honor the Scout movement. No. 460a contains 4 stamps similar to Nos. 457-460 with simulated perforations. Sold for 50f.

For overprint see No. RA19.

Soldiers on Maneuvers A109

**1968, Jan. 6 Photo. *Perf. 11½***

**461** A109 5f lt bl, brn & brt grn .40 .25
**462** A109 15f lt bl, ind & olive .65 .25

Issued for Army Day 1968.

White-cheeked Bulbul — A110

Birds: 10f, Hoopoe. 15f, Eurasian jay. 25f, Peregrine falcon. 30f, White stork. 40f, Black partridge. 50f, Marbled teal.

**1968, Jan. Litho. *Perf. 14***

**463** A110 5f org & black .70 .25
**464** A110 10f blue, blk & brn .90 .25
**465** A110 15f pink & multi 1.40 .25
**466** A110 25f dl org & multi 2.00 .50
**467** A110 30f emer, blk & brn 2.50 .50
**468** A110 40f rose lil & multi 3.25 .75
**469** A110 50f multicolored 4.75 1.25
*Nos. 463-469 (7)* 15.50 3.75

For overprint, see No. O311.

Fighting Soldiers A111

**1968, Feb. 8 *Perf. 11½***

**470** A111 15f blk, org & brt bl 3.50 .90

Revolution of Ramadan 14, 5th anniv.

Factories, Tractor and Grain — A112

**1968, May 1 Litho. *Perf. 13***

**471** A112 15f lt bl & multi .40 .25
**472** A112 25f multicolored .60 .25

Issued for Labor Day.

Soccer A113

5f, 25f, Goalkeeper holding ball, vert.

**1968, June 14** *Perf. 13½*

**473** A113 2f multicolored .40 .25
**474** A113 5f multicolored .40 .25
**475** A113 15f multicolored .50 .25
**476** A113 25f multicolored 2.25 .75
*a.* Souv. sheet, 70f, imperf. 9.00 *10.00*
*Nos. 473-476 (4)* 3.55 1.50

23rd C.I.S.M. (Conseil Internationale du Sports Militaire) Soccer Championships.
No. 476a shows badge of Military Soccer League.

Soldier, Flag, Chain and Rising Sun — A114

**1968, July 14** **Photo.** *Perf. 13½x14*

**478** A114 15f multicolored .50 .25

10th anniv. of the July 14, 1958 revolution.

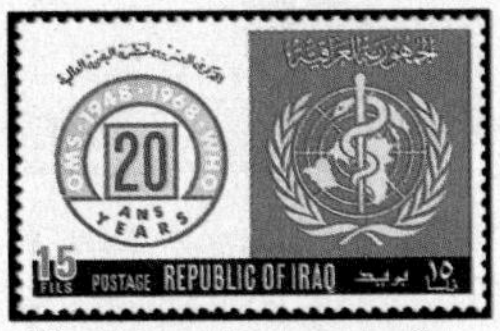
World Health Organization Emblem — A115

5f, 10f, Staff of Aesculapius over emblem, vert.

**1968, Nov. 29** **Litho.** *Perf. 13½*

**479** A115 5f multicolored .40 .25
**480** A115 10f multicolored .40 .25
**481** A115 15f blue, red & black .50 .25
**482** A115 25f yel grn, red & blk .75 .30
*Nos. 479-482 (4)* 2.05 1.05

WHO, 20th anniv. Exist imperf. Value $5.
For overprints, see Nos. O222-O224.

Human Rights Flame — A116

Mother and Children — A117

**1968, Dec. 22** **Litho.** *Perf. 13½*

**483** A116 10f lt bl, yel & car .40 .25
**484** A116 25f lt yel grn, yel & car .50 .25
*a.* Souv. sheet, 100f, imperf. 5.00 5.00

International Human Rights Year.
For overprint, see No. O232.

**1968, Dec. 31** **Litho.** *Perf. 13½*

**485** A117 15f multi .50 .25
**486** A117 25f bl & multi 1.25 .35
*a.* Souv. sheet, 100f, imperf 8.00 5.25

UNICEF. For overprints see Nos. 624-625, O234-O235.

Tanks A118

**1969, Jan. 6** **Photo.**

**487** A118 25f vio, car & brn 3.50 2.00

Issued for Army Day, Jan. 6.
For overprint, see No. O244.

Harvester A119

**1969, Feb.** **Photo.** *Perf. 13½*

**488** A119 15f yel brn & multi .50 .25

6th anniv. of the Revolution of Ramadan 14.

Mosque A119a

**1969, Mar. 19** **Photo.** *Perf. 13x13½*

**488A** A119a 15f multicolored 1.00 .75

Issued for Hajeer (pilgrimage) Year.

Emblem A120

**1969, Apr. 12** **Litho.** *Perf. 12½x12*

**489** A120 10f yel grn & multi .60 .30
**490** A120 15f orange & multi 1.00 .30

1st conference of the Arab Veterinary Union, Baghdad, Apr. 1969.

Barbus Grypus A121

Fish: 3f, Barbus puntius sharpeyi. 10f, Pampus argenteus. 100f, Barbus esocinus.

**1969, May 9** *Perf. 14*

**491** A121 2f multicolored 1.75 .45
**492** A121 3f multicolored 1.90 .45
**493** A121 10f multicolored 2.00 .45
**494** A121 100f multicolored 6.00 3.75
*Nos. 491-494 (4)* 11.65 5.10

For overprints, see Nos. O312-313.

Holy Kaaba, Mecca A122

**1969, May 28** **Photo.** *Perf. 12*

**495** A122 15f blue & multi 1.00 .50

Mohammed's 1,399th birthday.

ILO Emblem A123

**1969, June 6** **Litho.** *Perf. 13x12½*

**496** A123 5f lt vio, yel & blk .25 .25
**497** A123 15f grnsh gray, yel & black .25 .25
**498** A123 50f rose, yel & blk 1.25 .80
*a.* Souv. sheet, 100f, imperf. 6.00 *7.00*
*Nos. 496-498 (3)* 1.75 1.30

ILO, 50th anniv.
For overprint, see No. O297.

Weight Lifting — A124

Design: 5f, 35f, High jump.

**1969, June 20** *Perf. 13½x13*

**500** A124 3f org yel & multi .55 .25
**501** A124 5f blue & multi .55 .25
**502** A124 10f rose pink & multi .65 .30
**503** A124 35f yellow & multi 1.25 1.00
*a.* Souv. sheet of 4, #500-503, imperf. 12.00 12.00
*Nos. 500-503 (4)* 3.00 1.80

19th Olympic Games, Mexico City, Oct. 12-27, 1968. No. 503a sold for 100f.

Coat of Arms, Symbols of Industry — A125

**1969, July 14** **Photo.** *Perf. 13*

**504** A125 10f brn org & multi .40 .25
**505** A125 15f multicolored .60 .25

11th anniv. of the July 14, 1958 revolution.

Street Fighting A126

Pres. Ahmed Hassan al-Bakr — A127

Wheat and Fair Emblem — A128

Design: 20f, Baghdad International Airport.

**1969, July 17** *Perf. 13½*

**506** A126 10f yel & multi .50 .30
**507** A126 15f blue & multi .50 .30
**508** A126 20f blue & multi 1.60 .45
**509** A127 200f gold & multi 20.00 9.00
*Nos. 506-509 (4)* 22.60 10.05

Coup of July 17, 1968, 1st anniv. #508 also for the inauguration of Baghdad Intl. Airport. No. 509 exists imperf. Value $25.

**1969, Oct. 1** **Photo.** *Perf. 13½*

**510** A128 10f brt grn, gold & dl red .65 .25
**511** A128 15f ultra, gold & red .80 .35

6th International Fair, Baghdad.
For overprints see Nos. 567A-567B.

Motor Ship Al-Waleed A129

Designs: 15f, Floating crane Antara. 30f, Pilot ship Al-Rasheed. 35f, Suction dredge Hillah. 50f, Survey ship Al-Fao.

**1969, Oct. 8** **Litho.** *Perf. 12½*

**512** A129 15f black & multi .50 .25
**513** A129 20f black & multi .70 .45
**514** A129 30f black & multi 1.10 .55
**515** A129 35f black & multi 1.75 1.00
**516** A129 50f black & multi 5.25 2.25
*Nos. 512-516 (5)* 9.30 4.50

50th anniversary of Basrah Harbor.

Radio Tower and Map of Palestine A130

"Search for Knowledge" A131

**1969, Nov. 9** **Litho.** *Perf. 12½x13*

**517** A130 15f multicolored 3.50 .35
**518** A130 50f multicolored 6.50 .80

10th anniversary of Iraqi News Agency.
For overprints see Nos. 698-699.

**1969, Nov. 21** **Photo.** *Perf. 13*

**519** A131 15f blue & multi .35 .25
**520** A131 20f green & multi .50 .30

Campaign against illiteracy.

Front Page of First Baghdad Newspaper A132

**1969, Dec. 26** **Litho.** *Perf. 13½*

**521** A132 15f yel, org & black .70 .30

Centenary of the Iraqi press.
For overprint see No. 552.

Soldier, Map of Iraq and Plane — A133

**1970, Jan. 6** **Photo.** *Perf. 13*

**522** A133 15f lt vio & multi .70 .30
**523** A133 20f yellow & multi 1.40 .65

Issued for Army Day 1970.

Soldier, Farmer and Worker Shoring up Wall in Iraqi Colors — A134

Poppies — A135

**1970, Feb. 8 Photo. *Perf. 13***

**524** A134 10f multicolored .25 .25
**525** A134 15f brick red & multi .40 .25

7th anniv. of the Revolution of Ramadan 14.

**1970, June 12 Litho. *Perf. 13***

Flowers: 3f, Poet's narcissus. 5f, Tulip. 10f, 50f, Carnations. 15f, Rose.

**526** A135 2f emer & multi .40 .25
**527** A135 3f blue & multi .40 .25
**528** A135 5f multicolored .40 .25
**529** A135 10f lt grn & multi .60 .35
**530** A135 15f pale sal & multi 1.10 .55
**531** A135 50f lt grn & multi 3.25 1.25
*Nos. 526-531 (6)* 6.15 2.90

The overprinted sets Nos. 532-543 were released before Nos. 526-531.

For overprints see Nos. 621-623, RA20. For surcharge see No. 726.

Nos. 526-531 Overprinted in Ultramarine

**1970, Mar. 21**

**532** A135 2f emer & multi .60 .50
**533** A135 3f lt bl & multi .60 .50
**534** A135 5f multicolored .60 .50
**535** A135 10f lt grn & multi .60 .50
**536** A135 15f pale sal & multi 1.20 .80
**537** A135 50f lt grn & multi 3.50 1.25
*Nos. 532-537 (6)* 7.10 4.05

Issued for Novrooz (New Year).

Nos. 526-531 Overprinted in Black

**1970, Apr. 18**

**538** A135 2f emer & multi .50 .50
**539** A135 3f lt bl & multi .50 .50
**540** A135 5f multicolored .50 .50
**541** A135 10f lt grn & multi .50 .50
**542** A135 15f pale sal & multi 1.40 .90
**543** A135 50f lt grn & multi 3.00 1.10
*Nos. 538-543 (6)* 6.40 4.00

Issued for the Spring Festival, Mosul.

Map of Arab Countries, Slogans — A136

50f, 150f, People, flag, sun and map of Palestine.

**1970, Apr. 7 *Perf. 13x12½***

**544** A136 15f gold & multi .40 .25
**545** A136 35f sil & multi .60 .55
**546** A136 50f red & multi 2.00 .70
*a.* Souv. sheet, 150f, imperf. 11.00 11.00
*Nos. 544-546 (3)* 3.00 1.50

23rd anniversary of Al-Baath Party.

Workers and Cogwheel — A137

**1970, May 1**

**547** A137 10f silver & multi .40 .25
**548** A137 15f silver & multi .50 .35
**549** A137 35f silver & multi 1.50 .75
*Nos. 547-549 (3)* 2.40 1.35

Issued for Labor Day.

Kaaba, Mecca, and Koran A138

**1970, May 17 Photo. *Perf. 13***

**550** A138 15f brt bl & multi .40 .25
**551** A138 20f orange & multi .40 .25

Mohammed's 1,400th birthday.

No. 521 Overprinted "1970" and Arabic Inscription in Prussian Blue

**1970, June 15 Litho. *Perf. 13½***

**552** A132 15f yel, org & black .55 .55

Day of Iraqi press.

Revolutionists and Guns — A139

Designs: 35f, Revolutionist and rising sun.

**1970, June 30 Litho. *Perf. 13***

**553** A139 10f blk & apple grn .25 .25
**554** A139 15f black & gold .40 .25
**555** A139 35f blk & red org .90 .45
*a.* Souv. sheet, 100f, imperf. 5.50 5.50
*Nos. 553-555 (3)* 1.55 .95

50th anniversary, Revolution of 1920.

Broken Chain and New Dawn — A140

**1970, July 14 *Perf. 13x13½***

**557** A140 15f multicolored .35 .25
**558** A140 20f multicolored .50 .25

12th anniv. of the July 14, 1958 revolution.

Map of Arab Countries and Hands — A141

**1970, July 17 *Perf. 13***

**559** A141 15f gold & multi .30 .25
**560** A141 25f gold & multi .55 .25

2nd anniversary of coup of July 17, 1968.

Pomegranates A142

**1970, Aug. 21 *Perf. 14***

**561** A142 3f shown .40 .25
**562** A142 5f Grapefruit .40 .25
**563** A142 10f Grapes .40 .25
**564** A142 15f Oranges 1.10 .35
**565** A142 35f Dates 3.50 1.90
*Nos. 561-565 (5)* 5.80 3.00

The Latin inscriptions on the 5f and 10f have been erroneously transposed.

For overprints & surcharge see #613-615, 725, O240-O245.

Kaaba, Mecca, Moon over Mountain and Spider Web — A143

**1970, Sept. 4 Photo. *Perf. 13***

**566** A143 15f multicolored .40 .25
**567** A143 25f multicolored .55 .25

Issued for Hajeer (Pilgrimage) Year.

Nos. 510-511 Overprinted in Red

**1970, Sept. Photo. *Perf. 13½***

**567A** A128 10f multi 3.50 2.00
**567B** A128 15f multi 3.50 2.00

7th International Fair, Baghdad.

Intl. Education Year Emblem A144

**1970, Nov. 13 Photo. *Perf. 13***

**568** A144 5f yel green & multi .35 .25
**569** A144 15f brick red & multi .50 .25

Flag and Map of Arab League Countries A145

**1970 *Perf. 11***

**570** A145 15f olive & multi .40 .25
**571** A145 35f gray & multi .50 .40

25th anniversary of the Arab League.

Baghdad Hospital and Emblem A146

**1970, Dec. 7 Litho. *Perf. 12***

**572** A146 15f yellow & multi .40 .25
**573** A146 40f lt green & multi 1.10 .60

Iraqi Medical Society, 50th anniv.

Sugar Beet — A147

15f, Sugar factory, horiz. 30f, like 5f.

***Perf. 13x13½, 13½x13***

**1970, Dec. 25 Photo.**

**574** A147 5f ocher, grn & blk .30 .25
**575** A147 15f black & multi .50 .25
**576** A147 30f org ver, grn & blk 1.50 .75
*Nos. 574-576 (3)* 2.30 1.25

Publicity for Mosul sugar factory.

OPEC Emblem A148

**1970, Dec. 30 Litho. *Perf. 13x13½***

**577** A148 10f rose claret, bis & bl .75 .40
**578** A148 40f emer, bis & blue 3.25 1.25

OPEC, 10th anniversary.

Soldiers — A149

Soldiers, Maps of Arab Countries and Israel — A150

***Perf. 13½x14, 11½x12½***

**1971, Jan. 6**

**579** A149 15f multicolored 1.00 .40
**580** A150 40f red org & multi 4.00 1.50
*a.* Souv. sheet of 2, #579-580, imperf. 12.00 *12.00*

Army Day, 50th anniversary.
No. 580a sold for 100f.

Marchers and Map of Arab Countries — A151

**1971, Feb. 8 Litho. *Perf. 11½x12½***

**581** A151 15f yellow & multi .45 .25
**582** A151 40f pink & multi 1.25 .50

Revolution of Ramadan 14, 8th anniversary.

Spider Web, Pilgrims
A152

**1971, Feb. 26 Photo. *Perf. 13***

| | | |
|---|---|---|
| **583** A152 10f pink & multi | .25 | .25 |
| **584** A152 15f buff & multi | .45 | .25 |

Hajeer (New) Year.

President al-Bakr
A153

**1971, Mar. 11 Litho. *Perf. 14***

| | | |
|---|---|---|
| **585** A153 15f orange & multi | .70 | .40 |
| **586** A153 100f emer & multi | 3.25 | 1.50 |

First anniversary of Mar. 11th Manifesto.

Marshland
A154

Tourist Publicity: 10f, Stork flying over Baghdad. 15f, "Summer Resorts." 100f, Return of Sindbad the Sailor.

**1971, Mar. 15 *Perf. 13***

| | | |
|---|---|---|
| **587** A154 5f multicolored | .45 | .25 |
| **588** A154 10f lt grn & multi | .80 | .25 |
| **589** A154 15f pink & multi | 1.00 | .50 |
| **590** A154 100f multicolored | 5.25 | 3.00 |
| *Nos. 587-590 (4)* | 7.50 | 4.00 |

Blacksmith Taming Serpent — A155

**1971, Mar. 21 *Perf. 11½x12***

| | | |
|---|---|---|
| **591** A155 15f multicolored | .85 | .35 |
| **592** A155 25f yel & multi | 1.75 | .70 |

Novrooz Festival.

No. 455 Overprinted

**1971, Mar. 23 Litho. *Perf. 13***

| | | |
|---|---|---|
| **593** A107 15f rose red & multi | 3.25 | 1.25 |

World Meteorological Day. See No. C39.

Workers, Soldier, Map of Arab Countries — A156

**1971, Apr. 7**

| | | |
|---|---|---|
| **594** A156 15f yel & multi | .80 | .45 |
| **595** A156 35f multicolored | 1.60 | .75 |
| **596** A156 250f multicolored | 12.00 | 12.00 |
| *Nos. 594-596 (3)* | 14.40 | 13.20 |

24th anniv. of the Al Baath Party. No. 596 has circular perforation around vignette set within a white square of paper, perforated on 4 sides. The design of No. 596 is similar to Nos. 594-595, but with denomination within the circle and no inscriptions in margin.

Nos. 443-444, 448 Overprinted

**1971, Apr. 14**

| | | |
|---|---|---|
| **597** A105 2f pale brn & multi | .50 | .25 |
| **598** A105 5f ver & multi | .70 | .25 |
| **599** A105 25f lemon & multi | 2.25 | 1.00 |
| *Nos. 597-599 (3)* | 3.45 | 1.50 |

Mosul Festival.

Worker, Farm Woman with Torch
A157

**1971, May 1 Litho. *Perf. 13***

| | | |
|---|---|---|
| **600** A157 15f ocher & multi | .35 | .25 |
| **601** A157 40f olive & multi | 1.25 | .30 |

Labor Day.

Muslim Praying in Mecca
A158

**1971, May 7**

| | | |
|---|---|---|
| **602** A158 15f yellow & multi | .55 | .25 |
| **603** A158 100f pink & multi | 2.75 | 1.25 |

Mohammed's 1,401st birthday.

People, Fists, Map of Iraq
A159

**1971, July 14 Photo. *Perf. 14***

| | | |
|---|---|---|
| **604** A159 25f green & multi | .55 | .25 |
| **605** A159 50f lt bl & multi | 1.75 | .60 |

13th anniv. of the July 14, 1958 revolution.

Surveyor, Preacher, Rising Sun
A160

**1971, July 17 *Perf. 13***

| | | |
|---|---|---|
| **606** A160 25f multicolored | .60 | .30 |
| **607** A160 70f orange & multi | 1.90 | .75 |

3rd anniversary of July 17, 1968, coup.

Rafidain Bank Emblem
A161

**1971, Sept. 24 Photo. *Perf. 13½***

**Diameter: 27mm**

| | | |
|---|---|---|
| **608** A161 10f multicolored | .55 | *.55* |
| **609** A161 15f multicolored | .90 | .90 |
| **610** A161 25f multicolored | 1.75 | *1.75* |

**Diameter: 32mm**

| | | |
|---|---|---|
| **611** A161 65f multicolored | 8.50 | 6.50 |
| **612** A161 250f multicolored | 22.50 | 21.00 |
| *Nos. 608-612 (5)* | 34.20 | 30.70 |

30th anniversary of Rafidain Bank. Nos. 608-612 have circular perforation around design within a white square of paper, perforated on 4 sides.

Nos. 561, 564-565 Overprinted

**1971, Oct. 15 Litho. *Perf. 14***

| | | |
|---|---|---|
| **613** A142 3f bl grn & multi | 2.75 | 2.75 |
| **614** A142 15f red & multi | 2.75 | 2.75 |
| **615** A142 35f orange & multi | 2.75 | 2.75 |
| *Nos. 613-615 (3)* | 8.25 | 8.25 |

Agricultural census, Oct. 15, 1971.

Soccer
A162

Designs: 25f, Track and field. 35f, Table tennis. 75f, Gymnastics. 95f, Volleyball and basketball.

**1971, Nov. 17 Litho. *Perf. 13½***

| | | |
|---|---|---|
| **616** A162 15f green & multi | .30 | .30 |
| **617** A162 25f pink & multi | .80 | .40 |
| **618** A162 35f lt bl & multi | 1.00 | .90 |
| **619** A162 70f lt grn & multi | 4.25 | 1.50 |
| **620** A162 95f yel grn & multi | 7.50 | 2.50 |
| *a.* Souvenir sheet of 5 | 24.00 | 24.00 |
| *Nos. 616-620 (5)* | 13.85 | 5.60 |

4th Pan-Arab Schoolboys Sports Games, Baghdad. No. 620a contains 5 stamps similar to Nos. 616-620 with simulated perforations. Sold for 200f.

Nos. 527-528, 530 Overprinted and Surcharged

**1971, Nov. 23 Litho. *Perf. 13***

| | | |
|---|---|---|
| **621** A135 15f multicolored | 1.75 | .40 |
| **622** A135 25f on 5f multi | 2.50 | 1.25 |
| **623** A135 70f on 3f multi | 9.50 | 3.00 |
| *Nos. 621-623 (3)* | 13.75 | 4.65 |

Students' Day. The 15f has only first 3 lines of Arabic overprint.

Nos. 485-486 Overprinted

**1971, Dec. 11 Litho. *Perf. 13½***

| | | |
|---|---|---|
| **624** A117 15f multicolored | 2.75 | 1.00 |
| **625** A117 25f blue & multi | 7.25 | 3.25 |

25th anniv. of UNICEF.

Children Crossing Street — A162a

**1971, Dec. 17 Litho. *Perf. 13x12½***

| | | |
|---|---|---|
| **625A** A162a 15f yel & multi | 2.50 | .80 |
| **625B** A162a 25f brt rose & multi | 4.50 | 2.50 |

2nd Traffic Week. For overprints see #668-669.

Arab Postal Union Emblem
A163

**1971, Dec. 24 Photo. *Perf. 11½***

| | | |
|---|---|---|
| **626** A163 25f emer, yel & brn | .45 | .25 |
| **627** A163 70f vio bl, yel & red | 1.75 | .65 |

25th anniv. of the Conf. of Sofar, Lebanon, establishing Arab Postal Union.

Racial Equality Emblem — A164

**1971, Dec. 31 *Perf. 13½x14***

| | | |
|---|---|---|
| **628** A164 25f brt grn & multi | .25 | .25 |
| **629** A164 70f orange & multi | 1.00 | .90 |

Intl. Year Against Racial Discrimination.

Soldiers with Flag and Torch — A165

**1972, Jan. 6 Photo. *Perf. 14x13½***

| | | |
|---|---|---|
| **630** A165 25f blue & multi | 1.20 | .65 |
| **631** A165 70f brt grn & multi | 4.00 | 2.50 |

Army Day, Jan. 6.

Workers A166

**1972, Feb. 8**

| | | | | |
|---|---|---|---|---|
| **632** | A166 | 25f brt grn & multi | 2.50 | .60 |
| **633** | A166 | 95f lilac & multi | 4.50 | 2.50 |

Revolution of Ramadan 14, 9th anniv.

Mosque, Minaret, Crescent and Caravan A167

**1972, Feb. 26 Litho. *Perf. 12½x13***

| | | | | |
|---|---|---|---|---|
| **634** | A167 | 25f bl grn & multi | .35 | .25 |
| **635** | A167 | 35f purple & multi | .70 | .40 |

Hegira (Pilgrimage) Year.

Peace Symbols and "11" — A168

**1972, Mar. 11 Photo. *Perf. 11x12½***

| | | | | |
|---|---|---|---|---|
| **636** | A168 | 25f lt blue & blk | 1.50 | .30 |
| **637** | A168 | 70f brt lilac & blk | 4.25 | 1.25 |

2nd anniversary of Mar. 11 Manifesto.

Mountain Range and Flowers — A169

**1972, Mar. 21 *Perf. 11½x11***

| | | | | |
|---|---|---|---|---|
| **638** | A169 | 25f vio blue & multi | 1.25 | .25 |
| **639** | A169 | 70f vio blue & multi | 4.25 | 1.50 |

Novrooz, New Year Festival.

Party Emblem A170

Symbolic Design — A171

***Perf. 14 (A170), 13 (A171)***

**1972 Litho.**

| | | | | |
|---|---|---|---|---|
| **640** | A170 | 10f brn org & multi | .35 | .25 |
| **641** | A171 | 25f bister & multi | .80 | .40 |
| **642** | A170 | 35f brn org & multi | .90 | .50 |
| **643** | A171 | 70f red & multi | 2.75 | 2.10 |
| | | *Nos. 640-643 (4)* | 4.80 | 3.25 |

Iraqi Arab Baath Socialist Party, 25th anniv. Issued: 25f, 70f, Mar. 23; 10f, 35f, Apr. 7.

Emblem, Map, Weather Balloons and Chart — A172

**1972, Mar. 23 Photo. *Perf. 14x13½***

| | | | | |
|---|---|---|---|---|
| **644** | A172 | 25f multicolored | 1.90 | .50 |
| **645** | A172 | 35f yel & multi | 3.25 | 1.50 |

12th World Meteorological Day.

Cogwheel and Ship — A173

**1972, Mar. 25 *Perf. 11x11½***

| | | | | |
|---|---|---|---|---|
| **646** | A173 | 25f ocher & multi | .50 | .25 |
| **647** | A173 | 35f pink & multi | 1.00 | .40 |

Arab Chamber of Commerce.

Derrick and Flame A174

Quill Pens, Map of Arab Countries A175

**1972, Apr. 7 *Perf. 13x13½***

| | | | | |
|---|---|---|---|---|
| **648** | A174 | 25f multicolored | 1.40 | .30 |
| **649** | A174 | 35f multicolored | 1.90 | 1.00 |

Opening of North Rumaila (INOC, North Iraq Oil Fields).

**1972, Apr. 17 Photo. *Perf. 11x11½***

| | | | | |
|---|---|---|---|---|
| **650** | A175 | 25f orange & multi | .55 | .25 |
| **651** | A175 | 35f blue & multi | 1.75 | 1.00 |

3rd Congress of Arab Journalists.

Women's Federation Emblem A176

**1972, Apr. 22 Litho. *Perf. 13½***

| | | | | |
|---|---|---|---|---|
| **652** | A176 | 25f green & multi | .55 | .30 |
| **653** | A176 | 35f lilac & multi | 1.75 | 1.20 |

Iraqi Women's Federation, 4th anniversary.

Hand Holding Globe-shaped Wrench — A177

**1972, May 1 Photo. *Perf. 11½***

| | | | | |
|---|---|---|---|---|
| **654** | A177 | 25f yel grn & multi | .45 | .25 |
| **655** | A177 | 35f orange & multi | .80 | .40 |

Labor Day.

Kaaba, Mecca, and Crescent — A178

**1972, May 26**

| | | | | |
|---|---|---|---|---|
| **656** | A178 | 25f green & multi | .55 | .25 |
| **657** | A178 | 35f purple & multi | 1.75 | 1.10 |

Mohammed's 1,402nd birthday.

Soldier, Civilian and Guns — A179

**1972, July 14 Photo. *Perf. 13½x14***

| | | | | |
|---|---|---|---|---|
| **658** | A179 | 35f multicolored | .90 | .40 |
| **659** | A179 | 70f lilac & multi | 3.00 | 1.20 |

14th anniv. of July 14, 1958, revolution.

Dome of the Rock, Arab Countries' Map, Fists A180

**1972, July 17 *Perf. 13***

| | | | | |
|---|---|---|---|---|
| **660** | A180 | 25f citron & multi | 1.20 | .70 |
| **661** | A180 | 95f blue & multi | 3.25 | 3.00 |

4th anniv. of July 17, 1968 coup.

Congress Emblem, Scout Saluting Iraqi Flag — A182

**1972, Aug. 12 Photo. *Perf. 13½x14***

| | | | | |
|---|---|---|---|---|
| **664** | A182 | 20f multicolored | 2.25 | 1.00 |
| **665** | A182 | 25f lilac & multi | 3.25 | 1.10 |

10th Arab Boy Scouts Jamboree and Conference, Mosul, Aug. 10-19.

**1972, Aug. 24**

Congress emblem and Girl Guide in camp.

| | | | | |
|---|---|---|---|---|
| **666** | A182 | 10f yellow & multi | 1.50 | .65 |
| **667** | A182 | 45f multicolored | 4.75 | 1.40 |

4th Arab Guides Camp & Conf., Mosul, Aug. 24-30.

No. 625B Ovptd.

No. 625A Ovptd. and Srchd.

**1972, Oct. 4 Photo. *Perf. 13x12½***

| | | | | |
|---|---|---|---|---|
| **668** | A162a | 25f brt rose & multi | 6.75 | 3.00 |
| **669** | A162a | 70f on 15f multi | 8.50 | 7.00 |

Third Traffic Week.

Central Bank of Iraq A183

**1972, Nov. 16 Photo. *Perf. 13***

| | | | | |
|---|---|---|---|---|
| **670** | A183 | 25f lt blue & multi | .80 | .40 |
| **671** | A183 | 70f lt green & multi | 2.25 | .90 |

25th anniversary, Central Bank of Iraq.

UIC Emblem A184

**1972, Dec. 29**

| | | | | |
|---|---|---|---|---|
| **672** | A184 | 25f dp rose & multi | 1.75 | .70 |
| **673** | A184 | 45f brt vio & multi | 5.00 | 3.00 |

50th anniv., Intl. Railroad Union (UIC).

**Nos. 148-149, 151, 180 and Type of 1957-58 Overprinted with 3 Bars**

**1973, Jan. 29 Engr. *Perf. 11½x12***

| | | | | |
|---|---|---|---|---|
| **674** | A28 | 10f blue | 3.50 | 1.25 |
| **675** | A33 | 10f blue | 3.50 | 1.25 |
| **676** | A28 | 15f black | 3.50 | 1.25 |
| **677** | A33 | 15f black | 3.50 | 1.25 |
| **678** | A28 | 25f rose violet | 3.50 | 1.25 |
| **679** | A33 | 25f rose violet | 3.50 | 1.25 |
| | | *Nos. 674-679 (6)* | 21.00 | 7.50 |

The size and position of the bottom bar of overprint differs; the bar can be same size as 2 top bars, short and centered or moved to the right.

No. 455 Overprinted

**1973, Mar. 25 Litho. *Perf. 13***

**680** A107 15f rose red & multi 10.00 4.00

Intl. History Cong. See Nos. C52-C53.

Workers and Oil Wells A185

**1973, June 1 Litho. *Perf. 13***

**681** A185 25f yel & multi 2.00 .90
**682** A185 70f rose & multi 9.50 3.00

1st anniv. of nationalization of oil industry. For overprint, see No. O298.

Ram's-head Harp — A186

Designs: 25f, 35f, 45f, Minaret, Mosul, 50f, 70f, 95f, Statue of goddess. 10f, 20f, like 5f.

**1973, June Litho. *Perf. 13x12½***

**683** A186 5f orange & blk .25 .25
**684** A186 10f bister & blk .35 .25
**685** A186 20f brt rose & blk .35 .25
**686** A186 25f ultra & blk .35 .25
**687** A186 35f emer & blk .60 .30
**688** A186 45f blue & black .70 .30
**689** A186 50f olive & yel .95 .30
**690** A186 70f violet & yel 1.25 .50
**691** A186 95f brown & yel 2.25 .75
*Nos. 683-691 (9)* 7.05 3.15

For overprints see Nos. O299-O307, RA21.

People with Flags, Grain A187

**1973, July 14**

**692** A187 25f multicolored .70 .30
**693** A187 35f multicolored 1.40 .40

July Festivals.

Nos. 393 and 395 Surcharged

**1973 Litho. *Perf. 13½x14***

**694** A85 25f on 3f multi 4.00 2.25
**695** A85 70f on 15f multi 10.00 5.00

Festival of Date Trees.

INTERPOL Headquarters — A188

**1973, Sept. 20 Litho. *Perf. 12***

**696** A188 25f multicolored 1.00 .60
**697** A188 70f brt bl & multi 5.50 3.75

50th anniv. of Intl. Criminal Police Org.

Nos. 517-518 Overprinted in Silver

**1973, Sept. 29 Litho. *Perf. 12½x13***

**698** A130 15f multicolored 6.50 2.50
**699** A130 50f multicolored 12.00 3.50

Meeting of Intl. Org. of Journalists' Executive Committee, Sept. 26-29.

Flags and Fair Emblem — A189

WMO Emblem — A190

**1973, Oct. 10 Photo. *Perf. 11***

**700** A189 10f brt grn & dk brn .45 .25
**701** A189 20f ocher & multi .80 .30
**702** A189 65f blue & multi 1.75 .90
*Nos. 700-702 (3)* 3.00 1.45

10th International Baghdad Fair, Oct. 1-21.

**1973, Nov. 15 Litho. *Perf. 12***

**703** A190 25f org, blk & green .70 .25
**704** A190 35f brt rose, blk & grn 2.25 1.00

Intl. meteorological cooperation, cent.

Flags of Arab League and Iraq, Maghreb Emblem A191

**1973, Dec. 1 Photo. *Perf. 14***

**705** A191 20f dl org & multi .40 .25
**706** A191 35f blue & multi 1.40 .90

11th session of Civil Aviation Council of Arab States, Baghdad, Dec. 1973.

No. 360 Overprinted

**1973, Dec. 12 Photo. *Perf. 11***

**707** A67a 30f orange & blue 5.00 2.75

6th Executive Council Meeting of APU, Baghdad.

Human Rights Flame — A192

**1973, Dec. 25 *Perf. 11½***

**708** A192 25f multicolored .25 .25
**709** A192 70f ultra & multi .90 .50

Universal Declaration of Human Rights, 25th anniv.

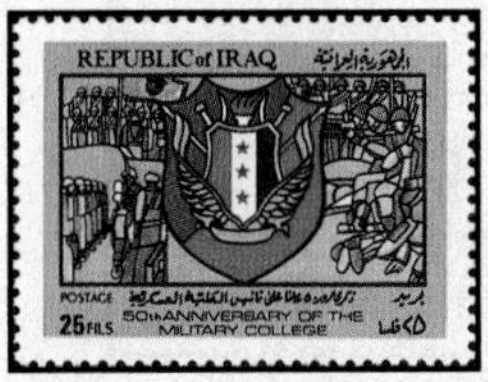


Military College Crest and Cadets A193

**1974, Jan. 6 *Perf. 12x11½***

**710** A193 25f ocher & multi .45 .25
**711** A193 35f ultra & multi 1.60 1.00

50th anniversary of the Military College.

UPU and Arab Postal Union Emblems A194

**1974, May 28 Photo. *Perf. 11½x12***

**712** A194 25f gold & multi .90 .25
**713** A194 35f gold & multi .90 .40
**714** A194 70f gold & multi 1.60 .90
*Nos. 712-714 (3)* 3.40 1.55

Centenary of the Universal Postal Union.

Symbols of Ancient Mesopotamia and Oil Industry — A195

**1974, June 1 Litho. *Perf. 12½***

**715** A195 10f blue & multi .40 .25
**716** A195 25f ocher & multi .85 .25
**717** A195 70f rose & multi 2.75 2.00
*Nos. 715-717 (3)* 4.00 2.50

Nationalization of the oil industry, 2nd anniv.

Festival A196

**1974, July 17 *Perf. 11½x12***

**718** A196 20f lilac & multi .35 .25
**719** A196 35f dull org & multi 1.00 .50

July Festivals.

National Front Emblem and People A197

**1974, July 17 *Perf. 12x11½***

**720** A197 25f blue & multi .65 .25
**721** A197 70f brt grn & multi 1.50 .75

1st anniv. of Progressive National Front.

Cement Plant and Brick Wall — A198

**1974, Oct. 19 *Perf. 11½x12***

**722** A198 20f gray bl & multi .45 .25
**723** A198 25f red & multi .65 .30
**724** A198 70f emerald & multi 1.40 1.00
*Nos. 722-724 (3)* 2.50 1.55

25th anniversary of Iraqi Cement Plant.

**Nos. 561 and 527 Surcharged**

a

b

**1975, Jan. 9 Litho. *Perf. 13, 14***

**725** A142 (a) 10f on 3f multi 3.50 2.50
**726** A135 (b) 25f on 3f multi 11.00 7.25

Globe and WPY Emblem A199

**1975, Jan. 30 *Perf. 11½x12***

**727** A199 25f dull bl & blk .60 .25
**728** A199 35f brt pink & ind 1.25 .65
**729** A199 70f yel grn & vio 3.50 1.40
*Nos. 727-729 (3)* 5.35 2.30

World Population Year 1974.

Festival Symbols — A200

**1975, July 17 Litho. *Perf. 12x11½***

| | | | | | |
|---|---|---|---|---|---|
| **730** | A200 | 5f lt brn & multi | .25 | .25 |
| **731** | A200 | 10f lt brn & multi | .25 | .25 |
| **732** | A200 | 35f lt brn & multi | 1.75 | .75 |
| | | *Nos. 730-732 (3)* | 2.25 | 1.25 |

Festivals, July 1975.

Map of Arab Countries A201

**1975, Aug. 5 Photo. *Perf. 13***

| | | | | |
|---|---|---|---|---|
| **733** | A201 | 25f rose & multi | .50 | .25 |
| **734** | A201 | 35f multicolored | .90 | .60 |
| **735** | A201 | 45f multicolored | 1.00 | .65 |
| | | *Nos. 733-735 (3)* | 2.40 | 1.50 |

Arab Working Org., 10th anniv.

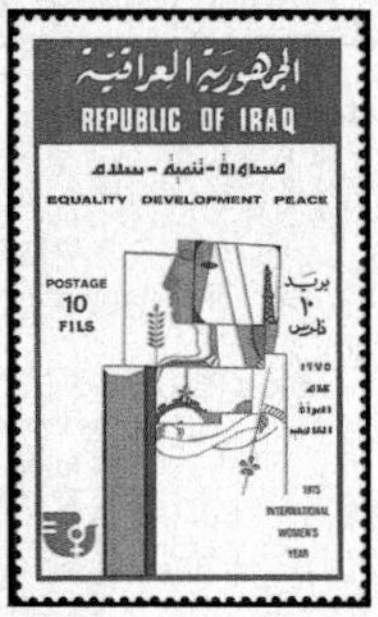

Symbols of Women, Oil Industry and Agriculture A202

**1975, Aug. 15 *Perf. 14***

| | | | | |
|---|---|---|---|---|
| **736** | A202 | 10f lilac & multi | .50 | .30 |
| **737** | A202 | 35f multicolored | 1.00 | .85 |
| **738** | A202 | 70f bl & multi | 4.25 | 1.50 |
| *a.* | | Souv. sheet, 100f, imperf. | 10.00 | *10.00* |
| | | *Nos. 736-738 (3)* | 5.75 | 2.65 |

International Women's Year.

Euphrates Dam and Causeway — A203

**1975, Sept. 5 Litho. *Perf. 12x11½***

| | | | | |
|---|---|---|---|---|
| **739** | A203 | 3f orange & multi | .25 | .25 |
| **740** | A203 | 25f purple & multi | .70 | .25 |
| **741** | A203 | 70f rose red & multi | 2.75 | 1.25 |
| | | *Nos. 739-741 (3)* | 3.70 | 1.75 |

Intl. Commission on Irrigation and Drainage, 25th anniv.

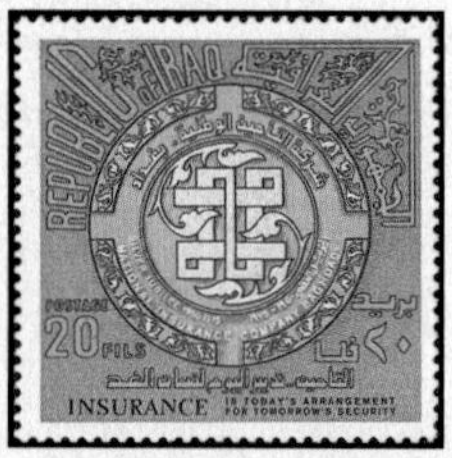

National Insurance Co. Seal A204

**1975, Oct. 11 Photo. *Perf. 13***

| | | | | |
|---|---|---|---|---|
| **742** | A204 | 20f brt bl & multi | .80 | .25 |
| **743** | A204 | 25f crim & multi | 1.00 | .40 |
| *a.* | | Souv. sheet, 100f, imperf. | 7.00 | *8.50* |

Natl. Insurance Co., Baghdad, 25th anniv.

Musician Entertaining King — A205

**1975, Nov. 21 *Perf. 14***

| | | | | |
|---|---|---|---|---|
| **744** | A205 | 25f silver & multi | .65 | .25 |
| **745** | A205 | 45f gold & multi | 1.50 | .90 |

Baghdad Intl. Music Conf., Nov. 1975.

Telecommunications Center — A206

**1975, Dec. 22 Litho. *Perf. 12½***

| | | | | |
|---|---|---|---|---|
| **746** | A206 | 5f lil rose & multi | .25 | .25 |
| **747** | A206 | 10f blue & multi | .30 | .25 |
| **748** | A206 | 60f green & multi | 1.90 | 1.20 |
| | | *Nos. 746-748 (3)* | 2.45 | 1.70 |

Inauguration of Telecommunications Center Building during July 1975 Festival.

Diesel Locomotive — A207

Conference Emblem and: 30f, Diesel passenger locomotive #511. 35f, 0-3-0 steam tank locomotive with passenger train. 50f, 2-3-0 German steam locomotive, c. 1914.

**1975, Dec. 22 Photo. *Perf. 14***

| | | | | |
|---|---|---|---|---|
| **749** | A207 | 25f tan & multi | 5.50 | 1.00 |
| **750** | A207 | 30f tan & multi | 8.50 | 2.00 |
| **751** | A207 | 35f yel grn & multi | 11.00 | 3.50 |
| **752** | A207 | 50f yel grn & multi | 16.00 | 9.50 |
| | | *Nos. 749-752 (4)* | 41.00 | 16.00 |

15th Taurus Railway Conference, Baghdad.

A208

Design: Soldier on guard.

**1976, Jan. 6 *Perf. 13***

| | | | | |
|---|---|---|---|---|
| **753** | A208 | 5f silver & multi | .25 | .25 |
| **754** | A208 | 25f silver & multi | .55 | .25 |
| **755** | A208 | 50f gold & multi | 1.60 | .60 |
| | | *Nos. 753-755 (3)* | 2.40 | 1.10 |

55th Army Day.

A209

Fingerprint crossed out, Arab world.

**1976, Jan. 8 Photo. *Perf. 13½x13***

| | | | | |
|---|---|---|---|---|
| **756** | A209 | 5f violet & multi | .25 | .25 |
| **757** | A209 | 15f blue & multi | .45 | .25 |
| **758** | A209 | 35f green & multi | 1.60 | 1.00 |
| | | *Nos. 756-758 (3)* | 2.30 | 1.50 |

Statue of Goddess — A210

20f-30f, Two female figures forming column. 35f-75f, Head of bearded man.

**1976, Jan. 1 Litho. *Perf. 13x12½***

| | | | | |
|---|---|---|---|---|
| **759** | A210 | 5f lilac & multi | .25 | .25 |
| **760** | A210 | 10f rose & multi | .25 | .25 |
| **761** | A210 | 15f yellow & multi | .30 | .25 |
| **762** | A210 | 20f bister & multi | .30 | .25 |
| **763** | A210 | 25f lt grn & multi | .45 | .25 |
| **764** | A210 | 30f blue & multi | .70 | .25 |
| **765** | A210 | 35f lil rose & multi | .80 | .30 |
| **766** | A210 | 50f citron & multi | 1.20 | .30 |
| **767** | A210 | 75f violet & multi | 1.75 | .70 |
| | | *Nos. 759-767 (9)* | 6.00 | 2.80 |

Iraq Earth Station A211

**1976, Feb. 8 *Perf. 13x13½***

| | | | | |
|---|---|---|---|---|
| **768** | A211 | 10f silver & multi | .40 | .25 |
| **769** | A211 | 25f silver & multi | 1.25 | .45 |
| **770** | A211 | 75f gold & multi | 4.50 | 2.00 |
| | | *Nos. 768-770 (3)* | 6.15 | 2.70 |

Revolution of Ramadan 14, 13th anniv.

Telephones 1876 and 1976 — A212

Map of Maghreb, ICATU Emblem — A213

**1976, Mar. 17 Litho. *Perf. 12x12½***

| | | | | |
|---|---|---|---|---|
| **771** | A212 | 35f multicolored | 1.25 | .45 |
| **772** | A212 | 50f multicolored | 2.50 | .70 |
| **773** | A212 | 75f multicolored | 4.00 | 1.00 |
| | | *Nos. 771-773 (3)* | 7.75 | 2.15 |

Centenary of first telephone call by Alexander Graham Bell, Mar. 10, 1876.

**1976, Mar. 24 Photo. *Perf. 13½***

| | | | | |
|---|---|---|---|---|
| **774** | A213 | 5f green & multi | .35 | .25 |
| **775** | A213 | 10f multicolored | .35 | .25 |
| | | *Nos. 774-775,C54 (3)* | 5.20 | 2.50 |

20th Intl. Conf. of Arab Workers Syndicates.

Map of Iraq, Family, Torch and Wreath — A214

**1976, Apr. 1 *Perf. 12½***

| | | | | |
|---|---|---|---|---|
| **776** | A214 | 5f multicolored | .25 | .25 |
| **777** | A214 | 15f lilac & multi | .45 | .25 |
| **778** | A214 | 35f multicolored | 2.25 | .90 |
| | | *Nos. 776-778 (3)* | 2.95 | 1.40 |

Police Day.

Pipeline, Map of Iraq — A215

Pres. A. H. al-Bakr Embracing Vice Pres. Saddam Hussein — A216

**1976, June 1 Photo. *Perf. 13***

| | | | | |
|---|---|---|---|---|
| **779** | A215 | 25f multicolored | 1.50 | .25 |
| **780** | A215 | 75f multicolored | 4.50 | 2.00 |

**Souvenir Sheet**

***Imperf***

| | | | | |
|---|---|---|---|---|
| **781** | A216 | 150f multicolored | 32.50 | 32.50 |

4th anniversary of oil nationalization.

"Festival" — A217

**1976, July 17 *Perf. 14***

| | | | | |
|---|---|---|---|---|
| **782** | A217 | 15f orange & multi | .35 | .25 |
| **783** | A217 | 35f orange & multi | 1.00 | .70 |

Festivals, July 1976.

Archbishop Capucci, Map of Palestine A218

**1976, Aug. 18 Litho. *Perf. 12***

| | | | | |
|---|---|---|---|---|
| **784** | A218 | 25f multicolored | .80 | .25 |
| **785** | A218 | 35f multicolored | 1.25 | .45 |
| **786** | A218 | 75f multicolored | 3.50 | 1.50 |
| | | *Nos. 784-786 (3)* | 5.55 | 2.20 |

Detention of Archbishop Hilarion Capucci in Israel, Aug. 18, 1974.

Common Kingfisher — A219

10f, Turtle dove. 15f, Pin-tailed sandgrouse. 25f, Blue rock thrush. 50f, Purple and gray herons.

**1976, Sept. 15 Litho.** ***Perf. 13½x14***

| | | | | |
|---|---|---|---|---|
| **787** | A219 | 5f multicolored | 2.75 | .85 |
| **788** | A219 | 10f multicolored | 2.75 | .85 |
| **789** | A219 | 15f multicolored | 3.75 | .85 |
| **790** | A219 | 25f multicolored | 7.25 | 1.10 |
| **791** | A219 | 50f multicolored | 11.00 | 1.50 |
| | | *Nos. 787-791 (5)* | 27.50 | 5.15 |

"15" — A220

**1976, Nov. 23 Photo.** ***Perf. 13½***

| | | | | |
|---|---|---|---|---|
| **792** | A220 | 30f multicolored | .75 | .25 |
| **793** | A220 | 70f multicolored | 2.50 | .75 |

15th anniv. of National Students Union.

Oil Tanker and Emblems A221

25f, 50f, Pier, refinery, pipeline.

**1976, Dec. 25** ***Perf. 12½x12***

| | | | | |
|---|---|---|---|---|
| **794** | A221 | 10f multicolored | .70 | .25 |
| **795** | A221 | 15f multicolored | .90 | .40 |
| **796** | A221 | 25f multicolored | 2.10 | .75 |
| **797** | A221 | 50f multicolored | 3.00 | 1.25 |
| | | *Nos. 794-797 (4)* | 6.70 | 2.65 |

1st Iraqi oil tanker (10f, 15f) and Nationalization of Basrah Petroleum Co. Ltd., 1st anniv. (25f, 50f).

Happy Children — A222

UNESCO Emblem and: 25f, Children with flowers and butterflies. 75f, Children planting flowers around flagpole.

**1976, Dec. 25** ***Perf. 12x12½***

| | | | | |
|---|---|---|---|---|
| **798** | A222 | 10f multicolored | .25 | .25 |
| **799** | A222 | 25f multicolored | 2.00 | .40 |
| **800** | A222 | 75f multicolored | 3.50 | 1.10 |
| | | *Nos. 798-800 (3)* | 5.75 | 1.75 |

30th anniv. of UNESCO, and Books for Children Campaign.

Ornament A223

**1977, Mar. 2 Photo.** ***Perf. 13½***

| | | | | |
|---|---|---|---|---|
| **801** | A223 | 25f gold & multi | .70 | .25 |
| **802** | A223 | 35f gold & multi | 1.00 | .30 |

Birthday of Mohammed (570-632).

Peace Dove — A224

**1977, Mar. 11** ***Perf. 14x13½***

| | | | | |
|---|---|---|---|---|
| **803** | A224 | 25f lt bl & multi | .35 | .25 |
| **804** | A224 | 30f buff & multi | .65 | .30 |

Peace Day.

Dahlia — A225

Flowers: 10f, Sweet peas. 35f, Chrysanthemums. 50f, Verbena.

**1977, Mar. 21 Litho.** ***Perf. 12½***

| | | | | |
|---|---|---|---|---|
| **805** | A225 | 5f multicolored | .25 | .25 |
| **806** | A225 | 10f multicolored | .45 | .25 |
| **807** | A225 | 35f multicolored | 1.10 | .30 |
| **808** | A225 | 50f multicolored | 2.25 | .65 |
| | | *Nos. 805-808 (4)* | 4.05 | 1.45 |

Spring Festivals, Baghdad.

Emblem with Doves A226

Designs: 75f, Emblematic Hindu "7" with flame. 100f, Dove with olive branch.

**1977, Apr. 7 Photo.** ***Perf. 13***

| | | | | |
|---|---|---|---|---|
| **809** | A226 | 25f yel & multi | .60 | .25 |
| **810** | A226 | 75f yel & multi | 2.25 | 1.00 |

**Souvenir Sheet**

***Imperf***

| | | | | |
|---|---|---|---|---|
| **811** | A226 | 100f multicolored | 6.00 | 6.00 |

Al Baath Party, 30th anniversary. No. 811 contains one 49x35mm stamp.

APU Emblem, Members' Flags A227

**1977, Apr. 12 Litho.** ***Perf. 14***

| | | | | |
|---|---|---|---|---|
| **812** | A227 | 25f orange & multi | .35 | .25 |
| **813** | A227 | 35f gray & multi | .70 | .40 |

25th anniversary of Arab Postal Union.

Cogwheel, Globe and "1" — A228

**1977, May 1 Litho.** ***Perf. 14½x14***

| | | | | |
|---|---|---|---|---|
| **814** | A228 | 10f multicolored | .25 | .25 |
| **815** | A228 | 30f multicolored | .55 | .25 |
| **816** | A228 | 35f multicolored | .70 | .60 |
| | | *Nos. 814-816 (3)* | 1.50 | 1.10 |

Labor Day.

Weight Lifting A229

75f, Weight lifter, standing up. 100f, Symbolic weight lifter with Iraqi flag, laurel wreath.

**1977, May 8 Photo.** ***Perf. 14***

| | | | | |
|---|---|---|---|---|
| **817** | A229 | 25f multicolored | .90 | .60 |
| **818** | A229 | 75f multicolored | 2.50 | 1.10 |

**Souvenir Sheet**

***Imperf***

| | | | | |
|---|---|---|---|---|
| **819** | A229 | 100f multicolored | 8.50 | *8.50* |

8th Asian Weight Lifting Championship, Baghdad, May 1977. No. 819 contains one 42x52mm stamp.

Arabian Garden A230

Arab Tourist Year: 10f, View of town with minarets, horiz. 30f, Landscape with bridge and waterfall. 50f, Hosts welcoming tourists, and drum, horiz.

***Perf. 11½x12, 12x11½***

**1977, June 15 Litho.**

| | | | | |
|---|---|---|---|---|
| **820** | A230 | 5f multicolored | .25 | .25 |
| **821** | A230 | 10f multicolored | .25 | .25 |
| **822** | A230 | 30f multicolored | .95 | .25 |
| **823** | A230 | 50f multicolored | 2.75 | 1.75 |
| | | *Nos. 820-823 (4)* | 4.20 | 2.50 |

Grain and Dove — A231

**1977, July 17 Photo.** ***Perf. 14***

| | | | | |
|---|---|---|---|---|
| **824** | A231 | 25f multicolored | .55 | .25 |
| **825** | A231 | 30f multicolored | .70 | .30 |

Festivals, July 1977.

Map of Arab Countries A232

**1977, Sept. 9 Photo.** ***Perf. 13½x14***

| | | | | |
|---|---|---|---|---|
| **826** | A232 | 30f multicolored | .80 | .45 |
| **827** | A232 | 70f multicolored | 2.40 | .90 |

UN Conference on Desertification, Nairobi, Kenya, Aug. 29-Sept. 9.

Census Emblem — A233

Festival Emblem — A234

**1977, Oct. 17 Litho.** ***Perf. 14x14½***

| | | | | |
|---|---|---|---|---|
| **828** | A233 | 20f ultra & multi | .30 | .25 |
| **829** | A233 | 30f brown & multi | .70 | .25 |
| **830** | A233 | 70f gray & multi | 1.40 | .80 |
| | | *Nos. 828-830 (3)* | 2.40 | 1.30 |

Population Census Day, Oct. 17.

**1977, Nov. 1 Photo.** ***Perf. 14***

| | | | | |
|---|---|---|---|---|
| **831** | A234 | 25f silver & multi | .30 | .25 |
| **832** | A234 | 50f gold & multi | .65 | .40 |

Al Mutanabby Festival, Nov. 1977.

A235

A236

Jumblatt, caricatures of Britain, US, Israel.

**1977, Nov. 16 Photo.** ***Perf. 14***

| | | | | |
|---|---|---|---|---|
| **833** | A235 | 20f multicolored | .40 | .25 |
| **834** | A235 | 30f multicolored | .55 | .25 |
| **835** | A235 | 70f multicolored | 1.25 | .60 |
| | | *Nos. 833-835 (3)* | 2.20 | 1.10 |

Kemal Junblatt, Druse leader, killed in Lebanese war.

**1977, Dec. 12 Photo.** ***Perf. 14***

| | | | | |
|---|---|---|---|---|
| **836** | A236 | 30f gold & multi | .40 | .25 |
| **837** | A236 | 35f silver & multi | .50 | .25 |

Hegira (Pilgrimage) Year.

Young People and Flags — A237

**1978, Apr. 7 Photo.** ***Perf. 11½x11***

| | | | | |
|---|---|---|---|---|
| **838** | A237 | 10f multicolored | .25 | .25 |
| **839** | A237 | 15f multicolored | .25 | .25 |
| **840** | A237 | 35f multicolored | .55 | .35 |
| | | *Nos. 838-840 (3)* | 1.05 | .85 |

Youth Day.

Coins and Coin Bank — A238

**1978, Apr. 15**

| | | | | |
|---|---|---|---|---|
| **841** | A238 | 15f multicolored | .30 | .25 |
| **842** | A238 | 25f multicolored | .50 | .25 |
| **843** | A238 | 35f multicolored | 1.00 | .40 |
| | | *Nos. 841-843 (3)* | 1.80 | .90 |

6th anniversary of postal savings law.

Microwave Transmission and Receiving A239

**1978, May 17** **Photo.** ***Perf. 14***

**844** A239 25f org & multi .40 .25
**845** A239 35f lilac & multi .40 .25
**846** A239 75f emer & multi 1.00 .60
*Nos. 844-846 (3)* 1.80 1.10

10th World Telecommunications Day and 1st anniversary of commissioning of national microwave network.

Emblems and Flags of Participants — A240

***Perf. 12½x11½***

**1978, June 19** **Litho.**

**847** A240 25f multicolored .55 .25
**848** A240 35f multicolored .85 .50

Conference of Postal Ministers of Arabian Gulf Countries, Baghdad (Saudi Arabia, United Arab Emirates, Qatar, Bahrain, Kuwait, Oman, People's Republic of Yemen).

Ancient Coin — A241

Designs: Ancient Iraqi coins. 75f vertical.

***Perf. 11½x12½***

**1978, June 25** **Photo.**

**849** A241 1f citron & multi .25 .25
**850** A241 2f blue & multi .25 .25
**851** A241 3f salmon & multi .25 .25
**852** A241 4f salmon & multi .25 .25
**853** A241 75f bl grn & multi 2.40 2.40
*Nos. 849-853 (5)* 3.40 3.40

Festival Emblem — A242

Festival Poster — A243

**1978, July 17** ***Perf. 13½x13***

**854** A242 25f multicolored .35 .25
**855** A242 35f multicolored .55 .25

**Souvenir Sheet**

***Perf. 13x13½***

**856** A243 100f multicolored 6.50 6.50

Festivals, July 1978.

WHO Emblem, Nurse, Hospital, Sick Child A244

**1978, Aug. 18** **Photo.** ***Perf. 14***

**857** A244 25f multicolored .25 .25
**858** A244 35f multicolored .65 .25
**859** A244 75f multicolored 1.75 .95
*Nos. 857-859 (3)* 2.65 1.45

Eradication of smallpox.

Maritime Union Emblem A245

**1978, Aug. 30** **Photo.** ***Perf. 11½x12***

**860** A245 25f multicolored .55 .30
**861** A245 75f multicolored 1.40 .55

1st World Maritime Day.

Workers A246

**1978, Sept. 12** ***Perf. 14***

**862** A246 10f multicolored .25 .25
**863** A246 25f multicolored .55 .25
**864** A246 35f multicolored 1.00 .65
*Nos. 862-864 (3)* 1.80 1.15

10th anniv. of People's Work Groups.

Fair Emblem with Atom Symbol — A247

Map of Iraq, Ruler and Globe — A248

**1978, Oct. 1**

**865** A247 25f multicolored .25 .25
**866** A247 35f multicolored .30 .25
**867** A247 75f multicolored 1.40 .85
*Nos. 865-867 (3)* 1.95 1.35

15th International Fair, Baghdad, Oct. 1-15.

**1978, Oct. 14**

**868** A248 25f multicolored .25 .25
**869** A248 35f multicolored .30 .25
**870** A248 75f multicolored 1.40 .85
*Nos. 868-870 (3)* 1.95 1.35

World Standards Day.

Altharthar-Euphrates Dam — A249

**1978** **Photo.** ***Perf. 11½***

**871** A249 5f multicolored .25 .25
**872** A249 10f multicolored .25 .25
**873** A249 15f multicolored .25 .25
**874** A249 25f multicolored .30 .25
**875** A249 35f multicolored .40 .25
**876** A249 50f multicolored .65 .30
*Nos. 871-876 (6)* 2.10 1.55

Arab Summit Conference A250

**1978, Nov. 2** **Photo.** ***Perf. 14***

**890** A250 25f multicolored .25 .25
**891** A250 35f multicolored .45 .25
**892** A250 75f multicolored 1.10 .85
*Nos. 890-892 (3)* 1.80 1.35

9th Arab Summit Conference, Baghdad, Nov. 2-5.

Surgeons' Conference Emblem — A251

**1978, Nov. 8** **Litho.** ***Perf. 12x11½***

**893** A251 25f multicolored .35 .25
**894** A251 75f multicolored 1.00 .65

4th Cong. of the Assoc. of Thoracic & Cardiovascular Surgeons of Asia, Baghdad, Nov. 6-10.

Pilgrims at Mt. Arafat and Holy Ka'aba A252

**1978, Nov. 9** **Photo.** ***Perf. 14***

**895** A252 25f multicolored .35 .25
**896** A252 35f multicolored .55 .25

Pilgrimage to Mecea.

Atom Symbol, Map of South America, Africa, Arabia A253

**1978, Nov. 11** ***Perf. 13½***

**897** A253 25f multicolored .25 .25
**898** A253 50f multicolored .55 .25
**899** A253 75f multicolored .90 .55
*Nos. 897-899 (3)* 1.70 1.05

Technical Cooperation Among Developing Countries Conf., Buenos Aires, Argentina, Sept. 1978.

Hands Holding Emblem — A254

**1978, Nov. 30** **Litho.** ***Perf. 13½x13***

**900** A254 25f multicolored .40 .25
**901** A254 50f multicolored .70 .30
**902** A254 75f multicolored 2.00 .65
*Nos. 900-902 (3)* 3.10 1.20

Anti-Apartheid Year.

Globe and Flame Emblem — A255

**1978, Dec. 20** ***Perf. 14***

**903** A255 25f multicolored .50 .25
**904** A255 75f multicolored 1.50 1.00

Declaration of Human Rights, 30th anniv.

Candle and Emblem — A256

**1979, Jan. 9** **Photo.** ***Perf. 14***

**905** A256 10f multicolored .35 .25
**906** A256 25f multicolored .35 .25
**907** A256 35f multicolored .65 .25
*Nos. 905-907 (3)* 1.35 .75

Police Day.

Book, Pencil and Flame — A257

**1979, Feb. 15** **Photo.** ***Perf. 14***

**908** A257 15f multicolored .25 .25
**909** A257 25f multicolored .35 .25
**910** A257 35f multicolored .90 .25
*Nos. 908-910 (3)* 1.50 .75

Application of Compulsory Education Law, anniversary.

Pupils, School and Teacher A258

**1979, Mar. 1** ***Perf. 13***

**911** A258 10f multicolored .25 .25
**912** A258 15f multicolored .25 .25
**913** A258 50f multicolored .80 .50
*Nos. 911-913 (3)* 1.30 1.00

Teacher's Day.

Pupils, Flag, Pencil — A259

**1979, Mar. 10** ***Perf. 13½x13***

**914** A259 15f multicolored .25 .25
**915** A259 25f multicolored .45 .25
**916** A259 35f multicolored .70 .25
*Nos. 914-916 (3)* 1.40 .75

National Comprehensive Compulsory Literacy Campaign.

Book, World Map, Arab Achievements A260

**1979, Mar. 22** ***Perf. 13***
**917** A260 35f multicolored .50 .25
**918** A260 75f multicolored 1.50 .65

Achievements of the Arabs.

Girl Playing Flute — A261

**1979, Apr. 15** **Litho.** ***Perf. 13½***
**919** A261 15f multicolored .35 .25
**920** A261 25f multicolored .55 .25
**921** A261 35f multicolored 1.00 .45
*Nos. 919-921 (3)* 1.90 .95

Mosul Spring Festival.

Iraqi Flag, Globe, UPU Emblem A262

**1979, Apr. 22** **Photo.** ***Perf. 13x13½***
**922** A262 25f multicolored .60 .25
**923** A262 35f multicolored .60 .25
**924** A262 75f multicolored 1.50 .65
*Nos. 922-924 (3)* 2.70 1.15

50th anniv. of Iraq's admission to the UPU.

Soccer Tournament Emblem A263

**1979, May 4** **Photo.** ***Perf. 13***
**925** A263 10f multicolored .25 .25
**926** A263 15f multicolored .30 .25
**927** A263 50f multicolored 1.00 .50
*Nos. 925-927 (3)* 1.55 1.00

5th Arabian Gulf Soccer Championship.

Child With Globe and Candle A264

Design: 100f, IYC emblem, boy and girl reaching for UN emblem, vert.

**1979, June 1** **Photo.** ***Perf. 13x13½***
**928** A264 25f multicolored .70 .30
**929** A264 75f multicolored 1.75 1.00

**Souvenir Sheet**

**930** A264 100f multicolored 30.00 27.50

International Year of the Child.
No. 930 contains one 30x42mm stamp.

Leaf and Flower — A265

**1979, July 17** **Litho.** ***Perf. 12½***
**931** A265 15f multicolored .25 .25
**932** A265 25f multicolored .35 .25
**933** A265 35f multicolored .35 .25
*Nos. 931-933 (3)* .95 .75

July festivals.

Students Holding Globe, UNESCO Emblem A266

**1979, July 25**
**934** A266 25f multicolored .50 .25
**935** A266 40f multicolored .90 .45
**936** A266 100f multicolored 2.00 .90
*Nos. 934-936 (3)* 3.40 1.60

Intl. Bureau of Education, Geneva, 50th anniv.

S. al Hosari, Philosopher A267

Designs: No. 938, Mustapha Jawad, historian. No. 939, Jawad Selim, sculptor.

**1979, Oct. 15** **Litho.** ***Perf. 12½***
**937** A267 25f multicolored .45 .25
**938** A267 25f multicolored .45 .25
**939** A267 25f multicolored .45 .25
*Nos. 937-939 (3)* 1.35 .75

Pilgrimage to Mecca A268

**1979, Oct. 25** **Litho.** ***Perf. 12½***
**940** A268 25f multicolored .60 .25
**941** A268 50f multicolored 1.25 .40

Iraqi News Agency, 20th Anniversary A269

**1979, Nov. 9** **Photo.** ***Perf. 11½***
**942** A269 25f multicolored .45 .25
**943** A269 50f multicolored 1.00 .25
**944** A269 75f multicolored 1.25 .40
*Nos. 942-944 (3)* 2.70 .90

Telecom 79 — A270

**1979, Nov. 20** **Litho.** ***Perf. 11½***
**945** A270 25f multicolored .45 .25
**946** A270 50f multicolored .70 .30
**947** A270 75f multicolored 1.25 .65
*Nos. 945-947 (3)* 2.40 1.20

3rd World Telecommunications Exhibition, Geneva, Sept. 20-26.

International Palestinian Solidarity Day — A271

**1979, Nov. 29** **Photo.** ***Perf. 11½x12***
**948** A271 25f multicolored 1.25 .25
**949** A271 50f multicolored 2.25 .45
**950** A271 75f multicolored 3.50 .85
*Nos. 948-950 (3)* 7.00 1.55

A272 A273

Designs: 25f, 75f, Ahmad Hassan Al-Bakr. 35f, 100f, Pres. Saddam Hussein.

**1979, Dec. 1** **Photo.** ***Perf. 13x13½***
**951** A272 25f multicolored .35 .25
**952** A272 35f multicolored .50 .25
**953** A272 75f multicolored 1.00 .40
**954** A272 100f multicolored 4.00 2.25
*Nos. 951-954 (4)* 5.85 3.15

**1979, Dec. 10** ***Perf. 14***

Vanguard Emblem and: 10f, Boy and violin. 15f, Children, map of Iraq. 25f, Youths. 35f, Vanguard emblem alone.

**955** A273 10f multicolored .25 .25
**956** A273 15f multicolored .25 .25
**957** A273 25f multicolored .40 .25
**958** A273 35f multicolored .50 .25
*Nos. 955-958 (4)* 1.40 1.00

World Meteorological Day — A274

**1980, Mar. 23** **Photo.** ***Perf. 14***
**959** A274 15f multicolored .25 .25
**960** A274 25f multicolored .30 .25
**961** A274 35f multicolored .70 .25
*Nos. 959-961 (3)* 1.25 .75

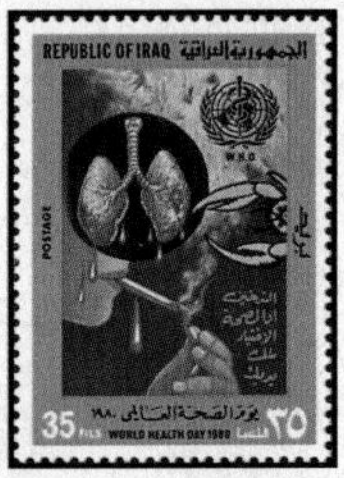


World Health Day — A275

**1980, Apr. 7** **Photo.** ***Perf. 14***
**962** A275 25f multicolored .35 .25
**963** A275 35f multicolored .50 .25
**964** A275 75f multicolored 1.90 .50
*Nos. 962-964 (3)* 2.75 1.00

Festivals Emblem — A276

Pres. Hussein — A277

**1980, July 17** **Photo.** ***Perf. 13½x13***
**965** A276 25f multicolored .50 .30
**966** A276 35f multicolored .75 .35

**Souvenir Sheet**

***Perf. 13½***

**967** A277 100f multicolored 14.00 12.00

July Festivals.

Hurdles, Moscow '80 Emblem A278

**1980, July 30** **Photo.** ***Perf. 14***
**968** A278 15f shown .25 .25
**969** A278 20f Weight lifting, vert. .45 .35
**970** A278 30f Boxing .85 .40
**971** A278 35f Soccer, vert. 1.75 .75
*Nos. 968-971 (4)* 3.30 1.75

**Souvenir Sheet**

**972** A278 100f Wrestling 10.50 10.50

22nd Summer Olympic Games, Moscow, July 19-Aug. 3.

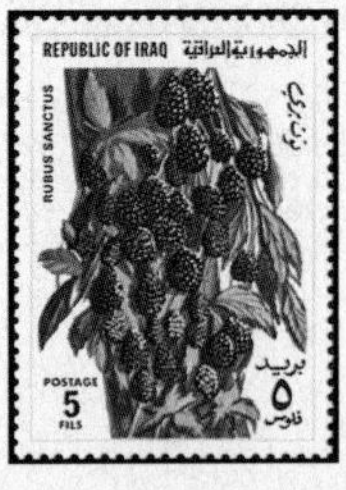


Fruits — A279

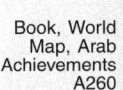

**1980, Aug. 15**
973 A279 5f Blackberries .25 .25
974 A279 15f Apricots .50 .25
975 A279 20f Pears .70 .25
976 A279 25f Apples .85 .25
977 A279 35f Plums 1.10 .35
*Nos. 973-977 (5)* 3.40 1.35

World Tourism Conference, Manila, Sept. 27 — A279a

**1980, Aug. 30 Litho. *Perf. 12½***
978 A279a 25f multicolored .35 .25
979 A279a 50f multicolored .85 .25
980 A279a 100f multicolored 1.75 .85
*Nos. 978-980 (3)* 2.95 1.35

Postal Union Emblem, Posthorn, Map of Arab States — A280

**1980, Sept. 8 *Perf. 12***
981 A280 10f multicolored .25 .25
982 A280 30f multicolored .35 .25
983 A280 35f multicolored .70 .25
*Nos. 981-983 (3)* 1.30 .75

Arab Postal Union, 11th Congress, Baghdad.

20th Anniversary of OPEC — A281

**1980, Sept. 30**
984 A281 30f multicolored 1.00 .25
985 A281 75f multicolored 1.60 .75

Papilio Machaon A282

**1980, Oct. 20 Photo. *Perf. 13½x14***
987 A282 10f shown 2.00 .35
988 A282 15f Danaus chrysippus 2.25 .65
989 A282 20f Vanessa atalanta 3.25 .80
990 A282 30f Colias croceus 5.25 1.25
*Nos. 987-990 (4)* 12.75 3.05

Hegira, 1,500th Anniv. A283

**1980, Nov. 9 Litho. *Perf. 11½x12***
991 A283 15f multicolored .40 .25
992 A283 25f multicolored .75 .25
993 A283 35f multicolored 1.00 .35
*Nos. 991-993 (3)* 2.15 .85

International Palestinian Solidarity Day — A284

**1980, Nov. 29**
994 A284 25f multicolored 1.25 .50
995 A284 35f multicolored 1.75 .50
996 A284 75f multicolored 3.50 2.00
*Nos. 994-996 (3)* 6.50 3.00

Army Day — A285

February Revolution, 18th Anniversary A286

**1981, Jan. 6 Photo. *Perf. 14x13½***
997 A285 5f multicolored .30 .25
998 A285 30f multicolored .55 .25
999 A285 75f multicolored 1.60 .70
*Nos. 997-999 (3)* 2.45 1.20

**1981, Feb. 8 *Perf. 12***
1000 A286 15f multicolored .25 .25
1001 A286 30f multicolored .45 .25
1002 A286 35f multicolored .70 .25
*Nos. 1000-1002 (3)* 1.40 .75

Map of Arab Countries A287

**1981, Mar. 22 Litho. *Perf. 12½***
1003 A287 5f multicolored .25 .25
1004 A287 25f multicolored .50 .25
1005 A287 35f multicolored .70 .25
*Nos. 1003-1005 (3)* 1.45 .75

Battle of Qadisiya — A288

**1981, Apr. 7 Photo. *Perf. 13½x13***
1006 A288 30f multicolored .45 .25
1007 A288 35f multicolored .60 .25
1008 A288 75f multicolored 1.10 .50
*Nos. 1006-1008 (3)* 2.15 1.00

**Souvenir Sheet**

1009 A288 100f multicolored 6.50 *6.50*

No. 1009 contains one horiz. stamp.

Helicopters and Tank A289

**1981, June 1 Photo.**
1010 A289 5f shown .25 .25
1011 A289 10f Plane .35 .25
1012 A289 15f Rocket .50 .25
*Nos. 1010-1012,C66 (4)* 5.10 3.25

Air Force, 50th anniv.

Natl. Assembly Election, First Anniv. — A290

**1981, June 20 *Perf. 12½***
1013 A290 30f multicolored .45 .25
1014 A290 35f multicolored .60 .25
1015 A290 45f multicolored .95 .35
*Nos. 1013-1015 (3)* 2.00 .85

July Festivals A291

**1981, July 17 Photo.**
1016 A291 15f multicolored .25 .25
1017 A291 25f multicolored .40 .25
1018 A291 35f multicolored .70 .25
*Nos. 1016-1018 (3)* 1.35 .75

Pottery Maker — A292

Designs: Popular industries.

**1981, Aug. 15 *Perf. 14***
1019 A292 5f Straw weaver .25 .25
1020 A292 30f Metal worker .55 .25
1021 A292 35f shown .75 .25
1022 A292 50f Rug maker, horiz. 1.00 .35
*Nos. 1019-1022 (4)* 2.55 1.10

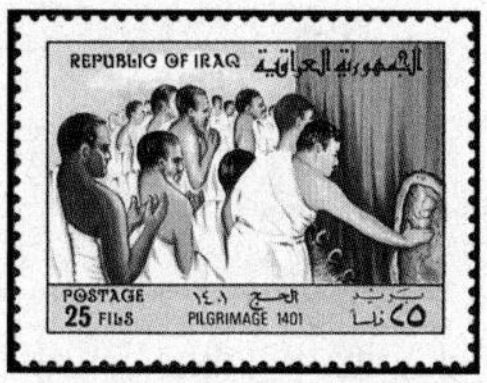

Islamic Pilgrimage — A293

**1981, Oct. 7 Photo. *Perf. 12x11½***
1023 A293 25f multicolored .55 .25
1024 A293 45f multicolored 1.00 .30
1025 A293 50f multicolored 1.00 .30
*Nos. 1023-1025 (3)* 2.55 .85

World Food Day A294

**1981, Oct. 16 Photo. *Perf. 14***
1026 A294 30f multicolored .55 .25
1027 A294 45f multicolored 1.00 .40
1028 A294 75f multicolored 1.50 .75
*Nos. 1026-1028 (3)* 3.05 1.40

Intl. Year of the Disabled — A295

**1981, Nov. 15**
1029 A295 30f multicolored .45 .25
1030 A295 45f multicolored .75 .30
1031 A295 75f multicolored 1.10 .60
*Nos. 1029-1031 (3)* 2.30 1.15

5th Anniv. of United Arab Shipping Co. A296

**1981, Dec. 2 *Perf. 13x13½***
1032 A296 50f multicolored 1.40 .60
1033 A296 120f multicolored 4.00 1.75

Saddam Hussein Gymnasium A297

**1981, Sept. 26 Litho. *Perf. 12x12½***
1034 A297 45f shown .70 .25
1035 A297 50f Palace of Conferences .70 .30
1036 A297 120f like #1035 2.10 1.25
1037 A297 150f like #1034 2.75 1.50
*Nos. 1034-1037 (4)* 6.25 3.30

For surcharges see Nos. 1097-1099.

35th Anniv. of Al Baath Party — A298

**1982, Apr. 7 Photo. *Perf. 13½x13***
1038 A298 25f Pres. Hussein, flowers .55 .25
1039 A298 30f "7 7 7" .55 .25
1040 A298 45f like 25f .90 .40
1041 A298 50f like 30f .90 .40
*Nos. 1038-1041 (4)* 2.90 1.30

**Souvenir Sheet**

***Imperf***

1042 A298 150f multicolored 6.75 6.75

Mosul Spring Festival — A299

**1982, Apr. 15 Litho. *Perf. 11½x12***
1043 A299 25f Birds 1.10 .25
1044 A299 30f Girl .70 .25
1045 A299 45f like 25f 1.10 .50
1046 A299 50f like 30f 1.10 .40
*Nos. 1043-1046 (4)* 4.00 1.40

Intl. Workers' Day
A300

**1982, May 1** ***Perf. 12½***
**1047** A300 25f multicolored .45 .25
**1048** A300 45f multicolored .70 .30
**1049** A300 50f multicolored .75 .40
*Nos. 1047-1049 (3)* 1.90 .95

14th World Telecommunications Day — A301

**1982, May 17 Photo.** ***Perf. 13x13½***
**1050** A301 5f multicolored .25 .25
**1051** A301 45f multicolored .70 .35
**1052** A301 100f multicolored 1.60 .90
*Nos. 1050-1052 (3)* 2.55 1.50

10th Anniv. of Oil Nationalization
A302

**1982, June 1 Litho.** ***Perf. 12½***
**1053** A302 5f Oil gusher .25 .25
**1054** A302 25f like 5f .60 .25
**1055** A302 45f Statue 1.25 .25
**1056** A302 50f like 45f 1.50 .35
*Nos. 1053-1056 (4)* 3.60 1.10

Martyrs' Day — A303

**1981, Dec. 1 Photo.** ***Perf. 14***
**1057** A303 45f multicolored .45 .35
**1058** A303 50f multicolored .55 .45
**1059** A303 120f multicolored 1.50 1.00
*Nos. 1057-1059,O339A-O339C (6)* 8.50 3.80

Women's Day — A304

**1982, Mar. 4 Litho.** ***Perf. 12½x13***
**1060** A304 25f multicolored .55 .25
**1061** A304 45f multicolored .90 .40
**1062** A304 50f multicolored .90 .50
*Nos. 1060-1062 (3)* 2.35 1.15

A305

**1982, Apr. 12** ***Perf. 12½***
**1063** A305 25f multicolored .55 .25
**1064** A305 45f multicolored .90 .30
**1065** A305 50f multicolored .90 .30
*Nos. 1063-1065 (3)* 2.35 .85

Arab Postal Union, 30th anniv.

A305a

**1982, June 7 Photo.** ***Perf. 14***
**1065A** A305a 30f Nuclear power emblem, lion .60 .30
**1065B** A305a 45f shown 1.00 .35
**1065C** A305a 50f like 30f 1.10 .50
**1065D** A305a 120f like 45f 2.40 1.50
*Nos. 1065A-1065D (4)* 5.10 2.65

First anniv. of attack on nuclear power reactor.

July Festivals — A306

**1982, July 17 Photo.** ***Perf. 14½x14***
**1066** A306 25f multicolored .50 .25
**1067** A306 45f multicolored .70 .25
**1068** A306 50f multicolored .80 .30
*Nos. 1066-1068 (3)* 2.00 .80

Lacerta Viridis
A307

**1982, Aug. 20 Litho.** ***Perf. 12½***
**1069** A307 25f shown 2.25 .75
**1070** A307 30f Vipera aspis 2.25 .75
**1071** A307 45f Lacerta virdis, diff. 3.00 1.10
**1072** A307 50f Natrix tessellata 3.50 1.50
*Nos. 1069-1072 (4)* 11.00 4.10

7th Non-aligned Countries Conference, Baghdad, Sept. — A308

#1073, Tito. #1074, Nehru. #1075, Nasser. #1076, Kwame Nkrumah. #1077, Hussein.

**1982, Sept. 6 Photo.** ***Perf. 13x13½***
**1073** A308 50f multicolored .85 .40
**1074** A308 50f multicolored .85 .40
**1075** A308 50f multicolored .85 .40
**1076** A308 50f multicolored .85 .40
**1077** A308 100f multicolored 1.90 .55
*Nos. 1073-1077 (5)* 5.30 2.15

TB Bacillus Centenary
A309

**1982, Oct. 1** ***Perf. 14x14½***
**1078** A309 20f multicolored .65 .25
**1079** A309 50f multicolored 1.10 .30
**1080** A309 100f multicolored 2.10 .85
*Nos. 1078-1080 (3)* 3.85 1.40

1982 World Cup — A310

Designs: Various soccer players. 150f horiz.

**1982, July 1 Litho.** ***Perf. 11½x12***
**1081** A310 5f multicolored .50 .25
**1082** A310 45f multicolored 1.00 .45
**1083** A310 50f multicolored 1.10 .50
**1084** A310 100f multicolored 2.00 1.00
*Nos. 1081-1084 (4)* 4.60 2.20

**Souvenir Sheet**
***Perf. 12½***
**1085** A310 150f multicolored 4.00 4.00

13th UPU Day
A311

**1982, Oct. 9** ***Perf. 12x11½***
**1086** A311 5f multicolored .25 .25
**1087** A311 45f multicolored .70 .30
**1088** A311 100f multicolored 1.60 .85
*Nos. 1086-1088 (3)* 2.55 1.40

Musical Instruments
A312

**1982, Nov. 15** ***Perf. 12½x13***
**1089** A312 5f Drums .25 .25
**1090** A312 10f Zither .25 .25
**1091** A312 35f Stringed instrument .85 .35
**1092** A312 100f Lute 2.75 .95
*Nos. 1089-1092 (4)* 4.10 1.80

Birth Anniv. of Mohammed — A313

Baghdad and Medina Mosque views.

**1982, Dec. 27 Litho.** ***Perf. 12x11½***
**1093** A313 25f multicolored .25 .25
**1094** A313 30f multicolored .40 .25
**1095** A313 45f multicolored .55 .25
**1096** A313 50f multicolored .70 .35
*Nos. 1093-1096 (4)* 1.90 1.10

Nos. 1034-1036 Surcharged

**1983, May 15 Litho.** ***Perf. 12x12½***
**1097** A297 60f on 50f multi 1.25 .50
**1098** A297 70f on 45f multi 1.75 .60
**1099** A297 160f on 120f multi 4.50 2.00
*Nos. 1097-1099 (3)* 7.50 3.10

July Festivals
A314

**1983, July 17 Litho.** ***Perf. 14½x14***
**1100** A314 30f multicolored .45 .25
**1101** A314 60f multicolored 1.00 .35
**1102** A314 70f multicolored 1.40 .45
*Nos. 1100-1102 (3)* 2.85 1.05

Local Flowers — A315

**1983, June 15 Photo.** ***Perf. 15x14***
**Border Color**
**1103** A315 10f shown, light blue .25 .25
**1104** A315 20f Flowers, diff., pale yellow .45 .25
**1105** A315 30f like 10f, yellow .55 .25
**1106** A315 40f like 20f, gray .95 .40
**1107** A315 50f like 10f, pale green 1.10 .50
**1108** A315 100f like 20f, pink 2.25 1.00
*a.* Bklt. pane of 6, #1103-1108 9.75
*Nos. 1103-1108 (6)* 5.55 2.65

Nos. 1103-1108 issued in booklets only. For surcharges see Nos. 1501-1506.

A316

Battle of Thi Qar — A317

**1983, Oct. 30 Photo.** ***Perf. 12½x13***
**1109** A316 20f silver & multi .25 .25
**1110** A317 50f silver & multi .75 .30
**1111** A316 60f gold & multi 1.00 .35
**1112** A317 70f gold & multi 1.10 .40
*Nos. 1109-1112 (4)* 3.10 1.30

World Communications Year — A318

25f, 70f show emblem and hexagons.

**1983, Oct. 20 Photo.** ***Perf. 11½x12***

| | | | | |
|---|---|---|---|---|
| **1113** | A318 | 5f brt yel grn & multi | .25 | .25 |
| **1114** | A318 | 25f rose lil & multi | .30 | .25 |
| **1115** | A318 | 60f brt org yel & multi | .90 | .35 |
| **1116** | A318 | 70f brt bl vio & multi | 1.10 | .40 |
| | | *Nos. 1113-1116 (4)* | 2.55 | 1.25 |

**Souvenir Sheet**

| | | | | |
|---|---|---|---|---|
| **1117** | A318 | 200f apple grn & multi | 4.25 | 4.25 |

Baghdad Intl. Fair — A319

**1983, Nov. 1 Photo.** ***Perf. 12½***

| | | | | |
|---|---|---|---|---|
| **1118** | A319 | 60f multicolored | .75 | .40 |
| **1119** | A319 | 70f multicolored | .95 | .50 |
| **1120** | A319 | 160f multicolored | 2.10 | 1.25 |
| | | *Nos. 1118-1120 (3)* | 3.80 | 2.15 |

Symbolic "9" — A320

9th Natl. Congress of Arab Baath Socialist Party: 30f, 70f, Symbols of development. 60f, 100f, Torch, eagle, globe, open book.

**1983, Nov. 10 Photo.** ***Perf. 14***

| | | | | |
|---|---|---|---|---|
| **1121** | A320 | 30f multicolored | .35 | .25 |
| **1122** | A320 | 60f multicolored | .75 | .40 |
| **1123** | A320 | 70f multicolored | .95 | .50 |
| **1124** | A320 | 100f multicolored | 1.40 | .70 |
| | | *Nos. 1121-1124 (4)* | 3.45 | 1.85 |

Festival Crowd — A321

Various Paintings.

**1983, Nov. 20 Litho.** ***Perf. 12½***

| | | | | |
|---|---|---|---|---|
| **1125** | A321 | 60f shown | 1.50 | .60 |
| **1126** | A321 | 60f Men hauling boat, vert. | 1.50 | .60 |
| **1127** | A321 | 60f Decorations | 1.50 | .60 |
| **1128** | A321 | 70f Village | 2.00 | .85 |
| **1129** | A321 | 70f Crowd | 2.00 | .85 |
| | | *Nos. 1125-1129 (5)* | 8.50 | 3.50 |

Sabra and Shattela Palestinian Refugee Camp Massacre A322

Various Victims.

**1983, Nov. 29** ***Perf. 11½x12***

| | | | | |
|---|---|---|---|---|
| **1130** | A322 | 10f multicolored | .25 | .25 |
| **1131** | A322 | 60f multicolored | 1.00 | .40 |
| **1132** | A322 | 70f multicolored | 1.25 | .50 |
| **1133** | A322 | 160f multicolored | 2.75 | 1.25 |
| | | *Nos. 1130-1133 (4)* | 5.25 | 2.40 |

Pres. Hussein, Map — A323

**1983 Photo.** ***Perf. 13½x13***

| | | | | |
|---|---|---|---|---|
| **1134** | A323 | 60f multicolored | .75 | .30 |
| **1135** | A323 | 70f multicolored | 1.00 | .50 |
| **1136** | A323 | 250f multicolored | 3.50 | 2.00 |
| | | *Nos. 1134-1136 (3)* | 5.25 | 2.80 |

Hussein as head of Al Baath Party, 4th anniv.

Modern Building — A324

Various buildings.

**1983, Dec. 31 Litho.** ***Perf. 14***

| | | | | |
|---|---|---|---|---|
| **1137** | A324 | 60f multicolored | .70 | .40 |
| **1138** | A324 | 70f multicolored | .90 | .50 |
| **1139** | A324 | 160f multicolored | 2.25 | 1.10 |
| **1140** | A324 | 200f multicolored | 2.75 | 1.40 |
| | | *Nos. 1137-1140,O340-O341 (6)* | 8.50 | 4.55 |

Medical Congress Emblem A325

**1984, Mar. 10** ***Perf. 13x12½***

| | | | | |
|---|---|---|---|---|
| **1141** | A325 | 60f multicolored | .80 | .40 |
| **1142** | A325 | 70f multicolored | 1.00 | .50 |
| **1143** | A325 | 200f multicolored | 3.00 | 1.40 |
| | | *Nos. 1141-1143 (3)* | 4.80 | 2.30 |

25th Intl. Congress of Military Medicine and Pharmacy, Baghdad, Mar. 10-15.

Pres. Hussein's Birthday — A326

Various portraits of Hussein.

**1984, Apr. 28 Litho.** ***Perf. 12½x13***

| | | | | |
|---|---|---|---|---|
| **1144** | A326 | 60f multicolored | .65 | .30 |
| **1145** | A326 | 70f multicolored | .70 | .40 |
| **1146** | A326 | 160f multicolored | 2.10 | 1.25 |
| **1147** | A326 | 200f multicolored | 2.50 | 1.60 |
| | | *Nos. 1144-1147 (4)* | 5.95 | 3.55 |

**Souvenir Sheet**

***Imperf***

| | | | | |
|---|---|---|---|---|
| **1148** | A326 | 250f multicolored | 6.50 | 6.50 |

Gold ink on Nos. 1144-1147 and dark green ink in "margin" of No. 1148 was applied by a thermographic process, producing a raised effect. No. 1148 has perf. 12½x13 label picturing Pres. Hussein.

1984 Summer Olympics, Los Angeles — A327

**1984, Aug. 12 Litho.** ***Perf. 12x11½***

| | | | | |
|---|---|---|---|---|
| **1149** | A327 | 50f Boxing | .70 | .50 |
| **1150** | A327 | 60f Weight lifting | .90 | .50 |
| **1151** | A327 | 70f like 50f | 1.10 | .60 |
| **1152** | A327 | 100f like 60f | 1.60 | .90 |

**Size: 80x60mm**

***Imperf***

| | | | | |
|---|---|---|---|---|
| **1153** | A327 | 200f Soccer | 5.00 | 5.00 |
| | | *Nos. 1149-1153 (5)* | 9.30 | 7.50 |

Nos. 1153 contains one 32x41mm perf. 12½ label within the stamp.

A328

50f, 70f, Pres. Hussein, flaming horses heads, map. 60f, 100f, Abstract of woman, sapling, rifle. 200f, Shield, heraldic eagle.

**1984, Sept. 22** ***Perf. 11½x12***

| | | | | |
|---|---|---|---|---|
| **1154** | A328 | 50f multicolored | .55 | .30 |
| **1155** | A328 | 60f multicolored | .70 | .40 |
| **1156** | A328 | 70f multicolored | .85 | .50 |
| **1157** | A328 | 100f multicolored | 1.25 | .65 |

**Size: 80x60mm**

***Imperf***

| | | | | |
|---|---|---|---|---|
| **1158** | A328 | 200f multicolored | 3.50 | 3.50 |
| | | *Nos. 1154-1158 (5)* | 6.85 | 5.35 |

Battle of Qadisiya. No. 1158 contains one 32x41mm perf. 12½ label within the stamp.

A329

Martyrs' Day: 50f, 70f, Natl. flag as flame. 60f, 100f, Woman holding rifle, medal.

**1984, Dec. 1** ***Perf. 13½***

| | | | | |
|---|---|---|---|---|
| **1159** | A329 | 50f multicolored | .45 | .35 |
| **1160** | A329 | 60f multicolored | .65 | .35 |
| **1161** | A329 | 70f multicolored | .75 | .40 |
| **1162** | A329 | 100f multicolored | 1.00 | .65 |
| | | *Nos. 1159-1162 (4)* | 2.85 | 1.75 |

Pres. Hussein's Visit to Al-Mustansiriyah University, 5th Anniv. — A330

**1985, Apr. 2 Photo.** ***Perf. 12x11½***

| | | | | |
|---|---|---|---|---|
| **1163** | A330 | 60f dk bl gray & dk pink | .55 | .35 |
| **1164** | A330 | 70f myr grn & dk pink | .65 | .40 |
| **1165** | A330 | 250f blk & dk pink | 2.50 | 1.40 |
| | | *Nos. 1163-1165 (3)* | 3.70 | 2.15 |

Iraqi Air Force, 54th Anniv. — A331

10f, 160f, Pres. Hussein, fighter planes, pilot's wings. 60f, 70f, 200f, Planes, flag, "54," horiz.

***Perf. 13x12½, 13½ (60f, 70f)***

**1985, Apr. 22** **Litho.**

| | | | | |
|---|---|---|---|---|
| **1166** | A331 | 10f multicolored | .30 | .25 |
| **1167** | A331 | 60f multicolored | 1.50 | .75 |
| **1168** | A331 | 70f multicolored | 1.60 | .75 |
| **1169** | A331 | 160f multicolored | 4.00 | 2.00 |
| | | *Nos. 1166-1169 (4)* | 7.40 | 3.75 |

**Souvenir Sheet**

***Perf. 12½***

| | | | | |
|---|---|---|---|---|
| **1170** | A331 | 200f multicolored | 6.75 | 6.75 |

Pres. Hussein, 48th Birthday — A332

30f, 70f, Pres. Hussein, sunflower. 60f, 100f, Pres., candle & flowers. 200f, Flowers & text.

**1985, Apr. 28** ***Perf. 13½***

| | | | | |
|---|---|---|---|---|
| **1171** | A332 | 30f multicolored | .35 | .25 |
| **1172** | A332 | 60f multicolored | .65 | .30 |
| **1173** | A332 | 70f multicolored | .75 | .40 |
| **1174** | A332 | 100f multicolored | 1.10 | .60 |
| | | *Nos. 1171-1174 (4)* | 2.85 | 1.55 |

**Souvenir Sheet**

***Perf. 13x12½***

| | | | | |
|---|---|---|---|---|
| **1175** | A332 | 200f multicolored | 4.50 | 4.50 |

Posts and Telecommunications Development Program — A333

Designs: 20f, 60f, Graph, woman in modern office. 50f, 70f, Satellite dish and graphs.

**1985, June 30** ***Perf. 12½***

| | | | | |
|---|---|---|---|---|
| **1176** | A333 | 20f multicolored | .35 | .25 |
| **1177** | A333 | 50f multicolored | .70 | .30 |
| **1178** | A333 | 60f multicolored | .70 | .30 |
| **1179** | A333 | 70f multicolored | .95 | .50 |
| | | *Nos. 1176-1179 (4)* | 2.70 | 1.35 |

Battle of Qadisiya A334

Designs: 10f, 60f, Shown. 20f, 70f, Pres. Hussein, Al-Baath Party emblem. 200f, Dove, natl. flag as shield, soldier.

**1985, Sept. 4** ***Perf. 11½x12***

| | | | | |
|---|---|---|---|---|
| **1180** | A334 | 10f multicolored | .25 | .25 |
| **1181** | A334 | 20f multicolored | .25 | .25 |
| **1182** | A334 | 60f multicolored | .90 | .40 |
| **1183** | A334 | 70f multicolored | 1.10 | .65 |
| | | *Nos. 1180-1183 (4)* | 2.50 | 1.55 |

**Souvenir Sheet**

***Perf. 12x12½***

| | | | | |
|---|---|---|---|---|
| **1184** | A334 | 200f multicolored | 3.25 | 3.25 |

No. 1184 contains one stamp 30x45mm.

Solar Energy Research Center A335

**1985, Sept. 19** *Perf. 13½*
1185 A335 10f multicolored .25 .25
1186 A335 50f multicolored .95 .40
1187 A335 100f multicolored 1.90 .95
*Nos. 1185-1187 (3)* 3.10 1.60

UN Child Survival Campaign A336

Designs: 10f, 50f, Stop Polio Campaign. 15f, 100f, Girl, infant.

**1985, Oct. 10**
1188 A336 10f multicolored .25 .25
1189 A336 15f multicolored .25 .25
1190 A336 50f multicolored .75 .30
1191 A336 100f multicolored 1.50 .85
*Nos. 1188-1191 (4)* 2.75 1.65

Al Sharif, Poet, Death Millennium A337

**1985, Oct. 20**
1192 A337 10f multicolored .25 .25
1193 A337 50f multicolored .55 .30
1194 A337 100f multicolored 1.25 .80
*Nos. 1192-1194 (3)* 2.05 1.35

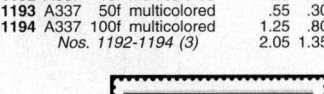

UN, 40th Anniv. A338

**1985, Oct. 24**
1195 A338 10f multicolored .25 .25
1196 A338 40f multicolored .55 .25
1197 A338 100f multicolored 1.40 .75
*Nos. 1195-1197 (3)* 2.20 1.25

Death of Iraqi Prisoners of War in Iran — A339

30f, 100f, Knife, Geneva Convention declaration, red crescent, red cross. 70f, 200f, POWs, gun shell, natl. flag, cherub & dove.

**1985, Nov. 10** *Perf. 14*
1198 A339 30f multicolored .35 .25
1199 A339 70f multicolored .75 .40
1200 A339 100f multicolored 1.10 .65
1201 A339 200f multicolored 2.50 1.25

**Size: 110x80mm**

***Imperf***

1202 A339 250f multicolored 5.00 5.00
*Nos. 1198-1202 (5)* 9.70 7.55

No. 1202 contains 2 perf. 14 labels similar to 100f and 200f designs within the stamp.

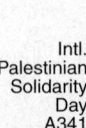

Intl. Palestinian Solidarity Day A341

**1985, Nov. 29** Litho. *Perf. 13½*
1207 A341 10f multicolored .25 .25
1208 A341 50f multicolored .95 .40
1209 A341 100f multicolored 2.10 .95
*Nos. 1207-1209 (3)* 3.30 1.60

Martyrs' Day — A342

**1985, Dec. 1** *Perf. 11½x12*
1210 A342 10f multicolored .25 .25
1211 A342 40f multicolored .45 .25
1212 A342 100f multicolored 1.40 .75
*Nos. 1210-1212 (3)* 2.10 1.25

Intl. Youth Year — A343

IYY emblem and: 40f, 100f, Soldier holding flag. 50f, 200f, Youths, flag. 250f, Flag, cogwheel, rifle muzzle, symbols of industry.

**1985, Dec. 12** Litho. *Perf. 11½x12*
1213 A343 40f multicolored .45 .25
1214 A343 50f multicolored .65 .30
1215 A343 100f multicolored 1.40 .75
1216 A343 200f multicolored 2.75 2.00
*Nos. 1213-1216 (4)* 5.25 3.30

**Souvenir Sheet**

***Perf. 12x12½***

1217 A343 250f multicolored 5.00 5.00

No. 1217 contains one stamp 30x45mm. Exists imperf.

Army Day A344

Pres. Hussein, "6" and: 10f, 50f, Soldier, flowers, vert. 40f, 100f, Flag, cogwheel, rockets. 200f, Al-Baath Party emblem, rifle, waves.

**1986, Jan. 6** *Perf. 11½x12, 12x11½*
1218 A344 10f multicolored .25 .25
1219 A344 40f multicolored .65 .25
1220 A344 50f multicolored .85 .30
1221 A344 100f multicolored 1.75 .95
*Nos. 1218-1221 (4)* 3.50 1.75

**Miniature Sheet**

***Perf. 12½x11½***

1222 A344 200f multicolored 5.00 5.00

No. 1222 contains one stamp 52x37mm.

Women's Day A345

Designs: 30f, 100f, Women in traditional and modern occupations, vert. 50f, 150f, Emblem, green flag, battle scene, grapes.

***Perf. 11½x12, 12x11½***

**1986, Mar. 8** Litho.
1223 A345 30f multicolored .45 .25
1224 A345 50f multicolored .65 .30
1225 A345 100f multicolored 1.40 .75
1226 A345 150f multicolored 2.25 1.00
*Nos. 1223-1226 (4)* 4.75 2.30

Pres. Hussein, 49th Birthday A346

Designs: 30f, 100f, Children greeting Pres. 50f, 150f, Portrait. 250f, Portrait, flag, flowers.

**1986, Apr. 28** Litho. *Perf. 11½x12*
1227 A346 30f multicolored .45 .25
1228 A346 50f multicolored .75 .25
1229 A346 100f multicolored 1.50 .45
1230 A346 150f multicolored 2.10 .65

**Size: 80x60mm**

***Imperf***

1231 A346 250f multicolored 5.00 5.00
*Nos. 1227-1231 (5)* 9.80 6.60

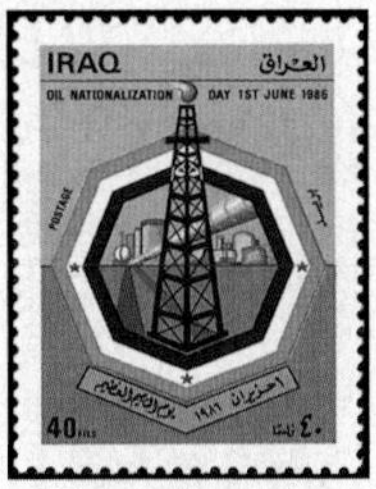


Oil Nationalization Day, June 1 — A347

Designs: 10f, 100f, Symbols of industry, horiz. 40f, 150f, Oil well, pipeline to refinery.

***Perf. 12x11½, 11½x12***

**1986, July 25** Litho.
1232 A347 10f multicolored .25 .25
1233 A347 40f multicolored .55 .25
1234 A347 100f multicolored 1.50 .75
1235 A347 150f multicolored 2.10 1.25
*Nos. 1232-1235 (4)* 4.40 2.50

Labor Day — A348

Designs: 10f, 100f, Laborer, cog wheel. 40f, 150f, May Day emblem.

**1986, July 28** *Perf. 11½x12*
1236 A348 10f multicolored .25 .25
1237 A348 40f multicolored .75 .25
1238 A348 100f multicolored 1.40 .65
1239 A348 150f multicolored 2.10 .95
*Nos. 1236-1239 (4)* 4.50 2.10

Iraqi Air Force, 55th Anniv. A349

Designs: 30f, 100f, Fighter plane, pilot's wings, natl. flag. 50f, 150f, Fighter planes. 250f, Medal, aircraft in flight.

**1986, July 28** *Perf. 12x11½*
1240 A349 30f multicolored .70 .25
1241 A349 50f multicolored 1.40 .30
1242 A349 100f multicolored 2.75 1.40
1243 A349 150f multicolored 4.25 1.90

**Size: 81x61mm**

***Imperf***

1244 A349 250f multicolored 5.00 5.00
*Nos. 1240-1244 (5)* 14.10 8.85

No. 1244 also exists perf.

July Festivals A350

Pres. Hussein and: 20f, 100f, Flag. 30f, 150f, "17." 250f, Inscription, portrait inside medal of honor.

**1986, July 29** *Perf. 11½x12*
1245 A350 20f multicolored .30 .25
1246 A350 30f multicolored .40 .25
1247 A350 100f multicolored 1.50 .75
1248 A350 150f multicolored 2.25 1.25

**Size: 81x61mm**

***Imperf***

1249 A350 250f multicolored 4.00 4.00
*Nos. 1245-1249 (5)* 8.45 6.50

1st Qadisiya Battle — A351

Designs: 20f, 70f, Warrior, shield, vert. 60f, 100f, Pres. Hussein, star, battle scene.

***Perf. 13x13½, 13½x13***

**1986, Sept. 4** Litho.
1250 A351 20f multicolored .35 .25
1251 A351 60f multicolored .80 .40
1252 A351 70f multicolored .95 .50
1253 A351 100f multicolored 1.60 .65
*Nos. 1250-1253 (4)* 3.70 1.80

Battle between the Arabs and Persian Empire.

Hussein's Battle of Qadisiya — A352

30f, 100f, Pres. Hussein, soldiers saluting peace, vert. 40f, 150f, Pres., armed forces. 250f, Pres., soldiers, flags, military scenes.

***Perf. 11½x12½, 12½x11½***

**1986, Sept. 4**
1254 A352 30f multicolored .90 .25
1255 A352 40f multicolored 1.25 .25
1256 A352 100f multicolored 2.50 .50
1257 A352 150f multicolored 4.25 .70

**Size: 80x60mm**

***Imperf***

1258 A352 250f multicolored 4.75 4.75
*Nos. 1254-1258 (5)* 13.65 6.45

Intl. Peace Year — A353

**1986, Nov. 15 Litho. *Perf. 11½x12***

**1259** A353 50f Dove, flag, G clef .65 .25
**1260** A353 100f Globe, dove, rifle 1.10 .60
**1261** A353 150f like 50f 1.75 1.00
**1262** A353 250f like 100f 2.50 1.40

**Size: 80x69mm**

***Imperf***

**1263** A353 200f Emblem, flag, map, fist 2.75 2.75
*Nos. 1259-1263 (5)* 8.75 6.00

Pres. Hussein
A354 A355

**1986 *Perf. 12½x12***

**1264** A354 30f multicolored .70 .25
**1265** A355 30f multicolored .70 .25
**1266** A354 50f multicolored .90 .25
**1267** A355 50f multicolored .90 .25
**1268** A354 100f multicolored 1.90 .65
**1269** A355 100f multicolored 1.90 .65
**1270** A354 150f multicolored 2.40 .85
**1271** A355 150f multicolored 2.60 .85
**1272** A354 250f multicolored 4.75 1.40
**1273** A354 350f multicolored 6.25 1.90
*Nos. 1264-1273 (10)* 23.00 7.30

For overprints & surcharges see #1347-1348, 1455, 1480-1481, 1484, 1499-1500, 1518-1519.

Army Day — A356

**1987, Jan. 6 Litho. *Perf. 12x12½***

**1274** A356 20f shown .25 .25
**1275** A356 40f Hussein, armed forces .35 .30
**1276** A356 90f like 20f .95 .90
**1277** A356 100f like 40f 1.00 1.00
*Nos. 1274-1277 (4)* 2.55 2.45

United Arab Shipping Co., 10th Anniv. (in 1986) A357

**1987, Apr. 3 Litho. *Perf. 12½***

**1278** A357 50f Cargo ship .55 .25
**1279** A357 100f Container ship Chaleb Ibn Al Waleeb 1.10 .60
**1280** A357 150f like 50f 1.75 .85
**1281** A357 250f like 100f 3.00 1.40

**Size: 102x91mm**

***Imperf***

**1282** A357 200f Loading cargo aboard the Waleeb 3.75 3.75
*Nos. 1278-1282 (5)* 10.15 6.85

Arab Baath Socialist Party, 40th Anniv. — A358

**1987, Apr. 7 Litho. *Perf. 12x12½***

**1283** A358 20f shown .25 .25
**1284** A358 40f Hussein, "7," map .35 .30
**1285** A358 90f like 20f .95 .90
**1286** A358 100f like 40f 1.00 1.00
*Nos. 1283-1286 (4)* 2.55 2.45

Pres. Hussein's 50th Birthday A359

**1987, Apr. 28 *Perf. 12½x12***

**1287** A359 20f shown .25 .25
**1288** A359 40f Portrait .35 .30
**1289** A359 90f like 20f .95 .90
**1290** A359 100f like 40f 1.10 1.00
*Nos. 1287-1290 (4)* 2.65 2.45

July Festivals — A360

**1987, July 17 *Perf. 12½x12, 12x12½***

**1291** A360 20f Hussein, star, flag, horiz. .25 .25
**1292** A360 40f shown .35 .30
**1293** A360 90f like 20f, horiz. .95 .90
**1294** A360 100f like 40f 1.00 1.00
*Nos. 1291-1294 (4)* 2.55 2.45

UNICEF, 40th Anniv. — A361

**1987, Oct. 4 *Perf. 12x12½, 12½x12***

**1295** A361 20f shown .25 .25
**1296** A361 40f "40," horiz. .35 .30
**1297** A361 90f like 20f .95 .90
**1298** A361 100f like 40f, horiz. 1.00 1.00
*Nos. 1295-1298 (4)* 2.55 2.45

Census Day A362

**1987, Nov. 1 *Perf. 12x11½***

**1299** A362 20f shown .25 .25
**1300** A362 30f Graph, Arabs, diff. .35 .25
**1301** A362 50f like 30f .55 .35
**1302** A362 500f like 20f 5.25 4.00
*Nos. 1299-1302 (4)* 6.40 4.85

Army Day A363

***Perf. 11½x12, 12x11½***

**1988, Jan. 6 Litho.**

**1303** A363 20f "6," Hussein, troops, vert. .25 .25
**1304** A363 30f shown .25 .25
**1305** A363 50f like 20f, vert. .55 .25
**1306** A363 150f like 30f 1.60 .60
*Nos. 1303-1306 (4)* 2.65 1.35

Art Day — A364

**1988, Jan. 8 Litho. *Perf. 11½x12***

**1307** A364 20f shown .35 .25
**1308** A364 30f Hussein, rainbow, gun barrel, music .50 .30
**1309** A364 50f like 20f .70 .35
**1310** A364 100f like 30f 1.25 .40

**Size: 60x80mm**

***Imperf***

**1311** A364 150f Notes, instruments, floral ornament 2.50 2.50
*Nos. 1307-1311 (5)* 5.30 3.80

A365

**1988, Feb. 8 *Perf. 11½x12, 12x11½***

**1312** A365 20f "8," troops, Hussein, horiz. .35 .25
**1313** A365 30f "8," Hussein, eagle .45 .25
**1314** A365 50f like 20f, horiz. .65 .35
**1315** A365 150f like 30f 2.10 .65
*Nos. 1312-1315 (4)* 3.55 1.50

Popular Army, 18th anniv. (20f, 50f); Feb. 8th Revolution, 25th anniv. (30f, 150f).

Al-Baath Arab Socialist Party, 50th Anniv. — A366

**1988, Apr. 7 *Perf. 12x12½, 12½x12***

**1316** A366 20f Flag, grain, convention, horiz. .35 .25
**1317** A366 30f shown .45 .30
**1318** A366 50f like 20f, horiz. .65 .30
**1319** A366 150f like 30f 2.10 .60
*Nos. 1316-1319 (4)* 3.55 1.45

President Hussein's 41st Birthday — A367

**1988, Apr. 28 *Perf. 12x12½***

**1320** A367 20f shown .40 .30
**1321** A367 30f Hussein, 3 hands, flowers .50 .40
**1322** A367 50f like 20f .75 .40
**1323** A367 100f like 50f 1.50 .60

**Size: 90x99mm**

***Imperf***

**1324** A367 150f Sun, Hussein, heart, flowers 4.25 4.25
*Nos. 1320-1324 (5)* 7.40 5.95

World Health Organization, 40th Anniv. — A368

**1988, June 1 *Perf. 12½x12, 12x12½***

**1325** A368 20f WHO anniv. emblem, horiz. .35 .25
**1326** A368 40f shown .45 .30
**1327** A368 90f like 20f, horiz. 1.25 .40
**1328** A368 100f like 40f 1.40 .40
*Nos. 1325-1328 (4)* 3.45 1.35

Regional Marine Environment Day, Apr. 4 — A369

**1988, Apr. 24 *Perf. 12x12½, 12½x12***

**1329** A369 20f shown .45 .25
**1330** A369 40f Flag in map, fish, horiz. .45 .30
**1331** A369 90f like 20f 1.25 .40
**1332** A369 100f like 40f, horiz. 1.25 .40
*Nos. 1329-1332 (4)* 3.40 1.35

Shuhada School Victims Memorial A370

A371

**1988, June 1 *Perf. 11½x12, 12x11½***

**1333** A370 20f shown .35 .25
**1334** A370 40f Girl caught in explosion, horiz. .45 .30
**1335** A370 90f like 20f 1.25 .40
**1336** A370 100f like 40f, horiz. 1.40 .40
*Nos. 1333-1336 (4)* 3.45 1.35

**Souvenir Sheet**

***Perf. 12½***

**1337** A371 150f red, blk & brt grn 3.00 3.00

Pilgrimage to Mecca — A372

**1988, July 24 Litho. *Perf. 13½***

**1338** A372 90f multicolored 1.25 .40
**1339** A372 100f multicolored 1.50 .60
**1340** A372 150f multicolored 2.25 .70
*Nos. 1338-1340 (3)* 5.00 1.70

Basra, 1350th Anniv. A373

**1988, Oct. 22** *Perf. 12x11½*
**1341** A373 100f multicolored 1.40 .60

Natl. Flag, Grip on Lightning — A374

Pres. Hussein, Natl. Flag — A375

**1988, July 17** *Perf. 12x12½*
**1342** A374 50f shown .75 .40
**1343** A374 90f Map, Hussein, desert 1.40 .50
**1344** A374 100f like 50f 1.50 .50
**1345** A374 150f like 90f 2.00 .60

**Size: 90x70mm**

***Imperf***

**1346** A375 250f shown 6.00 4.50
*Nos. 1342-1346 (5)* 11.65 6.50

July Festivals and 9th anniv. of Pres. Hussein's assumption of office.

Nos. 1272-1273 Overprinted

**1988, Aug. 7** **Litho.** *Perf. 12½x12*
**1347** A354 250f multicolored 6.00 2.00
**1348** A354 350f multicolored 8.50 4.00

Victory.

Navy Day — A376

**1988, Aug. 12** *Perf. 12x12½*
**1349** A376 50f shown 1.10 .40
**1350** A376 90f Map, boats 2.00 .60
**1351** A376 100f like 50f 2.25 .85
**1352** A376 150f like 90f 3.50 1.00

**Size: 91x70mm**

***Imperf***

**1353** A376 250f Emblem, Pres. Hussein decorating officers 9.00 9.00
*Nos. 1349-1353 (5)* 17.85 11.85

1988 Summer Olympics, Seoul — A377

**1988, Sept. 19** *Perf. 12x12½*
**1354** A377 100f Boxing, character trademark 2.25 .80
**1355** A377 150f Flag, emblems 3.50 1.10

**Size: 101x91mm**

***Imperf***

**1356** A377 500f Emblem, trademark, Hussein, trophy 17.00 17.00
*Nos. 1354-1356 (3)* 22.75 18.90

Liberation of Fao — A378

**1988, Sept. 1** *Perf. 12x11½*
**1357** A378 100f multicolored 2.00 .60
**1358** A378 150f multicolored 3.00 .95

**Size: 60x80mm**

***Imperf***

**1359** A378 500f Hussein, text 16.50 16.50
*Nos. 1357-1359 (3)* 21.50 18.05

Mosul A379

Baghdad A380

Ancient cities.

**1988, Oct. 22** *Perf. 12x11½, 11½x12*
**1360** A379 50f Fortress .95 .25
**1361** A380 150f Astrolabe, modern architecture 3.00 .95

Al-Hussein Missile — A381

**1988, Sept. 10** *Perf. 11½x12*
**1362** A381 100f multicolored 1.40 .50
**1363** A381 150f multicolored 2.25 .70

**Size: 80x60mm**

***Imperf***

**1364** A381 500f Hussein, map, missile 10.00 10.00
*Nos. 1362-1364 (3)* 13.65 11.20

2nd Intl. Festival, Babylon A382

**1988, Sept. 30** *Perf. 11½x12*
**1365** A382 100f multicolored 1.40 .60
**1366** A382 150f multicolored 2.00 .70

**Size: 60x80mm**

***Imperf***

**1367** A382 500f Medallions 8.50 8.50
*Nos. 1365-1367 (3)* 11.90 9.80

Victorious Iraq A383

**1988, Aug. 8** **Litho.** *Perf. 12x11½*
**1368** A383 50f multicolored 6.00 6.00
**1369** A383 100f multicolored 10.00 10.00
**1370** A383 150f multicolored 14.50 14.50
*Nos. 1368-1370 (3)* 30.50 30.50

Birthday of Mohammed A384

**1988, Oct. 23** **Litho.** *Perf. 11½x12*
**1371** A384 100f multicolored 1.50 .60
**1372** A384 150f multicolored 2.00 .90
**1373** A384 1d multicolored 14.00 5.25
*Nos. 1371-1373 (3)* 17.50 6.75

Martyrs' Day A385

**1988, Dec. 1** **Litho.** *Perf. 13½*
**1374** A385 100f multicolored 1.00 .40
**1375** A385 150f multicolored 1.90 .75
**1376** A385 500f multicolored 6.50 2.00
*Nos. 1374-1376 (3)* 9.40 3.15

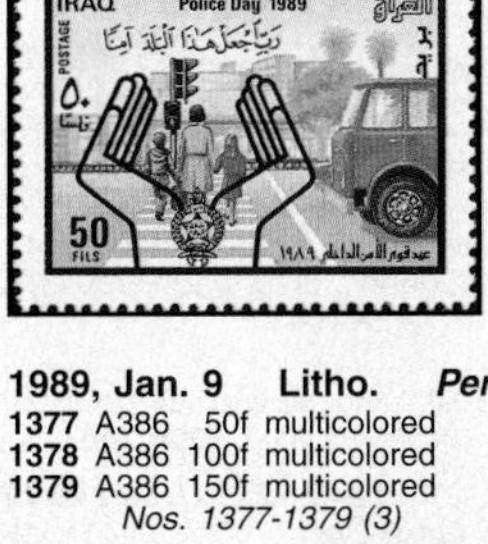


Police Day A386

**1989, Jan. 9** **Litho.** *Perf. 12x11½*
**1377** A386 50f multicolored .60 .40
**1378** A386 100f multicolored 1.40 .45
**1379** A386 150f multicolored 2.00 .90
*Nos. 1377-1379 (3)* 4.00 1.75

Postal Savings Bank — A387

a

**1988** **Litho.** *Perf. 11½x12*
**1380** A387 50f shown 1.60 .80

**Size: 23½x25mm**

***Perf. 13½x13***

**1381** A387(a) 100f multi 6.25 3.00
**1382** A387(a) 150f multi 6.75 3.25
*Nos. 1380-1382 (3)* 14.60 7.05

#1381-1382 have a line of Arabic at the top.

#1381-1382 without overprint are postal savings stamps.

For surcharges see #1507-1510, 1512-1514.

Arab Cooperation Council — A388

**1989, Feb. 12** **Litho.** *Perf. 12x11½*
**1383** A388 100f shown 1.40 .40
**1384** A388 150f Statesmen, diff. 2.00 .70

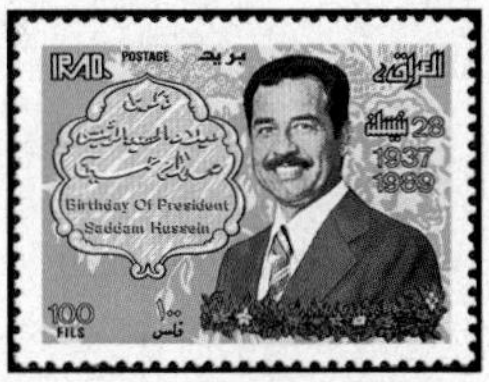


52nd Birthday of Pres. Hussein A392

**1989, Apr. 28** **Litho.** *Perf. 12x11½*
**1392** A392 100f multicolored 1.25 .50
**1393** A392 150f multicolored 1.75 .50

**Size: 60x81mm**

***Imperf***

**1394** A392 250f Hussein, diff. 6.00 6.00
*Nos. 1392-1394 (3)* 9.00 7.00

Fao Liberation, 1st Anniv. — A393

**1989, Apr. 18** *Perf. 12x11½*
**1395** A393 100f multi 1.25 .50
**1396** A393 150f multi 2.00 .50

**Size: 60x81mm**

***Imperf***

**1397** A393 250f Calendar 3.00 3.00
*Nos. 1395-1397 (3)* 6.25 4.00

Gen. Adnan Khairalla — A394

**1989, May 6** **Litho.** *Perf. 13½*
**1398** A394 50f gold & multi .80 .30
**1399** A394 100f copper & multi 1.60 .40
**1400** A394 150f silver & multi 2.40 .75
*Nos. 1398-1400 (3)* 4.80 1.45

Gen. Adnan Khairalla (1940-1989), deputy commander-in-chief of the armed forces and minister of defense.

Reconstruction of Basra — A395

**1989, June 14**

**1401** A395 100f multi 1.60 .40
**1402** A395 150f multi 2.40 .75

Reconstruction of Fao — A396

Women — A397

**1989, June 25**

**1403** A396 100f multi 1.60 .40
**1404** A396 150f multi 2.40 .75

**1989, June 25 Litho.** ***Perf. 11½x12***

**1405** A397 100f yel & multi 1.25 .35
**1406** A397 150f brt pink & multi 1.40 .55
**1407** A397 1d brt blue & multi 12.00 3.75
**1408** A397 5d white & multi 50.00 16.00
*Nos. 1405-1408 (4)* 64.65 20.65

For surcharges see Nos. 1485-1486, 1511, 1522.

July Festivals — A398

**1989, July 17 Litho.** ***Perf. 12x12½***

**1409** A398 50f multicolored .65 .30
**1410** A398 100f multicolored 1.25 .40
**1411** A398 150f multicolored 2.10 .65
*Nos. 1409-1411 (3)* 4.00 1.35

Election of Pres. Hussein, 10th anniv.

Family A399

**1989, July 19** ***Perf. 13½***

**1412** A399 50f multicolored 1.00 .45
**1413** A399 100f multicolored 1.75 .75
**1414** A399 150f multicolored 4.75 1.25
*Nos. 1412-1414 (3)* 7.50 2.45

A400

Victory Day — A401

**1989, Aug. 8** ***Perf. 12x12½***

**1415** A400 100f multicolored 1.25 .40
**1416** A400 150f multicolored 2.10 .65

**Size: 71x91mm**

***Imperf***

**1417** A401 250f multicolored 4.25 4.25
*Nos. 1415-1417 (3)* 7.60 5.30

Interparliamentary Union, Cent. — A402

**1989, Sept. 15** ***Perf. 12½x12***

**1418** A402 25f multicolored .35 .25
**1419** A402 100f multicolored 1.25 .40
**1420** A402 150f multicolored 2.10 .65
*Nos. 1418-1420 (3)* 3.70 1.30

Ancient Cities A403

**1989, Oct. 15** ***Perf. 11½x12½***

**1421** A403 100f Dhi Qar-ur 1.75 .55
**1422** A403 100f Erbil 1.75 .55
**1423** A403 100f An Najaf 1.75 .55
*Nos. 1421-1423 (3)* 5.25 1.65

5th Session of the Arab Ministers of Transport Council, Baghdad, Oct. 21 A404

Designs: 100f, Land, air and sea transport, diff. 150f, Modes of transport, flags, vert.

**1989, Oct. 21** ***Perf. 12x11½, 11½x12***

**1424** A404 50f shown 1.25 .55
**1425** A404 100f multicolored 2.60 .75
**1426** A404 150f multicolored 4.00 1.10
*Nos. 1424-1426 (3)* 7.85 2.40

Iraqi News Agency, 30th Anniv. A405

**1989, Nov. 9** ***Perf. 13½***

**1427** A405 50f multicolored .55 .30
**1428** A405 100f multicolored 1.10 .40
**1429** A405 150f multicolored 1.75 .65
*Nos. 1427-1429 (3)* 3.40 1.35

Declaration of Palestinian State, 1st Anniv. — A406

**1989, Nov. 15** ***Perf. 12x12½***

**1430** A406 25f shown .25 .25
**1431** A406 50f Palestinian uprising .65 .30
**1432** A406 100f like 25f 1.25 .40
**1433** A406 150f like 50f 2.10 .60
*Nos. 1430-1433 (4)* 4.25 1.55

Flowers — A407

**1989, Nov. 20** ***Perf. 13½x13***

**1434** A407 25f *Viola sp.* .35 .35
**1435** A407 50f *Antirrhinum majus* .75 .35
**1436** A407 100f *Hibiscus trionum* 1.50 .45
**1437** A407 150f *Mesembryanthemum sparkles* 2.40 .45
*Nos. 1434-1437 (4)* 5.00 1.60

**Miniature Sheet**

***Perf. 12½x11½***

**1438** Sheet of 4 9.25 9.25
*a.* A407 25f like No. 1434 2.10 2.10
*b.* A407 50f like No. 1435 2.10 2.10
*c.* A407 100f like No. 1436 2.10 2.10
*d.* A407 150f like No. 1437 2.10 2.10

No. 1438 has a continuous design. No. 1438 sold for 500f.

For overprints and surcharges see Nos. 1450-1451, 1456, 1516, 1524.

A408

**1989, Oct. 25 Litho.** ***Perf. 13½***

**1439** A408 100f multicolored 1.40 .40
**1440** A408 150f multicolored 2.10 .65

Reconstruction of Fao.

A409

**1989, Dec. 4 Litho.** ***Perf. 13½***

**1441** A409 50f multicolored .65 .30
**1442** A409 100f multicolored 1.25 .40
**1443** A409 150f multicolored 1.75 .65
*Nos. 1441-1443 (3)* 3.65 1.35

Martyrs' Day.

Iraqi Red Crescent Soc. — A410

**1989, Dec. 10 Litho.** ***Perf. 13½***

**1444** A410 100f multicolored .70 .35
**1445** A410 150f multicolored 2.00 .80
**1446** A410 500f multicolored 6.75 2.50
*Nos. 1444-1446 (3)* 9.45 3.65

Arab Cooperation Council, 1st Anniv. — A411

**1990, Feb. 16 Litho.** ***Perf. 13x13½***

**1447** A411 50f yellow & multi 1.00 .50
**1448** A411 100f orange & multi 2.75 .90

**Size: 80x62mm**

***Imperf***

**1449** A411 250f blue & multi 7.50 7.50
*Nos. 1447-1449 (3)* 11.25 8.90

For surcharge see No. 1523.

Nos. 1435, 1437 Ovptd.

**1990, May 28 Litho.** ***Perf. 13½x13***

**1450** A407 50f multicolored 1.10 .85
**1451** A407 150f multicolored 3.75 2.50

Arab League Summit Conf., Baghdad.

End of Iran-Iraq War, 2nd Anniv. — A412

**1990, Aug. 30 Litho.** ***Perf. 13½x13***

**1452** A412 50f purple & multi *.75*
**1453** A412 100f blue & multi *1.50*

***Imperf***

**Size: 59x81mm**

**1454** A412 250f Saddam Hussein, dove 5.00

For surcharge see No. 1525.

**The surcharged issues of 1992-97 have been extensively forged. Collectors are urged to purchase these stamps with certificates of authenticity or from expert sellers who can attest to their authenticity**

No. 1269 Surcharged

**1992(?) Litho. *Perf. 12½x12***

**1455** A355 1d on 100f #1269 *8.50*

**No. 1434 Surcharged**

Type I

عشرة دنانير

Type II

**1993, Aug. 1 Litho. *Perf. 13½x13***

**1456** A407 10d on 25f Type I *30.00*

*a.* Type II *40.00*

No. RA23 Surcharged

**1992 Photo. *Perf. 14***

**1457** PT3 100f on 5f multi *3.00*

Reconstruction of Iraq — A413

Designs: 250f, Satellite dish. 500f, Bridges. 750f, Power plant, horiz. 1d, Factory.

**1993, Sept. Photo. *Perf. 14***

**1459** A413 250f red & multi *.85*

**1460** A413 500f blue & multi *1.50*

**1461** A413 750f yellow & multi *2.25*

**1462** A413 1d multicolored *3.00*

*Nos. 1459-1462 (4)* 7.60

Stamps of this issue may be poorly centered or have perforations running through the design.

For surcharge see No. 1526.

Peace Ship A414

**1993 Photo. *Perf. 14***

**1463** A414 2d red & multi *2.50*

**1464** A414 5d green & multi *6.50*

**No. RA23 Surcharged**

b

c

d

e

f

g

h

i

j

k

l

m

n

o

p

q

r

٢٥ دينار

s

t

**1994, Feb. 5 Photo. *Perf. 14***

**1465** PT3(b) 500f on 5f multi, ovpt. 17mm wide *15.00*

*a.* Overprint 14½mm wide *40.00*

**1466** PT3(c) 1d on 5f multi *2.00*

**1467** PT3(d) 1d on 5f multi *3.50*

*a.* PT3(e) 1d on 5f multi *6.00*

*b.* PT3(f) 1d on 5f multi *3.00*

*c.* PT3(g) 1d on 5f multi *3.00*

**1468** PT3(h) 2d on 5f multi *7.00*

**1469** PT3(i) 2d on 5f multi *3.50*

**1470** PT3(j) 3d on 5f multi *2.00*

**1471** PT3(k) 3d on 5f multi *2.00*

**1472** PT3(l) 5d on 5f multi *3.00*

*a.* PT3(m) 5d on 5f multi *2.00*

*b.* PT3(n) 5d on 5f multi *4.50*

**1473** PT3(o) 5d on 5f multi *4.25*

**1474** PT3(p) 10d on 5f multi *4.25*

**1475** PT3(q) 25d on 5f multi *8.50*

*a.* PT3(r) 25d on 5f multi *14.00*

**1476** PT3(s) 25d on 10d on 5f *5.00*

**1477** PT3(t) 50d on 5f multi *28.00*

**No. 1273 Surcharged**

u

v

**1994, Apr. 28 Litho. *Perf. 12½x12***

**1480** A354(u) 5d on 350f #1273 *7.00*

**1481** A354(v) 5d on 350f #1273 *7.00*

*a.* Pair, #1480-1481 *22.50*

Alqa'id Two-Deck Bridge A415

**1994, July 17 *Perf. 14***

**1482** A415 1d pink & multi *3.50*

**1483** A415 3d blue & multi *3.50*

*a.* Pair, #1482-1483 *8.50*

No. 1273 Surcharged

**1994, Aug. 8 *Perf. 12½x12***

**1484** A354 5d on 350f #1273 *4.75*

**No. 1406 Surcharged**

w

x

**1995, Jan. 2 *Perf. 11½x12***

**1485** A397(w) 5d on 150f #1406 *5.00*

**1486** A397(x) 5d on 150f #1406 *5.00*

*a.* Pair *20.00*

Baghdad Clock — A416

Saddam Tower — A417

**1995, Feb. 28 *Perf. 11***

**1487** A416 7d blue & black *2.50*

**Size: 76x98mm**

***Imperf***

**1488** A416 25d multicolored *14.00*

**1995, Mar. 12 *Perf. 14***

**1489** A417 2d multicolored *1.00*

**1490** A417 5d multicolored *3.25*

*a.* Vert. pair, #1489-1490 *4.50*

Honoring Dead From Battle of Um Almariq (Mother of All Battles) — A418

**1995 *Imperf.***

**1491** A418 100d multicolored *14.00*

Saddam Hussein, 58th Birthday — A419

Design: No. 1492, Saddam seated, flowers & flag behind him, vert.

**1995, Apr. 28 *Imperf.***

**1492** A419 25d multicolored *16.00*

**1493** A419 25d multicolored *16.00*

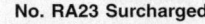

Saddam River Canal Project
A420

**1995, July 17** ***Perf. 11***

**1494** A420 4d olive yellow & blue 4.00
**1495** A420 4d red & blue 4.00

**Size: 97x57mm**

***Imperf***

**1496** A420 25d multicolored, denom. in black 13.50
*a.* Denomination in red 13.50

Embargo of Iraq — A421

**1995, Aug. 6** ***Perf. 11***

**1497** A421 10d blue green & rose lilac 3.00

**Size: 77x100mm**

***Imperf***

**1498** A421 25d multicolored 14.00

**No. 1273 Surcharged**

y

z

**1995, Oct. 15** **Litho.** ***Perf. 12½x12***

**1499** A354(y) 25d on 350f #1273 3.00
**1500** A354(z) 25d on 350f #1273 3.00
*a.* Pair 20.00

**Nos. 1103-1108 Surcharged**

aa

ab

**1995(?)** **Photo.** ***Perf. 15x14***

**1501** A315(aa) 100don 10f #1103 2.00
**1502** A315(ab) 25d on 20f #1104 2.00
**1503** A315(aa) 100don 30f #1105 2.00
**1504** A315(ab) 25d on 40f #1106 8.00
**1505** A315(aa) 100don 50f #1107 8.00
**1506** A315(ab) 25d on 100f #1108 8.00
*a.* Bklt. pane of 6, #1501-1506 32.00

**No. 1380, Postal Savings Stamps Similar to Type A387 Surcharged in Red or Black**

٢٥ دينار — ac
خمسون دينار — ad

ae

**1995(?)** **Litho.** ***Perf. 11½x12***

**Size: 23½x25mm**

**1507** A387(ac) 25d on 100f multi 2.00
**1508** A387(ac) 25d on 150f blue & multi 2.00
**1509** A387(ad) 50d on 250f yel & multi (R) 4.00
**1510** A387(ae) 50d on 50f #1380 4.00

The 250f postal savings stamp was also overprinted in denominations of 500f, 2500f and 5000f. These were not issued and were demonitized Feb. 1, 1996. They were subsequently surcharged with new values and with a bar obliterating the original overprint. See Nos. 1512-1514.

No. 1406 Surcharged

**1995(?)**

**1511** A397 100d on 150f multi 5.00

**Postal Savings Stamps Similar to Type A387 Surcharged in Red**

af

ag

ah

**1996** **Litho.** ***Perf. 11½x12***

**Size: 23½x25mm**

**On 250f Yellow & Multi**

**1512** A387(af) 25d on 500d 6.00
**1513** A387(ag) 25d on 5000d 5.00
**1514** A387(ah) 50d on 2500d 10.00
*Nos. 1512-1514 (3)* 21.00

A421a

A421b

Children, Bank — A421c

**1996** **Litho.** ***Perf. 13½***

**1514A** A421a 25d on 10f grn & multi 35.00
**1514B** A421b 25d on 25f bl & multi 2.00
**1514C** A421c 50d on 10f grn & multi 110.00

Children, Bank — A422

**1996** **Litho.** ***Perf. 13½***

**1515** A422 50d on 50f multi 3.00

No. 1515 without surcharge is a postal savings stamp.

No. 1435 Surcharged

**1996** ***Perf. 13½x13***

**1516** A407 100d on 50f multi 6.50

No. O341 Surcharged

**1996** ***Perf. 14***

**1517** A324 100d on 70f #O341 5.00

**No. 1273 Surcharged**

ak

al

**1996** **Litho.** ***Perf. 12½x12***

**1517A** A354(ak) 25d on 350f 1.25
**1519A** A354(al) 1000d on 350f 42.50

**No. 1273 Surcharged in Blue or Black**

ai

aj

**1996** ***Perf. 12½x12***

**1518** A354(ai) 250d on 350f (Bl) 7.50
**1519** A354(aj) 350d on 350f 18.00

No. O345 Surcharged

**1996** **Litho.** ***Perf. 13½***

**1519B** A329 100d on 60f 5.00

Battle of Um Al Maarik — A423

**1997, Feb. 13** **Photo.** ***Perf. 11***

**1520** A423 25d blk, red & green 1.00
**1521** A423 100d blue, red & grn 5.00
*a.* Arabic word at right center reversed 20.00

No. 1406 Surcharged

**1997, Apr. 22** **Litho.** ***Perf. 11½x12***

**1522** A397 25d on 150f #1406 4.25

Post Day.

**No. 1448 Surcharged**

**1997** ***Perf. 13x13½***

**1523** A411 25d on 100f #1448 2.00

Baath Party, 50th anniv.

No. 1450 Surcharged like No. 1516

**1997** **Litho.** ***Perf. 13½***

**1524** A407 100d on 50f multi 45.00

No. 1452 Surcharged

**1997** *Perf. 13½x13*
**1525** A412 100d on 50f multi 8.00

No. 1459 Surcharged

**1997** *Perf. 14*
**1526** A413 25d on 250f multi 1.25

Science Day.

A424

Referendum Day: 250d, Saddam Hussein, map of Arab nations.

**1997** *Perf. 14*
**1527** A424 25d shown 1.50
**1527A** A424 100d multicolored 6.00

***Imperf***

**Size: 91x77mm**

**1528** A424 250d multicolored 10.00

A425

Saddam Hussein and: 25d, 100d, #1531, Water irrigating trees, grain. #1532, Water pipeline, flowers, grain.

**1997, Dec. 19** *Perf. 14*

**Self-Adhesive (#1530)**

**1529** A425 25d multicolored 1.00
**1530** A425 100d multicolored 3.00

***Imperf***

**Size: 68x81mm**

**1531** A425 250d multicolored 6.00

**Size: 64x82mm**

**1532** A425 250d multicolored 6.00

Wafa'a Alqa'id project.

Saladin (1169-1250), Founder of Ayyubid Dynasty, Saddam Hussein — A426

**1998, Feb.** **Litho.** *Perf. 14*

**Self-Adhesive**

**1533** A426 25d multicolored 1.00
**1534** A426 100d multicolored 3.00

**Size: 79x67mm**

***Imperf***

**1535** A426 250d multicolored 18.00

Nos. 1533-1534 exist imperf. No. 1535 has water-activated gum.

New Year — A427

**1998, Mar. 21** *Imperf.*
**1536** A427 250d Zinnias 9.00
**1537** A427 250d Irises 9.00

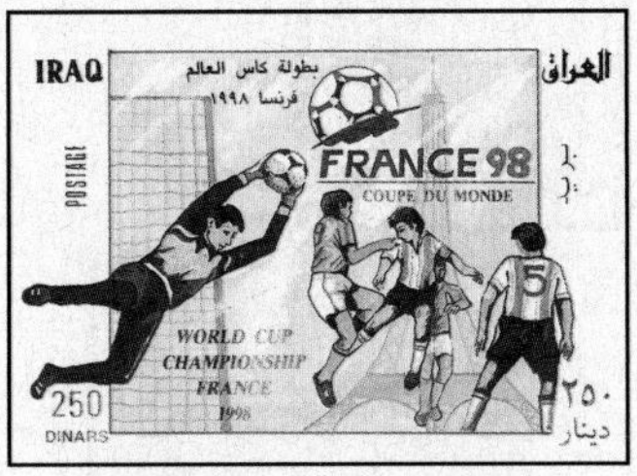


1998 World Cup Soccer Championship, France — A428

**1998, June** *Imperf.*
**1538** A428 250d shown 7.00

**Size: 63x76mm**

**1539** A428 250d Two players, vert. 6.00

Souvenir Sheet

Arab Police & Security Leaders Conf., 25th Anniv. — A429

**1998, July 12** **Litho.** *Imperf.*
**1540** A429 250d multicolored 6.00

A430

"Zad" Day (Arabic Alphabet) — A431

**1998, Oct. 25** *Perf. 14*
**1541** A430 25d multicolored .50
**1542** A431 100d multicolored 2.00

Flowers — A432

Designs: 25d, Chamomilla recutita. 50d, Helianthus annuus. 1000d, Carduus nutans.

**1998, Oct. 27**
**1543** A432 25d multicolored .40
**1544** A432 50d brown leaves .75
**1545** A432 50d green leaves —
**1546** A432 1000d multicolored 8.50

**Self-Adhesive**

**1547** A432 25d like #1543 7.50

No. 1547 is printed on glossy paper.

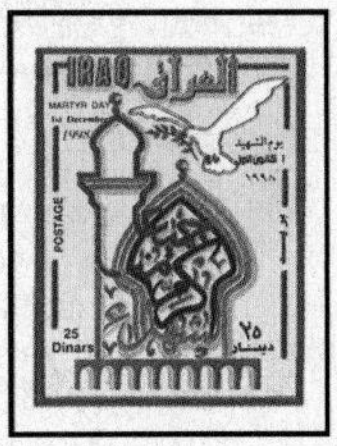

A433

Martyr's Day — A434

**1998, Dec. 1**
**1548** A433 25d multicolored .50
**1549** A434 100d multicolored 1.75

Nos. 1548-1549 exist imperf.

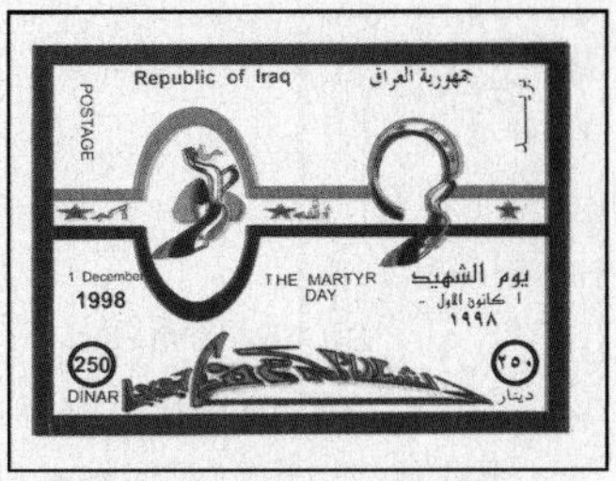


Martyr's Day — A434a

**1998, Dec. 1** **Litho.** *Imperf.*
**1550** A434a 250d multicolored 4.50

Anthocharis Euphome — A435

**1998, Dec. 20**
**1551** A435 100d Precis orithya 3.00
**1552** A435 150d shown 4.50

Exist imperf. Value, set $15.

Intl. Conference on Tower of Babel and Ziggurat of Borsippa — A436

**1999, Jan. 23** **Litho.** *Perf. 14*
**1553** A436 25d multicolored 1.00
**1554** A436 50d multicolored 2.00

***Imperf***

**Size: 71x89mm**

**1555** A436 250d multicolored 9.00

Great Dam — A437

**1999, Apr. 28** *Perf. 14*
**1556** A437 25d Dam 1.00
**1557** A437 100d Dam, Saddam Hussein 2.50

***Imperf***

**Size: 70x92mm**

**1558** A437 250d Like #1557 9.00

Saddamiya, Ath-therthar City A438

**1999, May 7** *Perf. 14*
**1559** A438 25d Saddam Hussein, emblem 1.00
**1560** A438 100d Al-Saddamiyah City 2.00

***Imperf***

**Size: 92x70mm**

**1561** A438 250d Clock tower 9.00

Saddam Hussein, 62nd Birthday — A439

**1999, May 17** *Perf. 14*

**1562** A439 25d multicolored .25
**1563** A439 50d multicolored .50
**1564** A439 150d multicolored 1.75
**1565** A439 500d multicolored 6.00
**1566** A439 1000d multicolored 14.00
**1567** A439 5000d multi, horiz. 55.00
*Nos. 1562-1567 (6)* 77.50

1998 World Cup, France — A440

**1999, July 17**

**1568** A440 25d Two players 1.75
**1569** A440 100d Goalie save, horiz. 4.00

Honey Bees — A441

**1999, Sept. 18**

**1570** A441 25d brown & multi 2.00
**1571** A441 50d black & multi 3.00

Al Fat'h Day A442

Saddam Hussein and: 25d, Eagle, flowers. 50d, People. 250d, Eagle, flag.

**1999, Dec. 12** **Litho.** *Perf. 14*

**1572-1573** A442 Set of 2 2.00

***Imperf***

**Size: 93x71mm**

**1574** A442 250d multi 6.75

A443

A444

A445

Jerusalem Day A446

**2000, Feb.** *Perf. 14*

**1575** A443 25d multi 1.00
**1576** A444 50d multi 1.25
**1577** A445 100d multi 2.50
**1578** A446 150d multi 3.50
*Nos. 1575-1578 (4)* 8.25

***Imperf***

**Size: 93x71mm**

**1579** A446 250d multi 10.00

A447

Saddam Hussein's Birthday A448

**2000, May 17** *Perf. 14*

**1580** A447 25d multi .50
**1581** A448 50d multi .75

***Imperf***

**Size: 92x71mm**

**1582** A448 500d Saddam Hussein, stars 9.00

Sculpture A449

Text "July Festivals 2000": a, At right. b, At left. c, At bottom center on two lines. d, At lower left. e, At bottom center on 3 lines.

**2000, July 12** *Perf. 14*

**1583** Horiz. strip of 5 2.00
*a.-e.* A449 25d Any single .35

Exists imperf. Value, strip $10.

Victory Day — A450

Designs: 25d, 250d, Saddam Hussein. 50d, Saddam Hussein, flag.

**2000, Aug. 8** *Perf. 14*

**1584-1585** A450 Set of 2 2.50

***Imperf***

**Size: 71x91mm**

**1586** A450 250d multi 4.50

Birds A451

Designs: 25d, Anas platyrhynchos. 50d, Passer domesticus. 150d, Porphyrio poliocephalus.

**2000, Aug. 28** *Perf. 14*

**1587-1589** A451 Set of 3 5.00

***Imperf***

**Size: 93x71mm**

**1590** A451 500d Carduelis carduelis 10.00

Prophet Mohammad's Birthday — A452

Designs: 25d, Green background. 50d, Tan background.

**2000, Oct. 11** *Perf. 14*

**1591-1592** A452 Set of 2 2.00

A453

Referendum Day — A454

**2000, Oct. 15** *Perf. 14*

**1593** A453 25d multi .35
**1594** A454 50d multi .75

***Imperf***

**Size: 93x72mm**

**1595** A453 250d Saddam Hussein, crowd 4.50

Baytol Hikma, 1200th Anniv. — A455

**2001, Jan.** *Perf. 14*

**1596-1597** A455 Set of 2 1.50
**1597a** Pair 4.50

A456

A457

Writing, 5th Millennium A458

**2001, Mar.** **Litho.** *Perf. 14*

**1598** A456 25d multi .30
**1599** A457 50d multi .55
**1600** A456 75d multi .80
**1601** A457 100d multi 1.10
**1602** A458 150d multi 1.75
**1603** A458 250d multi 2.75
*Nos. 1598-1603 (6)* 7.25

Bombing of Al Amiriya Shelter, 10th Anniv. A459

Designs: 25d, 150d, Mother, injured child, rescue workers. 50d, Doves, wreath, picture frames, vert.

**2001, Mar.** *Perf. 14*

**1604-1605** A459 Set of 2 1.50

***Imperf***

**Size: 91x71mm**

**Without Gum**

**1606** A459 150d multi 4.00

Al Baath Party, 54th Anniv. A460

Designs: 25d, People, torch. 50d, Al Baath Party founder Michel Aflaq, Saddam Hussein. 100d, Map of Middle East.

**2001, Apr. 7** *Perf. 14*

**1607-1609** A460 Set of 3 2.00

Saddam Hussein's 64th Birthday A461

Saddam Hussein: 25d, Seated, with flowers, vert. 50d, Seated. 100d, Seated, with people. 250d, Standing, with crowd.

**2001, Apr. 28** *Perf. 14*
**1610-1612** A461 Set of 3 *1.50*

***Imperf***
**Size: 89x69mm**
**Without Gum**

**1613** A461 250d multi *4.50*

Fish — A462

Designs: 25d, Barbus sharpeyi. 50d, Barbus esocinus. 100d, Barbus xanthopterus. 150d, Pampus argenteus.

**2001, Aug. 4** *Perf. 14*
**1614-1617** A462 Set of 4 *5.00*

Battle of Um Al Maarik, 10th Anniv. — A463

Frame color: 25d, Red. 100d, Black.

**2001, Aug.**
**1618-1619** A463 Set of 2 *1.25*

Mammals — A464

Designs: 100d, Gazella subgutturosa. 250d, Lepus europaeus. 500d, Camelus dromedarius.
1000d, Various mammals.

**2001, Aug.** *Perf. 14*
**1620-1622** A464 Set of 3 *7.50*

***Imperf***
**Size: 92x70mm**
**Without Gum**

**1623** A464 1000d multi *9.00*

Nationalization of Oil Industries, 29th Anniv. — A465

Designs: 25d, Oil rig, workers, soldier, Iraqi flag. 50d, Oil rig, refinery, pipeline.

**2001, Sept. 15** **Litho.** *Perf. 14*
**1624-1625** A465 Set of 2 *1.00*

Support for Palestinians — A466

Designs: No. 1626, 25d, Saddam Hussein, map of Israel and Iraq. No. 1627, 25d, Dome of the Rock, Palestinian flag, gunman, vert. 50d, Dome of the Rock, Palestinian flag, gunman with arms raised, vert.
No. 1629, 250d, Dome of the Rock, Israeli tank and Palestinian rock-thrower. No. 1630, 250d, Dome of the Rock, doves, Palestinian flag and Mohammad J. Durra and father.

**2001, Sept. 20**
**1626-1628** A466 Set of 3 *1.25*

***Imperf***
**Size: 88x67mm**
**Without Gum**

**1629-1630** A466 Set of 2 *5.00*

2001 Youth Soccer World Cup — A467

Designs: 25d, Players, map of world. 50d, Map of Asia, player, trophy, vert.

**2001, Oct. 7** *Perf. 14*
**1631-1632** A467 Set of 2 *1.00*

Iraqi Claim of Depleted Uranium US Bombs Dropped on Iraqi Citizens — A468

Falling bombs and: No. 1633, 25d, Woman and children. No. 1634, 25d, No. 1636, 250d, Disfigured people. 50d, People, Iraqi flag, horiz.

**2001, Nov.**
**1633-1635** A468 Set of 3 *4.00*

***Imperf***
**Size: 70x91mm**
**Without Gum**

**1636** A468 250d multi *7.00*

Army Day — A469

Designs: 25d, Iraqi flag, soldiers, airplanes, ship and tank. No. 1638, 50d, No. 1640, 250d, Monument, vert. 100d, Soldier, Iraqi flag, tank, vert.

**2002, Jan. 6** *Perf. 14*
**1637-1639** A469 Set of 3 *3.50*

***Imperf***
**Size: 73x91mm**
**Without Gum**

**1640** A469 250d multi *3.50*

Liberation of Fao — A470

Saddam Hussein and: 25d, Mosque. 100d, Soldier, map of Iraq, horiz.

**2002, Apr. 17** *Perf. 14*
**1641-1642** A470 Set of 2 *1.50*

February 8 Revolution, 39th Anniv. — A470a

February 8 Revolution, 39th Anniv. — A470b

**2002, Feb. 8** **Litho.** *Perf. 14*

| | | | | |
|---|---|---|---|---|
| **1642A** | A470a | 50d multi | 8.00 | — |
| **1642B** | A470b | 100d multi | 12.00 | — |

Jerusalem Day — A471

Frame color: 25d, Blue. 50d, Yellow. 100d, Pink.

**2002, Apr.**
**1643-1645** A471 Set of 3 *2.00*

Hegira, Year 1423 — A472

Designs: 25d, Mosques, Holy Kaaba. 50d, Minaret and mosque, vert. 75d, Bird, spider web.

**2002, Apr.**
**1646-1648** A472 Set of 3 *1.75*

Bombardment of Al Amirya Shelter, 11th Anniv. — A473

Frame color: 25d, Black. 50d, Red.

**2002, Apr.**
**1649-1650** A473 Set of 2 *1.00*

War Against Iraq, 11th Anniv. — A474

**2002, Apr.**
**1651** A474 100d multi *1.75*

Flowers — A475

Designs: 25d, Roses. 50d, Roses, diff. 150d, Poppies, carnations.
250d, Roses, diff.

**2002, Apr.** *Perf. 14*
**1652-1654** A475 Set of 3 *3.50*

***Imperf***
**Size: 73x91mm**
**Without Gum**

**1655** A475 250d multi *5.00*

Saddam Hussein's 65th Birthday — A476

Color of vignette frame and country name: 25d, Red. 50d, Purple. 75d, Green. 100d, Dark blue.
No. 1660, 250d, Saddam Huseein, hearts and flowers. No. 1661, 250d, Saddam Hussein with headdress.

**2002, Apr. 28** *Perf. 14*
**1656-1659** A476 Set of 4 *2.75*

***Imperf***
**Size: 74x91mm**
**Without Gum**

**1660-1661** A476 Set of 2 *6.00*

Palestinian Unity — A477

**2002** **Litho.** *Perf. 14*
**1662** A477 5000d multi *35.00*

Mosques — A478

Designs: 25d, Sheikh Maroof Mosque. 50d, Al-Mouiz Mosque. 75d, Um Al Marik Mosque.

**2002**
**1663-1665** A478 Set of 3 *2.00*

Post Day — A479

Air mail envelope and: 50d, Stamp with dove. 100d, Airplane, ship, train, map of world.
250d, Globe and dove.

**2002**
**1666-1667** A479 Set of 2 *2.00*

***Imperf***
**Size: 70x91mm**
**Without Gum**

**1668** A479 250d multi *4.50*

2002 World Cup Soccer Championships, Japan and Korea — A480

World Cup, various players and background color of: 50d, Blue. 100d, Yellow. 150d, Red violet.
250d, Purple.

| **2002** | | *Perf. 14* |
|---|---|---|
| **1669-1671** A480 | Set of 3 | *3.00* |

***Imperf***
**Size: 70x92mm**
**Without Gum**

**1672** A480 250d multi *4.00*

Ancient Ships A481

Various ships: 150d, 250d, 500d.

| **2002** | | *Perf. 14* |
|---|---|---|
| **1673-1675** A481 | Set of 3 | *9.00* |

Victory Day — A482

Frame color: 25d, Blue. 50d, Pink.
150d, Eagle, vert.

| **2002** | | *Perf. 14* |
|---|---|---|
| **1676-1677** A482 | Set of 2 | *1.75* |

***Imperf***
**Size: 71x90mm**
**Without Gum**

**1678** A482 150d multi *4.00*

A483

A484

A485

A486

Poets — A487

| **2002** | **Litho.** | *Perf. 14* |
|---|---|---|
| **1679** A483 | 25d multi | *.35* |
| **1680** A484 | 50d multi | *.50* |
| **1681** A485 | 75d multi | *1.00* |
| **1682** A486 | 100d multi | *1.25* |
| | *Nos. 1679-1682 (4)* | *3.10* |

***Imperf***
**Size: 70x92mm**
**Without Gum**

**1683** A487 150d multi *4.00*

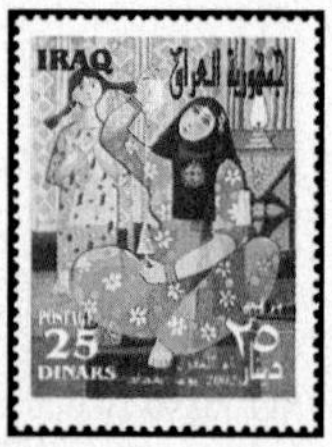

A488

A489

A490

Baghdad Day — A491

| **2002** | | *Perf. 14* |
|---|---|---|
| **1684** A488 | 25d multi | *.35* |
| **1685** A489 | 50d multi | *.50* |
| **1686** A490 | 75d multi | *1.00* |
| | *Nos. 1684-1686 (3)* | *1.85* |

***Imperf***
**Size: 91x70mm**
**Without Gum**

**1687** A491 250d multi *5.00*

Referendum Day — A492

Designs: 100d, 250d, Saddam Hussein, people, hands, heart and flowers. 150d, Fist, ballot box.

| **2002** | | *Perf. 14* |
|---|---|---|
| **1688-1689** A492 | Set of 2 | *2.50* |

***Imperf***
**Size: 71x92mm**
**Without Gum**

**1690** A492 250d multi *2.75*

Mammals A493

Designs: 25d, Oryx leucoryx. 50d, Acionyx jubatus, vert. 75d, 250d, Panthera leo persica, vert. 100d, Castor fiber. 150d, Equus hemionus hemippus.

| **2002** | | *Perf. 14* |
|---|---|---|
| **1691-1695** A493 | Set of 5 | *7.00* |

***Imperf***
**Size: 70x93mm**
**Without Gum**

**1696** A493 250d multi *8.00*

Saddam University A494

Background colors: 50d, Brown. 100d, Blue.

| **2002** | | *Perf. 14* |
|---|---|---|
| **1697-1698** A494 | Set of 2 | *2.00* |

Iraqi Coalition Provisional Authority postal officials have declared as illegal 13 Iraqi stamps of the Saddam Hussein regime with various overprints and surcharges that read "Iraq / In Coalition / Occupation."

**Issues of the Coalition Provisional Authority**

Transportation — A495

Designs: 50d, Raft. 100d, Horse-drawn carriage. 250d, Horse-drawn rail car. 500d, Boat. 5000d, Camel caravan.

| **2004, Jan. 15** | **Litho.** | *Perf. 14* |
|---|---|---|
| **1699-1703** A495 | Set of 5 | *9.75 9.75* |

Dated 2003.

New Year — A496

| **2006, Mar. 16** | **Litho.** | *Perf. 13* |
|---|---|---|
| **1704** A496 | 250d multi | 1.00 1.00 |

A497

June 30, 2004 Installation of Iraqi Interim Government A498

| **2006, Sept. 7** | **Litho.** | *Perf. 14½* |
|---|---|---|
| **1705** A497 | 100d multi | .35 .35 |
| **1706** A498 | 250d multi | .90 .90 |

Iraq Civilization A499

Designs: 100d, Mannequin with headdress. 150d, Golden bull. 200d, Stone carving.
250d, Paintings of horses on walls.

| **2006, Sept. 11** | **Litho.** | *Perf. 14½* |
|---|---|---|
| **1707-1709** A499 | Set of 3 | 1.75 1.75 |

***Imperf***
**Size: 80x61mm**

**1710** A499 250d multi 2.00 2.00

2004 Summer Olympics, Athens — A500

Designs: 100d, Soccer players. 150d, Runners.
500d, Various athletes.

**2006, Sept. 24** *Perf. 14¼*
**1711-1712** A500 Set of 2 1.50 1.50

***Imperf***

**Size: 100x70mm**

**1713** A500 500d multi 2.75 2.75

Paintings — A501

Unnamed paintings by: 100d, Akram Shukri. 150d, Hafidh Al Duroubi. 200d, Faiq Hassan.
250d, Atheer M. G.

**2006, Oct. 9** *Perf. 14¼*
**1714-1716** A501 Set of 3 2.00 2.00

***Imperf***

**Size: 88x70mm**

**1717** A501 250d multi 2.25 2.25

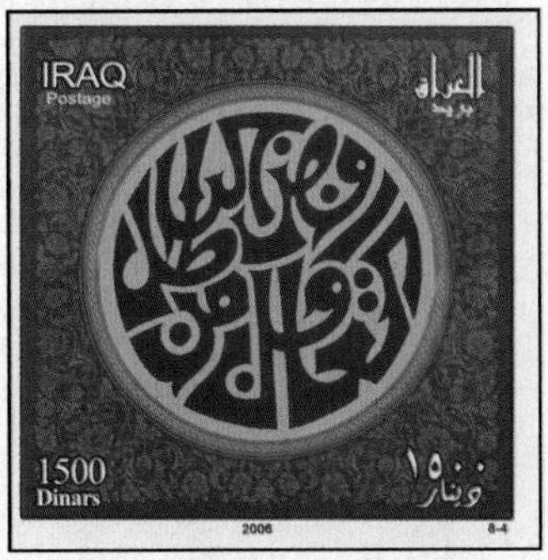


The items shown above were prepared in 2006 but not issued.

Flowers — A502

Designs: 250d, Anemone. 750d, Viola mammola. 1000d, Atropa belladonna.

**2007** **Litho.** ***Die Cut***

**Self-Adhesive**

**1718-1720** A502 Set of 3 3.50 3.50
*1720a* Souvenir sheet, #1718-1720 3.75 3.75

Issued: Nos. 1718-1720, 4/11; No. 1720a, 5/7.

Street Vendor A502a

Two Women A502b

**2007, Apr. 23** **Litho.** ***Perf. 13½x13¼***
**1720B** A502a 100d multi .30 .30
**1720C** A502b 250d multi .75 .75

Singers and Cat — A503

**2007, Apr. 23** ***Perf. 13½x13¼***
**1721** A503 5000d multi 15.00 15.00

Dated 2006.

Butterflies A504

Designs: 100d, Papilio demodocus. 250d, Precis orithua. 500d, Coitas croceus.
1000d, Papilio demodocus, diff.

**2007, Apr. 23** ***Perf. 13½x13¼***
**1722-1724** A504 Set of 3 2.50 2.50

**Size: 80x61mm**

***Imperf***

**1725** A504 1000d multi 2.75 2.75

Artisans — A505

Designs: 250d, Rug maker. 350d, Blanket maker. 500d, Basket maker.

**2007, May 22** **Litho.** ***Die Cut***

**Self-Adhesive**

**1726-1728** A505 Set of 3 3.50 3.50
*1728a* Miniature sheet, #1726-1728 4.00

Folklore — A506

**2007, June 7** ***Imperf.***
**1729** A506 1000d multi 2.75 2.75

Dated 2006.

Rafidain Bank, 65th Anniv. (in 2006) — A507

Background colors: 100d, Light blue. 150d, Orange red. 250d, Brown. 500d, Lilac.

**2007, July 10** ***Perf. 14***
**1730-1733** A507 Set of 4 2.75 2.75

Dated 2006.

Birds A508

Designs: 150d, Anser anser. 250d, Merops superciliosus. 500d, Pterocles alchata.
1500d, Ducks in flight.

**2007, Sept.** ***Perf. 14***
**1734-1736** A508 Set of 3 2.25 2.25

***Imperf***

**Size: 80x80mm**

**1737** A508 1500d multi 3.75 3.75

A509

Musicians and Actors A510

Designs: 250d, Mohammad al-Qubanchi, singer. 500d, Haqi al-Shibly, actor, horiz. 750d, Nazem al-Ghazaly, singer, horiz. 1000d, Munir Bashir, musician.

**2007, Oct. 1** ***Die Cut***

**Self-Adhesive**

**1738** A509 250d multi 1.25 1.25
**1739** A509 500d multi 2.25 2.25
**1740** A509 750d multi 3.25 3.25
**1741** A510 1000d multi 4.50 4.50
*a.* Miniature sheet, #1738-1741 12.00
*Nos. 1738-1741 (4)* 11.25 11.25

A511

A512

National Reconciliation — A513

**2008, Oct. 27** **Litho.** ***Perf. 12¾x13¼***
**1742** A511 250d multi .75 .75

***Perf. 13***

**1743** A512 500d multi 1.50 1.50
**1744** A513 750d multi 2.25 2.25
*Nos. 1742-1744 (3)* 4.50 4.50

Diplomatic Relations Between Iraq and People's Republic of China, 50th Anniv. — A514

**2008, Oct. 28** ***Perf. 12***
**1745** A514 500d multi 1.75 1.75

A three-dimensional souvenir sheet of one 500d stamp without white borders was presented as a gift to Chinese and Iraqi officials.

Wasit Poetry Festival — A515

**2008, Nov. 24** ***Perf. 13¼x13***
**1746** A515 5000d multi 12.00 12.00

Collective Cemeteries — A516

Rose and: 250d, Corpses and mourners. 500d, Skeletal remains.

**2008, Dec. 14**

**1747-1748** A516 Set of 2 2.10 2.10

Campaign to Regain Stolen Antiquities A517

Buildings and various antiquities: 250d, 500d, 750d.

**2009, Mar. 17** ***Perf. 13x13¼***

**1749-1751** A517 Set of 3 3.75 3.75

Environmental Protection — A518

**2009, Mar. 29**

**1752** A518 1000d multi 3.00 3.00

Campaign to Restore Marshes A519

**2009, Apr. 22**

**1753** A519 10,000d multi 32.50 32.50

Intl. Children's Day — A520

Children's art: No. 1754, 50d, Shown. No. 1755, 50d, Two women wearing traditional clothing. No. 1756, 50d, Three men, palm trees. No. 1757, 50d, Woman hugging daughter. No. 1758, 50d, Three women.

500d, Woman holding baby, horiz.

**2009, June 1 Litho.** ***Perf. 13¼x13***

**1754-1758** A520 Set of 5 2.50 2.50

***Imperf***

**Size:80x60mm**

**1759** A520 500d multi *3.00 3.00*

2009 FIFA Confederations Cup Soccer Tournament — A521

Emblem and: 100d, Goalie. 250d, Player dribbling ball. 500d, Player kicking ball.

750d, Emblem only.

**2009, June 13** ***Perf. 13x13¼***

**1760-1762** A521 Set of 3 2.50 2.50

***Imperf***

**Size: 80x80mm**

**1763** A521 750d multi 2.00 2.00

Iraqi Tourism Week (in 2008) — A522

No. 1764, 250d — "Iraqi Tourism Week" in white, with denomination at: a, Right (5-1). b, Left (5-2).

No. 1765, 250d — "Iraqi Tourism Week" in black, with denomination at: a, Right (5-3). b, Left (5-4).

500d, Horsemen (5-5).

**2009, July 14** ***Perf. 13¼x13***

**Horiz. Pairs, #a-b**

**1764-1765** A522 Set of 2 3.00 3.00

***Imperf***

**Size: 90x60mm**

**1766** A522 500d multi 1.50 1.50

Dated 2009.

Jerusalem, Capital of Arab Culture — A523

**2009, Aug. 2** ***Perf. 13¼x13***

**1767** A523 250d org brn & multi .80 .80

***Imperf***

**Size: 60x80mm**

**1768** A523 750d ol grn & multi 2.10 2.10

Emmanuel Baba Dawud (1934-2009), Soccer Player and Coach — A524

Dawud and: 250d, Pink frame. 500d, Green frame.

**2009, Dec. 30 Litho.** ***Perf. 13x13¼***

**1769-1770** A524 Set of 2 1.75 1.75

Iraqi Republic Railways — A525

Designs: 250d, Steam locomotive. 500d, Diesel locomotive. 750d, Steam locomotive, diff.

1000d, Diesel locomotive, building.

**2010, Jan. 25 Litho.** ***Perf. 13¼x13***

**1772-1774** A525 Set of 3 3.75 3.75

**Size: 80x80mm**

***Imperf***

**1775** A525 1000d multi 2.50 2.50

Elections — A526

Color of stylized people: 250d, Purple. 500d, Green. 1000d, Red.

**2010, Mar. 7** ***Perf. 13¼x13***

**1776-1778** A526 Set of 3 4.25 4.25

Arabian Brotherhood Scouts Day — A527

Designs: No. 1779, 250d, Bugler. No. 1780, 250d, Girls in field. No. 1781, 250d, Boys saluting flag. No. 1782, 250d, Girls standing at attention.

1000d, Scouts carrying flags.

**2010, Mar. 23** ***Perf. 13x13¼***

**1779-1782** A527 Set of 4 2.50 2.50

**Size: 80x60mm**

***Imperf***

**1783** A527 1000d multi 2.50 2.50

Iraqi Post Day — A528

Designs: 250d, Envelope in mail slot. 500d, Dove, envelope, clay tablet.

**2010, Apr. 27** ***Perf. 13¼x13***

**1784-1785** A528 Set of 2 1.90 1.90

A529

Prehistoric Animals — A530

No. 1786 — Various prehistoric animals with stamps numbered: a, 10-1. b, 10-2. c, 10-3. d, 10-4. e, 10-5. f, 10-6. g, 10-7. h, 10-8.

No. 1787, 500d, 10-9. No. 1788, 500d, 10-10.

**2010, June 28** ***Perf. 13¼x13***

**1786** Block of 8 7.25 7.25

*a.-h.* A529 250d Any single .90 .90

***Imperf***

**1787-1788** A530 Set of 2 2.50 2.50

2010 World Cup Soccer Championships, South Africa — A531

Emblem and various soccer players with frame in: 250d, Maroon. 500d, Brown. 750d, Purple. No. 1792, 1000d, Red.

No. 1793, Emblem and two soccer players.

**2010, July 13** ***Perf. 13¼x13***

**1789-1792** A531 Set of 4 6.25 6.25

**Size: 125x70mm**

***Imperf***

**1793** A531 1000d multi 2.50 2.50

Koran — A532

**2010, Aug. 11 Litho.** ***Perf. 13¼x13***

**1794** A532 250d multi .65 .65

**Size:90x70mm**

***Imperf***

**1795** A532 500d multi 1.25 1.25

Intl. Youth Year — A533

"2010," Arabic text and: No. 1796, 250d, Youths, candle, olive branch. No. 1797, 250d, Young woman and man, leaves.

**2010, Sept. 8** ***Perf. 13¼x13***

**1796-1797** A533 Set of 2 1.25 1.25

Organization of Petroleum Exporting Countries, 50th Anniv. — A534

Sites in Iraq, OPEC 50th anniversary emblem and: 250d, Map of Iraq. 500d, World map.

**2010, Sept. 14** ***Perf. 13x13¼***

**1798-1799** A534 Set of 2 1.90 1.90

Kirkuk, City of Iraqi Culture — A535

**2010, Oct. 4 Litho. *Perf. 13¼x13***
**1800** A535 1000d multi 2.50 2.50

Convention on the Rights of the Child, 20th Anniv. — A536

Stylized faces in oval and: 500d, Child holding adult's hand. 750d, Child solving math problem on blackboard. 1000d, Children on carousel.

**2010, Nov.**
**1801-1803** A536 Set of 3 5.50 5.50

Intl. Year of Biodiversity — A537

Designs: 250d, Coccinella septempunctata. 500d, Egretta alba. 750d, Persian gazelle, horiz. No. 1807, 1000d, Ophisops elegans, horiz.

No. 1808, 1000d, Butterfly, dragonfly, ladybug, frog, various birds, horiz.

***Perf. 13x13¼, 13¼x13***
**2011, Jan. 11 Litho.**
**1804-1807** A537 Set of 4 6.25 6.25

**Size: 150x75mm**

***Imperf***

**1808** A537 1000d multi 2.60 2.60

2011 Asian Cup Soccer Tournament, Qatar — A538

Designs: 250d, Goalie. 500d, Player. 750d, Player, diff. No. 1812, 1000d, Player scissor kicking ball.

No. 1813, 1000d, Silhouettes of players, vert.

**2011, Jan. 27 *Perf. 13¼x13***
**1809-1812** A538 Set of 4 6.25 6.25

**Size: 60x60mm**

***Imperf***

**1813** A538 1000d multi 2.60 2.60

Biodiversity of Shatt al-Arab and Persian Gulf — A539

Designs: 250d, Metapenaeus affinis. 500d, Torpedo panthera. 750d, Hermit crab. No. 1817, 1000d, Carp.

No. 1818, 1000d, Lionfish.

**2011, Feb. 13 *Perf. 13¼x13***
**1814-1817** A539 Set of 4 6.25 6.25

**Size: 80x61mm**

***Imperf***

**1818** A539 1000d multi 2.60 2.60

Desertification Control Day — A540

Desert and: 750d, Boy examining seedling. 1000d, Hands holding seedling.

**2011, Apr. 19 *Perf. 13x13¼***
**1819-1820** A540 Set of 2 4.25 4.25

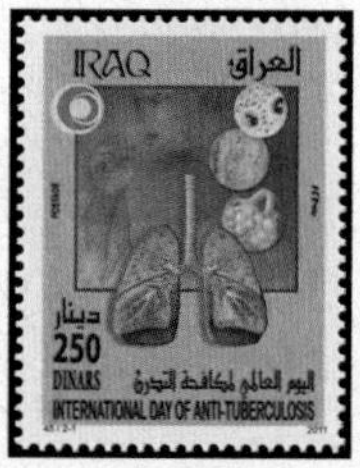


Intl. Day Against Tuberculosis A541

Frame color: 250d, Blue. 500d, Green.

**2011, June 21 *Perf. 13¼x13***
**1821-1822** A541 Set of 2 1.90 1.90

Archaeological Sites — A542

Designs: 250d, Babylon. 500d, Hatra. 750d, Ziggurat of Ur. No. 1826, 1000d, Nineveh.

No. 1827, 1000d, Spiral Minaret, vert.

**2011, June 29 *Perf. 13x13¼***
**1823-1826** A542 Set of 4 6.50 6.50

**Size: 60x80mm**

***Imperf***

**1827** A542 1000d multi 2.60 2.60

Poets — A543

Designs: 250d, Abdul al-Wahhab al-Bayati (1926-99). 500d, Muhammad Mahdi al-Jawahiri (1899-1997). 750d, Nazek al-Malaeka (1923-2007).

**2011, July 7 *Perf. 13¼x13***
**1828-1830** A543 Set of 3 3.75 3.75

Musical Instruments A544

Designs: 250d, Zarna. 500d, Rababa. 750d, Ud. 1000d, Qanun.

**2011, July 31**
**1831-1834** A544 Set of 4 6.50 6.50

Arabian Horses — A545

Designs: 250d, Two black horses. 500d, Two white horses. 750d, Gray and brown horses. No. 1838, 1000d, Gray and white horses.

No. 1839, 100d, Five horses.

**2011**
**1835-1838** A545 Set of 4 8.00 8.00

***Imperf***

**Size: 105x85mm**

**1839** A545 1000d multi 3.00 3.00

Halabja Chemical Attack, 23rd Anniv. A546

**2011, Oct. 24 *Perf. 13x13¼***
**1840** A546 1000d multi 2.75 2.75

Iraqi Philatelic and Numismatic Society, 60th Anniv. — A547

Designs: 250d, Emblem, stamps and coins. 500d, Coins, emblem and stamps, horiz.

**2011, Nov. 3 *Perf. 13x13¼, 13¼x13***
**1841-1842** A547 Set of 2 2.00 2.00

Traditional Iraqi Costumes A548

Various men and women in costumes with frame color of: No. 1843, 500d, Brown (6-1). No. 1844, 500d, Purple (6-2). No. 1845, 500d, Gray green (6-3). No. 1846, 500d, Bister (6-4). No. 1847, 500d, Pink (6-5).

No. 1848, 500d, Orange brown (6-6).

**2011, Nov. 3 *Perf. 13¼x13***
**1843-1847** A548 Set of 5 6.75 6.75

**Size: 80x80mm**

***Imperf***

**1848** A548 500d multi 1.40 1.40

Ramsar Convention, 40th Anniv. — A549

Various birds: 500d, 750d, 1000d. 1000d is vert.

***Perf. 13x13¼, 13¼x13***
**2011, Nov. 3 Litho.**
**1849-1851** A549 Set of 3 6.00 6.00

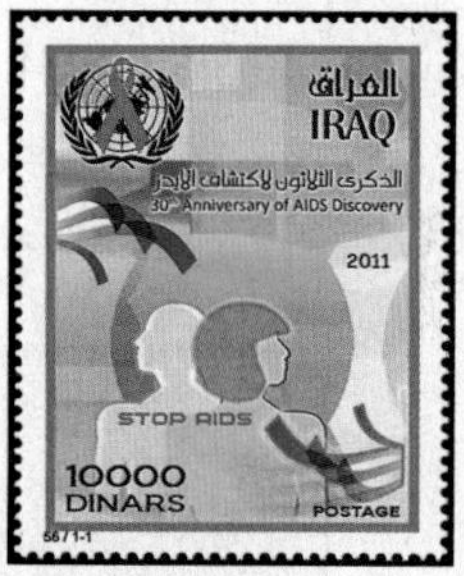


Discovery of AIDS, 30th Anniv. A550

**2012, Jan. 3 *Perf. 13x13¼***
**1852** A550 10,000d multi 26.00 26.00

Dated 2011.

Battle of Al-Taaf (Karbala), 680 — A551

Revolution of Imam Hussain — A552

No. 1853: a, Camel caravan. b, Riderless horse. c, Battle scene. d, Birds over battle camp, rider heading to battle.

**Litho. With Foil Application**
**2012, Jan. 11 *Perf. 13¼x13***

| | | | | |
|---|---|---|---|---|
| **1853** | | Horiz. strip of 4 | 6.75 | 6.75 |
| *a.* | A551 | 250d multi | .65 | .65 |
| *b.* | A551 | 500d multi | 1.40 | 1.40 |
| *c.* | A551 | 750d multi | 2.00 | 2.00 |
| *d.* | A551 | 1000d multi | 2.60 | 2.60 |

***Imperf***

**1854** A552 1000d multi 2.60 2.60

No. 1854 is dated 2011.

Martyr's Day A553

Emblem, doves and: 750d, Protesters with flag, coffins, two mourning women. 1000d, Coffins, mourning man.

**2012, Mar. 4 Litho. *Perf. 13x13¼***
**1855-1856** A553 Set of 2 4.75 4.75

Arab Summit Conference, Baghdad — A554

Emblem with background color of: 250d, Pink. 500d, Blue. 750d, Orange.

**2012, May 3 *Perf. 13¼x13***
**1857-1859** A554 Set of 3 5.75 5.75

Flowers — A555

Designs: No. 1860, 250d, Sunflowers. No. 1861, 500d, Gardenias. No. 1862, 750d, Weasel's snouts. No. 1863, 1000d, Carnations.
No. 1864, 1000d, Various flowers
No. 1865, 250d, Zinnias. No. 1866, 500d, Anemones. No. 1867, 750d, Roses. No. 1868, 1000d, Chrysanthemums.

**2012, May 6 *Perf. 13¼x13***
**1860-1863** A555 Set of 4 6.75 6.75

**Size: 80x80mm (#1864)**

***Imperf***

**1864** A555 1000d multi 2.75 2.75

**Self-Adhesive**

***Die Cut***

**1865-1868** A555 Set of 4 6.75 6.75

Al-Kadhimiya Mosque, Baghdad — A556

Various views of mosque numbered: No. 1869, 250d, 4-1. No. 1870, 250d, 4-2. No. 1871, 250d, 4-3.
500d, Mosque, doves, scroll, horiz (4-4).

**2012, June 12 *Perf. 13¼x13***
**1869-1871** A556 Set of 3 2.25 2.25

**Size: 100x70mm**

***Imperf***

**1872** A556 500d multi 1.50 1.50

Genocide of Kurdish Faylees — A557

Map of Iraq and various Kurdish refugees: 750d, 1000d.

**2012, June 19 *Perf. 13¼x13***
**1873-1874** A557 Set of 2 4.75 4.75

National Commission on Education, Culture and Science — A558

**2012, July 27**
**1875** A558 5000d multi 14.00 14.00

2012 Summer Olympics, London A559

Designs: 250d, Archery. 500d, Gymnastics. 750d, Fencing. No. 1879, 1000d, Hurdles.
No. 1880, 1000d, Olympic rings, torch bearer, runner, high jump, equestrian, kayaker, swimmer. No. 1881. 1000d, Olympic rings, torch, mascots, stadiums, flags, javelin.

**2012, Sept. 9 *Perf. 13x13¼***
**1876-1879** A559 Set of 4 7.00 7.00

**Size: 120x70mm**

***Imperf***

**1880-1881** A559 Set of 2 5.50 5.50

Kings of Iraq A560

Designs: 500d, King Faisal II (1935-1958). 750d, King Ghazi (1912-1939). No. 1884, 1000d, King Faisal I (1885-1933).
No. 1885, Kings Faisal I, Ghazi and Faisal II, equestrian statue, arms.

**2012, Oct. 2 *Perf. 14¼***
**1882-1884** A560 Set of 3 6.25 6.25

**Size: 90x70mm**
**On Thin Card Stock**
**Without Gum**

***Imperf***

**1885** A560 1000d multi 2.75 2.75

Arab Post Day A561

**2012, Nov. 26 *Perf. 13x13¼***
**1886** A561 250d multi .70 .70

Kirkuk Castle — A562

**2012, Nov. 26 *Perf. 13¼x13***
**1887** A562 500d multi 1.40 1.40

Water Wheel — A563

**2012, Dec. 4 *Perf. 13¼***
**1888** A563 10,000d multi 27.50 27.50

## AIR POST STAMPS

**Catalogue values for unused stamps in this section are for Never Hinged items.**

Basra Airport — AP1

Diyala Railway Bridge — AP2

Vickers Viking over: 4f, 20f, Kut Dam. 5f, 35f, Faisal II Bridge.

***Perf. 11½, 11½x12***

**1949, Feb. 1 Engr. Unwmk.**

| | | | | |
|---|---|---|---|---|
| **C1** | AP1 | 3f blue green | 1.00 | .25 |
| **C2** | AP1 | 4f red violet | 1.00 | .25 |
| **C3** | AP1 | 5f red brown | 1.00 | .25 |
| **C4** | AP1 | 10f carmine | 5.50 | 1.50 |
| **C5** | AP1 | 20f blue | 3.75 | .65 |
| **C6** | AP1 | 35f red orange | 3.75 | .65 |
| **C7** | AP2 | 50f olive | 5.00 | 1.10 |
| **C8** | AP2 | 100f violet | 9.75 | 2.25 |
| | | *Nos. C1-C8 (8)* | 30.75 | 6.90 |

Sheets exist, perf. and imperf., containing one each of Nos. C1-C8, with arms and Arabic inscription in blue green in upper and lower margin. Value (2 sheets), each $80.

### Republic

ICY Emblem — AP3

**1965, Aug. 13 Litho. *Perf. 13½***

| | | | | |
|---|---|---|---|---|
| **C9** | AP3 | 5f brn org & black | 1.00 | .25 |
| **C10** | AP3 | 10f citron & dk brn | 1.50 | .25 |
| **C11** | AP3 | 30f ultra & black | 3.50 | 1.10 |
| | | *Nos. C9-C11 (3)* | 6.00 | 1.60 |

International Cooperation Year.

Trident 1E Jet Plane AP4

**1965, Dec. 1 Photo. *Perf. 11½***

**Granite Paper**

| | | | | |
|---|---|---|---|---|
| **C12** | AP4 | 5f multicolored | .90 | .55 |
| **C13** | AP4 | 10f multicolored | .90 | .55 |
| **C14** | AP4 | 40f multicolored | 6.00 | 4.75 |
| | | *Nos. C12-C14 (3)* | 7.80 | 5.85 |

Introduction by Iraqi Airways of Trident 1E jet planes.

Arab International Tourist Union Emblem — AP5

Travelers on Magic Carpet AP6

**1966, Dec. 3 Litho. *Perf. 13½, 14***

| | | | | |
|---|---|---|---|---|
| **C15** | AP5 | 2f multicolored | 1.00 | .30 |
| **C16** | AP6 | 5f yellow & multi | 1.50 | .30 |
| **C17** | AP5 | 15f blue & multi | 1.75 | .50 |
| **C18** | AP6 | 50f multicolored | 3.00 | .80 |
| | | *Nos. C15-C18 (4)* | 7.25 | 1.90 |

Meeting of the Arab Intl. Tourist Union, Baghdad.
For overprint see No. RAC1.

### Costume Type of Regular Issue

Iraqi Costumes: 40f, Woman's head. 50f, Woman's costume. 80f, Man's costume.

**1967, Nov. 10 Litho. *Perf. 13***

| | | | | |
|---|---|---|---|---|
| **C19** | A105 | 40f multicolored | 2.50 | .90 |
| **C20** | A105 | 50f blue & multi | 3.50 | 1.25 |
| **C21** | A105 | 80f green & multi | 5.50 | 1.75 |
| | | *Nos. C19-C21 (3)* | 11.50 | 3.90 |

For overprints, see CO1-CO3.

### International Tourist Year Type of Regular Issue

Designs: 50f, Female statue, Temples of Hatra. 80f, Spiral Tower (Malwiye of Samarra). 100f, Adam's Tree. 200f, Aladdin's Cave. 500f, Golden Shiah Mosque of Kadhimain. 50f, 80f, 100f and 200f are vert.

**1967, Dec. 1 Litho.**

| | | | | |
|---|---|---|---|---|
| **C22** | A107 | 50f multicolored | 4.00 | .40 |
| **C23** | A107 | 80f multicolored | 4.25 | .65 |
| **C24** | A107 | 100f multicolored | 4.25 | .80 |
| **C25** | A107 | 200f ver & multi | 8.75 | 3.25 |
| **C26** | A107 | 500f brn & multi | 35.00 | 18.00 |
| | | *Nos. C22-C26 (5)* | 51.50 | 23.10 |

For overprints see Nos. C39, C52, C53, CO4.

Arabian AP7

Animals: 2f, Striped hyena. 3f, Leopard. 5f, Mountain gazelle. 200f, Arabian stallion.

**1969, Sept. 1 Litho. *Perf. 14***

| | | | | |
|---|---|---|---|---|
| **C27** | AP7 | 2f multicolored | .85 | .25 |
| **C28** | AP7 | 3f multicolored | .85 | .25 |
| **C29** | AP7 | 5f multicolored | .85 | .25 |
| **C30** | AP7 | 10f multicolored | 1.10 | .30 |
| **C31** | AP7 | 200f multicolored | 13.50 | 6.00 |
| | | *Nos. C27-C31 (5)* | 17.15 | 7.05 |

For overprints, see Nos. CO5-CO7.

Ross Smith's Vickers Vimy AP8

**1969, Dec. 4 Litho. *Perf. 14***

| | | | | |
|---|---|---|---|---|
| **C32** | AP8 | 15f dk bl & multi | 3.50 | 1.20 |
| **C33** | AP8 | 35f multicolored | 5.00 | 2.75 |
| *a.* | | Souv. sheet of 2, #C32-C33, imperf. | 15.00 | 13.00 |

50th anniv. of the first England to Australia flight of Capt. Ross Smith and Lt. Keith Smith. No. C33a sold for 100f.

View Across Euphrates — AP9

Iraqi Banknotes and Pres. Hassan al-Bakr AP10

**1970, Oct. 30 Litho. *Perf. 13***

| | | | | |
|---|---|---|---|---|
| **C34** | AP9 | 10f brt bl & multi | 2.25 | .50 |
| **C35** | AP9 | 15f multicolored | 3.50 | 1.10 |
| **C36** | AP10 | 1d multicolored | 70.00 | 24.00 |
| | | *Nos. C34-C36 (3)* | 75.75 | 25.60 |

National Development Plan.
For overprints see Nos. C42-C43.

Telecommunications Emblem — AP11

**1970, Dec. 15 Litho. *Perf. 14x13½***

| | | | | |
|---|---|---|---|---|
| **C37** | AP11 | 15f gray & multi | .90 | .25 |
| **C38** | AP11 | 25f lt bl & multi | 1.10 | .50 |

10th Conf. of Arab Telecommunications Union.

No. C23 Overprinted

**1971, Apr. 23 *Perf. 13***

| | | | | |
|---|---|---|---|---|
| **C39** | A107 | 80f multicolored | 10.00 | 5.50 |

World Meteorological Day.

Iraqi Philatelic Society Emblem — AP12

**1972, Feb. 25 Litho. *Perf. 13***

| | | | | |
|---|---|---|---|---|
| **C40** | AP12 | 25f multicolored | 1.25 | .95 |
| **C41** | AP12 | 70f pink & multi | 4.00 | 2.40 |

Iraqi Philatelic Society, 20th anniversary.

### Nos. C34-C35 Overprinted

**1972, Feb. 25**

| | | | | |
|---|---|---|---|---|
| **C42** | AP9 | 10f brt bl & multi | 2.50 | 2.40 |
| **C43** | AP9 | 15f multicolored | 2.50 | 2.40 |

9th Cong. of Natl. Union of Iraqi Students.

Soccer and C.I.S.M. Emblem AP13

20f, 35f, Players, soccer ball, C.I.S.M. emblem. 100f, Winged lion, Olympic & C.I.S.M. emblems.

**1972, June 9 Litho. *Perf. 13½***

| | | | | |
|---|---|---|---|---|
| **C46** | AP13 | 10f lt bl & multi | .75 | .30 |
| **C47** | AP13 | 20f dp bl & multi | 1.75 | .30 |
| **C48** | AP13 | 25f green & multi | 1.75 | .30 |
| **C49** | AP13 | 35f brt bl & multi | 4.75 | .80 |
| *a.* | | Souv. sheet, 100f, imperf. | 22.50 | 22.50 |
| | | *Nos. C46-C49 (4)* | 9.00 | 1.70 |

25th Military Soccer Championships (C.I.S.M.), Baghdad, June 9-19.

Statue of Athlete — AP14

Design: 70f, Mesopotamian archer on horseback, ancient and modern athletes.

**1972, Nov. 15 Photo. *Perf. 14x13½***

| | | | | |
|---|---|---|---|---|
| **C50** | AP14 | 25f multicolored | 1.50 | .65 |
| **C51** | AP14 | 70f multicolored | 3.75 | 2.10 |

Cong. of Asian and World Body Building Championships, Baghdad, Nov. 15-23, 1972.

Nos. C23, C26 Overprinted

**1973, Mar. 25 Litho. *Perf. 13***

| | | | | |
|---|---|---|---|---|
| **C52** | A107 | 80f multi | 21.00 | 7.25 |
| **C53** | A107 | 500f multi | 75.00 | *75.00* |

International History Congress.

### ICATU Type of 1976

**1976, Mar. 24 Photo. *Perf. 13½***

| | | | | |
|---|---|---|---|---|
| **C54** | A213 | 75f blue & multi | 4.50 | 2.00 |

Symbolic Eye AP15

Basketball AP16

**1976, June 20 Photo. *Perf. 14***

| | | | | |
|---|---|---|---|---|
| **C55** | AP15 | 25f ultra & dk brn | .40 | .25 |
| **C56** | AP15 | 35f brt grn & dk brn | .60 | .25 |
| **C57** | AP15 | 50f orange & multi | 1.25 | .60 |
| | | *Nos. C55-C57 (3)* | 2.25 | 1.10 |

World Health Day: Foresight prevents blindness.

**1976, July 30 Litho. *Perf. 12x12½***

Montreal Olympic Games Emblem and: 35f, Volleyball. 50f, Wrestling. 75f, Boxing. 100f, Target shooting, horiz.

| | | | | |
|---|---|---|---|---|
| **C58** | AP16 | 25f yel & multi | .75 | .25 |
| **C59** | AP16 | 35f blue & multi | 1.00 | .50 |
| **C60** | AP16 | 50f ver & multi | 1.25 | .95 |
| **C61** | AP16 | 75f yel grn & multi | 2.25 | 1.25 |
| | | *Nos. C58-C61 (4)* | 5.25 | 2.95 |

### Souvenir Sheet

***Imperf***

| | | | | |
|---|---|---|---|---|
| **C62** | AP16 | 100f grn & multi | 7.00 | 7.00 |

21st Olympic Games, Montreal, Canada, July 17-Aug. 1.

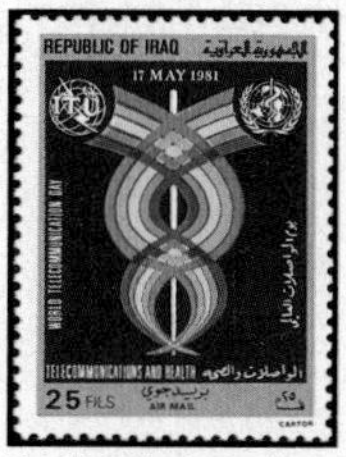


13th World Telecommunications Day — AP17

**1981, May 17 Photo. *Perf. 12½***

| | | | | |
|---|---|---|---|---|
| **C63** | AP17 | 25f multicolored | .50 | .25 |
| **C64** | AP17 | 50f multicolored | 1.00 | .40 |
| **C65** | AP17 | 75f multicolored | 1.75 | .85 |
| | | *Nos. C63-C65 (3)* | 3.25 | 1.50 |

### Air Force Type of 1981

**1981, June 1 Photo. *Perf. 14x13½***

| | | | | |
|---|---|---|---|---|
| **C66** | A289 | 120f Planes, vert. | 4.00 | 2.50 |

## AIR POST OFFICIAL STAMP

**Catalogue values for all unused stamps in this section are for Never Hinged items.**

Nos. C19-C22 Overprinted

**1971 Litho. *Perf. 13***

| | | | | |
|---|---|---|---|---|
| **CO1** | A105 | 40f multicolored | 4.75 | 1.40 |
| **CO2** | A105 | 50f multicolored | 6.00 | 1.40 |
| **CO3** | A105 | 80f multicolored | 5.50 | 1.40 |

### "Official" Reading Down

| | | | | |
|---|---|---|---|---|
| **CO4** | A107 | 50f multicolored | 5.25 | 3.25 |
| | | *Nos. CO1-CO4 (4)* | 21.50 | 7.45 |

Nos. C27-C28, C30 Overprinted or Surcharged

**1971 *Perf. 14***

| | | | | |
|---|---|---|---|---|
| **CO5** | AP7 | 10f multicolored | 7.50 | 5.00 |
| **CO6** | AP7 | 15f on 3f multi | 7.50 | 5.00 |
| **CO7** | AP7 | 25f on 2f multi | 7.50 | 5.00 |
| | | *Nos. CO5-CO7 (3)* | 22.50 | 15.00 |

No bar and surcharge on No. CO5.

## OFFICIAL STAMPS

### British Mandate

Regular Issue of 1923 Overprinted

k

l

**1923 Wmk. 4 *Perf. 12***

| | | | | |
|---|---|---|---|---|
| **O1** | A1(k) | ½a olive grn | 1.25 | .50 |
| **O2** | A2(k) | 1a brown | 1.50 | .25 |
| **O3** | A3(l) | 1½a car lake | 3.25 | .75 |
| **O4** | A4(k) | 2a brown org | 2.25 | .30 |
| **O5** | A5(k) | 3a deep blue | 4.00 | .75 |
| **O6** | A6(l) | 4a dull violet | 4.25 | .50 |
| **O7** | A7(k) | 6a blue green | 6.00 | 1.40 |
| **O8** | A6(l) | 8a olive bister | 6.50 | 1.30 |
| **O9** | A8(l) | 1r green & brn | 7.50 | 1.40 |
| **O10** | A1(k) | 2r black (R) | 22.50 | 9.00 |
| **O11** | A6(l) | 5r orange | 65.00 | 27.50 |
| **O12** | A7(k) | 10r carmine | 95.00 | 60.00 |
| | | *Nos. O1-O12 (12)* | 219.00 | 103.65 |

### Regular Issue of 1923-25 Overprinted

m

n

**1924-25**

| | | | | |
|---|---|---|---|---|
| **O13** | A1(m) | ½a olive green | 1.75 | .30 |
| **O14** | A2(m) | 1a brown | 1.50 | .30 |
| **O15** | A3(n) | 1½a car lake | 1.50 | .30 |
| **O16** | A4(m) | 2a brown org | 2.25 | .30 |
| **O17** | A5(m) | 3a deep blue | 2.75 | .30 |
| **O18** | A6(n) | 4a dull violet | 5.75 | .30 |
| **O19** | A7(m) | 6a blue green | 2.75 | .30 |
| **O20** | A6(n) | 8a olive bister | 5.75 | .40 |
| **O21** | A8(n) | 1r green & brn | 13.00 | 1.00 |
| **O22** | A1(m) | 2r bister ('25) | 42.50 | 4.50 |
| **O23** | A6(n) | 5r orange | 70.00 | 50.00 |
| **O24** | A7(m) | 10r brown red | 100.00 | 52.50 |
| | | *Nos. O13-O24 (12)* | 249.50 | 110.50 |

For overprint see Nos. O42, O47, O51-O53.

### No. 14 Overprinted Type "n"

**1927**

| | | | | |
|---|---|---|---|---|
| **O25** | A9 | 1r red brown | 10.00 | 2.00 |

### Regular Issue of 1931 Overprinted Vertically

o

**1931**

| | | | | |
|---|---|---|---|---|
| O26 | A10 | ½a green | .35 | *3.00* |
| O27 | A10 | 1a chestnut | .35 | .25 |
| O28 | A10 | 1½a carmine | 8.75 | *16.00* |
| O29 | A10 | 2a orange | .85 | .25 |
| O30 | A10 | 3a light blue | 1.50 | .70 |
| O31 | A10 | 4a purple brown | 1.75 | .90 |
| O32 | A10 | 6a Pruss blue | 5.75 | *12.50* |
| O33 | A10 | 8a dark green | 5.75 | 12.50 |

### Overprinted Horizontally

p

| | | | | |
|---|---|---|---|---|
| O34 | A11 | 1r dark brown | 11.00 | *12.50* |
| O35 | A11 | 2r yellow brown | 22.50 | *45.00* |
| O36 | A11 | 5r deep orange | 52.50 | *85.00* |
| O37 | A11 | 10r red | 95.00 | *140.00* |
| | | *Nos. O26-O37 (12)* | 206.05 | 328.60 |

### Overprinted Vertically Reading Up

| | | | | |
|---|---|---|---|---|
| O38 | A9(p) | 25r violet | 925.00 | *1,200.* |

For overprints see Nos. O39-O41, O43-O46, O48-O50, O54.

### Kingdom

Nos. O15, O19, O22-O24, O26-O31, O33-O35, O38 Surcharged with New Values in Fils and Dinars, like Nos. 28-43

**1932, Apr. 1**

| | | | | |
|---|---|---|---|---|
| O39 | A10 | 3f on ½a | 4.00 | 4.00 |
| O40 | A10 | 4f on 1a (G) | 2.75 | .25 |
| O41 | A10 | 5f on 1a | 2.75 | .25 |
| *a.* | | Inverted Arabic "5" | *52.50* | *35.00* |
| O42 | A3 | 8f on 1½a | 6.25 | .60 |
| O43 | A10 | 10f on 2a | 3.50 | .25 |
| O44 | A10 | 15f on 3a | 4.75 | 2.75 |
| O45 | A10 | 20f on 4a | 4.75 | 2.75 |
| O46 | A10 | 25f on 4a | 5.00 | 2.25 |
| O47 | A7 | 30f on 6a | 5.25 | 2.00 |
| O48 | A10 | 40f on 8a | 4.50 | 4.00 |
| *a.* | | "Flis" for "Fils" | *300.00* | *450.00* |
| O49 | A11 | 50f on 1r | 6.25 | 4.00 |
| O50 | A11 | 75f on 1r | 7.00 | 7.00 |
| O51 | A1 | 100f on 2r | 20.00 | 4.00 |
| O52 | A6 | 200f on 5r | 26.00 | 26.00 |
| O53 | A7 | ½d on 10r | 75.00 | *100.00* |
| *a.* | | Bar in "½" omitted | *850.00* | *975.00* |
| O54 | A9 | 1d on 25r | 140.00 | *210.00* |
| | | *Nos. O39-O54 (16)* | 317.75 | 370.10 |

Regular Issue of 1932 Overprinted Vertically like Nos. O26-O33

**1932, May 9**

| | | | | |
|---|---|---|---|---|
| O55 | A12 | 2f ultramarine | 1.00 | .25 |
| O56 | A12 | 3f green | 1.00 | .25 |
| O57 | A12 | 4f violet brn | 1.25 | .25 |
| O58 | A12 | 5f gray | 1.25 | .25 |
| O59 | A12 | 8f deep red | 1.25 | .25 |
| O60 | A12 | 10f yellow | 2.25 | .25 |
| O61 | A12 | 15f deep blue | 2.75 | .25 |
| O62 | A12 | 20f orange | 2.75 | .25 |
| O63 | A12 | 25f rose lilac | 2.75 | .40 |
| O64 | A12 | 30f olive grn | 4.00 | .40 |
| O65 | A12 | 40f dark violet | 5.75 | .40 |

### Overprinted Horizontally Like Nos. O34 to O37

| | | | | |
|---|---|---|---|---|
| O66 | A13 | 50f deep brown | 3.75 | .50 |
| O67 | A13 | 75f lt ultra | 2.75 | 1.00 |
| O68 | A13 | 100f deep green | 12.50 | 1.50 |
| O69 | A13 | 200f dark red | 22.50 | 8.75 |

### Overprinted Vertically like No. O38

| | | | | |
|---|---|---|---|---|
| O70 | A14 | ½d gray blue | 15.00 | 22.50 |
| O71 | A14 | 1d claret | 70.00 | *100.00* |
| | | *Nos. O55-O71 (17)* | 152.50 | *137.45* |

Regular Issue of 1934-38 Overprinted Type "o" Vertically Reading up in Black

**1934-38** **Unwmk.**

| | | | | |
|---|---|---|---|---|
| O72 | A15 | 1f purple ('38) | 1.10 | .50 |
| O73 | A15 | 2f ultramarine | 1.10 | .25 |
| O74 | A15 | 3f green | .65 | .25 |
| O75 | A15 | 4f purple brn | 1.10 | .25 |
| O76 | A15 | 5f gray green | 1.00 | .25 |
| O77 | A15 | 8f deep red | 4.50 | .25 |
| O78 | A15 | 10f yellow | .45 | .25 |
| O79 | A15 | 15f deep blue | 10.00 | 1.50 |
| O80 | A15 | 20f orange | 1.00 | .25 |
| O81 | A15 | 25f brown violet | 20.00 | 6.25 |
| O82 | A15 | 30f olive green | 4.50 | .25 |
| O83 | A15 | 40f dark violet | 5.75 | .40 |

### Overprinted Type "p"

| | | | | |
|---|---|---|---|---|
| O84 | A16 | 50f deep brown | 1.00 | .65 |
| O85 | A16 | 75f ultramarine | 6.75 | .90 |
| O86 | A16 | 100f deep green | 1.75 | 1.00 |
| O87 | A16 | 200f dark red | 4.50 | 2.75 |

### Overprinted Type "p" Vertically Reading Up

| | | | | |
|---|---|---|---|---|
| O88 | A17 | ½d gray blue | 11.00 | *18.00* |
| O89 | A17 | 1d claret | 45.00 | *55.00* |
| | | *Nos. O72-O89 (18)* | 121.15 | 88.95 |

**Catalogue values for unused stamps in this section, from this point to the end of the section, are for Never Hinged items.**

### Stamps of 1941-42 Overprinted in Black or Red

r

s

***Perf. 11½x13½, 13 to 14 and Compound***

**1941-42**

| | | | | |
|---|---|---|---|---|
| O90 | A18(r) | 1f dk vio ('42) | .50 | .25 |
| O91 | A18(r) | 2f choc ('42) | .50 | .25 |
| O92 | A19(r) | 3f brt grn ('42) | .50 | .25 |
| O93 | A19(r) | 4f pur (R) ('42) | .50 | .25 |
| O94 | A19(r) | 5f dk car rose ('42) | .50 | .25 |
| O95 | A20(s) | 8f carmine | 1.75 | .25 |
| O96 | A20(s) | 8f ocher ('42) | .50 | .25 |
| O97 | A20(s) | 10f ocher | 12.75 | .85 |
| O98 | A20(s) | 10f car ('42) | 1.40 | .25 |
| O99 | A20(s) | 15f dull blue | 12.75 | 1.50 |
| O100 | A20(s) | 15f blk (R) ('42) | 2.25 | .65 |
| O101 | A20(s) | 20f black (R) | 3.75 | .65 |
| O102 | A20(s) | 20f dl bl ('42) | 1.25 | .25 |
| O103 | A21(s) | 25f dark vio | 1.75 | .65 |
| O104 | A21(r) | 25f dk vio ('42) | 2.00 | .65 |
| O105 | A21(s) | 30f dp orange | 1.75 | .65 |
| O106 | A21(r) | 30f dk org ('42) | 1.75 | .65 |
| O107 | A21(s) | 40f brown org | 1.10 | .25 |
| O108 | A21(r) | 40f chnt ('42) | 1.75 | .65 |
| O109 | A21(r) | 50f ultra | 3.25 | .25 |
| O110 | A21(r) | 75f rose vio | 2.00 | .85 |
| O111 | A22(s) | 100f ol grn ('42) | 4.50 | .65 |
| O112 | A22(s) | 200f dp org ('42) | 6.00 | 1.75 |
| O113 | A23(r) | ½d blue ('42) | 20.00 | 20.00 |
| O114 | A23(r) | 1d grnsh bl ('42) | 32.50 | 29.00 |
| | | *Nos. O90-O114 (25)* | 117.25 | 61.90 |

The space between the English and Arabic on overprints "r" and "s" varies with the size of the stamps.

For overprints see Nos. O165, RA5.

Stamps of 1942 Overprinted in Black

**1942** **Unwmk.** ***Perf. 13x13½***

| | | | | |
|---|---|---|---|---|
| O115 | A24 | 1f violet & brown | .65 | .65 |
| O116 | A24 | 2f dark blue & brn | .65 | .65 |
| O117 | A24 | 3f lt green & brn | .65 | .65 |
| O118 | A24 | 4f dl brown & brn | .65 | .65 |
| O119 | A24 | 5f sage green & brn | .85 | .85 |
| O120 | A24 | 6f red orange & brn | .85 | .85 |
| O121 | A24 | 10f dl rose red & brn | 1.10 | 1.10 |
| O122 | A24 | 12f yel green & brn | 1.50 | 1.50 |
| | | *Nos. O115-O122 (8)* | 6.90 | 6.90 |

Stamps of 1948 Overprinted in Black

**1948, Jan. 15** ***Perf. 11½x12***

**Size: 17¾x20½mm**

| | | | | |
|---|---|---|---|---|
| O123 | A25 | 1f slate | .25 | .35 |
| O124 | A25 | 2f sepia | .25 | .45 |
| O125 | A25 | 3f emerald | .25 | .45 |
| O126 | A25 | 4f purple | .25 | .35 |
| O127 | A25 | 5f rose lake | .25 | .25 |
| O128 | A25 | 6f plum | .25 | .45 |
| O129 | A25 | 8f ocher | .25 | .45 |
| O130 | A25 | 10f rose red | .25 | .35 |
| O131 | A25 | 12f dark olive | .25 | .35 |
| O132 | A25 | 15f black | 4.00 | *6.75* |
| O133 | A25 | 20f blue | .25 | .25 |
| O134 | A25 | 25f rose violet | .25 | .25 |
| O135 | A25 | 30f red orange | .25 | .25 |
| O136 | A25 | 40f orange brn | .55 | .45 |

***Perf. 12x11½***

**Size: 22x27½mm**

| | | | | |
|---|---|---|---|---|
| O137 | A25 | 60f deep blue | .80 | .25 |
| O138 | A25 | 75f lilac rose | 1.40 | .40 |
| O139 | A25 | 100f olive grn | 1.40 | 1.00 |
| O140 | A25 | 200f dp orange | 2.25 | 1.00 |
| O141 | A25 | ½d blue | 19.00 | 16.00 |
| O142 | A25 | 1d green | 27.50 | 35.00 |
| | | *Nos. O123-O142 (20)* | 59.90 | 65.05 |

For overprints see Nos. O166-O177, O257, O272, O274, O277, O282, RA1, RA3, RA4.

Same Overprint on Nos. 133-138

**1949-51** ***Perf. 11½x12***

**Size: 17¾x20½mm**

| | | | | |
|---|---|---|---|---|
| O143 | A25 | 3f rose lake ('51) | 3.25 | 1.00 |
| O144 | A25 | 5f emerald ('51) | 3.50 | 1.00 |
| O145 | A25 | 14f dk olive ('50) | 1.75 | .35 |
| O146 | A25 | 16f rose red ('51) | 3.25 | .35 |
| O147 | A25 | 28f blue ('51) | 1.00 | .35 |

***Perf. 12x11½***

**Size: 22x27½mm**

| | | | | |
|---|---|---|---|---|
| O148 | A25 | 50f deep blue | 1.25 | .50 |
| | | *Nos. O143-O148 (6)* | 14.00 | 3.55 |

For overprints see #O258, O273, O275, O276.

Same Overprint in Black on Stamps and Type of 1954-57

**1955-59** ***Perf. 11½x12***

| | | | | |
|---|---|---|---|---|
| O148A | A28 | 1f blue ('56) | .25 | .25 |
| O149 | A28 | 2f chocolate | .25 | .25 |
| O150 | A28 | 3f rose lake | .25 | .25 |
| O151 | A28 | 4f violet | .25 | .25 |
| O152 | A28 | 5f emerald | .25 | .25 |
| O153 | A28 | 6f plum ('56) | .25 | .25 |
| O154 | A28 | 8f ocher ('56) | .25 | .25 |
| O155 | A28 | 10f blue | .25 | .25 |
| O155A | A28 | 16f brt rose ('57) | 22.50 | 22.50 |
| O156 | A28 | 20f olive | .45 | .25 |
| O157 | A28 | 25f rose violet | 2.25 | 1.00 |
| O158 | A28 | 30f vermilion | 1.00 | .25 |
| O159 | A28 | 40f orange brn | .45 | .25 |

**Size: 22½x27½mm**

| | | | | |
|---|---|---|---|---|
| O160 | A28 | 50f blue | 2.25 | .75 |
| O161 | A28 | 60f pale purple | 14.00 | 5.75 |
| O161A | A28 | 100f ol grn ('59) | 32.50 | 16.00 |
| | | *Nos. O148A-O161A (16)* | 77.40 | 48.75 |

Dates of issue for Nos. O155A and O161A are suppositional.

For overprints see Nos. O178-O191, O259-O260, O283-O291.

Same Ovpt. on Stamps of 1957-58

| | | | | |
|---|---|---|---|---|
| O162 | A33 | 1f blue | 4.25 | 1.75 |
| O162A | A33 | 2f chocolate | 5.00 | 3.75 |
| O162B | A33 | 3f dk carmine | 6.50 | 2.75 |
| O162C | A33 | 4f dull violet | 7.75 | 1.75 |
| O162D | A33 | 5f emerald | 4.25 | 1.75 |
| O163 | A33 | 6f plum | 4.25 | 2.75 |
| O164 | A33 | 10f blue | 4.25 | 1.40 |
| | | *Nos. O162-O164 (7)* | 36.25 | 15.90 |

For overprints see #O192-O199, O292-O293.

### Republic

Official Stamps of 1942-51 with Additional Overprint

***Perf. 13½x14***

**1958-59** **Engr.** **Unwmk.**

| | | | | |
|---|---|---|---|---|
| O165 | A22 | 200f dp orange | 10.00 | 5.75 |

***Perf. 11½x12, 12x11½***

| | | | | |
|---|---|---|---|---|
| O166 | A25 | 12f dk olive | 1.00 | .75 |
| O167 | A25 | 14f olive | 1.10 | .95 |
| O168 | A25 | 15f black | .95 | .50 |
| O169 | A25 | 16f rose red | 3.75 | 2.10 |
| O170 | A25 | 25f rose vio | 3.50 | 2.00 |
| O171 | A25 | 28f blue | 2.00 | 1.60 |
| O172 | A25 | 40f orange brn | 1.25 | .95 |
| O173 | A25 | 60f deep blue | 5.00 | 2.50 |
| O174 | A25 | 75f lilac rose | 2.25 | 1.90 |
| O175 | A25 | 200f dp orange | 2.75 | 2.40 |
| O176 | A25 | ½d blue | 17.00 | 6.25 |
| O177 | A25 | 1d green | 27.50 | 12.50 |
| | | *Nos. O166-O177 (12)* | 68.05 | 34.40 |

Other denominations of types A22 and A25 exist with this overprint, but these were probably not regularly issued.

Same Ovpt. on Nos. O148A-O161A

| | | | | |
|---|---|---|---|---|
| O178 | A28 | 1f blue | .60 | .25 |
| O179 | A28 | 2f chocolate | .60 | .25 |
| O180 | A28 | 3f rose lake | .60 | .25 |
| O181 | A28 | 4f violet | .60 | .25 |
| O181A | A28 | 5f emerald | .65 | .40 |
| O182 | A28 | 6f plum | .60 | .25 |
| O183 | A28 | 8f ocher | .55 | .25 |
| O183A | A28 | 10f blue | .80 | .25 |
| O184 | A28 | 16f bright rose | 7.50 | 7.00 |
| O185 | A28 | 20f olive | .65 | .25 |
| O186 | A28 | 25f rose violet | .65 | .25 |
| O187 | A28 | 30f vermilion | .70 | .40 |
| O188 | A28 | 40f orange brn | 1.00 | .40 |
| O189 | A28 | 50f blue | 1.00 | .50 |
| O190 | A28 | 60f pale purple | 1.00 | .60 |
| O191 | A28 | 100f olive grn | 2.10 | .60 |
| | | *Nos. O178-O191 (16)* | 19.60 | 12.15 |

Same Ovpts. on #O162-O164, 216

| | | | | |
|---|---|---|---|---|
| O192 | A33 | 1f blue | .25 | .25 |
| O193 | A33 | 2f chocolate | .25 | .25 |
| O194 | A33 | 3f dark carmine | .45 | .25 |
| O195 | A33 | 4f dull violet | .25 | .25 |
| O196 | A33 | 5f emerald | .25 | .25 |
| O197 | A33 | 6f plum | .25 | .25 |
| O198 | A33 | 8f ocher | .65 | .25 |
| O199 | A33 | 10f blue | .70 | .25 |
| | | *Nos. O192-O199 (8)* | 3.05 | 2.00 |

Nos. 232-233, 235-237, 242 Overprinted

**Litho. & Photo.**

**1961, Apr. 1** **Unwmk.** ***Perf. 11½***

| | | | | |
|---|---|---|---|---|
| O200 | A38 | 1f multi | .40 | .30 |
| O201 | A38 | 2f multi | .40 | .30 |
| O202 | A38 | 4f multi | .40 | .30 |
| O203 | A38 | 5f multi | .50 | .30 |
| O204 | A38 | 10f multi | .80 | .60 |
| O205 | A38 | 50f multi | 13.50 | 10.50 |
| | | *Nos. O200-O205 (6)* | 16.00 | 12.30 |

Nos. 232-247 Overprinted

### Emblem in Gold, Red and Blue; Blue Inscriptions

**1961**

| | | | | |
|---|---|---|---|---|
| O206 | A38 | 1f gray | .40 | .30 |
| O207 | A38 | 2f salmon | .40 | .30 |
| O208 | A38 | 3f pale violet | .40 | .30 |
| O209 | A38 | 4f bright yel | .40 | .30 |
| O210 | A38 | 5f light blue | .40 | .30 |
| O211 | A38 | 10f bright pink | .40 | .30 |
| O212 | A38 | 15f lt green | .40 | .30 |
| O213 | A38 | 20f bister brn | .40 | .30 |
| O214 | A38 | 30f light gray | .50 | .30 |
| O215 | A38 | 40f orange yel | .50 | .30 |
| O216 | A38 | 50f yel green | .60 | .30 |
| O217 | A38 | 75f pale green | .80 | .40 |
| O218 | A38 | 100f orange | .90 | .65 |
| O219 | A38 | 200f lilac | 3.25 | 1.40 |
| O220 | A38 | 500f bister | 11.50 | 5.50 |
| O221 | A38 | 1d brt green | 22.50 | 11.50 |
| | | *Nos. O206-O221 (16)* | 43.75 | 22.75 |

**Nos. 480-482 Overprinted**

**1971 Litho. *Perf. 13½***
**O222** A115 10f multicolored .80 1.50
**O223** A115 15f blue & multi 8.00 1.50
**O224** A115 25f multicolored 8.00 3.00
*Nos. O222-O224 (3)* 16.80 6.00

Overprint lines are spaced 16mm on No. O222, 32½mm on Nos. O223-O224.

Same Overprint on Nos. 453, 455-456

**1971 *Perf. 13***
**O225** A107 5f lilac & multi 6.00 .30
**O226** A107 15f rose red & multi 6.00 .50
**O227** A107 25f vio bl & multi 8.50 1.50
*Nos. O225-O227 (3)* 20.50 2.30

Overprint horizontal on Nos. O225 and O227; vertical, reading down on No. O226. Distance between English and Arabic words: 8mm.

Nos. 446, 448-449 Overprinted

**1971 Litho. *Perf. 13***
**O228** A105 15f multicolored 1.50 .65
**O229** A105 15f multi, wide ovpt. setting 62.50 7.50
*a.* Narrow setting 47.50
**O230** A105 25f multicolored 10.50 3.00
**O231** A105 30f multicolored 10.50 3.00
*Nos. O228-O231 (4)* 85.00 14.15

No. O229 overprinted "Official" horizontally. Two overprint settings on O229: wide, 6.5mm between English and Arab inscriptions; narrow, 2mm between inscriptions.

Same Overprint on Nos. 483-486

**1972 *Perf. 13½***
**O232** A116 10f multicolored 5.00 .50
**O233** A116 25f multicolored 5.00 1.00

**1972**
**O234** A117 15f multicolored 5.00 .50
**O235** A117 25f multicolored 5.00 1.00

Same Overprint, "Official" Reading Down on Nos. 562-565

**1972**
**O240** A142 5f multicolored 5.00 3.75
**O241** A142 10f multicolored 5.00 3.75
**O242** A142 15f multicolored 5.00 3.75
**O243** A142 35f multicolored 5.00 3.75
*Nos. O240-O243 (4)* 20.00 15.00

Latin inscription on Nos. O240-O241 obliterated with heavy bar.

No. 487 Overprinted "Official" like No. CO5

**1972 Photo. *Perf. 13½***
**O244** A118 25f multicolored 10.50 3.00

#O134, O148 Ovptd. with 3 Bars
***Perf. 11½x12, 12x11½***

**1973, Jan. 29 Engr.**
**O257** A25 25f rose violet 6.00 1.50
**O258** A25 50f deep blue 6.00 5.50

Same on Nos. O157 and O160
**O259** A28 25f rose violet 6.00 1.50
**O260** A28 50f blue 6.00 1.50

Type of 1957 Overprinted

**Size: 22x27½mm**
**O261** A33 50f rose violet 6.00 1.50
*Nos. O257-O261 (5)* 30.00 11.50

See note after No. 679. No. O261 not issued without overprints.

King Faisal Issues Overprinted

Two sizes of overprint: Arabic 6½mm or 9mm.

**1973**
**O263** A28 15f black (#149) 4.00 3.75
**O264** A33 15f black 4.00 1.00
**O265** A25 25f rose vio (#121) 15.00 6.00
**O266** A28 25f rose vio (#151) 4.00 1.00
**O267** A33 25f rose violet 4.00 1.00

Same Overprint on Nos. 674-677
**O268** A28 10f blue 3.75 3.75
**O269** A33 10f blue 52.50 60.00
**O270** A28 15f black 67.50 75.00
**O271** A33 15f black 2.50 2.00
*Nos. O263-O271 (9)* 157.25 153.50

Official Stamps of 1948-51 Overprinted

Overprint design faces left or right.

**1973**
**O272** A25 12f (#O131) 1.75 .30
**O273** A25 14f (#O145) 1.75 .50
**O274** A25 15f (#O132) 1.75 .50
**O275** A25 16f (#O146) 3.25 .85
**O276** A25 28f (#O147) 6.75 1.10
**O277** A25 30f (#O135) 6.75 .95
**O278** A25 40f (#O136) 6.75 1.40
**O279** A25 60f (#O137) 6.75 5.25
**O280** A25 100f (#O139) 22.50 8.50
**O281** A25 ½d (#O141) 57.50 22.50
**O282** A25 1d (#O142) 110.00 110.00
*Nos. O272-O282 (11)* 225.50 151.85

Same Overprint on Official Stamps of 1955-59
**O283** A28 3f (#O150) 1.75 .60
**O284** A28 6f (#O153) 1.75 .60
**O285** A28 8f (#O154) 1.75 .60
**O286** A28 16f (#O155A) *15.00 15.00*
**O287** A28 20f (#O156) 1.75 .60
**O288** A28 30f (#O158) 1.75 .95
**O289** A28 40f (#O159) 1.75 1.60
**O290** A28 60f (#O161) 8.75 2.00
**O291** A28 100f (#O161A) *27.50 8.00*
*Nos. O283-O291 (9)* *61.75 29.95*

Same Overprint on 1957-58 Issues
**O292** A33 3f dk car (#O162B) 5.00 1.25
**O293** A33 6f plum (#O163) 5.00 1.25
**O294** A33 8f ocher (#179) 5.00 1.25
**O295** A33 30f red orange 5.00 1.25
*Nos. O292-O295 (4)* 20.00 5.00

The overprint on Nos. O294-O295 includes the "On State Service" overprint; No. O295 was not issued without overprints. The overprint leaf design faces left or right and varies in size.

Nos. 403, 497, 681 Overprinted

***Perf. 12½, 13x12½, 13½***
**1974 (?) Photo., Litho.**
**O296** A89 2f multicolored 5.00
**O297** A123 15f multicolored 6.00 .50
**O298** A185 25f multicolored 3.75 1.00
*Nos. O296-O298 (3)* 14.75

Size of "Official" on Nos. O297-O298 9mm.

Nos. 683-691 Overprinted

**1974 Litho. *Perf. 13x12½***
**O299** A186 5f orange & blk .30 .30
**O300** A186 10f bister & blk .30 .30
**O301** A186 20f brt rose & blk .65 .30
**O302** A186 25f ultra & blk 1.25 1.25
**O303** A186 35f emerald & blk 1.25 .50
**O304** A186 45f blue & black 1.25 .60
**O305** A186 50f olive & yel 1.75 .65
**O306** A186 70f violet & yel 1.75 .95
**O307** A186 95f brown & yel 2.50 1.10
*Nos. O299-O307 (9)* 11.00 5.95

Nos. 455 and 467 Overprinted

**1975 Litho. *Perf. 13, 14***
**O308** A107 15f multicolored 3.50 3.50
**O311** A110 30f multicolored 6.25 4.25

Space between Arabic and English lines of overprint is 4mm on No. O308, 13mm on No. O311.

Nos. 491-493 Overprinted or Surcharged like Nos. CO5-CO7

**1975 *Perf. 14***
**O312** A121 10f multicolored 6.50 4.00
**O312A** A121 15f on 3f multi 6.50 4.00
**O313** A121 25f on 2f multi 6.50 4.00
*Nos. O312-O313 (3)* 19.50 12.00

Nos. 322-325 Overprinted

**Engr.; Engr. & Photo.**
**1975 *Perf. 12x11***
**O314** A57 10f rose red 8.00 .60
**O315** A57 15f brown & buff 8.00 .75
**O316** A57 20f violet blue 8.00 .75
**O317** A57 30f orange 15.00 .80
*Nos. O314-O317 (4)* 39.00 2.90

Arms of Iraq — O1

**1975 Photo. *Perf. 14***
**O318** O1 5f multicolored .30 .30
**O319** O1 10f blue & multi .30 .30
**O320** O1 15f yel & multi .40 .40
**O321** O1 20f ultra & multi .65 .65
**O322** O1 25f org & multi .90 .90
**O323** O1 30f rose & multi 1.00 1.00
**O324** O1 50f multicolored 1.75 1.75
**O325** O1 100f multicolored 3.25 3.25
*Nos. O318-O325 (8)* 8.55 8.55

Nos. 787-791 Overprinted "OFFICIAL" in English and Arabic

**1976, Sept. 15 Litho. *Perf. 13½x14***
**O327** A219 5f multicolored 1.25 .75
**O328** A219 10f multicolored 1.25 .95
**O329** A219 15f multicolored 1.40 .95
**O330** A219 25f multicolored 3.75 1.25
**O331** A219 50f multicolored 6.25 2.25
*Nos. O327-O331 (5)* 13.90 6.15

Altharthar - Euphrates Canal — O2

**1978 Photo. *Perf. 11½***
**O332** O2 5f multicolored .30 .30
**O333** O2 10f multicolored .30 .30
**O334** O2 15f multicolored .45 .30
**O335** O2 25f multicolored .90 .30
*Nos. O332-O335 (4)* 1.95 1.20

Baghdad University Entrance — O3

**1981, Oct. 21 Litho. *Perf. 12x12½***
**O336** O3 45f multicolored .65 .40
**O337** O3 50f multicolored .70 .50

Nos. O336-O337 Surcharged

**1983, May 15 Litho. *Perf. 12x12½***
**O338** O3 60f on 45f multi 2.50 .50
**O339** O3 70f on 50f multi 3.00 .75

Martyrs Type of 1981 Inscribed "OFFICIAL" in English and Arabic

**1981 Photo. *Perf. 14***
**O339A** A303 45f silver border 1.25 .40
**O339B** A303 50f gold border 1.25 .50
**O339C** A303 120f metallic bl border 3.50 1.10
*Nos. O339A-O339C (3)* 6.00 2.00

Building Type of 1983 Inscribed "OFFICIAL" in English and Arabic

**1982, Dec. 31 Litho. *Perf. 14***
**O340** A324 60f multicolored .90 .50
**O341** A324 70f multicolored 1.00 .65

For surcharge see No. 1517.

Martyr Type of 1984 Inscribed "OFFICIAL" in English and Arabic

**1984, Dec. 1 *Perf. 13½***
**O342** A329 20f multicolored .30 .30
**O343** A329 30f multicolored .30 .30
**O344** A329 50f multicolored .55 .40
**O345** A329 60f multicolored .70 .40
*Nos. O342-O345 (4)* 1.85 1.40

No. RA22 Overprinted

**1985 (?) Litho. *Perf. 13x12½***
**O346** PT2 5f bister, blk & yel 3.25 1.00

## POSTAL TAX STAMPS

**Catalogue values for unused stamps in this section are for Never Hinged items.**

Nos. O125 and 115 Surcharged in Carmine or Black

**1949 Unwmk. *Perf. 11½x12***
**RA1** A25 2f on 3f emer (C) *25.00 15.00*
**RA2** A25 2f on 6f plum *32.50 14.00*

Similar Overprint in Carmine or Black on Nos. O124, O127 and O94 Middle Arabic Line Omitted
***Perf. 11½x12***
**RA3** A25 2f sepia (C) *20.00 9.00*
**RA4** A25 5f rose lake *40.00 20.00*

***Perf. 12x13½, 14***
**RA5** A19 5f dark car rose *20.00 10.50*

Larger overprint on #RA5, 20½mm wide. Value $22.50.

No. 115 Surcharged in Black

*Perf. 11½x12*

| | | | | |
|---|---|---|---|---|
| **RA6** | A25 | 5f on 6f plum | 45.00 | 17.00 |

The tax on Nos. RA1-RA6 was to aid the war in Palestine.

Nos. 317, 322-326 Surcharged

**Engr.; Engr. & Photo.**

**1963** *Perf. 12x11*

| | | | | |
|---|---|---|---|---|
| **RA7** | A57 | 5f on 1f green | 3.75 | 4.50 |
| **RA8** | A57 | 5f on 10f rose red | 3.75 | 4.50 |
| **RA9** | A57 | 5f on 15f brn & buff | 3.75 | 4.50 |
| **RA10** | A57 | 5f on 20f vio blue | 3.75 | 4.50 |
| **RA11** | A57 | 5f on 30f orange | 3.75 | 4.50 |
| **RA12** | A57 | 5f on 40f brt green | 3.75 | 4.50 |
| | | *Nos. RA7-RA12 (6)* | 22.50 | 27.00 |

Surtax was for the Defense Fund.

PT1

**1967, Aug. Photo.** *Perf. 13½*

| | | | | |
|---|---|---|---|---|
| **RA13** | PT1 | 5f brown | .45 | .25 |

Surtax was for flood victims.

No. RA13 Overprinted

**1967, Nov.**

| | | | | |
|---|---|---|---|---|
| **RA14** | PT1 | 5f brown | .45 | .45 |

Surtax was for Defense Fund.

Nos. 305A-305B with Surcharge Similar to Nos. RA7-RA12

**1972 Litho.** *Perf. 13½x14*

| | | | | |
|---|---|---|---|---|
| **RA15** | A54a | 5f on 14f | 7.00 | 7.00 |
| **RA16** | A54a | 5f on 35f | 7.00 | 7.00 |

Surtax was for the Defense Fund. The 2 disks obliterating old denominations are on one line at the bottom. Size of Arabic inscription: 17x12mm.

No. 452 with Surcharge Similar to Nos. RA7-RA12, and Nos. 443, 457 and 526 Srchd.

**1973 Litho.** *Perf. 13*

| | | | | |
|---|---|---|---|---|
| **RA17** | A105 | 5f on 2f multi | 8.50 | 8.50 |
| **RA18** | A107 | 5f on 2f multi | 8.50 | 8.50 |
| **RA19** | A108 | 5f on 2f multi | 8.50 | 8.50 |
| **RA20** | A135 | 5f on 2f multi | 8.50 | 8.50 |
| | | *Nos. RA17-RA20 (4)* | 34.00 | 34.00 |

Surtax was for the Defense Fund. Surcharges on Nos. RA17-RA20 are adjusted to fit shape of stamps and to obliterate old denominations.

No 683 Overprinted

**1974 Litho.** *Perf. 13x12½*

| | | | | |
|---|---|---|---|---|
| **RA21** | A186 | 5f orange & blk | 6.00 | 4.00 |

Soldier — PT2

**1974**

| | | | | |
|---|---|---|---|---|
| **RA22** | PT2 | 5f bister, blk & yel | 2.50 | 3.00 |

Surtax of Nos. RA21-RA22 was for the Defense Fund.
For overprint see No. O346.

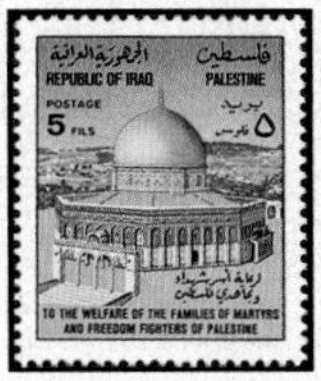

Dome of the Rock, Jerusalem — PT3

**1977 Photo.** *Perf. 14*

| | | | | |
|---|---|---|---|---|
| **RA23** | PT3 | 5f multicolored | 2.75 | 1.50 |

Surtax was for families of Palestinians.
For surcharges see Nos. 1457, 1465-1477.

## AIR POST POSTAL TAX STAMPS

**Catalogue values for unused stamps in this section are for Never Hinged items.**

#C15 Surcharged Like #RA17-RA20

**1973 Litho.** *Perf. 13½*

| | | | | |
|---|---|---|---|---|
| **RAC1** | AP5 | 5f on 2f multi | 8.50 | 8.50 |

Surtax was for the Defense Fund.

# IRELAND

'ir-lənd

(Eire)

LOCATION — Comprises the entire island of Ireland, except 5,237 square miles at the extreme north
GOVT. — Republic
AREA — 27,136 sq. mi.
POP. — 3,626,087 (1996)
CAPITAL — Dublin

12 Pence = 1 Shilling
100 Pence = 1 Pound (Punt) (1971)
100 Cents = 1 Euro (2002)

**Catalogue values for unused stamps in this country are for Never Hinged items, beginning with Scott 99 in the regular postage section, Scott C1 in the air post section, and Scott J5 in the postage due section.**

### Watermarks

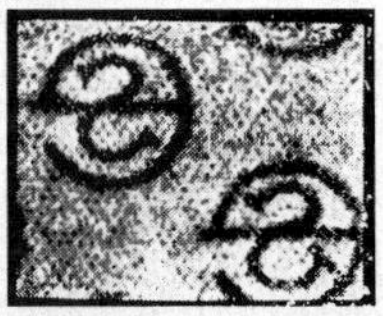

Wmk. 44 — SE in Monogram

The letters "SE" are the initials of "Saorstat Eireann" (Irish Free State).

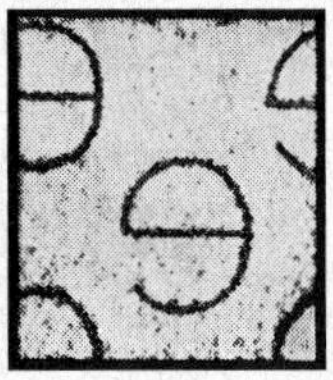

Wmk. 262 — Multiple "e"

### Overprinted by Dollard, Ltd.

Great Britain Nos. 159-167, 170-172, 179-181 Overprinted

Overprint means "Provisional Government of Ireland."

**Overprint measures 15x17½mm**
**Black or Gray Black Overprint**

**1922, Feb. 17 Wmk. 33** *Perf. 15x14*

| | | | | |
|---|---|---|---|---|
| **1** | A82 | ½p green | 1.50 | 1.50 |
| | | Never hinged | 2.50 | |
| *a.* | | Inverted overprint | 500.00 | 700.00 |
| | | Never hinged | 750.00 | |
| **2** | A83 | 1p scarlet | 1.75 | 1.50 |
| | | Never hinged | 2.50 | |
| *a.* | | Inverted overprint | 300.00 | 550.00 |
| *b.* | | Double overprint | | — |
| **3** | A86 | 2½p ultra | 3.75 | 16.00 |
| | | Never hinged | 7.50 | |
| **4** | A87 | 3p violet | 10.00 | 13.00 |
| | | Never hinged | 17.00 | |
| **5** | A88 | 4p slate green | 10.00 | 20.00 |
| | | Never hinged | 17.00 | |
| **6** | A89 | 5p yel brown | 10.00 | 22.50 |
| | | Never hinged | 17.50 | |
| **7** | A90 | 9p black brown | 29.00 | 40.00 |
| | | Never hinged | 47.50 | |
| **8** | A90 | 10p light blue | 17.50 | 32.50 |
| | | Never hinged | 30.00 | |
| | | *Nos. 1-8 (8)* | 83.50 | 147.00 |

The ½p with red overprint is a proof. Value, $150.

**Red or Carmine Overprint**

**1922, Apr.-July**

| | | | | |
|---|---|---|---|---|
| **9** | A86 | 2½p ultra | 2.50 | 9.50 |
| | | Never hinged | 5.00 | |
| **10** | A88 | 4p slate green (R) | 17.00 | 30.00 |
| | | Never hinged | 30.00 | |
| **10A** | A88 | 4p slate green (C) | 90.00 | 140.00 |
| | | Never hinged | 150.00 | |
| **11** | A90 | 9p black brown (R) | 35.00 | 40.00 |
| | | Never hinged | 62.50 | |
| **11A** | A90 | 9p black brown (C) | 150.00 | 175.00 |
| | | Never hinged | 225.00 | |
| | | *Nos. 9-11A (5)* | 294.50 | 394.50 |

### Overprinted in Black

There is a variation that is 21x14mm.
The "h" and "é" are 1mm apart.
See Nos. 36-38.

**Overprint measures 21½x14mm**

**1922, Feb. 17 Wmk. 34** *Perf. 11x12*

| | | | | |
|---|---|---|---|---|
| **12** | A91 | 2sh6p brown | 57.50 | 110.00 |
| | | Never hinged | 125.00 | |
| **13** | A91 | 5sh car rose | 100.00 | 200.00 |
| | | Never hinged | 225.00 | |
| **14** | A91 | 10sh gray blue | 250.00 | 400.00 |
| | | Never hinged | 450.00 | |
| | | *Nos. 12-14 (3)* | 407.50 | 710.00 |

### Overprinted by Alex. Thom & Co.

Overprinted in Black

TWO PENCE
Die I — Four horizontal lines above the head. Heavy colored lines above and below the bottom tablet. The inner frame line is closer to the central design than it is to the outer frame line.
Die II — Three lines above the head. Thinner lines above and below the bottom tablet. The inner frame line is midway between the central design and the outer frame line.

**Overprint measures 14½x16mm**

**1922, Feb. 17 Wmk. 33** *Perf. 15x14*

| | | | | |
|---|---|---|---|---|
| **15** | A84 | 1½p red brown | 3.00 | 3.00 |
| | | Never hinged | 5.00 | |
| *a.* | | "PENCF" | 400.00 | 350.00 |
| **16** | A85 | 2p orange (II) | 4.00 | 2.00 |
| | | Never hinged | 6.50 | |
| *a.* | | Inverted overprint (II) | 400.00 | 500.00 |
| *b.* | | 2p orange (I) | 4.00 | 2.00 |
| | | As "b," never hinged | 6.50 | |
| *c.* | | Inverted overprint (I) | 210.00 | 300.00 |
| **17** | A89 | 6p red violet | 17.50 | 12.50 |
| | | Never hinged | 30.00 | |
| **18** | A90 | 1sh bister | 25.00 | 22.50 |
| | | Never hinged | 47.50 | |
| | | *Nos. 15-18 (4)* | 49.50 | 40.00 |

**Important:** see Nos. 25-26, 31, 35.

### Overprinted by Harrison & Sons

Overprinted in Black in Glossy Black Ink

**Overprint measures 15¼x17mm**

**1922, June Coil Stamps**

| | | | | |
|---|---|---|---|---|
| **19** | A82 | ½p green | 6.00 | 25.00 |
| | | Never hinged | 7.50 | |
| **20** | A83 | 1p scarlet | 5.00 | 20.00 |
| | | Never hinged | 7.50 | |
| **21** | A84 | 1½p red brown | 8.00 | 57.50 |
| | | Never hinged | 12.00 | |
| **22** | A85 | 2p orange (I) | 30.00 | 50.00 |
| | | Never hinged | 47.50 | |
| *a.* | | 2p orange (II) | 30.00 | 47.50 |
| | | Never hinged | 50.00 | |
| | | *Nos. 19-22 (4)* | 49.00 | 152.50 |

In Harrison overprint, "i" of "Rialtas" extends below the base of the other letters.
The Harrison stamps were issued in coils, either horizontal or vertical. The paper is double where the ends of the strips were overlapped. Mint pairs with the overlap sell for about three times the price of a single. The perforations are often clipped.

### Overprinted by Alex. Thom & Co.

Stamps of Great Britain, 1912-22 Overprinted as Nos. 15 to 18, in Shiny to Dull Blue Black, or Red

Note: The blue black overprints can best be distinguished from the black by use of 50-power magnification with a light source behind the stamp.

**Overprint measures 14½x16mm**

**1922, July-Nov.** *Perf. 15x14*

| | | | | |
|---|---|---|---|---|
| **23** | A82 | ½p green | 1.50 | 2.00 |
| | | Never hinged | 5.00 | |
| **24** | A83 | 1p scarlet | 2.25 | 2.25 |
| | | Never hinged | 3.75 | |
| **25** | A84 | 1½p red brown | 6.50 | 10.00 |
| | | Never hinged | 15.00 | |
| **26** | A85 | 2p orange (II) | 4.25 | 2.25 |
| | | Never hinged | 7.25 | |
| *a.* | | Inverted overprint (II) | 275.00 | 500.00 |
| *b.* | | 2p orange (I) | 35.00 | 4.25 |
| | | Never hinged | 50.00 | |
| **27** | A86 | 2½p ultra (R) | 10.00 | 35.00 |
| | | Never hinged | 20.00 | |
| **28** | A87 | 3p violet | 3.00 | 7.25 |
| | | Never hinged | 6.50 | |
| **29** | A88 | 4p slate green (R) | 4.50 | 4.75 |
| | | Never hinged | 10.00 | |
| **30** | A89 | 5p yellow brown | 10.00 | 17.00 |
| | | Never hinged | 20.00 | |
| **31** | A89 | 6p red violet | 9.00 | 7.50 |
| | | Never hinged | 20.00 | |
| **32** | A90 | 9p blk brn (R) | 22.50 | 26.00 |
| | | Never hinged | 40.00 | |
| **33** | A90 | 9p ol grn (R) | 12.00 | 45.00 |
| | | Never hinged | 22.50 | |
| **34** | A90 | 10p light blue | 30.00 | 60.00 |
| | | Never hinged | 65.00 | |
| **35** | A90 | 1sh bister | 15.00 | 15.00 |
| | | Never hinged | 35.00 | |
| | | *Nos. 23-35 (13)* | 130.50 | 234.00 |

Nos. 23, 24, 28, 34 overprinted in dull black, rather than the normal blue-black, are believed to be proofs, pressed into use when supplies of the issued values ran low.

### Overprinted as Nos. 12 to 14 in Blue Black (Shiny to Dull)

The "h" and "é" are ½mm apart.

### Overprint measures 21x13½mm

**1922 Wmk. 34 *Perf. 11x12***

**36** A91 2sh6p gray brown 325. *450.*
Never hinged 550.
**37** A91 5sh car rose 325. *500.*
Never hinged 575.
**38** A91 10sh gray blue 1,900. *2,250.*
Never hinged 3,000.
*Nos. 36-38 (3)* 2,550. *3,200.*

Overprinted in Blue Black

### Overprint measures 15¾x16mm

**1922, Dec. Wmk. 33 *Perf. 15x14***

**39** A82 ½p green 1.50 *2.75*
Never hinged 2.75
**40** A83 1p scarlet 1.50 *5.00*
Never hinged 8.00
**41** A84 1½p red brown 3.50 *17.50*
Never hinged 8.00
**42** A85 2p orange (II) 15.00 15.00
Never hinged 25.00
**43** A90 1sh bister 50.00 *62.50*
Never hinged 67.50
*Nos. 39-43 (5)* 71.50 *102.75*

Stamps of Great Britain, 1912-22, Overprinted in Shiny to Dull Blue Black or Red

This overprint means "Irish Free State"

The inner loop of the "9" is an upright oval.

The measurement of "1922" is made across the bottom of the numerals and does not include the serif at the top of the "1."

There were 5 plates for printing the overprint on Nos. 44-55. In the impressions from plate I the 12th stamp in the 15th row has no accent on the 2nd "A" of "SAORSTAT." To correct this an accent was inserted by hand, sometimes this was in a reversed position.

On Nos. 56-58 the accent was omitted on the 2nd stamp in the 3rd and 8th rows. Damage to the plate makes the accent look reversed on the 4th stamp in the 7th row. The top of the "t" slants down in a line with the so-called accent.

### Overprint measures 15x8½mm "1922" is 6¼mm long

**1922-23 Wmk. 33 *Perf. 15x14***

**44** A82 ½p green 1.50 1.50
Never hinged 2.50
*a.* Accent omitted 1,300. *1,000.*
*b.* Accent added 125.00 *150.00*
**45** A83 1p scarlet 1.50 1.50
Never hinged 2.50
*a.* Accent omitted 14,000. *9,000.*
*b.* Accent added 150.00 *175.00*
*c.* Accent and final "t" omitted 12,000. *7,500.*
*d.* Accent and final "t" added 250.00 *300.00*
**46** A84 1½p red brown 3.50 *17.50*
Never hinged 10.00
**47** A85 2p orange (II) 3.00 *5.00*
Never hinged 7.50
**48** A86 2½p ultra (R) 5.00 *10.00*
Never hinged 9.00
*a.* Accent omitted 160.00 *200.00*
**49** A87 3p violet 10.00 *12.50*
Never hinged 22.50
*a.* Accent omitted 325.00 *425.00*
**50** A88 4p sl green (R) 5.00 *9.00*
Never hinged 10.00
*a.* Accent omitted 225.00 *300.00*
**51** A89 5p yel brown 5.75 *10.00*
Never hinged 9.50
**52** A89 6p dull violet 3.50 3.00
Never hinged 7.00
*a.* Accent added 900.00 *900.00*
**53** A90 9p ol green (R) 5.50 *12.50*
Never hinged 12.50
*a.* Accent omitted 275.00 *350.00*
**54** A90 10p lt blue 20.00 *57.50*
Never hinged 50.00
**55** A90 1sh bister 15.00 *15.00*
Never hinged 40.00
*a.* Accent omitted 9,000. *10,000.*
*b.* Accent added 825.00 *900.00*

**Perf. 11x12**
**Wmk. 34**

**56** A91 2sh6p lt brown 62.50 *100.00*
Never hinged 140.00
*a.* Accent omitted 450.00 *600.00*
**57** A91 5sh car rose 100.00 *200.00*
Never hinged 250.00
*a.* Accent omitted 600.00 *900.00*
**58** A91 10sh gray blue 225.00 *500.00*
Never hinged 500.00
*a.* Accent omitted 3,000. *4,000.*
*Nos. 44-58 (15)* 466.75 *955.00*

### Overprinted by Harrison & Sons
Coil Stamps
Same Ovpt. in Black or Blue Black

**1923 Wmk. 33 *Perf. 15x14***

**59** A82 ½p green 3.25 *15.00*
Never hinged 6.50
*a.* Tall "1" 10.00 55.00
Never hinged 27.50
**60** A83 1p scarlet 8.50 *21.00*
Never hinged 15.00
*a.* Tall "1" 45.00 160.00
Never hinged 95.00
**61** A84 1½p red brown 8.50 *50.00*
Never hinged 22.50
*a.* Tall "1" 95.00 250.00
Never hinged 190.00
**62** A85 2p orange (II) 12.00 *20.00*
Never hinged 17.00
*a.* Tall "1" 15.00 *55.00*
Never hinged 30.00
*Nos. 59-62 (4)* 32.25 *106.00*

These stamps were issued in coils, made by joining horizontal or vertical strips of the stamps. See 2nd paragraph after No. 22. In some strips there were two stamps with the "1" of "1922" 2½mm high and with serif at foot.

In this setting the middle "e" of "eireann" is a trifle above the line of the other letters, making the word appear slightly curved. The lower end of the "1" of "1922" is rounded on Nos. 59-62 instead of flat as on Nos. 44-47.

The inner loop of the "9" is round.

See Nos. 77b, 78b and 79b.

Booklet Panes

For very fine, the perforation holes at top or bottom of the pane should be visible, though not necessarily perfect half circles.

"Sword of Light" — A1

Map of Ireland — A2

Coat of Arms — A3

Celtic Cross — A4

***Perf. 15x14***

**1922-23 Typo. Wmk. 44**

**65** A1 ½p emerald 1.50 1.50
Never hinged 3.00
*a.* Booklet pane of 6 *350.00*
**66** A2 1p car rose 1.50 1.50
Never hinged 3.00
*a.* Booklet pane of 6 *350.00*
*b.* Booklet pane of 3 + 3 labels *400.00*
**67** A2 1½p claret 3.50 3.00
Never hinged 8.00
**68** A2 2p deep green 1.50 .75
Never hinged 2.50
*a.* Booklet pane of 6 *350.00*
*b.* Perf. 15 horiz. ('35) *12,500.* *2,000.*

No. 68b is valued in the grade of fine.

**69** A3 2½p chocolate 4.00 *8.50*
Never hinged 9.50
**70** A4 3p ultra 3.50 3.00
Never hinged 7.25
**71** A3 4p slate 6.25 *6.25*
Never hinged 12.50
**72** A1 5p deep violet 22.50 15.00
Never hinged 57.50
**73** A1 6p red violet 7.25 5.75
Never hinged 14.50
**74** A3 9p violet 35.00 25.00
Never hinged 125.00
**75** A4 10p brown 17.00 *35.00*
Never hinged 57.50
**76** A1 1sh light blue 35.00 17.00
Never hinged 110.00
*Nos. 65-76 (12)* 138.50 122.25

The 2p was issued in 1922; other denominations in 1923.

No. 68b is a vertical coil stamp.

See Nos. 87, 91-92, 105-117, 137-138, 225-226, 326. For types overprinted see Nos. 118-119.

### Overprinted by the Government Printing Office, Dublin Castle and British Board of Inland Revenue at Somerset House, London

Great Britain Nos. 179-181 Ovptd. in Black or Gray Black

The measurement of "1922" is made across the bottom of the numerals and does not include the serif at the top of the "1."

### "1922" is 5½mm long

**1925 Wmk. 34 *Perf. 11x12***

**77** A91 2sh6p gray brown 70.00 *175.00*
Never hinged 125.00
**78** A91 5sh rose red 95.00 *275.00*
Never hinged 160.00
**79** A91 10sh gray blue 225.00 *575.00*
Never hinged 425.00
*Nos. 77-79 (3)* 390.00 *1,025.*

In 1927 the 2sh6p, 5sh and 10sh stamps were overprinted from a plate in which the Thom and Castle clichés were combined, thus including wide and narrow "1922" in the same setting.

### Overprinted by British Board of Inland Revenue at Somerset House, London

Pair with "1922" Wide and Narrow

**1927**

*77a* A91 2sh6p 400.
Never hinged 775.
*78a* A91 5sh 700.
Never hinged 1,350.
*79a* A91 10sh 1,700.
Never hinged 3,750.
*Nos. 77a-79a (3)* 2,800.

### Wide "1922"
### "1922" is 6¼mm long

**1927-28**

*77b* A91 2sh6p 60.00 *60.00*
Never hinged 110.00
*78b* A91 5sh ('28) 90.00 *140.00*
Never hinged 225.00
*79b* A91 10sh ('28) 250.00 *425.00*
Never hinged 550.00
*Nos. 77b-79b (3)* 400.00 625.00

Daniel O'Connell — A5

***Perf. 15x14***

**1929, June 22 Wmk. 44**

**80** A5 2p dark green .60 .55
Never hinged 1.00
**81** A5 3p dark blue 4.25 *14.00*
Never hinged 15.00
**82** A5 9p dark violet 4.75 *13.50*
Never hinged 16.00
*Nos. 80-82 (3)* 9.60 *28.05*

Catholic Emancipation in Ireland, centenary.

Shannon River Hydroelectric Station — A6

**1930, Oct. 15**

**83** A6 2p black brown 1.25 *2.75*
Never hinged 4.25

Opening of the hydroelectric development of the River Shannon.

Farmer with Scythe A7

Cross of Cong and Chalice A8

**1931, June 12**

**84** A7 2p pale blue 1.00 *1.50*
Never hinged 2.50

Bicentenary of Royal Dublin Society.

**1932, May 12**

**85** A8 2p dark green 2.00 .85
Never hinged 3.00
**86** A8 3p bright blue 4.50 *8.00*
Never hinged 7.00

International Eucharistic Congress.

### Type of 1922-23 Issue
### Coil Stamp

**1933-34 *Perf. 15 Horizontally***

**87** A2 1p rose ('34) 27.50 *60.00*
Never hinged 45.00
*a.* 1p carmine rose 125.00 *300.00*
Never hinged 200.00

No. 87a has a single perforation at each side near the top, while No. 87 is perforated top and bottom only.

See No. 68b.

Adoration of the Cross A9

Hurling A10

**1933, Sept. 18 *Perf. 15x14***

**88** A9 2p slate green .65 .55
Never hinged 2.00
**89** A9 3p deep blue 3.00 *6.00*
Never hinged 8.75

Holy Year.

**1934, July 27**

**90** A10 2p green 1.00 1.50
Never hinged 2.50

50th anniv. of the Gaelic Athletic Assoc.

### Types of 1922-23
### Coil Stamps
### Wmk. 44 Sideways

**1934 *Perf. 14 Vertically***

**91** A1 ½p green 30.00 *75.00*
Never hinged 45.00
**92** A2 2p gray green 50.00 *125.00*
Never hinged 85.00

### Overprinted by Harrison & Sons
Great Britain Nos. 222-224
Overprinted in Black

**1935 Wmk. 34 *Perf. 11x12***

**93** A91 2sh6p brown 52.50 70.00
Never hinged 100.00
**94** A91 5sh carmine 200.00 225.00
Never hinged 350.00
**95** A91 10sh dark blue 400.00 *650.00*
Never hinged 1,100.
*Nos. 93-95 (3)* 652.50 945.00

Waterlow printing can be distinguished by the crossed lines in the background of portrait. Previous issues have horizontal lines only.

St. Patrick and Paschal Fire — A11

**1937, Sept. 8 Wmk. 44 *Perf. 14x15***

| | | | | |
|---|---|---|---|---|
| 96 | A11 2sh6p bright green | | 90.00 | 90.00 |
| | Never hinged | | 225.00 | |
| 97 | A11 5sh brown violet | | 110.00 | 110.00 |
| | Never hinged | | 250.00 | |
| 98 | A11 10sh dark blue | | 90.00 | 90.00 |
| | Never hinged | | 225.00 | |
| | *Nos. 96-98 (3)* | | 290.00 | 290.00 |

See Nos. 121-123.

**Catalogue values for unused stamps in this section, from this point to the end of the section, are for Never Hinged items.**

Allegory of Ireland and Constitution A12

**1937, Dec. 29 *Perf. 15x14***

| | | | |
|---|---|---|---|
| 99 | A12 2p plum | 2.00 | .30 |
| 100 | A12 3p deep blue | 7.00 | 7.00 |

Constitution Day.
See Nos. 169-170.

Father Theobald Mathew A13

**1938, July 1**

| | | | |
|---|---|---|---|
| 101 | A13 2p black brown | 2.00 | .45 |
| 102 | A13 3p ultramarine | 9.00 | 9.00 |

Temperance Crusade by Father Mathew, centenary.

Washington, US Eagle and Harp — A14

**1939, Mar. 1**

| | | | |
|---|---|---|---|
| 103 | A14 2p bright carmine | 1.50 | .50 |
| 104 | A14 3p deep blue | 13.00 | 12.00 |

US Constitution, 150th anniv.

### Type of 1922-23 Coil Stamp

**1940-46 Wmk. 262 *Perf. 15 Horiz.***

| | | | |
|---|---|---|---|
| 105 | A2 1p car rose ('46) | 40.00 | 32.50 |
| a. | Perf. 14 horiz. | 60.00 | 60.00 |

### Types of 1922-23

**1940-42 *Perf. 15x14***

**Size: 18x22mm**

| | | | |
|---|---|---|---|
| 106 | A1 ½p emerald ('41) | 2.75 | 1.40 |
| a. | Booklet pane of 6 | *350.00* | |
| 107 | A2 1p car rose ('41) | 2.00 | 1.40 |
| a. | Booklet pane of 6 | 6.00 | |
| b. | Bklt. pane of 3 + 3 labels | *3,500.* | |
| 108 | A2 1½p claret ('41) | 17.00 | 1.40 |
| a. | Booklet pane of 6 | 140.00 | |
| 109 | A2 2p deep green | 2.50 | 1.40 |
| a. | Booklet pane of 6 | 12.50 | |
| 110 | A3 2½p choc ('41) | 17.00 | 3.50 |
| a. | Booklet pane of 6 | 95.00 | |
| 111 | A4 3p dull blue ('41) | 2.75 | 1.40 |
| a. | Booklet pane of 6 | 40.00 | |
| 112 | A3 4p slate | 2.75 | 1.40 |
| a. | Booklet pane of 6 | 65.00 | |
| 113 | A1 5p deep violet | 2.75 | 1.40 |
| 114 | A1 6p red violet ('42) | 2.75 | 1.40 |
| 115 | A3 9p violet | 2.75 | 1.40 |
| 116 | A4 10p olive brown | 2.75 | 1.40 |
| 117 | A1 1sh blue | 175.00 | 42.50 |
| | *Nos. 106-117 (12)* | 232.75 | 60.00 |

Types of 1922-23 Overprinted in Green or Violet

Overprint reads: "In memory of the Rebellion of 1916."

**1941, Apr. 12 *Perf. 15x14***

| | | | |
|---|---|---|---|
| 118 | A2 2p yellow orange | 3.00 | .70 |
| 119 | A4 3p blue (V) | 50.00 | 40.00 |

Volunteer Soldier and Dublin Post Office A15

**1941, Oct. 27**

| | | | |
|---|---|---|---|
| 120 | A15 2½p bluish black | 3.00 | 1.75 |

Nos. 118-120 commemorate the 25th anniv. of the Easter Rebellion.

### St. Patrick Type of 1937

**1943-45 Wmk. 262 *Perf. 14x15***

| | | | |
|---|---|---|---|
| 121 | A11 2sh6p bright green | 7.00 | 2.75 |
| 122 | A11 5sh brown violet | 9.75 | 4.00 |
| 123 | A11 10sh dark blue ('45) | 17.00 | 8.75 |
| | *Nos. 121-123 (3)* | 33.75 | 15.50 |

Dr. Douglas Hyde A16

Sir Rowan Hamilton A17

**1943, July 31 *Perf. 15x14***

| | | | |
|---|---|---|---|
| 124 | A16 ½p green | 1.00 | 1.50 |
| 125 | A16 2½p red lilac | 2.25 | 1.25 |

50th anniv. of the Gaelic League.

**1943, Nov. 13 Typo. Wmk. 262**

| | | | |
|---|---|---|---|
| 126 | A17 ½p deep green | .75 | 1.50 |
| 127 | A17 2½p dk red brown | 2.25 | 1.25 |

Centenary of discovery of the mathematical formula of Quaternions by William Rowan Hamilton.

Brother Michael O'Clery — A18

**1944, June 30 *Perf. 14x15***

| | | | |
|---|---|---|---|
| 128 | A18 ½p emerald | .35 | .35 |
| a. | Booklet pane of 6 | 25.00 | |
| 129 | A18 1sh reddish brown | 1.75 | 1.75 |

300th anniv. of the death of Michael O'Clery, Irish historian.

Edmund Rice — A19

Sower — A20

**1944, Aug. 29 *Perf. 15x14***

| | | | |
|---|---|---|---|
| 130 | A19 2½p slate | 2.10 | 1.40 |

Death centenary of Edmund Ignatius Rice, founder of the Christian Brothers of Ireland.

**1945, Sept. 15**

| | | | |
|---|---|---|---|
| 131 | A20 2½p ultramarine | 1.50 | .25 |
| 132 | A20 6p red violet | 10.00 | 8.75 |

Commemorates the work of the Young Irelanders and the death centenary of Thomas Davis, Sept. 16, 1845.

Plowman A21

**1946, Sept. 16 Typo.**

| | | | |
|---|---|---|---|
| 133 | A21 2½p red | 2.00 | .25 |
| 134 | A21 3p dark blue | 6.50 | 6.75 |

Birth centenary of Charles Stewart Parnell and Michael Davitt, leaders in the struggle for Irish political independence.

Theobald Wolfe Tone A22

***Perf. 15x14***

**1948, Nov. 19 Wmk. 262**

| | | | |
|---|---|---|---|
| 135 | A22 2½p deep plum | 2.00 | .25 |
| 136 | A22 3p deep violet | 9.00 | 9.50 |

Insurrection of 1798, 150th anniversary.

### Types of 1922-23

**1949**

| | | | |
|---|---|---|---|
| 137 | A1 8p bright red | 2.00 | 1.50 |
| 138 | A4 11p carmine rose | 2.00 | 1.50 |

Leinster House, Dublin A23

**1949, Nov. 21**

| | | | |
|---|---|---|---|
| 139 | A23 2½p red brown | 2.00 | .75 |
| 140 | A23 3p violet blue | 8.50 | 7.75 |

International recognition of the Republic, Easter Monday, 1949.

James Clarence Mangan A24

Statue of St. Peter A25

**1949, Dec. 5**

| | | | |
|---|---|---|---|
| 141 | A24 1p dark green | 3.50 | 1.40 |

Mangan (1803-1849), poet.

**Wmk. 262**

**1950, Sept. 11 Engr. *Perf. 12½***

| | | | |
|---|---|---|---|
| 142 | A25 2½p violet | 1.50 | .50 |
| 143 | A25 3p blue | 11.50 | 12.50 |
| 144 | A25 9p brown | 11.50 | 14.00 |
| | *Nos. 142-144 (3)* | 24.50 | 27.00 |

Holy Year, 1950.

Thomas Moore — A26

Irish Harp — A27

**1952, Nov. 10 *Perf. 13***

| | | | |
|---|---|---|---|
| 145 | A26 2½p deep plum | .25 | .25 |
| 146 | A26 3½p dk olive green | 4.00 | 4.00 |

Death centenary of Thomas Moore (1779-1852), poet.

**1953, Feb. 9 Typo. *Perf. 14x15***

| | | | |
|---|---|---|---|
| 147 | A27 2½p bright green | 2.50 | .25 |
| 148 | A27 1sh4p bright blue | 30.00 | 32.50 |

Ireland's National festival "An Tostal."

Robert Emmet — A28

Madonna by della Robbia — A29

**1953, Sept. 21 Engr. *Perf. 12½x13***

| | | | |
|---|---|---|---|
| 149 | A28 3p deep green | 4.00 | .35 |
| 150 | A28 1sh3p carmine rose | 50.00 | 26.00 |

150th anniv. of the execution of Robert Emmet (1778-1803), Irish nationalist.

**1954, May 24 *Perf. 15***

| | | | |
|---|---|---|---|
| 151 | A29 3p blue | 1.10 | .25 |
| 152 | A29 5p deep green | 8.00 | 7.75 |

Marian Year, 1953-54.

John Henry Cardinal Newman A30

Statue of John Barry A31

**1954, July 19 Typo. *Perf. 15x14***

| | | | |
|---|---|---|---|
| 153 | A30 2p rose lilac | 3.00 | .25 |
| 154 | A30 1sh3p blue | 20.00 | 9.00 |

Opening of the Catholic University of Ireland, centenary.

**1956, Sept. 16 Engr. *Perf. 15***

| | | | |
|---|---|---|---|
| 155 | A31 3p dull purple | 1.00 | .25 |
| 156 | A31 1sh3p blue | 13.00 | 12.00 |

John Barry (1745-1803), "Father of the American Navy," on the occasion of the unveiling of a statue in Wexford, Ireland, his birthplace.

Redmond A32

O'Crohan A33

***Perf. 14x15***

**1957, June 11 Wmk. 262**

| | | | |
|---|---|---|---|
| 157 | A32 3p dark blue | 1.50 | .25 |
| 158 | A32 1sh3p rose lake | 17.50 | 17.50 |

Birth cent. of John Edward Redmond (1856-1918), Irish political leader.

**1957, July 1**

| | | | |
|---|---|---|---|
| 159 | A33 2p dull purple | 2.00 | .25 |
| 160 | A33 5p violet | 7.50 | 6.50 |

Birth cent. of Thomas O'Crohan (Tomas O'Criomhthain) (1856-1937), fisherman and author.

Brown A34

Father Luke Wadding A35

**1957, Sept. 23 Typo. *Perf. 15x14***
**161** A34 3p blue 3.75 .75
**162** A34 1sh3p carmine rose 45.00 30.00

Adm. William (Guillermo) Brown (1777-1857), founder of the Argentine Navy.

**1957, Nov. 25 Engr. *Perf. 15***
**163** A35 3p dark blue 2.00 .70
**164** A35 1sh3p deep claret 22.50 12.50

Luke Wadding (1588-1657), Irish Franciscan friar and historian.

Clarke
A36

Aikenhead
A37

**1958, July 28 Wmk. 262**
**165** A36 3p deep green 1.00 .25
**166** A36 1sh3p red brown 17.00 13.50

Thomas J. Clarke (1858-1916), patriot.

**1958, Oct. 20 *Perf. 15x14***
**167** A37 3p blue 1.50 .25
**168** A37 1sh3p carmine 20.00 15.00

Mother Mary Aikenhead (1787-1858), founder of the Irish Sisters of Charity.

**Constitution Type of 1937**

**1958, Dec. 29 Typo. Wmk. 262**
**169** A12 3p brown 1.10 .25
**170** A12 5p bright green 5.50 6.50

21st anniv. of the constitution.

Arthur Guinness — A38

**1959, July 20 Engr. *Perf. 15***
**171** A38 3p rose lake 3.50 .25
**172** A38 1sh3p dark blue 20.00 10.00

Bicentenary of Guinness Brewery.

Flight of the Holy Family A39

**1960, June 20 *Perf. 15***
**173** A39 3p rose violet .35 .25
**174** A39 1sh3p sepia 1.20 *2.50*

World Refugee Year, 7/1/59-6/30/60.

**Europa Issue**

Symbolic Wheel CD3

**1960, Sept. 19 Engr. *Perf. 15***
**175** CD3 6p orange brown *22.50* *2.00*
**176** CD3 1sh3p violet *52.50* *12.00*

No. 176 has fugitive ink.

De Havilland Dragon, Boeing 707 Jet and Dublin Airport
A41

**1961, June 26 *Perf. 15***
**177** A41 6p dull blue 1.75 2.50
**178** A41 1sh3p green 5.00 4.50

25th anniv. of the founding of Aer Lingus, Irish International Airlines.

St. Patrick — A42

**1961, Sept. 25 *Perf. 14½***
**179** A42 3p blue .80 .25
**180** A42 8p pale purple 2.25 *6.00*
**181** A42 1sh3p green 2.50 1.60
*Nos. 179-181 (3)* 5.55 7.85

1,500th anniv. of St. Patrick's death.

John O'Donovan and Eugene O'Curry A43

**1962, Mar. 26 *Perf. 15***
**182** A43 3p crimson .50 .25
**183** A43 1sh3p purple 4.50 5.00

Death centenaries of John O'Donovan (1806-1861) and Eugene O'Curry (1794-1862), Gaelic scholars and translators.

**Europa Issue**

19 Leaves on Young Tree CD5

**1962, Sept. 17 Engr. Wmk. 262**
**184** CD5 6p pink & dark red *.50* *.50*
**185** CD5 1sh3p bluish grn & dk blue grn *1.50* *1.00*

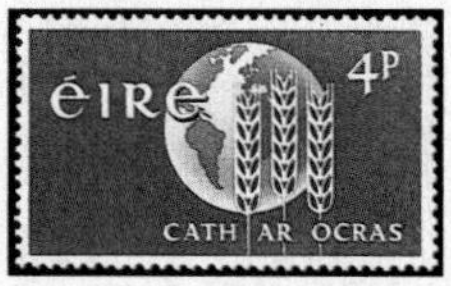


Wheat Emblem and Globe A45

**1963, Mar. 21 Wmk. 262**
**186** A45 4p violet .50 .25
**187** A45 1sh3p red 3.00 *3.00*

FAO "Freedom from Hunger" campaign.

**Europa Issue**

Stylized Links, Symbolizing Unity CD6

**1963, Sept. 16 *Perf. 15***
**188** CD6 6p rose carmine *1.25* *1.25*
**189** CD6 1sh3p dark blue *3.50* *2.00*

Centenary Emblem A47

**1963, Dec. 2 Photo. *Perf. 14½x14***
**190** A47 4p gray & red .60 .25
**191** A47 1sh3p brt green, gray & red 1.60 *2.75*

Centenary of the International Red Cross.

Wolfe Tone A48

**1964, Apr. 13 Engr. *Perf. 15***
**192** A48 4p black .50 .25
**193** A48 1sh3p dark blue 5.50 6.00

Birth bicentenary of Theobald Wolfe Tone (1763-1798), Irish revolutionist.

Irish Pavilion A49

**1964, July 20 Photo. *Perf. 14½x14***
**194** A49 5p multicolored .75 .25
*a.* Brown omitted 5,500.
**195** A49 1sh5p multicolored 6.00 6.00

New York World's Fair, 1964-65.

**Europa Issue**

CEPT Daisy (22 Petals) — CD7

***Perf. 14x14½***

**1964, Sept. 14 Litho. Wmk. 262**
**196** CD7 8p dull grn & ultra *4.00* *1.25*
**197** CD7 1sh5p red brown & org *16.00* *3.00*

ITU Emblem, Globe and Communication Waves — A51

**1965, May 17 Photo. *Perf. 14½x14***
**198** A51 3p dp blue & emerald .50 .25
**199** A51 8p black & emerald 4.00 *5.75*

ITU, cent.

William Butler Yeats — A52

**1965, June 14 *Perf. 15***
**200** A52 5p orange brn & blk .75 .30
**201** A52 1sh5p gray green, brn & black 6.00 5.75

Birth centenary of William Butler Yeats (1865-1939), poet and dramatist.

ICY Emblem A53

**1965, Aug. 16 Photo. *Perf. 15***
**202** A53 3p brt blue & vio bl .75 .70
**203** A53 10p redsh brn & dk brn 4.75 *5.00*

International Cooperation Year.

**Europa Issue**

Leaves and Fruit — CD8

**1965, Sept. 27 *Perf. 15***
**204** CD8 8p brick red & blk *5.50* *.60*
**205** CD8 1sh5p lt blue & claret *14.50* *2.75*

James Connolly A55

Designs: No. 207, Thomas J. Clarke. No. 208, Patrick Henry Pearse. No. 209, Symbolic of lives lost in fight for independence, and of Ireland marching into freedom. No. 210, Eamonn Ceannt. No. 211, Sean MacDiarmada. No. 212, Thomas MacDonagh. No. 213, Joseph Plunkett.

**1966, Apr. 12 Wmk. 262 *Perf. 15***
**206** A55 3p blue & black 1.60 .55
**207** A55 3p olive green 1.60 .55
*a.* Pair, #206-207 4.50 *2.25*
**208** A55 5p olive & black 2.00 .55
**209** A55 5p brt grn, blk & orange 2.00 .55
*a.* Pair, #208-209 5.00 *2.50*
**210** A55 7p dull org & blk 2.00 *4.00*
**211** A55 7p blue grn & blk 2.00 *4.00*
*a.* Pair, #210-211 5.75 *12.00*
**212** A55 1sh5p grnsh bl & blk 2.00 *3.50*
**213** A55 1sh5p emerald & blk 2.00 *3.50*
*a.* Pair, #212-213 8.00 *17.50*
*Nos. 206-213 (8)* 15.20 17.20

50th anniv. of the Easter Week Rebellion, and to honor the signers of the Proclamation of the Irish Republic.

Roger Casement — A56

**1966, Aug. 3 *Perf. 15***
**214** A56 5p black .40 .40
**215** A56 1sh dark red brown 2.40 1.75

50th death anniv. of Roger Casement (1864-1916), British consular agent and Irish rebel who was executed for treason.

**Europa Issue**

Symbolic Sailboat — CD9

**1966, Sept. 26 Photo. *Perf. 15***
**216** CD9 7p orange & green *2.00* *.40*
**217** CD9 1sh5p gray & green *5.00* *1.60*

Ballintubber Abbey A58

**1966, Nov. 8 *Perf. 15***
**218** A58 5p red brown .50 .50
**219** A58 1sh black 1.00 1.00

750th anniversary of Ballintubber Abbey.

**Cross and Sword Types of 1922**

**1966-67 Photo.** ***Perf. 15***

**Size: 17x20½mm**

**225** A4 3p blue ('67) 1.50 1.50
**226** A1 5p brt vio, type II ('68) 1.60 1.50
*a.* Booklet pane of 6, No. 226b 62.50
*b.* Type I ('66) 8.25 8.25

Type I has irregularly spaced lines in shading behind sword.

**Europa Issue**

Cogwheels — CD10

**1967, May 2**

**232** CD10 7p green & gold *1.90* *.80*
**233** CD10 1sh5p dk red & gold *4.25* *1.50*

Maple Leaves A60

**1967, Aug. 28** **Photo.**

**234** A60 5p multicolored .40 .40
**235** A60 1sh5p multicolored 1.00 1.00

Centenary of the Canadian Confederation.

Rock of Cashel A61

**1967, Sept. 25 Wmk. 262** ***Perf. 15***

**236** A61 7p sepia .40 .40
**237** A61 10p Prussian blue 1.00 1.00

International Tourist Year.

One Cent Fenian Fantasy — A62

Swift's Bust and St. Patrick's Cathedral, Dublin — A63

Design: 1sh, 24c Fenian fantasy.

**1967, Oct. 23 Photo.** ***Perf. 15***

**238** A62 5p lt green & slate grn .40 .40
**239** A62 1sh pale pink & gray 1.00 *1.00*

Fenian Rising, centenary. The Fenian fantasy was created by S. Allan Taylor.

**1967, Nov. 30** ***Perf. 15***

Design: 1sh5p, Gulliver, Lilliputian army.

**240** A63 3p gray & sepia .40 .40
**241** A63 1sh5p lt blue & sepia 1.00 1.00

Birth tercentenary of Jonathan Swift (1667-1745), author of Gulliver's Travels.

**Europa Issue**

Golden Key with CEPT Emblem CD11

**1968, Apr. 29 Photo. Wmk. 262**

**242** CD11 7p multicolored *1.00* *1.00*
**243** CD11 1sh5p multicolored *2.75* *2.00*

St. Mary's Cathedral, Limerick A65

**1968, Aug. 26 Engr.** ***Perf. 15***

**244** A65 5p dull blue .40 *.50*
**245** A65 10p olive 1.00 *2.00*

800th anniv. of the founding of St. Mary's Cathedral by Donal Mor O'Brien, last King of Munster.

Countess Markievicz A66

**1968, Sept. 23 Photo. Wmk. 262**

**246** A66 3p black .40 .40
**247** A66 1sh5p dark blue 1.25 1.25

Birth centenary of Countess Constance Markievicz (1868-1927), champion of Irish Independence and first Minister of Labor.

James Connolly — A67

**1968, Sept. 23** ***Perf. 15***

**248** A67 6p brown, dk brn & blk .50 .50
**249** A67 1sh dull grn, grn & blk .70 .50

Birth centenary of James Connolly (1868-1916), founder of the Irish Socialist Party, editor of "Workers' Republic" and Commander of the Irish Citizen Army.

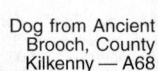

Dog from Ancient Brooch, County Kilkenny — A68

Winged Ox from Lichfield Gospel Book A69

Designs: ½p, 1p, 2p, 3p, 4p, 5p, 6p, Dog. 7p, 8p, 9p, 10p, 1sh, 1sh9p, Stag from ancient bowl, Kent. 2sh6p, 5sh, Winged ox. 10sh, Eagle, from ancient manuscript.

**1968-70 Photo. Wmk. 262** ***Perf. 15***

**250** A68 ½p orange .25 *.50*
**251** A68 1p yellow green .25 *.50*
**252** A68 2p ocher .25 *.50*
**253** A68 3p bright blue .25 *.50*
**254** A68 4p dark red .35 *.50*
**255** A68 5p deep green .40 *1.25*
**256** A68 6p brown .35 .50
*a.* Booklet pane of 6 ('70) 27.50
**257** A68 7p yel & brown .85 *3.25*
**258** A68 8p red org & blk .85 *3.00*
**259** A68 9p ol grn & dk bl .85 *1.50*
**260** A68 10p violet & dk brn .95 *3.00*
**261** A68 1sh dk red brn & brown .75 *2.25*
**262** A68 1sh9p grnsh bl & dk brown .75 *3.00*
**263** A69 2sh6p red org, bl, ol & dull yel 4.50 3.00
**264** A69 5sh ol, gray, bis & yel 5.00 1.40
**265** A69 10sh dk red brn, yel & dp org 11.00 2.50
*Nos. 250-265 (16)* 27.60 27.15

Issued: 2p, 8p, 2sh6p, 10sh, 10/14/68; 6p, 9p, 1sh9p, 5sh, 2/24/69; 4p, 5p, 10p, 1sh, 3/31/69; ½p, 1p, 3p, 7p, 6/9/69.

See Nos. 290-304, 343-359, 395-402, 466-475.

**1970 Coil Stamps** ***Perf. 14x15***

*251a* A68 1p yellow green 2.25 *4.25*
*252a* A68 2p ocher 2.25 *4.25*
*253a* A68 3p bright blue 2.25 *4.25*
*Nos. 251a-253a (3)* 6.75 *12.75*

Human Rights Flame — A70

**1968, Nov. 4 Wmk. 262** ***Perf. 15***

**266** A70 5p black, ocher & gold .30 .30
**267** A70 7p crim, ocher & gold .70 .70

International Human Rights Year.

First Meeting of Irish Parliament A71

**1969, Jan. 21** ***Perf. 15x14½***

**268** A71 6p dark slate green .30 .30
**269** A71 9p dark blue gray .70 .70

50th anniv. of the first meeting of the Dail Eireann at the Mansion House, Dublin, Jan. 21, 1919.

"EUROPA" and "CEPT" CD12

**1969, Apr. 28 Photo.** ***Perf. 15***

**270** CD12 9p ultra, gray & ocher *1.50* *.75*
**271** CD12 1sh9p car, gray & gold *2.50* *1.25*

Europa and CEPT, 10th anniv.

ILO Emblem — A73

**1969, July 14** ***Perf. 15***

**272** A73 6p gray & black .30 .30
**273** A73 9p yellow & black 1.00 1.00

ILO, 50th anniv.

Last Supper and Crucifixion, by Evie Hone A74

***Perf. 15x14½***

**1969, Sept. 1 Photo. Wmk. 262**

**274** A74 1sh multicolored 1.00 *2.50*

The design is after a stained-glass window by Evie Hone (1894-1955) in the Eton College Chapel.

Mahatma Gandhi A75

**1969, Oct. 2** ***Perf. 15***

**275** A75 6p dk yel grn & blk .50 .50
**276** A75 1sh9p yel, grn & black 1.50 *1.50*

Mohandas K. Gandhi (1869-1948), leader in India's fight for independence.

Stylized Bird, Tree and Shamrock A76

**1970, Feb. 23** ***Perf. 15***

**277** A76 6p olive bister & black .25 *.25*
**278** A76 9p violet & black 1.00 *1.00*

Nature Conservation Year.

**Europa Issue**

Interwoven Threads CD13

**1970, May 4 Photo.** ***Perf. 15***

**279** CD13 6p purple & silver *2.00* .30
**280** CD13 9p yel brn & silver *3.00* *1.25*
**281** CD13 1sh9p dk gray & sil *4.50* *1.75*
*Nos. 279-281 (3)* 9.50 3.30

Sailing Boats, by Peter Monamy (1670-1749) A78

**1970, July 13** ***Perf. 15***

**282** A78 4p gold & multi 1.00 1.00

250th anniv. of the Royal Cork Yacht Club.

Madonna of Eire, by Mainie Jellett (1896-1943) A79

Tomás MacCurtain A80

**1970, Sept. 1 Photo.** ***Perf. 15***

**283** A79 1sh violet blue & multi 1.00 1.00

**1970, Oct. 26** ***Perf. 15***

Nos. 285, 287, Terence MacSwiney.

**284** A80 9p violet & black 1.25 1.40
**285** A80 9p violet & black 1.25 1.40
*a.* Pair, #284-285 4.50 *4.75*
**286** A80 2sh9p brt blue & blk 3.00 4.00
**287** A80 2sh9p brt blue & blk 3.50 4.00
*a.* Pair, #286-287 9.50 *12.50*

50th anniv. of the deaths of Tomás MacCurtain (1884-1920) and Terence MacSwiney (1879-1920), lord mayors of Cork, who died during the Irish war of independence.

Kevin Barry
A81

**1970, Nov. 2**

**288** A81 6p olive green .50 .30
**289** A81 1sh2p violet blue 1.50 1.25

50th anniv. of the death of Kevin Barry (1902-1920), who was hanged during the Irish war of independence.

### Decimal Currency Issue

Types of 1968-69 (Numerals only)

Designs: ½p, 1p, 1½p, 2p, 2½p, 3p, 3½p, 4p, No. 298A, Dog. No. 298, 6p, 7p, 7½p, 9p, Stag. 10p, 12p, 20p, Winged ox. 50p, Eagle.

Two types of 10p:
I — Ox outlined in lilac
II — Outlined in brown

**1971-75 Wmk. 262 Photo. *Perf. 15***

**290** A68 ½p yellow green .25 .25
*a.* Booklet pane of 6 30.00
**291** A68 1p bright blue .90 .60
*a.* Booklet pane of 6 5.75
*c.* Bklt. pane of 5 + label ('74) 1.75
**292** A68 1½p brown red .30 .30
**293** A68 2p dark green .40 .40
*b.* Booklet pane of 5 + label ('75) 1.75
**294** A68 2½p sepia .45 .45
*a.* Booklet pane of 6 15.00
**295** A68 3p yel orange .40 .40
**296** A68 3½p deep orange .45 .45
**297** A68 4p violet .30 .30
**298** A68 5p ap grn & brn 1.25 1.25
**298A** A68 5p apple grn ('74) 2.00 1.25
*c.* Booklet pane of 6 ('74) 12.00
*d.* Bklt. pane of 5 + label ('74) 2.50
**299** A68 6p blue gray & dk brown 1.25 1.10
**299A** A68 7p ol green & ind ('74) 3.50 3.50
**300** A68 7½p rose vio & dk brown .60 .80
**301** A68 9p bl grn & blk 1.90 .90
**302** A69 10p lil & multi (I) 16.00 .90
*b.* Type II 20.00 6.50
**302A** A69 12p multi ('74) 1.10 1.25
**303** A69 20p slate & multi 4.00 .90
**304** A69 50p rose brn & multi 11.00 1.25
*Nos. 290-304 (18)* 46.05 16.25

Booklet panes have watermark sideways.
Issued: No. 298A, 7p, 12p, 1/29/74; others, 2/15/71.
See Nos. 343-359, 395-402, 466-475.

**1971-74 Coil Stamps *Perf. 14x15***

*291b* A68 1p bright blue .90 .50
*292a* A68 1½p brown red .25 .50
*293a* A68 2p dark green ('72) .30 .40
*294b* A68 2½p sepia .30 .75
*c.* Strip of 3 (1p, 1½p, 2½p) 2.50 1.50
*297a* A68 4p violet ('72) 1.25 1.00
*b.* Strip of 4 (1½p, 2p, 2½p, 4p) ('72) 2.50 2.00
*298b* A68 5p apple green ('74) 1.25 1.00
*e.* Strip of 4 (2x1½p, 2p, 5p) ('74) 2.50 2.00

Europa Issue, 1971 — CD14

Common Design Type

**1971, May 3 Wmk. 262 *Perf. 15***

**305** CD14 4p apple green & blk 1.00 .25
**306** CD14 6p blue & black 4.00 1.25

John M. Synge — A82

An Island Man, by Jack B. Yeats — A83

**1971, July 19 Photo. *Perf. 15***

**307** A82 4p gray, black & gold .30 .30
**308** A82 10p org, black & gold .90 .90

Birth cent. of John Millington Synge (1871-1909), poet and dramatist.

**1971, Aug. 30 *Perf. 15***

**309** A83 6p multicolored .90 .90

Jack Butler Yeats (1871-1957), painter.

Racial Equality Emblem
A84

Madonna, by John Hughes, Loughrea Cathedral
A85

***Perf. 14x14½***

**1971, Oct. 18 Litho. Unwmk.**

**310** A84 4p red .25 .25
**311** A84 10p black .50 .50

Intl. Year Against Racial Discrimination.

**1971, Nov. 15 Photo. *Perf. 15***

**312** A85 2½p dp bl grn, gold & slate .25 .25
**313** A85 6p ultra, gold & slate .75 .75

Christmas.

"Your Heart is your Health"
A86

**1972, Apr. 7 Photo. Wmk. 262**

**314** A86 2½p gold & brown .35 .35
**315** A86 12p silver & black 2.25 1.50

World Health Day.

### Europa Issue

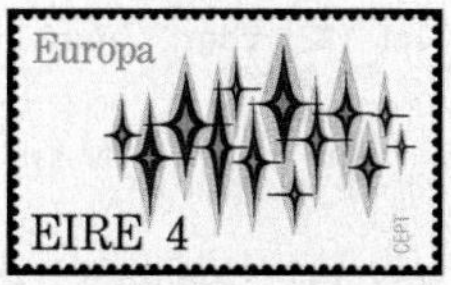

Sparkles, Symbolic of Communications — CD15

**1972, May 1 *Perf. 15***

**316** CD15 4p red, black & sil 3.50 .50
**317** CD15 6p blue, black & sil 9.50 4.00

Dove Soaring Past Rising Moon — A88

**1972, June 1 Photo.**

**318** A88 4p gray blue, org & dk bl .25 .25
**319** A88 6p olive, yel & dk green .90 .75

The patriot dead of 1922-23.

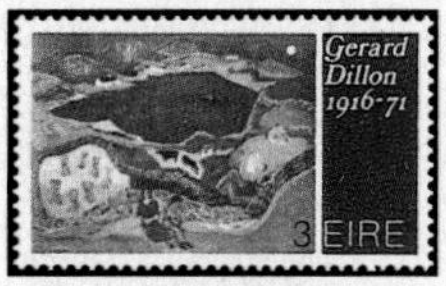

Black Lake, by Gerard Dillon
A89

**1972, July 10 *Perf. 15***

**320** A89 3p indigo & multi .75 .75

Rider from Clonmacnoise Slab and Olympic Rings — A90

**1972, Aug. 28 Photo. Wmk. 262**

**321** A90 3p yellow, black & gold .25 .25
**322** A90 6p salmon, black & gold .90 .90

20th Olympic Games, Munich, Aug. 26-Sept. 11, and 50th anniversary of the Olympic Council of Ireland.

Madonna and Child — A91

Ireland No. 68 — A92

**1972, Oct. 16 Unwmk. *Perf. 15***

**323** A91 2½p dk green & multi .25 .25
**324** A91 4p tan & multi .55 .35
**325** A91 12p multicolored 1.60 1.10
*Nos. 323-325 (3)* 2.40 1.70

Christmas. The design is after a miniature in the Book of Kells, 9th century.

**1972, Dec. 6 Photo.**

**326** A92 6p blue gray & dp grn .75 1.10
*a.* Souvenir sheet of 4 9.50 11.00

50th anniv. of 1st Irish postage stamp.

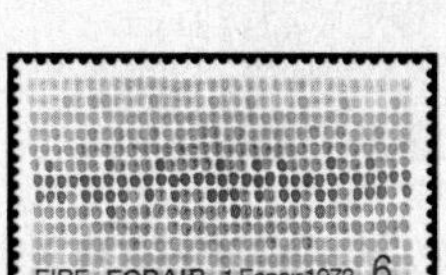

Recurrent Celtic Head Motif — A93

**1973, Jan. 1 Unwmk.**

**327** A93 6p orange & multi .50 .60
**328** A93 12p green & multi 1.50 1.40

Ireland's entry into the European Community.

### Europa Issue

Post Horn of Arrows CD16

**1973, Apr. 30**

**329** CD16 4p bright ultra 1.25 .25
**330** CD16 6p black 4.00 1.75

"Berlin Blues I," by William Scott
A95

***Perf. 15x14½***

**1973, Aug. 9 Photo. Unwmk.**

**331** A95 5p lt blue, blue & dk brn .70 .55

Weather Map of Northwest Europe — A96

**1973, Sept. 4 *Perf. 14½x15***

**332** A96 3½p ultra & multi .30 .25
**333** A96 12p lilac & multi 2.00 1.60

Intl. meteorological cooperation, cent.

Tractor Plowing and Birds
A97

**1973, Oct. 5 *Perf. 15x14½***

**334** A97 5p emerald & multi .35 .35
**335** A97 7p emerald & multi 1.90 1.10

World Plowing Championships, Wellington Bridge, County Wexford, Oct. 1-7.

Flight into Egypt, by Jan de Cock — A98

**1973, Nov. 1 *Perf. 15***

**336** A98 3½p black & multi .25 .25
**337** A98 12p gold & multi 1.25 .90

Christmas.

Rescue, by Bernard Gribble
A99

Design: Ballycotton lifeboat rescuing crew of Daunt Rock Lightship, 1936.

**1974, Mar. 28 Photo. Wmk. 262**

**338** A99 5p multicolored .50 .40

Sesquicentennial of the founding of the Royal National Lifeboat Institution.

### Europa Issue

Edmund Burke, by John Henry Foley — A100

***Perf. 14½x15***

**1974, Apr. 29 Unwmk.**

**339** A100 5p lt ultra & black 1.75 .25
**340** A100 7p lt green & black 9.50 1.25

Oliver Goldsmith, by John Henry Foley — A101

**1974, June 24** **Photo.**

**341** A101 3½p brt citron & blk .30 .25
**342** A101 12p emerald & black 1.75 1.50

Oliver Goldsmith (1728-1774), writer.

### Types of 1968-69

½p, 1p, 2p, 3p, 3½p, 5p, Nos. 350, 352, Dog. Nos. 349, 351, 8p, 9p, Stag. 10p, 15p, 20p, Winged ox. 50p, £1, Eagle.

Two types of 50p: I, fine screen. II, coarse screen.

**1974-78** **Unwmk.** ***Perf. 15***

**343** A68 ½p yel green ('78) .25 .25
**344** A68 1p brt blue ('75) .25 .25
**345** A68 2p dark green ('76) .25 .25
**346** A68 3p ocher ('75) .25 .25
**347** A68 3½p deep orange 4.00 *4.00*
**348** A68 5p apple green .60 .25
**349** A68 6p bl gray & dk brn 1.90 *2.00*
**350** A68 6p blue gray ('75) .50 .45
**351** A68 7p lt ol grn & indigo 2.75 2.75
**352** A68 7p olive green ('75) .70 .70
*a.* Bklt. pane of 5 + label ('77) 14.00 *16.00*
**353** A68 8p brown & dk brn ('75) 1.15 1.15
**354** A68 9p lt bl grn & black ('75) 1.75 .60
**355** A69 10p lil & multi ('75) 2.75 .80
**356** A69 15p multi ('75) 2.00 1.15
**357** A69 20p slate & multi 1.25 .40
**358** A69 50p rose brown & multi, type I ('74) 1.60 .55
*a.* Type II ('83) 3.25 3.25
**359** A69 £1 multi ('75) 4.00 1.50
*Nos. 343-359 (17)* 25.95 17.30

### Coil Stamps

**1977, Mar. 21** ***Perf. 14x15***

*344b* A68 1p bright blue .60 *.70*
*345b* A68 2p dark green .40 *.50*
*348b* A68 5p apple green 1.00 *1.25*
*c.* Strip of 4 (1p, 2x2p, 5p) 2.50 *2.75*

Kitchen Table, by Norah McGuinness A102

**1974, Aug. 19** **Photo.** ***Perf. 14x15***

**360** A102 5p multicolored .75 .75

Rugby A103

**1974, Sept. 2** **Engr.** ***Perf. 15x14***

**361** A103 3½p slate green .70 .70
*a.* 3½ deep slate green 9.00 9.00
**362** A103 12p multicolored 3.00 3.00

Centenary of Irish Rugby Union.

No. 361a was printed from a reengraved plate with more deeply engraved lines. The original printing (No. 361) was considered to be of unsatisfactory quality.

UPU "Postmark" A104

**1974, Oct. 9** **Photo.** ***Perf. 14½x15***

**363** A104 5p emerald & black .30 .30
**364** A104 7p ultra & black .90 .90

Centenary of Universal Postal Union.

Virgin and Child, by Bellini — A105

**1974, Nov. 14**

**365** A105 5p multicolored .45 .30
**366** A105 15p multicolored 1.50 *2.75*

Christmas.

"Peace" — A106

**1975, Mar. 25** **Photo.** ***Perf. 14½x15***

**367** A106 8p dp rose lil & ultra .35 .30
**368** A106 15p ultra & emerald 1.50 1.25

International Women's Year.

### Europa Issue

Castletown Hunt (detail), by Robert Healy A107

**1975, Apr. 28** **Photo.** ***Perf. 15x14½***

**369** A107 7p black *3.00 .25*
**370** A107 9p green *7.00 2.00*

Chipping from the Fringe A108

**1975, June 26** **Photo.** ***Perf. 15x14½***

**371** A108 6p shown .50 .30
**372** A108 9p Putting 2.50 1.60

9th European Amateur Golf Team Championships, Killarney.

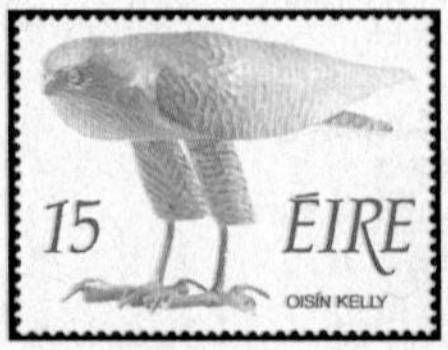


Bird of Prey, by Oisín Kelly A109

**1975, July 28**

**373** A109 15p ocher .90 *1.10*

Nano Nagle and Pupils, Engraving by Charles Turner — A110

**1975, Sept. 1** **Photo.** ***Perf. 14½x15***

**374** A110 5p light blue & black .25 .25
**375** A110 7p buff & black .90 .90

Presentation Order of Nuns, bicentenary.

Clock Tower, St. Ann's Church, Shandon — A111

Designs: 7p, 9p, Holycross Abbey.

**1975, Oct. 6** **Photo.** ***Perf. 12½***

**376** A111 5p sepia .35 .25
**377** A111 6p ultra & multi .50 *1.00*
**378** A111 7p sapphire .70 .35
**379** A111 9p multicolored 1.00 1.00
*Nos. 376-379 (4)* 2.55 2.60

European Architectural Heritage Year.

St. Oliver Plunkett, by Imogen Stuart — A112

Madonna and Child, by Fra Filippo Lippi — A113

**1975, Oct. 13** **Engr.** ***Perf. 14x14½***

**380** A112 7p black .35 .25
**381** A112 15p dull red 1.25 *1.40*

Canonization of Oliver Plunkett (1625-1681), Primate of Ireland.

**1975, Nov. 13** **Photo.** ***Perf. 15***

**382** A113 5p multicolored .40 .30
**383** A113 7p multicolored .50 .30
**384** A113 10p gold & multi 1.00 1.25
*Nos. 382-384 (3)* 1.90 1.85

Christmas.

James Larkin — A114

**1976 Jan. 21** **Photo.** ***Perf. 14½x15***

**385** A114 7p gray & slate grn .25 .25
**386** A114 11p ocher & brown 1.25 1.25

James Larkin (1876-1947), trade union leader.

Bell Making First Call — A115

**1976, Mar. 10** **Photo.** ***Perf. 14½x15***

**387** A115 9p multicolored .25 .25
**388** A115 15p multicolored 1.50 1.40

Centenary of first telephone call by Alexander Graham Bell, March 10, 1876.

13 Stars and Stripes A116

Designs: 8p, 50 stars, and stripes. 9p, 15p, Benjamin Franklin on Albany essay of 1847.

**1976, May 17** **Litho.** ***Perf. 15x14***

**389** A116 7p ultra, sil & red .35 .25
*a.* Silver (inscription) omitted *2,000. 1,200.*
**390** A116 8p ultra, sil & red .45 *.80*
*a.* Silver (inscription) omitted *2,000. 1,200.*
**391** A116 9p bl, sil & ocher .85 .40
*a.* Silver (inscription) omitted *2,000. 1,200.*
**392** A116 15p red, sil & bl .90 .80
*a.* Silver (inscription) omitted *950.00 1,200.*
*b.* Souvenir sheet of 4, #389-392 6.00 *10.00*
*Nos. 389-392 (4)* 2.55 2.25

American Bicentennial. No. 392b exists with silver omitted.

Irish Delft Spirit Barrel — A117

Europa: 11p, Bowl, Irish Delft. Designs show mark of Henry Delamain's Factory, Dublin, both pieces c. 1756.

**1976, July 1** **Photo.** ***Perf. 15x14½***

**393** A117 9p gray & magenta *2.50 .25*
**394** A117 11p gray & blue *4.50 1.00*

### Types of 1968

Designs: 8p, 9p, 9½p, No. 399, Dog. No. 398, 11p, 12p, Stag. 17p, Winged ox.

**1976-79** **Photo.** **Unwmk.** ***Perf. 15***

**395** A68 8p brown .50 .25
**396** A68 9p blue green .60 .25
**397** A68 9½p red ('79) .75 .25
**398** A68 10p lilac & black 1.50 .60
**399** A68 10p purple ('77) .60 .25
**400** A68 11p carmine & black .75 .60
**401** A68 12p emer & black ('77) .95 .25
**402** A69 17p ol, bl & ocher ('77) 1.50 .90
*Nos. 395-402 (8)* 7.15 3.35

The Lobster Pots, by Paul Henry A118

**1976, Aug. 30** **Photo.** ***Perf. 15***

**405** A118 15p gold & multi 1.25 1.00

Paul Henry (1876-1958), birth centenary.

Radio Waves A119

Radio Tower and Waves, Globe — A120

*Perf. 14½x14, 14x14½*

**1976, Oct. 5** **Litho.**
**406** A119 9p brt blue & black .25 .25
**407** A120 11p black & multi 1.00 *1.60*

Irish broadcasting, 50th anniversary.

Nativity, by Lorenzo Monaco A121

**1976, Nov. 11** *Perf. 15x14½*
**408** A121 7p multicolored .30 .25
**409** A121 9p multicolored .50 .30
**410** A121 15p multicolored 1.00 .85
*Nos. 408-410 (3)* 1.80 1.40

Christmas.

Irish Manuscript, 16th Century A122

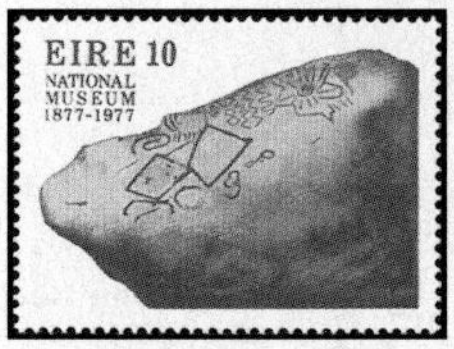

Stone from Newgrange Burial Mound A123

**1977, May 9** **Photo.** *Perf. 15x14½*
**411** A122 8p multicolored .35 .35
**412** A123 10p multicolored .75 .70

Centenaries of National Library (8p) and National Museum (10p).

**Europa Issue**

View of Ballynahinch A124

Lugalla Lake — A125

**1977, June 27** **Litho.** *Perf. 14x14½*
**413** A124 10p multicolored *2.25* .25
**414** A125 12p multicolored *8.00* *1.40*

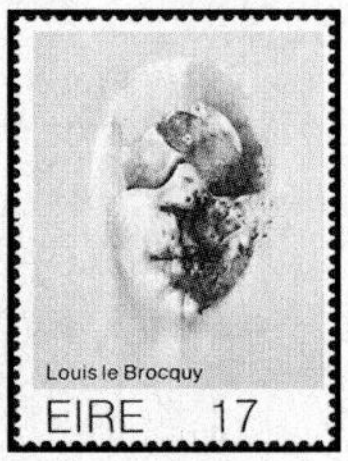

Head, by Louis le Brocquy, 1973 — A126

**1977, Aug. 8** *Perf. 14x14½*
**415** A126 17p multicolored 1.00 1.00

Girl Guide and Tents A127

Design: 17p, Boy Scout and tents.

**1977, Aug. 22** **Photo.** *Perf. 15x14½*
**416** A127 8p multicolored .50 .25
**417** A127 17p multicolored 1.25 *1.25*

European Scout and Guide Conference, Ireland, and 50th anniversary of Catholic Boy Scouts of Ireland.

The Shanachie, by Jack B. Yeats — A128

Eriugena A129

*Perf. 14x14½, 14½x14*

**1977, Sept. 12** **Litho.**
**418** A128 10p black .45 .35
**419** A129 12p black 1.00 *1.25*

Folklore of Ireland Society, 50th anniv. and 1100th death anniv. of Johannes Scottus Eriugena, philospher, poet and mystic.

"Electricity," Mural by Robert Ballagh — A130

Bulls, from Contemporary Coin — A131

Greyhound A132

**Litho. (10p, 17p); Photo. (12p)**
***Perf. 14½x14; 15x14½ (12p)***

**1977, Oct. 10**
**420** A130 10p multicolored .30 .25
**421** A131 12p multicolored .50 .50
**422** A132 17p multicolored .80 .80
*Nos. 420-422 (3)* 1.60 1.55

50th anniversaries of: Electricity Supply Board (10p); Agricultural Credit Act (12p); introduction of greyhound racing (17p).

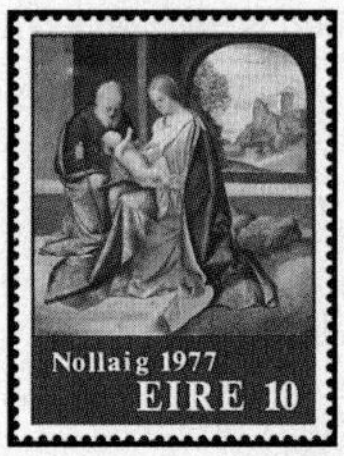

Holy Family, by Giorgione — A133

**1977, Nov. 3** **Photo.** *Perf. 14½x15*
**423** A133 8p multicolored .35 .25
**424** A133 10p multicolored .50 .50
**425** A133 17p multicolored .85 .85
*Nos. 423-425 (3)* 1.70 1.60

Christmas.

Bremen, Junkers Monoplane A134

**1978, Apr. 13** **Litho.** *Perf. 14*
**426** A134 10p ultra & black .30 .30
**427** A134 17p lt brown & black .90 .90

50th anniversary of first East-West transatlantic flight from Baldonnel, County Dublin, to Greenly Island, Gulf of St. Lawrence.

Spring Gentian — A135

Wild flowers: 10p, Strawberry tree. 11p, Large-flowered butterwort. 17p, St. Daboec's heath.

**1978, June 12** **Litho.** *Perf. 14x14½*
**428** A135 8p multicolored .30 .30
**429** A135 10p multicolored .45 .45
**430** A135 11p multicolored .60 *.80*
**431** A135 17p multicolored .75 *1.00*
*Nos. 428-431 (4)* 2.10 *2.55*

Catherine McAuley — A136

Vaccination, lithograph by Manigaud — A137

William Orpen, Self-portrait A138

**1978, Sept. 18** **Litho.** *Perf. 14*
**432** A136 10p multicolored .35 .25
**433** A137 11p multicolored .50 .50
**434** A138 17p multicolored 1.00 .75
*Nos. 432-434 (3)* 1.85 1.50

Catherine McAuley (1778-1841), founder of Sisters of Mercy (10p); eradication of smallpox (11p); William Orpen (1878-1931), painter (17p).

Offshore Oil Well — A139

**1978, Oct. 18** **Litho.** *Perf. 14*
**435** A139 10p multicolored .55 .35

First natural gas coming in off the Irish Coast at Kinsale.

Woodcock on Farthing A140

Coins: 10p, Salmon on florin. 11p, Hen and chicks on penny. 17p, Horse on half crown.

**1978, Oct. 26** **Photo.** *Perf. 15x14½*
**436** A140 8p multicolored .45 .25
**437** A140 10p multicolored .55 .25
**438** A140 11p multicolored .65 .60
**439** A140 17p multicolored 1.10 1.00
*Nos. 436-439 (4)* 2.75 2.10

Irish currency, 50th anniversary.

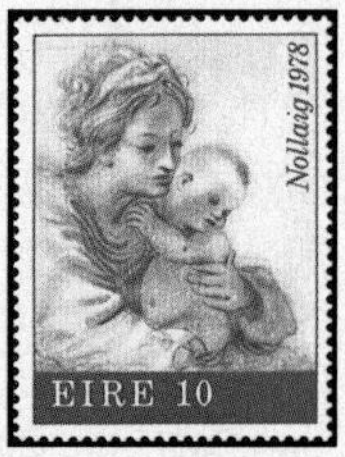

Virgin and Child, by Guercino — A141

**1978, Nov. 16** **Photo.** *Perf. 14½x15*
**440** A141 8p multicolored .25 .25
**441** A141 10p multicolored .35 .30
**442** A141 17p multicolored .65 .55
*Nos. 440-442 (3)* 1.25 1.10

Christmas.

Conolly Folly, Castletown
A142

Europa: 11p, Belvedere on Tower Hill at Dromoland.

**1978, Dec. 6** *Perf. 15x14½*

**443** A142 10p brown *2.00 .25*
**444** A142 11p dull green *8.00 1.00*

Cross-country Runners — A143

**1979, Aug. 20 Litho.** ***Perf. 14½x14***

**445** A143 8p multicolored .35 .35

7th World Cross-country Championships, Greenpark Racecourse, Limerick, March 25.

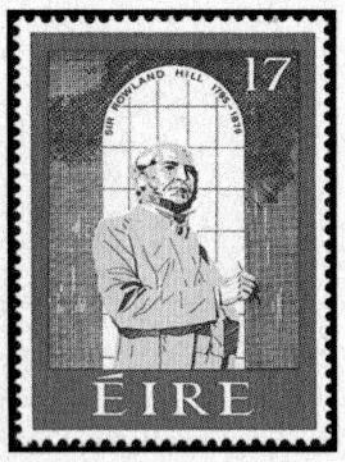


Rowland Hill, Bronze Statue — A144

**1979, Aug. 20** ***Perf. 14x14½***

**446** A144 17p multicolored .50 .50

Sir Rowland Hill (1795-1879), originator of penny postage.

"European Communities" (7 Languages)
A145

**1979, Aug. 20 Photo.** ***Perf. 14½x15***

**447** A145 10p lt greenish gray .35 .35
**448** A145 11p rose lilac .45 .45

European Parliament, first direct elections, June 7-10.

Wren
A146

Birds: 10p, Great crested grebe. 11p, Greenland white-fronted geese. 17p, Peregrine falcon.

**1979, Aug. 30 Litho.** ***Perf. 14½x14***

**449** A146 8p multicolored .35 .25
**450** A146 10p multicolored .50 .50
**451** A146 11p multicolored .60 .60
**452** A146 17p multicolored 1.00 1.00
*Nos. 449-452 (4)* 2.45 2.35

A Happy Flower
A147

Children's Drawings: 11p, "Me and my skipping rope," vert. 17p, "Swans on a lake."

***Perf. 14½x14, 14x14½***

**1979, Sept. 13** **Litho.**

**453** A147 10p multicolored .40 .30
**454** A147 11p multicolored .70 .45
**455** A147 17p multicolored 1.00 .60
*Nos. 453-455 (3)* 2.10 1.35

International Year of the Child.

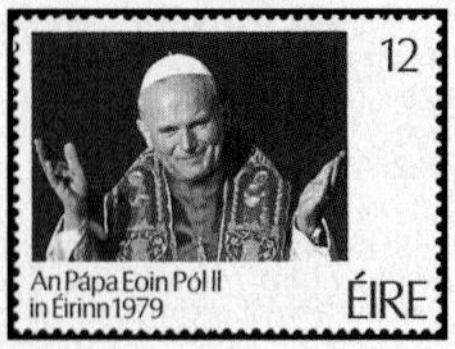


Pope John Paul II
A148

**1979, Sept. 29 Litho.** ***Perf. 14½x14***

**456** A148 12p multicolored .60 .45

Visit of Pope John Paul II to Ireland.

Hospitaller Brother Teaching Child
A149

**1979, Oct. 4**

**457** A149 9½p rose & black .55 .35

Hospitaller Order of St. John of God, centenary in Ireland.

Windmill and Sun — A150

**1979, Oct. 4 Photo.** ***Perf. 14½x15***

**458** A150 11p multicolored .55 .45

Energy conservation.

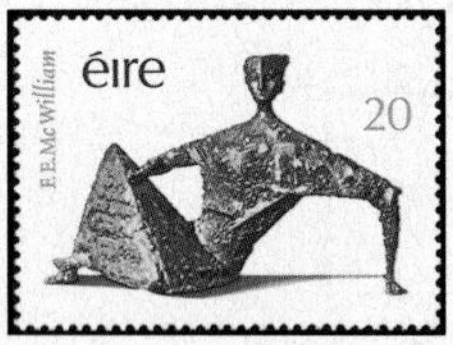


"Seated Figure," by F.E. McWilliam
A151

**1979, Oct. 4 Litho.** ***Perf. 14½x14***

**459** A151 20p multicolored 1.25 .75

Patrick Pearse
A152

**1979, Nov. 10 Photo.** ***Perf. 15x14½***

**460** A152 12p multicolored .55 .35

Patrick Henry Pearse (1879-1916), Irish writer and leader of Easter Rebellion.

Mother and Child, Panel, Domnach Argid Shrine — A153

**1979, Nov. 15 Photo.** ***Perf. 14½x15***

**461** A153 9½p multicolored .40 .25
**462** A153 20p multicolored 1.00 .85

Christmas.

## Europa Issue

Bianconi Long Car, 1836
A154

Laying Transatlantic Cable, Steamer William Cory, 1866 — A155

**1979, Dec. 6 Litho.** ***Perf. 15x14***

**463** A154 12p multicolored *1.50 .40*
**464** A155 13p multicolored *5.50 .85*

## Type of 1968

Designs: 13p, 16p, Stag; others, Dog.

**1980-82 Photo.** ***Perf. 15***

**466** A68 12p green .60 .60
**467** A68 13p red brown & dk brn 1.15 .30
**468** A68 15p ultra 1.00 .50
**469** A68 16p olive green & blk 1.15 .50

**Litho.**

***Perf. 14x15***

**470** A68 18p dull red brn ('81) 1.00 .60
**471** A68 19p dull blue ('81) 1.15 .55
**472** A68 22p gray blue ('81) 1.00 .25
**473** A68 24p brown olive ('81) 1.40 .40
**474** A68 26p bluish green ('82) 1.40 .65
**475** A68 29p dp rose lilac ('82) 1.60 .80
*Nos. 466-475 (10)* 11.45 5.15

Issued: 12p, 13p, 3/26/80; 15p, 16p, 7/10/80; 18p, 19p, 4/27/81; 22p, 9/1/81; 24p, 10/29/81; 26p, 29p, 4/1/82.

St. Jean Baptiste de la Salle — A156

**1980, Mar. 19 Litho.** ***Perf. 14x15***

**477** A156 12p multicolored .55 .35

The Brothers of the Christian School (founded by St. Jean Baptiste), centenary in Ireland.

## Europa Issue

George Bernard Shaw, by Alick Ritchie
A157

Oscar Wilde, by Toulouse-Lautrec
A158

**1980, May 7 Litho.** ***Perf. 14x15***

**478** A157 12p multicolored *2.50 .30*
**479** A158 13p multicolored *2.50 .65*

Irish Ermine — A159

**1980, July 30 Litho.** ***Perf. 14x15***

**480** A159 12p shown .35 .30
**481** A159 15p Irish hare .40 .35
**482** A159 16p Fox .40 .30
**483** A159 25p Red deer .90 .90
*a.* Miniature sheet of 4, #480-483 2.50 *3.50*
*Nos. 480-483 (4)* 2.05 1.85

Bodhran Drum and Whistle Players — A160

**1980, Sept. 25 Photo.** ***Perf. 14x15***

**484** A160 12p shown .40 .25
**485** A160 15p Piper, Uilleann pipes .60 .45
**486** A160 25p Irish jig .75 .65
*Nos. 484-486 (3)* 1.75 1.35

Sean O'Casey (1880-1964), Playwright
A161

**1980, Oct. 23 Litho.** ***Perf. 14x14½***

**487** A161 12p multicolored .35 .25

Gold Painting No. 57, by Patrick Scott — A162

**1980, Oct. 23** ***Perf. 14x15***

**488** A162 25p multicolored .75 .55

A163

**1980, Dec. 4 Photo.** ***Perf. 15x14½***

**489** A163 12p multicolored .30 .25
**490** A163 15p multicolored .55 .40
**491** A163 25p multicolored .95 .70
*Nos. 489-491 (3)* 1.80 1.35

Christmas.

A164

Scientists and Inventions: 12p, Robert Boyle (1627-1691), and Air Pump, 1659. 15p, Harry Ferguson (1884-1960), hydraulic tractor, 1936. 16p, Charles Parsons (1854-1931), Parsons' turbine, 1884. 25p, John Holland (1841-1914), Holland submarine, 1878.

**1981, Mar. 12 Litho.** ***Perf. 14x14½***

**492** A164 12p multicolored .25 .25
**493** A164 15p multicolored .35 .30
**494** A164 16p multicolored .45 .40
**495** A164 25p multicolored .95 .80
*Nos. 492-495 (4)* 2.00 1.75

The Cock and the Pot, Rubbing, 1841 — A165

Europa: 19p, The Scales of Judgment, rubbing, 1827.

**1981, May 4 Litho.** ***Perf. 14½x15***

**496** A165 18p multicolored *2.00* .30
**497** A165 19p multicolored *3.50* *.50*

Hiking A166

***Perf. 14x15, 15x14***

**1981, June 24 Litho.**

**498** A166 15p Bicycling, vert. .25 .25
**499** A166 18p shown .45 .45
**500** A166 19p Mountain climbing .50 .50
**501** A166 30p Rock climbing, vert. .85 .85
*Nos. 498-501 (4)* 2.05 2.05

Youth Hostel Assn., 50th anniv.

Jeremiah O'Donovan Rossa (1831-1915), Journalist — A167

Railway Embankment, by William John Leech (1881-1968) — A168

***Perf. 14½x15, 15x14½***

**1981, Aug. 31**

**502** A167 15p multicolored .45 .55
**503** A168 30p multicolored 1.00 1.00

James Hoban (1762-1831), White House Architect — A169

**1981, Sept. 29** ***Perf. 15x14***

**504** A169 18p multicolored .75 .70

Same design used for US Nos. 1935-1936.

Draft Horse King of Diamonds A170

Famous Horses: No. 505, Show-jumper Boomerang. No. 506, Steeplechaser Arkle. 24p, Flat racer Ballymoss. 36p, Connemara pony Coosheen Finn.

**1981, Oct. 23 Litho.** ***Perf. 15x14***

**505** A170 18p multicolored .70 .55
**506** A170 18p multicolored .70 .55
***a.*** Pair, #505-506 1.50 2.50
**507** A170 22p multicolored .85 .85
**508** A170 24p multicolored .70 *.85*
**509** A170 36p multicolored 1.40 1.40
*Nos. 505-509 (5)* 4.35 4.20

Nativity, by Federico Barocci — A171

**1981, Nov. 19 Litho.** ***Perf. 14x15***

**510** A171 18p multicolored .40 .25
**511** A171 22p multicolored .55 .35
**512** A171 36p multicolored 1.05 .70
*Nos. 510-512 (3)* 2.00 1.30

Christmas 1981.

A172

**1981, Dec. 10 Litho.** ***Perf. 14x14½***

**513** A172 18p multicolored .65 .55

Land Law Act centenary.

250th Anniv. of Royal Dublin Society A173

**1981, Dec. 10** ***Perf. 14½x14***

**514** A173 22p multicolored .75 .60

50th Anniv. of Killarney Natl. Park A174

**1982, Feb. 26 Litho.** ***Perf. 14½x14***

**515** A174 18p Upper Lake .55 .35
**516** A174 36p Eagle's Nest .95 1.25

The Stigmatization of St. Francis, by Sassetta — A175

Francis Makemie, Old Presbyterian Church, Ramelton — A176

**1982, Apr. 2** ***Perf. 14x15, 15x14***

**517** A175 22p multicolored .60 .50
**518** A176 24p brown .90 .90

800th birth anniv. of St. Francis of Assisi; 300th anniv. of Francis Makemie's ordination (father of American Presbyterianism).

**Europa Issue**

Great Famine of 1845-50 — A177

Conversion of Ireland to Christianity (St. Patrick and his Followers, by Vincenzo Valdre) A178

**1982, May 4**

**519** A177 26p tan & brown *5.50* *.75*
**520** A178 29p multicolored *7.50* *4.00*

Padraic O'Connaire (1882-1928), Writer — A179

Designs: 26p, James Joyce (1882-1941), writer and poet, by Brancusi. 29p, John Field (1782-1837), Composer and pianist, Nocturne score. 44p, Charles Joseph Kickham (1828-1882), journalist and writer. 29p, 44p by Colin Harrison.

**1982, June 16 Litho.** ***Perf. 14x15***

**521** A179 22p blue & black .45 .40
**522** A179 26p black & brown .70 .70
**523** A179 29p black & blue 1.00 1.00
**524** A179 44p gray green & black 1.60 1.60
*Nos. 521-524 (4)* 3.75 3.70

Porbeagle Shark A180

**1982, July 29** ***Perf. 15x14***

**525** A180 22p shown .55 .55
**526** A180 22p Oyster .55 .55
**527** A180 26p Salmon .85 .55
**528** A180 29p Dublin Bay prawn 1.10 1.10
*Nos. 525-528 (4)* 3.05 2.75

Currach A181

**1982, Sept. 21** ***Perf. 15x14, 14x15***

**529** A181 22p shown .55 .45
**530** A181 22p Galway hooker, vert. .55 .45
**531** A181 26p Asgard II training ship .85 .75
**532** A181 29p Howth 17-footer, vert. 1.20 1.20
*Nos. 529-532 (4)* 3.15 2.85

The Irish House of Commons, by Francis Wheatley A182

**1982, Oct. 14 Litho.** ***Perf. 14½x14***

**533** A182 22p multicolored .45 .45

Bicentenary of Grattan's Parliament.

A183

Eamon de Valera (1882-1975), President, by Robert Ballagh.

**1982, Oct. 14** ***Perf. 14x14½***

**534** A183 26p multicolored .60 .60

A183a — 535

Madonna and Child, by Andrea della Robbia (1435-1525)

**1982, Nov. 11 Litho.** ***Perf. 14½x15***

**535** A183a 22p lt violet & multi .45 .45
**536** A183a 26p gray & multi .60 .60

Christmas.

A184

A185

Killarney Cathedral, 1855 — A186

Designs: 1p-5p, Central Pavilion, Dublin Botanical Gardens. 6p, 7p, 10p, 12p, Dr. Steeven's Hospital, Dublin. 15p, 20p, 22p, Aughnanure Castle, Oughterard, 16th cent. 23p, 26p, Cormac's Chapel, 1134. 29p, 30p, St. Mac Dara's Church. 50p, Casino, Marino. £1, Cahir Castle, 15th century. £5 Central Bus Station, Dublin, 1953.
50p, £1, £5 horiz.

**1982-90 Litho. *Perf. 14x15, 15x14***

**537** A184 1p dull blue .30 .25
**538** A184 2p gray green .30 .25
**539** A184 3p black .30 .25
**540** A184 4p rose lake .30 .25
*a.* Perf. 13½ on 3 or 4 sides .95 .25
**541** A184 5p brown .45 .30
**542** A184 6p dull blue .45 .30
**543** A184 7p gray green .85 .45
**544** A184 10p black .85 .45
**545** A184 12p rose lake .85 .45
**546** A185 15p gray green 1.20 .55
**547** A185 20p rose lake 1.20 .55
**548** A185 22p dull blue 1.20 .55
*a.* Bklt. pane of 7+label (3 4p, 4 22p) ('83) 9.00
**549** A185 23p gray green 1.50 1.00
**550** A185 26p black 1.90 1.00
*a.* Bklt. pane, 2 ea 2p, 22p, 26p 10.50
*b.* Bklt. pane, 4 ea 2p, 22p, 26p 21.00
*c.* Bklt. pane, 3 4p, 5 22p, 4 26p ('88) 32.50
*d.* Perf. 13½ on 3 sides 4.50 2.00
**551** A184 29p gray green 2.25 1.25
**552** A184 30p black 1.40 .60
*a.* Perf. 13½ on 3 or 4 sides 2.50 .60

***Perf. 14x15, 15x14***

**553** A186 44p gray & black 2.25 1.25
**554** A186 50p gray & dull blue 2.25 .75
**555** A186 £1 gray & brown 7.50 2.50
**556** A186 £5 gray & rose lake 20.00 9.50
*Nos. 537-556 (20)* 47.30 22.45

Stamps from No. 550c imprinted "Booklet Stamp" in green on reverse side. No. 550c sold for £2.
Issued: 4p, 6p-7p, 20p, 23p, 30p, 50p, 3/16/83; 1p-3p, 5p, 10p-15p, 7/6/83; Nos. 540a, 550d, 552a, 5/3/90; others, 12/15/82.
See Nos. 638-645, 803a, 804b.

Dublin Chamber of Commerce Bicentenary A187

Bank of Ireland Bicentenary — A188

**1983, Feb. 23 Litho.**

**557** A187 22p Ouzel Galley goblet .45 .65
**558** A188 26p Bank .70 .85

Padraig Siochfhradha (1883-1964), Writer — A189

Boys' Brigade Centenary A190

**1983, Apr. 7 Litho. *Perf. 14x14½***

**559** A189 26p multicolored .60 .45
**560** A190 29p multicolored 1.00 .75

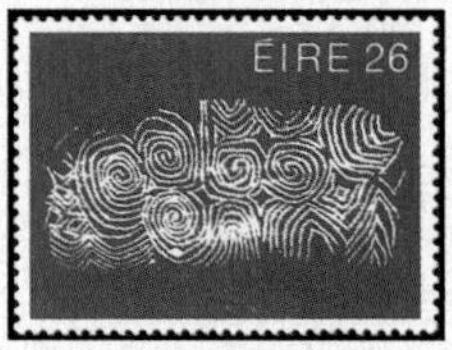

Europa A191

Design: 26p, Newgrange Winter Solstice, Neolithic Pattern Drawing by Louis le Brocquy. 29p, Quaternion formula, by William Rowan Hamilton (1805-1865).

**1983, May 4 Litho. *Perf. 14½x14***

**561** A191 26p black & gold *3.50* .65
**562** A191 29p multicolored *9.00 6.00*

Kerry Blue Terrier A192

Drawings of dogs by Wendy Walsh.

**1983, June 23**

**563** A192 22p shown .70 .70
**564** A192 26p Irish wolfhound .85 .85
**565** A192 26p Irish water spaniel .85 .85
**566** A192 29p Irish terrier 1.00 1.00
**567** A192 44p Irish setters 1.50 1.50
*a.* Miniature sheet of 5, #563-567 8.00 8.00
*Nos. 563-567 (5)* 4.90 4.90

Sean Mac Diarmada (1883-1916), Nationalist A193

Society for the Prevention of Cruelty to Animals A194

Society of St. Vincent de Paul Sesquicentennial A195

Industrial Credit Co., 50th Anniv. A196

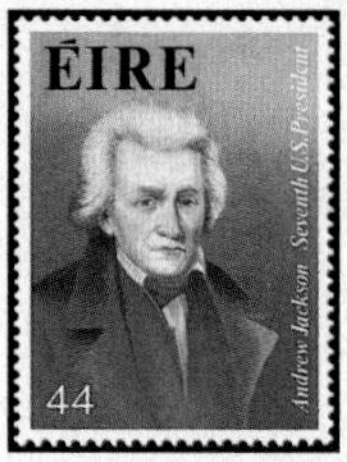

US Pres. Andrew Jackson (1767-1845) A197

***Perf. 14x14½, 14½x14***

**1983, Aug. 11**

**568** A193 22p multicolored .60 .50
**569** A194 22p multicolored .60 .50
**570** A195 26p multicolored .75 .70
**571** A196 26p multicolored .75 .70
**572** A197 44p gray 1.75 1.40
*Nos. 568-572 (5)* 4.45 3.80

WCY — A198

**1983, Sept. 15 Litho. *Perf. 14x15***

**573** A198 22p Mailman 1.00 1.00
**574** A198 29p Dish antenna 1.25 1.25

Handicrafts A199

**1983, Oct. 13 Litho. *Perf. 14x15***

**575** A199 22p Weaving .70 .45
**576** A199 26p Basketweaving .90 .50
**577** A199 29p Irish crochet 1.10 .70
**578** A199 44p Harpmaking 2.25 1.25
*Nos. 575-578 (4)* 4.95 2.90

La Natividad by Rogier van der Weyden — A200

**1983, Nov. 30 Litho. *Perf. 14x14½***

**579** A200 22p multicolored .60 .35
**580** A200 26p multicolored 1.20 .90

Christmas.

Irish Railways Sesquicentenary — A201

Locomotives: 23p, Princess, Dublin and Kingstown Railway. 26p, Macha, Great Southern Railways. 29p, Kestrel, Great Northern Railway. 44p, Link-Hoffman railcar, Coras Iompair Eireann.

**1984, Jan. 30 *Perf. 14½x14***

**581** A201 23p multicolored .95 .95
**582** A201 26p multicolored .55 .55
**583** A201 29p multicolored 1.10 1.10
**584** A201 44p multicolored 1.90 1.90
*a.* Souvenir sheet of 4, #581-584 6.00 *6.50*
*Nos. 581-584 (4)* 4.50 4.50

Private Overprints
Nos. 584a, 684a, 708a, 708b, 803a, 804a, 811a, 826a, 847a, 855a, 876b, and others, exist with privately applied show overprints.

Local Trees A202

**1984, Mar. 1 Litho. *Perf. 15x14***

**585** A202 22p Irish whitebeam .65 .55
**586** A202 26p Irish yew .80 .70
**587** A202 29p Irish willow 1.25 1.00
**588** A202 44p Birch 1.75 1.75
*Nos. 585-588 (4)* 4.45 4.00

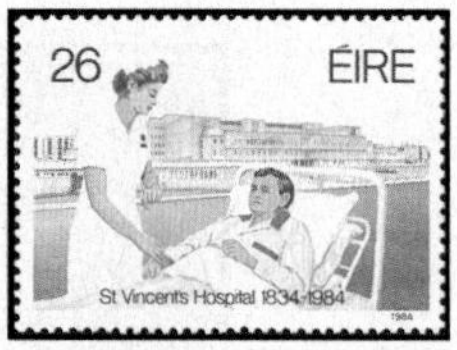

St. Vincent's Hospital, Dublin, Sesquicentenary — A203

Royal College of Surgeons in Ireland Bicentenary — A204

**1984, Apr. 12 Litho.**

**589** A203 26p multicolored .90 .70
**590** A204 44p multicolored 1.60 1.40

2nd European Parliament Election A205

**1984, May 10 Litho. *Perf. 15x14***

**591** A205 26p multicolored 1.50 1.40

Europa (1959-84) A206

**1984, May 10**

**592** A206 26p multicolored *4.75 3.00*
**593** A206 29p multicolored *10.00 3.75*

John McCormack (1884-1945), Singer — A207

**1984, June 6 Litho. *Perf. 14x14½***

**594** A207 22p multicolored 1.00 1.00

See US No. 2090.

1984 Summer Olympics A208

**1984, June 21 Litho. *Perf. 14½x14***

**595** A208 22p Hammer throw .60 .50
**596** A208 26p Hurdles .90 .70
**597** A208 29p Running 1.00 .95
*Nos. 595-597 (3)* 2.50 2.15

Gaelic Athletic Assoc. Centenary A209

**1984, Aug. 23 Litho. *Perf. 14x15***

**598** A209 22p Hurlers .80 .80
**599** A209 26p Soccer, vert. 1.25 1.25

Mayoral City of Galway, 500th Anniv. — A210

St. Brendan (484-577) A211

**1984, Sept. 18 *Perf. 14x15, 15x14***

**600** A210 26p Medal .60 .60
**601** A211 44p Portrait, manuscript 1.40 1.40

Post Office Bicentenary — A212

**1984, Oct. 19 *Perf. 15x14***

**602** A212 26p Handing sealed letter 1.00 1.00

A213

Virgin And Child by Sassoferrato A214

***Perf. 14½x14, 14x14½***

**1984, Nov. 26 Litho.**

**603** A213 17p multicolored .40 .40
**604** A214 22p multicolored .70 .70
**605** A214 26p multicolored 1.20 1.20
*Nos. 603-605 (3)* 2.30 2.30

Christmas.

Love A215

A216

**1985, Jan. 31 Litho. *Perf. 15x14***

**606** A215 22p Heart-shaped balloon .50 .50
**607** A216 26p Bouquet of hearts 1.10 1.10

Dunsink Observatory, 200th Anniv. — A217

Cork City Charter, 800th Anniv. A218

Royal Irish Academy, 200th Anniv. — A219

1st Manned Flight in Ireland, 200th Anniv. — A220

**1985, Mar. 14 Litho.**

**608** A217 22p black .55 .55
**609** A218 26p multicolored .75 .75
**610** A219 37p multicolored 1.25 1.25
**611** A220 44p multicolored 1.40 1.40
*Nos. 608-611 (4)* 3.95 3.95

Butterflies A221

**1985, Apr. 11 Litho. *Perf. 14x15***

**612** A221 22p Common blue 1.40 1.25
**613** A221 26p Red admiral 1.50 1.40
**614** A221 28p Brimstone 1.70 1.40
**615** A221 44p Marsh fritillary 2.50 2.25
*Nos. 612-615 (4)* 7.10 6.30

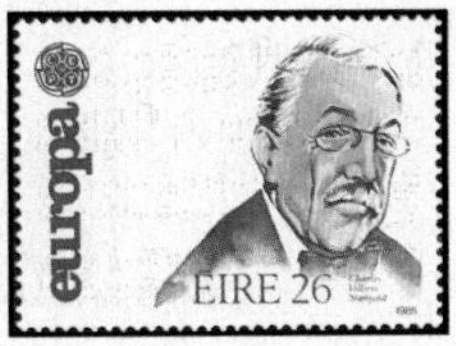


Europa A222

26p, Charles Villiers Stanford (1852-1924), composer. 37p, Turlough O'Carolan (1670-1738), Composer.

**1985, May 16 Litho. *Perf. 15x14***

**616** A222 26p multicolored *3.50* .*75*
**617** A222 37p multicolored *8.50* 6.50

European Music Year — A223

Composers: No. 618, Giuseppe Domenico Scarlatti (1685-1757). No. 619, George Frideric Handel (1685-1759). No. 620, Johann Sebastian Bach (1685-1750).

**1985, May 16 Litho. *Perf. 14x15***

**618** A223 22p multicolored 1.50 *2.10*
**619** A223 22p multicolored 1.50 *2.10*
*a.* Pair, #618-619 4.00 4.50
**620** A223 26p multicolored 1.50 *2.10*
*Nos. 618-620 (3)* 4.50 6.30

Irish UN Defense Forces in the Congo, 1960 A224

Thomas Ashe (1885-1917), Patriot and Educator — A225

Bishop George Berkeley (1685-1753), Philosopher and Educator — A226

***Perf. 15x14, 14x15***

**1985, June 20 Litho.**

**621** A224 22p multicolored .75 .75
**622** A225 26p multicolored .85 .85
**623** A226 44p multicolored 1.40 1.40
*Nos. 621-623 (3)* 3.00 3.00

Irish forces as part of the UN Defense Forces, 25th anniv. (22p).

Intl. Youth Year — A227

**1985, Aug. 1 Litho.**

**624** A227 22p multi, horiz. .75 .75
**625** A227 26p multicolored .95 .95

**Architecture Type of 1982**

Designs: 24p, 39p, Cormac's Chapel. 28p, 32p, 37p, St. Mac Dara's Church. 46p, Cahir Castle. £1, Killarney Cathedral. £2, Casino, Marino. 46p, £2, horiz.

***Perf. 15x14, 14x15 (A184, No. 644)***

**1985-88 Litho.**

**638** A185 24p brown 1.40 .70
**639** A184 28p rose lake 1.75 .40
*a.* Bklt. pane, 4 2p, 2 24p, 1 4p, 5 28p ('88) 8.00
*c.* Bklt. pane, 2 2p, 3 4p, 3 24p, 4 28p ('88) 8.50
**640** A184 32p brown 2.00 1.00
**641** A184 37p dull blue 3.50 3.50
**642** A185 39p rose lake 3.50 2.40
**643** A186 46p gray & gray grn 3.75 2.75
**644** A186 £1 gray & dull bl 6.50 2.00
**645** A186 £2 gray & gray grn 12.50 6.25
*Nos. 638-645 (8)* 34.90 19.00

Issued: 24p, 28p, 37p, £1, June 27, 1985; 32p, 39p, 46p, May 1, 1986; £2, July 26, 1988.

Industrial Innovations A228

Institution of Engineers, 150th Anniv. A229

**1985, Oct. 3 Litho. *Perf. 15x14***

**646** A228 22p Computer technology .60 .45
**647** A228 26p Peat production .85 .85
**648** A229 44p The Key Man, by Sean Keating 1.50 1.25
*Nos. 646-648 (3)* 2.95 2.55

Candle, Holly — A230

Virgin and Child in a Landscape, by Adrian van Ijsenbrandt A231

Christmas: No. 651, The Holy Family, by Murillo. 26p, Adoration of the Shepherds, by Louis Le Nain, horiz.

*Perf. 14x15, 15x14*

**1985, Nov. 26** **Litho.**

| | | | | |
|---|---|---|---|---|
| **649** | A230 22p shown | | 1.00 | 1.00 |
| **650** | A231 22p shown | | 1.00 | 1.00 |
| **651** | A231 22p multicolored | | 1.00 | 1.00 |
| *a.* | Pair, #650-651 | | 3.00 | 3.00 |
| **652** | A231 26p multicolored | | 1.40 | 1.40 |
| | *Nos. 649-652 (4)* | | 4.40 | 4.40 |

No. 649 was issued in discount sheets of 16 that sold for £3. Value $16.

Love — A232

**1986, Jan. 30** *Perf. 14x15*

| | | | |
|---|---|---|---|
| **653** | A232 22p shown | 1.00 | .80 |
| **654** | A232 26p Heart-shaped mailbox | 1.00 | 1.00 |

Ferns — A233

**1986, Mar. 20** **Litho.** *Perf. 14½x15*

| | | | |
|---|---|---|---|
| **655** | A233 24p Hart's tongue | .75 | .35 |
| **656** | A233 28p Rusty-back | 1.00 | .90 |
| **657** | A233 46p Killarney | 1.75 | 1.75 |
| | *Nos. 655-657 (3)* | 3.50 | 3.00 |

Europa — A234

**1986, May 1** *Perf. 14x15, 15x14*

| | | | |
|---|---|---|---|
| **658** | A234 28p Industry and nature | *7.50* | *1.25* |
| **659** | A234 39p Hedgerows, horiz. | *25.00* | *6.00* |

Aer Lingus, 50th Anniv. A235

**1986, May 27** *Perf. 15x14*

| | | | |
|---|---|---|---|
| **660** | A235 28p Jet, 1986 | 1.40 | 1.00 |
| **661** | A235 46p The Eagle, 1936 | 2.00 | 2.00 |

Inland Waterways A236

**1986, May 27** *Perf. 15x14, 14x15*

| | | | |
|---|---|---|---|
| **662** | A236 24p Robertstown Grand Canal | .90 | .90 |
| **663** | A236 28p Fishing, County Mayo, vert. | 1.25 | 1.25 |
| **664** | A236 30p Yachting, River Shannon | 1.50 | 1.50 |
| | *Nos. 662-664 (3)* | 3.65 | 3.65 |

British & Irish Steam Packet Co., 150th Anniv. A237

**1986, July 10** *Perf. 15x14*

| | | | |
|---|---|---|---|
| **665** | A237 24p Steamer Severn, 1836 | 1.25 | 1.00 |
| **666** | A237 28p M.V. Leinster, 1986 | 1.75 | 1.75 |

Lighthouses A238

**1986, July 10** *Perf. 14½x15*

| | | | |
|---|---|---|---|
| **667** | A238 24p Kish, helicopter | 1.40 | 1.40 |
| **668** | A238 30p Fastnet | 2.25 | 2.25 |

Dublin Council of Trade Unions, Cent. — A239

Arthur Griffith (1871-1922), Statesman A240

Women in Society, Construction Surveyor — A241

A242

Intl. Peace Year A242a

*Perf. 14½x15, 14x15 (#670, 672), 15x14½, 15x14*

**1986, Aug. 21**

| | | | |
|---|---|---|---|
| **669** | A239 24p multicolored | .70 | .55 |
| **670** | A240 28p multicolored | .90 | .80 |
| **671** | A241 28p multicolored | .90 | .80 |
| **672** | A242 30p multi, vert. | 1.00 | 1.00 |
| **673** | A242a 46p shown | 1.50 | 1.50 |
| | *Nos. 669-673 (5)* | 5.00 | 4.65 |

See Nos. 699, 711, 749, 807, 836.

William Mulready (1786-1863), Letter Sheet Designer — A243

Carriages by Charles Bianconi (1786-1875) — A244

*Perf. 15x14, 14x15*

**1986, Oct. 2** **Litho.**

| | | | |
|---|---|---|---|
| **674** | A243 24p multicolored | .70 | .70 |
| **675** | A244 28p multi, vert. | 1.25 | 1.25 |
| **676** | A244 39p shown | 1.75 | 1.75 |
| | *Nos. 674-676 (3)* | 3.70 | 3.70 |

Adoration of the Shepherds, by Francesco Pascucci A245

Adoration of the Magi, by Frans Francken III (1542-1616) A246

**1986, Nov. 20** *Perf. 15x14, 14½x15*

| | | | |
|---|---|---|---|
| **677** | A245 21p multicolored | .75 | .75 |
| **678** | A246 28p multicolored | 1.25 | 1.25 |

Christmas. No. 677 was issued in discount sheets of 12 that sold for £2.50. Vaue $30.

Love A247

*Perf. 15x14, 14x15*

**1987, Jan. 27** **Litho.**

| | | | |
|---|---|---|---|
| **679** | A247 24p Flowers, butterfly | .85 | .85 |
| **680** | A247 28p Postman, vert. | 1.25 | 1.25 |

Trolleys A248

**1987, Mar. 4** **Litho.** *Perf. 15x14*

| | | | |
|---|---|---|---|
| **681** | A248 24p Cork Electric | .70 | .70 |
| **682** | A248 28p Dublin Standard | .85 | .85 |
| **683** | A248 30p Howth (G.N.R.) | 1.00 | 1.00 |
| **684** | A248 46p Galway Horse | 1.50 | 1.50 |
| *a.* | Miniature sheet of 4, #681-684 | 5.50 | 5.50 |
| | *Nos. 681-684 (4)* | 4.05 | 4.05 |

See note following No. 584.

Waterford Chamber of Commerce, 200th Anniv. A249

Muintir Na Tire, 50th Anniv. A250

Trinity College Botanical Gardens, Dublin, 300th Anniv. — A251

Medical Missionaries of Mary, 50th Anniv. — A252

Anniversaries and events: 24p, Three ships, Chamber crest. 28p, Canon Hayes (1887-1957), founder, and symbols of Muintir Na Tire activities. 30p, College crest, Calceolaria burbidgei. 39p, Intl. Missionary Training Hospital, Drogheda, and Mother Mary Martin.

*Perf. 15x14, 14x15*

**1987, Apr. 9** **Litho.**

| | | | |
|---|---|---|---|
| **685** | A249 24p vio bl, blk & dk grn | .65 | .65 |
| **686** | A250 28p multicolored | .80 | .80 |
| **687** | A251 30p multicolored | .90 | .90 |
| **688** | A252 39p multicolored | 1.15 | 1.15 |
| | *Nos. 685-688 (4)* | 3.50 | 3.50 |

Europa A253

Modern architecture, art: 28p, Borda na Mona headquarters, Dublin, and The Turf Cutter, by sculptor John Behan. 39p, St. Mary's Church and ruins of Romanesque monastery at Cong.

**1987, May 14** *Perf. 15x14*

| | | | |
|---|---|---|---|
| **689** | A253 28p multicolored | *5.00* | *2.00* |
| **690** | A253 39p multicolored | *8.00* | *5.00* |

Cattle A254

**1987, July 2**

| | | | |
|---|---|---|---|
| **691** | A254 24p Kerry | .85 | .60 |
| **692** | A254 28p Friesian | 1.10 | 1.10 |
| **693** | A254 30p Hereford | 1.10 | 1.10 |
| **694** | A254 39p Shorthorn | 1.50 | 1.50 |
| | *Nos. 691-694 (4)* | 4.55 | 4.30 |

Festivals
A255

**1987, Aug. 27** *Perf. 14x15*

**695** A255 24p Fleadh Nua, Ennis .70 .70
**696** A255 28p Festival Queen, Tralee 1.00 1.00
**697** A255 30p Wexford opera festival 1.25 1.25
**698** A255 46p Ballinasloe horse fair 2.00 2.00
*Nos. 695-698 (4)* 4.95 4.95

Nos. 695-696 vert.

**Statesmen Type of 1986 and**

Ewer and Chalice, Company Crest
A256

Harp in Shield, Preamble Excerpt
A257

Woman Leading Board Meeting — A258

Design: No. 699, Cathal Brugha, vert.

*Perf. 14x15, 15x14*

**1987, Oct. 1** **Litho.**

**699** A240 24p black .80 .80
**700** A256 24p multicolored .80 .80
**701** A257 28p multicolored .90 .90
**702** A258 46p multicolored 1.50 1.50
*Nos. 699-702 (4)* 4.00 4.00

Company of Goldsmiths of Dublin, 350th anniv. (No. 700); Irish Constitution, 50th anniv. (28p); Women in Society, (46p).

A259

Christmas
A260

21p, 12 Days of Christmas (1st 3 days). 24p, Embroidery (detail), Waterford Vestments, 15th cent. 28p, Neapolitan creche (detail), 1850.

*Perf. 15x14, 14x15*

**1987, Nov. 17** **Litho.**

**703** A259 21p multicolored .65 .40
**704** A260 24p multicolored .85 .85
**705** A260 28p multicolored 1.10 1.10
*Nos. 703-705 (3)* 2.60 2.35

No. 703 issued in discount sheets of 14 + center label; sheet sold for £2.90. Value $22.50.

Love
A261

*Perf. 15x14½, 14½x15*

**1988, Jan. 27** **Litho.**

**706** A261 24p shown 1.00 1.00
**707** A261 28p Pillar box, vert. 1.20 1.20

Dublin Millennium
A262

**1988, Mar. 1** *Perf. 15x14*

**708** A262 28p multicolored 1.50 1.10
*a.* Booklet pane of 4, Gaelic 6.00
*b.* Booklet pane of 4, English 6.00

Nos. 708a, 708b consist of two vert. pairs separated by a history in Gaelic or English. See note following No. 584.

A263

Impact of the Irish Abroad
A264

Designs: No. 709, Robert O'Hara Burke (1820-1861), by Sir Sidney Nolan; 19th cent. map of Australia with Burke & Wills expedition route. 46p, Mural (detail) of the Eureka Stockade by Nolan.

**1988, Mar. 1**

**709** A263 24p multicolored 1.00 1.00
**710** A264 46p multicolored 2.00 2.00

**Statesmen Type of 1986 and**

1988 Summer Olympics, Seoul
A265

Order of Malta Ambulance Corps, 50th Anniv.
A266

Barry Fitzgerald (1888-1961), Actor — A267

Designs: 24p, William T. Cosgrave (1880-1965), president of the United Ireland and Fine Gael party. No. 713, Cycling.

*Perf. 14x15, 15x14*

**1988, Apr. 7** **Litho.**

**711** A240 24p black 1.00 1.00
**712** A265 28p multicolored 1.25 1.25
**713** A265 28p multicolored 1.25 1.25
*a.* Pair, #712-713 2.50 2.50
**714** A266 30p multicolored 1.60 1.60
**715** A267 50p multicolored 2.00 2.00
*Nos. 711-715 (5)* 7.10 7.10

Nos. 712-713 printed in sheets of 5 each plus two labels. Value, $16.50.

Sirius Sailing from Passage West, County Cork
A268

**1988, May 12** **Litho.** *Perf. 15x14*

**716** A268 24p multicolored 1.50 1.50

1st scheduled transatlantic crossing by steamship, sesquicentennial.

Europa
A269

28p, Air traffic controllers and A320 Airbus. 39p, Europe on globe, letters.

**1988, May 12** **Litho.** *Perf. 15x14*

**717** A269 28p multicolored *3.50* *1.00*
**718** A269 39p multicolored *6.00* *3.00*

Maia and Mercury Flying Boats in Foynes Harbor
A269a

**1988, May 12** **Litho.** *Perf. 15x14*

**719** A269a 46p multicolored 2.50 2.50

1st east-west transatlantic crossing by seaplane, 50th anniv.

Conservation of Flora — A270

**1988, June 21** **Litho.** *Perf. 14x15*

**720** A270 24p Otanthus maritimus 1.10 1.10
**721** A270 28p Saxifraga hartii 1.40 1.40
**722** A270 46p Astragalus danicus 2.25 2.25
*Nos. 720-722 (3)* 4.75 4.75

Irish Security Forces
A271

**1988, Aug. 23** **Litho.** *Perf. 15x14*

**723** A271 28p Garda Siochana (police) 1.50 1.00
**724** A271 28p Army 1.50 1.00
**725** A271 28p Navy, air corps 1.50 1.00
**726** A271 28p FCA, Slua Muiri 1.50 1.00
*a.* Strip of 4, #723-726 6.00 6.00

Institute of Chartered Accountants, Cent. — A272

Defeat of the Spanish Armada, 400th Anniv.
A273

*Perf. 14x15, 15x14*

**1988, Oct. 6** **Litho.**

**727** A272 24p multicolored 1.00 1.00
**728** A273 46p Duquesa Santa Ana off Donegal Coast 1.75 1.75

John F. Kennedy, Portrait by James Wyeth
A274

**1988, Nov. 24** **Litho.** *Perf. 15x14*

**729** A274 28p multicolored 2.00 1.50

A275

Christmas
A276

**1988, Nov. 24** *Perf. 14x15*

**730** A275 21p St. Kevin's Church, Glendalough .50 .40
**731** A276 24p Adoration of the Magi .70 .60
**732** A276 28p Flight into Egypt 1.10 1.10
**733** A276 46p Holy Family 1.75 1.75
*Nos. 730-733 (4)* 4.05 3.85

No. 730 issued only in discount sheets of 14. Sheet sold for £2.90. Value $20.

Love
A277

The Sonnet, by William Mulready (1786-1863)
A278

*Perf. 15x14, 14x15*

**1989, Jan. 24** **Litho.**

**734** A277 24p multicolored .90 .90
**735** A278 28p multicolored 1.10 1.10

Mulready, designer of Rowland Hill's first stamped envelope.

Classic Automobiles — A279

**1989, Apr. 11** **Litho.** ***Perf. 15x14***

**736** A279 24p Silver Stream .80 .80
**737** A279 28p Benz Comfortable 1.10 1.10
*a.* Booklet pane, 2 each 24p, 28p 4.00
**738** A279 39p Thomond Car 1.40 1.40
**739** A279 46p Chambers Car 1.60 1.60
*a.* Booklet pane of 4, #736-739 5.75
*Nos. 736-739 (4)* 4.90 4.90

Parks and Gardens
A280

**1989, Apr. 11**

**740** A280 24p Garinish Is. .70 .70
**741** A280 28p Glenveagh 1.00 1.00
**742** A280 32p Connemara Natl. Park 1.25 1.25
**743** A280 50p St. Stephen's Green 2.00 2.00
*Nos. 740-743 (4)* 4.95 4.95

Europa
A281

**1989, May 11**

**744** A281 28p Ring-a-ring-a-rosie *1.00 .90*
**745** A281 39p Hopscotch *1.50 1.50*

Irish Red Cross Soc., 50th Anniv. — A282

**1989, May 11** ***Perf. 14x15***

**746** A282 24p multicolored 1.00 1.00

European Parliament 3rd Elections — A283

**1989, May 11**

**747** A283 28p Stars from flag 1.00 1.00

Sts. Kilian, Colman and Totnan (d. 689), Martyred Missionaries, and Shamrock — A284

**1989, June 15** **Litho.** ***Perf. 13½***

**748** A284 28p multicolored 1.50 1.50
*a.* Booklet pane of 4, English 6.00
*b.* Booklet pane of 4, Gaelic 6.00
*c.* Booklet pane of 4, German 6.00
*d.* Booklet pane of 4, Latin 6.00

See Federal Republic of Germany No. 1580.

**Statesmen Type of 1986 and**

RIAI Emblem — A285

Dublin-Cork Coach, 1789 — A286

Singer, Scene from La Boheme
A287

Nehru — A288

Design: 24p, Sean Thomas O'Kelly (1883-1966), 2nd president.

*Perf. 14x15, 15x14*

**1989, July 25** **Litho.**

**749** A240 24p black 1.00 1.00
**750** A285 28p multicolored 1.00 1.00
**751** A286 28p multicolored 1.00 1.00
**752** A287 30p multicolored 1.15 1.15
**753** A288 46p red brown 1.75 1.75
*Nos. 749-753 (5)* 5.90 5.90

Royal Institute of Architects, 150th anniv.; Mail coach in Ireland, bicent.; Margaret Burke Sheridan (1889-1958), soprano; Jawaharlal Nehru, 1st prime minister of independent India.

Flags and Sail Ireland Yacht Rounding Cape Horn, by Des Fallon
A289

**1989, Aug. 31** **Litho.** ***Perf. 15x14***

**754** A289 28p multicolored 1.75 1.40

Whitbread round of the World Yacht Race 1989-90.

Wildlife: Game Birds — A290

**1989, Oct. 5** **Litho.** ***Perf. 13½***

**755** A290 24p Lagopus lagopus 1.40 .55
**756** A290 28p Vanellus vanellus 1.50 1.50
**757** A290 39p Scolopax rusticola 2.10 2.10
**758** A290 46p Phasianus colchicus 2.75 2.75
*a.* Miniature sheet of 4, #755-758 11.00 11.00
*Nos. 755-758 (4)* 7.75 6.90

Children and Creche — A291

Miniatures from a Flemish Psalter, 13th Cent. — A292

**1989, Nov. 14** **Litho.** ***Perf. 14x15***

**759** A291 21p multicolored .70 .70
**760** A292 24p Annunciation .70 .70
**761** A292 28p Nativity 1.00 1.00
**762** A292 46p Adoration of the Magi 1.50 1.50
*Nos. 759-762 (4)* 3.90 3.90

No. 759 issued only in discount sheets of 14. Sheet sold for £2.90. Value $15.

Ireland's Presidency of the European Communities — A293

European Tourism Year
A294

**1990, Jan. 9** **Litho.** ***Perf. 15x14***

**763** A293 30p multicolored 1.00 1.00
**764** A294 50p multicolored 2.00 2.00

Love Issue — A295

Love Issue — A296

**1990, Jan. 30** **Litho.** ***Perf. 14x15***

**765** A295 26p shown 1.50 1.50
**766** A296 30p "Love!" 1.50 1.50

Enamel Latchet Brooch — A297

Ardagh Chalice
A298

Art treasures of Ireland: 1p, 2p, Silver Kite Brooch, vert. 4p, 5p, Dunamase Food Vessel, vert. 10p, Derrinboy Armlets. 20p, Gold Dress Fastener. 26p, 28p, Lismore Crosier, vert. 32p, Broighter Collar. 34p, 37p, 38p, 40p, Gleninsheen Collar, vert. 41p, 44p, 45p, Silver thistle brooch, vert. 50p, 52p, Broighter boat, vert. £2, Tara Brooch. £5, St. Patrick's Bell Shrine, vert.

**1990-95** **Litho.** ***Perf. 15x14, 14x15***

**767** A297 1p blue & blk .30 .30
**768** A297 2p orange & blk .30 .30
**770** A297 4p violet & blk .40 .40
*a.* Perf. 13x13½ .40 .40
*b.* Photo. .40 .40
**771** A297 5p green & blk .50 .50
**774** A297 10p orange & blk .85 .85
**777** A297 20p yel & blk (I) 1.25 1.25
**778** A297 26p violet & blk 2.10 .85
*a.* Perf. 13½ on 3 or 4 sides 3.50 3.50
**779** A297 28p org & blk (I) 2.10 .90
*a.* Bklt. pane, 3 #770, 4 #779 + label 4.25
*b.* Photo. 2.75 2.75
**780** A297 30p brt blue & blk 2.10 1.00
*a.* Perf. 13½ 3.50 3.50
*b.* Bklt. pane, 3 #540a, 1 #550d, 2 #778a, 2 #780a 7.75
*c.* Bklt. pane, #768, 3 #770, #778, 2 #780 + label 5.50
**781** A297 32p green & blk 2.10 1.00
*a.* Bklt. pane, 2 #770b, #779b, 2 #781d 4.50
*b.* Perf. 13½x13 1.75 1.75
*c.* Bklt. pane, #770a, 3 #781b 5.25
*d.* Photo. 1.40 1.40
*e.* Booklet pane, 1 #770, 3 #781 5.25
**782** A297 34p yellow & blk 2.75 2.00
**783** A297 37p green & blk 3.50 2.50
**784** A297 38p purple & blk 3.50 2.50
**785** A297 40p blue & black 2.75 2.50
**786** A297 41p orange & blk 2.75 2.50
**787** A297 44p yellow & blk 3.50 2.50
**788** A297 45p violet & black 3.50 2.50
**789** A297 50p yellow & blk 2.75 2.00
**790** A297 52p blue & blk (I) 3.50 2.75
**791** A298 £1 yellow & blk (III) 6.00 3.00
**792** A298 £2 green & blk (III) 10.00 6.00
**793** A298 £5 blue & blk (III) 26.00 14.00

**Self-Adhesive**

***Die cut perf 11***

**Size: 27x21mm**

**794** A297 32p like #781 2.75 1.25
*a.* Die cut perf. 11½ 4.25 1.25
*b.* Die cut perf. 9½x9 2.75 1.25
*Nos. 767-794 (23)* 85.25 53.35

Issued: 26p, 30p, 32p, 41p, 50p, £1, 3/8; #780b, 5/3; 1p, 2p, 4p, 10p, 34p, £2, 7/26; #780c, 11/15; 5p, 20p, £5, 1/26/91; #781a, 5/14/91; 28p, 37p, 38p, 44p, 52p, 4/3/91;

#779a, 10/17/91; #794, 10/31/91; 40p, 45p, 5/14/92; #770a, 781b, 9/24/93; #781e, 11/16/95; No. 794b, 6/8/95.

#777, 779, 790, Type I - Coarse Dot Structure

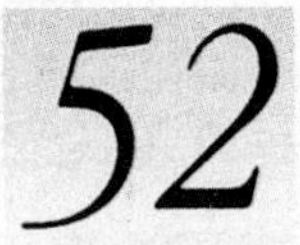


#777a, 779c, 790a, Type II - Fine Dot Structure

#791-793, Type III

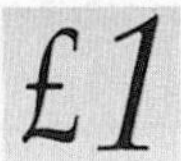


#791a-793a, Type IV

*Perf. 14x15, 15x14*

**1995, Nov. 15** **Litho.**

*777a* A297 20p Type II 3.75 3.75
*779c* A297 28p Type II 3.75 3.75
*790a* A297 52p Type II 5.50 5.50
*791a* A298 £1 Type IV 6.50 6.50
*792a* A298 £2 Type IV 13.50 13.50
*793a* A298 £5 Type IV 32.50 32.50
*Nos. 777a-793a (6)* 65.50 65.50

A299

**1990, Mar. 22** **Litho.** ***Perf. 14x15***

**Booklet Stamps**

**795** A299 26p Gift boxes 3.00 3.00
**796** A299 26p Nosegay 3.00 3.00
**797** A299 30p Horseshoe 3.00 3.00
**798** A299 30p Balloons 3.00 3.00
*a.* Bklt. pane of 4, #795-798 English labels 12.00
*b.* As "a," 4 English, 4 Gaelic labels 12.00

Greetings. Available only in discount booklets containing #798a, 798b. Bklts. sold for £1.98.

A300

**1990, Apr. 5** **Litho.** ***Perf. 14x15***

**799** A300 30p Tackle 2.00 2.00
**800** A300 30p Heading the ball 2.00 2.00
*a.* Pair, #799-800 4.50 4.50

1990 World Cup Soccer Championships, Italy.

Printed in sheets of 4 No. 800a plus label. Value, $25.

Williamite Wars, 300th Anniv. — A301

**1990, Apr. 5** **Litho.** ***Perf. 13½***

**801** A301 30p Siege of Limerick 1.75 1.75
**802** A301 30p Battle of the Boyne 1.75 1.75
*a.* Pair, #801-802 4.00 4.00

Penny Black, 150th Anniv. A302

**1990, May 3** **Litho.** ***Perf. 15x14***

**803** A302 30p #780 1.25 1.25
*a.* Bklt. pane, #803, 2 each #552a, 780a 8.00
**804** A302 50p #68, 255, 550, 780 1.75 1.75
*a.* Bklt. pane, 2 ea #803-804 9.50
*b.* Bklt. pane of 4, #552a, 780a, 803-804 8.00
Complete bklt., #803a, 804a, 804b, 780b 25.00

See note following No. 584.

Europa 1990 — A303

Post offices.

**1990, May 3** ***Perf. 14x15***

**805** A303 30p GPO, Dublin *1.50 1.25*
**806** A303 41p Westport P.O., County Mayo *1.75 1.50*

Printed in sheets of 10+2 labels. Value $35.

**Statesman Type of 1986**

**1990, June 21** **Litho.** ***Perf. 14x15***

**807** A240 30p Michael Collins 4.50 2.75

Irish Missionaries — A304

Design: 50p, Working at water pump.

**1990, June 21** ***Perf. 15x14***

**808** A304 26p multicolored 1.00 1.00
**809** A304 50p multicolored 2.00 2.00

Garden Flowers — A305

**1990, Aug. 30** **Litho.** ***Perf. 14x15***

**810** A305 26p Narcissus .70 .70
**811** A305 30p Rosa x hibernica .90 .90
*a.* Bklt. pane, 2 each #810-811 7.25
**812** A305 41p Primula 1.40 1.40
**813** A305 50p Erica erigena 1.50 1.50
*a.* Booklet pane of 4, #810-813 8.00
*Nos. 810-813 (4)* 4.50 4.50

See note following No. 584.

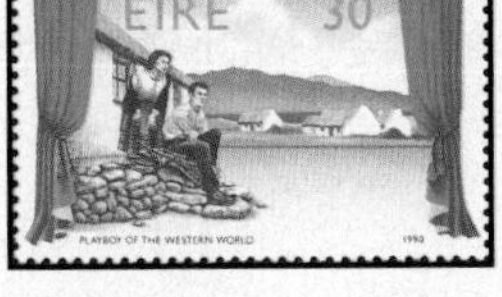


Theater A306

Designs: No. 814, Playboy of the Western World. No. 815, Juno and the Paycock. No. 816, The Field. No. 817, Waiting for Godot.

**1990, Oct. 18** **Litho.** ***Perf. 13½***

**814** A306 30p multicolored 1.75 1.75
**815** A306 30p multicolored 1.75 1.75
**816** A306 30p multicolored 1.75 1.75
**817** A306 30p multicolored 1.75 1.75
*a.* Block or strip of 4, #814-817 7.00 7.00

A307

Christmas A308

**1990, Nov. 15** **Litho.** ***Perf. 14x15***

**818** A307 26p Child praying .70 .70
**819** A308 26p Nativity scene .70 .70
**820** A308 30p Madonna and Child .90 .90
**821** A308 50p Adoration of the Magi 1.50 1.50
*Nos. 818-821 (4)* 3.80 3.80

No. 818 sold only in discount sheets of 12 for £2.86. Value $17.50.

Love — A309

**1991, Jan. 29** **Litho.** ***Perf. 14x15***

**822** A309 26p shown .90 .90
**823** A309 30p Boy, girl kissing 1.10 1.10

Irish Cycles — A310

**1991, Mar. 5**

**824** A310 26p Starley rover .95 .95
**825** A310 30p Child's horse tricycle 1.20 1.20
**826** A310 50p Penny farthing 1.90 1.90
*a.* Souvenir sheet of 3, #824-826 5.50 *5.50*
*Nos. 824-826 (3)* 4.05 4.05

See note following No. 584.

1916 Rising, 75th Anniv. A311

Design: Statue of Cuchulainn by Oliver Sheppard, 1916 Proclamation.

**1991, Apr. 3** **Litho.** ***Perf. 15x14***

**827** A311 32p multicolored 3.00 2.00

Dublin, European City of Culture A312

Designs: 28p, La Traviata, performed by Dublin Grand Opera Society. 32p, Dublin City Hall. 44p, St. Patrick's Cathedral, 800th anniv. 52p, Custom House, 200th anniv.

**1991, Apr. 11** ***Perf. 15x14***

**828** A312 28p multicolored .80 .80
**829** A312 32p multicolored 1.00 1.00
**830** A312 44p multicolored 1.40 1.40
*a.* Booklet pane of 3, #828-830 5.00 5.00

**Size: 41x25mm**

***Perf. 13½***

**831** A312 52p multicolored 1.60 1.60
*a.* Booklet pane of 4, #828-831 6.50
Complete booklet, #830a, 831a 11.50
*Nos. 828-831 (4)* 4.80 4.80

50th anniv. of Dublin Grand Opera Soc. (No. 828).

Europa A313

**1991, May 14** **Litho.** ***Perf. 15x14***

**832** A313 32p Giotto probe *1.00 .75*
**833** A313 44p Hubble telescope *1.75 1.75*

Williamite Wars, 300th Anniv. A314

**1991, May 14**

**834** A314 28p Siege of Athlone 1.50 1.50
**835** A314 28p Treaty of Limerick 1.50 1.50
*a.* Pair, #834-835 3.00 3.00

**Statesman Type of 1986 and**

Charles Stewart Parnell (1846-1891), Politician — A315

Society of United Irishmen, Bicent. A316

28p, John A. Costello (1891-1976), politician.

*Perf. 14x15, 15x14*

**1991, July 2** **Litho.**

**836** A240 28p black 1.15 1.15
**837** A315 32p multicolored 1.25 1.25
**838** A316 52p multicolored 2.10 2.10
*Nos. 836-838 (3)* 4.50 4.50

A317

***Perf. 15x14, 14x15***

**1991, Sept. 3** **Litho.**

**839** A317 28p Golfer putting, horiz. 1.25 1.25
**840** A317 32p shown 1.75 1.75

Walker Cup Competition, Portmarnock Golf Club (No. 839).

Irish Sheep — A318

**1991, Sept. 3** ***Perf. 14x15, 15x14***

**841** A318 32p Wicklow Cheviot 1.10 1.10
**842** A318 38p Donegal Blackface 1.75 1.75
**843** A318 52p Galway, horiz. 2.25 2.25
*Nos. 841-843 (3)* 5.10 5.10

Fishing Fleet A319

**1991, Oct. 17** **Litho.** ***Perf. 15x14***

**844** A319 28p Boatyard .65 .65
**845** A319 32p Inshore trawler .90 .90
*a.* Bklt. pane of 5, #845, 2 each #768, 783 5.00
*b.* Bklt. pane, 2 each #844, 845 5.75
**846** A319 44p Inshore potter 1.60 1.60
**847** A319 52p Factory ship 2.25 2.25
*a.* Booklet pane of 4, #844-847 8.00
*Nos. 844-847 (4)* 5.40 5.40

See note following No. 584.

A320

Christmas A321

**1991, Nov. 14** **Litho.** ***Perf. 14x15***

**848** A320 28p Wise men, star 1.00 1.00
**849** A321 28p Annunciation 1.10 1.10
**850** A321 32p Nativity 1.25 1.25
**851** A321 52p Adoration of the Magi 2.50 2.50
*Nos. 848-851 (4)* 5.85 5.85

No. 848 issued only in discount sheets of 13+2 labels which sold for £3.36. Value $17.50.

Love A322

Design: 32p, Rainbow over meadow, love etched in stone, vert.

***Perf. 15x14, 14x15***

**1992, Jan. 28** **Litho.**

**852** A322 28p shown 1.00 1.00
**853** A322 32p multicolored 1.50 1.50

1992 Summer Olympics, Barcelona A323

**1992, Feb. 25** **Litho.** ***Perf. 15x14***

**854** A323 32p Boxing 1.15 1.15
**855** A323 44p Sailing 1.40 1.40
*a.* Sheet of 4, 2 each #854-855 6.25 *6.50*

See note following No. 584.

Healthy Lifestyle — A324

**1992, Feb. 25** ***Perf. 14x15***

**856** A324 28p multicolored 1.50 1.50

Galway Chamber of Commerce and Industry, Bicent. A325

**1992, Apr. 2** **Litho.** ***Perf. 15x14***

**857** A325 28p multicolored 1.25 1.25

Intl. Maritime Heritage Year A326

***Perf. 15x14, 14x15***

**1992, Apr. 2** **Litho.**

**858** A326 32p Mari Cog 1.50 1.50
**859** A326 52p Ovoca, vert. 2.00 2.00

Greetings — A327

**1992, Apr. 2** ***Perf. 14x15***

**860** A327 28p Coastline 1.75 1.75
**861** A327 28p Mountain 1.75 1.75
**862** A327 32p Flowers 1.75 1.75
**863** A327 32p Pond 1.75 1.75
*a.* Bklt. pane of 4, #860-863, 8 English labels 7.00
*b.* Bklt. pane of 4, #860-863, 4 English labels + 4 Gaelic labels 7.00
*Nos. 860-863 (4)* 7.00 7.00

No. 863a contains Nos. 860-863 in order. No. 863b contains Nos. 862, 863, 860 and 861 in order.

Discovery of America, 500th Anniv. A328

Europa: 44p, Landing in New World.

**1992, May 14** **Litho.** ***Perf. 15x14***

**864** A328 32p multicolored *1.25 1.00*
**865** A328 44p multicolored *1.50 1.25*

Irish in the Americas — A329

Design: No. 867, The White House, bridge, railroad workers, musicians, workers.

**1992, May 14** ***Perf. 13½***

**866** A329 52p multicolored 2.00 2.00
**867** A329 52p multicolored 2.00 2.00
*a.* Pair, #866-867 4.00 4.00

Pine Marten A330

**1992, July 9** **Litho.** ***Perf. 15x14***

**868** A330 28p shown 1.15 1.15
**869** A330 32p In tree 1.40 1.40
**870** A330 44p With young 2.00 2.00
**871** A330 52p Holding bird 2.50 2.50
*Nos. 868-871 (4)* 7.05 7.05

World Wildlife Fund.

Trinity College, Dublin, 400th Anniv. — A331

**1992, Sept. 2** **Litho.** ***Perf. 13½***

**872** A331 32p Library 1.40 1.40
**873** A331 52p Main entrance 2.00 2.00

Views of Dublin by James Malton, Bicent. A332

**1992, Sept. 2** ***Perf. 15x14***

**874** A332 28p Rotunda, Assembly rooms 1.00 1.00
**875** A332 44p Charlemont House 1.25 1.25

Single European Market A333

**1992, Oct. 15** **Litho.** ***Perf. 15x14***

**876** A333 32p multicolored 1.50 1.50
*a.* Bklt. pane of 3 4.75
*b.* Bklt. pane of 4 6.50

No. 876b comes with stamps in three formats: four singles, two pairs, and block of four.

See note following No. 584.

Food and Farming — A334

**1992, Oct. 15** ***Perf. 14x15***

**877** A334 32p Fresh food 1.50 1.50
**878** A334 32p Cattle 1.50 1.50
**879** A334 32p Combine harvesting grain 1.50 1.50
**880** A334 32p Growing vegetables 1.50 1.50
*a.* Strip of 4, #877-880 5.00 5.00

A335

Christmas A336

Designs: No. 881, Rural churchyard. No. 882, The Annunciation, manuscript illustration, Chester Beatty Library, Dublin. 32p, Adoration of the Shepherds, by Jocopo da Empoli. 52p, Adoration of the Magi, by Johann Rottenhammer.

**1992, Nov. 19**

**881** A335 28p multicolored .95 .95
**882** A336 28p multicolored 1.00 1.00
**883** A336 32p multicolored 1.00 1.00
**884** A336 52p multicolored 1.90 1.90
*Nos. 881-884 (4)* 4.85 4.85

No. 881 issued only in discount sheets of 13+2 labels which sold for £3.36. Value $17.50.

Love A337

Design: 28p, Queen of Hearts, vert.

***Perf. 14x15, 15x14***

**1993, Jan. 26** **Litho.**

**885** A337 28p multicolored 1.00 1.00
**886** A337 32p multicolored 1.25 1.25

Irish Impressionist Paintings — A338

Designs: 28p, Evening at Tangier, by Sir John Lavery. 32p, The Goose Girl, by William J. Leech. 44p, La Jeune Bretonne, by Roderic O'Conor, vert. 52p, Lustre Jug, by Walter Osborne, vert.

**1993, Mar. 4** ***Perf. 13***

**887** A338 28p multicolored .90 .90
**888** A338 32p multicolored 1.10 1.10
*a.* Booklet pane of 2, #887-888 2.75
**889** A338 44p multicolored 1.25 1.25
**890** A338 52p multicolored 1.75 1.75
*a.* Booklet pane of 2, #889-890 3.50
*b.* Booklet pane of 4, #887-890 5.50
*Nos. 887-890 (4)* 5.00 5.00

No. 890b exists in two formats with different margin inscriptions.

Orchids — A339

**1993, Apr. 20** **Litho.** ***Perf. 14x15***

**891** A339 28p Bee orchid .85 .85
**892** A339 32p O'Kelly's orchid 1.10 1.10
**893** A339 38p Dark red helleborine 1.90 1.90
**894** A339 52p Irish lady's tresses 2.10 2.10
*a.* Souvenir sheet of 4, #891-894 7.50 7.50
*b.* As "a," with blue inscription 11.50 11.50
*Nos. 891-894 (4)* 5.95 5.95

No. 894b has a larger top margin than No. 894a. Added Inscription includes text and flags of Ireland and Thailand.

Contemporary Paintings — A340

Europa: 32p, Pears in a Copper Pan, by Hilda van Stockum. 44p, Arrieta Orzola, by Tony O'Malley.

**1993, May 18** **Litho.** ***Perf. 13x13½***

**895** A340 32p multicolored *1.25 1.25*
**896** A340 44p multicolored *1.75 1.75*

Issued in sheets of 10 + 2 labels.

Gaelic League, Cent. A341

Design: 52p, Illuminated manuscript presented to founder Douglas Hyde, vert.

***Perf. 15x14, 14x15***

**1993, July 8** **Litho.**

**897** A341 32p multicolored 1.25 1.25
**898** A341 52p multicolored 1.75 1.75

Irish Amateur Swimming Assoc., Cent. A342

Designs: No. 899, Swimmer diving into water. No. 900, Woman swimming.

**1993, July 8** ***Perf. 15x14***

**899** A342 32p multicolored 1.50 1.50
**900** A342 32p multicolored 1.50 1.50
*a.* Pair, #899-900 3.00 3.00

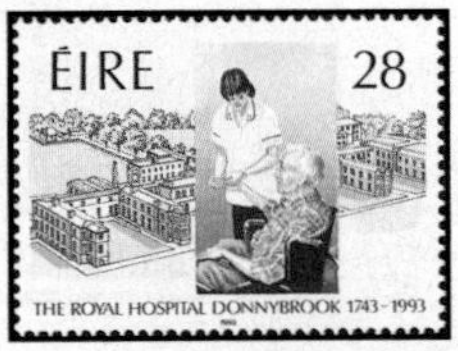


Royal Hospital Donnybrook, 250th Anniv. — A343

Carlow College, Bicent. — A344

Ceide Fields, County Mayo A345

Edward Bunting (1773-1843), Composer — A346

***Perf. 15x14, 14x15, 13½ (52p)***

**1993, Sept. 2** **Litho.**

**901** A343 28p multicolored 1.00 1.00
**902** A344 32p multicolored 1.25 1.25
**903** A345 44p multicolored 1.60 1.60
**904** A346 52p multicolored 2.10 2.10
*Nos. 901-904 (4)* 5.95 5.95

Irish Buses A347

Designs: 28p, Great Northern Railways Gardner. 32p, CIE Leyland Titan. No. 907, Horse-drawn omnibus. No. 908, Char-a-banc.

**1993, Oct. 12** **Litho.** ***Perf. 15x14***

**905** A347 28p multicolored 1.00 1.00
**906** A347 32p multicolored 1.00 1.00
*a.* Booklet pane, 2 each #905-906 5.25
**907** A347 52p multicolored 2.00 2.00
**908** A347 52p multicolored 2.00 2.00
*a.* Pair, #907-908 4.00 4.00
*b.* Booklet pane of 4, #905-908 6.00
*Nos. 905-908 (4)* 6.00 6.00

A348

Christmas A349

Designs: 32p, Mary placing infant Jesus in manger. 52p, Adoration of the shepherds.

***Perf. 14x15, 15x14***

**1993, Nov. 16** **Litho.**

**909** A348 28p multicolored .90 .90
**910** A349 28p multicolored .90 .90
**911** A349 32p multicolored 1.00 1.00
**912** A349 52p multicolored 2.25 2.25
*Nos. 909-912 (4)* 5.05 5.05

No. 909 issued only in discount sheets of 13+2 labels which sold for £3.36. Value $15.

Love A350

32p, Man, woman in shape of heart, vert.

***Perf. 15x14, 14x15***

**1994, Jan. 27** **Litho.**

**913** A350 28p multicolored .90 .90
**914** A350 32p multicolored 1.40 1.40

Greetings Stamps — A351

**1994, Jan. 27** ***Perf. 14x15***

**915** A351 32p Face in sun 2.25 2.25
**916** A351 32p Face in flower 2.25 2.25
**917** A351 32p Face in heart 2.25 2.25
*a.* Souv. sheet of 3, #915-917 7.00 7.00
**918** A351 32p Face in rose 3.75 3.75
*a.* Booklet pane of 4, #915-918, 4 English + 4 Gaelic labels 9.00
*b.* As "a," 8 English labels 9.00
*Nos. 915-918 (4)* 10.50 10.50

New Year 1994 (Year of the Dog), Hong Kong '94 (No. 917a).

No. 918a contains Nos. 915-918 in order. No. 918b contains Nos. 917, 918, 915, 916 in order.

Macra na Feirme, 50th Anniv. A352

The Taking of Christ, by Caravaggio A353

Irish Co-operative Organization Society, Cent. — A354

Irish Congress of Trade Unions, Cent. A355

**1994, Mar. 2** **Litho.** ***Perf. 15x14***

**919** A352 28p blue & gold 1.00 1.00
**920** A353 32p multicolored 1.25 1.25
**921** A354 38p multicolored 1.60 1.60
**922** A355 52p blue, blk & lt blue 1.90 1.90
*Nos. 919-922 (4)* 5.75 5.75

Voyages of St. Brendan (484-577) A356

Europa: 32p, St. Brendan, Irish monks sailing past volcano. 44p, St. Brendan on island with sheep, monks in boat.

**1994, Apr. 18** **Litho.** ***Perf. 15x14***

**923** A356 32p multicolored *1.25 1.25*
**924** A356 44p multicolored *1.75 1.75*
*a.* Miniature sheet of 2, #923-924 *3.00 3.00*

See Faroe Islands Nos. 264-265; Iceland Nos. 780-781.

Parliamentary Anniversaries — A357

#925, 1st meeting of the Dail, 1919. #926, 4th direct elections to European Parliament.

**1994, Apr. 27**

**925** A357 32p multicolored 1.25 1.25
**926** A357 32p multicolored 1.25 1.25
*a.* Booklet pane, 1 each #925-926 3.00
*b.* Booklet pane, 2 each #925-926 6.00
Complete booklet, #926a, 926b 9.00

1994 World Cup Soccer Championships, US — A358

Players from: No. 927, Argentina in striped shirt, Ireland in green. No. 928, Ireland, Germany.

**1994, May 31** ***Perf. 14x15***

**927** A358 32p multicolored 2.50 2.50
**928** A358 32p multicolored 2.50 2.50
*a.* Pair, #927-928 5.00 5.00

Printed in sheets of 4 No. 928a plus label. Value, $20.

Women's Hockey A359

32p, 1994 Women's Hockey World Cup, Dublin. 52p, Irish Ladies' Hockey Union, cent.

**1994, May 31** *Perf. 13x13½*

929 A359 32p multicolored 1.50 1.50
930 A359 52p multicolored 2.00 2.00

Moths A360

**1994, July 12 Litho.** *Perf. 14½x14*

931 A360 28p Garden tiger 1.40 1.40
932 A360 32p Burren green 1.50 1.50
933 A360 38p Emperor 1.90 1.90
934 A360 52p Elephant hawkmoth 2.40 2.40
*a.* Souvenir sheet of 4, #931-934 9.00 9.00
*b.* As "a," overprinted 12.00 12.00
*Nos. 931-934 (4)* 7.20 7.20

**Size: 34x23mm**

**Self-Adhesive**

***Die Cut Perf. 11½***

935 A360 32p like #932 3.00 3.00
936 A360 32p like #931 3.00 3.00
937 A360 32p like #934 3.00 3.00
938 A360 32p like #933 3.00 3.00
*a.* Strip of 4, #935-938 12.00 12.00

Overprint on No. 934b shows PHILAKOREA '94 exhibition emblem and Chinese inscription.

A361

A362

A363

Anniversaries and Events — A364

28p, Medieval view of Drogheda. No. 940, Edmund Ignatius Rice (1762-1844), philantropist. No. 941, Edmund Burke (1729-97), political commentator. No. 942, Eamonn Andrews (1922-87), broadcaster. No. 943, Vickers Vimy aircraft.

**1994, Sept. 6 Litho.** *Perf. 13½*

939 A361 28p multicolored 1.25 1.25

***Perf. 14x14½***

940 A362 32p multicolored 1.40 1.40

***Perf. 14x13½***

941 A363 32p multicolored 1.40 1.40
942 A363 52p multicolored 2.25 2.25

***Perf. 15x14***

943 A364 52p multicolored 2.25 2.25
*Nos. 939-943 (5)* 8.55 8.55

Drogheda, 800th anniv. (No. 939). First Newfoundland-Ireland transatlantic flight, 75th anniv. (No. 943).

Nobel Prize Winners A365

No. 944, George Bernard Shaw (1856-1950), dramatist, essayist. No. 945, Samuel Beckett (1906-89), playwright. 32p, Sean McBride (1904-88), statesman. 52p, William Butler Yeats (1865-1939), poet.

**1994, Oct. 18 Litho.** *Perf. 15x14*

944 A365 28p multicolored .85 .85
945 A365 28p multicolored .85 .85
*a.* Pair, #944-945 1.75 1.75
946 A365 32p multicolored .95 .95
*a.* Booklet pane of 3, #944-946 2.50
*b.* Bklt. pane, #944-945, 2 #946 3.50
947 A365 52p multicolored 1.40 1.40
*a.* Booklet pane, 1 #946, 2 #947 4.00
*b.* Booklet pane of 4, #944-947 4.50
Complete bklt., #946a-946b, 947a-947b 17.50
*Nos. 944-947 (4)* 4.05 4.05

A366

Christmas A367

#948, Stained glass nativity scene. #949, Annunciation, detail, 11th cent. ivory plaque. 32p, Flight Into Egypt, 15th cent. wood carving. 52p, Nativity, detail, 11th cent. ivory plaque.

**1994, Nov. 17 Litho.** *Perf. 14x15*

948 A366 28p multicolored .95 .95
949 A367 28p multicolored 1.05 1.05
950 A367 32p multicolored 1.10 1.10
951 A367 52p multicolored 1.90 1.90
*Nos. 948-951 (4)* 5.00 5.00

No. 948 issued only in discount sheets of 13 plus 2 labels which sold for £3.36. Value $16.50.

Greetings Stamps — A368

**1995, Jan. 24 Litho.** *Perf. 14x15*

952 A368 32p Tree of hearts 2.50 2.50

**Booklet Stamps**

953 A368 32p Teddy bear, balloon 2.50 2.50
954 A368 32p Clown juggling hearts 2.50 2.50
955 A368 32p Bouquet of flowers 2.50 2.50
*a.* Booklet pane, #952-955 + 4 English, 4 Gaelic labels 10.00
*b.* As "a," 8 English labels 10.00
Complete booklet, #955a-955b 20.00
*c.* Souvenir sheet, #952, 954-955 + 3 English, 3 Gaelic labels 8.50 8.50

New Year 1995 (Year of the Boar) (No. 955c).

No. 955a contains Nos. 953-954, 952, 955 in order. No. 955b contains Nos. 952, 955, 953-954 in order.

The falling heart on No. 952 has a black outline. The falling heart without an outline comes from Nos. 955a-955c.

Narrow Gauge Railways A369

**1995, Feb. 28 Litho.** *Perf. 15x14*

956 A369 28p West Clare .95 .95
957 A369 32p Co. Donegal 1.20 1.20
958 A369 38p Cork & Muskerry 1.40 1.40
959 A369 52p Cavan & Leitrim 1.90 1.90
*a.* Souvenir sheet of 4, #956-959 7.00 7.00
*Nos. 956-959 (4)* 5.45 5.45

No. 959a exists with Singapore '95 overprint in sheet margin. Value $10.

Peace & Freedom A370

Europa: Nos. 960, 962, Stylized dove, reconstructed city. 44p, No. 963, Stylized dove, map of Europe.

**1995, Apr. 6 Litho.** *Perf. 15x14*

960 A370 32p multicolored *.90 .90*
961 A370 44p multicolored *1.50 1.50*

**Size: 34½x23mm**

**Self-Adhesive Coil Stamps**

***Die Cut Perf. 11½***

962 A370 32p multicolored *2.00 2.00*
963 A370 32p multicolored *2.00 2.00*

Nos. 962-963 are coil stamps, printed in horizontal rolls of 100, with 50 of each design alternating.

1995 Rugby World Cup A371

**1995, Apr. 6** *Perf. 14*

964 A371 32p shown 1.00 1.00
965 A371 52p Player being tackled 2.00 2.00

**Souvenir Sheet**

966 A371 £1 like #964 6.00 *7.00*

No. 966 has a continuous design.

A372

A373

32p, Irish soldiers, Cross of Fontenoy.

**1995, May 15 Photo.** *Perf. 11½*

967 A372 32p multicolored 1.40 1.40

Battle of Fontenoy, 250th Anniv. See Belgium No. 1583.

**1995, May 15 Litho.** *Perf. 14x15*

Military uniforms: 28p, Irish Brigade, French Army, 1745. No. 969, Tercio Irlanda, Army of Flanders, 1605. No. 970, Royal Dublin Fusiliers, 1914. 38p, St. Patrick's Battalion, Papal Army, 1860. 52p, The Fighting 69th, Army of Potomac, 1861.

968 A373 28p multicolored .90 .90
969 A373 32p multicolored 1.05 1.05
*a.* Bklt. pane, 2 ea #968-969 3.75
970 A373 32p multicolored 1.00 1.00
971 A373 38p multicolored 1.25 1.25
*a.* Bklt. pane of 3, #968-969, #971 3.25
972 A373 52p multicolored 2.25 2.25
*a.* Bklt. pane of 3, #968-969, 972 3.00
*b.* Bklt. pane of 4, #968-969, 971-972 3.50
Complete booklet, #969a, 971a, 972a, 972b 16.50
*Nos. 968-972 (5)* 6.45 6.45

Radio, Cent. A374

Designs: No. 973, Guglielmo Marconi, transmitting equipment. No. 974, Radio channel dial.

**1995, June 8 Litho.** *Perf. 13½*

973 A374 32p multicolored *12.50 12.50*
974 A374 32p multicolored *12.50 12.50*
*a.* Pair, #973-974 *25.00 25.00*

See Germany No. 1900, Italy Nos. 2038-2039, San Marino No. 1336-1337, Vatican City No. 978-979.

A375

A376

A377

Anniversaries & Events A378

Designs: 28p, Dr. Bartholomew Mosse, Rotunda Hospital. No. 976, Piper, laurel wreath over map of Europe. No. 977, St. Patrick's College. 52p, Geological map of Ireland.

**1995, July 27 Litho.** *Perf. 14½x14*

975 A375 28p multicolored .90 .90
976 A376 32p multicolored 1.00 1.00

*Perf. 14½*

**977** A377 32p multicolored 1.00 1.00

*Perf. 13½*

**978** A378 52p multicolored 1.60 1.60
*Nos. 975-978 (4)* 4.50 4.50

Rotunda Hospital, 250th anniv. (No. 975). End of World War II, 50th anniv. (No. 976). St. Patrick's College, Maynooth, bicent. No. 977). Geological survey of Ireland, 150th anniv. (No. 978).

Reptiles & Amphibians — A379

**1995, Sept. 1 Litho. *Perf. 15x14***

**979** A379 32p Natterjack toad 1.25 1.25
**980** A379 32p Common lizard 1.25 1.25
**981** A379 32p Smooth newt 1.25 1.25
**982** A379 32p Common frog 1.25 1.25
*a.* Strip of 4, #979-982 12.50 12.50

***Die Cut Perf. 9¼***

**Size: 34½x22½mm**

**Self-Adhesive**

**982B** A379 32p like No. 979 3.00 3.00
**982C** A379 32p like No. 980 3.00 3.00
**982D** A379 32p like No. 981 3.00 3.00
**982E** A379 32p like No. 982 3.00 3.00
*f.* Strip of 4, Nos. 982B-982E 12.00 12.00

Natl. Botanic Gardens, Bicent. — A380

Designs: 32p, Crinum moorei. 38p, Sarracenia x moorei. 44p, Solanum crispum "glasnevin."

**1995, Oct. 9 Litho. *Perf. 14x15***

**983** A380 32p multicolored 1.00 1.00
**984** A380 38p multicolored 1.10 1.10
**985** A380 44p multicolored 1.40 1.40
*a.* Booklet pane of 3, #983-985 5.25
*b.* Bklt. pane of 4, #984-985, 2 #983 6.25
Complete booklet, #985a-985b 11.00
*Nos. 983-985 (3)* 3.50 3.50

UN, 50th Anniv. A381

**1995, Oct. 19 *Perf. 13x13½***

**986** A381 32p shown 1.00 1.00
**987** A381 52p UN, "50" emblem 2.00 2.00

A382

Christmas A383

Designs: No. 988, Adoration of the Magi. No. 989, Adoration of the Shepherds. 32p, Adoration of the Magi. 52p, Nativity.

**1995, Nov. 16 Litho. *Perf. 14½x14***

**988** A382 28p multicolored 1.25 1.25
**989** A383 28p multicolored 1.25 1.25
**990** A383 32p multicolored 1.60 1.60
**991** A383 52p multicolored 2.25 2.25
*Nos. 988-991 (4)* 6.35 6.35

No. 988 issued only in discount sheets of 13+2 labels, which sold for £3.36. Value $15.

Greetings/Love Stamps — A384

Television cartoon characters from "Zog, Zig and Zag:" No. 992, With hearts. No. 993, Waving hands. No. 994, In car, wearing space helmets. No. 995, Holding out hands, wearing hats.

**1996, Jan. 23 Litho. *Perf. 14x15***

**992** A384 32p multicolored 2.75 2.75

**Booklet Stamps**

**993** A384 32p multicolored 2.75 2.75
**994** A384 32p multicolored 2.75 2.75
**995** A384 32p multicolored 2.75 2.75
*a.* Booklet pane, Nos. 992-995, 5 English, 3 Gaelic labels 10.00
*b.* As "a," 7 English, 1 Gaelic label 10.00
Complete booklet, #995a-995b 22.00
*c.* Souvenir sheet, Nos. 992, 994-995 + 4 English, 2 Gaelic labels, 1 large label with Chinese inscription 7.50 7.50

No. 995a contains Nos. 993-995, 992 in order. No. 995b contains Nos. 995, 992-994 in order.

New Year 1996 (Year of the Rat) (No. 995c).

A385

1996 Summer/Paralympic Games, Atlanta — A386

**1996, Feb. 1**

**996** A385 28p show 1.00 1.00
**997** A386 32p Discus 1.00 1.00
**998** A386 32p Canoeing 1.00 1.00
**999** A386 32p Running 1.00 1.00
*a.* Strip of 3, Nos. 997-999 4.00 4.00

No. 999a printed in sheets of 9 stamps. Value $18.

L'Imaginaire Irlandais — A387

**1996, Mar. 12 Litho. *Perf. 15x14***

**1000** A387 32p multicolored 2.00 2.00

Irish Horse Racing A388

**1996, Mar. 12 Litho. *Perf. 15x14***

**1001** A388 28p Fairyhouse .85 .85
**1002** A388 32p Punchestown .95 .95
**1003** A388 32p The Curragh .95 .95
*a.* Pair, #1002-1003 1.90 1.90
*b.* Booklet pane, 2 #1001, 1 each #1002-1003 3.75
*c.* Souv. sheet, #1002-1003 16.00 16.00
**1004** A388 38p Galway 1.20 1.20
*a.* Booklet pane, 2 #1002, 1 #1004 3.50
**1005** A388 52p Leopardstown 1.50 1.50
*a.* Bklt. pane, #1005, 2 #1003 3.50
*b.* Bklt. pane, 1 ea #1002-1005 4.50
Complete bklt., Nos. 1003b, 1004a, 1005a, 1005b 16.00
*Nos. 1001-1005 (5)* 5.45 5.45

No. 1003c for China '96.

UNESCO World Heritage Site A389

UNICEF, 50th Anniv. A390

Designs: 28p, Passage tombs, Bru na Bóinne National Monument, Boyne Valley. 32p, Children.

**1996, Apr. 2 Litho. *Perf. 14***

**1006** A389 28p sepia & black 1.00 1.00
**1007** A390 32p multicolored 1.50 1.50

Europa A391

32p, Louie Bennett (1870-1956), Suffragette, trade unionist. 44p, Lady Augusta Gregory (1852-1932), playwright, co-founder of Abbey Theatre.

**1996, Apr. 2 *Perf. 15x14***

**1008** A391 32p violet *1.00 1.00*
**1009** A391 44p green *1.50 1.50*

***Die Cut 9¼***

**Self-Adhesive Coil Stamps**

**1009A** A391 32p like #1008 *2.50 2.50*
**1009B** A391 32p like #1009 *2.50 2.50*

Nos. 962-963 are coil stamps, printed in horizontal rolls with each value alternating.

Irish Winners of Tourist Trophy Motorcycle Races — A392

32p, Stanley Woods. 44p, Artie Bell. No. 1012, Alec Bennett. 52p, No. 1014, Robert & Joey Dunlop.

**1996, May 30 *Perf. 14***

**1010** A392 32p multicolored .90 .90
**1011** A392 44p multicolored 1.40 1.40
**1012** A392 50p multicolored 1.90 1.90
**1013** A392 52p multicolored 1.90 1.90
*Nos. 1010-1013 (4)* 6.10 6.10

**Souvenir Sheet**

**1014** A392 50p multicolored 3.00 3.00

See Isle of Man Nos. 701-705.

Michael Davitt (1846-1906), Nationalist Leader — A393

**1996, July 4 Litho. *Perf. 13½x13***

**1015** A393 28p multicolored .95 .95

Ireland's Presidency of the European Union A394

**1996, July 4 *Perf. 13x13½***

**1016** A394 32p multicolored 1.00 1.00

Thomas A. McLaughlin (1896-1971), Designer of Ardnacrusha Hydro-electric Power Station — A395

**1996, July 4**

**1017** A395 38p multicolored 1.25 1.25

Bord na Móna (Irish Peat Corp.), 50th Anniv. A396

**1996, July 4**

**1018** A396 52p multicolored 1.60 1.60

Irish Naval Service, 50th Anniv. A397

Designs: 32p, Coastal patrol vessel. 44p, Corvette. 52p, Motor torpedo boat, vert.

**1996, July 18 *Perf. 15x14***

**1019** A397 32p multicolored .90 .90
*a.* Booklet pane, 3 #1019 3.25
**1020** A397 44p multicolored 1.40 1.40
**1021** A397 52p multicolored 1.75 1.75
*a.* Booklet pane of 3, #1019-1021 6.25
Complete booklet, #1019a, 1021a 9.50
*Nos. 1019-1021 (3)* 4.05 4.05

People with Disabilities
A398

**1996, Sept. 3 Litho. *Perf. 14x15***

**1022** A398 28p Man in wheel-chair 1.40 1.40
**1023** A398 28p Blind woman, child 1.40 1.40
*a.* Pair, #1022-1023 3.00 3.00

Freshwater Ducks
A399

Designs: 32p, Anas crecca. 38p, Anas clypeata. 44p, Anas penelope. 52p, Anas platyrhynchos.

**1996, Sept. 24 *Perf. 15x14***

**1024** A399 32p multicolored 1.00 1.00
**1025** A399 38p multicolored 1.25 1.25
**1026** A399 44p multicolored 1.60 1.60
**1027** A399 52p multicolored 2.10 2.10
*a.* Souvenir sheet, #1024-1027 7.25 7.25
*Nos. 1024-1027 (4)* 5.95 5.95

No. 1027a is a continuous design.

Motion Pictures, Cent.
A400

**1996, Oct. 17 Litho. *Perf. 13½***

**1028** A400 32p Man of Aran 1.50 1.50
**1029** A400 32p My Left Foot 1.50 1.50
**1030** A400 32p The Commitments 1.50 1.50
**1031** A400 32p The Field 1.50 1.50
*a.* Strip of 4, #1028-1031 7.00 7.00

A401

Christmas
A402

No. 1032, Stained glass scene of Holy Family. No. 1033, Adoration of the Magi. 32p, The Annunciation. 52p, Shepherds receive news of Christ's birth.

**1996, Nov. 19 *Perf. 14***

**1032** A401 28p multicolored 1.00 1.00
**1033** A402 28p multicolored 1.00 1.00
**1034** A402 32p multicolored 1.10 1.10
**1035** A402 52p multicolored 2.00 2.00
*Nos. 1032-1035 (4)* 5.10 5.10

No. 1032 sold only in discount sheets of 15 for £3.92. Value $21.

Spideog Robin — A403

Greenland White-fronted Goose — A404

***Perf. 15x14, 14x15***

**1997, Jan. 16 Litho.**

**1036** A403 28p Blue tit. horiz. 2.00 2.00
**1037** A403 32p shown 2.50 2.50
*b.* Perf. 14 2.50 2.50
**1038** A403 44p Puffin 3.50 3.50
**1039** A403 52p Barn owl 4.00 4.00
**1040** A404 £1 shown 5.00 5.00

**Booklet Stamp**

**Size: 18x21mm, 21x18mm**

**1040A** A403 32p Like #1037 3.00 3.00
*b.* Booklet pane, 3 #1040A, 1 #770 14.00
Complete booklet, #1040b 14.00

**Size: 20x23mm**

***Perf. 14x15***

**1040C** A403 32p Like #1037, "Eire" 8½mm wide ('99) 3.00 3.00
*d.* Bklt. pane of 5 + 5 labels 15.00
Complete booklet 15.00
*Nos. 1036-1040C (7)* 23.00 23.00

On Nos. 1037,1037b "Eire" is 9mm wide, and size of design is 21x24mm.

See Nos. 1053-1054, 1067, 1076-1081A, 1094, 1105-1115C, 1314-1319B, 1340-1343.

Compare with Nos. 1353-1373.

Issued: No. 1040C, 6/30/99

Greetings Stamps — A405

Designs: No. 1041, Doves on tree limb. No. 1042, Cow jumping over moon. No. 1043, Pig going to market. No. 1044, Rooster on fence.

**1997, Jan. 28 Litho. *Perf. 14x15***

**1041** A405 32p multicolored 1.75 1.75

**Booklet Stamps**

**1042** A405 32p multicolored 1.75 1.75
**1043** A405 32p multicolored 1.75 1.75
**1044** A405 32p multicolored 1.75 1.75
*a.* Booklet pane, #1041-1044, 5 English, 3 Gaelic labels 7.00
*b.* As "a," #1041-1044, 7 English, 1 Gaelic label 7.00
Complete booklet, #1044a, 1044b 14.00
*c.* Souvenir sheet, 1042-1044, 3 English, 3 Gaelic labels + 1 large label with "Year of the Ox," Hong Kong '97 8.00 8.00

No. 1044a contains Nos. 1042, 1041, 1043-1044 in order. No. 1044b contains Nos. 1043-1044, 1041-1042 in order.

Irish State, 75th Anniv.
A406

Designs: No. 1045, Dáil, national flag, constitution. No. 1046, Defense forces, badges, UN flag. No. 1047, Four Courts, scales of justice. No. 1048, Garda badge, Garda Siochána.

**1997, Feb. 18 *Perf. 15x14***

**1045** A406 32p multicolored 1.25 1.25
**1046** A406 32p multicolored 1.25 1.25
*a.* Pair, #1045-1046 2.50 2.50
**1047** A406 52p multicolored 1.75 1.75
**1048** A406 52p multicolored 1.75 1.75
*a.* Pair, #1047-1048 3.50 3.50

See Nos. 1055-1058, 1082-1084, 1095-1096.

Marine Mammals
A407

Designs: 28p, Halichoerus grypus, vert. 32p, Tursiops truncatus, vert. 44p, Phocaena phocaena. 52p, Orcinus orca.

***Perf. 14x15, 15x14***

**1997, Mar. 6 Litho.**

**1049** A407 28p multicolored .85 .85
**1050** A407 32p multicolored .95 .95
**1051** A407 44p multicolored 1.40 1.40
**1052** A407 52p multicolored 1.75 1.75
*a.* Souvenir sheet, #1049-1052 7.00 7.00
*Nos. 1049-1052 (4)* 4.95 4.95

Bird Type of 1997

***Die Cut Perf. 9x9½***

**1997, Mar. 6 Litho.**

**Self-Adhesive Coil Stamps**

**1053** A403 32p Peregrine falcon 7.50 7.50
**1054** A403 32p like #1037 7.50 7.50
*a.* Pair, #1053-1054 17.50

***Die Cut Perf. 11x11¼***

**1054B** A403 32p Like #1053 *20.00 20.00*
**1054C** A403 32p Like #1054 *20.00 20.00*
*d.* Pair, #1054B-1054C *40.00*
*Nos. 1053-1054C (4)* 55.00 55.00

Issued: Nos. 1053-1054, 3/6/97; Nos. 1054B-1054C, 4/97.

**Irish State, 75th Anniv. Type of 1997**

No. 1055, Singer, violinist, bodhran player. No. 1056, Athlete, soccer and hurling players. No. 1057, Irish currency, blueprint, food processing plant. No. 1058, Abbey Theatre emblem, books, palette, paintbrushes, Séamus Heaney manuscript.

**1997, Apr. 3 *Perf. 15x14***

**1055** A406 32p multicolored 1.25 1.25
**1056** A406 32p multicolored 1.25 1.25
*a.* Pair, #1055-1056 2.50 2.50
**1057** A406 52p multicolored 1.75 1.75
**1058** A406 52p multicolored 1.75 1.75
*a.* Pair, #1057-1058 3.50 3.50

Irish Coinage, Millennium
A408

**1997, Apr. 3 *Perf. 15x14***

**1059** A408 32p First Irish coin 2.00 2.00

Stories and Legends
A409

Europa: 32p, "The Children of Lir" flying as swans. 44p, "Oisin & Niamh" on horse.

**1997, May 14 Litho. *Perf. 14***

**1060** A409 32p multicolored *1.00 1.00*
**1061** A409 44p multicolored *1.50 1.50*

***Die Cut Perf. 9x9½***

**Self-Adhesive Coil Stamps**

**1062** A409 32p like #1060 *2.50 2.50*
**1063** A409 32p like #1061 *2.50 2.50*
*a.* Pair, #1062-1063 *5.00*

The Great Famine, 150th Anniv.
A410

Designs: 28p, Passengers waiting to board emigrant ship. 32p, Family group attending dying child. 52p, Irish Society of Friends soup kitchen.

**1997, May 14 Litho. *Perf. 15x14***

**1064** A410 28p multicolored 1.20 1.20
**1065** A410 32p multicolored 1.25 1.25
**1066** A410 52p multicolored 2.10 2.10
*Nos. 1064-1066 (3)* 4.55 4.55

**Bird Type of 1997**

Souvenir Sheet

**1997, May 29 *Perf. 14***

**1067** A404 £2 Pintail, horiz. 11.00 11.00

PACIFIC 97.

No. 1067 shows the duck's head in brown. See No. 1111 for stamp with duck's head in black.

Kate O'Brien (1897-1974), Novelist — A411

**1997, July 1 Litho. *Perf. 14***

**1068** A411 28p multicolored 1.25 1.25

St. Columba (521-97), Irish Patron Saint — A412

**1997, July 1 *Perf. 14x15***

**1069** A412 28p multicolored 1.25 1.25

A413

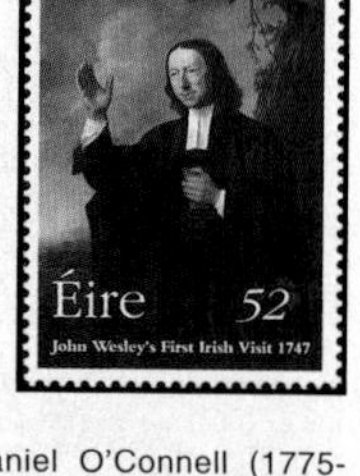


A414

Designs: 32p, Daniel O'Connell (1775-1847), politician. 52p, John Wesley (1703-91), founder of Methodism, first visit to Ireland, 250th anniv.

**1997, July 1 *Perf. 14x14½***

**1070** A413 32p multicolored 1.40 1.40
**1071** A414 52p multicolored 1.75 1.75

Lighthouses — A415

Designs: No. 1072, Baily. No. 1073, Tarbert. 38p, Hook Head, vert. 50p, Fastnet.

**1997, July 1** *Perf. 15x14, 14x15*

**1072** A415 32p multicolored 1.15 1.15
**1073** A415 32p multicolored 1.15 1.15
*a.* Pair, #1072-1073 2.25 2.25
*b.* Bklt. pane, #1073, 2 #1072 3.00
*c.* Bklt. pane, 2 ea #1072-1073 4.00
**1074** A415 38p multicolored 1.15 1.15
**1075** A415 50p multicolored 1.50 1.05
*a.* Booklet pane, #1074-1075 3.00
*b.* Bklt. pane of 4, #1073a, 1074-1075 5.00
Complete booklet, #1073b, 1073c, 1075a, 1075b 16.00

### Bird Type of 1997

*Perf. 14x15, 15x14*

**1997, Aug. 27** **Litho.**

**1076** A403 1p Magpie .75 .75
**1077** A403 2p Gannet .75 .75
**1078** A403 4p Corncrake .75 .75
**1079** A403 10p Kingfisher 1.00 1.00
**1080** A403 20p Lapwing 1.75 1.00
**1081** A404 £5 Shelduck 25.00 19.00

**Booklet Stamp**

**Size: 18x21mm**

**1081A** A403 4p Like #1078 4.00 4.00
*Nos. 1076-1081A (7)* 34.00 27.25

### Irish State, 75th Anniv. Type of 1997

28p, Quill, page from Annals of Four Masters, No. 128. 32p, Stained glass window, No. 82. 52p, Aer Lingus airplane, letter, No. C7.

**1997, Aug. 27** *Perf. 15x14*

**1082** A406 28p multicolored 1.10 1.10
**1083** A406 32p multicolored 1.25 1.25
**1084** A406 52p multicolored 2.25 2.25
*Nos. 1082-1084 (3)* 4.60 4.60

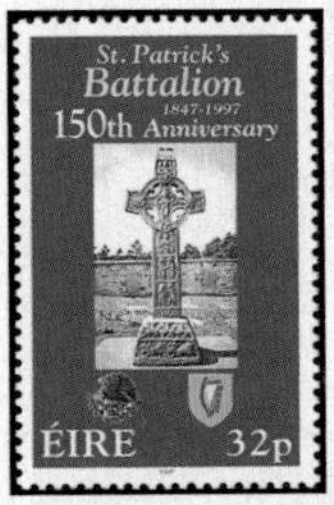


St. Patrick's Battalion, 150th Anniv. — A416

**1997, Sept. 12** **Litho.** *Perf. 14x13½*

**1085** A416 32p multicolored 2.00 2.00

See Mexico No. 2049.

Bram Stoker's "Dracula" A417

Scenes of Dracula: 28p, Being transformed into a bat, vert. 32p, With potential victim, vert. 38p, Emerging from coffin. 52p, With wolf.

**1997, Oct. 1** *Perf. 14x15, 15x14*

**1086** A417 28p multicolored 1.00 1.00
**1087** A417 32p multicolored 1.25 1.25
*a.* Souvenir sheet of 1 3.50 3.50
**1088** A417 38p multicolored 1.50 1.50
**1089** A417 52p multicolored 1.90 1.90
*a.* Souv. sheet of 4, #1086-1089 7.25 7.25
*Nos. 1086-1089 (4)* 5.65 5.65

Stamps from Nos. 1087a, 1089a have souvenir sheet background framing vignette.

A418

Christmas — A419

Nos. 1090-1092: Different images of Holy Family in stained glass. No. 1093, Christmas tree.

**1997, Nov. 18** **Litho.** *Perf. 14x15*

**1090** A418 28p multicolored 1.10 1.10
**1091** A418 32p multicolored 1.40 1.40
**1092** A418 52p multicolored 2.00 2.00
*Nos. 1090-1092 (3)* 4.50 4.50

**Self-Adhesive**

*Serpentine Die Cut 9x9½*

**1093** A419 28p multicolored 1.25 1.25
*a.* Booklet pane, 20 #1093 25.00

By its nature, No. 1093a is a complete booklet. The peelable paper backing serves as a booklet cover.

No. 1093 sold only in discount booklets for £5.32.

### Bird Type of 1997

*Perf. 15x14 (on 3 Sides)*

**1997, Dec. 6** **Litho.**

**Booklet Stamp**

**1094** A403 32p like #1053 3.00 3.00
*a.* Bklt. pane, #1081A, 3 #1094 12.50
Complete booklet, #1094a 13.50

### Irish State, 75th Anniv. Type of 1997

No. 1095, General Post Office, No. 68.

No. 1096: a, like No. 1048. b, like No. 1047. c, like No. 1057. d, like No. 1058. e, like No. 1082. f, like No. 1084.

**1997, Dec. 6** **Litho.** *Perf. 15x14*

**1095** A406 32p multicolored 2.00 2.00

**Sheet of 12**

**1096** A406 32p #a.-f. + #1045-1046, 1055-1056, 1083, 1095 15.00 15.00

Greetings Stamps — A420

Love is: No. 1097, "...from my heart." No. 1098, "...a birthday wish." No. 1099, "...thinking of you." No. 1100, "...keeping in touch."

**1998, Jan. 26** **Litho.** *Perf. 14x15*

**1097** A420 32p multicolored 2.00 2.00
**1098** A420 32p multicolored 2.00 2.00
**1099** A420 32p multicolored 2.00 2.00
**1100** A420 32p multicolored 2.00 2.00
*a.* Bklt. pane, #1097-1100 + 8 labels 8.00
Complete booklet, 2 #1100a 16.00
*b.* Souv. sheet, #1098-1100 + 7 labels 8.00 8.00

No. 1100a exists with stamps in two different orders. No. 1100b has 1 English, 4 Chinese, 1 Gaelic labels + 1 large label with "Year of the Tiger," in English and Chinese. Same value.

See Nos. 1120-1123.

Aviation Pioneers A421

28p, Lady Mary Heath (Sophie Catherine Pierce), 1st solo flight, Capetown-Croydon via Cairo, 1928. 32p, Col. James Fitzmaurice, navigator on "Bremen," 1st east-west Atlantic flight, 1928. 44p, Capt. J.P. (Paddy) Saul, navigator aboard Southern Cross, Dublin-Newfoundland, 1930. 52p, Capt. Charles Blair, 1st non-stop commercial flight Foynes-NYC, 1942.

**1998, Feb. 24** *Perf. 15x14*

**1101** A421 28p multicolored 1.25 1.25
**1102** A421 32p multicolored 1.60 1.60
*a.* Bklt. pane, 2 ea #1101-1102 4.50
**1103** A421 44p multicolored 1.90 1.90
*a.* Bklt. pane, #1103, 2 #1102 4.50
**1104** A421 52p multicolored 2.25 2.25
*a.* Bklt. pane, #1102, 2 #1104 5.25
*b.* Bklt. pane of 4, #1101-1104 5.75
Complete booklet, #1102a, 1103a, 1104a, 1104b 26.00
*Nos. 1101-1104 (4)* 7.00 7.00

### Bird Types of 1997

No. 1111A: b, Like No. 1107. c, Like No. 1080. d, Like No. 1077. e, Like No. 1078. f, Like No. 1076. g, Like No. 1106B, "Eire" 8½mm wide. h, Like No. 1079. i, Like No. 1053. j, Like No. 1039. k, Like No. 1037. l, Like No. 1109. m, Like No. 1106, "Eire" 8½mm wide. n, Wren. o, Pied wagtail. p, Like No. 1038.

**1998-99** **Litho.** *Perf. 15x14, 14x15*

**1105** A403 5p Woodpigeon, horiz. .90 .75
**1106** A403 30p Blackbird 1.50 1.10
*d.* Perf. 14 1.90 1.10
**1106B** A403 30p Goldcrest, bklt. stamp 1.90 1.90
*c.* Booklet pane, 5 each #1106, 1106B 18.00
Complete booklet, #1106Bc 18.00
**1107** A403 35p Stonechat 1.90 1.90
*a.* Perf. 14 2.25 2.25
**1108** A403 40p Ringed plover, horiz. 2.25 2.25
*a.* Perf. 14 2.75 2.75
**1109** A403 45p Song thrush 3.50 3.50
*a.* Perf. 14 3.75 3.75
**1110** A403 50p Sparrowhawk, horiz. 3.75 3.75
*a.* Perf. 14 4.25 4.25
**1111** A404 £2 Pintail 9.00 9.00

**Sheet of 15**

**1111A** A403 30p #b.-p. 25.00 25.00

See note under #1067.

**Booklet Stamps**

**Size: 18x21mm, 21x18mm**

**1112** A403 5p Like #1105 1.50 1.50
**1113** A403 30p Like #1106 1.90 1.90
*a.* Booklet pane, 2 #1112, 3 #1113 9.00
Complete booklet, #1113a 9.00
**1113B** A403 30p like #1106B 1.10 1.10
*c.* Bklt. pane, 2 #1112, 3 #1113B + label 4.50
Complete booklet, #1113c 4.50

**Size: 20x23mm**

**1113D** A403 45p Like #1109, "Eire" 8½mm wide 3.00 3.00
*e.* Booklet pane of 4 + 4 labels 12.00
Complete booklet 12.00

**Size: 21x24mm**

*Perf. 10¾x13 on 3 sides*

**1113F** A403 30p Like #1106, "Eire" 8½mm wide 2.00 2.00
*i.* Like #1113F, perf. 14¼x14¾ on 3 sides ('99) 2.00 2.00
**1113G** A403 30p Like #1106B, "Eire" 8½mm wide 2.00 2.00
*h.* Booklet pane, 5 each #1113F-1113G 20.00 —
Booklet, #1113Gh 20.00
*j.* Like #1113G, perf. 14¼x14¾ on 3 sides ('99) 2.00 2.00
*k.* Pair, #1113F-1113G 4.00 4.00

*Die Cut Perf. 9x9½*

**Self-Adhesive**

**1114** A403 30p like #1106 7.00 7.00
**1115** A403 30p like #1106B 7.00 7.00
*a.* Pair, #1114-1115 14.00 14.00

**Litho.**

*Die Cut Perf. 11x11¼*

**Self-Adhesive Coil Stamps**

**1115B** A403 30p Like #1114 7.00 7.00
**1115C** A403 30p Like #1115 7.00 7.00
*d.* Pair, #1115B-1115C 14.00 14.00

Issued: No. 1115B-1115C, 5/98; No. 1106B, 1113B, 9/4/98; No. 1111A, 2/16/99; No. 1113D, 6/30/99; No. 1113F, 1113G, 5/3/01.

Equestrian Sports A422

30p, Show jumping. 32p, Three-day event. 40p, Gymkhana. 45p, Dressage, vert.

**1998, Apr. 2**

**1116** A422 30p multicolored 1.40 1.25
**1117** A422 32p multicolored 1.50 1.25
**1118** A422 40p multicolored 2.00 2.00
**1119** A422 45p multicolored 2.25 2.25
*a.* Souvenir sheet, #1116-1119 7.50 7.50
*Nos. 1116-1119 (4)* 7.15 6.75

### Greetings Type of 1998

**1998, May 6** **Litho.** *Perf. 14x15*

**Booklet Stamps**

**1120** A420 30p like #1098 2.00 2.00
**1121** A420 30p like #1099 2.00 2.00
**1122** A420 30p like #1100 2.00 2.00
**1123** A420 30p like #1097 2.00 2.00
*a.* Bklt. pane, #1120-1123 + 8 labels 8.00 8.00
Complete booklet, 2 #1123a 16.00

No. 1123a exists with stamps in different order. Complete booklet contains two different panes.

Festivals A423

Europa: 30p, Crinniú na mBáid, Kinvara (sailboats). 40p, Puck Fair, Killorglin.

**1998, May 6** *Perf. 15x14*

**1124** A423 30p multicolored *1.25 1.25*
**1125** A423 40p multicolored *1.75 1.75*

*Serpentine Die Cut Perf 9x9½*

**Self-Adhesive**

**1126** A423 30p like #1124 *2.00 2.00*
**1127** A423 30p like #1125 *2.00 2.00*
*a.* Pair, #1126-1127 *4.00 4.00*
*Nos. 1124-1127 (4)* 7.00 7.00

1798 Rebellion, Bicent. A424

Battle scene and: No. 1128, "Liberty." No. 1129, Pikeman. No. 1130, French soldier. No. 1131, Wolfe Tone. No. 1132, Henry Joy McCracken.

**1998, May 6**

**1128** A424 30p multicolored 1.00 1.00
**1129** A424 30p multicolored 1.00 1.00
**1130** A424 30p multicolored 1.00 1.00
*a.* Strip of 3, #1128-1130 3.00 3.00
**1131** A424 45p multicolored 1.50 1.50
**1132** A424 45p multicolored 1.50 1.50
*a.* Pair, #1131-1132 3.00 3.00

Tour de France Bicycle Race A425

No. 1133, 4 cyclists. No. 1134, 2 cyclists, 1 wearing dark glasses. No. 1135, 2 cyclists, 1 wearing hat. No. 1136, Leading rider in yellow jersey.

**1998, June 2 Litho. *Perf. 15x14***

**1133** A425 30p multicolored 1.25 1.25
**1134** A425 30p multicolored 1.25 1.25
**1135** A425 30p multicolored 1.25 1.25
**1136** A425 30p multicolored 1.25 1.25
*a.* Strip of 4, #1133-1136 5.50 5.50

Democracy Stamps A426

Designs: 30p, Local government (Ireland Act), cent. 32p, Entrance into European Union, 25th anniv. 35p, Women's vote in local elections, cent. 45c, Republic of Ireland Act, 50th anniv.

**1998, June 2**

**1137** A426 30p multicolored .85 .85
**1138** A426 32p multicolored .85 .85
**1139** A426 35p multicolored 1.00 1.00
**1140** A426 45p multicolored 1.25 1.25
*Nos. 1137-1140 (4)* 3.95 3.95

1998 Tall Ships Race — A427

***Perf. 14x15, 15x14***

**1998, July 20 Litho.**

**1141** A427 30p Asgard II .70 .70
*a.* Perf. 15 1.00 1.00
**1142** A427 30p Eagle 1.00 1.00
*a.* Pair, #1141-1142 1.75 1.75
*b.* Perf. 15 2.50 2.50
*c.* Bklt. pane, #1142b, 2 #1141a 2.25
**1143** A427 45p Boa Esperanza, horiz. 1.25 1.25
*a.* Perf. 15 1.40 1.40
**1144** A427 £1 T.S. Royalist, horiz. 3.00 3.00
*a.* Perf. 15 5.00 5.00
*b.* Bklt. pane of 3, #1142b, 1143a, 1144a 9.00
Complete booklet, #1142c, 1144b 11.50
*Nos. 1141-1144 (4)* 5.95 5.95

**Souvenir Sheet**

**1145** A427 £2 like #1143 8.00 8.00

***Die Cut Perf. 9x9½, 9½x9***

**Self-Adhesive**

**1145A** A427 30p like #1143 2.50 2.50
**1145B** A427 30p like #1141 2.50 2.50
**1145C** A427 30p like #1142 2.50 2.50
**1145D** A427 30p like #1144 2.50 2.50
*e.* Strip of 4, #1145A-1145D 10.00 10.00

Portugal '98 (#1145).
Issued: £2, 9/4; others, 7/20.

Postboxes — A428

No. 1146, Ashworth, 1856. No. 1147, Wallbox, 1922. No. 1148, Double Pillarbox, 1899. No. 1149, Penfold, 1866.

**1998, Sept. 3**

**1146** A428 30p multicolored 1.25 1.25
**1147** A428 30p multicolored 1.25 1.25
**1148** A428 30p multicolored 1.25 1.25
**1149** A428 30p multicolored 1.25 1.25
*a.* Strip of 4, #1146-1149 5.00 5.00

Mary Immaculate College, Limerick, Cent. — A429

Newton School, Waterford, Bicent. — A430

**1998, Sept. 3 *Perf. 15x14, 14x15***

**1150** A429 30p multicolored 1.00 1.00
**1151** A430 40p multicolored 1.50 1.50

Universal Declaration of Human Rights, 50th Anniv. A431

**1998, Sept. 3 *Perf. 15x14***

**1152** A431 45p multicolored 1.50 1.50

Endangered Animals — A432

No. 1153, Cheetah. No. 1154, Scimitar-horned oryx. 40p, Golden lion tamarin. 45p, Tiger.

**1998, Oct. 8 Litho. *Perf. 14***

**1153** A432 30p multi 1.50 1.50
**1154** A432 30p multi 1.50 1.50
*a.* Pair, #1153-1154 3.00 3.00
**1155** A432 40p multi, vert. 1.50 1.50
**1156** A432 45p multi, vert. 1.75 1.75
*a.* Souvenir sheet, #1153-1156, perf. 15 10.00 10.00
*b.* As "a," inscription on extended margin 11.00 11.00
*Nos. 1153-1156 (4)* 6.25 6.25

Stamps on Nos. 1156a, 1156b have a white border. No. 1156b contains exhibition logo and "National Stamp Exhibition RDS-Dublin-6-8 November 1998" in sheet margin.

A433

Christmas — A434

No. 1157, Holy family. 32p, Adoration of the Shepherds. 45p, Adoration of the Magi.
No. 1160, Choir singers.

**1998, Nov. 17 Litho. *Perf. 14x15***

**1157** A433 30p multicolored 1.00 1.00
**1158** A433 32p multicolored 1.25 1.25
**1159** A433 45p multicolored 2.25 2.25
*Nos. 1157-1159 (3)* 4.50 4.50

**Booklet Stamp**

**Self-Adhesive**

***Serpentine Die Cut Perf. 11x11½***

**1160** A434 30p multicolored 1.50 1.50
*a.* Booklet pane of 20 30.00

No. 1160a is a complete booklet. The Peelable paper backing serves as a booklet cover.
No. 1160 sold only in discount booklets at £5.40.

A435

Pets greetings stamps.

**1999, Jan. 26 Litho. *Perf. 14x15***

**1161** A435 30p Dog 1.50 1.50

**Booklet Stamps**

**1162** A435 30p Cat 1.50 1.50
**1163** A435 30p Fish 1.50 1.50
**1164** A435 30p Rabbit 1.50 1.50
*a.* Booklet pane, #1161-1164 + 5 English, 3 Gaelic labels 6.00
*b.* Booklet pane, #1161-1164 + 7 English, 1 Gaelic label 6.00
Complete booklet, #1164a-1164b 12.00
*c.* Souvenir sheet, #1162-1164 (see footnote) 7.00 7.00

No. 1164a contains Nos. 1161-1164 in order. No. 1164b contains stamps in reverse order. No. 1164c has 1 English, 2 Chinese, 3 Gaelic labels + 1 large label with "Year of the Rabbit" in English and Chinese.
New Year 1999 (Year of the Rabbit) (No. 1164c).

A436

Irish Actors: 30p, Micheál Mac Liammóir (1899-1978). 45p, Siobhán McKenna (1923-86). 50p, Noel Purcell (1900-85).

**1999, Feb. 16 Litho. *Perf. 14x15***

**1165** A436 30p brown .70 .70
**1166** A436 45p green 1.25 1.25
**1167** A436 50p blue 1.50 1.50
*Nos. 1165-1167 (3)* 3.45 3.45

Irish Emigration A437

**1999, Feb. 26 Litho. *Perf. 15x14***

**1168** A437 45p multicolored 2.00 2.00

See US No. 3286.

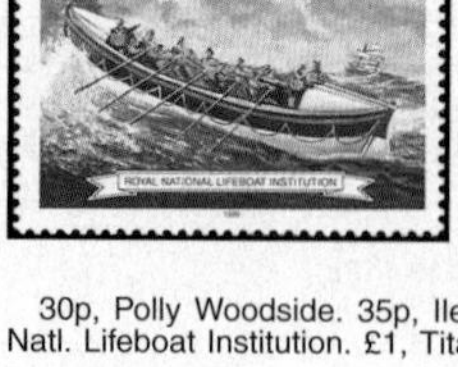

Maritime Heritage A438

30p, Polly Woodside. 35p, Ilen. 45p, Royal Natl. Lifeboat Institution. £1, Titanic.

**1999, Mar. 19 Litho. *Perf. 14***

**1169** A438 30p multi, vert. .85 .85
**1170** A438 35p multi, vert. .95 .95
**1171** A438 45p multi 1.40 1.40
**1172** A438 £1 multi 2.75 2.75
*a.* Souvenir sheet of 2 7.50 7.50
*b.* As "a" ovptd. in sheet margin 9.25 9.25
*Nos. 1169-1172 (4)* 5.95 5.95

**Souvenir Sheet**

***Perf. 14x14½***

**1173** Sheet of 2, #1173a, Australia #1729 6.00 6.00
*a.* A438 30p like #1169 2.75 .80

Australia '99, World Stamp Expo. (No. 1172b, No. 1173). See Australia No. 1729a. No. 1172b is overprinted in gold in sheet margin with Australia '99, World Stamp Expo exhibition emblem.
Sky is gray blue, country and denomination are 3mm high on No. 1169. Sky is blue, country and denomination are 4mm high on No. 1173a.

Natl. Parks A438a

Europa: #1174, 1176, Whooping swans, Kilcolman Nature Reserve. 40p, #1177, Fallow deer, Wellington Memorial Obelisk, Phoenix Park.

**1999, Apr. 29 Litho. *Perf. 15x14***

**1174** A438a 30p multicolored *1.00 1.00*
**1175** A438a 40p multicolored *1.25 1.25*

***Die Cut Perf. 9x9½***

**Self-adhesive**

**1176** A438a 30p Like #1174 *2.25 2.25*
**1177** A438a 30p Like #1175 *2.25 2.25*
*a.* Pair, #1176-1177 *4.50 4.50*

A439

**1999, Apr. 29 Litho. *Perf. 14x15***

**1178** A439 30p green & black 1.50 1.50

Prime Minister Sean Lemass (1899-1971).

A440

**1999, Apr. 29 *Perf. 15x14***

**1179** A440 30p multicolored 1.50 1.50

Introduction of the Euro. No. 1179 is denominated in both pence and euros.

A441

**1999, Apr. 29 *Perf. 14x15***

**1180** A441 45p multicolored 2.50 2.50

Council of Europe, 50th anniv.

Intl. Year of Older Persons A442

**1999, June 15** ***Perf. 15x14***

**1181** A442 30p multicolored 1.50 1.50

UPU, 125th Anniv. A443

**1999, June 15**

**1182** A443 30p Modern mail truck 1.75 1.75
**1183** A443 30p Early mail truck 1.75 1.75
*a.* Pair, #1182-1183 3.50 3.50

Pioneer Total Abstinence Assoc., Cent. — A444

**1999, June 15** ***Perf. 14x15***

**1184** A444 32p Fr. James Cullen 2.00 2.00

Gaelic Football Team of the Millennium A445

No. 1185: a, Danno Keeffe. b, Enda Colleran. c, Joe Keohane. d, Seán Flanagan. e, Seán Murphy. f, John Joe Reilly. g, Martin O'Connell. h, Mick O'Connell. i, Tommy Murphy. j, Seán O'Neill. k, Seán Purcell. l, Pat Spillane. m. Mikey Sheehy. n, Tom Langan. o, Kevin Heffernan.

***Perf. 14¾x14¼***

**1999, Aug. 17** **Litho.**

**1185** Sheet of 15 + label 30.00 30.00
*a.-o.* A445 30p any single 1.25 1.25

**Booklet Stamps**

**Size: 33x22mm**

**Self-Adhesive**

***Serpentine Die Cut Perf. 11¼x11½***

**1186** A445 30p like #1185a 1.75 1.75
**1187** A445 30p like #1185c 1.75 1.75
**1188** A445 30p like #1185e 1.75 1.75
**1189** A445 30p like #1185h 1.75 1.75
**1190** A445 30p like #1185l 1.75 1.75
**1191** A445 30p like #1185m 1.75 1.75
*a.* Bklt. pane, #1186-1189, 2 each #1190-1191 17.50
**1192** A445 30p like #1185d 1.75 1.75
**1193** A445 30p like #1185b 1.75 1.75
**1194** A445 30p like #1185n 1.75 1.75
**1195** A445 30p like #1185k 1.75 1.75
*a.* Bklt. pane, 2 ea #1192-1195 17.50
**1196** A445 30p like #1185o 1.75 1.75
**1197** A445 30p like #1185g 1.75 1.75
**1198** A445 30p like #1185i 1.75 1.75
*a.* Bklt. pane, 3 ea #1196-1197, 2 #1198 17.50
**1199** A445 30p like #1185f 1.75 1.75
**1200** A445 30p like #1185j 1.75 1.75
*a.* Bklt. pane, 4 ea #1199-1200 17.50

Nos. 1191a, 1195a, 1198a, 1200a are each complete booklets. The peelable paper backing serves as a booklet cover. No. 1185 exists imperf.

See Nos. 1246-1261.

Airplanes A446

Designs: 30p, Douglas DC-3. 32p, Britten Norman Islander. 40p, Boeing 707. 45p, Lockheed Constellation.

**1999, Sept. 9** **Litho.** ***Perf. 14¾x14¼***

**1201** A446 30p multicolored .90 .90
*a.* Booklet pane of 4 3.75
**1202** A446 32p multicolored 1.00 1.00
*a.* Bklt. pane, 2 ea #1201, 1202 4.00
**1203** A446 40p multicolored 1.25 1.25
*a.* Bklt. pane, #1203, 2 #1201 5.00
**1204** A446 45p multicolored 1.30 1.30
*a.* Booklet pane, #1201-1204 4.50
Complete bkt., #1201a-1204a 17.50
*Nos. 1201-1204 (4)* 4.45 4.45

Extinct Irish Animals A447

***Perf. 14¼x14¾, 14¾x14¼***

**1999, Oct. 11** **Litho.**

**1205** A447 30p Mammoth, vert. 1.25 1.25
**1206** A447 30p Giant deer, vert. 1.25 1.25
*a.* Pair, #1205-1206 2.50 2.50
**1207** A447 45p Wolf 2.00 2.00
**1208** A447 45p Brown bear 2.00 2.00
*a.* Pair, #1207-1208 4.00 4.00
*b.* Souvenir sheet, #1205-1208, perf. 14¾ 8.00 8.00

Stamps from No. 1208b do not have white border.

***Die Cut Perf. 9¼x9½, 9½x9¼***

**1999, Oct. 11** **Litho.**

**Self-Adhesive**

**1209** A447 30p Like #1208 2.00 2.00
**1210** A447 30p Like #1205 2.00 2.00
**1211** A447 30p Like #1207 2.00 2.00
**1212** A447 30p Like #1206 2.00 2.00
*a.* Strip, #1209-1212 8.00

Christmas A448

**1999, Nov. 4** **Litho.** ***Perf. 14¾x14¼***

**1213** A448 30p Holy Family .90 .90
**1214** A448 32p Shepherds 1.40 1.40
**1215** A448 45p Magi 2.00 2.00
*Nos. 1213-1215 (3)* 4.30 4.30

**Self-Adhesive Booklet Stamp**

**Size: 19x27mm**

***Die Cut 11x11¼***

**1216** A448 30p Angel, vert. 1.25 1.25
*a.* Booklet pane of 20 25.00 25.00

No. 1216a sold for £5.40 and is a complete booklet.

Millennium — A449

People of the 20th Century — No. 1217: a, Grace Kelly. b, Jesse Owens. c, John F. Kennedy. d, Mother Teresa. e, John McCormack. f, Nelson Mandela.

Irish Historic Events — No. 1218, horiz.: a, Norman invasion, 1169. b, Flight of the Earls, 1607. c, Irish Parliament, 1782. d, Land league. e, Irish independence. f, UN peacekeeping.

Discoveries — No. 1219: a, Rev. Nicholas Callan, electrical scientist. b, Birr Telescope. c, Thomas Edison. d, Albert Einstein. e, Marie Curie. f, Galileo.

The Arts — No. 1220: a, Ludwig van Beethoven. b, Dame Ninette de Valois, ballet director. c, James Joyce. d, Mona Lisa, by Leonardo da Vinci. e, Painting by Sir John Lavery. f, William Shakespeare.

World Events — No. 1221, horiz.: a, French Revolution, 1789. b, Industrial Revolution. c, Peace, 1945. d, Women's liberation. e, Fall of the Berlin Wall, 1989. f, Modern communications.

Epic Journeys — No. 1222, horiz.: a, Marco Polo. b, Capt. James Cook. c, Australian explorers Robert O'Hara Burke and William Wills. d, Antarctic explorer Ernest Shackleton. e, Charles Lindbergh. f, Astronaut on moon.

***Perf. 14¼x14¾, 14¾x14¼***

**1999-2001** **Litho.**

**1217** Sheet of 12, 2 ea #a.-f. 27.50 27.50
*a.-f.* A449 30p Any single 2.10 2.10
**1218** Sheet of 12, 2 ea #a.-f. 27.50 27.50
*a.-f.* A449 30p Any single 2.10 2.10
**1219** Sheet of 12, 2 each #a.-f. 27.50 27.50
*a.-f.* A449 30p Any single 2.10 2.10
**1220** Sheet of 12, 2 each #a.-f. 27.50 27.50
*a.-f.* A449 30p Any single 2.10 2.10
**1221** A449 Sheet of 12, 2 each #a-f 27.50 27.50
*a.-f.* 30p Any single 2.10 2.10
**1222** A449 Sheet of 12, 2 each #a-f 27.50 27.50
*a.-f.* 30p Any single 2.10 2.10

Issued: No. 1217, 12/31; No. 1218, 1/1/00; No. 1219, 2/29/00; No. 1220, 6/16/00; No. 1221, 12/31/00; No. 1222, 1/1/01.

Mythical Creatures — A450

**2000, Jan. 26** **Litho.** ***Perf. 14¼x14¾***

**1223** A450 30p Frog Prince 1.50 1.50
**1224** A450 30p Pegasus 1.50 1.50
**1225** A450 30p Unicorn 1.50 1.50
**1226** A450 30p Dragon 1.50 1.50
*a.* Booklet pane, #1223-1226, + 3 Gaelic, 5 English labels 6.00
*b.* Booklet pane, #1223-1226, + 2 Gaelic, 6 English labels 6.00
*c.* Booklet pane, #1223, 1226, + 14 labels 3.00
Complete booklet, #1226a-1226c 15.00
*d.* Souvenir sheet, #1224-1226, + 7 labels 7.00 7.00
*Nos. 1223-1226 (4)* 6.00 6.00

New Year 2000 (Year of the Dragon), No. 1226d.

Emigrant Ship Jeanie Johnston A451

**2000, Mar. 9** **Litho.** ***Perf. 14¾x14¼***

**1227** A451 30p multi 2.00 2.00

Europa, 2000

Common Design Type

**2000, May 9** **Litho.** ***Perf. 14¼x14¾***

**1230** CD17 32p multi 1.75 1.75

***Die Cut Perf 9½x9¼***

**Self-Adhesive**

**Size: 22x34mm**

**1231** CD17 30p multi 3.00 3.00

Oscar Wilde (1854-1900), Playwright — A453

No. 1232, Portrait. No. 1233, The Happy Prince. No. 1234, The Importance of Being Earnest. No. 1235, The Picture of Dorian Gray. No. 1236, £2, Like No. 1232, signature at left.

***Perf. 14¼x14¾, 14¼x14 (#1236)***

**2000, May 22** **Litho.**

**1232** A453 30p multi 1.50 1.50
**1233** A453 30p multi 1.50 1.50
**1234** A453 30p multi 1.50 1.50
**1235** A453 30p multi 1.50 1.50
*a.* Block, #1232-1235 6.00 6.00

**Size: 27x27mm**

**1236** A453 30p multi + label 13.50 13.50
Sheet of 20 275.00
*Nos. 1232-1236 (5)* 19.50 19.50

**Souvenir Sheet**

**1237** A453 £2 multi 8.00 8.00
*a.* With Stamp Show 2000 emblem in margin 8.00 8.00

No. 1237 contains one 30x40mm stamp.

No. 1236 was printed in sheets of 20 stamps and 20 labels for £10. These sheets were not available at Irish post offices, but were sold at the Irish Post booths at The Stamp Show 2000 in London and World Stamp Expo in Ahaheim, California. Labels were blank, but purchasers could provide Irish Post with photographic images or other artwork that would be reproduced on the labels.

2000 Summer Olympics, Sydney A454

**2000, July 7** **Litho.** ***Perf. 13¼***

**1238** A454 30p Running .90 .90
**1239** A454 30p Javelin 1.60 1.60
*a.* Pair, #1238-1239 2.50 2.50
**1240** A454 50p Long jump 1.25 1.25
**1241** A454 50p High jump 1.25 1.25
*a.* Pair, #1240-1241 2.50 2.50

Stampin' the Future A455

Children's Stamp Design Contest Winners: 30p, Marguerite Nyhan (rocket and flowers), vert. 32p, Kyle Staunton (2000). No. 1244, Jennifer Branagan (Earth, sun and moon). No. 1245, Diarmuid O'Ceochain (rocket, building on moon).

***Perf. 14¼x14¾, 14¾x14¼***

**2000, July 7**

**1242** A455 30p multi 1.25 1.25
**1243** A455 32p multi 1.25 1.25
**1244** A455 45p multi 2.10 2.10
**1245** A455 45p multi 2.10 2.10
*a.* Pair, #1244-1245 4.25 4.25
*Nos. 1242-1245 (4)* 6.70 6.70

**Team of the Millennium Type of 1999**

Hurling — No. 1246: a, Tony Reddin. b, Bobby Rackard. c, Nick O'Donnell. d, John Doyle. e, Brian Whelahan. f, John Keane. g,

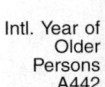

Paddy Phelan. h, Lory Meagher. i, Jack Lynch. j, Jim Langton. k, Mick Mackey. l, Christy Ring. m, Jimmy Doyle. n, Ray Cummins. o, Eddie Keher.

**2000, Aug. 2 Litho.** ***Perf. 14¾x14¼***

**1246** Sheet of 15 + label 15.00 15.00
*a.-o.* A445 30p Any single 1.00 1.00

No. 1246 exists imperf. Value, $125.

**Booklet Stamps**

**Self-Adhesive**

**Size: 33x22mm**

***Serpentine Die Cut 11¼x11½***

**1247** A445 30p Like #1246a 1.90 1.90
**1248** A445 30p Like #1246m 1.90 1.90
**1249** A445 30p Like #1246d 1.90 1.90
*a.* Booklet, 3 each #1247-1248, 4 #1249 15.00
**1250** A445 30p Like #1246b 1.90 1.90
**1251** A445 30p Like #1246c 1.90 1.90
*a.* Booklet, 5 each #1250-1251 15.00
**1252** A445 30p Like #1246k 1.90 1.90
**1253** A445 30p Like #1246e 1.90 1.90
**1254** A445 30p Like #1246f 1.90 1.90
*a.* Booklet, 4 #1252, 3 each #1253-1254 15.00
**1255** A445 30p Like #1246g 1.90 1.90
**1256** A445 30p Like #1246j 1.90 1.90
**1257** A445 30p Like #1246h 1.90 1.90
**1258** A445 30p Like #1246o 1.90 1.90
*a.* Booklet, 2 each #1255-1256, 3 each #1257-1258 15.00
**1259** A445 30p Like #1246i 1.90 1.90
**1260** A445 30p Like #1246n 1.90 1.90
**1261** A445 30p Like #1246l 1.90 1.90
*a.* Booklet, 3 each #1259-1260, 4 #1261 15.00
*Nos. 1247-1261 (15)* 28.50 28.50

No. 1246 exists imperf.

Butterflies A456

Designs: 30p, Peacock. 32p, Small tortoiseshell. 45p, Silver-washed fritillary. 50p, Orange-tip.

**2000, Sept. 6** ***Perf. 13¼x12¾***

**1262** A456 30p multi .70 .70
**1263** A456 32p multi 1.00 1.00
**1264** A456 45p multi 1.50 1.50
**1265** A456 50p multi 1.75 1.75
*a.* Souvenir sheet, #1262-1265 10.00 10.00

Stamps from No. 1265a lack year date.

Military Aircraft A457

Designs: No. 1266, Bristol F.2b Mk II fighter. No. 1267, Hawker Hurricane Mk IIc. No. 1268, Alouette III helicopter. No. 1269, De Havilland DH.115 Vampire T.55.

**2000, Oct. 9 Litho.** ***Perf. 14¾x14¼***

**1266** A457 30p multi .80 .80
**1267** A457 30p multi .80 .80
*a.* Pair, #1266-1267 1.75 1.75
*b.* Booklet pane, 2 each #1266-1267 3.50
**1268** A457 45p multi 1.75 1.75
*a.* Booklet pane, #1266-1268 3.50
**1269** A457 45p multi 1.75 1.75
*a.* Pair, #1268-1269 3.50 3.50
*b.* Booklet pane, 2 each #1268-1269 7.00
*c.* Booklet pane, #1266-1269 5.00
Booklet, #1267b, 1268a, 1269b, 1269c 20.00
*Nos. 1266-1269 (4)* 5.10 5.10

**Coil Stamps**

**Self-Adhesive**

***Die Cut Perf. 9¼x9½***

**1270** A457 30p Like #1266 2.50 2.50
**1271** A457 30p Like #1267 2.50 2.50
**1272** A457 30p Like #1269 2.50 2.50
**1273** A457 30p Like #1268 2.50 2.50
*a.* Strip, #1270-1273 10.00

Dept. of Agriculture, Cent. A458

**2000, Nov. 14 Litho.** ***Perf. 13½***

**1274** A458 50p multi 2.00 2.00

Christmas A459

Designs: No. 1275, Nativity. 32p, Adoration of the Magi. 45p, Adoration of the Shepherds. No. 1278, Flight to Egypt.

**2000, Nov. 14** ***Perf. 14¼x14¾***

**1275** A459 30p multi .85 .85
**1276** A459 32p multi 1.50 1.50
**1277** A459 45p multi 2.25 2.25

**Booklet Stamp**

**Self-Adhesive**

**Size: 21x26mm**

***Serpentine Die Cut 11¼***

**1278** A459 30p multi 1.50 1.50
*a.* Booklet of 24 35.00
*Nos. 1275-1278 (4)* 6.10 6.10

No. 1278 sold for £6.60.

Pets — A460

Designs: Nos. 1279, 1283, Goldfish, hearts. Nos. 1280a, 1284, Snake. Nos. 1280b, 1282, Frog, four-leaf clover. Nos. 1280c, 1285, Turtle, stars. No. 1281, Lizard, daisy.

**2001, Jan. 24 Litho.** ***Perf. 14¼x14¾***

**1279** A460 30p multi 2.00 2.00

**Souvenir Sheet**

**1280** Sheet of 3 7.50 7.50
*a.-c.* A460 30p Any single 2.50 2.50

**Booklet Stamps**

**Size: 25x30mm**

**Self-Adhesive**

***Serpentine Die Cut 12***

**1281** A460 30p multi 1.40 1.40
**1282** A460 30p multi 1.40 1.40
**1283** A460 30p multi 1.40 1.40
**1284** A460 30p multi 1.40 1.40
**1285** A460 30p multi 1.40 1.40
*a.* Booklet, 2 each #1281-1285 + 10 labels 14.00
*Nos. 1281-1285 (5)* 7.00 7.00

New Year 2001 (Year of the Snake), No. 1280.

Broadcasting in Ireland — A461

Designs: 30p, Camera, audience, man. 32p, Microphone, announcers. 45p, People listening to radio. 50p, Television.

**2001, Feb. 27** ***Perf. 14¾x14¼***

**1286** A461 30p multi .70 .70
**1287** A461 32p multi 1.00 1.00
**1288** A461 45p multi 1.50 1.50
**1289** A461 50p multi 1.75 1.75
*Nos. 1286-1289 (4)* 4.95 4.95

Literary Anniversaries A462

Designs: 30p, Marsh's Library, first public library in Ireland, 300th anniv. 32p, Book of Common Prayer, first book printed in Ireland, 450th anniv.

**2001, Mar. 14** ***Perf. 14¼x14¾***

**1290** A462 30p multi 1.00 1.00
**1291** A462 32p multi 2.00 2.00

Comhaltas Ceoltóirí Eirann, 50th Anniv. — A463

Musician with: No. 1292, Bagpipes. No. 1293, Tambourine. No. 1294, Flute, horiz. No. 1295, Violin, horiz.

***Perf. 14¼x14¾, 14¾x14¼***

**2001, Mar. 14**

**1292** A463 30p multi 1.00 1.00
**1293** A463 30p multi 1.00 1.00
*a.* Pair, #1292-1293 2.00 2.00
**1294** A463 45p multi 1.50 1.50
**1295** A463 45p multi 1.50 1.50
*a.* Pair, #1294-1295 3.00 3.00
*Nos. 1292-1295 (4)* 5.00 5.00

Race Cars A464

Designs: Nos. 1296, 1300, 1301, Jordan Grand Prix Formula 1. Nos. 1297, 1304, Hillman Imp, Tulip Rally. Nos. 1298, 1303, Mini Cooper S, Monte Carlo Rally. Nos. 1299, 1302, Mercedes SSK, Irish Grand Prix.

**2001, Apr. 26** ***Perf. 13¾x14¼***

**1296** A464 30p multi .65 .65
**1297** A464 32p multi .90 .90
**1298** A464 45p multi 1.40 1.40
**1299** A464 £1 multi 3.00 3.00
*Nos. 1296-1299 (4)* 5.95 5.95

**Souvenir Sheet**

**1300** A464 £2 multi 8.00 8.00
*a.* With Belgica show emblem in margin 10.00 10.00

**Booklet Stamps**

**Size: 36x24mm**

**Self-Adhesive**

***Serpentine Die Cut 11¾***

**1301** A464 30p multi 3.75 3.75
**1302** A464 30p multi 3.75 3.75
**1303** A464 30p multi 3.75 3.75
**1304** A464 30p multi 3.75 3.75
*a.* Booklet, 4 #1301, 2 each #1302-1304 37.50
*Nos. 1301-1304 (4)* 15.00 15.00

Issued: No. 1300a, 6/9/01.

Irish Heritage in Australia A465

**2001, May 3** ***Perf. 14¾x14¼***

**1305** A465 30p Ned Kelly 1.25 1.25
**1306** A465 30p Peter Lalor 1.25 1.25
*a.* Pair, #1305-1306 2.50 2.50
**1307** A465 45p Settlers 1.50 1.50
**1308** A465 45p Emigrants 1.50 1.50
*a.* Pair, #1307-1308 3.00 3.00
*Nos. 1305-1308 (4)* 5.50 5.50

**Souvenir Sheet**

**1309** A465 £1 Like #1305 4.00 4.00

Europa A466

**2001, May 16 Litho.** ***Perf. 14¾x14¼***

**1310** A466 30p Wading *.75 .75*
**1311** A466 32p Fishing *1.25 1.25*

**Coil Stamps**

**Self-Adhesive**

***Die Cut Perf. 9¼x9½***

**1312** A466 30p Wading *2.00 2.00*
**1313** A466 30p Fishing *2.00 2.00*
*a.* Strip, #1312-1313 *4.00*

**Bird Types of 1997 With Added Euro Denominations**

Designs: Nos. 1314, 1319A, Blackbird. 1319B, Goldcrest. 32p, Robin. 35p, Puffin. 40p, Wren. 45p, Song thrush. £1, Greenland white-fronted goose.

***Perf. 14¼x14¾***

**2001, June 11 Litho.**

**1314** A403 30p multi 1.60 1.60
**1315** A403 32p multi 2.25 2.25
**1316** A403 35p multi 2.75 2.75
**1317** A403 40p multi 3.25 3.25
**1318** A403 45p multi 4.00 4.00

***Perf. 14¾x14¼***

**1319** A404 £1 multi 6.00 6.00
*Nos. 1314-1319 (6)* 19.85 19.85

**Self-Adhesive**

**Coil Stamps**

**Size: 21x26mm**

**1319A** A403 30p multi 4.50 4.50
**1319B** A403 30p multi 4.50 4.50
*c.* Pair, #1319A-1319B 9.00

Battle of Kinsale, 400th Anniv. A467

Designs: No. 1320, Soldiers on horseback. No. 1321, Soldiers in stream. 32p, Soldiers and ramparts. 45p, View of Kinsale.

**2001, July 10** ***Perf. 13½***

**1320** A467 30p multi 1.10 1.10
**1321** A467 30p multi 1.10 1.10
*a.* Pair, #1320-1321 2.25 2.25
**1322** A467 32p multi 2.00 2.00
**1323** A467 45p multi 2.25 2.25
*Nos. 1320-1323 (4)* 6.45 6.45

Hall of Fame Athletes A468

Designs: Nos. 1324, 1328, Padraic Carney, soccer player. Nos. 1325, 1329, Frank Cummins, hurler. Nos. 1326, 1330, Jack O'Shea, soccer player. Nos. 1327, 1331, Nicky Rackard, hurler.

**2001, Sept. 5 Litho. *Perf. 14¾x14***

| | | | | |
|---|---|---|---|---|
| **1324** | A468 30p multi | | 1.25 | 1.25 |
| **1325** | A468 30p multi | | 1.25 | 1.25 |
| **1326** | A468 30p multi | | 1.25 | 1.25 |
| **1327** | A468 30p multi | | 1.25 | 1.25 |
| *a.* | Horiz. strip, #1324-1327 | | 5.00 | 5.00 |

**Booklet Stamps**

**Size: 33x22mm**

**Self-Adhesive**

***Serpentine Die Cut 11x11½***

| | | | |
|---|---|---|---|
| **1328** | A468 30p multi | 2.00 | 2.00 |
| **1329** | A468 30p multi | 2.00 | 2.00 |
| **1330** | A468 30p multi | 2.00 | 2.00 |
| **1331** | A468 30p multi | 2.00 | 2.00 |
| *a.* | Booklet, 2 each #1328, 1331, 3 each #1329-1330 | 20.00 | |
| | *Nos. 1324-1331 (8)* | 13.00 | 13.00 |

Sailboats — A469

Designs: No. 1332, Ruffian 23. No. 1333, Howth 17. No. 1334, 1720 Sportsboat. No. 1335, The Glen. No. 1336, Ruffian 23. No. 1337, Howth 17. No. 1338, The Glen. No. 1339, 1720 Sportsboat.

**2001, Sept. 5 *Perf. 14x14¾***

| | | | |
|---|---|---|---|
| **1332** | A469 30p multi | 1.25 | 1.25 |
| **1333** | A469 32p multi | 1.25 | 1.25 |
| **1334** | A469 45p multi | 1.75 | 1.75 |
| **1335** | A469 45p multi | 1.75 | 1.75 |
| *a.* | Horiz. pair, #1334-1335 | 3.50 | 3.50 |
| | *Nos. 1332-1335 (4)* | 6.00 | 6.00 |

**Coil Stamps**

**Self-Adhesive**

***Serpentine Die Cut 9½x9¼***

| | | | |
|---|---|---|---|
| **1336** | A469 30p multi | 2.50 | 2.50 |
| **1337** | A469 30p multi | 2.50 | 2.50 |
| **1338** | A469 30p multi | 2.50 | 2.50 |
| **1339** | A469 30p multi | 2.50 | 2.50 |
| *a.* | Strip of 4, #1336-1339 | 10.00 | |

**Bird Type of 1997**

***Serpentine Die Cut 11¼***

**2001, Oct. 9 Litho.**

**Booklet Stamps**

**Self-Adhesive**

| | | | |
|---|---|---|---|
| **1340** | A403 N Blackbird | 1.75 | 1.75 |
| **1341** | A403 N Goldcrest | 1.75 | 1.75 |
| *a.* | Booklet, 5 each #1340-1341 | 17.50 | 17.50 |
| **1342** | A403 E Robin | 1.90 | 1.90 |
| *a.* | Booklet of 10 + 10 etiquettes | 19.00 | |
| **1343** | A403 W Song thrush | 3.00 | 3.00 |
| *a.* | Booklet of 10 + 10 etiquettes | 30.00 | |
| | *Nos. 1340-1343 (4)* | 8.40 | 8.40 |

Fish A470

Designs: 30p, Perch. No. 1345, Arctic char. No. 1346, Pike. 45p, Common bream.

**2001, Oct. 9 *Perf. 14¾x14***

| | | | |
|---|---|---|---|
| **1344** | A470 30p multi | 1.25 | 1.25 |
| **1345** | A470 32p multi | 1.75 | 1.75 |
| **1346** | A470 32p multi | 1.75 | 1.75 |
| *a.* | Horiz. pair, #1345-1346 | 3.50 | 3.50 |
| **1347** | A470 45p multi | 2.50 | 2.50 |
| *a.* | Booklet pane, #1344-1347 | 6.25 | — |
| *b.* | Booklet pane, #1345, 1346, 2 #1347 | 8.75 | — |
| *c.* | Booklet pane, 2 each #1344, 1347 | 7.50 | — |
| | Booklet, #1347b, 1347c, 2 #1347a | 29.00 | |

No. 1347a exists with stamps in different order. The booklet contains the two different panes.

Governmental Support of Arts, 50th Anniv. — A471

**2001, Nov. 5 *Perf. 14x14¾***

| | | | |
|---|---|---|---|
| **1348** | A471 50p multi | 2.50 | 2.50 |

Christmas — A472

Designs: No. 1349, Nativity. 32p, Annunciation. 45p, Presentation in the Temple. No. 1352, Madonna and Child.

**2001, Nov. 5 *Perf. 14x14¾***

| | | | |
|---|---|---|---|
| **1349** | A472 30p multi | 1.00 | 1.00 |
| **1350** | A472 32p multi | 1.40 | 1.40 |
| **1351** | A472 45p multi | 2.50 | 2.50 |

**Booklet Stamp**

**Size: 21x27mm**

**Self-Adhesive**

***Serpentine Die Cut 11x11¼***

| | | | |
|---|---|---|---|
| **1352** | A472 30p multi | 1.50 | 1.50 |
| *a.* | Booklet of 24 | 35.00 | |
| | *Nos. 1349-1352 (4)* | 6.40 | 6.40 |

No. 1352a sold for £6.60.

100 Cents = 1 Euro (€)

A473

Birds (With Euro Denominations Only) — A474

Designs: 1c, Magpie. 2c, Gannet. 3c, Blue tit, horiz. 4c, Corncrake. 5c, Wood pigeon, horiz. Nos. 1358, 1370, 10c, Kingfisher. 20c, Lapwing. Nos. 1360, 1371, 1372, 38c, Blackbird. No. 1373, 38c, Goldcrest. 41c, Chaffinch. 44c, Robin. 50c, Gray heron, horiz. 51c, Roseate tern, horiz. 57c, Curlew. €1, Barnacle goose. €2, Greenland white-fronted goose, vert. €5, Pintail. €10, Shelduck, vert.

***Perf. 14x14¾, 14¾x14***

**2002, Jan. 1 Litho.**

| | | | | |
|---|---|---|---|---|
| **1353** | A473 | 1c multi | .25 | .25 |
| **1354** | A473 | 2c multi | .25 | .25 |
| **1355** | A473 | 3c multi | .25 | .25 |
| **1356** | A473 | 4c multi | .25 | .25 |
| **1357** | A473 | 5c multi | .25 | .25 |
| **1358** | A473 | 10c multi | .40 | .30 |
| **1359** | A473 | 20c multi | .75 | .65 |
| **1360** | A473 | 38c multi | 1.40 | 1.25 |
| **1361** | A473 | 41c multi | 1.60 | 1.40 |
| **1362** | A473 | 44c multi | 1.75 | 1.60 |
| **1363** | A473 | 50c multi | 1.90 | 1.75 |
| **1364** | A473 | 51c multi | 1.90 | 1.75 |
| **1365** | A473 | 57c multi | 2.25 | 1.90 |
| **1366** | A474 | €1 multi | 3.75 | 3.50 |
| **1367** | A474 | €2 multi | 7.50 | 7.00 |
| **1368** | A474 | €5 multi | 19.00 | 17.50 |
| **1369** | A474 | €10 multi | 37.50 | 35.00 |

**Booklet Stamps**

**Size: 18x20mm**

***Perf. 14¾x14¼ on 3 Sides***

| | | | | |
|---|---|---|---|---|
| **1370** | A473 | 10c multi | 1.25 | 1.25 |
| **1371** | A473 | 38c multi | 2.75 | 2.75 |
| *a.* | | Booklet pane, #1370, 5 #1371 | 14.00 | — |
| | | Booklet, #1371a | 14.00 | |

**Coil Stamps**

**Size: 21x26mm**

**Self-Adhesive**

***Serpentine Die Cut 11x11¼***

| | | | |
|---|---|---|---|
| **1372** | A473 38c multi | 5.75 | 5.75 |
| **1373** | A473 38c multi | 5.75 | 5.75 |
| *a.* | Pair, #1372-1373 | 14.00 | 14.00 |
| | *Nos. 1353-1373 (21)* | 96.45 | 90.35 |

See Nos. 1392-1398, 1421-1423, 1433-1434, 1447-1449, 1492-1495, 1511-1515, 1523-1526.

Introduction of the Euro A475

Designs: 38c, 1 euro coin introduced in 2002. 41c, 50p coin used from 1971-2001. 57c, 1p coin used from 1928-71.

**2002, Jan. 1 Litho. *Perf. 14¾x14¼***

| | | | |
|---|---|---|---|
| **1374** | A475 38c multi | 1.10 | 1.10 |
| **1375** | A475 41c multi | 1.25 | 1.25 |
| **1376** | A475 57c multi | 1.75 | 1.75 |
| | *Nos. 1374-1376 (3)* | 4.10 | 4.10 |

Toys — A476

Designs: Nos. 1377, 1379, Teddy bear. Nos. 1378a, 1381, Rocking horse. Nos. 1378b, 1382, Wooden locomotive. Nos. 1378c, 1380, Doll. No. 1383, Blocks.

**2002, Jan. 22 *Perf. 14¼x14¾***

| | | | |
|---|---|---|---|
| **1377** | A476 38c multi | 2.00 | 2.00 |

**Souvenir Sheet**

***Perf. 14¼x14¾ on 3 or 4 Sides***

| | | | |
|---|---|---|---|
| **1378** | Sheet of 3 | 9.00 | 9.00 |
| *a.-c.* | A476 38c Any single | 3.00 | 3.00 |

**Booklet Stamps**

**Self-Adhesive**

**Size: 21x27mm**

***Serpentine Die Cut 11¼***

| | | | |
|---|---|---|---|
| **1379** | A476 38c multi | 1.75 | 1.75 |
| **1380** | A476 38c multi | 1.75 | 1.75 |
| **1381** | A476 38c multi | 1.75 | 1.75 |
| **1382** | A476 38c multi | 1.75 | 1.75 |
| **1383** | A476 38c multi | 1.75 | 1.75 |
| *a.* | Booklet of 10, 2 each #1379-1383, + 10 labels | 17.50 | |
| | *Nos. 1379-1383 (5)* | 8.75 | 8.75 |

New Year 2002 (Year of the Horse), No. 1378.

Steeplechasing in Ireland, 250th Anniv. — A477

**2002, Mar. 12 *Perf. 14¾x14¼***

| | | | |
|---|---|---|---|
| **1384** | A477 38c Arkle | 1.25 | 1.25 |
| **1385** | A477 38c L'Escargot | 1.25 | 1.25 |
| **1386** | A477 38c Dawn Run | 1.25 | 1.25 |
| **1387** | A477 38c Istabraq | 1.25 | 1.25 |
| *a.* | Horiz. strip of 4, #1384-1387 | 5.00 | 5.00 |

Scouting A478

Designs: No. 1388, Scout with peg and mallet. No. 1389, Scouts and leader around camp fire. No. 1390, Scouts on hike. No. 1391, Scouts kayaking.

**2002, Mar. 12**

| | | | |
|---|---|---|---|
| **1388** | A478 41c multi | 1.25 | 1.25 |
| **1389** | A478 41c multi | 1.25 | 1.25 |
| *a.* | Horiz. pair, #1388-1389 | 2.50 | 2.50 |
| **1390** | A478 57c multi | 2.00 | 2.00 |
| **1391** | A478 57c multi | 2.00 | 2.00 |
| *a.* | Horiz. pair, #1390-1391 | 4.00 | 4.00 |
| | *Nos. 1388-1391 (4)* | 6.50 | 6.50 |

**Bird Type of 2002**

Designs: No. 1395, Chaffinch. No. 1396, Goldcrest. 44c, Robin. 47c, Kestrel, horiz. 55c, Oystercatcher. 57c, Song thrush. 60c, Jay, horiz.

**2002 Litho. *Perf. 14¾x14***

| | | | |
|---|---|---|---|
| **1392** | A473 47c multi | 4.25 | 4.25 |
| **1393** | A473 55c multi | 4.75 | 4.75 |
| **1394** | A473 60c multi | 6.00 | 6.00 |

**Self-Adhesive**

***Serpentine Die Cut 11x11¼***

**Size: 21x26mm**

| | | | |
|---|---|---|---|
| **1395** | A473 41c multi | 3.75 | 3.75 |
| **1396** | A473 41c multi | 3.75 | 3.75 |
| *a.* | Coil pair, #1395-1396 | 7.50 | |
| *b.* | Booklet of 10, 5 each #1395-1396 | 37.50 | |

**Booklet Stamps**

| | | | |
|---|---|---|---|
| **1397** | A473 44c multi | 2.50 | 2.50 |
| *a.* | Booklet of 10 | 25.00 | |
| **1398** | A473 57c multi | 2.75 | 2.75 |
| *a.* | Booklet of 10 | 27.50 | |
| | *Nos. 1392-1398 (7)* | 27.75 | 27.75 |

Issued: Nos. 1395-1398, 4/2. Nos. 1392-1394, 6/17.

Compare Nos. 1395-1396 with Nos. 1433-1434.

Mammals A479

Designs: 41c, Meles meles. 50c, €5, Lutra lutra. 57c, Sciurus vulgaris, vert. €1, Erinaceus europaeus, vert.

***Perf. 14¾x14¼, 14¼x14¾***

**2002, Apr. 23 Litho.**

| | | | |
|---|---|---|---|
| **1399** | A479 41c multi | 1.00 | 1.00 |
| **1400** | A479 50c multi | 1.25 | 1.25 |
| **1401** | A479 57c multi | 1.40 | 1.40 |
| **1402** | A479 €1 multi | 2.50 | 2.50 |
| | *Nos. 1399-1402 (4)* | 6.15 | 6.15 |

**Souvenir Sheet**

| | | | |
|---|---|---|---|
| **1403** | A479 €5 multi | 21.00 | 21.00 |

Europa A480

Designs: Nos. 1404, 1406, Clown. Nos. 1405, 1407, Equestrian act.

**2002, May 14 Litho. *Perf. 14¾x14***

| | | | |
|---|---|---|---|
| **1404** | A480 41c multi | *1.25* | *1.25* |
| **1405** | A480 44c multi | *1.40* | *1.40* |

**Coil Stamps**

**Size: 34x23mm**

**Self-Adhesive**

***Die Cut Perf. 9¼x9½***

| | | | |
|---|---|---|---|
| **1406** | A480 41c multi | *1.25* | *1.25* |
| **1407** | A480 41c multi | *1.25* | *1.25* |
| *a.* | Horiz. pair, #1406-1407 | *2.50* | *2.50* |
| | *Nos. 1404-1407 (4)* | 5.15 | 5.15 |

Soccer Stars A481

Designs: Nos. 1408, 1415, Packie Bonner. Nos. 1409, 1412, Roy Keane, vert. Nos. 1410, 1413, Paul McGrath, vert. Nos. 1411, 1414, David O'Leary, vert.

**2002, May 14** ***Perf. 14¾x14, 14x14¾***

1408 A481 41c multi 1.25 1.25
1409 A481 41c multi 1.25 1.25
1410 A481 41c multi 1.25 1.25
1411 A481 41c multi 1.25 1.25
a. Vert. strip of 3, #1409-1411 5.00 5.00

**Booklet Stamps**
**Sizes: 23x34, 34x23mm**
**Self-Adhesive**
***Serpentine Die Cut 11½x11¾, 11¾x11½***

1412 A481 41c multi 3.00 3.00
1413 A481 41c multi 3.00 3.00
1414 A481 41c multi 3.00 3.00
1415 A481 41c multi 3.00 3.00
a. Booklet, 3 #1412-1413, 2 #1414-1415 30.00

Canonization of St. Pio of Pietrelcina (1887-1968) A482

**2002, June 17 Litho.** ***Perf. 14x14¾***

1416 A482 41c multi 2.00 2.00

BrianBorú, 1000th Anniv of High Kingship A483

Designs: 41c, Leading troops into battle. 44c, Commanding ships. 57c, On throne. €1, Decreeing Armagh as the primacy of the Irish church.

**2002, July 9** ***Perf. 14¾x14***

1417 A483 41c multi 1.00 1.00
1418 A483 44c multi 1.25 1.25
1419 A483 57c multi 1.40 1.40
1420 A483 €1 multi 2.50 2.50
*Nos. 1417-1420 (4)* 6.15 6.15

**Bird Type of 2002**

Designs: No. 1421, Goldcrest. No. 1422, 36c, Wren. No. 1423, Chaffinch.

***Perf. 14x14¾ on 3 Sides***

**2002, Aug. 6** **Litho.**

**Booklet Stamps**

1421 A473 41c multi 2.25 2.25
a. Booklet pane of 10, 5 each #1361, 1421 22.50 —
Booklet, #1421a 22.50

**Size: 18x21mm**
***Perf. 14¾x14¼ on 3 Sides***

1422 A473 36c multi 2.25 2.25
1423 A473 41c multi 2.75 2.75
a. Booklet pane of 5, #1422, 4 #1423 + label 21.00 —
Booklet, #1423a 21.00

Paintings in National Gallery A484

Designs: No. 1424, Before the Start, by Jack B. Yeats. No. 1425, The Conjuror, by Nathaniel Hone. No. 1426, The Colosseum and Arch of Constantine, Rome, by Giovanni Paolo Panini. No. 1427, The Gleaners, by Jules Breton.

**2002, Aug. 29** ***Perf. 14¾x14***

1424 A484 41c multi 1.25 1.25
a. Booklet pane of 4 5.00 —
1425 A484 41c multi 1.25 1.25
a. Booklet pane of 4 5.00 —
1426 A484 41c multi 1.25 1.25
a. Booklet pane of 4 5.00 —
1427 A484 41c multi 1.25 1.25
a. Horiz. strip, #1424-1427 5.00 5.00
b. Booklet pane of 4 5.00 —
Booklet, #1424a, 1425a, 1426a, 1427b 20.00

See Nos. 1496-1499, 1572-1575.

Archbishop Thomas Croke (1823-1902) A485

**2002, Sept. 17** ***Perf. 14x14¾***

1428 A485 44c multi 2.00 2.00

**Hall of Fame Athletes Type of 2001**

Designs: No. 1429, Peter McDermott, soccer player. No. 1430, Jimmy Smyth, hurler. No. 1431, Matt Connor, soccer player. No. 1432, Seanie Duggan, hurler.

**2002, Sept. 17** ***Perf. 14¾x14***

1429 A468 41c multi 1.25 1.25
1430 A468 41c multi 1.25 1.25
1431 A468 41c multi 1.25 1.25
1432 A468 41c multi 1.25 1.25
a. Horiz. strip, #1429-1432 5.00 5.00

**Bird Type of 2002 Redrawn**

Designs: No. 1433, Chaffinch. No. 1434, Goldcrest

***Serpentine Die Cut 11x11¼***

**2002, Oct. 17** **Photo.**

**Coil Stamps**
**Self-Adhesive**

1433 A473 41c multi 5.00 5.00
1434 A473 41c multi 5.00 5.00
a. Coil pair, #1433-1434 10.00

Text appears grayer on Nos. 1433-1434 than on Nos. 1395-1396. On No. 1433, the second "h" of "Chaffinch" touches the branch, while it does not touch on No. 1395. On No. 1434, the points of the pine needles at the bottom of the stamp are shown, while they are cut off on No. 1396.

Irish Rock Musicians A486

Designs: Nos. 1435, 1439, U2. Nos. 1436, 1440, Phil Lynott. Nos. 1437, 1441, Van Morrison. Nos. 1438, 1442, Rory Gallagher.

**2002, Oct. 17 Litho.** ***Perf. 13¼x12¾***

1435 A486 41c multi 1.25 1.25
1436 A486 41c multi 1.25 1.25
a. Horiz. pair, #1435-1436 2.50 2.50
1437 A486 57c multi 1.75 1.75
1438 A486 57c multi 1.75 1.75
a. Horiz. pair, #1437-1438 3.50 3.50
*Nos. 1435-1438 (4)* 6.00 6.00

**Souvenir Sheets**
***Perf. 12¾x13¼***

1439 A486 €2 multi 12.00 12.00
1440 A486 €2 multi 12.00 12.00
1441 A486 €2 multi 12.00 12.00
1442 A486 €2 multi 12.00 12.00

Christmas — A487

Scenes from *Les Très Riches Heures du Duc de Berry*: No. 1443, Adoration of the Magi. 44c, The Annunciation. 57c, Angels Announcing Birth to Shepherds.
No. 1446, Adoration of the Shepherds.

**2002, Nov. 7 Litho.** ***Perf. 14¼x14¾***

1443 A487 41c multi .95 .95
1444 A487 44c multi 1.10 1.10
1445 A487 57c multi 1.50 1.50

**Booklet Stamp**
**Self-Adhesive**
**Size: 21x27mm**
***Serpentine Die Cut 11x11¼***

1446 A487 41c multi 1.50 1.50
a. Booklet pane of 24 37.50
*Nos. 1443-1446 (4)* 5.05 5.05

No. 1446a sold for €9.43.

**Bird Type of 2002**

Designs: 50c, Puffin. 75c, Ringed plover, horiz.. 95c, Sparrowhawk, horiz.

**2003, Jan. 6 Litho.** ***Perf. 14¾x14***

1447 A473 75c multi 2.50 2.50
1448 A473 95c multi 3.50 3.50

**Booklet Stamp**
**Self-Adhesive**
**Size: 21x27mm**
***Serpentine Die Cut 11x11¼***

1449 A473 50c multi 2.00 2.00
a. Booklet pane of 10 + 10 etiquettes 20.00

Baby Animals — A488

Designs: Nos. 1450, 1452, Puppies. Nos. 1451a, 1454, Goats. Nos. 1451b, 1453, Chicks. Nos. 1451c, 1455, Kittens. No. 1456, Rabbits.

**2003, Jan. 28** ***Perf. 14x14¾***

1450 A488 41c multi 2.00 2.00

**Souvenir Sheet**
***Perf. 14x14¾ on 3 or 4 Sides***

1451 Sheet of 3 7.00 7.00
a.-c. A488 50c Any single 2.25 2.25

**Booklet Stamps**
**Size: 22x28mm**
**Self-Adhesive**
***Serpentine Die Cut 11x11¼***

1452 A488 41c multi 1.75 1.75
1453 A488 41c multi 1.75 1.75
1454 A488 41c multi 1.75 1.75
1455 A488 41c multi 1.75 1.75
1456 A488 41c multi 1.75 1.75
a. Booklet pane of 10, 2 each #1452-1456 + 10 labels 17.50
*Nos. 1452-1456 (5)* 8.75 8.75

New Year 2003 (Year of the Goat), No. 1451.

St. Patrick's Day — A489

Designs: Nos. 1457, 1460, St. Patrick. Nos. 1458, 1461, St. Patrick's Day Parade, Dublin. Nos. 1459, 1462, St. Patrick's Day Parade, New York.

**2003, Feb. 28** ***Perf. 14x14¾***

1457 A489 41c multi 1.00 1.00
a. Booklet pane of 4 4.00
1458 A489 50c multi 1.25 1.25
a. Booklet pane of 4 5.00
1459 A489 57c multi 1.50 1.50
a. Booklet pane of 4 6.00
b. Booklet pane of 3, #1457-1459 3.75
Complete booklet, #1457a, 1458a, 1459a, 1459b 19.00
*Nos. 1457-1459 (3)* 3.75 3.75

**Booklet Stamps**
**Self-Adhesive**
**Size: 22x32mm**
***Serpentine Die Cut 11¼***

1460 A489 41c multi 3.50 3.50
a. Booklet pane of 10 35.00
1461 A489 50c multi 4.25 4.25
a. Booklet pane of 10 42.50
1462 A489 57c multi 4.75 4.75
a. Booklet pane of 10 47.50
*Nos. 1460-1462 (3)* 12.50 12.50

Beetles A490

Designs: 41c, €2, Seven-spotted ladybug. 50c, Great diving beetle. 57c, Leaf beetle. €1, Green tiger beetle.

**2003, Apr. 1** ***Perf. 13¾x14***

1463 A490 41c multi 1.00 1.00
1464 A490 50c multi 1.25 1.25
1465 A490 57c multi 1.40 1.40
1466 A490 €1 multi 2.50 2.50
*Nos. 1463-1466 (4)* 6.15 6.15

**Souvenir Sheet**

1467 A490 €2 multi 7.50 7.50

European Year of People With Disabilities A491

**2003, May 9** ***Perf. 14¾x14***

1468 A491 41c multi 1.75 1.75

Europa — A492

Posters by Paul Henry: 41c, Dingle Peninsula (Ireland for Holidays). 57c, Connemara (Ireland This Year).

**2003, May 9** ***Perf. 14x14¾***

1469 A492 41c multi *1.00 1.00*
1470 A492 57c multi *1.50 1.50*

11th Special Olympics World Summer Games A493

Designs: 41c, Competitors waving. 50c, Swimmer. 57c, Sprinter. €1, Shot put.

**2003, May 20** ***Perf. 13¾x14***

1471 A493 41c multi 1.00 1.00
1472 A493 50c multi 1.25 1.25
1473 A493 57c multi 1.40 1.40
1474 A493 €1 multi 2.50 2.50
*Nos. 1471-1474 (4)* 6.15 6.15

Ford Motor Company, Cent. A494

**2003, June 30 Litho.** ***Perf. 14¼x14***

1475 A494 41c multi 2.00 2.00

Gordon Bennett Race in Ireland, Cent. A495

Race map and 1903 automobiles: Nos. 1476, 1483, Napier. Nos. 1477, 1482, Mercedes. Nos. 1478, 1481, Mors. Nos. 1479, 1480, Winton.

**2003, June 30** *Perf. 14¼x14*
**1476** A495 41c multi 1.25 1.25
**1477** A495 41c multi 1.25 1.25
**1478** A495 41c multi 1.25 1.25
**1479** A495 41c multi 1.25 1.25
*a.* Horiz. strip of 4, #1476-1479 5.00 5.00

**Coil Stamps**
**Size: 33x22mm**
**Self-Adhesive**
***Serpentine Die Cut 11¼***

**1480** A495 41c multi 2.25 2.25
**1481** A495 41c multi 2.25 2.25
**1482** A495 41c multi 2.25 2.25
**1483** A495 41c multi 2.25 2.25
*a.* Strip of 4, #1480-1483 9.00

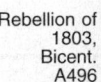

Rebellion of 1803, Bicent. A496

Designs: 41c, Robert Emmet (1778-1803), rebellion leader. 50c, Thomas Russell (1767-1803), rebellion leader. 57c, Anne Devlin (1780-1851), assistant to Emmet.

**2003, July 29** **Litho.** *Perf. 14¾x14*
**1484** A496 41c multi 1.50 1.50
**1485** A496 50c multi 1.75 1.75
**1486** A496 57c multi 2.25 2.25
*Nos. 1484-1486 (3)* 5.50 5.50

Powered Flight, Cent. A497

Designs: 41c, First Irish-built monoplane, built by Harry Ferguson, 1909. 50c, John Alcock & Arthur Brown's non-stop transatlantic flight, 1919. No. 1489, Lillian Bland, first female aircraft designer, 1910. Nos. 1490, 1491, Wright Flyer.

**2003, July 29**
**1487** A497 41c multi 1.50 1.50
**1488** A497 50c multi 1.75 1.75
**1489** A497 57c multi 2.00 2.00
**1490** A497 57c multi 2.00 2.00
*a.* Horiz. pair, #1489-1490 4.00 4.00

**Souvenir Sheet**

**1491** A497 €5 multi 15.00 15.00

**Bird Type of 2002**

Designs: 7c, Stonechat. 48c, No. 1494, Peregrine falcon. No. 1495, Pied wagtail.

**2003, Aug. 25** **Litho.** *Perf. 14x14¾*
**1492** A473 7c multi .40 .40
**1493** A473 48c multi 3.00 3.00

**Self-Adhesive**
***Serpentine Die Cut 11x11¼***

**1494** A473 N multi 2.00 2.00
**1495** A473 N multi 2.00 2.00
*a.* Coil pair, #1494-1495 4.00
*b.* Booklet pane, 5 each #1494-1495 20.00

Nos. 1494-1495 each sold for 48c on day of issue.

**National Gallery Paintings Type of 2002**

Designs: No. 1496, Self-portrait as Timanthes, by James Barry. No. 1497, Man Writing a Letter, by Gabriel Metsu. No. 1498, Woman Reading a Letter, by Metsu. No. 1499, Woman Seen From the Back, by Antoine Watteau.

**2003, Sept. 9** *Perf. 14x14¾*
**1496** A484 48c multi 1.25 1.25
*a.* Booklet pane of 4 5.00 —
**1497** A484 48c multi 1.25 1.25
**1498** A484 48c multi 1.25 1.25
*a.* Booklet pane, 2 each #1497-1498 5.00 —
**1499** A484 48c multi 1.25 1.25
*a.* Horiz. strip, #1496-1499 5.00 5.00
*b.* Booklet pane of 4 5.00 —
Complete booklet, #1496a, 1499b, 2 #1498a 28.00

Frank O'Connor (1903-66), Writer — A498

**2003, Sept. 16** **Litho.** *Perf. 14x14¼*
**1500** A498 50c multi 2.25 2.25

Ernest Thomas Sinton Walton (1903-95), 1951 Nobel Laureate in Physics — A499

**2003, Sept. 16**
**1501** A499 57c multi 2.50 2.50

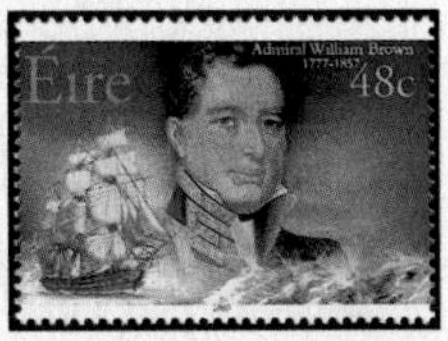

Mariners A500

Designs: Nos. 1502, 1507, Argentine Admiral William (Guillermo) Brown (1777-1857). Nos. 1503, 1506, 1510, American Commodore John Barry (1745-1803). Nos. 1504, 1508, Captain Robert Halpin (1836-94). Nos. 1505, 1509, Captain Richard Roberts (1803-41).

***Perf. 14¼x14 (#1502-1505, 1510)***
**2003, Sept. 30**
**1502** A500 48c multi 1.25 1.25
**1503** A500 48c multi 1.25 1.25
*a.* Horiz. pair, #1502-1503 2.50 2.50
**1504** A500 57c multi 1.50 1.50
**1505** A500 57c multi 1.50 1.50
*a.* Horiz. pair, #1504-1505 3.00 3.00

**Coil Stamps**
**Self-Adhesive (#1506-1509)**
**Size: 33x22mm (#1506-1509)**
***Serpentine Die Cut 11x11¼ (#1506-1509)***

**1506** A500 48c multi 2.50 2.50
**1507** A500 48c multi 2.50 2.50
**1508** A500 48c multi 2.50 2.50
**1509** A500 48c multi 2.50 2.50
*a.* Horiz. strip, #1506-1509 10.00 10.00
*Nos. 1502-1509 (8)* 15.50 15.50

**Souvenir Sheet**

**1510** A500 €5 multi 15.00 15.00

**Bird Type of 2002**

Designs: 4c, Corncrake. Nos. 1511, 1515, Pied wagtail. Nos. 1513, 1514, Peregrine falcon.

***Perf. 14x14¾ on 3 Sides***
**2003, Sept. 30** **Litho.**
**Booklet Stamps (#1511-1513)**
**1511** A473 48c multi 2.00 2.00
*a.* Booklet pane, 5 each #1493, 1511 20.00 —
Complete booklet, #1511a 20.00

**Size: 18x20mm**
***Perf. 15x14 on 3 Sides***

**1512** A473 4c multi .30 .30
**1513** A473 48c multi 2.50 2.50
*a.* Booklet pane, 2 #1512, 4 #1513 10.50 —
Complete booklet, #1513a 10.50
*Nos. 1511-1513 (3)* 4.80 4.80

**Self-Adhesive**
**Size: 20x25mm**
***Serpentine Die Cut 11x11¼***

**1514** A473 48c multi 2.00 2.00
**1515** A473 48c multi 2.00 2.00
*a.* Coil pair, #1514-1515 4.00
*b.* Booklet pane, 5 each #1514-1515 20.00

Examples of Nos. 1514-1515 from booklets are on a heavy, opaque paper, while those from coils are on a thinner, semi-transparent paper.

Election of Pope John Paul II, 25th Anniv. — A501

Pope John Paul II: 48c, In Ireland, 1979. 50c, At Vatican. 57c, At United Nations.

**2003, Oct. 16** *Perf. 14x14¾*
**1516** A501 48c multi 1.25 1.25
**1517** A501 50c multi 1.25 1.25
**1518** A501 57c multi 1.40 1.40
*Nos. 1516-1518 (3)* 3.90 3.90

Christmas A502

Designs: No. 1519, Flight into Egypt. 50c, Angel. 57c, Three Kings. No. 1522, Nativity.

**2003, Nov. 10** *Perf. 13¼*
**1519** A502 48c multi 1.50 1.50

**Size: 37x27mm**
***Perf. 14¾x14***

**1520** A502 50c multi 1.50 1.50
**1521** A502 57c multi 1.75 1.75
*Nos. 1519-1521 (3)* 4.75 4.75

**Booklet Stamp**
**Self-Adhesive**
**Size: 26x21mm**
***Serpentine Die Cut 11¼***

**1522** A502 48c multi 2.00 2.00
*a.* Booklet pane of 24 27.50

No. 1522a sold for €11.04.

**Bird Type of 2002**

Designs: Nos. 1523, 1525, Puffin. Nos. 1524, 1526, Song thrush.

**2004, Jan. 5** **Litho.** *Perf. 14x14¾*
**1523** A473 60c multi 2.50 2.50
**1524** A473 65c multi 2.50 2.50

**Booklet Stamps**
**Self-Adhesive**
**Size: 21x26mm**
***Serpentine Die Cut 11x11¼***

**1525** A473 60c multi 2.50 2.50
*a.* Booklet pane of 10 25.00
**1526** A473 65c multi 2.75 2.75
*a.* Booklet pane of 10 27.50

Irish Presidency of the European Union — A503

**2004, Jan. 15** *Perf. 14x14¾*
**1527** A503 48c multi 1.75 1.75

Love — A504

Designs: Nos. 1528, 1529a, 1530, Chimpanzees. Nos. 1529b, 1531, Panda. Nos. 1529c, 1532, Koala. No. 1533, Hippopotamus.

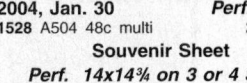

**2004, Jan. 30** *Perf. 14x14¾*
**1528** A504 48c multi 2.00 2.00

**Souvenir Sheet**
***Perf. 14x14¾ on 3 or 4 Sides***

**1529** Sheet of 3 6.00 6.00
*a.-c.* A504 60c Any single 2.00 2.00

**Booklet Stamps**
**Self-Adhesive**
**Size: 21x26mm**
***Serpentine Die Cut 11x11¼***

**1530** A504 48c multi 2.50 2.50
**1531** A504 48c multi 2.50 2.50
**1532** A504 48c multi 2.50 2.50
**1533** A504 48c multi 2.50 2.50
*a.* Booklet pane, 3 each #1530-1531, 2 each #1532-1533 + 10 labels 25.00
*Nos. 1530-1533 (4)* 10.00 10.00

New Year 2004 (Year of the Monkey), No. 1529.

Abbey Theater, Dublin, Cent. — A505

**2004, Feb. 27** *Perf. 14x14¾*
**1534** A505 48c multi 1.75 1.75

St. Patrick's Day — A506

**2004, Feb. 27**
**1535** A506 65c multi 2.00 2.00

Antarctic Expedition of Ernest Shackleton, 90th Anniv. A507

Designs: No. 1536, Ship's stern, expedition members, dogs. No. 1537, Ship's bow, expedition members, dogs. Nos. 1538, 1540a, Man emerging from tent. Nos. 1539, 1540b, Tents, expedition members.

**2004, Mar. 19** *Perf. 13½*
**1536** A507 48c multi 1.50 1.50
**1537** A507 48c multi 1.50 1.50
*a.* Horiz. pair, #1536-1537 3.00 3.00
*b.* Booklet pane, 2 #1537a 6.00 —
**1538** A507 65c multi 2.00 2.00
**1539** A507 65c multi 2.00 2.00
*a.* Horiz. pair, #1538-1539 4.00 4.00
*b.* Booklet pane, 2 #1539a 8.00 —
*c.* Booklet pane, #1537a, 1539a 7.00 —
Complete booklet, #1537b, 1539b, 2 #1539c 28.00
*Nos. 1536-1539 (4)* 7.00 7.00

**Souvenir Sheet**
***Perf. 13½ on 2 or 3 Sides***

**1540** Sheet of 2 7.00 7.00
*a.-b* A507 €1 Either single 3.50 3.50

No. 1539c exists with two different margins, both of which are in complete booklet.

FIFA (Fédération Internationale de Football Association), Cent. A508

**2004, Mar. 31** *Perf. 13½x13*
**1541** A508 60c multi 2.00 2.00

Expansion of the European Union A509

**2004, May 1 Litho.** *Perf. 14¾x14*
**1542** A509 65c multi 4.00 4.00

Europa — A510

Designs: 48c, Ross Castle. 65c, Cliffs of Moher .

**2004, May 11** *Perf. 14x13¾*
**1543** A510 48c multi *1.25 1.25*
**1544** A510 65c multi *1.75 1.75*

Ducks A511

Designs: 48c, Tufted duck. 60c, Red-breasted merganser. 65c, Gadwall. €1, Garganey.

**2004, May 11** *Perf. 13x13¼*
**1545** A511 48c multi 1.25 1.25
**1546** A511 60c multi 1.50 1.50
**1547** A511 65c multi 1.75 1.75
**1548** A511 €1 multi 2.50 2.50
*a.* Souvenir sheet, #1545-1548 7.00 7.00
*Nos. 1545-1548 (4)* 7.00 7.00

Intl. Year of the Family, 10th Anniv. — A512

**2004, May 15 Litho.** *Perf. 13¼x13*
**1549** A512 65c multi 2.00 2.00

Winning Artwork in Texaco Children's Art Competition A513

Designs: 48c, Untitled work (Frog), by Daire Lee. 60c, Marmalade Cat, by Cian Colman. 65c, Ralleshin Dipditch, by Daire O'Rourke. €1, Fish on a Dish, by Ailish Fitzpatrick, horiz.

**2004, May 19** *Perf. 14x14¾*
**1550** A513 48c multi 1.15 1.15
**1551** A513 60c multi 1.50 1.50
**1552** A513 65c multi 1.60 1.60

*Perf. 14¾x14*
**1553** A513 €1 multi 2.50 2.50
*Nos. 1550-1553 (4)* 6.75 6.75

Publication of *Ulysses*, by James Joyce, Cent. — A514

Designs: 48c, Caricature of Joyce, by Tullio Percoli. 65c, Photograph of Joyce.

**2004, June 16 Litho.** *Perf. 13¼*
**1554** A514 48c multi 1.25 1.25
**1555** A514 65c multi 1.50 1.50

Irish College, Paris, France — A515

**2004, June 26** *Perf. 14x14¾*
**1556** A515 65c multi 2.00 2.00

Inauguration of LUAS Tram System, Dublin A516

**2004, June 30** *Perf. 13¼*
**1557** A516 48c Environment 1.50 1.50
**1558** A516 48c Accessibility 1.50 1.50
*a.* Horiz. pair, #1557-1558 3.00 3.00

2004 Summer Olympics, Athens A517

Olympic flame, rings and: 48c, Javelin thrower. 60c, Myron's Discobolus.

**2004, July 22** *Perf. 13¾x14*
**1559** A517 48c multi 1.25 1.25
**1560** A517 60c multi 1.75 1.75

Camogie, Cent. A518

Camogie players and: No. 1561, Camogie Association emblem. No. 1562, Cup.

**2004, July 22** *Perf. 14¾x14*
**1561** A518 48c multi 1.25 1.25
**1562** A518 48c multi 1.25 1.25
*a.* Horiz. pair, #1561-1562 2.50 2.50

Flowers — A519

Designs: 4c, Common dog-violet. 5c, Dandelion. Nos. 1565, 1571, Primrose. Nos. 1569A, 1570, Daisy. 60c, Hawthorn. 65c, Bluebell. €2, Lords-and-ladies. €5, Dog-rose, horiz.

*Perf. 14x14¾, 14¾x14*

**2004, Sept. 9 Litho.**
**1563** A519 4c multi .25 .25
**1564** A519 5c multi .25 .25
**1565** A519 48c multi 1.50 1.50
**1566** A519 60c multi 1.90 1.90
**1567** A519 65c multi 2.00 2.00

**Size: 23x44mm**
**1568** A519 €2 multi 6.00 6.00

**Size: 44x23mm**
**1569** A519 €5 multi 15.00 15.00
*Nos. 1563-1569 (7)* 26.90 26.90

**Booklet Stamp**

*Perf. 14x14¾ on 3 Sides*
**1569A** A519 48c multi 1.50 1.50
*b.* Booklet pane 5 each #1565, 1569A 15.00 —
Complete booklet, #1569Ab 15.00

**Self-Adhesive**

**Size: 20x25mm**

*Serpentine Die Cut 11x11¼*
**1570** A519 48c multi 1.50 1.50
**1571** A519 48c multi 1.50 1.50
*a.* Vert. coil pair, #1570-1571 3.00 3.00
*b.* Booklet pane, 5 each #1570-1571 15.00

No. 1571 is on the left side of No. 1571b.

See Nos. 1606-1610, 1650-1655, 1708-1713, 1723-1729, 1770-1773, 1814, 1852, 1865.

**National Gallery Paintings Type of 2002**

Designs: No. 1572, The House Builders, by Walter Osborne. No. 1573, Kitchen Maid with the Supper at Emmaus, by Diego Velázquez. No. 1574, The Lamentation Over the Dead Christ, by Nicolas Poussin. No. 1575, The Taking of Christ, by Caravaggio.

**2004, Sept. 16** *Perf. 14¾x14*
**1572** A484 48c multi 1.25 1.25
*a.* Booklet pane of 4 5.00 —
**1573** A484 48c multi 1.25 1.25
*a.* Booklet pane of 4 5.00 —
**1574** A484 48c multi 1.25 1.25
*a.* Booklet pane of 4 5.00 —
**1575** A484 48c multi 1.25 1.25
*a.* Horiz. strip of 4, #1572-1575 5.00 5.00
*b.* Booklet pane of 4 5.00 —
Complete booklet, #1572a, 1573a, 1574a, 1575b 30.00

Complete booklet sold for €8.

Nobel Prize Winners for Literature — A520

Designs: No. 1576, William Butler Yeats (1865-1939), 1923 winner. No. 1577, George Bernard Shaw (1856-1950), 1925 winner. No. 1578, Samuel Beckett (1906-89), 1969 winner. No. 1579, Seamus Heaney (b. 1939), 1995 winner.

*Perf. 12½x13½*

**2004, Oct. 1 Litho. & Engr.**
**1576** A520 N multi 1.50 1.50
**1577** A520 N multi 1.50 1.50
**1578** A520 N multi 1.50 1.50
**1579** A520 N multi 1.50 1.50
*b.* Booklet pane of 4, #1576-1579 6.00 —
Complete booklet, #1579b 6.00

Nos. 1576-1579 each sold for 48c on day of issue. See Sweden No. 2492.

Patrick Kavanagh (1904-67), Poet A521

**2004, Oct. 21 Litho.** *Perf. 13x13¼*
**1580** A521 48c green & black 1.50 1.50

Quakerism in Ireland, 350th Anniv. A522

**2004, Oct. 21**
**1581** A522 60c multi 1.90 1.90

Christmas A523

Designs: 48c, Holy Family. 60c, Flight into Egypt. 65c, Adoration of the Magi.

**2004, Nov. 10 Litho.** *Perf. 14x14¾*
**1582** A523 48c multi 1.50 1.50
**1583** A523 60c multi 1.90 1.90
**1584** A523 65c multi 2.00 2.00
*Nos. 1582-1584 (3)* 5.40 5.40

**Booklet Stamp**

**Self-Adhesive**

*Serpentine Die Cut 11x11¼*

**Size: 21x27mm**
**1585** A523 48c multi 1.50 1.50
*a.* Booklet pane of 24 36.00

No. 1585a sold for €11.04.

Love A524

Birds: Nos. 1586, 1587b, 1590, Parrots. Nos. 1587a, 1588, Rooster. Nos. 1587c, 1591, Owl. No. 1589, Storks.

**2005, Jan. 28** *Perf. 14¾x14*
**1586** A524 48c multi 4.25 4.25
**1587** Sheet of 3 7.50 7.50
*a.-c.* A524 60c Any single 2.50 2.50

**Booklet Stamps**

**Self-Adhesive**

*Serpentine Die Cut 11¼x11*

**Size: 27x21mm**
**1588** A524 48c multi 1.75 1.75
**1589** A524 48c multi 1.75 1.75
**1590** A524 48c multi 1.75 1.75
**1591** A524 48c multi 1.75 1.75
*a.* Booklet pane, 3 each #1588, 1590, 2 each #1589, 1591 + 10 labels 17.50

New Year 2005 (Year of the Rooster).

St. Patrick's Day — A525

**2005, Feb. 17 Litho.** ***Perf. 14x14¾***

**1592** A525 65c multi 2.00 2.00

Works of Women Artists A526

Designs: No. 1593, Landscape, Co. Wicklow, by Evie Hone (1894-1955). No. 1594, Seabird and Landmarks, by Nano Reid (1905-81). No. 1595, Threshing, by Mildred Anne Butler (1858-1941), vert. No. 1596, Three Graces, by Gabriel Hayes (1909-78), vert.

**2005, Feb. 24** ***Perf. 14¾x14, 14x14¾***

**1593** A526 48c multi 1.25 1.25
**1594** A526 48c multi 1.25 1.25
*a.* Horiz. pair, #1593-1594 2.50 2.50
**1595** A526 65c multi 1.75 1.75
**1596** A526 65c multi 1.75 1.75
*a.* Horiz. pair, #1595-1596 3.50 3.50

Cork, 2005 European Cultural Capital A527

**2005, Mar. 7 Litho.** ***Perf. 13¼***

**1597** A527 48c shown 1.75 1.75
**1598** A527 48c Buildings, bridge 1.75 1.75
*a.* Horiz. pair, #1597-1598 3.50 3.50

Intl. Year of Physics — A528

Designs: 48c, William Rowan Hamilton (1805-65), mathematician and astronomer. 60c, UNESCO Headquarters, Paris. 65c, Albert Einstein (1879-1955), physicist.

**2005, Mar. 14**

**1599** A528 48c multi 1.10 1.10
**1600** A528 60c multi 1.40 1.40
**1601** A528 65c multi 1.50 1.50
*Nos. 1599-1601 (3)* 4.00 4.00

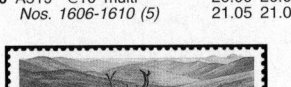

Dublin-Belfast Railway, 150th Anniv. — A529

Designs: No. 1602, Modern train. No. 1603, Steam locomotive at Connolly Station, Dublin. 60c, Steam locomotive on Boyne Valley Viaduct. 65c, Modern train at station platform.

**2005, Apr. 5 Litho.** ***Perf. 14¾x14***

**1602** A529 48c multi 1.50 1.50
*a.* Booklet pane of 4 6.00 —
**1603** A529 48c multi 1.50 1.50
*a.* Booklet pane of 4 6.00 —
*b.* Horiz. pair, #1602-1603 3.00 3.00
**1604** A529 60c multi 1.90 1.90
*a.* Booklet pane of 4 7.75 —
**1605** A529 65c multi 2.00 2.00
*a.* Booklet pane of 4 8.00 —
Complete booklet, #1602a, 1603a, 1604a, 1605a 27.75
*b.* Souvenir sheet, #1602-1605 8.50 8.50
*Nos. 1602-1605 (4)* 6.90 6.90

Complete booklet sold for €9.

### Flowers Type of 2004

Designs: 1c, Bloody crane's-bill. 2c, Irish orchid. 7c, Fly orchid. 10c, Mountain avens. €10, Spring gentian, horiz.

**2005, Apr. 12** ***Perf. 14x14¾***

**1606** A519 1c multi .25 .25
**1607** A519 2c multi .25 .25
**1608** A519 7c multi .25 .25
**1609** A519 10c multi .30 .30

**Size: 44x23mm**

**1610** A519 €10 multi 20.00 20.00
*Nos. 1606-1610 (5)* 21.05 21.05

Biosphere Reserves in Ireland and Canada — A530

Designs: 48c, Deer, Killarney National Park, Ireland. 65c, Saskatoon berries, Waterton Lakes National Park, Canada.

**2005, Apr. 22** ***Perf. 13¼x13***

**1611** A530 48c multi 1.25 1.25
**1612** A530 65c multi 1.75 1.75
*a.* Souvenir sheet, #1611-1612 5.00 5.00

See Canada Nos. 2105-2106.

Europa A531

**2005, May 9 Litho.** ***Perf. 14¼x14***

**1613** A531 48c Irish stew *1.50 1.50*
**1614** A531 65c Oysters *2.00 2.00*

Worldwide Fund for Nature (WWF) A532

Butterflies: 48c, Small copper. 60c, Green hairstreak. 65c, €5, Painted lady. €1, Pearl-bordered fritillary.

**2005, May 24** ***Perf. 13¼***

**1615** A532 48c multi 1.25 1.25
**1616** A532 60c multi 1.60 1.60
**1617** A532 65c multi 1.75 1.75
**1618** A532 €1 multi 2.50 2.50
*Nos. 1615-1618 (4)* 7.10 7.10

**Souvenir Sheet**

**1619** A532 €5 multi 14.00 14.00

Tall Ships A533

**2005, July 4 Litho.** ***Perf. 13½***

**1620** A533 48c Dunbrody 1.25 1.25
**1621** A533 60c Tenacious 1.60 1.60
**1622** A533 65c Eagle 1.75 1.75
*Nos. 1620-1622 (3)* 4.60 4.60

Round Towers — A534

**2005, July 27 Litho.** ***Perf. 13¼***

**1623** A534 48c Glendalough 1.25 1.25
**1624** A534 48c Ardmore 1.25 1.25
**1625** A534 48c Clones 1.25 1.25
**1626** A534 48c Kilmacduagh 1.25 1.25
*a.* Horiz. strip of 4, #1623-1626 5.00 5.00

Apimondia 2005 Apriarists Congress, Dublin — A535

**2005, Aug. 19** ***Perf. 13½x13***

**1627** A535 65c multi 2.25 2.25

2006 Ryder Cup Golf Tournament, K Club, Straffan — A536

Designs: No. 1628, Golfers Darren Clark, Paul McGinley, and Pádraig Harrington. No. 1629, Golfers Eamonn Darcy, Christy O'Connor, Jr., and Philip Walton. 60c, Golfers Harry Bradshaw, Ronan Rafferty, and Christy O'Connor, Sr. 65c, K Club.

**2005, Sept. 27 Litho.** ***Perf. 14¾x14***

**1628** A536 48c multi 1.50 1.50
*a.* Booklet pane of 4 6.00 —
**1629** A536 48c multi 1.50 1.50
*a.* Pair, #1628-1629 3.00 3.00
*b.* Booklet pane of 4 6.00 —
**1630** A536 60c multi 2.00 2.00
*a.* Booklet pane of 4 8.00 —
*b.* Booklet pane, 2 each #1628-1630 ('06) 10.00 —
**1631** A536 65c multi 2.00 2.00
*a.* Booklet pane of 4 8.00 —
*b.* Booklet pane, 2 #1631 ('06) 4.00 —
Complete booklet, #1628a, 1629b, 1630a, 1631a 28.00
*Nos. 1628-1631 (4)* 7.00 7.00

Nos. 1630b, 1631b issued 9/14/06.

Pres. Erskine Childers (1905-74) A537

**2005, Oct. 10** ***Perf. 14x14¾***

**1632** A537 48c multi 3.50 3.50

Ireland in the United Nations A538

Designs: No. 1633, Irish Defense Force member assisting man in East Timor. No. 1634, Medical worker aiding child in East Timor. 60c, F. H. Boland, Ireland's signer of United Nations Charter. 65c, Irish Defense Force member in classroom in Lebanon.

**2005, Oct. 14** ***Perf. 14¾x14***

**1633** A538 48c multi 1.50 1.50
**1634** A538 48c multi 1.50 1.50
*a.* Horiz. pair, #1633-1634 3.00 3.00
**1635** A538 60c multi 1.90 1.90
**1636** A538 65c multi 2.00 2.00
*Nos. 1633-1636 (4)* 6.90 6.90

Arthur Griffith's Policy Establishing Sinn Féin, Cent. — A539

**2005, Nov. 10** ***Perf. 13½***

**1637** A539 48c multi 2.00 2.00

Christmas A540

Designs: 48c, Nativity. 60c, Choir of angels. 65c, Choir of angels, diff.

**2005, Nov. 10** ***Perf. 14x14¾***

**1638** A540 48c multi 1.50 1.50
**1639** A540 60c multi 1.90 1.90
**1640** A540 65c multi 2.00 2.00
*Nos. 1638-1640 (3)* 5.40 5.40

**Booklet Stamp**
**Self-Adhesive**
**Size: 21x27mm**
***Serpentine Die Cut 11x11¼***

**1641** A540 48c multi 1.50 1.50
*a.* Booklet pane of 26 35.00 35.00

No. 1641a sold for €12.

Patrick Gallagher and Templecrone Cooperative Store — A541

**2006, Jan. 16 Litho.** ***Perf. 14¾x14***

**1642** A541 48c sepia 1.75 1.75

Templecrone Cooperative Agricultural Society, cent.

New Year 2006 (Year of the Dog) A542

Designs: Nos. 1643, 1644b, 1647, Dog, man and woman. Nos. 1644a, 1645, Two dogs, man. Nos. 1644c, 1646, Dog on leash, woman. No. 1648, Dog biting sneaker.

**2006, Jan. 16** ***Perf. 14¾x14***

**1643** A542 48c multi 1.75 1.75

**Souvenir Sheet**

**1644** Sheet of 3 7.50 7.50
*a.-c.* A542 65c Any single 2.50 2.50

**Booklet Stamps**
**Self-Adhesive**
**Size: 26x21mm**
***Serpentine Die Cut 11¼x11***

**1645** A542 48c multi 1.75 1.75
**1646** A542 48c multi 1.75 1.75
**1647** A542 48c multi 1.75 1.75
**1648** A542 48c multi 1.75 1.75
*a.* Booklet pane, 3 each #1645-1646, 2 each #1647-1648, + 10 labels 17.50
*Nos. 1645-1648 (4)* 7.00 7.00

St. Patrick Lights the Paschal Fire at Slane, by Sean Keating
A543

**2006, Feb. 16** ***Perf. 14¾x14***
**1649** A543 65c multi 2.25 2.25

St. Patrick's Day.

**Flowers Type of 2004**

Designs: 12c, Autumn gorse. 25c, Common knapweed. 75c, Navelwort. 90c, Viper's bugloss. €1, Foxglove.

**2006, Feb. 20** ***Perf. 14x14¾***
**1650** A519 12c multi .30 .30
**1651** A519 25c multi .60 .60
**1652** A519 75c multi 1.90 1.90
**1653** A519 90c multi 2.25 2.25

**Size: 23x44mm**

**1654** A519 €1 multi 2.50 2.50
*Nos. 1650-1654 (5)* 7.55 7.55

**Booklet Stamp**
**Self-Adhesive**
**Size: 21x27mm**
***Serpentine Die Cut 11x11¼***

**1655** A519 75c multi 2.25 2.25
*a.* Booklet pane of 10 22.50

Trees
A544

**2006, Mar. 7** ***Perf. 13¼***
**1656** A544 48c Sessile oak 1.25 1.25
**1657** A544 60c Yew 1.60 1.60
**1658** A544 75c Ash 2.00 2.00
**1659** A544 €1 Strawberry tree 2.50 2.50
*a.* Souvenir sheet, #1656-1659 8.00 8.00
*b.* As "a," with Washington 2006 World Philatelic Exhibition emblem in margin 9.00 9.00
*Nos. 1656-1659 (4)* 7.35 7.35

No. 1659b issued in June. No. 1659b sold for €3.

St. Hubert, Stained Glass Window by Harry Clarke (1889-1931)
A545

**2006, Mar. 21** ***Perf. 13¼***
**1660** A545 48c multi 1.40 1.40

Easter Rebellion, 90th Anniv. — A546

**2006, Apr. 12** ***Perf. 13½***
**1661** A546 48c multi 1.40 1.40

Adoption of European Union Flag, 20th Anniv.
A547

**2006, May 9** ***Perf. 14¼x14***
**1662** A547 48c multi 1.40 1.40

Europa — A548

Winning art in children's stamp design contest: 48c, People holding Irish and European Union flags, by Katie McMillan. 75c, Flowers with flags, by Sarah Naughter.

**2006, May 9** ***Perf. 14x14¼***
**1663** A548 48c multi 1.40 1.40
**1664** A548 75c multi 1.90 1.90

University Church, Dublin, 150th Anniv. — A549

**2006, May 25 Litho.** ***Perf. 14x14¾***
**1665** A549 48c multi 1.75 1.75

Department of the Gaeltacht, 50th Anniv. — A550

**2006, June 6** ***Perf. 13¼***
**1666** A550 48c multi 1.75 1.75

TG4 Television Channel, 10th Anniv.
A551

**2006, June 6**
**1667** A551 48c multi 1.75 1.75

Celtic Scholars — A552

Designs: No. 1668, Máirtín O Cadhain (1906-70), writer. No. 1669, Johann Caspar Zeuss (1806-56), philologist.

**2006, June 6** ***Perf. 14x14¾***
**1668** A552 48c multi 1.50 1.50
**1669** A552 48c multi 1.50 1.50
*a.* Pair, #1668-1669 3.00 3.00

Rosslare-Fishguard Ferry Service, Cent. — A553

Designs: No. 1670, Steam ferry. No. 1671, Modern ferry.

**2006, June 20** ***Perf. 14¾x14***
**1670** A553 48c multi 1.50 1.50
**1671** A553 48c multi 1.50 1.50
*a.* Pair, #1670-1671 3.00 3.00
*b.* Souvenir sheet, #1670-1671 3.50 3.50

Battle of the Somme, 90th Anniv.
A554

**2006, June 26** ***Perf. 13½x13¾***
**1672** A554 75c multi 2.50 2.50

Guide Dog — A555

**Litho. & Embossed**

**2006, July 7** ***Perf. 13¼x13***
**1673** A555 48c multi 1.75 1.75

A556

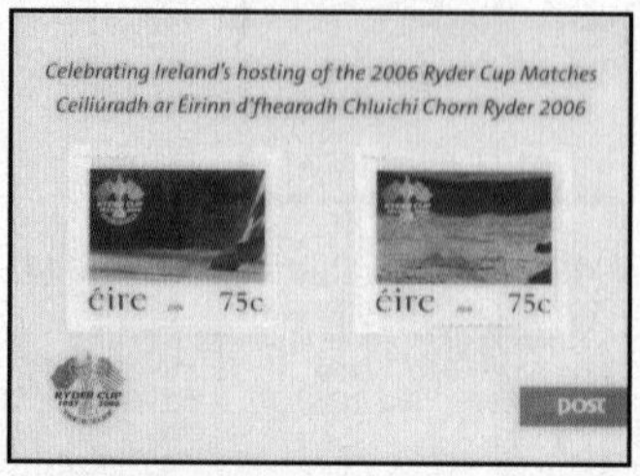
Celebrating Ireland's hosting of the 2006 Ryder Cup Matches
Ceiliúradh ar Éirinn d'fhearadh Chluichí Chorn Ryder 2006
éire 75c
éire 75c
2006 Ryder Cup Golf Tournament, K Club, Straffan — A557

Golf ball: Nos. 1674, 1678, On tee. Nos. 1675, 1679, In rough. Nos. 1676, 1680, In sand trap. Nos. 1677, 1681, Near green.
No. 1682: a, Tee shot. b, Sand trap shot.

**2006** **Litho.** ***Perf. 14x14¾***
**1674** A556 48c multi 1.25 1.25
**1675** A556 48c multi 1.25 1.25
**1676** A556 48c multi 1.25 1.25
**1677** A556 48c multi 1.25 1.25
*a.* Horiz. strip, #1674-1677 5.00 5.00
*b.* Souvenir sheet #1674-1677 5.50 5.50
*c.* Booklet pane, 2 each #1674-1677 10.00 —
*d.* Booklet pane, #1674-1677 5.00 —

**Coil Stamps**
**Self-Adhesive**
**Size: 21x27mm**
***Serpentine Die Cut 11x11¼***

**1678** A556 48c multi 1.25 1.25
**1679** A556 48c multi 1.25 1.25
**1680** A556 48c multi 1.25 1.25
**1681** A556 48c multi 1.25 1.25
*a.* Vert. strip, #1678-1681 5.00

**Souvenir Sheet**
**Self-Adhesive**
**Litho. With Three-Dimensional Plastic Affixed**
***Serpentine Die Cut 9¼***

**1682** A557 Sheet of 2 6.50
*a.-b.* 75c Either single 3.25 3.25
Complete booklet, #1630b, 1631b, 1677c, 1677d, and unbound #1682 40.00

Issued: Nos. 1674-1678, 7/25; No. 1682, 9/14. Complete booklet sold for €12. No. 1677b has Ryder Cup emblem in margin while No. 1677d does not.

Winning of Olympic 1500-Meter Running Gold Medal by Ronnie Delany, 50th Anniv. — A558

***Perf. 13¾x13½***

**2006, Aug. 16** **Litho.**
**1683** A558 48c multi 1.25 1.25

Michael Cusack (1847-1906), Sports Journalist
A559

**2006, Aug. 23** ***Perf. 14x14¾***
**1684** A559 48c multi 1.25 1.25

Michael Davitt (1846-1906), Founder of National Land League — A560

**2006, Sept. 5**
**1685** A560 48c multi 1.25 1.25

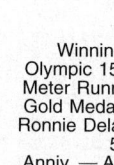

National Concert Hall, Dublin, 25th Anniv. — A561

**2006, Sept. 8**

**1686** A561 48c multi 1.25 1.25

Inland Waterways — A562

Designs: No. 1687, Barrow River at Graiguenamanagh. No. 1688, Belturbet Marina, Erne River. No. 1689, Grand Canal at Cornalaur. No. 1690, Meelick Pier, Shannon River.

**2006, Oct. 20 Litho.** ***Perf. 13½x13¾***

**1687** A562 75c multi 1.75 1.75
*a.* Booklet pane of 4 7.00 —
**1688** A562 75c multi 1.75 1.75
*a.* Booklet pane of 4 7.00 —
**1689** A562 75c multi 1.75 1.75
*a.* Booklet pane of 4 7.00 —
**1690** A562 75c multi 1.75 1.75
*a.* Booklet pane of 4 7.00 —
Complete booklet, #1687a-1690a 28.00

Traditional Irish Music Groups — A563

Designs: No. 1691, The Chieftains. No. 1692, The Dubliners. No. 1693, The Clancy Brothers and Tommy Makem. No. 1694, Altan.

**2006, Nov. 7 Litho.** ***Perf. 13½x13¾***

**1691** A563 48c multi 1.75 1.75
*a.* Booklet pane of 4 7.00 —
**1692** A563 48c multi 1.75 1.75
*a.* Booklet pane of 4 7.00 —
**1693** A563 75c multi 2.50 2.50
*a.* Booklet pane of 4 10.00 —
**1694** A563 75c multi 2.50 2.50
*a.* Booklet pane of 4 10.00 —
Complete booklet, #1691a, 1692a, 1693a, 1694a 34.00
*b.* Souvenir sheet, #1691-1694 7.00 7.00
*c.* As "b," with Belgica '06 emblem added in margin 7.00 7.00
*d.* As "b," with MonacoPhil 2006 emblem added in margin 7.00 7.00

Complete booklet sold for €10.
No. 1694c issued 11/16; No. 1694d, 12/1.

Christmas
A564 A565

Designs: No. 1695, Madonna and Child. 75c, Shepherd and lamb. No. 1697, Nativity.

**2006, Nov. 9** ***Perf. 14x14¾***

**1695** A564 48c multi 1.50 1.50
**1696** A564 75c multi 2.25 2.25

**Booklet Stamp**
**Self-Adhesive**
***Serpentine Die Cut 11x11¼***

**1697** A565 48c multi 1.50 1.50
*a.* Booklet pane of 26 39.00
*Nos. 1695-1697 (3)* 5.25 5.25

No. 1697a sold for €12.

Father Luke Wadding (1588-1657) A566

Irish Franciscan College, Louvain, 400th Anniv. — A567

**2007, Jan. 24 Litho.** ***Perf. 14x14¾***

**1698** A566 75c multi 2.25 2.25
**1699** A567 75c multi 2.25 2.25

Hands With Wedding Rings A568

Greetings A569

Designs: No. 1701, Stamp with hat, heart balloon. No. 1702, Birthday cake.

***Serpentine Die Cut 11¼***

**2007, Jan. 26 Booklet Stamps**
**Self-Adhesive**

**1700** A568 N multi 1.50 1.50
*a.* Booklet pane of 10 15.00
**1701** A569 N multi 1.50 1.50
**1702** A569 N multi 1.50 1.50
*a.* Booklet pane of 10, 5 each #1701-1702 15.00
*Nos. 1700-1702 (3)* 4.50 4.50

Nos. 1700-1702 each sold for 48c on day of issue.

New Year 2007 (Year of the Pig) A570

**2007, Feb. 9 Litho.** ***Perf. 14¾x14***

**1703** A570 75c grn & multi 2.00 2.00

**Souvenir Sheet**

**1704** Sheet of 3, #1704a, 2 #1703 7.50 7.50
*a.* A570 75c red & multi 2.50 2.50

St. Patrick's Day — A571

**2007, Feb. 9** ***Perf. 13½***

**1705** A571 75c multi 2.00 2.00

Flight of the Earls, 400th Anniv. — A572

Designs: No. 1706, Hugh O'Neill, Earl of Tyrone, and ship at right. No. 1707, Rory O'Donnell, Earl of Tyrconnell, and rowboat at left.

**2007, Feb. 23** ***Perf. 14x14¾***

**1706** A572 48c multi 1.50 1.50
**1707** A572 48c multi 1.50 1.50
*a.* Horiz. pair, #1706-1707 3.00 3.00
*b.* Souvenir sheet, #1707a 3.00 3.00

**Flowers Type of 2004**

Designs: 3c, Yellow flag. 55c, No. 1712, Large-flowered butterwort. 78c, Black bog-rush. 95c, Purple loosestrife. No. 1713, Blue-eyed grass.

**2007, Mar. 1 Litho.** ***Perf. 14x14¾***

**1708** A519 3c multi .25 .25
**1709** A519 55c multi 1.50 1.50
**1710** A519 78c multi 2.10 2.10
**1711** A519 95c multi 2.50 2.50
*Nos. 1708-1711 (4)* 6.35 6.35

**Self-Adhesive**
**Size: 21x26mm**
***Serpentine Die Cut 11x11¼***

**1712** A519 N multi 1.50 1.50
**1713** A519 N multi 1.50 1.50
*a.* Booklet pane, 5 each #1712-1713 15.00
*b.* Vert. coil pair, #1712-1713 3.00

Nos. 1712-1713 each sold for 55c on day of issue.

Castles A573

Designs: No. 1714, Trim Castle. No. 1715, Dunluce Castle. No. 1716, Lismore Castle. No. 1717, Portumna Castle.

**2007, Mar. 9** ***Perf. 14¾x14***

**1714** A573 55c multi 1.50 1.50
**1715** A573 55c multi 1.50 1.50
**1716** A573 55c multi 1.50 1.50
**1717** A573 55c multi 1.50 1.50
*b.* Souvenir sheet, #1714-1717 6.00 6.00

Treaty of Rome, 50th Anniv. — A574

**2007, Mar. 28** ***Perf. 14x14¾***

**1718** A574 55c multi 1.50 1.50

Planets — A575

Earth and: No. 1719, Jupiter. No. 1720, Neptune. No. 1721, Saturn. No. 1722, Uranus.

**2007, Apr. 20 Litho.** ***Perf. 13¼***

**1719** A575 55c multi 1.50 1.50
**1720** A575 55c multi 1.50 1.50
*a.* Horiz. pair, #1719-1720 3.00 3.00
**1721** A575 78c multi 2.25 2.25
**1722** A575 78c multi 2.25 2.25
*a.* Horiz. pair, #1721-1722 4.50 4.50
*b.* Souvenir sheet, #1719-1722 7.50 7.50
*c.* Booklet pane, #1719-1722 7.50 —
Complete booklet, 4 #1722c 30.00
*Nos. 1719-1722 (4)* 7.50 7.50

No. 1722c has stamps with straight edges at right. Complete booklet contains four examples of No. 1722c with different margins.

**Flower Type of 2004**

Designs: 5c, Dandelion. 25c, Common knapweed. 55c, Large-flowered butterwort. 78c, Black bog-rush.

***Die Cut Perf. 12¾***

**2007, Apr. 20 Litho.**

**Coil Stamp**
**Self-Adhesive (#1723, 1728-1729)**
**Size: 21x26mm**

**1723** A519 55c multi 1.50 1.50

**Booklet Stamps**
**Size: 17x20mm**
***Perf. 14¾x14 on 3 Sides***

**1724** A519 5c multi .25 .25
**1725** A519 25c multi .70 .70
**1726** A519 55c multi 1.50 1.50
*a.* Booklet pane of 6, #1725, 2 #1724, 3 #1726 5.75 —
Complete booklet, #1726a 5.75

**Size: 20x23mm**
***Perf. 14x14¾ on 3 Sides***

**1727** A519 55c multi 1.50 1.50
*a.* Booklet pane of 10 15.00 —
Complete booklet, #1727a 15.00

**Size: 21x26mm**
***Serpentine Die Cut 11x11¼***

**1728** A519 55c multi 1.50 1.50
*a.* Booklet pane of 10 15.00
**1729** A519 78c multi 2.25 2.25
*a.* Booklet pane of 10 22.50
*Nos. 1723-1729 (7)* 9.20 9.20

Europa A576

**2007, May 9** ***Perf. 14¼x14***

**1730** A576 55c Female Scout 1.50 1.50
**1731** A576 78c Male Scout 2.10 2.10

Scouting, cent.

Canonization of St. Charles of Mount Argus (1821-93) A577

**2007, June 5** ***Perf. 13¼***

**1732** A577 55c multi 1.50 1.50

Institute of Public Administration, 50th Anniv. — A578

**2007, June 13**

**1733** A578 55c multi 1.50 1.50

RTE Performing Groups A579

Designs: Nos. 1734, 1742, National Symphony Orchestra (Ceolfhoireann Shiansach

Náisiúnta). Nos. 1735, 1740, Concert Orchestra (Ceolfhoireann Cheolchoirme). Nos. 1736, 1743, Vanbrugh Quartet (Ceathairéad Vanbrugh). Nos. 1737, 1741, Philharmonic Choir (Cór Fiolarmónach). Nos. 1738, 1739, Children's Choir (Cór na nOg).

**2007, June 19** ***Perf. 13¼x13½***

| | | | | |
|---|---|---|---|---|
| **1734** | A579 55c multi | | 1.50 | 1.50 |
| **1735** | A579 55c multi | | 1.50 | 1.50 |
| **1736** | A579 55c multi | | 1.50 | 1.50 |
| *a.* | Booklet pane, 2 each #1734-1736 | | 9.00 | — |
| **1737** | A579 55c multi | | 1.50 | 1.50 |
| **1738** | A579 55c multi | | 1.50 | 1.50 |
| *a.* | Horiz. strip of 5, #1734-1738 | | 7.50 | 7.50 |
| *b.* | Booklet pane, 2 each #1737-1738 | | 6.00 | — |
| | Complete booklet, 2 each #1736a, 1738b | | 30.00 | |

**Booklet Stamps**
**Self-Adhesive**
***Serpentine Die Cut 11¼x11½***

| | | | |
|---|---|---|---|
| **1739** | A579 55c multi | 1.50 | 1.50 |
| **1740** | A579 55c multi | 1.50 | 1.50 |
| **1741** | A579 55c multi | 1.50 | 1.50 |
| **1742** | A579 55c multi | 1.50 | 1.50 |
| **1743** | A579 55c multi | 1.50 | 1.50 |
| *a.* | Booklet pane of 10, 2 each #1739-1743 | 15.00 | |
| | *Nos. 1734-1743 (10)* | 15.00 | 15.00 |

Revival of Honorable Society of King's Inns, 400th Anniv. — A580

**2007, July 10** ***Perf. 13¼***
**1744** A580 55c multi 1.50 1.50

Registry of Deeds Act, 300th Anniv. A581

**2007, July 10** ***Perf. 14¾x14***
**1745** A581 78c multi 2.25 2.25

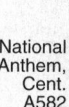

National Anthem, Cent. A582

**2007, July 17** **Litho.** ***Perf. 13½***
**1746** A582 55c multi 1.50 1.50

**Weddings Type of 2007**
***Serpentine Die Cut 11¼***
**2007, July 25** **Self-Adhesive**
**Booklet Stamp**

| | | | |
|---|---|---|---|
| **1747** | A568 55c multi | 1.50 | 1.50 |
| *a.* | Booklet pane of 10 | 15.00 | |

Viking Ship Skuldelev 2 — A583

Designs: 55c, Ship. €3, Ship on water.

**2007, Aug. 7** **Litho.** ***Perf. 14¾x14***
**1748** A583 55c multi 1.50 1.50

**Souvenir Sheet**
**1749** A583 €3 multi 7.50 7.50

2007 Rugby World Cup, France — A584

Designs: 55c, Player carrying ball. 78c, Player catching ball.

**2007, Aug. 20** ***Perf. 13¼***

| | | | |
|---|---|---|---|
| **1750** | A584 55c multi | 1.50 | 1.50 |
| *a.* | Souvenir sheet of 1 | 1.50 | 1.50 |
| **1751** | A584 78c multi | 2.25 | 2.25 |
| *a.* | Souvenir sheet of 1 | 2.25 | 2.25 |

Cat Caricatures by Martyn Turner — A585

Designs: Nos. 1752, 1756a, Fat Cat. Nos. 1753, 1756b, Celtic Tigress. Nos. 1754, 1756c, Cool Cats. Nos. 1755, 1756d, Kilkenny Cat.

**2007, Sept. 6** ***Perf. 14x14¾***

| | | | |
|---|---|---|---|
| **1752** | A585 55c multi | 1.50 | 1.50 |
| **1753** | A585 55c multi | 1.50 | 1.50 |
| *a.* | Horiz. pair, #1752-1753 | 3.00 | 3.00 |
| **1754** | A585 78c multi | 2.25 | 2.25 |
| **1755** | A585 78c multi | 2.25 | 2.25 |
| *a.* | Horiz. pair, #1754-1755 | 4.50 | 4.50 |

**Souvenir Sheet**
***Perf. 13¼***

| | | | |
|---|---|---|---|
| **1756** | Sheet of 4 | 7.50 | 7.50 |
| *a.-b.* | A585 55c Either single, 16x16mm | 1.50 | 1.50 |
| *c.-d.* | A585 78c Either single, 16x16mm | 2.25 | 2.25 |

Excavations of San Clemente Basilica, Rome, 150th Anniv. — A586

**2007, Sept. 12** ***Perf. 14¾x14***
**1757** A586 55c multi 1.60 1.60

James Fintan Lalor (1807-49), Political Writer — A587

**2007, Sept. 18** ***Perf. 14x14¾***
**1758** A587 55c multi 1.60 1.60

Natural History Museum, Dublin, 150th Anniv. — A588

**2007, Oct. 25** **Litho.** ***Perf. 13¼***
**1759** A588 55c multi 1.60 1.60

Christmas A589

Designs: No. 1760, Presentation in the Temple. No. 1761, Three Magi. No. 1762, Adoration of the Shepherds.

**2007, Nov. 8** ***Perf. 14¾x14***

| | | | |
|---|---|---|---|
| **1760** | A589 55c multi | 1.60 | 1.60 |
| **1761** | A589 78c multi | 2.40 | 2.40 |

**Self-Adhesive**
**Booklet Stamp**
**Size: 21x27mm**
***Serpentine Die Cut 11x11¼***

| | | | |
|---|---|---|---|
| **1762** | A589 55c multi | 1.60 | 1.60 |
| *a.* | Booklet pane of 26 | 42.50 | |

No. 1762a sold for €13.75.

Charles Wesley (1707-88), Hymn Writer — A590

**2007, Nov. 15** ***Perf. 14x14¾***
**1763** A590 78c multi 2.40 2.40

Bride and Groom A591

***Serpentine Die Cut 11¼***
**2008, Jan. 16** **Litho.**
**Booklet Stamp**
**Self-Adhesive**

| | | | |
|---|---|---|---|
| **1764** | A591 55c multi | 1.60 | 1.60 |
| *a.* | Booklet pane of 10 | 16.00 | |

Greetings — A592

***Serpentine Die Cut 11¼***
**2008, Jan. 16** **Self-Adhesive**
**Booklet Stamps**

| | | | |
|---|---|---|---|
| **1765** | A592 55c Frog | 1.60 | 1.60 |
| **1766** | A592 55c Elephant | 1.60 | 1.60 |
| *a.* | Booklet pane of 10, 5 each #1765-1766 | 16.00 | |

New Year 2008 (Year of the Rat) A593

**2008, Jan. 23** ***Perf. 14¾x14***

| | | | |
|---|---|---|---|
| **1767** | A593 78c multi | 2.40 | 2.40 |
| *a.* | Souvenir sheet of 3 | 7.25 | 7.25 |

Liam Whelan (1935-58), Soccer Player Killed in Airplane Crash — A594

**2008, Feb. 4** ***Perf. 13½x13¾***
**1768** A594 55c multi 2.00 2.00

St. Patrick's Day — A595

**2008, Feb. 11** ***Perf. 13¼x13***
**1769** A595 78c multi 2.40 2.40

**Flower Type of 2004**

Designs: 20c, Thrift. 50c, Biting stonecrop. 82c, Sea aster.

**2008, Mar. 3** **Litho.** ***Perf. 14x14¾***
**Size: 20x23mm**

| | | | |
|---|---|---|---|
| **1770** | A519 20c multi | .65 | .65 |
| **1771** | A519 50c multi | 1.60 | 1.60 |
| **1772** | A519 82c multi | 2.50 | 2.50 |
| *a.* | Booklet pane of 10 | 25.00 | — |
| | Complete booklet, #1772a | 25.00 | |
| | *Nos. 1770-1772 (3)* | 4.75 | 4.75 |

**Booklet Stamp**
**Self-Adhesive**
**Size: 21x25mm**
***Serpentine Die Cut 11x11¼***

| | | | |
|---|---|---|---|
| **1773** | A519 82c multi | 2.50 | 2.50 |
| *a.* | Booklet pane of 10 | 25.00 | |

European Year of Intercultural Dialogue — A596

**2008, Mar. 7** ***Perf. 13¼***
**1774** A596 55c multi 1.75 1.75

Hugh Lane, by Antonio Mancini — A597

**2008, Mar. 28** **Litho.** ***Perf. 13½***
**1775** A597 55c multi 1.75 1.75

Dublin City Gallery, cent. (founded by Lane).

Paintings by Paul Henry (1876-1958) A598

Designs: No. 1776, A Connemara Village (left half, "Paul Henry" in blue). No. 1777, A Connemara Village (right half, "Paul Henry" in white). No. 1778, West of Ireland Landscape (left half, "Paul Henry" in gray at left). No. 1779, West of Ireland Landscape (right half, "Paul Henry" in gray at right).

**2008, Apr. 17** *Perf. 13¼*

**1776** A598 55c multi 1.75 1.75
**1777** A598 55c multi 1.75 1.75
**1778** A598 55c multi 1.75 1.75
**1779** A598 55c multi 1.75 1.75
*a.* Horiz. strip of 4, #1776-1779 7.00 7.00
*b.* Booklet pane of 4, #1776-1779 7.00 —
Complete booklet, 4 #1779b 28.00

No. 1779b has example of No. 1779 with straight edge at right. The four examples of No. 1779b in the complete booklet have different margins. The complete booklet sold for €9.

Credit Union Movement, 50th Anniv. A599

**2008, Apr. 23** *Perf. 14¾x14*

**1780** A599 55c multi 1.75 1.75

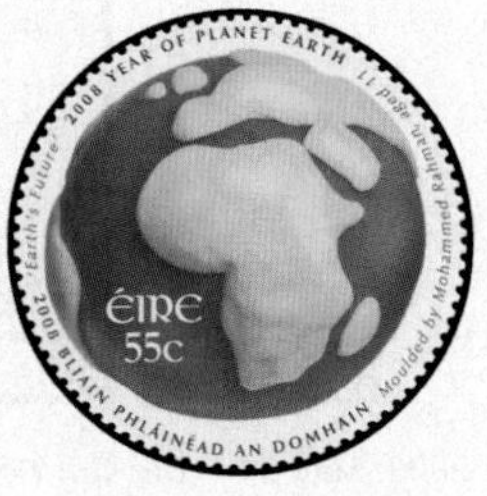


Intl. Year of Planet Earth A600

Plasticine sculptures of Earth created by children: No. 1781, Africa and Europe, by Mohammed Rahman. No. 1782, South and North America, by Conor Reid.

**2008, Apr. 28** *Die Cut Perf.*

**Self-Adhesive**

**1781** A600 55c red & multi 1.75 1.75
**1782** A600 55c blue & multi 1.75 1.75
*a.* Horiz. pair, #1781-1782, on backing paper without back printing 3.50
*b.* Booklet pane of 10, 5 each #1781-1782 17.50

Institute of Creative Advertising and Design, 50th Anniv. A601

**2008, May 23** *Perf. 13¼*

**1783** A601 55c multi 1.75 1.75

R. M. S. Leinster, 90th Anniv. of Sinking A602

**2008, May 30** *Perf. 14¾x14*

**1784** A602 55c multi 1.75 1.75

Europa — A603

Designs: 55c, Boy writing letter. 82c, Girl writing letter.

**2008, June 9** *Perf. 14x14¾*

**1785** A603 55c multi 1.75 1.75
**1786** A603 82c multi 2.50 2.50

Tidy Towns Competition, 50th Anniv. — A604

**2008, June 19**

**1787** A604 55c multi 1.75 1.75

Participation of Irish Defense Forces in UN Missions, 50th Anniv. — A605

**2008, June 26** *Perf. 14¾x14*

**1788** A605 55c multi 1.75 1.75

Movies Filmed in Ireland — A606

Designs: No. 1789, Kings. No. 1790, Cré na Cille. No. 1791, The Wind that Shakes the Barley. No. 1792, Garage.

**2008, July 8 Litho.** *Perf. 14¾x14*

**1789** A606 55c multi 1.75 1.75
**1790** A606 55c multi 1.75 1.75
**1791** A606 82c multi 2.60 2.60
**1792** A606 82c multi 2.60 2.60
*a.* Booklet pane of 4, #1789-1792 9.25 —
Complete booklet, 4 #1792a 37.50
*b.* Souvenir sheet of 4, #1789-1792 8.75 8.75
*Nos. 1789-1792 (4)* 8.70 8.70

No. 1792b has a printed margin. The complete booklet, which sold for €12, contains 4 examples of No. 1792a, each with a different order of stamps and without a printed margin.

2008 Summer Olympics, Beijing A607

Designs: 52c, Rowing. 82c, Shot put.

**2008, July 15**

**1793** A607 55c multi 1.75 1.75
**1794** A607 82c multi 2.60 2.60

**Souvenir Sheet**

**Stamps Inscribed "Olympex 2008"**

**1795** Sheet of 2 4.50 4.50
*a.* A607 55c multi 1.75 1.75
*b.* A607 82c multi 2.60 2.60

Mushrooms A608

Designs: No. 1796, Parasol. No. 1797, Orange birch bolete. 82c, Pink waxcap. 95c, Scarlet elfcup.

**2008, Aug. 1 Litho.** *Perf. 14x14¾*

**1796** A608 55c multi 1.75 1.75
**1797** A608 55c multi 1.75 1.75
*a.* Horiz. pair, #1796-1797 3.50 3.50
**1798** A608 82c multi 2.60 2.60
*Nos. 1796-1798 (3)* 6.10 6.10

**Souvenir Sheet**

**1799** A608 95c multi 3.00 3.00

First Transatlantic Cable Message From Europe to US, 150th Anniv. — A609

**2008, Aug. 15** *Perf. 13¼*

**1800** A609 82c multi 2.40 2.40

Old Age Pensions Act, Cent. — A610

**2008, Sept. 19 Litho.** *Perf. 13¼*

**1801** A610 55c multi 1.50 1.50

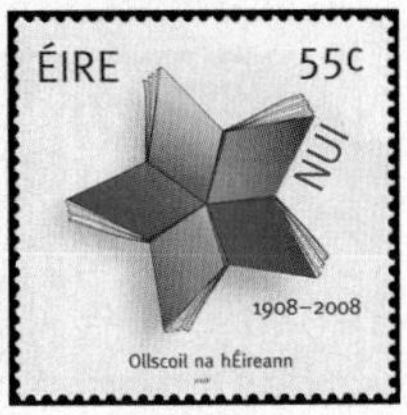


National University of Ireland, Cent. — A611

**2008, Sept. 19** *Perf. 13½*

**1802** A611 55c multi 1.50 1.50

Patrick Pearse (1879-1916), Patriot, and Founder of St. Enda's School — A612

Pearse and school buildings: No. 1803, Cullenswood House. No. 1804, The Hermitage.

**2008, Sept. 25** *Perf. 14¾x14¼*

**1803** A612 55c multi 1.50 1.50
**1804** A612 55c multi 1.50 1.50

Irish Bands A613

**2008, Oct. 10 Litho.** *Perf. 13½*

**1805** A613 55c Planxty 1.50 1.50
**1806** A613 55c De Danann 1.50 1.50
**1807** A613 82c Tulla Ceili Band 2.25 2.25
**1808** A613 82c Bothy Band 2.25 2.25
*a.* Souvenir sheet, #1805-1808 7.50 7.50
*Nos. 1805-1808 (4)* 7.50 7.50

Dancers — A614

**2008, Nov. 7 Litho.** *Perf. 13½*

**1809** A614 55c Irish dancer 1.40 1.40

**Souvenir Sheet**

**1810** Sheet of 2, #1809, 1810a 3.50 3.50
*a.* A614 82c Flamenco dancer 2.10 2.10

See Spain No. 3609.

A615

Christmas — A616

Creche figures: No. 1811, Flight into Egypt. 82c, Annunciation. No. 1813, Infant Jesus.

**2008, Nov. 7** *Perf. 14¾x14*

**1811** A615 55c multi 1.40 1.40
**1812** A615 82c multi 2.10 2.10

**Booklet Stamp**

**Self-Adhesive**

***Serpentine Die Cut 11x11¼***

**1813** A616 55c multi 1.40 1.40
*a.* Booklet pane of 26 37.50

No. 1813a sold for €13.75.

**Flowers Type of 2004**

Design: N, Yellow horned poppy.

***Serpentine Die Cut 14***

**2008, Dec. 5** **Litho.**

**Booklet Stamp**

**Self-Adhesive**

**Size: 17x21mm**

**1814** A519 N multi 1.40 1.40
*a.* Booklet pane of 10 14.00

No. 1814 sold for 55c on day of issue.

Eye — A617

**Litho. & Embossed**

**2009, Jan. 23** ***Perf. 14¼***
**1815** A617 55c black 1.50 1.50

Louis Braille (1809-52), educator of the blind.

Love A618

***Die Cut Perf. 13¼***

**2009, Jan. 23** **Litho.**

**Self-Adhesive**

**1816** A618 55c multi 1.50 1.50
*a.* Vert. pair on backing paper without back printing 3.00
*b.* Booklet pane of 10 15.00

All pairs from booklet pane are on backing paper with printing.

New Year 2009 (Year of the Ox) A619

**2009, Jan. 23** ***Perf. 14¾x14***
**1817** A619 82c multi 2.25 2.25
*a.* Souvenir sheet of 3 6.75 6.75

St. Patrick Climbs Croagh Patrick, by Margaret Clarke — A620

**2009, Feb. 19** ***Perf. 14x14¾***
**1818** A620 82c multi 2.10 2.10

St. Patrick's Day.

Greetings — A621

Designs: No. 1819, Man lifting girl with letter to mailbox slot. No. 1820, Woman with letter, dog.

**2009, Mar. 6** ***Die Cut Perf. 12¾x13¼***

**Self-Adhesive**

**1819** A621 55c multi 1.40 1.40
**1820** A621 55c multi 1.40 1.40
*a.* Horiz. pair, #1819-1820, on backing paper withour back printing 2.80
*b.* Booklet pane of 10, 5 each #1819-1820, + 10 stickers 14.00

All pairs from booklet pane are on backing paper with printing.

Charles Darwin (1809-82), Naturalist — A622

**2009, Mar. 20** ***Perf. 13½***
**1821** A622 82c multi 2.25 2.25

Scene from "The Playboy of the Western World" — A623

**2009, Mar. 24** ***Perf. 14x14¾***
**1822** A623 55c multi 1.50 1.50

John Millington Synge (1871-1909), writer.

Irish Times Newspaper, Cent. — A624

**2009, Mar. 27** ***Perf. 13¼***
**1823** A624 55c multi 1.50 1.50

A625 A626

A627 A628

A629 A630

A631 A632

An Post, 25th Anniv.
A633 A634

***Serpentine Die Cut 11x11¼***

**2009, Apr. 3** **Litho.**

**Coil Stamps**

**Self-Adhesive**

**Size: 25x30mm**

**1824** A625 55c multi 1.50 1.50
**1825** A626 55c multi 1.50 1.50
**1826** A627 55c multi 1.50 1.50
**1827** A628 55c multi 1.50 1.50
**1828** A629 55c multi 1.50 1.50
*a.* Vert. strip of 5, #1824-1828 7.50
**1829** A630 55c multi 1.50 1.50
**1830** A631 55c multi 1.50 1.50
**1831** A632 55c multi 1.50 1.50
**1832** A633 55c multi 1.50 1.50
**1833** A634 55c multi 1.50 1.50
*a.* Vert. strip of 5, #1829-1833 7.50
*b.* Vert. strip of 10, #1824-1833 15.00
*Nos. 1824-1833 (10)* 15.00 15.00

***Serpentine Die Cut 14***

**1834** Booklet pane of 10 15.00
*a.* A625 55c multi, 20x24mm 1.50 1.50
*b.* A626 55c multi, 20x24mm 1.50 1.50
*c.* A627 55c multi, 20x24mm 1.50 1.50
*d.* A628 55c multi, 20x24mm 1.50 1.50
*e.* A629 55c multi, 20x24mm 1.50 1.50
*f.* A630 55c multi, 20x24mm 1.50 1.50
*g.* A631 55c multi, 20x24mm 1.50 1.50
*h.* A632 55c multi, 20x24mm 1.50 1.50
*i.* A633 55c multi, 20x24mm 1.50 1.50
*j.* A634 55c multi, 20x24mm 1.50 1.50

No. 1833b was only available in a full roll of 100 stamps. The philatelic bureau sold Nos. 1828a and 1833a as a convenience to collectors rather than No. 1833b.

Paintings by Francis Bacon (1909-92) — A635

Designs: 55c, Self-portrait. 82c, Artist's Studio.

**2009, Apr. 24** ***Perf. 13½***
**1835** A635 55c multi 1.50 1.50

**Souvenir Sheet**

**1836** A635 82c multi 2.25 2.25

James Larkin (1875-1947), Union Organizer A636

**2009, Apr. 30** ***Perf. 13¼***
**1837** A636 55c multi 1.50 1.50

Irish Transport and General Workers' Union, cent.

Volvo Ocean Race Stopover in Galway A637

Designs: 55c, Green Dragon yacht. €3, Green Dragon and another yacht, vert.

**2009, May 8** ***Perf. 13¾x14***
**1838** A637 55c multi 1.60 1.60

**Souvenir Sheet**

**1839** A637 €3 multi 8.50 8.50

No. 1839 contains one 27x48mm stamp.

European Conference of Postal and Telecommunications Administrations, 50th Anniv. — A638

**2009, May 15** ***Perf. 13¼***
**1840** A638 82c multi 2.40 2.40

Europa A639

Designs: 55c, Crab Nebula. 82c, Jets from a brown dwarf.

**2009, May 15**
**1841** A639 55c multi 1.60 1.60
**1842** A639 82c multi 2.40 2.40

Intl. Year of Astronomy.

European Dog Show, Dublin — A640

**2009, May 21** ***Die Cut Perf. 13x13¼***

**Self-Adhesive**

**1843** A640 55c multi 1.60 1.60
*a.* Horiz. pair on backing paper without back printing 3.25
*b.* Booklet pane of 10 #1843 16.00

City Status of Kilkenny, 400th Anniv. — A641

**2009, June 16** ***Perf. 13½***
**1844** A641 55c multi 1.60 1.60

Anthony Trollope (1815-82), Writer — A642

**2009, June 26** ***Perf. 14x14¾***
**1845** A642 82c multi 2.40 2.40

Birrell Land Act, Cent. — A643

**2009, July 15** *Perf. 13¼*
**1846** A643 82c multi 2.40 2.40

Composers — A644

Designs: No. 1847, Wolfgang Amadeus Mozart (1756-91). No. 1848, George Frideric Handel (1685-1759). No. 1849, Joseph Haydn (1732-1809). No. 1850, Frédéric Chopin (1810-49).

**2009, Aug. 14** *Perf. 13¼x13*
**1847** A644 55c multi 1.60 1.60
**1848** A644 55c multi 1.60 1.60
*a.* Horiz. pair, #1847-1848 3.25 3.25
**1849** A644 82c multi 2.40 2.40
**1850** A644 82c multi 2.40 2.40
*a.* Horiz. pair, #1849-1850 5.00 5.00
*b.* Souvenir sheet of 4, #1847-1850 8.25 8.25
*c.* Booklet pane of 4, #1847-1850 8.50 —
Complete booklet, 4 #1850c 34.00
*Nos. 1847-1850 (4)* 8.00 8.00

On No. 1850b, stamps are at upper left with No. 1847 having straight edges at top and left, No. 1848 having straight edge at top and No. 1849 having straight edge at left. On No. 1850c, stamps are at right with Nos. 1848 and 1850 having straight edges at right. Complete booklet sold for €12 and contains four examples of No. 1850c, each with different margins.

Arthur Guinness (1725-1803), Founder of Guinness Brewery — A645

**2009, Aug. 28** *Perf. 14x14¾*
**1851** A645 82c multi 2.40 2.40

Guinness Brewery, 250th anniv.

**Flower Type of 2004**

Design: 82c, Sea aster.

**2009, Aug. 7** *Serpentine Die Cut 14*
**Booklet Stamp**
**Self-Adhesive**
**Size: 17x20mm**

**1852** A519 82c multi 2.40 2.40
*a.* Booklet pane of 10 24.00

Compare No. 1852 with No. 1773.

Plantation of Ulster, 400th Anniv. A646

Designs: No. 1853, English text. No. 1854, Gaelic text.

**2009, Sept. 4** *Perf. 14¾x14*
**1853** A646 55c multi 1.60 1.60
**1854** A646 55c multi 1.60 1.60
*a.* Horiz. pair, #1853-1854 3.20 3.20

Playwrights — A647

Designs: No. 1855, Brian Friel. No. 1856, Tom Murphy. No. 1857, Frank McGuinness.

**2009, Sept. 18**
**1855** A647 55c multi 1.60 1.60
**1856** A647 55c multi 1.60 1.60
**1857** A647 55c multi 1.60 1.60
*Nos. 1855-1857 (3)* 4.80 4.80

Dragonflies A648

Designs: No. 1858, Large red damselfly. No. 1859, Irish bluet. 82c, Four-spotted chaser, horiz.
95c, Banded demoiselle, horiz.

**2009, Oct. 16** **Litho.** *Perf. 14x14¾*
**1858** A648 55c multi 1.75 1.75
**1859** A648 55c multi 1.75 1.75
*a.* Horiz. pair, #1858-1859 3.50 3.50

*Perf. 14¾x14*

**1860** A648 82c multi 2.50 2.50
*Nos. 1858-1860 (3)* 6.00 6.00

**Souvenir Sheet**
*Perf. 13¼*

**1861** A648 95c multi 3.00 3.00

No. 1861 contains one 60x25mm stamp.

Illustrations From Gospel Book, Monastery of Gamaghiel, Armenia — A649

Virgin and Child, by Simon Bening — A650

Christmas: No. 1862, Nativity. 82c, Annunciation.

**2009, Nov. 6** *Perf. 14¾x14*
**1862** A649 55c multi 1.75 1.75
**1863** A649 82c multi 2.50 2.50

**Booklet Stamp**
**Self-Adhesive**
*Serpentine Die Cut 11x11¼*

**1864** A650 55c multi 1.75 1.75
*a.* Booklet pane of 26 46.00

No. 1864a sold for €13.75.

**Flowers Type of 2004**

Design: Large-flowered butterwort.

*Serpentine Die Cut 14*
**2009, Oct. 16** **Litho.**
**Booklet Stamp**
**Self-Adhesive**
**Size:17x21mm**

**1865** A519 55c multi 1.75 1.75
*a.* Booklet pane of 10 17.50

Compare with No. 1728.

Douglas Hyde (1860-1949), First President of Ireland — A651

**2010, Jan. 21** **Litho.** *Perf. 14x14¾*
**1866** A651 55c multi 1.60 1.60

Lovebirds A652

**2010, Jan. 21** *Die Cut Perf. 13¼*
**Self-Adhesive**

**1867** A652 55c multi 1.60 1.60
*a.* Vert. pair on backing paper without back printing 3.20
*b.* Booklet pane of 10 16.00

Greetings A653

Designs: No. 1868, Girl astronaut in spaceship, birthday cake. No. 1869, Boy astronaut, heart.

*Die Cut Perf. 13¼x12¾*
**2010, Jan. 28** **Self-Adhesive**
**1868** A653 55c multi 1.60 1.60
**1869** A653 55c multi 1.60 1.60
*a.* Vert. pair, #1868-1869, on backing paper without back printing 3.20
*b.* Booklet pane of 10, 5 each #1868-1869 16.00

New Year 2010 (Year of the Tiger) A654

**2010, Feb. 11** *Perf. 13¼*
**1870** A654 82c multi 2.25 2.25
*a.* Souvenir sheet of 3 6.75 6.75

St. Patrick's Day — A655

**2010, Feb. 18** *Perf. 14x14¾*
**1871** A655 82c multi 2.25 2.25

President's Award, 25th Anniv. A656

**2010, Mar. 11** **Litho.** *Perf. 13¼*
**1872** A656 55c multi 1.50 1.50

Irish Countrywoman's Association, Cent. — A657

**2010, Mar. 25**
**1873** A657 55c multi 1.50 1.50

Crosses — A658

Designs: No. 1874, Monasterboice Cross, County Louth. No. 1875, Carndonagh Cross, County Donegal. No. 1876, Drumcliffe Cross, County Sligo. No. 1877, Ahenny Cross, County Tipperary.

**2010, Apr. 8**
**1874** A658 55c black 1.50 1.50
**1875** A658 55c black 1.50 1.50
**1876** A658 55c black 1.50 1.50
**1877** A658 55c black 1.50 1.50
*a.* Horiz. strip of 4, #1874-1877 6.00 6.00
*Nos. 1874-1877 (4)* 6.00 6.00

Europa — A659

Scenes from children's books: 55c, The Happy Prince, by Oscar Wilde. 82c, Gulliver's Travels, by Jonathan Swift.

**2010, May 6**
**1878** A659 55c multi 1.40 1.40
**1879** A659 82c multi 2.10 2.10

Máirtín O Direáin (1910-88), Poet A660

**2010, May 27** *Perf. 14¾x14*
**1880** A660 55c multi 1.40 1.40

Paintings by Roderic O'Conor (1860-1940) — A661

Designs: No. 1881, The Breton Girl (shown). No. 1882, Self-portrait.

**2010, May 27** *Perf. 13¼*

**1881** A661 55c multi 1.40 1.40
**1882** A661 55c multi 1.40 1.40

Humanitarians — A662

Designs: No. 1883, Mother Teresa (1910-97), 1979 Nobel Laureate for Peace. No. 1884, Henry Dunant (1828-1910), founder of the Red Cross, 1901 Nobel Laureate for Peace.

**2010, June 17**

**1883** A662 55c multi 1.40 1.40
**1884** A662 55c multi 1.40 1.40
*a.* Horiz. pair, #1883-1884 2.80 2.80

Fashion Designers A663

Work of Irish designers: No. 1885, Paul Costelloe. No. 1886, Louise Kennedy. No. 1887, Lainey Keogh. No. 1888, John Rocha. No. 1889, Philip Treacy. No. 1890, Orla Kiely.

**Litho. & Embossed**

**2010, July 15** *Perf. 13¼*

**1885** A663 55c multi 1.50 1.50
*a.* Booklet pane of 3 4.50 —
**1886** A663 55c multi 1.50 1.50
*a.* Booklet pane of 3 4.50 —
**1887** A663 55c multi 1.50 1.50
*a.* Horiz. strip of 3, #1885-1887 4.50 4.50
*b.* Booklet pane of 3 4.50 —
**1888** A663 82c multi 2.25 2.25
*a.* Booklet pane of 3 6.75 —
**1889** A663 82c multi 2.25 2.25
*a.* Booklet pane of 3 6.75 —
**1890** A663 82c multi 2.25 2.25
*a.* Horiz. strip of 3, #1888-1890 6.75 6.75
*b.* Booklet pane of 3 6.75 —
Complete booklet, #1885a, 1886a, 1887b, 1888a, 1889a, 1890b 34.00
*Nos. 1885-1890 (6)* 11.25 11.25

Complete booklet sold for €13.

Birds — A664

**2010, July 29** **Litho.** *Perf. 13¼*

**1891** A664 55c Buzzard 1.50 1.50
**1892** A664 55c Golden eagle 1.50 1.50
*a.* Horiz. pair, #1891-1892 3.00 3.00
**1893** A664 82c Peregrine falcon 2.25 2.25
**1894** A664 95c Merlin 2.50 2.50
*a.* Souvenir sheet, #1891-1894 7.75 7.75
*Nos. 1891-1894 (4)* 7.75 7.75

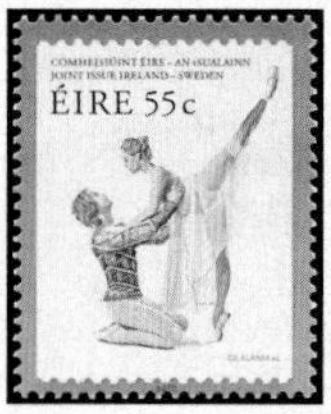


Romeo and Juliet (Vignette of Sweden No. 1141) — A665

**Litho. & Engr.**

**2010, Aug. 26** *Perf. 12¾*

**1895** A665 55c multi 1.40 1.40

Stamp engraving work of Czeslaw Slania. See Sweden No. 2642.

Irish Wheelchair Association, 50th Anniv. — A666

**2010, Sept. 8** **Litho.** *Perf. 14¾x14*

**1896** A666 55c multi 1.40 1.40

Showbands — A667

Designs: No. 1897, The Miami Showband. No. 1898, The Drifters Showband. No. 1899, The Royal Showband. No. 1900, The Freshmen.

**2010, Sept. 23** *Perf. 13½*

**1897** A667 55c multi 1.50 1.50
**1898** A667 55c multi 1.50 1.50
**1899** A667 82c multi 2.25 2.25
**1900** A667 82c multi 2.25 2.25
*a.* Souvenir sheet of 4, #1897-1900 7.50 7.50
*b.* Booklet pane of 4, #1897-1900 8.25 —
Complete booklet, 4 #1900b 33.00
*Nos. 1897-1900 (4)* 7.50 7.50

On No. 1900a, stamps are not near the edge of the sheet and stamps have perforations on all four sides. On No. 1900b, Nos, 1898 and 1900 are at the right side of the sheet and have a straight edge at right. The complete booklet sold for €12 and contains four examples of No. 1900b, each with different margins.

Ireland Automobile Association, Cent. — A668

**2010, Oct. 14** *Perf. 14¾x14*

**1901** A668 55c multi 1.60 1.60

Irishmen Involved With Chilean Independence A669

Designs: No. 1902, Commander General John Mackenna (1771-1814). No. 1903, Supreme Director Bernardo O'Higgins (1778-1842).

**2010, Oct. 28** *Perf. 13¼*

**1902** A669 82c multi 2.40 2.40
**1903** A669 82c multi 2.40 2.40
*a.* Horiz. pair, #1902-1903 4.80 4.80

See Chile No. 1562.

A670

Christmas A671

Stained-glass windows from churches in Roscommon: No. 1904, Holy Family. 82c, Joseph and Mary.

**2010, Nov. 4** *Perf. 13½*

**1904** A670 55c multi 1.60 1.60
**1905** A670 82c multi 2.40 2.40

**Self-Adhesive**

***Serpentine Die Cut 11¼x11***

**1906** A671 55c multi 1.60 1.60
*a.* Vert. pair on backing paper without printing on back 3.25
*b.* Booklet pane of 26 #1906 42.00

No. 1906b sold for €13.75 and all stamps have printing on the back of the backing paper.

Bride and Groom — A672

**2011, Jan. 20** *Die Cut Perf. 13¼*

**Self-Adhesive**

**1907** A672 55c multi 1.50 1.50
*a.* Horiz. pair on backing paper without printing on back 3.00
*b.* Booklet pane of 10 15.00

Tulips — A673

Balloons — A674

**2011, Jan. 27** *Die Cut Perf. 13¼x13*

**Self-Adhesive**

**1908** A673 55c multi 1.50 1.50
**1909** A674 55c multi 1.50 1.50
*a.* Vert. pair, #1908-1909 on backing paper without printing on back 3.00
*b.* Booklet pane of 10, 5 each #1908-1909, + 10 stickers 15.00

American Chamber of Commerce, Ireland, 50th Anniv. — A675

**2011, Feb. 3** *Perf. 14x14¾*

**1910** A675 55c multi 1.50 1.50

Pres. Cearbhall O Dáleaigh (Carroll O'Daly) (1911-78) A676

**2011, Feb. 10** *Perf. 13¾*

**1911** A676 55c multi 1.50 1.50

St. Patrick's Day — A677

**2011, Feb. 17** *Perf. 14¼x14¾*

**1912** A677 82c multi 2.40 2.40

A678

Women's Rights A679

**2011, Mar. 3** *Perf. 13¼*

**1913** A678 55c multi 1.60 1.60
**1914** A679 82c multi 2.40 2.40

Irish Amateur Boxing Association, Cent. — A680

**2011, Apr. 14** **Litho.** *Perf. 14¾x14*

**1915** A680 55c multi 1.60 1.60

Europa A681

Designs: 55c, Girl under tulip tree, Knockabbey Gardens. 82c, River Walk, Avondale Forest Park.

**2011, May 5**

| | | | | |
|---|---|---|---|---|
| **1916** | A681 | 55c multi | 1.60 | 1.60 |
| **1917** | A681 | 82c multi | 2.40 | 2.40 |

Intl. Year of Forests.

Year of Craft — A682

Craft object made of: No. 1918, Ceramics, by Deirdre McLoughlin. No. 1919, Glass, by Róisín de Buitléar. No. 1920, Metal, by Inga Reed. No. 1921, Textiles, by Helen McAllister. No. 1922, Wood, by Liam Flynn.

**2011, May 12** ***Perf. 13¼***

**Booklet Stamps**

| | | | | |
|---|---|---|---|---|
| **1918** | A682 | 55c multi | 1.60 | 1.60 |
| *a.* | | Booklet pane of 3 | 5.00 | — |
| **1919** | A682 | 55c multi | 1.60 | 1.60 |
| *a.* | | Booklet pane of 3 | 5.00 | — |
| **1920** | A682 | 55c multi | 1.60 | 1.60 |
| *a.* | | Booklet pane of 3 | 5.00 | — |
| **1921** | A682 | 55c multi | 1.60 | 1.60 |
| *a.* | | Booklet pane of 3 | 5.00 | — |
| **1922** | A682 | 55c multi | 1.60 | 1.60 |
| *a.* | | Booklet pane of 3 | 5.00 | — |
| | | Complete booklet, #1918a, 1919a, 1920a, 1921a, 1922a | 25.00 | |
| *b.* | | Booklet pane of 5, #1918-1922 | 8.00 | — |
| | | Complete booklet, #1922b | 8.00 | 8.00 |
| | | *Nos. 1918-1922 (5)* | 8.00 | 8.00 |

National Parks A683

Designs: No. 1923, Ballycroy National Park. No. 1924, The Burren National Park. No. 1925, Connemara National Park. No. 1926, Glenveagh National Park. No. 1927, Killarney National Park. No. 1928, Wicklow Mountains National Park.

**2011, June 6** ***Perf. 14¾x14***

| | | | | |
|---|---|---|---|---|
| **1923** | A683 | 55c multi | 1.60 | 1.60 |
| *a.* | | Booklet pane of 3 | 5.00 | — |
| **1924** | A683 | 55c multi | 1.60 | 1.60 |
| *a.* | | Booklet pane of 3 | 5.00 | — |
| **1925** | A683 | 55c multi | 1.60 | 1.60 |
| *a.* | | Booklet pane of 3 | 5.00 | — |
| *b.* | | Horiz. strip of 3, #1923-1925 | 4.80 | 4.80 |
| *c.* | | Souvenir sheet of 3, #1923-1925 | 4.80 | 4.80 |
| **1926** | A683 | 82c multi | 2.40 | 2.40 |
| *a.* | | Booklet pane of 3 | 7.50 | — |
| **1927** | A683 | 82c multi | 2.40 | 2.40 |
| *a.* | | Booklet pane of 3 | 7.50 | — |
| **1928** | A683 | 82c multi | 2.40 | 2.40 |
| *a.* | | Booklet pane of 3 | 7.50 | — |
| | | Complete booklet, #1923a, 1924a, 1925a, 1926a, 1927a, 1928a | 37.50 | |
| *b.* | | Horiz. strip of 3, #1926-1928 | 7.25 | 7.25 |
| *c.* | | Souvenir sheet of 3, #1926-1928 | 7.25 | 7.25 |
| | | *Nos. 1923-1928 (6)* | 12.00 | 12.00 |

Complete booklet sold for €13.

Amnesty International, 50th Anniv. A684

**2011, June 30** ***Perf. 13½***

| | | | | |
|---|---|---|---|---|
| **1929** | A684 | 55c multi | 1.60 | 1.60 |

Hermit Crab — A685

***Serpentine Die Cut 14***

**2011, June 22** **Litho.**

**Booklet Stamp**
**Self-Adhesive**

| | | | | |
|---|---|---|---|---|
| **1930** | A685 | 55c multi | 1.60 | 1.60 |
| *a.* | | Booklet pane of 10 | 16.00 | |
| *b.* | | Die cut perf. 14 | 1.50 | 1.50 |
| *c.* | | Booklet pane of 10 #1930b | 15.00 | |

Issued: No. 1930b, 5/1/12.

Renewable Energy A686

Designs: No. 1931, House with solar panels. No. 1932, Ardnacrusha Hydroelectric Station. No. 1933, Wind turbines. No. 1934, Ocean Energy Development Unit. No. 1935, Field of rape flowers for biofuel.

***Die Cut Perf. 13¼x13***

**2011, Aug. 5** **Litho.**

**Self-Adhesive**

| | | | | |
|---|---|---|---|---|
| **1931** | A686 | 55c multi | 1.60 | 1.60 |
| *a.* | | Booklet pane of 3 | 5.25 | |
| **1932** | A686 | 55c multi | 1.60 | 1.60 |
| *a.* | | Booklet pane of 3 | 5.25 | |
| **1933** | A686 | 55c multi | 1.60 | 1.60 |
| *a.* | | Booklet pane of 3 | 5.25 | |
| **1934** | A686 | 55c multi | 1.60 | 1.60 |
| *a.* | | Booklet pane of 3 | 5.25 | |
| **1935** | A686 | 55c multi | 1.60 | 1.60 |
| *a.* | | Booklet pane of 3 | 5.25 | |
| | | Complete booklet, #1931a, 1932a, 1933a, 1934a, 1935a | 27.00 | |
| *b.* | | Booklet pane of 10, 2 each #1931-1935 | 16.00 | |
| *c.* | | Horiz. strip of 5, #1931-1935, on backing paper without back printing | 8.00 | |
| | | *Nos. 1931-1935 (5)* | 8.00 | 8.00 |

Complete booklet sold for €9.

Horses A687

Designs: No. 1936, Colored horse. No. 1937, Irish draft horse. No. 1938, Thoroughbred. No. 1939, Connemara pony.

**2011, Sept. 1** **Litho.** ***Perf. 13¼***

| | | | | |
|---|---|---|---|---|
| **1936** | A687 | 55c multi | 1.50 | 1.50 |
| **1937** | A687 | 55c multi | 1.50 | 1.50 |
| **1938** | A687 | 55c multi | 1.50 | 1.50 |
| **1939** | A687 | 55c multi | 1.50 | 1.50 |
| *a.* | | Block of 4, #1936-1939 | 6.00 | 6.00 |
| *b.* | | Souvenir sheet of 4, #1936-1939 | 6.00 | 6.00 |
| | | *Nos. 1936-1939 (4)* | 6.00 | 6.00 |

2011 Solheim Cup Women's Golf Tournament, Killeen Castle Golf Course, Dunsany — A688

**2011, Sept. 15** ***Perf. 14¾x14¼***

| | | | | |
|---|---|---|---|---|
| **1940** | A688 | 55c multi | 1.50 | 1.50 |

Wildlife — A689

**Coil Stamps**

***Serpentine Die Cut 11x11¼***

**2011, Sept. 29** **Self-Adhesive**

| | | | | |
|---|---|---|---|---|
| **1941** | A689 | 55c Red squirrel | 1.50 | 1.50 |
| **1942** | A689 | 55c Bottlenose dolphin | 1.50 | 1.50 |
| *a.* | | Vert. pair, #1941-1942 | 3.00 | 3.00 |

Brian O'Nolan (1911-66), Writer — A690

**2011, Oct. 6** ***Perf. 13¾***

| | | | | |
|---|---|---|---|---|
| **1943** | A690 | 55c multi | 1.50 | 1.50 |

Christmas — A691

***Serpentine Die Cut 11x11¼***

**2011, Nov. 10**

**Self-Adhesive**

| | | | | |
|---|---|---|---|---|
| **1944** | A691 | 55c multi | 1.50 | 1.50 |
| *a.* | | Horiz. pair on backing paper without back printing | 3.00 | |
| *b.* | | Booklet pane of 26 | 39.00 | |

No. 1944b sold for €13.75.

Television Broadcasting in Ireland, 50th Anniv. — A692

Designs: No. 1945, Gay Byrne hosting *The Late Late Show.* No. 1946, Emma O'Driscoll and puppet on children's show *Hubble.* No. 1947, Newscaster Anne Doyle.

**2011, Nov. 24** ***Perf. 14¾x14***

| | | | | |
|---|---|---|---|---|
| **1945** | A692 | 55c multi | 1.50 | 1.50 |
| **1946** | A692 | 55c multi | 1.50 | 1.50 |
| **1947** | A692 | 55c multi | 1.50 | 1.50 |
| *a.* | | Horiz. strip of 3, #1945-1947 | 4.50 | 4.50 |
| | | *Nos. 1945-1947 (3)* | 4.50 | 4.50 |

Bride, Groom and Limousine A693

**2012, Jan. 19** ***Die Cut Perf. 13¼***

**Self-Adhesive**

| | | | | |
|---|---|---|---|---|
| **1948** | A693 | 55c multi | 1.50 | 1.50 |
| *a.* | | Vert. pair on backing paper without printing on back | 3.00 | |
| *b.* | | Booklet pane of 10 | 15.00 | |

Gift — A694

Birthday Candles — A695

***Die Cut Perf. 12¾x13½***

**2012, Jan. 26** **Self-Adhesive**

| | | | | |
|---|---|---|---|---|
| **1949** | A694 | 55c multi | 1.50 | 1.50 |
| **1950** | A695 | 55c multi | 1.50 | 1.50 |
| *a.* | | Horiz. pair, #1949-1950, on backing paper without printing on back | 3.00 | |
| *b.* | | Booklet pane of 10, 5 each #1949-1950 + 10 stickers | 15.00 | |

Ireland's Chairmanship of Organization for Security and Cooperation in Europe A696

**2012, Feb. 2** ***Perf. 13½x13¼***

| | | | | |
|---|---|---|---|---|
| **1951** | A696 | 55c multi | 1.50 | 1.50 |

St. Patrick's Day — A697

**2012, Feb. 9** ***Perf. 14x14¾***

| | | | | |
|---|---|---|---|---|
| **1952** | A697 | 82c multi | 2.25 | 2.25 |

Dancer From Fabulous Beast Dance Theater — A698

Dancers From Dance Theater of Ireland — A699

Dancer From Irish Modern Dance Theater — A700

Dancer from CoisCéim Dance Theater — A701

*Die Cut Perf. 13¼*

**2012, Mar. 22** **Litho.**

**Booklet Stamps Self-Adhesive**

| | | | |
|---|---|---|---|
| **1953** A698 55c multi | 1.50 | 1.50 |
| **1954** A699 55c multi | 1.50 | 1.50 |
| **1955** A700 55c multi | 1.50 | 1.50 |
| **1956** A701 55c multi | 1.50 | 1.50 |
| *a.* Block of 4, #1953-1956 | 6.00 | |
| *b.* Booklet pane of 8, 2 each #1953-1956 | 12.00 | |
| *Nos. 1953-1956 (4)* | 6.00 | 6.00 |

Sinking of the Titanic, Cent. — A702

Designs: No. 1957, Thomas Andrews, shipbuilder in charge of construction of the Titanic, and Titanic under construction. No. 1958, Father Frank Browne, amateur photographer and passenger on Titanic from Southampton to Cork, and Titanic off Cobh. No. 1959, Edward John Smith, ship's captain, and Titanic. No. 1960, Molly Brown, passenger, and Titanic's staircase.

**2012, Apr. 12** *Perf. 13¼*

| | | |
|---|---|---|
| **1957** A702 55c multi | 1.50 | 1.50 |
| **1958** A702 55c multi | 1.50 | 1.50 |
| *a.* Horiz. pair, #1957-1958 | 3.00 | 3.00 |
| **1959** A702 82c multi | 2.25 | 2.25 |
| **1960** A702 82c multi | 2.25 | 2.25 |
| *a.* Horiz. pair, #1959-1960 | 4.50 | 4.50 |
| *b.* Booklet pane of 4, #1957-1960 | 8.00 | — |
| Complete booklet, 4 #1960b | 32.00 | |
| *Nos. 1957-1960 (4)* | 7.50 | 7.50 |

On No. 1960b, Nos. 1958 and 1960 are at the right side of the pane and have a straight edge at right. The complete booklet sold for €12 and contains four examples of No. 1960b, each with different pane margins.

Bram Stoker (1847-1912), Writer — A703

Designs: No. 1961, Stoker. No. 1962, Count Dracula biting woman's neck.

**2012, Apr. 19** *Perf. 14x14¾*

| | | |
|---|---|---|
| **1961** A703 55c multi | 1.50 | 1.50 |
| **1962** A703 55c multi | 1.50 | 1.50 |
| *a.* Horiz. pair, #1961-1962 | 3.00 | 3.00 |
| *b.* Souvenir sheet of 2, #1961-1962 | 3.00 | 3.00 |

Europa A704

Designs: 55c, Little Skellig Island. 82c, Ha'penny Bridge, Dublin.

**2012, May 3** *Perf. 13½*

| | | |
|---|---|---|
| **1963** A704 55c multi | 1.50 | 1.50 |
| **1964** A704 82c multi | 2.25 | 2.25 |

50th Intl. Eucharistic Congress, Dublin — A705

Designs: 55c, Chalice and host. 82c, Monstrance and host.

**2012, June 7** *Perf. 14x14¾*

| | | |
|---|---|---|
| **1965** A705 55c multi | 1.40 | 1.40 |
| **1966** A705 82c multi | 2.00 | 2.00 |

Volvo Ocean Race A706

Designs: 55c, Sailboats. €3, Sailboats, diff., vert.

**2012, June 14** *Perf. 14¾x14¼*

| | | |
|---|---|---|
| **1967** A706 55c multi | 1.40 | 1.40 |

**Souvenir Sheet**

| | | |
|---|---|---|
| **1968** A706 €3 multi | 7.50 | 7.50 |

No. 1968 contains one 28x48mm stamp.

Common Frog — A707

**2012, May 1** *Die Cut Perf. 14x14¼*

**Booklet Stamp Self-Adhesive**

| | | |
|---|---|---|
| **1969** A707 82c multi | 2.25 | 2.25 |
| *a.* Booklet pane of 10 | 22.50 | |

Dublin Fire Brigade, 150th Anniv. — A708

Designs: No. 1970, Firefighter carrying baby. No. 1971, Firefighters in chemical suits. No. 1972, Firefighters at car accident. No. 1973, Firefighter rescuing drowning man.

**2012, June 28** *Perf. 13¼*

| | | |
|---|---|---|
| **1970** A708 55c multi | 1.40 | 1.40 |
| *a.* Booklet pane of 4 | 6.25 | 6.25 |
| **1971** A708 55c multi | 1.40 | 1.40 |
| *a.* Booklet pane of 4 | 6.25 | 6.25 |
| **1972** A708 55c multi | 1.40 | 1.40 |
| *a.* Booklet pane of 4 | 6.25 | 6.25 |
| **1973** A708 55c multi | 1.40 | 1.40 |
| *a.* Booklet pane of 4 | 6.25 | 6.25 |
| Complete booklet, #1970a, 1971a, 1972a, 1973a | 25.00 | |
| *b.* Horiz. strip of 4, #1970-1973 | 5.60 | 5.60 |
| *Nos. 1970-1973 (4)* | 5.60 | 5.60 |

Nos. 1970a-1973a each have straight edge at right. Complete booklet sold for €10.

Science — A709

Designs: No. 1974, Conference Center, Dublin, molecular structure of DNA. No. 1975, Robert Boyle (1627-91), chemist and physicist, formula and graph of Boyle's Law.

**2012, July 5**

| | | |
|---|---|---|
| **1974** A709 55c multi | 1.40 | 1.40 |
| **1975** A709 55c multi | 1.40 | 1.40 |
| *a.* Horiz. pair, #1974-1975 | 2.80 | 2.80 |
| *b.* Souvenir sheet of 2, #1974-1975 | 2.80 | 2.80 |

2012 City of Science Festival, Dublin (No. 1974); Boyle's Law, 350th anniv. (No. 1975).

2012 Summer Olympics, London — A710

Emblem of 2012 Summer Olympics and: 55c, Stylized winner's platform. 82c, Vertical bars.

**2012, July 19** *Perf. 14x14¾*

| | | |
|---|---|---|
| **1976** A710 55c multi | 1.40 | 1.40 |
| **1977** A710 82c | 2.10 | 2.10 |

Myths and Legends A711

Designs: No. 1978, The Children of Lir (swans in flight). No. 1979, Deirdre of the Sorrows (couple embracing). No. 1980, Fionn Mac Cumhaill (man in water, fish). No. 1981, Setanta (Setanta swinging hurling stick at dog).

*Perf. 14¾x14¼*

**2012, Sept. 13** **Litho.**

| | | |
|---|---|---|
| **1978** A711 55c multi | 1.50 | 1.50 |
| **1979** A711 55c multi | 1.50 | 1.50 |
| *a.* Horiz. pair, #1978-1979 | 3.00 | 3.00 |
| **1980** A711 82c multi | 2.10 | 2.10 |
| **1981** A711 82c multi | 2.10 | 2.10 |
| *a.* Horiz. pair, #1980-1981 | 4.20 | 4.20 |
| *Nos. 1978-1981 (4)* | 7.20 | 7.20 |

Barnardos Ireland Children's Charity, 50th Anniv. A712

**2012, Oct. 11** *Perf. 13¼*

| | | |
|---|---|---|
| **1982** A712 55c multi | 1.40 | 1.40 |

Christmas — A713

*Serpentine Die Cut 11x11¼*

**2012, Nov. 8** **Self-Adhesive**

| | | |
|---|---|---|
| **1983** A713 55c multi | 1.40 | 1.40 |
| *a.* Horiz. pair on backing paper without back printing | 2.80 | |
| *b.* Booklet pane of 26 | 36.50 | |

No. 1983b sold for €13.75.

Irish Presidency of Council of the European Union — A714

**2013, Jan. 17** *Perf. 14x14¾*

| | | |
|---|---|---|
| **1984** A714 55c multi | 1.50 | 1.50 |

The Gathering Ireland 2013 Tourism Initiative A715

**2013, Jan. 24** *Perf. 13¼*

| | | |
|---|---|---|
| **1985** A715 82c multi | 2.25 | 2.25 |

St. Patrick's Day A716

**2013, Feb. 7** *Perf. 14¾x14*

| | | |
|---|---|---|
| **1986** A716 82c multi | 2.25 | 2.25 |

---

**AIR POST STAMPS**

**Catalogue values for unused stamps in this section are for Never Hinged items.**

Angel over Rock of Cashel AP1

Designs: 1p, 1sh3p, 1sh5p, Rock of Cashel. 3p, 8p, Lough Derg. 6p, Croagh Patrick. 1sh, Glendalough.

***Perf. 15x14***

**1948-65 Wmk. 262 Engr.**

| | | | | | |
|---|---|---|---|---|---|
| **C1** | AP1 | 1p | dk brown ('49) | 6.50 | 6.50 |
| **C2** | AP1 | 3p | blue | 11.00 | 9.50 |
| **C3** | AP1 | 6p | rose lilac | 1.10 | .90 |
| **C4** | AP1 | 8p | red brown ('54) | 4.50 | 3.50 |
| **C5** | AP1 | 1sh | green ('49) | 2.25 | 1.15 |
| **C6** | AP1 | 1sh3p | ver ('54) | 5.50 | 1.15 |

***Perf. 15***

| | | | | | |
|---|---|---|---|---|---|
| **C7** | AP1 | 1sh5p | dark blue ('65) | 4.50 | .90 |
| | | | *Nos. C1-C7 (7)* | 35.35 | 23.60 |

## POSTAGE DUE STAMPS

D1

**1925 Typo. Wmk. 44 *Perf. 14x15***

| | | | | | |
|---|---|---|---|---|---|
| **J1** | D1 | ½p | emerald | 27.50 | 42.50 |
| | | | Never hinged | 140.00 | |
| **J2** | D1 | 1p | carmine | 17.00 | 12.50 |
| | | | Never hinged | 60.00 | |
| **J3** | D1 | 2p | dark green | 32.50 | 15.00 |
| | | | Never hinged | 125.00 | |
| **J4** | D1 | 6p | plum | 10.50 | 14.00 |
| | | | Never hinged | 45.00 | |
| | | | *Nos. J1-J4 (4)* | 87.50 | 84.00 |

**Catalogue values for unused stamps in this section, from this point to the end of the section, are for Never Hinged items.**

**1940-70 Wmk. 262**

| | | | | | |
|---|---|---|---|---|---|
| **J5** | D1 | ½p | emerald ('43) | 27.50 | 22.50 |
| **J6** | D1 | 1p | brt carmine ('41) | 1.10 | .50 |
| **J7** | D1 | 1½p | vermilion ('52) | 2.25 | *5.00* |
| **J8** | D1 | 2p | dark green | 1.25 | .55 |
| **J9** | D1 | 3p | blue ('52) | 2.25 | 2.00 |
| **J10** | D1 | 5p | royal purple ('43) | 3.50 | *7.50* |
| **J11** | D1 | 6p | plum ('60) | 4.00 | 1.75 |
| **J12** | D1 | 8p | orange ('62) | 7.50 | 7.50 |
| **J13** | D1 | 10p | red lilac ('65) | 8.50 | 7.00 |
| **J14** | D1 | 1sh | lt yel grn ('69) | 25.00 | 9.00 |
| | | | *Nos. J5-J14 (10)* | 82.85 | 63.30 |

**1971, Feb. 15 Typo. Wmk. 262**

| | | | | | |
|---|---|---|---|---|---|
| **J15** | D1 | 1p | sepia | 2.50 | *3.50* |
| **J16** | D1 | 1½p | bright green | 2.50 | *3.50* |
| **J17** | D1 | 3p | gray green | 2.50 | *3.50* |
| **J18** | D1 | 4p | orange | 2.50 | *3.50* |
| **J19** | D1 | 5p | bright blue | 2.50 | *3.50* |
| **J20** | D1 | 7p | yellow | 2.50 | *3.50* |
| **J21** | D1 | 8p | scarlet | 2.50 | *3.50* |
| | | | *Nos. J15-J21 (7)* | 17.50 | 24.50 |

**1978 Unwmk.**

| | | | | | |
|---|---|---|---|---|---|
| **J25** | D1 | 3p | gray green | 3.50 | *3.50* |
| **J26** | D1 | 4p | orange | 5.00 | *10.50* |
| **J27** | D1 | 5p | bright blue | 3.50 | *3.50* |
| | | | *Nos. J25-J27 (3)* | 12.00 | *17.50* |

Celtic Knot — D2

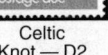

D3

**1980-85 Photo. *Perf. 15***

| | | | | | |
|---|---|---|---|---|---|
| **J28** | D2 | 1p | brt yel green | .75 | *1.25* |
| **J29** | D2 | 2p | ultramarine | .75 | *1.25* |
| **J30** | D2 | 4p | dark green | .75 | *1.25* |
| **J31** | D2 | 6p | yel orange | .75 | *1.25* |
| **J32** | D2 | 8p | violet blue | 1.00 | *2.00* |
| **J33** | D2 | 18p | green | 1.60 | *2.00* |
| **J33A** | D2 | 20p | org brown ('85) | 3.50 | *6.50* |
| **J34** | D2 | 24p | emerald | 2.25 | 1.90 |
| **J35** | D2 | 30p | violet blue ('85) | 7.00 | *9.00* |
| **J36** | D2 | 50p | rose pink ('85) | 4.00 | 4.00 |
| | | | *Nos. J28-J36 (10)* | 22.35 | 30.40 |

Issue dates: 1p, 2p, 4p, 6p, 8p, 18p, 24p, June 11; 20p, 30p, 50p, Aug. 22.

**1988, Oct. 6 Litho. *Perf. 14x15***

| | | | | | |
|---|---|---|---|---|---|
| **J37** | D3 | 1p | blk, dp yel & brt red | .80 | *1.25* |
| **J38** | D3 | 2p | blk, vio brn & brt red | .80 | *1.25* |
| **J39** | D3 | 3p | blk, dull vio & brt red | .80 | *1.25* |
| **J40** | D3 | 4p | blk, vio & brt red | .80 | *1.25* |
| **J41** | D3 | 5p | blk, vio bl & brt red | .80 | *1.25* |
| **J42** | D3 | 17p | blk, brt ol grn & brt red | 1.60 | *2.40* |
| **J43** | D3 | 20p | blk, bluish gray & brt red | 2.10 | *2.75* |
| **J44** | D3 | 24p | blk, bl grn & brt red | 2.40 | *3.25* |
| **J45** | D3 | 30p | blk & brt red | 2.40 | *3.25* |
| **J46** | D3 | 50p | blk, gray & brt red | 3.25 | *4.25* |
| **J47** | D3 | £1 | blk, dk ol brn & brt red | 6.75 | *8.25* |
| | | | *Nos. J37-J47 (11)* | 22.50 | 30.40 |

# ISRAEL

ˈiz-rē-əl

LOCATION — Western Asia, bordering on the Mediterranean Sea
GOVT. — Republic
AREA — 8,017 sq. mi.
POP. — 5,749,760 (1999 est.)
CAPITAL — Jerusalem

When the British mandate of Palestine ended in May 1948, the Jewish state of Israel was proclaimed by the Jewish National Council in Palestine.

1000 Mils = 1 Pound
1000 Prutot = 1 Pound (1949)
100 Agorot = 1 Pound (1960)
100 Agorot = 1 Shekel (1980)

**Catalogue values for all unused stamps in this country are for Never Hinged items.**

**Tabs**

**Stamps of Israel are printed in sheets with tabs (labels) usually attached below the bottom row, sometimes at the sides.**

**Tabs of the following numbers are in two parts, perforated between: 9, 15, 23-37, 44, 46-47, 50, 55, 62-65, 70-72, 74-77, 86-91, 94-99, 104-118, 123-126, 133-136B, 138-141, 143-151, 160-161, 165-167, 178-179, 182, 187-189, 203, 211-213, 222-223, 228-237, 243-244, 246-250, 256-258, 269-270, 272-273, 275, 294-295, 312, 337-339, 341-344, 346-347, 353-354, C1-C13, C22-C30. Both parts must be present to qualify for with tab value. Stamps with only one part sell for about one-quarter to one-third of full tab prices.**

**Watermarks**

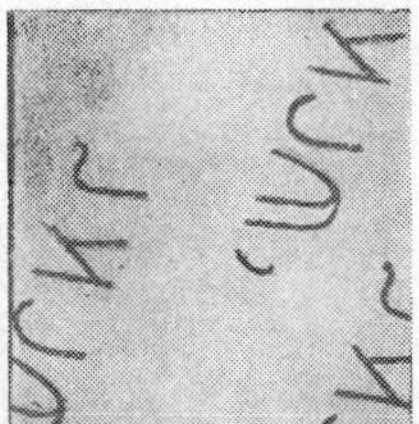

Wmk. 301 — ISRAEL in Hebrew

Wmk. 302 — Multiple Stag

Ancient Judean Coins
A1 A2

Designs: Nos. 1-6, Various coins.

***Perf. 10, 11 and Compound***

**1948, May 16 Typo. Unwmk.**

| | | | | | |
|---|---|---|---|---|---|
| **1** | A1 | 3m | orange | .30 | .25 |
| **2** | A1 | 5m | yellow grn | .30 | .25 |
| **3** | A1 | 10m | red violet | .50 | .25 |
| **4** | A1 | 15m | red | .75 | .25 |
| **5** | A1 | 20m | bright ultra | 2.25 | .35 |
| **6** | A1 | 50m | orange brown | 9.00 | 1.00 |
| | | | *Nos. 1-6 (6)* | 13.10 | 2.35 |
| | | | Nos. 1-6 (6) with tabs | 250.00 | |
| | | | Set, with tabs, hinged | 100.00 | |

**Size: 34½x22mm**

| | | | | | |
|---|---|---|---|---|---|
| **7** | A2 | 250m | dark sl grn | 32.50 | 10.00 |
| **8** | A2 | 500m | red brn, *cr* | 140.00 | 52.50 |

**Size: 36½x24mm**

| | | | | | |
|---|---|---|---|---|---|
| **9** | A2 | 1000m | blk bl, *pale bl* | 220.00 | 100.00 |
| | | | *Nos. 7-9 (3)* | 392.50 | 162.50 |
| | | | Nos. 7-9 with tabs | *6,500.* | |
| | | | Set, hinged | 175.00 | |

Nos. 1-9 exist imperf.
See design A6. For overprints see #J1-J5.

**Rouletted**

| | | | | | |
|---|---|---|---|---|---|
| *1a* | A1 | 3m | | .50 | .25 |
| *2b* | A1 | 5m | | .65 | .25 |
| *3b* | A1 | 10m | | 11.00 | .90 |
| | | | *Nos. 1a-3b (3)* | 12.15 | 1.40 |
| | | | Set, with tabs | 265.00 | |
| | | | Set with tabs, hinged | 110.00 | |

Flying Scroll — A3

**1948, Sept. 26 Litho. *Perf. 11½***

| | | | | | |
|---|---|---|---|---|---|
| **10** | A3 | 3m | brn red & ultra | .40 | .25 |
| **11** | A3 | 5m | dl grn & ultra | .40 | .25 |
| **12** | A3 | 10m | dp car & ultra | .40 | .25 |
| **13** | A3 | 20m | dp ultra & ultra | 1.50 | .75 |
| **14** | A3 | 65m | brown & red | 11.00 | 3.25 |
| | | | *Nos. 10-14 (5)* | 13.70 | 4.75 |
| | | | With tabs | 250.00 | |
| | | | With tabs, hinged | 100.00 | |

Jewish New Year, 5709.

Flag of Israel — A4

**1949, Mar. 31**

| | | | | | |
|---|---|---|---|---|---|
| **15** | A4 | 20m | bright blue | .50 | .25 |
| | | | With tab | 45.00 | |

Appointment of the government by the Knesset.

Souvenir Sheet

A5

**1949, May 1 *Imperf.***

| | | | | | |
|---|---|---|---|---|---|
| **16** | A5 | | Sheet of 4 | 80.00 | 27.50 |
| *a.* | | | 10m dark carmine rose | 15.00 | 4.00 |

1st anniv. of Israeli postage stamps.

The sheet was sold at "TABUL," First National Stamp Exhibition, in Tel Aviv, May 1-6, 1949. Tickets, costing 100 mils, covered the entrance fee and one sheet.

Bronze Half-Shekel of 67 A.D. — A6

Approach to Jerusalem — A8

Hebrew University, Jerusalem A7

"The Negev" by Reuven Rubin — A9

**1949-50 Unwmk. *Perf. 11½, 14***

| | | | | | |
|---|---|---|---|---|---|
| **17** | A6 | 3p | gray black | .25 | .25 |
| **18** | A6 | 5p | purple | .25 | .25 |
| **19** | A6 | 10p | green | .25 | .25 |
| **20** | A6 | 15p | deep rose | .25 | .25 |
| **21** | A6 | 30p | dark blue | .30 | .25 |
| **22** | A6 | 50p | brown | 1.25 | .25 |

**23** A7 100p Prus grn .40 .25
With tab 20.00
**24** A8 250p org brn & gray 1.25 .65
With tab 35.00
**25** A9 500p dp org & brown 7.50 5.50
With tab 230.00
*Nos. 17-25 (9)* 11.70 7.90
Nos. 17-22 with tabs (6) 70.00
Tete beche pairs, Nos. 18-21 80.00 80.00

Each of Nos. 17-22 portrays a different coin.
25th anniv. of the Hebrew University in Jerusalem (No. 23).
Issued: 250p, 2/16; 3p-50p, 12/18; 100p, 5/9/50; 500p, 12/26/50.
See Nos. 38-43, 56-61, 80-83, and design A1. For overprints see Nos. O1-O4.

Well at Petah Tikva — A10

**1949, Aug. 10** *Perf. 11*
**27** A10 40p dk grn & brn 7.50 .30
With tab 85.00

70th anniv. of Petah Tikva.

Arms and Service Insignia A11

**1949, Sept. 20** *Perf. 11½*
**28** A11 5p Air Force .35 .25
**29** A11 10p Navy .95 .40
**30** A11 35p Army 4.00 2.75
*Nos. 28-30 (3)* 5.30 3.40
With tabs 600.00

Jewish New Year, 5710.

Running Stag — A12

**1950, Mar. 26**
**31** A12 40p purple .55 .30
*a.* Booklet pane of 4 3.75
**32** A12 80p rose red .70 .35
*a.* Booklet pane of 4 7.50
Complete booklet, 1 ea. #31a, 32a 27.50
*b.* Nos. 31 and 32 tête bêche 45.00 25.00
With tabs 67.50

75th anniv. (in 1949) of the UPU.

Struggle for Free Immigration A13

Arrival of Immigrants A14

**1950, Apr. 23**
**33** A13 20p dull brown 2.25 1.50
**34** A14 40p dull green 4.75 3.50
With tabs 500.00

Independence Day, Apr. 22, 1950.

Fruit and Star of David — A15

**1950, Aug. 31** **Litho.** *Perf. 14*
**35** A15 5p vio blue & org .25 .25
**36** A15 15p red brn & grn .35 .25
With tabs 45.00

Jewish New Year, 5711.

Runner and Track A16

**1950, Oct. 1**
**37** A16 80p olive & sl blk 1.60 .60
With tab 62.50

3rd Maccabiah, Ramat Gan, Sept. 27, 1950.

**Coin Type of 1949 Redrawn**

Designs: Various coins.

**1950**
**38** A6 3p gray black .25 .25
**39** A6 5p purple .25 .25
*a.* Tête bêche pair 3.00 3.00
**40** A6 10p green .25 .25
*a.* Tête bêche pair 1.25 1.00
**41** A6 15p deep rose .25 .25
*a.* Tête bêche pair 2.00 1.75
**42** A6 30p dark blue .25 .25
*a.* Tête bêche pair 4.00 4.00
**43** A6 50p brown .25 .25
*Nos. 38-43 (6)* 1.50 1.50
With tabs 2.90

Inscription at left measures 11mm on Nos. 38-43; 9mm on Nos. 17-22.

Detail from Tablet, "Founding of Tel Aviv" A17

**1951, Mar. 22**
**44** A17 40p dark brown .30 .25
With tab 20.00

40th anniversary of Tel Aviv.

Young Man Holding Outline Map of Israel — A18

**1951, Apr. 30** **Litho.**
**45** A18 80p red brown .25 .25
With tab 3.75

Issued to promote the sale of Independence Bonds.

Metsudat Yesha A19

Hakastel A20

**1951, May 9** **Unwmk.**
**46** A19 15p red brown .30 .25
**47** A20 40p deep blue .60 .25
With tabs 45.00

Proclamation of State of Israel, 3rd anniv.

Tractor and Wheat — A21

Tree — A22

Plower and National Fund Stamp of 1902 — A23

**1951, June 24** *Perf. 14*
**48** A21 15p red brown .25 .25
**49** A22 25p Prussian green .25 .25
**50** A23 80p dull blue .35 .25
*Nos. 48-50 (3)* .85 .75
With tabs 90.00

Jewish National Fund, 50th anniversary.

Theodor Zeev Herzl — A24

Carrier Pigeons — A25

**1951, Aug. 14**
**51** A24 80p gray green .25 .25
With tab 4.00

23rd Zionist Congress, Jerusalem.

**1951, Sept. 16**

Designs: 15p, Girl holding dove and fruit. 40p, Scrolls of the law.

**52** A25 5p blue .25 .25
**53** A25 15p cerise .25 .25
**54** A25 40p rose violet .25 .25
*Nos. 52-54 (3)* .75 .75
With tabs 3.25

Jewish New Year, 5712.

Menorah and Emblems of Twelve Tribes — A26

**1952, Feb. 27**
**55** A26 1000p dk bl & gray 16.00 7.00
With tab 250.00

**Redrawn Coin Type of 1950**

Designs: Various coins.

**1952, Mar. 30**
**56** A6 20p orange .25 .25
*a.* Tête bêche pair 2.50 2.50
**57** A6 35p olive green .25 .25
**58** A6 40p orange brown .25 .25
**59** A6 45p red violet .25 .25
*a.* Tête bêche pair 4.50 4.50
**60** A6 60p carmine .25 .25
**61** A6 85p aquamarine .25 .25
*Nos. 56-61 (6)* 1.50 1.50
With tabs 12.00

Thistle and Yad Mordecai Battlefield A27

Battlefields: 60p, Cornflower and Deganya. 110p, Anemone and Safed.

**1952, Apr. 29**
**62** A27 30p lil rose & vio brn .25 .25
**63** A27 60p ultra & gray blk .25 .25
**64** A27 110p crimson & gray .35 .25
*Nos. 62-64 (3)* .85 .75
With tabs 20.00

Proclamation of State of Israel, 4th anniv.

Manhattan Skyline and American Zionists' House A28

**1952, May 13**
**65** A28 220p dark blue & gray .35 .25
With tab 11.00

Opening of American Zionists' House, Tel Aviv.

Figs — A29

**Unwmk.**
**1952, Sept. 3** **Litho.** *Perf. 14*
**66** A29 15p shown .30 .25
**67** A29 40p Lily .30 .25
**68** A29 110p Dove .30 .25
**69** A29 220p Nut cluster .50 .25
*Nos. 66-69 (4)* 1.40 1.00
With tabs 26.00

Jewish New Year, 5713.

Pres. Chaim Weizmann (1874-1952) and Presidential Standard — A30

**1952, Dec. 9**
**70** A30 30p slate .25 .25
**71** A30 110p black .25 .25
With tabs 9.00

Weizmann, president of Israel 1948-52.

Numeral Incorporating Agricultural Scenes — A31

**1952, Dec. 31**
**72** A31 110p brown, buff & emer .40 .25
With tab 8.50

70th anniversary of B.I.L.U. (Bet Yaakov Lechu Venelcha) immigration.

Five Anemones and State Emblem — A32

**1953, Apr. 19**

73 A32 110p grnsh bl, bl blk & red .25 .25
With tab 4.25

5th anniversary of State of Israel.

Rabbi Moshe ben Maimon (Maimonides) A33

Holy Ark, Jerusalem A34

**1953, Aug. 3 Wmk. 301** ***Perf. 14x13***

74 A33 110p brown .35 .35
With tab 8.25

7th International Congress of History of Science, Jerusalem, Aug. 4-11.

**1953, Aug. 11**

Holy Arks: 45p, Petah Tikva. 200p, Safed.

75 A34 20p sapphire .25 .25
76 A34 45p brown red .25 .25
77 A34 200p purple .25 .25
*Nos. 75-77 (3)* .75 .75
With tabs 9.75

Jewish New Year, 5714.

Combined Ball-Globe A35

Desert Rose A36

**Unwmk.**

**1953, Sept. 20 Litho.** ***Perf. 14***

78 A35 110p blue & dark brn .25 .25
With tab 4.25

4th Maccabiah, Sept. 20-29, 1953.

**1953, Sept. 22**

79 A36 200p multicolored .25 .25
With tab 4.50

Conquest of the Desert Exhib., 9/22-10/14.

**Redrawn Type of 1950**

Designs: Various coins.

**1954, Jan. 5**

80 A6 80p olive bister .25 .25
81 A6 95p blue green .25 .25
82 A6 100p fawn .25 .25
83 A6 125p violet blue .25 .25
*Nos. 80-83 (4)* 1.00 1.00
With tabs 3.00

Marigold and Ruins at Yehiam — A37

350p, Narcissus and bridge at Gesher.

**1954, May 5** **Litho.**

84 A37 60p dk bl, mag & ol gray .25 .25
85 A37 350p dk brn, grn & yel .25 .25
With tabs 2.25

Memorial Day and 6th anniversary of proclamation of State of Israel.

Theodor Zeev Herzl (1860-1904), Founder of Zionist Movement — A38

**1954, July 21** **Wmk. 302**

86 A38 160p dk bl, dk brn & cr .25 .25
With tab .85

Bearers with Grape Cluster A39

**1954, Sept. 8** ***Perf. 13x14***

87 A39 25p dark brown .25 .25
With tab .25

Jewish New Year, 5715.

19th Century Mail Coach and Jerusalem Post Office A40

200p, Mail truck & present G.P.O., Jerusalem.

**1954, Oct. 13** ***Perf. 14***

88 A40 60p blue, blk & yel .25 .25
89 A40 200p dk grn, blk & red .25 .25
With tabs 3.00

TABIM, National Stamp Exhibition, Jerusalem, Oct. 13-18.

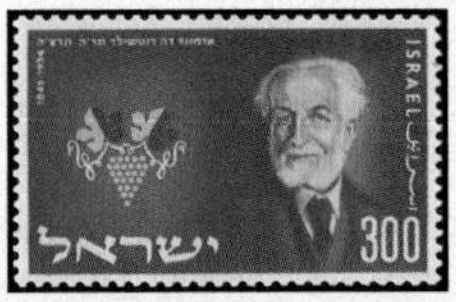

Baron Edmond de Rothschild (1845-1934) and Grape Cluster — A41

**1954, Nov. 23** ***Perf. 13x14***

90 A41 300p dark blue green .25 .25
With tab .85

Lighted Oil Lamp A42

**1955, Jan. 13** ***Perf. 13x14***

91 A42 250p dark blue .25 .25
With tab .75

Teachers' Association, 50th anniversary.

Parachutist and Barbed Wire — A43

**1955, Mar. 31 Litho.** ***Perf. 14***

92 A43 120p dk Prus green .25 .25
With tab .45

Jewish volunteers from Palestine who served in British army in World War II.

Lighted Menorah A44

**1955, Apr. 26**

93 A44 150p dk grn, blk & org .25 .25
With tab .35

Proclamation of State of Israel, 7th anniv.

Immigration by Ship — A45

Designs: 10p, Immigration by plane. 25p, Agricultural training. 30p, Gardening. 60p, Vocational training. 750p, Scientific education.

**1955, May 10 Unwmk.** ***Perf. 14***

94 A45 5p brt blue & black .25 .25
95 A45 10p red & black .25 .25
96 A45 25p deep grn & black .25 .25
97 A45 30p orange & black .25 .25
98 A45 60p lilac rose & blk .25 .25
99 A45 750p olive bis & blk .25 .25
*Nos. 94-99 (6)* 1.50 1.50
With tabs 1.75

Israel's Youth Immigration Institution, 20th anniv.

Musicians with Tambourine and Cymbals — A46

Musician with: 60p, Ram's Horn. 120p, Loud Trumpet. 250p, Harp.

**1955, Aug. 25 Photo. Wmk. 302**

100 A46 25p dark green & org .25 .25

**Unwmk.**

101 A46 60p dk gray & orange .25 .25
102 A46 120p dark blue & yel .25 .25
103 A46 250p red brn & org .25 .25
#100-103, with tabs .50

Jewish New Year, 5716.
See Nos. 121-123.

Ambulance A47

**1955, Nov. 1 Wmk. 301** ***Perf. 14***

104 A47 160p grn, red & blk .25 .25
With tab .30

Magen David Adom (Israeli Red Cross), 25th anniv.

Mandrake, Reuben — A48

Twelve Tribes: 20p, Gates of Sechem, Simeon. 30p, Ephod, Levi. 40p, Lion, Judah. 50p, Scales, Dan. 60p, Stag, Naphtali. 80p, Tents, Gad. 100p, Tree, Asher. 120p, Sun and stars, Issachar. 180p, Ship, Zebulon. 200p, Sheaf of wheat, Joseph. 250p, Wolf, Benjamin.

**1955-57 Wmk. 302** ***Perf. 13x14***

105 A48 10p bright green .25 .25
106 A48 20p red lilac ('56) .25 .25
107 A48 30p bright ultra .25 .25
108 A48 40p brown ('56) .25 .25
109 A48 50p grnsh bl ('56) .25 .25
110 A48 60p lemon .25 .25
111 A48 80p deep vio ('56) .25 .25
112 A48 100p vermilion .25 .25
113 A48 120p olive ('56) .25 .25
114 A48 180p lil rose ('56) .25 .25
115 A48 200p green ('56) .25 .25
116 A48 250p gray ('56) .25 .25
#105-116, with tabs 2.00

See Nos. 133-136B.

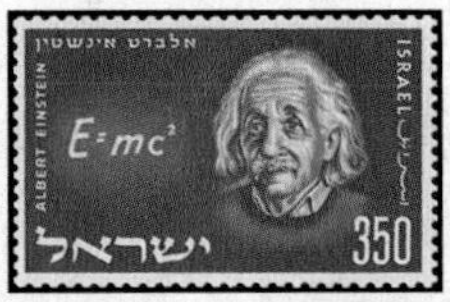

Albert Einstein (1879-1955) and Equation of his Relativity Theory — A49

**1956, Jan. 3** ***Perf. 13x14***

117 A49 350p brown .25 .25
With tab .60

Technion, Haifa A50

**1956, Jan. 3** **Wmk. 302**

118 A50 350p lt ol grn & blk .25 .25
With tab .25

Israel Institute of Technology, 30th anniv.

"Eight Years of Israel" — A51

Jaffa Oranges — A52

**1956, Apr. 12 Litho.** ***Perf. 14***

119 A51 150p multicolored .25 .25
With tab .25

Proclamation of State of Israel, 8th anniv.

**1956, May 20 Wmk. 302** ***Perf. 14***

120 A52 300p bl grn & orange .25 .25
With tab .25

4th Intl. Congress of Mediterranean Citrus Growers.

**New Year Type of 1955**

Musician with: 30p, Lyre. 50p, Cymbals. 150p, Double oboe, horiz.

**1956, Aug. 14 Photo.** ***Perf. 14x13***

121 A46 30p brown & brt blue .25 .25

*Perf. 14*

**122** A46 50p purple & orange .25 .25
**123** A46 150p dk bl grn & org .25 .25
#121-123, with tabs .25

Jewish New Year, 5717.

Haganah Insignia A54

Bezalel Museum and Antique Lamp A55

**1957, Jan. 1** *Perf. 13x14*

**124** A54 20p + 80p brt grn .25 .25
**125** A54 50p + 150p car rose .25 .25
**126** A54 50p + 350p ultra .25 .25
#124-126, with tabs .25

Defense issue. Divided denomination used to show increased postal rate.

**1957, Apr. 29 Litho.** *Perf. 14*

**127** A55 400p multicolored .25 .25
With tab .25

Bezalel Natl. Museum, Jerusalem, 50th anniv.

Jet Plane and "9" — A56

Horse and Seal — A57

**1957, Apr. 29**

**128** A56 250p deep bl & blk .25 .25
With tab .25

Proclamation of State of Israel, 9th anniv.

**1957, Sept. 4 Wmk. 302** *Perf. 14*

Ancient Seals: 160p, Lion. 300p, Gazelle.

**129** A57 50p ocher & blk, *lt bl* .25 .25

*Perf. 14x13*
**Photo. Unwmk.**

**130** A57 160p grn & blk, *bis brn* .25 .25
**131** A57 300p dp car & blk, *pink* .25 .25
#130-131, with tabs .25

Jewish New Year, 5718.

**TABIL**
Souvenir Sheet

Bet Alpha Synagogue Mosaic — A58

**1957, Sept. 17 Litho.** *Roulette 13*

**132** A58 Sheet of 4 .30 .30
*a.* 100p multicolored .25 .25
*b.* 200p multicolored .25 .25
*c.* 300p multicolored .25 .25
*d.* 400p multicolored .25 .25

1st Intl. stamp exhib. in Israel, Tel Aviv, 9/17-23.

**Tribes Type of 1955-57**
*Perf. 13x14*

**1957-59 Unwmk. Photo.**

**133** A48 10p brt grn ('58) .25 .25
**133A** A48 20p red lilac .25 .25
**133C** A48 40p brown ('59) .55 .45
**134** A48 50p greenish blue .25 .25
**135** A48 60p lemon .25 .25
**136** A48 100p vermilion .25 .25
**136B** A48 120p olive ('58) .25 .25
*Nos. 133-136B (7)* 2.05 1.95
With tabs 42.50

Hammer Thrower — A59

**1958, Jan. 20** *Perf. 14x13*

**137** A59 500p bister & car .25 .25
With tab .25

Maccabiah Games, 25th anniversary.

Ancient Ship — A60

Ships: 20p, Three-master used for "illegal immigration." 30p, Cargo ship "Shomron." 1000p, Passenger ship "Zion."

**Wmk. 302**

**1958, Jan. 27 Litho.** *Perf. 14*
**Size: 36½x22½mm**

**138** A60 10p ocher, red & blk .25 .25

*Perf. 13x14*
**Photo.**

**139** A60 20p brt grn, blk & brn .25 .25
**140** A60 30p red, blk & grnsh bl .25 .25

**Size: 56½x22½mm**

**141** A60 1000p brt bl, blk & grn .25 .25
#138-141, with tabs .35

Issued to honor Israel's merchant fleet.

Menorah and Olive Branch — A61

**Unwmk.**

**1958, Apr. 21 Litho.** *Perf. 14*

**142** A61 400p gold, blk & grn .25 .25
With tab .25

Memorial Day and 10th anniversary of proclamation of State of Israel.

Dancing Youths Forming "10" — A62

**1958, July 2**

**143** A62 200p dk org & dk grn .25 .25
With tab .25

First World Conference of Jewish Youth, Jerusalem, July 28-Aug. 1.

Convention Center, Jerusalem A63

**1958, July 2**

**144** A63 400p vio & org, *yellow* .25 .25
With tab .25

10th Anniversary of Independence Exhibition, Jerusalem, June 5-Aug. 21.

Wheat — A64

**1958, Aug. 27 Photo.** *Perf. 14x13*

**145** A64 50p shown .25 .25
**146** A64 60p Barley .25 .25
**147** A64 160p Grapes .25 .25
**148** A64 300p Figs .25 .25
#145-148, with tabs .30

Jewish New Year, 5719.

"Love Thy Neighbor . . ." — A65

**1958, Dec. 10 Litho.** *Perf. 14*

**149** A65 750p yel, gray & grn .25 .25
With tab .90

Universal Declaration of Human Rights, 10th anniversary.

Designing and Printing Stamps A66

Radio and Telephone — A67

120p, Mobile post office. 500p, Teletype.

**1959, Feb. 25 Wmk. 302** *Perf. 14*

**150** A66 60p olive, blk & red .25 .25
**151** A66 120p olive, blk & red .25 .25
**152** A67 250p olive, blk & red .25 .25
**153** A67 500p olive, blk & red .25 .25
#150-153, with tabs .45

Decade of postal activities in Israel.

Shalom Aleichem A68

Cyclamen A69

Portraits: No. 155, Chaim Nachman Bialik. No. 156, Eliezer Ben-Yehuda.

**1959 Unwmk. Photo.** *Perf. 14x13*

**154** A68 250p yel grn & red brn .25 .25
**155** A68 250p ocher & ol gray .25 .25
#154-155, with tabs .35

*Perf. 14*
**Litho.**

**156** A68 250p bl & vio bl .25 .25
With tab .40

Birth cent. of Aleichem (Solomon Rabinowitz), Yiddish writer (No. 154); 25th death anniv. of Bialik, Hebrew poet (No. 155); birth cent. of Ben-Yehuda, father of modern Hebrew (No. 156).

Issued: #154, 3/30; #155, 7/22; #156, 11/25.

**1959, May 11 Wmk. 302** *Perf. 14*

Flowers: 60p, Anemone. 300p, Narcissus.

**Flowers in Natural Colors**

**157** A69 60p deep green .25 .25
**158** A69 120p deep plum .25 .25
**159** A69 300p blue .25 .25
#157-159, with tabs .35

Memorial Day and 11th anniversary of proclamation of State of Israel.

Buildings, Tel Aviv — A70

**1959, May 4**

**160** A70 120p multicolored .25 .25
With tab .25

50th anniversary of Tel Aviv.

Bristol Britannia and Windsock A71

**1959, July 22**

**161** A71 500p multicolored .25 .25
With tab .30

Civil Aviation in Israel, 10th anniversary.

Pomegranates A72

*Perf. 14x13*

**1959, Sept. 9 Photo. Unwmk.**

**162** A72 60p shown .25 .25
**163** A72 200p Olives .25 .25
**164** A72 350p Dates .25 .25
*Nos. 162-164 (3)* .75 .75
With tabs 1.50

Jewish New Year, 5720.

Merhavya A73

Settlements: 120p, Yesud Ha-Maala. 180p, Deganya.

**1959, Nov. 25 Photo.** *Perf. 13x14*

**165** A73 60p citron & dk grn .25 .25
**166** A73 120p red brn & ocher .25 .25
**167** A73 180p blue & dk grn .25 .25
*Nos. 165-167 (3)* .75 .75
With tabs 1.90

Settlements of Merhavya and Deganya, 50th anniv.; Yesud Ha-Maala, 75th anniv.

Judean Coin (66-70 A.D.) — A74

**1960 Unwmk. *Perf. 13x14***

**Denominations in Black**

| | | | | |
|---|---|---|---|---|
| 168 | A74 | 1a brn, *pinkish* | .25 | .25 |
| *a.* | | On surface colored paper | .25 | .25 |
| | | As "a," with tab | .75 | |
| *b.* | | Black overprint omitted | | |
| 169 | A74 | 3a brt red, *pinkish* | .25 | .25 |
| 170 | A74 | 5a gray, *pinkish* | .25 | .25 |
| 171 | A74 | 6a brt grn, *lt bl* | .25 | .25 |
| 171A | A74 | 7a gray, *bluish* | .25 | .25 |
| 172 | A74 | 8a mag, *lt blue* | .25 | .25 |
| 173 | A74 | 12a grnsh bl, *lt bl* | .25 | .25 |
| *a.* | | Black overprint omitted | | |
| 174 | A74 | 18a orange | .25 | .25 |
| 175 | A74 | 25a blue | .25 | .25 |
| 176 | A74 | 30a carmine | .25 | .25 |
| 177 | A74 | 50a bright lilac | .25 | .25 |
| | | #168-177, with tabs | 2.00 | |

Issue dates: 7a, July 6; others, Jan. 6.

Operation "Magic Carpet" A75

Design: 50a, Resettled family in front of house, grapes and figs.

**1960, Apr. 7 Unwmk. *Perf. 13x14***

| | | | | |
|---|---|---|---|---|
| 178 | A75 | 25a red brown | .25 | .25 |
| 179 | A75 | 50a green | .25 | .25 |
| | | #178-179, with tabs | .35 | |

World Refugee Year, July 1, 1959-June 30, 1960.

Sand Lily — A76

Design: 32a, Evening primrose.

**1960, Apr. 27 Litho. *Perf. 14***

| | | | | |
|---|---|---|---|---|
| 180 | A76 | 12a multicolored | .25 | .25 |
| 181 | A76 | 32a brn, yel & grn | .25 | .25 |
| | | #180-181, with tabs | .55 | |

Memorial Day; proclamation of State of Israel, 12th anniv. See #204-206, 238-240.

Atom Diagram and Atomic Reactor A77

**1960, July 6 Wmk. 302 *Perf. 14***

| | | | | |
|---|---|---|---|---|
| 182 | A77 | 50a blue, red & blk | .25 | .25 |
| | | With tab | .60 | |

Installation of Israel's first atomic reactor.

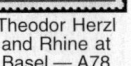

Theodor Herzl and Rhine at Basel — A78

King Saul — A79

**1960, Aug. 31 Litho. *Perf. 14***

| | | | | |
|---|---|---|---|---|
| 183 | A78 | 25a gray brown | .25 | .25 |
| | | With tab | .40 | |

**1960, Aug. 31 Wmk. 302**

Designs: 25a, King David. 40a, King Solomon.

**Kings in Multicolor**

| | | | | |
|---|---|---|---|---|
| 184 | A79 | 7a emerald | .25 | .25 |

**Unwmk.**

| | | | | |
|---|---|---|---|---|
| 185 | A79 | 25a brown | .25 | .25 |
| 186 | A79 | 40a blue | .25 | .25 |
| | | *Nos. 185-186 (2)* | .50 | .50 |
| | | With tabs | 1.25 | |

Jewish New Year, 5721. See Nos. 208-210.

Jewish Postal Courier, Prague, 18th Century A80

***Perf. 13x14***

**1960, Oct. 9 Photo. Unwmk.**

| | | | | |
|---|---|---|---|---|
| 187 | A80 | 25a olive blk, *gray* | .25 | .25 |
| | | With tab | 2.50 | |
| *a.* | | Souvenir sheet | 13.00 | 8.00 |

TAVIV Natl. Stamp Exhib., Tel Aviv, Oct. 9-19.

No. 187a sold only at Exhibition for 50a.

Henrietta Szold and Hadassah Medical Center A81

**1960, Dec. 14 *Perf. 13x14***

| | | | | |
|---|---|---|---|---|
| 188 | A81 | 25a turq bl & vio gray | .25 | .25 |
| | | With tab | .30 | |

Birth cent. of Henrietta Szold, founder of Hadassah, American Jewish women's organization.

Shields of Jerusalem and First Zionist Congress A82

**1960, Dec. 14 Unwmk. *Perf. 14***

| | | | | |
|---|---|---|---|---|
| 189 | A82 | 50a vio bl & turq blue | .25 | .25 |
| | | With tab | 1.10 | |

25th Zionist Congress, Jerusalem, 1960.

Ram — A83

Signs of Zodiac — A84

**1961, Feb. 27 Photo. *Perf. 13x14***

| | | | | |
|---|---|---|---|---|
| 190 | A83 | 1a Ram | .25 | .25 |
| 191 | A83 | 2a Bull | .25 | .25 |
| 192 | A83 | 6a Twins | .25 | .25 |
| 193 | A83 | 7a Crab | .25 | .25 |
| 194 | A83 | 8a Lion | .25 | .25 |
| *a.* | | Booklet pane of 6 ('65) | .45 | |
| 195 | A83 | 10a Virgin | .25 | .25 |
| 196 | A83 | 12a Scales | .25 | .25 |
| *a.* | | Booklet pane of 6 ('65) | .45 | |
| 197 | A83 | 18a Scorion | .25 | .25 |
| 198 | A83 | 20a Archer | .25 | .25 |
| 199 | A83 | 25a Goat | .25 | .25 |
| 200 | A83 | 32a Water bearer | .25 | .25 |
| 201 | A83 | 50a Fishes | .25 | .25 |

***Perf. 14***

**Litho.**

| | | | | |
|---|---|---|---|---|
| 202 | A84 | £1 dk bl, gold & lt bl | .25 | .25 |
| | | *Nos. 190-202 (13)* | 3.25 | 3.25 |
| | | With tabs | 5.25 | |

Booklet pane sheets (Nos. 194a, 196a) of 36 (9x4) contain 6 panes of 6, with gutters dividing the sheet in four sections. Each sheet yields 4 tete beche pairs and 4 tete beche gutter pairs, or strips. See Nos. 215-217.

Vertical strips of 6 of the 1a, 10a and No. 216 (5a) are from larger sheets from which coils were produced. Regular sheets of 50 are arranged 10x5.

Javelin Thrower and "7" — A85

**1961, Apr. 18 Litho. *Perf. 14***

| | | | | |
|---|---|---|---|---|
| 203 | A85 | 25a multicolored | .25 | .25 |
| | | With tab | .45 | |

7th Intl. Congress of the Hapoel Sports Org., Ramat Gan, May 1961.

**Flower Type of 1960**

7a, Myrtle. 12a, Sea onion. 32a, Oleander.

**1961, Apr. 18 Unwmk.**

**Flowers in Natural Colors**

| | | | | |
|---|---|---|---|---|
| 204 | A76 | 7a green | .25 | .25 |
| 205 | A76 | 12a rose carmine | .25 | .25 |
| 206 | A76 | 32a brt greenish bl | .25 | .25 |
| | | *Nos. 204-206 (3)* | .75 | .75 |
| | | With tabs | 1.00 | |

Memorial Day; proclamation of State of Israel, 13th anniv.

Scaffold Around "10" and Sapling — A86

**1961, June 14 Photo. *Perf. 14***

| | | | | |
|---|---|---|---|---|
| 207 | A86 | 50a Prussian blue | .25 | .25 |
| | | With tab | .55 | |

Israel bond issue 10th anniv.

**Type of 1960**

Designs: 7a, Samson. 25a, Judas Maccabaeus. 40a, Bar Cocheba.

**1961, Aug. 21 Litho. *Perf. 14***

**Multicolored Designs**

| | | | | |
|---|---|---|---|---|
| 208 | A79 | 7a red orange | .25 | .25 |
| 209 | A79 | 25a gray | .25 | .25 |
| 210 | A79 | 40a lilac | .25 | .25 |
| | | *Nos. 208-210 (3)* | .75 | .75 |
| | | With tabs | 1.25 | |

Jewish New Year, 5722.

Bet Hamidrash Synagogue, Medzibozh A87

**1961, Aug. 21 Photo. *Perf. 13x14***

| | | | | |
|---|---|---|---|---|
| 211 | A87 | 25a dk brn & yel | .25 | .25 |
| | | With tab | .40 | |

Bicentenary of death of Rabbi Israel Baal-Shem-Tov, founder of Hasidism.

Pine Cone A88

Design: 30a, Symbolic trees.

**1961, Dec. 26 Unwmk. *Perf. 13x14***

| | | | | |
|---|---|---|---|---|
| 212 | A88 | 25a green, yel & blk | .25 | .25 |
| 213 | A88 | 30a org, green & ind | .25 | .25 |
| | | #212-213, with tabs | 2.00 | |

Achievements of afforestation program.

Cello, Harp, French Horn and Kettle Drum — A89

**1961, Dec. 26 Litho. *Perf. 14***

| | | | | |
|---|---|---|---|---|
| 214 | A89 | 50a multicolored | .25 | .25 |
| | | With tab | 2.00 | |

Israel Philharmonic Orchestra, 25th anniv.

**Zodiac Type of 1961 Surcharged with New Value**

**1962, Mar. 18 Photo. *Perf. 13x14***

| | | | | |
|---|---|---|---|---|
| 215 | A83 | 3a on 1a lt lilac | .25 | .25 |
| *a.* | | Without overprint | 80.00 | |
| 216 | A83 | 5a on 7a gray | .25 | .25 |
| 217 | A83 | 30a on 32a emerald | .25 | .25 |
| *a.* | | Without overprint | 32.50 | |
| | | #215-217, with tabs | .25 | |

See note after No. 202.

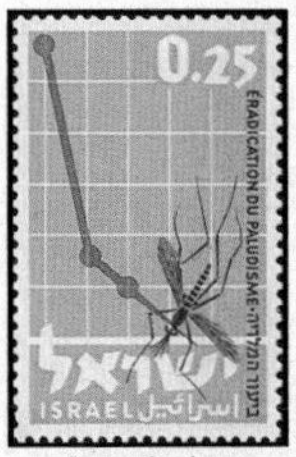

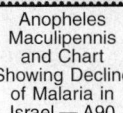

Anopheles Maculipennis and Chart Showing Decline of Malaria in Israel — A90

View of Rosh Pinna — A91

**1962, Apr. 30 *Perf. 14x13***

| | | | | |
|---|---|---|---|---|
| 218 | A90 | 25a ocher, red & blk | .25 | .25 |
| | | With tab | .50 | |

WHO drive to eradicate malaria.

**1962, Apr. 30 Unwmk.**

| | | | | |
|---|---|---|---|---|
| 219 | A91 | 20a yel, green & brn | .25 | .25 |
| | | With tab | .50 | |

Rosh Pinna agricultural settlement, 80th anniv.

Flame ("Hear, O Israel . . .") A92

Yellow Star of David and Six Candles A93

**1962, Apr. 30 Photo.**

| | | | | |
|---|---|---|---|---|
| 220 | A92 | 12a black, org & red | .25 | .25 |

***Perf. 14***

| | | | | |
|---|---|---|---|---|
| 221 | A93 | 55a multicolored | .25 | .25 |
| | | #220-221, with tabs | 1.40 | |

Heroes and Martyrs Day, in memory of the 6,000,000 Jewish victims of Nazi persecution.

Vautour Fighter-Bomber — A94

Design: 30a, Fighter-Bombers in formation.

**1962, Apr. 30** ***Perf. 13x14***

**222** A94 12a blue .25 .25
**223** A94 30a olive green .25 .25
#222-223, with tabs 1.75

Memorial Day; proclamation of the state of Israel, 14th anniv.

Symbolic Flags — A95

Wolf and Lamb, Isaiah 11:6 — A96

**1962, June 5** ***Perf. 14***

**224** A95 55a multicolored .25 .25
With tab 1.00

Near East Intl. Fair, Tel Aviv, June 5-July 5.

**1962, Sept. 5**

Designs: 28a, Leopard and kid, Isaiah 11:6. 43a, Child and asp, Isaiah 11:8.

**225** A96 8a buff, red & black .25 .25
**226** A96 28a buff, lilac & black .25 .25
**227** A96 43a buff, org & black .25 .25
*Nos. 225-227 (3)* .75 .75
With tabs 3.00

Jewish New Year, 5723.

Boeing 707 — A97

**1962, Nov. 7** ***Perf. 13x14***

**228** A97 55a bl, dk bl & rose lil .30 .25
With tab 1.25
*a.* Souvenir sheet 2.25 1.75

El Al Airlines; El Al Philatelic Exhibition, Tel Aviv, Nov. 7-14. Issued in sheets of 15.

No. 228a contains one stamp in greenish blue, dark blue & rose lilac with greenish blue color continuing into margin design (No. 228 has white perforations). Sold for £1 for one day at philatelic counters in Jerusalem, Haifa and Tel Aviv and for one week at the El Al Exhibition.

Cogwheel Symbols of UJA Activities A98

**1962, Dec. 26** **Unwmk.** ***Perf. 13x14***

**229** A98 20a org red, sil & bl .25 .25
With tab .50

25th anniv. of the United Jewish Appeal (United States) and its support of immigration, settlement, agriculture and care of the aged and sick.

Janusz Korczak A99

**1962, Dec. 26** **Photo.**

**230** A99 30a olive grn & blk .25 .25
With tab .45

Dr. Janusz Korczak (Henryk Goldszmit, 1879-1942), physician, teacher and writer, killed in Treblinka concentration camp.

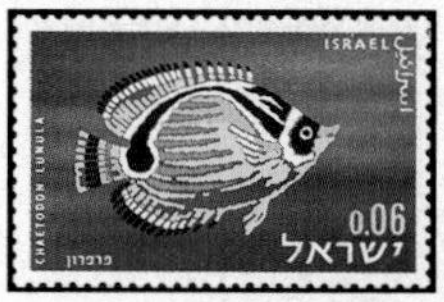


Orange butterflyfish A100

Red Sea fish: 3a, Pennant Coral Fish. 8a, Lionfish. 12a, Zebra-striped angelfish.

**1962, Dec. 26** **Litho.** ***Perf. 14***

**Fish in Natural Colors**

**231** A100 3a green .25 .25
**232** A100 6a purple .25 .25
**233** A100 8a brown .25 .25
**234** A100 12a dark blue .25 .25
#231-234, with tabs .60

See Nos. 246-249.

Stockade at Dawn A101

Design: 30a, Completed stockade at night.

**1963, Mar. 21** **Unwmk.** ***Perf. 14***

**235** A101 12a yel brn, blk & yel .25 .25
**236** A101 30a dp plum, blk & lt bl .25 .25
#235-236, with tabs .85

25th anniv. of the "Stockade and Tower" villages.

Hand Offering Food to Bird A102

**1963, Mar. 21** **Photo.** ***Perf. 13x14***

**237** A102 55a gray & black .25 .25
With tab .80
*a.* Booklet pane of 4 32.50

FAO "Freedom from Hunger" campaign.

Issued in sheets of 15 (5x3) with 5 tabs. The booklet pane sheet of 16 (4x4) is divided into 2 panes of 8 (4x2) by horizontal gutter. The 4 stamps at left in each pane are inverted in relation to the 4 at right, making 4 horizontal tete beche pairs down the center of the sheet.

**Flower Type of 1960**

8a, White lily. 30a, Hollyhock. 37a, Tulips.

**1963, Apr. 25** **Litho.** ***Perf. 14***

**Flowers in Natural Colors**

**238** A76 8a slate .25 .25
**239** A76 30a yellow green .25 .25
**240** A76 37a sepia .25 .25
*Nos. 238-240 (3)* .75 .75
With tabs 3.00

Memorial Day; proclamation of the State of Israel, 15th anniv.

Typesetter, 19th Century — A103

**1963, June 19** **Photo.** ***Perf. 14x13***

**241** A103 12a tan & vio brn .50 .40
With tab 1.60
*a.* Sheet of 16 45.00 *65.00*

Hebrew press in Palestine, cent. The background of the sheet shows page of 1st issue of "Halbanon" newspaper, giving each stamp a different background.

"The Sun Beat upon the Head of Jonah" — A104

Hoe Clearing Thistles — A105

Designs: 30a, "There was a mighty tempest in the sea." 55a, "Jonah was in the belly of the fish." 30a, 55a horiz.

**1963, Aug. 21** ***Perf. 14x13, 13x14***

**242** A104 8a org, lil & blk .25 .25
**243** A104 30a multicolored .25 .25
**244** A104 55a multicolored .25 .25
*Nos. 242-244 (3)* .75 .75
With tabs 2.75

Jewish New Year, 5724.

**1963, Aug. 21** ***Perf. 14***

**245** A105 37a multicolored .25 .25
With tab .90

80 years of agricultural settlements in Israel; "Year of the Pioneers."

**Fish Type of 1962**

Red Sea Fish: 2a, Undulate triggerfish. 6a, Radiate turkeyfish. 8a, Bigeye. 12a, Imperial angelfish.

**1963, Dec. 16** **Litho.** ***Perf. 14***

**Fish in Natural Colors**

**246** A100 2a violet blue .25 .25
**247** A100 6a green .25 .25
**248** A100 8a orange .25 .25
**249** A100 12a olive green .25 .25
*Nos. 246-249 (4)* 1.00 1.00
With tabs .90

S.S. Shalom, Sailing Vessel and Ancient Map of Coast Line — A106

**1963, Dec. 16** **Photo.** ***Perf. 13x14***

**250** A106 £1 ultra, brt grn & lil .85 .45
With tab 8.00

Maiden voyage of S.S. Shalom.

"Old Age and Survivors Insurance" A107

Pres. Izhak Ben-Zvi (1884-1963) A108

Designs (Insurance): 25a, Maternity. 37a, Large family. 50a, Workers' compensation.

**1964, Feb. 24** **Litho.** ***Perf. 14***

**251** A107 12a multicolored .25 .25
**252** A107 25a multicolored .25 .25
**253** A107 37a multicolored .25 .25
**254** A107 50a multicolored .30 .30
*Nos. 251-254 (4)* 1.05 1.05
With tabs 7.75

Natl. Insurance Institute 10th anniv.

**1964, Apr. 13** **Photo.** ***Perf. 14x13***

**255** A108 12a dark brown .25 .25
With tab .25

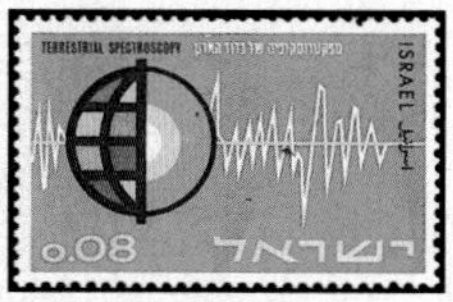


Terrestrial Spectroscopy — A109

Designs: 35a, Macromolecules of the living cell. 70a, Electronic computer.

**1964, Apr. 13** ***Perf. 14***

**256** A109 8a multicolored .25 .25
**257** A109 35a multicolored .25 .25
**258** A109 70a multicolored .25 .25
*Nos. 256-258 (3)* .75 .75
With tabs 3.50

Proclamation of the State of Israel, 16th anniv.; Israel's contribution to science.

Basketball Players A110

Serpent of Aesculapius and Menorah A111

8a, Runner. 12a, Discus thrower. 50a, Soccer.

**1964, June 24** ***Perf. 14x13***

**259** A110 8a brt brick red & dk brown .25 .25
**260** A110 12a rose lil & dk brn .25 .25
**261** A110 30a bl, car & dk brn .25 .25
**262** A110 50a yel grn, org red & dk brown .25 .25
*Nos. 259-262 (4)* 1.00 1.00
With tabs .90

Israel's participation in the 18th Olympic Games, Tokyo, Oct. 10-25.

**1964, Aug. 5** **Unwmk.**

**263** A111 £1 ol bis & slate grn .40 .30
With tab .75

6th World Congress of the Israel Medical Association, Haifa, Aug. 3-13.

Ancient Glass Vase — A112

Different glass vessels, 1st-3rd centuries.

**1964, Aug. 5** **Litho.**

**264** A112 8a vio, brn & org .25 .25
**265** A112 35a ol, grn & bl grn .25 .25
**266** A112 70a brt car rose, blue & violet blue .25 .25
*Nos. 264-266 (3)* .75 .75
With tabs .85

Jewish New Year, 5725.

Steamer Bringing Immigrants A113

Eleanor Roosevelt (1884-1962) A114

**1964, Nov. 2 Litho. *Perf. 14***

**267** A113 25a slate bl, bl grn & blk .25 .25
With tab .35

30th anniv. of the blockade runners bringing immigrants to Israel.

**1964, Nov. 2 Photo. *Perf. 14x13***

**268** A114 70a dull purple .25 .25
With tab .45

Chess Board, Knight and Emblem of Chess Olympics — A115

**1964, Nov. 2 *Perf. 13x14***

**269** A115 12a shown .25 .25
**270** A115 70a Rook .35 .30
With tabs 1.90

16th Chess Olympics, Tel Aviv, Nov. 1964.

"Africa-Israel Friendship" — A116

**1964, Nov. 30 Photo. *Perf. 14x13***

**271** A116 57a ol, blk, gold & red brown .35 .25
With tab 2.00
*a.* Souvenir sheet 1.40 1.40

TABAI, Natl. Stamp Exhibition, dedicated to African-Israel friendship, Haifa, Nov. 30-Dec. 6. No. 271a contains one imperf. stamp. Sold for £1.

View of Masada from West A117

Designs: 36a, Northern Palace, lower terrace. £1, View of Northern Palace, vert.

**1965, Feb. 3 Photo. *Perf. 13x14***

**272** A117 25a dull green .25 .25
**273** A117 36a bright blue .25 .25
**274** A117 £1 dark red brn .25 .25
*Nos. 272-274 (3)* .75 .75
With tabs 1.75

Ruins of Masada, the last stronghold in the war against the Romans, 66-73 A.D.

Book Fair Emblem A118

**1965, Mar. 24 Photo. *Perf. 13x14***

**275** A118 70a gray ol, brt bl & blk .25 .25
With tab .30

2nd Intl. Book Fair, Jerusalem, April.

Arms of Ashdod — A119

Town Emblems: 1a, Lydda (Lod). 2a, Qiryat Shemona. 5a, Petah Tikva. 6a, Nazareth. 8a, Beersheba. 10a Bet Shean. 12a, Tiberias. 20a, Elat. 25a, Acre (Akko). 35a, Dimona. 37a, Zefat. 50a, Rishon Leziyyon. 70a, Jerusalem. £1, Tel Aviv-Jaffa. £3, Haifa.

**Size: 17x22½mm**

**1965-66 *Perf. 13x14***

**276** A119 1a brown .25 .25
**277** A119 2a lilac rose .25 .25
**278** A119 5a gray .25 .25
**279** A119 6a violet .25 .25
**280** A119 8a orange .25 .25
*a.* Booklet pane of 6 .45
**281** A119 10a emerald .25 .25
**282** A119 12a dark purple .25 .25
*a.* Booklet pane of 6 .50
**283** A119 15a green .25 .25
**284** A119 20a rose red .25 .25
**285** A119 25a ultramarine .25 .25
**286** A119 35a magenta .25 .25
**287** A119 37a olive .25 .25
**288** A119 50a greenish bl .25 .25

***Perf. 14x13***

**Size: 22x27mm**

**289** A119 70a dark brown .25 .25
**290** A119 £1 dark green .25 .25
**291** A119 £3 dk carmine rose .55 .25
*Nos. 276-291 (16)* 4.30 4.00
With tabs 10.00

Issued: #283-286, 3/24/65; #290, 11/24/65; #291, 3/14/66; others, 2/2/66.

The uncut booklet pane sheets of 36 are divided into 4 panes (2 of 6 stamps, 2 of 12) by horizontal and vertical gutters. alf of the stamps in the 2 panes of 12 are inverted, causing 4 horizontal tête bêche pairs and 4 horizontal tête bêche gutter pairs.

Vertical strips of 6 of the 1a, 5a and 10a are from larger sheets, released Jan. 10, 1967, from which coils were produced. Regular sheets of 50 are arranged 10x5.

No. 290 also comes tagged (1975).

See Nos. 334-336, 386-393.

Hands Reaching for Hope, and Star of David — A120

"Irrigation of the Desert" — A121

**1965, Apr. 27 Unwmk. *Perf. 14x13***

**292** A120 25a gray, black & yel .25 .25
With tab .40

Liberation of Nazi concentration camps, 20th anniv.

**1965, Apr. 27 Photo.**

**293** A121 37a olive bister & blue .25 .25
With tab .25

Memorial Day; proclamation of the state of Israel, 17th anniv.

Telegraph Pole and Syncom Satellite A122

**1965, July 21 Unwmk. *Perf. 13x14***

**294** A122 70a vio, blk & grnsh bl .25 .25
With tab .45

ITU, centenary.

Symbol of Cooperation and UN Emblem A123

**1965, July 21 Litho. *Perf. 14***

**295** A123 36a gray, dp claret, bl, red & bis .25 .25
With tab .30

International Cooperation Year.

Dead Sea Extraction Plant A124

"Let There be Light . . ." A125

**1965, July 21**

**296** A124 12a Crane .25 .25
**297** A124 50a shown .25 .25
#296-297, with tabs .70

Dead Sea chemical industry.

**1965, Sept. 7 Photo. *Perf. 13x14***

Genesis 1, The Creation: 8a, Firmament and Waters. 12a, Dry land and vegetation. 25a, Heavenly lights. 35a, Fish and fowl. 70a, Man.

**298** A125 6a dk pur, lil & gold .25 .25
**299** A125 8a brt grn, dk bl & gold .25 .25
**300** A125 12a red brn, blk & gold .25 .25
**301** A125 25a dk pur, pink & gold .25 .25
**302** A125 35a lt & dk bl & gold .25 .25
**303** A125 70a dp cl, car & gold .35 .25
*Nos. 298-303 (6)* 1.60 1.50
With tabs 1.50

Jewish New Year, 5726. Sheets of 20 (10x2).

Charaxes Jasius A126

Flags over Rooftops A127

Butterflies & Moths: 6a, Papilio alexanor maccabaeus. 8a, Daphnis nerii. 12a, Zegris eupheme uarda.

**1965, Dec. 15 Litho. *Perf. 14***

**Butterflies in Natural Colors**

**304** A126 2a lt olive green .25 .25
**305** A126 6a lilac .25 .25
**306** A126 8a ocher .25 .25
**307** A126 12a blue .25 .25
#304-307, with tabs .60

**1966, Apr. 20 Litho. *Perf. 14***

Designs: 30a, Fireworks over Tel Aviv. 80a, Warships and Super Mirage jets, Haifa.

**308** A127 12a multi .25 .25
**309** A127 30a multi .25 .25
**310** A127 80a multi .25 .25
#308-310, with tabs .45

Proclamation of state of Israel, 18th anniv.

Memorial, Upper Galilee — A128

**1966, Apr. 20 Photo. *Perf. 14x13***

**311** A128 40a olive gray .25 .25
With tab .25

Issued for Memorial Day.

Knesset Building, Jerusalem — A129

**1966, June 22 Photo. *Perf. 13x14***

**312** A129 £1 deep blue .25 .25
With tab .50

Inauguration of the Knesset Building (Parliament). Sheets of 12.

Road Sign and Motorcyclist A130

Spice Box A131

Road Signs and: 5a, Bicyclist. 10a, Pedestrian. 12a, Child playing ball. 15a, Automobile.

**1966, June 22 *Perf. 14***

**313** A130 2a sl, red brn & lil rose .25 .25
**314** A130 5a ol bis, sl & lil rose .25 .25
**315** A130 10a vio, lt bl & lil rose .25 .25
**316** A130 12a bl, grn & lil rose .25 .25
**317** A130 15a grn, red & lil rose .25 .25
#313-317, with tabs .25

Issued to publicize traffic safety.

**1966, Aug. 24 Photo. *Perf. 13x14***

Ritual Art Objects: 15a, Candlesticks. 35a, Kiddush cup. 40a, Torah pointer. 80a, Hanging lamp.

**318** A131 12a sil, gold, blk & bl .25 .25
**319** A131 15a sil, gold, blk & lil .25 .25
**320** A131 35a sil, gold, blk & emer .25 .25
**321** A131 40a sil, gold, blk & vio bl .25 .25
**322** A131 80a sil, gold, blk & red .25 .25
#318-322, with tabs .75

Jewish New Year, 5727.

Bronze Panther, Avdat, 1st Century, B.C. — A132

30a, Stone menorah, Tiberias, 2nd Cent. 40a, Phoenician ivory sphinx, 9th cent., B.C. 55a, Gold earring (calf's head), Ashdod, 6th-4th cents. B.C. 80a, Miniature gold capital, Persia, 5th cent., B.C. £1.15, Gold drinking horn (ram's head), Persia, 5th cent., B.C., vert.

**1966, Oct. 26 Litho. *Perf. 14***

**323** A132 15a dp bl & yel brn .25 .25
**324** A132 30a vio brn & bister .25 .25
**325** A132 40a sepia & yel bis .30 .25
**326** A132 55a Prus grn, dp yel & brown .35 .25
**327** A132 80a lake, dp yel & brown .55 .25

***Perf. 13x14***

**328** A132 £1.15 vio, gold & brn 1.25 .70
*Nos. 323-328 (6)* 2.95 1.95
With tabs 6.00

Israel Museum, Jerusalem. Sheets of 12.

Coach and Mailman of Austrian Levant — A133

Microscope and Cells — A134

Designs: 15a, Turkish mailman and caravan. 40a, Palestinian mailman and locomotive. £1, Israeli mailman and jet liner.

**1966, Dec. 14 Photo. *Perf. 14***

**329** A133 12a ocher & green .25 .25
**330** A133 15a lt grn, brn & dp car .25 .25
**331** A133 40a brt rose & dk blue .25 .25
**332** A133 £1 grnsh bl & brown .25 .25
*Nos. 329-332 (4)* 1.00 1.00
With tabs .80

Issued for Stamp Day.

**1966, Dec. 14 *Perf. 14x13***

**333** A134 15a red & dark slate grn .25 .25
With tab .25

Campaign against cancer.

**Arms Type of 1965-66**

Town Emblems: 40a, Mizpe Ramon. 55a, Ashkelon. 80a, Rosh Pinna.

**1967, Feb. 8 Unwmk. *Perf. 13x14***

**334** A119 40a dark olive .25 .25
**335** A119 55a dk carmine rose .25 .25
**336** A119 80a red brown .25 .25
*Nos. 334-336 (3)* .75 .75
With tabs 1.75

Port of Acre A135

Ancient Ports: 40a, Caesarea. 80a, Jaffa.

**1967, Mar. 22 Photo. *Perf. 13x14***

**337** A135 15a dark brown .25 .25
**338** A135 40a dark blue grn .25 .25
**339** A135 80a deep blue .25 .25
*Nos. 337-339 (3)* .75 .75
With tabs 1.00

Page of Shulhan Aruk and Crowns — A136

**1967, Mar. 22 *Perf. 13½x13***

**340** A136 40a dk & lt bl, gray & gold .25 .25
With tab .25

400th anniv. of the publication (in 1565) of the Shulhan Aruk, a compendium of Jewish religious and civil law, by Joseph Karo (1488-1575).

War of Independence Memorial — A137

**1967, May 10 Unwmk. *Perf. 13x14***

**341** A137 55a lt bl, indigo & sil .25 .25
With tab .40

Issued for Memorial Day, 1967.

Auster Plane over Convoy on Jerusalem Road A138

Military Aircraft: 30a, Mystère IV jet fighter over Dead Sea area. 80a, Mirage jet fighters over Masada.

**1967, May 10 Photo.**

**342** A138 15a lt ol grn & dk bl grn .25 .25
**343** A138 30a ocher & dark brn .25 .25
**344** A138 80a grnsh bl & vio bl .25 .25
*Nos. 342-344 (3)* .75 .75
With tabs .80

Issued for Independence Day, 1967.

Israeli Ships in Straits of Tiran A139

15a, Star of David, sword & olive branch, vert. 80a, Wailing (Western) Wall, Jerusalem.

**1967, Aug. 16 *Perf. 14x13, 13x14***

**345** A139 15a dk red, blk & yel .25 .25
**346** A139 40a Prussian green .25 .25
**347** A139 80a deep violet .25 .25
#345-347, with tabs .25

Victory of the Israeli forces, June, 1967.

Torah, Scroll of the Law — A140

Various ancient, decorated Scrolls of the Law.

**1967, Sept. 13 *Perf. 13x14***

**348** A140 12a gold & multi .25 .25
**349** A140 15a silver & multi .25 .25
**350** A140 35a gold & multi .25 .25
**351** A140 40a silver & multi .25 .25
**352** A140 80a gold & multi .25 .25
#348-352, with tabs .70

Jewish New Year, 5728. Sheets of 20 (10x2).

Chaim Weizmann A141

Design: 40a, Lord Balfour.

**1967, Nov. 2 Photo. *Perf. 13x14***

**353** A141 15a dark green .25 .25
**354** A141 40a brown .25 .25
#353-354, with tabs .25

50th anniv. of the Balfour Declaration, which established the right to a Jewish natl. home in Palestine. Issued in sheets of 15.

Emblem and Doll — A142

Nubian Ibex — A143

Inscriptions: 30a, Hebrew. 40a, French.

**1967, Nov. 2 Litho. *Perf. 14***

**355** A142 30a yellow & multi .25 .25
**356** A142 40a brt bl & multi .25 .25
**357** A142 80a brt grn & multi .25 .25
#355-357, with tabs .45

Intl. Tourist Year. Issued in sheets of 15.

**1967, Dec. 27 Litho. *Perf. 13***

18a, Caracal lynx. 60a, Dorcas gazelles.

**Animal in Ocher & Brown**

**358** A143 12a dull purple .25 .25
**359** A143 18a bright green .25 .25
**360** A143 60a bright blue .25 .25
#358-360, with tabs .40

Flags Forming Soccer Ball — A144

**1968, Mar. 11 Photo. *Perf. 13***

**361** A144 80a ocher & multi .25 .25
With tab .25

Pre-Olympic soccer tournament.

Welcoming Immigrants A145

Resistance Fighter A146

Design: 80a, Happy farm family.

**1968, Apr. 24 Litho. *Perf. 14***

**362** A145 15a lt green & multi .25 .25
**363** A145 80a cream & multi .25 .25
#362-363, with tabs .25

Issued for Independence Day, 1968.

**1968, Apr. 24 Photo. *Perf. 14x13***

**364** A146 60a brown olive .25 .25
With tab .25

Warsaw Ghetto Uprising, 25th anniv. Design from Warsaw Ghetto Memorial.

Sword and Laurel A147

Rifles and Helmet A148

**1968, Apr. 24 Litho. *Perf. 14***

**365** A147 40a gold & multi .25 .25
**366** A148 55a black & multi .25 .25
#365-366, with tabs .30

Zahal defense army, Independence Day (No. 365); Memorial Day (No. 366).

Candle and Prison Window A149

Prime Minister Moshe Sharett (1894-1965) A150

**1968, June 5 Photo. *Perf. 14x13***

**367** A149 80a blk, gray & sepia .25 .25
With tab .25

Issued to honor those who died for freedom.

**1968, June 5 Unwmk.**

**368** A150 £1 deep brown .25 .25
With tab .25

27th Zionist Congress.

Knot Forming Star of David — A151

Dome of the Rock and Absalom's Tomb — A152

**1968, Aug. 21 Litho. *Perf. 13***

**369** A151 30a multi .25 .25
With tab .25

50 years of Jewish Scouting. Sheets of 15.

**1968, Aug. 21 Photo. *Perf. 14x13***

Views of Jerusalem: 15a, Church of the Resurrection. 35a, Tower of David and City Wall. 40a, Yemin Moshe District and Mount of Olives. 60a, Israel Museum and "Shrine of the Book."

**370** A152 12a gold & multi .25 .25
**371** A152 15a gold & multi .25 .25
**372** A152 35a gold & multi .25 .25
**373** A152 40a gold & multi .25 .25
**374** A152 60a gold & multi .25 .25
#370-374, with tabs .50

Jewish New Year, 5729. Sheets of 15.

Detail from Lions' Gate, Jerusalem (St. Stephen's Gate) A153

**1968, Oct. 8 Unwmk. *Perf. 13x14***

**375** A153 £1 brown org .25 .25
With tab .25
*a.* Souvenir sheet .35 .30

TABIRA Natl. Philatelic Exhibition. No. 375a contains one imperf. stamp. Sold only at exhibition for £1.50. No. 375 Issued in sheets of 15.

Abraham Mapu A154

Wheelchair Basketball A155

**1968, Oct. 8 Photo. *Perf. 14x13***

**376** A154 30a dark olive grn .25 .25
With tab .25

Mapu (1808-1867), novelist and historian.

**1968, Nov. 6 Photo. *Perf. 14x13***

**377** A155 40a green & yel grn .25 .25
With tab .25

17th Stoke-Mandeville Games for the Paralyzed, Nov. 4-13. Sheets of 15.

Port of Elat — A156

Ports of Israel: 60a, Ashdod. £1, Haifa.

**1969, Feb. 19 Unwmk. *Perf. 13x14***

**378** A156 30a deep magenta .25 .25
**379** A156 60a brown .25 .25
**380** A156 £1 dull green .25 .25
*Nos. 378-380 (3)* .75 .75
With tabs 2.00

Tank A157

**1969, Apr. 16 Photo. *Perf. 13x14***

**381** A157 15a shown .25 .25
**382** A157 80a Destroyer .25 .25
#381-382, with tabs .40

Issued for Independence Day 1969.

Israel's Flag at Half-mast — A158

**1969, Apr. 16**

**383** A158 55a vio, gold & bl .25 .25
With tab .25

Issued for Memorial Day.

Worker and ILO Emblem A159

**1969, Apr. 16**

**384** A159 80a dark blue grn .25 .25
With tab .25

ILO, 50th anniversary.

Hand Holding Torch A160

Arms of Hadera A161

**1969, July 9 Photo. *Perf. 14x13***

**385** A160 60a gold & multi .25 .25
With tab .60

Issued to publicize the 8th Maccabiah.

**1969-73 *Perf. 13x14***

Town Emblems: 3a, Hertseliya. 5a, Holon. 15a, Bat Yam. 18a, Ramla. 20a, Kefar Sava. 25a, Giv'atayim. 30a, Rehovot. 40a, Netanya. 50a, Bene Beraq. 60a, Nahariyya. 80a, Ramat Gan.

**386** A161 2a green .25 .25
**387** A161 3a deep magenta .25 .25
**388** A161 5a orange .25 .25
**389** A161 15a bright rose .25 .25
*c.* Bklt. pane of 6 (2 #389 + 4 #389A) ('71) .65
**389A** A161 18a ultra ('70) .25 .25
*d.* Bklt. pane of 6 ('71) .70
*e.* Bklt. pane of 6 (1 #281 + 5 #389A) ('73) .65
**389B** A161 20a brown ('70) .25 .25
*f.* Bklt. pane of 5 + label ('73) .90
**390** A161 25a dark blue .25 .25
**390A** A161 30a brt pink ('70) .25 .25
**391** A161 40a purple .25 .25
**392** A161 50a greenish bl .25 .25
**392A** A161 60a olive ('70) .25 .25
**393** A161 80a dark green .25 .25
*Nos. 386-393 (12)* 3.00 3.00
With tabs 3.75

Nos. 389c and 389d were also sold in uncut sheets of 36, No. 389e in uncut sheet of 18. See note after No. 291 about similar sheets.

Noah Building the Ark — A162

The Story of the Flood: 15a, Animals boarding the Ark. 35a, The Ark during the flood. 40a, Noah sending out the dove. 60a, Noah and the rainbow.

**1969, Aug. 13 Unwmk. *Perf. 14***

**394** A162 12a multicolored .25 .25
**395** A162 15a multicolored .25 .25
**396** A162 35a multicolored .25 .25
**397** A162 40a multicolored .25 .25
**398** A162 60a multicolored .25 .25
#394-398, with tabs .70

Jewish New Year, 5730. Sheets of 15.

King David by Marc Chagall A163

**1969, Sept. 24 Photo. *Perf. 14***

**399** A163 £3 multicolored .65 .55
With tab 1.25

Atom Diagram and Test Tube — A164

**1969, Nov. 3 *Perf. 14x13***

**400** A164 £1.15 vio bl & multi .70 .45
With tab 2.25

Weizmann Institute of Science, 25th anniv.

Joseph Trumpeldor A165

Dum Palms, Emeq Ha-Arava A166

**1970, Jan. 21 Photo. *Perf. 14x13***

**401** A165 £1 dark purple .25 .25
With tab .60

50th anniv. of the defense of Tel Hay under the leadership of Joseph Trumpeldor.

**1970, Jan. 21**

Views: 3a, Tahana Waterfall. 5a, Nahal Baraq Canyon, Negev. 6a, Cedars in Judean Hills. 30a, Soreq Cave, Judean Hills.

**402** A166 2a olive .25 .25
**403** A166 3a deep blue .25 .25
**404** A166 5a orange red .25 .25
**405** A166 6a slate green .25 .25
**406** A166 30a brt purple .25 .25
#402-406, with tabs .35

Issued to publicize nature reserves.

Magic Carpet Shaped as Airplane A167

Prime Minister Levi Eshkol (1895-1969) A168

**1970, Jan. 21 Litho. *Perf. 13***

**407** A167 30a multicolored .25 .25
With tab .25

20th anniv. of "Operation Magic Carpet" which airlifted the Yemeni Jews to Israel.

**1970, Mar. 11 Litho. *Perf. 14***

**408** A168 15a bl & multi .25 .25
With tab .25

Mania Shochat — A169

Camel and Train — A170

Portrait: 80a, Ze'ev Jabotinsky (1880-1940), writer and Zionist leader.

**1970, Mar. 11 Photo. *Perf. 14x13***

**409** A169 40a dp plum & buff .25 .25
**410** A169 80a green & cream .25 .25
#409-410, with tabs 1.10

Ha-Shomer (Watchmen defense organization), 60th anniv. (No. 409); defense of Jerusalem, 50th anniv. (No. 410)

**1970, Mar. 11 Litho. *Perf. 13***

**411** A170 80a orange & multi .40 .25
With tab .75

Opening of Dimona-Oron Railroad.

Scene from "The Dibbuk" — A171

**1970, Mar. 11 Photo. *Perf. 14x13***

**412** A171 £1 multicolored .25 .25
With tab .60

Habimah Natl. Theater, 50th anniv.

Memorial Flame A172

Orchis Laxiflorus A173

**1970, May 6 Photo. *Perf. 13x14***

**413** A172 55a vio, pink & blk .25 .25
With tab .25

Issued for Memorial Day, 1970.

**1970, May 6 Litho. *Perf. 14***

Flowers: 15a, Iris mariae. 80a, Lupinus pilosus.

**414** A173 12a pale gray, plum & grn .25 .25
**415** A173 15a multicolored .25 .25
**416** A173 80a pale bl & multi .30 .30
*Nos. 414-416 (3)* .80 .80
With tabs .95

Issued for Independence Day, 1970.

Charles Netter — A174

420 Class Yachts — A175

80a, Agricultural College (Mikwe Israel) & garden.

**1970, May 6 Photo. *Perf. 14x13***

**417** A174 40a lt grn, dk brn & gold .25 .25
**418** A174 80a gold & multi .25 .25
With tabs 1.25

Centenary of first agricultural college in Israel; its founder, Charles Netter.

**1970, July 8 Photo. *Perf. 14x13***

Designs: Various 420 Class yachts.

**419** A175 15a grnsh bl, blk & sil .25 .25
**420** A175 30a ol, red, blk & sil .25 .25
**421** A175 80a ultra, blk & silver .25 .25
*Nos. 419-421 (3)* .75 .75
With tabs 1.10

World "420" Class Sailing Championships.

Hebrew Letters Shaped Like Ship and Buildings A176

**1970, July 8** ***Perf. 13x14***

**422** A176 40a gold & multi .25 .25
With tab .25

Keren Hayesod, a Zionist Fund to maintain schools and hospitals in Palestine, 50th anniv.

Arava Plane A177

**1970, July 8**

**423** A177 £1 brt blue, blk & sil .25 .25
With tab .35

First Israeli designed and built aircraft.

Bird (Exiles) and Sun (Israel) A178

**1970, Sept. 7** **Litho.** ***Perf. 14***

**424** A178 80a yel & multi .25 .25
With tab .25

"Operation Ezra and Nehemiah," the exodus of Iraqi Jews.

Old Synagogue, Cracow — A179

Historic Synagogues: 15a, Great Synagogue, Tunis. 35a, Portuguese Synagogue, Amsterdam. 40a, Great Synagogue, Moscow. 60a, Shearith Israel Synagogue, New York.

***Perf. 14, 13 (15a)***

**1970, Sept. 7** **Photo.**

**425** A179 12a gold & multi .25 .25
**426** A179 15a gold & multi .25 .25
**427** A179 35a gold & multi .25 .25
**428** A179 40a gold & multi .25 .25
**429** A179 60a gold & multi .25 .25
#425-429, with tabs .40

Jewish New Year, 5731.

Tel Aviv Post Office, 1920 — A180

**1970, Oct. 18** **Photo.** ***Perf. 14***

**430** A180 £1 multicolored .25 .25
With tab .25
*a.* Souvenir sheet 1.50 1.50

TABIT Natl. Stamp Exhibition, Tel Aviv, Oct. 18-29. No. 430a contains an imperf. stamp similar to No. 430. Sold for £1.50.

Mother and Child A181

**1970, Oct. 18** ***Perf. 13x14***

**431** A181 80a dp grn, yel & gray .25 .25
With tab .45

WIZO, Women's Intl. Zionist Org., 50th anniv.

Paris Quai, by Camille Pissarro — A182

Paintings from Tel Aviv Museum: 85a, The Jewish Wedding, by Josef Israels. £2, Flowers in a Vase, by Fernand Leger.

**1970, Dec. 22** **Litho.** ***Perf. 14***

**432** A182 85a black & multi .25 .25
**433** A182 £1 black & multi .25 .25
**434** A182 £2 black & multi .50 .30
*Nos. 432-434 (3)* 1.00 .80
With tabs 1.75

Hammer and Menorah Emblem — A183

Persian Fallow Deer — A184

**1970, Dec. 22**

**435** A183 35a gold & multi .25 .25
With tab .25

General Federation of Labor in Israel (Histadrut), 50th anniversary.

**1971, Feb. 16** **Litho.** ***Perf. 13***

Animals of the Bible: 3a, Asiatic wild ass. 5a, White oryx. 78a, Cheetah.

**436** A184 2a multicolored .25 .25
**437** A184 3a multicolored .25 .25
**438** A184 5a multicolored .25 .25
**439** A184 78a multicolored .25 .25
#436-439, with tabs .45

"Samson and Dalila," Israel National Opera — A185

Theater Art in Israel: No. 441, Inn of the Ghosts, Cameri Theater. No. 442, A Psalm of David, Inbal Dance Theater.

**1971, Feb. 16** ***Perf. 14x13***

**440** A185 50a bister & multi .25 .25
**441** A185 50a lt grn & multi .25 .25
**442** A185 50a blue & multi .25 .25
*Nos. 440-442 (3)* .75 .75
With tabs .60

Basketball A186

Defense Forces Emblem A187

No. 444, Runner. No. 445, Athlete on rings.

**1971, Apr. 13** **Litho.** ***Perf. 14***

**443** A186 50a green & multi .25 .25
**444** A186 50a ocher & multi .25 .25
**445** A186 50a lt vio & multi .25 .25
#443-445, with tabs .50

9th Hapoel Games.

**1971, Apr. 13** **Photo.** ***Perf. 14x13***

**446** A187 78a multicolored .25 .25
With tab .25

Memorial Day, 1971, and the war dead.

Jaffa Gate, Jerusalem — A188

Gates of Jerusalem: 18c, New Gate. 35c, Damascus Gate. 85c, Herod's Gate.

**1971, Apr. 13** ***Perf. 14***

**Size: 41x41mm**

**447** A188 15a gold & multi .25 .25
**448** A188 18a gold & multi .25 .25
**449** A188 35a gold & multi .25 .25
**450** A188 85a gold & multi .60 .40
*a.* Souvenir sheet of 4 3.50 3.50
*Nos. 447-450 (4)* 1.35 1.15
With tabs 2.00

Independence Day, 1971. No. 450a contains 4 stamps similar to Nos. 447-450, but smaller (27x27mm). Sold at the Jerusalem Exhibition for £2.

See Nos. 488-491.

"He Wrote . . . Words of the Covenant" A189

"You shall rejoice in your feast" A190

85a, "First Fruits . . ." Exodus 23:19. £1.50, ". . . Feast of Weeks" Exodus 34:22. The quotation on 50a is from Exodus 34:28. The quotations are in English on the tabs.

**1971, May 25** **Photo.** ***Perf. 14x13***

**451** A189 50a yellow & multi .25 .25
**452** A189 85a yellow & multi .25 .25
**453** A189 £1.50 yellow & multi .45 .30
*Nos. 451-453 (3)* .95 .80
With tabs 1.75

For the Feast of Weeks (Shabuoth).

**1971, Aug. 24** **Photo.** ***Perf. 14x13***

Designs: 18a, "You shall dwell in booths for seven days . . ." Leviticus 23:42. 20a, "That I made the people of Israel dwell in booths . . ." Lev. 23:43. 40a, ". . . when you have gathered in the produce of the land" Lev. 23:39. 65a, ". . . then I will give you your rains in their season" Lev. 26:4. The quotation on 15a is from Deuteronomy 16:14. The quotations are in English on tabs.

**454** A190 15a yellow & multi .25 .25
**455** A190 18a yellow & multi .25 .25
**456** A190 20a yellow & multi .25 .25
**457** A190 40a yellow & multi .25 .25
**458** A190 65a yellow & multi .25 .25
#454-458, with tabs .75

For the Feast of Tabernacles (Sukkoth).

Sun Shining on Fields A191

**1971, Aug. 24** ***Perf. 14***

**459** A191 40a gold & multi .25 .25
With tab .25

1st cooperative settlement in Israel, at Emeq (Valley of Israel), 50th anniv.

Retort and Grain — A192

**1971, Oct. 25** **Litho.** ***Perf. 14***

**460** A192 £1 green & multi .25 .25
With tab .25

50th anniversary of Volcani Institute of Agricultural Research.

**Tagging**

Starting in 1975, vertical luminescent bands were overprinted on various regular and commemorative stamps.

In the 1971-75 regular series, values issued both untagged and tagged are: 20a, 25a, 30a, 35a, 45a, 50a, 65a, £1.10, £1.30, £2 and £3. Also No. 290 was re-issued with tagging in 1975.

Regular issues from 1975 onward, including the £1.70, are tagged unless otherwise noted.

Tagged commemoratives include Nos. 562-563 and all from Nos. 567-569 onward unless otherwise noted.

Negev — A193

Landscapes: 3a, Judean desert. 5a, Gan Ha-Shelosha. 18a, Kinneret. 20a, Tel Dan. 22a, Fishermen, Yafo. 25a, Arava. 30a, En Avedat. 35a, Brekhat Ram, Golan Heights. 45a, Grazing sheep, Mt. Hermon. 50a, Rosh Pinna. 55a, Beach and park, Netanya. 65a, Plain of Zebulun. 70a, Shore, Engedi. 80a, Beach at Elat. 88a, Boats in Akko harbor. 95a, Hamifratz Hane'elam. £1.10, Aqueduct near Akko. £1.30, Zefat. £1.70, Upper Nazareth. £2, Coral Island. £3, Haifa.

**1971-75** **Photo.** ***Perf. 13x14***

| | | | | | |
|---|---|---|---|---|---|
| **461** | A193 | 3a | deep blue | .25 | .25 |
| **462** | A193 | 5a | green | .25 | .25 |
| **463** | A193 | 15a | deep org | .25 | .25 |
| **464** | A193 | 18a | bright mag | .65 | .25 |
| **464A** | A193 | 20a | dark green | .25 | .25 |
| **465** | A193 | 22a | brt blue | 1.00 | .25 |
| **465A** | A193 | 25a | orange red | .25 | .25 |
| **466** | A193 | 30a | brt rose | .25 | .25 |
| **466A** | A193 | 35a | plum | .25 | .25 |
| **467** | A193 | 45a | dull vio blue | .25 | .25 |
| **468** | A193 | 50a | green | .25 | .25 |
| **469** | A193 | 55a | olive | .25 | .25 |
| **469A** | A193 | 65a | black | .25 | .25 |
| **470** | A193 | 70a | deep car | .25 | .25 |
| **470A** | A193 | 80a | deep ultra | .25 | .25 |
| **471** | A193 | 88a | greenish blue | 1.00 | .25 |
| **472** | A193 | 95a | org ver | .80 | .25 |
| **472A** | A193 | £1.10 | olive | .25 | .25 |
| **472B** | A193 | £1.30 | deep blue | .25 | .25 |
| **472C** | A193 | £1.70 | dark brown | .40 | .25 |
| **473** | A193 | £2 | brown | .40 | .25 |
| **474** | A193 | £3 | deep violet | .55 | .25 |
| | | | *Nos. 461-474 (22)* | 8.55 | 5.50 |
| | | | With tabs | 12.00 | |

Issued: 15a, 18a, 50a, 88a, 10/25; 22a, 55a, 70a, 1/4/72; 3a, 5a, 30a, £3, 11/7/72; 45a, 95a, £2, 1/16/73; 20a, 65a, 10/23/73; 35a, £1.10, 12/20/73; 25a, 80a, £1.30, 11/5/74; £1.70, 6/17/75.

See No. 592.

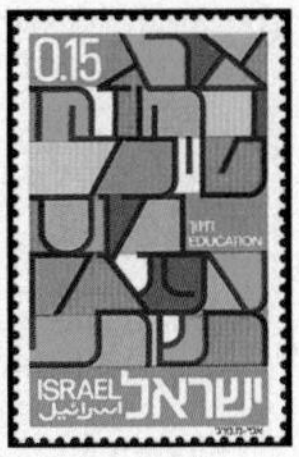

"Get Wisdom" Proverbs 4:7 — A194

Abstract Designs: 18a, Mathematical and scientific formula. 20a, Tools and engineering symbols. 40a, Abbreviations of various college degrees.

**1972, Jan. 4 Litho. *Perf. 14***

| | | | | |
|---|---|---|---|---|
| **475** | A194 | 15a brt grn & multi | .25 | .25 |
| **476** | A194 | 18a multicolored | .25 | .25 |
| **477** | A194 | 20a multicolored | .25 | .25 |
| **478** | A194 | 40a red, blk & gold | .25 | .25 |
| | | #475-478, with tabs | .30 | |

The Scribe, Sculpture by Boris Schatz A195

Works by Israeli Artists: 55a, Young Girl (Sarah), by Abel Pann. 70a, Zefat (landscape), by Menahem Shemi, horiz. 85a, Old Jerusalem, by Jacob Steinhardt. £1, Resurrection (abstract), by Aharon Kahana.

***Perf. 13x14 (40a, 85a), 14***

**1972, Mar. 7**

| | | | | |
|---|---|---|---|---|
| **479** | A195 | 40a black & tan | .25 | .25 |
| **480** | A195 | 55a red brn & multi | .25 | .25 |
| **481** | A195 | 70a lt grn & multi | .25 | .25 |
| **482** | A195 | 85a blk & yellow | .25 | .25 |
| **483** | A195 | £1 blk & multi | .30 | .25 |
| | | *Nos. 479-483 (5)* | 1.30 | 1.25 |
| | | With tabs | 1.40 | |

Exodus — A196

Passover: 45a, Baking unleavened bread. 95a, Seder.

**1972, Mar. 7 Litho. *Perf. 13***

| | | | | |
|---|---|---|---|---|
| **484** | A196 | 18a buff & multi | .25 | .25 |
| **485** | A196 | 45a buff & multi | .25 | .25 |
| **486** | A196 | 95a buff & multi | .30 | .25 |
| | | *Nos. 484-486 (3)* | .80 | .75 |
| | | With tabs | 1.25 | |

"Let My People Go" — A197

**1972, Mar. 7 *Perf. 14***

| | | | | |
|---|---|---|---|---|
| **487** | A197 | 55a blk, bl & yel grn | .45 | .30 |
| | | With tab | 3.00 | |

No. 487 inscribed in Hebrew, Arabic, Russian and English.

**Gate Type of 1971**

Gates of Jerusalem: 15a, Lions' Gate. 18a, Golden Gate. 45a, Dung Gate. 55a, Zion Gate.

**1972, Apr. 17 Photo. *Perf. 14***
**Size: 40x40mm**

| | | | | |
|---|---|---|---|---|
| **488** | A188 | 15a gold & multi | .25 | .25 |
| **489** | A188 | 18a gold & multi | .25 | .25 |
| **490** | A188 | 45a gold & multi | .25 | .25 |
| **491** | A188 | 55a gold & multi | .35 | .35 |
| *a.* | | Souvenir sheet of 4 | 2.60 | 2.60 |
| | | *Nos. 488-491 (4)* | 1.10 | 1.10 |
| | | With tabs | 2.25 | |

Independence Day. #491a contains 4 27x27mm stamps similar to #488-491. Sold for £2.

Jethro's Tomb — A198

**1972, Apr. 17 Litho. *Perf. 13***

| | | | | |
|---|---|---|---|---|
| **492** | A198 | 55a multicolored | .25 | .25 |
| | | With tab | .25 | |

Memorial Day — A199

**1972, Apr. 17 *Perf. 14***

| | | | | |
|---|---|---|---|---|
| **493** | A199 | 55a Flowers | .25 | .25 |
| | | With tab | .25 | |

Hebrew Words Emerging from Opened Ghetto — A200

**1972, June 6 *Perf. 13***

| | | | | |
|---|---|---|---|---|
| **494** | A200 | 70a blue & multi | .45 | .35 |
| | | With tab | 2.00 | |

Rabbi Isaac ben Solomon Ashkenazi Luria ("Ari") (1534-72), Palestinian cabalist.

International Book Year — A201

**1972, June 6 *Perf. 14x13***

| | | | | |
|---|---|---|---|---|
| **495** | A201 | 95a Printed page | .25 | .25 |
| | | With tab | .35 | |

Satellite Earth Station, Satellite and Rainbow — A202

**1972, June 6 *Perf. 13***

| | | | | |
|---|---|---|---|---|
| **496** | A202 | £1 tan & multi | .25 | .25 |
| | | With tab | .30 | |

Opening of satellite earth station in Israel.

17th Cent. Ark, Ancona — A203

Menorah and "25" — A204

Holy Arks from: 45a, Padua, 1729. 70a, Parma, 17th century. 95a, Reggio Emilia, 1756. Arks moved to Israel from Italian synagogues.

**1972, Aug. 8 Photo. *Perf. 14x13***

| | | | | |
|---|---|---|---|---|
| **497** | A203 | 15a deep brn & yel | .25 | .25 |
| **498** | A203 | 45a dp grn, yel grn & gold | .25 | .25 |
| **499** | A203 | 70a brn red, yel & bl | .25 | .25 |
| **500** | A203 | 95a magenta & gold | .25 | .25 |
| | | *Nos. 497-500 (4)* | 1.00 | 1.00 |
| | | With tabs | 1.50 | |

Jewish New Year, 5733.

**1972, Aug. 8**

| | | | | |
|---|---|---|---|---|
| **501** | A204 | £1 silver, bl & mag | .25 | .25 |
| | | With tab | .25 | |

25th anniversary of the State of Israel.

Brass Menorah, Morocco, 18th-19th Century A205

Menorahs: 25a, Brass, Poland, 18th century. 70a, Silver, Germany, 17th century.

**1972, Nov. 7 Litho. *Perf. 14x13***

| | | | | |
|---|---|---|---|---|
| **502** | A205 | 12a emer, blk & bl grn | .25 | .25 |
| **503** | A205 | 25a lil rose, blk & org | .25 | .25 |
| **504** | A205 | 70a blue, blk & vio | .25 | .25 |
| | | #502-504, with tabs | .55 | |

Hanukkah (Festival of Lights), 1972.

Child's Drawing — A206

Pendant — A207

Designs: Children's drawings.

**1973, Jan. 16 Litho. *Perf. 14***
**Sizes: 22½x37mm (2a, 55a); 17x48mm (3a)**

| | | | | |
|---|---|---|---|---|
| **505** | A206 | 2a blk & multi | .25 | .25 |
| **506** | A206 | 3a multicolored | .25 | .25 |
| **507** | A206 | 55a multicolored | .25 | .25 |
| | | #505-507, with tabs | .30 | |

Youth Wing of Israel Museum, Jerusalem (2a, 3a) and Youth Workshops, Tel Aviv Museum (55a).

**1973, Jan. 16 Photo. *Perf. 14x13***

| | | | | |
|---|---|---|---|---|
| **508** | A207 | 18a silver & multi | .25 | .25 |
| | | With tab | .25 | |

Immigration of North African Jews.

Levi, by Marc Chagall A208

Tribes of Israel: #510, Simeon. #511, Reuben. #512, Issachar. #513, Zebulun. **#514**, Judah. #515, Dan. #516, Gad. #517, **Asher.** #518, Naphtali. #519, Joseph. No.520, Benjamin.

**1973 Litho. *Perf. 14***

| | | | | |
|---|---|---|---|---|
| **509** | A208 | £1 multicolored | .40 | .40 |
| **510** | A208 | £1 gray grn & multi | .40 | .40 |
| **511** | A208 | £1 olive & multi | .40 | .40 |
| **512** | A208 | £1 gray bl & multi | .40 | .40 |
| **513** | A208 | £1 lemon & multi | .40 | .40 |
| **514** | A208 | £1 gray & multi | .40 | .40 |
| **515** | A208 | £1 bl grn & multi | .40 | .40 |
| **516** | A208 | £1 gray & multi | .40 | .40 |
| **517** | A208 | £1 yel grn & multi | .40 | .40 |
| **518** | A208 | £1 sepia & multi | .40 | .40 |
| **519** | A208 | £1 olive & multi | .40 | .40 |
| **520** | A208 | £1 tan & multi | .40 | .40 |
| | | *Nos. 509-520 (12)* | 4.80 | 4.80 |
| | | With tabs | 8.50 | |

Designs from stained glass windows by Marc Chagall, Hadassah-Hebrew University Medical Center Synagogue, Jerusalem.
Issued: #509-514, 3/26; #515-520, 8/21.

Israel's Declaration of Independence — A209

**1973, May 3 Photo. *Perf. 14***

| | | | | |
|---|---|---|---|---|
| **521** | A209 | £1 ocher & multi | .25 | .25 |
| | | With tab | .25 | |
| *a.* | | Souvenir sheet | .65 | .75 |

25 years of Independence. No. 521a sold for £1.50.

Star of David and Runners A210

**1973, May 3 Litho.**

| | | | | |
|---|---|---|---|---|
| **522** | A210 | £1.10 multicolored | .25 | .25 |
| | | With tab | .25 | |

9th Maccabiah.

Prison-cloth Hand — A211

**1973, May 3 Photo.**

| | | | | |
|---|---|---|---|---|
| **523** | A211 | 55a blue black | .25 | .25 |
| | | With tab | .25 | |

Heroes and martyrs of the Holocaust, 1933-1945.

Flame
A212

Prophets
A213

**1973, May 3** **Litho.**

**524** A212 65a multicolored .25 .25
With tab .25

Memorial Day.

**1973, Aug. 21** **Photo.** ***Perf. 13x14***

**525** A213 18a Isaiah .25 .25
**526** A213 65a Jeremiah .25 .25
**527** A213 £1.10 Ezekiel .25 .25
#525-527, with tabs .25

Jewish New Year, 5734.

Torch of Learning, Cogwheel — A214

**1973, Oct. 23** ***Perf. 14x13***

**528** A214 £1.25 slate & multi .25 .25
With tab .25

50th anniversary of the Technion, Israel Institute of Technology.

Rescue Boat and Danish Flag — A215

**1973, Oct. 23** ***Perf. 13x14***

**529** A215 £5 bister, red & blk .40 .30
With tab .50

30th anniversary of the rescue by the Danes of the Jews in Denmark.

Spectators at Stamp Show — A216

Design: £1, Spectators, different design.

**1973, Dec. 20** **Litho.** ***Perf. 13***

**530** A216 20a brown & multi .25 .25
**531** A216 £1 brown & multi .25 .25
#530-531, with tabs .20

JERUSALEM '73 Philatelic Exhibition, Mar. 25-Apr. 2, 1974.

Souvenir Sheets

Israel No. 7 — A217

Designs: £2, No. 8. £3, No. 9.

**1974, Mar. 25** **Photo.** ***Perf. 14x13***

**532** A217 £1 silver & dk slate grn .25 .25
**533** A217 £2 silver & red brn .25 .25
**534** A217 £3 silver & blk blue .25 .25
*Nos. 532-534 (3)* .75 .75

Jerusalem '73 Philatelic Exhibition, Mar. 25-Apr. 2, 1974 (postponed from Dec. 1973), 25th anniv. of State of Israel. Each sheet was sold with a 50 per cent surcharge.

Soldier with Prayer Shawl
A218

Quill and Inkwell with Hebrew Letters
A219

**1974, Apr. 23** ***Perf. 13x14***

**535** A218 £1 blk & light bl .25 .25
With tab .25

Memorial Day.

**1974, Apr. 23** ***Perf. 14x13***

**536** A219 £2 gold & black .25 .25
With tab .25

50th anniversary of Hebrew Writers Assn.

Lady in Blue, by Moshe Kisling
A220

Designs: £2, Mother and Child, Sculpture by Chana Orloff. £3, Girl in Blue, by Chaim Soutine.

**1974, June 11** **Litho.** ***Perf. 14***

**537** A220 £1.25 multicolored .25 .25
**538** A220 £2 multicolored .25 .25
**539** A220 £3 multicolored .30 .30
#537-539, with tabs 1.00

Art works from Tel Aviv, En Harod and Jerusalem Museums.

Wrench
A221

**1974, June 11**

**540** A221 25a multicolored .25 .25
With tab .25

50th anniv. of Working Youth Movement.

Istanbuli Synagogue, Jerusalem — A222

Designs: Interiors of restored synagogues in Jerusalem's Old City.

**1974, Aug. 6** **Photo.** ***Perf. 13x14***

**541** A222 25a shown .25 .25
**542** A222 70a Emtzai Synagogue .25 .25
**543** A222 £1 Rabbi Yohanan Synagogue .25 .25
#541-543, with tabs .25

Jewish New Year, 5735.

Lady Davis Technical Center "AMAL," Tel Aviv — A223

60a, Elias Sourasky Library, Tel Aviv University. £1.45, Mivtahim Rest Home, Zikhron Yaaqov.

**1974, Aug. 6** ***Perf. 13½x14***

**544** A223 25a violet black .25 .25
**545** A223 60a dark blue .25 .25
**546** A223 £1.45 maroon .25 .25
#544-546, with tabs .25

Modern Israeli architecture.

David Ben-Gurion — A224

**1974, Nov. 5** ***Perf. 14***

**547** A224 25a brown .25 .25
**548** A224 £1.30 slate green .25 .25
#547-549, with tabs .25

David Ben-Gurion (1886-1973), first Prime Minister and Minister of Defense of Israel.

Arrows on Globe — A225

Dove Delivering Letter — A226

**1974, Nov. 5** **Litho.** ***Perf. 14***

**549** A225 25a black & multi .25 .25

**Photo.**

**550** A226 £1.30 gold & multi .25 .25
#549-550, with tabs .25

Centenary of Universal Postal Union.

Hebrew University, Mount Scopus, Jerusalem — A227

**1975, Jan. 14** **Litho.** ***Perf. 13***

**551** A227 £2.50 multicolored .25 .25
With tab .25

Hebrew University, 50th anniv.

Girl Carrying Plant — A228

Welder — A229

Arbor Day: 35a, Bird singing in tree. £2, Boy carrying potted plant.

**1975, Jan. 14** ***Perf. 14***

**552** A228 1a multicolored .25 .25
**553** A228 35a multicolored .25 .25
**554** A228 £2 multicolored .25 .25
#552-554, with tabs .25

**1975, Jan. 14** **Photo.** ***Perf. 14x13***

80a, Tractor driver. £1.20, Electrical lineman.

**555** A229 30a multicolored .25 .25
**556** A229 80a multicolored .25 .25
**557** A229 £1.20 ultra & multi .25 .25
#555-557, with tabs .25

Occupational safety and publicity for the Institute for Safety and Hygiene.

Hebrew University Synagogue, Jerusalem — A230

Modern Israeli architecture: £1.30, Yad Mordecai Museum. £1.70, Bat Yam City Hall.

***Perf. 14, 13½x14 (#559)***

**1975, Mar. 4** **Photo.**

**558** A230 80a brown .25 .25
**559** A230 £1.30 slate green .25 .25
**560** A230 £1.70 brown olive .25 .25
#558-560, with tabs .40

US President Harry S Truman (1884-1972) — A231

**1975, Mar. 4** **Engr.** ***Perf. 14***

**561** A231 £5 dark brown .35 .25
With tab .40

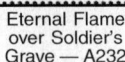

Eternal Flame over Soldier's Grave — A232

Memorial Tablet — A233

**1975, Apr. 10 Photo.** ***Perf. 14x13***

**562** A232 £1.45 black & multi .25 .25
With tab .25

Memorial Day.

**1975, Apr. 10**

**563** A233 £1.45 blk, red & gray .25 .25
With tab .25

In memory of soldiers missing in action.

Hurdling A234

**1975, Apr. 10** ***Perf. 13x14***

**564** A234 25a shown .25 .25
**565** A234 £1.70 Bicycling .25 .25
**566** A234 £3 Volleyball .25 .25
#564-566, with tabs .40

10th Hapoel Games; 50th anniv. of Hapoel Org.

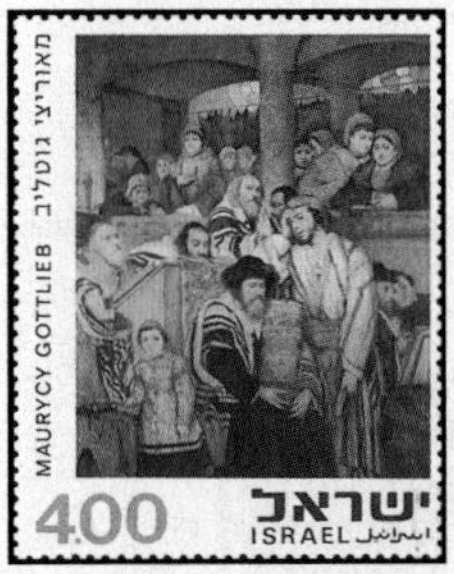

Yom Kippur, by Maurycy Gottlieb A235

Paintings of religious holidays: £1.00 Hanukkah, by Mortiz D. Oppenheim. 1.40, The Purim Players, by Jankel Adler, horiz.

**1975, June 17 Litho.** ***Perf. 14***

**567** A235 £1 multicolored .25 .25
**568** A235 £1.40 multicolored .25 .25
**569** A235 £4 multicolored .25 .25
#567-569, with tabs .50

Old Couple A236

**1975, June 17 Photo.** ***Perf. 13x14***

**570** A236 £1.85 multicolored .25 .25
With tab .25

International Gerontological Association, 10th triennial conference, Jerusalem.

Pres. Zalman Shazar (1889-1974) — A237

**1975, Aug. 5 Photo.** ***Perf. 14x13***

**571** A237 35a silver & blk .25 .25
With tab .25

Pioneer Women, 50th Anniv. — A238

**1975, Aug. 5** ***Perf. 14½***

**572** A238 £5 Emblem .30 .25
With tab .35

Judges of Israel — A239

**1975, Aug. 5** ***Perf. 13x14***

**573** A239 35a Gideon .25 .25
**574** A239 £1 Deborah .25 .25
**575** A239 £1.40 Jephthah .25 .25
#573-575, with tabs .35

Jewish New Year, 5736.

Hebrew University, Mt. Scopus — A240

**1975, Oct. 14 Photo.** ***Perf. 14x13***

**576** A240 £4 multicolored .25 .25
With tab .25

Return of Hadassah to Mt. Scopus, Jerusalem.

Collared Pratincoles A241

Protected Birds: £1.70, Spur-winged plover. £2, Black-winged stilts.

**1975, Oct. 14 Litho.** ***Perf. 13***

**577** A241 £1.10 pink & multi .25 .25
**578** A241 £1.70 lemon & multi .25 .25
**579** A241 £2 multicolored .25 .25
#577-579, with tabs .40

Butterfly and Factory (Air Pollution) — A242

Designs: 80a, Fish and tanker (water pollution). £1.70, Ear and jet (noise pollution).

**1975, Dec. 9 Photo.** ***Perf. 14***

**580** A242 50a car & multi .25 .25
**581** A242 80a green & multi .25 .25
**582** A242 £1.70 orange & multi .25 .25
With tabs .45

Environmental protection.

Star of David — A243

**1975-80** ***Perf. 13x14***

**583** A243 75a vio bl & car .25 .25
**584** A243 £1.80 violet bl & gray .25 .25
**585** A243 £1.85 vio bl & lt brn .25 .25
**586** A243 £2.45 vio bl & brt green .25 .25
**587** A243 £2.70 vio bl & purple .25 .25
**588** A243 £4.30 ultra & red .25 .25
**589** A243 £5.40 vio bl & ol .30 .25
**590** A243 £8 vio bl & bl .40 .25
*Nos. 583-590 (8)* 2.20 2.00
With tabs 2.75

Issued: £1.85, 12/9; £2.45, 6/22/76; 75a, 12/77; £5.40, 5/23/78; £1.80, £8, 5/22/79; £2.70, 12/25/79; £4.30, 5/26/80.

**Landscape Type of 1971-75**

Design: £10, View of Elat and harbor.

**1976, Aug. 17 Photo.** ***Perf. 14x14½***

**592** A193 £10 Prussian blue .85 .25
With tab 1.00

No. 592 issued both tagged and untagged.

"In the days of Ahasuerus." — A247

Designs (from Book of Esther): 80a, "He set the royal crown on her head." £1.60, "Thus shall it be done to the man whom the king delights to honor."

**1976, Feb. 17 Photo.** ***Perf. 14***

**593** A247 40a multicolored .25 .25
**594** A247 80a multicolored .25 .25
**595** A247 £1.60 multicolored .25 .25
*a.* Souv. sheet of 3, #593-595, perf 13x14 .35 .35
#593-595, with tabs .30

Purim Festival. No. 595a sold for £4.

Border Settlement, Barbed Wire — A248

**1976, Feb. 17**

**596** A248 £1.50 olive & multi .25 .25
With tab .25

Border settlements, part of Jewish colonization of Holy Land.

Symbolic Key — A249

**1976, Feb. 17**

**597** A249 £1.85 multicolored .25 .25
With tab .25

Bezalel Academy of Arts and Design, Jerusalem, 70th anniv.

"200" US Flag A250

**1976, Apr. 25 Photo.** ***Perf. 13x14***

**598** A250 £4 gold & multi .25 .25
With tab .30

American Bicentennial.

Dancers of Meron, by Reuven Rubin A251

**1976, Apr. 25 Litho.** ***Perf. 14***

**599** A251 £1.30 multicolored .25 .25
With tab .25

Lag Ba-Omer festival.

8th Brigade Monument, Ben-Gurion Airport — A252

**1976, Apr. 25 Photo.** ***Perf. 14x13***

**600** A252 £1.85 multicolored .25 .25
With tab .25

Memorial Day.

**Souvenir Sheet**

Tourism, Sport and Industry — A253

**1976, Apr. 25**

**601** A253 Sheet of 3 .60 .50
*a.* £1 multicolored .25 .25
*b.* £2 multicolored .25 .25
*c.* £4 multicolored .35 .25

No. 601 sold for £10.

High Jump A254

**1976, June 22** ***Perf. 13x14***

**602** A254 £1.60 shown .25 .25
**603** A254 £2.40 Diving .25 .25
**604** A254 £4.40 Gymnastics .30 .25
#602-604, with tabs .65

21st Olympic Games, Montreal, Canada, July 17-Aug. 1.

Tents and Suns — A255

**1976, June 22** ***Perf. 14***

**605** A255 £1.50 green & multi .25 .25
With tab .25

Israel Camping Union.

"Truth"
A256

Pawn
A257

Design: £1.50, "Judgment" (scales). £1.90, "Peace" (dove and olive branch).

**1976, Aug. 17 Photo. *Perf. 14x13***
**Tagged**

| | | | | |
|---|---|---|---|---|
| **606** | A256 | 45a gold & multi | .25 | .25 |
| **607** | A256 | £1.50 gold & multi | .25 | .25 |
| **608** | A256 | £1.90 gold & multi | .25 | .25 |
| | | #606-608, with tabs | .30 | |

Festivals 5737.

**1976, Oct. 19 Litho. *Perf. 14***

| | | | | |
|---|---|---|---|---|
| **609** | A257 | £1.30 shown | .25 | .25 |
| **610** | A257 | £1.60 Rook | .25 | .25 |
| | | #609-610, with tabs | .35 | |

22nd Men's and 7th Women's Chess Olympiad, Haifa, Oct. 24-Nov. 11.

Byzantine Building, 6th Century
A258

70a, City wall, 7th cent. B.C. £2.40, Robinson's Arch. £2.80, Steps to Gate of Hulda. Both from area leading to 2nd Temple, 1st cent. B.C. £5, Wall, Omayyad Palace, 8th cent. A.D.

**1976 Litho. *Perf. 14***

| | | | | |
|---|---|---|---|---|
| **611** | A258 | 70a multicolored | .25 | .25 |
| **612** | A258 | £1.30 multicolored | .25 | .25 |
| **613** | A258 | £2.40 multicolored | .25 | .25 |
| **614** | A258 | £2.80 multicolored | .35 | .25 |
| **615** | A258 | £5 multicolored | .45 | .40 |
| | | *Nos. 611-615 (5)* | 1.55 | 1.40 |
| | | With tabs | 1.75 | |

Excavations in Old Jerusalem.
Issued: #612-614, 10/19; #611, 615, 12/23.

Clearing the Land, 1890
A259

Designs: 10a, Building harbor wall. 60a, Road building, vert. £1.40, Plower and horse-drawn plow. £1.80, Planting trees.

**1976, Dec. 23 Photo. *Perf. 13***

| | | | | |
|---|---|---|---|---|
| **616** | A259 | 5a brown & gold | .25 | .25 |
| **617** | A259 | 10a purple & gold | .25 | .25 |
| **618** | A259 | 60a gold & car | .25 | .25 |
| **619** | A259 | £1.40 gold & blue | .25 | .25 |
| **620** | A259 | £1.80 green & gold | .25 | .25 |
| | | #616-620, with tabs | .40 | |

Work of the pioneers.

"Let's Pull up Grandfather's Carrot" — A260

**1977, Feb. 15 Litho. *Perf. 14***

| | | | | |
|---|---|---|---|---|
| **621** | A260 | £2.60 multicolored | .25 | .25 |
| | | With tab | .30 | |

Voluntary service.

Doves, Jew and Arab Shaking Hands
A261

£1.40, Arab & Jew holding hands, and flowers. £2.70, Peace dove, Arab and Jew dancing. Illustrations for the book "My Shalom-My Peace."

**1977, Feb. 15**

| | | | | |
|---|---|---|---|---|
| **622** | A261 | 50a multicolored | .25 | .25 |
| **623** | A261 | £1.40 multicolored | .25 | .25 |
| **624** | A261 | £2.70 multicolored | .25 | .25 |
| | | 622-#624, with tabs | .55 | |

Children's drawings for peace.

"By the Rivers of Babylon . . ." — A262

Drawings by Efraim Moshe Lilien: £1.80, Abraham, vert. £2.10, "May our eyes behold thee when thou returnest to Zion in compassion."

***Perf. 14x13, 13x14***
**1977, Feb. 15 Photo.**

| | | | | |
|---|---|---|---|---|
| **625** | A262 | £1.70 gray, brn & blk | .25 | .25 |
| **626** | A262 | £1.80 yel, blk & brn | .25 | .25 |
| **627** | A262 | £2.10 lt grn & dk grn | .25 | .25 |
| | | *Nos. 625-627 (3)* | .75 | .75 |
| | | With tabs | .75 | |

Souvenirs for 5th Zionist Congress, 1902.

Trumpet
A263

Embroidered Sabbath Cloth
A264

**1977, Apr. 19 Litho. *Perf. 14***

| | | | | |
|---|---|---|---|---|
| **628** | A263 | £1.50 shown | .25 | .25 |
| **629** | A263 | £2 Lyre | .25 | .25 |
| **630** | A263 | £5 Cymbals | .25 | .25 |
| | | #628-630, with tabs | .55 | |

Ancient musical instruments, Haifa Music Museum and Amli Library.

**1977, Apr. 19 *Perf. 13x14***

| | | | | |
|---|---|---|---|---|
| **631** | A264 | £3 buff & multi | .25 | .25 |
| | | With tab | .30 | |

Importance of Sabbath observation in Jewish life.

Parachutists' Memorial, Bilu-Gedera, Tel Aviv — A265

**1977, Apr. 19 *Perf. 13x14***

| | | | | |
|---|---|---|---|---|
| **632** | A265 | £3.30 gray, blk & grn | .30 | .25 |
| | | With tab | .40 | |

Memorial Day.

10th Maccabiah — A266

**1977, June 23 Photo. *Perf. 14x13***

| | | | | |
|---|---|---|---|---|
| **633** | A266 | £1 Fencing | .25 | .25 |
| **634** | A266 | £2.50 Shot put | .25 | .25 |
| **635** | A266 | £3.50 Judo | .25 | .25 |
| | | *Nos. 633-635 (3)* | .75 | .75 |
| | | With tabs | .70 | |

ZOA Convention Emblem — A267

**1977, June 23 *Perf. 14***

| | | | | |
|---|---|---|---|---|
| **636** | A267 | £4 silver & multi | .30 | .25 |
| | | With tab | .40 | |

Convention of Zionist Organization of America (ZOA), Jerusalem, June 1977.

Petah Tikva Centenary — A268

**1977, June 23 *Perf. 14x13***

| | | | | |
|---|---|---|---|---|
| **637** | A268 | £1.50 multicolored | .25 | .25 |
| | | With tab | .25 | |

Matriarchs of the Bible — A269

**1977, Aug. 16 Photo. *Perf. 14***

| | | | | |
|---|---|---|---|---|
| **638** | A269 | 70a Sarah | .25 | .25 |
| **639** | A269 | £1.50 Rebekah | .25 | .25 |
| **640** | A269 | £2 Rachel | .25 | .25 |
| **641** | A269 | £3 Leah | .25 | .25 |
| | | #638-641, with tabs | .75 | |

Jewish New Year, 5738.

Frontier Guards — A270

Illuminated Page — A271

**1977, Aug. 16 Litho. *Perf. 14***

| | | | | |
|---|---|---|---|---|
| **642** | A270 | £1 shown | .25 | .25 |
| **643** | A270 | £1 Police | .25 | .25 |
| **644** | A270 | £1 Civil Guard | .25 | .25 |
| | | #642-644, with tabs | .35 | |

Israel Police Force, established Mar. 26, 1948.

**1977, July 21 Photo. *Perf. 14x13***

| | | | | |
|---|---|---|---|---|
| **645** | A271 | £4 multicolored | .25 | .25 |
| | | With tab | .25 | |

4th cent. of Hebrew printing at Safad.

Farm Growing from Steel Helmet
A272

Koffler Accelerator
A273

**1977, Oct. 18 Litho. *Perf. 14***

| | | | | |
|---|---|---|---|---|
| **646** | A272 | £3.50 multicolored | .25 | .25 |
| | | With tab | .25 | |

Fighting Pioneer Youth (NAHAL), established 1949.

**1977, Oct. 18 Photo. *Perf. 14x13***

| | | | | |
|---|---|---|---|---|
| **647** | A273 | £8 black & blue | .60 | .40 |

Inauguration of Koffler accelerator at Weizmann Institute of Science, Rehovot. Untagged.

Caesarea — A274

Scenes: £1, Arava on the Dead Sea. £20, Rosh Pinna.

**1977-78 *Perf. 13½x14***
**Size: 27x22mm**

| | | | | |
|---|---|---|---|---|
| **649** | A274 | 10a violet blue | .25 | .25 |
| **664** | A274 | £1 olive bister | .25 | .25 |

***Perf. 14½x14***
**Size: 27½x26½mm**

| | | | | |
|---|---|---|---|---|
| **672** | A274 | £20 org & dk grn ('78) | .80 | .25 |
| | | #649-672, with tabs | 1.50 | |

The 10a is untagged. The £1, £20 issued tagged and untagged.
Issued: 10a, £1, 10/18/77; £20, 7/4/78.

First Holy Land Locomotive
A276

Locomotives: £1.50, Jezreel Valley train. £2, British Mandate period. £2.50, Israel Railways.

**1977, Dec. 13 Photo. *Perf. 13x14***

| | | | | | |
|---|---|---|---|---|---|
| **674** | A276 | | 65a multicolored | .25 | .25 |
| **675** | A276 | | £1.50 multicolored | .25 | .25 |
| **676** | A276 | | £2 multicolored | .25 | .25 |
| **677** | A276 | | £2.50 multicolored | .25 | .25 |
| | | *a.* | Souvenir sheet of 4, #674-677 | 1.50 | 1.25 |
| | | | #674-677, with tabs | .90 | |

Railways in the Holy Land. #677a sold for £10.

Cypraea Isabella — A277

Designs: Red Sea shells.

**1977, Dec. 13 Litho. *Perf. 14***

| | | | | |
|---|---|---|---|---|
| **678** | A277 | £2 shown | .25 | .25 |
| **679** | A277 | £2 Lioconcha castrensis | .25 | .25 |
| **680** | A277 | £2 Gloripallium pallium | .25 | .25 |
| **681** | A277 | £2 Malea pomum | .25 | .25 |
| | | #678-681, with tabs | .50 | |

Street in Jerusalem, by Haim Glicksberg (1904-1970)
A278

Paintings: £3.80, Thistles, by Leopold Krakauer (1890-1954). £4.40, An Alley in Zefat, by Mordekhai Levanon (1901-1968).

**1978, Feb. 14**

**682** A278 £3 multicolored .25 .25
**683** A278 £3.80 multicolored .25 .25
**684** A278 £4.40 multicolored .25 .25
*Nos. 682-684 (3)* .75 .75
With tabs .65

Marriage Contract, Netherlands, 1648 — A279

Marriage Contracts (Ketubah): £3.90, Morocco, 1897. £6, Jerusalem, 1846.

**1978, Feb. 14**

**685** A279 75a multicolored .25 .25
**686** A279 £3.90 multicolored .25 .25
**687** A279 £6 multicolored .30 .25
#685-687, with tabs .65

Eliyahu Golomb — A280

Designs: Portraits.

**1978, Apr. 23 Photo. *Perf. 14x13***

**688** A280 £2 shown .25 .25
**689** A280 £2 Dr. Moshe Sneh .25 .25
**690** A280 £2 David Raziel .25 .25
**691** A280 £2 Yitzhak Sadeh .25 .25
**692** A280 £2 Abraham Stern .25 .25
#688-692, with tabs .60

Heroes of underground movement. Nos. 688-692 issued in sheets of 15.

See Nos. 695-696, 699-700, 705-706, 712-714, 740-742.

Souvenir Sheet

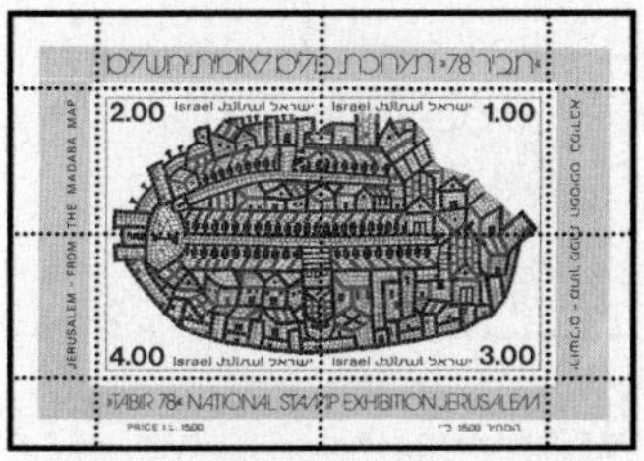


Jerusalem, Mosaic, from Madaba Map — A281

**1978, Apr. 23 Litho. *Perf. 14***

**693** A281 Sheet of 4 1.40 1.40
*a.* £1 multicolored .25 .25
*b.* £2 multicolored .25 .25
*c.* £3 multicolored .40 .35
*d.* £4 multicolored .50 .45

Tabir '78 National Stamp Exhibition, Jerusalem, Apr. 23. No. 693 sold for £15.

Flowers A282

Design: Flowers, after children's paintings on Memorial Wall in Yad-Lebanim Museum, Petah Tikva. Each stamp shows different flowers.

**1978, Apr. 23 *Perf. 14***

**694** Sheet of 15 1.40 1.25
*a.-o.* A282 £1.50 single stamp .25 .25

Memorial Day.

**Heroes Type**

Designs: No. 695, Theodor Herzl. No. 696, Chaim Weizmann.

**1978, July 5 Photo. *Perf. 14x13***

**695** A280 £2 gray & gray ol .25 .25
**696** A280 £2 buff & vio bl .25 .25
#695-696, with tabs .25

Herzl, founder of Zionism; Weizmann, 1st President of Israel.

Hatiqwa, 1st Verse A285

YMCA Building, Jerusalem A286

**1978, July 4 *Perf. 13x14***

**697** A285 £8.40 multicolored .45 .35
With tab .50

Centenary of Israeli National Anthem, Hatiqwa, by poet Naftali Herz Imber.

**1978, July 4 Litho. *Perf. 13***

**698** A286 £5.40 multicolored .25 .25
With tab .35

Centenary of YMCA in Jerusalem.

**Heroes Type**

Designs: No. 699, Rabbi Kook (1865-1935). No. 700, Rabbi Ouziel (1880-1963).

**1978, Aug. 22 Photo. *Perf. 14x13***

**699** A280 £2 pale gray & slate grn .25 .25
**700** A280 £2 pale gray & dk pur .25 .25
#699-700, with tabs .25

Patriarchs A288

**1978, Aug. 22 *Perf. 14***

**701** A288 £1.10 Abraham & Isaac .25 .25
**702** A288 £5.20 Isaac .25 .25
**703** A288 £6.60 Jacob .30 .30
#701-703, with tabs .70

Festivals 5739.

Families and Houses A289

**1978, Aug. 22 *Perf. 13x14***

**704** A289 £5.10 multicolored .30 .25
With tab .35

Social welfare.

**Heroes Type**

Designs: No. 705, David Ben-Gurion. No. 706, Ze'ev Jabotinsky.

**1978, Oct. 31 Photo. *Perf. 14x13***

**705** A280 £2 buff & vio brn .25 .25
**706** A280 £2 gray & indigo .25 .25
#705-706, with tabs .25

30 years of independence. Ben-Gurion, first Prime Minister, and Ze'ev Vladimir Jabotinsky (1880-1940), leader of World Union of Zionist Revisionists.

Star of David and Growing Tree — A291

**1978, Oct. 31 Litho. *Perf. 14***

**707** A291 £8.40 multicolored .45 .35
With tab .50

United Jewish Appeal, established 1939 in US to help Israel.

Old and New Hospital Buildings A292

**1978, Oct. 31**

**708** A292 £5.40 multicolored .25 .25
With tab .30

Opening of new Shaare Zedek Medical Center, Jerusalem.

Silver and Enamel Vase, India — A293

£3, Elephant with howdah, Persia, 13th cent. £4, Mosque lamp, glass and enamel, Syria, 14th cent.

**1978, Oct. 31**

**709** A293 £2.40 multicolored .25 .25
**710** A293 £3 multicolored .25 .25
**711** A293 £4 multicolored .25 .25
*Nos. 709-711 (3)* .75 .75
With tabs .65

Leo Arie Mayer Memorial Museum for Islamic Art, Jerusalem.

**Heroes Type**

#712, Menachem Ussishkin (1863-1941). #713, Berl Katzenelson (1878-1944). #714, Max Nordau (1849-1923).

**1978, Dec. 26 Photo. *Perf. 14x13***

**712** A280 £2 citron & sl grn .25 .25
**713** A280 £2 gray & vio blue .25 .25
**714** A280 £2 buff & black .25 .25
#712-714, with tabs .45

30th anniversary of independence.

Iris Lortetii — A295

Protected Wild Flowers: £5.40, Iris haynei. £8.40, Iris nazarena.

**1978, Dec. 26 Litho. *Perf. 14***

**715** A295 £1.10 multicolored .25 .25
**716** A295 £5.40 multicolored .30 .25
**717** A295 £8.40 multicolored .45 .35
*Nos. 715-717 (3)* 1.00 .85
With tabs .95

Agricultural Mechanization A296

Symbolic Designs: £2.40, Seawater desalination. £4.30, Electronics. £5, Chemical fertilizers.

**1979, Feb. 13 Litho. *Perf. 13***

**718** A296 £1.10 multicolored .25 .25
**719** A296 £2.40 multicolored .25 .25
**720** A296 £4.30 multicolored .25 .25
**721** A296 £5 multicolored .25 .25
#718-721, with tabs .70

Technological Achievements.

"Hope from Darkness" A297

**1979, Feb. 13**

**722** A297 £5.40 multicolored .30 .25
With tab .35

Salute to "the Righteous among Nations," an award to those who helped during Nazi period.

Jewish Brigade Flag — A298

**1979, Feb. 13 Photo. *Perf. 14***

**723** A298 £5.10 blue, yel & blk .25 .25
With tab .30

Jewish Brigade served with British Armed Forces during WWII.

Paper (Prayer for Peace) in Crevice of Western Wall — A299

**1979, Mar. 26 Photo. *Perf. 14x13***

**724** A299 £10 multicolored .35 .25
With tab .40
*a.* Souv. sheet of 1, imperf. .40 .45

Signing of peace treaty between Israel and Egypt, Mar. 26.

11th Hapoel Games — A300

**1979, Apr. 23 Litho. *Perf. 13***

**725** A300 £1.50 Weightlifting .25 .25
**726** A300 £6 Tennis .30 .25
**727** A300 £11 Gymnastics .50 .40
*Nos. 725-727 (3)* 1.05 .90
With tabs 1.00

"50" and Rotary Emblem — A301

**1979, Apr. 23 Photo. *Perf. 14x13***

| | | | | | |
|---|---|---|---|---|---|
| **728** | A301 | £7 multicolored | | .35 | .25 |
| | | With tab | | .40 | |

Rotary Intl. in Israel, 50th anniv.

Navy Memorial, Ashdod A302

**1979, Apr. 23**

| | | | | |
|---|---|---|---|---|
| **729** | A302 | £5.10 multicolored | .25 | .25 |
| | | With tab | .30 | |

Memorial Day.

Rabbi Yehoshua ben Hananya A303

Flag Colors as Search Light A304

Craftsmen-Sages: £8.50, Rabbi Meir Baal Ha-Ness, scribe. £13, Rabbi Johanan, sandal maker.

**1979, Sept. 4 Photo. *Perf. 14x13***

| | | | | |
|---|---|---|---|---|
| **730** | A303 | £1.80 multicolored | .25 | .25 |
| **731** | A303 | £8.50 multicolored | .25 | .25 |
| **732** | A303 | £13 multicolored | .35 | .30 |
| | | *Nos. 730-732 (3)* | .85 | .80 |
| | | With tabs | .75 | |

Jewish New Year 5740.

**1979, Sept. 4**

| | | | | |
|---|---|---|---|---|
| **733** | A304 | £10 multicolored | .25 | .25 |
| | | With tab | .30 | |

Jewish Agency, 50th anniversary.

Hot Springs, Tiberias A305

Boy Riding Rainbow A306

Design: £12, Dead Sea health resorts.

**1979, Sept. 4 Litho. *Perf. 14***

| | | | | |
|---|---|---|---|---|
| **734** | A305 | £8 multicolored | .25 | .25 |
| **735** | A305 | £12 multicolored | .30 | .25 |
| | | #734-735, with tabs | .55 | |

**1979, Nov. 13 Photo. *Perf. 13x14***

| | | | | |
|---|---|---|---|---|
| **736** | A306 | £8.50 multicolored | .25 | .25 |
| | | With tab | .25 | |

International Year of the Child.

Jerusalem — A307

Children's Drawings of Jerusalem: £4, People of different nationalities, horiz. £5, Praying at the Western Wall, horiz.

**1979, Nov. 13 *Perf. 14***

| | | | | |
|---|---|---|---|---|
| **737** | A307 | £1.80 multicolored | .25 | .25 |
| **738** | A307 | £4 multicolored | .25 | .25 |
| **739** | A307 | £5 multicolored | .25 | .25 |
| | | #737-739, with tabs | .30 | |

**Heroes Type**

Designs: £7, Arthur Ruppin (1876-1943). £9, Joseph Trumpeldor (1880-1920). £13, Aaron Aaronsohn (1876-1919).

**1979, Nov. 13 Photo. *Perf. 14x13***

| | | | | |
|---|---|---|---|---|
| **740** | A280 | £7 gray & magenta | .25 | .25 |
| **741** | A280 | £9 pale grn & Prus bl | .25 | .25 |
| **742** | A280 | £13 pale yel & dk ol | .35 | .35 |
| | | *Nos. 740-742 (3)* | .85 | .85 |
| | | With tabs | 1.10 | |

Sorek Cave — A308

**1980, Jan. 15 Litho. *Perf. 13x14***

| | | | | |
|---|---|---|---|---|
| **743** | A308 | £50 multicolored | 1.00 | .50 |
| | | With tab | 1.25 | |

Star of David in Cogwheel A309

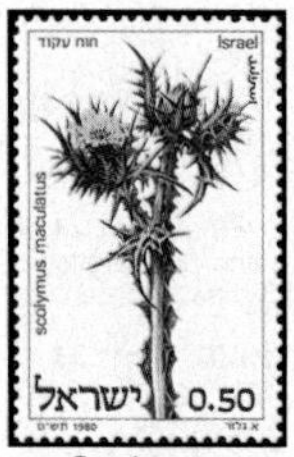

Scolymus Maculatus A310

**1980, Jan. 15 *Perf. 14***

| | | | | |
|---|---|---|---|---|
| **744** | A309 | £13 multicolored | .40 | .40 |
| | | With tab | .45 | |

Organization for Rehabilitation through Training (ORT), centenary.

**1980, Jan. 15**

Thistles: £5.50, Echinops viscosus. £8.50, Cynara syriaca.

| | | | | |
|---|---|---|---|---|
| **745** | A310 | 50a multicolored | .25 | .25 |
| **746** | A310 | £5.50 multicolored | .25 | .25 |
| **747** | A310 | £8.50 multicolored | .25 | .25 |
| | | #745-747, with tabs | .50 | |

Men and Drop of Blood — A311

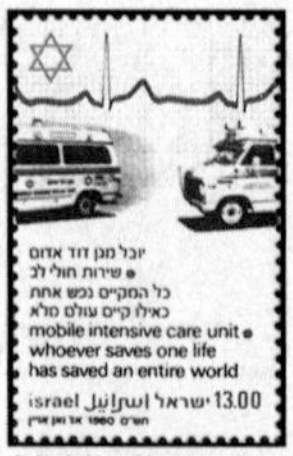

Mobile Intensive Care Unit — A312

**1980, Apr. 15 Photo. *Perf. 14x13***

| | | | | |
|---|---|---|---|---|
| **748** | A311 | £2.70 multicolored | .25 | .25 |
| **749** | A312 | £13 multicolored | .30 | .30 |
| *a.* | | Souv. sheet, 2 each #748-749 | 1.00 | 1.00 |
| | | #748-749, with tabs | .45 | |

Magen David Adom (Red Star of David), 50th anniv.

Road of Courage Monument A313

Sabbath Lamp, Netherlands, 18th Century A314

**1980, Apr. 15 Litho. *Perf. 14***

| | | | | |
|---|---|---|---|---|
| **750** | A313 | £12 multicolored | .30 | .25 |
| | | With tab | .35 | |

Memorial Day.

**1980, Aug. 5 Photo. *Perf. 13x14***

Sabbath Lamps: £20, Germany, 18th century. £30, Morocco, 19th century.

| | | | | |
|---|---|---|---|---|
| **751** | A314 | £4.30 multicolored | .25 | .25 |
| **752** | A314 | £20 multicolored | .30 | .30 |
| **753** | A314 | £30 multicolored | .50 | .50 |
| | | *Nos. 751-753 (3)* | 1.05 | 1.05 |
| | | With tabs | 1.10 | |

Yizhak Gruenbaum A315

Renewal of Jewish Settlement in Gush Etzion A316

**1980, Aug. 5 *Perf. 14x13***

| | | | | |
|---|---|---|---|---|
| **754** | A315 | £32 sepia | .80 | .70 |
| | | With tab | .85 | |

Yizhak Gruenbaum (1879-1970), first minister of the interior.

**1980, Aug. 5**

| | | | | |
|---|---|---|---|---|
| **755** | A316 | £19 multicolored | .35 | .30 |
| | | With tab | .40 | |

View of Haifa and Mt. Carmel, 17th Century — A317

**1980, Sept. 28 Litho. *Perf. 14x13***

| | | | | |
|---|---|---|---|---|
| **756** | A317 | Sheet of 2 | 2.00 | *2.25* |
| *a.* | | 2s multicolored | .75 | *.85* |
| *b.* | | 3s multicolored | 1.00 | *1.10* |

Haifa 80 National Stamp Exhibition, Haifa, Sept. 28-Oct. 7.

A318

**1980-81 Photo. *Perf. 13x14***

| | | | | | |
|---|---|---|---|---|---|
| **757** | A318 | 5a | brt yel grn & green | .25 | .25 |
| **758** | A318 | 10a | red & brt mag | .25 | .25 |
| **759** | A318 | 20a | grnsh bl & dk blue | .25 | .25 |
| **760** | A318 | 30a | lil & dp vio | .25 | .25 |
| **761** | A318 | 50a | red org & red brown | .25 | .25 |
| **762** | A318 | 60a | brt yel grn & dk brown | .25 | .25 |
| **762A** | A318 | 70a | Prus bl & black | .25 | .25 |
| **763** | A318 | 1s | brt mag & dk green | .25 | .25 |
| **764** | A318 | 2s | dk bl grn & brn red | .25 | .25 |
| **765** | A318 | 2.80s | brown & grn | .30 | .25 |
| **766** | A318 | 3.20s | gray & red | .35 | .25 |
| **767** | A318 | 4.20s | ultra & dk pur | .40 | .25 |
| **768** | A318 | 5s | green & blk | .55 | .25 |
| **769** | A318 | 10s | brn org & brn | 1.25 | .25 |
| | | | #757-769, with tabs | 5.00 | |

Issued: 70a, 5/5/81; others, 12/16/80.

See Nos. 784-786, 807-808

Prime Minister Golda Meir (1898-1978) — A319

**1981, Feb. 10 Photo. *Perf. 14x13***

| | | | | |
|---|---|---|---|---|
| **770** | A319 | 2.60s rose violet | .40 | .40 |
| | | With tab | .45 | |

View of Jerusalem, by Mordechai Ardon — A320

Paintings of Jerusalem by: 50a, Anna Ticho. 1.50s, Joseph Zaritsky, vert.

**1981, Feb. 10 Litho. *Perf. 14***

| | | | | |
|---|---|---|---|---|
| **771** | A320 | 50a multicolored | .25 | .25 |
| **772** | A320 | 1.50s multicolored | .25 | .25 |
| **773** | A320 | 2.50s multicolored | .40 | .35 |
| | | *Nos. 771-773 (3)* | .90 | .85 |
| | | With tabs | .95 | |

Hand Putting Coin in Light Bulb — A321

**1981, Mar. 17 Photo. *Perf. 14***

| | | | | |
|---|---|---|---|---|
| **774** | A321 | 2.60s shown | .25 | .25 |
| **775** | A321 | 4.20s Hand squeezing solar energy | .40 | .35 |
| | | #774-775, with tabs | .80 | |

Shmuel Yosef Agnon (1880-1970), Writer — A322

Wind Surfing — A323

Designs: 2.80s, Moses Montefiore (1784-1885), first knighted English Jew. 3.20s, Abba Hillel Silver (1893-1963), statesman.

***Perf. 14x13, 14 (3.20s)***

**1981, Mar. 17**

**776** A322 2s dk blue & blk .25 .25
**777** A322 2.80s dk bl grn & blk .30 .30
**778** A322 3.20s deep bis & blk .35 .30
*Nos. 776-778 (3)* .90 .85
With tabs 1.00

**1981, May 5** ***Perf. 14x13***

**779** A323 80a shown .25 .25
**780** A323 4s Basketball .55 .55
**781** A323 6s High jump .75 .75
*Nos. 779-781 (3)* 1.55 1.55
With tabs 1.50

11th Maccabiah Games, July 8-16.

Biq'at Hayarden Memorial A324

Jewish Family Heritage A325

**1981, May 5** ***Perf. 13x14***

**782** A324 1s red & black .25 .25
With tab .25

**1981, May 5** **Litho.** ***Perf. 14***

**783** A325 3s multicolored .40 .35
With tab .45

### Type of 1980

**1981, Aug. 25** **Photo.** ***Perf. 13x14***

**784** A318 90a dp vio & brn org .25 .25
**785** A318 3s red & dk blue .45 .30
**786** A318 4s dk brn vio & dp lil rose .50 .35
*Nos. 784-786 (3)* 1.20 .90
With tabs 1.25

The Burning Bush A326

Roses A327

Festivals 5742 (Book of Exodus): 1s "Let my people go . . ." 3s, Crossing of the Red Sea. 4s, Moses with Tablets.

**1981, Aug. 25**

**787** A326 70a multicolored .25 .25
**788** A326 1s multicolored .25 .25
**789** A326 3s multicolored .35 .35
**790** A326 4s multicolored .45 .40
*Nos. 787-790 (4)* 1.30 1.25
With tabs 1.25

**1981, Oct. 22** **Litho.** ***Perf. 14***

**791** A327 90a Rosa damascena .25 .25
**792** A327 3.50s Rosa phoenicia .40 .35
**793** A327 4.50s Rosa hybrida .50 .45
*Nos. 791-793 (3)* 1.15 1.05
With tabs 1.50

Ha-Shiv'a Interchange, Morasha-Ashod Highway — A328

**1981, Oct. 22** **Photo.** ***Perf. 14x13***

**794** A328 8s multicolored .70 .65
With tab .75

Elat Stone A329

Arbutus Andrachne A330

**1981, Dec. 29** **Litho.** ***Perf. 14***

**795** A329 2.50s shown .25 .25
**796** A329 5.50s Star sapphire .55 .55
**797** A329 7s Emerald .70 .70
*Nos. 795-797 (3)* 1.50 1.50
With tabs 2.25

**1981, Dec. 29**

**798** A330 3s shown .30 .30
**799** A330 3s Cercis siliquastrum .30 .30
**800** A330 3s Quercus ithaburensis .30 .30
*a.* Vert. or horiz. strip of 3, #798-800 1.00 1.00
#800a, horiz. strip of 3 with tabs 1.25

Sheets of 9.

Road Safety — A331

**1982, Mar. 2** **Photo.** ***Perf. 14x13***

**801** A331 7s multicolored .70 .70
With tab 1.00
*a.* Souvenir sheet 1.25 1.25

No. 801a sold for 10s.

Joseph Gedalyah Klausner — A331a (1874-1958), Historian and Philosopher

7s, Perez Bernstein (1890-1971), writer and editor. 8s, Rabbi Arys Levin (1885-1969).

**1982, Mar. 2**

**802** A331a 7s multi .50 .50
**803** A331a 8s multi .55 .55
**804** A331a 9s cream & dk bl .65 .65
*Nos. 802-804 (3)* 1.70 1.70
With tabs 1.90

### Type of 1980 and

Produce — A332

**1982-83** **Photo.** ***Perf. 13 x 14***

**805** A332 40a Prus bl & grn .25 .25
**806** A332 80a lt bl & pur .25 .25
**807** A318 1.10s ol & red .25 .25
**808** A318 1.20s bl & red .25 .25
**809** A332 1.40s ol grn & red .25 .25
**810** A332 6s red vio & brn org .25 .25
**811** A332 7s brn org & ol .25 .25
**812** A332 8s brt grn & red brn .25 .25
**813** A332 9s ol & brn .25 .25
**814** A332 15s ver & brt grn .40 .25
*Nos. 805-814 (10)* 2.65 2.50
With tabs 5.00

Issued: 1.10s, 2/11; 1.20s, 3/16; 1.40s, 6/22/82; 40a, 80a, 6s, 1/11/83; 7s-15s, 10/11/83.

See Nos. 876-879.

Tel Aviv Landscape, by Aryeh Lubin (d. 1980) — A333

Landscapes by: 8s, Sionah Tagger, vert. 15s, Israel Paldi (1892-1979).

**1982, Apr. 22** **Litho.** ***Perf. 14***

**815** A333 7s multicolored .50 .50
**816** A333 8s multicolored .50 .50
**817** A333 15s multicolored 1.00 1.00
*Nos. 815-817 (3)* 2.00 2.00
With tabs 3.00

Gedudei Nouar Youth Corps A334

Armour Memorial, En Zetim A335

**1982, Apr. 22** **Photo.** ***Perf. 14x13***

**818** A334 5s multicolored .40 .35
With tab .55

**1982, Apr. 22** **Litho.** ***Perf. 14***

**819** A335 1.50s multicolored .25 .25
With tab .25

Memorial Day.

Joshua Addressing Crowd — A336

Festivals 5743 (Book of Joshua): 5.50s, Crossing River Jordan. 7.50s, Blowing down walls of Jericho. 9.50s, Battle with five kings of Amorites.

**1982, Aug. 10** ***Perf. 14***

**820** A336 1.50s multicolored .25 .25
**821** A336 5.50s multicolored .30 .30
**822** A336 7.50s multicolored .45 .45
**823** A336 9.50s multicolored .55 .55
*Nos. 820-823 (4)* 1.55 1.55
With tabs 1.50

Hadassah, 70th Anniv. — A337

**1982, Aug. 10** **Litho.**

**824** A337 12s multicolored .85 .70
With tab 1.25

Rosh Pinna Settlement Centenary A338

**1982** **Photo.** ***Perf. 13x14***

**825** A338 2.50s shown .25 .25
**826** A338 3.50s Rishon Leziyyon .25 .25
**827** A338 6s Zikhron Yaaqov .35 .30
**828** A338 9s Mazkeret Batya .65 .60
*Nos. 825-828 (4)* 1.50 1.40
With tabs 1.50

Issued: 2.50s, 3.50s, Aug. 10; others, Oct. 5.

See Nos. 849-850.

Olive Branch A339

Emblem of Council for a Beautiful Israel A340

**1982, Sept. 12**

**829** A339 multicolored .25 .25
With tab .40
*a.* Booklet pane of 8 + 8 ('84) 3.00

Sold at various values.

**1982, Oct. 5** **Litho.** ***Perf. 14***

**830** A340 17s multicolored .90 .75
With tab 1.00
*a.* Souv. sheet of 1, imperf. 2.25 2.25

No. 830a was for Beer Sheva '82 National Stamp Exhibition. Sold for 25s.

Eliahu Bet Tzuri — A341

Independence Martyrs: b, Hannah Szenes. c, Shlomo Ben Yosef. d, Yosef Lishanski. e, Naaman Belkind. f, Eliezer Kashani. g, Yechiel Dresner. h, Dov Gruner. i, Mordechai Alkachi. j, Eliahu Hakim. k, Meir Nakar. l, Avshalom Haviv. m, Yaakov Weiss. n, Meir Feinstein. o, Moshe Barazani. p, Eli Cohen. q, Samuel Azaar. r, Moshe Marzouk. s, Shalom Salih. t, Yosef Basri.

**1982, Dec.** ***Perf. 14x13½***

**831** Sheet of 20 5.50 5.50
*a.-t.* A341 3s multicolored .25 .25

Anti-Smoking Campaign A342

**1983, Feb. 15** **Litho.** ***Perf. 13***

**832** A342 7s Candy in ash tray .35 .25
With tab .50

Beekeeping
A343

**1983, Feb. 15 Photo.** ***Perf. 13x14***

**833** A343 30s multi 1.60 1.50
With tab 1.75

A343a

**1983, Feb. 15 Litho.** ***Perf. 14***

**834** A343a 8s Golan .30 .30
**835** A343a 15s Galil .65 .55
**836** A343a 20s Yehuda and Shomeron .95 .70
*Nos. 834-836 (3)* 1.90 1.55
With tabs 3.00

Memorial Day (Apr. 17) — A344

**1983, Apr. 12** ***Perf. 13***

**837** A344 3s Division of Steel Memorial, Besor Region .25 .25
With tab .25

Independence Day — A345

**1983, Apr. 12** ***Perf. 14***

**838** A345 25s multicolored 1.25 1.00
With tab 1.40
*a.* Souvenir sheet, imperf. 2.50 2.25

No. 838a sold for 35s.

12th Hapoel Games — A346

**1983, Apr. 12** ***Perf. 14x13***

**839** A346 6s multicolored .25 .25
With tab .35

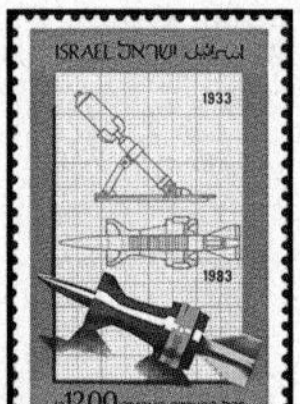

50th Anniv. of Israel Military Industries — A347

**1983, Apr. 12**

**840** A347 12s multicolored .55 .55
With tab .60

Souvenir Sheet

WWII Uprising Leaders — A348

Designs: a, Yosef Glazman (1908-1943), Founder of United Partisans Org. b, Text.1 c, Mordechai Anilewicz (1919-1943), leader of Warsaw Ghetto revolt. No. 841 sold for 45s.

**1983, June 7** ***Perf. 14***

**841** A348 Sheet of 3 2.75 2.75
*a.* 10s multicolored .75 .60
*b.* 10s multicolored .75 .60
*c.* 10s multicolored .75 .60

Raoul Wallenberg (1912-1945), Swedish Diplomat — A349

**1983, June 7** ***Perf. 14x13***

**842** A349 14s multicolored .65 .45
With tab 1.00

The Last Way, by Yosef Kuzkovski — A350

**1983, June 7** ***Perf. 14***

**843** A350 35s multicolored 1.10 1.10
With tab 1.25

Ohel Moed Synagogue, Tel Aviv
A351

**1983, Aug. 23**

**844** A351 3s shown .25 .25
**845** A351 12s Yeshurun Society, Jerusalem .35 .35
**846** A351 16s Ohel Aharon, Haifa .50 .50
**847** A351 20s Eliyahu Khakascni, Beer Sheva .60 .60
*Nos. 844-847 (4)* 1.70 1.70
With tabs 1.90

View of Afula, Jezreel Valley — A352

**1983, Aug. 23**

**848** A352 15s multicolored .65 .55
With tab .80

**Settlement Type of 1982**

**1983, Aug. 23**

**849** A338 11s Yesud Ha-Maala .45 .40
**850** A338 13s Nes Ziyyona .50 .45
#849-850, with tabs 1.25

Souvenir Sheet

Tel Aviv Seashore Promenade — A353

**1983, Sept. 25** ***Perf. 14x13***

**851** A353 Sheet of 2 8.00 8.00
*a.* 30s multicolored 2.50 2.25
*b.* 50s multicolored 4.00 3.75

Tel Aviv '83, 13th Natl. Stamp Show, Sept. Sold for 120s.

KFIR-C2 Tactical Fighter — A354

**1983, Dec. 13 Photo.** ***Perf. 14***

**852** A354 8s shown .25 .25
**853** A354 18s Reshef class missile boat .25 .25
**854** A354 30s Merkava-MK1 battle tank .45 .45
*Nos. 852-854 (3)* .95 .95
With tabs .90

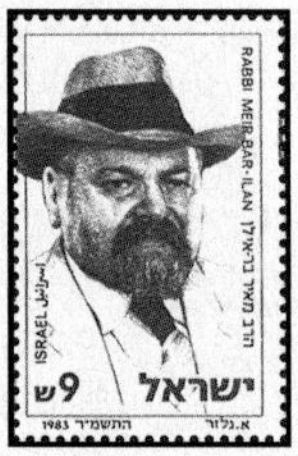

Rabbi Meir Bar-Ilan (1880-1949), Founder of Mizrachi Movement — A355

**1983, Dec. 13 Photo.** ***Perf. 14x13***

**855** A355 9s multicolored .25 .25
With tab .25

Jewish Immigration from Germany, 50th Anniv.
A356

**1983, Dec. 13 Photo.** ***Perf. 13x14***

**856** A356 14s multicolored .40 .35
With tab .45

Michael Halperin (1860-1919), Zionist — A357

Uri Zvi Grinberg (1896-1981), Poet — A358

15s, Yigal Allon (1918-1980), military commander, founder of Israel Labor Party.

**1984, Mar. 15 Photo.** ***Perf. 14x13***

**857** A357 7s multicolored .25 .25

**Litho.**

***Perf. 14***

**858** A357 15s multicolored .25 .25

***Perf. 13***

**859** A358 16s multicolored .30 .30
*Nos. 857-859 (3)* .80 .80
With tabs 1.00

Hevel Ha-Besor Settlement — A359

**1984, Mar. 15** ***Perf. 14***

**860** A359 12s shown .25 .25
**861** A359 17s Arava .30 .25
**862** A359 40s Gaza Strip .75 .50
*Nos. 860-862 (3)* 1.30 1.00
With tabs 1.50

Monument of Alexander Zaid, by David Polus
A360

Monuments: No. 864, Tel Hay Defenders (seated lion), by Abraham Melnikov (1892-1960). No. 865, Dov Gruner, by Chana Orloff (1888-1968).

**1984, Mar. 15** ***Perf. 13x14***

**863** A360 15s multicolored .35 .25
**864** A360 15s multicolored .35 .25
**865** A360 15s multicolored .35 .25
*Nos. 863-865 (3)* 1.05 .75
With tabs 1.35

Memorial Day — A361

Natl. Labor Fed., 50th Anniv. — A362

Design: Oliphant House (Druse military memorial), Dalyat Al Karmil.

**1984, Apr. 26 Photo.** ***Perf. 14x13***

**866** A361 10s multicolored .25 .25
With tab .25

**1984, Apr. 26**

**867** A362 35s multicolored .35 .25
With tab .40

**Produce Type of 1982-83**

**1984 Photo.** ***Perf. 13x14***

**876** A332 30s vio brn & red .35 .25
**877** A332 50s dp bis & rose mag .65 .40
**878** A332 100s gray & green 1.25 .80
**879** A332 500s dp org & bl blk 1.10 .90
*Nos. 876-879 (4)* 3.35 2.35
With tabs 7.00

Issued: 500s, 11/27; others 4/26.

Leon Pinsker (1821-91), A363

Gen. Charles O. Wingate (1903-44) A364

**1984, July 3** *Perf. 14x13*

**880** A363 20s Hovevei Zion founder .25 .25
**881** A364 20s British soldier .25 .25
#880-881, with tabs .50

Hearts, Stars — A365

**1984, July 3**

**882** A365 30s multicolored .25 .25
With tab .30

70th anniv. of American Jewish Joint Distribution Committee (philanthropic org. created during World War I).

1984 Summer Olympics A366

**1984, July 3** **Litho.** *Perf. 14*

**883** A366 80s Dove .70 .70
With tab .90

**Souvenir Sheet**

*Perf. 14x13*

**884** A366 240s like 80s 5.00 4.25

No. 884 contains one 23x32mm stamp. Sold for 350s.

Biblical Women A367

David Wolffsohn (1856-1914), Jewish Colonial Trust Founder A368

**1984, Sept. 4** **Photo.** *Perf. 13x14*

**885** A367 15s Hannah .25 .25
**886** A367 70s Ruth .35 .35
**887** A367 100s Huldah .60 .60
*Nos. 885-887 (3)* 1.20 1.20
With tabs 1.25

**1984, Sept. 4** *Perf. 14x14½*

**888** A368 150s multicolored .90 .60
With tab 1.25

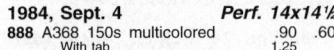

Nahalal Settlement (Founded 1921) A369

**1984, Sept. 4** *Perf. 14*

**889** A369 80s multicolored .50 .45
With tab .60

World Food Day, Oct. 16 — A370

**1984, Nov. 27** **Litho.**

**891** A370 200s Bread, wheat 1.00 .65
With tab 1.10

Rabbi Isaac Herzog (1888-1959), Statesman, Scholar — A371

**1984, Nov. 27** **Photo.** *Perf. 14½*

**892** A371 400s multicolored 1.60 1.40
With tab 1.75

A372

Children's Book Illustrations (Authors and their books): 20s, Apartment to Let, by Leah Goldberg (1911-70). 30s, Why is the Zebra Wearing Pajamas, by Omer Hillel (b. 1926) (30x30mm). 50s, Across the Sea, by Haim Nahman Bialik (1873-1934).

*Perf. 14, 13 (30s)*

**1984, Nov. 27** **Litho.**

**893** A372 20s multicolored .25 .25
**894** A372 30s multicolored .25 .25
**895** A372 50s multicolored .30 .25
*Nos. 893-895 (3)* .80 .75
With tabs .80

Birds of Prey — A373

**1985, Feb. 5** **Litho.** *Perf. 14*

**896** A373 100s Lappet faced vulture .35 .35
**897** A373 200s Bonelli's eagle .60 .60
**898** A373 300s Sooty falcon .80 .80
**899** A373 500s Griffon vulture 1.50 1.50
*Nos. 896-899 (4)* 3.25 3.25
With tabs 6.00

**Souvenir Sheet**

**899A** Sheet of 4 8.00 5.00
*b.* A373 100s like #896 .50 .40
*c.* A373 200s like #897 .90 .80
*d.* A373 300s like #898 1.25 1.10
*e.* A373 500s like #899 1.75 1.60

No. 899A sold for 1650s. Nos. 899Ab-899Ad do not have inscriptions below the design.

Aviation in the Holy Land A374

**1985, Apr. 2** **Litho.** *Perf. 14*

**900** A374 50s Bleriot XI, 1913 .25 .25
**901** A374 150s Scipio-Short S-17 Kent, 1931 .50 .40
**902** A374 250s Tiger Moth DH-82, 1934 .80 .70
**903** A374 300s Scion-Short S-16, 1937 .85 1.00
*Nos. 900-903 (4)* 2.40 2.35
With tabs 2.75

Natl. Assoc. of Nurses — A375

**1985, Apr. 2** **Litho.** *Perf. 14*

**904** A375 400s multicolored 1.00 .95
With tab 1.50

Golani Brigade Memorial and Museum — A376

**1985, Apr. 2** **Photo.** *Perf. 14x13*

**905** A376 50s multicolored .25 .25
With tab .45

Zivia (1914-1978) and Yitzhak (1915-1981) Zuckerman, Resistance Heroes, Warsaw Ghetto — A377

**1985, Apr. 2** **Photo.** *Perf. 13x14*

**906** A377 200s multicolored .65 .50
With tab .80

**Souvenir Sheets**

Dome of the Rock — A378

16th Cent. Bas-relief, Ottoman Period — A379

Adam, Eve and the Serpent (detail) — A380

#907b, The Western Wall. #907c, Church of the Holy Sepulchre. #908b, Hand, 18th cent. bas-relief, Jewish Quarter. #908c, Rosette carving, 12th-13th cent. Crusader capital. #909, Frontispiece and detail, Schocken Bible, South Germany, ca. 1290.

**1985, May 14** **Litho.** *Perf. 13x14*

**907** Sheet of 3 3.00 3.00
*a.-c.* A378 200s any single .80 .75

Sold for 900s.

*Perf. 14x13*

**908** Sheet of 3 4.00 4.00
*a.-c.* A379 350s any single 1.25 1.10

Sold for 1500s.

*Perf. 14*

**909** A380 800s multi 3.75 3.75
*Nos. 907-909 (3)* 10.75 10.75

Sold for 1200s.

The Israeli postal administration authorized the Intl. Philatelic Federation (FIP) to overprint a limited number of these souvenir sheets for sale exclusively at ISRAPHIL '85 to raise funds. The FIP overprints have control numbers and are inscribed "Under the Patronage of the Philatelic Federation" in the sheet margin. The sheets remained valid for postage but were not sold by the post office. Value for set of sheets $45.

12th Maccabiah Games A381

1985 Festivals A382

**1985, July 16** **Litho.** *Perf. 14*

**910** A381 400s Basketball .75 .75
**911** A381 500s Tennis .90 .90
**912** A381 600s Windsurfing 1.10 1.10
*Nos. 910-912 (3)* 2.75 2.75
With tabs 4.00

**1985, July 16** **Litho.** *Perf. 14*

Tabernacle utensils: 100sh, Ark of the Covenant. 150sh, Acacia showbread table. 200sh, Menora. 300sh, Incense altar.

**913** A382 100s multi .25 .25
**914** A382 150s multi .30 .30
**915** A382 200s multi .35 .35
**916** A382 300s multi .55 .55
*Nos. 913-916 (4)* 1.45 1.45
With tabs 2.25

A383

A384

**1985, July 16** **Litho.** *Perf. 14*

**917** A383 150s Emblem, badges .40 .25
With tab .55

Intl. Youth Year.

**1985, Nov. 5** **Litho.** *Perf. 14*

**918** A384 200s multi .80 .25
With tab .95

Leon Yehuda Recanati (1890-1945), financier and philanthropist.

Meir Dizengoff (1861-1936), Founder and Mayor of Tel Aviv — A385

**1985, Nov. 5**

919 A385 500s multi 1.00 .65
With tab 1.25

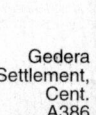

Gedera Settlement, Cent. A386

**1985, Nov. 5 Photo. *Perf. 13x14***

920 A386 600s multi 1.10 .80
With tab 1.40

The Kibbutz — A387

**1985, Nov. 5 Litho. *Perf. 14***

921 A387 900s multi 1.25 1.10
With tab 1.50

Theodor Herzl A388

Capital, Second Temple, Jerusalem A389

Designs: 1s, Corinthian, A.D. 1st cent. 3s, Ionic, 1st cent. B.C.

**1986, Jan. 1 Photo. *Perf. 13x14***

922 A388 1a red & ultra .25 .25
923 A388 2a green & ultra .25 .25
924 A388 3a brown & ultra .25 .25
925 A388 5a blue & ultra .25 .25
926 A388 10a org & ultra .25 .25
927 A388 20a pink & ultra .25 .25
928 A388 30a lemon & ultra .25 .25
929 A388 50a pur & ultra .45 .40
930 A389 1s multi 1.00 .95
931 A389 3s multi 2.75 2.75
*Nos. 922-931 (10)* 5.95 5.85
With tabs 6.25

1s and 3s designs with 1000a and 1500a values were not issued.

See Nos. 1014-1020, 1699.

Red Sea Coral A390

**1986, Mar. 4 Litho. *Perf. 14***

932 A390 30a Balanophyllia .35 .35
933 A390 40a Goniopora .50 .50
934 A390 50a Dendronephthya .65 .65
*Nos. 932-934 (3)* 1.50 1.50
With tabs 3.00

Arthur Rubinstein (1887-1982), Pianist — A391

**1986, Mar. 4 Photo. *Perf. 13x14***

935 A391 60a Picasso portraits .90 .80
With tab 1.25

Broadcasting from Jerusalem, 50th Anniv. — A392

**1986, Mar. 4 Litho. *Perf. 14***

936 A392 70a Map and microphone, 1936 .90 .90
With tab 1.10

Negev Brigade Memorial, Beer Sheva — A393

**1986, May 4 Litho. *Perf. 13***

937 A393 20a multicolored .30 .30
With tab .40

Memorial Day.

Al Jazzar Mosque, Akko — A394

**1986, May 4 Photo. *Perf. 14x13***

938 A394 30a multicolored .40 .40
With tab .50

Id Al-Fitr Feast.

Institutes of Higher Learning in the US — A395

Designs: No. 939, 942a, Hebrew Union College, Jewish Institute of Religion, 1875, Cincinnati. No. 940, 942b, Yeshiva University, 1886, NYC. No. 941, 942c, Jewish Theological Seminary of America, 1886, NYC.

**1986, May 4 Litho. *Perf. 14***

939 A395 50a multicolored .60 .60
940 A395 50a multicolored .60 .60
941 A395 50a multicolored .60 .60
*Nos. 939-941 (3)* 1.80 1.80
With tabs 2.75

**Souvenir Sheet**

942 Sheet of 3 + label 4.00 4.00
*a.-c.* A395 75a any single 1.25 1.25

AMERIPEX '86. Size of Nos. 942a-942c: 36x23mm. No. 942 sold for 3s.

Ben Gurion Airport, 50th Anniv. A396

**1986, July 22 *Perf. 14x13***

943 A396 90a Terminal from aircraft 1.25 1.25
With tab 1.50

"No to Racism" in Graffiti — A397

**1986, July 22 *Perf. 14***

944 A397 60a multicolored .90 .80
With tab 1.10

Druze Feast of Prophet Nabi Sabalan A398

**1986, July 22 Photo. *Perf. 14***

945 A398 40a Tomb, Hurfeish .50 .50
With tab .60

Joseph Sprinzak (1885-1959), 1st Speaker of Knesset — A399

**1986, July 22 Litho. *Perf. 13***

946 A399 80a multicolored 1.00 1.00
With tab 1.10

Worms Illuminated Mahzor, 13th Cent. — A400

**1986, Sept. 23 Litho. *Perf. 13x14***

947 A400 20a Gates of Heaven .25 .25
948 A400 40a Sheqalim, prayer .50 .50
949 A400 90a Rose flower prayer introduction 1.10 1.10
*Nos. 947-949 (3)* 1.85 1.85
With tabs 2.25

David Ben-Gurion (1886-1973) — A401

**1986, Oct. 19 Litho. *Perf. 14x13***

950 A401 1s multicolored 1.25 1.25
With tab 1.40

**Souvenir Sheet**

Map of the Holyland, by Gerard de Jode, 1578 — A402

**1986, Oct. 19 *Perf. 14½***

951 A402 2s multicolored 4.00 3.50

NATANYA '86 Stamp Exhibition; Organized philately in Natanya, 50th anniv. Sold for 3s.

Israel Meteorological Service, 50th Anniv. — A403

**1986, Dec. 18 Litho. *Perf. 13***

952 A403 50a multicolored .70 .70
With tab 1.25

Basilica of the Annunciation, Nazareth — A404

**1986, Dec. 18 Litho. *Perf. 14***

953 A404 70a multicolored .90 .90
With tab 1.60

Israel Philharmonic Orchestra, 50th Anniv. — A405

**1986, Dec. 18**

954 A405 1.50s Bronislaw Huberman, violinist 2.25 2.00
955 A405 1.50s Arturo Toscanini, conductor 2.25 2.00
*a.* Pair, #954-955 4.50 4.00
With tabs 6.75

Owls A406

**1987, Feb. 24 Litho. *Perf. 14x13***

956 A406 30a Bubo bubo .55 .55
957 A406 40a Otus brucei .70 .70
958 A406 50a Tyto alba .90 .90
959 A406 80a Strix butleri 1.50 1.50
*Nos. 956-959 (4)* 3.65 3.65
With tabs 8.00

**Souvenir Sheet**

960 Sheet of 4 10.00 10.00
*a.* A406 30a like #956 1.40 1.40
*b.* A406 40a like #957 1.75 1.75
*c.* A406 50a like #958 2.25 2.25
*d.* A406 80a like #959 3.50 3.50

Sold for 3s. Nos. 960a-960d do not have inscriptions below the design.

Ammunition Hill Memorial, Jerusalem A407

**1987, Apr. 16** **Litho.** ***Perf. 14***

**961** A407 30a multicolored .40 .40
With tab .65

Memorial Day.

13th Hapoel Games A408

**1987, Apr. 16**

**962** A408 90a multicolored 1.10 1.10
With tab 1.60

**Souvenir Sheet**

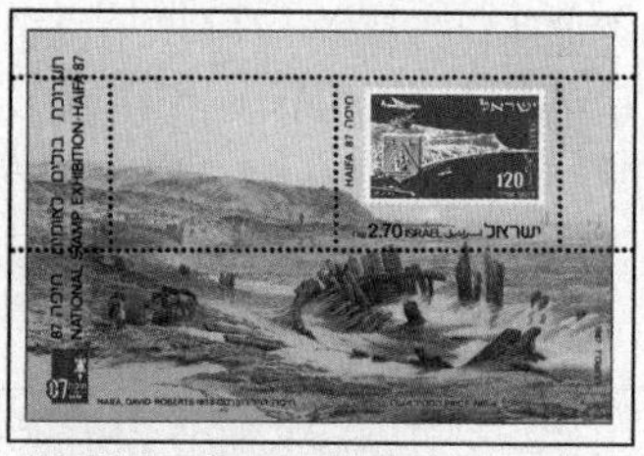

HAIFA '87 Stamp Exhibition — A409

**1987, Apr. 16** ***Perf. 14x13***

**963** A409 2.70s No. C8 6.00 6.00

Sold for 4s.

Amateur Radio Operators — A410

**1987, June 14** **Litho.** ***Perf. 14***

**964** A410 2.50s multi 3.75 3.75
With tab 4.50

World Dog Show, June 23-27 — A411

**1987, June 14**

**965** A411 40a Saluki .90 .70
**966** A411 50a Sloughi 1.10 .90
**967** A411 2s Canaan 5.00 4.00
*Nos. 965-967 (3)* 7.00 5.60
With tabs 9.00

Clean Environment A412

**1987, June 14** ***Perf. 13***

**968** A412 40a multicolored .75 .45
With tab .85

Rabbi Moshe Avigdor Amiel (1883-1945), Founder of Yeshivas — A413

**1987, Sept. 10** **Litho.** ***Perf. 14***

**969** A413 1.40s multi 1.40 1.40
With tab 1.50

Synagogue Models, Nahum Goldmann Museum, Tel Aviv A414

Kupat Holim Health Insurance Institute, 75th Anniv. A415

**1987, Sept. 10** ***Perf. 13x14***

**970** A414 30a Altneuschul, Prague, 13th cent. .40 .40
**971** A414 50a Aleppo, Syria, 9th cent. .60 .60
**972** A414 60a Florence, Italy, 19th cent. .75 .75
*Nos. 970-972 (3)* 1.75 1.75
With tabs 1.90

See Nos. 996-998.

**1987, Sept. 10** ***Perf. 14***

**973** A415 1.50s multi 1.50 1.50
With tab 1.75

Pinhas Rosen (1887-1978), First Minister of Justice — A416

**1987, Nov. 24** **Litho.** ***Perf. 13***

**974** A416 80a multicolored .90 .90
With tab 1.25

A417

Exploration of the Holy Land, 19th cent.: 30a, Thomas Howard Molyneux (1847) and Christopher Costigan (1835). 50a, William Francis Lynch (1848). 60a, John MacGregor (1868-1869).

**1987, Nov. 24** ***Perf. 14***

**975** A417 30a multi .45 .45
**976** A417 50a multi .70 .70
**977** A417 60a multi .85 .55
*Nos. 975-977 (3)* 2.00 1.70
With tabs 2.50

**Souvenir Sheet**

**978** Sheet of 3 4.00 4.00
*a.* A417 40a like #975 .85 .85
*b.* A417 50a like #976 1.25 1.25
*c.* A417 80a like #977 1.75 1.75

No. 978 sold for 2.50s.

A418

A419

**1988, Jan. 26**

**979** A418 10a Computer technology .25 .25
**980** A418 80a Genetic engineering .95 .95
**981** A418 1.40s Medical engineering 1.60 1.60
*Nos. 979-981 (3)* 2.80 2.80
With tabs 3.00

Industrialization of Israel, cent.

**1988, Jan. 26**

**982** A419 40a multicolored .50 .50
With tab .60

Water conservation.

Australia Bicentennial — A420

**1988, Jan. 26** ***Perf. 14***

**983** A420 1s multi 1.25 1.25
With tab 1.50

Sunflower — A421

**1988, Mar. 9** **Photo.** ***Perf. 13x14***

**984** A421 (30a) dk yel grn & yel .25 .25
With tab .35

A422

Design: Anne Frank (1929-45), Amsterdam house where she hid.

**1988, Apr. 19** **Litho.**

**985** A422 60a multicolored .50 .50
With tab .60

Independence 40 Stamp Exhibition, Jerusalem A423

Design: Modern Jerusalem.

**1988, Apr. 19**

**986** A423 1s shown .90 .90
With tab 1.00

**Souvenir Sheet**

**987** A423 2s detail from 1s 3.50 3.50

No. 987 sold for 3s.

Memorial Day A424

**1988, Apr. 19** ***Perf. 14x13***

**988** A424 40a multicolored .35 .35
With tab .45
*a.* Souvenir sheet of 1 .75 .75

Natl. independence, 40th anniv. No. 988a contains one stamp like No. 988 but without copyright inscription LR. Sold for 60a.

**Souvenir Sheet**

Israel's 40th Anniv. Exhibition, Tel Aviv — A425

Stamps on stamps: a, No. 245. b, No. 297. c, No. 120. d, No. 96. e, Like No. 794. f, No. 252. g, No. 333. h, No. 478.

**1988, June 9** **Litho.** ***Perf. 14***

**989** Sheet of 8 + label 2.75 2.75
*a.-h.* A425 20a any single .30 .30

Sold for 2.40s. Center label pictures Israel 40 emblem.

B'nai B'rith in Jerusalem, Cent. — A426

**1988, June 27** ***Perf. 14***

**990** A426 70a multicolored .70 .70
With tab .75

Nature Reserves in the Negev A427

**1988, June 27**

**991** A427 40a Ein Zin .50 .40
**992** A427 60a She'Zaf .70 .60
**993** A427 70a Ramon .90 .75
*Nos. 991-993 (3)* 2.10 1.75
With tabs 2.40

See Nos. 1052-1054, 1154-1156.

Agents Executed During World War II — A428

Portraits: 40a, Havivah Reik (1914-1944). 1.65s, Enzo Hayyim Sereni (1905-1944).

**1988, Sept. 1** **Litho.**

**994** A428 40a multicolored .35 .35
**995** A428 1.65s multicolored 1.40 1.40
#994-995, with tabs 1.90

**Synagogue Models Type of 1987**

Models in the Nahum Goldmann Museum, Tel Aviv: 35a, Kai-Feng Fu Synagogue, 12th cent., China. 60a, Zabludow Synagogue, 17th cent., Poland. 70a, Touro Synagogue, 1763,

Newport, Rhode Island, designed by Peter Harrison.

**1988, Sept. 1** *Perf. 13x14*

**996** A414 35a multicolored .30 .30
**997** A414 60a multicolored .55 .55
**998** A414 70a multicolored .65 .65
*Nos. 996-998 (3)* 1.50 1.50
With tabs 1.60

A429

**1988, Nov. 9** *Perf. 14*

**999** A429 80a multicolored .85 .85
With tab 1.00

Kristallnacht, Nazi pogrom in Germany, 50th anniv.

Moshe Dayan (1915-1981), Foreign Minister, Minister of Defense — A430

**1988, Nov. 9** *Perf. 13*

**1000** A430 40a multicolored .40 .40
With tab .50

Jewish Legion, 70th Anniv. A431

**1988, Nov. 9** *Perf. 14*

**1001** A431 2s yel brn, sepia & lem 1.60 1.60
With tab 1.75

Agricultural Achievements — A433

50a, Avocado (fruit-growing). 60a, Lilium longiflorum (horticulture). 90a, Irrigation.

**1988, Dec. 22** *Perf. 14*

**1004** A433 50a multicolored .45 .45
**1005** A433 60a multicolored .55 .55
**1006** A433 90a multicolored .85 .85
*Nos. 1004-1006 (3)* 1.85 1.85
With tabs 2.00

Natl. Tourism — A434

**1989, Mar. 12** **Litho.** *Perf. 13*

**1007** A434 40a Red Sea .45 .35
**1008** A434 60a Dead Sea .60 .50
**1009** A434 70a Mediterranean Sea .75 .55
**1010** A434 1.70s Sea of Galilee 1.75 1.40
*Nos. 1007-1010 (4)* 3.55 2.80
With tabs 3.75

Rabbi Judah Leib Maimon (1875-1962) — A435

**1989, Mar. 12** *Perf. 14*

**1011** A435 1.70s multi 1.75 1.25
With tab 2.00

Rashi, Rabbi Solomon Ben Isaac (b. 1039), Talmudic Commentator — A436

**1989, Mar. 12**

**1012** A436 4s buff & black 4.25 3.00
With tab 4.50

Memorial Day — A437

UNICEF — A438

Fallen Airmen's Memorial at Har Tayassim.

**1989, Apr. 30** **Litho.** *Perf. 14*

**1013** A437 50a multi .50 .45
With tab .60

**Archaeology Type of 1986**

Gates of Huldah, Temple Compound, Mt. Moriah: 40a, Rosettes and rhomboids, frieze and columns, facade of the eastern gate, 1st cent. B.C. 60a, Corinthian capital, 6th cent.

70a, Bas-relief from the Palace of Umayade Caliphs, 8th cent. 80a, Corinthian capital from the Church of Ascension on the Mount of Olives, 12-13th cent. 90a, Star of David, limestone relief, northern wall, near the new gate, Suleiman's Wall. 2s, Mamluk relief, 14th century. 10s, Carved frieze from a sepulcher entrance, end of the Second Temple Period.

**1988-90** **Litho.** *Perf. 14*

**1014** A389 40a multi .35 .30
**1015** A389 60a multi .50 .40
**1016** A389 70a multi .55 .40
**1017** A389 80a multi .65 .45
**1018** A389 90a multi .65 .45
**1019** A389 2s multi 1.40 .95
**1020** A389 10s multi 8.75 5.75
*Nos. 1014-1020 (7)* 12.85 8.70
With tabs 14.00

Issued: 40a, 60a, 12/22/88; 70a, 80a, 6/11/89; 10s, 4/30/89; 90a, 10/17/89; 2s, 6/12/90.

**1989, Apr. 30** *Perf. 14*

**1022** A438 90a multicolored .80 .65
With tab .90

Moshe Smoira (1888-1961), 1st Pres. of Israeli Supreme Court — A439

**1989, June 11** **Litho.** *Perf. 13*

**1023** A439 90a deep blue .80 .65
With tab .90

13th Maccabiah Games, July 3-13 A440

**1989, June 11** *Perf. 13x14*

**1024** A440 80a multi .80 .65
With tab .90

Ducks — A441

Designs: a, Garganey. b, Mallard. c, Teal. d, Shelduck.

**1989, July 18** **Litho.** *Perf. 14*

**1025** Strip of 4 5.75 5.75
With tabs 9.00
*a.-d.* A441 80a any single 1.25 .85

**Souvenir Sheet**

**1025E** Sheet of 4 7.00 7.00
*f.* A441 80a like No. 1025d 1.60 1.60
*g.* A441 80a like No. 1025b 1.60 1.60
*h.* A441 80a like No. 1025a 1.60 1.60
*i.* A441 80a like No. 1025c 1.60 1.60

World Stamp Expo '89. No. 1025E contains four 29x33mm stamps. Sold for 5s.

Graphic Design Industry — A442

**1989, July 18**

**1026** A442 1s multi 1.00 .75
With tab 1.10

Souvenir Sheet

French Revolution, Bicent. — A443

**1989, July 7**

**1027** A443 3.50s multi 8.50 8.50

Sold for 5s.

Hebrew Language Council, Cent. — A444

**1989, Sept. 3** **Litho.** *Perf. 13x14*

**1028** A444 1s multi .95 .70
With tab 1.10

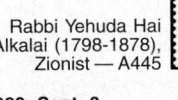

Rabbi Yehuda Hai Alkalai (1798-1878), Zionist — A445

**1989, Sept. 3** *Perf. 14*

**1029** A445 2.50s multi 5.00 1.75
With tab 6.50

Mizrah Festival A446

Paper cutouts: 50a, Menorah and lions, by Gadoliahu Neminsky, Holbenisk, Ukraine, 1921. 70a, Menorah and hands, Morocco, 19th-20th cent. 80a, "Misrah," hunting scene and deer, Germany, 1818.

**1989, Sept. 3** *Perf. 14x13*

**1030** A446 50a multi .45 .35
**1031** A446 70a multi .65 .50
**1032** A446 80a multi .75 .55
*Nos. 1030-1032 (3)* 1.85 1.40
With tabs 2.00

Tevel '89 Youth Stamp Exhibition, Oct. 15-21 A447

**1989, Oct. 12** **Photo.** *Perf. 13x14*

**1033** A447 50a multi .45 .30
With tab .60

1st Israeli Stamp Day — A448

**1989, Oct. 17** **Litho.** *Perf. 14*

**1034** A448 1s multi .85 .75
With tab .95

Special Occasions A449

**1989, Nov. 17** **Photo.** *Perf. 13½x14*

**1035** A449 (50a) Good luck .45 .35
**1036** A449 (50a) With love .45 .35
*a.* Booklet pane of 10 5.00
**1037** A449 (50a) See you again .45 .35
*a.* Booklet pane of 10 + 2 labels 5.75
*b.* Sheet of 20 + 5 labels 11.50
*Nos. 1035-1037 (3)* 1.35 1.05
With tabs 1.75

Nos. 1036a, 1037a contain 5 tete-beche pairs, No. 1037b contains 10 tete-beche pairs.

#1037a-1037b had value of 80a when released.

Issued: No. 1036a, Aug. 7, 1990. Nos. 1037a-1037b, June 22, 1993.

See Nos. 1059-1061, 1073-1075.

A450

Design: Tapestry and Rebab, a Stringed Instrument, from the Museum of Bedouin Culture.

**1990, Feb. 13 Litho. *Perf. 13***

**1038** A450 1.50s multicolored 1.25 .95
With tab 1.50

The Circassians in Israel — A451

Designs: Circassian folk dancers.

**1990, Feb. 13 Photo. *Perf. 14x13***

**1039** A451 1.50s multicolored 1.25 .95
With tab 1.50

Rehovot City, Cent. A452

**1990, Feb. 13 *Perf. 14***

**1040** A452 2s multicolored 1.90 1.40
With tab 2.25

Souvenir Sheet

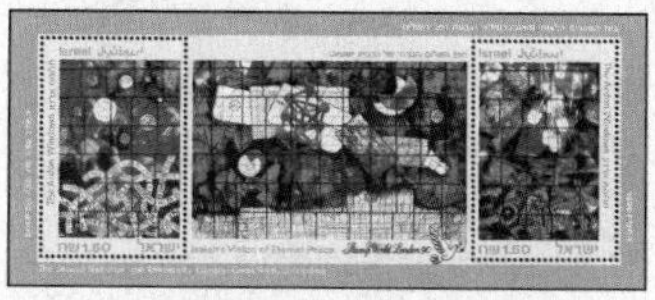
*Isaiah's Vision of Eternal Peace,* by Mordecai Ardon — A453

Series of 3 stained-glass windows, The Hall of Eternal Jewishness and Humanism, Hebrew University Library, Jerusalem: a, "Roads to Jerusalem" (inscription at L). b, Isaiah's prophecy of broken guns beaten into ploughshares (inscription at R).

**1990, Apr. 17 Litho. *Perf. 14***

**1041** Sheet of 2 7.00 7.00
***a.-b.*** A453 1.50s any single 3.00 3.00

Stamp World London '90. Sold for 4.50s.
Also exists imperf. Value $85.

Architecture — A454

Design: 75a, School, Deganya Kibbutz, 1930. 1.10s, Dining hall, Kibbutz Tel Yosef by Leopold Krakauer, 1933. 1.20s, Engel House by Ze'ev Rechter, 1933. 1.40s, Home of Dr. Chaim Weizmann, Rehovot by Erich Mendelsohn, 1936. 1.60s, Jewish Agency for Palestine, Jerusalem, by Yohanan Ratner, 1932.

**1990-92 Photo. *Perf. 14x13½***

**1044** A454 75a black, pale grn & buff .60 .55
**1045** A454 1.10s blk, yel & grn .95 .95
**1046** A454 1.20s blk, bl & yel 1.10 1.10
**1047** A454 1.40s blk, lt lil & buff 1.25 1.25
**1048** A454 1.60s multicolored 1.10 1.10
***a.*** Dotted rose lilac background 1.10 1.10
*Nos. 1044-1048 (5)* 5.00 4.95
With tabs 5.25

No. 1048 has a solid bluish lilac background.

Issued: 75a, 4/17; 1.10s, 1.20s, 12/12; 1.40s, 4/9/91; 1.60s, 4/26/92; #1048a, 7/14/96.

**Nature Reserves Type of 1988**

**1990, Apr. 17 Litho. *Perf. 14***

**1052** A427 60a Gamla, Yehudiyya .55 .45
**1053** A427 80a Huleh .75 .55
**1054** A427 90a Mt. Meron .90 .65
*Nos. 1052-1054 (3)* 2.20 1.65
With tabs 2.50

Memorial Day A456

**1990, Apr. 17 Photo. *Perf. 13x14***

**1055** A456 60a Artillery Corps Memorial .60 .45
With tab .80

Intl. Folklore Festival, Haifa — A457

**1990, June 12 Litho. *Perf. 14***

**1056** 1.90s Denom at UL 2.50 2.50
**1057** 1.90s Denom at UR 2.50 2.50
***a.*** A457 Pair, #1056-1057 5.00 5.00
With tabs 6.00

Hagana, 70th Anniv. — A459

**1990, June 12**

**1058** A459 1.50s multicolored 1.40 1.40
With tab 1.50

**Special Occasions Type of 1989**

**1990, June 12 *Perf. 13½x14***

**1059** A449 55a Good luck .50 .35
**1060** A449 80a See you again .75 .50
**1061** A449 1s With love .95 .60
*Nos. 1059-1061 (3)* 2.20 1.45
With tabs 2.50

Spice Boxes — A460

55a, Austro-Hungarian spice box, 19th cent. 80a, Italian, 19th cent. 1s, German, 18th cent.

**1990, Sept. 4 Litho. *Perf. 13x14***

**1062** A460 55a sil, gray & blk .40 .40
**1063** A460 80a sil, gray & blk .60 .60
**1064** A460 1s multicolored .75 .75
***a.*** Bklt. pane of 6 (3 #1062, 2 #1063, #1064) 7.50 7.50
*Nos. 1062-1064 (3)* 1.75 1.75
With tabs 1.90

A461

**1990, Sept. 4 *Perf. 13***

**1065** A461 1.10s Aliya absorption .85 .85
With tab .90

Electronic Mail — A462

**1990, Sept. 4 *Perf. 14x13***

**1066** A462 1.20s black & grn .90 .90
With tab 1.00

Souvenir Sheet

Beersheba '90 Stamp Exhibition — A463

**1990, Sept. 4 *Perf. 13x14***

**1067** A463 3s multicolored 5.50 5.50

Sold for 4s.

Computer Games — A464

**1990, Dec. 12 Litho. *Perf. 13x14***

**1068** A464 60a Basketball .45 .45
**1069** A464 60a Chess .45 .45
**1070** A464 60a Auto racing .45 .45
*Nos. 1068-1070 (3)* 1.35 1.35
With tabs 1.50

Ze'ev Jabotinsky (1880-1940), Zionist Leader — A465

**1990, Dec. 12 Litho. *Perf. 13x14***

**1071** A465 1.90s multicolored 1.40 1.40
With tab 1.50

Philately Day — A466

**1990, Dec. 12 *Perf. 14***

**1072** A466 1.20s P.O., Yafo, #5 .90 .90
With tab 1.00

**Special Occasions Type of 1989**

**1991, Feb. 19 Photo. *Perf. 13½x14***

**1073** A449 (60a) Happy birthday .45 .35
**1074** A449 (60a) Keep in touch .45 .35
***a.*** Booklet pane of 10 + 2 labels 5.75
***b.*** Sheet of 20 + 5 labels 11.50
**1075** A449 (60a) Greetings .45 .35
*Nos. 1073-1075 (3)* 1.35 1.05
With tabs 1.50

No. 1074a contains 5 tete-beche pairs. No. 1074b contains 10 tete-beche pairs.
Nos. 1074a-1074b had value of 85a when released.
Issued: Nos. 1074a-1074b, 4/18/94.

Famous Women A467

Designs: No. 1076, Sarah Aaronsohn (1890-1917), World War I heroine. No. 1077, Rahel Bluwstein (1890-1931), poet. No. 1078, Lea Goldberg (1911-1970), poet.

**1991, Feb. 19 *Perf. 14***

**1076** A467 1.30s multicolored 1.10 1.10
**1077** A467 1.30s multicolored 1.10 1.10
**1078** A467 1.30s multicolored 1.10 1.10
*Nos. 1076-1078 (3)* 3.30 3.30
With tabs 3.50

See Nos. 1096-1097, 1102-1103.

Hadera, Cent. — A468

**1991, Feb. 19 *Perf. 13***

**1079** A468 2.50s multicolored 2.00 2.00
With tab 2.25

Intelligence Services Memorial, G'lilot A469

**1991, Apr. 9 Litho. *Perf. 14***

**1080** A469 65a multicolored .60 .60
With tab .70

14th Hapoel Games A470

**1991, Apr. 9**

**1081** A470 60a multicolored .55 .50
**1082** A470 90a multicolored .75 .70
**1083** A470 1.10s multicolored .95 .90
*Nos. 1081-1083 (3)* 2.25 2.10
With tabs 2.50

Electrification
A471

Designs: 70a, First power station, Tel Aviv, 1923. 90a, Yarden Power Station, Naharayim, 1932. 1.20s, Rutenberg Power Station, Ashqelon, 1991.

**1991, June 11 Litho. *Perf. 13***

**1084** A471 70a multicolored .65 .60
**1085** A471 90a multicolored .80 .75
**1086** A471 1.20s multicolored 1.10 1.00
*Nos. 1084-1086 (3)* 2.55 2.35
With tabs 2.75

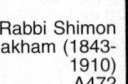

Rabbi Shimon Hakham (1843-1910)
A472

**1991, June 11**

**1087** A472 2.10s multicolored 1.90 1.50
With tab 2.00

Souvenir Sheet

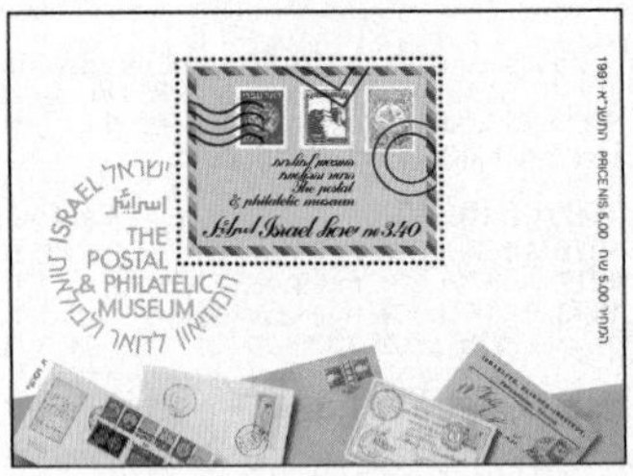

Postal and Philatelic Museum, Tel Aviv — A473

Israel #5, Palestine #70, Turkey #133.

**1991, June 11 *Perf. 14x13***

**1088** A473 3.40s multicolored 7.00 7.00

No. 1088 sold for 5s. Exists imperf. Value $90.

A474

Jewish Festivals: 65a, Man blowing ram's horn, Rosh Hashanah. 1s, Father blessing children, Yom Kippur. 1.20s, Family seated at harvest table, Sukkoth.

**1991, Aug. 27 Litho. *Perf. 14***

**1089** A474 65a multicolored .50 .50
**1090** A474 1s multicolored .75 .75
**1091** A474 1.20s multicolored .90 .90
*Nos. 1089-1091 (3)* 2.15 2.15
With tabs 2.50

Jewish Chronicle, 150th Anniv. — A475

**1991, Aug. 27**

**1092** A475 1.50s multicolored 1.10 1.10
With tab 1.25

Baron Maurice De Hirsch (1831-1896), Founder of Jewish Colonization Assoc. — A476

**1991, Aug. 27 *Perf. 14***

**1093** A476 1.60s multicolored 1.25 1.25
With tab 1.40

Souvenir Sheet

Haifa, by Gustav Bauernfeind — A477

**1991, Aug. 27 *Perf. 14x13***

**1094** A477 3s multicolored 6.25 5.00

Haifa '91, Israeli-Polish Philatelic Exhibition. Sold for 4s.

Philately Day — A478

**1991, Dec. 2 Litho. *Perf. 13***

**1095** A478 70a #2 on piece .50 .50
With tab .60

**Famous Women Type of 1991**

Designs: 1s, Rahel Yanait Ben-Zvi (1886-1979), politician. 1.10s, Dona Gracia (Nasi, 1510?-1569), philanthropist.

**1991, Dec. 2 Litho. *Perf. 14***

**1096** A467 1s multicolored .70 .70
**1097** A467 1.10s multicolored .75 .75
#1096-1097, with tabs 1.60

1992 Summer Olympics, Barcelona — A479

**1991, Dec. 2**

**1098** A479 1.10s multicolored .85 .85
With tab 1.40

Lehi — A480

Etzel — A481

**1991, Dec. 2 *Perf. 14***

**1099** A480 1.50s multicolored 1.00 1.00
With tab 1.25

**1991, Dec. 2**

**1100** A481 1.50s blk & red 1.00 1.00
With tab 1.25

Wolfgang Amadeus Mozart, Death Bicent. — A482

**1991, Dec. 2 *Perf. 13***

**1101** A482 2s multicolored 2.75 1.75
With tab 3.25
*a.* Booklet pane of 4 11.00

One pair in No. 1101a is tete beche.

**Famous Women Type of 1991**

80a, Hanna Rovina (1889-1980), actress. 1.30s, Rivka Guber (1902-81), educator.

**1992, Feb. 18 Litho. *Perf. 14***

**1102** A467 80a multicolored .50 .50
**1103** A467 1.30s multicolored .90 .90
#1102-1103, with tabs 1.50

Sea of Galilee
A483

Anemone
A483a

**1992, Feb. 18**

**1104** A483 85a Trees 1.50 .70
**1105** A483 85a Sailboat 1.50 .70
**1106** A483 85a Fish 1.50 .70
*a.* Strip of 3, #1104-1106 4.50 2.10
With tabs 5.00

**1992, Feb. 18 Photo. *Perf. 13x14***

**1107** A483a (75a) multi .50 .45
With tab .60

PALMAH, 50th Anniv.
A484

The Samaritans
A485

**1992, Feb. 18 Litho. *Perf. 14***

**1108** A484 1.50s multicolored 1.00 1.00
With tab 1.25

**1992, Feb. 18**

**1109** A485 2.60s multicolored 1.75 1.75
With tab 2.25

Rabbi Hayyim Joseph David Azulai (1724-1806)
A486

Rabbi Joseph Hayyim Ben Elijah (1834-1909)
A487

**1992, Apr. 26 *Perf. 13***

**1110** A486 85a multicolored .60 .60

***Perf. 14***

**1111** A487 1.20s multicolored .80 .80
#1110-1111, with tabs 1.75

Discovery of America, 500th Anniv.
A488

**1992, Apr. 26 *Perf. 14***

**1112** A488 1.60s multicolored 1.25 1.25
With tab 1.40

Memorial Day — A488a

**1992, Apr. 26 Litho. *Perf. 13***

**1113** A488a 85a multicolored .55 .55
With tab .60

Souvenir Sheet

Expulsion of Jews from Spain, 500th Anniv. — A489

Designs: No. 1114a, 80a, Map of Palestine. b, 1.10s, Map of Italy, Sicily, Greece and central Mediterranean. c, 1.40s, Map of Spain and Portugal.

**1992, Apr. 26 *Perf. 14***

**1114** A489 Sheet of 3, #a.-c. 3.75 3.75

Jaffa-Jerusalem Railway, Cent. — A490

Different train and four scenes on each stamp showing railroad equipment and memorabilia.

**1992**

**1115** A490 85a multicolored .65 .60
**1116** A490 1s multicolored .80 .75
**1117** A490 1.30s multicolored 1.00 .95
**1118** A490 1.60s multicolored 1.25 1.10
#1115-1118, with tabs 4.00
*a.* Bklt. pane of 4, #1115-1118 4.00

**Souvenir Sheet**

**1118B** Sheet of 4 + 4 labels 4.75 4.75
*c.* A490 50a like #1118 1.00 1.00
*d.* A490 50a like #1117 1.00 1.00
*e.* A490 50a like #1115 1.00 1.00
*f.* A490 50a like #1116 1.00 1.00

Nos. 1115 and 1118, 1116 and 1117 are tete beche in No. 1118a. Nos. 1118c and 1118f, 1118d and 1118e are tete beche in No. 1118B.

Issued: #1118B, Sept. 17; others June 16.

Rabbi Hayyim Benatar (1696-1743)
A491

Rabbi Shalom Sharabi (1720-1777)
A492

**1992, June 16** ***Perf. 13***
1119 A491 1.30s multicolored .90 .90
1120 A492 3s multicolored 2.00 2.00
#1119-1120, with tabs 3.25

Jewish Natl. & University Library, Jerusalem, Cent. — A493

85a, Parables, 1491. 1s, Italian manuscript, 15th cent. 1.20s, Bible translation by Martin Buber.

**1992, Sept. 17** **Litho.** ***Perf. 13x14***
1121 A493 85a multicolored .55 .55
1122 A493 1s multicolored .65 .65
1123 A493 1.20s multicolored .80 .80
*Nos. 1121-1123 (3)* 2.00 2.00
With tabs 2.25

Supreme Court A494

**1992, Sept. 17** ***Perf. 14***
1124 A494 3.60s multicolored 2.10 2.10
With tab 2.25

Wild Animals A495

#1125, Panthera pardus saxicolor. #1126, Elephas maximus. #1127, Pan troglodytes. #1128, Panthera leo persica.

**1992, Sept. 17**
1125 A495 50a multicolored .50 .50
1126 A495 50a multicolored .50 .50
1127 A495 50a multicolored .50 .50
1128 A495 50a multicolored .50 .50
*a.* Strip of 4, #1125-1128 2.25 2.25
With tabs 2.50

European Unification A496

**1992, Dec. 8** **Litho.** ***Perf. 13***
1129 A496 1.50s multicolored .90 .90
With tab 1.00

Stamp Day.

First Hebrew Film, 75th Anniv. — A497

Films: 80a, Liberation of the Jews, 1918. 2.70s, Oded, the Vagabond, 1932, first Hebrew feature film. 3.50s, The Promised Land, 1935, first Hebrew talkie.

**1992, Dec. 8**
1130 A497 80a multicolored .60 .60
1131 A497 2.70s multicolored 1.90 1.90
1132 A497 3.50s multicolored 2.50 2.50
*Nos. 1130-1132 (3)* 5.00 5.00
With tabs 5.25

Birds — A498

**1992-98** **Photo.** ***Perf. 13x14***
1133 A498 10a Wallcreeper .25 .25
1134 A498 20a Tristram's grackle .25 .25
1135 A498 30a White wagtail .25 .25
1137 A498 50a Palestine sunbird .30 .25
1141 A498 85a Sinai rosefinch .45 .30
1142 A498 90a Swallow .60 .60
1142A A498 1s Trumpeter finch .65 .65
*b.* Violet background .65 .65
1143 A498 1.30s Graceful warbler .70 .45
1144 A498 1.50s Black-eared wheatear .85 .55
1146 A498 1.70s Common bulbul .85 .55
*Nos. 1133-1146 (10)* 5.15 4.10
With tabs 5.25

No. 1142A has a gray background.

### Souvenir Sheet

Designs: a, like #1133. b, like #1137. c, like #1135. d, like #1134. e, like #1141. f, like #1144. g, like #1146. h, like #1142A. i, like #1143. j, like #1142.

**Litho.** ***Perf. 14***
1152 Sheet of 10 6.00 6.00
*a.-j.* A498 30a Any single .50 .50

Nos. 1152a-1152j, issued for China '96, 9th Asian Intl. Philatelic Exhibition, have color variations and a gray border.

Issued: 10a, 20a, 30a, 90a, 12/8; 1.30s, 1.70s, 12/9/93; 50a, 1.50s, 2/16/93; 85a, 2/8/94; 1s, 6/7/95; #1152, 4/17/96; #1142Ab, 11/22/98.

Menachem Begin (1913-92), Prime Minister 1977-83 — A499

**1993, Feb. 16** **Litho.** ***Perf. 13***
1153 A499 80a multicolored .45 .45
With tab .50

### Nature Reserves Type of 1988

**1993, Feb. 16** ***Perf. 14***
1154 A427 1.20s Hof Dor .70 .70
1155 A427 1.50s Nahal Ammud .90 .90
1156 A427 1.70s Nahal Ayun .95 .95
*Nos. 1154-1156 (3)* 2.55 2.55
With tabs 2.75

Baha'i World Center, Haifa — A500

**1993, Feb. 16** ***Perf. 13***
1157 A500 3.50s multicolored 3.25 2.25
With tab 5.25

Medical Corps Memorial — A501

**1993, Apr. 18** **Litho.** ***Perf. 13***
1158 A501 80a multicolored .45 .45
With tab .55

Scientific Concepts A502

Warsaw Ghetto Uprising, 50th Anniv. A503

**1993, Apr. 18** ***Perf. 14***
1159 A502 80a Principle of lift .50 .50
1160 A502 80a Waves .50 .50
1161 A502 80a Color mixing .50 .50
1162 A502 80a Eye's memory .50 .50
*a.* Strip of 4, #1159-1162 2.00 2.00
With tabs 2.25

**1993, Apr. 18** ***Perf. 14***
1163 A503 1.20s gray, black & yel .80 .80
With tab .85

See Poland No. 3151.

Independence, 45th Anniv. — A504

**1993, Apr. 18** ***Perf. 14***
1164 A504 3.60s multicolored 2.25 2.25
With tab 2.50

Giulio Racah (1909-1965), Physicist — A505

1.20s, Aharon Katchalsky-Katzir (1913-72), chemist.

**1993, June 29** **Photo.** ***Perf. 13x14***
1165 A505 80a magenta, bister & blue .45 .45
1166 A505 1.20s magenta, bister & blue .65 .65
#1165-1166, with tabs 1.25

Traffic Safety — A506

Fight Against Drugs — A507

Children's drawings: 80a, Family crossing street. 1.20s, Traffic signs. 1.50s, Traffic director with hand as face.

**1993, June 29** **Litho.** ***Perf. 14***
1167 A506 80a multicolored .50 .50
1168 A506 1.20s multicolored .80 .80
1169 A506 1.50s multicolored .95 .95
*Nos. 1167-1169 (3)* 2.25 2.25
With tabs 2.50

**1993, June 29** ***Perf. 14***
1170 A507 2.80s multicolored 1.75 1.75
With tab 1.90

14th Maccabiah Games A508

**1993, June 29** ***Perf. 14***
1171 A508 3.60s multicolored 2.25 2.25
With tab 2.50

Respect for the Elderly A509

Festivals A510

**1993, Aug. 22** **Litho.** ***Perf. 14***
1172 A509 80a multicolored .50 .50
With tab .55

**1993, Aug. 22** ***Perf. 14***
1173 A510 80a Wheat .55 .55
1174 A510 1.20s Grapes .75 .75
1175 A510 1.50s Olives .95 .95
*Nos. 1173-1175 (3)* 2.25 2.25
With tabs 2.50

Environmental Protection — A511

**1993, Aug. 22**
1176 A511 1.20s multicolored .80 .80
With tab .85

B'nai B'rith, 150th Anniv. — A512

**1993, Aug. 22** ***Perf. 13***
1177 A512 1.50s multicolored .90 .90
With tab 1.00

### Souvenir Sheet

Telafila '93, Israel-Romania Philatelic Exhibition — A513

3.60s, Immigrant Ship, by Marcel Janco.

**1993, Aug. 21** **Litho.** ***Perf. 14x13***
1178 A513 3.60s multicolored 2.50 2.50

Hebrew Magazines for Children, Cent. A514

**1993, Dec. 9 Litho.** ***Perf. 14***

**1179** A514 1.50s multicolored .90 .90
With tab 1.00

Philately Day.

Hanukkah A515

Hanukkah lamp with candles lit and: 90a, Oil lamp, Talmudic Period. 1.30s, Hanukkah Lamp, Eretz Israel carved stone, 20th cent. 2s, Lighting the Hanukkah Lamp, Rothschild Miscellany illuminated manuscript, c. 1470. #1183, Moroccan lamp, Mazagan. #1184: Folding Hanukkah Lamp, Lodz Ghetto, 1944. 2.10s, Coin of the Bar-Kokhba War. 1.80s, Cubic copper savivon (dreidel). 2.15s, Hanukkah lamp "Mattathias the Hasmonean," by Boris Schatz.

**1993-99**

**1180** A515 90a multicolored .55 .55
**1181** A515 1.30s multicolored .80 .80
**1182** A515 2s multicolored 1.25 1.25
**1183** A515 1.50s multicolored .90 .90
**1184** A515 1.50s multicolored 1.00 1.00
**1185** A515 2.10s multicolored 1.25 1.25
**1186** A515 1.80s multicolored 1.00 1.00
**1187** A515 2.15s multicolored 1.10 1.10
*Nos. 1180-1187 (8)* 7.85 7.85
With tabs 8.75

The numbering of this set reflects the lighting of the candles on the Menorah.

Issued: 90a, 1.30s, 2s, 12/9/93; #1183, 11/27/94; #1184, 12/14/95; #1185-1186, 12/23/97; 2.15s, 1/5/99.

Beetles A516

#1189, Graphopterus serrator. #1190, Potosia cuprea. #1191, Coccinella septempunctata. #1192, Chlorophorus varius.

**1994, Feb. 8 Litho.** ***Perf. 14***

**1189** A516 85a multicolored .45 .40
**1190** A516 85a multicolored .45 .40
**1191** A516 85a multicolored .45 .40
**1192** A516 85a multicolored .45 .40
***a.*** Bklt. pane, 2 each #1189-1192 4.25
*Nos. 1189-1192 (4)* 1.80 1.60
With tabs 1.90

Health — A517

**1994, Feb. 8** ***Perf. 13***

**1193** A517 85a Exercise .55 .40
**1194** A517 1.30s Don't smoke .75 .60
**1195** A517 1.60s Eat sensibly .95 .75
*Nos. 1193-1195 (3)* 2.25 1.75
With tabs 2.50

Mordecai Haffkine (1860-1930), Developer of Cholera Vaccine — A518

**1994, Feb. 8** ***Perf. 14***

**1196** A518 3.85s multicolored 2.25 1.75
With tab 2.50

Intl. Style Architecture in Tel Aviv, 1930-39 A519

#1197, Citrus House, by Karl Rubin, 1936-38. #1198, Assuta Hospital, by Yosef Neufeld, 1934-35. #1199, Cooperative Workers' Housing, by Arieh Sharon, 1934-36.

**1994, Apr. 5 Litho.** ***Perf. 14***

**1197** A519 85a multicolored .50 .50
**1198** A519 85a multicolored .50 .50
**1199** A519 85a multicolored .50 .50
*Nos. 1197-1199 (3)* 1.50 1.50
With tabs 1.60

Memorial Day — A520

85a, Monument to fallen soldiers of Communications, Electronics & Computer Corps, Yehud.

**1994, Apr. 5 Litho.** ***Perf. 14***

**1200** A520 85a multicolored .50 .50
With tab .55

Prevent Violence — A521

**1994, Apr. 5** ***Perf. 13***

**1201** A521 3.85s black & red 2.10 2.10
With tab 2.25

Saul Adler (1895-1966), Scientist — A522

**1994, Apr. 5** ***Perf. 14***

**1202** A522 4.50s multicolored 2.60 2.60
With tab 2.75

Hot Air Ballooning A523

#1203, Filling balloon. #1204, Balloons in flight. #1205, Marking target.

**1994, June 21 Litho.** ***Perf. 14***

**1203** A523 85a multicolored .50 .50
**1204** A523 85a multicolored .50 .50
**1205** A523 85a multicolored .50 .50
*Nos. 1203-1205 (3)* 1.50 1.50
With tabs 1.60

Tarbut Elementary Schools, 75th Anniv. A524

**1994, June 21**

**1206** A524 1.30s multicolored .80 .80
With tab .90

Antoine de St. Exupery (1900-44) A525

**1994, June 21**

**1207** A525 5s multicolored 3.00 3.00
With tab 3.25

Intl. Olympic Committee, Cent. — A526

Peace — A527

**1994, June 21**

**1208** A526 2.25s multicolored 1.40 1.40
With tab 1.50

**1994, Aug. 23 Litho.** ***Perf. 14***

**1209** A527 90a multicolored .55 .55
With tab .60

Peace Between Arabs and Israelis.

Children's Drawings of Bible Stories A528

Designs: 85a, Adam and Eve. 1.30s, Jacob's Dream. 1.60s, Moses in the Bulrushes. 4s, Parting of the Red Sea.

**1994, Aug. 23**

**1210** A528 85a multicolored .50 .50
**1211** A528 1.30s multicolored .80 .80
**1212** A528 1.60s multicolored .95 .95
*Nos. 1210-1212 (3)* 2.25 2.25
With tabs 2.50

**Souvenir Sheet**

***Perf. 13x14***

**1213** A528 4s multicolored 2.75 2.75

No. 1213 contains one 40x51mm stamp.

Immigration to Israel — A529

**1994, Aug. 23** ***Perf. 13***

**1214** A529 1.40s Third Aliya .80 .80
**1215** A529 1.70s Fourth Aliya .95 .95
#1214-1215, with tabs 1.90

Israel-Jordan Peace Treaty — A530

**1994, Oct. 26 Litho.** ***Perf. 14***

**1216** A530 3.50s multicolored 2.00 2.00
With tab 2.25

Public Transportation — A531

Designs: 90a, Ford Model T's, 1920's. 1.40s, White Super buses, 1940's. 1.70s, Leyland Royal Tiger buses, 1960's.

**1994, Nov. 27**

**1217** A531 90a multicolored .55 .55
**1218** A531 1.40s multicolored .90 .90
**1219** A531 1.70s multicolored 1.00 1.00
*Nos. 1217-1219 (3)* 2.45 2.45
With tabs 2.75

Computerization of Post Offices — A532

**1994, Nov. 27**

**1220** A532 3s multicolored 1.90 1.90
With tab 2.00

Dreyfus Affair, Cent. A533

**1994, Nov. 27**

**1221** A533 4.10s multicolored 2.50 2.50
With tab 2.75

Outdoor Sculpture A534

Designs: 90a, Serpentine, by Itzhak Danziger (1916-77), Yarkon Park, Tel Aviv. 1.40s, Stabile, by Alexander Calder (1898-1976), Mount Herzl, Jerusalem. 1.70s, Gate to the Hall of Remembrance, by David Palombo (1920-66), Yad Vashem, Jerusalem.

**1995, Feb. 7 Litho.** ***Perf. 14x13***

**1222** A534 90a multicolored .55 .55
**1223** A534 1.40s multicolored .90 .90
**1224** A534 1.70s multicolored 1.00 1.00
*Nos. 1222-1224 (3)* 2.45 2.45
With tabs 2.75

Jewish Composers A535

Title of work, composer: No. 1225, Schelomo, by Ernest Bloch (1880-1959). No. 1226, Symphony No. 1 - Jeremiah, by Leonard Bernstein (1918-90).

**1995, Feb. 7**

**1225** A535 4.10s multicolored 2.50 2.50
**1226** A535 4.10s multicolored 2.50 2.50
#1225-1226, with tabs 5.50

See Nos. 1231-1232, 1274-1275.

Ordnance Corps Monument, Netanya — A536

**1995, Apr. 25 Litho.** ***Perf. 13***

**1227** A536 1s multicolored .65 .65
With tab .70

End of World War II, Liberation of Concentration Camps, 50th Anniv. — A537

**1995, Apr. 25** *Perf. 14x13*

**1228** A537 1s multicolored .65 .65
With tab .70

### Souvenir Sheet

**1229** A537 2.50s like #1228 1.60 1.60

No. 1229 contains one 51x40mm stamp.

UN, 50th Anniv. A538

**1995, Apr. 25** *Perf. 14*

**1230** A538 1.50s multicolored .90 .90
With tab 1.00

### Composer Type of 1995

#1231, Arnold Schoenberg (1874-1951). #1232, Darius Milhaud (1892-1974).

**1995, Apr. 25**

**1231** A535 2.40s multicolored 1.50 1.50
**1232** A535 2.40s multicolored 1.50 1.50
#1231-1232, with tabs 3.25

Souvenir Sheet

Jewish Volunteers to British Army in World War II — A539

**1995, Apr. 25**

**1233** A539 2.50s multicolored 1.75 1.75
With tab 2.00

15th Hapoel Games, Ramat Gan A540

**1995, June 7** **Litho.** *Perf. 14*

**1234** A540 1s Kayak .65 .65
With tab .70

Kites — A541

Designs: No. 1235, Hexagonal "Tiara" kite, bird-shaped kite, rhombic Eddy kite. No. 1236, Drawing of kite glider, "Cody War Kite," box kite. No. 1237, Rhombic aerobatic kites, aerobatic "Delta" kite, drawing by Otto Lilienthal.

**1995, June 7**

**1235** 1s multicolored .65 .65
**1236** 1s multicolored .65 .65
**1237** 1s multicolored .65 .65
*a.* A541 Strip of 3, #1235-1237 2.00 2.00
With tabs 2.25

Children's Books A542

Designs: 1s, Stars in a Bucket, by Anda Amir-Pinkerfeld. 1.50s, Hurry, Run, Dwarfs, by Miriam Yallan-Stekelis. 1.80s, Daddy's Big Umbrella, by Levin Kipnis.

**1995, June 7**

**1238** A542 1s multicolored .65 .65
**1239** A542 1.50s multicolored 1.00 1.00
**1240** A542 1.80s multicolored 1.25 1.25
*Nos. 1238-1240 (3)* 2.90 2.90
With tabs 3.25

Zim Israel Navigation Co. Ltd., 50th Anniv. A543

**1995, June 7**

**1241** A543 4.40s multicolored 3.00 3.00
With tab 3.25

Festivals A544

Designs: 1s, Elijah's Chair for circumcision, linen cloth. 1.50s, Tallit bag, usually a Bar-Mitzvah gift. 1.80s, Marriage Stone for breaking glass at wedding, cloth.

**1995, Sept. 4** **Litho.** *Perf. 14*

**1242** A544 1s multicolored .65 .65
**1243** A544 1.50s multicolored 1.00 1.00
**1244** A544 1.80s multicolored 1.25 1.25
*Nos. 1242-1244 (3)* 2.90 2.90
With tabs 3.25

Jerusalem, 3000th Anniv. A545

Designs: 1s, 6th Cent. mosaic pavement, Gaza Synagogue. 1.50s, 19th Cent. illustration of city from map of Eretz Israel, by Rabbi Pinie of Safed. 1.80s, Aerial photograph of Knesset, Supreme Court.

**1995, Sept. 4**

**1245** A545 1s multicolored .65 .65
**1246** A545 1.50s multicolored 1.00 1.00
**1247** A545 1.80s multicolored 1.25 1.25
*Nos. 1245-1247 (3)* 2.90 2.90
With tabs 3.25

See Nos. 1862-1863.

Veterinary Services, 75th Anniv. A546

**1995, Sept. 4**

**1248** A546 4.40s multicolored 3.00 3.00
With tab 3.25

Yitzhak Rabin (1922-95), Prime Minister A547

**1995, Dec. 5**

**1249** A547 5s multicolored 3.25 3.25
With tab 3.50

Fire Fighting and Rescue Service, 70th Anniv. A548

Designs: No. 1250, Fighting fire. No. 1251, Rescue vehicle, fireman beside car.

**1995, Dec. 14**

**1250** A548 1s multicolored .65 .65
**1251** A548 1s multicolored .65 .65
#1250-1251, with tabs 1.50

Model Planes A549

**1995, Dec. 14**

**1252** A549 1.80s multicolored 1.25 1.25
With tab 1.40

Philately Day.

Motion Pictures, Cent. A550

Silhouettes of people in theater viewing: 4.40s, Marx Brothers, Simone Signoret, Peter Sellers, Danny Kaye, Al Jolson.

**1995, Dec. 14**

**1253** A550 4.40s multicolored 3.00 3.00
With tab 3.25

### Souvenir Sheet

Jerusalem, City of David, 3000th Anniv. — A551

Designs: a, Mosaic pavement of King David playing harp, Gaza Synagogue, 6th cent. CE. b, Map of Eretz Israel drawn by Rabbi Pinie, 19th cent. c, Present day aerial view of Knesset and Supreme Court.

**1995, Dec. 16**

**1254** Sheet of 3 2.75 2.75
*a.* A551 1s multicolored .60 .60
*b.* A551 1.50s multicolored .90 .90
*c.* A551 1.80s multicolored 1.25 1.25

Sports — A552

**1996-98** **Photo.** *Perf. 13x14*

**1256** A552 1.05s Mountain cycling .65 .65
**1257** A552 1.10s Horseback riding .65 .65
*a.* Booklet pane of 20 13.00
Complete booklet, #1257a 13.00
**1258** A552 1.80s Water skiing 1.00 1.00
**1259** A552 1.90s Paragliding 1.25 1.25
**1260** A552 2s Women's volleyball 1.25 1.25
**1261** A552 2.20s Whitewater rafting 1.25 1.25
**1262** A552 3s Beach bat & ball 1.75 1.75
**1263** A552 5s Archery 3.00 3.00
**1264** A552 10s Rappelling 5.75 5.75
*Nos. 1256-1264 (9)* 16.55 16.55
With tabs 18.50

Issued: 1.05s, 1.90s, 2s, 2/20/96; 1.10s, 5s, 2/13/97; 10s, 7/8/97; 3s, 9/23/97; 1258, 1261, 2/17/98.

### Souvenir Sheet

Synagogue, Dura-Europos, Syria, 3rd Century A.D. — A553

Murals from synagogue walls: a, Temple, walls of Jerusalem. b, Torah Ark niche. c, Anointing of David as king by Prophet Samuel.

**1996, Feb. 20** **Litho.** *Perf. 14x13*

**1266** A553 Sheet of 3 2.75 2.75
*a.* 1.05s multicolored .60 .60
*b.* 1.60s multicolored .90 .90
*c.* 1.90s multicolored 1.25 1.25

Jerusalem, 3000th anniv.

Israel Cattle Breeders' Assoc., 70th Anniv. A554

**1996, Feb. 20** *Perf. 14*

**1267** A554 4.65s multicolored 3.00 3.00
With tab 3.25

Hebrew Writers' Assoc., 75th Anniv. — A555

No. 1269: a, M.J. Berdyczewski. b, Yehuda Burla. c, Devorah Baron. d, Haim Hazaz. e, J.L. Gordon. f, Joseph Hayyim Brenner. g, Abraham Shlonsky. h, Yaakov Shabtai. i, I.L. Peretz. j, Nathan Alterman. k, Saul Tchernichowsky. l, Amir Gilboa. m, Yokheved Bat-Miriam. n, Mendele Mokher Sefarim.

**1996, Apr. 17** **Litho.** *Perf. 14*

**1269** Pane of 14 3.50 3.50
*a.-n.* A555 40a Any single .25 .25

Manufacturers Assoc. of Israel, 75th Anniv. — A556

**1996, Apr. 17**

**1271** A556 1.05s multicolored .65 .65
With tab .75

Monument to the Fallen Israel Police A557

**1996, Apr. 17**

**1272** A557 1.05s multicolored .65 .65
With tab .75

Settlement of Metulla, Cent. — A558

**1996, Apr. 17**

**1273** A558 1.90s multicolored 1.25 1.25
With tab 1.40

### Composer Type of 1995

Designs: No. 1274, Felix Mendelssohn (1809-47). No. 1275, Gustav Mahler (1860-1911).

**1996** **Litho.** ***Perf. 14***

| | | |
|---|---|---|
| **1274** A535 4.65s multicolored | 3.00 | 3.00 |
| **1275** A535 4.65s multicolored | 3.00 | 3.00 |
| #1274-1275, with tabs | 6.50 | |

Issued: #1275, 4/17/96; #1274, 6/25/96.

A559

A560

**1996, June 25**

| | | |
|---|---|---|
| **1276** A559 1.05s multicolored | .65 | .65 |
| With tab | .75 | |

Eleven Jewish settlements in Negev Desert, 50th Anniv.

**1996, June 25**

| | | |
|---|---|---|
| **1277** A560 1.05s Fencing | .65 | .65 |
| **1278** A560 1.60s Pole vault | 1.00 | 1.00 |
| **1279** A560 1.90s Wrestling | 1.25 | 1.25 |
| *a.* Booklet pane of 6, 1 #1277, 2 #1278, 3 #1279 | 6.50 | |
| Complete booklet, #1279a | 6.50 | |
| *Nos. 1277-1279 (3)* | 2.90 | 2.90 |
| With tabs | 3.25 | |

1996 Summer Olympics, Atlanta.

Fruit A561

1.05s, Orange, "sweety", kumquat, lemon. 1.60s, Avocado, persimmon, date, mango, grapes. 1.90s, Carambola, lychee, papaya.

**1996, June 25**

| | | |
|---|---|---|
| **1280** A561 1.05s multicolored | .65 | .65 |
| **1281** A561 1.60s multicolored | 1.00 | 1.00 |
| **1282** A561 1.90s multicolored | 1.25 | 1.25 |
| *Nos. 1280-1282 (3)* | 2.90 | 2.90 |
| With tabs | 3.25 | |

Public Works Department, 75th Anniv. — A562

**1996, Sept. 3** **Litho.** ***Perf. 14***

| | | |
|---|---|---|
| **1283** A562 1.05s multicolored | .65 | .65 |
| With tab | .75 | |

Festivals A563

Stylized designs: 1.05s, Bowl of honey, two lighted candles, Rosh Hashanah. 1.60s, Sukka booth, Sukkot. 1.90s, Inside of synagogue during Torah reading, Simchat Torah.

**1996, Sept. 3**

| | | |
|---|---|---|
| **1284** A563 1.05s multicolored | .65 | .65 |
| **1285** A563 1.60s multicolored | 1.00 | 1.00 |
| **1286** A563 1.90s multicolored | 1.25 | 1.25 |
| *Nos. 1284-1286 (3)* | 2.90 | 2.90 |
| With tabs | 3.25 | |

1st Zionist Congress, Cent. — A564

Designs: 4.65s, Tapestry of Theodore Herzl, David's Tower, shining sun. 5s, Casino building, Basel, site of first congress.

**1996, Sept. 3**

| | | |
|---|---|---|
| **1287** A564 4.65s multicolored | 3.00 | 3.00 |
| With tab | 3.25 | |

**Souvenir Sheet**

| | | |
|---|---|---|
| **1288** A564 5s multicolored | 3.00 | 3.00 |

No. 1288 contains one 40x51mm stamp. See No. 1867.

Hanukkah A565

***Serpentine Die Cut 11***

**1996, Oct. 22** **Photo.**

| | | |
|---|---|---|
| **1289** A565 2.50s multicolored | 1.50 | 1.50 |
| With tab | 1.60 | |

See US No. 3118.

Ha-Shilo'ah, Cent., edited by Ahad Ha'am (1856-1927) — A566

**1996, Dec. 5** **Litho.** ***Perf. 14***

| | | |
|---|---|---|
| **1290** A566 1.15s multicolored | .70 | .70 |
| With tab | .80 | |

Coexistence: Man and Animals — A567

**1996, Dec. 5**

| | | |
|---|---|---|
| **1291** A567 1.10s Birds, aircraft | .65 | .65 |
| **1292** A567 1.75s Pets | 1.10 | 1.10 |
| **1293** A567 2s Dolphins | 1.25 | 1.25 |
| *Nos. 1291-1293 (3)* | 3.00 | 3.00 |
| With tabs | 3.25 | |

Space Research in Israel A568

**1996, Dec. 5**

| | | |
|---|---|---|
| **1294** A568 2.05s multicolored | 1.25 | 1.25 |
| With tab | 1.40 | |

Philately Day.

UOAD (Umbrella Organization of Associations for the Disabled) — A569

**1996, Dec. 5**

| | | |
|---|---|---|
| **1295** A569 5s multicolored | 3.00 | 3.00 |
| With tab | 3.25 | |

**Souvenir Sheet**

Inventors — A570

Designs: a, 1.50s, Alexander Graham Bell (1847-1922). b, 2s, Thomas Alva Edison (1847-1931).

**1997, Feb. 13** **Litho.** ***Perf. 13***

| | | |
|---|---|---|
| **1296** A570 Sheet of 2, #a.-b. | 2.25 | 2.25 |

Hong Kong '97.

Ethnic Costumes A571

1.10s, Ethiopia. 1.70s, Kurdistan. 2s, Salonica.

**1997, Feb. 13** ***Perf. 14***

| | | |
|---|---|---|
| **1297** A571 1.10s multicolored | .65 | .65 |
| **1298** A571 1.70s multicolored | 1.00 | 1.00 |
| **1299** A571 2s multicolored | 1.25 | 1.25 |
| *Nos. 1297-1299 (3)* | 2.90 | 2.90 |
| With tabs | 3.25 | |

Miguel de Cervantes (1547-1616), Writer — A572

**1997, Feb. 13**

| | | |
|---|---|---|
| **1300** A572 3s multicolored | 1.75 | 1.75 |
| With tab | 2.00 | |

Mounument to the Fallen Soldiers of the Logistics Corps A573

**1997, Apr. 30** **Litho.** ***Perf. 14***

| | | |
|---|---|---|
| **1301** A573 1.10s multicolored | .65 | .65 |
| With tab | .70 | |

A574

A575

Jewish monuments in Prague: No. 1302, Tombstone of Rabbi Judah Loew MaHaRal. No. 1303, Altneuschul Synagogue.

**1997, Apr. 30**

| | | |
|---|---|---|
| **1302** A574 1.70s blue & multi | 1.00 | 1.00 |
| **1303** A574 1.70s red & multi | 1.00 | 1.00 |
| *a.* Sheet, 4 each, #1302-1303 | 8.00 | 8.00 |
| #1302-1303, with tabs | 2.25 | |

Stamps in No. 1303a do not have tabs. See Czech Republic Nos. 3009-3010.

**1997, Apr. 30**

Design: "The Vilna Gaon," Rabbi Elijah Ben Solomon Zalman (1720-97).

| | | |
|---|---|---|
| **1304** A575 2s multicolored | 1.25 | 1.25 |
| With tab | 1.40 | |

Organized Clandestine Immigration (1934-48) — A576

**1997, Apr. 30**

| | | |
|---|---|---|
| **1305** A576 5s multicolored | 3.00 | 3.00 |
| With tab | 3.25 | |

**Souvenir Sheet**

Discovery of the Cairo Geniza, Cent., Discovery of Dead Sea Scrolls, 50th Anniv. — A577

Designs: a, 2s, Ben Ezra Synagogue, Cairo. b, 3s, Cliffs, Dead Sea, Prof. Sukenik examining scrolls.

**1997, May 29** **Litho.** ***Perf. 13***

| | | |
|---|---|---|
| **1306** A577 Sheet of 2, #a.-b. | 3.00 | 3.00 |

Pacific '97.

Hello First Grade A578

**1997, July 8** **Litho.** ***Perf. 14***

| | | |
|---|---|---|
| **1307** A578 1.10s multicolored | .65 | .65 |
| With tab | .70 | |

Road Safety — A579

#1308, "Keep in Lane," car sinking into lake, fish. #1309, "Keep Your Distance," car with bird on front grille. #1310, "Don't Drink and Drive," man holding drink, car balanced on edge of cliff.

**1997, July 8** ***Perf. 13***

| | | |
|---|---|---|
| **1308** A579 1.10s multicolored | .65 | .65 |
| **1309** A579 1.10s multicolored | .65 | .65 |
| **1310** A579 1.10s multicolored | .65 | .65 |
| *Nos. 1308-1310 (3)* | 1.95 | 1.95 |
| With tabs | 2.25 | |

15th Maccabiah Games A580

**1997, July 8** ***Perf. 14***

| | | |
|---|---|---|
| **1311** A580 5s Ice skating | 3.00 | 3.00 |
| With tab | 3.25 | |

Festival Stamps — A581

The Visiting Patriarchs, Sukkot: 1.10s, Abraham. 1.70s, Isaac. 2s, Jacob.

**1997, Sept. 23 Litho. *Perf. 14***

**1312** A581 1.10s multicolored .60 .60
**1313** A581 1.70s multicolored .95 .95
**1314** A581 2s multicolored 1.10 1.10
*a.* Booklet pane, 1 #1312, 2 #1313, 3 #1314 5.75
Complete booklet, #1314a 5.75
*Nos. 1312-1314 (3)* 2.65 2.65
With tabs 3.00

Compare with Nos. 1375-1378.

Music and Dance in Israel — A582

Designs: 1.10s, Zimriya, World assembly of choirs. 2s, Karmiel Dance Festival. 3s, Festival of Klezmers (musical instruments).

**1997, Sept. 23 *Perf. 13***

**1315** A582 1.10s multicolored .60 .60
**1316** A582 2s multicolored 1.10 1.10
**1317** A582 3s multicolored 1.75 1.75
*Nos. 1315-1317 (3)* 3.45 3.45
With tabs 3.75

UN Resolution on Creation of Jewish State, 50th Anniv. — A583

**1997, Sept. 23 *Perf. 13x14***

**1318** A583 5s multicolored 2.75 2.75
With tab 3.00

Souvenir Sheet

Pushkin's "Eugene Onegin," Translated by Abraham Shlonsky — A584

**1997, Nov. 19 *Perf. 14x13***

**1319** A584 5s multicolored 2.75 2.75

See Russia No. 6418.

State of Israel, 50th Anniv. in 1998 — A585

**1997, Dec. 23 *Perf. 14***

**1320** A585 (1.10s) multicolored .60 .60
With tab .65
*a.* Size: 17x22mm .60 .60
With tab .65
*b.* Booklet pane, 20 #1320a 12.00
Complete booklet, #1320b 12.00
*c.* As "a," perf. 13x14, photo. .60 .60
With tab .65

No. 1320b consists of two blocks of 10 stamps, tete-beche in relationship to each other. No. 1320 is 18x23mm. No. 1320a has brighter blue stripes in flag.

Issued: #1320a, 2/17/98; #1320c, 5/3/98.

"MACHAL," Overseas Volunteers A586

Designs: 1.80s, "GACHAL," recruitment in the Diaspora.

**1997, Dec. 23**

**1321** A586 1.15s multicolored .65 .65
**1322** A586 1.80s multicolored 1.00 1.00
#1321-1322, with tabs 1.75

Chabad's Children of Chernobyl A587

**1997, Dec. 23**

**1323** A587 2.10s multicolored 1.10 1.10
With tab 1.25

A588

A589

**1997, Dec. 23**

**1324** A588 2.50s Julia Set Fractal 1.40 1.40
With tab 1.50

Philately Day.

**1998, Feb. 17 Litho. *Perf. 14x13***

Three battle fronts during war: Nos. 1325, 1328a (1.50s), Northern Front, photograph of people, Zefat, 1948. Nos. 1326, 1328b (2.50s), Central Front, drawing over photograph of vehicles coming down mountain, outskirts of Jerusalem, 1948. Nos. 1327, 1328c (3s), Southern Front, raising Israeli flag, Elat, 1949.

**1325** A589 1.15s multicolored .65 .65
**1326** A589 1.15s multicolored .65 .65
**1327** A589 1.15s multicolored .65 .65
*Nos. 1325-1327 (3)* 1.95 1.95
With tabs 2.25

**Souvenir Sheet**

**1328** A589 Sheet of 3, #a.-c. 3.90 3.90

War of Independence, 1947-49. No. 1328b is 51x40mm.

See No. 1861.

Chaim Herzog (1918-97), President of Israel A590

**1998, Feb. 17 *Perf. 14***

**1329** A590 5.35s multicolored 3.00 3.00
With tab 3.25

A591

A592

Jewish Contributions to Modern World Culture: a, Franz Kafka (1883-1924), writer. b, George Gershwin. c, Lev Davidovich Landau (1908-68), physicist. d, Albert Einstein. e, Leon Blum (1872-1950), statesman. f, Elizabeth Rachel Felix (1821-58), actress.

**1998, Apr. 27 Litho. *Perf. 14***

**1330** Sheet of 6 + 6 labels 3.00 3.00
*a.-f.* A591 90a Any single .50 .50

See No. 1362.

**1998, Apr. 27**

**1331** A592 1.15s multicolored .60 .60
With tab .65

Memorial Day.

A593

A594

**1998, Apr. 27**

**1332** A593 1.15s multicolored .60 .60
With tab .65

Declaration of the Establishment of the State of Israel, 50th anniv.

**1998, Apr. 27**

**1333** A594 5.35s multicolored 3.00 3.00
With tab 3.25

Israel Defense Forces, 50th anniv.

Holocaust Memorial Day — A595

Non-Jews who risked their lives to save Jews during Holocaust: Giorgio Perlasca, Aristides de Sousa Mendes, Carl Lutz, Sempo Sugihara, Selahattin Ulkumen.

**1998, Apr. 27 *Perf. 13***

**1334** A595 6s multicolored 3.25 3.25
With tab 3.50

Children's Pets — A596

Israel '98: a, Cat. b, Dog. c, Bird. d, Goldfish. e, Hamster. f, Rabbit.

**1998, May 13**

**1335** Sheet of 6 2.00 2.00
*a.-f.* A596 60a Any single .35 .35

No. 1335 contains diagonal perforations so that lower left corner of each stamp can be removed leaving denominated portion in shape of a pentagon.

Postal and Philatelic Museum A597

Illustrations by Kariel Gardosh featuring cartoon character, "Srulik:" a, At post office counter. b, Looking at stamp with magnifying glass. c, Putting mail into post box.

**1998, May 13 *Perf. 14***

**1336** Sheet of 3 3.75 3.75
*a.* A597 1.50s multicolored .80 .80
*b.* A597 2.50s multicolored 1.25 1.25
*c.* A597 3s multicolored 1.60 1.60

Aircraft Used in War of Independence, 1948 — A598

**1998, May 3 Litho. *Perf. 14***

**1337** A598 2.20s Dragon Rapide 1.25 1.25
**1338** A598 2.20s Spitfire 1.25 1.25
**1339** A598 2.20s B-17 Flying Fortress 1.25 1.25
*a.* Strip of 3, #1337-1339 3.75 3.75
With tabs 4.00 4.00

Israel '98.

No. 1339a was issued in sheets containing 2 strips printed tete beche separated by strip of three labels.

A limited-edition booklet exists. It contained the following panes: 1 #1305, 1 #1318, 1 #1320, 1 #1320b, 1 each #1321-1322, 1 each #1325-1327, 1 #1332, 1 #1333, 1 #1339a. Value, $85.

Souvenir Sheet

Mosaic of a Young Woman, Zippori — A599

**1998, May 13**

**1340** A599 5s multicolored 3.25 3.25

Israel '98. Sold for 6s

Souvenir Sheet

King Solomon's Temple — A600

a, Drawing of the temple. b, Inscribed ivory pomegranate.

**1998, May 13**

**1341** A600 Sheet of 2 4.00 4.00
*a.* 2s multicolored 1.60 1.60
*b.* 3s multicolored 2.40 2.40

Israel '98. Sold for 7s

Israel Jubilee Exhibition A601

**1998, Aug. 3 Litho. *Perf. 14x13***
**1342** A601 5.35s multicolored 2.50 2.50
With tab 2.75

Child's Drawing "Living in a World of Mutual Respect" A602

**1998, Sept. 8 *Perf. 14***
**1343** A602 1.15s multicolored .55 .55
With tab .60

Holy Cities A603

**1998, Sept. 8**
**1344** A603 1.80s Hebron .85 .85
**1345** A603 2.20s Jerusalem 1.00 1.00
#1344-1345, with tabs 2.10

See No. 1864.

**1999**
**1346** A603 1.15s Zefat .60 .60
**1347** A603 5.35s Tiberias 2.75 2.75
#1346-1347, with tabs 3.75

Festival Stamps A604

Holy ark curtains: 1.15s, Peacocks on both sides of menorah, text, Star of David. 1.80s, Menorah, text, two lions. 2.20s, Text surrounded by ornate floral pattern.

**1998, Sept. 8**
**1348** A604 1.15s multicolored .55 .55
**1349** A604 1.80s multicolored .85 .85
**1350** A604 2.20s multicolored 1.00 1.00
*Nos. 1348-1350 (3)* 2.40 2.40
With tabs 2.75

Natl. Flag A605

Hyacinth A606

**1998, Dec. 17 Litho. *Die Cut***
**Self-Adhesive**
**1351** A605 1.15s dk bl & bl .55 .55
**1352** A605 2.15s dk bl & grn 1.00 1.00
**1353** A605 3.25s dk bl & rose red 1.60 1.60
**1354** A605 5.35s dk bl & yel org 2.75 2.75
*Nos. 1351-1354 (4)* 5.90 5.90

**1999, Feb. 1 Photo. *Perf. 15***
**1355** A606 (1.15s) multicolored .60 .60
With tab .65

See Nos, 1492A, 1539D-1540.

Knesset, 50th Anniv. A607

**1999, Feb. 1 Litho. *Perf. 14***
**1356** A607 1.80s multicolored .90 .90
With tab 1.00

Manuscript of Rabbi Shalem Shabazi (1619-80), Poet — A608

**1999, Feb. 1**
**1357** A608 2.20s multicolored 1.10 1.10
With tab 1.25

Jewish Colonial Trust, Cent. A609

Drawings from one pound sterling share.

**1999, Feb. 16**
**1358** A609 1.80s multicolored .90 .90
With tab 1.00

Ethnic Costumes A610

Designs: 2.15s, Yemenite Jewry, Yemen. 3.25s, Bene Israel Community, India.

**1999, Feb. 16**
**1359** A610 2.15s multicolored 1.10 1.10
**1360** A610 3.25s multicolored 1.60 1.60
#1359-1360, with tabs 3.00

See Nos. 1373-1374.

Souvenir Sheet

Ancient Boat from Sea of Galilee — A611

a, 3s, Reconstructed boat. b, 5s, Ancient boat.

**1999, Mar. 19 Litho. *Perf. 13***
**1361** A611 Sheet of 2, #a.-b. 4.00 4.00

Australia '99, World Stamp Expo.

**Jewish Contributions to Modern World Culture Type of 1998**

Designs: a, Emile Durkheim (1858-1917), social scientist. b, Paul Ehrlich (1854-1915), medical researcher. c, Rosa Luxemburg (1870-1919), politician. d, Norbert Wiener (1894-1964), mathematician, developer of computer science. e, Sigmund Freud (1856-1939), psychologist, founder of psychoanalysis. f, Martin Buber (1878-1965), religious philosopher.

**1999, Apr. 18 Litho. *Perf. 14***
**1362** Sheet of 6 + 6 labels 2.75 2.75
***a.-f.*** A591 90a Any single .45 .45

Monument for Fallen Bedouin Soldiers A612

**1999, Apr. 18**
**1363** A612 1.20s multicolored .60 .60
With tab .65

Israel's Admission to UN, 50th Anniv. A613

**1999, Apr. 18**
**1364** A613 2.30s multicolored 1.10 1.10
With tab 1.25

Simcha Holtzberg (1924-94), Holocaust Survivor, "Father of Wounded Soldiers" A614

**1999, Apr. 18**
**1365** A614 2.50s multicolored 1.25 1.25
With tab 1.40

Painting, "My Favorite Room," by James Ensor (1860-1949) — A614a

**1999, May 16 Photo. *Perf. 11½***
**1365A** A614a 2.30s multi 1.10 1.10
With tab 1.25

See Belgium No. 1738.

"Lovely Butterfly," Children's Television Show A615

Puppets: No. 1366, Ouza, the goose. No. 1367, Nooly, the chick & Shabi, the snail. No. 1368, Batz, the tortoise, and Pingi, the penguin.

**1999, June 22 Litho. *Perf. 14***
**1366** A615 1.20s multicolored .60 .60
**1367** A615 1.20s multicolored .60 .60
**1368** A615 1.20s multicolored .60 .60
***a.*** Strip of 3, #1366-1368 1.80 1.80
With tabs 2.00

Pilgrimage to the Holy Land A616

**1999, June 22 *Perf. 14x13***
**1369** A616 3s Nazareth 1.50 1.50
**1370** A616 3s River Jordan 1.50 1.50
**1371** A616 3s Jerusalem 1.50 1.50
*Nos. 1369-1371 (3)* 4.50 4.50
With tabs 5.00

Rabbi Or Sharga (?-1794) — A617

Illustration from Musa-Nameh manuscript, by Shahin, depicting battle of Isreal over Amalek.

**1999, June 22 *Perf. 14***
**1372** A617 5.60s multicolored 2.75 2.75
With tab 3.00

**Ethnic Costumes Type of 1999**

Designs: 2.30s, Jewish woman in traditional Moroccan costume. 3.40s, Jewish man in traditional costume of Bukhara.

**1999, Sept. 1 Litho. *Perf. 14***
**1373** A610 2.30s multicolored 1.10 1.10
**1374** A610 3.40s multicolored 1.60 1.60
#1373-1374, with tab 3.00

"Ushpizin," Guests in the Sukkah, Festival of Sukkoth — A619

**1999, Sept. 1**
**1375** A619 1.20s Joseph .60 .60
**1376** A619 1.90s Moses .90 .90
**1377** A619 2.30s Aaron 1.10 1.10
**1378** A619 5.60s David 2.75 2.75
***a.*** Bklt. pane, #1376-1378, 3 #1375 6.75 6.75
Complete booklet, #1378a 6.75
*Nos. 1375-1378 (4)* 5.35 5.35
With tabs 6.00

Stamp Day A620

**1999, Sept. 1**
**1379** A620 5.35s multicolored 2.50 2.50
With tab 2.75

Ceramic Urns, Museum of Jewish Culture, Bratislava, Slovakia — A621

Designs: No. 1380, Urn from 1776 showing man on sick bed, denomination at UL. No. 1381, Urn from 1734 showing funeral procession, denomination at UR.

**1999, Nov. 23 Litho. *Perf. 14***
**1380** A621 1.90s multi .95 .95
**1381** A621 1.90s multi .95 .95
#1380-1381, with tabs 2.10

See Slovakia Nos. 344-345.

Kiryat Shemona, 50th Anniv. A622

**1999, Dec. 7**
**1382** A622 1.20s multicolored .60 .60
With tab .65

Proclamation of Jerusalem as Israel's Capital, 50th Anniv. — A623

**1999, Dec. 7 *Perf. 13x14***
**1383** A623 3.40s multicolored 1.60 1.60
With tab 1.75

Sidna "Baba Sali" The Admor, Israel Abihssira (1890-1984) A624

**1999, Dec. 7** *Perf. 13*

**1384** A624 4.40s multi 2.25 2.25
With tab 2.50

Millennium A625

Designs: 1.40s, Joggers in park. 1.90s, Researcher with flask. 2.30s, Man at computer. 2.80s, Astronaut in space.

**2000, Jan. 1**

**1385** A625 1.40s multi .70 .70
**1386** A625 1.90s multi .95 .95
**1387** A625 2.30s multi 1.10 1.10
**1388** A625 2.80s multi 1.40 1.40
*Nos. 1385-1388 (4)* 4.15 4.15
With tabs 4.75

Stampin' the Future Children's Stamp Design Contest Winners A626

Various children's drawings.

**2000, Jan. 1** *Perf. 13x13½*

**Background Colors**

**1389** A626 1.20s blue .60 .60
**1390** A626 1.90s yel org .95 .95
**1391** A626 2.30s red 1.10 1.10
**1392** A626 3.40s green 1.60 1.60
*Nos. 1389-1392 (4)* 4.25 4.25
With tabs 4.75

Fairy Tales of Hans Christian Andersen (1805-75) A627

1.20s, The Little Mermaid. 1.90s, The Emperor's New Clothes. 2.30s, The Ugly Duckling.

**2000, Feb. 15** **Litho.** *Perf. 13x14*

**1393** A627 1.20s multi .60 .60
**1394** A627 1.90s multi .95 .95
**1395** A627 2.30s multi 1.10 1.10
*Nos. 1393-1395 (3)* 2.65 2.65
With tabs 3.00

Pilgrimage to the Holy Land A628

Churches: 1.40s, All Apostles, Capernaum. 1.90s, St. Andrew's, Jerusalem. 2.30s, Church of the Visitation, Ein Kerem.

**2000, Feb. 15** *Perf. 14x13*

**1396** A628 1.40s multi .70 .70
**1397** A628 1.90s multi .95 .95
**1398** A628 2.30s multi 1.10 1.10
*Nos. 1396-1398 (3)* 2.75 2.75
With tabs 3.00

King Hussein of Jordan (1935-99) A629

Shuni Historic Site A630

**2000, Feb. 15** **Litho.** *Perf. 14*

**1399** A629 4.40s multi 2.25 2.25
With tab 2.50

***Perf. 14 Syncopated***

**2000, Feb. 15** **Photo.**

**1400** A630 2.30s multi 1.10 1.10
With tab 1.25

See #1409, 1427-1428, 1442, 1478, 1492, 1601.

A631

A632

Worldwide Fund for Nature: Various depictions of Blanford's fox.

**2000, May 3** **Litho.** *Perf. 14*

**Denomination Color**

**1401** A631 1.20s red violet .80 .80
**1402** A631 1.20s green .80 .80
**1403** A631 1.20s blue .80 .80
**1404** A631 1.20s yellow .80 .80
*a.* Strip, #1401-1404 + central label 4.00 4.00
With tabs 4.75

See Nos. 1435-1438.

**2000, May 3**

**1405** A632 1.20s multi .60 .60
With tab .65

Memorial Day.

Intl. Communications Day — A633

**2000, May 3** *Perf. 13*

**1406** A633 2.30s multi 1.10 1.10
With tab 1.25

Land of Three Religions A634

**2000, May 3**

**1407** A634 3.40s multi 1.60 1.60
With tab 1.75

See No. 1866.

Johann Sebastian Bach (1685-1750) A635

**2000, May 3**

**1408** A635 5.60s multi 2.75 2.75
With tab 3.00

**Historic Site Type of 2000**

***Perf. 14 Syncopated***

**2000, July 25** **Photo.**

**1409** A630 1.20s Juara .60 .60
With tab .70
*a.* Perf. 14¾x15 Syncopated .60 .60
With tab .70

The line containing the country name in English and Arabic is 10mm long on No. 1409, 11 mm long on No. 1409a.
Issued: #1409a, 2001.

2000 Summer Olympics, Sydney — A636

**2000, July 25** **Litho.** *Perf. 13*

**1410** A636 2.80s multi 1.40 1.40
With tab 1.50

A637

A638

**2000, July 25** *Perf. 14*

**1411** A637 4.40s multi 2.25 2.25
With tab 2.50

King Hassan II of Morocco (1929-99).

**2000, June 25** *Perf. 13½x13*

Israeli food.

**1412** A638 1.40s Couscous .70 .70
**1413** A638 1.90s Gefilte fish .95 .95
**1414** A638 2.30s Falafel 1.10 1.10
*a.* Booklet pane, #1412, 2 #1413, 3 #1414 6.00
Booklet, #1414a 6.00
*Nos. 1412-1414 (3)* 2.75 2.75
With tabs 3.00

Dental Health A639

**2000, Sept. 19** **Litho.** *Perf. 14*

**1415** A639 2.20s multi 1.10 1.10
With tab 1.25

Dohany Synagogue, Budapest A640

**2000, Sept. 19** *Perf. 13x14*

**1416** A640 5.60s multi 2.75 2.75
With tab 3.00

See Hungary No. 3710.

Jewish New Year Cards — A641

Designs: 1.20s, Boy giving girl a gift. 1.90s, Girl holding Zionist flag. 2.30s, Man giving flowers and greetings to woman.

**2000, Sept. 19** *Perf. 14*

**1417** A641 1.20s multi .60 .60
**1418** A641 1.90s multi .95 .95
**1419** A641 2.30s multi 1.10 1.10
*Nos. 1417-1419 (3)* 2.65 2.65
With tabs 3.00

See Nos. 1455-1457.

Aleppo Codex — A642

**2000, Dec. 5** *Perf. 13*

**1420** A642 4.40s multi 2.10 2.10
With tab 2.40

Dinosaurs A643

Designs: No. 1421, Struthiomimuses on beach. No. 1422, Struthiomimuses in forest. No. 1423. Struthiomimus on hill.

**2000, Dec. 5** **Litho.** *Perf. 13*

**1421** A643 2.20s multi 1.10 1.10
**1422** A643 2.20s multi 1.10 1.10
**1423** A643 2.20s multi 1.10 1.10
*a.* Strip of 3, #1421-1423 3.30 3.30
With tabs 3.50

Science Fiction A644

Designs: 2.80s, Robot. 3.40s, Time travel. 5.60s, Space flight.

**2000, Dec. 5** *Perf. 14*

**1424** A644 2.80s multi 1.40 1.40
**1425** A644 3.40s multi 1.75 1.75
**1426** A644 5.60s multi 2.75 2.75
*Nos. 1424-1426 (3)* 5.90 5.90
With tabs 6.50

**Historic Sites Type of 2000**

***Perf. 14 Syncopated***

**2000-2001** **Photo.**

**1427** A630 2.20s Mitzpe Revivim 1.10 1.10
With tab 1.25
**1428** A630 3.40s Ilaniyya 1.75 1.75
With tab 1.90

Issued: 2.20s, 12/5; 3.40s, 2/13/01.

Settlements, Cent. — A645

**2001, Feb. 13 Litho. *Perf. 14***

**1429** A645 2.50s Yavne'el 1.25 1.25
**1430** A645 4.70s Menahamia 2.25 2.25
**1431** A645 5.90s Kefar Tavor 3.00 3.00
*Nos. 1429-1431 (3)* 6.50 6.50
With tabs 7.25

Hebrew Letters Aleph and Beth — A646

No. 1432: a, Aleph. b, Beth. c, Gimel. d, Daleth. e, He. f, Waw. g, Zayin. h, Heth. i, Teth. j, Yod. k, Kaph. l, Lamed. m, Mem. n, Nun. o, Samekh. p, Ayin. q, Pe. r, Sadhe. s, Qoph. t, Resh. u, Sin. v, Taw.

No. 1433 — End-of-word letters: a, Kaph. b, Mem. c, Nun. d, Pe. e, Sadhe.

**2001, Feb. 13 Photo. *Perf. 15***

**1432** Sheet of 22 1.10 1.10
***a.-v.*** A646 10a Any single .25 .25

**Litho.**

***Perf. 14***

**1433** Horiz. strip of 5 .25 .25
***a.-e.*** A646 10a Any single .25 .25
**1434** A646 1s shown .50 .50
With tab .55

No. 1433 issued in sheets of two tete-beche strips. The horizontal strips of stamps in No. 1432 are printed tete-beche.

**Worldwide Fund for Nature Type of 2000 Without WWF Emblem**

Designs: 1.20s, Lesser kestrel. 1.70s, Kuhl's pipistrelle. 2.10s, Roe deer. 2.50s, Greek tortoise.

**2001, Mar. 18 Litho. *Perf. 14***

**1435** A631 1.20s multi .65 .65
**1436** A631 1.70s multi .85 .85
**1437** A631 2.10s multi 1.10 1.10
**1438** A631 2.50s multi 1.40 1.40
***a.*** Booklet pane, 2 each #1435-1438 8.00
*Nos. 1435-1438 (4)* 4.00 4.00
With tabs 4.25

Flowers — A647

No. 1439: a, Prairie gentian (purple). b, Barberton daisy (yellow) c, Star of Bethlehem (orange). d, Calla lily (white).

**2001, Mar. 18**

**1439** Horiz. strip of 4 + 6 labels 2.40 2.40
***a.-d.*** A647 1.20s Any single .60 .60

No. 1439 was printed in sheets of four strips. The second and fourth strips in the sheet have the stamps in reverse order. Sheets sold at the Jerusalem 2001 Stamp Exhibition could have their labels personalized by the purchaser.

See No. 1463.

Souvenir Sheet

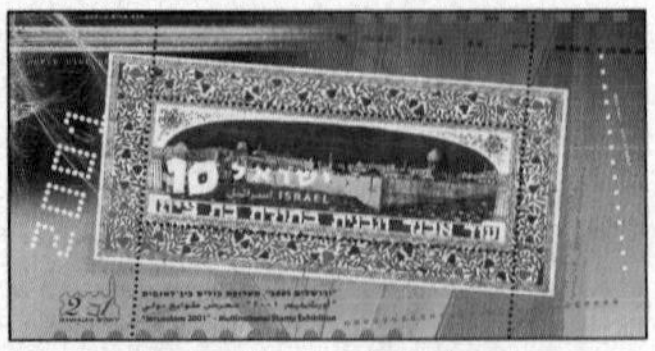

Jerusalem 2001 Stamp Exhibition — A648

**2001, Mar. 18**

**1440** A648 10s multi 5.00 5.00

Monument to Fallen Nahal Soldiers — A649

**2001, Apr. 18 Litho. *Perf. 13***

**1441** A649 1.20s multi .55 .55
With tab .60

Memorial Day.

**Historic Sites Type of 2000**

***Perf. 14 Syncopated***

**2001, May 23 Photo.**

**1442** A630 2s Sha'ar HaGay Inn .95 .95
With tab 1.10

Shrine of the Báb Terraces, Haifa — A650

**2001, May 23 *Perf. 13x13¼***

**1443** A650 3s multi 1.40 1.40
With tab 1.60

Karaite Jews — A651

**2001, May 23 Litho. *Perf. 14***

**1444** A651 5.60s multi 2.75 2.75
With tab 3.00

Souvenir Sheet

Belgica 2001 Intl. Stamp Exhibition, Brussels — A652

Cut diamonds: a, 1.40s, Marquise. b, 1.70s, Round. c, 4.70s, Square.

**2001, May 23 *Perf. 14¾x14½***

**1445** A652 Sheet of 3 4.75 4.75
***a.*** 1.40s multi .85 .85
***b.*** 1.70s multi 1.00 1.00
***c.*** 4.70s multi 2.75 2.75

No. 1445 sold for 10s.

Youth Movements — A653

**2001, July 17 *Perf. 14***

**1446** A653 5.60s multi 2.75 2.75
With tab 3.00

Bezalel School of Art Ceramic Facade Tiles — A654

Landscapes of: 1.20s, Hebron. 1.40s, Jaffa. 1.90s, Haifa. 2.30s, Tiberias.

**2001, July 17 *Perf. 13x14***

**1447** A654 1.20s multi .55 .55
**1448** A654 1.40s multi .65 .65
**1449** A654 1.90s multi .90 .90
**1450** A654 2.30s multi 1.10 1.10
*Nos. 1447-1450 (4)* 3.20 3.20
With tabs 3.50

Souvenir Sheet

Phila Nippon '01, Japan — A655

Children's stamp design contest winners: a, 1.20s, Balloons. b, 1.40s, Cat. c, 2.50s, Veterinarian with dog. d, 4.70s, Dolphins.

**2001, July 17 *Perf. 14¾***

**1451** A655 Sheet of 4 4.75 4.75
***a.*** 1.20s multi .55 .55
***b.*** 1.40s multi .70 .70
***c.*** 2.50s multi 1.25 1.25
***d.*** 4.70s multi 2.25 2.25

No. 1451 sold for 10s.

Shota Rustaveli (c. 1172-c. 1216), Georgian Poet — A656

**2001, Sept. 3 Litho. *Perf. 13x14***

**1452** A656 3.40s multi 1.60 1.60
With tab 1.75

Yehuda Amichai (1924-2000), Poet — A657

**2001, Sept. 3**

**1453** A657 5.60s multi 2.60 2.60
With tab 2.75

Jewish National Fund, Cent — A658

**2001, Sept. 3 *Perf. 14***

**1454** A658 5.60s multi 2.60 2.60
With tab 2.75

**Jewish New Year Cards Type of 2000**

Designs: 1.20s, Soldier, dove with olive branch. 1.90s, Two women. 2.30s, Boy with flowers.

**2001, Sept. 3**

**1455** A641 1.20s multi .55 .55
**1456** A641 1.90s multi .90 .90
**1457** A641 2.30s multi 1.10 1.10
*Nos. 1455-1457 (3)* 2.55 2.55
With tabs 2.75

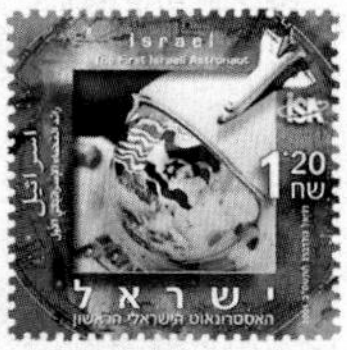

Selection of Col. Ilan Ramon as Israel's First Astronaut — A659

**2001, Dec. 11 Litho. *Perf. 13***

**1458** A659 1.20s multi .55 .55
With tab .65

Akim Association for the Rehabilitation of the Mentally Handicapped, 50th Anniv. — A660

**2001, Dec. 11 *Perf. 13x14***

**1459** A660 2.20s multi 1.00 1.00
With tab 1.10

Heinrich Heine (1797-1856), Poet — A661

**2001, Dec. 11**

**1460** A661 4.40s multi 2.10 2.10
With tab 2.40

Institute for the Blind, Jerusalem, Cent. — A662

**Litho. & Embossed**

**2001, Dec. 11 *Perf. 14¾***

**1461** A662 5.60s multi 2.60 2.60
With tab 3.00

Coastal Conservation — A663

**2001, Dec. 11 Litho. *Perf. 13***

**1462** A663 10s multi 4.75 4.75
With tab 5.25

**Flower Type of 2001**

**2002, Feb. 24 Litho. *Perf. 14***

**1463** A647 1.20s Yellow lily .55 .55
With tab .60

No. 1463 has small picture of flower at left, while No. 1439b has small picture of flower at right.

Languages
A664

**2002, Feb. 24** *Perf. 13x14*

**1464** A664 2.10s Yiddish .90 .90
**1465** A664 2.10s Ladino .90 .90
With tabs 2.00

Mushrooms
A665

Designs: 1.90s, Agaricus campester. 2.20s, Amanita muscaria. 2.80s, Suillus granulatus.

**2002, Feb. 24**

**1466** A665 1.90s multi .80 .80
**1467** A665 2.20s multi .95 .95
**1468** A665 2.80s multi 1.25 1.25
*Nos. 1466-1468 (3)* 3.00 3.00
With tabs 3.50

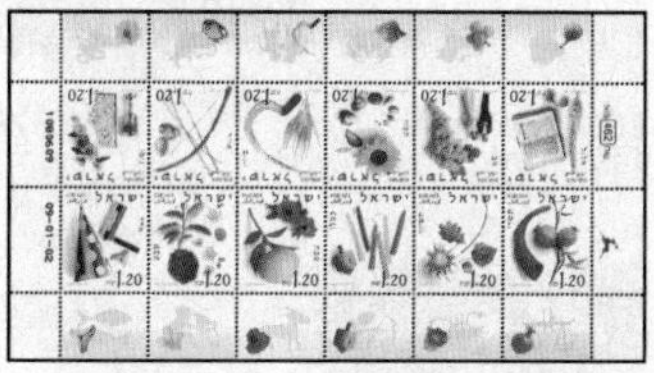

Months of the Year — A666

Designs: a, Tishrei (shofar, pomegranates). b, Heshvan (dried leaves). c, Kislev (dreidel, Hanukkah candles). d, Tevet (orange, flowers). e, Shevat (seedling, flowers, seeds). f, Adar (party hat, noisemaker, hamentashen). g, Nisan (cup, matzoh, flowers). h, Iyyar (bow and arrows, seeds). i, Sivan (wheat, sickle). j, Tammuz (flower, shells). k, Av (bride, groom, grapes). l, Elul, (cotton, dates, prayer book).

**2002, Feb. 24 Photo.** *Perf. 14x14¼*

**1469** A666 Sheet of 12 6.25 6.25
*a.-l.* 1.20s Any single .50 .50

**Self-Adhesive**

***Serpentine Die Cut 16***

**1470** A666 Booklet of 12 6.25
*a.-l.* 1.20s Any single .50 .50

Monument to Fallen Military Police
A667

**2002, Apr. 10 Litho.** *Perf. 14*

**1471** A667 1.20s multi .50 .50
With tab .60

Hakhel Le Yisrael — A668

**2002, Apr. 10** *Perf. 13x14*

**1472** A668 4.70s multi 2.00 2.00
With tab 2.25
*a.* Perf. 13¼x13 (1830a) 3.25 3.25

Issued: No. 1472a, 11/21/10.

Israel Foundation for Handicapped Children, 50th Anniv. — A669

**2002, Apr. 10**

**1473** A669 5.90s multi 2.50 2.50
With tab 2.75

Historians — A670

Designs: No. 1474, Heinrich Graetz (1817-91). No. 1475, Simon Dubnow (1860-1941). No. 1476, Benzion Dinur (1884-1973). No. 1477, Yitzhak Baer (1888-1980).

**2002, Apr. 10** *Perf. 14*

**1474** A670 2.20s multi .90 .90
**1475** A670 2.20s multi .90 .90
**1476** A670 2.20s multi .90 .90
**1477** A670 2.20s multi .90 .90
*Nos. 1474-1477 (4)* 3.60 3.60
With tabs 4.00

See Nos. 1553-1555.

**Historic Sites Type of 2000**

***Perf. 14 Syncopated***

**2002, June 18 Photo.**

**1478** A630 3.30s Hatsar Kinneret 1.40 1.40
With tab 1.60

Cable Cars — A671

**2002, June 18 Litho.** *Perf. 14*

**1479** A671 2.20s Haifa .95 .95
**1480** A671 2.20s Massada .95 .95
**1481** A671 2.20s Menara .95 .95
**1482** A671 2.20s Rosh Haniqra .95 .95
*Nos. 1479-1482 (4)* 3.80 3.80
With tabs 4.25

Souvenir Sheet

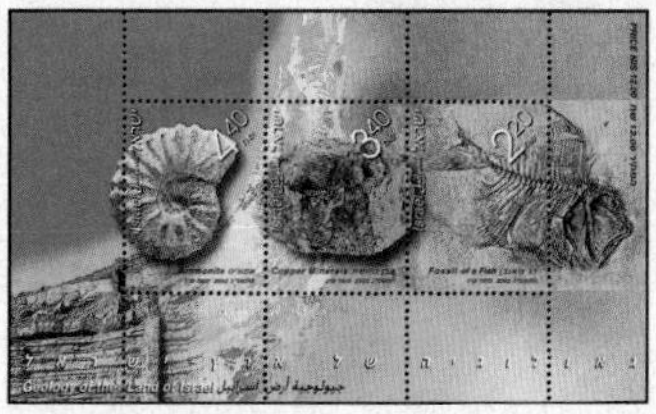

Geology — A672

**2002, June 18**

**1483** A672 Sheet of 3 5.00 5.00
*a.* 2.20s Fish fossil 1.10 1.10
*b.* 3.40s Copper minerals 1.75 1.75
*c.* 4.40s Ammonite 2.10 2.10

No. 1483 sold for 12s.

Rechavam Ze'evy (1926-2001), Assassinated Tourism Minister
A673

Baruch Spinoza (1632-77), Philosopher
A674

**2002, Aug. 27 Litho.** *Perf. 14*

**1484** A673 1.20s multi .50 .50
With tab .60

**2002, Aug. 27** *Perf. 13x14*

**1485** A674 5.90s multi 2.50 2.50
With tab 2.75 2.75

Wine — A675

Designs: 1.20s, Clippers, bunch of grapes. 1.90s, Corkscrew, cork. 2.30s, Wine glass, bottle.

**2002, Aug. 27** *Perf. 14*

**1486** A675 1.20s multi .50 .50
**1487** A675 1.90s multi .80 .80
**1488** A675 2.30s multi 1.00 1.00
*Nos. 1486-1488 (3)* 2.30 2.30
With tabs 2.60

Birds of the Jordan Valley
A676

**2002, Aug. 27** *Perf. 14½x14*

**1489** A676 2.20s Golden eagle .95 .95
**1490** A676 2.20s Black stork .95 .95
**1491** A676 2.20s Common crane .95 .95
*Nos. 1489-1491 (3)* 2.85 2.85
With tabs 3.25

**Historic Sites Type of 2000**

***Perf. 14 Syncopated***

**2002, Aug. 27 Photo.**

**1492** A630 4.60s Kadoorie School 2.00 2.00
With tab 2.25

**Hyacinth Type of 1999**

***Perf. 14 Syncopated***

**2002, Oct. 21 Photo.**

**1492A** A606 (1.20s) multi .55 .55
With tab .60

Political Journalists
A677

Designs: 1.20s, Abba Ahimeir (1897-1962). 3.30s, Israel Eldad (1910-96). 4.70s, Moshe Beilinson (1890-1936). 5.90s, Rabbi Binyamin (1880-1957).

**2002, Nov. 26 Litho.** *Perf. 14*

**1493** A677 1.20s multi .50 .50
**1494** A677 3.30s multi 1.40 1.40
**1495** A677 4.70s multi 2.00 2.00
**1496** A677 5.90s multi 2.50 2.50
*Nos. 1493-1496 (4)* 6.40 6.40
With tabs 7.25

Toys
A678

Menorah
A679

**2002, Nov. 26**

**1497** A678 2.20s Five Stones .95 .95
**1498** A678 2.20s Marbles .95 .95
**1499** A678 2.20s Spinning top .95 .95
**1500** A678 2.20s Yo-yo .95 .95
*Nos. 1497-1500 (4)* 3.80 3.80
With tabs 4.25

**2002-03 Photo.** *Perf. 15x14¾*

**1501** A679 20a red .25 .25
**1502** A679 30a gray olive .25 .25
**1503** A679 40a gray green .25 .25
**1504** A679 50a gray brown .25 .25
**1505** A679 1s purple .40 .40
**1506** A679 1.30s blue .50 .50
*Nos. 1501-1506 (6)* 1.90 1.90
With tabs 1.90

Issued: 30a, 1s, 11/26/02; 20a, 40a, 50a, 1.30s, 2/11/03.

See Nos. 1758-1760.

Yeshivot Hahesder, 50th Anniv. (in 2004)
A680

**2003, Feb. 11 Litho.** *Perf. 14*

**1507** A680 1.20s multi .50 .50
With tab .60

11 September 2001, by Michael Gross — A681

**2003, Feb. 11** *Perf. 13x14*

**1508** A681 2.30s multi .95 .95
With tab 1.10

Monument for the Victims of Hostile Acts, Jerusalem
A682

**2003, Feb. 11** *Perf. 14x13*

**1509** A682 4.70s multi 1.90 1.90
With tab 2.25

Powered Flight, Cent.
A683

Designs: 2.30s, Wright Flyer in flight. 3.30s, Engine, propellor, Wright brothers. 5.90s, Orville Wright piloting Wright Flyer.

**2003, Feb. 11** *Perf. 14*

**1510** A683 2.30s multi .95 .95
**1511** A683 3.30s multi 1.40 1.40
**1512** A683 5.90s multi 2.40 2.40
*Nos. 1510-1512 (3)* 4.75 4.75
With tabs 5.25

Memorial Day — A684

**2003, Apr. 27 Litho. *Perf. 14***
**1513** A684 1.20s multi .55 .55
With tab .65

Holocaust Memorial Day — A685

**2003, Apr. 27 *Perf. 13***
**1514** A685 2.20s multi 1.00 1.00
With tab 1.10

Yemeni Jewish Immigration A686

**2003, Apr. 27 *Perf. 14***
**1515** A686 3.30s multi 1.50 1.50
With tab 1.60

Israeli Aircraft Industries, 50th Anniv. A687

**2003, Apr. 27**
**1516** A687 3.30s multi 1.50 1.50
With tab 1.60

Independence, 55th Anniv. — A688

**2002, Apr. 27**
**1517** A688 5.90s multi 2.75 2.75
With tab 3.00

Famous Men — A689

Designs: 1.90s, Ya'akov Meridor (1913-95), government minister. 2.20s, Ya'akov Dori (1899-1973), first chief of staff of the Israel Defense Forces. 2.80s, Sheikh Ameen Tarif (1898-1993), President of Druse Religious Court.

**2003, Apr. 27 *Perf. 13***
**1518** A689 1.90s multi .85 .85
**1519** A689 2.20s multi 1.00 1.00
**1520** A689 2.80s multi 1.25 1.25
*Nos. 1518-1520 (3)* 3.10 3.10
With tabs 3.50

Greetings — A690

Designs: No. 1521, Open box, Hebrew letters. No. 1522, Bride and groom. No. 1523, Heart as flower.No. 1524, Hot air balloon, flowers. No. 1525, Flowers and ladybug. No. 1526, Boy and teddy bear.

**2003 *Perf. 14***
**1521** A690 (1.20s) multi .55 .55
*a.* Sheet of 12 + 12 labels 9.50 9.50
**1522** A690 (1.20s) multi .55 .55
*a.* Sheet of 12 + 12 labels 9.50 9.50
**1523** A690 (1.20s) multi .55 .55
*a.* Sheet of 12 + 12 labels 9.50 9.50
*Nos. 1521-1523 (3)* 1.65 1.65
With tabs 1.90
**1524** A690 (1.20s) multi .55 .55
*a.* Sheet of 12 + 12 labels 9.50 9.50
**1525** A690 (1.20s) multi .55 .55
*a.* Sheet of 12 + 12 labels 9.50 9.50
**1526** A690 (1.20s) multi .55 .55
*a.* Sheet of 12 + 12 labels 9.50 9.50
*Nos. 1524-1526 (3)* 1.65 1.65
With tabs 1.90

Issued: Nos. 1521-1523, 4/27; Nos. 1524-1526, 6/24; Nos. 1521a-1523a, 1524a-1526a, 10/19. Nos. 1521a-1526a each sold for 21.20s. Labels could be personalized.

Self-adhesive examples of Nos. 1521, 1523, 1524-1526 come from sheets issued in 1999 that sold for much more than face value.

Village Centenaries A691

**2003, June 24 Litho. *Perf. 14***
**1527** A691 3.30s Atlit 1.50 1.50
**1528** A691 3.30s Givat-Ada 1.50 1.50
**1529** A691 3.30s Kfar-Saba 1.50 1.50
*Nos. 1527-1529 (3)* 4.50 4.50
With tabs 5.00

Evolution of the Israeli Flag A692

Designs: 1.90s, Flag of the Prague Jewish community, 15th cent. 2.30s, Ness Ziona flag, 1891. 4.70s, Theodor Herzl's "Der Judenstaat" flag design, 1896. 5.90s, Israeli flag, 1948.

**2003, June 24**
**1530** A692 1.90s multi .90 .90
**1531** A692 2.30s multi 1.10 1.10
**1532** A692 4.70s multi 2.10 2.10
**1533** A692 5.90s multi 2.75 2.75
*Nos. 1530-1533 (4)* 6.85 6.85
With tabs 7.50

Yad Vashem, 50th Anniv. — A693

Stars of David and: No. 1534, List of Jewish forced laborers. No. 1535, Teddy bear, page of testimony.

**2003, Sept. 9 Litho. *Perf. 14***
**1534** A693 2.20s multi 1.00 1.00
**1535** A693 2.20s multi 1.00 1.00
*a.* Pair, #1534-1535 2.00 2.00
Pair with tabs 2.25
*b.* Miniature sheet, 3 #1535a 6.00 6.00

No. 1535b issued 2004.

Olive Oil — A694

Designs: 1.30s, Olives. 1.90s, Olive press. 2.30s, Jars of oil.

**2003, Sept. 9**
**1536** A694 1.30s multi .55 .55
**1537** A694 1.90s multi .85 .85
**1538** A694 2.30s multi 1.00 1.00
*a.* Booklet pane, #1536, 2 #1537, 3 #1538 5.25 —
Complete booklet, #1538a 5.25
*Nos. 1536-1538 (3)* 2.40 2.40
With tabs 2.75

Souvenir Sheet

Armenian Ceramics in Jerusalem — A695

No. 1539: a, Deer, by Karakashian-Balian Studio, 1930s-1940s. b, Bird, by Stepan Karakashian, 1980s. c, Tree of Life, by Marie Balian, 1990s.

**2003, Sept. 9 *Perf.***
**1539** A695 Sheet of 3 6.50 6.50
*a.* 2.30s multi 1.40 1.40
*b.* 3.30s multi 2.10 2.10
*c.* 4.70s multi 3.00 3.00

No. 1539 contains three 31mm diameter stamps and sold for 15s.

### Hyacinth Type of 1999

**2003 Photo. *Perf. 15 Syncopated***
**1539D** A606 (1.20s) multi .60 .60

### Booklet Stamp
### Self-Adhesive
***Serpentine Die Cut 13½x14***

**1540** A606 (1.30s) multi .60 .60
*a.* Booklet pane of 20 12.00

Issued: 1.20s, 10/8; 1.30s, 12/4.

Immigrants to Israel — A696

Designs: 2.10s, Leibowitch family, clerical house, Zikhron Ya'acov. 6.20s, Second Aliya immigrants, Rothschild Ave., Tel Aviv.

**2003, Dec. 9 Litho. *Perf. 13***
**1541** A696 2.10s multi .95 .95
**1542** A696 6.20s multi 3.00 3.00
With tabs 4.50

Famous Men — A697

Designs: 3.30s, Aharon David Gordon (1856-1922), laborer. 4.90s, Emile Habiby (1921-96), journalist, politician. 6.20s, Yehoshua Hankin (1865-1945), land developer.

**2003, Dec. 9 *Perf. 14***
**1543** A697 3.30s multi 1.50 1.50
**1544** A697 4.90s multi 2.25 2.25
**1545** A697 6.20s multi 3.00 3.00
*Nos. 1543-1545 (3)* 6.75 6.75
With tabs 7.50

Children on Wheels — A698

No. 1546: a, Boy on bicycle. b, Girl on roller blades. c, Girl on scooter. d, Boy on skateboard.

**2003, Dec. 9 *Perf. 13¾***
**1546** Horiz. strip of 4 2.40 2.40
*a.-d.* A698 1.30s Any single .60 .60
Strip with tabs 2.75

Philately Day.

Red Sea Fish A699

Designs: No. 1547, Amphiprion bicinctus. No. 1548, Pseudanthias squamipinnis. No. 1549, Pseudochromis fridmani. No. 1550, Chaetodon paucifasciatus.

**2004, Jan. 30 Litho. *Perf. 14***
**1547** A699 1.30s multi .60 .60
**1548** A699 1.30s multi .60 .60
**1549** A699 1.30s multi .60 .60
**1550** A699 1.30s multi .60 .60
*a.* Souvenir sheet, #1547-1550 3.50 3.50
*Nos. 1547-1550 (4)* 2.40 2.40
With tabs 2.75

2004 Hong Kong Stamp Expo (#1550a). No. 1550a sold for 7.50s.

Menachem Begin Heritage Center, Jerusalem A700

**2004, Feb. 24 *Perf. 13***
**1551** A700 2.50s multi 1.10 1.10
With tab 1.25

Col. Ilan Ramon (1954-2003), First Israeli Astronaut A701

**2004, Feb. 24**
**1552** A701 2.60s multi 1.25 1.25
With tab 1.40

### Historians Type of 2002

Designs: 2.40s, Emanuel Ringelblum (1900-44). 3.70s, Jacob Talmon (1916-80). 6.20s, Jacob Herzog (1921-72).

**2004, Feb. 24 *Perf. 14***
**1553** A670 2.40s multi 1.10 1.10
**1554** A670 3.70s multi 1.60 1.60
**1555** A670 6.20s multi, Type I 2.75 2.75
*a.* Type II — —
*Nos. 1553-1555 (3)* 5.45 5.45
With tabs 6.00

Type II has thicker shadows behind the Hebrew characters and numerals, with the shadow at the top of the "6" with a projection, the shadow is visible below, to the right, and above the horizontal line of the "2," and a shadow all around the "0." The background and face are greener, and the width of the color band at the bottom is wider.

Type I has thin shadows behind the Hebrew characters and numerals, with the shadow at the top of the "6" without a projection, the shadow visible below and to the right only of the horizontal line of the "2," and a partial shadow around the "0." The background and face have a lighter shade. The width of the color band at the bottom is narrower.

Memorial Day A702

**2004, Apr. 20 Litho. *Perf. 14***
**1556** A702 1.30s multi .60 .60
With tab .65

FIFA (Fédération Internationale de Football Association), Cent. — A703

**2004, May 3** *Perf. 13*

| | | | | |
|---|---|---|---|---|
| **1557** | A703 2.10s multi | | .95 | .95 |
| | With tab | | 1.10 | |

Printed in sheets of 12 + 4 central labels.

UEFA (European Football Union), 50th Anniv. A704

**2004, May 3** *Perf. 14*

| | | | |
|---|---|---|---|
| **1558** | A704 6.20s multi | 2.75 | 2.75 |
| | With tab | 3.00 | |

Ottoman Clock Towers — A705

**2004, May 3** *Perf. 13x14*

| | | | |
|---|---|---|---|
| **1559** | A705 1.30s Acre | .60 | .60 |
| **1560** | A705 1.30s Safed | .60 | .60 |
| **1561** | A705 1.30s Jaffa | .60 | .60 |
| **1562** | A705 1.30s Jerusalem | .60 | .60 |
| **1563** | A705 1.30s Haifa | .60 | .60 |
| | *Nos. 1559-1563 (5)* | 3.00 | 3.00 |
| | With tabs | 3.25 | |

**Booklet Stamps**

| | | | |
|---|---|---|---|
| **1563A** | A705 3.10s Safed | 1.40 | 1.40 |
| *f.* | Booklet pane of 1 | 1.40 | — |
| **1563B** | A705 3.70s Acre | 1.60 | 1.60 |
| *g.* | Booklet pane of 1 | 1.60 | — |
| **1563C** | A705 5.20s Haifa | 2.25 | 2.25 |
| *h.* | Booklet pane of 1 | 2.25 | — |
| **1563D** | A705 5.50s Jerusalem | 2.40 | 2.40 |
| *i.* | Booklet pane of 1 | 2.40 | — |
| **1563E** | A705 7s Jaffa | 3.00 | 3.00 |
| *j.* | Booklet pane of 1 | 3.40 | — |
| *k.* | Booklet pane, #1563A-1563E | 11.00 | — |
| | Complete booklet, #1563Af, 1563Bg, 1563Ch, 1563Di, 1563Ej, 1563Ek | 22.00 | |
| | *Nos. 1563A-1563E (5)* | 10.65 | 10.65 |

A706

Great Synagogue of Rome — A707

**2004, May 20 Litho.** *Perf. 13x14*

| | | | |
|---|---|---|---|
| **1564** | A706 2.10s multi | .95 | .95 |
| **1565** | A707 2.10s multi | .95 | .95 |
| | With tabs | 2.25 | |

See Italy Nos. 2607-2608.

Theodor Herzl (1860-1904), Zionist Leader — A708

**2004, July 6** *Perf. 13*

| | | | |
|---|---|---|---|
| **1566** | A708 2.50s multi | 1.10 | 1.10 |
| | With tab | 1.25 | |

See Austria No. 1960, Hungary No. 3903.

National Insurance Institute, 50th Anniv. — A709

**2004, July 6**

| | | | |
|---|---|---|---|
| **1567** | A709 7s multi | 3.25 | 3.25 |
| | With tab | 3.75 | |

2004 Summer Olympics, Athens A710

Medals won by Israeli athletes in previous Olympics: 1.50s, 1992 Silver medal, Judo. 2.40s, 1996 Bronze medal, Men's Mistral (windsurfing). 6.90s, 2000 Bronze medal, Kayaking.

**2004, July 6** *Perf. 14*

| | | | |
|---|---|---|---|
| **1568** | A710 1.50s multi | .65 | .65 |
| **1569** | A710 2.40s multi | 1.10 | 1.10 |
| **1570** | A710 6.90s multi | 3.25 | 3.25 |
| | *Nos. 1568-1570 (3)* | 5.00 | 5.00 |
| | With tabs | 5.50 | |

Founding of Herzliya Hebrew High School, Tel Aviv, Cent. (in 2005) — A711

**2004, Aug. 31 Litho.** *Perf. 13x14*

| | | | |
|---|---|---|---|
| **1571** | A711 2.20s multi | 1.00 | 1.00 |
| | With tab | 1.10 | |

Ben-Gurion Heritage Institute — A712

**2004, Aug. 31** *Perf. 13*

| | | | |
|---|---|---|---|
| **1572** | A712 2.50s multi | 1.10 | 1.10 |
| | With tab | 1.25 | |

Adventure Stories — A713

Designs: 2.20s, Eight on the Trail of One, by Yemima Avidar-Tchernovitz (parachutist). 2.50s, The "Hasamba" Series, by Igal Mossinsohn (children, donkey). 2.60s, Our Gang, by Pucho (four people).

**2004, Aug. 31**

| | | | |
|---|---|---|---|
| **1573** | A713 2.20s multi | 1.00 | 1.00 |
| **1574** | A713 2.50s multi | 1.10 | 1.10 |
| **1575** | A713 2.60s multi | 1.25 | 1.25 |
| | *Nos. 1573-1575 (3)* | 3.35 | 3.35 |
| | With tabs | 3.75 | |

Festivals A714

Bread making: 1.50s, Wheat ears, sickle. 2.40s, Mill, wooden fork. 2.70s, Oven, bread shovel.

**2004, Aug. 31** *Perf. 14x13*

| | | | |
|---|---|---|---|
| **1576** | A714 1.50s multi | .65 | .65 |
| **1577** | A714 2.40s multi | 1.10 | 1.10 |
| **1578** | A714 2.70s multi | 1.25 | 1.25 |
| | *Nos. 1576-1578 (3)* | 3.00 | 3.00 |
| | With tabs | 3.25 | |

Opening of Third Terminal at Ben-Gurion Airport A715

**2004, Nov. 2 Litho.** *Perf. 14x13*

| | | | |
|---|---|---|---|
| **1579** | A715 2.70s multi | 1.25 | 1.25 |
| | With tab | 1.40 | |

Winning Design of Telabul 2004 Stamp Designing Contest A716

**2004, Dec. 14**

| | | | |
|---|---|---|---|
| **1580** | A716 1.30s multi | .60 | .60 |
| | With tab | .70 | |

Bank of Israel, 50th Anniv. A717

**2004, Dec. 14**

| | | | |
|---|---|---|---|
| **1581** | A717 6.20s multi | 3.00 | 3.00 |
| | With tab | 3.25 | |

Philately Day A718

Designs: 2.10s, Mailbox of Austrian Postal Services, Jerusalem Post Office. 2.20s, Mailbox of British Mandate era, Lilienblum St. Post Office, Tel Aviv. 3.30s, Modern mailbox, Main Post Office, Tel Aviv.

**2004, Dec. 14**

| | | | |
|---|---|---|---|
| **1582** | A718 2.10s multi | .95 | .95 |
| **1583** | A718 2.20s multi | 1.00 | 1.00 |
| **1584** | A718 3.30s multi | 1.60 | 1.60 |
| | *Nos. 1582-1584 (3)* | 3.55 | 3.55 |
| | With tabs | 4.00 | |

Ancient Water Systems A719

Designs: 2.10s, Hazor water tunnel and ivory cosmetics spoon. 2.20s, Megiddo water system and seal. 3.30s, Caesarea Aqueduct, coin from Caesarea. 6.20s, Hezekiah's tunnel, pool of Siloam, Jerusalem, and imprinted piece of clay.

**2005, Feb. 22 Litho.** *Perf. 14x13*

| | | | |
|---|---|---|---|
| **1585** | A719 2.10s multi | .95 | .95 |
| **1586** | A719 2.20s multi | 1.00 | 1.00 |
| **1587** | A719 3.30s multi | 1.50 | 1.50 |
| **1588** | A719 6.20s multi | 3.00 | 3.00 |
| | *Nos. 1585-1588 (4)* | 6.45 | 6.45 |
| | With tabs | 7.25 | |

Animals in the Bible A720

Designs: Nos. 1589, 1593a, Ostrich. Nos. 1590, 1593b, Brown bear. Nos. 1591, 1593c, Wolf. Nos. 1592, 1592d, Nile crocodile.

**2005, Feb. 22** *Perf. 14x13*

| | | | |
|---|---|---|---|
| **1589** | A720 1.30s yel & multi | .60 | .60 |
| **1590** | A720 1.30s blue & multi | .60 | .60 |
| **1591** | A720 2.20s org & multi | 1.00 | 1.00 |
| **1592** | A720 2.20s pink & multi | 1.00 | 1.00 |
| | *Nos. 1589-1592 (4)* | 3.20 | 3.20 |
| | With tabs | 3.50 | |

**Souvenir Sheet**

*Perf. 14*

| | | | |
|---|---|---|---|
| **1593** | Sheet of 4 | 5.50 | 5.50 |
| *a.* | A720 1.30s yel & multi | .85 | .85 |
| *b.* | A720 2.10s blue & multi | 1.40 | 1.40 |
| *c.* | A720 2.30s org & multi | 1.50 | 1.50 |
| *d.* | A720 2.80s pink & multi | 1.75 | 1.75 |

No. 1593 sold for 12s and contains four 40x25mm stamps.

Memorial Day A721

**2005, May 3 Litho.** *Perf. 14x13½*

| | | | |
|---|---|---|---|
| **1594** | A721 1.50s multi | .70 | .70 |
| | With tab | .80 | |

Reserve Force A722

**2005, May 3**

| | | | |
|---|---|---|---|
| **1595** | A722 2.20s multi | 1.00 | 1.00 |
| | With tab | 1.10 | |

Bar-Ilan University, 50th Anniv. A723

**2005, May 3**

| | | | |
|---|---|---|---|
| **1596** | A723 2.20s multi | 1.00 | 1.00 |
| | With tab | 1.10 | |

End of World War II, 60th Anniv. — A724

No. 1597: a, Jewish partisan and underground fighters. b, Jewish soldiers in Allied forces.

**2005, May 3**

**1597** A724 Horiz. pair 3.00 3.00
*a.-b.* 3.30s Either single 1.50 1.50
With tab 3.25

Schools — A725

Designs: 2.10s, Hebrew kindergarden, Rishon Le-Zion. 6.20s, Lemel Elementary School, Jerusalem.

**2005, May 3** ***Perf. 13½x14***

**1598** A725 2.10s multi 1.00 1.00
**1599** A725 6.20s multi 3.00 3.00
With tabs 4.50 4.50

Pope John Paul II (1920-2005) A726

**2005, May 18 Litho.** ***Perf. 13¾x14***

**1600** A726 3.30s multi 1.50 1.50
With tab 1.75

See No. 1865.

**Historic Sites Type of 2000**

***Serpentine Die Cut 11¼x11***

**2005, June 7 Litho.**

**Booklet Stamp**

**Self-Adhesive**

**1601** A630 2.20s Mitzpe Revimim 1.00 1.00
*a.* Booklet pane of 12 12.00

2005 Maccabiah Games — A727

**2005, July 11** ***Perf. 13¾x14***

**1602** A727 3.30s multi 1.50 1.50
With tab 1.75

Gagea Commutate — A728

***Perf. 14 Syncopated***

**2005, July 26 Photo.**

**1603** A728 (1.30s) multi .60 .60
With tab .70

See Nos. 1618, 1656D.

Maimonides (1138-1204), Rabbi, Philosopher A729

**2005, July 26 Litho.** ***Perf. 13¾x14***

**1604** A729 8.20s multi 3.75 3.75
With tab 4.25

Paintings — A730

Designs: 2.20s, Agrippas Street, by Arie Aroch. 4.90s, Tablets of the Covenant, by Moshe Castel. 6.20s, The Rift in Time, No. 7, by Moshe Kupferman.

**2005, July 26** ***Perf. 13¾x14***

**1605** A730 2.20s multi 1.00 1.00
**1606** A730 4.90s multi 2.25 2.25
**1607** A730 6.20s multi 2.75 2.75
*Nos. 1605-1607 (3)* 6.00 6.00
With tabs 6.75

Prime Minister Yitzhak Rabin (1922-95) and Yitzhak Rabin Center, Tel Aviv — A731

**2005, Sept. 27 Litho.** ***Perf. 13***

**1608** A731 2.20s multi .95 .95
With tab 1.10

Albert Einstein (1879-1955), Physicist — A732

**2005, Sept. 27**

**1609** A732 3.30s multi 1.50 1.50
With tab 1.60

Intl. Year of Physics.
See No. 1620.

Priestly Blessing at Western Wall — A733

**2005, Sept. 27** ***Perf. 13½x14***

**1610** A733 6.20s multi 2.75 2.75
With tab 3.00
*a.* Perf. 13½ (1866a) 4.25 4.25

Issued: No. 1610a, 11/21/10.

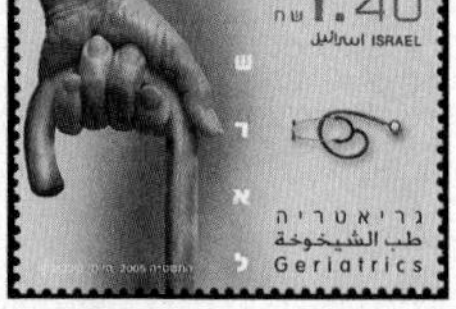

Medicine in Israel A734

**2005, Sept. 27** ***Perf. 14x13½***

**1611** A734 1.40s Geriatrics .65 .65
**1612** A734 2.20s Pediatrics .95 .95
**1613** A734 2.20s Rehabilitation .95 .95
**1614** A734 6.20s Mental Health 2.75 2.75
*Nos. 1611-1614 (4)* 5.30 5.30
With tabs 6.00

Orders of the Mishnah A735

**2005, Sept. 27**

**1615** A735 1.30s Zeraim .60 .60
**1616** A735 2.10s Moed .90 .90
**1617** A735 2.30s Nashim 1.00 1.00
*Nos. 1615-1617 (3)* 2.50 2.50
With tabs 2.75

See Nos. 1653-1655.

**Gagea Commutate Type of 2005**

***Serpentine Die Cut 13½x14***

**2005, Nov. 3 Photo.**

**1618** A728 (1.30s) multi .60 .60
*a.* Booklet pane of 20 12.00

Diplomatic Relations With Germany, 40th Anniv. — A736

**2005, Nov. 3 Litho.** ***Perf. 13***

**1619** A736 2.10s multi .90 .90
With tab 1.00

See Germany No. 2359.

**Einstein Type of 2005**

Souvenir Sheet

**2005, Dec. 27**

**1620** A732 8.20s multi 5.25 5.25

Philately Day, Jerusalem 2006 National Stamp Exhibition. No. 1620 sold for 12s.

Children's Rights — A737

Inscriptions: No. 1621, Childhood is happiness. No. 1622, Indifference hurts. No. 1623, A warm home.

**2005, Dec. 27** ***Perf. 13½x14***

**1621** A737 1.30s multi .60 .60
**1622** A737 1.30s multi .60 .60
**1623** A737 1.30s multi .60 .60
*Nos. 1621-1623 (3)* 1.80 1.80
With tabs 2.00

Theater Personalities A738

Designs: No. 1624, Joseph Millo (1916-97), director. No. 1625, Moshe Halevy (1895-1974), director. No. 1626, Shai K. Ophir (1928-87), actor. No. 1627, Nissim Aloni (1926-88), playwright.

**2005, Dec. 27**

**1624** A738 2.20s multi .95 .95
**1625** A738 2.20s multi .95 .95
**1626** A738 6.20s multi 2.75 2.75
**1627** A738 6.20s multi 2.75 2.75
*Nos. 1624-1627 (4)* 7.40 7.40
With tabs 8.25

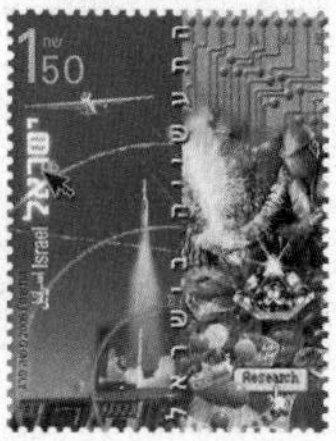

Manufacturers Association of Israel, 85th Anniv. — A739

**2005, Dec. 29 Litho.** ***Perf. 13¾x14***

**1628** A739 1.50s multi .65 .65
With tab .75

Emblem of Israel Post A740

**2006** ***Perf. 14x13¾***

**1629** A740 1.50s multi .65 .65
With tab .75

**Souvenir Sheet**

***Imperf***

**1630** A740 5.90s multi 3.50 3.50

Issued: 1.50s, 2/28; 5.90s, 5/8. Jerusalem 2006 National Stamp Exhibition (#1630). No. 1630 sold for 7.50s. Embossed and numbered examples of No. 1630 were given as gifts and were not available for sale.

Headquarters of Chabad Lubavitch Hasidism, Brooklyn, NY — A741

**2006, Feb. 28** ***Perf. 14x13¾***

**1631** A741 2.50s multi 1.10 1.10
With tab 1.25

Pres. Ezer Weizman (1924-2005) A742

**2005, Feb. 28** ***Perf. 13¾x14***

**1632** A742 7.40s multi 3.25 3.25
With tab 3.50

Children's Art A743

Contest-winning art by Jewish children in US: Nos. 1633, 1637a, Desert Bloom, by Yael Bildner. Nos. 1634, 1637c, Harmony, by Michela T. Janower. Nos. 1635, 1637d, Together in Israel, by Jessica Deutsch. Nos. 1636, 1637b, Colors of Israel, by Marissa Galin.

**2006** ***Perf. 14x13¾***

**1633** A743 1.50s multi .65 .65
**1634** A743 2.40s multi 1.00 1.00
**1635** A743 3.60s multi 1.60 1.60
**1636** A743 7.40s multi 3.25 3.25
*Nos. 1633-1636 (4)* 6.50 6.50
With tabs 7.25

### Souvenir Sheet

*Perf. 14*

| | | | |
|---|---|---|---|
| **1637** | Sheet of 4 | 6.75 | 6.75 |
| *a.* | A743 2.20s multi | 1.10 | 1.10 |
| *b.* | A743 2.40s multi | 1.25 | 1.25 |
| *c.* | A743 3.60s multi | 1.75 | 1.75 |
| *d.* | A743 5.10s multi | 2.60 | 2.60 |

Issued: Nos. 1633-1636, 2/28; No. 1637, 5/28. Washington 2006 World Philatelic Exhibition (#1637). No. 1637 sold for 15s and contains four 40x35mm stamps.

Yad Lashiron Armored Corps Memorial, Latrun A744

**2006, Apr. 11** *Perf. 14x13¾*

| | | | |
|---|---|---|---|
| **1638** | A744 1.50s multi | .70 | .70 |
| | With tab | .80 | |

Memorial Day.

Tel Aviv University, 50th Anniv. A745

**2006, May 8**

| | | | |
|---|---|---|---|
| **1639** | A745 3.60s multi | 1.60 | 1.60 |
| | With tab | 1.75 | |

Tulips — A746

**2006, May 8** *Perf. 14x14¼*

| | | | |
|---|---|---|---|
| **1640** | A746 1.50s shown | .70 | .70 |
| *a.* | Sheet of 12 + 12 labels | 12.50 | 12.50 |
| **1641** | A746 1.50s Columbines | .70 | .70 |
| | With tabs | 1.60 | |
| *a.* | Sheet of 12 + 12 labels | 12.50 | 12.50 |

Nos. 1640a and 1641a each sold for 27s. Labels could be personalized.

Compare with type A647.

### Souvenir Sheet

Jerusalem 2006 National Stamp Exhibition — A747

**2006, May 8** *Perf. 14*

| | | | |
|---|---|---|---|
| **1642** | A747 10s multi | 6.75 | 6.75 |

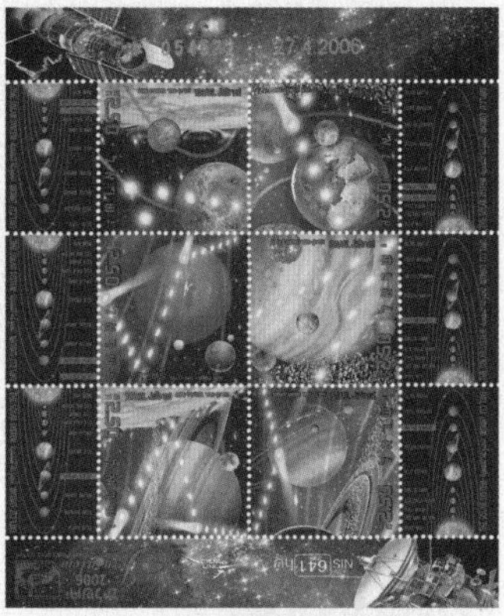

The Solar System — A748

Designs: Nos. 1643a, 1644d, Sun, Mercury and Venus. Nos. 1643b, 1644c, Earth, Moon and Mars. Nos. 1643c, 1644e, Neptune, Pluto, and moons. Nos. 1643d, 1644b, Jupiter, moons and asteroids. Nos. 1643e, 1644f, Saturn, moon, Sun and asteroids. Nos. 1643f, 1644a, Uranus, moons, asteroids, part of Saturn.

**2006, May 8** *Perf. 13*

| | | | |
|---|---|---|---|
| **1643** | A748 Sheet of 6 | 6.75 | 6.75 |
| *a.-f.* | 2.50s Any single | 1.10 | 1.10 |

### Self-Adhesive

*Serpentine Die Cut 11*

| | | | |
|---|---|---|---|
| **1644** | A748 Booklet pane of 6 | 6.75 | |
| *a.-f.* | 2.50s Any single | 1.10 | 1.10 |

Jerusalem 2006 National Stamp Exhibition. The six individual stamps, when separated, could be rearranged to produce a Star of David over the planets.

Religious Zionist Education, Cent. — A749

**2006, July 25** *Perf. 13¾x14*

| | | | |
|---|---|---|---|
| **1645** | A749 3.60s multi | 1.60 | 1.60 |
| | With tab | 1.75 | |

Rabbis of Jerusalem A750

Rabbis: 1.50s, Jacob Saul Eliachar (1817-1906). 2.20s, Samuel Salant (1816-1909). 2.40s, Jacob Meir (1856-1939).

**2006, July 25**

| | | | |
|---|---|---|---|
| **1646** | A750 1.50s multi | .70 | .70 |
| **1647** | A750 2.20s multi | 1.00 | 1.00 |
| **1648** | A750 2.40s multi | 1.10 | 1.10 |
| | *Nos. 1646-1648 (3)* | 2.80 | 2.80 |
| | With tabs | 3.00 | |

Silver Khamsas A751

Khamsa from: 1.50s, Morocco, 1920. 2.50s, Tunisia, 1930. 7.40s, Iran, 1925.

**2006, July 26**

| | | | |
|---|---|---|---|
| **1649** | A751 1.50s multi | .70 | .70 |
| **1650** | A751 2.50s multi | 1.10 | 1.10 |
| **1651** | A751 7.40s multi | 3.50 | 3.50 |
| | *Nos. 1649-1651 (3)* | 5.30 | 5.30 |
| | With tabs | 5.75 | |

Abba Eban (1915-2002), Foreign Minister — A752

**2006, Sept. 12** *Perf. 14x13¾*

| | | | |
|---|---|---|---|
| **1652** | A752 7.30s multi | 3.50 | 3.50 |
| | With tab | 4.00 | |

### Orders of the Mishnah Type of 2005

**2006, Sept. 12**

| | | | |
|---|---|---|---|
| **1653** | A735 1.50s Nezikin | .70 | .70 |
| **1654** | A735 2.20s Kodashim | 1.00 | 1.00 |
| **1655** | A735 2.40s Tohorot | 1.10 | 1.10 |
| | *Nos. 1653-1655 (3)* | 2.80 | 2.80 |
| | With tabs | 3.00 | |

Bezalel Academy of Arts and Design, Cent. — A753

**2006, Sept. 12** *Perf. 13*

| | | | |
|---|---|---|---|
| **1656** | Horiz. strip of 3 | 3.50 | 3.50 |
| *a.* | A753 2.50s green | 1.10 | 1.10 |
| *b.* | A753 2.50s blue | 1.10 | 1.10 |
| *c.* | A753 2.50s orange | 1.10 | 1.10 |
| | Strip with tabs | 4.00 | |

### Gagea Commutate Type of 2005 Redrawn With Two Leaves at Right

**2006, Sept. 20 Litho.** *Perf. 14*

| | | | |
|---|---|---|---|
| **1656D** | A728 (1.50s) multi | .70 | .70 |

Medicinal Herbs and Spices — A754

Designs: 1.50s, Coriandrum sativum. 2.50s, Micromeria fruticosa. 3.30s, Mentha piperita.

**2006, Dec. 17 Litho.** *Perf. 14¼x14*

| | | | |
|---|---|---|---|
| **1657** | A754 1.50s multi | .70 | .70 |
| **1658** | A754 2.50s multi | 1.25 | 1.25 |
| **1659** | A754 3.30s multi | 1.60 | 1.60 |
| | *Nos. 1657-1659 (3)* | 3.55 | 3.55 |
| | With tabs | 4.00 | |

See Nos. 1700-1701, 1747.

Creation of Esperanto Language, 120th Anniv. A755

**2006, Dec. 17** *Perf. 14x13¾*

| | | | |
|---|---|---|---|
| **1660** | A755 3.30s multi | 1.60 | 1.60 |
| | With tab | 1.75 | |

Israeli Fashions A756

Women's fashions from: 1.50s, 1882-1948. 2.50s, 1948-73. 3.30s, 1973-90. 7.30s, 1990-2005.

**2006, Dec. 17** *Perf. 13*

| | | | |
|---|---|---|---|
| **1661** | A756 1.50s multi | .70 | .70 |
| **1662** | A756 2.50s multi | 1.25 | 1.25 |
| **1663** | A756 3.30s multi | 1.60 | 1.60 |
| **1664** | A756 7.30s multi | 3.50 | 3.50 |
| | *Nos. 1661-1664 (4)* | 7.05 | 7.05 |
| | With tabs | 7.75 | |

Crusader Sites in Israel A757

**2006, Dec. 17 Litho.** *Perf. 14x13¾*

| | | | |
|---|---|---|---|
| **1665** | A757 2.50s Atlit | 1.25 | 1.25 |
| **1666** | A757 2.50s Caesarea | 1.25 | 1.25 |
| **1667** | A757 2.50s Montfort | 1.25 | 1.25 |
| **1668** | A757 2.50s Belvoir | 1.25 | 1.25 |
| | *Nos. 1665-1668 (4)* | 5.00 | 5.00 |
| | With tabs | 5.50 | |

Development — A758

Development of the: 2.50s, Negev. 3.30s, Galilee.

**2007, Feb. 20 Litho.** *Perf. 14x13¾*

| | | | |
|---|---|---|---|
| **1669** | A758 2.50s multi | 1.25 | 1.25 |
| **1670** | A758 3.30s multi | 1.60 | 1.60 |
| | With tabs | 3.25 | |

Sports and Physical Education A759

Inscriptions: 2.90s, Physical education in schools. 3s, Wingate Institute. 7.30s, Sport for all.

**2007, Feb. 20**

| | | | |
|---|---|---|---|
| **1671** | A759 2.90s multi | 1.40 | 1.40 |
| **1672** | A759 3s multi | 1.50 | 1.50 |
| **1673** | A759 7.30s multi | 3.50 | 3.50 |
| | *Nos. 1671-1673 (3)* | 6.40 | 6.40 |
| | With tabs | 7.25 | |

Educational Television A760

Designs: Nos. 1674a, 1675, Ma Pit'om (green panel). Nos. 1674b, 1676, Krovim Krovim (blue panel). Nos. 1674c, 1677, No Secrets (orange panel).

**2007, Feb. 20** *Perf. 13¾x14*

| | | | |
|---|---|---|---|
| **1674** | Strip of 3 | 3.75 | 3.75 |
| *a.-c.* | A760 2.50s Any single | 1.25 | 1.25 |
| | Strip with tabs | 4.25 | |

### Booklet Stamps

### Self-Adhesive

*Serpentine Die Cut 10¾x11*

| | | | |
|---|---|---|---|
| **1675** | A760 2.50s multi | 1.25 | 1.25 |
| **1676** | A760 2.50s multi | 1.25 | 1.25 |
| **1677** | A760 2.50s multi | 1.25 | 1.25 |
| *a.* | Booklet pane, 2 each #1675-1677 | 7.50 | |

Memorial Day A761

**2007, Apr. 17 Litho.** *Perf. 14x13¾*
1678 A761 1.50s multi .75 .75
With tab .85

Scouting, Cent. A762

**2007, Apr. 17**
1679 A762 2.50s multi 1.25 1.25
With tab 1.40

Regional Development Towns — A763

Towns in: 2.50s, Northern region. 3.30s, Central region. 7.30s, Southern region.

**2007, Apr. 17**
1680 A763 2.50s multi 1.25 1.25
1681 A763 3.30s multi 1.75 1.75
1682 A763 7.30s multi 3.75 3.75
*Nos. 1680-1682 (3)* 6.75 6.75
With tabs 7.50

Souvenir Sheet

Neve-Tzedek Neighborhood of Tel Aviv, 120th Anniv. — A764

**2007, Apr. 17** *Perf. 13¾x14*
1683 A764 Sheet of 3 7.50 7.50
*a.* 2.20s Founders 1.50 1.50
*b.* 3.30s Neve-Tzedek 2.25 2.25
*c.* 5.80s Intellectuals 3.75 3.75

No. 1683 sold for 15s.

Reunification of Jerusalem, 40th Anniv. — A765

**2007, May 16**
1684 A765 1.50s multi .75 .75
With tab .85

Volunteer Organizations A766

**2007, June 20** *Perf. 13*
1685 A766 1.50s multi .75 .75
With tab .85

Israel Prison Service — A767

**2007, June 20** *Perf. 13¾x14*
1686 A767 2.50s multi 1.25 1.25
With tab 1.40

Dance — A768

No. 1687: a, Ballet. b, Ethnic dance. c, Israeli folk dance. d, Modern dance.

**2007, June 20**
1687 Horiz. strip of 4 4.25 4.25
*a.-d.* A768 2.20s Any single 1.00 1.00
Strip with tabs 4.75

UNESCO World Heritage Sites A769

Designs: 3.30s, Akko (Acre). 5s, 10s, Tel Aviv. 5.80s, Masada.

**2007** *Perf. 14x13¾*
1688 A769 3.30s multi 1.60 1.60
1689 A769 5s multi 2.40 2.40
1690 A769 5.80s multi 2.75 2.75
*Nos. 1688-1690 (3)* 6.75 6.75
With tabs 7.50

**Souvenir Sheet**

1691 A769 10s multi 7.25 7.25

Issued: 3.30s, 5s, 5.80s, 6/20; 10s, 8/27. Tel Aviv, cent. (#1691). No. 1691 sold for 15s.

Beach — A770

**2007, Aug. 27** *Perf. 14*
1692 A770 (1.50s) multi .75 .75
With tab .85
*a.* Miniature sheet of 12 + 12 labels 13.50 13.50

No. 1692a sold for 27s. Labels could be personalized. Self-adhesive examples of No. 1692 come from sheets issued in 1999 that sold for much more than face value.

Hashomer A771

**2007, Aug. 27** *Perf. 14x13¾*
1693 A771 3.30s multi 1.60 1.60
With tab 1.75

Israel Reserve Forces — A772

**2007, Aug. 27** *Perf. 13¾x14*
1694 A772 7.30s multi 3.75 3.75
With tab 4.25

Chalom Messas (1909-2003), Chief Rabbi of Morocco and Jerusalem A773

**2007, Aug. 27**
1695 A773 7.30s multi 3.75 3.75
With tab 4.25

Women of the Bible — A774

**2007, Aug. 27**
1696 A774 1.50s Jael .75 .75
1697 A774 2.20s Esther 1.10 1.10
1698 A774 2.40s Miriam 1.25 1.25
*Nos. 1696-1698 (3)* 3.10 3.10
With tabs 3.50

**Theodor Herzl Type of 1986**
***Serpentine Die Cut 13½x13¾***
**2007, Nov. 1** **Litho.**
**Self-Adhesive**
1699 A388 5a blue & ultra .25 .25

**Medicinal Herbs and Spices Type of 2006**

Designs: 1.55s, Laurus nobilis. 2.25s, Coridothymus capitatus.

**2007, Nov. 5** *Perf. 14*
1700 A754 1.55s multi .80 .80
1701 A754 2.25s multi 1.25 1.25
With tabs 2.25

Rabbi Itzhak Kaduri (1902-2006) A775

**2007, Dec. 5** *Perf. 13½x14*
1702 A775 8.15s multi 4.25 4.25
With tab 4.75

Tel Aviv Movie Theaters A776

Designs: 4.50s, Eden Cinema. 4.60s, Mograbi Cinema.

**2007, Dec. 5** *Perf. 14x13½*
1703 A776 4.50s multi 2.40 2.40
1704 A776 4.60s multi 2.40 2.40
With tabs 5.25

Family Love — A777

Designs: 1.55s, Boy giving flower to mother. 2.25s, Girl with baby brother. 3.55s. Father and son.

**2007, Dec. 5** *Perf. 13½x14*
1705 A777 1.55s multi .80 .80
1706 A777 2.25s multi 1.25 1.25
1707 A777 3.55s multi 1.90 1.90
*Nos. 1705-1707 (3)* 3.95 3.95
With tabs 4.50

Hula Nature Reserve A778

Designs: Nos. 1708a, 1710, Pelicans, Caspian terrapins, iris (denomination in yellow). Nos. 1708b, 1709, Water buffalos, marbled duck, reed warbler, wildcat, wild raspberry (denomination in red violet). Nos. 1708c, 1711, Otter, catfish, cranes, willow herb (denomination in orange).

**2007, Dec. 5** *Perf. 14x13½*
1708 Strip of 3 3.75 3.75
*a.-c.* A778 2.25s Any single 1.25 1.25
Strip with tabs 4.25

**Booklet Stamps**
**Self-Adhesive**
***Serpentine Die Cut 11x10¼***
1709 A778 2.25s multi 1.25 1.25
1710 A778 2.25s multi 1.25 1.25
1711 A778 2.25s multi 1.25 1.25
*a.* Booklet pane, 2 each #1709-1711 7.50
*Nos. 1709-1711 (3)* 3.75 3.75

Miniature Sheet

Noah's Ark — A779

No. 1712: a, Dove and olive branch. b, Noah and family, animals, leaving ark. c, Camels, giraffes, zebra, elephants, whale. d, Peafowl, bears, tiger. e, Lions, wolf. f, Wolf, leopards, goats, kangaroos.

**2007, Dec. 5** *Perf. 14*
1712 A779 Sheet of 6 8.50 8.50
*a.-f.* 2.25s Any single 1.40 1.40

World Stamp Championship Israel 2008. No. 1712 sold for 16s. A limited edition booklet containing two self-adhesive examples of Nos. 1712a-1712f sold at the Israel 2008 World Stamp Championship Philatelic Exhibtion, Tel Aviv.

Israel Rokach (1896-1959), Mayor of Tel Aviv — A780

**2008, Jan. 27 Litho.** ***Perf. 14x13¾***

**1713** A780 2.25s multi 1.25 1.25
With tab 1.40

Tel Aviv Land Lottery, Cent. (in 2009) — A781

**2008, Jan. 27** ***Perf. 13***

**1714** A781 4.50s multi 2.50 2.50
With tab 2.75

Intl. Holocaust Remembrance Day — A782

**2008, Jan. 27** ***Perf. 14***

**1715** A782 4.60s multi 2.60 2.60
With tab 3.00

See United Nations No.948, United Nations Offices in Geneva No.479, United Nations Offices in Vienna No. 412.

Mekorot, National Water System, 70th Anniv. — A783

**2008, Jan. 27** ***Perf. 13¾x14***

**1716** A783 5.80s multi 3.25 3.25
With tab 3.75

Akiva Aryeh Weiss (1868-1947), Tel Aviv Builder and Developer — A784

**2008, Jan. 27** ***Perf. 14x13¾***

**1717** A784 8.15s multi 4.75 4.75
With tab 5.25

UNESCO World Heritage Sites A785

Designs: 2.25s, Biblical Tels. 3.40s, Incense Route.

**2008, Jan. 27**

**1718** A785 2.25s multi 1.25 1.25
**1719** A785 3.40s multi 1.90 1.90
With tabs 3.50

Israeli Boy and Flag — A786

Flowers — A787

**2008, Apr. 28 Litho.** ***Perf. 14***

**1720** A786 (1.55s) multi .90 .90
With tab 1.00

**Booklet Stamp**
**Self-Adhesive**
***Serpentine Die Cut 13½x14***

**1721** A786 (1.55s) multi .90 .90
*a.* Booklet pane of 20 18.00

**2008, Apr. 28** ***Perf. 14***

**1722** A787 (1.55s) White roses .90 .90
**1723** A787 (1.55s) Cyclamen persicum .90 .90
With tabs 2.00

Self-adhesive examples of Nos. 1722-1723 come from sheets issued in 1999 that sold for much more than face value.

Independence, 60th Anniv. — A788

**2008, Apr. 28** ***Perf. 14x13¾***

**1724** A788 1.55s multi .90 .90
With tab 1.00

Memorial Day — A789

**2008, Apr. 28** ***Perf. 13¾x14***

**1725** A789 1.55s multi .90 .90
With tab 1.00

Israel Export Institute, 50th Anniv. A790

**2008, Apr. 28** ***Perf. 14x13¾***

**1726** A790 2.80s multi 1.60 1.60
With tab 1.75

Souvenir Sheet

Hatikva (National Anthem), 120th Anniv. — A791

**2008, Apr. 28** ***Perf. 13¾***

**1727** A791 10s multi 8.75 8.75

No. 1727 sold for 15s.

Miniature Sheet

Independence Day Posters — A792

No. 1728 — Poster from: a, 1981 (green panel). b, 1991 (brown panel). c, 2006 (blue panel). d, 1971 (purple panel). e, 1965 (dark red panel). f, 1952 (orange panel).

**2008, Apr. 28** ***Perf. 13¾x14***

**1728** A792 Sheet of 6 8.00 8.00
*a.-f.* 2.25s Any single 1.25 1.25

Children's Art — A793

Designs: No. 1729, I Love Israel (numbers, symbols, Hebrew and Roman letters), by Etai Epstein. No. 1730, Israel is My Home (Hebrew letters, house and map of Israel), by Yuval Sulema and Eden Vilker. No. 1731, Israel's 60th, (girl, telescope, cat, butterflies, flowers and "60"), by Daniel Hazan.

**2008, May 14 Litho.** ***Perf. 13½x14***

**1729** A793 2.25s multi 1.40 1.40
**1730** A793 2.25s multi 1.40 1.40
**1731** A793 2.25s multi 1.40 1.40
*Nos. 1729-1731 (3)* 4.20 4.20
With tabs 4.75

Souvenir Sheet

Jerusalem of Gold — A794

**Litho. & Embossed With Foil Application**

**2008, May 14** ***Perf. 14½x14¼***

**1732** A794 18s multi 13.50 13.50

No. 1732 sold for 22.50s.

Souvenir Sheet

Tel Aviv, Cent. (in 2009) — A795

No. 1733 — Sketches of Tel Aviv life by Nahum Gutman: a, The First Concert. b, The First Lamp Post. c, Dr. Hisin.

**2008, May 14 Litho.** ***Perf. 14x13¾***

**1733** A795 Sheet of 3 11.00 11.00
*a.* 3.50s multi 2.75 2.75
*b.* 4.50s multi 3.75 3.75
*c.* 5.50s multi 4.50 4.50

2008 World Stamp Championships, Israel. No. 1733 sold for 18s.

Gush Katif, 1970-2005 Gaza Strip Settlement A796

**2008, July 14 Litho.** ***Perf. 14x13***

**1734** A796 1.55s multi .90 .90
With tab 1.00

Promenades — A797

Designs: 4.50s, Tabgha Promenade (on Sea of Galilee), Capernaum. 4.60s, Armon Hanatziv Promenade, Jerusalem. 8.15s, Rishonim Promenade, Netanya.

**2008, July 14**

**1735** A797 4.50s multi 2.60 2.60
**1736** A797 4.60s multi 2.75 2.75
**1737** A797 8.15s multi 4.75 4.75
*Nos. 1735-1737 (3)* 10.10 10.10
With tabs 11.00

2008 Summer Olympics, Beijing A798

**2008, July 14**

**1738** A798 1.55s Swimming .90 .90
**1739** A798 1.55s Gymnastics .90 .90
**1740** A798 2.25s Sailing 1.40 1.40
**1741** A798 2.25s Tennis 1.40 1.40
*Nos. 1738-1741 (4)* 4.60 4.60
With tabs 5.00

Rabbis A799

Designs: 2.30s, Rabbi Samuel Mohilewer (1824-98). 8.50s, Rabbi Zvi Hirsch Kalischer (1795-1874).

**2008, Sept. 17** ***Perf. 12½x13***

**1742** A799 2.30s multi 1.40 1.40
**1743** A799 8.50s multi 5.00 5.00
With tabs 7.00

Torah Crowns A800

Torah crown from: 1.60s, Aden, late 19th cent. No. 1737, Turkey, 19th cent. No. 1738, Poland, 1729.

**2008, Sept. 17** ***Perf. 14x13***

**1744** A800 1.60s multi .95 .95
**1745** A800 3.80s multi 2.25 2.25
**1746** A800 3.80s multi 2.25 2.25
*Nos. 1744-1746 (3)* 5.45 5.45
With tabs 6.00

**Herbs and Spices Type of 2006 and**

Salvia Fruticosa — A801

Design: 1.60s, Artemisia arborescens.

**2008-09** *Perf. 13*

**1747** A754 1.60s multi .95 .95
**1748** A801 (2.90s) multi 1.75 1.75
With tabs 3.00

**Self-Adhesive**
**Booklet Stamps**
*Serpentine Die Cut 11x10¾*

**1749** A801 (2.90s) multi 1.75 1.75
*a.* Booklet pane of 10 + 10 etiquettes 17.50

**With Different Arabic Inscription and Dash Before "24"**

**1749B** A801 (2.90s) multi 1.50 1.50
*c.* Booklet pane of 10 + 10 etiquettes 15.00

Issued: Nos. 1747-1749, 9/17/08. No. 1749B, 1/25/09.

Landmarks of France and Israel — A802

Airplane, stamped first flight cover and: 1.60s, Haifa waterfront, Israel. 3.80s, Eiffel Tower, Paris.

**2008, Nov. 6** **Litho.** *Perf. 14*

**1750** A802 1.60s multi .85 .85
**1751** A802 3.80s multi 2.00 2.00
With tabs 3.25

First flight between France and Israel, 60th anniv. See France Nos. 3533-3534.

2008 Census A803

**2008, Dec. 17** *Perf. 14x13*

**1752** A803 1.60s multi .85 .85
With tab .95

Israeli Defense Forces Radio A804

**2008, Dec. 17** *Perf. 14x13¾*

**1753** A804 2.30s multi 1.25 1.25
With tab 1.40

Taglit-Birthright Israel — A805

**2008, Dec. 17** *Perf. 14x13*

**1754** A805 5.60s multi 3.00 3.00
With tab 3.25

Ancient Letters A806

Designs: 1.60s, Bar Kokhba letters, A.D. 134. 2.30s, Lachish letters, 589 B.C. 8.50s, Letter from Ugarit, 1230 B.C.

**2008, Dec. 17**

**1755** A806 1.60s multi .85 .85
**1756** A806 2.30s multi 1.25 1.25
**1757** A806 8.50s multi 4.50 4.50
*Nos. 1755-1757 (3)* 6.60 6.60
With tabs 7.25

**Menorah Type of 2002-03**

**2009** *Serpentine Die Cut 13½x13¾*
**Self-Adhesive**

**1758** A679 30a gray olive .25 .25
**1758A** A679 40a gray green .25 .25
**1759** A679 50a gray brown .25 .25
**1760** A679 1s purple .50 .50
*Nos. 1758-1760 (3)* 1.00 1.00

Issued: 30a, 50a, 1s, 2/17; 40a, 9/8.

Tel Aviv, Cent. A807

People and: 1.60s, Boardwalk and beaches. 2.30s, Buildings with different architectural styles. 3.80s, Parks.

**2009** *Perf. 14x13¾*

**1761** A807 1.60s multi .80 .80
**1762** A807 2.30s multi 1.10 1.10
**1763** A807 3.80s multi 1.90 1.90
*Nos. 1761-1763 (3)* 3.80 3.80
With tabs 4.25

Extreme Sports A808

**2009, Feb. 17**

**1764** A808 4.40s Mountain biking 2.10 2.10
**1765** A808 5.40s Skydiving 2.60 2.60
**1766** A808 5.60s Surfing 2.75 2.75
*Nos. 1764-1766 (3)* 7.45 7.45
With tabs 8.25

Fruit — A809

No. 1767: a, Grapes. b, Lemons. c, Avocados. d, Oranges. e, Pomegranates.

**2009, Feb. 17** *Perf. 14*

**1767** Vert. strip of 5 4.00 4.00
*a.-e.* A809 (1.60s) Any single .80 .80
Strip with tabs 4.50

See Nos. 1792-1796.

Memorial Day A810

**2009, Apr. 22** *Perf. 14x13¾*

**1768** A810 1.60s multi .75 .75
With tab .85

Intl. Year of Astronomy A811

Designs: 2.30s, Gersonides using Jacob's staff. 3.80s, Gravitational lensing. 8.50s, Laser Interferometer Space Antenna.

**2009, Apr. 22**

**1769** A811 2.30s multi 1.10 1.10
**1770** A811 3.80s multi 1.90 1.90
**1771** A811 8.50s multi 4.00 4.00
*Nos. 1769-1771 (3)* 7.00 7.00
With tabs 7.75

Souvenir Sheet

Berek Joselewicz, A Jewish Fighter for Polish Freedom's Last Battle, Kock, by Juliusz Kossak — A812

**2009, Apr. 22** *Perf. 14*

**1772** A812 6.10s multi 3.00 3.00

See Poland No. 3935.

Miniature Sheet

Israeli Musicians — A813

No. 1773: a, Zohar Argov (1955-87). b, Sasha Argov (1914-95). c, Meir Ariel (1942-99). d, Yossi Banai (1932-2006). e, Naomi Shemer (1930-2004). f, Shoshana Damari (1923-2006). g, Yair Rosenblum (1944-96). h, Moshe Wilensky (1910-97). i, Ehud Manor (1941-2005). j, Arik Lavie (1927-2004). k, Uzi Hitman (1952-2004). l, Ofra Haza (1957-2000).

**2009, Apr. 22** *Perf. 13*

**1773** A813 Sheet of 12 + 4 labels 9.00 9.00
*a.-l.* 1.60s Any single .75 .75

Love — A814

**2009, June 30** *Perf. 14*

**1774** A814 (1.60s) multi .85 .85
With tab .95

Dead Sea — A815

**2009, June 30** *Perf. 13¾x14*

**1775** A815 2.30s multi 1.25 1.25
With tab 1.40

18th Maccabiah Games — A816

**2009, June 30**

**1776** A816 5.60s multi 3.00 3.00
With tab 3.25

Intl. Harp Contest, 50th Anniv. — A817

**2009, June 30**

**1777** A817 8.50s multi 4.50 4.50
With tab 5.00

Environmental Quality — A818

No. 1778: a, Geothermal energy (Earth as teakettle, 31x31mm). b, Global warming (Earth melting in frying pan, 62x31mm). c, Solar energy (house with solar panels on Earth, 31x31mm).

**2009, June 30** *Perf. 13*

**1778** Horiz. strip of 3 3.75 3.75
*a.-c.* A818 2.30s Any single 1.25 1.25
Strip with tabs 4.25

Leumit Health Fund, 75th Anniv. A819

**2009, Sept. 8** *Perf. 14x13¾*

**1779** A819 8.80s multi 4.75 4.75
With tab 5.25

Honey A820

Honeycomb and: 1.60s, Bee on flower. 4.60s, Honeycomb on plate. 6.70s, Honey dripping on apple slice.

**2009, Sept. 8**

**1780** A820 1.60s multi .85 .85
**1781** A820 4.60s multi 2.50 2.50
**1782** A820 6.70s multi 3.75 3.75
*Nos. 1780-1782 (3)* 7.10 7.10
With tabs 8.00

Virtual Communications — A821

Designs: 2.40s, Instant messaging software. 5.30s, USB flash drive. 6.50s, Voice over Internet protocol.

**2009, Sept. 8**

| | | | | |
|---|---|---|---|---|
| **1783** | A821 2.40s multi | 1.25 | 1.25 |
| **1784** | A821 5.30s multi | 3.00 | 3.00 |
| **1785** | A821 6.50s multi | 3.50 | 3.50 |
| | *Nos. 1783-1785 (3)* | 7.75 | 7.75 |
| | With tabs | 8.50 | |

Animal Assisted Therapy A822

Designs: Nos. 1786, 1789, Woman and dog. Nos. 1787, 1790, Girl and horse. Nos. 1788, 1791, Girl and dolphin.

**2009, Sept. 8** ***Perf. 14x13¾***

| | | | |
|---|---|---|---|
| **1786** | A822 2.40s multi | 1.25 | 1.25 |
| **1787** | A822 2.40s multi | 1.25 | 1.25 |
| **1788** | A822 2.40s multi | 1.25 | 1.25 |
| | *Nos. 1786-1788 (3)* | 3.75 | 3.75 |
| | With tabs | 4.25 | |

**Booklet Stamps**

**Self-Adhesive**

***Serpentine Die Cut 11x10¼***

| | | | |
|---|---|---|---|
| **1789** | A822 2.40s multi | 1.25 | 1.25 |
| **1790** | A822 2.40s multi | 1.25 | 1.25 |
| **1791** | A822 2.40s multi | 1.25 | 1.25 |
| ***a.*** | Booklet pane of 6, 2 each #1789-1791 | 7.50 | |
| | *Nos. 1789-1791 (3)* | 3.75 | 3.75 |

**Fruit Type of 2009**

***Serpentine Die Cut 14¼x13***

**2009, Nov. 26** **Litho.**

**Booklet Stamps**

**Self-Adhesive**

| | | | |
|---|---|---|---|
| **1792** | A809 (1.60s) Lemons | .85 | .85 |
| **1793** | A809 (1.60s) Grapes | .85 | .85 |
| **1794** | A809 (1.60s) Pomegranates | .85 | .85 |
| **1795** | A809 (1.60s) Oranges | .85 | .85 |
| **1796** | A809 (1.60s) Avocados | .85 | .85 |
| ***a.*** | Booklet pane of 20, 4 each #1792-1796 | 17.00 | |
| | *Nos. 1792-1796 (5)* | 4.25 | 4.25 |

Yiddish Theater, Iasi, Romania A823

**2009, Nov. 26** **Litho.** ***Perf. 14***

| | | | |
|---|---|---|---|
| **1797** | A823 4.60s multi | 2.50 | 2.50 |
| | With tab | 2.75 | |

See Romania No. 5142.

Lighthouses — A824

Lighthouses at: 4.60s, Jaffa. 6.70s, Tel Aviv. 8.80s, Ashdod.

**2009, Nov. 26** ***Perf. 14x13¾***

| | | | |
|---|---|---|---|
| **1798** | A824 4.60s multi | 2.50 | 2.50 |
| **1799** | A824 6.70s multi | 3.75 | 3.75 |
| **1800** | A824 8.80s multi | 4.75 | 4.75 |
| | *Nos. 1798-1800 (3)* | 11.00 | 11.00 |
| | With tabs | 12.00 | |

Maritime Archaeology — A825

Diver and: No. 1801, Earthenware jugs. No. 1802, Figurines. 3.60s, Weapons. 5s, Anchors.

**2009, Nov. 26**

| | | | |
|---|---|---|---|
| **1801** | A825 2.40s multi | 1.25 | 1.25 |
| **1802** | A825 2.40s multi | 1.25 | 1.25 |
| **1803** | A825 3.60s multi | 1.90 | 1.90 |
| **1804** | A825 5s multi | 2.75 | 2.75 |
| | *Nos. 1801-1804 (4)* | 7.15 | 7.15 |
| | With tabs | 8.00 | |

Arava Valley Settlements, 50th Anniv. — A826

**2010, Jan. 27** **Litho.** ***Perf. 14x13¾***

| | | | |
|---|---|---|---|
| **1805** | A826 1.60s multi | .85 | .85 |
| | With tab | .95 | |

Lions Club of Israel, 50th Anniv. A827

**2010, Jan. 27**

| | | | |
|---|---|---|---|
| **1806** | A827 4.60s multi | 2.50 | 2.50 |
| | With tab | 2.75 | |

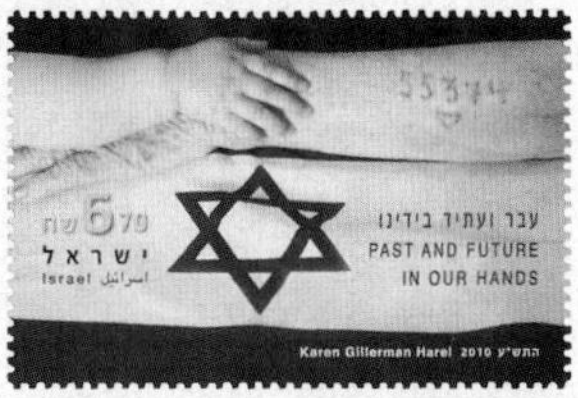


Intl. Holocaust Remembrance Day — A828

**2010, Jan. 27** ***Perf. 14***

| | | | |
|---|---|---|---|
| **1807** | A828 6.70s multi | 3.75 | 3.75 |
| | With tab | 4.25 | |

Alliance Israelite Universelle, 150th Anniv. — A829

**2010, Jan. 27** ***Perf. 14x13¾***

| | | | |
|---|---|---|---|
| **1808** | A829 8.80s multi | 4.75 | 4.75 |
| | With tab | 5.25 | |

Birds — A830

No. 1809: a, Carduelis carduelis. b, Upupa epops. c, Prinia gracilis.

**2010, Jan. 27** ***Perf. 13¾x14***

| | | | |
|---|---|---|---|
| **1809** | Strip of 3, #a-c | 4.00 | 4.00 |
| ***a.-c.*** | A830 2.40s Any single | 1.25 | 1.25 |
| | Strip with tabs | 4.50 | |

Memorial Day — A831

**2010, Apr. 14** **Litho.** ***Perf. 13¾x14***

| | | | |
|---|---|---|---|
| **1810** | A831 1.60s multi | .85 | .85 |
| | With tab | .95 | |

Tribute to World Trade Center Victims, by Eliezer Weishoff, Jerusalem A832

**2010, Apr. 14**

| | | | |
|---|---|---|---|
| **1811** | A832 2.40s multi | 1.40 | 1.40 |
| | With tab | 1.60 | 1.60 |

Friendship Between Israel and Canada, 60th Anniv. A833

**2010, Apr. 14** ***Perf. 14x13¾***

| | | | |
|---|---|---|---|
| **1812** | A833 4.60s multi | 2.50 | 2.50 |
| | With tab | 2.75 | |

See Canada No. 2379.

Israeli Innovations A834

Designs: No. 1813, Drip irrigation dripper and farm field. No. 1814, Computer chip and computer. No. 1815, Gastrointestinal camera and intestines.

**2010, Apr. 14** ***Perf. 14x13¼***

| | | | |
|---|---|---|---|
| **1813** | A834 2.40s multi | 1.40 | 1.40 |
| **1814** | A834 2.40s multi | 1.40 | 1.40 |
| **1815** | A834 2.40s multi | 1.40 | 1.40 |
| | *Nos. 1813-1815 (3)* | 4.20 | 4.20 |
| | With tabs | 4.75 | |

Expo 2010, Shanghai.

Souvenir Sheet

Children's Books — A835

No. 1816: a, Alice's Adventures in Wonderland, by Lewis Carroll. b, Peter Pan, by Sir James M. Barrie. c, Gulliver's Travels, by Jonathan Swift.

**2010, Apr. 14** ***Perf. 14¾x14***

| | | | |
|---|---|---|---|
| **1816** | A835 Sheet of 3 | 7.50 | 7.50 |
| ***a.-c.*** | 4.60s Any single | 2.50 | 2.50 |

London 2010 International Stamp Exhibition.

Souvenir Sheet

Theodor Herzl (1860-1904), Zionist Leader — A836

No. 1817: a, Herzl leaning on railing, settlers. b, Settlers at settlement. c, Boy waving Israeli flag, adults, city skyline.

**2010, Apr. 14**

| | | | |
|---|---|---|---|
| **1817** | A836 Sheet of 3 | 8.25 | 8.25 |
| ***a.*** | 3.70s multi | 2.00 | 2.00 |
| ***b.*** | 4.60s multi | 2.50 | 2.50 |
| ***c.*** | 6.70s multi | 3.75 | 3.75 |

Kibbutzim, Cent. A837

**2010, June 14** **Litho.** ***Perf. 14x13½***

| | | | |
|---|---|---|---|
| **1818** | A837 2.50s multi | 1.40 | 1.40 |
| | With tab | 1.60 | |

Rabbi Nachman of Breslev (1772-1810), Philosopher — A838

**2010, June 14** ***Perf. 13½x14***

| | | | |
|---|---|---|---|
| **1819** | A838 3.70s multi | 1.90 | 1.90 |
| | With tab | 2.10 | |

Simon Wiesenthal (1908-2005), Hunter of Nazi War Criminals — A839

**2010, June 14** ***Perf. 12½***

| | | | |
|---|---|---|---|
| **1820** | A839 5s multi | 2.60 | 2.60 |
| | With tab | 3.00 | |

The Star of David is made up of tiny holes made by a laser. See Austria No. 2264.

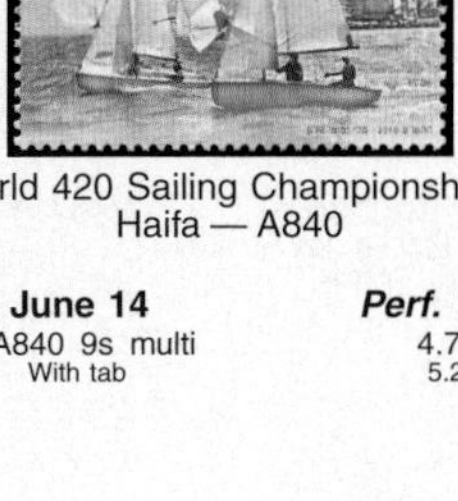

World 420 Sailing Championships, Haifa — A840

**2010, June 14** ***Perf. 14x15***

| | | | |
|---|---|---|---|
| **1821** | A840 9s multi | 4.75 | 4.75 |
| | With tab | 5.25 | |

Story Gardens, Holon — A841

Sculptures based on children's stories: No. 1822, Where is Pluto? (Dog). No. 1823, Shmuel the Hedgehog. No. 1824, Soul Bird.

**2010, June 14** ***Perf. 14x13½***

**1822** A841 2.50s multi 1.40 1.40
**1823** A841 2.50s multi 1.40 1.40
**1824** A841 2.50s multi 1.40 1.40
*Nos. 1822-1824 (3)* 4.20 4.20
With tabs 4.75

Musical Instruments — A842

No. 1825: a, Zoma and oboe. b, Rebab and violin. c, Darbouka and drum. d, Qanun and piano. e, Oud and guitar.

**2010, June 14** ***Perf. 13½x14***

**1825** Horiz. strip of 5 4.50 4.50
*a.-e.* A842 1.70s Any single .90 .90
Strip with tabs 5.00

Tzevet (Israel Defense Forces Veterans Association), 50th Anniv. — A843

**2010, Aug. 25** **Litho.** ***Perf. 13¼x13***

**1826** A843 2.50s multi 1.40 1.40
With tab 1.60

Settlements Outside of Jerusalem's Old City Walls, 150th Anniv. — A844

**2010, Aug. 25** ***Perf. 13¼***

**1827** A844 3.70s multi 2.00 2.00
With tab 2.25
*a.* Booklet pane of 2 5.00 —

Issued: No. 1827a, 11/21/10.

Urban Renaissance — A845

**2010, Aug. 25** ***Perf. 13x13¼***

**1828** A845 8.90s multi 4.75 4.75
With tab 5.25

Shofars — A846

Shofar blower and shofar made of: 1.70s, Ram's horn. 4.20s, Kudu horn. 6.10s, Ram's horn, diff.

**2010, Aug. 25** ***Perf. 13¼x13***

**1829** A846 1.70s multi .90 .90
**1830** A846 4.20s multi 2.25 2.25
*a.* Booklet pane of 2, #1427a, 1830 6.00 —
**1831** A846 6.10s multi 3.25 3.25
*Nos. 1829-1831 (3)* 6.40 6.40
With tabs 7.00

Issued: No. 1830a, 11/21/10.

Greetings
A847 A848

**2010, Aug. 25** ***Perf. 13¾x14***

**1832** A847 (1.70s) multi .90 .90
With tab 1.00
*a.* Sheet of 12 + 12 labels 15.00 15.00
**1833** A848 (1.70s) multi .90 .90
With tab 1.00
*a.* Sheet of 12 +12 labels 15.00 15.00

**Booklet Stamps**
**Self-Adhesive**
***Serpentine Die Cut 12½x12¾***

**1834** A847 (1.70s) multi .90 .90
**1835** A848 (1.70s) multi .90 .90
*a.* Booklet pane of 12, 6 each #1834-1835 11.00

Nos. 1832a and 1833a each sold for 28s. Labels could be personalized.

Miniature Sheet

Animals and Their Young — A849

No. 1836: a, Chicks. b, Hen. c, Kitten with ball of yarn. d, Cat. e, Rabbit kit, flower, carrot. f, Rabbit.

**2010, Aug. 25** ***Perf. 13x13¼***

**1836** A849 Sheet of 6 + 3 labels 5.50 5.50
*a.-f.* 1.70s Any single .90 .90

Garden of Gethsemane, Jerusalem — A850

**2010, Nov. 15** **Litho.** ***Perf. 13x13¼***

**1837** A850 4.20s multi 2.40 2.40
With tab 2.75

Printed in sheets of 4. See Vatican City No. 1456.

Flag of Israel — A851

**2010, Nov. 21** ***Perf. 13¾x14***

**1838** A851 (1.70s) multi .95 .95
With tab 1.10
*1838a* Sheet of 12 + 12 labels 15.50 15.50

No. 1838a sold for 28s. Labels could be personalized.
See No. 1877.

Movie Theaters — A852

Designs: 4.20s, Armon Cinema, Haifa. 9s, Zion Cinema, Jerusalem.

**2010, Nov. 21** ***Perf. 13x13¼***

**1839** A852 4.20s multi 2.40 2.40
**1840** A852 9s multi 5.00 5.00
With tabs 8.25

Bible Stories — A853

Designs: No. 1841, Adam and Eve. No. 1842, Samson and the Lion. No. 1843, Jonah and the Fish.
6s, Moses parting the Red Sea, vert.

**2010, Nov. 21** ***Perf. 14½x14¼***

**1841** A853 1.70s multi .95 .95
*a.* Miniature sheet of 6 5.75 5.75
**1842** A853 1.70s multi .95 .95
*a.* Miniature sheet of 6 5.75 5.75
**1843** A853 1.70s multi .95 .95
*a.* Miniature sheet of 6 5.75 5.75
*Nos. 1841-1843 (3)* 2.85 2.85
With tabs 3.25

**Souvenir Sheet**
***Perf. 13½x13***

**1844** A853 6s multi 3.50 3.50

Jerusalem 2010 Intl. Philatelic Exhibition (No. 1844). No. 1844 contains one 30x40mm stamp.

A854

A855

A856

A857

A858

A859

A860

A861

A862

A863

A864

A865

A866

A867

Animation
A868

**2010, Nov. 21 Litho. *Perf. 13x13¼***

**1845** Sheet of 15 14.50 14.50
*a.* A854 1.70s multi .95 .95
*b.* A855 1.70s multi .95 .95
*c.* A856 1.70s multi .95 .95
*d.* A857 1.70s multi .95 .95
*e.* A858 1.70s multi .95 .95
*f.* A859 1.70s multi .95 .95
*g.* A860 1.70s multi .95 .95
*h.* A861 1.70s multi .95 .95
*i.* A862 1.70s multi .95 .95
*j.* A863 1.70s multi .95 .95
*k.* A864 1.70s multi .95 .95
*l.* A865 1.70s multi .95 .95
*m.* A866 1.70s multi .95 .95
*n.* A867 1.70s multi .95 .95
*o.* A868 1.70s multi .95 .95

**Booklet Panes of 1**
**Self-Adhesive**

***Serpentine Die Cut 6¼***

**1846** A854 1.70s multi .95 .95
**1847** A855 1.70s multi .95 .95
**1848** A856 1.70s multi .95 .95
**1849** A857 1.70s multi .95 .95
**1850** A858 1.70s multi .95 .95
**1851** A859 1.70s multi .95 .95
**1852** A860 1.70s multi .95 .95
**1853** A861 1.70s multi .95 .95
**1854** A862 1.70s multi .95 .95
**1855** A863 1.70s multi .95 .95
**1856** A864 1.70s multi .95 .95
**1857** A865 1.70s multi .95 .95
**1858** A866 1.70s multi .95 .95
**1859** A867 1.70s multi .95 .95
**1860** A868 1.70s multi .95 .95
Complete booklet, #1846-1860 14.50
*Nos. 1846-1860 (15)* 14.25 14.25

**Types of 1995-2010 Redrawn or In Different Sizes**

**2010, Nov. 21 Litho. *Perf. 13½x13***

**Booklet Stamps**

**1861** A589 1.15s Like #1326, 30x40mm (1863a) .75 .75

***Perf. 13x13½***

**1862** A545 1.50s Like #1246, 40x30mm (1866a) 1.00 1.00
**1863** A545 1.80s Like #1247, 40x30mm (1863a) 1.25 1.25
*a.* Booklet pane of 2, #1861, 1863 2.00 —
**1864** A603 2.20s Like #1345, 40x30mm (1867a) 1.50 1.50

***Perf. 13½***

**1865** A726 3.30s Like #1600, redrawn, 30x40mm (1866a) 2.25 2.25

***Perf. 13½x13¼***

**1866** A634 3.40s Like #1866, redrawn, 30x30mm (1866a) 2.25 2.25
*a.* Booklet pane of 4, #1610a, 1862, 1865, 1866 9.75 —

***Perf. 13½***

**1867** A564 4.65s Like #1287, 30x40mm (1867a) 3.25 3.25
*a.* Booklet pane of 2, #1864, 1867 4.75 —
Complete booklet, #1827a, 1830a, 1863a, 1866a, 1867a 27.50
*Nos. 1861-1867 (7)* 12.25 12.25

Complete booklet sold for 49s.

Intl. Year of Chemistry
A869

Chemical models of: 4.20s, Ubiquitin, protein destroyer. 6.10s, Ribosome, protein constructor.

**2011, Jan. 4 Litho. *Perf. 14x13½***

**1868** A869 4.20s multi 2.40 2.40
**1869** A869 6.10s multi 3.50 3.50
With tabs 6.50

Roots of the Hebrew Language
A870

**2011, Feb. 7 *Perf. 13½x14***

**1870** A870 3.70s multi 2.00 2.00
With tab 2.25

Clalit Health Services, Cent.
A871

**2011, Feb. 7 *Perf. 14x13½***

**1871** A871 9s multi 5.00 5.00
With tab 5.50

Building Projects of King Herod — A872

**2011, Feb. 7 *Perf. 13½x14***

**1872** A872 1.70s Masada .95 .95
**1873** A872 1.70s Caesarea .95 .95
**1874** A872 2.50s Jerusalem 1.40 1.40
**1875** A872 2.50s Herodian 1.40 1.40
*Nos. 1872-1875 (4)* 4.70 4.70
With tabs 5.25

Worldwide Fund for Nature (WWF) — A873

No. 1876 — Panthera pardus saxicolor: a, Leaping. b, Standing on hill with rams. c, Drinking. d, With cub.

**2011, Feb. 7 *Perf. 14x13½***

**1876** A873 Block of 4 3.80 3.80
*a.-d.* 1.70s Any single .95 .95
Nos. 1876a-1876d, with tabs 4.25

**Flag of Israel Type of 2010**

***Serpentine Die Cut 13x14¼***

**2011, Apr. 12 Litho.**

**Booklet Stamp**
**Self-Adhesive**

**1877** A851 (1.70s) multi 1.00 1.00
*a.* Booklet pane of 20 20.00

Memorial Day — A874

**2011, Apr. 12 *Perf. 13½x13***

**1878** A874 1.70s multi 1.00 1.00
With tab 1.10

Aliyah of Ethiopian Jews — A875

**2011, Apr. 12 *Perf. 14¼***

**1879** A875 2.50s multi 1.50 1.50
With tab 1.75

Mount Carmel Training Center, 50th Anniv.
A876

**2011, Apr. 12 *Perf. 13x13½***

**1880** A876 5s multi 3.00 3.00
With tab 3.50

Pres. Ephraim Katzir (1916-2009) — A877

**2011, Apr. 12 *Perf. 13x13½***

**1881** A877 9s multi 5.25 5.25
With tab 5.75

Tourism
A878

Designs: 4.20s, Sea of Galilee. 6s, Tower of David and Old City Wall, Jerusalem. 6.10s, Red Sea clownfish near Eilat.

**2011, Apr. 12 *Perf. 14x13½***

**1882** A878 4.20s multi 2.50 2.50
**1883** A878 6s multi 3.50 3.50
**1884** A878 6.10s multi 3.75 3.75
*Nos. 1882-1884 (3)* 9.75 9.75
With tabs 11.00

Miniature Sheet

Butterflies — A879

Designs: Nos. 1885a, 1888, Anaphaeis aurota. Nos. 1885b, 1887, Vanessa atalanta. Nos. 1885c, 1886, Papilio machaon syracus. Nos. 1885d, 1889, Apharitis acamas. Nos. 1885e, 1890, Danaus chrysippus. Nos. 1885f, 1891, Polyommatus icarus zelleri.

**2011 *Perf. 13¾x14***

**1885** A879 Sheet of 6 6.00 6.00
*a.-f.* (1.70s) Any single 1.00 1.00

**Booklet Stamps**
**Self-Adhesive**

***Serpentine Die Cut 13x14¼***

**1886** A879 (1.70s) multi 1.00 1.00
**1887** A879 (1.70s) multi 1.00 1.00
**1888** A879 (1.70s) multi 1.00 1.00
**1889** A879 (1.70s) multi 1.00 1.00
**1890** A879 (1.70s) multi 1.00 1.00
**1891** A879 (1.70s) multi 1.00 1.00
*a.* Booklet pane of 20, 4 each #1886-1889, 2 each #1890-1891 20.00
*Nos. 1886-1891 (6)* 6.00 6.00

Issued: No. 1885, 4/12; Nos. 1886-1891, 6/27.

Rabbi Shlomo Goren (1917-94), Chief Rabbi of Israel
A880

**2011, June 27 *Perf. 13x13½***

**1892** A880 1.70s multi 1.00 1.00
With tab 1.10

Doctor in Clown Costume Treating Child
A881

**2011, June 27 Litho.**

**1893** A881 9s multi 5.25 5.25
With tab 5.75

Israeli Agricultural Achievements — A882

Designs: No. 1894, Medjool date trees nourished by saline water in pots. No. 1895, Tomatoes growing in hothouse. No. 1896, Water purification pool, Dan Region Wastewater Treatment Facility.

**2011, June 27**

| | | | |
|---|---|---|---|
| **1894** | A882 2.50s multi | 1.50 | 1.50 |
| **1895** | A882 2.50s multi | 1.50 | 1.50 |
| **1896** | A882 2.50s multi | 1.50 | 1.50 |
| | *Nos. 1894-1896 (3)* | 4.50 | 4.50 |
| | With tabs | 5.00 | |

Miniature Sheet

Beaches — A883

No. 1897: a, Sea of Galilee Beach, hot air balloons. b, Sea of Galilee Beach, no balloons. c, Caesarea Beach, no kites. d, Caesarea Beach, kites. e, Tel Aviv Beach, sailboats. f, Tel Aviv Beach, jetty. g, Dead Sea Beach, no airplane. h, Dead Sea Beach, airplane. i, Eilat Beach, speedboats. j, Eilat Beach, no speedboats.

**2011, June 27** *Perf. 14x13½*

| | | | |
|---|---|---|---|
| **1897** | A883 Sheet of 10 | 10.00 | 10.00 |
| *a.-j.* | 1.70s Any single | 1.00 | 1.00 |

Admission of Israel to Organization for Economic Cooperation and Development — A884

**2011, Sept. 13**

| | | | |
|---|---|---|---|
| **1898** | A884 9.30s multi | 5.00 | 5.00 |
| | With tab | 5.50 | |

Items at Rosh Hashanah Feast A885

Designs: 1.70s, Apples and honey. 4s, Fish head. 5.90s, Pomegranates.

**2011, Sept. 13**

| | | | |
|---|---|---|---|
| **1899** | A885 1.70s multi | .95 | .95 |
| **1900** | A885 4s multi | 2.25 | 2.25 |
| **1901** | A885 5.90s multi | 3.25 | 3.25 |
| | *Nos. 1899-1901 (3)* | 6.45 | 6.45 |
| | With tabs | 7.25 | |

Children's Games A886

Designs: Nos. 1902, 1905, Hopscotch. Nos. 1903, 1906, Hide and seek. Nos. 1904, 1907, Tag.

**2011, Sept. 13** *Perf. 14x13½*

| | | | |
|---|---|---|---|
| **1902** | A886 2.60s multi | 1.40 | 1.40 |
| **1903** | A886 2.60s multi | 1.40 | 1.40 |
| **1904** | A886 2.60s multi | 1.40 | 1.40 |
| | *Nos. 1902-1904 (3)* | 4.20 | 4.20 |
| | With tabs | 4.75 | |

**Booklet Stamps Self-Adhesive**

***Serpentine Die Cut 12½***

| | | | |
|---|---|---|---|
| **1905** | A886 2.60s multi | 1.40 | 1.40 |
| **1906** | A886 2.60s multi | 1.40 | 1.40 |
| **1907** | A886 2.60s multi | 1.40 | 1.40 |
| *a.* | Booklet pane of 6, 2 each #1905-1907 | 8.50 | |
| | *Nos. 1905-1907 (3)* | 4.20 | 4.20 |

Miniature Sheet

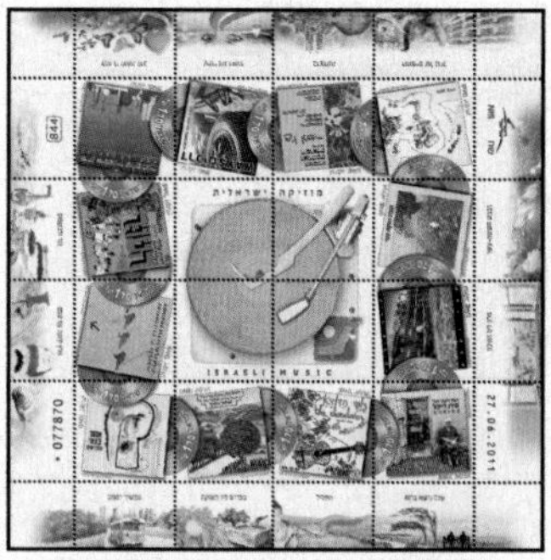

Israeli Record Albums — A887

No. 1908: a, *Why Should I Take it to Heart,* by Arik Einstein and Shalom Hanoch, 1979. b, *Ways,* by Shlomo Artzi, 1979. c, *Barcelona,* by Israel Andalusian Orchestra and Jo Amar, 2000. d, *Poogy Tales,* by Kaveret, 1973. e, *To the Candle and the Spices,* by Lehakat Tsliley Ha'Ud, 1975. f, *HaKeves HaShisha Asar,* by HaKeves Ha Shisha Asar (tree in field with white calf), 1978. g, *Antarctica,* by Corinne Allal, 1989. h, *Ashes and Dust,* by Yehuda Poliker (boy watching train pass), 1988. i, *Continuing to Ride,* by Ehud Banai and the Refugees (abstract head), 1987. j, *The Middle of the Road,* by Yehoram Gaon, 1984. k, *The Flute,* by the Doodaim, 1959. l, *Out of the Depths,* by The Idan Raichel Project (woman sitting by door), 2005.

**2011, Sept. 13** *Perf. 13¼x14*

| | | | |
|---|---|---|---|
| **1908** | A887 Sheet of 12 + 4 central labels | 11.50 | 11.50 |
| *a.-l.* | 1.70s Any single | .95 | .95 |

Valley Railroad A888

**2011, Dec. 6** *Perf. 14x13¼*

| | | | |
|---|---|---|---|
| **1909** | A888 2.60s multi | 1.40 | 1.40 |
| | With tab | 1.60 | |

Tribute to Rescue Forces — A889

**2011, Dec. 6** *Perf. 13¼x14*

| | | | |
|---|---|---|---|
| **1910** | A889 3.80s red & yel grn | 2.00 | 2.00 |
| | With tab | 2.25 | |

Israel Philharmonic Orchestra, 75th Anniv. — A890

**2011, Dec. 6**

| | | | |
|---|---|---|---|
| **1911** | A890 4s multi | 2.10 | 2.10 |
| | With tab | 2.40 | |

Miniature Sheet

Israeli Soccer Legends — A891

No. 1912: a, Avi Cohen (1956-2010). b, Menachem Ashkenazi (1934-2000). c, Nahum Stelmach (1936-99). d, Jerry Beit Halevi (1912-97). e, Eli Fuchs (1924-92). f, Shmuel Ben-Dror (1924-2009). g, Natan Panz (1917-48). h, Ya'akov Grundman (1939-2004). i, Avi Ran (1963-87). j, Ya'akov Hodorov (1927-2006). English translations of names are on tabs adjacent to stamps.

**2011, Dec. 6** *Perf. 14x13¼*

| | | | |
|---|---|---|---|
| **1912** | A891 Sheet of 10 | 9.00 | 9.00 |
| *a.-j.* | 1.70s Any single | .90 | .90 |

Memorial Candle — A892

**2012, Feb. 7** *Perf. 13¾*

| | | | |
|---|---|---|---|
| **1913** | A892 (1.70s) multi | .90 | .90 |
| | With tab | 1.00 | |
| *a.* | Sheet of 12 + 12 labels | 15.00 | 15.00 |

No. 1913a sold for 28s. Labels could be personalized.

Rabbi Shneur Zalman of Lidai (1745-1812), Founder of Chabad Hasidism — A893

**2012, Feb. 7** *Perf. 13x13¼*

| | | | |
|---|---|---|---|
| **1914** | A893 1.70s multi | .90 | .90 |
| | With tab | 1.00 | |

Technion (Israel Institute of Technology), Cent. — A894

**2012, Feb. 7**

| | | | |
|---|---|---|---|
| **1915** | A894 2.60s multi | 1.40 | 1.40 |
| | With tab | 1.60 | |

Trial, Sentencing and Execution of Nazi War Criminal Adolf Eichmann, 50th Anniv. — A895

**2012, Feb. 7** *Perf. 13¼x13*

| | | | |
|---|---|---|---|
| **1916** | A895 9.30s multi | 5.00 | 5.00 |
| | With tab | 5.50 | |

Famous Women A896

Designs: 4s, Bracha Zefira (1910-90), singer. 5.90s, Batia Makov (1841-1912), business entrepreneur.

**2012, Feb. 7** *Perf. 13x13¼*

| | | | |
|---|---|---|---|
| **1917** | A896 4s multi | 2.10 | 2.10 |
| **1918** | A896 5.90s multi | 3.25 | 3.25 |
| | With tabs | 6.00 | |

Gemstones From High Priest's Breastplate — A897

Gemstones and inscribed tribe: No. 1919, Carnelian, Reuven. No. 1920, Topaz, Shimon. No. 1921, Emerald, Levi. No. 1922, Turquoise, Yehuda.

**2012, Feb. 7 Litho.** *Perf. 13x13¼*

| | | | |
|---|---|---|---|
| **1919** | A897 2.60s multi | 1.40 | 1.40 |
| **1920** | A897 2.60s multi | 1.40 | 1.40 |
| **1921** | A897 2.60s multi | 1.40 | 1.40 |
| **1922** | A897 2.60s multi | 1.40 | 1.40 |
| | *Nos. 1919-1922 (4)* | 5.60 | 5.60 |
| | With tabs | 6.25 | |

See Nos. 1925-1928, 1935-1938.

Diplomatic Relations Between Israel and People's Republic of China, 20th Anniv. — A898

Designs: 2s, Waxwing, five-pointed star. 3s, White dove, Star of David.

**2012, Mar. 20 Litho.** *Perf. 13¼x14*

| | | | |
|---|---|---|---|
| **1923** | A898 2s multi | 1.10 | 1.10 |
| **1924** | A898 3s multi | 1.60 | 1.60 |
| | Wit tabs | 3.00 | |

See People's Republic of China Nos. 3986-3987.

**Gemstones From High Priest's Breastplate Type of 2012**

Gemstones and inscribed tribe: No. 1925, Lazurite, Issachar. No. 1926, Quartz, Zevulun. No. 1927, Zircon, Dan. No. 1928, Amethyst, Naftali.

**2012, Apr. 17** *Perf. 14x13¼*

| | | | |
|---|---|---|---|
| **1925** | A897 3s multi | 1.60 | 1.60 |
| **1926** | A897 3s multi | 1.60 | 1.60 |
| **1927** | A897 3s multi | 1.60 | 1.60 |
| **1928** | A897 3s multi | 1.60 | 1.60 |
| | *Nos. 1925-1928 (4)* | 6.40 | 6.40 |
| | With tabs | 7.25 | |

Memorial Day A899

**2012, Apr. 17**
**1929** A899 1.70s multi .90 .90
With tab 1.00

Chain of Generations Center, Western Wall Plaza, Jerusalem A900

**2012, Apr. 17** *Perf. 13¼x14*
**1930** A900 9.30s multi 5.00 5.00
With tab 5.50

Jewish Seamanship — A901

Designs: No. 1931, Hehalutz in Jaffa Harbor, 1919. No. 1932, Sara A in Haifa Harbor, 1935, and Jeremiah Helpern. No. 1933, Har Zion in Tel-Aviv Harbor, 1935, and Captain Erich Hirschfeld.

**2012, Apr. 17** *Perf. 14x13¼*
**1931** A901 3s multi 1.60 1.60
**1932** A901 3s multi 1.60 1.60
**1933** A901 3s multi 1.60 1.60
*Nos. 1931-1933 (3)* 4.80 4.80
With tabs 5.25

Miniature Sheet

Children's Books — A902

No. 1934 — Books and illustrations: a, A Tale of Five Balloons, by Miriam Roth (girl holding blue balloon). b, Raspberry Juice, by Haya Shenhav (lion and giraffe). c, Caspion the Little Fish, by Paul Kor (fish). d, The Absent-minded Guy from Kefar Azar, by Leah Goldberg (man with glasses holding umbrellas). e, Itamar Walks on Walls, by David Grossman (Itamar walking on wall). f, Hot Sweet Corn, by Miriam Roth (five children eating corn on the cob). g, The Lion that Loved Strawberries, by Tirtza Atar (lion and strawberries). h, Come to Me, Nice Butterfly, by Fania Bergstein (child reaching for butterfly in fenced garden).

**2012, Apr. 17**
**1934** A902 Sheet of 8 9.00 9.00
***a.-h.*** 2s Any single 1.10 1.10

### Gemstones From High Preist's Breasplate Type of 2012

Gemstone and inscribed tribe: No. 1935, Agate, Gad. No. 1936, Aquamarine, Asher. No. 1937, Onyx, Yosef. No. 1938, Jasper, Binyamin.

**2012, June 26** *Perf. 13x13¼*
**1935** A897 3s multi 1.60 1.60
**1936** A897 3s multi 1.60 1.60
**1937** A897 3s multi 1.60 1.60
**1938** A897 3s multi 1.60 1.60
*Nos. 1935-1938 (4)* 6.40 6.40
With tabs 7.25

Teddy Kollek (1911-2007), Mayor of Jerusalem A903

**2012, June 26** *Perf. 13¼x13*
**1939** A903 9.40s multi 4.75 4.75
With tab 5.25

2012 Summer Olympics, London A904

London landmarks, 2012 Olympic Games emblem and: No. 1940, High jump. No. 1941, Artistic gymnastics. 4.50s, Taekwondo.

**2012, June 26** *Perf. 13x13¼*
**1940** A904 2s multi 1.00 1.00
**1941** A904 2s multi 1.00 1.00
**1942** A904 4.50s multi 2.40 2.40
*Nos. 1940-1942 (3)* 4.40 4.40
With tabs 5.00

Israeli Membership in Intl. Police Association, 50th Anniv. — A905

**2012, Sept. 4**
**1943** A905 4.20s multi 2.25 2.25
With tab 2.50

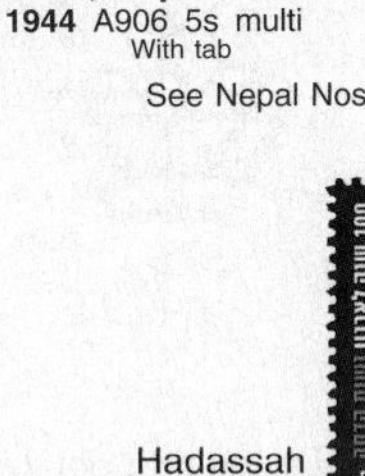

Dead Sea, Mt. Everest, Flags of Israel and Nepal — A906

**2012, Sept. 4** *Perf. 13¼x13*
**1944** A906 5s multi 2.60 2.60
With tab 3.00

See Nepal Nos. 874-875.

Hadassah (Women's Zionist Organization of America), Cent. — A907

**2012, Sept. 4**
**1945** A907 6.20s multi 3.25 3.25
With tab 3.75



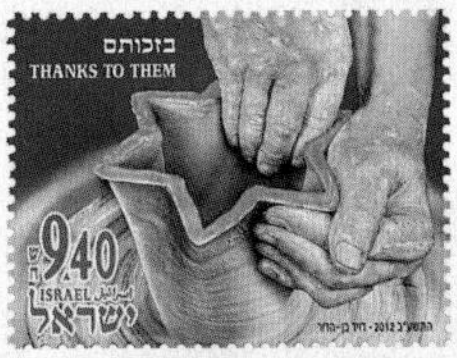

Contribution of Senior Citizens — A908

**2012, Sept. 4** *Perf. 13x13¼*
**1946** A908 9.40s multi 4.75 4.75
With tab 5.25

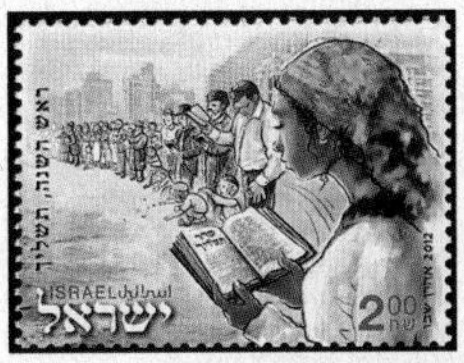

Worshipers Casting Away Sins at Water's Edge on Rosh Hashanah A909

Synagogue Members Reciting Kol Nidrei Prayer on Yom Kippur A910

Worshipers Holding Palm Fronds on Succoth A911

**2012, Sept. 4**
**1947** A909 2s multi 1.00 1.00
**1948** A910 4.20s multi 2.25 2.25
**1949** A911 6.20s multi 3.25 3.25
*Nos. 1947-1949 (3)* 6.50 6.50
With tabs 7.25

Tourist Attractions A912

Designs: Nos. 1950, 1953, Grotto, Rosh Hanikra. Nos. 1951, 1954, Jaffa. Nos. 1952, 1955, Solomon's Pillars, Timna Park.

**2012, Sept. 4** *Perf. 13x13¼*
**1950** A912 3s multi 1.50 1.50
**1951** A912 3s multi 1.50 1.50
**1952** A912 3s multi 1.50 1.50
*Nos. 1950-1952 (3)* 4.50 4.50
With tabs 5.00

### Booklet Stamps Self-Adhesive

*Serpentine Die Cut 12½*

**1953** A912 3s multi 1.50 1.50
**1954** A912 3s multi 1.50 1.50
**1955** A912 3s multi 1.50 1.50
***a.*** Booklet pane of 6, 2 each #1953-1955 9.00
*Nos. 1953-1955 (3)* 4.50 4.50

## AIR POST STAMPS

Doves Pecking at Grapes — AP1

Marisa Eagle — AP2

Designs: 30p, Beth Shearim eagle. 40p, Mosaic bird. 50p, Stylized dove. 250p, Mosaic dove and olive branch.

*Perf. 11½*

**1950, June 25** **Unwmk.** **Litho.**
**C1** AP1 5p brt grnsh bl .60 .25
**C2** AP1 30p gray .30 .25
**C3** AP1 40p dark green .30 .25
**C4** AP1 50p henna brown .30 .25
**C5** AP2 100p rose car 11.00 11.00
**C6** AP2 250p dk gray bl 1.50 .50
*Nos. C1-C6 (6)* 14.00 12.50
With tabs 275.00

Haifa Bay and City Seal AP3

120p, Haifa, Mt. Carmel and city seal.

**1952, Apr. 13** *Perf. 14*

**Seal in Gray**

**C7** AP3 100p ultramarine .30 .25
**C8** AP3 120p purple .25 .25
#C7-C8, with tabs 15.00

Stamps were available only on purchase of a ticket to the National Stamp Exhibition, Haifa. Price, including ticket, 340p.

Olive Tree — AP4

Tanur Cascade AP5

Coast at Tel Aviv-Jaffa AP6

70p, En Gev, Sea of Galilee. 100p, Road to Jerusalem. 150p, Lion Rock. 350p, Bay of Elat, Red Sea. 750p, Lake Hule. 3000p, Tomb of Rabbi Meir Baal Haness, Tiberias.

**1953-56 Litho.**

| | | | | | |
|---|---|---|---|---|---|
| **C9** | AP4 | 10p olive grn | .25 | .25 |
| **C10** | AP4 | 70p violet | .25 | .25 |
| **C11** | AP4 | 100p green | .25 | .25 |
| **C12** | AP4 | 150p orange brn | .25 | .25 |
| **C13** | AP4 | 350p car rose | .25 | .25 |
| **C14** | AP5 | 500p dull & dk bl | .25 | .25 |
| **C15** | AP6 | 750p brown | .25 | .25 |
| **C16** | AP6 | 1000p deep bl grn | 4.50 | .75 |
| | | With tab | 95.00 | |
| **C17** | AP6 | 3000p claret | .25 | .25 |
| | | *Nos. C9-C17 (9)* | 6.50 | 2.75 |
| | | Nos. C9-C15, C17 with tabs | 5.00 | |

Issued: 1000p, 3/16/53; 10p, 100p, 500p, 3/2/54; 70p, 150p, 350p, 4/6/54; 750p, 8/21/56; 3000p, 11/13/56.

Old Town, Zefat — AP7

Designs: 20a, Ashkelon, Afridar Center. 25a, Acre, tower and boats. 30a, Haifa, view from Mt. Carmel. 35a, Capernaum, ancient synagogue, horiz. 40a, Jethro's tomb, horiz. 50a, Jerusalem, horiz. 65a, Tiberias, tower and lake, horiz. £1, Jaffa, horiz.

**1960-61 Photo. *Perf. 13x14, 14x13***

| | | | | |
|---|---|---|---|---|
| **C18** | AP7 | 15a light lil & blk | .25 | .25 |
| **C19** | AP7 | 20a brt yel grn & blk | .25 | .25 |
| **C20** | AP7 | 25a orange & blk ('61) | .25 | .25 |
| **C21** | AP7 | 30a grnsh bl & blk ('61) | .25 | .25 |
| **C22** | AP7 | 35a yel grn & blk ('61) | .25 | .25 |
| **C23** | AP7 | 40a lt vio & blk ('61) | .25 | .25 |
| **C24** | AP7 | 50a olive & blk ('61) | .25 | .25 |
| **C25** | AP7 | 65a lt ultra & black | .25 | .25 |
| **C26** | AP7 | £1 pink & blk ('61) | .40 | .30 |
| | | *Nos. C18-C26 (9)* | 2.40 | 2.30 |
| | | With tabs | 11.00 | |

Issued: #C18, C19, C25, 2/24/60; #C20-C22, 6/14/61; #C23, C24, C26, 10/26/61.

Port of Elat ('Aqaba) — AP8

**Wmk. 302**

**1962, Feb. 21 Litho. *Perf. 14***

| | | | | |
|---|---|---|---|---|
| **C27** | AP8 | £3 multicolored | 1.60 | 1.00 |
| | | With tab | 9.00 | |

Houbara Bustard — AP9

Birds: 5a, Sinai rose finch, horiz. 20a, White-breasted kingfisher, horiz. 28a, Mourning wheatear, horiz. 30a, Blue-cheeked bee eater. 40a, Graceful prinia. 45a, Palestine sunbird. 70a, Scops owl. £1, Purple heron. £3, White-tailed Sea eagle.

***Perf. 13x14, 14x13***

**1963 Unwmk. Photo.**

| | | | | |
|---|---|---|---|---|
| **C28** | AP9 | 5a dp vio & multi | .25 | .25 |
| **C29** | AP9 | 20a red & multi | .25 | .25 |
| **C30** | AP9 | 28a emerald & multi | .25 | .25 |
| **C31** | AP9 | 30a orange & multi | .25 | .25 |
| **C32** | AP9 | 40a multicolored | .25 | .25 |
| **C33** | AP9 | 45a yellow & multi | .25 | .25 |
| **C34** | AP9 | 55a multicolored | .25 | .25 |
| **C35** | AP9 | 70a black & multi | .25 | .25 |
| **C36** | AP9 | £1 multicolored | .35 | .35 |
| **C37** | AP9 | £3 ultra & multi | .85 | .70 |
| | | *Nos. C28-C37 (10)* | 3.20 | 3.05 |
| | | With tabs | 5.75 | |

Issue dates: #C28-C30, Apr. 15; #C31-C33, June 19; #C34-C36, Feb. 13; #C37, Oct. 23.

Diamond and Boeing 707 AP10

Boeing 707 and: 10a, Textiles. 30a, Symbolic stamps. 40a, Vase, jewelry. 50a, Chick, egg. 55a, Melon, avocado, strawberries. 60a, Gladioli. 80a, Electronic equipment, chart. £1, Heavy oxygen isotopes (chemical apparatus). £1.50, Women's fashions.

**1968 Photo. *Perf. 13x14***

| | | | | |
|---|---|---|---|---|
| **C38** | AP10 | 10a ultra & multi | .25 | .25 |
| **C39** | AP10 | 30a gray & multi | .25 | .25 |
| **C40** | AP10 | 40a multicolored | .25 | .25 |
| **C41** | AP10 | 50a multicolored | .25 | .25 |
| **C42** | AP10 | 55a multicolored | .25 | .25 |
| **C43** | AP10 | 60a sl grn, lt grn & red | .25 | .25 |
| **C44** | AP10 | 80a yel, brn & lt bl | .25 | .25 |
| **C45** | AP10 | £1 dark bl & org | .25 | .25 |
| **C46** | AP10 | £1.50 multicolored | .25 | .25 |
| **C47** | AP10 | £3 pur & lt bl | .30 | .25 |
| | | *Nos. C38-C47 (10)* | 2.55 | 2.50 |
| | | With tabs | 3.00 | |

Israeli exports. Sheets of 15 (5x3).
Issued: #C38-C41, 3/11; #C47, 2/7; #C42-C43, C45, 11/6; #C44, C46, 12/23.

### POSTAGE DUE STAMPS

Types of Regular Issue Overprinted in Black

Various coins, as on postage denominations.

**Unwmk.**

**1948, May 28 Typo. *Perf. 11***

**Yellow Paper**

| | | | | |
|---|---|---|---|---|
| **J1** | A1 | 3m orange | 3.00 | 1.25 |
| **J2** | A1 | 5m yellow green | 4.00 | 1.75 |
| **J3** | A1 | 10m red violet | 7.00 | 4.00 |
| **J4** | A1 | 20m ultramarine | 13.00 | 8.00 |
| **J5** | A1 | 50m orange brown | 52.50 | 47.50 |
| | | *Nos. J1-J5 (5)* | 79.50 | 62.50 |
| | | With tabs (blank) | *2,750.* | |

The 3m, 20m and 50m are known with overprint omitted.
Nos. J1-J5 exist imperf.

D1

Running Stag — D2

**1949, Dec. 18 Litho. *Perf. 11½***

| | | | | |
|---|---|---|---|---|
| **J6** | D1 | 2p orange | .25 | .25 |
| **J7** | D1 | 5p purple | .25 | .25 |
| **J8** | D1 | 10p yellow green | .25 | .25 |
| **J9** | D1 | 20p vermilion | .25 | .25 |
| **J10** | D1 | 30p violet blue | .25 | .25 |
| **J11** | D1 | 50p orange brown | .45 | .25 |
| | | *Nos. J6-J11 (6)* | 1.70 | 1.50 |
| | | With tabs (blank) | 125.00 | |

**1952, Nov. 30 Unwmk. *Perf. 14***

| | | | | |
|---|---|---|---|---|
| **J12** | D2 | 5p orange brown | .25 | .25 |
| **J13** | D2 | 10p Prussian blue | .25 | .25 |
| **J14** | D2 | 20p magenta | .25 | .25 |
| **J15** | D2 | 30p gray black | .25 | .25 |
| **J16** | D2 | 40p green | .25 | .25 |
| **J17** | D2 | 50p brown | .25 | .25 |
| **J18** | D2 | 60p purple | .25 | .25 |
| **J19** | D2 | 100p red | .25 | .25 |
| **J20** | D2 | 250p blue | .25 | .25 |
| | | *Nos. J12-J20 (9)* | 2.25 | 2.25 |
| | | With tabs (blank) | 5.00 | |

### OFFICIAL STAMPS

Redrawn Type of 1950 Overprinted in Black

**1951, Feb. 1 Unwmk. *Perf. 14***

| | | | | |
|---|---|---|---|---|
| **O1** | A6 | 5p bright red violet | .25 | .25 |
| **O2** | A6 | 15p vermilion | .25 | .25 |
| **O3** | A6 | 30p ultramarine | .25 | .25 |
| **O4** | A6 | 40p orange brown | .25 | .25 |
| | | *Nos. O1-O4 (4)* | 1.00 | 1.00 |
| | | With tabs | 20.00 | |

## ITALIAN COLONIES

ə-ˈtal-yən ˈkä-lə-nēz

General Issues for all Colonies

100 Centesimi = 1 Lira

**Used values in italics are for postaly used stamps. Cancelled-to-order copies sell for about the same as unused, hinged stamps.**

**Watermark**

Wmk. 140

**Type of Italy, Dante Alighieri Society Issue, in New Colors**

Overprinted in Red or Black

**1932, July 11 Wmk. 140 *Perf. 14***

| | | | | |
|---|---|---|---|---|
| **1** | A126 | 10c gray blk | 1.50 | *3.75* |
| **2** | A126 | 15c olive brn | 1.50 | *3.75* |
| **3** | A126 | 20c slate grn | 1.50 | 2.25 |
| **4** | A126 | 25c dk grn | 1.50 | 2.25 |
| **5** | A126 | 30c red brn (Bk) | 1.50 | 2.25 |
| **6** | A126 | 50c bl blk | 1.50 | 1.50 |
| **7** | A126 | 75c car rose (Bk) | 2.00 | 6.00 |
| **8** | A126 | 1.25 l dk bl | 2.00 | *9.00* |
| **9** | A126 | 1.75 l violet | 2.00 | *13.50* |
| **10** | A126 | 2.75 l org (Bk) | 2.00 | *22.50* |
| **11** | A126 | 5 l + 2 l ol grn | 2.00 | *26.00* |
| **12** | A126 | 10 l + 2.50 l dp bl | 2.00 | *42.50* |
| | | *Nos. 1-12,C1-C6 (18)* | 42.00 | *248.25* |

**Types of Italy, Garibaldi Issue, in New Colors and Inscribed: "POSTE COLONIALI ITALIANE"**

**1932, July 1 Photo.**

| | | | | |
|---|---|---|---|---|
| **13** | A138 | 10c green | 4.50 | *16.50* |
| **14** | A138 | 20c car rose | 4.50 | *10.50* |
| **15** | A138 | 25c green | 4.50 | *10.50* |
| **16** | A138 | 30c green | 4.50 | *16.50* |
| **17** | A138 | 50c car rose | 4.50 | *10.50* |
| **18** | A141 | 75c car rose | 4.50 | *18.00* |
| **19** | A141 | 1.25 l deep blue | 4.50 | *18.00* |
| **20** | A141 | 1.75 l + 25c dp bl | 9.00 | *24.00* |
| **21** | A144 | 2.55 l + 50c ol brn | 9.00 | *42.50* |
| **22** | A145 | 5 l + 1 l dp bl | 9.00 | *52.50* |
| | | *Nos. 13-22,C8-C12 (15)* | 94.50 | *356.50* |

See Nos. CE1-CE2.

Plowing with Oxen — A1

Pack Camel — A2

Lioness — A3

**1933, Mar. 27 Wmk. 140**

| | | | | |
|---|---|---|---|---|
| **23** | A1 | 10c ol brn | 16.00 | *22.50* |
| **24** | A2 | 20c dl vio | 16.00 | *22.50* |
| **25** | A3 | 25c green | 16.00 | *22.50* |
| **26** | A1 | 50c purple | 16.00 | *22.50* |
| **27** | A2 | 75c carmine | 16.00 | *26.00* |
| **28** | A3 | 1.25 l blue | 16.00 | *26.00* |
| **29** | A1 | 2.75 l red orange | 26.00 | 47.50 |
| **30** | A2 | 5 l + 2 l gray grn | 35.00 | *95.00* |
| **31** | A3 | 10 l + 2.50 l org brn | 35.00 | *145.00* |
| | | *Nos. 23-31,C13-C19 (16)* | 381.00 | *864.50* |

Annexation of Eritrea by Italy, 50th anniv.

Agricultural Implements A4

Arab and Camel — A5

"Eager with New Life" — A7

Steam Roller — A6

**1933 Photo. *Perf. 14***

| | | | | |
|---|---|---|---|---|
| **32** | A4 | 5c orange | 9.50 | *13.50* |
| **33** | A5 | 25c green | 9.50 | *13.50* |
| **34** | A6 | 50c purple | 9.50 | 12.00 |
| **35** | A4 | 75c carmine | 9.50 | *22.50* |
| **36** | A5 | 1.25 l deep blue | 9.50 | *22.50* |
| **37** | A6 | 1.75 l rose red | 9.50 | *22.50* |
| **38** | A4 | 2.75 l dark blue | 9.50 | *34.00* |
| **39** | A5 | 5 l brnsh blk | 18.00 | *45.00* |
| **40** | A6 | 10 l bluish blk | 18.00 | *57.50* |
| **41** | A7 | 25 l gray black | 22.50 | *90.00* |
| | | *Nos. 32-41,C20-C27 (18)* | 244.50 | *657.50* |

10th anniversary of Fascism. Each denomination bears a different inscription.

Issue dates: 25 l, Dec. 26; others, Oct. 5.

Mercury and Fasces — A8

**1934, Apr. 18**

| | | | | |
|---|---|---|---|---|
| **42** | A8 | 20c red orange | 2.40 | *8.00* |
| **43** | A8 | 30c slate green | 2.40 | *8.00* |
| **44** | A8 | 50c indigo | 2.40 | *8.00* |
| **45** | A8 | 1.25 l blue | 2.40 | *16.00* |
| | | *Nos. 42-45 (4)* | 9.60 | *40.00* |

15th annual Trade Fair, Milan.

Scoring a Goal — A9

Soccer Kickoff — A10

**1934, June 5**

| | | | | |
|---|---|---|---|---|
| **46** | A9 | 10c olive green | 27.50 | *45.00* |
| **47** | A9 | 50c purple | 55.00 | 30.00 |
| **48** | A9 | 1.25 l blue | 55.00 | *110.00* |
| **49** | A10 | 5 l brown | 80.00 | *350.00* |
| **50** | A10 | 10 l gray blue | 80.00 | *350.00* |
| | | *Nos. 46-50,C29-C35 (12)* | 592.00 | *1,725.* |

2nd World Soccer Championship.

SEMI-POSTAL STAMPS

Many issues of Italy and Italian Colonies include one or more semi-postal denominations. To avoid splitting sets, these issues are generally listed as regular postage, airmail, etc., unless all values carry a surtax.

**AIR POST STAMPS**

**Italian Air Post Stamps for Dante Alighieri Society Issue in New Colors and Overprinted in Red or Black Like #1-12**

**1932, July 11 Wmk. 140 *Perf. 14***

| | | | | |
|---|---|---|---|---|
| **C1** | AP10 | 50c gray blk (R) | 3.00 | *8.00* |
| **C2** | AP11 | 1 l indigo (R) | 3.00 | *8.00* |
| **C3** | AP11 | 3 l gray (R) | 3.75 | *12.00* |
| **C4** | AP11 | 5 l ol brn (R) | 3.75 | *17.50* |
| **C5** | AP10 | 7.70 l + 2 l car rose | 3.75 | *22.50* |
| **C6** | AP11 | 10 l + 2.50 l org | 3.75 | *45.00* |
| | | *Nos. C1-C6 (6)* | 17.80 | *108.00* |

Leonardo da Vinci — AP1

**1932, Sept. 7 Photo. *Perf. 14½***

| | | | | |
|---|---|---|---|---|
| **C7** | AP1 | 100 l dp grn & brn | 13.50 | *120.00* |

**Types of Italian Air Post Stamps, Garibaldi Issue, in New Colors and Inscribed: "POSTE AEREA COLONIALE ITALIANA"**

**1932, July 1**

| | | | | |
|---|---|---|---|---|
| **C8** | AP13 | 50c car rose | 4.50 | *18.00* |
| **C9** | AP14 | 80c green | 4.50 | *18.00* |
| **C10** | AP13 | 1 l + 25c ol brn | 9.00 | *28.00* |
| **C11** | AP13 | 2 l + 50c ol brn | 9.00 | *28.00* |
| **C12** | AP14 | 5 l + 1 l ol brn | 9.00 | *45.00* |
| | | *Nos. C8-C12 (5)* | 28.25 | *122.00* |

Eagle AP2

Savoia Marchetti 55 — AP3

Savoia Marchetti 55 Over Map of Eritrea AP4

**1933 *Perf. 14***

| | | | | |
|---|---|---|---|---|
| **C13** | AP2 | 50c org brn | 14.50 | *22.50* |
| **C14** | AP2 | 1 l blk vio | 14.50 | *22.50* |
| **C15** | AP3 | 3 l carmine | 27.50 | *45.00* |
| **C16** | AP3 | 5 l olive brn | 27.50 | *45.00* |
| **C17** | AP2 | 7.70 l + 2 l slate | 35.00 | *100.00* |
| **C18** | AP3 | 10 l + 2.50 l dp bl | 35.00 | *100.00* |
| **C19** | AP4 | 50 l dk vio | 35.00 | *100.00* |
| | | *Nos. C13-C19 (7)* | 154.50 | *387.50* |

50th anniv. of Italian Government of Eritrea.

Issue dates: 50 l, June 1; others, Mar. 27.

Macchi-Costoldi Seaplane — AP5

Savoia S73 — AP6

Winding Propeller AP7

"More Efficient Machinery" AP8

**1933-34**

| | | | | |
|---|---|---|---|---|
| **C20** | AP5 | 50c org brn | 12.00 | 19.50 |
| **C21** | AP6 | 75c red vio | 12.00 | 19.50 |
| **C22** | AP5 | 1 l bis brn | 12.00 | 19.50 |
| **C23** | AP6 | 3 l olive gray | 12.00 | *38.00* |
| **C24** | AP5 | 10 l dp vio | 12.00 | *38.00* |
| **C25** | AP6 | 12 l bl grn | 12.00 | *57.50* |
| **C26** | AP7 | 20 l gray blk | 17.50 | *67.50* |
| **C27** | AP8 | 50 l blue ('34) | 30.00 | *65.00* |
| | | *Nos. C20-C27 (8)* | 109.50 | *300.00* |

Tenth anniversary of Fascism.

Issue dates: 50 1, Dec. 26; others, Oct. 5.

Natives Hailing Dornier Wal — AP9

**1934, Apr. 24**

| | | | | |
|---|---|---|---|---|
| **C28** | AP9 | 25 l brown olive | 26.00 | *240.00* |

Issued in honor of Luigi Amadeo, Duke of the Abruzzi (1873-1933).

Airplane over Stadium AP10

Goalkeeper Leaping — AP11

Seaplane and Soccer Ball AP12

**1934, June**

| | | | | |
|---|---|---|---|---|
| **C29** | AP10 | 50c yel brn | 16.00 | *45.00* |
| **C30** | AP10 | 75c dp vio | 16.00 | *45.00* |
| **C31** | AP11 | 5 l brn blk | 55.00 | *110.00* |
| **C32** | AP11 | 10 l red org | 55.00 | *110.00* |
| **C33** | AP10 | 15 l car rose | 55.00 | *110.00* |
| **C34** | AP11 | 25 l green | 55.00 | 260.00 |
| **C35** | AP12 | 50 l bl grn | 55.00 | 260.00 |
| | | *Nos. C29-C35 (7)* | 307.00 | *940.00* |

World Soccer Championship Games, Rome.

Issued: 50 l, June 21; others, June 5.

**AIR POST SPECIAL DELIVERY STAMPS**

**Garibaldi Type of Italy**

**Wmk. 140**

**1932, Oct. 6 Photo. *Perf. 14***

| | | | | |
|---|---|---|---|---|
| **CE1** | APSD1 | 2.25 l + 1 l dk vio & sl | 10.50 | *28.00* |
| **CE2** | APSD1 | 4.50 l + 1.50 l dk brn & grn | 10.50 | *45.00* |

## ITALIAN EAST AFRICA

ə-ˈtal-yən ˈēst ˈa-fri-kə

LOCATION — In eastern Africa, bordering on the Red Sea and Indian Ocean
GOVT. — Italian Colony
AREA — 665,977 sq. mi. (estimated)
POP. — 12,100,000 (estimated)
CAPITAL — Asmara

This colony was formed in 1936 and included Ethiopia and the former colonies of Eritrea and Italian Somaliland.

For previous issues see listings under these headings.

100 Centesimi = 1 Lira

**Used values in italics are for postaly used stamps. Cancelled-to-order copies sell for about the same as unused, hinged stamps.**

Grant's Gazelle — A1

Eagle and Lion — A2

Victor Emmanuel III — A3

Fascist Legionary — A5

Statue of the Nile — A4

Desert Road — A6

**Wmk. 140**

**1938, Feb. 7 Photo. *Perf. 14***

| | | | | |
|---|---|---|---|---|
| **1** | A1 | 2c red orange | 1.60 | *1.10* |
| **2** | A2 | 5c brown | 1.60 | .25 |
| **3** | A3 | 7½c dk violet | 2.40 | *4.75* |
| **4** | A4 | 10c olive brown | 2.40 | .25 |
| **5** | A5 | 15c slate green | 1.60 | .40 |
| **6** | A3 | 20c crimson | 1.60 | .25 |
| **7** | A6 | 25c green | 2.40 | .25 |
| **8** | A1 | 30c olive brown | 1.75 | .80 |
| **9** | A2 | 35c sapphire | 2.50 | *12.00* |
| **10** | A3 | 50c purple | 1.60 | .25 |
| | | **Engr.** | | |
| **11** | A5 | 75c carmine lake | 2.50 | .40 |
| **12** | A6 | 1 l olive green | 1.75 | .25 |
| **13** | A3 | 1.25 l deep blue | 2.50 | .40 |
| **14** | A4 | 1.75 l orange | 17.00 | .25 |
| **15** | A2 | 2 l cerise | 2.50 | .40 |
| **16** | A6 | 2.55 l dark brown | 20.00 | *32.50* |
| **17** | A1 | 3.70 l purple | 55.00 | *65.00* |
| **18** | A5 | 5 l purple | 20.00 | 4.75 |
| **19** | A2 | 10 l henna brown | 22.50 | 20.00 |
| **20** | A4 | 20 l dull green | 32.50 | 32.50 |
| | | *Nos. 1-20,C1-C11,CE1-CE2 (33)* | 410.45 | 323.40 |

Augustus Caesar (Octavianus) A7

Goddess Abundantia A8

**1938, Apr. 25 Photo. *Perf. 14***

| | | | | | |
|---|---|---|---|---|---|
| **21** | A7 | 5c bister brn | .85 | *2.00* |
| **22** | A8 | 10c copper red | .85 | 1.25 |
| **23** | A7 | 25c deep green | 1.60 | 1.25 |
| **24** | A8 | 50c purple | 1.60 | .85 |
| **25** | A7 | 75c crimson | 1.60 | 3.00 |
| **26** | A8 | 1.25 l deep blue | 1.60 | 8.50 |
| | | *Nos. 21-26,C12-C13 (8)* | 9.70 | *24.85* |

Bimillenary of the birth of Augustus Caesar (Octavianus), first Roman emperor.

Rome-Berlin Axis.

Four stamps of type AP8, without "Posta Aerea," were prepared in 1941, but not issued. Value, each $2,400.

Native Boat — A9

Native Soldier — A10

Statue Suggesting Italy's Conquest of Ethiopia — A11

**1940, May 11 Wmk. 140**

| | | | | | |
|---|---|---|---|---|---|
| **27** | A9 | 5c olive brown | .85 | *1.20* |
| **28** | A10 | 10c red orange | .85 | *1.20* |
| **29** | A11 | 25c green | 2.25 | 2.00 |
| **30** | A9 | 50c purple | 2.25 | 1.20 |
| **31** | A10 | 75c rose red | 2.25 | *7.50* |
| **32** | A11 | 1.25 l dark blue | 2.25 | 6.00 |
| **33** | A10 | 2 l + 75c carmine | 2.25 | *22.50* |
| | | *Nos. 27-33,C14-C17 (11)* | 23.45 | *56.60* |

Issued in connection with the first Triennial Overseas Exposition held at Naples.

Hitler and Mussolini ("Two Peoples, One War") A12

**1941, June 19**

| | | | | |
|---|---|---|---|---|
| **34** | A12 | 5c ocher | 2.50 |
| **35** | A12 | 10c chestnut | 2.50 |
| **36** | A12 | 20c black | 4.50 |
| **37** | A12 | 25c turquoise grn | 4.50 |
| **38** | A12 | 50c rose lilac | 4.50 |
| **39** | A12 | 75c rose car | 4.50 |
| **40** | A12 | 1.25 l brt ultra | 4.50 |
| | | *Nos. 34-40,C18-C19 (9)* | 173.00 |

SEMI-POSTAL STAMPS

Many issues of Italy and Italian Colonies include one or more semi-postal denominations. To avoid splitting sets, these issues are generally listed as regular postage, airmail, etc., unless all values carry a surtax.

## AIR POST STAMPS

Plane Flying over Mountains AP1

Mussolini Carved in Stone Cliff — AP2

Airplane over Lake Tsana AP3

Bataleur Eagle — AP4

**Wmk. Crowns (140)**

**1938, Feb. 7 Photo. *Perf. 14***

| | | | | | |
|---|---|---|---|---|---|
| **C1** | AP1 | 25c slate green | 3.25 | *4.75* |
| **C2** | AP2 | 50c olive brown | 72.50 | .25 |
| **C3** | AP3 | 60c red orange | 3.25 | *13.50* |
| **C4** | AP1 | 75c orange brn | 4.00 | 2.50 |
| **C5** | AP4 | 1 l slate blue | 1.25 | .25 |

**Engr.**

| | | | | | |
|---|---|---|---|---|---|
| **C6** | AP2 | 1.50 l violet | 1.75 | .40 |
| **C7** | AP3 | 2 l slate blue | 1.75 | 1.75 |
| **C8** | AP1 | 3 l carmine lake | 2.50 | 6.75 |
| **C9** | AP4 | 5 l red brown | 72.50 | 35.00 |
| **C10** | AP2 | 10 l violet brn | 12.00 | 14.50 |
| **C11** | AP1 | 25 l slate blue | 24.00 | 35.00 |
| | | *Nos. C1-C11 (11)* | 173.75 | 95.55 |

Eagle Attacking Serpent — AP5

**1938, Apr. 25 Photo.**

| | | | | | |
|---|---|---|---|---|---|
| **C12** | AP5 | 50c bister brown | .80 | 2.75 |
| **C13** | AP5 | 1 l purple | .80 | *5.25* |

Bimillenary of the birth of Augustus Caesar (Octavianus), first Roman emperor.

**Triennial Overseas Exposition Type**

#C14, C16, Tractor. #C15, C17, Plane over city.

**1940, May 11**

| | | | | | |
|---|---|---|---|---|---|
| **C14** | A10 | 50c olive gray | 2.25 | *7.50* |
| **C15** | A9 | 1 l purple | 2.25 | *7.50* |
| **C16** | A10 | 2 l + 75c gray blue | 3.00 | — |
| **C17** | A9 | 5 l + 2.50 l red brn | 3.00 | — |
| | | *Nos. C14-C17 (4)* | 7.20 | *13.00* |

Hitler and Mussolini ("Two Peoples, One War") AP8

AP9

**1941, Apr. 24**

| | | | | |
|---|---|---|---|---|
| **C18** | AP8 | 1 l slate blue | 135.00 |
| **C19** | AP9 | 1 l slate blue | 10.50 |

Rome-Berlin Axis.

## AIR POST SPECIAL DELIVERY STAMPS

Plow and Airplane — APSD1

**Wmk. 140**

**1938, Feb. 7 Engr. *Perf. 14***

| | | | | | |
|---|---|---|---|---|---|
| **CE1** | APSD1 | 2 l slate blue | 8.00 | *12.00* |
| **CE2** | APSD1 | 2.50 l dark brown | 8.00 | *20.00* |

## SPECIAL DELIVERY STAMPS

Victor Emmanuel III — SD1

**Wmk. 140**

**1938, Apr. 16 Engr. *Perf. 14***

| | | | | | |
|---|---|---|---|---|---|
| **E1** | SD1 | 1.25 l dark green | 12.00 | 12.00 |
| **E2** | SD1 | 2.50 l dark carmine | 12.00 | *35.00* |

## POSTAGE DUE STAMPS

Italy, Nos. J28 to J40, Overprinted in Black

**1941 Wmk. 140 *Perf. 14***

| | | | | |
|---|---|---|---|---|
| **J1** | D6 | 5c brown | 1.60 |
| **J2** | D6 | 10c blue | 1.60 |
| **J3** | D6 | 20c rose red | 3.25 |
| **J4** | D6 | 25c green | 3.25 |
| **J5** | D6 | 30c red orange | 8.00 |
| **J6** | D6 | 40c black brown | 8.00 |
| **J7** | D6 | 50c violet | 8.00 |
| **J8** | D6 | 60c slate black | 11.00 |
| **J9** | D7 | 1 l red orange | 22.50 |
| **J10** | D7 | 2 l green | 22.50 |
| **J11** | D7 | 5 l violet | 35.00 |
| **J12** | D7 | 10 l blue | 22.50 |
| **J13** | D7 | 20 l carmine rose | 22.50 |
| | | *Nos. J1-J13 (13)* | 169.70 |

In 1943 a set of 11 "Segnatasse" stamps, picturing a horse and rider and inscribed "A. O. I.," was prepared but not issued. Value, $17.50.

# ITALIAN STATES

ə-ˈtal-yən ˈstāts

**Watermarks**

Wmk. 157 — Large Letter "A"

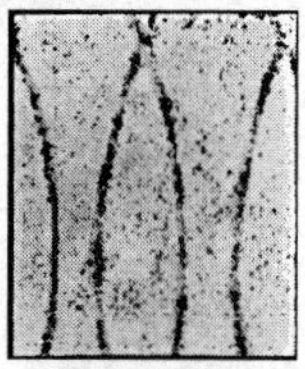
Wmk. 184 — Interlaced Wavy Lines

Wmk. 184 has double lined letters diagonally across the sheet readiing: "II R R POSTE TOSCANE."

Wmk. 185 — Crowns in the sheet

The watermark consists of twelve crowns, arranged in four rows of three, with horizontal and vertical lines between them. Only parts of the watermark appear on each stamp.

Wmk. 186 — Fleurs-de-Lis in Sheet

# MODENA

LOCATION — In northern Italy
GOVT. — Duchy
AREA — 1,003 sq. mi.
POP. — 448,000 (approx.)
CAPITAL — Modena

In 1852, when the first postage stamps were issued, Modena was under the rule of Duke Francis V of the House of Este-Lorraine. In June, 1859, he was overthrown and the Duchy was annexed to the Kingdom of Sardinia which on March 17, 1861, became the Kingdom of Italy.

100 Centesimi = 1 Lira

Values of Modena stamps vary tremendously according to condition. Values are for very fine examples, and values for unused stamps are for examples with original gum as defined in the catalogue introduction. Extremely fine or superb examples sell at much higher prices, and fine or poor examples sell at greatly reduced prices. In addition, very fine unused examples without gum sell for about 20% of the values shown.

Coat of Arms — A1

**1852-57 Unwmk. Typo. *Imperf.***

**Without Period After Figures of Value**

| | | | | | |
|---|---|---|---|---|---|
| **1** | A1 | 5c blk, *green* | 2,375. | 125.00 |
| **2** | A1 | 10c blk, *rose* | 600.00 | 80.00 |
| | *a.* | "EENT. 10" | *9,000.* | *2,650.* |
| | *b.* | "1" of "10" inverted | *9,000.* | *2,650.* |
| | *c.* | "CNET" | *1,475.* | *1,650.* |
| | *d.* | No period after "CENT" | *2,100.* | 725.00 |
| **3** | A1 | 15c blk, *yellow* | 70.00 | 32.50 |
| | *a.* | "CETN 15." | *9,000.* | *1,000.* |
| | *b.* | No period after "CENT" | 325.00 | *525.00* |
| **4** | A1 | 25c blk, *buff* | 120.00 | 45.00 |
| | *a.* | No period after "CENT" | 650.00 | *1,000.* |
| | *b.* | "ENT.25" omitted | *1,000.* | — |

| | | | | |
|---|---|---|---|---|
| c. | | 25c black, *green* (error) | 3,600. | 2,250. |
| d. | | "N" of "CENT" omitted | 725.00 | 1,650. |
| 5 | A1 | 40c blk, *blue* | 450.00 | 110.00 |
| a. | | 40c black, *pale blue* | *16,500.* | 1,650. |
| b. | | No period after "CENT" | *1,900.* | *1,500.* |
| c. | | As "a," no period after "CENT" | — | — |

Unused examples of No. 5a lack gum.

Used examples of No. 4c have a green administrative cancellation.

See Nos. PR3-PR4.

### With Period After Figures of Value

| | | | | |
|---|---|---|---|---|
| 6 | A1 | 5c blk, *green* | 42.50 | *47.50* |
| a. | | 5c black, *olive green* ('55) | 475.00 | 145.00 |
| b. | | "ENT" | — | *2,750.* |
| c. | | "CNET" | *4,350.* | *3,600.* |
| d. | | As "a," "CNET" | *2,250.* | *2,175.* |
| e. | | "E" of "CENT" sideways | — | *5,750.* |
| f. | | As "a," "CEN1" | *2,750.* | *2,500.* |
| g. | | As "a," no period after "5" | 725.00 | 575.00 |
| h. | | Double impression, no gum | *1,200.* | — |
| i. | | As "a," double impression | *1,200.* | — |
| j. | | Pair, #6a, 6g | 1,300. | *2,350.* |
| 7 | A1 | 10c blk, *rose* ('57) | 475.00 | 350.00 |
| a. | | "CENE" | 1,500. | *1,700.* |
| b. | | "CNET" | 650.00 | *900.00* |
| c. | | "CE6T" | 1,500. | *1,700.* |
| d. | | "N" of "CENT" sideways | *11,500.* | *4,350.* |
| e. | | Double impression | 1,200. | *4,400.* |
| f. | | Raised period after "10" | 1,500. | 1,825. |
| 8 | A1 | 40c blk, *blue* ('54) | 50.00 | *125.00* |
| a. | | "CNET" | 290.00 | *800.00* |
| b. | | "CENE" | 650.00 | *1,700.* |
| c. | | "CE6T" | 650.00 | *1,700.* |
| d. | | "49" | 290.00 | *900.00* |
| e. | | "4C" | 650.00 | *1,700.* |
| f. | | "CEN.T" | *37,500.* | — |
| g. | | Space between "T" and period | 290.00 | *825.00* |
| h. | | Pair, one with no period after value | 725.00 | *2,500.* |

### Wmk. 157

| | | | | |
|---|---|---|---|---|
| 9 | A1 | 1 l black ('53) | 57.50 | *2,250.* |
| a. | | With period after "LIRA" | 165.00 | *4,250.* |
| b. | | No period after "1" | 145.00 | *3,600.* |

### Provisional Government

Coat of Arms — A2

**1859** **Unwmk.**

| | | | | |
|---|---|---|---|---|
| 10 | A2 | 5c green | 1,450. | *700.00* |
| a. | | 5c emerald | 1,525. | *800.00* |
| b. | | 5c dark green | 1,525. | 800.00 |
| 11 | A2 | 15c brown | 2,325. | *4,000.* |
| a. | | 15c gray brown | 325.00 | |
| b. | | 15c black brown | 2,625. | 5,000. |
| c. | | No period after "15" | *3,000.* | *4,750.* |
| d. | | Period before "CENT" | *4,000.* | *6,500.* |
| e. | | Double impression (#11a) | *1,650.* | |
| 12 | A2 | 20c lilac | 75.00 | *1,350.* |
| a. | | 20c violet | 4,000. | 180.00 |
| b. | | 20c blue violet | 2,400. | 180.00 |
| c. | | As #12, no period after "20" | 100.00 | *1,500.* |
| d. | | As #12, "ECNT" | 250.00 | *3,250.* |
| e. | | As #12, "N" inverted | 200.00 | *2,250.* |
| f. | | Double impression (#12b) | | *6,500.* |
| 13 | A2 | 40c carmine | 190.00 | *1,350.* |
| a. | | 40c brown rose | 190.00 | *1,350.* |
| b. | | No period after "40" | 365.00 | *2,275.* |
| c. | | Period before "CENT" | 365.00 | *2,275.* |
| d. | | Inverted "5" before the "C", no gum | *36,000.* | *45,000.* |
| 14 | A2 | 80c buff | 190.00 | *21,000.* |
| a. | | 80c brown orange | 190.00 | *21,000.* |
| b. | | "CENT 8" | 365.00 | — |
| c. | | "CENT 0" | 1,200. | — |
| d. | | No period after "80" | 365.00 | — |
| e. | | "N" inverted | 365.00 | — |

### NEWSPAPER TAX STAMPS

NT1

Type I

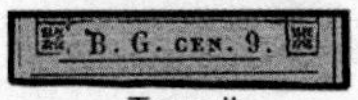

Type II

**1853** **Unwmk.** **Typo.** ***Imperf.***

| | | | | |
|---|---|---|---|---|
| PR1 | NT1 | 9c blk, *violet* (I) | — | *3,000.* |
| PR2 | NT1 | 9c blk, *violet* (II) | 725.00 | 80.00 |
| a. | | No period after "9" | 1,100. | 275.00 |

All known unused examples of #PR1 lack gum.

**1855-57**

| | | | | |
|---|---|---|---|---|
| PR3 | A1 | 9c blk, *violet* | 3.65 | |
| a. | | No period after "9" | 7.25 | |
| b. | | No period after "CENT" | 11.00 | |
| PR4 | A1 | 10c blk, *gray vio* ('57) | 72.50 | *250.00* |
| a. | | "CEN1" | 365.00 | *1,450.* |

No. PR3 was never placed in use.

NT2

**1859**

| | | | | |
|---|---|---|---|---|
| PR5 | NT2 | 10c black | 1,100. | *2,100.* |
| a. | | Double impression | *16,250.* | *20,000.* |
| b. | | Vert. guidelines between stamps | 1,150. | |

### Values for unused pairs

*PR5* NT2 10c black 2,750.

## PARMA

LOCATION — Comprising the present provinces of Parma and Piacenza in northern Italy.

GOVT. — Independent Duchy

AREA — 2,750 sq. mi. (1860)

POP. — 500,000 (1860)

CAPITAL — Parma

Parma was annexed to Sardinia in 1860.

100 Centesimi = 1 Lira

Values of Parma stamps vary tremendously according to condition. Values are for very fine examples, and values for unused stamps are for examples with original gum as defined in the catalogue introduction except for No. 8 which is known only without gum. Extremely fine or superb copies sell at much higher prices, and fine or poor stamps sell at greatly reduced prices. In addition, very fine unused stamps without gum sell for about 20% of the values shown.

Crown and Fleur-de-lis

A1 A2

**1852** **Unwmk.** **Typo.** ***Imperf.***

| | | | | |
|---|---|---|---|---|
| 1 | A1 | 5c blk, *yellow* | 130.00 | *150.00* |
| 2 | A1 | 10c blk, *white* | 130.00 | *150.00* |
| 3 | A1 | 15c blk, *pink* | 4,200. | 95.00 |
| a. | | Tête bêche pair, horiz. | | *100,000.* |
| b. | | Double impression | | *4,750.* |
| 4 | A1 | 25c blk, *violet* | *16,500.* | 235.00 |
| 5 | A1 | 40c blk, *blue* | 3,500. | 540.00 |
| a. | | 40c black, *pale blue* | *6,000.* | 800.00 |

**1854-55**

| | | | | |
|---|---|---|---|---|
| 6 | A1 | 5c org yel | *9,500.* | 800.00 |
| a. | | 5c lemon yellow | *12,000.* | 1,000. |
| b. | | Double impression | | *19,000.* |
| 7 | A1 | 15c red | *12,000.* | 300.00 |
| 8 | A1 | 25c red brn ('55) | — | *450.00* |
| a. | | Double impression | | *38,000.* |

No. 8 unused is without gum.

**1857-59**

| | | | | |
|---|---|---|---|---|
| 9 | A2 | 15c red ('59) | 385.00 | 360.00 |
| 10 | A2 | 25c red brown | 650.00 | 210.00 |
| 11 | A2 | 40c bl, wide "0" ('58) | 90.00 | *550.00* |
| a. | | Narrow "0" in "40" | 95.00 | *650.00* |

### Provisional Government

A3

**1859**

| | | | | |
|---|---|---|---|---|
| 12 | A3 | 5c yel grn | 600.00 | *30,000.* |
| a. | | 5c blue green | 3,000. | *5,400.* |
| 13 | A3 | 10c brown | 1,200. | *650.00* |
| a. | | 10c deep brown | 1,200. | *650.00* |
| b. | | "1" of "10" inverted | 2,400. | *5,000.* |
| c. | | Thick "0" in "10" | 1,500. | *775.00* |
| 14 | A3 | 20c pale blue | 1,200. | 240.00 |
| a. | | 20c deep blue | 1,200. | 265.00 |
| b. | | Thick "0" in "20" | 1,450. | 265.00 |
| 15 | A3 | 40c red | 650.00 | *10,000.* |
| a. | | 40c brown red | *24,000.* | *15,000.* |
| b. | | Thick "0" in "40" (#15) | 775.00 | *11,250.* |
| c. | | Thick "0" in "40," (#15a) | *28,000.* | *17,000.* |
| 16 | A3 | 80c olive yellow | 8,000. | *250,000.* |
| a. | | 80c orange yellow | 11,000. | — |
| b. | | 80c bister | 9,000. | |
| c. | | 80c orange bister | 9,750. | |

Nos. 12-16 exist in two other varieties: with spelling "CFNTESIMI" and with small "A" in "STATI." These are valued about 50 per cent more than normal stamps.

See Nos. PR1-PR2.

### NEWSPAPER TAX STAMPS

**Type of 1859**

**Normal Paper ('53)**

**1853-57** **Unwmk.** **Typo.** ***Imperf.***

| | | | | |
|---|---|---|---|---|
| PR1 | A3 | 6c black, *deep rose* | 2,100. | 325.00 |
| PR2 | A3 | 9c black, *blue* | 1,100. | *12,750.* |

**Thin, Semitransparent Paper ('57)**

| | | | |
|---|---|---|---|
| *PR1a* | A3 | 6c black, *rose* ('57) | 140.00 |
| *PR2a* | A3 | 9c black, *blue* | 72.50 |

These stamps belong to the same class as the Newspaper Tax Stamps of Modena, Austria, etc.

Note following #16 also applies to #PR1-PR2.

Nos. PR1a-PR2a were not issued.

The stamps of Parma were superseded by those of Sardinia in 1860.

## ROMAGNA

LOCATION — Comprised the present Italian provinces of Forli, Ravenna, Ferrara and Bologna.

GOVT. — One of the Roman States

AREA — 5,626 sq. mi.

POP. — 1,341,091 (1853)

CAPITAL — Ravenna

Postage stamps were issued when a provisional government was formed pending the unification of Italy. In 1860 Romagna was annexed to Sardinia and since 1862 the postage stamps of Italy have been used.

100 Bajocchi = 1 Scudo

Values of Romagna stamps vary tremendously according to condition. Values are for very fine examples, and values for unused stamps are for examples with original gum as defined in the catalogue introduction. Extremely fine or superb stamps sell at much higher prices, and fine or poor stamps sell at greatly reduced prices. In addition, very fine unused stamps without gum sell for about 20% of the values shown.

A1

**1859** **Unwmk.** **Typo.** ***Imperf.***

| | | | | |
|---|---|---|---|---|
| 1 | A1 | ½b blk, *straw* | 30.00 | *350.00* |
| a. | | Half used as ¼b on cover | | *16,500.* |
| 2 | A1 | 1b blk, *drab* | 30.00 | *180.00* |
| 3 | A1 | 2b blk, *buff* | 42.50 | *210.00* |
| a. | | Half used as 1b on cover | | 6,250. |
| 4 | A1 | 3b blk, *dk grn* | 50.00 | *360.00* |
| 5 | A1 | 4b blk, *fawn* | 550.00 | 165.00 |
| a. | | Half used as 2b on cover | | *30,000.* |
| 6 | A1 | 5b blk, *gray vio* | 60.00 | *400.00* |
| 7 | A1 | 6b blk, *yel grn* | 400.00 | *8,500.* |
| a. | | Half used as 3b on cover | | *150,000.* |
| 8 | A1 | 8b blk, *rose* | 200.00 | *1,800.* |
| a. | | Half used as 4b on cover | | *150,000.* |
| 9 | A1 | 20b blk, *gray grn* | 200.00 | *2,400.* |

Forged cancellations are plentiful.

Bisects used Oct. 12, 1859 to Mar. 1, 1860.

*These stamps have been reprinted several times. The reprints usually resemble the originals in the color of the paper but there are impressions on incorrect colors and also in colors on white paper. They often show broken letters and other injuries. The Y shaped ornaments between the small circles in the corners are broken and blurred and the dots outside the circles are often missing or joined to the circles.*

The stamps of Romagna were superseded by those of Sardinia in February, 1860.

## ROMAN STATES

LOCATION — Comprised most of the central Italian Peninsula, bounded by the former Kingdom of Lombardy-Venetia and Modena on the north, Tuscany on the west, and the Kingdom of Naples on the southeast.
GOVT. — Under the direct government of the See of Rome.
AREA — 16,000 sq. mi.
POP. — 3,124,758 (1853)
CAPITAL — Rome

Upon the formation of the Kingdom of Italy, the area of the Roman States was greatly reduced and in 1870 they disappeared from the political map of Europe. Postage stamps of Italy have been used since that time.

100 Bajocchi = 1 Scudo
100 Centesimi = 1 Lira (1867)

Values of Roman States stamps vary tremendously according to condition. Values are for very fine examples, and values for unused stamps are for examples with original gum as defined in the catalogue introduction. Extremely fine or superb stamps sell at much higher prices, and fine or poor stamps sell at greatly reduced prices. In addition, very fine unused stamps without gum sell for about 20% of the values shown.

Papal Arms
A1 A2

A3

A4

A5

A6

A7

A8

A9

A10

A11

**1852 Unwmk. Typo. *Imperf.***

| No. | Type | Description | Unused | Used |
|---|---|---|---|---|
| 1 | A1 | ½b black, *dull violet* | 65.00 | *150.00* |
| a. | | ½b black, *gray blue* | 800.00 | 100.00 |
| b. | | ½b black, *gray lilac* | 800.00 | 400.00 |
| c. | | ½b black, *gray* | 800.00 | 100.00 |
| d. | | ½b black, *reddish violet* | 4,250. | 3,000. |
| e. | | ½b black, *dark violet* | 325.00 | 350.00 |
| f. | | Tête bêche pair | | 32,500. |
| h. | | As "a," half used as ¼b on wrapper | | *60,000.* |
| | | As "h," pen canceled | | *10,000.* |
| i. | | As #1, double impression | — | *6,750.* |
| j. | | Impression on both sides | — | *14,500.* |
| 2 | A2 | 1b black, *gray green* | 360.00 | 10.00 |
| a. | | 1b black, *blue green* | 900.00 | 60.00 |
| b. | | As "a," half used as ½b on cover | | 475.00 |
| c. | | Grayish oily ink | 1,300. | 32.50 |
| d. | | Double impression | | *6,500.* |
| e. | | Impression on both sides | — | *14,250.* |
| 3 | A3 | 2b black, *greenish white* | 18.00 | *72.50* |
| a. | | 2b black, *yellow green* | 265.00 | 18.00 |
| b. | | As #3, half used as 1b on cover | | *6,000.* |
| c. | | As "a," half used as 1b on cover | | 400.00 |
| d. | | Grayish oily ink | 1,425. | 37.50 |
| e. | | No period after "BAJ" | 165.00 | 37.50 |
| f. | | As "a" and "e" | 540.00 | 35.00 |
| g. | | Double impression | | *6,500.* |
| 4 | A4 | 3b black, *brown* | 300.00 | 60.00 |
| a. | | 3b black, *light brown* | 6,000. | 180.00 |
| b. | | 3b black, *yellow brown* | 2,675. | 45.00 |
| c. | | 3b black, *yellow buff* | 2,675. | *45.00* |
| d. | | 3b black, *chrome yellow* | 47.50 | *180.00* |
| e. | | One-third used as 1b on circular | | *3,750.* |
| f. | | Two-thirds used as 2b on circular | | *11,500.* |
| g. | | Grayish oily ink | 7,750. | 235.00 |
| h. | | Impression on both sides | — | *12,000.* |
| i. | | Double impression | — | *6,600.* |
| j. | | Half used as 1½b on cover | | *12,500.* |
| 5 | A5 | 4b black, *lemon* | 265.00 | 80.00 |
| a. | | 4b black, *yellow* | 265.00 | 80.00 |
| b. | | 4b black, *rose brown* | 12,500. | 130.00 |
| c. | | 4b black, *gray brown* | 10,000. | 80.00 |
| d. | | Half used as 2b on cover | | 2,500. |
| e. | | One-quarter used as 1b on cover | | *24,000.* |
| f. | | Impression on both sides | — | *12,000.* |
| g. | | Ribbed paper | 325.00 | 90.00 |
| h. | | Grayish oily ink | 24,000. | 360.00 |
| i. | | As "a," half used as 2b on cover | | 4,250. |
| j. | | As "a," one-quarter used as 1b on cover | | *23,500.* |
| 6 | A6 | 5b black, *rose* | 250.00 | 16.00 |
| a. | | 5b black, *pale rose* | 265.00 | 17.50 |
| c. | | Impression on both sides | | *12,500.* |
| d. | | Double impression | | *6,500.* |
| e. | | Grayish oily ink | 1,550. | 40.00 |
| f. | | Half used as 2½b on cover | | *60,000.* |
| 7 | A7 | 6b black, *greenish gray* | 1,075. | 75.00 |
| a. | | 6b black, *gray* | 1,650. | 80.00 |
| b. | | 6b black, *grayish lilac* | 1,575. | 240.00 |
| c. | | Grayish oily ink | 4,250. | 300.00 |
| d. | | Double impression | — | *6,500.* |
| e. | | Half used as 3b on cover | | 4,750. |
| f. | | One-third used as 2b on cover | | *18,000.* |
| 8 | A8 | 7b black, *blue* | 1,700. | 80.00 |
| a. | | Half used as 3¼b on cover | | *30,000.* |
| b. | | Double impression | — | 6,500. |
| c. | | Grayish oily ink | 5,500. | 150.00 |
| 9 | A9 | 8b black | 625.00 | 45.00 |
| a. | | Half used as 4b on cover | | 9,000. |
| b. | | Quarter used as 2b on cover | | *90,000.* |
| c. | | Double impression | — | — |
| d. | | Grayish oily ink | 2,500. | 225.00 |
| 10 | A10 | 50b dull blue | *16,000.* | 1,800. |
| a. | | 50b deep blue (worn impression) | *30,000.* | 3,250. |
| 11 | A11 | 1sc rose | *4,000.* | *3,600.* |

Counterfeits exist of Nos. 10-11. Fraudulent cancellations are found on No. 11.

A12

A13

A14

A15

A16

A17

A18

**1867 Glazed Paper *Imperf.***

| No. | Type | Description | Unused | Used |
|---|---|---|---|---|
| 12 | A12 | 2c black, *green* | 95.00 | *350.00* |
| a. | | No period after "Cent" | 120.00 | *390.00* |
| 13 | A13 | 3c black, *gray* | 1,500. | *9,000.* |
| a. | | 3c black, *lilac gray* | 3,600. | *2,400.* |
| 14 | A14 | 5c black, *light blue* | 210.00 | *240.00* |
| a. | | No period after "5" | 415.00 | *500.00* |
| 15 | A15 | 10c black, *vermilion* | 2,100. | 105.00 |
| a. | | Double impression | | 6,500. |
| 16 | A16 | 20c black, *copper red (unglazed)* | 210.00 | 135.00 |
| a. | | No period after "20" | 600.00 | 400.00 |
| b. | | No period after "CENT" | 600.00 | 400.00 |
| 17 | A17 | 40c black, *yellow* | 225.00 | *180.00* |
| a. | | No period after "40" | 285.00 | 225.00 |
| 18 | A18 | 80c black, *lilac rose* | 200.00 | *500.00* |
| a. | | No period after "80" | 300.00 | *750.00* |

Imperforate stamps on unglazed paper, or in colors other than listed, are unfinished remainders of the 1868 issue.
Fraudulent cancellations are found on Nos. 13, 14, 17, 18.

**1868 Glazed Paper *Perf. 13***

| No. | Type | Description | Unused | Used |
|---|---|---|---|---|
| 19 | A12 | 2c black, *green* | 9.00 | *90.00* |
| a. | | No period after "CENT" | 11.00 | *110.00* |
| 20 | A13 | 3c black, *gray* | 55.00 | *3,250.* |
| a. | | 3c black, *lilac gray* | *10,000.* | *18,000.* |
| 21 | A14 | 5c black, *light blue* | 60.00 | *60.00* |
| a. | | No period after "5" | 75.00 | *72.50* |
| b. | | No period after "Cent" | 150.00 | *350.00* |
| c. | | 5c black, *lt bl* (unglazed, imperf., without gum) | 120.00 | — |
| 22 | A15 | 10c black, *orange ver* | 3.00 | *15.00* |
| a. | | 10c black, *vermilion* | 60.00 | 15.00 |
| b. | | 10c black, *ver* (unglazed) | 1.25 | — |
| c. | | 10c black, *ver* (unglazed, imperf., without gum) | 1.25 | — |
| 23 | A16 | 20c black, *deep crimson* | 4.75 | *30.00* |
| a. | | 20c black, *magenta* | 6.00 | *42.50* |
| b. | | 20c black, *magenta* (unglazed) | 300.00 | *35.00* |
| c. | | 20c black, *magenta* (imperf., without gum) | 2.50 | — |
| d. | | 20c black, *copper red* (unglazed) | 1,950. | 42.50 |
| e. | | 20c black, *deep crimson* (imperf., without gum) | 2.50 | — |
| f. | | No period after "20" *(copper red)* | *2,800.* | 350.00 |
| g. | | No period after "20" *(mag)* | 24.00 | *180.00* |
| h. | | No period after "20" *(deep crimson)* | 25.00 | *180.00* |
| i. | | No period after "CENT" *(copper red)* | *2,800.* | 375.00 |
| j. | | No period after "CENT" *(magenta)* | 24.00 | *180.00* |
| k. | | No period after "CENT" *(deep crimson)* | 24.00 | *180.00* |
| 24 | A17 | 40c black, *green-ish yellow* | 11.00 | *125.00* |
| a. | | 40c black, *yellow* | 210.00 | *75.00* |
| b. | | 40c black, *orange yellow* | 90.00 | *750.00* |
| c. | | No period after "40" | 15.00 | *95.00* |
| 25 | A18 | 80c black, *rose lilac* | 210.00 | *415.00* |
| a. | | 80c black, *bright rose* | *6,500.* | *60,000.* |
| b. | | 80c black, *rose* (unglazed) | 65.00 | — |
| c. | | No period after "80" *(rose lilac)* | 110.00 | — |
| d. | | 80c black, *pale rose lilac* (unglazed) | 77.50 | — |
| e. | | 80c black, *pale rose* | 55.00 | 425.00 |
| f. | | As "e," no period after "80" | 65.00 | 650.00 |
| g. | | As "a," no period after "80" | 7,000. | — |
| h. | | As "e," double impression | — | — |
| | | *Nos. 19-25 (7)* | 352.75 | 3,985. |

All values except the 3c are known imperforate vertically or horizontally. and in vertical and horizontal pairs, imperf between. See the *Scott Specialized Catalogue of Stamps and Covers* for detailed listings.
Double impressions are known of the 5c, 10c, 20c (all three colors), 40c and 80c.
Fraudulent cancellations are found on Nos. 20, 24 and 25.
*The stamps of the 1867 and 1868 issues have been privately reprinted; many of these reprints are well executed and it is difficult to distinguish them from the originals. Most reprints show more or less pronounced defects of the design. On the originals the horizontal lines between stamps are unbroken, while on most of the reprints these lines are broken. Most of the perforated reprints gauge 11½.*

Roman States stamps were replaced by those of Italy in 1870.

## SARDINIA

LOCATION — An island in the Mediterranean Sea off the west coast of Italy and a large area in northwestern Italy, including the cities of Genoa, Turin and Nice.
GOVT. — Kingdom

As a result of war and revolution, most of the former independent Italian States were joined to the Kingdom of Sardinia in 1859 and 1860. On March 17, 1861, the name was changed to the Kingdom of Italy.

100 Centesimi = 1 Lira

Values of Sardinia stamps vary tremendously according to condition. Values are for very fine examples, and values for unused stamps are for examples with original gum as defined in the catalogue introduction. Extremely fine or superb stamps sell at much higher prices, and fine or poor stamps sell at greatly reduced prices. In addition, very fine unused stamps without gum sell for about 20-30% of the values shown.

King Victor Emmanuel II — A1

**1851 Unwmk. Litho. *Imperf.***

| No. | Type | Description | Unused | Used |
|---|---|---|---|---|
| 1 | A1 | 5c gray black | 13,000. | 2,200. |
| a. | | 5c black | 13,000. | 2,200. |
| 2 | A1 | 20c blue | 9,000. | 235.00 |
| a. | | 20c deep blue | 9,000. | 235.00 |
| b. | | 20c pale blue | 9,000. | 325.00 |
| 3 | A1 | 40c rose | 19,000. | *4,100.* |
| a. | | 40c violet rose | 19,000. | *5,850.* |

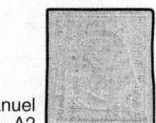
King Victor Emmanuel II — A2

**Vignette & Inscriptions Embossed**
**1853**

| No. | Type | Description | Unused | Used |
|---|---|---|---|---|
| 4 | A2 | 5c *blue green* | *18,000.* | 1,200. |
| a. | | Double embossing | | *3,250.* |
| 5 | A2 | 20c *dull blue* | *19,000.* | 180.00 |
| a. | | Double embossing | | *1,350.* |
| 6 | A2 | 40c *pale rose* | *10,750.* | 900.00 |
| b. | | Double embossing | | *2,400.* |

King Victor Emmanuel II — A3

### Lithographed Frame in Color, Colorless Embossed Vignette

**1854**

| | | | | |
|---|---|---|---|---|
| 7 | A3 | 5c yellow green | 32,500. | 650.00 |
| a. | | Double embossing | | 1,350. |
| b. | | 5c grayish green | 3,600. | |
| 8 | A3 | 20c blue | 17,500. | 175.00 |
| a. | | Double embossing | | 540.00 |
| b. | | 20c indigo | 800.00 | |
| 9 | A3 | 40c rose | *90,000.* | 3,250. |
| a. | | Double embossing | | 6,000. |
| b. | | 40c brown rose | 200.00 | — |

Nos. 7b, 8b and 9b, differing in shade from the original stamps, were prepared but not issued.

King Victor Emmanuel II — A4

Stamps of this issue vary greatly in color, paper and sharpness of embossing as between the early (1855-59) printings and the later (1860-63) ones. Year dates after each color name indicate whether the stamp falls into the Early or Late printing group.

As a rule, early printings are on smooth thick paper with sharp embossing, while later printings are usually on paper varying from thick to thin and of inferior quality with embossing less distinct and printing blurred. The outer frame shows a distinct design on the early printings, while this design is more or less blurred or even a solid line on the later printings.

### Typographed Frame in Color, Colorless Embossed Vignette

**1855-63 Unwmk. *Imperf.***

| | | | | |
|---|---|---|---|---|
| 10 | A4 | 5c green ('62-63) | 5.00 | *12.00* |
| a. | | 5c yellow green ('62-63) | 36.00 | 18.00 |
| b. | | 5c olive green ('60-61) | 450.00 | 75.00 |
| c. | | 5c yellow green ('55-59) | 1,000. | 175.00 |
| d. | | 5c myrtle green ('57) | 6,500. | 525.00 |
| e. | | 5c emerald ('55-57) | 3,900. | 425.00 |
| f. | | Head inverted | — | 3,400. |
| g. | | Double head, one inverted | — | *3,400.* |
| 11 | A4 | 10c bister ('63) | 5.00 | *24.00* |
| a. | | 10c ocher ('62) | 100.00 | 24.00 |
| b. | | 10c olive bister ('62) | 210.00 | 24.00 |
| c. | | 10c olive green ('61) | 210.00 | 32.50 |
| d. | | 10c reddish brown ('61) | 1,650. | 175.00 |
| e. | | 10c gray brown ('61) | 150.00 | 45.00 |
| f. | | 10c olive gray ('60-61) | 400.00 | 60.00 |
| g. | | 10c gray ('60) | 1,500. | 200.00 |
| h. | | 10c grayish brown ('59) | 145.00 | 235.00 |
| i. | | 10c violet brown ('59) | 650.00 | 325.00 |
| j. | | 10c dark brown ('58) | *825.00* | 400.00 |
| k. | | Head inverted | — | 4,000. |
| l. | | Double head, one inverted | — | 4,000. |
| m. | | Pair, one without embossing | *2,250.* | — |
| n. | | Half used as 5c on cover (15c rate) | | *115,000.* |
| 12 | A4 | 20c indigo ('62) | 95.00 | 42.50 |
| a. | | 20c blue ('61) | 180.00 | 18.00 |
| b. | | 20c light blue ('60-61) | 180.00 | 18.00 |
| c. | | 20c Prussian bl ('59-60) | 840.00 | 30.00 |
| d. | | 20c indigo ('57-58) | 510.00 | 42.50 |
| e. | | 20c sky blue ('55-56) | 6,500. | 190.00 |
| f. | | 20c cobalt ('55) | 3,400. | 110.00 |
| g. | | Head inverted | 3,250. | 1,600. |
| h. | | Double head, one inverted | — | — |
| i. | | Pair, one without embossing | 1,200. | — |
| j. | | Half used as 10c on cover | | *150,000.* |
| 13 | A4 | 40c red ('63) | 19.00 | *42.50* |
| a. | | 40c rose ('61-62) | 150.00 | 65.00 |
| b. | | 40c carmine ('60) | 775.00 | 385.00 |
| c. | | 40c light red ('57) | 3,600. | 120.00 |
| d. | | 40c vermilion ('55-57) | 6,500. | 380.00 |
| e. | | Head inverted | — | 5,500. |
| f. | | Double head, one inverted | — | *5,900.* |
| g. | | Pair, one without embossing | 1,800. | — |
| h. | | Half used as 20c on cover | | *76,000.* |
| 14 | A4 | 80c orange yellow ('62) | 24.00 | *410.00* |
| a. | | 80c yellow ('60-61) | 27.50 | *400.00* |
| b. | | 80c yellow ocher ('59) | 950.00 | 760.00 |
| c. | | 80c ocher ('58) | 225.00 | *600.00* |
| d. | | 80c brown orange ('58) | 240.00 | *650.00* |
| e. | | Head inverted | — | *22,000.* |
| f. | | Half used as 40c on cover | | — |
| 15 | A4 | 3 l bronze, thin paper ('61) | 425.00 | *3,650.* |
| | | *Nos. 10-15 (6)* | 573.00 | 4,181. |

Forgeries of the inverted and double head varieties have been made by applying a faked head embossing to printer's waste without head. These forgeries are plentiful.

Fraudulent cancellations are found on #13-15.

*The 5c, 20c and 40c have been reprinted; the embossing of the reprints is not as sharp as that of the originals,the colors are dull and blurred.*

---

### NEWSPAPER STAMPS

N1

### Typographed and Embossed

**1861 Unwmk. *Imperf.***

| | | | | |
|---|---|---|---|---|
| P1 | N1 | 1c black | 6.75 | *15.00* |
| a. | | Numeral "2" | 600.00 | *2,500.* |
| b. | | Figure of value inverted | 2,400. | *34,000.* |
| c. | | Double impression | 2,750. | — |
| P2 | N1 | 2c black | 180.00 | 105.00 |
| a. | | Numeral "1" | *13,000.* | *32,500.* |
| b. | | Figure of value inverted | *2,400.* | *34,000.* |

Forgeries of the varieties of the embossed numerals have been made from printer's waste without numerals.

See Italy No. P1 for 2c buff.

The stamps of Sardinia were superseded in 1862 by those of Italy, which were identical with the 1855 issue of Sardinia, but perforated. Until 1863, imperforate and perforated stamps were issued simultaneously.

---

## TUSCANY

LOCATION — In the north central part of the Apennine Peninsula.

GOVT. — Grand Duchy

AREA — 8,890 sq. mi.

POP. — 2,892,000 (approx.)

CAPITAL — Florence

Tuscany was annexed to Sardinia in 1860.

60 Quattrini = 20 Soldi = 12 Crazie = 1 Lira

100 Centesimi = 1 Lira (1860)

---

Values of Tuscany stamps vary tremendously according to condition. Values are for very fine examples, and values for unused stamps are for examples with original gum as defined in the catalogue introduction. Extremely fine or superb stamps sell at much higher prices, and fine or poor stamps sell at greatly reduced prices.

---

Dangerous counterfeits exist of #1-PR1c.

Lion of Tuscany — A1

**1851-52 Typo. Wmk. 185 *Imperf.***

**Blue, Grayish Blue or Gray Paper**

| | | | | |
|---|---|---|---|---|
| 1 | A1 | 1q black ('52) | 17,500. | 2,250. |
| 2 | A1 | 1s ocher, *grayish* | 22,000. | 2,600. |
| a. | | 1s orange, *grayish* | 24,000. | 2,600. |
| b. | | 1s yellow, *bluish* | 26,000. | 2,900. |
| 3 | A1 | 2s scarlet | *65,000.* | 10,500. |
| 4 | A1 | 1cr carmine | 11,000. | 180.00 |
| a. | | 1cr brown carmine | 14,500. | 180.00 |
| 5 | A1 | 2cr blue | 6,500. | 200.00 |
| a. | | 2cr greenish blue | 14,000. | 200.00 |
| 6 | A1 | 4cr green | 11,000. | 225.00 |
| a. | | 4cr bluish green | 11,000. | 225.00 |
| 7 | A1 | 6cr slate blue | 12,000. | 350.00 |
| a. | | 6cr blue | 11,000. | 350.00 |
| b. | | 6cr indigo | 12,000. | 375.00 |
| 8 | A1 | 9cr gray lilac | 26,000. | 375.00 |
| a. | | 9cr deep violet | 26,000. | 375.00 |
| 9 | A1 | 60cr red ('52) | *120,000.* | *32,500.* |

The first paper was blue, later paper more and more grayish. Stamps on distinctly blue paper sell about 20 percent higher, except Nos. 3 and 9 which were issued on blue paper only. Examples without watermark are proofs.

*Reprints of Nos. 3 and 9 have re-engraved value labels, color is too brown and impressions blurred and heavy. Paper same as originals.*

No. 14a

**1857-59 Wmk. 184**

**White Paper**

| | | | | |
|---|---|---|---|---|
| 10 | A1 | 1q black | 2,200. | 1,150. |
| 11 | A1 | 1s yellow | *65,000.* | 7,500. |
| 12 | A1 | 1cr carmine | 14,500. | 950.00 |
| 13 | A1 | 2cr blue | 4,800. | 200.00 |
| 14 | A1 | 4cr green | 11,000. | 225.00 |
| a. | | Inverted value tablet | | *1,100,000.* |
| 15 | A1 | 6cr deep blue | *15,500.* | 375.00 |
| 16 | A1 | 9cr gray lilac ('59) | *65,000.* | *7,500.* |

### Provisional Government

Coat of Arms — A2

**1860**

| | | | | |
|---|---|---|---|---|
| 17 | A2 | 1c brn lilac | 4,150. | 1,200. |
| a. | | 1c red lilac | 5,250. | 1,350. |
| b. | | 1c gray lilac | 4,250. | 1,200. |
| 18 | A2 | 5c green | 16,000. | 325.00 |
| a. | | 5c olive green | 18,000. | 350.00 |
| b. | | 5c yellow green | 22,000. | 450.00 |
| 19 | A2 | 10c deep brown | 5,750. | 75.00 |
| a. | | 10c gray brown | 5,000. | 75.00 |
| b. | | 10c purple brown | 5,000. | 75.00 |
| 20 | A2 | 20c blue | 14,500. | 225.00 |
| a. | | 20c deep blue | 14,500. | 275.00 |
| b. | | 20c gray blue | 15,000. | 275.00 |
| 21 | A2 | 40c rose | 22,000. | 440.00 |
| a. | | 40c carmine | 22,000. | 440.00 |
| b. | | Half used as 20c on cover | | *300,000.* |
| 22 | A2 | 80c pale red brn | *40,000.* | 1,900. |
| a. | | 80c brown orange | *40,000.* | 1,900. |
| 23 | A2 | 3 l ocher | *300,000.* | *130,000.* |

---

### NEWSPAPER TAX STAMPS

NT1

**1854 Unwmk. Typo. *Imperf.***

**Yellowish Pelure Paper**

| | | | | |
|---|---|---|---|---|
| PR1 | NT1 | 2s black | 100.00 | |
| a. | | Tête bêche pair | 950.00 | |
| b. | | As "a," one stamp on back | 950.00 | |
| c. | | Double impression | 700.00 | |

This stamp represented a fiscal tax on newspapers coming from foreign countries. It was not canceled when used.

The stamps of Tuscany were superseded by those of Sardinia in 1861.

---

## TWO SICILIES

LOCATION — Formerly comprised the island of Sicily and the lower half of the Apennine Peninsula.

GOVT. — Independent Kingdom

CAPITAL — Naples

The Kingdom was annexed to Sardinia in 1860.

200 Tornesi = 100 Grana = 1 Ducat

---

Values of Two Sicilies stamps vary tremendously according to condition. Values are for very fine examples, and values for unused stamps are for examples with original gum as defined in the catalogue introduction. Extremely fine or superb copies sell at much higher prices, and fine or poor copies sell at greatly reduced prices. In addition, very fine unused stamps without gum sell for about 20%-30% of the values shown.

### Naples

Coat of Arms

A1 A2

A3

A4

A5

A6

A7

**1858 Engr. Wmk. 186 *Imperf.***

| | | | | |
|---|---|---|---|---|
| 1 | A1 | ½g pale lake | 2,100. | 360.00 |
| a. | | ½g rose lake | 2,100. | 360.00 |
| b. | | ½g lake | 2,700. | 600.00 |
| c. | | ½g carmine lake | 3,275. | 800.00 |
| d. | | Half used as ¼g on newspaper | | *240,000.* |
| 2 | A2 | 1g pale lake | 1,050. | 42.50 |
| a. | | 1g rose lake | 725.00 | 45.00 |
| b. | | 1g brown lake | 1,800. | 90.00 |
| c. | | 1g carmine lake | 1,050. | 72.50 |
| d. | | Printed on both sides | | 2,000. |
| e. | | Printed on both sides, one inverted | | 1,000. |
| 3 | A3 | 2g pale lake | 450.00 | 16.00 |
| a. | | 2g rose lake | 450.00 | 16.00 |
| b. | | 2g lake | 750.00 | 25.00 |
| c. | | 2g carmine lake | 900.00 | 25.00 |
| d. | | Impression of 1g on reverse | | *1,800.* |
| e. | | Double impression | | *10,000.* |
| f. | | Printed on both sides | | 2,000. |
| 4 | A4 | 5g brown lake | 3,600. | 75.00 |
| a. | | 5g rose lake | 3,000. | 75.00 |
| b. | | 5g carmine lake | 4,500. | 75.00 |
| d. | | Printed on both sides | | *5,000.* |
| e. | | 5g rose carmine | 6,000. | 180.00 |
| f. | | 5g bright carmine | 6,500. | 210.00 |
| g. | | 5g dark carmine | 7,750. | 300.00 |
| 5 | A5 | 10g rose lake | 6,500. | 210.00 |
| a. | | 10g lake | 7,250. | 350.00 |
| b. | | 10g carmine lake | 7,250. | 350.00 |
| c. | | Printed on both sides | | 16,250. |
| d. | | Double impression | | *17,000.* |
| 6 | A6 | 20g rose lake | 6,000. | 750.00 |
| a. | | 20g lake | 6,000. | 900.00 |
| b. | | Double impression | *60,000.* | |
| c. | | 20g pale rose | *9,000.* | 1,500. |
| d. | | 20g pale car rose | *10,000.* | 1,800. |
| 7 | A7 | 50g rose lake | *12,000.* | 2,700. |
| a. | | 50g lake | *12,000.* | 2,700. |

Nos. 1-2, 4-7 have been reprinted in bright rose and Nos. 1, 7 in dull brown. The reprints are on thick unwatermarked paper. Value $8 each.

### Provisional Government

A8

A9

**1860**

| | | | | |
|---|---|---|---|---|
| 8 | A8 | ½t deep blue | 235,000. | 11,000. |
| 9 | A9 | ½t blue | 47,500. | 3,250. |
| a. | | ½t deep blue | 47,500. | 3,250. |

100 varieties of each.

No. 8 was made from the plate of No. 1, which was altered by changing the "G" to "T."

No. 9 was made from the same plate after a second alteration erasing the coat of arms and inserting the Cross of Savoy. Dangerous counterfeits exist of Nos. 8-9.

## Sicily

Ferdinand II — A10

**1859 Unwmk. Engr. *Imperf.***

**Soft Porous Paper, Brownish Gum**

**(Naples consignment)**

| | | | | |
|---|---|---|---|---|
| 10g | A10 | ½g orange | 575.00 | *4,000.* |
| c. | | Printed on both sides | — | *40,000.* |
| 11 | A10 | 1g dark brown | 17,500. | 700.00 |
| 12h | A10 | 1g pale olive green (III) | 200.00 | *180.00* |
| c. | | Double impression | 4,400. | 4,400. |
| 13g | A10 | 2g blue | 180.00 | 120.00 |
| b. | | Printed on both sides | — | 26,000. |
| 14 | A10 | 5g deep rose | 725.00 | 600.00 |
| 15 | A10 | 5g vermilion | 600.00 | *1,600.* |
| 16 | A10 | 10g dark blue | 800.00 | 375.00 |
| 17 | A10 | 20g dk gray vio | 800.00 | 625.00 |
| 18 | A10 | 50g dk brn red | 800.00 | *4,750.* |

There were three plates each for the 1g and 2g, two each for the ½g and 5g and one plate each for the other values.

Nos. 10a, 10b, 11, 11a, 14, 14a, 14b and 15 are printed from Plate I on which the stamps are 2 to 2½mm apart. On almost all stamps from Plate I, the S and T of POSTA touch.

Nos. 12a, and 15a are from Plate II and No. 12 is from Plate III. On both Plates II and III stamps are spaced 1½mm apart. Most stamps from Plate II have a white line about 1mm long below the beard.

Nos. 10-18 are on soft, porous paper with brownish gum, while Nos. 10, 12 and 13 exist also on hard white paper, with white gum. Color shades exist, some on both types of paper. For detailed listings, see the *Scott Classic Specialized Catalogue of Stamps and Covers.*

The ½g blue is stated to be a proof of which two examples are known. Both originated on the same cover. One stamp is sound and still on its original partial cover. This item was sold at auction in 2011, where it realized $2.6 million. The second stamp is a faulty, loose single.

Fraudulent cancellations are known on Nos. 10, 15, 15a and 18.

## Neapolitan Provinces

King Victor Emmanuel II — A11

**Lithographed, Center Embossed**

**1861 Unwmk. *Imperf.***

| | | | | |
|---|---|---|---|---|
| 19 | A11 | ½t green | 18.50 | *325.00* |
| a. | | ½t yellow green | 500.00 | 440.00 |
| b. | | ½t emerald | 8,750. | 1,450. |
| c. | | ½t black (error) | *160,000.* | *180,000.* |
| d. | | Head inverted (green) | 255.00 | |
| e. | | Head inverted (yel grn) | | 14,500. |
| f. | | Printed on both sides | | 40,000. |
| 20 | A11 | ½g bister | 215.00 | *290.00* |
| a. | | ½g brown | 215.00 | *400.00* |
| b. | | ½g gray brown | 255.00 | *290.00* |
| c. | | Head inverted | 2,350. | — |
| 21 | A11 | 1g black | 400.00 | 37.50 |
| a. | | Head inverted | | *2,175.* |
| 22 | A11 | 2g blue | 145.00 | 14.50 |
| a. | | 2g deep blue | 145.00 | 14.50 |
| b. | | Head inverted | *500.00* | *1,275.* |
| c. | | 2g black (error) | | *180,000.* |
| 23 | A11 | 5g car rose | 290.00 | 165.00 |
| a. | | 5g vermilion | 290.00 | 200.00 |
| b. | | 5g lilac rose | 325.00 | 325.00 |
| c. | | Head inverted | 1,450. | *11,000.* |
| e. | | Printed on both sides | | 25,000. |
| 25 | A11 | 10g orange | 115.00 | *365.00* |
| a. | | 10g ocher | *1,450.* | 800.00 |
| b. | | 10g bister | 135.00 | *365.00* |
| 26 | A11 | 20g yellow | 550.00 | *3,650.* |
| a. | | Head inverted | | 50,000. |
| 27 | A11 | 50g gray | 45.00 | *11,000.* |
| a. | | 50g slate | 50.00 | *11,000.* |
| b. | | 50g slate blue | 57.50 | *14,500.* |
| | | *Nos. 19-27 (8)* | 1,778. | 15,847. |

Counterfeits of the inverted head varieties of this issue are plentiful. See note on forgeries after Sardinia No. 15.

Fraudulent cancellations are found on Nos. 19-20, 23-27.

Stamps similar to those of Sardinia 1855-61, type A4 but with inscriptions in larger, clearer lettering, were prepared in 1861 for the Neapolitan Provinces. They were not officially issued although a few are known postally used. Denominations: 5c, 10c, 20c, 40c and 80c.

Stamps of Two Sicilies were replaced by those of Italy in 1862.

# ITALY

'i-tᵊl-ē

LOCATION — Southern Europe
GOVT. — Republic
AREA — 119,764 sq. mi.
POP. — 56,735,130 (1999 est.)
CAPITAL — Rome

Formerly a kingdom, Italy became a republic in June 1946

100 Centesimi = 1 Lira
100 Cents = 1 Euro (2002)

**Catalogue values for unused stamps in this country are for Never Hinged items, beginning with Scott 691 in the regular postage section, Scott B47 in the semi-postal section, Scott C129 in the airpost section, Scott D21 in the pneumatic post section, Scott E32 in the special delivery section, Scott EY11 in the authorized delivery section, Scott J83 in the postage due section, Scott Q77 in the parcel post section, Scott QY5 in the parcel post authorized delivery section, Scott 1N1 in the A.M.G. section, Scott 1LN1 in the Venezia Giulia section, 1LNC1 in the occupation air post section, 1LNE1 in the occupation special delivery section, and all of the items in the Italian Social Republic area.**

### Watermarks

Wmk. 87 — Honeycomb

Wmk. 140 — Crown

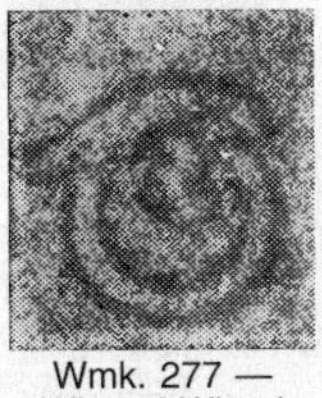

Wmk. 277 — Winged Wheel

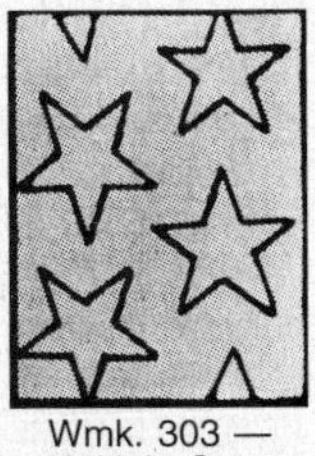

Wmk. 303 — Multiple Stars

Values of Italy stamps vary tremendously according to condition. Quotations are for very fine examples, and values for unused stamps are for examples with original gum as defined in the catalogue introduction. Extremely fine or superb copies sell at much higher prices, and fine or poor copies sell at greatly reduced prices. In addition, unused examples without gum are discounted severely.

Very fine examples of Nos. 17-21, 24-75, J2-J27, O1-O8 and Q1-Q6 will have perforations barely clear of the frame-line or design due to the narrow spacing of the stamps on the plates.

King Victor Emmanuel II — A4

### Typographed; Head Embossed

**1862 Unwmk. *Perf. 11½x12***

| | | | | |
|---|---|---|---|---|
| **17** | A4 | 10c bister | *9,500.* | 360.00 |
| *g.* | | Vert. half used as 5c on cover | | *160,000.* |
| **19** | A4 | 20c dark blue | 24.00 | *40.00* |
| *f.* | | Vert. half used as 10c on cover | | *210,000.* |
| **20** | A4 | 40c red | 325.00 | 200.00 |
| **21** | A4 | 80c orange | 65.00 | *2,400.* |

The outer frame shows a distinct design on the early printings, while this design is more or less blurred, or even a solid line, on the later printings.

Numerous shades of Nos. 17-21 exist. Some are very expensive. For listings, see the *Scott Classic Catalogue.*

The 20c and 40c exist perf. 11½. These are remainders of Sardinia with forged perforations.

Counterfeit cancellations are often found on No. 21.

### Lithographed; Head Embossed

**1863 *Imperf.***

| | | | | |
|---|---|---|---|---|
| **22** | A4 | 15c blue | 80.00 | 55.00 |
| *a.* | | Head inverted | | *92,000.* |
| *b.* | | Double head | 160.00 | 87.50 |
| *c.* | | Head omitted | 800.00 | *55,000.* |
| *j.* | | Triple head | 360.00 | *560.00* |

See note after Sardinia No. 15.
No. 22c is valued with original gum only.

King Victor Emmanuel II — A5

Type I — First "C" in bottom line nearly closed.
Type II — "C" open. Line broken below "Q."

**1863 Litho.**

| | | | | |
|---|---|---|---|---|
| **23** | A5 | 15c blue, Type II | 10.00 | *16.00* |
| *a.* | | Type I | 400.00 | 27.50 |
| | | No gum | 47.50 | |
| *c.* | | As "a," double impression | | *5,250.* |
| *f.* | | As "a," printed on both sides | | 24,000. |

One example of No. 23f is known used, cancelled "Milano, 25-VII-1863." Unused examples always lack gum and are from printer's waste. They are of little value.

A6

A7

A8

A13

**1863-77 Typo. Wmk. 140 *Perf. 14***

| | | | | |
|---|---|---|---|---|
| **24** | A6 | 1c gray green | 8.00 | 4.00 |
| *a.* | | Imperf., pair | | *12,000.* |
| **25** | A7 | 2c org brn ('65) | 32.50 | 2.75 |
| *a.* | | Imperf., pair | 150.00 | *200.00* |
| **26** | A8 | 5c slate grn | 2,400. | 4.50 |
| **27** | A8 | 10c buff | 4,000. | 5.50 |
| *a.* | | 10c orange brown | 4,000. | 5.50 |
| **28** | A8 | 10c blue ('77) | 7,500. | 6.50 |
| **29** | A8 | 15c blue | 3,000. | 4.00 |
| *a.* | | Imperf, single | | *5,500.* |
| **30** | A8 | 30c brown | 12.00 | 12.00 |
| *a.* | | Imperf, single | | — |
| **31** | A8 | 40c carmine | 8,750. | 8.00 |
| *a.* | | 40c rose | 8,750. | 8.00 |
| **32** | A8 | 60c lilac | 12.00 | *19.00* |
| **33** | A13 | 2 l vermilion | 32.50 | *125.00* |

Nos. 26 to 32 have the head of type A8 but with different corner designs for each value.

Early printings of Nos. 24-27, 29-33 were made in London by De La Rue, later printings in Turin. Used examples can be determined by cancellation date. Unused singles cannot be distinguished.

For overprints see Italian Offices Abroad Nos. 1-5, 8-11.

No. 29 Surcharged in Brown

**1865**

Type I — Dots flanking stars in oval, and dot in eight check-mark ornaments in corners.
Type II — Dots in oval, none in corners.
Type III — No dots.

| | | | | |
|---|---|---|---|---|
| **34** | A8 | 20c on 15c bl (I) | 750.00 | 4.75 |
| *a.* | | Type II | 10,500. | 20.00 |
| *b.* | | Type III | 2,100. | 8.00 |
| *c.* | | Inverted surcharge (I) | | *80,000.* |

A15

**1867-77 Typo.**

| | | | | |
|---|---|---|---|---|
| **35** | A15 | 20c blue | 800.00 | 1.60 |
| **36** | A15 | 20c orange ('77) | 5,500. | 4.00 |

For overprints see Italian Offices Abroad #9-10.

Official Stamps Surcharged in Blue

**1878**

| | | | | |
|---|---|---|---|---|
| **37** | O1 | 2c on 2c lake | 200.00 | 32.50 |
| **38** | O1 | 2c on 5c lake | 240.00 | 40.00 |
| **39** | O1 | 2c on 20c lake | 875.00 | 4.75 |
| **40** | O1 | 2c on 30c lake | 800.00 | 16.00 |
| **41** | O1 | 2c on 1 l lake | 650.00 | 4.75 |
| **42** | O1 | 2c on 2 l lake | 650.00 | 12.00 |
| **43** | O1 | 2c on 5 l lake | 875.00 | 16.00 |
| **44** | O1 | 2c on 10 l lake | 650.00 | 20.00 |
| | | *Nos. 37-44 (8)* | 4,940. | 146.00 |

### Inverted Surcharge

| | | | | |
|---|---|---|---|---|
| *37a* | O1 | 2c on 2c | | 2,000. |
| *38a* | O1 | 2c on 5c | | 1,600. |
| *39a* | O1 | 2c on 20c | *47,500.* | 1,000. |
| *40a* | O1 | 2c on 30c | | 1,600. |
| *41a* | O1 | 2c on 1 l | *55,000.* | 1,400. |
| *42a* | O1 | 2c on 2 l | *55,000.* | 1,600. |
| *43a* | O1 | 2c on 5 l | | 1,600. |
| *44a* | O1 | 2c on 10 l | | 1,600. |

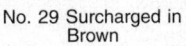

King Humbert I — A17

**1879 Typo. *Perf. 14***

| | | | | |
|---|---|---|---|---|
| **45** | A17 | 5c blue green | 9.50 | 1.60 |
| **46** | A17 | 10c claret | 475.00 | 1.75 |
| **47** | A17 | 20c orange | 450.00 | 1.60 |
| **48** | A17 | 25c blue | 800.00 | 9.50 |
| **49** | A17 | 30c brown | 175.00 | *2,800.* |
| **50** | A17 | 50c violet | 24.00 | 27.50 |
| **51** | A17 | 2 l vermilion | 65.00 | *400.00* |

Nos. 45-51 have the head of type A17 with different corner designs for each value.

Beware of forged cancellations on No. 49, on or off cover.

For surcharges and overprints see Nos. 64-66, Italian Offices Abroad 12-17.

Arms of Savoy — A24

Humbert I — A25

A26

A27

A28

A29

**1889**

| | | | | |
|---|---|---|---|---|
| **52** | A24 | 5c dark green | 875.00 | 3.25 |
| **53** | A25 | 40c brown | 14.50 | 20.00 |
| **54** | A26 | 45c gray green | 2,600. | 9.50 |
| **55** | A27 | 60c violet | 19.00 | *47.50* |
| **56** | A28 | 1 l brown & yel | 19.00 | 24.00 |
| *a.* | | 1 l brown & orange | 21.00 | 30.00 |
| **57** | A29 | 5 l grn & claret | 30.00 | *1,200.* |

Forged cancellations exist on #51, 57.

Parcel Post Stamps of 1884-86 Surcharged in Black

**1890**

| | | | | |
|---|---|---|---|---|
| **58** | PP1 | 2c on 10c ol gray | 6.00 | *8.00* |
| *a.* | | Inverted surcharge | 550.00 | *3,600.* |
| **59** | PP1 | 2c on 20c blue | 6.00 | *8.00* |
| **60** | PP1 | 2c on 50c claret | 65.00 | 47.50 |
| *a.* | | Inverted surcharge | | *52,500.* |
| **61** | PP1 | 2c on 75c blue grn | 6.00 | *8.00* |
| **62** | PP1 | 2c on 1.25 l org | 55.00 | 40.00 |
| *a.* | | Inverted surcharge | *95,000.* | *47,500.* |
| **63** | PP1 | 2c on 1.75 l brn | 24.00 | *60.00* |
| | | *Nos. 58-63 (6)* | 162.00 | 171.50 |

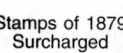

Stamps of 1879 Surcharged

**1890-91**

| | | | | |
|---|---|---|---|---|
| **64** | A17 | 2c on 5c bl grn ('91) | 22.50 | 55.00 |
| *a.* | | "2" with thin tail | 140.00 | 325.00 |
| **65** | A17 | 20c on 30c brown | 475.00 | 12.00 |
| **66** | A17 | 20c on 50c violet | 550.00 | 47.50 |
| | | *Nos. 64-66 (3)* | 1,047. | 114.50 |

Arms of Savoy — A33

Humbert I — A34

A35

A36

A37

A38

**1891-96** **Typo.**

| | | | | |
|---|---|---|---|---|
| **67** | A33 | 5c green | 550.00 | 2.40 |
| **68** | A34 | 10c claret ('96) | 9.50 | 2.40 |
| **69** | A35 | 20c orange ('95) | 9.50 | 2.40 |
| **70** | A36 | 25c blue | 9.50 | 10.00 |
| **71** | A37 | 45c ol grn ('95) | 9.50 | 10.00 |
| **72** | A38 | 5 l blue & rose | 95.00 | *240.00* |

Arms of Savoy — A39

A40

A41

**1896-97**

| | | | | |
|---|---|---|---|---|
| **73** | A39 | 1c brown | 11.00 | 8.00 |
| *a.* | | Half used as ½c on cover | | 1,600. |
| **74** | A40 | 2c orange brown | 11.00 | 2.00 |
| **75** | A41 | 5c green ('97) | 40.00 | 2.00 |
| | | *Nos. 73-75 (3)* | 62.00 | 12.00 |

A42

Coat of Arms
A43 A44

Victor Emmanuel III
A45 A46

**1901-26**

| | | | | |
|---|---|---|---|---|
| **76** | A42 | 1c brown | 1.60 | .40 |
| *a.* | | Imperf, single | 450.00 | *725.00* |
| **77** | A43 | 2c org brn | 1.60 | .40 |
| *a.* | | Double impression | 125.00 | *225.00* |
| *b.* | | Imperf, single | 125.00 | *175.00* |
| **78** | A44 | 5c blue grn | 87.50 | .60 |
| *a.* | | Imperf, single | 2,000. | |
| **79** | A45 | 10c claret | 120.00 | 1.25 |
| *a.* | | Imperf, single | — | *10,500.* |
| **80** | A45 | 20c orange | 24.00 | 1.25 |
| **81** | A45 | 25c ultra | 275.00 | 4.00 |
| *a.* | | 25c dp blue | 275.00 | 4.00 |
| **82** | A46 | 25c grn & pale grn ('26) | 1.60 | .35 |
| **83** | A45 | 40c brown | 800.00 | 9.50 |
| **84** | A45 | 45c olive grn | 12.50 | .40 |
| *a.* | | Imperf, single | 160.00 | *225.00* |
| **85** | A45 | 50c violet | 950.00 | 17.50 |
| **86** | A46 | 75c dk red & rose ('26) | 4.75 | .35 |
| **87** | A46 | 1 l brown & grn | 4.75 | .40 |
| *a.* | | Imperf, single | 80.00 | *120.00* |
| *b.* | | Floral design (green) omitted | 160.00 | |
| *c.* | | Double impression of vignette (brown) | 80.00 | *110.00* |
| **88** | A46 | 1.25 l bl & ultra ('26) | 12.50 | .35 |
| **89** | A46 | 2 l dk grn & org ('23) | 24.00 | 8.00 |
| **90** | A46 | 2.50 l dk grn & org ('26) | 65.00 | 8.00 |
| **91** | A46 | 5 l blue & rose | 32.50 | 7.25 |
| | | *Nos. 76-91 (16)* | 2,417. | 60.00 |

Nos. 83, 85, unused, are valued in fine condition.

The borders of Nos. 79-81, 83-85, 87, 89 and 91 differ slightly for each denomination.

On Nos. 82, 86, 88 and 90, the value is expressed as "Cent. 25," etc.

See No. 87d in set following No. 174G.

For surcharges and overprints see Nos. 148-149, 152, 158, 174F-174G, B16; Austria N20-N21, N27, N30, N52-N53, N58, N60, N64-N65, N71, N74; Dalmatia 1, 6-7.

**Overprints & Surcharges See Offices in China, Crete, Africa, Turkish Empire (Albania to Valona) and Aegean Islands for types A36-A58 overprinted or surcharged.**

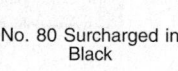

No. 80 Surcharged in Black

**1905**

| | | | | |
|---|---|---|---|---|
| **92** | A45 | 15c on 20c org | 80.00 | 2.00 |
| *a.* | | Double surcharge | | *5,000.* |

A47

No. 93

No. 111

No. 123

**1906** **Unwmk.** **Engr.** ***Perf. 12***

| | | | | |
|---|---|---|---|---|
| **93** | A47 | 15c slate | 80.00 | 1.00 |
| *a.* | | Vert. pair, imperf horiz. | 200.00 | 200.00 |
| *b.* | | Horiz. pair, imperf vert. | 200.00 | 200.00 |
| *c.* | | Booklet pane of 6 | *3,750.* | |
| | | Complete bklt., 4 #93c | *15,000.* | |

A48

A49

**1906-19** **Wmk. 140** **Typo.** ***Perf. 14***

| | | | | |
|---|---|---|---|---|
| **94** | A48 | 5c green | 1.60 | .35 |
| *a.* | | Imperf, single | 40.00 | 40.00 |
| *b.* | | Printed on both sides | 250.00 | |
| **95** | A48 | 10c claret | 3.25 | .35 |
| *a.* | | Imperf, single | 40.00 | 40.00 |
| *b.* | | Printed on both sides | 250.00 | |
| **96** | A48 | 15c slate ('19) | 3.25 | .40 |
| *a.* | | Imperf, single | 140.00 | *225.00* |
| | | *Nos. 94-96 (3)* | 8.10 | 1.10 |

The frame of #95 differs in several details.

See Nos. 96b-96d following No. 174G.

For overprints and surcharge see Nos. 142A-142B, 150, 174A, B5, B9-B10; Austria N22-N23, N31, N54-N55, N61-N62, N66-N67; Dalmatia 2-5.

**1908-27**

| | | | | |
|---|---|---|---|---|
| **97** | A49 | 20c brn org ('25) | 1.60 | 1.00 |
| **98** | A49 | 20c green ('25) | .40 | .25 |
| **99** | A49 | 20c lil brn ('26) | 3.20 | .35 |
| **100** | A49 | 25c blue | 2.40 | .35 |
| *a.* | | Imperf., pair | 72.50 | 72.50 |
| *b.* | | Printed on both sides | 225.00 | *360.00* |
| **101** | A49 | 25c lt grn ('27) | 6.50 | *16.00* |
| **102** | A49 | 30c org brn ('22) | 3.20 | .80 |
| *a.* | | Imperf, single | 250.00 | — |
| **103** | A49 | 30c gray ('25) | 4.75 | .25 |
| **104** | A49 | 40c brown | 4.00 | .35 |
| *a.* | | Imperf., pair | 95.00 | 95.00 |
| **105** | A49 | 50c violet | 1.60 | .35 |
| *a.* | | Imperf., pair | 87.50 | 87.50 |
| **106** | A49 | 55c dl vio ('20) | 19.00 | *27.50* |
| **107** | A49 | 60c car ('17) | 2.40 | .40 |
| **108** | A49 | 60c blue ('23) | 9.50 | *80.00* |
| **109** | A49 | 60c brn org ('26) | 12.50 | .60 |
| **110** | A49 | 85c red brn ('20) | 24.00 | 22.50 |
| | | *Nos. 97-110 (14)* | 95.05 | *150.70* |

The upper panels of Nos. 104 and 105 are in solid color with white letters. A body of water has been added to the background.

See Nos. 100c-105j following No. 174G.

For overprints & surcharges see #142C-142D,147, 151, 153-157, 174B-174E, B7-B8, B12-B15A; Austria N24-N26, N28-N29, N32, N56-N57, N59, N63, N68-N70, N72-N73.

A50

A51

**Redrawn**

***Perf. 13x13½, 13½x14***

**1909-17** **Typo.** **Unwmk.**

| | | | | |
|---|---|---|---|---|
| **111** | A50 | 15c slate black | 300.00 | 2.40 |
| **112** | A50 | 20c brown org ('16) | 65.00 | 4.75 |

No. 111 is similar to No. 93, but the design has been redrawn and the stamp is 23mm high instead of 25mm. There is a star at each side of the coat collar, but one is not distinct. See illustrations next to A47.

For overprints see Nos. B6, B11.

**Wmk. 140** ***Perf. 14***

| | | | | |
|---|---|---|---|---|
| **113** | A50 | 20c brn org ('17) | 8.00 | .40 |
| *a.* | | Imperf., pair | 32.50 | *40.00* |

Stamps overprinted "Prestito Nazionale, 1917," or later dates, are Thrift or Postal Savings Stamps.

**1910, Nov. 1**

| | | | | |
|---|---|---|---|---|
| **114** | A51 | 10 l gray grn & red | 80.00 | 35.00 |
| *a.* | | Red inverted | | *5,500.* |

For surcharge see Dalmatia No. 8.

Giuseppe Garibaldi
A52 A53

***Perf. 14x13½***

**1910, Apr. 15** **Unwmk.**

| | | | | |
|---|---|---|---|---|
| **115** | A52 | 5c green | 32.50 | 27.50 |
| **116** | A52 | 15c claret | 55.00 | 55.00 |

50th anniversary of freedom of Sicily.

**1910, Dec. 1**

| | | | | |
|---|---|---|---|---|
| **117** | A53 | 5c claret | 140.00 | 140.00 |
| **118** | A53 | 15c green | 250.00 | 200.00 |

50th anniversary of the plebiscite of the southern Italian provinces in 1860.

Nos. 115-118 sold for 5c above face value to benefit the anniversary committee. The stamps were valid only on mail to addresses within the Kingdom of Italy. Nos. 115-116 were valid to June 30, 1910; Nos. 117-118 were valid to Jan. 31, 1911.

**Used values in italics are for postally used stamps. CTO's sell for about the same as unused, hinged stamps.**

Symbols of Rome and Turin — A54

Symbol of Valor — A55

Genius of Italy — A56

Glory of Rome — A57

**1911, May 1** **Engr.** ***Perf. 14x13½***

| | | | | |
|---|---|---|---|---|
| **119** | A54 | 2c brown | 3.25 | *6.50* |
| *a.* | | Vert. pair, imperf horiz. | 95.00 | 95.00 |
| *b.* | | Horiz. pair, imperf vert. | 95.00 | 95.00 |
| **120** | A55 | 5c deep green | 45.00 | 40.00 |
| **121** | A56 | 10c carmine | 32.50 | *60.00* |
| *a.* | | Vert. pair, imperf horiz. | — | — |
| *b.* | | Horiz. pair, imperf vert. | 200.00 | 200.00 |
| **122** | A57 | 15c slate | 42.25 | *80.00* |
| | | *Nos. 119-122 (4)* | 123.25 | *186.50* |

50th anniv. of the union of Italian States to form the Kingdom of Italy.

Nos. 119 to 122 were sold at a premium over their face value to benefit the anniversary committee. They were valid to Dec. 31, 1911. The stamps were valid only for mail to addresses within the Kingdom of Italy. They were used by military post offices in Libya. After 1913, No. 119 was sold without the premium.

For surcharges see Nos. 126-128.

Victor Emmanuel III
A58

Campanile, Venice
A59

**1911, Oct. Re-engraved** *Perf. 13½*

| | | | | |
|---|---|---|---|---|
| **123** | A58 | 15c slate | 32.50 | 1.25 |
| *a.* | | Imperf., single | 95.00 | *125.00* |
| *b.* | | Printed on both sides | 400.00 | *525.00* |
| *c.* | | Bklt. pane of 6 | *1,500.* | |
| | | Cplt. bklt., 4 #123c | *6,000.* | |

The re-engraved stamp is 24mm high. The stars at each side of the coat collar show plainly and the "C" of "Cent" is nearer the frame than in No. 93. See illustrations next to A47.

For surcharge see No. 129.

**1912, Apr. 25** *Perf. 14x13½*

| | | | | |
|---|---|---|---|---|
| **124** | A59 | 5c indigo | 9.50 | *14.50* |
| **125** | A59 | 15c dk brn | 52.50 | *67.50* |

Re-erection of the Campanile at Venice.

Nos. 124-125 were sold only in Venice and were valid to Dec. 31, 1912. The stamps were valid only for mail within Italy.

Nos. 120-121 Surcharged in Black

**1913, Mar. 1**

| | | | | |
|---|---|---|---|---|
| **126** | A55 | 2c on 5c dp grn | 2.40 | *6.75* |
| **127** | A56 | 2c on 10c car | 2.40 | *6.75* |

No. 122 Surcharged in Violet

| | | | | |
|---|---|---|---|---|
| **128** | A57 | 2c on 15c slate | 2.40 | *6.75* |
| | | *Nos. 126-128 (3)* | 7.20 | *20.25* |
| | | Set, never hinged | 18.00 | |

No. 123 Surcharged

**1916, Jan. 8**

| | | | | |
|---|---|---|---|---|
| **129** | A58 | 20c on 15c slate | 17.50 | 1.25 |
| | | Never hinged | 45.00 | |
| *a.* | | Bklt. pane of 6 | *750.00* | |
| | | Cplt. bklt., 4 #129a | *3,000.* | |
| *b.* | | Inverted surcharge | 350.00 | 350.00 |
| *c.* | | Double surcharge | 225.00 | 225.00 |
| *e.* | | Vert. pair, one without surcharge | 1,300. | |
| *g.* | | Imperf, single | 160.00 | *200.00* |

Old Seal of Republic of Trieste
A60

Allegory of Dante's Divine Comedy
A61

Italy Holding Laurels for Dante — A62

Dante Alighieri — A63

**Wmk. 140**

**1921, June 5 Litho.** *Perf. 14*

| | | | | |
|---|---|---|---|---|
| **130** | A60 | 15c blk & rose | 7.25 | *55.00* |
| *a.* | | Horiz. pair, imperf btwn. | 950.00 | |
| **131** | A60 | 25c bl & rose | 7.25 | *55.00* |
| **132** | A60 | 40c brn & rose | 7.25 | *55.00* |
| | | *Nos. 130-132 (3)* | 21.75 | *165.00* |
| | | Set, never hinged | 48.00 | |

Reunion of Venezia Giulia with Italy.

**1921, Sept. 28** **Typo.**

| | | | | |
|---|---|---|---|---|
| **133** | A61 | 15c vio brn | 7.25 | *35.00* |
| *a.* | | Imperf, single | 40.00 | 40.00 |
| **134** | A62 | 25c gray grn | 7.25 | *35.00* |
| *a.* | | Imperf, single | 40.00 | 40.00 |
| **135** | A63 | 40c brown | 7.25 | *35.00* |
| *a.* | | Imperf, single | 40.00 | 40.00 |
| | | *Nos. 133-135 (3)* | 21.75 | *105.00* |
| | | Set, never hinged | 48.00 | |

600th anniversary of the death of Dante.

A 15c gray was not issued. Value: hinged $160, never hinged $400, used $550.

Nos. 133-135 exist in part perforate pairs.

"Victory" — A64

**1921, Nov. 1 Engr.** *Perf. 14*

| | | | | |
|---|---|---|---|---|
| **136** | A64 | 5c olive green | 1.60 | *2.00* |
| *b.* | | Imperf, single | 250.00 | 275.00 |
| **137** | A64 | 10c red | 2.40 | 2.40 |
| *c.* | | Imperf, single | 250.00 | 525.00 |
| **138** | A64 | 15c slate green | 4.00 | *9.50* |
| **139** | A64 | 25c ultra | 2.40 | *6.50* |
| *c.* | | Imperf, single | 190.00 | 190.00 |
| *d.* | | As "c," double impression | 650.00 | — |
| | | *Nos. 136-139 (4)* | 10.40 | *20.40* |
| | | Set, never hinged | 19.00 | |

3rd anniv. of the victory on the Piave.

For surcharges see Nos. 171-174.

Flame of Patriotism Tempering Sword of Justice — A65

Giuseppe Mazzini — A66

Mazzini's Tomb
A67

**1922, Sept. 20 Typo.** *Perf. 14*

| | | | | |
|---|---|---|---|---|
| **140** | A65 | 25c maroon | 13.00 | *35.00* |
| **141** | A66 | 40c vio brn | 25.00 | *45.00* |
| **142** | A67 | 80c dk bl | 13.00 | *55.00* |
| | | *Nos. 140-142 (3)* | 51.00 | *135.00* |
| | | Set, never hinged | 127.50 | |

Mazzini (1805-1872), patriot and writer.

Nos. 95, 96, 100 and 104 Overprinted in Black

**1922, June 4 Wmk. 140** *Perf. 14*

| | | | | |
|---|---|---|---|---|
| **142A** | A48 | 10c claret | 475.00 | 475.00 |
| **142B** | A48 | 15c slate | 250.00 | 250.00 |
| **142C** | A49 | 25c blue | 250.00 | 250.00 |
| **142D** | A49 | 40c brown | 400.00 | 400.00 |
| | | *Nos. 142A-142D (4)* | 1,375. | 1,375. |
| | | Set, never hinged | 3,300. | |

9th Italian Philatelic Congress, Trieste. Nos. 142A-142D were on sale to Sept. 30, 1922. Counterfeits exist.

Christ Preaching The Gospel — A68

Portrait at upper right and badge at lower right differ on each value. Portrait at upper left is of Pope Gregory XV. Others: 20c, St. Theresa. 30c, St. Dominic. 50c, St. Francis of Assisi. 1 l, St. Francis Xavier.

**1923, June 11**

| | | | | |
|---|---|---|---|---|
| **143** | A68 | 20c ol grn & brn org | 6.50 | *175.00* |
| *a.* | | Imperf, single | 475.00 | 650.00 |
| *b.* | | Vert. pair, imperf btwn. | 1,000. | 1,450. |
| **144** | A68 | 30c claret & brn org | 6.50 | *175.00* |
| *a.* | | Imperf, single | 475.00 | 650.00 |
| *c.* | | Horiz. pair, imperf btwn. | 1,000. | 1,450. |
| **145** | A68 | 50c vio & brn org | 6.50 | *175.00* |
| *a.* | | Imperf, single | 475.00 | 650.00 |
| *c.* | | Horiz. pair, imperf btwn. | 1,200. | 1,600. |
| *d.* | | Vert. pair, imperf btwn. | 1,000. | 1,450. |
| **146** | A68 | 1 l bl & brn org | 6.50 | *175.00* |
| *a.* | | | 475.00 | 650.00 |
| *c.* | | Horiz. pair, imperf btwn. | 1,000. | 1,450. |
| *d.* | | Vert. pair, imperf btwn. | 1,000. | 1,450. |
| | | *Nos. 143-146 (4)* | 26.00 | *700.00* |
| | | Set, never hinged | 64.00 | |

Forged cancellations exist on Nos. 143-146.

300th anniv. of the Propagation of the Faith. Practically the entire issue was delivered to speculators.

**Stamps of Previous Issues, Surcharged**

a

b

c

d

e

**1923-25**

| | | | | |
|---|---|---|---|---|
| **147** | A49(a) | 7½c on 85c | .40 | *1.25* |
| *a.* | | Double surcharge | — | *1,600.* |
| **148** | A42(b) | 10c on 1c | .40 | .35 |
| *a.* | | Inverted surcharge | 24.00 | *40.00* |
| **149** | A43(b) | 10c on 2c | .40 | .35 |
| *a.* | | Inverted surcharge | 60.00 | *95.00* |
| **150** | A48(c) | 10c on 15c | .40 | .35 |
| *a.* | | Vert. pair, one without surcharge | *875.00* | — |
| **151** | A49(a) | 20c on 25c | .40 | .35 |
| **152** | A45(d) | 25c on 45c | 1.60 | *16.00* |
| *a.* | | Vert. pair, one without surcharge | *875.00* | |
| **153** | A49(a) | 25c on 60c | 3.25 | 1.00 |
| *a.* | | Vert. pair, one without surcharge | *725.00* | — |
| **154** | A49(a) | 30c on 50c | .40 | .35 |
| **155** | A49(a) | 30c on 55c | 1.60 | .35 |
| **156** | A49(a) | 50c on 40c | 6.50 | .40 |
| *a.* | | Inverted surcharge | 240.00 | *360.00* |
| *b.* | | Double surcharge | 130.00 | *150.00* |
| **157** | A49(a) | 50c on 55c | 22.50 | 12.00 |
| *a.* | | Inverted surcharge | 1,100. | *2,200.* |
| **158** | A51(e) | 1.75 l on 10 l | 16.00 | *32.50* |
| *a.* | | Vert. pair, one without surcharge | *1,250.* | |
| | | *Nos. 147-158 (12)* | 53.85 | 65.25 |
| | | Set, never hinged | 133.00 | |

Years of issue: Nos. 148-149, 156-157, 1923; Nos. 147, 152-153, 1924; others, 1925.

Emblem of the New Government A69

Wreath of Victory, Eagle and Fasces A70

Symbolical of Fascism and Italy — A71

**Unwmk.**

**1923, Oct. 24 Engr. *Perf. 14***

| | | | | |
|---|---|---|---|---|
| **159** | A69 | 10c dark green | 4.75 | *11.00* |
| *a.* | | Imperf, single | 800.00 | *950.00* |
| **160** | A69 | 30c dark violet | 4.75 | *11.00* |
| **161** | A69 | 50c brown carmine | 9.50 | *20.00* |
| | | **Wmk. 140 Typo.** | | |
| **162** | A70 | 1 l blue | 16.00 | *20.00* |
| **163** | A70 | 2 l brown | 19.00 | *24.00* |
| **164** | A71 | 5 l blk & bl | 32.50 | *65.00* |
| *a.* | | Imperf, single | 325.00 | — |
| | | *Nos. 159-164 (6)* | 86.50 | *151.00* |
| | | Set, never hinged | 225.50 | |

Anniv. of the March of the Fascisti on Rome.

Fishing Scene A72

Designs: 15c, Mt. Resegone. 30c, Fugitives bidding farewell to native mountains. 50c, Part of Lake Como. 1 l, Manzoni's home, Milan. 5 l, Alessandro Manzoni. The first four designs show scenes from Manzoni's work "I Promessi Sposi."

**1923, Dec. 29 *Perf. 14***

| | | | | |
|---|---|---|---|---|
| **165** | A72 | 10c brn red & blk | 24.00 | *200.00* |
| **166** | A72 | 15c bl grn & blk | 24.00 | *200.00* |
| **167** | A72 | 30c blk & slate | 24.00 | *200.00* |
| *a.* | | Imperf, single | *3,000.* | |
| | | Imperf, pair | — | |
| **168** | A72 | 50c org brn & blk | 24.00 | *200.00* |
| **169** | A72 | 1 l blue & blk | 160.00 | *800.00* |
| *a.* | | Imperf, single, no gum | 160.00 | *875.00* |
| **170** | A72 | 5 l vio & blk | 800.00 | *4,400.* |
| *a.* | | Imperf, single | 950.00 | |
| | | Imperf, pair | — | |
| | | *Nos. 165-170 (6)* | 1,056. | *6,000.* |
| | | Set, never hinged | 2,640. | |

50th anniv. of the death of Alessandro Manzoni.

Nos. 136-139 Surcharged

**1924, Feb.**

| | | | | |
|---|---|---|---|---|
| **171** | A64 | 1 l on 5c ol grn | 25.00 | *250.00* |
| **172** | A64 | 1 l on 10c red | 16.00 | *250.00* |
| **173** | A64 | 1 l on 15c slate grn | 25.00 | *250.00* |
| **174** | A64 | 1 l on 25c ultra | 16.00 | *250.00* |
| | | *Nos. 171-174 (4)* | 82.00 | *1,000.* |
| | | Set, never hinged | 200.00 | |

Surcharge forgeries exist.

***Perf. 14x13½***

| | | | | |
|---|---|---|---|---|
| *171a* | A64 | 1 l on 5c | 35.00 | *300.00* |
| *172a* | A64 | 1 l on 10c | 20.00 | *300.00* |
| *173a* | A64 | 1 l on 15c | 35.00 | *300.00* |
| *174h* | A64 | 1 l on 25c | 20.00 | *300.00* |
| | | *Nos. 171a-174h (4)* | 110.00 | *1,200.* |
| | | Set, never hinged | 220.00 | |

Nos. 95, 102, 105, 108, 110, 87 and 89 Overprinted in Black or Red

**1924, Feb. 16**

| | | | | |
|---|---|---|---|---|
| **174A** | A48 | 10c claret | 2.40 | *47.50* |
| **174B** | A49 | 30c org brn | 2.40 | *47.50* |
| **174C** | A49 | 50c violet | 2.40 | *47.50* |
| **174D** | A49 | 60c bl (R) | 14.50 | *140.00* |
| **174E** | A49 | 85c choc (R) | 6.50 | *140.00* |
| **174F** | A46 | 1 l brn & grn | 47.50 | *450.00* |
| **174G** | A46 | 2 l dk grn & org | 35.00 | *450.00* |
| | | *Nos. 174A-174G (7)* | 110.70 | *1,322.* |
| | | Set, never hinged | 275.00 | |

These stamps were sold on an Italian merchant ship which made a cruise to South American ports in 1924.

Overprint forgeries exist of #174D-174G.

### Stamps of 1901-22 with Advertising Labels Attached

***Perf. 14 all around, Imperf. between***

**1924-25**

| | | | | |
|---|---|---|---|---|
| *96b* | A48 | 15c + Bitter Campari | 4.00 | *24.00* |
| *96c* | A48 | 15c + Cordial Campari | 4.00 | *20.00* |
| *96d* | A48 | 15c + Columbia | 65.00 | 52.50 |
| *100c* | A49 | 25c + Abrador | 125.00 | 125.00 |
| *100d* | A49 | 25c + Coen | 240.00 | 65.00 |
| *100e* | A49 | 25c + Piperno | 1,600. | 1,000. |
| *100f* | A49 | 25c + Reinach | 125.00 | 87.50 |
| *100g* | A49 | 25c + Tagliacozzo | 950.00 | 1,000. |
| *102b* | A49 | 30c + Columbia | 32.50 | *40.00* |
| *105b* | A49 | 50c + Coen | 1,600. | 87.50 |
| *105c* | A49 | 50c + Columbia | 24.00 | 16.00 |
| *105d* | A49 | 50c + De Montel | 4.00 | *16.00* |
| *105e* | A49 | 50c + Piperno | 2,200. | 325.00 |
| *105f* | A49 | 50c + Reinach | 240.00 | 65.00 |
| *105g* | A49 | 50c + Siero Casali | 24.00 | *47.50* |
| *105h* | A49 | 50c + Singer | 4.00 | *9.50* |
| *105i* | A49 | 50c + Tagliacozzo | *2,400.* | 650.00 |
| *105j* | A49 | 50c + Tantal | 400.00 | 200.00 |
| *87d* | A46 | 1 l + Columbia | 950.00 | 950.00 |
| | | *Nos. 96b-87d (19)* | 10,991. | 4,780. |
| | | Set, never hinged | 22,700. | |

No. 113 with Columbia label and No. E3 with Cioccolato Perugina label were prepared but not issued. Values: Columbia, unused $55, never hinged $140; Cioccolato, unused $20, never hinged $47.50.

King Victor Emmanuel III — A78

**1925-26 Engr. Unwmk. *Perf. 11***

| | | | | |
|---|---|---|---|---|
| **175** | A78 | 60c brn car | 1.60 | .80 |
| *a.* | | Perf. 13½ | 8.00 | 2.40 |
| *b.* | | Imperf., pair | 275.00 | — |
| **176** | A78 | 1 l dk bl | 1.60 | .80 |
| *a.* | | Perf. 13½ | 16.00 | 11.00 |
| *b.* | | Imperf., pair | 275.00 | — |
| | | ***Perf. 13½*** | | |
| **177** | A78 | 1.25 l dk bl ('26) | 4.75 | 2.40 |
| *a.* | | Perf. 11 | 110.00 | 120.00 |
| *b.* | | Imperf., pair | 600.00 | — |
| | | *Nos. 175-177 (3)* | 7.95 | 4.00 |
| | | Set, never hinged | 20.00 | |

25th year of the reign of Victor Emmanuel III.

Nos. 175 to 177 exist with sideways watermark of fragments of letters or a crown, which are normally on the sheet margin.

St. Francis and His Vision A79

Monastery of St. Damien A80

Assisi Monastery A81

St. Francis' Death A82

St. Francis — A83

**1926, Jan. 30 Wmk. 140 *Perf. 14***

| | | | | |
|---|---|---|---|---|
| **178** | A79 | 20c gray grn | .80 | *1.00* |
| *a.* | | Imperf single | 950.00 | 950.00 |
| **179** | A80 | 40c dk vio | .80 | *1.00* |
| **180** | A81 | 60c red brn | .80 | *1.00* |
| *a.* | | Imperf single | 475.00 | 475.00 |
| | | **Unwmk. *Perf. 11*** | | |
| **181** | A83 | 30c slate blk | .80 | *1.00* |
| *a.* | | Perf. 13½ | 12.00 | *20.00* |
| | | Never hinged | 30.00 | |
| **182** | A82 | 1.25 l dark blue | 4.00 | 1.00 |
| *a.* | | Perf. 13½ | 475.00 | 40.00 |
| | | Never hinged | 1,200. | |
| | | ***Perf. 13½*** | | |
| **183** | A83 | 5 l + 2.50 l dk brn | 11.00 | *120.00* |
| | | *Nos. 178-183 (6)* | 18.20 | *125.00* |
| | | Set, never hinged | 45.00 | |

700th anniv. of the death of St. Francis of Assisi.

Alessandro Volta — A84

**1927 Wmk. 140 Typo. *Perf. 14***

| | | | | |
|---|---|---|---|---|
| **188** | A84 | 20c dk car | 3.25 | 1.25 |
| **189** | A84 | 50c grnsh blk | 3.25 | .80 |
| **190** | A84 | 60c chocolate | 4.75 | 4.75 |
| **191** | A84 | 1.25 l ultra | 16.00 | 8.00 |
| | | *Nos. 188-191 (4)* | 27.25 | 14.80 |
| | | Set, never hinged | 68.00 | |

Cent. of the death of Alessandro Volta.

The 20c in purple is Cyrenaica No. 25 with overprint omitted. Values: $4,000 unused; $6,000 never hinged.

A85

**1927-29 Size: 17½x22mm *Perf. 14***

| | | | | |
|---|---|---|---|---|
| **192** | A85 | 50c brn & slate | 3.25 | .40 |
| *a.* | | Imperf, pair | — | — |
| | | **Unwmk. Engr. *Perf. 11*** | | |
| | | **Size: 19x23mm** | | |
| **193** | A85 | 1.75 l dp brn | 4.00 | .35 |
| *a.* | | Perf. 13½ ('29) | *35,000.* | *3,250.* |
| | | Never hinged | *55,000.* | |
| *b.* | | Perf. 11x13½ ('29) | — | 2,250. |
| *c.* | | Perf. 13½x11 ('29) | — | 2,250. |
| *d.* | | Imperf, single | *2,750.* | |
| **194** | A85 | 1.85 l black | 3.25 | .70 |
| **195** | A85 | 2.55 l brn car | 4.00 | *9.50* |
| **196** | A85 | 2.65 l dp vio | 6.50 | *80.00* |
| *a.* | | Imperf, single | 2,100. | |
| | | *Nos. 192-196 (5)* | 21.00 | *90.95* |
| | | Set, never hinged | 45.00 | |

A86

**1928-29 Wmk. 140 Typo. *Perf. 14***

| | | | | |
|---|---|---|---|---|
| **197** | A86 | 7½c lt brown | 3.25 | *12.00* |
| **198** | A86 | 15c brown org ('29) | 3.25 | .35 |
| **199** | A86 | 35c gray blk ('29) | 8.75 | 14.50 |
| **200** | A86 | 50c dull violet | 19.00 | .35 |
| *a.* | | Imperf single | 250.00 | |
| | | *Nos. 197-200 (4)* | 34.25 | *27.20* |
| | | Set, never hinged | 85.50 | |

Emmanuel Philibert, Duke of Savoy — A87

Statue of Philibert, Turin — A88

Philibert and Italian Soldier of 1918 — A89

**1928 *Perf. 11***

| | | | | |
|---|---|---|---|---|
| **201** | A87 | 20c red brn & ultra | 9.50 | *16.00* |
| *a.* | | Perf. 13½ | 240.00 | 240.00 |
| **202** | A87 | 25c dp red & bl grn | 9.50 | *16.00* |
| *a.* | | Perf. 13½ | 47.50 | *52.50* |
| **203** | A87 | 30c bl grn & red brn | 16.00 | *32.00* |
| *a.* | | Center inverted | *57,500.* | *7,600.* |
| *b.* | | Perf. 13½ | 35.00 | 35.00 |
| | | ***Perf. 14*** | | |
| **204** | A89 | 50c org brn & bl | 4.00 | 1.25 |
| **205** | A89 | 75c dp red | 4.75 | 4.00 |
| **206** | A88 | 1.25 l bl & blk | 4.75 | 4.00 |
| **207** | A89 | 1.75 l bl grn | 32.50 | *40.00* |
| **208** | A87 | 5 l vio & bl grn (Perf. 11) | 29.00 | *110.00* |
| **209** | A89 | 10 l blk & pink | 35.00 | *225.00* |
| **210** | A88 | 20 l vio & blk | 70.00 | *725.00* |
| | | *Nos. 201-210 (10)* | 215.00 | *1,173.* |
| | | Set, never hinged | 535.00 | |

400th anniv. of the birth of Emmanuel Philibert, Duke of Savoy; 10th anniv. of the victory of 1918; Turin Exhibition.

She-wolf Suckling Romulus and Remus

A90 A95a

Julius Caesar A91

Augustus Caesar A92

"Italia" — A93

A94

A95

**1929-42 Wmk. 140 Photo. *Perf. 14***

| | | | | |
|---|---|---|---|---|
| **213** | A90 | 5c olive brn | .25 | .25 |
| **214** | A91 | 7½c deep vio | 1.60 | .25 |
| **215** | A92 | 10c dark brown | .25 | .25 |
| **216** | A93 | 15c slate grn | .25 | .25 |
| **217** | A91 | 20c rose red | .25 | .25 |
| **218** | A94 | 25c dp green | .25 | .25 |
| **219** | A95 | 30c olive brn | .25 | .25 |
| *a.* | | Imperf., pair | 1,100. | |
| **220** | A93 | 35c dp blue | .25 | .25 |
| **221** | A95 | 50c purple | .25 | .25 |
| *a.* | | Imperf., pair | 725.00 | *875.00* |
| **222** | A94 | 75c rose red | .25 | .25 |
| **222A** | A91 | 1 l dk pur ('42) | .25 | .25 |
| **223** | A94 | 1.25 l dp blue | .25 | .25 |
| **224** | A92 | 1.75 l red org | .25 | .25 |
| **225** | A93 | 2 l car lake | .25 | .25 |
| **226** | A95a | 2.55 l slate grn | .25 | .80 |
| **226A** | A95a | 3.70 l pur ('30) | .25 | .80 |
| **227** | A95a | 5 l rose red | .25 | .25 |
| **228** | A93 | 10 l purple | 4.00 | 4.00 |
| **229** | A91 | 20 l lt green | 4.75 | *12.00* |
| **230** | A92 | 25 l bluish sl | 11.00 | *35.00* |
| **231** | A94 | 50 l dp violet | 13.00 | *40.00* |
| | | *Nos. 213-231 (21)* | 38.35 | *96.35* |
| | | Set, never hinged | 94.00 | |

Stamps of the 1929-42 issue overprinted "G.N.R." are 1943 local issues of the Guardia Nazionale Republicana.

See Nos. 427-438, 441-459.

For surcharge and overprints see Nos. 460, M1-M13, 1N10-1N13, 1LN1-1LN1A, 1LN10; Italian Social Republic 1-5A; Yugoslavia-Ljubljana N36-N54.

Courtyard of Monte Cassino A96

Monks Laying Cornerstone — A98

St. Benedict of Nursia — A100

Designs: 25c, Fresco, "Death of St. Benedict." 75c+15c, 5 l+1 l, Monte Cassino Abbey.

**1929, Aug. 1 Photo. Wmk. 140**

| | | | | |
|---|---|---|---|---|
| **232** | A96 | 20c red orange | 1.60 | 1.60 |
| **233** | A96 | 25c dk green | 1.60 | 1.60 |
| **234** | A98 | 50c + 10c ol brn | 4.00 | *30.00* |
| **235** | A98 | 75c + 15c crim | 4.75 | *40.00* |
| **236** | A96 | 1.25 l + 25c saph | 6.50 | *45.00* |
| **237** | A98 | 5 l + 1 l dk vio | 9.50 | *100.00* |

**Unwmk.**

**Engr.**

| | | | | |
|---|---|---|---|---|
| **238** | A100 | 10 l + 2 l slate grn | 14.50 | *260.00* |
| | | *Nos. 232-238 (7)* | 42.45 | *478.20* |
| | | Set, never hinged | 105.00 | |

14th cent. of the founding of the Abbey of Monte Cassino by St. Benedict in 529 A.D. The premium on some of the stamps was given to the committee for the celebration of the centenary.

Prince Humbert and Princess Marie José A101

**1930, Jan. 8 Photo. Wmk. 140**

| | | | | |
|---|---|---|---|---|
| **239** | A101 | 20c orange red | .80 | .60 |
| **240** | A101 | 50c + 10c ol brn | 2.40 | *4.00* |
| **241** | A101 | 1.25 l + 25c dp bl | 5.50 | *13.00* |
| | | *Nos. 239-241 (3)* | 8.70 | *17.60* |
| | | Set, never hinged | 22.00 | |

Marriage of Prince Humbert of Savoy with Princess Marie José of Belgium.

The surtax on Nos. 240 and 241 was for the benefit of the Italian Red Cross Society.

The 20c in green is Cyrenaica No. 35 with overprint omitted. Values: $35,000 unused; $52,500 never hinged.

Ferrucci Leading His Army A102

Fabrizio Maramaldo Killing Ferrucci A103

Francesco Ferrucci — A104

**1930, July 10**

| | | | | |
|---|---|---|---|---|
| **242** | A102 | 20c rose red | .80 | .80 |
| **243** | A103 | 25c deep green | 1.40 | .80 |
| **244** | A103 | 50c purple | .80 | .40 |
| **245** | A103 | 1.25 l deep blue | 11.00 | 4.75 |
| **246** | A104 | 5 l + 2 l org red | 22.50 | *140.00* |
| | | *Nos. 242-246 (5)* | 36.50 | *146.75* |
| | | Set, never hinged | 90.00 | |
| | | *Nos. 242-246,C20-C22 (8)* | 60.50 | *314.75* |
| | | Set, never hinged | 150.00 | |

4th cent. of the death of Francesco Ferrucci, Tuscan warrior.

**Overprints**
**See Aegean Islands for types A103-A145 Overprinted.**

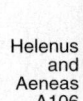

Helenus and Aeneas A106

Designs: 20c, Anchises and Aeneas watch passing of Roman Legions. 25c, Aeneas feasting in shade of Albunea. 30c, Ceres and her children with fruits of Earth. 50c, Harvesters at work. 75c, Woman at loom, children and calf. 1.25 l, Anchises and his sailors in sight of Italy. 5 l+1.50 l, Shepherd piping by fireside. 10 l+2.50 l, Aeneas leading his army.

**1930, Oct. 21 Photo. *Perf. 14***

| | | | | |
|---|---|---|---|---|
| **248** | A106 | 15c olive brn | 2.40 | 2.40 |
| **249** | A106 | 20c orange | 2.40 | 1.60 |
| **250** | A106 | 25c green | 3.20 | 1.60 |
| **251** | A106 | 30c dull vio | 9.50 | 4.00 |
| **252** | A106 | 50c violet | 16.00 | .80 |
| **253** | A106 | 75c rose red | 4.00 | *12.00* |
| **254** | A106 | 1.25 l blue | 4.00 | *12.00* |

**Unwmk. Engr.**

| | | | | |
|---|---|---|---|---|
| **255** | A106 | 5 l +1.50 l red brn | 60.00 | *400.00* |
| **256** | A106 | 10 l +2.50 l gray grn | 60.00 | *550.00* |
| | | *Nos. 248-256 (9)* | 161.50 | *984.40* |
| | | Set, never hinged | 405.00 | |
| | | *Nos. 248-256,C23-C26 (13)* | 332.00 | *2,019.* |
| | | Set, never hinged | 835.00 | |

Bimillenary of the birth of Virgil. Surtax on Nos. 255-256 was for the National Institute Figli del Littorio.

Arms of Italy (Fascist Emblems Support House of Savoy Arms) — A115

**1930, Dec. 16 Photo. Wmk. 140**

| | | | | |
|---|---|---|---|---|
| **257** | A115 | 2c deep orange | 1.60 | .25 |
| | | Never hinged | 4.00 | |

St. Anthony being Installed as a Franciscan A116

Olivares Hermitage, Portugal A118

St. Anthony Freeing Prisoners A120

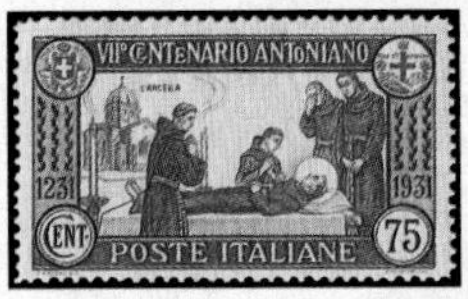
St. Anthony's Death A121

St. Anthony Succoring the Poor — A122

Designs: 25c, St. Anthony preaching to the fishes. 50c, Basilica of St. Anthony, Padua.

**Wmk. 140**

**1931, Mar. 9 Photo. *Perf. 14***

| | | | | |
|---|---|---|---|---|
| **258** | A116 | 20c dull violet | 4.00 | 1.25 |
| **259** | A116 | 25c gray green | 2.40 | 1.25 |
| **260** | A118 | 30c brown | 6.50 | 2.40 |
| **261** | A118 | 50c violet | 2.00 | .80 |
| **262** | A120 | 1.25 l blue | 20.00 | 9.50 |

**Unwmk. Engr.**

| | | | | |
|---|---|---|---|---|
| **263** | A121 | 75c brown red | 9.50 | *16.00* |
| *a.* | | Perf. 12 | 100.00 | *300.00* |
| | | Never hinged | 240.00 | |
| **264** | A122 | 5 l + 2.50 l ol grn | 40.00 | *250.00* |
| | | *Nos. 258-264 (7)* | 84.40 | *281.20* |
| | | Set, never hinged | 210.00 | |

7th centenary of the death of Saint Anthony of Padua.

Tower of Meloria — A123

Training Ship "Amerigo Vespucci" A124

Cruiser "Trento" A125

**1931, Nov. 29 Photo. Wmk. 140**

| | | | | |
|---|---|---|---|---|
| **265** | A123 | 20c rose red | 8.75 | 2.00 |
| **266** | A124 | 50c purple | 8.75 | 1.60 |
| **267** | A125 | 1.25 l dk bl | 24.00 | 4.75 |
| | | *Nos. 265-267 (3)* | 41.50 | 8.35 |
| | | Set, never hinged | 165.00 | |

Royal Naval Academy at Leghorn (Livorno), 50th anniv.

Giovanni Boccaccio A126

Designs: 15c, Niccolo Machiavelli. 20c, Paolo Sarpi. 25c, Count Vittorio Alfieri. 30c, Ugo Foscolo. 50c, Count Giacomo Leopardi. 75c, Giosue Carducci. 1.25 l, Carlo Giuseppe Botta. 1.75 l, Torquato Tasso. 2.75 l, Francesco Petrarca. 5 l+2 l, Ludovico Ariosto. 10 l+2.50 l, Dante Alighieri.

**1932, Mar. 14 *Perf. 14***

| | | | | |
|---|---|---|---|---|
| **268** | A126 | 10c olive brn | 3.25 | 1.60 |
| **269** | A126 | 15c slate green | 3.25 | 2.00 |
| **270** | A126 | 20c rose red | 3.25 | 1.60 |
| **271** | A126 | 25c dp green | 3.25 | 1.25 |
| **272** | A126 | 30c olive brn | 4.00 | 1.60 |
| **273** | A126 | 50c violet | 2.40 | .80 |
| **274** | A126 | 75c car rose | 16.00 | 8.00 |
| **275** | A126 | 1.25 l dp blue | 4.75 | 4.00 |
| **276** | A126 | 1.75 l orange | 12.00 | 8.00 |
| **277** | A126 | 2.75 l gray | 24.00 | *40.00* |
| **278** | A126 | 5 l + 2 l car rose | 29.00 | *225.00* |
| **279** | A126 | 10 l + 2.50 l ol grn | 35.00 | *350.00* |
| | | *Nos. 268-279 (12)* | 140.15 | *643.85* |
| | | Set, never hinged | 350.00 | |
| | | *Nos. 268-279,C28-C33,C34 (19)* | 239.15 | *2,096.* |
| | | Set, never hinged | 600.00 | |

Dante Alighieri Society, a natl. literary association founded to promote development of the Italian language and culture. The surtax was added to the Society funds to help in its work.

View of Caprera A138

Garibaldi Carrying His Dying Wife A141

Garibaldi Memorial A144

Giuseppe Garibaldi A145

Designs: 20c, 30c, Garibaldi meeting Victor Emmanuel II. 25c, 50c, Garibaldi at Battle of Calatafimi. 1.25 l, Garibaldi's tomb. 1.75 l+25c, Rock of Quarto.

**1932, Apr. 6**

| | | | | |
|---|---|---|---|---|
| **280** | A138 | 10c gray blk | 2.40 | 1.60 |
| **281** | A138 | 20c olive brn | 2.40 | 1.25 |
| **282** | A138 | 25c dull grn | 3.25 | 1.60 |
| **283** | A138 | 30c orange | 3.25 | 2.40 |
| **284** | A138 | 50c violet | 1.60 | .40 |
| **285** | A141 | 75c rose red | 16.00 | 9.50 |
| **286** | A141 | 1.25 l dp blue | 32.50 | 4.00 |
| **287** | A141 | 1.75 l + 25c bl gray | 40.00 | *87.50* |

| | | | | |
|---|---|---|---|---|
| **288** | A144 | 2.55 l + 50c red brn | 32.50 | *125.00* |
| **289** | A145 | 5 l + 1 l cop red | 32.50 | *130.00* |
| | | *Nos. 280-289 (10)* | 166.40 | *363.25* |
| | | Set, never hinged | 410.00 | |
| | | *Nos. 280-289,C35-C39,CE1-CE2 (17)* | 242.40 | *619.25* |
| | | Set, never hinged | 600.00 | |

50th anniv. of the death of Giuseppe Garibaldi, patriot.

Plowing with Oxen and Tractor A146

10c, Soldier guarding mountain pass. 15c, Marine, battleship & seaplane. 20c, Head of Fascist youth. 25c, Hands of workers & tools. 30c, Flags, Bible & altar. 35c, "New roads for the new Legions." 50c, Mussolini statue, Bologna. 60c, Hands with spades. 75c, Excavating ruins. 1 l, Steamers & galleons. 1.25 l, Italian flag, map & points of compass. 1.75 l, Flag, athlete & stadium. 2.55 l, Mother & child. 2.75 l, Emblems of drama, music, art & sport. 5 l+2.50 l, Roman emperor.

**1932, Oct. 27** **Photo.**

| | | | | |
|---|---|---|---|---|
| **290** | A146 | 5c dk brown | 2.40 | 1.25 |
| **291** | A146 | 10c dk brown | 2.40 | .80 |
| **292** | A146 | 15c dk gray grn | 2.40 | 1.25 |
| **293** | A146 | 20c car rose | 2.40 | .60 |
| **294** | A146 | 25c dp green | 2.40 | .40 |
| **295** | A146 | 30c dk brown | 3.25 | 2.40 |
| **296** | A146 | 35c dk blue | 8.00 | *9.50* |
| **297** | A146 | 50c purple | 1.60 | .40 |
| **298** | A146 | 60c orange brn | 12.00 | 8.00 |
| **299** | A146 | 75c car rose | 4.00 | 4.00 |
| **300** | A146 | 1 l black vio | 16.00 | 6.50 |
| **301** | A146 | 1.25 l dp blue | 4.00 | 1.60 |
| **302** | A146 | 1.75 l orange | 24.00 | 2.00 |
| **303** | A146 | 2.55 l dk gray | 29.00 | *40.00* |
| **304** | A146 | 2.75 l slate grn | 29.00 | *40.00* |
| **305** | A146 | 5 l + 2.50 l car rose | 40.00 | *300.00* |
| | | *Nos. 290-305 (16)* | 182.85 | *418.70* |
| | | Set, never hinged | 455.00 | |
| | | *Nos. 290-305,C40-C41,E16-E17 (20)* | 202.25 | *617.45* |
| | | Set, never hinged | 520.00 | |

10th anniv. of the Fascist government and the March on Rome.

Statue of Athlete — A162

Cross in Halo, St. Peter's Dome — A163

**1933, Aug. 16** ***Perf. 14***

| | | | | |
|---|---|---|---|---|
| **306** | A162 | 10c dk brown | .80 | .80 |
| **307** | A162 | 20c rose red | .80 | .80 |
| **308** | A162 | 50c purple | .80 | .40 |
| **309** | A162 | 1.25 l blue | 4.75 | *6.50* |
| | | *Nos. 306-309 (4)* | 7.15 | 8.50 |
| | | Set, never hinged | 18.00 | |

Intl. University Games at Turin, Sept., 1933.

**1933, Oct. 23**

Designs: 25c, 50c, Angel with cross. 1.25 l, as 20c. 2.55 l, + 2.50 l, Cross with doves.

| | | | | |
|---|---|---|---|---|
| **310** | A163 | 20c rose red | 4.75 | 1.25 |
| **311** | A163 | 25c green | 12.00 | 1.60 |
| **312** | A163 | 50c purple | 4.75 | .40 |
| **313** | A163 | 1.25 l dp blue | 12.00 | 4.75 |
| **314** | A163 | 2.55 l + 2.50 l blk | 8.00 | *175.00* |
| | | *Nos. 310-314 (5)* | 41.50 | *183.00* |
| | | Set, never hinged | 105.00 | |
| | | *Nos. 310-314,CB1-CB2 (7)* | 47.90 | *309.00* |
| | | Set, never hinged | 121.00 | |

Issued at the solicitation of the Order of the Holy Sepulchre of Jerusalem to mark the Holy Year.

Anchor of the "Emanuele Filiberto" A166

Antonio Pacinotti A172

Designs: 20c, Anchor. 50c, Gabriele d'Annunzio. 1.25 l, St. Vito's Tower. 1.75 l, Symbolizing Fiume's annexation. 2.55 l+2 l, Victor Emmanuel III arriving aboard "Brindisi." 2.75 l+2.50 l, Galley, gondola and battleship.

**1934, Mar. 12**

| | | | | |
|---|---|---|---|---|
| **315** | A166 | 10c dk brown | 8.00 | 4.00 |
| **316** | A166 | 20c rose red | 1.60 | 1.60 |
| **317** | A166 | 50c purple | 1.60 | 1.60 |
| **318** | A166 | 1.25 l blue | 1.60 | *6.50* |
| **319** | A166 | 1.75 l + 1 l indigo | 1.60 | *35.00* |
| **320** | A166 | 2.55 l + 2 l dull vio | 1.60 | *55.00* |
| **321** | A166 | 2.75 l + 2.50 l ol grn | 1.60 | *55.00* |
| | | *Nos. 315-321 (7)* | 17.60 | *158.70* |
| | | Set, never hinged | 44.00 | |
| | | *Nos. 315-321,C56-C61,CE5-CE7 (16)* | 29.95 | *312.10* |
| | | Set, never hinged | 66.50 | |

10th anniversary of annexation of Fiume.

**1934, May 23**

| | | | | |
|---|---|---|---|---|
| **322** | A172 | 50c purple | .80 | .40 |
| **323** | A172 | 1.25 l sapphire | 1.25 | *2.75* |
| | | Set, never hinged | 5.00 | |

75th anniv. of invention of the dynamo by Antonio Pacinotti (1841-1912), scientist.

Guarding the Goal — A173

Players — A175

Soccer Players A174

**1934, May 23**

| | | | | |
|---|---|---|---|---|
| **324** | A173 | 20c red orange | 6.50 | *8.00* |
| **325** | A174 | 25c green | 6.50 | 2.40 |
| **326** | A174 | 50c purple | 6.50 | 1.25 |
| **327** | A174 | 1.25 l blue | 16.00 | 16.00 |
| **328** | A175 | 5 l + 2.50 l brn | 95.00 | *550.00* |
| | | *Nos. 324-328 (5)* | 130.50 | *577.65* |
| | | Set, never hinged | 330.00 | |
| | | *Nos. 324-328,C62-C65 (9)* | 264.00 | *1,465.* |
| | | Set, never hinged | 625.00 | |

2nd World Soccer Championship.
For overprints see Aegean Islands Nos. 31-35.

Luigi Galvani — A176

**1934, Aug. 16**

| | | | | |
|---|---|---|---|---|
| **329** | A176 | 30c brown, *buff* | 1.00 | .80 |
| **330** | A176 | 75c carmine, *rose* | 1.40 | 3.25 |
| | | Set, never hinged | 6.00 | |

Intl. Congress of Electro-Radio-Biology.

Carabinieri Emblem — A177

Cutting Barbed Wire A178

Designs: 20c, Sardinian Grenadier and soldier throwing grenade. 25c, Alpine Infantry. 30c, Military courage. 75c, Artillery. 1.25 l, Acclaiming the Service. 1.75 l+1 l, Cavalry. 2.55 l+2 l, Sapping Detail. 2.75 l+2 l, First aid.

**1934, Sept. 6** **Photo.** **Wmk. 140**

| | | | | |
|---|---|---|---|---|
| **331** | A177 | 10c dk brown | 2.40 | 2.40 |
| **332** | A178 | 15c olive grn | 2.40 | *4.00* |
| **333** | A178 | 20c rose red | 2.40 | 1.60 |
| **334** | A177 | 25c green | 4.00 | 1.60 |
| **335** | A178 | 30c dk brown | 4.00 | *8.00* |
| **336** | A178 | 50c purple | 2.40 | .80 |
| **337** | A178 | 75c car rose | 40.00 | 12.00 |
| **338** | A178 | 1.25 l dk blue | 40.00 | 8.00 |
| **339** | A177 | 1.75 l + 1 l red org | 17.50 | *52.50* |
| **340** | A178 | 2.55 l + 2 l dp cl | 17.50 | *67.50* |
| **341** | A178 | 2.75 l + 2 l vio | 21.00 | *72.50* |
| | | *Nos. 331-341 (11)* | 153.60 | *230.90* |
| | | Set, never hinged | 385.00 | |
| | | *Nos. 331-341,C66-C72 (18)* | 202.10 | *379.90* |
| | | Set, never hinged | 505.00 | |

Centenary of Military Medal of Valor.
For overprints see Aegean Islands Nos. 36-46.

Man Holding Fasces A187

Standard Bearer, Bayonet Attack A188

Design: 30c, Eagle and soldier.

**1935, Apr. 23** ***Perf. 14***

| | | | | |
|---|---|---|---|---|
| **342** | A187 | 20c rose red | .80 | .80 |
| **343** | A187 | 30c dk brown | 6.50 | 8.00 |
| **344** | A188 | 50c purple | .80 | .40 |
| | | *Nos. 342-344 (3)* | 8.10 | 9.20 |
| | | Set, never hinged | 20.00 | |

Issued in honor of the University Contests.

Fascist Flight Symbolism A190

Leonardo da Vinci — A191

**1935, Oct. 1**

| | | | | |
|---|---|---|---|---|
| **345** | A190 | 20c rose red | 20.00 | 2.00 |
| **346** | A190 | 30c brown | 35.00 | 6.50 |
| **347** | A191 | 50c purple | 72.50 | 1.25 |
| **348** | A191 | 1.25 l dk blue | 80.00 | 7.25 |
| | | *Nos. 345-348 (4)* | 207.50 | 17.00 |
| | | Set, never hinged | 830.00 | |

International Aeronautical Salon, Milan.

Vincenzo Bellini — A192

Bellini's Villa — A194

Bellini's Piano A193

**1935, Oct. 15**

| | | | | |
|---|---|---|---|---|
| **349** | A192 | 20c rose red | 16.00 | 4.00 |
| **350** | A192 | 30c brown | 24.00 | 12.00 |
| **351** | A192 | 50c violet | 24.00 | 1.60 |
| **352** | A192 | 1.25 l dk blue | 40.00 | 16.00 |
| **353** | A193 | 1.75 l + 1 l red org | 35.00 | *240.00* |
| **354** | A194 | 2.75 l + 2 l ol blk | 65.00 | *260.00* |
| | | *Nos. 349-354 (6)* | 204.00 | *533.60* |
| | | Set, never hinged | 510.00 | |
| | | *Nos. 349-354,C79-C83 (11)* | 287.00 | *1,021.* |
| | | Set, never hinged | 710.00 | |

Bellini (1801-35), operatic composer.

Map of Italian Industries A195

Designs: 20c, 1.25 l, Map of Italian Industries. 30c, 50c, Cogwheel and plow.

**1936, Mar. 23**

| | | | | |
|---|---|---|---|---|
| **355** | A195 | 20c red | .80 | .40 |
| **356** | A195 | 30c brown | .80 | 1.25 |
| **357** | A195 | 50c purple | .80 | .35 |
| **358** | A195 | 1.25 l blue | 4.75 | 3.25 |
| | | *Nos. 355-358 (4)* | 7.15 | 5.25 |
| | | Set, never hinged | 18.00 | |

The 17th Milan Trade Fair.

Flock of Sheep A197

Ajax Defying the Lightning A199

Bust of Horace A200

Designs: 20c, 1.25 l+1 l, Countryside in Spring. 75c, Capitol. 1.75 l+1 l, Pan piping. 2.55 l+1 l, Dying warrior.

**Wmk. Crowns (140)**

**1936, July 1** **Photo.** ***Perf. 14***

| | | | | |
|---|---|---|---|---|
| **359** | A197 | 10c dp green | 6.50 | 1.25 |
| **360** | A197 | 20c rose red | 4.75 | .80 |
| **361** | A199 | 30c olive brn | 6.50 | 2.25 |
| **362** | A200 | 50c purple | 6.50 | .40 |
| **363** | A197 | 75c rose red | 16.00 | 9.50 |
| **364** | A197 | 1.25 l + 1 l dk bl | 27.50 | *130.00* |
| **365** | A199 | 1.75 l + 1 l car rose | 32.50 | *240.00* |
| **366** | A197 | 2.55 l + 1 l sl blk | 40.00 | *275.00* |
| | | *Nos. 359-366 (8)* | 140.25 | *659.20* |
| | | Set, never hinged | 350.00 | |
| | | *Nos. 359-366,C84-C88 (13)* | 202.00 | *1,153.* |
| | | Set, never hinged | 500.00 | |

2000th anniv. of the birth of Quintus Horatius Flaccus (Horace), Roman poet.

Child Holding Wheat — A204

Child Giving Salute — A205

Child and Fasces — A206

"Il Bambino" by della Robbia — A207

**1937, June 28**

**367** A204 10c yellow brn 3.25 1.60
**368** A205 20c car rose 3.25 1.25
**369** A204 25c green 3.25 2.00
**370** A206 30c dk brown 4.75 4.00
**371** A205 50c purple 3.25 .40
**372** A207 75c rose red 16.00 *17.50*
**373** A205 1.25 l dk blue 20.00 17.50
**374** A206 1.75 l + 75c org 40.00 *175.00*
**375** A207 2.75 l + 1.25 l dk bl grn 32.50 *200.00*
**376** A205 5 l + 3 l bl gray 40.00 *275.00*
*Nos. 367-376 (10)* 166.25 *694.25*
Set, never hinged 415.00
*Nos. 367-376,C89-C94 (16)* 262.25 *1,377.*
Set, never hinged 655.00

Summer Exhibition for Child Welfare. The surtax on Nos. 374-376 was used to support summer camps for children.

Rostral Column — A208

15c, Army Trophies. 20c, Augustus Caesar (Octavianus) offering sacrifice. 25c, Cross Roman Standards. 30c, Julius Caesar and Julian Star. 50c, Augustus receiving acclaim. 75c, Augustus Caesar. 1.25 l, Symbolizing maritime glory of Rome. 1.75 l+1 l, Sacrificial Altar. 2.55 l+2 l, Capitol.

**1937, Sept. 23**

**377** A208 10c myrtle grn 3.25 .80
**378** A208 15c olive grn 3.25 1.25
**379** A208 20c red 3.25 .60
**380** A208 25c green 3.25 .60
**381** A208 30c olive bis 4.00 .80
**382** A208 50c purple 3.25 .35
**383** A208 75c scarlet 3.25 4.75
**384** A208 1.25 l dk blue 8.00 5.50
**385** A208 1.75 l + 1 l plum 40.00 *160.00*
**386** A208 2.55 l + 2 l sl blk 52.50 *225.00*
*Nos. 377-386 (10)* 124.00 *399.65*
Set, never hinged 300.00
*Nos. 377-386,C95-C99 (15)* 259.00 *812.65*
Set, never hinged 625.00

Bimillenary of the birth of Emperor Augustus Caesar (Octavianus) on the occasion of the exhibition opened in Rome by Mussolini, Sept. 22, 1937.
For overprints see Aegean Islands #47-56.

Gasparo Luigi Pacifico Spontini A218

Antonius Stradivarius A219

Count Giacomo Leopardi A220

Giovanni Battista Pergolesi A221

Giotto di Bondone — A222

**1937, Oct. 25**

**387** A218 10c dk brown 1.60 .80
**388** A219 20c rose red 1.60 .80
**389** A220 25c dk green 1.60 .80
**390** A221 30c dk brown 1.60 1.60
**391** A220 50c purple 1.60 .80
**392** A221 75c crimson 2.25 *4.75*
**393** A222 1.25 l dp blue 3.25 *4.75*
**394** A218 1.75 l dp orange 3.25 *4.75*
**395** A219 2.55 l + 2 l gray grn 16.00 *200.00*
**396** A222 2.75 l + 2 l red brn 16.00 *240.00*
*Nos. 387-396 (10)* 48.75 *459.05*
Set, never hinged 125.00

Centennials of Spontini, Stradivarius, Leopardi, Pergolesi and Giotto.
For overprints see Aegean Islands #57-58.

Guglielmo Marconi A223

Augustus Caesar (Octavianus) A224

**1938, Jan. 24**

**397** A223 20c rose pink 3.25 .80
**398** A223 50c purple .80 .35
**399** A223 1.25 l blue 3.25 5.50
*Nos. 397-399 (3)* 7.30 6.65
Set, never hinged 18.00

Guglielmo Marconi (1874-1937), electrical engineer, inventor of wireless telegraphy.

**1938, Oct. 28**

10c, Romulus Plowing. 25c, Dante. 30c, Columbus. 50c, Leonardo da Vinci. 75c, Victor Emmanuel II and Garibaldi. 1.25 l, Tomb of Unknown Soldier, Rome. 1.75 l, Blackshirts' March on Rome, 1922. 2.75 l, Map of Italian East Africa and Iron Crown of Monza. 5 l, Victor Emmanuel III.

**400** A224 10c brown 2.40 .80
**401** A224 20c car rose 2.40 .80
**402** A224 25c dk green 2.40 .80
**403** A224 30c olive brn 2.40 2.00
**404** A224 50c lt violet 2.40 .80
**405** A224 75c rose red 3.25 3.25
**406** A224 1.25 l dp blue 6.50 3.25
**407** A224 1.75 l vio blk 8.00 4.00
**408** A224 2.75 l slate grn 26.00 *47.50*
**409** A224 5 l lt red brn 32.50 *52.50*
*Nos. 400-409 (10)* 88.25 *115.70*
Set, never hinged 220.00
*Nos. 400-409,C100-C105 (16)* 142.25 *286.20*
Set, never hinged 350.00

Proclamation of the Empire.

Wood-burning Engine and Streamlined Electric Engine — A234

**1939, Dec. 15 Photo. *Perf. 14***

**410** A234 20c rose red .80 .60
**411** A234 50c brt violet 1.60 .80
**412** A234 1.25 l dp blue 4.00 4.00
*Nos. 410-412 (3)* 6.40 5.40
Set, never hinged 16.00

Centenary of Italian railroads.

Adolf Hitler and Benito Mussolini A235

Hitler and Mussolini A236

**1941 Wmk. 140**

**413** A235 10c dp brown 2.25 2.25
**414** A235 20c red orange 2.25 2.25
**415** A235 25c dp green 7.50 2.25
**416** A236 50c violet 6.00 1.90
**417** A236 75c rose red 7.50 6.00
**418** A236 1.25 l deep blue 9.00 9.00
*Nos. 413-418 (6)* 34.50 23.65
Set, never hinged 75.00

Rome-Berlin Axis.
Stamps of type A236 in the denominations and colors of Nos. 413-415 were prepared but not issued. They were sold for charitable purposes in 1948. Value $35 each.

Galileo Teaching Mathematics at Padua — A237

Designs: 25c, Galileo presenting telescope to Doge of Venice. 50c, Galileo Galilei (1564-1642). 1.25 l, Galileo studying at Arcetri.

**1942, Sept. 28**

**419** A237 10c dk org & lake .75 .60
**420** A237 25c gray grn & grn .75 .60
**421** A237 50c brn vio & vio .75 .60
*a.* Frame missing 825.00
**422** A237 1.25 l Prus bl & ultra .75 2.75
*Nos. 419-422 (4)* 3.00 4.55
Set, never hinged 5.75

Statue of Rossini — A241

Gioacchino Rossini — A242

**1942, Nov. 23 Photo.**

**423** A241 25c deep green .75 .75
**424** A241 30c brown .75 .75
**425** A242 50c violet .75 .75
**426** A242 1 l blue .75 2.00
*Nos. 423-426 (4)* 3.00 4.25
Set, never hinged 5.75

Gioacchino Antonio Rossini (1792-1868), operatic composer.

"Victory for the Axis" A243

"Discipline is the Weapon of Victory" A244

"Everything and Everyone for Victory" A245

"Arms and Hearts Must Be Stretched Out Towards the Goal" A246

***Perf. 14 all around, Imperf. between***
**1942 Photo. Wmk. 140**

**427** A243 25c deep green .40 *1.00*
**428** A244 25c deep green .40 *1.00*
**429** A245 25c deep green .40 *1.00*
**430** A246 25c deep green .40 *1.00*
**431** A243 30c olive brown .40 *3.75*
**432** A244 30c olive brown .40 *3.75*
**433** A245 30c olive brown .40 *3.75*
**434** A246 30c olive brown .40 *3.75*
**435** A243 50c purple .40 *1.00*
**436** A244 50c purple .40 *1.00*
**437** A245 50c purple .40 *1.00*
**438** A246 50c purple .40 *1.00*
*Nos. 427-438 (12)* 4.80 *23.00*
Set, never hinged 11.50

Issued in honor of the Italian Army.
The left halves of #431-438 are type A95.
For overprints see Italian Social Republic #6-17.

She-Wolf Suckling Romulus and Remus — A247

***Perf. 10½x11½, 11x11½, 11½, 14***
**1944, Jan. Litho. Wmk. 87**
**Without Gum**

**439** A247 50c rose vio & bis rose 2.25 *3.75*

**Unwmk.**

**440** A247 50c rose vio & pale rose .40 *1.50*

Nos. 439-440 exist imperf., part perf.

### Types of 1929

**1945, May Unwmk. *Perf. 14***

| | | | | |
|---|---|---|---|---|
| **441** | A93 | 15c slate green | .25 | .25 |
| **442** | A93 | 35c deep blue | .25 | .30 |
| **443** | A91 | 1 l deep violet | .45 | .25 |
| | | *Nos. 441-443 (3)* | .95 | .80 |
| | | Set, never hinged | 2.00 | |

### Types of 1929 Redrawn Fasces Removed

Victor Emmanuel III A248

Julius Caesar A249

Augustus Caesar A250

"Italia" A251

A252

**1944-45 Wmk. 140 Photo. *Perf. 14***

| | | | | |
|---|---|---|---|---|
| **444** | A248 | 30c dk brown | .25 | .25 |
| **445** | A248 | 50c purple | 3.00 | *4.75* |
| **446** | A248 | 60c slate grn ('45) | .25 | 1.15 |
| **447** | A249 | 1 l dp violet ('45) | .25 | .25 |
| | | *Nos. 444-447 (4)* | 3.75 | 6.40 |
| | | Set, never hinged | 7.50 | |

**1945 Unwmk. *Perf. 14***

| | | | | |
|---|---|---|---|---|
| **448** | A250 | 10c dk brown | .25 | *1.50* |
| **448A** | A249 | 20c rose red | .25 | .25 |
| **449** | A251 | 50c dk violet | .25 | .25 |
| **450** | A248 | 60c slate grn | .25 | .25 |
| **451** | A251 | 60c red org | .25 | .25 |
| **452** | A249 | 1 l dp violet | .25 | .25 |
| **452A** | A249 | 1 l dp vio, redrawn | .25 | .25 |
| **452B** | A251 | 2 l dp car | 1.50 | 1.15 |
| **452C** | A251 | 10 l purple | 4.50 | *8.50* |
| | | *Nos. 448-452C (9)* | 7.75 | *12.65* |
| | | Set, never hinged | 15.00 | |

**1945 Wmk. 277**

| | | | | |
|---|---|---|---|---|
| **453** | A249 | 20c rose red | .25 | *.75* |
| **454** | A248 | 60c slate grn | .25 | *.75* |
| **455** | A249 | 1 l dp violet | .25 | .25 |
| **456** | A251 | 1.20 l dk brown | .25 | *.75* |
| **457** | A251 | 2 l dk red | .25 | .25 |
| **458** | A252 | 5 l dk red | .25 | *.75* |
| **459** | A251 | 10 l purple | 5.25 | *9.50* |
| | | *Nos. 453-459 (7)* | 6.75 | *13.00* |
| | | Set, never hinged | 17.00 | |

Nos. 452A and 457 are redrawings of types A249 and A251. In the redrawn 1 l, the "L" of "LIRE" extends under the "IRE" and the letters of "POSTE ITALIANE" are larger. In the original the "L" extends only under the "I."

In the redrawn 2 l, the "2" is smaller and thinner, and the design is less distinct.

For overprints see Nos. 1LN2-1LN8.

No. 224 Surcharged in Black

**1945, Mar. Wmk. 140**

| | | | | |
|---|---|---|---|---|
| **460** | A92 | 2.50 l on 1.75 l red org | .25 | *.50* |
| | | Never hinged | .30 | |
| *a.* | | Six bars at left | 1.50 | 1.50 |

Loggia dei Mercanti, Bologna A253

Basilica of San Lorenzo, Rome A254

### Stamps of Italian Social Republic Surcharged in Black

**1945, May 2 Photo. *Perf. 14***

| | | | | |
|---|---|---|---|---|
| **461** | A253 | 1.20 l on 20c crim | .25 | .25 |
| **462** | A254 | 2 l on 25c green | .25 | .25 |
| *a.* | | 2½ mm between "2" and "LIRE" | 1.50 | 1.50 |
| | | Set, never hinged | .75 | |

Breaking Chain A255

United Family and Scales A256

Planting Tree — A257

Tying Tree — A258

Torch A259

"Italia" and Sprouting Oak Stump A260

**1945-47 Wmk. 277 Photo. *Perf. 14***

| | | | | |
|---|---|---|---|---|
| **463** | A255 | 10c rose brown | .25 | .25 |
| **464** | A256 | 20c dk brown | .25 | .25 |
| **464A** | A259 | 25c brt bl grn ('46) | .25 | .25 |
| **465** | A257 | 40c slate | .25 | .25 |
| **465A** | A255 | 50c dp vio ('46) | .25 | .25 |
| **466** | A258 | 60c dk green | .25 | *.40* |
| **467** | A255 | 80c car rose | .25 | .25 |
| **468** | A257 | 1 l dk green | .25 | .25 |
| **469** | A259 | 1.20 l chestnut | .25 | *1.15* |
| **470** | A258 | 2 l dk claret brn | .25 | .40 |
| **471** | A259 | 3 l red | .25 | .25 |
| **471A** | A259 | 4 l red org ('46) | .25 | .25 |
| **472** | A256 | 5 l deep blue | .30 | .25 |
| **472A** | A257 | 6 l dp vio ('47) | 6.00 | .25 |
| **473** | A255 | 10 l slate | .80 | .25 |
| **473A** | A257 | 15 l dp bl ('46) | 7.50 | .25 |
| **474** | A259 | 20 l dk red vio | 2.40 | .25 |
| **475** | A260 | 25 l dk grn | 22.50 | .25 |
| **476** | A260 | 50 l dk vio brn | 7.50 | .25 |
| | | *Nos. 463-476 (19)* | 50.00 | 5.95 |
| | | Set, never hinged | 140.00 | |

See Nos. 486-488.

For overprints see Nos. 1LN11-1LN12, 1LN14-1N19, Trieste 1-13, 15-17, 30-32, 58-68, 82-83.

United Family and Scales A261

**1946, July 29 Engr. *Perf. 14***

| | | | | |
|---|---|---|---|---|
| **477** | A261 | 100 l car lake | 175.00 | 2.00 |
| | | Never hinged | 440.00 | |
| *a.* | | Perf. 14x13½ | 180.00 | 2.50 |
| | | Never hinged | 450.00 | |

For overprints see #1LN13, Trieste 14, 69.

Forgeries exist perf. 11¼ and perf. 11½ on unwatermarked paper.

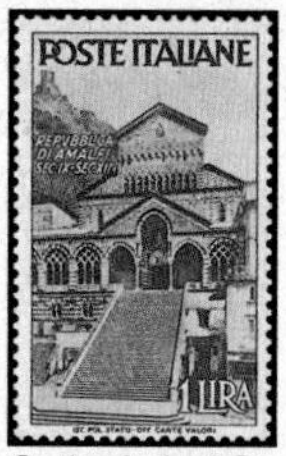
Cathedral of St. Andrea, Amalfi — A262

Church of St. Michael, Lucca — A263

"Peace" from Fresco at Siena A264

Signoria Palace, Florence A265

View of Cathedral Domes, Pisa A266

Republic of Genoa A267

"Venice Crowned by Glory," by Paolo Veronese A268

Oath of Pontida A269

**1946, Oct. 30**

| | | | | |
|---|---|---|---|---|
| **478** | A262 | 1 l brown | .25 | .25 |
| **479** | A263 | 2 l dk blue | .25 | .25 |
| **480** | A264 | 3 l dk bl grn | .25 | .25 |
| **481** | A265 | 4 l dp org | .25 | .25 |
| **482** | A266 | 5 l dp violet | .25 | .25 |
| **483** | A267 | 10 l car rose | .25 | .25 |
| **484** | A268 | 15 l dp ultra | .60 | .60 |
| **485** | A269 | 20 l red brown | .25 | .25 |
| | | *Nos. 478-485 (8)* | 2.35 | 2.35 |
| | | Set, never hinged | 3.00 | |

Proclamation of the Republic.

### Types of 1945

**1947-48 Wmk. 277 Photo. *Perf. 14***

| | | | | |
|---|---|---|---|---|
| **486** | A255 | 8 l dk green ('48) | 2.40 | .25 |
| **487** | A256 | 10 l red orange | 27.00 | .25 |
| **488** | A259 | 30 l dk blue ('48) | 165.00 | .25 |
| | | *Nos. 486-488 (3)* | 194.40 | .75 |
| | | Set, never hinged | 500.00 | |

St. Catherine Giving Mantle to Beggar — A270

5 l, St. Catherine carrying cross. 10 l, St. Catherine, arms outstretched. 30 l, St. Catherine & scribe.

**1948, Mar. 1 Photo.**

| | | | | |
|---|---|---|---|---|
| **489** | A270 | 3 l yel grn & gray grn | .25 | .25 |
| **490** | A270 | 5 l vio & bl | .25 | .30 |
| **491** | A270 | 10 l red brn & vio | 1.50 | *3.75* |
| **492** | A270 | 30 l bis & gray brn | 10.50 | *26.00* |
| | | *Nos. 489-492 (4)* | 12.50 | *30.30* |
| | | Set, never hinged | 30.00 | |
| | | *Nos. 489-492,C127-C128 (6)* | 68.50 | 90.30 |
| | | Set, never hinged | 165.00 | |

600th anniv. of the birth of St. Catherine of Siena, Patroness of Italy.

"Constitutional Government" — A271

**1948, Apr. 12**

| | | | | |
|---|---|---|---|---|
| **493** | A271 | 10 l rose vio | .80 | *1.00* |
| **494** | A271 | 30 l blue | 1.75 | *3.00* |
| | | Set, never hinged | 6.50 | |

Proclamation of the constitution of 1/1/48.

Uprising at Palermo, Jan. 12, 1848 A272

Designs (Revolutionary scenes): 4 l, Rebellion at Padua. 5 l, Proclamation of statute, Turin. 6 l, "Five Days of Milan." 8 l, Daniele Manin proclaming the Republic of Venice. 10 l, Defense of Vicenza. 12 l, Battle of Curtatone. 15 l, Battle of Gioto. 20 l, Insurrection at Bologna. 30 l, "Ten Days of Brescia." 50 l, Garibaldi in Rome fighting. 100 l, Death of Goffredo Mameli.

**1948, May 3**

| | | | | |
|---|---|---|---|---|
| **495** | A272 | 3 l dk brown | .55 | *1.15* |
| **496** | A272 | 4 l red violet | .55 | *1.15* |
| **497** | A272 | 5 l dp blue | 3.75 | 1.15 |
| **498** | A272 | 6 l dp yel grn | 1.00 | 1.15 |
| **499** | A272 | 8 l brown | 1.00 | 1.15 |
| **500** | A272 | 10 l orange red | 1.50 | 1.15 |
| **501** | A272 | 12 l dk gray grn | 4.50 | 3.00 |
| **502** | A272 | 15 l gray blk | 10.50 | 2.00 |
| **503** | A272 | 20 l car rose | 24.00 | 13.50 |
| **504** | A272 | 30 l brt ultra | 5.25 | 2.00 |
| **505** | A272 | 50 l violet | 52.50 | 5.25 |
| **506** | A272 | 100 l blue blk | 97.50 | 27.50 |
| | | *Nos. 495-506 (12)* | 202.60 | *60.15* |
| | | Set, never hinged | 405.00 | |
| | | *Nos. 495-506,E26 (13)* | 270.10 | 79.15 |
| | | Set, never hinged | 540.00 | |

Centenary of the Risorgimento, uprisings of 1848-49 which led to Italian unification.

For overprints see Trieste Nos. 18-29, E5.

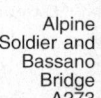

Alpine Soldier and Bassano Bridge A273

**1948, Oct. 1 Wmk. 277 *Perf. 14***

| | | | | |
|---|---|---|---|---|
| **507** | A273 | 15 l dark green | 1.50 | *2.25* |
| | | Never hinged | 3.00 | |

Bridge of Bassano, re-opening, Oct. 3, 1948.

For overprint see Trieste No. 33.

Gaetano Donizetti — A274

**1948, Oct. 23 Photo.**

| | | | | |
|---|---|---|---|---|
| **508** | A274 | 15 l dark brown | 1.15 | *2.10* |
| | | Never hinged | 2.25 | |

Death cent. of Gaetano Donizetti, composer.

For overprint see Trieste No. 34.

Fair Buildings A275

**1949, Apr. 12**
**509** A275 20 l dark brown 3.00 *3.75*
Never hinged 9.00

27th Milan Trade Fair, April 1949.
For overprint see Trieste No. 35.

Standard of Doges of Venice — A276

15 l, Clock strikers, Lion Tower and Campanile of St. Mark's. 20 l, Lion standard and Venetian galley. 50 l, Lion tower and gulls.

**1949, Apr. 12** **Buff Background**
**510** A276 5 l red brown .25 .25
**511** A276 15 l dk green 2.25 2.25
**512** A276 20 l dp red brn 4.50 .25
**513** A276 50 l dk blue 24.00 2.25
*Nos. 510-513 (4)* 31.00 5.00
Set, never hinged 77.50

Biennial Art Exhibition of Venice, 50th anniv.
For overprints see Trieste Nos. 36-39.

"Transportation" and Globes — A277

**1949, May 2** **Wmk. 277** ***Perf. 14***
**514** A277 50 l brt ultra 26.00 9.00
Never hinged 52.50

75th anniv. of the UPU.
For overprint see Trieste No. 40.

Workman and Ship — A278

**1949, May 30** **Photo.**
**515** A278 5 l dk green 4.50 *7.50*
**516** A278 15 l violet 11.50 *22.50*
**517** A278 20 l brown 21.00 22.50
*Nos. 515-517 (3)* 37.00 *52.50*
Set, never hinged 92.50

European Recovery Program.
For overprints see Trieste Nos. 42-44.

The Vascello, Rome A279

**1949, May 18**
**518** A279 100 l brown 130.00 120.00
Never hinged 255.00

Centenary of Roman Republic.
For overprint see Trieste No. 41.

Giuseppe Mazzini — A280

Vittorio Alfieri — A281

**1949, June 1**
**519** A280 20 l gray 3.75 4.50
Never hinged 11.50

Erection of a monument to Giuseppe Mazzini (1805-72), Italian patriot and revolutionary.
For overprint see Trieste No. 45.

**1949, June 4** **Photo.**
**520** A281 20 l brown 3.00 3.50
Never hinged 9.00

200th anniv. of the birth of Vittorio Alfieri, tragic dramatist.
For overprint see Trieste No. 46.

Basilica of St. Just, Trieste A282

**1949, June 8**
**521** A282 20 l brown red 9.00 *19.00*
Never hinged 13.50

Trieste election, June 12, 1949.
For overprint see Trieste No. 47.

Staff of Aesculapius, Globe — A283

**1949, June 13** **Wmk. 277** ***Perf. 14***
**522** A283 20 l violet 15.00 15.00
Never hinged 37.50

2nd World Health Cong., Rome, 1949.
For overprint see Trieste No. 49.

Lorenzo de Medici A284

Andrea Palladio A285

**1949, Aug. 4**
**523** A284 20 l violet blue 3.75 3.75
Never hinged 11.50

Birth of Lorenzo de Medici, 500th anniv.
For overprint see Trieste No. 50.

**1949, Aug. 4**
**524** A285 20 l violet 6.00 *9.00*
Never hinged 15.00

Andrea Palladio (1518-1580), architect.
For overprint see Trieste No. 51.

Tartan and Fair Buildings A286

**1949, Aug. 16**
**525** A286 20 l red 2.60 *3.00*
Never hinged 7.50

133th Levant Fair, Bari, September, 1949.
For overprint see Trieste No. 52.

Voltaic Pile — A287

Alessandro Volta — A288

**1949, Sept. 14** **Engr.** ***Perf. 14***
**526** A287 20 l rose car 3.00 2.00
*a.* Perf. 13x14 12.00 9.50
**527** A288 50 l deep blue 30.00 35.00
*a.* Perf. 13x14 150.00 65.00
Set, never hinged 97.50

Invention of the Voltaic Pile, 150th anniv.
For overprints see Trieste Nos. 53-54.

Holy Trinity Bridge — A289

**1949, Sept. 19** **Photo.**
**528** A289 20 l deep green 3.75 3.50
Never hinged 9.00

Issued to publicize plans to reconstruct Holy Trinity Bridge, Florence.
For overprint see Trieste No. 55.

Gaius Valerius Catullus A290

Domenico Cimarosa A291

**1949, Sept. 19** **Wmk. 277** ***Perf. 14***
**529** A290 20 l brt blue 4.50 3.50
Never hinged 11.50

2000th anniversary of the death of Gaius Valerius Catullus, Lyric poet.
For overprint see Trieste No. 56.

**1949, Dec. 28**
**530** A291 20 l violet blk 3.75 3.00
Never hinged 10.50

Bicentenary of the birth of Domenico Cimarosa, composer.
For overprint see Trieste No. 57.

Milan Fair Scene A292

**1950, Apr. 12** **Photo.**
**531** A292 20 l brown 2.25 3.00
Never hinged 4.50

The 28th Milan Trade Fair.
For overprint see Trieste No. 70.

Flags and Italian Automobile A293

**1950, Apr. 29**
**532** A293 20 l vio gray 4.25 2.75
Never hinged 11.50

32nd Intl. Auto Show, Turin, May 4-14, 1950.
For overprint see Trieste No. 71.

Pitti Palace, Florence A294

"Perseus" by Cellini — A295

Composite of Italian Cathedrals and Churches — A296

**1950, May 22**
**533** A294 20 l olive grn 3.00 3.00
**534** A295 55 l blue 29.00 16.50
Set, never hinged 80.00

5th General Conf. of UNESCO.
For overprints see Trieste Nos. 72-73.

**1950, May 29**
**535** A296 20 l violet 6.00 .75
**536** A296 55 l blue 30.00 3.00
Set, never hinged 95.00

Holy Year, 1950.
For overprints see Trieste Nos. 74-75.

Gaudenzio Ferrari A297

Radio Mast and Tower of Florence A298

**1950, July 1** **Wmk. 277** ***Perf. 14***
**537** A297 20 l gray grn 7.50 3.25
Never hinged 19.00

Issued to honor Gaudenzio Ferrari.
For overprint see Trieste No. 76.

**1950, July 15** **Photo.**
**538** A298 20 l purple 9.00 6.00
**539** A298 55 l blue 70.00 *90.00*
Set, never hinged 200.00

Intl. Shortwave Radio Conf., Florence, 1950.
For overprints Trieste see Nos. 77-78.

Ludovico A. Muratori A299

Guido d'Arezzo A300

**1950, July 22**
**540** A299 20 l brown 2.25 2.60
Never hinged 6.75

200th anniv. of the death of Ludovico A. Muratori, writer.
For overprint see Trieste No. 79.

**1950, July 29**
**541** A300 20 l dark green 7.50 3.00
Never hinged 22.50

900th anniv. of the death of Guido d'Arezzo, music teacher and composer.
For overprint see Trieste No. 80.

Tartan and Fair Buildings A301

**1950, Aug. 21**

**542** A301 20 l chestnut brown 3.75 2.60
Never hinged 11.50

Levant Fair, Bari, September, 1950.
For overprint see Trieste No. 81.

G. Marzotto and A. Rossi — A302

Tobacco Plant — A303

**1950, Sept. 11**

**543** A302 20 l indigo 2.25 2.00
Never hinged 4.50

Pioneers of the Italian wool industry.
For overprint see Trieste No. 84.

**1950, Sept. 11**

Designs: 20 l, Mature plant, different background. 55 l, Girl holding tobacco plant.

**544** A303 5 l dp claret & grn 1.50 *3.75*
**545** A303 20 l brown & grn 2.40 1.15
**546** A303 55 l dp ultra & brn 32.50 30.00
*Nos. 544-546 (3)* 36.40 34.90
Set, never hinged 92.50

Issued to publicize the European Tobacco Conference, Rome, 1950.
For overprints see Trieste Nos. 85-87.

Arms of the Academy of Fine Arts — A304

Augusto Righi — A305

**1950, Sept. 16**

**547** A304 20 l ol brn & red brn 2.60 2.60
Never hinged 6.00

200th anniv. of the founding of the Academy of Fine Arts, Venice.
For overprint see Trieste No. 88.

**1950, Sept. 16**

**548** A305 20 l cream & gray blk 2.60 2.60
Never hinged 6.00

Centenary of the birth of Augusto Righi, physicist.
For overprint see Trieste No. 89.

Blacksmith, Aosta Valley — A306

1851 Stamp of Tuscany — A307

Designs: 1 l, Auto mechanic. 2 l, Mason. 5 l, Potter. 6 l, Lace-making. 10 l, Weaving, 12 l, Sailor steering boat. 15 l, Shipbuilding. 20 l, Fisherman. 25 l, Sorting oranges. 30 l, Woman carrying grapes. 35 l, Olive picking. 40 l, Wine cart. 50 l, Shepherd and flock. 55 l, Plowing. 60 l, Grain cart. 65 l, Girl worker in hemp field. 100 l, Husking corn. 200 l, Woodcutter.

**1950, Oct. 20 Wmk. 277 *Perf. 14***

**549** A306 50c vio blue .25 .25
**550** A306 1 l dk bl vio .25 .25
**551** A306 2 l sepia .25 .25
**552** A306 5 l dk gray .25 .25
**553** A306 6 l chocolate .25 .25
**554** A306 10 l dp green 3.75 .25
**555** A306 12 l dp blue grn 1.90 .25
**556** A306 15 l dk gray bl 1.25 .25
**557** A306 20 l blue vio 9.00 .25
**558** A306 25 l brn org 1.50 .25
**559** A306 30 l magenta 1.25 .25
**560** A306 35 l crimson 7.50 1.15
**561** A306 40 l brown .30 .25
**562** A306 50 l violet 10.50 .25
**563** A306 55 l dp blue .65 .25
**564** A306 60 l red 2.10 .25
**565** A306 65 l dk grn .65 .25

***Perf. 13x14, 14x13***
**Engr.**

**566** A306 100 l brn org 30.00 .25
*a.* Perf. 13 30.00 .25
*b.* Perf. 14 32.50 .25
**567** A306 200 l ol brn 9.00 3.00
*a.* Perf. 14 9.00 3.00
*Nos. 549-567 (19)* 80.60 8.40
Set, never hinged 210.00

See Nos. 668-673A. For overprints see Trieste Nos. 90-108, 122-124, 178-180.

**1951, Mar. 27 Photo. *Perf. 14***

Design: 55 l, Tuscany 6cr.

**568** A307 20 l red vio & red 1.50 .95
**569** A307 55 l ultra & blue 18.00 37.50
Set, never hinged 50.00

Centenary of Tuscany's first stamps.
For overprints see Trieste Nos. 109-110.

Italian Automobile A308

**1951, Apr. 2**

**570** A308 20 l dk green 5.25 3.50
Never hinged 15.00

33rd Intl. Automobile Exhib., Turin, Apr. 4-15, 1951.
For overprint see Trieste No. 111.

Altar of Peace, Medea A309

**1951, Apr. 11**

**571** A309 20 l blue vio 3.00 3.00
Never hinged 9.00

Consecration of the Altar of Peace at Redipuglia Cemetery, Medea.
For overprint see Trieste No. 112.

Helicopter over Leonardo da Vinci Heliport — A310

P. T. T. Building, Milan Fair — A311

**1951, Apr. 12 Photo.**

**572** A310 20 l brown 9.80 1.90
**573** A311 55 l dp blue 30.00 *65.00*
Set, never hinged 97.50

29th Milan Trade Fair.
For overprints see Trieste Nos. 113-114.

Symbols of the International Gymnastic Festival A312

Statue of Diana, Spindle and Turin Tower A313

**Wmk. 277**
**1951, May 18 Photo. *Perf. 14***
**Fleur-de-lis in Red**

**574** A312 5 l dk brown 22.50 *575.00*
**575** A312 10 l Prus green 22.50 *575.00*
**576** A312 15 l vio blue 22.50 *575.00*
*Nos. 574-576 (3)* 67.50 *1,725.*
Set, never hinged 90.00

International Gymnastic Festival and Meet, Florence, 1951.
Fake cancellations exist on Nos. 574-576.
For overprints see Trieste Nos. 115-117.

**1951, Apr. 26**

**577** A313 20 l purple 9.50 4.25
Never hinged 26.00

Tenth International Exhibition of Textile Art and Fashion, Turin, May 2-16.
For overprint see Trieste No. 118.

Landing of Columbus A314

**1951, May 5**

**578** A314 20 l Prus green 4.50 3.75
Never hinged 15.00

500th anniversary of birth of Columbus.
For overprint see Trieste No. 119.

Reconstructed Abbey of Montecassino — A315

Design: 55 l, Montecassino Ruins.

**1951, June 18**

**579** A315 20 l violet 3.00 1.90
**580** A315 55 l brt blue 30.00 50.00
Set, never hinged 82.50

Issued to commemorate the reconstruction of the Abbey of Montecassino.
For overprints see Trieste Nos. 120-121.

Pietro Vannucci (Il Perugino) A316

Stylized Vase A317

Cartouche of Amenhotep III and Pitcher A318

**1951, July 23**

**581** A316 20 l brn & red brn 2.60 *3.75*
Never hinged 4.50

500th anniversary (in 1950) of the birth of Pietro Vannucci, painter.
For overprint see Trieste No. 125.

**1951, July 23**

**582** A317 20 l grnsh gray & blk 7.75 3.75
**583** A318 55 l vio bl & pale sal 27.50 52.50
Set, never hinged 52.50

Triennial Art Exhibition, Milan, 1951.
For overprints see Trieste Nos. 126-127.

Cyclist — A319

**1951, Aug. 23**

**584** A319 25 l gray black 5.25 5.25
Never hinged 10.50

World Bicycle Championship Races, Milan, Aug.-Sept. 1951.
For overprint see Trieste No. 128.

Tartan and Globes A320

**1951, Sept. 8 Photo.**

**585** A320 25 l deep blue 3.00 3.00
Never hinged 7.50

15th Levant Fair, Bari, September 1951.
For overprint see Trieste No. 129.

"La Figlia di Jorio" by Michetti A321

**1951, Sept. 15 Wmk. 277 *Perf. 14***

**586** A321 25 l dk brown 3.00 3.00
Never hinged 7.50

Centenary of the birth of Francesco Paolo Michetti, painter.
For overprint see Trieste No. 130.

Sardinia Stamps of 1851 A322

**1951, Oct. 5**

**587** A322 10 l shown 1.05 3.00
**588** A322 25 l 20c stamp 1.60 1.50
**589** A322 60 l 40c stamp 10.50 *14.50*
*Nos. 587-589 (3)* 13.15 19.00
Set, never hinged 19.00

Centenary of Sardinia's 1st postage stamp.
For overprints see Trieste Nos. 131-133.

Mercury — A323

Roman Census A324

**1951, Oct. 31**

**590** A323 10 l green .85 1.90
**591** A324 25 l vio gray 2.60 1.90
Set, never hinged 7.50

3rd Industrial and the 9th General Italian Census.
For overprints see Trieste Nos. 134-135.

Winter Scene — A325

Trees A326

**1951, Nov. 21**

**592** A325 10 l ol & dl grn 1.50 *4.25*
**593** A326 25 l dull grn 4.50 1.15
Set, never hinged 9.00

Issued to publicize the Festival of Trees.
For overprints see Trieste Nos. 136-137.

Giuseppe Verdi A327

Portraits of Verdi, various backgrounds.

**1951, Nov. 19** **Engr.**

**594** A327 10 l vio brn & dk grn 2.00 *3.75*
**595** A327 25 l red brn & dk brn 5.50 1.50
**596** A327 60 l dp grn & indigo 22.50 19.00
*Nos. 594-596 (3)* 30.00 24.25
Set, never hinged 60.00

50th anniversary of the death of Giuseppe Verdi, composer.
For overprints see Trieste Nos. 138-140.

Vincenzo Bellini — A328

**Wmk. 277**

**1952, Jan. 28** **Photo.** ***Perf. 14***

**597** A328 25 l gray & gray blk 1.90 1.50
Never hinged 5.75

150th anniversary of the birth of Vincenzo Bellini, composer.
For overprint see Trieste No. 141.

Palace of Caserta and Statuary A329

**1952, Feb. 1**

**598** A329 25 l dl grn & ol bis 1.50 1.15
Never hinged 4.50

Issued to honor Luigi Vanvitelli, architect.
For overprint see Trieste No. 142.

Statues of Athlete and River God Tiber — A330

**1952, Mar. 22**

**599** A330 25 l brn & sl blk .95 1.05
Never hinged 1.90

Issued on the occasion of the first International Exhibition of Sports Stamps.
For overprint see Trieste No. 143.

Milan Fair Buildings A331

**1952, Apr. 12** **Engr.**

**600** A331 60 l ultra 26.00 22.50
Never hinged 52.50

30th Milan Trade Fair.
For overprint see Trieste No. 144.

Leonardo da Vinci — A332

Virgin of the Rocks — A332a

**1952** **Wmk. 277** **Photo.** ***Perf. 14***

**601** A332 25 l deep orange .25 .25

**Unwmk.**
**Engr.** ***Perf. 13***

**601A** A332a 60 l ultra 2.25 *8.75*

**Wmk. 277**

**601B** A332 80 l brn car 11.50 .40
*c.* Perf. 14x13 9.50 .40
Set, never hinged 40.00

Leonardo da Vinci, 500th birth anniv.
For overprints see Trieste #145, 163-164.

First Stamps and Cathedral Bell Towers of Modena and Parma A333

**1952, May 29** ***Perf. 14***

**602** A333 25 l blk & red brn 1.25 1.15
**603** A333 60 l blk & ultra 5.00 *14.00*
Set, never hinged 9.50

Cent. of the 1st postage stamps of Modena and Parma.
For overprints see Trieste Nos. 146-147.

Globe and Torch — A334

Lion of St. Mark — A335

**1952, June 7**

**604** A334 25 l bright blue .95 1.15
Never hinged 2.50

Issued to honor the Overseas Fair at Naples and Italian labor throughout the world.
For overprint see Trieste No. 148.

**1952, June 14**

**605** A335 25 l black & yellow 1.15 1.15
Never hinged 2.75

26th Biennial Art Exhibition, Venice.
For overprint see Trieste No. 149.

"P" and Basilica of St. Anthony A336

Flag and Basilica of St. Just A337

**1952, June 19**

**606** A336 25 l bl gray, red & dk bl 1.90 1.50
Never hinged 5.75

30th International Sample Fair of Padua.
For overprint see Trieste No. 150.

**1952, June 28**

**607** A337 25 l dp grn, dk brn & red 1.30 1.30
Never hinged 3.00

4th International Sample Fair of Trieste.
For overprint see Trieste No. 151.

Fair Entrance and Tartan A338

**1952, Sept. 6** **Wmk. 277** ***Perf. 14***

**608** A338 25 l dark green .95 1.15
Never hinged 2.10

16th Levant Fair, Bari, Sept. 1952.
For overprint see Trieste No. 152.

Girolamo Savonarola A339

Mountain Peak and Climbing Equipment A340

**1952, Sept. 20**

**609** A339 25 l purple 1.50 .95
Never hinged 3.75

500th anniversary of the birth of Girolamo Savonarola.
For overprint see Trieste No. 153.

**1952, Oct. 4**

**610** A340 25 l gray .55 .55
Never hinged 1.15

Issued to publicize the National Exhibition of the Alpine troops, Oct. 4, 1952.
For overprint see Trieste No. 154.

Colosseum and Plane A341

**1952, Sept. 29**

**611** A341 60 l vio bl & dk bl 6.00 *11.50*
Never hinged 8.25

Issued to publicize the first International Civil Aviation Conference, Rome, Sept. 1952.
For overprint see Trieste No. 155.

Guglielmo Cardinal Massaia and Map A342

**1952, Nov. 21** **Engr.** ***Perf. 13***

**612** A342 25 l brn & dk brn 1.15 *1.75*
Never hinged 1.90

Centenary of the establishment of the first Catholic mission in Ethiopia.
For overprint see Trieste No. 156.

Symbols of Army, Navy and Air Force A343

Sailor, Soldier and Aviator A344

Design: 60 l, Boat, plane and tank.

**1952, Nov. 3** **Photo.** ***Perf. 14***

**613** A343 10 l dk green .25 .25
**614** A344 25 l blk & dk brn .40 .25
**615** A344 60 l black & blue 4.00 *6.50*
*Nos. 613-615 (3)* 4.65 7.00
Set, never hinged 9.00

Armed Forces Day, Nov. 4, 1952.
For overprints see Trieste Nos. 157-159.

Antonio Mancini — A345

Vincenzo Gemito — A346

**1952, Dec. 6**

**616** A345 25 l dark green .55 *.95*
**617** A346 25 l brown .55 *.95*
Set, never hinged 2.25

Birth centenaries of Antonio Mancini, painter, and Vincenzo Gemito, sculptor.
For overprints see Trieste Nos. 160-161.

Martyrs, Jailer and Artist Boldini A347

**1952, Dec. 31**

**618** A347 25 l gray blk & dk blue .75 .75
Never hinged 2.75

Centenary of the deaths of the five Martyrs of Belfiore.
For overprint see Trieste No. 162.

Antonello da Messina — A349

**1953, Feb. 21 Photo. *Perf. 14***

**621** A349 25 l car lake .75 .75
Never hinged 2.50

Messina Exhibition of the paintings of Antonello and his 15th cent. contemporaries.
For overprint see Trieste No. 165.

Racing Cars A350

**1953, Apr. 24**

**622** A350 25 l violet .60 .75
Never hinged 1.25

20th 1,000-mile auto race.
For overprint see Trieste No. 166.

Decoration "Knights of Labor" Bee and Honeycomb A351

Arcangelo Corelli A352

**1953, Apr. 30**

**623** A351 25 l violet .55 *.75*
Never hinged 1.05

For overprint see Trieste No. 167.

**1953, May 30**

**624** A352 25 l dark brown .55 *.75*
Never hinged 1.15

300th anniv. of the birth of Arcangelo Corelli, composer.
For overprint see Trieste No. 168.

St. Clare of Assisi and Convent of St. Damien A353

"Italia" after Syracusean Coin A354

**1953, June 27**

**625** A353 25 l brown & dull red .35 *.45*
Never hinged .75

St. Clare of Assisi, 700th death anniv.
For overprint see Trieste No. 169.

**1953-54 Wmk. 277 *Perf. 14***

**Size: 17x21mm**

**626** A354 5 l gray .25 .25
**627** A354 10 l org ver .25 .25
**628** A354 12 l dull green .25 .25
**628A** A354 13 l brt lil rose ('54) .25 .25
**629** A354 20 l brown 2.25 .25
**630** A354 25 l purple 3.00 .25
**631** A354 35 l rose car .35 .25
**632** A354 60 l blue 19.00 7.50
**633** A354 80 l orange brn 37.50 .75
*Nos. 626-633 (9)* 63.10 10.00
Set, never hinged 120.00

See Nos. 661-662, 673B-689, 785-788, 998A-998W, 1288-1290. For overprints see Trieste Nos. 170-177.

Mountain Peaks — A355

Tyche, Goddess of Fortune — A356

**1953, July 11**

**634** A355 25 l blue green .45 .45
Never hinged 1.50

Festival of the Mountain.
For overprint see Trieste No. 181.

**1953, July 16**

**635** A356 25 l dark brown .45 .25
**636** A356 60 l deep blue 2.25 *3.25*
Set, never hinged 6.75

Intl. Exposition of Agriculture, Rome, 1953.
For overprints see Trieste Nos. 182-183.

Continents Joined by Rainbow A357

**1953, Aug. 6**

**637** A357 25 l org & Prus bl 1.25 .25
**638** A357 60 l lil rose & dk vio bl 3.50 3.50
Set, never hinged 14.50

Signing of the North Atlantic Treaty, 4th anniv.
For overprints see Trieste Nos. 184-185.

Luca Signorelli A358

Agostino Bassi A359

**1953, Aug. 13**

**639** A358 25 l dk brn & dull grn .40 .40
Never hinged 1.10

Issued to publicize the opening of an exhibition of the works of Luca Signorelli, painter.
For overprint see Trieste No. 186.

**1953, Sept. 5**

**640** A359 25 l dk gray & brown .35 .35

6th International Microbiology Congress, Rome, Sept. 6-12, 1953.
For overprint see Trieste No. 187.

Siena — A360

Rapallo A361

Views: 20 l, Seaside at Gardone. 25 l, Mountain, Cortina d'Ampezzo. 35 l, Roman ruins, Taormina. 60 l, Rocks and sea, Capri.

**1953, Dec. 31 *Perf. 14***

**641** A360 10 l dk brn & red brn .25 .25
**642** A361 12 l lt blue & gray .25 .25
**643** A361 20 l brn org & dk brn .25 .25
**644** A360 25 l dk grn & pale bl .45 .25
**645** A361 35 l cream & brn .60 .40
**646** A361 60 l bl grn & ind 1.15 1.75
*Nos. 641-646 (6)* 2.95 3.15
Set, never hinged 7.50

For overprints see Trieste Nos. 188-193, 204-205.

Lateran Palace, Rome — A362

Television Screen and Aerial — A363

**1954, Feb. 11**

**647** A362 25 l dk brown & choc .35 .25
**648** A362 60 l blue & ultra 1.75 *2.50*
Set, never hinged 4.50

Signing of the Lateran Pacts, 25th anniv.
For overprints see Trieste Nos. 194-195.

**1954, Feb. 25**

**649** A363 25 l purple .75 .25
**650** A363 60 l dp blue grn 3.25 *4.50*
Set, never hinged 8.25

Introduction of regular natl. television service.
For overprints see Trieste Nos. 196-197.

"Italia" and Quotation from Constitution A364

**1954, Mar. 20**

**651** A364 25 l purple .50 .25
Never hinged 2.00

Propaganda for the payment of taxes.
For overprint see Trieste No. 198.

Vertical Flight Trophy — A365

Eagle Perched on Ruins — A366

**1954, Apr. 24**

**652** A365 25 l gray black .45 *.70*
Never hinged .90

Issued to publicize the experimental transportation of mail by helicopter, April 1954.
For overprint see Trieste No. 199.

**1954, June 1**

**653** A366 25 l gray, org brn & blk .25 *.35*
Never hinged .40

10th anniv. of Italy's resistance movement.
For overprint see Trieste No. 200.

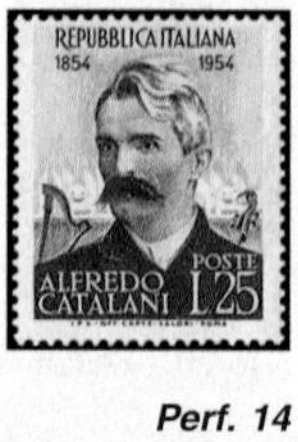


Alfredo Catalani, Composer, Birth Centenary — A367

**1954, June 19 *Perf. 14***

**654** A367 25 l dk grnsh gray .25 *.30*
Never hinged .40

For overprint see Trieste No. 201.

Marco Polo, Lion of St. Mark and Dragon A368

**1954, July 8 Engr. *Perf. 14***

**655** A368 25 l red brown .25 .25

***Perf. 13***

**656** A368 60 l gray green 2.60 *5.25*
*a.* Perf. 13x12 5.75 5.75
Set, never hinged 5.25

700th anniv. of the birth of Marco Polo.
For overprints see Trieste Nos. 202-203.

Automobile and Cyclist A369

**1954, Sept. 6 Photo. *Perf. 14***

**657** A369 25 l dp green & red .30 .30
Never hinged .60

Italian Touring Club, 60th anniv.
For overprint see Trieste No. 206.

St. Michael Overpowering the Devil — A370

**1954, Oct. 9**

**658** A370 25 l rose red .25 .25
**659** A370 60 l blue 1.10 2.00
Set, never hinged 1.75

23rd general assembly of the International Criminal Police, Rome 1954.
For overprints see Trieste Nos. 207-208.

Pinocchio and Group of Children — A371

**1954, Oct. 26**

**660** A371 25 l rose red .40 .30
Never hinged .75

Carlo Lorenzini, creator of Pinocchio.

**Italia Type of 1953-54**

**1954, Dec. 28 Engr. *Perf. 13***

**Size: 22½x27½mm**

**661** A354 100 l brown 65.00 .30
**662** A354 200 l dp blue 3.00 .50
Set, never hinged 150.00

Madonna, Perugino A372

Amerigo Vespucci and Map A373

60 l, Madonna of the Pieta, Michelangelo.

**1954, Dec. 31 Photo. *Perf. 14***

| | | | | |
|---|---|---|---|---|
| **663** | A372 | 25 l brown & bister | .25 | .25 |
| **664** | A372 | 60 l black & cream | 1.50 | *2.50* |
| | | Set, never hinged | 3.00 | |

Issued to mark the end of the Marian Year.

**1954, Dec. 31 Engr. *Perf. 13***

| | | | | |
|---|---|---|---|---|
| **665** | A373 | 25 l dp plum | .25 | .25 |
| *a.* | | Perf. 13x14 | 4.50 | .75 |
| **666** | A373 | 60 l blue blk | 1.60 | *2.75* |
| *a.* | | Perf. 13x14 | 1.00 | *2.75* |
| | | Set, never hinged | 3.50 | |

500th anniv. of the birth of Amerigo Vespucci, explorer, 1454-1512.

Silvio Pellico (1789-1854), Dramatist — A374

**Wmk. 277**

**1955, Jan. 24 Photo. *Perf. 14***

| | | | | |
|---|---|---|---|---|
| **667** | A374 | 25 l brt blue & vio | .30 | .25 |
| | | Never hinged | .40 | |

**Italy at Work Type of 1950**

**1955-57 Wmk. 303**

| | | | | |
|---|---|---|---|---|
| **668** | A306 | 50c vio bl | .25 | .25 |
| **669** | A306 | 1 l dk bl vio | .25 | .25 |
| **670** | A306 | 2 l sepia | .25 | .25 |
| **671** | A306 | 15 l dk gray bl | .30 | .25 |
| **672** | A306 | 30 l magenta | 30.00 | .25 |
| **673** | A306 | 50 l violet | 11.50 | .25 |
| **673A** | A306 | 65 l dk grn ('57) | 16.00 | *42.50* |
| | | *Nos. 668-673A (7)* | 58.55 | 44.00 |
| | | Set, never hinged | 125.00 | |

**Italia Type of 1953-54 and**

St. George, by Donatello — A374a

**1955-58 Wmk. 303 Photo. *Perf. 14***

**Size: 17x21mm**

| | | | | |
|---|---|---|---|---|
| **673B** | A354 | 1 l gray ('58) | .25 | .25 |
| **674** | A354 | 5 l slate | .25 | .25 |
| **675** | A354 | 6 l ocher ('57) | .25 | .25 |
| **676** | A354 | 10 l org ver | .25 | .25 |
| **677** | A354 | 12 l dull green | .25 | .25 |
| **678** | A354 | 13 l brt lil rose | .25 | .25 |
| **679** | A354 | 15 l gray vio ('56) | .25 | .25 |
| **680** | A354 | 20 l brown | .25 | .25 |
| **681** | A354 | 25 l purple | .25 | .25 |
| **682** | A354 | 35 l rose car | .25 | .25 |
| **683** | A354 | 50 l olive ('58) | .25 | .25 |
| **685** | A354 | 60 l blue | .25 | .25 |
| **686** | A354 | 80 l brown org | .25 | .25 |
| **687** | A354 | 90 l lt red brn ('58) | .25 | .25 |

**Size: 22½x28mm**

**Engr. *Perf. 13½***

| | | | | |
|---|---|---|---|---|
| **688** | A354 | 100 l brn ('56) | 4.25 | .25 |
| *a.* | | Perf. 13½x12 | 4.25 | .25 |
| *b.* | | Perf. 13½x14 | *1,225.* | 22.50 |
| **689** | A354 | 200 l gray bl ('57) | 3.75 | .25 |
| **690** | A374a | 500 l grn ('57) | 1.50 | .25 |
| *b.* | | Perf. 14x13½ | .75 | .25 |
| **690A** | A374a | 1000 l rose car ('57) | 2.50 | .60 |
| *c.* | | Perf. 14x13½ | 1.50 | .25 |
| | | *Nos. 673B-690A (18)* | 15.50 | 4.85 |
| | | Set, never hinged | 40.00 | |

Nos. 690-690A were printed on ordinary and fluorescent paper.

See Nos. 785-788. See Nos. 998A-998W for small-size set.

**Catalogue values for unused stamps in this section, from this point to the end of the section, are for Never Hinged items.**

"Italia" A375

Oil Derrick and Old Roman Aqueduct A376

**1955, Mar. 15 Photo. *Perf. 14***

| | | | | |
|---|---|---|---|---|
| **691** | A375 | 25 l rose vio | 1.75 | .25 |

Issued as propaganda for the payment of taxes.

**1955, June 6**

60 l, Marble columns and oil field on globe.

| | | | | |
|---|---|---|---|---|
| **692** | A376 | 25 l olive green | .35 | .25 |
| **693** | A376 | 60 l henna brown | 1.30 | *1.50* |

4th World Petroleum Cong., Rome, June 6-15, 1955.

Antonio Rosmini, Philosopher, Death Centenary — A377

**1955, July 1 Wmk. 303 *Perf. 14***

| | | | | |
|---|---|---|---|---|
| **694** | A377 | 25 l sepia | .75 | .25 |

Girolamo Fracastoro and Stadium at Verona A378

**1955, Sept. 1**

| | | | | |
|---|---|---|---|---|
| **695** | A378 | 25 l gray blk & brn | .60 | .25 |

Intl. Medical Congress, Verona, Sept. 1-4.

Basilica of St. Francis, Assisi A379

**1955, Oct. 4**

| | | | | |
|---|---|---|---|---|
| **696** | A379 | 25 l black & cream | .40 | .25 |

Issued in honor of St. Francis and for the 7th centenary (in 1953) of the Basilica in Assisi.

Young Man at Drawing Board — A380

**1955, Oct. 15**

| | | | | |
|---|---|---|---|---|
| **697** | A380 | 25 l Prus green | .40 | .25 |

Centenary of technical education in Italy.

Harvester — A381

FAO Headquarters, Rome — A382

**1955, Nov. 3**

| | | | | |
|---|---|---|---|---|
| **698** | A381 | 25 l rose red & brn | .30 | .25 |
| **699** | A382 | 60 l blk & brt pur | 1.50 | 1.15 |

Intl. Institute of Agriculture, 50th anniv. and FAO, successor to the Institute, 10th anniv.

A383

A384

**1955, Nov. 10**

| | | | | |
|---|---|---|---|---|
| **700** | A383 | 25 l rose brown | .75 | .25 |

70th anniversary of the birth of Giacomo Matteotti, Italian socialist leader.

**1955, Nov. 19**

| | | | | |
|---|---|---|---|---|
| **701** | A384 | 25 l dark green | .35 | .25 |

Death of Battista Grassi, zoologist, 30th anniv.

"St. Stephen Giving Alms" — A385

"St. Lorenzo Giving Alms" A386

**1955, Nov. 26**

| | | | | |
|---|---|---|---|---|
| **702** | A385 | 10 l black & cream | .25 | .25 |
| **703** | A386 | 25 l ultra & cream | .40 | .25 |

Death of Fra Angelico, painter, 500th anniv.

Giovanni Pascoli A387

**1955, Dec. 31**

| | | | | |
|---|---|---|---|---|
| **704** | A387 | 25 l gray black | .30 | .25 |

Centenary of the birth of Giovanni Pascoli, poet.

Ski Jump "Italia" A388

Stadiums at Cortina: 12 l, Skiing. 25 l, Ice skating. 60 l, Ice racing, Lake Misurina.

**1956, Jan. 26 Photo.**

| | | | | |
|---|---|---|---|---|
| **705** | A388 | 10 l blue grn & org | .25 | .25 |
| **706** | A388 | 12 l yellow & blk | .25 | .25 |
| **707** | A388 | 25 l vio blk & org brn | .35 | .25 |
| **708** | A388 | 60 l sapphire & org | 1.60 | 2.25 |
| | | *Nos. 705-708 (4)* | 2.45 | 3.00 |

VII Winter Olympic Games at Cortina d'Ampezzo, Jan. 26-Feb. 5, 1956.

Mail Coach and Tunnel Exit A389

**1956, May 19 Wmk. 303 *Perf. 14***

| | | | | |
|---|---|---|---|---|
| **709** | A389 | 25 l dk blue grn | 4.50 | .75 |

50th anniv. of the Simplon Tunnel.

Arms of Republic and Symbols of Industry A390

**1956, June 2**

| | | | | |
|---|---|---|---|---|
| **710** | A390 | 10 l gray & slate bl | .30 | .25 |
| **711** | A390 | 25 l pink & rose red | .35 | .25 |
| **712** | A390 | 60 l lt bl & brt bl | 4.50 | *5.25* |
| **713** | A390 | 80 l orange & brn | 6.00 | .25 |
| | | *Nos. 710-713 (4)* | 11.15 | 6.00 |

Tenth anniversary of the Republic.

Amedeo Avogadro A391

**1956, Sept. 8**

| | | | | |
|---|---|---|---|---|
| **714** | A391 | 25 l black vio | .25 | .25 |

Centenary of the death of Amedeo Avogadro, physicist.

**Europa Issue**

"Rebuilding Europe" — A392

**1956, Sept. 15**

| | | | | |
|---|---|---|---|---|
| **715** | A392 | 25 l dark green | *1.50* | .25 |
| **716** | A392 | 60 l blue | *10.00* | *1.00* |

Issued to symbolize the cooperation among the six countries comprising the Coal and Steel Community.

Globe and Satellites A393

**1956, Sept. 22**

| | | | | |
|---|---|---|---|---|
| **717** | A393 | 25 l intense blue | .25 | .25 |

7th Intl. Astronautical Cong., Rome, Sept. 17-22.

Globe — A394

**1956, Dec. 29 Litho. Unwmk.**
**718** A394 25 l red & bl grn, *pink* .30 .25
**719** A394 60 l bl grn & red, *pale bl grn* .40 .25

Italy's admission to the United Nations. The design, viewed through red and green glasses, becomes three-dimensional.

Postal Savings Bank and Notes A395

**1956, Dec. 31 Photo. Wmk. 303**
**720** A395 25 l sl bl & dp ultra .25 .25

80th anniversary of Postal Savings.

Ovid A396

Antonio Canova A397

Paulina Borghese as Venus A398

**1957, June 10** ***Perf. 14***
**721** A396 25 l ol grn & blk .30 .25

2000th anniversary of the birth of the poet Ovid (Publius Ovidius Naso).

**1957, July 15 Engr.**

60 l, Sculpture: Hercules and Lichas.

**722** A397 25 l brown .25 .25
**723** A397 60 l gray .25 .55
**724** A398 80 l vio blue .25 .25
*Nos. 722-724 (3)* .75 1.05

Birth of Antonio Canova, sculptor, 200th anniv.

Traffic Light A399

"United Europe" A400

**Wmk. 303**
**1957, Aug. 7 Photo.** ***Perf. 14***
**725** A399 25 l green, blk & red .35 .25

Campaign for careful driving.

**1957, Sept. 16 Litho.** ***Perf. 14***
**Flags in Original Colors**
**726** A400 25 l light blue *.75* .25
***Perf. 13***
**727** A400 60 l violet blue *5.50* *.60*

United Europe for peace and prosperity.

Giosue Carducci A401

Filippino Lippi A402

**1957, Oct. 14 Engr.** ***Perf. 14***
**728** A401 25 l brown .30 .25

Death of the poet Giosue Carducci, 50th anniv.

**1957, Nov. 25 Wmk. 303** ***Perf. 14***
**729** A402 25 l reddish brown .30 .25

Birth of Filippino Lippi, painter, 500th anniv.

2000th Anniv. of the Death of Marcus Tullius Cicero, Roman Statesman and Writer — A403

**1957, Nov. 30 Photo.**
**730** A403 25 l brown red .25 .25

St. Domenico Savio and Students of Various Races A404

**1957, Dec. 14**
**731** A404 15 l brt lil & blk .25 .25

Cent. of the death of St. Domenico Savio.

St. Francis of Paola A405

Giuseppe Garibaldi A406

**1957, Dec. 21 Engr.**
**732** A405 25 l black .25 .25

450th anniv. of the death of St. Francis of Paola, patron saint of seafaring men.

**1957, Dec. 14** ***Perf. 14x13, 13x14***

Design: 110 l, Garibaldi monument, horiz.

**733** A406 15 l slate green .25 .25
**734** A406 110 l dull purple .35 .25

150th anniv. of the birth of Giuseppe Garibaldi.

Peasant, Dams and Map of Sardinia A407

**1958, Feb. 1 Engr.** ***Perf. 14***
**738** A407 25 l bluish grn .25 .25

Completion of the Flumendosa-Mulargia irrigation system.

Immaculate Conception Statue, Rome, and Lourdes Basilica — A408

**1958, Apr. 16 Wmk. 303** ***Perf. 14***
**739** A408 15 l rose claret .25 .25
**740** A408 60 l blue .25 .25

Apparition of the Virgin Mary at Lourdes, cent.

Book and Symbols of Labor Industry and Agriculture A409

Designs: 60 l, "Tree of Freedom," vert. 110 l, Montecitorio Palace.

**1958, May 9 Photo.** ***Perf. 14***
**741** A409 25 l bl grn & ocher .25 .25
**742** A409 60 l blk brn & bl .25 .25
**743** A409 110 l ol bis & blk brn .25 .25
*Nos. 741-743 (3)* .75 .75

10th anniversary of the constitution.

Brussels Fair Emblem A410

Prologue from Pagliacci A411

**1958, June 12**
**744** A410 60 l blue & yellow .25 .25

Intl. and Universal Exposition at Brussels.

**1958, July 10**
**745** A411 25 l dk bl & dk red .25 .25

Birth of Ruggiero Leoncavallo, composer, cent.

Scene from La Bohème A412

**1958, July 10 Engr. Unwmk.**
**746** A412 25 l dark blue .25 .25

Birth of Giacomo Puccini, composer, cent.

Giovanni Fattori, Self-portrait A413

"Ave Maria on the Lake" by Giovanni Segantini A414

**1958, Aug. 7 Wmk. 303** ***Perf. 13x14***
**747** A413 110 l redsh brown .40 .30

Death of Giovanni Fattori, painter, 50th anniv.

**1958, Aug. 7** ***Perf. 14***
**748** A414 110 l slate, *buff* .40 .30

Birth of Giovanni Segantini, painter, cent.

Map of Brazil, Plane and Arch of Titus A415

**1958, Aug. 23 Photo.** ***Perf. 14***
**749** A415 175 l Prus green .75 *1.15*

Italo-Brazilian friendship on the occasion of Pres. Giovanni Gronchi's visit to Brazil.

Common Design Types pictured following the introduction.

**Europa Issue, 1958**
Common Design Type
**1958, Sept. 13 Size: 20½x35½mm**
**750** CD1 25 l red & blue *.60* .25
**751** CD1 60 l blue & red *1.25* *.35*

Issued to show the European Postal Union at the service of European integration.

½g Stamp of Naples A416

Evangelista Torricelli A417

Design: 60 l, 1g Stamp of Naples.

***Perf. 14x13½, 13½***
**1958, Oct. 4 Engr. Unwmk.**
**752** A416 25 l brown red .25 .25
**753** A416 60 l blk & red brn .25 .25

Centenary of the stamps of Naples.

**1958, Oct. 20 Wmk. 303** ***Perf. 14***
**754** A417 25 l rose claret .60 .35

350th anniv. of the birth of Evangelista Torricelli, mathematician and physicist.

"The Triumph of Caesar," Montegna A418

Persian Style Bas-relief, Sorrento A419

25 l, Coats of Arms of Trieste, Rome & Trento, horiz. 60 l, War memorial bell of Rovereto.

**1958, Nov. 3 Engr. *Perf. 14x13½***

**755** A418 15 l green .25 .25
**756** A418 25 l gray .25 .25
**757** A418 60 l rose claret .25 .25
*Nos. 755-757 (3)* .75 .75

40th anniv. of Italy's victory in World War I.

**1958, Nov. 27 Photo.**

**758** A419 25 l sepia, *bluish* .25 .25
**759** A419 60 l vio bl, *bluish* .50 .65

Visit of the Shah of Iran to Italy.

Eleonora Duse — A420

Dancers and Antenna — A421

**Unwmk.**

**1958, Dec. 11 Engr. *Perf. 14***

**760** A420 25 l brt ultra .25 .25

Cent. of the birth of Eleonora Duse, actress.

**1958, Dec. 29 Photo. Wmk. 303**

Design: 60 l, Piano, dove and antenna.

**761** A421 25 l red, bl & blk .25 .25
**762** A421 60 l ultra & blk .25 .25

10th anniv. of the Prix Italia (International Radio and Television Competitions).

Stamp of Sicily — A422

Design: 60 l, Stamp of Sicily, 5g.

***Perf. 14x13½***

**1959, Jan. 2 Engr. Unwmk.**

**763** A422 25 l Prus green .25 .25
**764** A422 60 l dp orange .25 .25

Centenary of the stamps of Sicily.

Dome of St. Peter's and Tower of Lateran Palace A423

**Wmk. 303**

**1959, Feb. 11 Photo. *Perf. 14***

**765** A423 25 l ultra .25 .25

30th anniversary of the Lateran Pacts.

Map of North Atlantic and NATO Emblem A424

**1959, Apr. 4**

**766** A424 25 l dk bl & ocher .25 .25
**767** A424 60 l dk bl & green .25 .25

10th anniv. of NATO.

Arms of Paris and Rome A425

**1959, Apr. 9**

**768** A425 15 l blue & red .25 .25
**769** A425 25 l blue & red .25 .25

Cultural ties between Rome and Paris.

"A Gentle Peace Has Come" — A426

Statue of Lord Byron — A427

**1959, Apr. 13 Engr. Unwmk.**

**770** A426 25 l olive green .25 .25

International War Veterans Association convention, Rome.

**1959, Apr. 21**

**771** A427 15 l black .25 .25

Unveiling in Rome of a statue of Lord Byron by Bertel Thorvaldson, Danish sculptor.

Camillo Prampolini — A428

**1959, Apr. 27 Unwmk. *Perf. 14***

**772** A428 15 l car rose 7.00 .40

Camillo Prampolini, socialist leader and reformer, birth centenary.

Fountain of Dioscuri and Olympic Rings — A429

Baths of Carcalla A430

Designs: 25 l, Capitoline tower. 60 l, Arch of Constantine. 110 l, Ruins of Basilica of Massentius.

**1959, June 23 Photo. Wmk. 303**

**Designs in Dark Sepia**

**773** A429 15 l red orange .25 .25
**774** A429 25 l blue .25 .25
**775** A430 35 l bister .25 .25
**776** A430 60 l rose lilac .25 .30
**777** A430 110 l yellow .30 .25
*Nos. 773-777 (5)* 1.30 1.30

1960 Olympic Games in Rome.

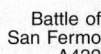

Victor Emanuel II, Garibaldi, Cavour, Mazzini A431

Battle of San Fermo A432

25 l, "After the Battle of Magenta" by Fattori and Red Cross, vert. 60 l, Battle of Palestro. 110 l, "Battle of Magenta" by Induno, vert.

**Engr., Cross Photo. on 25 l**

**1959, June 27 Unwmk.**

**778** A431 15 l gray .25 .25
**779** A431 25 l brn & red .25 .25
**780** A432 35 l dk violet .25 .25
**781** A432 60 l ultra .25 .25
**782** A432 110 l magenta .25 .25
*Nos. 778-782 (5)* 1.25 1.25

Cent. of the war of independence. No. 779 for the centenary of the Red Cross idea.

Labor Monument, Geneva A433

Stamp of Romagna A434

**1959, July 20 *Perf. 14x13, 14***

**783** A433 25 l violet .25 .25
**784** A433 60 l brown .30 .25

40th anniv. of the ILO.

**Italia Type of 1953-54**

**Photo.; Engr. (100 l, 200 l)**

**1959-66 Wmk. 303 *Perf. 14***

**Size: 17x21mm**

**785** A354 30 l bis brn ('60) .25 .25
**786** A354 40 l lil rose ('60) 1.25 .25
**786A** A354 70 l Prus grn ('60) .35 .25
**787** A354 100 l brown .65 .25
**787A** A354 130 l gray & dl red ('66) .25 .25
**788** A354 200 l dp blue .65 .25
*Nos. 785-788 (6)* 3.40 1.50

**1959, Sept. 1 Photo.**

Design: 60 l, Stamp of Romagna, 20b.

**789** A434 25 l pale brn & blk .25 .25
**790** A434 60 l gray grn & blk .25 .25

Centenary of the stamps of Romagna.

**Europa Issue, 1959**

Common Design Type

**1959, Sept. 19 Size: 22x27½mm**

**791** CD2 25 l olive green *.40* .25
**792** CD2 60 l blue *.40* .25

Stamp of 1953 with Facsimile Cancellation A435

Aeneas Fleeing with Father and Son, by Raphael A436

**1959, Dec. 20 Wmk. 303 *Perf. 14***

**793** A435 15 l gray, rose car & blk .25 .25

Italy's first Stamp Day, Dec. 20, 1959.

**1960, Apr. 7 Engr. Unwmk.**

**794** A436 25 l lake .25 .25
**795** A436 60 l gray violet .25 .25

World Refugee Year, 7/1/59-6/30/60. Design is detail from "The Fire in the Borgo."

Garibaldi's Proclamation to the Sicilians — A437

King Victor Emmanuel and Garibaldi Meeting at Teano — A438

60 l, Volunteers embarking, Quarto, Genoa.

**Wmk. 303**

**1960, May 5 Photo. *Perf. 14***

**796** A437 15 l brown .25 .25

***Perf. 13x14, 14x13***

**Engr. Unwmk.**

**797** A438 25 l rose claret .25 .25
**798** A437 60 l ultramarine .25 .25

Cent. of the liberation of Southern Italy (Kingdom of the Two Sicilies) by Garibaldi.

Emblem of 17th Olympic Games — A439

Olympic Stadium A440

Statues: 15 l, Roman Consul on way to the games. 35 l, Myron's Discobolus. 110 l, Seated boxer. 200 l, Apoxyomenos by Lysippus.

Stadia: 25 l, Velodrome. 60 l, Sports palace. 150 l, Small sports palace.

**Photogravure, Engraved**

***Perf. 14x13½, 13½x14***

**1960 Wmk. 303, Unwmk.**

**799** A439 5 l yellow brn .25 .25
**800** A440 10 l dp org & dk bl .25 .25
**801** A439 15 l ultra .25 .25
**802** A440 25 l lt vio & brn .25 .25
**803** A439 35 l rose cl .25 .25
**804** A440 60 l bluish grn & brn .25 .25
**805** A439 110 l plum .25 .25
**806** A440 150 l blue & brn 1.50 *2.75*
**807** A439 200 l green .75 .25
*Nos. 799-807 (9)* 4.00 4.75

17th Olympic Games, Rome, 8/25-9/11.

The photo. denominations (5-10, 25, 60, 150 l) are wmkd.; the engraved (15, 35, 110, 200 l) are unwmkd.

Bottego Statue, Parma
A441

Michelangelo da Caravaggio
A442

**1960 Unwmk. Engr. *Perf. 14***

**808** A441 30 l brown .25 .25

Birth cent. of Vittorio Bottego, explorer.

### Europa Issue, 1960
Common Design Type

**1960 Photo. Wmk. 303**
**Size: 37x27mm**

**809** CD3 30 l dk grn & bis brn *.30* .25
**810** CD3 70 l dk bl & salmon *.40* .25

**1960 Unwmk. Engr. *Perf. 13x13½***

**811** A442 25 l orange brn .25 .25

350th anniv. of the death of Michelangelo da Caravaggio (Merisi), painter.

Mail Coach and Post Horn
A443

**1960 Wmk. 303 Photo. *Perf. 14***

**812** A443 15 l blk brn & org brn .25 .25

Issued for Stamp Day, Dec. 20.

Slave, by Michelangelo — A444

Designs from Sistine Chapel by Michelangelo: 5 l, 10 l, 115 l, 150 l, Heads of various "slaves." 15 l, Joel. 20 l, Libyan Sybil. 25 l, Isaiah. 30 l, Eritrean Sybil. 40 l, Daniel. 50 l, Delphic Sybil. 55 l, Cumaean Sybil. 70 l, Zachariah. 85 l, Jonah. 90 l, Jeremiah. 100 l, Ezekiel. 200 l, Self-portrait. 500 l, Adam. 1000 l, Eve.

**Wmk. 303**
**1961, Mar. 6 Photo. *Perf. 14***
**Size: 17x21mm**

**813** A444 1 l gray .25 .25
**814** A444 5 l brown org .25 .25
**815** A444 10 l red org .25 .25
**816** A444 15 l brt lil .25 .25
**817** A444 20 l Prus grn .25 .25
**818** A444 25 l brown .30 .25
**819** A444 30 l purple .25 .25
**820** A444 40 l rose red .25 .25
**821** A444 50 l olive .45 .25
**822** A444 55 l red brn .25 .25
**823** A444 70 l blue .25 .25
**824** A444 85 l slate grn .25 .25
**825** A444 90 l lil rose .40 .25
**826** A444 100 l vio gray .65 .25
**827** A444 115 l ultra .25 .25

**Engr.**

**828** A444 150 l chocolate .75 .25
**829** A444 200 l dark blue 1.50 .25
*a.* Perf. 13½ 1.50 .25

***Perf. 13½***
**Size: 22x27mm**

**830** A444 500 l blue grn 3.75 .25
**831** A444 1000 l brown red 4.50 *5.50*
*Nos. 813-831 (19)* 15.05 10.00

Map Showing Flight from Italy to Argentina
A445

185 l, Italy to Uruguay. 205 l, Italy to Peru.

**1961, Apr. Photo. *Perf. 14***

**832** A445 170 l ultra 4.50 4.50
**833** A445 185 l dull green 4.50 4.50
**834** A445 205 l violet blk 15.00 14.00
*a.* 205 l rose lilac 1,500. *2,250.*
*Nos. 832-834 (3)* 24.00 23.00

Visit of Pres. Gronchi to South America, 4/61.

Nos. 832-833 and 834a were issued Apr. 4, to become valid on Apr. 6. The map of Peru on No. 834a was drawn incorrectly and the stamp was therefore withdrawn on Apr. 4. A corrected design in new color (No. 834) was issued Apr. 6. Forgeries of No. 834a exist.

Statue of Pliny, Como Cathedral
A446

Ippolito Nievo (1831-61), Writer
A447

**1961, May 27**

**835** A446 30 l brown .25 .25

1900th anniversary of the birth of Pliny the Younger, Roman consul and writer.

**1961, June 8 Wmk. 303 *Perf. 14***

**836** A447 30 l multi .25 .25

St. Paul Aboard Ship
A448

**1961, June 28**

**837** A448 30 l multi .25 .25
**838** A448 70 l multi .30 .30

1,900th anniversary of St. Paul's arrival in Rome. The design is after a miniature from the Bible of Borso D'Este.

Cavalli Gun and Gaeta Fortress
A449

Cent. of Italian unity: 30 l, Carignano palace, Turin. 40 l, Montecitorio palace, Rome. 70 l, Palazzo Vecchio, Florence. 115 l, Villa Madama, Rome. 300 l, Steel construction, Italia '61 Exhibition, Turin.

**1961, Aug. 12 Photo.**

**839** A449 15 l dk bl & redsh brn .25 .25
**840** A449 30 l dk bl & red brn .25 .25
**841** A449 40 l bl & brn .35 .25
**842** A449 70 l brn & pink .45 .25
**843** A449 115 l org brn & dk bl 1.60 .25
**844** A449 300 l brt grn & red 7.00 8.25
*Nos. 839-844 (6)* 9.90 9.50

### Europa Issue, 1961
Common Design Type

**1961, Sept. 18 Wmk. 303 *Perf. 14***
**Size: 36½x21mm**

**845** CD4 30 l carmine *.25* .25
**846** CD4 70 l yel grn *.30* .25

Giandomenico Romagnosi — A450

***Perf. 13½***
**1961, Nov. 28 Unwmk. Engr.**

**847** A450 30 l green .25 .25

Bicentenary of the birth of Giandomenico Romagnosi, jurist and philosopher.

Design from 1820 Sardinia Letter Sheet
A451

**Wmk. 303**
**1961, Dec. 3 Photo. *Perf. 14***

**848** A451 15 l lil rose & blk .25 .25

Issued for Stamp Day 1961.

Family Scene "I am the Lamp that Glows so Gently . . ."
A452

**1962, Apr. 6 Wmk. 303 *Perf. 14***

**849** A452 30 l red .25 .25
**850** A452 70 l blue .25 .30

Death of Giovanni Pascoli, poet, 50th anniv.

Pacinotti's Dynamo
A453

**1962, June 12**

**851** A453 30 l rose & blk .25 .25
**852** A453 70 l ultra & blk .25 .30

Antonio Pacinotti (1841-1912), physicist and inventor of the ring winding dynamo.

St. Catherine of Siena, by Andrea Vanni — A454

Lion of St. Mark — A455

70 l, St. Catherine, 15th century woodcut.

**1962, June 26 Photo.**

**853** A454 30 l black .25 .25

**Engraved and Photogravure**

**854** A454 70 l red & blk .25 .40

500th anniversary of the canonization of St. Catherine of Siena, Patroness of Italy.

**1962, Aug. 25 Photo.**

Design: 30 l, Stylized camera eye.

**855** A455 30 l bl & blk .25 .25
**856** A455 70 l red org & blk .25 .25

Intl. Film Festival in Venice, 30th anniv.

Motorcyclist and Bicyclist
A456

70 l, Group of cyclists. 300 l, Bicyclist.

**1962, Aug. 30**

**857** A456 30 l grn & blk .25 .25
**858** A456 70 l bl & blk .25 .25
**859** A456 300 l dp org & blk 4.25 4.25
*Nos. 857-859 (3)* 4.75 4.75

World Bicycle Championship Races.

### Europa Issue, 1962
Common Design Type

**1962, Sept. 17 Size: 37x21mm**

**860** CD5 30 l carmine *.45* .25
**861** CD5 70 l blue *.90* .30

Swiss and Italian Flags, Eugenio and Angela Lina Balzan Medal
A457

**1962, Oct. 25 Wmk. 303 *Perf. 14***

**862** A457 70 l rose red, grn & brn .55 .35

1st distribution of the Balzan Prize by the Intl. Balzan Foundation for Italian-Swiss Cooperation.

Malaria Eradication Emblem — A458

Stamps of 1862 and 1961 — A459

**1962, Oct. 31 Photo.**

**863** A458 30 l light violet .25 .25
**864** A458 70 l light blue .25 .25

WHO drive to eradicate malaria.

**1962, Dec. 2**

**865** A459 15 l pur, buff & bister .25 .25

Stamp Day and cent. of Italian postage stamps.

A460

A461

Holy Spirit Descending on Apostles.

**1962, Dec. 8**

**866** A460 30 l org & dk bl grn, *buff* .25 .25
**867** A460 70 l dk bl grn & org, *buff* .25 .30

21st Ecumenical Council of the Roman Catholic Church, Vatican II. The design is an illumination from the Codex Syriacus.

**1962, Dec. 10 Engr. Unwmk.**

Statue of Count Camillo Bensi di Cavour.

**868** A461 30 l dk grn .25 .25

Centenary of Court of Accounts.

Count Giovanni Pico della Mirandola A462

Gabriele D'Annunzio A463

**Wmk. 303**

**1963, Feb. 25 Photo. *Perf. 14***

**869** A462 30 l gray blk .25 .25

Mirandola (1463-94), Renaissance scholar.

**1963, Mar. 12 Engr. Unwmk.**

**870** A463 30 l dk grn .25 .25

Issued to commemorate the centenary of the birth of Gabriele d'Annunzio, author and soldier.

Sower — A464

Design: 70 l, Harvester tying sheaf, sculpture from Maggiore Fountain, Perugia.

**1963, Mar. 21 Photo. Wmk. 303**

**871** A464 30 l rose car & brn .25 .25
**872** A464 70 l bl & brn .30 .30

FAO "Freedom from Hunger" campaign.

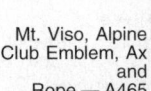

Mt. Viso, Alpine Club Emblem, Ax and Rope — A465

Map of Italy and "INA" Initials — A466

**1963, Mar. 30 Wmk. 303 *Perf. 14***

**873** A465 115 l dk brn & brt bl .25 .25

Italian Alpine Club founding, cent.

**1963, Apr. 4**

**874** A466 30 l grn & blk .25 .25

50th anniv. of the Natl. Insurance Institute.

Globe and Stamp A467

**1963, May 7 Photo. *Perf. 14***

**875** A467 70 l bl & grn .25 .25

1st Intl. Postal Conf., Paris, 1863.

Crosses and Centenary Emblem on Globe — A468

**1963, June 8 Wmk. 303 *Perf. 14***

**876** A468 30 l dk gray & red .25 .25
**877** A468 70 l dl bl & red .25 .25

International Red Cross founding, cent.

Roman Column, Globe and Highways A469

**1963, Aug. 21 Wmk. 303 *Perf. 14***

**878** A469 15 l gray ol & dk bl .25 .25
**879** A469 70 l dl bl & brn .25 .25

UN Tourist Conf., Rome, Aug. 21-Sept. 5.

**Europa Issue, 1963**

Common Design Type

**1963, Sept. 16 Size: 27½x23mm**

**880** CD6 30 l rose & brn *.30* .25
**881** CD6 70 l brn & grn *.35* .25

Bay of Naples, Vesuvius and Sailboats A470

Athlete on Greek Vase A471

**1963, Sept. 21 Wmk. 303 *Perf. 14***

**882** A470 15 l bl & org .25 .25
**883** A471 70 l dk grn & org brn .25 .30

4th Mediterranean Games, Naples, Sept. 21-29.

Giuseppe Gioachino Belli (1791-1863), Poet — A472

Stamps Forming Flower — A473

**1963, Nov. 14 Wmk. 303 *Perf. 14***

**884** A472 30 l red brn .25 .25

**1963, Dec. 1**

**885** A473 15 l bl & car .25 .25

Issued for Stamp Day.

Pietro Mascagni and Old Costanzi Theater, Rome — A474

#886, Giuseppe Verdi & La Scala, Milan.

**1963 Photo.**

**886** A474 30 l gray grn & yel brn .25 .25
**887** A474 30 l yel brn & gray grn .25 .25

Verdi (1813-1901), and Mascagni (1863-1945), composers. Issued: #886, Oct. 10; #887, Dec. 7.

Galileo Galilei A475

Nicodemus by Michelangelo A476

**1964, Feb. 15 Wmk. 303 *Perf. 14***

**888** A475 30 l org brn .25 .25
**889** A475 70 l black .25 .25

Galilei (1564-1642), astronomer & physicist.

**1964, Feb. 18 Photo.**

**890** A476 30 l brown .25 .25

Michelangelo Buonarroti (1475-1564), artist. Head of Nicodemus (self-portrait?) from the Pieta, Florence Cathedral. See No. C137.

Carabinieri A477

70 l, Charge of Pastrengo, 1848, by De Albertis.

**1964, June 5 Wmk. 303 *Perf. 14***

**891** A477 30 l vio bl & red .25 .25
**892** A477 70 l brown .25 .25

150th anniv. of the Carabinieri (police corps).

Giambattista Bodoni — A478

***Perf. 14x13***

**1964, July 30 Engr. Unwmk.**

**893** A478 30 l carmine .25 .25
*a.* Perf. 13 .25 .25

Death of Giambattista Bodoni (1740-1813), printer & type designer (Bodoni type), 150th anniv.

**Europa Issue, 1964**

Common Design Type

**Wmk. 303**

**1964, Sept. 14 Photo. *Perf. 14***

**Size: 21x37mm**

**894** CD7 30 l brt rose lilac *.25* .25
**895** CD7 70 l blue green *.30* .25

Walled City — A479

Left Arch of Victor Emmanuel Monument, Rome — A480

**1964, Oct. 15 Photo. *Perf. 14***

**896** A479 30 l emer & dk brn .25 .25
**897** A479 70 l bl & dk brn .25 .25

**Unwmk. Engr.**

**898** A479 500 l red 1.50 1.75
*Nos. 896-898 (3)* 2.00 2.25

7th Congress of European Towns. The buildings in design are: Big Ben, London; Campodoglio, Rome; Town Hall, Bruges; Römer, Frankfurt; Town Hall, Paris; Belfry, Zurich; Gate, Kampen (Holland).

**1964, Nov. 4 Photo. Wmk. 303**

**899** A480 30 l dk red brn .25 .25
**900** A480 70 l blue .25 .25

Pilgrimage to Rome of veterans living abroad.

Giovanni da Verrazano and Verrazano-Narrows Bridge, New York Bay — A481

**1964, Nov. 21 Wmk. 303 *Perf. 14***

**901** A481 30 l blk & brn .25 .25

Opening of the Verrazano-Narrows Bridge connecting Staten Island and Brooklyn, NY, and to honor Giovanni da Verrazano (1485-1528), discoverer of New York Bay. See No. C138.

Italian Sports Stamps, 1934-63 — A482

**1964, Dec. 6 Photo. *Perf. 14***

**902** A482 15 l gldn brn & dk brn .25 .25

Issued for Stamp Day.

Italian Soldiers in Concentration Camp — A483

Victims Trapped by Swastika A484

15 l, Italian soldier, sailor and airman fighting for the Allies. 70 l, Guerrilla fighters in the mountains. 115 l, Marchers with Italian flag. 130 l, Ruins of city and torn Italian flag.

**1965, Apr. 24 Photo. Wmk. 303**

**903** A483 10 l black .25 .25
**904** A483 15 l grn & rose car .25 .25
**905** A484 30 l plum .25 .25
**906** A483 70 l deep blue .25 .25
**907** A484 115 l rose car .25 .25
**908** A484 130 l grn, sepia & red .25 .25
*Nos. 903-908 (6)* 1.50 1.50

Italian resistance movement during World War II, 20th anniv.

Antonio Meucci, Guglielmo Marconi and ITU Emblem A485

**1965, May 17 *Perf. 14***

**909** A485 70 l red & dk grn .25 .25

Cent. of the ITU.

Sailboats of Flying Dutchman Class
A486

Designs: 70 l, Sailboats of 5.5-meter class, vert. 500 l, Sailboats, Lightning class.

**1965, May 31 Photo. Wmk. 303**

| | | | | |
|---|---|---|---|---|
| **910** | A486 | 30 l blk & dl rose | .25 | .25 |
| **911** | A486 | 70 l blk & ultra | .25 | .25 |
| **912** | A486 | 500 l blk & gray bl | .55 | .35 |
| | | *Nos. 910-912 (3)* | 1.05 | .85 |

Issued to publicize the World Yachting Championships, Naples and Alassio.

Mont Blanc and Tunnel
A487

**1965, June 16 Wmk. 303 *Perf. 14***

| | | | | |
|---|---|---|---|---|
| **913** | A487 | 30 l black | .25 | .25 |

Opening of the Mont Blanc Tunnel connecting Entrayes, Italy, and Le Polerins, France.

Alessandro Tassoni and Scene from "Seccia Rapita" — A488

**Unwmk.**

**1965, Sept. 20 Photo. *Perf. 14***

| | | | | |
|---|---|---|---|---|
| **914** | A488 | 40 l blk & multi | .25 | .25 |

Tassoni (1565-1635), poet. Design is from 1744 engraving by Bartolomeo Soliani.

**Europa Issue, 1965**

Common Design Type

**1965, Sept. 27 Wmk. 303**

**Size: 36½x27mm**

| | | | | |
|---|---|---|---|---|
| **915** | CD8 | 40 l ocher & ol grn | .25 | .25 |
| **916** | CD8 | 90 l ultra & ol grn | .25 | .25 |

Dante, 15th Century Bust — A489

Designs (from old Manuscripts): 40 l, Dante in Hell. 90 l, Dante in Purgatory led by Angel of Chastity. 130 l, Dante in Paradise interrogated by St. Peter on faith, horiz.

***Perf. 13½x14, 14x13½***

**1965, Oct. 21 Photo. Unwmk.**

| | | | | |
|---|---|---|---|---|
| **917** | A489 | 40 l multi | .25 | .25 |
| **918** | A489 | 90 l multi | .25 | .25 |
| **919** | A489 | 130 l multi | .25 | .25 |

**Wmk. 303 *Perf. 14***

| | | | | |
|---|---|---|---|---|
| **920** | A489 | 500 l slate grn | .55 | .35 |
| | | *Nos. 917-920 (4)* | 1.30 | 1.10 |

Dante Alighieri (1265-1321), poet.

House under Construction — A490

**1965, Oct. 31 Wmk. 303 *Perf. 14***

| | | | | |
|---|---|---|---|---|
| **921** | A490 | 40 l buff, blk & org brn | .25 | .25 |

Issued for Savings Day.

Jet Plane, Moon and Airletter Border
A491

Design: 40 l, Control tower and plane.

**1965, Nov. 3**

| | | | | |
|---|---|---|---|---|
| **922** | A491 | 40 l dk Prus bl & red | .25 | .25 |

**Unwmk.**

| | | | | |
|---|---|---|---|---|
| **923** | A491 | 90 l red, grn, dp bl & buff | .25 | .25 |

Night air postal network.

Map of Italy with Milan-Rome Highway — A492

**1965, Dec. 5 Photo. *Perf. 13x14***

| | | | | |
|---|---|---|---|---|
| **924** | A492 | 20 l bl, blk, ocher & gray | .25 | .25 |

Issued for Stamp Day.

Two-Man Bobsled — A493

Design: 90 l, Four-man bobsled.

**1966, Jan. 24 Wmk. 303 *Perf. 14***

| | | | | |
|---|---|---|---|---|
| **925** | A493 | 40 l dl bl, gray & red | .25 | .25 |
| **926** | A493 | 90 l vio & bl | .25 | .25 |

Intl. Bobsled Championships, Cortina d'Ampezzo.

Woman Skater — A494

Benedetto Croce — A495

Winter University Games: 40 l, Skier holding torch, horiz. 500 l, Ice hockey.

**1966, Feb. 5 Photo.**

| | | | | |
|---|---|---|---|---|
| **927** | A494 | 40 l blk & red | .25 | .25 |
| **928** | A494 | 90 l vio & red | .25 | .25 |
| **929** | A494 | 500 l brn & red | .55 | .35 |
| | | *Nos. 927-929 (3)* | 1.05 | .85 |

**1966, Feb. 25 Wmk. 303 *Perf. 14***

| | | | | |
|---|---|---|---|---|
| **930** | A495 | 40 l brown | .25 | .25 |

Benedetto Croce (1866-1952), philosopher, statesman and historian.

Arms of Venice and Other Cities in Venezia — A496

**1966, Mar. 22 Photo. Unwmk.**

| | | | | |
|---|---|---|---|---|
| **932** | A496 | 40 l gray & multi | .25 | .25 |

Centenary of Venezia's union with Italy.

Battle of Bezzecca — A497

**1966, July 21 Wmk. 303 *Perf. 14***

| | | | | |
|---|---|---|---|---|
| **933** | A497 | 90 l ol grn | .25 | .25 |

Centenary of the unification of Italy and of the Battle of Bezzecca.

Umbrella Pine — A498

Carnations62
A499

25 l, Apples. 50 l, Florentine iris. 55 l, Cypresses. 90 l, Daisies. 170 l, Olive tree. 180 l, Juniper.

**1966-68 Unwmk. *Perf. 13½x14***

| | | | | |
|---|---|---|---|---|
| **934** | A498 | 20 l multi | .25 | .25 |
| **934A** | A498 | 25 l multi ('67) | .25 | .25 |
| **935** | A499 | 40 l multi | .25 | .25 |
| **935A** | A498 | 50 l multi ('67) | .25 | .25 |
| **935B** | A498 | 55 l multi ('68) | .25 | .25 |
| **936** | A499 | 90 l multi | .25 | .25 |
| **937** | A498 | 170 l multi | .25 | .25 |
| **937A** | A498 | 180 l multi ('68) | .25 | .25 |
| | | *Nos. 934-937A (8)* | 2.00 | 2.00 |

Tourist Attractions
A500

**1966, May 28 Wmk. 303 *Perf. 14***

| | | | | |
|---|---|---|---|---|
| **938** | A500 | 20 l yel, org & blk | .25 | .25 |

Issued for tourist publicity and in connection with the National Conference on Tourism, Rome.

"I" in Flag Colors — A501

***Perf. 13½x14***

**1966, June 2 Photo. Unwmk.**

| | | | | |
|---|---|---|---|---|
| **939** | A501 | 40 l multi | .25 | .25 |
| **940** | A501 | 90 l multi | .25 | .25 |

20th anniversary of the Republic of Italy.

Singing Angels, by Donatello — A502

***Perf. 13½x14***

**1966, Sept. 24 Photo. Unwmk.**

| | | | | |
|---|---|---|---|---|
| **941** | A502 | 40 l multi | .25 | .25 |

Donatello (1386-1466), sculptor.

**Europa Issue, 1966**

Common Design Type

**1966, Sept. 26 Wmk. 303 *Perf. 14***

**Size: 22x38mm**

| | | | | |
|---|---|---|---|---|
| **942** | CD9 | 40 l brt pur | .25 | .25 |
| **943** | CD9 | 90 l brt bl | .25 | .25 |

Madonna, by Giotto — A503

***Perf. 13½x14***

**1966, Oct. 20 Photo. Unwmk.**

| | | | | |
|---|---|---|---|---|
| **944** | A503 | 40 l multi | .25 | .25 |

700th anniversary of the birth of Giotto di Bondone (1266?-1337), Florentine painter.

Italian Patriots
A504

**1966, Nov. 3 Wmk. 303 *Perf. 14***

| | | | | |
|---|---|---|---|---|
| **945** | A504 | 40 l gray & dl grn | .25 | .25 |

50th anniv. of the execution by Austrians of 4 Italian patriots: Fabio Filzi, Cesare Battisti, Damiano Chiesa and Nazario Sauro.

Postrider — A505

*Perf. 14x13½*

**1966, Dec. 4 Photo. Unwmk.**

**946** A505 20 l multi .25 .25

Issued for Stamp Day.

Globe and Compass Rose A506

**1967, Mar. 20 Photo. Wmk. 303**

**947** A506 40 l dull blue .25 .25

Centenary of Italian Geographical Society.

Arturo Toscanini (1867-1957), Conductor — A507

**1967, Mar. 25** ***Perf. 14***

**948** A507 40 l dp vio & cream .25 .25

Seat of Parliament on Capitoline Hill, Rome A508

**1967, Mar. 25** ***Perf. 14***

**949** A508 40 l sepia .25 .25
**950** A508 90 l rose lil & blk .25 .25

10th anniv. of the Treaty of Rome, establishing the European Common Market.

**Europa Issue, 1967**

Common Design Type

**1967, Apr. 10 Wmk. 303** ***Perf. 14***

**Size: 22x28mm**

**951** CD10 40 l plum & pink .25 .25
**952** CD10 90 l ultra & pale gray .35 .25

Alpine Ibex, Grand Paradiso Park — A509

National Parks: 40 l, Brown bear, Abruzzi Apennines, horiz. 90 l, Red deer, Stelvio Pass, Ortler Mountains, horiz. 170 l, Oak and deer, Circeo.

*Perf. 13½x14, 14x13½*

**1967, Apr. 22 Photo.**

**953** A509 20 l multi .25 .25
**954** A509 40 l multi .25 .25
**955** A509 90 l multi .25 .25
**956** A509 170 l multi .30 .30
*Nos. 953-956 (4)* 1.05 1.05

Claudio Monteverdi and Characters from "Orfeo" A510

**1967, May 15** ***Perf. 14***

**957** A510 40 l bis brn & brn .25 .25

Monteverdi (1567-1643), composer.

Bicyclists and Mountains A511

50th Bicycle Tour of Italy: 90 l. Three bicyclists on the road. 500 l, Group of bicyclists.

*Perf. 14x13½*

**1967, May 15 Photo. Unwmk.**

**958** A511 40 l multi .25 .25
**959** A511 90 l brt bl & multi .25 .25
**960** A511 500 l yel grn & multi 1.50 .85
*Nos. 958-960 (3)* 2.00 1.35

Luigi Pirandello and Stage A512

**1967, June 28** ***Perf. 14x13***

**961** A512 40 l blk & multi .25 .25

Pirandello (1867-1936), novelist & dramatist.

Stylized Mask A513

**1967, June 30 Wmk. 303** ***Perf. 14***

**962** A513 20 l grn & blk .25 .25
**963** A513 40 l car rose & blk .25 .25

10th "Festival of Two Worlds," Spoleto.

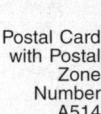

Postal Card with Postal Zone Number A514

Design: 40 l, 50 l, Letter addressed with postal zone number.

**Wmk. 303, Unwmkd, (20 l, 40 l)**

**1967-68**

**964** A514 20 l multi .25 .25
**965** A514 25 l multi ('68) .25 .25
**966** A514 40 l multi .25 .25
**967** A514 50 l multi ('68) .25 .25
*Nos. 964-967 (4)* 1.00 1.00

Introduction of postal zone numbers, 7/1/67.

Pomilio PC-1 Biplane and 1917 Airmail Postmark A515

**1967, July 18 Photo. Wmk. 303**

**968** A515 40 l blk & lt bl .25 .25

1st airmail stamp, Italy #C1, 50th anniv.

St. Ivo Church, Rome — A516

Umberto Giordano and "Improvisation" from Opera Andrea Chenier — A517

**1967, Aug. 2 Unwmk.** ***Perf. 14***

**969** A516 90 l multi .25 .25

Francesco Borromini (1599-1667), architect.

**1967, Aug. 28 Wmk. 303**

**970** A517 20 l blk & org brn .25 .25

Umberto Giordano (1867-1948), composer.

Oath of Pontida, by Adolfo Cao — A518

**1967, Sept. 2**

**971** A518 20 l dk brn .25 .25

800th anniv. of the Oath of Pontida, which united the Lombard League against Emperor Frederick I.

ITY Emblem — A519

*Perf. 13½x14*

**1967, Oct. 23 Photo. Unwmk.**

**972** A519 20 l blk, cit & brt bl .25 .25
**973** A519 50 l blk, org & brt bl .25 .25

Issued for International Tourist Year, 1967.

Lions Emblem — A520

Soldier at the Piave — A521

**1967, Oct. 30** ***Perf. 14x13½***

**974** A520 50 l multi .25 .25

50th anniversary of Lions International.

**1967, Nov. 9** ***Perf. 13x14***

**975** A521 50 l multi .25 .25

50th anniversary of Battle of the Piave.

Enrico Fermi at Los Alamos and Model of 1st Atomic Reactor — A522

**Wmk. 303**

**1967, Dec. 2 Photo.** ***Perf. 14***

**976** A522 50 l org brn & blk .25 .25

25th anniv. of the 1st atomic chain reaction under Enrico Fermi (1901-54), Chicago, IL.

"Day and Night" and Pigeon Carrying Italy No. 924 — A523

**1967, Dec. 3 Unwmk.** ***Perf. 13½x14***

**977** A523 25 l multi .25 .25

Issued for Stamp Day, 1967.

Scouts at Campfire — A524

**1968, Apr. 23** ***Perf. 13x14***

**978** A524 50 l multi .25 .25

Issued to honor the Boy Scouts.

**Europa Issue, 1968**

Common Design Type

***Perf. 14x13***

**1968, Apr. 29 Wmk. 303**

**Size: 36½x26mm**

**979** CD11 50 l blk, rose & sl grn .25 .25
**980** CD11 90 l blk, bl & brn .25 .25

St. Aloysius Gonzaga, by Pierre Legros — A525

***Perf. 13½x14***

**1968, May 28 Photo. Wmk. 303**

**981** A525 25 l red brn & dl vio .25 .25

Aloysius Gonzaga (1568-1591), Jesuit priest who ministered to victims of the plague.

Arrigo Boito and Mephistopheles — A526

**1968, June 10 Unwmk.** ***Perf. 14***

**982** A526 50 l multi .25 .25

Boito (1842-1918), composer and librettist.

Francesco Baracca and "Planes," by Giacomo Balla A527

**1968, June 19**

**983** A527 25 l multi .25 .25

Major Francesco Baracca (1888-1918), World War I aviator.

Giambattista Vico — A528

Bicycle Wheel and Velodrome, Rome — A529

Designs: No. 985, Tommaso Campanella. No. 986, Gioacchino Rossini.

***Perf. 14x13½***

**1968 Engr. Wmk. 303**

**984** A528 50 l ultra .25 .25
**985** A528 50 l black .25 .25
*a.* Perf. 13½ .80 .25
**986** A528 50 l car rose .25 .25
*Nos. 984-986 (3)* .75 .75

Vico (1668-1744), philosopher; Campanella (1568-1639), Dominican monk, philosopher poet and teacher; Rossini (1792-1868), composer.

Issued: #984, 6/24; #985, 9/5; #986, 10/25.

***Perf. 13x14***

**1968, Aug. 26 Photo. Unwmk.**

90 l, Bicycle and Sforza Castle, Imola.

**987** A529 25 l slate, rose & brown .25 .25
**988** A529 90 l slate, blue & ver .25 .25

Bicycling World Championships: 25 l for the track championships at the Velodrome in Rome; 90 l, the road championships at Imola.

"The Small St. Mark's Place," by Canaletto — A531

**1968, Sept. 30 Unwmk. *Perf. 14***

**989** A531 50 l pink & multi .25 .25

Canaletto (Antonio Canale, 1697-1768), Venetian painter.

"Mobilization" — A533

Symbolic Designs: 25 l, Trench war. 40 l, The Navy. 50 l, The Air Force. 90 l, The Battle of Vittorio Veneto. 180 l, The Unknown Soldier.

**1968, Nov. 2 Photo. Unwmk.**

**990** A533 20 l brn & multi .25 .25
**991** A533 25 l bl & multi .25 .25
**992** A533 40 l multi .25 .25
**993** A533 50 l multi .25 .25
**994** A533 90 l grn & multi .25 .25
**995** A533 180 l bl & multi .30 .30
*Nos. 990-995 (6)* 1.55 1.55

50th anniv. of the Allies' Victory in WW I.

Emblem — A534

**1968, Nov. 20 *Perf. 14x13½***

**996** A534 50 l blk, bl grn & red .25 .25

50th anniv. of the Postal Checking Service.

Parabolic Antenna, Fucino A535

**1968, Nov. 25 Photo. *Perf. 14***

**997** A535 50 l multi .25 .25

Issued to publicize the expansion of the space communications center at Fucino.

Development of Postal Service — A536

**1968, Dec. 1 Wmk. 303**

**998** A536 25 l car & yel .25 .25

Issued for the 10th Stamp Day.

Fluorescent Paper was introduced in 1968 for regular and special delivery issues. These stamps are about 1mm. smaller each way than the non-fluorescent ones they replaced, except Nos. 690-690A which remained the same size.

Commemorative or nonregular stamps issued only on fluorescent paper are Nos. 935B, 937A, 965, 967 and from 981 onward unless otherwise noted.

**Italia Type of 1953-54**

Small Size: 16x19½-20mm

**Photo.; Engr. (100, 150, 200-400 l)**

**1968-76 Wmk. 303 *Perf. 14***

**998A** A354 1 l dk gray .25 .25
**998B** A354 5 l slate .25 .25
**998C** A354 6 l ocher .25 .25
**998D** A354 10 l org ver .25 .25
**998E** A354 15 l gray vio .25 .25
**998F** A354 20 l brown .25 .25
**998G** A354 25 l purple .25 .25
**998H** A354 30 l bis brn .25 .25
**998I** A354 40 l lil rose .25 .25
**998J** A354 50 l olive .25 .25
**998K** A354 55 l vio ('69) .25 .25
**998L** A354 60 l blue .25 .25
**998M** A354 70 l Prus grn .25 .25
**998N** A354 80 l brn org .25 .25
**998O** A354 90 l lt red brn .25 .25
**998P** A354 100 l redsh brn .25 .25
**998Q** A354 125 l ocher & lil ('74) .25 .25
**998R** A354 130 l gray & dl red .25 .25
**998S** A354 150 l vio ('76) .25 .25
**998T** A354 180 l gray & vio brn ('71) .30 .25
**998U** A354 200 l slate blue .35 .25
**998V** A354 300 l Prus grn ('72) .50 .25
**998W** A354 400 l dull red ('76) .65 .25
*Nos. 998A-998W (23)* 6.55 5.75

Memorial Medal — A537

**Unwmk.**

**1969, Apr. 22 Photo. *Perf. 14***

**999** A537 50 l pink & blk .25 .25

Centenary of the State Audit Bureau.

**Europa Issue, 1969**

Common Design Type

**1969, Apr. 28 *Perf. 14x13***

**Size: 35½x25½mm**

**1000** CD12 50 l mag & multi *.25* .25
**1001** CD12 90 l bl & multi *.45* .25

Niccolo Machiavelli A538

ILO Emblem A539

**1969, May 3 *Perf. 14x13½***

**1002** A538 50 l blue & multi .25 .25

Niccolo Machiavelli (1469-1527), statesman and political philosopher.

**Wmk. 303**

**1969, June 7 Photo. *Perf. 14***

**1003** A539 50 l grn & blk .25 .25
**1004** A539 90 l car & blk .25 .25

50th anniv. of the ILO.

Federation Emblem, Tower of Superga Basilica and Matterhorn A540

**1969, June 26 Unwmk. *Perf. 14***

**1005** A540 50 l gold, bl & car .25 .25

Federation of Italian Philatelic Societies, 50th anniv.

Sondrio-Tirano Stagecoach, 1903 — A541

**1969, Dec. 7 Engr. Wmk. 303**

**1006** A541 25 l violet blue .25 .25

Issued for the 11th Stamp Day.

Downhill Skier — A542

90 l, Sassolungo & Sella Group, Dolomite Alps.

***Perf. 13x14***

**1970, Feb. 6 Unwmk. Photo.**

**1007** A542 50 l blue & multi .25 .25
**1008** A542 90 l blue & multi .25 .25

World Alpine Ski Championships, Val Gardena, Bolzano Province, Feb. 6-15.

Galatea, by Raphael A543

Painting: 50 l, Madonna with the Goldfinch (detail), by Raphael, 1483-1520.

**1970, Apr. 6 Photo. *Perf. 14x13***

**1009** A543 20 l multi .25 .25
**1010** A543 50 l multi .25 .25

Symbol of Flight, Colors of Italy and Japan A544

**1970, May 2 Unwmk. *Perf. 14***

**1011** A544 50 l multi .25 .25
**1012** A544 90 l multi .25 .25

50th anniv. of Arturo Ferrarin's flight from Rome to Tokyo, Feb. 14-May 31, 1920.

**Europa Issue, 1970**

Common Design Type

**1970, May 4 Wmk. 303**

**Size: 36x20mm**

**1013** CD13 50 l red & org *.25* .25
**1014** CD13 90 l bl grn & org *.40* .25

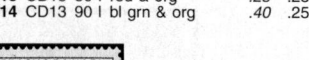

Gattamelata, Bust by Donatello — A545

**1970, May 30 Engr. *Perf. 14x13***

**1015** A545 50 l slate green .25 .25

Erasmo de' Narni, called Il Gattamelata (1370-1443), condottiere.

Runner A546

**Unwmk.**

**1970, Aug. 26 Photo. *Perf. 14***

**1016** A546 20 l shown .25 .25
**1017** A546 180 l Swimmer .30 .25

1970 World University Games, Turin, 8/26-9/6.

Dr. Maria Montessori and Children A547

**1970, Aug. 31 *Perf. 14x13***

**1018** A547 50 l multi .25 .25

Montessori (1870-1952), educator & physician.

Map of Italy and Quotation of Count Camillo Cavour — A548

**1970, Sept. 19 Unwmk. *Perf. 14***
**1019** A548 50 l multi .25 .25

Union of the Roman States with Italy, cent.

Loggia of St. Mark's Campanile, Venice A549

***Perf. 14x13½***
**1970, Sept. 26 Engr. Wmk. 303**
**1020** A549 50 l red brown .25 .25

Iacopo Tatti "Il Sansovino" (1486-1570), architect.

Garibaldi at Battle of Dijon A550

**1970, Oct. 15 Photo. *Perf. 14***
**1021** A550 20 l gray & dk bl .25 .25
**1022** A550 50 l brt rose lil & dk bl .25 .25

Cent. of Garibaldi's participation in the Franco-Prussian War during Battle of Dijon.

Tree and UN Emblem — A551

**1970, Oct. 24 Unwmk. *Perf. 13x14***
**1023** A551 25 l blk, sep & grn .25 .25
**1024** A551 90 l blk, brt bl & yel grn .25 .25

25th anniversary of the United Nations.

Rotary Emblem A552

**1970, Nov. 12 Wmk. 303 *Perf. 14***
**1025** A552 25 l bluish vio & org .25 .25
**1026** A552 90 l bluish vio & org .25 .25

Rotary International, 65th anniversary.

Telephone Dial and Trunk Lines A553

**1970, Nov. 24**
**1027** A553 25 l yel grn & dk red .25 .25
**1028** A553 90 l ultra & dk red .25 .25

Issued to publicize the completion of the automatic trunk telephone dialing system.

"Man Damaging Nature" — A554

**1970, Nov. 28 Wmk. 303 *Perf. 14***
**1029** A554 20 l car lake & grn .25 .25
**1030** A554 25 l dk bl & emer .25 .25

For European Nature Conservation Year.

Mail Train A555

**1970, Dec. 6 Engr.**
**1031** A555 25 l black .25 .25

For the 12th Stamp Day.

Virgin and Child, by Fra Filippo Lippi — A556

**1970, Dec. 12 Photo. Unwmk.**
**1032** A556 25 l multi .25 .25

Christmas 1970. See No. C139.

Saverio Mercadante (1795-1870), Composer — A557

**1970, Dec. 17 Wmk. 303**
**1033** A557 25 l vio & gray .25 .25

Mercury, by Benvenuto Cellini — A558

Bramante's Temple, St. Peter in Montorio — A559

**1971, Mar. 20 Photo. *Perf. 14***
**1034** A558 50 l Prussian blue .25 .25

Benvenuto Cellini (1500-1571), sculptor.

**Photogravure and Engraved**
**1971, Apr. 8 *Perf. 13x14***
**1035** A559 50 l ocher & blk .25 .25

Honoring Bramante (Donato di Angelo di Antonio, 1444-1514), architect.

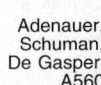

Adenauer, Schuman, De Gasperi A560

***Perf. 14x13½***
**1971, Apr. 28 Photo. Wmk. 303**
**1036** A560 50 l blk & lt grnsh bl .25 .25
**1037** A560 90 l blk & lil rose .25 .25

European Coal & Steel Community, 20th anniv.

**Europa Issue, 1971**
Common Design Type
**1971, May 3 *Perf. 14***
**1038** CD14 50 l ver & dk red *.25* .25
**1039** CD14 90 l brt rose lil & dk lil *.40* .25

Giuseppe Mazzini, Italian Flag — A561

***Perf. 14x13½***
**1971, June 12 Unwmk.**
**1040** A561 50 l multi .25 .25
**1041** A561 90 l multi .25 .25

25th anniversary of the Italian Republic.

Kayak Passing Between Poles A562

Design: 90 l, Kayak in free descent.

**1971, June 16 Photo. *Perf. 14***
**1042** A562 25 l multi .25 .25
**1043** A562 90 l multi .25 .25

Canoe Slalom World Championships, Merano.

Skiing, Basketball, Volleyball — A563

50 l, Gymnastics, cycling, track and swimming.

***Perf. 13½x14***
**1971, June 26 Photo. Unwmk.**
**1044** A563 20 l emer, ocher & blk .25 .25
**1045** A563 50 l dl bl, org & blk .25 .25

Youth Games.

Plane Circling Globe and "A" — A564

Designs: 50 l, Ornamental "A." 150 l, Tail of B747 in shape of "A."

**1971, Sept. 16 *Perf. 14x13½***
**1046** A564 50 l multi .25 .25
**1047** A564 90 l multi .25 .25
**1048** A564 150 l multi .25 .25
*Nos. 1046-1048 (3)* .75 .75

ALITALIA, Italian airlines founding, 25th anniv.

Grazia Deledda (1871-1936), Novelist — A565

**Photogravure and Engraved**
***Perf. 13½x14***
**1971, Sept. 28 Wmk. 303**
**1049** A565 50 l blk & salmon .25 .25

Child in Barrel Made of Banknote — A566

***Perf. 13x14***
**1971, Oct. 27 Photo. Unwmk.**
**1050** A566 25 l blk & multi .25 .25
**1051** A566 50 l multi .25 .25

Publicity for postal savings bank.

UNICEF Emblem and Children A567

90 l, Children hailing UNICEF emblem.

**1971, Nov. 26 *Perf. 14x13***
**1052** A567 25 l pink & multi .25 .25
**1053** A567 90 l multi .25 .25

25th anniv. of UNICEF.

Packet Tirrenia and Postal Ensign A568

**1971, Dec. 5 Wmk. 303 *Perf. 14***
**1054** A568 25 l slate green .25 .25

Stamp Day.

Nativity A569

Christmas: 90 l, Adoration of the Kings. Both designs are from miniatures in Evangelistary of Matilda in Nonantola Abbey, 12th-13th centuries.

***Perf. 14x13***
**1971, Dec. 10 Photo. Unwmk.**
**1055** A569 25 l gray & multi .25 .25
**1056** A569 90 l gray & multi .25 .25

Giovanni Verga and Sicilian Cart A570

**1972, Jan. 27**

**1057** A570 25 l org & multi .25 .25
**1058** A570 50 l multi .25 .25

Verga (1840-1922), writer & playwright.

Giuseppe Mazzini (1805-1872), Patriot and Writer — A571

**Wmk. 303**

**1972, Mar. 10 Engr. *Perf. 13***

**1059** A571 25 l blk & Prus grn .25 .25
**1060** A571 90 l black .25 .25
**1061** A571 150 l blk & rose red .25 .25
*Nos. 1059-1061 (3)* .75 .75

Flags, Milan Fair A572

Designs: 50 l, 90 l, Different abstract views.

***Perf. 14x13½***

**1972, Apr. 14 Photo. Unwmk.**

**1062** A572 25 l emer & blk .25 .25
**1063** A572 50 l dp org & blk .25 .25
**1064** A572 90 l bl & blk .25 .25
*Nos. 1062-1064 (3)* .75 .75

50th anniversary of the Milan Sample Fair.

**Europa Issue 1972**

Common Design Type

**1972, May 2 *Perf. 13x14***

**Size: 26x36mm**

**1065** CD15 50 l multi .25 .25
**1066** CD15 90 l multi .40 .25

Alpine Soldier and Pack Mule A573

50 l, Mountains, Alpinist's hat, pick & laurel. 90 l, Alpine soldier & mountains.

**1972, May 10 *Perf. 14x13***

**1067** A573 25 l ol & multi .25 .25
**1068** A573 50 l bl & multi .25 .25
**1069** A573 90 l grn & multi .25 .25
*Nos. 1067-1069 (3)* .75 .75

Centenary of the Alpine Corps.

Brenta Mountains, Society Emblem A574

Emblem and: 50 l, Mountain climber & Brenta Mountains. 180 l, Sunset over Mt. Crozzon.

***Perf. 14x13***

**1972, Sept. 2 Photo. Unwmk.**

**1070** A574 25 l multi .25 .25
**1071** A574 50 l multi .25 .25
**1072** A574 180 l multi .30 .25
*Nos. 1070-1072 (3)* .80 .75

Tridentine Alpinist Society centenary.

Conference Emblem, Seating Diagram A575

**1972, Sept. 21**

**1073** A575 50 l multi .25 .25
**1074** A575 90 l multi .25 .25

60th Conference of the Inter-Parliamentary Union, Montecitorio Hall, Rome.

St. Peter Damian, by Giovanni di Paoli, c. 1445 A576

**1972, Sept. 21 Photo.**

**1075** A576 50 l multi .25 .25

St. Peter Damian (1007-72), church reformer, cardinal, papal legate.

The Three Graces, by Antonio Canova (1757-1822), Sculptor — A577

**1972, Oct. 13 Engr. Wmk. 303**

**1076** A577 50 l black .25 .25

Page from Divine Comedy, Foligno Edition A578

Designs (Illuminated First Pages): 90 l, Mantua edition, vert. 180 l, Jesina edition.

***Perf. 14x13½, 13½x14***

**1972, Nov. 23 Photo. Unwmk.**

**1077** A578 50 l ocher & multi .25 .25
**1078** A578 90 l multi .25 .25
**1079** A578 180 l multi .30 .25
*Nos. 1077-1079 (3)* .80 .75

500th anniversary of three illuminated editions of Dante's Divine Comedy.

Angel — A579

Christmas: 25 l, Christ Child in cradle, horiz. 150 l, Angel. All designs from 18th century Neapolitan crèche.

***Perf. 13x14, 14x13***

**1972, Dec. 6 Photo.**

**1080** A579 20 l multi .25 .25
**1081** A579 25 l multi .25 .25
**1082** A579 150 l multi .25 .25
*Nos. 1080-1082 (3)* .75 .75

Passenger and Mail Autobus A580

**1972, Dec. 16 Engr. Wmk. 303**

**1083** A580 25 l magenta .25 .25

Stamp Day.

Leòn Battista Alberti — A581

Lorenzo Perosi — A582

**1972, Dec. 16 *Perf. 14***

**1084** A581 50 l ultra & ocher .25 .25

Leòn Battista Alberti (1404-1472), architect, painter, organist and writer.

**1972, Dec. 20 Photo. Unwmk.**

**1085** A582 50 l dk vio brn & org .25 .25
**1086** A582 90 l blk & yel grn .25 .25

Lorenzo Perosi (1872-1956), priest & composer.

Luigi Orione and Boys — A583

Ship Exploring Ocean Floor — A584

**1972, Dec. 30**

**1087** A583 50 l lt bl & dk bl .25 .25
**1088** A583 90 l ocher & slate grn .25 .25

Orione (1872-1940), founder of CARITAS; Catholic Welfare Organization.

**1973, Feb. 15 Photo. *Perf. 13x14***

**1089** A584 50 l multi .25 .25

Cent. of the Naval Hydrographic Institute.

Palace Staircase, Caserta A585

**1973, Mar. 1 Engr. *Perf. 14x13½***

**1090** A585 25 l gray olive .25 .25

Luigi Vanvitelli (1700-1773), architect.

Schiavoni Shore — A586

The Tetrarchs, 4th Century Sculpture — A587

50 l, "Triumph of Venice," by Vittore Carpaccio. 90 l, Bronze horses from St. Mark's. 300 l, St. Mark's Square covered by flood.

**1973 Photo. *Perf. 14***

**1091** A586 20 l ultra & multi .25 .25
**1092** A587 25 l ultra & multi .25 .25
**1093** A586 50 l ultra & multi .25 .25
**1094** A587 90 l ultra & multi .25 .25
**1095** A586 300 l ultra & multi .40 .35
*Nos. 1091-1095 (5)* 1.40 1.35

Save Venice campaign. Issued: #1091, 3/5; others 4/10.

Verona Fair Emblem — A588

**1973, Mar. 10 *Perf. 13x14***

**1096** A588 50 l multi .25 .25

75th International Fair, Verona.

Title Page for Book about Rosa — A589

**1973, Mar. 15 *Perf. 14***

**1097** A589 25 l org & blk .25 .25

Salvator Rosa (1615-1673), painter & poet.

G-91 Jet Fighters A590

Designs: 25 l, Formation of S-55 seaplanes. 50 l, G-91Y fighters. 90 l, Fiat CR-32's flying figure 8. 180 l, Camprini-Caproni jet, 1940.

**1973, Mar. 28 *Perf. 14x13½***

**1098** A590 20 l multi .25 .25
**1099** A590 25 l multi .25 .25
**1100** A590 50 l multi .25 .25
**1101** A590 90 l multi .25 .25
**1102** A590 180 l multi .30 .25
*Nos. 1098-1102,C140 (6)* 1.60 1.50

50th anniversary of military aviation.

Soccer Field and Ball A591

Design: 90 l, Soccer players and goal.

**1973, May 19 Photo. *Perf. 14x13½***

**1103** A591 25 l ol, blk & lt grn .25 .25
**1104** A591 90 l grn & multi .55 .55

75th anniv. of Italian Soccer Federation.

Alessandro Manzoni, by Francisco Hayez — A592

Villa Rotunda, by Andrea Palladio (1508-80), Architect. — A593

**1973, May 22** **Engr.**

**1105** A592 25 l blk & brn .25 .25

Manzoni (1785-1873), novelist and poet.

**1973, May 30** **Photo.** **Unwmk.**

***Perf. 13x14***

**1106** A593 90 l blk, yel & lem .25 .25

Spiral and Cogwheels A594

**1973, June 20** ***Perf. 14x13***

**1107** A594 50 l gold & multi .25 .25

50th anniversary of the State Supply Office.

**Europa Issue 1973**

Common Design Type

**1973, June 30** **Litho.** ***Perf. 14***

**Size: 36x20mm**

**1108** CD16 50 l lil, gold & yel *.25* .25
**1109** CD16 90 l lt bl grn, gold & yel *.40* .25

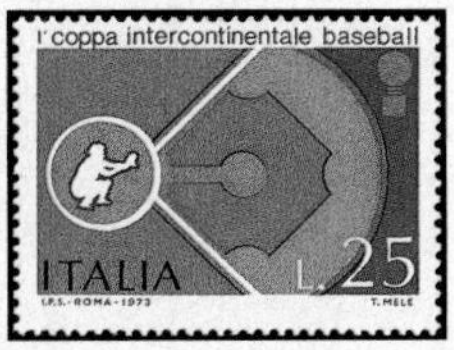


Catcher and Diamond A595

Design: 90 l, Diamond and batter.

**1973, July 21** **Photo.** ***Perf. 14x13½***

**1110** A595 25 l multi .25 .25
**1111** A595 90 l multi .25 .25

International Baseball Cup.

Viareggio by Night — A596

**1973, Aug. 10** **Photo.** ***Perf. 13x14***

**1112** A596 25 l blk & multi .25 .25

Viareggio Carnival.

Assassination of Giovanni Minzoni — A597

**1973, Aug. 23** ***Perf. 14x13***

**1113** A597 50 l multi .25 .25

Minzoni (1885-1923), priest & social worker.

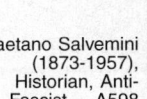

Gaetano Salvemini (1873-1957), Historian, Anti-Fascist — A598

**1973, Sept. 8** ***Perf. 14x13½***

**1114** A598 50 l pink & multi .25 .25

Palazzo Farnese, Caprarola, by Vignola A599

**1973, Sept. 21** **Engr.** ***Perf. 14x13½***

**1115** A599 90 l choc & yel .25 .25

Giacomo da Vignola (real name, Giacomo Barocchio), 1507-1573, architect.

St. John the Baptist, by Caravaggio A600

**Lithographed & Engraved**

**1973, Sept. 28** ***Perf. 14***

**1116** A600 25 l blk & dl yel .25 .25

400th anniversary of the birth of Michelangelo da Caravaggio (1573-1610?), painter.

Tower of Pisa — A601

**1973, Oct. 8** **Photo.**

**1117** A601 50 l multi .25 .25

8th century of Leaning Tower of Pisa.

Famous Men — A602

Designs: No. 1118, Sandro Botticelli. No. 1119, Giambattista Piranesi. No. 1120, Paolo Veronese. No. 1121, Andrea del Verrocchio. No. 1122, Giovanni Battista Tiepolo. No. 1123, Francesco Borromini. No. 1124, Rosalba Carriera. No. 1125, Giovanni Bellini (Giambellino). No. 1126, Andrea Mantegna. No. 1127, Raphael (Raffaello).

**1973-74** **Photo.** ***Perf. 14x13½***

**1118** A602 50 l multi .25 .25
**1119** A602 50 l multi .25 .25
**1120** A602 50 l multi .25 .25
**1121** A602 50 l multi .25 .25
**1122** A602 50 l multi .25 .25
**1123** A602 50 l multi .25 .25
**1124** A602 50 l multi .25 .25
**1125** A602 50 l multi .25 .25
**1126** A602 50 l multi .25 .25
**1127** A602 50 l multi .25 .25
*Nos. 1118-1127 (10)* 2.50 2.50

Famous artists.

Issued: #1118-1122, 11/5; #1123-1127, 5/25/74.

See #1204-1209, 1243-1247, 1266-1270.

Trevi Fountain, Rome — A603

Designs: No. 1129, Immacolatella Fountain, Naples. No. 1130, Pretoria Fountain, Palermo.

**Photogravure and Engraved**

**1973, Nov. 10** ***Perf. 13½x14***

**1128** A603 25 l blk & multi .25 .25
**1129** A603 25 l blk & multi .25 .25
**1130** A603 25 l blk & multi .25 .25
*Nos. 1128-1130 (3)* .75 .75

See Nos. 1166-1168, 1201-1203, 1251-1253, 1277-1279, 1341-1343, 1379-1381.

Angels, by Agostino di Duccio — A604

Sculptures by Agostino di Duccio: 25 l, Virgin and Child. 150 l, Angels with flute and trumpet.

**1973, Nov. 26**

**1131** A604 20 l yel grn & blk .25 .25
**1132** A604 25 l lt bl & blk .25 .25
**1133** A604 150 l yel & blk .25 .25
*Nos. 1131-1133 (3)* .75 .75

Christmas 1973.

Map of Italy, Rotary Emblems — A605

**1973, Nov. 28** **Photo.**

**1134** A605 50 l red, grn & dk bl .25 .25

50th anniv. of Rotary International of Italy.

Caravelle A606

**Wmk. 303**

**1973, Dec. 2** **Engr.** ***Perf. 14***

**1135** A606 25 l Prussian blue .25 .25

15th Stamp Day.

Gold Medal of Valor, 50th Anniv. — A607

***Perf. 13½x14***

**1973, Dec. 10** **Photo.** **Unwmk.**

**1136** A607 50 l gold & multi .25 .25

Enrico Caruso (1873-1921), Operatic Tenor — A608

Design: 50 l, Caruso as Duke in Rigoletto.

**1973, Dec. 15** **Engr.**

**1137** A608 50 l magenta .25 .25

Christ Crowning King Roger — A609

Norman art in Sicily: 50 l, King William II offering model of church to the Virgin, mosaic from Monreale Cathedral. The design of 20 l, is from a mosaic in Martorana Church, Palermo.

**Lithographed and Engraved**

**1974, Mar. 4** ***Perf. 13½x14***

**1138** A609 20 l ind & buff .25 .25
**1139** A609 50 l red & lt grn .25 .25

Luigi Einaudi (1874-1961), Pres. of Italy — A610

**1974, Mar. 23** **Engr.** ***Perf. 14x13½***

**1140** A610 50 l green .25 .25

Guglielmo Marconi (1874-1937), Italian Inventor and Physicist — A611

Design: 90 l, Marconi and world map.

**1974, Apr. 24** **Photo.** ***Perf. 14x13½***

**1141** A611 50 l bl grn & gray .25 .25
**1142** A611 90 l vio & multi .25 .25

David, by Giovanni L. Bernini — A612

Europa: 90 l, David, by Michelangelo.

**1974, Apr. 29** **Photo.** ***Perf. 13½x14***

**1143** A612 50 l sal, ultra & gray *.50* .25
**1144** A612 90 l grn, ultra & buff *.50* .25

Customs Frontier Guards, 1774, 1795, 1817
A613

Uniforms of Customs Service: 50 l, Lombardy Venetia, 1848, Sardinia, 1815, Tebro Battalion, 1849. 90 l, Customs Guards, 1866, 1880 and Naval Marshal, 1892. 180 l, Helicopter pilot, Naval and Alpine Guards, 1974. All bordered with Italian flag colors.

**1974, June 21 Photo. *Perf. 14***

**1145** A613 40 l multi .25 .25
**1146** A613 50 l multi .25 .25
**1147** A613 90 l multi .25 .25
**1148** A613 180 l multi .30 .25
*Nos. 1145-1148 (4)* 1.05 1.00

Customs Frontier Guards bicentenary.

Sprinter
A614

**1974, June 28 Photo. *Perf. 14x13***

**1149** A614 40 l shown .25 .25
**1150** A614 50 l Pole vault .25 .25

European Athletic Championships, Rome.

Sharpshooter — A615

Design: 50 l, Bersaglieri emblem.

**1974, June 27**

**1151** A615 40 l multi .25 .25
**1152** A615 50 l grn & multi .25 .25

Bersaglieri Veterans Association, 50th anniv.

View of Portofino — A616

**1974, July 10 *Perf. 14***

**1153** A616 40 l shown .25 .25
**1154** A616 40 l View of Gradara .25 .25

Tourist publicity.

See Nos. 1190-1192, 1221-1223, 1261-1265, 1314-1316, 1357-1360, 1402-1405, 1466-1469, 1520-1523, 1563A-1563D, 1599-1602, 1630-1633, 1708-1711, 1737-1740, 1776-1779, 1803-1806, 1830-1833, 1901-1904.

Petrarch (1304-74), Poet — A617

50 l, Petrarch at his desk (from medieval manuscript).

**Lithographed and Engraved**

**1974, July 19 *Perf. 13½x14***

**1155** A617 40 l ocher & multi .25 .25
**1156** A617 50 l ocher, yel & bl .25 .25

Niccolo Tommaseo (1802-1874), Writer, Venetian Education Minister — A618

Tommaseo Statue, by Ettore Ximenes, Shibenik.

**1974, July 19**

**1157** A618 50 l grn & pink .25 .25

Giacomo Puccini (1858-1924), Composer
A619

**1974, Aug. 16 Photo.**

**1158** A619 40 l multi .25 .25

Lodovico Ariosto (1474-1533), Poet — A620

**1974, Sept. 9 Engr. *Perf. 14x13½***

**1159** A620 50 l King Roland, woodcut .25 .25

The design is from a contemporary illustration of Ariosto's poem "Orlando Furioso."

Quotation from Menippean Satire by Varro
A621

**1974, Sept. 21**

**1160** A621 50 l ocher & dk red .25 .25

Marcus Terentius Varro (116-27 BC), Roman scholar and writer.

"October," 15th Century Mural
A622

**1974, Sept. 28 Photo. *Perf. 14***

**1161** A622 50 l multi .25 .25

14th International Wine Congress, Trento.

"UPU" and Emblem
A623

Design: 90 l, Letters, "UPU" and emblem.

**1974, Oct. 19 Photo. *Perf. 14***

**1162** A623 50 l multi .25 .25
**1163** A623 90 l multi .25 .25

Centenary of Universal Postal Union.

St. Thomas Aquinas, by Francesco Traini — A624

**1974, Oct. 25 *Perf. 13x14***

**1164** A624 50 l multi .25 .25

St. Thomas Aquinas (1225-1274), scholastic philosopher, 700th death anniversary.

Bas-relief from Ara Pacis — A625

**1974, Oct. 26**

**1165** A625 50 l multi .25 .25

Centenary of the Ordini Forensi (Bar Association).

**Fountain Type of 1973**

Designs: No. 1166, Oceanus Fountain, Florence. No. 1167, Neptune Fountain, Bologna. No. 1168, Fontana Maggiore, Perugia.

**Photogravure and Engraved**

**1974, Nov. 9 *Perf. 13x14***

**1166** A603 40 l blk & multi .25 .25
**1167** A603 40 l blk & multi .25 .25
**1168** A603 40 l blk & multi .25 .25
*Nos. 1166-1168 (3)* .75 .75

St. Francis Adoring Christ Child, Anonymous — A626

**Photogravure and Engraved**

**1974, Nov. 26 *Perf. 14x13½***

**1169** A626 40 l multi .25 .25

Christmas 1974.

Masked Dancers — A627

**1974, Dec. 1 Photo. *Perf. 13½x14***

**1170** A627 40 l Pulcinella .25 .25
**1171** A627 50 l shown .25 .25
**1172** A627 90 l Pantaloon .25 .25
*Nos. 1170-1172 (3)* .75 .75

16th Stamp Day 1974.

God Admonishing Adam, by Jacopo della Quercia — A628

Courtyard, Uffizi Gallery, Florence, by Giorgio Vasari
A629

**1974, Dec. 20 Engr. *Perf. 14***

**1173** A628 90 l dk vio bl .25 .25

**Lithographed and Engraved**

**1174** A629 90 l multi .25 .25

Italian artists: Jacopo della Quercia (1374-c. 1438), sculptor, and Giorgio Vasari (1511-1574), architect, painter and writer.

Angel with Tablet — A630

Angel with Cross — A632

Angels' Bridge, Rome — A631

Holy Year 1975: 50 l, Angel holding column. 150 l, Angel holding Crown of Thorns. The angels are statues by Giovanni Bernini on the Angels' Bridge (San Angelo).

**1975, Mar. 25 Photo. *Perf. 14***

**1175** A630 40 l multi .25 .25
**1176** A630 50 l bl & multi .25 .25
**1177** A631 90 l bl & multi .25 .25
**1178** A630 150 l vio & multi .25 .25
**1179** A632 180 l multi .30 .25
*Nos. 1175-1179 (5)* 1.30 1.25

Pitti Madonna, by Michelangelo
A633

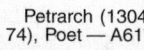

Works of Michelangelo: 50 l, Niche in Vatican Palace. 90 l, The Flood, detail from Sistine Chapel.

**1975, Apr. 18 Engr. *Perf. 13½x14***

**1180** A633 40 l dl grn .25 .25
**1181** A633 50 l sepia .25 .25
**1182** A633 90 l red brn .25 .25
*Nos. 1180-1182 (3)* .75 .75

Michelangelo Buonarroti (1475-1564), sculptor, painter and architect.

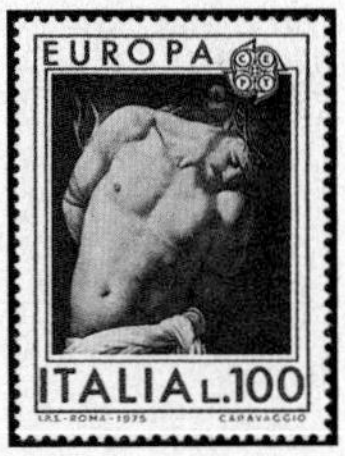


Flagellation of Jesus, by Caravaggio A634

Europa: 150 l, Apparition of Angel to Hagar and Ishmael, by Tiepolo (detail).

**1975, Apr. 29 Photo. *Perf. 13x14***

**1183** A634 100 l multi *.30* .25
**1184** A634 150 l multi *.30* .25

Four Days of Naples, by Marino Mazzacurati A635

Resistance Fighters of Cuneo, by Umberto Mastroianni A636

Design: 100 l, Martyrs of Ardeatine Caves, by Francesco Coccia.

**1975, Apr. 23**

**1185** A635 70 l multi .25 .25
**1186** A636 100 l ol & multi .25 .25
**1187** A636 150 l multi .25 .25
*Nos. 1185-1187 (3)* .75 .75

Resistance movement victory, 30th anniv.

Globe and IWY Emblem A637

**1975, May *Perf. 14x13½***

**1188** A637 70 l multi .25 .25

International Women's Year 1975.

Satellite, San Rita Launching Platform — A638

**1975, May 28 *Perf. 13½x14***

**1189** A638 70 l multi .25 .25

San Marco satellite project.

**Tourist Type of 1974**

Paintings: No. 1190, View of Isola Bella. No. 1191, Baths of Montecatini. No. 1192, View of Cefalù.

**1975, June 16 Photo. *Perf. 14***

**1190** A616 150 l grn & multi .25 .25
**1191** A616 150 l bl grn & multi .25 .25
**1192** A616 150 l red brn & multi .25 .25
*Nos. 1190-1192 (3)* .75 .75

Artist and Model, Armando Spadini A640

Painting: No. 1194, Flora, by Guido Reni.

**1975, June 20 Engr. *Perf. 14***

**1193** A640 90 l blk & multi .25 .25
**1194** A640 90 l multi .25 .25

50th death anniv. of Armando Spadini and 400th birth anniv. of Guido Reni.

Giovanni Pierluigi da Palestrina (1525-94), Composer of Sacred Music — A641

**1975, June 27 Engr. *Perf. 13½x14***

**1195** A641 100 l magenta & tan .25 .25

Emmigrants and Ship A642

**1975, June 30 Photo. *Perf. 14x13½***

**1196** A642 70 l multi .25 .25

Italian emigration centenary.

Emblem of United Legal Groups A643

**1975, July 25 Photo. *Perf. 14x13½***

**1197** A643 100 l yel, grn & red .25 .25

Unification of Italian legal organizations, cent.

Locomotive Wheels A644

**1975, Sept. 15 Photo. *Perf. 14x13½***

**1198** A644 70 l multi .25 .25

Intl. Railroad Union, 21st cong., Bologna.

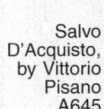

Salvo D'Acquisto, by Vittorio Pisano A645

**1975, Sept. 23**

**1199** A645 100 l multi .25 .25

D'Acquisto died in 1943 saving 22 people.

Stylized Syracusean Italia — A646

**1975, Sept. 26 Photo. *Perf. 13½x14***

**1200** A646 100 l org & multi .25 .25

Cent. of unification of the State Archives.

**Fountain Type of 1973**

Designs: No. 1201, Rosello Fountain, Sassari. No. 1202, Fountain of the 99 Faucets, Aquila. No. 1203, Piazza Fontana, Milan.

**Photogravure and Engraved**

**1975, Oct. 30 *Perf. 13x14***

**1201** A603 70 l blk & multi .25 .25
**1202** A603 70 l blk & multi .25 .25
**1203** A603 70 l blk & multi .25 .25
*Nos. 1201-1203 (3)* .75 .75

**Famous Men Type of 1973-74**

Designs: No. 1204, Alessandro Scarlatti. No. 1205, Antonio Vivaldi. No. 1206, Gaspare Spontini. No. 1207, Ferruccio Busoni. No. 1208, Francesco Cilea. No. 1209, Franco Alfano.

**1975, Nov. 14 Photo. *Perf. 14x13½***

**1204** A602 100 l multi .25 .25
**1205** A602 100 l multi .25 .25
**1206** A602 100 l multi .25 .25
**1207** A602 100 l multi .25 .25
**1208** A602 100 l multi .25 .25
**1209** A602 100 l multi .25 .25
*Nos. 1204-1209 (6)* 1.50 1.50

Famous musicians.

Annunciation to the Shepherds A648

Christmas: 100 l, Nativity. 150 l, Annunciation to the Kings. Designs from painted wood panels, portal of Alatri Cathedral, 14th century.

**Lithographed and Engraved**

**1975, Nov. 25 *Perf. 13½x14***

**1210** A648 70 l grn & multi .25 .25
**1211** A648 100 l ultra & multi .25 .25
**1212** A648 150 l brn & multi .25 .25
*Nos. 1210-1212 (3)* .75 .75

"The Magic Orchard" — A649

Children's Drawings: 70 l, Children on Horseback, horiz. 150 l, Village and procession, horiz.

***Perf. 14x13½, 13½x14***

**1975, Dec. 7 Photo.**

**1213** A649 70 l multi .25 .25
**1214** A649 100 l multi .25 .25
**1215** A649 150 l multi .25 .25
*Nos. 1213-1215 (3)* .75 .75

17th Stamp Day.

Boccaccio, by Andrea del Castagno — A650

Design: 150 l, Frontispiece for "Fiammetta," 15th century woodcut.

**Engraved and Lithographed**

**1975, Dec. 22 *Perf. 13½x14***

**1216** A650 100 l yel grn & blk .25 .25
**1217** A650 150 l buff & multi .25 .25

Giovanni Boccaccio (1313-1375), writer.

State Advocate's Office, Rome — A651

**1976, Jan. 30 Photo. *Perf. 13½x14***

**1218** A651 150 l multi .25 .25

State Advocate's Office, centenary.

ITALIA 76 Emblem — A652

Design: 180 l, Milan Fair pavilion.

**1976, Mar. 27 Photo. *Perf. 13½x14***

**1219** A652 150 l blk, red & grn .25 .25
**1220** A652 180 l blk, red, grn & bl .25 .25

ITALIA 76 International Philatelic Exhibition, Milan, Oct. 14-24.

**Tourist Type of 1974**

Tourist publicity: #1221, Fenis Castle. #1222, View of Ischia. #1223, Itria Valley.

**1976, May 21 Photo. *Perf. 14***

**1221** A616 150 l grn & multi .25 .25
**1222** A616 150 l plum & multi .25 .25
**1223** A616 150 l yel & multi .25 .25
*Nos. 1221-1223 (3)* .75 .75

Majolica Plate, Deruta — A653

Europa: 180 l, Ceramic vase in shape of woman's head, Caltagirone.

**1976, May 22 *Perf. 13½x14***

**1224** A653 150 l multi .25 .25
**1225** A653 180 l brn & multi .30 .25

Italian Flags — A654

Italian Presidents A655

**1976, June 1**

| | | | | | |
|---|---|---|---|---|---|
| **1226** | A654 | 100 l | multi | .25 | .25 |
| **1227** | A655 | 150 l | multi | .25 | .25 |

30th anniversary of Italian Republic.

Fortitude, by Giacomo Serpotta, 1656-1732 A656

Paintings: No. 1229, Woman at Table, by Umberto Boccioni, 1882-1916. No. 1230, The Gunner's Letter, by F. T. Marinetti, 1876-1944.

**1976, July 26 Engr. *Perf. 14***

| | | | | | |
|---|---|---|---|---|---|
| **1228** | A656 | 150 l | blue | .25 | .25 |

**Lithographed and Engraved**

| | | | | | |
|---|---|---|---|---|---|
| **1229** | A656 | 150 l | multi | .25 | .25 |
| **1230** | A656 | 150 l | blk & red | .25 | .25 |
| | | | *Nos. 1228-1230 (3)* | .75 | .75 |

Italian art.

Paintings by Vittore Carpaccio (1460-1526), Venetian Painter — A657

Designs: No. 1231, St. George. No. 1232, Dragon, after painting in Church of St. George Schiavoni, Venice.

**1976, July 30 Engr. *Perf. 14x13½***

| | | | | | |
|---|---|---|---|---|---|
| **1231** | A657 | 150 l | rose lake | .25 | .25 |
| **1232** | A657 | 150 l | rose lake | .25 | .25 |
| ***a.*** | | | Pair, #1231-1232 + label | .50 | .25 |

Flora, by Titian A658

**1976, Sept. 15 Engr. *Perf. 14***

| | | | | | |
|---|---|---|---|---|---|
| **1233** | A658 | 150 l | carmine | .25 | .25 |

Titian (1477-1576), Venetian painter.

St. Francis, 13th Century Fresco — A659

**1976, Oct. 2 Engr. *Perf. 14***

| | | | | | |
|---|---|---|---|---|---|
| **1234** | A659 | 150 l | brown | .25 | .25 |

St. Francis of Assisi, 750th death anniv.

Cart, from Trajan's Column A660

100 l, Emblem of Kingdom of Sardinia. 150 l, Marble mask, 19th cent. mail box. 200 l, Hand canceler, 19th cent. 400 l, Automatic letter sorting machine.

**1976, Oct. 14 Photo. *Perf. 14x13½***

| | | | | | |
|---|---|---|---|---|---|
| **1235** | A660 | 70 l | multi | .25 | .25 |
| **1236** | A660 | 100 l | multi | .25 | .25 |
| **1237** | A660 | 150 l | multi | .25 | .25 |
| **1238** | A660 | 200 l | multi | .30 | .25 |
| **1239** | A660 | 400 l | multi | .35 | .25 |
| | | | *Nos. 1235-1239 (5)* | 1.40 | 1.25 |

ITALIA 76 International Philatelic Exhibition, Milan, Oct. 14-24.

Girl and Animals — A661

Designs (Children' Drawings): 100 l, Trees, rabbit and flowers. 150 l, Boy healing tree.

**1976, Oct. 17 *Perf. 13½x14***

| | | | | | |
|---|---|---|---|---|---|
| **1240** | A661 | 40 l | multi | .25 | .25 |
| **1241** | A661 | 100 l | multi | .25 | .25 |
| **1242** | A661 | 150 l | multi | .25 | .25 |
| | | | *Nos. 1240-1242 (3)* | .75 | .75 |

18th Stamp Day and nature protection.

**Famous Men Type of 1973-74**

Designs: No. 1243, Lorenzo Ghiberti. No. 1244, Domenico Ghirlandaio. No. 1245, Sassoferrato. No. 1246, Carlo Dolci. No. 1247, Giovanni Piazzetta.

**1976, Nov. 22 Photo. *Perf. 14x13½***

| | | | | | |
|---|---|---|---|---|---|
| **1243** | A602 | 170 l | multi | .25 | .25 |
| **1244** | A602 | 170 l | multi | .25 | .25 |
| **1245** | A602 | 170 l | multi | .25 | .25 |
| **1246** | A602 | 170 l | multi | .25 | .25 |
| **1247** | A602 | 170 l | multi | .25 | .25 |
| | | | *Nos. 1243-1247 (5)* | 1.25 | 1.25 |

Famous painters.

The Visit, by Silvestro Lega A662

**1976, Dec. 7 Photo. *Perf. 14x13½***

| | | | | | |
|---|---|---|---|---|---|
| **1248** | A662 | 170 l | multi | .25 | .25 |

Silvestro Lega (1826-1895), painter.

Adoration of the Kings, by Bartolo di Fredi — A663

Christmas: 120 l, Nativity, by Taddeo Gaddi.

**1976, Dec. 11 *Perf. 13½x14***

| | | | | | |
|---|---|---|---|---|---|
| **1249** | A663 | 70 l | multi | .25 | .25 |
| **1250** | A663 | 120 l | multi | .25 | .25 |

**Fountain Type of 1973**

Designs: No. 1251, Antique Fountain, Gallipoli. No. 1252, Madonna Fountain, Verona. No. 1253, Silvio Cosini Fountain, Palazzo Doria, Genoa.

**Lithographed and Engraved**

**1976, Dec. 21 *Perf. 13½x14***

| | | | | | |
|---|---|---|---|---|---|
| **1251** | A603 | 170 l | blk & multi | .25 | .25 |
| **1252** | A603 | 170 l | blk & multi | .25 | .25 |
| **1253** | A603 | 170 l | blk & multi | .25 | .25 |
| | | | *Nos. 1251-1253 (3)* | .75 | .75 |

Snakes Forming Net A664

Design: 170 l, Drug addict and poppy.

**1977, Feb. 28 Photo. *Perf. 14x13½***

| | | | | | |
|---|---|---|---|---|---|
| **1254** | A664 | 120 l | multi | .25 | .25 |
| **1255** | A664 | 170 l | multi | .25 | .25 |

Fight against drug abuse.

Micca Setting Fire A665

**1977, Mar. 5**

| | | | | | |
|---|---|---|---|---|---|
| **1256** | A665 | 170 l | multi | .25 | .25 |

Pietro Micca (1677-1706), patriot who set fire to the powder magazine of Turin Citadel.

Globe with Cross in Center — A666

Design: 120 l, People of the World united as brothers by St. John Bosco.

**1977, Mar. 29 Photo. *Perf. 13x13½***

| | | | | | |
|---|---|---|---|---|---|
| **1257** | A666 | 70 l | multi | .25 | .25 |
| **1258** | A666 | 120 l | multi | .25 | .25 |

Honoring the Salesian missionaries.

Italian Constitution, Article 53 — A667

**1977, Apr. 14 Photo. *Perf. 14***

| | | | | | |
|---|---|---|---|---|---|
| **1259** | A667 | 120 l | bis, brn & blk | .25 | .25 |
| **1260** | A667 | 170 l | lt grn, grn & blk | .25 | .25 |

"Pay your taxes."

**Tourist Type of 1974**

Europa (Europa Emblem and): 170 l, Taormina. 200 l, Castle del Monte.

**1977, May 2**

| | | | | | |
|---|---|---|---|---|---|
| **1261** | A616 | 170 l | multi | *.65* | .25 |
| **1262** | A616 | 200 l | multi | *.85* | .25 |

**Tourist Type of 1974**

Paintings: No. 1263, Canossa Castle. No. 1264, Fermo. No. 1265, Castellana Caves.

**1977, May 30 Photo. *Perf. 14***

| | | | | | |
|---|---|---|---|---|---|
| **1263** | A616 | 170 l | brn & multi | .25 | .25 |
| **1264** | A616 | 170 l | vio & multi | .25 | .25 |
| **1265** | A616 | 170 l | gray & multi | .25 | .25 |
| | | | *Nos. 1263-1265 (3)* | .75 | .75 |

**Famous Men Type of 1973-74**

Designs: No. 1266, Filippo Brunelleschi. No. 1267, Pietro Aretino. No. 1268, Carlo Goldoni. No. 1269, Luigi Cherubini. No. 1270, Eduardo Bassini.

**1977, June 27 *Perf. 14x13½***

| | | | | | |
|---|---|---|---|---|---|
| **1266** | A602 | 70 l | multi | .25 | .25 |
| **1267** | A602 | 70 l | multi | .25 | .25 |
| **1268** | A602 | 70 l | multi | .25 | .25 |
| **1269** | A602 | 70 l | multi | .25 | .25 |
| **1270** | A602 | 70 l | multi | .25 | .25 |
| | | | *Nos. 1266-1270 (5)* | 1.25 | 1.25 |

Famous artists, writers and scientists.

Justice, by Andrea Delitio A669

Painting: No. 1272, Winter, by Giuseppe Arcimboldi, 1527-c.1593.

**Engraved and Lithographed**

**1977, Sept. 5 *Perf. 14***

| | | | | | |
|---|---|---|---|---|---|
| **1271** | A669 | 170 l | multi | .25 | .25 |
| **1272** | A669 | 170 l | multi | .25 | .25 |

Corvette Caracciolo — A670

Italian Ships: No. 1274, Hydrofoil gunboat Sparviero. No. 1275, Paddle steamer Ferdinando Primo. No. 1276, Passenger liner Saturnia.

**Photogravure and Engraved**

**1977, Sept. 23 *Perf. 14x13½***

| | | | | |
|---|---|---|---|---|
| **1273** | 170 l | multi | .25 | .25 |
| **1274** | 170 l | multi | .25 | .25 |
| **1275** | 170 l | multi | .25 | .25 |
| **1276** | 170 l | multi | .25 | .25 |
| ***a.*** | | A670 Block or strip of 4, #1273-1276 + 2 labels | 1.00 | .50 |

See #1323-1326, 1382-1385, 1435-1438.

**Fountain Type of 1973**

Designs: No. 1277, Pacassi Fountain, Gorizia. No. 1278, Fraterna Fountain, Isernia. No. 1279, Palm Fountain, Palmi.

**Lithographed and Engraved**

**1977, Oct. 18 *Perf. 13x14***

| | | | | | |
|---|---|---|---|---|---|
| **1277** | A603 | 120 l | blk & multi | .25 | .25 |
| **1278** | A603 | 120 l | blk & multi | .25 | .25 |
| **1279** | A603 | 120 l | blk & multi | .25 | .25 |
| | | | *Nos. 1277-1279 (3)* | .75 | .75 |

Volleyball — A671

Designs (Children's Drawings): No. 1281, Butterflies and net. No. 1282, Flying kites.

**1977, Oct. 23 Photo. *Perf. 13x14***

**1280** A671 120 l multi .25 .25
**1281** A671 120 l multi .25 .25
**1282** A671 120 l multi .25 .25
*a.* Block of 3, #1280-1282 + label .50 .30

19th Stamp Day.

Symbolic Blood Donation A672

Design: 70 l, Blood donation symbolized.

**1977, Oct. 26 *Perf. 14x13½***

**1283** A672 70 l multi .25 .25
**1284** A672 120 l multi .30 .25

Blood donors.

Quintino Sella and Italy No. 24 — A673

**1977, Oct. 23 *Perf. 13½x14***

**1285** A673 170 l olive & blk brn .30 .25

Quintino Sella (1827-1884), statesman, engineer, mineralogist, birth sesquicentenary.

**Italia Type of 1953-54 and**

Italia — A674

**1977-87 Wmk. 303 *Perf. 14***

**Size: 16x20mm**

**Photo.**

**1288** A354 120 l dk bl & emer .25 .25

**Photo. & Engr.**

**1289** A354 170 l grn & ocher .25 .25

**Litho. & Engr.**

**1290** A354 350 l red, ocher & pur .55 .25

***Perf. 14x13½***

**Engr. Unwmk.**

**1291** A674 1500 l multi 2.25 .25
**1292** A674 2000 l multi 3.00 .25
**1293** A674 3000 l multi 4.00 .25
**1294** A674 4000 l multi 5.75 .25
**1295** A674 5000 l multi 8.00 .65
**1296** A674 10,000 l multi 14.00 2.00
**1297** A674 20,000 l multi 30.00 12.00
*Nos. 1288-1297 (10)* 68.05 16.40

Issued: 120 l, 170 l, 350l, 11/22/77; 5,000 l, 12/4/78; 4,000 l, 2/12/79; 3,000 l, 3/12/79; 2,000 l, 4/12/79; 1,500 l, 5/14/79; 10,000 l, 6/27/83; 20,000 l, 1/5/87.

Dina Galli (1877-1951), Actress — A675

***Perf. 13½x14***

**1977, Dec. 2 Photo. Unwmk.**

**1309** A675 170 l multi .25 .25

Adoration of the Shepherds, by Pietro Testa — A676

Christmas: 120 l, Adoration of the Shepherds, by Gian Jacopo Caraglio.

**Lithographed and Engraved**

**1977, Dec. 13 *Perf. 14***

**1310** A676 70 l blk & ol .25 .25
**1311** A676 120 l blk & bl grn .25 .25

La Scala Opera House, Milan, Bicent. — A677

Designs: 170 l, Facade. 200 l, Auditorium.

**1978, Mar. 15 Litho. *Perf. 13½x14***

**1312** A677 170 l multi .25 .25
**1313** A677 200 l multi .30 .25

**Tourist Type of 1974**

Paintings: 70 l, Gubbio. 200 l, Udine. 600 l, Paestum.

**1978, Mar. 30 Photo. *Perf. 14***

**1314** A616 70 l multi .25 .25
**1315** A616 200 l multi .30 .25
**1316** A616 600 l multi .75 .45
*Nos. 1314-1316 (3)* 1.30 .95

Giant Grouper A678

Designs (outline of "Amerigo Vespucci" in background): No. 1318, Leatherback turtle. No. 1319, Mediterranean monk seal. No. 1320, Audouin's gull.

**1978, Apr. 3 *Perf. 14x13***

**1317** A678 170 l multi .40 .25
**1318** A678 170 l multi .40 .25
**1319** A678 170 l multi .40 .25
**1320** A678 170 l multi .40 .25
*a.* Strip of 4, #1317-1320 + label 1.60 1.00

Endangered species in Mediterranean.

Castel Nuovo, Angevin Fortifications, Naples — A679

Europa: 200 l, Pantheon, Rome.

**1978, Apr. 29 Litho. *Perf. 14x13½***

**1321** A679 170 l multi *.45* .25
**1322** A679 200 l multi *.55* .25

**Ship Type of 1977**

Designs: No. 1323, Cruiser Benedetto Brin. No. 1324, Frigate Lupo. No. 1325, Ligurian brigantine Fortuna. No. 1326, Container ship Africa.

**1978, May 8 Litho. & Engr.**

**1323** 170 l multi .50 .25
**1324** 170 l multi .50 .25
**1325** 170 l multi .50 .25
**1326** 170 l multi .50 .25
*a.* A670 Block of 4, #1323-1326 + 2 labels 2.00 .75

Matilde Serao — A680

Designs: Portraits of famous Italians.

**1978, May 10 Engr. *Perf. 14x13½***

**1327** A680 170 l shown .25 .25
**1328** A680 170 l Vittorino da Feltre .25 .25
**1329** A680 170 l Victor Emmanuel II .25 .25
**1330** A680 170 l Pope Pius IX .25 .25
**1331** A680 170 l Marcello Malpighi .25 .25
**1332** A680 170 l Antonio Meucci .25 .25
*a.* Block of 6, #1327-1332 1.50 .75

Constitution, 30th Anniv. — A681

**1978, June 2 Litho. *Perf. 13½x14***

**1333** A681 170 l multi .25 .25

Telegraph Wires and Lens — A682

**1978, June 30 Photo.**

**1334** A682 120 l lt bl & gray .25 .25

Photographic information.

The Lovers, by Tranquillo Cremona (1837-1878) — A683

Design: 520 l, The Cook (woman with goose), by Bernardo Strozzi (1581-1644).

**Engraved and Lithographed**

**1978, July 12 *Perf. 14***

**1335** A683 170 l multi .50 .25
**1336** A683 520 l multi 2.00 .75

Holy Shroud of Turin, by Giovanni Testa, 1578 — A684

**1978, Sept. 8 Photo. *Perf. 14***

**1337** A684 220 l yel, red & blk .45 .25

400th anniversary of the transfer of the Holy Shroud from Savoy to Turin.

Volleyball — A685

Design: 120 l, Volleyball, diff.

**1978, Sept. 20**

**1338** A685 80 l multi .45 .25
**1339** A685 120 l multi .45 .25

Men's Volleyball World Championship.

Mother and Child, by Masaccio — A686

**1978, Oct. 18 Engr. *Perf. 13½x14***

**1340** A686 170 l indigo .25 .25

Masaccio (real name Tommaso Guidi; 1401-28), painter.

**Fountain Type of 1973**

Designs: No 1341, Neptune Fountain, Trent. No. 1342, Fortuna Fountain, Fano. No. 1343, Cavallina Fountain, Genzano di Lucania.

**1978, Oct. 25 Litho. & Engr.**

**1341** A603 120 l blk & multi .25 .25
**1342** A603 120 l blk & multi .25 .25
**1343** A603 120 l blk & multi .25 .25
*Nos. 1341-1343 (3)* .75 .75

Virgin and Child, by Giorgione — A687

Adoration of the Kings, by Giorgione — A688

**1978, Nov. 8 Engr. *Perf. 13x14***

| | | | | | |
|---|---|---|---|---|---|
| **1344** | A687 | 80 l | dark red | .25 | .25 |

**Photo. *Perf. 14x13½***

| | | | | | |
|---|---|---|---|---|---|
| **1345** | A688 | 120 l | multi | .25 | .25 |

Christmas 1978.

Flags as Flowers — A689

Designs: No. 1347, European flags. No. 1348, "People hailing Europe."

**1978, Nov. 26 Photo. *Perf. 13x14***

| | | | | | |
|---|---|---|---|---|---|
| **1346** | A689 | 120 l | multi | .25 | .25 |
| **1347** | A689 | 120 l | multi | .25 | .25 |
| **1348** | A689 | 120 l | multi | .25 | .25 |
| | | | *Nos. 1346-1348 (3)* | .75 | .75 |

20th Stamp Day on theme "United Europe."

State Printing Office, Stamps A690

Design: 220 l, Printing press and stamps.

**1979, Jan. 6 Photo. *Perf. 14x13½***

| | | | | | |
|---|---|---|---|---|---|
| **1349** | A690 | 170 l | multi | .25 | .25 |
| **1350** | A690 | 220 l | multi | .35 | .25 |

1st stamps printed by State Printing Office, 50 anniv.

St. Francis Washing Lepers, 13th Century Painting A691

**1979, Jan. 22**

| | | | | | |
|---|---|---|---|---|---|
| **1351** | A691 | 80 l | multi | .25 | .25 |

Leprosy relief.

Bicyclist Carrying Bike — A692

**1979, Jan. 27 *Perf. 13½x14***

| | | | | | |
|---|---|---|---|---|---|
| **1352** | A692 | 170 l | multi | .25 | .25 |
| **1353** | A692 | 220 l | multi | .35 | .25 |

World Crosscountry Bicycle Championships.

Virgin Mary, by Antonello da Messina A693

Painting: 520 l, Haystack, by Ardengo Soffici (1879-1964).

**1979, Feb. 15 Engr. *Perf. 14***

| | | | | | |
|---|---|---|---|---|---|
| **1354** | A693 | 170 l | multi | .30 | .25 |
| **1355** | A693 | 520 l | multi | .70 | .70 |

Albert Einstein (1879-1955), Theoretical Physicist and His Equation. — A694

**Lithographed and Engraved**

**1979, Mar. 14 *Perf. 13x14***

| | | | | | |
|---|---|---|---|---|---|
| **1356** | A694 | 120 l | multi | .25 | .25 |

**Tourist Type of 1974**

Paintings: 70 l, Asiago. 90 l, Castelsardo. 170 l, Orvieto. 220 l, Scilla.

**1979, Mar. 30 Photo. *Perf. 14***

| | | | | | |
|---|---|---|---|---|---|
| **1357** | A616 | 70 l | grn & multi | .25 | .25 |
| **1358** | A616 | 90 l | car & multi | .25 | .25 |
| **1359** | A616 | 170 l | ultra & multi | .25 | .25 |
| **1360** | A616 | 220 l | gray & multi | .35 | .25 |
| | | | *Nos. 1357-1360 (4)* | 1.10 | 1.00 |

Famous Italians — A695

No. 1361, Carlo Maderno (1556-1629), architect. No. 1362, Lazzaro Spallanzani (1729-1799), physiologist. No. 1363, Ugo Foscolo (1778-1827), writer. No. 1364 Massimo Bontempelli (1878-1960), journalist. No. 1365, Francesco Severi (1879-1961), mathematician.

**1979, Apr. 23 Engr. *Perf. 14x13½***

| | | | | | |
|---|---|---|---|---|---|
| **1361** | A695 | 170 l | multi | .25 | .25 |
| **1362** | A695 | 170 l | multi | .25 | .25 |
| **1363** | A695 | 170 l | multi | .25 | .25 |
| **1364** | A695 | 170 l | multi | .25 | .25 |
| **1365** | A695 | 170 l | multi | .25 | .25 |
| | | | *Nos. 1361-1365 (5)* | 1.25 | 1.25 |

Telegraph A696

Europa: 220 l, Carrier pigeons.

**1979, Apr. 30 Photo. *Perf. 14***

| | | | | | |
|---|---|---|---|---|---|
| **1366** | A696 | 170 l | multi | .65 | .25 |
| **1367** | A696 | 220 l | multi | .65 | .30 |

Flags and "E" — A697

**1979, May 5 *Perf. 14x13½***

| | | | | | |
|---|---|---|---|---|---|
| **1368** | A697 | 170 l | multi | .25 | .25 |
| **1369** | A697 | 220 l | multi | .35 | .25 |

European Parliament, first direct elections, June 7-10.

Exhibition Emblem, Dome of Milan A698

**1979, June 22 Photo. *Perf. 14***

| | | | | | |
|---|---|---|---|---|---|
| **1370** | A698 | 170 l | multi | .25 | .25 |
| **1371** | A698 | 220 l | multi | .35 | .25 |

3rd World Machine Tool Exhib., Milan, Oct. 10-18.

Aeneas and Rotary Emblem — A699

**1979, June 9 *Perf. 13½x14***

| | | | | | |
|---|---|---|---|---|---|
| **1372** | A699 | 220 l | multi | .35 | .25 |

70th World Rotary Cong., Rome, June 1979.

Basket — A700

**1979, June 13 *Perf. 14***

| | | | | | |
|---|---|---|---|---|---|
| **1373** | A700 | 80 l | shown | .25 | .25 |
| **1374** | A700 | 120 l | Basketball players | .30 | .25 |

21st European Basketball Championship, June 9-20.

A701

Patient & Physician, 16th cent. woodcut.

**1979, June 16 Photo. & Engr.**

| | | | | | |
|---|---|---|---|---|---|
| **1375** | A701 | 120 l | multi | .25 | .25 |

Digestive Ailments Study Week.

A702

Design: Ottorino Respighi (1879-1936), composer, Roman landscape.

**Lithographed and Engraved**

**1979, July 9 *Perf. 13x14***

| | | | | | |
|---|---|---|---|---|---|
| **1376** | A702 | 120 l | multi | .25 | .25 |

Woman Making Phone Call A703

200 l, Woman with old-fashioned phone.

**1979, Sept. 20 Photo. *Perf. 14***

| | | | | | |
|---|---|---|---|---|---|
| **1377** | A703 | 170 l | red & gray | .25 | .25 |
| **1378** | A703 | 220 l | grn & slate | .35 | .25 |

3rd World Telecommunications Exhibition, Geneva, Sept. 20-26.

**Fountain Type of 1973**

Designs: No. 1379, Great Fountain, Viterbo. No. 1380, Hot Springs, Acqui Terme. No. 1381, Pomegranate Fountain, Issogne Castle.

**Lithographed and Engraved**

**1979, Sept. 22 *Perf. 13x14***

| | | | | | |
|---|---|---|---|---|---|
| **1379** | A603 | 120 l | multi | .30 | .25 |
| **1380** | A603 | 120 l | multi | .30 | .25 |
| **1381** | A603 | 120 l | multi | .30 | .25 |
| | | | *Nos. 1379-1381 (3)* | .90 | .75 |

**Ship Type of 1977**

Designs: No. 1382, Cruiser Enrico Dandolo. No. 1383, Submarine Carlo Fecia. No. 1384, Freighter Cosmos. No. 1385, Ferry Deledda.

**1979, Oct. 12 *Perf. 14x13½***

| | | | | |
|---|---|---|---|---|
| **1382** | 170 l | multi | .30 | .25 |
| **1383** | 170 l | multi | .30 | .25 |
| **1384** | 170 l | multi | .30 | .25 |
| **1385** | 170 l | multi | .30 | .25 |
| ***a.*** | | A670 Block of 4, #1382-1385 + 2 labels | 1.60 | .75 |

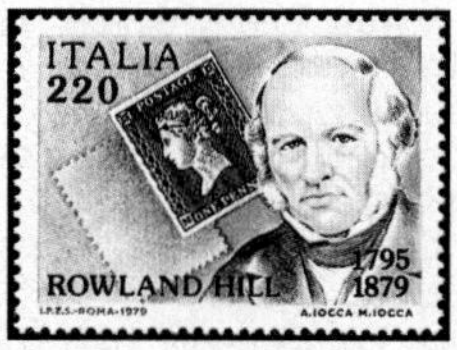


Penny Black, Rowland Hill A704

**1979, Oct. 25 Photo.**

| | | | | | |
|---|---|---|---|---|---|
| **1386** | A704 | 220 l | multi | .35 | .25 |

Minstrels and Church A705

**1979, Nov. 7 Photo. *Perf. 14x13½***

| | | | | | |
|---|---|---|---|---|---|
| **1387** | A705 | 120 l | multi | .25 | .25 |

Christmas 1979.

Black and White Boys Holding Hands A706

Children's Drawings: 120 l, Children of various races under umbrella map, vert. 150 l, Children and red balloons.

***Perf. 14x13½, 13½x14***

| **1979, Nov. 25** | | **Photo.** | |
|---|---|---|---|
| **1388** A706 | 70 l multi | .25 | .25 |
| **1389** A706 | 120 l multi | .25 | .25 |
| **1390** A706 | 150 l multi | .25 | .25 |
| | *Nos. 1388-1390 (3)* | .75 | .75 |

21st Stamp Day.

Solar Energy Panels A707

Energy Conservation: 170 l, Sun & pylon.

| **1980, Feb. 25** | **Photo.** | ***Perf. 14x13½*** | |
|---|---|---|---|
| **1391** A707 | 120 l multi | .25 | .25 |
| **1392** A707 | 170 l multi | .25 | .25 |

St. Benedict of Nursia, 1500th Birth Anniv. — A708

| **1980, Mar. 21** | **Engr.** | ***Perf. 13½x14*** | |
|---|---|---|---|
| **1393** A708 | 220 l dark blue | .35 | .25 |

Royal Palace, Naples — A709

**Lithographed and Engraved**

| **1980, Apr. 16** | | ***Perf. 13½x14*** | |
|---|---|---|---|
| **1394** A709 | 220 l multi | .35 | .25 |

20th International Philatelic Exhibition, Europa '80, Naples, Apr. 26-May 4.

Antonio Pigafetta, Caravel A710

Europa: 220 l, Antonio Lo Surdo (1880-1949) geophysicist.

| **1980, Apr. 28** | **Litho.** | ***Perf. 14x13½*** | |
|---|---|---|---|
| **1395** A710 | 170 l multi | *.40* | .25 |
| **1396** A710 | 220 l multi | *.70* | .30 |

St. Catherine, Reliquary Bust — A711

| **1980, Apr. 29** | | **Photo.** | |
|---|---|---|---|
| **1397** A711 | 170 l multi | .25 | .25 |

St. Catherine of Siena (1347-1380).

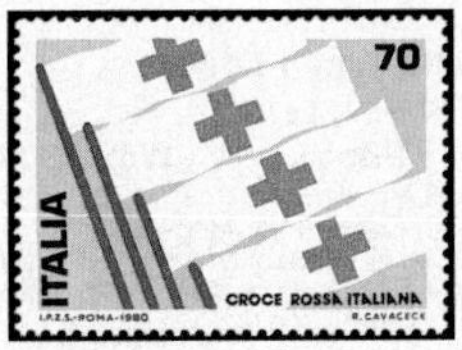


Italian Red Cross A712

| **1980, May 15** | **Photo.** | ***Perf. 14x13½*** | |
|---|---|---|---|
| **1398** A712 | 70 l multi | .25 | .25 |
| **1399** A712 | 80 l multi | .25 | .25 |

Temples of Philae, Egypt — A713

| **1980, May 20** | | | |
|---|---|---|---|
| **1400** | Pair + label | .70 | .25 |
| *a.* | A713 220 l shown | .35 | .25 |
| *b.* | A713 220 l Temple of Philae, diff. | .35 | .25 |

Italian civil engineering achievements (Temples of Philae saved from ruin by Italian engineers).

Soccer Player A714

| **1980, June 11** | | | |
|---|---|---|---|
| **1401** A714 | 80 l multi | 2.00 | 1.25 |

European Soccer Championships, Milan, Turin, Rome, Naples, June 9-22.

**Tourist Type of 1974**

Paintings: 80 l, Erice. 150 l, Villa Rufolo, Ravello. 200 l, Roseto degli Abruzzi. 670 l, Public Baths, Salsomaggiore Terme.

| **1980, June 28** | | ***Perf. 14*** | |
|---|---|---|---|
| **1402** A616 | 80 l multi | .25 | .25 |
| **1403** A616 | 150 l multi | .30 | .25 |
| **1404** A616 | 200 l multi | .35 | .25 |
| **1405** A616 | 670 l multi | .95 | .95 |
| | *Nos. 1402-1405 (4)* | 1.85 | 1.70 |

Cosimo I with his Artists, by Giorgio Vasari, and Armillary sphere — A715

| **1980, July 2** | | ***Perf. 13½x14*** | |
|---|---|---|---|
| **1406** A715 | Pair + label | .50 | .50 |
| *a.* | 170 l Cosimo I | .25 | .25 |
| *b.* | 170 l Armillary sphere | .25 | .25 |

The Medici in Europe of the 16th Century Exhibition, Florence.

Fonte Avellana Monastery Millennium A716

| **1980, Sept. 3** | **Engr.** | ***Perf. 14x13½*** | |
|---|---|---|---|
| **1407** A716 | 200 l grn & brn | .30 | .25 |

Castles — A717

Designs: No. 1408, St. Angelo Castle, Rome. No. 1409, Sforzesco, Milan. No. 1410, Del Monte, Andria. No. 1411, Ursino, Catania. No. 1412, Rocca di Calascio. No. 1413, Norman Tower, St. Mauro Fort. No. 1414, Isola Capo Rizzuto. No. 1415, Aragonese, Ischia. No. 1416, Estense, Ferrarra. No. 1417, Miramare, Trieste. No. 1418, Ostia, Rome. No. 1419, Gavarone, Savona. No. 1420, Cerro al Volturno, Isernia. No. 1421, Rocca di Mondavio. No. 1422, Svevo, Bari. No. 1423, Mussomelli, Caltanissetta. No. 1424, Imperatore-Prato, Florence. No. 1425, Bosa, Nuoro. No. 1426, Rovereto, Trento. No. 1427, Scaligero, Sirmione. No. 1428, Ivrea, Turin. No. 1429, Rocca Maggiore, Assisi. No. 1430, St. Pierre, Aosta. No. 1431 Montagnana, Padua. No. 1432, St. Severna, Rome. No. 1433, Lombardia, Enna. No. 1434, Serralunga d'Alba, Cuneo.

**Photo. (#1408-1417), Litho. and Engr. (#1418-1422, 1425, 1427-1428), Engr. (#1423-1424, 1426, 1429-1434)**

***Perf. 14x13½***

| **1980, Sept. 22** | | **Wmk. 303** | |
|---|---|---|---|
| **1408** A717 | 5 l multi | .25 | .25 |
| **1409** A717 | 10 l multi | .25 | .25 |
| **1410** A717 | 20 l multi | .25 | .25 |
| **1411** A717 | 40 l multi | .25 | .25 |
| **1412** A717 | 50 l multi | .25 | .25 |
| **1413** A717 | 60 l multi | .25 | .25 |
| **1414** A717 | 90 l multi | .25 | .25 |
| **1415** A717 | 100 l multi | .25 | .25 |
| **1416** A717 | 120 l multi | .25 | .25 |
| **1417** A717 | 150 l multi | .25 | .25 |
| **1418** A717 | 170 l multi | .25 | .25 |
| **1419** A717 | 180 l multi | .75 | *1.00* |
| **1420** A717 | 200 l multi | .30 | .25 |
| **1421** A717 | 250 l multi | .35 | .25 |
| **1422** A717 | 300 l multi | .40 | .25 |
| **1423** A717 | 350 l multi | .45 | .25 |
| **1424** A717 | 400 l multi | .55 | .25 |
| **1425** A717 | 450 l multi | .60 | .25 |
| **1426** A717 | 500 l multi | .70 | .25 |
| **1427** A717 | 600 l multi | .90 | .25 |
| **1428** A717 | 700 l multi | 1.00 | .25 |
| **1429** A717 | 800 l multi | 1.10 | .25 |
| **1430** A717 | 900 l multi | 1.25 | .25 |
| **1431** A717 | 1000 l multi | 1.40 | .25 |
| | *Nos. 1408-1431 (24)* | 12.50 | 6.75 |

**Coil Stamps**
***Perf. 14 Vert.***

**Size: 16x21mm**

| | | | |
|---|---|---|---|
| **1432** A717 | 30 l multi | .25 | .25 |
| **1433** A717 | 120 l multi | .25 | .25 |
| *a.* | Pair, Nos. 1432-1433 | .40 | .25 |
| **1434** A717 | 170 l multi | .30 | .25 |
| *a.* | Pair, Nos. 1432, 1434 | .75 | .75 |
| | *Nos. 1432-1434 (3)* | .80 | .75 |

No. 1412 exists dated "1980."

See Nos. 1475-1484, 1657-1666, 1862-1866.

**Ship Type of 1977**

#1435, Corvette Gabbiano. #1436, Torpedo boat Audace. #1437, Sailing ship Italia. #1438, Floating dock Castoro Sei.

**Lithographed and Engraved**

| **1980, Oct. 11** | | ***Perf. 14x13½*** | |
|---|---|---|---|
| **1435** | 200 l multi | *1.25* | .40 |
| **1436** | 200 l multi | *1.25* | .40 |
| **1437** | 200 l multi | *1.25* | .40 |
| **1438** | 200 l multi | *1.25* | .40 |
| *a.* | A670 Block of 4, #1435-1438 + 2 labels | *7.00* | 7.00 |

Philip Mazzei (1730-1816), Political Writer in US — A718

| **1980, Oct. 18** | **Photo.** | ***Perf. 13½x14*** | |
|---|---|---|---|
| **1439** A718 | 320 l multi | .50 | .30 |

Villa Foscari Malcontenta, Venezia — A719

Villas: 150 l, Barbaro Maser, Treviso. 170 l, Godi Valmarana, Vicenza.

**Lithographed and Engraved**

| **1980, Oct. 31** | | ***Perf. 14x13½*** | |
|---|---|---|---|
| **1440** A719 | 80 l multi | .40 | .40 |
| **1441** A719 | 150 l multi | .50 | .25 |
| **1442** A719 | 170 l multi | .60 | .25 |
| | *Nos. 1440-1442 (3)* | 1.50 | .90 |

See Nos. 1493-1495, 1528-1530, 1565-1568, 1606-1609, 1646-1649, 1691-1695.

St. Barbara, by Palma the Elder (1480-1528) — A720

Design: No. 1444, Apollo and Daphne, by Gian Lorenzo Bernini (1598-1680).

| **1980, Nov. 20** | | ***Perf. 14*** | |
|---|---|---|---|
| **1443** A720 | 520 l multi | .80 | .55 |
| **1444** A720 | 520 l multi | .80 | .55 |

Nativity Sculpture by Federico Brandini, 16th Cent. — A721

| **1980, Nov. 22** | | **Engr.** | |
|---|---|---|---|
| **1445** A721 | 120 l brn org & blk | .25 | .25 |

Christmas 1980.

View of Verona A722

22nd Stamp Day: Views of Verona drawings by school children.

**1980, Nov. 30 Photo. *Perf. 14x13½***

**1446** A722 70 l multi .25 .25
**1447** A722 120 l multi .25 .25
**1448** A722 170 l multi .25 .25
*Nos. 1446-1448 (3)* .75 .75

Daniele Comboni (1831-1881), Savior of the Africans — A723

**1981, Mar. 14 Engr.**

**1449** A723 80 l multi .25 .25

Alcide de Gasperi (1881-1954), Statesman A724

**1981, Apr. 3 *Perf. 13½x14***

**1450** A724 200 l olive green .30 .25

International Year of the Disabled — A725

**1981, Apr. 11 Photo.**

**1451** A725 300 l multi .45 .35

A726

**1981, Apr. 27 Photo. *Perf. 13½x14***

**1452** A726 200 l Roses .35 .30
**1453** A726 200 l Anemones .35 .30
**1454** A726 200 l Oleanders .35 .30
*Nos. 1452-1454 (3)* 1.05 .90

See Nos. 1510-1512, 1555-1557.

Europa — A727

Designs: No. 1455, Chess game with human pieces, Marostica. No. 1456, Horse race, Siena.

**1981, May 4**

**1455** A727 300 l shown *1.00* .40
**1456** A727 300 l multicolored *1.00* .40

St. Rita Offering Thorn — A728

**1981, May 22**

**1457** A728 600 l multi .85 .40

St. Rita of Cascia, 600th birth anniversary.

Ciro Menotti (1798-1831), Patriot — A729

**1981, May 26 Engr. *Perf. 14x13½***

**1458** A729 80 l brn & blk .25 .25

G-222 Aeritalia Transport Plane — A730

**1981, June 1 Photo.**

**1459** 200 l shown .30 .30
**1460** 200 l MB-339 Aermacchi jet .30 .30
**1461** 200 l A-109 Agusta helicopter .30 .30
**1462** 200 l P-68 Partenavia transport plane .30 .30
*a.* A730 Block of 4, #1459-1462 + 2 labels 1.50 1.50

See Nos. 1505-1508, 1550-1553.

Hydro-geological Research — A731

**1981, June 8 *Perf. 13½x14***

**1463** A731 80 l multi .25 .25

Sao Simao Dam and Power Station, Brazil — A732

Civil Engineering Works Abroad: No. 1465, High Island Reservoir, Hong Kong.

**1981, June 26 Engr. *Perf. 14x13½***

**1464** A732 300 l dark blue .45 .25
**1465** A732 300 l red .45 .25
*a.* Pair, #1464-1465 + label 1.05 .35

See Nos. 1516-1517, 1538-1539.

**Tourist Type of 1974**

**1981, July 4 Photo. *Perf. 14***

**1466** A616 80 l View of Matera .25 .25
**1467** A616 150 l Lake Garda .35 1.10
**1468** A616 300 l St. Teresa di Gallura beach .50 .50
**1469** A616 900 l Tarquinia 1.75 .55
*Nos. 1466-1469 (4)* 2.85 2.40

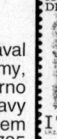

Naval Academy, Livorno and Navy Emblem A735

Naval Academy of Livorno Centenary: 150 l, View. 200 l, Cadet with sextant, training ship Amerigo Vespucci.

**1981, July 24 *Perf. 14x13½***

**1472** A735 80 l multi .25 .25
**1473** A735 150 l multi .25 .25
**1474** A735 200 l multi .30 .25
*Nos. 1472-1474 (3)* .80 .75

**Castle Type of 1980**

***Perf. 14x13½***

**1981-84 Photo. Wmk. 303**

**1475** A717 30 l Aquila .25 .25
**1476** A717 70 l Aragonese, Reggio Calabria .25 .25
**1477** A717 80 l Sabbionara, Avio .25 .25

***Perf. 13½***

**1478** A717 550 l Rocca Sinibalda .90 .25

**Engr.**

**1479** A717 1400 l Caldoresco, Vasto 2.00 .50
*Nos. 1475-1479 (5)* 3.65 1.50

Issue dates: Nos. 1475-1477, Aug. 20, 1981; Nos. 1478-1479, Feb. 14, 1984.

**Coil Stamps**

**1981-88 Engr. *Perf. 14 Vert.***

**Size: 16x21mm**

**1480** A717 50 l Scilla .25 .25
**1481** A717 200 l Angionia, Lucera *2.75 2.00*
**1482** A717 300 l Norman Castle, Melfi .60 .25
**1483** A717 400 l Venafro .65 .25
**1484** A717 450 l Piobbico Pesaro .75 .25
*a.* Pair, #1480, 1484 1.00 .50
*Nos. 1480-1484 (5)* *5.00 3.00*

Issued: #1481-1482, 9/30; #1483, 6/25/83; #1480, 1484, 7/25/85; #1484a, 3/1/88.

Palazzo Spada, Rome (Council Seat) A736

**1981, Aug. 31 Engr. Unwmk.**

**1485** A736 200 l multi .30 .25

State Council sesquicentennial.

World Cup Races — A737

**1981, Sept. 4 Photo. *Perf. 13½x14***

**1486** A737 300 l multi .50 .35

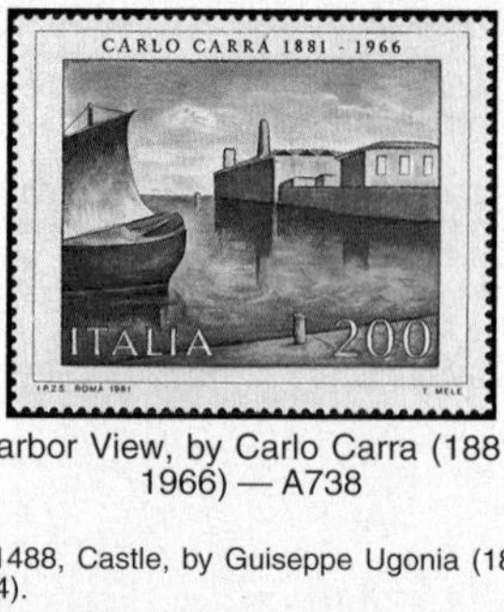


Harbor View, by Carlo Carra (1881-1966) — A738

#1488, Castle, by Guiseppe Ugonia (1881-1944).

**Lithographed and Engraved**

**1981, Sept. 7 *Perf. 14***

**1487** A738 200 l multi .30 .25
**1488** A738 200 l multi .30 .25

See #1532-1533, 1638-1639, 1697-1698, 1732.

Riace Bronze, 4th Cent. B.C. — A739

**1981, Sept. 9 Photo. *Perf. 13½x14***

**1489** 200 l Statue .30 .25
**1490** 200 l Statue, diff. .30 .25
*a.* A739 Pair, #1489-1490 .65 .30

Greek statues found in 1972 in sea near Reggio di Calabria.

Virgil, Mosaic, Treviri A740

**1981, Sept. 19 *Perf. 14***

**1491** A740 600 l multi .75 .50

Virgil's death bimillennium.

Food and Wine, by Gregorio Sciltian A741

**1981, Oct. 16 Litho. *Perf. 14***

**1492** A741 150 l multi .40 .25

World Food Day.

**Villa Type of 1980**

**Lithographed and Engraved**

**1981, Oct. 17 *Perf. 14x13½***

**1493** A719 100 l Villa Campolieto, Ercolano .25 .25
**1494** A719 200 l Cimbrone, Ravello .30 .25
**1495** A719 300 l Pignatelli, Naples .50 .50
*Nos. 1493-1495 (3)* 1.05 1.00

Adoration of the Magi, by Giovanni de Campione d'Italia (Christmas 1981) — A743

**1981, Nov. 21 Engr. *Perf. 14***

| | | | |
|---|---|---|---|
| **1496** | A743 200 l multi | .35 | .25 |

Pope John XXIII (1881-1963) A744

**1981, Nov. 25 Photo. *Perf. 13½x14***

| | | | |
|---|---|---|---|
| **1497** | A744 200 l multi | .30 | .25 |

Stamp Day — A745

**Photogravure, Photogravure and Engraved (200 l)**

***Perf. 14x13½, 13½x14***

**1981, Nov. 29**

| | | | |
|---|---|---|---|
| **1498** | A745 120 l Letters, horiz. | .25 | .25 |
| **1499** | A745 200 l Angel, letter chest | .50 | .55 |
| **1500** | A745 300 l Letter seal | .65 | .30 |
| | *Nos. 1498-1500 (3)* | 1.40 | 1.10 |

St. Francis of Assisi, 800th Birth Anniv. — A746

Design: St. Francis Receiving the Stigmata, by Pietro Cavaro.

**1982, Jan. 6 *Perf. 13½x14***

| | | | |
|---|---|---|---|
| **1501** | A746 300 l dk bl & brn | .50 | .30 |

Niccolo Paganini (1782-1840), Composer, Violinist — A748

**1982, Feb. 19 Photo. *Perf. 13½x14***

| | | | |
|---|---|---|---|
| **1503** | A748 900 l multi | 1.25 | 1.25 |

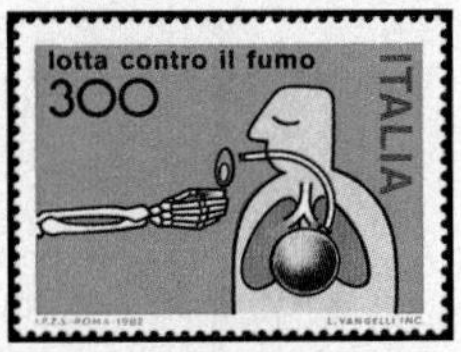


Anti-smoking Campaign — A749

**1982, Mar. 2 Photo. *Perf. 14x13½***

| | | | |
|---|---|---|---|
| **1504** | A749 300 l multi | .40 | .30 |

**Aircraft Type of 1981**

**1982, Mar. 27 Litho. *Perf. 14x13½***

| | | | |
|---|---|---|---|
| **1505** | 300 l Aeritalia MRCA | .55 | .55 |
| **1506** | 300 l SIAI 260 Turbo | .55 | .55 |
| **1507** | 300 l Piaggio 166-dl3 Turbo | .55 | .55 |
| **1508** | 300 l Nardi NH-500 | .55 | .55 |
| *a.* | A730 Block of 4, #1505-1508 + 2 labels | 4.50 | |

Sicilian Vespers, 700th Anniv. — A750

**1982, Mar. 31 Engr. *Perf. 13½x14***

| | | | |
|---|---|---|---|
| **1509** | A750 120 l multi | .25 | .25 |

**Flower Type of 1981**

**1982, Apr. 10 Photo.**

| | | | |
|---|---|---|---|
| **1510** | A726 300 l Cyclamens | .65 | .50 |
| **1511** | A726 300 l Camellias | .65 | .50 |
| **1512** | A726 300 l Carnations | .65 | .50 |
| | *Nos. 1510-1512 (3)* | 1.95 | 1.50 |

Europa — A751

**Photogravure and Engraved**

**1982, May 3 *Perf. 13½x14***

| | | | |
|---|---|---|---|
| **1513** | A751 200 l Coronation of Charlemagne, 799 | *.85* | .45 |
| **1514** | A751 450 l Treaty of Rome signatures, 1957 | *1.00* | .55 |

**Engineering Type of 1981**

**1982, May 29 Photo. *Perf. 14x13½***

| | | | |
|---|---|---|---|
| **1516** | A732 450 l Microwaves across Red Sea | .75 | .30 |
| **1517** | A732 450 l Automatic letter sorting | .75 | .30 |
| *a.* | Pair, #1516-1517 + label | 1.50 | 1.50 |

Giuseppe Garibaldi (1807-82) A753

**1982, June 2 *Perf. 13½x14***

| | | | |
|---|---|---|---|
| **1518** | A753 200 l multi | .60 | .60 |

Game of the Bridge, Pisa — A754

**1982, June 5**

| | | | |
|---|---|---|---|
| **1519** | A754 200 l multi | .35 | .35 |

See Nos. 1562, 1603, 1628-1629, 1655, 1717, 1749, 1775, 1807.

**Tourist Type of 1974**

**1982, June 28 *Perf. 14***

| | | | |
|---|---|---|---|
| **1520** | A616 200 l Frasassi Caves | .55 | .90 |
| **1521** | A616 200 l Paganella Valley | .55 | .90 |
| **1522** | A616 450 l Temple of Agrigento | .75 | .35 |
| **1523** | A616 450 l Rodi Garganico Beach | .75 | .35 |
| | *Nos. 1520-1523 (4)* | 2.60 | 2.50 |

World Junior Canoeing Championship — A755

**1982, Aug. 4 Photo. *Perf. 14***

| | | | |
|---|---|---|---|
| **1524** | A755 200 l multi | .45 | .45 |

Duke Federico da Montefeltro (1422-1482) — A756

**Photogravure and Engraved**

**1982, Sept. 10 *Perf. 14x13½***

| | | | |
|---|---|---|---|
| **1525** | A756 200 l Urbino Palace, Gubbio Council House | .30 | .30 |

Italy's Victory in 1982 World Cup A757

**1982, Sept. 12 Photo. *Perf. 14***

| | | | |
|---|---|---|---|
| **1526** | A757 1000 l World Cup | 2.00 | 1.75 |

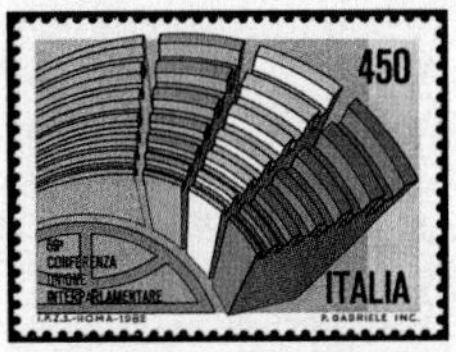


69th Inter-Parliamentary Conference, Rome — A758

**1982, Sept. 14 *Perf. 14x13½***

| | | | |
|---|---|---|---|
| **1527** | A758 450 l multi | .55 | .30 |

**Villa Type of 1980**

Designs: 150 l, Temple of Aesculapius, Villa Borghese, Rome. 250 l, Villa D'Este, Tivoli, Rome. 350 l, Villa Lante, Bagnaia, Viterbo.

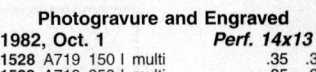

**Photogravure and Engraved**

**1982, Oct. 1 *Perf. 14x13½***

| | | | |
|---|---|---|---|
| **1528** | A719 150 l multi | .35 | .35 |
| **1529** | A719 250 l multi | .85 | .25 |
| **1530** | A719 350 l multi | 1.25 | 1.10 |
| | *Nos. 1528-1530 (3)* | 2.45 | 1.70 |

Thurn and Taxis Family Postal Service — A759

**1982, Oct. 23 Engr. *Perf. 13½x14***

| | | | |
|---|---|---|---|
| **1531** | A759 300 l Franz von Taxis (1450-1517) | .40 | .25 |

**Art Type of 1981**

Paintings: No. 1532, The Fortune Teller by G.B. Piazzetta (1682-1754). No. 1533, Antonietta Negroni Prati Morosini as a Little Girl by Francesco Hayez (1791-1882).

**Lithographed and Engraved**

**1982, Nov. 3 *Perf. 14***

| | | | |
|---|---|---|---|
| **1532** | A738 300 l multi | .50 | .50 |
| **1533** | A738 300 l multi | .50 | .50 |

24th Stamp Day A761

Children's Drawings.

**1982, Nov. 28 Photo. *Perf. 14x13½***

| | | | |
|---|---|---|---|
| **1534** | A761 150 l multi | .35 | .35 |
| **1535** | A761 250 l multi | .50 | .35 |
| **1536** | A761 350 l multi | .65 | .65 |
| | *Nos. 1534-1536 (3)* | 1.50 | 1.35 |

Cancer Research — A762

**1983, Jan. 14 Photo. *Perf. 13½x14***

| | | | |
|---|---|---|---|
| **1537** | A762 400 l multi | .55 | .35 |

**Engineering Type of 1981**

**1983, Jan. 20 *Perf. 13½***

| | | | |
|---|---|---|---|
| **1538** | A732 400 l Globe, factories | .55 | .35 |
| **1539** | A732 400 l Automated assembly line | .55 | .35 |
| *a.* | Pair, #1538-1539 | 1.30 | 1.30 |

Crusca Academy, 400th Anniv. — A763

**1983, Jan. 25 Engr. *Perf. 14x13½***

| | | | |
|---|---|---|---|
| **1540** | A763 400 l Emblem | .55 | .35 |

World Biathlon Championship — A764

**1983, Feb. 5 Photo. *Perf. 14***

| | | | |
|---|---|---|---|
| **1541** | A764 200 l multi | .45 | .45 |

Gabriele Rossetti (1783-1854), Writer — A765

**1983, Feb. 28 Engr. *Perf. 14x13½***
**1542** A765 300 l dk brn & dk bl .40 .30

Francesco Guicciardini (1483-1540), Historian — A766

**1983, Mar. 5 Engr. *Perf. 13½x14***
**1543** A766 450 l sepia .60 .35

Umberto Saba (1883-1957), Poet — A767

**1983, Mar. 9 Photo. *Perf. 14x13½***
**1544** A767 600 l multi .75 .55

Pope Pius XII (1876-1958) A768

**1983, Mar. 21 Engr. *Perf. 13½x14***
**1545** A768 1400 l dark blue 2.00 .90

Holy Year — A769

**1983, Mar. 25 Photo. *Perf. 14***
**1546** A769 250 l St. Paul's Basilica .35 .35
**1547** A769 300 l St. Maria Maggiore Church .50 .25
**1548** A769 400 l San Giovanni Church .55 .25
**1549** A769 500 l St. Peter's Church .90 .25
*Nos. 1546-1549 (4)* 2.30 1.10

**Aircraft Type of 1981**

**1983, Mar. 28 Litho. *Perf. 14x13½***
**1550** 400 l Caproni C22J glider .50 .50
**1551** 400 l Aeritalia Macchi jet fighter .50 .50
**1552** 400 l SIAI-211 jet trainer .50 .50
**1553** 400 l A-129 Agusta helicopter .50 .50
*a.* A730 Block or strip of 4, #1550-1553 + 2 labels 2.75 2.75

Intl. Workers' Day (May 1) — A770

**1983, Apr. 29 Engr. *Perf. 14x13½***
**1554** A770 1200 l blue 1.50 .90

**Flower Type of 1981**

**1983, Apr. 30 Photo. *Perf. 13½x14***
**1555** A726 200 l Mimosa .65 .65
**1556** A726 200 l Rhododendron .65 .65
**1557** A726 200 l Gladiolus .65 .65
*Nos. 1555-1557 (3)* 1.95 1.95

Europa 1983 A771

**Litho. & Engr.**

**1983, May 2 *Perf. 14x13½***
**1558** A771 400 l Galileo, telescope, 160l *4.00 1.00*
**1559** A771 500 l Archimedes and his screw *4.00 .40*

Ernesto T. Moneta (1833-1918), Nobel Peace Prize Winner, 1907 — A772

**1983, May 5 Engr. *Perf. 14x13½***
**1560** A772 500 l multi .80 .35

Monument, Globe, Computer Screen A773

20th Natl. Eucharistic Congress A775

**1983, May 9 Photo. *Perf. 13½x14***
**1561** A773 500 l multi .80 .35

3rd Intl. Congress of Jurisdicial Information.

**Folk Celebration Type of 1982**

#1562, La Corsa Dei Ceri Procession, Gubbio.

**1983, May 13 *Perf. 13½***
**1562** A754 300 l multi .55 .35

**1983, May 14 *Perf. 14***
**1563** A775 300 l multi .40 .30

**Tourist Type of 1974**

**1983, July 30 Photo. *Perf. 14***
**1563A** A616 250 l Alghero .75 1.75
**1563B** A616 300 l Bardonecchia .75 .75
**1563C** A616 400 l Riccione .75 .35
**1563D** A616 500 l Taranto 1.25 .35
*Nos. 1563A-1563D (4)* 3.50 3.20

Girolamo Frescobaldi (1583-1643), Composer A776

**1983, Sept. 14 Engr. *Perf. 13½x14***
**1564** A776 400 l brn & grn .55 .30

**Villa Type of 1980**

Designs: 250 l, Fidelia, Spello. 300 l, Imperiale, Pesaro. 400 l, Michetti Convent, Francavilla al Mare. 500 l, Riccia.

**Photogravure and Engraved**

**1983, Oct. 10 *Perf. 14x13½***
**1565** A719 250 l multi .85 1.50
**1566** A719 300 l multi .65 .45
**1567** A719 400 l multi .90 .45
**1568** A719 500 l multi 1.25 .35
*Nos. 1565-1568 (4)* 3.65 2.75

Francesco de Sanctis (1817-1883), Writer — A777

**1983, Oct. 28 Photo.**
**1569** A777 300 l multi .40 .35

Christmas 1983 — A778

Raphael Paintings: 250 l, Madonna of the Chair. 400 l, Sistine Madonna. 500 l, Madonna of the Candelabra.

**1983, Nov. 10 *Perf. 13½x14***
**1570** A778 250 l multi .50 .35
**1571** A778 400 l multi .65 .25
**1572** A778 500 l multi .80 .30
*Nos. 1570-1572 (3)* 1.95 .90

25th Stamp Day, World Communications Year — A779

Children's Drawings. 200 l, 400 l horiz.

***Perf. 14x13½, 13½x14***
**1983, Nov. 27**
**1573** A779 200 l Letters holding hands .35 .35
**1574** A779 300 l Spaceman .60 .25
**1575** A779 400 l Flag train, globe .80 .30
*Nos. 1573-1575 (3)* 1.75 .90

Road Safety A780

***Perf. 13½x14, 14x13½***
**1984, Jan. 20 Photo.**
**1576** A780 300 l Bent road sign, vert. .55 .55
**1577** A780 400 l Accident .65 .55

Promenade in Bois de Boulogne, by Giuseppe de Nittis (1846-1884) — A781

Design: 400 l, Portrait of Paul Guillaume, 1916, by Amedeo Modigliani (1884-1920).

**Lithographed and Engraved**

**1984, Jan. 25 *Perf. 14***
**1578** A781 300 l multi .55 .45
**1579** A781 400 l multi .75 .65

Galaxy-Same Tractor — A782

Italian-made vehicles.

**1984, Mar. 10 Photo. *Perf. 14x13½***
**1580** A782 450 l shown .70 .70
**1581** A782 450 l Alfa-33 car .70 .70
**1582** A782 450 l Maserati Biturbo car .70 .70
**1583** A782 450 l Iveco 190-38 truck .70 .70
*a.* Block of 4, #1580-1583 + 2 labels 6.00 6.00

See Nos. 1620-1623, 1681-1684.

A783

**1984, Apr. 10**
**1584** A783 300 l Mosaic, furnace .50 .50
**1585** A783 300 l Glass Blower .50 .50
*a.* Pair, #1584-1585 + label 1.25 1.25

2nd European Parliament Elections — A784

**1984, Apr. 16**
**1586** A784 400 l Parliament Strasbourg .75 .75

Forest Preservation — A785

**1984, Apr. 24 Photo. *Perf. 14x13½***

**1587** A785 450 l Helicopter fire patrol .75 .75
**1588** A785 450 l Hedgehog, squirrel, badger .75 .75
**1589** A785 450 l Riverside waste dump .75 .75
**1590** A785 450 l Plant life, animals .75 .75
*a.* Block of 4, #1587-1590 10.00 10.00

Italia '85 A786

**1984, Apr. 26 *Perf. 14***

**1591** A786 450 l Ministry of Posts, Rome .80 .30
**1592** A786 550 l Via Appia Antiqua, Rome 1.00 .35

Rome Pacts, 40th Anniv. A787

Trade Unionists: Giuseppe di Vittorio, Bruno Buozzi, Achille Grandi.

**1984, Apr. 30 *Perf. 14x13½***

**1593** A787 450 l multi .75 .75

Europa (1959-84) A788

**1984, May 5**

**1594** A788 450 l multi *5.00* .90
**1595** A788 550 l multi *8.50* 3.25

Intl. Telecommunications Symposium, Florence, May — A789

**1984, May 7 *Perf. 14***

**1596** A789 550 l multi 1.10 .65

Italian Derby Centenary A790

**Lithographed and Engraved**

**1984, May 12 *Perf. 14x13½***

**1597** A790 250 l Racing 1.25 1.50
**1598** A790 400 l Racing, diff. 1.75 .75

**Tourist Type of 1974**

**1984, May 19 Photo. *Perf. 14***

**1599** A616 350 l Campione d'Italia 2.00 2.60
**1600** A616 400 l Chianciano Terme baths 1.50 .85
**1601** A616 450 l Padula 1.60 .75
**1602** A616 550 l Greek ampitheater, Syracuse 1.60 .90
*Nos. 1599-1602 (4)* 6.70 5.10

**Folk Celebration Type of 1982**

Design: La Macchina Di Santa Rosa.

**1984, Sept. 3 Photo. *Perf. 13½x14***

**1603** A754 400 l multi .70 .35

Peasant Farming A792

**1984, Oct. 1 Photo. *Perf. 14x13½***

**1604** A792 250 l Grain harvester, thresher .55 .75
**1605** A792 350 l Cart, hand press .55 .35

**Villa Type of 1980**

Designs: 250 l, Villa Caristo, Stignano. 350 l, Villa Doria Pamphili, Genoa. 400 l, Villa Reale, Stupinigi. 450 l, Villa Mellone, Lecce.

**Lithographed and Engraved**

**1984, Oct. 6 *Perf. 14x13½***

**1606** A719 250 l multi 1.05 1.25
**1607** A719 350 l multi 1.05 1.00
**1608** A719 400 l multi 1.25 .35
**1609** A719 450 l multi 1.25 .35
*Nos. 1606-1609 (4)* 4.60 2.95

Italia '85 — A793

**1984, Nov. 9 *Perf. 13½x14***

**1610** A793 550 l Etruscan bronze statue .55 .45
**1611** A793 550 l Italia '85 emblem .55 .45
**1612** A793 550 l Etruscan silver mirror .55 .45
*a.* Strip of 3, #1610-1612 3.75 3.75

Journalistic Information A794

**1985, Jan. 15 Photo. *Perf. 13½x14***

**1613** A794 350 l Globe, paper tape, microwave dish .60 .35

Modern Problems — A795

**1985, Jan. 23 Photo. *Perf. 13½x14***

**1614** A795 250 l Aging .45 .45

A796

Italia '85. No. 1615, The Hunt, by Raphael (1483-1520). No. 1616, Emblem. No. 1617, Detail from fresco by Baldassare Peruzzi (1481-1536) in Bishop's Palace, Ostia Antica.

**Photo. and Engr., Photo. (#1616)**

**1985, Feb. 13 *Perf. 13½x14***

**1615** A796 600 l multi .90 .40
**1616** A796 600 l multi .90 .40
**1617** A796 600 l multi .90 .40
*a.* Strip of 3, #1615-1617 3.75 3.75

Faience Tiles, Plate, Flask and Covered Bowl — A797

Italian ceramics: No. 1619, Tile mural, gladiators in combat.

**1985, Mar. 2 Photo. *Perf. 14x13½***

**1618** A797 600 l multi .75 .40
**1619** A797 600 l multi .75 .40
*a.* Pair, #1618-1619 + label 2.50 2.50

**Italian Vehicle Type of 1984**

**1985, Mar. 21**

**1620** A782 450 l Lancia Thema .70 .55
**1621** A782 450 l Fiat Abarth .70 .55
**1622** A782 450 l Fiat Uno .70 .55
**1623** A782 450 l Lamborghini .70 .55
*a.* Block of 4, #1620-1623 + 2 labels 11.00 11.00

A799

Italia '85: No. 1624, Church of St. Mary of Peace, Rome, by Pietro de Cortona (1596-1669). No. 1625, Exhibition emblem. No. 1626, Church of St. Agnes, Rome, fountain and obelisk.

**Photo. and Engr., Photo. (#1625)**

**1985, Mar. 30 *Perf. 13½x14***

**1624** A799 250 l multi .30 .30
**1625** A799 250 l multi .30 .30
**1626** A799 250 l multi .30 .30
*a.* Strip of 3, #1624-1626 1.75 1.75

Pope Sixtus V, (1520-1590), 400th Anniv. of Papacy — A800

Sixtus V, dome of St. Peter's Basilica, Rome.

**1985, Apr. 24 Litho. and Engr.**

**1627** A800 1500 l multi 2.25 1.10

**Folk Celebration Type of 1982**

Folktales: No. 1628, The March of the Turks, Potenza. No. 1629, San Marino Republican Regatta, Amalti.

**1985, May 29 Photo.**

**1628** A754 250 l multi .75 .60
**1629** A754 350 l multi 1.10 .60

**Tourist Type of 1974**

Scenic views: 350 l, Bormio town center. 400 l, Mt. Vesuvius from Castellamare di Stabia. 450 l, Stromboli Volcano from the sea. 600 l, Beach, old town at Termoli.

**1985, June 1 *Perf. 14***

**1630** A616 350 l multi .75 1.60
**1631** A616 400 l multi .80 .35
**1632** A616 450 l multi .90 .35
**1633** A616 600 l multi 2.00 .60
*Nos. 1630-1633 (4)* 4.45 2.90

Nature Conservation A803

**1985, June 5 *Perf. 13½x14***

**1634** A803 500 l European beaver .60 .30
**1635** A803 500 l Primula .60 .30
**1636** A803 500 l Nebrodi pine .60 .30
**1637** A803 500 l Italian sandpiper .60 .30
*a.* Block of 4, #1634-1637 12.00 12.00

**Art Type of 1981**

Designs: No. 1638, Madonna bu Il Sassoferrato, G.B. Salvi, 1609-1685. No. 1639, Pride of the Work by Mario Sironi, 1885-1961.

**Lithographed and Engraved**

**1985, June 15 *Perf. 14***

**1638** A738 350 l multi .85 .95
**1639** A738 400 l multi 1.10 .95

Europa — A805

Tenors and Composers: 500 l, Aureliano Pertile (1885-1969) and Giovanni Martinelli (1885-1962). 600 l, Johann Sebastian Bach (1685-1750) and Vincenzo Bellini (1801-1835).

**1985, June 20 Photo. *Perf. 13½x14***

**1640** A805 500 l multi *4.50* *.60*
**1641** A805 600 l multi *8.00* *1.10*

San Salvatore Abbey, Monte Amiata, 950th Anniv. A806

**Lithographed and Engraved**

**1985, Aug. 1 *Perf. 14x13½***

**1642** A806 450 l multi .60 .35

World Cycling Championships — A807

**1985, Aug. 21 Photo.**

**1643** A807 400 l multi 1.10 .35

7th Intl. Congress for Crime Prevention, Milan, Aug. 26-Sept. 6 — A808

**1985, Aug. 26**
**1644** A808 600 l multi 1.40 .45

Intl. Youth Year A809

**1985, Sept. 3**
**1645** A809 600 l multi 1.40 .45

### Villa Type of 1980

Designs: 300 l, Nitti, Maratea. 400 l, Aldrovandi Mazzacorati, Bologna. 500 l, Santa Maria, Pula. 600 l, De Mersi, Villazzano.

### Lithographed and Engraved

**1985, Oct. 1** ***Perf. 14x13½***
**1646** A719 300 l multi 1.10 .35
**1647** A719 400 l multi 1.50 .35
**1648** A719 500 l multi 1.75 .30
**1649** A719 600 l multi 2.25 .35
*Nos. 1646-1649 (4)* 6.60 1.35

Natl. and Papal Arms, Treaty Document A810

**1985, Oct. 15** **Photo.**
**1650** A810 400 l multi .75 .35

Ratification of new Concordat with the Vatican.

Souvenir Sheets

Parma #10, View of Parma — A812

A813

Sardinia #1, Great Britain #1 — A814

No. 1651: b, Two Sicilies #3, Naples. c, Two Sicilies #10, Palermo. d, Modena #3, Modena. e, Roman States #8, Rome. f, Tuscany #5, Florence. g, Sardinia #15, Turin. h, Romagna #7, Bologna. i, Lombardy-Venetia #4, Milan.
No. 1652a, Switzerland #3L1. b, Japan #1. c, US #2. d, Western Australia #1. e, Mauritius #4.

### Lithographed and Engraved

**1985, Oct. 25** ***Perf. 14***
**1651** Sheet of 9 5.50 5.50
*a.-i.* A812 300 l, any single .50 .50

***Perf. 14x13½***

**1652** Sheet of 5 + label 6.00 3.75
*a.-e.* A813 500 l, any single .90 .55

***Imperf***

**1653** A814 4000 l multi 6.00 4.00

Italia '85, Rome, Oct. 25-Nov. 3.

Long-distance Skiing — A815

**1986, Jan. 25 Photo.** ***Perf. 14x13½***
**1654** A815 450 l multi .90 .45

### Folk Celebration Type of 1982

Design: Procession of St. Agnes, Le Candelore Folk Festival, Catania.

**1986, Feb. 3** ***Perf. 13½x14***
**1655** A754 450 l multi .85 .30

Amilcare Ponchielli (1834-1886), Composer — A816

### Photogravure and Engraved

**1986, Mar. 8** ***Perf. 14x13½***
**1656** A816 2000 l Scene from La Giaconda 3.00 .55

### Castle Type of 1980

Designs: 380 l, Vignola, Modena. 650 l, Montecchio Castle, Castiglion Fiorentino. 750 l, Rocca di Urbisaglia.

***Perf. 14x13½***

**1986-90 Photo. Wmk. 303**
**1657** A717 380 l multi ('87) .55 .30
**1658** A717 650 l multi .90 .30

**Engr.**

**1659** A717 750 l multi ('90) 1.10 .30
*Nos. 1657-1659 (3)* 2.55 .90

Issue date: 750 l, Sept. 20.

### Coil Stamps

***Perf. 14 Vert.***

**1988-91 Engr. Wmk. 303**

**Size: 16x21mm**

**1661** A717 100 l St. Severa .25 .25
**1662** A717 500 l Norman Castle, Melfi .80 .40
**1663** A717 600 l Scaligero, Sirmione 1.10 .55
**1664** A717 650 l Serralunga D'Alba 1.10 .50
**1665** A717 750 l Venafro 1.25 .60
**1666** A717 800 l Rocca Maggiore, Assisi 1.50 .75
*Nos. 1661-1666 (6)* 6.00 3.05

Issued: 600 l, 800 l, 2/20/91; others, 3/1/88.

Giovanni Battista Pergolesi (1710-1736), Musician — A817

***Perf. 13½x14***

**1986, Mar. 15 Photo. Unwmk.**
**1667** A817 2000 l multi 3.25 1.00

The Bay, Acitrezza — A818

**1986, Mar. 24** ***Perf. 14***
**1668** A818 350 l shown .65 .50
**1669** A818 450 l Piazetta, Capri .90 .50
**1670** A818 550 l Kursaal, Merano 1.00 .35
**1671** A818 650 l Lighthouse, San Benedetto del Tronto 1.25 .45
*Nos. 1668-1671 (4)* 3.80 1.80

Europa 1986 — A819

Trees in special shapes: a, Heart (life). b, Star (poetry). c, Butterfly (color). d, Sun (energy).

**1986, Apr. 28 Photo.** ***Perf. 13x14***
**1672** Block of 4 *12.00 12.00*
*a.-d.* A819 650 l, any single *1.10 .45*

25th Intl. Opthalmological Congress, Rome, May 4-10 — A820

**1986, May 3 Photo.** ***Perf. 14***
**1673** A820 550 l multi .90 .40

Police in Uniform — A821

**1986, May 10**
**1674** A821 550 l multi 1.60 .55
**1675** A821 650 l multi 1.90 .90

European Police Conference, Chianciano Terme, May 10-12. Nos. 1674-1675 printed se-tenant with labels picturing male or female police.

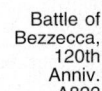

Battle of Bezzecca, 120th Anniv. A822

**1986, May 31** ***Perf. 14x13½***
**1676** A822 550 l multi .95 .35

Memorial Day for Independence Martyrs — A823

**1986, May 31** ***Perf. 14***
**1677** A823 2000 l multi 3.50 1.00

Bersaglieri Corps of Mountain Troops, 150th Anniv. — A824

**1986, June 1** ***Perf. 13½x14***
**1678** A824 450 l multi 1.10 .35

Telecommunications — A825

**1986, June 16** ***Perf. 14x13½***
**1679** A825 350 l multi .55 .35

Sacro Monte di Varallo Monastery — A826

**1986, June 28 Engr.** ***Perf. 14***
**1680** A826 2000 l Prus bl & sage grn 3.25 1.00

### Italian Vehicle Type of 1984

**1986, July 4 Photo.** ***Perf. 14x13½***
**1681** A782 450 l Alfa Romeo AR8 Turbo .70 .40
**1682** A782 450 l Innocenti 650 SE .70 .40
**1683** A782 450 l Ferrari Testarossa .70 .40
**1684** A782 450 l Fiatallis FR 10B .70 .40
*a.* Block of 4, #1681-1684 + 2 labels *12.00* 10.00

Ladies' Fashions — A827

Breda Heavy Industry — A828

Olivetti Computer Technology — A829

**1986, July 14**

**1685** A827 450 l shown 1.30 .45
**1686** A827 450 l Men's fashions 1.30 .45
*a.* Pair, #1685-1686 + label *7.50* 7.50
**1687** A828 650 l shown *3.25* .45
**1688** A829 650 l shown *3.25* .45
*Nos. 1685-1688 (4)* *9.10* 1.80

Alitalia, Italian Airlines, 40th Anniv. A830

**1986, Sept. 16 Photo. *Perf. 14x13½***

**1689** A830 550 l Anniv. emblem 1.00 .40
**1690** A830 650 l Jet, runway lights 1.25 .50

**Villa Type of 1980**

**1986, Oct. 1 Photo. & Engr.**

**1691** A719 350 l Necker, Trieste .65 .45
**1692** A719 350 l Borromeo, Cassano D'Adda .65 .45
**1693** A719 450 l Palagonia, Bagheria .85 .35
**1694** A719 550 l Medicea, Poggio a Caiano 1.00 .40
**1695** A719 650 l Castello d'Issogne, Issogne 1.25 .50
*Nos. 1691-1695 (5)* 4.40 2.15

Christmas — A831

Madonna and Child, bronze sculpture by Donatello, Basilica del Santo, Padua.

**1986, Oct. 10 Engr. *Perf. 14***

**1696** A831 450 l brown olive .75 .35

**Art Type of 1981**

Designs: 450 l, Seated Woman Holding a Book, drawing by Andrea del Sarto, Uffizi, Florence, vert. 550 l, Daphne at Pavarola, painting by Felice Casorati, Museum of Modern Art, Turin, vert.

**1986, Oct. 11 Litho. & Engr.**

**1697** A738 450 l blk & pale org 1.50 .35
**1698** A738 550 l multi 2.00 .40

Memorial, Globe, Plane — A832

Plane, Cross, Men — A833

**1986, Nov. 11 Photo. *Perf. 13½x14***

**1699** A832 550 l multi 1.05 .45
**1700** A833 650 l multi 1.20 .55

Intl. Peace Year, memorial to Italian airmen who died at Kindu, Zaire, while on a peace mission.

Stamp Day A834

**1986, Nov. 29 *Perf. 14x13½***

**1701** A834 550 l Die of Sardinia No. 2 1.50 .40

Francesco Matraire, printer of first Sardinian stamps.

A835

Industries — A836

***Perf. 14½x13½***

**1987, Feb. 27 Photo.**

**1702** A835 700 l Marzotto Textile, 1836 1.20 .55
**1703** A836 700 l Italgas Energy Corp., 1837 1.20 .55

Environmental Protection — A837

Designs: a, Volturno River. b, Garda Lake. c, Trasimeno Lake. d, Tirso River.

**1987, Mar. 6 Litho. *Perf. 14x13½***

**1704** Block of 4 8.50 8.50
*a.-d.* A837 500 l, any single .85 .40

Antonio Gramsci (1891-1937), Author and Artist — A838

**1987, Apr. 27 Litho. *Perf. 14x13½***

**1705** A838 600 l scar & gray black 1.00 .50

Europa 1987 A839

Modern architecture: 600 l, Church of Sun Motorway, Florence, designed by Michelucci. 700 l, Railway station, Rome, designed by Nervi.

**1987, May 4 Photo.**

**1706** A839 600 l multi *2.50* *.60*
**1707** A839 700 l multi *3.25* *.60*

**Tourist Type of 1974**

**1987, May 9 *Perf. 14***

**1708** A616 380 l Verbania Pallanza .75 .60
**1709** A616 400 l Palmi .85 .60
**1710** A616 500 l Vasto 1.10 .50
**1711** A616 600 l Villacidro 1.40 .50
*Nos. 1708-1711 (4)* 4.10 2.20

Naples Soccer Club, Nat'l. Champions A840

**1987, May 18 Litho. *Perf. 13½x14***

**1712** A840 500 l multi 2.25 1.75

The Absinthe Drinkers, by Degas — A841

**1987, May 29**

**1713** A841 380 l multi .90 .45

Fight against alcoholism.

St. Alfonso M. de Liguori (1696-1787) and Gulf of Naples — A842

**1987, Aug. 1 *Perf. 14x13½***

**1714** A842 400 l multi .75 .40

Events A843

Emblems and natl. landmarks: No. 1715, OLYMPHILEX '87, Intl. Olympic Committee Building, Foro Italico, Rome. No. 1716, World Athletics Championships, Olympic Stadium, Rome.

**1987, Aug. 29 Photo. *Perf. 14x14½***

**1715** A843 700 l multi 1.10 .45
**1716** A843 700 l multi 1.10 .45

**Folk Celebration Type of 1982**

Design: Quintana Joust, Foligno.

***Perf. 13½x14½***

**1987, Sept. 12 Photo.**

**1717** A754 380 l multi .75 .35

Piazzas A844

380 l, Piazza del Popolo, Ascoli Piceno. 500 l, Piazza Giuseppe Verdi, Palermo. 600 l, Piazza San Carlo, Turin. 700 l, Piazza dei Signori, Verona.

**Litho. & Engr.**

**1987, Oct. 10 *Perf. 14x13½***

**1718** A844 380 l multi .75 .45
**1719** A844 500 l multi 1.00 .35
**1720** A844 600 l multi 1.25 .45
**1721** A844 700 l multi 1.40 .50
*Nos. 1718-1721 (4)* 4.40 1.75

See Nos. 1747-1748, 1765-1766.

Christmas A845

Paintings by Giotto: 500 l, Adoration in the Manger, Basilica of St. Francis, Assisi. 600 l, The Epiphany, Scrovegni Chapel, Padua.

**1987, Oct. 15 Photo. *Perf. 13½x14***

**1722** A845 500 l multi 1.05 .40
**1723** A845 600 l multi 1.25 .40

Battle of Mentana, 120th Anniv. A846

**Litho. & Engr.**

**1987, Nov. 3 *Perf. 14x13½***

**1724** A846 380 l multi .85 .35

Il Pantocrator (Christ), Mosaic, Monreale Cathedral — A847

Coat of Arms and San Carlo Theater, Naples, from an 18th Cent. Engraving — A848

**1987, Nov. 4 *Perf. 14***

**1725** A847 500 l multi 1.50 .50
**1726** A848 500 l multi 1.50 .50

Artistic heritage. See Nos. 1768-1769.

Nunziatella Military School, 200th Anniv.
A849

**1987, Nov. 14** ***Perf. 14x13½***
**1727** A849 600 l multi 1.05 .40

Stamp Day — A850

Philatelist Marco DeMarchi (d. 1936) holding magnifying glass and stamp album, Milan Cathedral.

**1987, Nov. 20 Photo.** ***Perf. 13½x14***
**1728** A850 500 l multi 1.60 .50

Homo Aeserniensis (Flint Knapper) — A851

**Photo. & Engr.**

**1988, Feb. 6** ***Perf. 13½x14***
**1729** A851 500 l multi .90 .55

Remains of Isernia Man, c. 736,000 years-old, discovered near Isernia.

E. Quirino Visconti School, Rome
A852

**Litho. & Engr.**

**1988, Mar. 1 Unwmk.** ***Perf. 14x13½***
**1730** A852 500 l multi .75 .40

See Nos. 1764, 1824, 1842.

St. John Bosco (1815-1888), Educator — A853

**1988, Apr. 2 Photo.** ***Perf. 13½x14***
**1731** A853 500 l multi .75 .55

**Art Type of 1981**

Painting: *The Archaeologists,* by Giorgio de Chirico (1888-1978).

**1988, Apr. 7 Engr.** ***Perf. 14***
**1732** A738 650 l multi, vert. 1.90 .65

1st Printed Hebrew Bible, 500th Anniv.
A854

Soncino Bible excerpt, 15th cent.

**1988, Apr. 22 Photo.** ***Perf. 14x13½***
**1733** A854 550 l multi .90 .50

Epilepsy Foundation
A855

Design: St. Valentine, electroencephalograph readout, epileptic in seizure and medieval crest.

**1988, Apr. 23**
**1734** A855 500 l multi .85 .55

Europa 1988
A856

Transport and communication: 650 l, ETR 450 locomotive. 750 l, Electronic mail, map of Italy.

**1988, May 2**
**1735** A856 650 l multi *1.75 .60*
**1736** A856 750 l multi *2.25 .85*

**Tourist Type of 1974**

Scenic views: 400 l, Castiglione della Pescaia. 500 l, Lignano Sabbiadoro. 650 l, Noto. 750 l, Vieste.

**1988, May 7 Photo.** ***Perf. 14***
**1737** A616 400 l multi .60 .85
**1738** A616 500 l multi .80 .65
**1739** A616 650 l multi 1.10 .75
**1740** A616 750 l multi 1.25 1.10
*Nos. 1737-1740 (4)* 3.75 3.35

A858

**1988, May 16**
**1741** A858 500 l Golf .80 .45

1990 World Cup Soccer Championships — A859

**1988, May 16 Litho.** ***Perf. 14x13½***
**1742** A859 3150 l blk, grn & dark red 3.75 2.75

1988 Natl. Soccer Championships, Milan — A860

**1988, May 23** ***Perf. 13½x14***
**1743** A860 650 l multi .90 .55

Bronze Sculpture, Pergola — A861

**1988, June 4 Engr.** ***Perf. 14***
**1744** A861 500 l Horse .95 .95
**1745** A861 650 l Woman 1.00 1.00

Bologna University, 900th Anniv. — A862

**1988, June 10 Engr.** ***Perf. 13½x14***
**1746** A862 500 l violet .75 .50

**Piazza Type of 1987**

Designs: 400 l, Piazza del Duomo, Pistoia. 550 l, Piazza del Unita d'Italia, Trieste.

**Litho. & Engr.**

**1988, July 2** ***Perf. 14x13½***
**1747** A844 400 l multi .70 .55
**1748** A844 550 l multi .95 .50

**Folk Celebration Type of 1982**

Discesa Dei Candelieri, Sassari: Man wearing period costume, column and bearers.

**1988, Aug. 13 Photo.** ***Perf. 13½x14***
**1749** A754 550 l multi 1.30 .40

Intl. Gastroenterology and Digestive Endoscopy Congress, Rome — A863

**1988, Sept. 5**
**1750** A863 750 l multi 1.25 .65

Neorealistic Films — A864

Italian films amd directors: 500 l, *Ossessione,* 1942, by Luchino Visconti. 650 l, *Ladri di Biciclette,* 1948, by Vittorio DeSica. 2400 l, *Roma Citta Aperta,* 1945, by Roberto Rossellini. 3050 l, *Riso Amaro,* 1949, by Giuseppe DeSantis.

**1988, Oct. 13 Litho.** ***Perf. 14x13½***
**1751** A864 500 l multi .85 1.10
**1752** A864 650 l multi 1.10 1.30
**1753** A864 2400 l multi 4.50 1.75
**1754** A864 3050 l multi 6.00 2.25
*Nos. 1751-1754 (4)* 12.45 6.40

Elsag — A865

Aluminia — A866

State Mint and Polygraphic Insitute — A867

Italian Industries.

**1988, Oct. 19** **Photo.**
**1755** A865 750 l multi 1.10 .60
**1756** A866 750 l multi 1.10 .60

**Photo. & Engr.**

**1757** A867 750 l multi 1.10 .60
*Nos. 1755-1757 (3)* 3.30 1.80

Christmas: *Nativity,* by Pasquale Celommi, Church of the Virgin's Assumption
A868

**1988, Oct. 29 Photo.** ***Perf. 13½x14***
**1758** A868 650 l multi 1.50 .45

Christmas
A869

**Photo. & Engr.**

**1988, Nov. 12** ***Perf. 14x13½***
**1759** A869 500 l dark blue grn & chest brn 1.40 .50

St. Charles Borromeo (1538-1584), Ecclesiastical Reformer — A870

**1988, Nov. 4** **Litho. & Engr.**
**1760** A870 2400 l multi 3.50 1.75

Stamp Day — A871

Japan #69 & stamp designer Edoardo Chiossone.

**1988, Dec. 9 Photo. *Perf. 13½x14***
**1761** A871 500 l multi .80 .40

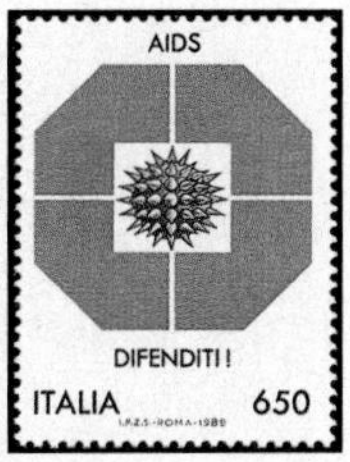


Campaign Against AIDS — A872

**1989, Jan. 13**
**1762** A872 650 l multi 1.00 .35

Paris-Peking Rally — A873

**1989, Jan. 21 *Perf. 14½x13½***
**1763** A873 3150 l Map, Itala race car 4.50 4.50

**School Type of 1988**

**1989 Photo. & Engr. *Perf. 14x13½***
**1764** A852 650 l multi .85 .40

**Piazza Type of 1987**

No. 1765, Piazza Del Duomo, Catanzaro. No. 1766, Piazza Di Spagna, Rome.

**Litho. & Engr.**

**1989, Apr. 10 *Perf. 14x13½***
**1765** A844 400 l multi .75 .75
**1766** A844 400 l multi .75 .75

Velo World Yachting Championships A875

**1989, Apr. 8 Photo. *Perf. 14***
**1767** A875 3050 l multi 4.25 1.25

**Artistic Heritage Type of 1987**

Art and architecture: 500 l, King with scepter and orb, Palazzo Della Ragione, Padova, vert. 650 l, Crypt of St. Nicolas, St. Nicolas Basilica, Bari, vert.

**1989, Apr. 8 Litho. & Engr., Engr.**
**1768** A847 500 l multi .85 .75
**1769** A847 650 l indigo 1.30 .75

Europa 1989 — A876

Children's games.

***Perf. 14x13½, 13½x14***

**1989, May 8 Photo.**
**1770** A876 500 l Leapfrog, horiz. *1.10* *.50*
**1771** A876 650 l shown *1.60* *.50*
**1772** A876 750 l Sack race, horiz. *1.60* *.50*
*Nos. 1770-1772 (3)* 4.30 1.50

European Parliament 3rd Elections — A877

**1989, June 3 *Perf. 13½x14***
**1773** A877 500 l multi 1.10 .55

No. 1773 also inscribed in European Currency Units "ECU 0,31."

Pisa University — A878

**1989, May 29 Engr. *Perf. 14x13½***
**1774** A878 500 l violet .80 .40

**Folk Celebration Type of 1982**

Priest and Flower Feast street scene.

**1989, May 27 Photo. *Perf. 13½x14***
**1775** A754 400 l multi .65 .55

**Tourist Type of 1974**

**1989, June 10 Photo. *Perf. 14***
**1776** A616 500 l Naxos Gardens 1.00 .65
**1777** A616 500 l Spotorno 1.00 .65
**1778** A616 500 l Pompei 1.00 .65
**1779** A616 500 l Grottammare 1.00 .65
*Nos. 1776-1779 (4)* 4.00 2.60

Ministry of Posts, Cent. A879

**1989, June 24 *Perf. 14x13½***
**1780** A879 500 l Posthorn, No. 52 .90 1.25
**1781** A879 2400 l Posthorn, Earth 3.75 1.00

INTER Soccer Championships — A880

**1989, June 26**
**1782** A880 650 l multi .85 .55

Interparliamentary Union, Cent. — A881

**1989, June 28**
**1783** A881 750 l multi 1.00 .65

French Revolution, Bicent. — A882

**1989, July 7 Photo. *Perf. 14***
**1784** A882 3150 l multi 4.25 4.25

*Fortified Walls of Corinaldo,* by Francesco di Giorgio Martini (1439-1502) — A883

**Litho. & Engr.**

**1989, Sept. 2 *Perf. 14***
**1785** A883 500 l multi .90 .45

Charlie Chaplin (1889-1977) — A884

**1989, Sept. 23 Engr. *Perf. 14x13½***
**1786** A884 750 l black & sepia 1.40 .55

Naples-Portici Railway, 150th Anniv. — A885

**1989, Oct. 3 Litho. & Engr.**
**1787** 550 l Denom at UL .55 .30
**1788** 550 l Denom at UR .55 .30
***a.*** A885 Pair, #1787-1788 1.50 1.50

*Adoration of the Kings,* by Correggio — A887

**1989, Oct. 21 Photo. *Perf. 13½x14***
**1789** 500 l multicolored .75 .35
**1790** 500 l multicolored .75 .35
***a.*** A887 Pair, #1789-1790 1.75 1.75

Christmas.

Fidardo Castle, the Stradella, Accordion — A889

Industries.

**1989, Oct. 14 Photo. *Perf. 14x13½***
**1791** A889 450 l Music .75 .50
**1792** A889 450 l Arnoldo World Publishing .75 .50

Stamp Day — A890

**1989, Nov. 24 *Perf. 13½x14***
**1793** A890 500 l Emilio Diena 1.00 .45

1990 World Soccer Championships, Italy — A891

**1989, Dec. 9 Engr. *Perf. 13½x14***
**1794** A891 450 l multicolored .65 .40

Columbus's First Voyage, 1474-1484 — A892

**1990, Feb. 24 Photo.**
**1795** 700 l Denom at UL 1.10 .55
**1796** 700 l Denom at UR 1.10 .55
***a.*** A892 Pair, #1795-1796 2.10 1.90

**Souvenir Sheets**

1990 World Cup Soccer Championships, Italy — A894

Soccer club emblems and stadiums in Italy.

No. 1797: a, Italy. b, US. c, Olympic Stadium, Rome. d, Municipal Stadium, Florence. e, Austria. f, Czechoslovakia.

No. 1798: a, Argentina. b, Russia. c, St. Paul Stadium, Naples. d, New Stadium, Bari. e, Cameroun. f, Romania.

No. 1799: a, Brazil. b, Costa Rica. c, Alps Stadium, Turin. d, Ferraris Stadium, Genoa. e, Sweden. f, Scotland.

No. 1800: a, UAE. b, West Germany. c, Dall'ara Stadium, Bologna. d, Meazza Stadium, Milan. e, Colombia. f, Yugoslavia.

No. 1801: a, Belgium. b, Uruguay. c, Bentegodi Stadium, Verona. d, Friuli Stadium, Udine. e, South Korea. f, Spain.

No. 1802: a, England. b, Netherlands. c, Sant'elia Stadium, Cagliari. d, La Favorita Stadium, Palermo. e, Ireland. f, Egypt.

**1990, Mar. 24** ***Perf. 14x13½***

**1797** Sheet of 6 2.75 5.00
*a.-f.* A894 450 l any single .45 .85
**1798** Sheet of 6 4.00 5.00
*a.-f.* A894 600 l any single .65 .85
**1799** Sheet of 6 5.00 3.75
*a.-f.* A894 650 l any single .80 .65
**1800** Sheet of 6 5.25 3.75
*a.-f.* A894 700 l any single .85 .65
**1801** Sheet of 6 6.50 3.75
*a.-f.* A894 800 l any single 1.00 .65
**1802** Sheet of 6 8.75 8.00
*a.-f.* A894 1200 l any single 1.40 1.25
*Nos. 1797-1802 (6)* 32.25 29.25

See No. 1819.

### Tourist Type of 1974

**1990, Mar. 30** **Photo.** ***Perf. 14***

**1803** A616 600 l Sabbioneta .75 .45
**1804** A616 600 l Montepulciano .75 .45
**1805** A616 600 l Castellammare del Golfo .75 .45
**1806** A616 600 l San Felice Circeo .75 .45
*Nos. 1803-1806 (4)* 3.00 1.80

### Folk Celebration Type of 1982

Design: Horse race, Merano.

**1990, Apr. 9** ***Perf. 13½x14***

**1807** A754 600 l multicolored .80 .45

Aurelio Saffi, Death Cent. A895

**1990, Apr. 10** ***Perf. 14***

**1808** A895 700 l multicolored .85 .45

Giovanni Giorgi (1871-1950) — A896

**1990, Apr. 23** ***Perf. 14x13½***

**1809** A896 600 l multicolored .75 .45

Metric System in Italy, 55th. anniv.

Labor Day, Cent. — A897

**1990, Apr. 28** **Photo.** ***Perf. 13½x14***

**1810** A897 600 l multicolored .90 .45

Naples Soccer Club, Italian Champions A898

**1990, Apr. 30** ***Perf. 13½x14***

**1811** A898 700 l multicolored 1.25 .30

Europa A899

Post Offices: 700 l, San Silvestro Piazza, Rome. 800 l, Fondaco Tedeschi, Venice.

**1990, May 7** ***Perf. 14x13½***

**1812** A899 700 l multicolored *1.50 .60*
**1813** A899 800 l multicolored *2.25 .75*

Giovanni Paisiello (1740-1816), Composer A900

**1990, May 9** ***Perf. 14x13½***

**1814** A900 450 l multicolored .65 .65

Dante Alighieri (1265-1321), Poet — A901

**1990, May 12** ***Perf. 14x13½***

**1815** A901 700 l multicolored .85 .45

Dante Alighieri Soc., cent.

Mosaic (Detail) — A902

Sculpture — A903

**Photo. (#1816), Litho. & Engr. (#1817)**

**1990, May 19** ***Perf. 13½x14***

**1816** A902 450 l multicolored .55 .85
**1817** A903 700 l multicolored .85 .55

Malatestiana Music Festival, Rimini, 40th Anniv. — A904

**1990, June 15** **Photo.** ***Perf. 14***

**1818** A904 600 l multicolored .75 .45

### World Cup Soccer Type of 1990 Inscribed "Campione Del Mondo"

**1990, July 9** **Litho.** ***Perf. 14x13½***

**1819** A894 600 l like No. 1800b 1.25 1.00

Still Life, by Giorgio Morandi (1890-1964) — A905

**1990, July 20** **Engr.** ***Perf. 14***

**1820** A905 750 l black 1.00 .65

Greco-Roman Wrestling, World Championships — A906

**1990, Oct. 11** **Litho.** ***Perf. 14x13½***

**1821** A906 3200 l multicolored 4.25 1.50

Christmas — A907

Paintings of the Nativity by: 600 l, Emidio Vangelli. 750 l, Pellegrino.

**1990, Oct. 26** ***Perf. 14***

**1822** A907 600 l multicolored .75 .40
**1823** A907 750 l multicolored 1.10 .50

### School Type of 1988 and

Italian Schools — A908

Designs: 600 l, Bernardino Telesio gymnasium, Cosenza. 750 l, University of Catania.

**Litho. & Engr.**

**1990, Nov. 5** ***Perf. 14x13½***

**1824** A852 600 l multicolored .75 .40

**Engr.**

**1825** A908 750 l multicolored 1.10 .50

Stamp Day — A909

Self-portrait, Corrado Mezzana (1890-1952).

**1990, Nov. 16** **Litho.** ***Perf. 13½x14***

**1826** A909 600 l multicolored .85 .45

A910

**1991, Jan. 5** **Litho.** ***Perf. 13½x14***

**1827** A910 600 l The Nativity .85 .45

Genoa Flower Show — A911

**1991, Jan. 10** ***Perf. 14***

**1828** A911 750 l multicolored 1.00 .50

Seal of the Univ. of Siena — A912

**1991, Jan. 15** **Photo.** ***Perf. 13½x14***

**1829** A912 750 l multicolored .90 .50

### Tourist Type of 1974

**1991** **Photo.**

**1830** A616 600 l San Remo .85 .45
**1831** A616 600 l Roccaraso .85 .45
**1832** A616 600 l La Maddalena .85 .45
**1833** A616 600 l Calgi .85 .45
*Nos. 1830-1833 (4)* 3.40 1.80

United Europe — A913

***Perf. 14x13½***

**1991, Mar. 12** **Photo.** **Unwmk.**

**1834** A913 750 l multi 1.00 .30

#1834 also carries .48 ECU denomination.

Discovery of America, 500th Anniv. (in 1992) — A914

**1991, Mar. 22** **Litho.**

**1835** 750 l Ships leaving port 1.00 .50
**1836** 750 l Columbus, Queen's court 1.00 .50
*a.* A914 Pair, #1835-1836 2.00 2.00

Giuseppe Gioachino Belli (1791-1863), Poet — A916

**1991, Apr. 15 Litho.** ***Perf. 14x13½***

**1837** A916 600 l bl & gray blk .75 .45

Church of St. Gregory, Rome — A917

**1991, Apr. 20 Photo.** ***Perf. 14x13½***

**1838** A917 3200 l multicolored 4.00 1.50

Europa A918

**1991, Apr. 29 Photo.** ***Perf. 14x13½***

**1839** A918 750 l DRS satellite *1.60 .70*

**1840** A918 800 l Hermes space shuttle *1.60 .70*

Santa Maria Maggiore Church, Lanciano — A919

**1991, May 2 Engr.** ***Perf. 13½x14***

**1841** A919 600 l brown .75 .45

**Schools Type of 1988**

Design: D. A. Azuni school, Sassari.

**Litho. & Engr.**

**1991, May 3** ***Perf. 14x13½***

**1842** A852 600 l multicolored .75 .45

Team Genoa, Italian Soccer Champions, 1990-91 — A920

**1991, May 27 Photo.** ***Perf. 13½x14***

**1843** A920 3000 l multicolored 4.00 2.50

Basketball, Cent. — A921

**1991, June 5**

**1844** A921 500 l multicolored .65 .55

Children's Rights — A922

**1991, June 14**

**1845** A922 600 l shown .90 .35

**1846** A922 750 l Man, child with balloon 1.10 .65

Art and Culture A923

Designs: 600 l, Sculpture by Pericle Fazzini (b. 1913). 3200 l, Exhibition Hall, Turin, designed by Pier Luigi Nervi (1891-1979).

**Litho. & Engr.**

**1991, June 21** ***Perf. 14***

**1847** A923 600 l multicolored .70 .70

**1848** A923 3200 l multicolored 4.00 1.00

Egyptian Museum, Turin — A924

**1991, Aug. 31 Litho.** ***Perf. 13½x14***

**1849** A924 750 l grn, yel & gold 1.10 .50

Luigi Galvani (1737-1798), Electrophysicist — A925

**1991, Sept. 24** ***Perf. 14x13½***

**1850** A925 750 l multicolored 1.10 .40

Radio, cent. (in 1995). See Nos. 1873, 1928, 1964.

Nature Protection A926

**1991, Oct. 10 Photo.** ***Perf. 14x13½***

**1851** A926 500 l Marevivo posidonia 1.00 .60

**1852** A926 500 l Falco pellegrino 1.00 .60

**1853** A926 500 l Cervo sardo 1.00 .60

**1854** A926 500 l Orso marsicano 1.00 .60

*Nos. 1851-1854 (4)* 4.00 2.40

World Wildlife Fund.

Wolfgang Amadeus Mozart, Death Bicent. — A927

**1991, Oct. 7** ***Perf. 13½x14***

**1855** A927 800 l multicolored 1.10 .50

Christmas A928

**1991, Oct. 18**

**1856** A928 600 l multicolored .80 .40

Giulio and Alberto Bolaffi, Philatelists — A929

**1991, Oct. 25** ***Perf. 14***

**1857** A929 750 l multicolored 1.00 .50

Stamp Day.

Pietro Nenni (1891-1980), Politician — A930

**1991, Oct. 30**

**1858** A930 750 l multicolored 1.00 .50

Fountain of Neptune, Florence, by Bartolomeo Ammannati (1511-1592) A931

**1992, Feb. 6 Photo.** ***Perf. 13½x14***

**1859** A931 750 l multicolored 1.00 .50

22nd European Indoor Track Championships — A932

**1992, Jan. 30** ***Perf. 14x13½***

**1860** A932 600 l multicolored .90 .55

University of Ferrara, 600th Anniv. — A933

**1992, Mar. 4 Photo.** ***Perf. 13½x14***

**1861** A933 750 l multicolored .90 .55

**Castle Type of 1980**

***Perf. 14x13½***

**1992-94 Photo. Wmk. 303**

**1862** A717 200 l Cerro al Volturno .30 .25

**1863** A717 250 l Mondavio .35 .25

**1864** A717 300 l Bari .40 .25

**1865** A717 450 l Bosa .65 .35

**1866** A717 850 l Arechi, Salerno 1.25 .50

*Nos. 1862-1866 (5)* 2.95 1.60

Issued: 200 l, 250 l, 300 l, 450 l, 2/24/94; 850 l, 3/7/92.

This is an expanding set. Numbers will change if necessary.

University of Naples — A934

**1992, Mar. 9 Unwmk.** ***Perf. 14x13½***

**1872** A934 750 l multicolored 1.00 .50

**Radio Cent. Type of 1991**

Alessandro Volta (1745-1827), Italian physicist.

**1992, Mar. 26**

**1873** A925 750 l multicolored 1.10 .55

Radio, cent. (in 1995).

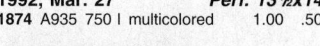

Genoa '92 Intl. Philatelic Exhibition — A935

**1992, Mar. 27** ***Perf. 13½x14***

**1874** A935 750 l multicolored 1.00 .50

Lorenzo de Medici (1449-1492) A936

**1992, Apr. 8** ***Perf. 14***

**1875** A936 750 l bl & org brn 1.00 .50

Filippini Institute, 300th Anniv. — A937

**1992, May 2 Photo. *Perf. 13½x14***
**1876** A937 750 l multicolored 1.00 .50

Discovery of America, 500th Anniv. A938

#1877, Columbus seeking Queen Isabella's support. #1878, Columbus' fleet. #1879, Sighting land. #1880, Landing in New World.

**1992, Apr. 24 Photo. *Perf. 14x13½***
**1877** A938 500 l multicolored .80 .60
**1878** A938 500 l multicolored .80 .60
**1879** A938 500 l multicolored .80 .60
**1880** A938 500 l multicolored .80 .60
*a.* Block of 4, #1877-1880 3.25 3.00

See US Nos. 2620-2623.

Discovery of America, 500th Anniv. — A939

Designs: 750 l, Monument to Columbus, Genoa. 850 l, Globe, Genoa '92 Exhibition emblem.

**1992, May 2 *Perf. 13½x14***
**1881** A939 750 l multicolored *1.40 .65*
**1882** A939 850 l multicolored *1.75 .75*

Europa.

Miniature Sheets

Voyages of Columbus — A940

Columbus: #1883: a, Presenting natives. b, Announcing his discovery. c, In chains.
#1884: a, Welcomed at Barcelona. b, Restored to favor. c, Describing his 3rd voyage.
#1885: a, In sight of land. b, Fleet. c, Queen Isabella pledging her jewels.
#1886: a, Soliciting aid from Isabella. b, At La Rabida. c, Recall.
#1887: a, Landing. b, Santa Maria. c, Queen Isabella and Columbus. #1888, Columbus.
#1883-1888 are similar in design to US #230-245.

**1992, May 22 Engr. *Perf. 10½***
**1883** A940 Sheet of 3 6.75 6.00
*a.* 50 l olive black .25 .25
*b.* 300 l dark blue green .40 .25
*c.* 4000 l red violet 5.25 3.75
**1884** A940 Sheet of 3 5.50 5.00
*a.* 100 l brown violet .25 .25
*b.* 800 l magenta .85 .60
*c.* 3000 l green 3.75 3.25
**1885** A940 Sheet of 3 3.75 3.50
*a.* 200 l dark blue .25 .25
*b.* 900 l ultra 1.10 1.10
*c.* 1500 l orange 1.75 1.75
**1886** A940 Sheet of 3 3.00 3.00
*a.* 400 l chocolate .55 .55
*b.* 700 l vermillion 1.00 .60
*c.* 1000 l slate blue 1.30 1.30
**1887** A940 Sheet of 3 4.25 4.25
*a.* 500 l brown violet .65 .50
*b.* 600 l dark green .70 .60
*c.* 2000 l crimson lake 2.40 2.40
**1888** A940 5000 l Sheet of 1 7.00 7.00
*Nos. 1883-1888 (6)* 30.25 28.75

See US Nos. 2624-2629, Portugal Nos. 1918-1923 and Spain Nos. 2677-2682.

Tour of Italy Bicycle Race A941

**1992, May 23 Photo. *Perf. 14x13½***
**1889** A941 750 l Ocean 1.10 .50
**1890** A941 750 l Mountains 1.10 .50
*a.* Pair, #1889-1890 2.25 2.00

No. 1890a printed in continuous design.

Milan, Italian Soccer Champions A942

**1992, May 25 *Perf. 13½x14***
**1891** A942 750 l black, red & grn 1.10 .50

Beach Resorts A943

**1992 *Perf. 14x13½***
**1892** A943 750 l Viareggio .90 .50
**1893** A943 750 l Rimini .90 .50

Issued: #1892, May 30; #1893, June 13.

Tazio Nuvolari (1892-1953), Race Car Driver — A944

**1992, June 5 *Perf. 14x13½***
**1900** A944 3200 l multicolored 4.75 2.25

**Tourism Type of 1974**

**1992, June 30 *Perf. 14***
**1901** A616 600 l Arcevia .70 .55
**1902** A616 600 l Maratea .70 .55
**1903** A616 600 l Braies .70 .55
**1904** A616 600 l Pantelleria .70 .55
*Nos. 1901-1904 (4)* 2.80 2.20

The Shepherds, by Jacopo da Ponte — A945

**Litho. & Engr.**

**1992, Sept. 5 *Perf. 14***
**1905** A945 750 l multicolored .90 .50

Discovery of America, 500th Anniv. — A946

500 l, Columbus' house, Genoa. 600 l, Columbus' fleet. 750 l, Map. 850 l, Columbus pointing to land. 1200 l, Coming ashore. 3200 l, Columbus, art by Michelangelo.

**1992, Sept. 18 Photo. *Perf. 13½x14***
**1906** A946 500 l multicolored .60 .50
**1907** A946 600 l multicolored .75 .40
**1908** A946 750 l multicolored 1.00 .55
**1909** A946 850 l multicolored 1.10 .60
**1910** A946 1200 l multicolored 1.50 .85
**1911** A946 3200 l multicolored 4.00 2.00
*Nos. 1906-1911 (6)* 8.95 4.90

Genoa '92.

Stamp Day — A947

**1992, Sept. 22 *Perf. 14***
**1912** A947 750 l multicolored 1.00 .50

**Self-Adhesive**
***Perf. 13½***

**1913** A947 750 l multicolored 4.00 4.00

Lions Intl., 75th Anniv. A948

**1992, Sept. 24 *Perf. 14x13½***
**1914** A948 3000 l multicolored 3.75 1.60

Single European Market A949

**1992, Oct. 5 Photo. *Perf. 14x13½***
**1915** A949 600 l multicolored 1.00 .50

Intl. Conference on Nutrition, Rome A950

**1992, Oct. 16 Photo. *Perf. 14x13½***
**1916** A950 500 l multicolored .65 .40

Christmas A951

**1992, Oct. 31**
**1917** A951 600 l multicolored 1.00 .50

Miniature Sheet

United Europe — A952

Buildings on natl. flags, inscriptions in native language: a, Italy (Benvenuta). b, Belgium (Vienvenue, Welkom). c, Denmark (Velkommen). d, France (Bienvenue L'Europe). e, Germany (Willkommen). f, Greece. g, Ireland (Failte). h, Luxembourg (Bienvenue Europe). i, Netherlands (Welkom). j, Portugal (Bem-Vinda). k, United Kingdom (Welcome). l, Spain (Bienvenida).

**1993, Jan. 20 Photo. *Perf. 13½x14***
**Sheet of 12**
**1918** A952 750 l #a.-l. 13.50 11.00

Meeting of Veterans of 1943 Battle of Nikolajewka, Russia — A953

**1993, Jan. 23 Litho. *Perf. 14x13½***
**1919** A953 600 l multicolored 1.25 .50

Carlo Goldoni (1707-93), Playwright A954

Paintings depicting scenes from plays: No. 1920, Man in harlequin costume leaning on picture. No. 1921, Woman seated in front of harlequins.

**1993, Feb. 6 Photo. *Perf. 13½x14***
**1920** A954 500 l multicolored .70 .55
**1921** A954 500 l multicolored .70 .55

Mosaic from the Piazza Armerina A955

**Photo. & Engr.**

**1993, Feb. 20** *Perf. 14*
**1922** A955 750 l multicolored 1.00 .50

Natl. Health Day Promoting a Healthy Heart A956

**1993, Mar. 5 Photo.** *Perf. 14x13½*
**1923** A956 750 l multicolored 1.00 .50

Cats A957

**1993, Mar. 6** *Perf. 14x13½,13½x14*
**1924** A957 600 l European .85 .55
**1925** A957 600 l Maine coon, vert. .85 .55
**1926** A957 600 l Devon Rex, vert. .85 .55
**1927** A957 600 l White Persian .85 .55
*Nos. 1924-1927 (4)* 3.40 2.20

**Radio Cent. Type of 1991**

Design: 750 l, Temistocle Calzecchi Onesti.

**1993, Mar. 26 Litho.** *Perf. 14x13½*
**1928** A925 750 l multicolored 1.00 .50

Radio cent. (in 1995).

City Scene, by Francesco Guardi (1712-1793) — A958

**Photo. & Engr.**

**1993, Apr. 6** *Perf. 14*
**1929** A958 3200 l multicolored 5.25 2.50

Horace (Quintus Horatius Flaccus), Poet and Satirist, 2000th Anniv. of Death — A959

**1993, Apr. 19 Photo.** *Perf. 13½x14*
**1930** A959 600 l multicolored .75 .40

Contemporary Paintings — A960

Europa: 750 l, Carousel Animals, by Lino Bianchi Barriviera. 850 l, Abstract, by Gino Severini.

**1993, May 3**
**1931** A960 750 l multicolored *1.25* .60
**1932** A960 850 l multicolored *1.40* .70

Natl. Soccer Champions, Milan — A961

**1993, May 24**
**1933** A961 750 l multicolored 1.00 .50

Natl. Academy of St. Luke, 400th Anniv. — A962

**1993, May 31** **Photo.**
**1934** A962 750 l multicolored 1.00 .50

St. Giuseppe Benedetto Cottolengo (1786-1842) A963

**1993, May** **Photo. & Engr.**
**1935** A963 750 l multicolored 1.00 .50

Family Fest '93 — A964

**1993, June 5 Photo.** *Perf. 14x13½*
**1936** A964 750 l multicolored 1.00 .55

Tourism A965

**1993, June 28 Photo.** *Perf. 14x13½*
**1937** A965 600 l Palmanova .75 .45
**1938** A965 600 l Senigallia .75 .45
**1939** A965 600 l Carloforte .75 .45
**1940** A965 600 l Sorrento .75 .45
*Nos. 1937-1940 (4)* 3.00 1.80

See Nos. 1972-1975, 2032-2035.

1993 World Kayaking Championships, Trentino — A966

**1993, July 1** *Perf. 13½x14*
**1941** A966 750 l multicolored 1.00 .50

Regina Margherita Observatory, Cent. — A967

**1993, Sept. 4 Photo.** *Perf. 14x13½*
**1942** A967 500 l multicolored .75 .40

Museum Treasures A968

Designs: No. 1943, Concert, by Bartolomeo Manfredi. No. 1944, Ancient map of Foggia. 750 l, Illuminated page with "S," vert. 850 l, The Death of Adonis, by Sebastiano Del Piombo.

*Perf. 14x13½, 13½x14*

**1993, Nov. 27** **Litho.**
**1943** A968 600 l multicolored 1.00 .45
**1944** A968 600 l multicolored 1.00 .45
**1945** A968 750 l multicolored 1.25 .50
**1946** A968 850 l multicolored 1.40 .60
*Nos. 1943-1946 (4)* 4.65 2.00

Holy Stairway, Veroli — A969

**1993, Sept. 25 Photo.** *Perf. 13½x14*
**1947** A969 750 l multicolored 1.00 .50

World War II — A970

Events of 1943: No. 1948, Deportation of Jews from Italy, Oct. 16, 1943. No. 1949, Soldiers, helmet (Battle of Naples). No. 1950, Execution of the Cervi Brothers.

**1993, Sept. 25**
**1948** A970 750 l multicolored 1.00 .50
**1949** A970 750 l multicolored 1.00 .50
**1950** A970 750 l multicolored 1.00 .50
*Nos. 1948-1950 (3)* 3.00 1.50

See Nos. 1984-1986.

Thurn and Taxis Postal History A971

#1951, Coach. #1952, Coat of arms. # 1953, Cart. #1954, Post rider on galloping horse. #1955, Post rider on walking horse.

**1993, Oct. 2** *Perf. 14x13½*
**1951** A971 750 l multicolored 1.00 .40
**1952** A971 750 l multicolored 1.00 .40
**1953** A971 750 l multicolored 1.00 .40
**1954** A971 750 l multicolored 1.00 .40
**1955** A971 750 l multicolored 1.00 .40
*Nos. 1951-1955 (5)* 5.00 2.00

*Perf. 14 Horiz.*

*1951a* A971 750 l 1.10 .65
*1952a* A971 750 l 1.10 .65
*1953a* A971 750 l 1.10 .65
*1954a* A971 750 l 1.10 .65
*1955a* A971 750 l 1.10 .65
*b.* Booklet pane of 5, #1951a-1955a 5.00

Bank of Italy, Cent. A972

**1993, Oct. 15** *Perf. 14x13½*
**1956** A972 750 l Bank exterior 1.50 .60
**1957** A972 1000 l 1000 Lire note 2.00 .80

Christmas A973

Designs: 600 l, Living Creche in the town of Corchiano. 750 l, Detail of The Annunciation, by Piero Della Francesca.

**1993, Oct. 26 Litho.** *Perf. 13½x14*
**1958** A973 600 l multicolored .90 .45
**1959** A973 750 l multicolored 1.10 .50

Stamp Day A974

**1993, Nov. 12 Photo.** *Perf. 14*
**1960** A974 600 l blue & red .75 .45

First Italian colonial postage stamps, cent.

Circus — A975

**1994, Jan. 8 Litho.** *Perf. 13½x14*
**1961** A975 600 l Acrobat, horses .90 .40
**1962** A975 750 l Clown performing 1.10 .50

Presence of Women in the Home A976

**1994, Feb. 14 Photo.** *Perf. 14*
**1963** A976 750 l multicolored 1.00 .45

**Radio Cent. Type of 1991**

750 l, Augusto Righi (1850-1920), physicist.

*Perf. 14x13½*

**1994, Mar. 11 Photo. Unwmk.**
**1964** A925 750 l multicolored 1.00 .45

Radio cent. (in 1995).

Dogs
A977

**1994, Mar. 12** *Perf. 14x13*

**1965** A977 600 l German shepherd .85 .55
**1966** A977 600 l Abruzzi sheepdog .85 .55
**1967** A977 600 l Boxer .85 .55
**1968** A977 600 l Dalmatian .85 .55
*Nos. 1965-1968 (4)* 3.40 2.20

Italian Cuisine — A978

**1994, Mar. 24** *Perf. 13x14*

**1969** A978 500 l Breads .70 .45
**1970** A978 600 l Pasta .90 .40

Procession Honoring Apparition of Christ, Tarquinia — A979

**1994, Apr. 2** *Perf. 13½*

**1971** A979 750 l multicolored 1.25 .50

### Tourism Type of 1993

**1994, Apr. 23 Photo.** *Perf. 14x13½*

**1972** A965 600 l Orta San Giulio .85 .45
**1973** A965 600 l Santa Marinella .85 .45
**1974** A965 600 l Messina .85 .45
**1975** A965 600 l Monticchio, Potenza .85 .45
*Nos. 1972-1975 (4)* 3.40 1.80

A981

Nobel Prize Winners: 750 l, Camillo Golgi (1844-1926), Physician, Medicine, 1906. 850 l, Guilio Natta (1903-), Chemistry, 1963.

**1994, May 2 Photo.** *Perf. 13½x14*

**1976** A981 750 l multicolored *1.25 .60*
**1977** A981 850 l multicolored *1.40 .70*

Publication of "Summa de Arithemtica, Geometria, Proportioni et Proportionalita," 500th Anniv. — A982

Fra Luca Pacioli (c. 1445-1514), mathematician.

**1994, May 2 Photo.** *Perf. 14x13*

**1978** A982 750 l multicolored 1.00 .50

Lajos Kossuth (1802-94) — A983

**1994, Apr. 30 Photo.** *Perf. 13½x14*

**1979** A983 3750 l multicolored 4.50 1.75

Milan, Winners of 1993-94 Italian Soccer Championships — A984

**1994, May 2** *Perf. 14x13½*

**1980** A984 750 l multicolored 1.10 .50

World Swimming Championships A985

**1994, May 2 Photo.** *Perf. 13½x14*

**1981** A985 600 l Diving .75 .45
**1982** A985 750 l Water polo 1.00 .45

Archaeology Exhibition, Rimini — A986

**1994, May 6**

**1983** A986 750 l multicolored 1.00 .50

### World War II Type of 1993

Events of 1944: No. 1984, Destruction of Monte Cassino. No. 1985, Massacre of the Ardeatine Caves. No. 1986, Massacre at Marzabotto.

**1994, May 18**

**1984** A970 750 l multicolored 1.00 .50
**1985** A970 750 l multicolored 1.00 .50
**1986** A970 750 l multicolored 1.00 .50
*Nos. 1984-1986 (3)* 3.00 1.50

22nd Natl. Eucharistic Congress, Siena — A987

**1994, May 28 Photo.** *Perf. 13½x14*

**1987** A987 600 l multicolored .75 .40

Ariadne, Venus and Bacchus, by Tintoretto (1518-94) — A988

**1994, May 31** *Perf. 14*

**1988** A988 750 l multicolored 1.00 .50

Brotherhood of Mercy, Florence, 700th Anniv. — A989

**1994, June 4** *Perf. 14x13½*

**1989** A989 750 l multicolored 1.00 .50

European Parliamentary Elections — A990

**1994, June 11 Photo.** *Perf. 13½x14*

**1990** A990 600 l multicolored .85 .40

Natl. Museums — A991

#1991, Attic Krater, Natl. Archaeological Museum. #1992, Ancient drawing, Natl. Archives. 750 l, Statue, Natl. Roman Museum. 850 l, Medallion, Natl. Archives.

**1994, June 16**

**1991** A991 600 l multicolored .75 .45
**1992** A991 600 l multicolored .75 .45
**1993** A991 750 l multicolored 1.00 .45
**1994** A991 850 l multicolored 1.10 .45
*Nos. 1991-1994 (4)* 3.60 1.80

Intl. Olympic Committee, Cent. — A992

**1994, June 23**

**1995** A992 850 l multicolored 1.40 .70

G-7 Summit, Naples — A993

**1994, July 8**

**1996** A993 600 l multicolored .30 .40

A 750 l in this design was printed in error but not issued. Value, *$17,000.*

A995

A996

**1994, Sept. 8 Photo.** *Perf. 14*

**1998** A995 500 l multicolored .80 .35

Basilica of Loreto, 500th anniv.

**1994, Sept. 19**

**1999** A996 750 l multicolored .90 .40

Frederick II (1194-1250), Holy Roman Emperor.

Stamp Day — A998

Designs: 600 l, Pietro Miliani (1744-1817), paper manufacturer. 750 l, Convent of San Domenico.

**1994, Sept. 16 Photo.** *Perf. 13½x14*

**2001** A998 600 l multicolored .75 .45
**2002** A998 750 l multicolored 1.00 .45

Basilica of St. Mark, 900th Anniv. A999

**1994, Oct. 8 Photo.** *Perf. 13½x13*

**2003** A999 750 l multicolored 1.10 1.10
*a.* Souvenir sheet of 2, tete beche 2.25 2.25

No. 2003 printed with se-tenant label. No. 2003a contains one each No. 2003 and San Marino No. 1314. Only No. 2003 was valid for postage in Italy. See San Marino No. 1314.

Christmas A1000

600 l, The Annunciation, by Melozzo da Forli. 750 l, Madonna and Child, by Lattanzio da Rimini.

**1994, Nov. 5 Photo.** *Perf. 13½x14*

**2004** A1000 600 l multicolored .75 .40
**2005** A1000 750 l multicolored 1.00 .50

Italian Touring Club, Cent. — A1001

**1994, Nov. 8**
**2006** A1001 600 l multicolored .80 .40

CREDIOP, 75th Anniv. — A1002

**1994, Nov. 11**
**2007** A1002 750 l multicolored 1.00 .40

Giovanni Gentile (1875-1944), Philosopher A1003

**1994, Nov. 21**
**2008** A1003 750 l multicolored 1.10 .50

Querini Dubois Palace, Venice — A1004

**1994** ***Perf. 13½x14***
**2009** A1004 600 l red & silver .85 .40

New Italian Postal Emblem A1005

**1994** ***Perf. 14x13½***
**2010** A1005 750 l red, black & green 1.50 .50
**2011** A1005 750 l red brown 1.50 .50
*a.* Pair, #2010-2011 3.00 2.50

See Nos. 2059-2060.

World Speed Skating Championships — A1006

**1995, Feb. 6 Photo.** ***Perf. 14x13½***
**2012** A1006 750 l multicolored 1.10 .50

Achille Beltrame (1871-1945) A1007

Design: 500 l, Cover of first issue of LA DOMENICA DEL CORRIERE.

**1995, Feb. 18 Photo.** ***Perf. 13½x14***
**2013** A1007 500 l multicolored 1.10 .40

Italian Food — A1008

**1995, Mar. 4**
**2014** A1008 500 l Rice .80 .50
**2015** A1008 750 l Olives, olive oil 1.25 .40

See Nos. 2068-2069.

Birds A1009

**1995, Mar. 11 Photo.** ***Perf. 14x13½***
**2016** A1009 600 l Heron 1.00 .50
**2017** A1009 600 l Vulture 1.00 .50
**2018** A1009 600 l Royal eagle 1.00 .50
**2019** A1009 600 l Alpine chaffinch 1.00 .50
*Nos. 2016-2019 (4)* 4.00 2.00

UN, 50th Anniv. A1010

**1995, Mar. 24 Photo.** ***Perf. 14x13½***
**2020** A1010 850 l multicolored 1.40 .60

Fifth Day of Milan War Memorial, by Giuseppe Grandi, Cent. A1011

**1995, Mar. 25 Photo.** ***Perf. 14x13½***
**2021** A1011 750 l gold, black & blue 1.10 .50

Miniature Sheet

End of World War II, 50th Anniv. — A1012

Designs: a, Mafalda de Savoy, concentration camp, barbed wire. b, Allied DUKW, Battles of Anzio and Nettuno. c, Women in World War II, Teresa Gullace. d, Gold Medal of Valor, Palazzo Vecchio, Florence. e, Gold Medal of Valor, building, Vittorio Veneto. f, Gold Medal of Valor, Cathedral, Cagliari. g. Mountain Battalion. h, Air dropping supplies, Balkans. i, Atlantic fleet.

**1995, Mar. 31 Photo.** ***Perf. 14x13½***
**2022** A1012 750 l Sheet of 9, #a.-i. 10.00 7.00

Natl. Treasures A1013

Designs: No. 2023, Illuminated manuscript with "P," State Archives, Rome. No. 2024, Painting of Port of Naples, by Tavola Strozzi, Natl. Museum of San Martino, horiz. No. 2025, Illuminated manuscript with "I," Christ, State Archives, Mantua. No. 2026, Painting, Sacred and Profane Love, by Titian, Borghese Gallery and Museum, Rome, horiz.

***Perf. 13½x14, 14x13½***
**1995, Apr. 28** **Photo.**
**2023** A1013 500 l multicolored .65 .40
**2024** A1013 500 l multicolored .65 .40
**2025** A1013 750 l multicolored 1.00 .50
**2026** A1013 850 l multicolored 1.10 .60
*Nos. 2023-2026 (4)* 3.40 1.90

Venice Biennial, Cent. — A1014

**1995, Apr. 29** ***Perf. 13½x14***
**2027** A1014 750 l multicolored 1.00 .40

Basilica of Santa Croce, Florence A1015

**1995, May 3** **Engr.**
**2028** A1015 750 l deep brn blk 1.00 .40

Peace & Freedom A1016

Europa: 750 l, Family, liberating soldiers, Italian flag. 850 l, Stars of European flag, church, mosque.

**1995, May 5 Photo.** ***Perf. 13½x14***
**2029** A1016 750 l multicolored 1.50 .50
**2030** A1016 850 l multicolored 1.50 .60

Volleyball, Cent. — A1017

**1995, May 8**
**2031** A1017 750 l multicolored 1.00 .50

**Tourism Type of 1993**

**1995, May 12 Photo.** ***Perf. 14x13½***
**2032** A965 750 l Nuoro .90 .45
**2033** A965 750 l Susa .90 .45
**2034** A965 750 l Alatri .90 .45
**2035** A965 750 l Venosa .90 .45
*Nos. 2032-2035 (4)* 3.60 1.80

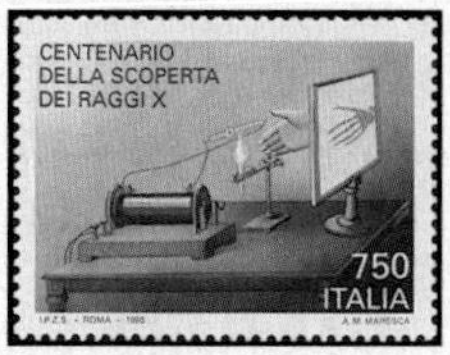


Discovery of the X-Ray, Cent. A1018

**1995, June 2**
**2036** A1018 750 l multicolored 1.00 .40

1994-95 Natl. Soccer Championship Team, Juventus A1019

**1995, June 5** ***Perf. 13½x14***
**2037** A1019 750 l multicolored 1.10 .50

Radio, Cent. A1020

Designs: 750 l, Griffone House. 850 l, Guglielmo Marconi, transmitting equipment.

**1995, June 8** ***Perf. 14x13½***
**2038** A1020 750 multicolored 1.25 .50

***Perf. 14***
**2039** A1020 850 l multicolored 1.40 .60

No. 2039 is 36x21mm. See Germany No. 1900, Ireland No. 974a, San Marino Nos. 1336-1337, Vatican City Nos. 978-979.

A1021

St. Anthony of Padua (1195-1231) — A1022

*Perf. 13½x14, 14x13½*

**1995, June 13**

**2040** A1021 750 l multicolored 1.25 .50
**2041** A1022 850 l multicolored 1.40 .60

See Brazil No. 2539 and Portugal Nos. 2054-2057.

Historical Public Gardens A1023

Designs: No. 2042, Durazzo Pallavicini, Pegli. No. 2043, Boboli, Firenze. No. 2044, Ninfa, Cisterna di Latina. No. 2045, Royal Park, Caserta.

**Litho. & Engr.**

**1995, June 24** *Perf. 14x13½*

**2042** A1023 750 l multicolored 1.00 .40
**2043** A1023 750 l multicolored 1.00 .40
**2044** A1023 750 l multicolored 1.00 .40
**2045** A1023 750 l multicolored 1.00 .40
*Nos. 2042-2045 (4)* 4.00 1.60

Congress of European Society of Ophthalmology A1024

**1995, June 24 Litho.** *Perf. 13½x14*

**2046** A1024 750 l multicolored 1.00 .40

The Sailors' Wives, by Massimo Campigli (1895-1971) — A1025

**1995, July 4 Photo.** *Perf. 14*

**2047** A1025 750 l multicolored 1.25 .50

14th World Conference on Relativity, Florence A1026

**1995, Aug. 7 Litho.** *Perf. 14x13*

**2048** A1026 750 l Galileo, Einstein 1.75 .50

Motion Pictures, Cent. — A1027

#2049, Son of the Shiek, Rudolph Valentino. #2050, L'oro Di Napoli, Toto. #2051, Le Notti Di Cabiria, F. Fellini. #2052, Cinecitta '95.

**Litho. & Engr.**

**1995, Aug. 29** *Perf. 13½x14*

**2049** A1027 750 l multicolored 1.25 .50
**2050** A1027 750 l multicolored 1.25 .50
**2051** A1027 750 l multicolored 1.25 .50
**2052** A1027 750 l multicolored 1.25 .50
*Nos. 2049-2052 (4)* 5.00 2.00

See #2099-2101, 2170-2172, 2269-2271.

FAO, 50th Anniv. A1028

**1995, Sept. 1 Photo.** *Perf. 14x13½*

**2053** A1028 850 l multicolored 1.25 .50

Basilica of Pontida & Death of St. Albert of Prezzate, 900th Anniv. A1029

**1995, Sept. 2** **Engr.**

**2054** A1029 1000 l blue & brown 1.60 .70

ROMA '95, First World Military Games — A1030

**1995, Sept. 6 Photo.** *Perf. 13½x14*

**2055** A1030 850 l multicolored 1.40 .70

Italian News Agency (ANSA), 50th Anniv. A1031

**1995, Oct. 27 Photo.** *Perf. 14x13½*

**2056** A1031 750 l multicolored 1.25 .60

Christmas A1032

Designs: 750 l, Nativity figurines, Cathedral of Polignano a Mare, by Stefano da Putignano. 850 l, Adoration of the Magi, by Fra Angelico.

**1995, Nov. 18**

**2057** A1032 750 l multicolored 1.75 .60
**2058** A1032 850 l multicolored 2.25 .70

**New Italian Postal Emblem Type of 1994**

**1995, Dec. 9 Photo.** *Perf. 13½x14*

**Size: 26x18mm**

**2059** A1005 750 l like No. 2011 1.25 .60
*a.* Booklet pane of 8 10.00
Complete booklet, #2059a 10.00
**2060** A1005 850 l like No. 2010 1.40 .70
*a.* Booklet pane of 8 11.50
Complete booklet, #2060a 11.50

Renato Mondolfo A1033

**1995, Dec. 9 Photo.** *Perf. 14x13½*

**2061** A1033 750 l multicolored 1.10 .50

Philately Day.

F.T. Marinetti (1876-1944), Poet and Ideologue — A1034

**1996, Jan. 19 Photo.** *Perf. 14*

**2062** A1034 750 l multicolored 1.25 .60

Collections from Natl. Museum and Archives A1035

#2063, Arms of the Academy of Georgofili, Florence. #2064, Illuminated manuscript from Lucca (1372), vert. #2065, Manuscript of Gabriele D'Annunzio (1863-1938), author, soldier, political leader. #2066, French miniature, c. 1486.

**1996, Feb. 26** *Perf. 14x13½, 13½x14*

**2063** A1035 750 l multicolored 1.25 .50
**2064** A1035 750 l multicolored 1.25 .50
**2065** A1035 850 l multicolored 1.40 .60
**2066** A1035 850 l multicolored 1.40 .60
*Nos. 2063-2066 (4)* 5.30 2.20

Sarah and the Angel, by Tiepolo (1696-1770) — A1036

**1996, Mar. 5** *Perf. 14*

**2067** A1036 1000 l multicolored 2.00 .80

**Italian Food Type of 1995**

**1996, Mar. 20** *Perf. 13½x14*

**2068** A1008 500 l White wine, grapes .80 .40
**2069** A1008 750 l Red wine, grapes 1.75 .40

CHINA '96, 9th Asian Intl. Philatelic Exhibition A1037

**1996, Mar. 22** *Perf. 14x13½*

**2070** A1037 1250 l multicolored 2.00 1.00

Marco Polo's return from China, 700th anniv. (in 1995).

See San Marino No. 1350.

Cathedral of Milan — A1038

No. 2071, Front entrance. No. 2072, Corner, side view.

**1996, Mar. 23** *Perf. 13½x14*

**2071** A1038 750 l multicolored 1.25 .40
**2072** A1038 750 l multicolored 1.25 .40
*a.* Pair, #2071-2072 2.50 1.50
*b.* Booklet pane, 4 #2072a 11.50
Complete booklet, #2072b 11.50

No. 2072a is a continuous design.

ITALIA '98, Intl. Philatelic Exhibition, Milan.

A1039

**1996, Apr. 3** *Perf. 13½x14, 14x13½*

**2073** A1039 750 l shown 1.25 .60
**2074** A1039 750 l Globe, "100" 1.25 .60

Natl. Press Federation, 50th anniv. (#2073). "La Gazzetta dello Sport," cent. (#2074), horiz.

Intl. Museum of Postal Images, Belvedere Ostrense A1040

**1996, Apr. 13 Photo.** *Perf. 13½x14*

**2075** A1040 500 l multicolored 1.00 .40

Academy of Finance Police, Cent. — A1040a

**1996, Apr. 13**

**2076** A1040a 750 l multicolored 1.40 .60

RAMOGE Agreement Between France, Italy, Monaco, 20th Anniv. A1041

**Photo. & Engr.**

**1996, May 14** *Perf. 14x13½*

**2077** A1041 750 l multicolored 1.60 .60

See France No. 2524, Monaco No. 1998.

Rome-New York Trans-Continental Drive — A1042

**1996, Apr. 13 Photo. *Perf. 13½x14***
**2078** A1042 4650 l multicolored 8.00 4.00

Europa (Famous Women) A1043

750 l, Carina Negrone, pilot. 850 l, Adelaide Ristori, actress.

**1996, Apr. 29 Photo. *Perf. 13½x14***
**2079** A1043 750 l multicolored 1.25 .60
**2080** A1043 850 l multicolored 1.40 .70

St. Celestine V (1215-96) A1044

**Litho. & Engr.**
**1996, May 18 *Perf. 14x13½***
**2081** A1044 750 l multicolored 1.25 .60

Tourism A1045

#2082, Pienza Cathedral. #2083, St. Anthony's Church, Diano Marina. #2084, Belltower of Church of St. Michael the Archangel, Monte Sant'Angelo. #2085, Prehistoric stone dwelling, Lampedusa.

**1996, May 18 Photo. *Perf. 14x13½***
**2082** A1045 750 l multicolored 1.40 .60
**2083** A1045 750 l multicolored 1.40 .60
**2084** A1045 750 l multicolored 1.40 .60
**2085** A1045 750 l multicolored 1.40 .60
*Nos. 2082-2085 (4)* 5.60 2.40

Consecration of Reconstructed Farfa Abbey, 500th Anniv. — A1046

**1996, May 18 Photo. *Perf. 13½x14***
**2086** A1046 1000 l multicolored 1.60 .80

Mediterranean Fair, Palermo — A1047

**1996, May 25 *Perf. 14x13½***
**2087** A1047 750 l multicolored 1.25 .60

Italian Republic, 50th Anniv. — A1048

**1996, June 1 *Perf. 13½x14***
**2088** A1048 750 l multicolored 1.50 .60

Production of Vespa Motor Scooters, 50th Anniv. — A1049

**1996, June 20**
**2089** A1049 750 l multicolored 1.50 .60

First Meeting of European Economic Community, Messina and Venice, 40th Anniv. — A1050

**1996, June 21 *Perf. 14***
**2090** A1050 750 l multicolored 1.25 .60

Modern Olympic Games, Cent. A1051

Designs: 500 l, Runners, 1896. 750 l, Discus, Atlanta skyline, vert. 850 l, Gymnast on rings, basketball, Atlanta stadium. 1250 l, 1896 stadium, Athens, 1996 stadium, Atlanta, vert.

***Perf. 14x13½, 13½x14***
**1996, July 1 Photo.**
**2091** A1051 500 l multicolored .75 .35
**2092** A1051 750 l multicolored 1.10 .50
**2093** A1051 850 l multicolored 1.25 .60
**2094** A1051 1250 l multicolored 1.75 .80
*Nos. 2091-2094 (4)* 4.85 2.25

Butterflies A1052

#2095, Melanargia arge. #2096, Papilio hospiton. #2097, Zygaena rubicundus. #2098, Acanthobrahmaea europaea.

**1996, Aug. 26 *Perf. 14x13½***
**2095** A1052 750 l multicolored 1.25 .50
**2096** A1052 750 l multicolored 1.25 .50
**2097** A1052 750 l multicolored 1.25 .50
**2098** A1052 750 l multicolored 1.25 .50
*Nos. 2095-2098 (4)* 5.00 2.00

**Motion Picture Type of 1995**

#2099, Massimo Troisi in "Scusate Il Ritardo." #2100, Aldo Fabrizi in "Prima Comunione." #2101, Bartolomeo Pagano as Maciste in "Cabiria."

**Photo. & Engr.**
**1996, Aug. 30 *Perf. 13½x14***
**2099** A1027 750 l multicolored 1.50 .60
**2100** A1027 750 l multicolored 1.50 .60
**2101** A1027 750 l multicolored 1.50 .60
*Nos. 2099-2101 (3)* 4.50 1.80

A1054

**1996, Sept. 7 Photo. *Perf. 13½x14***
**2102** A1054 750 l multicolored 2.00 .50

Milan, 1995-96 national soccer champions.

The Duomo, Cathedral of Santa Maria del Fiore, Florence, 700th Anniv. A1055

**1996, Sept. 7 Engr. *Perf. 14x13½***
**2103** A1055 750 l dark blue 1.40 .60

13th Intl. Congress of Prehistoric Science — A1056

**1996, Sept. 9 Photo. *Perf. 13½x14***
**2104** A1056 850 l multicolored 1.25 .60

Levant Fair, Bari A1057

**1996, Sept. 13 Photo. *Perf. 14x13½***
**2105** A1057 750 l multicolored 1.25 .60

1997 Mediterranean Games, Bari — A1058

**1996, Sept. 13 *Perf. 13½x14***
**2106** A1058 750 l multicolored 1.25 .60

Juventus, 1995-96 European Soccer Champions A1059

**1996, Sept. 14**
**2107** A1059 750 l multicolored 1.50 .60

Alessandro Pertini (1896-1990), Former President A1060

**1996, Sept. 25 Photo. *Perf. 13½x14***
**2108** A1060 750 l multicolored 1.25 .60

Eugenio Montale (1896-1981), Poet — A1061

**1996, Oct. 12 Litho. & Engr.**
**2109** A1061 750 l blue & brown 1.25 .60

Annunciation, by Pietro da Cortona (1596-1669) A1062

**1996, Oct. 31 Photo.**
**2110** A1062 500 l multicolored 1.00 .40

Invitation to Philately A1063

Designs: 750 l, Tex Willer, western scene. 850 l, Seagulls, gondola, city, Corto Maltese.

**Litho. & Engr.**
**1996, Oct. 31 *Perf. 14x13½***
**2111** A1063 750 l multicolored 1.40 .60
**2112** A1063 850 l multicolored 1.60 .70

Stamp Day — A1064

**1996, Nov. 8 Photo. *Perf. 13½x14***
**2113** A1064 750 l multicolored 1.25 .60

Universities of Italy — A1065

Designs: No. 2114, Agrarian School, cent., University of Perugia. No. 2115, University of Sassari (1562-1996), horiz. No. 2116, University of Salerno

***Perf. 13½x14, 14x13½***

**1996, Nov. 9 Engr.**

| | | | | | |
|---|---|---|---|---|---|
| **2114** | A1065 | 750 l | brown | 1.25 | .60 |
| **2115** | A1065 | 750 l | green | 1.25 | .60 |
| **2116** | A1065 | 750 l | blue | 1.25 | .60 |
| | *Nos. 2114-2116 (3)* | | | 3.75 | 1.80 |

World Food Day — A1066

**1996, Nov. 13 Photo. *Perf. 14x13½***
**2117** A1066 850 l green & black 1.40 .70

Christmas A1067

Designs: 750 l, Madonna and Child, by Pisanello. 850 l, Santa, toys, horiz.

***Perf. 13½x14, 14x13½***

**1996, Nov. 15**

| | | | | | |
|---|---|---|---|---|---|
| **2118** | A1067 | 750 l | multicolored | 1.40 | .60 |
| **2119** | A1067 | 850 l | multicolored | 1.60 | .70 |

UNESCO, 50th Anniv. — A1068

850 l, UNICEF 50th Anniv., baby, globe, emblem.

**1996, Nov. 20 *Perf. 13½x14***

| | | | | | |
|---|---|---|---|---|---|
| **2120** | A1068 | 750 l | multicolored | 1.25 | .60 |
| **2121** | A1068 | 850 l | multicolored | 1.40 | .70 |

Natl. Institute of Statistics, 70th Anniv. — A1069

**1996, Nov. 26**
**2122** A1069 750 l multicolored 1.25 .60

"Strega" Literary Award 50th Anniv. — A1070

**1996, Nov. 29**
**2123** A1070 3400 l multicolored 5.50 2.75

First Natl. Flag, Bicent. — A1071

**1997, Jan. 7 Photo. *Perf. 13½x14***
**2124** A1071 750 l multicolored 1.25 .60

Sestrieres '97, World Alpine Skiing Championships A1072

**1997, Feb. 1 Photo. *Perf. 13½x14***

| | | | | | |
|---|---|---|---|---|---|
| **2125** | A1072 | 750 l | shown | 1.25 | .60 |
| **2126** | A1072 | 850 l | Ski of colors | 1.40 | .70 |

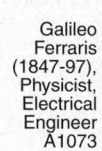

Galileo Ferraris (1847-97), Physicist, Electrical Engineer A1073

**1997, Feb. 7 *Perf. 14x13½***
**2127** A1073 750 l multicolored 1.25 .60

Emanuela Loi (1967-92),Police Woman Killed by Mafia — A1074

**1997, Mar. 8**
**2128** A1074 750 l multicolored 1.25 .60

Italia '98, World Philatelic Exhibition, Milan — A1075

Designs: a, Airmail philately. b, Topical philately. c, Postal history. d, Philatelic literature.

**1997, Mar. 21 Litho. *Perf. 13½x14***

| | | | |
|---|---|---|---|
| **2129** | Sheet of 4 | 5.00 | 2.50 |
| ***a.-d.*** | A1075 750 l any single | 1.25 | .60 |

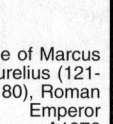

Statue of Marcus Aurelius (121-180), Roman Emperor A1076

**1997, Mar. 25 Photo.**
**2130** A1076 750 l multicolored 1.25 .60

Treaty of Rome, 40th anniv.

St. Ambrose (339-397), Bishop of Milan — A1077

**Litho. & Engr.**

**1997, Apr. 4 *Perf. 14***
**2131** A1077 1000 l multicolored 1.60 .80

St. Geminian, 1600th Death Anniv. — A1078

**1997, Apr. 4 Photo. *Perf. 13½x14***
**2132** A1078 750 l multicolored 1.25 .60

University of Rome A1079

Design: No. 2134, University of Padua.

**1997, Apr. 14 Engr. *Perf. 14x13½***

| | | | | | |
|---|---|---|---|---|---|
| **2133** | A1079 | 750 l | claret | 1.25 | .60 |
| **2134** | A1079 | 750 l | blue | 1.25 | .60 |

Founding of Rome, 2750th Anniv. A1080

**1997, Apr. 21 Photo. *Perf. 14x13½***
**2135** A1080 850 l multicolored 1.40 .70

Timoleontee Wall, Gela — A1081

**1997, Apr. 24**
**2136** A1081 750 l multicolored 1.25 .60

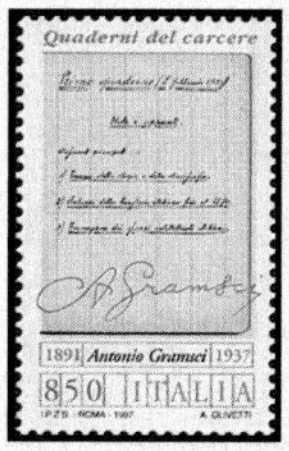

Antonio Gramsci (1891-1937), Politician — A1082

**1997, Apr. 26 Photo. *Perf. 14***
**2137** A1082 850 l multicolored 1.40 .70

Monastery Church, Pavia, 500th Anniv. — A1083

**1997, May 3 *Perf. 13½x14***
**2138** A1083 1000 l multicolored 1.60 .80

Stories and Legends A1084

Europa: 800 l, Cobbler's workshop. 900 l, Street singer, vert.

***Perf. 14x13, 13x14***

**1997, May 5 Photo.**

| | | | | | |
|---|---|---|---|---|---|
| **2139** | A1084 | 800 l | multicolored | 1.25 | .60 |
| **2140** | A1084 | 900 l | multicolored | 1.50 | .75 |

Massimo Theatre, Palermo, Cent. — A1085

**1997, May 16 Photo. *Perf. 13½x14***
**2141** A1085 800 l multicolored 1.25 .60

Tourism A1086

Designs: No. 2142, St. Vitalian Basilica, Ravenna. No. 2143, Tomb of Marcus Tullius Cicero (106-43BC), Formia. No. 2144, College of Assumption of the Holy Mary, Positano. No. 2145, St. Sebastian Church, Acireale.

**1997, May 17 Photo. *Perf. 14x13***

| | | | | | |
|---|---|---|---|---|---|
| **2142** | A1086 | 800 l | multicolored | 1.25 | .60 |
| **2143** | A1086 | 800 l | multicolored | 1.25 | .60 |
| **2144** | A1086 | 800 l | multicolored | 1.25 | .60 |
| **2145** | A1086 | 800 l | multicolored | 1.25 | .60 |
| | *Nos. 2142-2145 (4)* | | | 5.00 | 2.40 |

Book Fair, Turin — A1087

**1997, May 22** ***Perf. 13½x14***
**2146** A1087 800 l multicolored 1.25 .60

Queen Paola of Belgium, 60th Birthday A1088

**1997, May 23 Photo.** ***Perf. 14x13½***
**2147** A1088 750 l San Angelo Castle 1.25 .60

See Belgium No. 1652.

Rome Fair A1089

**1997, May 24 Photo.** ***Perf. 14x13½***
**2148** A1089 800 l multicolored 1.25 .60

Cathedral of Orvieto — A1090

**1997, May 31 Engr.** ***Perf. 13x14***
**2149** A1090 450 l deep violet .75 .35

Fr. Giuseppe Morosini (1913-44) A1091

**1997, June 4** **Photo.**
**2150** A1091 800 l multicolored 1.25 .60

Bologna Fair A1092

**1997, June 7** ***Perf. 14x13***
**2151** A1092 800 l multicolored 1.25 .60

Juventus, 1996-97 Italian Soccer Champions A1093

**1997, June 7** ***Perf. 13½x14***
**2152** A1093 800 l multicolored 1.50 .60

Abruzzo Natl. Park, 75th Anniv. — A1094

**1997, June 7 Photo.** ***Perf. 13½x14***
**2153** A1094 800 l multicolored 1.40 .60

Italian Naval League, Cent. — A1095

**1997, June 10 Photo.** ***Perf. 13½x14***
**2154** A1095 800 l multicolored 1.25 .60

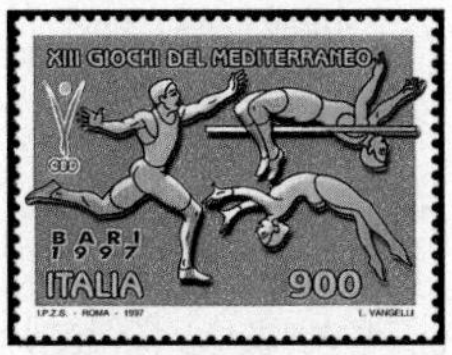

13th Mediterranean Games, Bari — A1096

**1997, June 13** ***Perf. 14x13½***
**2155** A1096 900 l multicolored 1.50 .75

Public Gardens A1097

Designs: No. 2156, Miramare-Trieste Park. No. 2157, Cavour-Santena. No. 2158, Villa Sciarra, Rome. No. 2159, Orto Botanical Gardens, Palermo.

**Photo. & Engr.**

**1997, June 14** ***Perf. 14x13½***
**2156** A1097 800 l multicolored 1.25 .60
**2157** A1097 800 l multicolored 1.25 .60
**2158** A1097 800 l multicolored 1.25 .60
**2159** A1097 800 l multicolored 1.25 .60
*Nos. 2156-2159 (4)* 5.00 2.40

Italian Labor Force — A1098

***Perf. 13½x14, 14x13½***

**1997, June 20**
**2160** A1098 800 l Industry 1.25 .60
**2161** A1098 900 l Agriculture, horiz. 1.50 .75

John Cabot's Voyage to Canada, 500th Anniv. A1099

**1997, June 24 Litho.** ***Perf. 14***
**2162** A1099 1300 l multicolored 2.10 1.60

See Canada No. 1649.

Pietro Verri (1728-97), Economist, Journalist A1100

**1997, June 28** ***Perf. 13½x14***
**2163** A1100 3600 l multicolored 6.00 3.00

Madonna of the Rosary by Pomarancio il Vecchio (Niccolo Cercignani)(d. 1597) — A1101

650 l, The Miracle of Ostia, by Paolo de Dono Uccello (1397-1475).

**1997, July 19 Photo.** ***Perf. 13½x14***
**2164** A1101 450 l multicolored .75 .40

**Size: 26x37mm**

**2165** A1101 650 l multicolored 1.25 .60

Varia di Palmi Festival — A1102

**1997, Aug. 2** ***Perf. 13½x14***
**2166** A1102 800 l multicolored 1.25 .60

Universiade 97, Sicily A1103

**1997, Aug. 19 Photo.** ***Perf. 14x13½***
**2167** A1103 450 l Basketball .75 .35
**2168** A1103 800 l High jump 1.25 .60

Antonio Rosmini (1797-1855), Priest, Philosopher — A1104

**1997, Aug. 26**
**2169** A1104 800 l multicolored 1.25 .60

**Motion Picture Type of 1995**

#2170, Pietro Germi in "The Railway Man." #2171, Anna Magnani in "Mamma Roma." #2172, Ugo Tognazzi in "My Dear Friends."

**Photo. & Engr.**

**1997, Aug. 27** ***Perf. 13½x14***
**2170** A1027 800 l multicolored 1.25 .60
**2171** A1027 800 l multicolored 1.25 .60
**2172** A1027 800 l multicolored 1.25 .60
*Nos. 2170-2172 (3)* 3.75 1.80

Viareggio Literary Prize A1106

**1997, Aug. 30 Photo.** ***Perf. 14x13½***
**2173** A1106 4000 l multicolored 6.50 3.25

Intl. Fair, Bolzano A1107

**1997, Sept. 1**
**2174** A1107 800 l multicolored 1.25 .60

A1108

Artifacts and Paintings from Natl. Museums and Galleries: 450 l, Bronze head, 500BC, National Museum, Reggio Calabria. 650 l, Madonna and Child with Two Vases of Roses, by Ercole di Roberti, Natl. Picture Gallery, Ferrara. 800 l, Miniature of troubadour, Sordello da Goito, Arco Palace Museum, Manta. 900 l, St. George and the Dragon, Vitale da Bologna, Natl. Picture Gallery, Bologna.

**1997, Sept. 13 Photo.** ***Perf. 13½x14***
**2175** A1108 450 l multicolored .75 .35
**2176** A1108 650 l multicolored 1.00 .50
**2177** A1108 800 l multicolored 1.25 .60
**2178** A1108 900 l multicolored 1.50 .75
*Nos. 2175-2178 (4)* 4.50 2.20

Pope Paul VI (1897-1978) A1109

**1997, Sept. 26 Engr.** ***Perf. 13x14***
**2179** A1109 4000 l dark blue 6.50 3.00

Milan Fair
A1110

**1997, Sept. 30 Photo.** ***Perf. 14x13***
**2180** A1110 800 l multicolored 1.25 .60

Marshall Plan, 50th Anniv. — A1111

**1997, Oct. 17**
**2181** A1111 800 l multicolored 1.25 .60

Christmas
A1112

Nativity scenes: 800 l, Molded polychrome, from Church of St. Francis, Leonessa. 900 l, Fresco, from Baglioni Chapel, St. Mother Mary Church, Spello.

**1997, Oct. 18**
**2183** A1112 800 l multicolored 1.50 .50
**2184** A1112 900 l multicolored 1.50 .50

Aristide Merloni (1897-1970)
A1113

**1997, Oct. 24** ***Perf. 13x14***
**2185** A1113 800 l multicolored 1.25 .60

Giovanni Battista Cavalcaselle (1819-97), Art Historian
A1114

**Litho. & Engr.**
**1997, Oct. 31** ***Perf. 13½x14***
**2186** A1114 800 l multicolored 1.25 .60

Philately Day — A1115

**1997, Dec. 5** **Photo.**
**2187** A1115 800 l multicolored 1.25 .60

Emigration of Italian Population of Dalmatia, Istria & Fiume, 50th Anniv.
A1116

**1997, Dec. 6** ***Perf. 14x13½***
**2188** A1116 800 l multicolored 1.25 .60

State Highway Police, 50th Anniv.
A1117

**1997, Dec. 12**
**2189** A1117 800 l multicolored 1.25 .60

Constitution, 50th Anniv. — A1118

**1998, Jan. 2 Photo.** ***Perf. 13½x14***
**2190** A1118 800 l multicolored 1.25 .60

Hercules and the Hydra, by Antonio Del Pollaiolo (1429-98)
A1119

**1998, Jan. 3** ***Perf. 14***
**2191** A1119 800 l multicolored 1.25 .60

See Nos. 2278, 2319.

Famous Writers
A1120

450 l, Bertolt Brecht (1898-1956), playwright. 650 l, Federico Garcia Lorca (1898-1936), poet, dramatist. 800 l, Curzio Malaparte (Kurt Suckert) (1898-1957), journalist, writer. 900 l, Leonida Repaci (1898-1985), writer.

**1998, Feb. 2** ***Perf. 14x13½***
**2192** A1120 450 l multi .75 .40
**2193** A1120 650 l multi 1.00 .60
**2194** A1120 800 l multi 1.25 .50
**2195** A1120 900 l multi, vert. 1.50 .50
*Nos. 2192-2195 (4)* 4.50 2.00

Verona Fair, Cent.
A1121

**1998, Feb. 11 Photo.** ***Perf. 14x13½***
**2196** A1121 800 l multicolored 1.40 .60

Jewish Emancipation, 150th Anniv. — A1122

**1998, Mar. 28** ***Perf. 14***
**2197** A1122 800 l multicolored 1.40 .60

National Festivals
A1123

**1998, Apr. 3 Litho.** ***Perf. 13½x14***
**2198** A1123 800 l Umbria Jazz 1.25 .60
**2199** A1123 900 l Giffoni Film 1.50 .75

Europa.

Completion of "The Last Supper," by Leonardo da Vinci (1452-1519), 500th Anniv. — A1124

**1998, Apr. 4 Engr.** ***Perf. 14x13½***
**2200** A1124 800 l red brown 1.75 .60

Gaetano Donizetti (1797-1848), Composer — A1125

**1998, Apr. 8** **Photo.**
**2201** A1125 800 l multicolored 1.40 .60

Italian Opera, 400th Anniv. — A1126

**1998, Apr. 8** ***Perf. 13½x14***
**2202** A1126 800 l multicolored 1.40 .60

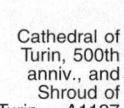

Cathedral of Turin, 500th anniv., and Shroud of Turin — A1127

**1998, Apr. 18 Photo.** ***Perf. 13½x14***
**2203** A1127 800 l multicolored 1.40 .60

Tourism
A1128

#2204, Castle, Otranto. #2205, Mori Fountain and Castle, Marino. #2206, Village and chapel, Livigno. #2207, Marciana Marina, Elba Island.

**1998, Apr. 18 Litho.** ***Perf. 14x13½***
**2204** A1128 800 l multicolored 1.25 .60
**2205** A1128 800 l multicolored 1.25 .60
**2206** A1128 800 l multicolored 1.25 .60
**2207** A1128 800 l multicolored 1.25 .60
*Nos. 2204-2207 (4)* 5.00 2.40

See Nos. 2283-2286.

Sardinia Intl. Fair
A1129

**1998, Apr. 23 Photo.** ***Perf. 14x13½***
**2208** A1129 800 l multicolored 1.40 .60

The Charge of Carabinieri at Pastrengo, by Sebastiano de Albertis (1828-97)
A1130

**1998, Apr. 30** ***Perf. 13½x14***
**2209** A1130 800 l multicolored 1.40 .60

A1131

**1998, May 11 Photo.** ***Perf. 13½x14***
**2210** A1131 800 l Padua Fair 1.25 .60

Juventus, 1997-98 Italian Soccer Champions
A1132

**1998, May 18**
**2211** A1132 800 l multicolored 1.75 .60

Polytechnical School, Turin — A1133

**1998, May 18 Engr. *Perf. 14x13½***
**2212** A1133 800 l dark blue 1.25 .60

World Food Program — A1134

**1998, May 22 Photo.**
**2213** A1134 900 l multicolored 1.50 .75

4th Intl. Convention on Fossils, Evolution, and Environment, Pergola — A1135

**1998, May 30 Photo. *Perf. 14x13½***
**2214** A1135 800 l multicolored 1.40 .60

Carthusian Monastery of Santa Maria di Pesio, 825th Anniv. A1136

**1998, May 30**
**2215** A1136 800 l multicolored 1.25 .60

A1137

**1998, June 2 *Perf. 13½x14***
**2216** A1137 800 l multicolored 1.40 .60

Honoring the fallen of the Italian police corps.

6th World Congress of Endoscopic Surgery — A1138

**1998, June 3**
**2217** A1138 900 l multicolored 1.50 .75

Italian Museums A1139

#2218, Regional Archeological Museum, Agrigento. #2219, Natl. Museum of the Risorgimento, Turin. #2220, Peggy Guggenheim Collection, Venier Dei Leoni Palace, Venice.

**1998, June 6 *Perf. 13½x14, 14x13½***
**2218** A1139 800 l multi 1.25 .60
**2219** A1139 800 l multi, horiz. 1.25 .60
**2220** A1139 800 l multi, horiz. 1.25 .60
*Nos. 2218-2220 (3)* 3.75 1.80

A1140

**1998, June 13 *Perf. 13½x14***
**2221** A1140 800 l Vicenza Fair 1.25 .60

Giacomo Leopardi (1798-1837), Poet — A1141

**1998, June 29 Photo. *Perf. 14x13½***
**2222** A1141 800 l dark brn & sep 1.25 .60

Women in Art — A1142

Paintings: 100 l, "Young Velca," Etruscan tomb. 450 l, Detail from, "Herod's Feast," by Filippo Lippi. 650 l, Woman in profile, by Fra Benci. 800 l, "Lady with the Unicorn," by Raphael. 1000 l, sculpture of Constanza Buonarelli, by Gian Lorenzo Bernini.

**1998, July 8 Photo. *Perf. 14x13½***
**2223** A1142 100 l blk & multi .40 .25
**2224** A1142 450 l vio & multi .85 .30
**2225** A1142 650 l gray grn & multi 1.15 .40

**Engr.**
**Wmk. 303**

**2226** A1142 800 l red brn & multi 1.50 .50
**2227** A1142 1000 l grn bl & multi 1.90 .70
*Nos. 2223-2227 (5)* 5.80 2.15

**Denominated in Lira and Euros**

**1999, Jan. 28 Photo. *Perf. 14x13½***
**2228** A1142 100 l blk & multi .40 .25
**2229** A1142 450 l vio & multi .80 .30
**2230** A1142 650 l gray grn & multi 1.10 .40

**Engr.**
**Wmk. 303**

**2231** A1142 800 l red brn & multi 1.25 .45
**2232** A1142 1000 l grn bl & multi 1.75 .65
*Nos. 2228-2232 (5)* 5.30 2.05

See Nos. 2436-2453.

33rd World Baseball Cup A1143

***Perf. 14x13½***
**1998, July 21 Photo. Unwmk.**
**2251** A1143 900 l multicolored 1.50 .75

Columbus' Landing in Venezuela and Exploration of Amerigo Vespucci, 500th Anniv. A1144

**1998, Aug. 12**
**2252** A1144 1300 l multicolored 2.10 1.00

See Venezuela No. 1595.

Riccione Intl. Stamp Fair, 50th Anniv. — A1145

**1998, Aug. 28 *Perf. 13½x14***
**2253** A1145 800 l multicolored 1.25 .60

Mother Teresa (1910-97) A1146

**1998, Sept. 5 *Perf. 14x13½, 13½x14***
**2254** A1146 800 l shown 1.25 .60
**2255** A1146 900 l Portrait, vert. 1.75 .60

See Albania Nos. 2578-2579.

Father Pio da Pietrelcina (1887-1968) — A1147

**1998, Sept. 23 Engr. *Perf. 14x13½***
**2256** A1147 800 l deep blue 1.25 .60

1998 World Equestrian Championships, Rome — A1148

**1998, Oct. 2 Photo. *Perf. 14x13½***
**2257** A1148 4000 l multicolored 6.50 3.00

School of Higher Education in Telecommunications, Rome — A1149

**1998, Oct. 9 Engr. *Perf. 14x13½***
**2258** A1149 800 l deep blue 1.25 .60

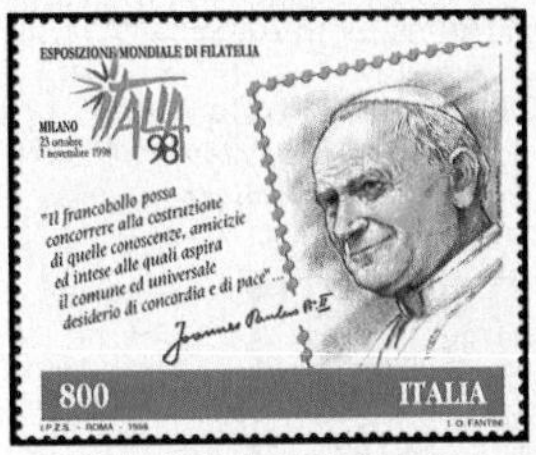


Italia '98, Intl. Philatelic Exhibition — A1150

**1998, Oct. 23 Photo. *Perf. 14***
**2259** A1150 800 l Pope John Paul II 2.00 .50

See San Marino No. 1430 and Vatican City No. 1085.

Armed Forces Day A1151

Emblem from branch of the military and: No. 2260, Aircraft carrier "Giuseppe Garibaldi," Navy. No. 2261, Eurofighter 2000, Air Force. No. 2262, Officer, Carabinieri (police force), vert. No. 2263, Italian monument, El Alamein battlefield, vert.

***Perf. 14x13½, 13½x14***
**1998, Oct. 24 Photo.**
**2260** A1151 800 l multicolored 1.10 .50
**2261** A1151 800 l multicolored 1.10 .50
**2262** A1151 800 l multicolored 1.10 .50
**2263** A1151 800 l multicolored 1.10 .50
*Nos. 2260-2263 (4)* 4.40 2.00

Nos. 2260-2263 were printed se-tenant with Italia '98 label. Air Force, 75th anniv. (#2261).

Art Day — A1152

**1998, Oct. 25 *Perf. 13½x14***
**2264** A1152 800 l Dionysus 1.25 .60

Italia '98.

Enzo Ferrari (1898-1988) Automobile Manufacturer — A1153

a, 1931 Bobbio-Passo del Penice. b, 1952 Ferrari F1. c, 1963 Ferrari GTO. d, 1998 Ferrari F1.

**1998, Oct. 26 Litho.** ***Perf. 13½***
**2265** A1153 800 l Sheet of 4, #a.-d. 6.50 5.50

Italia '98.

Universal Declaration of Human Rights, 50th Anniv. — A1154

**1998, Oct. 27 Photo.** ***Perf. 14x13½***
**2266** A1154 1400 l multicolored 2.25 1.10

Printed se-tenant with a label. Italia '98.

Europe Day — A1155

**1998, Oct. 28** ***Perf. 13½x14***
**2267** A1155 800 l multicolored 1.25 .40

***Die Cut Perf. 11***

**Self-Adhesive**

**Booklet Stamp**

**2268** A1155 800 l multicolored 1.25 1.25
*a.* Booklet pane of 6 7.50
Complete booklet, #2268a 7.50

**Motion Picture Type of 1995**

Motion pictures, stars: 450 l, "Ti Conosco Mascherina," Eduardo de Filippo. 800 l, "Fantasmi a Roma," Antonio Pietrangeli. 900 l, "Il Signor Max," Mario Camerini.

**1998, Oct. 29 Litho. & Engr.**
**2269** A1027 450 l multicolored .75 .35
**2270** A1027 800 l multicolored 1.25 .50
**2271** A1027 900 l multicolored 1.50 .65
*Nos. 2269-2271 (3)* 3.50 1.50

Nos. 2269-2271 each printed se-tenant with label. Italia '98.

Communications Day — A1156

**1998, Oct. 31 Photo.**
**2272** A1156 800 l multicolored 1.25 .60

Souvenir Sheet

Stamp Day — A1157

**1998, Nov. 1 Litho.**
**2273** A1157 4000 l multicolored 6.50 4.00

Italia '98.

Christmas A1158

800 l, Sculpture, "The Epiphany," Church of St. Mark, Seminara, vert. 900 l, Adoration of the shepherds, drawing by Giulio Romano.

***Perf. 13½x14, 14x13½***

**1998, Nov. 28 Engr.**
**2274** A1158 800 l deep blue 1.25 .60
**2275** A1158 900 l brown 1.50 .75

The Ecstasy of St. Teresa, Sculpture by Gian Lorenzo Bernini — A1159

**1998, Dec. 1 Photo.** ***Perf. 13½x14***
**2276** A1159 900 l multicolored 1.50 .75

Emancipation of Valdesi, 150th Anniv. — A1160

**1998, Dec. 4** ***Perf. 14***
**2277** A1160 800 l multicolored 1.25 .60

**Art Type of 1998**

Conception of Space, by Lucio Fontana (1899-1968).

**1999, Feb. 19 Photo.** ***Perf. 14***
**2278** A1119 450 l multicolored .90 .35

National Parks A1162

Europa: 800 l, Wolf, Calabria, vert. 900 l, Birds, Tuscan Archipelago.

***Perf. 13¼x14, 14x13¼***

**1999, Mar. 12 Photo.**
**2279** A1162 800 l multicolored 1.25 .60
**2280** A1162 900 l multicolored 1.50 .75

Holy Year 2000 — A1163

**1999, Mar. 13** ***Perf. 13¼x13¾***
**2281** A1163 1400 l Holy Door 2.25 1.10

St. Egidio Church, Cellere A1164

**1999, Apr. 10 Engr.** ***Perf. 13¾x13½***
**2282** A1164 800 l brown lake 1.25 .60

**Tourism Type of 1998**

#2283, Earthen pyramids, Segonzano. #2284, Waterfalls, river, Terni. #2285, Buildings, Lecce. #2286, Walls around Lipari.

**1999, Apr. 17 Photo.** ***Perf. 14x13¼***
**2283** A1128 800 l multicolored 1.40 .60
**2284** A1128 800 l multicolored 1.40 .60
**2285** A1128 800 l multicolored 1.40 .60
**2286** A1128 800 l multicolored 1.40 .60
*Nos. 2283-2286 (4)* 5.60 2.40

Museums A1165

#2287, Swan on Lake, Casina della Civette, Rome. #2288, "Iulia Bela," International Ceramics Museaum, Faenza, vert. #2289, Bells, Marinelli Historic Bell Museum, Agnone.

***Perf. 14x13¼, 13¼x14***

**1999, Apr. 17 Photo.**
**2287** A1165 800 l multicolored 1.40 .60
**2288** A1165 800 l multicolored 1.40 .60
**2289** A1165 800 l multicolored 1.40 .60
*Nos. 2287-2289 (3)* 4.20 1.80

Constitutional Court — A1166

***Perf. 13¾x13¼***

**1999, Apr. 23 Photo.**
**2290** A1166 800 l multicolored 1.25 .60

Natl. Firefighting Service A1167

**1999, Apr. 29**
**2291** A1167 800 l multicolored 1.50 .60

Military Academy of Modena — A1168

**1999, May 3 Photo.** ***Perf. 13¼x14***
**2292** A1168 800 l multicolored 1.40 .60

50th Anniv. of Death of Grande Torino Soccer Team in Airplane Crash A1169

**1999, May 4 Photo.** ***Perf. 14x13¼***
**2293** A1169 800 l Plane, team members 1.40 .60
**2294** A1169 900 l Superga Basilica, names 1.75 .75

Council of Europe, 50th Anniv. A1170

**1999, May 5 Photo.** ***Perf. 14x13¼***
**2295** A1170 800 l multicolored 1.25 .60

Milan, 1998-99 Italian Soccer Champions A1171

**1999, June 7 Photo.** ***Perf. 13¼x14***
**2296** A1171 800 l multicolored 1.25 .60

Elections for European Parliament, 20th Anniv. A1172

**1999, June 10 Photo.** ***Perf. 14x13¼***
**2297** A1172 800 l multicolored 1.25 .60

Priority Mail A1173

**Typo. & Silk-screened**

**1999, June 14** ***Die Cut 11¼***

**Self-Adhesive**

**2298** A1173 1200 l multicolored 2.00 1.00
*a.* Bklt. pane of 4 + 4 etiquettes 8.00
Complete booklet, #2298a 8.00
*b.* Bklt. pane of 8, no etiquettes 16.00
Complete booklet, #2298b 16.00

No. 2298 was intended for Priority Mail service. Self-adhesive blue etiquettes to be used with each stamp on mail were provided on the sheets and in booklets of 4 stamps.

The backing paper from the sheet stamps is rouletted, while the backing paper in the booklets is not.

See No. 2324.

Fausto Coppi (1919-60), Cyclist A1174

**1999, June 12 Photo.** ***Perf. 14x13¼***
**2299** A1174 800 l multi 1.25 .60

Fiat Automobile Co., Cent. — A1175

**1999, July 10 Photo.** ***Perf. 13¼x14***
**2300** A1175 4800 l multi 8.00 2.75

Statue of Our Lady of the Snows, Mt. Rocciamelone, Cent. — A1176

**1999, July 19**
**2301** A1176 800 l multi 1.25 .60

Eleonora de Fonseca Pimentel (1752-1799), Writer — A1177

**1999, Aug. 20** ***Perf. 14x13¼***
**2302** A1177 800 l multi 1.25 .60

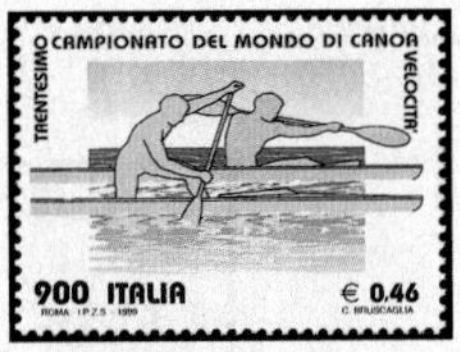


30th World Canoe Championships — A1178

**1999, Aug. 26**
**2303** A1178 900 l multi 1.50 .75

Johann Wolfgang von Goethe (1749-1832), German Poet — A1179

**1999, Aug. 28**
**2304** A1179 4000 l multi 6.75 2.50

World Cycling Championships A1180

**1999, Sept. 15 Photo.** ***Perf. 13¼x14***
**2305** A1180 1400 l multi 2.25 .90

Stamp Day — A1181

**1999, Sept. 25 Photo.** ***Perf. 13¼x14***
**2306** A1181 800 l multi 1.25 .60

Basilica of St. Francis, Assisi — A1182

**Litho. & Engr.**

**1999, Sept. 25** ***Perf. 14x13¼***
**2307** A1182 800 l multi 1.25 .60

Giuseppe Parini (1729-99), Poet — A1183

**1999, Oct. 2 Engr.** ***Perf. 13¼x14***
**2308** A1183 800 l blue gray 1.25 .60

Alessandro Volta's Pile, Bicent. — A1184

**1999, Oct. 11 Photo.**
**2309** A1184 3000 l multi 5.00 2.25

UPU, 125th Anniv. A1185

**1999, Oct. 18** ***Perf. 14x13¼***
**2310** A1185 900 l multi 1.50 .70

Goffredo Mameli (1827-49), Lyricist of Natl. Anthem, Nos. 506, 518 — A1186

**1999, Oct. 22** ***Perf. 14***
**2311** A1186 1500 l multi 2.40 1.10

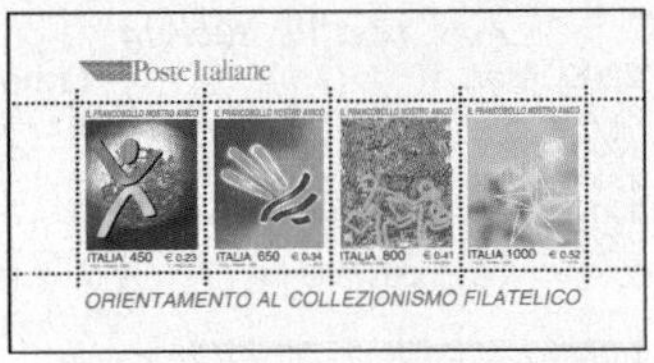


"Stamps, Our Friends" — A1187

Various abstract designs: a, 450 l. b, 650 l. c, 800 l. d, 1000 l.

**1999, Oct. 23** ***Perf. 13¼x14***
**2312** A1187 Sheet of 4, #a.-d. 4.75 2.25

A1188

**1999, Nov. 4**
**2313** A1188 900 l 1899 Military Conscript 1.50 .70

Christmas A1189

Designs: 800 l, Santa Claus, reindeer and sleigh. 1000 l, Nativity, By Dosso Dossi.

**1999, Nov. 5 Photo.**
**2314** A1189 800 l multi 1.25 .60
**2315** A1189 1000 l multi 1.75 .75

See Finland Nos. 1117-1119.

Holy Year 2000 A1190

#2316, Map by Conrad Peutinger, 1507. #2317, 18th cent. print of pilgrims in Rome. #2318, Bas-relief, facade of Fidenza Duomo.

**1999, Nov. 24 Photo.** ***Perf. 14x13¼***
**2316** A1190 1000 l multi 1.60 .75
**2317** A1190 1000 l multi 1.60 .75
**2318** A1190 1000 l multi 1.60 .75
*Nos. 2316-2318 (3)* 4.80 2.25

**Art Type of 1998**

Design: Restless Leopard, by Antonio Ligabue (1899-1965), horiz.

**1999, Nov. 27 Photo.** ***Perf. 14***
**2319** A1119 1000 l multi 1.75 .75

Schools A1191

Designs: 450 l, State Institute of Art, Urbino. 650 l, Normal Superior School, Pisa.

**1999, Nov. 27 Engr.** ***Perf. 14x13¼***
**2320** A1191 450 l black .75 .35
**2321** A1191 650 l brown 1.00 .45

Year 2000 A1192

**1999, Nov. 27 Photo.**
**2322** A1192 4800 l multi 7.75 3.50

**Souvenir Sheet**

Millennium — A1193

Designs: a, The past. b, The future.

**2000, Jan. 1 Litho.** ***Perf. 14x13¼***
**2323** A1193 Sheet of 2 6.50 5.00
*a.-b.* A1193 2000 l Any single 3.25 1.50

See #2330-2332, 2365-2366.

**Priority Mail Type of 1999 Redrawn With Yellow Rectangle at Center**

**Typo. & Silk-Screened**

**2000, Jan. 10** ***Die Cut 11¼***

**Self-Adhesive**

**2324** A1173 1200 l multi 3.50 .90

No. 2324 was intended for Priority Mail service. A self-adhesive blue etiquette is adjacent to the stamp. See No. 2393 for similar stamp with Posta Prioritaria in lower case letters.

First Performance of Opera "Tosca," Cent. — A1194

**Litho. & Engr.**

**2000, Jan. 14** ***Perf. 14x13¼***
**2325** A1194 800 l multi 1.25 .50

Basilica of St. Paul — A1195

**2000, Jan. 18 Photo.** ***Perf. 13¼x14***
**2326** A1195 1000 l multi 1.75 .70

Holy Year 2000.

Six Nation Rugby Tournament — A1196

**2000, Feb. 5** ***Perf. 14x13¼***
**2327** A1196 800 l multi 1.25 .50

5th Symposium on Breast Diseases
A1197

**2000, Feb. 12** ***Perf. 13¼x14***

**2328** A1197 800 l shown 1.25 .50
**2329** A1197 1000 l Woman holding rose 1.60 .70

**Millennium Type of 2000**

Souvenir Sheet

No. 2330: a, Art. b, Science.
No. 2331: a, Nature. b, The city.
No. 2332: a, Generations. b, Space.

**2000** **Litho.** ***Perf. 14x13¼***

**2330** Sheet of 2 3.00 3.00
*a.-b.* A1193 800 l Any single 1.50 .60
**2331** Sheet of 2 3.00 3.00
*a.-b.* A1193 800 l Any single 1.50 .60
**2332** Sheet of 2 3.00 3.00
*a.-b.* A1193 800 l Any single 1.50 .60

Issued: #2330, 3/4; #2331, 5/4; #2332, 7/4.

Skiing World Cup — A1198

**2000, Mar. 7** **Photo.** ***Perf. 13¼x14***

**2333** A1198 4800 l multi 7.75 3.00

Souvenir Sheet

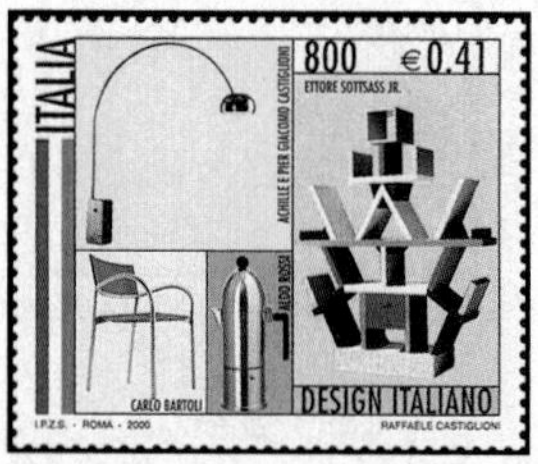


Italian Design — A1199

Household furnishings designed by:

a, Achille & Pier Giacomo Castiglioni, Ettore Sottsass, Jr. Carlo Bartoli, Aldo Rossi. b, Mario Bellini, Alessandro Mendini, Vico Magistretti, Alberto Meda & Paolo Rizzatto. c, Gio Ponti, Gatti Paolini Teodoro, Massimo Morozzi, Tobia Scarpa. d, Pietro Chiesa, Joe Colombo, Cini Boeri & Tomu Katayanagi, Lodovico Acerbis & Giotto Stoppino. e, Gaetano Pesce, Antonio Citterio & Oliver Loew, Enzo Mari, De Pas D'Urbino Lomazzi. f, Marco Zanuso, Anna Castelli Ferrieri, Michele de Lucchi & Giancarlo Fassina, Bruno Munari.

**2000, Mar. 9** **Litho.** ***Perf. 13¼***

**2334** Sheet of 6 8.00 8.00
*a.-f.* A1199 800 l Any single 1.25 .50

Holy Year 2000
A1200

Paintings depicting the life of Jesus:

450 l, The Adoration of the Shepherds, by Ghirlandaio. 650 l, The Baptism and Temptation of Christ, by Veronese, vert. 800 l, The Last Supper, by Ghirlandaio, vert. 1000 l, Fresco from Episodes of the Life of the Virgin Mary and Christ, by Giotto. 1200 l, The Resurrection of Christ, by Piero della Francesca, vert.

***Perf. 14x13¼, 13¼x14***

**2000, Mar. 10** **Litho.**

**2335** A1200 450 l multi .75 .35
**2336** A1200 650 l multi 1.00 .40
**2337** A1200 800 l multi 1.25 .50
**2338** A1200 1000 l multi 1.75 .70
**2339** A1200 1200 l multi 2.25 .90
*Nos. 2335-2339 (5)* 7.00 2.85

La Civiltá Cattolica, 150th Anniv.
A1201

**2000, Apr. 6** **Photo.** ***Perf. 14x13¼***

**2340** A1201 800 l multi 1.25 .50

San Giuseppe de Merode College, Rome, 150th Anniv.
A1202

**2000, Apr. 8**

**2341** A1202 800 l multi 1.25 .50

Intl. Cycling Union, Cent. — A1203

**2000, Apr. 14** **Photo.** ***Perf. 13¼x14***

**2342** A1203 1500 l multi 2.40 1.00

Tourism — A1204

Designs: No. 2343, Terre di Franciacorta, Brescia. No. 2344, Dunarobba Petrified Forest, Avigliano Umbro. No. 2345, Ercolano. No. 2346, Bella di Taormina Island.

**2000, Apr. 14** ***Perf. 14x13¼***

**2343** A1204 800 l multi 1.40 .50
**2344** A1204 800 l multi 1.40 .50
**2345** A1204 800 l multi 1.40 .50
**2346** A1204 800 l multi 1.40 .50
*Nos. 2343-2346 (4)* 5.60 2.00

Little Holy Society, Caltanissetta — A1205

**2000, Apr. 19**

**2347** A1205 800 l multi 1.40 .50

Niccolò Piccinni (1728-1800), Opera Composer
A1206

**2000, May 6** ***Perf. 13¼x14***

**2348** A1206 4000 l multi 6.50 2.75

**Europa, 2000**

Common Design Type

**2000, May 9**

**2349** CD17 800 l multi 1.25 .50

Post and Telecommunications Historical Museum — A1207

No. 2350, Ship, telecommunications equipment. No. 2351, #19, 20.

**2000, May 9** **Litho.** ***Perf. 14x13¼***

**2350** A1207 800 l multi 1.25 .50
**2351** A1207 800 l multi 1.25 .50

Lazio, 1999-2000 Soccer Champions
A1208

**2000, May 20** **Photo.** ***Perf. 13¼x14***

**2352** A1208 800 l multi 1.25 .50

Monza Cathedral
A1209

**2000, May 31**

**2353** A1209 800 l multi 1.25 .50

Rome, Headquarters of UN Food and Agriculture Agencies
A1210

**2000, June 17** **Photo.** ***Perf. 13¼x14***

**2354** A1210 1000 l multi 1.60 .70

Jesus the Redeemer Monument, Nuoro, Cent. — A1211

**2000, June 24**

**2355** A1211 800 l multi 1.25 .50

Società Italiana per Condotte d'Acqua, Construction Company, 120th Anniv. — A1212

**2000, June 28** ***Perf. 14x13¼***

**2356** A1212 800 l multi 1.25 .50

Stampin' the Future Children's Stamp Design Contest Winner — A1213

**2000, July 7** ***Perf. 13¼x14***

**2357** A1213 1000 l multi 1.60 .70

Archery World Championships, Campagna
A1214

**2000, July 8**

**2358** A1214 1500 l multi 2.75 1.00

World Cycling Championships
A1215

**2000, July 31** **Photo.** ***Perf. 13¼x14***

**2359** A1215 800 l multi 1.40 .50

Madonna and Child, by Carlo Crivelli
A1216

**Litho. & Engr.**

**2000, Aug. 8** ***Perf. 14***
**2360** A1216 800 l multi 1.25 .50

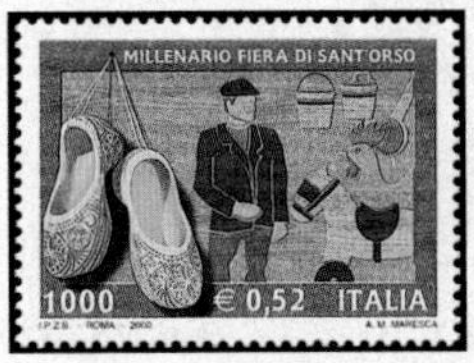


Sant'Orso Fair, 1000th Anniv. A1217

**2000, Aug. 8 Photo.** ***Perf. 14x13¼***
**2361** A1217 1000 l multi 1.60 .70

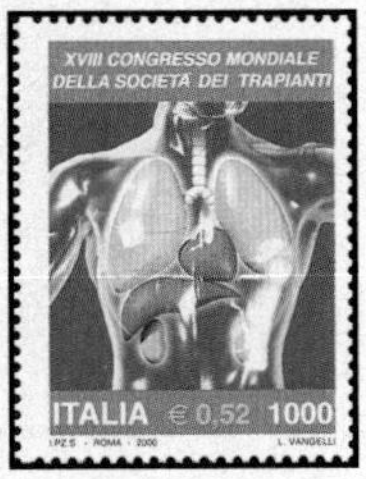


18th World Congress of Transplantation Society A1218

**2000, Aug. 26 Photo.** ***Perf. 13¼x14***
**2362** A1218 1000 l multi 1.60 .70

2000 Summer Olympics, Sydney — A1219

Designs: 800 l, Celebrating athlete, Olympic stadium, Sydney. 1000 l, Myron's Discobolus, Sydney skyline.

**2000, Sept. 1**
**2363** A1219 800 l multi 1.25 .50
**2364** A1219 1000 l multi 1.60 .70

**Millennium Type of 2000**
**Souvenir Sheet**

No. 2365, vert.: a, War. b, Peace.

**2000 Litho.** ***Perf. 13¼x14***
**2365** Sheet of 2 3.00 3.00
***a.-b.*** A1193 800 l Any single 1.50 .60

Issued: No. 2365, 9/4.

**Millennium Type of 2000**

No. 2366: a, Meditation. b, Expression.

**2000, Nov. 4 Litho.** ***Perf. 14x13¼***
**2366** Sheet of 2 3.00 3.00
***a.-b.*** A1193 800 l Any single 1.50 .60

Issued: No. 2366, 11/4.

Battle of Marengo, Bicent. — A1220

**2000, Sept. 8 Photo.** ***Perf. 13¼x14***
**2367** A1220 800 l multi 1.25 .50

Fellini Film Year — A1221

**2000, Sept. 20 Photo.** ***Perf. 13¼x14***
**2368** A1221 800 l multi 1.25 .50

Philately Day A1222

**2000, Sept. 23 Photo.** ***Perf. 14x13¼***
**2369** A1222 800 l multi 1.25 .50

Father Luigi Maria Monti (1825-1900) — A1223

**2000, Sept. 30 Photo.** ***Perf. 14x13¼***
**2370** A1223 800 l multi 1.25 .50

Antonio Salieri (1750-1825), Composer A1224

**2000, Sept. 30** ***Perf. 13¼x14***
**2371** A1224 4800 l multi 8.00 3.00

2000 Paralympics, Sydney — A1225

**2000, Oct. 2 Photo.** ***Perf. 13¼x14***
**2372** A1225 1500 l multi 2.60 .90

World Mathematics Year — A1226

**2000, Oct. 14 Photo.** ***Perf. 14x13¼***
**2373** A1226 800 l multi 1.25 .50

Voluntarism A1227

**2000, Oct. 18** ***Perf. 13¼x14***
**2374** A1227 800 l multi 1.25 .50

Giordano Bruno (1548-1600), Philosopher — A1228

**2000, Oct. 20** ***Perf. 14x13¼***
**2375** A1228 800 l multi 1.25 .50

Madonna and Child, by Luca Della Robbia A1229

**Litho. & Engr.**

**2000, Oct. 25** ***Perf. 14***
**2376** A1229 800 l multi 1.25 .50

Accademia Roveretana Degli Agiati, 250th Anniv. — A1230

**2000, Oct. 26 Photo.** ***Perf. 13¼x14***
**2377** A1230 800 l multi 1.25 .50

Gaetano Martino (1900-67), Statesman — A1231

**2000, Nov. 3 Photo.** ***Perf. 14***
**2378** A1231 800 l multi 1.25 .50

Perseus, by Benvenuto Cellini (1500-71), Sculptor — A1232

**Litho. & Engr.**

**2000, Nov. 3** ***Perf. 14***
**2379** A1232 1200 l multi 2.00 .85

Schools A1233

Designs: 800 l, Camerino University. 1000 l, Calabria University, Cosenza.

**2000, Nov. 6 Engr.** ***Perf. 14x13¼***
**2380** A1233 800 l blue 1.25 .50
**2381** A1233 1000 l blue 1.60 .70

Christmas A1234

Designs: 800 l, Snowflakes. 1000 l, Creche, Matera Cathedral, horiz.

***Perf. 13¼x14, 14x13¼***

**2000, Nov. 6 Photo.**
**2382** A1234 800 l multi 1.25 .50
**2383** A1234 1000 l multi 1.60 .70

World Snowboarding Championships A1235

**2001, Jan. 15 Photo.** ***Perf. 13¼x14***
**2384** A1235 1000 l multi 1.60 .70

The Annunciation, by Botticelli — A1236

**2001, Jan. 18** ***Perf. 14***
**2385** A1236 1000 l multi 1.60 .70

Exhibit of Italian art at Natl. Museum of Western Art, Tokyo.

Souvenir Sheet

Opera Composers — A1237

No. 2386: a, Vincenzo Bellini (1801-35). b, Domenico Cimarosa (1749-1801). c, Gaspare Luigi Pacifico Spontini (1774-1851). d, Giuseppe Verdi (1813-1901).

**2001, Jan. 27 Litho. *Perf. 13¼x14***

**2386** A1237 Sheet of 4 5.00 5.00
***a.-d.*** 800 l Any single 1.25 .50

St. Rose of Viterbo (1235-1252) A1238

**2001, Mar. 6 Photo. *Perf. 13¼x14***

**2387** A1238 800 l multi 1.25 .50

Souvenir Sheet

Ferrari, 2000 Formula 1 World Champions — A1239

**2001, Mar. 9 Litho. *Perf. 14x13¼***

**2388** A1239 5000 l multi 8.25 8.25

Santa Maria Abbey, Sylvis — A1240

**2001, Mar. 10 Engr. *Perf. 14***

**2389** A1240 800 l blue 1.25 .50

Postage Stamp Sesquicentennials — A1241

Designs: No. 2390, Tuscany #1. No. 2391, Sardinia #1. No. 2392, Lombardy-Venetia #1.

**2001, Mar. 31 Photo. *Perf. 13¼x14***

**2390** A1241 800 l multi 1.50 .50
**2391** A1241 800 l multi 1.50 .50
**2392** A1241 800 l multi 1.50 .50
*Nos. 2390-2392 (3)* 4.50 1.50

Priority Mail A1242

***Serpentine Die Cut 11***
**Typo & Silk Screened**

**2001, Apr. 10 Self-Adhesive**

**2393** A1242 1200 l multi 2.00 .85
***a.*** Booklet pane of 4 + 4 etiquettes 8.00
Booklet, #2393a 8.00

Compare with No. 2324. No. 2393 was intended for Priority Mail service. A self-adhesive blue etiquette is adjacent to the stamp.

See Nos. 2466-2471, 2582-2585B, 2613A-2615, 2691A-2691B.

Tourism A1243

**2001, Apr. 14 Photo. *Perf. 14x13¼***

**2394** A1243 800 l Stintino 1.40 .50
**2395** A1243 800 l Comacchio 1.40 .50
**2396** A1243 800 l Diamante 1.40 .50
**2397** A1243 800 l Pioraco 1.40 .50
*Nos. 2394-2397 (4)* 5.60 2.00

Nature and the Environment A1244

Designs: 450 l, Campanula. 650 l, Marmots. 800 l, Storks. 1000 l, World Day Against Desertification.

**2001, Apr. 21 *Perf. 13¼x14***

**2398** A1244 450 l multi .75 .35
**2399** A1244 650 l multi 1.00 .40
**2400** A1244 800 l multi 1.25 .50
**2401** A1244 1000 l multi 1.60 .70
*Nos. 2398-2401 (4)* 4.60 1.95

General Agricultural Confederation A1245

**2001, Apr. 24 Photo. *Perf. 13¼x14***

**2402** A1245 800 l multi 1.25 .50

Gorizia, 1000th Anniv. A1246

**2001, Apr. 28 *Perf. 14x13¼***

**2403** A1246 800 l multi 1.25 .50

Europa A1247

**2001, May 4 Photo. *Perf. 14x13¼***

**2404** A1247 800 l multi 1.25 .50

European Union's Charter of Fundamental Rights — A1248

**2001, May 9 Photo. *Perf. 14x13¼***

**2405** A1248 800 l multi 1.25 .50

Order of the Knights of Labor, Cent. — A1249

**2001, May 9 Photo. *Perf. 13¼x14***

**2406** A1249 800 l multi 1.25 .50

Workplace Injury Memorial Day — A1250

**2001, May 19**

**2407** A1250 800 l multi 1.25 .50

Art and Student Creativity Day A1251

Children's art by: No. 2408, Lucia Catena. No. 2409, Luigi Di Cristo. No. 2410, Barbara Grilli. No. 2411, Rita Vergari, vert.

**2001, May 26 *Perf. 13¼x14, 14x13¼***

**2408** A1251 800 l multi 1.40 .50
**2409** A1251 800 l multi 1.40 .50
**2410** A1251 800 l multi 1.40 .50
**2411** A1251 800 l multi 1.40 .50
*Nos. 2408-2411 (4)* 5.60 2.00

Masaccio (1401-28), Painter — A1252

**2001, June 1 *Perf. 13¼x14***

**2412** A1252 800 l multi 1.25 .50

Madonna of Senigallia, by Piero della Francesca A1253

**Litho. & Engr.**

**2001, June 9 *Perf. 14***

**2413** A1253 800 l multi 1.25 .50

Panathlon International, 50th Anniv. — A1254

**2001, June 12 Photo. *Perf. 13¼x14***

**2414** A1254 800 l multi 1.25 .50

Republic of San Marino, 1700th Anniv. — A1255

**2001, June 23**

**2415** A1255 800 l multi 1.25 .50

Rome, 2000-2001 Soccer Champions A1256

**2001, June 23 Photo. *Perf. 13¼x14***

**2416** A1256 800 l multi 1.25 .50

Harbormaster's Corps and Coast Guard — A1257

**2001, July 20 Photo. *Perf. 14x13¼***

**2417** A1257 800 l multi 1.25 .50

Salvatore Quasimodo (1901-68), Writer — A1258

**2001, Aug. 20** *Perf. 13¼x14*

2418 A1258 1500 l multi 2.60 1.00

Octagonal Room, Domus Aurea (Golden House of Nero), Rome — A1259

**2001, Aug. 31** **Engr.** *Perf. 14*

2419 A1259 1000 l multi 1.75 .70

Italian Design A1260

Household furnishings designed by: a, Piero Lissoni, Patricia Urquiola and Anna Bartoli. b, Monica Graffeo and Rodolfo Dordoni. c, Ferruccio Laviani and Massimo Iosa Ghini. d, Anna Gili and Miki Astori. e, Marco Ferreri, M. Cananzi and R. Semprini. f, Stefano Giovannoni and Massimiliano Datti.

**2001, Sept. 1** **Litho.** *Perf. 13¼*

2420 Sheet of 6 8.50 8.50
*a.-f.* A1260 800 l Any single 1.40 .50

Cent. of Il Quarto Stato, Painting by Giuseppe Pellizza da Volpedo — A1261

**2001, Sept. 15** **Engr.** *Perf. 14x13¼*

2421 A1261 1000 l brown 1.75 .70

Discovery of Mummified Man "Otzi" in Melting Glacier, 10th Anniv. — A1262

**2001, Sept. 19** **Photo.** *Perf. 13¼x14*

2422 A1262 800 l multi 1.25 .50

Stamp Day A1263

**2001, Sept. 22** *Perf. 14x13¼*

2423 A1263 800 l multi 1.25 .50

Enrico Fermi (1901-54), Physicist — A1264

**2001, Sept. 29** *Perf. 13¼x14*

2424 A1264 800 l multi 1.25 .50

Schools A1265

Designs: No. 2425, Pavia University. No. 2426, Bari University, vert. No. 2427, Camilo Cavour State Science High School, Rome.

*Perf. 14x13¼, 13¼x14*

**2001, Sept. 29** **Engr.**

2425 A1265 800 l blue 1.25 .50
2426 A1265 800 l red brown 1.25 .50
2427 A1265 800 l Prus blue 1.25 .50
*Nos. 2425-2427 (3)* 3.75 1.50

Latin Union A1266

**2001, Oct. 12** **Photo.** *Perf. 14x13¼*

2428 A1266 800 l multi 1.25 .50

Natl. Archaeological Museum, Taranto — A1267

**2001, Oct. 12** **Photo.** *Perf. 14x13¼*

2429 A1267 1000 l multi 1.75 .70

Intl. Food and Agriculture Organizations A1268

Wheat and emblem of: a, Intl. Fund for Agricultural Development. b, Food and Agriculture Organization and farmer (49x27mm). c, World Food Program.

**2001, Oct. 16** **Photo.** *Perf. 14x13¼*

2430 Horiz. strip of 3 3.75 3.75
*a.-c.* A1268 800 l Any single 1.25 .50

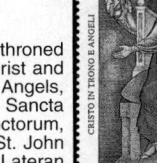

Enthroned Christ and Angels, Sancta Sanctorum, St. John Lateran Basilica A1269

**Litho. & Engr.**

**2001, Oct. 19** *Perf. 14*

2431 A1269 800 l multi 1.25 .50

Madonna and Child, by Macrino d'Alba A1270

**2001, Oct. 20**

2432 A1270 800 l multi 1.25 .50

A1271

Christmas A1272

**2001, Oct. 30** **Photo.** *Perf. 14x13¼*

2433 A1271 800 l multi 1.25 .50
2434 A1272 1000 l multi 1.60 .70

**Souvenir Sheet**

Italian Silk Industry — A1273

**Silk-screened on Silk**

**2001, Nov. 29** *Imperf.*

2435 A1273 5000 l multi 9.00 9.00

100 Cents = 1 Euro (€)

**Women in Art Type of 1998 With Denominations in Euros Only**

Designs: 1c, Hebe, sculpture by Antonio Canova. 2c, Profile of woman from Syracuse tetradrachm. 3c, Queen of Sheba from "The Meeting of King Solomon and the Queen of Sheba," painting by Piero della Francesa. 5c, "Young Velca," Etruscan tomb. 10c, Head of terra cotta statue, 3rd cent. BC. 20c, Danae, painting by Correggio. 23c, Detail from "Herod's Feast," by Fra Filippo Lippi. 41c, "Lady with the Unicorn," by Raphael. 45c, "Venus of Urbina," by Titian. 50c, "Antea," by Parmigianino. 65c, "Princess of Trebizonde," by Antonio Pisano. 70c, "Neptune Gives to Venice," by Giovanni Battista Tiepolo. 77c, "Primavera," by Botticelli. 85c, "Courtesan," by Vittore Carpaccio.

*Perf. 14x13¼, 13¼x13½ (#2447, 2449, 2450, 2452, 2453)*

**2002-04** **Photo.**

2436 A1142 1c multi .25 .25
*a.* Perf. 13¼x13½ .25 .25
2437 A1142 2c multi .25 .25
*a.* Perf. 13¼x13½ .25 .25
2438 A1142 3c multi .25 .25
*a.* Perf. 13¼x13½ .25 .25
2440 A1142 5c multi .25 .25
*a.* Perf. 13¼x13½ .25 .25
2441 A1142 10c multi .25 .25
*a.* Perf. 13¼x13½ ('04) .30 .25
2443 A1142 20c multi .60 .25
*a.* Perf. 13¼x13½ .60 .25
2444 A1142 23c multi .70 .25

**Engr.**

**Wmk. 303**

2446 A1142 41c multi 1.25 .45
*a.* Perf. 13¼x13½ 1.00 .35
2447 A1142 45c multi 1.40 .50
2448 A1142 50c multi 1.50 .55
*a.* Perf. 13¼x13½ 1.50 .55
2449 A1142 65c multi 1.90 .70
2450 A1142 70c multi 2.10 .75
2451 A1142 77c multi 2.25 .80
*a.* Perf. 13¼x13½ 2.25 .80
2452 A1142 85c multi 2.50 .90
2453 A1142 90c multi 2.75 1.00
*Nos. 2436-2453 (15)* 18.20 7.40

Issued: 2c, 5c, 10c, 23c, 41c, 50c, No. 2451, 1/1. 1c, 3c, 20c, 3/1. Nos. 2437a, 2438a, 2004; No. 2446a, 2003. No. 2451a, 2004 (?); Nos. 2436a, 2440a, 2448a, 2004; 45c, 1/27/04; 65c, 3/20/04; 85c, 2/17/04; No. 2443a, 2004; 70c, 7/31/04; 90c, 6/26/04; No. 2441a, 2004. This is an expanding set.

No. 2446 was reprinted in 2003 with imprint "I.P.Z.S. S.p.A.-Roma."

Italia — A1274

*Perf. 14x13¼, 13¼x13½ (#2460, 2461A, 2462)*

**2002-04** **Engr.** **Unwmk.**

2454 A1274 €1 multi 3.00 1.50
2455 A1274 €1.24 multi 3.75 1.75
2457 A1274 €1.55 multi 4.50 2.25
2459 A1274 €2.17 multi 6.50 3.25
2460 A1274 €2.35 multi 7.00 3.50
2461 A1274 €2.58 multi 7.75 3.75
2461A A1274 €2.80 multi 8.50 4.25
2462 A1274 €3 multi 9.00 4.50
2463 A1274 €3.62 multi 10.50 5.25
2465 A1274 €6.20 multi 18.00 9.00
*Nos. 2454-2465 (10)* 78.50 39.00

Issued: €1, €1.24, €1.55, €2.17, €2.58, €3.62, 1/2. €6.20, 3/1. €2.35, 5/7/04; €2.80, 2/3/04; €3, 5/22/04.

Compare Type A1274 with Type A1407.

**Priority Mail Type of 2001 with Euro Denominations Only**

**Typo. & Silk Screened**

**2002, Jan. 2** ***Serpentine Die Cut 11***

**Self-Adhesive**

**Background Color**

2466 A1242 62c yellow 1.90 .95
Booklet, 4 #2466 7.50
2467 A1242 77c blue green 2.50 1.10
2468 A1242 €1 blue 3.00 1.50
2469 A1242 €1.24 yel green 3.75 1.75
2470 A1242 €1.86 rose 5.50 2.75
2471 A1242 €4.13 lilac 12.50 6.00
*Nos. 2466-2471 (6)* 29.15 14.05

A self-adhesive etiquette is adjacent to each stamp.

No. 2466-2471 were reprinted in 2003 with imprint "I.P.Z.S. S.p.A.-Roma-2003." No. 2468 was reprinted in 2004 with imprint "I.P.Z.S. S.p.A. - Roma - 2004."

Introduction of the Euro — A1275

No. 2472: a, 1285 Venetian ducat. b, 1252 Genoan genovino and Florentine florin.

No. 2473: a, Euro symbol and flags. b, 1946 Italian 1-lira coin and new 1-euro coin.

**2002, Jan. 2 Photo. *Perf. 14x13¼***
**2472** A1275 Horiz. pair 2.50 .90
*a.-b.* 41c Either single 1.25 .45
**2473** A1275 Horiz. pair 2.50 .90
*a.-b.* 41c Either single 1.25 .45

Blessed Josemaría Escrivá (1902-75), Founder of Opus Dei A1276

**2002, Jan. 9**
**2474** A1276 41c multi 2.00 .45

Luigi Bocconi and Luigi Bocconi Commercial University, Milan A1277

**2002, Jan. 24**
**2475** A1277 41c multi 1.40 .45

Parma Stamps, 150th Anniv. — A1278

**2002, Jan. 26 *Perf. 13¼x14***
**2476** A1278 41c No. 1 1.40 .45

Intl. Year of Mountains A1279

**2002, Feb. 1**
**2477** A1279 41c multi 1.75 .45

2006 Winter Olympics, Turin — A1280

**2002, Feb. 23**
**2478** A1280 41c multi 1.40 .45

Malato Alla Fonte, Sculpture by Arnolfo de Cambio — A1281

**2002, Mar. 8 Engr. *Perf. 14***
**2479** A1281 41c red lilac 1.40 .45

Tourism A1282

Designs: No. 2480, Venaria Reale. No. 2481, San Gimignano. No. 2482, Sannicandro di Bari. No. 2483, Capo d'Orlando.

**2002, Mar. 23 Photo. *Perf. 14x13¼***
**2480** A1282 41c multi 1.40 .45
**2481** A1282 41c multi 1.40 .45
**2482** A1282 41c multi 1.40 .45
**2483** A1282 41c multi 1.40 .45
*Nos. 2480-2483 (4)* 5.60 1.80

See Nos. 2598-2600.

Santa Maria Della Grazie Sanctuary, Spezzano Albanese — A1283

**2002, Apr. 3 Engr. *Perf. 14***
**2484** A1283 41c red brown 1.40 .45

State Police, 150th Anniv. A1284

**2002, Apr. 12 Photo. *Perf. 14x13¼***
**2485** A1284 41c multi 1.40 .45

Fr. Matteo Ricci (1552-1610), Missionary in China, Geographer — A1285

**2002, Apr. 20**
**2486** A1285 41c multi 1.40 .45

Europa A1286

**2002, May 4 Photo. *Perf. 14x13¼***
**2487** A1286 41c multi 1.25 .45

Francesco Morosini Naval School, Venice A1287

**2002, May 4**
**2488** A1287 41c multi 1.40 .45

Italian Cinema — A1288

Designs: No. 2489, Umberto D., directed by Vittorio De Sica. No. 2490, Miracle in Milan, written by Cesare Zavattini.

**Litho. & Engr.**

**2002, May 10 *Perf. 13¼x14***
**2489** A1288 41c multi 1.40 .45
**2490** A1288 41c multi 1.40 .45

Juventus, 2001-02 Italian Soccer Champions A1289

**2002, May 18 Photo.**
**2491** A1289 41c multi 1.40 .45

Giovanni Falcone (1939-92) and Paolo Borsellino (1940-92), Judges Assassinated by Mafia — A1290

**2002, May 23 *Perf. 14x13¼***
**2492** A1290 62c multi 2.10 .75

NATO-Russia Summit Meeting, Rome — A1291

**2002, May 28 Photo. *Perf. 14x13¼***
**2493** A1291 41c multi 1.40 .45

World Kayak Championships, Valsesia — A1292

**2002, May 30 *Perf. 13¼x14***
**2494** A1292 52c multi 1.75 .60

Italian Military Forces in Peace Missions — A1293

**2002, June 1**
**2495** A1293 41c multi 1.40 .45

Modena Stamps, 150th Anniv. — A1294

**2002, June 1 Photo. *Perf. 13¼x14***
**2496** A1294 41c multi 1.40 .45

Alfredo Binda (1902-86), Cyclist — A1295

**2002, June 14 Photo. *Perf. 13¼x14***
**2497** A1295 41c multi 1.40 .45

St. Pio of Pietrelcina (1887-1968) — A1296

**2002, June 16 *Perf. 14***
**2498** A1296 41c multi 1.40 .45

Monument to the Massacre of the Acqui Division — A1297

**2002, June 21 *Perf. 13¼x14***
**2499** A1297 41c multi 1.40 .45

The Crucifixion, by Cimabue A1298

**Litho. & Engr.**

**2002, June 22 *Perf. 14***
**2500** A1298 €2.58 multi 8.25 2.75

Prefectural Institute, Bicent. A1299

**2002, June 24 Photo. *Perf. 14x13¼***
**2501** A1299 41c multi 1.40 .45

St. Maria Goretti (1890-1902) A1300

**2002, July 6** ***Perf. 13¼x14***
**2502** A1300 41c multi 1.40 .45

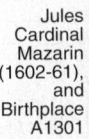

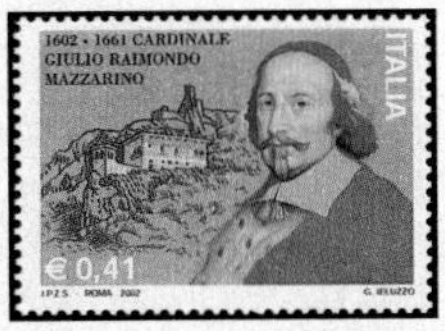


Jules Cardinal Mazarin (1602-61), and Birthplace A1301

**2002, July 13** **Photo.** ***Perf. 14x13¼***
**2503** A1301 41c multi 1.40 .45

Italians Around the World — A1302

**2002, Aug. 8** ***Perf. 13¼x14***
**2504** A1302 52c multi 1.75 .60

Monument to Sant'Anna di Stazzema Massacre A1303

**2002, Aug. 17**
**2505** A1303 41c multi 1.40 .45

UNESCO World Heritage Sites — A1304

Designs: 41c, Pisa. 52c, Aeolian Islands.

**2002, Aug. 30** ***Perf. 14***
**2506** A1304 41c multi + label 1.40 .45
**2507** A1304 52c multi + label 1.75 .60

Italian Design A1305

Apparel by: a, Krizia. b, Dolce e Gabbana. c, Gianfranco Ferre. d, Giorgio Armani. e, Laura Biagiotti. f, Prada.

**2002, Aug. 30** **Litho.**
**2508** Sheet of 6 8.50 8.50
*a.-f.* A1305 41c Any single 1.40 .45

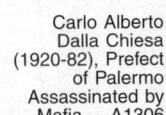

Carlo Alberto Dalla Chiesa (1920-82), Prefect of Palermo Assassinated by Mafia — A1306

**2002. Sept. 3** **Photo.** ***Perf. 13¼x14***
**2509** A1306 41c multi 1.40 .45

Concordia Theater, Monte Castello de Vibio — A1307

**Litho. & Engr.**

**2002, Sept. 7** ***Perf. 14***
**2510** A1307 41c multi 1.40 .45

Sailboat Gathering, Imperia A1308

**2002, Sept. 11** **Photo.** ***Perf. 14x13¼***
**2511** A1308 41c multi 1.40 .45

Santa Giulia Museum, Brescia — A1309

Palazzo Altemps, Roman Natl. Museum A1310

***Perf. 13¼x14, 14x13¼***

**2002, Oct. 4** **Photo.**
**2512** A1309 41c multi 1.50 .45
**2513** A1310 41c multi 1.50 .45

Roman States Postage Stamps, 150th Anniv. — A1311

**2002, Oct. 4** **Photo.** ***Perf. 13¼x14***
**2514** A1311 41c Roman States #6 1.40 .45

Flora and Fauna — A1312

**2002, Oct. 11**
**2515** A1312 23c Orchid .80 .30
**2516** A1312 52c Lynx 1.60 .60
**2517** A1312 77c Stag beetle 2.60 .90
*Nos. 2515-2517 (3)* 5.00 1.80

World Food Day — A1313

**2002, Oct. 16** **Photo.** ***Perf. 13¼x14***
**2518** A1313 41c multi 1.40 .45

Forestry Corps — A1314

**2002, Oct. 22**
**2519** A1314 41c multi 1.40 .45

Father Carlo Gnocchi (1902-56), Founder of Fondazione Pro Juventute A1315

**2002, Oct. 25**
**2520** A1315 41c multi 1.40 .45

2002 Muscular Dystrophy Telethon A1316

**2002, Oct. 31** ***Perf. 14x13¼***
**2521** A1316 41c multi 1.40 .45

Christmas A1317

Designs: 41c, Nativity. 62c, Child with candle, Christmas tree, vert.

***Perf. 14x13¼, 13¼x14***

**2002, Oct. 31** **Photo.**
**2522** A1317 41c multi 1.40 .45
**2523** A1317 62c multi 2.10 .75

Women's Sports — A1318

**2002, Nov. 20** **Photo.** ***Perf. 13¼x14***
**2524** A1318 41c multi 1.40 .45

Stamp Day A1319

**2002, Nov. 29** ***Perf. 14x13¼***
**2525** A1319 62c multi 2.10 .75

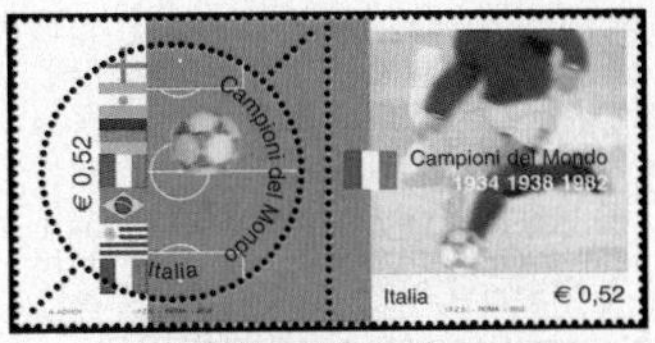


2002 World Cup Soccer Championships, Japan and Korea — A1320

No. 2526: a, Flags, soccer ball and field (33mm diameter). b, Soccer player, years of Italian championships.

**2002, Nov. 29** **Litho.** ***Perf. 14***
**2526** A1320 Horiz. pair 3.50 1.50
*a.-b.* 52c Either single 1.75 .60

See Argentina No. 2184, Brazil No. 2840, France No. 2891, Germany No. 2163 and Uruguay No. 1946.

Vittorio Emanuele Orlando (1860-1952), Politician — A1321

**2002, Dec. 4** **Photo.** ***Perf. 13¼x14***
**2527** A1321 41c multi 1.40 .45

2003 Winter Universiade Games, Tarvisio — A1322

**2003, Jan. 16** **Photo.** ***Perf. 13½x14***
**2528** A1322 52c multi 1.75 .60

"La Repubblica Italiana" Philatelic Exhibition, Rome A1323

**2003, Jan. 16** ***Perf. 14***
**2529** A1323 62c multi 2.25 .75
*a.* Booklet pane of 5 *120.00* *135.00*
Complete booklet, #2529a *120.00*

World Cyclocross Championships, Monopoli — A1324

**2003, Feb. 1 Photo.** ***Perf. 13¼x14***
**2530** A1324 41c multi 1.40 .60

Alinari Brothers Photographic Studio, 150th Anniv. — A1325

**2003, Feb. 1** ***Perf. 14x13¼***
**2531** A1325 77c multi + label 2.75 1.10

European Year of the Disabled A1326

**2003, Feb. 14**
**2532** A1326 41c multi 1.40 .60

World Nordic Skiing Championships, Val di Fiemme — A1327

**2003, Feb. 18 Photo.** ***Perf. 14x13¼***
**2533** A1327 41c multi 1.40 .60

National Civil Service — A1328

**2003, Feb. 25 Photo.** ***Perf. 14x13¼***
**2534** A1328 62c multi + label 2.10 .75

Duel of Barletta, 500th Anniv. A1329

**2003, Mar. 6**
**2535** A1329 41c multi 1.40 .60

Torquato Tasso High School, Rome — A1330

**2003, Mar. 11 Photo.** ***Perf. 14***
**2536** A1330 41c multi 1.40 .60

Encounter at the Golden Door, by Giotto A1331

**2003, Mar. 20 Litho. & Engr.**
**2537** A1331 41c multi 1.40 .60

Gian Rinaldo Carli High School, Pisino d'Istria — A1332

**2003, Mar. 24 Photo.**
**2538** A1332 41c multi 1.40 .60

Lincei Academy, 400th Anniv. — A1333

**Litho. & Engr.**
**2003, Mar. 26** ***Perf. 13¼x14***
**2539** A1333 41c multi 1.40 .60

World Junior Fencing Championships, Trapani — A1334

**2003, Apr. 4 Photo.** ***Perf. 14x13¼***
**2540** A1334 41c multi 1.40 .60

Acquasanta Golf Club, Rome, Cent. A1335

**2003, Apr. 5**
**2541** A1335 77c multi 2.25 1.10

**Tourism Type of 2002**

**2003, Apr. 5**
**2542** A1282 41c Sestri Levante 1.50 .60
**2543** A1282 41c Lanciano 1.50 .60
**2544** A1282 41c Procida 1.50 .60
*Nos. 2542-2544 (3)* 4.50 1.80

La Sapienza University, Rome, 700th Anniv. — A1336

**2003, Apr. 10 Photo.** ***Perf. 14***
**2545** A1336 41c multi 1.40 .60

Natl. Pasta Museum, Rome — A1337

**2003, Apr. 17** ***Perf. 13¼x14***
**2546** A1337 41c multi 1.40 .60

Guido Carli Free Intl. University for Social Studies — A1338

**2003, Apr. 23 Photo.** ***Perf. 14***
**2547** A1338 €2.58 multi 8.25 3.25

Europa — A1339

Poster art by Marcello Dudovich: 41c, Woman in blue dress. 52c, Women in white dresses.

**2003, May 5 Photo.** ***Perf. 13¼x14***
**2548** A1339 41c multi 1.25 .60
**2549** A1339 52c multi 1.50 .75

Central State Archives, 50th Anniv. A1340

**2003, May 8** ***Perf. 14x13¼***
**2550** A1340 41c multi 1.40 .60

Veronafil Philatelic Exhibition, Verona A1341

**2003, May 9**
**2551** A1341 41c multi 1.40 .60

Aldo Moro (1916-78), Premier — A1342

**2003, May 9** ***Perf. 13¼x14***
**2552** A1342 62c multi 2.10 .95

**Souvenir Sheet**

Antonio Meucci (1808-96), Telephone Pioneer — A1343

**2003, May 28 Litho.**
**2553** A1343 52c multi 2.00 1.50

Father Eugenio Barsanti and Felice Matteucci, Internal Combustion Engine Pioneers A1344

**2003, May 31 Photo.** ***Perf. 14x13¼***
**2554** A1344 52c multi 1.75 .75

Post Office, Latina A1345

**2003, June 30 Engr.** ***Perf. 14***
**2555** A1345 41c blue 1.40 .60

City of Latina, 70th anniv.

Italian Presidency of the Council of the European Union A1346

**2003, July 1 Photo.** ***Perf. 14x13¼***
**2556** A1346 41c multi 1.40 .60

Ezio Vanoni (1903-56), Economist A1347

**2003, July 1** ***Perf. 13¼x14***
**2557** A1347 €2.58 multi 8.25 3.25

The Assumption, by Corrado Giaquinto (c. 1694-1765)
A1348

**2003, July 2** ***Perf. 14***
**2558** A1348 77c multi 2.75 .90

Eugenio Balzan (1874-1953), Journalist — A1349

**2003, July 15 Photo.** ***Perf. 14x13¼***
**2559** A1349 41c multi 1.40 .60

Francesco Mazzola "Il Parmigianino," (1503-40), Painter — A1350

**2003, Aug. 23 Photo.** ***Perf. 14x14¼***
**2560** A1350 41c multi 1.75 .60

Juventus, 2002-03 Italian Soccer Champions
A1351

**2003, Aug. 30** ***Perf. 13¼x14***
**2561** A1351 41c multi 1.75 .60

Abbey of St. Sylvester I, Nonantola — A1352

**Litho. & Engr.**

**2003, Sept. 6** ***Perf. 14***
**2562** A1352 41c multi 1.40 .60

Italian Aviation Pioneers
A1353

**2003, Sept. 12 Photo.** ***Perf. 13x13¼***
**2563** A1353 52c Mario Calderara 1.60 .75
**2564** A1353 52c Mario Cobianchi 1.60 .75
**2565** A1353 52c Gianni Caproni 1.60 .75
**2566** A1353 52c Alessandro Marchetti 1.60 .75
*a.* Souvenir sheet, #2563-2566 7.00 7.00
*Nos. 2563-2566 (4)* 6.40 3.00

Giovanni Giolitti (1842-1928), Premier — A1354

**2003, Sept. 13 Photo.** ***Perf. 14x13¼***
**2567** A1354 41c multi 1.40 .60

Europalia Italia Festival, Belgium
A1355

Designs: 41c, Still Life, by Giorgio Morandi. 52c, 1947 Cisitalia 202, designed by Battista Pininfarina.

**2003, Sept. 13**
**2568** A1355 41c multi 1.40 .60
**2569** A1355 52c multi 1.75 .75

See Belgium Nos. 1980-1981.

Cent. of First Publication of Leonardo Magazine, by Attilio Vallecchi (1880-1946)
A1356

**2003, Sept. 27 Photo.** ***Perf. 13x13¼***
**2570** A1356 41c multi 1.40 .60

The Family — A1357

**2003, Oct. 3** ***Perf. 13¼x13***
**2571** A1357 77c multi 2.50 1.10

Maestà, by Duccio di Buoninsegna
A1358

**2003, Oct. 4**
**2572** A1358 41c multi 1.40 .60

Exhibition of paintings by Duccio di Buoninsegna, Siena.

Vittorio Alfieri (1749-1803), Poet — A1359

**2003, Oct. 8** ***Perf. 13x13¼***
**2573** A1359 41c multi 1.40 .60

Ugo La Malfa (1903-79), Government Minister — A1360

**2003, Oct. 13** ***Perf. 13¼x13***
**2574** A1360 62c multi 2.10 .95

Bernardino Ramazzini (1633-1714), Physician — A1361

**2003, Oct. 15** ***Perf. 13x13¼***
**2575** A1361 41c multi 1.40 .60

Confedilizia Property Owner's Organization, 120th Anniv. — A1362

**2003, Oct. 15** ***Perf. 13¼x13***
**2576** A1362 €2.58 multi 7.75 3.25

Nativity, by Gian Paolo Cavagna — A1363

Poinsettia
A1364

**2003, Oct. 24**
**2577** A1363 41c multi 1.40 .50
**2578** A1364 62c multi 2.10 .80

Christmas.

Futurist Art by Giacomo Balla
A1365

Designs: 41c, Forme Grido Viva L'Italia. 52c, Linee-Forza del Pugno di Boccioni.

**2003, Nov. 26 Photo.** ***Perf. 13x13¼***
**2579** A1365 41c multi 1.40 .60
**2580** A1365 52c multi 1.75 .75

Philately Day
A1366

**2003, Nov. 28 Photo.** ***Perf. 13x13¼***
**2581** A1366 41c multi 1.40 .60

**Priority Mail Type of 2001 With Euro Denominations Only**

**Typo. & Silk Screened**

**2004** ***Serpentine Die Cut 11***

**Self-Adhesive**

**Background Color**

**2582** A1242 60c orange (gold frame) 2.00 .85
**2583** A1242 80c yellow brown 2.60 1.25
**2584** A1242 €1.40 green 4.25 2.00
**2585** A1242 €1.50 gray 4.50 2.25

**Photo.**

**2585A** A1242 60c dull orange (bronze frame) 1.75 .85
**2585B** A1242 80c dull brn (bronze frame) 2.40 1.25
*Nos. 2582-2585B (6)* 17.50 8.45

Issued: 60c, 1/2; €1.40, 1/10; 80c, €1.50, No. 2585A, 3/19/04. A self-adhesive etiquette is adjacent to each stamp.

The frame has a splotchy appearance on Nos. 2585A and 2585B.

No. 2585A exists dated 2005. Undated examples of No. 2585B were issued in 2008.

See No. 2613A.

A1367

Television Transmissions in Italy, 50th Anniv. — A1368

**2004, Jan. 3 Photo.** ***Perf. 13x13¼***
**2586** A1367 41c multi 1.40 .60
**2587** A1368 62c multi 2.10 .95

Giorgio La Pira (1904-77), Judge
A1369

**2004, Jan. 9 Photo.** ***Perf. 13x13¼***
**2588** A1369 41c multi 1.40 .60

Genoa, 2004 European Cultural Capital — A1370

**2004, Feb. 12 Photo. *Perf. 13¼x13***

2589 A1370 45c multi 1.40 .60

2006 Winter Olympics, Turin — A1371

Designs: 23c, Santa Maria Assunta Church, Pragelato. 45c, San Pietro Apostolo Church, Bardonecchia. 62c, Mole Antonelliana, Turin. 65c, Fountain, Sauze d'Oulx.

**2004, Mar. 9**

2590 A1371 23c multi .80 .35
2591 A1371 45c multi 1.40 .60
2592 A1371 62c multi 2.10 .95
2593 A1371 65c multi 2.10 .95
*Nos. 2590-2593 (4)* 6.40 2.85

Petrarch (1304-74), Poet — A1372

**2004, Mar. 18**

2594 A1372 45c multi 1.40 .60

Giorgio Amarelli Licorice Museum, Rossano — A1373

**2004, Apr. 3 *Perf. 14***

2595 A1373 45c multi 1.40 .60

Road Safety A1374

Designs: 60c, Car dashboard, traffic signs. 62c, Seat belt, map of Italy, vert.

**2004, Apr. 7 *Perf. 13x13¼, 13¼x13***

2596 A1374 60c multi 1.90 .85
2597 A1374 62c multi 2.10 .95

**Tourism Type of 2002**

**2004, Apr. 10 Photo. *Perf. 13x13¼***

2598 A1282 45c Vignola 1.40 .60
2599 A1282 45c Viterbo 1.40 .60
2600 A1282 45c Isole Egadi 1.40 .60
*Nos. 2598-2600 (3)* 4.20 1.80

Casa del Fascio, Como, Designed by Giuseppe Terragni (1904-43), Architect A1375

**2004, Apr. 17 *Perf. 13x13¼***

2601 A1375 85c multi 2.75 1.00

Souvenir Sheet

Rome-Bangkok Foundation — A1376

No. 2602: a, Wat Saket, Bangkok. b, Colosseum, Rome.

**2004, Apr. 21 Litho. *Perf. 14x13¼***

2602 A1376 Sheet of 2 4.00 4.00
*a.-b.* 65c Either single 2.00 .95

See Thailand No. 2125.

Martyrdom of St. George, 1700th Anniv. — A1377

**2004, Apr. 23 Photo. *Perf. 14***

2603 A1377 €2.80 multi 8.50 3.75

Europa A1378

Map of Europe and: 45c, Closed suitcase. 62c, Open suitcase.

**2004, May 7 *Perf. 13x13¼***

2604 A1378 45c multi 1.25 .60
2605 A1378 62c multi 1.90 .95

Souvenir Sheet

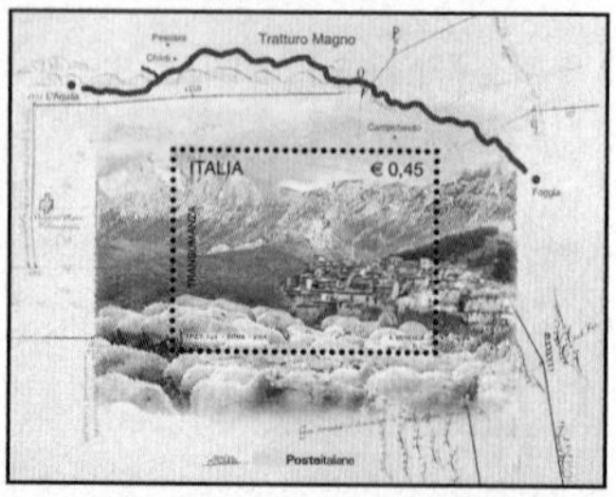


L'Aquila - Foggia Livestock Trail — A1379

**2004, May 8 Litho. *Perf. 14x13¼***

2606 A1379 45c multi 2.00 2.00

Great Synagogue, Rome — A1380

**2004, May 20 Photo. *Perf. 13¼x14***

2607 A1380 60c shown 1.90 .85
2608 A1380 62c Synagogue, diff. 2.10 .95

See Israel Nos. 1564-1565.

Milan, 2003-04 Italian Soccer Champions A1381

**2004, May 22 *Perf. 13x13¼***

2609 A1381 45c multi 1.50 .60

50th Puccini Festival — A1382

**2004, May 28 Photo. *Perf. 13¼x13***

2610 A1382 60c multi 2.00 .85

University of Turin, 600th Anniv. — A1383

**2004, June 3 Engr. *Perf. 14***

2611 A1383 45c brown 1.50 .60

Achille Varzi (1904-48), Automobile and Motorcycle Racer A1384

**2004, June 5 Photo. *Perf. 13x13¼***

2612 A1384 45c multi 1.50 .60

Penitentiary Police Corps — A1385

**2004, June 16 Photo. *Perf. 13x13¼***

2613 A1385 45c multi 1.50 .60

**Priority Mail Type of 2001 With Euro Denominations Only**

***Serpentine Die Cut 11***

**2004, June 16 Photo.**

**Self-Adhesive**

**Background Color**

2613A A1242 €1.40 blue green 4.75 1.50
2614 A1242 €2 slate grn (bronze frame) 6.50 2.50
2615 A1242 €2.20 rose 7.00 2.75
*Nos. 2613A-2615 (3)* 18.25 6.75

Issued: €2, 6/16; €1.40, July; €2.20, 6/26.

A self-adhesive etiquette is adjacent to each stamp.

No. 2613A has a less obvious coating over the circled "P" that shines most when viewed from an oblique angle. No. 2613A exists dated 2006. Undated examples of No. 2613A were issued in 2007. Undated examples of Nos. 2614 and 2615 were issued in 2008.

Ascent of K2 By Italian Mountaineers, 50th Anniv. — A1386

**2004, July 31 Photo. *Perf. 13¼x13***

2616 A1386 65c multi 2.10 .95

Italian Regions A1387

**2004, Aug. 27 *Perf. 14x13¼***

2617 A1387 45c Liguria 1.50 .60
2618 A1387 45c Emilia Romagna 1.50 .60
2619 A1387 45c Abruzzo 1.50 .60
2620 A1387 45c Basilicata 1.50 .60
*Nos. 2617-2620 (4)* 6.00 2.40

See Nos. 2654-2657, 2746-2749, 2796-2799, 2876-2879.

Apparition of Madonna of Tirano, 500th Anniv. — A1388

**2004, Sept. 4 *Perf. 13¼x13***

2621 A1388 45c multi 1.40 .60

St. Nilus of Rossano (c. 905-1005), Abbot — A1389

**2004, Sept. 25 Photo. *Perf. 14¼x14***

2622 A1389 45c multi 1.40 .60

State Archives, Florence — A1390

**2004, Sept. 30 Photo.** ***Perf. 14¼x14***
**2623** A1390 45c multi 1.40 .60

Lacemaking — A1391

**2004, Oct. 8 Embroidered** ***Imperf.***
**Self-Adhesive**
**2624** A1391 €2.80 blue & gray 9.00 3.25

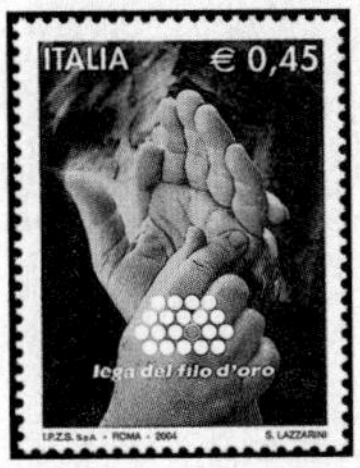

Filo d'Oro Society — A1392

**2004, Oct. 9 Photo.** ***Perf. 13¼x13***
**2625** A1392 45c multi 1.40 .60

Victor Emmanuel III State Technical Institute, Lucera A1393

**2004, Oct. 16** ***Perf. 14x14¼***
**2626** A1393 45c multi 1.40 .60

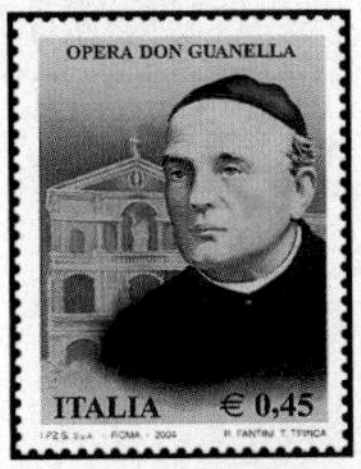

Father Luigi Guanella (1842-1915) A1394

**2004, Oct. 19 Photo.** ***Perf. 13¼x13***
**2627** A1394 45c multi 1.40 .60

Return of Trieste to Italy, 50th Anniv. A1395

**2004, Oct. 26** ***Perf. 13x13¼***
**2628** A1395 45c multi 1.50 .60
*a.* Booklet pane of 4 6.00 —
Complete booklet, #2628a 6.00

Military Information and Security Service A1396

**2004, Oct. 27 Photo.** ***Perf. 13x13¼***
**2629** A1396 60c multi 1.90 .85

European Constitution — A1397

**2004, Oct. 29**
**2630** A1397 62c multi 2.25 .95

Venice Dockyards, 900th Anniv. A1398

**2004, Oct. 30 Photo.** ***Perf. 13x13¼***
**2631** A1398 €2.80 multi 9.00 3.75

Live Nativity Scene, Tricase A1399

Christmas Tree — A1400

**2004, Oct. 30 Photo.** ***Perf. 13x13¼***
**2632** A1399 45c multi 1.40 .60

**Photo. & Embossed**
***Perf. 13¼x13***
**2633** A1400 62c multi 2.10 .95

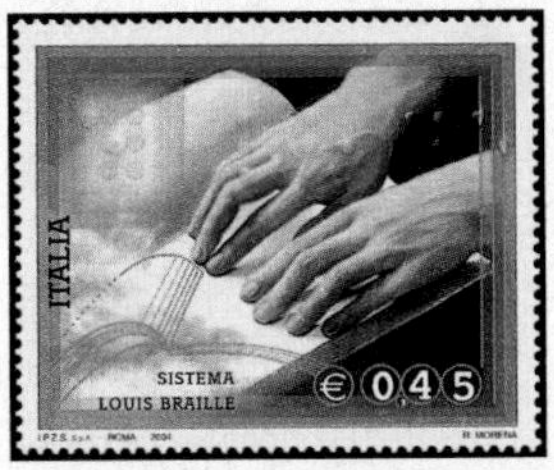

Hands and Braille Book — A1401

**Photo. & Embossed**
**2004, Nov. 6** ***Perf. 14***
**2634** A1401 45c multi 2.00 .60

Martyrdom of St. Lucy, 1700th Anniv. — A1402

**2004, Nov. 6 Photo.** ***Perf. 13¼x13***
**2635** A1402 45c multi 1.25 .60

Philately Day — A1403

**2004, Nov. 12** ***Perf. 13¼x14***
**2636** A1403 45c multi 1.40 .60

Tenth "Sport For All" World Congress A1404

**2004, Nov. 12 Photo.** ***Perf. 13¼x13***
**2637** A1404 65c multi 2.10 .95

Maria Santissima Assunta Free University, Rome — A1405

**2004, Nov. 15** ***Perf. 14***
**2638** A1405 45c multi 1.40 .60

Souvenir Sheet

Italian-made Footwear — A1406

No. 2639: a, Woman's shoe by Casadei. b, Men's shoes by Moreschi. c, Men's shoe by Fratelli Rosetti. d, Athletic shoe by Superga.

**2004, Nov. 27 Photo.** ***Perf. 13¼x13***
**2639** A1406 Sheet of 4 6.00 6.00
*a.-d.* 45c Any single 1.50 .60

Italia With Large Numerals — A1407

***Perf. 13¼x13½***
**2005, Jan. 21 Engr. Unwmk.**
**2640** A1407 €1 multi 3.00 1.50

Compare type A1407 with type A1274.

Italian Auto Club, Cent. — A1408

**2005, Jan. 21 Photo.** ***Perf. 13¼x13***
**2648** A1408 45c multi 1.40 .60

Luigi Calabresi (1937-72), Assassinated Police Commissioner A1409

**2005, Jan. 26**
**2649** A1409 45c multi 1.40 .60

Exodus of Italians From Istria, Fiume and Dalmatia, 60th Anniv. A1410

**2005, Feb. 10 Photo.** ***Perf. 14x13¼***
**2650** A1410 45c multi 1.50 .60

Rotary International, Cent. — A1411

**2005, Feb. 23** ***Perf. 13¼x14***
**2651** A1411 65c multi 1.90 .95

Sassari Brigade A1412

**2005, Mar. 1** ***Perf. 14x13¼***
**2652** A1412 45c multi 1.40 .60

14th Art Quadrennial, Rome — A1413

**2005, Mar. 4**
**2653** A1413 45c multi 1.40 .60

**Italian Regions Type of 2004**

**2005, Mar. 18** ***Perf. 13x13¼***

| | | | | |
|---|---|---|---|---|
| **2654** | A1387 | 45c Lombardy | 1.50 | .60 |
| **2655** | A1387 | 45c Friuli-Venezia Giulia | 1.50 | .60 |
| **2656** | A1387 | 45c Campania | 1.50 | .60 |
| **2657** | A1387 | 45c Calabria | 1.50 | .60 |
| | | *Nos. 2654-2657 (4)* | 6.00 | 2.40 |

2006 Winter Olympics, Turin — A1414

Turin Olympics emblem and: 23c, Pinerolo. 45c, Cesana Torinese. 60c, Mascots Neve and Gliz. 62c, Sestriere.

**2005, Mar. 21** ***Perf. 13¼x13***

| | | | | |
|---|---|---|---|---|
| **2658** | A1414 | 23c multi | .80 | .35 |
| **2659** | A1414 | 45c multi | 1.40 | .60 |
| **2660** | A1414 | 60c multi | 2.00 | .85 |
| **2661** | A1414 | 62c multi | 2.25 | .95 |
| | | *Nos. 2658-2661 (4)* | 6.45 | 2.75 |

Intl. Year of Physics A1415

**2005, Mar. 29** ***Perf. 14x13¼***
**2662** A1415 85c multi 2.75 1.25

Opening of New Milan Fair Complex A1416

**2005, Mar. 31**
**2663** A1416 45c multi 1.40 .60

State Railways, Cent. A1417

**2005, Apr. 22 Photo.** ***Perf. 13x13¼***
**2664** A1417 45c multi 1.40 .60

Italian Army — A1418

**2005, Apr. 29** ***Perf. 13¼x13***
**2665** A1418 45c multi 1.40 .60

Europa — A1419

**2005, May 9 Photo.** ***Perf. 13¼x13***

| | | | | |
|---|---|---|---|---|
| **2666** | A1419 | 45c Wheat | 1.10 | .55 |
| **2667** | A1419 | 62c Grapes | 1.90 | .95 |

St. Ignatius of Làconi (1701-81) A1420

**2005, May 11 Photo.** ***Perf. 13¼x13***
**2668** A1420 45c multi 1.40 .60

Commercial Confederation, 60th Anniv. — A1421

**2005, May 18**
**2669** A1421 60c multi 2.00 .85

Tommaso Campanella High School, Reggio Calabria — A1422

**2005, May 20 Photo.** ***Perf. 13x13¼***
**2670** A1422 45c multi 1.40 .60

San Giuseppe da Copertino Basilica A1423

**2005, May 21 Engr.** ***Perf. 14***
**2671** A1423 45c blue gray 1.40 .60

Tourism — A1424

**2005, May 26** **Photo.**

| | | | | |
|---|---|---|---|---|
| **2672** | A1424 | 45c Asolo | 1.50 | .60 |
| **2673** | A1424 | 45c Rocchetta a Volturno | 1.50 | .60 |
| **2674** | A1424 | 45c Amalfi | 1.50 | .60 |
| | | *Nos. 2672-2674 (3)* | 4.50 | 1.80 |

See Nos. 2734-2736, 2803-2806, 2887-2890, 2948-2951, 3080-3083, 3126-3129.

St. Gerardo Maiella (1726-55) A1425

**2005, May 28** ***Perf. 13x13¼***
**2675** A1425 45c multi 1.40 .60

Juventus, 2004-05 Italian Soccer Champions A1426

**2005, June 6** ***Perf. 13¼x13***
**2676** A1426 45c multi 1.40 .60

Ratification of Modifications to Italy-Vatican Concordat, 20th Anniv. — A1427

Arms of Vatican City and Italy and: 45c, Map. €2.80, Pen.

**2005, June 9** ***Perf. 13x13¼***

| | | | | |
|---|---|---|---|---|
| **2677** | A1427 | 45c multi | 1.40 | .60 |
| **2678** | A1427 | €2.80 multi | 9.00 | 3.75 |

See Vatican City Nos. 1301-1302.

First Italian Dirigible Flight by Almerico da Schio, Cent. A1428

**2005, June 17 Photo.** ***Perf. 13x13¼***
**2679** A1428 €3 multi 9.00 4.25

European Youth Olympic Festival, Lignano Sabbiadoro — A1429

**2005, June 20 Photo.** ***Perf. 13¼x13***
**2680** A1429 62c multi 2.00 .95

Intl. Day Against Illegal Drugs A1430

**2005, June 25 Photo.** ***Perf. 13x13¼***
**2681** A1430 45c multi 1.40 .60

Institute for Maritime Trades Social Insurance A1431

**2005, June 28**
**2682** A1431 45c multi 1.40 .60

Leo Longanesi (1905-57), Writer — A1432

**2005, Aug. 26 Engr.** ***Perf. 13¼x14***
**2683** A1432 45c dark blue 1.40 .60

Alberto Ascari (1918-55), Race Car Driver A1433

**2005, Sept. 2 Photo.** ***Perf. 13x13¼***
**2684** A1433 €2.80 multi 9.00 3.75

A1434

National Military Aerobatic Team A1435

**2005, Sept. 3 Photo.** ***Perf. 13x13¼***
**2685** A1434 45c multi 1.40 .60
**2686** A1435 60c multi 2.00 .85

Pietro Savorgnan di Brazzà (1852-1905), Explorer of Africa — A1436

**2005, Sept. 14 Photo.** ***Perf. 13¼x13***
**2687** A1436 45c multi 1.40 .60

Guido Gonella (1905-82), Politician, Journalist A1437

**2005, Sept. 17**
**2688** A1437 45c multi 1.40 .60

Italian Participation in Exploration of Mars — A1438

**Photo. With Hologram Applied**
**2005, Sept. 21** ***Die Cut***
**Self-Adhesive**
**2689** A1438 80c multi 2.50 1.25

Printed in sheets of 4.

Intercultura, 50th Anniv. — A1439

**2005, Sept. 23 Photo.** ***Perf. 13x13¼***
**2690** A1439 60c multi 2.00 .85

Souvenir Sheet

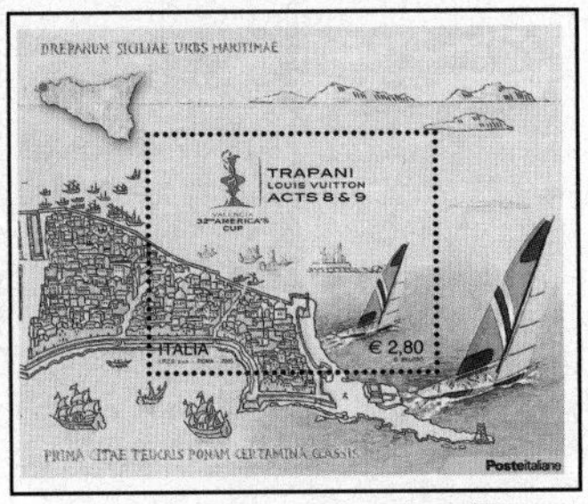


Louis Vuitton Cup Acts 8 & 9 (Races to Determine America's Cup Challenger), Trapani — A1440

**2005, Sept. 28 Photo.** ***Perf. 13¼x13***
**2691** A1440 €2.80 multi 8.50 8.50

**Priority Mail Type of 2001 With Euro Denominations Only Inscribed "I. P. Z. S. S. p. A. - ROMA 2005" at Bottom**

**2005 Photo.** ***Serpentine Die Cut 11***
**Self-Adhesive**
**Background Color**
**2691A** A1242 62c yellow 2.10 .95
**2691B** A1242 €1.50 gray 5.00 2.25

Issued: 62c, Oct.; €1.50, Dec.

Nos. 2466 and 2585 have different printer's inscriptions and have a more easily seen coating over the circled "P" than on Nos. 2691A and 2691B. The coating over the circled "P" on Nos. 2691A and 2691B shines most when viewed from an oblique angle. A self-adhesive etiquette is adjacent to each stamp. Nos. 2691A and 2691B have self-adhesive selvage surrounding the stamp and etiquette. This selvage is not found on Nos. 2466 and 2585.

No. 2691B exists without year date and without etiquette, issued in 2007.

Stamp Day — A1441

**2005, Oct. 7 Photo.** ***Perf. 13¼x13***
**2692** A1441 45c multi 1.40 .60

Italian Organ Donation Association A1442

**2005, Oct. 7 Photo.** ***Perf. 13¼x13***
**2693** A1442 60c multi 1.90 .85

National Association of Communities A1443

**2005, Oct. 19**
**2694** A1443 45c multi 1.40 .60

Story of Sts. Stephan and John The Baptist, by Fra Filippo Lippi A1444

**2005, Oct. 25** ***Perf. 13x13¼***
**2695** A1444 45c shown 1.50 .60
**2696** A1444 €1.50 Four men 4.75 2.25

A1445

Christmas A1446

**2005, Oct. 31 Photo.** ***Perf. 13x13¼***
**2697** A1445 45c multi 1.40 .60

***Perf. 13¼x13***
**2698** A1446 62c multi 2.10 .95

Alcide De Gasperi (1881-1954), Prime Minister — A1447

**2005, Nov. 9 Photo.** ***Perf. 13¼x13***
**2699** A1447 62c multi 2.00 .95

Giuseppe Mazzini (1805-72), Revolution Leader A1448

**2005, Nov. 10 Photo.** ***Perf. 13x13¼***
**2700** A1448 45c multi 1.40 .60

National Civil Protection A1449

**2005, Nov. 16 Photo.** ***Perf. 13¼x13***
**2701** A1449 45c multi 1.50 .60

Italian Red Cross — A1450

**2005, Nov. 16**
**2702** A1450 45c multi 1.50 .60

Admission to United Nations, 50th Anniv. A1451

**2005, Nov. 23** ***Perf. 13x13¼***
**2703** A1451 70c multi 2.50 1.00

Popes Reigning in 2005 A1452

Designs: 45c, Pope John Paul II (1920-2005). 65c, Pope Benedict XVI.

**2005, Nov. 26 Photo.** ***Perf. 13x13¼***
**2704** A1452 45c multi 1.50 .60
**2705** A1452 65c multi 2.25 .95

Reconstitution of Caserta Province, 60th Anniv. — A1453

**2005, Dec. 5 Photo.** ***Perf. 13x13¼***
**2706** A1453 45c multi 1.40 .60

Opening of Enrico Toti Submarine Exhibit at Natl. Museum of Science and Technology, Milan A1454

**2005, Dec. 7**
**2707** A1454 82c multi 2.40 1.25

Eighteenth Birthday Greetings A1455

**2006, Jan. 1 Photo.** ***Perf. 13½x13***
**2708** A1455 45c blue & multi 1.50 .60
**2709** A1455 45c pink & multi 1.50 .60

Souvenir sheets of 1 of redrawn stamps similar to Nos. 2708-2709 exist from a limited printing. Value, set of two sheets *$1,500.*

Panini, Soccer Card and Sticker Creators A1456

**2006, Jan. 30 Photo.** ***Perf. 13x13¼***
**2710** A1456 €2.80 multi 8.75 3.75

Quattroruote Magazine, 50th Anniv. — A1457

**2006, Feb. 1** ***Perf. 13¼x13***
**2711** A1457 62c multi 2.00 .95

Carlo Bo University, Urbino, 500th Anniv. — A1458

Ernesto Cairoli State High School, Varese — A1459

Alessandron Tassoni State Science High School, Modena — A1460

Agostino Nifo State High School, Sessa Aurunca — A1461

**2006, Feb. 6**
**2712** A1458 45c multi 1.50 .60
**2713** A1459 45c multi 1.50 .60
**2714** A1460 45c multi 1.50 .60
**2715** A1461 45c multi 1.50 .60
*Nos. 2712-2715 (4)* 6.00 2.40

2006 Winter Olympics, Turin A1462

**2006, Feb. 8** ***Perf. 13x13¼***
**2716** A1462 23c Biathlon .75 .35
**2717** A1462 45c Figure skating 1.40 .60
**2718** A1462 65c Ice hockey 2.10 .95
**2719** A1462 70c Curling 2.25 1.00
**2720** A1462 85c Bobsled 2.75 1.25
**2721** A1462 90c Alpine skiing 3.00 1.90
**2722** A1462 €1 Torch 3.25 1.50
**2723** A1462 €1.30 Luge 4.25 2.00
**2724** A1462 €1.70 Medals 5.50 2.50
*a.* Souvenir sheet, #2716-2724 25.00 20.00
*Nos. 2716-2724 (9)* 25.25 12.05

Nos. 23, 45, 79 and 239 — A1463

**2006, Feb. 9 Photo.** ***Perf. 13¼x13***
**2725** A1463 60c multi 2.00 .85
*a.* Booklet pane of 4 8.00 —
Complete booklet, #2725a 8.00

Kingdom of Italy Stamp Show, Rome.

Dalmatian Historical Society, 80th Anniv. A1464

**2006, Feb. 10 Engr.** ***Perf. 13x13¼***
**2726** A1464 45c red vio & dk bl 1.50 .60

Detail of Fresco From Mantua Castle Bridal Chamber, by Andrea Mantegna (1431-1506) — A1465

**2006, Feb. 25 Photo.** ***Perf. 13x13¼***
**2727** A1465 45c multi 1.50 .60

2006 Winter Paralympics, Turin — A1466

**2006, Mar. 9** ***Perf. 13¼x13***
**2728** A1466 60c multi 2.10 .85

Items Made in Italy A1467

**2006, Mar. 11** ***Perf. 13x13¼***
**2729** A1467 60c Gelato 1.75 .85
**2730** A1467 €2.80 Carrara marble 8.50 4.25

National Singers Association, 25th Anniv. — A1468

**2006, Mar. 17**
**2731** A1468 45c multi 1.50 .60

Aircraft Carrier "Cavour" A1469

**2006, Mar. 17**
**2732** A1469 60c multi 2.00 .85

Opening of Sempione Tunnel — A1470

**2006, Mar. 18** ***Perf. 13¼x13***
**2733** A1470 62c multi 2.00 .95

### Tourism Type of 2005

**2006, Mar. 24**
**2734** A1424 45c Lago di Como 1.50 .60
**2735** A1424 45c Marina di Pietrasanta 1.50 .60
**2736** A1424 45c Pozzuoli 1.50 .60
*Nos. 2734-2736 (3)* 4.50 1.80

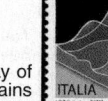

Intl. Day of Mountains A1471

**2006, Mar. 30** ***Perf. 13x13¼***
**2737** A1471 60c multi 2.00 .85

Madonna and Child Icon, Mondragone Basilica — A1472

**2006, Apr. 1**
**2738** A1472 45c multi 1.50 .60

First Vote for Italian Citizens Abroad — A1473

**2006, Apr. 3** ***Perf. 13¼x13***
**2739** A1473 62c multi 2.00 .95

"Two Republics" Philatelic Exhibition A1474

**2006, Apr. 5 Photo.** ***Perf. 13x13¼***
**2740** A1474 62c multi 2.00 .95
*a.* Souvenir sheet, #2740, San Marino #1676a 4.00 4.00

See San Marino No. 1676. On No. 2740a, the Italian stamp is on the left. On San Marino No. 1676, the Italian stamp is on the right. Both stamps in No. 2740a have text printed on reverse.

Matterhorn Ski School, 70th Anniv. — A1475

**2006, Apr. 13 Photo.** ***Perf. 13¼x13***
**2741** A1475 45c multi 1.50 .60

Madonna of Humility, by Gentile da Fabriano
A1476

**2006, Apr. 20 Photo. *Perf. 13x13¼***
**2742** A1476 €2.80 multi 8.75 4.00

Il Giorno Newspaper, 50th Anniv. — A1477

**2006, Apr. 21 *Perf. 13¼x13***
**2743** A1477 45c multi 1.50 .60

Constitutional Court, 50th Anniv. — A1478

**2006, Apr. 22 Engr.**
**2744** A1478 45c blue 1.50 .60

Enrico Mattei (1906-62), Public Administrator
A1479

**2006, Apr. 29 Photo. *Perf. 13¼x13***
**2745** A1479 45c multi 1.50 .60

**Italian Regions Type of 2004**

**2006, Apr. 29 *Perf. 13x13¼***
**2746** A1387 45c Piedmont 1.50 .60
**2747** A1387 45c Tuscany 1.50 .60
**2748** A1387 45c Lazio 1.50 .60
**2749** A1387 45c Puglia 1.50 .60
*Nos. 2746-2749 (4)* 6.00 2.40

Targa Floria Automobile Race Track, Cent. — A1480

**2006, May 6 Photo. *Perf. 13¼x13***
**2750** A1480 60c multi 2.00 .85

Christopher Columbus (1451-1506), Explorer — A1481

**2006, May 6 Photo. *Perf. 13x13¼***
**2751** A1481 62c multi 2.00 .95

Europa
A1482

People sitting on wall: 45c, View of faces. 62c, View of backs.

**2006, May 8**
**2752** A1482 45c multi 1.40 .60
**2753** A1482 62c multi 2.10 .95

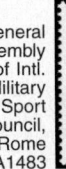

General Assembly of Intl. Military Sport Council, Rome
A1483

**2006, May 9**
**2754** A1483 45c multi 1.40 .60

2006 World Team Chess Championships, Turin — A1484

**2006, May 20 Photo. *Perf. 13¼x13***
**2755** A1484 62c multi 2.00 .95

Constituent Assembly, 60th Anniv.
A1485

**2006, June 1 *Perf. 13x13¼***
**2756** A1485 60c multi 2.00 .85

Woman Suffrage, 60th Anniv. — A1486

**2006, June 1 *Perf. 13¼x13***
**2757** A1486 60c multi 2.00 .85

2006 World Bridge Championships, Verona — A1487

**2006, June 9 *Perf. 13x13¼***
**2758** A1487 65c multi 2.10 .95

Salto di Quirra Proving Grounds, 50th Anniv. — A1488

**2006, June 13 *Perf. 13¼x13***
**2759** A1488 60c multi 2.00 .85

Customs Department General Headquarters, Cent. — A1489

Customs Cadet Legion, Cent.
A1490

**2006, June 21 *Perf. 13¼x13***
**2760** A1489 60c multi 2.00 .85

***Perf. 13x13¼***
**2761** A1490 60c multi 2.00 .85

Reopening of Greek Theater, Tindari, 50th Anniv. — A1491

**2006, July 6 *Perf. 13¼x13***
**2762** A1491 €1.50 multi 4.75 2.25

Autostrada del Sole, 50th Anniv.
A1492

**2006, July 10 *Perf. 13x13¼***
**2763** A1492 60c multi 2.00 .85

Terrorist Bombing in Bologna, 26th Anniv. — A1493

**2006, Aug. 2 *Perf. 13¼x13***
**2764** A1493 60c multi 2.00 .85

Italian Philatelic Union, 40th Anniv. — A1494

**2006, Sept. 1 *Perf. 13x13¼***
**2765** A1494 60c multi + label 2.00 .85

St. Gregory the Great (540-604)
A1495

**2006, Sept. 2 *Perf. 13¼x13***
**2766** A1495 60c multi 2.00 .85

Victory of Italian 2006 World Cup Soccer Team
A1496

**2006, Sept. 9 Photo. *Perf. 13x13¼***
**2767** A1496 €1 multi 3.00 1.50

Victims of Terrorism
A1497

**2006, Sept. 16**
**2768** A1497 60c multi 2.25 .85

Ettore Majorana (1906-38?), Physicist
A1498

**2006, Sept. 18 *Perf. 13¼x13***
**2769** A1498 60c multi 2.00 .85

Saints
A1499

Designs: No. 2770, St. Ignatius of Loyola (1491-1556). No. 2771, St. Francis Xavier (1506-52).

**2006, Sept. 27** *Perf. 13x13¼*
**2770** A1499 60c multi 1.90 .85
**2771** A1499 60c multi 1.90 .85

World Fencing Championships, Turin — A1500

**2006, Sept. 29**
**2772** A1500 65c multi 2.10 .95

Lottery, 500th Anniv. A1501

**2006, Oct. 6** **Photo.** *Perf. 13x13¼*
**2773** A1501 60c multi 2.00 .85

Philately Day
A1502

**2006, Oct. 6**
**2774** A1502 60c multi 2.00 .85

Land and Marine Area Protection System
A1503

**2006, Oct. 6**
**2775** A1503 65c multi 2.10 .95

Luchino Visconti (1906-76), Film Director — A1504

**2006, Oct. 13** *Perf. 13¼x13*
**2776** A1504 60c multi 2.00 .85

Dino Buzzati (1906-72), Writer
A1505

**2006, Oct. 16** *Perf. 13x13¼*
**2777** A1505 60c multi 2.00 .75

Adoration of the Magi, by Jacopo Bassano
A1506

Christmas Tree — A1507

**2006, Oct. 28** **Engr.** *Perf. 13x13¼*
**2778** A1506 60c rose 2.00 .80

**Photo.**
*Perf. 13¼x13*
**2779** A1507 65c multi 2.00 .85

Vittoriano Building, Tomb of the Unknown Soldier, Rome
A1508

**2006, Nov. 11** **Photo.** *Perf. 13x13¼*
**2780** A1508 60c multi 2.00 .80

Cathedral of St. Evasius, Casale Monteferrato — A1509

**2007, Jan. 4** **Engr.** *Perf. 13x13¼*
**2781** A1509 60c rose 2.00 .80

First Montessori School, Cent. — A1510

**2007, Jan. 5** **Photo.** *Perf. 13¼x13*
**2782** A1510 60c multi 2.00 .80

School for Public Administration, 50th Anniv. — A1511

**2007, Jan. 10** **Photo.** *Perf. 13x13¼*
**2783** A1511 65c multi 2.00 .85

Parma Cathedral — A1512

**2007, Jan. 13** **Engr.** *Perf. 13¼x13*
**2784** A1512 60c green 2.00 .80

Arturo Toscanini (1867-1957), Conductor
A1513

**2007, Jan. 16** **Photo.**
**2785** A1513 60c multi 2.00 .80

St. Francis of Paola (1416-1507) — A1514

**2007, Jan. 27** *Perf. 13x13¼*
**2786** A1514 60c multi 2.00 .80

Ferrante Gonzaga (1507-57), Soldier
A1515

**2007, Jan. 27**
**2787** A1515 €1 multi 3.25 1.40

Antonio Genovesi Salerno Foundation, 20th Anniv. — A1516

**2007, Jan. 29** **Photo.** *Perf. 13x13¼*
**2788** A1516 60c multi 1.90 .80

Relocation of Istrian Area Refugees to Giuliana di Fertilia District, Sardinia, 60th Anniv.
A1517

**2007, Feb. 10** **Photo.** *Perf. 13x13¼*
**2789** A1517 60c multi 1.90 .80

Father Lodovico Acernese (1835-1916)
A1518

**2007, Feb. 16** **Photo.** *Perf. 13¼x13*
**2790** A1518 23c multi .90 .30

Giosuè Carducci (1835-1907), 1906 Nobel Laureate in Literature — A1519

**2007, Feb. 16** **Photo.** *Perf. 13x13¼*
**2791** A1519 60c multi 1.90 .80

University of Brescia — A1520

**2007, Feb. 26** *Perf. 13¼x13*
**2792** A1520 60c multi 2.00 .80

European Equal Opportunity Year — A1521

**2007, Mar. 1** **Photo.** *Perf. 13¼x13*
**2793** A1521 60c multi 2.00 .80

Scipione Maffei State High School, Verona — A1522

**2007, Mar. 14** **Photo.** *Perf. 13¼x13*
**2794** A1522 60c multi 2.00 .80

Nicolò Carosio (1907-84), Radio Sportscaster — A1523

**2007, Mar. 15** *Perf. 13x13¼*

**2795** A1523 65c multi 2.10 .85

### Italian Regions Type of 2004

**2007, Mar. 16 Photo.** *Perf. 13x13¼*

**2796** A1387 60c Trentino-Alto Adige 2.00 .80
**2797** A1387 60c Marche 2.00 .80
**2798** A1387 60c Umbria 2.00 .80
**2799** A1387 60c Sardinia 2.00 .80
*Nos. 2796-2799 (4)* 8.00 3.20

Venice, UNESCO World Heritage Site — A1524

**2007, Mar. 16 Engr.** *Perf. 13¼x13*

**2800** A1524 60c black 2.25 .80

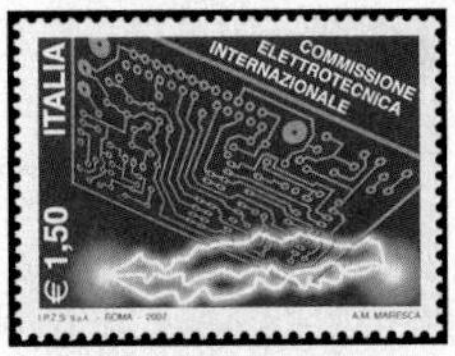


Intl. Electrotechnical Commission — A1525

**2007, Mar. 16 Photo.** *Perf. 13x13¼*

**2801** A1525 €1.50 multi 4.00 2.00

### Souvenir Sheet

Treaty of Rome, 50th Anniv. — A1526

**2007, Mar. 25 Photo.** *Perf. 13x13¼*

**2802** A1526 Sheet of 2 4.00 4.00
*a.* 60c Stars and "50" 1.75 .80
*b.* 65c "Insieme dal 1957" 2.00 .85

### Tourism Type of 2005

**2005, Apr. 13** *Perf. 13¼x13*

**2803** A1424 60c Brunico-Bruneck 1.90 .85
**2804** A1424 60c Gaeta 1.90 .85
**2805** A1424 60c Massafra 1.90 .85
**2806** A1424 60c Cattolica Eraclea 1.90 .85
*Nos. 2803-2806 (4)* 7.60 3.40

Giuseppe Tomasi di Lampedusa (1896-1957), Writer — A1527

**2007, Apr. 14 Photo.** *Perf. 13¼x13*

**2807** A1527 60c multi 2.00 .85

Forum, Rome A1528

**2007, Apr. 21** *Perf. 13x13¼*

**2808** A1528 60c multi 2.00 .85

Europa — A1529

Scouts: 60c, In canoe. 65c, At campfire.

**2007, Apr. 23** *Perf. 13¼x13*

**2809** A1529 60c multi 1.90 .85
**2810** A1529 65c multi 2.10 .95
*a.* Souvenir sheet, #2809-2810 4.00 3.00

Duccio Galamberti (1906-44), World War II Resistance Leader — A1530

**2007, Apr. 24**

**2811** A1530 60c multi 2.50 .85

School of Economics and Finance, Rome, 50th Anniv. A1531

**2007, Apr. 27** *Perf. 13x13¼*

**2812** A1531 €2.80 multi 8.75 3.75

Cinecittà Film Studios, Rome, 70th Anniv. A1532

**2007, Apr. 28**

**2813** A1532 65c multi 2.00 .85

Polirone Monastery, San Benedetto Po, 1000th Anniv. — A1533

**2007, May 5 Engr.** *Perf. 13¼x13*

**2814** A1533 60c blue & blk 1.90 .80

Malatesta Castle, Montefiore Conca — A1534

**2007, May 12**

**2815** A1534 60c brown 1.90 .80

Bancarella Musica Folk Music Project — A1535

**2007, May 23** **Photo.**

**2816** A1535 60c multi 1.90 .80

Emblem of Lamborghini Automobiles A1536

**2007, May 23**

**2817** A1536 85c multi 2.75 1.25

F. C. Internazionale, 2006-07 Italian Soccer Champions A1537

**2007, June 4 Photo.** *Perf. 13¼*

**2818** A1537 60c multi 2.25 .80

Chianca Dolmen — A1538

**2007, June 9 Engr.** *Perf. 13¼x13*

**2819** A1538 60c brown 1.90 .85

Luigi Ganna, (1883-1957), Cyclist — A1539

**2007, June 9 Photo.** *Perf. 13¼x13*

**2820** A1539 60c multi 1.90 .80

Altiero Spinelli (1907-86), Writer and Politician A1540

**2007, June 21** *Perf. 13x13¼*

**2821** A1540 60c multi 1.90 .80

Two Worlds Festival, 50th Anniv. A1541

**2007, June 29 Photo.** *Perf. 13x13¼*

**2822** A1541 60c multi 2.00 .85

San Vincenzo Basilica, Galliano — A1542

**2007, July 2 Litho.** *Rouletted 7*

**On Wood Veneer**

**Self-Adhesive**

**2823** A1542 €2.80 black 8.75 3.75

Fiat 500 Automobile A1543

**2007, July 4 Photo.** *Perf. 13x13¼*

**2824** A1543 60c multi 2.00 .85

Giuseppe Garibaldi (1807-82), Patriot
A1544

**2007, July 4**
**2825** A1544 65c multi 2.10 .95

Capt. Maurizio Poggiali (1965-97), Pilot
A1545

**2007, July 6**
**2826** A1545 60c multi 1.90 .85

Roman Speleology Club
A1546

**2007, July 9**
**2827** A1546 €1.40 multi 4.50 2.00

Primo Carnera (1906-67), Boxer
A1547

**2007, July 13**
**2828** A1547 60c multi 1.90 .85

Marco Foscarini School, Venice — A1548

St. Pius V Institute for Political Studies, Rome — A1549

Salerno Medical College — A1550

**2007, Sept. 17 Photo.** ***Perf. 13¼x13***
**2829** A1548 60c multi 2.00 .85
**2830** A1549 60c multi 2.00 .85
**2831** A1550 60c multi 2.00 .85
*Nos. 2829-2831 (3)* 6.00 2.55

Protected Donkey Breeds
A1551

**2007, Sept. 22** ***Perf. 13x13¼***
**2832** A1551 60c multi 2.00 .85

31st European Women's Basketball Championships
A1552

**2007, Sept. 22** ***Perf. 13¼x13***
**2833** A1552 65c multi 2.10 .95

Sacra di San Michele Abbey, Sant'Ambroglio di Torino — A1553

**2007, Sept. 29** **Engr.**
**2834** A1553 60c red brown 2.00 .85

Concetto Marchesi (1878-1957), Historian
A1554

**2007, Oct. 1** **Photo.**
**2835** A1554 60c multi 1.90 .85

Jacopo Barozzi (Il Vignola) (1507-73), Architect
A1555

**2007, Oct. 1** ***Perf. 13x13¼***
**2836** A1555 €2.80 multi 8.50 3.75

Grandparent's Day — A1556

**2007, Oct. 2**
**2837** A1556 60c multi 1.90 .85

Philately Day — A1557

**2007, Oct. 12** ***Perf. 13¼x13***
**2838** A1557 60c multi 1.90 .85

Cupid and Psyche, Sculpture by Antonio Canova (1757-1822) — A1558

**2007, Oct. 12 Engr.** ***Perf. 13x13¼***
**2839** A1558 €1.50 black 4.75 2.10

Miniature Sheet

Entertainers — A1559

No. 2840: a, Beniamino Gigli (1890-1957), opera singer. b, Maria Callas (1923-77), opera singer. c, Amedeo Nazzari (1907-79), actor.

**2007, Oct. 18 Photo.** ***Perf. 13¼x13***
**2840** A1559 Sheet of 3 5.75 3.75
***a.-c.*** 60c Any single 1.90 .85

Giuseppe Di Vittorio (1892-1957), Union Leader — A1560

**2007, Nov. 3** ***Perf. 13x13¼***
**2841** A1560 60c multi 1.90 .85

Mondadori Publishing House, Cent.
A1561

**2007, Nov. 12**
**2842** A1561 60c multi 1.90 .85

Madonna and Child, by Giovan Battista Cima da Conegliano
A1562

Snow-covered House and Trees — A1563

**2007, Nov. 20 Engr.** ***Perf. 13¼x13***
**2843** A1562 60c green 2.00 .85

**Photo.**

**2844** A1563 65c multi 2.10 .95

Christmas.

Italian 2007-08 Term on UN Security Council
A1564

**2007, Dec. 1 Photo.** ***Perf. 13x13¼***
**2845** A1564 85c multi 2.75 1.25

Governor's Palace, Fiume (Rijeka, Croatia)
A1565

**2007, Dec. 10**
**2846** A1565 65c multi 2.10 .95

Italian Constitution, 60th Anniv. — A1566

**2008, Jan. 2** ***Perf. 13¼x13***
**2847** A1566 60c multi 1.90 .90

Italian Red Cross Volunteer Nursing Corps, Cent. — A1567

**2008, Jan. 29**
**2848** A1567 60c multi 1.90 .90

Amintore Fanfani (1908-99), Politician A1568

**2008, Feb. 6** ***Perf. 13x13¼***
**2849** A1568 €1 multi 3.25 1.50

Italian Stock Exchange, Bicent. — A1569

**2008, Feb. 8** ***Perf. 13¼x13***
**2850** A1569 65c multi 2.10 1.00

Olivetti Typewriter and First Olivetti Factory A1570

**2008, Feb. 12** ***Perf. 13x13¼***
**2851** A1570 60c multi 2.00 .95

Olivetti Corporation, Cent.

Villa Reale, Monza, Designed by Giuseppe Piermarini A1571

**2008, Feb. 18 Engr.** ***Perf. 13x13¼***
**2852** A1571 €1.40 black & blue 4.50 2.10

Natl. Council of Economics and Labor, 50th Anniv. A1572

**2008, Feb. 20 Photo.**
**2853** A1572 €1.50 multi 4.75 2.40

Dorando Pietri (1885-1942), Marathon Runner — A1573

**2008, Feb. 23**
**2854** A1573 60c multi 2.00 .95

Souvenir Sheet

Song, "Nel Blu, Dipinto di Blu," 50th Anniv. — A1574

**2008, Feb. 25** ***Perf. 13¼x13***
**2855** A1574 60c multi 2.25 1.75

Anna Magnani (1908-73), Actress — A1575

**2008, Mar. 7**
**2856** A1575 60c multi 2.00 .95

Emblem of Ricordi Publishing House and La Scala Theater, Milan A1576

**2008, Mar. 7 Photo.** ***Perf. 13x13¼***
**2857** A1576 60c indigo & gray 2.00 .95

Ricordi Music Publishing House, bicent.

Italia 2009 Intl. Philatelic Exhibition, Rome — A1577

Exhibition emblem and: 60c, Congress Center. 65c, Colosseum.

**2008, Mar. 7 Photo.** ***Perf. 13¼x13***
**2858** A1577 60c multi 2.00 .95
**2859** A1577 65c multi 2.00 1.00

Carlo Combi High School, Capodistria — A1578

**2008, Mar. 8**
**2860** A1578 60c multi 2.00 .95

Edmondo de Amicis (1846-1908), Writer — A1579

**2008, Mar. 11 Photo.** ***Perf. 13¼x13***
**2861** A1579 60c multi 2.00 .95

Self-portrait, by Bernardino di Betto (Pintoricchio, c. 1454-1513) — A1580

**2008, Mar. 14** ***Perf. 13x13¼***
**2862** A1580 60c multi 2.00 .95

Running of the Madonna, Sulmona — A1581

**2008, Mar. 15** ***Perf. 13¼x13***
**2863** A1581 60c multi 2.00 .95

Italian Rowing Federation, 120th Anniv. A1582

**2008, Mar. 31 Photo.** ***Perf. 13x13¼***
**2864** A1582 65c multi 2.10 1.10

Confirmation of the Rule, by Giotto — A1583

**2008, Apr. 16 Photo.** ***Perf. 13x13¼***
**2865** A1583 60c multi 2.00 .95

Rule of life of St. Francis of Assisi, 700th anniv.

Imperial Forum, Rome A1584

**2008, Apr. 21**
**2866** A1584 60c multi 2.00 .95

Italian National Press Federation, Cent. — A1585

**2008, Apr. 23** ***Perf. 13¼x13***
**2867** A1585 60c multi 2.00 .95

Flight, Sculpture by Pasquale Basile A1586

**2008, Apr. 23** ***Perf. 13x13¼***
**2868** A1586 €1.40 multi 4.50 2.25

Intl. Decade of Education for Sustainable Development.

Giovannino Guareschi (1908-68), Journalist A1587

**2008, May 1 Photo.** ***Perf. 13¼x13***
**2869** A1587 60c multi 2.00 .95

Ludovico Geymonat (1908-91), Philosopher — A1588

**2008, May 8** ***Perf. 13x13¼***
**2870** A1588 60c multi 2.00 .95

Europa — A1589

Designs: 60c, Red mailbox. 65c, Brown mailbox.

**2008, May 9 Photo.** ***Perf. 13¼x13***

**2871** A1589 60c multi 2.00 .95
**2872** A1589 65c multi 2.10 1.00

Works of Andrea Palladio (1508-80), Architect A1590

Designs: 60c, Alpini Bridge, Bassano. 65c, Palladian Basilica, Vicenza.

**2008, May 10 Engr.** ***Perf. 13x13¼***

**2873** A1590 60c multi 1.90 .95
**2874** A1590 65c multi 2.10 1.10

St. Francis Caracciolo (1563-1608) — A1591

**2008, May 23 Photo.** ***Perf. 13x13¼***

**2875** A1591 60c multi 2.00 .95

**Italian Regions Type of 2004**

**2008, May 23 Photo.** ***Perf. 13x13¼***

**2876** A1387 60c Valle d'Aosta 2.00 .95
**2877** A1387 60c Veneto 2.00 .95
**2878** A1387 60c Molise 2.00 .95
**2879** A1387 60c Sicily 2.00 .95
*Nos. 2876-2879 (4)* 8.00 3.80

Guastalla School, Monza — A1592

**2008, May 24 Photo.** ***Perf. 13¼x13***

**2880** A1592 60c dk & lt blue 2.00 .95

Ducati Desmosedici GP7 Motorcycle — A1593

**2008, May 31** ***Perf. 13x13¼***

**2881** A1593 60c multi 2.00 .95

Giacomo Puccini (1858-1924), Composer A1594

**2008, June 21 Photo.** ***Perf. 13¼x13***

**2882** A1594 €1.50 multi 4.75 2.40

F. C. Internazionale, 2007-08 Italian Soccer Champions — A1595

**2008, July 4 Photo.** ***Perf. 13x13¼***

**2883** A1595 60c multi 2.00 .95

2008 Summer Olympics, Beijing A1596

Olympic rings and: 60c, Torch bearer and map. 85c, Greek and Chinese athletes.

**2008, July 7 Photo.** ***Perf. 13x13¼***

**2884** A1596 60c multi 1.90 .95
**2885** A1596 85c multi 2.75 1.40

Tommaso Landolfi (1908-79), Writer A1597

**2008, July 19 Photo.** ***Perf. 13x13¼***

**2886** A1597 60c multi 2.00 .95

**Tourism Type of 2005**

**2008, July 24 Photo.** ***Perf. 13¼x13***

**2887** A1424 60c Tre Cime di Lavaredo 2.00 .95
**2888** A1424 60c Introdacqua 2.00 .95
**2889** A1424 60c Casamicciola Terme 2.00 .95
**2890** A1424 60c Mamoiada 2.00 .95
*Nos. 2887-2890 (4)* 8.00 3.80

Bowl of Saffron and Crocuses — A1598

Ingredients for Spaghetti all'Amatriciana — A1599

**2008 Photo.** ***Perf. 13¼x13***

**2891** A1598 60c multi 2.00 .95

***Perf. 13x13¼***

**2892** A1599 60c multi 2.00 .95

Issued: No. 2891, 7/26; No. 2892, 8/29.

Bell Tower, Treviglio A1600

**2008, Aug. 30 Engr.** ***Perf. 13x13¼***

**2893** A1600 60c multi 2.00 .85

Dante Alighieri High School, Gorizia — A1601

Seal of the University of Perugia — A1602

**2008, Sept. 8 Photo.** ***Perf. 13¼x13***

**2894** A1601 60c multi 2.00 .85
**2895** A1602 60c multi 2.00 .85

Cesare Pavese (1908-50), Writer — A1603

**2008, Sept. 9**

**2896** A1603 65c multi 2.00 .95

Alberico Gentili (1552-1608), Jurist — A1604

**2008, Sept. 13** ***Perf. 13x13¼***

**2897** A1604 65c multi 2.00 .95

Malatestiana Library, Cesena — A1605

**2008, Sept. 19 Engr.** ***Perf. 13¼x13***

**2898** A1605 60c black 2.00 .85

World Road Cycling Championships, Varese — A1606

**2008, Sept. 22 Photo.** ***Perf. 13x13¼***

**2899** A1606 60c multi 1.90 .85

Philately Day — A1607

**2008, Oct. 10** ***Perf. 13¼x13***

**2900** A1607 60c multi 1.90 .80

Italia 2009 Intl. Philatelic Exhibition, Rome A1608

**2008, Oct. 10 Photo.** ***Perf. 13x13¼***

**2901** A1608 85c multi 2.75 1.25

**Litho. on Gold Foil**
**Self-Adhesive**
***Rouletted 8***

**2902** A1608 €2.80 multi 8.75 3.75

Local Police — A1609

**2008, Oct. 23 Photo.** ***Perf. 13¼x13***

**2903** A1609 60c multi 1.90 .80

Oath of the Plebian Tribune, 2500th Anniv. A1610

**2008, Oct. 24** *Perf. 13x13¼*
**2904** A1610 60c multi 1.90 .80

Madonna and Child Enthroned with Two Angels, by Lorenzo di Credi — A1611

Wreath — A1612

**2008, Oct. 30 Photo.** *Perf. 13¼x13*
**2905** A1611 60c multi 2.00 .80

**Litho. on Gold Foil**
**Self-Adhesive**
***Rouletted 8***
**2906** A1612 €2.80 multi 8.50 3.75

Christmas.

UNESCO World Heritage Sites — A1613

Designs: 60c, Val d'Orcia. €2.80, Historic Center of Urbino.

**2008, Oct. 31 Engr.** *Perf. 13¼x13*
**2907** A1613 60c multi 1.90 .80
**2908** A1613 €2.80 blue & black 8.50 3.75

Messina Earthquake, Cent. — A1614

**2008, Nov. 3 Photo.** *Perf. 13x13¼*
**2909** A1614 60c multi 1.90 .80

Corriere dei Piccoli Comic Strips, Cent. A1615

**2008, Nov. 8**
**2910** A1615 60c multi 1.90 .80

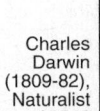

Charles Darwin (1809-82), Naturalist A1616

**2009, Feb. 12**
**2911** A1616 65c multi 2.00 .85

Souvenir Sheet

Song, "Tintarella di Luna," 50th Anniv. — A1617

**2009, Feb. 17** *Perf. 13¼x13*
**2912** A1617 60c multi 1.90 .80

5th Natl. Conference on Drugs, Trieste — A1618

**2009, Mar. 12**
**2913** A1618 60c multi 1.90 .80

Valle Camonica Rock Drawing UNESCO World Heritage Site — A1619

**2009, Mar. 27** **Engr.**
**2914** A1619 €2.80 brown 8.25 3.75

Italia 2009 Intl. Philatelic Exhibition, Rome — A1620

People and: 60c, Italian stamps. €1, Map of Europe.

**2009, Mar. 27** **Photo.**
**2915** A1620 60c multi 1.90 .80
**2916** A1620 €1 multi 3.00 1.40

Father Primo Mazzolari (1890-1959), Writer on Social and Religious Issues — A1621

**2009, Apr. 14** *Perf. 13x13¼*
**2917** A1621 60c multi 1.90 .80

Sardinia Grenadier Corps, 350th Anniv. A1622

**2009, Apr. 16**
**2918** A1622 60c multi 1.90 .80

Piazza di Spagna, Spanish Steps, Fontana della Barcaccia, Rome A1623

**2009, Apr. 21**
**2919** A1623 60c multi 1.90 .80

Indro Montanelli (1909-2001), Journalist A1624

**2009, Apr. 22** *Perf. 13¼x13*
**2920** A1624 60c multi 1.90 .80

Bulgari Jewelers, 125th Anniv. — A1625

**2009, Apr. 24**
**2921** A1625 60c multi 2.00 .80

Italy-Switzerland Chamber of Commerce, Cent. — A1626

**2009, May 2** *Perf. 13x13¼*
**2922** A1626 60c multi 1.90 .85

Carabinieri Command for Cultural Heritage Protection A1627

**2009, May 4**
**2923** A1627 60c multi 1.90 .85

16th Mediterranean Games, Pescara — A1628

**2009, May 5**
**2924** A1628 60c multi 1.90 .85

European Parliament Elections A1629

**2009, May 7**
**2925** A1629 60c multi 2.50 .85

Europa A1630

Designs: 60c, Galileo National Telescope, La Palma, Canary Islands. 65c, AGILE astronomical satellite.

**2009, May 7**
**2926** A1630 60c multi 1.90 .85
**2927** A1630 65c multi 2.00 .95

Intl. Year of Astronomy.

Giro d'Italia Bicycle Race, Cent. — A1631

**2009, May 9** *Perf. 13¼x13*
**2928** A1631 60c multi 1.90 .85

Academy of Italian-German Studies, Merano, 50th Anniv. — A1632

**2009, May 9** *Perf. 13x13¼*
**2929** A1632 60c multi 1.90 .85

Mille Miglia Auto Race
A1633

**2009, May 14** ***Perf. 13x13¼***
**2930** A1633 60c multi 1.90 .85

Festival of Mysteries, Campobasso
A1634

**2009, May 22** ***Perf. 13¼***
**2931** A1634 60c multi 1.90 .85

See Nos. 3041, 3160.

Cathedral of Santa Maria Madre di Dio, Rieti — A1635

**2009, May 27** **Engr.** ***Perf. 13¼x13***
**2932** A1635 60c black 1.90 .85

Giovanni Palatucci (1909-45), Police Official Who Saved Jews From Deportation
A1636

**2009, May 29** **Photo.**
**2933** A1636 60c multi 2.50 .85

Gilera Motorbikes, Cent. — A1637

**2009, June 6** ***Perf. 13x13¼***
**2934** A1637 60c multi 1.90 .85

Postage Stamps of Sicily, 150th Anniv.
A1638

**2009, June 18** **Photo.** ***Perf. 13x13¼***
**2935** A1638 60c multi 1.90 .85

Souvenir Sheet

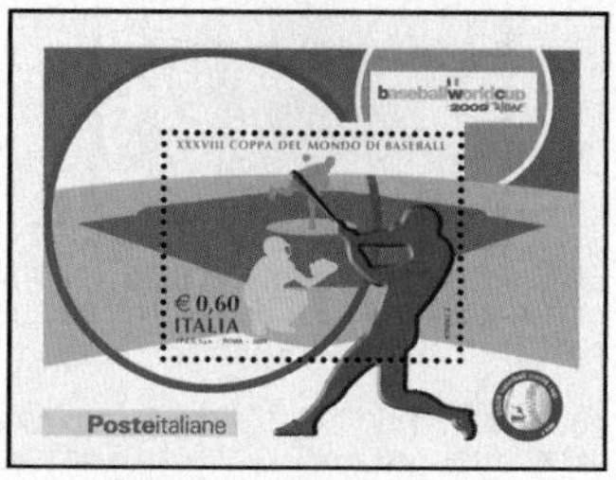


2009 Baseball World Cup Tournament — A1639

**2009, June 20** **Photo.** ***Perf. 13x13¼***
**2936** A1639 60c multi 2.00 2.00

St. Giovanni Leonardi (1541-1609)
A1640

**2009, June 23** ***Perf. 13¼x13***
**2937** A1640 60c multi 1.90 .85

F. C. Internazionale, 2008-09 Italian Soccer Champions
A1641

**2009, June 25**
**2938** A1641 60c multi 1.90 .85

San Daniele Prosciutto, 500th Anniv. of Historical Documentation of Production — A1642

**2009, June 26** ***Perf. 13x13¼***
**2939** A1642 60c multi 1.90 .85

St. Mark's Square, Venice
A1643

**2009, July 2**
**2940** A1643 60c multi 2.00 .85

Envelope
A1644

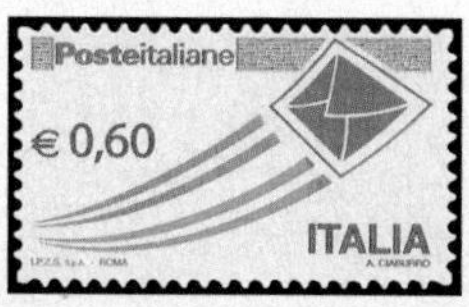


**2009** **Engr.** ***Serpentine Die Cut 11***
**Self-Adhesive**
**Denomination Color**

**2941** A1644 60c blue 1.90 .85
**2942** A1644 €1.40 red 4.25 2.00
**2943** A1644 €1.50 green 4.50 2.10
**2944** A1644 €2 brown 6.25 2.75
**2945** A1644 €3.30 black 10.50 5.00
*Nos. 2941-2945 (5)* 27.40 12.70

Issued: Nos. 2941-2944, 7/7. No. 2945, 10/31. See No. 3074.

Insurrection of the Women of Carrara, 65th Anniv. — A1645

**2009, July 7** **Photo.** ***Perf. 13x13¼***
**2946** A1645 €1.50 multi 4.50 2.10

G8 Summit, L'Aquila — A1646

**2009, July 8** **Photo.** ***Perf. 13¼x13***
**2947** A1646 65c multi 2.00 .95

**Tourism Type of 2005**

**2009, July 10** **Photo.** ***Perf. 13¼x13***
**2948** A1424 60c Verezzi 1.90 .85
**2949** A1424 60c Isola del Giglio 1.90 .85
**2950** A1424 60c Costa degli Dei, Capo Vaticano 1.90 .85
**2951** A1424 60c Gole dell'Alcantara 1.90 .85
*Nos. 2948-2951 (4)* 7.60 3.40

La Nazione Newspaper, Florence, 150th Anniv. — A1647

**2009, July 14**
**2952** A1647 60c multi 1.90 .85

13th World Aquatics Championships, Rome — A1648

**2009, July 18** **Engr. & Embossed**
**2953** A1648 €1.50 blue 4.50 2.10

Forest Fire Prevention
A1649

**2009, Aug. 1** **Photo.**
**2954** A1649 60c multi 1.90 .85

30th Rimini Meeting
A1650

**2009, Aug. 25**
**2955** A1650 60c green & black 1.90 .85

Montebello Lancers Cavalry Regiment, 150th Anniv. — A1651

**2009, Sept. 4**
**2956** A1651 60c multi 1.90 .85

Painting by Francesco Solimena
A1652

**2009, Sept. 17** **Photo.** ***Perf. 13x13¼***
**2957** A1652 60c multi 1.90 .90

Portrait of a Woman, by Giovanni Ambrogio de Predis, and Ambrosian Academy Library and Gallery, Milan — A1653

**2009, Sept. 21** **Engr.** ***Perf. 13¼x13***
**2958** A1653 €1.40 black 4.25 2.10

Emilio Alessandrini (1942-79), Magistrate Killed by Terrorists A1654

**2009, Sept. 26 Photo.** ***Perf. 13¼x13***

| | | | |
|---|---|---|---|
| **2959** A1654 60c multi | | 1.90 | .85 |

Souvenir Sheet

Christian Roots of Europe — A1655

No. 2960: a, Green cross, yellow brown map. b, Yellow brown cross, green map.

**2009, Oct. 7** ***Perf. 13x13¼***

| | | | |
|---|---|---|---|
| **2960** A1655 | Sheet of 2 | 3.75 | 1.90 |
| *a.* | 60c multi | 1.75 | .90 |
| *b.* | 65c multi | 2.00 | 1.00 |

L'Unione Sarda Newspaper, 120th Anniv. — A1656

**2009, Oct. 13** ***Perf. 13¼x13***

| | | | |
|---|---|---|---|
| **2961** A1656 60c multi | | 1.90 | .90 |

Father Luigi Sturzo (1871-1959), Politician A1657

**2009, Oct. 14**

| | | | |
|---|---|---|---|
| **2962** A1657 €1.50 multi | | 4.50 | 2.25 |

Norberto Bobbio (1909-2004), Historian A1658

**2009, Oct. 16**

| | | | |
|---|---|---|---|
| **2963** A1658 65c multi | | 2.00 | 1.00 |

Fathers Giovanni Minozzi (1884-1959) and Giovanni Semeria (1867-1931), Founders of Natl. Institute of Southern Italy — A1659

**2009, Oct. 19**

| | | | |
|---|---|---|---|
| **2964** A1659 60c multi | | 1.90 | .90 |

Philately Day A1660

**2009, Oct. 21** ***Perf. 13x13¼***

| | | | |
|---|---|---|---|
| **2965** A1660 60c multi | | 1.90 | .90 |

Italian Language Day — A1661

**2009, Oct. 21 Photo.** ***Perf. 13¼x13***

| | | | |
|---|---|---|---|
| **2966** A1661 60c multi + label | | 2.10 | .90 |

Printed in sheets of 5 + 5 labels. See San Marino No. 1801; Vatican City No. 1426.

Sports Day at Italia 2009 Intl. Philatelic Exhibition, Rome — A1662

Sports figures: 60c, Gino Bartali (1914-2000), cyclist. 65c, Valentino Mazzola (1919-49), soccer player. €1.40, Michele Alboreto (1956-2001), race car driver.

**2009, Oct. 22 Photo.** ***Perf. 13¼x13***

| | | | |
|---|---|---|---|
| **2967** A1662 | 60c multi | 1.75 | .90 |
| **2968** A1662 | 65c multi | 2.00 | 1.00 |
| **2969** A1662 | €1.40 multi | 4.25 | 2.10 |
| | *Nos. 2967-2969 (3)* | 8.00 | 4.00 |

Souvenir Sheet

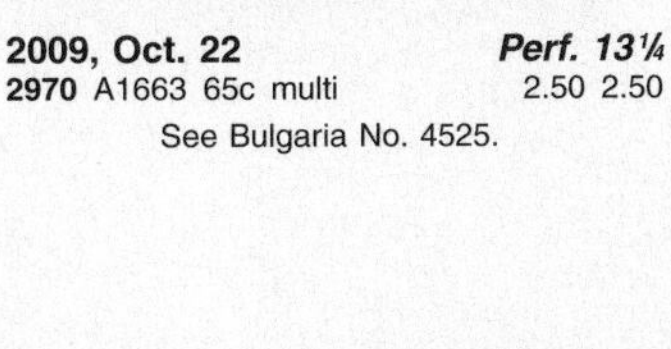

Diplomatic Relations Between Italy and Bulgaria, 130th Anniv. — A1663

**2009, Oct. 22** ***Perf. 13¼***

| | | | |
|---|---|---|---|
| **2970** A1663 65c multi | | 2.50 | 2.50 |

See Bulgaria No. 4525.

Adoration of the Shepherds, by Domenico Piola (1627-1703) — A1664

Ornaments — A1665

**2009, Oct. 23** ***Perf. 13¼x13***

| | | | |
|---|---|---|---|
| **2971** A1664 60c multi | | 1.90 | .90 |

**Self-Adhesive**

***Serpentine Die Cut 11***

| | | | |
|---|---|---|---|
| **2972** A1665 60c multi | | 1.90 | .90 |

Christmas.

Souvenir Sheet

Comic Strips — A1666

No. 2973: a, Cocco Bill, by Benito Jacovitti. b, Diabolik, by Angela and Luciana Giussani. c, Lupo Alberto, by Silver.

**2009, Oct. 23** ***Perf. 13x13¼***

| | | | |
|---|---|---|---|
| **2973** A1666 | Sheet of 3 | 9.25 | 7.50 |
| *a.-c.* | €1 Any single | 3.00 | 1.50 |

Collector's Day at Italia 2009 Intl. Philatelic Exhibition, Rome.

Music Day at Italia 2009 Intl. Philatelic Exhibition, Rome — A1667

Designs: 65c, Luciano Pavarotti (1935-2007), singer. €1, Mino Reitano (1944-2009), singer. €1.50, Nino Rota (1911-79), composer.

**2009, Oct. 24** ***Perf. 13¼***

| | | | |
|---|---|---|---|
| **2974** A1667 | 65c multi | 2.10 | 1.00 |
| **2975** A1667 | €1 multi | 3.25 | 1.50 |
| **2976** A1667 | €1.50 multi | 4.75 | 2.25 |
| | *Nos. 2974-2976 (3)* | 10.10 | 4.75 |

Europe Day at Italia 2009 Intl. Philatelic Exhibition, Rome A1668

No. 2977 — Roman architectural works: a, Pont du Gard, France. b, Hadrian's Wall, Great Britain. c, Odeon of Patras, Greece. d, Porta Nigra, Trier, Germany. e, Segovia Aqueduct, Spain.

**2009, Oct. 25** ***Serpentine Die Cut 11***

**Self-Adhesive**

| | | | |
|---|---|---|---|
| **2977** | Booklet pane of 5 + label | 10.00 | |
| *a.-e.* | A1668 65c Any single | 2.00 | 1.00 |
| | Complete booklet, #2977 | 10.00 | |

Art of the 20th Century — A1669

Designs: 60c, Guantanamera, sculpture by Giacomo Manzù (1908-91). 65c, Danza dell'Orzo (The Bear Dance), by Gino Severini (1883-1966). 85c, Donna e Ambiente, by Federico de Pistoris (1898-1975).

**2009, Oct. 30** ***Perf. 13¼x13***

| | | | |
|---|---|---|---|
| **2978** A1669 | 60c multi | 1.90 | .90 |
| **2979** A1669 | 65c multi | 2.10 | 1.00 |
| **2980** A1669 | 85c multi | 2.75 | 1.25 |
| | *Nos. 2978-2980 (3)* | 6.75 | 3.15 |

Giorgio Perlasca (1910-92), Rescuer of Jews in World War II — A1670

**2010, Jan. 31 Photo.** ***Perf. 13x13¼***

| | | | |
|---|---|---|---|
| **2981** A1670 60c multi | | 2.40 | .85 |

Souvenir Sheet

Santa Maria de Collemaggio Basilica, L'Aquila — A1671

**2010, Feb. 10 Photo.** ***Perf. 13¼x13***

| | | | |
|---|---|---|---|
| **2982** A1671 60c multi | | 1.60 | 1.60 |

**Folk Festivals Type of 2009**

Designs: No. 2983, Acireale Carnival. No. 2984, Jousting tournament, Sa Sartiglia, Oristano.

**2010, Feb. 12 Photo.** ***Perf. 13½***

| | | | |
|---|---|---|---|
| **2983** A1634 60c multi | | 1.50 | .85 |
| **2984** A1634 60c multi | | 1.50 | .85 |

2010 Winter Olympics, Vancouver A1672

***Serpentine Die Cut 11***

**2010, Feb. 12** **Self-Adhesive**

| | | | |
|---|---|---|---|
| **2985** A1672 85c multi | | 2.10 | 1.00 |

2010 Youth Olympics, Singapore — A1673

**2010, Feb. 12** **Photo.**

**Self-Adhesive**

**2986** A1673 85c multi 2.10 1.00

Mario Pannunzio (1910-68), Journalist A1674

**2010, Mar. 5** ***Perf. 13x13¼***

**2987** A1674 60c multi 1.50 .85

Ennio Flaiano (1910-72), Screenwriter A1675

**2010, Mar. 5** **Photo.** ***Perf. 13¼x13***

**2988** A1675 60c multi 1.50 .85

Madonna dei Miracoli Basilica, Motta di Livenza — A1676

**2010, Mar. 9**

**2989** A1676 60c black 1.60 .80

Massimo D'Azeglio, First President of Province of Milan, and Isimbardi Palace A1677

**2010, Mar. 19** ***Perf. 13x13¼***

**2990** A1677 60c multi 1.60 .80

Province of Milan, 150th anniv.

Alfa Romeo Automobiles, Cent. — A1678

No. 2991: a, 1910 24HP. b, 2010 Giulietta.

**2010, Mar. 20**

**2991** Horiz. pair + central label 3.25 1.60
***a.-b.*** A1678 60c Either single 1.60 .80

Burial of Christ with Three Angels Holding the Shroud, by Gerolamo della Rovere — A1679

**2010, Mar. 22** ***Perf. 13¼x13***

**2992** A1679 60c multi 1.60 .80

Confindustria (Federation of Employers), Cent. — A1680

**2010, May 5** ***Perf. 13x13¼***

**2993** A1680 €1.40 multi 3.75 1.90

Miniature Sheet

Expedition of the Thousand, 150th Anniv. — A1681

No. 2994 — Paintings: a, Garibaldi Sets Sail From Quarto, by V. Azzola. b, Landing at Marsala, by unknown artist. c, Battle of Calatafimi, by Remigio Legat. d, Encounter in Teano of Garibaldi and Victor Emmanuel II, by Pietro Aldi.

**2010, May 5**

**2994** A1681 Sheet of 4 8.00 4.00
***a.*** 60c multi 1.50 .75
***b.*** 65c multi 1.75 .85
***c.*** 85c multi 2.25 1.10
***d.*** €1 multi 2.50 1.25

Rhaetian Railway in the Albula - Bernina Landscapes UNESCO World Heritage Site — A1682

**2010, May 6** ***Perf. 13¼x13***

**2995** A1682 65c multi 1.75 .85

Pinocchio, by Carlo Collodi — A1683

Geronimo Stilton, by Elisabetta Dami — A1684

**2010, May 7**

**2996** A1683 60c multi 1.50 .75
**2997** A1684 65c multi 1.75 .85

Europa.

Sister Maria Domenica Brun Barbentini (1789-1868), Founder of the Congregation of the Sister Servants of the Sick of St. Camillus — A1685

**2010, May 22** ***Perf. 13x13¼***

**2998** A1685 60c multi 1.50 .75

Hanbury Botanic Gardens, Ventimiglia A1686

**2010, May 29**

**2999** A1686 60c multi 1.50 .75

**Tourism Type of 2005 and**

1955 Tourism Poster — A1687

**2010, June 4** ***Perf. 13¼x13***

**3000** A1424 60c Courmayeur 1.50 .75
**3001** A1424 60c Todi 1.50 .75
**3002** A1424 60c Viggiano 1.50 .75
**3003** A1424 60c Isole Tremiti 1.50 .75
*Nos. 3000-3003 (4)* 6.00 3.00

**Self-Adhesive**

***Serpentine Die Cut 11***

**3004** A1687 60c multi 1.50 .75

Camilo Benso, Count of Cavour (1810-61), Statesman A1688

**2010, June 6** ***Perf. 13¼x13***

**3005** A1688 60c multi 1.50 .75

Association of Italian Joint Stock Companies, Cent. A1689

**2010, June 17** **Photo.** ***Perf. 13x13¼***

**3006** A1689 60c multi 1.60 .75

F.C. Internazionale, 2009-10 Italian Soccer Champions A1690

**2010, June 24** ***Perf. 13¼x13***

**3007** A1690 60c multi 1.60 .75

Federacciai Iron and Steel Plant, Bagnoli, Cent. — A1691

**Litho. & Silk-Screened**

**2010, June 28** ***Perf. 13¼x14***

**3008** A1691 €3.30 black 10.00 4.25

No. 3008 is coated with a varnish producing a rough surface, and is printed with a special ink that allows the stamp to be lifted by a magnet.

Envelope A1692

***Serpentine Die Cut 11x11¼***

**2010, July 1** **Photo.**

**Self-Adhesive**

**Color of Denomination**

**3009** A1692 5c dark blue .30 .25
**3010** A1692 10c black .30 .25
**3011** A1692 20c blue green .60 .25
*Nos. 3009-3011 (3)* 1.20 .75

Giovanni Virginio Schiaparelli (1835-1910), Astronomer — A1693

**2010, July 2** ***Perf. 13x13¼***

**3012** A1693 65c multi 1.75 .85

Pope Benedict XVI, Statue of Pope Celestine V — A1694

**2010, July 4** ***Perf. 13¼x13***
**3013** A1694 60c multi 1.60 .75

Celestinian Jubliee Year.

David with the Head of Goliath, by Caravaggio (1571-1610) — A1695

**2010, July 16** ***Perf. 13x13¼***
**3014** A1695 60c multi 2.00 .80

Ettore Paratore (1907-2000), Latin Scholar, Mosaic and Theater Mask — A1696

**2010, July 17** ***Perf. 13¼x13***
**3015** A1696 65c multi 1.75 .85

50th Plautus Festival, Sarsina.

Samnite Theater, Pietrabbondante — A1697

**2010, July 31** **Engr.**
**3016** A1697 60c brown 1.60 .80

Joe Petrosino (1860-1909), New York City Policeman, Statue of Liberty, Brooklyn Bridge — A1698

**2010, Aug. 30** **Photo.** ***Perf. 13x13¼***
**3017** A1698 85c multi 2.25 1.10

1960 Summer Olympics, Rome, 50th Anniv. A1699

**2010, Sept. 7**
**3018** A1699 60c multi 1.60 .80

First National Gathering of Fire Brigades, Cortina d'Ampezzo A1700

**2010, Sept. 10** ***Perf. 13x13¼***
**3019** A1700 60c multi 1.60 .80

National Aerobatic Team, 50th Anniv. A1701

**2010, Sept. 11**
**3020** A1701 60c multi 1.75 .85

Piazzale di Porta Pia, Rome A1702

**2010, Sept. 20**
**3021** A1702 60c multi 1.75 .85

Men's Volleyball World Championships, Italy — A1703

**Engr. & Embossed**

**2010, Sept. 24** ***Perf. 13x13¼***
**3022** A1703 85c blue 2.40 1.25

Torre Del Greco Coral — A1704

**2010, Sept. 30** **Photo.** ***Perf. 13¼x13***
**3023** A1704 60c multi 2.00 .85

Souvenir Sheet

Turin-Salerno High Speed Rail Line — A1705

**2010, Oct. 2** ***Perf. 13x13¼***
**3024** A1705 60c multi 1.75 .85

Corriere Adriatico Newspaper, Ancona, 150th Anniv. — A1706

**2010, Oct. 5** ***Perf. 13¼x13***
**3025** A1706 60c multi 1.75 .85

National Anti-trust Authority, 20th Anniv. A1707

**2010, Oct. 10** ***Perf. 13x13¼***
**3026** A1707 €1.40 multi 4.00 2.00

School of Oenology, Conegliano A1708

**2010, Oct. 21** ***Perf. 13x13¼***
**3027** A1708 60c multi 2.00 .85

Leonardo Sciascia (1921-89), Writer A1709

**2010, Oct. 23** **Engr.**
**3028** A1709 60c black 1.75 .85

Italian Tennis Federation, Cent. A1710

**2010, Oct. 25** **Photo.**
**3029** A1710 60c multi 1.75 .85

Self-Portrait of Pietro Annigoni (1910-88) — A1711

**2010, Oct. 27** ***Perf. 13¼x13***
**3030** A1711 60c multi 1.75 .85

Souvenir Sheet

Italian Film Personalities — A1712

No. 3031: a, Federico Fellini (1920-93), director. b, Vittorio Gassman (1922-2000), actor, director. c, Alberto Sordi (1920-2003), actor, director.

**2010, Oct. 28**
**3031** A1712 Sheet of 3 5.25 2.60
*a.-c.* 60c Any single 1.75 .85

Philately Day — A1713

**2010, Oct. 29**
**3032** A1713 60c multi 1.75 .85

Frette Textiles, 150th Anniv. — A1714

**2010, Oct. 29**
**3033** A1714 60c multi 1.75 .85

Adoration of the Magi, by Sandro Botticelli — A1715

Toy Train A1716

**2010, Oct. 29** ***Perf. 13¼x13***
**3034** A1715 60c multi 1.75 .85

***Perf. 13x13¼***

**3035** A1716 65c multi 1.90 .95

Christmas.

Mario Mazzuca (1910-83), Rugby Player A1717

**2010, Oct. 30** ***Perf. 13x13¼***
**3036** A1717 60c multi 1.75 .85

Gentilini Cookies, 120th Anniv. — A1718

**2010, Oct. 31** ***Perf. 13¼x13***
**3037** A1718 60c multi 1.75 .85

Berlucchi Wines, 50th Anniv. (in 2011) — A1719

**2010, Nov. 5**
**3038** A1719 60c multi 1.75 .85

A1720

Italian Flag, 150th Anniv. — A1721

**2011, Jan. 7** **Photo.** ***Perf. 13x13¼***

**Souvenir Sheet**

**3039** A1720 60c multi 1.60 .80

**Self-Adhesive**

***Serpentine Die Cut 11***

**3040** A1721 60c multi 1.60 .80

Unification of Italy, 150th anniv.

**Folk Festivals Type of 2009**

Design: No. 3041, Battle of the Oranges, Carnival of Ivrea.

**2011, Feb. 20** **Photo.** ***Perf. 13½***
**3041** A1634 60c multi 1.75 .85

Antonio Fogazzaro (1842-1911), Writer — A1722

**2011, Mar. 7** ***Perf. 13x13¼***
**3042** A1722 60c multi 1.75 .85

Intl. Women's Day A1723

**2011, Mar. 8**
**3043** A1723 75c multi 2.10 1.10

Miniature Sheet

Taxation Agencies, 10th Anniv. — A1724

No. 3044: a, Territorio (Land Registry). b, Dogane (Customs). c, Demanio (State Property). d, Entrate (Revenue).

**2011, Mar. 10**
**3044** A1724 Sheet of 4 7.00 3.50
*a.-d.* 60c Any single 1.75 .85

Souvenir Sheet

Proclamation of the Kingdom of Italy, 150th Anniv. — A1725

**2011, Mar. 17** **Photo.** ***Perf. 13x13¼***
**3045** A1725 60c multi 1.75 .85

Souvenir Sheet

Piazza del Popolo, Rome — A1726

**2011, Mar. 21** ***Perf. 13¼x13***
**3046** A1726 €1.50 multi 4.50 2.25

Unification of Italy, 150th anniv. See Vatican City No. 1470.

Cheeses Made in Italy — A1727

Designs: No. 3047, Gorgonzola. No. 3048, Parmigiano Reggiano. No. 3049, Mozzarella di Bufala Campana (buffalo milk mozzarella). No. 3050, Ragusano.

**2011, Mar. 25**
**3047** A1727 60c multi 1.75 .85
**3048** A1727 60c multi 1.75 .85
**3049** A1727 60c multi 1.75 .85
**3050** A1727 60c multi 1.75 .85
*Nos. 3047-3050 (4)* 7.00 3.40

World Theater Day — A1728

***Serpentine Die Cut 11***

**2011, Mar. 27** **Self-Adhesive**
**3051** A1728 60c multi 1.75 .85

Italy No. 22 — A1729

***Serpentine Die Cut 11¼***

**2011, Mar. 29** **Photo.**

**Self-Adhesive**

**3052** A1729 60c aqua &dk blue 1.75 .85
*a.* Booklet pane of 10 17.50
Complete booklet, #3052a 17.50

First Man in Space, 50th Anniv. A1730

***Serpentine Die Cut 11***

**2011, Apr. 12** **Photo.**

**Self-Adhesive**

**3054** A1730 75c multi 2.25 1.10

Quadriga on King Victor Emmanuel II Monument, Rome — A1731

**2011, Apr. 21** ***Perf. 13¼x13***
**3055** A1731 60c multi 1.75 .85

Emilion Salgari (1862-1911), Writer — A1732

**2011, Apr. 23** ***Perf. 13x13¼***
**3056** A1732 60c multi 1.75 .85

Beatification of Pope John Paul II — A1733

***Serpentine Die Cut 11***

**2011, Apr. 29** **Self-Adhesive**
**3057** A1733 60c multi 1.75 .85

Europa — A1734

Forest and: 60c, Mushrooms, squirrel. 75c, Bird, flowers.

**2011, May 9** ***Perf. 13¼x13***
**3058** A1734 60c multi 1.75 .85
**3059** A1734 75c multi 2.25 1.10

Intl. Year of Forests.

Amnesty International, 50th Anniv. — A1735

***Serpentine Die Cut 11¼***

**2011, May 28** **Photo.**

**Self-Adhesive**

**3060** A1735 60c multi 1.75 .85

National Emigration Museum, Rome
A1736

**2011, June 1** ***Perf. 13x13¼***
**3061** A1736 60c multi 1.75 .85

Souvenir Sheets

Unification of Italy, 150th Anniv. — A1737

Famous people and artwork: No. 3062, Camillo Benso, Conte di Cavour (1810-61), statesman, scene from 1856 Congress of Paris. No. 3063, Carlo Cattaneo (1801-69), writer, scene from 1848 Milan Revolt. No. 3064, Giuseppe Garibaldi (1807-82), military leader, scene of Garibaldi entering Naples, Sept. 7, 1860. No. 3065, Vincenzo Gioberti (1801-52), politician, scene of people celebrating in Naples. No. 3066, Clara Maffei (1814-86), Cristina Trivulzio Belgiojoso (1808-71), advocates of independence, scene of soldiers carrying injured Luciano Manara at Villa Spada, 1850. No. 3067, Giuseppe Mazzini (1805-72), politician, cover page of Giovine Italia, and Unione, Forza e Liberta flag. No. 3068, Carlo Pisacane (1818-57), patriot, and depiction of his murder. No. 3069, King Victor Emmanuel II (1820-78), and depiction of him on horseback

**2011, June 2**

| | | | | |
|---|---|---|---|---|
| **3062** | A1737 60c multi | | 1.75 | .85 |
| **3063** | A1737 60c multi | | 1.75 | .85 |
| **3064** | A1737 60c multi | | 1.75 | .85 |
| **3065** | A1737 60c multi | | 1.75 | .85 |
| **3066** | A1737 60c multi | | 1.75 | .85 |
| **3067** | A1737 60c multi | | 1.75 | .85 |
| **3068** | A1737 60c multi | | 1.75 | .85 |
| **3069** | A1737 60c multi | | 1.75 | .85 |
| | *Nos. 3062-3069 (8)* | | 14.00 | 6.80 |

Souvenir Sheet

Anita and Giuseppe Garibaldi, First Tower of San Marino — A1738

**2011, June 4**
**3070** A1738 €1.50 multi 4.50 2.25

Granting of San Marino citizenship to Garibaldis. See San Marino No. 1851.

Miniature Sheet

Italian Navy, 150th Anniv. — A1739

No. 3071: a, Arms of the Savoia family, Navy arms and pennant. b, Naval Academy, Livorno. c, Training ship Amerigo Vespucci. d, Emblems of Italian Sailor's Union and National Association of Italian Sailors

**2011, June 10**
**3071** A1739 Sheet of 4 7.00 3.50
***a.-d.*** 60c Any single 1.75 .85

Italian Referees Association, Cent. — A1740

**2011, June 18**
**3072** A1740 60c multi 1.75 .85

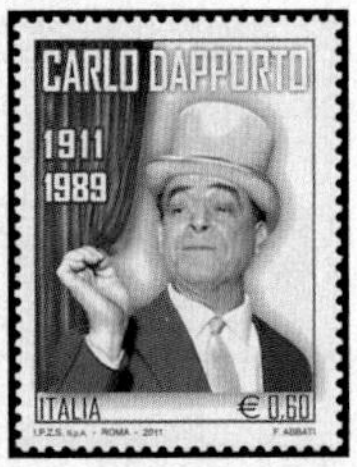


Carlo Dapporto (1911-89), Actor — A1741

**2011, June 25** ***Perf. 13¼x13***
**3073** A1741 60c multi 1.75 .85

**Envelope Type of 2009**

***Serpentine Die Cut 11***

**2011, June 28** **Engr.**

**Self-Adhesive**

**Denomination Color**

**3074** A1644 75c lilac 2.10 1.10

Parks and Gardens — A1742

Designs: No. 3075, Flower Garden, Appenninica di Capracotta. No. 3076, Padua Botanical Gardens.

**2011, July 4** **Photo.** ***Perf. 13¼x13***
**3075** A1742 60c multi 1.75 .85
**3076** A1742 60c multi 1.75 .85

Holy Trinity Benedictine Abbey, Cava de'Tirreni, 1000th Anniv. — A1743

**2011, July 7** **Engr.** ***Perf. 13¼x13***
**3077** A1743 60c black 1.75 .85

Compasso d'Oro Award for Industrial Design — A1744

**2011, July 12** **Photo.** ***Perf. 13½***
**3078** A1744 60c multi 1.75 .85

Hadrian's Villa, Tivoli — A1745

**2011, July 14** ***Perf. 13¼x13***
**3079** A1745 60c multi 1.75 .85

**Tourism Type of 2005 and**

1955 Tourism Poster — A1746

**2011, July 23** **Photo.** ***Perf. 13¼x13***

| | | | | |
|---|---|---|---|---|
| **3080** | A1424 60c Tarvisio | | 1.75 | .85 |
| **3081** | A1424 60c Riviera del Conero, Sirolo | | 1.75 | .85 |
| **3082** | A1424 60c Sepino | | 1.75 | .85 |
| **3083** | A1424 60c Bosa | | 1.75 | .85 |
| | *Nos. 3080-3083 (4)* | | 7.00 | 3.40 |

**Self-Adhesive**

***Serpentine Die Cut 11***

**3084** A1746 60c multi 1.75 .85

Souvenir Sheet

St. Luke Painting the Virgin, by Giorgio Vasari (1511-74) — A1747

**2011, July 30** ***Perf. 13x13¼***
**3085** A1747 €1.40 multi 4.00 2.00

**Folk Festivals Type of 2009**

Design: Mastrogiurato Festival, Lanciano.

**2011, Aug. 26** ***Perf. 13½***
**3086** A1634 60c multi 1.75 .85

Milan, 2010-11 Italian Soccer Champions
A1748

F. C. Internazionale, 2010-11 Italy Cup Soccer Champions — A1749

**2011, Aug. 27** ***Perf. 13¼x13***
**3087** A1748 60c multi 1.75 .85

***Perf. 13x13¼***

**3088** A1749 60c multi 1.75 .85

World Sports Fishing Championships, Italy — A1750

***Serpentine Die Cut 11***

**2011, Aug. 27** **Self-Adhesive**
**3089** A1750 60c multi 1.75 .85

2011 European Field Archery Championships, Montevarchi — A1751

***Serpentine Die Cut 11***

**2011, Aug. 27** **Self-Adhesive**
**3090** A1751 75c multi 2.10 1.10

25th National Eucharistic Congress — A1752

**2011, Sept. 3** **Photo.**

**Self-Adhesive**

**3091** A1752 60c multi 1.75 .85

Arch of Trajan, Benevento A1753

**2011, Sept. 9** **Engr.** ***Perf. 13x13¼***

**3092** A1753 60c black 1.75 .85

Intl. Year of Chemistry A1754

***Serpentine Die Cut 11***

**2011, Sept. 11** **Photo.**

**Self-Adhesive**

**3093** A1754 €1.40 multi 4.00 2.00

Council of State, 180th Anniv. — A1755

***Serpentine Die Cut 11***

**2011, Sept. 13** **Engr.**

**Self-Adhesive**

**3094** A1755 60c black 1.75 .85

Organization for Economic Cooperation and Development, 50th Anniv. — A1756

**2011, Sept. 30** **Photo.**

**Self-Adhesive**

**3095** A1756 60c multi 1.75 .85

European Year of Volunteers A1757

**Self-Adhesive**

**2011, Oct. 4** ***Serpentine Die Cut 11***

**3096** A1757 75c multi 2.10 1.10

Marzotto Textiles, 175th Anniv. A1758

**2011, Oct. 14** **Photo.**

**Self-Adhesive**

**3097** A1758 60c multi 1.75 .85

Italo Svevo (1861-1928), Writer — A1759

**Self-Adhesive**

**2011, Oct. 28** ***Serpentine Die Cut 11***

**3098** A1759 60c multi 1.75 .85

Equestrian Order of the Holy Sepulchre of Jerusalem A1760

**2011, Nov. 3** **Photo.**

**Self-Adhesive**

**3099** A1760 60c multi 2.10 .85

Souvenir Sheets

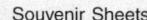

Battles — A1761

No. 3100: a, Battle of Pastrengo, 1848. b, Battle of Solferino, 1859. c, Battle of Volturno, 1860.

No. 3101: a, Battle of Bezzecca, 1866. b, Breach of Porta Pia, 1870. c, Battles of the Isonzo, 1915-17.

**2011, Nov. 4** ***Perf. 13x13¼***

| | | | | |
|---|---|---|---|---|
| **3100** | A1761 | Sheet of 3 | 5.25 | 2.60 |
| ***a.-c.*** | | 60c Any single | 1.75 | .85 |
| **3101** | A1761 | Sheet of 3 | 5.25 | 2.60 |
| ***a.-c.*** | | 60c Any single | 1.75 | .85 |

Italian Military Missions in Foreign Countries A1762

***Serpentine Die Cut 11***

**2011, Nov. 12** **Self-Adhesive**

**3102** A1762 75c multi 2.10 1.00

Philately Day — A1763

**Self-Adhesive**

**2011, Nov. 18** **Photo.**

**3103** A1763 60c multi 1.60 .80

Italian Mint, Cent. — A1764

**2011, Nov. 18** **Self-Adhesive**

**3104** A1764 60c multi 1.60 .80

Postal Savings Booklets A1765

Designs: 60c, Old postal savings booklets. 75c, Modern postal savings booklets.

**2011, Nov. 18** **Self-Adhesive**

**3105** A1765 60c multi 1.60 .80

**3106** A1765 75c multi 2.00 1.00

Fratelli Carli Olive Oil, Cent. — A1766

**2011, Nov. 19** **Self-Adhesive**

**3107** A1766 60c multi 1.60 .80

Madonna and Child with Pomegranate, by Unknown Artist — A1767

Flying Reindeer A1768

**2011, Nov. 19** **Self-Adhesive**

**3108** A1767 60c multi 1.60 .80

**3109** A1768 60c multi 1.60 .80

Christmas.

Russian-Italian Year of Culture — A1769

**2011, Dec. 10** **Self-Adhesive**

**3110** A1769 75c multi 2.00 1.00

See Russia No. 7326.

Italian Olympic Committee Library and Stylized Athletes A1770

**Self-Adhesive**

**2012, Jan. 4** ***Serpentine Die Cut 11***
**3111** A1770 60c multi 1.60 .80

Giulio Onesti (1912-81), Member of Italian Olympic Committee and collector of books on sports.

Souvenir Sheet

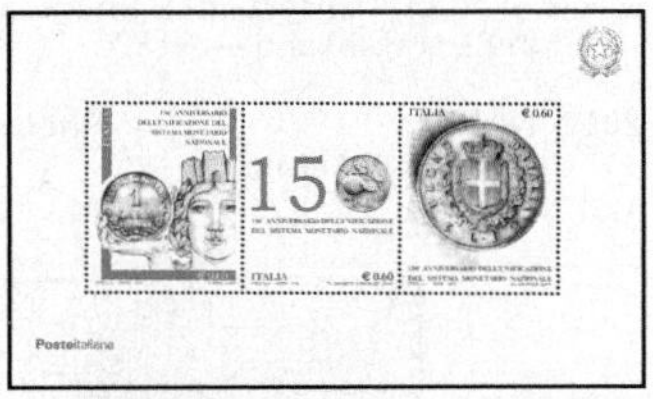

Introduction of the Italian Lira, 150th Anniv. — A1771

No. 3112: a, Italia holding lira coin. b, "150" with coin as zero. c, Coin.

**2012, Mar. 23** ***Perf. 13x13¼***
**3112** A1771 Sheet of 3 5.00 2.50
***a.-c.*** 60c Any single 1.60 .80

Italian Regional Wine Grapes and Vineyards A1772

No. 3113 — Grapes and vineyards for wines guaranteed to be from specific regions: a, Aglianico del Vulture Superiore. b, Cannellino di Frascati. c, Barolo. d, Greco di Tufo. e, Brunello di Montalcino. f, Montepulciano d'Abruzzo Colline Teramane. g, Colli Orientali del Fruili Picolit. h, Montefalco Sagrantino. i, Prosecco Conegliano Valdobbiadene Superiore. j, Vernaccia di Serrapetrona. k, Cerasuolo di Vittoria. l, Vermentino di Gallura. m, Moscato di Scanzo. n, Romagna Albana. o, Primitivo di Manduria Dolce Naturale.

***Serpentine Die Cut 11***
**2012, Mar. 24** **Self-Adhesive**
**3113** Sheet of 15 24.00
***a.-o.*** A1772 60c Any single 1.60 .80

Milanofil 2012 Intl. Philatelic Exhibition, Milan.

Le Fracchie di San Marco — A1773

**2012, Mar. 31** ***Perf. 13¼***
**3114** A1773 60c multi 1.60 .80

Giovanni Pascoli (1855-1912), Poet — A1774

**Self-Adhesive**

**2012, Apr. 6** ***Serpentine Die Cut 11***
**3115** A1774 60c multi 1.60 .80

Savings Banks Association (ACRI), Cent. — A1775

**2012, Apr. 11** **Self-Adhesive**
**3116** A1775 60c multi 1.60 .80

Publication of Lunario Barbanera (Almanac), 250th Anniv. A1776

**2012, Apr. 11** **Self-Adhesive**
**3117** A1776 60c multi 1.60 .80

Balsamic Vinegar From Modena A1777

**2012, Apr. 17** **Self-Adhesive**
**3118** A1777 60c multi 1.60 .80

Europa A1779

Woman and: 60c, Field of sunflowers, building, building pillars. 75c, Dancer, coastal village.

***Serpentine Die Cut 11***
**2012, May 9** **Photo.**
**Self-Adhesive**
**3120** A1779 60c multi 1.50 .75
**3121** A1779 75c multi 1.90 .95

Santa Maria Novella Perfumes and Pharmaceuticals Shop, Florence, 400th Anniv. — A1780

**2012, May 10** ***Serpentine Die Cut 11***
**Self-Adhesive**
**3122** A1780 75c multi 1.90 .95

Trani Cathedral A1781

**2012, June 1** **Engr.** ***Perf. 13x13¼***
**3123** A1781 60c black 1.50 .75

Pres. Luigi Einaudi (1874-1961) A1782

***Serpentine Die Cut 11***
**2012, July 2** **Photo.**
**Self-Adhesive**
**3124** A1782 60c multi 1.50 .75

Horse Battle, by Aligi Sassu (1912-2000) — A1783

**2012, July 17** ***Perf. 13¼x13***
**3125** A1783 60c multi 1.50 .75

**Tourism Type of 2005 and**

Travel Poster — A1784

***Serpentine Die Cut 11***
**2012, July 19** **Self-Adhesive**
**3126** A1424 60c Baveno 1.50 .75
**3127** A1424 60c Maiori 1.50 .75
**3128** A1424 60c Monte Cassino 1.50 .75
**3129** A1424 60c Ustica 1.50 .75
**3130** A1784 60c multi 1.50 .75
*Nos. 3126-3130 (5)* 7.50 3.75

Juventus, 2011-12 Italian Soccer Champions A1785

**2012, July 21** **Photo.**
**Self-Adhesive**
**3131** A1785 60c multi 1.50 .75

Expo 2015, Milan A1786

**2012, Aug. 1** ***Serpentine Die Cut 11***
**Self-Adhesive**
**3132** A1786 60c multi 1.50 .75

Boniface VIII Baths, Fiuggi — A1787

**2012, Aug. 4** **Engr.**
**Self-Adhesive**
**3133** A1787 €1.50 black 4.00 2.00

Fermo Cathedral A1788

**2012, Aug. 14** ***Perf. 13x13¼***
**3134** A1788 60c black 1.60 .80

Roma Newspaper, 150th Anniv. A1789

***Serpentine Die Cut 11***
**2012, Sept. 10** **Photo.**
**Self-Adhesive**
**3135** A1789 60c multi 1.60 .80

Souvenir Sheet

Battle of the Milvian Bridge, 1700th Anniv. — A1790

**2012, Sept. 13** ***Perf. 13x13¼***
**3136** A1790 €1.40 multi 3.75 1.90

See Vatican City No. 1507.

Anti-Mafia Investigation Department A1791

***Serpentine Die Cut 11***
**2012, Sept. 21** **Self-Adhesive**
**3137** A1791 60c multi 1.60 .80

Italian Surgery Congress, Rome — A1792

**2012, Sept. 23** **Photo.**

**Self-Adhesive**

**3138** A1792 60c red & green 1.60 .80

Botanical Gardens — A1793

Botianical Gardens in: No. 3139, Rome. No. 3140, Catania.

***Serpentine Die Cut 11***

**2012, Sept. 28** **Self-Adhesive**

**3139** A1793 75c multi 2.00 1.00
**3140** A1793 75c multi 2.00 1.00

Court of Auditors, 150th Anniv. A1794

**2012, Oct. 1** **Engr.**

**Self-Adhesive**

**3141** A1794 60c green & black 1.60 .80

Cusano Milanino, Cent. A1795

**2012, Oct. 6** **Photo.**

**Self-Adhesive**

**3142** A1795 60c multi 1.60 .80

Second Vatican Council (Vatican II), 50th Anniv. — A1796

**2012, Oct. 11** ***Serpentine Die Cut 11***

**Self-Adhesive**

**3143** A1796 60c multi 1.60 .80

National Corps of Scouts and Guides, Cent. A1797

**2012, Oct. 12** **Photo.**

**Self-Adhesive**

**3144** A1797 60c multi 1.60 .80

Philately Day — A1798

No. 3145 — Steps in the creation of an Italian stamp: a, Philatelic consultation group (Consulta filatelica). b, Signing of decree (Decretazione). c, Graphic design (Ideazione grafica). d, Philatelic commision inspecting designs (Commissione filatelica). e, Printing of stamps (Produzione carte valori).

**2012, Oct. 12** ***Perf. 13¼x13***

**3145** Horiz. strip of 5 8.00 4.00
*a.-e.* A1798 60c Any single 1.60 .80

Manger with Saints John the Baptist and Bartholomew, by Antonio del Massaro — A1799

Christmas Tree — A1800

**2012, Oct. 12** ***Serpentine Die Cut 11***

**Self-Adhesive**

**3146** A1799 60c multi 1.60 .80
**3147** A1800 60c multi 1.60 .80

Christmas.

Guzzini Housewares — A1801

**2012, Oct. 13** **Photo.**

**Self-Adhesive**

**3148** A1801 60c multi 1.60 .80

Ceramics A1802

No. 3149: a, Castelli ceramic plate. b, Caltagirone ceramic tiles. c, Ceramic tiles with inscription "Arte della ceramica" in square. d, Castellamonte ceramic stoves. e, Squillace ceramic plate.

**2012, Oct. 14** ***Perf. 13¼x13***

**3149** Horiz. strip of 5 8.00 4.00
*a.-e.* A1802 60c Any single 1.60 .80

Pope John Paul I (1912-78) — A1803

**2012, Oct. 17** ***Serpentine Die Cut 11***

**Self-Adhesive**

**3150** A1803 60c multi 1.60 .80

Luigi Carlo Farini (1812-66), Prime Minister — A1805

***Serpentine Die Cut 11***

**2012, Oct. 22** **Photo.**

**Self-Adhesive**

**3153** A1805 60c multi 1.60 .80

Italian El Alamein War Memorial, Italian Base Q33, Emblem of Folgore Parachute Brigade A1806

**2012, Oct. 23** ***Serpentine Die Cut 11***

**Self-Adhesive**

**3154** A1806 €1.40 multi 3.75 1.90

Battle of El Alamein, 70th anniv.

81st General Assembly of Interpol, Rome A1807

**2012, Nov. 3** **Photo.**

**Self-Adhesive**

**3155** A1807 60c multi 1.60 .80

Italian National Electricity Company, 50th Anniv. — A1808

**2012, Nov. 5** ***Serpentine Die Cut 11***

**Self-Adhesive**

**3156** A1808 60c multi 1.60 .80

Elimination of Architectural Barriers to the Handicapped — A1809

**2012, Nov. 9** **Photo.**

**Self-Adhesive**

**3157** A1809 60c multi 1.60 .80

Primo Levi (1919-87), Writer A1810

***Serpentine Die Cut 11***

**2012, Nov. 10** **Self-Adhesive**

**3158** A1810 75c multi 2.00 1.00

Emblem of Health and Anti-Adulteration Center, 50th Anniv. — A1811

**2012, Nov. 29** **Photo.**

**Self-Adhesive**

**3159** A1811 60c multi 1.60 .80

**Folk Festival Type of 2009**

Design: Ndocciata Christmas Festival, Agnone.

**2012, Dec. 7** ***Perf. 13¼***

**3160** A1634 60c multi 1.60 .80

Awarding of 2012 Nobel Peace Prize to the European Union — A1812

**2012, Dec. 10** ***Perf. 13¼x13***

**3161** A1812 75c multi 2.00 1.00

## SEMI-POSTAL STAMPS

Many issues of Italy and Italian Colonies include one or more semi-postal denominations. To avoid splitting sets, these issues are generally listed as regular postage, airmail, etc., unless all values carry a surtax.

Italian Flag — SP1

Italian Eagle Bearing Arms of Savoy — SP2

**1915-16 Typo. Wmk. 140 *Perf. 14***

| | | | |
|---|---|---|---|
| **B1** | SP1 10c + 5c rose | 8.50 | 11.00 |
| **B2** | SP2 15c + 5c slate | 6.75 | 9.00 |
| **B3** | SP2 20c + 5c orange | 32.50 | 60.00 |
| | *Nos. B1-B3 (3)* | 47.75 | *80.00* |
| | Set, never hinged | 125.00 | |

No. B2 Surcharged

**1916**

| | | | |
|---|---|---|---|
| **B4** | SP2 20c on 15c + 5c | 21.00 | 52.50 |
| | Never hinged | 52.50 | |
| *a.* | Double overprint | 675.00 | — |
| | Never hinged | — | |
| *b.* | Inverted overprint | 675.00 | 1,200. |
| | Never hinged | — | |
| *c.* | Pair, one without surcharge | 1,725. | |
| | Never hinged | 2,500. | |

Regular Issues of 1906-16 Overprinted in Blue or Red

**1921**

| | | | |
|---|---|---|---|
| **B5** | A48 10c claret (Bl) | 1,275. | 1,500. |
| *a.* | Double overprint | 1,500. | |
| **B6** | A50 20c brn org (Bl) | 1,875. | 450.00 |
| **B7** | A49 25c blue (R) | 250.00 | 180.00 |
| *a.* | Double overprint | 425.00 | |
| **B8** | A49 40c brn (Bl) | 100.00 | 21.00 |
| *a.* | Inverted overprint | 170.00 | 150.00 |
| | *Nos. B5-B8 (4)* | 3,500. | 2,151. |
| | Set, never hinged | 5,500. | |

Regular Issues of 1901-22 Overprinted in Black, Blue, Brown or Red

**1922-23**

| | | | |
|---|---|---|---|
| **B9** | A48 10c cl ('23) (Bk) | 105.00 | 82.50 |
| *a.* | Blue ovpt. | 105.00 | 82.50 |
| | Never hinged | 225.00 | |
| *b.* | Brown ovpt. | 105.00 | 82.50 |
| | Never hinged | 225.00 | |
| *d.* | Blk ovpt. double | 170.00 | |
| *e.* | As "b," ovpt. double | 185.00 | |
| **B10** | A48 15c slate (Org) | 375.00 | *500.00* |
| *a.* | Blue ovpt. | 1,000. | 925.00 |
| | Never hinged | 2,000. | |
| *b.* | Red overprint | 450.00 | *600.00* |
| | Never hinged | 950.00 | |
| **B11** | A50 20c brn org (Bk) | 425.00 | *500.00* |
| *a.* | Blue ovpt. | 850.00 | 450.00 |
| | Never hinged | 1,700. | |
| **B12** | A49 25c blue (BK; '23) | 140.00 | 110.00 |
| *b.* | Red Overprint | 375.00 | 500.00 |
| | Never hinged | 750.00 | |
| *c.* | Orange ovpt. | 375.00 | 500.00 |
| | Never hinged | 750.00 | |
| **B12A** | A49 30c org brn (Bk) | 275.00 | 200.00 |
| **B13** | A49 40c brn (Bl) | 210.00 | 110.00 |
| *a.* | Black ovpt. | 210.00 | 110.00 |
| | Never hinged | 450.00 | |
| *b.* | As "a," invtd. ovpt. | — | — |
| **B14** | A49 50c vio ('23) (Bk) | 750.00 | 750.00 |
| *a.* | Blue overprint | | — |
| **B15** | A49 60c car (Bk) | 2,700. | 2,425. |
| **B15A** | A49 85c choc (Bk) | 375.00 | *500.00* |
| **B16** | A46 1 l brn & grn ('23) (Bk) | 4,650. | 2,800. |
| *a.* | Inverted overprint | *5,250.* | |
| | Never hinged | *6,000.* | |
| | *Nos. B9-B16 (10)* | 10,005. | 7,977. |
| | Set, never hinged | 14,250. | |

The stamps overprinted "B. L. P." were sold by the Government below face value to the National Federation for Assisting War Invalids. Most of them were affixed to special envelopes (Buste Lettere Postali) which bore advertisements. The Federation was permitted to sell these envelopes at a reduction of 5c from the face value of each stamp. The profits for the war invalids were derived from the advertisements.

Values of Nos. B5-B16 unused are for stamps with original gum. Most copies without gum or with part gum sell for about a quarter of values quoted. Uncanceled stamps affixed to the special envelopes usually sell for about half value.

The overprint on Nos. B9-B16 is wider (13½mm) than that on Nos. B5-B8 (11mm). The 1922-23 overprint exists both typo. and litho. on 10c, 15c, 20c and 25c; only litho. on 40c, 50c, 60c and 1 l; and only typo. on 30c and 85c.

Counterfeits of the B.L.P. overprints exist.

Administering Fascist Oath — SP3

**1923, Oct. 29 *Perf. 14x14½***

| | | | |
|---|---|---|---|
| **B17** | SP3 30c + 30c brown | 32.50 | *135.00* |
| **B18** | SP3 50c + 50c violet | 32.50 | *135.00* |
| *a.* | Horiz. pair, imperf between | 1,100. | |
| **B19** | SP3 1 l + 1 l gray | 32.50 | *135.00* |
| | *Nos. B17-B19 (3)* | 97.50 | *405.00* |
| | Set, never hinged | 250.00 | |

The surtax was given to the Benevolent Fund of the Black Shirts (the Italian National Militia).

Anniv. of the March of the Fascisti on Rome.

St. Maria Maggiore SP4

Pope Opening Holy Door SP8

Designs: 30c+15c, St. John Lateran. 50c+25c, St. Paul's Church. 60c+30c, St. Peter's Basilica. 5 l+2.50 l, Pope closing Holy Door.

**1924, Dec. 24 *Perf. 12***

| | | | |
|---|---|---|---|
| **B20** | SP4 20c + 10c dk grn & brn | 4.50 | *12.50* |
| **B21** | SP4 30c + 15c dk brn & brn | 4.50 | *12.50* |
| **B22** | SP4 50c + 25c vio & brn | 4.50 | *12.50* |
| **B23** | SP4 60c + 30c dp rose & brn | 4.50 | *37.50* |
| **B24** | SP8 1 l + 50c dp bl & vio | 7.50 | *37.50* |
| **B25** | SP8 5 l + 2.50 l org brn & vio | 9.00 | *75.00* |
| | *Nos. B20-B25 (6)* | 34.50 | *187.50* |
| | Set, never hinged | 80.00 | |

The surtax was contributed toward the Holy Year expenses.

Castle of St. Angelo SP10

Designs: 50c+20c, 60c+30c, Aqueduct of Claudius. 1.25 l+50c, 1.25 l+60c, Capitol, Roman Forum. 5 l+2 l, 5 l+2.50 l, People's Gate.

**Unwmk.**

**1926, Oct. 26 Engr. *Perf. 11***

| | | | |
|---|---|---|---|
| **B26** | SP10 40c + 20c dk brn & blk | 3.50 | *22.50* |
| **B27** | SP10 60c + 30c brn red & ol brn | 3.50 | *22.50* |
| **B28** | SP10 1.25 l + 60c bl grn & blk | 3.50 | *62.50* |
| **B29** | SP10 5 l + 2.50 l dk bl & blk | 6.00 | *190.00* |
| | *Nos. B26-B29 (4)* | 16.50 | *297.50* |
| | Set, never hinged | 37.50 | |

**Stamps inscribed "Poste Italiane" and "Fiere Campionaria di Tripoli" are listed in Libya.**

**1928, Mar. 1**

| | | | |
|---|---|---|---|
| **B30** | SP10 30c + 10c dl vio & blk | 12.00 | *55.00* |
| **B31** | SP10 50c + 20c ol grn & sl | 20.00 | *55.00* |
| **B32** | SP10 1.25 l + 50c dp bl & blk | 25.00 | *110.00* |
| **B33** | SP10 5 l + 2 l brn red & blk | 55.00 | *375.00* |
| | *Nos. B30-B33 (4)* | 112.00 | *595.00* |
| | Set, never hinged | 275.00 | |

The tax on Nos. B26 to B33 was devoted to the charitable work of the Voluntary Militia for National Defense.

See Nos. B35-B38.

Victor Emmanuel II — SP14

**1929, Jan. 4 Photo. *Perf. 14***

| | | | |
|---|---|---|---|
| **B34** | SP14 50c + 10c ol grn | 4.50 | *9.25* |
| | Never hinged | 11.00 | |

50th anniv. of the death of King Victor Emmanuel II. The surtax was for veterans.

**Type of 1926 Issue**

Designs in same order.

**1930, July 1 Engr.**

| | | | |
|---|---|---|---|
| **B35** | SP10 30c + 10c dk grn & vio | 2.50 | *37.50* |
| **B36** | SP10 50c + 10c dk grn & bl grn | 3.50 | *28.00* |
| **B37** | SP10 1.25 l + 30c ind & grn | 8.50 | *90.00* |
| **B38** | SP10 5 l + 1.50 l blk brn & ol brn | 17.00 | *375.00* |
| | *Nos. B35-B38 (4)* | 31.50 | *530.50* |
| | Set, never hinged | 77.50 | |

The surtax was for the charitable work of the Voluntary Militia for National Defense.

Militiamen at Ceremonial Fire with Quotation from Leonardo da Vinci — SP15

Symbolical of Pride for Militia — SP16

Symbolical of Militia Guarding Immortality of Italy SP17

Militia Passing Through Arch of Constantine SP18

**1935, July 1 Photo. Wmk. 140**

| | | | |
|---|---|---|---|
| **B39** | SP15 20c + 10c rose red | 10.00 | *12.00* |
| **B40** | SP16 25c + 15c green | 10.00 | *19.00* |
| **B41** | SP17 50c + 30c purple | 10.00 | *24.00* |
| **B42** | SP18 1.25 l + 75c blue | 10.00 | *35.00* |
| | *Nos. B39-B42 (4)* | 40.00 | *90.00* |
| | Set, never hinged | 100.00 | |
| | *Nos. B39-B42,CB3 (5)* | 50.00 | *125.00* |
| | Set, never hinged | 117.50 | |

The surtax was for the Militia.

Roman Battle SP19

Roman Warriors SP20

**1941, Dec. 13**

| | | | |
|---|---|---|---|
| **B43** | SP19 20c + 10c rose red | .75 | *1.50* |
| **B44** | SP19 30c + 15c brown | .75 | *1.90* |
| **B45** | SP20 50c + 25c violet | .75 | *1.90* |
| **B46** | SP20 1.25 l + 1 l blue | 1.50 | *3.00* |
| | *Nos. B43-B46 (4)* | 3.75 | *8.30* |
| | Set, never hinged | 7.50 | |

2,000th anniv. of the birth of Livy (59 B.C.-17 A.D.), Roman historian.

**Catalogue values for unused stamps in this section, from this point to the end of the section, are for Never Hinged items.**

Aid for Flood Victims — SP21

**1995, Jan. 2 Photo. *Perf. 13½x14***

| | | | |
|---|---|---|---|
| **B47** | SP21 750 l +2250 l multi | 6.00 | 4.25 |

Queen Helen (1873-1952) SP22

**2002, Mar. 2 Photo. *Perf. 13¼x14***

| | | | |
|---|---|---|---|
| **B48** | SP22 41c + 21c multi | 1.75 | .90 |

Surtax for breast cancer research and prevention.

Intl. Commission on Occupational Health, 28th Congress — SP23

**2006, Mar. 8 Photo. *Perf. 13x13¼***

| | | | |
|---|---|---|---|
| **B49** | SP23 60c +30c multi | 2.75 | 1.90 |

Surtax for breast cancer research.

Nursing — SP24

*Serpentine Die Cut 11*

**2010, May 16** **Photo.**

**Self-Adhesive**

**B50** SP24 60c +30c multi 2.25 2.25

Surtax for breast cancer research.

## AIR POST STAMPS

Used values for Nos. C1-C105 are for postally used stamps with legible cancellations. Forged cancels on these issues abound, and expertization is srongly recommended.

### Special Delivery Stamp No. E1 Overprinted

**1917, May** **Wmk. 140** ***Perf. 14***

**C1** SD1 25c rose red 22.50 *42.50*
Never hinged 55.00

Type of SD3 Surcharged in Black

**1917, June 27**

**C2** SD3 25c on 40c violet 22.50 *50.00*
Never hinged 55.00

Type SD3 was not issued without surcharge.

AP2

**1926-28** **Typo.**

**C3** AP2 50c rose red ('28) 18.00 12.50
**C4** AP2 60c gray 5.00 *12.50*
**C5** AP2 80c brn vio & brn ('28) 32.50 *125.00*
**C6** AP2 1 l blue 12.00 *12.50*
**C7** AP2 1.20 l brn ('27) 29.00 *125.00*
**C8** AP2 1.50 l buff 18.00 32.50
**C9** AP2 5 l gray grn 42.50 *115.00*
*Nos. C3-C9 (7)* 157.00 *435.00*
Set, never hinged 375.00

Nos. C4 and C6 Surcharged

**1927, Sept. 16**

**C10** AP2 50c on 60c gray 22.50 *82.50*
*a.* Pair, one without surcharge 1,950.
**C11** AP2 80c on 1 l blue 57.50 *375.00*
Set, never hinged 190.00

Pegasus AP3

Wings AP4

Spirit of Flight — AP5

Arrows AP6

**1930-32** **Photo.** **Wmk. 140**

**C12** AP4 25c dk grn ('32) .25 .25
**C13** AP3 50c olive brn .25 .25
**C14** AP5 75c org brn ('32) .40 .25
**C15** AP4 80c org red .25 *.70*
**C16** AP5 1 l purple .25 .25
**C17** AP6 2 l deep blue .40 .25
**C18** AP3 5 l dk green .80 *1.60*
**C19** AP3 10 l dp car 1.60 *6.50*
*Nos. C12-C19 (8)* 4.20 10.05
Set, never hinged 10.00

The 50c, 1 l and 2 l were reprinted in 1942 with labels similar to those of Nos. 427-438, but were not issued. Value, set of 3: unused $550; never hinged $1,100.

For overprints see Nos. MC1-MC5. For overprints and surcharges on design AP6 see Nos. C52-C55; Yugoslavia-Ljubljana NB9-NB20, NC11-NC17.

### Ferrucci Type of Postage

Statue of Ferrucci.

**1930, July 10**

**C20** A104 50c purple 4.00 *18.00*
**C21** A104 1 l orange brn 4.00 *20.00*
**C22** A104 5 l + 2 l brn vio 16.00 *130.00*
*Nos. C20-C22 (3)* 24.00 *168.00*
Set, never hinged 60.00

For overprinted types see Aegean Islands Nos. C1-C3.

### Virgil Type of Postage

Jupiter sending forth his eagle.

**1930, Oct. 21** **Photo.** **Wmk. 140**

**C23** A106 50c lt brown 24.00 *40.00*
**C24** A106 1 l orange 24.00 *45.00*

**Engr.**

**Unwmk.**

**C25** A106 7.70 l + 1.30 l vio brn 57.50 *475.00*
**C26** A106 9 l + 2 l indigo 65.00 *525.00*
*Nos. C23-C26 (4)* 170.50 *1,085.*
Set, never hinged 430.00

The surtax on Nos. C25-C26 was for the National Institute Figli del Littorio.

For overprinted types see Aegean Islands Nos. C4-C7.

Trans-Atlantic Squadron — AP9

**1930, Dec. 15** **Photo.** **Wmk. 140**

**C27** AP9 7.70 l Prus bl & gray 450.00 *1,350.*
Never hinged 900.00
*a.* Seven stars instead of six 1,850. —
Never hinged 3,750.

Flight by Italian aviators from Rome to Rio de Janeiro, Dec. 1930-Jan. 12, 1931.

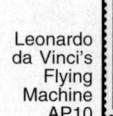

Leonardo da Vinci's Flying Machine AP10

Leonardo da Vinci AP11

Leonardo da Vinci — AP12

**1932**

**C28** AP10 50c olive brn 5.00 *14.50*
**C29** AP11 1 l violet 6.50 *16.00*
**C30** AP11 3 l brown red 8.00 *40.00*
**C31** AP11 5 l dp green 13.00 *47.50*
**C32** AP10 7.70 l + 2 l dk bl 10.00 *160.00*
**C33** AP11 10 l + 2.50 l blk brn 11.50 *275.00*
*Nos. C28-C33 (6)* 54.00 *553.00*
Set, never hinged 135.00

**Engr.**

**Unwmk.**

**C34** AP12 100 l brt bl & grnsh blk 45.00 *900.00*
Never hinged 110.00
*a.* Thin paper 225.00 *1,650.*

Dante Alighieri Soc. and especially Leonardo da Vinci, to whom the invention of a flying machine has been attributed. Surtax was for the benefit of the Society.

Inscription on No. C34: "Man with his large wings by beating against the air will be able to dominate it and lift himself above it".

Issued: #C28-C33, Mar. 14; #C34, Aug. 6.

For overprinted types see Aegean Islands Nos. C8-C13.

Garibaldi's Home at Caprera AP13

Farmhouse where Anita Garibaldi Died AP14

50c, 1 l+25c, Garibaldi's home, Caprera. 2 l+50c, Anita Garibaldi. 5 l+1 l, Giuseppe Garibaldi.

**1932, Apr. 6** **Photo.** **Wmk. 140**

**C35** AP13 50c copper red 5.00 *8.00*
**C36** AP14 80c deep green 5.00 *13.00*
**C37** AP13 1 l + 25c red brn 8.00 *32.50*
**C38** AP13 2 l + 50c dp bl 13.00 *45.00*
**C39** AP14 5 l + 1 l dp grn 13.00 *52.50*
*Nos. C35-C39 (5)* 44.00 *151.00*
Set, never hinged 110.00

50th anniv. of the death of Giuseppe Garibaldi, patriot. The surtax was for the benefit of the Garibaldi Volunteers.

For overprinted types see Aegean Islands Nos. C15-C19.

### March on Rome Type of Postage

50c, Eagle sculpture and airplane. 75c, Italian buildings from the air.

**1932, Oct. 27** ***Perf. 14***

**C40** A146 50c dark brown 3.25 *10.00*
**C41** A146 75c orange brn 10.00 *32.50*
Set, never hinged 32.50

### Graf Zeppelin Issue

Zeppelin over Pyramid of Caius Cestius AP19

5 l, Tomb of Cecilia Metlella. 10 l, Stadium of Mussolini. 12 l, St. Angelo Castle and Bridge. 15 l, Roman Forum. 20 l, Imperial Avenue.

**1933, Apr. 24**

**C42** AP19 3 l black & grn 23.00 *105.00*
**C43** AP19 5 l green & brn 23.00 *120.00*
**C44** AP19 10 l car & dl bl 23.00 *275.00*
**C45** AP19 12 l dk bl & red org 23.00 *475.00*
**C46** AP19 15 l dk brn & gray 23.00 *625.00*
**C47** AP19 20 l org brn & bl 23.00 *675.00*
*a.* Vertical pair, imperf. between 9,000.
Never hinged 14,000.
*Nos. C42-C47 (6)* 138.00 *2,275.*
Set, never hinged 325.00

### Balbo's Trans-Atlantic Flight Issue

Italian Flag

King Victor Emmanuel III

Allegory "Flight" — AP25

#C49, Colosseum at Rome, Chicago skyline. #C48-C49 consist of 3 parts; Italian flag, Victor Emmanuel III, & scene arranged horizontally.

**1933, May 20**

**C48** AP25 5.25 l + 19.75 l red, grn & ultra 125.00 *1,875.*
Never hinged 250.00
*a.* Left stamp without ovpt. *31,500.*
Never hinged *47,000.*
**C49** AP25 5.25 l + 44.75 l grn, red & ultra 160.00 *1,875.*
Never hinged 325.00

Transatlantic Flight, Rome-Chicago, of 24-seaplane squadron led by Gen. Italo Balbo. Center and right sections paid postage. At left is registered air express label overprinted "APPARECCHIO" and abbreviated pilot's name. Twenty triptychs of each value differ in name overprint.

No. C49 overprinted "VOLO DI RITORNO/ NEW YORK-ROMA" was not issued; flight canceled. Value: unused $32,500; never hinged $50,000.

For overprints see Nos. CO1, Aegean Islands C26-C27.

### Type of Air Post Stamp of 1930 Surcharged in Black

**1934, Jan. 18**

**C52** AP6 2 l on 2 l yel 9.75 *82.50*
**C53** AP6 3 l on 2 l yel grn 9.75 *120.00*
**C54** AP6 5 l on 2 l rose 9.75 *240.00*
**C55** AP6 10 l on 2 l vio 9.75 *330.00*
*Nos. C52-C55 (4)* 39.00 *772.50*
Set, never hinged 92.00

For use on mail carried on a special flight from Rome to Buenos Aires.

### Annexation of Fiume Type

25c, 75c, View of Fiume Harbor. 50c, 1 l+50c, Monument to the Dead. 2 l+1.50 l, Venetian Lions. 3 l+2 l, Julian wall.

**1934, Mar. 12**

**C56** A166 25c green .95 *4.00*
**C57** A166 50c brown .95 *2.40*
**C58** A166 75c org brn .95 *10.00*
**C59** A166 1 l + 50c dl vio .95 *16.00*
**C60** A166 2 l + 1.50 l dl bl .95 *21.00*
**C61** A166 3 l + 2 l blk brn .95 *23.00*
*Nos. C56-C61 (6)* 4.80 *76.40*
Set, never hinged 14.40

Airplane and View of Stadium AP32

Soccer Player and Plane AP33

Airplane and Stadium Entrance AP35

Airplane over Stadium AP34

**1934, May 24**

| | | | | |
|---|---|---|---|---|
| **C62** | AP32 | 50c car rose | 11.00 | *45.00* |
| **C63** | AP33 | 75c gray blue | 17.50 | *55.00* |
| **C64** | AP34 | 5 l + 2.50 l ol grn | 52.50 | *350.00* |
| **C65** | AP35 | 10 l + 5 l brn blk | 52.50 | *550.00* |
| | | *Nos. C62-C65 (4)* | 133.50 | *1,000.* |
| | | Set, never hinged | 332.50 | |

2nd World Soccer Championships.

For overprinted types see Aegean Islands Nos. C28-C31.

Zeppelin under Fire AP36

Air Force Memorial — AP40

Designs: 25c, 80c, Zeppelin under fire. 50c, 75c, Motorboat patrol. 1 l+50c, Desert infantry. 2 l+1 l, Plane attacking troops.

**1934, Apr. 24**

| | | | | |
|---|---|---|---|---|
| **C66** | AP36 | 25c dk green | 3.25 | *6.50* |
| **C67** | AP36 | 50c gray | 3.25 | *8.00* |
| **C68** | AP36 | 75c dk brown | 3.25 | *10.00* |
| **C69** | AP36 | 80c slate blue | 3.25 | *12.00* |
| **C70** | AP36 | 1 l + 50c red brn | 8.00 | *30.00* |
| **C71** | AP36 | 2 l + 1 l brt bl | 11.50 | *37.50* |
| **C72** | AP40 | 3 l + 2 l brn blk | 16.00 | *45.00* |
| | | *Nos. C66-C72 (7)* | 48.50 | *149.00* |
| | | Set, never hinged | 120.00 | |

Cent. of the institution of the Military Medal of Valor.

For overprinted types see Aegean Islands Nos. C32-C38.

King Victor Emmanuel III — AP41

**1934, Nov. 5**

| | | | | |
|---|---|---|---|---|
| **C73** | AP41 | 1 l purple | 3.25 | *75.00* |
| **C74** | AP41 | 2 l brt blue | 3.25 | *82.50* |
| **C75** | AP41 | 4 l red brown | 7.50 | *275.00* |
| **C76** | AP41 | 5 l dull green | 7.50 | *350.00* |
| **C77** | AP41 | 8 l rose red | 23.00 | *450.00* |
| **C78** | AP41 | 10 l brown | 25.00 | *675.00* |
| | | *Nos. C73-C78 (6)* | 69.50 | *1,907.* |
| | | Set, never hinged | 160.00 | |

65th birthday of King Victor Emmanuel III and the nonstop flight from Rome to Mogadiscio.

For overprint see No. CO2.

Muse Playing Harp AP42

Angelic Dirge for Bellini AP43

Scene from Bellini Opera, La Sonnambula — AP44

**1935, Sept. 24**

| | | | | |
|---|---|---|---|---|
| **C79** | AP42 | 25c dull yellow | 4.75 | *13.00* |
| **C80** | AP42 | 50c brown | 4.75 | *11.00* |
| **C81** | AP42 | 60c rose carmine | 16.00 | *29.00* |
| **C82** | AP43 | 1 l + 1 l purple | 25.00 | *200.00* |
| **C83** | AP44 | 5 l + 2 l green | 32.50 | *275.00* |
| | | *Nos. C79-C83 (5)* | 83.00 | *528.00* |
| | | Set, never hinged | 200.00 | |

Vincenzo Bellini, (1801-35), operatic composer.

### Quintus Horatius Flaccus Type

25c, Seaplane in Flight. 50c, 1 l+1 l, Monoplane over valley. 60c, Oak and eagle. 5 l+2 l, Ruins of ancient Rome.

**1936, July 1**

| | | | | |
|---|---|---|---|---|
| **C84** | A197 | 25c dp green | 3.25 | *12.00* |
| **C85** | A197 | 50c dk brown | 5.00 | *12.00* |
| **C86** | A197 | 60c scarlet | 8.50 | *20.00* |
| **C87** | A197 | 1 l + 1 l vio | 20.00 | *200.00* |
| **C88** | A197 | 5 l + 2 l slate bl | 25.00 | *300.00* |
| | | *Nos. C84-C88 (5)* | 61.75 | *544.00* |
| | | Set, never hinged | 150.00 | |

Child of the Balilla AP49

Heads of Children AP50

**1937, June 28**

| | | | | |
|---|---|---|---|---|
| **C89** | AP49 | 25c dk bl grn | 8.00 | *22.50* |
| **C90** | AP50 | 50c brown | 16.00 | 15.00 |
| **C91** | AP49 | 1 l purple | 12.00 | *30.00* |
| **C92** | AP50 | 2 l + 1 l dk bl | 16.00 | *160.00* |
| **C93** | AP49 | 3 l + 2 l org | 20.00 | *240.00* |
| **C94** | AP50 | 5 l + 3 l rose lake | 24.00 | *275.00* |
| | | *Nos. C89-C94 (6)* | 96.00 | *742.50* |
| | | Set, never hinged | 240.00 | |

Summer Exhibition for Child Welfare. The surtax on Nos. C92-C94 was used to support summer camps for poor children.

Prosperous Italy AP51

50c, Prolific Italy. 80c, Apollo's steeds. 1 l+1 l, Map & Roman Standard. 5 l+1 l, Augustus Caesar.

**1937, Sept. 23**

| | | | | |
|---|---|---|---|---|
| **C95** | AP51 | 25c red vio | 8.00 | *13.50* |
| **C96** | AP51 | 50c olive brn | 8.00 | *11.00* |
| **C97** | AP51 | 80c orange brn | 24.00 | *16.50* |
| **C98** | AP51 | 1 l + 1 l dk bl | 30.00 | *150.00* |
| **C99** | AP51 | 5 l + 1 l dl vio | 65.00 | *275.00* |
| | | *Nos. C95-C99 (5)* | 135.00 | *466.00* |
| | | Set, never hinged | 325.00 | |

Bimillenary of the birth of Augustus Caesar (Octavianus) on the occasion of the exhibition opened in Rome by Mussolini on Sept. 22nd, 1937.

For overprinted types see Aegean Islands Nos. C39-C43.

King Victor Emmanuel III — AP56

25c, 3 l, King Victor Emmanuel III. 50c, 1 l, Dante Alighieri. 2 l, 5 l, Leonardo da Vinci.

**1938, Oct. 28**

| | | | | |
|---|---|---|---|---|
| **C100** | AP56 | 25c dull green | 5.00 | 6.50 |
| **C101** | AP56 | 50c dk yel brn | 5.00 | 6.50 |
| **C102** | AP56 | 1 l violet | 8.00 | *10.00* |
| **C103** | AP56 | 2 l royal blue | 8.00 | *37.50* |
| **C104** | AP56 | 3 l brown car | 13.00 | *45.00* |
| **C105** | AP56 | 5 l dp green | 15.00 | *65.00* |
| | | *Nos. C100-C105 (6)* | 54.00 | *170.50* |
| | | Set, never hinged | 135.00 | |

Proclamation of the Empire.

Plane and Clasped Hands AP59

Swallows in Flight AP60

**1945-47 Wmk. 277 Photo. *Perf. 14***

| | | | | |
|---|---|---|---|---|
| **C106** | AP59 | 1 l slate bl | .25 | .25 |
| **C107** | AP60 | 2 l dk blue | .25 | .25 |
| **C108** | AP59 | 3.20 l red org | .25 | .25 |
| **C109** | AP60 | 5 l dk green | .25 | .25 |
| **C110** | AP59 | 10 l car rose | .25 | .25 |
| **C111** | AP60 | 25 l dk bl ('46) | 6.50 | 13.00 |
| **C112** | AP60 | 25 l brown ('47) | .25 | .25 |
| **C113** | AP59 | 50 l dk grn ('46) | 14.00 | 20.00 |
| **C114** | AP59 | 50 l violet ('47) | .25 | .25 |
| | | *Nos. C106-C114 (9)* | 22.25 | 34.75 |
| | | Set, never hinged | 40.00 | |

Issued: #C111, C113, 7/13/46; #C112, C114, 4/21/47.

See Nos. C130-C131. For surcharges and overprints see Nos. C115, C136, 1LNC1-1LNC7, Trieste C1-C6, C17-C22.

No. C108 Surcharged in Black

**1947, July 1**

| | | | | |
|---|---|---|---|---|
| **C115** | AP59 | 6 l on 3.20 l | .25 | .25 |
| | | Never hinged | .25 | |
| *a.* | | Horiz. pair, one without surcharge | *1,400.* | |
| *b.* | | Inverted surcharge | | *26,000.* |

Radio on Land — AP61

Plane over Capitol Bell Tower — AP65

Designs: 6 l, 25 l, Radio on land. 10 l, 35 l, Radio at sea. 20 l, 50 l, Radio in the skies.

**1947, Aug. 1 Photo. *Perf. 14***

| | | | | |
|---|---|---|---|---|
| **C116** | AP61 | 6 l dp violet | .25 | .25 |
| **C117** | AP61 | 10 l dk car rose | .25 | .25 |
| **C118** | AP61 | 20 l dp orange | .75 | 1.10 |
| **C119** | AP61 | 25 l aqua | 1.10 | 1.60 |
| **C120** | AP61 | 35 l brt blue | 1.10 | 2.40 |
| **C121** | AP61 | 50 l lilac rose | 3.00 | 5.00 |
| | | *Nos. C116-C121 (6)* | 6.45 | 10.60 |
| | | Set, never hinged | 10.00 | |

50th anniv. of radio.

For overprints see Trieste Nos. C7-C12.

**1948**

| | | | | |
|---|---|---|---|---|
| **C123** | AP65 | 100 l green | 1.50 | .25 |
| **C124** | AP65 | 300 l lilac rose | .25 | .60 |
| **C125** | AP65 | 500 l ultra | .45 | 1.20 |

**Engr.**

| | | | | |
|---|---|---|---|---|
| **C126** | AP65 | 1000 l dk brown | .80 | 2.40 |
| *a.* | | Vert. pair, imperf. btwn. | *275.00* | *275.00* |
| *b.* | | Perf. 14x13 | .90 | 2.40 |
| | | *Nos. C123-C126 (4)* | 3.00 | 4.45 |
| | | Set, never hinged | 11.00 | |

See No. C132-C135. For overprints see Trieste Nos. C13-C16, C23-C26.

St. Catherine Carrying Cross AP66

200 l, St. Catherine with outstretched arms.

**1948, Mar. 1** **Photo.**

**C127** AP66 100 l bl vio & brn org 35.00 37.50
**C128** AP66 200 l dp blue & bis 21.00 22.50
Set, never hinged 135.00

600th anniversary of the birth of St. Catherine of Siena, patroness of Italy.

**Catalogue values for unused stamps in this section, from this point to the end of the section, are for Never Hinged items.**

Giuseppe Mazzini (1805-1872), Patriot — AP67

**1955, Dec. 31** **Wmk. 303** ***Perf. 14***
**C129** AP67 100 l Prus green 2.00 1.40

### Types of 1945-46, 1948

**1955-62** **Wmk. 303** ***Perf. 14***
**C130** AP60 5 l green ('62) .25 .25
**C131** AP59 50 l vio ('57) .25 .25
**C132** AP65 100 l green .75 .25
**C133** AP65 300 l lil rose .85 .55
**C134** AP65 500 l ultra ('56) 1.00 .90

**Engr.**

***Perf. 13½***

**C135** AP65 1000 l maroon ('59) 2.00 2.00
*Nos. C130-C135 (6)* 5.10 4.20

Fluorescent Paper
See note below No. 998.
No. C132 was issued on both ordinary and fluorescent paper. The design of the fluorescent stamp is smaller.
Airmail stamps issued only on fluorescent paper are Nos. C139-C140.

### Type of 1945-46 Surcharged in Ultramarine

**1956, Feb. 24**
**C136** AP59 120 l on 50 l mag 1.25 *1.90*

Visit of Pres. Giovanni Gronchi to the US and Canada.

Madonna of Bruges, by Michelangelo AP68

**Wmk. 303**

**1964, Feb. 18** **Photo.** ***Perf. 14***
**C137** AP68 185 l black .30 .30

Michelangelo Buonarroti (1475-1564), artist.

### Verrazano Type of Regular Issue

**1964, Nov. 21** **Wmk. 303** ***Perf. 14***
**C138** A481 130 l blk & dull grn .25 .25

See note after No. 901.

Adoration of the Kings, by Gentile da Fabriano — AP69

**1970, Dec. 12** **Photo.** **Unwmk.**
**C139** AP69 150 l multicolored .30 .25

Christmas 1970.

### Aviation Type of Regular Issue

Design: F-140S Starfighter over Aeronautical Academy, Pozzuoli.

**1973, Mar. 28** **Photo.** ***Perf. 14x13½***
**C140** A590 150 l multicolored .30 .25

## AIR POST SEMI-POSTAL STAMPS

### Holy Year Type of Postage

Dome of St. Peter's, dove with olive branch, Church of the Holy Sepulcher.

**Wmk. 140**

**1933, Oct. 23** **Photo.** ***Perf. 14***
**CB1** A163 50c + 25c org brn 2.40 *26.00*
**CB2** A163 75c + 50c brn vio 4.00 *100.00*
Set, never hinged 16.00

Symbolical of Military Air Force — SPAP2

**1935, July 1**
**CB3** SPAP2 50c + 50c brown 10.00 *37.50*

The surtax was for the Militia.

## AIR POST SPECIAL DELIVERY STAMPS

Garibaldi, Anita Garibaldi, Plane APSD1

**Wmk. 140**

**1932, June 2** **Photo.** ***Perf. 14***
**CE1** APSD1 2.25 l + 1 l 16.00 *52.50*
**CE2** APSD1 4.50 l + 1.50 l 16.00 *52.50*
Set, never hinged 80.00

Death of Giuseppe Garibaldi, 50th anniv.
For overprinted types see Aegean Islands Nos. CE1-CE2.

Airplane and Sunburst APSD2

**1933-34**
**CE3** APSD2 2 l gray blk ('34) .25 *3.00*
**CE4** APSD2 2.25 l gray blk 6.50 *180.00*
Set, never hinged 17.00

For overprint and surcharge see Nos. MCE1, Yugoslavia-Ljubljana NCE1.

### Annexation of Fiume Type

Flag raising before Fascist headquarters.

**1934, Mar. 12**
**CE5** A166 2 l + 1.25 l 4.75 *29.00*
**CE6** A166 2.25 l + 1.25 l .95 *23.00*
**CE7** A166 4.50 l + 2 l .95 *25.00*
*Nos. CE5-CE7 (3)* 5.60 *77.00*
Set, never hinged 17.00

Triumphal Arch in Rome APSD4

**1934, Aug. 31**
**CE8** APSD4 2 l + 1.25 l brown 16.00 *40.00*
**CE9** APSD4 4.50 l + 2 l cop red 20.00 *40.00*
Set, never hinged 90.00

Centenary of the institution of the Military Medal of Valor.
For overprinted types see Aegean Islands Nos. CE3-CE4.

## AIR POST OFFICIAL STAMPS

### Balbo Flight Type of Air Post Stamp of 1933 Overprinted

**1933** **Wmk. 140** ***Perf. 14***
**CO1** AP25 5.25 l + 44.75 l red, grn & red vio 3,100. *13,000.*
Never hinged 4,750.

Air Post Stamp of 1934 Overprinted in Gold

**1934**
**CO2** AP41 10 l blue blk 825.00 *13,000.*
Never hinged 1,650.

65th birthday of King Victor Emmanuel III and the non-stop flight from Rome to Mogadiscio.

## PNEUMATIC POST STAMPS

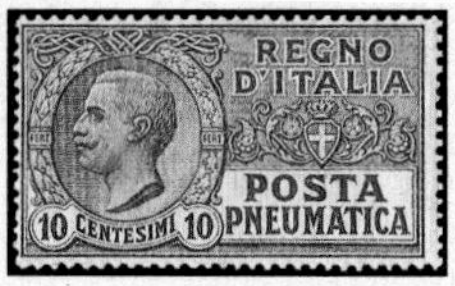


PN1

**1913-28** **Wmk. 140** **Typo.** ***Perf. 14***
**D1** PN1 10c brown 2.75 *28.00*
**D2** PN1 15c brn vio ('28) 2.40 *12.50*
*a.* 15c dull violet ('21) 3.25 *22.50*
**D3** PN1 15c rose red ('28) 8.00 *20.00*
**D4** PN1 15c claret ('28) 2.40 *12.50*
**D5** PN1 20c brn vio ('25) 18.00 *40.00*
**D6** PN1 30c blue ('23) 8.00 *125.00*
**D7** PN1 35c rose red ('27) 20.00 *200.00*
**D8** PN1 40c dp red ('26) 24.00 *290.00*
*Nos. D1-D8 (8)* 85.55 *728.00*

Nos. D1, D2a, D5-D6, D8 Surcharged Like Nos. C10-C11

**1924-27**
**D9** PN1 15c on 10c 4.50 *34.00*
**D10** PN1 15c on 20c ('27) 9.00 *62.50*
**D11** PN1 20c on 10c ('25) 9.00 *67.50*
**D12** PN1 20c on 15c ('25) 12.00 *40.00*
**D13** PN1 35c on 40c ('27) 21.00 *325.00*
**D14** PN1 40c on 30c ('25) 12.00 *350.00*
*Nos. D9-D14 (6)* 67.50 *879.00*

Dante Alighieri PN2

Galileo Galilei PN3

**1933, Mar. 29** **Photo.**
**D15** PN2 15c dark violet .45 *1.60*
**D16** PN3 35c rose red .45 *6.75*

Similar to Types of 1933, Without "REGNO"

**1945, Oct. 22** **Wmk. 277**
**D17** PN2 60c dull brown .25 *3.25*
**D18** PN3 1.40 l dull blue .25 *3.25*

Minerva — PN6

**1947, Nov. 15**
**D19** PN6 3 l rose lilac 6.50 *10.50*
**D20** PN6 5 l aqua .25 .25
Set, never hinged 8.50

**Catalogue values for unused stamps in this section, from this point to the end of the section, are for Never Hinged items.**

**1958-66** **Wmk. 303**
**D21** PN6 10 l rose red .25 .25
**D22** PN6 20 l sapphire ('66) .25 .25

## SPECIAL DELIVERY STAMPS

Victor Emmanuel III — SD1

**1903-26** **Typo.** **Wmk. 140** ***Perf. 14***
**E1** SD1 25c rose red 50.00 1.20
*a.* Imperf., pair 500.00 625.00
**E2** SD1 50c dl red ('20) 5.00 1.75
**E3** SD1 60c dl red ('22) 9.00 1.20
**E4** SD1 70c dl red ('25) 1.50 .35
**E5** SD1 1.25 l dp bl ('26) .75 .25
*Nos. E1-E5 (5)* 66.25 4.75

No. E1 is almost always found poorly centered, and it is valued thus.
For overprints and surcharges see Nos. C1, E11, E13, Austria NE1-NE2, Dalmatia E1, Offices in Crete, Offices in Africa, Offices in Turkish Empire.

Victor Emmanuel III — SD2

**1908-26**
**E6** SD2 30c blue & rose 2.10 *4.00*
**E7** SD2 2 l bl & red ('25) 8.00 *130.00*
**E8** SD2 2.50 l bl & red ('26) 3.00 *10.50*
*Nos. E6-E8 (3)* 13.10 *144.50*

The 1.20 lire blue and red (see No. E12) was prepared in 1922, but not issued. Value: unused $200; never hinged $400.
For surcharges and overprints see Nos. E10, E12, Austria NE3, Dalmatia E2, Offices in China, Offices in Africa, Offices in Turkish Empire.

SD3

**1917, Nov.**
**E9** SD3 25c on 40c violet 37.50 *110.00*

Type SD3 not issued without surcharge.
For surcharge see No. C2.

**No. E6 Surcharged**

**1921, Oct.**
**E10** SD2 1.20 l on 30c 2.25 *26.00*
*a.* Comma in value omitted 12.50 *52.50*
*b.* Double surcharge 340.00

No. E2 Surcharged

**1922, Jan. 9**
**E11** SD1 60c on 50c dull red 45.00 2.00
*a.* Inverted surcharge 290.00 290.00
*b.* Double surcharge 1,850.
*c.* Imperf., pair 500.00 *625.00*

**Type of 1908 Surcharged**

**1924, May**
**E12** SD2 1.60 l on 1.20 l bl & red 3.00 *135.00*
*a.* Double surch., one inverted 340.00

**No. E3 Surcharged like No. E11**

**1925, Apr. 11**
**E13** SD1 70c on 60c dull red 1.50 1.20
*a.* Inverted surcharge 340.00 *400.00*

Victor Emmanuel III — SD4

**1932-33** **Photo.**
**E14** SD4 1.25 l green .30 .25
**E15** SD4 2.50 l dp org ('33) .30 *6.00*

For overprints and surcharges see Italian Social Republic Nos. E1-E2; Yugoslavia-Ljubljana NB5-NB8, NE1.

**March on Rome Type of Postage**

1.25 l Ancient Pillars and Entrenchments. 2.50 l, Head of Mussolini, trophies of flags, etc.

**1932, Oct. 27**
**E16** A146 1.25 l deep green 2.40 1.75
**E17** A146 2.50 l deep orange 8.00 *160.00*
Set, never hinged 34.00

"Italia" SD7

**1945, Aug. Wmk. 277 *Perf. 14***
**E18** SD7 5 l rose carmine .25 1.00

Winged Foot SD8

Rearing Horse and Torch-Bearer — SD9

**1945-51**

| | | | | |
|---|---|---|---|---|
| **E19** | SD8 | 5 l henna brn | .25 | .25 |
| **E20** | SD9 | 10 l deep blue | .25 | .25 |
| **E21** | SD9 | 15 l dk car rose ('47) | 1.60 | .25 |
| **E22** | SD8 | 25 l brt red org ('47) | 22.50 | .25 |
| **E23** | SD8 | 30 l dp vio ('46) | 3.00 | 3.25 |
| **E24** | SD8 | 50 l lil rose ('51) | 22.50 | .25 |
| **E25** | SD9 | 60 l car rose ('48) | 35.00 | .25 |
| | | *Nos. E19-E25 (7)* | 85.10 | 4.75 |
| | | Set, never hinged | 160.00 | |

See No. E32. For overprints see Nos. 1LNE1-1LNE2, Trieste E1-E4, E6-E7.

**Type of Regular Issue of 1948 Inscribed: "Espresso"**

**1948, Sept. 18 Photo. *Perf. 14***
**E26** A272 35 l violet *(Naples)* 67.50 19.00
Never hinged 135.00

**Catalogue values for unused stamps in this section, from this point to the end of the section, are for Never Hinged items.**

**Type of 1945-51**

**1955, July 7 Wmk. 303 *Perf. 14***
**E32** SD8 50 l lilac rose 5.75 .25

Etruscan Winged Horses SD10

**1958-76 Photo.**

**Size: 36½x20¼mm**
**E33** SD10 75 l magenta .25 .25

**Size: 36x20mm**
**E34** SD10 150 l dl bl grn ('68) .25 .25
*a.* Size: 36½x20¼mm ('66) .40 .25
**E35** SD10 250 l blue ('74) .30 .25
**E36** SD10 300 l brown ('76) .40 .25
*Nos. E33-E36 (4)* 1.20 1.00

Nos. E34-E36 are fluorescent.

---

**AUTHORIZED DELIVERY STAMPS**

For the payment of a special tax for the authorized delivery of correspondence privately instead of through the post office.

AD1

Coat of Arms — AD2

**1928 Wmk. 140 Typo. *Perf. 14***
**EY1** AD1 10c dull blue 9.00 .60
*a.* Perf. 11 35.00 4.50

**1930 Photo. *Perf. 14***
**EY2** AD2 10c dark brown .25 .25

For surcharge and overprint see Nos. EY3, Italian Social Republic EY1.

No. EY2 Surcharged in Black

**1945**
**EY3** AD2 40c on 10c dark brown .50 1.50

Coat of Arms — AD3

"Italia" — AD4

**1945-46 Photo. Wmk. 277**
**EY4** AD3 40c dark brown .25 1.00
**EY5** AD3 1 l dk brown ('46) 3.25 6.00

For overprint see Trieste No. EY1.

**1947-52 Size: 27½x22½mm**
**EY6** AD4 1 l brt grnsh bl .25 .35
**EY7** AD4 8 l brt red ('48) 12.00 .35

**Size: 20½x16½mm**
**EY8** AD4 15 l violet ('49) 31.00 .30
**EY9** AD4 20 l rose vio ('52) 2.00 .25
*Nos. EY6-EY9 (4)* 45.25 1.25
Set, never hinged 125.00

For overprints see Trieste Nos. EY2-EY5.

**Catalogue values for unused stamps in this section, from this point to the end of the section, are for Never Hinged items.**

**Italia Type of 1947**

**1955-90 Wmk. 303 Photo. *Perf. 14***

**Size: 20½x16½mm**

| | | | | |
|---|---|---|---|---|
| **EY11** | AD4 | 20 l rose vio | .25 | .25 |
| **EY12** | AD4 | 30 l Prus grn ('65) | .25 | .25 |
| **EY13** | AD4 | 35 l ocher ('74) | .25 | .25 |
| **EY14** | AD4 | 110 l lt ultra ('77) | .25 | .25 |
| **EY15** | AD4 | 270 l brt pink ('84) | .75 | .25 |

**Size: 19½x16½mm**

| | | | | |
|---|---|---|---|---|
| **EY16** | AD4 | 300 l rose & grn ('87) | .60 | .40 |
| **EY17** | AD4 | 370 l tan & brn vio | .65 | .40 |
| | | *Nos. EY11-EY17 (7)* | 3.00 | 2.05 |

Issue date: 370 l, Sept. 24, 1990.

---

**POSTAGE DUE STAMPS**

Unused values for Postage Due stamps are for examples with full original gum. Stamps with part gum or privately gummed sell for much less.

D1

D2

**1863 Unwmk. Litho. *Imperf.***
**J1** D1 10c yellow 2,000. 225.00
No gum 85.00
*a.* 10c yellow orange 2,100. 250.00
No gum 90.00

**1869 Wmk. 140 Typo. *Perf. 14***
**J2** D2 10c buff 5,000. 65.00

D3

**1870-1925**

| | | | | |
|---|---|---|---|---|
| **J3** | D3 | 1c buff & mag | 4.00 | 12.50 |
| **J4** | D3 | 2c buff & mag | 13.00 | 25.00 |
| **J5** | D3 | 5c buff & mag | 1.60 | .80 |
| **J6** | D3 | 10c buff & mag ('71) | 1.60 | .80 |
| *b.* | | Imperf, single | | *2,100.* |
| **J7** | D3 | 20c buff & mag ('94) | 16.00 | .80 |
| *a.* | | Imperf., pair | 250.00 | *250.00* |
| **J8** | D3 | 30c buff & mag | 5.00 | 1.25 |
| *b.* | | Imperf, pair | *2,900.* | 1,600. |
| **J9** | D3 | 40c buff & mag | 5.00 | 2.40 |
| **J10** | D3 | 50c buff & mag | 5.00 | 1.25 |
| *b.* | | Imperf, single | | *1,800.* |
| **J11** | D3 | 60c buff & mag | 950.00 | 4.00 |
| **J12** | D3 | 60c buff & brn ('25) | 40.00 | 15.00 |
| **J13** | D3 | 1 l lt bl & brn | 5,300. | 20.00 |
| **J14** | D3 | 1 l bl & mag ('94) | 40.00 | 1.25 |
| *a.* | | Imperf., pair | 160.00 | 180.00 |
| **J15** | D3 | 2 l lt bl & brn | 5,300. | 32.50 |
| **J16** | D3 | 2 l bl & mag ('03) | 57.50 | 6.50 |
| **J17** | D3 | 5 l bl & brn ('74) | 540.00 | 37.50 |
| **J18** | D3 | 5 l bl & mag ('03) | 200.00 | 32.50 |
| **J19** | D3 | 10 l bl & brn ('74) | *6,500.* | 37.50 |
| **J20** | D3 | 10 l bl & mag ('94) | 200.00 | 6.50 |

Early printings of 5c, 10c, 30c, 40c, 50c and 60c were in buff and magenta, later ones (1890-94) in stronger shades. The earlier, paler shades and their inverted-numeral varieties sell for considerably more than those of the later shades. Values are for the later shades.

For surcharges and overprints see Nos. J25-J27, Offices in China, Offices in Turkish Empire.

**Numeral Inverted**

| | | | | |
|---|---|---|---|---|
| *J3a* | D3 | 1c | 4,500. | 2,900. |
| *J4a* | D3 | 2c | *11,500.* | 4,000. |
| *J5a* | D3 | 5c | 6.50 | 12.50 |
| *J6a* | D3 | 10c | 8.00 | 16.00 |
| *J7b* | D3 | 20c | 65.00 | 60.00 |
| *J8a* | D3 | 30c | 12.50 | *25.00* |
| *J9a* | D3 | 40c | 540.00 | *650.00* |
| *J10a* | D3 | 50c | 60.00 | 80.00 |
| *J11a* | D3 | 60c | 540.00 | 400.00 |
| *J13a* | D3 | 1 l | | — |
| *J14b* | D3 | 1 l | 4,500. | 3,250. |
| *J15a* | D3 | 2 l | | *2,900.* |
| *J16a* | D3 | 2 l | *3,750.* | *3,750.* |
| *J17a* | D3 | 5 l | | 1,450. |
| *J19a* | D3 | 10 l | *17,500.* | 325.00 |

D4

**1884-1903**
**J21** D4 50 l green 90.00 80.00
**J22** D4 50 l yellow ('03) 100.00 50.00
**J23** D4 100 l claret 90.00 40.00
**J24** D4 100 l blue ('03) 80.00 20.00
*Nos. J21-J24 (4)* 360.00 190.00

Nos. J3 & J4 Surcharged in Black

**1890-91**
**J25** D3 10c on 2c 130.00 37.50
**J26** D3 20c on 1c 540.00 29.00
*a.* Inverted surcharge *10,000.*
**J27** D3 30c on 2c 1,800. 12.50
*a.* Inverted surcharge *2,700.*
*Nos. J25-J27 (3)* 2,470. 79.00

Coat of Arms
D6 D7

**1934 Photo.**
**J28** D6 5c brown .80 .40
**J29** D6 10c blue .80 .40
**J30** D6 20c rose red .80 .40

**J31** D6 25c green .80 .40
**J32** D6 30c red org .80 .40
**J33** D6 40c blk brn .80 *4.50*
**J34** D6 50c violet .80 .40
**J35** D6 60c slate blk .80 *13.50*
**J36** D7 1 l red org .80 .40
**J37** D7 2 l green .80 .40
**J38** D7 5 l violet 1.60 .80
**J39** D7 10 l blue 6.50 *11.00*
**J40** D7 20 l car rose 12.50 *37.50*
*Nos. J28-J40 (13)* 28.60 70.50

For overprints and surcharges see Italian Social Republic #J1-J13, Yugoslavia-Ljubljana NJ14-NJ22.

D8

D9

**1945-46 Unwmk. *Perf. 14***
**J41** D8 5c brn, *grayish* ('46) 2.40 *7.50*
**J42** D8 10c blue .45 *1.50*
**J43** D8 20c rose red, *grayish* ('46) 2.00 *1.50*
**J44** D8 25c dk grn .45 *1.50*
**J45** D8 30c red org .45 *1.50*
**J46** D8 40c blk brn .45 *1.50*
**J47** D8 50c violet .45 *1.50*
**J48** D8 60c black .45 *7.50*
**J49** D9 1 l red org .45 *1.50*
**J50** D9 2 l green .45 *1.50*
**J51** D9 5 l violet .45 *1.50*
**J52** D9 10 l blue .45 *1.50*
**J53** D9 20 l car rose .45 *6.00*
*Nos. J41-J53 (13)* 9.35 *36.00*

Nos. J41 and J43 have yellow gum.

**Wmk. 277**
**J54** D8 10c dark blue .25 5.00
**J55** D8 25c dk grn 1.25 5.75
**J56** D8 30c red org 1.25 11.00
**J57** D8 40c blk brn .25 .25
**J58** D8 50c vio ('46) 5.75 8.00
**J59** D8 60c bl blk ('46) 7.50 26.00
**J60** D9 1 l red org .25 .25
**J61** D9 2 l dk grn .25 .25
**J62** D9 5 l violet 12.00 11.00
**J63** D9 10 l dark blue 18.00 11.00
**J64** D9 20 l car rose 29.00 30.00
*Nos. J54-J64 (11)* 75.75 108.50
Set, never hinged 190.00

For overprints see Trieste Nos. J1, J3-J5.

D10

**1947-54 Photo. *Perf. 14***
**J65** D10 1 l red orange .25 .25
**J66** D10 2 l dk green .25 .25
**J67** D10 3 l carmine .50 2.40
**J68** D10 4 l brown .30 1.25
**J69** D10 5 l violet .65 .25
**J70** D10 6 l vio blue 2.00 3.25
**J71** D10 8 l rose vio 8.50 4.00
**J72** D10 10 l deep blue .75 .25
**J73** D10 12 l golden brn 3.25 3.25
**J74** D10 20 l lil rose 35.00 .25
**J75** D10 25 l dk red ('54) 35.00 .80
**J76** D10 50 l aqua 25.00 .25
**J77** D10 100 l org yel ('52) 8.00 .25

**Engr.**
***Perf. 13½x14***
**J78** D10 500 l dp bl & dk car ('52) 8.50 .40
*a.* Perf. 11x13 10.00 .40
*b.* Perf. 13 10.00 .40
*Nos. J65-J78 (14)* 127.95 17.10
Set, never hinged 325.00

For overprints see Trieste Nos. J2, J6-J29.

**Catalogue values for unused stamps in this section, from this point to the end of the section, are for Never Hinged items.**

**1955-91 Wmk. 303 Photo. *Perf. 14***
**J83** D10 5 l violet .25 .25
**J85** D10 8 l rose vio 200.00 225.00
**J86** D10 10 l deep blue .25 .25
**J87** D10 20 l lil rose .25 .25
**J88** D10 25 l dk red .25 .25
**J89** D10 30 l gray brn ('61) .30 .25
**J90** D10 40 l dl brn ('66) .25 .25
**J91** D10 50 l aqua .30 .25
*a.* Type II .30 .25
**J92** D10 100 l org yel ('58) .25 .25

**Engr.**
**J93** D10 500 l dp bl & dk car ('61) 3.25 .25
**J94** D10 900 l dp car & gray grn ('84) 1.20 .25
**J95** D10 1500 l brown & orange 3.00 1.60
*Nos. J83,J86-J95 (11)* 9.55 4.10

Type I imprint on No. J91 reads: "1ST POL. STATO OFF. CARET VALORI". Type II imprint reads: "I.P.Z.S. OFF. CARTE VALORI" (1992). No. J91 has lighter background with more distinguishable lettering and design.

No. J92 exists with both Type I & Type II imprints.

Nos. J92 and J93 exist with "I. P. Z. S. ROMA" imprint.

Issue date: 1500 l, Feb. 20, 1991.

## MILITARY STAMPS

Regular Stamps, 1929-42, Overprinted

**1943 Wmk. 140 *Perf. 14***
**M1** A90 5c ol brn .50 .80
**M2** A92 10c dk brn .50 .80
**M3** A93 15c slate grn .50 .80
**M4** A91 20c rose red .50 .80
**M5** A94 25c dp grn .50 .80
**M6** A95 30c ol brn .50 .80
**M7** A95 50c purple .50 .40
**M8** A91 1 l dk pur 3.75 *20.00*
**M9** A94 1.25 l deep blue .50 *1.00*
**M10** A92 1.75 l red org .50 *.80*
**M11** A93 2 l car lake .50 *1.00*
**M12** A95a 5 l rose red .50 *3.25*
**M13** A93 10 l purple 3.75 *29.00*
*Nos. M1-M13 (13)* 13.00 *60.25*

Due to a shortage of regular postage stamps during 1944-45, this issue was used for ordinary mail. "P. M." stands for "Posta Militare."

## MILITARY AIR POST STAMPS

**Air Post Stamps, 1930 Overprinted Like Nos. M1-M13 in Black**

**1943 Wmk. 140 *Perf. 14***
**MC1** AP3 50c olive brown .45 *.80*
**MC2** AP5 1 l purple .45 *.80*
**MC3** AP6 2 l deep blue .45 *15.00*
**MC4** AP3 5 l dark green 3.75 *25.00*
**MC5** AP3 10 l deep carmine 3.75 *32.50*
*Nos. MC1-MC5 (5)* 8.85 *74.10*

## MILITARY AIR POST SPECIAL DELIVERY STAMPS

**#CE3 Overprinted Like #M1-M13**

**1943 Wmk. 140 *Perf. 14***
**MCE1** APSD2 2 l gray black 3.50 *29.00*

## MILITARY SPECIAL DELIVERY STAMPS

**#E14 Overprinted Like #M1-M13**

**1943 Wmk. 140 *Perf. 14***
**ME1** SD4 1.25 l green 1.00 *1.60*

## OFFICIAL STAMPS

O1

**1875 Wmk. 140 Typo. *Perf. 14***
**O1** O1 2c lake 3.00 *5.00*
**O2** O1 5c lake 3.00 *5.00*
**O3** O1 20c lake 1.50 *1.60*
**O4** O1 30c lake 1.50 *3.25*
**O5** O1 1 l lake 4.50 *19.00*
**O6** O1 2 l lake 30.00 *55.00*
**O7** O1 5 l lake 52.50 *200.00*
**O8** O1 10 l lake 90.00 150.00
*Nos. O1-O8 (8)* 186.00 *438.85*

For surcharges see Nos. 37-44.

Stamps inscribed "Servizio Commissioni" were used in connection with the postal service but not for the payment of postage.

## NEWSPAPER STAMP

N1

**Typographed, Numeral Embossed**
**1862 Unwmk. *Imperf.***
**P1** N1 2c buff 52.50 *110.00*
*a.* Numeral double 475.00 *1,650.*
*b.* Printed on gummed side 500.00

Black 1c and 2c stamps of similar type are listed under Sardinia.

## PARCEL POST STAMPS

King Humbert I — PP1

**1884-86 Wmk. 140 Typo. *Perf. 14***
**Various Frames**
**Q1** PP1 10c olive gray 125.00 110.00
**Q2** PP1 20c blue 250.00 170.00
**Q3** PP1 50c claret 10.00 15.00
**Q4** PP1 75c blue grn 10.00 15.00
**Q5** PP1 1.25 l orange 20.00 32.50
**Q6** PP1 1.75 l brown 25.00 *125.00*
*Nos. Q1-Q6 (6)* 440.00 467.50

For surcharges see Nos. 58-63.

Parcel Post stamps from No. Q7 onward were used by affixing them to the waybill so that one half remained on it following the parcel, the other half staying on the receipt given the sender. Most used halves are right halves. Complete stamps were and are obtainable canceled, probably to order.

Both unused and used values are for complete stamps.

PP2

**1914-22 Wmk. 140 *Perf. 13***
**Q7** PP2 5c brown 5.00 *11.50*
**Q8** PP2 10c deep blue 5.00 *11.50*
**Q9** PP2 20c black ('17) 20.00 *11.50*
**Q10** PP2 25c red 25.00 *11.50*
**Q11** PP2 50c orange 32.50 *25.00*
**Q12** PP2 1 l violet 37.50 10.00
**Q13** PP2 2 l green 40.00 10.00
**Q14** PP2 3 l bister 50.00 32.50
**Q15** PP2 4 l slate 57.50 50.00
**Q16** PP2 10 l rose lil ('22) 100.00 50.00
**Q17** PP2 12 l red brn ('22) 160.00 *310.00*
**Q18** PP2 15 l ol grn ('22) 150.00 *310.00*
**Q19** PP2 20 l brn vio ('22) 125.00 *310.00*
*Nos. Q7-Q19 (13)* 807.50 *1,153.*

**Halves Used**
Q7-Q14, each .40
Q15 .80
Q16 1.60
Q17 4.00
Q18 4.00
Q19 6.50

Imperfs exist. Value per pair: 20c, 25c, 50c, 2 l, 3l, 4 l: $50 each; 10l $225.

**No. Q7 Surcharged**

**Q20** PP2 30c on 5c brown 1.60 *16.00*
Half stamp 3.25
**Q21** PP2 60c on 5c brown 1.60 *16.00*
Half stamp 3.25
**Q22** PP2 1.50 l on 5c brown 5.50 *140.00*
Half stamp 6.50
*a.* Double surcharge 250.00

**No. Q16 Surcharged**

**Q23** PP2 3 l on 10 l rose lilac 5.50 *55.00*
Half stamp 3.25
*Nos. Q20-Q23 (4)* 14.20 *227.00*

PP3

**1927-39 Wmk. 140**
**Q24** PP3 5c brn ('38) .80 *2.00*
**Q25** PP3 10c dp bl ('39) .80 *2.00*
**Q26** PP3 25c red ('32) .80 *2.00*
**Q27** PP3 30c ultra .80 *2.90*
**Q28** PP3 50c org ('32) .80 *2.00*
**Q29** PP3 60c red .80 *2.90*
**Q30** PP3 1 l lilac ('31) .80 *2.90*
**Q31** PP3 1 l brn vio ('36) 24.00 72.50
**Q32** PP3 2 l grn ('32) .80 *2.90*
**Q33** PP3 3 l yel bister .80 *6.50*
*a.* Printed on both sides 65.00
**Q34** PP3 4 l gray .80 *6.50*
**Q35** PP3 10 l rose lil ('34) 2.40 *40.00*
**Q36** PP3 20 l lil brn ('33) 3.25 *57.50*
*Nos. Q24-Q36 (13)* 37.65 *202.60*

Value of used halves: Nos. Q24-Q34, each 40c; Q35 80c; Q36 $4.

For overprints see Italian Social Republic Nos. Q1-Q12.

**Nos. Q24-Q30, Q32-Q36 Overprinted Between Halves in Black**

**1945 Wmk. 140 *Perf. 13***
**Q37** PP3 5c brown 1.50 9.00
**Q38** PP3 10c dp blue 1.50 9.00
**Q39** PP3 25c red 1.50 9.00
**Q40** PP3 30c ultra 18.00 35.00
**Q41** PP3 50c orange 1.50 9.00
**Q42** PP3 60c red 1.50 9.00
**Q43** PP3 1 l lilac 1.50 9.00
**Q44** PP3 2 l green 1.50 9.00
**Q45** PP3 3 l yel bister 1.50 9.00
**Q46** PP3 4 l gray 1.50 9.00
**Q47** PP3 10 l rose lilac 16.50 *72.50*
**Q48** PP3 20 l lilac brn 37.50 *160.00*
*Nos. Q37-Q48 (12)* 85.50 *348.50*
Set, never hinged 200.00

**Halves Used**
Q37-48, each .25

**Type of 1927**
**With Fasces Removed**

**1946 Typo.**
**Q55** PP3 1 l lilac 2.25 5.75
**Q56** PP3 2 l green 1.50 5.75
**Q57** PP3 3 l yellow org 2.25 9.25
**Q58** PP3 4 l gray 4.50 9.25
**Q59** PP3 10 l rose lilac 45.00 85.00
**Q60** PP3 20 l lilac brn 60.00 290.00
*Nos. Q55-Q60 (6)* 115.50 405.00
Set, never hinged 260.00

**Halves Used**
Q55-Q58, each .25
Q59 .80
Q60 1.25

PP4

PP5

*Perf. 13¼, 13¼x14, 12¼x13x13¼*

**1946-54 Photo. Wmk. 277**

| No. | Design | Description | Unused | Used |
|---|---|---|---|---|
| Q61 | PP4 | 25c dl vio bl ('48) | .25 | .30 |
| Q62 | PP4 | 50c brown ('47) | .40 | .30 |
| Q63 | PP4 | 1 l golden brn ('47) | .40 | .30 |
| Q64 | PP4 | 2 l lt bl grn ('47) | .80 | .75 |
| Q65 | PP4 | 3 l red org ('47) | .40 | .30 |
| Q66 | PP4 | 4 l gray blk ('47) | 6.50 | *11.00* |
| Q67 | PP4 | 5 l lil rose ('47) | .40 | .30 |
| a. | | Perf. 13¼ | .40 | .30 |
| Q68 | PP4 | 10 l violet | 8.00 | .40 |
| a. | | Perf. 13¼ | 8.00 | 2.00 |
| Q69 | PP4 | 20 l lilac brn | 3.25 | .60 |
| a. | | Perf. 13¼ | 5.00 | 1.00 |
| Q70 | PP4 | 30 l plum ('52) | 4.00 | 5.00 |
| a. | | Perf. 13¼ | 4.00 | *5.00* |
| Q71 | PP4 | 50 l rose red | 16.00 | 2.40 |
| a. | | Perf. 13¼ | 16.00 | 2.40 |
| Q72 | PP4 | 100 l sapphire | 40.00 | 45.00 |
| a. | | Perf. 13¼ | 140.00 | 45.00 |
| Q73 | PP4 | 200 l green ('48) | 55.00 | 80.00 |
| a. | | Perf. 13¼ | 55.00 | 80.00 |
| Q74 | PP4 | 300 l brn car ('48), perf 13¼ | 725.00 | 1,050. |
| Q75 | PP4 | 500 l brown ('48) | 40.00 | 35.00 |
| a. | | Perf. 12¼x13¼ | 100.00 | 100.00 |

**Engr.**

*Perf. 13*

| No. | Design | Description | Unused | Used |
|---|---|---|---|---|
| Q76 | PP5 | 1000 l ultra ('54) | 2,800. | 3,100. |
| | | *Nos. Q61-Q76 (16)* | 3,700. | 4,331. |
| | | Set, never hinged | 5,500. | |

**Halves Used**

| | |
|---|---|
| Q61-Q73, each | .25 |
| Q74 | 8.00 |
| Q75 | 3.25 |
| Q76 | 22.50 |

For overprints see Trieste Nos. Q1-Q26.

**Catalogue values for unused stamps in this section, from this point to the end of the section, are for Never Hinged items.**

*Perf. 12½x13*

**1955-59 Wmk. 303 Photo.**

**Without Imprint**

| No. | Design | Description | Unused | Used |
|---|---|---|---|---|
| Q77 | PP4 | 25c vio bl | .25 | *.25* |
| Q77A | PP4 | 50c brn ('56) | 3.00 | *3.00* |
| Q78 | PP4 | 5 l lil rose ('59) | .25 | .25 |
| Q79 | PP4 | 10 l violet | .25 | .25 |
| Q80 | PP4 | 20 l lil brn | .25 | .25 |
| Q81 | PP4 | 30 l plum ('56) | .25 | .25 |
| Q82 | PP4 | 40 l dl vio ('57) | .25 | .25 |
| Q83 | PP4 | 50 l rose red | .25 | .25 |
| Q84 | PP4 | 100 l sapphire | .25 | .25 |
| Q85 | PP4 | 150 l org brn ('57) | .25 | .25 |
| Q86 | PP4 | 200 l grn ('56) | .30 | .25 |
| Q87 | PP4 | 300 l brn car ('58) | .45 | .40 |
| Q88 | PP4 | 400 l gray blk ('57) | .55 | .45 |
| Q89 | PP4 | 500 l brn ('57) | 1.00 | .60 |

**Engr.**

*Perf. 13*

| No. | Design | Description | Unused | Used |
|---|---|---|---|---|
| Q90 | PP5 | 1000 l ultra ('57) | 1.25 | .95 |
| Q91 | PP5 | 2000 l red brn & car ('57) | 4.50 | 4.50 |
| | | *Nos. Q77-Q91 (16)* | 13.30 | *12.40* |

**Halves Used**

| | |
|---|---|
| Q77-Q89, each | .25 |
| Q90-Q91, each | .40 |

**1960-66 Photo. *Perf. 12½x13***

| No. | Design | Description | Unused | Used |
|---|---|---|---|---|
| Q92 | PP4 | 60 l bright lilac | .25 | .25 |
| Q93 | PP4 | 140 l dull red | .25 | .30 |
| Q94 | PP4 | 280 l yellow | .60 | .45 |
| Q95 | PP4 | 600 l olive bister | .70 | .75 |
| Q96 | PP4 | 700 l blue ('66) | 1.75 | .75 |
| Q97 | PP4 | 800 l dp org ('66) | 2.10 | .95 |
| | | *Nos. Q92-Q97 (6)* | 5.65 | 3.45 |

**Halves Used**

| | |
|---|---|
| Q92-Q93, each | .25 |
| Q94 | .25 |
| Q95 | .40 |
| Q96-Q97, each | .25 |

**Imprint: "I.P.S.-Off. Carte Valori-Roma"**

**1973, Mar. Photo. Wmk. 303**

| No. | Design | Description | Unused | Used |
|---|---|---|---|---|
| Q98 | PP4 | 20 l lilac brown | .25 | .25 |
| Q99 | PP4 | 30 l plum | .25 | .25 |

## PARCEL POST AUTHORIZED DELIVERY STAMPS

For the payment of a special tax for the authorized delivery of parcels privately instead of through the post office.

PAD1

**1953 Wmk. 277 Photo. *Perf. 13***

| No. | Design | Description | Unused | Used |
|---|---|---|---|---|
| QY1 | PAD1 | 40 l orange red | 12.50 | *12.50* |
| QY2 | PAD1 | 50 l ultra | 160.00 | *160.00* |
| QY3 | PAD1 | 75 l brown | 80.00 | *80.00* |
| QY4 | PAD1 | 110 l lil rose | 80.00 | *80.00* |
| | | *Nos. QY1-QY4 (4)* | 332.50 | *332.50* |
| | | Set, never hinged | 450.00 | |

**Halves Used**

| | |
|---|---|
| QY1 | .35 |
| QY2 | 1.25 |
| QY3 | 3.25 |
| QY4 | 3.25 |

For overprints see Trieste Nos. QY1-QY4.

**Catalogue values for unused stamps in this section, from this point to the end of the section, are for Never Hinged items.**

**1956-58 Wmk. 303 *Perf. 12½x13***

| No. | Design | Description | Unused | Used |
|---|---|---|---|---|
| QY5 | PAD1 | 40 l orange red | 1.60 | .90 |
| QY6 | PAD1 | 50 l ultra | 3.25 | 2.25 |
| QY7 | PAD1 | 60 l brt vio bl ('58) | 9.00 | 5.25 |
| QY8 | PAD1 | 75 l brown | 375.00 | 160.00 |
| QY9 | PAD1 | 90 l lil ('58) | .35 | *.75* |
| QY10 | PAD1 | 110 l lil rose | 375.00 | 140.00 |
| QY11 | PAD1 | 120 l grnsh bl ('58) | .35 | *.75* |
| | | *Nos. QY5-QY11 (7)* | 764.55 | 309.90 |

**Halves Used**

| | |
|---|---|
| QY5-QY6, each | .25 |
| QY7 | .90 |
| QY8,QY10 | 8.00 |
| QY9 | .30 |
| QY11 | .25 |

**1960-81**

| No. | Design | Description | Unused | Used |
|---|---|---|---|---|
| QY12 | PAD1 | 70 l green ('66) | 45.00 | 9.00 |
| QY13 | PAD1 | 80 l brown | .40 | .40 |
| QY14 | PAD1 | 110 l org yel | .40 | .40 |
| QY15 | PAD1 | 140 l black | .45 | .50 |
| QY16 | PAD1 | 150 l car rose ('68) | .30 | .50 |
| QY17 | PAD1 | 180 l red ('66) | .40 | .60 |
| QY18 | PAD1 | 240 l dk bl ('66) | .45 | .70 |

**Engr. *Perf. 13½***

| No. | Design | Description | Unused | Used |
|---|---|---|---|---|
| QY19 | PAD1 | 500 l ocher ('76) | 1.40 | 1.40 |
| QY20 | PAD1 | 600 l bl grn ('79) | 1.40 | 1.40 |
| QY21 | PAD1 | 900 l ultra ('81) | 1.10 | 1.40 |
| | | *Nos. QY12-QY21 (10)* | 51.30 | 16.30 |

**Halves Used**

| | |
|---|---|
| QY12 | 4.00 |
| QY13-QY15, QY18, QY21, each | .25 |
| QY16, QY17, QY19, each | .25 |
| QY20 | .35 |

PAD2

***Perf. 14x13½***

**1984 Photo. Wmk. 303**

| No. | Design | Description | Unused | Used |
|---|---|---|---|---|
| QY22 | PAD2 | 3000 l multi | 3.50 | 2.50 |

## OCCUPATION STAMPS

**Issued under Austrian Occupation**

Emperor Karl of Austria
OS1 OS2

**Austria #M49-M67 Surcharged in Black**

**1918 Unwmk. *Perf. 12½***

| No. | Design | Description | Unused | Used |
|---|---|---|---|---|
| N1 | OS1 | 2c on 1h grnsh bl | .25 | *.45* |
| N2 | OS1 | 3c on 2h red org | .25 | *.40* |
| N3 | OS1 | 4c on 3h ol gray | .25 | *.45* |
| N4 | OS1 | 6c on 5h ol grn | .25 | *.40* |
| N5 | OS1 | 7c on 6h vio | .25 | *.45* |
| a. | | Perf. 12½x11½ | 16.00 | *45.00* |
| N6 | OS1 | 11c on 10h org brn | .25 | *.45* |
| N7 | OS1 | 13c on 12h blue | .25 | *.45* |
| N8 | OS1 | 16c on 15h brt rose | .25 | *.40* |
| N9 | OS1 | 22c on 20h red brn | .25 | *.45* |
| a. | | Perf. 11½ | 22.50 | *75.00* |
| N10 | OS1 | 27c on 25h ultra | .60 | *1.20* |
| N11 | OS1 | 32c on 30h slate | .60 | *1.10* |
| N12 | OS1 | 43c on 40h ol bis | .60 | *.85* |
| a. | | Perf. 11½ | 15.00 | *67.50* |
| N13 | OS1 | 53c on 50h dp grn | .60 | *.80* |
| N14 | OS1 | 64c on 60h rose | .60 | *1.20* |
| N15 | OS1 | 85c on 80h dl bl | .60 | *.80* |
| N16 | OS1 | 95c on 90h dk vio | .60 | *.80* |
| N17 | OS2 | 2 l 11c on 2k rose, *straw* | .60 | 1.60 |
| N18 | OS2 | 3 l 16c on 3k grn, *bl* | 1.10 | 3.00 |
| N19 | OS2 | 4 l 22c on 4k rose, *grn* | 2.25 | 3.75 |
| | | *Nos. N1-N19 (19)* | 10.40 | *19.00* |

Emperor Karl — OS3

**Austria #M69-M81 Surcharged in Black**

**1918**

| No. | Design | Description | Unused |
|---|---|---|---|
| N20 | OS3 | 2c on 1h grnsh bl | 5.75 |
| N21 | OS3 | 3c on 2h orange | 5.75 |
| N22 | OS3 | 4c on 3h ol gray | 5.75 |
| N23 | OS3 | 6c on 5h yel grn | 5.75 |
| N24 | OS3 | 11c on 10h dk brn | 5.75 |
| N25 | OS3 | 22c on 20h red | 5.75 |
| N26 | OS3 | 27c on 25h blue | 5.75 |
| N27 | OS3 | 32c on 30h bister | 5.75 |
| N28 | OS3 | 48c on 45h dk sl | 5.75 |
| N29 | OS3 | 53c on 50h dp grn | 5.75 |
| N30 | OS3 | 64c on 60h violet | 5.75 |
| N31 | OS3 | 85c on 80h rose | 5.75 |
| N32 | OS3 | 95c on 90h brn vio | 5.75 |
| N33 | OS2 | 1 l 6c on 1k ol grn, *grnish* | 5.75 |
| | | *Nos. N20-N33 (14)* | 80.50 |

Nos. N20 to N33 inclusive were never placed in use in the occupied territory. They were, however, on sale at the Post Office in Vienna for a few days before the Armistice.

## OCCUPATION SPECIAL DELIVERY STAMPS

Bosnia #QE1-QE2 Surcharged

**1918 Unwmk. *Perf. 12½***

| No. | Design | Description | Unused | Used |
|---|---|---|---|---|
| NE1 | SH1 | 3c on 2h ver | 11.00 | *19.00* |
| NE2 | SH1 | 6c on 5h dp grn | 11.00 | *19.00* |

Nos. NE1-NE2 are on yellowish paper. Reprints on white paper sell for about 70 cents a set.

## OCCUPATION POSTAGE DUE STAMPS

**Bosnia #J16, J18-J19, J21-J24 Surcharged Like Nos. NE1-NE2**

**1918 Unwmk. *Perf. 12½***

| No. | Design | Description | Unused | Used |
|---|---|---|---|---|
| NJ1 | D2 | 6c on 5h red | 3.25 | *7.25* |
| a. | | Perf. 11½ | 7.50 | *12.00* |
| NJ2 | D2 | 11c on 10h red | 2.40 | *6.00* |
| a. | | Perf. 11½ | 5.50 | *12.00* |
| NJ3 | D2 | 16c on 15h red | .80 | *4.00* |
| NJ4 | D2 | 27c on 25h red | .80 | *4.00* |
| NJ5 | D2 | 32c on 30h red | .80 | *4.00* |
| NJ6 | D2 | 43c on 40h red | .80 | *4.00* |
| NJ7 | D2 | 53c on 50h red | .80 | *4.00* |
| | | *Nos. NJ1-NJ7 (7)* | 9.65 | *33.25* |

## OCCUPATION NEWSPAPER STAMPS

Austrian #MP1-MP4 Surcharged

**1918 Unwmk. *Perf. 12½***

| No. | Design | Description | Unused | Used |
|---|---|---|---|---|
| NP1 | MN1 | 3c on 2h blue | .25 | *.40* |
| a. | | Perf. 11½ | 11.00 | *37.50* |
| NP2 | MN1 | 7c on 6h org | .95 | *1.20* |
| NP3 | MN1 | 11c on 10h car | .95 | *1.20* |
| NP4 | MN1 | 22c on 20h brn | .95 | *1.20* |
| a. | | Perf. 11½ | 110.00 | *225.00* |
| | | *Nos. NP1-NP4 (4)* | 3.10 | *4.00* |

# A.M.G.

Issued jointly by the Allied Military Government of the United States and Great Britain, for civilian use in areas under Allied occupation.

**Catalogue values for unused stamps in this section are for Never Hinged items.**

OS4

**Offset Printing**

**"Italy Centesimi" (or "Lira") in Black**

**1943 Unwmk. *Perf. 11***

| No. | Design | Description | Unused | Used |
|---|---|---|---|---|
| 1N1 | OS4 | 15c pale orange | 1.60 | 1.00 |
| 1N2 | OS4 | 25c pale citron | 1.60 | 1.00 |
| 1N3 | OS4 | 30c light gray | 1.60 | 1.00 |
| 1N4 | OS4 | 50c light violet | 1.60 | 1.00 |
| 1N5 | OS4 | 60c orange yellow | 1.60 | 2.00 |
| 1N6 | OS4 | 1 l lt yel green | 1.60 | 1.00 |
| 1N7 | OS4 | 2 l deep rose | 2.50 | 2.00 |
| 1N8 | OS4 | 5 l light blue | 3.50 | *3.25* |
| 1N9 | OS4 | 10 l buff | 3.50 | *5.00* |
| | | *Nos. 1N1-1N9 (9)* | 19.10 | *17.25* |

Italy Nos. 217, 220 and 221 Overprinted in Blue, Vermilion, Carmine or Orange

**1943, Dec. 10 Wmk. 140 *Perf. 14***

| No. | Design | Description | Unused | Used |
|---|---|---|---|---|
| 1N10 | A91 | 20c rose red (Bl) | 1.50 | *3.00* |
| 1N11 | A93 | 35c dp blue (C) | 17.50 | *19.00* |
| a. | | 35c deep blue (V) | 35.00 | *60.00* |
| 1N13 | A95 | 50c purple (C) | .75 | *1.10* |
| a. | | 50c purple (O) | .90 | *2.00* |
| | | *Nos. 1N10-1N13 (3)* | 19.75 | *23.10* |

Nos. 1N1-1N9 were for use in Sicily, Nos. 1N10-1N13 for use in Naples.

## VENEZA GIULIA

**Catalogue values for unused stamps in this section are for Never Hinged items.**

**Stamps of Italy, 1929 to 1945 Overprinted in Black**

a

b

### On Stamps of 1929

| 1945-47 | Wmk. 140 | | Perf. 14 | |
|---|---|---|---|---|
| 1LN1 | A92 (a) | 10c dk brown | .30 | .35 |
| 1LN1A | A91 (a) | 20c rose red ('47) | .40 | .50 |

### On Stamps of 1945

| 1945 | Wmk. 277 | | Perf. 14 | |
|---|---|---|---|---|
| 1LN2 | A249 (a) | 20c rose red | .35 | .50 |
| 1LN3 | A248 (a) | 60c sl grn | .45 | .35 |
| 1LN4 | A249 (a) | 1 l dp vio | .30 | .35 |
| 1LN5 | A251 (a) | 2 l dk red | .35 | .35 |
| 1LN6 | A252 (b) | 5 l dk red | .65 | .50 |
| 1LN7 | A251 (a) | 10 l purple | .90 | *1.25* |
| | *Nos. 1LN2-1LN7 (6)* | | 3.00 | *3.30* |

### On Stamps of 1945

| 1945-46 | | Unwmk. | | |
|---|---|---|---|---|
| 1LN7A | A250(a) | 10c dk brn ('46) | .30 | .25 |
| 1LN7B | A249(a) | 20c rose red ('46) | .25 | *.50* |
| 1LN8 | A251(a) | 60c red org | .25 | .25 |
| | *Nos. 1LN7A-1LN8 (3)* | | .80 | *1.00* |

### On Air Post Stamp of 1930

| 1945 | Wmk. 140 | | Perf. 14 | |
|---|---|---|---|---|
| 1LN9 | AP3 (a) | 50c olive brn | .25 | .50 |

### On Stamp of 1929

| 1946 | | | | |
|---|---|---|---|---|
| 1LN10 | A91 (a) | 20 l lt green | 2.25 | *6.50* |

### On Stamps of 1945

**Wmk. 277**

| | | | | |
|---|---|---|---|---|
| 1LN11 | A260 (a) | 25 l dk green | 8.00 | *9.00* |
| 1LN12 | A260 (a) | 50 l dk vio brn | 8.00 | *15.00* |

### Italy No. 477 Overprinted in Black

| | | | | |
|---|---|---|---|---|
| 1LN13 | A261 | 100 l car lake | 29.00 | *90.00* |
| | *Nos. 1LN10-1LN13 (4)* | | 47.25 | *120.50* |

### Stamps of Italy, 1945-47 Overprinted Type "a" in Black

| 1947 | | | | |
|---|---|---|---|---|
| 1LN14 | A259 | 25c brt bl grn | .25 | 1.00 |
| 1LN15 | A258 | 2 l dk claret brn | .60 | *.35* |
| 1LN16 | A259 | 3 l red | .45 | .25 |
| 1LN17 | A259 | 4 l red org | .70 | .25 |
| 1LN18 | A257 | 6 l deep violet | 2.00 | *1.90* |
| 1LN19 | A259 | 20 l dk red vio | *55.00* | 7.50 |
| | *Nos. 1LN14-1LN19 (6)* | | *59.00* | *11.25* |

Some denominations of the Venezia Giulia A.M.G. issues exist with inverted overprint; several values exist in horizontal and vertical pairs, one stamp without overprint.

## OCCUPATION AIR POST STAMPS

**Catalogue values for unused stamps in this section are for Never Hinged items.**

### Italy Nos. C106-C107 and C109-C113 Overprinted Like 1LN13 in Black

| 1946-47 | Wmk. 277 | | Perf. 14 | |
|---|---|---|---|---|
| 1LNC1 | AP59 | 1 l sl blue ('47) | .40 | *5.00* |
| 1LNC2 | AP60 | 2 l dk blue ('47) | .40 | *2.50* |
| 1LNC3 | AP60 | 5 l dk green ('47) | 3.00 | *1.50* |
| 1LNC4 | AP59 | 10 l car rose ('47) | 3.00 | *1.50* |
| 1LNC5 | AP60 | 25 l dk blue | 3.00 | *1.50* |
| 1LNC6 | AP60 | 25 l brown ('47) | 35.00 | *47.50* |
| 1LNC7 | AP59 | 50 l dk green | 6.50 | *11.00* |
| | *Nos. 1LNC1-1LNC7 (7)* | | 51.30 | *70.50* |

Nos. 1LNC5 and 1LNC7 exist with inverted overprint; No. 1LNC5 with double overprint, one inverted.

## OCCUPATION SPECIAL DELIVERY STAMPS

**Catalogue values for unused stamps in this section are for Never Hinged items.**

### Italy Nos. E20 and E23 Overprinted Like 1LN13 in Black

| 1946 | Wmk. 277 | | Perf. 14 | |
|---|---|---|---|---|
| 1LNE1 | SD9 | 10 l deep blue | 4.00 | *1.60* |
| 1LNE2 | SD8 | 30 l deep violet | 8.75 | *19.00* |

# ITALIAN SOCIAL REPUBLIC

On Sept. 15, 1943, Mussolini proclaimed the establishment of a Republican fascist party and a new fascist government. This government's authority covered only the Northern Italy area occupied by the Germans.

**Catalogue values for unused stamps in this section are for hinged stamps. Never hinged examples are valued at 2-2.5 times the values shown.**

### Italy Nos. 218, 219, 221 to 223 and 231 Overprinted in Black or Red

a

b

c

| 1944 | Wmk. 140 | | Perf. 14 | |
|---|---|---|---|---|
| 1 | A94(a) | 25c deep grn | .30 | *2.00* |
| 2 | A95(b) | 30c ol brn (R) | .30 | *2.00* |
| 3 | A95(c) | 50c pur (R) | .30 | *2.00* |
| 4 | A94(a) | 75c rose red | .30 | *2.00* |
| 5 | A94(b) | 1.25 l dp bl (R) | .30 | *2.00* |
| 5A | A94(b) | 50 l dp vio (R) | 250.00 | *4,500.* |
| | *Nos. 1-5 (5)* | | 1.50 | 10.00 |

Nos. 1 to 5 exist with overprint inverted. Value, each: unused $30; used $37.50.

No. 1 exists with overprint "b." Value: unused, $60; used $800.

Counterfeits of No. 5A exist.

### Italy Nos. 427 to 438 Overprinted Same in Black or Red

| | | | | |
|---|---|---|---|---|
| 6 | A243(a) | 25c deep green | .45 | *4.50* |
| 7 | A244(a) | 25c deep green | .45 | *4.50* |
| 8 | A245(a) | 25c deep green | .45 | *4.50* |
| 9 | A246(a) | 25c deep green | .45 | *4.50* |
| 10 | A243(b) | 30c olive brown (R) | .45 | *37.50* |
| 11 | A244(b) | 30c olive brown (R) | .45 | *37.50* |
| 12 | A245(b) | 30c olive brown (R) | .45 | *37.50* |
| 13 | A246(b) | 30c olive brown (R) | .45 | *37.50* |
| 14 | A243(c) | 50c purple (R) | .45 | *4.50* |
| 15 | A244(c) | 50c purple (R) | .45 | *4.50* |
| 16 | A245(c) | 50c purple (R) | .45 | *4.50* |
| 17 | A246(c) | 50c purple (R) | .45 | *4.50* |
| | *Nos. 6-17 (12)* | | 5.40 | *186.00* |

Loggia dei Mercanti, Bologna — A1

Basilica of San Lorenzo, Rome — A2

Drummer Boy — A3

| 1944 | Photo. | | Perf. 14 | |
|---|---|---|---|---|
| 18 | A1 | 20c crimson | .25 | *.60* |
| 19 | A2 | 25c green | .25 | *.60* |
| 20 | A3 | 30c brown | .25 | *.60* |
| 21 | A3 | 75c dark red | .25 | *1.60* |
| | *Nos. 18-21 (4)* | | 1.00 | 3.40 |

For surcharges see Italy Nos. 461-462.

Church of St. Ciriaco, Ancona A4

Monte Cassino Abbey A5

Loggia dei Mercanti, Bologna A6

Basilica of San Lorenzo, Rome A7

Statue of "Rome" A8

Basilica of St. Maria delle Grazie, Milan A9

| 1944 | | | Unwmk. | |
|---|---|---|---|---|
| 22 | A4 | 5c brown | .25 | *.35* |
| 23 | A5 | 10c brown | .25 | .25 |
| 24 | A6 | 20c rose red | .25 | .25 |
| 25 | A7 | 25c deep green | .25 | .25 |
| 26 | A3 | 30c brown | .25 | .25 |
| 27 | A8 | 50c purple | .25 | .25 |
| 28 | A3 | 75c dark red | 1.25 | *26.00* |
| 29 | A5 | 1 l purple | .25 | .25 |
| 30 | A9 | 1.25 l blue | .80 | *16.50* |
| 31 | A9 | 3 l deep green | .80 | *50.00* |
| | *Nos. 22-31 (10)* | | 4.60 | *94.35* |

Bandiera Brothers — A10

| 1944, Dec. 6 | | | | |
|---|---|---|---|---|
| 32 | A10 | 25c deep green | .35 | *.55* |
| 33 | A10 | 1 l purple | .35 | *.55* |
| 34 | A10 | 2.50 l rose red | .35 | *7.50* |
| | *Nos. 32-34 (3)* | | 1.05 | *8.60* |

Cent. of the execution of Attilio (1811-44) and Emilio Bandiera (1819-44), revolutionary patriots who were shot at Cosenza, July 23, 1844, by Neapolitan authorities after an unsuccessful raid.

This set was overprinted in 1945 by the committee of the National Philatelic Convention to publicize that gathering at Venice.

## SPECIAL DELIVERY STAMPS

### Italy Nos. E14 and E15 Overprinted in Red or Black

| 1944 | Wmk. 140 | | Perf. 14 | |
|---|---|---|---|---|
| E1 | SD4 | 1.25 l green (R) | .25 | *.60* |
| E2 | SD4 | 2.50 l deep orange | .25 | *25.00* |

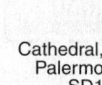

Cathedral, Palermo SD1

| 1944 | | | Photo. | |
|---|---|---|---|---|
| E3 | SD1 | 1.25 l green | .25 | *1.00* |

## AUTHORIZED DELIVERY STAMP

**Catalogue values for unused stamps in this section are for Never Hinged items.**

Italy No. EY2 Overprinted

| 1944 | Wmk. 140 | | Perf. 14 | |
|---|---|---|---|---|
| EY1 | AD2 | 10c dark brown | .25 | *.80* |

Italy No. EY2 with overprint type a and type b were prepared but not issued. Values: type a, unused $135, never hinged $425; type b, unused $250, never hinged $800.

## POSTAGE DUE STAMPS

### Italy #J28-J40 Overprinted Like #EY1

| 1944 | Wmk. 140 | | Perf. 14 | |
|---|---|---|---|---|
| J1 | D6 | 5c brown | 5.00 | *9.00* |
| J2 | D6 | 10c blue | 5.00 | *7.50* |
| J3 | D6 | 20c rose red | 5.00 | *7.50* |
| J4 | D6 | 25c green | 5.00 | *7.50* |
| J5 | D6 | 30c red org | 5.00 | *13.50* |
| J6 | D6 | 40c blk brn | 5.00 | *19.00* |
| J7 | D6 | 50c violet | 5.00 | *6.00* |
| J8 | D6 | 60c slate blk | 25.00 | *60.00* |
| J9 | D7 | 1 l red org | 5.00 | *6.00* |
| J10 | D7 | 2 l green | 16.00 | *37.50* |
| J11 | D7 | 5 l violet | 45.00 | *260.00* |
| J12 | D7 | 10 l blue | 80.00 | *600.00* |
| J13 | D7 | 20 l car rose | 80.00 | *1,000.* |
| | *Nos. J1-J13 (13)* | | 286.00 | *2,033.* |

## PARCEL POST STAMPS

Both unused and used values are for complete stamps.

### Italian Parcel Post Stamps and Types of 1927-39 Overprinted

| 1944 | Wmk. 140 | | Perf. 13 | |
|---|---|---|---|---|
| Q1 | PP3 | 5c brown | 6.50 | *75.00* |
| Q2 | PP3 | 10c deep blue | 6.50 | *75.00* |
| Q3 | PP3 | 25c carmine | 6.50 | *82.50* |
| Q4 | PP3 | 30c ultra | 6.50 | *82.50* |
| Q5 | PP3 | 50c orange | 6.50 | *75.00* |
| Q6 | PP3 | 60c red | 6.50 | *525.00* |
| Q7 | PP3 | 1 l lilac | 6.50 | *75.00* |
| Q8 | PP3 | 2 l green | 375.00 | *2,400.* |
| Q9 | PP3 | 3 l yel bister | 50.00 | *825.00* |
| Q10 | PP3 | 4 l gray | 90.00 | *975.00* |
| Q11 | PP3 | 10 l rose lilac | 190.00 | *3,500.* |
| Q12 | PP3 | 20 l lilac brn | 500.00 | *5,000.* |
| | *Nos. Q1-Q12 (12)* | | 1,250. | 13,690. |

No parcel post service existed in 1944. Nos. Q1-Q12 were used undivided, for regular postage.

## ITALIAN OFFICES ABROAD

Stamps listed under this heading were issued for use in the Italian Post Offices which, for various reasons, were maintained from time to time in foreign countries.

100 Centesimi = 1 Lira

### GENERAL ISSUE

Values of Italian Offices Abroad stamps vary tremendously according to condition. Quotations are for very fine examples, and values for unused stamps are for examples with original gum as defined in the catalogue introduction. Extremely fine or superb examples sell at much higher prices, and fine or poor examples sell at greatly reduced prices. In addition, unused examples without gum are discounted severely.

Very fine examples of Nos. 1-17 will have perforations barely clear of the frameline or design due to the narrow spacing of the stamps on the plates.

Italian Stamps with Corner Designs Slightly Altered and Overprinted

**1874-78 Wmk. 140 *Perf. 14***

1 A6 1c ol grn 26.00 *45.00*
 a. Inverted overprint *35,000.*
 c. 2 dots in lower right corner 82.50 *260.00*
 d. Three dots in upper right corner 875.00 *1,650.*
 e. Without overprint 70,000.
2 A7 2c org brn 27.50 *52.50*
 a. Without overprint 70,000.
3 A8 5c slate grn 875.00 52.50
 a. Lower right corner not altered *22,500.* 2,400.
4 A8 10c buff 1,500. 110.00
 a. Upper left corner not altered *28,500.* 1,650.
 b. None of the corners altered — *67,500.*
 c. Lower corners not altered *11,250.*
5 A8 10c blue ('78) 500.00 34.00
6 A15 20c blue 2,150. 52.50
7 A15 20c org ('78) 8,500. 30.00
8 A8 30c brown 7.00 *30.00*
 a. None of the corners altered *47,500.*
 b. Right lower corner not altered — —
 c. Double overprint —
9 A8 40c rose 7.00 *30.00*
10 A8 60c lilac 17.00 *300.00*
11 A13 2 l vermilion 215.00 *975.00*

**1881**

12 A17 5c green 21.00 19.00
13 A17 10c claret 7.00 *15.00*
14 A17 20c orange 7.00 *9.00*
 a. Double overprint, on piece —
15 A17 25c blue 7.00 *22.50*
16 A17 50c violet 17.50 *75.00*
17 A17 2 l vermilion 21.50 —
 *Nos. 12-17 (6)* 81.00
 *Nos. 12-16 (5)* 149.50

The "Estero" stamps were used in various parts of the world, South America, Africa, Turkey, etc.

Forged cancellations exist on Nos. 1-2, 9-11, 16.

### OFFICES IN CHINA

100 Cents = 1 Dollar

### PEKING

Italian Stamps of 1901-16 Handstamped

**Wmk. 140, Unwmk.**

**1917 *Perf. 12, 13½, 14***

1 A48 2c on 5c green 375.00 260.00
 a. Inverted surcharge 325.00 240.00
 b. Double surcharge, one inverted 975.00 750.00
 c. 4c on 5c green *8,000.*
3 A48 4c on 10c claret (No. 95) 675.00 400.00
 a. Inverted surcharge 600.00 375.00
 b. Double surcharge, one inverted 1,500. 1,000.
 c. 4c on 10c claret (No. 79) —
5 A58 6c on 15c slate 1,350. 975.00
 b. 8c on 15c slate 4,875. 4,500.
 c. Pair, one without surcharge —
7 A58 8c on 20c on 15c slate 5,250. 3,750.
 a. Inverted surcharge 4,875. 3,350.
8 A50 8c on 20c brn org (No. 112) *10,500.* 3,900.
 a. Inverted surcharge *9,750.* *3,500.*
9 A49 20c on 50c vio *52,500.* *33,500.*
 a. Inverted surcharge *45,000.* *30,000.*
 b. 40c on 50c violet *21,000.* *21,000.*
 c. As "b," inverted surcharge *18,500.* *18,500.*
11 A46 40c on 1 l brn & grn *315,000.* *52,500.*
 a. Inverted surcharge 275,000. 45,000.

Excellent forgeries exist of the higher valued stamps of Offices in China.

Italian Stamps of 1901-16 Overprinted

**1917-18**

12 A42 1c brown 37.50 *60.00*
13 A43 2c orange brown 37.50 *60.00*
 a. Double overprint 375.00 —
14 A48 5c green 11.00 *22.50*
 a. Double overprint 240.00 —
15 A48 10c claret 11.00 *22.50*
16 A50 20c brn org (No. 112) 260.00 *300.00*
17 A49 25c blue 11.00 *30.00*
18 A49 50c violet 11.00 *30.00*
19 A46 1 l brown & grn 26.00 *60.00*
20 A46 5 l blue & rose 52.50 *97.50*
21 A51 10 l gray grn & red 300.00 *550.00*
 *Nos. 12-21 (10)* 757.50 *1,232.*

Italy No. 113, the watermarked 20c brown orange, was also overprinted "Pechino," but not issued. Value: hinged $20; never hinged $50.

Italian Stamps of 1901-16 Surcharged

Type I

Type II

TWO DOLLARS:
Type I — Surcharged "2 dollari Pechino"
Type II — Surcharged "2 DOLLARI."
Type III — Surcharged "2 dollari." "Pechino" measures 11½mm wide, instead of 13mm.

**1918-19 *Perf. 14***

22 A42 ½c on 1c brown 300.00 *300.00*
 a. Surcharged "1 cents" 900.00 1,000.
23 A43 1c on 2c org brn 11.00 *22.50*
 a. Surcharged "1 cents" 450.00 525.00
24 A48 2c on 5c green 11.00 *22.50*
25 A48 4c on 10c claret 11.00 *22.50*
26 A50 8c on 20c brn org (No. 112) 60.00 *45.00*
 a. "8 CENTS" doubled 475.00 475.00
27 A49 10c on 25c blue 22.50 *45.00*
 a. "10 CENTS" doubled 475.00 475.00
28 A49 20c on 50c violet 22.50 *45.00*
29 A46 40c on 1 l brown & green 300.00 *375.00*
30 A46 $2 on 5 l bl & rose (type I) 525.00 *900.00*
 a. Type II *100,000.* *80,000.*
 b. Type III *16,000.* *12,000.*
 *Nos. 22-30 (9)* 1,263. *1,777.*

Italy No. 100 Surcharged

**1919**

32 A49 10c on 25c blue 9.00 *22.50*

Imperf. examples of No. 32 are proofs.

### PEKING SPECIAL DELIVERY STAMPS

Italian Special Delivery Stamp 1908 Ovptd.

**1917 Wmk. 140 *Perf. 14***

E1 SD2 30c blue & rose 15.00 *55.00*

No. E1 Surcharged

**1918**

E2 SD2 12c on 30c bl & rose 120.00 *400.00*

### PEKING POSTAGE DUE STAMPS

Italian Postage Due Stamps Overprinted Like Nos. 12-21

**1917 Wmk. 140 *Perf. 14***

J1 D3 10c buff & magenta 5.25 *13.50*
 a. Double overprint 375.00
J2 D3 20c buff & magenta 5.25 *13.50*
J3 D3 30c buff & magenta 5.25 *13.50*
J4 D3 40c buff & magenta 10.50 *13.50*
 *Nos. J1-J4 (4)* 26.25 *54.00*

Nos. J1-J4 Surcharged Like No. E2

**1918**

J5 D3 4c on 10c *112,500.* *90,000.*
J6 D3 8c on 20c 45.00 *97.50*
 a. Pair, one without surcharge 1,800.
J7 D3 12c on 30c 110.00 *225.00*
J8 D3 16c on 40c 450.00 *825.00*

In 1919, the same new values were surcharged on Italy Nos. J6-J9 in a different style: four lines to cancel the denomination, and "-PECHINO- 4 CENTS." These were not issued. Value $10 each, never hinged $25 each.

### TIENTSIN

Italian Stamps of 1906 Handstamped

**Wmk. 140, Unwmk.**

**1917 *Perf. 12, 13½, 14***

1 A48 2c on 5c green 550.00 550.00
 a. Surcharge inverted 525.00 525.00
 b. Double surcharge 1,000. 750.00
 c. 4c on 5c green *14,500.*
 d. Double surcharge, one inverted 1,100. 750.00
2 A48 4c on 10c claret 1,000. 900.00
 a. Surcharge inverted 975.00 825.00
 b. Double surcharge 1,650. 975.00
 c. Double surcharge, one inverted 1,800. 1,000.
4 A58 6c on 15c slate 2,250. 1,800.
 a. Surcharge inverted 2,000. 1,650.
 b. 4c on 15c slate 7,500. 6,750.
 *Nos. 1-4 (3)* 3,800. 3,250.

Italian Stamps of 1901-16 Overprinted

**1917-18**

5 A42 1c brown 37.50 *60.00*
 a. Inverted overprint 475.00 475.00
6 A43 2c orange brn 37.50 *60.00*
7 A48 5c green 11.00 *22.50*
8 A48 10c claret 11.00 *22.50*
 a. Double overprint 525.00
9 A50 20c brn org (#112) 250.00 *300.00*
10 A49 25c blue 11.00 *30.00*
11 A49 50c violet 11.00 *30.00*
12 A46 1 l brown & grn 26.00 *60.00*
13 A46 5 l blue & rose 52.50 *97.50*
14 A51 10 l gray grn & red 310.00 *550.00*
 *Nos. 5-14 (10)* 757.50 *1,232.*

Italy No. 113, the watermarked 20c brown orange was also overprinted "Tientsin," but not issued. Value: hinged $30; never hinged $75.

Italian Stamps of 1901-16 Surcharged

Type I

TWO DOLLARS:
Type I — Surcharged "2 Dollari Tientsin"
Type II — Surcharged "2 dollari."
Type III — Surcharged "2 Dollari." "Tientsin" measures 10mm wide instead of 13mm.

**1918-21** *Perf. 14*

15 A42 ½c on 1c brown 300.00 *300.00*
a. Inverted surcharge 550.00 550.00
b. Surcharged "1 cents" 900.00 1,000.
16 A43 1c on 2c org brn 11.00 *22.50*
a. Surcharged "1 cents" 450.00 525.00
b. Inverted surcharge 550.00 550.00
17 A48 2c on 5c green 11.00 *22.50*
18 A48 4c on 10c claret 11.00 *22.50*
19 A50 8c on 20c brn org (#112) 60.00 45.00
20 A49 10c on 25c blue 22.50 *45.00*
21 A49 20c on 50c violet 30.00 *45.00*
22 A46 40c on 1 l brn & grn 300.00 *375.00*
23 A46 $2 on 5 l bl & rose (type I) 525.00 *900.00*
a. Type II *17,250. 13,500.*
b. Type III ('21) *16,000. 13,500.*
*Nos. 15-23 (9)* 1,270. *1,777.*

### SPECIAL DELIVERY STAMPS

Italian Special Delivery Stamp of 1908 Overprinted

**1917** **Wmk. 140** *Perf. 14*
E1 SD2 30c blue & rose 15.00 *55.00*

No. E1 Surcharged

**1918**
E2 SD2 12c on 30c bl & rose 120.00 *400.00*

### POSTAGE DUE STAMPS

Italian Postage Due Stamps Overprinted

**1917** **Wmk. 140** *Perf. 14*
J1 D3 10c buff & magenta 5.25 *13.50*
a. Double overprint 375.00
J2 D3 20c buff & magenta 5.25 *13.50*
J3 D3 30c buff & magenta 5.25 *13.50*
a. Double overprint 375.00
J4 D3 40c buff & magenta 10.50 *13.50*
*Nos. J1-J4 (4)* 26.25 *54.00*

Nos. J1-J4 Surcharged

**1918**
J5 D3 4c on 10c *8,250. 8,250.*
J6 D3 8c on 20c 45.00 *97.50*
a. "8 CENTS" double 2,400.
J7 D3 12c on 30c 110.00 *225.00*
J8 D3 16c on 40c 460.00 *825.00*

In 1919, the same new values were surcharged on Italy Nos. J6-J9 in a different style: four lines to cancel the denomination, and "-TIENTSIN- 4 CENTS." These were not issued. Value $8 each, never hinged $20 each.

## OFFICES IN CRETE

40 Paras = 1 Piaster
100 Centesimi = 1 Lira (1906)

**Italy Nos. 70 and 81 Surcharged in Red or Black**

a

b

**1900-01** **Wmk. 140** *Perf. 14*
1 A36(a) 1pi on 25c blue 7.50 *82.50*
2 A45(b) 1pi on 25c dp bl (Bk) ('01) 4.50 *11.00*

Italian Stamps Overprinted

**1906**
**On Nos. 76-79, 92, 81, 83-85, 87, 91**
3 A42 1c brown 2.25 *4.50*
a. Pair, one without ovpt. 1,350.
b. Double overprint 375.00
4 A43 2c org brn 2.25 *4.50*
a. Imperf., pair 2,600.
b. Double overprint 375.00
5 A44 5c bl grn 3.75 *6.00*
6 A45 10c claret 375.00 300.00
7 A45 15c on 20c org 3.75 *6.00*
8 A45 25c blue 13.50 *26.00*
9 A45 40c brown 13.50 *26.00*
10 A45 45c ol grn 11.00 *26.00*
11 A45 50c violet 13.50 *32.50*
12 A46 1 l brn & grn 75.00 *120.00*
13 A46 5 l bl & rose 475.00 *525.00*
*Nos. 3-13 (11)* 988.50 *1,076.*

On Nos. 94-95, 100, 104-105

**1907-10**
14 A48 5c green 2.25 2.25
a. Inverted overprint 340.00
15 A48 10c claret 2.25 2.25
a. Double overprint —
16 A49 25c blue 3.75 *15.00*
17 A49 40c brown 34.00 *40.00*
18 A49 50c violet 3.75 *13.50*
*Nos. 14-18 (5)* 46.00 *73.00*

On No. 111 in Violet

**1912** **Unwmk.** *Perf. 13x13½*
19 A50 15c slate black 3.75 *4.50*

### SPECIAL DELIVERY STAMPS

Special Delivery Stamp of Italy Overprinted

**1906** **Wmk. 140** *Perf. 14*
E1 SD1 25c rose red 10.50 *22.50*

## OFFICES IN AFRICA

40 Paras = 1 Piaster
100 Centesimi = 1 Lira (1910)

**BENGASI**

Italy No. 81 Surcharged in Black

**1901** **Wmk. 140** *Perf. 14*
1 A45 1pi on 25c dp bl 60.00 *150.00*

Same Surcharge on Italy No. 100

**1911**
1A A49 1pi on 25c blue 60.00 *150.00*

**TRIPOLI**

Italian Stamps of 1901-09 Overprinted in Black or Violet

**1909** **Wmk. 140**
2 A42 1c brown 4.50 3.00
a. Inverted overprint 260.00
3 A43 2c orange brn 2.25 *3.00*
4 A48 5c green 160.00 9.00
a. Double overprint 300.00
5 A48 10c claret 3.00 3.00
a. Double overprint 210.00 *210.00*
6 A49 25c blue 2.25 *3.00*
7 A49 40c brown 7.50 7.50
8 A49 50c violet 9.00 9.00

*Perf. 13½x14*
**Unwmk.**
9 A50 15c slate blk (V) 4.50 4.50
*Nos. 2-9 (8)* 193.00 *42.00*

Italian Stamps of 1901 Overprinted

**1909** **Wmk. 140** *Perf. 14*
10 A46 1 l brown & grn 135.00 97.50
11 A46 5 l blue & rose 45.00 290.00

**Same Overprint on Italy Nos. 76-77**

**1915**
12 A42 1c brown 3.25
13 A43 2c orange brown 3.25

Nos. 12-13 were prepared but not issued. No. 12 exists as a pair, one without overprint, value $2,250 hinged, $3,500 never hinged. No. 12 also exists with inverted overprint.

### SPECIAL DELIVERY STAMPS

Italy Nos. E1, E6 Ovptd. Like Nos. 10-11

**1909** **Wmk. 140** *Perf. 14*
E1 SD1 25c rose red 18.00 11.00
E2 SD2 30c blue & rose 6.00 *15.00*

Tripoli was ceded by Turkey to Italy in Oct., 1912, and became known as the Colony of Libia. Later issues will be found under Libya.

## OFFICES IN TURKISH EMPIRE

40 Paras = 1 Piaster

Various powers maintained post offices in the Turkish Empire before World War I by authority of treaties which ended with the signing of the Treaty of Lausanne in 1923. The foreign post offices were closed Oct. 27, 1923.

**GENERAL ISSUE**

Italian Stamps of 1906-08 Surcharged

**Printed at Turin**

**1908** **Wmk. 140**
1 A48 10pa on 5c green 7.50 4.50
2 A48 20pa on 10c claret 7.50 4.50
3 A49 40pa on 25c blue 2.25 2.25
4 A49 80pa on 50c violet 6.00 4.50

See Janina Nos. 1-4.

Surcharged in Violet

**Unwmk.**
5 A47 30pa on 15c slate 2.25 2.25
*Nos. 1-5 (5)* 25.50 18.00

Nos. 1, 2, 3 and 5 were first issued in Janina, Albania, and subsequently for general use. They can only be distinguished by the cancellations.

**Italian Stamps of 1901-08 Surcharged**

Nos. 6-8

No. 9

Nos. 10-12

**Printed at Constantinople**

**1908** **First Printing**
6 A48 10pa on 5c green 325.00 400.00
a. Vert. pair, one without surcharge 3,350.
7 A48 20pa on 10c claret 325.00 400.00
8 A47 30pa on 15c slate 1,000. *1,225.*
9 A49 1pi on 25c blue 1,000. *1,225.*
a. "PIASTRE" 1,800. 1,800.
10 A49 2pi on 50c violet 2,800. *3,350.*
11 A46 4pi on 1 l brn & grn *16,500. 10,000.*
12 A46 20pi on 5 l bl & rose *37,500. 30,000.*

On Nos. 8, 9 and 10 the surcharge is at the top of the stamp. No. 11 has the "4" closed at the top. No. 12 has the "20" wide.

**Second Printing**

Italian Stamps of 1901-08 Surcharged

Nos. 13-15

No. 16

Nos. 17-19

**13** A48 10pa on 5c green 34.00 *45.00*
**14** A48 20pa on 10c claret 34.00 *45.00*
**15** A47 30pa on 15c slate 135.00 *105.00*
*a.* Double surcharge 300.00 300.00
*b.* Triple surcharge 675.00 675.00
**16** A49 1pi on 25c blue 34.00 *45.00*
*a.* "PIPSTRA" 240.00 240.00
*b.* "1" omitted 240.00 240.00
**17** A49 2pi on 50c violet 210.00 210.00
*a.* Surcharged "20 PIASTRE" 2,250. 2,250.
*b.* "20" with "0" scratched out 750.00 750.00
*c.* "2" 5mm from "PIASTRE" 550.00 550.00
**18** A46 4pi on 1 l brn & grn 1,350. 1,350.
**19** A46 20pi on 5 l bl & rose 9,000. 4,800.
*Nos. 13-19 (7)* 10,797. 6,600.

On No. 18 the "4" is open at the top.

### Third Printing

Surcharged in Red

**20** A47 30pa on 15c slate 9.00 *9.00*
*a.* Double surcharge 225.00 225.00

### Fourth Printing

**20B** A46 4pi on 1 l brn & grn 60.00 90.00
*c.* Inverted "S" 190.00 190.00
**20D** A46 20pi on 5 l bl & rose 190.00 *225.00*
*i.* Inverted "S" 525.00 525.00

### Fifth Printing

**20E** A46 4pi on 1 l brn & grn 52.50 67.50
*f.* Surch. "20 PIASTRE" 2,600.
**20G** A46 20pi on 5 l bl & rose 52.50 67.50
*h.* Double surcharge 1,500. 1,500.

Italian Stamps of 1906-19 Surcharged

**1921**
**21** A48 1pi on 5c green 300.00 *400.00*
**22** A48 2pi on 15c slate 6.00 *9.00*
**23** A50 4pi on 20c brn org (No. 113) 67.50 *82.50*
**24** A49 5pi on 25c blue 67.50 *82.50*
*a.* Double surcharge 300.00
**25** A49 10pi on 60c carmine 3.75 *6.00*
*Nos. 21-25 (5)* 444.75 *580.00*

No. 21 is almost always found poorly centered, and it is valued thus.

On No. 25 the "10" is placed above "PIASTRE."

### Italian Stamps of 1901-19 Surcharged

n

o

**1922**
**26** A42(n) 10pa on 1c brown 2.25 *2.60*
**27** A43(n) 20pa on 2c org brn 2.25 *2.60*
**28** A48(n) 30pa on 5c green 6.00 *6.00*
**29** A48(o) 1pi20pa on 15c slate 6.75 *2.60*
**30** A50(n) 3pi on 20c brn org (#113) 9.00 *16.50*
**31** A49(o) 3pi30pa on 25c blue 4.50 *2.60*
**32** A49(o) 7pi20pa on 60c carmine 9.00 *6.00*
**33** A46(n) 15pi on 1 l brn & grn 26.00 *45.00*
*Nos. 26-33 (8)* 65.75 *83.90*

On No. 32, the distance between the two lines is 2mm. See note after No. 58A.

Italy No. 100 Surcharged

**34** A49 3.75pi on 25c blue 2.25 2.60

### Italian Stamps of 1901-20 Surcharged

q

r

**1922**
**35** A48 30pi on 5c green 3.75 *16.50*
**36** A49 1.50pi on 25c blue 2.25 *9.00*
**37** A49 3.75pi on 40c brown 3.00 *10.50*
*a.* Double surcharge 300.00
**38** A49 4.50pi on 50c violet 7.50 *22.50*
**39** A49 7.50pi on 60c carmine 6.00 *16.50*
*a.* Double surcharge 375.00
*b.* Pair, one without surcharge 1,650.
**40** A49 15pi on 85c red brn 11.00 *37.50*
**41** A46 18.75pi on 1 l brn & grn 5.25 *30.00*

On No. 40 the numerals of the surcharge are above "PIASTRE."

Italian Stamps of 1901-20 Surcharged

**42** A46 45pa on 5 l bl & rose 400.00 *675.00*
**43** A51 90pa on 10 l gray grn & red 450.00 *825.00*

On No. 42 the figure "4" is open at top. See note after No. 61.

On No. 43 the figure "9" has a curved or arched bottom. See note after No. 62.

Italian Stamps of 1901-17 Surcharged Type "q" or:

**44** A43 30pa on 2c org brn 2.25 *6.00*
**45** A50 1.50pi on 20c brn org (#113) 2.25 *6.00*
*Nos. 35-45 (11)* 893.25 *1,654.*

Italian Stamps of 1901-20 Surcharged in Black or Red

**46** A48 30pa on 5c green 2.25 *3.75*
**47** A48 1½pi on 10c claret 2.25 *3.75*
**48** A49 3pi on 25c blue 19.00 7.50
**49** A49 3¾pi on 40c brown 3.75 *3.75*
**50** A49 4½pi on 50c violet 45.00 40.00
**51** A49 7½pi on 85c red brn 9.00 *11.00*
*a.* "PIASIRE" 45.00 *45.00*
**52** A46 7½pi on 1 l brn & grn (R) 11.00 *13.50*
*a.* Double surcharge 160.00
*b.* "PIASIRE" 52.50 *52.50*
**53** A46 15pi on 1 l brn & grn 67.50 *160.00*
**54** A46 45pi on 5 l blue & rose 100.00 *100.00*
**55** A51 90pi on 10 l gray grn & red 82.50 *190.00*
*Nos. 46-55 (10)* 342.25 *533.25*

### Italian Stamps of 1901-20 Surcharged Type "o" or

No. 58

No. 59

Nos. 61-62

**1923**
**56** A49 1pi20pa on 25c blue 13.50
**57** A49 3pi30pa on 40c brown 13.50
**58** A49 4pi20pa on 50c violet 13.50
**58A** A49 7pi20pa on 60c car 37.50
**59** A49 15pi on 85c red brn 13.50
**60** A46 18pi30pa on 1 l brn & grn 13.50
*a.* Double surcharge *300.00*
**61** A46 45pi on 5 l bl & rose 37.50
**62** A51 90pi on 10 l gray grn & red 34.00
*Nos. 56-62 (8)* 176.50

On No. 58A the distance between the lines is 1.5mm. On No. 61 the figure "4" is closed at top. On No. 62 the figure "9" is nearly rectilinear at bottom.

Nos. 56-62 were not issued.

---

## SPECIAL DELIVERY STAMPS

Italian Special Delivery Stamps Surcharged

**1908** **Wmk. 140** ***Perf. 14***
**E1** SD1 1pi on 25c rose red 3.00 *4.50*

Surcharged

**1910**
**E2** SD2 60pa on 30c blue & rose 6.00 *7.50*

Surcharged

**1922**
**E3** SD2 15pi on 1.20 l on 30c bl & rose 32.50 *82.50*

On No. E3, lines obliterate the first two denominations.

Surcharged

**1922**
**E4** SD2 15pi on 30c bl & rose 475.00 *975.00*

Surcharged

**1923**
**E5** SD2 15pi on 1.20 l blue & red 15.00

No. E5 was not regularly issued.

---

## ALBANIA

Stamps of Italy Surcharged in Black

**1902** **Wmk. 140** ***Perf. 14***
**1** A44 10pa on 5c green 4.50 2.25
**2** A45 35pa on 20c orange 6.75 7.50
**3** A45 40pa on 25c blue 13.50 7.50
*Nos. 1-3 (3)* 24.75 17.25

Nos. 1-3 with red surcharges are proofs.

**1907**
**4** A48 10pa on 5c green 52.50 *60.00*
**5** A48 20pa on 10c claret 34.00 *26.00*
**6** A45 80pa on 50c violet 34.00 *26.00*
*Nos. 4-6 (3)* 120.50 *112.00*

No. 5 is almost always found poorly centered, and it is valued thus.

---

## CONSTANTINOPLE

Stamps of Italy Surcharged in Black or Violet

**Wmk. 140, Unwmk. (#3)**

**1909-11** *Perf. 14, 12*

| | | | |
|---|---|---|---|
| **1** | A48 10pa on 5c green | 2.25 | *2.25* |
| **2** | A48 20pa on 10c claret | 2.25 | *2.25* |
| **3** | A47 30pa on 15c slate (V) | 2.25 | *2.25* |
| **4** | A49 1pi on 25c blue | 2.25 | *2.25* |
| *a.* | Double surcharge | 195.00 | *195.00* |
| **5** | A49 2pi on 50c violet | 4.50 | *3.00* |

Surcharged

| | | | |
|---|---|---|---|
| **6** | A46 4pi on 1 l brn & grn | 4.50 | 3.75 |
| **7** | A46 20pi on 5 l bl & rose | 67.50 | 67.50 |
| **8** | A51 40pi on 10 l gray grn & red | 7.50 | *30.00* |
| | *Nos. 1-8 (8)* | 93.00 | *113.25* |

**Italian Stamps of 1901-19 Surcharged**

Nos. 10, 12-13

Nos. 9, 11

**1922**

| | | | |
|---|---|---|---|
| **9** | A48 20pa on 5c green | 19.00 | *30.00* |
| **10** | A48 1pi20pa on 15c slate | 2.25 | 2.25 |
| **11** | A49 3pi on 30c org brn | 2.25 | 2.25 |
| **12** | A49 3pi30pa on 40c brown | 2.25 | 2.25 |
| **13** | A46 7pi20pa on 1 l brn & grn | 2.25 | 2.25 |
| | *Nos. 9-13 (5)* | 28.00 | 39.00 |

Italian Stamps of 1901-20 Surcharged

**1923**

| | | | |
|---|---|---|---|
| **14** | A48 30pa on 5c green | 3.00 | 2.25 |
| **15** | A49 1pi20pa on 25c blue | 3.00 | 2.25 |
| **16** | A49 3pi30pa on 40c brown | 3.00 | 1.90 |
| **17** | A49 4pi20pa on 50c violet | 3.00 | 1.90 |
| **18** | A49 7pi20pa on 60c car | 3.00 | 1.90 |
| **19** | A49 15pi on 85c red brn | 3.00 | 3.00 |
| **20** | A46 18pi30pa on 1 l brn & grn | 3.00 | 3.00 |
| **21** | A46 45pi on 5 l bl & rose | 3.00 | *6.75* |
| **22** | A51 90pi on 10 l gray grn & red | 3.00 | *7.50* |
| | *Nos. 14-22 (9)* | 27.00 | 30.45 |

## CONSTANTINOPLE SPECIAL DELIVERY STAMP

Unissued Italian Special Delivery Stamp of 1922 Surcharged in Black

**1923** **Wmk. 140** *Perf. 14*

| | | | |
|---|---|---|---|
| **E1** | SD2 15pi on 1.20 l bl & red | 7.50 | *40.00* |

## CONSTANTINOPLE POSTAGE DUE STAMPS

Italian Postage Due Stamps of 1870-1903 Overprinted

**1922** **Wmk. 140** *Perf. 14*

| | | | |
|---|---|---|---|
| **J1** | D3 10c buff & mag | 75.00 | *105.00* |
| **J2** | D3 30c buff & mag | 75.00 | *105.00* |
| **J3** | D3 60c buff & mag | 75.00 | *105.00* |
| **J4** | D3 1 l blue & mag | 75.00 | *105.00* |
| **J5** | D3 2 l blue & mag | 1,800. | *3,000.* |
| **J6** | D3 5 l blue & mag | 825.00 | *1,125.* |
| | *Nos. J1-J6 (6)* | 2,925. | *4,545.* |

A circular control mark with the inscription "Poste Italiane Constantinopoli" and with the arms of the Kingdom of Italy (Savoy Cross) in the center was applied to each block of four of these stamps in black. Value, set of 6 blocks of four with control marks, $18,500.

## DURAZZO

Stamps of Italy Surcharged in Black or Violet

**Wmk. 140, Unwmk. (#3)**

**1909-11** *Perf. 14, 12*

| | | | |
|---|---|---|---|
| **1** | A48 10pa on 5c green | 1.50 | *3.00* |
| **2** | A48 20pa on 10c claret | 1.50 | *3.00* |
| **3** | A47 30pa on 15c slate (V) | 75.00 | 3.75 |
| **4** | A49 1pi on 25c blue | 2.25 | *3.75* |
| **5** | A49 2pi on 50c violet | 2.25 | *3.75* |

Surcharged

| | | | |
|---|---|---|---|
| **6** | A46 4pi on 1 l brn & grn | 3.75 | *4.50* |
| **7** | A46 20pi on 5 l bl & rose | 315.00 | 260.00 |
| **8** | A51 40pi on 10 l gray grn & red | 19.00 | *130.00* |
| | *Nos. 1-8 (8)* | 420.25 | 411.75 |

No. 3 Surcharged

**1916** **Unwmk.** *Perf. 12*

| | | | |
|---|---|---|---|
| **9** | A47 20c on 30pa on 15c slate | 4.75 | *19.00* |

## JANINA

Stamps of Italy Surcharged

**1902-07** **Wmk. 140** *Perf. 14*

| | | | |
|---|---|---|---|
| **1** | A44 10pa on 5c green | 10.50 | 3.75 |
| **2** | A45 35pa on 20c orange | 7.50 | *4.75* |
| **3** | A45 40pa on 25c blue | 37.50 | 12.00 |
| **4** | A45 80pa on 50c vio ('07) | 62.50 | *45.00* |
| | *Nos. 1-4 (4)* | 118.00 | *65.50* |

Surcharged in Black or Violet

**Wmk. 140, Unwmk. (#7)**

**1909-11** *Perf. 14, 12*

| | | | |
|---|---|---|---|
| **5** | A48 10pa on 5c green | 1.50 | *3.00* |
| **6** | A48 20pa on 10c claret | 1.50 | *3.00* |
| **7** | A47 30pa on 15c slate (V) | 1.50 | *3.00* |
| **8** | A49 1pi on 25c blue | 1.50 | *3.00* |
| **9** | A49 2pi on 50c violet | 1.50 | *3.75* |

Surcharged

| | | | |
|---|---|---|---|
| **10** | A46 4pi on 1 l brn & grn | 3.75 | *4.50* |
| **11** | A46 20pi on 5 l bl & rose | 350.00 | 400.00 |
| **12** | A51 40pi on 10 l gray grn & red | 19.00 | *110.00* |
| | *Nos. 5-12 (8)* | 380.25 | 530.25 |

## JERUSALEM

Stamps of Italy Surcharged in Black or Violet

**Wmk. 140, Unwmk. (#3)**

**1909-11** *Perf. 14, 12*

| | | | |
|---|---|---|---|
| **1** | A48 10pa on 5c green | 7.50 | *19.00* |
| **2** | A48 20pa on 10c claret | 7.50 | *19.00* |
| **3** | A47 30pa on 15c slate (V) | 7.50 | *26.00* |
| **4** | A49 1pi on 25c blue | 7.50 | *19.00* |
| **5** | A49 2pi on 50c violet | 26.00 | *60.00* |

Surcharged

| | | | |
|---|---|---|---|
| **6** | A46 4pi on 1 l brn & grn | 34.00 | *82.50* |
| **7** | A46 20pi on 5 l bl & rose | 1,200. | *1,300.* |
| **8** | A51 40pi on 10 l gray grn & red | 45.00 | *550.00* |
| | *Nos. 1-8 (8)* | 1,335. | *2,075.* |

Forged cancellations exist on Nos. 1-8.

## SALONIKA

Stamps of Italy Surcharged in Black or Violet

**Wmk. 140, Unwmk. (#3)**

**1909-11** *Perf. 14, 12*

| | | | |
|---|---|---|---|
| **1** | A48 10pa on 5c green | 1.50 | *3.00* |
| **2** | A48 20pa on 10c claret | 1.50 | *3.00* |
| **3** | A47 30pa on 15c slate (V) | 2.25 | *3.00* |
| **4** | A49 1pi on 25c blue | 2.25 | *3.00* |
| **5** | A49 2pi on 50c violet | 2.25 | *3.75* |

Surcharged

| | | | |
|---|---|---|---|
| **6** | A46 4pi on 1 l brn & grn | 3.75 | *4.50* |
| **7** | A46 20pi on 5 l bl & rose | 525.00 | 700.00 |
| **8** | A51 40pi on 10 l gray grn & red | 19.00 | *120.00* |
| | *Nos. 1-8 (8)* | 557.50 | 840.25 |

## SCUTARI

Stamps of Italy Surcharged in Black or Violet

**Wmk. 140, Unwmk. (#3)**

**1909-11** *Perf. 14, 12*

| | | | |
|---|---|---|---|
| **1** | A48 10pa on 5c green | 1.50 | *3.00* |
| **2** | A48 20pa on 10c claret | 1.50 | *3.00* |
| **3** | A47 30pa on 15c slate (V) | 26.00 | 6.00 |
| **4** | A49 1pi on 25c blue | 1.50 | *3.00* |
| **5** | A49 2pi on 50c violet | 1.50 | *4.50* |

Surcharged

| | | | |
|---|---|---|---|
| **6** | A46 4pi on 1 l brn & grn | 3.00 | *4.50* |
| **7** | A46 20pi on 5 l bl & rose | 34.00 | *52.50* |
| **8** | A51 40pi on 10 l gray grn & red | 70.00 | *165.00* |
| | *Nos. 1-8 (8)* | 139.00 | *241.50* |

**Surcharged like Nos. 1-5**

**1915**

| | | | |
|---|---|---|---|
| **9** | A43 4pa on 2c orange brn | 2.25 | *5.25* |

No. 3 Surcharged

**1916** **Unwmk.** *Perf. 12*

| | | | |
|---|---|---|---|
| **10** | A47 20c on 30pa on 15c slate | 6.00 | *26.00* |

## SMYRNA

Stamps of Italy Surcharged in Black or Violet

**Wmk. 140, Unwmk. (#3)**

**1909-11** *Perf. 14, 12*

| | | | |
|---|---|---|---|
| **1** | A48 10pa on 5c green | 1.50 | 1.50 |
| **2** | A48 20pa on 10c claret | 1.50 | 1.50 |
| **3** | A47 30pa on 15c slate (V) | 3.00 | *4.50* |
| **4** | A49 1pi on 25c blue | 3.00 | *4.50* |
| **5** | A49 2pi on 50c violet | 3.75 | *6.00* |

Surcharged

| | | | |
|---|---|---|---|
| **6** | A46 4pi on 1 l brn & grn | 4.50 | *7.50* |
| **7** | A46 20pi on 5 l bl & rose | 180.00 | 225.00 |
| **8** | A51 40pi on 10 l gray grn & red | 19.00 | *110.00* |
| | *Nos. 1-8 (8)* | 216.25 | *360.50* |

**Italian Stamps of 1901-22 Surcharged**

Nos. 10, 12-13

Nos. 9, 11

**1922**

| | | | |
|---|---|---|---|
| **9** | A48 20pa on 5c green | 30.00 | |
| **10** | A48 1pi20pa on 15c slate | 1.50 | |
| **11** | A49 3pi on 30c org brn | 1.50 | |

**12** A49 3pi30pa on 40c brown 3.75
**13** A46 7pi20pa on 1 l brn & grn 3.75
*Nos. 9-13 (5)* 40.50

Nos. 9-13 were not issued.

### VALONA

Stamps of Italy Surcharged in Black or Violet

**Wmk. 140, Unwmk. (#3)**

**1909-11** ***Perf. 14, 12***

**1** A48 10pa on 5c green 1.50 *3.25*
**2** A48 20pa on 10c claret 1.50 *3.00*
**3** A47 30pa on 15c slate (V) 19.00 6.00
**4** A49 1pi on 25c blue 2.25 *3.00*
**5** A49 2pi on 50c violet 2.25 *3.75*

Surcharged

**6** A46 4pi on 1 l brn & grn 2.25 *3.75*
**7** A46 20pi on 5 l bl & rose 52.50 60.00
**8** A51 40pi on 10 l gray grn & red 60.00 *165.00*
*Nos. 1-8 (8)* 141.25 *247.75*

Italy No. 123 Surcharged in Violet or Red Violet

**1916**

**9** A58 30pa on 15c slate (V) 4.75 *13.50*
*a.* Red violet surcharge 10.50 *30.00*

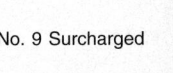

No. 9 Surcharged

**10** A58 20c on 30pa on 15c slate 2.25 *19.00*

# AEGEAN ISLANDS

## (Dodecanese)

A group of islands in the Aegean Sea off the coast of Turkey. They were occupied by Italy during the Tripoli War and were ceded to Italy by Turkey in 1924 by the Treaty of Lausanne. Stamps of Italy overprinted with the name of the island were in use at the post offices maintained in the various islands.

Rhodes, on the island of the same name, was capital of the entire group.

100 Centesimi = 1 Lira

### GENERAL ISSUE

Italian Stamps of 1907-08 Overprinted

**1912** **Wmk. 140** ***Perf. 14***

**1** A49 25c blue 52.50 *34.00*
*a.* Inverted overprint 275.00 *275.00*
**2** A49 50c violet 52.50 *34.00*
*a.* Inverted overprint 275.00 *275.00*

### Virgil Issue

Italian Stamps of 1930 Ovptd. in Red or Blue

**1930** **Photo.** **Wmk. 140** ***Perf. 14***

**3** A106 15c vio blk 1.50 *19.00*
**4** A106 20c org brn 1.50 *19.00*
**5** A106 25c dk green 1.50 *9.00*
**6** A106 30c lt brown 1.50 *9.00*
**7** A106 50c dull vio 1.50 *9.00*
**8** A106 75c rose red 1.50 *19.00*
**9** A106 1.25 l gray bl 1.50 *26.00*

**Engr.**

**Unwmk.**

**10** A106 5 l + 1.50 l dk vio 4.50 *47.50*
**11** A106 10 l + 2.50 l ol brn 4.50 *47.50*
*Nos. 3-11,C4-C7 (13)* *33.00* 402.50

### St. Anthony of Padua Issue

Italian Stamps of 1931 Ovptd. in Blue or Red

**1932** **Photo.** **Wmk. 140** ***Perf. 14***

**12** A116 20c black brn 30.00 26.00
**13** A116 25c dull grn 30.00 26.00
**14** A118 30c brown org 30.00 30.00
**15** A118 50c dull vio 30.00 22.50
**16** A120 1.25 l gray bl 30.00 34.00

**Engr.**

**Unwmk.**

**17** A121 75c lt red 30.00 *45.00*
**18** A122 5 l + 2.50 l dp org 30.00 *160.00*
*Nos. 12-18 (7)* 210.00 *343.50*

### Dante Alighieri Society Issue

Italian Stamps of 1932 Overprinted

**1932** **Photo.** **Wmk. 140**

**19** A126 10c grnsh gray 1.50 *7.50*
**20** A126 15c black vio 1.50 *7.50*
**21** A126 20c brown org 1.50 *7.50*
**22** A126 25c dp green 1.50 7.50
**23** A126 30c dp org 1.50 *7.50*
**24** A126 50c dull vio 1.50 3.75
**25** A126 75c rose red 1.50 *10.50*
**26** A126 1.25 l blue 1.50 *9.00*
**27** A126 1.75 l ol brn 3.00 *10.50*
**28** A126 2.75 l car rose 3.00 *10.50*
**29** A126 5 l + 2 l dp vio 3.00 *24.00*
**30** A126 10 l + 2.50 l dk brn 3.00 *40.00*
*Nos. 19-30 (12)* 24.00 *145.75*

See Nos. C8-C14.

### Soccer Issue

Types of Italy, "Soccer" Issue, Overprinted in Black or Red

**1934**

**31** A173 20c brn rose (Bk) 82.50 97.50
**32** A174 25c green (R) 82.50 97.50
**33** A174 50c violet (R) 300.00 75.00
**34** A174 1.25 l gray bl (R) 82.50 *175.00*
**35** A175 5 l +2.50 l bl (R) 82.50 *400.00*
*Nos. 31-35 (5)* 630.00 *845.00*

See Nos. C28-C31.

Same Overprint on Types of Medal of Valor Issue of Italy, in Red or Black

**1935**

**36** A177 10c sl gray (R) 45.00 *90.00*
**37** A178 15c brn (Bk) 45.00 *90.00*
**38** A178 20c red org (Bk) 45.00 *90.00*
**39** A177 25c dp grn (R) 45.00 *90.00*
**40** A178 30c lake (Bk) 45.00 *90.00*
**41** A178 50c ol grn (Bk) 45.00 *90.00*
**42** A178 75c rose red (Bk) 45.00 *90.00*
**43** A178 1.25 l dp bl (R) 45.00 *90.00*
**44** A177 1.75 l + 1 l pur (R) 45.00 *90.00*
**45** A178 2.55 l + 2 l dk car (Bk) 45.00 *90.00*
**46** A178 2.75 l + 2 l org brn (Bk) 45.00 *90.00*
*Nos. 36-46 (11)* 495.00 *990.00*

See Nos. C32-C38, CE3-CE4.

Types of Italy, 1937, Overprinted in Blue or Red

**1938** **Wmk. 140** ***Perf. 14***

**47** A208 10c dk brn (Bl) 3.75 9.00
**48** A208 15c pur (R) 3.75 9.00
**49** A208 20c yel bis (Bl) 3.75 9.00
**50** A208 25c myr grn (R) 3.75 9.00
**51** A208 30c dp cl (Bl) 3.75 9.00
**52** A208 50c sl grn (R) 3.75 15.00
**53** A208 75c rose red (Bl) 3.75 15.00
**54** A208 1.25 l dk bl (R) 3.75 15.00
**55** A208 1.75 l + 1 l dp org (Bl) 6.00 *28.00*
**56** A208 2.55 l + 2 l ol brn (R) 6.00 *28.00*
*Nos. 47-56 (10)* 42.00 146.00

Bimillenary of birth of Augustus Caesar (Octavianus), first Roman emperor.

See Nos. C39-C43.

Same Overprint of Type of Italy, 1937, in Red

**1938**

**57** A222 1.25 l deep blue 1.50 *2.25*
**58** A222 2.75 l + 2 l brown 1.75 *9.00*

600th anniversary of the death of Giotto di Bondone, Italian painter.

Statue of Roman Wolf — A1

Arms of Rhodes — A2

Dante's House, Rhodes A3

**1940** **Photo.**

**59** A1 5c lt brown .75 1.10
**60** A2 10c pale org .75 1.10
**61** A3 25c blue grn 1.50 1.90
**62** A1 50c rose vio 1.50 1.90
**63** A2 75c dull ver 1.50 3.75
**64** A3 1.25 l dull blue 1.50 3.75
**65** A2 2 l + 75c rose 1.50 26.00
*Nos. 59-65,C44-C47 (11)* 18.00 79.00

Triennial Overseas Exposition, Naples.

### AIR POST STAMPS

**Ferrucci Issue**

Types of Italian Air Post Stamps of 1930 Overprinted in Blue or Red Like Nos. 12-18

**1930** **Wmk. 140** ***Perf. 14***

**C1** A104 50c brn vio (Bl) 10.50 *22.50*
**C2** A104 1 l dk bl (R) 10.50 *22.50*
**C3** A104 5 l + 2 l dp car (Bl) 19.00 *62.50*
*Nos. C1-C3 (3)* 40.00 *107.50*

Nos. C1-C3 were sold at Rhodes only.

**Virgil Issue**

Types of Italian Air Post Stamps of 1930 Overprinted in Red or Blue Like Nos. 3-11

**1930** **Photo.**

**C4** A106 50c dp grn (R) 2.25 *37.50*
**C5** A106 1 l rose red (Bl) 2.25 *37.50*

**Engr.**

**Unwmk.**

**C6** A106 7.70 l + 1.30 l dk brn (R) 4.50 *47.50*
**C7** A106 9 l + 2 l gray (R) 4.50 *75.00*
*Nos. C4-C7 (4)* 13.50 *197.50*

**Dante Alighieri Society Issue**

Types of Italian Air Post Stamps of 1932 Overprinted Like Nos. 19-30

**1932** **Wmk. 140**

**C8** AP10 50c car rose 1.50 *6.00*
**C9** AP11 1 l dp grn 1.50 *6.00*
**C10** AP11 3 l dl vio 1.50 *9.00*
**C11** AP11 5 l dp org 1.50 *9.00*
**C12** AP10 7.70 l + 2 l ol brn 4.50 *21.00*
**C13** AP11 10 l + 2.50 l dk bl 4.50 *28.00*
*Nos. C8-C13 (6)* 15.00 *79.00*

Leonardo da Vinci — AP12

**1932** **Photo.** ***Perf. 14½***

**C14** AP12 100 l dp bl & grnsh gray 19.00 *135.00*

Garibaldi Types of Italian Air Post Stamps of 1932 Overprinted in Red or Blue

**1932**

**C15** AP13 50c deep green 52.50 *125.00*
**C16** AP14 80c copper red 52.50 *125.00*
**C17** AP13 1 l + 25c dl bl 52.50 *125.00*
**C18** AP13 2 l + 50c red brn 52.50 *125.00*
**C19** AP14 5 l + 1 l bluish sl 52.50 *125.00*
*Nos. C15-C19 (5)* 262.50 *625.00*

See Nos. CE1-CE2.

Graf Zeppelin over Rhodes AP17

**1933** ***Perf. 14***

**C20** AP17 3 l olive brn 82.50 *225.00*
**C21** AP17 5 l dp vio 82.50 *260.00*
**C22** AP17 10 l dk green 82.50 *400.00*
**C23** AP17 12 l dk blue 82.50 *450.00*
**C24** AP17 15 l car rose 82.50 *450.00*
**C25** AP17 20 l gray blk 82.50 *450.00*
*Nos. C20-C25 (6)* 495.00 *2,235.*

**Balbo Flight Issue**

Italian Air Post Stamps of 1933 Ovptd.

**1933 Wmk. 140 *Perf. 14***

**C26** AP25 5.25 l + 19.75 l grn, red & bl gray 55.00 *155.00*
**C27** AP25 5.25 l + 44.75 l red, grn & bl gray 55.00 *155.00*

**Soccer Issue**

Types of Italian Air Post Stamps of 1934 Overprinted in Black or Red Like #31-35

**1934**

**C28** AP32 50c brown (R) 19.00 *75.00*
**C29** AP33 75c rose red) 19.00 *75.00*
**C30** AP34 5 l + 2.50 l red org 30.00 *150.00*
**C31** AP35 10 l + 5 l grn (R) 30.00 *175.00*
*Nos. C28-C31 (4)* 98.00 *475.00*

Types of Medal of Valor Issue of Italy Overprinted in Red or Black Like #31-35

**1935**

**C32** AP36 25c dp grn 62.50 *110.00*
**C33** AP36 50c blk brn (R) 62.50 *110.00*
**C34** AP36 75c rose 62.50 *110.00*
**C35** AP36 80c dk brn 62.50 *110.00*
**C36** AP36 1 l + 50c ol grn 45.00 *110.00*
**C37** AP36 2 l + 1 l dp bl (R) 45.00 *110.00*
**C38** AP40 3 l + 2 l vio (R) 45.00 *110.00*
*Nos. C32-C38 (7)* 385.00 *770.00*

Types of Italy Air Post Stamps, 1937, Overprinted in Blue or Red Like #47-56

**1938 Wmk. 140 *Perf. 14***

**C39** AP51 25c dl gray vio (R) 4.50 9.00
**C40** AP51 50c grn (R) 4.50 9.00
**C41** AP51 80c brt bl (R) 4.50 28.00
**C42** AP51 1 l + 1 l rose lake 9.00 28.00
**C43** AP51 5 l + 1 l rose red 12.00 *55.00*
*Nos. C39-C43 (5)* 34.50 129.00

Bimillenary of the birth of Augustus Caesar (Octavianus).

Statues of Stag and Roman Wolf AP18

Plane over Government Palace, Rhodes — AP19

**1940 Photo.**

**C44** AP18 50c olive blk 2.25 3.75
**C45** AP19 1 l dk vio 2.25 3.75
**C46** AP18 2 l + 75c dk bl 2.25 11.00
**C47** AP19 5 l + 2.50 l cop brn 2.25 21.00
*Nos. C44-C47 (4)* 9.00 39.50

Triennial Overseas Exposition, Naples.

**AIR POST SPECIAL DELIVERY STAMPS**

Type of Italian Garibaldi Air Post Special Delivery Stamps Overprinted in Blue or Ocher Like Nos. 12-18

**1932 Wmk. 140 *Perf. 14***

**CE1** APSD1 2.25 l + 1 l bl & rose & (Bl) 82.50 *225.00*
**CE2** APSD1 4.50 l + 1.50 l ocher & gray (O) 82.50 *225.00*

Type of Medal of Valor Issue of Italy, Ovptd. in Black

**1935**

**CE3** APSD4 2 l + 1.25 l dp bl 45.00 *110.00*
**CE4** APSD4 4.50 l + 2 l grn 45.00 *110.00*

**ISSUES FOR THE INDIVIDUAL ISLANDS**

Italian Stamps of 1901-20 Overprinted with Names of Various Islands as

a

b

c

The 1912-22 issues of each island have type "a" overprint in black on all values except 15c (type A58) and 20c on 15c, which have type "b" overprint in violet.

The 1930-32 Ferruci and Garibaldi issues are types of the Italian issues overprinted type "c."

**CALCHI**

Overprinted "Karki" in Black or Violet

**1912-22 Wmk. 140 *Perf. 13½, 14***

1 A43 2c orange brn 7.50 7.50
*a.* Double overprint 325.00 *550.00*
2 A48 5c green 4.50 *7.50*
3 A48 10c claret 1.50 *7.50*
4 A48 15c slate ('22) 3.75 *40.00*
*a.* Double overprint 325.00
5 A50 20c brn org ('21) 3.75 *37.50*
6 A49 25c blue 1.50 *7.50*
7 A49 40c brown 1.50 *7.50*
8 A49 50c violet 1.50 *16.00*

**Unwmk.**

9 A58 15c slate (V) 37.50 16.00
10 A50 20c brn org ('17) 120.00 *150.00*
*Nos. 1-10 (10)* 183.00 *297.00*

No. 9 Surcharged

**1916 *Perf. 13½***

11 A58 20c on 15c slate 2.25 *26.00*

**Ferrucci Issue**

Types of Italy

Overprinted in Red or Blue

**1930 Wmk. 140 *Perf. 14***

12 A102 20c vio (R) 3.75 *9.00*
13 A103 25c dk grn (R) 3.75 *9.00*
14 A103 50c blk (R) 3.75 *15.00*
15 A103 1.25 l dp bl (R) 3.75 *15.00*
16 A104 5 l + 2 l dp car (Bl) 10.50 *25.00*
*Nos. 12-16 (5)* 25.50 *73.00*

**Garibaldi Issue**

Types of Italy

Overprinted "CARCHI" in Red or Blue

**1932**

17 A138 10c brown 18.00 *34.00*
18 A138 20c red brn (Bl) 18.00 *34.00*
19 A138 25c dp grn 18.00 *34.00*
20 A138 30c bluish sl 18.00 *34.00*
21 A138 50c red vio (Bl) 18.00 *34.00*
22 A141 75c cop red (Bl) 18.00 *34.00*
23 A141 1.25 l dl bl 18.00 *34.00*
24 A141 1.75 l + 25c brn 18.00 *34.00*
25 A144 2.55 l + 50c org (Bl) 18.00 *34.00*
26 A145 5 l + 1 l dl vio 18.00 *34.00*
*Nos. 17-26 (10)* 180.00 *340.00*

**CALINO**

Overprinted "Calimno" in Black or Violet

**1912-21 Wmk. 140 *Perf. 13½, 14***

1 A43 2c orange brn 7.50 7.50
2 A48 5c green 3.00 *7.50*
3 A48 10c claret 1.50 *7.50*
4 A48 15c slate ('21) 3.75 *45.00*
5 A50 20c brn org ('21) 3.75 *45.00*
6 A49 25c blue 7.50 *7.50*
7 A49 40c brown 1.50 *7.50*
8 A49 50c violet 1.50 *16.00*

**Unwmk.**

9 A58 15c slate (V) 32.50 16.00
10 A50 20c brn org ('17) 82.50 *190.00*
*Nos. 1-10 (10)* 145.00 *349.50*

No. 9 Surcharged Like Calchi No. 11

**1916 *Perf. 13½***

11 A58 20c on 15c slate 15.00 *30.00*

**Ferrucci Issue**

Types of Italy

Overprinted in Red or Blue

**1930 Wmk. 140 *Perf. 14***

12 A102 20c violet (R) 3.75 *9.00*
13 A103 25c dk green (R) 3.75 *9.00*
14 A103 50c black (R) 3.75 *15.00*
15 A103 1.25 l dp bl (R) 3.75 *15.00*
16 A104 5 l + 2 l dp car (Bl) 10.50 *25.00*
*Nos. 12-16 (5)* 25.50 *73.00*

**Garibaldi Issue**

Types of Italy

Overprinted in Red or Blue

**1932**

17 A138 10c brown 18.00 *34.00*
18 A138 20c red brn (Bl) 18.00 *34.00*
19 A138 25c dp grn 18.00 *34.00*
20 A138 30c bluish sl 18.00 *34.00*
21 A138 50c red vio (Bl) 18.00 *34.00*
22 A141 75c cop red (Bl) 18.00 *34.00*
23 A141 1.25 l dull blue 18.00 *34.00*
24 A141 1.75 l + 25c brn 18.00 *34.00*
25 A144 2.55 l + 50c org (Bl) 18.00 *34.00*
26 A145 5 l + 1 l dl vio 18.00 *34.00*
*Nos. 17-26 (10)* 180.00 *340.00*

**CASO**

Overprinted "Caso" in Black or Violet

**1912-21 Wmk. 140 *Perf. 13½, 14***

1 A43 2c orange brn 7.50 7.50
2 A48 5c green 4.50 *7.50*
3 A48 10c claret 1.50 *7.50*
4 A48 15c slate ('21) 3.75 *40.00*
5 A50 20c brn org ('20) 3.00 *30.00*
6 A49 25c blue 1.50 *7.50*
7 A49 40c brown 1.50 *7.50*
8 A49 50c violet 1.50 *16.00*

**Unwmk.**

9 A58 15c slate (V) 37.50 *16.00*
10 A50 20c brn org ('17) 120.00 *190.00*
*Nos. 1-10 (10)* 182.25 *329.50*

No. 9 Surcharged Like Calchi No. 11

**1916 *Perf. 13½***

11 A58 20c on 15c slate 1.50 *22.50*

**Ferrucci Issue**

Types of Italy

Overprinted in Red or Blue

**1930 Wmk. 140 *Perf. 14***

12 A102 20c violet (R) 3.75 *9.00*
13 A103 25c dk green (R) 3.75 *9.00*
14 A103 50c black (R) 3.75 *15.00*
15 A103 1.25 l dp bl (R) 3.75 *15.00*
16 A104 5 l + 2 l dp car (Bl) 10.50 *25.00*
*Nos. 12-16 (5)* 25.50 *73.00*

**Garibaldi Issue**

Types of Italy

Overprinted in Red or Blue

**1932**

17 A138 10c brown 18.00 *34.00*
18 A138 20c red brn (Bl) 18.00 *34.00*
19 A138 25c dp grn 18.00 *34.00*
20 A138 30c bluish sl 18.00 *34.00*
21 A138 50c red vio (Bl) 18.00 *34.00*
22 A141 75c cop red (Bl) 18.00 *34.00*
23 A141 1.25 l dull blue 18.00 *34.00*
24 A141 1.75 l + 25c brn 18.00 *34.00*
25 A144 2.55 l + 50c org (Bl) 18.00 *34.00*
26 A145 5 l + 1 l dl vio 18.00 *34.00*
*Nos. 17-26 (10)* 180.00 *340.00*

**COO**

**(Cos, Kos)**

Overprinted "Cos" in Black or Violet

**1912-22 Wmk. 140 *Perf. 13½, 14***

1 A43 2c orange brn 7.50 7.50
2 A48 5c green 8.25 7.50
3 A48 10c claret 4.50 *7.50*
4 A48 15c slate ('22) 3.75 *47.50*
5 A50 20c brn org ('21) 3.00 *30.00*
6 A49 25c blue 34.00 7.50
7 A49 40c brown 1.50 *7.50*
8 A49 50c violet 1.50 *16.00*

**Unwmk.**

9 A58 15c slate (V) 52.50 16.50
10 A50 20c brn org ('17) 52.50 *190.00*
*Nos. 1-10 (10)* 169.00 *337.50*

No. 9 Surcharged Like Calchi No. 11

**1916 *Perf. 13½***

11 A58 20c on 15c slate 15.00 *34.00*

**Ferrucci Issue**

Types of Italy

Overprinted in Red or Blue

**1930 Wmk. 140 *Perf. 14***

12 A102 20c violet (R) 3.75 *9.00*
13 A103 25c dk green (R) 3.75 *9.00*
14 A103 50c black (R) 3.75 *15.00*
15 A103 1.25 l dp bl (R) 3.75 *15.00*
16 A104 5 l + 2 l dp car (Bl) 10.50 25.00
*Nos. 12-16 (5)* 25.50 *73.00*

**Garibaldi Issue**

Types of Italy

Overprinted in Red or Blue

**1932**

17 A138 10c brown 18.00 *34.00*
18 A138 20c red brn (Bl) 18.00 *34.00*
19 A138 25c dp grn 18.00 *34.00*
20 A138 30c bluish sl 18.00 *34.00*
21 A138 50c red vio (Bl) 18.00 *34.00*
22 A141 75c cop red (Bl) 18.00 *34.00*
23 A141 1.25 l dull blue 18.00 *34.00*
24 A141 1.75 l + 25c brn 18.00 *34.00*
25 A144 2.55 l + 50c org (Bl) 18.00 *34.00*
26 A145 5 l + 1 l dl vio 18.00 *34.00*
*Nos. 17-26 (10)* 180.00 *340.00*

**LERO**

Overprinted "Leros" in Black or Violet

**1912-22 Wmk. 140 *Perf. 13½, 14***

1 A43 2c orange brn 9.00 7.50
2 A48 5c green 7.50 7.50
3 A48 10c claret 3.00 *7.50*
4 A48 15c slate ('22) 3.75 *34.00*
5 A50 20c brn org ('21) 150.00 100.00
6 A49 25c blue 60.00 7.50
7 A49 40c brown 4.50 *7.50*
8 A49 50c violet 1.50 *16.00*

**Unwmk.**

9 A58 15c slate (V) 75.00 16.00
10 A50 20c brn org ('17) 52.50 *190.00*
*Nos. 1-10 (10)* 366.75 *393.50*

No. 9 Surcharged Like Calchi No. 11

**1916 *Perf. 13½***

11 A58 20c on 15c slate 15.00 *34.00*

**Ferrucci Issue**

Types of Italy

Overprinted in Red or Blue

**1930 *Perf. 14***

12 A102 20c violet (R) 3.75 *9.00*
13 A103 25c dk green (R) 3.75 *9.00*
14 A103 50c black (R) 3.75 *15.00*
15 A103 1.25 l dp bl (R) 3.75 *15.00*
16 A104 5 l + 2 l dp car (Bl) 10.50 *25.00*
*Nos. 12-16 (5)* 25.50 *73.00*

**Garibaldi Issue**

Types of Italy

Overprinted in Red or Blue

**1932**

17 A138 10c brown 18.00 *34.00*
18 A138 20c red brn (Bl) 18.00 *34.00*
19 A138 25c dp grn 18.00 *34.00*

| | | | | |
|---|---|---|---|---|
| 20 | A138 | 30c bluish sl | 18.00 | *34.00* |
| 21 | A138 | 50c red vio (Bl) | 18.00 | *34.00* |
| 22 | A141 | 75c cop red (Bl) | 18.00 | *34.00* |
| 23 | A141 | 1.25 l dull blue | 18.00 | *34.00* |
| 24 | A141 | 1.75 l + 25c brn | 18.00 | *34.00* |
| 25 | A144 | 2.55 l + 50c org (Bl) | 18.00 | *34.00* |
| 26 | A145 | 5 l + 1 l dl vio | 18.00 | *34.00* |
| | | *Nos. 17-26 (10)* | 180.00 | *340.00* |

## LISSO

Overprinted "Lipso" in Black or Violet

**1912-22 Wmk. 140 *Perf. 13½, 14***

| | | | | |
|---|---|---|---|---|
| 1 | A43 | 2c orange brn | 7.50 | 7.50 |
| 2 | A48 | 5c green | 4.50 | *7.50* |
| 3 | A48 | 10c claret | 3.00 | *7.50* |
| 4 | A48 | 15c slate ('22) | 3.75 | *34.00* |
| 5 | A50 | 20c brn org ('21) | 3.75 | *40.00* |
| 6 | A49 | 25c blue | 1.50 | *7.50* |
| 7 | A49 | 40c brown | 3.00 | *7.50* |
| 8 | A49 | 50c violet | 1.50 | *16.00* |

**Unwmk.**

| | | | | |
|---|---|---|---|---|
| 9 | A58 | 15c slate (V) | 37.50 | 16.00 |
| 10 | A50 | 20c brn org ('17) | 82.50 | *190.00* |
| | | *Nos. 1-10 (10)* | 148.50 | *333.50* |

No. 9 Surcharged Like Calchi No. 11

**1916 *Perf. 13½***

| | | | | |
|---|---|---|---|---|
| 11 | A58 | 20c on 15c slate | 1.50 | *26.00* |

**Ferrucci Issue**

Types of Italy
Overprinted in Red or Blue

**1930 Wmk. 140 *Perf. 14***

| | | | | |
|---|---|---|---|---|
| 12 | A102 | 20c violet (R) | 3.75 | *9.00* |
| 13 | A103 | 25c dk green (R) | 3.75 | *9.00* |
| 14 | A103 | 50c black (R) | 3.75 | *15.00* |
| 15 | A103 | 1.25 l dp bl (R) | 3.75 | *15.00* |
| 16 | A104 | 5 l + 2 l dp car (Bl) | 10.50 | *25.00* |
| | | *Nos. 12-16 (5)* | 25.50 | *73.00* |

**Garibaldi Issue**

Types of Italy
Overprinted "LIPSO" in Red or Blue

**1932**

| | | | | |
|---|---|---|---|---|
| 17 | A138 | 10c brown | 18.00 | *34.00* |
| 18 | A138 | 20c red brn (Bl) | 18.00 | *34.00* |
| 19 | A138 | 25c dp grn | 18.00 | *34.00* |
| 20 | A138 | 30c bluish sl | 18.00 | *34.00* |
| 21 | A138 | 50c red vio (Bl) | 18.00 | *34.00* |
| 22 | A141 | 75c cop red (Bl) | 18.00 | *34.00* |
| 23 | A141 | 1.25 l dull blue | 18.00 | *34.00* |
| 24 | A141 | 1.75 l + 25c brn | 18.00 | *34.00* |
| 25 | A144 | 2.55 l + 50c org (Bl) | 18.00 | *34.00* |
| 26 | A145 | 5 l + 1 l dl vio | 18.00 | *34.00* |
| | | *Nos. 17-26 (10)* | 180.00 | *340.00* |

## NISIRO

Overprinted "Nisiros" in Black or Violet

**1912-22 Wmk. 140 *Perf. 13½, 14***

| | | | | |
|---|---|---|---|---|
| 1 | A43 | 2c orange brn | 7.50 | 7.50 |
| 2 | A48 | 5c green | 4.50 | *7.50* |
| 3 | A48 | 10c claret | 1.50 | *7.50* |
| 4 | A48 | 15c slate ('22) | 26.00 | *47.50* |
| 5 | A50 | 20c brn org ('21) | 97.50 | *110.00* |
| 6 | A49 | 25c blue | 3.00 | *7.50* |
| 7 | A49 | 40c brown | 1.50 | *7.50* |
| 8 | A49 | 50c violet | 3.75 | *16.00* |

**Unwmk.**

| | | | | |
|---|---|---|---|---|
| 9 | A58 | 15c slate (V) | 37.50 | 16.00 |
| 10 | A50 | 20c brn org ('17) | 120.00 | *190.00* |
| | | *Nos. 1-10 (10)* | 302.75 | *417.00* |

No. 9 Surcharged Like Calchi No. 11

**1916 *Perf. 13½***

| | | | | |
|---|---|---|---|---|
| 11 | A58 | 20c on 15c slate | 1.50 | *30.00* |

**Ferrucci Issue**

Types of Italy
Overprinted in Red or Blue

**1930 Wmk. 140 *Perf. 14***

| | | | | |
|---|---|---|---|---|
| 12 | A102 | 20c violet (R) | 3.75 | *9.00* |
| 13 | A103 | 25c dk green (R) | 3.75 | *9.00* |
| 14 | A103 | 50c black (R) | 3.75 | *15.00* |
| 15 | A103 | 1.25 l dp bl (R) | 3.75 | *15.00* |
| 16 | A104 | 5 l + 2 l dp car (Bl) | 10.50 | *25.00* |
| | | *Nos. 12-16 (5)* | 25.50 | *73.00* |

**Garibaldi Issue**

Types of Italy
Overprinted in Red or Blue

**1932**

| | | | | |
|---|---|---|---|---|
| 17 | A138 | 10c brown | 18.00 | *34.00* |
| 18 | A138 | 20c red brn (Bl) | 18.00 | *34.00* |
| 19 | A138 | 25c dp grn | 18.00 | *34.00* |
| 20 | A138 | 30c bluish sl | 18.00 | *34.00* |
| 21 | A138 | 50c red vio (Bl) | 18.00 | *34.00* |
| 22 | A141 | 75c cop red (Bl) | 18.00 | *34.00* |
| 23 | A141 | 1.25 l dull blue | 18.00 | *34.00* |
| 24 | A141 | 1.75 l + 25c brn | 18.00 | *34.00* |
| 25 | A144 | 2.55 l + 50c org (Bl) | 18.00 | *34.00* |
| 26 | A145 | 5 l + 1 l dl vio | 18.00 | *34.00* |
| | | *Nos. 17-26 (10)* | 180.00 | *340.00* |

## PATMO

Overprinted "Patmos" in Black or Violet

**1912-22 Wmk. 140 *Perf. 13½, 14***

| | | | | |
|---|---|---|---|---|
| 1 | A43 | 2c orange brn | 7.50 | 7.50 |
| 2 | A48 | 5c green | 4.50 | *7.50* |
| 3 | A48 | 10c claret | 3.00 | *7.50* |
| 4 | A48 | 15c slate ('22) | 3.75 | *45.00* |
| 5 | A50 | 20c brn org ('21) | 150.00 | 190.00 |
| 6 | A49 | 25c blue | 1.50 | *7.50* |
| 7 | A49 | 40c brown | 3.75 | *7.50* |
| 8 | A49 | 50c violet | 1.50 | *16.00* |

**Unwmk.**

| | | | | |
|---|---|---|---|---|
| 9 | A58 | 15c slate (V) | 37.50 | 16.00 |
| 10 | A50 | 20c brn org ('17) | 82.50 | *190.00* |
| | | *Nos. 1-10 (10)* | 295.50 | *494.50* |

No. 9 Surcharged Like Calchi No. 11

**1916 *Perf. 13½***

| | | | | |
|---|---|---|---|---|
| 11 | A58 | 20c on 15c slate | 15.00 | *34.00* |

**Ferrucci Issue**

Types of Italy
Overprinted in Red or Blue

**1930 Wmk. 140 *Perf. 14***

| | | | | |
|---|---|---|---|---|
| 12 | A102 | 20c violet (R) | 3.75 | *9.00* |
| 13 | A103 | 25c dk green (R) | 3.75 | *9.00* |
| 14 | A103 | 50c black (R) | 3.75 | *15.00* |
| 15 | A103 | 1.25 l dp bl (R) | 3.75 | *15.00* |
| 16 | A104 | 5 l + 2 l dp car (Bl) | 10.50 | *25.00* |
| | | *Nos. 12-16 (5)* | 25.50 | *73.00* |

**Garibaldi Issue**

Types of Italy
Overprinted in Red or Blue

**1932**

| | | | | |
|---|---|---|---|---|
| 17 | A138 | 10c brown | 18.00 | *34.00* |
| 18 | A138 | 20c red brn (Bl) | 18.00 | *34.00* |
| 19 | A138 | 25c dp grn | 18.00 | *34.00* |
| 20 | A138 | 30c bluish sl | 18.00 | *34.00* |
| 21 | A138 | 50c red vio (Bl) | 18.00 | *34.00* |
| 22 | A141 | 75c cop red (Bl) | 18.00 | *34.00* |
| 23 | A141 | 1.25 l dull blue | 18.00 | *34.00* |
| 24 | A141 | 1.75 l + 25c brn | 18.00 | *34.00* |
| 25 | A144 | 2.55 l + 50c org (Bl) | 18.00 | *34.00* |
| 26 | A145 | 5 l + 1 l dl vio | 18.00 | *34.00* |
| | | *Nos. 17-26 (10)* | 180.00 | *340.00* |

## PISCOPI

Overprinted "Piscopi" in Black or Violet

**1912-21 Wmk. 140 *Perf. 13½, 14***

| | | | | |
|---|---|---|---|---|
| 1 | A43 | 2c orange brn | 7.50 | 7.50 |
| 2 | A48 | 5c green | 4.50 | *7.50* |
| 3 | A48 | 10c claret | 1.50 | *7.50* |
| 4 | A48 | 15c slate ('21) | 15.00 | *45.00* |
| 5 | A50 | 20c brn org ('21) | 52.50 | *60.00* |
| 6 | A49 | 25c blue | 1.50 | *7.50* |
| 7 | A49 | 40c brown | 1.50 | *7.50* |
| 8 | A49 | 50c violet | 1.50 | *16.00* |

**Unwmk.**

| | | | | |
|---|---|---|---|---|
| 9 | A58 | 15c slate (V) | 37.50 | 16.00 |
| 10 | A50 | 20c brn org ('17) | 82.50 | *190.00* |
| | | *Nos. 1-10 (10)* | 205.50 | *364.50* |

No. 9 Surcharged Like Calchi No. 11

**1916 *Perf. 13½***

| | | | | |
|---|---|---|---|---|
| 11 | A58 | 20c on 15c slate | 1.50 | *30.00* |

**Ferrucci Issue**

Types of Italy
Overprinted in Red or Blue

**1930 Wmk. 140 *Perf. 14***

| | | | | |
|---|---|---|---|---|
| 12 | A102 | 20c violet (R) | 3.75 | *9.00* |
| 13 | A103 | 25c dk green (R) | 3.75 | *9.00* |
| 14 | A103 | 50c black (R) | 3.75 | *15.00* |
| 15 | A103 | 1.25 l dp bl (R) | 3.75 | *15.00* |
| 16 | A104 | 5 l + 2 l dp car (Bl) | 10.50 | *25.00* |
| | | *Nos. 12-16 (5)* | 25.50 | *73.00* |

**Garibaldi Issue**

Types of Italy
Overprinted in Red or Blue

**1932**

| | | | | |
|---|---|---|---|---|
| 17 | A138 | 10c brown | 18.00 | *34.00* |
| 18 | A138 | 20c red brn (Bl) | 18.00 | *34.00* |
| 19 | A138 | 25c dp grn | 18.00 | *34.00* |
| 20 | A138 | 30c bluish sl | 18.00 | *34.00* |
| 21 | A138 | 50c red vio (Bl) | 18.00 | *34.00* |
| 22 | A141 | 75c cop red (Bl) | 18.00 | *34.00* |
| 23 | A141 | 1.25 l dull blue | 18.00 | *34.00* |
| 24 | A141 | 1.75 l + 25c brn | 18.00 | *34.00* |
| 25 | A144 | 2.55 l + 50c org (Bl) | 18.00 | *34.00* |
| 26 | A145 | 5 l + 1 l dl vio | 18.00 | *34.00* |
| | | *Nos. 17-26 (10)* | 180.00 | *340.00* |

## RHODES

**(Rodi)**

Overprinted "Rodi" in Black or Violet

**1912-24 Wmk. 140 *Perf. 13½, 14***

| | | | | |
|---|---|---|---|---|
| 1 | A43 | 2c org brn | 1.50 | *7.50* |
| 2 | A48 | 5c green | 4.50 | *7.50* |
| a. | | Double overprint | 340.00 | *550.00* |
| 3 | A48 | 10c claret | 1.50 | *7.50* |
| 4 | A48 | 15c slate ('21) | 150.00 | 60.00 |
| 5 | A45 | 20c org ('16) | 3.00 | *7.50* |
| 6 | A50 | 20c brn org ('19) | 6.00 | *15.00* |
| a. | | Double overprint | 82.50 | |
| 7 | A49 | 25c blue | 4.50 | *7.50* |
| 8 | A49 | 40c brown | 6.00 | *7.50* |
| 9 | A49 | 50c violet | 1.50 | *16.00* |
| 10 | A49 | 85c red brn ('22) | 82.50 | *115.00* |
| 11 | A46 | 1 l brn & grn ('24) | 3.00 | |

No. 11 was not regularly issued.

**Unwmk.**

| | | | | |
|---|---|---|---|---|
| 12 | A58 | 15c slate (V) | 37.50 | 16.00 |
| 13 | A50 | 20c brn org ('17) | 190.00 | 190.00 |
| | | *Nos. 1-13 (13)* | 491.50 | 457.00 |

No. 12 Surcharged Like Calchi No. 11

**1916 *Perf. 13½***

| | | | | |
|---|---|---|---|---|
| 14 | A58 | 20c on 15c slate | 120.00 | *150.00* |

Windmill, Rhodes — A1

Medieval Galley — A2

Christian Knight — A3

Crusader Kneeling in Prayer — A4

Crusader's Tomb — A5

No Imprint

**1929 Unwmk. Litho. *Perf. 11***

| | | | | |
|---|---|---|---|---|
| 15 | A1 | 5c magenta | 10.50 | 2.25 |
| 16 | A2 | 10c olive brn | 10.50 | 1.50 |
| 17 | A3 | 20c rose red | 10.50 | .75 |
| 18 | A3 | 25c green | 10.50 | .75 |
| 19 | A4 | 30c dk blue | 62.50 | 2.25 |
| 20 | A5 | 50c dk brown | 10.50 | .75 |
| 21 | A5 | 1.25 l dk blue | 10.50 | 2.25 |
| 22 | A4 | 5 l magenta | 75.00 | *120.00* |
| 23 | A4 | 10 l olive brn | 225.00 | *285.00* |
| | | *Nos. 15-23 (9)* | 425.50 | *415.50* |

Visit of the King and Queen of Italy to the Aegean Islands. The stamps are inscribed "Rodi" but were available for use in all the Aegean Islands.

Nos. 15-23 and C1-C4 were used in eastern Crete in 1941-42 with Greek postmarks.

See Nos. 55-63.

**Ferrucci Issue**

Types of Italy
Overprinted in Red or Blue

**1930 Wmk. 140 *Perf. 14***

| | | | | |
|---|---|---|---|---|
| 24 | A102 | 20c violet (R) | 3.75 | *9.00* |
| 25 | A103 | 25c dk green (R) | 3.75 | *9.00* |
| 26 | A103 | 50c black (R) | 3.75 | *15.00* |
| 27 | A103 | 1.25 l dp blue (R) | 3.75 | *15.00* |
| 28 | A104 | 5 l + 2 l dp car (Bl) | 10.50 | *25.00* |
| | | *Nos. 24-28 (5)* | 25.50 | *73.00* |

**Hydrological Congress Issue**

Rhodes Issue of 1929 Overprinted

**1930 Unwmk. *Perf. 11***

| | | | | |
|---|---|---|---|---|
| 29 | A1 | 5c magenta | 60.00 | 52.50 |
| 30 | A2 | 10c olive brn | 60.00 | 52.50 |
| 31 | A3 | 20c rose red | 67.50 | 52.50 |
| 32 | A3 | 25c green | 75.00 | 52.50 |
| 33 | A4 | 30c dk blue | 60.00 | 52.50 |
| 34 | A5 | 50c dk brown | 560.00 | 90.00 |
| 35 | A5 | 1.25 l dk blue | 400.00 | 135.00 |
| 36 | A4 | 5 l magenta | 375.00 | *560.00* |
| 37 | A4 | 10 l olive grn | 375.00 | *600.00* |
| | | *Nos. 29-37 (9)* | 2,032. | *1,647.* |

Rhodes Issue of 1929 Overprinted in Blue or Red

**1931**

| | | | | |
|---|---|---|---|---|
| 38 | A1 | 5c mag (Bl) | 9.00 | *21.00* |
| 39 | A2 | 10c ol brn (R) | 9.00 | *21.00* |
| 40 | A3 | 20c rose red (Bl) | 9.00 | *35.00* |
| 41 | A3 | 25c green (R) | 9.00 | *35.00* |
| 42 | A4 | 30c dk blue (R) | 9.00 | *35.00* |
| 43 | A5 | 50c dk brown (R) | 60.00 | *82.50* |
| 44 | A5 | 1.25 l dk bl (R) | 52.50 | *120.00* |
| | | *Nos. 38-44 (7)* | 157.50 | 349.50 |

Italian Eucharistic Congress, 1931.

**Garibaldi Issue**

Types of Italy
Overprinted in Red or Blue

**1932 Wmk. 140 *Perf. 14***

| | | | | |
|---|---|---|---|---|
| 45 | A138 | 10c brown | 18.00 | *34.00* |
| 46 | A138 | 20c red brn (Bl) | 18.00 | *34.00* |
| 47 | A138 | 25c dp grn | 18.00 | *34.00* |
| 48 | A138 | 30c bluish sl | 18.00 | *34.00* |
| 49 | A138 | 50c red vio (Bl) | 18.00 | *34.00* |
| 50 | A141 | 75c cop red (Bl) | 18.00 | *34.00* |
| 51 | A141 | 1.25 l dl bl | 18.00 | *34.00* |
| 52 | A141 | 1.75 l + 25c brn | 18.00 | *34.00* |
| 53 | A144 | 2.55 l + 50c org (Bl) | 18.00 | *34.00* |
| 54 | A145 | 5 l + 1 l dl vio | 18.00 | *34.00* |
| | | *Nos. 45-54 (10)* | 180.00 | *340.00* |

Types of Rhodes Issue of 1929
Imprint: "Officina Carte-Valori Roma"

**1932**

| | | | | |
|---|---|---|---|---|
| 55 | A1 | 5c rose lake | 1.50 | .25 |
| 56 | A2 | 10c dk brn | 1.50 | .25 |
| 57 | A3 | 20c red | 1.50 | .25 |
| 58 | A3 | 25c dl grn | 1.50 | .25 |
| 59 | A4 | 30c dl bl | 1.50 | .25 |
| 60 | A5 | 50c blk brn | 1.50 | .25 |
| 61 | A5 | 1.25 l dp bl | 1.50 | .25 |
| 62 | A4 | 5 l rose lake | 1.50 | 2.25 |
| 63 | A4 | 10 l ol brn | 3.75 | *4.50* |
| | | *Nos. 55-63 (9)* | 15.75 | 8.50 |

Aerial View of Rhodes A6

Map of Rhodes — A7

Deer and Palm — A8

**1932 Wmk. 140 Litho. *Perf. 11***

**Shield in Red**

| | | | | |
|---|---|---|---|---|
| **64** | A6 | 5c blk & grn | 9.00 | *22.50* |
| **65** | A6 | 10c blk & vio bl | 9.00 | *19.00* |
| **66** | A6 | 20c blk & dl yel | 9.00 | *19.00* |
| **67** | A6 | 25c lil & blk | 9.00 | *19.00* |
| **68** | A6 | 30c blk & pink | 9.00 | *19.00* |

**Shield and Map Dots in Red**

| | | | | |
|---|---|---|---|---|
| **69** | A7 | 50c blk & gray | 9.00 | *19.00* |
| **70** | A7 | 1.25 l red brn & gray | 9.00 | *37.50* |
| **71** | A7 | 5 l dk bl & gray | 22.50 | *92.50* |
| **72** | A7 | 10 l dk grn & gray | 60.00 | *170.00* |
| **73** | A7 | 25 l choc & gray | 250.00 | *1,125.* |
| | | *Nos. 64-73 (10)* | 395.50 | *1,542.* |

20th anniv. of the Italian occupation and 10th anniv. of Fascist rule.

**1935, Apr. Photo. Wmk. 140**

| | | | | |
|---|---|---|---|---|
| **74** | A8 | 5c orange | 25.00 | *34.00* |
| **75** | A8 | 10c brown | 25.00 | *34.00* |
| **76** | A8 | 20c car rose | 25.00 | *40.00* |
| **77** | A8 | 25c green | 25.00 | *40.00* |
| **78** | A8 | 30c purple | 25.00 | *47.50* |
| **79** | A8 | 50c red brn | 25.00 | *47.50* |
| **80** | A8 | 1.25l blue | 25.00 | *110.00* |
| **81** | A8 | 5 l yellow | 225.00 | *400.00* |
| | | *Nos. 74-81 (8)* | 400.00 | *753.00* |

Holy Year.

The above overprints on No. 55 are stated to have been prepared locally for use on German military correspondence, but banned by postal authorities in Berlin.

## RHODES SEMI-POSTAL STAMPS

Rhodes Nos. 55-62 Surcharged in Black or Red

**1943 Wmk. 140 *Perf. 14***

| | | | | |
|---|---|---|---|---|
| **B1** | A1 | 5c + 5c rose lake | 3.75 | 4.50 |
| **B2** | A2 | 10c + 10c dk brn | 3.75 | 4.50 |
| **B3** | A3 | 20c + 20c red | 3.75 | 4.50 |
| **B4** | A3 | 25c + 25c dl grn | 3.75 | 4.50 |
| **B5** | A4 | 30c + 30c dl bl (R) | 6.00 | 7.50 |
| **B6** | A5 | 50c + 50c blk brn | 6.00 | 7.50 |
| **B7** | A5 | 1.25 l + 1.25 l dp bl (R) | 7.50 | 11.00 |
| **B8** | A4 | 5 l + 5 l rose lake | 150.00 | 250.00 |
| | | *Nos. B1-B8 (8)* | 184.50 | 294.00 |

The surtax was for general relief.

Rhodes Nos. 55-58, 60 and 61 Surcharged in Black or Red

**1944**

| | | | | |
|---|---|---|---|---|
| **B9** | A1 | 5c + 3 l rose lake | 4.50 | *10.50* |
| **B10** | A2 | 10c + 3 l dk brn (R) | 4.50 | *10.50* |
| **B11** | A3 | 20c + 3 l red | 4.50 | *10.50* |
| **B12** | A3 | 25c +3 l dl grn (R) | 4.50 | *10.50* |
| **B13** | A5 | 50c + 3 l blk brn (R) | 4.50 | *10.50* |
| **B14** | A5 | 1.25 l + 5 l dp bl (R) | 37.50 | *70.00* |
| | | *Nos. B9-B14 (6)* | 60.00 | *122.50* |

The surtax was for war victims.

Rhodes Nos. 62 and 63 Surcharged in Red

**1945**

| | | | | |
|---|---|---|---|---|
| **B17** | A4 | 5 l + 10 l rose lake | 15.00 | *34.00* |
| **B18** | A4 | 10 l + 10 l ol brn | 15.00 | *34.00* |

The surtax was for the Red Cross.

## RHODES AIR POST STAMPS

Symbolical of Flight — AP18

**Wmk. 140 Upright (No. C1), Sideways (No. C2a-C4a)**

**1935-38 Typo. *Perf. 14***

| | | | | |
|---|---|---|---|---|
| **C1** | AP18 | 50c black & yel | .75 | .40 |
| **C2a** | AP18 | 80c black & mag | .75 | *2.25* |
| **C3a** | AP18 | 1 l black & green | .75 | .40 |
| **C4a** | AP18 | 5 l black & red vio | 1.50 | *4.50* |
| | | *Nos. C1-C4a (4)* | 4.25 | 8.30 |

Nos. C2a-C4a were issued in 1937-38, on paper with sideways watermark. The 1935 first printing, which includes C1, is on paper within which the watermark is upright. For detailed listings, see the *Scott Classic Specialized Catalogue.*

## RHODES AIR POST SEMI-POSTAL STAMPS

Rhodes Nos. C1-C4 Surcharged in Silver

**1944 Wmk. 140 *Perf. 14***

| | | | | |
|---|---|---|---|---|
| **CB1** | AP18 | 50c + 2 l | 12.00 | 3.75 |
| **CB2** | AP18 | 80c + 2 l | 12.00 | 7.50 |
| **CB3** | AP18 | 1 l + 2 l | 16.00 | 9.00 |
| **CB4** | AP18 | 5 l + 2 l | 100.00 | *110.00* |
| | | *Nos. CB1-CB4 (4)* | 140.00 | *130.25* |

The surtax was for war victims.

## RHODES SPECIAL DELIVERY STAMPS

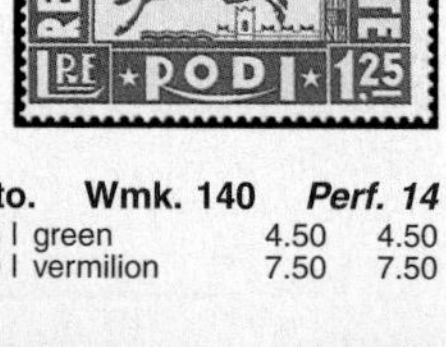


Stag — SD1

**1936 Photo. Wmk. 140 *Perf. 14***

| | | | | |
|---|---|---|---|---|
| **E1** | SD1 | 1.25 l green | 4.50 | 4.50 |
| **E2** | SD1 | 2.50 l vermilion | 7.50 | 7.50 |

Nos. 58 and 57 Surcharged in Black

**1943**

| | | | | |
|---|---|---|---|---|
| **E3** | A3 | 1.25 l on 25c dl grn | 1.50 | *3.75* |
| **E4** | A3 | 2.50 l on 20c red | 1.50 | *3.75* |

## RHODES SEMI-POSTAL SPECIAL DELIVERY STAMPS

Rhodes Nos. E1 and E2 Srchd. in Red or Black

**1943 Wmk. 140 *Perf. 14***

| | | | | |
|---|---|---|---|---|
| **EB1** | SD1 | 1.25 l + 1.25 l (R) | 82.50 | 92.50 |
| **EB2** | SD1 | 2.50 l + 2.50 l | 97.50 | 150.00 |

The surtax was for general relief.

## RHODES POSTAGE DUE STAMPS

Maltese Cross PD1

Immortelle PD2

**1934 Photo. Wmk. 140 *Perf. 13***

| | | | | |
|---|---|---|---|---|
| **J1** | PD1 | 5c vermilion | 4.50 | 7.50 |
| **J2** | PD1 | 10c carmine | 4.50 | 7.50 |
| **J3** | PD1 | 20c dk grn | 4.50 | 6.00 |
| **J4** | PD1 | 30c purple | 4.50 | 6.00 |
| **J5** | PD1 | 40c dk bl | 4.50 | 12.00 |
| **J6** | PD2 | 50c vermilion | 4.50 | 6.00 |
| **J7** | PD2 | 60c carmine | 4.50 | 22.50 |
| **J8** | PD2 | 1 l dk grn | 4.50 | 22.50 |
| **J9** | PD2 | 2 l purple | 4.50 | 12.00 |
| | | *Nos. J1-J9 (9)* | 40.50 | 102.00 |

## RHODES PARCEL POST STAMPS

Both unused and used values are for complete stamps.

PP1

PP2

**1934 Photo. Wmk. 140 *Perf. 13***

| | | | | |
|---|---|---|---|---|
| **Q1** | PP1 | 5c vermilion | 6.00 | 11.00 |
| **Q2** | PP1 | 10c carmine | 6.00 | 11.00 |
| **Q3** | PP1 | 20c dk green | 6.00 | 11.00 |
| **Q4** | PP1 | 25c purple | 6.00 | 11.00 |
| **Q5** | PP1 | 50c dk blue | 6.00 | 11.00 |
| **Q6** | PP1 | 60c black | 6.00 | 11.00 |
| **Q7** | PP2 | 1 l vermilion | 6.00 | 11.00 |
| **Q8** | PP2 | 2 l carmine | 6.00 | 11.00 |
| **Q9** | PP2 | 3 l dk green | 6.00 | 11.00 |
| **Q10** | PP2 | 4 l purple | 6.00 | 11.00 |
| **Q11** | PP2 | 10 l dk blue | 6.00 | 11.00 |
| | | *Nos. Q1-Q11 (11)* | 66.00 | 121.00 |

Value of used halves, Nos. Q1-Q11, each 80 cents.

See note preceding No. Q7 of Italy.

## SCARPANTO

Overprinted "Scarpanto" in Black or Violet

**1912-22 Wmk. 140 *Perf. 13½, 14***

| | | | | |
|---|---|---|---|---|
| **1** | A43 | 2c org brn | 9.00 | 7.50 |
| **2** | A48 | 5c green | 3.00 | *7.50* |
| **3** | A48 | 10c claret | 1.50 | *7.50* |
| **4** | A48 | 15c slate ('22) | 15.00 | *45.00* |
| **5** | A50 | 20c brn org ('21) | 52.50 | 52.50 |
| **6** | A49 | 25c blue | 9.00 | 7.50 |
| **7** | A49 | 40c brown | 1.50 | *7.50* |
| **8** | A49 | 50c violet | 3.00 | *16.00* |

**Unwmk.**

| | | | | |
|---|---|---|---|---|
| **9** | A58 | 15c slate (V) | 30.00 | 16.00 |
| **10** | A50 | 20c brn org ('17) | 120.00 | *190.00* |
| | | *Nos. 1-10 (10)* | 244.50 | *357.00* |

No 9 Surcharged Like Calchi No. 11

**1916 *Perf. 13½***

| | | | | |
|---|---|---|---|---|
| **11** | A58 | 20c on 15c slate | 1.50 | *30.00* |

**Ferrucci Issue**

Types of Italy

Overprinted in Red or Blue

**1930 Wmk. 140 *Perf. 14***

| | | | | |
|---|---|---|---|---|
| **12** | A102 | 20c violet (R) | 3.75 | *9.00* |
| **13** | A103 | 25c dk green (R) | 3.75 | *9.00* |
| **14** | A103 | 50c black (R) | 3.75 | *15.00* |
| **15** | A103 | 1.25 l dp bl (R) | 3.75 | *15.00* |
| **16** | A104 | 5 l + 2 l dp car (Bl) | 10.50 | *25.00* |
| | | *Nos. 12-16 (5)* | 25.50 | *73.00* |

**Garibaldi Issue**

Types of Italy

Overprinted in Red or Blue

**1932**

| | | | | |
|---|---|---|---|---|
| **17** | A138 | 10c brown | 18.00 | *34.00* |
| **18** | A138 | 20c red brn (Bl) | 18.00 | *34.00* |
| **19** | A138 | 25c dp grn | 18.00 | *34.00* |
| **20** | A138 | 30c bluish sl | 18.00 | *34.00* |
| **21** | A138 | 50c red vio (Bl) | 18.00 | *34.00* |
| **22** | A141 | 75c cop red (Bl) | 18.00 | *34.00* |
| **23** | A141 | 1.25 l dull blue | 18.00 | *34.00* |
| **24** | A141 | 1.75 l + 25c brn | 18.00 | *34.00* |
| **25** | A144 | 2.55 l + 50c org (Bl) | 18.00 | *34.00* |
| **26** | A145 | 5 l + 1 l dl vio | 18.00 | *34.00* |
| | | *Nos. 17-26 (10)* | 180.00 | *340.00* |

## SIMI

Overprinted "Simi" in Black or Violet

**1912-21 Wmk. 140 *Perf. 13½, 14***

| | | | | |
|---|---|---|---|---|
| **1** | A43 | 2c org brn | 15.00 | 7.50 |
| **2** | A48 | 5c green | 30.00 | 7.50 |
| **3** | A48 | 10c claret | 1.50 | *7.50* |
| **4** | A48 | 15c slate ('21) | 120.00 | 60.00 |
| **5** | A50 | 20c brn org ('21) | 60.00 | 34.00 |
| **6** | A49 | 25c blue | 9.00 | *7.50* |
| **7** | A49 | 40c brown | 1.50 | *7.50* |
| **8** | A49 | 50c violet | 1.50 | *16.00* |

**Unwmk.**

| | | | | |
|---|---|---|---|---|
| **9** | A58 | 15c slate (V) | 60.00 | 16.00 |
| **10** | A50 | 20c brn org ('17) | 60.00 | *105.00* |
| | | *Nos. 1-10 (10)* | 358.50 | *268.50* |

No. 9 Surcharged Like Calchi No. 11

**1916 *Perf. 13½***

| | | | | |
|---|---|---|---|---|
| **11** | A58 | 20c on 15c slate | 7.50 | *26.00* |

**Ferrucci Issue**

Types of Italy

Overprinted in Red or Blue

**1930 Wmk. 140 *Perf. 14***

| | | | | |
|---|---|---|---|---|
| **12** | A102 | 20c violet (R) | 3.75 | *9.00* |
| **13** | A103 | 25c dk green (R) | 3.75 | *9.00* |
| **14** | A103 | 50c black (R) | 3.75 | *15.00* |
| **15** | A103 | 1.25 l dp bl (R) | 3.75 | *15.00* |
| **16** | A104 | 5 l + 2 l dp car (Bl) | 10.50 | *25.00* |
| | | *Nos. 12-16 (5)* | 25.50 | *73.00* |

**Garibaldi Issue**

Types of Italy

Overprinted in Red or Blue

**1932**

| | | | | |
|---|---|---|---|---|
| **17** | A138 | 10c brown | 18.00 | *34.00* |
| **18** | A138 | 20c red brn (Bl) | 18.00 | *34.00* |
| **19** | A138 | 25c dp grn | 18.00 | *34.00* |
| **20** | A138 | 30c bluish sl | 18.00 | *34.00* |
| **21** | A138 | 50c red vio (Bl) | 18.00 | *34.00* |
| **22** | A141 | 75c cop red (Bl) | 18.00 | *34.00* |
| **23** | A141 | 1.25 l dull blue | 18.00 | *34.00* |
| **24** | A141 | 1.75 l + 25c brn | 18.00 | *34.00* |
| **25** | A144 | 2.55 l + 50c org (Bl) | 18.00 | *34.00* |
| **26** | A145 | 5 l + 1 l dl vio | 18.00 | *34.00* |
| | | *Nos. 17-26 (10)* | 180.00 | *340.00* |

## STAMPALIA

Overprinted "Stampalia" in Black or Violet

**1912-21 Wmk. 140** *Perf. 13½, 14*

| | | | | |
|---|---|---|---|---|
| 1 | A43 | 2c org brn | 9.00 | 7.50 |
| 2 | A48 | 5c green | 1.50 | *7.50* |
| 3 | A48 | 10c claret | 1.50 | *7.50* |
| 4 | A48 | 15c slate ('21) | 10.50 | *34.00* |
| 5 | A50 | 20c brn org ('21) | 45.00 | *60.00* |
| 6 | A49 | 25c blue | 1.50 | *7.50* |
| 7 | A49 | 40c brown | 4.50 | *7.50* |
| 8 | A49 | 50c violet | 1.50 | *16.00* |

**Unwmk.**

| | | | | |
|---|---|---|---|---|
| 9 | A58 | 15c slate (V) | 37.50 | 16.00 |
| 10 | A50 | 20c brn org ('17) | 82.50 | *105.00* |
| | | *Nos. 1-10 (10)* | 195.00 | *268.50* |

No. 9 Surcharged Like Calchi No. 11

**1916** *Perf. 13½*

| | | | | |
|---|---|---|---|---|
| 11 | A58 | 20c on 15c slate | 1.50 | *26.00* |

**Ferrucci Issue**

Types of Italy

Overprinted in Red or Blue

**1930 Wmk. 140** *Perf. 14*

| | | | | |
|---|---|---|---|---|
| 12 | A102 | 20c violet (R) | 3.75 | *9.00* |
| 13 | A103 | 25c dk green (R) | 3.75 | *9.00* |
| 14 | A103 | 50c black (R) | 3.75 | *15.00* |
| 15 | A103 | 1.25 l dp bl (R) | 3.75 | *15.00* |
| 16 | A104 | 5 l + 2 l dp car (Bl) | 10.50 | *25.00* |
| | | *Nos. 12-16 (5)* | 25.50 | *73.00* |

**Garibaldi Issue**

Types of Italy

Overprinted in Red or Blue

**1932**

| | | | | |
|---|---|---|---|---|
| 17 | A138 | 10c brown | 18.00 | *34.00* |
| 18 | A138 | 20c red brn (Bl) | 18.00 | *34.00* |
| 19 | A138 | 25c dp grn | 18.00 | *34.00* |
| 20 | A138 | 30c bluish sl | 18.00 | *34.00* |
| 21 | A138 | 50c red vio (Bl) | 18.00 | *34.00* |
| 22 | A141 | 75c cop red (Bl) | 18.00 | *34.00* |
| 23 | A141 | 1.25 l dull blue | 18.00 | *34.00* |
| 24 | A141 | 1.75 l + 25c brn | 18.00 | *34.00* |
| 25 | A144 | 2.55 l + 50c org (Bl) | 18.00 | *34.00* |
| 26 | A145 | 5 l + 1 l dl vio | 18.00 | *34.00* |
| | | *Nos. 17-26 (10)* | 180.00 | *340.00* |

## TRIESTE

A free territory (1947-1954) on the Adriatic Sea between Italy and Yugoslavia. In 1954 the territory was divided, Italy acquiring the northern section and seaport, Yugoslavia the southern section (Zone B).

**Catalogue values for all unused stamps in this country are for Never Hinged items.**

### ZONE A

**Issued jointly by the Allied Military Government of the United States and Great Britain**

Stamps of Italy 1945-47 Overprinted

a

b

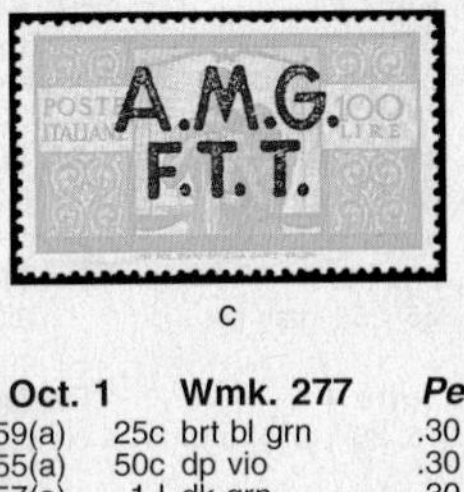

c

**1947, Oct. 1 Wmk. 277** *Perf. 14*

| | | | | |
|---|---|---|---|---|
| 1 | A259(a) | 25c brt bl grn | .30 | *1.60* |
| 2 | A255(a) | 50c dp vio | .30 | *1.60* |
| 3 | A257(a) | 1 l dk grn | .30 | .25 |
| 4 | A258(a) | 2 l dk cl brn | .30 | .25 |
| 5 | A259(a) | 3 l red | .30 | .25 |
| 6 | A259(a) | 4 l red org | .30 | .25 |
| 7 | A256(a) | 5 l deep blue | .30 | .25 |
| 8 | A257(a) | 6 l dp vio | .30 | .25 |
| 9 | A255(a) | 10 l slate | .30 | .25 |
| 10 | A257(a) | 15 l deep blue | 2.75 | .25 |
| 11 | A259(a) | 20 l dk red vio | 4.50 | .25 |
| 12 | A260(b) | 25 l dk grn | 6.00 | *13.00* |
| 13 | A260(b) | 50 l dk vio brn | 7.00 | *8.00* |

*Perf. 14x13½*

| | | | | |
|---|---|---|---|---|
| 14 | A261(c) | 100 l car lake | 55.00 | 45.00 |
| | | *Nos. 1-14 (14)* | 77.95 | *71.45* |

The letters "F. T. T." are the initials of "Free Territory of Trieste."

**Italy Nos. 486-488 Ovptd. Type "a"**

**1948, Mar. 1** *Perf. 14*

| | | | | |
|---|---|---|---|---|
| 15 | A255 | 8 l dk green | 6.00 | *11.00* |
| 16 | A256 | 10 l red org | 19.00 | .30 |
| 17 | A259 | 30 l dk blue | 275.00 | 19.00 |
| | | *Nos. 15-17 (3)* | 300.00 | 30.30 |

Italy Nos. 495 to 506 Overprinted — d

**1948, July 1**

| | | | | |
|---|---|---|---|---|
| 18 | A272 | 3 l dk brn | .45 | .45 |
| 19 | A272 | 4 l red vio | .45 | .45 |
| 20 | A272 | 5 l deep blue | .45 | .45 |
| 21 | A272 | 6 l dp yel grn | .90 | .45 |
| 22 | A272 | 8 l brown | .45 | .45 |
| 23 | A272 | 10 l org red | .90 | .45 |
| 24 | A272 | 12 l dk gray grn | .90 | *1.40* |
| 25 | A272 | 15 l gray blk | 19.00 | 16.50 |
| 26 | A272 | 20 l car rose | 35.00 | 16.50 |
| 27 | A272 | 30 l brt ultra | 2.75 | 2.75 |
| 28 | A272 | 50 l violet | 22.50 | *32.50* |
| 29 | A272 | 100 l bl blk | 52.50 | *80.00* |
| | | *Nos. 18-29 (12)* | 136.25 | *152.35* |

Italy, Nos. 486 to 488, Overprinted in Carmine

**1948, Sept. 8**

| | | | | |
|---|---|---|---|---|
| 30 | A255 | 8 l dk green | .30 | .25 |
| 31 | A256 | 10 l red org | .30 | .25 |
| 32 | A259 | 30 l dk blue | 2.00 | 2.00 |
| | | *Nos. 30-32,C17-C19 (3)* | 2.60 | 2.50 |

The overprint is embossed.

**Italy, No. 507, Overprinted Type "d" in Carmine**

**1948, Oct. 15**

| | | | | |
|---|---|---|---|---|
| 33 | A273 | 15 l dk green | 4.75 | 4.75 |

Italy, No. 508, Overprinted in Green — e

**1948, Nov. 15**

| | | | | |
|---|---|---|---|---|
| 34 | A274 | 15 l dk brown | 16.00 | 4.00 |

**Italy, No. 509, Overprinted Type "d" in Red**

**1949, May 2 Wmk. 277** *Perf. 14*

| | | | | |
|---|---|---|---|---|
| 35 | A275 | 20 l dk brown | 16.00 | 8.00 |

Italy, Nos. 510 to 513, Overprinted — f

**1949, May 2 Buff Background**

| | | | | |
|---|---|---|---|---|
| 36 | A276 | 5 l red brown | .80 | *1.60* |
| 37 | A276 | 15 l dk green | 13.00 | *24.00* |
| 38 | A276 | 20 l dp red brn | 7.25 | 1.60 |
| 39 | A276 | 50 l dk blue | 16.00 | 12.00 |
| | | *Nos. 36-39 (4)* | 37.05 | *39.20* |

**Italy, No. 514, Overprinted Type "d" in Red**

**1949, May 2**

| | | | | |
|---|---|---|---|---|
| 40 | A277 | 50 l brt ultra | 5.50 | 5.50 |

**Italy, No. 518, Overprinted Type "d" in Red**

**1949, May 30**

| | | | | |
|---|---|---|---|---|
| 41 | A279 | 100 l brown | 72.50 | *120.00* |

**Italy, Nos. 515-517, Ovptd. Type "f"**

**1949, June 15**

| | | | | |
|---|---|---|---|---|
| 42 | A278 | 5 l dk green | 14.50 | 9.50 |
| 43 | A278 | 15 l violet | 14.50 | *17.50* |
| 44 | A278 | 20 l brown | 14.50 | 14.50 |
| | | *Nos. 42-44 (3)* | 43.50 | 41.50 |

**Italy, Nos. 519 and 520, Overprinted Type "e" in Carmine**

**1949, July 16**

| | | | | |
|---|---|---|---|---|
| 45 | A280 | 20 l gray | 14.50 | 8.00 |
| 46 | A281 | 20 l brown | 14.50 | 8.00 |

Italy, No. 521 Ovptd. in Green — g

**1949, June 8**

| | | | | |
|---|---|---|---|---|
| 47 | A282 | 20 l brown red | 8.00 | 8.00 |

**Italy, No. 522, Overprinted Type "f" in Carmine**

**1949, July 8**

| | | | | |
|---|---|---|---|---|
| 49 | A283 | 20 l violet | 22.50 | 16.00 |

**Italy, No. 523 Overprinted Type "e", without Periods, in Black**

**1949, Aug. 27**

| | | | | |
|---|---|---|---|---|
| 50 | A284 | 20 l violet blue | 16.00 | 8.00 |

**Italy, No. 524 Ovptd. Type "f"**

**1949, Aug. 27**

| | | | | |
|---|---|---|---|---|
| 51 | A285 | 20 l violet | 24.00 | 24.00 |

**Italy, No. 525, Overprinted Type "d" in Green**

**1949, Sept. 10**

| | | | | |
|---|---|---|---|---|
| 52 | A286 | 20 l red | 14.50 | 8.00 |

Italy Nos. 526 and 527 Overprinted — h

**Wmk. 277**

**1949, Nov. 7 Photo.** *Perf. 14*

| | | | | |
|---|---|---|---|---|
| 53 | A287 | 20 l rose car | 6.50 | 6.50 |
| 54 | A288 | 50 l deep blue | 24.00 | *26.00* |

**Same Overprint on No. 528**

**1949, Nov. 7**

| | | | | |
|---|---|---|---|---|
| 55 | A289 | 20 l dp grn | 8.75 | 6.50 |

**Same Overprint on No. 529**

**1949, Nov. 7**

| | | | | |
|---|---|---|---|---|
| 56 | A290 | 20 l brt blue | 5.50 | 4.75 |

**Same Overprint in Red on No. 530**

**1949, Dec. 28**

| | | | | |
|---|---|---|---|---|
| 57 | A291 | 20 l violet blk | 7.25 | 4.00 |

**Same Overprint in Black on Italian Stamps of 1945-48**

**1949-50 Photo.**

| | | | | |
|---|---|---|---|---|
| 58 | A257 | 1 l dk green | .25 | *1.00* |
| 59 | A258 | 2 l dk cl brn | .25 | .25 |
| 60 | A259 | 3 l red | .25 | .25 |
| 61 | A256 | 5 l deep blue | .25 | .25 |
| 62 | A257 | 6 l dp violet | .25 | .25 |
| 63 | A255 | 8 l dk green | 55.00 | 35.00 |
| 64 | A256 | 10 l red org | .25 | .25 |
| 65 | A257 | 15 l deep blue | 4.00 | .80 |
| 66 | A259 | 20 l dk red vio | 2.40 | .25 |
| 67 | A260 | 25 l dk grn ('50) | 40.00 | 4.75 |
| 68 | A260 | 50 l dk vio brn ('50) | 60.00 | 4.00 |

**Engr.**

| | | | | |
|---|---|---|---|---|
| 69 | A261 | 100 l car lake | 120.00 | 24.00 |
| | | *Nos. 58-69 (12)* | 282.90 | 71.05 |

Issued: 3 l, 20 l, 10/21; 5 l, 11/5; 10 l, 11/7; 100 l, 11/23; 15 l, 11/28; 1 l, 2 l, 6 l, 8 l, 12/28; 50 l, 1/19; 25 l, 2/25.

**Italy, No. 531, Overprinted Type "g" in Carmine**

**1950, Apr. 12**

| | | | | |
|---|---|---|---|---|
| 70 | A292 | 20 l brown | 7.25 | 4.00 |

**Same Overprint in Carmine on Italy, No. 532**

**1950, Apr. 29**

| | | | | |
|---|---|---|---|---|
| 71 | A293 | 20 l vio gray | 4.00 | 4.00 |

**Same Overprint in Carmine on Italy, Nos. 533 and 534**

**1950, May 22**

| | | | | |
|---|---|---|---|---|
| 72 | A294 | 20 l olive green | 4.75 | 4.75 |
| 73 | A295 | 55 l blue | 17.50 | 17.50 |

**Italy, Nos. 535 and 536, Overprinted Type "h" in Black**

**1950, May 29**

| | | | | |
|---|---|---|---|---|
| 74 | A296 | 20 l violet | 4.75 | 4.75 |
| 75 | A296 | 55 l blue | 17.50 | 17.50 |

**Italy, No. 537, Overprinted Type "g" in Carmine**

**1950, July 10**

| | | | | |
|---|---|---|---|---|
| 76 | A297 | 20 l gray grn | 4.75 | 4.00 |

**Same Overprint in Carmine on Italy, Nos. 538-539**

**1950, July 15**

| | | | | |
|---|---|---|---|---|
| 77 | A298 | 20 l purple | 8.00 | 4.75 |
| 78 | A298 | 55 l blue | 27.50 | *32.50* |

**Italy, No. 540, Overprinted Type "h"**

**1950, July 22**

| | | | | |
|---|---|---|---|---|
| 79 | A299 | 20 l brown | 8.75 | 5.50 |

Italy, No. 541 Overprinted in Carmine — i

**1950, July 29**

| | | | | |
|---|---|---|---|---|
| 80 | A300 | 20 l dk grn | 7.25 | 5.50 |

**Italy, No. 542, Overprinted Type "g"**

**1950, Aug. 21**

| | | | | |
|---|---|---|---|---|
| 81 | A301 | 20 l chnt brn | 4.00 | 4.00 |

Italy, Nos. 473A and 474, Overprinted

**1950, Aug. 27**

| | | | | |
|---|---|---|---|---|
| 82 | A257 | 15 l deep blue | 6.50 | 4.75 |
| 83 | A259 | 20 l dk red vio | 6.50 | 2.40 |

Trieste Fair.

**Italy, No. 543, Overprinted Type "i" in Carmine**

**1950, Sept. 11**

| | | | | |
|---|---|---|---|---|
| 84 | A302 | 20 l indigo | 4.00 | 3.25 |

**Italy Nos. 544-546, Ovptd. Type "h"**

**1950, Sept. 16 Wmk. 277** *Perf. 14*

| | | | | |
|---|---|---|---|---|
| 85 | A303 | 5 l dp cl & grn | 1.60 | *4.00* |
| 86 | A303 | 20 l brn & grn | 4.00 | 4.00 |
| 87 | A303 | 55 l dp ultra & brn | 30.00 | *35.00* |
| | | *Nos. 85-87 (3)* | 35.60 | *43.00* |

**Same, in Black, on Italy No. 547**

**1950, Sept. 16**

| | | | | |
|---|---|---|---|---|
| 88 | A304 | 20 l ol brn & red brn | 4.50 | 4.00 |

**Same, in Black, on Italy No. 548**

**1950, Sept. 16**

| | | | | |
|---|---|---|---|---|
| 89 | A305 | 20 l cr & gray blk | 7.25 | 4.75 |

**Italy, Nos. 549 to 565, Overprinted Type "g" in Black**

**1950, Oct. 20**

**90** A306 50c violet blue .25 .25
**91** A306 1 l dk blue vio .25 .25
**92** A306 2 l sepia .25 .25
**93** A306 5 l dk gray .25 .25
**94** A306 6 l chocolate .25 .25
**95** A306 10 l deep green .80 .25
**96** A306 12 l dp blue grn 2.40 .80
**97** A306 15 l dk gray bl 2.40 .25
**98** A306 20 l blue vio 2.40 .25
**99** A306 25 l brown org 3.25 .25
**100** A306 30 l magenta 1.60 .80
**101** A306 35 l crimson 2.75 1.60
**102** A306 40 l brown 1.75 1.60
**103** A306 50 l violet .80 .80
**104** A306 55 l deep blue .80 .80
**105** A306 60 l red 9.50 *11.00*
**106** A306 65 l dk green .80 .80

Italy Nos. 566 and 567 Overprinted — k

***Perf. 14, 14x13½***

**Engr.**

**107** A306 100 l brown org 7.25 .25
**108** A306 200 l olive brn 5.50 *8.00*
*Nos. 90-108 (19)* 43.25 *28.70*

**Italy Nos. 568 and 569 Overprinted Type "k" in Black**

**1951, Mar. 27 Photo. *Perf. 14***

**109** A307 20 l red vio & red 4.75 4.75
**110** A307 55 l ultra & bl 55.00 55.00

**Italy No. 570 Overprinted Type "g"**

**1951, Apr. 2**

**111** A308 20 l dk grn 3.25 3.25

**Same, on Italy No. 571**

**1951, Apr. 11**

**112** A309 20 l bl vio 4.00 3.25

**Italy Nos. 572 and 573 Overprinted**

**1951, Apr. 12**

**113** A310(h) 20 l brown 4.00 4.00
**114** A311(g) 55 l deep blue 5.50 5.50

**Italy Nos. 574 to 576 Overprinted Type "h" in Black**

**1951, May 18 Fleur-de-Lis in Red**

**115** A312 5 l dk brown 8.75 *50.00*
**116** A312 10 l Prus grn 8.75 *50.00*
**117** A312 15 l vio bl 8.75 *50.00*
*Nos. 115-117 (3)* 26.25 *150.00*

Italy No. 577 Overprinted — m

**1951, Apr. 26**

**118** A313 20 l purple 4.00 4.00

**Italy No. 578 Overprinted Type "h"**

**1951, May 5**

**119** A314 20 l Prus green 4.00 4.00

**Italy Nos. 579-580 Ovptd. Type "g"**

**1951, June 18**

**120** A315 20 l violet 1.60 1.60
**121** A315 55 l brt blue 4.00 4.00

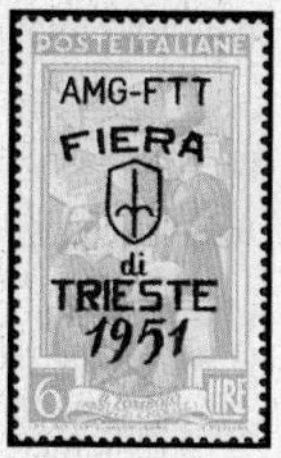


Nos. 94, 98 and 104 Overprinted

**1951, June 24**

**122** A306 6 l chocolate .80 *1.75*
**123** A306 20 l blue violet 1.75 .80
**124** A306 55 l deep blue 1.75 1.75
*Nos. 122-124 (3)* 4.30 4.30

Issued to publicize the Trieste Fair, 1951.

Italy No. 581 Overprinted — n

**1951, July 23**

**125** A316 20 l brn & red brn 3.25 3.25

**Italy Nos. 582 and 583 Overprinted Types "n" and "h" in Red**

**1951, July 23**

**126** A317(n) 20 l grnsh gray & blk 2.40 2.40
**127** A318(h) 55 l vio bl & pale sal 4.00 4.00

**Italy No. 584 Overprinted Type "g" in Carmine**

**1951, Aug. 23**

**128** A319 25 l gray blk 14.50 5.50

**Overprint "g" on Italy No. 585**

**1951, Sept. 8**

**129** A320 25 l deep blue 3.25 3.25

**Italy No. 586 Overprinted Type "h" in Red**

**1951, Sept. 15**

**130** A321 25 l dk brn 3.25 3.25

Italy Nos. 587-589 Ovptd. in Blue — o

**1951, Oct. 11**

**131** A322 10 l dk brn & gray 1.60 1.60
**132** A322 25 l rose red & bl grn 1.60 1.60
**133** A322 60 l vio bl & red org 3.25 3.25
*Nos. 131-133 (3)* 6.45 6.45

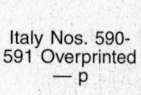

Italy Nos. 590-591 Overprinted — p

**Overprint Spaced to Fit Design**

**1951, Oct. 31 Photo.**

**134** A323 10 l green 2.00 2.00
**135** A324 25 l vio gray 2.00 2.00

**Italy Nos. 592-593 Ovptd. Type "k"**

**1951, Nov. 21**

**136** A325 10 l ol & dull grn 2.00 2.00
**137** A326 25 l dull green 2.00 2.00

**Italy Nos. 594-596 Overprinted Types "k" or "p" in Black Overprint "p" Spaced to Fit Design**

**1951, Nov. 23**

**138** A327(p) 10 l vio brn & dk grn 1.60 1.60
**139** A327(k) 25 l red brn & dk brn 1.60 .80
**140** A327(p) 60 l dp grn & ind 3.25 3.25
*Nos. 138-140 (3)* 6.45 5.65

**Italy No. 597 Overprinted Type "p" Overprint Spaced to Fit Design**

**1952, Jan. 28 Wmk. 277 *Perf. 14***

**141** A328 25 l gray & gray blk 3.25 2.40

**Italy No. 598 Overprinted Type "k"**

**1952, Feb. 2**

**142** A329 25 l dl grn & ol bis 3.25 2.40

**Same on Italy No. 599**

**1952, Mar. 26**

**143** A330 25 l brn & sl blk 3.25 2.40

**Same on Italy No. 600**

**1952, Apr. 12**

**144** A331 60 l ultra 3.25 *4.00*

**Same on Italy No. 601**

**1952, Apr. 16**

**145** A332 25 l dp orange .80 .40

**Stamps of Italy Overprinted "AMG FTT" in Various Sizes and Arrangements**

**On Nos. 602-603**

**1952, June 14 Wmk. 277 *Perf. 14***

**146** A333 25 l blk & red brn 1.60 1.60
**147** A333 60 l blk & ultra 2.40 2.40

**1952, June 7 On No. 604**

**148** A334 25 l bright blue 3.25 2.40

**1952, June 14 On No. 605**

**149** A335 25 l black & yellow 3.25 2.40

**1952, June 19 On No. 606**

**150** A336 25 l bl gray, red & dk bl (R) 3.25 2.40

**1952, June 28 On No. 607**

**151** A337 25 l dp grn, dk brn & red 3.25 2.40

**1952, Sept. 6 On No. 608**

**152** A338 25 l dark green 3.25 2.40

**On No. 609 in Bronze**

**1952, Sept. 20**

**153** A339 25 l purple 3.25 2.40

**1952, Oct. 4 On No. 610**

**154** A340 25 l gray 3.25 2.40

**1952, Oct. 1 On No. 611**

**155** A341 60 l vio bl & dk bl 4.00 4.00

**On No. 612**

**1952, Nov. 21 *Perf. 13***

**156** A342 25 l brn & dk brn 3.25 2.40

**On Nos. 613-615**

**1952, Nov. 3 *Perf. 14***

**157** A343 10 l dk green .80 .40
**158** A344 25 l blk & dk brn 1.60 .30
**159** A344 60 l blk & blue 1.60 *2.00*
*Nos. 157-159 (3)* 4.00 *2.70*

**1952, Dec. 6 On Nos. 616-617**

**160** A345 25 l dk green 3.25 2.40
**161** A346 25 l brown 3.25 2.40

**1953, Jan. 5 On No. 618**

**162** A347 25 l gray blk & dk bl (Bl) 3.25 2.40

**On Nos. 601A-601B**

**1952, Dec. 31**

**163** A332a 60 l ultra (G) 2.40 *3.25*
**164** A332 80 l brown car 3.25 2.40

**1953, Feb. 21 On No. 621**

**165** A349 25 l car lake 3.25 2.40

**1953, Apr. 24 On No. 622**

**166** A350 25 l violet 3.25 2.40

**1953, Apr. 30 On No. 623**

**167** A351 25 l violet 3.25 2.40

**1953, May 30 On No. 624**

**168** A352 25 l dark brown 3.25 2.40

**1953, June 27 On No. 625**

**169** A353 25 l brn & dull red 3.25 2.40

**1953-54 On Nos. 626-633**

**170** A354 5 l gray .25 *.30*
**171** A354 10 l org ver .25 .25
**172** A354 12 l dull grn .25 .25
**172A** A354 13 l brt lil rose ('54) .25 .25
**173** A354 20 l brown .80 .80
**174** A354 25 l purple .80 .90
**175** A354 35 l rose car 3.25 2.40
**176** A354 60 l blue 4.00 3.25
**177** A354 80 l org brn 11.00 8.00
*Nos. 170-177 (9)* 20.85 16.40

Issue dates: 13 l, Feb. 1. Others, June 16.

Italy, Nos. 554, 558 and 564 Overprinted in Red or Green

**1953, June 27**

**178** A306 10 l dp green (R) .80 .80
**179** A306 25 l brown org .80 .40
**180** A306 60 l red 2.40 2.00
*Nos. 178-180 (3)* 4.00 3.20

5th International Sample Fair of Trieste.

**1953, July 11 On No. 634**

**181** A355 25 l blue green 3.25 2.40

**1953, July 16 On Nos. 635-636**

**182** A356 25 l dark brown 1.60 *.80*
**183** A356 60 l deep blue 2.40 *3.25*

**1953, Aug. 6 On Nos. 637-638**

**184** A357 25 l org & Prus bl 1.60 1.60
**185** A357 60 l lil rose & dk vio bl 3.25 3.25

**1953, Aug. 13 On No. 639**

**186** A358 25 l dk brn & dl grn 3.25 2.40

**1953, Sept. 5 On No. 640**

**187** A359 25 l dk gray & brn 3.25 2.40

**1954, Jan. 26 On Nos. 641-646**

**188** A360 10 l dk brn & red brn .40 .40
**189** A361 12 l lt bl & gray .40 .40
**190** A361 20 l brn org & dk brn .40 .40
**191** A360 25 l dk grn & pale bl .40 .40
**192** A361 35 l cream & brn 2.40 2.40
**193** A361 60 l bl grn & ind 2.40 2.40
*Nos. 188-193 (6)* 6.40 6.40

**1954, Feb. 11 On Nos. 647-648**

**194** A362 25 l dk brn & choc 1.60 .80
**195** A362 60 l bl & ultra 2.40 *3.25*

**1954, Feb. 25 On Nos. 649-650**

**196** A363 25 l purple 1.60 .80
**197** A363 60 l dp bl grn 2.40 *3.25*

**1954, Mar. 20 On No. 651**

**198** A364 25 l purple 3.25 2.40

**1954, Apr. 24 On No. 652**

**199** A365 25 l gray blk 3.25 2.40

**1954, June 1 On No. 653**

**200** A366 25 l gray, org brn & blk 3.25 2.40

**1954, June 19 On No. 654**

**201** A367 25 l dk grnsh gray 3.25 2.40

**1954, July 8** **On Nos. 655-656**

| | | | | |
|---|---|---|---|---|
| 202 | A368 | 25 l red brown | 1.60 | 1.60 |
| 203 | A368 | 60 l gray green | 2.40 | 2.40 |

Nos. 644, 646 With Additional Overprint

**1954, June 17**

| | | | | |
|---|---|---|---|---|
| 204 | A360 | 25 l dk grn & pale bl | 1.60 | 1.60 |
| 205 | A361 | 60 l bl grn & indigo | 2.40 | 2.40 |

International Sample Fair of Trieste.

**1954, Sept. 6** **On No. 657**

| | | | | |
|---|---|---|---|---|
| 206 | A369 | 25 l dp grn & red | 3.25 | 2.40 |

**1954, Oct. 30** **On Nos. 658-659**

| | | | | |
|---|---|---|---|---|
| 207 | A370 | 25 l rose red | 1.60 | 1.60 |
| 208 | A370 | 60 l blue | 2.40 | 2.40 |

## OCCUPATION AIR POST STAMPS

### Air Post Stamps of Italy, 1945-47, Overprinted Type "c" in Black

**1947, Oct. 1** **Wmk. 277** ***Perf. 14***

| | | | | |
|---|---|---|---|---|
| C1 | AP59 | 1 l slate bl | .25 | .25 |
| C2 | AP60 | 2 l dk blue | .25 | .25 |
| C3 | AP60 | 5 l dk green | 8.00 | 6.50 |
| C4 | AP59 | 10 l car rose | 8.00 | 6.50 |
| C5 | AP60 | 25 l brown | 24.00 | 16.00 |
| C6 | AP59 | 50 l violet | 115.00 | 24.00 |
| | | *Nos. C1-C6 (6)* | 155.50 | 53.50 |

### Italy, Nos. C116 to C121, Overprinted Type "b" in Black

**1947, Nov. 19**

| | | | | |
|---|---|---|---|---|
| C7 | AP61 | 6 l dp violet | 2.40 | *4.00* |
| C8 | AP61 | 10 l dk car rose | 2.40 | *4.00* |
| C9 | AP61 | 20 l dp org | 21.00 | 16.00 |
| C10 | AP61 | 25 l aqua | 3.25 | *4.75* |
| C11 | AP61 | 35 l brt blue | 3.25 | *6.50* |
| C12 | AP61 | 50 l lilac rose | 21.00 | 12.50 |
| | | *Nos. C7-C12 (6)* | 53.30 | *47.75* |

### Italy, Nos. C123 to C126, Overprinted Type "f" in Black

**1948**

| | | | | |
|---|---|---|---|---|
| C13 | AP65 | 100 l green | 120.00 | 8.00 |
| C14 | AP65 | 300 l lil rose | 27.50 | *37.50* |
| C15 | AP65 | 500 l ultra | 50.00 | *52.50* |
| C16 | AP65 | 1000 l dk brown | 260.00 | *350.00* |
| | | *Nos. C13-C16 (4)* | 457.50 | *448.00* |

Issue date: Nos. C13-C15, Mar. 1.

Italy, No. C110, C113 and C114, Ovptd. in Black

**1948, Sept. 8**

| | | | | |
|---|---|---|---|---|
| C17 | AP59 | 10 l carmine rose | .40 | .40 |
| C18 | AP60 | 25 l brown | .80 | .80 |
| C19 | AP59 | 50 l violet | 1.20 | 1.20 |
| | | *Nos. C17-C19 (3)* | 2.40 | 2.40 |

The overprint is embossed.

### Italy Air Post Stamps of 1945-48 Overprinted Type "h" in Black

**1949-52**

| | | | | |
|---|---|---|---|---|
| C20 | AP59 | 10 l car rose | .25 | .25 |
| C21 | AP60 | 25 l brown ('50) | .25 | .25 |
| C22 | AP59 | 50 l violet | .25 | .25 |
| C23 | AP65 | 100 l green | .80 | .25 |
| C24 | AP65 | 300 l lil rose ('50) | 19.00 | *32.50* |
| C25 | AP65 | 500 l ultra ('50) | 50.00 | 37.50 |
| C26 | AP65 | 1000 l dk brn ('52) | 75.00 | *95.00* |
| | | *Nos. C20-C26 (7)* | 145.55 | *166.00* |

No. C26 is found in two perforations: 14 and 14x13.

Issued: 100 l, 11/7; 50 l, 12/5; 10 l, 12/28; 25 l, 1/23; 300 l, 500 l, 11/25; 1000 l, 2/18.

## OCCUPATION SPECIAL DELIVERY STAMPS

### Special Delivery Stamps of Italy 1946-48 Overprinted Type "c"

**1947-48** **Wmk. 277** ***Perf. 14***

| | | | | |
|---|---|---|---|---|
| E1 | SD9 | 15 l dk car rose | .25 | .30 |
| E2 | SD8 | 25 l brt red org ('48) | 90.00 | 27.50 |
| E3 | SD8 | 30 l dp vio | .60 | .60 |
| E4 | SD9 | 60 l car rose ('48) | 90.00 | 40.00 |
| | | *Nos. E1-E4 (4)* | 180.85 | 68.40 |

Issue dates: Oct. 1, 1947. Mar. 1, 1948.

### Italy No. E26, Overprinted Type "d"

**1948, Sept. 24**

| | | | | |
|---|---|---|---|---|
| E5 | A272 | 35 l violet | 4.00 | 4.00 |

### Italy No. E25, Overprinted Type "h"

**1950, Sept. 27**

| | | | | |
|---|---|---|---|---|
| E6 | SD9 | 60 l car rose | 8.75 | 3.25 |

### Italy No. E32 Overprinted Type "k"

**1952, Feb. 4**

| | | | | |
|---|---|---|---|---|
| E7 | SD8 | 50 l lilac rose | 8.75 | 3.25 |

## OCCUPATION AUTHORIZED DELIVERY STAMPS

### Authorized Delivery Stamp of Italy, 1946 Overprinted Type "a" in Black

**1947, Oct. 1** **Wmk. 277** ***Perf. 14***

| | | | | |
|---|---|---|---|---|
| EY1 | AD3 | 1 l dark brown | .80 | *1.60* |

Italy, No. EY7 Overprinted in Black

**1947, Oct. 29**

| | | | | |
|---|---|---|---|---|
| EY2 | AD4 | 8 l bright red | 14.50 | 4.75 |

### Italy, No. EY8, Overprinted Type "a" in Black

**1949, July 30**

| | | | | |
|---|---|---|---|---|
| EY3 | AD4 | 15 l violet | 80.00 | 40.00 |

### Same, Overprinted Type "h" in Black

**1949, Nov. 7**

| | | | | |
|---|---|---|---|---|
| EY4 | AD4 | 15 l violet | 1.60 | *2.00* |

### Italy No. EY9 Overprinted Type "h" in Black

**1952, Feb. 4**

| | | | | |
|---|---|---|---|---|
| EY5 | AD4 | 20 l rose violet | 14.50 | 2.40 |

## OCCUPATION POSTAGE DUE STAMPS

### Postage Due Stamps of Italy, 1945-47, Overprinted Type "a"

**1947, Oct. 1** **Wmk. 277** ***Perf. 14***

| | | | | |
|---|---|---|---|---|
| J1 | D9 | 1 l red orange | .80 | .80 |
| J2 | D10 | 2 l dk green | .40 | .80 |
| J3 | D9 | 5 l violet | 8.00 | 1.60 |
| J4 | D9 | 10 l dk blue | 15.00 | 7.00 |
| J5 | D9 | 20 l car rose | 30.00 | 9.50 |
| J6 | D10 | 50 l aqua | 2.40 | 1.60 |
| | | *Nos. J1-J6 (6)* | 56.60 | 21.30 |

### Same Overprint on Postage Due Stamps of Italy, 1947

**1949**

| | | | | |
|---|---|---|---|---|
| J7 | D10 | 1 l red orange | .40 | *.80* |
| J8 | D10 | 3 l carmine | .80 | *3.25* |
| J9 | D10 | 4 l brown | 17.50 | *32.50* |
| J10 | D10 | 5 l violet | 140.00 | 45.00 |
| J11 | D10 | 6 l vio blue | 47.50 | *65.00* |
| J12 | D10 | 8 l rose vio | 95.00 | *160.00* |
| J13 | D10 | 10 l deep blue | 210.00 | 45.00 |
| J14 | D10 | 12 l golden brn | 32.50 | *47.50* |
| J15 | D10 | 20 l lilac rose | 32.50 | 14.50 |
| | | *Nos. J7-J15 (9)* | 576.20 | 413.55 |

Issued: 3 l, 4 l, 6 l, 8 l, 12 l, 1/24; others, 4/15.

### Postage Due Stamps of Italy, 1947-54, Overprinted Type "h"

**1949-54**

| | | | | |
|---|---|---|---|---|
| J16 | D10 | 1 l red orange | .25 | .25 |
| J17 | D10 | 2 l dk green | .25 | .25 |
| J18 | D10 | 3 l car ('54) | .25 | .50 |
| J20 | D10 | 5 l violet | 1.25 | .25 |
| J21 | D10 | 6 l vio bl ('50) | .25 | .25 |
| J22 | D10 | 8 l rose vio ('50) | .25 | *1.00* |
| J23 | D10 | 10 l deep blue | .35 | *1.00* |
| J24 | D10 | 12 l gldn brn ('50) | 1.60 | 1.00 |
| J25 | D10 | 20 l lilac rose | 4.00 | .25 |
| J26 | D10 | 25 l dk red ('54) | 5.50 | 3.25 |
| J27 | D10 | 50 l aqua ('50) | 6.50 | .25 |
| J28 | D10 | 100 l org yel ('52) | 10.00 | 1.75 |
| J29 | D10 | 500 l dp bl & dk car ('52) | 115.00 | 90.00 |
| | | *Nos. J16-J29 (13)* | 145.45 | 100.00 |

Issued: 5 l, 10 l, 11/7; 1 l, 11/22; 2 l, 20 l, 12/28; 6 l, 8 l, 12 l, 5/16; 50 l, 11/25; 100 l, 11/11; 500 l, 6/19; 3 l, 1/24; 25 l, 2/1.

## OCCUPATION PARCEL POST STAMPS

See note preceding Italy No. Q7.

### Parcel Post Stamps of Italy, 1946-48, Overprinted

**1947-48** **Wmk. 277** ***Perf. 13½***

| | | | | |
|---|---|---|---|---|
| Q1 | PP4 | 1 l golden brn | .80 | *2.40* |
| Q2 | PP4 | 2 l lt bl grn | 1.00 | *4.00* |
| Q3 | PP4 | 3 l red org | .80 | *4.00* |
| Q4 | PP4 | 4 l gray blk | 1.25 | *4.75* |
| Q5 | PP4 | 5 l lil rose ('48) | 27.50 | *35.00* |
| Q6 | PP4 | 10 l violet | 8.00 | *20.00* |
| Q7 | PP4 | 20 l lilac brn | 8.00 | *20.00* |
| Q8 | PP4 | 50 l rose red | 12.00 | *37.50* |
| Q9 | PP4 | 100 l sapphire | 17.50 | *47.50* |
| Q10 | PP4 | 200 l grn ('48) | 575.00 | *1,000.* |
| Q11 | PP4 | 300 l brn car ('48) | 350.00 | *525.00* |
| Q12 | PP4 | 500 l brn ('48) | 200.00 | *300.00* |
| | | *Nos. Q1-Q12 (12)* | 1,201. | *2,000.* |

**Halves Used**

| | |
|---|---|
| Q1-Q4 | .40 |
| Q5 | .40 |
| Q6-Q7 | .40 |
| Q8 | .40 |
| Q9 | .40 |
| Q10 | .80 |
| Q11 | .60 |
| Q12 | .60 |

Issued: #Q1-Q4, Q6-Q9, Oct. 1; others, Mar. 1.

### Parcel Post Stamps of Italy, 1946-54, Overprinted

**1949-54**

| | | | | |
|---|---|---|---|---|
| Q13 | PP4 | 1 l gldn brn ('50) | 1.75 | 1.60 |
| Q14 | PP4 | 2 l lt bl grn ('51) | .85 | *1.00* |
| Q15 | PP4 | 3 l red org ('51) | .85 | *1.00* |
| Q16 | PP4 | 4 l gray blk ('51) | .85 | 1.00 |
| Q17 | PP4 | 5 l lilac rose | .85 | *1.00* |
| Q18 | PP4 | 10 l violet | 2.25 | 2.25 |
| Q19 | PP4 | 20 l lil brn | 2.25 | 2.25 |
| Q20 | PP4 | 30 l plum ('52) | .85 | *1.00* |
| Q21 | PP4 | 50 l rose red ('50) | 1.75 | *2.00* |
| Q22 | PP4 | 100 l saph ('50) | 4.00 | *7.00* |
| Q23 | PP4 | 200 l green | 27.50 | *70.00* |
| Q24 | PP4 | 300 l brn car ('50) | 140.00 | *200.00* |
| Q25 | PP4 | 500 l brn ('51) | 77.50 | *110.00* |

***Perf. 13x13½***

| | | | | |
|---|---|---|---|---|
| Q26 | PP5 | 1000 l ultra ('54) | 325.00 | *475.00* |
| | | *Nos. Q13-Q26 (14)* | 586.25 | *875.10* |

**Halves Used**

| | |
|---|---|
| Q13-Q18, Q20 | .40 |
| Q19, Q22 | .40 |
| Q21 | .40 |
| Q23 | .80 |
| Q24 | .80 |
| Q25 | .80 |
| Q26 | 2.00 |

Pairs of Q18 exist with 5mm between overprints instead of 11mm. Value $2,000.

Issued: 20 l, 200 l, 11/22; 5 l, 10 l, 11/28; 300 l, 1/19; 50 l, 3/10; 1 l, 10/7; 100 l, 11/9; 500 l, 11/25; 2 l, 3 l, 4 l, 8/1; 30 l, 3/6; 1000 l, 8/12.

## PARCEL POST AUTHORIZED DELIVERY STAMPS

For the payment of a special tax for the authorized delivery of parcels privately instead of through the post office. Both unused and used values are for complete stamps.

### Parcel Post Authorized Delivery Stamps of Italy 1953 Overprinted in Black like Nos. Q13-Q26

**1953, July 8** **Wmk. 277**

| | | | | |
|---|---|---|---|---|
| QY1 | PAD1 | 40 l org red | 21.00 | *7.00* |
| QY2 | PAD1 | 50 l ultra | 21.00 | *7.00* |
| QY3 | PAD1 | 75 l brown | 21.00 | *13.00* |
| QY4 | PAD1 | 110 l lilac rose | 21.00 | *13.00* |
| | | *Nos. QY1-QY4 (4)* | 84.00 | *40.00* |

**Halves Used**

| | |
|---|---|
| QY1 | .25 |
| QY2 | .25 |
| QY3-QY4, each | .35 |

# IVORY COAST

'iv-rē 'kōst

LOCATION — West coast of Africa, bordering on Gulf of Guinea
GOVT. — Republic
AREA — 127,520 sq. mi.
POP. — 15,818,068 (1999 est.)
CAPITAL — Yamoussoukro

The former French colony of Ivory Coast became part of French West Africa and used its stamps, starting in 1945. On December 4, 1958, Ivory Coast became a republic, with full independence on August 7, 1960.

100 Centimes = 1 Franc

**Catalogue values for unused stamps in this country are for Never Hinged items, beginning with Scott 167 in the regular postage section, Scott B15 in the semi-postal section, Scott C14 in the airpost section, Scott J19 in the postage due section, Scott M1 in the military section, and Scott O1 in the official section.**

Navigation and Commerce — A1

*Perf. 14x13½*

**1892-1900 Typo. Unwmk.**

**Colony Name in Blue or Carmine**

| | | | | |
|---|---|---|---|---|
| 1 | A1 | 1c black, *lil bl* | 2.00 | 2.40 |
| 2 | A1 | 2c brown, *buff* | 2.75 | 3.25 |
| 3 | A1 | 4c claret, *lav* | 4.75 | 4.75 |
| 4 | A1 | 5c green, *grnsh* | 13.50 | 9.00 |
| 5 | A1 | 10c black, *lavender* | 20.00 | 12.50 |
| 6 | A1 | 10c red ('00) | 130.00 | 110.00 |
| 7 | A1 | 15c blue, quadrille paper | 32.50 | 13.50 |
| 8 | A1 | 15c gray ('00) | 20.00 | 5.75 |
| 9 | A1 | 20c red, *green* | 21.00 | 16.00 |
| 10 | A1 | 25c black, *rose* | 24.00 | 6.50 |
| 11 | A1 | 25c blue ('00) | 40.00 | 37.50 |
| 12 | A1 | 30c brown, *bister* | 35.00 | 27.50 |
| 13 | A1 | 40c red, *straw* | 27.50 | 16.00 |
| 14 | A1 | 50c car, *rose* | 80.00 | 65.00 |
| 15 | A1 | 50c brn, *azure* ('00) | 37.50 | 32.50 |
| 16 | A1 | 75c deep vio, *org* | 32.50 | 32.50 |
| 17 | A1 | 1fr brnz grn, *straw* | 52.50 | 45.00 |
| | | *Nos. 1-17 (17)* | 575.50 | 439.65 |

Perf. 13½x14 stamps are counterfeits.
For surcharges see Nos. 18-20, 37-41.

Nos. 12, 16-17 Surcharged in Black

**1904**

| | | | | |
|---|---|---|---|---|
| 18 | A1 | 0,05c on 30c brn, *bis* | 87.50 | 87.50 |
| 19 | A1 | 0,10c on 75c vio, *org* | 18.00 | 18.00 |
| 20 | A1 | 0,15c on 1fr brnz grn, *straw* | 26.00 | 26.00 |
| | | *Nos. 18-20 (3)* | 131.50 | 131.50 |

Gen. Louis Faidherbe A2

Oil Palm — A3

Dr. N. Eugène Ballay A4

**1906-07**

**Name of Colony in Red or Blue**

| | | | | |
|---|---|---|---|---|
| 21 | A2 | 1c slate | 2.00 | 2.00 |
| a. | | "CÔTE D'IVOIRE" omitted | 160.00 | 160.00 |
| 22 | A2 | 2c chocolate | 2.00 | 2.00 |
| 23 | A2 | 4c choc, *gray bl* | 2.40 | 2.40 |
| a. | | "CÔTE D'IVOIRE" double | 225.00 | |
| b. | | "CÔTE D'IVOIRE" omitted | 190.00 | |
| 24 | A2 | 5c green | 4.00 | 2.75 |
| a. | | "CÔTE D'IVOIRE" omitted | 110.00 | 92.50 |
| 25 | A2 | 10c carmine (B) | 9.50 | 6.50 |
| a. | | "CÔTE D'IVOIRE" double | 210.00 | 400.00 |
| b. | | "CÔTE D'IVOIRE" omitted | | 400.00 |
| 26 | A3 | 20c black, *azure* | 10.00 | 9.50 |
| 27 | A3 | 25c bl, *pinkish* | 9.50 | 6.00 |
| 28 | A3 | 30c choc, *pnksh* | 12.50 | 8.75 |
| 30 | A3 | 35c black, *yel* | 12.50 | 5.75 |
| a. | | "CÔTE D'IVOIRE" omitted | 225.00 | |
| 31 | A3 | 45c choc, *grnsh* | 18.00 | 12.50 |
| 32 | A3 | 50c deep violet | 16.00 | 12.50 |
| 33 | A3 | 75c blue, *org* | 16.00 | 12.50 |
| 34 | A4 | 1fr black, *azure* | 40.00 | 35.00 |
| 35 | A4 | 2fr blue, *pink* | 52.50 | 50.00 |
| 36 | A4 | 5fr car, *straw* (B) | 100.00 | 95.00 |
| | | *Nos. 21-36 (15)* | 306.90 | 263.15 |

**Stamps of 1892-1900 Surcharged in Carmine or Black**

**1912**

| | | | | |
|---|---|---|---|---|
| 37 | A1 | 5c on 15c gray (C) | 1.60 | 1.60 |
| 38 | A1 | 5c on 30c brn, *bis* (C) | 2.40 | 2.75 |
| 39 | A1 | 10c on 40c red, *straw* | 2.40 | 2.75 |
| a. | | Pair, one without surcharge | 75.00 | 75.00 |
| 40 | A1 | 10c on 50c brn, *az* (C) | 4.00 | 4.75 |
| 41 | A1 | 10c on 75c dp vio, *org* | 9.00 | 10.00 |
| | | *Nos. 37-41 (5)* | 19.40 | 21.85 |

Two spacings between the surcharged numerals are found on Nos. 37 to 41. For detailed listings, see the *Scott Classic Specialized Catalogue of Stamps and Covers.*

River Scene A5

**1913-35**

| | | | | |
|---|---|---|---|---|
| 42 | A5 | 1c vio brn & vio | .25 | .25 |
| 43 | A5 | 2c brown & blk | .25 | .25 |
| 44 | A5 | 4c vio & vio brn | .30 | .30 |
| 45 | A5 | 5c yel grn & bl grn | 1.10 | .50 |
| 46 | A5 | 5c choc & ol brn ('22) | .30 | .30 |
| 47 | A5 | 10c red org & rose | 2.00 | .95 |
| 48 | A5 | 10c yel grn & bl grn ('22) | .70 | .70 |
| 49 | A5 | 10c car rose, *bluish* ('26) | .30 | .30 |
| 50 | A5 | 15c org & rose ('17) | 1.75 | .80 |
| 51 | A5 | 20c black & gray | .80 | .55 |
| 52 | A5 | 25c ultra & bl | 11.00 | 6.50 |
| 53 | A5 | 25c blk & vio ('22) | .55 | .55 |
| 54 | A5 | 30c choc & brn | 2.40 | 2.00 |
| 55 | A5 | 30c red org & rose ('22) | 2.75 | 2.75 |
| 56 | A5 | 30c lt bl & rose red ('26) | .50 | .50 |
| 57 | A5 | 30c dl grn & grn ('27) | .80 | .80 |
| 58 | A5 | 35c vio & org | .95 | .80 |
| 59 | A5 | 40c gray & bl grn | 1.60 | .80 |
| 60 | A5 | 45c red org & choc | 1.00 | .80 |
| 61 | A5 | 45c dp rose & mar ('34) | 6.25 | 5.00 |
| 62 | A5 | 50c black & vio | 5.00 | 3.50 |
| 63 | A5 | 50c ultra & bl ('22) | 2.00 | 2.00 |
| 64 | A5 | 50c ol grn & bl ('25) | .80 | .80 |
| 65 | A5 | 60c vio, *pnksh* ('25) | .80 | .80 |
| 66 | A5 | 65c car rose & ol grn ('26) | 1.60 | 1.60 |
| 67 | A5 | 75c brn & rose | 1.00 | .80 |
| 68 | A5 | 75c ind & ultra ('34) | 4.50 | 4.00 |
| 69 | A5 | 85c red vio & blk ('26) | 1.60 | 1.60 |
| 70 | A5 | 90c brn red & rose ('30) | 17.50 | 13.50 |
| 71 | A5 | 1fr org & black | 1.10 | 1.00 |
| 72 | A5 | 1.10fr dl grn & dk brn ('28) | 7.75 | 7.00 |
| 73 | A5 | 1.50fr lt bl & dp bl ('30) | 10.00 | 7.50 |
| 74 | A5 | 1.75fr lt ultra & mag ('35) | 17.50 | 9.50 |
| 75 | A5 | 2fr brn & blue | 6.00 | 2.90 |
| 76 | A5 | 3fr red vio ('30) | 11.00 | 7.50 |
| 77 | A5 | 5fr dk bl & choc | 10.00 | 5.75 |
| | | *Nos. 42-77 (36)* | 133.70 | 95.15 |

Nos. 45, 47, 50, 52, 56 and 58 exist on both ordinary and chalky paper. See the *Scott Classic Specialized Catalogue of Stamps & Covers 1840-1940* for listings.
For surcharges see Nos. 78-91, B1.
Nos. 45, 47 and 52, pasted on cardboard and overprinted "Valeur d'echange" and value of basic stamp, were used as emergency currency in 1920.

Stamps and Type of 1913-34 Srchd.

**1922-34**

| | | | | |
|---|---|---|---|---|
| 78 | A5 | 50c on 45c dp rose & maroon ('34) | 4.00 | 2.75 |
| 79 | A5 | 50c on 75c indigo & ultra ('34) | 2.40 | 2.00 |
| 80 | A5 | 50c on 90c brn red & rose ('34) | 2.40 | 2.40 |
| 81 | A5 | 60c on 75c vio, *pnksh* | .65 | .65 |
| a. | | Surcharge omitted | 160.00 | *175.00* |
| 82 | A5 | 65c on 15c orange & rose ('25) | 1.25 | 1.25 |
| 83 | A5 | 85c on 75c brown & rose ('25) | 1.60 | 1.25 |
| | | *Nos. 78-83 (6)* | 12.30 | 10.30 |

Stamps and Type of 1913 Surcharged with New Value and Bars

**1924-27**

| | | | | |
|---|---|---|---|---|
| 84 | A5 | 25c on 2fr (R) | 1.10 | 1.10 |
| 85 | A5 | 25c on 5fr | 1.10 | 1.10 |
| 86 | A5 | 90c on 75c brn red & cer ('27) | 2.00 | 1.60 |
| a. | | Surcharge omitted | 240.00 | |
| 87 | A5 | 1.25fr on 1fr dk bl & ultra (R) ('26) | 1.25 | 1.25 |
| 88 | A5 | 1.50fr on 1fr lt bl & dk blue ('27) | 2.00 | 2.00 |
| 89 | A5 | 3fr on 5fr brn red & bl grn ('27) | 6.00 | 6.00 |
| a. | | Double surcharge | 160.00 | |
| 90 | A5 | 10fr on 5fr dl red & rose lil ('27) | 17.50 | 16.00 |
| 91 | A5 | 20fr on 5fr bl grn & ver ('27) | 21.00 | 19.00 |
| | | *Nos. 84-91 (8)* | 51.95 | 48.05 |

Common Design Types pictured following the introduction.

**Colonial Exposition Issue**

Common Design Types
Name of Country in Black

**1931 Engr. *Perf. 12½***

| | | | | |
|---|---|---|---|---|
| 92 | CD70 | 40c deep green | 4.00 | 4.00 |
| 93 | CD71 | 50c violet | 6.50 | 6.50 |
| 94 | CD72 | 90c red orange | 5.50 | 5.50 |
| 95 | CD73 | 1.50fr dull blue | 6.50 | 6.50 |
| | | *Nos. 92-95 (4)* | 22.50 | 22.50 |

Stamps of Upper Volta 1928, Overprinted

**1933 *Perf. 13½x14***

| | | | | |
|---|---|---|---|---|
| 96 | A5 | 2c brown & lilac | .25 | .25 |
| a. | | Inverted overprint | 27.50 | |
| b. | | Double overprint | 40.00 | 47.50 |
| 97 | A5 | 4c blk & yellow | .35 | .35 |
| a. | | Inverted overprint | 100.00 | |
| b. | | Double overprint | 65.00 | 72.50 |
| 98 | A5 | 5c ind & gray bl | .65 | .50 |
| a. | | Inverted overprint | 47.50 | |
| b. | | Double overprint | 65.00 | |
| 99 | A5 | 10c indigo & pink | .50 | .50 |
| 100 | A5 | 15c brown & blue | 1.25 | 1.00 |
| 101 | A5 | 20c brown & green | 1.25 | 1.00 |
| 102 | A6 | 25c brn & yellow | 2.25 | 1.90 |
| 103 | A6 | 30c dp grn & brn | 2.75 | 2.00 |
| a. | | Double overprint | 75.00 | |
| 104 | A6 | 45c brown & blue | 10.00 | 6.50 |
| a. | | Inverted overprint | 80.00 | |
| b. | | Double overprint | 120.00 | |
| 105 | A6 | 65c indigo & bl | 4.00 | 2.90 |
| a. | | Double overprint | 95.00 | |
| 106 | A6 | 75c black & lilac | 4.75 | 2.50 |
| a. | | Double overprint | 95.00 | |
| 107 | A6 | 90c brn red & lil | 4.00 | 2.90 |

Burkina Faso Nos. 58 & 60 Ovptd.

| | | | | |
|---|---|---|---|---|
| 108 | A7 | 1fr brown & green | 4.75 | 3.25 |
| a. | | Inverted overprint | 150.00 | 160.00 |
| 109 | A7 | 1.50fr ultra & grysh | 4.50 | 2.90 |
| a. | | Inverted overprint | 150.00 | |
| b. | | Double overprint | 95.00 | |

Burkina Faso Nos. 52 & 54 Surcharged

| | | | | |
|---|---|---|---|---|
| 110 | A6 | 1.25fr on 40c blk & pink | 3.00 | 2.25 |
| a. | | Double overprint | 100.00 | |
| 111 | A6 | 1.75fr on 50c blk & green | 5.25 | 3.25 |
| a. | | Double overprint | 100.00 | |
| | | *Nos. 96-111 (16)* | 49.50 | 33.95 |

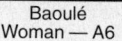

Baoulé Woman — A6

Rapids on Comoe River — A9

Mosque at Bobo-Dioulasso — A7

Coastal Scene A8

**1936-44** *Perf. 13*

| | | | | |
|---|---|---|---|---|
| 112 | A6 | 1c carmine rose | .25 | .25 |
| 113 | A6 | 2c ultramarine | .25 | .25 |
| 114 | A6 | 3c dp grn ('40) | .25 | .25 |
| 115 | A6 | 4c chocolate | .25 | .25 |
| 116 | A6 | 5c violet | .25 | .25 |
| 117 | A6 | 10c Prussian bl | .25 | .25 |
| 118 | A6 | 15c copper red | .25 | .25 |
| 119 | A7 | 20c ultramarine | .35 | .25 |
| 120 | A7 | 25c copper red | .50 | .25 |
| 121 | A7 | 30c blue green | .35 | .35 |
| 122 | A7 | 30c brown ('40) | .25 | .25 |
| 123 | A6 | 35c dp grn ('38) | .85 | .65 |
| 124 | A7 | 40c carmine rose | .50 | .35 |
| 125 | A7 | 45c brown | .65 | .65 |
| 126 | A7 | 45c blue grn ('40) | .35 | .35 |
| 127 | A7 | 50c plum | .50 | .50 |
| 128 | A7 | 55c dark vio ('38) | .60 | .60 |
| 129 | A8 | 60c car rose ('40) | .40 | .40 |
| 130 | A8 | 65c red brown | .65 | .50 |
| 131 | A8 | 70c red brn ('40) | .65 | .65 |
| 132 | A8 | 75c dark violet | 1.25 | .75 |
| 133 | A8 | 80c blk brn ('38) | 1.50 | .95 |
| 134 | A8 | 90c carmine rose | 10.00 | 5.50 |
| 135 | A8 | 90c dk grn ('39) | .85 | .80 |
| 136 | A8 | 1fr dark green | 5.00 | 2.75 |
| 137 | A8 | 1fr car rose ('38) | 1.75 | .95 |
| 138 | A8 | 1fr dk vio ('40) | .65 | .65 |
| 139 | A8 | 1.25fr copper red | .50 | .40 |
| 140 | A8 | 1.40fr ultra ('40) | .65 | .65 |
| 141 | A8 | 1.50fr ultramarine | .60 | .40 |
| 141A | A8 | 1.50fr grnsh blk ('42) | 2.25 | 2.00 |
| 142 | A8 | 1.60fr blk brn ('40) | 1.25 | 1.00 |
| 143 | A9 | 1.75fr carmine rose | .65 | .40 |
| 144 | A9 | 1.75fr dull bl ('38) | 1.25 | .85 |
| 145 | A9 | 2fr ultramarine | .85 | .60 |
| 146 | A9 | 2.25fr dark bl ('39) | 1.25 | 1.25 |
| 147 | A9 | 2.50fr rose red ('40) | 1.75 | 1.40 |
| 148 | A9 | 3fr green | .95 | .60 |
| 149 | A9 | 5fr chocolate | 1.00 | .65 |
| 150 | A9 | 10fr violet | 1.50 | 1.00 |
| 151 | A9 | 20fr copper red | 2.75 | 1.80 |
| | | *Nos. 112-151 (41)* | 46.55 | 32.85 |

For types A7, A8 and A9 without "RF," see Nos. 166A-166D.

For surcharges see Nos. B8-B11.

### Paris International Exposition Issue

Common Design Types

**1937** *Perf. 13*

| | | | | |
|---|---|---|---|---|
| 152 | CD74 | 20c deep violet | 2.00 | 2.00 |
| 153 | CD75 | 30c dark green | 2.00 | 2.00 |
| 154 | CD76 | 40c carmine rose | 2.00 | 2.00 |
| 155 | CD77 | 50c dk brn & bl | 1.60 | 1.60 |
| 156 | CD78 | 90c red | 1.60 | 1.60 |
| 157 | CD79 | 1.50fr ultra | 2.00 | 2.00 |
| | | *Nos. 152-157 (6)* | 11.20 | 11.20 |

### Colonial Arts Exhibition Issue

Souvenir Sheet

Common Design Type

**1937** *Imperf.*

| | | | | |
|---|---|---|---|---|
| 158 | CD76 | 3fr sepia | 8.75 | *10.00* |

Louis Gustave Binger A10

**1937** *Perf. 13*

| | | | | |
|---|---|---|---|---|
| 159 | A10 | 65c red brown | .65 | .65 |

Death of Governor General Binger; 50th anniv. of his exploration of the Niger.

### Caillie Issue

Common Design Type

**1939** **Engr.** *Perf. 12½x12*

| | | | | |
|---|---|---|---|---|
| 160 | CD81 | 90c org brn & org | .80 | .80 |
| 161 | CD81 | 2fr bright violet | 1.20 | 1.20 |
| 162 | CD81 | 2.25fr ultra & dk bl | 1.20 | 1.20 |
| | | *Nos. 160-162 (3)* | 3.20 | 3.20 |

### New York World's Fair Issue

Common Design Type

**1939**

| | | | | |
|---|---|---|---|---|
| 163 | CD82 | 1.25fr carmine lake | 1.50 | 1.50 |
| 164 | CD82 | 2.25fr ultramarine | 1.50 | 1.50 |

Ebrié Lagoon and Marshal Pétain A11

**1941**

| | | | | |
|---|---|---|---|---|
| 165 | A11 | 1fr green | .80 | — |
| 166 | A11 | 2.50fr deep blue | .85 | — |

For surcharges, see Nos. B14A-B14B.

### Types of 1936-40 Without "RF"

**1944** *Perf. 13*

| | | | |
|---|---|---|---|
| 166A | A7 | 30c brown | 1.60 |
| 166B | A8 | 60c car rose | 1.75 |
| 166C | A8 | 1fr dark violet | 1.75 |
| 166D | A9 | 20fr copper red | 3.75 |
| | | *Nos. 166A-166D (4)* | 8.85 |

Nos. 166A-166D were issued by the Vichy government in France, but were not placed on sale in Ivory Coast.

For other stamps inscribed Cote d'Ivoire and Afrique Occidental Francaise see French West Africa Nos. 58, 72, 77.

**Catalogue values for unused stamps in this section, from this point to the end of the section, are for Never Hinged items.**

### Republic

Elephant — A12

**1959, Oct. 1** **Engr.** *Perf. 13*

| | | | | |
|---|---|---|---|---|
| 167 | A12 | 10fr black & emerald | .85 | .35 |
| 168 | A12 | 25fr vio brn & olive | 1.25 | .50 |
| 169 | A12 | 30fr ol blk & grnsh bl | 1.50 | 1.00 |
| | | *Nos. 167-169 (3)* | 3.60 | 1.85 |

Imperforates

Most Ivory Coast stamps from 1959 onward exist imperforate in issued and trial colors, and also in small presentation sheets in issued colors.

President Felix Houphouet-Boigny A13

**1959, Dec. 4** **Unwmk.**

| | | | | |
|---|---|---|---|---|
| 170 | A13 | 25fr violet brown | 1.00 | .60 |

Proclamation of the Republic, 1st anniv.

Bété Mask — A14

Designs: Masks of 5 tribes: Bété, Gueré, Baoulé, Senufo and Guro. #174-176 horiz.

**1960** *Perf. 13*

| | | | | |
|---|---|---|---|---|
| 171 | A14 | 50c pale brn & vio brn | .25 | .25 |
| 172 | A14 | 1fr violet & mag | .25 | .25 |
| 173 | A14 | 2fr ultra & bl grn | .25 | .25 |
| 174 | A14 | 4fr dk grn & org | .25 | .25 |
| 175 | A14 | 5fr ver & brown | .40 | .30 |
| 176 | A14 | 6fr dark brn & vio | .50 | .40 |
| 177 | A14 | 45fr dk grn & brn vio | 1.80 | 1.00 |
| 178 | A14 | 50fr dk brn & grnsh bl | 2.75 | 1.20 |
| 179 | A14 | 85fr car & slate grn | 5.00 | 2.25 |
| | | *Nos. 171-179 (9)* | 11.45 | 6.15 |

### C.C.T.A. Issue

Common Design Type

**1960, May 16** **Engr.** *Perf. 13*

| | | | | |
|---|---|---|---|---|
| 180 | CD106 | 25fr grnsh bl & vio | 1.10 | .50 |

Emblem of the Entente — A14a

**1960, May 29** **Photo.** *Perf. 13x13½*

| | | | | |
|---|---|---|---|---|
| 181 | A14a | 25fr multicolored | 1.10 | 1.00 |

1st anniv. of the Entente (Dahomey, Ivory Coast, Niger and Upper Volta).

Young Couple with Olive Branch and Globe — A15

**1961, Aug. 7** **Engr.** *Perf. 13*

| | | | | |
|---|---|---|---|---|
| 182 | A15 | 25fr emer, bister & blk | 1.00 | .50 |

First anniversary of Independence.

Blood Lilies — A16

Designs: Various Local Plants & Orchids.

**1961-62**

| | | | | |
|---|---|---|---|---|
| 183 | A16 | 5fr dk grn, red & orange ('62) | 1.00 | .35 |
| 184 | A16 | 10fr ultra, claret & yel | .60 | .35 |
| 185 | A16 | 15fr org, rose lil & green ('62) | 1.80 | .50 |
| 186 | A16 | 20fr brn, dk red & yel | 1.00 | .50 |
| 187 | A16 | 25fr grn, red brn & yel | 1.00 | .50 |
| 188 | A16 | 30fr blk, car & green | 1.25 | .75 |
| 189 | A16 | 70fr green, ver & yel | 3.25 | 1.60 |
| 190 | A16 | 85fr brn, lil, yel & grn | 5.25 | 2.00 |
| | | *Nos. 183-190 (8)* | 15.15 | 6.55 |

Early Letter Carrier and Modern Mailman — A17

**1961, Oct. 14** **Unwmk.** *Perf. 13*

| | | | | |
|---|---|---|---|---|
| 191 | A17 | 25fr choc, emer & bl | 1.00 | .70 |

Issued for Stamp Day.

Ayamé Dam — A18

**1961, Nov. 18** **Engr.**

| | | | | |
|---|---|---|---|---|
| 192 | A18 | 25fr grnsh bl, blk & grn | 1.10 | .50 |

Swimming Race A19

**1961, Dec. 23** **Unwmk.** *Perf. 13*

| | | | | |
|---|---|---|---|---|
| 193 | A19 | 5fr shown | .45 | .25 |
| 194 | A19 | 20fr Basketball | .65 | .30 |
| 195 | A19 | 25fr Soccer | 1.10 | .45 |
| | | *Nos. 193-195 (3)* | 2.20 | 1.00 |

Abidjan Games, Dec. 24-31. See No. C17.

Palms — A20

**1962, Feb. 5** **Photo.** *Perf. 12x12½*

| | | | | |
|---|---|---|---|---|
| 196 | A20 | 25fr brn, blue & org | 1.10 | .45 |

Commission for Technical Co-operation in Africa South of the Sahara, 17th session, Abidjan, 2/5-16.

Fort Assinie and Assinie River — A21

**1962, May 26** **Engr.** *Perf. 13*

| | | | | |
|---|---|---|---|---|
| 197 | A21 | 85fr Prus grn, grn & dl red brn | 3.25 | 1.50 |

Centenary of the Ivory Coast post.

### African and Malagasy Union Issue

Common Design Type

**1962, Sept. 8** **Photo.** *Perf. 12½x12*

| | | | | |
|---|---|---|---|---|
| 198 | CD110 | 30fr multicolored | 2.10 | .75 |

African and Malagasy Union, 1st anniv.

Fair Emblem, Cotton and Spindles — A22

**1963, Jan. 26** **Engr.** *Perf. 13*

| | | | | |
|---|---|---|---|---|
| 199 | A22 | 50fr grn, brn org & sepia | 2.75 | 1.25 |

Bouake Fair, Jan. 26-Feb. 4.

Stylized Map of Africa A23

**1963, May 25** **Photo.** *Perf. 12½x12*

| | | | | |
|---|---|---|---|---|
| 200 | A23 | 30fr ultra & emerald | 1.10 | .90 |

Conference of African heads of state for African unity, Addis Ababa.

Hartebeest — A24

Designs: 1fr, Yellow-backed duiker, horiz. 2fr, Potto. 4fr, Beecroft's hyrax, horiz. 5fr, Water chevrotain. 15fr, Forest hog, horiz. 20fr, Wart hog, horiz. 25fr, Bongo (antelope).

45fr, Cape hunting dogs, or hyenas, horiz. 50fr, Black-and-white colobus (monkey).

**1963-64 Engr. *Perf. 13***

| | | | | |
|---|---|---|---|---|
| **201** | A24 | 1fr choc, grn & yellow ('64) | .75 | .25 |
| **202** | A24 | 2fr blk, dk bl, gray ol & brown ('64) | .75 | .25 |
| **203** | A24 | 4fr red brn, dk bl, brn & black ('64) | .65 | .30 |
| **204** | A24 | 5fr sl grn, brn & citron ('64) | .65 | .30 |
| **205** | A24 | 10fr ol grn & ocher | .85 | .30 |
| **206** | A24 | 15fr red brn, grn & black ('64) | 1.40 | .45 |
| **207** | A24 | 20fr red org grn & blk | 1.75 | .45 |
| **208** | A24 | 25fr red brn & green | 2.40 | .60 |
| **209** | A24 | 45fr choc, bl grn & yel green | 5.00 | 1.50 |
| **210** | A24 | 50fr red brn, grn & blk | 7.00 | 2.00 |
| *a.* | | Min. sheet of 4, #205, 207, 209-210 | 25.00 | 25.00 |
| | | *Nos. 201-210 (10)* | 21.20 | 6.40 |

See Nos. 218-220.

UNESCO Emblem, Scales and Globe — A25

**1963, Dec. 10 Unwmk.**

**211** A25 85fr dk bl, blk & org 2.25 .80

Universal Declaration of Human Rights, 15th anniv.

Sun Radiating from Ivory Coast over Africa — A26

**1964, Mar. 17 Photo. *Perf. 12x12½***

**212** A26 30fr grn, dl vio & red 1.10 .45

Inter-African Conference of Natl. Education Ministers.

Weather Station and Balloon — A27

**1964, Mar. 23 *Perf. 13x12½***

**213** A27 25fr multicolored 1.25 .60

World Meteorological Day, Mar. 23.

Physician Vaccinating Child — A28

**1964, May 8 Engr. *Perf. 13***

**214** A28 50fr dk brn, bl & red 1.90 .70

Issued to honor the National Red Cross.

Wrestlers, Globe and Torch — A29

**1964, June 27 Unwmk. *Perf. 13***

| | | | | |
|---|---|---|---|---|
| **215** | A29 | 35fr Globe, torch, athletes, vert. | 1.50 | .55 |
| **216** | A29 | 65fr shown | 2.75 | 1.10 |

18th Olympic Games, Tokyo, Oct. 10-25.

**Europafrica Issue, 1964**

Common Design Type

Design: 30fr, White man and black man beneath tree of industrial symbols.

**1964, July 20 Photo. *Perf. 12x13***

**217** CD116 30fr multicolored 1.10 .35

**Animal Type of 1963-64**

Designs: 5fr, Manatee, horiz. 10fr, Pygmy hippopotamus, horiz. 15fr, Royal antelope.

**1964, Oct. 17 Engr. *Perf. 13***

| | | | | |
|---|---|---|---|---|
| **218** | A24 | 5fr yel grn, sl grn & brn | .75 | .30 |
| **219** | A24 | 10fr sep, Prus grn & dp cl | 2.00 | .45 |
| **220** | A24 | 15fr lil rose, grn & org brn | 3.00 | .45 |
| | | *Nos. 218-220 (3)* | 5.75 | 1.20 |

**Co-operation Issue**

Common Design Type

**1964, Nov. 7 Unwmk. *Perf. 13***

**221** CD119 25fr grn, dk brn & red 1.10 .35

Korhogo Mail Carriers with Guard, 1914 — A30

**1964, Nov. 28 Engr.**

**222** A30 85fr blk, brn, bl & brn red 2.75 1.40

Issued for Stamp Day.

Potter A31

Artisans: 10fr, Wood carvers. 20fr, Ivory carver. 25fr, Weaver.

**1965, Mar. 27 Engr. *Perf. 13***

| | | | | |
|---|---|---|---|---|
| **223** | A31 | 5fr mag, green & blk | .40 | .25 |
| **224** | A31 | 10fr red lil, grn & blk | .50 | .25 |
| **225** | A31 | 20fr bis, dp bl & dk brn | .90 | .30 |
| **226** | A31 | 25fr brn, olive & car | 1.10 | .45 |
| | | *Nos. 223-226 (4)* | 2.90 | 1.25 |

Unloading Mail, 1900 A32

**1965, Apr. 24 Unwmk. *Perf. 13***

**227** A32 30fr multicolored 1.25 .70

Issued for Stamp Day.

A32a

ITU emblem, old and new telecommunication equipment.

**1965, May 17**

**228** A32a 85fr mar, brt grn & dk bl 2.25 .70

ITU, centenary.

Abidjan Railroad Station A33

**1965, June 12 Engr. *Perf. 13***

**229** A33 30fr magenta, bl & brn ol 1.60 .80

Pres. Felix Houphouet-Boigny and Map of Ivory Coast — A34

**1965, Aug. 7 Photo. *Perf. 12½x13***

**230** A34 30fr multicolored 1.00 .45

Fifth anniversary of Independence.

Hammerhead Stork — A35

Birds: 1fr, Bruce's green pigeon, horiz. 2fr, Spur-winged goose, horiz. 5fr, Stone partridge. 15fr, White-breasted guinea fowl. 30fr, Namaqua dove, horiz. 50fr, Lizard buzzard, horiz. 75fr, Yellow-billed stork. 90fr, Forest (or Latham's) francolin.

**1965-66 Engr. *Perf. 13***

| | | | | |
|---|---|---|---|---|
| **231** | A35 | 1fr yel grn, pur & yellow ('66) | 1.00 | .30 |
| **232** | A35 | 2fr slate grn, blk & red ('66) | 1.00 | .40 |
| **233** | A35 | 5fr dk ol, dk brn & brn red ('66) | 1.25 | .45 |
| **234** | A35 | 10fr red lil, blk & red brown | 1.40 | .30 |
| **235** | A35 | 15fr sl grn, gray & ver | 1.50 | .40 |
| **236** | A35 | 30fr sl grn, mar & red brown | 2.00 | .65 |
| **237** | A35 | 50fr brn, blk & chlky bl | 3.50 | 1.00 |
| **238** | A35 | 75fr org, mar & sl grn | 6.25 | 1.50 |
| **239** | A35 | 90fr emerald, blk & brown ('66) | 7.25 | 3.00 |
| | | *Nos. 231-239 (9)* | 25.15 | 8.00 |

Mail Train, 1906 — A36

**1966, Mar. 26 Engr. *Perf. 13***

**240** A36 30fr grn, blk & mar 2.75 1.00

Issued for Stamp Day.

Baoulé Mother and Child, Carved in Wood — A37

Designs: 10fr, Unguent vessel, Wamougo mask lid, 20fr, Atié carved drums. 30fr, Bété female ancestral figure.

**1966, Apr. 9 Unwmk.**

| | | | | |
|---|---|---|---|---|
| **241** | A37 | 5fr blk & emerald | .45 | .25 |
| **242** | A37 | 10fr purple & blk | .75 | .30 |
| **243** | A37 | 20fr orange & blk | 2.00 | .75 |
| **244** | A37 | 30fr red & black | 2.50 | 1.00 |
| | | *Nos. 241-244 (4)* | 5.70 | 2.30 |

Intl. Negro Arts Festival, Dakar, Senegal, 4/1-24.

Hotel Ivoire A38

**1966, Apr. 30 Engr. *Perf. 13***

**245** A38 15fr bl, grn, red & olive .90 .40

Farm Tractor A39

**1966, Aug. 7 Photo. *Perf. 12½x12***

**246** A39 30fr multicolored 1.00 .55

6th anniversary of independence.

Uniformed Teacher and Villagers A40

**1966, Sept. 1 Engr. *Perf. 13***

**247** A40 30fr dk red, indigo & dk brn 1.00 .50

National School of Administration.

Veterinarian Treating Cattle A41

**1966, Oct. 22 Engr. *Perf. 13***

**248** A41 30fr ol, bl & dp brn 1.10 .50

Campaign against cattle plague.

Man, Waves, UNESCO Emblem — A42

Delivery of Gift Parcels — A43

**1966, Nov. 14 Engr. *Perf. 13***
**249** A42 30fr dp bl & vio brn 1.00 .55

UNESCO, 20th anniv.

**1966, Dec. 11 Engr. *Perf. 13***
**250** A43 30fr dk bl, brn & blk 1.00 .55

UNICEF, 20th anniv.

Bouaké Hospital and Red Cross A44

**1966, Dec. 20**
**251** A44 30fr red brn, red & lilac 1.00 .55

Sikorsky S-43 Seaplane and Boats — A45

**1967, Mar. 25 Engr. *Perf. 13***
**252** A45 30fr indigo, bl grn & brn 3.00 1.20

Stamp Day. 30th anniv. of the Sikorsky S-43 flying boat route.

Pineapple Harvest A46

| **1967** | **Engr.** | ***Perf. 13*** | |
|---|---|---|---|
| **253** A46 | 20fr shown | .60 | .40 |
| **254** A46 | 30fr Cabbage tree | .85 | .45 |
| **255** A46 | 100fr Bananas | 3.50 | 1.10 |
| | *Nos. 253-255 (3)* | 4.95 | 1.95 |

Issue dates: 30fr, June 24; others, Mar. 25.

Genie, Protector of Assamlangangan A47

**1967, July 31 Engr. *Perf. 13***
**256** A47 30fr grn, blk & maroon 1.00 .55

Intl. PEN Club (writers' organization), 25th Congress, Abidjan, July 31-Aug. 5.

Old and New Houses A48

**1967, Aug. 7 Photo. *Perf. 12½x12***
**257** A48 30fr multicolored 1.00 .55

7th anniversary of independence.

Lions Emblem and Elephant's Head A49

**1967, Sept. 2 Photo. *Perf. 12½x13***
**258** A49 30fr lt bl & multi 1.50 .60

50th anniversary of Lions International.

**Monetary Union Issue**
Common Design Type

**1967, Nov. 4 Engr. *Perf. 13***
**259** CD125 30fr car, slate grn & blk .85 .40

Allegory of French Recognition of Ivory Coast — A50

Tabou Radio Station — A51

**1967, Nov. 17 Photo. *Perf. 13x12½***
**260** A50 90fr multicolored 2.50 .95

Days of Recognition, 20th anniv. See No. 298.

**1968, Mar. 9 Engr. *Perf. 13***
**261** A51 30fr dk grn, brn & brt grn 1.10 .55

Issued for Stamp Day.

Cotton Mill — A52

Designs: 5fr, Palm oil extraction plant. 15fr, Abidjan oil refinery. 20fr, Unloading raw cotton and spinning machine, vert. 30fr, Flour mill. 50fr, Cacao butter extractor. 70fr, Instant coffee factory, vert. 90fr, Saw mill and timber.

| **1968** | **Engr.** | ***Perf. 13*** | |
|---|---|---|---|
| **262** A52 | 5fr ver, slate grn & blk | .40 | .25 |
| **263** A52 | 10fr dk grn, gray & ol bis | .70 | .25 |
| **264** A52 | 15fr ver, lt ultra & blk | 1.50 | .65 |
| **265** A52 | 20fr Prus blue & choc | 1.10 | .55 |
| **266** A52 | 30fr dk grn, brt bl & brown | 1.10 | .65 |
| **267** A52 | 50fr red, brt grn & blk | 1.90 | .90 |
| **268** A52 | 70fr dk brn, bl & brn | 2.50 | 1.00 |
| **269** A52 | 90fr dp bl, blk & brn | 3.25 | 1.60 |
| | *Nos. 262-269 (8)* | 12.45 | 5.85 |

Issued: 5fr, 15fr, June 8; 10fr, 20fr, 90fr, Mar. 23; others, Oct. 5.

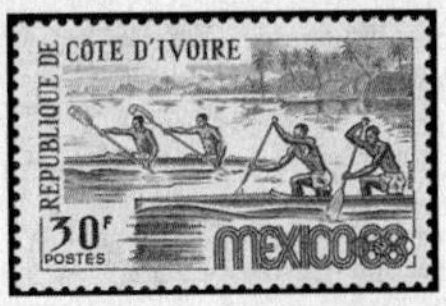


Canoe Race A53

| **1968, Apr. 6** | **Engr.** | ***Perf. 13*** | |
|---|---|---|---|
| **270** A53 | 30fr shown | 1.00 | .50 |
| **271** A53 | 100fr Runners | 3.00 | .90 |

19th Olympic Games, Mexico City, 10/12-27.

Queen Pokou Sacrificing her Son — A54

**1968, Aug. 7 Photo. *Perf. 12½x12***
**272** A54 30fr multicolored 1.10 .50

8th anniversary of independence.

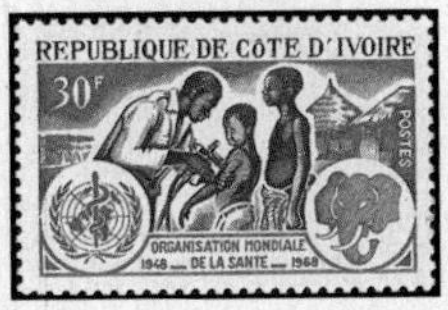


Vaccination, WHO Emblem and Elephant's Head A55

**1968, Sept. 28 Engr. *Perf. 13***
**273** A55 30fr choc, brt bl & maroon 1.00 .50

WHO, 20th anniversary.

Antelope in Forest — A56

**1968, Oct. 26 Engr. *Perf. 13***
**274** A56 30fr ultra, brn & olive 5.75 1.25

Protection of fauna and flora.

Abidjan Anthropological Museum and Carved Screen — A57

**1968, Nov. 2**
**275** A57 30fr vio bl, ol & rose mag 1.00 .50

Human Rights Flame and Statues of "Justitia" A58

**1968, Nov. 9 Engr. *Perf. 13***
**276** A58 30fr slate, org & dk brn 1.00 .50

International Human Rights Year.

"Ville de Maranhao" at Grand Bassam A59

**1969, Mar. 8 Engr. *Perf. 13***
**277** A59 30fr brn, brt bl & grn 1.75 .55

Issued for Stamp Day.

Opening of Hotel Ivoire, Abidjan — A60

**1969, Mar. 29**
**278** A60 30fr ver, bl & grn 1.25 .50

Carved Figure — A61

Mountains and Radio Tower, Man — A62

**1969, July 5 Engr. *Perf. 13***
**279** A61 30fr red lil, blk & red org 1.10 .60

Ivory Coast art exhibition, Fine Arts Museum, Vevey, Switzerland, 7/12-9/22.

**1969, Aug. 7 Engr. *Perf. 13***
**280** A62 30fr dl brn, sl & grn 1.25 .50

9th anniversary of independence.

**Development Bank Issue**
Common Design Type

Design: Development Bank emblem and Ivory Coast coat of arms.

**1969, Sept. 6**
**281** CD130 30fr ocher, grn & mar .70 .40

Arms of Bouake — A63

Coats of Arms: 15fr, Abidjan. 30fr, Ivory Coast.

| **1969** | **Photo.** | ***Perf. 13*** | |
|---|---|---|---|
| **282** A63 | 10fr multicolored | .40 | .25 |
| **283** A63 | 15fr multicolored | .50 | .25 |
| **284** A63 | 30fr multicolored | .85 | .25 |
| | *Nos. 282-284 (3)* | 1.75 | .75 |

Issued: 10fr, 10/25; 15fr, 12/27; 30fr, 12/20.
See Nos. 335-336, 378-382, design A297.

Sport Fishing and SKAL Emblem A64

**1969, Nov. 22 Engr. *Perf. 13***

**285** A64 30fr shown 4.00 .55
**286** A64 100fr Vacation village, SKAL emblem 5.00 1.40

1st Intl. Congress in Africa of the SKAL Tourist Assoc., Abidjan, Nov. 23-28.

**ASECNA Issue**
Common Design Type

**1969, Dec. 13 Engr. *Perf. 13***

**287** CD132 30fr vermilion .90 .40

University Center, Abidjan — A65

**1970, Feb. 26 Engr. *Perf. 13***

**288** A65 30fr indigo & yel grn .90 .50

Higher education in Ivory Coast, 10th anniv.

Gabriel Dadié and Telegraph Operator A66

**1970, Mar. 7 Engr. *Perf. 13***

**289** A66 30fr dk red, sl grn & blk .70 .35

Stamp Day; Gabriel Dadié (1891-1953) 1st native-born postal administrator.

University of Abidjan — A67

**1970, Mar. 21 Photo.**

**290** A67 30fr Prus bl, dk pur & dk yel grn .90 .50

3rd General Assembly of the Assoc. of French-language Universities (A.U.P.E.L.F.).

Safety Match Production — A68

**1970, May 9 Engr. *Perf. 13***

**291** A68 5fr shown .40 .45
**292** A68 20fr Textile industry .60 .40
**293** A68 50fr Shipbuilding 1.60 .50
*Nos. 291-293 (3)* 2.60 1.35

Radar, Classroom with Television — A69

**1970, May 17**

**294** A69 40fr red, grn & gray olive 1.10 .55

Issued for World Telecommunications Day.

**UPU Headquarters Issue**
Common Design Type

**1970, May 20**

**295** CD133 30fr lil, brt grn & olive 1.10 .50

UN Emblem, Lion, Antelopes and Plane A70

**1970, June 27 Engr. *Perf. 13***

**296** A70 30fr dk red brn, ultra & dk green 3.25 1.25

25th anniversary of the United Nations.

Coffee Branch and Bags Showing Increased Production A71

**1970, Aug. 7 Engr. *Perf. 13***

**297** A71 30fr org, bluish grn & gray 1.50 .50

Tenth anniversary of independence.

**Type of 1967**

**1970, Oct. 29 Photo. *Perf. 12x12½***

**298** A50 40fr multicolored 1.00 .50

Ivory Coast Democratic Party, 5th Congress.

Power Plant at Uridi — A73

**1970, Nov. 21 Engr. *Perf. 13***

**299** A73 40fr multicolored 2.00 .40

Independence, 10th Anniv. — A73a

Designs: Nos. 299A, 299D, Pres. Houphouet-Boigny, Gen. Charles DeGaulle. Nos. 299B, 299F, Pres. Houphouet-Boigny, elephants. Nos. 299C, 299E, Coat of arms.

**1970, Nov. 27 Embossed *Perf. 10½***
**Die Cut**

**299A** A73a 300fr Silver *15.00 15.00*
**299B** A73a 300fr Silver *15.00 15.00*
**299C** A73a 300fr Silver *15.00 15.00*
*g.* Pair, #299B-299C *35.00 35.00*
**299D** A73a 1000fr Gold *45.00 45.00*
**299E** A73a 1000fr Gold *45.00 45.00*

**Litho. & Embossed**

**299F** A73a 1200fr Gold & multi *45.00 45.00*
*h.* Pair, #299E-299F *100.00 100.00*

Nos. 299B, 299F are airmail.

Postal Service Autobus, 1925 A74

**1971, Mar. 6 Engr. *Perf. 13***

**300** A74 40fr dp grn, dk brn & gldn brn 2.75 .50

Stamp Day.

Marginella Desjardini A75

Marine Life: 1fr, Aporrhaispes gallinae. 5fr, Neptunus validus. 10fr, Hermodice carunculata, vert. No. 305, Natica fanel, vert. No. 306, Goniaster cuspidatus, vert. No. 307, Xenorhora digitata. 25fr, Conus prometheus. 35fr, Polycheles typhlops, vert. No. 310, Conus genuanus. No. 311, Chlamys flabellum. 45fr, Strombus bubonius. 50fr, Enoplometopus callistus, vert. 65fr, Cypraea stercoraria.

**1971-72 Engr. *Perf. 13***

**301** A75 1fr olive & multi .50 .25
**302** A75 5fr red & multi .50 .30
**303** A75 10fr emer & multi 1.00 .30
**304** A75 15fr brt bl & multi 1.00 .35
**305** A75 15fr dp car & multi 1.50 .40
**306** A75 20fr ocher & car 1.90 .50
**307** A75 20fr ver & multi 2.25 .65
**308** A75 25fr dk car, rose brn & black 1.25 .35
**309** A75 35fr yel & multi 2.50 .75
**310** A75 40fr emer & multi 4.00 1.25
**311** A75 40fr brown & multi 3.25 1.10
**312** A75 45fr multi 4.50 1.50
**313** A75 50fr green & multi 5.00 1.60
**314** A75 65fr bl, rose brn & sl grn 3.50 1.50
*Nos. 301-314 (14)* 32.65 10.80

Issued: #304, 306, 310, 4/24/71; 5fr, 35fr, 50fr, 6/5/71; 1fr, 10fr, #311, 10/23/71; 25fr, 65fr, 1/29/72; #305, 307, 45fr, 4/3/72.

Submarine Cable Station, 1891 A76

**1971, May 17**

**315** A76 100fr bl, ocher & olive 2.25 .85

3rd World Telecommunications Day.

Apprentice and Lathe — A77

**1971, June 19 Engr. *Perf. 13***

**316** A77 35fr grn, slate & org brn .90 .40

Technical instruction and professional training.

Map of Africa and Telecommunications System — A78

**1971, June 26 *Perf. 13x12½***

**317** A78 45fr magenta & multi .85 .40

Pan-African Telecommunications system.

Bondoukou Market — A79

**1971, Aug. 7 Engr. *Perf. 13***
**Size: 48x27mm**

**318** A79 35fr ultra, brn & slate 1.00 .45

11th anniv. of independence. See No. C46.

White, Black and Yellow Girls — A80

**1971, Oct. 10 Photo. *Perf. 13***

**319** A80 40fr shown .80 .25
**320** A80 45fr Boys around globe .80 .25

Intl. Year Against Racial Discrimination.

Gaming Table and Lottery Tickets A81

**1971, Nov. 13 *Perf. 12½***

**321** A81 35fr green & multi 1.00 .50

National lottery.

Electric Power Installations — A82

**1971, Dec. 18 *Perf. 13***

**322** A82 35fr red brn & multi 2.00 .50

Cogwheel and Workers A83

**1972, Mar. 18 Engr. *Perf. 13***

**323** A83 35fr org, bl & dk brn .70 .40

Technical Cooperation Week.

"Your Heart is Your Health" — A84

**1972, Apr. 7 Photo. *Perf. 12½x13***
**324** A84 40fr blue, olive & red .85 .50

World Health Day.

Girls Reading, Book Year Emblem — A85

***Perf. 12½x13, 13x12½***
**1972, Apr. 22 Engr.**
**325** A85 35fr Boys reading, horiz. .70 .25
**326** A85 40fr shown .90 .40

International Book Year.

Postal Sorting Center, Abidjan A86

**1972, May 13 *Perf. 13***
**327** A86 40fr dk grn, rose lil & bis 1.10 .40

Stamp Day.

Radio Tower, Abobo, and ITU Emblem — A87

**1972, May 17 Engr. *Perf. 13***
**328** A87 40fr blue, red & grn 2.00 .65

4th World Telecommunications Day.

Computer Operator, Punch Card A88

**1972, June 24**
**329** A88 40fr brt grn, bl & red 2.00 .60

Development of computerized information.

View of Odienné — A89

**1972, Aug. 7 Engr. *Perf. 13***
**330** A89 35fr bl, grn & brn 1.00 .60

12th anniversary of independence.

### West African Monetary Union Issue
Common Design Type

**1972, Nov. 2 Engr. *Perf. 13***
**331** CD136 40fr brn, gray & red lilac 1.00 .50

Diamond and Diamond Mine — A90

**1972, Nov. 4**
**332** A90 40fr Prus bl, slate & org brn 3.25 1.60

Pasteur Institute, Louis Pasteur A91

**1972, Nov. 21**
**333** A91 35fr vio bl, grn & brn 1.10 .50

Pasteur (1822-1895), chemist and bacteriologist.

Children at Village Pump A92

**1972, Dec. 9 Engr. *Perf. 13***
**334** A92 35fr dk red, grn & blk 1.25 .40

Water campaign. See No. 360.

### Arms Type of 1969

**1973 Photo. *Perf. 12***
**335** A63 5fr Daloa .45 .25
**336** A63 10fr Gagnoa .45 .25

Nos. 335-336 are 16½-17x22mm and have "DELRIEU" below design at right. Nos. 282-284 are 17x23mm and have no name at lower right.

Dr. Armauer G. Hansen — A93

**1973, Feb. 3 Engr. *Perf. 13***
**342** A93 35fr lil, dp bl & brn 1.10 .40

Centenary of the discovery of the Hansen bacillus, the cause of leprosy.

Lake Village Bletankoro — A94

**1973, Mar. 10 Engr. *Perf. 13***
**343** A94 200fr choc, bl & grn 4.75 2.00

Balistes Capriscus A95

Fish: 20fr, Pseudupeneus prayensis. 25fr, Cephalopholis taeniops. 35fr, Priacanthus arenatus. 50fr, Xyrichthys novacula.

**1973-74 Engr. *Perf. 13***
**344** A95 15fr ind & slate grn 1.50 .60
**345** A95 20fr lilac & multi 2.50 .75
**346** A95 25fr slate grn & rose ('74) 3.75 .80
**347** A95 35fr rose red & slate grn 2.75 1.10
**348** A95 50fr blk, ultra & rose red 4.00 1.20
*Nos. 344-348 (5)* 14.50 4.45

Issued: 50fr, 3/24; 15fr, 20fr, 7/7; 35fr, 12/1; 25fr, 3/2.

Children A96

**1973, Apr. 7 Engr. *Perf. 13***
**354** A96 40fr grn, blk & dl red 1.10 .45

Establishment of first children's village in Africa (SOS villages for homeless children).

Parliament, Abidjan — A97

**1973, Apr. 24 Photo. *Perf. 13x12½***
**355** A97 100fr multicolored 1.25 .45

112th session of the Inter-parliamentary Council.

Teacher and PAC Store A98

**1973, May 12 Photo. *Perf. 13x12½***
**356** A98 40fr multicolored .70 .25

Commercial Action Program (PAC).

Mother, Typist, Dress Form and Pot — A99

**1973, May 26**
**357** A99 35fr multicolored .90 .40

Technical instruction for women.

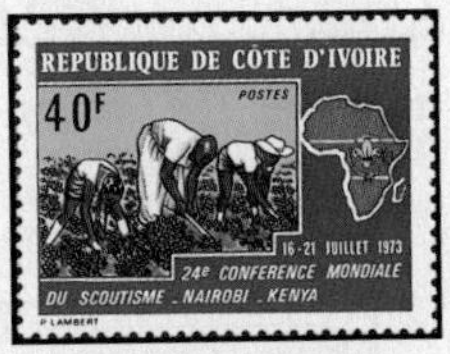

Farmers, African Scout Emblem A100

**1973, July 16 Photo. *Perf. 13x12½***
**358** A100 40fr multicolored 1.00 .60

24th Boy Scout World Conference, Nairobi, Kenya, July 16-21.

Party Headquarters, Yamoussokro — A101

**1973, Aug. 7 Photo. *Perf. 13***
**359** A101 35fr multicolored .70 .50

Children at Dry Pump A102

**1973, Aug. 16 Engr.**
**360** A102 40fr multicolored 1.25 .45

African solidarity in drought emergency.

### African Postal Union Issue
Common Design Type

**1973, Sept. 12 Engr. *Perf. 13***
**361** CD137 100fr pur, blk & red 2.50 1.00

Decorated Arrow Heads, Abidjan Museum — A103

**1973, Sept. 15 Photo. *Perf. 12½x13***
**362** A103 5fr blk, brn red & brn .55 .25

Ivory Coast No. 1 — A104

**1973, Oct. 9 Engr. *Perf. 13***
**363** A104 40fr emer, blk & org 1.25 .60

Stamp Day.

Highway Intersection A105

**1973, Oct. 13**
**364** A105 35fr blue, blk & grn .90 .45

Indenie-Abidjan intersection.

Map of Africa, Federation Emblem — A106

Elephant Emblem — A107

**1973, Oct. 26 Photo. *Perf. 13***
**365** A106 40fr ultra, red brn & vio bl .65 .30

Intl. Social Security Federation, 18th General Assembly, Abidjan, Oct. 26-Nov. 3.

**1973, Nov. 19**
**366** A107 40fr blk & bister .75 .30

7th World Congress of the Universal Federation of World Travel Agents' Associations, Abidjan.

Kong Mosque — A108

**1974, Mar. 9**
**367** A108 35fr bl, grn & brn 1.10 .60

People and Sun A109

**1974, Apr. 20 Photo. *Perf. 13***
**368** A109 35fr multicolored .65 .35

Permanent Mission to UN.

Grand Lahou Post Office — A110

**1974, May 17 Engr. *Perf. 13***
**369** A110 35fr multicolored 1.00 .60

Stamp Day.

Map and Flags of Members A110a

**1974, May 29 Photo. *Perf. 13x12½***
**370** A110a 40fr blue & multi .70 .25

15th anniversary of the Council of Accord.

Pres. Houphouet-Boigny
A111 A112

**1974-76 Engr. *Perf. 13***
**371** A111 25fr grn, org & brn .65 .25
 *a.* Booklet pane of 10 6.50
 *b.* Booklet pane of 20 13.00
**373** A112 35fr org, grn & brn 1.00 .25
 *a.* Booklet pane of 10 10.00
 *b.* Booklet pane of 20 20.00
**374** A112 40fr grn, org & brn 1.00 .25
 *a.* Booklet pane of 10 10.00
**375** A112 60fr bl, car & brn ('76) .90 .40
**376** A112 65fr car, bl & brn ('76) .90 .40
 *Nos. 371-376 (5)* 4.45 1.55

See Nos. 783-792.

**Ivory Coast Arms Type of 1969 with smaller "P" and "s" in "Postes"**

**1974, June 29 Photo. *Perf. 12***
**378** A63 35fr brn, emer & gold .70 .25
 *a.* Booklet pane of 10 7.50
 *b.* Booklet pane of 20 15.00
**379** A63 40fr vio, bl, emer & gold .90 .25
 *a.* Booklet pane of 10 10.00
 *b.* Booklet pane of 20 20.00

**Inscribed: "COTE D'IVOIRE"**

**1976, Jan.**
**380** A63 60fr car, gold & emer .90 .25
**381** A63 65fr grn, gold & emer .90 .30
**382** A63 70fr bl, gold & emer 1.00 .40
 *Nos. 378-382 (5)* 4.40 1.45

See design A297.

WPY Emblem — A114

**1974, Aug. 19 Engr. *Perf. 13***
**383** A114 40fr emerald & blue .80 .30

World Population Year.

Cotton Harvest — A115

**1974, Sept. 21 Litho. *Perf. 12½x13***
**384** A115 50fr multicolored 1.10 .50

UPU Centenary A116

**1974, Oct. 9 Engr. *Perf. 13***
**385** A116 40fr multicolored .80 .30

See Nos. C59-C60.

Plowing Farmer, Service Emblem A117

**1974, Dec. 7 Photo. *Perf. 13***
**386** A117 35fr multicolored .75 .30

14th anniversary of independence.

National Library, First Anniv. — A118

**1975, Jan. 9 Photo. *Perf. 13***
**387** A118 40fr multicolored .70 .30

Raoul Follereau and Blind Students — A119

**1975, Jan. 26 Engr. *Perf. 13***
**388** A119 35fr multicolored 1.75 .80

Follereau, educator of the blind and lepers.

Congress Emblem — A120

**1975, Mar. 4 Photo. *Perf. 12½x13***
**389** A120 40fr blk & emerald .75 .30

52nd Congress of the Intl. Assoc. of Seed Crushers, Abidjan, Mar. 2-7.

Coffee Cultivation A121

**1975, Mar. 15 *Perf. 13½x13***
**390** A121 5fr Flowering branch .35 .25
**391** A121 10fr Branch with beans .65 .25

Sassandra Wharf — A122

**1975, Apr. 19 Engr. *Perf. 13***
**392** A122 100fr multicolored 2.25 1.25

Letter Sorting A123

**1975, Apr. 26 Photo. *Perf. 13***
**393** A123 40fr multicolored 1.10 .60

Stamp Day.

Cotton Flower — A124

Cotton Bolls — A125

**1975, May 3 Photo. *Perf. 13***
**394** A124 5fr multicolored .45 .35
**395** A125 10fr multicolored .70 .35

Cotton cultivation.

Marie Kore, Women's Year Emblem — A126

**1975, May 19 Engr. *Perf. 13***
**396** A126 45fr lt bl, yel grn & brn .75 .50

International Women's Year.

Fort Dabou — A127

**1975, June 7 Engr. *Perf. 13***
**397** A127 50fr multicolored .90 .60

Abidjan Harbor — A128

40fr, Grand Bassam wharf, 1906. 100fr, Planned harbor expansion on Locodjro.

**1975, July 1 Photo. *Perf. 13***
**398** A128 35fr multicolored 1.10 .60

**Miniature Sheet**

**399** Sheet of 3 9.50 9.50
 *a.* A128 40fr multi, vert. 3.75 3.75
 *b.* A128 100fr multi 4.00 4.00

25th anniversary of Abidjan Harbor. No. 399 contains Nos. 398, 399a, 399b.

Cacao Pods on Tree — A129

**1975, Aug. 2**
**400** A129 35fr multicolored 2.25 .65

Farm Workers A130

**1975, Oct. 4** **Photo.** ***Perf. 13x12½***
**401** A130 50fr multicolored .85 .60

Natl. Org. for Rural Development.

Railroad Bridge, N'zi River — A131

**1975, Dec. 7** **Photo.** ***Perf. 13***
**402** A131 60fr multicolored 4.75 1.25

15th anniversary of independence.

Baoulé Mother and Child, Carved in Wood — A132

**1976, Jan. 24** **Litho.** ***Perf. 13***
**403** A132 65fr black & multi 2.00 .65

Baoulé Mask A133

Chief Abron's Chair A133a

**1976, Feb. 7** **Photo.** ***Perf. 12½***
**404** A133 20fr multicolored .60 .30
**405** A133a 150fr multicolored 3.00 1.00

Senufo Statuette — A134

**1976, Feb. 21** ***Perf. 13x13½***
**406** A134 25fr ocher & multi .75 .45

Telephones 1876 and 1976 — A135

**1976, Mar. 10** **Litho.** ***Perf. 12***
**407** A135 70fr multicolored 1.10 .65

Centenary of first telephone call by Alexander Graham Bell, Mar. 10, 1876.

Ivory Coast Map, Pigeon, Carving A136

**1976, Apr. 10** **Photo.** ***Perf. 12½***
**408** A136 65fr multicolored 1.25 .60

20th Stamp Day.

Smiling Trees and Cat — A137

**1976, June 5** **Litho.** ***Perf. 12½***
**409** A137 65fr multicolored 1.25 .60

Nature protection.

Children with Books — A138

**1976, July 3** **Photo.** ***Perf. 12½x13***
**410** A138 65fr multicolored 1.10 .60

Runner, Maple Leaf, Olympic Rings — A139

**1976, July 17** **Litho.** ***Perf. 12***
**411** A139 60fr Javelin, vert. 1.00 .55
**412** A139 65fr shown 1.00 .55

21st Olympic Games, Montreal, Canada, July 17-Aug. 1.

Mohammad Ali Jinnah — A139a

**1976, Aug. 14** **Litho.** ***Perf. 13***
**412A** A139a 50fr multicolored *65.00 15.00*

1st Governor-General of Pakistan.

Cashew A140

**1976, Sept. 18** ***Perf. 12½***
**413** A140 65fr blue & multi 1.90 .70

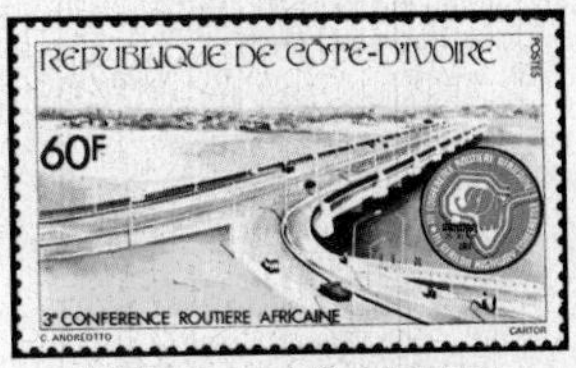


Highway and Conference Emblem — A141

**1976, Oct. 25** **Litho.** ***Perf. 12½x12***
**414** A141 60fr multicolored .90 .50

3rd African Highway Conference, Abidjan, July 25-30.

Pres. Houphouet-Boigny A142

**1976-77** **Photo.** ***Perf. 13½x12½***
**415** A142 35fr brn, red lil & blk ('77) *125.00* —
**416** A142 40fr brt grn, ocher & brn blk 4.50 .75
*a.* Bklt. pane of 12 (8#416, 4#417) 55.00
**417** A142 45fr ocher, brt grn & brn blk 4.50 1.00
**418** A142 60fr brn, mag & brn blk 6.00 1.00
**419** A142 65fr grn, org & brn blk 7.00 1.50
*Nos. 416-419 (4)* 22.00 4.25

The 40fr and 45fr issued in booklet and coil; 35fr, 60fr and 65fr in coil only. No. 416 coil sells for about the same as No. 415.

Stamps from booklets are imperf. on one side or two adjoining sides. Coils have control number on back of every 10th stamp.

John Paul Jones, American Marine and Ship — A143

American Bicentennial: 125fr, Count de Rochambeau and grenadier of Touraine Regiment. 150fr, Admiral Count Jean Baptiste d'Estaing and French marine. 175fr, Lafayette and grenadier of Soissons Regiment. 200fr, Jefferson, American soldier, Declaration of Independence. 500fr, Washington, US flag, Continental officer.

**1976, Nov. 27** **Litho.** ***Perf. 11***
**421** A143 100fr multicolored 1.50 .30
**422** A143 125fr multicolored 1.75 .45
**423** A143 150fr multicolored 2.00 .55
**424** A143 175fr multicolored 2.00 .70
**425** A143 200fr multicolored 2.50 .75
*Nos. 421-425 (5)* 9.75 2.75

**Souvenir Sheet**

**426** A143 500fr multicolored 7.00 2.50

"Development and Solidarity" — A144

**1976, Dec. 7** **Photo.** ***Perf. 13***
**427** A144 60fr multicolored .90 .60

16th anniversary of independence.

Benin Head, Ivory Coast Arms — A145

**1977, Jan. 15** **Photo.** ***Perf. 13***
**428** A145 65fr gold, dk brn & grn 1.10 .75

2nd World Black and African Festival, Lagos, Nigeria, Jan. 15-Feb. 12.

Musical Instruments — A146

**1977, Mar. 5** **Engr.** ***Perf. 13***
**429** A146 5fr Baoule bells .35 .25
**430** A146 10fr Senufo balafon .35 .25
**431** A146 20fr Dida drum .55 .25
*Nos. 429-431 (3)* 1.25 .75

Air Afrique Plane Unloading Mail A147

**1977, Apr. 9** **Litho.** ***Perf. 13***
**432** A147 60fr multicolored 1.25 .60

Stamp Day.

Sassenage Castle, Grenoble — A148

**1977, May 21 Litho. *Perf. 12½***

**433** A148 100fr multicolored 2.00 .75

Intl. French Language Council, 10th anniv.

Orville and Wilbur Wright, "Wright Flyer," 1903 — A149

History of Aviation: 75fr, Louis Bleriot crossing English Channel, 1909. 100fr, Ross Smith and Vickers-Vimy (flew England-Australia, 1919). 200fr, Charles A. Lindbergh and "Spirit of St. Louis" (flew New York-Paris, 1927). 300fr, Supersonic jet Concorde, 1976. 500fr, Lindbergh in flying suit and "Spirit of St. Louis."

**1977, June 27 Litho. *Perf. 14***

| | | | | | |
|---|---|---|---|---|---|
| **434** | A149 | 60fr multi | | 1.00 | .30 |
| **435** | A149 | 75fr multi | | 1.10 | .30 |
| **436** | A149 | 100fr multi | | 1.25 | .30 |
| **437** | A149 | 200fr multi | | 3.00 | .75 |
| **438** | A149 | 300fr multi | | 4.00 | 1.25 |
| | | *Nos. 434-438 (5)* | | 10.35 | 2.90 |

**Souvenir Sheet**

**439** A149 500fr multi 6.50 2.00

Santos Dumont's "Ville de Paris," 1907 — A150

65fr, LZ1 at takeoff. 150fr,"Schwaben" LZ10 over Germany. 200fr, "Bodensee" LZ120, 1919. 300fr, LZ127 over Sphinx & pyramids.

**1977, Sept. 3 Litho. *Perf. 11***

| | | | | |
|---|---|---|---|---|
| **440** | A150 | 60fr multi | 1.00 | .25 |
| **441** | A150 | 65fr multi | 1.00 | .35 |
| **442** | A150 | 150fr multi | 2.00 | .55 |
| **443** | A150 | 200fr multi | 3.00 | 1.00 |
| **444** | A150 | 300fr multi | 4.00 | 1.25 |
| | | *Nos. 440-444 (5)* | 11.00 | 3.40 |

History of the Zeppelin. Exist imperf.

See No. C63.

Congress Emblem — A151

**1977, Sept. 12 Photo. *Perf. 12½***

**445** A151 60fr lt & dk grn .80 .50

17th Intl. Congress of Administrative Sciences in Africa, Abidjan, Sept. 12-16.

A152

**1977, Nov. 12 Photo. *Perf. 13½x14***

**446** A152 65fr multicolored 3.25 .75

Yamoussoukro, 1st Ivory Coast container ship.

Butterflies A152a

Designs: 30fr, Epiphora rectifascia boolana. 60fr, Charaxes jasius epijasius. 65fr, Imbrasia arata. 100fr, Palla decius.

**1977, Nov. Photo. *Perf. 14x13***

| | | | | |
|---|---|---|---|---|
| **446A** | A152a | 30fr multi | — | *2.25* |
| **446B** | A152a | 60fr multi | — | *17.50* |
| **446C** | A152a | 65fr multi | — | *4.00* |
| **446D** | A152a | 100fr multi | — | *6.00* |
| | | *Nos. 446A-446D (4)* | | *29.75* |
| | | Set, unused | 280.00 | |

A153

Hand Holding Produce, Generators, Factories.

**1977, Dec. 7 Photo. *Perf. 13½***

**447** A153 60fr multicolored .90 .65

17th anniversary of independence.

Flowers — A153a

5fr, Strophanthus hispidus. 20fr, Anthurium cultorum. 60fr, Arachnis flos-aeris. 65fr, Renanthera storiei.

**1977 Photo. *Perf. 13x14***

| | | | | |
|---|---|---|---|---|
| **447A** | A153a | 5fr multi | *125.00* | *62.50* |
| **447B** | A153a | 20fr multi | *125.00* | *62.50* |
| **447C** | A153a | 60fr multi | *125.00* | *62.50* |
| **447D** | A153a | 65fr multi | *125.00* | *62.50* |
| | | *Nos. 447A-447D (4)* | *500.00* | *250.00* |

Presidents Giscard d'Estaing and Houphouet-Boigny — A154

**1978, Jan. 11 *Perf. 13***

| | | | | |
|---|---|---|---|---|
| **448** | A154 | 60fr multicolored | 1.00 | .35 |
| **449** | A154 | 65fr multicolored | 1.25 | .35 |
| **450** | A154 | 100fr multicolored | 1.60 | .75 |
| *a.* | | Souvenir sheet, 500fr | 9.25 | 9.25 |
| | | *Nos. 448-450 (3)* | 3.85 | 1.45 |

Visit of Pres. Valery Giscard d'Estaing. No. 450a contains one stamp.

St. George and the Dragon, by Rubens A155

Paintings by Peter Paul Rubens (1577-1640): 150fr, Child's head. 250fr, Annunciation. 300fr, The Birth of Louis XIII. 500fr, Virgin & Child.

**1978, Mar. 4 Litho. *Perf. 13½***

| | | | | |
|---|---|---|---|---|
| **451** | A155 | 65fr gold & multi | .90 | .35 |
| **452** | A155 | 150fr gold & multi | 2.00 | .60 |
| **453** | A155 | 250fr gold & multi | 3.00 | 1.00 |
| **454** | A155 | 300fr gold & multi | 4.25 | 1.50 |
| | | *Nos. 451-454 (4)* | 10.15 | 3.45 |

**Souvenir Sheet**

**455** A155 500fr gold & multi 7.00 3.25

Royal Guards — A156

**1978, Apr. 1 Litho. *Perf. 12½***

| | | | | |
|---|---|---|---|---|
| **456** | A156 | 60fr shown | 1.25 | .40 |
| **457** | A156 | 65fr Cosmological figures | 1.25 | .40 |

Rural Postal Center — A157

**1978, Apr. 8**

**458** A157 60fr multicolored 1.00 .60

Stamp Day.

Antenna, ITU Emblem A158

**1978, May 17 *Perf. 13***

**459** A158 60fr multicolored .90 .50

10th World Telecommunications Day.

Svante August Arrhenius, Electrolytic Apparatus — A159

Nobel Prize Winners: 75fr, Jules Bordet, child, mountains, eagle and Petri dish. 100fr, André Gide, and St. Peter's, Rome. 200fr, John Steinbeck and horse farm. 300fr, Children with flowers and UNICEF emblem. 500fr, Max Planck, rockets and earth.

**1978, May 27 Litho. *Perf. 13½***

| | | | | |
|---|---|---|---|---|
| **460** | A159 | 60fr multi | .75 | .25 |
| **461** | A159 | 75fr multi | 1.00 | .30 |
| **462** | A159 | 100fr multi | 1.00 | .35 |
| **463** | A159 | 200fr multi | 2.00 | .70 |
| **464** | A159 | 300fr multi | 4.00 | 1.00 |
| | | *Nos. 460-464 (5)* | 8.75 | 2.60 |

**Souvenir Sheet**

**465** A159 500fr multi 5.50 2.00

Soccer Ball, Player and Argentina '78 Emblem — A160

Soccer Ball, Argentina '78 Emblem and: 65fr, Player, vert. 100fr, Player, diff. 150fr, Goalkeeper. 300fr, Ball as sun, and player, vert. 500fr, Ball as globe with Argentina on map of South America.

**1978, June 17**

| | | | | |
|---|---|---|---|---|
| **466** | A160 | 60fr multi | .70 | .25 |
| **467** | A160 | 65fr multi | .85 | .30 |
| **468** | A160 | 100fr multi | 1.00 | .55 |
| **469** | A160 | 150fr multi | 1.50 | .60 |
| **470** | A160 | 300fr multi | 3.00 | .95 |
| | | *Nos. 466-470 (5)* | 7.05 | 2.65 |

**Souvenir Sheet**

**471** A160 500fr multi 5.00 2.00

11th World Cup Soccer Championship, Argentina, June 1-25.

Miniodes Discolor A161

Butterflies: 65fr, Charaxes lactetinctus. 100fr, Papilio zalmoxis. 200fr, Papilio antimachus.

**1978, July 8 Photo. *Perf. 14x13***

| | | | | |
|---|---|---|---|---|
| **472** | A161 | 60fr multicolored | 3.75 | 1.00 |
| **473** | A161 | 65fr multicolored | 3.75 | 1.00 |
| **474** | A161 | 100fr multicolored | 5.50 | 1.75 |
| **475** | A161 | 200fr multicolored | 10.00 | 4.00 |
| | | *Nos. 472-475 (4)* | 23.00 | 7.75 |

Cricket A162

Insects: 20fr, 60fr, Various hemiptera. 65fr, Goliath beetle.

**1978, Aug. 26 Litho. *Perf. 12½***

| | | | | |
|---|---|---|---|---|
| **476** | A162 | 10fr multicolored | 1.10 | .40 |
| **477** | A162 | 20fr multicolored | 1.75 | .40 |
| **478** | A162 | 60fr multicolored | 3.50 | 1.00 |
| **479** | A162 | 65fr multicolored | 5.00 | 1.25 |
| | | *Nos. 476-479 (4)* | 11.35 | 3.05 |

Stylized Figures Emerging from TV Screen
A163

65fr, Passengers on train made up of TV sets.

**1978, Sept. 18** *Perf. 13*

**480** A163 60fr multicolored .90 .30
**481** A163 65fr multicolored 1.10 .35

Educational television programs.

Map of Ivory Coast, Mobile Drill Platform Ship
A164

Map of Ivory Coast, Ram at Discovery Site and: 65fr, Gold goblets. 500fr, Pres. Houphouet-Boigny holding gold goblets.

**1978, Oct. 18** **Litho.** *Perf. 12½x12*

**482** A164 60fr multicolored 1.40 .50
**483** A164 65fr multicolored 1.40 .50

**Souvenir Sheet**

**484** A164 500fr multicolored 12.00 12.00

Announcement of oil discovery off the coast of Ivory Coast, 1st anniv.

National Assembly, Paris, UPU Emblem
A165

**1978, Dec. 2** **Litho.** *Perf. 13½*

**485** A165 200fr multicolored 2.00 .90

Congress of Paris, centenary.

Drummer
A166

**1978, Dec. 7** **Photo.** *Perf. 12½x13*

**486** A166 60fr multicolored 1.10 .60

18th anniversary of independence.

Poster — A167

Design: 65fr, Arrows made of flags, and television screen.

**1978, Dec. 12**

**487** A167 60fr multicolored .90 .40
**488** A167 65fr multicolored .90 .40

Technical cooperation among developing countries with the help of educational television.

Plowing — A168

**1979, Jan. 27** **Photo.** *Perf. 13*

**489** A168 100fr multicolored 2.00 .60

King Hassan II, Pres. Houphouet-Boigny, Flags and Map of Morocco and Ivory Coast — A169

**1979, Jan. 27** **Photo.** *Perf. 13*

**490** A169 60fr multicolored *2.50* 1.00
**491** A169 65fr multicolored *3.50* 1.25
**492** A169 500fr multicolored *17.50* 7.50
*Nos. 490-492 (3)* *23.50* 9.75

Visit of King Hassan of Morocco to Ivory Coast. The visit never took place and the stamps were not issued. To recover the printing costs the stamps were sold in Paris for one day.

Horus — A170

**1979, Feb. 17** **Litho.** *Perf. 12½*

**493** A170 200fr multi 3.00 1.25
**494** A170 500fr Vulture with ankh, car-touches 6.50 3.25

UNESCO drive to save Temples of Philae.

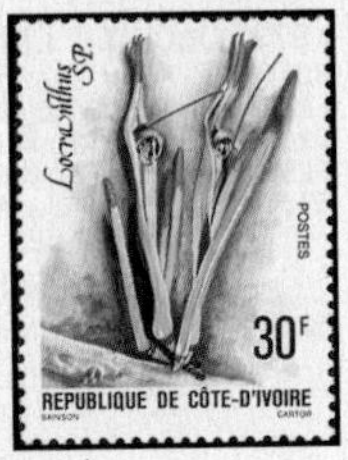


Flowers — A171

**1979, Feb. 24**

**495** A171 30fr Locranthus 1.00 .50
**496** A171 60fr Vanda Josephine 1.50 .60
**497** A171 65fr Renanthera storiei 1.75 .80
*Nos. 495-497 (3)* 4.25 1.90

Wildlife Protection
A172

**1979, Mar. 24** **Photo.** *Perf. 13x13½*

**498** A172 50fr Hippopotamus 2.25 .70

Globe and Emblem — A173

Child Riding Dove — A174

**1979, Apr. 1** **Litho.** *Perf. 12x12½*

**499** A173 60fr multicolored .60 .45
**500** A174 65fr multicolored .70 .50
**501** A173 100fr multicolored 1.50 .90
**502** A174 500fr multicolored 5.50 3.00
*Nos. 499-502 (4)* 8.30 4.85

International Year of the Child.

Rural Mail Delivery — A175

**1979, Apr. 7** *Perf. 12½*

**503** A175 60fr multicolored 1.10 .35

Stamp Day.

Korhogo Cathedral — A176

**1979, Apr. 9** *Perf. 13*

**504** A176 60fr multicolored .90 .45

Arrival of Catholic missionaries, 75th anniv.

Crying Child — A177

**1979, May 17** **Litho.** *Perf. 12½*

**505** A177 65fr multicolored .90 .50

10th anniv. of SOS Village (for homeless children).

Euphaedra Xypete
A178

Butterflies: 65fr, Pseudacraea bois duvali. 70fr, Auchenisa schausi.

**1979, May 26** *Perf. 13x13½*

**506** A178 60fr multicolored 2.50 1.00
**507** A178 65fr multicolored 3.00 1.00
**508** A178 70fr multicolored 4.50 1.50
*Nos. 506-508 (3)* 10.00 3.50

Endangered Animals — A179

**1979, June 2**

**509** A179 5fr Antelopes .75 .35
**510** A179 20fr Duikerbok 1.25 .45
**511** A179 60fr Aardvark 4.00 1.40
*Nos. 509-511 (3)* 6.00 2.20

UPU Emblem, Radar, Truck and Ship — A180

#513, Ancestral figure & antelope, vert.

**1979, June 8** **Engr.** *Perf. 13*

**512** A180 70fr multi 3.00 2.00

**Photo.**

**513** A180 70fr multi 3.00 2.00

Philexafrique II, Libreville, Gabon, June 8-17. Nos. 512, 513 each printed in sheets of 10 with 5 labels showing exhibition emblem.

Rowland Hill, Steam Locomotive, Great Britain No. 75 — A181

Rowland Hill, Locomotives and: 75fr, Ivory Coast #125. 100fr, Hawaii #4. 150fr, Japan #30, syll. 3. 300fr, France #2. 500fr, Ivory Coast #123.

**1979, July 7 Litho. *Perf. 13½***

| | | | | |
|---|---|---|---|---|
| **514** | A181 | 60fr multi | .70 | .25 |
| **515** | A181 | 75fr multi | .80 | .30 |
| **516** | A181 | 100fr multi | 1.25 | .40 |
| **517** | A181 | 150fr multi | 1.50 | .65 |
| **518** | A181 | 300fr multi | 3.25 | .85 |
| | | *Nos. 514-518 (5)* | 7.50 | 2.45 |

**Souvenir Sheet**

| | | | | |
|---|---|---|---|---|
| **519** | A181 | 500fr multi | 6.75 | 3.00 |

Sir Rowland Hill (1795-1879), originator of penny postage.

Insects — A181a

**1979 Photo. *Perf. 14x13, 13x14***

| | | | | |
|---|---|---|---|---|
| **519A** | A181a | 30fr Wasp | *15.00* | *2.50* |
| **519B** | A181a | 60fr Praying mantis, vert. | *30.00* | *4.00* |
| **519C** | A181a | 65fr Cricket | *40.00* | *4.00* |
| | | *Nos. 519A-519C (3)* | *85.00* | *10.50* |

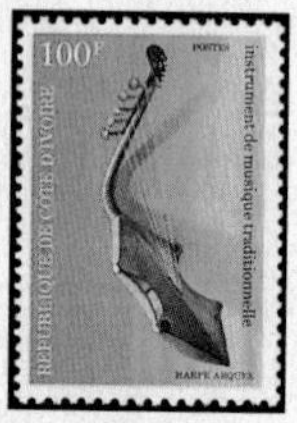


A181b

Musical instruments.

**1979 Photo. *Perf. 13x14***

| | | | | |
|---|---|---|---|---|
| **519D** | A181b | 100fr Harp | *35.00* | *14.00* |
| **519E** | A181b | 150fr Whistles | *50.00* | *20.00* |

"TELECOM 79" — A182

Culture Day — A183

**1979, Sept. 20 Litho. *Perf. 13x12½***

| | | | | |
|---|---|---|---|---|
| **520** | A182 | 60fr multicolored | .90 | .40 |

3rd World Telecommunications Exhibition, Geneva, Sept. 20-26.

**1979, Oct. 13 *Perf. 12½***

| | | | | |
|---|---|---|---|---|
| **521** | A183 | 65fr multicolored | .90 | .40 |

Fish — A183a

**1979 Photo. *Perf. 14x13***

| | | | | |
|---|---|---|---|---|
| **521A** | A183a | 60fr Pterois volitans | *150.00* | — |
| **521B** | A183a | 65fr Coelacanth | *150.00* | — |

Boxing — A184

**1979, Oct. 27 Litho. *Perf. 14x13½***

| | | | | |
|---|---|---|---|---|
| **522** | A184 | 60fr shown | .60 | .25 |
| **523** | A184 | 65fr Running | .65 | .25 |
| **524** | A184 | 100fr Soccer | 1.00 | .35 |
| **525** | A184 | 150fr Bicycling | 1.50 | .45 |
| **526** | A184 | 300fr Wrestling | 3.25 | 1.25 |
| | | *Nos. 522-526 (5)* | 7.00 | 2.55 |

**Souvenir Sheet**

| | | | | |
|---|---|---|---|---|
| **527** | A184 | 500fr Gymnastics | 6.00 | 2.00 |

Pre-Olympic Year.

Wildlife Fund Emblem and Jentink's Duiker — A185

Wildlife Protection: 60fr, Colobus Monkey. 75fr, Manatees. 100fr, Epixerus ebii. 150fr, Hippopotamus. 300fr, Chimpanzee.

**1979, Nov. 3 Litho. *Perf. 14½***

| | | | | |
|---|---|---|---|---|
| **528** | A185 | 40fr multi | *3.00* | .30 |
| **529** | A185 | 60fr multi | *3.25* | .50 |
| **530** | A185 | 75fr multi | *4.00* | .60 |
| **531** | A185 | 100fr multi | *4.75* | .85 |
| **532** | A185 | 150fr multi | *6.50* | 1.25 |
| **533** | A185 | 300fr multi | *15.00* | 2.50 |
| | | *Nos. 528-533 (6)* | *36.50* | 6.00 |

Raoul Follerau Institute, Adzope — A186

**1979, Dec. 6 Litho. *Perf. 12½***

| | | | | |
|---|---|---|---|---|
| **534** | A186 | 60fr multi | 1.40 | .60 |

Independence, 19th Anniversary A187

**1979, Dec. 7 Litho. *Perf. 14x13½***

| | | | | |
|---|---|---|---|---|
| **535** | A187 | 60fr multicolored | 1.10 | .35 |

Fireball A188

Local Flora: 5fr, Clerodendron thomsonae, vert. 50fr, Costus incanusiamus, vert. 60fr, Ficus elastica abidjan, vert.

**1980 Litho. *Perf. 12½***

| | | | | |
|---|---|---|---|---|
| **536** | A188 | 5fr multicolored | .30 | .25 |
| **537** | A188 | 10fr multicolored | .40 | .25 |
| **538** | A188 | 50fr multicolored | 1.10 | .30 |
| **539** | A188 | 60fr multicolored | 1.25 | .30 |
| | | *Nos. 536-539 (4)* | 3.05 | 1.10 |

Issued: 5fr, 10fr, Jan. 26; 50fr, 60fr, Feb. 16.

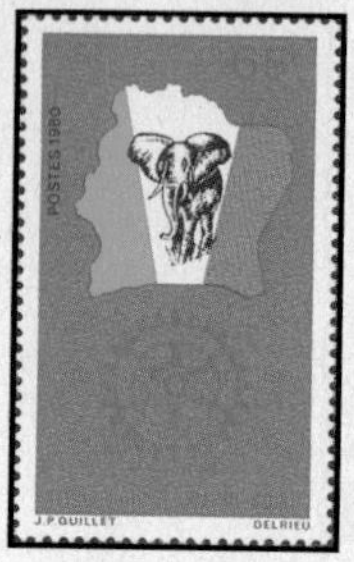

Rotary Intl., 75th Anniv. — A189

**1980, Feb. 23 Photo. *Perf. 13½***

| | | | | |
|---|---|---|---|---|
| **540** | A189 | 65fr multicolored | .90 | .50 |

International Archives Day — A190

**1980, Feb. 26 Litho.**

| | | | | |
|---|---|---|---|---|
| **541** | A190 | 65fr multicolored | .90 | .50 |

Astronaut Shaking Hands with Boy — A191

Path of Apollo 11 — A192

**1980, July 6 Photo.**

| | | | | |
|---|---|---|---|---|
| **542** | A191 | 60fr multicolored | .90 | .50 |
| **543** | A192 | 65fr multicolored | .90 | .50 |
| **544** | A191 | 70fr multicolored | 1.75 | .75 |
| **545** | A192 | 150fr multicolored | 3.00 | 1.75 |
| | | *Nos. 542-545 (4)* | 6.55 | 3.50 |

Apollo 11 moon landing, 10th anniv. (1979).

Jet and Map of Africa A193

**1980, Mar. 22 *Perf. 12½***

| | | | | |
|---|---|---|---|---|
| **546** | A193 | 60fr multicolored | .90 | .45 |

ASECNA (Air Safety Board), 20th anniv.

Boys and Stamp Album, Globe — A194

**1980, Apr. 12 Litho. *Perf. 12½***

| | | | | |
|---|---|---|---|---|
| **547** | A194 | 65fr bl grn & red brn | 1.10 | .50 |

Stamp Day; Youth philately.

Missionary and Church, Aboisso A195

**1980, Apr. 26 Photo. *Perf. 13x13½***

| | | | | |
|---|---|---|---|---|
| **548** | A195 | 60fr multicolored | 1.10 | .50 |

Settlement of the Holy Fathers at Aboisso, 75th anniversary.

Fight Against Cigarette Smoking A196

**1980, May 3 *Perf. 12½***

| | | | | |
|---|---|---|---|---|
| **549** | A196 | 60fr multicolored | 1.10 | .50 |

Pope John Paul II, Pres. Houphouet-Boigny — A197

**1980, May 10 Photo. *Perf. 13***

| | | | | |
|---|---|---|---|---|
| **550** | A197 | 65fr multicolored | 2.50 | 1.00 |

Visit of Pope John Paul II to Ivory Coast.

Le Belier Locomotive A198

**1980, May 17 Litho. *Perf. 13***

| | | | | |
|---|---|---|---|---|
| **551** | A198 | 60fr shown | .70 | .35 |
| **552** | A198 | 65fr Abidjan Railroad Station, 1904 | .80 | .35 |
| **553** | A198 | 100fr Passenger car, 1908 | 1.60 | .60 |
| **554** | A198 | 150fr Steam locomotive, 1940 | 2.00 | 1.00 |
| | | *Nos. 551-554 (4)* | 5.10 | 2.30 |

Central Bank of West African States, 1st Anniversary A199

**1980, May 26 Litho. *Perf. 12x12½***

| | | | | |
|---|---|---|---|---|
| **555** | A199 | 60fr multicolored | .90 | .50 |

Lujtanus Sebae A200

**1980, Apr. 19** **Photo.** ***Perf. 14***

**556** A200 60fr shown 3.25 .65
**557** A200 65fr Monodactylus sebae, vert. 3.50 1.00
**558** A200 100fr Colisa fasciata 3.75 1.40
*Nos. 556-558 (3)* 10.50 3.05

Snake — A201

**1980, July 12** **Litho.** ***Perf. 12½***

**559** A201 60fr shown 2.00 .75
**560** A201 150fr Toad 4.75 1.75

Tourists in Village, by K. Ehouman Pierre A202

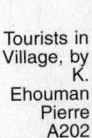

Conference Emblem — A203

**1980, Aug. 9**

**561** A202 60fr multicolored .75 .30
**562** A203 65fr multicolored .75 .30

National Tourist Office, Abidjan; World Tourism Conference, Manila.

Forticula Auricularia A204

***Perf. 14x13, 13x14***

**1980, Sept. 6** **Photo.**

**563** A204 60fr shown 5.00 2.00
**564** A204 65fr Praying mantis, vert. 5.00 2.00

***Perf. 13½x13, 13x13½***

**1980, Oct. 11** **Photo.**

Designs: 60fr, 200fr, Various grasshoppers.

**565** A204 60fr multi, vert. 2.50 1.25
**566** A204 200fr multi 7.50 3.50

Hands Free from Chain, Map of Ivory Coast, Pres. Houphouet-Boigny — A205

Pres. Houphouet-Boigny, Symbols of Development — A206

***Perf. 12½x13, 14x14½ (A206)***

**1980, Oct. 18**

**567** A205 60fr shown 1.25 .75
**568** A206 65fr shown 1.25 .75
**569** A205 70fr Map, colors, document 1.75 1.00
**570** A205 150fr like #567 4.25 2.75
**571** A206 300fr like #568 7.50 4.25
*Nos. 567-571 (5)* 16.00 9.50

Pres. Houphouet-Boigny, 75th birthday.

7th PDCI and RDA Congress A207

**1980, Oct. 25** ***Perf. 12½***

**572** A207 60fr multicolored .90 .40
**573** A207 65fr multicolored .90 .40

River Cruise Boat Sotra A208

**1980, Dec. 6** **Litho.** ***Perf. 13x13½***

**574** A208 60fr multicolored 1.10 .60

View of Abidjan — A209

**1980, Dec. 7** ***Perf. 13x12½***

**575** A209 60fr multicolored .90 .30

20th anniversary of independence.

Universities Association Emblem — A210

**1980, Dec. 16** ***Perf. 12½***

**576** A210 60fr multicolored .90 .50

African Universities Assoc., 5th General Conf.

African Postal Union, 5th Anniversary A211

**1980, Dec. 24** **Photo.** ***Perf. 13½***

**577** A211 150fr multi 1.50 .60

Herichtys Cyanoguttatum — A212

**1981, Mar. 14** **Litho.** ***Perf. 12½***

**578** A212 60fr shown 1.10 .65
**579** A212 65fr Labeo bicolor 1.25 .75
**580** A212 200fr Tetraodon fluviatilis 3.25 1.75
*Nos. 578-580 (3)* 5.60 3.15

Birds — A212a

**1980, Dec. 30** **Photo.** ***Perf. 14½x14***

**580A** A212a 60fr Spreo superbus *100.00 40.00*
**580B** A212a 65fr Tockus camurus *100.00 40.00*
**580C** A212a 65fr Balearica pavonina *100.00 40.00*
**580D** A212a 100fr Ephippiorhynchus *200.00 175.00*
*Nos. 580A-580D (4)* *500.00 295.00*

Post Office, Grand Lahou A213

25th Anniv. of Ivory Coast Philatelic Club A214

**1981, May 2** **Litho.** ***Perf. 12½***

**581** A213 60fr multicolored .90 .30
**582** A214 65fr multicolored .90 .30

Stamp Day.

13th World Telecommunications Day — A215

**1981, May 17**

**583** A215 30fr multicolored .45 .25
**584** A215 60fr multicolored .90 .35

Viking Satellite Landing, 1976 — A216

Space Conquest: Columbia space shuttle.

**1981, June 13** **Litho.** ***Perf. 13½***

**585** A216 60fr multi .65 .25
**586** A216 75fr multi .85 .30
**587** A216 125fr multi 1.25 .55
**588** A216 300fr multi 2.75 1.25
*Nos. 585-588 (4)* 5.50 2.35

**Souvenir Sheet**

**589** A216 500fr multi 5.25 1.25

Local Flowers — A217

**1981, July 4** **Photo.** ***Perf. 14½x14***

**590** A217 50fr Amorphophallus 1.60 .55
**591** A217 60fr Sugar Cane 1.90 1.00
**592** A217 100fr Heliconia ivoirea 3.75 1.50
*Nos. 590-592 (3)* 7.25 3.05

Prince Charles and Lady Diana, Coach — A218

Royal Wedding: Couple and coaches.

**1981, Aug. 8** **Litho.** ***Perf. 12½***

**593** A218 80fr multi .80 .25
**594** A218 100fr multi 1.00 .50
**595** A218 125fr multi 1.50 .85
*Nos. 593-595 (3)* 3.30 1.60

**Souvenir Sheet**

**596** A218 500fr multi 5.50 2.00

For overprints see Nos. 642-645.

Elephant on Flag and Map — A219

**1981, Sept.** **Litho.** ***Perf. 12½***

**597** A219 80fr multicolored .75 .25
**598** A219 100fr multicolored 1.00 .50
**599** A219 125fr multicolored 1.25 .60
*Nos. 597-599 (3)* 3.00 1.35

See Nos. 662-666, 833.

Soccer Players A220

Soccer players.

**1981, Sept. 19** ***Perf. 14***

**600** A220 70fr multi, horiz. .65 .35
**601** A220 80fr multi, horiz. .75 .45
**602** A220 100fr multi .90 .55

**603** A220 150fr multi 1.25 .85
**604** A220 350fr multi 3.25 1.60
*Nos. 600-604 (5)* 6.80 3.80

**Souvenir Sheet**

**605** A220 500fr multi, horz. 4.75 2.00

ESPANA '82 World Cup Soccer Championship.
For overprints see Nos. 651-656.

West African Rice Development Assoc., 10th Anniv. — A221

**1981, Oct. 3** ***Perf. 12½***
**606** A221 80fr multicolored 1.10 .50

World Food Day A222

**1981, Oct. 18**
**607** A222 100fr multicolored 1.10 .60

Post Day — A223

**1981, Oct. 9** **Litho.** ***Perf. 12½***
**608** A223 70fr multicolored .65 .30
**609** A223 80fr multicolored .75 .45
**610** A223 100fr multicolored .95 .55
*Nos. 608-610 (3)* 2.35 1.30

75th Anniv. of Grand Prix — A224

Designs: Winners and their cars.

**1981, Nov. 21** ***Perf. 14***
**611** A224 15fr Felice Nazarro, 1907 .25 .25
**612** A224 40fr Jim Clark, 1962 .50 .25
**613** A224 80fr Fiat, 1907 1.00 .45
**614** A224 100fr Auto Union, 1936 1.25 .50
**615** A224 125fr Ferrari, 1961 1.50 .60
*Nos. 611-615 (5)* 4.50 2.05

**Souvenir Sheet**

**616** A224 500fr 1933 car 5.75 2.75

21st Anniv. of Independence — A225

**1981, Dec. 7** ***Perf. 13x12½***
**617** A225 50fr multicolored .60 .30
**618** A225 80fr multicolored 1.10 .50

Traditional Hairstyle — A226

Designs: Various hairstyles.

**1981, Dec. 19** **Photo.** ***Perf. 14½x14***
**619** A226 80fr multicolored 1.50 .75
**620** A226 100fr multicolored 2.50 1.10
**621** A226 125fr multicolored 3.25 1.50
*Nos. 619-621 (3)* 7.25 3.35

Stamp Day Africa — A227

**1982, Apr. 3** **Litho.** ***Perf. 12½x12***
**622** A227 100fr Bingerville P.O., 1902 1.10 .60

Rotary Emblem on Map of — A228

**1982, Apr. 13** ***Perf. 12½***
**623** A228 100fr ultra & gold 1.10 .60

Pres. Houphouet-Boigny's Rotary Goodwill Conference, Abidjan, Apr. 13-15.

250th Birth Anniv. of George Washington — A229

Anniversaries: 100fr, Auguste Piccard (1884-1962), Swiss physicist. 350fr, Goethe (1749-1832). 450fr, 500fr, Princess Diana, 21st birthday (portraits).

**1982, May 15** **Litho.** ***Perf. 13***
**624** A229 80fr multi .75 .35
**625** A229 100fr multi 1.00 .50
**626** A229 350fr multi 3.75 1.25
**627** A229 450fr multi 4.50 1.50
*Nos. 624-627 (4)* 10.00 3.60

**Souvenir Sheet**

**628** A229 500fr multi 4.50 2.00

Visit of French Pres. Mitterand, May 21-24 — A230

**1982, May 21** **Photo.** ***Perf. 13½***
**629** A230 100fr multicolored 1.40 .55

14th World Telecommunications Day — A231

**1982, May 29** **Litho.** ***Perf. 13***
**630** A231 80fr multicolored .85 .30

Scouting Year — A232

Scouts sailing, diff. 80fr, 150fr, 350fr, 500fr vert.

**1982, May 29** ***Perf. 12½***
**631** A232 80fr multi .85 .30
**632** A232 100fr multi 1.25 .35
**633** A232 150fr multi 1.50 .60
**634** A232 350fr multi 3.50 1.25
*Nos. 631-634 (4)* 7.10 2.50

**Souvenir Sheet**

**635** A232 500fr multi 6.00 2.50

TB Bacillus Centenary A233

**1982, June 5** **Photo.** ***Perf. 13x13½***
**636** A233 30fr brown & multi .70 .30
**637** A233 80fr lt grn & multi 1.10 .50

UN Conference on Human Environment, 10th Anniv. — A234

**1982, July** **Photo.** ***Perf. 13½x13***
**638** A234 40fr multicolored .70 .30
**639** A234 80fr multicolored 1.25 .45

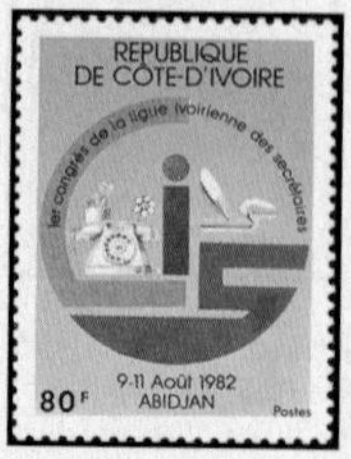


League of Ivory Coast Secretaries, First Congress — A235

**1982, Aug. 9** **Litho.** ***Perf. 12½x13***
**640** A235 80fr tan & multi 1.00 .40
**641** A235 100fr silver & multi 1.25 .50

593-596 Overprinted in Blue: "NAISSANCE / ROYALE 1982"

**1982, Aug. 21** ***Perf. 12½***
**642** A218 80fr multi .85 .45
**643** A218 100fr multi 1.00 .55
**644** A218 125fr multi 1.25 .65
*Nos. 642-644 (3)* 3.10 1.65

**Souvenir Sheet**

**645** A218 500fr multi 4.50 4.50

Birth of Prince William of Wales, June 21.

La Colombe de l'Avenir, 1962, by Pablo Picasso (1881-1973) — A236

Picasso Paintings: 80fr, Child with Dove, 1901. 100fr, Self-portrait, 1901. 185fr, Les Demoiselles d'Avignon, 1907. 350fr, The Dream, 1932. Nos. 646-649 vert.

**1982, Sept. 4** **Litho.** ***Perf. 13***
**646** A236 80fr multi .85 .35
**647** A236 100fr multi 1.00 .40
**648** A236 185fr multi 2.50 .65
**649** A236 350fr multi 4.00 1.25
**650** A236 500fr multi 6.00 1.75
*Nos. 646-650 (5)* 14.35 4.40

Nos. 600-605 Overprinted with World Cup Winners 1966-1982 in Black on Silver

**1982, Oct. 9** **Litho.** ***Perf. 14***
**651** A220 70fr multi .65 .30
**652** A220 80fr multi .80 .50
**653** A220 100fr multi 1.00 .55
**654** A220 150fr multi 1.50 .90
**655** A220 350fr multi 3.50 1.50
*Nos. 651-655 (5)* 7.45 3.75

**Souvenir Sheet**

**656** A220 500fr multi 5.50 5.50

Italy's victory in 1982 World Cup.

13th World UPU Day — A237

Designs: 80fr, P.O. counter. 100fr, Postel-2001 building, Abidjan, vert. 350fr, Postal workers. 500fr, Postel-2001 interior.

**1982, Oct. 23** ***Perf. 12½***
**657** A237 80fr multi .75 .45
**658** A237 100fr multi 1.25 .50
**659** A237 350fr multi 3.25 1.50

**Size: 48x37mm**

***Perf. 13***

**660** A237 500fr multi 4.50 2.25
*Nos. 657-660 (4)* 9.75 4.70

22nd Anniv. of Independence — A238

**1982, Dec. 7** ***Perf. 13***
**661** A238 100fr multicolored 1.10 .60

**Elephant Type of 1981**

**1982-84**

| | | | | |
|---|---|---|---|---|
| **662** | A219 | 5fr multicolored | .25 | .25 |
| **662A** | A219 | 10fr multi ('84) | .45 | .25 |
| **662B** | A219 | 20fr multicolored | .45 | .25 |
| **663** | A219 | 25fr multicolored | .35 | .25 |
| **664** | A219 | 30fr multicolored | .35 | .25 |
| **665** | A219 | 40fr multicolored | .55 | .25 |
| **666** | A219 | 50fr multicolored | .55 | .25 |
| | | *Nos. 662-666 (7)* | 2.95 | 1.75 |

Man Waterfall A238a

**1982 Photo. *Perf. 15x14***

| | | | | |
|---|---|---|---|---|
| **666A** | A238a | 80fr shown | *20.00* | *2.00* |
| **666B** | A238a | 80fr Boisee Savanna | *30.00* | *1.75* |
| **666C** | A238a | 500fr like #666A | *65.00* | *7.00* |
| | | *Nos. 666A-666C (3)* | 115.00 | 10.75 |

Issued: #666B, Dec. 18; others, Nov. 27.

20th Anniv. of West African Monetary Union A239

**1982, Dec. 21 Litho. *Perf. 12½***

| | | | | |
|---|---|---|---|---|
| **667** | A239 | 100fr Emblem | 1.10 | .55 |

Abouissa Children's Village A240

**1983, Mar. 5 Photo. *Perf. 13½x13***

| | | | | |
|---|---|---|---|---|
| **668** | A240 | 125fr multicolored | 1.50 | .60 |

Anteater A241

**1983, Mar. 12 Litho. *Perf. 12½x13***

| | | | | |
|---|---|---|---|---|
| **669** | A241 | 35fr Pangolin, vert. | .55 | .40 |
| **670** | A241 | 90fr shown | 1.00 | .50 |
| **671** | A241 | 100fr Colobus monkey, vert. | 1.25 | .60 |
| **672** | A241 | 125fr Buffalo | 1.50 | .75 |
| | | *Nos. 669-672 (4)* | 4.30 | 2.25 |

Stamp Day — A242

**1983, Mar. 19 Litho. *Perf. 12½***

| | | | | |
|---|---|---|---|---|
| **673** | A242 | 100fr Grand Bassam P.O., 1903 | 1.10 | .60 |

Easter 1983 A243

Paintings by Rubens (1577-1640). 100fr, 400fr, 500fr vert.

**1983, Apr. 9 *Perf. 13***

| | | | | |
|---|---|---|---|---|
| **674** | A243 | 100fr Descent from the Cross | 1.00 | .30 |
| **675** | A243 | 125fr Resurrection | 1.25 | .45 |
| **676** | A243 | 350fr Crucifixion | 3.25 | 1.00 |
| **677** | A243 | 400fr Piercing of the Sword | 4.00 | 1.25 |
| **678** | A243 | 500fr Descent, diff. | 4.75 | 1.50 |
| | | *Nos. 674-678 (5)* | 14.25 | 4.50 |

25th Anniv. of UN Economic Commission for Africa — A244

**1983, Apr. 29 Litho. *Perf. 13x12½***

| | | | | |
|---|---|---|---|---|
| **679** | A244 | 100fr multicolored | 1.10 | .55 |

Gray Parakeet A245

**1983, June 11**

| | | | | |
|---|---|---|---|---|
| **680** | A245 | 100fr Fish eagle, vert. | 2.00 | 1.00 |
| **681** | A245 | 125fr shown | 2.75 | .75 |
| **682** | A245 | 150fr Touracoes | 4.25 | 1.00 |
| | | *Nos. 680-682 (3)* | 9.00 | 2.75 |

World Communications Year — A245a

Designs: 100fr, Tower, telephone, operators. 125fr, Buildings, satellite dish.

**1983, July 16 *Perf. 12½x13***

| | | | | |
|---|---|---|---|---|
| **682A** | A245a | 100fr multi | *125.00* | — |
| **682B** | A245a | 125fr multi | *125.00* | — |

A246

**1983, Sept. 3 Litho. *Perf. 12½***

| | | | | |
|---|---|---|---|---|
| **683** | A246 | 50fr Flali, Gouro | .50 | .30 |
| **684** | A246 | 100fr Masked dancer, Guere | 1.10 | .45 |
| **685** | A246 | 125fr Stilt dancer, Yacouba | 1.50 | .55 |
| | | *Nos. 683-685 (3)* | 3.10 | 1.30 |

20th Anniv. of the Ivory Hotel, Abidjan — A249

**1983, Sept. 7 *Perf. 13***

| | | | | |
|---|---|---|---|---|
| **693** | A249 | 100fr multicolored | 1.10 | .60 |

Ecology in Action A250

**1983, Oct. 24 Litho.**

| | | | | |
|---|---|---|---|---|
| **694** | A250 | 25fr Forest after fire | .65 | .35 |
| **695** | A250 | 100fr Animals fleeing | 1.75 | .75 |
| **696** | A250 | 125fr Animals grazing | 2.25 | 1.10 |
| | | *Nos. 694-696 (3)* | 4.65 | 2.20 |

Raphael (1483-1520), 500th Birth Anniv. — A252

Paintings: 100fr, Christ and St. Peter. 125fr, Study for St. Joseph, vert. 350fr, Virgin of the House of Orleans, vert. 500fr, Virgin with the Blue Diadem, vert.

**1983, Nov. 5 Litho. *Perf. 13***

| | | | | |
|---|---|---|---|---|
| **698** | A252 | 100fr multi | 1.00 | .35 |
| **699** | A252 | 125fr multi | 1.25 | .50 |
| **700** | A252 | 350fr multi | 3.00 | 1.50 |
| **701** | A252 | 500fr multi | 4.50 | 2.00 |
| | | *Nos. 698-701 (4)* | 9.75 | 4.35 |

Auto Race A253

**1983, Oct. 24 Litho. *Perf. 12½***

| | | | | |
|---|---|---|---|---|
| **702** | A253 | 100fr Car, map | 1.25 | .60 |

Flowers — A254

**1983, Nov. 26 Photo. *Perf. 14x15***

| | | | | |
|---|---|---|---|---|
| **703** | A254 | 100fr Fleurs d'Ananas | *150.00* | — |
| **704** | A254 | 125fr Heliconia Rostrata | *10.00* | *3.00* |
| **705** | A254 | 150fr Rose de Porcelaine | *10.00* | *3.00* |
| | | *Nos. 703-705 (3)* | *170.00* | |

23rd Anniv. of Independence — A255

**1983, Dec. 7**

| | | | | |
|---|---|---|---|---|
| **706** | A255 | 100fr multicolored | 1.10 | .50 |

First Audio-visual Forum, Abidjan — A256

**1984, Jan. 25 Litho. *Perf. 13x12½***

| | | | | |
|---|---|---|---|---|
| **707** | A256 | 100fr Screen, arrow | 1.10 | .50 |

14th African Soccer Cup — A257

**1984, Mar. 4 Photo. *Perf. 12½***

| | | | | |
|---|---|---|---|---|
| **708** | A257 | 100fr Emblem | 1.00 | .40 |
| **709** | A257 | 200fr Maps shaking hands | 2.00 | .85 |

Local Insects A258

**1984, Mar. 24 Litho. *Perf. 13***

| | | | | |
|---|---|---|---|---|
| **710** | A258 | 100fr Argiope, vert. | 2.00 | .70 |
| **711** | A258 | 125fr Polistes gallicus | 2.25 | .90 |

Stamp Day — A259

**1984, Apr. 7 Litho. *Perf. 12½***

| | | | | |
|---|---|---|---|---|
| **712** | A259 | 100fr Abidjan P.O., 1934 | 1.10 | .55 |

Lions Emblem A260

**1984, Apr. 27 *Perf. 13½x13***

| | | | | |
|---|---|---|---|---|
| **713** | A260 | 100fr multicolored | 1.00 | .50 |
| **714** | A260 | 125fr multicolored | 1.50 | .65 |

3rd Convention of Multi-district 403, Abidjan, Apr. 27-29.

16th World Telecommunications Day — A261

**1984, May 17** *Perf. 12½*
**715** A261 100fr multi 1.10 .55

Council of Unity, 25th Anniv. — A262

**1984, May 29**
**716** A262 100fr multicolored 1.00 .35
**717** A262 125fr multicolored 1.25 .45

First Governmental Palace, Grand-Bassam — A263

**1984, July 14** **Litho.** *Perf. 12½*
**718** A263 100fr shown 1.00 .35
**719** A263 125fr Palace of Justice, Grand-Bassam 1.25 .50

Men Playing Eklan — A264

**1984, Aug. 11** *Perf. 13*
**720** A264 100fr Board 1.40 .35
**721** A264 125fr shown 1.50 .55

Locomotive "Gazelle" — A265

**1984** *Perf. 12½*
**722** A265 100fr shown 1.00 .40
**723** A265 100fr Cargo ship 1.00 .40
**724** A265 125fr Superpacific 1.75 .50
**725** A265 125fr Cargo ship, diff. 1.25 .50
**726** A265 350fr Pacific type 10 4.00 1.25
**727** A265 350fr Ocean liner 3.50 1.25
**728** A265 500fr Mallet class GT2 5.50 1.75
**729** A265 500fr Ocean liner, diff. 5.50 1.75
*Nos. 722-729 (8)* 23.50 7.80

Issue dates: trains, Aug. 25; ships, Sept. 1.

Stamp Day A266

**1984, Oct. 20** **Litho.** *Perf. 12½*
**730** A266 100fr Map, post offices 1.50 .60

10th Anniv., West African Union A267

**1984, Oct. 27** **Litho.** *Perf. 13½*
**731** A267 100fr Map, member nations 1.00 .50

Wildlife — A267a

**1984, Nov. 3** **Photo.** *Perf. 14½x15*
**731A** A267a 100fr Tragelaphus scriptus *75.00 12.00*
**731B** A267a 150fr Felis serval *75.00 12.00*

Tourism A267b

**1984, Nov. 10** **Photo.** *Perf. 15x14½*
**731C** A267b 50fr Le Club Valtur *65.00 11.00*
**731D** A267b 100fr Grand Lahou *65.00 11.00*

Flowers — A267c

**1984, Nov. 17** **Photo.** *Perf. 14½x15*
**731E** A267c 100fr Allamanda carthartica *75.00 12.00*
**731F** A267c 125fr Baobob *75.00 12.00*

90th Anniv., Ivory Coast Postage Stamps A268

**1984, Nov. 23** **Litho.** *Perf. 12½*
**732** A268 125fr Book cover 1.40 .75

24th Anniv. of Independence — A269

**1984, Dec. 7** **Litho.** *Perf. 12½*
**733** A269 100fr Citizens, outline map 1.00 .60

Rotary Intl. Conf. — A270

**1985, Jan. 16** **Litho.** *Perf. 12½x13*
**734** A270 100fr multicolored .90 .50
**735** A270 125fr multicolored 1.10 .55

Traditional Costumes A271

**1985, Feb. 16** **Litho.** *Perf. 13½*
**736** A271 90fr Dan le Babou 1.50 .45
**737** A271 100fr Post-natal gown 1.50 .55

Birds — A271a

**1985** **Photo.** *Perf. 14½x15*
**737A** A271a 25fr Marabout *150.00 17.50*
**737B** A271a 100fr Jacana *150.00 17.50*
**737C** A271a 350fr Ibis *150.00 17.50*
*Nos. 737A-737C (3)* 450.00

Issued: Nos. 737A, 737B, Mar. No. 737C, 8/17.

Stamp Day — A272

**1985, Apr. 13** **Litho.** *Perf. 12½*
**738** A272 100fr Riverboat Adjame 2.25 .80

18th District of Zonta Intl., 7th Conference, Abidjan, Apr. 25-27 — A273

**1985, Apr. 25** **Litho.** *Perf. 13½*
**739** A273 125fr Zonta Intl. emblem 1.25 .60

Bondoukou — A273a

100fr, Marche de Bondoukou. 125fr, Mosque, Samatiguila.

**1985** **Litho.** *Perf. 14½x13½*
**739A** A273a 100fr multi *140.00 9.00*
**739B** A273a 125fr multi *140.00 9.00*
**739C** A273a 200fr multi *140.00 9.00*
*Nos. 739A-739C (3)* *420.00 27.00*

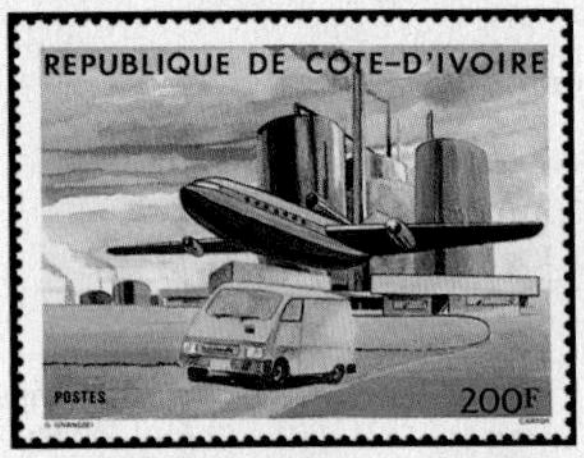


PHILEXAFRICA '85, Lome — A274

**1985, May 15** *Perf. 13*
**740** A274 200fr Factory, jet, van 2.00 1.10
**741** A274 200fr Youth sports, farming 2.00 1.10
*a.* Pair, Nos. 740-741 + label 6.00 6.00

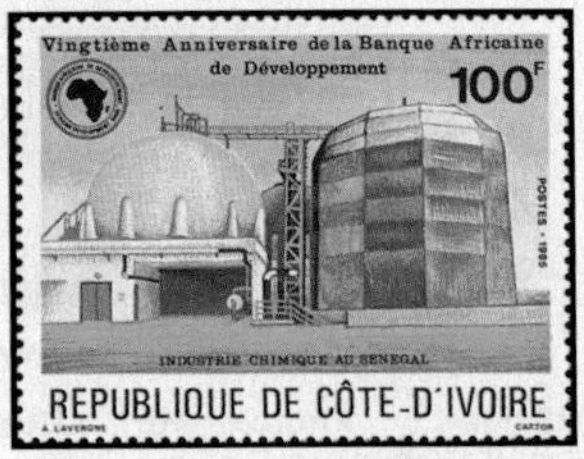


African Development Bank, 20th Anniv. — A275

**1985, June 18**
**742** A275 100fr Senegal chemical industry .95 .45
**743** A275 125fr Gambian tree nursery 1.10 .65

Intl. Youth Year — A276

**1985, July 20** *Perf. 12½*
**744** A276 125fr Map, profiles, dove 1.20 .65

Natl. Armed Forces, 25th Anniv. — A277

Emblems: No. 745, Presidential Guard. No. 746, F.A.N.C.I. 125fr, Air Transport & Liaison Group, G.A.T.L. 200fr, National Marines. 350fr, National Gendarmerie.

**1985, July 27** *Perf. 12½x13*
**745** A277 100fr dp rose lil & gold .85 .45
**746** A277 100fr dark bl & gold .90 .50
**747** A277 125fr blk brn & gold 1.10 .55
**748** A277 200fr blk brn & gold 1.75 1.00
**749** A277 350fr brt ultra & sil 2.75 1.75
*Nos. 745-749 (5)* 7.35 4.25

1986 World Cup Soccer Preliminaries, Mexico — A279

**1985, Aug.** *Perf. 13*
**751** A279 100fr Heading the ball .80 .45
**752** A279 150fr Tackle 1.25 .75
**753** A279 200fr Dribbling 1.50 1.00
**754** A279 350fr Passing 3.00 1.75
*Nos. 751-754 (4)* 6.55 3.95

**Souvenir Sheet**
**755** A279 500fr Power shot 4.25 2.00

Ivory Coast — Sovereign Military Order of Malta Postal Convention, Dec. 19, 1984 — A280

**1985, Aug. 31** *Perf. 13x12½*
**756** A280 125fr Natl. arms 1.00 .65
**757** A280 350fr S.M.O.M. arms 3.00 1.75

Visit of Pope John Paul II — A281

**1985, Sept. 24** *Perf. 13*
**Overprint in Black**
**758** A281 100fr Portrait, St. Paul's Cathedral, Abidjan 2.00 1.00

The overprint, "Consecration de la Cathedrale Saint Paul d'Abidjon," was added to explain the reason for the visit of the Pope. Copies without overprint exist but were not issued.

UN Child Survival Campaign A282

**1985, Oct. 5** **Litho.** *Perf. 13½x14*
**759** A282 100fr Breast-feeding .90 .50
**760** A282 100fr Oral rehydration therapy .90 .50
**761** A282 100fr Mother and child .90 .50
**762** A282 100fr Vaccination .90 .50
*Nos. 759-762 (4)* 3.60 2.00

UN 40th Anniv. — A283

**1985, Oct. 31** *Perf. 13*
**763** A283 100fr multicolored 1.00 .60

Admission to UN, 25th anniv.

World Wildlife Fund — A284

Striped antelopes.

**1985, Nov. 30**
**764** A284 50fr multicolored *7.00* 1.00
**765** A284 60fr multicolored *9.00* 2.00
**766** A284 75fr multicolored *18.00* 3.00
**767** A284 100fr multicolored *27.50* 5.00
*Nos. 764-767 (4)* *61.50* 11.00

City Skyline — A285

**1985, Nov. 21** **Litho.** *Perf. 13*
**768** A285 125fr multicolored 1.25 .65

Expo '85 national industrial exhibition.

Return to the Land Campaign A286

**1985, Dec. 7** *Perf. 12½*
**769** A286 125fr multicolored 1.25 .65

Natl. independence, 25th anniv.

Flowers — A286a

100fr, L'Amorphophallus staudtii. 125fr, Crinum scillifolium. 200fr, Triphyophyllum peltatum.

**1985, Dec. 28** **Litho.** *Perf. 14x15*
**769A** A286a 100fr multi *140.00* *10.00*
**769B** A286a 125fr multi *140.00* *10.00*
**769C** A286a 200fr multi *140.00* *10.00*
*Nos. 769A-769C (3)* *420.00* *30.00*

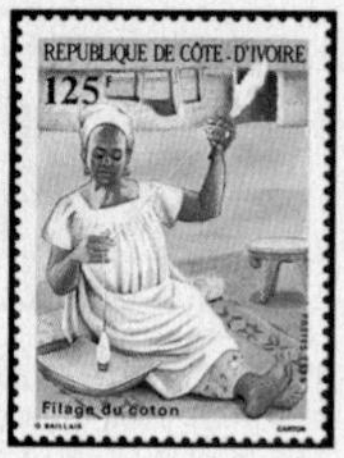

Handicrafts A287

**1986, Jan.** *Perf. 13½*
**770** A287 125fr Spinning thread 1.25 .55
**771** A287 155fr Painting 1.50 .75

Flora — A288

**1986, Feb. 22** **Litho.** *Perf. 13½*
**772** A288 40fr Omphalocarpum elatum .45 .25
**773** A288 50fr Momordica charantia .55 .30
**774** A288 125fr Millettia takou 1.25 .75
**775** A288 200fr Costus afer 2.00 1.00
*Nos. 772-775 (4)* 4.25 2.30

Cooking Utensils, Natl. Museum, Abidjan — A289

**1986, Mar. 6** *Perf. 13x12½, 12½x13*
**776** A289 20fr We bowl .25 .25
**777** A289 30fr Baoule bowl .30 .25
**778** A289 90fr Baoule platter 1.00 .45
**779** A289 125fr Dan scoop 1.25 .65
**780** A289 440fr Baoule lidded pot 4.00 2.25
*Nos. 776-780 (5)* 6.80 3.85

Nos. 776-778 horiz.

Natl. Pedagogic and Vocational School, 10th Anniv. — A290

**1986, Mar. 20** *Perf. 13½*
**781** A290 125fr multicolored 1.40 .60

Cable Ship Stephan, 1910 — A291

**1986, Apr. 12** **Litho.** *Perf. 12½*
**782** A291 125fr multicolored 2.25 .60

Stamp Day.

**Houphouet-Boigny Type of 1974-76**

**1986, Apr.** **Engr.** *Perf. 13*
**783** A112 5fr dk red, dp rose lil & brn .25 .25
**784** A112 10fr gray grn, brt bl & brn .25 .25
**785** A112 20fr brt ver, blk brn & brn .25 .25
**786** A112 25fr bl, dp rose lil & brn .30 .25
**787** A112 30fr brt ver, blk brn & brn .30 .25
**789** A112 50fr lake, dk vio & brn .50 .25
**790** A112 90fr dk brn vio, rose lake & brn .90 .40
**791** A112 125fr brt lil rose, brt ver & brn 1.25 .50
**792** A112 155fr dk brn vio, Prus bl & brn 1.25 .60
*Nos. 783-792 (9)* 5.25 3.00

The 1986 printing of the 40fr is in slightly darker colors than No. 374.

Natl. Youth and Sports Institute, 25th Anniv. — A293

**1986, May 9** **Litho.** *Perf. 12½*
**793** A293 125fr brt org & dk yel grn 1.10 .60

Fish A294

5fr, Polypterus endlicheri. 125fr, Synodontis punctifer. 150fr, Protopterus annectens. 155fr, Synodontis koensis. 440fr, Malapterurus electricus.

**1986, July 5** **Litho.** *Perf. 14½x13½*
**794** A294 5fr multi .25 .25
**795** A294 125fr multi 1.25 .55
**796** A294 150fr multi 1.75 .75
**797** A294 155fr multi 2.00 .75
**798** A294 440fr multi 5.00 2.00
*Nos. 794-798 (5)* 10.25 4.30

Enthronement of a Chief, Agni District — A295

**1986, July 19** *Perf. 13½x14½*
**799** A295 50fr Drummer, vert. .45 .40
**800** A295 350fr Chief in litter 3.50 2.00
**801** A295 440fr Royal entourage 4.50 3.00
*Nos. 799-801 (3)* 8.45 5.40

Rural Houses — A296

**1986, Aug. 2** **Litho.** *Perf. 14x15*
**802** A296 125fr Baoule aoulo 1.25 .60
**803** A296 155fr Upper Antiam eva 1.50 .80
**804** A296 350fr Lobi soukala 3.00 1.75
*Nos. 802-804 (3)* 5.75 3.15

Coat of Arms
A297

Coastal Landscapes
A298

**1986-87** **Engr.** ***Perf. 13***

**807** A297 50fr bright org .40 .25
**808** A297 125fr dark green 1.25 .35
**809** A297 155fr crimson 1.50 .35
**810** A297 195fr blue ('87) 1.75 .35
*Nos. 807-810 (4)* 4.90 1.30

Issue dates: 50fr, 125fr, 155fr, Aug. 23.

***Perf. 14x15, 15x14***

**1986, Aug. 30** **Litho.**

**820** A298 125fr Grand Bereby 1.50 .75
**821** A298 155fr Sableux Boubele, horiz. 2.00 1.00

Oceanographic Research Center — A299

***Perf. 14½x13½***

**1986, Sept. 13** **Litho.**

**822** A299 125fr Fishing grounds 1.10 .60
**823** A299 155fr Net fishing 1.50 .80

Intl. Peace Year — A300

**1986, Oct. 16** **Litho.** ***Perf. 14x13½***

**824** A300 155fr multicolored 1.40 .75

Research and Development — A301

**1986, Nov. 15** ***Perf. 13½x14***

**825** A301 125fr Bull 1.50 .90
**826** A301 155fr Wheat 1.50 .90

Natl. Independence, 26th Anniv. — A302

**1986, Dec. 6** **Litho.** ***Perf. 13½x14***

**827** A302 155fr multicolored 1.50 .75

Rural Housing
A303

**1987, Mar. 14** **Litho.** ***Perf. 13½x14***

**828** A303 190fr Guesseple Dan 2.00 1.10
**829** A303 550fr M'Bagui Senoufo 5.50 3.00

Stamp Day — A304

Jean Mermoz College, 25th Anniv. — A305

**1987, Apr. 4** ***Perf. 13x13½***

**830** A304 155fr Mailman, 1918 1.40 .80

**1987, Apr. 9** ***Perf. 13***

**831** A305 40fr Cock, elephant .40 .30
**832** A305 155fr Dove, children 1.50 .70

**Elephant Type of 1981**

**1987, Apr. 9**

**833** A219 35fr multicolored .50 .25

Fouilles, by Krah N'Guessan
A306

Paintings by local artists: 500fr, Cortege Ceremonial, by Santoni Gerard.

**1987, Aug. 14** **Litho.** ***Perf. 14½x15***

**841** A306 195fr multi 1.75 1.00
**842** A306 500fr multi 4.50 2.75

World Post Day, Express Mail Service
A307

**1987, Oct. 9** ***Perf. 13½***

**843** A307 155fr multi 1.50 .95
**844** A307 195fr multi 1.75 1.00

Intl. Trade Cent.
A308

**1987, Oct. 24**

**845** A308 155fr multi 2.10 1.00

A309

**1987, Dec. 5** **Litho.** ***Perf. 14x13½***

**846** A309 155fr multicolored 1.40 .90

Natl. Independence, 27th anniv.

A310

**1988, Feb. 20** **Litho.** ***Perf. 14x13½***

**847** A310 155fr multicolored 1.40 .85

Lions Club for child survival.

The Modest Canary, by Monne Bou
A311

Paintings by local artists: 20fr, The Couple, by K.J. Houra, vert. 150fr, The Eternal Dance, by Bou, vert. 155fr, La Termitiere, by Mathilde Moro, vert. 195fr, The Sun of Independence, by Michel Kodjo, vert.

**1988, Jan. 30** ***Perf. 12½x13, 13x12½***

**848** A311 20fr multi .30 .25
**849** A311 30fr shown .30 .25
**850** A311 150fr multi 1.50 .75
**851** A311 155fr multi 1.60 .85
**852** A311 195fr multi 2.00 1.00
*Nos. 848-852 (5)* 5.70 3.10

Stamp Day
A312

**1988, Apr. 4** **Litho.** ***Perf. 13***

**853** A312 155fr Bereby P.O., c. 1900 1.40 .90

A313

**1988, Apr. 18** **Litho.** ***Perf. 15x14***

**854** A313 195fr blk & dark red 2.25 1.40

15th French-Language Nations Cardiology Congress, Abidjan, Apr. 18-20.

A314

**1988, May 21** **Litho.** ***Perf. 12x13***

**855** A314 195fr multicolored 2.00 1.00

Intl. Fund for Agricultural Development (IFAD), 10th anniv.

1st Intl. Day for the Campaign Against Drug Abuse and Drug Trafficking
A315

**1988, Aug. 27** **Litho.** ***Perf. 13½***

**856** A315 155fr multi 1.75 1.00

Stone Heads — A316

Various stone heads from the Niangoran-Bouah Archaeological Collection.

**Litho. & Engr.**

**1988, July 9** ***Perf. 13x14½***

**857** A316 5fr beige & sep .25 .25
**858** A316 10fr buff & sep .25 .25
**859** A316 30fr pale grn & sep .30 .25
**860** A316 155fr pale yel & sep 1.50 .85
**861** A316 195fr pale yel grn & sep 2.00 .95
*Nos. 857-861 (5)* 4.30 2.55

World Post Day — A317

**1988, Oct. 15** **Litho.** ***Perf. 14***

**862** A317 155fr multi 1.50 .90

Natl. Independence 28th Anniv. — A318

Year of the Forest: 40fr, Healthy trees. No. 864, Stop forest fires. No. 865, Planting trees.

**1988, Dec. 6** ***Perf. 11½x12***

**863** A318 40fr multi .50 .25
**864** A318 155fr multi 1.75 .90
**865** A318 155fr multi 1.75 .90
*Nos. 863-865 (3)* 4.00 2.05

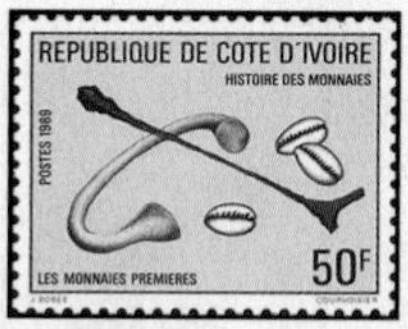


History of Money
A319

**1989, Feb. 25 Litho. *Perf. 12x11½***

**Granite Paper**

| | | | | |
|---|---|---|---|---|
| **866** | A319 | 50fr shown | 1.00 | .25 |
| **867** | A319 | 195fr Senegal bank notes, 1854, 1901 | 2.50 | 1.25 |

See Nos. 885-886, 896-898, 915. For surcharges see Nos. 904-905.

"Valeur d'echange 0fr.25" on 25c Type A5, 1920
A320

**1989, Apr. *Perf. 12½***

| | | | | |
|---|---|---|---|---|
| **868** | A320 | 155fr multi | 1.75 | .95 |

Stamp Day.

Jewelry from the National Museum Collection
A321

**1989, Mar. 25 Litho. *Perf. 14***

| | | | | |
|---|---|---|---|---|
| **869** | A321 | 90fr Voltaic bracelets | 1.00 | .60 |
| **870** | A321 | 155fr Anklets | 2.00 | 1.25 |

Sculptures by Christian Lattier
A322

***Perf. 11½x12, 12x11½***

**1989, May 13 Granite Paper**

| | | | | |
|---|---|---|---|---|
| **871** | A322 | 40fr *The Old Man and the Infant*, vert. | .50 | .25 |
| **872** | A322 | 155fr *The Saxophone Player*, vert. | 1.75 | 1.00 |
| **873** | A322 | 550fr *The Panther* | 4.25 | 2.75 |
| | | *Nos. 871-873 (3)* | 6.50 | 4.00 |

For surcharge see No. 903.

Council for Rural Development, 30th Anniv. — A323

**1989, May 29 *Perf. 15x14***

| | | | | |
|---|---|---|---|---|
| **874** | A323 | 75fr Flags, well, tractor, field | 1.00 | .50 |

See Togo No. 1526.

Intl. Peace Congress — A324

**1989, June Litho. *Perf. 13***

| | | | | |
|---|---|---|---|---|
| **875** | A324 | 195fr multi | 1.75 | 1.00 |

Rural Habitat
A325

**1989, June 10 Litho. *Perf. 14***

| | | | | |
|---|---|---|---|---|
| **876** | A325 | 155fr Hut, Sirikukube Dida | 1.75 | 1.00 |

For surcharge see No. 902.

Sekou Watara, King of Kong (1710-1745) — A326

Designs: No. 878, Bastille, Declaration of Human Rights and Citizenship.

**1989, July 7 Litho. *Perf. 13***

| | | | | |
|---|---|---|---|---|
| **877** | A326 | 200fr shown | 2.75 | 1.50 |
| **878** | A326 | 200fr multi | 2.75 | 1.50 |
| *a.* | | Pair, Nos. 877-878 + label | 8.50 | 7.50 |

PHILEXFRANCE '89, French revolution bicent.

Endangered Species — A327

**1989, Sept. 16 *Perf. 12x11½***

**Granite Paper**

| | | | | |
|---|---|---|---|---|
| **879** | A327 | 25fr *Varanus niloticus* | .50 | .30 |
| **880** | A327 | 100fr *Crocodylus niloticus* | 2.00 | .90 |

World Post Day
A328

**1989, Oct. 9 Litho. *Perf. 12½x13***

| | | | | |
|---|---|---|---|---|
| **881** | A328 | 195fr multi | 1.75 | .90 |

CAPTEAO, 30th Anniv.
A329

**1989, Oct. 28 Litho. *Perf. 12½***

| | | | | |
|---|---|---|---|---|
| **882** | A329 | 155fr multicolored | 1.50 | .90 |

Conference of Postal and Telecommunication Administrations of West African Nations.

A330

**1989, Dec. 7 *Perf. 13***

| | | | | |
|---|---|---|---|---|
| **883** | A330 | 155fr multicolored | 1.50 | .85 |

Natl. independence, 29th anniv.

A331

**1990, Jan. 18 Litho. *Perf. 13***

| | | | | |
|---|---|---|---|---|
| **884** | A331 | 155fr multicolored | 1.25 | .85 |

Pan-African Union, 10th anniv.

**History of Money Type of 1989**

**1990, Mar. 17 Litho. *Perf. 12x11½***

**Granite Paper**

| | | | | |
|---|---|---|---|---|
| **885** | A319 | 155fr 1923 25fr note | 1.50 | .85 |
| **886** | A319 | 195fr 1, 2, 5fr notes | 2.50 | 1.25 |

Stamp Day
A332

**1990, Apr. 21 Litho. *Perf. 13x12½***

| | | | | |
|---|---|---|---|---|
| **887** | A332 | 155fr Packet Africa | 1.75 | .90 |

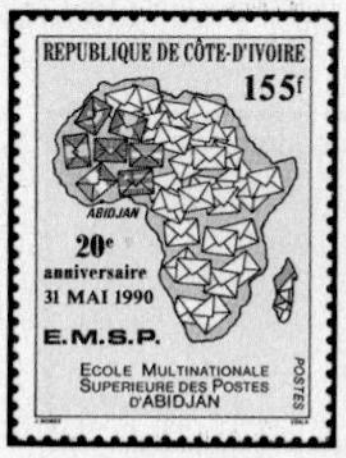


Multinational Postal School, 20th Anniv. — A333

**1990, May 31 *Perf. 12½***

| | | | | |
|---|---|---|---|---|
| **888** | A333 | 155fr multicolored | 1.50 | .80 |

Rural Village
A334

**1990, June 30 *Perf. 14***

| | | | | |
|---|---|---|---|---|
| **889** | A334 | 155fr multicolored | 1.50 | .60 |

Intl. Literacy Year
A335

**1990, July 28 *Perf. 15x14***

| | | | | |
|---|---|---|---|---|
| **890** | A335 | 195fr multicolored | 1.75 | .90 |

Dedication of Basilica of Notre Dame of Peace, Yamoussoukro — A336

**1990, Sept. 8 *Perf. 14½x13½***

| | | | | |
|---|---|---|---|---|
| **891** | A336 | 155fr shown | 1.50 | .80 |
| **892** | A336 | 195fr Basilica, diff. | 2.50 | 1.25 |

Visit of Pope John Paul II — A337

**1990, Sept. 9 *Perf. 13***

| | | | | |
|---|---|---|---|---|
| **893** | A337 | 500fr multicolored | 5.00 | 2.75 |

World Post Day — A338

**1990, Oct. 9 Litho. *Perf. 14x15***

| | | | | |
|---|---|---|---|---|
| **894** | A338 | 195fr multicolored | 3.25 | 1.50 |

Independence, 30th Anniv. — A339

**1990, Dec. 6 Litho. *Perf. 13½x14½***

| | | | | |
|---|---|---|---|---|
| **895** | A339 | 155fr multicolored | 1.75 | .90 |

**History of Money Type of 1989**

**1991, Mar. 1 Litho. *Perf. 11½***

**Granite Paper**

| | | | | |
|---|---|---|---|---|
| **896** | A319 | 40fr French West Africa 1942 5fr, 100fr notes | .45 | .25 |
| **897** | A319 | 155fr like #896 | 1.60 | .85 |
| **898** | A319 | 195fr French West Africa & Togo 50fr, 500fr notes | 2.00 | 1.25 |
| | | *Nos. 896-898 (3)* | 4.05 | 2.35 |

For surcharges see Nos. 904-905.

Stamp Day A340

**1991, May 18 Litho. *Perf. 13½***

| | | | | | |
|---|---|---|---|---|---|
| **899** | A340 | 150fr | multicolored | 1.50 | .55 |

Miniature Sheets

French Open Tennis Championships, Cent. — A341

Tennis Players: No. 900a, Henri Cochet. b, Rene Lacoste. c, Jean Borotra. d, Don Budge. e, Marcel Bernard. f, Ken Rosewall. g, Rod Laver. h, Bjorn Borg. i, Yannick Noah.

No. 901a, Suzanne Lenglen. b, Helen Wills Moody. c, Simone Mathieu. d, Maureen Connolly. e, Francoise Durr. f, Margaret Court. g, Chris Evert. h, Martina Navratilova. i, Steffi Graf.

**1991, May 24 Litho. *Perf. 13½***

| | | | | | |
|---|---|---|---|---|---|
| **900** | A341 | 200fr | #a.-i. | 22.50 | 22.50 |
| **901** | A341 | 200fr | #a.-i. | 22.50 | 22.50 |

**Nos. 872, 876, 897-898 Surcharged**

***Perfs. as Before***

**1991, July 15 Litho.**

| | | | | | |
|---|---|---|---|---|---|
| **902** | A325 | 150fr on 155fr #876 | | 1.75 | .55 |

**Granite Paper**

| | | | | | |
|---|---|---|---|---|---|
| **903** | A322 | 150fr on 155fr #872 | | 1.75 | .55 |
| **904** | A319 | 150fr on 155fr #897 | | 1.75 | .65 |
| **905** | A319 | 200fr on 195fr #898 | | 2.25 | .80 |
| | | *Nos. 902-905 (4)* | | 7.50 | 2.55 |

Location of obliterator and surcharge varies.

Packet Boats A342

**1991, June 28 Litho. *Perf. 12x11½***

**Granite Paper**

| | | | | | |
|---|---|---|---|---|---|
| **906** | A342 | 50fr | Europe | .55 | .25 |
| **907** | A342 | 550fr | Asia | 5.25 | 2.75 |

World Post Day A343

**1991, Oct. 9 *Perf. 13***

| | | | | | |
|---|---|---|---|---|---|
| **908** | A343 | 50fr | shown | .55 | .25 |
| **909** | A343 | 100fr | SIPE, globe | .95 | .50 |

Tribal Drums — A344

**1991 Litho. *Perf. 14x15***

| | | | | | |
|---|---|---|---|---|---|
| **910** | A344 | 5fr | We | .25 | .25 |
| **911** | A344 | 25fr | Krou, Soubre region | .25 | .25 |
| **912** | A344 | 150fr | Sinematiali | 1.75 | 1.10 |
| **913** | A344 | 200fr | Akye, Alepe region | 2.00 | 1.25 |
| | | | *Nos. 910-913 (4)* | 4.25 | 2.85 |

Independence, 31st Anniv. — A345

**1991, Dec. 7 Litho. *Perf. 13½x14½***

| | | | | | |
|---|---|---|---|---|---|
| **914** | A345 | 150fr | multicolored | 1.75 | .80 |

**History of Money Type of 1989**

**1991, Dec. 8 *Perf. 12x11½***

**Granite Paper**

| | | | | | |
|---|---|---|---|---|---|
| **915** | A319 | 100fr | like #898 | 1.00 | .70 |

Flowers A346

Various flowers.

**1991, Dec. 20 Engr. *Perf. 13***

| | | | | | |
|---|---|---|---|---|---|
| **916** | A346 | 150fr | grn, blk & mag, vert. | 1.50 | .50 |
| **917** | A346 | 200fr | grn, olive & rose car | 1.90 | .85 |

African Soccer Championships — A347

Designs: 150fr, Elephants holding trophy, map, soccer ball, vert.

**1992, Apr. 22 Litho. *Perf. 13***

| | | | | | |
|---|---|---|---|---|---|
| **918** | A347 | 20fr | multicolored | .35 | .25 |
| **919** | A347 | 150fr | multicolored | 1.75 | 1.25 |

Animals A348

**1992, May 5 Engr. *Perf. 13x12½***

| | | | | | |
|---|---|---|---|---|---|
| **920** | A348 | 5fr | Viverra civetta | .25 | .25 |
| **921** | A348 | 40fr | Nandinia binotata | .55 | .25 |
| **922** | A348 | 150fr | Tragelaphus euryceros | 2.00 | .80 |
| **923** | A348 | 500fr | Panthera pardus | 5.00 | 3.25 |
| | | | *Nos. 920-923 (4)* | 7.80 | 4.55 |

World Post Day — A349

**1992, Oct. 7 Litho. *Perf. 13***

| | | | | | |
|---|---|---|---|---|---|
| **924** | A349 | 150fr | black & blue | 1.50 | .80 |

First Ivory Coast Postage Stamp, Cent. — A350

Designs: a, #3, #197. b, #182, #909 with mail trucks, post office boxes.

**1992, Oct. 7**

| | | | | | |
|---|---|---|---|---|---|
| **925** | A350 | 150fr | Pair, #a.-b. + label | 5.00 | 3.50 |

Funeral Monuments A351

Various grave site monuments.

**1992, Dec. 30 Engr. *Perf. 13***

| | | | | | |
|---|---|---|---|---|---|
| **926** | A351 | 5fr | multicolored | .25 | .25 |
| **927** | A351 | 50fr | multicolored | .65 | .25 |
| **928** | A351 | 150fr | multicolored | 1.60 | .80 |
| **929** | A351 | 400fr | multicolored | 3.75 | 1.75 |
| | | | *Nos. 926-929 (4)* | 6.25 | 3.05 |

Intl. Abidjan Marathon A351a

**1992, Nov. 20 Litho. *Perf. 11½***

**Granite Paper**

| | | | | | |
|---|---|---|---|---|---|
| **929A** | A351a | 150fr | Flags, runners | 1.10 | .50 |
| **929B** | A351a | 200fr | Runners | 2.25 | .75 |

Nos. 929A-929B were not available in the philatelic market until Apr. 1994.

Gold Mine of Ity, 1st Anniv. — A351b

**1992, Nov. 8 Litho. *Perf. 14x15***

| | | | | | |
|---|---|---|---|---|---|
| **929C** | A351b | 200fr | multicolored | 2.00 | .75 |

No. 929C was not available in the philatelic market until Apr. 1994.

32nd Anniv. of Independence A351c

150fr, People, flag, Statue of Liberty, map.

**1992, Dec. 4**

| | | | | | |
|---|---|---|---|---|---|
| **929D** | A351c | 30fr | shown | .35 | .35 |
| **929E** | A351c | 150fr | multicolored | 1.75 | .75 |

Nos. 929D-929E were not available in the philatelic market until Apr. 1994.

Tourist Attractions — A351d

***Perf. 14x15, 15x14***

**1992, Sept. 4 Litho.**

| | | | | | |
|---|---|---|---|---|---|
| **929F** | A351d | 10fr | Modern hotel, horiz. | — | — |
| **929G** | A351d | 25fr | Dent de Man | *35.00* | — |
| **929H** | A351d | 100fr | Resort, horiz. | *45.00* | — |
| **929I** | A351d | 200fr | Map of tourist sites | *65.00* | — |

Environmental Summit — A351e

200fr, Prevent water pollution, horiz.

***Perf. 11½x12, 12x11½***

**1992, June 5 Litho.**

**Granite Paper**

| | | | | | |
|---|---|---|---|---|---|
| **929J** | A351e | 150fr | multicolored | *70.00* | — |
| **929K** | A351e | 200fr | multicolored | *70.00* | — |

Stamp Day A352

Designs showing children interested in philately: No. 930, Girl, stamp collection, #169. No. 931, Girl, #431, #446B, #186, and #920. 150fr, Boy sitting under tree, stamp exhibition.

**1993, Apr. 17 Litho. *Perf. 13½***

| | | | | | |
|---|---|---|---|---|---|
| **930** | A352 | 50fr | multicolored | .45 | .25 |
| **931** | A352 | 50fr | multicolored | .45 | .25 |
| **932** | A352 | 150fr | multicolored | 1.75 | .75 |
| | | | *Nos. 930-932 (3)* | 2.65 | 1.25 |

A353

A354

Medicinal plants.

**1993, May 14 Litho. *Perf. 11½x12***

**Granite Paper**

933 A353 5fr Argemone mexicana .35 .25
934 A353 20fr Hibiscus esculentus .45 .25
935 A353 200fr Cassia alata 2.00 1.25
*Nos. 933-935 (3)* 2.80 1.75

**1993, Aug. 27 Photo. *Perf. 12x11½***

Orchids: 10fr, Calyptrochilum emarginatum. 50fr, Plectrelminthus caudathus. 150fr, Eulophia guineensis.

**Granite Paper**

936 A354 10fr multicolored .25 .25
937 A354 50fr multicolored .40 .30
938 A354 150fr multicolored 1.50 .90
*Nos. 936-938 (3)* 2.15 1.45

Ivory Coast Colony, Cent. A355

25fr, Organization charter. 100fr, Colonial Governor Louis Gustave Binger, Pres. F. Houphouet-Boigny. 500fr, Natives selecting goods for trade.

**1993, Sept. 17 *Perf. 13x12½***

939 A355 25fr green & black .35 .25
940 A355 100fr blue & black 1.10 .75
941 A355 500fr brown & black 5.00 3.50
*Nos. 939-941 (3)* 6.45 4.50

Elimination Round of 1994 World Cup Soccer Championships, US — A356

Designs: 150fr, Cartoon soccer players. 200fr, Three players. 300fr, Two players. 400fr, Cartoon players, diff.

**1993, Sept. 24 Litho. *Perf. 14x15***

942 A356 150fr multicolored 1.10 .45
943 A356 200fr multicolored 2.25 .85
944 A356 300fr multicolored 3.00 1.75
945 A356 400fr multicolored 4.00 2.25
*Nos. 942-945 (4)* 10.35 5.30

World Post Day A357

Designs: 30fr, Map of Ivory Coast. 200fr, Post office, Bouake.

**1993, Oct. 9 *Perf. 13x13½***

946 A357 30fr multicolored .35 .25
947 A357 200fr multicolored 2.00 1.25

African Biennial of Plastic Arts, Abidjan A358

***Perf. 14½x13½***

**1993, Nov. 24 Litho.**

948 A358 200fr multicolored 1.75 .90

Independence, 33rd Anniv. — A359

**1993, Dec. 7 Litho. *Perf. 13½x13***

950 A359 200fr multicolored 2.00 .95

Pres. Felix Houphouet-Boigny (1905-93) — A360

Pres. Houphouet-Boigny and: Nos. 951a, 952a, 953a, Modern buildings, technology. Nos. 951b, 952b, 953b, Agriculture, shipping. Nos. 951c, 952c, 953c, Dove, rainbow, Presidential palace.

**1994, Feb. 5 Litho. *Perf. 13***

951 A360 150fr Strip of 3, #a.-c. 3.00 2.00
952 A360 200fr Strip of 3, #a.-c. 4.00 3.00

**Souvenir Sheet**

***Perf. 12***

953 A360 500fr Sheet of 3, #a.-c. 10.00 10.00

Raoul Follereau, Campaign Against Leprosy A361

**1994, Feb. 20 Litho. *Perf. 13***

954 A361 150fr multicolored 1.10 .85

RASCOM (Regional African Satellite Communications Organization), 1st Meeting, Abidjan — A362

**1994, Jan. 19 Litho. *Perf. 14x13***

955 A362 150fr multicolored .85 .50

Woman Carrying Basket — A363

**Litho. & Engr.**

**1994-95 *Perf. 13½x13***

**Color of Border**

956 A363 5fr orange .25 .25
956A A363 10fr green .25 .25
956B A363 20fr red .25 .25
957 A363 25fr blue .25 .25
957A A363 30fr olive bister .25 .25
958 A363 40fr yellow green .25 .25
959 A363 50fr brown .25 .25
960 A363 75fr lilac rose .30 .25
961 A363 150fr bright green .70 .35
961A A363 180fr pale lake .95 .50
961B A363 280fr gray 1.40 .70
962 A363 300fr violet 1.40 .70
*Nos. 956-962 (12)* 6.50 4.25

Issued: 30fr, 180fr, 280fr, 5/16/95, dated 1994; others, 11/4/94.

Stained Glass Windows, Basilica of Notre Dame of Peace, Yamoussoukro A364

Designs: 25fr, Christ, world map. 150fr, Christ, fishermen. 200fr, Madonna and Child. 600fr, Aerial view of Cathedral, Yamoussoukro.

**1994, Nov. 18 Litho. *Perf. 14***

963 A364 25fr lilac rose & multi .35 .25
964 A364 150fr pale orange & multi 1.00 .60
965 A364 200fr yellow & mulit 1.25 .80
*Nos. 963-965 (3)* 2.60 1.65

**Souvenir Sheet**

966 A364 600fr multicolored 5.00 5.00

Natl. Independence, 34th Anniv. — A365

**1994, Dec. 6 Litho. *Perf. 12***

967 A365 150fr multicolored 1.00 .40

Snakes A366

Designs: 10fr, Python regius. 20fr, Philothamnus semivariegatus. 100fr, Dendroaspis veridis. 180fr, Bitis arietans. 500fr, Bitis nasicornis.

**1995, June 23 Litho. *Perf. 13***

968 A366 10fr multicolored .25 .25
969 A366 20fr multicolored .25 .25
970 A366 100fr multicolored .65 .25
971 A366 180fr multicolored 1.40 .75
972 A366 500fr multicolored 3.00 1.50
*Nos. 968-972 (5)* 5.55 3.00

FAO, 50th Anniv. — A367

UN, 50th Anniv. — A368

**1995, Aug. 4 Litho. *Perf. 11½***

973 A367 100fr multicolored .75 .35
974 A368 280fr multicolored 2.50 .75

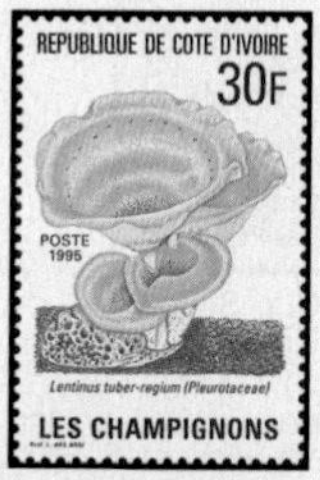

Mushrooms A369

Designs: 30fr, Lentinus tuber-regium. 50fr, Volvariella volvacea. 180fr, Dictyophora indusiata. 250fr, Termitomyces schimperi.

**1995, Sept. 8 *Perf. 14x13½***

975 A369 30fr multicolored .45 .35
976 A369 50fr multicolored .85 .70
977 A369 180fr multicolored 2.50 1.00
978 A369 250fr multicolored 2.75 2.00
*a.* Block of 4, #975-978 8.50 6.00
*b.* Dated "1997" —

#978a was issued in sheets of 16 stamps.

Louis Pasteur (1822-95) A370

**1995, Sept. 28 *Perf. 11½***

979 A370 280fr multicolored 1.50 .80

School Philatelic Clubs A371

**1995, Oct. 6 *Perf. 13½***

980 A371 50fr GSR .50 .25
981 A371 180fr LBP 1.75 .80

Butterflies

Designs: 180fr, Pala decius. 280fr, Papilio dardanus. 550fr, Papilio menestheus.

**1995 Litho. *Perf. 15x14***

981A A371a 180fr multicolored *13.50* *2.00*
981B A371a 280fr multicolored *19.00* *3.00*
981C A371a 550fr multicolored *24.00* *4.00*
*Nos. 981A-981C (3)* *56.50* *9.00*

Transportation in Abidjan — A372

Designs: 180fr, People pushing, pulling cart of grain, automobiles, bus on street. 280fr, People getting into bus in middle of traffic.

**1996, May 24 *Perf. 13½***

982 A372 180fr multicolored 1.10 .60
983 A372 280fr multicolored 1.75 1.00

Fish A373

Designs: 50fr, Heterotis niloticus. 180fr, Auchenoglanis occidentalis. 700fr, Schilbe mandibularis.

**1996, June**

984 A373 50fr multicolored .35 .30
985 A373 180fr multicolored 1.10 .65
986 A373 700fr multicolored 4.25 2.50
*Nos. 984-986 (3)* 5.70 3.45

A374

Orchids: 40fr, Cyrtorchis arcuata. 100fr, Eulophia horsfalii. 180fr, Eulophidium maculatum. 200fr, Ansellia africana.

**1996, July 12 Litho. *Perf. 13½x13***

**987** A374 40fr multicolored .35 .30
**988** A374 100fr multicolored .75 .45
**989** A374 180fr multicolored 1.50 1.00
**990** A374 200fr multicolored 1.60 1.10
*Nos. 987-990 (4)* 4.20 2.85

A375

**1996, Nov. 19**

**991** A375 200fr Boxing 1.10 .60
**992** A375 280fr Running 1.75 1.00
**993** A375 400fr Long jump 2.25 1.25
**994** A375 500fr Natl. Olympic Committee emblem 2.75 1.75
*Nos. 991-994 (4)* 7.85 4.60

1996 Summer Olympic Games, Atlanta.

Carved Canes A376

180fr, Cane of Birifor hunter. 200fr, Cane of Chief Lobi. 280fr, Cane of Chief Lobi (Gbobéri).

**1996, Sept. 20 Litho. *Perf. 11½***

**995** A376 180fr black & green 1.10 .60
**996** A376 200fr black & org yel 1.10 .70
**997** A376 280fr black & lilac 1.75 1.00
*Nos. 995-997 (3)* 3.95 2.30

Water Flowers A377

Designs: 50fr, Nelumbo nucifera. 180fr, Nymphea lotus. 280fr, Nymphea capensis. 700fr, Nymphea alba.

**1997, June 20 Litho. *Perf. 13½x14***

**998** A377 50fr multicolored .30 .25
**999** A377 180fr multicolored 1.10 .60
**1000** A377 280fr multicolored 1.75 1.00
**1001** A377 700fr multicolored 4.00 2.50
*Nos. 998-1001 (4)* 7.15 4.35

Basilica of Our Lady of Peace, Yamoussoukro — A378

a, 180fr, Pres. Felix Houphouet-Boigny, exterior view of basilica. b, 200fr, Interior view. c, 280fr, Aerial view, Pope John Paul II.

**1997, July 8 Litho. *Perf. 13***

**1002** A378 Strip of 3, #a.-c. 5.00 4.00

Traditional Jewelry — A379

Various beaded necklaces.

**1997, Aug. 22 *Perf. 11½***

**1003** A379 50fr plum & black .35 .25
**1004** A379 100fr plum & black .55 .50
**1005** A379 180fr plum & black 1.10 .75
*Nos. 1003-1005 (3)* 2.00 1.50

A379a

Various stone heads of Gohitafla.

**1997, Oct. 10 Litho. *Perf. 11½***
**Granite Paper**

**1006** A379a 100fr red & multi .55 .25
**1007** A379a 180fr blue & multi 1.10 .75
**1008** A379a 500fr green & multi 2.75 1.50
*Nos. 1006-1008 (3)* 4.40 2.50

A380

Work tools: 180fr, Pulley. 280fr, Comb. 300fr, Navette, horiz.

**1997, Nov. 28 *Perf. 13½***

**1009** A380 180fr orange & multi 1.10 .50
**1010** A380 280fr green & multi 1.50 .75
**1011** A380 300fr blue & multi 1.60 .75
*Nos. 1009-1011 (3)* 4.20 2.00

Endangered Species A381

Designs: 180fr, African manatee. 280fr, Jentink's duiker. 400fr, Kob antelope.

**1997, Dec. 19 Photo. *Perf. 11½***

**1012** A381 180fr multicolored 1.60 1.00
**1013** A381 280fr multicolored 1.75 1.00
**1014** A381 400fr multicolored 2.25 1.25
*Nos. 1012-1014 (3)* 5.60 3.25

1998 World Cup Soccer Championships, France — A382

Paris landmarks in background and: 180fr, Player, ball depicted with angry face. 280fr, Flags of nations inside outline of player. 400fr, Player taking shot on goal. 500fr, Two players, mascot, vert.

***Perf. 13x13½, 13½x13***

**1998, June 5 Litho.**

**1015** A382 180fr multicolored 1.10 .55
**1016** A382 280fr multicolored 1.60 1.00
**1017** A382 400fr multicolored 2.25 1.25
**1018** A382 500fr multicolored 2.75 1.40
*Nos. 1015-1018 (4)* 7.70 4.20

Mushrooms A383

50fr, Agaricus bingensis. 180fr, Lactarius gymnocarpus. 280fr, Termitomyces le testui.

**1998, June 26 Litho. *Perf. 13½x13***

**1019** A383 50fr multicolored .60 .40
**1020** A383 180fr multicolored 1.25 1.00
**1021** A383 280fr multicolored 2.10 1.25
*Nos. 1019-1021 (3)* 3.95 2.65

See No. B20A.

Endemic Plants — A384

Designs: 40fr, Hutchinsonia barbata. 100fr, Synsepalum aubrevillei. 180fr, Cola lorougnonis.

**1998, July 10 *Perf. 12***
**Granite Paper**

**1022** A384 40fr multicolored .45 .25
**1023** A384 100fr multicolored .75 .50
**1024** A384 180fr multicolored 1.10 .75
*Nos. 1022-1024 (3)* 2.30 1.50

Traditional Costumes from Grand-Bassam Museum — A385

**1998, Nov. 13 Litho. *Perf. 13½x13***

**1025** A385 180fr Tapa 1.10 .75
**1026** A385 280fr Raffia 1.60 1.10

Trains of Africa A386

180fr, South African Railway, 1918. 280fr, Garret 2-8-2+2-8-2 Beyer Peacock, 1925. 500fr, Cecil Rhodes.

**1999, Feb. 26 Litho. *Perf. 13½***

**1027** A386 180fr multicolored 1.10 .75
**1028** A386 280fr multicolored 1.75 1.10

**Souvenir Sheet**

**1029** A386 500fr multicolored 2.50 2.50

See No. B20B.

PhilexFrance '99, World Philatelic Exhibition — A387

Animals: 180fr+20fr, Loxodonta africana. 250fr, Syncerus caffer. 280fr, Pan troglodytes. 400fr, Cercopithecus aethiops.

**1999, July 2 Litho. *Perf. 13x13¼***

**1030** A387 180fr +20fr multi 1.50 1.10
**1031** A387 250fr multicolored 1.60 1.25
**1032** A387 280fr multicolored 1.75 1.25
**1033** A387 400fr multicolored 2.25 1.75
*Nos. 1030-1033 (4)* 7.10 5.35

UPU, 125th Anniv. A388

UPU emblem and: 180fr+20fr, Carved heads. 280fr, Methods of delivering mail.

**1999, June 25 *Perf. 11¾x11½***

**1034** A388 180fr +20fr multi 1.10 .75
**1035** A388 280fr multicolored 1.50 1.10

Flowers A389

Ahouakro Rock Formations A390

Designs: 100fr, Ancistrochilus rothschilianus. 180fr+20fr, Brachycorythis pubescens. 200fr, Bulbophyllum barbigerum. 280fr, Habenaria macrandra.

**1999, July 27 Litho. *Perf. 13¼x13***

**1036** A389 100fr multicolored .55 .35
**1037** A389 180fr +20fr multi 1.40 1.00
**1038** A389 200fr multicolored 1.50 1.10
**1039** A389 280fr multicolored 1.75 1.25
*Nos. 1036-1039 (4)* 5.20 3.70

***Perf. 13¼x14, 14x13¼***

**1999, Aug. 6 Litho.**

Various rock formations.

**1040** A390 180fr +20fr multi, horiz. 1.60 .75
**1041** A390 280fr multi, horiz. 1.60 1.00
**1042** A390 400fr multi 2.40 1.50
*Nos. 1040-1042 (3)* 5.60 3.25

PhilexFrance 99 — A391

**1999, July 2 Litho. *Perf. 13***

**1043** A391 280fr multicolored 2.75 2.75

No. 1043 has a holographic image. Soaking in water may affect hologram.

Birds — A392

Designs: 50fr, Oriolus auratus. 180fr + 20fr, Nectarinia cinnyris venusta. 280fr, Trenon vinago australis. 300fr, Psittacus eithacus.

**1999, Oct. 29 Litho. *Perf. 13¼x13***

**1044** A392 50fr multi .45 .25
**1045** A392 180fr + 20fr multi 1.50 1.00
**1046** A392 280fr multi 2.25 1.25
**1047** A392 300fr multi 2.25 1.25
*Nos. 1044-1047 (4)* 6.45 3.75

Fish A393

Designs: 100fr, Synodontis schall. 180fr + 20fr, Chromidotilapia guntheri. 280fr, Distichodus rostratus.

**1999, Nov. 19 *Perf. 13½x13¼***

**1048** A393 100fr multi .75 .35
**1049** A393 180fr +20fr multi 1.50 1.00
**1050** A393 280fr multi 2.25 1.50
*Nos. 1048-1050 (3)* 4.50 2.85

Challenges for Ivory Coast in Third Millennium — A394

Designs: 100fr, Education. 180fr +20fr, Agriculture. 200fr, Industry. 250fr, Information. 280fr, Peace. 400fr, Culture.

**1999, Dec. 10 *Perf. 13½x13¾***

**1051** A394 100fr multi .55 .35
**1052** A394 180fr +20fr multi 1.10 .75
**1053** A394 200fr multi 1.10 .75
**1054** A394 250fr multi 1.40 1.00
**1055** A394 280fr multi 1.50 1.00
**1056** A394 400fr multi 1.75 1.50
*Nos. 1051-1056 (6)* 7.40 5.35

Native Masks A395

***Perf. 13½x13¼, 13¼x13½***

**2000, June 30 Litho.**

**1057** A395 30fr Wambélé .35 .25
**1058** A395 180fr +20fr Djè 1.25 .80
**1059** A395 400fr Korobla, vert. 2.25 1.75
*Nos. 1057-1059 (3)* 3.85 2.80

Edible Plants — A396

Designs: 30fr, Blighia sapida. 180fr+20fr, Ricinodendron heudelotii. 300fr, Telfaira occidentalis. 400fr, Napoleonaea vogelii.

**2000, July 14 *Perf. 13¼x13½***

**1060** A396 30fr multi .35 .25
**1061** A396 180fr +20fr multi 1.40 .80
**1062** A396 300fr multi 1.75 1.25
**1063** A396 400fr multi 2.25 2.00
*Nos. 1060-1063 (4)* 5.75 4.30

Pres. Robert Guei, Elephant, Map and Dove — A397

**2000, Aug. 4 *Perf. 13¾x13¼***

**1064** A397 180fr +20fr red & multi 1.50 .80
**1065** A397 400fr yel & multi 2.75 1.75

Independence, 40th anniv., coup d'etat of Robert Guei.

Cacao — A398

Frame colors: 5fr, Dark blue green. 10fr, Light brown. 20fr, Claret. 25fr, Blue. 30fr, Greenish black. 40fr, Cerise. 50fr, Golden brown. 100fr, Brown. 180fr+20fr, Orange. 300fr, Blue violet. 350fr, Prussian blue. 400fr, Emerald. 600fr, Olive green.

***Perf. 11½x11¾***

**2000, Aug. 25 Photo.**

**Granite Paper**

**1066-1078** A398 Set of 13 11.50 8.00

National Lottery, 30th Anniv. — A399

Denominations: 180fr+20fr, 400fr.

**2000, Aug. 30 Litho. *Perf. 13¼x13***

**1079-1080** A399 Set of 2 4.25 2.75

2000 Summer Olympics, Sydney A400

Designs: 180fr+20fr, Soccer. 400fr, Kangaroo. 600fr, Runners. 750fr, Bird over stadium.

**2000, Sept. 8 *Perf. 13½x13¼***

**1081-1084** A400 Set of 4 12.00 9.00

Hairstyles — A401

Various hairstyles: 180fr+20fr, 300fr, 400fr, 500fr.

**2000, Sept. 22 *Perf. 13¾x13¼***

**1085-1088** A401 Set of 4 8.50 6.50

Release of Nelson Mandela, 10th Anniv. — A402

**2000, Oct. 6 Photo. *Perf. 12x11¾***

**1089** A402 300fr multi 2.10 1.25

Historic Monuments A403

Designs: 180fr+20fr, Queen Pokou. 400fr, Akwaba. 600fr, Invocation of the Spirits.

**2000, Nov. 10 Litho. *Perf. 13½x13***

**1090-1092** A403 Set of 3 7.00 6.00

UN High Commisioner for Refugees, 50th Anniv. — A404

**2000, Dec. 8 Photo. *Perf. 11¾x12***

**1093** A404 400fr multi 2.50 1.75

Abokouamekro Animal Park — A405

Designs: 50fr, Cattle. 100fr, Rhinoceroses. 180fr+20fr, Rhinoceros. 400fr+20fr, Cattle.

**2001, May 14 Litho. *Perf. 13½x13¼***

**1094-1097** A405 Set of 4 6.50 3.25

Sculpted Columns in National Museum — A406

Designs: 100fr, Alingué, Wouo Anouman. 180fr+20fr, Blolo Bian, Blolo B1a. 300fr+20fr, Botoumo. 400fr+20fr, Odi Oka.

**2001, June 18 *Perf. 13¼x13***

**1098-1101** A406 Set of 4 5.00 5.00

Elimination Rounds for World Cup Soccer Championships — A407

Various soccer plays: 180fr + 20fr, 400fr + 20fr, 600fr + 20fr, 700fr.

**2001, Aug. 21 Litho. *Perf. 13x13¼***

**1102-1105** A407 Set of 4 10.00 10.00

The following items inscribed "Republique de Cote d'Ivoire" have been declared "illegal" by Ivory Coast postal authorities:

Sheets of nine 100fr stamps: Marilyn Monroe (2 different).

Sheets of six 100fr stamps: Shells and Rotary emblem (2 different), Dogs and Scouting emblem (2 different), Butterflies and Scouting emblem (2 different), Orchids (2 different), Motorbike races and Rotary emblem (2 different), Table tennis players (2 different), Old fire engines (2 different), Elvis Presley (2 different), Marilyn Monroe, Pope John Paul II.

Sheets of six stamps: Trains (4 different).

Souvenir sheets of one stamp: Trains (4 different).

Sheet of ten 200fr Stamps: Birds.

Sheets of nine stamps of various denominations: Japanese Women, Earle K. Bergey, Julie Bell, Michael Möbius, Nudes.

Sheet of eight stamps of various denominations: Nature Conservancy.

Sheets of eight 300fr stamps: Owls and Mushrooms, Lighthouses and Penguins.

Sheets of eight 100fr stamps: Anthony Hopkins, Ben Affleck, Eminem.

Sheets of six stamps of various denominations: Spirited Away, Nature Conservancy, Nudes

Sheets of six 500fr stamps: History of World Aircraft (5 different), Red Cross and Rotary emblem, Japanese Women, Actresses, Women Tennis Players, Marilyn Monroe.

Sheet of six 450fr stamps: The Lord of the Rings.

Sheets of six 400fr stamps: Beatles (2 different).

Sheets of six 350fr stamps: Uniforms of World War II (5 different).

Sheets of Six 300fr stamps: Harry Potter (3 different), Fire Engines (2 different), Owls and Mushrooms.

Sheets of six 200fr stamps: Dogs and Scouting emblem, Lighthouses and Rotary emblem.

Sheets of six 100fr stamps: Pope John Paul II, Celine Dion, Pierce Brosnan, Classic Automobiles.

Sheets of four 100fr stamps: AC/DC, Backstreet Boys, Bee Gees, Beatles, Doors, Freddie Mercury, KISS, Madonna, Metallica, Queen, Rolling Stones.

Sheets of three stamps of various denominations: Nature Conservancy (2 different), Fairy Tales, Fantasy Tales, Dinosaurs, Steam Railways.

Sheet of two 1000fr stamps: Pope John Paul II.

Sheets of Two 500fr stamps: Nature Conservancy, Mother Teresa and Pope John Paul II.

Sheets of two 250fr stamps: Pope John Paul II (3 different).

Souvenir sheets of one 1000fr stamp: Dinosaurs, Fish, Owl and Scouting emblem.

Souvenir sheets of one 500fr stamp: Snow White, Nature Conservancy, Pope John Paul II.

Souvenir sheets of one 300fr stamp: Harry Potter (2 different).

Souvenir sheets of one 250fr stamp: Disney Cartoons and Scouting emblem (10 different).

Souvenir sheets of one 150fr stamp: Fire Engines and Scouting emblem (5 different).

Souvenir sheets of one 100fr stamp: Sorayama (5 different), Locomotives (2 different).

Korhogo Art
A408

Designs: 100fr, Shown. 180fr+20fr, Hunters and wildlife. 400fr+20fr, Painter, vert.

**2001, Nov. 27 Litho. *Perf. 14***

**1106-1108** A408 Set of 3 4.00 4.00

A409

2002 World Cup Soccer Championships, Japan and Korea — A410

Design: 300fr+20fr, Caricatures of soccer players in action, horiz.

***Perf. 13¾, 13x13¼ (#1110), 13¼x13 (#1112)***

**2002, June 6 Litho.**

**1109** A409 180fr +20fr grn & multi 1.25 1.25
**1110** A410 300fr +20fr multi 2.25 2.25
**1111** A409 400fr +20fr red & multi 2.75 2.75
Complete booklet, 10 #1111 30.00 30.00
**1112** A410 600fr +20fr shown 4.00 4.00

**Souvenir Sheet**

**1113** A409 500fr red & multi 3.50 3.50

Ivory Coast — People's Republic of China Diplomatic Relations, 20th Anniv.
A411

**2003, July 9 Litho. *Perf. 12***

**1114** A411 180fr grn & multi 1.25 1.25
**1115** A411 400fr org & multi 2.25 2.25
**1116** A411 650fr red & multi 3.75 3.75
*Nos. 1114-1116 (3)* 7.25 7.25

Sculpted Columns in Museum of Civilizations
A412

Designs: 20fr, Alinguè Bia column. 100fr, Laliè column. 180fr+20fr, Tre Ni Tre column. 300fr+20fr, Golikplé-Kplé column.

**2003, Nov. 27 Litho. *Perf. 13½x13***

**1117** A412 20fr multi .25 .25
**1118** A412 100fr multi .50 .50
**1119** A412 180fr +20fr shown 1.00 1.00
**1120** A412 300fr +20fr multi 1.50 1.50
*Nos. 1117-1120 (4)* 3.25 3.25

Paintings by Unknown Artists — A413

Designs: 50fr, Au Revoir. 100fr, Ballet. 250fr, Le Chef, horiz. 500fr, Ligne de Main, horiz. 825fr, Appel, horiz.

***Perf. 13¼x13, 13x13¼***

**2004, June 15 Litho.**

**1121-1125** A413 Set of 5 — —

Independence, 44th Anniv. — A414

Denominations: 100fr, 250fr.

**2004, Aug. 7 *Perf. 13¼x13***

**1126-1127** A414 Set of 2 — —

2004 Summer Olympics, Athens
A415

Designs: 50fr, Sprint race. 100fr, Greco-Roman wrestling, vert. 250fr, Torch bearer, vert. 825fr, Discus throw, vert. 1000fr, Sprint race.

***Perf. 13x13¼, 13¼x13***

**2004, Aug. 13**

**1128-1131** A415 Set of 4 — —

**Souvenir Sheet**

**1131A** A415 1000fr multi 8.25 8.25

National Reconciliation
A416

**2004, Sept. 28 Litho. *Perf. 13¼x13***

**1132** A416 50fr shown *3.50* —
**1133** A416 250fr multi *9.00* —

Promotion of Women
A417

**2004, Nov. 26 Litho. *Perf. 14x13½***

**1134** A417 250fr multi — —

Molothrus Bonariensis
A418

***Perf. 14¼x13½***

**2004, Dec. 22 Litho.**

**1135** A418 50fr multi —

Trichosurus Vulpecula
A419

**2004, Dec. 22 *Perf. 14x13¼***

**1136** A419 100fr multi 2.25 2.25

Flora — A420

Design: 250fr, Cassia tuhovaliana.

**2004, Dec. 22 *Perf. 13½x14¼***

**1137** A420 250fr multi —

An additional stamp was issued in this set. The editors would like to examine any example.

Tenth General Assembly of African Organization of Supreme Audit Institutions
A421

Frame color: 250fr, Blue. 350fr, Purple.

**2005, July 18 Litho. *Perf. 13¼***

**1139-1140** A421 Set of 2 *10.00* —

"Culture and Excellence" — A422

Designs: 100fr, Dan spoon. 250fr, Sénoufo cane, vert.

**2005, July 25 *Perf. 13x13½, 13½x13***

**1141-1142** A422 Set of 2 — —

World Summit on the Information Society, Tunis — A423

Frame color: 30fr, Red. 220fr, Green.

**2005, Sept. 28 *Perf. 13¼***

**1143-1144** A423 Set of 2 — —

Women's Hairstyles
A424

Various hairstyles: 70fr, 100fr, 250fr, 350fr.

**2005, Nov. 3**

**1145-1148** A424 Set of 4 — —

Kings and Chiefs — A425

Designs: 30fr, Tchaman chief standing. 70fr, Tchaman chief, diff. 80fr, Yacouba, Baoulé and Abron chiefs, horiz. 250fr, Akan king and staff-bearer, horiz. 1000fr, Yacouba, Baoulé, and Abron chiefs, horiz.

**2005, Nov. 22**

**1149-1152** A425 Set of 4 — —

**Souvenir Sheet**

**1152A** A425 1000fr multi 8.25 8.25

Masks — A426

Designs: 70fr, Dan. 220fr, Gu. 250fr, Zamblé.

**2005, Dec. 22**

**1153-1155** A426 Set of 3 — —

Europa Stamps, 50th Anniv. (in 2006) — A427

Map of Ivory Coast and: 30fr, Corn and map of Ireland. 70fr, Rubber tree and map of Germany. 80fr, Cotton plant and map of Poland. 220fr, Bananas and map of Netherlands. 250fr, Pineapple and map of Czech Republic. 350fr, Cacao and map of Belgium. 400fr, Sweet potatoes and map of Great Britain. 650fr, Coffee beans and map of Italy. 1000fr, Peanuts and map of Portugal. 2775fr, Palm nut and map of Spain.

**2005, Dec. 23 Litho. *Perf. 13¼***

**1156-1165** A427 Set of 10 22.00 22.00
*1160a* Miniature sheet, #1156-1160 2.40 2.40
*1165a* Miniature sheet, #1161-1165 19.50 19.50
*1165b* Miniature sheet, #1156-1165 22.00 22.00

Coffee Branches, Flowers and Cherries — A428

Designs: 220fr, Coffea arabusta. 250fr, Coffea liberica.

**2005, Dec. 28 Litho. *Perf. 13¼***
**1166-1167** A428 Set of 2 — —

Mushrooms A429

Designs: 220fr, Marasmius zenkeri. 250fr, Cantharellus rufopunctatus.

**2005, Dec. 28**
**1168-1169** A429 Set of 2 4.75 4.75

Endangered Plants — A430

Designs: 30fr, Dorstenia astyanactis. 70fr, Monosalpinx guillaumetii. 80fr, Monanthotaxis capea. 100fr, Okoubaka aubrevillei.

**2005, Dec. 28 Litho. *Perf. 13¼***
**1170** A430 30fr multi — —
**1171** A430 70fr multi — —
**1172** A430 80fr multi — —
**1173** A430 100fr multi — —

Urban Transportation — A431

Designs: 30fr, Buses, automobiles, ferry. 80fr, Buses, automobiles, ferry, diff.

**2005, Dec. 29 Litho. *Perf. 13¼***
**1174-1175** A431 Set of 2 — —

Léopold Sédar Senghor (1906-2001), First President of Senegal — A432

Denominations: 50fr, 250fr.

**2006, Mar. 20 Litho. *Perf. 13½***
**1176-1177** A432 Set of 2 2.40 2.40

A433

2006 World Cup Soccer Championships, Germany — A434

Designs: 50fr, Emblem. 100fr, Goalie making save. 200fr, World Cup. 250fr, Mascot. 1000fr, Mascot.

**2006, June 9 Litho. *Perf. 13x13¼***
**1178** A433 50fr multi — —
**1179** A434 100fr multi — —
**1180** A433 200fr multi — —
**1181** A433 250fr multi — —

**Souvenir Sheet**

***Perf. 13¾***

**1182** A433 1000fr multi — —

China-Africa Forum, Beijing A435

Designs: 250fr, Map of Africa and China. 650fr, Forum venue.

**2006, Nov. 28 *Perf. 12x12¼***
**1183-1184** A435 Set of 2 7.50 7.50

Pardon A436

Denominations: 50fr, 250fr.

**2008, June 25 *Perf. 13x13¼***
**1185-1186** A436 Set of 2 3.00 3.00

## SEMI-POSTAL STAMPS

No. 47 Surcharged in Red

**1915 Unwmk. *Perf. 14x13½***
**B1** A5 10c + 5c 1.60 1.60
*a.* Double surcharge 80.00 80.00

Issued on ordinary and chalky paper.

**Curie Issue**
Common Design Type

**1938 *Perf. 13***
**B2** CD80 1.75fr + 50c brt ultra 11.00 9.50

**French Revolution Issue**
Common Design Type

**1939 Photo.**
**Name and Value Typo. in Black**

**B3** CD83 45c + 25c grn 8.75 8.75
**B4** CD83 70c + 30c brn 8.75 8.75
**B5** CD83 90c + 35c red org 8.75 8.75
**B6** CD83 1.25fr + 1fr rose pink 8.75 8.75
**B7** CD83 2.25fr + 2fr blue 8.75 8.75
*Nos. B3-B7 (5)* 43.75 43.75

Stamps of 1936-38 Surcharged in Red or Black

**1941**
**B8** A7 50c + 1fr plum (Bk) 2.50 2.50
**B9** A8 80c + 2fr blk brn (R) 10.50 10.50
**B10** A8 1.50fr + 2fr ultra (R) 11.50 11.50
**B11** A9 2fr + 3fr ultra (Bk) 12.50 12.50
*Nos. B8-B11 (4)* 37.00 37.00

**Common Design Type and**

Native Engineer SP1

Senegalese Light Artillery SP2

**1941 Photo. *Perf. 13½***
**B12** SP1 1fr + 1fr red 1.25
**B13** CD86 1.50fr + 3fr claret 1.25
**B14** SP2 2.50fr + 1fr blue 1.25
*Nos. B12-B14 (3)* 3.75

Nos. B12-B14 were issued by the Vichy government in France, but were not placed on sale in Ivory Coast.

Nos. 165-166 Surcharged in Black or Red

**1944 Engr. *Perf. 12½x12***
**B14A** 50c + 1.50fr on 2.50fr deep blue (R) .80
**B14B** + 2.50fr on 1fr green .80

Colonial Development Fund.

Nos. B14A-B14B were issued by the Vichy government in France, but were not placed on sale in Ivory Coast.

**Catalogue values for unused stamps in this section, from this point to the end of the section, are for Never Hinged items.**

**Republic**
**Anti-Malaria Issue**
Common Design Type

**1962, Apr. 7 Engr. *Perf. 12½x12***
**B15** CD108 25fr + 5fr ol grn 1.25 1.25

**Freedom from Hunger Issue**
Common Design Type

**1963, Mar. 21 *Perf. 13***
**B16** CD112 25fr + 5fr red lil, dk vio & brn 1.50 1.50

Red Cross - Red Crescent Soc., Child Survival Campaign — SP3

**1987, May 8 Litho. *Perf. 13½***
**B17** SP3 195fr +5fr multi 2.50 2.50

No. B17 surcharged "+5fr" in red. Not issued without surcharge. Surtax for the Red Cross - Red Crescent Soc.

Organization of African Unity, 25th Anniv. — SP4

**1988, Nov. 19 Litho. *Perf. 12½x13***
**B18** SP4 195fr +5fr multi 2.25 2.25

Marie Therese Houphouet-Boigny and N'Daya Intl. Emblem — SP5

**1988, Dec. 9 Litho. *Perf. 13***
**B19** SP5 195fr +5fr multi 2.25 2.25

N'Daya Intl., 1st anniv.

See postage issues, beginning with #1030, for semi-postal stamps that are part of sets with regular postage stamps.

Council of Understanding, Solidarity & Rural Development, 40th Anniv. — SP6

**1999, May 29 Litho. *Perf. 13x13½***
**B20** SP6 180fr +20fr multi 1.20 1.20

**Postage Types of 1998-99 With Added Surtax**

**1999 ? Litho. *Perf. 12***
**Granite Paper (#B20A)**

**B20A** A383 180fr +20fr Like #1024 —

***Perf. 13½***

**B20B** A386 180fr +20fr Like #1027 —

Nos. B20A-B20B apparently were not issued with Nos. 1022-1024 and 1027-1029.

Independence, 41st Anniv. — SP7

**2001, Aug. 7 Litho.** ***Perf. 13¼x13½***
**B21** SP7 180fr +20fr multi 1.10 1.10

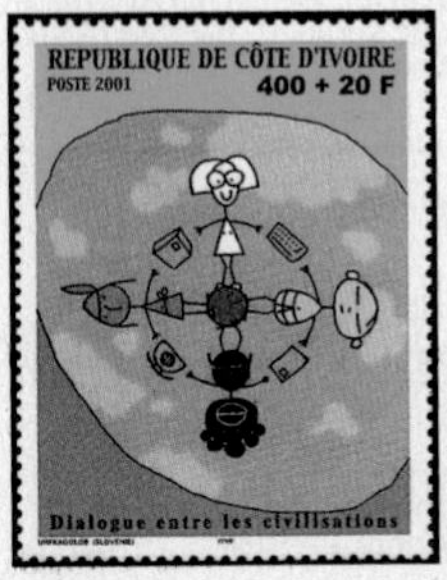


Year of Dialogue Among Civilizations SP8

**2001, Oct. 9** ***Perf. 13x13¼***
**B22** SP8 400fr +20fr multi 2.25 2.25

Second Republic, 1st Anniv. SP9

**2001, Oct. 26**
**B23** SP9 180fr +20fr multi 1.10 1.10

Planned 2004 Universal Postal Union Congress, Abidjan — SP10

Vignette size: 180fr+20fr, 23x37mm. 400fr+20fr, 26x37mm. 600fr+20fr, 36x49mm.

***Perf. 13, 13¼x13 (#B25)***

**2001, Dec. 21 Litho.**
**B24** SP10 180fr +20fr multi 1.00 1.00
*a.* Souvenir sheet of 1 5.00 5.00
**B25** SP10 400fr +20fr multi 2.25 2.25
**B26** SP10 600fr +20fr multi 3.25 3.25

On Nos. B24-B26 and B24a portions of the design were applied by a thermographic process producing a shiny raised effect. No. B24a sold for 1000fr and contains imperforate examples of Nos. B25 and B26 in the margin, which are surmised to be invalid for postage as the face value of these two stamps exceeds the selling price of the sheet. The 2004 UPU Congress was moved from Abidjan to Bucharest, Romania due to political unrest in the Ivory Coast.

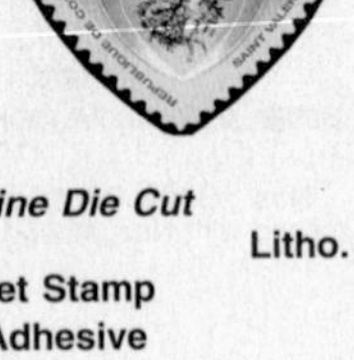

St. Valentine's Day — SP11

***Serpentine Die Cut***

**2002, Feb. 14 Litho.**

**Booklet Stamp**

**Self-Adhesive**

**B27** SP11 180fr +20fr multi 1.10 1.10
*a.* Booklet pane of 8 9.00

Jean Mermoz Intl. College, Abidjan, 40th Anniv. SP12

Panel color: 180fr+20fr, Tan. 400fr+20fr, Red.

**2002, Apr. 19** ***Perf. 13½x13¼***
**B28-B29** SP12 Set of 2 3.00 3.00

Decentralization SP14

Denomination color: 180fr+20fr, Green. 400fr+20fr, Blue.

**2002, Dec. 4 Litho.** ***Perf. 13¼x13***
**B34-B35** SP14 Set of 2 3.00 3.00

SP15

Campaign Against AIDS — SP16

**2003, Dec. 22 Litho.** ***Perf. 13¼***
**B36** SP15 180fr +20fr multi 1.00 1.00

***Perf. 13¾***

**B37** SP16 400fr +20fr multi 2.00 2.00

Values for No. B37 are for stamps with surrounding selvage.

## AIR POST STAMPS

Common Design Type

**1940 Unwmk. Engr.** ***Perf. 12½x12***
**C1** CD85 1.90fr ultramarine .40 .40
**C2** CD85 2.90fr dark red .40 .40
**C3** CD85 4.50fr dk gray grn .75 .75
**C4** CD85 4.90fr yel bister 1.00 1.00
**C5** CD85 6.90fr deep orange 1.50 1.50
*Nos. C1-C5 (5)* 4.05 4.05

Common Design Types

**1942**
**C6** CD88 50c car & blue .25
**C7** CD88 1fr brn & black .50
**C8** CD88 2fr dk grn & red brn .80
**C9** CD88 3fr dk blue & scar .85
**C10** CD88 5fr vio & dk red .85

**Frame Engraved, Center Typographed**
**C11** CD89 10fr multicolored 1.10
**C12** CD89 20fr multicolored 1.50
**C13** CD89 50fr multicolored 2.10
*Nos. C6-C13 (8)* 7.95

There is doubt whether Nos. C6-C12 were officially placed in use.

**Catalogue values for unused stamps in this section, from this point to the end of the section, are for Never Hinged items.**

**Republic**

Lapalud Place and Post Office, Abidjan — AP1

Designs: 200fr, Houphouet-Boigny Bridge. 500fr, Ayamê dam.

**1959, Oct. 1 Engr.** ***Perf. 13***
**C14** AP1 100fr multicolored 3.00 .75
**C15** AP1 200fr multicolored 5.00 2.25
**C16** AP1 500fr multicolored 11.00 4.50
*Nos. C14-C16 (3)* 19.00 7.50

**Sports Type of 1961**

**1961, Dec. 23**
**C17** A19 100fr High jump 4.50 2.25

**Air Afrique Issue**

Common Design Type

**1962, Feb. 17 Unwmk.** ***Perf. 13***
**C18** CD107 50fr Prus bl, choc & org brn 2.00 1.25

Village in Man Region — AP2

**1962, June 23 Engr.** ***Perf. 13***
**C19** AP2 200fr Street in Odienne, vert. 5.50 2.75
**C20** AP2 500fr shown 11.00 5.00

UN Headquarters, New York — AP3

**1962, Sept. 20** ***Perf. 13***
**C21** AP3 100fr multi 2.75 1.25

Admission to the UN, 2nd anniv.

Sassandra Bay — AP4

**1963 Unwmk.** ***Perf. 13***
**C22** AP4 50fr Moossou bridge 2.25 .75
**C23** AP4 100fr shown 3.25 1.75
**C24** AP4 200fr Comoe River 6.00 2.75
*Nos. C22-C24 (3)* 11.50 5.25

**African Postal Union Issue**

Common Design Type

**1963, Sept. 8 Photo.** ***Perf. 12½***
**C25** CD114 85fr org brn, ocher & red 2.50 1.50

**1963 Air Afrique Issue**

Common Design Type

**1963, Nov. 19 Unwmk.** ***Perf. 13x12***
**C26** CD115 25fr crim, gray, blk & grn 1.00 .50

Ramses II and Queen Nefertari — AP5

**1964, Mar. 7 Engr.** ***Perf. 13***
**C27** AP5 60fr car, blk & red brn 2.50 1.50

UNESCO campaign to save historic monuments in Nubia.

Arms of Republic — AP6

**1964, June 13 Photo.**
**C28** AP6 200fr ultra, yel grn & gold 5.00 2.25

President John F. Kennedy (1917-63) — AP7

**1964, Nov. 14 Unwmk.** ***Perf. 12½***
**C29** AP7 100fr gray, cl brn & blk 2.75 1.50
*a.* Souvenir sheet of 4 13.00 13.00

Liana Bridge, Lieupleu — AP8

**1965, Dec. 4 Engr.** ***Perf. 13***
**C30** AP8 100fr ol grn, dk grn & dk red brn 3.50 1.75

Street in Kong — AP9

**1966, Mar. 5 Engr.** ***Perf. 13***
**C31** AP9 300fr brt bl, bis brn & vio brn 9.00 5.00

**Air Afrique Issue, 1966**
Common Design Type

**1966, Aug. 20 Photo. *Perf. 13***
**C32** CD123 30fr dk grn, blk & gray 1.00 .60

Air Afrique Headquarters AP10

**1967, Feb. 4 Engr. *Perf. 13***
**C33** AP10 500fr emer, ind & ocher 11.50 5.50

Opening of Air Afrique headquarters in Abidjan.

**African Postal Union Issue, 1967**
Common Design Type

**1967, Sept. 9 Engr. *Perf. 13***
**C34** CD124 100fr blk, vio & car lake 3.50 1.50

Senufo Village — AP11

**1968 Engr. *Perf. 13***
**C35** AP11 100fr shown 3.25 1.25
**C36** AP11 500fr Tiegba village 11.50 4.50

Issue dates: 100fr, Feb. 17; 500fr, Apr. 27.

**PHILEXAFRIQUE Issue**

Street in Grand Bassam, by Achalme — AP12

**1969, Jan. 11 Photo. *Perf. 12x12½***
**C37** AP12 100fr grn & multi 4.25 4.25

PHILEXAFRIQUE Phil. Exhib., Abidjan, Feb. 14-23. Printed with alternating green label. Value, single with attached label, $6.

**2nd PHILEXAFRIQUE Issue**
Common Design Type

50fr, Ivory Coast #130 & view of San Pedro. 100fr, Ivory Coast #149 & man wearing chief's garments, vert. 200fr, Ivory Coast #77 # Exhibition Hall, Abidjan.

**1969, Feb. 14 Engr. *Perf. 13***
**C38** CD128 50fr grn, brn red & deep bl 3.00 3.00
**C39** CD128 100fr brn, org & dp blue 4.50 4.50
**C40** CD128 200fr brn, gray & dp blue 7.00 7.00
*a.* Min. sheet of 3, #C38-C40 18.50 18.50
*Nos. C38-C40 (3)* 14.50 14.50

Opening of PHILEXAFRIQUE.

Man Waterfall — AP13

Mount Niangbo — AP14

**1970 Engr. *Perf. 13***
**C41** AP13 100fr multicolored 3.25 1.50
**C42** AP14 200fr multicolored 4.25 2.00

Issue dates: 100fr, Jan. 6; 200fr, July 18.

San Pedro Harbor — AP15

**1971, Mar. 21 Engr. *Perf. 13***
**C43** AP15 100fr multicolored 2.25 1.00

Treichville Swimming Pool — AP16

**1971, May 29 Photo. *Perf. 12½***
**C44** AP16 100fr multicolored 3.00 1.25

Aerial View of Coast Line — AP17

**1971, July 3 Engr. *Perf. 13***
**C45** AP17 500fr multi 12.00 6.00

Tourist publicity for the African Riviera.

**Bondoukou Market Type of Regular Issue**

Design: 200fr, Similar to No. 318, but without people at left and in center.

**Embossed on Gold Paper**

**1971, Aug. 7 *Perf. 12½***
**Size: 36x26mm**
**C46** A79 200fr gold, ultra & blk 4.75 2.50

**African Postal Union Issue, 1971**
Common Design Type

Design: 100fr, Ivory Coast coat of arms and UAMPT building, Brazzaville, Congo.

**1971, Nov. 13 Photo. *Perf. 13x13½***
**C47** CD135 100fr bl & multi 2.00 1.00

Lion of St. Mark AP18

**1972, Feb. 5 Photo. *Perf. 12½***
**C48** AP18 100fr shown 3.50 1.75
**C49** AP18 200fr Waves, St. Mark's Basilica, Venice 6.00 3.25

UNESCO campaign to save Venice.

Kawara Mosque — AP19

**1972, Apr. 29 Engr. *Perf. 13***
**C50** AP19 500fr bl, brn & ocher 12.00 6.00

View of Gouessesso — AP20

**1972 Engr. *Perf. 13***
**C51** AP20 100fr shown 3.25 1.25
**C52** AP20 200fr Jacqueville Lake 4.75 1.75
**C53** AP20 500fr Kossou Dam 10.00 6.00
*Nos. C51-C53 (3)* 18.00 9.00

Issued: 100fr, 6/10; 200fr, 1/8; 500fr, 11/17.

Akakro Radar Earth Station — AP21

**1972, Nov. 27 Engr. *Perf. 13***
**C54** AP21 200fr brt bl, sl grn & choc 4.50 1.75

The Judgment of Solomon, by Nandjui Legue — AP22

**1973, Aug. 26 Photo. *Perf. 13***
**C55** AP22 500fr multi 12.00 5.75

6th World Peace Conference for Justice.

Sassandra River Bridge — AP23

**1974, May 4 Engr. *Perf. 13***
**C56** AP23 100fr blk & yel grn 2.25 .75
**C57** AP23 500fr slate grn & brn 12.00 4.25

Vridi Soap Factory, Abidjan — AP24

**1974, July 6 Photo. *Perf. 13***
**C58** AP24 200fr multi 3.50 1.75

UPU Emblem, Ivory Coast Flag, Post Runner and Jet — AP25

**1974, Oct. 9 Photo. *Perf. 13***
**C59** AP25 200fr multi 5.00 3.00
**C60** AP25 300fr multi 6.00 4.00

Centenary of Universal Postal Union.

Fly Whisk and Panga Knife, Symbols of Akans Royal Family — AP26

**1976, Apr. 3 Photo. *Perf. 12½x13***
**C61** AP26 200fr brt bl & multi 4.75 2.00

Tingrela Mosque — AP27

**1977, May 7 Engr. *Perf. 13***
**C62** AP27 500fr multi 7.50 4.50

**Zeppelin Type of 1977**
Souvenir Sheet

"Graf Zeppelin" LZ 127 over New York.

**1977, Sept. 3 Litho. *Perf. 11***
**C63** A150 500fr multi 6.25 1.90

Exists imperf.

**Philexafrique II - Essen Issue**
Common Design Types

#C64, Elephant and Ivory Coast No. 239. #C65, Pheasant and Bavaria No. 1.

**1978, Nov. 1 Litho. *Perf. 13x12½***
**C64** CD138 100fr multi 3.50 2.50
**C65** CD139 100fr multi 3.50 2.50
*a.* Pair, #C64-C65 + label 9.00 9.00

Gymnast, Olympic Rings — AP28

Various gymnasts. 75fr, 150fr, 350fr, vert.

**1980, July 24 Litho. *Perf. 14½***

C66 AP28 75fr multi .90 .25
C67 AP28 150fr multi 1.25 .45
C68 AP28 250fr multi 3.00 1.00
C69 AP28 350fr multi 3.50 1.25
*Nos. C66-C69 (4)* 8.65 2.95

**Souvenir Sheet**

C70 AP28 500fr multi 5.50 2.00

22nd Summer Olympic Games, Moscow, July 19-Aug. 3.

President Houphouet-Boigny, 75th Birthday AP28a

**Embossed Die Cut**

**1980, Oct. 18 *Perf. 10½***

C70A AP28a 2000fr Silver *20.00 20.00*
C70B AP28a 3000fr Gold *35.00 35.00*

Manned Flight Bicentenary — AP29

Various balloons. 100fr, 125fr, 350fr vert.

**1983, Apr. 2 Litho. *Perf. 13***

C71 AP29 100fr Montgolfier, 1783 1.00 .35
C72 AP29 125fr Hydrogen, 1783 1.50 .45
C73 AP29 150fr Mail transport, 1870 1.75 .50
C74 AP29 350fr Double Eagle II, 1978 4.50 1.00
C75 AP29 500fr Dirigible 6.50 1.75
*Nos. C71-C75 (5)* 15.25 4.05

Pre-Olympic Year — AP30

Various swimming events.

**1983, July 9 Litho. *Perf. 14***

C76 AP30 100fr Crawl .95 .35
C77 AP30 125fr Diving 1.25 .45
C78 AP30 350fr Backstroke 2.00 .75
C79 AP30 400fr Butterfly 4.00 1.40
*Nos. C76-C79 (4)* 8.20 2.95

**Souvenir Sheet**

C80 AP30 500fr Water polo 5.50 2.00

1984 Summer Olympics — AP31

Pentathlon.

**1984, Mar. *Perf. 12½***

C81 AP31 100fr Swimming 1.00 .30
C82 AP31 125fr Running 1.25 .40
C83 AP31 185fr Shooting 1.75 .60
C84 AP31 350fr Fencing 3.75 1.25
*Nos. C81-C84 (4)* 7.75 2.55

**Souvenir Sheet**

C85 AP31 500fr Equestrian 5.50 2.00

Los Angeles Olympics Winners AP32

**1984, Dec. 15 Litho. *Perf. 13***

C86 AP32 100fr Tiacoh, silver 1.00 .25
C87 AP32 150fr Lewis, gold 1.50 .40
C88 AP32 200fr Babers, gold 2.00 .75
C89 AP32 500fr Cruz, gold 4.25 1.50
*Nos. C86-C89 (4)* 8.75 2.90

Christmas AP33

Paintings: 100fr, Virgin and Child, by Correggio. 200fr, Holy Family with Angels, by Andrea del Sarto. 400fr, Virgin and Child, by Bellini.

**1985, Jan. 12 *Perf. 13***

C90 AP33 100fr multi 1.00 .35
C91 AP33 200fr multi 1.75 .85
C92 AP33 400fr multi 3.75 1.75
*Nos. C90-C92 (3)* 6.50 2.95

Nos. C91-C92 have incorrect frame inscriptions.

Audubon Birth Bicentenary — AP34

Birds: 100fr, Mergus serrator. 150fr, Pelecanus erythrorhynchos. 200fr, Mycteria americana. 350fr, Melanitta deglandi.

**1985, June 8 Litho. *Perf. 13***

C93 AP34 100fr multi 1.00 .45
C94 AP34 150fr multi, vert. 1.50 .70
C95 AP34 200fr multi, vert. 2.50 1.00
C96 AP34 350fr multi 3.50 1.75
*Nos. C93-C96 (4)* 8.50 3.90

PHILEXAFRICA '85, Lome, Togo — AP35

**1985, Nov. 16 Litho. *Perf. 13***

C97 AP35 250fr shown 3.00 2.00
C98 AP35 250fr Soccer, boys and deer 3.00 2.00
*a.* Pair, #C97-C98 + label 9.00 6.00

Edmond Halley, Computer Drawing of Comet — AP36

Return of Halley's Comet: 155fr, Sir William Herschel, Uranus. 190fr, Space probe, comet. 350fr, MS T-5 probe, comet. 440fr, Skylab, Kohoutek comet.

**1986, Jan. Litho. *Perf. 13***

C99 AP36 125fr shown 1.00 .50
C100 AP36 155fr multi 1.25 .75
C101 AP36 190fr multi 1.75 .90
C102 AP36 350fr multi 3.00 1.60
C103 AP36 440fr multi 3.75 2.10
*Nos. C99-C103 (5)* 10.75 5.85

1986 World Cup Soccer Championships, Mexico — AP37

Various soccer plays.

**1986, Apr. 26 Litho. *Perf. 13***

C104 AP37 90fr multi .80 .40
C105 AP37 125fr multi 1.25 .60
C106 AP37 155fr multi 1.50 .70
C107 AP37 440fr multi 4.00 2.10
C108 AP37 500fr multi 4.50 2.50
*Nos. C104-C108 (5)* 12.05 6.30

**Souvenir Sheet**

***Perf. 13½x13***

C109 AP37 600fr multi 6.25 2.50

AP38

1988 Summer Olympics, Seoul — AP39

Sailing sports.

**1987, May 23 Litho. *Perf. 12½***

C110 AP38 155fr Soling Class 1.50 .60
C111 AP38 195fr Windsurfing 2.25 .75
C112 AP38 250fr 470 Class 3.00 1.00
C113 AP38 550fr Windsurfing, diff. 6.00 2.50
*Nos. C110-C113 (4)* 12.75 4.85

**Souvenir Sheet**

C114 AP39 650fr 470 Class, diff. 7.00 2.25

1988 Summer Olympics, Seoul — AP40

**1988, June 18 Litho. *Perf. 13***

C115 AP40 100fr Gymnastic rings .90 .40
C116 AP40 155fr Women's handball 1.25 .60
C117 AP40 195fr Boxing 2.00 .75
C118 AP40 500fr Parallel bars 5.00 2.00
*Nos. C115-C118 (4)* 9.15 3.75

**Souvenir Sheet**

C119 AP40 500fr Horizontal bar *14.00* 2.00

1990 World Cup Soccer Championships, Italy — AP41

Italian monuments and various athletes.

**1989, Nov. 25 Litho. *Perf. 13***

C120 AP41 195fr Milan Cathedral 1.75 .75
C121 AP41 300fr Columbus Monument, Genoa 2.50 1.25
C122 AP41 450fr Turin 3.50 1.75
C123 AP41 550fr Bologna 5.00 2.00
*Nos. C120-C123 (4)* 12.75 5.75

World Cup Soccer Championships, Italy — AP42

Various plays.

**1990, May 31 Litho. *Perf. 13***

C124 AP42 155fr multicolored 1.50 .60
C125 AP42 195fr multicolored 1.75 .85
C126 AP42 500fr multicolored 4.25 2.00
C127 AP42 600fr multicolored 5.75 2.50
*Nos. C124-C127 (4)* 13.25 5.95

## AIR POST SEMI-POSTAL STAMPS

**Types of Dahomey Air Post Semi-Postal Issue**

***Perf. 13½x12½, 13 (#CB3)***

**Photo, Engr. (#CB3)**

**1942, June 22**

CB1 SPAP1 1.50fr + 3.50fr green 1.00 *5.50*
CB2 SPAP2 2fr + 6fr brown 1.00 *5.50*
CB3 SPAP2 3fr + 9fr car red 1.00 *5.50*
*Nos. CB1-CB3 (3)* 3.00 *16.50*

Native children's welfare fund.

**Colonial Education Fund**

Common Design Type

***Perf. 12½x13½***

**1942, June 22 Engr.**

CB4 CD86a 1.20fr + 1.80fr blue & red 1.00 *5.50*

## POSTAGE DUE STAMPS

Natives — D1

D2

*Perf. 14x13½*

**1906-07 Unwmk. Typo.**

| | | | |
|---|---|---|---|
| **J1** D1 | 5c grn, *greenish* | 4.00 | 4.00 |
| **J2** D1 | 10c red brown | 4.00 | 4.00 |
| **J3** D1 | 15c dark blue | 6.50 | 6.50 |
| **J4** D1 | 20c blk, *yellow* | 9.50 | 9.50 |
| **J5** D1 | 30c red, *straw* | 9.50 | 9.50 |
| **J6** D1 | 50c violet | 7.25 | 7.25 |
| **J7** D1 | 60c black, *buff* | 32.50 | 32.50 |
| **J8** D1 | 1fr blk, *pinkish* | 35.00 | 35.00 |
| | *Nos. J1-J8 (8)* | 108.25 | 108.25 |

**1914**

| | | | |
|---|---|---|---|
| **J9** D2 | 5c green | .25 | .25 |
| **J10** D2 | 10c rose | .30 | .30 |
| **J11** D2 | 15c gray | .30 | .30 |
| **J12** D2 | 20c brown | .55 | .55 |
| **J13** D2 | 30c blue | .55 | .55 |
| **J14** D2 | 50c black | .90 | .90 |
| **J15** D2 | 60c orange | 1.25 | 1.25 |
| **J16** D2 | 1fr violet | 1.50 | 1.50 |
| | *Nos. J9-J16 (8)* | 5.60 | 5.60 |

Type of 1914 Issue Surcharged

**1927**

| | | | |
|---|---|---|---|
| **J17** D2 | 2fr on 1fr lilac rose | 2.75 | 2.75 |
| **J18** D2 | 3fr on 1fr org brown | 2.75 | 2.75 |

**Catalogue values for unused stamps in this section, from this point to the end of the section, are for Never Hinged items.**

### Republic

Guéré Mask — D3

Mask — D4

**1960 Engr. *Perf. 14x13***

**Denomination Typographed in Black**

| | | | |
|---|---|---|---|
| **J19** D3 | 1fr purple | .25 | .25 |
| **J20** D3 | 2fr bright green | .25 | .25 |
| **J21** D3 | 5fr orange yellow | .50 | .50 |
| **J22** D3 | 10fr ultramarine | .90 | .90 |
| **J23** D3 | 20fr lilac rose | 1.60 | 1.60 |
| | *Nos. J19-J23 (5)* | 3.50 | 3.50 |

**1962, Nov. 3 Typo. *Perf. 13½x14***

Designs: Various masks and heads, Bingerville school of art.

| | | | |
|---|---|---|---|
| **J24** D4 | 1fr org & brt blue | .25 | .25 |
| **J25** D4 | 2fr black & red | .30 | .30 |
| **J26** D4 | 5fr red & dark grn | .40 | .40 |
| **J27** D4 | 10fr green & lilac | .90 | .90 |
| **J28** D4 | 20fr dark pur & blk | 1.60 | 1.60 |
| | *Nos. J24-J28 (5)* | 3.45 | 3.45 |

Baoulé Weight — D5

Gold Weight — D6

Designs: Various Baoulé weights.

**1968, May 18 Photo. *Perf. 13***

| | | | |
|---|---|---|---|
| **J29** D5 | 5fr cit, brn & bl grn | .25 | .25 |
| **J30** D5 | 10fr lt bl, brn & bl grn | .30 | .30 |
| **J31** D5 | 15fr sal, brn & bl grn | .80 | .80 |
| **J32** D5 | 20fr gray, car & bl grn | 1.10 | 1.10 |
| **J33** D5 | 30fr bis, brn & bl grn | 1.50 | 1.50 |
| | *Nos. J29-J33 (5)* | 3.95 | 3.95 |

**1972, May 27 Engr.**

Designs: Various gold weights.

| | | | |
|---|---|---|---|
| **J34** D6 | 20fr vio bl & org red | .90 | .90 |
| **J35** D6 | 40fr ver & ocher | 1.50 | 1.50 |
| **J36** D6 | 50fr orange & chocolate | 2.00 | 2.00 |
| **J37** D6 | 100fr slate grn & ocher | 4.00 | 4.00 |
| | *Nos. J34-J37 (4)* | 8.40 | 8.40 |

It has been reported that Nos. J34-J37 were used briefly as regular postage for domestic use. Examples of use as postage to foreign addresses exists.

## MILITARY STAMP

**The catalogue value for the unused stamp in this section is for Never Hinged.**

Coat of Arms — M1

*Perf. 13x14*

**1967, Jan. 1 Unwmk. Typo.**

| | | | |
|---|---|---|---|
| **M1** M1 | multi | 3.50 | 3.50 |

## OFFICIAL STAMPS

**Catalogue values for unused stamps in this section are for Never Hinged items.**

Ivory Coast Coat of Arms — O1

**1974, Jan. 1 Photo. *Perf. 12***

| | | | |
|---|---|---|---|
| **O1** O1 | (35fr) green & multi | .75 | .25 |
| **O2** O1 | (75fr) orange & multi | 1.20 | .45 |
| **O3** O1 | (100fr) lil rose & multi | 1.50 | .80 |
| **O4** O1 | (250fr) violet & multi | 4.00 | 1.50 |
| | *Nos. O1-O4 (4)* | 7.45 | 3.00 |

## PARCEL POST STAMPS

**Postage Due Stamps of French Colonies Overprinted**

Overprinted In Black

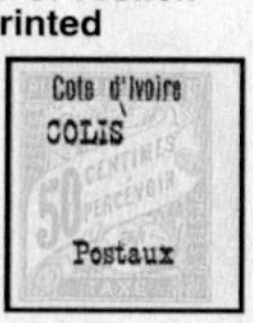

**1903 Unwmk. *Imperf.***

| | | | |
|---|---|---|---|
| **Q1** D1 | 50c lilac | 42.50 | 40.00 |
| **Q2** D1 | 1fr rose, *buff* | 42.50 | 40.00 |

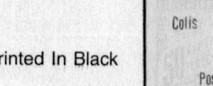

Overprinted In Black

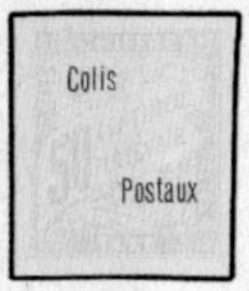

| | | | |
|---|---|---|---|
| **Q3** D1 | 50c lilac | 3,300. | 3,400. |
| **Q4** D1 | 1fr rose, *buff* | 3,300. | 3,400. |

**Accents on "O" of "COTE"**

Nos. Q7-Q8, Q11-Q12, Q15, Q17-Q18, Q21-Q22, Q24-Q25 exist with or without accent.

Overprinted In Red and Black

**Red Overprint**

| | | | |
|---|---|---|---|
| **Q5** D1 | 50c lilac | 120.00 | 120.00 |
| *a.* | Inverted overprint | 425.00 | 425.00 |

**Blue Black Overprint**

| | | | |
|---|---|---|---|
| **Q6** D1 | 1fr rose, *buff* | 87.50 | 87.50 |
| *a.* | Inverted overprint | 350.00 | 350.00 |

Surcharged in Black

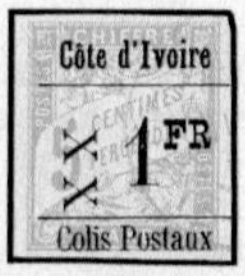

a

b

c

d

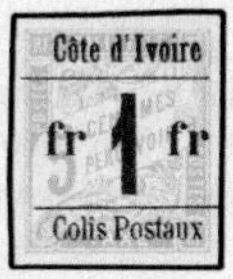

e

f

g

h

**1903**

| | | | |
|---|---|---|---|
| **Q7** D1 | 50c on 15c pale grn | 16.00 | 16.00 |
| *a.* | Inverted surcharge | 225.00 | 225.00 |
| **Q8** D1 | 50c on 60c brn, *buff* | 35.00 | 35.00 |
| *a.* | Inverted surcharge | 225.00 | 225.00 |
| **Q9** | (a) 1fr on 5c blue | *4,400.* | *3,600.* |
| **Q10** | (b) 1fr on 5c blue | *4,400.* | *2,800.* |
| **Q11** | (c) 1fr on 5c blue | 18.00 | 16.00 |
| *a.* | Inverted surcharge | 950.00 | 950.00 |
| **Q12** | (d) 1fr on 5c blue | 27.50 | 24.00 |
| **Q13** | (e) 1fr on 5c blue | *4,800.* | *4,000.* |
| **Q14** | (f) 1fr on 5c blue | *12,000.* | *9,500.* |
| **Q15** | (g) 1fr on 5c blue | 110.00 | 110.00 |
| **Q16** | (h) 1fr on 5c blue | *3,750.* | *3,850.* |
| **Q17** | (c) 1fr on 10c gray brn | 27.50 | 24.00 |
| *a.* | Inverted surcharge | 325.00 | 325.00 |
| **Q18** | (d) 1fr on 10c gray brn | 47.50 | 45.00 |
| *a.* | Inverted surcharge | 475.00 | 475.00 |
| **Q19** | (g) 1fr on 10c gray brn | *4,000.* | *3,850.* |
| **Q20** | (h) 1fr on 10c gray brn | *46,000.* | |

Some authorities regard Nos. Q9 and Q10 as essays. A sub-type of type "a" has smaller, bold "XX" without serifs.

**Surcharged in Black**

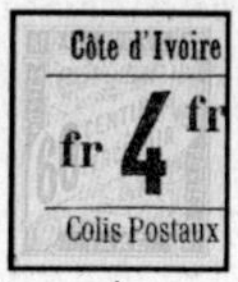

j

k

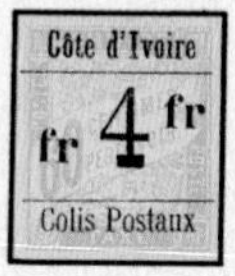

l

| | | | |
|---|---|---|---|
| **Q21** | (j) 4fr on 60c brn, *buff* | 140.00 | 140.00 |
| *a.* | Double surcharge | | 5,600. |
| **Q22** | (k) 4fr on 60c brn, *buff* | 375.00 | 375.00 |
| **Q23** | (l) 4fr on 60c brn, *buff* | 1,200. | 1,000. |

Surcharged in Black

| | | | |
|---|---|---|---|
| **Q24** D1 | 4fr on 15c green | 130.00 | 130.00 |
| *a.* | One large star | 525.00 | 525.00 |
| *b.* | Two large stars | 300.00 | 300.00 |
| **Q25** D1 | 4fr on 30c rose | 130.00 | 130.00 |
| *a.* | One large star | 525.00 | 525.00 |
| *b.* | Two large stars | 300.00 | 300.00 |

Overprinted in Black

**1904**

| | | | |
|---|---|---|---|
| **Q26** D1 | 50c lilac | 45.00 | 45.00 |
| *a.* | Inverted overprint | | |
| **Q27** D1 | 1fr rose, *buff* | 45.00 | 45.00 |
| *a.* | Inverted overprint | | |

Overprinted in Black

| | | | |
|---|---|---|---|
| **Q28** D1 | 50c lilac | 42.50 | 42.50 |
| *a.* | Inverted overprint | 225.00 | 225.00 |
| **Q29** D1 | 1fr rose, *buff* | 42.50 | 42.50 |
| *a.* | Inverted overprint | 225.00 | 225.00 |

Surcharged in Black

| | | | |
|---|---|---|---|
| **Q30** D1 | 4fr on 5c blue | 240.00 | 240.00 |
| **Q31** D1 | 8fr on 15c green | 240.00 | 240.00 |

Overprinted in Black

**1905**

| | | | |
|---|---|---|---|
| **Q32** D1 | 50c lilac | 92.50 | 92.50 |
| **Q33** D1 | 1fr rose, *buff* | 92.50 | 92.50 |

Surcharged in Black

| | | | |
|---|---|---|---|
| **Q34** | D1 2fr on 1fr rose, *buff* | 240.00 | 240.00 |
| **Q35** | D1 4fr on 1fr rose, *buff* | 240.00 | 240.00 |
| *a.* | Italic "4" | 2,200. | 2,200. |
| **Q36** | D1 8fr on 1fr rose, *buff* | 700.00 | 700.00 |

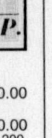

# SHOWGARD MOUNTS

Showgard mounts are manufactured with the highest archival qualities in mind. The foil used to produce the mounts is acid free and stronger than other mounts for maximum protection and durability. Selecting the right size mount for your stamp is easy. Simply use a millimeter ruler to measure the stamps width then the height. Showgard incorporates these measurements into their product numbers to insure you get the right size. Mounts available with clear (c) or black (b) backgrounds. Please specify background preference when ordering.

| *Item* | *Description* | *Mounts* | *Retail* | *AA** |
|---|---|---|---|---|
| SGC50/31 | 50/31 U.S. Jumbo Singles - Horizontal | 40 | $3.85 | **$2.75** |
| SGCV31/50 | 31/50 U.S. Jumbo Singles - Vertical | 40 | $3.85 | **$2.75** |
| SGJ40/25 | 40/25 U.S. Commem. - Horizontal | 40 | $3.85 | **$2.75** |
| SGJV25/40 | 25/40 U.S. Commem. - Vertical | 40 | $3.85 | **$2.75** |
| SGE22/25 | 22/25 U.S. Regular Issues - Vertical | 40 | $3.85 | **$2.75** |
| SGEH25/22 | 25/22 U.S. Regular Issues - Horizontal | 40 | $3.85 | **$2.75** |
| SGT25/27 | 25/27 U.S. Famous Americans | 40 | $3.85 | **$2.75** |
| SGU33/27 | 33/27 U.N., Germany | 40 | $3.85 | **$2.75** |
| SGN40/27 | 40/27 United Nations | 40 | $3.85 | **$2.75** |
| SGAH41/31 | 41/31 U.S. Semi Jumbo - Horizontal | 40 | $3.85 | **$2.75** |
| SGAV31/41 | 31/41 U.S. Semi Jumbo - Vertical | 40 | $3.85 | **$2.75** |
| SGDH52/36 | 52/36 U.S. Duck Stamps | 30 | $3.85 | **$2.75** |
| SGS31/31 | 31/31 U.S. Celebrate the Century | 30 | $3.85 | **$2.75** |
| SGUS2 | Cut Style with Tray-8 Sizes | 320 | $29.50 | **$21.25** |
| SGUS3 | Strip Style w/Tray-No. 22 thru No. 52 | 75 | $43.95 | **$31.50** |
| SGUS1 | U.S. Strip Sizes No. 22 thru No. 52 | 50 | $22.50 | **$16.25** |
| SG50VPB | 50th Anniversary Value Pack | 50 | $24.95 | **$19.96** |
| SG67/25 | 67/25 U.S. Coil Strips of 3 | 40 | $7.50 | **$5.50** |
| SG57/55 | 57/55 U.S. Regular Issue | 25 | $7.50 | **$5.50** |
| SG106/55 | 106/55 U.S. 3¢, 4¢ Commemoratives | 20 | $7.50 | **$5.50** |
| SG105/57 | 105/57 U.S. Giori Press Issues | 20 | $7.50 | **$5.50** |
| SG127/70 | 127/70 U.S. Jumbo Issues | 10 | $7.50 | **$5.50** |
| SG140/89 | 140/89 Postcards, Souvenir Sheets | 10 | $7.50 | **$5.50** |
| SG165/94 | 165/94 First Day Covers | 10 | $7.50 | **$5.50** |
| SG20 | 215/20 U.S. Mini Stamps, etc. | 22 | $8.95 | **$6.50** |
| SG22 | 215/22 Narrow U.S. Airs | 22 | $8.95 | **$6.50** |
| SG24 | 215/24 U.K. and Canada, early U.S. | 22 | $8.95 | **$6.50** |
| SG25 | 215/25 U.S. Commem. & Regular Issues | 22 | $8.95 | **$6.50** |
| SG27 | 215/27 U.S. Famous Americans, U.N. | 22 | $8.95 | **$6.50** |
| SG28 | 215/28 Switzerland, Liechtenstein | 22 | $8.95 | **$6.50** |
| SG30 | 215/30 U.S. Special Stamps, Jamestown | 22 | $8.95 | **$6.50** |
| SG31 | 315/31 U.S. Squares & Semi Jumbo | 22 | $8.95 | **$6.50** |
| SG33 | 215/33 U.K. Issues, Misc. Foreign | 22 | $8.95 | **$6.50** |
| SG36 | 215/36 Duck Stamps, Misc. Foreign | 15 | $8.95 | **$6.50** |
| SG39 | 215/39 U.S. Magsaysay, Misc. Foreign | 15 | $8.95 | **$6.50** |
| SG41 | 215/41 U.S. Vertical Commem. Israel Tabs | 15 | $8.95 | **$6.50** |
| SG44 | 215/44 Booklet Panes, Hatteras Quartet | 15 | $8.95 | **$6.50** |
| SG48 | 215/48 Canada Reg. Issue & Comm Blocks | 15 | $8.95 | **$6.50** |
| SG50 | 215/50 U.S. Plain Blocks of 4 | 15 | $8.95 | **$6.50** |
| SG52 | 215/52 France Paintings, Misc. Foreign | 15 | $8.95 | **$6.50** |
| SG57 | 215/57 U.S. Commem. Plate Blocks | 15 | $8.95 | **$6.50** |
| SG61 | 215/61 Souvenir Sheets, Tab Singles, etc. | 15 | $8.95 | **$6.50** |
| SG63 | 240/63 U.S. Semi Jumbo Blocks | 10 | $11.25 | **$8.25** |
| SG66 | 240/66 U.S. ATM Panes, SA Duck Panes | 10 | $11.25 | **$8.25** |
| SG68 | 240/68 Canadian Plate Blocks, etc. | 10 | $11.25 | **$8.25** |
| SG74 | 240/74 U.N. Inscription Blocks of 4 | 10 | $11.25 | **$8.25** |
| SG80 | 240/80 U.S. Commem. Blocks | 10 | $11.25 | **$8.25** |
| SG82 | 240/82 U.N. Chagall SS, Canada Plate Blocks | 10 | $11.25 | **$8.25** |
| SG84 | 240/84 Israel Plate Blocks, etc. | 10 | $11.25 | **$8.25** |
| SG89 | 240/89 U.N. Inscription Blocks of 6 | 10 | $11.25 | **$8.25** |
| SG100 | 240/100 U.S. Squares Plate Blocks | 7 | $11.25 | **$8.25** |
| SG120 | 240/120 Miniature Sheets | 7 | $11.25 | **$8.25** |
| SG70 | 264/70 U.S. Jumbo Plate Blocks | 10 | $14.85 | **$10.65** |
| SG91 | 264/91 U.K. Souvenir Sheets | 10 | $14.85 | **$10.65** |
| SG105 | 264/105 U.K. Blocks, Covers, etc. | 10 | $14.85 | **$10.65** |
| SG107 | 264/107 U.S. Plate No. Strip of 20 | 10 | $14.85 | **$10.65** |
| SGMPK | Assortment No. 22 thru No. 41 | 12 | $7.15 | **$5.25** |
| SGMPK2 | Assortment No. 76 thru No. 171 | 15 | $29.95 | **$22.50** |
| SGAB | U.S. SS to 1975-except White Plains | 11 | $7.65 | **$5.50** |
| SGWSE | World Stamp Expo Souvenir Sheets | 3 | $2.50 | **$1.75** |
| SG265/231 | 265/231 U.S. Full Sheets & Souvenir Cards | 5 | $21.25 | **$15.25** |
| SGRP94 | U.S. 1994 Souvenir Sheets | 5 | $9.75 | **$6.95** |
| SGRPAC97 | Pacific 97 Issues | 7 | $4.75 | **$3.50** |
| SGDC2006 | Washington 2006 Souvenir Sheets (4) | 11 | $7.75 | **$5.50** |
| SGTM | Trans-Mississippi Issues | 11 | $4.75 | **$3.50** |
| SGSPC | Space Exploration Sheets | 5 | $6.50 | **$4.75** |
| SG111 | 264/111 U.S. Floating Plate No. Strips of 20 | 5 | $9.75 | **$6.95** |
| SG127 | 264/127 Modern U.S. Definitive Sheets of 20 | 5 | $10.75 | **$7.75** |

| *Item* | *Description* | *Mounts* | *Retail* | *AA** |
|---|---|---|---|---|
| SG137 | 264/137 U.N. SS, U.K. Coronation | 5 | $11.75 | **$8.50** |
| SG158 | 264/158 Miniature Sheets, Apoll Soyuz PB | 5 | $13.50 | **$9.75** |
| SG175 | 264/175 U.S. Sheets-Pan American Reissues | 5 | $14.50 | **$10.50** |
| SG188 | 264/188 U.S. Miniature Sheets-Hollywood, etc. | 5 | $15.25 | **$10.95** |
| SG198 | 264/198 U.S. Miniature Sheets | 5 | $15.95 | **$11.50** |
| SG260/25 | 260/25 U.S. Coil Strips of up to 11 stamps | 25 | $11.95 | **$8.50** |
| SG293/30 | 293/30 U.S. American Eagle Coil Strips of up to 11 stamps | 5 | $3.50 | **$2.50** |
| SG260/40 | 260/40 U.S. Postal People Full Strip | 10 | $9.75 | **$6.95** |
| SG260/46 | 260/46 U.S. Vending Booklets | 10 | $9.75 | **$6.95** |
| SG260/55 | 260/55 U.S. 13¢ Eagle Full Strip | 10 | $9.75 | **$6.95** |
| SG260/59 | 260/59 U.S. Double Press Reg. Iss. Strips of 20 | 10 | $9.75 | **$6.95** |
| SG111/91 | 111/91 U.S. Columbian Souvenir Sheets | 6 | $4.50 | **$3.25** |
| SG229/131 | 229/131 U.S. WWII Sheets, Looney Tunes | 5 | $9.87 | **$7.00** |
| SG187/144 | 187/144 U.N. Flag Sheetlets | 10 | $17.50 | **$12.50** |
| SG204/153 | 204/153 U.S. Commem. Sheets, Bicentennial | 5 | $10.25 | **$7.25** |
| SG120/207 | 120/207 U.S. Ameripex Presidential Sheetlets | 4 | $5.75 | **$4.25** |
| SG192/201 | 192/201 U.S. Classics Mini-Sheets | 5 | $12.50 | **$8.95** |
| SG280/228 | 280/228 U.S. Greetings From America Sheets | 5 | $18.50 | **$13.25** |
| SG191/229 | 191/229 U.S. Celebrate The Century Sheets | 5 | $14.50 | **$10.50** |
| SG76 | 264/76 BEP SS, Booklets, Plate Blocks | 5 | $10.95 | **$7.50** |
| SG96 | 264/96 Souvenir Sheets, Panes | 5 | $10.95 | **$7.50** |
| SG109 | 264/109 Foreign Miniature Sheets | 5 | $10.95 | **$7.50** |
| SG115 | 264/115 Foreign Miniature Sheets | 5 | $10.95 | **$7.95** |
| SG117 | 264/117 Foreign Miniature Sheets | 5 | $10.95 | **$7.95** |
| SG121 | 264/121 Foreign Miniature Sheets | 5 | $10.95 | **$7.95** |
| SG131 | 264/131 Looney Toons, Misc. Sheetlets | 5 | $10.95 | **$7.95** |
| SG135 | 264/135 Foreign Miniature Sheets | 5 | $10.95 | **$7.95** |
| SG139 | 264/139 White House Pane, etc. | 5 | $10.95 | **$7.95** |
| SG143 | 264/143 Victorian Love, Misc. Sheets | 5 | $10.95 | **$7.95** |
| SG147 | 264/147 Cinco de Mayo, etc. | 5 | $13.95 | **$9.97** |
| SG151 | 264/151 Antique Auto, Communication, etc. | 5 | $13.95 | **$9.97** |
| SG163 | 264/163 Tropical Flowers, UN Human Rights | 5 | $13.95 | **$9.97** |
| SG167 | 264/167 Misc. U.S. Sheetlets | 5 | $13.95 | **$9.97** |
| SG171 | 264/171 Helping Children Learn, etc. | 5 | $13.95 | **$9.97** |
| SG181 | 264/181 U.S. Sheets– Calder, All Aboard, etc. | 5 | $16.95 | **$12.25** |
| SG201 | 264/201 Dinosaurs, etc. | 5 | $16.95 | **$12.25** |
| SG215 | 264/215 U.S. Sheets–Arctic Animals, Ballet, etc. | 5 | $16.95 | **$12.25** |

**7" LIGHTHOUSE STAMP MOUNT CUTTER**

This affordable and versatile mount cutter features an attachable measuring scale up to 7" (180mm) with an adjustable stop for accurate and clean cuts every time.

| *Item* | *Retail* | *AA* |
|---|---|---|
| LH180MC | $20.95 | **$18.99** |

Call **1-800-572-6885**

Visit **www.amosadvantage.com**

ORDER ONLINE Get the AMOS ADVANTAGE Discount

**ORDERING INFORMATION**

*AA prices apply to paid subscribers of Amos Hobby titles and orders placed online. Prices, terms and product availability subject to change.

**Shipping & Handling:**

United States: 10% of order total. Minimum charge $7.99 Maximum charge $45.00
Canada: 20% of order total. Minimum charge $19.99 Maximum charge $200.00
Foreign orders are shipped via FedEx Economny Intl. and billed actual freight.

# Illustrated Identifier

This section pictures stamps or parts of stamp designs that will help identify postage stamps that do not have English words on them.

Many of the symbols that identify stamps of countries are shown here as well as typical examples of their stamps.

See the Index and Identifier on the previous pages for stamps with inscriptions such as "sen," "posta," "Baja Porto," "Helvetia," "K.S.A.", etc.

*Linn's Stamp Identifier* is now available. The 144 pages include more than 2,000 inscriptions and more than 500 large stamp illustrations. Available from Linn's Stamp News, P.O. Box 29, Sidney, OH 45365-0029.

## 1. HEADS, PICTURES AND NUMERALS

### GREAT BRITAIN

Great Britain stamps never show the country name, but, except for postage dues, show a picture of the reigning monarch.

Victoria

Edward VII George V Edward VIII

George VI

Elizabeth II

Some George VI and Elizabeth II stamps are surcharged in annas, new paisa or rupees. These are listed under Oman.

Silhouette (sometimes facing right, generally at the top of stamp)

The silhouette indicates this is a British stamp. It is not a U.S. stamp.

### VICTORIA

Queen Victoria

### INDIA

Other stamps of India show this portrait of Queen Victoria and the words "Service" (or "Postage") and "Annas."

### AUSTRIA

### YUGOSLAVIA

(Also BOSNIA & HERZEGOVINA if imperf.)

### BOSNIA & HERZEGOVINA

Denominations also appear in top corners instead of bottom corners.

### HUNGARY

Another stamp has posthorn facing left

### BRAZIL

### AUSTRALIA

Kangaroo and Emu

### GERMANY

### Mecklenburg-Vorpommern

### SWITZERLAND

### PALAU

## 2. ORIENTAL INSCRIPTIONS

### CHINA

中 中

Any stamp with this one character is from China (Imperial, Republic or People's Republic). This character appears in a four-character overprint on stamps of Manchukuo. These stamps are local provisionals, which are unlisted. Other overprinted Manchukuo stamps show this character, but have more than four characters in the overprints. These are listed in People's Republic of China.

Some Chinese stamps show the Sun.

中華民國郵票

Most stamps of Republic of China show this series of characters.

Stamps with the China character and this character are from People's Republic of China. 人

中国人民邮政
T.34(5-1)

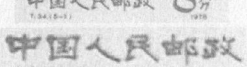

Calligraphic form of People's Republic of China

| (一) | (二) | (三) | (四) | (五) | (六) |
|---|---|---|---|---|---|
| 1 | 2 | 3 | 4 | 5 | 6 |
| (七) | (八) | (九) | (十) | (一十) | (二十) |
| 7 | 8 | 9 | 10 | 11 | 12 |

### Chinese stamps without China character

### REPUBLIC OF CHINA

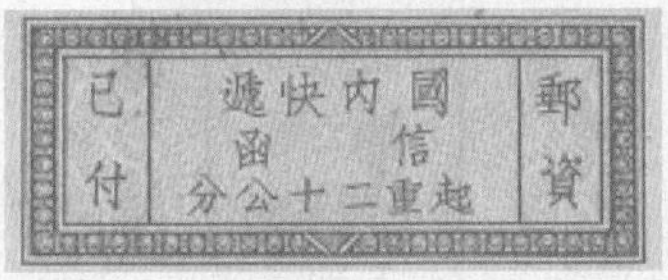

### PEOPLE'S REPUBLIC OF CHINA

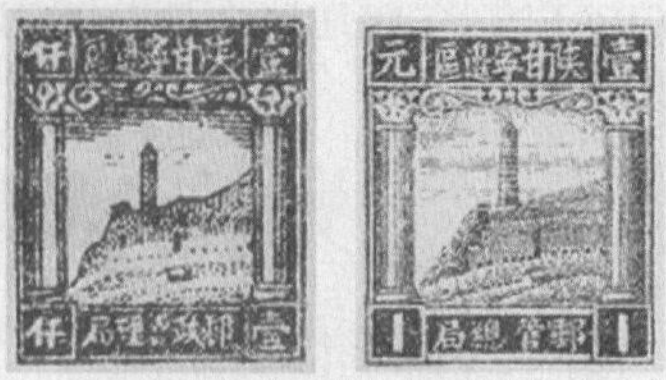

Mao Tse-tung

## MANCHUKUO

Temple

Emperor Pu-Yi

The first 3 characters are common to many Manchukuo stamps.

The last 3 characters are common to other Manchukuo stamps.

Orchid Crest

Manchukuo stamp without these elements

## JAPAN

Chrysanthemum Crest

Country Name

Japanese stamps without these elements

The number of characters in the center and the design of dragons on the sides will vary.

## RYUKYU ISLANDS

Country Name

## PHILIPPINES (Japanese Occupation)

Country Name

## NETHERLANDS INDIES (Japanese Occupation)

## JAVA

## SUMATRA

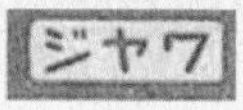

Java

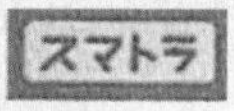

Sumatra

## MOLUCCAS, CELEBES AND SOUTH BORNEO

## NORTH BORNEO (Japanese Occupation)

Indicates Japanese Occupation

Country Name

## MALAYA (Japanese Occupation)

Indicates Japanese Occupation

Country Name

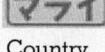

## BURMA

### Union of Myanmar

ပြည်ထောင်စုမြန်မာနိုင်ငံတော်

Union of Myanmar

### (Japanese Occupation)

Indicates Japanese Occupation

Country Name

Other Burma Japanese Occupation stamps without these elements

Burmese Script

## KOREA

These two characters, in any order, are common to stamps from the Republic of Korea (South Korea) or of the People's Democratic Republic of Korea (North Korea).

This series of four characters can be found on the stamps of both Koreas. Most stamps of the Democratic People's Republic of Korea (North Korea) have just this inscription.

Indicates Republic of Korea (South Korea)

South Korean postage stamps issed after 1952 do not show currency expressed in Latin letters. Stamps wiith " HW," "HWAN," "WON," "WN," "W" or "W" with two lines through it, if not illustrated in listings of stamps before this date, are revenues. North Korean postage stamps do not have currency expressed in Latin letters.

Yin Yang appears on some stamps.

South Korean stamps show Yin Yang and starting in 1966, 'KOREA" in Latin letters

Example of South Korean stamps lacking Latin text, Yin Yang and standard Korean text of country name. North Korean stamps never show Yin Yang and starting in 1976 are inscribed "DPRK" or "DPR KOREA" in Latin letters.

## THAILAND

Country Name

King Chulalongkorn

King Prajadhipok and Chao P'ya Chakri

## 3. CENTRAL AND EASTERN ASIAN INSCRIPTIONS

### INDIA - FEUDATORY STATES

#### Alwar

#### Bhor

## Bundi

Similar stamps come with different designs in corners and differently drawn daggers (at center of circle).

## Dhar

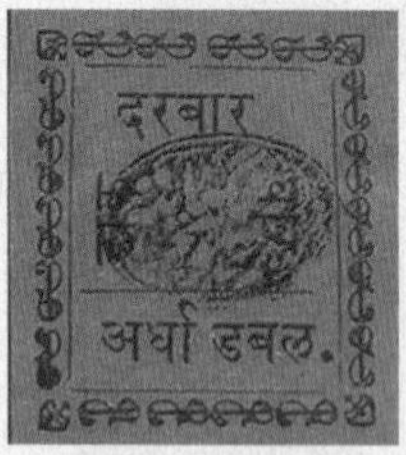

## Duttia

## Faridkot

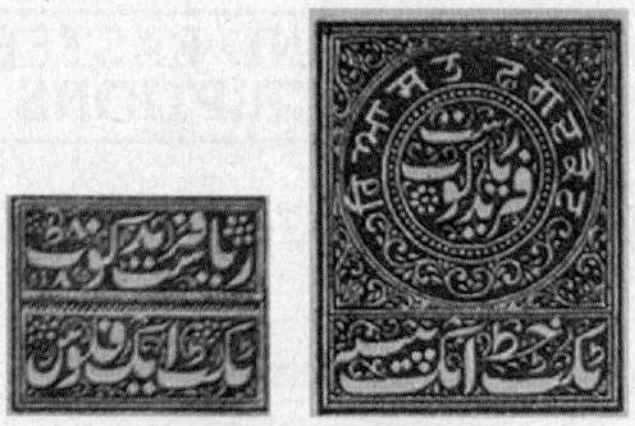

## Hyderabad

Similar stamps exist with different central design which is inscribed "Postage" or "Post & Receipt."

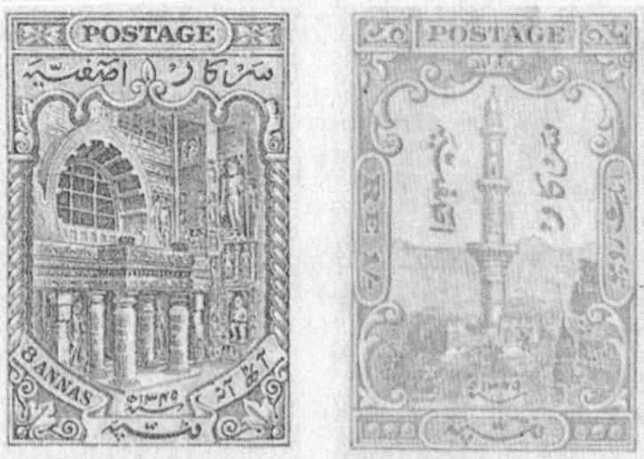

## Indore

## Jammu & Kashmir

Text varies.

## Jasdan

## Jhalawar

## Kotah

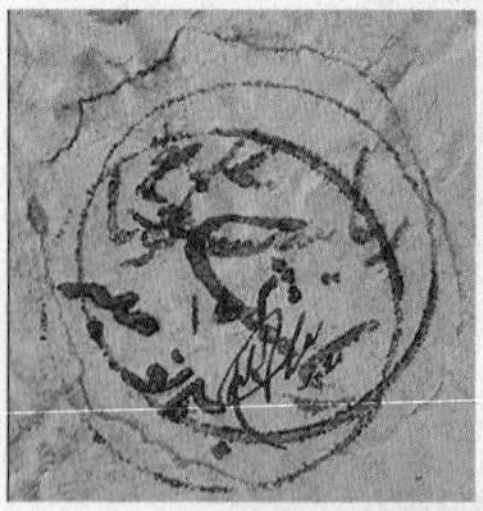

Size and text varies

## Nandgaon

## Nowanuggur

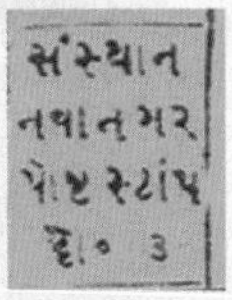

## Poonch

Similar stamps exist
in various sizes with different text

## Rajasthan

## Rajpeepla

## Soruth

## Tonk

## BANGLADESH

Country Name

## NEPAL

Similar stamps are smaller, have squares in upper corners and have five or nine characters in central bottom panel.

## TANNU TUVA

## ISRAEL

## GEORGIA

This inscription is found on other pictorial stamps.

Country Name

## ARMENIA

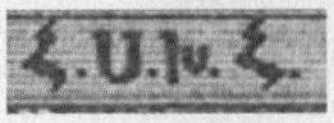

The four characters are found somewhere on pictorial stamps. On some stamps only the middle two are found.

## 4. AFRICAN INSCRIPTIONS

### ETHIOPIA

## 5. ARABIC INSCRIPTIONS

١ ٢ ٣ ٤ ٥
1 2 3 4 5

٦ ٧ ٨ ٩ ٠
6 7 8 9 0

### AFGHANISTAN

Many early Afghanistan stamps show Tiger's head, many of these have ornaments protruding from outer ring, others show inscriptions in black.

Arabic Script

Crest of King Amanullah

Mosque Gate & Crossed Cannons

افغانستان

The four characters are found somewhere on pictorial stamps. On some stamps only the middle two are found.

### BAHRAIN

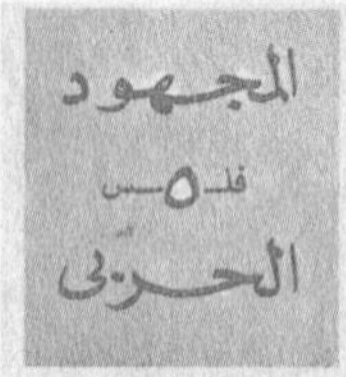

## EGYPT

Postage

## IRAN

Country Name

Royal Crown

Lion with Sword

Symbol

Emblem

## IRAQ

## JORDAN

## LEBANON

Similar types have denominations at top and slightly different design.

## LIBYA

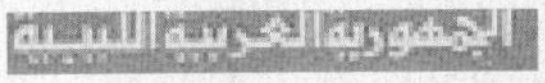

Country Name in various styles

Other Libya stamps show Eagle and Shield (head facing either direction) or Red, White and Black Shield (with or without eagle in center).

Without Country Name

## SAUDI ARABIA

Tughra (Central design)

Palm Tree and Swords

## SYRIA

## Arab Government Issues

THRACE

YEMEN

## PAKISTAN

## PAKISTAN - BAHAWALPUR

Country Name in top panel, star and crescent

## TURKEY

Star & Crescent is a device found on many Turkish stamps, but is also found on stamps from other Arabic areas (see Pakistan-Bahawalpur)

Tughra (similar tughras can be found on stamps of Turkey in Asia, Afghanistan and Saudi Arabia)

Mohammed V

Mustafa Kemal

Plane, Star and Crescent

## TURKEY IN ASIA

Other Turkey in Asia pictorials show star & crescent.
Other stamps show tughra shown under Turkey.

## 6. GREEK INSCRIPTIONS

### GREECE

Country Name in various styles
(Some Crete stamps overprinted with the Greece country name are listed in Crete.)

Lepta

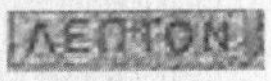


Drachma Drachmas Lepton

Abbreviated Country Name 

Other forms of Country Name

No country name

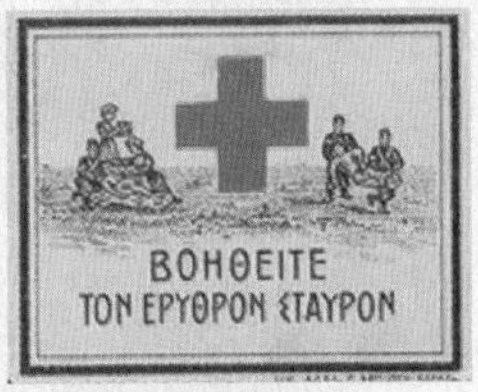

### CRETE

Country Name

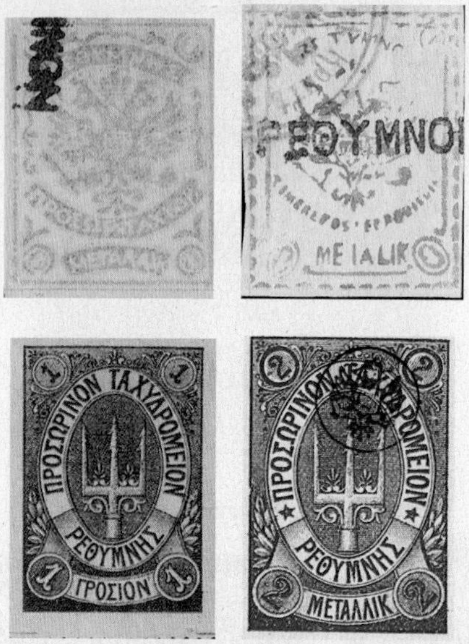

Crete stamps with a surcharge that have the year "1922" are listed under Greece.

## EPIRUS

Similar stamps have text above the eagle.

## IONIAN IS.

# 7. CYRILLIC INSCRIPTIONS

## RUSSIA

Postage Stamp Imperial Eagle

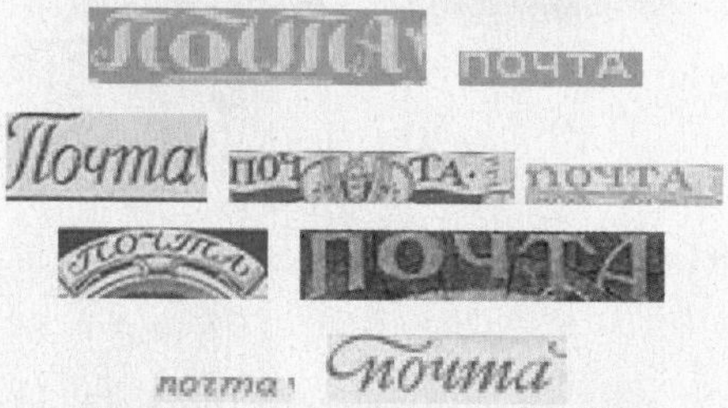

Postage in various styles

Abbreviation for Kopeck Abbreviation for Ruble Russia

Abbreviation for Russian Soviet Federated Socialist Republic RSFSR stamps were overprinted (see below)

Abbreviation for Union of Soviet Socialist Republics

This item is footnoted in Latvia

## RUSSIA - Army of the North

"OKCA"

## RUSSIA - Wenden

## RUSSIAN OFFICES IN THE TURKISH EMPIRE

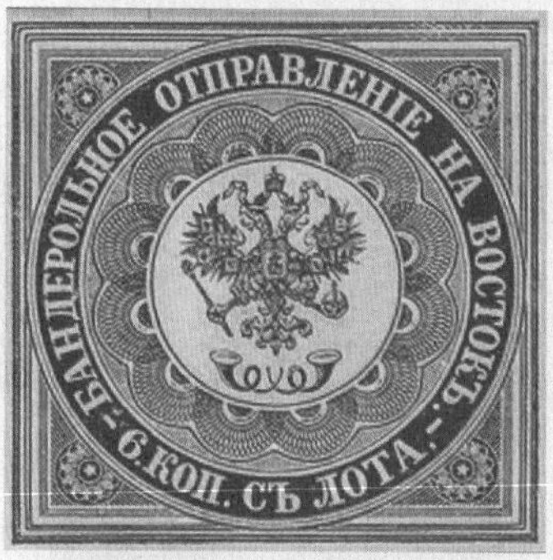

These letters appear on other stamps of the Russian offices.

The unoverprinted version of this stamp and a similar stamp were overprinted by various countries (see below).

## ARMENIA

## BELARUS

## FAR EASTERN REPUBLIC

Country Name

## FINLAND

Circles and Dots on stamps similar to Imperial Russia issues

## SOUTH RUSSIA

Country Name

## BATUM

Forms of Country Name

## TRANSCAUCASIAN FEDERATED REPUBLICS

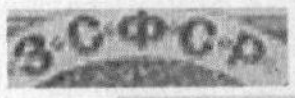

Abbreviation for Country Name

## KAZAKHSTAN

ҚАЗАҚСТАН

Country Name

## KYRGYZSTAN

КЫРГЫЗСТАН

КЫРГЫЗСТАН

Country Name

## ROMANIA

## TAJIKISTAN

Country Name & Abbreviation

## UKRAINE

Country Name in various forms

The trident appears on many stamps, usually as an overprint.

Abbreviation for Ukrainian Soviet Socialist Republic

## WESTERN UKRAINE

Abbreviation for Country Name

## AZERBAIJAN

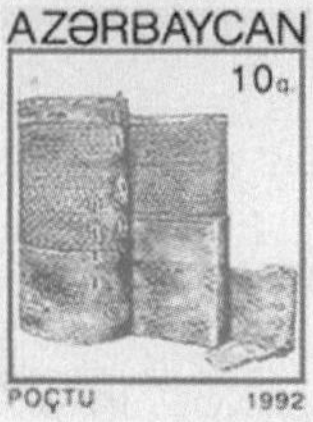


AZƏRBAYCAN

Country Name

А.С.С.Р.

Abbreviation for Azerbaijan Soviet Socialist Republic

## MONTENEGRO

ЦРНЕГОРЕ

ЦРНА ГОРА

Country Name in various forms

ЦР. ГОРЕ

Abbreviation for country name

No country name (A similar Montenegro stamp without country name has same vignette.)

## SERBIA

СРПСКА СРБИЈА

Country Name in various forms

СРП. К.С.

Abbreviation for country name

No country name

## MACEDONIA

МАКЕДОНИЈА

МАКЕДОНИЈА

Country Name

МАКЕДОНСКИ
11 Октомври 1997

Different form of Country Name

## SERBIA & MONTENEGRO

## YUGOSLAVIA

ЈУГОСЛАВИЈА

Showing country name

No Country Name

## BOSNIA & HERZEGOVINA (Serb Administration)

РЕПУБЛИКА СРПСКА

Country Name

РЕПУБЛИКЕ СРПСКЕ

Different form of Country Name

No Country Name

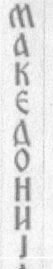

**BULGARIA**

Country Name Postage

Stotinka

Stotinki (plural) Abbreviation for Stotinki

Country Name in various forms and styles

No country name

Abbreviation for Lev, leva

**MONGOLIA**

Country name in one word Tugrik in Cyrillic

Country name in two words Mung in Cyrillic

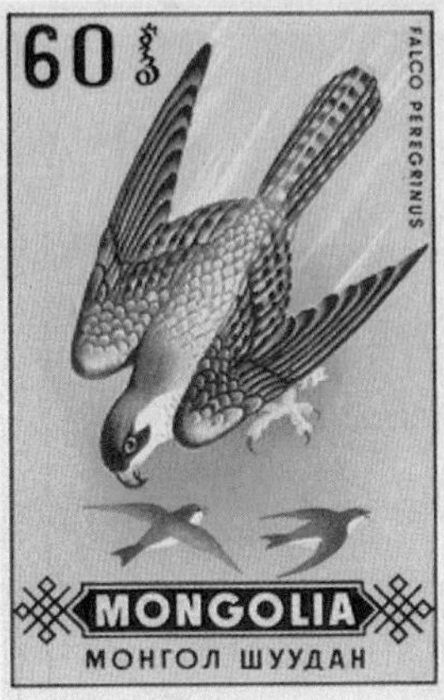

Mung in Mongolian

Tugrik in Mongolian

Arms

No Country Name

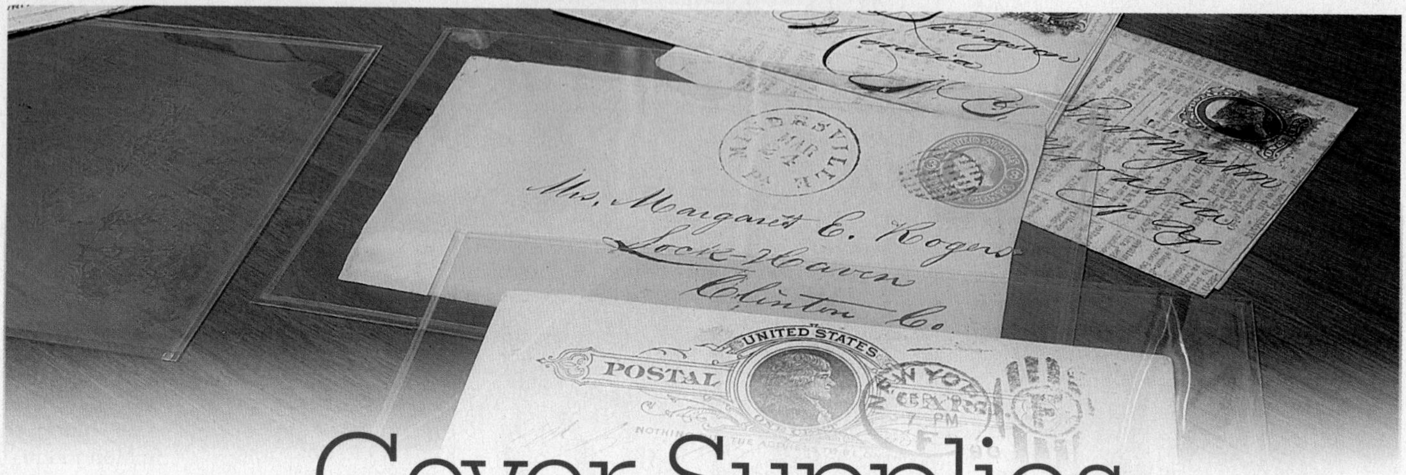

# Cover Supplies

**COVER SLEEVES**
Protect your covers with clear polyethylene sleeves.
**Sold in packages of 100.**

**U.S. POSTAL CARD**

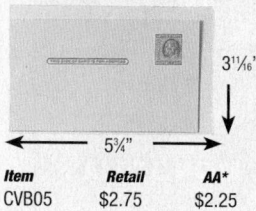

3¹¹⁄₁₆"
5¾"

| *Item* | *Retail* | *AA** |
|---|---|---|
| CVB05 | $2.75 | $2.25 |

**U.S. FIRST DAY COVER #6**

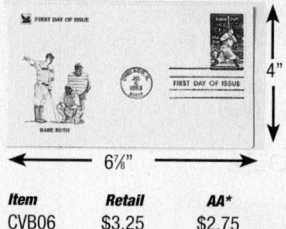

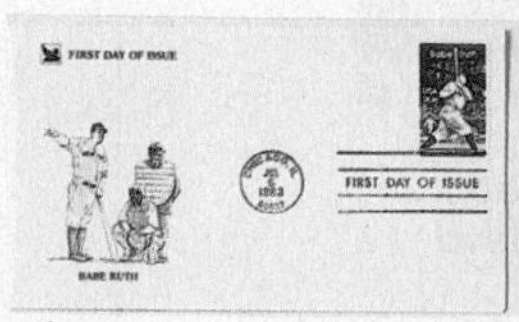

4"
6⅞"

| *Item* | *Retail* | *AA** |
|---|---|---|
| CVB06 | $3.25 | $2.75 |

**CONTINENTAL POSTCARD**

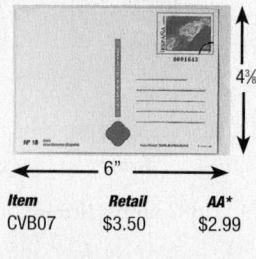

4⅜"
6"

| *Item* | *Retail* | *AA** |
|---|---|---|
| CVB07 | $3.50 | $2.99 |

**EUROPEAN FIRST DAY COVER**

5⅛"
7"

| *Item* | *Retail* | *AA** |
|---|---|---|
| CVB09 | $4.25 | $3.95 |

**#10 BUSINESS ENVELOPE**

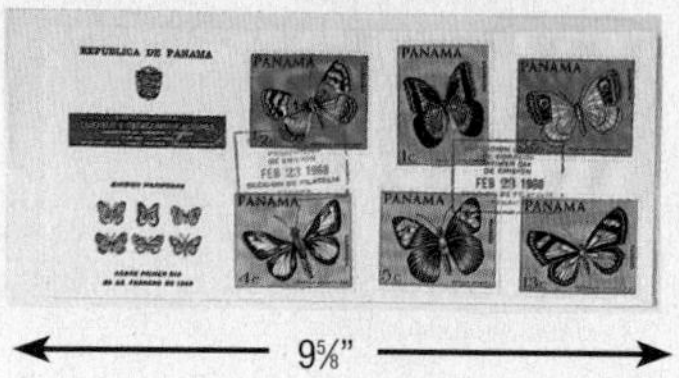

4¼"
9⅝"

| *Item* | *Retail* | *AA** |
|---|---|---|
| CVB10 | $5.75 | $4.95 |

**COVER BINDERS AND PAGES**
Padded, durable, 3-ring binders will hold up to 100 covers. Features the "D" ring mechanism on the right hand side of album so you don't have to worry about creasing or wrinkling covers when opening or closing binder. Cover pages sold separately. Available in black with 1 or 2 pockets. Sold in packages of 10.

| *Item* | | *Retail* | *AA** |
|---|---|---|---|
| CBRD | Burgundy | $11.99 | $9.59 |
| CBBL | Blue | $11.99 | $9.59 |
| CBCA | Candy Apple | $11.99 | $9.59 |
| CBGY | Gray | $11.99 | $9.59 |
| CBBK | Black | $11.99 | $9.59 |
| SS2PGB | Pgs. 2-Pock. | $4.95 | $4.50 |
| SS2PG1B | Pgs. 1-Pock. | $4.95 | $4.50 |

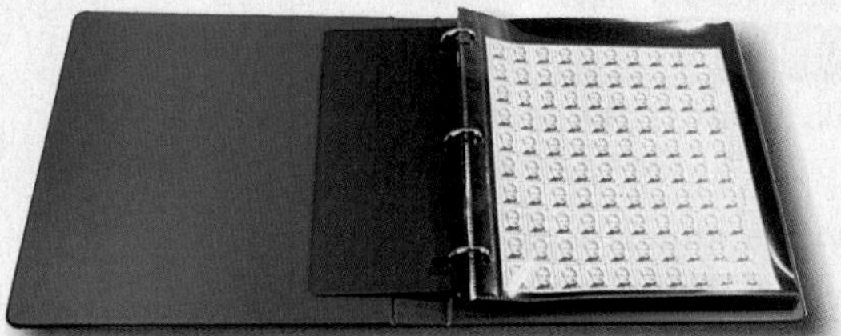

**MINT SHEET BINDERS & PAGES**
Keep those mint sheets intact in a handsome, 3-ring binder. Just like the cover album, the Mint Sheet album features the "D" ring mechanism on the right hand side of binder so you don't have to worry about damagaing your stamps when turning the pages.

| *Item* | | | *Retail* | *AA** |
|---|---|---|---|---|
| MBRD | Red (Burgundy) | | $18.99 | $15.25 |
| MBBL | Blue | | $18.99 | $15.25 |
| MBGY | Gray | | $18.99 | $15.25 |
| MBBK | Black | | $18.99 | $15.25 |
| SSMP3B | Mint Sheet Pages | (Black 12 per pack) | $8.75 | $7.95 |
| SSMP3C | Mint Sheet Pages | (Clear 12 per pack) | $8.75 | $7.95 |

**PRINZ CORNER MOUNTS**
Clear, self-adhesive corner mounts are ideal for postal cards and covers. Mounts measure ⅞" each side and are made from transparent glass foil. There are 250 mounts in each pack.

| *Item* | *Retail* | *AA** |
|---|---|---|
| ACC176 | $9.95 | **$7.96** |

1. AA* prices apply to paid subscribers of *Linn's and orders placed online.*
2. Prices, terms and product availability subject to change.
3. **Shipping & Handling:**
   United States: 10% of order total. Minimum charge $7.99 Maximum charge $45.00.
   Canada: 20% of order total. Minimum charge $19.99 Maximum charge $200.00.
   Foreign orders are shipped via FedEx Intl and billed actual freight. Credit cards only.

# Call 1-800-572-6885

## www.amosadvantage.com

# INDEX AND IDENTIFIER

All page numbers shown are those in this Volume 3.

Postage stamps that do not have English words on them are shown in the Illustrated Identifier.

# Vol. 3 Number Additions, Deletions & Changes

| Number in 2013 Catalogue | Number in 2014 Catalogue |
|---|---|
| **Georgia** | |
| 12 | 1 |
| 13 | 2 |
| 14 | 3 |
| 15 | 4 |
| 16 | 5 |
| 17 | 6 |
| 18 | 13 |
| 19 | 14 |
| 20 | 15 |
| new | 7-12 |
| new | 8a |
| new | 16-18 |
| **German States** | |
| **Bavaria** | |
| new | 257b |
| new | 258a |
| new | 262a |
| new | 264a |
| **Great Britain** | |
| 158Bg | 158Be |
| new | 353h |
| new | 353php |
| new | 354g |
| new | 354h |
| new | 354php |
| new | 355e |
| new | 355f |
| new | 355pfp |
| new | 357i |
| new | 382a |
| new | 398pa |
| new | 417a |
| new | 438a |
| new | 514b |
| new | 574a |
| MH383a | deleted |
| MH384a | deleted |
| MH391a | deleted |
| MH392a | deleted |
| **Jersey** | |
| 786a | deleted |
| 787a | deleted |
| 788a | deleted |
| 789a | deleted |
| 789c | deleted |
| new | 854b-857b |
| new | 857c |
| new | 854d-857d |
| new | 857e |
| new | 854f-857f |
| new | 857g |
| new | 854h-857h |
| new | 857i |
| new | 1144f-1144k |
| new | 1144l-1144q |
| new | 1145f-1145k |
| new | 1145l-1145q |
| **Isle of Man** | |
| 352a | deleted |
| 355a | deleted |
| new | 766a |
| new | 941b |

| Number in 2013 Catalogue | Number in 2014 Catalogue |
|---|---|
| **Greenland** | |
| 423a | deleted |
| 468a | deleted |
| 510a | deleted |
| 532a | deleted |
| 558a | deleted |
| 581a | deleted |
| 590a | deleted |
| **Guinea** | |
| 2267-2276 | 2269-2278 |
| **Hong Kong** | |
| 502dc | deleted |
| 502ca | 502e |
| 502da | 502f |
| 502db | 502g |
| **Hungary** | |
| new | 1035a |
| new | 1042a |
| new | 1174a |
| new | 1175a |
| 1N40 | 1N41 |
| new | 1N40 |
| **Iceland** | |
| new | O28f |
| **Iran** | |
| 14a | 14b |
| 14b | 14c |
| **Italy** | |
| new | 1684a |

# INDEX TO ADVERTISERS
# 2014 VOLUME 3

# STOCKBOOKS

Stockbooks are a classic and convenient storage alternative for many collectors. These 9" x 12" Lighthouse stockbooks feature heavyweight archival quality paper with 9 pockets on each page and include double glassine interleaving between the pages for added protection.

| *Item* | *Color* | *Pg Count* | *Retail* | *AA** |
|---|---|---|---|---|
| LS4/8BK | Black | 16 pgs | $17.95 | **$15.95** |
| LS4/8BL | Blue | 16 pgs | $17.95 | **$15.95** |
| LS4/8GR | Green | 16 pgs | $17.95 | **$15.95** |
| LS4/8RD | Red | 16 pgs | $17.95 | **$15.95** |
| LS4/16BK | Black | 32 pgs | $27.95 | **$23.95** |
| LS4/16BL | Blue | 32 pgs | $27.95 | **$23.95** |
| LS4/16GR | Green | 32 pgs | $27.95 | **$23.95** |
| LS4/16RD | Red | 32 pgs | $27.95 | **$23.95** |

| *Item* | *Color* | *Pg Count* | *Retail* | *AA** |
|---|---|---|---|---|
| LS4/32BK | Black | 64 pgs | $53.95 | **$46.95** |
| LS4/32BL | Blue | 64 pgs | $53.95 | **$46.95** |
| LS4/32GR | Green | 64 pgs | $53.95 | **$46.95** |
| LS4/32RD | Red | 64 pgs | $53.95 | **$46.95** |

AMOS HOBBY PUBLISHING

1. *AA prices apply to paid subscribers of Amos Hobby publications, or orders placed online.
2. Prices, terms and product availability subject to change.
3. **Shipping & Handling:**
   United States: 10% of order total.
   Minimum charge $7.99 Maximum charge $45.00
   Canada: 20% of order total.
   Minimum charge $19.99 Maximum charge $200.00
   Foreign orders are shipped via FedEx Intl. and billed actual freight. Credit cards only.

**To Order Call:**

**1-800-572-6885**

**www.amosadvantage.com**

# 2014
# VOLUME 3
# DEALER DIRECTORY
# YELLOW PAGE LISTINGS

**This section of your Scott Catalogue contains advertisements to help you conveniently find what you need, when you need it...!**

## Accessories

**BROOKLYN GALLERY COIN & STAMP, INC.**
8725 4th Ave.
Brooklyn, NY 11209
PH: 718-745-5701
FAX: 718-745-2775
info@brooklyngallery.com
www.brooklyngallery.com

## Appraisals

**PHILIP WEISS AUCTIONS**
1 Neil Ct.
Oceanside, NY 11572
PH: 516-594-0731
FAX: 516-594-9414
phil@prwauctions.com
www.prwauctions.com

## Asia

**MICHAEL ROGERS, INC.**
Suite 4-1
415 S. Orlando Ave.
Winter Park, FL 32789-3683
PH: 407-644-2290
PH: 800-843-3751
FAX: 407-645-4434
Stamps@michaelrogersinc.com
www.michaelrogersinc.com

**THE STAMP ACT**
PO Box 1136
Belmont, CA 94002
PH: 650-703-2342
PH: 650-592-3315
FAX: 650-508-8104
thestampact@sbcglobal.net

## Auctions

**DANIEL F. KELLEHER AUCTIONS LLC**
PMB 44
60 Newtown Rd
Danbury, CT 06810
PH: 203-297-6056
FAX: 203-297-6059
info@kelleherauctions.com
www.kelleherauctions.com

**DUTCH COUNTRY AUCTIONS**
4115 Concord Pike
Wilmington, DE 19803
PH: 302-478-8740
FAX: 302-478-8779
auctions@dutchcountryauctions.com
www.dutchcountryauctions.com

## Auctions

**MICHAEL ROGERS, INC.**
Suite 4-1
415 S. Orlando Ave.
Winter Park, FL 32789-3683
PH: 407-644-2290
PH: 800-843-3751
FAX: 407-645-4434
Stamps@michaelrogersinc.com
www.michaelrogersinc.com

**PHILIP WEISS AUCTIONS**
1 Neil Ct.
Oceanside, NY 11572
PH: 516-594-0731
FAX: 516-594-9414
phil@prwauctions.com
www.prwauctions.com

**R. MARESCH & SON LTD.**
5th Floor - 6075 Yonge St.
Toronto, ON M2M 3W2
CANADA
PH: 416-363-7777
FAX: 416-363-6511
www.maresch.com

## Auctions - Public

**ALAN BLAIR AUCTIONS, L.L.C.**
Suite 1
5405 Lakeside Ave.
Richmond, VA 23228-6060
PH: 800-689-5602
FAX: 804-262-9307
alanblair@verizon.net
www.alanblairstamps.com

## British Commonwealth

**ARON R. HALBERSTAM PHILATELISTS, LTD.**
PO Box 150168
Van Brunt Station
Brooklyn, NY 11215-0168
PH: 718-788-3978
FAX: 718-965-3099
arh@arhstamps.com
www.arhstamps.com

## Central America

**GUY SHAW**
PO Box 27138
San Diego, CA 92198
PH/FAX: 858-485-8269
guyshaw@guyshaw.com
www.guyshaw.com

## China

**MICHAEL ROGERS, INC.**
Suite 4-1
415 S. Orlando Ave.
Winter Park, FL 32789-3683
PH: 407-644-2290
PH: 800-843-3751
FAX: 407-645-4434
Stamps@michaelrogersinc.com
www.michaelrogersinc.com

**THE STAMP ACT**
PO Box 1136
Belmont, CA 94002
PH: 650-703-2342
PH: 650-592-3315
FAX: 650-508-8104
thestampact@sbcglobal.net

## Ducks

**MICHAEL JAFFE**
PO Box 61484
Vancouver, WA 98666
PH: 360-695-6161
PH: 800-782-6770
FAX: 360-695-1616
mjaffe@brookmanstamps.com
www.brookmanstamps.com

## German Colonies

**COLONIAL STAMP COMPANY**
5757 Wilshire Blvd. PH #8
Los Angeles, CA 90036
PH: 323-933-9435
FAX: 323-939-9930
Toll Free in North America
PH: 877-272-6693
FAX: 877-272-6694
info@colonialstampcompany.com
www.colonialstampcompany.com

## German E. Africa (B & G)

**COLONIAL STAMP COMPANY**
5757 Wilshire Blvd. PH #8
Los Angeles, CA 90036
PH: 323-933-9435
FAX: 323-939-9930
Toll Free in North America
PH: 877-272-6693
FAX: 877-272-6694
info@colonialstampcompany.com
www.colonialstampcompany.com

## German New Guinea (B & G)

**COLONIAL STAMP COMPANY**
5757 Wilshire Blvd. PH #8
Los Angeles, CA 90036
PH: 323-933-9435
FAX: 323-939-9930
Toll Free in North America
PH: 877-272-6693
FAX: 877-272-6694
info@colonialstampcompany.com
www.colonialstampcompany.com

## British Commonwealth

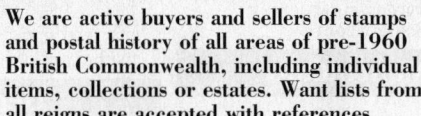

## British Commonwealth

### German So. West Africa

**COLONIAL STAMP COMPANY**
5757 Wilshire Blvd. PH #8
Los Angeles, CA 90036
PH: 323-933-9435
FAX: 323-939-9930
Toll Free in North America
PH: 877-272-6693
FAX: 877-272-6694
info@colonialstampcompany.com
www.colonialstampcompany.com

### German States

**COLONIAL STAMP COMPANY**
5757 Wilshire Blvd. PH #8
Los Angeles, CA 90036
PH: 323-933-9435
FAX: 323-939-9930
Toll Free in North America
PH: 877-272-6693
FAX: 877-272-6694
info@colonialstampcompany.com
www.colonialstampcompany.com

### Germany

**HENRY GITNER PHILATELISTS, INC.**
PO Box 3077-S
Middletown, NY 10940
PH: 845-343-5151
PH: 800-947-8267
FAX: 845-343-0068
hgitner@hgitner.com
www.hgitner.com

### Gold Coast

**COLONIAL STAMP COMPANY**
5757 Wilshire Blvd. PH #8
Los Angeles, CA 90036
PH: 323-933-9435
FAX: 323-939-9930
Toll Free in North America
PH: 877-272-6693
FAX: 877-272-6694
info@colonialstampcompany.com
www.colonialstampcompany.com

### Great Britain

**ARON R. HALBERSTAM PHILATELISTS, LTD.**
PO Box 150168
Van Brunt Station
Brooklyn, NY 11215-0168
PH: 718-788-3978
FAX: 718-965-3099
arh@arhstamps.com
www.arhstamps.com

**COLONIAL STAMP COMPANY**
5757 Wilshire Blvd. PH #8
Los Angeles, CA 90036
PH: 323-933-9435
FAX: 323-939-9930
Toll Free in North America
PH: 877-272-6693
FAX: 877-272-6694
info@colonialstampcompany.com
www.colonialstampcompany.com

### Hong Kong

**ARON R. HALBERSTAM PHILATELISTS, LTD.**
PO Box 150168
Van Brunt Station
Brooklyn, NY 11215-0168
PH: 718-788-3978
FAX: 718-965-3099
arh@arhstamps.com
www.arhstamps.com

**COLONIAL STAMP COMPANY**
5757 Wilshire Blvd. PH #8
Los Angeles, CA 90036
PH: 323-933-9435
FAX: 323-939-9930
Toll Free in North America
PH: 877-272-6693
FAX: 877-272-6694
info@colonialstampcompany.com
www.colonialstampcompany.com

**THE STAMP ACT**
PO Box 1136
Belmont, CA 94002
PH: 650-703-2342
PH: 650-592-3315
FAX: 650-508-8104
thestampact@sbcglobal.net

### India & States

**COLONIAL STAMP COMPANY**
5757 Wilshire Blvd. PH #8
Los Angeles, CA 90036
PH: 323-933-9435
FAX: 323-939-9930
Toll Free in North America
PH: 877-272-6693
FAX: 877-272-6694
info@colonialstampcompany.com
www.colonialstampcompany.com

### Germany



### Iraq

**COLONIAL STAMP COMPANY**
5757 Wilshire Blvd. PH #8
Los Angeles, CA 90036
PH: 323-933-9435
FAX: 323-939-9930
Toll Free in North America
PH: 877-272-6693
FAX: 877-272-6694
info@colonialstampcompany.com
www.colonialstampcompany.com

### Israel

**HENRY GITNER PHILATELISTS, INC.**
PO Box 3077-S
Middletown, NY 10940
PH: 845-343-5151
PH: 800-947-8267
FAX: 845-343-0068
hgitner@hgitner.com
www.hgitner.com

### Italy

**HENRY GITNER PHILATELISTS, INC.**
PO Box 3077-S
Middletown, NY 10940
PH: 845-343-5151
PH: 800-947-8267
FAX: 845-343-0068
hgitner@hgitner.com
www.hgitner.com

### Japan

**MICHAEL ROGERS, INC.**
Suite 4-1
415 S. Orlando Ave.
Winter Park, FL 32789-3683
PH: 407-644-2290
PH: 800-843-3751
FAX: 407-645-4434
Stamps@michaelrogersinc.com
www.michaelrogersinc.com

### Korea

**MICHAEL ROGERS, INC.**
Suite 4-1
415 S. Orlando Ave.
Winter Park, FL 32789-3683
PH: 407-644-2290
PH: 800-843-3751
FAX: 407-645-4434
Stamps@michaelrogersinc.com
www.michaelrogersinc.com

**THE STAMP ACT**
PO Box 1136
Belmont, CA 94002
PH: 650-703-2342
PH: 650-592-3315
FAX: 650-508-8104
thestampact@sbcglobal.net

### Latin America

**GUY SHAW**
PO Box 27138
San Diego, CA 92198
PH/FAX: 858-485-8269
guyshaw@guyshaw.com
www.guyshaw.com

### Manchukuo

**MICHAEL ROGERS, INC.**
Suite 4-1
415 S. Orlando Ave.
Winter Park, FL 32789-3683
PH: 407-644-2290
PH: 800-843-3751
FAX: 407-645-4434
Stamps@michaelrogersinc.com
www.michaelrogersinc.com

### Middle East-Arab

**MICHAEL ROGERS, INC.**
Suite 4-1
415 S. Orlando Ave.
Winter Park, FL 32789-3683
PH: 407-644-2290
PH: 800-843-3751
FAX: 407-645-4434
Stamps@michaelrogersinc.com
www.michaelrogersinc.com

### New Issues

**DAVIDSON'S STAMP SERVICE**
PO Box 36355
Indianapolis, IN 46236-0355
PH: 317-826-2620
ed-davidson@earthlink.net
www.newstampissues.com

### South America

**GUY SHAW**
PO Box 27138
San Diego, CA 92198
PH/FAX: 858-485-8269
guyshaw@guyshaw.com
www.guyshaw.com

## Stamp Stores

### Arizona

**A TO Z STAMPS & COINS**
4950 E. Thomas Rd.
Phoenix, AZ 85018
OFFICE: 480-844-9878
CELL: 248-709-8939
michael@azstampcoin.com
www.WorldwideStamps.com

### California

**BROSIUS STAMP, COIN & SUPPLIES**
2105 Main St.
Santa Monica, CA 90405
PH: 310-396-7480
FAX: 310-396-7455
brosius.stamp.coin@hotmail.com

**COAST PHILATELICS**
Suite D
1113 Baker St.
Costa Mesa, CA 92626
PH: 714-545-1791
chizz5@aol.com

**COLONIAL STAMP COMPANY**
5757 Wilshire Blvd. PH #8
Los Angeles, CA 90036
PH: 323-933-9435
FAX: 323-939-9930
Toll Free in North America
PH: 877-272-6693
FAX: 877-272-6694
info@colonialstampcompany.com
www.colonialstampcompany.com

**FISCHER-WOLK PHILATELICS**
Suite 211
22762 Aspan St.
Lake Forest, CA 92630
PH: 949-837-2932
fischerwolk@fw.occoxmail.com

### Georgia

**STAMPS UNLIMITED OF GEORGIA, INC.**
Suite 1460
100 Peachtree St. NW
Atlanta, GA 30303
PH: 404-688-9161
tonyroozen@yahoo.com
www.stampsunlimitedofga.com

# Stamp Stores

## Illinois

**DR. ROBERT FRIEDMAN & SONS**
2029 W. 75th St.
Woodridge, IL 60517
PH: 800-588-8100
FAX: 630-985-1588
drbobstamps@comcast.net
www.drbobfriedmanstamps.com

## Indiana

**KNIGHT STAMP & COIN CO.**
237 Main St.
Hobart, IN 46342
PH: 219-942-4341
PH: 800-634-2646
knight@knightcoin.com
www.knightcoin.com

## New Jersey

**BERGEN STAMPS & COLLECTIBLES**
306 Queen Anne Rd.
Teaneck, NJ 07666
PH: 201-836-8987

**TRENTON STAMP & COIN CO**
Thomas DeLuca
Store: Forest Glen Plaza
1804 Highway 33
Hamilton Square, NJ 08690
Mail: PO Box 8574
Trenton, NJ 08650
PH: 609-584-8100
PH: 800-446-8664
FAX: 609-587-8664
TOMD4TSC@aol.com

## New York

**CHAMPION STAMP CO., INC.**
432 W. 54th St.
New York, NY 10019
PH: 212-489-8130
FAX: 212-581-8130
championstamp@aol.com
www.championstamp.com

## Ohio

**HILLTOP STAMP SERVICE**
Richard A. Peterson
PO Box 626
Wooster, OH 44691
PH: 330-262-8907 (0)
PH: 330-262-5378
hilltop@bright.net
www.hilltopstamps.com

## Ohio

**THE LINK STAMP CO.**
3461 E. Livingston Ave.
Columbus, OH 43227
PH/FAX: 614-237-4125
PH/FAX: 800-546-5726

## Virginia

**LATHEROW & CO., INC.**
5054 Lee Hwy.
Arlington, VA 22207
PH: 703-538-2727
PH: 800-647-4624
FAX: 703-538-5210
latherows@gmail.com

## Topicals

**E. JOSEPH McCONNELL, INC.**
PO Box 683
Monroe, NY 10949
PH: 845-783-9791
FAX: 845-782-0347
ejstamps@gmail.com
www.EJMcConnell.com

## Topicals-Columbus

**MR. COLUMBUS**
PO Box 1492
Fennville, MI 49408
PH: 269-543-4755
David@MrColumbus1492.com
MrColumbus1492.com

## United Nations

**BRUCE M. MOYER**
Box 99
East Texas, PA 18046
PH: 610-395-8410
FAX: 610-395-8537
moyer@unstamps.com
www.unstamps.com

## United States

**ACS STAMP COMPANY**
13650 Via Varra #210
Broomfield, CO 80020
PH: 303-841-8666
ACS@ACSStamp.com
www.acsstamp.com

## United States

**BROOKMAN STAMP CO.**
PO Box 90
Vancouver, WA 98666
PH: 360-695-1391
PH: 800-545-4871
FAX: 360-695-1616
info@brookmanstamps.com
www.brookmanstamps.com

## U.S.-Classics/Moderns

**A TO Z STAMPS & COINS**
4950 E. Thomas Rd.
Phoenix, AZ 85018
OFFICE: 480-844-9878
CELL: 248-709-8939
michael@azstampcoin.com
www.WorldwideStamps.com

## U.S.-Collections Wanted

**DR. ROBERT FRIEDMAN & SONS**
2029 W. 75th St.
Woodridge, IL 60517
PH: 800-588-8100
FAX: 630-985-1588
drbobstamps@comcast.net
www.drbobfriedmanstamps.com

**DUTCH COUNTRY AUCTIONS**
4115 Concord Pike
Wilmington, DE 19803
PH: 302-478-8740
FAX: 302-478-8779
auctions@dutchcountryauctions.com
www.dutchcountryauctions.com

## Want Lists-British Empire 1840-1935 German Cols./Offices

**COLONIAL STAMP COMPANY**
5757 Wilshire Blvd. PH #8
Los Angeles, CA 90036
PH: 323-933-9435
FAX: 323-939-9930
Toll Free in North America
PH: 877-272-6693
FAX: 877-272-6694
info@colonialstampcompany.com
www.colonialstampcompany.com

## Wanted-Estates

**A TO Z STAMPS & COINS**
4950 E. Thomas Rd.
Phoenix, AZ 85018
OFFICE: 480-844-9878
CELL: 248-709-8939
michael@azstampcoin.com
www.WorldwideStamps.com

## Wanted-Worldwide Collections

**DANIEL F. KELLEHER AUCTIONS LLC**
PMB 44
60 Newtown Rd
Danbury, CT 06810
PH: 203-297-6056
FAX: 203-297-6059
info@kelleherauctions.com
www.kelleherauctions.com

## Worldwide



# Stamp Shows

## Wanted-Worldwide Collections

**DR. ROBERT FRIEDMAN & SONS**
2029 W. 75th St.
Woodridge, IL 60517
PH: 800-588-8100
FAX: 630-985-1588
drbobstamps@comcast.net
www.drbobfriedmanstamps.com

**DUTCH COUNTRY AUCTIONS**
4115 Concord Pike
Wilmington, DE 19803
PH: 302-478-8740
FAX: 302-478-8779
auctions@dutchcountryauctions.com
www.dutchcountryauctions.com

## Websites

**ACS STAMP COMPANY**
13650 Via Varra #210
Broomfield, CO 80020
PH: 303-841-8666
ACS@ACSStamp.com
www.acsstamp.com

## Worldwide Stamps

**A TO Z STAMPS & COINS**
4950 E. Thomas Rd.
Phoenix, AZ 85018
OFFICE: 480-844-9878
CELL: 248-709-8939
michael@azstampcoin.com
www.WorldwideStamps.com